BOOK REVIEW INDEX

1997 CUMULATION

ISSN 0524-0581

BOOK REVIEW INDEX

1997 CUMULATION

Beverly Baer
Editor

GALE

DETROIT • NEW YORK • TORONTO • LONDON

Managing Editor: Ann V. Evory
Project Editor: Beverly Baer
Editors: Shelly Dickey, Debra Kirby, Kelly Sprague
Associate Editors: Victoria A. Coughlin, Paula Cutcher-Jackson, Kathleen Dallas, Lydia Fink,
Nancy Franklin, William H. Harmer, Arlene M. Johnson, Rebecca A. Mansour, Dana Shonta
Assistant Editors: Prindle LaBarge, Sharon M. McGilvray

Research Manager: Victoria B. Cariappa

Production Director: Mary Beth Trimper
External Production Assistant: Deborah Milliken
Product Design Manager: Cynthia Baldwin
Desktop Publisher: Gary Leach

Manager, Data Entry Services: Eleanor Allison
Data Entry Coordinator: Ken D. Benson, Jr.
Data Entry Associates: Maleka Imrana, Arlene Ann Kevonian,
Shanitta L. Watkins, Constance J. Wells

Manager, Technical Support Services: Theresa Rocklin
Senior Programmer/Analyst: Piotr Luczycki
Programmer/Analysts: Flavio Bezerra, Sheila Printup
Program Design: Donald G. Dillaman

While every effort has been made to ensure the reliability of the information presented in this publication, Gale Research does not guarantee the accuracy of the data contained herein. Gale accepts no payment for listing; and inclusion in the publication of any organization, agency, institution, publication, service, or individual does not imply endorsement of the publisher. Errors brought to the attention of the publisher and verified to the satisfaction of the publisher will be corrected in future editions.

Three paperbound issues are published in February, May and September. The annual cumulation includes all citations from the three issues.

This book is printed on acid-free paper that meets the minimum requirements of American National Standard for Information Sciences—Permanence Paper for Printed Library Materials, ANSI Z39.48-1984.

Library of Congress Catalog Card Number 65-9908
ISBN 0-7876-1209-X
ISSN 0524-0581

Printed in the United States of America

Contents

Introduction

Book Review Index (BRI) is a master key providing access to reviews of thousands of books, periodicals, and books-on-tape. Representing a wide range of popular, academic, and professional interests, *BRI* guides readers and researchers to reviews appearing in more than 600 publications, including reviewing journals such as *Choice, Booklist,* and *School Library Journal*; national publications of general interest like *Time* and *Newsweek*; and scholarly and literary journals such as *American Ethnologist* and *Sewanee Review*.

BRI includes citations for reviews of any type of book, periodical, or reference work that has been or is about to be published and is at least 50 pages long. (Poetry, children's, and song books are exceptions to the 50-page rule.) *BRI*'s definition of "review" is broad, citing reviews that provide a critical comment, a description of the book's contents, or a recommendation regarding the type of library collection for which a book is suited. Reviews of audio books or electronic media are cited if they are presentations of previously published books.

Highlights

● **Up-to-Date**—The *BRI* editorial staff compiles citations on an ongoing basis, as journals arrive. By publishing several issues a year plus the cumulation, the *BRI* user is provided with up-to-date citations.

● **Comprehensive**—*BRI* cites more reviews from a wider variety of publications than any other resource of its kind. (For a complete list of the periodicals indexed in *BRI* see Publications Indexed following this Introduction.)

● **Accurate**—Each entry is double-checked for accuracy.

● **Easy-to-Use**—Entries are arranged by author's name, or by title if there is no primary author, in a single alphabetical sequence with citations listed in an easy-to-read format. A Title Index aids readers who do not have complete author information.

Form and Content of Entries

[1] **Sattler, Helen R -** [2] *The Book of Eagles*
[3] *(Illus. by Jean D Zallinger)*
[4] *c* [5] CCB-B - [6] v50 - O '96 - [7] p43+ [51-250]

[1] Author or Editor of work being reviewed
[2] Title of work being reviewed
[3] Illustrator (if applicable)
[4] Age or Type code (see explanation below)
[5] Abbreviation of reviewing periodical title (see Publications Indexed for complete list of abbreviations)
[6] Volume number and date or issue number
[7] Page on which review appears (see explanation below)

Works published in several editions over the years may have the name of the editor, translator, or publisher added in parentheses after the title to clarify which version is under review.

Explanation of Letter Codes—Some entries in *BRI* include age and/or type codes that help define the kind of work being reviewed.

● Age codes: Age designations are determined by the reviewer or publisher.
   "c" denotes a book for children (up to age ten)
   "y" denotes a book written for young adults (ages eleven and up)

● Type codes:
  "p" indicates a review of a periodical or newspaper
  "r" indicates a review of a reference work

Page Number Designations:

"R" before a page number in a citation: the page number appears as a roman numeral in the periodical.

"*" (an asterisk) following a page number: a page within a special section of a periodical that was not numbered sequentially with the main section.

"+" (plus sign) following the page number: indicates a review that continues on a succeeding page(s).

"[51-250]" following the page number: denotes the approximate word-count of the review. Ranges used are 1-50, 51-250, 251-500, and 501+.

Arrangement of Entries

A user searching for a particular entry in the author or title indexes should note the following guidelines.

● Roman and arabic numerals file in numerical order before the letter A. For example, the title *30-Minute Meals* would file at the beginning of the Title Index; *Thirty-Minute Meals* would file in the T's.

● Acronyms and initialisms file as single words unless periods or spaces divide the letters. Letters following a period or space file as new words. Users should note that variant forms of initialisms would file separately under this arrangement. For example, U.S.A. would appear near the beginning of the U section, while USA would file just before the word "Use."

● Corporate authors and titles with no author are interfiled with authors in the main entry section.

Title Index Aids Main Entry Search

The Title Index, which follows the main entry Author Index, allows the user access to the citations by way of the title. This index is useful when the name of the author is unknown. Listings in the title index refer the user to the main entry section. When a title appears without an author it is an indication that the title itself is the main entry form.

Available in Electronic Formats

● **Diskette/Magnetic Tape:** *BRI* is available for licensing on magnetic tape or diskette in a standard or customized fielded format. The database is available for internal data processing and nonpublishing only. For more information, call 800-977-GALE.

● **Online:** *BRI* is also available online (File 137 on DIALOG).

Acknowledgements

The editors of *BRI* would like to thank individuals from other Gale Research editorial teams who contributed to the completion of the 1997 *BRI Cumulation*.

Comments and Suggestions Are Welcome

The editors welcome comments or suggestions on the scope and coverage of *BRI*. Please address correspondence to: The Editor, *Book Review Index*, Gale Research, 835 Penobscot Bldg., Detroit, MI 48226-4094; Fax 313-961-6741; or call 1-800-347-GALE toll-free.

Publications Indexed

The periodical abbreviations used in *Book Review Index* citations are arranged here alphabetically in letter-by-letter sequence. The full periodical title appears to the right of the abbreviation. The following information is also provided for each publication: frequency, ISSN, and subscription address.

A

AAAGA: *Association of American Geographers. Annals*
Quarterly ISSN 0004-5608
Journals Dept.
Blackwell Publishers
350 Main Street
Malden, MA 02148

A Anth: *American Anthropologist*
Quarterly ISSN 0002-7294
American Anthropological Association
4350 N. Fairfax Dr., Ste.640
Arlington, VA 22203-1621

AAPSS-A: *American Academy of Political and Social Science. Annals*
Bimonthly ISSN 0002-7162
Sage Publications, Inc.
2455 Teller Rd.
Thousand Oaks, CA 91320

A Arch: *American Archivist*
Quarterly ISSN 0360-9081
600 S. Federal, Ste. 504
Chicago, IL 60605

A Art: *American Artist*
Monthly ISSN 0002-7375
P.O. Box 1944
Marion, OH 43305-1944

AB: *AB Bookman's Weekly*
Weekly ISSN 0001-0340
P.O. Box AB
Clifton, NJ 07015

ABA Jour: *ABA Journal*
Monthly ISSN 0747-0088
American Bar Association
750 N. Lake Shore Dr.
Chicago, IL 60611

ABE: *Adult Basic Education*
3/yr ISSN 1052-231X
P.O. Box 592053
Orlando, FL 32859-2053

ABR: *American Book Review*
Bimonthly ISSN 0149-9408
Unit for Contemporary Literature
Campus Box 4241
Illinois St. Univ.
Normal, IL 61790-4241

ACI: *Advancing the Consumer Interest*
Semi-annual ISSN 1044-7385
American Council on Consumer Interests
240 Stanley Hall
University of Missouri
Columbia, MO 65211

ACM: *Another Chicago Magazine*
Semiannual ISSN 0272-4359
Left Field Press
3709 N. Kenmore
Chicago, IL 60613

Adoles: *Adolescence*
Quarterly ISSN 0001-8449
Libra Publishers, Inc.
3089C Clairemont Dr., Ste. 383
San Diego, CA 92117

Adult L: *Adult Learning*
Bimonthly ISSN 1045-1595
American Association for Adult and Continuing Education
1200 19th St., NW
Suite 300
Washington, DC 20036

Advocate: *Advocate*
Biweekly ISSN 0001-8996
P.O. Box 541
Mount Morris, IL 61054-0541

AE: *Adult Education Quarterly*
Quarterly ISSN 0741-7136
American Association for Adult and Continuing Education
1200 19th St., NW
Suite 300
Washington, DC 20036

Aethlon: *Aethlon: The Journal of Sport Literature*
Biannual ISSN 1048-3756
Department of English
East Tennessee State University
Box 70683
Johnson City, TN 37614-0683

AF: *American Forests*
Bimonthly ISSN 0002-8541
American Forestry Association
P.O. Box 2000
Washington, DC 20013

Afr Am R: *African American Review*
Quarterly ISSN 1062-4783
Dept. of English
Indiana State University
Terre Haute, IN 47809

Africa T: *Africa Today*
Quarterly ISSN 0001-9887
Lynne Rienner Publishers
1800 30th St., Ste. 314
Boulder, CO 80301-1026

Afr Rep: *Africa Report*
Bimonthly ISSN 0001-9836
Subscription Services
P.O. Box 3000, Dept. AR
Denville, NJ 07834

Afterimage: *Afterimage*
10 issues/year ISSN 0300-7472
31 Prince St.
Rochester, NY 14607

Agenda: *Agenda*
Quarterly ISSN 0002-0796
Agenda and Editions Charitable Trust
5 Cranbourne Ct.
Albert Bridge Rd.
London SW11 4PE, England

AH: *American Heritage*
8 issues/year ISSN 0002-8738
American Heritage Subscription Dept.
P.O. Box 5022
Harlan, IA 51593-0522

AHR: *American Historical Review*
5 issues/year ISSN 0002-8762
American Historical Association
400 A St. S.E.
Washington, DC 20003

AJA: *American Journal of Archaeology*
Quarterly ISSN 0002-9114
Archaeological Institute of America
Boston University
656 Beacon St.
Boston, MA 02215-2010

AJCH: *American Journal of Clinical Hypnosis*
Quarterly ISSN 0002-9157
2200 E. Devon Ave.
Ste. 291
Des Plaines, IL 60018

AJE: *American Journal of Education*
Quarterly ISSN 0195-6744
University of Chicago Press
Journals Division
P.O. Box 37005
Chicago, IL 60637

AJMR: *American Journal on Mental Retardation*
Bimonthly ISSN 0895-8017
c/o AAMR office
444 N. Capitol St., NW, Ste. 846
Washington, DC 20001-1512

AJN: *American Journal of Nursing*
Monthly ISSN 0002-936X
Subscriptions
P.O. Box 50480
Boulder, CO 80322-0480

AJP: *American Journal of Philology*
Quarterly ISSN 0002-9475
Johns Hopkins University Press
Journals Publishing Division
2715 N. Charles Street
Baltimore, MD 21218-4319

A J Psy: *American Journal of Psychology*
Quarterly ISSN 0002-9556
Subscription Dept.
University of Illinois Press
1325 South Oak St.
Champaign, IL 61820

AJPsych: *American Journal of Psychiatry*
Monthly ISSN 0002-953X
Circulation Dept.
American Psychiatric Assn.
1400 K St., N.W.
Washington, DC 20005

AJR: *AJR: American Journalism Review*
10 issues/year ISSN 1067-8654
Subscription Department
P.O. Box 561
Mount Morris, IL 61054

AJS: *American Journal of Sociology*
Bimonthly ISSN 0002-9602
University of Chicago Press
Journals Division
P.O. Box 37005
Chicago, IL 60637

AL: *American Literature*
Quarterly ISSN 0002-9831
Duke University Press
Box 90660
Duke University
Durham, NC 27708-0660

Albion: *Albion*
Quarterly ISSN 0095-1390
Department of History
Appalachian State University
Boone, NC 28608

ALBR: *Academic Library Book Review*
Bimonthly ISSN 0894-933X
Subscription Dept.
290 Broadway
Lynbrook, NY 11563

A Lib: *American Libraries*
Monthly ISSN 0002-9769
Subscription Services
American Library Association
50 E. Huron St.
Chicago, IL 60611

Alt Pr R: *Alternative Press Review*
Quarterly ISSN 1072-7299
C.A.L. Press
POB 1446
Columbia, MO 65205-1446

Am: *America*
Weekly ISSN 0002-7049
America Press, Inc.
106 W. 56th St.
New York, NY 10019

Am Ant: *American Antiquity*
Quarterly ISSN 0002-7316
Society for American Archaeology
900 Second St. N.E. Ste 12
Washington, DC 20002-3557

Ambio: *Ambio*
8/yr. ISSN 0044-7447
P.O. Box 1897
Lawrence, KS 66044-8897

Am Craft: *American Craft*
Bimonthly ISSN 0194-8008
American Craft Council
P.O. Box 3000
Denville, NJ 07834

Amerasia J: *Amerasia Journal*
3/yr. ISSN 0044-7471
3230 Campbell Hall
UCLA Asian American Studies Ctr.
405 Hilgard Ave.
Los Angeles, CA 90095-1546

Amer R: *Americas Review: A Review of Hispanic Literature and Art of the USA*
Quarterly ISSN 1042-6213
University of Houston
Houston, TX 77204-2090

Am Ethnol: *American Ethnologist*
Quarterly ISSN 0094-0496
4350 North Fairfax Drive
Suite 640
Arlington, VA 22203-1620

Am Geneal: *American Genealogist*
Quarterly ISSN 0002-8592
P.O. Box 398
Demorest, GA 30535-0398

Am Hist: *American History*
Bimonthly ISSN 1076-8866
P.O. Box 1776
Mt. Morris, IL 61054

Am Ind CRJ: *American Indian Culture and Research Journal*
Quarterly ISSN 0161-6463
American Indian Studies Center
3220 Campbell Hall
University of California, Los Angeles
Box 951548
Los Angeles, CA 90095-1548

Am M: *American Music*
Quarterly ISSN 0734-4392
University of Illinois Press
1325 S. Oak St.
Champaign, IL 61820

Am MT: *American Music Teacher*
Bimonthly ISSN 0003-0112
The Carew Tower
441 Vine St., Suite 505
Cincinnati, OH 45202-2814

Am Phil: *American Philatelist*
Monthly ISSN 0003-0473
American Philatelic Society, Inc.
P.O. Box 8000
100 Oakwood Ave.
State College, PA 16801

Am Q: *American Quarterly*
Quarterly ISSN 0003-0678
Johns Hopkins University Press
Journals Publishing Division
2715 North Charles St.
Baltimore, MD 21218-4319

Ams: *Americas: A Quarterly Review of Inter-American Cultural History*
Quarterly ISSN 0003-1615
Journal Division, CUA Press
303 Administration Bldg.
Catholic University of America
Washington, DC 20064

Am Sci: *American Scientist*
Bimonthly ISSN 0003-0996
Sigma Xi
P.O. Box 13975
Research Triangle Park, NC 27709

Am Spect: *American Spectator*
Monthly ISSN 0148-8414
P.O. Box 1978
Marion, OH 43305-1978

Am Theat: *American Theatre*
10 issues/year ISSN 8750-3255
355 Lexington Ave.
New York, NY 10017

Am Vis: *American Visions*
Bimonthly ISSN 0884-9390
P.O. Box 614
Mt. Morris, IL 61054

Analog: *Analog Science Fiction and Fact*
Monthly ISSN 1059-2113
P.O. Box 54625
Boulder, CO 80322-4625

ANQ:QJ: *ANQ: A Quarterly Journal of Short Articles, Notes, and Reviews*
Quarterly ISSN 0895-769X
Heldref Publications
1319 Eighteenth St. NW
Washington, DC 20036-1802

Ant & CM: *Antiques & Collecting Magazine*
Monthly ISSN 0884-6294
1006 S. Michigan Ave.
Chicago, IL 60605

Antiq J: *Antiquaries Journal*
3 issues/year ISSN 0003-5815
Journals Subscriptions Dept.
Oxford University Press
Pinkhill House, Southfield Rd.
Eynsham, Oxford OX8 1JJ, England

Ant R: *Antioch Review*
Quarterly ISSN 0003-5769
Subscriptions
P.O. Box 148
Yellow Springs, OH 45387

APH: *Air Power History*
Quarterly ISSN 1044-016X
George C. Marshall Library
Virginia Military Institute
Lexington, VA 24450

Apo: *Apollo*
Monthly ISSN 0003-6356
P.O. Box 47
North Hollywood, CA 91603-0047

Appalachia: *Appalachia*
Quarterly ISSN 0003-6595
Appalachian Regional Commission
1666 Connecticut Ave., N.W.
Washington, DC 20235

APR: *American Poetry Review*
Bimonthly ISSN 0360-3709
1721 Walnut St.
Philadelphia, PA 19103

APSR: *American Political Science Review*
Quarterly ISSN 0003-0554
Membership Secretary
American Political Science Association
1527 New Hampshire Ave. N.W.
Washington, DC 20036

AR: *Accounting Review*
Quarterly ISSN 0001-4826
American Accounting Association
5717 Bessie Dr.
Sarasota, FL 34233-2399

ARBA: *American Reference Books Annual*
Annual ISSN 0065-9959
Libraries Unlimited, Inc.
P.O. Box 6633
Englewood, CO 80155-6633

Arch: *Archaeology*
Bimonthly ISSN 0003-8113
Subscription Service
P.O. Box 420427
Palm Coast, FL 32142-0427

Archiv: *Archivaria*
Semiannual ISSN 0318-6954
Association of Canadian Archivists
P.O. Box 2596, Station D
Ottawa, ON, Canada K1P 5W6

Arena: *Arena Magazine*
Bimonthly ISSN 1039-1010
P.O. Box 18
North Carlton 3054, Australia

Arm Det: *Armchair Detective*
Quarterly ISSN 0004-217Z
TAD
549 Park Ave., Suite 252
Scotch Plains, NJ 07076-1705

Arm F&S: *Armed Forces and Society*
Quarterly ISSN 0095-327-X
Dept. 4010
Transaction Periodicals Consortium
Rutgers University
New Brunswick, NJ 08903

Art Am: *Art in America*
Monthly ISSN 0004-3214
P.O. Box 11292
Des Moines, IA 50340

Art Asiae: *Artibus Asiae*
Quarterly ISSN 0004-3648
Museum Rietberg Zurich
Gablerstrasse 15
CH-8002 Zurich, Switzerland

Art Bull: *Art Bulletin*
Quarterly ISSN 0004-3079
College Art Association
275 7th Ave.
New York, NY 10001

Art Dir: *Art Direction*
Monthly ISSN 0004-3109
10 E. 39th St.
New York, NY 10016

Art J: *Art Journal*
Quarterly ISSN 0004-3249
College Art Association
275 7th Ave.
New York, NY 10001

Art N: *ARTnews*
10 issues/year ISSN 0004-3273
Subscription Service
P.O. Box 2083
Knoxville, IA 50197-2083

A & S Sm: *Air & Space/Smithsonian*
Bimonthly ISSN 0886-2257
P.O. Box 420113
Palm Coast, FL 32142-0113

AS: *American Scholar*
Quarterly ISSN 0003-0937
1811 Q St. N.W.
Washington, DC 20009

ASBYP: *Appraisal: Science Books for Young People*
Quarterly ISSN 0003-7052
605 Commonwealth Ave.
Boston, MA 02215

ASInt: *American Studies International*
Semiannual ISSN 0883-105X
Editor, American Studies International
The George Washington University
Washington, DC 20052

Astron: *Astronomy*
Monthly ISSN 0091-6358
21027 Crossroads Circle
P.O. Box 1612
Waukesha, WI 53187-1612

Atl: *Atlantic Monthly*
Monthly ISSN 0276-9077
Atlantic Subscription Processing Center
Box 52661
Boulder, CO 80322

Atl BT: *Atlantic Books Today*
Quarterly ISSN 1192-3652
2085 Maitland Street
Suite 202
Halifax, NS, Canada B3K 2Z8

Aud: *Audubon*
Bimonthly ISSN 0097-7136
National Audubon Society
P.O. Box 52529
Boulder, CO 80322-2529

Aust Bk R: *Australian Book Review*
10 issues/year ISSN 0155-2864
Suite 3
21 Drummond Place
Carlton 3053, Australia

B

Barron's: *Barron's*
Weekly ISSN 0005-6073
200 Burnett Rd.
Chicopee, MA 01020

BAS: *Bulletin of the Atomic Scientists*
6 issues/year ISSN 0096-3402
6042 S. Kimbark Ave.
Chicago, IL 60637

BC: *Book Collector*
Quarterly ISSN 0006-7237
20 Maple Grove
London NW9 8QY, England

Beav: *Beaver*
Bimonthly ISSN 0005-7517
c/o H.A. & J.L. Wood, Inc.
Box 329
Pembina, ND 58271-0329

Belles Let: *Belles Lettres*
3 issues/year ISSN 0884-2957
Karen T. Jenkins
P.O. Box 372068
Satellite Beach, FL 32937-0068

B Ent: *Black Enterprise*
Monthly ISSN 0006-4165
Circulation Center
P.O. Box 3009
Harlan, IA 51537-4100

BHR: *Business History Review*
Quarterly ISSN 0007-6805
Business Manager
Harvard Business School
Boston, MA 02163

BIC: *Books in Canada*
9 issues/year ISSN 0045-2564
Canadian Review of Books Ltd.
Circulation Dept.
130 Spadina Ave., Ste. 603
Toronto, ON, Canada M5V 2L4

Biography: *Biography: An Interdisciplinary Quarterly*
Quarterly ISSN 0162-4962
University of Hawaii Press
2840 Kolowalu St.
Honolulu, HI 96822

BioSci: *BioScience*
11 issues/year ISSN 0006-3568
Circulation
AIBS
1313 Dolley Madison Blvd., Suite 402
McLean, VA 22101

Bkbird: *Bookbird*
Quarterly ISSN 0006-7377
Subscriptions
P.O. Box 807
Highland Park, IL 60035-0807

Bks & Cult: *Books & Culture*
Bimonthly ISSN 1082-8931
P.O. Box 37060
Boone, IA 50037-0060

Bks Keeps: *Books for Keeps*
Bimonthly ISSN 0143-909X
6 Brightfield Rd., Lee
London SE12 8QF, England

BL: *Booklist*
22 issues/year ISSN 0006-7385
434 W. Downer
Aurora, IL 60506

Bloom Rev: *Bloomsbury Review*
Bimonthly ISSN 0276-1564
1762 Emerson St.
Denver, CO 80218-1012

Bl S: *Black Scholar*
Quarterly ISSN 0006-4246
P.O. Box 2869
Oakland, CA 94618

BM: *Burlington Magazine*
Monthly ISSN 0007-6287
14-16 Duke's Road
London WC1H 9AD, England

Books: *Books Magazine*
Bimonthly ISSN 0006-7423
43 Museum St.
London WC1A 1LY, England

Boston R: *Boston Review*
Bimonthly ISSN 0734-2306
E53-407
30 Wadsworth St.
M.I.T.
Cambridge, MA 02139

B Rpt: *Book Report*
5 issues/year ISSN 0731-4388
Linworth Publishing, Inc.
480 East Wilson Bridge Rd., Suite L
Worthington, OH 43085-2372

BSA-P: *Bibliographical Society of America. Papers*
Quarterly ISSN 0006-128X
P.O. Box 397
Grand Central Station
New York, NY 10163-0397

BTB: *Biblical Theology Bulletin*
Quarterly ISSN 0146-1079
P.O. Box 1038
South Orange, NJ 07079

Bus Bk R: *Business Book Review*
Quarterly ISSN 0741-8132
1549 Clairmont Rd.
Suite 203
Decatur, GA 30033

BusLR: *Business Library Review*
Quarterly ISSN 1045-7798
P.O. Box 27542
Newark, NJ 07101-8472

Bus Soc: *Business and Society*
3 issues/year ISSN 0007-6503
c/o 2455 Teller Road
Thousand Oaks, CA 91320

Bus W: *Business Week*
Weekly ISSN 0007-7135
P.O. Box 430
Hightstown, NJ 08520

Buzz E J: *Buzzworm's Earth Journal*
Bimonthly ISSN 0898-2996
P.O. Box 6853
Syracuse, NY 13217

BW: *Book World*
Weekly ISSN 0006-7369
Washington Post
1150 15th St. N.W.
Washington, DC 20071

BWatch: *Bookwatch*
Monthly ISSN 0896-6521
James A Cox
278 Orchard Dr.
Oregon, WI 53575

BYTE: *BYTE*
12 issues/year ISSN 0360-5280
BYTE Subscription Dept.
P.O. Box 552
Hightstown, NJ 08520

C

Callaloo: *Callaloo*
Quarterly ISSN 0161-2492
Johns Hopkins University Press
Journals Publishing Division
2715 N. Charles St.
Baltimore, MD 21218-4319

Can CL: *Canadian Children's Literature*
Quarterly ISSN 0319-0080
Depts. of English and French
University of Guelph
Guelph, ON, Canada N1G 2W1

Can Hist R: *Canadian Historical Review*
Quarterly ISSN 0008-3755
IMS of New York
P.O. Box 1518
Champlain, NY 12919

Can Lit: *Canadian Literature*
Quarterly ISSN 0008-4360
Circulation Manager, Canadian
Literature
#167-1855 West Mall
University of British Columbia
Vancouver, BC, Canada V6T 1Z2

Can Mat: *CM: A Reviewing Journal of Canadian Materials for Young People*
Bimonthly ISSN 0821-1450
Canadian Library Association
200 Elgin St., Suite 602
Ottawa, ON, Canada K2P 1L5

Car DisAb: *Careers and the DisAbled*
3/year ISSN 0891-5202
Circulation Dept.
Equal Opportunity Publications, Inc.
150 Motor Pky., Ste. 420
Hauppauge, NY 11788-5145

Car Wom: *Career Woman*
3/year ISSN 1051-1075
Circulation Dept.
Equal Opportunity Publications, Inc.
150 Motor Pky., Ste. 420
Hauppauge, NY 11788-5145

Cat Fan: *Cat Fancy*
Monthly ISSN 0892-6514
Subscription Service Dept.
P.O. Box 52864
Boulder, CO 80322-2864

Cath W: *Catholic World*
Bimonthly ISSN 1042-3494
Paulist Press
997 Macarthur Blvd.
Mahwah, NJ 07430

CAY: *Come-All-Ye*
Quarterly ISSN 0736-6132
P.O. Box 494
Hatboro, PA 19040-0494

CBR: *Computer Book Review*
Quarterly ISSN 0737-0334
P.O. Box 61067
Honolulu, HI 96839

CBRA: *Canadian Book Review Annual*
Annual ISSN 0383-770X
44 Charles Street West, Suite 3205
Toronto, ON, Canada M4Y 1R8

CBRS: *Children's Book Review Service*
Monthly ISSN 0090-7987
220 Berkeley Place
Brooklyn, NY 11217

CC: *Christian Century*
Weekly ISSN 0009-5281
Subscription Service
407 S. Dearborn St.
Chicago, IL 60605-1150

CCB-B: *Center for Children's Books. Bulletin*
11 issues/year ISSN 0008-9036
The Bulletin of the Center for Children's Books
University of Illinois Press
1325 S. Oak
Champaign, IL 61820

CE: *Childhood Education*
5 issues/year ISSN 0009-4056
Childhood Education
11501 Georgia Ave. Suite 315
Wheaton, MD 20902

CEH: *Central European History*
Quarterly ISSN 0008-9389
Humanities Press International, Inc.
165 First Avenue
Atlantic Highlands, NJ 07716-1289

Ceram Mo: *Ceramics Monthly*
Monthly ISSN 0009-0328
P.O. Box 6102
Westerville, OH 43086-6102

CF: *Canadian Forum*
Monthly ISSN 0008-3631
Circulation Dept.
5502 Atlantic St.
Halifax, NS, Canada B3H 1G4

CG: *Canadian Geographic*
Bimonthly ISSN 0706-2168
Box 1182
Lewiston, NY 14092-8182

CH: *Church History*
Quarterly ISSN 0009-6407
Henry W. Bowden
P.O. Box 8517
Red Bank, NJ 07701

Cha Men: *Changing Men*
3/year ISSN 0889-7174
P.O. Box 908
Madison, WI 53701

Ch Bk News: *Children's Book News*
Quarterly ISSN 0075-9938
Canadian Children's Book Centre
35 Spadina Rd.
Toronto, ON, Canada M5R 2S9

Ch BWatch: *Children's Bookwatch*
Monthly ISSN 0896-4521
James A. Cox
278 Orchard Drive
Oregon, WI 53575

CHE: *Chronicle of Higher Education*
Weekly ISSN 0009-5982
P.O. Box 1955
Marion, OH 43305

Chel: *Chelsea*
Semiannual ISSN 0009-2185
Box 773, Cooper Station
New York, NY 10276-0773

Chess L: *Chess Life*
Monthly ISSN 0197-260X
3054 NYS Rte. 9W
New Windsor, NY 12553

Child Lit: *Children's Literature*
Annual ISSN 0092-8208
Yale University Press
P.O. Box 209040
New Haven, CT 06520-9040

China T: *China Today*
Monthly ISSN 1003-0905
China Books and Periodicals, Inc.
2929 24th St.
San Francisco, CA 94110

ChLAQ: *Children's Literature Association Quarterly*
Quarterly ISSN 0885-0429
ChLA
P.O. Box 138
Battle Creek, MI 49016

Ch Lit Ed: *Children's Literature in Education*
Quarterly ISSN 0045-6713
Human Sciences Press, Inc.
Subscription Dept.
233 Spring St.
New York, NY 10013-1578

Choice: *Choice*
11 issues/year ISSN 0009-4978
100 Riverview Center
Middletown, CT 06457

CHR: *Catholic Historical Review*
Quarterly ISSN 0008-8080
Business Officer
Catholic University of America
Leahy Hall, Room 240
620 Michigan Ave. N.E.
Washington, DC 20064

Ch Rev Int: *China Review International*
Semiannual ISSN 1069-5834
University of Hawai'i Press
2840 Kolowalu St.
Honolulu, HI 96822

ChrPhil: *Chronicle of Philanthropy*
Bi-Weekly ISSN 1040-676X
P.O. Box 1989
Marion, OH 43305

Ch Today: *Christianity Today*
14 issues/year ISSN 0009-5753
P.O. Box 11618
Des Moines, IA 50340-1618

Civil Lib: *Civil Liberties: The National Newsletter of the ACLU*
Quarterly ISSN 0009-790X
American Civil Liberties Union
132 W. 43rd St.
New York, NY 10036

CJ: *Classical Journal*
4 issues/year ISSN 0009-8353
Classical Association of the Middle West and South
c/o Dr. Gregory N. Daugherty
Dept of Classics, Randolph Macon College
P.O. Box 5005
Ashland, VA 23005-5505

CJR: *Columbia Journalism Review*
Bimonthly ISSN 0010-194X
P.O. Box 578
Mt. Morris, IL 61054

Class Out: *Classical Outlook*
Quarterly ISSN 0009-8361
Business Manager
American Classical League
Miami University
Oxford, OH 45056

Class R: *Classical Review*
Semiannual ISSN 0009-840X
Journals Subscriptions Dept.
Oxford University Press
Great Clarendon Street
Oxford OX2 6DP, England

Clio: *Clio: A Journal of Literature, History and the Philosophy of History*
Quarterly ISSN 0884-2043
Indiana University-Purdue University at Fort Wayne
Fort Wayne, IN 46805

CLR: *Columbia Law Review*
8/year ISSN 0010-1958
435 W. 116th St.
New York, NY 10027

CLS: *Comparative Literature Studies*
Quarterly ISSN 0010-4132
Penn State University Press
Suite C, University Support Building 1
820 N. University Dr.
University Park, PA 16802

CLW: *Catholic Library World*
Bimonthly ISSN 0008-820X
Catholic Library Association
5005 Jamieson Ave.
St. Louis, MO 63109

CML: *Classical and Modern Literature*
Quarterly ISSN 0197-2227
CML, Inc.
P.O. Box 629
Terre Haute, IN 47808-0629

Cng: *Change*
Bimonthly ISSN 0009-1383
Heldref Publications
1319 Eighteenth St. N.W.
Washington, DC 20036-1802

Coin W: *Coin World*
Weekly ISSN 0010-0447
P.O. Box 4315
Sidney, OH 45365-9943

Col Comp: *College Composition and Communication*
Quarterly ISSN 0010-096X
National Council of Teachers of English
1111 W. Kenyon Rd.
Urbana, IL 61801-1096

Col Lit: *College Literature*
3 issues/year ISSN 0093-3139
Editor, College Literature
210-211 Philips Hall
West Chester University
West Chester, PA 19383

Comp Dr: *Comparative Drama*
Quarterly ISSN 0010-4078
Western Michigan University
Kalamazoo, MI 49008-3801

Comp L: *Comparative Literature*
Quarterly ISSN 0010-4124
Dept. of Romance Languages
1233 University of Oregon
Eugene, OR 97403-1233

Compt & H: *Computers and the Humanities*
Bimonthly ISSN 0010-4817
P.O. Box 358
Accord Station
Hingham, MA 02018-0358

Comt: *Commentary*
Monthly ISSN 0010-2601
165 E. 56th St.
New York, NY 10022

Comw: *Commonweal*
Biweekly ISSN 0010-3330
Commonweal Foundation
15 Dutch St.
New York, NY 10038

Cons: *Conscience*
Quarterly ISSN 0740-6835
Catholics for a Free Choice
1436 U St. NW
Washington, DC 20009-3997

Cont Ed: *Contemporary Education*
Quarterly ISSN 0010-7476
School of Education
Indiana State University
Terre Haute, IN 47809

Cont Pac: *Contemporary Pacific*
Semiannual ISSN 1043-898X
University of Hawai'i Press
Journals Dept.
2840 Kolowalu St.
Honolulu, HI 96822-1888

CP: *Contemporary Psychology*
Monthly ISSN 0010-7549
750 First St. NE
Washington, DC 20002-4242

CPR: *Canadian Philosophical Reviews*
Bimonthly ISSN 0228-491X
Academic Printing & Publishing
P.O. Box 4218
Edmonton, AB, Canada T6E 4T2

CQ: *Carolina Quarterly*
3 issues/year ISSN 0008-6797
Greenlaw Hall CB #3520
University of North Carolina
Chapel Hill, NC 27599-3520

CR: *Contemporary Review*
Monthly ISSN 0010-7565
Mercury Airfreight International Ltd., Inc.
2323 Randolph Ave.
Avenel, NJ 07001

Cres: *Cresset*
9 issues/year ISSN 0011-1198
Valparaiso University
#10 Huegli Hall
Valparaiso, IN 46383

Crim J & B: *Criminal Justice and Behavior*
Quarterly ISSN 0093-8548
2455 Teller Road
Thousand Oaks, CA 91320

Critiq: *Critique*
Quarterly ISSN 0011-1619
Heldref Publications
1319 Eighteenth St., N. W.
Washington, DC 20036-1802

Critm: *Criticism*
Quarterly ISSN 0011-1589
Wayne State University Press
Leonard N. Simons Bldg.
4809 Woodward Ave.
Detroit, MI 48201-1309

Crit Q: *Critical Quarterly*
Quarterly ISSN 0011-1562
Journals Marketing Manager
Blackwell Publishers
350 Main Street
Malden, MA 02148

Crit R: *Critical Review*
Quarterly ISSN 0891-3811
Business Office
P.O. Box 1254
Dept. 129
Danbury, CT 06813

CRL: *College & Research Libraries*
Bimonthly ISSN 0010-0870
Subscription Dept.
c/o Choice Magazine
100 Riverview Center
Middletown, CT 06457-3445

CS: *Contemporary Sociology*
Bimonthly ISSN 0094-3061
American Sociological Association
1722 N St. N.W.
Washington, DC 20036

CSM: *Christian Science Monitor*
Daily ISSN 0882-7729
P.O. Box 11202
Des Moines, IA 50340-1202

C&U: *College and University*
3/yr ISSN 0010-0889
AACRAO
1 Dupont Circle N.W. Suite 330
Washington, DC 20036-1171

Cu H: *Current History*
9 issues/year ISSN 0011-3530
4225 Main St.
Philadelphia, PA 19127

Cur R: *Curriculum Review*
9 issues/year ISSN 0147-2453
Lawrence Ragan Communications, Inc.
212 W. Superior St.
Suite 200
Chicago, IL 60610

CW: *Classical World*
Bimonthly ISSN 0009-8418
Classical Assn. of the Atlantic States
Dept. of Classics
Duquesne University
Pittsburgh, PA 15282-1704

D

Dal R: *Dalhousie Review*
Quarterly ISSN 0011-5827
Office Manager
Dalhousie University
Halifax, NS, Canada B3H 3J5

Dance: *Dance Magazine*
Monthly ISSN 0011-6009
P.O. Box 50470
Cicero, IL 60804-9901

Dance RJ: *Dance Research Journal*
Semiannual ISSN 0149-7677
CORD
Dept. of Dance, SUNY
College at Brockport
Brockport, NY 14420

Dbt: *Downbeat*
Monthly ISSN 0012-5768
P.O. Box 906
Elmhurst, IL 60126-0906

Dialogue: *Dialogue: Canadian Philosophical Review*
Quarterly ISSN 0012-2173
Wilfrid Laurier University Press
Waterloo, ON, Canada N2L 3C5

Dis: *Dissent*
Quarterly ISSN 0012-3846
Foundation for the Study of Independent Social Ideas, Inc.
521 5th Ave., Ste. 1700
New York, NY 10017

Dog Fan: *Dog Fancy*
Monthly ISSN 0892-6522
P.O. Box 53264
Boulder, CO 80328-3264

DOMES: *Digest of Middle East Studies*
Quarterly ISSN 1060-4367
Editor, DOMES
School of Library and Information Science
University of Wisconsin-Milwaukee
Box 413
Milwaukee, WI 53201

E

ECEJ: *Early Childhood Education Journal*
Quarterly ISSN 1082-3301
Subscription Dept.
Human Sciences Press, Inc.
233 Spring Street
New York, NY 10013-1578

ECOL: *Ecology*
8 times/year ISSN 0012-9658
Business Manager
Ecological Society of America
Arizona State University
Box 873211
Tempe, AZ 85287-3211

Econ: *Economist*
Weekly ISSN 0013-0613
P.O. Box 58524
Boulder, CO 80322-8524

Econ J: *Economic Journal*
Bimonthly ISSN 0013-0133
Mercury Airfreight International Ltd. Inc.
2323 E-F Randolph Ave.
Avenel, NJ 07001

Ed F: *Educational Forum*
Quarterly ISSN 0013-1725
Post Office Box A
West Lafayette, IN 47906-0576

Ed Theory: *Educational Theory*
Quarterly ISSN 0013-2004
Education Building
University of Illinois at Urbana-Champaign
1310 South Sixth Street
Champaign, IL 61820

EG: *Economic Geography*
Quarterly ISSN 0013-0095
Clark University
950 Main St.
Worcester, MA 01610

EGH: *Everton's Genealogical Helper*
Bimonthly ISSN 0016-6359
Everton Publishers, Inc.
P.O. Box 368
Logan, UT 84323-0368

EHR: *English Historical Review*
5/yr ISSN 0013-8266
c/o Mercury Airfreight International, Ltd.
2323 Randolph Ave.
Avenel, NJ 07001

Eight-C St: *Eighteenth-Century Studies*
Quarterly ISSN 0013-2586
Journals Div.
Johns Hopkins University Press
2715 N. Charles St.
Baltimore, MD 21218-4319

EJ: *English Journal*
8 issues/year ISSN 0013-8274
NCTE
1111 W. Kenyon Road
Urbana, IL 61801-1096

EL: *Educational Leadership*
8 issues/year ISSN 0013-1784
Membership Dept.
1250 N. Pitt St.
Alexandria, VA 22314-1453

ELT: *English Literature in Transition 1880-1920*
Quarterly ISSN 0013-8339
Dept. of English
University of North Carolina at Greensboro
Greensboro, NC 27412-5001

E Mag: *E Magazine*
Bimonthly ISSN 1046-8021
Subscription Dept.
P.O. Box 2047
Marion, OH 43306

Emerg Lib: *Emergency Librarian*
5 issues/year ISSN 0315-8888
Transborder Mail
Box 6016
Federal Way, WA 98063-6016

Emmy: *Emmy*
Bimonthly ISSN 0164-3495
5220 Lankershim Blvd.
North Hollywood, CA 91601-3109

En Jnl: *Energy Journal*
Quarterly ISSN 0195-6574
International Assn. for Energy Economics
The Energy Journal Subscription Dept.
28790 Chagrin Blvd., Ste. 210
Cleveland, OH 44122

Ent W: *Entertainment Weekly*
Weekly ISSN 1049-0434
P.O. Box 30608
Tampa, FL 33630-0608

Env: *Environment*
10 issues/year ISSN 0013-9157
Heldref Publications
1319 Eighteenth St., N.W.
Washington, DC 20036-1802

Equal Opp: *Equal Opportunity*
3/year ISSN 0071-1039
Circulation Dept.
Equal Opportunity Publications, Inc.
150 Motor Pky., Ste. 420
Hauppauge, NY 11788-5145

ER: *Ecumenical Review*
Quarterly ISSN 0013-0796
World Council of Churches
P.O. Box 9907
Church St. Station
New York, NY 10249

ES: *Educational Studies (American Educational Studies Assn.)*
Quarterly ISSN 0013-1946
Dept. of Educational Foundations and Curriculum
LB 8144
Georgia Southern University
Statesboro, GA 30460

Esq: *Esquire*
Monthly ISSN 0194-9535
P.O. Box 7146
Red Oak, IA 51591

Essays CW: *Essays On Canadian Writing*
3 issues/year ISSN 0313-0300
2120 Queen St. East, Ste. 200
Toronto, ON, Canada M4E 1E2

Essence: *Essence*
Monthly ISSN 0014-0880
P.O. Box 53400
Boulder, CO 80322-3400

Ethics: *Ethics*
Quarterly ISSN 0014-1704
University of Chicago Press
Journals Division
P.O. Box 37005
Chicago, IL 60637

Ex Child: *Exceptional Children*
6/yr. ISSN 0014-4029
1920 Association Dr.
Reston, VA 20191-1589

Ext: *Extrapolation*
Quarterly ISSN 0014-5483
Journals Dept.
Kent State University Press
Kent, OH 44242

F

Fam in Soc: *Families in Society*
Monthly ISSN 1044-3894
Subscription Dept.
11700 W. Lake Park Dr.
Milwaukee, WI 53224-3099

Fam Relat: *Family Relations*
Quarterly ISSN 0197-6664
National Council on Family Relations
3989 Central Ave. NE, Suite 550
Minneapolis, MN 55421

FC: *Film Comment*
Bimonthly ISSN 0015-119X
P.O. Box 3000
Denville, NJ 07834-9925

Fed Prob: *Federal Probation*
Quarterly ISSN 0014-9128
Administrative Office of the U.S. Courts
Washington, DC 20544

FEER: *Far Eastern Economic Review*
Weekly ISSN 0014-7591
c/o YellowStone International Corp.
2375 Pratt Blvd.
Elk Grove Village, IL 60007-5937

FF: *Fanfare*
Bimonthly ISSN 0148-9364
P.O. Box 720
Tenafly, NJ 07670

FHB: *Fine Homebuilding*
Bimonthly ISSN 0273-1398
The Taunton Press, Inc.
63 S. Main St.
P.O. Box 5506
Newtown, CT 06470-5506

Fic Int: *Fiction International*
Semiannual ISSN 0092-1912
San Diego State University Press
San Diego State University
San Diego, CA 92182

Film Cr: *Film Criticism*
3 issues/year ISSN 0163-5069
Allegheny College
Meadville, PA 16335

Fine Gard: *Fine Gardening*
Bimonthly ISSN 0896-6281
The Taunton Press, Inc.
63 S. Main St.
P.O. Box 5506
Newtown, CT 06470-5506

FIR: *Films in Review*
Bimonthly ISSN 0015-1688
P.O. Box 970
Wantagh, NY 11793

Five Owls: *Five Owls*
5 issues/year ISSN 0892-6735
Hamline Univ. Crossroads Ctr. MS-C1924
1536 Hewitt Ave.
St. Paul, MN 55104

Fly: *Flying*
Monthly ISSN 0015-4806
P.O. Box 53647
Boulder, CO 80322

Folkl: *Folklore*
Annual ISSN 0015-587X
University College London
Gower Street
London WC1E 6BT, England

For Aff: *Foreign Affairs*
6 issues/year ISSN 0015-7120
P.O. Box 420235
Palm Coast, FL 32142-0235

Fortune: *Fortune*
Biweekly ISSN 0015-8259
P.O. Box 30604
Tampa, FL 33630-0604

FQ: *Film Quarterly*
Quarterly ISSN 0015-1386
University of California Press
Journals Dept.
2120 Berkeley Way
Berkeley, CA 94720

FR: *French Review*
Bimonthly ISSN 0016-111X
57 E. Armory Ave.
Champaign, IL 61820

FSM: *Finescale Modeler*
9/yr. ISSN 0277-979X
Kalmbach Publishing Co.
21027 Crossroads Circle
P.O. Box 1612
Waukesha, WI 53187-1612

Fut: *Futurist*
Bimonthly ISSN 0016-3317
7910 Woodmont Ave., Ste. 450
Bethesda, MD 20814

G

Games: *Games*
Bimonthly ISSN 0199-9788
P.O. Box 469077
Escondido, CA 92046-9077

Ga R: *Georgia Review*
Quarterly ISSN 0016-8386
University of Georgia
Athens, GA 30602-9009

Garbage: *Garbage: The Independent Environmental Quarterly*
Quarterly ISSN 1044-3061
P.O. Box 56519
Boulder, CO 80322

Generation: *Generations*
Quarterly ISSN 0738-7806
American Society on Aging
833 Market St., Ste. 511
San Francisco, CA 94103-1824

Geog: *Geographical*
Monthly ISSN 0016-741X
c/o Mercury Airfreight International
2323 Randolph Ave.
Avenel, NJ 07001

Ger Q: *German Quarterly*
Quarterly ISSN 0016-8831
American Association of Teachers of German
112 Haddontowne Court, #104
Cherry Hill, NJ 08034-3662

GJ: *Geographical Journal*
3 issues/year ISSN 0016-7398
Royal Geographical Society
1 Kensington Gore
London SW7 2AR, England

GW: *Guardian Weekly*
Weekly ISSN 0025-200X
19 West 44th St.
Suite 1613
New York, NY 10036-6101

H

HAHR: *Hispanic American Historical Review*
Quarterly ISSN 0018-2168
Duke University Press
Box 90660
Durham, NC 27708-0660

Har Bus R: *Harvard Business Review*
Bimonthly ISSN 0017-8012
Subscription Service
P.O. Box 52623
Boulder, CO 80328-2623

Hast Cen R: *Hastings Center Report*
Bimonthly ISSN 0093-0334
The Hastings Center
255 Elm Road
Briarcliff Manor, NY 10510

HB: *Horn Book Magazine*
Bimonthly ISSN 0018-5078
Circulation Dept.
11 Beacon St., Ste. 1000
Boston, MA 02108

HB Guide: *Horn Book Guide*
Semiannual ISSN 1044-405X
The Horn Book, Inc.
Circulation Dept.
11 Beacon St., Ste. 1000
Boston, MA 02108

HE: *Human Events*
Weekly ISSN 0018-7194
Subscription Services Dept.
7811 Montrose Rd.
Potomac, MD 20854

HeartsongR: *Heartsong Review*
Semiannual ISSN 0889-5252
P.O. Box 5716
Eugene, OR 97405

Heaven B: *Heaven Bone*
Semiannual ISSN 1042-5381
P.O. Box 486
Chester, NY 10918

HER: *Harvard Educational Review*
Quarterly ISSN 0017-8055
Gutman Library, Ste. 349
6 Appian Way
Cambridge, MA 02138-3752

HG&LRev: *Harvard Gay & Lesbian Review*
Quarterly ISSN 1077-6591
P.O. Box 180300
Boston, MA 02118

HIR: *Harvard International Review*
Quarterly ISSN 0739-1854
Subscription Services Dept.
P.O. Box 3000
Denville, NJ 07834-9452

Hisp: *Hispania*
Quarterly ISSN 0018-2133
AATSP
Frasier Hall - Room 8
University of Northern Colorado
Greeley, CO 80639

Hispanic: *Hispanic*
Monthly ISSN 0898-3097
98 San Jacinto Blvd., Ste. 1150
Austin, TX 78701

Historian: *Historian*
Quarterly ISSN 0018-2370
Phi Alpha Theta
50 College Drive
Allentown, PA 18104

Hist & T: *History and Theory*
Quarterly ISSN 0018-2656
Blackwell Publishers
Subscriber Services Coordinator
350 Main St.
Malden, MA 02148

HJAS: *Harvard Journal of Asiatic Studies*
Semiannual ISSN 0073-0548
2 Divinity Ave.
Cambridge, MA 02138

HLR: *Harvard Law Review*
8 issues/year ISSN 0017-811X
Gannett House
1511 Massachusetts Ave.
Cambridge, MA 02138

HM: *Harper's Magazine*
Monthly ISSN 0017-789X
P.O. Box 7511
Red Oak, IA 51591-0511

HMR: *Hungry Mind Review*
Quarterly ISSN 0887-5499
1648 Grand Ave.
St. Paul, MN 55105

Horoscope: *Horoscope*
Monthly ISSN 0018-5116
P.O. Box 54625
Boulder, CO 80328-4625

Hort: *Horticulture*
10 issues/year ISSN 0018-5329
Subscription Service
P.O. Box 53880
Boulder, CO 80322

HR: *Hudson Review*
Quarterly ISSN 0018-702X
684 Park Ave.
New York, NY 10021

HR Mag: *HR Magazine*
Monthly ISSN 1047-3149
Circulation Dept.
606 N. Washington St.
Alexandria, VA 22314

HRNB: *History: Reviews of New Books*
Quarterly ISSN 0361-2759
Heldref Publications
1319 Eighteenth St. N.W.
Washington, DC 20036-1802

H Sch M: *High School Magazine*
4/yr ISSN 1070-9533
NASSP
1904 Association Dr.
Reston, VA 20191-1537

HT: *History Today*
Monthly ISSN 0018-2753
M.A.I. Ltd.
2323 Randolph Ave.
Avenel, NJ 07001

Hum: *Humanist*
Bimonthly ISSN 0018-7399
7 Harwood Dr.
P.O. Box 1188
Amherst, NY 14226-7188

Humor: *Humor*
Quarterly ISSN 0933-1719
Mercury Airfreight International, Ltd.
Inc.
2323 Randolph Ave.
Avenel, NJ 07001

I

IEEE Exp: *IEEE Expert: Intelligent Systems and Their Applications*
Bimonthly ISSN 0885-9000
10662 Los Vaqueros Circle
P.O. Box 3014
Los Alamitos, CA 90720

ILN: *Illustrated London News*
6 issues/year ISSN 0019-2422
Orient-Express Magazine
c/o Mercury Airfreight International, Ltd.
2323 Randolph Ave.
Avenel, NJ 07001

ILR: *International Labour Review*
Bimonthly ISSN 0020-7780
ILO Publications
International Labour Office
CH-1211 Geneva 22, Switzerland

ILRR: *Industrial and Labor Relations Review*
Quarterly ISSN 0019-7939
201 ILR Research Bldg.
Cornell University
Ithaca, NY 14853-3901

ILS: *Irish Literary Supplement*
Semiannual ISSN 0733-3390
Irish Studies
114 Paula Blvd.
Selden, NY 11784

Inc.: *Inc.*
Monthly ISSN 0162-8968
P.O. Box 54129
Boulder, CO 80322-4129

Indexer: *Indexer*
Semiannual ISSN 0019-4131
Bournham
Burington Green
Tenbury Wells
Worcestershire WR15 8TQ, England

IndRev: *Independent Review: A Journal of Political Economy*
Quarterly ISSN 1086-1653
The Independent Institute
134 Ninety-Eighth Ave.
Oakland, CA 94603-1004

Info Out: *Information Outlook*
Monthly ISSN 1091-0808
Special Libraries Assn.
1700 Eighteenth St., NW
Washington, DC 20009-2514

Inst: *Instructor*
8 issues/year ISSN 1049-5851
P.O. Box 53896
Boulder, CO 80322-3896

Intpr: *Interpretation: A Journal of Bible and Theology*
Quarterly ISSN 0020-9643
3401 Brook Rd.
Richmond, VA 23227

IPQ: *International Philosophical Quarterly*
Quarterly ISSN 0019-0365
Canisius Hall
Fordham University
Bronx, NY 10458

IRLA: *Information Retrieval & Library Automation*
Monthly ISSN 0020-0220
P.O. Box 88
Mt. Airy, MD 21771

Isis: *Isis*
Quarterly ISSN 0021-1753
University of Chicago Press
Journals Division
P.O. Box 37005
Chicago, IL 60637

J

JAAC: *Journal of Aesthetics and Art Criticism*
Quarterly ISSN 0021-8529
Journal Division
University of Wisconsin Press
114 N. Murray St.
Madison, WI 53715

JAAL: *Journal of Adolescent & Adult Literacy*
8 issues/year ISSN 1081-3004
International Reading Association
P.O. Box 8139
Newark, DE 19714-8139

JAAR: *Journal of the American Academy of Religion*
Quarterly ISSN 0002-7189
P.O. Box 15399
Atlanta, GA 30333-0399

J Account: *Journal of Accountancy*
Monthly ISSN 0021-8448
Fulfillment Manager
Harborside Financial Center
201 Plaza III
Jersey City, NJ 07311-3881

J Aes Ed: *Journal of Aesthetic Education*
Quarterly ISSN 0021-8510
University of Illinois Press
1325 S. Oak St.
Champaign, IL 61820

JAF: *Journal of American Folklore*
Quarterly ISSN 0021-8715
American Folklore Society
4350 North Fairfax Drive, Ste. 640
Arlington, VA 20035

JAH: *Journal of American History*
Quarterly ISSN 0021-8723
Business Office]
Organization of American Historians
112 North Bryan St.
Bloomington, IN 47408-4199

JAL: *Journal of Academic Librarianship*
Bimonthly ISSN 0099-1333
JAI Press
55 Old Post Rd., No. 2
P.O. Box 1678
Greenwich, CT 06836-1678

J Am Cult: *Journal of American Culture*
Quarterly ISSN 0191-1813
American Culture Association
Bowling Green State University
Bowling Green, OH 43403

JAML: *Journal of Arts Management, Law & Society*
Quarterly ISSN 1063-2921
Heldref Publications
1319 Eighteenth St. N.W.
Washington, DC 20036-1802

J Am St: *Journal of American Studies*
3 issues/year ISSN 0021-8758
Cambridge University Press
Journals Dept.
40 W. 20th St.
New York, NY 10011-4211

JAS: *Journal of Asian Studies*
Quarterly ISSN 0021-9118
Association for Asian Studies
1 Lane Hall
University of Michigan
Ann Arbor, MI 48109

JB: *Junior Bookshelf*
Bimonthly ISSN 0022-6505
Marsh Hall
Thurstonland
Huddersfield HD4 6XB, England

JBL: *Journal of Biblical Literature*
Quarterly ISSN 0021-9231
SBL Membership Services
Scholars Press
P.O. Box 15399
Atlanta, GA 30333-0399

J Bl St: *Journal of Black Studies*
Bimonthly ISSN 0021-9347
Sage Publications, Inc.
2455 Teller Rd.
Thousand Oaks, CA 91320

J Broadcst: *Journal of Broadcasting and Electronic Media*
Quarterly ISSN 0883-8151
Broadcast Education Association
1771 N Street, NW
Washington, DC 20036-2891

JC: *Journal of Communication*
Quarterly ISSN 0021-9916
Journals Dept.
Oxford University Press
2001 Evans Rd.
Cary, NC 27513

J Car P&E: *Journal of Career Planning and Employment*
Quarterly ISSN 0884-5352
National Assn. of Colleges and Employers
62 Highland Ave.
Bethlehem, PA 18017

J Chem Ed: *Journal of Chemical Education*
Monthly ISSN 0021-9584
Subscription Dept.
P.O. Box 606
Vineland, NJ 08360

J Ch St: *Journal of Church and State*
Quarterly ISSN 0021-969X
P.O. Box 97308
Waco, TX 76798-7308

J ClinPsyc: *Journal of Clinical Psychiatry*
Monthly ISSN 0160-6689
Circulartion Dept.
Physicians Postgraduate Press, Inc.
P.O. Box 752870
Memphis, TN 38175-2870

J Con A: *Journal of Consumer Affairs*
Semiannual ISSN 0022-0078
American Council on Consumer Interests
240 Stanley Hall
University of Missouri
Columbia, MO 65211

JE: *Journal of Education*
3 issues/year ISSN 0022-0574
Boston University School of Education
605 Commonwealth Ave.
Boston, MA 02215

JEGP: *Journal of English and Germanic Philology*
Quarterly ISSN 0363-6941
University of Illinois Press
1325 S. Oak St.
Champaign, IL 61820

JEH: *Journal of Economic History*
Quarterly ISSN 0022-0507
Cambridge University Press
110 Midland Ave.
Port Chester, NY 10573-9864

JEL: *Journal of Economic Literature*
Quarterly ISSN 0022-0515
2014 Broadway, Ste. 305
Nashville, TN 37203

J Film & Vid: *Journal of Film & Video*
Quarterly ISSN 0724-4671
Dept. of Communication
Georgia State University
University Plaza
Atlanta, GA 30303-3080

J Gov Info: *Journal of Government Information*
Quarterly ISSN 1352-0237
Elsevier Science, Customer Support Dept.
P.O. Box 945
New York, NY 10010

JHI: *Journal of the History of Ideas*
Quarterly ISSN 0022-5037
Johns Hopkins University Press
Journals Publishing Division
2715 N. Charles St.
Baltimore, MD 21218-4319

J Hi E: *Journal of Higher Education*
Bimonthly ISSN 0022-1546
Ohio State University Press
1070 Carmack Rd.
Columbus, OH 43210-1002

J Hist G: *Journal of Historical Geography*
Quarterly ISSN 0305-7488
Publications Expediting Inc.
200 Meacham Ave.
Elmont, NY 11003

J Homosex: *Journal of Homosexuality*
Quarterly ISSN 0091-8369
Subscription Dept.
The Haworth Press, Inc.
10 Alice St.
Binghamton, NY 13904-1580

JIB: *Journal of International Business Studies*
Quarterly
Editorial Coordinator, JIBS
Richard Ivey School of Business
University of Western Ontario
London, ON, Canada N6A 3K7

JIH: *Journal of Interdisciplinary History*
Quarterly ISSN 0022-1953
MIT Press Journals
55 Hayward St.
Cambridge, MA 02142

JM: *Journal of Marketing*
Quarterly ISSN 0022-2429
American Marketing Association
250 S. Wacker Dr., Suite 200
Chicago, IL 60606-5819

JMCQ: *Journalism & Mass Communication Quarterly*
Quarterly ISSN 1077-6990
Association for Education in Journalism & Mass Communication
USC, LeConte College
Room 121
Columbia, SC 29208-0251

JMF: *Journal of Marriage and the Family*
Quarterly ISSN 0022-2445
National Council on Family Relations
3989 Central Ave. NE Suite 550
Minneapolis, MN 55421

JMH: *Journal of Modern History*
Quarterly ISSN 0022-2801
University of Chicago Press
P.O. Box 37005
Chicago, IL 60637

J Mil H: *Journal of Military History*
Quarterly ISSN 0899-3718
George C. Marshall Library
Virginia Military Institute
Lexington, VA 24450-1600

JMSW: *Journal of Multicultural Social Work*
Quarterly ISSN 1042-8224
Subscription Dept.
The Haworth Press, Inc.
10 Alice St.
Binghamton, NY 13904-1580

JNE: *Journal of Negro Education*
Quarterly ISSN 0022-2984
Circulation Dept.
P.O. Box 311
Howard University
Washington, DC 20059

JOYS: *Journal of Youth Services in Libraries*
Quarterly ISSN 0894-2498
American Library Association
Subscription Dept.
50 E. Huron St.
Chicago, IL 60611

JP: *Journal of Parapsychology*
Quarterly ISSN 0022-3387
402 N. Buchanan Blvd.
Durham, NC 27701-1728

JPC: *Journal of Popular Culture*
Quarterly ISSN 0022-3840
Popular Press
Bowling Green State University
Bowling Green, OH 43403

JPE: *Journal of Political Economy*
Bimonthly ISSN 0022-3808
University of Chicago Press
5720 S. Woodlawn Ave.
Chicago, IL 60637

J Phil: *Journal of Philosophy*
Monthly ISSN 0022-362X
1150 Amsterdam Ave., MC 4971
Columbia University
New York, NY 10027

J Pol: *Journal of Politics*
Quarterly ISSN 0022-3816
Journals Division
University of Texas Press
P.O. Box 7819
Austin, TX 78713-7819

J Pop F&TV: *Journal of Popular Film and Television*
Quarterly ISSN 0195-6051
Heldref Publications
1319 Eighteenth St., N.W.
Washington, DC 20036-1802

JPR: *Journal of Peace Research*
Quarterly ISSN 0022-3433
c/o Mercury Airfreight International Ltd., Inc.
2323 Randolph Ave.
Avenel, NJ 07001

JR: *Journal of Religion*
Quarterly ISSN 0022-4189
University of Chicago Press
Journals Division
P.O. Box 37005
Chicago, IL 60637

J Rehab RD: *Journal of Rehabilitation Research and Development*
Quarterly ISSN 0007-506X
Scientific and Technical Publications Section
103 S. Gay St.
Baltimore, MD 21202-4051

JSH: *Journal of Southern History*
Quarterly ISSN 0022-4642
Dept. of History
University of Georgia
Athens, GA 30602

J Soc H: *Journal of Social History*
Quarterly ISSN 0022-4529
Carnegie-Mellon University
Schenley Park
Pittsburgh, PA 15213

JSS: *Jewish Social Studies*
Quarterly ISSN 0021-6704
Indiana University Press
601 North Morton
Bloomington, IN 47404

J Teach Ed: *Journal of Teacher Education*
5 issues/year ISSN 0022-4871
Publications Dept., AACTE
1 Dupont Circle, Suite 610
Washington, DC 20036-1186

JTWS: *Journal of Third World Studies*
Bi-annual ISSN 8755-3449
Association of Third World Studies, Inc.
P.O. Box 1232
Americus, GA 31709

J Urban H: *Journal of Urban History*
6 issues/year ISSN 0096-1442
Sage Publications, Inc.
2455 Teller Rd.
Thousand Oaks, CA 91320

JWD: *Journal of Workforce Diversity*
Annual
Circulation Dept.
Equal Opportunity Publications, Inc.
150 Motor Pky., Ste. 420
Hauppauge, NY 11788-5145

JWomHist: *Journal of Women's History*
Quarterly ISSN 1042-7961
Indiana University Press
Journals Division
601 N. Morton St.
Bloomington, IN 47404-3797

K

Ken R: *Kenyon Review*
Quarterly ISSN 0163-075X
Kenyon College
Gambier, OH 43022

Kiplinger: *Kiplinger's Personal Finance Magazine*
Monthly ISSN 1056-697X
Dept. CA
Editors Park, MD 20782

Kliatt: *Kliatt Young Adult Paperback Book Guide*
6 issues/year ISSN 1065-8602
33 Bay State Road
Wellesley, MA 02181

KR: *Kirkus Reviews*
Semi-Monthly ISSN 0042-6598
200 Park Ave. S.
New York, NY 10003

L

LA: *Language Arts*
8 issues/year ISSN 0360-9170
NCTE
1111 W. Kenyon Rd.
Urbana, IL 61801-1096

LA Ant: *Latin American Antiquity*
Quarterly ISSN 1045-6635
Society for American Archaeology
900 Second St., N.E., Suite 12
Washington, DC 20002-3557

Lam Bk Rpt: *Lambda Book Report*
Bimonthly ISSN 1048-9487
Lambda Rising, Inc.
1625 Connecticut Avenue, NW
Washington, DC 20009-1013

Lang Soc: *Language in Society*
Quarterly ISSN 0047-4045
Journals Dept.
Cambridge University Press
110 Midland Ave.
Port Chester, NY 10573-4930

LAR: *Library Association Record*
Monthly ISSN 0024-2195
World Wide Subscription Service Ltd.
Unit 4 Gibbs Reed Farm
Ticehurst, East Sussex TN5 7HE, England

LATBR: *Los Angeles Times Book Review*
Weekly ISSN 0458-3035
Los Angeles Times, Inc.
Times Mirror Square
Los Angeles, CA 90053

Law Q Rev: *Law Quarterly Review*
Quarterly ISSN 0023-933X
Customer Service Department
Sweet & Maxwell Ltd.
North Way, Andover
Hants SP10 5BE, England

Learning: *Learning*
6 issues/year ISSN 0090-3167
P.O. Box 54293
Boulder, CO 80322-4293

Lect Y V: *Lectura Y Vida*
Quarterly ISSN 0325-8637
Asociacion Internacional de Lectura
P.O. Box 8139
Newark, DE 19714

Legacy: *Legacy: A Journal of American Women Writers*
Semiannually ISSN 0748-4321
Penn State Press
820 N. University Dr.
University Park, PA 16802

L'Esprit: *L'Esprit Createur*
Quarterly ISSN 0014-0767
Dept. of French
1015 Patterson Tower
University of Kentucky
Lexington, KY 40506

LHTN: *Library Hi Tech News*
10 issues/year ISSN 0741-9058
Pierian Press
P.O. Box 1808
Ann Arbor, MI 48106

Lib: *Library*
Quarterly ISSN 0024-2160
Dept. of History
DP 20
University of Washington
Seattle, WA 98195

Lib & Cul: *Libraries & Culture*
(Formerly Journal of Library History)
Quarterly ISSN 0894-8631
University of Texas Press
P.O. Box 7819
Austin, TX 78713-7819

LJ: *Library Journal*
20 issues/year ISSN 0363-0277
P.O. Box 59690
Boulder, CO 80322-9690

LMR: *Literary Magazine Review*
Quarterly ISSN 0732-6637
English Language and Literature
Un. of Northern Iowa
Cedar Falls, IA 50614-0502

Locus: *Locus*
Monthly ISSN 0047-4959
Locus Publications
P.O. Box 13305
Oakland, CA 94661

Lon R Bks: *London Review of Books*
24 issues/year ISSN 0260-9592
P.O. Box 1953
Marion, OH 43305-1953

LQ: *Library Quarterly*
Quarterly ISSN 0024-2519
University of Chicago Press
P.O. Box 37005
Chicago, IL 60637

LR: *Library Review*
Bimonthly ISSN 0024-2535
MCB University Press Limited
P.O. Box 10812
Birmingham, AL 35201-0812

LRTS: *Library Resources & Technical Services*
Quarterly ISSN 0024-2527
50 E. Huron St.
Chicago, IL 60611

LT: *Library Talk*
5 issues/year ISSN 1043-237X
Linworth Publishing
480 East Wilson Bridge Rd., Suite L
Worthington, OH 43085-2373

M

MA: *Modern Age*
Quarterly ISSN 0026-7457
ISI
P.O. Box 4431
Wilmington, DE 19807-0431

Mac: *Maclean's*
Weekly ISSN 0024-9262
P.O. Box 1600
Postal Station A
Toronto, ON, Canada M5W 2B8

Mag Antiq: *Magazine Antiques*
Monthly ISSN 0161-9284
P.O. Box 37009
Boone, IA 50037-0009

Mag Bl: *Magical Blend*
Quarterly ISSN 1040-4287
P.O. Box 600
Chico, CA 95927-0600

Magpies: *Magpies*
5 issues/year ISSN 0817-0088
Subscription
P.O. Box 563
Hamilton, Queensland 4007, Australia

Mar Crp G: *Marine Corps Gazette*
Monthly ISSN 0025-3170
Box 1775
Quantico, VA 22134

Math T: *Mathematics Teacher*
9 issues/year ISSN 0025-5769
1906 Association Dr.
Reston, VA 20191-1593

McCall Nee: *McCall's Needlework*
Bimonthly ISSN 1069-2894
P.O. Box 56634
Boulder, CO 80322

Meanjin: *Meanjin*
Quarterly ISSN 0025-6293
99 Barry Street
Carlton, Victoria 3053, Australia

Media M: *Media and Methods*
Bimonthly ISSN 0025-6897
1429 Walnut St.
Philadelphia, PA 19102

M Ed J: *Music Educators Journal*
6 issues/year ISSN 0027-4321
1806 Robert Fulton Drive
Reston, VA 20191-4348

MEJ: *Middle East Journal*
Quarterly ISSN 0026-3141
Circulation Dept.
Middle East Journal
1761 N Street NW
Washington, DC 20036-2882

Men's J: *Men's Journal*
10/year ISSN 1063-4657
P.O. Box 57055
Boulder, CO 80322-7055

MEP: *Middle East Policy*
Quarterly ISSN 1061-1924
Circulation Dept.
1730 M St. N.W., Suite 512
Washington, DC 20036

MEQ: *Middle East Quarterly*
Quarterly ISSN 1073-9467
AM & M
P.O. Box 1897
Lawrence, KS 66044-8897

Meridian: *Meridian*
Semiannual ISSN 1040-7421
Subscription Manager
Map Collection
University of Arizona Library
Tucson, AZ 85721

MFS: *Modern Fiction Studies*
Quarterly ISSN 0026-7724
Johns Hopkins University Press
Journals Division
2715 N. Charles St.
Baltimore, MD 21218

MFSF: *Magazine of Fantasy and Science
Fiction*
11 issues/year ISSN 0024-984X
143 Cream Hill Rd.
West Cornwall, CT 06796

MHR: *Medical Humanities Review*
Semiannual ISSN 0892-2772
Institute for the Medical Humanities
University of Texas Medical Branch
Galveston, TX 77555-1311

Mid-Am: *Mid-America: An Historical
Review*
3 issues/year ISSN 0026-2927
Loyola University of Chicago
6525 N. Sheridan Rd.
Chicago, IL 60626

Mil Rev: *Military Review*
Bimonthly ISSN 0026-4148
CGSC
Fort Leavenworth, KS 66027-1231

M Lab R: *Monthly Labor Review*
Monthly ISSN 0098-1818
Superintendent of Documents
Government Printing Office
Washington, DC 20402

MLJ: *Modern Language Journal*
Quarterly ISSN 0026-7902
University of Wisconsin Press
Journal Division
114 N. Murray St.
Madison, WI 53715

MLN: *MLN (Modern Language Notes)*
5 issues/year ISSN 0026-7910
Johns Hopkins University Press
Journals Publishing Division
2715 North Charles Street
Baltimore, MD 21218-4319

MLR: *Modern Language Review*
Quarterly ISSN 0026-7937
Modern Humanities Research
Association
King's College London, Strand
London WC2R 2LS, England

Model R: *Model Railroader*
Monthly ISSN 0026-7341
Kalmbach Publishing Co.
21027 Crossroads Circle
P.O. Box 1612
Waukesha, WI 53187

M of Hist: *Magazine of History*
Quarterly ISSN 0882-228X
Organization of American Historians
112 North Bryan St.
Bloomington, IN 47408-4199

Money: *Money*
13 issues/year ISSN 0149-4953
P.O. Box 60001
Tampa, FL 33660-0001

Moth Jones: *Mother Jones*
Bimonthly ISSN 0362-8841
P.O. Box 469024
Escondido, CA 92046-9024

MP: *Modern Philology*
Quarterly ISSN 0026-8232
University of Chicago Press
Journals Division
P.O. Box 37005
Chicago, IL 60637

MQ: *Musical Quarterly*
Quarterly ISSN 0027-4631
Oxford University Press
Journals Fulfillment Dept.
2001 Evans Rd.
Cary, NC 27513

MQR: *Michigan Quarterly Review*
Quarterly ISSN 0026-2420
3032 Rackham Bldg.
915 E. Washington St.
Ann Arbor, MI 48109-1070

MR: *Minnesota Review*
Semiannual ISSN 0026-5667
Dept. of English
East Carolina University
Greenville, NC 27858-4353

Ms: *Ms.*
Bimonthly ISSN 0047-8318
P.O. Box 5299
Harlan, IA 51593

MultiCul R: *MultiCultural Review*
Quarterly ISSN 1058-9236
P.O. Box 5007
Westport, CT 06881-5007

N

Names: *Names*
Quarterly ISSN 0027-7738
Wayne H. Finke, Secretary-Treasurer
Dept. of Modern Languages
Baruch College
17 Lexington Ave.
New York, NY 10010

NAR: *North American Review*
Bimonthly ISSN 0029-2397
University of Northern Iowa
1222 W. 27th St.
Cedar Falls, IA 50614-0516

NASSP-B: *National Association of
Secondary School Principals. Bulletin*
9 issues/year ISSN 0192-6365
1904 Association Dr.
Reston, VA 20191-1537

Nat: *Nation*
Weekly ISSN 0027-8378
P.O. Box 37072
Boone, IA 50037

Nat For: *National Forum*
Quarterly ISSN 0162-1831
Honor Society of Phi Kappa Phi
Box 16000
Louisiana State University
Baton Rouge, LA 70893

Nat Peop: *Native Peoples*
Quarterly ISSN 0895-7606
P.O. Box 36820
Phoenix, AZ 85067-6820

Nat R: *National Review*
Biweekly ISSN 0028-0038
Circulation Dept.
P.O. Box 668
Mt. Morris, IL 61054-0668

Nature: *Nature*
Weekly ISSN 0028-0836
345 Park Ave. S.
New York, NY 10010-1707

NCR: *National Civic Review*
Quarterly ISSN 0027-9013
Jossey Bass
Subscription Manager
350 Sansome St.
San Francisco, CA 94104

Necro: *Necrofile*
Quarterly ISSN 1077-8187
Necronomicon Press
P.O. Box 1304
West Warwick, RI 02893

NEQ: *New England Quarterly*
Quarterly ISSN 0028-4866
Meserve Hall 239
Northeastern University
360 Huntington Ave.
Boston, MA 02115

New Ad: *New Advocate*
Quarterly ISSN 0895-1381
480 Washington Street
Norwood, MA 02062

New Age: *New Age Journal*
Bimonthly ISSN 0746-3618
P.O. Box 53275
Boulder, CO 80321-3275

New ER: *New England Review*
Quarterly ISSN 1053-1297
University Press of New England
23 South Main St..
Hanover, NH 03775-2048

New R: *New Republic*
Weekly ISSN 0028-6583
Subscription Service Dept.
P.O. Box 37298
Boone, IA 50037-0298

New Sci: *New Scientist*
Weekly ISSN 0262-4079
c/o M.A.I.L. America
2323 Randolph Ave.
Avenel, NJ 07001

New York: *New York Magazine*
Weekly ISSN 0028-7369
Subscription Dept.
Box 54661
Boulder, CO 80322-4661

NGSQ: *National Genealogical Society
Quarterly*
Quarterly ISSN 0027-934X
4527 17th St. N.
Arlington, VA 22207-2399

NH: *Natural History*
Monthly ISSN 0028-0712
P.O. Box 5000
Harlan, IA 51537-5000

Nine-C Lit: *Nineteenth-Century Literature*
Quarterly ISSN 0891-9356
Periodicals Dept.
University of California Press
2120 Berkeley Way
Berkeley, CA 94720

NL: *New Leader*
Biweekly ISSN 0028-6044
275 7th Ave.
New York, NY 10001

Notes: *Notes (Music Library Association)*
Quarterly ISSN 0027-4380
P.O. Box 487
Canton, MA 02021

NP: *National Parks*
Bimonthly ISSN 0276-8186
1776 Mass. Ave. N.W.
Washington, DC 20036

NRJ: *Natural Resources Journal*
Quarterly ISSN 0028-0739
School of Law
University of New Mexico
Albuquerque, NM 87131-1431

NS: *New Statesman*
Weekly ISSN 0954-2361
C & C Mailers International Inc.
900 Lincoln Boulevard
P.O. Box 177
Middlesex, NJ 08846

NW: *Newsweek*
Weekly ISSN 0028-9604
P.O. Box 59968
Boulder, CO 80328-9968

NWCR: *Naval War College Review*
Quarterly ISSN 0028-1484
Code 32S
Naval War College
686 Cushing Rd.
Newport, RI 02841-1207

NWSA Jnl: *NWSA Journal*
3/year ISSN 1040-0656
Journals Manager
Indiana University Press
601 N. Morton
Bloomington, IN 47404

NY: *New Yorker*
Weekly ISSN 0028-792X
Box 56447
Boulder, CO 80328-6447

NYRB: *New York Review of Books*
20 issues/year ISSN 0028-7504
Subscription Service Dept.
P.O. Box 420384
Palm Coast, FL 32142-0384

NYTBR: *New York Times Book Review*
Weekly ISSN 0028-7806
P.O. Box 3009
South Hackensack, NJ 07606-3009

NYTLa: *New York Times (Late Ed.)*
Daily ISSN 0362-4331
P.O. Box 3009
South Hackensack, NJ 07606-1009

O

Obs: *Observer (London)*
Weekly ISSN 0029-7712
Observer, Ltd.
Chelsea Bridge House,
Queenstown Rd.,
London SW8 4NN, England

ON: *Opera News*
17 issues/year ISSN 0030-3607
Circulation Dept.
70 Lincoln Center Plaza
New York, NY 10023-6593

OnIssues: *On the Issues*
Quarterly ISSN 0895-6014
The Progressive Women's Quarterly
P.O. Box 3000, Dept. OTI
Denville, NJ 07834

OOB: *Off Our Backs*
Monthly ISSN 0030-0071
2337-B 18th St. N.W.
Washington, DC 20009

OS: *Other Side*
Bimonthly ISSN 0145-7675
Subscription Dept.
The Other Side
Box 2007
Hagerstown, MD 21742

P

Pac A: *Pacific Affairs*
Quarterly ISSN 0030-851X
University of British Columbia
Vancouver, BC, Canada V6T 1Z2

Pac S: *Pacific Studies*
Quarterly ISSN 0275-3596
Institute for Polynesian Studies
Brigham Young University-Hawaii
Laie, HI 96762-1294

Par: *Parents Magazine*
Monthly ISSN 0195-0967
P.O. Box 3042
Harlan, IA 51537-0207

PAR: *Public Administration Review*
Bimonthly ISSN 0033-3352
1120 G St. N.W., Suite 700
Washington, DC 20005-3885

Parabola: *Parabola*
Quarterly ISSN 0362-1596
P.O. Box 3000
Denville, NJ 07834

Parameters: *Parameters: US Army War
College Quarterly*
Quarterly ISSN 0031-1723
U.S. Army War College
Carlisle Barracks
Carlisle, PA 17013-5050

Par Ch: *Parents' Choice*
Quarterly ISSN 0161-8164
Box 185
Waban, MA 02168

Parnassus: *Parnassus: Poetry in Review*
Semiannual ISSN 0048-3028
205 W. 89th St. #8F
New York, NY 10024

Per A J: *Performing Arts Journal*
3 issues/year ISSN 0735-8393
Johns Hopkins University Press
Journals Publishing Division
2715 N. Charles St.
Baltimore, MD 21218-4319

Per Psy: *Personnel Psychology*
Quarterly ISSN 0031-5826
745 Haskins Rd., Ste. A
Bowling Green, OH 43402

Pers PS: *Perspectives on Political Science*
Quarterly ISSN 1045-7097
Heldref Publications
1319 Eighteenth St.,N.W.
Washington, DC 20036-1802

Pet PM: *Petersen's Photographic
Magazine*
Monthly ISSN 0199-4913
Subscriber Services
P.O. Box 56495
Boulder, CO 80322-6495

Phil Lit R: *Philatelic Literature Review*
Quarterly ISSN 0270-1707
American Philatelic Research Library,
Inc.
P.O. Box 8000
State College, PA 16803

Phil R: *Philosophical Review*
Quarterly ISSN 0031-8108
Cornell University
327 Goldwin Smith Hall
Ithaca, NY 14853-3201

PHR: *Pacific Historical Review*
Quarterly ISSN 0030-8684
University of California Press
2120 Berkeley Way
Berkeley, CA 94720

Phys Today: *Physics Today*
Monthly ISSN 0031-9228
Subscription Fulfillment
c/o American Institute of Physics
500 Sunnyside Blvd.
Woodbury, NY 11797

PIR: *Philosophy in Review*
6/year ISSN 1206-5269
Academic Printing & Publishing
P.O. Box 4218
Edmonton, AB, Canada T6E 4T2

PMS: *Popular Music and Society*
Quarterly ISSN 0300-7766
Bowling Green State University Popular
Press
Bowling Green, OH 43403

Poet: *Poetry*
Monthly ISSN 0032-2032
60 W. Walton St.
Chicago, IL 60610

Poetics T: *Poetics Today*
Quarterly ISSN 0333-5372
Duke University Press
Box 90660
Durham, NC 27708-0660

Pol Res Q: *Political Research Quarterly*
Quarterly ISSN 1065-9129
252 Orson Spencer Hall
University of Utah
Salt Lake City, UT 84112

Pol Stud J: *Policy Studies Journal*
Quarterly ISSN 0190-292X
Policy Studies Organization
University of Illinois at Urbana-
Champaign
Urbana, IL 61801-3696

Post Script: *Post Script: Essays in Film
and the Humanities*
3 issues/year ISSN 0277-9897
Literature and Languages Dept.
Texas A & M University-Commerce
Commerce, TX 75429

PQ: *Philological Quarterly*
Quarterly ISSN 0031-7977
Publication Order Dept.
University of Iowa
100 Oakdale Campus M1050H
Iowa City, IA 52242-5000

P&R: *Parks & Recreation*
Monthly ISSN 0031-2215
National Recreation and Park
Association
2775 S. Quincy St.
Ste. 300
Arlington, VA 22206

PR: *Partisan Review*
Quarterly ISSN 0031-2525
236 Bay State Rd.
Boston, MA 02215

Pres SQ: *Presidential Studies Quarterly*
Quarterly ISSN 0360-4918
c/o Cesar Rossi
208 East 75th St.
New York, NY 10021

Prog: *Progressive*
Monthly ISSN 0033-0736
P.O. Box 421
Mount Morris, IL 61054-0421

Prog Arch: *Progressive Architecture*
Monthly ISSN 0033-0752
Reinhold Publishing
1100 Superior Ave.
Cleveland, OH 44114-2543

PS: *Prairie Schooner*
Quarterly ISSN 0032-6682
201 Andrews Hall
University of Nebraska
Lincoln, NE 68588-0334

PSM: *Physician and Sportsmedicine*
Monthly ISSN 0091-3847
Box 462
Hightstown, NJ 08520-9205

PSQ: *Political Science Quarterly*
Quarterly ISSN 0032-3195
475 Riverside Dr., Suite 1274
New York, NY 10115-1274

PSR: *Political Science Reviewer*
Annual ISSN 0091-3715
3901 Centerville Rd.
P.O. Box 4431
Wilmington, DE 19807-0431

PT: *Psychology Today*
Bi-monthly ISSN 0033-3107
P.O. Box 55046
Boulder, CO 80322-5046

Pub Hist: *Public Historian*
Quarterly ISSN 0272-3433
University of California Press
Berkeley, CA 94720

Pub Int: *Public Interest*
Quarterly ISSN 0033-3557
Subscription Office
Dept. PI,
P.O. Box 3000
Denville, NJ 07834

Pub Op Q: *Public Opinion Quarterly*
Quarterly ISSN 0033-362X
University of Chicago Press
P.O. Box 37005
Chicago, IL 60637

Pub Rel J: *Public Relations Journal*
Monthly ISSN 0033-3670
33 Irving Place
New York, NY 10003-2376

PW: *Publishers Weekly*
Weekly ISSN 0000-0019
P.O. Box 6457
Torrance, CA 90504

Q

QJS: *Quarterly Journal of Speech*
Quarterly ISSN 0033-5630
5105 Backlick Rd. #F
Annandale, VA 22003

QRB: *Quarterly Review of Biology*
Quarterly ISSN 0033-5770
P.O. Box 37005
University of Chicago Press
Journals Division
Chicago, IL 60637

Quad: *Quadrant*
Monthly ISSN 0033-5002
P.O. Box 1495
Collingwood, Victoria 3066, Australia

Queens Q: *Queen's Quarterly*
Quarterly ISSN 0033-6041
Queen's University
Kingston, ON, Canada K7L 3N6

Quill & Q: *Quill & Quire*
Monthly ISSN 0033-6491
Customer Service
35 Riviera Dr., Unit 17
Markham, ON, Canada L3R 8N4

R

RA: *Reviews in Anthropology*
Quarterly ISSN 0093-8157
International Publishers Distributor
820 Town Center Dr.
Langhorne, PA 19047

RAH: *Reviews in American History*
Quarterly ISSN 0048-7511
Journals Publishing Division
John Hopkins University Press
2715 North Charles Street
Baltimore, MD 21218-4319

Rapport: *Rapport: The Modern Guide to
Books, Music & More*
Bimonthly ISSN 1061-6861
Rapport Publishing Co., Inc.
5265 Fountain Ave.
Los Angeles, CA 90029

RCF: *Review of Contemporary Fiction*
3 issues/year ISSN 0276-0045
Campus Box 4241
Normal, IL 61790-4241

Readings: *Readings: A Journal of Reviews
and Commentary in Mental Health*
Quarterly ISSN 0886-3784
c/o 49 Sheridan Ave.
P.O. Box 1413
Albany, NY 12201-1413

Reason: *Reason*
11 issues/year ISSN 0048-6906
P.O. Box 526
Mount Morris, IL 61054

Ref Bk R: *Reference Book Review*
Semiannual ISSN 0272-1988
P.O. Box 190954
Dallas, TX 75219

Rel Ed: *Religious Education*
Quarterly ISSN 0034-4087
409 Prospect St.
New Haven, CT 06511-2177

Rel St: *Religious Studies*
Quarterly ISSN 0034-4125
Cambridge University Press
110 Midland Ave.
Port Chester, NY 10573-4930

Rel St Rev: *Religious Studies Review*
Quarterly ISSN 0319-485X
CSSR Executive Office
Valparaiso University
Valparaiso, IN 46383

Ren Q: *Renaissance Quarterly*
Quarterly ISSN 0034-4338
Renaissance Society of America, Inc.
24 West 12th Street
New York, NY 10011

Ren & Ref: *Renaissance and Reformation*
Quarterly ISSN 0034-429X
Dept. of French Studies
Univesity of Guelph
Guelph, ON, Canada N1G 2W1

RES: *Review of English Studies*
Quarterly ISSN 0034-6551
c/o M.A.I.L. America
2323 Randolph Ave.
Arenel, NJ 07001

Res & Exp: *Research and Exploration*
Quarterly ISSN 8755-724X
Research & Exploration Subscriptions
National Geographic Society
P.O. Box 2174
Washington, DC 20013-2174

RM: *Review of Metaphysics*
Quarterly ISSN 0034-6632
Catholic University of America
Washington, DC 20064

RMR: *Rocky Mountain Review of Language & Literature*
Biannually ISSN 0361-1299
Rocky Mountain Modern Language Association
English Dept.
Boise State University
Boise, ID 83725

RocksMiner: *Rocks & Minerals*
Bimonthly ISSN 0035-7529
Heldref Publications
1319 Eighteenth St., N.W.
Washington, DC 20036-1802

Roundup M: *Roundup Magazine*
Bimonthly
James Crutchfield
1012 Fair St.
Franklin, TN 37064-2718

RP: *Review of Politics*
Quarterly ISSN 0034-6705
University of Notre Dame
P.O. Box B
Notre Dame, IN 46556

Robotica: *Robotica*
Bi-Monthly ISSN 0263-5747
Cambridge University Press
110 Midland Avenue
Port Chester
New York, NY 10573-4930

RQ: *RQ*
Quarterly ISSN 0033-7072
S & S Computer Services, Inc.
434 W. Downer
Aurora, IL 60506

R&R Bk N: *Reference & Research Book News*
8 times/year ISSN 0887-3763
5739 NE Sumner St.
Portland, OR 97218

RR: *Review for Religious*
Bimonthly ISSN 0034-639X
P.O. Box 6070
Duluth, MN 55806

RSR: *Reference Services Review*
Quarterly ISSN 0090-7324
Pierian Press
P.O. Box 1808
Ann Arbor, MI 48106

RT: *Reading Teacher*
8 issues/year ISSN 0034-0561
International Reading Association
P.O. Box 8139
Newark, DE 19714-8139

Russ Rev: *Russian Review*
Quarterly ISSN 0036-0341
Ohio State University Press
1070 Carmack Road
Columbus, OH 43210-1002

S

SA: *Scientific American*
Monthly ISSN 0036-8733
P.O. Box 3187
Harlan, IA 51537

Sailing: *Sailing*
Monthly ISSN 0036-2719
P.O. Box 249
Port Washington, WI 53074

Salm: *Salmagundi*
Quarterly ISSN 0036-3529
Skidmore College
Saratoga Springs, NY 12866

SAQ: *South Atlantic Quarterly*
Quarterly ISSN 0038-2876
Duke University Press
Box 90660
Durham, NC 27708-0676

SB: *Science Books & Films*
9 issues/year ISSN 0098-342X
P.O. Box 3000, Dept. SBF
Denville, NJ 07834

Sch Arts: *School Arts*
9 issues/year ISSN 0036-6463
50 Portland St.
Worcester, MA 01608

Sch Lib: *School Librarian*
Quarterly ISSN 0036-6595
School Library Association
Liden Library, Barrington Close
Liden, Swindon SN3 6HF, England

Sci: *Science*
Weekly ISSN 0036-8075
P.O. Box 1811
Danbury, CT 06813-1811

SciTech: *SciTech Book News*
10 issues/year ISSN 0196-6006
Book News, Inc.
5739 NE Sumner St.
Portland, OR 97218

Sculpt R: *Sculpture Review*
Quarterly ISSN 0747-5284
1177 Avenue of the Americas
New York, NY 10036

SDA: *Studies in the Decorative Arts*
Semiannual ISSN 1069-8825
P.O. Box 3000
Denville, NJ 07834-3000

SE: *Social Education*
7 issues/year ISSN 0037-7724
3501 Newark St., N.W.
Washington, DC 20016-3167

Sea H: *Sea History*
Quarterly ISSN 0146-9312
5 John Walsh Blvd.
P.O. Box 68
Peekskill, NY 10566

SEP: *Saturday Evening Post*
Bimonthly ISSN 0048-9239
Subscription Offices
P.O. Box 420235
Palm Coast, FL 32142-0235

Ser R: *Serials Review*
Quarterly ISSN 0098-7913
Pierian Press
P.O. Box 1808
Ann Arbor, MI 48106

Sev Cent N: *Seventeenth-Century News*
Quarterly ISSN 0037-3028
Harrison T. Meserole
English Dept.
Texas A&M University
College Station, TX 77843-4227

Sew R: *Sewanee Review*
Quarterly ISSN 0037-3052
Sewanee, TN 37383-1000

SF: *Social Forces*
Quarterly ISSN 0037-7732
Subscriptions
University of North Carolina Press
P.O. Box 2288
Chapel Hill, NC 27515

SF Chr: *Science Fiction Chronicle*
Monthly ISSN 0195-5365
P.O. Box 22730
Brooklyn, NY 11202-0056

SFR: *San Francisco Review*
Bimonthly ISSN 0194-0724
877 Bryant St., Ste. 210
San Francisco, CA 94103

SFS: *Science-Fiction Studies*
3 issues/year ISSN 0091-7729
East College
DePauw University
Greencastle, IN 46135

Shakes Q: *Shakespeare Quarterly*
Quarterly ISSN 0037-3222
201 E. Capitol St. S.E.
Washington, DC 20003-1094

Shen: *Shenandoah*
Quarterly ISSN 0037-3583
Box 722
Lexington, VA 24450

SIAM Rev: *SIAM Review*
Quarterly ISSN 0036-1445
3600 University City Science Center
Philadelphia, PA 19104-2688

Sierra: *Sierra*
Bimonthly ISSN 0161-7362
Sierra Club Member Services
P.O. Box 52968
Boulder, CO 80322-2968

Signs: *Signs: Journal of Women in Culture and Society*
Quarterly ISSN 0097-9740
University of Chicago Press
Journals Division
P.O. Box 37005
Chicago, IL 60637

Si & So: *Sight and Sound*
Monthly ISSN 0037-4806
c/o Mercury Airfreight International Ltd., Inc.
2323 Randolph Ave.
Avenel, NJ 07001

Six Ct J: *Sixteenth Century Journal*
Quarterly ISSN 0361-0160
MC 111-L
Truman State University
100 E. Normal St.
Kirksville, MO 63501-4211

Skeptic: *Skeptic*
Quarterly ISSN 1063-9330
P.O. Box 338
Altadena, CA 91001

SL: *Special Libraries*
Quarterly ISSN 0038-6723
Special Libraries Association
1700 18th St. N.W.
Washington, DC 20009-2514

Slav R: *Slavic Review*
Quarterly ISSN 0037-6779
AAASS
8 Story Street
Cambridge, MA 02138

S Liv: *Southern Living*
Monthly ISSN 0038-4305
Customer Service
P.O. Box 830119
Birmingham, AL 35283

SLJ: *School Library Journal*
Monthly ISSN 0362-8930
P.O. Box 57559
Boulder, CO 80322-7559

SLMQ: *School Library Media Quarterly*
Quarterly ISSN 0278-4823
Subscription Dept.
American Library Association
50 E. Huron St.
Chicago, IL 60611

Sm Bus Rep: *Small Business Reports*
Monthly ISSN 0164-5382
Fulfillment Dept.
Small Business Reports
P.O. Box 53140
Boulder, CO 80322-3140

Smith: *Smithsonian*
Monthly ISSN 0037-7333
P.O. Box 420312
Palm Coast, FL 32142-0312

Sm Pr: *Small Press*
Quarterly ISSN 0000-0485
Kymbolde Way
Wakefield, RI 02879

Sm Pr R: *Small Press Review*
Monthly ISSN 0037-7228
Dustbooks
P.O. Box 100
Paradise, CA 95967

SN: *Saturday Night*
10 issues/year ISSN 0036-4975
P.O. Box 1518
Champlain, NY 12919

Soc: *Society*
Bimonthly ISSN 0147-2011
Transaction Publishers
Rutgers-The State University
New Brunswick, NJ 08903

Socio R: *Sociological Review*
Quarterly ISSN 0038-0261
c/o Mercury Airfreight International Ltd., Inc.
2323 E-F Randolph Ave.
Avenel, NJ 07001

SocSciComR: *Social Science Computer Review*
Quarterly ISSN 0894-4393
c/o 2455 Teller Road
Thousand Oaks, CA 91320

Soc Ser R: *Social Service Review*
Quarterly ISSN 0037-7961
University of Chicago Press
Journals Division
P.O. Box 37005
Chicago, IL 60637

Soc W: *Social Work*
Bimonthly ISSN 0037-8046
NASW
750 1st., N.E., Ste. 700
Washington, DC 20002-4241

South CR: *South Carolina Review*
Semiannual ISSN 0038-3163
Dept. of English
Strode Tower, Box 341503
Clemson University
Clemson, SC 29634-1503

South Cul: *Southern Cultures*
Quarterly ISSN 1068-8218
Duke University Press
Box 90660
Durham, NC 27708-0660

South HR: *Southern Humanities Review*
Quarterly ISSN 0038-4186
9088 Haley Center
Auburn University
Auburn, AL 36849

South R: *Southern Review*
Quarterly ISSN 0038-4534
43 Allen Hall
Louisiana State University
Baton Rouge, LA 70803-5005

Spec: *Spectator*
Weekly ISSN 0038-6952
Subscriptions Dept.
P.O. Box 14, Harold Hill
Romford, Essex RM3 8EQ, England

Specu: *Speculum*
Quarterly ISSN 0038-7134
Medieval Academy of America
1430 Massachusetts Ave.
Cambridge, MA 02138

Spitball: *Spitball*
Quarterly ISSN 8755-741X
5560 Fox Rd.
Cincinnati, OH 45239

S&S: *Science & Society*
Quarterly ISSN 0036-8237
Guilford Publications
72 Spring St.
New York, NY 10012

SS: *Social Studies*
Bimonthly ISSN 0037-7996
Heldref Publications
1319 Eighteenth St.,N.W.
Washington, DC 20036-1802

SSF: *Studies in Short Fiction*
Quarterly ISSN 0039-3789
Newberry College
Newberry, SC 29108

SSQ: *Social Science Quarterly*
Quarterly ISSN 0038-4941
University of Texas Press
P.O. Box 7819
Austin, TX 78713-7819

S&T: *Sky & Telescope*
Monthly ISSN 0037-6604
P.O. Box 9111
Belmont, MA 02178-9111

Stand: *Stand Magazine*
Quarterly ISSN 0038-9366
179 Wingrove Rd.
Newcastle Upon Tyne NE4 9DA,
England

Stereo: *Stereo Review*
Monthly ISSN 0039-1220
P.O. Box 55627
Boulder, CO 80322-5627

Sulfur: *Sulfur*
Semiannual ISSN 0730-305X
English Dept.
Eastern Michigan University
Ypsilanti, MI 48197

Surface DJ: *Surface Design Journal*
Quarterly ISSN 0197-4483
P.O. Box 20799
Oakland, CA 94620-0799

SWR: *Southwest Review*
Quarterly ISSN 0038-4712
307 Fondren Library West
Southern Methodist University
Dallas, TX 75275

T

T&C: *Technology and Culture*
Quarterly ISSN 0040-165X
University of Chicago Press
P.O. Box 37005
Chicago, IL 60637

TCI: *TCI: The Business of Entertainment
Technology and Design*
10 issues/year ISSN 0040-5469
TCI
P.O. Box 470
Mount Morris, IL 61054-0470

TCR: *Teachers College Record*
Quarterly ISSN 0161-4691
525 W. 120th St.
Box 103
New York, NY 10027

TDR: *TDR: The Drama Review*
Quarterly ISSN 0012-5962
Journals Dept.
MIT Press
55 Hayward St.
Cambridge, MA 02142

Teach Mus: *Teaching Music*
Monthly ISSN 1069-7446
1806 Robert Fulton Drive
Reston, VA 22091-4348

Tec R: *Technology Review*
8 issues/year ISSN 0040-1692
P.O. Box 489
Mount Morris, IL 61054

TES: *Times Educational Supplement*
Weekly ISSN 0040-7887
Priory House
St. John's Lane
London EC1M 4BX, England

Theat J: *Theatre Journal*
Quarterly ISSN 0192-2882
Johns Hopkins University Press
Journals Division
2715 North Charles St.
Baltimore, MD 21218-4319

Theol St: *Theological Studies*
Quarterly ISSN 0040-5639
P.O. Box 465
Hanover, PA 17331

THS: *Theatre History Studies*
Annual ISSN 0733-2033
Editor
Theatre Dept.
Central College
Pella, IA 50219

Tikkun: *Tikkun*
Bimonthly ISSN 0887-9982
P.O. Box 460926
Escondido, CA 92046

Time: *Time*
Weekly ISSN 0040-781X
Time
P.O. Box 30601
Tampa, FL 33630-0601

TLS: *Times Literary Supplement*
Weekly ISSN 0040-7895
P. O. Box 3000
Denville, NJ 07834

TPR: *Threepenny Review*
Quarterly ISSN 0275-1410
P.O. Box 9131
Berkeley, CA 94709

TranslRev: *Translation Review*
3 issues/year ISSN 0737-4836
University of Texas at Dallas
Box 830688 - MC35
Richardson, TX 75083-0688

TranslRevS: *Translation Review
Supplement*
2 issues/year ISSN 0737-4836
University of Texas at Dallas
Box 830688 - MC35
Richardson, TX 75083-0688

Trav: *Travel-Holiday*
Monthly ISSN 0199-025X
P.O. Box 5233
Harlan, IA 51593

Treas Seek: *Treasure Seekers*
bimonthly ISSN 1078-1471
Subscription Dept.
P.O. Box 1395
Agoura Hills, CA 91376-1395

Trial: *Trial*
Monthly ISSN 0041-2538
ATLA
P.O. Box 3717
Washington, DC 20007-4499

Trib Bks: *Tribune Books (Chicago)*
Weekly
Mail Subscription Div.
777 W. Chicago Ave.
Chicago, IL 60610

Tric: *Tricycle: The Buddhist Review*
Quarterly ISSN 1055-484X
Subscription Dept.
TRI Box 3000
Denville, NJ 07834

Trop F H: *Tropical Fish Hobbyist*
Monthly ISSN 0041-3259
One Tropical Fish Plz.
Neptune City, NJ 07753

TSWL: *Tulsa Studies in Women's
Literature*
Semiannual ISSN 0732-7730
600 S. College
Tulsa, OK 74104-3189

TT: *Theology Today*
Quarterly ISSN 0040-5736
P.O. Box 29
Princeton, NJ 08542

TV Q: *Television Quarterly*
Quarterly ISSN 0040-2796
National Academy of Television Arts
and Sciences
111 West 57th Street
New York, NY 10019

U

Under Nat: *Underwater Naturalist*
Quarterly ISSN 0041-6606
American Littoral Society
Sandy Hook
Highlands, NJ 07732

Univ Bkmn: *University Bookman*
Quarterly ISSN 0041-9265
F.M. Kirby Campus
3901 Centerville Rd.
P.O. Box 4431
Wilmington, DE 19807-0431

Urban Ed: *Urban Education*
Quarterly ISSN 0042-0859
2455 Teller Rd.
Thousand Oaks, CA 91320

Urb For: *Urban Forests*
Bimonthly ISSN 1052-2484
American Forests
P.O. Box 2000
Washington, DC 20013

Utne R: *Utne Reader*
Bimonthly ISSN 8750-0256
Box 7460
Red Oak, IA 51591-0460

V

VLS: *Village Voice Literary Supplement*
10 issues/year ISSN 0887-8633
P.O. Box 3000, Dept. VLS
Denville, NJ 07834-9891

VOYA: *Voice of Youth Advocates*
Bimonthly ISSN 0160-4201
Scarecrow Press, Inc.
4720A Boston Way
Lanham, MD 20706

VQR: *Virginia Quarterly Review*
Quarterly ISSN 0042-675X
Business Manager
1 W. Range
Charlottesville, VA 22903

VS: *Victorian Studies*
Quarterly ISSN 0042-5222
Journals Division
Indiana University Press
601 N. Morton
Bloomington, IN 47404-3797

VV: *Village Voice*
Weekly ISSN 0042-6180
P.O. Box 3000
Denville, NJ 07834

W

WAL: *Western American Literature*
Quarterly ISSN 0043-3462
Utah State University
Logan, UT 84322-3200

Wash M: *Washington Monthly*
10 issues/year ISSN 0043-0633
Box 587
Mount Morris, IL 61054

WB: *Workbench*
Bimonthly ISSN 0043-8057
P.O. Box 7506
Red Oak, IA 51591-0506

WER: *Whole Earth Review*
Quarterly ISSN 0749-5056
P.O. Box 3000
Denville, NJ 07834

WestFolk: *Western Folklore*
Quarterly ISSN 0043-373X
Dept. of Anthropology
California State University-Chico
Chico, CA 95292-0400

Who Cares: *Who Cares*
Quarterly ISSN 1070-7255
P.O. Box 3000
Denville, NJ 07834

WHQ: *Western Historical Quarterly*
Quarterly ISSN 0043-3810
Utah State University
Logan, UT 84322-0740

WHR: *Western Humanities Review*
Quarterly ISSN 0043-3845
University of Utah Mailing Bureau
Bldg. 50
Salt Lake City, UT 84112

W&I: *World & I*
Monthly ISSN 0887-9346
3400 New York Ave., N.E.
Washington, DC 20002

Wildbird: *WildBird*
Monthly ISSN 0892-5534
Subscription Dept.
P.O. Box 52898
Boulder, CO 80322-2898

Wil Q: *Wilson Quarterly*
Quarterly ISSN 0363-3276
Subscriber Service
P.O. Box 420406
Palm Coast, FL 32142-0406

WLT: *World Literature Today*
Quarterly ISSN 0196-3570
110 Monnet Hall
University of Oklahoma
Norman, OK 73069

W&M Q: *William and Mary Quarterly*
Quarterly ISSN 0043-5597
Editor
Box 8781
Williamsburg, VA 23187-8781

WOC: *Work and Occupations*
Quarterly ISSN 0730-8884
c/o 2455 Teller Road
Thousand Oaks, CA 91320

Woman's J: *Woman's Journal*
Monthly ISSN 0043-7344
Southbank Publishing Group
IPC Magazines Ltd.
King's Reach Tower
Stamford St.
London SE1 9LS, England

Wom R Bks: *Women's Review of Books*
11 issues/yr. ISSN 0738-1433
Wellesley College
Center for Research on Women
Wellesley, MA 02181

Workbook: *Workbook*
Quarterly ISSN 0195-4636
Southwest Research and Information
Center
P.O. Box 4524
Albuquerque, NM 87106

WorldV: *WorldViews: A Quarterly Review
of Resources for Education and Action*
Quarterly ISSN 1084-7559
464 19 Street
Oakland, CA 94612-2297

WP: *World Politics*
Quarterly ISSN 0043-8871
Johns Hopkins University Press
Journals Publishing Division
2715 N. Charles St.
Baltimore, MD 21218-4319

WSJ-Cent: *Wall Street Journal (Central
Ed.)*
Daily ISSN 099-9660
200 Burnett Rd.
Chicopee, MA 01020

WSJ-MW: *Wall Street Journal (Midwest
Ed.)*
Daily ISSN 0163-089X
200 Burnett Rd.
Chicopee, MA 01020

Y

Yacht: *Yachting*
Monthly ISSN 0043-9940
P.O. Box 56349
Boulder, CO 80322-6349

YLJ: *Yale Law Journal*
8 issues/year ISSN 0044-0094
P.O. Box 208215
New Haven, CT 06520-8215

YR: *Yale Review*
Quarterly ISSN 0044-0124
Journals Subscriptions Dept.
Blackwell Publishers
350 Main St.
Malden, MA 02148

Z

Zygon: *Zygon*
Quarterly ISSN 0591-2385
Journals Dept.
Blackwell Publishers, Inc.
350 Main St.
Malden, MA 02148

A

2 Cuddly Ducks
 c Ch BWatch - v6 - My '96 - p3 [1-50]
2 Cuddly Lambs
 c Ch BWatch - v6 - My '96 - p3 [1-50]
3D Design
 p LJ - v121 - O 15 '96 - p95 [51-250]
V Centenario Do Livro Impresso Em Portugal 1487-1987
 Lib - v18 - S '96 - p273 [1-50]
10 Years of Dolce and Gabbana
 LATBR - D 8 '96 - p30 [51 250]
The 11th Commandment
 c BL - v93 - O 1 '96 - p337 [51-250]
 c HB Guide - v8 - Spr '97 - p86 [51-250]
 c PW - v243 - N 4 '96 - p47 [51-250]
The 20th-Century Art Book
 r LJ - v122 - F 1 '97 - p78 [51-250]
 NYTBR - v101 - D 8 '96 - p19 [51-250]
20th Century Composers Series
 TES - Ag 30 '96 - p32 [501+]
24 Hours (Collective Effort)
 Arena - O '96 - p53+ [501+]
 Aust Bk R - Je '96 - p51+ [501+]
30 Years of Regional Trends. Electronic Media Version
 r LAR - v99 - Mr '97 - p160 [51-250]
75 Years of All-Time Favorites
 BL - v93 - Mr 15 '97 - p1202 [51-250]
The 100 Best Mutual Funds You Can Buy 1995
 r ARBA - v28 - '97 - p92 [51-250]
100 Nursery Rhymes (Francis). Book and Audio Version
 c TES - Jl 19 '96 - pR8 [51-250]
101 American English Idioms
 c Ch BWatch - v6 - O '96 - p2 [51-250]
The 101 Times
 p Sm Pr R - v29 - F '97 - p19 [501+]
1001 Hints and Tips for Your Garden
 r BL - v93 - Ja '97 - p898 [51-250]
 r LJ - v122 - Ja '97 - p130+ [51-250]
A. Bacus
 p Sm Pr R - v28 - D '96 - p13+ [501+]
Aadnoy, Bernt S - *Modern Well Design*
 SciTech - v20 - D '96 - p70 [51-250]
Aamodt, Bjorn - *Samlede Dikt 1973-1994*
 WLT - v70 - Aut '96 - p976+ [251-500]
Aardema, Verna - *Borreguita and the Coyote (Illus. by Petra Mathers)*
 c SS - v88 - Ja '97 - p29+ [501+]
 How the Ostrich Got Its Long Neck (Illus. by Marcia Brown)
 c Inst - v105 - My '96 - p69 [1-50]
 The Lonely Lioness and the Ostrich Chicks (Illus. by Yumi Heo)
 c BL - v93 - N 15 '96 - p589 [51-250]
 c CCB-B - v50 - F '97 - p198 [51-250]
 c HB - v73 - Ja '97 - p71+ [51-250]
 c HB Guide - v8 - Spr '97 - p99 [51-250]
 c KR - v64 - S 1 '96 - p1318 [51-250]
 c LATBR - S 1 '96 - p11 [51-250]
 c NYTBR - v101 - O 27 '96 - p44 [1-50]
 c Par Ch - v20 - O '96 - p28 [51-250]
 c PW - v243 - O 7 '96 - p73 [51-250]
 c SLJ - v42 - O '96 - p110 [51-250]
 c Time - v148 - D 9 '96 - p78 [51-250]
 This for That (Illus. by Victoria Chess)
 c BL - v93 - Mr 15 '97 - p1244 [51-250]
 c CCB-B - v50 - Mr '97 - p238 [51-250]
 c KR - v64 - D 1 '96 - p1732 [51-250]
 c PW - v243 - N 25 '96 - p74+ [51-250]
Aaron, Henry J - *Economic Effects of Fundamental Tax Reform*
 Econ - v341 - D 7 '96 - p9* [51-250]

The Problem That Won't Go Away
 Choice - v34 - S '96 - p163 [51-250]
 JEL - v34 - S '96 - p1441 [51-250]
Aaron, Moses - *Lily and Me*
 c Magpies - v11 - S '96 - p31 [51-250]
Aaron, William - *Mot Pour Mot. Book and Electronic Media Version*
 MLJ - v81 - Spr '97 - p127+ [251-500]
Aarons, Leroy - *Prayers for Bobby*
 LATBR - O 27 '96 - p11 [51 250]
Aarons, Victoria - *A Measure of Memory*
 Choice - v34 - O '96 - p274+ [51-250]
Aaronsohn, Elizabeth - *Going against the Grain*
 Learning - v25 - S '96 - p47 [51-250]
Aaronson, Susan Ariel - *Trade and the American Dream*
 BHR - v70 - Aut '96 - p418+ [501+]
 Choice - v34 - O '96 - p328 [51-250]
 JEL - v35 - Mr '97 - p267+ [51-250]
Aarts, Leo J M - *Curing the Dutch Disease*
 JEL - v35 - Mr '97 - p236+ [51-250]
Aaseng, Nathan - *American Dinosaur Hunters*
 y BL - v93 - N 15 '96 - p578 [51-250]
 c HB Guide - v8 - Spr '97 - p161 [51-250]
 c SLJ - v42 - D '96 - p125+ [51-250]
 Genetics: Unlocking the Secrets of Life
 c CBRS - v25 - S '96 - p10 [51-250]
 y CCB-B - v50 - O '96 - p46+ [51-250]
 y HB Guide - v8 - Spr '97 - p115 [51-250]
 Head Injuries
 y BL - v92 - Ag '96 - p1892 [51-250]
 c HB Guide - v7 - Fall '96 - p347 [51-250]
 y SB - v33 - Ja '97 - p13 [51-250]
 Meat-Eating Plants
 c HB Guide - v7 - Fall '96 - p340 [51-250]
 c SB - v33 - Ja '97 - p18 [251-500]
 The O.J. Simpson Trial
 y HB Guide - v7 - Fall '96 - p313 [51-250]
 You Are the President
 c Ch BWatch - v7 - Ja '97 - p6 [51-250]
 You Are the President II
 c Ch BWatch - v7 - Ja '97 - p6 [51-250]
Aasht, Darshan Singh - *Punjabi Bal Sahit Da Aalochanatmak Muhandra*
 Bkbird - v34 - Spr '96 - p56+ [1-50]
AASL Electronic Library. 1st Ed. Electronic Media Version
 r CLW - v66 - Je '96 - p55 [51-250]
Abad Fociolince, Hector Joaquin - *The Joy of Being Awake*
 BW - v26 - D 22 '96 - p9 [251-500]
Abadinsky, Howard - *Probation and Parole. 6th Ed.*
 R&R Bk N - v11 - D '96 - p45 [51-250]
Abadzis, Nick - *The Amazing Mr. Pleebus*
 c Bks Keeps - N '96 - p9 [51-250]
 The Freaky Beastie of Hill Road School
 c Bks Keeps - N '96 - p9 [51-250]
Abanes, Richard - *American Militias*
 Bks & Cult - v2 - N '96 - p18+ [501+]
 Nat - v264 - F 24 '97 - p28+ [501+]
Abarbanel, Henry D I - *Analysis of Observed Chaotic Data*
 Am Sci - v85 - Mr '97 - p191 [251-500]
 Phys Today - v49 - N '96 - p86+ [501+]
Abarca Vasquez, Carlos - *Rodrigo Carazo Y La Utopia De La Dignidad 1970-1983*
 BL - v93 - S 15 '96 - p227 [1-50]
Abbate, Vincenzo - *Maestri Del Disegno Nelle Collezioni Di Palazzo Abatellis*
 BM - v138 - O '96 - p712+ [501+]
Abbey, Edward - *The Serpents of Paradise*
 Bloom Rev - v16 - Jl '96 - p22 [1-50]

Abbink, Emily - *Missions of the Monterey Bay Area*
 c HB Guide - v8 - Spr '97 - p172 [51-250]
Abbot, Laura - *This Christmas*
 LJ - v121 - N 15 '96 - p47 [51-250]
Abbott, Don Paul - *Rhetoric in the New World*
 Choice - v34 - O '96 - p271+ [51-250]
Abbott, Donald - *How the Wizard Came to Oz (Illus. by Donald Abbott)*
 c Ch BWatch - v7 - F '97 - p1 [51-250]
 The Speckled Rose of Oz
 c Ch BWatch - v7 - F '97 - p1 [51-250]
Abbott, Edwin - *Flatland. 2nd Ed.*
 VS - v39 - Win '96 - p129+ [501+]
Abbott, H Porter - *Beckett Writing Beckett*
 Choice - v34 - N '96 - p452 [51-250]
 VQR - v73 - Win '97 - p10* [51-250]
Abbott, Jeff - *Distant Blood*
 PW - v243 - O 14 '96 - p81 [51-250]
Abbott, Lee K - *Love Is the Crooked Thing*
 NYTBR - v101 - O 27 '96 - p48 [1-50]
 Strangers in Paradise
 NYTBR - v101 - O 27 '96 - p48 [1-50]
Abbott, Mary - *Family Ties*
 JMH - v68 - S '96 - p678+ [501+]
Abbs, Peter - *The Polemics of Imagination*
 AJE - v104 - Ag '96 - p319+ [501+]
 TES - N 29 '96 - p9* [501+]
Abdallah, Mohammed Ben - *Ananse and the Golden Drum*
 c Bkbird - v34 - Spr '96 - p53 [1-50]
Abd Al-Majid, Isam Mohammed - *Modeling Methods for Environmental Engineers*
 SciTech - v21 - Mr '97 - p81 [51-250]
Abd-Elfattah, Anwar-Saad A - *Purines and Myocardial Protection*
 SciTech - v20 - N '96 - p47 [51-250]
Abdulai, David - *Sankofa: Stories, Proverbs and Poems of an African Childhood*
 Bloom Rev - v17 - Ja '97 - p18 [51-250]
Abdul-Baki, Kathryn K - *Tower of Dreams*
 WLT - v70 - Sum '96 - p754+ [501+]
Abdul-Jabbar, Kareem - *Black Profiles in Courage*
 y BL - v93 - Ja '97 - p762 [1-50]
 KR - v64 - Ag 15 '96 - p1197 [251-500]
 y LJ - v121 - S 15 '96 - p78 [51-250]
Abe, Etsuo - *The Origins of Japanese Industrial Power*
 TLS - O 25 '96 - p13 [251-500]
Abe, Kobo - *Kangaroo Notebook*
 PW - v244 - My 5 '97 - p206 [1-50]
 TranslRevS - v2 - D '96 - p28+ [51-250]
 WLT - v71 - Win '97 - p228 [51-250]
Abe, Masao - *Buddhism and Interfaith Dialogue*
 Rel St Rev - v23 - Ja '97 - p48 [51-250]
Abegaz, Berhanu - *The Challenge of European Integration*
 EG - v72 - O '96 - p458+ [501+]
Abel, Kenneth - *The Blue Wall*
 BW - v26 - Ag 4 '96 - p8 [51-250]
Abel, Sam - *Opera in the Flesh*
 Choice - v34 - O '96 - p290 [51-250]
 ON - v61 - D 28 '96 - p52 [501+]
Abella, Alex - *The Great American*
 BL - v93 - Mr 1 '97 - p1108 [51-250]
 KR - v65 - Ja 15 '97 - p74 [251-500]
 LJ - v122 - Ja '97 - p141 [51-250]
 PW - v244 - Ja 6 '97 - p63 [51-250]
Abelmann, Nancy - *Echoes of the Past, Epics of Dissent*
 Choice - v34 - Mr '97 - p1244 [51-250]

Abelson, Harold - *Structure and Interpretation of Computer Programs. 2nd Ed.*
  Choice - v34 - F '97 - p998 [51-250]
  New Sci - v153 - Mr 1 '97 - p46+ [501+]
Abelson, Peter - *Project Appraisal and Valuation of the Environment*
  R&R Bk N - v11 - D '96 - p23 [51-250]
Abelson, Robert P - *Statistics as Principled Argument*
  A J Psy - v110 - Spr '97 - p146+ [501+]
Abensur, Nadine - *The Art of Vegetarian Cooking*
  Books - v10 - Je '96 - p21 [1-50]
  Secrets from a Vegetarian Kitchen
  BL - v93 - Mr 15 '97 - p1215 [51-250]
  PW - v244 - Mr 24 '97 - p77+ [51-250]
Aberbach, Moshe - *Labor, Crafts and Commerce in Ancient Israel*
  Rel St Rev - v23 - Ap '97 - p193 [51-250]
Abercrombie, Stanley - *George Nelson: The Design of Modern Design*
  Am Craft - v56 - Ag '96 - p28 [1-50]
  TLS - My 24 '96 - p21 [501+]
Abernethy, Francis Edward - *Juneteenth Texas*
  AB - v99 - F 17 '97 - p527+ [501+]
  BWatch - v17 - D '96 - p5 [51-250]
  CAY - v17 - Win '96 - p2 [51-250]
  The Texas Folklore Society 1943-1971. Vol. 2
  J Am Cult - v18 - Win '95 - p106 [51-250]
Aberth, John - *Criminal Churchmen in the Age of Edward III*
  Choice - v34 - D '96 - p666 [51-250]
  TLS - S 6 '96 - p30 [501+]
  Univ Bkmn - v36 - Win '96 - p3+ [501+]
Ab Hugh, Dafydd - *The Mountain*
  y Kliatt - v30 - S '96 - p6 [51-250]
Abingdon Clergy Income Tax Guide. 1997 Ed.
  r CC - v114 - Mr 12 '97 - p275 [51-250]
Abiodun, Rowland - *The Yoruba Artist*
  Africa T - v44 - 1 '97 - p102+ [251-500]
Abitbol, M Maurice - *Birth and Human Evolution*
  SciTech - v20 - N '96 - p32 [51-250]
Able, Allen - *Flatbush Odyssey*
  VQR - v72 - Aut '96 - p141* [1-50]
Ablow, Keith - *Denial*
  KR - v65 - My 1 '97 - p658 [251-500]
Abner, Allison - *Finding Our Way*
  y BL - v93 - Ja '97 - p764 [1-50]
Abo, Tetsuo - *Hybrid Factory*
  BHR - v70 - Aut '96 - p420+ [501+]
Aborough, Jez - *It's the Bear!*
  c Bks Keeps - N '96 - p6 [51-250]
Abortion and Reproductive Rights. Electronic Media Version
  r LJ - v122 - Mr 15 '97 - p96 [51-250]
Abosh, Beverley - *Mental Illness in the Family*
  SciTech - v20 - S '96 - p32 [51-250]
Aboud, Jehad - *Die Rolle Des Konigs Und Seiner Familie Nach Den Texten Von Ugaret*
  Rel St Rev - v23 - Ja '97 - p56 [51-250]
Abou-El-Haj, Barbara Fay - *The Medieval Cult of Saints*
  CHR - v82 - Jl '96 - p524+ [501+]
Abousleiman, Y - *Computer Methods and Water Resources III*
  SciTech - v20 - D '96 - p2 [51-250]
Abracadabra! The Ultimate Magic Kit
  c PW - v244 - Ap 7 '97 - p94 [51-250]
Abraham, A J - *The Lebanon War*
  Choice - v34 - S '96 - p205 [51-250]
  MEJ - v51 - Win '97 - p127+ [501+]
Abraham, Julie - *Are Girls Necessary?*
  Wom R Bks - v14 - N '96 - p14+ [501+]
Abraham, Ken - *Who Are the Promise Keepers?*
  BL - v93 - My 15 '97 - p1545 [51-250]
  PW - v244 - Ap 28 '97 - p68+ [51-250]
Abraham, Laurie Kaye - *Mama Might Be Better Off Dead*
  Hast Cen R - v26 - Jl '96 - p39+ [501+]
Abraham, Marilyn J - *First We Quit Our Jobs*
  BL - v93 - F 1 '97 - p922 [51-250]
  KR - v64 - D 1 '96 - p1709 [251-500]
  LJ - v122 - F 15 '97 - p152+ [51-250]
  PW - v244 - Ja 20 '97 - p388 [251-500]
Abraham, Nader G - *Molecular Biology of Hematopoiesis 5*
  SciTech - v21 - Mr '97 - p56 [51-250]
Abraham, Nicolas - *Rhythms: On the Work, Translation, and Psychoanalysis*
  MLN - v111 - D '96 - p1037+ [501+]

Abraham, Pearl - *The Romance Reader*
  Ent W - O 4 '96 - p57 [51-250]
  y Kliatt - v31 - Ja '97 - p5 [251-500]
  LATBR - O 13 '96 - p15 [51-250]
  NYTBR - v101 - S 1 '96 - p24 [1-50]
Abrahams, Ray - *After Socialism*
  R&R Bk N - v12 - F '97 - p39 [51-250]
Abrahamson, Mark - *Urban Enclaves*
  CS - v25 - N '96 - p781+ [501+]
  Soc Ser R - v70 - D '96 - p662+ [501+]
Abram, Dave - *Scotland. 2nd Ed.*
  r BL - v93 - S 15 '96 - p212 [1-50]
Abram, David - *The Spell of the Sensuous*
  ABR - v18 - D '96 - p3+ [501+]
  Bloom Rev - v16 - S '96 - p14 [251-500]
  BW - v27 - Mr 23 '97 - p12 [51-250]
  Parabola - v21 - N '96 - p94+ [501+]
  Sci - v275 - Ja 10 '97 - p174 [501+]
  Utne R - My '96 - p18+ [51-250]
Abramovitz, Mimi - *Regulating the Lives of Women. Rev. Ed.*
  BWatch - v17 - N '96 - p6 [51-250]
Abrams, Elliott - *Faith or Fear*
  BL - v93 - My 15 '97 - p1545 [51-250]
  LJ - v122 - My 1 '97 - p127 [51-250]
  WSJ-Cent - v99 - My 27 '97 - pA16 [51-250]
Abrams, Elliott M - *How the Maya Built Their World*
  LA Ant - v7 - Je '96 - p172+ [501+]
Abrams, Michael - *Eddie's Monster (Illus. by Nicolas Van Pallandt)*
  c HB Guide - v8 - Spr '97 - p56 [51-250]
Abramson, Charles I - *Russian Contributions to Invertebrate Behavior*
  SciTech - v20 - S '96 - p20 [51-250]
Abramson, Glenda - *The Oxford Book of Hebrew Short Stories*
  BL - v93 - N 15 '96 - p572 [51-250]
  LJ - v121 - S 15 '96 - p99 [51-250]
  TLS - Mr 7 '97 - p23 [501+]
Abramson, Jeffrey - *Postmortem: The O.J. Simpson Case*
  Bl S - v26 - Fall '96 - p100 [51-250]
  KR - v64 - My 1 '96 - p651 [251-500]
Abramson, Joanne - *The Large Macaws*
  Choice - v34 - O '96 - p306 [51-250]
Abramson, Leslie - *The Defense Is Ready*
  y BL - v93 - D 15 '96 - p690 [51-250]
  KR - v64 - D 1 '96 - p1709 [251-500]
  LATBR - F 16 '97 - p7 [501+]
  LJ - v122 - Ja '97 - p122 [51-250]
  NYTBR - v102 - Mr 16 '97 - p20 [51-250]
  PW - v243 - D 16 '96 - p50 [51-250]
  The Defense Is Ready (Abramson). Audio Version
  PW - v244 - Mr 3 '97 - p31 [51-250]
Abramson, Michael - *Further and Higher Education Partnerships*
  R&R Bk N - v11 - N '96 - p55 [51-250]
Abramson, Nils H - *Light in Flight or the Holodiagram*
  SciTech - v21 - Mr '97 - p80 [51-250]
Abramson, Paul R - *Value Change in Global Perspective*
  APSR - v90 - S '96 - p665+ [501+]
  CS - v25 - S '96 - p638+ [501+]
  J Pol - v58 - Ag '96 - p909+ [501+]
  Pub Op Q - v60 - Sum '96 - p322+ [501+]
Abramson, Paul R, 1949- - *Sexual Nature, Sexual Culture*
  Am Ethnol - v24 - F '97 - p213+ [501+]
  Am Sci - v84 - My '96 - p301 [501+]
Abramson, Rudy - *Hallowed Ground*
  BL - v93 - F 15 '97 - p996+ [51-250]
  BW - v26 - D 8 '96 - p12 [51-250]
Abrial, Jean-Raymond - *The B-Book: Assigning Programs to Meanings*
  Choice - v34 - Mr '97 - p1195 [51-250]
Abrons, Richard - *Every Day a Visitor*
  PW - v243 - O 14 '96 - p79 [51-250]
Abruzzese, Roberta Straessle - *Nursing Staff Development. 2nd Ed.*
  SciTech - v20 - S '96 - p43 [51-250]
Absalom, Roger - *Italy since 1800*
  Historian - v58 - Sum '96 - p890+ [501+]
Abse, Leo - *The Man behind the Smile*
  TLS - D 20 '96 - p29 [501+]
Abshire, David - *Putting America's House in Order*
  JEL - v34 - D '96 - p2036 [51-250]
Abu-Jamal, Mumia - *Death Blossoms*
  BL - v93 - F 15 '97 - p977 [51-250]
  LJ - v122 - Ap 1 '97 - p108+ [51-250]
  OS - v33 - Mr '97 - p35 [51-250]
  Live from Death Row
  Hum - v56 - S '96 - p47 [251-500]
Abukhanfusa, Kerstin - *The Principle of Provenance*
  Archiv - Spr '96 - p249+ [501+]

Abulafia, Anna Sapir - *Christians and Jews in the Twelfth-Century Renaissance*
  AHR - v101 - D '96 - p1532+ [251-500]
Abulafia, David - *The French Descent into Renaissance Italy 1494-95*
  Six Ct J - v27 - Win '96 - p1084+ [501+]
  A Mediterranean Emporium
  EHR - v111 - S '96 - p958+ [251-500]
Abu Mashar - *The Abbreviation of the Introduction to Astrology*
  Isis - v87 - S '96 - p541 [251-500]
Abu-Rabi, Ibrahim M - *Intellectual Origins of Islamic Resurgence in the Modern Arab World*
  MEJ - v50 - Sum '96 - p443+ [501+]
  Rel St Rev - v23 - Ap '97 - p200 [51-250]
Aburish, Said K - *The Rise, Corruption, and Coming Fall of the House of Saud*
  MEP - v5 - 1 '97 - p199+ [501+]
  WorldV - v12 - O '96 - p9+ [51-250]
Abu Shouk, Ahmad Ibrahim - *The Public Treasury of the Muslims*
  MEJ - v50 - Aut '96 - p631 [51-250]
Abu-Taleb, Samy - *Conversational Arabic in 7 Days*
  MLJ - v80 - Win '96 - p544 [501+]
Abzug, Robert H - *Cosmos Crumbling*
  Am Q - v48 - D '96 - p724+ [501+]
  JR - v76 - O '96 - p646+ [251-500]
  Rel St Rev - v23 - Ja '97 - p92 [51-250]
Academic American Encyclopedia 1996. Vols. 1-21
  yr BL - v93 - S 15 '96 - p265+ [501+]
Academic Press Dictionary of Science and Technology. Version 1.0. Electronic Media Version
  r Am Sci - v85 - Ja '97 - p91+ [501+]
  yr BL - v93 - D 1 '96 - p677 [251-500]
  r Choice - v34 - N '96 - p440 [251-500]
  r LJ - v122 - My 1 '97 - p147 [51-250]
  yr SLJ - v42 - N '96 - p54 [51-250]
Accad, Evelyne - *Wounding Words*
  LJ - v121 - N 1 '96 - p73 [51-250]
  PW - v243 - O 14 '96 - p79+ [51-250]
Accampo, Elinor A - *Gender and the Politics of Social Reform in France 1870-1914*
  JEH - v56 - D '96 - p940+ [501+]
Accardo, Pasquale - *The Invisible Disability*
  EL - v54 - S '96 - p105 [51-250]
Access New York Restaurants 96/97
  r BL - v93 - S 15 '96 - p206 [1-50]
Access San Francisco Restaurants. 2nd Ed.
  r BL - v93 - S 15 '96 - p206 [1-50]
Access to Air Travel for People with Reduced Mobility
  J Gov Info - v23 - S '96 - p666 [51-250]
Accessible Meetings in North Dakota
  J Gov Info - v23 - S '96 - p590 [51-250]
Accidents in North American Mountaineering 1995
  HM - v293 - Ag '96 - p64+ [501+]
Accinelli, Robert - *Crisis and Commitment*
  PHR - v66 - F '97 - p141+ [501+]
Accorsi, William - *Rachel Carson (Illus. by William Accorsi)*
  c SLJ - v42 - D '96 - p45 [51-250]
Accounting Horizons
  p JEL - v34 - S '96 - p1504 [51-250]
Accredited Institutions of Postsecondary Education, Programs, Candidates 1995-96
  r R&R Bk N - v11 - N '96 - p53 [51-250]
Achard, Guy - *La Femme A Rome*
  Choice - v34 - D '96 - p566 [1-50]
Achberger, Karen R - *Understanding Ingeborg Bachmann*
  MLR - v92 - Ap '97 - p534+ [501+]
Achenbach, Thomas M - *Empirically Based Assessment of Child and Adolescent Psychopathology. 2nd Ed.*
  SciTech - v21 - Mr '97 - p65 [51-250]
Achenbaum, W Andrew - *Crossing Frontiers*
  AJS - v102 - Ja '97 - p1220+ [501+]
  Choice - v34 - O '96 - p366 [51-250]
  MHR - v10 - Fall '96 - p88+ [501+]
  RAH - v24 - D '96 - p701+ [501+]
Acheng - *Ma Shi De Dong Yu*
  BL - v93 - N 1 '96 - p484 [1-50]
Acheson, Alison - *Thunder Ice*
  y BIC - v25 - N '96 - p33+ [501+]
  c Can CL - v22 - Fall '96 - p125+ [501+]
  c Ch BWatch - v6 - D '96 - p5 [51-250]
  c Quill & Q - v62 - Ag '96 - p41+ [251-500]
Acheson, James - *Contemporary British Poetry*
  Choice - v34 - F '97 - p964 [51-250]
  R&R Bk N - v12 - F '97 - p84 [1-50]
Achilles-Syndram, Kathrin - *Kunst Des Sammelns*
  BM - v138 - Ag '96 - p551 [501+]

Achinstein, Sharon - *Milton and the Revolutionary Reader*
AHR - v101 - O '96 - p1204 [501+]
EHR - v112 - Ap '97 - p473+ [501+]
MLR - v91 - O '96 - p971+ [501+]
Ren Q - v49 - Win '96 - p887+ [501+]
RES - v48 - F '97 - p107+ [501+]
Achor, Amy Blount - *Animal Rights. Rev. Ed.*
BWatch - v17 - S '96 - p4 [51-250]
Choice - v34 - Ja '97 - p781 [51-250]
Achtemeier, Paul J - *1 Peter*
Am - v176 - Mr 8 '97 - p29 [51-250]
Aciman, Andre - *Out of Egypt*
NS - v125 - N 1 '96 - p45 [501+]
Salm - Sum '96 - p182+ [501+]
Spec - v277 - N 23 '96 - p43 [1-50]
TLS - N 29 '96 - p12 [51-250]
TLS - D 27 '96 - p31 [501+]
Acker, Kathy - *Pussy, King of the Pirates*
LATBR - Mr 24 '96 - p10 [51-250]
Ackerman, Al - *Maitre Ling and Autres Histoires*
Sm Pr R - v28 - Jl '96 - p18 [1-50]
Ackerman, Diane - *A Natural History of the Senses (Porter). Audio Version*
y Kliatt - v30 - S '96 - p58 [51-250]
The Rarest of the Rare
y Kliatt - v31 - My '97 - p29+ [251-500]
NYTBR - v102 - F 16 '97 - p32 [1-50]
PW - v243 - D 30 '96 - p64 [1-50]
A Slender Thread
y BL - v93 - D 1 '96 - p623 [51-250]
Ent W - Ja 17 '97 - p58 [51-250]
KR - v64 - N 15 '96 - p1641 [251-500]
LJ - v122 - Ja '97 - p125 [51-250]
NW - v129 - F 10 '97 - p66 [51-250]
NY - v73 - Mr 24 '97 - p83 [51-250]
NYTBR - v102 - Mr 2 '97 - p11 [501+]
PW - v243 - N 25 '96 - p64 [51-250]
Trib Bks - Ja 19 '97 - p6+ [501+]
Ackerman, Forrest J - *Ackermanthology!*
PW - v244 - Mr 31 '97 - p69 [51-250]
Ackerman, Frank - *Why Do We Recycle?*
PW - v244 - Ja 6 '97 - p60 [51-250]
Ackerman, Jennifer - *Notes from the Shore*
S Liv - v31 - Jl '96 - p80 [51-250]
Ackerman, Karen - *Bingleman's Midway (Illus. by Barry Moser)*
c RT - v50 - D '96 - p342+ [51-250]
Song and Dance Man
c New Ad - v9 - Fall '96 - p267+ [501+]
Ackerman, Lillian A - *A Song to the Creator*
LJ - v121 - N 1 '96 - p66 [51-250]
Ackerman, Marc J - *Does Wednesday Mean Mom's House or Dad's?*
PW - v243 - O 21 '96 - p80 [51-250]
Readings - v12 - Mr '97 - p30 [51-250]
Ackermann, Ernest - *Learning to Use the World Wide Web*
Choice - v34 - F '97 - p998 [51-250]
Ackermann, Robert John - *Heterogeneities: Race, Gender, Class, Nation, and State*
CC - v113 - N 20 '96 - p1177+ [51-250]
WorldV - v12 - O '96 - p6 [51-250]
Acklen, Laura - *WordPerfect 7 for Windows 95 and Windows NT Essentials*
Quill & Q - v62 - N '96 - p30+ [51-250]
Ackroyd, Peter - *Blake*
Ant R - v54 - Fall '96 - p487+ [251-500]
BL - v93 - Ja '97 - p759 [1-50]
Choice - v34 - My '97 - p1493 [51-250]
NY - v72 - My 27 '96 - p126+ [501+]
NYTBR - v101 - D 8 '96 - p85 [1-50]
PW - v243 - N 4 '96 - p42 [1-50]
W&I - v11 - Ag '96 - p260+ [501+]
Chatterton
NYTBR - v101 - N 3 '96 - p28 [1-50]
First Light
NYTBR - v101 - N 3 '96 - p28 [1-50]
Milton in America
BL - v93 - Mr 15 '97 - p1224 [51-250]
KR - v65 - F 15 '97 - p236 [251-500]
LJ - v122 - Ap 1 '97 - p120 [51-250]
NS - v125 - S 27 '96 - p60 [501+]
NYTBR - v102 - Ap 6 '97 - p14 [501+]
NYTLa - v146 - My 14 '97 - pC17 [501+]
Obs - S 1 '96 - p16* [501+]
PW - v244 - F 24 '97 - p62 [51-250]
Spec - v277 - S 7 '96 - p34+ [501+]
TLS - Ag 30 '96 - p23 [501+]
WSJ-Cent - v99 - My 6 '97 - pA20 [501+]
The Trial of Elizabeth Cree
WLT - v71 - Win '97 - p149 [501+]

Acland, Charles R - *Youth, Murder, Spectacle*
J Am Cult - v18 - Win '95 - p116+ [51-250]
Acock, Alan C - *Family Diversity and Well-Being*
CS - v26 - Ja '97 - p80+ [51-250]
Acosta, Anibal A - *Human Spermatozoa in Assisted Reproduction. 2nd Ed.*
SciTech - v20 - D '96 - p51 [51-250]
Acosta, Oscar - *Oscar Zeta Acosta: The Uncollected Works*
Choice - v34 - D '96 - p616 [251-500]
Acquaviva, Sabino - *La Ragazza Del Ghetto*
BL - v93 - D 1 '96 - p644 [1-50]
Acronyms, Initialisms and Abbreviations Dictionary 1997. Vol. 1, Pts. 1-3
r R&R Bk N - v11 - D '96 - p59 [51-250]
Acs, Zoltan J - *Small Firms and Economic Growth. Vols. 1-2*
Econ J - v107 - Ja '97 - p279 [251-500]
JEL - v34 - S '96 - p1451 [51-250]
R&R Bk N - v11 - N '96 - p37 [51-250]
Acton, David - *Hand of a Craftsman*
Am Craft - v56 - Ag '96 - p26 [1-50]
Choice - v34 - Ja '97 - p782 [51-250]
R&R Bk N - v11 - N '96 - p61 [51-250]
Acton, Lesley - *Repairing Pottery and Porcelain*
Ceram Mo - v44 - N '96 - p26 [251-500]
Acuna, Rodolfo F - *Anything but Mexican*
Choice - v34 - O '96 - p344 [51-250]
WHQ - v28 - Spr '97 - p101 [1-50]
Aczel, Amir D - *Fermat's Last Theorem*
Choice - v34 - Ap '97 - p1375 [51-250]
KR - v64 - S 1 '96 - p1283 [251-500]
LJ - v121 - O 15 '96 - p86 [51-250]
Nature - v383 - O 31 '96 - p774 [501+]
NY - v72 - D 9 '96 - p118 [51-250]
NYTLa - v146 - D 16 '96 - pC16 [501+]
PW - v243 - S 2 '96 - p106 [51-250]
SciTech - v21 - Mr '97 - p13 [51-250]
Utne R - Ja '97 - p96 [1-50]
WSJ-MW - v78 - N 25 '96 - pA14 [501+]
Ada, Alma Flor - *Dear Peter Rabbit (Illus. by Leslie Tryon)*
c PW - v244 - F 3 '97 - p108 [1-50]
Gathering the Sun (Illus. by Simon Silva)
c PW - v244 - Mr 31 '97 - p76 [51-250]
c SLJ - v43 - Mr '97 - p169+ [51-250]
The Gold Coin (Illus. by N Waldman)
c SS - v88 - Ja '97 - p29+ [501+]
Jordi's Star (Illus. by Susan Gaber)
c BL - v93 - Ja '97 - p651 [51-250]
c CBRS - v25 - F '97 - p73 [51-250]
c CCB-B - v50 - D '96 - p126 [51-250]
c HB Guide - v8 - Spr '97 - p17 [51-250]
c PW - v243 - N 4 '96 - p75 [51-250]
c SLJ - v42 - D '96 - p84 [51-250]
Mediopollito (Illus. by Kim Howard)
c RT - v50 - F '97 - p426 [51-250]
c SS - v88 - Ja '97 - p29+ [501+]
Adab, B J - *Annotated Texts for Translation: English-French*
r R&R Bk N - v12 - F '97 - p78 [51-250]
Adair, Gene - *Thomas Alva Edison: Inventing the Electric Age*
y HB Guide - v7 - Fall '96 - p370 [51-250]
Adair, Gilbert - *Flickers: An Illustrated Celebration of 100 Years of Cinema*
New R - v215 - D 2 '96 - p58+ [501+]
Adair, Richard - *Courtship, Illegitimacy, and Marriage in Early Modern England*
Choice - v34 - N '96 - p515 [51-250]
R&R Bk N - v11 - N '96 - p41 [51-250]
Adair, Virginia Hamilton - *Ants on the Melon*
Ken R - v18 - Sum '96 - p186+ [501+]
NY - v72 - D 16 '96 - p108 [51-250]
NYTBR - v101 - D 8 '96 - p76 [1-50]
South R - v33 - Win '97 - p136+ [501+]
Time - v148 - D 23 '96 - p86 [51-250]
TLS - N 29 '96 - p12 [51-250]
WAL - v31 - Fall '96 - p274+ [251-500]
Adam, A K M - *Making Sense of New Testament Theology*
Intpr - v51 - Ap '97 - p204+ [501+]
Rel St Rev - v23 - Ja '97 - p69 [51-250]
Adam, Adolf - *Foundations of Liturgy*
CH - v65 - S '96 - p557+ [501+]
Adam, Barry D - *Experiencing HIV*
R&R Bk N - v12 - F '97 - p97 [51-250]
SciTech - v21 - Mr '97 - p56 [51-250]
Adam, Magda - *Documents Diplomatiques Francais Sur L'Histoire Du Bassin Des Carpates 1918-1932. Vol. 1*
EHR - v111 - N '96 - p1341+ [251-500]

Adamec, Ludwig W - *Dictionary of Afghan Wars, Revolutions, and Insurgencies*
r ARBA - v28 - '97 - p56+ [51-250]
Adamovics, John A - *Chromatographic Analysis of Pharmaceuticals. 2nd Ed.*
SciTech - v21 - Mr '97 - p68 [51-250]
Adams, Adrian - *A Claim to Land by the River*
Lon R Bks - v19 - Mr 6 '97 - p20+ [501+]
Adams, Alice - *Medicine Men*
BL - v93 - F 15 '97 - p971 [51-250]
KR - v65 - F 15 '97 - p236 [251-500]
LJ - v122 - Mr 15 '97 - p87 [51-250]
NYTBR - v102 - Ap 13 '97 - p26 [501+]
PW - v244 - F 24 '97 - p61+ [51-250]
A Southern Exposure
Ent W - D 6 '96 - p59 [51-250]
y Kliatt - v31 - Mr '97 - p6 [51-250]
NYTBR - v101 - D 22 '96 - p20 [51-250]
Sew R - v104 - Jl '96 - p468+ [501+]
WLT - v70 - Sum '96 - p689 [501+]
Adams, Alice E - *Reproducing the Womb*
Signs - v22 - Win '97 - p488+ [501+]
Adams, Anna - *Green Resistance*
y Sch Lib - v45 - F '97 - p41 [51-250]
Adams, Annmarie - *Architecture in the Family Way*
Choice - v34 - N '96 - p442 [51-250]
Adams, Anthony - *Hard at It*
Quill & Q - v62 - Jl '96 - p42 [501+]
Adams, Arthur G - *The Hudson River Guidebook*
r Sea H - Win '96 - p47 [51-250]
The Hudson through the Years
Sea H - Win '96 - p47 [51-250]
Adams, Bruce F - *The Politics of Punishment*
Choice - v34 - My '97 - p1555 [51-250]
Adams, Carmen - *The Claw*
y VOYA - v19 - O '96 - p202 [501+]
Adams, Carol A - *Financial Reporting by Multinationals*
JEL - v35 - Mr '97 - p255 [51-250]
R&R Bk N - v11 - D '96 - p35 [51-250]
Adams, Carol J - *Animals and Women*
NWSA Jnl - v8 - Fall '96 - p175+ [501+]
Ecofeminism and the Sacred
Signs - v22 - Win '97 - p496+ [501+]
Neither Man nor Beast
NWSA Jnl - v9 - Spr '97 - p131+ [501+]
Violence against Women and Children
Rel St Rev - v23 - Ja '97 - p47 [51-250]
Adams, Clinton - *Second Impressions*
AB - v99 - Mr 3 '97 - p694 [51-250]
Adams, David Wallace - *Education for Extinction*
AHR - v102 - F '97 - p165 [251-500]
AJE - v104 - Ag '96 - p328+ [501+]
ES - v27 - Sum '96 - p168+ [501+]
Adams, Douglas - *The Hitchhiker's Guide to the Galaxy*
y Kliatt - v30 - S '96 - p4 [1-50]
Adams, Geoffrey - *The Huguenots and French Opinion 1685-1787*
Rel St Rev - v23 - Ja '97 - p84 [51-250]
Adams, Georgie - *The First Christmas (Illus. by Anna C Leplar)*
c Bks Keeps - N '96 - p19 [1-50]
c JB - v60 - D '96 - p226 [51-250]
Nanny Fox and the Christmas Surprise (Illus. by Selina Young)
c BL - v93 - N 1 '96 - p506 [51-250]
c Ch BWatch - v6 - D '96 - p1 [1-50]
c HB Guide - v8 - Spr '97 - p17 [51-250]
c PW - v243 - S 30 '96 - p91 [51-250]
c SLJ - v42 - O '96 - p33 [51-250]
c Smith - v27 - N '96 - p166 [1-50]
Nanny Fox and the Three Little Pigs (Illus. by Selina Young)
c JB - v60 - D '96 - p226 [51-250]
c Sch Lib - v45 - F '97 - p17 [51-250]
The Nursery Storybook (Illus. by Peter Utton)
c Bks Keeps - Ja '97 - p19 [1-50]
c JB - v60 - D '96 - p244 [51-250]
c Sch Lib - v45 - F '97 - p17 [51-250]
Adams, Gerald R - *Psychosocial Development during Adolescence*
R&R Bk N - v11 - D '96 - p41 [51-250]
Adams, Gerry - *Before the Dawn*
BL - v93 - Ja '97 - p811 [51-250]
BW - v27 - Ja 26 '97 - p5 [501+]
KR - v64 - N 15 '96 - p1641 [251-500]
Nat - v264 - F 24 '97 - p25+ [501+]
NYTBR - v102 - F 16 '97 - p12 [501+]
PW - v244 - Ja 27 '97 - p91 [51-250]
Spec - v277 - O 12 '96 - p51 [501+]
TLS - N 15 '96 - p14 [501+]

Adams, Glenda - *The Tempest of Clemenza*
BL - v93 - O 1 '96 - p320 [51-250]
Econ - v341 - N 16 '96 - p18*+ [501+]
LJ - v121 - S 15 '96 - p93 [51-250]

Adams, Graham C - *The Ottoneum Theater*
Shakes Q - v47 - Fall '96 - p344+ [251-500]

Adams, Harold - *Hatchet Job*
Arm Det - v30 - Win '97 - p100 [251-500]
BL - v93 - N 15 '96 - p573 [51-250]
BW - v27 - Ja 19 '97 - p11 [251-500]
KR - v64 - N 1 '96 - p1564+ [51-250]
LATBR - D 15 '96 - p12 [251-500]
PW - v243 - O 14 '96 - p67 [51-250]

Adams, J N - *Pelagonius and Latin Veterinary Terminology in the Roman Empire*
Isis - v87 - D '96 - p717 [501+]

Adams, James, 1951- - *Sellout: Aldrich Ames and the Corruption of the CIA*
CR - v270 - F '97 - p111 [1-50]

Adams, James Eli - *Dandies and Desert Saints*
ELT - v39 - 3 '96 - p404 [51-250]
Nine-C Lit - v51 - Mr '97 - p550+ [501+]

Adams, Jane - *The Transformation of Rural Life*
JEH - v56 - S '96 - p743+ [501+]
JIH - v27 - Aut '96 - p347+ [501+]

Adams, Janus - *Glory Days*
yr Kliatt - v31 - Mr '97 - p30 [51-250]

Adams, John, 1735-1826 - *A Defence of the Constitutions of Government of the United States of America. Vols. 1-3*
RP - v58 - Sum '96 - p531+ [501+]

Adams, John, 1938- - *The Institutional Economics of the International Economy*
JEL - v35 - Mr '97 - p210 [51-250]
Risk
GJ - v162 - Jl '96 - p242 [51-250]

Adams, Jonathan S - *The Myth of Wild Africa*
NYTBR - v102 - Mr 9 '97 - p28 [51-250]

Adams, Kevin - *Wildflowers of the Southern Appalachians*
Choice - v34 - S '96 - p153+ [51-250]

Adams, Laurie Schneider - *The Methodologies of Art*
Choice - v34 - My '97 - p1484 [51-250]
LJ - v121 - S 15 '96 - p63 [51-250]

Adams, Michael - *Sex in the Snow*
Mac - v110 - Mr 3 '97 - p66 [501+]
Quill & Q - v63 - Ja '97 - p13 [51-250]
Quill & Q - v63 - Ja '97 - p33 [251-500]

Adams, Nicholas D - *Warehouse and Distribution Automation Handbook*
SciTech - v20 - D '96 - p85 [51-250]

Adams, Nick - *Heartbreaker*
y VOYA - v19 - O '96 - p202 [501+]

Adams, Noah - *Piano Lessons*
NY - v72 - My 27 '96 - p132 [51-250]
PW - v244 - F 24 '97 - p88 [1-50]
SLJ - v42 - D '96 - p42+ [51-250]
Trib Bks - Ap 6 '97 - p8 [1-50]

Adams, P F - *Health-Risk Behaviors Among Our Nation's Youth*
J Gov Info - v23 - S '96 - p547+ [51-250]

Adams, Paul - *Reinventing Human Services*
Soc Ser R - v70 - D '96 - p670 [51-250]

Adams, Richard - *Tales from Watership Down*
y BL - v93 - S 1 '96 - p5 [51-250]
LJ - v121 - O 15 '96 - p92 [51-250]
NYTBR - v101 - D 1 '96 - p23 [51-250]
PW - v243 - S 23 '96 - p54 [51-250]
y SLJ - v43 - Ja '97 - p139 [51-250]
Spec - v277 - S 7 '96 - p36 [501+]

Adams, Robert McCormick - *Paths of Fire*
Choice - v34 - Mr '97 - p1200 [51-250]
New Sci - v153 - F 8 '97 - p42+ [501+]
Sci - v275 - Ja 10 '97 - p174 [501+]

Adams, Robert Merrihew - *Leibniz: Determinist, Theist, Idealist*
RM - v50 - S '96 - p143+ [501+]

Adams, Roy J - *Industrial Relations under Liberal Democracy*
ILRR - v50 - Ja '97 - p361+ [501+]

Adams, Scott - *The Dilbert Principle*
Bus W - D 16 '96 - p19+ [51-250]
CSM - v88 - N 7 '96 - p14 [51-250]
CSM - v89 - D 12 '96 - p14 [51-250]
CSM - v89 - Ja 9 '97 - p14 [51-250]
Ent W - Ja 31 '97 - p51+ [501+]
LJ - v122 - Mr 15 '97 - p37 [1-50]
Prog - v61 - Ja '97 - p36 [51-250]
The Dilbert Principle (Adams). Audio Version
BWatch - v17 - D '96 - p10 [1-50]

Dogbert's Top Secret Management Handbook
BL - v93 - N 15 '96 - p556 [51-250]
CSM - v88 - N 7 '96 - p14 [51-250]
CSM - v89 - D 12 '96 - p14 [51-250]
CSM - v89 - Ja 9 '97 - p14 [51-250]
CSM - v89 - F 6 '97 - p14 [51-250]
Ent W - Ja 31 '97 - p51+ [501+]
Fugitive from the Cubicle Police
BWatch - v17 - N '96 - p11 [51-250]

Adams, Simon - *20th Century: A Visual History*
y Sch Lib - v45 - F '97 - p49 [51-250]
The DK Visual Timeline of the 20th Century
cr BL - v93 - D 1 '96 - p647 [51-250]
cr Ch BWatch - v7 - Ja '97 - p7 [1-50]
cr SLJ - v43 - Ja '97 - p118 [51-250]

Adams, Steven G - *Maple Talk*
SciTech - v20 - D '96 - p7 [51-250]

Adams, Thomas Randolph - *English Maritime Books Printed before 1801*
r BC - v46 - Spr '97 - p150+ [501+]
r RQ - v35 - Sum '96 - p484+ [51-250]

Adams, W M - *The Physical Geography of Africa*
GJ - v163 - Mr '97 - p95 [501+]

Adams, William D - *Commonsense Vegetable Gardening for the South*
r Hort - v74 - Ag '96 - p67+ [251-500]

Adams, William J - *Finite Mathematics, Models, and Structure*
SciTech - v20 - S '96 - p3 [51-250]
Get a Firmer Grip on Your Math
Math T - v90 - Mr '97 - p248 [51-250]
Get a Grip on Your Math
Math T - v90 - Mr '97 - p248 [51-250]

Adamson, Donald - *Blaise Pascal: Mathematician, Physicist, and Thinker about God*
Isis - v87 - S '96 - p545 [251-500]

Adamson, Jean - *Topsy and Tim Have Itchy Heads*
c Bks Keeps - N '96 - p6 [51-250]
Topsy and Tim Meet the Ambulance Crew
c Bks Keeps - N '96 - p6 [51-250]

Adamson, Joseph - *Melville, Shame, and the Evil Eye*
Choice - v34 - Ap '97 - p1332 [51-250]
R&R Bk N - v12 - F '97 - p89 [51-250]

Adamson, Lydia - *A Cat on a Beach Blanket*
PW - v244 - Ap 21 '97 - p63 [51-250]
A Cat under the Mistletoe
y SLJ - v43 - Ja '97 - p139 [51-250]
WSJ-MW - v78 - D 9 '96 - pA12 [1-50]

Adamson, Lynda G - *Recreating the Past*
r New Ad - v9 - Fall '96 - p347+ [51-250]
r RQ - v36 - Win '96 - p216 [51-250]

Adamson, Seabron - *Energy Use, Air Pollution, and Environmental Policy in Krakow*
JEL - v34 - D '96 - p2131 [51-250]

Adang, Camilla - *Muslim Writers on Judaism and the Hebrew Bible*
Rel St Rev - v23 - Ap '97 - p199 [51-250]

Adas, William Michael - *Technology and European Overseas Enterprises*
SciTech - v20 - S '96 - p46 [51-250]

Aday, Lu Ann - *Designing and Conducting Health Surveys. 2nd Ed.*
r SciTech - v21 - Mr '97 - p45 [51-250]

Adcock, Betty - *The Difficult Wheel*
HR - v49 - Sum '96 - p341+ [501+]

Adcock, Fleur - *Hugh Primas and the Archpoet*
Specu - v71 - O '96 - p925+ [501+]
The Oxford Book of Creatures
BW - v26 - Ag 25 '96 - p13 [51-250]
ELT - v40 - 1 '97 - p125 [51-250]

Addelson, Kathryn Pyne - *Moral Passages*
Ethics - v107 - O '96 - p176+ [51-250]

Addleson, Mark - *Equilibrium Versus Understanding*
JEL - v34 - S '96 - p1407 [51-250]

Addleton, Jonathan S - *Some Far and Distant Place*
KR - v65 - F 1 '97 - p179 [251-500]
LJ - v122 - Ap 1 '97 - p100 [51-250]
PW - v244 - Ja 27 '97 - p86 [51-250]

Addonizio, Kim - *Jimmy and Rita*
BW - v27 - Ja 26 '97 - p8 [251-500]
LJ - v122 - Mr 15 '97 - p66 [51-250]
PW - v243 - D 30 '96 - p61 [51-250]

Addy, Sharon H - *A Visit with Great-Grandma*
c Learning - v25 - Mr '97 - p54 [1-50]

Adedjouma, Davida - *The Palm of My Heart (Illus. by Gregory Christie)*
c BL - v93 - F 15 '97 - p1024+ [51-250]
c CBRS - v25 - N '96 - p29 [51-250]
c CCB-B - v50 - D '96 - p127 [51-250]
c HB Guide - v8 - Spr '97 - p149 [51-250]
c KR - v64 - Ag 15 '96 - p1232 [51-250]
c SLJ - v43 - Ja '97 - p95 [51-250]

Adeeb, Hassan - *Nigeria: One Nation, Many Cultures*
c HB Guide - v7 - Fall '96 - p384 [51-250]

Adelman, Alan - *An International Student's Guide to Mexican Universities*
yr ARBA - v28 - '97 - p143+ [51-250]

Adelman, Clifford - *Lessons of a Generation*
TCR - v97 - Sum '96 - p651+ [501+]

Adelman, Irma - *Dynamics and Income Distribution*
Econ J - v106 - S '96 - p1467+ [501+]
Institutions and Development Strategies
Econ J - v106 - S '96 - p1480 [51-250]

Adelman, Jeremy - *Frontier Development*
EHR - v112 - F '97 - p251+ [501+]
JIH - v27 - Aut '96 - p363+ [501+]

Adelman, M A - *The Genie out of the Bottle*
BHR - v70 - Sum '96 - p279+ [501+]
JEL - v35 - Mr '97 - p183+ [501+]

Adelsberger, Lucie - *Auschwitz: A Doctor's Story*
TranslRevS - v2 - D '96 - p6+ [51-250]

Adelson, Roger - *London and the Invention of the Middle East*
AAPSS-A - v550 - Mr '97 - p178+ [501+]
Albion - v28 - '96 - p745+ [501+]
For Aff - v75 - S '96 - p155 [51-250]
HT - v47 - Ja '97 - p59 [501+]

Adepoju, Aderanti - *Gender, Work and Population in Sub-Saharan Africa*
Signs - v22 - Aut '96 - p227+ [501+]

Ades, Dawn - *Dali*
HAHR - v77 - My '97 - p294+ [251-500]

Adewale, Maja-Pearce - *Directory of African Media*
r Africa T - v43 - 4 '96 - p405+ [501+]

Adey, Robert - *Locked Room Murders and Other Impossible Crimes*
r RQ - v36 - Win '96 - p223 [51-250]

Adinolfi, JoAnn - *Tina's Diner (Illus. by JoAnn Adinolfi)*
c PW - v244 - Ap 28 '97 - p74 [51-250]

Adint, Victor - *Working Together against Crime*
c SLJ - v43 - F '97 - p107+ [51-250]

Adireks, Paul - *Until the Karma Ends*
FEER - v159 - N 21 '96 - p66 [501+]

Adizes, Ichak - *The Pursuit of Prime*
BL - v93 - D 1 '96 - p626 [51-250]

Adjaye, Joseph K - *Time in the Black Consciousness*
J Bl St - v27 - N '96 - p292+ [501+]

Adjibolosoo, Senyo B-S K - *Human Factor Engineering and the Political Economy of African Development*
JEL - v35 - Mr '97 - p268+ [51-250]
R&R Bk N - v11 - D '96 - p30 [51-250]
The Human Factor in Developing Africa
JTWS - v13 - Fall '96 - p247+ [501+]

Adkin, Mark - *The Charge: Why the Light Brigade Was Lost*
TLS - F 28 '97 - p29 [501+]

Adkins, Lisa - *Gendered Work*
CS - v25 - N '96 - p799+ [501+]
Sexualizing the Social
R&R Bk N - v11 - N '96 - p40 [51-250]

Adkins, Mark - *Be Strong for Me*
PW - v244 - Mr 31 '97 - p55+ [51-250]
Be Strong for Me (Rubinstein). Audio Version
PW - v244 - F 3 '97 - p42+ [51-250]

Adkins, Susan L - *Legacy: General Aviation Highlights from 8 Decades of NACA/NASA Research. Electronic Media Version*
r J Gov Info - v23 - S '96 - p569 [51-250]

Adler, C S - *More than a Horse*
c BL - v93 - Mr 15 '97 - p1241 [51-250]
c CCB-B - v50 - Mr '97 - p238+ [51-250]
What's to Be Scared Of, Suki?
c BL - v93 - N 1 '96 - p497 [51-250]
c Ch BWatch - v6 - D '96 - p5 [51-250]
c HB Guide - v8 - Spr '97 - p61 [51-250]
c SLJ - v42 - O '96 - p120 [51-250]

Adler, David, 1962- - *The Life and Cuisine of Elvis Presley*
J Am Cult - v19 - Sum '96 - p151+ [501+]

Adler, David A - *Calculator Riddles (Illus. by Cynthia Fisher)*
c BL - v93 - Ap 1 '97 - p1341 [1-50]
c Inst - v105 - My '96 - p71 [1-50]

Cam Jansen and the Ghostly Mystery (Illus. by Susanna Natti)
c BL - v93 - Ja '97 - p855 [251-500]
c HB Guide - v8 - Spr '97 - p56 [51-250]
c SLJ - v42 - D '96 - p84 [51-250]
Easy Math Puzzles (Illus. by Cynthia Fisher)
c BL - v93 - Mr 1 '97 - p1156 [51-250]
c CCB-B - v50 - My '97 - p310 [51-250]
Fraction Fun (Illus. by Nancy Tobin)
c CCB-B - v50 - D '96 - p127 [51-250]
c HB Guide - v8 - Spr '97 - p110 [51-250]
c Learning - v25 - Ja '97 - p56 [1-50]
c PW - v243 - S 9 '96 - p84 [51-250]
c SLJ - v42 - N '96 - p95 [51-250]
The Kids' Catalog of Jewish Holidays
c BL - v93 - D 15 '96 - p722 [51-250]
c SLJ - v43 - Mr '97 - p170 [51-250]
Lou Gehrig: The Luckiest Man (Illus. by Terry Widener)
c BL - v93 - My 15 '97 - p1575 [51-250]
c CBRS - v25 - Mr '97 - p91 [51-250]
c CCB-B - v50 - Ap '97 - p270 [51-250]
c KR - v65 - F 1 '97 - p218 [51-250]
c PW - v244 - F 24 '97 - p91 [51-250]
c Trib Bks - Mr 30 '97 - p4+ [51-250]
Lucky Stars
c BL - v92 - Ag '96 - p1899+ [51-250]
One Yellow Daffodil (Illus. by Lloyd Bloom)
c RT - v50 - N '96 - p258 [51-250]
c RT - v50 - Mr '97 - p478 [51-250]
A Picture Book of Davy Crockett (Illus. by John Wallner)
c HB Guide - v7 - Fall '96 - p370 [251-500]
A Picture Book of Sojourner Truth (Illus. by Gershom Griffith)
c SLJ - v42 - D '96 - p45 [51-250]
A Picture Book of Thomas Alva Edison (Illus. by John Wallner)
c HB Guide - v8 - Spr '97 - p155 [51-250]
c Inst - v106 - O '96 - p67 [51-250]
c SB - v33 - Ja '97 - p21 [51-250]
c SLJ - v42 - D '96 - p110+ [51-250]
Young Cam Jansen and the Dinosaur Game (Illus. by Susanna Natti)
c BL - v92 - Ag '96 - p1909+ [51-250]
c HB Guide - v7 - Fall '96 - p283 [51-250]
Young Cam Jansen and the Lost Tooth (Illus. by Susanna Natti)
c BL - v93 - My 1 '97 - p1502 [51-250]
Young Cam Jansen and the Missing Cookie (Illus. by Susanna Natti)
c BL - v92 - Ag '96 - p1909+ [51-250]
c HB Guide - v7 - Fall '96 - p283 [1-50]
Adler, David Gray - *The Constitution and the Conduct of American Foreign Policy*
   Choice - v34 - Mr '97 - p1239 [51-250]
   For Aff - v75 - N '96 - p154 [51-250]
Adler, Elizabeth - *Now or Never*
   BL - v93 - F 15 '97 - p1005 [51-250]
   KR - v64 - D 15 '96 - p1748 [251-500]
   LJ - v122 - Ja '97 - p141 [51-250]
   PW - v244 - Ja 27 '97 - p78 [51-250]
The Secret of the Villa Mimosa
   Books - v9 - S '95 - p24 [1-50]
Adler, Franklin Hugh - *Italian Industrialists from Liberalism to Fascism*
   Ant R - v54 - Fall '96 - p491+ [251-500]
   Choice - v34 - O '96 - p337+ [51-250]
   JEL - v34 - D '96 - p2097+ [51-250]
Adler, Freda - *The Legacy of Anomie Theory*
   SF - v75 - S '96 - p360+ [251-500]
Adler, Mortimer J - *How to Think about War and Peace*
   Rapport - v19 - 6 '96 - p33 [251-500]
Adler, Nancy J - *Competitive Frontiers*
   JIB - v27 - 4 '96 - p802+ [501+]
Adler, Naomi - *The Barefoot Book of Animal Tales from around the World (Illus. by Amanda Hall)*
c JB - v60 - D '96 - p244+ [51-250]
c Sch Lib - v44 - Ag '96 - p102 [51-250]
c TES - D 6 '96 - p16* [501+]
The Dial Book of Animal Tales from around the World (Illus. by Amanda Hall)
c BL - v93 - O 1 '96 - p356 [51-250]
c CCB-B - v50 - N '96 - p90+ [51-250]
c HB Guide - v8 - Spr '97 - p99 [1-50]
c KR - v64 - S 1 '96 - p1318 [51-250]
c PW - v243 - O 21 '96 - p85 [51-250]
c SLJ - v42 - D '96 - p110 [51-250]
Adler, William M - *Land of Opportunity*
   LATBR - O 20 '96 - p15 [251-500]

Adlerman, Dan - *Africa Calling (Illus. by Kimberly M Adlerman)*
c BL - v93 - O 1 '96 - p356 [51-250]
c CBRS - v25 - Win '97 - p61 [51-250]
c HB Guide - v8 - Spr '97 - p17 [51-250]
c PW - v243 - O 14 '96 - p82 [51-250]
c SLJ - v42 - S '96 - p170 [51-250]
Adoff, Arnold - *I Am the Darker Brother. Rev. Ed. (Illus. by Benny Andrews)*
y BL - v93 - F 15 '97 - p1013 [51-250]
y CCB-B - v50 - My '97 - p311 [51-250]
y Kliatt - v31 - Mr '97 - p22 [51-250]
c PW - v243 - D 9 '96 - p69 [51-250]
In for Winter, Out for Spring (Illus. by Jerry Pinkney)
c PW - v244 - F 24 '97 - p93 [1-50]
Love Letters (Illus. by Lisa Desimini)
c BL - v93 - Ja '97 - p863 [251-500]
c CBRS - v25 - Mr '97 - p91+ [51-250]
c CCB-B - v50 - Mr '97 - p239 [51-250]
c KR - v64 - D 1 '96 - p1732 [51-250]
c PW - v243 - D 2 '96 - p60+ [51-250]
c SLJ - v43 - Mr '97 - p195 [51-250]
Slow Dance Heart Break Blues (Illus. by William Cotton)
y Emerg Lib - v24 - S '96 - p23 [1-50]
c RT - v50 - D '96 - p343 [51-250]
Adorian, Simon - *Trojans*
c Sch Lib - v44 - N '96 - p166 [51-250]
Adorni-Braccesi, Simonetta - *Una Citta Infetta*
   CHR - v82 - O '96 - p706+ [501+]
Adorno, Theodor W - *Aesthetic Theory*
   PW - v243 - D 2 '96 - p50 [51-250]
The Stars down to Earth and Other Essays on the Irrational in Culture
   RM - v49 - Je '96 - p909+ [501+]
Adriance, Madeleine Cousineau - *Promised Land*
   CS - v25 - S '96 - p627+ [501+]
Adriani, Gotz - *Cezanne Paintings*
   Art J - v55 - Win '96 - p95+ [501+]
Adshead, Paul - *The Red Herring Mystery*
c HB Guide - v7 - Fall '96 - p285 [51-250]
Adshead, S A M - *China in World History. 2nd Ed.*
   Historian - v58 - Sum '96 - p878+ [251-500]
Adsorption: Journal of the International Adsorption Society
p Nature - v383 - S 5 '96 - p41 [251-500]
Advanced Computational Methods in Heat Transfer IV
   SciTech - v20 - D '96 - p24 [51-250]
Advanced Telecommunications in U.S. Public Elementary and Secondary Schools 1995
   EL - v54 - O '96 - p91 [51-250]
   SLMQ - v24 - Sum '96 - p220 [51-250]
Advances in Applied Microeconomics. Vol. 6
   JEL - v35 - Mr '97 - p199+ [51-250]
Advances in Behavioral Economics. Vol. 3
   JEL - v35 - Mr '97 - p199 [51-250]
Advances in Bioengineering 1996
   SciTech - v21 - Mr '97 - p44 [51-250]
Advances in Chemical Physics. Vol. 95
   SciTech - v20 - N '96 - p23 [51-250]
Advances in Chemical Physics. Vol. 96
   SciTech - v20 - D '96 - p28 [1-50]
Advances in Chemical Physics. Vol. 99
   SciTech - v21 - Mr '97 - p31 [51-250]
Advances in Collection Development and Resource Management. Vol. 1
   LAR - v98 - Jl '96 - p373 [51-250]
Advances in Cryogenic Engineering. Vol. 41, Pts. A-B
   SciTech - v20 - D '96 - p83 [51-250]
Advances in Futures and Options Research. Vol. 8
   JEL - v34 - S '96 - p1434+ [51-250]
Advances in Group Processes. Vol. 13
   JEL - v34 - D '96 - p2142 [51-250]
Advances in Heat and Mass Transfer in Biotechnology 1996
   SciTech - v21 - Mr '97 - p34 [51-250]
Advances in International Accounting. Vol. 9
   JEL - v35 - Mr '97 - p255+ [51-250]
Advances in International Comparative Management. Vol. 11
   JEL - v34 - D '96 - p2092 [51-250]
, 1959- - *Advances in Nuclear Dynamics*
   SciTech - v20 - N '96 - p20 [51-250]
Advances in Nuclear Dynamics 2
   SciTech - v20 - D '96 - p25 [51-250]
Advances in Taxation. Vol. 8
   JEL - v35 - Mr '97 - p256 [51-250]
Advances in the Theory of Computation and Computational Mathematics. Vol. 1
   SciTech - v20 - D '96 - p16 [51-250]

Advances in Turbulence VI
   SciTech - v20 - D '96 - p61 [51-250]
Advances in Working Capital Management. Vol. 3
   JEL - v34 - S '96 - p1463 [51-250]
Adverse Reactions to HIV Vaccines
   J Gov Info - v23 - S '96 - p558 [51-250]
Aebi, Robert - *Schrodinger Diffusion Processes*
   SciTech - v20 - S '96 - p9 [51-250]
Aelfric - *Aelfric's Prefaces*
   MLR - v91 - O '96 - p952+ [501+]
Aellen, Christian - *A La Recherche De L'Ordre Cosmique. Vols. 1-2*
   AJA - v100 - Jl '96 - p626+ [501+]
Aer, Anneli - *Patents in Imperial Russia*
   Russ Rev - v55 - O '96 - p714 [251-500]
   Slav R - v55 - Sum '96 - p482+ [501+]
Aercke, Kristiaan P - *Gods of Play*
   Ren Q - v49 - Win '96 - p913+ [501+]
Aeronautical Information Manual/Federal Aviation Regulations 1997
   A & S Sm - v11 - F '97 - p87 [1-50]
Aertsen, A - *Brain Theory*
   SciTech - v21 - Mr '97 - p41 [51-250]
Aeschlimann, Jean-Christopher - *Ethique Et Responsabilite--Paul Ricoeur*
   Dialogue - v35 - Fall '96 - p836+ [501+]
Aeschylus - *Persians (Hall)*
   Choice - v34 - D '96 - p609 [51-250]
Aesop - *Aesop's Fables (Illus. by Heidi Holder)*
c ECEJ - v24 - Fall '96 - p37 [51-250]
Aesop's Fables (Kent). Audio Version
y Kliatt - v31 - My '97 - p35 [51-250]
Aesoph, Lauri - *How to Eat Away Arthritis*
   LJ - v121 - N 1 '96 - p100 [51-250]
Afary, Janet - *The Iranian Constitutional Revolution 1906-1911*
   Choice - v34 - Ja '97 - p860 [51-250]
Affordable Bed and Breakfasts in Quebec 96-97
r Quill & Q - v62 - S '96 - p25 [51-250]
Affron, Charles - *Sets in Motion*
   Film Cr - v21 - Fall '96 - p91+ [501+]
Afgan, Naim - *New Developments in Heat Exchangers*
   SciTech - v21 - Mr '97 - p85 [51-250]
Afkhami, Mahnaz - *Women in Exile*
   MEJ - v50 - Sum '96 - p457 [51-250]
Africa Faith and Justice Network - *The African Synod*
   WorldV - v12 - Jl '96 - p5 [51-250]
Africa On File. Vols. 1-2
cr SLJ - v42 - Ag '96 - p180 [51-250]
Africa: The Art of a Continent
   Choice - v34 - Ja '97 - p782 [51-250]
   LJ - v121 - N 15 '96 - p58 [51-250]
The African Business Handbook. Vol. 3
r R&R Bk N - v12 - F '97 - p20 [51-250]
African Development Indicators 1996
r Choice - v34 - Ja '97 - p765 [51-250]
r JEL - v34 - D '96 - p2121 [51-250]
African Exodus
   For Aff - v75 - S '96 - p161 [51-250]
African Rights (Organization) - *Facing Genocide*
   For Aff - v76 - My '97 - p147+ [51-250]
African Statistical Yearbook. 1992 Ed., Vol. 1, Pt. 2
r R&R Bk N - v11 - D '96 - p26 [51-250]
Afshar, Haleh - *Women and Politics in the Third World*
   TLS - S 13 '96 - p32 [251-500]
After the Flood
   J Gov Info - v23 - S '96 - p582 [1-50]
Afterimage
p Sm Pr R - v28 - Jl '96 - p27+ [501+]
Afterman, Allan B - *International Accounting, Financial Reporting, and Analysis*
r AR - v72 - Ja '97 - p177+ [501+]
Afton, Jean - *Cheyenne Dog Soldiers*
   PW - v244 - Ap 21 '97 - p57 [51-250]
The Aga Khan Rural Support Program: A Third Evaluation
   JEL - v35 - Mr '97 - p279 [51-250]
Agard, John - *A Caribbean Dozen (Illus. by Cathie Felstead)*
c Bks Keeps - Ja '97 - p24 [51-250]
Get Back, Pimple! (Illus. by Point)
c JB - v60 - Ag '96 - p153 [51-250]
We Animals Would Like a Word with You (Illus. by Satoshi Kitamura)
c Bks Keeps - Mr '97 - p23 [51-250]
c TES - D 13 '96 - p32 [51-250]
Why Is the Sky? (Illus. by Andrzej Klimowski)
c JB - v60 - O '96 - p189+ [51-250]
c Sch Lib - v45 - F '97 - p41 [51-250]
c TES - Jl 26 '96 - pR8 [51-250]

Agarwal, Bina - *A Field of One's Own*
  CS - v26 - Ja '97 - p50+ [501+]
  TLS - Ja 17 '97 - p29 [501+]
Agarwal, R P - *Dynamical Systems and Applications*
  SIAM Rev - v38 - D '96 - p713 [1-50]
Agarwal, V K - *Principles of Seed Pathology. 2nd Ed.*
  SciTech - v21 - Mr '97 - p70 [51-250]
Agasso, Domenico - *Saint Mary Mazzarello: The Spirit of Joy*
  RR - v56 - Ja '97 - p107 [1-50]
Agawu, Kofi - *African Rhythm*
  Notes - v53 - Mr '97 - p818+ [501+]
Agee, James - *Agee: Selected Literary Documents*
  Choice - v34 - Mr '97 - p1157+ [51-250]
Agee, Jon - *Dmitri the Astronaut (Illus. by Jon Agee)*
  c CBRS - v25 - O '96 - p13 [51-250]
  c HB Guide - v8 - Spr '97 - p17 [51-250]
  c NYTBR - v102 - Mr 2 '97 - p25 [1-50]
  c NYTLa - v146 - D 9 '96 - pC18 [51-250]
  c SLJ - v42 - N '96 - p76 [51-250]
  So Many Dynamos! and Other Palindromes
  c PW - v244 - F 24 '97 - p93 [1-50]
Agee, M J - *Heaven Found*
  Rapport - v19 - 4 '96 - p40 [51-250]
Agel, Jerome - *Words That Make America Great*
  r BL - v93 - Mr 15 '97 - p1262 [51-250]
  LJ - v122 - Ap 1 '97 - p105 [51-250]
Agenor, Pierre-Richard - *Development Macroeconomics*
  Choice - v34 - N '96 - p504+ [51-250]
  JEL - v34 - S '96 - p1475 [51-250]
Ager, Derek - *The New Catastrophism*
  Am Sci - v84 - N '96 - p602 [251-500]
Aggarwal, Vinod K - *Debt Games*
  JEL - v35 - Mr '97 - p217 [51-250]
Aggor, F Komla - *Eros En La Poesia De Miguel Hernandez*
  Hisp - v79 - S '96 - p439+ [501+]
Agha, Shahid Ali - *The Country without a Post Office*
  PW - v244 - F 24 '97 - p87 [1-50]
Aghion, Irene - *Gods and Heroes of Classical Antiquity*
  r Choice - v34 - My '97 - p1471 [51-250]
Agnew, Jean - *Belfast Merchant Families in the Seventeenth Century*
  ILS - v16 - Spr '97 - p36 [1-50]
Agnew, John - *Human Geography*
  TES - O 18 '96 - pR6 [251-500]
  Mastering Space
  EG - v73 - Ja '97 - p137+ [501+]
Agnew, Palmer - *Distributed Multimedia*
  CBR - v14 - N '96 - p37 [51-250]
Agni
  p Sm Pr R - v28 - O '96 - p13+ [501+]
Agonafer, Mulugeta - *Africa in the Contemporary International Disorder*
  JEL - v35 - Mr '97 - p284 [51-250]
Agoos, Julie - *Calendar Year*
  PW - v243 - D 30 '96 - p62 [51-250]
Agosin, Manuel R - *Foreign Direct Investment in Latin America*
  JEL - v34 - D '96 - p2045 [51-250]
Agosin, Marjorie - *Happiness: Stories*
  TranslRevS - v1 - My '95 - p28 [51-250]
  Starry Night
  LJ - v122 - F 1 '97 - p84 [51-250]
  Tapestries of Hope, Threads of Love
  Bloom Rev - v16 - N '96 - p7+ [501+]
  LATBR - S 1 '96 - p11 [51-250]
  R&R Bk N - v11 - D '96 - p42 [51-250]
  What Is Secret
  Choice - v34 - S '96 - p134 [51-250]
Agosta, William - *Bombardier Beetles and Fever Trees*
  BioSci - v47 - Mr '97 - p187+ [51-250]
Agosti, Maristella - *Information Retrieval and Hypertext*
  SciTech - v20 - S '96 - p8 [51-250]
Agostino, Marc - *Le Pape Pie XI Et L'Opinion 1922-1939*
  CHR - v83 - Ja '97 - p122+ [501+]
Agrest, Diana - *The Sex of Architecture*
  Ms - v7 - N '96 - p81 [251-500]
Agricultural and Resource Economics Review
  p JEL - v35 - Mr '97 - p307 [51-250]
Agricultural Economics
  p JEL - v34 - S '96 - p1504 [51-250]
The Agricultural Outlook. 1996 Ed.
  r JEL - v34 - D '96 - p2130 [51-250]
Agricultural Policies, Markets and Trade in OECD Countries 1996. Vols. 1-2
  JEL - v35 - Mr '97 - p296+ [51-250]
Agriculture, Trade, and the Environment
  J Gov Info - v23 - S '96 - p554 [51-250]

Aguero, Felipe - *Soldiers, Civilians, and Democracy*
  APSR - v90 - D '96 - p928+ [501+]
  Arm F&S - v23 - Fall '96 - p126+ [501+]
  Choice - v34 - S '96 - p202 [51-250]
  JPR - v33 - Ag '96 - p377 [251-500]
Agueros, Jack - *Sonnets from the Puerto Rican*
  BWatch - v17 - S '96 - p9 [1-50]
  y Kliatt - v30 - N '96 - p19 [51-250]
  LJ - v121 - S 15 '96 - p71+ [51-250]
  Sm Pr R - v29 - Ja '97 - p5 [51-250]
Aguilar, Rosario - *The Lost Chronicles of Terra Firma*
  BL - v93 - D 15 '96 - p707+ [51-250]
  KR - v64 - D 15 '96 - p1767 [51-250]
  NYTBR - v102 - Mr 2 '97 - p18 [51-250]
Aguilera Garramuno, Marco Tulio - *Las Noches De Ventura*
  WLT - v70 - Aut '96 - p919 [251-500]
Aguinis, Marcos - *La Conspiracion De Los Idiotas*
  BL - v93 - Mr 15 '97 - p1232 [1-50]
Aguirre, Erick - *Pasado Meridiano*
  BL - v93 - S 15 '96 - p227 [1-50]
Aguirre, Rafael A - *Amanecer*
  BL - v93 - Ap 1 '97 - p1284 [1-50]
Aguirre Beltran, Gonzalo - *Cuatro Nobles Titulados En Contienda Por La Tierra*
  HAHR - v76 - N '96 - p778+ [251-500]
  El Negro Esclavo En Nueva Espana
  HAHR - v77 - F '97 - p109+ [251-500]
Aguirre Gandarias, Sabino - *Lope Garcia De Salazar: El Primer Historiados De Bizkaia 1399-1476*
  EHR - v111 - N '96 - p1261 [51-250]
Agutter, Paul S - *The Meaning of Nucleocytoplasmic Transport*
  SciTech - v20 - D '96 - p31 [51-250]
A H Ahmad Sarji - *The Civil Service of Malaysia*
  J Gov Info - v23 - S '96 - p659 [1-50]
Ahearn, Edward J - *Visionary Fictions*
  Choice - v34 - My '97 - p1490 [51-250]
Ahearne, Jeremy - *Michel De Certeau: Interpretation and Its Other*
  CS - v26 - Mr '97 - p251+ [501+]
Ahenakew, Freda - *Our Grandmothers' Lives as Told in Their Own Words*
  JWomHist - v8 - Fall '96 - p205+ [501+]
Ahl, Diane Cole - *Benozzo Gozzoli*
  Choice - v34 - Mr '97 - p1149+ [51-250]
  LJ - v122 - F 15 '97 - p130 [51-250]
  Spec - v277 - D 14 '96 - p76 [51-250]
  Leonardo Da Vinci's Sforza Monument Horse
  BM - v138 - O '96 - p699 [251-500]
Ahl, Frederick - *The Odyssey Re-Formed*
  Choice - v34 - D '96 - p609 [51-250]
  New R - v216 - F 24 '97 - p30+ [501+]
Ahl, Valerie - *Hierarchy Theory*
  R&R Bk N - v11 - D '96 - p67 [51-250]
Ahlander, Ann-Mari Satre - *Environmental Problems in the Shortage Economy*
  Env - v38 - O '96 - p25 [51-250]
Ahlberg, Allan - *The Better Brown Stories (Illus. by Fritz Wegner)*
  c Bks Keeps - Ja '97 - p23 [51-250]
  c Bks Keeps - Ja '97 - p23 [51-250]
  c HB - v72 - S '96 - p590+ [51-250]
  c HB Guide - v7 - Fall '96 - p289 [51-250]
  c Magpies - v11 - My '96 - p41 [251-500]
  c Smith - v27 - N '96 - p174 [1-50]
  The Giant Baby (Illus. by Fritz Wegner)
  c Bks Keeps - Jl '96 - p12 [51-250]
  c Magpies - v11 - S '96 - p45 [1-50]
  Master Bun the Bakers' Boy (Illus. by Fritz Wegner)
  c Bks Keeps - N '96 - p4+ [501+]
  Master Money the Millionaire (Illus. by Andre Amstutz)
  c Bks Keeps - N '96 - p4+ [501+]
  Master Salt the Sailors' Son (Illus. by Andre Amstutz)
  c Bks Keeps - N '96 - p4+ [501+]
  Miss Brick the Builders' Baby (Illus. by Colin McNaughton)
  c Bks Keeps - N '96 - p4+ [501+]
  Miss Dirt the Dustman's Daughter (Illus. by Tony Ross)
  c Bks Keeps - N '96 - p4+ [501+]
  Miss Dose the Doctor's Daughter (Illus. by Faith Jaques)
  c Bks Keeps - N '96 - p4+ [501+]
  Miss Jump the Jockey (Illus. by Andre Amstutz)
  c Bks Keeps - N '96 - p4+ [501+]
  Mr. and Mrs. Hay the Horse (Illus. by Colin McNaughton)
  c Bks Keeps - N '96 - p4+ [501+]
  Mr. Biff the Boxer (Illus. by Janet Ahlberg)
  c Bks Keeps - N '96 - p4+ [501+]

  Mr. Buzz the Beeman (Illus. by Faith Jaques)
  c Bks Keeps - N '96 - p4+ [501+]
  Mr. Cosmo the Conjuror (Illus. by Joe Wright)
  c Bks Keeps - N '96 - p4+ [501+]
  Mr. Creep the Crook (Illus. by Andre Amstutz)
  c Bks Keeps - N '96 - p4+ [501+]
  Mr. Tick the Teacher (Illus. by Faith Jaques)
  c Bks Keeps - N '96 - p4+ [501+]
  Mrs. Jolly's Joke Shop (Illus. by Colin McNaughton)
  c Bks Keeps - N '96 - p4+ [501+]
  Mrs. Lather's Laundry (Illus. by Andre Amstutz)
  c Bks Keeps - N '96 - p4+ [501+]
  Mrs. Plug the Plumber (Illus. by Joe Wright)
  c Bks Keeps - N '96 - p4+ [501+]
  Mrs. Vole the Vet (Illus. by Emma Chichester Clark)
  c Bks Keeps - N '96 - p4+ [501+]
  Mrs. Wobble the Waitress (Illus. by Janet Ahlberg)
  c Bks Keeps - N '96 - p4+ [501+]
  Put on a Show! (Illus. by Colin McNaughton)
  c Bks Keeps - N '96 - p8 [51-250]
  Who Stole the Pie? (Illus. by Colin McNaughton)
  c Bks Keeps - N '96 - p8 [51-250]
Ahlberg, Janet - *Each Peach Pear Plum*
  c Bks Keeps - Mr '97 - p7 [1-50]
  The Jolly Pocket Postman
  c RT - v50 - S '96 - p54 [51-250]
Ahlbrandt, Calvin D - *Discrete Hamiltonian Systems*
  SciTech - v21 - Mr '97 - p21 [51-250]
Ahlbrandt, Roger S - *The Renaissance of American Steel*
  LJ - v122 - F 1 '97 - p92 [51-250]
  WSJ-MW - v78 - D 19 '96 - pA16 [501+]
Ahlburg, Dennis A - *The Impact of Population Growth on Well-Being in Developing Countries*
  JEL - v34 - D '96 - p2066 [51-250]
Ahles, Carol Laflin - *Fine Machine Sewing*
  LJ - v121 - D '96 - p91 [51-250]
Ahlgren, Gillian T W - *Teresa of Avila and the Politics of Sanctity*
  Bks & Cult - v2 - S '96 - p38 [501+]
  Choice - v34 - D '96 - p666 [51-250]
Ahlstrom, Goran - *Technological Development and Industrial Exhibitions 1850-1914*
  JEL - v34 - S '96 - p1471 [51-250]
  T&C - v38 - Ja '97 - p251+ [501+]
Ahmad, Nyla - *CyberSurfer: The OWL Internet Guide for Kids (Illus. by Martha Newbigging)*
  c Ch Bk News - v19 - Spr '96 - p21 [251-500]
  c Ch BWatch - v6 - Jl '96 - p2 [1-50]
  c Emerg Lib - v24 - Mr '97 - p26 [1-50]
  c Quill & Q - v63 - F '97 - p51 [51-250]
  c SLJ - v42 - S '96 - p208+ [51-250]
Ahmad, Rukhsana - *The Hope Chest*
  Obs - D 22 '96 - p17* [51-250]
  TLS - D 6 '96 - p23 [251-500]
Ahmed, Akbar S - *Living Islam*
  MEJ - v50 - Aut '96 - p621+ [501+]
  Postmodernism and Islam
  MEJ - v50 - Aut '96 - p621+ [501+]
Ahmed, Iftikhar - *Beyond Rio*
  JEL - v34 - S '96 - p1475+ [51-250]
Ahmed, Ishtiaq - *State, Nation and Ethnicity in Contemporary South Asia*
  Choice - v34 - S '96 - p202 [51-250]
Ahmed, Zafar U - *International Business Education Development*
  JEL - v34 - D '96 - p2063 [51-250]
Aho, James A - *This Thing of Darkness*
  J Ch St - v38 - Aut '96 - p913+ [251-500]
Ahrensdorf, Peter J - *The Death of Socrates and the Life of Philosophy*
  APSR - v90 - S '96 - p638+ [501+]
  RP - v58 - Fall '96 - p811+ [501+]
Ahsan, Aitzaz - *The Indus Saga and the Making of Pakistan*
  Choice - v34 - My '97 - p1554 [51-250]
Ahsanullah, M - *Applied Statistical Science I*
  SciTech - v21 - Mr '97 - p251+ [51-250]
Ahuis, Ferdinand - *Exodus 11,1-13,16 Und Die Bedeutung Der Tragergruppen Fur Das Verstandnis Des Passa*
  Rel St Rev - v23 - Ja '97 - p57 [51-250]
Ahuja, Satinder - *Chiral Separations*
  SciTech - v21 - Mr '97 - p95 [51-250]
Ahuja, Vijay - *Network and Internet Security*
  CBR - v14 - S '96 - p31 [1-50]
  Secure Commerce on the Internet
  CBR - v15 - Spr '97 - p7 [51-250]
Aidley, David J - *Ion Channels*
  Choice - v34 - Mr '97 - p1181 [51-250]
  Nature - v385 - Ja 16 '97 - p218 [51-250]

Aidoo, Ama Ata - *No Sweetness Here and Other Stories*
 ABR - v17 - Ag '96 - p16+ [501+]
 WLT - v71 - Win '97 - p205+ [501+]
AIDS Funding. 4th Ed.
 r ARBA - v28 - '97 - p310 [251-500]
Aiginger, Karl - *Applied Industrial Organization*
 JEL - v35 - Mr '97 - p163+ [501+]
Aikema, Bernard - *Jacopo Bassano and His Public*
 AB - v99 - Mr 3 '97 - p692 [251-250]
 Choice - v34 - Ja '97 - p782 [51-250]
 TLS - N 8 '96 - p33 [251-500]
 Tiepolo and His Circle
 NYRB - v44 - F 6 '97 - p35+ [501+]
Aiken, Joan - *The Cockatrice Boys*
 y BL - v93 - S 1 '96 - p69 [51-250]
 y BW - v26 - O 27 '96 - p11 [251-500]
 y BWatch - v17 - N '96 - p8 [51-250]
 y JB - v60 - Ag '96 - p162+ [51-250]
 y Sch Lib - v44 - Ag '96 - p117 [51-250]
 y SLJ - v43 - Mr '97 - p214 [51-250]
 c TES - Ag 30 '96 - p28 [51-250]
 y VOYA - v19 - F '97 - p333+ [251-500]
 Cold Shoulder Road
 c Bks Keeps - N '96 - p10 [51-250]
 y BL - v93 - Ap 1 '97 - p1302 [1-50]
 y Ch BWatch - v6 - My '96 - p2 [51-250]
 c CLW - v67 - D '96 - p55+ [251-500]
 c HB Guide - v7 - Fall '96 - p289 [51-250]
 c Obs - v54 - O 13 '96 - p18* [51-250]
 c PW - v244 - Ap 7 '97 - p94 [1-50]
 y VOYA - v19 - O '96 - p205 [51-250]
 A Creepy Company (Karpf). Audio Version
 c Ch BWatch - v6 - O '96 - p2 [1-50]
 Emma Watson
 y BL - v93 - S 15 '96 - p218 [51-250]
 LATBR - S 15 '96 - p10 [251-500]
 Fog Hounds. Wind Cat. Sea Mice (Illus. by Peter Bailey)
 c Books - v11 - Ap '97 - p24 [1-50]
 Jane Fairfax
 PW - v244 - Mr 31 '97 - p72 [1-50]
Aiken, Lewis R - *Rating Scales and Checklists*
 Per Psy - v50 - Spr '97 - p263+ [501+]
Aikman, David - *Hope: The Heart's Great Quest*
 Bks & Cult - v2 - My '96 - p23 [501+]
Aiming High
 TES - Mr 14 '97 - p20* [1-50]
Ainley, Janet - *Enriching Primary Mathematics with IT*
 TES - Ja 3 '97 - p47U [1-50]
 TES - Ja 17 '97 - p14* [501+]
Ainsworth, Catherine Harris - *Folktales of America. Vol. 4*
 CAY - v16 - Fall '95 - p2 [51-250]
Ainsworth, M - *Theory and Numerics of Ordinary and Partial Differential Equations*
 SIAM Rev - v38 - D '96 - p715 [251-500]
Ainsworth, Maryan W - *Petrus Christus: Renaissance Master of Bruges*
 Ren Q - v49 - Win '96 - p909+ [501+]
AIP Conference on Chaotic, Fractal, and Nonlinear Signal Processing (1995: Mystic, CT) - *Chaotic, Fractal, and Nonlinear Signal Processing*
 SciTech - v20 - D '96 - p75 [51-250]
Air Pollution IV
 SciTech - v20 - D '96 - p27 [51-250]
Air Pollution Modeling and Its Application XI
 SciTech - v21 - Mr '97 - p82 [51-250]
Aird, Catherine - *After Effects*
 Arm Det - v30 - Win '97 - p105 [251-500]
 BL - v92 - Ag '96 - p1884 [51-250]
Aisner, Joseph - *Comprehensive Textbook of Thoracic Oncology*
 SciTech - v20 - S '96 - p31 [51-250]
Aitchison, Jean - *International Thesaurus of Refugee Terminology. 2nd Ed.*
 r ARBA - v28 - '97 - p319 [251-500]
 r Choice - v34 - Mr '97 - p1133 [251-500]
 r R&R Bk N - v12 - F '97 - p55 [51-250]
 The Language Web
 Spec - v278 - F 8 '97 - p41+ [501+]
 The Seeds of Speech
 Choice - v34 - F '97 - p960 [51-250]
Aitchison, N B - *Armagh and the Royal Centres in Early Medieval Ireland*
 CHR - v82 - Jl '96 - p512+ [501+]
 EHR - v112 - Ap '97 - p425+ [501+]
Aitchison, John - *A Geography of the Welsh Language 1961-1991*
 GJ - v162 - Jl '96 - p230 [251-500]
Aitken, Adam - *In One House*
 Aust Bk R - Ag '96 - p56 [501+]

Aitken, M J - *The Origin of Modern Humans and the Impact of Chronometric Dating*
 RA - v25 - 4 '96 - p265+ [501+]
Aitken, Peter - *Microsoft Office 97 Professional 6-in-One*
 r CBR - v15 - Spr '97 - p8 [51-250]
Aitken, Robert - *The Ground We Share*
 BL - v92 - Ag '96 - p1858+ [51-250]
 Parabola - v21 - Ag '96 - p120 [1-50]
 Original Dwelling Place
 PW - v244 - Ap 21 '97 - p69 [1-50]
 Tric - v6 - Fall '96 - p131+ [501+]
 The Practice of Perfection
 PW - v244 - Ap 21 '97 - p69 [1-50]
Aitkens, Maggi - *Kerry, a Teenage Mother*
 y Emerg Lib - v24 - S '96 - p26 [1-50]
Aiyengar, Devi S - *I Am Hindu*
 c SLJ - v43 - Ja '97 - p95+ [51-250]
Aizpurua, Ramon - *Curazao Y La Costa De Caracas*
 HAHR - v76 - N '96 - p786+ [251-500]
Ajilvsgi, Geyata - *Butterfly Gardening for the South*
 LJ - v121 - D '96 - p66 [1-50]
Ajzenberg-Selove, Fay - *A Matter of Choices*
 Isis - v87 - D '96 - p695+ [51-250]
Ajzenstat, Janet - *Canada's Origins*
 BIC - v25 - N '96 - p13+ [501+]
Akagi, Cynthia G - *Dear Michael*
 y BL - v93 - Ja '97 - p828 [251-500]
Akaha, Tsuneo - *Japan in the Posthegemonic World*
 Pac A - v69 - Fall '96 - p413+ [501+]
Akbulut, Nazire - *Das Türkenbild In Der Neueren Deutschen Literatur 1970-1990*
 Ger Q - v69 - Spr '96 - p227+ [501+]
Ake, Claude - *Democracy and Development in Africa*
 Africa T - v43 - 4 '96 - p405+ [501+]
 For Aff - v75 - S '96 - p160+ [51-250]
 JEL - v34 - D '96 - p2113 [51-250]
 WorldV - v12 - Jl '96 - p5+ [51-250]
Akehurst, F R P - *A Handbook of the Troubadours*
 Notes - v53 - D '96 - p430+ [501+]
Akenside, Mark - *The Poetical Works of Mark Akenside*
 TLS - D 27 '96 - p13 [501+]
Akhtar, Salman - *Quest for Answers*
 J ClinPsyc - v57 - O '96 - p490+ [501+]
Akiko, Yosano - *River of Stars*
 PW - v244 - Ap 28 '97 - p72 [51-250]
Akiner, Shirin - *Political and Economic Trends in Central Asia*
 JTWS - v13 - Fall '96 - p235+ [501+]
Akinsha, Konstantin - *Beautiful Loot*
 Am - v175 - S 14 '96 - p27+ [501+]
Akivis, Maks A - *Conformal Differential Geometry and Its Generalizations*
 SciTech - v20 - N '96 - p15 [51-250]
Akiyama, Nobuo - *2001 Japanese and English Idioms*
 r ARBA - v28 - '97 - p394+ [251-500]
Akkermans, Antoon D L - *Molecular Microbial Ecology Manual*
 SciTech - v20 - S '96 - p24 [51-250]
Akkermans, E - *Physique Quantique Mesoscopique*
 SciTech - v20 - N '96 - p18 [51-250]
Aklaey, Airat - *Interethnic Conflict and Political Change in the Former USSR*
 r JPR - v34 - F '97 - p107 [51-250]
Akst, Daniel - *St. Burl's Obituary*
 Bloom Rev - v16 - Jl '96 - p16 [251-500]
 LATBR - Ag 11 '96 - p8 [251-500]
 PW - v244 - Mr 3 '97 - p72 [1-50]
 VV - v41 - N 12 '96 - p85 [51-250]
Aksyonov, Vassily - *The Winter's Hero*
 CSM - v88 - O 21 '96 - p12 [501+]
 SFR - v21 - Jl '96 - p5 [251-500]
Aktrin Research Institute - *The Furniture Industry in China and Hong Kong*
 R&R Bk N - v11 - N '96 - p33 [51-250]
Alagappa, Muthiah - *Political Legitimacy in Southeast Asia*
 PSQ - v111 - Win '96 - p740+ [501+]
Alan-Williams, Gregory - *Boys to Men*
 y BL - v93 - F 15 '97 - p986 [51-250]
 KR - v64 - D 15 '96 - p1775 [251-500]
 LJ - v122 - Ap 1 '97 - p112+ [51-250]
 PW - v243 - D 30 '96 - p50 [51-250]
 A Gathering of Heroes
 Bl S - v26 - Fall '96 - p107 [51-250]
 y Kliatt - v31 - Ja '97 - p20 [51-250]
Alaolmolki, Nozar - *The Persian Gulf Region in the Twenty First Century*
 MEJ - v51 - Spr '97 - p312 [51-250]
Alarcon, Francisco X - *Laughing Tomatoes (Illus. by Maya Christina Gonzalez)*
 c KR - v65 - Mr 15 '97 - p458 [51-250]

Alarcon, Karen Beaumont - *Louella Mae, She's Run Away! (Illus. by Rosanne Litzinger)*
 c CBRS - v25 - Mr '97 - p85 [51-250]
 c HB - v73 - My '97 - p300 [51-250]
 c KR - v65 - F 15 '97 - p296 [51-250]
 c PW - v244 - Mr 31 '97 - p73 [51-250]
Alasuutari, Pertti - *Researching Culture*
 CS - v25 - S '96 - p706+ [501+]
Alazraki, Jaime - *Hacia Cortazar*
 Hisp - v79 - S '96 - p450+ [501+]
Albahari, David - *Words Are Something Else*
 BW - v26 - S 8 '96 - p12 [51-250]
 CSM - v88 - O 31 '96 - pB1+ [501+]
 LJ - v121 - N 1 '96 - p109 [51-250]
 NYTBR - v101 - Ag 25 '96 - p19 [51-250]
 TranslRevS - v2 - D '96 - p30 [51-250]
Albalak, Ramon J - *Polymer Devolatilization*
 SciTech - v20 - S '96 - p61 [51-250]
Alban, Laureano - *Encyclopedia of Wonders. Vol. 1*
 r TranslRevS - v2 - D '96 - p32 [51-250]
Albarelli, Dean - *Cheaters and Other Stories*
 HR - v49 - Win '97 - p687+ [501+]
 LJ - v121 - N 1 '96 - p109 [51-250]
 NYTBR - v101 - Ag 25 '96 - p19 [51-250]
Albee, Edward - *A Delicate Balance*
 Trib Bks - Ja 19 '97 - p8 [1-50]
Albee, George W - *Primary Prevention Works*
 SciTech - v21 - Mr '97 - p46 [51-250]
Albee, Sarah - *Big Words for Little Scientists (Illus. by Bruce McNally)*
 c Emerg Lib - v24 - S '96 - p43 [1-50]
Albelda, Randy - *The War on the Poor*
 y Kliatt - v31 - Ja '97 - p25 [251-500]
 LATBR - My 26 '96 - p11 [51-250]
 y VOYA - v19 - O '96 - p224 [251-500]
Alberigo, Giuseppe - *History of Vatican II. Vol. 1*
 Bks & Cult - v3 - Ja '97 - p37 [251-500]
 CC - v113 - N 13 '96 - p1119+ [501+]
 CH - v65 - D '96 - p765+ [501+]
 Choice - v34 - O '96 - p297 [51-250]
 Comw - v123 - S 13 '96 - p33+ [501+]
 Theol St - v57 - D '96 - p757+ [501+]
Albers, Robert H - *Shame: A Faith Perspective*
 Bks & Cult - v2 - Mr '96 - p3+ [501+]
Albert, Bill - *Castle Garden*
 PW - v243 - N 11 '96 - p72 [1-50]
Albert, Burton - *Journey of the Nightly Jaguar (Illus. by Robert Roth)*
 c HB Guide - v7 - Fall '96 - p319 [51-250]
 The Pirates of Bat Cave Island (Illus. by Margeaux Lucas)
 c PW - v244 - Ap 28 '97 - p77 [1-50]
Albert, Daniel M - *The History of Ophthalmology*
 SciTech - v21 - Mr '97 - p61 [51-250]
Albert, Katherine - *Get a Good Night's Sleep*
 PW - v243 - N 4 '96 - p72 [51-250]
Albert, Kristiane - *Mallorca*
 r BL - v93 - S 15 '96 - p210 [1-50]
Albert, Marjorie - *Picnic in the Park*
 c Ch BWatch - v6 - S '96 - p2 [51-250]
Albert, Neil - *Appointment in May*
 Arm Det - v30 - Win '97 - p112+ [251-500]
Albert, Richard N - *An Annotated Bibliography of Jazz Fiction and Jazz Fiction Criticism*
 r ARBA - v28 - '97 - p431+ [251-500]
 r Choice - v34 - Mr '97 - p1133 [51-250]
 r R&R Bk N - v12 - F '97 - p83 [1-50]
Albert, Susan Wittig - *Rosemary Remembered*
 BWatch - v17 - S '96 - p1+ [51-250]
 Rueful Death
 Arm Det - v30 - Win '97 - p97 [51-250]
 BL - v93 - O 1 '96 - p324 [51-250]
 KR - v64 - S 1 '96 - p1270+ [51-250]
 LJ - v121 - O 1 '96 - p131 [1-50]
 PW - v243 - S 16 '96 - p73 [51-250]
 Writing from Life
 LJ - v121 - N 15 '96 - p69 [51-250]
 PW - v243 - D 2 '96 - p52 [51-250]
Alberta. Lotteries Review Committee - *New Directions for Lotteries and Gaming*
 J Gov Info - v23 - S '96 - p624 [51-250]
Albertine, Susan - *A Living of Words*
 TSWL - v15 - Fall '96 - p371+ [501+]
Alberto Vargas: The Esquire Years
 BWatch - v18 - Mr '97 - p3 [1-50]

Alberts, Laurie - *The Price of Land in Shelby*
  BL - v93 - S 15 '96 - p218 [51-250]
  KR - v64 - Ag 15 '96 - p1166 [251-500]
  LJ - v121 - S 15 '96 - p93 [51-250]
  LJ - v122 - Ap 1 '97 - p156 [51-250]
  NYTBR - v101 - N 10 '96 - p56 [51-250]
  PW - v243 - S 9 '96 - p66 [51-250]
Albertus, Magnus, Saint - *De Vegetabilibus. Bk. 6, Pts. 1-2*
  Isis - v87 - D '96 - p720 [501+]
Alberty, Robert A - *Physical Chemistry. 2nd Ed.*
  SB - v33 - Ja '97 - p7 [51-250]
  SciTech - v20 - D '96 - p28 [51-250]
Albertz, Rainer - *A History of Israelite Religion in the Old Testament Period. Vols. 1-2*
  Intpr - v51 - Ja '97 - p73+ [501+]
Albery, Nicholas - *The Book of Visions*
  r Utne R - S '96 - p93 [1-50]
DIY Futures
  New Sci - v151 - S 14 '96 - p45 [51-250]
Albiston, Jordie - *Botany Bay Document*
  Aust Bk R - D '96 - p69+ [501+]
Albizurez Palma, Francisco - *Grandes Momentos De La Literatura Guatemalteca*
  BL - v93 - S 15 '96 - p227 [1-50]
Alborough, Jez - *Can You Jump like a Kangaroo?*
  c Ch BWatch - v6 - S '96 - p1 [51-250]
  c TES - N 29 '96 - p13* [51-250]
Can You Peck like a Hen?
  c Ch BWatch - v6 - S '96 - p1 [51-250]
Where's My Teddy?
  c PW - v244 - F 10 '97 - p85 [1-50]
Albrecht, Donald - *World War II and the American Dream*
  Arm F&S - v23 - Win '96 - p308+ [501+]
Albrecht, Gloria - *The Character of Our Communities*
  Rel St Rev - v23 - Ap '97 - p159 [51-250]
Albrecht, Sally K - *The Night the Reindeer Rocked. Book and Audio Version*
  c CAY - v16 - Fall '95 - p11 [51-250]
Albrecht, Theodore - *Letters to Beethoven and Other Correspondence. Vols. 1-3*
  Choice - v34 - My '97 - p1508 [51-250]
Albrecht, V - *Figur Und Raum*
  Apo - v144 - O '96 - p60 [251-500]
Alcala, Kathleen - *Spirits of the Ordinary*
  BL - v93 - F 1 '97 - p924+ [51-250]
  KR - v64 - D 1 '96 - p1684 [251-500]
  LJ - v121 - D '96 - p141 [51-250]
  PW - v243 - D 30 '96 - p54+ [51-250]
Alcalay, Ammiel - *Keys to the Garden*
  TranslRevS - v2 - D '96 - p3 [51-250]
Alciato, Andrea - *Emblemata: Lyons 1550*
  r R&R Bk N - v12 - F '97 - p83 [1-50]
Alcock, Ian - *Deer: A Personal View*
  New Sci - v153 - Mr 8 '97 - p45 [1-50]
Alcock, Leslie - *Cadbury Castle, Somerset*
  EHR - v112 - Ap '97 - p424+ [501+]
  Specu - v71 - O '96 - p926+ [501+]
Alcock, Susan E - *Placing the Gods*
  AJA - v100 - Jl '96 - p618+ [501+]
Alcock, Vivien - *The Face at the Window*
  c Bks Keeps - Jl '96 - p12 [51-250]
  y Can Lit - Spr '97 - p250+ [501+]
The Red-Eared Ghosts
  c BL - v93 - Mr 1 '97 - p1160 [51-250]
  c CCB-B - v50 - Ap '97 - p270+ [51-250]
  c KR - v65 - Ap 1 '97 - p548 [51-250]
  c Par Ch - v21 - Mr '97 - p8 [1-50]
  c PW - v244 - Mr 3 '97 - p76 [51-250]
Time Wreck
  c Sch Lib - v45 - F '97 - p44 [51-250]
  y TES - Ja 3 '97 - p22 [51-250]
The Trial of Anna Cotman
  c SLJ - v42 - N '96 - p40 [51-250]
Alcoff, Linda Martin - *Real Knowing*
  CPR - v16 - D '96 - p385+ [501+]
Alcoloumbre, Thierry - *Mallarmé: La Poetique Du Theatre Et L'Ecriture*
  FR - v70 - D '96 - p332+ [501+]
Alcorn, Alfred - *Murder in the Museum of Man*
  KR - v65 - Mr 15 '97 - p418 [51-250]
  LJ - v122 - Ap 1 '97 - p132+ [51-250]
  PW - v244 - Mr 31 '97 - p66 [51-250]
  Trib Bks - My 4 '97 - p4 [51-250]
Alcorn, Marshall W, Jr. - *Narcissism and the Literary Libido*
  MP - v94 - N '96 - p201+ [501+]
Alcorn, Paul A - *Social Issues in Technology. 2nd Ed.*
  SciTech - v20 - D '96 - p58 [51-250]

Alcott, Louisa May - *Behind a Mask*
  NYTBR - v102 - Ap 13 '97 - p32 [1-50]
The Chase
  Obs - Ag 18 '96 - p19* [51-250]
Eight Cousins
  c Ch BWatch - v6 - Jl '96 - p3 [1-50]
  c HB Guide - v7 - Fall '96 - p289 [1-50]
Good Wives (King). Audio Version
  y BL - v92 - Ag '96 - p1917 [51-250]
The Inheritance
  y BL - v93 - F 15 '97 - p971 [51-250]
  y Cur R - v36 - F '97 - p13 [51-250]
  PW - v244 - Ja 13 '97 - p54 [51-250]
The Inheritance. Audio Version
  BWatch - v18 - Mr '97 - p6 [1-50]
Little Men (Herbert). Audio Version
  LJ - v121 - N 15 '96 - p106 [51-250]
Little Women
  y EJ - v85 - S '96 - p110 [501+]
Little Women (Harper). Audio Version
  c TES - Ag 30 '96 - p28 [51-250]
Little Women (King). Audio Version
  y BL - v92 - Ag '96 - p1917 [51-250]
A Long Fatal Love Chase
  NYTBR - v102 - Ap 13 '97 - p32 [51-250]
Louisa May Alcott on Race, Sex, and Slavery
  LJ - v122 - My 1 '97 - p102 [51-250]
Louisa May Alcott Unmasked
  Nine-C Lit - v51 - D '96 - p419 [51-250]
A Modern Mephistopheles (Herbert). Audio Version
  LJ - v122 - My 1 '97 - p154 [51-250]
Rose in Bloom
  c Ch BWatch - v6 - My '96 - p7 [51-250]
  c HB Guide - v7 - Fall '96 - p289 [1-50]
The Selected Letters of Louisa May Alcott
  Nine-C Lit - v50 - Mr '96 - p552 [1-50]
Alcraft, Rob - *Mexico*
  c TES - Mr 21 '97 - p18* [251-500]
Alda, Arlene - *Pig, Horse, or Cow, Don't Wake Me Now*
  c PW - v243 - Jl 22 '96 - p243 [1-50]
Aldama, A A - *Computational Methods in Water Resources XI. Vols. 1-2*
  SciTech - v20 - D '96 - p69 [51-250]
Aldana, Patricia - *Jade and Iron (Illus. by Luis Garay)*
  c BL - v93 - D 1 '96 - p650 [51-250]
  y CCB-B - v50 - Ja '97 - p162 [51-250]
  c Emerg Lib - v24 - Mr '97 - p28 [1-50]
  c HB - v73 - Ja '97 - p72 [51-250]
  c HB Guide - v8 - Spr '97 - p99 [51-250]
  c Quill & Q - v62 - Jl '96 - p57 [251-500]
Aldape, Virginia Tortorica - *Nicole's Story (Illus. by Lillian S Kossacoff)*
  c Cur R - v36 - N '96 - p12 [51-250]
  c HB Guide - v8 - Spr '97 - p95 [1-50]
  c SLJ - v42 - S '96 - p195 [51-250]
Aldcroft, Derek H - *Economic Change in Eastern Europe since 1918*
  Econ J - v106 - N '96 - p1801+ [501+]
  EHR - v112 - Ap '97 - p540 [51-250]
  JEH - v56 - S '96 - p722+ [501+]
Enterprise and Management
  JEH - v56 - S '96 - p714+ [501+]
The European Economy 1750-1914
  BHR - v70 - Aut '96 - p429+ [501+]
  EHR - v111 - N '96 - p1312+ [501+]
  JEH - v56 - S '96 - p713+ [501+]
Rich Nations, Poor Nations
  JEL - v34 - S '96 - p1463+ [501+]
  R&R Bk N - v11 - N '96 - p25 [51-250]
Alden, Chris - *Apartheid's Last Stand*
  Choice - v34 - N '96 - p529 [51-250]
Alden, Dauril - *The Making of an Enterprise*
  Am - v176 - Mr 22 '97 - p31 [51-250]
  Choice - v34 - F '97 - p1018 [51-250]
Alden, John R - *George Washington: A Biography*
  LJ - v122 - Ja '97 - p155 [1-50]
Alden, Patricia - *African Studies and the Undergraduate Curriculum*
  JTWS - v13 - Spr '96 - p285+ [501+]
Alden, Paulette Bates - *Crossing the Moon*
  BL - v93 - S 1 '96 - p50 [51-250]
Alder, Elizabeth - *The King's Shadow*
  y Emerg Lib - v24 - S '96 - p24 [1-50]
  y Kliatt - v30 - S '96 - p3 [1-50]
  y SLJ - v42 - N '96 - p40 [1-50]
Alderman, Ellen - *The Right to Privacy*
  PW - v244 - Ja 27 '97 - p103 [1-50]
Alderman, Geoffrey - *Modern British Jewry*
  Rel St Rev - v22 - O '96 - p355 [51-250]
Alders, Koos - *Monetary Policy in a Converging Europe*
  JEL - v34 - S '96 - p1431 [51-250]

Alderson, Daniel - *Talking Back to Poems*
  y Kliatt - v30 - N '96 - p17 [51-250]
Alderton, David - *Looking after Cage Birds*
  BL - v93 - S 1 '96 - p48 [51-250]
Rodents of the World
  SciTech - v20 - D '96 - p33 [1-50]
Aldiss, Brian W - *Common Clay*
  VQR - v73 - Win '97 - p22* [51-250]
The Detached Retina
  Ext - v37 - Fall '96 - p285+ [501+]
Aldous, Richard - *Harold Macmillan and Britain's World Role*
  Albion - v28 - '96 - p737+ [501+]
Aldous Huxley Centenary Symposium (1994: University of Munster) - *Now More than Ever*
  R&R Bk N - v12 - F '97 - p86 [51-250]
Aldrich, Gary - *Unlimited Access*
  Atl - v278 - O '96 - p112+ [251-500]
  BL - v93 - S 1 '96 - p29 [1-50]
  W&I - v11 - N '96 - p258+ [501+]
Aldrich, John H - *Why Parties?*
  AJS - v102 - Jl '96 - p288+ [501+]
  J Pol - v58 - N '96 - p1214+ [501+]
Aldrich, Megan Brewster - *A.W.N. Pugin: Master of Gothic Revival*
  Albion - v28 - '96 - p716+ [501+]
  Am Craft - v56 - Ag '96 - p62 [1-50]
  BM - v139 - Ja '97 - p48 [501+]
Aldrich, Richard - *Education for the Nation*
  TES - D 6 '96 - p7* [501+]
Aldrich, Robert - *Greater France*
  Choice - v34 - Ja '97 - p854 [51-250]
Aldridge, A Owen - *The Dragon and the Eagle*
  AL - v68 - S '96 - p639+ [251-500]
Aldridge, Susan - *The Thread of Life*
  Choice - v34 - O '96 - p302 [51-250]
Aldrin, Buzz - *Encounter with Tiber*
  Analog - v117 - Ap '97 - p147+ [251-500]
  A & S Sm - v11 - Ag '96 - p83+ [51-250]
  MFSF - v92 - Ja '97 - p22 [51-250]
  y VOYA - v19 - D '96 - p275 [251-500]
Aldroubi, Akram - *Wavelets in Medicine and Biology*
  Choice - v34 - Mr '97 - p1194 [51-250]
Alefeld, G - *Scientific Computing and Validated Numerics*
  SciTech - v20 - N '96 - p4 [51-250]
Alegria, Claribel - *Death of Somoza*
  TranslRevS - v2 - D '96 - p15 [51-250]
Thresholds
  TranslRevS - v2 - D '96 - p32 [51-250]
Tunnel to Canto Grande
  Bloom Rev - v16 - N '96 - p7 [501+]
  TranslRevS - v2 - D '96 - p15 [51-250]
Umbrales
  BWatch - v17 - N '96 - p9 [51-250]
  LJ - v121 - O 15 '96 - p63 [51-250]
  PW - v243 - S 30 '96 - p81 [51-250]
  TranslRevS - v2 - D '96 - p32 [51-250]
Aleksander, Igor - *Impossible Minds*
  Nature - v383 - O 17 '96 - p592 [501+]
  New Sci - v152 - N 9 '96 - p41 [501+]
Alekseev, Victor R - *Diapause in the Crustacea*
  SciTech - v20 - D '96 - p32 [51-250]
Alen, Paule - *Charlie Fait Du Sport*
  c BL - v93 - N 1 '96 - p500 [1-50]
Alers, Rochelle - *Hidden Agenda*
  LJ - v122 - F 15 '97 - p125 [51-250]
Love Letters
  LJ - v122 - F 15 '97 - p125 [51-250]
Alesina, Alberto - *Partisan Politics, Divided Government, and the Economy*
  Econ J - v106 - N '96 - p1787+ [501+]
Alessandra, Tony - *The Platinum Rule*
  BL - v92 - Ag '96 - p1865 [51-250]
The Platinum Rule (Alessandra). Audio Version
  Quill & Q - v62 - Ag '96 - p37 [1-50]
Alexakis, Vassilis - *La Langue Maternelle*
  FR - v70 - O '96 - p137+ [251-500]
Alexander, of Aphrodisias - *Quaestiones. Vol. 2*
  RM - v49 - Je '96 - p946+ [501+]
Trattato Sulla Febre
  Isis - v87 - S '96 - p536 [501+]
Alexander, Bevin - *The Future of Warfare*
  JPR - v33 - Ag '96 - p377 [251-500]
Alexander, Bruce - *Watery Grave*
  y BL - v93 - S 15 '96 - p223 [51-250]
  BW - v26 - S 15 '96 - p6 [251-500]
  NYTBR - v101 - N 10 '96 - p62 [51-250]
Alexander, Charles C - *John McGraw*
  Aethlon - v13 - Fall '95 - p131+ [251-500]
Rogers Hornsby: A Biography
  Aethlon - v13 - Fall '95 - p131+ [251-500]

Alexander, Christine - *The Art of the Brontes*
  MLR - v91 - O '96 - p982+ [501+]
  Nine-C Lit - v51 - S '96 - p240+ [501+]
  RES - v47 - N '96 - p616+ [501+]
  VS - v39 - Aut '95 - p55+ [501+]
Alexander, Christopher J - *Gay and Lesbian Mental Health*
  SciTech - v20 - D '96 - p44 [51-250]
Alexander, Claire E - *The Art of Being Black*
  Choice - v34 - Mr '97 - p1201 [51-250]
Alexander, Doris - *Creating Literature out of Life*
  AB - v98 - N 25 '96 - p1830+ [501+]
  Choice - v34 - My '97 - p1490 [51-250]
Alexander, Earl - *My Dad Has HIV (Illus. by Ronnie Walter Shipman)*
  c HB Guide - v7 - Fall '96 - p246 [51-250]
Alexander, Edward - *The Jewish Wars*
  Rapport - v19 - 5 '96 - p46 [251-500]
Alexander, Elizabeth - *Body of Life*
  BW - v27 - F 16 '97 - p12 [51-250]
  Trib Bks - Ap 20 '97 - p3 [501+]
Alexander, Franz - *Psychoanalytic Pioneers*
  AJPsych - v153 - O '96 - p1363 [251-500]
Alexander, Harriet Semmes - *American and British Poetry*
  r AL - v68 - D '96 - p885 [51-250]
  r ARBA - v28 - '97 - p464 [51-250]
  r Choice - v34 - D '96 - p585 [51-250]
Alexander, Herbert E - *Financing the 1992 Election*
  J Pol - v58 - Ag '96 - p881+ [501+]
Alexander, Jenny - *Miss Fischer's Jewels (Illus. by Michael Reid)*
  c Sch Lib - v45 - F '97 - p22 [51-250]
Alexander, Jonathan J G - *Medieval Illuminators and Their Methods of Work*
  AB - v99 - Mr 3 '97 - p685+ [501+]
  The Painted Page
  AB - v99 - Mr 3 '97 - p685+ [501+]
Alexander, Joseph H - *The Final Campaign*
  Mar Crp G - v81 - Ja '97 - p76 [501+]
  Utmost Savagery
  NWCR - v50 - Win '97 - p164+ [501+]
Alexander, Ken - *Towards Freedom*
  y Quill & Q - v63 - F '97 - p58 [1-50]
Alexander, Lloyd - *The Iron Ring*
  y BL - v93 - My 15 '97 - p1572+ [51-250]
  c KR - v65 - My 1 '97 - p716 [51-250]
  c PW - v244 - Ap 14 '97 - p76+ [51-250]
  c Trib Bks - My 4 '97 - p7 [51-250]
Alexander, Loveday - *The Preface to Luke's Gospel*
  Rel St Rev - v23 - Ap '97 - p183 [51-250]
Alexander, Lucy - *Fathoms*
  Aust Bk R - F '97 - p47+ [501+]
Alexander, Lydia Lewis - *Wearing Purple*
  KR - v64 - O 15 '96 - p1501 [251-500]
  Ms - v7 - Ja '97 - p82 [1-50]
  PW - v243 - O 14 '96 - p69 [51-250]
Alexander, Marc R - *Church and Ministry in the Works of G.H. Tavard*
  Theol St - v57 - Mr '96 - p158+ [501+]
Alexander, Marianne - *The Centaur Pholus*
  Horoscope - v63 - F '97 - p18 [251-500]
Alexander, Marilyn Bennett - *We Were Baptized Too*
  TT - v53 - Ja '97 - p508+ [501+]
Alexander, Martha - *You're a Genius, Blackboard Bear (Illus. by Martha Alexander)*
  c Bks Keeps - v100 - S '96 - p8 [51-250]
  c RT - v50 - S '96 - p54 [51-250]
Alexander, Meena - *Fault Lines*
  Amerasia J - v22 - 2 '96 - p164+ [501+]
  Manhattan Music
  BW - v27 - Ap 6 '97 - p9 [501+]
  KR - v65 - Ja 15 '97 - p74 [251-500]
  Ms - v7 - Mr '97 - p83 [1-50]
  PW - v244 - F 10 '97 - p68 [51-250]
  Trib Bks - My 25 '97 - p1+ [501+]
  The Shock of Arrival
  PW - v243 - O 21 '96 - p76 [51-250]
Alexander, Michael - *Beowulf*
  Agenda - v34 - Sum '96 - p173+ [501+]
Alexander, Pat - *Star of Wonder (Illus. by Robin Laurie)*
  c Bks Keeps - N '96 - p19 [1-50]
Alexander, Patrick - *Images, Reflections*
  Aust Bk R - Je '96 - p67 [1-50]
Alexander, Paul - *Sri Lankan Fishermen*
  Pac A - v69 - Fall '96 - p440+ [501+]
Alexander, R McNeill - *Optima for Animals. Rev. Ed.*
  Choice - v34 - My '97 - p1525 [51-250]
  Nature - v386 - Ap 10 '97 - p567 [1-50]

Alexander, Robert, 1949- - *The Party Train*
  Bloom Rev - v16 - S '96 - p11 [51-250]
  HMR - Spr '97 - p11 [51-250]
Alexander, Robert J - *Presidents of Central America, Mexico, Cuba, and Hispaniola*
  HAHR - v77 - F '97 - p165+ [251-500]
Alexander, Ruth M - *The Girl Problem*
  J Soc H - v30 - Spr '97 - p781+ [501+]
Alexander, Sally Hobart - *On My Own*
  y BL - v93 - My 1 '97 - p1485 [51-250]
  y CCB-B - v50 - My '97 - p311 [51-250]
Alexander, Scott - *The People vs. Larry Flynt*
  NYRB - v44 - F 6 '97 - p25+ [501+]
Alexander, Stephen B - *Optical Communication Receiver Design*
  SciTech - v21 - Mr '97 - p87 [51-250]
Alexander, Sue - *What's Wrong Now, Millicent? (Illus. by David Scott Meier)*
  c HB Guide - v7 - Fall '96 - p246 [51-250]
  c LATBR - Jl 7 '96 - p11 [51-250]
Alexander, Thomas G - *Utah, the Right Place*
  WHQ - v27 - Win '96 - p540+ [501+]
Alexander, Titus - *Unravelling Global Apartheid*
  Choice - v34 - D '96 - p684 [51-250]
Alexander, Victoria D - *Museums and Money*
  Choice - v34 - F '97 - p954 [51-250]
  ChrPhil - v9 - N 14 '96 - p39 [51-250]
Alexander-Moegerle, Gil - *James Dobson's War on America*
  BL - v93 - F 1 '97 - p908 [51-250]
  PW - v244 - F 10 '97 - p80 [51-250]
Alexander-Roberts, Colleen - *Does My Child Need a Therapist?*
  PW - v244 - Mr 3 '97 - p70 [51-250]
Alexie, Sherman - *Indian Killer*
  y BL - v93 - S 1 '96 - p5 [51-250]
  CSM - v89 - Ja 6 '97 - p13 [251-500]
  NYTBR - v101 - N 24 '96 - p19 [501+]
  NYTBR - v101 - D 8 '96 - p80 [1-50]
  Prog - v61 - Ja '97 - p36 [51-250]
  VV - v41 - O 22 '96 - p57+ [501+]
  Indian Killer (Alexie). Audio Version
  Bloom Rev - v17 - Ja '97 - p22 [51-250]
  y Kliatt - v31 - My '97 - p40 [51-250]
  LJ - v122 - F 1 '97 - p126 [51-250]
  LJ - v122 - F 15 '97 - p114 [1-50]
  Reservation Blues
  BW - v26 - S 22 '96 - p12 [51-250]
  y Kliatt - v30 - N '96 - p4 [51-250]
  LATBR - O 6 '96 - p15 [51-250]
  NYTBR - v101 - S 22 '96 - p40 [51-250]
  PW - v243 - S 9 '96 - p80 [1-50]
  Trib Bks - Ja 12 '97 - p2 [1-50]
  The Summer of Black Widows
  Bloom Rev - v17 - Ja '97 - p7 [501+]
  LJ - v121 - N 1 '96 - p70+ [51-250]
  PW - v243 - S 30 '96 - p82+ [51-250]
Alfabetizacion Por Todos Y Para Todos
  Lect Y V - v17 - Je '96 - p41+ [501+]
Alfieri, Nereo - *Spina E La Ceramica Attica*
  AJA - v101 - Ja '97 - p194+ [251-500]
Alford, B W E - *Britain in the World Economy since 1880*
  CR - v269 - S '96 - p168 [51-250]
  Econ J - v106 - S '96 - p1478 [51-250]
  British Economic Performance 1945-1975
  JEL - v34 - D '96 - p2094 [51-250]
Alford, C Fred - *Group Psychology and Political Theory*
  RP - v58 - Sum '96 - p632+ [501+]
Alford, Norman - *The Rhymers' Club*
  Nine-C Lit - v50 - Mr '96 - p535+ [501+]
Alford, William P - *To Steal a Book Is an Elegant Offense*
  AHR - v101 - D '96 - p1596+ [501+]
  Ch Rev Int - v4 - Spr '97 - p55+ [501+]
  FEER - v159 - N 28 '96 - p63 [251-500]
  Historian - v58 - Sum '96 - p879+ [501+]
  HLR - v110 - D '96 - p559 [51-250]
  JIH - v27 - Aut '96 - p379+ [501+]
Alfred, Gerald R - *Heeding the Voices of Our Ancestors*
  PSQ - v111 - Win '96 - p732+ [501+]
Alger, Elizabeth - *Bertie at the Horse Show (Illus. by Elizabeth Alger)*
  c Magpies - v11 - S '96 - p30 [51-250]
Algosaibi, Ghazi - *An Apartment Called Freedom*
  Spec - v277 - N 16 '96 - p44 [1-50]
Algra, Keimpe - *Concepts of Space in Greek Thought*
  Isis - v87 - S '96 - p532+ [251-500]
Algren, Nelson - *Nonconformity: Writing on Writing*
  BL - v93 - S 1 '96 - p33 [51-250]
  BW - v26 - S 15 '96 - p11 [501+]
  LATBR - O 20 '96 - p14+ [251-500]

Alhadeff, Gini - *The Sun at Midday*
  KR - v64 - D 1 '96 - p1710 [251-500]
  LATBR - F 9 '97 - p4 [501+]
  LJ - v122 - Ja '97 - p108 [51-250]
  NYTBR - v102 - Ap 13 '97 - p23 [501+]
  NYTLa - v146 - Mr 4 '97 - pC16 [501+]
  PW - v243 - D 9 '96 - p55 [51-250]
Ali, Khanh - *Hinh Nhu La Tinh Yen*
  BL - v93 - My 15 '97 - p1568 [1-50]
Ali, Sharifah Enayat - *Afghanistan*
  c HB Guide - v7 - Fall '96 - p383 [1-50]
Aliboni, Roberto - *Security Challenges in the Mediterranean Region*
  Choice - v34 - Ja '97 - p871+ [51-250]
  MEJ - v50 - Aut '96 - p630 [51-250]
  R&R Bk N - v11 - F '97 - p51 [51-250]
Alicea, Gil - *The Air Down Here*
  y Emerg Lib - v24 - S '96 - p26 [1-50]
Aliki - *The Gods and Goddesses of Olympus (Illus. by Aliki)*
  c SLJ - v42 - N '96 - p38 [1-50]
  Hello! Good-Bye! (Illus. by Aliki)
  c CCB-B - v50 - D '96 - p127 [51-250]
  c HB Guide - v8 - Spr '97 - p98 [51-250]
  c KR - v64 - S 1 '96 - p1318 [51-250]
  c SLJ - v42 - S '96 - p170 [51-250]
  Manners (Illus. by Aliki)
  c PW - v244 - My 12 '97 - p77 [1-50]
  My Five Senses
  c Inst - v106 - S '96 - p92 [1-50]
  Those Summers (Illus. by Aliki)
  c CLW - v67 - D '96 - p55 [51-250]
  c HB Guide - v7 - Fall '96 - p246 [51-250]
  c KR - v64 - My 1 '96 - p684 [51-250]
  c RT - v50 - My '97 - p686 [51-250]
  c SLJ - v42 - Ag '96 - p115 [51-250]
  The Two of Them
  c HMR - Win '96 - p45 [1-50]
  Wild and Woolly Mammoths
  c HB Guide - v7 - Fall '96 - p333 [1-50]
Alinder, Mary Street - *Ansel Adams: A Biography*
  Bloom Rev - v16 - N '96 - p20 [501+]
  LATBR - Jl 7 '96 - p10 [51-250]
Aline, Countess of Romanones - *The Spy Wore Red (Conlin). Audio Version*
  y Kliatt - v30 - S '96 - p59 [51-250]
Alinhac, Serge - *Blowup for Nonlinear Hyperbolic Equations*
  SciTech - v20 - N '96 - p14 [1-50]
Aliotti, Shelley - *My Pen Pal Scrapbook (Illus. by Shelley Aliotti)*
  c Learning - v25 - N '96 - p81+ [51-250]
Aliprantis, Charalambos D - *Problems in Equilibrium Theory*
  JEL - v34 - D '96 - p2027 [51-250]
Alison, James - *Raising Abel*
  Theol St - v57 - D '96 - p765+ [501+]
Alker, Hayward R - *Rediscoveries and Reformulations*
  For Aff - v76 - Mr '97 - p176 [51-250]
Alkon, Amy - *Free Advice, by the Advice Ladies*
  Wom R Bks - v14 - Ja '97 - p11+ [51-250]
All about Beer
  p LJ - v122 - Ap 1 '97 - p63 [1-50]
All in It Together
  NCR - v85 - Spr '96 - p65 [51-250]
All Roads Are Good
  New R - v216 - Ap 21 '97 - p28+ [501+]
  Pub Hist - v18 - Sum '96 - p43+ [501+]
Allaby, Michael - *Enciclopedia Visual: El Planeta Tierra*
  cr BL - v93 - Mr 1 '97 - p1196 [51-250]
Allan, J A - *Water in the Middle East*
  GJ - v162 - N '96 - p332+ [501+]
  Water, Peace, and the Middle East
  MEQ - v4 - Mr '97 - p93 [51-250]
Allan, J W - *Islamic Art in the Ashmolean. Pts. 1-2*
  BM - v139 - Ja '97 - p45 [501+]
Allan, James R - *In the Trade of War*
  J Mil H - v61 - Ap '97 - p404+ [251-500]
Allan, John J - *Computers in Railways V. Vols. 1-2*
  SciTech - v21 - Mr '97 - p83 [51-250]
Allan, Nicholas - *Heaven (Illus. by Nicholas Allan)*
  c JB - v60 - O '96 - p181 [51-250]
  c KR - v64 - D 1 '96 - p1732 [51-250]
  c PW - v243 - D 2 '96 - p59 [51-250]
  c Sch Lib - v44 - N '96 - p145 [51-250]
  c TES - S 6 '96 - p7* [501+]
  Jesus' Christmas Party
  c Bks Keeps - N '96 - p20 [1-50]
Allan, Sean - *The Plays of Heinrich Von Kleist*
  Choice - v34 - Ap '97 - p1342 [51-250]

Allan, Tuzyline Jita - *Womanist and Feminist Aesthetics*
   AL - v68 - S '96 - p663 [51-250]
Allard, Denise - *The Egyptians*
   c TES - Jl 5 '96 - pR5 [251-500]
   Greece
   c HB Guide - v8 - Spr '97 - p168 [51-250]
   c SLJ - v43 - F '97 - p86 [51-250]
   The Greeks
   c TES - Jl 5 '96 - pR5 [251-500]
   India
   c HB Guide - v8 - Spr '97 - p169 [51-250]
   Israel
   c HB Guide - v8 - Spr '97 - p169 [51-250]
   Peru
   c HB Guide - v8 - Spr '97 - p178+ [1-50]
   Poland
   c HB Guide - v8 - Spr '97 - p168 [51-250]
   The Romans
   c TES - Jl 5 '96 - pR5 [251-500]
   The United States
   c HB Guide - v8 - Spr '97 - p172 [1-50]
   Vietnam
   c HB Guide - v8 - Spr '97 - p169 [51-250]
   The Vikings
   c TES - Jl 5 '96 - pR5 [251-500]
Allard, Harry - *Miss Nelson Is Missing! (Illus. by James Marshall)*
   c HB - v73 - Mr '97 - p188 [1-50]
   c New Ad - v9 - Fall '96 - p309+ [501+]
Allardice, Bruce S - *More Generals in Gray*
   r JSH - v62 - N '96 - p859+ [51-250]
Allchin, F R - *The Archaeology of Early Historic South Asia*
   Choice - v34 - O '96 - p322 [51-250]
Allcorn, Seth - *The Human Cost of a Management Failure*
   SciTech - v20 - S '96 - p29 [51-250]
Alldritt, Keith - *W.B. Yeats: The Man and the Milieu*
   BL - v93 - My 15 '97 - p1556 [51-250]
   KR - v65 - Ap 1 '97 - p511 [251-500]
   LJ - v122 - My 1 '97 - p102 [51-250]
   PW - v244 - Mr 24 '97 - p67 [251-500]
Allee, Mark A - *Law and Local Society in Late Imperial China*
   AHR - v101 - O '96 - p1259 [501+]
   Ch Rev Int - v3 - Fall '96 - p347+ [501+]
Allegretti, Joseph G - *The Lawyer's Calling*
   BL - v93 - N 1 '96 - p460 [51-250]
   CLW - v67 - Mr '97 - p48+ [501+]
Allemand-Cosneau, Claud - *Henry Moore: From the Inside Out*
   BM - v138 - S '96 - p624+ [501+]
Allen, Benjamin W - *Better Homes and Gardens Step-by-Step Wiring*
   BL - v93 - Mr 15 '97 - p1212+ [51-250]
   Step-by-Step Plumbing
   BL - v93 - Mr 15 '97 - p1212+ [51-250]
   PW - v244 - F 3 '97 - p104 [51-250]
Allen, Brian - *British Art Treasures from Russian Imperial Collections in the Hermitage*
   Choice - v34 - My '97 - p1484+ [51-250]
   LJ - v122 - Ap 1 '97 - p88 [51-250]
   Towards a Modern Art World
   Albion - v28 - Sum '96 - p363+ [501+]
   BM - v138 - Ag '96 - p549+ [501+]
Allen, Bryce L - *Information Tasks*
   SciTech - v21 - Mr '97 - p11 [51-250]
Allen, Catherine A - *Smart Cards*
   R&R Bk N - v12 - F '97 - p42 [51-250]
Allen, Charles Wesley - *Autobiography of Red Cloud*
   LJ - v122 - My 1 '97 - p116 [51-250]
Allen, Charlotte Vale - *Claudia's Shadow*
   Quill & Q - v62 - Jl '96 - p45 [251-500]
Allen, Craig - *Eisenhower and the Mass Media*
   JC - v46 - Sum '96 - p176+ [501+]
Allen, David G - *Subjects on the World's Stage*
   Ren Q - v50 - Spr '97 - p272+ [501+]
Allen, David S - *Freeing the First Amendment*
   APSR - v90 - D '96 - p904+ [501+]
Allen, David T - *Pollution Prevention for Chemical Processes*
   Choice - v34 - My '97 - p1527 [51-250]
   SciTech - v21 - Mr '97 - p81 [51-250]
Allen, Dick - *Ode to the Cold War*
   BL - v93 - Mr 1 '97 - p1106 [51-250]
   LJ - v122 - My 1 '97 - p107 [51-250]
   PW - v244 - F 24 '97 - p86 [51-250]
Allen, Donna - *Women Transforming Communications*
   R&R Bk N - v11 - D '96 - p59 [51-250]
Allen, Garrison - *Baseball Cat*
   BL - v93 - My 15 '97 - p1565 [51-250]
   PW - v244 - Ap 28 '97 - p53 [51-250]

Allen, Gay Wilson - *Walt Whitman and the World*
   AL - v68 - S '96 - p665 [51-250]
   J Am St - v30 - D '96 - p493 [251-500]
Allen, George - *How to Find, Buy, Manage and Sell a Manufactured Home Community*
   SciTech - v20 - D '96 - p87 [51-250]
Allen, James - *Simple Annals*
   PW - v244 - F 24 '97 - p87 [51-250]
Allen, Janet - *It's Never Too Late*
   EJ - v85 - D '96 - p82+ [501+]
Allen, John - *Geographical Worlds*
   GJ - v163 - Mr '97 - p102+ [501+]
   A Shrinking World?
   GJ - v163 - Mr '97 - p102+ [501+]
Allen, John C - *Against All Odds*
   SSQ - v77 - S '96 - p718+ [501+]
Allen, John P - *Assessing Alcohol Problems*
   J Gov Info - v23 - S '96 - p549 [51-250]
Allen, Jonathan - *Chicken Licken*
   c Magpies - v11 - Jl '96 - p24+ [51-250]
   Fowl Play
   c Sch Lib - v45 - F '97 - p17 [51-250]
Allen, Judy - *Amsterdam Quest*
   y JB - v60 - Ag '96 - p163 [251-500]
   Paris Quest
   y JB - v60 - Ag '96 - p163 [501+]
Allen, Kate - *Takes One to Know One*
   KR - v64 - Ag 15 '96 - p1187 [251-500]
Allen, Laura Jean - *Rollow and Tweedy and the Ghost at Dougal Castle. Book and Audio Version*
   c Ch BWatch - v7 - Ja '97 - p5 [1-50]
Allen, Lee - *The Special Guest*
   KR - v64 - S 1 '96 - p1269 [51-250]
   PW - v243 - S 16 '96 - p68 [51-250]
Allen, Maury - *Memories of the Mick*
   PW - v244 - Mr 31 '97 - p55 [51-250]
Allen, Michael J B - *Nuptial Arithmetic*
   Isis - v87 - D '96 - p719+ [501+]
   Ren Q - v49 - Aut '96 - p671+ [501+]
   Plato's Third Eye
   Six Ct J - v27 - Fall '96 - p954+ [501+]
Allen, Murray E - *Musculoskeletal Pain Emanating from the Head and Neck*
   SciTech - v21 - Mr '97 - p59 [51-250]
Allen, Pamela - *Waddle Giggle Gargle (Illus. by Pamela Allen)*
   c Aust Bk R - D '96 - p91+ [501+]
   Who Sank the Boat? (Illus. by Pamela Allen)
   c Magpies - v11 - Jl '96 - p10+ [501+]
Allen, Paul - *American Crawl*
   PW - v243 - D 30 '96 - p62 [51-250]
Allen, Paula Gunn - *As Long as the Rivers Flow*
   c BL - v93 - D 1 '96 - p645 [51-250]
   c HB Guide - v8 - Spr '97 - p176 [51-250]
   c KR - v64 - S 15 '96 - p1396 [51-250]
   c SLJ - v43 - Ja '97 - p118 [51-250]
   Song of the Turtle
   y BL - v92 - Ag '96 - p1875 [51-250]
   y BL - v92 - Ag '96 - p1890 [1-50]
   BL - v93 - Ja '97 - p808 [1-50]
Allen, Roberta - *Certain People and Other Stories*
   NYTBR - v102 - Mr 23 '97 - p18 [51-250]
   PW - v243 - D 16 '96 - p43 [51-250]
Allen, Roger MacBride - *Isaac Asimov's Utopia*
   y Kliatt - v31 - Mr '97 - p14 [51-250]
   LJ - v121 - N 15 '96 - p92 [51-250]
Allen, Ronald J - *Holy Root, Holy Branches*
   Theol St - v57 - Mr '96 - p181+ [251-500]
Allen, Steve - *Wake Up to Murder*
   BL - v93 - N 15 '96 - p573 [51-250]
   KR - v64 - S 15 '96 - p1355 [51-250]
   LJ - v121 - N 1 '96 - p111 [1-50]
   PW - v243 - S 23 '96 - p60 [51-250]
Allen, Sue - *Decorated Cloth in America*
   BC - v44 - Win '95 - p494+ [501+]
Allen, Thomas B - *Code-Name Downfall*
   PHR - v65 - Ag '96 - p500 [251-500]
   Possessed: The True Story of an Exorcism
   Bks & Cult - v3 - Ja '97 - p17+ [501+]
   Shadows in the Sea
   BW - v26 - D 29 '96 - p12 [51-250]
   LJ - v121 - N 15 '96 - p85 [51-250]
Allen, Tim - *I'm Not Really Here*
   CSM - v89 - D 12 '96 - p14 [51-250]
   CSM - v89 - Ja 9 '97 - p14 [51-250]
   Ent W - N 22 '96 - p129 [51-250]
Allen, Trevor - *The Storm Passed By*
   Choice - v34 - My '97 - p1555 [51-250]
   ILS - v16 - Spr '97 - p36 [1-50]
Allen, Ward S - *The Coming of the King James Gospels*
   Bks & Cult - v2 - S '96 - p22 [51-250]

Allen, William Francis - *Slave Songs of the United States*
   CAY - v17 - Fall '96 - p9 [51-250]
Allen, Woody - *Woody Allen on Woody Allen*
   TES - Ag 2 '96 - pR6 [51-250]
Allen, Zita - *Black Women Leaders of the Civil Rights Movement*
   y BL - v93 - F 15 '97 - p1009 [51-250]
   y HB Guide - v8 - Spr '97 - p92 [51-250]
   y SLJ - v43 - Ja '97 - p118 [51-250]
Allenbaugh, Kay - *Chocolate for a Woman's Soul*
   PW - v244 - Ap 28 '97 - p68 [51-250]
Allende, Isabel - *La Casa De Los Espiritus*
   CLS - v33 - 4 '96 - p372+ [501+]
   Paula
   Books - v9 - S '95 - p23 [51-250]
   WLT - v70 - Sum '96 - p671 [501+]
Alleton, Viviane - *Notions Et Perceptions Du Changement En Chine*
   Ch Rev Int - v3 - Fall '96 - p351+ [501+]
Alley, Robert S - *Without a Prayer*
   Choice - v34 - F '97 - p1034+ [51-250]
Alleyne, Mark D - *News Revolution*
   BL - v93 - F 15 '97 - p974 [51-250]
   PW - v244 - Ja 6 '97 - p58+ [51-250]
Alliance for Technology Access - *Computer Resources for People with Disabilities. 2nd Ed., Fully Rev.*
   yr Kliatt - v31 - My '97 - p23 [51-250]
Allison, A F - *The Contemporary Printed Literature of the English Counter-Reformation between 1558 and 1640. Vol. 2*
   r BC - v44 - Win '95 - p581+ [251-500]
Allison, David B - *Sade and the Narrative of Transgression*
   MLR - v91 - O '96 - p995+ [251-500]
Allison, Dorothy - *Two or Three Things I Know for Sure*
   y Kliatt - v30 - N '96 - p21 [51-250]
   LATBR - S 8 '96 - p11 [51-250]
Allison, Graham T - *Avoiding Nuclear Anarchy*
   SB - v32 - O '96 - p198 [51-250]
   The Greek Paradox
   For Aff - v76 - My '97 - p136 [51-250]
Allison, Jenene J - *Revealing Difference*
   MLR - v91 - O '96 - p994+ [251-500]
Allison, Jonathan - *Yeats's Political Identities*
   ILS - v15 - Fall '96 - p31 [1-50]
   ILS - v16 - Spr '97 - p6 [51-250]
Allison, Karen Hubert - *How I Gave My Heart to the Restaurant Business*
   BL - v93 - Mr 1 '97 - p1108 [51-250]
   PW - v244 - F 3 '97 - p92 [51-250]
Allison, Kathleen Cahill - *American Medical Association Complete Guide to Women's Health*
   r BL - v93 - N 1 '96 - p532+ [501+]
   r BL - v93 - F 1 '97 - p959 [1-50]
   r LJ - v121 - O 1 '96 - p68 [51-250]
Allison, Robert J - *The Crescent Obscured*
   J Ch St - v38 - Aut '96 - p919+ [251-500]
   JIH - v27 - Spr '97 - p714+ [501+]
   MEJ - v50 - Aut '96 - p623+ [501+]
   MEQ - v3 - S '96 - p81+ [251-500]
Allison, Roy - *Challenges for the Former Soviet South*
   JEL - v35 - Mr '97 - p289 [51-250]
Allison, Stacy - *Beyond the Limits*
   HM - v293 - Ag '96 - p64+ [501+]
Alliston, April - *Virtue's Faults*
   Choice - v34 - D '96 - p610 [51-250]
Allman, Barbara - *Her Piano Sang (Illus. by Shelly O Haas)*
   c BL - v93 - Ja '97 - p848 [251-500]
   c Ch BWatch - v7 - Ja '97 - p5 [51-250]
   c KR - v64 - D 1 '96 - p1733 [51-250]
   c SLJ - v43 - Ja '97 - p96 [51-250]
Alloy Digest 1952-1995. Electronic Media Version
   r Choice - v34 - My '97 - p1529 [51-250]
Alloy Finder: Version 2.0. Electronic Media Version
   r Choice - v34 - My '97 - p1529 [51-250]
Allport, Susan - *A Natural History of Parenting*
   y BL - v93 - F 1 '97 - p914 [51-250]
   KR - v65 - Ja 1 '97 - p29 [251-500]
   LJ - v122 - F 1 '97 - p100 [51-250]
   NYTBR - v102 - Ap 6 '97 - p15 [501+]
   PW - v244 - Ja 13 '97 - p62 [51-250]
Allrich, Steve - *Oil Painting for the Serious Beginner*
   A Art - v60 - O '96 - p80 [51-250]
Allsopp, Richard - *Dictionary of Caribbean English Usage*
   r ARBA - v28 - '97 - p384 [251-500]
   r Choice - v34 - My '97 - p1473 [501+]
   yr Sch Lib - v44 - Ag '96 - p127+ [51-250]
   r TES - D 27 '96 - p16 [1-50]

Allsopp, Vicky - *Understanding Economics*
    JEL - v34 - D '96 - p2010 [51-250]
Allston, Frank J - *Ready for Sea*
    R&R Bk N - v11 - D '96 - p73 [51-250]
Allum, Dianne J - *Cochlear Implant Rehabilitation in Children and Adults*
    SciTech - v20 - D '96 - p51 [51-250]
Allyn, Doug - *Black Water*
    Arm Det - v29 - Sum '96 - p359 [51-250]
    The Cheerio Killings
    Arm Det - v29 - Sum '96 - p309 [51-250]
Almaguer, Tomas - *Racial Fault Lines*
    Amerasia J - v22 - 2 '96 - p178+ [501+]
The Almanac of American Employers 1996-97
    r ARBA - v28 - '97 - p120+ [251-500]
    r R&R Bk N - v11 - D '96 - p33 [51-250]
The Almanac of British Politics 1983-
    r Econ - v342 - Mr 22 '97 - p106 [501+]
The Almanac of European Politics 1995
    r ARBA - v28 - '97 - p272+ [251-500]
Almarode, Jay - *Multi-User Smalltalk*
    SciTech - v21 - Mr '97 - p5 [51-250]
Almeida, Anna Luiza Ozorio De - *Sustainable Settlement in the Brazilian Amazon*
    Choice - v34 - D '96 - p673 [51-250]
    JEL - v34 - S '96 - p1480 [51-250]
Almeida, Ileana - *Estudios Basicos De Derechos Humanos*
    BL - v93 - S 15 '96 - p227 [1-50]
Almeida, Miguel Vale De - *The Hegemonic Male*
    Choice - v34 - Mr '97 - p1201 [51-250]
Almodovar, Pedro - *Almodovar on Almodovar*
    TES - Ag 2 '96 - pR6 [51-250]
Almon, Bert - *Earth Prime*
    WAL - v31 - Fall '96 - p269+ [251-500]
Almond, Barbara - *The Therapeutic Narrative*
    Choice - v34 - Ap '97 - p1330 [51-250]
    R&R Bk N - v12 - F '97 - p79 [51-250]
Almond, Brenda - *AIDS: A Moral Issue. 2nd Ed.*
    Choice - v34 - My '97 - p1532 [51-250]
Almond, Mark - *Revolution: 500 Years of Struggle for Change*
    LJ - v121 - N 1 '96 - p76+ [51-250]
    Obs - S 8 '96 - p18* [51-250]
    PW - v243 - N 25 '96 - p67 [1-50]
Almond, Philip C - *Heaven and Hell in Enlightenment England*
    EHR - v112 - F '97 - p204+ [501+]
Alogoskoufis, George - *Unemployment: Choices for Europe*
    Econ J - v106 - N '96 - p1841 [251-500]
Al-Omar, Fuad - *Islamic Banking*
    Choice - v34 - F '97 - p1009+ [51-250]
Alonso, Fernando - *Mateo Y Los Reyes Magos (Illus. by Alberto Urdiales)*
    c BL - v93 - F 15 '97 - p1032 [1-50]
Alonso, Luis Ricardo - *La Estrella Que Cayo Una Noche En El Mar*
    BL - v93 - Ap 1 '97 - p1284 [1-50]
    WLT - v70 - Aut '96 - p919+ [501+]
Alouf, James L - *American History Smart Junior*
    y Kliatt - v31 - My '97 - p24 [251-500]
Alper, Ann Fitzpatrick - *A Brief History of Planet Earth*
    c SB - v32 - N '96 - p238 [51-250]
Alperi, Victor - *La Novela De Un Pintor*
    Hisp - v79 - S '96 - p471+ [501+]
    Los Suenos De Un Portugues Y Otras Historias
    WLT - v70 - Sum '96 - p672 [51-250]
Alperovitz, Gar - *The Decision to Use the Atomic Bomb and the Architecture of an American Myth*
    Books - v9 - S '95 - p23 [51-250]
    y Kliatt - v31 - Ja '97 - p26 [51-250]
    RAH - v24 - S '96 - p529+ [501+]
Alpers, Paul J - *What Is Pastoral?*
    Choice - v34 - N '96 - p448 [51-250]
    Nine-C Lit - v51 - D '96 - p419 [51-250]
    R&R Bk N - v11 - N '96 - p65 [51-250]
Alpers, Svetlana - *The Making of Rubens*
    PW - v243 - D 30 '96 - p64 [1-50]
Alperson, Myra - *Foundations for a New Democracy*
    JEL - v34 - S '96 - p1459 [51-250]
    The International Adoption Handbook
    BL - v93 - My 1 '97 - p1463 [51-250]
Alpert, Barbara - *No Friend like a Sister*
    PW - v243 - N 11 '96 - p71 [51-250]
Alpert, Judith L - *Sexual Abuse Recalled*
    Soc Ser R - v70 - D '96 - p667 [1-50]
Alphabet Songs (Illus. by David Pace). Book and Audio Version
    c Sch Lib - v45 - F '97 - p17 [51-250]
    c TES - Ja 17 '97 - p13* [51-250]

Alphin, Elaine Marie - *A Bear for Miguel (Illus. by Joan Sandin)*
    c BL - v92 - Ag '96 - p1910 [51-250]
    c HB Guide - v7 - Fall '96 - p283 [51-250]
Als, Hilton - *The Women*
    Advocate - D 10 '96 - p79+ [501+]
    KR - v64 - S 15 '96 - p1363 [251-500]
    NY - v72 - D 16 '96 - p108 [51-250]
    NYTBR - v102 - Ja 5 '97 - p7 [501+]
    NYTLa - v146 - Ja 1 '97 - p33 [501+]
    PW - v243 - S 23 '96 - p65 [51-250]
Alschuler, Liora - *ABCD...SGML*
    BYTE - v21 - S '96 - p34 [251-500]
    CBR - v14 - Jl '96 - p20 [51-250]
Alson, Peter - *Confessions of an Ivy League Bookie*
    Obs - S 1 '96 - p17* [501+]
    Rapport - v19 - 4 '96 - p39 [251-500]
Alspach, JoAnn Grif - *The Educational Process in Nursing Staff Development*
    AJN - v96 - D '96 - p16M [51-250]
Alston, Julian M - *Making Science Pay*
    SciTech - v20 - N '96 - p57 [51-250]
Alston, Lee J - *Empirical Studies in Institutional Change*
    JEL - v35 - Mr '97 - p204 [51-250]
Alston, R C - *Books with Manuscript*
    r RES - v47 - Ag '96 - p396+ [501+]
Alston, Richard - *Soldier and Society in Roman Egypt*
    J Mil H - v60 - O '96 - p767+ [501+]
Alston, William P - *A Realist Conception of Truth*
    Choice - v34 - S '97 - p140 [51-250]
    J Phil - v94 - F '97 - p103+ [501+]
Alsup, Jerry David - *Alsop's Tables. Vol. 2*
    r EGH - v50 - N '96 - p192 [51-250]
Alt, Betty - *Weeping Violins*
    Choice - v34 - O '96 - p334 [51-250]
Alt, David - *Northwest Exposures*
    Choice - v34 - S '96 - p158 [51-250]
Altchek, Albert - *Diagnosis and Management of Ovarian Disorders*
    SciTech - v20 - N '96 - p51 [51-250]
Altea, Rosemary - *The Eagle and the Rose*
    Books - v9 - S '95 - p23 [1-50]
Altemose, Charlene - *What You Should Know about Angels*
    RR - v55 - S '96 - p554 [1-50]
Alten, Steve - *Meg*
    LJ - v122 - My 1 '97 - p136 [51-250]
    PW - v244 - Mr 24 '97 - p56 [51-250]
Alter, Judy - *Callie Shaw, Stable Boy*
    c BL - v93 - F 1 '97 - p939 [51-250]
    Cherokee Rose
    Roundup M - v3 - Ag '96 - p28 [251-500]
    Rodeos: The Greatest Show on Dirt
    c SLJ - v43 - Mr '97 - p195 [51-250]
Alter, Michael J - *Science of Flexibility. 2nd Ed.*
    r SciTech - v20 - S '96 - p22 [51-250]
Alter, Nora M - *Vietnam Protest Theatre*
    Choice - v34 - N '96 - p471 [51-250]
Alter, Robert - *The Pleasures of Reading*
    PW - v243 - S 30 '96 - p79 [1-50]
Alterman, Seymour L - *How to Control Diabetes*
    BL - v93 - S 15 '96 - p194 [51-250]
    BWatch - v17 - D '96 - p3 [51-250]
Alternative Library Literature 1994/1995
    r LJ - v122 - F 1 '97 - p114 [1-50]
    r R&R Bk N - v11 - N '96 - p80 [51-250]
Alternative Medicine Digest
    p LJ - v121 - N 15 '96 - p94 [51-250]
Alternative Press Index 1969-
    r RQ - v36 - Fall '96 - p53+ [51-250]
Alternative Press Index 1991-June 1996. Electronic Media Version
    r WorldV - v12 - O '96 - p23 [251-500]
Alternative Press Index 1995
    yr ARBA - v28 - '97 - p30+ [51-250]
Alternatives to the Peace Corps. 7th Ed.
    r BL - v92 - Ag '96 - p1922 [1-50]
Alth, Max - *Do-It-Yourself Plumbing*
    r LJ - v122 - F 1 '97 - p53 [51-250]
Altham, J E J - *World, Mind, and Ethics*
    CPR - v16 - Ag '96 - p231+ [501+]
    Ethics - v107 - Ja '97 - p351+ [501+]
Althea - *Alone at Home (Illus. by Karin Littlewood)*
    c JB - v60 - O '96 - p190 [51-250]
    c Sch Lib - v44 - Ag '96 - p109 [51-250]
    The Birthday Party (Illus. by Karin Littlewood)
    c JB - v60 - O '96 - p190 [51-250]
    c Sch Lib - v44 - Ag '96 - p109 [51-250]
    The Bullies (Illus. by Karin Littlewood)
    c Sch Lib - v44 - Ag '96 - p109 [51-250]

    Gita Gets Lost (Illus. by Karin Littlewood)
    c Sch Lib - v44 - Ag '96 - p109 [51-250]
Altheide, David L - *An Ecology of Communication*
    CS - v25 - N '96 - p807+ [501+]
    JMCQ - v73 - Aut '96 - p752+ [501+]
Altholz, Josef L - *Anatomy of a Controversy*
    EHR - v111 - N '96 - p1320 [251-500]
    VS - v39 - Win '96 - p293+ [501+]
Althusius, Johannes - *Politica*
    Univ Bkmn - v36 - Fall '96 - p10+ [501+]
Altman, Billy - *Laughter's Gentle Soul*
    BL - v93 - My 1 '97 - p1474 [51-250]
    KR - v65 - F 15 '97 - p263 [251-500]
    LJ - v122 - My 1 '97 - p102 [51-250]
    NY - v73 - Ap 7 '97 - p88+ [501+]
    NYTBR - v102 - Ap 20 '97 - p24 [501+]
    PW - v244 - F 24 '97 - p76 [51-250]
    WSJ-Cent - v99 - Ap 14 '97 - pA13 [501+]
Altman, Gail S - *Beethoven: A Man of His Word*
    Rapport - v19 - 6 '96 - p33 [251-500]
Altman, Irwin - *Polygamous Families in Contemporary Society*
    Choice - v34 - Mr '97 - p1244 [51-250]
    Sci - v274 - N 22 '96 - p1321 [1-50]
Altman, Linda Jacobs - *California*
    c BL - v93 - F 1 '97 - p937 [51-250]
    c Ch BWatch - v6 - D '96 - p6 [1-50]
    c HB Guide - v8 - Spr '97 - p172 [51-250]
    c SLJ - v43 - F '97 - p108 [51-250]
    Cesar Chavez
    c HB Guide - v7 - Fall '96 - p370 [1-50]
    Life on an Israeli Kibbutz
    y HB Guide - v7 - Fall '96 - p383 [51-250]
    Women Inventors
    y BL - v93 - My 1 '97 - p1485 [51-250]
    c KR - v65 - F 1 '97 - p218 [51-250]
Altman, Mark - *Deep Space Nine*
    Lon R Bks - v18 - My 23 '96 - p34+ [501+]
Altman, Neil - *The Analyst in the Inner City*
    Tikkun - v11 - My '96 - p59+ [501+]
Altman, Roberta - *The Cancer Dictionary*
    r LJ - v122 - Ja '97 - p56 [51-250]
    Every Woman's Handbook for Preventing Cancer
    LJ - v122 - Ja '97 - p58 [51-250]
    PW - v243 - S 16 '96 - p80 [51-250]
    Waking Up, Fighting Back
    Choice - v34 - N '96 - p490 [51-250]
    Nat - v263 - D 9 '96 - p33+ [501+]
    Wom R Bks - v13 - S '96 - p22 [501+]
Altman, Susan - *The Encyclopedia of African-American Heritage*
    r BL - v93 - Mr 15 '97 - p1256 [51-250]
Altringham, John D - *Bats: Biology and Behaviour*
    Choice - v34 - My '97 - p1525 [51-250]
Altshuler, Bruce - *The Avant-Garde in Exhibition*
    Art J - v55 - Win '96 - p105+ [501+]
Altstadt, Audrey L - *The Azerbaijani Turks*
    Historian - v58 - Sum '96 - p891+ [251-500]
Alumenda, Stephen - *Thandiwe's Spirit and the River*
    c Bkbird - v34 - Spr '96 - p53 [1-50]
Alva, Mike - *Numismatica Mexicana Hecha Facil*
    Coin W - v38 - Ap 28 '97 - p18 [1-50]
Alva, Walter - *Royal Tombs of Sipan*
    LA Ant - v7 - Mr '96 - p81+ [501+]
Alvarez, Cynthia - *Classic Star Wars (Illus. by Isidre Mones)*
    c HB Guide - v7 - Fall '96 - p246 [51-250]
Alvarez, Jose - *Living in Paris*
    PW - v244 - Mr 31 '97 - p58 [51-250]
Alvarez, Julia - *The Other Side*
    NYTBR - v101 - D 22 '96 - p20 [1-50]
    Trib Bks - Ja 19 '97 - p8 [1-50]
    Yo!
    Atl - v279 - F '97 - p110 [51-250]
    BL - v93 - S 15 '96 - p180 [51-250]
    BW - v27 - Ja 19 '97 - p9 [501+]
    KR - v64 - N 1 '96 - p1546 [251-500]
    LJ - v121 - O 1 '96 - p124 [51-250]
    Ms - v7 - Mr '97 - p82 [251-500]
    NYTBR - v102 - F 9 '97 - p19 [501+]
    PW - v243 - O 14 '96 - p62 [251-500]
    Trib Bks - Ja 26 '97 - p2 [501+]
Alvarez, Roman - *Translation, Power, Subversion*
    R&R Bk N - v11 - D '96 - p59 [51-250]
Alvarez, Tom - *How to Create Action, Fantasy, and Adventure Comics*
    LJ - v121 - N 15 '96 - p60 [51-250]
Alvarez, Walter - *T. Rex and the Crater of Doom*
    KR - v65 - Mr 15 '97 - p425 [251-500]
Alverson, Hoyt - *Semantics and Experience*
    Am Ethnol - v23 - N '96 - p935+ [501+]

Alverson, William S - *Wild Forest Conservation Biology and Public Policy*
  BioSci - v46 - O '96 - p697+ [501+]
Alves, Abel A - *Brutality and Benevolence*
  Choice - v34 - Ap '97 - p1399 [51-250]
  R&R Bk N - v12 - F '97 - p27 [51-250]
Alves, Dora - *New Perspectives for U.S.-Asia Pacific Security Strategy*
  RSR - v24 - 3 '96 - p45 [51-250]
Alves, Pericles Gasparini - *Evolving Trends in the Dual Use of Satellites*
  R&R Bk N - v12 - F '97 - p100 [51-250]
Alvi, Moniza - *A Bowl of Warm Air*
  TLS - D 6 '96 - p14 [501+]
Alwitt, Linda F - *The Low-Income Consumer*
  Choice - v34 - S '96 - p170 [51-250]
Alwood, Edward - *Straight News*
  Advocate - N 26 '96 - p69+ [501+]
  AJR - v18 - N '96 - p49 [501+]
  BL - v93 - S 15 '96 - p185 [51-250]
  Choice - v34 - F '97 - p959 [51-250]
  JMCQ - v73 - Aut '96 - p768+ [501+]
  LJ - v121 - S 15 '96 - p76+ [51-250]
  NYTBR - v101 - N 3 '96 - p23 [501+]
  NYTBR - v101 - D 8 '96 - p93 [1-50]
Aly, Gotz - *Cleansing the Fatherland*
  JMH - v68 - D '96 - p1028+ [501+]
Alzheimer's Research
  p Nature - v383 - S 5 '96 - p35 [251-500]
Amadeo, Edward J - *Institutions, Inflation and Unemployment*
  JEL - v34 - S '96 - p1346+ [501+]
Amalric, F - *People, the Environment and Responsibility*
  R&R Bk N - v11 - D '96 - p26 [51-250]
Aman, Reinhold - *Opus Maledictorum*
  Utne R - Jl '96 - p106 [51-250]
Amann, Herbert - *Linear and Quasilinear Parabolic Problems. Vol. 1*
  SIAM Rev - v39 - Mr '97 - p153+ [501+]
Amateur Astronomy
  p S&T - v93 - Mr '97 - p96 [51-250]
Amato, Carol J - *The World's Easiest Guide to Using the APA*
  Sm Pr R - v28 - Je '96 - p12 [51-250]
Amato, Ivan - *Stuff: The Materials the World Is Made Of*
  BL - v93 - My 1 '97 - p1469 [51-250]
  KR - v65 - Mr 15 '97 - p425 [251-500]
  LJ - v122 - Ap 1 '97 - p116+ [51-250]
  PW - v244 - Mr 10 '97 - p54 [51-250]
Ambegaokar, Vinay - *Reasoning about Luck*
  Choice - v34 - D '96 - p648 [51-250]
  Phys Today - v49 - D '96 - p54 [501+]
  Sci - v274 - O 25 '96 - p523 [1-50]
  SciTech - v20 - D '96 - p23 [1-50]
Ambegaonkar, Prakash - *Intranet Resource Kit*
  LJ - v122 - My 1 '97 - p132 [51-250]
Amberry, Tom - *Free Throw*
  Esq - v126 - D '96 - p40 [1-50]
Ambler, Tim - *The Financial Times Guide to Marketing*
  Choice - v34 - O '96 - p324 [51-250]
Ambraseys, Nicolas - *The Security of Turkey and Adjacent Areas*
  GJ - v162 - Jl '96 - p239 [51-250]
Ambrose, Brendalyn P - *Democratization and the Protection of Human Rights in Africa*
  JTWS - v13 - Fall '96 - p253+ [501+]
  JTWS - v13 - Fall '96 - p255+ [501+]
Ambrose, David - *Mother of God*
  Arm Det - v30 - Win '97 - p91+ [251-500]
  KR - v64 - S 1 '96 - p1252 [251-500]
  LJ - v121 - O 1 '96 - p124 [51-250]
  PW - v243 - S 23 '96 - p56 [51-250]
Ambrose, Delorese - *Healing the Downsized Organization*
  BL - v93 - N 1 '96 - p465 [51-250]
  LJ - v121 - N 15 '96 - p69 [51-250]
Ambrose, James E - *Simplified Design of Concrete Structures. 7th Ed.*
  SciTech - v21 - Mr '97 - p79 [51-250]
Ambrose, Stephen E - *D-Day, June 6, 1944*
  Pres SQ - v26 - Fall '96 - p1174+ [501+]

Undaunted Courage
  BL - v93 - Ja '97 - p759 [51-250]
  BL - v93 - Ap 1 '97 - p1285 [1-50]
  CSM - v88 - N 7 '96 - p14 [51-250]
  CSM - v89 - Ja 9 '97 - p14 [51-250]
  LATBR - D 29 '96 - p9 [51-250]
  LJ - v122 - Ja '97 - p48 [1-50]
  NYTBR - v101 - D 8 '96 - p93 [1-50]
  Roundup M - v4 - F '97 - p22 [51-250]
  Sea H - Aut '96 - p42 [251-500]
  y SLJ - v42 - D '96 - p33 [1-50]
  SLJ - v42 - D '96 - p43 [51-250]
  Trib Bks - My 25 '97 - p8 [1-50]
  VQR - v73 - Win '97 - p183+ [501+]
  WAL - v31 - Win '97 - p403+ [251-500]
  W&M Q - v54 - Ja '97 - p273+ [501+]
Undaunted Courage (Smith). Audio Version
  BL - v93 - N 15 '96 - p604 [501+]
  y Kliatt - v30 - N '96 - p51+ [51-250]
Ambrose's Chronology of World Leaders and Rulers
  r BL - v93 - S 1 '96 - p166 [1-50]
Ambrosia, Gloria - *Gloria's Gourmet Low-Fat Muffins*
  PW - v243 - D 16 '96 - p57 [51-250]
Ambrosiani, Bjorn - *Developments around the Baltic and the North Sea in the Viking Age*
  AJA - v100 - Jl '96 - p639+ [251-500]
Amdahl, Kenn - *Algebra Unplugged*
  Math T - v89 - S '96 - p512 [251-500]
Amdam, Rolv Petter - *Management Education and Competitiveness*
  JEL - v35 - Mr '97 - p229+ [51-250]
  R&R Bk N - v11 - D '96 - p27 [51-250]
Amell, Samuel - *The Contemporary Spanish Novel*
  r ARBA - v28 - '97 - p464 [51-250]
  r TranslRevS - v2 - D '96 - p4 [51-250]
Amen, Karen - *The Bottom Line*
  Books - v10 - Je '96 - p22 [1-50]
Amend, Bill - *At Least This Place Sells T-Shirts*
  y BL - v93 - Ap 1 '97 - p1306 [1-50]
Amende, Coral - *Hollywood Confidential*
  Ent W - Mr 28 '97 - p62 [51-250]
Amer, Ramses - *Peace-Keeping in a Peace Process*
  Pac A - v69 - Fall '96 - p450+ [501+]
Amerasekera, Ajith - *ESD in Silicon Integrated Circuits*
  SciTech - v20 - S '96 - p57 [51-250]
America, Richard F - *Soul in Management*
  BL - v93 - N 15 '96 - p556 [51-250]
  BWatch - v18 - Mr '97 - p3 [51-250]
  PW - v243 - O 21 '96 - p67 [51-250]
America: History and Life 1965-
  r ASInt - v34 - O '96 - p16+ [51-250]
America Preserved
  r J Gov Info - v23 - S '96 - p551 [51-250]
American Association of University Women. Thousand Oaks California Branch - *Profiles of Women Past and Present. Vol. 2*
  y VOYA - v19 - D '96 - p289 [251-500]
The American Bar Association Guide to Consumer Law
  BL - v93 - D 15 '96 - p695 [51-250]
The American Bibliography of Slavic and East European Studies for 1993
  r ARBA - v28 - '97 - p60+ [251-500]
  r R&R Bk N - v11 - D '96 - p9 [51-250]
American Business Locations Directory. Vols. 1-5
  r ARBA - v28 - '97 - p79+ [251-500]
American Chemical Society Directory of Graduate Research 1995
  r J Chem Ed - v73 - Je '96 - pA136 [51-250]
American Federation of Labor - *American Federation of Labor: History, Encyclopedia, Reference Book. Vols. 1-3*
  r RQ - v36 - Fall '96 - p49 [51-250]
American Fiction. Vol. 7
  LMR - v15 - Fall '96 - p33+ [501+]
American Forest and Paper Association - *Standard for Load Resistance Factor Design (LRFD) for Engineered Wood Construction*
  r SciTech - v20 - S '96 - p50 [51-250]
American Girl
  cp Par Ch - v20 - O '96 - p15 [1-50]
American Heart Association - *American Heart Association Guide to Heart Attack Treatment*
  LJ - v121 - O 15 '96 - p82 [51-250]
American Heart Association around the World Cookbook
  BL - v93 - N 15 '96 - p559 [51-250]
The American Heritage Talking Dictionary. Electronic Media Version
  r Choice - v34 - Mr '97 - p1147 [501+]
  yr Kliatt - v30 - S '96 - p39 [51-250]

American Heritage: The History of the United States for Young People. Electronic Media Version
  c PW - v244 - F 24 '97 - p36 [51-250]
The American Heritage Thesaurus
  cr CLW - v67 - D '96 - p59 [51-250]
The American Historical Association's Guide to Historical Literature. 3rd Ed., Vols. 1-2
  r ASInt - v34 - O '96 - p7 [51-250]
  yr CLW - v67 - D '96 - p52 [251-500]
  r RQ - v35 - Sum '96 - p485 [51-250]
  r Six Ct J - v27 - Fall '96 - p905+ [501+]
American Horticultural Society Pruning and Training
  BL - v93 - S 1 '96 - p51 [51-250]
  Fine Gard - Ja '97 - p66+ [251-500]
  Hort - v94 - F '97 - p64+ [501+]
The American Humanities Index for 1995. Pts. 1-2
  r ARBA - v28 - '97 - p343 [51-250]
American Images SBC Communications
  LJ - v121 - N 15 '96 - p58 [51-250]
American Institute of Chemical Engineers. Center for Chemical Process Safety - *Guidelines for Use of Vapor Cloud Dispersion Models*
  SciTech - v21 - Mr '97 - p26 [51-250]
American Jewish Historical Society - *An Index to American Jewish Historical Quarterly/American Jewish History: Volumes 51-80. Vols. 1-2*
  r ARBA - v28 - '97 - p161 [251-250]
American Jewish Year Book 1996
  r ARBA - v28 - '97 - p554 [51-250]
The American Journals CD. Electronic Media Version
  yr VOYA - v19 - D '96 - p294+ [251-500]
American Justice. Vols. 1-3
  yr ARBA - v28 - '97 - p220 [51-250]
  r BL - v93 - O 1 '96 - p366 [251-500]
  r Choice - v34 - N '96 - p425 [51-250]
  r RQ - v36 - Win '96 - p287+ [251-500]
The American Labor Press
  r RQ - v36 - Fall '96 - p53 [51-250]
American Labor Unions' Constitutions and Proceedings 1836-
  r RQ - v36 - Fall '96 - p51+ [51-250]
The American Labor Who's Who 1925-
  r RQ - v36 - Fall '96 - p54 [1-50]
The American Labor Year Book. 1916-1932 Eds.
  r RQ - v36 - Fall '96 - p49 [51-250]
American Library Association. Evaluation of Reference and Adult Service Committee - *The Reference Assessment Manual*
  LQ - v66 - O '96 - p487+ [501+]
American Library Association. Office for Intellectual Freedom - *Intellectual Freedom Manual. 5th Ed.*
  r ARBA - v28 - '97 - p244+ [251-500]
  r Emerg Lib - v24 - S '96 - p39 [51-250]
  SLMQ - v24 - Sum '96 - p219+ [51-250]
American Library Association. Reference and Adult Services Division. Notable Books Council - *Fifty Years of Notable Books*
  r A Lib - v27 - Ag '96 - p70 [51-250]
  r BL - v93 - S 15 '96 - p184 [501+]
American Literary Scholarship 1993
  Nine-C Lit - v50 - Mr '96 - p558 [501+]
American Literary Scholarship 1994
  Nine-C Lit - v51 - Mr '97 - p563 [501+]
American Management Association - *AMA Style Guide for Business Writing*
  r BL - v93 - My 1 '97 - p1514 [1-50]
American Mathematical Society - *Combined Membership List 1996-1997*
  r ARBA - v28 - '97 - p640 [51-250]
American Medical Association Manual of Style. 8th Ed.
  r BL - v93 - My 1 '97 - p1511 [1-50]
American Military Power
  RSR - v24 - 3 '96 - p48 [51-250]
American Nature Writing 1997
  PW - v244 - F 17 '97 - p207 [51-250]
  Trib Bks - My 4 '97 - p8 [1-50]
The American Presidency. Electronic Media Version
  r BL - v93 - F 15 '97 - p1040 [251-500]
  cr Ch BWatch - v6 - N '96 - p5 [51-250]
  cr LJ - v122 - Mr 15 '97 - p96 [51-250]
American Psychiatric Association - *DSM-IV Primary Care Version*
  J ClinPsyc - v58 - F '97 - p90 [501+]
American Psychiatric Association Practice Guidelines
  J ClinPsyc - v58 - Ja '97 - p34+ [501+]
American Psychiatric Press Review of Psychiatry. Vol. 15
  AJPsych - v153 - O '96 - p1358 [501+]
American Psychological Association. Practice Directorate - *Marketing Your Practice*
  SciTech - v20 - N '96 - p43 [51-250]

Organizing Your Practice through Automation
SciTech - v20 - N '96 - p42 [1-50]

American Society for Testing and Materials - *ASTM Standards on Color and Appearance Measurement. 5th Ed.*
r SciTech - v20 - S '96 - p49 [51-250]

American Society of Civil Engineers. Committee on Ground Water Quality - *Quality of Ground Water*
SciTech - v20 - D '96 - p69 [51-250]

American Society of Civil Engineers. Task Committee on Fasteners - *Mechanical Connections in Wood Structures*
SciTech - v20 - S '96 - p50 [51-250]

American Society of Civil Engineers. Task Committee on Hazardous Waste Site Assessment Manual - *Environmental Site Investigation Guidance Manual*
SciTech - v20 - S '96 - p52 [51-250]

American Society of Civil Engineers. Task Committee on Pipeline Crossings - *Pipeline Crossings*
SciTech - v20 - D '96 - p64 [51-250]

American Society of Civil Engineers. Task Committee on Pumped Storage - *Hydroelectric Pumped Storage Technology*
SciTech - v20 - S '96 - p54 [51-250]

American Society of Civil Engineers. Urban Transportation Division. Committee of Advanced Technology - *Applications of Advanced Technologies in Transportation Engineering: Proceedings of the 4th International Conference, Capri, Italy, June 27-30, 1995*
SciTech - v20 - S '96 - p50 [51-250]

American Society of Mechanical Engineers Fluids Engineering Division. Summer Meeting (1996: San Diego, CA) - *Proceedings of the ASME Fluids Engineering Division Summer Meeting. Vols. 1-4*
SciTech - v20 - D '96 - p61 [51-250]

American Society of Mechanical Engineers. History and Heritage Committee - *Landmarks in Mechanical Engineering*
LJ - v121 - D '96 - p140 [51-250]
New Sci - v153 - Mr 8 '97 - p42 [51-250]
y SB - v33 - My '97 - p108 [51-250]

American Southwest Travel-Smart Trip Planner. 1st Ed.-
r BL - v93 - S 15 '96 - p210 [1-50]

American Sport Education Program - *Coaching Youth Volleyball. 2nd Ed.*
BL - v93 - S 15 '96 - p202 [51-250]

American Treasures in the Library of Congress
PW - v244 - Ap 21 '97 - p57 [51-250]

American Visions: The Magazine of Afro-American Culture
p LJ - v122 - Mr 15 '97 - p95 [51-250]

American Writers. 4th Suppl., Vols. 1-2
yr ARBA - v28 - '97 - p438+ [251-500]
r BL - v93 - F 15 '97 - p1042 [51-250]

American Writing
p Sm Pr R - v28 - O '96 - p13+ [501+]

America's Corporate Families 1995. Vols. 1-3
r ARBA - v28 - '97 - p80 [251-500]

The Americas Review
p Sm Pr R - v29 - Ja '97 - p13+ [501+]

America's Top Jobs on CD-ROM. Electronic Media Version
r LJ - v122 - F 15 '97 - p168 [51-250]

Americas Watch Committee (U.S.) - *Silencing a People*
JTWS - v13 - Spr '96 - p369+ [501+]

Amerika, Mark - *In Memoriam to Postmodernism*
ABR - v17 - Ag '96 - p8+ [501+]

Amerikaner, Susan - *Mi Pequeno Libro De Numeros (Illus. by Judy Ziegler)*
c SLJ - v42 - N '96 - p132 [51-250]

Ameriks, Karl - *The Modern Subject*
CPR - v16 - Ag '96 - p236+ [501+]
R&R Bk N - v12 - F '97 - p3 [1-50]

Ameringer, Charles D - *The Caribbean Legion*
HAHR - v76 - N '96 - p843+ [251-500]

Amery, Heather - *Castle Tales (Illus. by Stephen Cartwright)*
c Books - v10 - Je '96 - p25 [51-250]

Ames, Andrea L - *The VRML 2.0 Sourcebook. 2nd Ed.*
SciTech - v21 - Mr '97 - p10 [51-250]
The VRML Sourcebook
Quill & Q - v62 - Ag '96 - p23 [51-250]

Ames, Glenn J - *Colbert, Mercantilism, and the French Quest for Asian Trade*
J Mil H - v61 - Ja '97 - p155+ [251-500]

Ames, Jim - *Color Theory Made Easy*
A Art - v60 - D '96 - p80 [51-250]

Ames, John Edward - *Soldier's Heart*
Roundup M - v4 - D '96 - p23 [51-250]

Ames, Roger T - *The Art of Rulership*
RM - v50 - D '96 - p383+ [501+]
Self and Deception
R&R Bk N - v11 - N '96 - p3 [51-250]

Amic, Peter J - *Computer Numerical Control Programming*
SciTech - v21 - Mr '97 - p85 [51-250]

Amichai, Yehuda - *The Selected Poetry of Yehuda Amichai*
BW - v27 - Ap 13 '97 - p12 [51-250]
NYTBR - v101 - O 27 '96 - p48 [51-250]
TranslRevS - v2 - D '96 - p5 [51-250]

Amico, Leonard N - *Bernard Palissy: In Search of Earthly Paradise*
Choice - v34 - F '97 - p954 [51-250]

Amigoni, David - *Victorian Biography*
Biography - v19 - Fall '96 - p429 [1-50]

Amigoni, Ferdinando - *La Piu Semplice Macchina*
MLR - v92 - Ja '97 - p220+ [501+]

Amin, Ash - *Behind the Myth of European Union*
JEL - v34 - D '96 - p2038 [51-250]

Amin, Shahid - *Event, Metaphor, Memory*
Lon R Bks - v19 - Ja 2 '97 - p28+ [501+]

Amin, Tahir - *Mass Resistance in Kashmir*
Pac A - v69 - Fall '96 - p438+ [501+]

Amirahmadi, Hooshang - *Small Islands, Big Politics*
MEJ - v51 - Win '97 - p150 [51-250]

Amis, Kingsley - *The King's English*
NS - v126 - Mr 21 '97 - p51+ [501+]
Spec - v278 - Mr 22 '97 - p43+ [501+]
TES - Mr 14 '97 - p9* [501+]
You Can't Do Both (Shelley). Audio Version
BL - v93 - Mr 15 '97 - p1253 [51-250]
LJ - v121 - O 15 '96 - p103 [51-250]

Amis, Martin - *The Information*
Ant R - v54 - Sum '96 - p380 [51-250]
Spec - v277 - N 16 '96 - p42 [1-50]
Spec - v277 - N 16 '96 - p43 [1-50]

Amiss, John Milton - *Machinery's Handbook Guide. 25th Ed.*
SciTech - v20 - S '96 - p52 [1-50]

Amitai-Preiss, Reuven - *Mongols and Mamluks*
EHR - v112 - Ap '97 - p444+ [501+]

Amith, Jonathan D - *The Amate Tradition*
R&R Bk N - v11 - D '96 - p18 [51-250]

Ammon, Bette DeBruyne - *Worth a Thousand Words*
r BL - v93 - Ja '97 - p901 [251-500]
r Cur R - v36 - N '96 - p3* [51-250]
r R&R Bk N - v12 - F '97 - p103 [51-250]
r SLJ - v43 - Ja '97 - p38 [51-250]

Ammon, Richard - *An Amish Christmas (Illus. by Pamela Patrick)*
c BL - v93 - S 1 '96 - p135 [51-250]
c CBRS - v25 - O '96 - p18 [51-250]
c HB Guide - v8 - Spr '97 - p17 [51-250]
c NYTBR - v101 - D 22 '96 - p16 [1-50]
c PW - v243 - S 30 '96 - p91 [51-250]
c SLJ - v42 - O '96 - p33 [51-250]

Ammonius, Hermiae - *On Aristotle's On Interpretation 1-8*
RM - v50 - D '96 - p384+ [501+]

Ammons, A R - *Brink Road*
Am - v175 - O 26 '96 - p26 [251-500]
HR - v49 - Win '97 - p659+ [501+]
LJ - v122 - Ap 1 '97 - p94 [1-50]
VQR - v73 - Win '97 - p30* [51-250]
Selected Poems
LJ - v122 - Ap 1 '97 - p94 [1-50]

Ammons, David N - *Municipal Benchmarks*
Choice - v34 - D '96 - p680 [51-250]
R&R Bk N - v11 - D '96 - p23 [51-250]

Ammons, Elizabeth - *Tricksterism in Turn-of-the-Century American Literature*
Am Q - v48 - S '96 - p542+ [501+]

Ammons, Kevin - *Good Girl, Bad Girl*
Advocate - S 17 '96 - p60 [1-50]
Advocate - O 29 '96 - p70+ [501+]

Amoia, Alba - *20th-Century Italian Women Writers*
Choice - v34 - Mr '97 - p1169 [51-250]

Amoss, Berthe - *The Cajun Gingerbread Boy (Illus. by Berthe Amoss)*
c R&R - v50 - O '96 - p130 [1-50]

Amphibians and Reptiles. Book and Electronic Media Version
c LATBR - D 22 '96 - p6 [51-250]

Amphoux, Christian-Bernard - *L'Evangile Selon Matthieu*
Rel St Rev - v23 - Ap '97 - p182 [51-250]

Ampo - *Voices from the Japanese Women's Movement*
Choice - v34 - S '96 - p184 [51-250]

Ampuero, Fernando - *Bicho Raro*
BL - v93 - Mr 15 '97 - p1232 [1-50]

Amrein, Werner O - *CO-Groups, Commutator Methods and Spectral Theory of N-Body Hamiltonians*
SciTech - v20 - S '96 - p14 [51-250]

Amrine, Frederick - *Goethe in the History of Science. Vol. 1*
r R&R Bk N - v12 - F '97 - p91 [51-250]

AMS-IMS-SIAM Joint Summer Research Conference on Matroid Theory (1995: University of Washington) - *Matroid Theory*
SciTech - v20 - D '96 - p15 [51-250]

AMS-SIAM Summer Seminar in Applied Mathematics (1995: Park City, Utah) - *The Mathematics of Numerical Analysis*
SciTech - v20 - D '96 - p17 [51-250]

Amsler, Cory - *Pioneering Americana*
Mag Antiq - v151 - Mr '97 - p384 [251-500]

Amstutz, Andre - *Tom's Hats (Illus. by Andre Amstutz)*
c Bks Keeps - Jl '96 - p8 [51-250]

Amt, Emilie - *The Accession of Henry II in England*
Specu - v72 - Ja '97 - p101+ [501+]

Amundsen, Darrel W - *Medicine, Society, and Faith in the Ancient and Medieval Worlds*
AHR - v102 - F '97 - p95 [51-250]
Am Sci - v85 - Ja '97 - p89+ [501+]
Hast Cen R - v26 - Jl '96 - p38+ [501+]
MHR - v10 - Fall '96 - p101+ [501+]
Rel St Rev - v23 - Ap '97 - p160 [51-250]

Anaerobe
p Nature - v383 - S 5 '96 - p40 [251-500]

Analysis, Design and Evaluation of Man-Machine Systems 1995
SciTech - v20 - N '96 - p61 [51-250]

Analysis of Status Indians in British Columbia. Vol. 3
J Gov Info - v23 - S '96 - p625+ [51-250]

Analytical Profiles of Drug Substances and Excipients. Vol. 24
r SciTech - v20 - N '96 - p56 [51-250]

Anand, Mulk Raj - *Conversations in Bloomsbury*
ELT - v40 - 2 '97 - p251 [51-250]

Anand, Sushila - *Indian Sahib*
Spec - v277 - S 21 '96 - p48+ [501+]

Anargyros, Isabelle - *Croqu'sandwich--Super Et Geant*
c BL - v93 - N 1 '96 - p500 [1-50]

Anastalpo, George - *The Amendments to the Constitution*
CH - v65 - D '96 - p724+ [501+]

Anastas, Paul T - *Green Chemistry*
Choice - v34 - N '96 - p486 [51-250]
SciTech - v20 - S '96 - p58 [51-250]

Anastasio, Dina - *Twenty Mini Mysteries You Can Solve (Illus. by Kevin Faerber)*
c Bks Keeps - Jl '96 - p7 [51-250]

Anatomic Pathology Slide Seminar (60th: 1994: Washington, D.C.) - *Urological Pathology*
SciTech - v20 - D '96 - p43 [51-250]

Anawalt, Sasha - *The Joffrey Ballet*
Advocate - D 10 '96 - p76+ [501+]
y BL - v93 - S 15 '96 - p199 [251-500]
BW - v26 - N 3 '96 - p1+ [501+]
LATBR - N 17 '96 - p8+ [501+]
LJ - v121 - N 1 '96 - p68 [51-250]
Nat - v264 - F 24 '97 - p32+ [501+]
NYTBR - v102 - F 9 '97 - p9 [501+]
NYTLa - v146 - Ja 15 '97 - pC17 [501+]

Anaya, Rudolfo - *The Farolitos of Christmas (Illus. by Edward Gonzales)*
c Emerg Lib - v23 - My '96 - p56 [51-250]
c JOYS - v9 - Sum '96 - p414 [51-250]
Jalamanta: A Message from the Desert
WLT - v70 - Aut '96 - p957+ [501+]
Maya's Children (Illus. by Maria Baca)
c BL - v93 - My 1 '97 - p1500 [51-250]
Rio Grande Fall
BL - v93 - S 1 '96 - p66 [51-250]
LJ - v122 - Ja '97 - p51 [1-50]

Anaya, S James - *Indigenous Peoples in International Law*
r APSR - v91 - Mr '97 - p227+ [501+]

Ancelet, Barry Jean - *Cajun and Creole Folktales*
FR - v70 - D '96 - p377+ [251-500]
Cris Sur Le Bayou
FR - v70 - F '97 - p439+ [501+]

Ancell, R Manning - *The Biographical Dictionary of World War II Generals and Flag Officers*
r ARBA - v28 - '97 - p189 [51-250]
r Choice - v34 - O '96 - p247+ [51-250]
r J Mil H - v60 - O '96 - p789+ [501+]

Ancient Art from the Shumei Family Collection
Choice - v34 - D '96 - p600 [51-250]
LJ - v121 - O 1 '96 - p72 [51-250]
R&R Bk N - v11 - N '96 - p59 [51-250]

Ancient Egyptian Art. Electronic Media Version
LJ - v121 - S 15 '96 - p105+ [501+]

Ancill, R J - *Schizophrenia: Exploring the Spectrum of Psychosis*
AJPsych - v153 - O '96 - p1359 [251-500]

Ancona, George - *Fiesta U.S.A. (Illus. by George Ancona)*
c HB Guide - v7 - Fall '96 - p318 [51-250]

Ancona, Ronnie - *Time and the Erotic in Horace's Odes*
AJP - v117 - Win '96 - p657+ [501+]

Anderman, Gunilla M - *Words, Words, Words*
R&R Bk N - v11 - N '96 - p63 [51-250]
TranslRevS - v2 - D '96 - p14 [51-250]

Anders, George - *Health against Wealth*
BL - v93 - N 1 '96 - p458 [51-250]
BW - v26 - N 17 '96 - p11 [251-500]
Choice - v34 - Mr '97 - p1192 [51-250]
KR - v64 - S 1 '96 - p1283+ [251-500]
LJ - v121 - O 1 '96 - p114+ [51-250]
NYTBR - v101 - N 24 '96 - p13 [501+]
PW - v243 - S 16 '96 - p58 [51-250]

Anders CD-ROM Guide. 2nd Ed.
r ARBA - v28 - '97 - p10 [251-500]

Andersdatter, Karla - *Wild Onions*
PW - v243 - N 18 '96 - p63 [51-250]

Andersen, Christopher - *Jack and Jackie*
LATBR - S 8 '96 - p4+ [501+]
NYTBR - v101 - S 1 '96 - p5 [501+]

Andersen, Hans Christian - *The Emperor's New Clothes (Illus. by Dorothee Duntze)*
c PW - v244 - Ap 7 '97 - p94 [1-50]
The Emperor's New Clothes (Gielgud). Audio Version
c Ch BWatch - v6 - N '96 - p7 [51-250]
Fairy Tales of Hans Christian Andersen (Illus. by Isabelle Brent)
c ECEJ - v24 - Fall '96 - p41 [51-250]
The Fir Tree
c TES - D 6 '96 - p16* [1-50]
Listen and Read The Ugly Duckling and Other Fairy Tales (Brill). Book and Audio Version
c BL - v93 - Mr 15 '97 - p1253 [51-250]
c Ch BWatch - v6 - Jl '96 - p7 [1-50]
New Danish Plays
TranslRevS - v2 - D '96 - p3 [51-250]

Andersen, Ib - *On the Art of Doing Field Studies*
JEL - v34 - S '96 - p1403 [51-250]

Andersen, Jorgen Ellegaard - *Geometry and Physics*
SciTech - v21 - Mr '97 - p20 [51-250]

Andersen, Martin Edwin - *Dossier Secreto*
JTWS - v13 - Spr '96 - p354+ [501+]

Andersen, Robin - *Consumer Culture and TV Programming*
FQ - v50 - Win '96 - p51+ [501+]

Andersen, Ronald - *Changing the U.S. Health Care System*
BWatch - v18 - Mr '97 - p2 [51-250]
SciTech - v21 - Mr '97 - p45 [51-250]

Andersen, Torben M - *Price Rigidity*
JEL - v34 - D '96 - p1960+ [501+]

Anderson, Alan - *Geology Crafts for Kids*
c HB Guide - v8 - Spr '97 - p113 [51-250]
c SLJ - v43 - F '97 - p108+ [51-250]

Anderson, Alex - *Simply Stars*
BL - v93 - Ja '97 - p805 [51-250]

Anderson, Alison - *Hidden Latitudes*
KR - v64 - My 1 '96 - p616 [251-500]
NYTBR - v101 - Jl 21 '96 - p11 [501+]

Anderson, Andrew D M - *Seeking Common Ground*
r AAPSS-A - v549 - Ja '97 - p185+ [251-500]

Anderson, Bob - *Stretching at Your Computer or Desk*
Kiplinger - v51 - My '97 - p115 [51-250]
PW - v244 - Ja 27 '97 - p100+ [51-250]

Anderson, Brian - *Algarve and Southern Portugal*
r BL - v93 - S 15 '96 - p212 [1-50]
Northern Portugal
r BL - v93 - S 15 '96 - p212 [1-50]

Anderson, Catherine - *Simply Love*
PW - v244 - F 24 '97 - p87 [51-250]

Anderson, Catherine Corley - *Jackie Kennedy Onassis: Woman of Courage*
c HB Guide - v7 - Fall '96 - p370+ [51-250]

Anderson, Charles D - *Bluebloods and Rednecks*
Beav - v77 - F '97 - p47 [1-50]

Anderson, Christopher - *Hollywood TV*
FQ - v49 - Fall '95 - p50+ [501+]

Anderson, Christopher L - *Primitives, Patriarchy, and the Picaresque in Blasco Ibanez's Canas Y Barro*
Hisp - v79 - D '96 - p781 [501+]

Anderson, Claude - *Black Labor White Wealth*
Bl S - v26 - Sum '96 - p63 [1-50]

Anderson, D T - *Atlas of Invertebrate Anatomy*
r SciTech - v20 - D '96 - p32 [1-50]

Anderson, Dave - *The Story of the Olympics*
c Cur R - v35 - S '96 - p12 [51-250]
y HB Guide - v7 - Fall '96 - p359 [51-250]
c KR - v64 - My 1 '96 - p684 [51-250]

Anderson, David G - *The Savannah River Chiefdoms*
Am Ant - v61 - Ap '96 - p437+ [501+]
Site Destruction in Georgia and the Carolinas
Am Ant - v61 - O '96 - p813+ [501+]

Anderson, Deborah Y - *Gender, Identity, and Self-Esteem*
Choice - v34 - My '97 - p1582 [51-250]

Anderson, Dee - *Amazingly Easy Puppet Plays*
BL - v93 - Mr 1 '97 - p1175 [51-250]

Anderson, Digby - *Gentility Recalled*
Nat R - v49 - Mr 10 '97 - p52+ [501+]

Anderson, Doris - *Rebel Daughter*
BIC - v26 - Mr '97 - p21 [501+]
CF - v75 - Mr '97 - p38+ [501+]
Mac - v109 - O 21 '96 - p89 [501+]
Quill & Q - v62 - S '96 - p70 [251-500]

Anderson, Douglas - *The Radical Enlightenments of Benjamin Franklin*
LJ - v122 - Mr 15 '97 - p68 [51-250]

Anderson, E N - *Ecologies of the Heart*
Choice - v34 - O '96 - p300 [51-250]

Anderson, Elizabeth - *Value in Ethics and Economics*
J Con A - v31 - Sum '97 - p165+ [501+]

Anderson, Frank W - *A Dance with Death*
Beav - v76 - D '96 - p47 [51-250]

Anderson, Gerald H - *Mission Legacies*
Bks & Cult - v2 - Ja '96 - p30 [51-250]

Anderson, Graham - *Sage, Saint, and Sophist*
R&R Bk N - v11 - D '96 - p4 [51-250]

Anderson, Greg - *Living Life on Purpose*
PW - v243 - D 30 '96 - p53 [51-250]

Anderson, J - *A Global World?*
GJ - v163 - Mr '97 - p102+ [501+]

Anderson, J L - *Explaining Long-Term Economic Change*
JEL - v34 - D '96 - p2094 [51-250]

Anderson, Jack - *Art without Boundaries*
PW - v244 - My 5 '97 - p186 [51-250]

Anderson, James A - *Communication Theory*
Choice - v34 - Ja '97 - p786 [51-250]
SciTech - v20 - N '96 - p5 [51-250]
An Introduction to Neural Networks
Am Sci - v84 - S '96 - p502+ [501+]

Anderson, Jaynie - *Giorgione*
Apo - v144 - D '96 - p13 [51-250]

Anderson, Jervis - *Bayard Rustin: Troubles I've Seen*
y BL - v93 - F 15 '97 - p977 [51-250]
BW - v27 - F 16 '97 - p3 [501+]
KR - v64 - N 15 '96 - p1642 [251-500]
LJ - v122 - Ja '97 - p108 [51-250]
New R - v216 - Ap 21 '97 - p34+ [501+]
NY - v73 - Mr 24 '97 - p83 [501+]
NYTBR - v102 - Mr 2 '97 - p13+ [501+]
PW - v243 - D 30 '96 - p49 [251-500]
Trib Bks - F 16 '97 - p3+ [501+]
WSJ-Cent - v99 - Ja 30 '97 - pA14 [501+]

Anderson, Joan - *The American Family Farm (Illus. by George Ancona)*
c PW - v244 - Ap 21 '97 - p74 [1-50]
Batboy: An Inside Look at Spring Training (Illus. by Matthew Cavanaugh)
c HB Guide - v7 - Fall '96 - p359 [51-250]
c Trib Bks - Mr 30 '97 - p4+ [51-250]
Cowboys: Roundup on an American Ranch (Illus. by George Ancona)
c BL - v93 - Ja '97 - p765 [1-50]
c HB Guide - v7 - Fall '96 - p352 [51-250]
c SLJ - v42 - D '96 - p27 [1-50]

Anderson, Joan Wester - *Where Angels Walk*
CSM - v89 - Ja 23 '97 - p12 [51-250]
Where Wonders Prevail
LJ - v121 - O 1 '96 - p85 [51-250]

Anderson, John - *The Official Gladiators Training Programme*
Books - v9 - S '95 - p24 [1-50]

Anderson, Jon Lee - *Che Guevara: A Revolutionary Life*
BL - v93 - Mr 15 '97 - p1202 [51-250]
KR - v65 - Mr 1 '97 - p343 [251-500]
LJ - v122 - Ap 15 '97 - p88 [51-250]
PW - v244 - Mr 10 '97 - p54 [51-250]

Anderson, Jon W - *The Culture of Bible Belt Catholics*
CLW - v66 - Je '96 - p29 [51-250]

Anderson, Judith H - *Spenser's Life and the Subject of Biography*
Choice - v34 - My '97 - p1500 [51-250]
Words That Matter
Choice - v34 - My '97 - p1490 [51-250]

Anderson, Karen - *Changing Woman*
AB - v99 - Mr 17 '97 - p868+ [501+]
BWatch - v17 - S '96 - p4 [51-250]
Choice - v34 - D '96 - p674 [51-250]
R&R Bk N - v11 - D '96 - p14 [51-250]

Anderson, Kate - *There's a Pig in the Closet!*
c Ch BWatch - v7 - F '97 - p2 [1-50]

Anderson, Kay J - *Vancouver's Chinatown*
AAAGA - v86 - D '96 - p794+ [501+]

Anderson, Ken - *Hitler and the Occult*
Skeptic - v3 - '95 - p103 [51-250]

Anderson, Kent - *Night Dogs*
PW - v244 - Ja 6 '97 - p65 [251-500]

Anderson, Kevin, 1948- - *Lenin, Hegel, and Western Marxism*
APSR - v91 - Mr '97 - p163+ [501+]
CS - v25 - N '96 - p823+ [501+]
Russ Rev - v56 - Ja '97 - p147+ [501+]

Anderson, Kevin J - *The Darkest Knight*
c Books - v11 - Ap '97 - p24 [51-250]
Darkest Knight
y Kliatt - v30 - N '96 - p11+ [51-250]
Darksaber
y Kliatt - v31 - Ja '97 - p11 [51-250]
Ground Zero (Anderson). Audio Version
y Kliatt - v30 - S '96 - p55 [51-250]
Ignition
y BL - v93 - D 15 '96 - p691 [51-250]
KR - v65 - Ja 15 '97 - p75 [251-500]
LJ - v122 - Ja '97 - p141 [51-250]
PW - v244 - F 10 '97 - p67+ [51-250]
Jedi Under Siege
c Books - v11 - Ap '97 - p24 [51-250]
Lightsaber
c Books - v11 - Ap '97 - p24 [51-250]
Ruins
y VOYA - v19 - O '96 - p214 [251-500]
Shards of Alderaan
y Kliatt - v31 - Mr '97 - p14 [51-250]
Star Wars: Jabba's Palace Pop-Up Book (Illus. by Ralph McQuarrie)
c BL - v93 - D 15 '96 - p732 [1-50]
Tales of the Bounty Hunters
BWatch - v18 - Mr '97 - p9 [1-50]
Virtual Destruction
SF Chr - v18 - O '96 - p78 [51-250]
War of the Worlds
SF Chr - v18 - O '96 - p76 [51-250]
y VOYA - v19 - O '96 - p222 [51-250]

Anderson, Laurie Halse - *Ndito Runs (Illus. by Anita Van Der Merwe)*
c HB Guide - v7 - Fall '96 - p246 [51-250]
Turkey Pox (Illus. by Dorothy Donohue)
c BL - v93 - S 1 '96 - p135 [51-250]
c CCB-B - v50 - N '96 - p89+ [51-250]
c HB Guide - v8 - Spr '97 - p17 [51-250]
c PW - v243 - S 30 '96 - p87 [51-250]
c SLJ - v42 - O '96 - p84 [51-250]

Anderson, Lee - *The Spirit of Voluntarism*
Pub Hist - v18 - Sum '96 - p73+ [501+]

Anderson, Linda - *Women and Autobiography in the Twentieth Century*
Choice - v34 - Ap '97 - p1332 [51-250]

Anderson, Lorin W - *International Encyclopedia of Teaching and Teacher Education. 2nd Ed.*
r ARBA - v28 - '97 - p138 [251-500]
r MLJ - v81 - Spr '97 - p110+ [501+]

Anderson, M C - *Integrated Colposcopy. 2nd Ed.*
SciTech - v20 - D '96 - p51 [51-250]

Anderson, M T - *Thirsty*
y CCB-B - v50 - Ap '97 - p269+ [501+]
y HB - v73 - My '97 - p313 [51-250]
y KR - v65 - Ja 1 '97 - p56 [51-250]
y PW - v244 - Ja 27 '97 - p108 [51-250]
y SLJ - v43 - Mr '97 - p184 [51-250]

Anderson, Malcolm - *Frontiers: Territory and State Formation in the Modern World*
Choice - v34 - S '96 - p205 [51-250]

Anderson, Margaret C - *Forbidden Fires*
LJ - v122 - F 1 '97 - p104 [51-250]

Anderson, Margaret J - *Bizarre Insects*
c HB Guide - v7 - Fall '96 - p340 [51-250]
c SB - v32 - Ag '96 - p180 [51-250]
Children of Summer (Illus. by Marie LeGlatin Keis)
c BL - v93 - Mr 1 '97 - p1160+ [51-250]
c KR - v65 - Mr 1 '97 - p376 [51-250]

Isaac Newton: The Greatest Scientist of All Time
y CLW - v67 - Mr '97 - p58+ [251-500]
c HB Guide - v8 - Spr '97 - p155 [51-250]
c SB - v32 - Ag '96 - p182 [51-250]
c SLJ - v42 - D '96 - p126 [51-250]
y VOYA - v19 - F '97 - p342 [251-500]
Anderson, Martin - *Impostors in the Temple*
C&U - v72 - Fall '96 - p29 [501+]
J Am Cult - v19 - Sum '96 - p154+ [501+]
Anderson, Mary Alice - *Teaching Information Literacy Using Electronic Resources for Grades 6-12*
Emerg Lib - v24 - Mr '97 - p42 [51-250]
SLJ - v43 - F '97 - p43 [51-250]
VOYA - v19 - F '97 - p363+ [251-500]
Anderson, Mary Ann - *The Long-Term Care Nursing Assistant Training Manual. 2nd Ed.*
SciTech - v20 - D '96 - p56 [51-250]
Anderson, Neil T - *Extreme Faith*
y VOYA - v19 - D '96 - p284 [251-500]
Purity under Pressure
y VOYA - v19 - D '96 - p284 [251-500]
Reality Check
y VOYA - v19 - D '96 - p284 [251-500]
Anderson, Norman H - *A Functional Theory of Cognition*
Choice - v34 - Ja '97 - p878 [51-250]
Anderson, Orson L - *Equations of State of Solids for Geophysics and Ceramic Science*
Am Sci - v84 - My '96 - p296+ [501+]
Anderson, Patricia J - *When Passion Reigned*
SFR - v21 - S '96 - p7 [251-500]
Anderson, Patricia June - *All of Us*
y BL - v93 - S 1 '96 - p34 [51-250]
Anderson, Peggy Perry - *To the Tub (Illus. by Peggy Perry Anderson)*
c HB Guide - v8 - Spr '97 - p17 [51-250]
c SLJ - v42 - O '96 - p84 [51-250]
Anderson, Peter - *The Pony Express*
c HB Guide - v8 - Spr '97 - p172 [51-250]
The Transcontinental Railroad
c HB Guide - v7 - Fall '96 - p384 [51-250]
Anderson, Peter J - *The Global Politics of Power, Justice and Death*
Choice - v34 - D '96 - p685 [51-250]
Anderson, Philip J - *Scandinavian Immigrants and Education in North America*
Choice - v34 - S '96 - p198 [51-250]
Anderson, Poul - *All One Universe*
New Sci - v153 - Ja 4 '97 - p40 [51-250]
The Fleet of Stars
y BL - v93 - Mr 1 '97 - p1114 [51-250]
BW - v27 - Ja 26 '97 - p6 [251-500]
KR - v65 - Ja 1 '97 - p26 [51-250]
LJ - v122 - F 15 '97 - p165 [51-250]
PW - v244 - F 24 '97 - p69 [51-250]
Anderson, Rachel - *Black Water*
y Kliatt - v31 - Ja '97 - p5+ [51-250]
The Doll's House
c Magpies - v11 - My '96 - p47 [251-500]
Anderson, Robert - *TVTV: The Debate*
Quill & Q - v62 - D '96 - p30 [501+]
Anderson, Robert Charles - *The Great Migration Begins. Vols. 1-3*
Am Geneal - v71 - O '96 - p252+ [501+]
J Am St - v30 - Ag '96 - p298+ [501+]
NGSQ - v85 - Mr '97 - p72+ [501+]
Anderson, Robert H - *Universal Access to E-mail*
J Gov Info - v23 - S '96 - p738+ [501+]
Anderson, Robert M, Jr. - *Practitioner's Guide to Clinical Neuropsychology*
r AJPsych - v153 - Ag '96 - p1107 [251-500]
Anderson, Robert Mads - *To Everest Via Antarctica*
New Sci - v152 - O 5 '96 - p46 [1-50]
Anderson, Ronald W - *Banking Sector Development in Central and Eastern Europe*
JEL - v34 - D '96 - p2125 [51-250]
Anderson, Sarah - *Anderson's Travel Companion*
r ARBA - v28 - '97 - p176 [51-250]
The Virago Book of Spirituality
TLS - N 22 '96 - p14 [501+]
Anderson, Scott - *Distant Fires*
y Emerg Lib - v23 - My '96 - p57+ [1-50]
Anderson, Scoular - *A Puzzling Day in the Land of the Pharaohs (Illus. by Scoular Anderson)*
c Ch BWatch - v6 - S '96 - p1 [1-50]
c HB Guide - v8 - Spr '97 - p142 [51-250]
c SLJ - v42 - O '96 - p120 [51-250]
Anderson, Sherwood - *Sherwood Anderson's Winesburg, Ohio*
LJ - v122 - Ja '97 - p155 [51-250]
Winesburg, Ohio (Guidall). Audio Version
y Kliatt - v30 - S '96 - p54+ [51-250]

Anderson, Stephanie - *Le Discours Feminin De Marguerite Duras*
FR - v70 - F '97 - p477+ [501+]
MLR - v91 - Jl '96 - p742 [251-500]
Anderson, Terry J - *The Privatization Process*
Choice - v34 - N '96 - p508 [51-250]
JEL - v34 - D '96 - p2082 [51-250]
Anderson, Terry Lee - *Sovereign Nations or Reservations?*
JEL - v34 - D '96 - p2098 [51-250]
Anderson, Victor - *Beyond Ontological Blackness*
TT - v53 - Ja '97 - p527+ [51-250]
Anderson, Walt - *Evolution Isn't What It Used to Be*
Analog - v116 - D '96 - p145+ [251-500]
NYTBR - v101 - O 13 '96 - p28 [501+]
Reason - v28 - N '96 - p71+ [501+]
SF Chr - v18 - O '96 - p82 [1-50]
y VOYA - v19 - O '96 - p224 [251-500]
Anderson, Walter, 1944- - *The Confidence Course*
BL - v93 - D 15 '96 - p690 [51-250]
PW - v244 - Ja 27 '97 - p92 [51-250]
Anderson, Warren H - *Rocks and Minerals of Kentucky*
RocksMiner - v71 - S '96 - p358+ [251-500]
Anderson, Warrigal - *Warrigal's Way*
Aust Bk R - F '97 - p59 [51-250]
Anderson, Wayne - *The Perfect Match*
y Emerg Lib - v24 - S '96 - p26 [1-50]
Wayne Anderson's Horrorble Book
c HB Guide - v8 - Spr '97 - p18 [51-250]
c PW - v243 - S 30 '96 - p86 [51-250]
Anderson, William - *The Face of Glory*
PW - v244 - Ja 13 '97 - p65 [51-250]
Anderson, William, 1805-1866 - *The Scottish Nation. Vols G-S*
r EGH - v50 - N '96 - p158 [51-250]
Anderson, William M - *Multicultural Perspectives in Music Education. 2nd Ed.*
Teach Mus - v3 - Ap '96 - p21 [51-250]
Anderson, William Scovil, 1927- - *Barbarian Play*
CW - v89 - Jl '96 - p495+ [501+]
Anderson, Wolseley - *Caribbean Immigrants*
Quill & Q - v63 - F '97 - p58 [1-50]
Anderson-Dargatz, Gail - *The Cure for Death by Lightning*
BIC - v25 - S '96 - p36+ [501+]
Mac - v109 - D 9 '96 - p64 [1-50]
Obs - Ja 19 '97 - p15* [51-250]
y SLJ - v42 - S '96 - p239 [51-250]
TES - F 14 '97 - p8* [51-250]
TLS - Ja 24 '97 - p22 [501+]
Andersson, Thomas - *Trading with the Environment*
Econ J - v106 - N '96 - p1852 [51-250]
Ando, Tadao - *The Colours of Light (Illus. by Richard Pare)*
NYTBR - v101 - D 8 '96 - p59 [51-250]
WSJ-MW - v78 - D 5 '96 - pA18 [51-250]
Andouze, Jean - *The Cambridge Atlas of Astronomy*
r Am Sci - v84 - My '96 - p293+ [501+]
Andrade, Carlos Drummond De - *Travelling in the Family*
TranslRevS - v2 - D '96 - p30 [51-250]
Andrade, Ernest - *Unconquerable Rebel*
Choice - v34 - N '96 - p523 [51-250]
Andrade, Juan M - *The TUXEDO System*
SciTech - v20 - D '96 - p7 [51-250]
Andrain, Charles F - *Political Protest and Social Change*
APSR - v90 - D '96 - p874+ [501+]
CS - v25 - S '96 - p634+ [501+]
J Pol - v58 - Ag '96 - p863+ [501+]
Andral, Jean-Louis - *Soulages: Noir Lumiere*
BM - v138 - Ag '96 - p563+ [501+]
Andre, Carl - *Carl Andre, Sculptor 1996*
BM - v138 - Jl '96 - p474+ [501+]
Andre, Pierre - *The Gardens of Versailles*
Hort - v74 - O '96 - p74+ [251-500]
Andre, Rae - *Researchers Hooked on Teaching*
R&R Bk N - v12 - F '97 - p67 [51-250]
Andreae, Christine - *A Small Target*
Arm Det - v30 - Win '97 - p94 [251-500]
KR - v64 - S 1 '96 - p1271 [51-250]
Andreae, Christopher - *Lines of Country*
Beav - v76 - O '96 - p46 [51-250]
Mary Newcomb
CSM - v89 - F 19 '97 - p13 [501+]
CSM - v89 - Ap 3 '97 - p14 [501+]
Andreopoulos, George J - *The Aftermath of Defeat*
EHR - v112 - F '97 - p267+ [51-250]
Andreotti, Giulio - *Cosa Loro*
TLS - Jl 19 '96 - p7 [501+]
Andreu, Guillemette - *Egypt in the Age of Pyramids*
y BL - v93 - My 1 '97 - p1475 [251-500]

Andrew, Christopher - *For the President's Eyes Only*
AHR - v101 - D '96 - p1646+ [501+]
J Am St - v30 - Ap '96 - p183+ [501+]
J Mil H - v61 - Ap '97 - p376+ [501+]
Andrew, Douglas - *A Trainer's Companion to Advanced Automotive Emissions Systems*
SciTech - v20 - D '96 - p80 [51-250]
Andrew, Dudley - *Mists of Regret*
AS - v66 - Win '97 - p145+ [501+]
J Pop F&TV - v24 - Win '97 - p188 [501+]
Andrew, Ian - *Pompeii*
y Kliatt - v31 - Mr '97 - p2+ [251-500]
Andrews, Alice - *The Atlas of American Society*
r SSQ - v78 - Mr '97 - p241+ [501+]
Andrews, Cecile - *The Circle of Simplicity*
LJ - v122 - F 15 '97 - p150 [51-250]
PW - v244 - F 17 '97 - p216 [51-250]
Andrews, Claudia Emerson - *Pharaoh, Pharaoh*
PW - v244 - Ap 28 '97 - p71 [51-250]
Andrews, Colman - *Flavors of the Riviera*
BL - v93 - Ja '97 - p758 [1-50]
BL - v93 - S 15 '96 - p196 [51-250]
LJ - v121 - N 15 '96 - p83 [51-250]
PW - v243 - S 2 '96 - p123 [51-250]
Andrews, E M - *The ANZAC Illusion*
EHR - v111 - S '96 - p1018 [251-500]
Andrews, George Reid - *The Afro-Argentines of Buenos Aires 1800-1900*
JPC - v29 - Spr '96 - p227+ [501+]
Blacks and Whites in Sao Paulo, Brazil 1888-1988
J Urban H - v22 - My '96 - p509+ [501+]
Andrews, Gregg - *City of Dust*
Choice - v34 - Mr '97 - p1226 [51-250]
R&R Bk N - v12 - F '97 - p26 [1-50]
Andrews, Jan - *Keri*
y Quill & Q - v62 - My '96 - p33+ [501+]
Andrews, Lew - *Story and Space in Renaissance Art*
Choice - v34 - O '96 - p264 [51-250]
Andrews, Lori - *Black Power, White Blood*
BW - v26 - Ag 25 '96 - p4+ [501+]
KR - v64 - My 1 '96 - p651+ [251-500]
Andrews, Malcolm - *Dickens and the Grown-Up Child*
TLS - Ag 30 '96 - p32 [251-500]
Andrews, Mark - *Learn Visual C++ Now*
CBR - v14 - S '96 - p31+ [1-50]
SciTech - v20 - N '96 - p9 [51-250]
Migrating to Windows 95
CBR - v14 - Jl '96 - p23 [1-50]
Andrews, Nigel - *True Myths*
y BL - v93 - S 15 '96 - p199 [51-250]
Andrews, Pat - *Voices of Diversity*
R&R Bk N - v11 - N '96 - p39 [51-250]
Andrews, Paul M - *We're Poor Little Lambs*
APH - v44 - Spr '97 - p58+ [251-500]
Andrews, Peggy - *Sisters Listening to Sisters*
R&R Bk N - v12 - F '97 - p53 [51-250]
Andrews, Richard - *Interpreting the New National Curriculum*
LAR - v99 - Mr '97 - p164 [51-250]
Andrews, Richard, 1953- - *The Tomb of God*
NS - v125 - D 20 '96 - p120+ [501+]
Andrews, Richard Mowery - *Law, Magistracy, and Crime in Old Regime Paris 1735-1789. Vol. 1*
AHR - v101 - D '96 - p1553+ [501+]
JIH - v27 - Aut '96 - p314+ [251-500]
Andrews, Robert - *Cassell Dictionary of Contemporary Quotations*
r LJ - v122 - Ap 1 '97 - p82 [51-250]
England. 2nd Ed.
r BL - v93 - S 15 '96 - p212 [1-50]
Famous Lines
r BL - v93 - Ap 1 '97 - p1354+ [251-500]
r BWatch - v18 - F '97 - p1 [51-250]
r Choice - v34 - My '97 - p1471 [51-250]
Sicily: The Rough Guide. 3rd Ed.
r BL - v93 - S 15 '96 - p212 [1-50]
Andrews, Sarah - *Mother Nature*
BL - v93 - My 15 '97 - p1565 [51-250]
KR - v65 - My 1 '97 - p679+ [251-500]
PW - v244 - Ap 14 '97 - p59 [51-250]
Andrews, Tim - *Raku: A Review of Contemporary Work*
Am Craft - v56 - O '96 - p51 [51-250]
Andrews, Tom - *The Point Where All Things Meet*
VQR - v72 - Aut '96 - p118* [51-250]
Andrews, V C - *All That Glitters*
Books - v9 - S '95 - p22 [1-50]
Ruby
Books - v9 - S '95 - p27 [1-50]

Andrews, William L - *The Oxford Companion to African American Literature*
  r BL - v93 - F 15 '97 - p1042+ [51-250]
  r LJ - v122 - Ap 15 '97 - p70 [51-250]
  r PW - v244 - Ja 27 '97 - p93 [51-250]
Andrien, Kenneth J - *The Kingdom of Quito 1690-1830*
    Choice - v34 - S '96 - p189 [51-250]
    JEL - v34 - S '96 - p1464 [51-250]
Andries, Lise - *Le Grand Livre Des Secrets*
    FR - v70 - O '96 - p130+ [501+]
Andrieu, Gabriel - *Le Roman De La Rose, ou, De Guillaume De Dole De Jean Renart*
    Specu - v71 - O '96 - p907+ [501+]
Andronico, Michael P - *Men in Groups*
    R&R Bk N - v12 - F '97 - p7 [51-250]
Androunas, Elena - *Soviet Media in Transition*
    JC - v46 - Aut '96 - p171+ [501+]
Andrus, Jeff - *Neighborhood Watch*
    Arm Det - v29 - Sum '96 - p369 [251-500]
    VQR - v72 - Aut '96 - p131* [251-250]
Andrychuk, Kristin - *The Swing Tree*
    BIC - v26 - Mr '97 - p40 [51-250]
Andryczuk, Hartmut - *Visuelle Poesie Aus Den USA*
    Sm Pr R - v28 - D '96 - p10 [251-500]
    Sm Pr R - v29 - F '97 - p14+ [501+]
Andryszewski, Tricia - *Abortion: Rights, Options, and Choices*
  y HB Guide - v7 - Fall '96 - p315+ [51-250]
  y VOYA - v19 - O '96 - p224 [51-250]
The Amazing Life of Moe Berg
  y HB Guide - v7 - Fall '96 - p371 [51-250]
  y VOYA - v19 - O '96 - p224+ [251-500]
The March on Washington 1963
  c BL - v93 - F 15 '97 - p1009 [51-250]
  c HB Guide - v8 - Spr '97 - p92 [51-250]
  c SLJ - v43 - Mr '97 - p195+ [51-250]
The Militia Movement in America
  y BL - v93 - F 15 '97 - p1009 [51-250]
  y KR - v65 - Ja 1 '97 - p56 [51-250]
  y SLJ - v43 - Mr '97 - p196 [51-250]
Aneau, Barthelemy - *Alector Ou Le Coq. Vols. 1-2*
    Ren Q - v50 - Spr '97 - p251+ [501+]
Anema, Durlynn - *Harriet Chalmers Adams: Adventurer and Explorer*
  y BL - v93 - Mr 1 '97 - p1154 [51-250]
  c KR - v65 - Mr 1 '97 - p376 [51-250]
Ang, Isabelle - *Nombres, Astres, Plantes Et Visceres*
    Ch Rev Int - v4 - Spr '97 - p62+ [501+]
Angel, George - *The Fifth Season*
    KR - v64 - My 1 '96 - p640 [51-250]
Angel, Jonathan - *Web Publisher's Construction Kit with Netscape Plug-Ins*
    BYTE - v22 - Mr '97 - p34 [51-250]
    LJ - v122 - Ja '97 - p138 [51-250]
Angel, Marie - *An Animated Alphabet (Illus. by Marie Angel)*
  c AB - v98 - N 18 '96 - p1730 [51-250]
  c BL - v93 - F 1 '97 - p910 [1-50]
Woodland Christmas
  c Bks Keeps - N '96 - p20 [51-250]
Angel, Ralph - *Neither World*
    Ant R - v54 - Sum '96 - p376 [251-500]
Angeles, Peter A - *Critiques of God*
    BL - v93 - Mr 15 '97 - p1207 [51-250]
Angelflesh
  p LMR - v15 - Fall '96 - p39 [51-250]
  p Sm Pr R - v28 - D '96 - p19 [51-250]
Angell, Marcia - *Science on Trial*
    KR - v64 - My 1 '96 - p652 [251-500]
    LATBR - Ag 11 '96 - p11 [251-500]
    Nat R - v48 - N 11 '96 - p56+ [501+]
    Nature - v383 - O 31 '96 - p784+ [501+]
    NYTBR - v101 - D 8 '96 - p92 [1-50]
    TLS - N 8 '96 - p31 [501+]
Angell, Roger - *Nothing but You*
    BL - v93 - Ja '97 - p809 [51-250]
    KR - v64 - D 1 '96 - p1702 [51-250]
    LJ - v122 - F 1 '97 - p109+ [51-250]
    PW - v243 - D 16 '96 - p42 [51-250]
    Trib Bks - F 9 '97 - p6+ [501+]
Angelou, Maya - *And Still I Rise*
    LJ - v121 - O 15 '96 - p94 [1-50]
And Still I Rise (Angelou). Audio Version
    Trib Bks - F 2 '97 - p6 [51-250]
I Know Why the Caged Bird Sings
    LJ - v121 - O 15 '96 - p94 [1-50]
Kofi and His Magic (Illus. by Margaret Courtney-Clarke)
  c BL - v93 - Mr 1 '97 - p1168 [51-250]
  c SLJ - v43 - Mr '97 - p170 [51-250]
  c Trib Bks - Ja 12 '97 - p5 [51-250]

My Painted House, My Friendly Chicken and Me
  c Emerg Lib - v24 - Mr '97 - p47 [51-250]
Angenent, Huub - *Background Factors of Juvenile Delinquency*
    R&R Bk N - v12 - F '97 - p57 [1-50]
Angerhofer, Paul J - *In Aedibus Aldi*
    BC - v45 - Sum '96 - p256 [51-250]
Anghelescu, Hermina G B - *Libraries and Culture: 25 Year Cumulative Index*
  r LQ - v67 - Ja '97 - p87+ [501+]
Angier, Natalie - *The Beauty of the Beastly*
    Books - v9 - S '95 - p24 [1-50]
  y Kliatt - v30 - N '96 - p29 [51-250]
Anglads, Edouard - *Non De Code*
    BL - v93 - F 1 '97 - p930 [1-50]
Anglesey, George Charles Henry Victor Paget, Marquis of - *A History of the British Cavalry 1816-1919. Vol. 8*
    Spec - v278 - F 1 '97 - p34+ [501+]
    TLS - F 7 '97 - p29 [501+]
One Leg
    Spec - v277 - D 14 '96 - p66 [501+]
The Anglo-Saxon Chronicle (Swanton)
    TLS - S 20 '96 - p31 [501+]
Anglund, Joan Walsh - *Little Angels' Alphabet of Love (Illus. by Joan Walsh Anglund)*
  c PW - v243 - D 30 '96 - p68 [1-50]
Poems of Childhood (Illus. by Joan Walsh Anglund)
  c HB Guide - v8 - Spr '97 - p151 [1-50]
  c KR - v64 - S 15 '96 - p1396 [51-250]
Angold, Michael - *Church and Society in Byzantium under the Commeni 1081-1261*
    AHR - v102 - F '97 - p96 [501+]
Angulo, Maria-Elena - *Magic Realism*
    Hisp - v79 - S '96 - p452+ [501+]
Anh, N H - *Analysis and Mechanics of Continuous Media*
    SIAM Rev - v38 - D '96 - p712+ [51-250]
Anholt, Catherine - *Sophie and the New Baby (Illus. by Catherine Anholt)*
  c Bks Keeps - N '96 - p6 [51-250]
Anholt, Laurence - *Billy Beast (Illus. by Arthur Robins)*
  c Books - v10 - Je '96 - p25 [1-50]
Cinderboy (Illus. by Arthur Robins)
  c Bks Keeps - Mr '97 - p22 [51-250]
Daft Jack and the Bean Stack (Illus. by Arthur Robins)
  c Bks Keeps - Mr '97 - p22 [51-250]
Degas and the Little Dancer (Illus. by Laurence Anholt)
  c JB - v60 - Ag '96 - p145 [51-250]
  c NW - v128 - D 2 '96 - p88 [1-50]
  c Sch Lib - v44 - Ag '96 - p98 [51-250]
The Magpie Song (Illus. by Dan Williams)
  c BL - v93 - S 1 '96 - p140 [51-250]
  c CBRS - v25 - S '96 - p6+ [51-250]
  c Ch BWatch - v6 - N '96 - p6 [1-50]
  c HB Guide - v8 - Spr '97 - p18 [51-250]
  c TES - S 6 '96 - p7* [501+]
Rumply Crumply Stinky Pin (Illus. by Arthur Robin)
  c Books - v10 - Je '96 - p25 [1-50]
Animal Families (Snapshot Books)
  c Ch BWatch - v6 - D '96 - p8 [1-50]
  c PW - v243 - N 4 '96 - p78 [51-250]
Animal People
  p Sm Pr R - v28 - D '96 - p16 [51-250]
Anink, David - *Handbook of Sustainable Buildings*
    New Sci - v151 - S 28 '96 - p48 [51-250]
Anjou, Gustave - *Ulster County, New York Probate Records*
  r EGH - v50 - N '96 - p196 [51-250]
Ankersmit, Frank - *A New Philosophy of History*
    HRNB - v25 - Win '97 - p92+ [501+]
    R&R Bk N - v11 - N '96 - p9 [51-250]
Ankrapp, Betty - *Health Care Software Sourcebook*
  r SciTech - v20 - S '96 - p28 [51-250]
Annan, Noel - *Changing Enemies*
    J Mil H - v61 - Ap '97 - p411+ [501+]
    LJ - v121 - D '96 - p114 [51-250]
    NYRB - v44 - Ja 9 '97 - p49+ [501+]
    NYTBR - v102 - F 2 '97 - p30 [501+]
    PW - v243 - S 16 '96 - p62 [51-250]
L'Annee Balzacienne 1994
    MLR - v91 - O '96 - p998+ [251-500]
Anner, John - *Beyond Identity Politics*
    BWatch - v17 - S '96 - p10 [51-250]
    Choice - v34 - Ja '97 - p881 [51-250]
Annerino, John - *Adventuring in Arizona. 2nd Ed.*
  r BL - v93 - S 15 '96 - p212 [1-50]
People of Legend
    LATBR - D 8 '96 - p5 [1-50]
Annesley, George - *The Rise of Modern Egypt*
    EHR - v112 - Ap '97 - p513 [51-250]

Anning, Angela - *A National Curriculum for the Early Years*
    TES - Mr 21 '97 - p7* [501+]
Annino, Antonio - *De Los Imperios A Las Naciones*
    HAHR - v76 - N '96 - p793+ [501+]
Annis, J Lee, Jr. - *Howard Baker: Conciliator in an Age of Crisis*
    AHR - v101 - O '96 - p1313 [501+]
Anno, Mitsumasa - *Anno's Counting House (Illus. by Mitsumasa Anno)*
  c BL - v93 - Ap 1 '97 - p1340 [1-50]
Annotations: A Directory of Periodicals Listed in the Alternative Press Index 1996
  r ARBA - v28 - '97 - p33 [51-250]
  r LJ - v122 - Ja '97 - p158 [51-250]
Annual '96: Fiction
    CCB-B - v50 - S '96 - p40 [51-250]
Annual '96: Non Fiction
    CCB-B - v50 - S '96 - p40 [51-250]
Annual Bulletin of Statistics of World Trade in Steel 1995
  r SciTech - v20 - N '96 - p82 [51-250]
Annual Bulletin of Steel Statistics for Europe. Vol. 21
  r ARBA - v28 - '97 - p596 [51-250]
  r SciTech - v20 - D '96 - p81 [1-50]
Annual Bulletin of Trade in Chemical Products
  r ARBA - v28 - '97 - p629 [51-250]
The Annual Register 1995
  r MEJ - v51 - Win '97 - p149 [51-250]
Annual Review of Astronomy and Astro-Physics. Vol. 34
    S&T - v93 - Mr '97 - p66 [1-50]
Annual Review of Cell and Development Biology. Vol. 12
    SciTech - v21 - Mr '97 - p37 [51-250]
Annual Review of Nursing Research. Vol. 13
    AJN - v96 - N '96 - p16G [51-250]
Annual Review of Psychology. Vol. 47
    Per Psy - v49 - Aut '96 - p773+ [501+]
Annual World Bank Conference on Development Economics 1995
    JEL - v34 - D '96 - p2108 [51-250]
Anonymous - *Primary Colors*
    Am - v175 - D 28 '96 - p26+ [501+]
    CSM - v88 - S 19 '96 - p14 [51-250]
    JPR - v33 - N '96 - p497 [51-250]
    LJ - v121 - O 1 '96 - p46 [51-250]
    NYTBR - v101 - N 3 '96 - p28 [51-250]
    NYTBR - v101 - D 8 '96 - p82 [1-50]
    Obs - D 1 '96 - p16* [51-250]
    Quad - v40 - Je '96 - p85+ [501+]
    TES - D 27 '96 - p16 [51-250]
Primary Colors (James). Audio Version
  y Kliatt - v31 - My '97 - p43 [51-250]
    LJ - v122 - Ap 15 '97 - p138 [51-250]
Anosike, Benji O - *How to Do Your Own Divorce without a Lawyer. Vol. 1*
  r BL - v93 - S 15 '96 - p280+ [251-500]
How to Plan Your Total Estate with a Will and Living Will, without the Lawyer's Fees
    ACI - v7 - Fall '95 - p32 [251-500]
How to Properly Plan Your Total Estate with a Living Trust, without the Lawyer's Fees
    ACI - v7 - Fall '95 - p32 [251-500]
Anquetil, Jacques - *Silk*
    LJ - v121 - O 1 '96 - p72 [51-250]
Ansa, Tina McElroy - *The Hand I Fan With*
    BL - v92 - Ag '96 - p1852+ [251-500]
    Bloom Rev - v17 - Ja '97 - p19 [1-50]
    BW - v26 - D 1 '96 - p7 [501+]
    Ent W - O 25 '96 - p108+ [51-250]
    LATBR - O 27 '96 - p4+ [501+]
    LJ - v121 - N 1 '96 - p82 [1-50]
    NYTBR - v101 - N 24 '96 - p18 [51-250]
The Hand I Fan With (Ralph). Audio Version
  y Kliatt - v31 - My '97 - p40 [51-250]
    LJ - v122 - Ap 1 '97 - p144+ [51-250]
    PW - v244 - Ja 6 '97 - p29 [51-250]
Ansari, Shahid L - *Target Costing*
    Choice - v34 - F '97 - p1009 [51-250]
    R&R Bk N - v12 - F '97 - p38 [51-250]
Ansay, A Manette - *Read This and Tell Me What It Says*
    PS - v70 - Fall '96 - p182+ [501+]
Sister
    KR - v64 - My 1 '96 - p616 [251-500]
    NL - v79 - O 7 '96 - p19+ [501+]
    NYTBR - v101 - S 1 '96 - p9 [501+]
    NYTBR - v101 - D 8 '96 - p82 [1-50]

Anscombe, Roderick - *Shank*
    Arm Det - v30 - Win '97 - p93+ [251-500]
    BL - v93 - S 15 '96 - p180 [51-250]
    Ent W - N 29 '96 - p84 [51-250]
    PW - v243 - S 2 '96 - p109+ [51-250]
    Spec - v278 - Ap 5 '97 - p38 [51-250]
Ansel, Talvikki - *My Shining Archipelago*
    LJ - v122 - My 1 '97 - p107 [51-250]
    PW - v244 - Mr 31 '97 - p71 [51-250]
Ansell, George - *Complications in Diagnostic Imaging and Interventional Radiology. 3rd Ed.*
    SciTech - v21 - Mr '97 - p49 [51-250]
Anselm, Saint, Archbishop of Canterbury - *The Letters of Saint Anselm of Canterbury. Vols. 1-3*
    EHR - v112 - F '97 - p160+ [501+]
Anselment, Raymond A - *The Realms of Apollo*
    Albion - v28 - Fall '96 - p481+ [501+]
    Ren Q - v50 - Spr '97 - p335+ [501+]
Anselmo, Reverge - *The Cadillac of Six-By's*
    KR - v65 - Mr 15 '97 - p396 [251-500]
    PW - v244 - Ap 28 '97 - p48 [51-250]
Anshaw, Carol - *Seven Moves*
    BL - v93 - S 15 '96 - p219 [51-250]
    BW - v26 - N 17 '96 - p6 [251-500]
    LJ - v121 - S 15 '96 - p93 [51-250]
    NYTBR - v101 - N 10 '96 - p55 [501+]
    PW - v243 - S 9 '96 - p64 [51-250]
    Rapport - v19 - 6 '96 - p26 [251-500]
Ansky, S - *The Dybbuk and Other Writings*
    TranslRevS - v1 - My '95 - p34 [51-250]
Ansolabehere, Stephen - *Going Negative*
    Pub Op Q - v60 - Fall '96 - p456+ [501+]
Anson Navarro, Arturo - *Francisco Bayeu*
    BM - v138 - Jl '96 - p479+ [501+]
Anson-Weber, Joan - *Snuffles (Illus. by Judith Russell)*
    c HB Guide - v7 - Fall '96 - p247 [1-50]
Ansorge, Wilehlm - *DNA Sequencing Strategies*
    r SciTech - v21 - Mr '97 - p42 [1-50]
Anstall, Harold B - *Practical Aspects of the Transfusion Service*
    SciTech - v20 - D '96 - p54 [51-250]
Anstee, Margaret Joan - *Orphan of the Cold War*
    For Aff - v76 - My '97 - p148 [51-250]
Anstey, Robert G - *Songs My Neighbours Taught Me*
    Sm Pr R - v28 - S '96 - p9 [51-250]
Antao, Brian - *Modeling and Simulation of Mixed Analog-Digital Systems*
    SciTech - v21 - Mr '97 - p92 [51-250]
Antczak, Frederick J - *Rhetoric and Pluralism*
    QJS - v82 - Ag '96 - p318+ [501+]
Anthes, Richard A - *Meteorology. 7th Ed.*
    SciTech - v20 - D '96 - p27 [51-250]
Anthony, John W - *Mineralogy of Arizona. 3rd Ed.*
    AB - v97 - Je 17 '96 - p2397 [51-250]
Anthony, Martin - *Mathematics for Economics and Finance*
    Choice - v34 - F '97 - p1010 [51-250]
Anthony, Michael - *In the Heat of the Day*
    Bl S - v26 - Fall '96 - p100 [51-250]
    KR - v64 - My 1 '96 - p617 [251-500]
Anthony, Patricia - *Cradle of Splendor*
    Analog - v116 - Jl '96 - p273+ [251-500]
    BWatch - v17 - S '96 - p8 [51-250]
    God's Fires
    KR - v65 - F 15 '97 - p260 [251-500]
    PW - v244 - Mr 24 '97 - p63 [51-250]
Anthony, Piers - *Balook*
    y Kliatt - v31 - My '97 - p10+ [251-250]
    Bearing an Hourglass (Guidall). Audio Version
    y Kliatt - v31 - My '97 - p35 [51-250]
    Hope of Earth
    KR - v65 - Mr 1 '97 - p341 [51-250]
    LJ - v122 - Ap 15 '97 - p123 [51-250]
    PW - v244 - Ap 28 '97 - p54 [51-250]
    On a Pale Horse (Guidall). Audio Version
    y Kliatt - v31 - Mr '97 - p44 [51-250]
    Roc and a Hard Place
    y Kliatt - v31 - Mr '97 - p14+ [51-250]
    The Willing Spirit
    KR - v64 - O 15 '96 - p1500 [51-250]
    LJ - v121 - N 15 '96 - p92 [51-250]
    PW - v243 - N 18 '96 - p67 [51-250]
    With a Tangled Skein (Guidall). Audio Version
    y Kliatt - v31 - My '97 - p35 [51-250]
    Yon Ill Wind
    y BL - v93 - S 15 '96 - p225+ [51-250]
    LJ - v121 - S 15 '96 - p100 [51-250]
    PW - v243 - S 16 '96 - p75 [51-250]
    Rapport - v19 - 6 '96 - p22 [51-250]
Anti-Semitism Worldwide 1995/6
    r MEQ - v3 - D '96 - p83+ [251-500]

Antinori, Aloisio - *Scipione Borghese E L'Architettura*
    BM - v138 - O '96 - p699 [251-500]
The Antioch Review
    p Sm Pr R - v28 - N '96 - p19 [51-250]
Antiviral Chemotherapy 4
    SciTech - v20 - S '96 - p42 [51-250]
Antle, Nancy - *Sam's Wild West Show (Illus. by Simms Taback)*
    c RT - v50 - O '96 - p135 [1-50]
Antler, Joyce - *The Journey Home*
    CHE - v43 - Ap 18 '97 - pA19 [251-250]
    LJ - v122 - Ap 1 '97 - p104 [251-250]
    Ms - v7 - Mr '97 - p83 [1-50]
    NYTBR - v102 - Mr 23 '97 - p19 [51-250]
    PW - v244 - Ja 20 '97 - p386 [51-250]
Antlov, Hans - *Leadership on Java*
    JTWS - v13 - Fall '96 - p233+ [501+]
Antoine, Heloise - *Curious Kids Go to Preschool (Illus. by Ingrid Godon)*
    c HB Guide - v8 - Spr '97 - p10 [51-250]
    c PW - v243 - S 9 '96 - p84 [51-250]
    c SLJ - v42 - N '96 - p76 [51-250]
Antoloni, Bianca Maria - *La Musica A Roma Attraverso Le Fonti D'Archivio*
    Notes - v53 - D '96 - p454+ [501+]
Anton, John P - *The Poetry and Poetics of Constantine P. Cavafy*
    WLT - v70 - Aut '96 - p1003 [51-250]
Anton, Ted - *Eros, Magic, and the Murder of Professor Culianu*
    BW - v26 - O 20 '96 - p4+ [501+]
    KR - v64 - S 15 '96 - p1363+ [251-500]
    LJ - v121 - O 15 '96 - p75 [51-250]
    NYRB - v44 - Ap 10 '97 - p4+ [501+]
    NYTLa - v146 - N 27 '96 - pC21 [501+]
    PW - v243 - S 2 '96 - p103 [51-250]
    Trib Bks - Ja 5 '97 - p4+ [501+]
Antonaccio, Maria - *Iris Murdoch and the Search for Human Goodness*
    Choice - v34 - Ap '97 - p1336+ [51-250]
    LJ - v121 - O 15 '96 - p62+ [51-250]
Antonelli, Cristiano - *The Economics of Localized Technological Change and Industrial Dynamics*
    JEL - v34 - S '96 - p1380+ [501+]
Antoni, Robert - *Blessed Is the Fruit*
    BL - v93 - Mr 15 '97 - p1226 [51-250]
    KR - v65 - F 1 '97 - p154 [251-500]
    PW - v244 - F 10 '97 - p64 [51-250]
Antonioni, Michelangelo - *The Architecture of Vision*
    Choice - v34 - N '96 - p467 [51-250]
    J Film & Vid - v48 - Win '96 - p54+ [501+]
    Utne R - Jl '96 - p109 [51-250]
Antrim, Donald - *The Hundred Brothers*
    BL - v93 - Ja '97 - p815 [51-250]
    Ent W - F 21 '97 - p120 [51-250]
    KR - v64 - D 15 '96 - p1748 [251-500]
    LJ - v122 - Ja '97 - p141 [51-250]
    NW - v129 - F 10 '97 - p66 [51-250]
    NYTBR - v102 - Mr 30 '97 - p10 [501+]
    PW - v244 - Ja 6 '97 - p64 [51-250]
    Time - v149 - Ap 14 '97 - p89+ [501+]
    Trib Bks - F 16 '97 - p6+ [501+]
Anuff, Ed - *Java Sourcebook*
    CBR - v14 - Jl '96 - p22 [1-50]
    Quill & Q - v62 - My '96 - p20+ [501+]
Anuta, Michael J - *Ships of Our Ancestors*
    LJ - v122 - Ap 15 '97 - p125 [1-50]
Anxo, Dominique - *Work Patterns and Capital Utilisation*
    r JEL - v34 - D '96 - p1961+ [501+]
Any, Carol - *Boris Eikhenbaum: Voices of a Russian Formalist*
    Russ Rev - v56 - Ja '97 - p133+ [501+]
    WLT - v71 - Win '97 - p179+ [501+]
Anzaldua, Gloria - *Friends from the Other Side*
    c Learning - v25 - Mr '97 - p54 [1-50]
    Prietita and the Ghost Woman (Illus. by Christina Gonzalez)
    c Ch BWatch - v6 - My '96 - p4 [1-50]
    c HB Guide - v7 - Fall '96 - p326 [51-250]
    c Smith - v27 - N '96 - p169 [1-50]
Aoki, Masahiko - *Corporate Governance in Transitional Economies*
    Econ J - v106 - N '96 - p1851 [251-500]
    The Japanese Main Bank System
    Econ J - v107 - Ja '97 - p235+ [501+]
    JEL - v34 - S '96 - p1363+ [501+]
Aparac-Gazivoda, Tatjana - *Wounded Libraries in Croatia*
    Slav R - v55 - Sum '96 - p462+ [501+]

Apel, Lorelei - *Dealing with Weapons at School and at Home*
    c Ch BWatch - v7 - F '97 - p6 [1-50]
Apfel, Roberta J - *Minefields in Their Hearts*
    Choice - v34 - Ap '97 - p1379 [51-250]
Apgar, Garry - *L'Art Singulier De Jean Huber, Voir Voltaire*
    BM - v138 - S '96 - p608 [501+]
Apollo, 1980- - *Concrete Candy*
    Bl S - v26 - Sum '96 - p63 [1-50]
Apollonius, Rhodius - *Argonautika: The Story of Jason and the Argonauts (Stevenson). Audio Version*
    BL - v93 - Ja '97 - p879 [51-250]
    y Kliatt - v31 - Ja '97 - p37 [51-250]
Apostolos-Cappadona, Diane - *Encyclopedia of Women in Religious Art*
    r ARBA - v28 - '97 - p366 [51-250]
    r LJ - v121 - N 15 '96 - p54 [51-250]
Apostolou, Spyros - *O Anorthoghrafos Epighrafopios*
    WLT - v70 - Sum '96 - p741 [251-500]
    To Imeroloyio Tou Ekmayiou
    WLT - v70 - Sum '96 - p741 [251-500]
Apotheloz, Denis - *Role Et Fonctionnement De L'Anaphore Dans La Dynamique Textuelle*
    FR - v70 - O '96 - p151+ [251-500]
Appel, John Wilton - *Francisco Jose De Caldas: A Scientist at Work in Nueva Granada*
    HAHR - v77 - F '97 - p123 [251-500]
Appel, Marty - *Slide, Kelly, Slide*
    Choice - v34 - N '96 - p498 [51-250]
Appel, Stephen - *Positioning Subjects*
    Choice - v34 - My '97 - p1550 [51-250]
Appelbaum, David - *Disruption*
    R&R Bk N - v12 - F '97 - p2 [51-250]
Appelfeld, Aharon - *Unto the Soul*
    TLS - N 29 '96 - p14 [1-50]
Appelfeld, Aron - *Ad She-Yaaleh Amud Ha-Shahar*
    BL - v93 - Mr 1 '97 - p1115 [1-50]
    WLT - v70 - Aut '96 - p1022 [501+]
Appelt, Kathi - *Bat Jamboree (Illus. by Melissa Sweet)*
    c CBRS - v24 - Ag '96 - p157 [51-250]
    c Ch BWatch - v6 - S '96 - p7+ [1-50]
    c HB Guide - v8 - Spr '97 - p18 [51-250]
    c SLJ - v42 - S '96 - p170 [51-250]
    I See the Moon (Illus. by Debra Reid Jenkins)
    c BL - v93 - Mr 15 '97 - p1244 [51-250]
    c CCB-B - v50 - My '97 - p311+ [51-250]
    c PW - v244 - Ja 27 '97 - p97 [51-250]
    A Red Wagon Year (Illus. by Laura McGee Kvasnosky)
    c BL - v93 - O 1 '96 - p356+ [51-250]
    c HB Guide - v8 - Spr '97 - p10 [51-250]
    c SLJ - v42 - D '96 - p84 [51-250]
    The Thunderherd (Illus. by Elizabeth Sayles)
    c HB Guide - v7 - Fall '96 - p247 [1-50]
    c SLJ - v42 - Ag '96 - p115 [51-250]
    Watermelon Day (Illus. by Dale Gottlieb)
    c HB Guide - v7 - Fall '96 - p247 [51-250]
Appiah, Anthony - *Color Conscious*
    y BL - v93 - N 1 '96 - p463 [251-500]
    BW - v26 - N 10 '96 - p13 [51-250]
    Choice - v34 - Ap '97 - p1422 [51-250]
    NS - v125 - D 13 '96 - p45+ [501+]
    Obs - Ja 5 '97 - p16* [501+]
    PW - v243 - S 16 '96 - p58 [51-250]
    The Dictionary of Global Culture
    r BL - v93 - My 1 '97 - p1520+ [251-500]
    r Econ - v342 - Mr 15 '97 - p5* [501+]
    r For Aff - v76 - My '97 - p122 [51-250]
    r NYRB - v44 - F 6 '97 - p30+ [501+]
    r NYTBR - v102 - F 2 '97 - p7 [501+]
    r PW - v243 - D 2 '96 - p50+ [51-250]
    Identities
    Bl S - v26 - Fall '96 - p103 [1-50]
    Bl S - v26 - Sum '96 - p63 [1-50]
Appignanesi, Richard - *Post-Modernism for Beginners (Appignanesi). Audio Version*
    Obs - Ap 13 '97 - p18* [51-250]
Apple, Michael - *Symptoms and Early Warning Signs*
    r BL - v93 - F 1 '97 - p958 [1-50]
Apple, Michael W - *Cultural Politics and Education*
    Choice - v34 - N '96 - p510 [51-250]
Apple, Rima D - *Vitamania: Vitamins in American Culture*
    Choice - v34 - D '96 - p643 [51-250]
    Nature - v383 - O 17 '96 - p589+ [501+]
    New Sci - v152 - O 5 '96 - p46 [1-50]
Applebee, Arthur N - *Curriculum as Conversation*
    AJE - v105 - My '97 - p108+ [501+]
    Choice - v34 - N '96 - p510 [51-250]
    R&R Bk N - v11 - N '96 - p54 [51-250]

Applebome, Peter - *Dixie Rising*
   Barron's - v76 - D 23 '96 - p51 [501+]
   Bus W - D 2 '96 - p22 [501+]
   BW - v27 - Ja 26 '97 - p11 [501+]
   Econ - v342 - F 15 '97 - p11*+ [501+]
   KR - v64 - S 1 '96 - p1284 [251-500]
   LJ - v121 - S 15 '96 - p82 [51-250]
   NYTBR - v101 - D 1 '96 - p26 [501+]
   NYTLa - v146 - D 20 '96 - pC37 [501+]
   PW - v243 - S 23 '96 - p62 [51-250]
   VV - v41 - D 17 '96 - p51+ [501+]
Appleby, A - *Saskatchewan's Protected Areas*
   J Gov Info - v23 - S '96 - p640+ [51-250]
Appleby, Joyce - *Knowledge and Postmodernism in
Historical Perspective*
   CPR - v16 - D '96 - p387+ [501+]
Appleby, R Scott - *Church and Age Unite!*
   CH - v65 - S '96 - p531+ [501+]
   Spokesmen for the Despised
   BL - v93 - D 1 '96 - p623 [51-250]
   Econ - v341 - N 16 '96 - p8* [51-250]
   Econ - v342 - Mr 15 '97 - p6*+ [501+]
   For Aff - v76 - My '97 - p141 [51-250]
   LJ - v121 - D '96 - p119 [51-250]
   PW - v244 - Ja 13 '97 - p69 [51-250]
Appleby, Stephen - *A Box of Secret Thoughts*
   Spec - v277 - D 7 '96 - p55 [51-250]
Applefield, David - *Once Removed*
   LJ - v121 - D '96 - p141 [51-250]
Applegate, Edd - *Literary Journalism*
   r BL - v93 - Ja '97 - p898 [51-250]
   r Choice - v34 - Ap '97 - p1305 [51-250]
   r R&R Bk N - v12 - F '97 - p82 [51-250]
   Print and Broadcast Journalism
   Choice - v34 - F '97 - p959 [51-250]
   R&R Bk N - v11 - D '96 - p62 [51-250]
Applegate, Katherine - *The Invasion*
   y VOYA - v19 - D '96 - p275+ [251-500]
   Listen to My Heart
   y VOYA - v19 - D '96 - p261 [51-250]
   Sharing Sam
   y Emerg Lib - v24 - S '96 - p26 [1-50]
   Tales from Agrabah (Illus. by Fred Marvin)
   c RT - v50 - O '96 - p138 [1-50]
Appleman, Daniel - *PC Magazine Visual Basic
Programmer's Guide to the Win32 API*
   SciTech - v21 - Mr '97 - p9 [51-250]
Appleman, Philip - *New and Selected Poems 1956-1996*
   Nat - v263 - D 23 '96 - p29+ [251-500]
   PW - v243 - Jl 22 '96 - p237+ [51-250]
Appleton, Andrew M - *State Party Profiles*
   r Choice - v34 - My '97 - p1578 [51-250]
Applewhite, Ashton - *Cutting Loose*
   KR - v65 - Ap 1 '97 - p511 [251-500]
   LJ - v122 - My 1 '97 - p126 [51-250]
   PW - v244 - Mr 24 '97 - p66+ [251-500]
Applewhite, Harriet B - *Political Alignment in the French
National Assembly 1789-1791*
   EHR - v111 - S '96 - p999+ [251-500]
**Application-Specific Systems, Architectures and
Processors 1996**
   SciTech - v20 - D '96 - p6 [51-250]
**Applications and Developments in New Engine Design
and Components**
   SciTech - v20 - D '96 - p73 [51-250]
Applications of Artificial Intelligence in Engineering XI
   SciTech - v21 - Mr '97 - p3 [51-250]
**Applications of Synchrotron Radiation Techniques to
Materials Science III**
   SciTech - v21 - Mr '97 - p76 [51-250]
Applied Geography and Development
   p JEL - v34 - D '96 - p2143 [51-250]
Appraisal Institute (U.S.) - *Directory of Designated
Members 1996*
   r ARBA - v28 - '97 - p129 [251-500]
Apps, Peter - *Smithers' Mammals of Southern Africa*
   r New Sci - v153 - Mr 8 '97 - p45 [1-50]
Apps, Roy - *Elizabeth Fry and the Forger's Daughter
(Illus. by Amy Burch)*
   c Bks Keeps - N '96 - p9+ [51-250]
   c Sch Lib - v44 - N '96 - p148 [51-250]
   The Haunting
   c Sch Lib - v44 - N '96 - p148 [51-250]
   Melvin and the Deadheads
   c JB - v60 - D '96 - p245 [251-500]
   *My Barmy Aunt Boomerang, the Coolest Act in School
(Illus. by Jamie Smith)*
   c Bks Keeps - Jl '96 - p11 [51-250]
Apraku, Kofi K - *Outside Looking In*
   Bl S - v26 - Sum '96 - p63 [1-50]
   Choice - v34 - S '96 - p217 [51-250]

Apt, Jay - *Orbit: NASA Astronauts Photograph the Earth*
   Astron - v25 - Mr '97 - p102+ [51-250]
   BL - v93 - Ja '97 - p810 [51-250]
   Choice - v34 - My '97 - p1520+ [51-250]
   LJ - v122 - F 1 '97 - p100 [51-250]
   SciTech - v21 - Mr '97 - p97 [51-250]
   WSJ-MW - v78 - D 5 '96 - pA18 [51-250]
Apt, Krzysztof R - *From Logic Programming to Prolog*
   SciTech - v21 - Mr '97 - p6 [51-250]
Apte, Vasudco Govind - *Hippocrene Concise Sanskrit-
English Dictionary*
   r ARBA - v28 - '97 - p399 [51-250]
Apter, Terri - *The Confident Child*
   PW - v244 - Mr 24 '97 - p78 [51-250]
   Secret Paths
   NYTBR - v102 - Mr 30 '97 - p24 [1-50]
   PW - v243 - D 30 '96 - p64 [1-50]
   Trib Bks - Mr 9 '97 - p8 [1-50]
Aquatic Geochemistry
   p Nature - v383 - S 5 '96 - p42 [251-500]
Aquila, Richard - *Wanted Dead or Alive*
   Nine-C Lit - v51 - Mr '97 - p554 [51-250]
   SFR - v21 - N '96 - p28+ [51-250]
   VQR - v73 - Win '97 - p25* [51-250]
Aquino, Maria Pilar - *Our Cry for Life*
   JAAR - v64 - Win '96 - p895+ [501+]
Arabic Short Stories
   TranslRevS - v1 - My '95 - p1 [51-250]
Arafat, K W - *Pausanias' Greece*
   Choice - v34 - N '96 - p523+ [51-250]
   TLS - N 1 '96 - p30 [501+]
Arakin, Vladimir Dmitrievich - *NTC's New College
Russian and English Dictionary*
   r Choice - v34 - Ja '97 - p772 [51-250]
Aral, M M - *Advances in Groundwater Pollution Control
and Remediation*
   SciTech - v20 - D '96 - p69 [51-250]
Arancibia, Juana Alcira - *La Nueva Mujer En La
Escritura De Autoras Hispanicas*
   Hisp - v79 - S '96 - p451+ [501+]
Arango, Gloria Mercedes - *La Mentalidad Religiosa En
Antioquia*
   HAHR - v76 - Ag '96 - p589+ [501+]
Arango Durling, Virginia - *Derechos Humanos De La
Mujer*
   BL - v93 - S 15 '96 - p227 [1-50]
Aranson, S Kh. - *Introduction to the Qualitative Theory of
Dynamical Systems on Surfaces*
   SciTech - v20 - N '96 - p15 [51-250]
Arasaratnam, Sinnappah - *Ceylon and the Dutch
1600-1800*
   R&R Bk N - v11 - N '96 - p15 [51-250]
   Maritime India in the Seventeenth Century
   Historian - v59 - Fall '96 - p167+ [251-500]
Arase, David - *Buying Power*
   J Pol - v59 - F '97 - p314+ [501+]
Arasse, Daniel - *Vermeer: Faith in Painting*
   Obs - D 29 '96 - p28 [51-250]
Arata, Stephen - *Fictions of Loss in the Victorian Fin De
Siecle*
   VQR - v73 - Win '97 - p10* [51-250]
Araujo, Carlos - *O Aldrabista*
   WLT - v71 - Win '97 - p131 [501+]
Araya Monge, Rolando - *Promesas De La Nueva Historia*
   BL - v93 - S 15 '96 - p227 [51-250]
Arbel, Benjamin - *Intercultural Contacts in the Medieval
Mediterranean*
   R&R Bk N - v11 - D '96 - p9 [51-250]
Arbuckle, Scott - *Zeb, the Cow's on the Roof Again! and
Other Tales of Early Texas Dwellings (Illus. by Scott
Arbuckle)*
   c HB Guide - v8 - Spr '97 - p61 [51-250]
   c KR - v64 - N 1 '96 - p1598 [51-250]
Arcand, Bernard - *The Jaguar and the Anteater*
   TranslRevS - v1 - My '95 - p7 [51-250]
Arceneaux, Jean - *Je Suis Cadien*
   TranslRevS - v2 - D '96 - p19 [51-250]
Archambault, John - *The Birth of a Whale (Illus. by Janet
Skiles)*
   c HB Guide - v7 - Fall '96 - p247 [51-250]
   Grandmother's Garden (Illus. by Raul Colon)
   c CCB-B - v50 - O '96 - p47 [51-250]
   c HB Guide - v8 - Spr '97 - p18 [51-250]
   c SLJ - v42 - N '96 - p76 [51-250]
Archbold, Lawrence - *French Organ Music*
   Notes - v53 - D '96 - p470+ [501+]
   TLS - O 4 '96 - p24 [501+]
Archbold, Rick - *Last Dinner on the Titanic*
   LJ - v122 - Ap 1 '97 - p104+ [51-250]

   Robert Bateman: Natural Worlds
   Aud - v98 - N '96 - p137 [1-50]
   y BL - v93 - D 1 '96 - p636 [51-250]
   PW - v243 - S 16 '96 - p64 [51-250]
L'Arche Daybreak Community - *Living the Beatitudes*
   RR - v56 - Ja '97 - p105 [1-50]
Archer, Clive - *The European Union. 2nd Ed.*
   JEL - v34 - S '96 - p1423 [51-250]
Archer, Ellen - *Under His Spell*
   SF Chr - v18 - O '96 - p80 [1-50]
Archer, Isaac - *Two East Anglian Diaries 1641-1729*
   CH - v65 - S '96 - p505+ [501+]
Archer, Jeffrey - *The Fourth Estate*
   Lon R Bks - v18 - Jl 18 '96 - p13+ [501+]
   Rapport - v19 - 6 '96 - p19 [251-500]
   TLS - Jl 7 '96 - p25 [251-500]
   The Fourth Estate (Jarvis). Audio Version
   BWatch - v17 - D '96 - p10 [1-50]
   y Kliatt - v31 - Ja '97 - p40 [51-250]
   The Fourth Estate (Prebble). Audio Version
   y Kliatt - v31 - Ja '97 - p40 [51-250]
Archer, John Michael - *Sovereignty and Intelligence*
   Ren Q - v49 - Win '96 - p865+ [501+]
Archer, Jules - *Breaking Barriers*
   y Kliatt - v30 - S '96 - p25 [51-250]
   A House Divided
   y CLW - v66 - Je '96 - p54 [51-250]
   They Had a Dream
   y Kliatt - v30 - S '96 - p25 [51-250]
Archer, Margaret S - *Realist Social Theory*
   Choice - v34 - S '96 - p217 [51-250]
Archer, Nathan - *Martian Deathtrap*
   SF Chr - v18 - O '96 - p79 [51-250]
Archer, R Douglas - *An Introduction to Aerospace
Propulsion*
   SciTech - v20 - N '96 - p77 [51-250]
Archer, Simon - *Gerry Anderson: The Authorised
Biography*
   New Sci - v152 - D 7 '96 - p46 [1-50]
Archer, Wesley L - *Industrial Solvents Handbook*
   r SciTech - v20 - S '96 - p59 [51-250]
Archibald, Elizabeth - *A Companion to Malory*
   Choice - v34 - My '97 - p1494 [51-250]
Archibald, J David - *Dinosaur Extinction and the End of
an Era*
   Choice - v34 - S '96 - p158 [51-250]
   Nature - v385 - Ja 2 '97 - p36 [501+]
   Sci - v273 - S 27 '96 - p1807+ [501+]
Archibold, O W - *Ecology of World Vegetation*
   GJ - v162 - Jl '96 - p237 [51-250]
**Archivists of the Ecclesiastical Province of British
Columbia and Yukon** - *A Guide to the Archives of the
Ecclesiastical Province of British Columbia and Yukon*
   Archiv - Fall '94 - p183+ [501+]
Arcilla, Rene Vincente - *For the Love of Perfection*
   TCR - v98 - Win '96 - p354+ [501+]
Arcudi, John - *Predator: Big Game*
   p Quill & Q - v62 - Ag '96 - p26 [51-250]
Ardagh, John - *Ireland and the Irish*
   NYTBR - v102 - Mr 16 '97 - p32 [1-50]
   PW - v244 - F 24 '97 - p88 [1-50]
Ardagh, Philip - *History's Travellers and Explorers (Illus.
by Chris Mould)*
   c JB - v60 - Ag '96 - p145 [51-250]
   c Sch Lib - v44 - Ag '96 - p110 [51-250]
   Why Do Humans Have Two Legs?
   c JB - v60 - D '96 - p245+ [51-250]
   Why Don't Fish Have Fingers?
   c Sch Lib - v45 - F '97 - p36 [51-250]
Ardelius, Lars - *Resandes Ensak*
   WLT - v70 - Sum '96 - p716 [251-500]
Arden, John - *Jack Juggler and the Emperor's Whore*
   Obs - O 27 '96 - p18* [51-250]
   Obs - D 15 '96 - p18* [51-250]
Arden, John Boghosian - *Consciousness, Dreams, and
Self*
   Choice - v34 - Ja '97 - p878 [51-250]
Arden, Lynie - *Work-at-Home Sourcebook. 6th Ed.*
   r LJ - v122 - My 1 '97 - p53 [1-50]
Ardener, Edwin - *Kingdom on Mount Cameroon*
   Choice - v34 - Ja '97 - p838 [51-250]
Ardito, Stefano - *Trekking in Africa*
   r New Sci - v153 - Mr 22 '97 - p47 [1-50]
Arditti, Fred D - *Derivatives: A Comprehensive Resource
for Options, Futures, Interest Rate Swaps, and Mortgage
Securities*
   Choice - v34 - S '96 - p174 [51-250]
   JEL - v34 - S '96 - p1434 [51-250]
   R&R Bk N - v12 - F '97 - p50 [51-250]
Arditti, Michael - *The Celibate*
   PW - v244 - My 5 '97 - p200 [51-250]

Pagan's Father
  BL - v93 - S 15 '96 - p218 [51-250]
  Ent W - S 13 '96 - p126 [51-250]
  NY - v72 - S 23 '96 - p95 [51-250]
  NYTBR - v101 - O 20 '96 - p22 [51-250]
Ardley, Bridget - *The Human Body*
  cr Sch Lib - v44 - Ag '96 - p110 [51-250]
Ardley, Neil - *How Things Work*
  c HB Guide - v7 - Fall '96 - p328 [51-250]
  The Science Book of Color
  c Inst - v106 - Ja '97 - p4* [1-50]
  The Science Book of the Senses
  c Inst - v106 - S '96 - p92 [1-50]
  A Young Person's Guide to Music
  c Am MT - v46 - D '96 - p54+ [501+]
  yr RQ - v35 - Sum '96 - p567 [251-500]
  cr Sch Lib - v44 - Ag '96 - p110 [51-250]
Ardolino, Frank - *Apocalypse and Armada in Kyd's Spanish Tragedy*
  CH - v65 - D '96 - p708+ [501+]
Ardonne, Marcus - *Arena of Lust*
  Quill & Q - v62 - Jl '96 - p42 [501+]
Arebi, Saddeka - *Women and Words in Saudi Arabia*
  MEJ - v51 - Spr '97 - p292+ [501+]
Arena, Felice - *Dolphin Boy Blue*
  y Sch Lib - v44 - Ag '96 - p117 [51-250]
Arenas, Reinaldo - *Adios A Mama*
  BL - v93 - Ap 1 '97 - p1284 [1-50]
  WLT - v70 - Aut '96 - p920 [501+]
  Before Night Falls
  TranslRevS - v1 - My '95 - p28 [251-250]
  La Loma Del Angel
  WLT - v70 - Sum '96 - p664 [501+]
  El Mundo Alucinante
  Hisp - v79 - D '96 - p762+ [501+]
Arendell, Terry - *Fathers and Divorce*
  SSQ - v78 - Mr '97 - p246 [251-500]
Arendt, Hannah - *Between Friends*
  VV - v42 - Ja 7 '97 - p44 [51-250]
  Love and Saint Augustine
  RP - v59 - Spr '97 - p368+ [501+]
Arens, Edmund - *Christopraxis: A Theology of Action*
  JR - v77 - Ja '97 - p160+ [501+]
  Theol St - v57 - Je '96 - p369+ [501+]
  TT - v53 - Ja '97 - p566 [51-250]
Arens, Katherine - *Austria and Other Margins*
  Choice - v34 - My '97 - p1502 [51-250]
Arens, Moshe - *Broken Covenant*
  Pres SQ - v26 - Fall '96 - p1186 [251-500]
Aretz, Jurgen - *Zeitgeschichte In Lebensbildern. Vol. 7*
  CHR - v82 - O '96 - p733+ [501+]
Arevalo, Teresa - *Rafael Arevalo Martinez: Biografia De 1926 Hasta Su Muerte En 1975*
  Hisp - v79 - S '96 - p453+ [501+]
  WLT - v70 - Sum '96 - p669+ [251-500]
Argall, Randal A - *1 Enoch and Sirach*
  Rel St Rev - v23 - Ja '97 - p86+ [51-250]
Argandona, Antonio - *The Ethical Dimensions of Financial Institutions and Markets*
  JEL - v34 - D '96 - p2054 [51-250]
Argentina Company Handbook. 1995/96 Ed.
  r ARBA - v28 - '97 - p116 [251-500]
Argersinger, Peter H - *The Limits of Agrarian Radicalism*
  PHR - v65 - Ag '96 - p491+ [251-500]
Argueta, Manlio - *Magic Dogs of the Volcanoes (Illus. by E Simmons)*
  c SS - v88 - Ja '97 - p29+ [501+]
  Milagro De La Paz
  BL - v93 - S 15 '96 - p227 [1-50]
Argyle, Charlotte - *Countdown to Christmas*
  c PW - v243 - S 30 '96 - p93 [1-50]
Argyridou-Peonidou, Elli - *Heures*
  WLT - v70 - Aut '96 - p1002+ [51-250]
Ariail, Dan - *The Carpenter's Apprentice*
  Bks & Cult - v3 - Mr '97 - p16+ [501+]
Arian, Asher - *Security Threatened*
  MEJ - v50 - Aut '96 - p598+ [501+]
  Pub Op Q - v60 - Fall '96 - p464+ [501+]
Arias Sanchez, Oscar - *Los Desaffos Del Siglo XXI Desde America Latina*
  BL - v93 - S 15 '96 - p227 [1-50]
Aridjis, Homero - *En Quien Piensas Cuando Haces El Amor?*
  LJ - v122 - Ja '97 - p78 [51-250]
Arieff, Allen I - *Fluid, Electrolyte, and Acid-Base Disorders. 2nd Ed.*
  SciTech - v20 - S '96 - p35 [51-250]
Aries, Elizabeth - *Men and Women in Interaction*
  Readings - v11 - S '96 - p25 [51-250]
Ariew, Robert - *Par Ici*
  FR - v70 - F '97 - p487+ [501+]

Ariew, Roger - *Descartes and His Contemporaries*
  RM - v50 - D '96 - p386+ [501+]
Arikha, Avigdor - *On Depiction. Rev. Ed.*
  TLS - N 8 '96 - p33 [251-500]
Arino, Ovide - *Mathematical Population Dynamics*
  SIAM Rev - v39 - Mr '97 - p175 [51-250]
Arion, Frank Martinus - *De Laatste Vrijheid*
  WLT - v70 - Aut '96 - p1012+ [501+]
Ariosto, Lodovico - *Five Cantos*
  Choice - v34 - O '96 - p284 [51-250]
Aristide, Jean-Bertrand - *Dignity*
  Choice - v34 - N '96 - p522 [51-250]
  TranslRevS - v2 - D '96 - p7 [51-250]
  WorldV - v12 - O '96 - p5 [51-250]
Aristophanes - *Clouds*
  SAQ - v95 - Fall '96 - p881+ [501+]
Aristotle - *Nicomachean Ethics*
  JHI - v58 - Ap '97 - p331+ [501+]
Arizona Charter Schools Handbook
  J Gov Info - v23 - S '96 - p578 [51-250]
Arizona Traveler's Handbook. 6th Ed.
  r BL - v93 - S 15 '96 - p212 [1-50]
  r BWatch - v17 - N '96 - p12 [51-250]
Arizpe, Lourdes - *Culture and Global Change*
  Env - v39 - Ja '97 - p25 [51-250]
Arjouni, Jakob - *One Death to Die*
  BL - v93 - Mr 15 '97 - p1228 [51-250]
  KR - v65 - F 1 '97 - p176 [51-250]
  NYTBR - v102 - Mr 30 '97 - p23 [51 250]
  PW - v244 - F 10 '97 - p71 [51-250]
  Trib Bks - Mr 2 '97 - p5 [51-250]
Arkeologjia: Materiale, Studime Dhe Informacione Arkeologjike
  p AJA - v101 - Ja '97 - p191 [251-500]
Arkin, Alan - *Some Fine Grandpa! (Illus. by Dirk Zimmer)*
  c LA - v73 - S '96 - p354+ [51-250]
Arkush, Brooke S - *The Archaeology of CA-MNO-2122*
  Am Ant - v61 - Jl '96 - p629+ [251-500]
ARL Statistics 1994-95
  r ARBA - v28 - '97 - p238 [51-250]
Arlacchi, Pino - *Il Processo*
  Choice - v34 - D '96 - p568 [1-50]
  TLS - Jl 19 '96 - p7 [51-250]
Arlen, Michael J - *Passage to Ararat*
  LATBR - My 26 '96 - p11 [51-250]
Arlinghaus, Sandra Lach - *Practical Handbook of Spatial Statistics*
  Choice - v34 - O '96 - p316 [51-250]
Arluke, Arnold - *Regarding Animals*
  Choice - v34 - F '97 - p954 [51-250]
Arma, Tom - *Baby Bugs (Illus. by Tom Arma)*
  c SLJ - v43 - Ja '97 - p75 [51-250]
  Funny Farm (Illus. by Tom Arma)
  c SLJ - v43 - Ja '97 - p75 [51-250]
  Jingle Babies (Illus. by Tom Arma)
  c KR - v64 - S 1 '96 - p1330 [51-250]
  c PW - v243 - S 30 '96 - p93 [51-250]
  c SLJ - v42 - O '96 - p33 [51-250]
Armacost, Michael H - *Friends or Rivals?*
  Choice - v34 - S '96 - p205 [51-250]
  FEER - v159 - S 19 '96 - p53 [501+]
  JEL - v34 - D '96 - p2040 [51-250]
Armanno, Venero - *Strange Rain*
  Aust Bk R - S '96 - p30+ [501+]
Armarego, W L F - *Purification of Laboratory Chemicals. 4th Ed.*
  SciTech - v21 - Mr '97 - p83 [51-250]
Armbrust, Walter - *Mass Culture and Modernism in Egypt*
  Choice - v34 - F '97 - p1004+ [51-250]
Armbruster, Ann - *Floods*
  c BL - v93 - Ja '97 - p848 [251-500]
  c HB Guide - v8 - Spr '97 - p113 [51-250]
  Lake Huron
  c SLJ - v43 - Mr '97 - p170 [51-250]
  Lake Michigan
  c SLJ - v43 - Mr '97 - p170 [51-250]
  Lake Superior
  c SLJ - v43 - Mr '97 - p170 [51-250]
  Wildfires
  c BL - v93 - Ja '97 - p848 [251-500]
  c HB Guide - v8 - Spr '97 - p116 [51-250]
The Armchair Detective
  p RQ - v36 - Win '96 - p226+ [51-250]
Arming Our Allies
  RSR - v24 - 3 '96 - p40 [51-250]
Armistead, John - *Cruel as the Grave*
  BL - v92 - Ag '96 - p1884 [51-250]
Armitage, Peter - *Advances in Biometry*
  SciTech - v20 - N '96 - p26 [51-250]

Armitage, Shelley - *Kewpies and Beyond*
  Humor - v9 - 3 '96 - p410+ [501+]
Armitage, Simon - *The Dead Sea Poems*
  Ant R - v54 - Sum '96 - p378 [251-500]
  Moon Country
  NS - v125 - N 15 '96 - p45 [501+]
Armony, Ariel C - *Argentina, the United States and the Anti-Communist Crusade in Central America 1977-1984*
  LJ - v122 - My 1 '97 - p124 [51-250]
Armor, David J - *Forced Justice*
  JSH - v62 - N '96 - p842+ [501+]
Armour, David A - *100 Years at Mackinac*
  Pub Hist - v19 - Win '97 - p86+ [501+]
Armour, Leslie - *Being and Idea*
  Dialogue - v35 - Fall '96 - p805+ [501+]
Armour, Margaret-Ann - *Hazardous Laboratory Chemicals Disposal Guide. 2nd Ed.*
  Choice - v34 - F '97 - p991 [51-250]
  SciTech - v21 - Mr '97 - p28 [51-250]
Armour, Tommy - *How to Play Your Best Golf All the Time*
  LJ - v121 - O 1 '96 - p52 [1-50]
Armpriester, K E - *Do Your Own Wiring*
  LJ - v122 - F 1 '97 - p53 [1-50]
Armstrong, C J - *World Databases in Agriculture*
  r ARBA - v28 - '97 - p568 [251-500]
  World Databases in Biosciences and Pharmacology
  r ARBA - v28 - '97 - p565 [51-250]
  r Choice - v34 - F '97 - p951 [51-250]
  r SciTech - v20 - N '96 - p25 [51-250]
  World Databases in Chemistry
  r ARBA - v28 - '97 - p629 [51-250]
  World Databases in Company Information
  r ARBA - v28 - '97 - p86 [251-500]
  r Choice - v34 - Ja '97 - p777 [51-250]
  r R&R Bk N - v11 - D '96 - p28 [51-250]
  World Databases in Humanities
  r Choice - v34 - D '96 - p597 [51-250]
  World Databases in Social Sciences
  r ARBA - v28 - '97 - p431 [51 250]
  r Choice - v34 - N '96 - p440 [51-250]
Armstrong, Campbell - *Silencer*
  Books - v11 - Ap '97 - p22 [51-250]
Armstrong, Carole - *Lives and Legends of the Saints*
  c BL - v93 - O 1 '96 - p338 [1-50]
  c LATBR - Mr 17 '96 - p11 [1-50]
Armstrong, D M - *Dispositions: A Debate*
  R&R Bk N - v12 - F '97 - p4 [51-250]
  TLS - D 27 '96 - p26 [501+]
Armstrong, David - *The Silver Cord*
  PW - v244 - Mr 24 '97 - p73 [1-50]
Armstrong, Isobel - *Nineteenth-Century Women Poets*
  NS - v125 - D 6 '96 - p53+ [501+]
  TLS - Mr 21 '97 - p5+ [501+]
  Victorian Poetry
  CR - v269 - S '96 - p167+ [51-250]
  Nine-C Lit - v51 - S '96 - p247+ [501+]
Armstrong, J A - *Forest Insect Pests in Canada*
  J Gov Info - v23 - S '96 - p613 [51-250]
Armstrong, J D, 1945- - *From Versailles to Maastricht*
  Choice - v34 - Ja '97 - p870 [51-250]
Armstrong, Jennifer - *Black-Eyed Susan (Illus. by Emily Martindale)*
  c LA - v73 - O '96 - p429 [51-250]
  The Dreams of Mairhe Mehan
  y BL - v93 - Ja '97 - p842 [251-500]
  y CCB-B - v50 - N '96 - p91 [51-250]
  y HMR - Spr '97 - p34 [501+]
  y KR - v64 - S 1 '96 - p1318+ [51-250]
  y SLJ - v42 - O '96 - p144 [51-250]
  Patrick Doyle Is Full of Blarney (Illus. by Krista Brauckmann-Towns)
  c HB Guide - v7 - Fall '96 - p285 [51-250]
  c SLJ - v42 - Ag '96 - p115 [51-250]
  The Snowball (Illus. by Jean Pidgeon)
  c BL - v93 - F 1 '97 - p949 [51-250]
  Sunshine, Moonshine (Illus. by Lucia Washburn)
  c BL - v93 - My 1 '97 - p1502+ [51-250]
Armstrong, Joe - *Concurrent Programming in ERLANG. 2nd Ed.*
  SciTech - v20 - S '96 - p6 [51-250]
Armstrong, John - *Looking at Pictures*
  TES - Ja 3 '97 - p23 [51-250]
Armstrong, Judith - *The Christesen Romance*
  Aust Bk R - D '96 - p22+ [501+]
Armstrong, Karen - *A History of God*
  CSM - v89 - N 25 '96 - p12 [51-250]

In the Beginning
  BL - v93 - S 15 '96 - p181+ [51-250]
  BW - v26 - D 8 '96 - p5 [501+]
  CSM - v88 - N 6 '96 - p12 [51-250]
  LJ - v121 - S 15 '96 - p72 [51-250]
  Nat R - v48 - D 9 '96 - p61+ [501+]
  PW - v243 - S 2 '96 - p127 [51-250]
Jerusalem: One City, Three Faiths
  Am - v176 - Mr 8 '97 - p25 [51-250]
  BL - v93 - Ja '97 - p756 [1-50]
  BW - v26 - Jl 7 '96 - p4 [501+]
  CR - v270 - F '97 - p105+ [251-500]
  LATBR - Jl 14 '96 - p1+ [501+]
  LATBR - D 29 '96 - p3+ [501+]
  Lon R Bks - v18 - O 31 '96 - p16+ [501+]
  MEQ - v4 - Mr '97 - p75+ [501+]
  NY - v72 - S 9 '96 - p91 [51-250]
  NYTBR - v101 - D 8 '96 - p13+ [501+]
  WSJ-MW - v78 - O 14 '96 - pA12 [501+]
Jerusalem: One City, Three Faiths (Armstrong). Audio Version
  Kliatt - v30 - N '96 - p49+ [51-250]
Armstrong, Louise - *Of Sluts and Bastards*
  NWSA Jnl - v8 - Fall '96 - p129+ [501+]
Armstrong, Luanne - *Annie*
  y Can CL - v22 - Fall '96 - p117+ [51-250]
Armstrong, Mark - *Regulatory Reform*
  JEL - v34 - D '96 - p1983+ [501+]
Armstrong, Pam - *Sea Searcher's Handbook*
  c SB - v33 - My '97 - p110 [51-250]
Armstrong, Pat - *Wasting Away*
  Choice - v34 - Mr '97 - p1192 [51-250]
Armstrong, Philip - *A More Perfect Legacy*
  CHR - v83 - Ja '97 - p147+ [251-500]
Armstrong, Robb - *Drew and the Bub Daddy Showdown (Illus. by Robb Armstrong)*
  c BL - v93 - S 15 '96 - p236 [51-250]
  c HB Guide - v7 - Fall '96 - p289 [51-250]
  c SLJ - v42 - Ag '96 - p142 [51-250]
Armstrong, Robert P - *Ghana Country Assistance Review*
  JEL - v34 - D '96 - p2047 [51-250]
Armstrong, William H - *Trueno*
  c BL - v93 - F 15 '97 - p1032 [1-50]
Arnaldez, Roger - *Three Messengers for One God*
  MEJ - v51 - Win '97 - p148 [501+]
  Theol St - v57 - Je '96 - p365+ [501+]
Arndt, Heinz W - *Essays in International Economics 1944-1994*
  JEL - v35 - Mr '97 - p217 [1-50]
Arne, Finn - *Norge: Helpostkatalog. 1996/97 Ed.*
  r Am Phil - v110 - D '96 - p1088 [51-250]
Arneil, Barbara - *John Locke and America*
  Choice - v34 - Ja '97 - p872 [51-250]
Arnesen, Eric - *Waterfront Workers of New Orleans*
  S&S - v60 - Win '96 - p500+ [501+]
Arnett, David - *Supernovae and Nucleosynthesis*
  Choice - v34 - O '96 - p301 [51-250]
  Nature - v381 - My 16 '96 - p204 [251-500]
  New Sci - v151 - S 28 '96 - p52 [51-250]
  Phys Today - v49 - O '96 - p68+ [501+]
  Sci - v274 - N 22 '96 - p1320+ [501+]
Arnett, Eric - *Nuclear Weapons after the Comprehensive Test Ban*
  Choice - v34 - Mr '97 - p1235+ [51-250]
Arnett, Peter - *Live from the Battlefield*
  Parameters - v26 - Win '96 - p148+ [501+]
Arnett, Robert - *India Unveiled*
  LJ - v122 - My 1 '97 - p128+ [51-250]
Arnheim, Rudolf - *The Split and the Structure*
  LJ - v121 - D '96 - p87 [1-50]
Arnold, A James - *Monsters, Tricksters, and Sacred Cows*
  Choice - v34 - O '96 - p324 [51-250]
Arnold, Alan - *Mastering AS/400 Performance*
  SciTech - v21 - Mr '97 - p10 [51-250]
Arnold, Caroline - *African Animals*
  c BL - v93 - Mr 15 '97 - p1236 [51-250]
  c SLJ - v43 - Mr '97 - p170 [51-250]
Bat (Illus. by Richard Hewett)
  c BL - v92 - Ag '96 - p1897 [51-250]
  c CCB-B - v50 - O '96 - p47 [51-250]
  c Emerg Lib - v24 - Mr '97 - p44 [1-50]
  c HB Guide - v8 - Spr '97 - p126 [51-250]
  c SLJ - v42 - S '96 - p210 [51-250]
Fox (Illus. by Richard Hewett)
  c BL - v92 - Ag '96 - p1897 [51-250]
  c CCB-B - v50 - O '96 - p47 [51-250]
  c HB Guide - v8 - Spr '97 - p126 [51-250]
  c SLJ - v42 - S '96 - p210 [51-250]
Hawk Highway in the Sky (Illus. by Robert Kruidenier)
  c KR - v65 - Ap 1 '97 - p548 [51-250]

Lion (Illus. by Richard Hewett)
  c RT - v50 - S '96 - p57 [51-250]
Rhino (Illus. by Richard Hewett)
  c RT - v50 - S '96 - p57 [51-250]
Stone Age Farmers beside the Sea (Illus. by Arthur P Arnold)
  c CCB-B - v50 - Ap '97 - p271 [51-250]
  c KR - v65 - F 15 '97 - p296 [51-250]
Stories in Stone (Illus. by Richard Hewett)
  c BL - v93 - D 15 '96 - p722 [51-250]
  c CCB-B - v50 - Ja '97 - p163 [51-250]
  c HB Guide - v8 - Spr '97 - p136 [51-250]
  c KR - v64 - O 15 '96 - p1528 [51-250]
  c SLJ - v42 - D '96 - p126 [51-250]
Arnold, Clinton E - *The Colossian Syncretism*
  Rel St Rev - v23 - Ap '97 - p185 [51-250]
Arnold, David - *Nature, Culture, Imperialism*
  JIH - v27 - Spr '97 - p746+ [501+]
The Problem of Nature
  New Sci - v153 - F 15 '97 - p44 [51-250]
  Socio R - v45 - My '97 - p354+ [501+]
Arnold, David M - *Abelian Groups and Modules*
  SciTech - v20 - D '96 - p15 [51-250]
Arnold, Guy - *Historical Dictionary of Aid and Development Organizations*
  r ARBA - v28 - '97 - p277 [51-250]
  r Choice - v34 - Ap '97 - p1305 [51-250]
Wars in the Third World Since 1945. 2nd Ed.
  r ARBA - v28 - '97 - p256 [51-250]
Arnold, Helen - *Egypt*
  c HB Guide - v8 - Spr '97 - p171 [51-250]
  c SLJ - v43 - F '97 - p86 [51-250]
Ireland
  c HB Guide - v8 - Spr '97 - p168 [51-250]
Italy
  c HB Guide - v8 - Spr '97 - p168 [51-250]
Kenya
  c HB Guide - v8 - Spr '97 - p171 [51-250]
  c SLJ - v43 - Mr '97 - p170 [51-250]
The West Indies
  c HB Guide - v8 - Spr '97 - p178 [1-50]
Arnold, James R - *The American West*
  HT - v46 - O '96 - p58 [1-50]
  LJ - v122 - Mr 15 '97 - p72 [51-250]
Napoleon Conquers Austria
  Historian - v59 - Win '97 - p455+ [501+]
Settling the West
  LJ - v122 - Mr 15 '97 - p72 [51-250]
Arnold, Johann Christoph - *I Tell You a Mystery*
  BL - v93 - F 1 '97 - p908+ [51-250]
  PW - v244 - Ja 27 '97 - p96 [51-250]
A Plea for Purity
  CC - v113 - N 6 '96 - p1091 [51-250]
Arnold, John - *Australia: A Reader's Guide*
  r ARBA - v28 - '97 - p59 [51-250]
Arnold, Karen D - *Lives of Promise*
  EL - v54 - D '96 - p86+ [251-500]
Arnold, Katya - *Baba Yaga (Illus. by Katya Arnold)*
  c Bks Keeps - Jl '96 - p7 [51-250]
Duck, Duck, Goose? (Illus. by Katya Arnold)
  c PW - v244 - My 5 '97 - p208 [51-250]
Katya's Book of Mushrooms (Illus. by Katya Arnold)
  c BL - v93 - Ap 1 '97 - p1326 [51-250]
  c CCB-B - v50 - Ap '97 - p271+ [51-250]
  c HB - v73 - My '97 - p336+ [51-250]
  c KR - v65 - F 15 '97 - p296 [51-250]
  c PW - v244 - Mr 3 '97 - p75+ [51-250]
Arnold, Matthew - *Culture and Anarchy*
  JAAC - v54 - Fall '96 - p403 [501+]
The Letters of Matthew Arnold. Vol. 1
  BW - v26 - D 29 '96 - p13 [51-250]
  Choice - v34 - Ja '97 - p791 [51-250]
Arnold, Nick - *Flying Machines (Illus. by Martin John)*
  c PW - v243 - D 30 '96 - p68 [51-250]
Arnold, Stephen E - *Publishing on the Internet*
  LAR - v98 - S '96 - p479 [251-500]
Arnold, Tedd - *No More Water in the Tub (Illus. by Tedd Arnold)*
  c RT - v50 - O '96 - p134 [1-50]
No Se Salta En La Cama! (Illus. by Tedd Arnold)
  c BL - v93 - My 1 '97 - p1506 [1-50]
Arnoldi, Mary Jo - *African Material Culture*
  Bl S - v26 - Fall '96 - p100 [51-250]
Crowning Achievements
  Am Craft - v56 - Ag '96 - p27 [1-50]
Playing with Time
  TDR - v40 - Fall '96 - p202 [51-250]

Arnosky, Jim - *All about Deer (Illus. by Jim Arnosky)*
  c BL - v93 - S 15 '96 - p243 [51-250]
  c Emerg Lib - v24 - Mr '97 - p44 [1-50]
  c HB Guide - v8 - Spr '97 - p126 [1-50]
  c SLJ - v42 - S '96 - p195 [51-250]
Bring 'Em Back Alive!
  c BL - v93 - My 1 '97 - p1489 [51-250]
Crinkleroot's Guide to Knowing Butterflies and Moths
  c HB Guide - v7 - Fall '96 - p340+ [51-250]
I See Animals Hiding (Illus. by Jim Arnosky)
  c RT - v50 - S '96 - p55 [51-250]
Little Champ (Illus. by Jim Arnosky)
  c RT - v50 - S '96 - p56 [51-250]
Nearer Nature (Illus. by Jim Arnosky)
  y BL - v92 - Ag '96 - p1892 [51-250]
  c HB Guide - v8 - Spr '97 - p116 [51-250]
  y SLJ - v42 - N '96 - p127+ [51-250]
  c Smith - v27 - N '96 - p168 [1-50]
Rabbits and Raindrops (Illus. by Jim Arnosky)
  c BL - v93 - Mr 1 '97 - p1168 [51-250]
  c CBRS - v25 - Ap '97 - p97 [1-50]
  c CCB-B - v50 - Mr '97 - p239 [51-250]
  c KR - v64 - D 15 '96 - p1796 [51-250]
  c PW - v243 - D 30 '96 - p66 [51-250]
  c SLJ - v43 - Mr '97 - p148 [51-250]
Arnot, Bob - *Dr. Bob Arnot's Program for Perfect Weight Control for Men and Women*
  PW - v244 - Ap 21 '97 - p68 [51-250]
Arnott, Susi - *Indonesia*
  c TES - Mr 21 '97 - p18* [251-500]
Arnove, Robert F - *Education as Contested Terrain*
  CS - v26 - Mr '97 - p179+ [501+]
Arnulf, Von Mailand - *Liber Gestorum Recentium*
  Specu - v71 - Jl '96 - p676+ [501+]
Arnup, Katherine - *Education for Motherhood*
  JWomHist - v8 - Fall '96 - p219+ [501+]
Aron, Lewis - *A Meeting of Minds*
  AJPsych - v153 - N '96 - p1501 [251-500]
Aron, Raymond - *In Defense of Decadent Europe. 2nd Ed.*
  JEL - v34 - D '96 - p2128 [51-250]
Aroneanu, Eugene - *Inside the Concentration Camps*
  BL - v93 - S 15 '96 - p214+ [51-250]
  LJ - v121 - N 15 '96 - p73 [51-250]
  R&R Bk N - v12 - F '97 - p14 [51-250]
Aronowitz, Stanley - *Dead Artists, Live Theories and Other Cultural Problems*
  SSQ - v77 - Je '96 - p456+ [501+]
The Death and Rebirth of American Radicalism
  LJ - v121 - N 1 '96 - p92 [51-250]
  PW - v243 - N 18 '96 - p68 [51-250]
The Jobless Future
  HER - v67 - Spr '97 - p148+ [501+]
  S&S - v60 - Win '96 - p504+ [501+]
  YR - v84 - O '96 - p137+ [501+]
Arons, Arnold B - *Teaching Introductory Physics*
  Choice - v34 - F '97 - p1000+ [51-250]
  SciTech - v20 - D '96 - p23 [51-250]
Aronson, Billy - *Betting on Forever (Illus. by John Quinn)*
  c HB Guide - v8 - Spr '97 - p61 [51-250]
  c SLJ - v43 - Mr '97 - p148 [51-250]
Eclipses: Nature's Blackouts
  c HB Guide - v8 - Spr '97 - p111 [51-250]
  c SLJ - v43 - Mr '97 - p196 [51-250]
Meteors: The Truth behind Shooting Stars
  c BL - v93 - F 15 '97 - p1016 [51-250]
  c BL - v93 - My 1 '97 - p1489 [51-250]
  c HB Guide - v8 - Spr '97 - p111 [51-250]
  c SLJ - v43 - Mr '97 - p196 [51-250]
Aronson, J Richards - *Management Policies in Local Government Finance. 4th Ed.*
  JEL - v35 - Mr '97 - p303+ [51-250]
Aronson, Jodi - *Inside Managed Care*
  SB - v33 - My '97 - p103 [251-500]
Aronson, Larry - *HTML 3 Manual of Style*
  r CBR - v14 - S '96 - p29 [1-50]
Aronson, Theo - *Princess Margaret: A Biography*
  Books - v11 - Ap '97 - p20 [51-250]
  TLS - F 14 '97 - p32 [501+]
  Woman's J - F '97 - p16 [51-250]
Arora, A K - *Ordering and Phase Transitions in Charged Colloids*
  SciTech - v20 - S '96 - p17 [51-250]
Arostegui, Martin C - *Twilight Warriors*
  y BL - v93 - F 1 '97 - p909 [51-250]
  KR - v64 - D 15 '96 - p1775 [251-500]
  LJ - v122 - Ap 1 '97 - p110 [51-250]
  PW - v244 - Ja 13 '97 - p66 [51-250]
Arozena, Steven - *Best Books for Public Libraries*
  r RQ - v36 - Win '96 - p213 [51-250]

Arranga, Edmund C - *Object-Oriented COBOL*
  SciTech - v20 - N '96 - p9 [51-250]
Arraras, Maria Celeste - *Selena's Secret*
  PW - v244 - Ja 27 '97 - p90+ [51-250]
Arredondo, Ines - *Underground River and Other Stories*
  NYTBR - v102 - Mr 23 '97 - p18 [51-250]
  TranslRevS - v2 - D '96 - p32 [51-250]
Arredondo, Patricia - *Successful Diversity Management Initiatives*
  Choice - v34 - N '96 - p502 [51-250]
Arreghini, Louis - *La Nouvelle-Caledonie Au Tournant Des Annees 1990*
  Cont Pac - v8 - Fall '96 - p470+ [501+]
Arreguin Manon, Jose P - *Dos Testimonios Sobre Historia De Los Aprovechamientos Hidraulicos En Mexico*
  HAHR - v76 - N '96 - p799 [251-500]
Arriens, Jan - *Welcome to Hell*
  LJ - v122 - My 1 '97 - p123 [51-250]
  PW - v244 - F 17 '97 - p207 [51-250]
Arrivi, Francisco - *Canticle for a Memory*
  TranslRevS - v1 - My '95 - p28 [1-50]
Arrizabalaga, Jon - *The Great Pox*
  KR - v65 - F 1 '97 - p179 [251-500]
  LJ - v122 - Mr 15 '97 - p72 [51-250]
  Nature - v386 - Mr 27 '97 - p343 [501+]
  New Sci - v153 - Ja 18 '97 - p40 [51-250]
  Obs - F 23 '97 - p15* [501+]
Arrow, Kenneth J - *Barriers to Conflict Resolution*
  JEL - v34 - D '96 - p1953+ [501+]
  Education in a Research University
  JEL - v34 - D '96 - p2063 [51-250]
  R&R Bk N - v11 - N '96 - p75 [51-250]
  The Rational Foundations of Economic Behaviour
  JEL - v34 - D '96 - p2022 [51-250]
Arrows for Change: Women's and Gender Perspectives in Health Policies and Programmes
  p WorldV - v12 - O '96 - p11 [51-250]
Arrowsmith
  p Sm Pr R - v29 - Ja '97 - p19 [51-250]
Arrowsmith, William - *Antonioni: The Poet of Images*
  AB - v98 - D 9 '96 - p1997 [501+]
Arroyo, Stephen - *Exploring Jupiter*
  Horoscope - v62 - N '96 - p28+ [501+]
Arru, Angiolina - *Il Servo: Storia Di Una Carriera Nel Settecento*
  AHR - v101 - O '96 - p1241 [251-500]
  Choice - v34 - D '96 - p566 [1-50]
Ars Poetica
  p Aust Bk R - Jl '96 - p57 [251-500]
Arseniev, V K - *Dersu the Trapper*
  BW - v26 - Ag 25 '96 - p12 [51-250]
Arsenijevic, Vladimir - *In the Hold*
  BL - v93 - S 1 '96 - p60 [51-250]
  BW - v26 - D 8 '96 - p7 [1-50]
  CSM - v89 - F 12 '97 - p12 [501+]
  NY - v72 - D 23 '96 - p146 [51-250]
  NYTBR - v101 - S 22 '96 - p21 [501+]
  NYTBR - v101 - D 8 '96 - p80 [1-50]
  SFR - v21 - S '96 - p29 [501+]
  TLS - N 15 '96 - p24 [501+]
  VV - v41 - S 24 '96 - p41 [251-500]
  U Potpalublju
  WLT - v70 - Sum '96 - p729 [501+]
The Art Book
  yr Kliatt - v31 - My '97 - p30 [51-250]
  TES - Ja 3 '97 - p23 [51-250]
Art Index 1929-
  r ASInt - v34 - O '96 - p19 [1-50]
The Art of Construction
  c Books - v9 - S '95 - p26 [1-50]
Art Papers
  p Sm Pr R - v28 - Jl '96 - p27+ [501+]
Artaud, Antonin - *Watchfiends and Rack Screams*
  ABR - v18 - D '96 - p26+ [501+]
Artaud, Denise - *Les Etats-Unis Et Leur Arriere-Cour*
  AHR - v102 - F '97 - p223 [501+]
Artemyev, V E - *Geochemistry of Organic Matter in River-Sea Systems*
  Choice - v34 - Mr '97 - p1187 [51-250]
  SciTech - v20 - D '96 - p2 [51-250]
Arter, David - *Parties and Democracy in the Post-Soviet Republics*
  Choice - v34 - My '97 - p1567 [51-250]
Arthritis and Allied Conditions. 13th Ed., Vols. 1-2
  New Sci - v153 - F 1 '97 - p48 [1-50]
  SciTech - v21 - Mr '97 - p59 [51-250]
Arthur, Christopher J - *Engels Today*
  TLS - F 28 '97 - p4 [501+]
Arthur, John - *Campus Wars*
  Ethics - v107 - Ja '97 - p398 [51-250]

Color Class Identity
  Bl S - v26 - Fall '96 - p100 [1-50]
Words That Bind
  CPR - v16 - Ag '96 - p238+ [501+]
Arthur, Shirley - *Surviving Teen Pregnancy. Rev. Ed.*
  y HB Guide - v7 - Fall '96 - p310 [51-250]
  y Kliatt - v30 - S '96 - p29+ [51-250]
Artificial Intelligence in Design '96
  SciTech - v21 - Mr '97 - p74 [51-250]
Artis, M J - *The UK Economy (Prest and Coppock). 14th Ed.*
  CR - v269 - D '96 - p334 [51-250]
Artists Communities
  r Ceram Mo - v45 - Ap '97 - p30 [251-500]
Arts and Humanities Citation Index 1981-
  r ASInt - v34 - O '96 - p17+ [51-250]
ArtWord Quarterly
  p LMR - v15 - Fall '96 - p40 [51-250]
Arundale, Justin - *Getting Your S/NVQ*
  LAR - v98 - Je '96 - p318 [251-500]
Aruri, Naseer H - *The Obstruction of Peace*
  Choice - v34 - S '96 - p205 [51-250]
Arx: World Journal of Prehistoric and Ancient Studies
  p AJA - v100 - O '96 - p809 [251-500]
Arzt, Donna E - *Refugees into Citizens*
  For Aff - v76 - My '97 - p142 [51-250]
Arzt, Noam H - *The Business of Higher Education*
  JEL - v34 - S '96 - p1442 [51-250]
Asaad, Ghazi - *Psychosomatic Disorders*
  SciTech - v20 - S '96 - p30 [51-250]
Asala, Joanne - *Recipes from Ireland*
  CAY - v17 - Fall '96 - p2 [51-250]
  Scandinavian Ghost Stories and Other Tales of the Supernatural
  c CAY - v17 - Fall '96 - p9 [51-250]
  Tales of the Slav Peasants and Herdsmen
  CAY - v17 - Fall '96 - p9 [51-250]
Asante, Clement E - *The Press in Ghana*
  JMCQ - v73 - Win '96 - p1012+ [501+]
Asante, Molefi K - *African Intellectual Heritage*
  Bloom Rev - v17 - Ja '97 - p20 [51-250]
  LJ - v121 - N 1 '96 - p84 [1-50]
Asaro, Catherine - *Catch the Lightning*
  KR - v64 - O 15 '96 - p1500 [51-250]
  LJ - v121 - N 15 '96 - p92 [51-250]
  PW - v243 - N 18 '96 - p66 [51-250]
Asbury, Kelly - *Bonnie's Blue House (Illus. by Kelly Asbury)*
  c BL - v93 - Mr 1 '97 - p1168 [51-250]
  c KR - v65 - Mr 1 '97 - p376 [51-250]
  c PW - v244 - Ap 7 '97 - p90 [51-250]
  Rusty's Red Vacation (Illus. by Kelly Asbury)
  c BL - v93 - Mr 1 '97 - p1168 [51-250]
  c PW - v244 - Ap 7 '97 - p90 [51-250]
  Yolanda's Yellow School (Illus. by Kelly Asbury)
  c BL - v93 - Mr 1 '97 - p1168 [51-250]
  c PW - v244 - Ap 7 '97 - p90 [51-250]
ASCE Specialty Conference on Robotics for Challenging Environments (2nd: 1996: Albuquerque, N.M.) - *Robotics for Challenging Environments*
  SciTech - v20 - D '96 - p72 [51-250]
Asch, Frank - *Moonbear's Pet*
  c PW - v244 - Ap 21 '97 - p73 [1-50]
  Sawgrass Poems (Illus. by Ted Levin)
  c HB Guide - v7 - Fall '96 - p366 [51-250]
  c LA - v73 - D '96 - p622 [51-250]
  c RT - v50 - My '97 - p685 [51-250]
  c SB - v33 - Ja '97 - p20 [251-500]
Asch, Ronald G - *Der Hof Karls I Von England*
  EHR - v111 - N '96 - p1280+ [501+]
Ascherson, Neal - *Black Sea*
  CR - v269 - N '96 - p277 [1-50]
  LATBR - D 29 '96 - p3 [51-250]
  Slav R - v55 - Sum '96 - p477+ [501+]
  TES - D 27 '96 - p16 [51-250]
Aschheim, Steven E - *Culture and Catastrophe*
  Tikkun - v11 - My '96 - p69+ [501+]
  TLS - Mr 21 '97 - p30 [501+]
Ascoli, Albert Russell - *Machiavelli and the Discourse of Literature*
  Specu - v71 - Jl '96 - p677+ [501+]
Asen, Dennis - *Deadly Impression*
  Arm Det - v30 - Win '97 - p107 [251-500]
Ash, Andrew - *The Future of Tropical Savannas*
  Choice - v34 - My '97 - p1522 [51-250]
Ash, John - *Selected Poems*
  Econ - v342 - Mr 29 '97 - p92 [51-250]
Ash, Lee - *Subject Collections. 7th Ed., Vols. 1-2*
  r ASInt - v34 - O '96 - p12 [1-50]

Ash, Michael - *Handbook of Paint and Coating Raw Materials. Vols. 1-2*
  r SciTech - v20 - D '96 - p83 [51-250]
  Handbook of Pharmaceutical Additives
  r SciTech - v20 - D '96 - p55 [51-250]
  Handbook of Plastic and Rubber Additives
  r ARBA - v28 - '97 - p629+ [51-250]
  Handbook of Water Treatment Chemicals
  r SciTech - v21 - Mr '97 - p82 [51-250]
  The Index of Antimicrobials
  r SciTech - v21 - Mr '97 - p67 [51-250]
Ash, Mitchell G - *Forced Migration and Scientific Change*
  Choice - v34 - N '96 - p512 [51-250]
Ash, Russell - *Apples and Oranges*
  c BL - v93 - D 1 '96 - p688 [51-250]
  Dante Gabriel Rossetti
  AB - v99 - Mr 3 '97 - p692+ [51-250]
  Incredible Comparisons
  c BL - v93 - D 1 '96 - p659 [51-250]
  c Ch BWatch - v6 - O '96 - p1 [1-50]
  c HB Guide - v8 - Spr '97 - p109 [51-250]
  c JB - v60 - D '96 - p263 [251-500]
  c Par Ch - v21 - Mr '97 - p5 [1-50]
  c Sch Lib - v45 - F '97 - p36 [51-250]
  c SLJ - v43 - Mr '97 - p196 [51-250]
  c TES - D 6 '96 - p22* [51-250]
  Sir John Everett Millais
  BL - v93 - Ap 1 '97 - p1274 [51-250]
  The Top 10 of Everything
  r LJ - v122 - Ja '97 - p82 [51-250]
Ash, Sarah - *Moths to a Flame*
  Books - v10 - Je '96 - p24 [51-250]
Ash, Stephen V - *When the Yankees Came*
  JSH - v63 - F '97 - p179+ [501+]
  RAH - v24 - S '96 - p426+ [501+]
Ashabranner, Brent - *The Lion's Whiskers and Other Ethiopian Tales (Illus. by Helen Siegl)*
  c PW - v244 - Ap 21 '97 - p73 [1-50]
  Our Beckoning Borders (Illus. by Paul Conklin)
  c Ch BWatch - v6 - Jl '96 - p7 [1-50]
  c HB Guide - v7 - Fall '96 - p311 [51-250]
  A Strange and Distant Shore
  c HB - v72 - S '96 - p606+ [51-250]
  c HB Guide - v8 - Spr '97 - p176+ [51-250]
  c SB - v33 - Ja '97 - p21 [251-500]
  y SLJ - v42 - S '96 - p230 [51-250]
  To Seek a Better World (Illus. by Paul Conklin)
  c BL - v93 - My 15 '97 - p1569 [51-250]
Ashbery, John - *Can You Hear, Bird*
  Lon R Bks - v18 - Ag 22 '96 - p25+ [501+]
  NYTBR - v102 - Ap 20 '97 - p32 [1-50]
  WLT - v70 - Aut '96 - p961 [501+]
  Selected Poems
  LJ - v122 - Ap 1 '97 - p94 [1-50]
  Self-Portrait in a Convex Mirror
  LJ - v122 - Ap 1 '97 - p94 [1-50]
Ashburn, Elizabeth - *Lesbian Art*
  Aust Bk R - Je '96 - p48+ [501+]
Ashby, Michael F - *Engineering Materials 1. 2nd Ed.*
  SciTech - v20 - D '96 - p62 [1-50]
  SciTech - v21 - Mr '97 - p76 [51-250]
Ashby, Ruth - *Herstory: Women Who Changed the World*
  cr RT - v50 - D '96 - p344+ [51-250]
Ashe, Arthur - *Days of Grace*
  y BL - v93 - D 15 '96 - p716 [1-50]
Ashelford, Jane - *The Art of Dress*
  BL - v93 - D 15 '96 - p695 [51-250]
  LJ - v122 - Ap 1 '97 - p88 [51-250]
  Mag Antiq - v151 - Mr '97 - p394 [51-250]
Ashenfelter, Orley C - *The Economics of Training. Vols. 1-2*
  JEL - v35 - Mr '97 - p237 [51-250]
Asher, Abigail - *Treasures of the Uffizi Florence*
  CSM - v89 - D 24 '96 - p16 [51-250]
Asher, Gerald - *Vineyard Tales*
  LJ - v122 - Ap 1 '97 - p64 [1-50]
Asher, Jane - *The Longing*
  TLS - O 11 '96 - p27 [51-250]
  Woman's J - Ja '97 - p13 [1-50]
Asher, Kenneth - *T.S. Eliot and Ideology*
  J Am St - v30 - Ap '96 - p150+ [251-500]
  TLS - Jl 7 '96 - p13 [501+]
Asher, Michael - *The Last of the Bedu*
  Spec - v277 - N 23 '96 - p51+ [501+]
  TLS - Ap 11 '97 - p29 [501+]
  Thesiger: A Biography
  GJ - v163 - Mr '97 - p106+ [251-500]
Asher, Robert - *Autowork*
  Historian - v59 - Win '97 - p417+ [251-500]
Asher, Sandy - *But That's Another Story*
  y HB Guide - v7 - Fall '96 - p363 [51-250]

Asheri, Ehud - *Zeh Yigamer Be-Bekhi*
BL - v93 - Mr 1 '97 - p1115 [1-50]
Ashford, Jane - *The Marriage Wager*
PW - v243 - S 30 '96 - p80 [51-250]
Ashford, Janet - *Start with a Scan*
CBR - v15 - Spr '97 - p9 [51-250]
LJ - v121 - O 1 '96 - p120 [1-50]
Ashley, Bernard - *I Forgot! Said Troy (Illus. by Derek Brazell)*
c   Sch Lib - v44 - Ag '96 - p98 [51-250]
A Present for Paul (Illus. by David Mitchell)
c   Bks Keeps - N '96 - p7 [51-250]
Ashley, Kathleen - *Autobiography and Postmodernism*
Can Lit - Win '96 - p137+ [501+]
Ashley, Maureen - *Touring in Wine Country: Northwest Italy*
r   LJ - v122 - Ap 1 '97 - p113 [51-250]
Ashley, Mike - *The Merlin Chronicles*
SF Chr - v18 - O '96 - p80 [1-50]
Space Stories
y   New Sci - v153 - F 8 '97 - p46 [51-250]
Ashman, John - *Disaster Planning for Library and Information Service*
LR - v45 - 5 '96 - p67+ [501+]
Ashpole, Edward - *Where Is Everybody?*
New Sci - v153 - Ja 18 '97 - p39 [1-50]
Ashton, Charles - *Billy's Drift*
c   Magpies - v11 - My '96 - p53 [1-50]
Jet Smoke and Dragon Fire
c   Bks Keeps - v100 - S '96 - p10 [51-250]
Ashton, David - *Education, Training, and the Global Economy*
Choice - v34 - O '96 - p328 [51-250]
JEL - v34 - D '96 - p2070 [51-250]
R&R Bk N - v11 - N '96 - p31 [51-250]
Ashton, Jay - *Keeping Cats*
c   TES - Mr 7 '97 - p12* [51-250]
Ashton, John - *Studying John*
Cres - v59 - S '96 - p40+ [501+]
JR - v76 - O '96 - p620+ [501+]
Ashton, Nigel John - *Eisenhower, Macmillan and the Problem of Nasser*
Choice - v34 - Ap '97 - p1412 [51-250]
TLS - Mr 28 '97 - p28 [501+]
Ashton, Owen - *The Chartist Movement*
r   R&R Bk N - v11 - D '96 - p31 [51-250]
r   VS - v39 - Win '96 - p256 [51-250]
Ashton, Robert - *Counter-Revolution: The Second Civil War and Its Origins 1646-8*
Historian - v58 - Sum '96 - p892+ [251-500]
Ashton, Rosemary - *George Eliot: A Life*
Econ - v341 - N 23 '96 - p103+ [501+]
KR - v65 - Mr 15 '97 - p426 [251-500]
Obs - D 1 '96 - p16* [51-250]
PW - v244 - Mr 24 '97 - p65 [51-250]
Spec - v277 - N 16 '96 - p55+ [501+]
TLS - N 22 '96 - p25 [501+]
Wil Q - v21 - Spr '97 - p106 [51-250]
Ashwell, Miranda - *Foundation Geography in Action. Bks. 1-3*
TES - Mr 28 '97 - pR7 [501+]
Ashwell, Rachel - *Shabby Chic*
LJ - v121 - S 15 '96 - p66 [51-250]
Ashworth, Gregory J - *War and the City*
J Urban H - v22 - S '96 - p720+ [501+]
Ashworth, John - *Slavery, Capitalism, and Politics in the Antebellum Republic. Vol. 1*
Choice - v34 - S '96 - p191 [51-250]
JEH - v57 - Mr '97 - p238+ [501+]
RAH - v24 - D '96 - p607+ [501+]
Ashworth, Liz - *Teaching the Bairns to Cook*
c   Sch Lib - v45 - F '97 - p36 [51-250]
Ashworth, Mary - *Teaching the World's Children*
MLJ - v80 - Fall '96 - p411+ [501+]
Ashworth, Sherry - *No Fear*
Woman's J - O '96 - p12 [1-50]
Asia Pacific Business Review
p   JEL - v34 - S '96 - p1504+ [51-250]
Asian American Coalition (Chicago, Ill.) - *Children of Asian America (Illus. by Gene H Mayeda)*
c   HB Guide - v7 - Fall '96 - p363 [51-250]
Asian Journal of Women's Studies
p   WorldV - v3 - Ja '97 - p13 [51-250]
Asian Markets. 4th Ed.
r   ARBA - v28 - '97 - p110+ [251-500]
Asian Test Symposium - *Proceedings of the 1996 Asian Test Symposium*
SciTech - v21 - Mr '97 - p90 [51-250]
Asikinack, Bill - *Exploration into North America*
c   HB Guide - v8 - Spr '97 - p172 [51-250]
c   SLJ - v42 - S '96 - p210 [51-250]

Asikoglu, Yaman - *Finance, Exchange Rates and Financial Liberalization*
JEL - v34 - D '96 - p2051 [51-250]
Asilomar Conference on Signals, Systems and Computers (29th: 1995: Pacific Grove, Ca.) - *Conference Record. Vols. 1-2*
SciTech - v20 - S '96 - p54 [51-250]
Asimakopulos, N - *The Plate Flaws of the Hermes Heads of Greece 1861-1886*
Phil Lit R - v46 - 1 '97 - p72+ [251-500]
Asimov, Isaac - *Foundation*
Reason - v28 - D '96 - p42+ [51-250]
Yours, Isaac Asimov
Ext - v37 - Fall '96 - p285+ [501+]
Asimov, Janet - *Norby and the Court Jester*
y   Kliatt - v30 - S '96 - p15 [51-250]
Aska, Warabe - *Aska's Sea Creatures (Illus. by Warabe Aska)*
c   RT - v50 - O '96 - p136 [1-50]
Askeland, Luther - *Ways in Mystery*
BL - v93 - F 1 '97 - p909 [51-250]
PW - v244 - Ja 13 '97 - p69 [51-250]
Askenasy, Hans - *Cannibalism: From Sacrifice to Survival*
Ant R - v54 - Sum '96 - p360+ [251-500]
Askew, Henry R - *Treatment of Behavior Problems in Dogs and Cats*
SciTech - v21 - Mr '97 - p39 [51-250]
Askew, Mike - *Number at Key Stage 2*
TES - O 4 '96 - p16* [1-50]
TES - F 21 '97 - p13* [51-250]
Askin, Frank - *Defending Rights*
BL - v93 - D 1 '96 - p623 [51-250]
LJ - v122 - Mr 15 '97 - p75 [51-250]
PW - v244 - Ja 6 '97 - p59 [51-250]
Aslanbeigui, Nahid - *Women in the Age of Economic Transformation*
NWSA Jnl - v8 - Sum '96 - p134+ [501+]
Aslett, Michael - *The Grolier Library of Environmental Concepts and Issues. Vols. 1-8*
yr   ARBA - v28 - '97 - p647 [51-250]
cr   SLJ - v42 - Ag '96 - p181 [51-250]
Aslund, Anders - *How Russia Became a Market Economy*
JEL - v34 - S '96 - p1388+ [501+]
Russian Economic Reform at Risk
JEL - v35 - Mr '97 - p180+ [501+]
ASM Handbook Comprehensive Index. Electronic Media Version
r   Choice - v34 - N '96 - p487 [51-250]
ASME Proceedings of the 31st National Heat Transfer Conference. Vol. 6
SciTech - v21 - Mr '97 - p24 [51-250]
ASME Proceedings of the 31st National Heat Transfer Conference. Vols. 1-5, 7-8
SciTech - v21 - Mr '97 - p23 [51-250]
Asmuss, Burkhard - *Republik Ohne Chance?*
EHR - v112 - Ap '97 - p524+ [251-500]
Aspler, Tony - *The Beast of Barbaresco*
Books - v10 - Je '96 - p10 [1-50]
Asprey, Robert B - *At Belleau Wood*
TLS - Ja 17 '97 - p33 [251-500]
Aspromourgos, Tony - *On the Origins of Classical Economics*
JEL - v34 - D '96 - p2010+ [51-250]
R&R Bk N - v11 - N '96 - p24 [51-250]
Asquith, Ros - *Nora Normal and the Great Shark Rescue*
c   Sch Lib - v44 - Ag '96 - p102+ [51-250]
The Teenage Worrier's Christmas Survival Guide
y   Bks Keeps - N '96 - p21 [51-250]
Assagioli, Roberto - *Transpersonal Development*
Rel St Rev - v23 - Ap '97 - p141+ [501+]
Assayas, Michka - *The Beatles and the Sixties*
y   SLJ - v43 - Mr '97 - p196 [51-250]
Assel, Heinrich - *Der Andere Aufbruch*
Six Ct J - v27 - Fall '96 - p952+ [501+]
Asser, Stuart M - *Microcomputer Servicing. 3rd Ed.*
r   SciTech - v21 - Mr '97 - p92 [51-250]
Microcomputer Theory and Servicing. 3rd Ed.
r   SciTech - v21 - Mr '97 - p92 [1-50]
Assessment Standards for School Mathematics
Math T - v89 - S '96 - p512 [51-250]
Assire, Jerome - *The Book of Bread*
CSM - v89 - D 13 '96 - p10 [51-250]
LJ - v122 - Ja '97 - p136 [51-250]
Assis, Andre Koch Torres - *Weber's Electrodynamics*
Isis - v87 - D '96 - p735+ [501+]
Assiter, Alison - *Enlightened Women*
Choice - v34 - S '96 - p218 [51-250]
CPR - v16 - D '96 - p389+ [501+]
Assmann, Jan - *Egyptian Solar Religion in the New Kingdom*
JR - v76 - O '96 - p671+ [501+]

Association of British Philatelic Societies Year Book and Directory 1995
r   Am Phil - v110 - S '96 - p829 [51-250]
Association of Nepalis in the Americas - *The Nepal Cookbook*
LJ - v121 - S 15 '96 - p90 [51-250]
Association of the Bar of the City of New York - *The Elsinore Appeal*
LJ - v121 - O 15 '96 - p75 [51-250]
VV - v41 - D 31 '96 - p47 [251-500]
Associations Unlimited. Electronic Media Version
r   BL - v93 - D 1 '96 - p677+ [501+]
r   Choice - v34 - Ap '97 - p1319 [251-500]
Assouline, Pierre - *Simenon: A Biography*
PW - v244 - Ap 28 '97 - p56 [251-500]
The ASTD Training and Development Handbook. 4th Ed.
r   Choice - v34 - Ja '97 - p840 [51-250]
R&R Bk N - v12 - F '97 - p45 [51-250]
Astell, Ann W - *Chaucer and the Universe of Learning*
Choice - v34 - F '97 - p963 [51-250]
Astfalk, Greg - *Applications on Advanced Architecture Computers*
SciTech - v21 - Mr '97 - p10 [1-50]
Astle, Richard M - *The Commonsense MBA (Astle). Audio Version*
LJ - v122 - F 1 '97 - p125 [51-250]
Astley, Neil - *Biting My Tongue*
WLT - v71 - Win '97 - p164 [251-500]
Astley, Thea - *The Multiple Effects of Rainshadow*
Aust Bk R - O '96 - p13+ [501+]
ASTM Standards on Electrical Protective Equipment for Workers. 10th Ed.
SciTech - v20 - D '96 - p74 [51-250]
ASTM Standards on Ground Water and Vadose Zone Investigations
r   SciTech - v20 - S '96 - p1 [1-50]
ASTM Standards on Whole Building Functionality and Serviceability
SciTech - v20 - D '96 - p71 [51-250]
Astolfi, Valter - *Occupazioni Ed Annessioni Italiane Nella Seconda Guerra Mondiale*
r   Am Phil - v110 - O '96 - p912 [51-250]
r   Phil Lit R - v45 - 3 '96 - p251+ [501+]
Aston, Margaret - *The King's Bedpost*
CH - v66 - Mr '97 - p197+ [251-500]
The Panorama of the Renaissance
y   BL - v93 - N 1 '96 - p478 [251-500]
KR - v64 - O 1 '96 - p1459 [51-250]
NYTBR - v101 - D 8 '96 - p19 [251-500]
PW - v243 - O 7 '96 - p48 [51-250]
y   SLJ - v43 - F '97 - p136 [51-250]
TLS - D 6 '96 - p26 [501+]
Aston, Philip J - *Nonlinear Mathematics and Its Applications*
SciTech - v20 - D '96 - p20 [1-50]
Astor, Gerald - *Crisis in the Pacific*
R&R Bk N - v11 - N '96 - p10 [1-50]
The Mighty Eighth
BL - v93 - My 15 '97 - p1558 [51-250]
LJ - v122 - My 1 '97 - p118 [51-250]
Astro, Alan - *Discourses of Jewish Identity in Twentieth Century France*
FR - v70 - Mr '97 - p627+ [501+]
Astrologo, Sergio - *Gli Occhi Colore Del Tempo*
WLT - v71 - Win '97 - p127 [501+]
Astronomical Almanac. 1996 Ed.
r   S&T - v92 - S '96 - p52 [51-250]
Aswad, Barbara C - *Family and Gender among American Muslims*
Choice - v34 - Ja '97 - p882 [51-250]
Atasoy, Nurhan - *Iznik: The Pottery of Ottoman Turkey*
SDA - v4 - Fall '96 - p133+ [501+]
Atchison, Lee - *Object-Oriented Test and Measurement Software Development in C++*
SciTech - v20 - D '96 - p10 [51-250]
Atchity, Kenneth John - *The Classical Greek Reader*
BWatch - v18 - F '97 - p2 [51-250]
LJ - v121 - O 1 '96 - p76 [51-250]
Atencia, Maria Victoria - *Poeziia*
WLT - v71 - Win '97 - p126 [51-250]
Athanasiou, Tom - *Slow Reckoning*
New Sci - v153 - Ja 25 '97 - p44 [251-500]
NS - v126 - Mr 7 '97 - p46+ [501+]
Atherly, Sara - *Math in the Bath and Other Fun Places, Too!*
c   HB Guide - v7 - Fall '96 - p329 [1-50]
Atherton, Ian - *Norwich Cathedral*
Choice - v34 - N '96 - p520 [51-250]

Atherton, Nancy - *Aunt Dimity's Good Deed*
  BL - v93 - S 15 '96 - p223 [51-250]
  KR - v64 - Ag 15 '96 - p1187+ [251-500]
Athkins, D E - *The Bride*
  y BL - v93 - Ap 1 '97 - p1310 [1-50]
  y Kliatt - v30 - N '96 - p4 [51-250]
Atiya, Nayra - *Out El Kouloub*
  BL - v93 - Ja '97 - p822 [51-250]
Atiyeh, George N - *The Book in the Islamic World*
  LQ - v66 - O '96 - p476+ [501+]
  MEJ - v50 - Sum '96 - p454 [51-250]
  Rel St Rev - v23 - Ap '97 - p200 [51-250]
Atkin, S Beth - *Voices from the Streets*
  y BL - v93 - N 1 '96 - p485 [51-250]
  y BL - v93 - Ap 1 '97 - p1286 [1-50]
  y BL - v93 - Ap 1 '97 - p1306 [1-50]
  c CBRS - v25 - O '96 - p20 [51-250]
  c HB - v72 - N '96 - p755+ [51-250]
  c HB Guide - v8 - Spr '97 - p95 [51-250]
  y LATBR - D 8 '96 - p17 [501+]
  c PW - v243 - S 9 '96 - p85 [51-250]
  y SLJ - v42 - O '96 - p152 [51-250]
  y VOYA - v19 - D '96 - p284 [251-500]
Atkins, G Pope - *Encyclopedia of the Inter-American System*
  r BL - v93 - My 15 '97 - p1612 [51-250]
Atkins, Harold N - *Highway Materials, Soils, and Concretes. 3rd Ed.*
  SciTech - v20 - D '96 - p70 [51-250]
Atkins, Martyn - *Informal Empire in Crisis*
  Ch Rev Int - v4 - Spr '97 - p66+ [501+]
Atkins, P W - *Concepts in Physical Chemistry*
  r J Chem Ed - v73 - Je '96 - pA136 [51-250]
  The Periodic Kingdom
  J Chem Ed - v73 - Ag '96 - pA177 [501+]
  New Sci - v152 - N 9 '96 - p43 [1-50]
  The Second Law. Rev. Ed.
  J Chem Ed - v73 - Je '96 - pA135+ [501+]
Atkins, Robert - *From Media to Metaphor*
  Art J - v54 - Win '95 - p87+ [501+]
Atkins, Ronald - *All That Jazz*
  LJ - v121 - O 15 '96 - p59+ [51-250]
Atkinson, A B - *Incomes and the Welfare State*
  JEL - v34 - S '96 - p1412 [51-250]
  Public Economics in Action
  JEL - v34 - S '96 - p1366+ [501+]
Atkinson, David J - *New Dictionary of Christian Ethics and Pastoral Theology*
  r ARBA - v28 - '97 - p549 [51-250]
Atkinson, Diana - *Highways and Dancehalls*
  KR - v65 - Ap 1 '97 - p476 [251-500]
  PW - v244 - Ap 7 '97 - p74 [51-250]
Atkinson, Diane - *The Suffragettes in Pictures*
  HT - v46 - O '96 - p58 [1-50]
Atkinson, Jay - *Caveman Politics*
  BL - v93 - Mr 1 '97 - p1108 [51-250]
  LJ - v122 - Mr 15 '97 - p87 [51-250]
  PW - v244 - F 17 '97 - p210 [51-250]
Atkinson, Kate - *Behind the Scenes at the Museum*
  BL - v93 - Ap 1 '97 - p1285 [1-50]
  Comw - v123 - D 6 '96 - p21 [1-50]
  Comw - v123 - D 6 '96 - p29 [51-250]
  LJ - v121 - O 1 '96 - p46 [1-50]
  NYTBR - v101 - D 8 '96 - p76 [1-50]
  NYTBR - v102 - F 16 '97 - p32 [51-250]
  TES - Jl 19 '96 - pR6 [1-50]
  TES - D 27 '96 - p16 [1-50]
  Trib Bks - Mr 9 '97 - p8 [1-50]
  Human Croquet
  KR - v65 - F 15 '97 - p237 [251-500]
  NS - v126 - Mr 21 '97 - p53 [501+]
  Obs - Mr 9 '97 - p17* [501+]
  PW - v244 - F 10 '97 - p63+ [51-250]
  Spec - v278 - Mr 8 '97 - p31 [501+]
  TLS - Mr 7 '97 - p21 [501+]
Atkinson, Leland - *Cocina!*
  BL - v93 - F 15 '97 - p987 [51-250]
Atkinson, Mary - *Diggers and Dumpers (Illus. by Richard Chasemore)*
  c Ch BWatch - v6 - Jl '96 - p4 [1-50]
  Racers and Roadsters (Illus. by Richard Chasemore)
  c Ch BWatch - v6 - Jl '96 - p4 [1-50]
Atkinson, Michael - *The Secret Marriage of Sherlock Holmes and Other Eccentric Readings*
  CHE - v43 - O 18 '96 - pA20 [51-250]
  Choice - v34 - F '97 - p963 [51-250]
Atkinson, Rick - *Crusade: The Untold Story of the Gulf War (Riggenbach). Audio Version*
  BL - v93 - N 1 '96 - p522 [51-250]
  y Kliatt - v31 - Ja '97 - p48 [51-250]

Atkinson, Robert S - *Stereoselective Synthesis*
  J Chem Ed - v73 - Ap '96 - pA93 [51-250]
Atkinson, W Patrick - *Theatrical Design in the Twentieth Century*
  r Choice - v34 - D '96 - p585 [51-250]
  r R&R Bk N - v11 - N '96 - p67 [51-250]
Atlan, Liliane - *Bonheur Mais Sur Quel Ton Le Dire*
  WLT - v71 - Win '97 - p107 [501+]
Atlanta Regional Commission - *Atlanta Region Outlook 1994*
  J Gov Info - v23 - S '96 - p599 [51-250]
Atlas, Nava - *Vegetarian Soups for All Seasons*
  LJ - v121 - O 15 '96 - p86 [51-250]
  PW - v243 - S 2 '96 - p124 [51-250]
Atlas Des Sites Du Proche Orient 14000-5700 BP
  r AJA - v100 - Jl '96 - p634 [501+]
The Atlas of Literature
  r BL - v93 - D 15 '96 - p745 [251-500]
  r Bloom Rev - v17 - Ja '97 - p15 [51-250]
  r BW - v26 - D 8 '96 - p15 [51-250]
  r Econ - v341 - D 7 '96 - p15* [51-250]
  Spec - v277 - S 28 '96 - p51+ [501+]
  r TES - S 27 '96 - p7* [501+]
  r TLS - N 1 '96 - p12+ [501+]
An Atlas of U.S. Economy, Technology, and Growth
  r ARBA - v28 - '97 - p324+ [51-250]
ATSDR's Toxicological Profiles on CD-ROM. Electronic Media Version
  r Choice - v34 - My '97 - p1532 [251-500]
Attacks on the Freedom to Learn. 14th Ed.
  ChrPhil - v9 - N 14 '96 - p39 [51-250]
Attanasio, A A - *The Dragon and the Unicorn*
  y VOYA - v19 - F '97 - p334 [251-500]
Attard-Montalto, Simon - *Paediatric MCQs for Postgraduate Examinations. Vol. 2*
  SciTech - v20 - N '96 - p52 [1-50]
Attenborough, David - *The Private Life of Plants*
  Fine Gard - S '96 - p68 [501+]
Attenborough, Robert D - *Human Biology in Papua New Guinea*
  Cont Pac - v8 - Fall '96 - p473+ [501+]
Attig, Thomas - *How We Grieve*
  Choice - v34 - My '97 - p1578 [51-250]
  Readings - v12 - Mr '97 - p22 [51-250]
Atton, Chris - *Alternative Literature*
  r Choice - v34 - O '96 - p248 [51-250]
  r LAR - v98 - Jl '96 - p369 [251-500]
  r R&R Bk N - v12 - F '97 - p102 [51-250]
Attwater, Donald - *The Penguin Dictionary of Saints. 3rd Ed.*
  r ARBA - v28 - '97 - p535 [51-250]
Attwood, Bain - *In the Age of Mabo*
  Aust Bk R - Je '96 - p12+ [501+]
  Choice - v34 - Ja '97 - p853 [51-250]
Attwood, Dennis A - *The Office Relocation Sourcebook*
  R&R Bk N - v12 - F '97 - p38 [51-250]
Atwell, Debby - *Barn (Illus. by Debby Atwell)*
  c BL - v93 - O 1 '96 - p357 [51-250]
  c CBRS - v25 - D '96 - p37 [1-50]
  c HB Guide - v8 - Spr '97 - p18 [51-250]
  c PW - v243 - S 2 '96 - p129+ [51-250]
  c SLJ - v42 - Ag '96 - p115 [51-250]
  c SLJ - v42 - D '96 - p27 [1-50]
Atwell, John E - *Schopenhauer on the Character of the World*
  RM - v49 - Je '96 - p910+ [501+]
  TLS - D 27 '96 - p27 [501+]
Atwell, Nancie - *In the Middle*
  New Ad - v9 - Fall '96 - p309+ [501+]

Atwood, Margaret - *Alias Grace*
  BIC - v25 - D '96 - p10+ [501+]
  BL - v93 - Ja '97 - p760 [51-250]
  BL - v93 - S 15 '96 - p180 [51-250]
  Bloom Rev - v17 - Ja '97 - p8 [501+]
  BW - v26 - D 22 '96 - p1+ [501+]
  CF - v75 - Ja '97 - p39+ [501+]
  CSM - v89 - Ja 16 '97 - p14 [51-250]
  CSM - v89 - F 20 '97 - p10 [51-250]
  CSM - v89 - F 21 '97 - p14 [501+]
  Ent W - N 29 '96 - p83 [51-250]
  KR - v64 - S 15 '96 - p1338 [251-500]
  LATBR - D 15 '96 - p2 [501+]
  LATBR - D 29 '96 - p11 [1-50]
  LJ - v122 - Ja '97 - p48 [51-250]
  LJ - v121 - N 1 '96 - p106 [51-250]
  Mac - v109 - D 9 '96 - p64 [1-50]
  Ms - v7 - Ja '97 - p79 [251-500]
  Nat - v263 - D 9 '96 - p25+ [501+]
  Nat R - v49 - F 10 '97 - p58 [251-500]
  NY - v72 - Ja 27 '97 - p76 [51-250]
  NYRB - v43 - D 19 '96 - p4+ [501+]
  NYTBR - v101 - D 29 '96 - p6 [501+]
  NYTLa - v146 - D 12 '96 - pC19 [501+]
  PW - v243 - O 7 '96 - p58 [251-500]
  PW - v243 - N 4 '96 - p37 [51-250]
  Quill & Q - v62 - S '96 - p63 [251-500]
  Quill & Q - v63 - F '97 - p50 [51-250]
  Spec - v277 - S 14 '96 - p36 [501+]
  Spec - v277 - N 16 '96 - p42 [1-50]
  Spec - v277 - N 30 '96 - p58 [51-250]
  TES - N 15 '96 - p8* [51-250]
  Time - v149 - D 16 '96 - p76 [501+]
  TLS - S 13 '96 - p23 [501+]
  Trib Bks - Ja 19 '97 - p1+ [501+]
  W&I - v12 - F '97 - p262+ [501+]
  Woman's J - O '96 - p12 [51-250]
  WSJ-MW - v78 - N 15 '96 - pA12 [501+]
  Alias Grace (McGovern). Audio Version
  BWatch - v18 - Mr '97 - p7 [1-50]
  y Kliatt - v31 - My '97 - p35 [51-250]
  Quill & Q - v62 - N '96 - p41 [1-50]
  Bluebeard's Egg
  y Kliatt - v31 - Mr '97 - p21 [1-50]
  Cat's Eye
  y BL - v93 - Ja '97 - p832 [1-50]
  The Handmaid's Tale
  Critiq - v38 - Win '97 - p83+ [501+]
  Princess Prunella and the Purple Peanut
  c Ch BWatch - v6 - My '96 - p4 [1-50]
Atwood, Richard - *Mary Magdalene in the New Testament Gospels and Early Tradition*
  Rel St Rev - v23 - Ap '97 - p186+ [51-250]
Atxaga, Bernardo - *The Lone Man*
  BL - v93 - Ja '97 - p815 [51-250]
  KR - v65 - Ja 15 '97 - p75 [251-500]
  LJ - v122 - F 1 '97 - p104 [51-250]
  NYTBR - v102 - Ap 20 '97 - p20 [51-250]
  PW - v243 - D 30 '96 - p55 [51-250]
  TLS - Ag 2 '96 - p22 [501+]
  Obabakoak
  TranslRevS - v1 - My '95 - p14 [51-250]
Atzeni, Sergio - *Passavamo Sulla Terra Leggeri*
  BL - v93 - D 1 '96 - p644 [1-50]
Au, Wilkie - *Urgings of the Heart*
  RR - v55 - S '96 - p541+ [251-500]
Aubert, Jean-Jacques - *Business Managers in Ancient Rome*
  AHR - v101 - D '96 - p1526+ [501+]
  AJP - v117 - Fall '96 - p501+ [501+]
Aubert, Rosemary - *Free Reign*
  LJ - v122 - F 1 '97 - p111 [51-250]
  NYTBR - v102 - Mr 30 '97 - p23 [51-250]
  PW - v244 - F 10 '97 - p70 [51-250]
Aubrey, Elizabeth - *The Music of the Troubadours*
  AB - v98 - D 9 '96 - p1994 [501+]
  Choice - v34 - Mr '97 - p1171 [51-250]
  Choice - v34 - Ap '97 - p1346 [51-250]
  FF - v20 - Mr '97 - p423+ [501+]
Auch, Mary Jane - *Eggs Mark the Spot*
  c HB Guide - v7 - Fall '96 - p247 [51-250]
  c PW - v244 - F 17 '97 - p220 [1-50]
  Hen Lake (Illus. by Mary Jane Auch)
  c PW - v243 - Jl 22 '96 - p243 [1-50]
  c RT - v50 - Mr '97 - p503 [51-250]
  Journey to Nowhere
  c KR - v65 - Mr 1 '97 - p376+ [51-250]
  c PW - v244 - My 12 '97 - p77 [51-250]
  Peeping Beauty. Book and Audio Version
  c Ch BWatch - v6 - N '96 - p7 [51-250]

Auchincloss, Louis - *La Gloire: The Roman Empire of Corneille and Racine*
  LJ - v122 - F 1 '97 - p78 [51-250]
  PW - v243 - O 21 '96 - p63 [51-250]
The Man behind the Book
  BL - v93 - D 1 '96 - p639 [51-250]
  KR - v64 - O 15 '96 - p1501+ [251-500]
  LJ - v121 - N 15 '96 - p61 [51-250]
  NYTBR - v101 - D 22 '96 - p14 [51-250]
  PW - v243 - O 21 '96 - p63 [51-250]
Auden, W H - *As I Walked Out One Evening*
  Obs - Ja 5 '97 - p17* [51-250]
  TES - F 21 '97 - p7* [51-250]
Essays and Reviews and Travel Books in Prose and Verse
  Obs - Mr 16 '97 - p15* [501+]
In Solitude for Company
  Choice - v34 - S '96 - p121 [51-250]
The Language of Learning and the Language of Love
  RES - v48 - F '97 - p134+ [501+]
Prose and Travel Books in Prose and Verse. Vol. 1
  BL - v93 - N 1 '96 - p476 [51-250]
  LJ - v121 - N 15 '96 - p61 [51-250]
  NYRB - v44 - Ap 10 '97 - p50+ [501+]
  PW - v243 - D 16 '96 - p53 [51-250]
Audi, Robert - *The Cambridge Dictionary of Philosophy*
  r ARBA - v28 - '97 - p528 [51-250]
  r Ethics - v107 - Ja '97 - p381+ [501+]
  r Rel St - v32 - D '96 - p529 [251-500]
  r TES - Ag 23 '96 - p27 [251-500]
Audin, Michele - *Spinning Tops*
  Choice - v34 - Ap '97 - p1375 [51-250]
  SciTech - v20 - D '96 - p18 [1-50]
AudioFile
  p LJ - v122 - F 15 '97 - p167 [51-250]
Auditory Neuroscience
  p Nature - v383 - S 5 '96 - p34 [251-500]
Audretsch, David B - *Innovation and Industry Evolution*
  JEL - v34 - D '96 - p1985+ [501+]
Audry-Llyic, Francoise - *Mes Premiers Chiffres*
  c BL - v93 - N 1 '96 - p500 [1-50]
Auerbach, Alan - *The World of Work*
  Per Psy - v49 - Win '96 - p1039+ [501+]
Auerbach, Ann Hagedorn - *Wild Ride*
  Aethlon - v13 - Fall '95 - p165+ [251-500]
Auerbach, Jessica - *Catch Your Breath*
  BWatch - v17 - D '96 - p6 [51-250]
Auerbach, Jonathan - *Male Call*
  Choice - v34 - My '97 - p1493 [51-250]
Auerbach, Judith D - *AIDS and Behavior*
  AJPsych - v154 - F '97 - p279 [501+]
Auerbach, Michael - *Conversations about Cancer*
  LJ - v122 - Ja '97 - p56 [1-50]
Auerbach, Nina - *Our Vampires, Ourselves*
  ABR - v18 - O '96 - p10 [501+]
  Choice - v34 - S '96 - p110 [51-250]
  ELT - v39 - 4 '96 - p491+ [501+]
  Lon R Bks - v18 - S 19 '96 - p17 [501+]
  Necro - Sum '96 - p5+ [501+]
Auerochs, Bernd - *Erzahlte Gesellschaft*
  Ger Q - v69 - Sum '96 - p356+ [501+]
Augarde, A J - *Oxford Primary School Dictionary*
  cr Bks Keeps - v100 - S '96 - p22+ [501+]
Augarde, Steve - *The Hokey Pokey and Other Party Rhymes*
  c PW - v243 - D 16 '96 - p61 [51-250]
The Itsy Bitsy Spider and Other Hand Rhymes
  c PW - v243 - D 16 '96 - p61 [51-250]
Augenbraum, Harold - *The Latino Reader*
  y BL - v93 - Mr 1 '97 - p1104 [51-250]
  LJ - v122 - Mr 15 '97 - p64 [51-250]
  PW - v244 - F 17 '97 - p207 [51-250]
  Trib Bks - Ap 20 '97 - p8 [1-50]
Latinos in English
  r RQ - v36 - Win '96 - p222 [51-250]
Aughey, Arthur - *Northern Ireland Politics*
  Choice - v34 - O '96 - p355 [51-250]
  TLS - S 20 '96 - p11 [501+]
Augustin, Ernst - *Gutes Geld*
  WLT - v71 - Win '97 - p135 [251-500]
Augustin, George - *Gott Eint--Trennt Christus?*
  Theol St - v57 - Mr '96 - p166+ [501+]
Augustine, Saint, Bishop of Hippo - *Arianism and Other Heresies*
  CHR - v83 - Ja '97 - p159 [51-250]
Augustine: De Doctrina Christiana (Green)
  Rel St Rev - v23 - Ap '97 - p189 [51-250]
The Confessions
  Cres - v60 - Christmas '96 - p9+ [501+]

The Confessions of Saint Augustine (Rotelle)
  BL - v93 - D 15 '96 - p694 [51-250]
  LJ - v122 - Ja '97 - p106 [51-250]
Augustine, Dolores L - *Patricians and Parvenus*
  EHR - v112 - F '97 - p249+ [501+]
Augustine, Jane - *Ecce Kosti*
  Sm Pr R - v28 - D '96 - p10 [251-500]
Augustinus, Aurelius - *Teaching Christianity*
  CLW - v67 - D '96 - p37 [51-250]
Auksi, Peter - *Christian Plain Style*
  CH - v65 - D '96 - p784+ [501+]
  JR - v77 - Ap '97 - p349+ [251-500]
  Six Ct J - v27 - Win '96 - p1162+ [501+]
  Theol St - v57 - D '96 - p776+ [251-500]
Auletta, Ken - *The Highwaymen: Warriors on the Information Superhighway*
  PW - v244 - Ap 14 '97 - p67 [51-250]
Aulin, Arvid - *Causal and Stochastic Elements in Business Cycles*
  JEL - v34 - D '96 - p2034 [51-250]
Aumann, Robert J - *Repeated Games with Incomplete Information*
  JEL - v35 - Mr '97 - p126+ [501+]
Aune, James Arnt - *Rhetoric and Marxism*
  QJS - v82 - N '96 - p402+ [501+]
Aune, Michael B - *Religious and Social Ritual*
  R&R Bk N - v12 - F '97 - p8 [51-250]
Aura, Alejandro - *The Other Side (Illus. by Julia Gukova)*
  c JB - v60 - O '96 - p181 [51-250]
  c Sch Lib - v44 - Ag '96 - p104 [51-250]
Aurelio, John R - *Earth Stories*
  BL - v93 - Mr 1 '97 - p1111 [51-250]
Ause, Wayne - *Instant HTML Web Page*
  Quill & Q - v62 - N '96 - p32 [51-250]
Auslander, Leora - *Taste and Power*
  Choice - v34 - N '96 - p515 [51-250]
  TLS - D 13 '96 - p8 [501+]
Aust, Patricia H - *Benni and Victoria (Illus. by Robert Sprouse)*
  c Ch BWatch - v6 - D '96 - p5 [51-250]
  c SLJ - v43 - Ja '97 - p75 [51-250]
Austad, Carol Shaw - *Is Long-Term Psychotherapy Unethical?*
  Readings - v12 - Mr '97 - p6+ [501+]
  SciTech - v20 - N '96 - p43 [51-250]
Austad, Steven N - *Why We Age*
  KR - v65 - My 1 '97 - p687 [251-500]
  PW - v244 - My 12 '97 - p70 [251-500]
Austell, Diane - *While the Music Plays*
  PW - v243 - S 9 '96 - p81 [51-250]
  PW - v243 - N 4 '96 - p40 [1-50]
Austen, Carol D - *Perspectives on Case Management Practice*
  Fam in Soc - v77 - S '96 - p449+ [501+]
Austen, Eric - *All That I Was*
  TES - D 27 '96 - p22 [51-250]
Austen, Jane - *Emma*
  Books - v11 - Ap '97 - p23 [1-50]
  LJ - v122 - Mr 15 '97 - p94 [1-50]
  W&I - v11 - S '96 - p270+ [501+]
Emma (Agutter). Audio Version
  LJ - v122 - F 15 '97 - p174 [51-250]
Emma (Keith). Audio Version
  TLS - Ag 2 '96 - p24 [501+]
Emma (Page). Audio Version
  y Kliatt - v31 - My '97 - p38 [51-250]
Emma (Scales). Audio Version
  TLS - Ag 2 '96 - p24 [501+]
Emma (Shaw). Audio Version
  TLS - Ag 2 '96 - p24 [501+]
Emma (Thompson). Audio Version
  BL - v93 - Ja '97 - p879 [51-250]
Jane Austen's Letters
  Obs - Ap 6 '97 - p18* [51-250]
Mansfield Park
  W&I - v11 - S '96 - p268
Mansfield Park. Audio Version
  BWatch - v18 - Mr '97 - p6 [1-50]
Northanger Abbey
  W&I - v11 - S '96 - p272+ [501+]
Persuasion
  RES - v48 - F '97 - p125+ [251-500]
  W&I - v11 - S '96 - p271+ [501+]
Persuasion (Scacchi). Audio Version
  BL - v92 - Ag '96 - p1917 [51-250]
The Poetry of Jane Austen and the Austen Family
  LJ - v122 - My 1 '97 - p102 [51-250]
Pride and Prejudice
  W&I - v11 - S '96 - p264+ [501+]
Sense and Sensibility
  W&I - v11 - S '96 - p266+ [501+]

Sense and Sensibility (Harker). Audio Version
  BL - v93 - Mr 15 '97 - p1253 [51-250]
  y Kliatt - v31 - Ja '97 - p45 [51-250]
  LJ - v121 - N 1 '96 - p122 [51-250]
Austen, K Frank - *Therapeutic Immunology*
  SciTech - v20 - N '96 - p55 [51-250]
Austen-Leigh, Joan - *Later Days at Highbury*
  LJ - v122 - Ap 1 '97 - p156 [51-250]
  NYTBR - v101 - D 1 '96 - p23 [51-250]
  PW - v243 - O 21 '96 - p72 [51-250]
  y SLJ - v43 - Mr '97 - p214 [51-250]
Auster, Ethel - *Managing Information for the Competitive Edge*
  R&R Bk N - v12 - F '97 - p37 [51-250]
Auster, Paul - *Why Write?*
  PW - v243 - S 23 '96 - p72 [51-250]
Austin, Guy - *Contemporary French Cinema*
  Choice - v34 - Mr '97 - p1170 [51-250]
Austin, Mary C - *Literature for Children and Young Adults about Oceania*
  r ARBA - v28 - '97 - p73 [251-500]
  r JOYS - v10 - Fall '96 - p96 [251-500]
Austin, Mary Hunter - *Beyond Borders*
  AL - v69 - Mr '97 - p248 [51-250]
A Mary Austin Reader
  Ant R - v54 - Fall '96 - p493+ [251-500]
  Choice - v34 - N '96 - p457 [51-250]
  WHQ - v27 - Win '96 - p551+ [1-50]
Austin, Norman - *Helen of Troy and Her Shameless Phantom*
  Class Out - v74 - Fall '96 - p39 [251-500]
Austin, Paul Britten - *The Great Retreat*
  TLS - N 29 '96 - p12 [1-50]
Austin, Timothy R - *Poetic Voices*
  MLR - v92 - Ja '97 - p145+ [501+]
Austin, Tom - *The O'Malley Saga. Bk. 1*
  Roundup M - v4 - F '97 - p26 [51-250]
Austin, Virginia - *Say Please*
  c ECEJ - v24 - Win '96 - p108 [1-50]
Austin Locations (Demographics and Forecasting Group, Austin, Texas)
  r J Gov Info - v23 - S '96 - p599+ [51-250]
Australia: A Continent Revealed
  Nature - v384 - N 28 '96 - p326 [51-250]
Australia Handbook
  r FEER - v160 - Mr 27 '97 - p52+ [501+]
Australia Productivity Commission - *International Cooperation on Competition Policy*
  JEL - v35 - Mr '97 - p247 [51-250]
The Australia-U.S. Trade and Investment Review
  J Gov Info - v23 - S '96 - p651 [51-250]
Australian-Pacific Conference on Contaminants and Soil Environment in the Australasia-Pacific Region (1st: 1996: Adelaide, S. Aust.) - *Contaminants and the Soil Environment in the Australasia-Pacific Region*
  SciTech - v20 - D '96 - p70 [51-250]
Australian Software Engineering Conference (1996: Melbourne, Vic.) - *1996 Australian Software Engineering Conference*
  SciTech - v20 - N '96 - p9 [51-250]
Australia's Welfare and Services Assistance 1995
  Soc Ser R - v71 - Mr '97 - p166+ [51-250]
Autonomous Robots
  p Nature - v383 - S 5 '96 - p43+ [251-500]
Autry, James A - *Confessions of an Accidental Businessman*
  BL - v93 - O 1 '96 - p310 [51-250]
  LJ - v121 - O 1 '96 - p94 [51-250]
  LJ - v122 - Mr 15 '97 - p35 [1-50]
Auty, Richard M - *Challenging the Orthodoxies*
  Choice - v34 - F '97 - p1010 [51-250]
Patterns of Development
  GJ - v162 - Jl '96 - p234 [251-500]
Avakian, Arlene Voski - *Through the Kitchen Window*
  BL - v93 - My 15 '97 - p1554 [51-250]
  PW - v244 - Ap 14 '97 - p65 [51-250]
Avec
  p Sm Pr R - v28 - D '96 - p13+ [501+]
Avedon, Richard - *In the American West*
  LJ - v121 - O 15 '96 - p94 [1-50]
  Obs - D 1 '96 - p18* [1-50]
Avellan De Tamayo, Nieves - *Los Escribanos De Venezuela*
  HAHR - v77 - My '97 - p317+ [251-500]
Avellaneda Navas, Jose Ignacio - *The Conquerers of the New Kingdom of Granada*
  JIH - v27 - Spr '97 - p733+ [251-500]
Avena, Thomas - *Dream of Order*
  LJ - v122 - Ap 1 '97 - p97 [51-250]
Jerome: After the Pagent
  LJ - v121 - D '96 - p87 [51-250]

Avenhaus, Rudolf - *Compliance Quantified*
  SciTech - v20 - D '96 - p6 [51-250]
Aveni, Anthony F - *Ancient Astronomers*
  Isis - v88 - Mr '97 - p131+ [501+]
  Behind the Crystal Ball
  y   BL - v92 - Ag '96 - p1858 [51-250]
  y   BL - v92 - Ag '96 - p1890 [1-50]
      Nature - v385 - Ja 30 '97 - p405+ [501+]
      New Sci - v152 - N 16 '96 - p45 [51-250]
      NYTBR - v101 - N 17 '96 - p32+ [501+]
      TLS - D 27 '96 - p30 [501+]
Avery, Charles - *David Le Marchand 1674-1726*
  BM - v138 - D '96 - p838+ [501+]
Avery, Gillian - *Behold the Child*
  AHR - v101 - O '96 - p1266+ [501+]
  AL - v69 - Mr '97 - p211+ [251-500]
  ChLAQ - v21 - Fall '96 - p142+ [501+]
  J Am Cult - v18 - Win '95 - p106 [51-250]
  JOYS - v9 - Sum '96 - p408 [251-500]
Avery, Martha - *Women of Mongolia*
  NH - v106 - F '97 - p13 [1-50]
  WorldV - v13 - Ja '97 - p12 [251-500]
Aves, Jonathan - *Workers against Lenin*
  HRNB - v25 - Win '96 - p83 [251-500]
Avi - *Beyond the Western Sea. Bk. 1*
  y   BL - v93 - Ja '97 - p764 [1-50]
  y   BL - v93 - Ap 1 '97 - p1288 [1-50]
  y   Emerg Lib - v24 - S '96 - p43 [1-50]
  c   HB Guide - v7 - Fall '96 - p289 [51-250]
  Beyond the Western Sea. Bk. 2
  y   CCB-B - v50 - D '96 - p128 [51-250]
  y   CLW - v67 - D '96 - p65 [51-250]
  y   CSM - v88 - N 21 '96 - pB4 [51-250]
  c   HB - v72 - N '96 - p731+ [251-500]
  c   HB Guide - v8 - Spr '97 - p61 [51-250]
  y   SLJ - v42 - O '96 - p144 [51-250]
  y   VOYA - v19 - D '96 - p267 [251-500]
  Beyond the Western Sea. Bks. 1-2
  y   BW - v26 - D 8 '96 - p21 [51-250]
  y   Learning - v25 - N '96 - p30 [51-250]
  Finding Providence (Illus. by James Watling)
  c   BL - v93 - F 1 '97 - p949 [51-250]
  c   CCB-B - v50 - Mr '97 - p240 [51-250]
  c   HB - v73 - My '97 - p313+ [51-250]
  c   KR - v65 - Ja 1 '97 - p56 [51-250]
  c   SLJ - v43 - Mr '97 - p170 [51-250]
  The Man Who Was Poe
  y   JAAL - v40 - S '96 - p317 [51-250]
  Poppy (Illus. by Brian Floca)
  c   LA - v73 - O '96 - p431+ [51-250]
  c   PW - v244 - F 3 '97 - p108 [1-50]
  c   RT - v50 - O '96 - p158 [51-250]
  c   SLJ - v42 - N '96 - p40 [1-50]
  Smugglers' Island (Guidall). Audio Version
  c   HB - v72 - S '96 - p566+ [501+]
  The True Confessions of Charlotte Doyle (Illus. by Ruth E Murray)
  c   JOYS - v10 - Fall '96 - p35+ [501+]
  c   JOYS - v10 - Fall '96 - p92+ [501+]
  y   Kliatt - v30 - S '96 - p2 [1-50]
  c   SLJ - v42 - N '96 - p40 [51-250]
  Wolf Rider
  y   JAAL - v40 - D '96 - p317 [51-250]
Avila, Maria Regina - *Cartas A Maria Regina*
  BL - v93 - Mr 15 '97 - p1232 [1-50]
Aviles Farre, Juan - *Pasion Y Farsa*
  EHR - v111 - S '96 - p1023+ [501+]
Aviram, J - *Masada: The Yigael Yadin Excavations 1963-1965. Vols. 1-5*
  Rel St Rev - v23 - Ap '97 - p193+ [51-250]
Avis, Kenneth E - *Biotechnology and Biopharmaceutical Manufacturing, Processing, and Preservation*
  SciTech - v20 - N '96 - p56 [51-250]
Avis, Nick - *Bending with the Wind*
  Can Lit - Win '96 - p142+ [501+]
Avis, Patricia - *Playing the Harlot or Mostly Coffee*
  TLS - Jl 19 '96 - p21 [501+]
Avitov, Yaron - *Adon Ha-Selihot*
  BL - v93 - Mr 1 '97 - p1115 [1-50]
Avramovic, Mila - *An Affordable Development?*
  SciTech - v20 - S '96 - p59 [51-250]
Avrich, Paul - *Anarchist Voices*
  BW - v26 - Ag 18 '96 - p12 [51-250]
  Historian - v58 - Sum '96 - p854+ [251-500]
  J Am St - v30 - Ap '96 - p165+ [251-500]
Avriel, Mordecai - *Mathematical Programming for Industrial Engineers*
  SciTech - v20 - S '96 - p46 [1-50]
Avruch, Kevin - *Critical Essays on Israeli Society, Religion, and Government. Vol. 4*
  MEJ - v51 - Spr '97 - p309 [51-250]

Al-Awadhi, N - *Restoration and Rehabilitation of the Desert Environment*
  SciTech - v21 - Mr '97 - p82 [51-250]
Awalt, Barbe - *Charlie Carrillo: Tradition and Soul*
  Bloom Rev - v16 - Jl '96 - p17+ [501+]
Awan, Shaila - *Fabulous Faces*
  c   CCB-B - v50 - Ja '97 - p169 [51-250]
The Awards Almanac 1996
  r   ARBA - v28 - '97 - p317+ [251-500]
Awdry, Christopher - *Learn with Thomas*
  c   HB Guide - v7 - Fall '96 - p236 [51-250]
Awe, Bolanle - *Nigerian Women in Historical Perspective*
  Africa T - v43 - '96 - p323+ [501+]
Awmiller, Craig - *This House on Fire*
  y   CCB-B - v50 - S '96 - p5 [51-250]
  c   HB Guide - v7 - Fall '96 - p357 [51-250]
  y   Kliatt - v31 - Mr '97 - p35 [51-250]
  y   VOYA - v19 - F '97 - p343 [251-500]
  Wynton Marsalis: Gifted Trumpet Player
  c   BL - v92 - Ag '96 - p1897 [51-250]
  c   HB Guide - v7 - Fall '96 - p371 [51-250]
  c   SLJ - v42 - Ag '96 - p148 [51-250]
Axelrod, Alan - *Cops, Crooks, and Criminologists*
  r   ARBA - v28 - '97 - p226+ [251-500]
  yr SLJ - v43 - Ja '97 - p142 [51-250]
Axelrod, Amy - *Pigs in the Pantry (Illus. by Sharon McGinley-Nally)*
  c   BL - v93 - Mr 1 '97 - p1168 [51-250]
  c   CCB-B - v50 - My '97 - p312 [51-250]
  c   KR - v65 - Mr 15 '97 - p458 [51-250]
  Pigs on a Blanket (Illus. by Sharon McGinley-Nally)
  c   HB Guide - v7 - Fall '96 - p247 [51-250]
Axford, J S - *Medicine*
  SciTech - v20 - D '96 - p41 [51-250]
Axler, Leo - *Separated by Death*
  Arm Det - v29 - Fall '96 - p498+ [251-500]
Axline, W Andrew - *The Political Economy of Regional Cooperation*
  Cont Pac - v8 - Fall '96 - p467+ [501+]
Axtell, Horace P - *A Little Bit of Wisdom*
  LJ - v121 - O 15 '96 - p65 [51-250]
Ayala, Victor - *Falling through the Cracks*
  Choice - v34 - S '96 - p161 [51-250]
Ayalon, Ami - *The Press in the Arab Middle East*
  AHR - v101 - D '96 - p1590+ [501+]
  Rel St Rev - v23 - Ap '97 - p201+ [51-250]
Ayalon, David - *Islam and the Abode of War*
  Rel St Rev - v22 - O '96 - p356 [51-250]
Ayalti, Hanan J - *The Presence Is in Exile, Too*
  PW - v244 - Ap 28 '97 - p51 [251-500]
Ayan, Jordan - *Aha! 10 Ways to Free Your Creative Spirit and Find Your Great Ideas*
  LJ - v122 - Ap 1 '97 - p102+ [51-250]
  PW - v244 - Ja 13 '97 - p68 [1-50]
Ayanoglu, Byron - *The New Vegetarian Gourmet*
  Quill & Q - v62 - Ag '96 - p30 [51-250]
Aycliffe, Jonathan - *The Lost*
  KR - v64 - Ag 15 '96 - p1166 [251-500]
  PW - v243 - S 16 '96 - p72 [51-250]
  y   VOYA - v19 - F '97 - p334 [251-500]
Ayd, Frank - *Lexicon of Psychiatry, Neurology and the Neurosciences*
  r   J ClinPsyc - v57 - Jl '96 - p313 [251-500]
Ayer, Eleanor H - *Adolf Hitler*
  c   HB Guide - v7 - Fall '96 - p370 [1-50]
  Everything You Need to Know about Teen Marriage
  y   SLJ - v42 - O '96 - p45 [1-50]
  Germany: In the Heartland of Europe
  c   HB Guide - v7 - Fall '96 - p381+ [51-250]
  Homeless Children
  y   HB Guide - v8 - Spr '97 - p95 [51-250]
  Parallel Journeys
  y   Emerg Lib - v24 - S '96 - p23 [1-50]
  y   RT - v50 - Mr '97 - p479+ [501+]
  Poland: A Troubled Past, a New Start
  c   HB Guide - v8 - Spr '97 - p168 [51-250]
Ayers, Edward L - *All over the Map*
  JSH - v63 - F '97 - p217+ [501+]
  WHQ - v27 - Win '96 - p518+ [251-500]
  The Oxford Book of the American South
  y   BL - v93 - My 1 '97 - p1475 [51-250]
  LJ - v122 - Ap 15 '97 - p82 [51-250]
Ayers, Tom - *The Illustrated Rules of Ice Hockey*
  c   Ch BWatch - v6 - O '96 - p6 [51-250]
Ayers, William - *City Kids, City Teachers*
  JAAL - v40 - S '96 - p79 [1-50]
  NASSP-B - v80 - O '96 - p117+ [501+]
  A Kind and Just Parent
  y   BL - v93 - My 1 '97 - p1465 [501+]

Aylesworth, Jim - *My Sister's Rusty Bike (Illus. by Richard Hull)*
  c   BL - v93 - N 15 '96 - p592+ [51-250]
  c   Ch BWatch - v7 - F '97 - p2 [51-250]
  c   HB Guide - v8 - Spr '97 - p18 [51-250]
  c   KR - v64 - S 1 '96 - p1319 [51-250]
  c   SLJ - v42 - O '96 - p84 [51-250]
  One Crow
  c   BL - v93 - Ap 1 '97 - p1340 [1-50]
  Teddy Bear Tears (Illus. by Jo Ellen McAllister-Stammen)
  c   BL - v93 - Ap 1 '97 - p1336 [51-250]
  Wake Up, Little Children (Illus. by Walter Lyon Krudop)
  c   HB Guide - v7 - Fall '96 - p247 [51-250]
Aylett, J F - *The Cold War and After*
  y   Sch Lib - v45 - F '97 - p49 [51-250]
Ayllon, Candido - *Spanish Composition through Literature. 3rd Ed.*
  MLJ - v81 - Spr '97 - p143 [501+]
Aylmer, Gerald - *Constitutional Royalism and the Search for Settlement c. 1640-9*
  EHR - v111 - N '96 - p1284+ [251-500]
Ayoob, Mohammed - *The Third World Security Predicament*
  SSQ - v77 - Je '96 - p467+ [501+]
Ayres, Becky Hickox - *Matreshka (Illus. by Alexi Natchev)*
  c   PW - v243 - N 18 '96 - p78 [51-250]
Ayres, E C - *Night of the Panther*
  BL - v93 - My 1 '97 - p1481 [51-250]
  LJ - v122 - My 1 '97 - p144 [1-50]
  PW - v244 - My 12 '97 - p62 [51-250]
Ayres, James E - *The Archaeology of Spanish and Mexican Colonialism in the American Southwest*
  Am Ant - v62 - Ja '97 - p162+ [501+]
  The Historical Archaeology of Dam Construction Camps in Central Arizona. Vol. 2A
  Pub Hist - v18 - Fall '96 - p162+ [501+]
Ayres, Katherine - *Family Tree*
  c   BL - v93 - N 15 '96 - p585 [51-250]
  c   CBRS - v25 - F '97 - p81 [51-250]
  c   CCB-B - v50 - F '97 - p198+ [51-250]
  c   HB Guide - v8 - Spr '97 - p62 [51-250]
  c   KR - v64 - O 15 '96 - p1528 [51-250]
  c   PW - v243 - N 18 '96 - p76 [51-250]
  c   SLJ - v42 - N '96 - p103 [51-250]
Ayres, Pam - *The Nubbler*
  c   TES - Mr 7 '97 - p12* [501+]
Ayres, Stephen M - *Health Care in the United States*
  Choice - v34 - N '96 - p490 [51-250]
Ayres-Bennett, Wendy - *A History of the French Language through Texts*
  FR - v70 - F '97 - p482+ [501+]
  Syntax and the Literary System
  MLR - v92 - Ja '97 - p184 [251-500]
Ayto, John - *The Oxford Dictionary of Modern Slang*
  r   CAY - v17 - Fall '96 - p9 [51-250]
Ayton, Andrew - *Knights and Warhorses*
  EHR - v112 - Ap '97 - p446 [251-500]
  Specu - v71 - O '96 - p927+ [501+]
Azaroff, Leonid V - *Physics over Easy*
  Choice - v34 - D '96 - p648 [51-250]
Azikiwe, Uche - *Women in Nigeria*
  r   ARBA - v28 - '97 - p331 [251-500]
  r   Choice - v34 - D '96 - p585 [51-250]
  r   R&R Bk N - v11 - N '96 - p42 [51-250]
Aziz, Nurjehan - *Her Mother's Ashes and Other Stories by South Asian Women in Canada and the United States*
  Can Lit - Win '96 - p178+ [501+]
Azkoul, Michael - *St. Gregory of Nyssa and the Tradition of the Fathers*
  Rel St Rev - v23 - Ja '97 - p78 [51-250]
Azua, Felix De - *Diary of a Humiliated Man*
  BW - v26 - D 22 '96 - p9 [51-250]
  Choice - v34 - My '97 - p1503 [51-250]
  LJ - v121 - O 1 '96 - p126 [51-250]
  PW - v243 - N 4 '96 - p37 [1-50]
Azwell, Tara - *Report Card on Report Cards*
  Learning - v25 - S '96 - p48+ [51-250]
Azzopardi, Mario - *Naked as Water*
  Sm Pr R - v28 - N '96 - p9 [501+]
  TranslRevS - v2 - D '96 - p29 [51-250]
  WLT - v71 - Win '97 - p197+ [501+]
Azzouni, Jody - *Metaphysical Myths, Mathematical Practice*
  Phil R - v105 - Ja '96 - p89+ [501+]

B

Baal-Teshuva, Jacob - *Chagall: A Retrospective*
  Bloom Rev - v16 - N '96 - p25 [51-250]
Baantjer, A C - *DeKok and Murder on the Menu*
  Rapport - v19 - 4 '96 - p24 [51-250]
Baar, Mirjam De - *Choosing the Better Part*
  R&R Bk N - v12 - F '97 - p91 [51-250]
Baars, Bernard J - *In the Theater of Consciousness*
  PW - v244 - F 3 '97 - p89 [51-250]
Babb, Lawrence A - *Absent Lord*
  Choice - v34 - Ja '97 - p810 [51-250]
  Rel St Rev - v23 - Ap '97 - p103+ [501+]
Babbel, David F - *Valuation of Interest-Sensitive
  Financial Instruments*
  R&R Bk N - v12 - F '97 - p48 [51-250]
Babbitt, Irving - *Character and Culture*
  Univ Bkmn - v36 - Fall '96 - p7+ [501+]
Babbitt, Natalie - *Kneeknock Rise (Toren). Audio Version*
  c BL - v93 - D 15 '96 - p740 [51-250]
  c BL - v93 - My 15 '97 - p1595 [1-50]
  c Emerg Lib - v24 - Mr '97 - p21 [51-250]
Babbitt, Susan E - *Impossible Dreams*
  Choice - v34 - S '96 - p140 [51-250]
  CPR - v16 - O '96 - p309+ [501+]
Babcock, Elise NeeDell - *When Life Becomes Precious*
  LJ - v122 - Ja '97 - p57 [1-50]
  PW - v243 - D 2 '96 - p58 [51-250]
Babenko, Hry Horri - *Shliakhom Burkhlyvym*
  BL - v93 - N 15 '96 - p577 [1-50]
Baber, Zaheer - *The Science of Empire*
  Choice - v34 - D '96 - p632 [51-250]
  TLS - O 11 '96 - p33 [501+]
Babich, Babette E - *Continental and Postmodern
  Perspectives in the Philosophy of Science*
  IPQ - v36 - D '96 - p502+ [501+]
  SciTech - v20 - D '96 - p3 [51-250]
Babington, Bruce - *Biblical Epics*
  r FQ - v49 - Fall '95 - p62+ [251-500]
Babson, Marian - *Break a Leg, Darlings*
  KR - v65 - Ja 15 '97 - p96 [51-250]
  LJ - v122 - F 1 '97 - p111 [1-50]
  PW - v244 - F 17 '97 - p214 [51-250]
  Even Yuppies Die
  Arm Det - v29 - Sum '96 - p367 [251-500]
  Rapport - v19 - 4 '96 - p28 [251-500]
Babur, Emperor of Hindustan - *The Baburnama:
  Memoirs of Babur, Prince and Emperor*
  MEJ - v51 - Spr '97 - p296+ [501+]
  MEP - v4 - 4 '96 - p156+ [501+]
  New R - v216 - Ja 6 '97 - p34+ [501+]
Baby Bugs' Favorite Things
  c PW - v244 - F 3 '97 - p108 [51-250]
Baby Tweety
  c Ch BWatch - v7 - F '97 - p1 [1-50]
Babybug
  cp Par Ch - v20 - O '96 - p15 [1-50]
Baca, Elmo - *Romance of the Mission*
  BL - v93 - S 15 '96 - p201 [51-250]
  LJ - v121 - S 15 '96 - p67 [51-250]
Bacarro, Joseph P - *Getting Started in Human Resource
  Management*
  HR Mag - v42 - Ja '97 - p148 [51-250]
Bach, C P E - *Organ Sonatas*
  Am MT - v46 - D '96 - p57+ [251-500]
Bach, Eric - *Algorithmic Number Theory. Vol. 1*
  SciTech - v20 - D '96 - p15 [51-250]
Bach, Johann Sebastian - *Handbook to Bach's Sacred
  Cantata Texts*
  r Choice - v34 - Ap '97 - p1305+ [51-250]
Bach, John R - *Pulmonary Rehabilitation*
  SciTech - v20 - S '96 - p36 [51-250]

Bache, Carl - *Tense, Aspect and Action*
  MLR - v92 - Ap '97 - p404+ [501+]
Bache, Ellyn - *The Activist's Daughter*
  KR - v65 - Mr 1 '97 - p316 [51-250]
  LJ - v122 - Mr 15 '97 - p87 [51-250]
  PW - v244 - Ap 7 '97 - p76 [51-250]
Bacher, Lutz - *Max Ophuls in the Hollywood Studios*
  Afterimage - v24 - N '96 - p16 [51-250]
  Choice - v34 - My '97 - p1506 [51-250]
Bachman, Richard - *The Regulators*
  Bks & Cult - v3 - Mr '97 - p14+ [501+]
  BW - v26 - S 22 '96 - p5 [501+]
  CSM - v88 - N 14 '96 - p14 [501+]
  Ent W - O 4 '96 - p54+ [501+]
  LATBR - S 22 '96 - p9 [501+]
  Necro - Win '97 - p9+ [501+]
  NYTBR - v101 - O 20 '96 - p16+ [501+]
  The Regulators (Nelligan). Audio Version
  y Kliatt - v31 - Mr '97 - p44+ [51-250]
  LJ - v122 - F 1 '97 - p127 [51-250]
Bachmann, Dieter - *So Many Worlds*
  LJ - v122 - Ja '97 - p92 [51-250]
  NS - v126 - Ja 10 '97 - p47 [1-50]
Bachmann, Heinz - *Implementing Deregulation and
  Promoting Foreign Direct Investment in Africa*
  JEL - v35 - Mr '97 - p215 [51-250]
Bachmann, Ingeborg - *Three Paths to the Lake*
  PW - v244 - F 24 '97 - p88 [1-50]
Bachmann, Michael - *Sunder Oder Ubertreter*
  Rel St Rev - v23 - Ap '97 - p185 [51-250]
Bachner, Bryan S - *Commercial Laws in the People's
  Republic of China*
  Ch Rev Int - v4 - Spr '97 - p134+ [501+]
Bachrach, Bernard S - *The Anatomy of a Little War*
  AHR - v101 - O '96 - p1195+ [501+]
  Historian - v59 - Fall '96 - p175+ [501+]
  J Mil H - v61 - Ap '97 - p359+ [251-500]
Bachrach, Stephen M - *The Internet: A Guide for
  Chemists*
  New Sci - v151 - S 28 '96 - p57 [51-250]
Bacik, James J - *Spirituality in Transition*
  CLW - v67 - D '96 - p36+ [251-500]
Back, Allan - *On Reduplication*
  R&R Bk N - v12 - F '97 - p4 [51-250]
Back, George - *Arctic Artist*
  Can Hist R - v77 - S '96 - p436+ [501+]
  Can Lit - Win '96 - p156+ [501+]
Back, Les - *New Ethnicities*
  Socio R - v45 - F 1 '97 - p165+ [501+]
The Back Door Guidebook 1997
  r J Car P&E - v57 - Win '97 - p19 [251-500]
Backhouse, Christopher J - *Concurrent Engineering*
  SciTech - v20 - D '96 - p84 [51-250]
Backhouse, Janet - *Books of Hours*
  AB - v99 - Mr 3 '97 - p685+ [501+]
  The Illuminated Manuscript
  AB - v99 - Mr 3 '97 - p685+ [501+]
  The Lindisfarne Gospels
  AB - v99 - Mr 3 '97 - p685+ [501+]
  LR - v45 - 8 '96 - p46+ [501+]
Backman, Clifford R - *The Decline and Fall of Medieval
  Sicily*
  CHR - v83 - Ja '97 - p86+ [251-500]
  JIH - v27 - Spr '97 - p693+ [251-500]
Backscheider, Paula R - *Popular Fiction by Women
  1660-1730*
  TLS - Mr 21 '97 - p8 [501+]
  Spectacular Politics
  MP - v94 - Ag '96 - p100+ [501+]
Backus, Anna Jean - *Mountain Meadows Witness*
  WHQ - v27 - Win '96 - p542+ [251-500]

Backus, Georgia - *Foundations of Geomagnetism*
  Nature - v384 - N 14 '96 - p128 [51-250]
Backus, Irena - *Le Miracle De Laon*
  CH - v65 - S '96 - p485+ [501+]
Bacon, Edwin - *The Gulag at War*
  AHR - v101 - D '96 - p1586 [251-500]
  Historian - v59 - Fall '96 - p177 [251-500]
  Russ Rev - v55 - O '96 - p718+ [501+]
Bacon, Ethel - *To See the Moon (Illus. by David Ray)*
  c HB Guide - v8 - Spr '97 - p18 [51-250]
  c KR - v64 - O 15 '96 - p1528 [51-250]
Bacon, Francis - *Francis Bacon (Vickers)*
  Choice - v34 - D '96 - p611 [51-250]
  NS & S - v9 - Ap 26 '96 - p35 [1-50]
  TLS - O 11 '96 - p3+ [501+]
  The History of the Reign of King Henry the Seventh
  VQR - v73 - Win '97 - p9* [51-250]
Bacon, Jean - *Life Lines*
  Trib Bks - My 25 '97 - p9 [501+]
Bacon, Robert - *Britain's Economic Problem Revisited.
  3rd Ed.*
  Econ J - v107 - Ja '97 - p278+ [51-250]
  TLS - S 20 '96 - p6+ [501+]
Bacon, Tony - *Classic Guitars of the '50s*
  Ant & CM - v101 - D '96 - p31 [51-250]
Bacon's International Media Directory 1996
  r ARBA - v28 - '97 - p350 [51-250]
Bacque, Raphaelle - *Chirac President*
  FR - v70 - Mr '97 - p631+ [501+]
Badami, Anita Rau - *Tamarind Mem*
  BIC - v25 - O '96 - p39 [251-500]
  Mac - v109 - S 9 '96 - p53 [501+]
  Quill & Q - v63 - F '97 - p60 [51-250]
Badash, Lawrence - *Scientists and the Development of
  Nuclear Weapons*
  Isis - v88 - Mr '97 - p158+ [501+]
  JPR - v33 - N '96 - p497 [51-250]
Baddiel, David - *Time for Bed*
  TLS - S 20 '96 - p25 [501+]
Baden, Robert - *And Sunday Makes Seven (Illus. by M
  Edwards)*
  c SS - v88 - Ja '97 - p29+ [501+]
Bader, Hilary - *Klingon (Dorn). Audio Version*
  y Kliatt - v30 - N '96 - p46 [51-250]
Bader, M J - *Images in Weather Forecasting*
  Choice - v34 - O '96 - p320 [51-250]
Bader, Ted - *Desire and Duty*
  PW - v244 - Ap 28 '97 - p55 [1-50]
Badger, David P - *Frogs*
  AB - v97 - Je 17 '96 - p2397 [51-250]
Badger, Reid - *A Life in Ragtime*
  AB - v98 - D 9 '96 - p1994 [51-250]
  AHR - v101 - O '96 - p1285+ [501+]
Badian, E - *From Plataea to Potidaea*
  Rel St Rev - v23 - Ap '97 - p170+ [51-250]
Badinter, Elisabeth - *XY: On Masculine Identity*
  Bks & Cult - v1 - N '95 - p31 [51-250]
Badiru, Adediji Bodunde - *Project Management in
  Manufacturing and High Technology Operations. 2nd
  Ed.*
  SciTech - v20 - S '96 - p46 [51-250]
Badley, Linda - *Writing Horror and the Body*
  Choice - v34 - Ja '97 - p791 [51-250]
  Necro - Win '97 - p11+ [501+]
  R&R Bk N - v11 - N '96 - p72 [1-50]
Badran, Margot - *Feminists, Islam, and Nation*
  APSR - v90 - D '96 - p929+ [501+]
  J Pol - v58 - Ag '96 - p870+ [501+]
  Rel St Rev - v23 - Ap '97 - p201 [51-250]
  TLS - Ja 10 '97 - p24+ [501+]

Badura-Triska, Eva - *Franz West: Proforma*
  BM - v138 - Ag '96 - p564+ [501+]
Baecque, Antoine De - *Francois Truffaut*
  TLS - Ja 17 '97 - p4+ [501+]
Baer, Ann - *Down the Common*
  KR - v65 - Ap 1 '97 - p476 [251-500]
  PW - v244 - Ap 14 '97 - p57 [251-250]
Baer, Barbara L - *Cartwheels on the Faultline*
  Sm Pr R - v28 - O '96 - p7 [51-250]
Baer, Gene - *Thump, Thump, Rat-a-Tat-Tat (Illus. by Lois Ehlert)*
  c HB Guide - v7 - Fall '96 - p236 [51-250]
Baer, George W - *One Hundred Years of Sea Power*
  JIH - v27 - Aut '96 - p355+ [251-250]
  Mar Crp G - v80 - S '96 - p93+ [501+]
Baer, Judy - *Broken Promises*
  y VOYA - v19 - D '96 - p260 [1-50]
  Cedar River Daydreams
  y VOYA - v19 - D '96 - p259+ [501+]
  Dear Judy, Did You Ever Like a Boy (Who Didn't Like You?)
  y VOYA - v19 - F '97 - p318 [51-250]
  Dear Judy, What's It like at Your House?
  y VOYA - v19 - F '97 - p318 [51-250]
  The Discovery
  y VOYA - v19 - D '96 - p260 [1-50]
  Fill My Empty Heart
  y VOYA - v19 - D '96 - p260 [1-50]
  The Intruder
  y VOYA - v19 - D '96 - p260 [1-50]
  Jennifer's Secret
  y VOYA - v19 - D '96 - p260 [1-50]
  Journey to Nowhere
  y VOYA - v19 - D '96 - p260 [1-50]
  Lonely Girl
  y VOYA - v19 - D '96 - p260 [1-50]
  Lost and Found
  y VOYA - v19 - D '96 - p260 [1-50]
  More than Friends
  y VOYA - v19 - D '96 - p260 [1-50]
  Never Too Late
  y VOYA - v19 - D '96 - p260 [1-50]
  New Girl in Town
  y VOYA - v19 - D '96 - p260 [1-50]
  No Turning Back
  y VOYA - v19 - D '96 - p260 [1-50]
  Second Chance
  y VOYA - v19 - D '96 - p260 [1-50]
  Silent Tears No More
  y VOYA - v19 - D '96 - p260 [1-50]
  Something Old, Something New
  y VOYA - v19 - D '96 - p260 [1-50]
  Special Kind of Love
  y VOYA - v19 - D '96 - p260 [1-50]
  Three's a Crowd
  y VOYA - v19 - D '96 - p260 [1-50]
  Tomorrow's Promise
  y VOYA - v19 - D '96 - p260 [1-50]
  Trouble with a Capital T
  y VOYA - v19 - D '96 - p260 [1-50]
  Unheard Voices
  y VOYA - v19 - D '96 - p260 [1-50]
  Vanishing Star
  y VOYA - v19 - D '96 - p260 [1-50]
  Yesterday's Dream
  y VOYA - v19 - D '96 - p260 [1-50]
Baer, Martha - *As Francesca*
  Advocate - Ap 1 '97 - p62 [51-250]
  BL - v93 - F 15 '97 - p1001 [51-250]
  Ent W - Mr 14 '97 - p75 [51-250]
  KR - v64 - D 1 '96 - p1684 [251-500]
  LJ - v122 - Ap 15 '97 - p116 [51-250]
  NYTBR - v102 - F 23 '97 - p15 [501+]
  PW - v243 - D 30 '96 - p53+ [51-250]
  VV - v42 - F 18 '97 - p55 [251-250]
Baer, Nancy - *Leader of the Pack*
  Dog Fan - v28 - Ja '97 - p37 [51-250]
Baer, Werner - *The Brazilian Economy. 4th Ed.*
  HAHR - v76 - Ag '96 - p594+ [501+]
Baer's 1996 Agricultural Almanac and Gardener's Guide
  r CAY - v16 - Fall '95 - p2 [51-250]
Baeten, Elizabeth M - *The Magic Mirror*
  Choice - v34 - Ap '97 - p1322 [51-250]
  R&R Bk N - v12 - F '97 - p8 [51-250]
Bagarozzi, Dennis A - *The Couple and Family in Managed Care*
  SciTech - v20 - N '96 - p43 [51-250]

Bagert, Brod - *The Gooch Machine (Illus. by Tim Ellis)*
  c CBRS - v25 - Mr '97 - p92 [51-250]
  c CCB-B - v50 - Mr '97 - p240 [51-250]
  c KR - v65 - Ja 1 '97 - p56+ [51-250]
Baggs, Sydney - *The Healthy House*
  New Sci - v152 - D 21 '96 - p72 [251-500]
Baghdasarian, Louisa - *Armenian (Eastern)-English Dictionary*
  r ARBA - v28 - '97 - p388+ [251-500]
Bagley, Bruce M - *Drug Trafficking in the Americas*
  SSQ - v77 - D '96 - p934+ [501+]
Bagnall, Roger S - *The Demography of Roman Egypt*
  CW - v89 - Jl '96 - p516+ [251-500]
  Egypt in Late Antiquity
  EHR - v112 - F '97 - p154+ [501+]
Bagnasco, Marcella Barra - *Locri Epizefiri IV*
  AJA - v100 - O '96 - p777+ [501+]
Bagshawe, Louise - *Career Girls*
  Books - v10 - Je '96 - p24 [51-250]
  Triple Feature
  KR - v65 - Mr 1 '97 - p316 [51-250]
  LJ - v122 - Ap 1 '97 - p120 [51-250]
  PW - v244 - Mr 10 '97 - p50 [51-250]
  Trib Bks - My 11 '97 - p11 [51-250]
Baguley, David - *Zola Et Les Genres*
  MLR - v92 - Ap '97 - p473+ [251-500]
Bahadur, Shyam - *Effect of Surface Coatings and Treatments on Wear*
  SciTech - v20 - D '96 - p63 [51-250]
Bahan, Ben - *My ABC Signs of Animal Friends (Illus. by Patricia Pearson)*
  c Ch BWatch - v7 - Ja '97 - p1 [51-250]
Baher, H - *Microelectronic Switched-Capacitor Filters with ISICAP*
  SciTech - v20 - S '96 - p56 [51-250]
Bahl, Roy - *The Guatemalan Tax Reform*
  JEL - v35 - Mr '97 - p224 [51-250]
  R&R Bk N - v12 - F '97 - p50 [51-250]
Bahl, Vinay - *The Making of the Indian Working Class*
  CS - v26 - Ja '97 - p56+ [501+]
Bahlke, Joachim - *Regionalismus Und Staatsintegration Im Widerstreit*
  EHR - v112 - F '97 - p189+ [501+]
Bahn, Paul G - *The Cambridge Illustrated History of Archaeology*
  y BL - v93 - S 15 '96 - p213 [51-250]
  HT - v46 - O '96 - p55 [51-250]
  New Sci - v152 - D 21 '96 - p75 [51-250]
  R&R Bk N - v11 - D '96 - p6 [51-250]
  Tombs, Graves and Mummies
  New Sci - v152 - D 21 '96 - p72 [1-50]
Bahr, Donald - *The Short Swift Time of Gods on Earth*
  CH - v66 - Mr '97 - p207+ [51-250]
Bahr, Howard - *The Black Flower*
  KR - v65 - F 1 '97 - p154 [251-500]
  PW - v244 - Mr 10 '97 - p52 [51-250]
Bahti, Timothy - *Allegories of History*
  Comp L - v48 - Fall '96 - p365+ [501+]
  Ends of the Lyric
  MLN - v111 - D '96 - p1010+ [501+]
  Jewish Writers, German Literature
  Choice - v34 - S '96 - p131+ [51-250]
Bai, Xinghua - *Acupuncture in Clinical Practice*
  SciTech - v20 - N '96 - p55 [51-250]
Baider, Lea - *Cancer and the Family*
  R&R Bk N - v12 - F '97 - p96 [51-250]
Baier, Kurt - *The Rational and the Moral Order*
  CPR - v16 - Ap '96 - p79+ [51-250]
  RM - v49 - Je '96 - p912+ [501+]
Baierlacher, Monika - *Wild Animals (Illus. by Christoph Scholl)*
  c Ch BWatch - v6 - My '96 - p1 [51-250]
Baigell, Renee - *Soviet Dissident Artists*
  Russ Rev - v55 - O '96 - p709+ [51-250]
Baigrie, Brian S - *Picturing Knowledge*
  Choice - v34 - F '97 - p984 [51-250]
  SciTech - v20 - N '96 - p4 [51-250]
Bail, Kathy - *DIY Feminism*
  Aust Bk R - D '96 - p43+ [501+]
Bail, Paul - *John Saul: A Critical Companion*
  Arm Det - v30 - Win '97 - p104+ [251-500]
  SFS - v24 - Mr '97 - p176+ [251-250]
  y SLJ - v42 - O '96 - p152 [51-250]
Bailer, Darice - *The Last Rail (Illus. by Bill Farnsworth). Book and Audio Version*
  c PW - v244 - F 3 '97 - p46 [51-250]
Bailey, Beth - *The First Strange Place*
  Arm F&S - v22 - Sum '96 - p655+ [501+]
Bailey, Dennis - *Khetho*
  y VOYA - v19 - O '96 - p199+ [501+]

  Thatha
  y VOYA - v19 - O '96 - p199+ [501+]
Bailey, Douglass W - *Prehistoric Bulgaria*
  AJA - v100 - O '96 - p782+ [501+]
Bailey, Elizabeth E - *The Political Economy of Privatization and Deregulation*
  Econ J - v106 - N '96 - p1844 [501+]
Bailey, F G - *The Civility of Indifference*
  Choice - v34 - S '96 - p168 [51-250]
  The Kingdom of Individuals
  Am Ethnol - v24 - F '97 - p218+ [501+]
Bailey, Hilary - *Miles and Flora*
  Spec - v278 - F 15 '97 - p26+ [501+]
  TLS - Mr 28 '97 - p22 [251-500]
Bailey, James - *After Thought*
  Choice - v34 - D '96 - p646 [51-250]
  KR - v64 - My 1 '96 - p652 [251-500]
  Nature - v382 - Ag 15 '96 - p593+ [501+]
  NYTBR - v102 - F 16 '97 - p22 [501+]
Bailey, Jill - *How Fish Swim*
  c Ch BWatch - v7 - Ja '97 - p3 [1-50]
  c HB Guide - v8 - Spr '97 - p124 [1-50]
  c SB - v33 - My '97 - p112 [51-250]
  c SLJ - v43 - F '97 - p86 [51-250]
  How Spiders Make Their Webs
  c Ch BWatch - v7 - Ja '97 - p3 [1-50]
  c HB Guide - v8 - Spr '97 - p121 [51-250]
  c SB - v33 - My '97 - p112 [51-250]
  c SLJ - v43 - F '97 - p86 [51-250]
  The Young Oxford Book of the Prehistoric World
  y HB Guide - v7 - Fall '96 - p333 [51-250]
  yr Par Ch - v21 - Mr '97 - p5 [1-50]
Bailey, Lee - *Lee Bailey's the Way I Cook*
  BL - v93 - N 15 '96 - p559 [51-250]
  LJ - v121 - N 15 '96 - p84 [51-250]
  PW - v243 - O 21 '96 - p81 [51-250]
  The Near Death Experience
  New Sci - v152 - O 26 '96 - p45 [51-250]
Bailey, Linda - *How Can a Frozen Detective Stay Hot on the Trail?*
  c HB Guide - v8 - Spr '97 - p62 [51-250]
  c Quill & Q - v62 - S '96 - p74 [251-500]
  How Can I Be a Detective if I Have to Baby-Sit?
  c CLW - v67 - D '96 - p55 [51-250]
  c HB Guide - v7 - Fall '96 - p289 [51-250]
  c TES - Jl 5 '96 - pR8 [51-250]
  How Come the Best Clues Are Always in the Garbage?
  c Bks Keeps - v100 - S '96 - p13 [51-250]
  c CLW - v67 - D '96 - p55 [51-250]
  c HB Guide - v7 - Fall '96 - p289 [51-250]
  c TES - Jl 5 '96 - pR8 [51-250]
  Who's Got Gertie? and How Do We Get Her Back?
  c HB Guide - v8 - Spr '97 - p62 [51-250]
Bailey, Michele - *Dreadful Lies*
  Arm Det - v30 - Win '97 - p88 [251-500]
Bailey, Patrick - *Geography Teachers' Handbook*
  GJ - v163 - Mr '97 - p109 [51-250]
  Sch Lib - v44 - N '96 - p176 [51-250]
Bailey, Paul - *The Oxford Book of London*
  CSM - v88 - N 21 '96 - pB2 [51-250]
  ELT - v40 - 1 '97 - p125 [51-250]
Bailey, Randall C - *The Recovery of Black Presence*
  TT - v53 - O '96 - p430+ [51-250]
Bailey, Richard W - *Huntin' and Shootin'*
  Obs - F 9 '97 - p15* [501+]
Bailey, Stephen - *An Innovative Economic Incentive Model for Improvement of the Working Environment in Europe*
  J Gov Info - v23 - S '96 - p667 [51-250]
Bailey, William Everett - *The Invisible Drug*
  BL - v93 - D 1 '96 - p626 [51-250]
  LJ - v121 - N 1 '96 - p100 [51-250]
Bailie, Gil - *Violence Unveiled*
  Rel St Rev - v22 - O '96 - p341 [51-250]
  Theol St - v57 - Mr '96 - p174+ [501+]
Bailin, Miriam - *The Sickroom in Victorian Fiction*
  Isis - v87 - D '96 - p740+ [501+]
Baillie, Allan - *Dragonquest (Illus. by Wayne Harris)*
  c Aust Bk R - N '96 - p63+ [501+]
  Old Magic (Illus. by Di Wu)
  c Aust Bk R - F '97 - p54+ [501+]
  Secrets of Walden Rising
  y Aust Bk R - S '96 - p58+ [501+]
  c BL - v93 - Ap 1 '97 - p1333 [51-250]
  y CCB-B - v50 - My '97 - p312 [51-250]
Baillie, Kate - *Provence and the Cote D'Azur. 3rd Ed.*
  r BL - v93 - S 15 '96 - p212 [1-50]
Baillie, Marilyn - *Side by Side (Illus. by Romi Caron)*
  c BL - v93 - My 15 '97 - p1576 [51-250]
  c Quill & Q - v63 - F '97 - p54 [251-500]
  Wild Talk (Illus. by Romi Caron)
  c Quill & Q - v62 - S '96 - p76 [251-500]

Baillie, Michael G L - *A Slice through Time*
AJA - v101 - Ja '97 - p192 [251-500]
Baillie, Robert - *Chez Albert*
FR - v70 - D '96 - p343+ [501+]
Bailyn, Bernard - *On the Teaching and Writing of History*
Biography - v19 - Fall '96 - p429 [1-50]
Bain, Barbara J - *Blood Cells: A Practical Guide. 2nd Ed.*
r SciTech - v20 - S '96 - p29 [51-250]
Bone Marrow Pathology. 2nd Ed.
SciTech - v20 - N '96 - p46 [51-250]
Bain, Donald - *A Deadly Judgment*
Arm Det - v29 - Fall '96 - p486 [51-250]
Arm Det - v29 - Sum '96 - p338 [51-250]
Bain, Elspeth - *The Grammar Book*
TES - Ja 10 '97 - p10* [501+]
Bain, F W - *The Ashes of a God. Electronic Media Version*
SF Chr - v18 - O '96 - p79 [51-250]
A Digit of the Moon. Electronic Media Version
SF Chr - v18 - O '96 - p79 [51-250]
Bain, Robert - *Whitman's and Dickinson's Contemporaries*
AL - v68 - S '96 - p669+ [51-250]
Choice - v34 - S '96 - p131 [51-250]
Nine-C Lit - v51 - S '96 - p270 [51-250]
Bainbridge, Beryl - *Every Man for Himself*
Atl - v278 - D '96 - p125 [51-250]
BL - v93 - N 1 '96 - p480+ [51-250]
BW - v26 - N 24 '96 - p7 [501+]
KR - v64 - Ag 15 '96 - p1167 [251-500]
LATBR - N 24 '96 - p6 [501+]
Lon R Bks - v18 - O 17 '96 - p16 [501+]
NS - v125 - S 13 '96 - p46 [251-500]
NYTBR - v101 - D 22 '96 - p8 [501+]
Obs - D 1 '96 - p16* [1-50]
Spec - v277 - S 14 '96 - p35 [501+]
Spec - v277 - N 23 '96 - p44 [1-50]
Spec - v277 - N 23 '96 - p45 [51-250]
Spec - v277 - N 23 '96 - p46 [51-250]
Spec - v277 - N 30 '96 - p58 [1-50]
TES - O 4 '96 - p7* [51-250]
TLS - S 6 '96 - p21 [501+]
TLS - N 29 '96 - p12 [1-50]
Woman's J - N '96 - p12 [1-50]
WSJ-MW - v78 - N 15 '96 - pA12 [501+]
Bainbridge, Simon - *Napoleon and English Romanticism*
VQR - v72 - Aut '96 - p122* [51-250]
Baines, M J - *Moving Finite Elements*
SIAM Rev - v38 - S '96 - p530+ [501+]
Baioni, Giuliano - *Kafka: Literatur Und Judentum*
MLR - v92 - Ap '97 - p518+ [501+]
Bair, Bruce - *Good Land*
KR - v65 - Ja 15 '97 - p105 [51-250]
LJ - v122 - F 15 '97 - p140 [51-250]
PW - v244 - F 3 '97 - p88+ [51-250]
Bair, Deirdre - *Anais Nin: A Biography*
NYTBR - v101 - Jl 21 '96 - p28 [51-250]
Baird, Anne - *The U.S. Space Camp Book of Astronauts*
c HB Guide - v7 - Fall '96 - p351+ [51-250]
c SB - v32 - O '96 - p212 [51-250]
Baird, Colin - *Environmental Chemistry*
J Chem Ed - v73 - N '96 - pA276+ [501+]
Baird, George - *The Space of Appearance*
BIC - v25 - N '96 - p9+ [501+]
Baird, Robert M - *Same-Sex Marriage*
LJ - v122 - Mr 15 '97 - p79 [51-250]
Baird, William - *History of New Testament Research. Vol. 1*
CH - v65 - D '96 - p733+ [501+]
Baiul, Oksana - *Oksana: My Own Story*
c BL - v93 - My 1 '97 - p1489+ [51-250]
c CCB-B - v50 - My '97 - p312+ [51-250]
Bajaj, Anil K - *Nonlinear Dynamics and Controls*
SciTech - v21 - Mr '97 - p17 [51-250]
Bajohr, Frank - *Zivilization Und Barbarei*
JMH - v68 - S '96 - p629+ [501+]
Bak, Per - *How Nature Works*
Choice - v34 - F '97 - p1001 [51-250]
Nature - v383 - O 31 '96 - p772+ [501+]
New Sci - v152 - N 30 '96 - p44+ [501+]
Bak, Richard - *Casey Stengel: A Splendid Baseball Life*
LJ - v122 - F 1 '97 - p82 [1-50]
PW - v243 - N 25 '96 - p61 [51-250]
Baka, Istvan - *Tajkep Fohasszal*
WLT - v71 - Win '97 - p191+ [501+]
Bakalar, Nicholas - *American Satire*
BW - v27 - Ap 6 '97 - p12 [51-250]
Bakari, Imruh - *African Experiences of Cinema*
TES - N 22 '96 - p8* [1-50]

Bakeless, John - *Lewis and Clark*
y Ch BWatch - v7 - F '97 - p7 [1-50]
Baker, A D, III - *The Naval Institute Guide to Combat Fleets of the World. Book and Electronic Media Version*
For Aff - v75 - N '96 - p151+ [51-250]
The Naval Institute Guide to Combat Fleets of the World. Electronic Media Version
r Choice - v34 - F '97 - p952 [251-500]
Baker, Alan - *Gray Rabbit's Odd One Out (Illus. by Alan Baker)*
c RT - O '96 - p130 [1-50]
I Thought I Heard--
c LA - v73 - D '96 - p619 [251-500]
c RT - v50 - Ap '97 - p591 [51-250]
c TES - S 27 '96 - p12* [501+]
Little Rabbit's First Word Book
c BL - v93 - N 1 '96 - p502 [51-250]
c HB Guide - v8 - Spr '97 - p10 [51-250]
Mouse's Christmas
c PW - v243 - S 30 '96 - p90 [51-250]
Baker, Alison - *How I Came West and Why I Stayed*
WAL - v31 - Win '97 - p410+ [501+]
Loving Wanda Beaver
WAL - v31 - Win '97 - p410+ [501+]
Baker, Calvin - *Naming the New World*
y BL - v93 - Ja '97 - p815 [51-250]
KR - v64 - D 1 '96 - p1685 [251-500]
LJ - v122 - Ja '97 - p141 [51-250]
NYTBR - v102 - Mr 23 '97 - p18 [51-250]
PW - v243 - N 25 '96 - p56 [51-250]
Time - v149 - Mr 3 '97 - p78 [251-500]
VV - v42 - F 25 '97 - p52 [501+]
Baker, Carin Greenberg - *Attack of the Slime Monster*
c Ch BWatch - v6 - Jl '96 - p5 [1-50]
Baker, Carlos - *Emerson among the Eccentrics*
Am - v175 - O 19 '96 - p26+ [501+]
Bloom Rev - v16 - N '96 - p19+ [501+]
CC - v113 - O 9 '96 - p943+ [251-500]
CR - v269 - D '96 - p332+ [251-500]
NEQ - v70 - Mr '97 - p160+ [501+]
NYTBR - v101 - D 8 '96 - p87 [1-50]
Spec - v277 - O 19 '96 - p48 [501+]
TLS - D 6 '96 - p5+ [501+]
VQR - v72 - Aut '96 - p125*+ [51-250]
Baker, Carolyn - *The Beginners Bible for Toddlers (Illus. by Danny Brooks Dalby)*
c HB Guide - v7 - Fall '96 - p308 [51-250]
Baker, Christina Looper - *The Conversation Begins*
Wom R Bks - v13 - S '96 - p7+ [501+]
In a Generous Spirit
Choice - v34 - F '97 - p963 [51-250]
Wom R Bks - v14 - Mr '97 - p24+ [501+]
Baker, Christopher P - *Costa Rica Handbook. 2nd Ed.*
r BL - v93 - S 15 '96 - p212 [1-50]
World Travel
SB - v32 - Ag '96 - p171 [51-250]
Baker, Christopher W - *How Did They Do It?*
FQ - v49 - Fall '95 - p61+ [51-250]
Baker, David - *Adolf Galland: The Authorised Biography*
Choice - v34 - Ap '97 - p1395+ [51-250]
TLS - Ja 10 '97 - p28 [251-500]
Ideology of Obsession
Choice - v34 - D '96 - p666+ [501+]
Baker, David, 1944- - *Spaceflight and Rocketry*
r ARBA - v28 - '97 - p593 [251-500]
Baker, David, 1954- - *Meter in English*
LJ - v122 - Ja '97 - p99 [51-250]
PW - v243 - N 25 '96 - p68 [51-250]
Baker, Dean - *Getting Prices Right*
NYRB - v44 - Mr 6 '97 - p19+ [501+]
Baker, Deborah Lesko - *The Subject of Desire*
Choice - v34 - Ja '97 - p801 [51-250]
Baker, Denise Nowakowski - *Julian of Norwich's Showings*
JR - v77 - Ja '97 - p139+ [501+]
MP - v94 - F '97 - p357+ [501+]
RES - v48 - F '97 - p81+ [501+]
Specu - v72 - Ja '97 - p105+ [501+]
Baker, Derek W - *The Flowers of William Morris*
BW - v26 - D 15 '96 - p13 [1-50]
BWatch - v18 - F '97 - p5 [51-250]
Choice - v34 - Ap '97 - p1324 [51-250]
Baker, Emerson W - *American Beginnings*
Can Hist R - v77 - S '96 - p463+ [501+]
GJ - v163 - Mr '97 - p96+ [501+]
Baker, Felicity - *Toys Ahoy!*
c TES - N 29 '96 - p13* [51-250]
Baker, H F - *Abelian Functions*
SciTech - v20 - S '96 - p11 [51-250]
Baker, Harry F - *Prion Diseases*
Sci - v273 - Ag 23 '96 - p1052+ [501+]

Baker, Houston A, Jr. - *Black Studies, Rap and the Academy*
CAY - v17 - Fall '96 - p9 [51-250]
Baker, Jean H - *The Stevensons: A Biography of an American Family*
CR - v269 - O '96 - p220+ [251-500]
Baker, Jeffrey P - *The Machine in the Nursery*
Choice - v34 - D '96 - p643 [51-250]
SciTech - v20 - N '96 - p52 [51-250]
Baker, Jennifer - *The Lying Game*
y VOYA - v19 - D '96 - p262 [51-250]
Baker, Jenny - *Kettle Broth to Gooseberry Fool*
TLS - F 7 '97 - p32 [251-500]
The Student's Cookbook
TES - S 27 '96 - p8* [51-250]
Baker, Karen Lee - *Seneca (Illus. by Karen Lee Baker)*
c BL - v93 - Ap 1 '97 - p1336+ [51-250]
c CCB-B - v50 - Mr '97 - p240+ [51-250]
c PW - v244 - Ja 27 '97 - p106 [51-250]
Baker, Keith - *The Magic Fan*
c PW - v244 - F 24 '97 - p93 [1-50]
Baker, Keith Michael - *The Terror*
EHR - v112 - Ap '97 - p496+ [501+]
Baker, Kenneth - *The Faber Book of War Poetry*
Obs - Ja 12 '97 - p15* [501+]
TES - O 18 '96 - p7* [501+]
TLS - D 13 '96 - p24 [501+]
The Kings and Queens
CR - v269 - O '96 - p218+ [251-500]
Baker, Kim - *The RVer's Bible*
LJ - v122 - Ap 15 '97 - p104 [51-250]
Baker, Liva - *The Second Battle of New Orleans*
BWatch - v17 - S '96 - p10 [51-250]
Choice - v34 - O '96 - p359 [51-250]
Nat - v264 - Ja 13 '97 - p28+ [501+]
Baker, Lynne Rudder - *Explaining Attitudes*
A J Psy - v109 - Fall '96 - p491+ [501+]
Baker, Mark Allen - *Collector's Guide to Celebrity Autographs*
r ARBA - v27 - '96 - p357 [251-500]
Baker, Maureen - *Canadian Family Policies*
JEL - v34 - S '96 - p1443+ [51-250]
Baker, Nicholson - *The Mezzanine*
Reason - v28 - D '96 - p38 [51-250]
Reason - v28 - D '96 - p42 [51-250]
SFR - v22 - Ja '97 - p48 [51-250]
The Size of Thoughts
LATBR - D 29 '96 - p4 [51-250]
NY - v72 - D 16 '96 - p108 [51-250]
NYTBR - v101 - D 8 '96 - p92+ [1-50]
NYTBR - v102 - Ap 20 '97 - p32 [51-250]
PW - v244 - F 3 '97 - p100 [1-50]
RCF - v16 - Fall '96 - p201 [251-500]
Trib Bks - My 4 '97 - p8 [1-50]
VLS - Win '96 - p8 [51-250]
Baker, Peter - *Deconstruction and the Ethical Turn*
FR - v70 - F '97 - p460+ [501+]
Baker, Robert A - *Mind Games*
Choice - v34 - F '97 - p1039 [51-250]
SciTech - v21 - Mr '97 - p52 [51-250]
Baker, Robin - *Sperm Wars*
BL - v93 - O 1 '96 - p313 [51-250]
KR - v64 - Ag 15 '96 - p1197+ [251-500]
LJ - v121 - N 1 '96 - p103 [51-250]
Baker, Ronald L - *From Needmore to Prosperity*
r Names - v45 - Mr '97 - p57+ [501+]
Baker, Russell - *The Good Times*
Parameters - v26 - Win '96 - p148+ [501+]
Growing Up
Parameters - v26 - Win '96 - p148+ [501+]
Baker, Sanna Anderson - *Mississippi Going North (Illus. by Bill Farnsworth)*
c HB Guide - v8 - Spr '97 - p172 [51-250]
c SLJ - v42 - O '96 - p111 [51-250]
Baker, Shirley K - *The Future of Resource Sharing*
LAR - v98 - Ag '96 - p428 [51-250]
Baker, T Lindsay - *The First Polish Americans*
LJ - v121 - N 15 '96 - p93 [1-50]
The WPA Oklahoma Slave Narratives
Choice - v34 - S '96 - p200 [51-250]
WHQ - v27 - Win '96 - p522+ [251-500]
Baker, Terry - *Economic Implications for Ireland of EMU*
JEL - v35 - Mr '97 - p211+ [51-250]
Baker, Wendy - *Experimenta Con La Electricidad (Illus. by Jon Barnes)*
c SLJ - v42 - Ag '96 - p178 [51-250]
Baker, William, 1944- - *Recent Work in Critical Theory 1989-1995*
r ARBA - v28 - '97 - p405+ [251-500]
r Choice - v34 - F '97 - p939 [51-250]
r R&R Bk N - v12 - F '97 - p80 [51-250]

Baker, William R - *Personal Speech-Ethics in the Epistle of James*
    Theol St - v57 - Je '96 - p343+ [501+]
Bakhtiar, Laleh - *Encyclopedia of Islamic Law*
    r MEQ - v3 - D '96 - p82+ [51-250]
Bakis, Kirsten - *Lives of the Monster Dogs*
    BL - v93 - Ja '97 - p815 [51-250]
    KR - v64 - N 15 '96 - p1616 [251-500]
    LATBR - F 16 '97 - p2 [501+]
    LJ - v122 - Ja '97 - p141+ [51-250]
    NYTBR - v102 - Mr 9 '97 - p4 [501+]
    PW - v243 - D 16 '96 - p41 [51-250]
    Time - v149 - Mr 3 '97 - p76 [251-500]
    Trib Bks - F 9 '97 - p1+ [501+]
    WSJ-Cent - v99 - Mr 3 '97 - pA16 [51-250]
Bakish, David - *Jimmy Durante: His Show Business Career*
    JPC - v30 - Fall '96 - p199 [51-250]
Bakker, Isabella - *Rethinking Restructuring*
    Choice - v34 - N '96 - p548 [51-250]
    JEL - v34 - D '96 - p2066 [51-250]
Bakker, J W De - *Control Flow Semantics*
    SciTech - v20 - S '96 - p6 [51-250]
Bakker, Jim - *I Was Wrong*
    BL - v93 - N 15 '96 - p548 [1-50]
    Ch Today - v40 - D 9 '96 - p44 [501+]
    CSM - v89 - N 25 '96 - p12 [51-250]
Bakker, Robert T - *Raptor Red*
    y Kllatt - v30 - S '96 - p4 [1-50]
    y Kliatt - v30 - N '96 - p12 [51-250]
Bakos, Adrinna E - *Politics, Ideology and the Law in Early Modern Europe*
    EHR - v112 - Ap '97 - p466 [51-250]
Baksh, Ishmael - *Out of Darkness*
    y Can CL - v22 - Sum '96 - p82+ [501+]
Bakshi, Parminder - *Distant Desire*
    R&R Bk N - v11 - N '96 - p70 [51-250]
Baktiari, Bahman - *Parliamentary Politics in Revolutionary Iran*
    Choice - v34 - F '97 - p1029+ [51-250]
Balaban, John - *Locusts at the Edge of Summer*
    PW - v244 - Ap 28 '97 - p72 [51-250]
Vietnam
    BW - v26 - Ag 18 '96 - p12 [51-250]
    TranslRevS - v2 - D '96 - p4 [51-250]
Balakian, Anna - *The Snowflake on the Belfry*
    Comp L - v49 - Win '97 - p78+ [501+]
Balakian, Peter - *Black Dog of Fate*
    KR - v65 - Ap 1 '97 - p512 [251-500]
    LJ - v122 - My 1 '97 - p102 [51-250]
    PW - v244 - Ap 7 '97 - p80 [251-500]
Dyer's Thistle
    y Kliatt - v30 - S '96 - p23 [51-250]
    WLT - v71 - Win '97 - p164+ [251-500]
Balakrishnan, Gopal - *Mapping the Nation*
    For Aff - v76 - Mr '97 - p175+ [51-250]
Baland, Jean-Marie - *Halting Degradation of Natural Resources*
    JEL - v35 - Mr '97 - p297 [51-250]
Balanis, Constantine A - *Antenna Theory. 2nd Ed.*
    SciTech - v20 - N '96 - p75 [51-250]
Balard, M - *La Circulation Des Nouvelles Au Moyen Age*
    EHR - v111 - N '96 - p1258+ [251-500]
Balay, Robert - *Guide to Reference Books. 11th Ed.*
    r ARBA - v28 - '97 - p6+ [501+]
    r LAR - v99 - Ja '97 - p50 [1-50]
Guide to Reference Books: Supplement to the Tenth Edition
    r ASInt - v34 - O '96 - p6 [51-250]
Balbir, Nalini - *Avasyaka-Studien: Introduction Generale Et Traductions*
    Rel St Rev - v23 - Ap '97 - p113+ [501+]
Balcells, Albert - *Catalan Nationalism*
    HRNB - v25 - Fall '96 - p31 [251-500]
Balcerowicz, Leszek - *Socialism, Capitalism, Transformation*
    JEL - v35 - Mr '97 - p289+ [51-250]
Balcom, Ted - *Book Discussions for Adults*
    RQ - v36 - Win '96 - p209 [51-250]
Baldacchini, Lorenzo - *Incunaboli E Cinquecentine In Romagna*
    r Lib - v19 - Mr '97 - p98+ [51-250]
Baldacci, David - *Absolute Power*
    Ent W - N 22 '96 - p131 [1-50]
Absolute Power (Guidall). Audio Version
    y LJ - v121 - N '96 - p36 [51-250]
Absolute Power (Heald). Audio Version
    Arm Det - v29 - Fall '96 - p472 [51-250]
Absolute Power (Kramer). Audio Version
    LJ - v121 - S 15 '96 - p112 [51-250]

Total Control
    BL - v93 - N 15 '96 - p548 [51-250]
    CSM - v89 - F 20 '97 - p10 [51-250]
    CSM - v89 - Mr 20 '97 - p14 [51-250]
    Ent W - F 21 '97 - p120+ [51-250]
    KR - v64 - N 1 '96 - p1546 [251-500]
    LJ - v122 - Ja '97 - p142 [51-250]
    PW - v243 - D 2 '96 - p41 [51-250]
    Quill & Q - v63 - Ja '97 - p20 [1-50]
Total Control (Dukes). Audio Version
    BWatch - v18 - Mr '97 - p8 [1-50]
Baldasano, J M - *Urban Transport and the Environment II*
    SciTech - v21 - Mr '97 - p2 [51-250]
Baldassarri, Mario - *The 1990s Slump*
    JEL - v34 - D '96 - p2033+ [51-250]
Equity, Efficiency and Growth
    JEL - v34 - D '96 - p2064 [51-250]
International Problems of Economic Interdependence
    Econ J - v106 - N '96 - p1835+ [51-250]
The International System Between New Integration and Neo-Protectionism
    JEL - v34 - D '96 - p2047 [51-250]
Balderrama, Francisco E - *Decade of Betrayal*
    AHR - v102 - F '97 - p237+ [501+]
    PHR - v65 - Ag '96 - p497+ [501+]
Baldinetti, Anna - *Carte Private Di Carlo Alfonso E Maria Nallino*
    r MEJ - v51 - Win '97 - p149 [51-250]
Baldizzone, Tiziana - *Tibet: On the Paths of the Gentlemen Brigands*
    BL - v93 - Mr 1 '97 - p1107 [51-250]
    PW - v244 - F 24 '97 - p80 [1-50]
Baldridge, Cates - *The Dialogics of Dissent in the English Novel*
    MLR - v91 - Jl '96 - p711+ [501+]
    VS - v39 - Aut '95 - p105+ [501+]
Baldrige, Letitia - *Letitia Baldrige's More than Manners!*
    BL - v93 - Mr 1 '97 - p1100 [51-250]
    PW - v244 - F 17 '97 - p216 [51-250]
Baldwin, Anna - *Platonism and the English Imagination*
    RES - v47 - Ag '96 - p452+ [501+]
Baldwin, David - *Track and Field Record Holders*
    r ARBA - v28 - '97 - p302 [51-250]
    r Choice - v34 - Mr '97 - p1133 [51-250]
    r R&R Bk N - v12 - F '97 - p31 [51-250]
Baldwin, David A - *Humanistic Management by Teamwork*
    r RQ - v36 - Win '96 - p314+ [501+]
Baldwin, Frank - *Balling the Jack*
    KR - v65 - My 1 '97 - p658 [251-500]
Baldwin, J, 1933- - *BuckyWorks: Buckminster Fuller's Ideas for Today*
    Am Sci - v84 - N '96 - p1933 [501+]
    Choice - v34 - S '96 - p148 [51-250]
    New Sci - v151 - S 21 '96 - p53 [51-250]
Baldwin, J F - *Fuzzy Logic*
    Choice - v34 - Ap '97 - p1373 [51-250]
    SciTech - v21 - Mr '97 - p84 [51-250]
Baldwin, John R - *The Dynamics of Industrial Competition*
    Econ J - v106 - S '96 - p1432+ [501+]
Baldwin, John W - *The Language of Sex*
    EHR - v112 - F '97 - p166+ [51-250]
Baldwin, Lewis V - *Toward the Beloved Community*
    Rel St Rev - v22 - O '96 - p358 [51-250]
Baldwin, Louis - *Women of Strength*
    r ARBA - v28 - '97 - p334+ [251-500]
    r Choice - v34 - My '97 - p1483 [51-250]
    r LJ - v122 - Ja '97 - p82+ [51-250]
Baldwin, Michael - *The First Mrs. Wordsworth*
    Books - v11 - Ap '97 - p22 [51-250]
Baldwin, Patricia - *Covering the Campus*
    Choice - v34 - S '96 - p179 [51-250]
Baldwin, Robert E - *Political Economy of U.S.-Taiwan Trade*
    JEL - v34 - S '96 - p1425 [51-250]
Baldwin, Robert F - *New England Whaler (Illus. by Richard Erickson)*
    c HB Guide - v7 - Fall '96 - p384 [51-250]
Baldwin, Shauna Singh - *English Lessons and Other Stories*
    BIC - v26 - Mr '97 - p10 [501+]
Baldwin, Sherman - *Ironclaw: A Navy Carrier Pilot's Gulf War Experience*
    A & S Sm - v11 - D '96 - p95+ [251-500]
    y BL - v93 - S 1 '96 - p58 [51-250]
    WSJ-MW - v77 - S 17 '96 - pA14 [501+]
Baldy, Marian W - *The University Wine Course. 2nd Ed.*
    LJ - v122 - Ap 1 '97 - p62 [51-250]

Balgassi, Haemi - *Peacebound Trains (Illus. by Chris K Soentpiet)*
    c BL - v93 - S 15 '96 - p236+ [51-250]
    c CBRS - v25 - N '96 - p29+ [1-50]
    c CCB-B - v50 - O '96 - p48 [51-250]
    c HB Guide - v8 - Spr '97 - p56 [51-250]
    c NYTBR - v102 - Mr 30 '97 - p18 [1-50]
    c SLJ - v43 - Ja '97 - p75 [51-250]
    c Smith - v27 - N '96 - p171 [1-50]
Bali (Knopf Guides)
    r BL - v93 - S 15 '96 - p210 [1-50]
Balick, Michael J - *Medicinal Resources of the Tropical Forest*
    Choice - v34 - S '96 - p154 [51-250]
    Nature - v382 - Ag 1 '96 - p412+ [501+]
Plants, People, and Culture
    CAY - v17 - Fall '96 - p2 [51-250]
    Choice - v34 - N '96 - p482+ [51-250]
    Nature - v382 - Ag 1 '96 - p412+ [501+]
    y SB - v32 - N '96 - p236 [51-250]
Balin, Arthur K - *The Life of the Skin*
    y BL - v93 - My 1 '97 - p1470 [51-250]
    KR - v65 - Ap 1 '97 - p512 [251-500]
Baliozian, Ara - *Pages from My Diary 1986-1995*
    WLT - v71 - Win '97 - p214 [501+]
Undiplomatic Observations
    WLT - v71 - Win '97 - p214+ [251-500]
Balisacan, Arsenio M - *Perspectives on Philippine Poverty*
    JTWS - v13 - Spr '96 - p249+ [501+]
Baljekar, Mridula - *The Real Balti Cookbook*
    BL - v93 - D 15 '96 - p701 [51-250]
Balkany: Mezhdu Proshlym I Budushchim
    Slav R - v55 - Sum '96 - p459+ [501+]
Balkwill, Fran - *The Incredible Human Body (Illus. by Mic Rolph)*
    c HB Guide - v8 - Spr '97 - p129 [51-250]
Microbes, Bugs and Wonder Drugs
    y Sch Lib - v44 - Ag '96 - p123 [51-250]
Ball, Barbara - *Task Maths. Bks. 1-3*
    y TES - Mr 21 '97 - pR11 [251-500]
Ball, Brian - *Bella and the Beanstalk*
    c TES - Jl 5 '96 - pR6 [1-50]
Ball, Deirdre - *Argentina. 3rd Ed.*
    r BL - v93 - S 15 '96 - p210 [1-50]
Ball, Desmond - *The Transformation of Security in the Asia/Pacific Region*
    R&R Bk N - v11 - N '96 - p79 [51-250]
Ball, Donna - *Exposure*
    Arm Det - v29 - Fall '96 - p500 [51-250]
Ball, Duncan - *Selby Spacedog (Illus. by Allan Stomann)*
    c Magpies - v11 - S '96 - p31 [51-250]
Selby: The Secret Adventures of a Talking Dog (Illus. by M K Brown)
    c BL - v93 - F 1 '97 - p939 [51-250]
    c PW - v244 - Ja 13 '97 - p76 [51-250]
    c SLJ - v43 - Mr '97 - p148 [51-250]
Ball, Frances - *Supporting Special Needs in the Secondary School Library*
    Sch Lib - v45 - F '97 - p53 [51-250]
Ball, Howard - *Hugo L. Black: Cold Steel Warrior*
    Choice - v34 - Mr '97 - p1238 [51-250]
Ball, Joanne Dubbs - *Fragrance Bottle Masterpieces*
    Ant & CM - v101 - F '97 - p32 [51-250]
Ball, Larry - *Multimedia Network Integration and Management*
    CBR - v14 - N '96 - p38 [51-250]
Ball, Lucille - *Love, Lucy*
    BW - v26 - O 20 '96 - p13 [51-250]
    CSM - v88 - N 7 '96 - p14 [51-250]
    Ent W - S 27 '96 - p68+ [501+]
    NYTBR - v101 - N 24 '96 - p19 [251-500]
Ball, Marion J - *Nursing Informatics*
    AJN - v96 - D '96 - p16N [51-250]
Ball, Norman R - *Ferranti-Packard: Pioneers in Canadian Electrical Manufacturing*
    Can Hist R - v77 - S '96 - p460+ [501+]
Ball, Pamela - *Lava*
    BL - v93 - Ap 1 '97 - p1280 [51-250]
    KR - v65 - F 1 '97 - p155 [251-500]
    PW - v244 - F 3 '97 - p92 [51-250]
    Trib Bks - Ap 13 '97 - p1+ [501+]
Ball, Philip - *Designing the Molecular World*
    Nature - v385 - Ja 2 '97 - p36 [1-50]
Ball, Stuart - *The Heath Government 1970-1974*
    HT - v46 - O '96 - p58 [1-50]
    TLS - F 28 '97 - p12+ [501+]
Ball, William Bentley - *Mere Creatures of the State?*
    Bks & Cult - v1 - N '95 - p5+ [501+]
Ballantine, D S - *Acoustic Wave Sensors*
    SciTech - v21 - Mr '97 - p89 [51-250]

Ballard, Carol - *The Heart and Circulatory System*
  c Sch Lib - v44 - N '96 - p173 [51-250]
  c TES - F 28 '97 - p16* [51-250]
  The Stomach and Digestive System
  c Sch Lib - v44 - N '96 - p173 [51-250]
  c TES - F 28 '97 - p16* [51-250]
Ballard, Donna - *Doing It for Ourselves*
  BL - v93 - F 15 '97 - p982 [51-250]
  Bus W - Mr 3 '97 - p14 [501+]
Ballard, J G - *Cocaine Nights*
  ILN - Christmas '96 - p90 [51-250]
  Obs - S 15 '96 - p18* [501+]
  Spec - v277 - S 21 '96 - p51+ [501+]
  TLS - S 20 '96 - p23 [501+]
  Crash
  Obs - N 24 '96 - p15* [501+]
  Rushing to Paradise
  NYTBR - v101 - Jl 21 '96 - p28 [51-250]
  A User's Guide to the Millennium
  Ent W - Je 28 '96 - p100 [51-250]
Ballard, James - *Cemeteries of the Dwight Mission, London and Scotia Areas of Pope County, Arkansas*
  r EGH - v50 - N '96 - p163 [51-250]
Ballard, Robert D - *Explorations: My Quest for Adventure and Discovery under the Sea*
  NWCR - v49 - Aut '96 - p163 [51-250]
Balle, Solvej - *According to the Law*
  KR - v64 - N 15 '96 - p1632 [51-250]
Ballen, Roger - *Platteland: Images from Rural South Africa*
  Afterimage - v24 - Ja '97 - p21 [501+]
Balliett, Whitney - *American Musicians II*
  r Choice - v34 - Ap '97 - p1346+ [51-250]
  NY - v72 - D 16 '96 - p109 [51-250]
  r NYTBR - v102 - Ap 6 '97 - p20 [51-250]
  WSJ-MW - v78 - N 20 '96 - pA20 [501+]
Ballinger, Erich - *Monster Manual*
  yr Emerg Lib - v24 - S '96 - p26 [1-50]
Ballobar, Antonio De La Cierva Lewita, Conde De - *Diario De Jerusalem En 1914-1919*
  MEJ - v51 - Spr '97 - p311 [51-250]
Ballyn, Susan - *Douglas Stewart: A Bibliography*
  r Aust Bk R - Je '96 - p67 [51-250]
Balm, Randall - *Grant Us Courage*
  Comw - v123 - S 13 '96 - p32+ [501+]
Balog, James - *James Balog's Animals A to Z*
  c HB Guide - v7 - Fall '96 - p236 [51-250]
Balogh, Jolan - *Katalog Der Auslandischen Bildwerke Des Museums Der Bildenden Kunste In Budapest, IV.-XVIII. Jahrhundert. Vol. 3*
  BM - v138 - Ag '96 - p552 [251-500]
Balogh, Mary - *Indiscreet*
  PW - v243 - D 2 '96 - p55 [51-250]
Balosky, Andrea - *Transitions: Unlocking the Creative Quilter Within*
  LJ - v122 - Ap 15 '97 - p79 [51-250]
Baloyra, Enrique A - *Conflict and Change in Cuba*
  Parameters - v26 - Win '96 - p157 [1-50]
Balsamo, Anne - *Technologies of the Gendered Body*
  Afterimage - v24 - Ja '97 - p23 [1-50]
  Bks & Cult - v3 - Ja '97 - p14+ [501+]
  SFS - v24 - Mr '97 - p124+ [501+]
  Socio R - v45 - My '97 - p334+ [501+]
  Wom R Bks - v13 - S '96 - p20+ [501+]
Baltas, Joyce - *Scholastic Guide to Balanced Reading*
  EL - v54 - D '96 - p92 [51-250]
Baltes, Paul B - *Interactive Minds*
  Choice - v34 - D '96 - p692 [51-250]
Balty, Jean Charles - *Portrat Und Gesellschaft In Der Romischen Welt*
  AJA - v100 - O '96 - p795+ [501+]
Balykin, V I - *Atom Optics with Laser Light*
  New Sci - v151 - S 28 '96 - p54+ [501+]
  Phys Today - v49 - S '96 - p88+ [501+]
Balz, Dan - *Storming the Gates*
  NYRB - v43 - Je 6 '96 - p11+ [501+]
Balzac, Honore De - *La Peau De Chagrin*
  FR - v70 - Mr '97 - p543+ [501+]
Balze, Felipe A M De La - *Remaking the Argentine Economy*
  HAHR - v76 - N '96 - p816+ [251-500]
Balzer, Marjorie Mandelstam - *Culture Incarnate*
  Am Ethnol - v23 - Ag '96 - p655 [501+]
Bambace, Anthony - *Will H. Bradley: His Work*
  r AB - v98 - N 25 '96 - p1832 [501+]
Bambach, Charles R - *Heidegger, Dilthey, and the Crisis of Historicism*
  AHR - v102 - F '97 - p90+ [501+]

Bambara, Toni Cade - *Deep Sightings and Rescue Missions*
  BL - v93 - S 15 '96 - p178 [51-250]
  KR - v64 - O 1 '96 - p1435 [251-500]
  LJ - v121 - D '96 - p92 [51-250]
  PW - v243 - O 7 '96 - p59+ [51-250]
Bambaren, Sergio - *Beach of Dreams*
  Aust Bk R - O '96 - p69 [1-50]
Bamberger, Michael - *The Design and Management of Poverty Reduction Programs and Projects in Anglophone Africa*
  JEL - v35 - Mr '97 - p232 [51-250]
Bamberger, Michelle - *Help! The Quick Guide to First Aid for Your Cat*
  r ARBA - v28 - '97 - p573 [51-250]
Bambrick, Susan - *The Cambridge Encyclopedia of Australia*
  r AB - v98 - Ag 19 '96 - p576+ [501+]
Bamford, Christopher - *Celtic Christianity*
  RR - v55 - S '96 - p553 [1-50]
Bamford, W H - *Service Experience and Design in Pressure Vessels and Piping*
  SciTech - v20 - D '96 - p85 [51-250]
Bamforth, Iain - *Open Workings*
  TLS - F 7 '97 - p24 [251-500]
Bammel, Caroline P Hammond - *Der Romerbriefkommentar Des Origenes*
  Rel St Rev - v22 - O '96 - p301+ [501+]
Ban, A W Van Den - *Agricultural Extension. 2nd Ed.*
  SciTech - v21 - Mr '97 - p69 [1-50]
Banaszak, Grzegorz - *Algebraic K-Theory*
  SciTech - v20 - D '96 - p19 [51-250]
Banaszak, Lee Ann - *Why Movements Succeed or Fail*
  TLS - Mr 21 '97 - p13 [251-500]
Ban Breathnach, Sarah - *Simple Abundance*
  CSM - v88 - N 7 '96 - p14 [51-250]
Banchoff, Thomas F - *Beyond the Third Dimension*
  Math T - v90 - Ja '97 - p70 [51-250]
Bancquart, Marie-Claire - *Enigmatiques*
  WLT - v70 - Sum '96 - p655+ [501+]
Bancroft, Henrietta - *Animals in Winter (Illus. by Helen K Davie)*
  c BL - v93 - D 1 '96 - p662 [51-250]
  c KR - v64 - D 1 '96 - p1733 [51-250]
  c SB - v33 - My '97 - p112 [251-500]
  c SLJ - v43 - Mr '97 - p170+ [51-250]
Bancroft, Nancy H - *Implementing SAP R/3*
  SciTech - v20 - S '96 - p62 [51-250]
Bandem, I Made - *Balinese Dance in Transition. 2nd Ed.*
  Choice - v34 - N '96 - p471+ [51-250]
Bandemer, Hans - *Fuzzy Sets, Fuzzy Logic, Fuzzy Methods with Applications*
  Choice - v34 - Mr '97 - p1195 [51-250]
  SciTech - v20 - N '96 - p13 [51-250]
Bandini, Raffaello - *Ad Nota*
  TLS - Jl 19 '96 - p12 [501+]
Bandon, Alexandra - *Dominican Americans*
  y JOYS - v9 - Sum '96 - p414+ [51-250]
Bandow, Doug - *Tripwire: Korea and U.S. Foreign Policy in a Changed World*
  Choice - v34 - D '96 - p685 [51-250]
  NYTBR - v101 - S 22 '96 - p30 [501+]
Bandyopadhyay, Pratul - *Geometry, Topology and Quantization*
  SciTech - v21 - Mr '97 - p13 [51-250]
Banerjee, Ajit K - *Rehabilitation of Degraded Forests in Asia*
  J Gov Info - v23 - S '96 - p688 [51-250]
Banerjee, Anindya - *Co-Integration, Error Correction, and the Econometric Analysis of Non-Stationary Data*
  Econ J - v106 - N '96 - p1813+ [501+]
Banerjee, Jacqueline P - *Through the Northern Gate*
  R&R Bk N - v12 - F '97 - p87 [51-250]
Banerjee, Utpal - *Dependence Analysis*
  SciTech - v21 - Mr '97 - p9 [51-250]
Baneth, Jean - *Selecting Development Projects for the World Bank*
  JEL - v34 - D '96 - p2113+ [51-250]
Bang, Elizabeth - *Christmas Doughcrafts*
  LJ - v121 - O 15 '96 - p56 [51-250]
  PW - v243 - S 2 '96 - p125 [51-250]
Bang, Molly - *Chattanooga Sludge (Illus. by Molly Bang)*
  c HB Guide - v7 - Fall '96 - p247+ [51-250]
  c SB - v32 - O '96 - p207 [51-250]
  c SLJ - v42 - Ag '96 - p148 [51-250]

Goose (Illus. by Molly Bang)
  c BL - v93 - S 15 '96 - p239 [51-250]
  c CBRS - v25 - Ja '97 - p49 [51-250]
  c CCB-B - v50 - D '96 - p128 [51-250]
  c Ch BWatch - v7 - F '97 - p2 [1-50]
  c HB - v72 - N '96 - p718+ [51-250]
  c HB Guide - v8 - Spr '97 - p18 [51-250]
  c KR - v64 - Ag 15 '96 - p1232 [51-250]
  c SLJ - v42 - N '96 - p76 [51-250]
  c SLJ - v42 - D '96 - p27 [1-50]
Ten, Nine, Eight
  c BL - v93 - Ap 1 '97 - p1340 [1-50]
  c HB Guide - v8 - Spr '97 - p10 [51-250]
  c Par - v72 - F '97 - p149 [1-50]
Wiley and the Hairy Man
  c HB Guide - v8 - Spr '97 - p100 [51-250]
Bangs, Carl - *Phineas F. Bresee: His Life in Methodism, the Holiness Movement, and the Church of the Nazarene*
  CC - v113 - S 25 '96 - p903+ [251-500]
Bangs, Edward - *Steven Kellogg's Yankee Doodle (Illus. by Steven Kellogg)*
  c KR - v64 - My 1 '96 - p690 [51-250]
Bangs, John Kendrick - *The Autobiography of Methuselah. Electronic Media Version*
  SF Chr - v18 - O '96 - p79 [51-250]
Banham, Martin - *The Cambridge Guide to Theatre*
  r Hisp - v79 - D '96 - p800+ [251-500]
Banham, Reyner - *A Critic Writes*
  LJ - v121 - N 1 '96 - p63 [51-250]
  Obs - F 2 '97 - p18* [501+]
Banim, Lisa - *Drums at Saratoga*
  c Ch BWatch - v6 - N '96 - p3 [51-250]
  The Hessian's Secret Diary (Illus. by James Watling)
  c BL - v93 - My 1 '97 - p1492 [51-250]
  c CBRS - v25 - F '97 - p81 [1-50]
  c Ch BWatch - v6 - Jl '96 - p3 [51-250]
Bank of Portugal - *Annual Report 1994. Abridged Ed.*
  JEL - v34 - D '96 - p2036 [51-250]
Bank of Spain - *Annual Report 1995*
  JEL - v35 - Mr '97 - p208 [51-250]
Bankart, C Peter - *Talking Cures*
  SciTech - v20 - D '96 - p44 [51-250]
Banker, Mark T - *Presbyterian Missions and Cultural Interaction in the Far Southwest 1850-1950*
  CH - v65 - S '96 - p539+ [501+]
Bankier, William - *The Last Act Was Deadly and Other Stories (Rubinek). Audio Version*
  y Kliatt - v30 - S '96 - p49 [51-250]
  y SLJ - v42 - O '96 - p79 [51-250]
Banks, Daibo Bill - *And Zen Some*
  Tric - v6 - Fall '96 - p142 [1-50]
Banks, Iain - *Whit: Or, Isis amongst the Unsaved*
  Obs - Ag 18 '96 - p19 [51-250]
Banks, Iain M - *Excession*
  BL - v93 - F 1 '97 - p929 [51-250]
  y Kliatt - v31 - My '97 - p12 [51-250]
  KR - v64 - D 1 '96 - p1706 [51-250]
  PW - v244 - Ja 27 '97 - p82 [51-250]
  Feersum Endjinn
  y Kliatt - v30 - N '96 - p12 [51-250]
Banks, Jack - *Monopoly Television*
  Ant R - v55 - Spr '97 - p238+ [251-500]
  Choice - v34 - D '96 - p623 [51-250]
Banks, James A - *Handbook of Research on Multicultural Education*
  TCR - v98 - Fall '96 - p153+ [501+]
  Multicultural Education, Transformative Knowledge, and Action
  Adoles - v31 - Win '96 - p991 [51-250]
  Choice - v34 - Ja '97 - p850 [51-250]
  EL - v54 - F '97 - p84 [251-500]
Banks, Jeri - *All of Us Together*
  J Rehab RD - v33 - Jl '96 - p337 [251-500]
Banks, Kate - *Baboon (Illus. by Georg Hallensleben)*
  c BL - v93 - Mr 1 '97 - p1166 [51-250]
  c CCB-B - v50 - Ap '97 - p272 [51-250]
  c HB - v73 - My '97 - p300+ [251-500]
  c KR - v65 - Mr 1 '97 - p377 [51-250]
  c PW - v244 - F 3 '97 - p105 [51-250]
  c SLJ - v43 - Mr '97 - p148 [51-250]
  Spider Spider (Illus. by Georg Hallensleben)
  c HB Guide - v8 - Spr '97 - p18 [51-250]
  c KR - v64 - O 1 '96 - p1464 [51-250]
  c SLJ - v42 - N '96 - p76 [51-250]
Banks, Lynne Reid - *Angela and Diabola*
  c KR - v65 - My 1 '97 - p716 [51-250]
  c PW - v244 - Ap 7 '97 - p92 [51-250]
  Broken Bridge
  c Bks Keeps - Mr '97 - p27 [51-250]
  Harry the Poisonous Centipede. Audio Version
  c TES - Ag 30 '96 - p28 [51-250]

Harry the Poisonous Centipede (Illus. by Tony Ross)
  c   Bks Keeps - N '96 - p9 [51-250]
  c   Sch Lib - v44 - N '96 - p148+ [51-250]
Banks, Marcus - *Organizing Jainism in India and England*
  Rel St Rev - v23 - Ap '97 - p103+ [501+]
Banks, Martin - *Conserving Rain Forests*
  y   SLJ - v42 - O '96 - p45 [1-50]
Banks, Paul - *The Making of Peter Grimes. Vols. 1-2*
  TLS - S 13 '96 - p6+ [501+]
Banks, Robert - *Paul's Idea of Community. Rev. Ed.*
  Rel St Rev - v23 - Ja '97 - p73 [51-250]
Banks, Russell - *The New World*
  NYTBR - v101 - O 27 '96 - p48 [1-50]
Rule of the Bone
  y   Emerg Lib - v24 - S '96 - p24 [1-50]
  NS & S - v9 - My 24 '96 - p40 [1-50]
Banks, Sara Harrell - *A Net to Catch Time (Illus. by Scott Cook)*
  c   BL - v93 - D 1 '96 - p668 [51-250]
  c   HB Guide - v8 - Spr '97 - p19 [51-250]
  c   KR - v64 - N 15 '96 - p1666 [51-250]
  c   PW - v243 - D 2 '96 - p59+ [51-250]
  c   SLJ - v43 - Ja '97 - p75 [51-250]
Under the Shadow of Wings
  c   BL - v93 - My 15 '97 - p1573 [51-250]
  c   KR - v65 - Ap 1 '97 - p548 [51-250]
Banks, William M - *Black Intellectuals*
  Bl S - v26 - Sum '96 - p63 [51-250]
  BW - v26 - N 17 '96 - p9 [501+]
  Choice - v34 - Ap '97 - p1402 [51-250]
  KR - v64 - Ag 15 '96 - p1198 [251-500]
  LJ - v121 - O 15 '96 - p70 [51-250]
  LJ - v121 - N 1 '96 - p84 [1-50]
  NYTBR - v101 - N 10 '96 - p21 [501+]
  Obs - Mr 2 '97 - p16* [501+]
  PW - v243 - S 2 '96 - p103 [51-250]
  W&I - v12 - Ap '97 - p276+ [501+]
Banks-Payne, Ruby - *Ruby's Low-Fat Soul Food Cookbook*
  y   Kliatt - v31 - Mr '97 - p36 [51-250]
Bann, Stephen - *Romanticism and the Rise of History*
  BM - v138 - O '96 - p700 [51-250]
  Hist & T - v35 - 3 '96 - p384+ [501+]
Under the Sign
  AJA - v100 - O '96 - p769+ [501+]
  BM - v139 - Ja '97 - p52 [501+]
Bannai, E - *Progress in Algebraic Combinatorics*
  SciTech - v20 - N '96 - p15 [51-250]
Banner, Adrian - *Addictive Behaviour*
  SciTech - v20 - D '96 - p46 [51-250]
Banner, James M - *The Elements of Teaching*
  BL - v93 - F 15 '97 - p977 [51-250]
  KR - v65 - Ja 15 '97 - p105 [251-500]
  PW - v244 - F 24 '97 - p80 [51-250]
Bannerji, Himani - *Thinking Through*
  Can Lit - Spr '97 - p251+ [501+]
  CF - v75 - O '96 - p39+ [501+]
Bannerman, Helen - *The Story of Little Babaji (Illus. by Fred Marcellino)*
  c   BL - v93 - Ja '97 - p767 [1-50]
  c   BL - v93 - S 1 '96 - p126 [51-250]
  c   BL - v93 - Ap 1 '97 - p1296 [1-50]
  c   CBRS - v25 - O '96 - p13 [51-250]
  c   CCB-B - v50 - S '96 - p5+ [51-250]
  c   Ch BWatch - v6 - N '96 - p6 [51-250]
  c   HB - v72 - S '96 - p536+ [501+]
  c   HB Guide - v8 - Spr '97 - p19 [51-250]
  c   LATBR - D 8 '96 - p19 [51-250]
  c   Learning - v25 - N '96 - p29 [51-250]
  c   NY - v72 - N 18 '96 - p98+ [51-250]
  c   NYTBR - v101 - N 10 '96 - p34 [501+]
  c   NYTLa - v146 - D 9 '96 - pC18 [51-250]
  c   Par - v71 - D '96 - p252 [51-250]
  c   SLJ - v42 - O '96 - p84 [51-250]
  c   Time - v148 - S 9 '96 - p72 [251-500]
  c   VV - v41 - S 17 '96 - p49 [501+]
The Story of Little Black Sambo
  c   HB - v72 - S '96 - p536+ [501+]
Banning, Lance - *Jefferson and Madison*
  AHR - v102 - F '97 - p170+ [251-500]
  JSH - v62 - N '96 - p799+ [251-500]
The Sacred Fire of Liberty
  APSR - v90 - D '96 - p884 [501+]
  AS - v66 - Spr '97 - p310+ [501+]
  HRNB - v25 - Fall '96 - p5 [501+]
  JSH - v63 - F '97 - p151+ [501+]
  RAH - v24 - S '96 - p401+ [501+]
  TLS - My 24 '96 - p11+ [501+]
  VQR - v72 - Aut '96 - p745+ [501+]
Bannister, Barbara A - *Infectious Disease*
  SciTech - v20 - S '96 - p30 [51-250]

Bannister, Jo - *No Birds Sing*
  BL - v92 - Ag '96 - p1884+ [51-250]
Bannister, Sybil - *I Lived under Hitler*
  HT - v46 - Ag '96 - p60 [51-250]
Bansak, Edward G - *Fearing the Dark*
  FQ - v50 - Win '96 - p61+ [251-500]
Banta, Martha - *Taylored Lives*
  T&C - v37 - O '96 - p846+ [501+]
Bantas, Andrei - *NTC's Romanian and English Dictionary*
  r   ARBA - v28 - '97 - p398 [251-500]
Bantock, Nick - *The Venetian's Wife*
  BW - v27 - Ja 5 '97 - p11 [501+]
  Mac - v109 - D 9 '96 - p66 [1-50]
  MFSF - v92 - F '97 - p42 [251-500]
  PW - v243 - S 2 '96 - p114+ [51-250]
  Quill & Q - v62 - O '96 - p42 [251-500]
Banton, Michael - *International Action against Racial Discrimination*
  Choice - v34 - My '97 - p1571 [51-250]
Banuazizi, Ali - *The New Geopolitics of Central Asia and Its Borderlands*
  MEP - v5 - 1 '97 - p211+ [501+]
Banulescu, Daniel - *Te Pup In Fund Conducator Iubit!*
  BL - v93 - D 15 '96 - p714 [1-50]
Banville, John - *Athena*
  WLT - v70 - Aut '96 - p958 [251-500]
The Untouchable
  KR - v65 - Mr 15 '97 - p396 [251-500]
  LATBR - Ap 20 '97 - p2 [501+]
  LJ - v122 - Ap 15 '97 - p116 [51-250]
  PW - v244 - Ap 14 '97 - p52 [51-250]
  WSJ-Cent - v99 - My 9 '97 - pA16 [501+]
Banyai, Istvan - *Re-Zoom (Illus. by Istvan Banyai)*
  y   Emerg Lib - v24 - S '96 - p26 [1-50]
  c   RT - v50 - O '96 - p137 [1-50]
  c   RT - v50 - D '96 - p345+ [1-50]
REM--Rapid Eye Movement (Illus. by Istvan Banyai)
  c   CCB-B - v50 - Ap '97 - p272 [51-250]
  c   HB - v73 - My '97 - p302 [51-250]
  c   KR - v65 - My 1 '97 - p716 [51-250]
  c   PW - v244 - Ap 14 '97 - p73 [51-250]
Zoom (Illus. by Istvan Banyai)
  c   RT - v50 - O '96 - p138 [1-50]
Banziger, Hans - *Institutionen--Literarische Feindbilder?*
  Ger Q - v69 - Fall '96 - p435+ [501+]
Baquero, Gaston - *Poemas Invisibles*
  BL - v93 - Ap 1 '97 - p1284 [1-50]
Barabba, Vincent P - *Meeting of the Minds*
  Choice - v34 - S '96 - p170 [51-250]
Barach, Jeffrey A - *Leadership and the Job of the Executive*
  HR Mag - v42 - Mr '97 - p136 [51-250]
  R&R Bk N - v11 - D '96 - p28 [51-250]
Baraka, Imamu Amiri - *The Autobiography of LeRoi Jones*
  Trib Bks - Ap 6 '97 - p8 [1-50]
Eulogies
  KR - v64 - O 15 '96 - p1502 [251-500]
  LJ - v121 - D '96 - p92 [51-250]
  LJ - v121 - N 1 '96 - p84 [1-50]
  PW - v243 - O 7 '96 - p48 [51-250]
Funk Lore
  BL - v93 - Ja '97 - p807+ [51-250]
  LJ - v121 - N 1 '96 - p84 [1-50]
  LJ - v121 - N 15 '96 - p65 [51-250]
  PW - v243 - D 30 '96 - p61+ [51-250]
Transbluesency: The Selected Poems of Amiri Baraka/ LeRoi Jones 1961-1995
  LJ - v122 - Ap 1 '97 - p94 [1-50]
  WLT - v71 - Win '97 - p154+ [501+]
Barakat, Huda - *The Stone of Laughter*
  Choice - v34 - N '96 - p451 [51-250]
  MEJ - v50 - Sum '96 - p454 [51-250]
Barakat, Salim - *Sonne Du Cor!*
  WLT - v70 - Aut '96 - p1023 [501+]
Baranczak, Stanislaw - *Pegaz Zdebiat*
  WLT - v70 - Aut '96 - p989 [501+]
Baranelli, Luca - *Album Calvino*
  TLS - O 4 '96 - p39 [501+]
Baranosky, Edward - *A Foot in Both Worlds*
  Sm Pr R - v28 - D '96 - p9 [251-500]
Baranowski, Shelley - *The Sanctity of Rural Life*
  AHR - v102 - F '97 - p126+ [251-500]
  JMH - v68 - S '96 - p629+ [501+]
Baranski, Zygmunt G - *The New Italian Novel*
  MLR - v92 - Ap '97 - p488+ [501+]
Barany, Michael - *Biochemistry of Smooth Muscle Contraction*
  Sci - v274 - O 18 '96 - p367+ [501+]
Barash, Carol - *English Women's Poetry 1649-1714*
  TLS - Mr 21 '97 - p8 [501+]

Barash, Joseph Andrew - *Heidegger Et Son Siecle*
  CPR - v16 - Ap '96 - p81+ [501+]
Baratta, Tommy - *Cooking for Jack*
  BL - v93 - S 15 '96 - p178 [51-250]
Barazangi, Nimat Hafez - *Islamic Identity and the Struggle for Justice*
  Choice - v34 - S '96 - p144 [51-250]
  MEJ - v50 - Aut '96 - p630+ [51-250]
  WorldV - v12 - Jl '96 - p8+ [51-250]
Barbanera, Marcello - *Il Guerriero Di Agrigento*
  AJA - v100 - Jl '96 - p637+ [251-500]
Barbara, Daniel - *Databases and Mobile Computing*
  SciTech - v20 - D '96 - p8 [51-250]
Barbash, Jack E - *Pesticides in Ground Water*
  SciTech - v20 - D '96 - p69 [51-250]
Barbeau, Arthur E - *The Unknown Soldiers*
  TLS - Ja 10 '97 - p28 [251-500]
Barbeau, Edward J - *Five Hundred Mathematical Challenges*
  Math T - v89 - O '96 - p606 [51-250]
Barber, Anthony - *Taking the Tide*
  TLS - N 15 '96 - p14 [501+]
Barber, Antonia - *The Mousehole Cat (Illus. by Nicola Bayley)*
  c   PW - v243 - O 14 '96 - p85 [1-50]
Barber, Barbara E - *Allie's Basketball Dream (Illus. by Darryl Ligasan)*
  c   BL - v93 - Ja '97 - p866 [251-500]
  c   CBR3 - v25 - Ja '97 - p54 [51-250]
  c   CCB-B - v50 - F '97 - p199 [51-250]
  c   Emerg Lib - v24 - Mr '97 - p66 [1-50]
  c   HB Guide - v8 - Spr '97 - p19 [51-250]
  c   PW - v243 - N 11 '96 - p73+ [51-250]
  c   SLJ - v42 - N '96 - p78 [51-250]
Barber, Benjamin R - *Jihad vs. McWorld*
  CS - v25 - S '96 - p588+ [501+]
Barber, Bruce - *Voices of Fire*
  Choice - v34 - Ap '97 - p1328 [51-250]
  Quill & Q - v62 - O '96 - p38 [251-500]
Barber, Cicely Mary - *The Little Green Book*
  c   IIB Guide - v7 - Fall '96 - p366 [1-50]
Barber, Connie - *Enter Your House with Care*
  Aust Bk R - Jl '96 - p56 [51-250]
Barber, Elizabeth Wayland - *Women's Work*
  JPC - v29 - Spr '96 - p229+ [501+]
Barber, John M - *John M. Barber's Chesapeake*
  Sea H - Win '96 - p45 [51-250]
Barber, Joseph - *Hypnosis and Suggestion in the Treatment of Pain*
  SciTech - v20 - D '96 - p41 [51-250]
Barber, Kathleen L - *Proportional Representation and Election Reform in Ohio*
  APSR - v90 - S '96 - p643 [501+]
Barber, Kim - *Career Success with Pets*
  Dog Fan - v28 - Ja '97 - p26 [251-500]
Barber, Malcolm - *Crusaders and Heretics 12th-14th Centuries*
  CHR - v82 - Jl '96 - p535+ [501+]
The New Knighthood
  Specu - v71 - Jl '96 - p679+ [501+]
Barber, Michael - *The Learning Game*
  NS - v125 - N 15 '96 - p44+ [501+]
  TES - N 8 '96 - p8* [501+]
  TLS - Ja 24 '97 - p10 [501+]
Raising Educational Standards in the Inner Cities
  Choice - v34 - O '96 - p333 [501+]
Barber, Nicky - *The Kingfisher Young People's Book of Music*
  cr   CSM - v88 - N 21 '96 - pB4 [51-250]
  c   HB Guide - v8 - Spr '97 - p140 [51-250]
  c   JB - v60 - D '96 - p263+ [51-250]
  cr   PW - v243 - S 16 '96 - p85 [51-250]
  c   SLJ - v43 - Mr '97 - p212 [51-250]
Barber, Nicola - *The Mind (Illus. by Ross Collins)*
  c   Sch Lib - v44 - N '96 - p173 [51-250]
Barber, Phil - *Football America*
  y   BL - v93 - N 15 '96 - p565 [51-250]
  LJ - v121 - N 15 '96 - p67 [51-250]
Barber, Phyllis - *How I Got Cultured*
  y   BL - v93 - D 15 '96 - p719 [1-50]
Barber, Richard - *The Knight and Chivalry*
  HT - v47 - F '97 - p60+ [51-250]
Barber, Stephen - *Weapons of Liberation*
  TLS - O 18 '96 - p28 [501+]
Barber, Theodore X - *Hypnosis: A Scientific Approach*
  AJCH - v39 - Ja '97 - p225+ [501+]
Barber, William J - *Designs within Disorder*
  Choice - v34 - My '97 - p1545 [51-250]
  JEL - v35 - Mr '97 - p172+ [501+]
  JEL - v35 - Mr '97 - p257 [51-250]

Barbera, Carmen - *Juana La Loca*
Hisp - v79 - S '96 - p472+ [501+]
Barberis, Peter - *The Elite of the Elite*
Choice - v34 - D '96 - p682 [51-250]
R&R Bk N - v12 - F '97 - p60 [51-250]
Barbero, Alessandro - *Bella Vita E Guerre Altrui Di Mr. Pyle, Gentiluomo*
BL - v93 - D 1 '96 - p644 [1-50]
Barbershop Collectibles
r Ant & CM - v101 - N '96 - p31 [1-50]
Barbet, Alix - *Les Peintures Des Necropoles Romaines D'Abila Et Du Nord De La Jordanie. Vols. 1-2*
AJA - v100 - Jl '96 - p629+ [501+]
Barbiellini Amidei, Gaspare - *L'Amore E Salvo*
BL - v93 - D 1 '96 - p644 [1-50]
Barbier, Frederic - *L'Empire Du Livre*
AHR - v101 - D '96 - p1565+ [501+]
BC - v45 - Aut '96 - p404+ [501+]
Barbier, Jean-Paul - *Ma Bibliotheque Poetique*
r Ren & Ref - v19 - Fall '96 - p99+ [501+]
Barbieri, Maureen - *Sounds from the Heart*
EJ - v85 - D '96 - p82+ [501+]
Barbolini, Anna Rosa Venturi - *Girolamo Tiraboschi: Mostra Documentario Bibliografica*
Lib - v19 - Mr '97 - p100 [51-250]
Barbosa, Rogerio Andrade - *African Animal Tales (Illus. by Cica Fittipaldi)*
c TranslRevS - v1 - My '95 - p10 [51-250]
Barbosa, Valmir C - *An Introduction to Distributed Algorithms*
Choice - v34 - My '97 - p1535 [51-250]
New Sci - v153 - Mr 1 '97 - p46+ [501+]
Barbosa-Canovas, Gustavo V - *Dehydration of Foods*
SciTech - v20 - N '96 - p80 [51-250]
Barbour, Alan G - *Lyme Disease*
r BL - v93 - F 1 '97 - p960 [1-50]
Sci - v274 - O 25 '96 - p523 [1-50]
SciTech - v21 - Mr '97 - p50 [51-250]
Barbour, Allen B - *Caring for Patients*
AJPsych - v153 - Ag '96 - p1106+ [501+]
Barbour, Andrew - *Fodor's South Africa. 1996 Ed.*
r BWatch - v17 - S '96 - p6 [51-250]
Barbour, Anne - *A Rake's Reform*
LJ - v121 - N 15 '96 - p47 [51-250]
Barbour, Daphne - *Saint-Porchaire Ceramics*
Ceram Mo - v44 - N '96 - p27 [51-250]
Barbour, Galen L - *Quality in the Veterans Health Administration*
SciTech - v20 - D '96 - p87 [51-250]
Redefining a Public Health System
R&R Bk N - v11 - D '96 - p72 [51-250]
SciTech - v21 - Mr '97 - p100 [51-250]
Barbour, Hugh - *Quaker Crosscurrents*
Rel St Rev - v22 - O '96 - p358 [51-250]
Barbour, James - *Biographies of Books*
AL - v68 - S '96 - p664 [51-250]
Nine-C Lit - v51 - Mr '97 - p554 [51-250]
TLS - Ja 3 '97 - p25 [501+]
Barbour, John D - *Versions of Deconversion*
Biography - v20 - Win '97 - p103+ [501+]
Rel St Rev - v23 - Ja '97 - p53 [51-250]
Theol St - v57 - Mr '96 - p177+ [501+]
Barbour, Robin S - *The Kingdom of God and Human Society*
Rel St Rev - v23 - Ja '97 - p69 [51-250]
Barbour, Sarah - *Nathalie Sarraute and the Feminist Reader*
Signs - v22 - Aut '96 - p254+ [501+]
Barbour, Scott - *Health and Fitness*
y Ch BWatch - v6 - Jl '96 - p2 [1-50]
y SLJ - v42 - Ag '96 - p167 [51-250]
y VOYA - v19 - O '96 - p232 [251-500]
Barbuto, Domenica M - *Guide to Civil War Books*
r LAR - v98 - N '96 - p595 [1-50]
Barbuto, Gennaro Maria - *Il Principe E L'Antichristo*
CH - v66 - Mr '97 - p122+ [501+]
Barcelona Conference on Algebraic Topology (1994: San Feliu De Guixols, Spain) - *Algebraic Topology*
SciTech - v20 - S '96 - p12 [51-250]
Barck, Simone - *Lexikon Sozialistischer Literatur*
MLR - v92 - Ja '97 - p256+ [501+]
Barclay, Donald A - *Into the Wilderness Dream*
J Am St - v30 - Ap '96 - p172+ [501+]
Barclay, Tony - *The Shop on Danforth Avenue*
y JB - v60 - O '96 - p197 [251-500]
Bard, Christine - *Les Filles De Marianne*
Choice - v34 - D '96 - p567 [1-50]
Bard, Kathryn A - *From Farmers to Pharaohs*
AJA - v101 - Ja '97 - p165+ [501+]
Bard, Mitchell G - *Forgotten Victims*
Pres SQ - v26 - Fall '96 - p1187+ [251-500]

Bardaglio, Peter W - *Reconstructing the Household*
JSH - v63 - F '97 - p166+ [501+]
J Soc H - v30 - Win '96 - p533+ [501+]
RAH - v24 - S '96 - p412+ [501+]
Bardana, Emil J - *Indoor Air Pollution and Health*
SciTech - v21 - Mr '97 - p46 [51-250]
Barden, Cindy - *Love to Write!*
Learning - v25 - S '96 - p89 [51-250]
Bardon, Jonathan - *A Shorter Illustrated History of Ulster*
HT - v46 - O '96 - p58 [1-50]
Barefoot, Daniel W - *General Robert F. Hoke: Lee's Modest Warrior*
Choice - v34 - Ja '97 - p861 [51-250]
Bar-El, Dalyah - *Nesuah: Ela Mah?*
BL - v93 - Mr 1 '97 - p1115 [1-50]
Barer, Burl - *The Saint: A Complete History in Print, Radio, Film and Television of Leslie Charteris' Robin Hood of Modern Crime, Simon Templar 1928-1992*
r JPC - v29 - Spr '96 - p230+ [251-500]
Bares, R - *Clinical PET*
SciTech - v21 - Mr '97 - p49 [51-250]
Barfield, Ray - *Listening to Radio 1920-1950*
Choice - v34 - Ja '97 - p786 [51-250]
R&R Bk N - v11 - D '96 - p61 [51-250]
Barford, J P - *Fundamental and Applied Aspects of Animal Cell Cultivation*
Choice - v34 - D '96 - p642 [51-250]
Barger, Jan - *Wake Up Piglet*
c Bks Keeps - v100 - S '96 - p9 [51-250]
Bargum, Johan - *Charlie Boy*
WLT - v70 - Aut '96 - p977+ [501+]
Barham, Bradford L - *Prosperity's Promise*
R&R Bk N - v11 - D '96 - p31 [51-250]
Baricco, Alessandro - *Seta*
BL - v93 - D 1 '96 - p644 [1-50]
Econ - v339 - My 18 '96 - p16*+ [501+]
Silk
Obs - Mr 9 '97 - p18* [251-500]
Barich, Bill - *Carson Valley*
KR - v65 - Ja 15 '97 - p75+ [251-500]
NYTBR - v102 - Ap 6 '97 - p22+ [501+]
PW - v244 - Ja 13 '97 - p52+ [51-250]
Time - v149 - Mr 31 '97 - p80 [251-500]
Barilla, Jean - *The Nutrition Superbook. Vol. 2*
BWatch - v17 - S '96 - p10 [51-250]
Barillari, Diana - *Istanbul 1900*
BL - v93 - Mr 15 '97 - p1217 [51-250]
Baring-Gould, Sabine - *A Book of Folklore*
Folkl - v107 - '96 - p126 [51-250]
Bar-Joseph, Uri - *Intelligence Intervention in the Politics of Democratic States*
AHR - v102 - F '97 - p90 [251-500]
PSQ - v111 - Fall '96 - p533+ [501+]
Barka, Vasyl - *Sudnyi Step*
BL - v93 - N 15 '96 - p577 [1-50]
Barkai, Haim - *The Lessons of Israel's Great Inflation*
Econ J - v107 - Ja '97 - p265 [251-500]
MEJ - v51 - Win '97 - p123+ [501+]
MEQ - v3 - S '96 - p83+ [251-500]
Barkan, Elazar - *The Retreat of Scientific Racism*
Am Ethnol - v23 - Ag '96 - p659+ [501+]
Barkan, Joanne - *Help! It's Halloween! (Illus. by Kathryn Mitter)*
c PW - v243 - S 30 '96 - p86 [51-250]
The Strangest Halloween (Illus. by Kathryn Mitter)
c PW - v243 - S 30 '96 - p86 [51-250]
Barkan, Stanley H - *O Jerusalem*
Sm Pr R - v28 - N '96 - p5 [251-500]
Barkan, Steven E - *Criminology: A Sociological Understanding*
R&R Bk N - v12 - F '97 - p51 [51-250]
Barker, Andrew - *Telegrams from the Soul*
R&R Bk N - v11 - N '96 - p75 [51-250]
Barker, Anthony J - *Slavery and Antislavery in Mauritius 1810-33*
Choice - v34 - Mr '97 - p1218 [51-250]
Barker, Cicely Mary - *The Little Lilac Book*
c HB Guide - v7 - Fall '96 - p366 [1-50]
Barker, Clive - *The Inhuman Condition (Steele). Audio Version*
BL - v93 - N 1 '96 - p522 [51-250]
BWatch - v18 - Mr '97 - p8 [1-50]
Sacrament
Necro - Win '97 - p11+ [501+]
PW - v243 - N 4 '96 - p42 [1-50]
y VOYA - v19 - D '96 - p276 [251-500]
Sacrament (Keith). Audio Version
y Kliatt - v31 - My '97 - p44 [51-250]
Barker, Elsa - *Letters from the Light (Ryan). Audio Version*
y Kliatt - v30 - N '96 - p50 [51-250]

Barker, Francis - *Colonial Discourse/Postcolonial Theory*
AL - v69 - Mr '97 - p254 [51-250]
The Culture of Violence
MLR - v92 - Ap '97 - p421+ [501+]
MP - v94 - Ag '96 - p89+ [501+]
Barker, Graeme - *The Biferno Valley Survey*
AJA - v101 - Ja '97 - p184+ [501+]
Am Ant - v62 - Ja '97 - p170 [501+]
A Mediterranean Valley
AJA - v101 - Ja '97 - p184+ [501+]
Am Ant - v62 - Ja '97 - p170 [501+]
Barker, J Craig - *The Abuse of Diplomatic Privileges and Immunities*
R&R Bk N - v11 - D '96 - p49 [51-250]
Barker, Juliet - *The Brontes*
HR - v49 - Sum '96 - p301+ [501+]
Nine-C Lit - v51 - S '96 - p240+ [501+]
NYTBR - v101 - N 17 '96 - p40 [51-250]
Trib Bks - Ja 5 '97 - p2 [51-250]
VS - v39 - Aut '95 - p55+ [501+]
Barker, L Randol - *Interactive Ambulatory Medicine. Electronic Media Version*
SciTech - v21 - Mr '97 - p49 [51-250]
Barker, Lewis M - *Learning and Behavior. 2nd Ed.*
R&R Bk N - v12 - F '97 - p6 [51-250]
Barker, Malcolm E - *More San Francisco Memoirs*
BWatch - v17 - S '96 - p6+ [51-250]
Barker, Martin - *The Lasting of the Mohicans*
AL - v69 - Mr '97 - p213+ [251-500]
Choice - v34 - O '96 - p275 [51-250]
Barker, Nicola - *Heading Inland*
NS - v125 - Ag 30 '96 - p48 [251-500]
Small Holdings
Books - v9 - S '95 - p24 [1-50]
Barker, Nicolas - *A Potencie of Life*
Lib - v18 - S '96 - p251+ [501+]
Barker, Pat - *Blow Your House Down*
NS - v125 - D 20 '96 - p117 [51-250]
The Eye in the Door (Firth). Audio Version
y Kliatt - v31 - My '97 - p43 [51-250]
The Ghost Road
Books - v9 - S '95 - p22 [1-50]
HR - v49 - Sum '96 - p316+ [501+]
LATBR - D 29 '96 - p6 [51-250]
NYTBR - v101 - D 1 '96 - p36 [51-250]
NYTBR - v101 - D 8 '96 - p80 [1-50]
Trib Bks - Ja 5 '97 - p2 [51-250]
Woman's J - Ag '96 - p11 [51-250]
The Ghost Road (Crossley). Audio Version
BL - v93 - My 15 '97 - p1596 [51-250]
The Ghost Road (Firth). Audio Version
y Kliatt - v31 - My '97 - p43 [51-250]
Regeneration
Spec - v277 - N 16 '96 - p44 [1-50]
Trib Bks - Ja 19 '97 - p8 [1-50]
Regeneration (Crossley). Audio Version
BWatch - v18 - Mr '97 - p7 [1-50]
Regeneration (Firth). Audio Version
y Kliatt - v31 - My '97 - p43 [51-250]
Barker, Paul - *The View from the Top*
Obs - Mr 30 '97 - p16* [51-250]
Barker, Rodney - *And the Waters Turned to Blood*
LJ - v122 - Ap 15 '97 - p112 [51-250]
Nature - v386 - Ap 10 '97 - p565 [501+]
PW - v244 - Mr 10 '97 - p59+ [51-250]
Trib Bks - Ap 20 '97 - p5 [501+]
And the Waters Turned to Blood (Gaines). Audio Version
PW - v244 - My 5 '97 - p41 [51-250]
Dancing with the Devil (Patton). Audio Version
y Kliatt - v30 - N '96 - p47+ [51-250]
Barker, Steven - *Excavations and Their Objects*
Rel St Rev - v23 - Ap '97 - p149+ [51-250]
Barker, Theo - *A Merseyside Town in the Industrial Revolution*
HT - v47 - Mr '97 - p55 [251-500]
Barkhoff, Jurgen - *Magnetische Fiktionen*
MLR - v92 - Ap '97 - p504+ [501+]
Barkhouse, Joyce - *Yesterday's Children (Illus. by Kevin Sollows)*
c Can CL - v22 - Fall '96 - p124 [51-250]
Barkley, Brad - *Circle View*
BL - v93 - Ja '97 - p815+ [51-250]
NYTBR - v102 - F 2 '97 - p21 [51-250]
PW - v243 - D 16 '96 - p44+ [51-250]
Barkovskii, V - *Chechenskii Tranzit*
BL - v93 - O 1 '96 - p327 [1-50]
Barkun, Michael - *Religion and the Racist Right*
Rel St Rev - v22 - O '96 - p358+ [51-250]

Barla, G - *Prediction and Performance in Rock Mechanics and Rock Engineering. Vols. 1-3*
　　SciTech - v21 - Mr '97 - p79 [51-250]
Barley, Janet Crane - *Winter in July*
　　LR - v45 - 4 '96 - p65+ [501+]
Barley, Nigel - *Smashing Pots*
　　Am Craft - v56 - Ag '96 - p62+ [1-50]
Barlow, Bernyce - *Sacred Sites of the West*
　　BL - v93 - O 1 '96 - p296 [51-250]
　　BWatch - v17 - N '96 - p4 [51-250]
　　LJ - v121 - N 1 '96 - p96 [51-250]
Barlow, Hugh D - *Crime and Public Policy*
　　CS - v26 - Ja '97 - p89+ [501+]
Barlow, Jeffrey G - *Revolt of the Admirals*
　　NWCR - v50 - Win '97 - p155+ [501+]
Barlow, Maude - *Class Warfare*
　　Dal R - v75 - Spr '95 - p102+ [501+]
Barlow, Richard E - *Mathematical Theory of Reliability*
　　SciTech - v20 - S '96 - p48 [51-250]
Barlow, Steve - *Mind the Door (Illus. by Tony Ross)*
　c　Sch Lib - v45 - F '97 - p22 [51-250]
　c　TES - N 15 '96 - p7* [51-250]
Barlow, William - *From Swing to Soul*
　　CAY - v16 - Fall '95 - p2 [51-250]
Barman, Jean - *Children, Teachers and Schools in the History of British Columbia*
　　Can Hist R - v78 - Mr '97 - p179+ [501+]
　　The West beyond the West. 2nd Ed.
　　JEL - v35 - Mr '97 - p261 [51 250]
Barmash, Isadore - *A Not-So-Tender Offer*
　　Rapport - v19 - 4 '96 - p37 [51-250]
Barme, Geremie - *Shades of Mao*
　　Ch Rev Int - v4 - Spr '97 - p68+ [501+]
　　FEER - v159 - D 19 '96 - p57+ [501+]
Barme, Scot - *Kulap in Oz*
　　Aust Bk R - Jl '96 - p29+ [501+]
Barmeier, Jim - *The Brain*
　y　HB Guide - v7 - Fall '96 - p347 [51-250]
Bar-Moha, Josef - *Kedoshim Be-Arvon Mugbal*
　　BL - v93 - Mr 1 '97 - p1115 [1-50]
Barna, Ed - *Covered Bridges of Vermont*
　　BWatch - v17 - S '96 - p6 [1-50]
Barnard, Alan - *Encyclopedia of Social and Cultural Anthropology*
　r　ARBA - v28 - '97 - p148 [51-250]
　r　Choice - v34 - Mr '97 - p1136 [51-250]
　r　LAR - v99 - F '97 - p104 [51-250]
　r　LJ - v122 - F 1 '97 - p70+ [51-250]
　r　New Sci - v153 - F 1 '97 - p45 [51-250]
Barnard, Christiaan - *The Donor*
　　Books - v10 - Je '96 - p9 [51-250]
Barnard, Jill - *People's Playground*
　　Aust Bk R - Jl '96 - p22+ [501+]
Barnard, Melanie - *365 More Ways to Cook Chicken*
　　Books - v11 - Ap '97 - p20 [51-250]
　　Marinades: The Secret of Great Grilling
　　BL - v93 - Mr 15 '97 - p1215 [51-250]
Barnard, Rita - *The Great Depression and the Culture of Abundance*
　　AL - v68 - D '96 - p864+ [501+]
Barnard, Robert - *The Bad Samaritan (Graham). Audio Version*
　　LJ - v122 - Mr 15 '97 - p101 [51-250]
　　The Habit of Widowhood
　　BL - v92 - Ag '96 - p1885 [51-250]
Barnard, Susan M - *Reptile Keeper's Handbook*
　　SciTech - v20 - S '96 - p45 [51-250]
Barnard, Timothy - *South American Cinema*
　r　ARBA - v28 - '97 - p513 [51-250]
　r　R&R Bk N - v11 - D '96 - p61 [51-250]
Barnbrook, Geoff - *Language and Computers*
　　New Sci - v153 - Mr 1 '97 - p45 [1-50]
Barneby, Rupert C - *Silk Tree, Guanacaste, Monkey's Earring. Pt. 1*
　　SciTech - v20 - D '96 - p31 [51-250]
Barner, Wilfried - *Geschichte Der Deutschen Literatur Von 1945 Bis Zur Gegenwart*
　　MLR - v91 - Jl '96 - p807+ [501+]
Barnes, Barry - *The Elements of Social Theory*
　　AJS - v102 - S '96 - p593+ [501+]
　　APSR - v90 - S '96 - p619+ [501+]
　　CS - v25 - N '96 - p825+ [501+]
　　Scientific Knowledge
　　Choice - v34 - D '96 - p631 [51-250]
　　Isis - v87 - D '96 - p764+ [501+]
　　Socio R - v45 - F 1 '97 - p185+ [501+]
Barnes, Christine - *Central Oregon*
　　BWatch - v17 - S '96 - p5 [51-250]
Barnes, David S - *The Making of a Social Disease*
　　JIH - v27 - Win '97 - p519+ [251-500]
　　JMH - v69 - Mr '97 - p158+ [501+]

Barnes, Djuna - *Collected Stories*
　　BW - v26 - O 27 '96 - p13 [51-250]
　　Poe's Mother
　　ABR - v18 - O '96 - p24 [501+]
Barnes, J W, 1921- - *Basic Geological Mapping. 3rd Ed.*
　　GJ - v162 - Jl '96 - p241 [51-250]
Barnes, Jim - *On Native Ground*
　　LJ - v122 - Mr 15 '97 - p63 [51-250]
Barnes, John, 1957- - *Kaleidoscope Century*
　y　Kliatt - v30 - N '96 - p12 [51-250]
　　One for the Morning Glory
　　Analog - v116 - Jl '96 - p273+ [251-500]
Barnes, John C - *Dante and the Middle Ages*
　　CR - v269 - N '96 - p280 [51-250]
Barnes, Joyce Annette - *Promise Me the Moon*
　c　BL - v93 - N 15 '96 - p585 [51-250]
　y　CCB-B - v50 - F '97 - p199+ [51-250]
　c　KR - v64 - N 1 '96 - p1598 [51-250]
　c　PW - v243 - D 16 '96 - p60 [51-250]
　c　SLJ - v43 - F '97 - p100 [51-250]
Barnes, Julian - *Cross Channel*
　　BW - v27 - Ap 6 '97 - p12 [51-250]
　　Ent W - Mr 28 '97 - p63 [1-50]
　　LATBR - Mr 17 '96 - p2 [501+]
　　LATBR - D 29 '96 - p11 [1-50]
　　NY - v72 - D 16 '96 - p109 [51-250]
　　NYTBR - v101 - D 8 '96 - p79 [1-50]
　　NYTBR - v102 - Mr 30 '97 - p24 [51-250]
　　Obs - D 1 '96 - p17* [1-50]
　　PW - v244 - Ja 13 '97 - p73 [1-50]
　　VQR - v72 - Aut '96 - p132* [51-250]
　　WLT - v71 - Win '97 - p149+ [251-500]
　　Letters from London 1990-5
　　TES - D 27 '96 - p16 [1-50]
Barnes, Kim - *In the Wilderness*
　　Trib Bks - Mr 16 '97 - p8 [1-50]
Barnes, Linda - *Cold Case*
　　KR - v65 - F 1 '97 - p173 [51-250]
　　PW - v244 - F 17 '97 - p213 [51-250]
　　Trib Bks - Ap 13 '97 - p5 [51-250]
Barnes, Philip - *Indonesia: The Political Economy of Energy*
　　JEL - v34 - S '96 - p1499 [51-250]
Barnes, Rik - *Complete Guide to Amerian Bed and Breakfast. 4th Ed.*
　r　ARBA - v28 - '97 - p177 [51-250]
Barnes, Robert M - *Trading in Choppy Markets*
　　R&R Bk N - v12 - F '97 - p49 [51-250]
Barnes, Robert W - *Baltimore County Families 1659-1759*
　r　EGH - v50 - N '96 - p170 [51-250]
Barnes, Simon - *Rogue Lion Safaris*
　　Spec - v278 - F 8 '97 - p40 [501+]
Barnes, Steven - *Blood Brothers*
　　BL - v93 - N 15 '96 - p575+ [51-250]
　　KR - v64 - O 1 '96 - p1432+ [51-250]
Barnes, Timothy D - *Athanasius and Constantius*
　　JAAR - v64 - Win '96 - p881+ [501+]
Barnes, Trevor J - *Logics of Dislocation*
　　JEL - v34 - S '96 - p1500 [51-250]
Barnes-Murphy, Frances - *Kings and Queens of Britain (Illus. by Rowan Barnes-Murphy)*
　c　KR - v64 - N 1 '96 - p1598 [51-250]
Barnes-Svarney, Patricia - *Asteroid: Earth Destroyer or New Frontier?*
　　Choice - v34 - F '97 - p984+ [51-250]
Barnet, Peter - *Images in Ivory*
　　Mag Antiq - v151 - Mr '97 - p382+ [501+]
Barnet, Richard J - *Global Dreams*
　　CS - v25 - S '96 - p610+ [501+]
Barnett, James - *Guide to Netscape Navigator 2.0*
　　CBR - v14 - S '96 - p29 [1-50]
Barnett, Louise - *Touched by Fire*
　　HRNB - v25 - Win '97 - p60+ [251-500]
　　KR - v64 - My 1 '96 - p653 [251-500]
Barnett, Michael - *Images of Earth: A Teachers Guide to Remote Sensing in Geography at Key Stage 2*
　　GJ - v162 - N '96 - p339 [251-500]
　　Images of Earth: A Teachers Guide to Remote Sensing in Geography at Key Stage 3 and GCSE
　　GJ - v162 - N '96 - p339 [251-500]
Barnett, Michael N - *Israel in Comparative Perspective*
　　MEJ - v50 - Sum '96 - p452 [51-250]
　　R&R Bk N - v12 - F '97 - p19 [51-250]
Barnett, Raymond A - *Applied Mathematics. 6th Ed.*
　　SciTech - v20 - D '96 - p6 [51-250]
Barnett, Robert - *Resistance and Reform in Tibet*
　　Historian - v59 - Fall '96 - p168+ [251-500]

Barnett, Rosalind C - *She Works/He Works*
　　NYRB - v43 - N 28 '96 - p22+ [501+]
　　NYTBR - v101 - S 22 '96 - p27 [501+]
　　Wom R Bks - v14 - N '96 - p5+ [501+]
Barnett, Victoria - *For the Soul of the People*
　　CH - v65 - S '96 - p536+ [501+]
Barnett, Vivian Endicott - *Vasily Kandinsky: A Colourful Life*
　　Art J - v55 - Fall '96 - p84+ [501+]
Barnett, William A - *Social Choice, Welfare, and Ethics*
　　Econ J - v106 - N '96 - p1833 [251-500]
Barnett, William K - *The Emergence of Pottery*
　　Ceram Mo - v44 - D '96 - p28 [51-250]
　　Choice - v34 - My '96 - p500 [51-250]
　　SB - v32 - O '96 - p202 [251-500]
Barnette, Martha - *Ladyfingers and Nun's Tummies*
　y　BL - v93 - My 15 '97 - p1551 [51-250]
　　KR - v65 - Mr 15 '97 - p426 [251-500]
Barnhardt, Wilton - *Gospel*
　　EJ - v85 - N '96 - p137+ [501+]
Barnhart, Michael A - *Japan and the World since 1868*
　　AHR - v101 - D '96 - p1597+ [501+]
　　Historian - v59 - Win '97 - p448+ [251-500]
Barnhart, Robert K - *The Barnhart Concise Dictionary of Etymology*
　r　ARBA - v28 - '97 - p380 [251-500]
Barnie, John - *No Hiding Place*
　　New Sci - v152 - O 19 '96 - p48 [1-50]
Barnouw, Dagmar - *Critical Realism*
　　JAAC - v54 - Fall '96 - p397+ [501+]
　　Germany 1945
　　Choice - v34 - My '97 - p1555 [51-250]
　　LJ - v122 - F 15 '97 - p145 [51-250]
　　PW - v244 - Ja 13 '97 - p67 [51-250]
Barnouw, Erik - *Media Marathon*
　　RAH - v24 - D '96 - p676+ [501+]
Barnstone, Aliki - *Madly in Love*
　　PW - v244 - Mr 31 '97 - p70 [51-250]
Barnstone, Willis - *The Secret Reader*
　　VQR - v72 - Aut '96 - p136* [51-250]
　　Six Masters of the Spanish Sonnet
　　TranslRevS - v1 - My '95 - p4 [51-250]
Barnum, Barbara Stevens - *Spirituality in Nursing*
　　Choice - v34 - S '96 - p161 [51-250]
Barocchi, P - *Il Carteggio Indiretto Di Michelangelo. Vol. 2*
　　Six Ct J - v27 - Fall '96 - p919+ [501+]
Barolsky, Paul - *The Faun in the Garden*
　　Ren Q - v49 - Win '96 - p906+ [501+]
Baron, Alan - *Little Pig's Bouncy Ball*
　c　HB Guide - v7 - Fall '96 - p236 [51-250]
　　Red Fox and the Baby Bunnies (Illus. by Alan Baron)
　c　BL - v93 - F 1 '97 - p944 [51-250]
　c　CCB-B - v50 - Ap '97 - p273 [51-250]
　c　SLJ - v43 - Mr '97 - p148 [51-250]
　　Red Fox Dances
　c　Ch BWatch - v6 - My '96 - p5 [1-50]
　c　HB Guide - v7 - Fall '96 - p236 [51-250]
　　The Red Fox Monster (Illus. by Alan Baron)
　c　HB Guide - v8 - Spr '97 - p10 [51-250]
　c　SLJ - v42 - N '96 - p78 [51-250]
Baron, Beth - *The Women's Awakening in Egypt*
　　JC - v46 - Aut '96 - p177+ [501+]
Baron, Deborah G - *Asian American Chronology*
　cr　ARBA - v28 - '97 - p151 [51-250]
　yr　SLJ - v43 - F '97 - p128 [51-250]
Baron, Georg - *Comparative Neurobiology in Chiroptera. Vol. 1*
　r　SciTech - v20 - S '96 - p21 [51-250]
Baron, James N - *Social Differentiation and Social Inequality*
　　R&R Bk N - v11 - N '96 - p39 [51-250]
Baron, Marcia W - *Kantian Ethics Almost without Apology*
　　Choice - v34 - O '96 - p292+ [51-250]
　　CPR - v16 - O '96 - p313+ [501+]
　　Theol Stu - v57 - D '96 - p783 [501+]
　　TLS - D 20 '96 - p27 [501+]
Baron, Marcie - *Your Own ABC (Illus. by June Bradford)*
　c　Quill & Q - v62 - N '96 - p48 [251-500]
Bar-On, Mordechai - *In Pursuit of Peace*
　　Choice - v34 - F '97 - p1030 [51-250]
Baron, Morgana - *Slave-Mistress of Vixania*
　　Quill & Q - v62 - Jl '96 - p42 [501+]
Baron, Robert A - *Social Psychology. 8th Ed.*
　　R&R Bk N - v11 - D '96 - p38 [51-250]
Baron, Stanley N - *Digital Image and Audio Communications*
　　Choice - v34 - D '96 - p641 [51-250]
Baron-Cohen, Simon - *Synaesthesia*
　　New Sci - v153 - F 1 '97 - p44 [51-250]

Barone, Dennis - *Beyond the Red Notebook*
　　AL - v68 - D '96 - p881 [51-250]
　The Returns
　　RCF - v16 - Fall '96 - p191 [251-500]
Baron-Faust, Rita - *Breast Cancer*
　　LJ - v122 - Ja '97 - p56 [1-50]
　Mental Wellness for Women
　　LJ - v121 - D '96 - p124 [51-250]
　　PW - v243 - D 2 '96 - p57 [51-250]
Baros, Aurel Maria - *La Furat De Fete Mari*
　　BL - v93 - D 15 '96 - p714 [1-50]
Barquin, Ramon C - *Planning and Designing the Data
　Warehouse*
　　SciTech - v20 - D '96 - p14 [51-250]
Barr, Helen - *Signes and Sothe*
　　MLR - v91 - O '96 - p958+ [501+]
　　RES - v48 - F '97 - p85+ [501+]
Barr, John - *The Hundred Fathom Curve*
　　BL - v93 - Mr 1 '97 - p1106 [51-250]
Barr, Kevin J - *Fire on the Earth*
　　RR - v56 - Mr '97 - p221 [1-50]
Barr, Nevada - *Endangered Species*
　y BL - v93 - F 15 '97 - p1006 [51-250]
　　KR - v65 - Ja 1 '97 - p21 [51-250]
　　LJ - v122 - F 1 '97 - p111 [1-50]
　　NYTBR - v102 - Ap 13 '97 - p24 [51-250]
　　PW - v244 - Ja 6 '97 - p67 [51-250]
　Firestorm
　　PW - v244 - Ap 21 '97 - p69 [1-50]
　y SLJ - v42 - S '96 - p239 [51-250]
Barr, Robert - *The American Frontier*
　c HB Guide - v7 - Fall '96 - p384 [51-250]
Barracca, Debra - *Las Aventuras De Maxi, El Perro
　Taxista (Illus. by Mark Buehner)*
　c BL - v93 - My 1 '97 - p1506 [1-50]
Barraclough, John - *Jamaica*
　c Sch Lib - v44 - Ag '96 - p110 [51-250]
　South Africa
　c Sch Lib - v44 - Ag '96 - p110 [51-250]
Barragan, Luis - *Barragan: The Complete Works*
　　VLS - Win '96 - p22 [51-250]
Barrass, Robert - *European Economic Integration and
　Sustainable Development*
　　Econ J - v107 - Ja '97 - p286 [51-250]
　　JEL - v34 - S '96 - p1423+ [51-250]
Barratt, David - *The Discerning Reader*
　　Bks & Cult - v2 - My '96 - p5 [1-50]
Barratt Brown, Michael - *The Blair Revelation*
　　TLS - Ja 31 '97 - p25 [501+]
Barre, Richard - *Bearing Secrets*
　　BWatch - v17 - S '96 - p1 [51-250]
　　KR - v64 - My 1 '96 - p640 [51-250]
Barreca, Regina - *Fay Weldon's Wicked Fictions*
　　Signs - v22 - Win '97 - p458+ [501+]
　The Penguin Book of Women's Humor
　y Kliatt - v30 - S '96 - p24 [51-250]
Barresi, Dorothy - *The Post-Rapture Diner*
　y Kliatt - v30 - S '96 - p23 [51-250]
Barrett, Andrea - *Ship Fever and Other Stories*
　　BL - v93 - Ap 1 '97 - p1285 [1-50]
　　BW - v26 - D 8 '96 - p6 [1-50]
　　CSM - v88 - N 12 '96 - p14 [51-250]
　　Ent W - N 29 '96 - p82+ [251-500]
　　NYTBR - v102 - Mr 2 '97 - p28 [51-250]
　　PW - v243 - N 4 '96 - p37 [51-250]
　　Sci - v274 - N 29 '96 - p1478 [251-500]
　　Trib Bks - F 23 '97 - p8 [1-50]
Barrett, Anthony A - *Agrippina: Sex, Power, and Politics
　in the Early Empire*
　　Choice - v34 - Ja '97 - p853 [51-250]
　　Class Out - v74 - Spr '97 - p122 [251-500]
　　HRNB - v25 - Win '97 - p92 [501+]
　　KR - v64 - Ag 15 '96 - p1198+ [251-500]
　　LJ - v121 - N 1 '96 - p78 [51-250]
Barrett, C K - *A Critical and Exegetical Commentary on
　the Acts of the Apostles 1*
　　Theol St - v57 - Mr '96 - p145+ [501+]
Barrett, Daniel - *Bandits on the Information
　Superhighway*
　　New Sci - v151 - S 14 '96 - p46 [51-250]
Barrett, Deirdre - *Trauma and Dreams*
　　Choice - v34 - Ap '97 - p1421 [51-250]
　　SciTech - v21 - Mr '97 - p55 [51-250]
Barrett, Edward - *Contextual Media*
　　SocSciComR - v14 - Win '96 - p491+ [501+]
Barrett, Julia - *The Third Sister*
　y BL - v92 - Ag '96 - p1879 [51-250]
　y BL - v92 - Ag '96 - p1891 [1-50]
　　BW - v26 - N 10 '96 - p10 [251-500]
　　Ent W - Ag 23 '96 - p118+ [51-250]
　　LATBR - S 15 '96 - p10+ [251-500]

Barrett, Maria - *Dishonored*
　　KR - v64 - Ag 15 '96 - p1167 [251-500]
　　LJ - v121 - S 15 '96 - p93 [51-250]
Barrett, Neal - *Bad Eye Blues*
　　KR - v65 - My 1 '97 - p680 [251-500]
　　PW - v244 - Mr 31 '97 - p65 [51-250]
Batman: The Ultimate Evil. Bks. 1-2
　yp VOYA - v19 - O '96 - p203+ [251-500]
　The Touch of Your Shadow, the Whisper of Your Name
　　SF Chr - v18 - O '96 - p77 [51-250]
Barrett, Neil - *The State of the Cybernation*
　　TES - O 18 '96 - p41U [1-50]
　　TES - Ja 3 '97 - p47U [251-500]
Barrett, Norman S - *The Olympic Spirit*
　c Bks Keeps - Jl '96 - p23 [51-250]
　Sports Facts
　yr Kliatt - v30 - N '96 - p31 [51-250]
Barrett, Richard S - *Fair Employment Strategies in
　Human Resource Management*
　　J Car P&E - v57 - Win '97 - p16 [251-500]
　　R&R Bk N - v12 - F '97 - p40 [51-250]
Barrett, Robert G - *Guns 'n' Rose*
　　Aust Bk R - D '96 - p80+ [501+]
Barrett, Stan - *Play It for Reul*
　y TES - Mr 21 '97 - p27* [51-250]
Barrett, Stanley R - *Anthropology: A Student's Guide to
　Theory and Method*
　　R&R Bk N - v11 - N '96 - p21 [51-250]
Barrett, T H - *Li Ao: Buddhist, Taoist, or Neo-Confucian?*
　　HJAS - v56 - 2 '96 - p485+ [501+]
Barrett, Tracy - *Virginia*
　c Ch BWatch - v6 - D '96 - p6 [1-50]
　c HB Guide - v8 - Spr '97 - p172 [51-250]
Barrett, Victoria - *Upon a Mystic Tide*
　　PW - v243 - N 11 '96 - p72 [51-250]
Barrette, Greg - *The Tao of Unity. Audio Version*
　　BWatch - v18 - Mr '97 - p8 [1-50]
Barrette, Johanne - *La Couronne Du Roi Ludovic (Illus.
　by Isabelle Beaudin)*
　c Can CL - v22 - Sum '96 - p101+ [251-500]
Barrie, J M - *The Admirable Crichton. Peter Pan. When
　Wendy Grew Up. What Every Woman Knows. Mary
　Rose*
　　ELT - v39 - 4 '96 - p504+ [501+]
Barrie, Thomas - *Spiritual Path, Sacred Place*
　r Choice - v34 - N '96 - p443 [51-250]
Barringer, Howard - *The Imperative Future*
　　SciTech - v21 - Mr '97 - p9 [51-250]
Barrington, Judith - *Writing the Memoir*
　　BL - v93 - F 1 '97 - p920 [51-250]
　　LJ - v122 - F 15 '97 - p143 [51-250]
Barrios, Richard - *A Song in the Dark*
　　Choice - v34 - S '96 - p135 [51-250]
Barriskill, Janet - *Visiting the Mino Kilns*
　　Ceram Mo - v45 - Ja '97 - p24 [251-500]
Barro, Robert J - *Economic Growth*
　　JEL - v34 - S '96 - p1486 [51-250]
　Getting It Right
　　Bus W - Je 10 '96 - p14 [501+]
　　JEL - v34 - D '96 - p2057 [51-250]
Barron, Ann E - *The Internet and Instruction*
　　SLMQ - v24 - Sum '96 - p220+ [51-250]
Barron, Caroline M - *Medieval London Widows
　1300-1500*
　　EHR - v111 - N '96 - p1256 [251-500]
Barron, James W - *Impact of Managed Care on
　Psychodynamic Treatment*
　　SciTech - v20 - N '96 - p44 [51-250]
Barron, John, 1930- - *Operation Solo*
　　NS - v126 - Mr 14 '97 - p48 [501+]
Barron, John M - *Consumer Attitudes toward Credit
　Insurance*
　　R&R Bk N - v11 - N '96 - p37 [51-250]
Barron, Kathryn - *Critter Crackers (Illus. by Kathryn
　Barron)*
　c HB Guide - v7 - Fall '96 - p366 [1-50]
Barron, Marlene - *Ready, Set, Count*
　　SLJ - v42 - Ag '96 - p36 [51-250]
　Ready, Set, Read and Write
　　SLJ - v42 - Ag '96 - p36 [51-250]
Barron, Neil - *Anatomy of Wonder 4*
　　Ext - v37 - Sum '96 - p172+ [501+]
　　RQ - v36 - Win '96 - p211+ [51-250]
　Fantasy Literature
　r RQ - v36 - Win '96 - p212 [51-250]
　Horror Literature
　r RQ - v36 - Win '96 - p210 [51-250]
Barron, Pattie - *The First-Time Gardener*
　y Kliatt - v30 - N '96 - p30 [51-250]

Barron, Robert - *Thomas Aquinas: Spiritual Master*
　　Am - v175 - N 2 '96 - p27+ [51-250]
　　RR - v56 - Ja '97 - p106 [1-50]
　　Theol St - v57 - D '96 - p777 [251-500]
Barron, Stephanie - *Jane and the Man of the Cloth*
　　BL - v93 - Ja '97 - p823 [51-250]
　　Ent W - Ja 31 '97 - p55 [51-250]
　　KR - v64 - D 1 '96 - p1704 [251-500]
　　LJ - v121 - D '96 - p151 [51-250]
　　NYTBR - v102 - Ja 19 '97 - p22 [51-250]
　　PW - v243 - N 11 '96 - p59 [51-250]
　Jane and the Unpleasantness at Scargrave Manor
　　LJ - v122 - Ja '97 - p51 [1-50]
　　NYTBR - v101 - S 8 '96 - p23 [51-250]
　　Quill & Q - v62 - O '96 - p30 [51-250]
Barron, Stephanie, 1950- - *Exiles + Emigres*
　　LJ - v122 - Ap 15 '97 - p76 [51-250]
Barron, T A - *The Lost Years of Merlin*
　y BL - v93 - S 1 '96 - p118 [51-250]
　y BL - v93 - Ap 1 '97 - p1288 [1-50]
　c HB Guide - v8 - Spr '97 - p62 [51-250]
　c NYTBR - v101 - N 24 '96 - p20 [1-50]
　c SLJ - v42 - S '96 - p201 [51-250]
　y VOYA - v19 - O '96 - p216 [251-500]
Barron, Thomas J - *Constitutions and National Identity*
　　EHR - v112 - Ap '97 - p549+ [251-500]
Barros, James - *Double Deception*
　　AHR - v102 - F '97 - p142+ [501+]
Barrow, Adam - *Blind Spot*
　　KR - v64 - D 1 '96 - p1685 [251-500]
　　LJ - v122 - Ja '97 - p142 [51-250]
　　PW - v243 - D 2 '96 - p40 [51-250]
Barrow, Andrew - *The Man in the Moon*
　　Spec - v277 - N 23 '96 - p45 [1-50]
　　Spec - v277 - N 23 '96 - p46 [1-50]
Barrow, C J - *Developing the Environment*
　　GJ - v162 - Jl '96 - p233 [251-500]
　y New Sci - v151 - S 28 '96 - p50+ [501+]
Barrow, Deborah J - *The Federal Judiciary and
　Institutional Change*
　　Choice - v34 - Ja '97 - p873 [51-250]
Barrow, John D - *The Anthropic Cosmological Principle*
　　New Sci - v152 - O 12 '96 - p42 [1-50]
　　PSR - v25 - '96 - p273+ [501+]
Barrow, Logie - *Democratic Ideas and the British Labour
　Movement 1880-1914*
　　Choice - v34 - Mr '97 - p1218 [51-250]
Barrow-Green, June - *Poincare and the Three Body
　Problem*
　　SciTech - v21 - Mr '97 - p18 [51-250]
Barrowman, Fergus - *The Picador Book of Contemporary
　New Zealand Fiction*
　　Meanjin - v55 - '96 - p704+ [501+]
　　TLS - Jl 19 '96 - p22 [501+]
Barrowman, Rachel - *The Turnbull: A Library and Its
　World*
　　Lib - v19 - Mr '97 - p88+ [501+]
Barrows, Allison - *The Artist's Model (Illus. by Allison
　Barrows)*
　c CCB-B - v50 - O '96 - p48 [51-250]
　c HB Guide - v8 - Spr '97 - p19 [51-250]
　c SLJ - v42 - Ag '96 - p115 [51-250]
Barry, Andrew - *Foucault and Political Reason*
　　APSR - v91 - Mr '97 - p164+ [501+]
　　Choice - v34 - My '96 - p534 [51-250]
　　R&R Bk N - v11 - N '96 - p47 [51-250]
Barry, Brian - *Justice as Impartiality*
　　APSR - v90 - D '96 - p884+ [501+]
Barry, Dave - *Dave Barry in Cyberspace*
　y BL - v93 - S 1 '96 - p2 [51-250]
　　BYTE - v21 - D '96 - p34 [51-250]
　　Ent W - O 18 '96 - p74 [51-250]
　　KR - v64 - S 1 '96 - p1284 [51-250]
　　LJ - v121 - S 15 '96 - p68 [51-250]
　　New Sci - v152 - N 30 '96 - p48 [51-250]
　　NYTBR - v101 - O 13 '96 - p20 [51-250]
　y SLJ - v43 - F '97 - p134 [51-250]
　Dave Barry's Book of Bad Songs
　　KR - v65 - Ap 1 '97 - p542 [51-250]
　　PW - v244 - Mr 31 '97 - p48 [51-250]
Barry, David - *Women and Political Insurgency*
　　Choice - v34 - D '96 - p667 [51-250]
　　R&R Bk N - v11 - N '96 - p42 [51-250]
Barry, Donald K - *Forms of Life and Following Rules*
　　R&R Bk N - v12 - F '97 - p4 [51-250]

Barry, John M - *Rising Tide*
BL - v93 - Mr 15 '97 - p1222 [51-250]
KR - v65 - F 1 '97 - p180 [251-500]
LATBR - Ap 6 '97 - p10 [501+]
NYTBR - v102 - Ap 13 '97 - p34 [501+]
NYTLa - v146 - Mr 24 '97 - pC15 [501+]
PW - v244 - Ja 27 '97 - p86 [251-500]
Wil Q - v21 - Spr '97 - p97+ [501+]
Barry, Jonathan - *The Tudor and Stuart Town*
J Urban H - v22 - My '96 - p516+ [501+]
Barry, Michael - *Design and Color in Islamic Architecture*
Choice - v34 - Mr '97 - p1150 [51-250]
NYTBR - v101 - D 8 '96 - p56+ [51-250]
Barry, Tom - *The Next Fifty Years*
Workbook - v21 - Fall '96 - p127+ [251-500]
Barry, William A - *Who Do You Say I Am?*
Am - v176 - Mr 8 '97 - p26 [51-250]
RR - v55 - N '96 - p651+ [251-500]
Barsky, Robert F - *Noam Chomsky: A Life of Dissent*
BL - v93 - Mr 15 '97 - p1211 [51-250]
PW - v244 - F 3 '97 - p89 [51-250]
Barstow, Anne Llewellyn - *Witchcraze: A New History of the European Witch Hunts*
Ren Q - v50 - Spr '97 - p341+ [501+]
Barta, Peter I - *Bely, Joyce, and Doblin*
Choice - v34 - Mr '97 - p1155 [51-250]
Russian Literature and the Classics
Choice - v34 - O '96 - p288 [51-250]
Barteau, Harry C - *Historical Dictionary of Luxembourg*
r ARBA - v28 - '97 - p62 [51-250]
r R&R Bk N - v12 - F '97 - p16 [51-250]
Bartell, Ernest - *Business and Democracy in Latin America*
PSQ - v111 - Win '96 - p735+ [501+]
Bartelmus, Peter - *Environment, Growth and Development*
GJ - v163 - Mr '97 - p105 [51-250]
Bartels, Dennis A - *When the North Was Red*
Am Ethnol - v24 - F '97 - p238+ [501+]
Bartels, Emily C - *Spectacles of Strangeness*
Ren Q - v49 - Aut '96 - p648+ [501+]
Bartelson, Jens - *A Genealogy of Sovereignty*
APSR - v91 - Mr '97 - p228+ [501+]
Barth, John - *The Friday Book*
Critiq - v37 - Sum '96 - p261+ [501+]
Letters
Critiq - v37 - Sum '96 - p261+ [501+]
Lost in the Funhouse
Critiq - v37 - Sum '96 - p261+ [501+]
On with the Story
KR - v64 - My 1 '96 - p617 [251-500]
NYTBR - v101 - D 8 '96 - p82 [1-50]
Sabbatical: A Romance
LJ - v121 - S 15 '96 - p102 [1-50]
Barth, Karl - *The Theology of John Calvin*
Intpr - v51 - Ap '97 - p210 [51-250]
Rel St Rev - v22 - O '96 - p349 [51-250]
Barth, Peter - *Logic-Based 0-1 Constraint Programming*
SciTech - v20 - D '96 - p8 [51-250]
Bartha, Laszlo - *The Chemistry of Non-Sag Tungsten*
SciTech - v20 - N '96 - p78 [51-250]
Barthel, Diane - *Historic Preservation*
Choice - v34 - Ap '97 - p1392 [51-250]
Barthelme, Frederick - *Painted Desert*
BW - v27 - Ap 6 '97 - p12 [51-250]
PW - v244 - Mr 17 '97 - p81 [1-50]
Trib Bks - Ap 20 '97 - p8 [1-50]
Bartholomeusz, Tessa - *Women under the Bo Tree*
JAAR - v64 - Win '96 - p867+ [501+]
Bartholomew, David J - *Uncertain Belief*
Choice - v34 - D '96 - p625 [51-250]
Bartholomew, James - *Yew and Non-Yew*
ILN - Christmas '96 - p89 [51-250]
Bartholomew, Rebecca - *Audacious Women*
CH - v65 - D '96 - p737+ [501+]
WHQ - v28 - Spr '97 - p81+ [501+]
Bartlett, Alison - *Cat among the Cabbages (Illus. by Alison Bartlett)*
c BL - v93 - F 1 '97 - p944+ [51-250]
c KR - v64 - D 1 '96 - p1733 [51-250]
c SLJ - v43 - Ja '97 - p75+ [51-250]
Bartlett, Anne Clark - *Male Authors, Female Readers*
JR - v77 - Ja '97 - p137+ [501+]
Vox Mystica
CH - v65 - D '96 - p706+ [501+]
Bartlett, Charlene B - *Cemetery Inscriptions and Revolutionary, War of 1812, and Civil War Veterans of Bowdoin, Maine*
r Am Geneal - v71 - Jl '96 - p188+ [251-500]
Bartlett, Elizabeth Ann - *Journey of the Heart*
PW - v243 - S 30 '96 - p76 [51-250]

Bartlett, Gillian - *Great Careers for People Interested in Art and Design*
y SLJ - v42 - S '96 - p230 [51-250]
Bartlett, Jonathan - *The Cook's Dictionary and Culinary Reference*
r ARBA - v28 - '97 - p568 [51-250]
r BL - v93 - D 15 '96 - p701 [51-250]
r LJ - v122 - F 15 '97 - p127 [51-250]
Bartlett, Laurence - *William Congreve: An Annotated Bibliography 1978-1994*
r ARBA - v28 - '97 - p453 [51-250]
Bartlett, Linda - *Feast for Life*
LJ - v121 - O 15 '96 - p86 [51-250]
PW - v243 - S 2 '96 - p126 [51-250]
Bartlett, Neil - *Cutting-Edge Java Game Programming*
y LJ - v122 - F 1 '97 - p102 [51-250]
Bartlett, Neil, 1958- - *The House on Brooke Street*
Advocate - Mr 4 '97 - p59 [51-250]
BL - v93 - Ja '97 - p816 [51-250]
KR - v64 - N 15 '96 - p1616 [251-500]
LJ - v122 - Ja '97 - p142 [51-250]
NYTBR - v102 - F 23 '97 - p16 [51-250]
PW - v243 - D 2 '96 - p41+ [51-250]
Mr. Clive and Mr. Page
Spec - v277 - N 23 '96 - p46 [51-250]
Bartlett, Robert - *The Making of Europe*
CH - v65 - S '96 - p468+ [501+]
J Soc H - v30 - Win '96 - p546+ [501+]
Wil Q - v21 - Win '97 - p37 [1-50]
Bartlett, Rosamund - *Wagner and Russia*
Russ Rev - v55 - O '96 - p706+ [501+]
Slav R - v55 - Sum '96 - p505+ [501+]
Bartlett, Thomas - *A Military History of Ireland*
Choice - v34 - O '96 - p340 [51-250]
For Aff - v76 - Mr '97 - p181 [51-250]
ILS - v15 - Fall '96 - p17+ [501+]
r J Mil H - v60 - O '96 - p770+ [501+]
TLS - Ag 2 '96 - p30 [501+]
Bartlett, Wynne - *Beatrix Potter's Derwentwater. Rev. Ed.*
r RSR - v24 - 3 '96 - p26 [51-250]
Bartlett's Roget's Thesaurus
r BL - v93 - S 15 '96 - p280 [251-500]
Bartley, Numan V - *The New South 1945-1980*
AB - v98 - Ag 5 '96 - p364 [501+]
JSH - v62 - N '96 - p767+ [501+]
RAH - v25 - Mr '97 - p136+ [501+]
VQR - v73 - Win '97 - p33* [1-50]
Bartok, Bela - *Bela Bartok Studies in Ethnomusicology*
LJ - v122 - F 15 '97 - p136 [51-250]
Bartoletti, Susan Campbell - *Dancing with Dziadziu (Illus. by Annika Nelson)*
c BL - v93 - Mr 15 '97 - p1238 [51-250]
c CCB-B - v50 - My '97 - p313 [51-250]
c KR - v65 - Mr 1 '97 - p377 [51-250]
c PW - v244 - F 10 '97 - p83 [51-250]
Growing Up in Coal Country
c BL - v93 - Ja '97 - p765 [1-50]
c BL - v93 - D 1 '96 - p651 [51-250]
c BL - v93 - Ap 1 '97 - p1298 [1-50]
c CBRS - v25 - N '96 - p33 [51-250]
y CCB-B - v50 - F '97 - p200 [51-250]
c HB - v73 - Mr '97 - p210+ [51-250]
c SLJ - v43 - F '97 - p109 [51-250]
Bartolomei De La Cruz, Hector G - *The International Labor Organization*
For Aff - v75 - N '96 - p148+ [51-250]
ILR - v135 - 2 '96 - p241+ [251-500]
JEL - v34 - D '96 - p2074 [251-500]
Barton, Anne - *Essays: Mainly Shakespearean*
MLR - v92 - Ap '97 - p453+ [501+]
Barton, Byron - *Big Machines*
c HB Guide - v7 - Fall '96 - p236 [1-50]
Dinosaurs
c HB Guide - v7 - Fall '96 - p236 [1-50]
The Little Red Hen (Illus. by Byron Barton)
c Ch BWatch - v6 - My '96 - p3 [51-250]
c PW - v244 - Ja 27 '97 - p108 [1-50]
Tools
c HB Guide - v7 - Fall '96 - p236 [1-50]
Zoo Animals
c HB Guide - v7 - Fall '96 - p236 [1-50]
Barton, Cynthia H - *Transcendental Wife*
Choice - v34 - Ap '97 - p1402 [51-250]
Barton, Geoff - *Genres*
y TES - F 28 '97 - pR7 [501+]
Stories from Europe
y TES - S 20 '96 - pR6 [251-500]
Ten Short Plays
y TES - S 20 '96 - pR6 [251-500]
Two Centuries
y TES - F 28 '97 - pR7 [501+]

Barton, Phoebe Linsey - *Colorado Medicaid Reform Study. Phase 2*
J Gov Info - v23 - S '96 - p579 [51-250]
Barton, William - *Acts of Conscience*
Analog - v117 - F '97 - p145+ [251-500]
KR - v64 - N 1 '96 - p1569 [51-250]
LJ - v121 - D '96 - p152 [51-250]
NYTBR - v102 - Ja 26 '97 - p22 [51-250]
PW - v243 - N 4 '96 - p68 [51-250]
Bartone, Elisa - *American Too (Illus. by Ted Lewin)*
c BL - v92 - Ag '96 - p1903+ [51-250]
c CBRS - v25 - Ja '97 - p54 [51-250]
c CCB-B - v50 - D '96 - p128+ [51-250]
c CSM - v88 - S 26 '96 - pB3 [51-250]
c HB Guide - v8 - Spr '97 - p19 [51-250]
c Inst - v106 - S '96 - p55 [51-250]
c SLJ - v42 - D '96 - p84 [51-250]
c Trib Bks - Ja 12 '97 - p5 [51-250]
Peppe the Lamplighter (Illus. by Ted Lewin)
c Inst - v106 - S '96 - p55 [1-50]
Bartoszynski, Robert - *Probability and Statistical Inference*
Choice - v34 - Ja '97 - p833 [51-250]
Bartram, William - *Travels and Other Writings*
Hort - v74 - Ag '96 - p64+ [501+]
New R - v215 - D 9 '96 - p42+ [501+]
NYRB - v43 - O 17 '96 - p4+ [501+]
Bartrum, Giulia - *German Renaissance Prints 1490-1550*
AB - v99 - Mr 3 '97 - p694 [51-250]
Ren Q - v50 - Spr '97 - p327+ [501+]
Bartsch, Richard A - *Chemical Separations with Liquid Membranes*
SciTech - v21 - Mr '97 - p95 [51-250]
Bartsch, William H - *Doomed at the Start*
APH - v43 - Win '96 - p58 [251-500]
Bartusiak, Marcia - *Through a Universe Darkly*
S&T - v92 - S '96 - p53 [51-250]
Bar-Yosef, Ofer - *Late Quarternary Chronology and Paleoclimates of the Eastern Mediterranean*
Am Ant - v61 - Ap '96 - p432+ [501+]
Barzel, Yoram - *Productivity Change, Public Goods and Transaction Costs*
Econ J - v106 - S '96 - p1466 [51-250]
Barzilai, Gad - *Wars, Internal Conflicts, and Political Order*
Choice - v34 - D '96 - p682 [51-250]
R&R Bk N - v11 - N '96 - p14 [51-250]
Bar-Zohar, Michael - *Bitter Scent*
BL - v93 - N 15 '96 - p558 [51-250]
KR - v64 - S 15 '96 - p1364 [251-500]
LJ - v121 - N 15 '96 - p72 [51-250]
PW - v243 - O 7 '96 - p56+ [51-250]
Bosem Mar
BL - v93 - Mr 1 '97 - p1115 [1-50]
Bar-Zvi, David - *Tropical Gardening*
Fine Gard - S '96 - p70 [51-250]
Hort - v94 - Mr '97 - p78 [251-500]
Bas, Ed - *Indoor Air Quality*
R&R Bk N - v12 - F '97 - p97 [51-250]
Basch, Michael Franz - *Doing Brief Psychotherapy*
AJPsych - v154 - Mr '97 - p431 [251-500]
Basch, Miguel - *Expanding Access to Financial Services in Latin America*
JEL - v34 - D '96 - p2107 [51-250]
Basch, Reva - *Secrets of the Super Net Searchers*
IRLA - v32 - N '96 - p11 [51-250]
LJ - v122 - Ja '97 - p138 [51-250]
LJ - v122 - F 1 '97 - p114 [51-250]
New Sci - v153 - F 15 '97 - p45 [1-50]
SciTech - v21 - Mr '97 - p89 [1-50]
Basco, Monica Ramirez - *Cognitive-Behavioral Therapy for Bipolar Disorder*
SB - v32 - N '96 - p231 [251-500]
SciTech - v20 - S '96 - p33 [51-250]
Base, Graeme - *Animalia (Illus. by Graeme Base)*
c Magpies - v11 - Jl '96 - p10+ [501+]
c PW - v243 - O 21 '96 - p85 [1-50]
The Discovery of Dragons (Illus. by Graeme Base)
c Aust Bk R - N '96 - p63+ [501+]
c BL - v93 - N 15 '96 - p585+ [51-250]
y BL - v93 - Ap 1 '97 - p1310 [1-50]
c HB Guide - v8 - Spr '97 - p57 [51-250]
c KR - v64 - O 15 '96 - p1528+ [51-250]
c PW - v243 - N 18 '96 - p74 [51-250]
c SLJ - v42 - N '96 - p103 [51-250]
The Sign of the Seahorse
c Magpies - v11 - Jl '96 - p45 [1-50]
Baseball Guide. 1996 Ed.
r ARBA - v28 - '97 - p296 [251-500]

Bash, Barbara - *In the Heart of the Village (Illus. by Barbara Bash)*
  c BL - v93 - S 15 '96 - p234 [51-250]
  c HB Guide - v8 - Spr '97 - p120+ [51-250]
  c Inst - v106 - Mr '97 - p27 [51-250]
  c SLJ - v42 - N '96 - p96 [51-250]
  c Smith - v27 - N '96 - p166+ [1-50]

Bash, Harry H - *Social Problems and Social Movements*
  SF - v75 - S '96 - p355+ [501+]
  Socio R - v45 - F 1 '97 - p147+ [501+]

Basinger, David - *The Case for Freewill Theism*
  BL - v93 - S 15 '96 - p182 [51-250]

Basista, Jakub - *Anglia, Swiat I Gwiazdy*
  EHR - v112 - F '97 - p196 [251-500]

Baskin, Ellen - *Serials on British Television 1950-1994*
  r ARBA - v28 - '97 - p504 [51-250]
  r Choice - v34 - O '96 - p248 [51-250]
  r LAR - v99 - F '97 - p102 [51-250]
  r R&R Bk N - v12 - F '97 - p81 [51-250]

Baskin, Yvonne - *The Work of Nature*
  PW - v244 - Mr 10 '97 - p59 [51-250]

Baskin-Salzberg, Anita - *Turtles*
  c BL - v93 - S 1 '96 - p120 [51-250]
  c HB Guide - v7 - Fall '96 - p342 [1-50]

Baskwill, Jane - *Somewhere (Illus. by Trish Hill)*
  c HB Guide - v7 - Fall '96 - p248 [51-250]

Baskysand, Andrius - *Brain Mechanisms and Psychotropic Drugs*
  SciTech - v20 - D '96 - p55 [51-250]

Basmajian, John V - *Clinical Decision Making in Rehabilitation*
  SciTech - v20 - D '96 - p55 [51-250]

Bass, Althea - *Cherokee Messenger*
  Roundup M - v4 - F '97 - p22 [251-500]

Bass, Cynthia - *Maiden Voyage*
  y SLJ - v42 - S '96 - p239 [51-250]
  y VOYA - v19 - F '97 - p326 [251-500]

Bass, Dorothy C - *Practicing Our Faith*
  PW - v244 - Ja 13 '97 - p68 [51-250]

Bass, Ellen - *Free Your Mind*
  y LATBR - Jl 14 '96 - p11 [51-250]

Bass, Rick - *The Book of Yaak*
  Aud - v98 - N '96 - p137 [1-50]
  BW - v27 - F 9 '97 - p13 [51-250]
  KR - v64 - S 15 '96 - p1364 [251-500]
  LATBR - Ja 26 '97 - p8 [501+]
  LJ - v122 - Ja '97 - p136+ [51-250]
  NYTBR - v101 - D 1 '96 - p31+ [501+]
  Utne R - Mr '97 - p84 [1-50]
  The Deer Pasture
  LATBR - S 8 '96 - p11 [51-250]
  The Lost Grizzlies
  BL - v93 - D 1 '96 - p630 [1-50]
  Obs - O 6 '96 - p18* [501+]
  WAL - v31 - Sum '96 - p161+ [501+]

Bass, Robin - *French Film Noir*
  TES - Ag 2 '96 - pR6 [1-50]

Bass, Scott A - *Older and Active*
  SSQ - v77 - D '96 - p940+ [501+]

Bass, Thomas A - *Vietnamerica*
  Choice - v34 - O '96 - p344 [51-250]
  Econ - v340 - S 14 '96 - p7*+ [501+]

Bass, Tom - *Tom Bass: Totem Maker*
  Aust Bk R - D '96 - p26+ [501+]

Bassett, Jan - *Great Explorations*
  Aust Bk R - D '96 - p13+ [501+]
  Wrecked! Mysteries and Disasters at Sea
  c Magpies - v11 - Jl '96 - p39 [51-250]
  y Sch Lib - v45 - F '97 - p52 [51-250]

Bassett, John Earl - *Thomas Wolfe: An Annotated Critical Bibliography*
  r ARBA - v28 - '97 - p446 [251-500]
  r Choice - v34 - F '97 - p939 [51-250]
  r R&R Bk N - v12 - F '97 - p90 [51-250]

Bassett, Paul G - *Framing Software Reuse*
  SciTech - v20 - N '96 - p9 [51-250]

Bassford, Christopher - *Clausewitz in English*
  Albion - v28 - Sum '96 - p342+ [501+]
  EHR - v111 - N '96 - p1328+ [501+]

Bassie-Sweet, Karen - *At the Edge of the World*
  Choice - v34 - F '97 - p1005 [51-250]

Bassiouni, M Cherif - *The Law of the International Criminal Tribunal for the Former Yugoslavia*
  R&R Bk N - v12 - F '97 - p62 [51-250]

Basso, Ellen B - *The Last Cannibals*
  AHR - v102 - F '97 - p243+ [501+]
  Am Ethnol - v23 - N '96 - p925+ [501+]

Basso, Keith H - *Wisdom Sits in Places*
  LJ - v121 - O 1 '96 - p88 [51-250]

Basso, Michael J - *The Underground Guide to Teenage Sexuality*
  LJ - v122 - Ap 15 '97 - p106 [51-250]

Bassuk, Ellen L - *The Doctor-Activist: Physicians Fighting for Social Change*
  Choice - v34 - O '96 - p313 [51-250]
  Readings - v12 - Mr '97 - p29+ [51-250]

Basta, Lofty L - *A Graceful Exit*
  Choice - v34 - D '96 - p643 [51-250]

Bastable, Bernard - *Too Many Notes, Mr. Mozart*
  Arm Det - v29 - Fall '96 - p490 [251-500]
  BWatch - v17 - N '96 - p10 [51-250]
  KR - v64 - My 1 '96 - p640+ [51-250]

Basten, Fred E - *The Lost Artwork of Hollywood*
  LATBR - N 10 '96 - p2 [51-250]
  PW - v243 - N 11 '96 - p68 [51-250]

Bastian, Jean-Pierre - *Protestantismos Y Modernidad Latinoamericana*
  HAHR - v77 - My '97 - p285+ [501+]

Bastian, John - *Home-School Work in Multicultural Settings*
  TES - F 28 '97 - p7* [51-250]

Bastien, Joseph W - *Drum and Stethoscope*
  RA - v4 '96 - p233+ [501+]

Bastien, Pierre - *Le Buste Monetaire Des Empereurs Romains. Vols. 1-3*
  AJA - v100 - O '96 - p798+ [501+]

Bastos, Maria Ines - *Politics of Technology in Latin America*
  R&R Bk N - v12 - F '97 - p36 [51-250]

Bastyra, Judy - *Cookie Fun*
  c PW - v244 - Ap 7 '97 - p94 [51-250]
  Cooking with Dad (Illus. by Paul Daviz)
  c Sch Lib - v44 - Ag '96 - p113 [51-250]
  Hanukkah Fun (Illus. by Catherine Ward)
  c PW - v243 - S 30 '96 - p88 [1-50]
  I Can Cook (Illus. by Michael Evans)
  c Sch Lib - v44 - N '96 - p161 [51-250]
  c TES - Jl 19 '96 - pR8 [1-50]
  Pizza Fun
  c PW - v244 - Ap 7 '97 - p94 [51-250]

Basu, Amrita - *The Challenge of Local Feminisms*
  CS - v25 - S '96 - p590+ [501+]
  JTWS - v13 - Fall '96 - p358+ [501+]
  NWSA Jnl - v8 - Fall '96 - p157+ [501+]
  Wom R Bks - v13 - S '96 - p15+ [501+]

Basu, Anuradha - *Public Expenditure Decision Making*
  JEL - v34 - D '96 - p2058 [51-250]

Basu, Aparna - *Mridula Sarabhai: Rebel with a Cause*
  Choice - v34 - S '96 - p183 [51-250]

Basu, Asish - *Earth Processes*
  SciTech - v20 - S '96 - p18 [51-250]

Basu, Kaushik - *Of People, of Places*
  Econ J - v106 - S '96 - p1461 [51-250]

Basu, Ron - *Total Manufacturing Solutions*
  SciTech - v21 - Mr '97 - p98 [51-250]

Basu, Tapan K - *Vitamins in Human Health and Disease*
  Choice - v34 - My '97 - p1532 [51-250]

Baswell, Christopher - *Virgil in Medieval England*
  Albion - v28 - Sum '96 - p287+ [501+]
  Specu - v72 - Ja '97 - p106+ [501+]

Bataille, Christophe - *Annam*
  BL - v93 - S 15 '96 - p218 [51-250]
  LATBR - S 22 '96 - p14+ [51-250]
  NYTBR - v101 - O 20 '96 - p13+ [501+]
  NYTBR - v101 - D 8 '96 - p76 [1-50]
  TranslRevS - v2 - D '96 - p21 [51-250]

Bataille, Gretchen M - *Ethnic Studies in the United States*
  r ARBA - v28 - '97 - p149+ [251-500]

Al-Batal, Mahmoud - *The Teaching of Arabic as a Foreign Language*
  MEJ - v50 - Sum '96 - p454+ [51-250]

Bat-Ami, Miriam - *Dear Elijah*
  c RT - v50 - S '96 - p58+ [51-250]

Batchelor, George - *The Life and Legacy of G.I. Taylor*
  Choice - v34 - F '97 - p982 [51-250]
  Nature - v385 - Ja 30 '97 - p406+ [501+]
  New Sci - v152 - D 21 '96 - p70 [501+]
  Sci - v274 - D 13 '96 - p1846 [501+]

Batchelor, John, 1942- - *The Art of Literary Biography*
  RES - v48 - F '97 - p72+ [501+]
  The Life of Joseph Conrad
  RES - v47 - Ag '96 - p440+ [501+]

Batchelor, John Calvin - *Ain't You Glad You Joined the Republicans?*
  HRNB - v25 - Win '97 - p53+ [501+]
  American Falls
  NYTBR - v101 - S 15 '96 - p44 [1-50]
  Peter Nevsky and the True Story of the Russian Moon Landing
  NYTBR - v101 - S 15 '96 - p44 [51-250]

Batchelor, Martine - *Walking on Lotus Flowers*
  Tric - v6 - Win '96 - p116 [1-50]

Batchelor, R E - *Using Spanish Synonyms*
  r MLR - v92 - Ja '97 - p222+ [501+]

Batchelor, Ray - *Henry Ford: Mass Production, Modernism and Design*
  T&C - v38 - Ja '97 - p258+ [501+]

Batchelor, Stephen - *The Awakening of the West*
  Rel St Rev - v22 - O '96 - p340 [51-250]
  Buddhism without Beliefs
  PW - v244 - Ap 14 '97 - p70 [51-250]

Bate, Jonathan - *Shakespeare: An Illustrated Stage History*
  Choice - v34 - O '96 - p292 [51-250]
  Shakespeare and Ovid
  Class Out - v74 - Win '97 - p80+ [251-500]
  Obs - D 1 '96 - p17* [1-50]
  Shakespeare and the English Romantic Imagination
  Obs - D 1 '96 - p17* [1-50]

Bate, Paul - *Strategies for Cultural Change*
  R&R Bk N - v11 - F '97 - p30 [51-250]

Bateman, Bradley W - *Keynes's Uncertain Revolution*
  Choice - v34 - F '97 - p1010 [51-250]
  JEL - v35 - Mr '97 - p192 [51-250]
  TLS - Ja 17 '97 - p28 [501+]

Bateman, Colin - *Empire State*
  TLS - Ap 11 '97 - p26 [51-250]
  Of Wee Sweetie Mice and Men
  KR - v65 - Ap 1 '97 - p477 [251-500]
  LJ - v122 - Ap 1 '97 - p120 [51-250]
  PW - v244 - Mr 31 '97 - p60 [51-250]

Bateman, Dick - *Geography*
  cr Sch Lib - v44 - N '96 - p161 [51-250]

Bateman, Robert - *Natural Worlds*
  Atl - v279 - Ja '97 - p97+ [501+]

Bateman, Teresa - *The Ring of Truth (Illus. by Omar Rayyan)*
  c CBRS - v25 - Mr '97 - p85 [51-250]
  c CCB-B - v50 - My '97 - p313 [51-250]
  c KR - v65 - F 1 '97 - p218 [51-250]
  c PW - v244 - F 24 '97 - p91 [51-250]

Bates, Bud - *Voice and Data Communications Handbook*
  CBR - v14 - S '96 - p31 [1-50]
  SciTech - v20 - S '96 - p54 [51-250]

Bates, Daniel G - *Case Studies in Human Ecology*
  R&R Bk N - v11 - D '96 - p20 [51-250]

Bates, David - *England and Normandy in the Middle Ages*
  EHR - v112 - Ap '97 - p437+ [501+]

Bates, David V - *Environmental Health Risks and Public Policy*
  Env - v38 - O '96 - p26 [51-250]

Bates, Don - *Knowledge and the Scholarly Medical Traditions*
  Am Ethnol - v24 - F '97 - p221+ [501+]

Bates, H E - *Through the Woods*
  Hort - v74 - N '96 - p61+ [251-500]

Bates, Irene M - *Lost Legacy*
  WHQ - v27 - Win '96 - p552 [1-50]

Bates, Jonathan - *Shakespearean Constitutions*
  Obs - D 1 '96 - p17* [1-50]

Bates, Karen Grigsby - *Basic Black*
  B Ent - v27 - F '97 - p215 [1-50]
  y BL - v93 - D 15 '96 - p695 [51-250]
  LJ - v121 - N 1 '96 - p73 [51-250]
  LJ - v122 - Ap 15 '97 - p37 [51-250]
  PW - v243 - N 18 '96 - p73 [51-250]

Bates, Larry M - *Conservative Systems and Quantum Chaos*
  SciTech - v20 - S '96 - p14 [51-250]

Bates, Mary Ellen - *The Online Deskbook*
  A Lib - v27 - Ag '96 - p70 [51-250]
  LJ - v121 - N 1 '96 - p104 [51-250]
  r SLMQ - v25 - Fall '96 - p61 [51-250]

Bates, Michael - *Reckless*
  y Emerg Lib - v24 - S '96 - p26 [1-50]
  Wicked
  y VOYA - v19 - O '96 - p202 [501+]

Bates, Milton J - *The Wars We Took to Vietnam*
  Choice - v34 - Mr '97 - p1158 [51-250]

Bateson, Mary Catherine - *Peripheral Visions*
  ES - v27 - Fall '96 - p292+ [501+]

Bateson, Robert N - *Introduction to Control System Technology. 5th Ed.*
  SciTech - v20 - N '96 - p70 [51-250]

Bateson-Hill, Margaret - *Lao Lao of Dragon Mountain* (*Illus. by Francesca Pelizzoli*)
c   BL - v93 - D 15 '96 - p730 [51-250]
c   CBRS - v25 - O '96 - p18+ [51-250]
c   CCB-B - v50 - Ja '97 - p164 [51-250]
c   HB Guide - v8 - Spr '97 - p19 [51-250]
c   NW - v128 - D 2 '96 - p88 [51-250]
c   Sch Lib - v44 - N '96 - p148 [251-500]
c   SLJ - v43 - Ja '97 - p76 [51-250]
c   TES - D 6 '96 - p17* [501+]

Bath, Michael - *Speaking Pictures*
Ren Q - v49 - Aut '96 - p643+ [501+]
Ren & Ref - v19 - Fall '96 - p88+ [501+]
RES - v47 - Ag '96 - p406+ [501+]

Baths: Your Guide to Planning and Remodeling
LJ - v121 - S 15 '96 - p66 [51-250]

Batinski, Michael C - *Jonathan Belcher, Colonial Governor*
Choice - v34 - O '96 - p344 [51-250]
NEQ - v70 - Mr '97 - p153+ [501+]
R&R Bk N - v11 - N '96 - p19 [1-50]

Batllori, Miguel - *El Abate Viscardo. Rev. Ed.*
HAHR - v77 - My '97 - p343+ [251-500]

Batra, Ravi - *The Great American Deception*
Barron's - v76 - N 18 '96 - p71 [501+]
Choice - v34 - My '97 - p1545+ [51-250]
JEL - v35 - Mr '97 - p209 [51-250]

Batstone, David - *New Visions for the Americas*
JAAR - v64 - Fall '96 - p696+ [501+]

Battacharyya, Shuvra S - *Software Synthesis from Dataflow Graphs*
SciTech - v21 - Mr '97 - p87 [51-250]

Battcock, Gregory - *New Artists' Video*
Afterimage - v24 - N '96 - p4 [1-50]

Batten, Jack - *Hoopla! Inside the Toronto Raptors' First Season*
Quill & Q - v62 - N '96 - p39 [251-500]

Battenberg, Friedrich - *Quellen Zur Geschichte Der Juden Im Hessischen Staatsarchiv Darmstadt 1080-1650*
Six Ct J - v27 - Win '96 - p1057+ [501+]

Battenhouse, Roy - *Shakespeare's Christian Dimension*
JAAR - v64 - Sum '96 - p446+ [501+]
Ren & Ref - v20 - Win '96 - p79+ [501+]

Battin, M Pabst - *Drug Use in Assisted Suicide and Euthanasia*
SB - v32 - N '96 - p228 [51-250]
SciTech - v20 - S '96 - p26 [51-250]
Ethical Issues in Suicide
MHR - v10 - Fall '96 - p68+ [501+]

Battista, Giovanni - *Correspondance De Giovanni Battista De Rossi Et De Louis Duchesne 1873-1894*
CHR - v83 - Ja '97 - p119+ [501+]

Battista, Vicente - *Sucesos Argentinos*
WLT - v71 - Win '97 - p115 [251-500]

Battle, Kemp - *Hearts of Fire*
y   BL - v93 - Mr 1 '97 - p1107 [51-250]
KR - v65 - Ja 15 '97 - p106 [251-500]
LJ - v122 - Mr 15 '97 - p68 [51-250]
PW - v244 - Ja 13 '97 - p64 [51-250]

Battle, Lois - *Bed and Breakfast*
BL - v93 - S 1 '96 - p5 [51-250]
KR - v64 - S 1 '96 - p1252 [251-500]
LJ - v121 - O 1 '96 - p124 [51-250]
NYTBR - v101 - D 15 '96 - p25 [51-250]
PW - v243 - S 16 '96 - p68 [51-250]
S Liv - v32 - F '97 - p80 [51-250]

Battle, Stafford L - *The African American Resource Guide to the Internet and Online Services*
r   BL - v92 - Ag '96 - p1922 [51-250]
r   Choice - v34 - Ja '97 - p765 [51-250]

Baty, S Paige - *American Monroe*
CS - v25 - N '96 - p813+ [501+]
FQ - v50 - Win '96 - p46+ [501+]

Bat Ye'or - *The Decline of Eastern Christianity under Islam*
Choice - v34 - Ap '97 - p1401 [51-250]
MEJ - v51 - Win '97 - p155 [51-250]

Baubock, Rainer - *Transnational Citizenship*
CS - v25 - S '96 - p593+ [501+]

Bauby, Jean-Dominique - *The Diving Bell and the Butterfly*
BL - v93 - My 1 '97 - p1458 [51-250]
KR - v65 - My 1 '97 - p711 [51-250]
Obs - Ap 13 '97 - p15* [501+]
PW - v244 - Ap 28 '97 - p61 [251-500]

Bauckham, Richard - *The Theology of Jurgen Moltmann*
Theol St - v57 - S '96 - p544+ [501+]

Baucum, Don - *Barron's EZ-101 Study Keys*
r   SLMQ - v25 - Fall '96 - p62 [1-50]

Baud, Michiel - *Peasants and Tobacco in the Dominican Republic 1870-1930*
AHR - v102 - F '97 - p232 [251-500]
HAHR - v77 - F '97 - p143+ [501+]

Baudelaire, Charles - *Baudelaire, Les Fleurs Du Mal*
MLR - v91 - Jl '96 - p578+ [501+]
Baudelaire: Selected Poems from Les Fleurs Du Mal
MLR - v92 - Ap '97 - p473 [251-500]
Les Fleurs Du Mal
MLR - v91 - O '96 - p999+ [251-500]
MLR - v92 - Ja '97 - p198+ [251-500]

Baudez, Claude-Francois - *Maya Sculpture of Copan*
r   LA Ant - v7 - Je '96 - p169+ [501+]

Baudino, Gael - *Spires of Spirit*
y   Kliatt - v31 - My '97 - p12 [51-250]

Baudot, Georges - *Utopia and History in Mexico*
Choice - v34 - O '96 - p342 [51-250]

Baudrillard, Jean - *Cool Memories II*
SFS - v24 - Mr '97 - p164+ [501+]
The Gulf War Did Not Take Place
CS - v26 - Mr '97 - p138+ [501+]
Symbolic Exchange and Death
MLR - v91 - Jl '96 - p689+ [501+]

Bauer, Caroline Feller - *Leading Kids to Books through Magic*
BL - v93 - S 15 '96 - p253 [51-250]
Emerg Lib - v24 - Mr '97 - p42 [51-250]
JOYS - v10 - Fall '96 - p97 [251-500]
SLMQ - v24 - Sum '96 - p219 [51-250]
The Poetry Break
Inst - v106 - N '96 - p26 [1-50]

Bauer, Dale M - *Edith Wharton's Brave New Politics*
AL - v68 - S '96 - p647+ [251-500]
J Am St - v30 - Ag '96 - p317+ [501+]

Bauer, David G - *The Complete Grants Sourcebook for Higher Education. 3rd Ed.*
r   ARBA - v28 - '97 - p310 [251-500]

Bauer, David R - *Treasures New and Old*
Rel St Rev - v23 - Ap '97 - p180 [51-250]
R&R Bk N - v11 - N '96 - p7 [51-250]

Bauer, Erwin A - *Bears: Behavior, Ecology, Conservation*
y   BL - v93 - Mr 1 '97 - p1098+ [501+]
Elk: Behavior, Ecology, Conservation
Choice - v34 - Mr '97 - p1185 [51-250]
SciTech - v20 - D '96 - p33 [1-50]
Mule Deer
AB - v97 - Je 17 '96 - p2404 [51-250]
y   Choice - v34 - N '96 - p484 [51-250]
Whitetails: Behavior, Ecology, Conservation
AB - v97 - Je 17 '96 - p2404 [51-250]

Bauer, Eugene E - *Contrails: A Boeing Salesman Reminisces*
A & S Sm - v11 - O '96 - p88 [1-50]

Bauer, Joan - *Squashed*
y   SLJ - v30 - S '96 - p3 [1-50]
y   TES - Mr 21 '97 - p14* [251-500]
Sticks
c   HB Guide - v7 - Fall '96 - p289 [51-250]
c   KR - v64 - My 1 '96 - p684 [51-250]
Sticks (Paris). Audio Version
y   Kliatt - v31 - Ja '97 - p46 [51-250]
Thwonk
y   Emerg Lib - v24 - S '96 - p24 [1-50]
y   Kliatt - v30 - S '96 - p15 [51-250]

Bauer, Marion Dane - *Alison's Puppy*
c   BL - v93 - My 1 '97 - p1492+ [51-250]
Alison's Wings (Illus. by Roger Roth)
c   HB Guide - v7 - Fall '96 - p285 [51-250]
c   SLJ - v42 - Ag '96 - p115+ [51-250]
On My Honor
c   HMR - Win '96 - p45 [1-50]
Our Stories
c   HB Guide - v8 - Spr '97 - p147 [51-250]
y   Kliatt - v31 - Ja '97 - p17 [251-500]
y   SLJ - v42 - D '96 - p140 [51-250]
y   VOYA - v19 - D '96 - p284+ [51-250]
A Question of Trust
c   SLJ - v43 - Mr '97 - p112 [1-50]

Bauer, Michael - *The San Francisco Chronicle Cookbook*
PW - v244 - Ja 6 '97 - p68+ [51-250]

Bauer, S Wise - *The Revolt*
BL - v93 - N 15 '96 - p571 [501+]
Ch Today - v41 - Mr 3 '97 - p47 [51-250]

Bauer, Yehuda - *Jews for Sale?*
PW - v244 - N 11 '96 - p72 [1-50]

Bauermeister, Erica - *Let's Hear It for the Girls*
r   BL - v93 - Mr 1 '97 - p1176 [51-250]
yr   Kliatt - v31 - My '97 - p17 [51-250]
r   PW - v243 - D 16 '96 - p61 [51-250]

Baughman, D R - *Neural Networks in Bioprocessing and Chemical Engineering*
SciTech - v20 - S '96 - p60 [51-250]

Baughman, Judith S - *American Decades 1920-1929*
yr   ARBA - v28 - '97 - p195 [51-250]

Baughman, T H - *Before the Heroes Came*
EHR - v111 - S '96 - p1011+ [251-500]

Baum, Dan - *Smoke and Mirrors*
BW - v26 - Ag 18 '96 - p6 [501+]
For Aff - v75 - N '96 - p153 [51-250]
KR - v64 - My 1 '96 - p653 [251-500]
Trib Bks - My 18 '97 - p8 [1-50]

Baum, Jan A - *Low Flow Anaesthesia*
SciTech - v20 - S '96 - p38 [51-250]

Baum, L Frank - *Our Landlady*
AL - v69 - Mr '97 - p247 [1-50]
Nine-C Lit - v51 - D '96 - p419 [1-50]
Roundup M - v4 - O '96 - p25 [51-250]
WHQ - v28 - Spr '97 - p98+ [251-500]
The Scarecrow of Oz (Illus. by John R Neill)
c   PW - v244 - Mr 31 '97 - p77 [1-50]
Tik-Tok of Oz (Illus. by John R Neill)
c   Ch BWatch - v6 - Jl '96 - p3 [1-50]
c   HB Guide - v7 - Fall '96 - p289 [51-250]
The Wizard of Oz (Illus. by Lisbeth Zwerger)
c   AB - v98 - N 18 '96 - p1726 [501+]
c   BW - v26 - N 3 '96 - p10 [251-500]
c   HB Guide - v8 - Spr '97 - p62 [51-250]
c   KR - v64 - Ag 15 '96 - p1232 [51-250]
c   NW - v128 - D 2 '96 - p86 [1-50]
c   NYTBR - v101 - N 10 '96 - p31 [501+]
c   PW - v243 - O 14 '96 - p85 [51-250]
c   SLJ - v42 - N '96 - p103 [51-250]
c   TES - N 8 '96 - p11* [251-500]

Baum, Lawrence - *The Supreme Court. 5th Ed.*
SSQ - v77 - S '96 - p711+ [501+]

Baum, Richard, 1930- - *In Search of Planet Vulcan*
BL - v93 - My 15 '97 - p1549 [51-250]

Baum, Richard, 1940- - *Burying Mao*
AAPSS-A - v546 - Jl '96 - p159+ [501+]
Ch Rev Int - v3 - Fall '96 - p357+ [501+]

Baum, Thomas - *Out of Body*
KR - v65 - Ap 1 '97 - p477 [251-500]
LJ - v122 - Ap 1 '97 - p120 [51-250]
PW - v244 - Mr 17 '97 - p75 [51-250]

Bauman, Michael - *Historians of the Christian Tradition*
Rel St Rev - v23 - Ja '97 - p82 [51-250]

Bauman, Richard W - *Critical Legal Studies*
r   ARBA - v28 - '97 - p221+ [51-250]
r   Choice - v34 - S '96 - p93 [51-250]

Bauman, Robert P - *From Promise to Performance*
BL - v93 - F 15 '97 - p982+ [51-250]

Bauman, Thomas - *Opera and the Enlightenment*
Eight-C St - v30 - Win '96 - p199+ [501+]
Notes - v53 - D '96 - p464+ [501+]

Bauman, Zygmunt - *Postmodern Ethics*
MLR - v92 - Ja '97 - p152+ [501+]

Baumann, Gerd - *Mathematica in Theoretical Physics*
Choice - v34 - O '96 - p319 [51-250]

Baumbach, Gerald F - *Experiencing Mystagogy*
CLW - v67 - D '96 - p53+ [251-500]

Baumeister, Roy F - *Evil: Inside Human Cruelty and Violence*
BL - v93 - N 15 '96 - p551 [51-250]
Choice - v34 - My '97 - p1578+ [51-250]
New Sci - v153 - F 1 '97 - p40+ [501+]
PW - v243 - O 14 '96 - p74 [51-250]

Baumel, Judith Tydor - *Kibbutz Buchenwald*
BL - v93 - D 15 '96 - p706 [51-250]
LJ - v122 - F 1 '97 - p93 [51-250]

Baumgardner, James - *Medicare and Graduate Medical Education*
J Gov Info - v23 - S '96 - p559+ [51-250]

Baumgart, Winfried - *Englishe Akten Zur Geschichte Des Krimkriegs. Vol. 3*
EHR - v111 - S '96 - p1004+ [501+]

Baumgarten, E Lee - *Price Guide and Bibliographic Check List for Children's and Illustrated Books 1880-1960. 1996 Ed.*
r   AB - v98 - N 18 '96 - p1732 [251-500]

Baumgarten, Jean - *Introduction A La Litterature Yiddish Ancienne*
Specu - v71 - Jl '96 - p682+ [501+]

Baumgartner, Frederic J - *France in the Sixteenth Century*
Six Ct J - v27 - Win '96 - p1065+ [501+]
Louis XII
EHR - v112 - Ap '97 - p454+ [501+]
HT - v47 - Mr '97 - p54 [501+]
Specu - v71 - Jl '96 - p683+ [501+]

Baumgartner, James E - *National Guide to Funding for Elementary and Secondary Education. 3rd Ed.*
  r ARBA - v28 - '97 - p139 [251-500]
National Guide to Funding for Libraries and Information Services. 3rd Ed.
  r ARBA - v27 - '96 - p239 [251-500]
National Guide to Funding in Religion. 3rd Ed.
  r ARBA - v28 - '97 - p539 [51-250]
Bauml, Franz H - *Attila: The Man and His Image*
  Slav R - v55 - Sum '96 - p455+ [501+]
Baumohl, Jim - *Homelessness in America*
  R&R Bk N - v12 - F '97 - p56 [51-250]
Baumrind, Diana - *Child Maltreatment and Optimal Caregiving in Social Contexts*
  Readings - v12 - Mr '97 - p23 [51-250]
Baumslag, Naomi - *Milk, Money, and Madness*
  Wom R Bks - v14 - O '96 - p25+ [501+]
Baun, Michael J - *An Imperfect Union*
  Choice - v34 - O '96 - p356 [51-250]
  Wil Q - v21 - Win '97 - p38 [51-250]
Baur, John E - *Christmas in Early America 1800-1900*
  CAY - v16 - Fall '95 - p2 [51-250]
Christmas on the American Frontier 1800-1900
  r JPC - v29 - Spr '96 - p258+ [51-250]
Baur, Susan - *The Intimate Hour*
  BL - v93 - D 15 '96 - p700 [51-250]
  KR - v64 - O 15 '96 - p1502 [51-250]
  LJ - v121 - D '96 - p124 [51-250]
  NYTBR - v102 - Ja 19 '97 - p16 [501+]
  NYTLa - v146 - Ja 20 '97 - pC18 [501+]
  PW - v243 - N 11 '96 - p65 [51-250]
Baur-Heinhold, Margarite - *Decorative Ironwork*
  Ant & CM - v101 - N '96 - p31 [51-250]
Bausch, Heather Anne - *Something's Buggy? (Illus. by Heather Anne Bausch)*
  c E Mag - v8 - Ja '97 - p48+ [51-250]
Bausch, Richard - *Good Evening Mr. and Mrs. America, and All the Ships at Sea*
  BL - v92 - Ag '96 - p1880 [251-500]
  NYTBR - v101 - O 27 '96 - p15 [501+]
  NYTLa - v146 - S 25 '96 - pC15 [501+]
  PW - v243 - N 4 '96 - p37 [51-250]
  Shen - v47 - Spr '97 - p113+ [501+]
  W&I - v12 - Mr '97 - p271+ [501+]
The Selected Stories of Richard Bausch
  Ant R - v54 - Fall '96 - p495 [251-500]
  BL - v92 - Ag '96 - p1880 [251-500]
  VQR - v73 - Win '97 - p20* [51-250]
Bausch, William J - *Storytelling the Word*
  CLW - v67 - Mr '97 - p36 [51-250]
Bauschinger, Sigrid - *Ich Habe Etwas Zu Sagen*
  Ger Q - v69 - Sum '96 - p355+ [501+]
Bautista, Renato G - *Emerging Separation Technologies for Metals II*
  SciTech - v20 - N '96 - p62 [51-250]
Bavin-Mizzi, Jill - *Ravished: Sexual Violence in Victorian Australia*
  Aust Bk R - Jl '96 - p66 [251-500]
Bawden, Juliet - *Rag Rug Inspirations*
  LJ - v122 - F 15 '97 - p133 [51-250]
Bawden, Nina - *Granny the Pag*
  y BL - v93 - Ap 1 '97 - p1302 [1-50]
  c CLW - v67 - Mr '97 - p52 [51-250]
  c HB - v72 - S '96 - p591+ [51-250]
  y HB Guide - v7 - Fall '96 - p300 [51-250]
  c LA - v73 - S '96 - p354 [51-250]
  c Magpies - v11 - My '96 - p41+ [51-250]
  c SLJ - v42 - D '96 - p27+ [1-50]
A Nice Change
  Spec - v278 - Mr 15 '97 - p40+ [501+]
The Real Plato Jones
  y Kliatt - v31 - Mr '97 - p6 [51-250]
  c PW - v243 - N 25 '96 - p78 [1-50]
  c RT - v50 - F '97 - p423 [51-250]
  y SLJ - v43 - Mr '97 - p112 [1-50]
Bawer, Bruce - *Beyond Queer*
  BL - v93 - Ja '97 - p808 [1-50]
  Dis - v43 - Fall '96 - p136+ [501+]
  HG&LRev - v3 - Fall '96 - p46 [501+]
Prophets and Professors
  New ER - v18 - Spr '97 - p163+ [501+]
  WLT - v71 - Win '97 - p159 [501+]
Bax, Mart - *Medjugorje: Religion, Politics, and Violence in Rural Bosnia*
  Am Ethnol - v24 - F '97 - p241+ [501+]
Baxandall, Michael - *Shadows and Enlightenment*
  Art J - v56 - Spr '97 - p103 [501+]
  Eight-C St - v30 - Fall '96 - p102+ [501+]
Baxendale, John - *Narrating the Thirties*
  Albion - v28 - '96 - p730+ [501+]
  R&R Bk N - v11 - N '96 - p11 [51-250]

Baxt, George - *The Fred Astaire and Ginger Rogers Murder Case*
  BL - v93 - F 15 '97 - p1006 [51-250]
  KR - v64 - D 15 '96 - p1772 [51-250]
  PW - v243 - D 30 '96 - p58 [51-250]
The William Powell and Myrna Loy Murder Case
  Arm Det - v29 - Sum '96 - p371 [251-500]
Baxter, Catherine S - *Stedman's Radiology and Oncology Words. 2nd Ed.*
  SciTech - v20 - N '96 - p40 [51-250]
Baxter, Charles - *Believers: A Novella and Stories*
  NYTBR - v102 - Ap 6 '97 - p7 [501+]
Burning Down the House
  KR - v65 - F 1 '97 - p180 [251-500]
  LJ - v122 - Mr 15 '97 - p64 [51-250]
  PW - v244 - Mr 10 '97 - p56 [51-250]
Baxter, Charles, 1947- - *Believers: A Novella and Stories*
  KR - v65 - Ja 15 '97 - p76 [251-500]
  LATBR - Mr 30 '97 - p10 [501+]
  Nat - v264 - Ap 7 '97 - p33+ [501+]
  PW - v244 - F 24 '97 - p65 [51-250]
Harmony of the World
  PW - v244 - F 24 '97 - p88 [1-50]
  Trib Bks - My 4 '97 - p8 [1-50]
Baxter, Colin F - *The War in North Africa 1940-1943*
  r ARBA - v28 - '97 - p209 [51-250]
  r Choice - v34 - O '96 - p248 [51-250]
Baxter, Craig - *Government and Politics in South Asia*
  Pac A - v69 - Sum '96 - p271+ [501+]
Baxter, Daniel J - *The Least of These My Brethren*
  y BL - v93 - F 1 '97 - p911 [51-250]
  KR - v65 - Ja 1 '97 - p29 [51-250]
  LJ - v122 - Ja '97 - p132 [51-250]
  PW - v243 - D 16 '96 - p46 [51-250]
  Trib Bks - Mr 23 '97 - p3 [51-250]
Baxter, James C - *The Meiji Unification through the Lens of Ishikawa Prefecture*
  AHR - v102 - F '97 - p156 [501+]
Baxter, John - *Bunuel*
  TES - Ag 30 '96 - p25 [51-250]
Steven Spielberg
  KR - v65 - F 1 '97 - p181 [251-500]
  PW - v244 - F 24 '97 - p78 [51-250]
Baxter, L - *Applications of Advanced Technology to Ash-Related Problems in Boilers*
  SciTech - v21 - Mr '97 - p85 [51-250]
Baxter, Larry K - *Capacitive Sensors*
  SciTech - v20 - D '96 - p77 [51-250]
Baxter, Lesley - *Oliver Twist (Illus. by Christian Birmingham)*
  c BL - v93 - S 1 '96 - p125 [51-250]
  c HB Guide - v8 - Spr '97 - p65 [51-250]
  c PW - v243 - N 11 '96 - p77 [51-250]
Baxter, Mary Lynn - *Southern Fires*
  PW - v243 - S 9 '96 - p81 [51-250]
Baxter, Maurice G - *Henry Clay and the American System*
  Historian - v59 - Fall '96 - p143 [251-500]
  JSH - v63 - F '97 - p161+ [251-500]
Baxter, Nicola - *Autumn (Illus. by Kim Woolley)*
  c HB Guide - v8 - Spr '97 - p109 [51-250]
Babies (Illus. by Michael Evans)
  c HB Guide - v7 - Fall '96 - p310+ [1-50]
  c SLJ - v42 - Ag '96 - p132 [51-250]
The Children's Classic Poetry Collection (Illus. by Cathie Shuttleworth)
  c PW - v243 - D 2 '96 - p62 [51-250]
Families
  c HB Guide - v7 - Fall '96 - p310+ [1-50]
Friends (Illus. by Michael Evans)
  c HB Guide - v7 - Fall '96 - p307 [1-50]
  c SLJ - v42 - Ag '96 - p132 [51-250]
Homes
  c HB Guide - v7 - Fall '96 - p318 [51-250]
Spring (Illus. by Kim Woolley)
  c HB Guide - v8 - Spr '97 - p109 [51-250]
Summer (Illus. by Kim Woolley)
  c HB Guide - v8 - Spr '97 - p109 [51-250]
Winter (Illus. by Kim Woolley)
  c HB Guide - v8 - Spr '97 - p109 [51-250]
Baxter, Stephen - *Voyage*
  BW - v27 - Mr 30 '97 - p8 [501+]
  KR - v64 - D 1 '96 - p1685+ [251-500]
  LJ - v122 - Ja '97 - p142 [51-250]
  New Sci - v152 - N 23 '96 - p48 [51-250]
  PW - v243 - D 9 '96 - p61 [51-250]
Baxter, Sylvester - *The Southwest in the American Imagination*
  Nine-C Lit - v51 - Mr '97 - p558 [51-250]

Bay, Ann Phillips - *A Kid's Guide to the Smithsonian (Illus. by Steven Rotblatt)*
  c BL - v93 - S 1 '96 - p120 [51-250]
  c PW - v243 - Jl 22 '96 - p243 [51-250]
Bay, Jeanette Graham - *A Treasury of Flannelboard Stories*
  c CLW - v66 - Je '96 - p44 [51-250]
Bay, William - *You Can Teach Yourself Guitar. Electronic Media Version*
  Teach Mus - v4 - D '96 - p48 [51-250]
Bay Windows
  p Sm Pr R - v28 - Je '96 - p19 [51-250]
Bayard, Thomas O - *Reciprocity and Retaliation in U.S. Trade Policy*
  BusLR - v21 - 3 '96 - p192+ [501+]
Bayertz, Kurt - *Sanctity of Life and Human Dignity*
  SciTech - v20 - D '96 - p37 [51-250]
Bayless, Martha - *Parody in the Middle Ages*
  Choice - v34 - My '97 - p1490 [51-250]
Bayless, Rick - *Rick Bayless's Mexican Kitchen*
  BL - v93 - N 15 '96 - p559 [51-250]
  LJ - v121 - N 15 '96 - p83 [51-250]
  PW - v243 - O 7 '96 - p71+ [51-250]
  PW - v243 - N 4 '96 - p47 [1-50]
Bayley, John - *George's Lair*
  Spec - v277 - N 30 '96 - p57 [501+]
  TLS - D 13 '96 - p23 [501+]
Bayley, Lesley - *Understanding Your Horse*
  y BL - v93 - Ja '97 - p795+ [51-250]
Baylis, John - *Ambiguity and Deterrence*
  Choice - v34 - S '96 - p184 [51-250]
Baylis, William E - *Clifford (Geometric) Algebras with Applications to Physics, Mathematics, and Engineering*
  SciTech - v20 - D '96 - p22 [1-50]
Bayly, Joseph - *Winterflight*
  HM - v293 - S '96 - p64+ [501+]
Baym, Nina - *American Women Writers and the Work of History 1790-1860*
  AHR - v101 - D '96 - p1614+ [501+]
  Legacy - v13 - 2 '96 - p156+ [501+]
  W&M Q - v53 - O '96 - p845+ [501+]
Bayne, Kathryn A L - *Current Issues and New Frontiers in Animal Research*
  Hast Cen R - v26 - Mr '96 - p48 [1-50]
Bayne-Smith, Marcia - *Race, Gender, and Health*
  NWSA Jnl - v9 - Spr '97 - p89+ [501+]
Baynham, Mike - *Literacy Practices*
  MLJ - v80 - Fall '96 - p397+ [501+]
Baynton, Douglas C - *Forbidden Signs*
  CHE - v43 - Ja 17 '97 - pA20 [51-250]
  Choice - v34 - Ap '97 - p1422 [51-250]
  Nat - v264 - Mr 10 '97 - p30+ [501+]
  NYTBR - v102 - Ja 26 '97 - p30 [501+]
Bayor, Ronald H - *The New York Irish*
  ILS - v15 - Fall '96 - p28 [501+]
Race and the Shaping of Twentieth-Century Atlanta
  Choice - v34 - O '96 - p344 [51-250]
  VQR - v73 - Win '97 - p166+ [501+]
Bazak Guide to Israel and Jordan 1996-1997
  r BL - v93 - S 15 '96 - p206 [1-50]
Bazalgette, Cary - *In Front of the Children*
  J Pop F&TV - v24 - Win '97 - p182+ [251-500]
Bazant, Jan - *Roman Portraiture*
  AJA - v100 - O '96 - p795+ [501+]
Bazillion, Richard J - *Academic Libraries as High-Tech Gateways*
  r LRTS - v40 - Ap '96 - p188+ [501+]
Bazirjian, Rosann - *New Automation Technology for Acquisitions and Collection Development*
  LR - v45 - 8 '96 - p41+ [501+]
Bea, Holly - *Where Does God Live? (Illus. by Kim Howard)*
  c PW - v244 - Ja 27 '97 - p98 [51-250]
Beach, Cecilia - *French Women Playwrights of the Twentieth Century*
  r ARBA - v28 - '97 - p431 [51-250]
  r Choice - v34 - N '96 - p425 [51-250]
Beach, Charles M - *Are We Becoming Two Societies?*
  JEL - v34 - S '96 - p1412 [51-250]
Beach, D N - *The Shona and Their Neighbours*
  EHR - v111 - S '96 - p1043 [251-500]
  GJ - v162 - N '96 - p333 [501+]
Beach, Dore - *The Responsible Conduct of Research*
  Choice - v34 - N '96 - p478 [51-250]
  New Sci - v151 - S 28 '96 - p55 [1-50]
  R&R Bk N - v11 - N '96 - p76 [51-250]
Beach, Eric - *Weeping for Lost Babylon*
  Aust Bk R - Jl '96 - p54+ [501+]
Beach, Milo Cleveland - *King of the World*
  FEER - v160 - Ap 10 '97 - p46+ [501+]

Beachey, R W - *A History of East Africa 1592-1902*
HRNB - v25 - Win '97 - p85+ [501+]

Beachy, John A - *Abstract Algebra. 2nd Ed.*
SciTech - v20 - D '96 - p15 [51-250]

Beadle, Richard - *The Cambridge Companion to Medieval English Theatre*
MLR - v92 - Ja '97 - p170+ [501+]
New Science out of Old Books
BC - v45 - Aut '96 - p407+ [501+]

Beagan, Glenda - *Changes and Dreams*
KR - v65 - Ap 1 '97 - p477+ [251-500]

Beagle, Peter S - *Immortal Unicorn*
SF Chr - v18 - O '96 - p80 [1-50]
The Unicorn Sonata
Analog - v117 - Ja '97 - p141+ [51-250]
y BL - v92 - Ag '96 - p1853 [251-500]
LJ - v121 - S 15 '96 - p100 [51-250]

Beal, Eileen - *Choosing a Career in the Restaurant Industry*
y SLJ - v43 - Mr '97 - p196+ [51-250]

Beal, George - *The Kingfisher Illustrated Thesaurus. New and Rev. Ed.*
cr CLW - v67 - D '96 - p58 [251-500]
cr SLJ - v42 - Ag '96 - p180 [51-250]

Bealer, Alex W - *Only the Names Remain. 2nd Ed. (Illus. by Kristina Rodanas)*
c HB Guide - v7 - Fall '96 - p390 [51-250]
y VOYA - v19 - O '96 - p226 [51-250]

Beales, Peter - *Visions of Roses*
Books - v10 - Je '96 - p21 [1-50]
LJ - v121 - N 1 '96 - p99 [51-250]
TES - Ag 23 '96 - p22 [51-250]

Beall, Michael E - *Inside AutoCAD LT for Windows 95*
SciTech - v20 - D '96 - p59 [51-250]

Beall, Pamela Conn - *Wee Sing Baby (Illus. by Tammy Daniel-Biske). Book and Audio Version*
PW - v243 - N 11 '96 - p35 [51-250]
Wee Sing Baby Band Sounds and Songs (Illus. by Tammy Daniel-Biske). Book and Audio Version
c Ch BWatch - v6 - Jl '96 - p5 [1-50]
Wee Sing Farm Animals (Illus. by Kurt R Kress). Book and Audio Version
c Ch BWatch - v6 - Jl '96 - p5 [1-50]
Wee Sing Toys (Illus. by Patrick O Chapin). Book and Audio Version
c Ch BWatch - v6 - Jl '96 - p5 [1-50]
Wee Sing Wheels (Illus. by Diana Fisher). Book and Audio Version
c Ch BWatch - v6 - Jl '96 - p5 [1-50]

Beals, Ivan A - *Our Racist Legacy*
LJ - v122 - Ap 15 '97 - p86 [51-250]

Beam, Joan - *The Native American in Long Fiction*
r ARBA - v28 - '97 - p437+ [51-250]
yr BL - v93 - My 1 '97 - p1533 [251-500]

Bean, Fred - *Lorena*
LJ - v121 - D '96 - p141 [51-250]
PW - v243 - N 11 '96 - p58+ [51-250]

Bean, Gerard M D - *Fiduciary Obligations and Joint Ventures*
Law Q Rev - v113 - Ap '97 - p341+ [501+]

Bean, Gregory - *A Death in Victory*
BL - v93 - My 15 '97 - p1566 [51-250]
PW - v244 - Ap 28 '97 - p53+ [51-250]

Bean, Jonathan J - *Beyond the Broker State*
Choice - v34 - My '97 - p1543 [51-250]
JEL - v35 - Mr '97 - p265 [51-250]

Beans, Bruce E - *Eagle's Plume*
Aud - v98 - N '96 - p134+ [501+]
y BL - v93 - S 1 '96 - p47 [51-250]
BL - v93 - D 1 '96 - p630 [1-50]
New Sci - v152 - N 16 '96 - p50 [51-250]
y SB - v32 - O '96 - p203 [251-500]

Bear, Greg - *New Legends*
y Kliatt - v30 - N '96 - p20 [51-250]
Songs of Earth and Power
y Kliatt - v31 - Mr '97 - p16 [51-250]

Bear, John - *College Degrees by Mail*
r J Car P&E - v57 - Fall '96 - p15 [51-250]

Bear, Mark F - *Neuroscience: Exploring the Brain*
SciTech - v20 - N '96 - p32 [51-250]

Beard, Barrett Thomas - *Wonderful Flying Machines*
APH - v44 - Spr '97 - p57 [51-250]
SciTech - v21 - Mr '97 - p100 [51-250]

Beard, Jane A - *Births, Deaths, and Marriages from El Paso Area Newspapers 1891-1895. Vol. 3*
r EGH - v50 - N '96 - p196 [51-250]

Beard, Mary - *Classics: A Very Short Introduction*
Class Out - v74 - Win '97 - p84 [251-500]

Beard, Patricia - *Growing Up Republican*
BW - v26 - S 8 '96 - p4 [251-500]

Beard, Peter - *Resist and Masking Techniques*
Ceram Mo - v45 - Ja '97 - p24+ [251-500]

Beard, Richard - *X20*
Obs - D 8 '96 - p17* [51-250]
TLS - D 27 '96 - p22 [251-500]

Beard, Sam - *Restoring Hope in America*
NYRB - v43 - D 19 '96 - p68+ [501+]

Beardsley, John - *Gardens of Revelation*
CAY - v16 - Fall '95 - p3 [51-250]

Beardstown Ladies' Investment Club - *The Beardstown Ladies' Guide to Smart Spending for Big Savings*
BL - v93 - N 15 '96 - p546 [51-250]
PW - v243 - N 4 '96 - p56+ [51-250]
The Beardstown Ladies' Stitch-in-Time Guide to Growing Your Nest Egg
PW - v243 - D 30 '96 - p64 [1-50]

Bearman, Robert - *Charters of the Redvers Family and the Earldom of Devon 1090-1217*
EHR - v112 - F '97 - p164+ [501+]

Bears at Work. Electronic Media Version
c PW - v244 - Ja 27 '97 - p37 [51-250]

Beasley, Donna - *Family Pride*
LJ - v122 - F 15 '97 - p140 [51-250]

The Beat Experience. Electronic Media Version
LJ - v121 - N 1 '96 - p114+ [501+]

Beate, Allert - *Languages of Visuality*
R&R Bk N - v11 - N '96 - p5 [51-250]

Beaton, M C - *Agatha Raisin and the Murderous Marriage*
BL - v93 - N 15 '96 - p573+ [51-250]
KR - v64 - S 1 '96 - p1271 [51-250]
LJ - v121 - N 1 '96 - p111 [1-50]
PW - v243 - O 7 '96 - p64 [51-250]
Agatha Raisin and the Potted Gardener
Arm Det - v29 - Sum '96 - p365 [251-500]
Death of a Macho Man
KR - v64 - My 1 '96 - p641 [251-500]

Beattie, Andrew - *Ordinary Jack*
c Sch Lib - v44 - Ag '96 - p115 [51-250]

Beattie, Ann - *Another You*
NYTBR - v101 - S 8 '96 - p36 [51-250]
My Life, Starring Dara Falcon
BL - v93 - Mr 15 '97 - p1203 [51-250]
KR - v65 - Mr 15 '97 - p397 [251-500]
NYTLa - v146 - Ap 24 '97 - pC16 [501+]
PW - v244 - Ap 7 '97 - p71+ [51-250]
Trib Bks - My 25 '97 - p7 [501+]

Beattie, Geoffrey - *On the Ropes*
Books - v11 - Ap '97 - p21 [1-50]
NS & S - v9 - My 24 '96 - p36+ [501+]

Beattie, L Elisabeth - *Conversations with Kentucky Writers*
PW - v243 - S 23 '96 - p70 [51-250]

Beattie, Melody - *Stop Being Mean to Yourself*
PW - v244 - Ap 21 '97 - p55+ [51-250]

Beatty, Barbara - *Preschool Education in America*
r AHR - v102 - F '97 - p163+ [51-250]
HER - v66 - Fall '96 - p675+ [501+]

Beatty, Grace Joely - *Microsoft Works for Windows 95*
BL - v92 - Ag '96 - p1868 [501+]

Beatty, Jan - *Mad River*
Choice - v34 - S '96 - p121+ [51-250]

Beatty, Monica Driscoll - *Blueberry Eyes*
c Ch BWatch - v6 - Jl '96 - p5 [1-50]

Beatty, Paul - *The White Boy Shuffle*
LJ - v121 - O 1 '96 - p46 [1-50]
Obs - D 8 '96 - p17* [51-250]
VLS - Win '96 - p8 [51-250]

Beaty, Barry J - *The Biology of Disease Vectors*
Choice - v34 - N '96 - p481 [51-250]
SciTech - v20 - S '96 - p28 [51-250]

Beaty, Jerome - *Misreading Jane Eyre*
Choice - v34 - F '97 - p963 [51-250]

Beauboeuf-Lafontant, Tamara - *Facing Racism in Education. 2nd Ed.*
JNE - v64 - Fall '95 - p479+ [501+]

Beauchamp, Cari - *Without Lying Down*
BL - v93 - Mr 15 '97 - p1220 [51-250]
BW - v27 - Ap 13 '97 - p3+ [501+]
Ent W - Ap 4 '97 - p78 [51-250]
KR - v65 - F 1 '97 - p181 [251-500]
LJ - v122 - Ap 15 '97 - p64+ [51-250]
PW - v244 - F 10 '97 - p76 [51-250]

Beauchamp, Dan E - *Health Care Reform and the Battle for the Body Politic*
Hast Cen R - v26 - S '96 - p40 [1-50]

Beauchamp, Tom L - *Intending Death*
CPR - v16 - Je '96 - p157+ [501+]
MHR - v10 - Fall '96 - p68+ [501+]

Beaudreau, Bernard C - *Mass Production, the Stock Market Crash, and the Great Depression*
R&R Bk N - v12 - F '97 - p39 [51-250]

Beaujot, Roderic - *Family over the Life Course*
J Gov Info - v23 - S '96 - p613 [51-250]

Beaulieu, Lionel - *Investing in People*
CS - v26 - Ja '97 - p64+ [501+]

Beaulieu, Trace - *The Mystery Science Theater 3000 Amazing Colossal Episode Guide*
r SF Chr - v18 - O '96 - p82 [1-50]

Beauman, Sally - *Sextet*
Books - v11 - Ap '97 - p21 [51-250]

Beaumarchais, Pierre Augustin Caron De - *Le Barbier De Seville*
MLR - v92 - Ja '97 - p194 [51-250]

Beaumont, Francis - *The Dramatic Works in the Beaumont and Fletcher Canon. Vol. 9*
Six Ct J - v27 - Fall '96 - p823+ [501+]
The Dramatic Works in the Beaumont and Fletcher Canon. Vol. 10
Choice - v34 - Mr '97 - p1158 [51-250]

Beaumont, J Graham - *The Blackwell Dictionary of Neuropsychology*
r ARBA - v28 - '97 - p284 [51-250]
r Choice - v34 - N '96 - p541 [51-250]
r Nature - v386 - Ap 17 '97 - p667+ [501+]

Beaumont, Jeanette - *Letters from Louisa*
Aust Bk R - Jl '96 - p33+ [501+]

Beaumont, Joan - *Australia's War 1939-45*
Aust Bk R - Je '96 - p23+ [501+]

Beaumont, P B - *The Future of Employment Relations*
ILRR - v50 - Ja '97 - p343+ [501+]

Beaumont, Peter - *Drylands: Environmental Management and Development*
JPR - v34 - F '97 - p107 [251-500]

Beaumont, Roger - *War, Chaos, and History*
AHR - v101 - O '96 - p1185+ [501+]

Beauregard, David N - *Virtue's Own Feature*
IPQ - v37 - Je '97 - p239+ [501+]
Ren Q - v50 - Spr '97 - p283+ [501+]

Beauvert, Thierry - *Opera Houses of the World*
BL - v93 - D 15 '96 - p702 [51-250]

Beavers, Herman - *Wrestling Angels into Song*
Critiq - v37 - Sum '96 - p314+ [501+]

Beccaria, Cesare, Marchese Di - *On Crimes and Punishments and Other Writings*
Ethics - v107 - O '96 - p182+ [51-250]

Bechard, Margaret - *Star Hatchling*
c JB - v60 - Ag '96 - p153 [51-250]
c RT - v50 - D '96 - p342 [51-250]
y Sch Lib - v44 - N '96 - p168 [51-250]

Bechko, P A - *The Tin-Pan Man*
Roundup M - v4 - Ap '97 - p25 [51-250]

Bechler, Zev - *Aristotle's Theory of Actuality*
CPR - v16 - D '96 - p392+ [501+]
RM - v50 - S '96 - p144+ [501+]

Bechtel, Guy - *La Chair, Le Diable Et Le Confesseur*
FR - v70 - D '96 - p378+ [501+]

Bechtel, Stefan - *The Good Luck Book*
PW - v244 - Mr 3 '97 - p58 [51-250]

Beck, Astrid B - *Fortunate the Eyes That See*
BTB - v26 - Win '96 - p172+ [251-500]

Beck, Hans-Ulrich - *Jan Van Goyen 1596-1656*
BM - v139 - Ja '97 - p63+ [501+]

Beck, Hartmut - *Raum Und Bewegung*
MLR - v91 - Jl '96 - p777+ [501+]

Beck, Hermann - *The Origins of the Authoritarian Welfare State in Prussia*
AHR - v102 - F '97 - p121+ [501+]
J Soc H - v30 - Spr '97 - p769+ [501+]

Beck, Ian - *Ian Beck's Picture Book (Illus. by Ian Beck)*
c Bks Keeps - Mr '97 - p17 [51-250]
The Oxford Nursery Book (Illus. by Ian Beck)
c Bks Keeps - N '96 - p7 [51-250]
c Emerg Lib - v24 - Mr '97 - p45 [1-50]

Beck, Jane - *Vermont Recollections*
CAY - v17 - Win '96 - p10 [51-250]

Beck, Kathrine - *Bad Neighbors*
BL - v93 - S 1 '96 - p60 [51-250]
BW - v27 - Ja 19 '97 - p8 [251-500]
Ent W - N 22 '96 - p131 [51-250]
KR - v64 - Ag 15 '96 - p1167+ [251-500]
NYTBR - v101 - N 3 '96 - p19 [51-250]

Beck, Norman A - *Mature Christianity in the 21st Century. Expanded and Rev. Ed.*
Rel Ed - v91 - Fall '96 - p601 [1-50]

Beck, Rainer - *Solar Astronomy Handbook*
S&T - v93 - Mr '97 - p63+ [501+]

Beck, Roy - *The Case against Immigration*
    BW - v26 - D 15 '96 - p4 [1-50]
    Choice - v34 - S '96 - p167 [51-250]
    Nat R - v48 - N 25 '96 - p65+ [501+]
    NYTBR - v101 - S 1 '96 - p18 [501+]
Beck, Susan P - *Elegant Beading for Sewing Machine and Serger*
    LJ - v122 - Ap 15 '97 - p79 [51-250]
    Quick Sewing Projects from Placemats
    LJ - v122 - Ap 15 '97 - p79 [51-250]
Beck, Tony - *The Experience of Poverty*
    Pac A - v69 - Sum '96 - p270+ [501+]
Beck, Ulrich - *The Normal Chaos of Love*
    CS - v26 - Ja '97 - p78+ [501+]
    Reflexive Modernization
    Ethics - v107 - O '96 - p190+ [51-250]
    SF - v75 - Mr '97 - p1119+ [501+]
Becker, A L - *Beyond Translation*
    Am Ethnol - v23 - N '96 - p904+ [501+]
Becker, Carol - *Zones of Contention*
    R&R Bk N - v11 - N '96 - p59 [1-50]
    Wom R Bks - v14 - D '96 - p27+ [501+]
Becker, Charles M - *Beyond Urban Bias in Africa*
    JTWS - v13 - Spr '96 - p299+ [501+]
Becker, Christine - *Gross Anatomy*
    c Ch BWatch - v6 - O '96 - p1 [1-50]
Becker, Gary Stanley - *Accounting for Tastes*
    JEL - v35 - Mr '97 - p199 [51-250]
    TLS - Ja 24 '97 - p31 [501+]
    WSJ-MW - v78 - N 19 '96 - pA20 [501+]
    The Economics of Life
    WSJ-MW - v78 - N 19 '96 - pA20 [501+]
    The Essence of Becker
    JEL - v34 - S '96 - p1444 [51-250]
Becker, Geoffrey, 1959- - *Bluestown*
    PW - v244 - Mr 24 '97 - p81 [1-50]
    Dangerous Men
    Ant R - v54 - Sum '96 - p367 [251-500]
Becker, Gerhold K - *Changing Nature's Course*
    SciTech - v20 - S '96 - p60 [51-250]
    Ethics in Business and Society
    JEL - v34 - D '96 - p2008 [51-250]
Becker, Jasper - *Hungry Ghosts*
    BL - v93 - D 15 '96 - p695 [51-250]
    Econ - v341 - O 19 '96 - p8* [51-250]
    FEER - v159 - Ag 15 '96 - p54+ [501+]
    KR - v64 - N 15 '96 - p1642 [251-500]
    LATBR - F 2 '97 - p3 [501+]
    LJ - v122 - Ja '97 - p117 [51-250]
    Lon R Bks - v18 - Jl 18 '96 - p3+ [501+]
    NY - v73 - Ap 14 '97 - p85 [51-250]
    NYTBR - v102 - F 16 '97 - p6+ [501+]
    NYTLa - v146 - F 4 '97 - pC15 [501+]
    PW - v244 - Ja 13 '97 - p65 [51-250]
    TLS - O 25 '96 - p3+ [501+]
    WSJ-Cent - v99 - F 7 '97 - pA14 [501+]
Becker, Jeffrey M - *Biotechnology: A Laboratory Course.
2nd Ed.*
    SciTech - v20 - S '96 - p59 [51-250]
Becker, Jim - *Scented Geraniums*
    r BWatch - v17 - N '96 - p5 [51-250]
Becker, Jurek - *Ende Des Grossenwahns*
    WLT - v71 - Win '97 - p144+ [501+]
    Jacob the Liar
    NY - v72 - Ja 13 '97 - p79 [51-250]
    NYTBR - v101 - N 17 '96 - p22 [501+]
Becker, Leslee - *The Sincere Cafe*
    KR - v64 - S 15 '96 - p1338 [251-500]
    PW - v243 - S 30 '96 - p79 [51-250]
Becker, Lucille Frackman - *Pierre Boulle*
    Choice - v34 - S '96 - p132 [51-250]
    WLT - v70 - Aut '96 - p918 [51-250]
Becker, Marion Rombauer - *The Joy of Cooking*
    BW - v26 - D 8 '96 - p4 [51-250]
Becker, Marjorie - *Setting the Virgin on Fire*
    HAHR - v77 - My '97 - p327+ [501+]
Becker, Robert - *Alzheimer Disease*
    SciTech - v21 - Mr '97 - p55 [51-250]
Becker, Theodore L - *Teaching Democracy by Being
Democratic*
    R&R Bk N - v12 - F '97 - p58 [51-250]
Becker, Thorsten - *Schones Deutschland*
    Econ - v341 - O 19 '96 - p16*+ [501+]
Becker, Uwe - *VUV and Soft X-Ray Photoionization*
    SciTech - v20 - D '96 - p25 [51-250]
Becker, William E - *Assessing Educational Practices*
    ILRR - v50 - Ap '97 - p524+ [501+]
    JEL - v35 - Mr '97 - p146+ [501+]
Becker, Yechiel - *Molecular Evolution of Viruses*
    SciTech - v20 - D '96 - p37 [51-250]

Becker-Cantarino, Barbara - *Berlin in Focus*
    R&R Bk N - v11 - D '96 - p9 [51-250]
Beckerman, Wilfred - *Growth, the Environment and the
Distribution of Incomes*
    Econ J - v106 - S '96 - p1483 [251-500]
    Through Green-Colored Glasses
    For Aff - v76 - Mr '97 - p177+ [51-250]
    LJ - v121 - D '96 - p137 [51-250]
Beckett, John - *The Rise and Fall of the Grenvilles*
    EHR - v111 - N '96 - p1315+ [251-500]
    VS - v39 - Spr '96 - p422+ [501+]
Beckett, Samuel - *Bande Et Sarabande*
    TLS - S 6 '96 - p4+ [501+]
    Dream of Fair to Middling Women
    Obs - S 29 '96 - p18* [501+]
    Eleutheria: A Play in Three Acts
    Am Theat - v14 - F '97 - p56 [51-250]
    NYRB - v43 - N 14 '96 - p24+ [501+]
    TLS - S 6 '96 - p4+ [501+]
    TranslRevS - v2 - D '96 - p21 [501+]
    Eleutheria (Minuit)
    TLS - S 6 '96 - p4+ [501+]
    Eleutheria (Wright)
    Lon R Bks - v18 - N 14 '96 - p8+ [501+]
    NS - v125 - S 27 '96 - p58+ [501+]
    TLS - S 6 '96 - p4+ [501+]
    Endgame
    Lon R Bks - v18 - N 14 '96 - p8+ [501+]
    Krapp's Last Tape
    Lon R Bks - v18 - N 14 '96 - p8+ [501+]
    Nohow On
    NYRB - v43 - N 14 '96 - p24+ [501+]
    Samuel Beckett: The Complete Short Prose 1929-1989
    Am Theat - v13 - D '96 - p21 [1-50]
    NYRB - v43 - N 14 '96 - p24+ [501+]
    Samuel Beckett's Mal Vu Mal Dit
    R&R Bk N - v12 - F '97 - p83 [51-250]
    Waiting for Godot
    Lon R Bks - v18 - N 14 '96 - p8+ [501+]
Beckett, Wendy - *A Child's Book of Prayer in Art*
    c BL - v93 - O 1 '96 - p338 [1-50]
    Mystery of Love
    BWatch - v18 - Mr '97 - p3 [51-250]
    Sister Wendy's Grand Tour
    y BL - v93 - N 1 '96 - p471 [51-250]
    LJ - v122 - F 15 '97 - p130 [51-250]
Beckham, Barry - *The Black Student's Guide to Colleges.
4th Ed.*
    yr BL - v93 - Mr 15 '97 - p1254 [51-250]
    The Black Student's Guide to Scholarships
    yr BL - v93 - Mr 15 '97 - p1254 [51-250]
Beckham, Joseph - *Meeting Legal Challenges*
    H Sch M - v4 - S '96 - p49 [51-250]
Beckham, Nancy - *Family Guide to Natural Therapies*
    BWatch - v17 - S '96 - p10 [51-250]
Beckham, Stephen Dow - *Requiem for a People*
    LJ - v121 - N 1 '96 - p112 [1-50]
Becking, Bob - *On Reading Prophetic Texts*
    Rel St Rev - v23 - Ap '97 - p166 [51-250]
Beckman, Gary - *Hittite Diplomatic Texts*
    Rel St Rev - v23 - Ja '97 - p55 [51-250]
Beckman, Pat Ramsey - *From the Ashes*
    y Ch BWatch - v6 - My '96 - p2 [51-250]
    y Kliatt - v31 - Ja '97 - p6 [51-250]
Beckman, Peter R - *Women, Gender, and World Politics*
    J Pol - v58 - Ag '96 - p870+ [501+]
Beckmann, Janet Pitts - *Nursing Negligence*
    Choice - v34 - S '96 - p161 [51-250]
Beckmann, Max - *Self-Portrait in Words*
    KR - v64 - N 15 '96 - p1643 [251-500]
    NYRB - v43 - N 28 '96 - p13+ [501+]
Beckner, Steven K - *Back from the Brink*
    Barron's - v77 - Ja 13 '97 - p58 [501+]
    BL - v93 - F 15 '97 - p977 [51-250]
    Bus W - Mr 3 '97 - p14 [501+]
    BW - v27 - F 16 '97 - p6 [251-500]
    Choice - v34 - My '97 - p1546 [51-250]
    KR - v64 - D 15 '96 - p1776 [251-500]
    LJ - v122 - Mr 15 '97 - p35 [1-50]
    PW - v243 - D 2 '96 - p45 [51-250]
Beckwith, Harry - *Selling the Invisible*
    BL - v93 - Mr 1 '97 - p1096 [51-250]
    PW - v244 - Ja 27 '97 - p91 [51-250]
Becnel, Thomas A - *Senator Allen Ellender of Louisiana*
    JSH - v63 - F '97 - p200+ [501+]
Bedani, Gino - *Politics and Ideology in the Italian
Workers' Movement*
    AHR - v101 - O '96 - p1242+ [501+]
Bedard, Michael - *A Darker Magic*
    y Can CL - v22 - Sum '96 - p8+ [501+]

    Painted Devil
    y Can CL - v22 - Sum '96 - p8+ [501+]
Bedarida, Francois - *L'Histoire Et Le Metier D'Historien
En France 1945-1995*
    JMH - v69 - Mr '97 - p166+ [501+]
    Touvier, Vichy Et Le Crime Contre L'Humanite
    TLS - O 4 '96 - p10+ [501+]
Bedau, Hugo A - *The Death Penalty in America*
    LJ - v122 - Mr 15 '97 - p75 [51-250]
Beddow, Michael - *Thomas Mann: Doctor Faustus*
    MLR - v92 - Ja '97 - p245+ [501+]
Bede, the Venerable, Saint - *Bede: On the Tabernacle*
    CW - v90 - S '96 - p68 [251-500]
Bede and His World. Vols. 1-2
    CHR - v82 - Jl '96 - p515+ [501+]
    Lib & Cul - v32 - Win '97 - p132+ [501+]
Bedel, Henri - *An Introduction to the History of the
Institute of the Brothers of the Christian Schools*
    RR - v56 - Mr '97 - p221 [1-50]
Bedell, Geraldine - *Party Tricks*
    NS - v126 - Ja 24 '97 - p45+ [251-500]
    Obs - F 2 '97 - p17* [501+]
Bederman, Gail - *Manliness and Civilization*
    CS - v26 - Mr '97 - p156+ [501+]
    Historian - v59 - Win '97 - p418+ [501+]
    J Am St - v30 - Ag '96 - p291+ [251-500]
    RAH - v24 - S '96 - p448+ [501+]
Bedford, Martyn - *Acts of Revision*
    Books - v11 - Ap '97 - p8 [51-250]
    NYTBR - v101 - S 1 '96 - p25 [501+]
Bedient, Cal - *Candy Necklace*
    PW - v244 - Ja 27 '97 - p94 [51-250]
Bedini, Silvio A - *Science and Instruments in Seventeenth-
Century Italy*
    T&C - v37 - Ap '96 - p346+ [501+]
    The Trail of Time
    Ch Rev Int - v3 - Fall '96 - p360+ [501+]
Bednarczyk, Angela - *Happy Birthday!*
    c PW - v244 - Ja 6 '97 - p74 [51-250]
    Opposites: A Beginner's Book of Signs
    c PW - v244 - Ja 6 '97 - p74 [51-250]
Bedson, Jack - *Sheep Dogs*
    c Magpies - v11 - My '96 - p53 [1-50]
Bedtime for Laura (Illus. by Renee Graef)
    c HB Guide - v8 - Spr '97 - p12 [51-250]
Beebee, T J C - *Ecology and Conservation of Amphibians*
    Choice - v34 - Ja '97 - p821 [51-250]
Beeby, Dean - *Cargo of Lies*
    Beav - v76 - D '96 - p42 [51-250]
    Can Hist R - v78 - Mr '97 - p137+ [501+]
Beech, George - *Le Conventum (Vers 1030)*
    EHR - v112 - Ap '97 - p428+ [501+]
Beeghley, Leonard - *What Does Your Wife Do?*
    ASInt - v34 - O '96 - p119+ [251-500]
    JMF - v59 - F '97 - p236 [251-500]
Beehler, Bruce M - *Birds of New Guinea*
    r AB - v97 - Je 17 '96 - p2398 [51-250]
Beekes, Robert S P - *Comparative Indo-European
Linguistics*
    Rel St Rev - v23 - Ap '97 - p172+ [51-250]
Beekman, E M - *Troubled Pleasures*
    Choice - v34 - D '96 - p618 [51-250]
Beekman, Sharon - *Enticed by the Light*
    PW - v244 - F 24 '97 - p82 [51-250]
Beem, John K - *Global Lorentzian Geometry. 2nd Ed.*
    SciTech - v20 - S '96 - p12 [51-250]
Beeman, Marsha Lynn - *Where Am I?*
    LJ - v122 - F 15 '97 - p153 [51-250]
Beemer, C Britt - *Predatory Marketing*
    BL - v93 - D 15 '96 - p698 [51-250]
    LJ - v122 - Ja '97 - p112+ [51-250]
Beenhakker, Henri L - *Investment Decision Making in the
Private and Public Sectors*
    R&R Bk N - v12 - F '97 - p48 [51-250]
Beer, Cecilia - *Temple-Boys: A Study of Cypriote Votive
Sculpture. Pt. 1*
    AJA - v100 - O '96 - p789+ [501+]
Beer, David F - *A Guide to Writing as an Engineer*
    SciTech - v20 - D '96 - p58 [51-250]
Beer, Ferdinand Pierre - *Vector Mechanics for Engineers.
6th Ed.*
    SciTech - v20 - D '96 - p61 [51-250]
Beer, Gillian - *Open Fields*
    Nine-C Lit - v51 - Mr '97 - p554 [51-250]
    NS - v126 - Ja 24 '97 - p46+ [501+]
    TLS - D 13 '96 - p5+ [501+]
Beer: The Magazine
    p LJ - v122 - Ap 1 '97 - p63 [1-50]
Beerbohm, Max - *Collected Verse*
    Nine-C Lit - v50 - Mr '96 - p535+ [501+]

Beers, David - *Blue Sky Dream*
  BL - v93 - Ja '97 - p756 [1-50]
  BL - v93 - S 1 '96 - p40 [51-250]
  Ent W - O 11 '96 - p86 [51-250]
  HMR - Spr '97 - p6+ [501+]
  LATBR - O 6 '96 - p6 [501+]
  NYTBR - v101 - O 27 '96 - p25 [501+]
  Reason - v28 - D '96 - p53+ [501+]
Beers, Henry Putney - *Bibliographies in American History*
  r ASInt - v34 - O '96 - p20 [1-50]
  Bibliographies in American History 1942-1978
  r ASInt - v34 - O '96 - p20 [1-50]
Beers, Terry - *...A Thousand Graceful Subtleties*
  RMR - v50 - 2 '96 - p214+ [501+]
Beers, W H - *The History of Brown County, Ohio*
  r EGH - v50 - N '96 - p179 [51-250]
Beeson, Dan L - *Assembling and Repairing Personal Computers*
  SciTech - v20 - D '96 - p78 [51-250]
Beeth, Howard - *Black Dixie*
  Lib & Cul - v32 - Win '97 - p146+ [501+]
Beetz, Kirk H - *Beacham's Encyclopedia of Popular Fiction. Vols. 1-11*
  r BL - v93 - Mr 1 '97 - p1183 [501+]
Beezley, William H - *Rituals of Rule, Rituals of Resistance*
  Am Ethnol - v23 - Ag '96 - p643 [501+]
Begay, Shonto - *Navajo: Visions and Voices across the Mesa (Illus. by Shonto Begay)*
  y Emerg Lib - v24 - S '96 - p23 [1-50]
  c RT - v50 - O '96 - p155+ [51-250]
  c RT - v50 - Mr '97 - p478 [51-250]
Begelman, Mitchell C - *Gravity's Fatal Attraction*
  Nature - v382 - Jl 25 '96 - p312 [251-500]
  Phys Today - v49 - O '96 - p70+ [501+]
  SciTech - v20 - N '96 - p16 [51-250]
  S&T - v92 - N '96 - p56+ [501+]
Begg, Paul - *The Jack the Ripper A-Z*
  r LJ - v121 - O 15 '96 - p94 [51-250]
Begiebing, Robert J - *The Strange Death of Mistress Coffin*
  NYTBR - v101 - Jl 21 '96 - p28 [1-50]
The Beginning of Heaven and Earth
  Choice - v34 - Mr '97 - p1178 [51-250]
Begley, Louis - *About Schmidt*
  BL - v92 - Ag '96 - p1879+ [51-250]
  BW - v26 - S 15 '96 - p5 [501+]
  Ent W - O 4 '96 - p57 [51-250]
  LATBR - S 15 '96 - p3 [501+]
  LJ - v122 - Ja '97 - p48 [51-250]
  NY - v72 - N 25 '96 - p117 [51-250]
  NYRB - v43 - O 31 '96 - p63+ [501+]
  NYTBR - v101 - S 22 '96 - p13 [501+]
  PW - v243 - N 4 '96 - p37 [51-250]
  Time - v148 - S 16 '96 - p82 [251-500]
  W&I - v12 - F '97 - p273+ [501+]
Bego, Mark - *The Rock and Roll Almanac*
  r BL - v93 - S 15 '96 - p284+ [51-250]
Begon, Michael - *Ecology: Individuals, Populations, and Communities. 3rd Ed.*
  y New Sci - v151 - S 28 '96 - p50+ [501+]
  SciTech - v20 - S '96 - p19 [1-50]
  Population Ecology. 3rd Ed.
  y New Sci - v151 - S 28 '96 - p50+ [501+]
  R&R Bk N - v12 - F '97 - p94 [51-250]
Behan, Brendan - *The King of Ireland's Son (Illus. by P J Lynch)*
  c Bks Keeps - Mr '97 - p20 [51-250]
  c CCB-B - v50 - Ap '97 - p273 [51-250]
  c KR - v65 - F 1 '97 - p219 [51-250]
  c PW - v244 - Mr 17 '97 - p84 [51-250]
  c Sch Lib - v45 - F '97 - p17 [51-250]
  c TES - Mr 14 '97 - p10* [501+]
Behan, Eileen - *Meals That Heal for Babies, Toddlers and Children*
  PW - v243 - S 2 '96 - p125 [51-250]
Behan, Tom - *The Camorra*
  R&R Bk N - v11 - D '96 - p44 [1-50]
Behar, Ruth - *Bridges to Cuba*
  HAHR - v77 - My '97 - p293+ [251-500]
  Hisp - v79 - D '96 - p799+ [501+]
  Translating Woman
  LATBR - D 29 '96 - p10 [51-250]
  The Vulnerable Observer
  BL - v93 - Ja '97 - p785 [51-250]
  CHE - v43 - Ja 31 '97 - pA16 [51-250]
  Choice - v34 - My '97 - p1540 [51-250]
  KR - v64 - N 1 '96 - p1571 [251-500]
  LJ - v122 - Ja '97 - p108 [51-250]
  NYTBR - v102 - Mr 23 '97 - p19 [51-250]
  PW - v243 - N 11 '96 - p63 [51-250]

  Women Writing Culture
  Am Ethnol - v23 - N '96 - p906+ [501+]
  CS - v26 - Ja '97 - p116+ [501+]
  NWSA Jnl - v8 - Fall '96 - p164+ [501+]
Behboodi, Rambod - *Industrial Subsidies and Friction in World Trade*
  Econ J - v107 - Ja '97 - p266 [51-250]
Behdad, Ali - *Belated Travelers*
  Ant R - v54 - Sum '96 - p374+ [251-500]
Behe, Michael J - *Darwin's Black Box*
  Bks & Cult - v2 - N '96 - p10+ [501+]
  Nat R - v48 - S 16 '96 - p62+ [501+]
  Nature - v383 - S 19 '96 - p227+ [501+]
  New Sci - v151 - S 14 '96 - p44+ [501+]
  Pub Int - Win '97 - p108+ [501+]
  Sci - v273 - Ag 30 '96 - p1180 [51-250]
  Skeptic - v4 - 3 '96 - p104 [251-500]
Behind the Scenes Series
  c Cur R - v35 - S '96 - p13 [51-250]
Behling, Sophia - *Sol Power*
  New Sci - v151 - S 28 '96 - p48 [51-250]
  TLS - N 29 '96 - p21 [501+]
Behme, Thomas - *Samuel Von Pufendorf: Naturrecht Und Staat*
  AHR - v101 - O '96 - p1184+ [501+]
Behn, Aphra - *The Works of Aphra Behn. Vols. 5-7*
  TLS - D 6 '96 - p18 [51-250]
Behne, Adolf - *The Modern Functional Building*
  Choice - v34 - F '97 - p954 [51-250]
  LJ - v122 - F 15 '97 - p130 [51-250]
  R&R Bk N - v12 - F '97 - p72 [51-250]
Behr, Edward - *Prohibition: Thirteen Years That Changed America*
  LJ - v121 - O 1 '96 - p97 [51-250]
  NYTBR - v101 - O 20 '96 - p23 [251-500]
Behrens, June - *Missions of the Central Coast*
  c HB Guide - v8 - Spr '97 - p172 [51-250]
Behrman, Jere R - *From Parent to Child*
  CS - v25 - S '96 - p620+ [501+]
  Human Resources in Latin America and the Caribbean
  JEL - v35 - Mr '97 - p269 [51-250]
Beider, Alexander - *A Dictionary of Jewish Surnames from the Kingdom of Poland*
  r Choice - v34 - D '96 - p585 [51-250]
Beier, Ross C - *Immunoassays for Residue Analysis*
  SciTech - v20 - S '96 - p63 [51-250]
Beifuss, John - *Armadillo Ray (Illus. by Peggy Turley)*
  c RT - v50 - Mr '97 - p500 [51-250]
Beifuss, Will - *The Psychedelic Sourcebook*
  r Mag Bl - Mr '97 - p57+ [51-250]
Beik, Mildred Allen - *The Miners of Windber*
  Choice - v34 - Mr '96 - p1226 [51-250]
  JEL - v35 - Mr '97 - p261+ [51-250]
Beilharz, Peter - *Postmodern Socialism*
  Aust Bk R - v - Ag '96 - p21+ [501+]
Beiner, Ronald - *Kant and Political Philosophy*
  CPR - v16 - Ag '96 - p241+ [501+]
  Ger Q - v69 - Spr '96 - p196+ [501+]
  Theorizing Citizenship
  RP - v59 - Win '97 - p127+ [501+]
Beinert, Wolfgang - *Handbook of Catholic Theology*
  r Am - v175 - D 7 '96 - p29 [251-500]
  r Theol St - v57 - D '96 - p760+ [501+]
Beinhart, Larry - *How to Write a Mystery*
  Arm Det - v29 - Fall '96 - p469 [51-250]
  Arm Det - v29 - Fall '96 - p491+ [51-250]
Beinin, Joel - *Political Islam*
  For Aff - v76 - Mr '97 - p195 [51-250]
Beirne, Barbara - *Children of the Ecuadorean Highlands*
  c BL - v93 - O 1 '96 - p344 [51-250]
  c Ch BWatch - v6 - O '96 - p5+ [1-50]
  c HB Guide - v8 - Spr '97 - p179 [51-250]
  c SLJ - v42 - N '96 - p111+ [51-250]
Beisel, Nicola - *Imperiled Innocents*
  LJ - v122 - Ja '97 - p118 [51-250]
Beith, Richard - *The Italian South Atlantic Air Mail Service 1939-1941*
  Phil Lit R - v45 - 3 '96 - p249+ [251-500]
Beit-Hallahmi, Benjamin - *Psychoanalytic Studies of Religion*
  r Choice - v34 - Mr '97 - p1133+ [51-250]
  r R&R Bk N - v12 - F '97 - p5 [51-250]
Beja, Morris - *Joyce in the Hibernian Metropolis*
  ILS - v15 - Fall '96 - p31 [1-50]
Bejczy, Istvan - *Pape Jansland En Utopia*
  Ren Q - v50 - Spr '97 - p297+ [501+]
Bekey, George A - *Neural Networks in Robotics*
  Robotica - v14 - S '96 - p585 [501+]
Bekke, Hans - *Civil Service Systems in Comparative Perspective*
  Econ - v341 - N 16 '96 - p9*+ [251-500]

Bekkers, Victor - *Emerging Electronic Highways*
  R&R Bk N - v11 - D '96 - p51 [51-250]
Beland, Pierre - *Beluga: A Farewell to Whales*
  Choice - v34 - D '96 - p637+ [51-250]
Belanger, Marcel - *D'Ou Surgi*
  Can Lit - Win '96 - p180+ [501+]
  Orf Effendi, Chroniqueur
  FR - v70 - F '97 - p490+ [501+]
Belbin, David - *The Beat: Smokescreen*
  c Bks Keeps - Jl '96 - p12 [51-250]
Belbin, Meredith - *The Coming Shape of Organization*
  R&R Bk N - v11 - N '96 - p30 [51-250]
Belchem, John - *Popular Radicalism in Nineteenth-Century Britain*
  Albion - v28 - '96 - p712+ [501+]
Belcher, John G, Jr. - *How to Design and Implement a Results-Oriented Variable Pay System*
  HR Mag - v41 - Ag '96 - p122+ [51-250]
Belenky, Mary Field - *A Tradition That Has No Name*
  PW - v244 - Ap 21 '97 - p53+ [51-250]
Beletsky, Les - *Red-Winged Blackbirds*
  New Sci - v153 - Mr 22 '97 - p46 [251-500]
Belford, Barbara - *Bram Stoker: A Biography of the Author of Dracula*
  CR - v269 - N '96 - p278 [51-250]
  NYTBR - v101 - Ap 7 '96 - p20 [501+]
  SFS - v24 - Mr '97 - p171+ [501+]
  VQR - v72 - Aut '96 - p124* [501+]
Belford, Ros - *Italy. 3rd Ed.*
  r BL - v93 - S 15 '96 - p212 [1-50]
Bel Geddes, Joan - *Childhood and Children*
  r BL - v93 - My 15 '97 - p1611 [51-250]
  r LJ - v122 - Ap 1 '97 - p82 [51-250]
Belgum, Erik - *Star Fiction*
  ABR - v17 - Ag '96 - p22 [501+]
Belieu, Erin - *Infanta*
  Ant R - v54 - Sum '96 - p375+ [251-500]
  Chel - 61 '96 - p125+ [501+]
  HR - v49 - Aut '96 - p503+ [501+]
Belin, Christian - *L'Oeuvre De Pierre Charron 1541-1603. Rev. Ed.*
  MLR - v92 - Ap '97 - p467+ [251-500]
  MLR - v92 - Ap '97 - p467+ [251-500]
Belitt, Ben - *The Forged Feature*
  Salm - Fall '96 - p237+ [501+]
Bell, Brian - *Channel Islands*
  r BL - v93 - S 15 '96 - p210 [1-50]
Bell, Caryn Cosse - *Revolution, Romanticism, and the Afro-Creole Protest Tradition in Louisiana 1718-1868*
  Nat - v264 - Mr 31 '97 - p28+ [501+]
Bell, Chip R - *Managers as Mentors*
  BL - v92 - Ag '96 - p1865 [51-250]
  Bus Bk R - v13 - 4 '96 - p112+ [501+]
Bell, Christine - *The Seven-Year Atomic Make-Over Guide and Other Stories*
  Ant R - v55 - Spr '97 - p245 [251-500]
  LATBR - Jl 7 '96 - p11 [51-250]
Bell, Daniel - *The Cultural Contradictions of Capitalism*
  NL - v79 - D 16 '96 - p14+ [501+]
  NY - v72 - Ja 13 '97 - p72+ [501+]
  Marxian Socialism in the United States
  NL - v79 - D 16 '96 - p14+ [501+]
Bell, Daniel A - *Towards Illiberal Democracy in Pacific Asia*
  APSR - v90 - S '96 - p666+ [501+]
Bell, David Scott - *The French Communist Party in the Fifth Republic*
  EHR - v112 - F '97 - p268+ [251-500]
  Historian - v59 - Fall '96 - p178 [251-500]
Bell, Derrick - *Gospel Choirs*
  Bl S - v26 - Fall '96 - p100 [51-250]
  NYTBR - v101 - Jl 21 '96 - p22 [501+]
Bell, Diane - *Radically Speaking*
  LJ - v121 - N 15 '96 - p77 [51-250]
  Ms - v - N '96 - p82 [1-50]
  Wom R Bks - v14 - O '96 - p9+ [501+]
Bell, Graham - *The Basics of Selection*
  Nature - v384 - D 12 '96 - p526+ [501+]
  SciTech - v21 - Mr '97 - p35 [1-50]
  Selection: The Mechanism of Evolution
  Choice - v34 - My '97 - p1522 [51-250]
  Nature - v384 - D 12 '96 - p526+ [501+]
  SciTech - v21 - Mr '97 - p35 [51-250]
Bell, Helen - *Idjhil (Illus. by Helen Bell)*
  c Aust Bk R - Jl '96 - p61+ [501+]
  c Magpies - v11 - Jl '96 - p29 [51-250]
Bell, Julie - *Hard Curves*
  BWatch - v18 - F '97 - p5 [51-250]
Bell, Krista - *Where Do You Get Your Great Ideas?*
  c Magpies - v11 - S '96 - p43 [51-250]

Bell, Landon C - *The Old Free State. Vols. 1-2*
  r EGH - v50 - N '96 - p190 [51-250]
Bell, Lili - *The Sea Maidens of Japan (Illus. by Erin McGonigle Brammer)*
  c CCB-B - v50 - My '97 - p314 [51-250]
  c KR - v65 - Ap 1 '97 - p548+ [51-250]
  c PW - v244 - Mr 24 '97 - p83 [51-250]
Bell, Madison Smartt - *All Souls' Rising*
     HR - v49 - Sum '96 - p316+ [501+]
     NYTBR - v101 - D 1 '96 - p36 [51-250]
     PW - v243 - S 30 '96 - p79 [1-50]
     Sew R - v104 - Jl '96 - p476+ [501+]
     VV - v42 - Ja 7 '97 - p42 [51-250]
  Ten Indians
  y BL - v93 - Ja '97 - p834 [501+]
  y BL - v93 - S 1 '96 - p5+ [51-250]
     KR - v64 - S 1 '96 - p1253 [251-500]
     LATBR - D 15 '96 - p9 [501+]
     NYTBR - v101 - N 24 '96 - p12 [501+]
     NYTBR - v101 - D 8 '96 - p84 [1-50]
     S Liv - v32 - F '97 - p80 [51-250]
     Time - v148 - O 28 '96 - p110 [251-500]
     Trib Bks - Ja 12 '97 - p3 [501+]
     W&I - v12 - Mr '97 - p262+ [501+]
Bell, Mark R - *The Mac Web Server Book*
     SciTech - v20 - D '96 - p76 [51-250]
Bell, Martin - *In Harm's Way*
     CR - v269 - N '96 - p278 [1-50]
     Woman's J - O '96 - p12 [1-50]
  In Harm's Way (Bell). Audio Version
  y Kliatt - v30 - N '96 - p49 [51-250]
Bell, Mary Hayley - *Whistle Down the Wind*
     PW - v244 - My 12 '97 - p60 [51-250]
Bell, Michael Davitt - *The Problem of American Realism*
     MP - v94 - N '96 - p262+ [501+]
Bell, Millicent - *The Cambridge Companion to Edith Wharton*
     J Am St - v30 - Ag '96 - p317+ [501+]
Bell, Nancy - *Biggie and the Mangled Mortician*
     PW - v244 - Ap 14 '97 - p60 [51-250]
  Biggie and the Poisoned Politician
     Arm Det - v29 - Sum '96 - p359 [51-250]
Bell, Peter, 1944- - *Victorian Biography*
  r ELT - v39 - 4 '96 - p523+ [501+]
Bell, Peter, 1949- - *Chamberlain, Germany and Japan 1933-4*
     Choice - v34 - D '96 - p667 [51-250]
Bell, Peter Alan - *Accidental Justice*
     PW - v244 - F 24 '97 - p76 [51-250]
Bell, Quentin - *Bloomsbury Recalled*
     Ant R - v54 - Sum '96 - p358+ [251-500]
     Bloom Rev - v16 - N '96 - p20 [501+]
     ELT - v40 - 2 '97 - p181+ [501+]
     NYTBR - v101 - D 8 '96 - p85 [1-50]
     NYTBR - v102 - Ap 6 '97 - p32 [51-250]
  Virginia Woolf: A Biography
     CR - v269 - S '96 - p168 [51-250]
     SFR - v21 - Jl '96 - p48 [1-50]
Bell, Robert H - *Jocoserious Joyce*
     ELT - v40 - 1 '97 - p125+ [51-250]
Bell, Robert M - *Lipid Second Messengers*
     SciTech - v20 - S '96 - p24 [51-250]
Bell, Stephen H - *Program Applicants as a Comparison Group in Evaluating Training Programs*
     ILRR - v50 - Ja '97 - p366+ [501+]
Bell, Steve - *Live Briefs*
     Obs - D 15 '96 - p17* [51-250]
Bell, Virginia - *The Best Friends Approach to Alzheimer's Care*
     BL - v93 - N 15 '96 - p554 [51-250]
Bell, Wendell - *Foundations of Futures Studies. Vol. 1*
     Choice - v34 - Mr '97 - p1199+ [51-250]
     Fut - v31 - Mr '97 - p49+ [501+]
     JEL - v35 - Mr '97 - p282 [51-250]
     R&R Bk N - v12 - F '97 - p12 [51-250]
Bell, William - *River My Friend (Illus. by Ken Campbell)*
  c Ch Bk News - v20 - Win '97 - p28 [51-250]
  c Quill & Q - v62 - S '96 - p73 [251-500]
  Sans Signature
  y Can CL - v22 - Sum '96 - p103+ [501+]
Bellah, Robert N - *Habits of the Heart. Rev. Ed.*
     BL - v93 - O 1 '96 - p308 [1-50]
Bellamann, Henry - *Kings Row*
     Nat R - v48 - D 23 '96 - p53 [51-250]
Bellamy, Christopher - *Knights in White Armour*
     Econ - v342 - Mr 15 '97 - p8* [51-250]
Bellamy, Elizabeth J - *Translations of Power*
     Ren Q - v49 - Win '96 - p915+ [501+]
Bellamy, Guy - *The Mystery of Men*
     Books - v10 - Je '96 - p23 [51-250]

Bellamy, Joe David - *Literary Luxuries*
     Choice - v34 - S '96 - p122 [51-250]
Bellamy, Robert V - *Television and the Remote Control*
     Choice - v34 - Ja '97 - p786 [51-250]
Bellanca, James - *Valuing Diversity in the School System*
     EL - v54 - D '96 - p92 [51-250]
Bellavia, Regina M - *Cultural Landscape Report for Sagamore Hill National Historic Site*
     J Gov Info - v23 - S '96 - p549+ [51-250]
Bellber, Philip - *Cook, Eat, Cha Cha Cha*
     PW - v244 - Ap 7 '97 - p88+ [51-250]
Belle, Jennifer - *Going Down*
     Ent W - Je 28 '96 - p100+ [51-250]
     KR - v64 - My 1 '96 - p617+ [51-250]
     LJ - v122 - Mr 15 '97 - p41 [51-250]
Bellear, Lisa - *Dreaming in Urban Areas*
     Aust Bk R - N '96 - p54 [501+]
Belleau, Remy - *Oeuvres Poetiques. Vol. 1*
     Ren Q - v50 - Spr '97 - p251+ [501+]
     Six Ct J - v27 - Win '96 - p1149+ [501+]
Bellenir, Karen - *Genetic Disorders Sourcebook*
  r Choice - v34 - Ja '97 - p827+ [51-250]
  r SciTech - v20 - D '96 - p41 [51-250]
  Mental Health Disorders Sourcebook
  r Readings - v11 - S '96 - p26 [51-250]
  r RQ - v36 - Win '96 - p302 [251-500]
  Substance Abuse Sourcebook
  r BWatch - v18 - Mr '97 - p2 [51-250]
  r Choice - v34 - Mr '97 - p1193+ [51-250]
  r R&R Bk N - v11 - D '96 - p70 [51-250]
Beller, Steven - *Francis Joseph*
     TLS - Mr 28 '97 - p27 [501+]
Beller, Thomas - *Seduction Theory*
     LATBR - My 12 '96 - p11 [51-250]
Belles Lettres
  p Sm Pr R - v28 - S '96 - p14 [51-250]
Bellesiles, Michael A - *Revolutionary Outlaws*
     ASInt - v34 - O '96 - p100+ [501+]
Bellessi, Diana - *The Twins, the Dream*
     BL - v93 - F 1 '97 - p921 [51-250]
     LJ - v122 - Ja '97 - p104 [51-250]
     PW - v243 - D 30 '96 - p62 [51-250]
Belleto, Rene - *Machine*
     TranslRevS - v1 - My '95 - p18 [51-250]
Bell-Fialkoff, Andrew - *Ethnic Cleansing*
     BW - v26 - N 17 '96 - p5 [51-250]
     Choice - v34 - Ap '97 - p1413 [51-250]
Bell-Gadsby, Cheryl - *Reclaiming Herstory*
     AJCH - v39 - Jl '96 - p71+ [501+]
     Readings - v11 - S '96 - p31 [51-250]
     SB - v32 - Ag '96 - p169 [51-250]
Bellini, Mario - *Mario Bellini, Architecture 1984-1995*
     R&R Bk N - v11 - N '96 - p60 [51-250]
Bellis, Alice Ogden - *The Structure and Composition of Jeremiah 50:2-51:58*
     Rel St Rev - v23 - Ap '97 - p166 [51-250]
Bellis, Teri James - *Assessment and Management of Central Auditory Processing Disorders in the Educational Setting*
     SciTech - v20 - S '96 - p31 [51-250]
Belliveau, Jeannette - *An Amateur's Guide to the Planet*
     LJ - v121 - O 15 '96 - p80 [51-250]
Bellocq, E J - *Bellocq: Photographs from Storyville, the Red-Light District of New Orleans*
     LATBR - N 3 '96 - p11 [51-250]
     NYRB - v44 - Ja 9 '97 - p12+ [501+]
     WSJ-MW - v78 - D 5 '96 - pA18 [51-250]
Bellomo, Manilo - *The Common Legal Past of Europe 1000-1800*
     Theol St - v57 - S '96 - p537+ [501+]
Bellomo, Nicola - *Modelling Mathematical Methods and Scientific Computation*
     SIAM Rev - v39 - Mr '97 - p154+ [501+]
Bellos, David - *Georges Perec: A Life in Words*
     MLN - v111 - S '96 - p797+ [501+]
Bellow, Gary - *Law Stories*
     Choice - v34 - Ap '97 - p1418 [51-250]
Bellow, Saul - *The Actual*
     BL - v93 - My 1 '97 - p1460 [51-250]
     KR - v65 - Mr 1 '97 - p317 [51-250]
     LJ - v122 - My 1 '97 - p136 [51-250]
     NYTLa - v146 - Ap 25 '97 - pC28 [501+]
     PW - v244 - Mr 24 '97 - p57 [51-250]
     WSJ-Cent - v99 - My 21 '97 - pA12 [51-250]
  The Victim
     SAQ - v95 - Fall '96 - p979+ [501+]
Bellowing Ark
  p Sm Pr R - v29 - F '97 - p13+ [51-250]
Bell-Villada, Gene H - *Art for Art's Sake and Literary Life*
     Choice - v34 - S '96 - p118 [51-250]

Beloff, Jim - *The Ukulele: A Visual History*
     LJ - v122 - My 1 '97 - p105 [51-250]
Beloff, Max Beloff, Baron - *Britain and European Union*
     Choice - v34 - My '97 - p1571 [51-250]
     Econ - v342 - F 15 '97 - p5*+ [51-250]
     For Aff - v76 - Mr '97 - p185+ [51-250]
     TLS - Ja 3 '97 - p5+ [501+]
     TLS - Ja 3 '97 - p5+ [501+]
Beloit Poetry Journal
  p Sm Pr R - v28 - D '96 - p14 [51-250]
  p Sm Pr R - v29 - F '97 - p16 [51-250]
Belousov, Vladimir - *Delo IAkubovskogo. Tochny: Udar*
     BL - v93 - O 1 '96 - p327 [1-50]
Belpre, Pura - *Firefly Summer*
  y HB Guide - v8 - Spr '97 - p77 [51-250]
  c SLJ - v43 - F '97 - p100 [51-250]
Bels, Alberts - *Saule Merktie*
     WLT - v71 - Win '97 - p194 [251-500]
Belsey, Catherine - *Desire: Love Stories in Western Culture*
     MLR - v91 - O '96 - p987+ [501+]
Belsky, R G - *Loverboy*
     Trib Bks - Mr 2 '97 - p4 [51-250]
Belting, Hans - *Die Erfindung Des Gemaldes*
     Art Bull - v78 - D '96 - p733+ [501+]
  Likeness and Presence
     CHR - v82 - Jl '96 - p481+ [251-500]
     JR - v76 - O '96 - p680+ [501+]
Beltman, Brian W - *Dutch Farmer in the Missouri Valley*
     Choice - v34 - D '96 - p674+ [51-250]
Belton, Robert J - *The Beribboned Bomb*
     Art J - v56 - Spr '97 - p95+ [51-250]
Belton, Sandra - *Ernestine and Amanda*
  c BL - v93 - Ja '97 - p855+ [251-500]
  c CBRS - v25 - Win '97 - p68 [51-250]
  c CCB-B - v50 - Ja '97 - p164 [51-250]
  c HB Guide - v8 - Spr '97 - p62 [51-250]
  c LATBR - S 15 '96 - p11 [51-250]
  c PW - v243 - O 21 '96 - p84 [51-250]
  c SLJ - v42 - N '96 - p103 [51-250]
Beltran, Antonio - *Revolucion Cientifica, Renacimiento E Historia De La Ciencia*
     Isis - v87 - S '96 - p547 [501+]
Bement, Leland C - *Hunter-Gatherer Mortuary Practices during the Central Texas Archaic*
     Am Ant - v61 - Jl '96 - p620+ [501+]
Bemporad, Jack - *Our Age*
     LJ - v121 - N 1 '96 - p72 [51-250]
Benaars, G A - *Theory and Practice of Education*
     JTWS - v13 - Spr '96 - p292+ [501+]
Benabib, Kim - *Obscene Bodies*
     Advocate - S 17 '96 - p60 [1-50]
     BW - v26 - D 1 '96 - p6 [51-250]
     CSM - v88 - N 13 '96 - p15 [51-250]
     NYTBR - v101 - S 29 '96 - p20 [51-250]
     PW - v243 - Jl 22 '96 - p226 [51-250]
Benabou, Marcel - *Why I Have Not Written Any of My Books*
     PW - v243 - N 4 '96 - p42 [1-50]
     RCF - v16 - Fall '96 - p202+ [251-500]
     TLS - Ja 24 '97 - p25 [501+]
     TranslRevS - v2 - D '96 - p21 [51-250]
     WLT - v71 - Win '97 - p113+ [501+]
Benadusi, Giovanna - *A Provincial Elite in Early Modern Tuscany*
     Choice - v34 - D '96 - p667+ [51-250]
     R&R Bk N - v11 - N '96 - p50 [51-250]
Benad-Wagenhoff, Volker - *Industrialisierung: Begriffe und Prozesse*
     T&C - v37 - Ap '96 - p349+ [501+]
  Industrieller Maschinenbau Im 19. Jahrhundert
     T&C - v37 - O '96 - p848+ [501+]
Ben-Amos, Ilana Krausman - *Adolescence and Youth in Early Modern England*
     EHR - v111 - S '96 - p974+ [501+]
Ben-Artzi Pelossof, Noa - *In the Name of Sorrow and Hope (Ben-Artzi Pelossof). Audio Version*
     BL - v93 - N 1 '96 - p522 [51-250]
Benbassa, Esther - *Haim Nahum, a Sephardic Chief Rabbi in Politics 1892-1923*
     Rel St Rev - v23 - Ap '97 - p197 [51-250]
  The Jews of the Balkans
     Rel St Rev - v23 - Ap '97 - p197 [51-250]
Benbrook, Charles M - *Pest Management at the Crossroads*
     Am Sci - v85 - Mr '97 - p195+ [501+]
     BioSci - v47 - Ap '97 - p260 [51-250]
     Choice - v34 - Ap '97 - p1362+ [51-250]
     Workbook - v21 - Win '96 - p184+ [501+]
Bencastro, Mario - *Arbol De La Vida*
     BL - v93 - S 15 '96 - p227 [1-50]

A Shot in the Cathedral
 BWatch - v17 - N '96 - p10 [51-250]
 Choice - v34 - Mr '97 - p1169 [51-250]
 PW - v243 - Jl 22 '96 - p228 [51-250]
The Tree of Life
 PW - v244 - Ap 21 '97 - p61 [51-250]
Bence-Jones, Mark - *Life in an Irish Country House*
 HT - v46 - O '96 - p58 [1-50]
 Spec - v278 - F 8 '97 - p39+ [501+]
Bencivenga, Ermanno - *My Kantian Ways*
 IPQ - v36 - S '96 - p379+ [1-50]
Bend, Marybeth - *Gutsy Women*
 r BL - v93 - S 15 '96 - p212 [1-50]
Bendall, Derek S - *Protein Electron Transfer*
 Choice - v34 - Mr '97 - p1188 [51-250]
Bendana, Alejandro - *La Mistica De Sandino*
 HAHR - v76 - N '96 - p802+ [501+]
Power Lines
 BL - v93 - O 1 '96 - p293+ [51-250]
Ben David, Arieh - *Safad*
 Am Phil - v110 - Jl '96 - p636 [51-250]
Bendazzi, Giannalberto - *Cartoons: One Hundred Years of Cinema Animation*
 JPC - v30 - Fall '96 - p199 [51-250]
Bender, Barbara - *Landscape: Politics and Perspectives*
 AJA - v100 - Jl '96 - p607+ [501+]
Bender, Bert - *The Descent of Love*
 AL - v69 - Mr '97 - p225+ [251-500]
 Choice - v34 - N '96 - p452 [51-250]
Bender, Carrie - *A Golden Sunbeam*
 BL - v93 - O 1 '96 - p304 [501+]
 LJ - v122 - Ap 1 '97 - p78 [51-250]
Bender, Edward A - *Mathematical Methods in Artificial Intelligence*
 Choice - v34 - O '96 - p315 [51-250]
Bender, Gary - *Call of the Game*
 Aethlon - v13 - Fall '95 - p181 [251-500]
Bender, Henry V - *Catullus: Advanced Placement Edition*
 Class Out - v74 - Spr '97 - p121 [51-250]
Bender, Michael - *Waiting for Filippo*
 c Can CL - v22 - Fall '96 - p114 [51-250]
Bender, Norman J - *Winning the West for Christ*
 Choice - v34 - D '96 - p627 [51-250]
 R&R Bk N - v11 - D '96 - p6 [1-50]
Bender, Paula Stone - *How to Keep Your Kids from Driving You Crazy*
 LJ - v122 - F 1 '97 - p100 [51-250]
 PW - v243 - D 16 '96 - p57 [51-250]
Bender, Richard W - *Herbal Bonsai*
 BL - v92 - Ag '96 - p1870 [51-250]
Bender, Robert - *The A to Z Beastly Jamboree (Illus. by Robert Bender)*
 c CBRS - v24 - Ag '96 - p157 [51-250]
 c HB Guide - v7 - Fall '96 - p326 [51-250]
 c Inst - v106 - Ag '96 - p42+ [1-50]
 c KR - v64 - My 1 '96 - p684 [51-250]
Bender, Sheila - *The Writer's Journal*
 BL - v93 - Ja '97 - p807 [51-250]
 KR - v64 - N 15 '96 - p1643 [251-500]
 LJ - v121 - D '96 - p94+ [51-250]
 PW - v243 - D 2 '96 - p53+ [51-250]
Bender, Steve - *Callaway Gardens*
 Pet PM - v25 - S '96 - p8 [51-250]
Bender, Thomas - *Budapest and New York*
 AHR - v101 - O '96 - p1176+ [501+]
Benderly, Beryl Lieff - *In Her Own Right*
 LJ - v122 - My 1 '97 - p133 [51-250]
Bendix, Deanna Marohn - *Diabolical Designs*
 Art J - v55 - Win '96 - p99+ [501+]
Benedek, Istvan - *Pressure-Sensitive Adhesives Technology*
 SciTech - v20 - D '96 - p83 [51-250]
Benedetti, Mario - *Blood Pact and Other Stories*
 KR - v65 - Mr 1 '97 - p334+ [51-250]
Benedetti, Paul - *Forward through the Rearview Mirror*
 KR - v65 - Ja 1 '97 - p52 [51-250]
 LJ - v122 - My 1 '97 - p132 [51-250]
 Quill & Q - v63 - F '97 - p30 [251-500]
Benedetto, John - *Harmonic Analysis and Applications*
 Choice - v34 - Ja '97 - p833 [51-250]
 SciTech - v20 - N '96 - p15 [51-250]
Benedict, Barbara M - *Making the Modern Reader*
 Choice - v34 - Ja '97 - p791 [51-250]
Benedict, Elizabeth - *The Joy of Writing Sex*
 BW - v26 - Ag 18 '96 - p13 [51-250]
 VLS - Win '96 - p25+ [501+]
Benedict, Helen - *Bad Angel*
 y Kliatt - v31 - My '97 - p5 [251-500]
Benedict, M G - *Super-Radiance: Multiatomic Coherent Emission*
 SciTech - v21 - Mr '97 - p24 [51-250]

Beneduce, Ann - *The Tempest (Illus. by Gennady Spirin)*
 c CSM - v88 - N 21 '96 - pB4 [51-250]
 c HB Guide - v7 - Fall '96 - p287+ [51-250]
 c SFR - v21 - S '96 - p47 [501+]
Benericetti, Ruggero - *Il Pontificale Di Ravenna*
 CH - v65 - S '96 - p456+ [251-500]
Benevolo, Leonardo - *The European City*
 J Urban H - v22 - S '96 - p720+ [501+]
Benezra, Neal - *Bruce Nauman*
 Art J - v54 - Win '95 - p93+ [501+]
Benford, Gregory - *Foundation's Fear*
 BL - v93 - Mr 1 '97 - p1114 [51-250]
 BW - v27 - Mr 30 '97 - p8 [501+]
 KR - v65 - Ja 15 '97 - p102+ [51-250]
 LJ - v122 - Mr 15 '97 - p93 [51-250]
 NYTBR - v102 - Ap 6 '97 - p24 [251-500]
 PW - v244 - F 24 '97 - p67+ [51-250]
In the Ocean of Night
 Books - v11 - Ap '97 - p22 [51-250]
Matter's End
 Books - v10 - Je '96 - p22 [1-50]
Matters End
 New Sci - v153 - Ja 4 '97 - p40 [51-250]
Bengelsdorf, Carolee - *The Problem of Democracy in Cuba*
 Parameters - v26 - Win '96 - p158 [1-50]
Bengeyfield, Pete - *Mountains and Mesas*
 WAL - v31 - Win '97 - p404+ [251-500]
Bengtson, Bradley P - *Photographic Atlas of Civil War Injuries*
 r AB - v99 - Mr 31 '97 - p1047+ [51-250]
Benguigui, Yamina - *Femmes D'Islam*
 BL - v93 - F 1 '97 - p930 [1-50]
Benhabib, Seyla - *Feminist Contentions*
 CS - v26 - Ja '97 - p123+ [501+]
Benian, Silvia - *From Renaissance to Revolution*
 Wil Q - v21 - Win '97 - p37 [1-50]
Benin. Direction Des Forets Et Des Ressources Naturelles - *Le Secteur Forestier National*
 J Gov Info - v23 - S '96 - p656 [1-50]
Bening, Guy R - *Carved Erosion*
 Sm Pr R - v28 - Je '96 - p13+ [501+]
Benink, Harald A - *Coping with Financial Fragility and Systemic Risk*
 JEL - v34 - S '96 - p1436 [51-250]
Benioff, Ron - *Vulnerability and Adaptation Assessments*
 SciTech - v21 - Mr '97 - p26 [51-250]
Benison, C C - *Death at Buckingham Palace*
 Arm Det - v29 - Sum '96 - p308 [51-250]
Beniston, Martin - *Mountain Environments in Changing Climates*
 GJ - v162 - Jl '96 - p237 [51-250]
Benito-Vessels, Carmen - *The Picaresque: A Symposium on the Rogue's Tale*
 MLR - v91 - Jl '96 - p774+ [251-500]
Benivieni, Antonio - *De Abditis Nonnullis Ac Mirandis Morborum Et Sanationum Causis*
 Isis - v88 - Mr '97 - p139+ [501+]
Benjafield, John G - *A History of Psychology*
 Isis - v88 - Mr '97 - p127+ [501+]
Benjamin, A H - *The Show-Off Mouse (Illus. by Val Biro)*
 c Bks Keeps - Jl '96 - p6+ [51-250]
What If! (Illus. by Jane Chapman)
 c Sch Lib - v44 - N '96 - p145 [51-250]
What's Up the Coconut Tree? (Illus. by Val Biro)
 c Bks Keeps - Jl '96 - p6+ [51-250]
Benjamin, Betsy Sterling - *The World of Rozome*
 Surface DJ - v21 - Fall '96 - p34 [51-250]
Benjamin, Carol Lea - *This Dog for Hire*
 BWatch - v18 - F '97 - p7 [1-50]
 KR - v64 - S 15 '96 - p1355 [51-250]
 LJ - v121 - N 1 '96 - p111 [51-250]
 PW - v243 - O 7 '96 - p64 [51-250]
 y VOYA - v19 - F '97 - p326 [251-500]
Benjamin, Clinton L - *Human Biology*
 SciTech - v20 - N '96 - p31 [51-250]
Benjamin, Cynthia - *I Am an Astronaut (Illus. by Miriam Sagasti)*
 c HB Guide - v7 - Fall '96 - p236 [1-50]
 c SB - v32 - O '96 - p209 [51-250]
Benjamin, Floella - *Skip across the Ocean (Illus. by Sheila Moxley)*
 c RT - v50 - F '97 - p425 [51-250]
Benjamin, Gail R - *Japanese Lessons*
 PW - v244 - Ja 13 '97 - p65 [51-250]
Benjamin, L Ann - *Family Literacy*
 JAAL - v40 - D '96 - p328 [51-250]
 J Gov Info - v23 - S '96 - p545 [51-250]
Benjamin, Lorna Smith - *Interpersonal Diagnosis and Treatment of Personality Disorders. 2nd Ed.*
 SciTech - v20 - N '96 - p45 [51-250]

Benjamin, Michael - *Cultural Diversity, Educational Equity, and the Transformation of Higher Education*
 R&R Bk N - v11 - D '96 - p54 [51-250]
Benjamin, Walter - *Selected Writings. Vol. 1*
 BL - v93 - F 1 '97 - p921 [51-250]
 BW - v27 - Mr 2 '97 - p13 [51-250]
 KR - v64 - O 1 '96 - p1435 [251-500]
 LJ - v122 - F 15 '97 - p134+ [51-250]
 Obs - Mr 23 '97 - p17* [501+]
Benjamini, Eli - *Immunology: A Short Course. 3rd Ed.*
 SciTech - v20 - S '96 - p24 [51-250]
Benjamins, Hendrik S - *Eingeordnete Freiheit*
 Rel St Rev - v22 - O '96 - p301+ [501+]
Benjaminson, Peter - *Secret Police*
 KR - v65 - Ja 15 '97 - p106 [251-500]
 PW - v244 - Ja 20 '97 - p386 [51-250]
Benkirane, A - *Nonlinear Partial Differential Equations*
 SIAM Rev - v39 - Mr '97 - p176 [51-250]
Benko, Stephen - *The Virgin Goddess*
 JAAR - v65 - Spr '97 - p221+ [501+]
 Rel St Rev - v23 - Ap '97 - p186 [51-250]
Ben-Lesser, Jay - *A Foxy Old Woman's Guide to Traveling Alone*
 OOB - v26 - Ag '96 - p24 [51-250]
Benn, Caroline - *Thirty Years On*
 TES - F 28 '97 - p7* [51-250]
Benn, Melissa - *Public Lives*
 Woman's J - S '96 - p10 [1-50]
Benne, Robert - *The Paradoxical Vision*
 JR - v77 - Ap '97 - p314+ [501+]
Benner, Erica - *Really Existing Nationalisms*
 AJS - v102 - Ja '97 - p1236+ [501+]
 APSR - v90 - D '96 - p885+ [501+]
Benner, J A - *Uncle Comanche*
 y VOYA - v19 - O '96 - p205 [251-500]
Bennet, Rick - *The Lost Brother*
 PW - v243 - S 16 '96 - p69 [51-250]
Bennett, Alan - *Writing Home*
 Obs - Mr 16 '97 - p18* [51-250]
Bennett, Allegra - *Renovating Woman*
 BL - v93 - Mr 15 '97 - p1212 [51-250]
 LJ - v122 - Ap 1 '97 - p119 [51-250]
 PW - v244 - F 3 '97 - p104 [51-250]
Bennett, Andrea T - *Apples, Bubbles, and Crystals (Illus. by Melody Sarecky)*
 c SB - v32 - Ag '96 - p177 [51-250]
 c SLJ - v42 - Ag '96 - p132 [51-250]
Bennett, Betty T - *Shelley: Poet and Legislator of the World*
 Nine-C Lit - v51 - S '96 - p270 [51-250]
Bennett, Bridget - *The Damnation of Harold Frederic*
 LJ - v122 - My 1 '97 - p102+ [51-250]
Bennett, Bruce - *Crossing Cultures*
 Aust Bk R - D '96 - p20+ [501+]
Bennett, Cherie - *Angel Kisses*
 y VOYA - v19 - D '96 - p262 [51-250]
Heaven Help Us
 y VOYA - v19 - D '96 - p262 [51-250]
Bennett, Christopher - *Yugoslavia's Bloody Collapse*
 AHR - v101 - D '96 - p1580+ [501+]
 Historian - v59 - Win '97 - p457+ [251-500]
 J Ch St - v38 - Sum '96 - p666+ [251-500]
Bennett, Douglas W - *Designing Hard Software*
 SciTech - v21 - Mr '97 - p9 [51-250]
Bennett, G H - *British Foreign Policy during the Curzon Period 1919-24*
 AHR - v102 - F '97 - p112+ [501+]
 Albion - v28 - Fall '96 - p532+ [501+]
Bennett, Gill - *The Indus Valley Civilisation*
 TES - D 13 '96 - p43 [51-250]
Bennett, Gillian - *Contemporary Legend*
 R&R Bk N - v12 - F '97 - p30 [51-250]
Bennett, Hal - *Lord of Dark Places*
 PW - v244 - Ap 21 '97 - p69 [1-50]
Bennett, Jack - *Voyage of the Lucky Dragon*
 y JAAL - v40 - D '96 - p319 [51-250]
Bennett, James W - *The Squared Circle*
 y EJ - v85 - N '96 - p130+ [251-500]
 y Emerg Lib - v24 - S '96 - p24 [1-50]
Bennett, Jay - *Coverup*
 y JAAL - v40 - D '96 - p316 [51-250]
Bennett, Jennifer - *The Tomato Handbook*
 Quill & Q - v63 - Mr '97 - p22 [251-500]
Bennett, Jill - *Playtime Poems (Illus. by Nick Sharratt)*
 c Magpies - v11 - S '96 - p45 [1-50]
Poems for Christmas (Illus. by Ian Beck)
 c Bks Keeps - N '96 - p24 [51-250]
Bennett, John W - *Settling the Canadian-American West 1890-1915*
 PHR - v66 - F '97 - p117+ [501+]

Bennett, Jonathan - *The Act Itself*
  IPQ - v37 - Mr '97 - p110+ [501+]
  TLS - Ja 10 '97 - p27 [501+]
Bennett, Judith - *Sex Signs. Rev. and Updated Ed.*
  LJ - v122 - F 1 '97 - p96 [51-250]
Bennett, Judith M - *Ale, Beer, and Brewsters in England*
  Choice - v34 - My '97 - p1555+ [51-250]
Bennett, Larry - *Fragments of Cities*
  J Urban H - v22 - S '96 - p750+ [501+]
Bennett, Mark - *TV Sets*
  NYTBR - v102 - Mr 30 '97 - p17 [51-250]
Bennett, Martyn - *The Civil Wars in Britain and Ireland 1638-1651*
  Choice - v34 - My '97 - p1556 [51-250]
Bennett, Michael - *Discovering and Restoring Antique Furniture*
  LJ - v121 - S 15 '96 - p66+ [51-250]
Bennett, Michael J - *When Dreams Came True*
  Choice - v34 - My '97 - p1561 [51-250]
  KR - v64 - O 1 '96 - p1436 [251-500]
  LJ - v122 - Ja '97 - p118 [51-250]
Bennett, Nigel - *Keeper of the King*
  KR - v64 - N 15 '96 - p1638+ [51-250]
  PW - v243 - D 9 '96 - p64 [51-250]
Bennett, Oliver - *Culture Policy and Management in the United Kingdom*
  JAML - v26 - Win '97 - p315+ [501+]
Bennett, Ralph - *Behind the Battle*
  EHR - v111 - S '96 - p1026 [251-500]
  Settlements in the Americas
  W&M Q - v53 - O '96 - p801+ [501+]
Bennett, Rodney - *Angel Voice*
  y JB - v60 - O '96 - p197+ [251-500]
  y Obs - v54 - O 13 '96 - p18* [51-250]
  y Sch Lib - v45 - F '97 - p44 [51-250]
  c TES - S 13 '96 - p7* [501+]
Bennett, Roy - *Fortissimo!*
  TES - Ja 31 '97 - p17* [51-250]
Bennett, Stewart - *An Historical Atlas of Lincolnshire*
  r EHR - v111 - S '96 - p1038+ [51-250]
Bennett, Susan - *Performing Nostalgia*
  Theat J - v48 - O '96 - p391+ [501+]
Bennett, Tegan - *Bombora*
  Aust Bk R - Je '96 - p46+ [501+]
Bennett, Tony - *The Birth of the Museum*
  AJA - v100 - O '96 - p769+ [501+]
  LQ - v67 - Ja '97 - p78+ [501+]
Bennett, Tony, 1926- - *Tony Bennett: What My Heart Has Seen*
  CSM - v88 - N 21 '96 - pB3 [51-250]
  LATBR - D 8 '96 - p12 [51-250]
Bennett, Vivienne - *The Politics of Water*
  AHR - v102 - F '97 - p238+ [501+]
  APSR - v90 - D '96 - p931+ [501+]
  J Pol - v58 - N '96 - p1248+ [501+]
Bennett, William John - *Body Count*
  y BL - v93 - S 15 '96 - p178 [51-250]
  KR - v64 - S 1 '96 - p1285 [251-500]
  LJ - v121 - O 15 '96 - p75+ [51-250]
  Nat R - v48 - N 11 '96 - p52+ [501+]
  NYTBR - v101 - N 3 '96 - p21 [501+]
  Pub Int - Win '97 - p102+ [501+]
  TLS - Ja 10 '97 - p9+ [501+]
  W&I - v12 - Mr '97 - p276+ [501+]
  WSJ-MW - v78 - N 11 '96 - pA12 [501+]
Benni, Stefano - *Elianto*
  BL - v93 - D 1 '96 - p644 [1-50]
  Econ - v339 - My 18 '96 - p16*+ [501+]
  WLT - v71 - Win '97 - p127+ [51-250]
Bennington, Geoffrey - *Legislations: The Politics of Deconstruction*
  South HR - v30 - Fall '96 - p372+ [501+]
Bennis, Phyllis - *Calling the Shots*
  Pres SQ - v27 - Win '97 - p160+ [501+]
  WorldV - v12 - Jl '96 - p5 [51-250]
Bennis, Warren - *Organizing Genius*
  Fortune - v135 - Mr 17 '97 - p150 [501+]
  LJ - v122 - Ja '97 - p114 [51-250]
  NYTBR - v102 - Mr 9 '97 - p21 [501+]
  PW - v243 - N 25 '96 - p61 [51-250]
Benoit, Philippe - *Project Finance at the World Bank*
  JEL - v34 - D '96 - p2114 [51-250]
Benoit, William L - *Candidates in Conflict*
  Choice - v34 - F '97 - p959 [51-250]
Ben-Rafael, Eliezer - *Language, Identity, and Social Division*
  Lang Soc - v25 - S '96 - p476+ [501+]
Bensaude-Vincent, Bernadette - *A History of Chemistry*
  Nature - v386 - Mr 6 '97 - p34 [501+]
  Lavoisier: Memoires D'Une Revolution
  Isis - v87 - D '96 - p688+ [501+]

Bensch, Stephen P - *Barcelona and Its Rulers 1096-1291*
  AHR - v101 - O '96 - p1196 [501+]
  EHR - v112 - Ap '97 - p434+ [501+]
BenShea, Noah - *Jacob's Ladder*
  PW - v244 - Mr 31 '97 - p58 [51-250]
Benski, Claude - *The Mars Effect*
  Horoscope - v62 - S '96 - p14+ [501+]
Benson, Allen C - *Connecting Kids and the Internet*
  LJ - v121 - D '96 - p156 [51-250]
  VOYA - v19 - F '97 - p355 [251-500]
Benson, Angela - *A Family Wedding*
  LJ - v122 - F 15 '97 - p125 [51-250]
  The Way Home
  PW - v244 - F 17 '97 - p217 [51-250]
Benson, Anna Bruni - *Solo Dolci*
  PW - v243 - O 7 '96 - p70+ [51-250]
Benson, E F - *The Collected Ghost Stories of E.F. Benson*
  BW - v26 - N 3 '96 - p12 [51-250]
Benson, Elaine - *Unmentionables: A Brief History of Underwear*
  BL - v93 - F 1 '97 - p911 [51-250]
  NYTBR - v101 - D 15 '96 - p24 [51-250]
  PW - v243 - S 23 '96 - p69+ [51-250]
Benson, Elizabeth P - *Olmec Art of Ancient Mexico*
  Choice - v34 - D '96 - p603+ [51-250]
  LJ - v121 - N 1 '96 - p64+ [51-250]
  Mag Antiq - v150 - Ag '96 - p142 [501+]
  PW - v243 - S 9 '96 - p77 [51-250]
  Time - v148 - N 18 '96 - p109 [1-50]
Benson, Herbert - *Timeless Healing*
  Sci - v276 - Ap 18 '97 - p369+ [501+]
Benson, Jackson J - *Wallace Stegner: His Life and Work*
  Aud - v99 - Ja '97 - p106+ [501+]
  BL - v93 - N 1 '96 - p473+ [51-250]
  Bloom Rev - v16 - N '96 - p17 [501+]
  BW - v26 - D 22 '96 - p4+ [51-250]
  KR - v64 - S 1 '96 - p1285 [251-500]
  LATBR - D 1 '96 - p7+ [501+]
  LJ - v121 - O 1 '96 - p88 [51-250]
  NYTBR - v101 - N 10 '96 - p69 [501+]
  PW - v243 - S 16 '96 - p58 [51-250]
  SN - v111 - D '96 - p12 [251-500]
  Trib Bks - Ja 5 '97 - p3 [501+]
  WAL - v31 - Win '97 - p381+ [501+]
Benson, John - *The Rise of Consumer Society in Britain 1880-1980*
  EHR - v112 - F '97 - p263 [501+]
Benson, Judi - *The Long Pale Corridor*
  NS & S - v9 - My 17 '96 - p37 [51-250]
  y Sch Lib - v44 - N '96 - p166+ [51-250]
Benson, Marjorie - *Awesome Almanac--Ohio*
  r ARBA - v28 - '97 - p48 [51-250]
Benson, Maxine - *1001 Colorado Place Names*
  r Names - v44 - S '96 - p241+ [501+]
Benson, Michael - *Dale Earnhardt*
  c HB Guide - v7 - Fall '96 - p359 [51-250]
Benson, Morton - *Dictionary of Russian Personal Names*
  r Slav R - v55 - Sum '96 - p523+ [501+]
Benson, Obert Louis - *Venona: Soviet Espionage and the American Response 1939-1957*
  For Aff - v76 - Mr '97 - p180 [51-250]
Benson, Raymond - *Zero Minus Ten*
  KR - v65 - Ap 1 '97 - p478 [251-500]
  Obs - Mr 30 '97 - p15* [51-250]
  PW - v244 - Ap 21 '97 - p61 [51-250]
Benson, Robert - *Between the Dreaming and the Coming True*
  BL - v93 - O 1 '96 - p297 [251-500]
Benson, Thomas A - *Copying and Duplicating. 2nd Ed.*
  Pet PM - v25 - F '97 - p60 [51-250]
Benson, Thomas W - *Landmark Essays on Rhetorical Criticism*
  QJS - v82 - Ag '96 - p302+ [501+]
Bensoussan, Albert - *Les Anges De Sodome*
  WLT - v71 - Win '97 - p201 [501+]
  L'Oeil De La Sultane
  WLT - v70 - Aut '96 - p1009 [501+]
Benstock, Shari - *On Fashion*
  Signs - v22 - Win '97 - p475+ [501+]
Bent, James A - *Effective Project Management through Applied Cost and Schedule Control*
  r SciTech - v20 - S '96 - p48 [51-250]
Bent, Jenny - *How Anansi Captured Tiger's Stories (Illus. by Jenny Bent)*
  c JB - v60 - Ag '96 - p140 [51-250]
  c Sch Lib - v44 - Ag '96 - p98 [51-250]
The Bent Guide to Gay/Lesbian Canada 1995/96
  r Quill & Q - v62 - S '96 - p24 [51-250]

Bentley, Dawn - *If You Were a Bug (Illus. by Jack Graber)*
  c BL - v93 - D 15 '96 - p732 [1-50]
  c HB Guide - v7 - Fall '96 - p341 [51-250]
Bentley, EElizabeth Petty - *Directory of Family Associations. 3rd Ed.*
  r ARBA - v28 - '97 - p165 [51-250]
Bentley, James - *The Most Beautiful Villages of the Dordogne*
  BL - v93 - O 1 '96 - p317 [51-250]
Bentley, Judith - *Dear Friend*
  c BL - v93 - F 15 '97 - p1017 [51-250]
  c CCB-B - v50 - F '97 - p200 [51-250]
  c KR - v64 - N 15 '96 - p1666 [51-250]
Bentley, Karen - *The Unsers*
  c HB Guide - v7 - Fall '96 - p359 [51-250]
Bentley, Michael L - *Astronomy Smart Junior*
  y Kliatt - v31 - My '97 - p24 [51-250]
Bentley, Nancy - *Putting on a Play (Illus. by Katy Keck Arnsteen)*
  c BL - v93 - F 1 '97 - p936 [51-250]
  c KR - v64 - D 15 '96 - p1796 [51-250]
  c SLJ - v43 - Mr '97 - p197 [51-250]
Bentley, Nancy, 1961- - *The Ethnography of Manners*
  ASInt - v34 - O '96 - p109+ [501+]
  Col Lit - v23 - O '96 - p203+ [501+]
  J Am St - v30 - D '96 - p490+ [251-500]
Bentley, Sean - *Grace and Desolation*
  Sm Pr R - v28 - N '96 - p8 [501+]
Bentley, Ursula - *The Angel of Twickenham*
  Obs - Mr 2 '97 - p18* [501+]
  Spec - v278 - F 15 '97 - p32 [501+]
  Woman's J - F '97 - p16 [51-250]
Benton, Barbara - *Soldiers for Peace*
  LJ - v122 - Ap 15 '97 - p101 [51-250]
Benton, D A - *How to Think Like a CEO*
  B Ent - v27 - O '96 - p36 [51-250]
  How to Think Like a CEO (Benton). Audio Version
  Quill & Q - v62 - Jl '96 - p52 [1-50]
Benton, Hope - *Best Friends*
  c SLJ - v43 - F '97 - p100 [51-250]
  A Thousand Lights
  c SLJ - v43 - Mr '97 - p184 [51-250]
Benton, M J - *The Penguin Historical Atlas of the Dinosaurs*
  r ARBA - v28 - '97 - p637 [51-250]
  yr Kliatt - v31 - My '97 - p30 [51-250]
Benton, Tim - *The Pitcairn Islands*
  GJ - v163 - Mr '97 - p109 [51-250]
Benvenisti, Meron - *City of Stone*
  Choice - v34 - My '97 - p1560 [51-250]
  For Aff - v76 - Mr '97 - p195 [51-250]
  KR - v64 - S 1 '96 - p1285+ [251-500]
  LJ - v121 - N 15 '96 - p72 [51-250]
  MEQ - v4 - Mr '97 - p75+ [501+]
  NYRB - v44 - Mr 27 '97 - p4+ [501+]
  NYTBR - v101 - D 8 '96 - p13+ [501+]
  PW - v243 - S 30 '96 - p70 [51-250]
  TLS - Mr 7 '97 - p8+ [501+]
  Intimate Enemies
  Am - v175 - N 30 '96 - p27+ [501+]
  JPR - v33 - N '96 - p497+ [51-250]
Benvenuto, Bice - *Concerning the Rites of Psychoanalysis*
  Rel St Rev - v22 - O '96 - p333+ [51-250]
Ben-Yehuda, Nachman - *The Masada Myth*
  AJS - v102 - Ja '97 - p1222+ [501+]
  For Aff - v75 - S '96 - p155 [51-250]
Benyus, Janine M - *Biomimicry: Innovation Inspired by Nature*
  KR - v65 - My 1 '97 - p687 [251-500]
Benz, Stephen Connely - *Guatemalan Journey*
  Parameters - v26 - Win '96 - p156 [1-50]
Benz, Wolfgang - *Encyclopedia of German Resistance to the Nazi Movement*
  r Choice - v34 - My '97 - p1474 [251-500]
  r LJ - v121 - D '96 - p84 [51-250]
  r PW - v243 - N 11 '96 - p64 [51-250]
Benzie, Alex - *The Year's Midnight*
  TLS - S 13 '96 - p23 [501+]
Ben-Zvi, Linda - *Theater in Israel*
  Choice - v34 - O '96 - p292 [51-250]
  Theat J - v49 - Mr '97 - p88+ [501+]
Beon, Yves - *Planet Dora*
  PW - v244 - Mr 10 '97 - p60 [51-250]
Bepko, Claudia - *The Heart's Progress*
  KR - v65 - F 1 '97 - p182 [251-500]
  LJ - v122 - Mr 15 '97 - p68 [51-250]
  PW - v244 - F 24 '97 - p73 [51-250]
Bequele, Assefa - *First Things First in Child Labour*
  J Gov Info - v23 - S '96 - p671 [51-250]

Beranek, Leo - *Concert and Opera Halls*
　Sci - v274 - N 15 '96 - p1149 [1-50]
Beratan, Kathi K - *Reconstructing the History of Basin and Range Extension Using Sedimentology and Stratigraphy*
　SciTech - v21 - Mr '97 - p33 [51-250]
Berberoglu, Berch - *The National Question*
　CS - v25 - N '96 - p741+ [501+]
Berberova, Nina - *Aleksandr Blok: A Life*
　LJ - v121 - S 15 '96 - p68 [51-250]
Berce, Yves-Marie - *The Birth of Absolutism*
　Six Ct J - v27 - Win '96 - p1065+ [501+]
Berchtold, Jacques - *L'Etreinte Abhorree*
　MLR - v91 - Jl '96 - p746 [51-250]
Bercuson, David Jay - *Significant Incident*
　BIC - v25 - N '96 - p11+ [501+]
　CF - v75 - Ja '97 - p44+ [501+]
　Quill & Q - v62 - O '96 - p39 [251-500]
　True Patriot
　Can Hist R - v77 - D '96 - p630+ [501+]
Berebitsky, William - *A Very Long Weekend*
　BL - v93 - F 1 '97 - p923 [51-250]
Berek, Jonathan S - *Novak's Gynecology. 12th Ed.*
　SciTech - v20 - N '96 - p51 [51-250]
Berenbaum, May R - *Bugs in the System*
　BW - v26 - Ag 25 '96 - p12 [51-250]
　BWatch - v17 - S '96 - p11 [51-250]
　Nature - v384 - D 5 '96 - p426 [1-50]
Berendt, John - *Midnight in the Garden of Good and Evil (Woodman). Audio Version*
　y Kliatt - v31 - Mr '97 - p49 [51-250]
Berenger, Jean - *A History of the Habsburg Empire*
　EHR - v111 - S '96 - p975+ [251-500]
Berens, Carol - *Hotel Bars and Lobbies*
　PW - v243 - N 18 '96 - p60 [51-250]
Berenson, Kathryn - *Quilts of Provence*
　LJ - v121 - N 15 '96 - p58 [51-250]
Berenson, Laurien - *Dog Eat Dog*
　KR - v64 - S 1 '96 - p1271+ [51-250]
　LJ - v121 - N 1 '96 - p111 [1-50]
　PW - v243 - S 9 '96 - p68 [51-250]
Berenstain, Stan - *The Berenstain Bears at the Teen Rock Cafe*
　c HB Guide - v8 - Spr '97 - p57 [51-250]
　The Berenstain Bears Draw-It!
　c HB Guide - v8 - Spr '97 - p19 [51-250]
　The Berenstain Bears Fly-It!
　c HB Guide - v8 - Spr '97 - p19 [51-250]
　The Berenstain Bears in Big Bear City
　c HB Guide - v7 - Fall '96 - p236 [1-50]
　The Berenstain Bears in Maniac Mansion
　c HB Guide - v8 - Spr '97 - p57 [51-250]
　Yike! Yike! Where's My Trike?
　c HB Guide - v7 - Fall '96 - p236+ [51-250]
Beresford, David - *Ten Men Dead*
　NYTBR - v102 - Mr 16 '97 - p32 [51-250]
　Trib Bks - Mr 23 '97 - p6 [1-50]
Beresford, Elisabeth - *Lizzie Fights On (Illus. by James Mayhew)*
　c Sch Lib - v45 - F '97 - p22 [51-250]
　The Smallest Whale (Illus. by Susan Field)
　c Sch Lib - v44 - Ag '96 - p98 [51-250]
Beresford-Kroeger, Diana - *An Ecological Guide to a North Temperate Garden*
　Quill & Q - v62 - S '96 - p69 [251-500]
Beretta, Marco - *Bibliotheca Lavoisieriana*
　r Isis - v88 - Mr '97 - p147+ [501+]
Berezhkov, Vasilii - *Vnutri I Vne Bollshogo Domall*
　BL - v93 - O 1 '96 - p327 [1-50]
Berg, Adriane - *Gifting to People You Love*
　PW - v243 - Jl 22 '96 - p224 [51-250]
Berg, Elizabeth - *Joy School*
　y BL - v93 - Mr 1 '97 - p1108+ [51-250]
　BW - v27 - Ap 13 '97 - p6 [251-500]
　KR - v65 - F 1 '97 - p155 [251-500]
　PW - v244 - F 10 '97 - p66 [51-250]
　Trib Bks - My 18 '97 - p9 [501+]
　The Pull of the Moon
　LATBR - My 12 '96 - p10 [51-250]
　Range of Motion
　Ent W - N 15 '96 - p67 [1-50]
　Woman's J - O '96 - p12 [1-50]
Berg, Frances M - *Afraid to Eat*
　Choice - v34 - Ap '97 - p1372 [51-250]
　LJ - v121 - N 15 '96 - p75 [251-500]
Berg, Leila - *Flickerbook*
　Lon R Bks - v19 - Ja 23 '97 - p30+ [501+]
　NS - v126 - Ja 10 '97 - p45+ [501+]
　Obs - Ja 26 '97 - p18* [501+]
Berg, Leo Van Den - *Urban Tourism*
　R&R Bk N - v12 - F '97 - p28 [51-250]

Berg, Maxine - *A Woman in History*
　Choice - v34 - Ja '97 - p854 [51-250]
　Lon R Bks - v18 - S 5 '96 - p23+ [501+]
Berg, Nancy E - *Exile from Exile*
　R&R Bk N - v11 - N '96 - p65 [51-250]
Berg, Stephen - *The Steel Cricket*
　PW - v244 - Mr 31 '97 - p71 [51-250]
Bergad, Laird W - *The Cuban Slave Market 1790-1880*
　AHR - v102 - F '97 - p231 [251-500]
　HAHR - v77 - F '97 - p119+ [501+]
　JEH - v56 - S '96 - p727+ [501+]
Bergado, D T - *Soft Ground Improvement in Lowland Environment*
　SciTech - v20 - N '96 - p65 [51-250]
Bergan, Helen - *Where the Information Is*
　r ChrPhil - v8 - Je 13 '96 - p38 [51-250]
Bergan, Ronald - *Jean Renoir: Projections of Paradise*
　FR - v70 - D '96 - p367+ [251-500]
Berge, Jean-Michel - *Hardware Component Modeling*
　SciTech - v21 - Mr '97 - p93 [51-250]
　Meta-Modeling: Performance and Information Modeling
　SciTech - v20 - N '96 - p75 [51-250]
　Object-Oriented Modeling
　SciTech - v21 - Mr '97 - p11 [51-250]
Bergeijk, Peter A G Van - *Privatization, Deregulation and the Macroeconomy*
　Choice - v34 - D '96 - p656 [51-250]
　JEL - v35 - Mr '97 - p209 [51-250]
Bergelson, David - *The Stories of David Bergelson*
　Choice - v34 - Ap '97 - p1331 [51-250]
　KR - v64 - D 15 '96 - p1767 [51-250]
　LJ - v121 - D '96 - p149 [51-250]
　NYTBR - v102 - Mr 9 '97 - p19 [51-250]
Bergemann, Thomas - *Q Auf Dem Prufstand*
　Rel St Rev - v23 - Ja '97 - p71 [51-250]
Bergen, David - *A Year of Lesser*
　BIC - v25 - O '96 - p40 [51-250]
　Choice - v34 - Ap '97 - p1333 [51-250]
　KR - v65 - Ja 1 '97 - p4 [251-500]
　LJ - v122 - F 1 '97 - p104 [51-250]
　NYTBR - v102 - Ap 6 '97 - p29 [501+]
Bergen, Doris L - *Twisted Cross*
　CC - v113 - N 6 '96 - p1091 [51-250]
Bergen, Raquel Kennedy - *Wife Rape*
　Choice - v34 - N '96 - p544+ [51-250]
　R&R Bk N - v11 - N '96 - p45 [51-250]
Berger, Alan L - *Children of Job*
　LJ - v122 - Ap 15 '97 - p95 [51-250]
Berger, Arthur Asa - *Bloom's Morning*
　KR - v64 - N 1 '96 - p1571 [251-500]
　New Sci - v153 - Mr 15 '97 - p42 [51-250]
　PW - v243 - N 4 '96 - p60+ [51-250]
　The Genius of the Jewish Joke
　PW - v243 - N 11 '96 - p68 [51-250]
　Manufacturing Desire
　Choice - v34 - O '96 - p270 [51-250]
　Narratives in Popular Culture, Media, and Everyday Life
　Choice - v34 - F '97 - p954 [51-250]
　R&R Bk N - v12 - F '97 - p76 [51-250]
Berger, Barbara - *Grandfather Twilight*
　c New Ad - v9 - Fall '96 - p309+ [501+]
　When the Sun Rose (Illus. by Barbara Berger)
　c PW - v244 - F 3 '97 - p108 [1-50]
Berger, Bob - *Beating Murphy's Law*
　y BL - v93 - Ap 1 '97 - p1342 [1-50]
　The Risk of Heaven
　Arm Det - v29 - Fall '96 - p484+ [51-250]
Berger, Bruce - *Facing the Music*
　WAL - v31 - Fall '96 - p286+ [51-250]
Berger, Charles R - *Communication and Social Influence Processes*
　QJS - v83 - F '97 - p122+ [501+]
Berger, John - *G: A Novel*
　Obs - D 1 '96 - p18* [51-250]
　A Painter of Our Time
　BW - v26 - O 27 '96 - p12 [51-250]
　Photocopies
　LATBR - S 22 '96 - p15 [51-250]
　NYTBR - v102 - Ja 12 '97 - p10 [501+]
　To the Wedding
　SFR - v21 - S '96 - p48 [1-50]
　TES - Jl 26 '96 - pR5 [51-250]
Berger, John J - *Charging Ahead*
　BL - v93 - My 1 '97 - p1467 [51-250]
　KR - v65 - Mr 15 '97 - p426+ [251-500]
　PW - v244 - Ap 7 '97 - p84 [51-250]
Berger, Joseph - *Theoretical Research Programs*
　SF - v75 - S '96 - p339+ [501+]
Berger, Klaus - *The Truth under Lock and Key?*
　Rel St Rev - v23 - Ap '97 - p174+ [51-250]

Berger, Mark T - *Under Northern Eyes*
　APSR - v90 - D '96 - p952 [501+]
Berger, Melvin - *Animal Senses*
　c Inst - v106 - S '96 - p92 [1-50]
　Call of the Wolves
　c SB - v32 - O '96 - p210 [251-500]
　How Do Airplanes Fly? (Illus. by Paul Babb)
　c HB Guide - v7 - Fall '96 - p349 [1-50]
　c SLJ - v42 - Ag '96 - p132 [51-250]
　How Do Animals Sleep?
　c SB - v32 - O '96 - p210 [251-500]
　Light
　c SB - v32 - N '96 - p239+ [251-500]
　Macmillan Early Science Big Books
　c Learning - v25 - Ag '96 - p95 [51-250]
　The Mighty Ocean
　c SB - v33 - Ja '97 - p16 [51-250]
Berger, Phil - *Blood Season*
　NYTBR - v101 - Ap 7 '96 - p24 [51-250]
Berger, Rainer - *SPD Und Grune*
　Choice - v34 - D '96 - p568 [1-50]
Berger, Robert W - *A Royal Passion*
　EHR - v112 - Ap '97 - p480 [501+]
　MLR - v91 - O '96 - p988+ [501+]
　Sev Cent N - v54 - Fall '96 - p74+ [501+]
Berger, Sidney E - *The Design of Bibliographies*
　Lib & Cul - v32 - Win '97 - p155+ [501+]
Berger, Stefan - *The British Labour Party and the German Social Democrats 1900-1931*
　AHR - v101 - D '96 - p1545 [501+]
　Albion - v28 - Sum '96 - p351+ [501+]
　EHR - v112 - Ap '97 - p523+ [501+]
　J Soc H - v30 - Win '96 - p524+ [501+]
　The Force of Labour
　Choice - v34 - Mr '97 - p1220 [51-250]
Berger, Suzanne - *National Diversity and Global Capitalism*
　Choice - v34 - O '96 - p330 [51-250]
　JEL - v34 - D '96 - p2040+ [501+]
Berger, Suzanne E - *Horizontal Woman*
　BL - v92 - Ag '96 - p1874 [51-250]
　NYTBR - v101 - D 1 '96 - p22 [51-250]
　Wom R Bks - v14 - Mr '97 - p8+ [501+]
Berger, Teresa - *Theology in Hymns?*
　Theol St - v58 - Mr '97 - p191 [251-500]
Berger, Thomas - *Suspects*
　BW - v26 - S 29 '96 - p5 [501+]
　NYTBR - v101 - S 29 '96 - p19 [501+]
　NYTBR - v101 - D 8 '96 - p82 [1-50]
　NYTLa - v145 - S 13 '96 - pC33 [501+]
　VQR - v73 - Win '97 - p23* [51-250]
　WSJ-MW - v78 - O 15 '96 - pA18 [51-250]
Berger, Yves - *Immobile Dans Le Courant Du Fleuve*
　FR - v70 - O '96 - p138+ [501+]
Berger Andreadakis, Katya - *Titian: Nymph and Shepherd*
　Nat - v264 - F 3 '97 - p27+ [501+]
Bergere, Marie-Claire - *Sun Yat-Sen*
　Ch Rev Int - v4 - Spr '97 - p71+ [501+]
Bergeron, Gerard - *Tout Etait Dans Montesquieu*
　CPR - v16 - Ag '96 - p243+ [501+]
Berger-Prossdorf, Tamara - *Die Funktion Der Heilsarmeegeistlichen In Den Dramen Brechts*
　Ger Q - v69 - Sum '96 - p357+ [501+]
Bergerud, Eric - *Touched with Fire*
　KR - v64 - My 1 '96 - p654 [251-500]
　LATBR - Jl 7 '96 - p4+ [501+]
　Mar Crp G - v80 - O '96 - p77 [501+]
　NL - v79 - Ag 12 '96 - p16+ [501+]
　NYTBR - v101 - S 1 '96 - p20 [501+]
Bergh, Jeroen C J M Van Den - *Ecological Economics and Sustainable Development*
　Choice - v34 - O '96 - p328 [51-250]
　JEL - v34 - S '96 - p1496 [51-250]
Berghahn, Volker - *Imperial Germany 1871-1914*
　HT - v46 - Jl '96 - p54+ [501+]
Berghall, Pii Elina - *Habitat II and the Urban Economy*
　J Gov Info - v23 - S '96 - p683 [51-250]
Berghaus, Gunter - *Fascism and Theatre*
　Choice - v34 - F '97 - p976 [51-250]
　TLS - Ja 17 '97 - p12 [501+]
Berghe, L Van Den - *Financial Conglomerates*
　R&R Bk N - v12 - F '97 - p47 [51-250]
Bergheim, Laura - *The Look-It-Up Guide to Washington Libraries and Archives*
　r RQ - v36 - Fall '96 - p132+ [251-500]
Bergin, Joseph - *The Making of the French Episcopate 1589-1661*
　Choice - v34 - My '97 - p1514 [51-250]
　TLS - F 28 '97 - p30+ [501+]

Bergland, Martha - *Idle Curiosity*
  BL - v93 - My 1 '97 - p1477 [51-250]
  KR - v65 - Mr 1 '97 - p317 [51-250]
  PW - v244 - Ap 28 '97 - p49 [251-500]
Bergman, Charles - *Orion's Legacy*
  BW - v26 - S 29 '96 - p13 [51-250]
Bergman, Ingmar - *Images: My Life in Film*
  J Film & Vid - v48 - Spr '96 - p96+ [501+]
  Private Confessions
  BL - v93 - Ja '97 - p816 [51-250]
  KR - v64 - N 15 '96 - p1617 [251-500]
  LJ - v122 - Ja '97 - p142 [51-250]
  NYTBR - v102 - Ja 12 '97 - p11 [501+]
  Obs - Ja 5 '97 - p18* [51-250]
  PW - v243 - N 25 '96 - p57 [51-250]
  Spec - v278 - Ja 25 '97 - p42+ [501+]
  TLS - F 7 '97 - p21 [501+]
Bergman, Jed I - *Managing Change in the Nonprofit Sector*
  Afterimage - v24 - Ja '97 - p23 [51-250]
Bergman, Paul - *Reel Justice*
  AB - v98 - D 9 '96 - p1997 [51-250]
  ABA Jour - v83 - F '97 - p90 [501+]
  Arm Det - v30 - Win '97 - p71 [51-250]
Bergman, Susan - *Martyrs: Contemporary Writers on Modern Lives of Faith*
  Bks & Cult - v3 - Mr '97 - p4 [51-250]
  BL - v93 - Ja '97 - p808 [1-50]
  BL - v93 - S 15 '96 - p183 [51-250]
  CC - v114 - F 19 '97 - p202+ [501+]
  Ch Today - v40 - N 11 '96 - p53+ [51-250]
  Comw - v124 - Ja 17 '97 - p23+ [501+]
Bergman, Yolanda - *Diet 911*
  BL - v93 - Mr 15 '97 - p1215 [51-250]
  PW - v244 - F 17 '97 - p216 [51-250]
Bergman-Carton, Janis - *The Woman of Ideas in French Art 1830-1848*
  AHR - v101 - D '96 - p1556+ [501+]
  Apo - v144 - Ag '96 - p73+ [501+]
  Art Bull - v78 - S '96 - p568+ [501+]
Bergmann, Barbara R - *In Defense of Affirmative Action*
  Econ - v341 - N 16 '96 - p6*+ [501+]
  ILRR - v50 - Ap '97 - p516+ [501+]
  JEL - v34 - D '96 - p2078 [51-250]
  JEL - v35 - Mr '97 - p153+ [501+]
  y Kliatt - v31 - My '97 - p26 [51-250]
  NY - v72 - N 25 '96 - p106+ [501+]
  NYTBR - v102 - Ap 13 '97 - p32 [1-50]
Bergmann, Hans - *God in the Street*
  Choice - v34 - S '96 - p122 [51-250]
Bergmann, Marianne - *Der Koloss Neros*
  AJA - v100 - O '96 - p802+ [501+]
Bergmans, Jan W M - *Digital Baseband Transmission and Recording*
  SciTech - v21 - Mr '97 - p88 [51-250]
Bergmeier, Horst J P - *Hitler's Airwaves*
  PW - v244 - My 12 '97 - p66 [51-250]
Bergoffen, Debra B - *The Philosophy of Simone De Beauvoir*
  R&R Bk N - v12 - F '97 - p3 [51-250]
Bergonzi, Bernard - *Heroes' Twilight*
  ELT - v40 - 1 '97 - p83+ [501+]
Bergounioux, Pierre - *Le Chevron*
  WLT - v71 - Win '97 - p112+ [251-500]
Bergreen, Laurence - *Capone: The Man and His Era*
  Books - v9 - S '95 - p27 [1-50]
Bergsten, C Fred - *Dilemmas of the Dollar. 2nd Ed.*
  R&R Bk N - v12 - F '97 - p47 [51-250]
  Korea-United States Cooperation in the New World Order
  JEL - v34 - S '96 - p1425+ [501+]
Bergum, Vangie - *A Child on Her Mind*
  BL - v93 - Ja '97 - p785 [51-250]
Berinstain, Valerie - *Great Carpets of the World*
  BL - v93 - D 15 '96 - p704+ [51-250]
Berinstein, Paula - *Finding Images Online*
  IRLA - v32 - N '96 - p11+ [51-250]
  LJ - v121 - N 1 '96 - p104 [51-250]
  SciTech - v21 - Mr '97 - p10 [51-250]
Beriou, Nicole - *Modern Questions about Medieval Sermons*
  CH - v66 - Mr '97 - p101+ [501+]
Berkenkotter, Carol - *Genre Knowledge in Disciplinary Communication*
  Col Comp - v47 - O '96 - p437 [1-50]
  Col Comp - v47 - D '96 - p605+ [501+]
Berkewicz, Ulla - *Angels Are Black and White*
  Choice - v34 - My '97 - p1502 [51-250]
  KR - v64 - N 15 '96 - p1632+ [51-250]

Berkhofer, Robert F, Jr. - *Beyond the Great Story*
  PHR - v65 - Ag '96 - p474+ [501+]
  RM - v50 - D '96 - p387+ [501+]
Berkin, Carol - *First Generations*
  y BL - v93 - S 15 '96 - p185 [51-250]
  LJ - v121 - S 15 '96 - p78 [51-250]
  NYRB - v43 - O 31 '96 - p66+ [501+]
  Wom R Bks - v14 - D '96 - p26+ [501+]
Berkley, George E - *Jews*
  LJ - v122 - Ap 1 '97 - p105 [51-250]
  PW - v244 - Ja 27 '97 - p87 [51-250]
Berkmann, Marcus - *Rain Men*
  NS & S - v9 - Ap 26 '96 - p32 [1-50]
Berkovski, B - *Magnetic Fluids and Applications Handbook*
  SciTech - v20 - N '96 - p19 [51-250]
Berkow, Ira - *To the Hoop*
  KR - v65 - Ap 1 '97 - p512+ [251-500]
  PW - v244 - Mr 24 '97 - p68+ [51-250]
Berkowitz, Allan L - *Embracing the Covenant*
  BL - v92 - Ag '96 - p1859 [51-250]
Berkowitz, Bob - *His Secret Life*
  KR - v65 - Ap 1 '97 - p513 [251-500]
  PW - v244 - Ap 7 '97 - p79 [51-250]
Berkowitz, Gerald - *New Broadways*
  TCI - v30 - O '96 - p55 [51-250]
Berkowitz, Michael - *Zionist Culture and West European Jewry before the First World War*
  Nat - v263 - N 11 '96 - p25+ [501+]
Berkowitz, Peter - *Nietzsche: The Ethics of an Immoralist*
  APSR - v90 - S '96 - p620+ [501+]
  RM - v50 - S '96 - p145+ [501+]
  RP - v58 - Sum '96 - p634+ [501+]
Berkowitz, Samuel - *Cleft Lip and Palate. Vols. 1-2*
  SciTech - v20 - N '96 - p49 [51-250]
Berkson, Carmel - *The Divine and the Demoniac*
  Rel St Rev - v23 - Ja '97 - p95 [51-250]
Berlage, Hendrik Petrus - *Hendrik Petrus Berlage: Thoughts on Style 1886-1909*
  Choice - v34 - O '96 - p264 [51-250]
Berland, Jody - *Theory Rules*
  R&R Bk N - v12 - F '97 - p8 [51-250]
Berleant, Arnold - *The Aesthetics of Environment*
  Rel St Rev - v22 - O '96 - p344 [51-250]
Berlekamp, Elwyn - *Mathematical Go*
  SIAM Rev - v38 - S '96 - p543+ [501+]
Berlet, Chip - *Eyes Right!*
  CS - v26 - Ja '97 - p26+ [501+]
Berleur, Jacques - *Des Roles Et Missions De L'Universite*
  IPQ - v36 - S '96 - p368+ [501+]
Berlin, Elois Ann - *Medical Ethnobiology of the Highland Maya of Chiapas, Mexico*
  Choice - v34 - D '96 - p637 [51-250]
  Nature - v382 - Ag 1 '96 - p413 [1-50]
Berlin, Ira - *Families and Freedom*
  Am Vis - v12 - F '97 - p26+ [51-250]
  KR - v64 - O 15 '96 - p1503 [51-250]
  LJ - v121 - N 1 '96 - p78 [51-250]
  PW - v243 - D 2 '96 - p48+ [51-250]
Berlin, Isaiah - *The Crooked Timber of Humanity*
  MA - v38 - Fall '96 - p392+ [501+]
  The Proper Study of Mankind
  Obs - F 23 '97 - p17* [501+]
Berlin, Isaiah, Sir - *The Proper Study of Mankind*
  Spec - v278 - Mr 8 '97 - p34+ [501+]
Berlin, Isaiah - *The Sense of Reality*
  KR - v65 - Mr 1 '97 - p343+ [51-250]
  LJ - v122 - My 1 '97 - p103 [51-250]
  NS - v125 - D 13 '96 - p48 [501+]
Berlin, Isaiah, Sir - *The Sense of Reality*
  Obs - N 3 '96 - p15* [501+]
Berlin, Isaiah - *The Sense of Reality*
  PW - v244 - F 17 '97 - p200 [51-250]
  Spec - v277 - N 23 '96 - p52 [501+]
  TLS - N 22 '96 - p4+ [501+]
  Wil Q - v21 - Spr '97 - p104 [251-500]
Berliner, David C - *Handbook of Educational Psychology*
  r BL - v93 - F 1 '97 - p965 [51-250]
  r Choice - v34 - F '97 - p944 [51-250]
  r LJ - v121 - D '96 - p112+ [51-250]
  r R&R Bk N - v12 - F '97 - p67 [51-250]
  The Manufactured Crisis
  ES - v27 - Sum '96 - p186+ [501+]
  JNE - v64 - Fall '95 - p481+ [501+]
Berliner, Don - *Aviation: Reaching for the Sky*
  y BL - v93 - My 1 '97 - p1485 [51-250]
Berlinski, David - *The Body Shop*
  Rapport - v19 - 5 '96 - p34 [251-500]

A Tour of the Calculus
  Choice - v34 - S '96 - p165 [51-250]
  Math T - v89 - D '96 - p782+ [251-500]
  NYTBR - v101 - D 8 '96 - p93 [1-50]
  NYTBR - v102 - F 23 '97 - p24 [51-250]
  PW - v244 - Ja 27 '97 - p103 [1-50]
Berlioz, Hector - *Selected Letters of Berlioz*
  PW - v244 - Mr 17 '97 - p72 [51-250]
Berlioz, Jacques - *Identifier Sources Et Citations*
  r Specu - v71 - Jl '96 - p685+ [501+]
The Berlitz Travellers Guide to Canada. 6th Ed.
  r Quill & Q - v63 - F '97 - p40 [51-250]
Berlo, Janet Catherine - *Plains Indian Drawings 1865-1935*
  BL - v93 - D 1 '96 - p637 [51-250]
  Choice - v34 - F '97 - p957 [51-250]
  LJ - v122 - F 15 '97 - p132 [51-250]
Berlow, Alan - *Dead Season*
  BW - v26 - O 6 '96 - p6+ [501+]
  Comw - v124 - D 14 '97 - p19+ [501+]
  FEER - v160 - F 20 '97 - p49 [501+]
  NYTBR - v101 - O 20 '96 - p32 [501+]
Berman, Allen G - *Warman's Coins and Currency. 2nd Ed.*
  Coin W - v38 - Ja 6 '97 - p98 [51-250]
Berman, Daniel M - *Who Owns the Sun?*
  BL - v93 - Ja '97 - p785 [51-250]
  Choice - v34 - My '97 - p1529 [51-250]
  KR - v64 - N 1 '96 - p1572 [251-500]
  LJ - v122 - Ja '97 - p137 [51-250]
  PW - v243 - D 30 '96 - p51 [51-250]
Berman, David - *George Berkeley: Idealism and the Man*
  JR - v77 - Ja '97 - p141+ [501+]
Berman, Eleanor - *The Laboratory Practice of Clinical Toxicology*
  SciTech - v20 - N '96 - p38 [51-250]
Berman, Harold J - *The Nature and Functions of Law. 5th Ed.*
  R&R Bk N - v11 - N '96 - p52 [51-250]
Berman, Jude - *Study Guide to the American Psychiatric Press Textbook of Psychiatry. 2nd Ed.*
  AJPsych - v153 - O '96 - p1357+ [251-500]
Berman, Matt - *What Else Should I Read?. Vol. 2*
  KR - v64 - Ag 15 '96 - p1246 [51-250]
  r SLJ - v43 - Ja '97 - p38 [51-250]
Berman, Paul - *A Tale of Two Utopias*
  Econ - v341 - O 19 '96 - p3*+ [501+]
  KR - v64 - My 1 '96 - p654 [251-500]
  NL - v79 - Ag 12 '96 - p8+ [501+]
  NYRB - v43 - O 17 '96 - p39+ [501+]
  NYTBR - v101 - D 8 '96 - p93 [1-50]
  VQR - v73 - Win '97 - p26* [51-250]
Berman, Peter - *Health Sector Reform in Developing Countries*
  JEL - v34 - D '96 - p2107+ [51-250]
Berman, Phillip L - *The Journey Home*
  BL - v93 - Ja '97 - p781 [51-250]
  LJ - v121 - N 1 '96 - p72 [51-250]
Berman, Ronald - *The Great Gatsby and Modern Times*
  AL - v68 - S '96 - p649+ [251-500]
  ASInt - v34 - O '96 - p110+ [251-500]
Berman, Ruth - *Ants (Illus. by William Munoz)*
  c BL - v92 - Ag '96 - p1902 [51-250]
  c HB Guide - v7 - Fall '96 - p341 [51-250]
  c SB - v32 - O '96 - p210+ [51-250]
  Peacocks (Illus. by Richard R Hewett)
  c Ch BWatch - v6 - My '96 - p3 [1-50]
  c HB Guide - v7 - Fall '96 - p343 [1-50]
Berman, Samuel A - *Midrass Tanhuma-Yelammedenu*
  Rel St Rev - v23 - Ap '97 - p196 [51-250]
Berman, Tzeporah - *Clayoquot and Dissent*
  Dal R - v75 - Spr '95 - p104+ [501+]
Bermingham, Ann - *The Consumption of Culture 1600-1800*
  Choice - v34 - Ja '97 - p781 [51-250]
  LR - v45 - 4 '96 - p60+ [251-500]
  R&R Bk N - v11 - D '96 - p38 [51-250]
Bernadac, Marie-Laure - *Femininmasculin*
  Art J - v55 - Win '96 - p88+ [51-250]
  Louise Bourgeois
  Choice - v34 - S '96 - p111 [51-250]
Bernal, Martin - *Black Athena*
  JHI - v57 - O '96 - p705+ [501+]
Bernanos, Georges - *Essais Et Ecrits De Combat*
  TLS - O 4 '96 - p8 [501+]
Bernard, Bruce D - *Selecting the Right Form of Business*
  R&R Bk N - v12 - F '97 - p65 [51-250]
Bernard, Charlotte - *Caesar and Rome*
  y HB Guide - v8 - Spr '97 - p165 [51-250]
  y SLJ - v42 - D '96 - p140+ [51-250]

Bernard, Robert W - *Surgical Restoration of the Aging Face*
    SciTech - v20 - N '96 - p49 [51-250]
Bernard, Robin - *Juma and the Honey Guide (Illus. by Nneka Bennett)*
    c   BL - v92 - Ag '96 - p1906 [51-250]
    c   CBRS - v24 - Ag '96 - p157 [1-50]
    c   HB Guide - v8 - Spr '97 - p19 [51-250]
    c   SLJ - v42 - Ag '96 - p121 [51-250]
Bernard, Ryan - *Corporate Intranet*
    CBR - v14 - S '96 - p28 [1-50]
  Weaving the Corporate Web
    Quill & Q - v62 - My '96 - p22+ [501+]
Bernard-Donals, Michael F - *Mikhail Bakhtin: Between Phenomenology and Marxism*
    Slav R - v55 - Sum '96 - p513+ [501+]
Bernardi, Daniel - *The Birth of Whiteness*
    Choice - v34 - F '97 - p972 [51-250]
Bernardin, Claude - *Rocket Man*
    r   LJ - v121 - N 1 '96 - p58 [51-250]
Bernardin, Joseph Louis - *A Blessing to Each Other*
    PW - v244 - F 10 '97 - p81 [51-250]
  The Gift of Peace
    Am - v176 - Mr 22 '97 - p28 [51-250]
    LJ - v122 - My 1 '97 - p109 [51-250]
    PW - v244 - Ja 27 '97 - p97 [51-250]
  Growing in Wisdom, Age and Grace
    CLW - v67 - Mr '97 - p36 [51-250]
Bernardini, Robert - *Christmas All Over (Illus. by Ruth Hunter McAnespy)*
    c   HB Guide - v8 - Spr '97 - p19 [51-250]
    c   PW - v243 - S 30 '96 - p91 [51-250]
Bernardo, Anilu - *Fitting In*
    y   BL - v93 - D 15 '96 - p721 [51-250]
    c   CBRS - v25 - Ja '97 - p54 [51-250]
    y   HB Guide - v8 - Spr '97 - p77 [51-250]
    y   PW - v243 - S 16 '96 - p84 [51-250]
    y   SLJ - v42 - N '96 - p120 [51-250]
  Jumping Off to Freedom
    y   HB Guide - v7 - Fall '96 - p300 [51-250]
    y   JAAL - v40 - S '96 - p71 [51-250]
Bernardo, Jose M - *Bayesian Theory*
    SIAM Rev - v39 - Mr '97 - p142+ [501+]
Bernardo, Jose Raul - *The Secret of the Bulls*
    PW - v244 - Ja 13 '97 - p73 [1-50]
    Trib Bks - Mr 16 '97 - p8 [1-50]
Bernd, Clifford Albrecht - *Poetic Realism in Scandinavia and Central Europe 1820-1895*
    MLR - v92 - Ap '97 - p540+ [501+]
    RMR - v50 - 2 '96 - p181+ [501+]
Berne, Suzanne - *A Crime in the Neighborhood*
    KR - v65 - Mr 15 '97 - p397 [251-500]
    LJ - v122 - Ap 1 '97 - p120 [51-250]
    PW - v244 - Mr 31 '97 - p59 [51-250]
Berner, A - *The Best of OPL II*
    Emerg Lib - v24 - S '96 - p42 [1-50]
Bernhard, Emery - *Happy New Year! (Illus. by Durga Bernhard)*
    c   BL - v93 - S 1 '96 - p134 [51-250]
    c   CCB-B - v50 - O '96 - p48+ [51-250]
    c   HB Guide - v8 - Spr '97 - p98 [51-250]
    c   PW - v243 - S 9 '96 - p85 [51-250]
    c   SLJ - v42 - S '96 - p195 [51-250]
  A Ride on Mother's Back (Illus. by Durga Bernhard)
    c   CBRS - v25 - Ja '97 - p49 [51-250]
    c   Emerg Lib - v24 - Mr '97 - p47 [51-250]
    c   HB Guide - v8 - Spr '97 - p98 [51-250]
    c   SLJ - v42 - O '96 - p111 [51-250]
  The Way of the Willow Branch (Illus. by Durga Bernhard)
    c   HB Guide - v7 - Fall '96 - p248 [51-250]
Bernhard, Michael - *From the Polish Underground*
    CS - v26 - Ja '97 - p41+ [501+]
Bernhard, Thomas - *The Loser*
    BWatch - v17 - D '96 - p6 [51-250]
Bernhardsen, Tor - *Geographic Information Systems*
    GJ - v163 - Mr '97 - p104 [251-500]
Bernhardson, Wayne - *Argentina, Uruguay and Paraguay. 2nd Ed.*
    r   BL - v93 - S 15 '96 - p210 [1-50]
Bernhardt, William - *Naked Justice*
    y   BL - v93 - Ja '97 - p778 [51-250]
    KR - v64 - D 1 '96 - p1686 [251-500]
    LJ - v122 - Ja '97 - p142 [51-250]
    PW - v243 - N 18 '96 - p60+ [51-250]
Bernheimer, Charles - *Comparative Literature in the Age of Multiculturalism*
    Col Lit - v23 - O '96 - p190+ [501+]
    Comp L - v49 - Win '97 - p76+ [501+]

Bernikow, Louise - *The American Woman's Almanac*
    r   PW - v244 - F 17 '97 - p207 [51-250]
    r   Trib Bks - Mr 30 '97 - p2 [1-50]
  The American Women's Almanac
    r   PW - v244 - F 17 '97 - p207 [51-250]
Bernlef, J - *Cellojaren*
    WLT - v70 - Aut '96 - p971+ [501+]
Bernotas, Bob - *Spike Lee: Filmmaker*
    y   BL - v93 - D 15 '96 - p716 [1-50]
Bernoulli, Daniel - *Die Werke Von Daniel Bernoulli. Vol. 7*
    Isis - v87 - S '96 - p550+ [501+]
Bernoulli: Official Journal of the Bernoulli Society for Mathematical Statistics and Probability
    p   Nature - v383 - S 5 '96 - p40 [51-250]
Bernstein, Andrew D - *NBA Hoop Shots*
    Pet PM - v25 - N '96 - p12 [51-250]
Bernstein, Basil B - *Pedagogy, Symbolic Control, and Identity*
    R&R Bk N - v11 - N '96 - p56 [51-250]
Bernstein, Bruce - *Modern by Tradition*
    Nat Peop - v9 - Sum '96 - p81+ [501+]
Bernstein, Carl - *His Holiness*
    Am - v175 - N 23 '96 - p24+ [501+]
    BL - v93 - O 1 '96 - p292 [1-50]
    BW - v26 - S 22 '96 - p1+ [501+]
    Comw - v124 - Ja 17 '97 - p16+ [501+]
    CSM - v89 - N 25 '96 - p12 [51-250]
    CSM - v89 - Ja 23 '97 - p12 [51-250]
    Econ - v341 - N 16 '96 - p5* [251-500]
    LATBR - O 13 '96 - p1+ [501+]
    New R - v216 - Ja 6 '97 - p40+ [501+]
    NS - v125 - O 18 '96 - p46+ [501+]
    NY - v72 - D 2 '96 - p107+ [501+]
    NYRB - v43 - O 31 '96 - p8+ [501+]
    NYTBR - v101 - S 29 '96 - p10 [501+]
    PW - v243 - N 4 '96 - p42 [51-250]
    TLS - D 27 '96 - p3+ [501+]
    Trib Bks - Ja 19 '97 - p11 [501+]
  His Holiness (Hockenberry). Audio Version
    y   Kliatt - v31 - My '97 - p47 [51-250]
    PW - v243 - N 4 '96 - p32 [51-250]
Bernstein, Irving - *Guns or Butter*
    APH - v43 - Win '96 - p64 [251-500]
    J Am St - v30 - D '96 - p477+ [251-500]
Bernstein, Jeremy - *Albert Einstein and the Frontiers of Physics*
    y   BL - v93 - S 1 '96 - p71 [51-250]
    c   SLJ - v42 - D '96 - p142 [51-250]
    y   VOYA - v19 - O '96 - p226 [251-500]
  Hitler's Uranium Club
    Choice - v34 - S '96 - p149 [51-250]
    Isis - v87 - S '96 - p569+ [501+]
  A Theory for Everything
    Choice - v34 - Mr '97 - p1198 [51-250]
    LJ - v121 - O 1 '96 - p118 [51-250]
    Nature - v384 - D 5 '96 - p425 [501+]
    New Sci - v152 - D 21 '96 - p66+ [501+]
Bernstein, Jon - *Pretty in Pink*
    y   BL - v93 - F 15 '97 - p990 [51-250]
    y   LJ - v122 - F 1 '97 - p79 [51-250]
Bernstein, Judith - *When the Bough Breaks*
    BL - v93 - My 15 '97 - p1544 [51-250]
Bernstein, Laurie - *Sonia's Daughters*
    Slav R - v55 - Fall '96 - p685+ [501+]
Bernstein, Matthew - *Visions of the East*
    LJ - v122 - F 1 '97 - p81 [51-250]
  Walter Wanger, Hollywood Independent
    FQ - v49 - Sum '96 - p61+ [501+]
Bernstein, Michael Andre - *Foregone Conclusions*
    MP - v94 - N '96 - p276+ [501+]
Bernstein, Peter L - *Against the Gods*
    Barron's - v76 - O 28 '96 - p62 [501+]
    BL - v93 - S 15 '96 - p185 [51-250]
    Bus W - O 21 '96 - p20 [501+]
    Bus W - D 16 '96 - p104 [51-250]
    CSM - v89 - Mr 4 '97 - p12 [501+]
    Econ - v341 - N 16 '96 - p13* [501+]
    KR - v64 - S 1 '96 - p1286 [251-500]
    LJ - v121 - N 1 '96 - p103 [51-250]
    Nature - v385 - Ja 9 '97 - p129+ [501+]
    New Sci - v152 - O 19 '96 - p46+ [501+]
    NS - v125 - D 20 '96 - p117 [51-250]
    NYTBR - v102 - F 16 '97 - p19 [51-250]
    Obs - N 3 '96 - p17* [501+]
    PW - v243 - S 9 '96 - p72 [51-250]
    TLS - F 21 '97 - p4+ [501+]
    WSJ-MW - v78 - O 21 '96 - pA20 [501+]

Bernstein, Richard - *The Coming Conflict with China*
    BL - v93 - F 15 '97 - p977+ [51-250]
    Bus W - Mr 24 '97 - p18 [501+]
    CSM - v89 - Mr 19 '97 - p14 [501+]
    Econ - v342 - Mr 15 '97 - p8* [51-250]
    For Aff - v76 - My '97 - p144 [51-250]
    LATBR - F 23 '97 - p6 [501+]
    LJ - v122 - F 15 '97 - p148 [51-250]
    NYTBR - v102 - Mr 16 '97 - p13 [501+]
    NYTLa - v146 - Mr 10 '97 - pC16 [501+]
    PW - v244 - Ja 20 '97 - p389 [251-500]
    WSJ-Cent - v99 - Mr 5 '97 - p4 [501+]
Bernstein, Richard J - *Hannah Arendt and the Jewish Question*
    Choice - v34 - Ap '97 - p1392 [51-250]
Bernstein, Richard K - *Dr. Bernstein's Diabetes Solution*
    BL - v93 - My 1 '97 - p1470 [51-250]
    LJ - v122 - My 1 '97 - p133 [51-250]
Bernstein, Robin - *Generation Q*
    Advocate - S 17 '96 - p82+ [251-500]
Bernstein, Terry - *Internet Security for Business*
    CBR - v14 - S '96 - p29 [1-50]
    R&R Bk N - v11 - N '96 - p29 [51-250]
Bernstein, Walter - *Inside Out*
    HMR - Win '96 - p17 [501+]
    LATBR - N 3 '96 - p1+ [501+]
    LJ - v121 - S 15 '96 - p75 [51-250]
    Nat - v263 - N 25 '96 - p28+ [501+]
    NYTBR - v101 - N 24 '96 - p22 [501+]
    NYTLa - v146 - N 22 '96 - pC30 [501+]
    PW - v243 - S 2 '96 - p100 [51-250]
    Rapport - v19 - 6 '96 - p27 [251-500]
    Trib Bks - Ja 26 '97 - p4 [501+]
    VV - v41 - D 10 '96 - p59+ [501+]
Berofsky, Bernard - *Liberation from Self*
    Choice - v34 - O '96 - p293 [501+]
    J Phil - v94 - Ap '97 - p212+ [501+]
Berolah, Lorraine - *Betty and Bala and the Proper Big Pumpkin (Illus. by Noel Cristaudo)*
    c   Aust Bk R - F '97 - p54+ [501+]
Berquist, Jon L - *Judaism in Persia's Shadow*
    BTB - v27 - Spr '97 - p28 [501+]
    Choice - v34 - N '96 - p474 [51-250]
    Rel St Rev - v23 - Ap '97 - p194+ [51-250]
Berrada, Mohamed - *The Game of Forgetting*
    MEJ - v51 - Win '97 - p152+ [51-250]
Berressem, Hanjo - *Pynchon's Poetics*
    Poetics T - v18 - Spr '97 - p95+ [501+]
Berriault, Gina - *Women in Their Beds*
    LATBR - My 26 '96 - p7 [501+]
    PW - v244 - Ap 14 '97 - p72 [1-50]
Berrick, Jill Duerr - *Faces of Poverty*
    NWSA Jnl - v8 - Fall '96 - p129+ [501+]
Berridge, Elizabeth - *Touch and Go (Phillips). Audio Version*
    y   Kliatt - v31 - Mr '97 - p47 [51-250]
Berridge, Virginia - *AIDS in the UK*
    New Sci - v152 - D 7 '96 - p50 [1-50]
Berrigan, Dan - *Isaiah: Spirit of Courage, Gift of Tears*
    OS - v32 - N '96 - p33 [51-250]
Berrigan, Philip - *Fighting the Lamb's War*
    BL - v93 - D 1 '96 - p624 [51-250]
    NYTBR - v102 - F 9 '97 - p16 [501+]
Berrigan, Ted - *On the Level Everyday*
    PW - v244 - Ap 28 '97 - p72+ [51-250]
Berrios, German E - *The History of Mental Symptoms*
    Choice - v34 - N '96 - p540 [51-250]
Berry, Adrian - *The Next 500 Years*
    Analog - v117 - Ja '97 - p141+ [251-500]
    Choice - v34 - N '96 - p478 [51-250]
    TES - Ag 2 '96 - p15 [51-250]
Berry, Dawn Bradley - *The 50 Most Influential Women in American Law*
    LJ - v122 - Ja '97 - p122 [51-250]
Berry, Donald A - *Bayesian Analysis in Statistics and Econometrics*
    SIAM Rev - v38 - S '96 - p544 [1-50]
Berry, Ellen - *Gifts That Save the Animals*
    r   E Mag - v8 - Ja '97 - p49 [51-250]
Berry, Elliot - *Topspin: Ups and Downs in Big-Time Tennis*
    NYTBR - v101 - Jl 21 '96 - p18 [51-250]
Berry, Holly - *Busy Lizzie*
    c   PW - v243 - O 14 '96 - p85 [1-50]
Berry, Ian - *Living Apart*
    B Ent - v27 - F '97 - p215 [1-50]
Berry, James - *Don't Leave an Elephant to Go and Chase a Bird (Illus. by Ann Grifalconi)*
    c   HB Guide - v7 - Fall '96 - p319 [51-250]

Everywhere Faces Everywhere (Illus. by Reynold Ruffins)
  y BL - v93 - My 1 '97 - p1496 [51-250]
  y CCB-B - v50 - Ap '97 - p273+ [51-250]
  y KR - v65 - Mr 15 '97 - p458 [51-250]
Hot Earth Cold Earth
    WLT - v70 - Aut '96 - p1015+ [501+]
Rough Sketch Beginning (Illus. by Robert Florczak)
  c HB Guide - v7 - Fall '96 - p366 [51-250]
  c RT - v50 - My '97 - p684 [51-250]
We Couldn't Provide Fish Thumbs (Illus. by Colin McNaughton)
  c TES - F 14 '97 - p7* [501+]
Berry, Liz - *The China Garden*
  y BL - v93 - Ap 1 '97 - p1288+ [1-50]
  y HB Guide - v7 - Fall '96 - p300 [51-250]
Berry, Margaret - *Meaning and Form*
    R&R Bk N - v11 - N '96 - p63 [51-250]
Berry, Mary - *Mary Berry's Complete Cookbook*
    Books - v9 - S '95 - p22 [1-50]
Berry, Mary Clay - *Voices from the Century Before*
    BW - v26 - N 24 '96 - p3 [501+]
    KR - v64 - S 15 '96 - p1365 [251-500]
    LJ - v121 - O 15 '96 - p70 [51-250]
    PW - v243 - O 7 '96 - p58 [51-250]
Berry, Mary Elizabeth - *The Culture of Civil War in Kyoto*
    JIH - v27 - Aut '96 - p381+ [501+]
Berry, Paul - *The Christian Inscription at Pompeii*
    Rel St Rev - v23 - Ja '97 - p68 [51-250]
Vera Brittain: A Life
    Albion - v28 - '96 - p723+ [501+]
    CR - v269 - N '96 - p277 [1-50]
Berry, R J - *God and the Biologist*
    New Sci - v153 - F 22 '97 - p44 [51-250]
Berry, Susan - *Decorating Entrances, Stairways and Landings*
    BL - v92 - Ag '96 - p1873 [51-250]
Guia Completa De Jardineria En Macetas
    LJ - v122 - Ja '97 - p78 [51-250]
Berry, Venise T - *Mediated Messages and African-American Culture*
    BWatch - v17 - D '96 - p5 [51-250]
    JMCQ - v73 - Win '96 - p1013+ [501+]
So Good
    Bloom Rev - v17 - Ja '97 - p19 [1-50]
    BW - v26 - N 3 '96 - p8 [251-500]
Berry, Vern - *Roots and Recipes*
    EGH - v50 - N '96 - p154 [51-250]
Berry, Wendell - *Another Turn of the Crank*
    Bks & Cult - v1 - N '95 - p30 [51-250]
    HR - v49 - Sum '96 - p323+ [501+]
    PW - v243 - S 9 '96 - p81 [1-50]
    Sew R - v104 - O '96 - p701+ [501+]
A World Lost
    Atl - v278 - N '96 - p122 [51-250]
    BL - v93 - Ja '97 - p760 [1-50]
    BL - v93 - S 15 '96 - p219 [51-250]
    KR - v64 - Ag 15 '96 - p1168+ [251-500]
    LJ - v121 - O 15 '96 - p89 [51-250]
    LJ - v122 - F 1 '97 - p136 [51-250]
    NYTBR - v101 - N 3 '96 - p19 [51-250]
    OS - v32 - N '96 - p33 [51-250]
    PW - v243 - S 2 '96 - p112 [51-250]
    W&I - v12 - F '97 - p233+ [501+]
    W&I - v12 - F '97 - p243+ [501+]
Berry, William A - *Justice for Sale*
    Rapport - v19 - 6 '96 - p28 [251-500]
Berryman, Phillip - *Religion in the Megacity*
    BL - v93 - D 15 '96 - p694 [51-250]
Stubborn Hope
    Workbook - v21 - Fall '96 - p137+ [501+]
Berryman-Fink, Cynthia - *The Manager's Desk Reference. 2nd Ed.*
  r ARBA - v28 - '97 - p123 [251-500]
  r Bus Bk R - v14 - 1 '97 - p123+ [51-250]
Bersani, Leo - *Arts of Impoverishment*
    CLS - v33 - 4 '96 - p422+ [251-500]
Homos
    Lon R Bks - v18 - My 23 '96 - p24+ [501+]
    Obs - D 1 '96 - p16* [1-50]
Berseneva, Anna - *Smiatenie Chuvstv*
    BL - v93 - O 1 '96 - p327 [1-50]
Berson, Alex - *Client/Server Architecture. 2nd Ed.*
    SciTech - v20 - S '96 - p7 [51-250]
Berson, Jon - *Foamers*
    PW - v244 - My 5 '97 - p202 [51-250]
Berson, Ruth - *The New Painting. Vols. 1-2*
    Choice - v34 - F '97 - p957 [51-250]
    LJ - v122 - Ja '97 - p94 [51-250]

Berst, Charles A - *Pygmalion: Shaw's Spin on Myth and Cinderella*
    ELT - v39 - 3 '96 - p379+ [501+]
Bersuker, Isaac B - *Electronic Structure and Properties of Transition Metal Compounds*
    Choice - v34 - S '96 - p156 [51-250]
Bertagna, Julie - *The Spark Gap*
  c Bks Keeps - Mr '97 - p26 [51-250]
Bertaud, Madeleine - *Le Genre Des Memoires, Essai De Definition*
    FR - v70 - D '96 - p321+ [501+]
Bertematti, Richard - *Project Death*
    LJ - v122 - My 1 '97 - p143 [51-250]
    PW - v244 - Mr 31 '97 - p66 [51-250]
Berthelemy, Jean-Claude - *Growth and Crisis in Cote D'Ivoire*
    JEL - v34 - D '96 - p2119 [51-250]
Berthold, P - *Control of Bird Migration*
    Choice - v34 - S '96 - p155 [51-250]
Berthold-Bond, Annie - *The Green Kitchen Handbook*
    BL - v93 - Mr 15 '97 - p1213 [51-250]
Berthoud, Joy - *Pecking Order*
    Econ - v341 - D 7 '96 - p4*+ [501+]
    NS - v126 - Ja 10 '97 - p48 [501+]
Berthrong, John H - *All under Heaven*
    Theol St - v57 - Mr '96 - p164+ [501+]
Bertin, G - *Spiral Structure in Galaxies*
    Choice - v34 - Ja '97 - p816 [51-250]
    SB - v32 - N '96 - p230 [51-250]
Bertini, Jo - *A Man and His Camel*
  c Magpies - v11 - My '96 - p40 [51-250]
Bertino, Joseph R - *Encyclopedia of Cancer. Vols. 1-3*
  r BL - v93 - Ja '97 - p892 [251-500]
  r BL - v93 - F 1 '97 - p958 [51-250]
  r LJ - v122 - Ja '97 - p56 [1-50]
  r LJ - v122 - Ap 15 '97 - p38 [51-250]
Bertius, P - *Nomenclator: The First Printed Catalogue of Leyden University Library 1595*
    LR - v45 - 7 '96 - p56+ [501+]
Bertocchi, Marida - *Modelling Techniques for Financial Markets and Bank Management*
    JEL - v35 - Mr '97 - p221 [51-250]
Bertoin, Jean - *Levy Processes*
    SciTech - v20 - D '96 - p16 [51-250]
Bertolucci, Attilio - *Selected Poems*
    TranslRevS - v1 - My '95 - p24 [51-250]
Berton, Pierre - *Attack on Montreal (Illus. by Paul McCusker)*
  y Can CL - v22 - Fall '96 - p101+ [501+]
The Battle of Lake Erie (Illus. by Paul McCusker)
  y Can CL - v22 - Fall '96 - p101+ [501+]
Before the Gold Rush (Illus. by Paul McCusker)
  y Can CL - v22 - Fall '96 - p101+ [501+]
The Death of Tecumseh (Illus. by Paul McCusker)
  y Can CL - v22 - Fall '96 - p101+ [501+]
Farewell to the Twentieth Century
    Quill & Q - v62 - Jl '96 - p50 [251-500]
The Great Lakes
    Beav - v76 - O '96 - p46 [51-250]
    Beav - v76 - D '96 - p41 [51-250]
    LJ - v121 - S 15 '96 - p85 [51-250]
    Mac - v109 - D 9 '96 - p66 [1-50]
    Quill & Q - v63 - Ja '97 - p31 [51-250]
Kings of the Klondike (Illus. by Paul McCusker)
  y Can CL - v22 - Fall '96 - p101+ [501+]
The Men in Sheepskin Coats (Illus. by Paul McCusker)
  y Can CL - v22 - Fall '96 - p101+ [501+]
Niagara: A History of the Falls
    LJ - v122 - F 1 '97 - p93+ [51-250]
    NYTBR - v102 - F 16 '97 - p8+ [501+]
    PW - v243 - D 2 '96 - p46 [51-250]
The Railway Pathfinders (Illus. by Paul McCusker)
  y Can CL - v22 - Fall '96 - p101+ [501+]
Steel across the Shield (Illus. by Paul McCusker)
  y Can CL - v22 - Fall '96 - p101+ [501+]
Bertoni, Franco - *Robert Wilson*
    TCI - v30 - O '96 - p59 [1-50]
Bertorelli, Victoria - *Air Quality A to Z*
  r J Gov Info - v23 - S '96 - p643 [1-50]
Bertram, Anne - *NTC's Dictionary of Folksy, Regional, and Rural Sayings*
  r ARBA - v28 - '97 - p385 [251-500]
Bertram, Eva - *Drug War Politics*
    Choice - v34 - Ja '97 - p874 [51-250]
    Utne R - Jl '96 - p109 [51-250]
Bertram, Jerome - *Monumental Brasses as Art and History*
    CR - v269 - D '96 - p335 [51-250]
Bertrand, Diane Gonzales - *Alicia's Treasure*
  c HB Guide - v7 - Fall '96 - p289 [51-250]

Sip, Slurp, Soup, Soup (Illus. by Alex Pardo DeLange)
  c PW - v244 - My 12 '97 - p75 [51-250]
Bertrand, Guy - *Enough Is Enough*
    Quill & Q - v63 - Ja '97 - p30 [51-250]
Bertrand, Lynne - *Dragon Naps (Illus. by Janet Street)*
  c HB Guide - v7 - Fall '96 - p248 [51-250]
Bertrand, Yves - *Contemporary Theories and Practice in Education*
    Choice - v34 - Ja '97 - p848 [51-250]
Bertschik, Julia - *Maulwurfsarchaologie: Zum Verhaltnis Von Geschichte Und Anthropologie In Wilhelm Raabes Historischen Erzahltexten*
    Ger Q - v70 - Win '97 - p81+ [501+]
Bertuca, David J - *The World's Columbian Exposition*
  r ARBA - v28 - '97 - p187 [51-250]
  r Choice - v34 - N '96 - p425 [51-250]
  r R&R Bk N - v11 - N '96 - p19 [51-250]
Berube, Michael - *Higher Education under Fire*
    J Hi E - v68 - Ja '97 - p106+ [501+]
Life as We Know It
    LATBR - O 27 '96 - p10 [51-250]
    Nat - v263 - O 28 '96 - p30+ [501+]
    NYTBR - v101 - O 27 '96 - p22+ [501+]
    NYTBR - v101 - D 8 '96 - p88 [1-50]
Berumen, Frank Javier Garcia - *The Chicano/Hispanic Image in American Film*
    HER - v66 - Fall '96 - p681+ [501+]
Berven, Dikka - *Montaigne: A Collection of Essays. Vols. 1-5*
    Six Ct J - v27 - Fall '96 - p850+ [501+]
Berwald, Olaf - *Philipp Melanchthons Sicht Der Rhetorik*
    Ren Q - v49 - Win '96 - p840+ [501+]
Berz, Martin - *Computational Differentiation*
    SciTech - v21 - Mr '97 - p15 [51-250]
Berzon, Betty - *The Intimacy Dance*
    LJ - v121 - O 1 '96 - p107 [51-250]
    PW - v243 - Jl 22 '96 - p220 [51-250]
Besanko, David - *The Economics of Strategy*
    JEL - v34 - S '96 - p1451 [51-250]
Besharov, Douglas J - *Enhancing Early Childhood Programs*
    ChrPhil - v8 - S 5 '96 - p46 [51-250]
    Soc Ser R - v71 - Mr '97 - p166 [51-250]
Besinger, Curtis - *Working with Mr. Wright*
    ASInt - v34 - O '96 - p91+ [501+]
Beskrovny, L G - *The Russian Army and Fleet in the Nineteenth Century*
    Choice - v34 - F '97 - p1020 [51-250]
    R&R Bk N - v11 - D '96 - p9 [1-50]
Besner, Hilda F - *Gay and Lesbian Students*
    Choice - v34 - D '96 - p660 [51-250]
Besnier, Niko - *Literacy, Emotion, and Authority*
    Pac A - v69 - Fall '96 - p457+ [501+]
Bessel, Richard - *Germany after the First World War*
    JMH - v68 - S '96 - p629+ [501+]
Besser, Gretchen Rous - *Germaine De Stael Revisited*
    FR - v70 - O '96 - p116 [501+]
Besser, Terry L - *Team Toyota*
    R&R Bk N - v12 - F '97 - p41 [51-250]
Besserman, Lawrence - *The Challenge of Periodization*
    R&R Bk N - v11 - D '96 - p63 [51-250]
Bessette, Alan E - *Mushrooms of North America in Color*
    ARBA - v28 - '97 - p581+ [51-250]
Bessie Smith Songbook
    CAY - v16 - Fall '95 - p9 [51-250]
Best, Anthony - *Britain, Japan, and Pearl Harbor*
    J Mil H - v61 - Ja '97 - p191+ [251-500]
Best, Cari - *Getting Used to Harry (Illus. by Diane Palmisciano)*
  c BL - v93 - N 1 '96 - p506 [51-250]
  c CCB-B - v50 - O '96 - p49 [51-250]
  c HB Guide - v8 - Spr '97 - p20 [51-250]
  c PW - v243 - S 2 '96 - p130 [51-250]
  c SLJ - v42 - O '96 - p84 [51-250]
Top Banana (Illus. by Erika Oller)
  c CBRS - v25 - Mr '97 - p85 [51-250]
  c KR - v65 - F 15 '97 - p296 [51-250]
  c PW - v244 - Mr 10 '97 - p66 [51-250]
Best, Judith - *The Choice of the People?*
    Pres SQ - v27 - Win '97 - p176 [51-250]
Best, Steven - *The Politics of Historical Vision*
    APSR - v90 - S '96 - p621+ [501+]
Best, Thomas F - *So We Believe, So We Pray*
    Rel St Rev - v23 - Ja '97 - p45 [51-250]
The Best American Erotica 1996
    VV - v41 - S 24 '96 - p43 [251-500]

The Best American Essays 1996
CSM - v89 - D 30 '96 - p13 [501+]
y Kliatt - v31 - My '97 - p20 [51-250]
KR - v64 - S 15 '96 - p1389 [251-500]
LJ - v121 - N 15 '96 - p61+ [51-250]
PW - v243 - S 30 '96 - p77 [51-250]
Trib Bks - Ja 5 '97 - p2 [51-250]
Best American Gay Fiction 1996
Advocate - S 17 '96 - p60 [1-50]
The Best American Poetry 1996
BL - v93 - S 1 '96 - p57 [51-250]
LJ - v121 - O 1 '96 - p82 [51-250]
Trib Bks - Ja 5 '97 - p2 [51-250]
VV - v41 - O 8 '96 - p49 [501+]
The Best American Short Plays 1995-1996
BL - v93 - Mr 1 '97 - p1104 [51-250]
The Best American Short Stories 1996
BL - v93 - N 15 '96 - p569 [51-250]
CSM - v89 - D 30 '96 - p13 [501+]
KR - v64 - O 1 '96 - p1425+ [251-500]
LJ - v121 - O 1 '96 - p129 [51-250]
PW - v243 - S 23 '96 - p71 [51-250]
Trib Bks - Ja 5 '97 - p2 [51-250]
The Best American Sports Writing 1996
y BL - v93 - O 1 '96 - p316+ [51-250]
Econ - v342 - F 15 '97 - p15* [501+]
y Kliatt - v31 - Mr '97 - p36 [51-250]
KR - v64 - S 15 '96 - p1370+ [251-500]
PW - v243 - O 14 '96 - p78 [51-250]
Best Bread Machine Recipes
BL - v93 - F 15 '97 - p987 [51-250]
Best Canadian Stories 96
Quill & Q - v63 - Ja '97 - p34 [501+]
Best Gay Erotica 1996
Quill & Q - v62 - Jl '96 - p42 [501+]
Best Gay Erotica 1997
PW - v244 - F 24 '97 - p65+ [51-250]
Best Lesbian Erotica 1996
Quill & Q - v62 - Jl '96 - p42 [501+]
Best Lesbian Erotica 1997
PW - v244 - F 24 '97 - p66 [51-250]
Best-Loved Recipes: Celebrating 75 Years of Great
Baking
BWatch - v18 - Mr '97 - p5+ [51-250]
The Best New Horror 6
Necro - Sum '96 - p15+ [501+]
The Best New Horror 7
KR - v64 - N 1 '96 - p1555 [251-500]
The Best New Science Fiction 1996
New Sci - v153 - Ja 4 '97 - p40 [51-250]
The Best of Sports Illustrated
CSM - v89 - D 5 '96 - pB4 [51-250]
Best of the Best 1995
Dog Fan - v28 - Ja '97 - p38 [51-250]
Best of Young American Novelists
TES - S 6 '96 - p8* [51-250]
The Best Plays of 1995-1996
TCI - v30 - O '96 - p58 [51-250]
Best Practices Report
Per Psy - v50 - Spr '97 - p227+ [501+]
The Best Resources for College Choice and Admissions
yr BL - v93 - Ja '97 - p896 [51-250]
The Best Treasury of Stories for Children (Illus. by A
Lewis)
c JB - v60 - D '96 - p246 [251-500]
c Sch Lib - v45 - F '97 - p17 [51-250]
Besteman, Catherine - *The Struggle for Land in Southern
Somalia*
R&R Bk N - v11 - N '96 - p31 [51-250]
Bester, Alfred - *The Demolished Man*
BW - v26 - Ag 4 '96 - p12 [51-250]
The Stars My Destination
BW - v26 - Ag 4 '96 - p12 [51-250]
Besterman, Theodore - *A World Bibliography of
Bibliographies and of Bibliographical Catalogues,
Calenders, Abstracts, Digests, Indexes, and the Like. 4th
Ed., Rev. and Greatly Enl. Throughout, Vols. 1-5*
r ASInt - v34 - O '96 - p20 [1-50]
Bestul, Thomas H - *Texts of the Passion*
Choice - v34 - My '97 - p1490 [51-250]
Betances, Emelio - *State and Society in the Dominican
Republic*
CS - v26 - Ja '97 - p55+ [501+]
HAHR - v77 - F '97 - p143+ [501+]
Betancourt, Philip P - *The Minoan Buildings on the West
Side of Area A*
AJA - v101 - Ja '97 - p173+ [501+]
Bethell, Leslie - *The Cambridge History of Latin America.
Vol. 6, Pt. 1*
r JEH - v56 - S '96 - p725+ [501+]

*The Cambridge History of Latin America. Vol. 6, Pts.
1-2*
CH - v66 - Mr '97 - p174+ [501+]
HAHR - v77 - F '97 - p77+ [501+]
The Cambridge History of Latin America. Vol. 11
r HAHR - v76 - Ag '96 - p537+ [251-500]
Bethlen, Julianna - *Dracula Junior and the Fake Fangs
(Illus. by Korky Paul)*
c BL - v93 - D 15 '96 - p732 [1-50]
c LATBR - O 20 '96 - p8 [51-250]
c PW - v243 - S 30 '96 - p85 [51-250]
The Ghost Pirate (Illus. by Brian Lee)
c BL - v93 - D 15 '96 - p732 [1-50]
c PW - v243 - S 23 '96 - p78 [51-250]
c SLJ - v42 - S '96 - p170 [51-250]
Bethune, James D - *Introduction to Electrical-Mechanical
Drafting with CAD*
SciTech - v20 - D '96 - p59 [51-250]
Betjeman, John, Sir - *John Betjeman: Letters. Vol. 2*
Obs - D 1 '96 - p18* [51-250]
John Betjeman: Letters. Vols. 1-2
Sew R - v104 - O '96 - p687+ [501+]
Betser, Muki - *Secret Soldier*
KR - v64 - My 1 '96 - p655 [251-500]
Betsky, Aaron - *Queer Space*
PW - v244 - Mr 10 '97 - p61 [51-250]
Better Buys for Business. Vols. 1-10
r ARBA - v28 - '97 - p93 [251-500]
Better Ceramics through Chemistry VII
SciTech - v21 - Mr '97 - p78 [51-250]
Better Homes and Gardens Eat and Stay Slim
PW - v243 - D 16 '96 - p56 [51-250]
Bettmann, Otto L - *Johann Sebastian Bach as His World
Knew Him*
Notes - v53 - D '96 - p456+ [501+]
Betts, Christopher - *Montesquieu: Lettres Persanes*
MLR - v91 - O '96 - p992 [51-250]
Betts, Doris - *The River to Pickle Beach*
NYTBR - v101 - N 24 '96 - p32 [51-250]
The Sharp Teeth of Love
y BL - v93 - My 1 '97 - p1477 [51-250]
KR - v65 - Mr 1 '97 - p317+ [51-250]
LJ - v122 - My 1 '97 - p136 [51-250]
PW - v244 - Mr 3 '97 - p62+ [51-250]
Souls Raised from the Dead
Sew R - v104 - Jl '96 - pR57+ [501+]
Betts, Richard K - *Military Readiness*
AAPSS-A - v549 - Ja '97 - p186+ [501+]
Soc - v34 - N '96 - p108+ [501+]
Betz, Cecily - *Mosby's Pediatric Nursing Reference. 3rd
Ed.*
r SciTech - v20 - S '96 - p41 [51-250]
Betz, Hans Dieter - *The Sermon on the Mount*
Rel St Rev - v23 - Ja '97 - p72 [51-250]
Theol St - v57 - D '96 - p736+ [501+]
TT - v53 - O '96 - p392+ [501+]
Betz, Hans-Georg - *Radical Right-Wing Populism in
Western Europe*
WP - v49 - O '96 - p130+ [501+]
Betz, Otto - *Jesus, Qumran, and the Vatican*
Rel St Rev - v23 - Ap '97 - p174+ [51-250]
Betz, Randal R - *The Child with a Spinal Cord Injury*
SciTech - v20 - S '96 - p39 [51-250]
Betzina, Sandra - *No Time to Sew*
BL - v93 - D 15 '96 - p700 [51-250]
LJ - v121 - D '96 - p91 [51-250]
Beudert, Monique - *German and American Art from
Beuys and Warhol*
Choice - v34 - Mr '97 - p1152 [51-250]
R&R Bk N - v12 - F '97 - p72 [51-250]
Beuken, W A M - *The Book of Job*
Rel St Rev - v23 - Ap '97 - p167+ [51-250]
Beuvery, E C - *Animal Cell Technology*
SciTech - v20 - S '96 - p59 [51-250]
Bevan, John - *The Infernal Diver*
Nature - v383 - O 24 '96 - p681 [51-250]
Beven, A R - *The Sanctuary Man*
Books - v10 - Je '96 - p24 [51-250]
Bever, Edward - *Africa*
r Choice - v34 - My '97 - p1471+ [51-250]
R&R Bk N - v12 - F '97 - p21 [51-250]
Beveridge, Craig - *Scotland after Enlightenment*
Obs - Ap 6 '97 - p18* [501+]
Beveridge, Judith - *Accidental Grace*
Aust Bk R - O '96 - p56+ [501+]
Aust Bk R - O '96 - p58 [501+]
Beveridge, Malcolm C M - *Cage Aquaculture. 2nd Ed.*
r SciTech - v20 - S '96 - p45 [51-250]
Beverley, John - *The Postmodernism Debate in Latin
America*
HAHR - v77 - F '97 - p87+ [501+]

Bevilacqua, Alberto - *Eros*
KR - v64 - O 1 '96 - p1436 [251-500]
LJ - v121 - O 15 '96 - p57 [51-250]
Nat - v263 - D 2 '96 - p30+ [501+]
PW - v243 - S 30 '96 - p70 [51-250]
VLS - Win '96 - p25+ [501+]
Bevington, Helen - *The Third and Only Way*
LJ - v121 - O 15 '96 - p57 [51-250]
NYTBR - v102 - Ja 5 '97 - p19 [51-250]
Bevis, William W - *Borneo Log*
Pac A - v69 - Sum '96 - p292+ [501+]
WAL - v31 - Sum '96 - p174+ [251-500]
Beyala, Calixthe - *Loukoum: The Little Prince of Belleville*
W&I - v11 - N '96 - p270+ [501+]
WLT - v70 - Aut '96 - p1011 [501+]
The Sun Hath Looked upon Me
y Kliatt - v30 - S '96 - p6 [51-250]
WLT - v71 - Win '97 - p203+ [251-500]
Your Name Shall Be Tanga
WLT - v71 - Win '97 - p204 [251-500]
Beye, Charles Rowan - *Ancient Epic Poetry*
CLS - v33 - 3 '96 - p303+ [501+]
Beyer, Anders - *The Music of Per Norgard*
Choice - v34 - Ja '97 - p806 [51-250]
FF - v20 - Mr '97 - p425+ [501+]
Beyer, Hans - *Handbook of Organic Chemistry*
Choice - v34 - N '96 - p485 [51-250]
r SciTech - v20 - S '96 - p16 [51-250]
Beyer, Jinny - *Christmas with Jinny Beyer*
BL - v92 - Ag '96 - p1873 [501+]
Beyer, Marcel - *Flughunde*
WLT - v70 - Aut '96 - p945 [251-500]
Beyer, Peter - *Religion and Globalization*
J Ch St - v38 - Aut '96 - p906+ [251-500]
Beyer, W Nelson - *Environmental Contaminants in
Wildlife*
SciTech - v20 - D '96 - p40 [51-250]
Beynon, Peter H - *Manual of Psittacine Birds*
SciTech - v20 - S '96 - p45 [51-250]
Manual of Raptors, Pigeons and Waterfowl
SciTech - v20 - D '96 - p33 [51-250]
Beze, Theodore De - *Correspondance De Theodore De
Beze. Vols. 17-18*
CH - v66 - Mr '97 - p116+ [501+]
Bezic, Sandra - *The Passion to Skate*
y BL - v93 - D 15 '96 - p705 [51-250]
Mac - v109 - D 9 '96 - p66 [1-50]
BFI Film and Television Handbook 1996
r LAR - v98 - D '96 - p652 [51-250]
BHA: Bibliography of the History of Art 1996.
Electronic Media Version
r ARBA - v28 - '97 - p363+ [251-500]
BHA: Bibliography of the History of Art: Subject
Headings
r ARBA - v28 - '97 - p363+ [251-500]
Bhagwati, Jagdish N - *Fair Trade and Harmonization.
Vol. 1*
JEL - v34 - D '96 - p2041 [51-250]
Fair Trade and Harmonization. Vol. 2
JEL - v34 - D '96 - p2079 [51-250]
Fair Trade and Harmonization. Vols. 1-2
Choice - v34 - N '96 - p506 [51-250]
R&R Bk N - v12 - F '97 - p43 [51-250]
Bhalla, A S - *Facing the Technological Challenge*
ILR - v135 - '96 - p117 [51-250]
JEL - v34 - S '96 - p1483+ [51-250]
SciTech - v20 - D '96 - p58 [51-250]
*Uneven Development in the Third World. 2nd (Rev. and
Enlarged) Ed.*
JTWS - v13 - Fall '96 - p219+ [501+]
Bhandari, Jagdeep S - *Corporate Bankruptcy*
JEL - v34 - D '96 - p2055 [51-250]
Bharadwaj, Veeravalli - *Scheduling Divisible Loads in
Parallel and Distributed Systems*
SciTech - v20 - D '96 - p8 [51-250]
Bhat, Vasanthakumar N - *The Green Corporation*
r Choice - v34 - Ja '97 - p840 [51-250]
R&R Bk N - v11 - D '96 - p27 [51-250]
Bhathal, Ragbir - *Australian Astronomers*
Sci - v274 - N 15 '96 - p1149 [1-50]
S&T - v93 - F '97 - p60 [51-250]
Bhatia, Shobha K - *Recent Developments in Geotextile
Filters and Prefabricated Drainage Geocomposites*
SciTech - v20 - D '96 - p63 [51-250]
Bhatt, Sujata - *The Stinking Rose*
WLT - v70 - Aut '96 - p1037 [51-250]
Bhatt, Vinayak V - *Financial Systems, Innovations and
Development*
JEL - v35 - Mr '97 - p269 [51-250]
Bhattacharya, Amit - *Occupational Ergonomics*
SciTech - v20 - S '96 - p46 [51-250]

Bhattacharya, Keron - *The Pearls on Coromandel*
BW - v26 - Jl 14 '96 - p7 [501+]
Bhattacharya, Pallab - *Semiconductor Optoelectronic Devices. 2nd Ed.*
SciTech - v21 - Mr '97 - p93 [51-250]
Bheldon, Riobard - *Riobard Bheldon: Amhrain Agus Danta*
ILS - v16 - Spr '97 - p28 [501+]
Bhugra, Dinesh - *Homelessness and Mental Health*
Readings - v12 - Mr '97 - p29 [51-250]
Psychiatry and Religion
SciTech - v21 - Mr '97 - p51 [51-250]
Bi, Feiyu - *Yao Ya Yao Yao Dao Wai Po Qiao*
BL - v93 - My 1 '97 - p1484 [1-50]
Biagini, Eugenio F - *Currents of Radicalism*
J Soc H - v30 - Fall '96 - p229+ [501+]
Liberty, Retrenchment and Reform
J Soc H - v30 - Fall '96 - p229+ [501+]
Biagini, Mary K - *A Handbook of Contemporary Fiction for Public Libraries and School Libraries*
yr RQ - v36 - Win '96 - p226 [51-250]
Biagioli, Mario - *Galileo, Courtier*
JMH - v68 - S '96 - p657+ [501+]
Bial, Raymond - *Mist over the Mountains (Illus. by Raymond Bial)*
c BL - v93 - Mr 1 '97 - p1156+ [51-250]
c CBRS - v25 - Ap '97 - p104+ [51-250]
c KR - v65 - F 15 '97 - p297 [51-250]
The Underground Railroad
c LA - v73 - O '96 - p442 [51-250]
y RT - v50 - N '96 - p248 [51-250]
With Needle and Thread
y HB Guide - v7 - Fall '96 - p355 [1-50]
Bialkowski, Stephen E - *Photothermal Spectroscopy Methods for Chemical Analysis*
Phys Today - v49 - O '96 - p76 [501+]
Bialosky, Jill - *The End of Desire*
NL - v80 - F 24 '97 - p14+ [251-500]
PW - v244 - Ja 27 '97 - p94 [51-250]
Bialostosky, Don H - *Rhetorical Traditions and British Romantic Literature*
Critm - v39 - Win '97 - p155+ [501+]
Bialystok, Ellen - *In Other Words*
MLJ - v81 - Spr '97 - p112+ [501+]
Bian, Yanjie - *Work and Inequality in Urban China*
SF - v75 - S '96 - p362+ [251-500]
Bianchi, Anne - *Zuppa! Soups from the Italian Countryside*
BL - v93 - D 15 '96 - p701 [51-250]
LJ - v121 - D '96 - p136 [51-250]
PW - v243 - S 2 '96 - p123 [51-250]
VLS - Win '96 - p14 [501+]
Bianchi, John - *The Lab Rats of Doctor Eclair (Illus. by John Bianchi)*
c Quill & Q - v63 - F '97 - p59 [51-250]
Welcome Back to Pokeweed Public School
c BL - v93 - F 1 '97 - p945 [51-250]
Bianchi, Lino - *Iconografia Palestriniana*
Notes - v53 - S '96 - p66+ [501+]
Bianciotto, Gabriel - *Le Roman De Troyle. Vols. 1-2*
Specu - v72 - Ja '97 - p108+ [501+]
Bianco, Anthony - *Faith and Fortune*
BL - v93 - Mr 1 '97 - p1107 [501+]
CSM - v89 - Mr 5 '97 - p14 [501+]
Econ - v342 - F 15 '97 - p13*+ [501+]
KR - v65 - Ja 1 '97 - p30 [251-500]
LATBR - F 9 '97 - p9 [501+]
Mac - v110 - Mr 10 '97 - p60+ [501+]
NYTBR - v102 - F 9 '97 - p6+ [501+]
PW - v244 - Ja 13 '97 - p64 [251-500]
Quill & Q - v63 - Mr '97 - p72 [251-500]
Trib Bks - F 23 '97 - p6 [501+]
WSJ-Cent - v99 - Ja 28 '97 - pA14 [501+]
Bianco-Mathis, Virginia - *The Adjunct Faculty Handbook*
R&R Bk N - v11 - N '96 - p55 [51-250]
Bianculli, David - *Dictionary of Teleliteracy*
r ARBA - v28 - '97 - p507 [51-250]
r Choice - v34 - D '96 - p585+ [51-250]
yr CLW - v67 - D '96 - p50 [51-250]
Biasin, Gian-Paolo - *The Flavors of Modernity*
MLR - v91 - Jl '96 - p762+ [251-500]
Bibby, Brian - *The Fine Art of California Indian Basketry*
BWatch - v17 - N '96 - p2 [1-50]
LJ - v121 - D '96 - p87+ [501+]
Bibby, Michael - *Hearts and Minds*
Choice - v34 - D '96 - p611 [51-250]
Biberdorf, Daryl - *Powerbuilder 5 How-To*
SciTech - v21 - Mr '97 - p9 [51-250]
Bible and Culture Collective - *The Postmodern Bible*
Rel St Rev - v23 - Ja '97 - p54 [51-250]

Bible. English. Authorized. 1997 - *The Bible: Authorised King James Version*
Obs - Mr 30 '97 - p16* [501+]
Bible. English. Living Translation. 1996 - *Holy Bible: The New Living Translation*
BIC - v25 - D '96 - p43 [51-250]
Bible. English. New Living Translation. 1996 - *Holy Bible: New Living Translation*
Time - v148 - S 9 '96 - p58+ [501+]
Bible. English. New Revised Standard. 1995 - *The Holy Bible: With Illustrations from the Vatican Library*
LATBR - D 8 '96 - p8 [51-250]
Bible. N.T. English. Lattimore. 1996 - *The New Testament*
BW - v26 - O 20 '96 - p13 [51-250]
LJ - v122 - F 15 '97 - p139 [51-250]
Bible. N.T. English. Luke. Tyndale. Selections. 1996 - *A Medieval Christmas*
c Bks Keeps - N '96 - p19 [1-50]
c JB - v60 - D '96 - p236 [1-50]
Bible. N.T. English. New Revised Standard. 1995 - *The New Testament and Psalms*
JAAR - v65 - Spr '97 - p141+ [501+]
Bible. N.T. English. Tyndale. 1995 - *Tyndale's New Testament*
Six Ct J - v27 - Win '96 - p1236+ [501+]
Bible. N.T. Gospels. English (Old English). 1994 - *The Old English Version of the Gospels. Vol. 1*
RES - v47 - N '96 - p555+ [501+]
Bible. N.T. Gospels. English. Scholars. 1993 - *The Five Gospels*
Bks & Cult - v1 - N '95 - p3+ [501+]
Bible. N.T. Gospels. English. Scholars. 1994 - *The Complete Gospels. Rev. and Expanded Ed.*
Intpr - v50 - O '96 - p428+ [251-500]
Bible. N.T. Greek. 1995 - *New Testament Greek Manuscripts. Vols. 1-4*
Rel St Rev - v23 - Ap '97 - p173+ [251-500]
Bible. N.T. James. English. Johnson. 1995 - *The Letter of James*
Rel St Rev - v23 - Ja '97 - p75 [51-250]
Bible. N.T. Mark. English. Price. 1996 - *Three Gospels*
BL - v93 - Ja '97 - p756 [1-50]
NYTBR - v101 - D 8 '96 - p93 [1-50]
OS - v32 - S '96 - p59 [51-250]
Bible. N.T. Matthew. English. Revised Standard. Selections. 1993 - *The Nativity: From the Gospels of Matthew and Luke (Illus. by Ruth Sanderson)*
c HB Guide - v8 - Spr '97 - p89 [51-250]
c JB - v60 - D '96 - p240 [51-250]
c PW - v243 - S 30 '96 - p92 [1-50]
Bible. N.T. Matthew. English. Selections. 1966. Authorized - *The Christmas Story from the Gospels of Matthew and Luke*
c TES - D 6 '96 - p16* [1-50]
Bible. O.T. English. Authorized. 1996 - *The Old Testament*
LATBR - Ja 5 '97 - p8+ [501+]
Bible. O.T. English. Authorized. Selections. 1996 - *Stories from the Old Testament*
c BL - v93 - O 1 '96 - p336+ [51-250]
c HB Guide - v8 - Spr '97 - p88 [51-250]
c JB - v60 - D '96 - p275 [51-250]
c Sch Lib - v44 - N '96 - p165+ [251-500]
c SLJ - v42 - O '96 - p136 [51-250]
Bible. O.T. Genesis. English. Alter. 1996 - *Genesis*
BL - v93 - S 1 '96 - p38 [51-250]
BW - v26 - D 8 '96 - p5 [501+]
Comw - v124 - Mr 14 '97 - p28+ [501+]
CSM - v88 - N 6 '96 - p12 [51-250]
Nat R - v48 - D 9 '96 - p61+ [501+]
NYTBR - v101 - D 15 '96 - p7+ [501+]
PW - v243 - N 4 '96 - p46 [51-250]
Wil Q - v21 - Win '97 - p101+ [501+]
Bible. O.T. Genesis. English. Mitchell. 1996 - *Genesis: A New Translation of the Classic Biblical Stories*
BW - v26 - D 8 '96 - p5 [501+]
Nat R - v48 - D 9 '96 - p61+ [501+]
NYTBR - v101 - D 15 '96 - p7+ [501+]
Parabola - v21 - N '96 - p120 [1-50]
Wil Q - v21 - Win '97 - p101+ [501+]
Bible. O.T. Genesis. English. Young. 1995 - *Genesis (Illus. by Ed Young)*
c BL - v93 - F 1 '97 - p944 [51-250]
c CCB-B - v50 - Mr '97 - p241 [51-250]
c KR - v65 - Ja 15 '97 - p148 [51-250]
c PW - v244 - Ja 13 '97 - p71+ [51-250]
c SLJ - v43 - Ja '97 - p96+ [51-250]
Bible. O.T. Job. English. Mitchell. 1992 - *The Book of Job*
VV - v42 - Ja 7 '97 - p44 [251-500]

Bible. O.T. Joel. English. Crenshaw. 1995 - *Joel*
Theol St - v57 - S '96 - p563+ [251-500]
Bible. O.T. Pentateuch. English. Fox. 1995 - *The Five Books of Moses*
CLW - v67 - D '96 - p34 [251-500]
Lon R Bks - v18 - My 23 '96 - p12+ [501+]
TLS - S 6 '96 - p31 [501+]
Bible. O.T. Psalms. English. 1996 - *The Psalms in English*
Agenda - v34 - Spr '96 - p182+ [501+]
BL - v93 - O 1 '96 - p300 [501+]
Bible. O.T. Psalms. English. Le Tord. Selections. 1997 - *Sing a New Song (Illus. by Bijou Le Tord)*
c BL - v93 - D 15 '96 - p730 [51-250]
c PW - v244 - Ja 27 '97 - p97+ [51-250]
c SLJ - v43 - Mr '97 - p171 [51-250]
Bible. O.T. Psalms. English. Slavitt. Selections. 1996 - *Sixty-One Psalms of David*
Am - v176 - F 15 '97 - p32+ [51-250]
BL - v93 - O 1 '96 - p300 [501+]
Bible. O.T. Song of Solomon. Hebrew. 1994 - *The Song of Songs*
Tikkun - v11 - Jl '96 - p65+ [501+]
Bible. O.T. Zephaniah. English. Berlin. 1994 - *Zephaniah: A New Translation with Introduction and Commentary*
Intpr - v50 - O '96 - p424+ [501+]
Biblio
p BC - v45 - Aut '96 - p381+ [51-250]
Bibliographic Index 1938-
r ASInt - v34 - O '96 - p20 [1-50]
Biblioteca Colombina - *Catalogo Concordado De La Biblioteca De Hernando Colon. Vol. 1*
r Lib - v18 - S '96 - p273 [51-250]
Bibliotheek Arnhem - *Catalogus Van De Pamfletten Aanwezig In De Bibliotheek Arnhem 1537-1795*
r Lib - v19 - Mr '97 - p98 [51-250]
Bicchieri, Cristina - *Rationality and Coordination*
Phil R - v105 - Ja '96 - p105+ [501+]
Bicerano, Jozef - *Prediction of Polymer Properties. 2nd Ed.*
SciTech - v20 - D '96 - p63 [51-250]
Bickel, Warren K - *Drug Policy and Human Nature*
R&R Bk N - v11 - D '96 - p43 [51-250]
Bicker, Lyn - *Private Banking in Europe*
JEL - v34 - D '96 - p2054+ [51-250]
R&R Bk N - v11 - D '96 - p36 [51-250]
Bickerstaff, Gordon F - *Immobilization of Enzymes and Cells*
SciTech - v21 - Mr '97 - p96 [51-250]
Bickersteth, John - *The Bickersteth Diaries 1914-1918*
Mac - v110 - F 10 '97 - p59+ [501+]
Bickerton, Derek - *Language and Human Behavior*
QJS - v83 - My '97 - p263+ [501+]
Bickford, Maggie - *Ink Plum*
Choice - v34 - F '97 - p955 [51-250]
Bickford-Smith, Vivian - *Ethnic Pride and Racial Prejudice in Victorian Cape Town*
Historian - v59 - Fall '96 - p134+ [501+]
JIH - v27 - Spr '97 - p741+ [501+]
Bickham, Jack M - *The Davis Cup Conspiracy*
Aethlon - v13 - Fall '95 - p139+ [251-500]
y Kliatt - v31 - Ja '97 - p6 [51-250]
Bicos, Olga - *Wrapped in Wishes*
PW - v243 - N 4 '96 - p40 [1-50]
Biddiscombe, Richard - *The End-User Revolution*
LAR - v98 - N '96 - p593 [501+]
Biddle, Alan - *Key Strategies: Music*
TES - S 13 '96 - pR11 [501+]
Biddle, Mark E - *Polyphony and Symphony in Prophetic Literature*
R&R Bk N - v11 - D '96 - p5 [51-250]
Biddle, Stanton F - *The African-American Yellow Pages*
r ARBA - v28 - '97 - p152+ [51-250]
r B Ent - v27 - F '97 - p215 [1-50]
yr BL - v93 - S 15 '96 - p280 [251-500]
r LJ - v121 - O 15 '96 - p50 [251-500]
Biddle, Wayne - *A Field Guide to Germs*
LATBR - S 22 '96 - p15 [51-250]
Biddlecombe, Peter - *I Came, I Saw, I Lost My Luggage*
Books - v11 - Ap '97 - p21 [51-250]
Bideleux, Robert - *European Integration and Disintegration*
Choice - v34 - Ap '97 - p1413 [51-250]
Bidima, Jean Godefroy - *La Philosophie Negro-Africaine*
Choice - v34 - D '96 - p565 [51-250]
Bidwai, Pravul - *Testing Times*
JPR - v34 - F '97 - p107+ [251-500]
Biebow, Natascha - *Eleonora (Illus. by Britta Teckentrup)*
c RT - v50 - Mr '97 - p502 [51-250]

Biebuyck, Daniel P - *African Ethnonyms*
   r ARBA - v28 - '97 - p147 [51-250]
Bieder, Robert E - *Native American Communities in Wisconsin 1600-1960*
     AHR - v102 - F '97 - p178+ [501+]
     PHR - v66 - F '97 - p121+ [501+]
Biehl, Janet - *Ecofascism: Lessons from the German Experience*
     Workbook - v21 - Win '96 - p170 [251-500]
Biel, Jackie - *Video*
   c Ch BWatch - v6 - My '96 - p6 [51-250]
   c HB Guide - v7 - Fall '96 - p349+ [51-250]
   c SB - v32 - Ag '96 - p181 [51-250]
   c SLJ - v42 - Ag '96 - p148+ [51-250]
Biel, Steven - *Down with the Old Canoe*
     BW - v26 - N 24 '96 - p7 [501+]
     Ent W - N 8 '96 - p62 [51-250]
     LJ - v121 - S 15 '96 - p78 [51-250]
     NY - v72 - O 14 '96 - p94+ [501+]
     NYTBR - v102 - Ja 26 '97 - p19 [251-500]
     NYTLa - v146 - O 29 '96 - pC16 [501+]
Bielecki, Tessa - *Teresa of Avila: Ecstasy and Common Sense*
     Bloom Rev - v16 - N '96 - p13 [51-250]
     PW - v243 - S 2 '96 - p126 [51-250]
Bielefield, Arlene - *Technology and Copyright Law*
     BWatch - v18 - Mr '97 - p5 [51-250]
     LJ - v122 - My 1 '97 - p146 [51-250]
Bien, Jeff - *America and Other Poems*
     Quill & Q - v62 - D '96 - p34 [251-500]
  Prosody at the Cafe Du Coin
     Quill & Q - v62 - D '96 - p34 [251-500]
Bien, Z - *Fuzzy Logic and Its Applications to Engineering, Information Sciences, and Intelligent Systems*
     SciTech - v20 - D '96 - p72 [51-250]
Bierbaum, Esther Green - *Museum Librarianship*
     LRTS - v40 - Jl '96 - p292+ [501+]
Bierce, Ambrose - *Poems of Ambrose Bierce*
     Nine-C Lit - v50 - Mr '96 - p552 [1-50]
Bierhorst, John - *The Dancing Fox (Illus. by Mary K Okheena)*
   c HB - v73 - My '97 - p332+ [51-250]
   c KR - v65 - Ap 1 '97 - p549 [51-250]
  Mythology of the Lenape
   r CAY - v17 - Fall '96 - p9 [51-250]
Bierman, John - *Righteous Gentile. Rev. Ed.*
   y Kliatt - v30 - N '96 - p21 [51-250]
     Obs - Mr 9 '97 - p18* [51-250]
Biermann, Christopher J - *Handbook of Pulping and Papermaking. 2nd Ed.*
     Choice - v34 - F '97 - p992+ [51-250]
     SciTech - v20 - D '96 - p86 [51-250]
Biernacki, Richard - *The Fabrication of Labor*
     J Soc H - v30 - Spr '97 - p774+ [501+]
Biersteker, Thomas J - *State Sovereignty as Social Construct*
     Choice - v34 - Mr '97 - p1238 [51-250]
Biesiot, Elizabeth - *Natural Treasures Field Guide for Kids (Illus. by Elizabeth Biesiot)*
   c BL - v93 - S 1 '96 - p120 [51-250]
   cr SB - v32 - O '96 - p210 [51-250]
Biespiel, David - *Shattering Air*
     Chel - 61 '96 - p146+ [501+]
     Choice - v34 - D '96 - p611 [51-250]
Biesty, Stephen - *Stephen Biesty's Incredible Explosions (Illus. by Stephen Biesty)*
   y BL - v93 - Ap 1 '97 - p1308 [1-50]
   c HB Guide - v8 - Spr '97 - p132 [51-250]
   c ILN - Christmas '96 - p88 [1-50]
   y Sch Lib - v45 - F '97 - p49+ [51-250]
   c SLJ - v42 - O '96 - p138 [51-250]
   c TES - D 6 '96 - p22* [51-250]
Biethahn, Jorg - *Evolutionary Algorithms in Management Applications*
     JEL - v34 - S '96 - p1461 [51-250]
Biffle, Christopher - *A Guided Tour of Five Works by Plato. 2nd Ed.*
     CPR - v16 - Ag '96 - p245+ [501+]
Big Animals (Ladybird First Explorers)
   c PW - v243 - S 9 '96 - p84 [51-250]
The Big Book of Library Grant Money 1996/97
   r Choice - v34 - S '96 - p93 [51-250]
   r SLMQ - v24 - Sum '96 - p219 [51-250]
The Big Emerging Markets 1996
   r J Gov Info - v24 - Ja '97 - p70+ [501+]
Bigelow, Brian J - *Learning the Rules*
     Choice - v34 - Ja '97 - p881+ [51-250]
     Readings - v12 - Mr '97 - p30 [51-250]
Bigelow, Stephen J - *Troubleshooting and Repairing Computer Printers. 2nd Ed.*
     SciTech - v21 - Mr '97 - p93 [51-250]

Biger, Gideon - *The Encyclopedia of International Boundaries*
   r BL - v92 - Ag '96 - p1920 [51-250]
   yr RQ - v35 - Sum '96 - p555+ [251-500]
Bigger, Charles P - *Kant's Methodology*
     Choice - v34 - S '96 - p140 [51-250]
Biggers, John - *Ananse: The Web of Life in Africa*
     LJ - v122 - Ap 15 '97 - p125 [1-50]
Biggins, John - *The Two-Headed Eagle*
     BL - v93 - S 15 '96 - p218 [51-250]
     LJ - v121 - S 15 '96 - p93+ [51-250]
Biggs, Deb R - *ProCite in Libraries*
     CLW - v67 - D '96 - p51 [51-250]
Biggs, Lindy - *The Rational Factory*
     Choice - v34 - Ap '97 - p1359 [51-250]
Biggs, Mary - *Women's Words*
   r ARBA - v28 - '97 - p36+ [251-500]
   r BL - v93 - D 1 '96 - p680+ [501+]
   r BWatch - v17 - S '96 - p3 [1-50]
   r Choice - v34 - Ja '97 - p765 [251-500]
Biggs, Melissa E - *French Films 1945-1993*
   r ARBA - v28 - '97 - p509 [51-250]
   r BL - v93 - S 1 '96 - p166 [51-250]
   r Choice - v34 - N '96 - p425 [51-250]
Biggs, Tyler - *Africa Can Compete!*
     JEL - v35 - Mr '97 - p270 [51-250]
  Structural Aspects of Manufacturing in Sub-Saharan Africa
     JEL - v35 - Mr '97 - p269+ [51-250]
  Technological Capabilities and Learning in African Enterprises
     JEL - v34 - S '96 - p1476 [51-250]
Biggs, Vicki - *Mother Superior*
     Sm Pr R - v28 - O '96 - p9 [51-250]
Bigham, Steven - *The Image of God the Father in Orthodox Theology and Iconography and Other Studies*
     Rel St Rev - v23 - Ap '97 - p190 [51-250]
Bigler, Erin D - *Neuroimaging. Vol. 1*
     SciTech - v20 - D '96 - p43 [51-250]
  Neuroimaging. Vol. 2
     SciTech - v21 - Mr '97 - p40 [51-250]
Bigsby, Christopher - *Pearl*
     PW - v243 - S 9 '96 - p67 [51-250]
  Still Lives
     TLS - S 27 '96 - p24 [501+]
Bigus, Joseph P - *Data Mining with Neural Networks*
     CBR - v14 - N '96 - p37 [51-250]
     SciTech - v20 - S '96 - p7 [51-250]
Bijker, Wiebe E - *Of Bicycles, Bakelites, and Bulbs*
     CS - v25 - N '96 - p811+ [501+]
     New Sci - v153 - Mr 22 '97 - p44 [1-50]
     T&C - v37 - O '96 - p853+ [501+]
Bijvoet, O L M - *Bisphosphonate on Bones*
     SciTech - v20 - S '96 - p37 [51-250]
Bike Culture Quarterly
   p Utne R - My '96 - p112 [51-250]
Biklen, Sari Knopp - *School Work*
     NWSA Jnl - v8 - Sum '96 - p152+ [501+]
Biko, Steve - *I Write What I Like*
     LJ - v122 - F 15 '97 - p166 [51-250]
Bikson, T K - *Preserving the Present*
     Archiv - Spr '96 - p247+ [501+]
Bildkatalog Der Skulpturen Des Vatikanischen Museums. Vol. 1, Pts. 1-3
     AJA - v100 - Jl '96 - p632
Biles, Roger - *Richard J. Daley: Politics, Race, and the Governing of Chicago*
     Historian - v59 - Win '97 - p420 [251-500]
Bilezikian, John P - *Principles of Bone Biology*
     SciTech - v21 - Mr '97 - p39 [51-250]
Bilitewski, Bernd - *Waste Management*
     Choice - v34 - My '97 - p1529 [51-250]
Bill, James A - *George Ball: Behind the Scenes in U.S. Foreign Policy*
     BL - v93 - Mr 15 '97 - p1222 [51-250]
     For Aff - v76 - My '97 - p133 [51-250]
     KR - v65 - Ja 15 '97 - p107 [251-500]
     LJ - v122 - Mr 15 '97 - p75 [51-250]
     PW - v244 - Ja 27 '97 - p89+ [251-500]
Billatos, Samir B - *Design for Manufacturing and Assembly*
     SciTech - v21 - Mr '97 - p99 [51-250]
Biller, Peter - *Heresy and Literacy 1000-1530*
     HT - v46 - Jl '96 - p55+ [501+]
     MLR - v92 - Ap '97 - p406+ [501+]
Billgren, Jan - *Svensk Posthistorisk 1855-1925*
     Phil Lit R - v45 - '96 - p347+ [501+]
Billig, Michael - *Banal Nationalism*
     RP - v58 - Fall '96 - p852+ [501+]

Billing, G D - *Introduction to Molecular Dynamics and Chemical Kinetics*
     Phys Today - v49 - O '96 - p74+ [501+]
Billing, Peter - *Hegemonins Decennier*
     AHR - v101 - D '96 - p1575 [501+]
Billingham, Richard - *Ray's a Laugh*
     LJ - v122 - Ja '97 - p92 [51-250]
Billings, Chris - *Rapid Application Development with Oracle Designer/2000*
     SciTech - v20 - D '96 - p11 [51-250]
Billings, Malcolm - *The Crusades: Five Centuries of Holy Wars*
     LATBR - O 13 '96 - p15 [51-250]
Billingsley, Franny - *Well Wished*
   c CCB-B - v50 - Ap '97 - p274 [251-500]
   c HB - v73 - My '97 - p314 [251-500]
   c KR - v65 - My 1 '97 - p716+ [51-250]
   c PW - v244 - Ap 7 '97 - p92 [51-250]
Billington, David P - *The Innovators: The Engineering Pioneers Who Made America Modern*
     Choice - v34 - O '96 - p310+ [51-250]
     Reason - v28 - D '96 - p42 [51-250]
     SB - v32 - Ag '96 - p170+ [501+]
     SciTech - v20 - N '96 - p60 [51-250]
Billington, Michael - *The Life and Work of Harold Pinter*
     BL - v93 - Mr 15 '97 - p1220+ [51-250]
     KR - v65 - F 1 '97 - p182 [251-500]
     Lon R Bks - v18 - N 14 '96 - p11+ [501+]
     NS - v125 - O 11 '96 - p48 [501+]
     Obs - N 10 '96 - p15* [501+]
     PW - v244 - Ja 20 '97 - p385 [51-250]
     Spec - v277 - O 12 '96 - p42+ [501+]
     Spec - v277 - N 23 '96 - p44 [1-50]
     TES - O 18 '96 - p7* [501+]
     TLS - O 25 '96 - p20 [501+]
Billington, Michael, 1939- - *One Night Stands*
     Theat J - v49 - Mr '97 - p96+ [501+]
Billington, Rachel - *The Life of Jesus (Illus. by Lee Stinson)*
   c Sch Lib - v45 - F '97 - p36 [51-250]
  Perfect Happiness
     Obs - S 29 '96 - p15* [501+]
     Spec - v277 - S 14 '96 - p45 [501+]
  Perfect Happiness. Audio Version
     Quill & Q - v62 - S '96 - p71 [1-50]
  Perfect Happiness (Beckinsale). Audio Version
     Quill & Q - v63 - Mr '97 - p75 [51-250]
Billinton, Roy - *Reliability Evaluation of Power Systems. 2nd Ed.*
   r SciTech - v20 - D '96 - p74 [51-250]
Billot, Antoine - *Economic Theory of Fuzzy Equilibria. 2nd Ed.*
     JEL - v34 - D '96 - p2028 [51-250]
Bills, David B - *The New Modern Times*
     ILRR - v50 - O '96 - p166+ [501+]
Bills, Greg - *Fearful Symmetry*
     KR - v64 - My 1 '96 - p618 [251-500]
Billson, Anne - *Stiff Lips*
     Spec - v277 - N 2 '96 - p50+ [501+]
     TLS - O 11 '96 - p26 [501+]
Billson, Janet Mancini - *Pathways to Manhood*
     Bl S - v26 - Fall '96 - p100 [1-50]
Billy, Dennis J - *Spirituality and Morality*
     Am - v175 - N 2 '96 - p28 [251-500]
     RR - v56 - Mr '97 - p218+ [501+]
Billy, Pierre-Henri - *Atlas Linguae Gallicae*
   r Names - v44 - S '96 - p237+ [501+]
  Thesaurus Linguae Gallicae
   r Names - v44 - S '96 - p237+ [501+]
Bilstein, Roger E - *The American Aerospace Industry*
     JEL - v35 - Mr '97 - p249 [51-250]
Bimbenet-Privat, Michele - *L'Orfevrerie Parisienne De La Renaissance*
     BM - v138 - Jl '96 - p466 [501+]
Bimber, Bruce A - *The Politics of Expertise in Congress*
     Choice - v34 - Ja '97 - p873+ [51-250]
     R&R Bk N - v11 - D '96 - p71 [51-250]
Bimson, John J - *Baker Encyclopedia of Bible Places*
   r Rel St Rev - v23 - Ja '97 - p68 [51-250]
Bina, Cyrus - *Beyond Survival*
     Choice - v34 - N '96 - p502 [51-250]
     JEL - v34 - D '96 - p2074 [51-250]
     R&R Bk N - v11 - N '96 - p32 [51-250]
Binch, Caroline - *Gregory Cool (Illus. by Caroline Binch)*
   c Emerg Lib - v24 - Mr '97 - p46 [51-250]
   c RT - v50 - F '97 - p420+ [51-250]
Binchy, Maeve - *Echoes*
     PW - v244 - F 24 '97 - p88 [1-50]

Evening Class
 BW - v27 - Mr 2 '97 - p5 [501+]
 CSM - v89 - Mr 20 '97 - p14 [51-250]
 KR - v65 - Ja 1 '97 - p4 [251-500]
 LJ - v122 - F 1 '97 - p104 [51-250]
 NYTBR - v102 - Ap 6 '97 - p21 [51-250]
 PW - v244 - Ja 6 '97 - p62 [251-500]
 Woman's J - N '96 - p12 [1-50]
This Year It Will Be Different
 CSM - v89 - D 19 '96 - p14 [51-250]
 CSM - v89 - Ja 16 '97 - p14 [51-250]
 NYTBR - v101 - D 8 '96 - p102 [51-250]
 Time - v148 - N 18 '96 - p114 [1-50]
Bindas, Kenneth J - *All of This Music Belongs to the Nation*
 Choice - v34 - S '96 - p136+ [51-250]
 HRNB - v25 - Fall '96 - p11+ [251-500]
 Notes - v53 - Mr '97 - p808+ [501+]
Binder, Frederick M - *All the Nations under Heaven*
 AHR - v102 - F '97 - p201 [251-500]
Binder, K - *Cohesion and Structure of Surfaces*
 SciTech - v20 - N '96 - p17 [51-250]
 Monte Carlo and Molecular Dynamics Simulations in Polymer Science
 Am Sci - v84 - N '96 - p614+ [501+]
Binder, Sarah A - *Politics or Principle?*
 LJ - v122 - Ja '97 - p123 [51-250]
Binder, Wolfgang - *American Contradictions*
 AL - v68 - S '96 - p666 [51-250]
 Ethnic Cultures in the 1920s in North America
 Can Lit - Win '96 - p140+ [501+]
Binding, Tim - *A Perfect Execution*
 KR - v64 - My 1 '96 - p618+ [251-500]
 Lon R Bks - v18 - Ag 22 '96 - p23+ [501+]
 NS & S - v9 - My 24 '96 - p40 [251-500]
Bindman, David - *Roubiliac and the Eighteenth-Century Monument*
 Albion - v28 - Fall '96 - p503+ [501+]
 Art Bull - v78 - S '96 - p565+ [501+]
 Eight-C St - v29 - Sum '96 - p436+ [501+]
Bindon, Annette - *Into Technology*
 TES - N 29 '96 - p12* [251-500]
Binford, Leigh - *The El Mozote Massacre*
 Choice - v34 - Ap '97 - p1399+ [51-250]
 LJ - v121 - O 15 '96 - p65 [51-250]
Bing, Elisabeth - *Laughter and Tears*
 BL - v93 - F 1 '97 - p911 [51-250]
 LJ - v122 - Ja '97 - p125 [51-250]
 PW - v243 - D 16 '96 - p56 [51-250]
Bing, Gordon - *Due Diligence Techniques and Analysis*
 R&R Bk N - v11 - D '96 - p29 [51-250]
Bingham, Alfred M - *The Tiffany Fortune and Other Chronicles of a Connecticut Family*
 BL - v93 - S 15 '96 - p213 [51-250]
Bingham, Caroline, 1938- - *Darnley: A Life of Henry Stuart, Lord Darnley, Consort of Mary Queen of Scots*
 TLS - Ag 30 '96 - p25 [501+]
Bingham, Caroline, 1962- - *Big Rig*
 c CLW - v67 - D '96 - p61 [51-250]
 c HB Guide - v7 - Fall '96 - p350 [1-50]
 Race Car
 c CLW - v67 - D '96 - p61 [51-250]
 c HB Guide - v7 - Fall '96 - p350 [1-50]
Bingham, Clara - *Women on the Hill*
 y BL - v93 - Ja '97 - p785 [51-250]
 KR - v64 - N 1 '96 - p1572 [251-500]
 LATBR - Ja 12 '97 - p14 [501+]
 LJ - v121 - D '96 - p122 [51-250]
 NYTBR - v102 - Mr 30 '97 - p17 [51-250]
Bingham, Dennis - *Acting Male*
 Can Lit - Spr '97 - p221+ [501+]
Bingham, Jane - *Usborne Illustrated Dictionary*
 cr Bks Keeps - v100 - S '96 - p22+ [501+]
Bingham, Mindy - *Things Will Be Different for My Daughter*
 VOYA - v19 - D '96 - p256 [1-50]
Bingham, Sallie - *Straight Man*
 BL - v93 - O 1 '96 - p320+ [51-250]
 LATBR - D 15 '96 - p15 [51-250]
 NYTBR - v102 - F 9 '97 - p22 [501+]
Bingham, Sam - *The Last Ranch*
 Atl - v278 - D '96 - p126 [51-250]
 BL - v93 - S 1 '96 - p40 [51-250]
 BW - v26 - O 27 '96 - p6 [501+]
 CSM - v89 - F 5 '97 - p15 [501+]
 NYTBR - v101 - O 20 '96 - p19 [501+]
Binkley, Marilyn R - *Reading Literacy in the United States*
 JAAL - v40 - N '96 - p238 [51-250]

Binkley, Thomas - *Spanish Romances of the Sixteenth Century*
 Hisp - v79 - D '96 - p782 [501+]
Binney, George - *Leaning into the Future*
 Per Psy - v50 - Spr '97 - p206+ [501+]
Binni, Walter - *Lezioni Leopardiane*
 MLR - v91 - O '96 - p1010+ [501+]
Binns, Brigit Legere - *Polenta*
 PW - v243 - D 2 '96 - p56+ [51-250]
Binns, John - *Ascetics and Ambassadors of Christ*
 Rel St Rev - v23 - Ja '97 - p79 [51-250]
Binns, Margaret - *Guinea*
 r ARBA - v28 - '97 - p53 [51-250]
 r R&R Bk N - v12 - F '97 - p21 [51-250]
Bin Sayeed, Khalid - *Western Dominance and Political Islam*
 MEP - v4 - 4 '96 - p144+ [501+]
Binski, Paul - *Medieval Death*
 Choice - v34 - Ap '97 - p1396 [51-250]
 TLS - N 29 '96 - p16 [1-50]
 Westminster Abbey and the Plantagenets
 Albion - v28 - Sum '96 - p288+ [501+]
 EHR - v111 - S '96 - p941+ [501+]
 Lon R Bks - v19 - Ja 2 '97 - p24+ [501+]
 SDA - v4 - Spr '97 - p133+ [501+]
Binstock, R C - *The Soldier*
 LJ - v122 - F 1 '97 - p136 [51-250]
 Tree of Heaven
 NYTBR - v101 - N 17 '96 - p40 [51-250]
 PW - v243 - N 25 '96 - p70 [1-50]
Binstock, Robert H - *The Future of Long-Term Care*
 Choice - v34 - F '97 - p996 [51-250]
 Hast Cen R - v27 - Ja '97 - p46 [51-250]
 JEL - v35 - Mr '97 - p228 [51-250]
 SciTech - v20 - D '96 - p40 [51-250]
Binswanger, Hans P - *The World Bank's Strategy for Reducing Poverty and Hunger*
 J Gov Info - v23 - S '96 - p690 [51-250]
Biochemical Society (Great Britain). Symposium (61st: 1994: University of Sussex) - *Free Radicals and Oxidative Stress*
 SciTech - v20 - N '96 - p26 [51-250]
A Biographical Dictionary of Artists. Rev. Ed.
 yr RQ - v35 - Sum '96 - p546+ [501+]
Biographical Dictionary of European Labor Leaders. Vols. 1-2
 r ARBA - v28 - '97 - p77 [251-500]
Biography
 p LJ - v122 - My 1 '97 - p42 [51-250]
Biography and Genealogy Master Index. 2nd Ed., Vols. 1-8. Book and Electronic Media Version
 r ASInt - v34 - O '96 - p12 [51-250]
Biography Database 1680-1830. Electronic Media Version
 r Choice - v34 - Ap '97 - p1319 [501+]
 r TLS - F 7 '97 - p12 [501+]
Biography Today: Profiles of People of Interest to Young Readers
 cr SLJ - v42 - Ag '96 - p181+ [51-250]
Biography Today: Scientists and Inventors Series. Vol. 1
 cr SLJ - v43 - F '97 - p128+ [51-250]
Biologically Based Technologies for Pest Control
 J Gov Info - v23 - S '96 - p556 [1-50]
Biospectroscopy
 p Nature - v383 - S 5 '96 - p37 [251-500]
Biotechnology Abstracts. Electronic Media Version
 r Choice - v34 - Ap '97 - p1363 [501+]
Biow, Douglas - *Mirabile Dictu*
 Choice - v34 - D '96 - p606 [51-250]
Birand, Mehmet Ali - *Shirts of Steel*
 JTWS - v13 - Spr '96 - p384+ [501+]
Biraschi, Anna Maria - *Geographia Antiqua*
 GJ - v162 - Jl '96 - p234+ [51-250]
Birbalsingh, Frank - *Frontiers of Caribbean Literature in English*
 AL - v69 - Mr '97 - p255 [1-50]
 Choice - v34 - O '96 - p277 [51-250]
 WLT - v70 - Aut '96 - p1014+ [501+]
 Novels and the Nation
 WLT - v71 - Win '97 - p165 [251-500]
Birch, Carol L - *Who Says?*
 BL - v93 - S 15 '96 - p254 [51-250]
Birch, Charles - *Feelings*
 Aust Bk R - Jl '96 - p67 [251-500]
 Choice - v34 - S '96 - p213 [51-250]
 Queens Q - v103 - Fall '96 - p607+ [501+]
Birch, Cyril - *Scenes for Mandarins*
 Ch Rev Int - v3 - Fall '96 - p364+ [501+]
Birch, Paul - *Imagination Engineering*
 LJ - v121 - O 1 '96 - p94 [51-250]

Birch, Sarah - *Christine Brooke-Rose and Contemporary Fiction*
 RES - v47 - N '96 - p631 [501+]
Birchall, Johnston - *Co-Op: The People's Business*
 VS - v39 - Aut '95 - p97+ [501+]
Birchfield, D L - *The Encyclopedia of North American Indians. Vols. 1-11*
 r LJ - v122 - My 1 '97 - p96 [51-250]
 Rabbit (Illus. by Diana Magnuson)
 c SLJ - v42 - Ag '96 - p132+ [51-250]
Birchman, David F - *Jigsaw Jackson (Illus. by Daniel San Souci)*
 c HB Guide - v7 - Fall '96 - p248 [51-250]
 The Raggly Scraggly No-Soap No-Scrub Girl (Illus. by Guy Portirio)
 c RT - v50 - D '96 - p345 [51-250]
Birchmore, Fred - *Around the World on a Bicycle*
 BWatch - v17 - N '96 - p12 [51-250]
Birchwood, Max - *Psychological Management of Schizophrenia*
 AJPsych - v153 - O '96 - p1361 [251-500]
Bird, Anat - *Supercommunity Banking Strategies*
 R&R Bk N - v12 - F '97 - p47 [51-250]
Bird, Carmel - *Automatic Teller*
 Aust Bk R - N '96 - p47 [501+]
 Dear Writer. Rev. and Expanded Ed.
 Aust Bk R - O '96 - p69 [1-50]
Bird, David - *Receiving the Vision*
 Rel St Rev - v22 - O '96 - p339 [51-250]
 Theol St - v57 - Mr '96 - p193 [251-500]
Bird, E - *Geology and Scenery of Dorset*
 GJ - v162 - N '96 - p341 [51-250]
Bird, Eric C F - *Beach Management*
 Choice - v34 - Mr '97 - p1188 [51-250]
 SciTech - v20 - D '96 - p67 [51-250]
Bird, Frederick Bruce - *The Muted Conscience*
 Choice - v34 - My '97 - p1543 [51-250]
Bird, Graham - *International Debt. Vols. 1-2*
 JEL - v35 - Mr '97 - p217 [51-250]
Bird, J O - *Higher Engineering Mathematics. 2nd Ed.*
 SciTech - v20 - N '96 - p61 [51-250]
Bird, John - *The Long Johns*
 Spec - v277 - D 7 '96 - p54 [51-250]
Bird, Jon - *Nancy Spero*
 LJ - v121 - O 15 '96 - p55 [51-250]
Bird, Jonathan - *Beneath the North Atlantic*
 LJ - v122 - Ap 1 '97 - p117 [51-250]
Bird, Julia - *Country Fabric Style*
 BL - v93 - Ap 1 '97 - p1275 [51-250]
Bird, Lydia - *Sonnet: One Woman's Voyage from Maryland to Greece*
 BL - v93 - My 15 '97 - p1558 [51-250]
 KR - v65 - Mr 1 '97 - p344 [51-250]
 LJ - v122 - Ap 15 '97 - p104 [51-250]
 PW - v244 - F 24 '97 - p70+ [51-250]
Bird, R Curtis - *Nuclear Structure and Gene Expression*
 SciTech - v21 - Mr '97 - p36 [51-250]
Bird, Richard Miller - *Decentralization of the Socialist State*
 J Gov Info - v23 - S '96 - p684 [51-250]
Bird, Richard W - *Coins of New Brunswick*
 Coin W - v37 - O 28 '96 - p66 [51-250]
Bird, S Elizabeth - *Dressing in Feathers*
 Choice - v34 - N '96 - p500 [51-250]
Bird (Eyewitness Virtual Reality Series). Electronic Media Version
 y SB - v33 - Mr '97 - p56 [51-250]
Bird Watcher's Digest
 p LJ - v121 - D '96 - p67 [51-250]
Birder's World
 p LJ - v121 - D '96 - p67 [1-50]
Birds and Blooms
 p LJ - v121 - D '96 - p67 [1-50]
Birdseye, Debbie Holsclaw - *What I Believe (Illus. by Robert Crum)*
 c BL - v93 - D 15 '96 - p722 [51-250]
 c HB Guide - v8 - Spr '97 - p87 [1-50]
 c KR - v64 - D 1 '96 - p1733 [51-250]
 c PW - v244 - Ja 13 '97 - p71 [51-250]
 c SLJ - v43 - F '97 - p109 [51-250]
Birdwhistell, Anne D - *Li Yong 1627-1705 and Epistemological Dimensions of Confucian Philosophy*
 Choice - v34 - S '96 - p140 [51-250]
 Rel St Rev - v23 - Ap '97 - p204 [51-250]
Birdwood, Vere - *So Dearly Loved, So Much Admired*
 EHR - v111 - N '96 - p1297 [51-250]
Birenbaum, Halina - *Hope Is the Last to Die*
 LJ - v122 - F 1 '97 - p112 [1-50]
 R&R Bk N - v12 - F '97 - p19 [1-50]
Biriukova, Nina - *Historicism in Russia*
 BM - v139 - Ja '97 - p52 [51-250]

Birke, Lynda - *Reinventing Biology*
 NWSA Jnl - v8 - Fall '96 - p183+ [501+]
Birken, Lawrence - *Hitler as Philosophe*
 AHR - v101 - D '96 - p1570+ [251-500]
Birkenhager, Willem H - *Practical Management of Hypertension. 2nd Ed.*
 SciTech - v20 - D '96 - p47 [51-250]
Birkerts, Sven - *The Gutenberg Elegies*
 NS - v125 - S 13 '96 - p46+ [501+]
 Quad - v40 - Jl '96 - p100+ [501+]
 SFR - v21 - N '96 - p48 [1-50]
 Tolstoy's Dictaphone
 BL - v93 - Ja '97 - p808 [1-50]
 BL - v93 - S 15 '96 - p191 [51-250]
 LATBR - D 1 '96 - p4 [501+]
 Utne R - S '96 - p96+ [251-500]
Birkinshaw, Patrick - *Grievances, Remedies and the State. 2nd Ed.*
 Law Q Rev - v113 - Ja '97 - p173+ [501+]
Birkner, Michael J - *James Buchanan and the Political Crisis of the 1850s*
 Choice - v34 - F '97 - p1025 [251-500]
Birley, Derek - *Playing the Game*
 Choice - v34 - O '96 - p320+ [51-250]
Birmingham, Stephen - *Life at the Dakota*
 VQR - v72 - Aut '96 - p141* [1-50]
 The Wrong Kind of Money
 BL - v93 - My 1 '97 - p1460 [251-500]
Birnbaum, Pierre - *The Jews of the Republic*
 Choice - v34 - Ap '97 - p1396 [51-250]
 Paths of Emancipation
 JIH - v27 - Win '97 - p568+ [251-500]
Birnbaum, Stephen - *Birnbaum's Disneyland*
 r LJ - v121 - D '96 - p128 [51-250]
Birnbaum's Canada 97
 r Quill & Q - v63 - F '97 - p40 [51-250]
Birnbaum's United States 97
 yr LJ - v122 - Mr 15 '97 - p79 [51-250]
Birnbaum's Walt Disney World without Kids 1997
 r LJ - v121 - D '96 - p128 [51-250]
Birney, Betty G - *Let's Play Hide and Seek! (Illus. by Dara Goldman)*
 c PW - v244 - Ap 28 '97 - p77 [51-250]
 Pie's in the Oven (Illus. by Holly Meade)
 c CBRS - v25 - Win '97 - p61 [51-250]
 c HB Guide - v8 - Spr '97 - p20 [51-250]
 c SLJ - v42 - S '96 - p170 [51-250]
Birnie, Lisa Hobbs - *Western Lights*
 Quill & Q - v62 - My '96 - p29 [501+]
Biro, Val - *Bears Can't Fly*
 c Sch Lib - v44 - N '96 - p145 [51-250]
 Rub-a-Dub-Dub (Illus. by Val Biro)
 c Bks Keeps - Ja '97 - p18 [51-250]
Birrell, Susan - *Women, Sport, and Culture*
 Aethlon - v13 - Fall '95 - p151+ [251-500]
Birren, Bruce - *Nonmammalian Genomes Analysis*
 SciTech - v20 - D '96 - p30 [51-250]
Birren, James E - *Encyclopedia of Gerontology. Vols. 1-2*
 r ARBA - v28 - '97 - p304 [251-500]
 r BL - v93 - D 1 '96 - p682 [251-500]
 r BL - v93 - F 1 '97 - p957 [1-50]
 r Choice - v34 - Mr '97 - p1136 [51-250]
 r LJ - v122 - Ap 15 '97 - p38 [51-250]
Bischoff, Bernhard - *Biblical Commentaries from the Canterbury School of Theodore and Hadrian*
 Albion - v28 - Win '96 - p660+ [501+]
 EHR - v111 - N '96 - p1216+ [501+]
 JR - v76 - O '96 - p631+ [501+]
Bishop, Arthur - *Our Bravest and Our Best*
 Beav - v76 - O '96 - p44+ [501+]
Bishop, Chris - *The Vital Guide to Combat Guns and Infantry Weapons*
 yr ARBA - v28 - '97 - p261 [51-250]
Bishop, Donald H - *Mysticism and the Mystical Experience*
 JR - v76 - O '96 - p662+ [501+]
Bishop, Elizabeth - *Exchanging Hats*
 BL - v93 - D 15 '96 - p702 [51-250]
 Bloom Rev - v16 - N '96 - p5 [51-250]
 CSM - v88 - N 21 '96 - pB3 [51-250]
 NYTBR - v101 - D 8 '96 - p19 [51-250]
 NYTLa - v146 - D 2 '96 - pC16 [51-250]
 PW - v243 - O 14 '96 - p75 [51-250]
 WSJ-MW - v78 - D 5 '96 - pA18 [51-250]
 One Art
 HMR - Win '96 - p8+ [501+]
Bishop, Gavin - *Maui and the Sun (Illus. by Gavin Bishop)*
 c HB Guide - v7 - Fall '96 - p319 [51-250]
Bishop, Keith - *Environment*
 c Sch Lib - v44 - N '96 - p161 [51-250]

Bishop, Michael - *At the City Limits of Fate*
 BW - v26 - D 29 '96 - p6 [251-500]
 NYTBR - v102 - F 23 '97 - p20 [51-250]
Contemporary French Women Poets. Vol. 1
 FR - v70 - F '97 - p458+ [251-500]
Contemporary French Women Poets. Vols. 1-2
 WLT - v70 - Sum '96 - p661+ [501+]
Bishop, Nic - *The Secrets of Animal Flight (Illus. by Nic Bishop)*
 c BL - v93 - Mr 15 '97 - p1236 [51-250]
 c HB - v73 - My '97 - p337 [51-250]
 c KR - v65 - F 1 '97 - p219 [51-250]
Bishop, Roma - *Easter Babies (Illus. by Roma Bishop)*
 c Ch BWatch - v6 - My '96 - p2 [1-50]
 Easter Counting (Illus. by Roma Bishop)
 c Ch BWatch - v6 - My '96 - p2+ [1-50]
 Easter Egg Hunt (Illus. by Roma Bishop)
 c Ch BWatch - v6 - My '96 - p2+ [1-50]
 Easter Sunday (Illus. by Roma Bishop)
 c Ch BWatch - v6 - My '96 - p2 [1-50]
Bishop, Victoria - *Landform Systems*
 TES - Mr 28 '97 - pR5+ [251-500]
Bisio, Attilio - *Wiley Encyclopedia of Energy and the Environment. Vols. 1-2*
 r Choice - v34 - Mr '97 - p1144+ [51-250]
 r SciTech - v20 - D '96 - p72 [51-250]
Biskupic, Joan - *The Supreme Court and Individual Rights. 3rd Ed.*
 BWatch - v18 - F '97 - p11+ [51-250]
Bissell, Richard M - *Reflections of a Cold Warrior*
 BW - v26 - Jl 14 '96 - p1+ [501+]
 Choice - v34 - O '96 - p359+ [251-500]
 HRNB - v25 - Win '97 - p90 [251-500]
 TLS - D 27 '96 - p6 [501+]
Bisson, Terry - *Pirates of the Universe*
 NYTBR - v101 - D 8 '96 - p94 [1-50]
 y SLJ - v42 - O '96 - p162 [51-250]
Bissonette, Bruce - *Travel Air*
 FSM - v15 - Ja '97 - p79 [1-50]
Bissoondath, Neil - *Selling Illusions*
 Can Lit - Win '96 - p171+ [501+]
Biswas, Suddhendu - *Applied Stochastic Processes*
 SIAM Rev - v39 - Mr '97 - p144 [251-500]
Bitel, Lisa M - *Land of Women*
 Choice - v34 - N '96 - p515+ [51-250]
Bitterer, Andreas - *AS/400 Application Development with VisualAge for Smalltalk*
 SciTech - v20 - D '96 - p12 [51-250]
Bittnar, Zdenek - *Numerical Methods in Structural Mechanics*
 SciTech - v20 - D '96 - p64 [51-250]
Bittner, Rosanne - *Tame the Wild Wind*
 PW - v243 - S 9 '96 - p81 [51-250]
 Texas Embrace
 PW - v244 - Mr 17 '97 - p81 [51-250]
Bittner, Wolfgang - *Wake Up, Grizzly! (Illus. by Gustavo Rosemffet)*
 c BL - v92 - Ag '96 - p1906 [51-250]
 c HB Guide - v7 - Fall '96 - p248 [1-50]
 c RT - v50 - F '97 - p424 [51-250]
Bitton-Jackson, Livia - *I Have Lived a Thousand Years*
 y BL - v93 - Mr 15 '97 - p1233 [51-250]
 y CCB-B - v50 - Ap '97 - p274+ [51-250]
 y PW - v244 - F 3 '97 - p108 [51-250]
Bixler, Susan - *Take Action!*
 BL - v93 - Ja '97 - p793 [51-250]
Bizer, Marc - *La Poesie Au Miroir*
 Ren & Ref - v20 - Win '96 - p84+ [501+]
Bizony, Piers - *2001: Filming the Future*
 SF Chr - v18 - O '96 - p80 [1-50]
 Island in the Sky
 Nature - v383 - O 31 '96 - p780 [1-50]
Bizzocchi, Roberto - *Genealogie Incredibili*
 Ren Q - v49 - Aut '96 - p598+ [501+]
Bizzotto, Elisa - *Walter Pater 1839-1894*
 Nine-C Lit - v51 - Mr '97 - p554 [51-250]
Bjarkman, Peter C - *Baseball with a Latin Beat*
 Aethlon - v13 - Spr '96 - p226 [251-500]
 Sports Great Dominique Wilkins
 c HB Guide - v8 - Spr '97 - p143 [1-50]
 Sports Great Scottie Pippen
 c HB Guide - v8 - Spr '97 - p143 [1-50]
 Top 10 Basketball Slam Dunkers
 y BL - v93 - Ap 1 '97 - p1306 [1-50]
Bjerke, Gene - *Writing for Video*
 LJ - v122 - Ap 1 '97 - p102 [51-250]
Bjojani, Namas - *Bombay: A Contemporary Account of Mumbai*
 FEER - v159 - D 19 '96 - p59 [501+]

Bjorck, Ake - *Numerical Methods for Least Squares Problems*
 Choice - v34 - N '96 - p496 [51-250]
 SciTech - v20 - S '96 - p9 [51-250]
Bjordal, Asmund - *Longlining*
 SciTech - v20 - D '96 - p58 [1-50]
Bjorhovde, Reidar - *Connections in Steel Structures III*
 SciTech - v20 - D '96 - p64 [51-250]
Bjork, Elizabeth Ligon - *Memory*
 Choice - v34 - Mr '97 - p1243 [51-250]
Bjork, Robert E - *Cynewulf: Basic Readings*
 R&R Bk N - v11 - N '96 - p69 [51-250]
Bjorling, Anna-Lisa - *Jussi*
 AB - v98 - D 9 '96 - p1994 [51-250]
 BL - v93 - S 15 '96 - p199 [51-250]
 LJ - v121 - D '96 - p95 [51-250]
 ON - v61 - Ja 25 '97 - p51+ [251-500]
Bjorn, Claus - *Nations, Nationalism and Patriotism in the European Past*
 EHR - v112 - F '97 - p275+ [501+]
Bjornson, Richard - *The African Quest for Freedom and Identity*
 Dal R - v75 - Spr '95 - p132+ [501+]
Bjornstad, David J - *The Contingent Valuation of Environmental Resources*
 Econ J - v107 - Ja '97 - p287 [251-500]
 JEL - v34 - S '96 - p1496 [51-250]
 R&R Bk N - v11 - N '96 - p21 [51-250]
Blach, James - *Prescription for Nutritional Healing. 2nd Ed.*
 BWatch - v17 - D '96 - p3 [1-50]
Black, Allida M - *Casting Her Own Shadow*
 SE - v60 - S '96 - p302 [51-250]
 Casting Her Own Shadow (Schraf). Audio Version
 LJ - v121 - N 15 '96 - p104 [51-250]
 What I Hope to Leave Behind
 SE - v60 - S '96 - p302 [51-250]
Black, Ayanna - *Voices: Canadian Writers of African Descent*
 y Quill & Q - v63 - F '97 - p58 [1-50]
Black, Baxter - *Hey, Cowboy, Wanna Get Lucky?*
 Aethlon - v13 - Fall '95 - p137 [251-500]
Black, C Clifton - *Mark: Images of an Apostolic Interpreter*
 JAAR - v64 - Fall '96 - p680+ [501+]
Black, Charles L, Jr. - *A New Birth of Freedom*
 PW - v244 - My 12 '97 - p66 [51-250]
Black, David - *An Impossible Life*
 PW - v244 - F 3 '97 - p95+ [51-250]
Black, Duncan - *Formal Contributions to the Theory of Public Choice*
 JEL - v34 - S '96 - p1414+ [51-250]
 R&R Bk N - v11 - N '96 - p25 [51-250]
Black, Fischer - *Exploring General Equilibrium*
 JEL - v35 - Mr '97 - p127+ [501+]
Black, Gregory D - *Hollywood Censored*
 CLW - v66 - Je '96 - p40+ [251-500]
Black, Jeffrey M - *Partnerships in Birds*
 Sci - v276 - Ap 11 '97 - p216 [501+]
Black, Jeremy - *British Foreign Policy in an Age of Revolution 1783-1793*
 EHR - v111 - N '96 - p1300+ [251-500]
 Cambridge Illustrated Atlas, Warfare: Renaissance to Revolution 1492-1792
 r ARBA - v28 - '97 - p251 [51-250]
 r J Mil H - v61 - Ja '97 - p151+ [501+]
 yr Sch Lib - v44 - Ag '96 - p127 [51-250]
 r Six Ct J - v27 - Win '96 - p1116+ [501+]
 r SLMQ - v25 - Fall '96 - p62 [51-250]
 European Warfare 1660-1815
 JMH - v68 - D '96 - p972+ [501+]
 A History of the British Isles
 r HT - v46 - O '96 - p59 [1-50]
 NS - v125 - S 20 '96 - p44+ [501+]
 TES - S 20 '96 - p8* [501+]
 TLS - F 14 '97 - p29 [501+]
 An Illustrated History of Eighteenth-Century Britain
 HT - v46 - O '96 - p58 [1-50]
Black, Kathryn - *In the Shadow of Polio*
 Bloom Rev - v16 - S '96 - p20 [501+]
 Choice - v34 - N '96 - p490+ [51-250]
 Wom R Bks - v14 - Mr '97 - p8+ [51-250]
Black, Maggie, 1945- - *Children First*
 Choice - v34 - Ap '97 - p1422 [51-250]
 In the Twilight Zone
 J Gov Info - v23 - S '96 - p671+ [51-250]
Black, Nancy B - *The Perilous Cemetery*
 Specu - v72 - Ja '97 - p110+ [501+]
 TranslRevS - v1 - My '95 - p21 [51-250]
Black, Paul - *Changing the Subject*
 SciTech - v21 - Mr '97 - p3 [51-250]

Black, Thom - *Kicking Your Kid Out of the Nest*
  Adoles - v31 - Fall '96 - p751 [51-250]
Black, Uyless - *Mobile and Wireless Networks*
  SciTech - v20 - S '96 - p55 [51-250]
Black, Veronica - *A Vow of Poverty*
  y BL - v93 - N 15 '96 - p574 [51-250]
     KR - v64 - S 15 '96 - p1355+ [51-250]
     LJ - v121 - N 1 '96 - p111 [1-50]
     PW - v243 - S 16 '96 - p74 [51-250]
Black Girl Talk Collective - *Black Girl Talk*
  y Ch Bk News - v19 - Spr '96 - p22 [251-500]
Black Literature 1827-1940. Electronic Media Version
  r Choice - v34 - Ap '97 - p1319+ [251-500]
The Black Pearl. Vol. 3
  Quill & Q - v62 - Jl '96 - p42 [501+]
Black Public Sphere Collective - *The Black Public Sphere*
  Bl S - v26 - Sum '96 - p63 [51-250]
  CS - v25 - N '96 - p817+ [501+]
Black Renaissance/Renaissance Noire
  p LJ - v122 - My 1 '97 - p42 [51-250]
Black Studies on CD-ROM. Electronic Media Version
  r WorldV - v12 - Jl '96 - p23 [51-250]
Blackaby, Mark - *Look What They've Done to the Blues*
  TLS - Mr 28 '97 - p22 [251-500]
Blackbridge, Persimmon - *Sunnybrook: A True Story with Lies*
  BIC - v26 - Mr '97 - p40 [51-250]
  Bloom Rev - v17 - Ja '97 - p14 [251-500]
  HMR - Spr '97 - p43+ [501+]
  Quill & Q - v62 - D '96 - p34 [251-500]
Blackburn, George G - *The Guns of Victory*
  Quill & Q - v62 - O '96 - p37 [251-500]
Blackburn, Julia - *The Book of Color*
  NYTBR - v101 - S 8 '96 - p36 [51-250]
  Trib Bks - Ja 19 '97 - p8 [1-50]
  The Book of Colour
  Books - v9 - S '95 - p9 [51-250]
Blackburn, Ken - *Kids' Paper Airplane Book*
  c PW - v243 - D 2 '96 - p62 [51-250]
  c SB - v33 - Mr '97 - p53 [51-250]
  The World Record Paper Airplane Book
  c Inst - v106 - S '96 - p87 [1-50]
Blackburn, Robert T - *Faculty at Work*
  CS - v26 - Mr '97 - p230+ [501+]
  J Hi E - v67 - N '96 - p716+ [501+]
  TCR - v98 - Spr '97 - p537+ [501+]
Blackburn, Robin - *The Making of New World Slavery*
  LATBR - Mr 16 '97 - p11 [501+]
  LJ - v122 - Ja '97 - p118 [51-250]
  Nat - v264 - Mr 31 '97 - p25+ [501+]
  NS - v126 - Mr 14 '97 - p44+ [501+]
  Obs - Mr 23 '97 - p17* [501+]
Blackburn, Simon - *The Oxford Dictionary of Philosophy*
  r Phil R - v105 - Ap '96 - p250+ [501+]
Blackburn, Stuart - *Inside the Drama-House*
  Choice - v34 - N '96 - p472 [51-250]
Blackburn, Virginia - *Blonde with Attitude*
  Books - v11 - Ap '97 - p23 [51-250]
Blacker, Terence - *Dream Team*
  c Books - v11 - Ap '97 - p24 [51-250]
  On the Wing
  c Books - v11 - Ap '97 - p24 [51-250]
  Pride and Penalties
  c Books - v11 - Ap '97 - p24 [51-250]
  Revenance
  Obs - F 2 '97 - p18* [51-250]
  Shooting Star
  c Books - v11 - Ap '97 - p24 [51-250]
  You're Kidding, Ms. Wiz (Illus. by Tony Ross)
  c Bks Keeps - N '96 - p9 [51-250]
  c JB - v60 - D '96 - p246 [51-250]
Blackford, Mansel G - *BFGoodrich: Tradition and Transformation 1870-1995*
  BL - v93 - Ja '97 - p793 [51-250]
Blackhurst, Hector - *East and Northeast Africa Bibliography*
  r ARBA - v28 - '97 - p50 [251-500]
  r Choice - v34 - Mr '97 - p1134 [251-500]
  r R&R Bk N - v12 - F '97 - p21 [51-250]
Blacking, John - *Music, Culture and Experience*
  TLS - S 13 '96 - p9+ [501+]
  WestFolk - v55 - Spr '96 - p163+ [51-250]
Blackman, Malorie - *A.N.T.I.D.O.T.E.*
  c Sch Lib - v44 - Ag '96 - p104 [51-250]
  Betsey's Birthday Surprise (Illus. by Lis Toft)
  c JB - v60 - Ag '96 - p145+ [51-250]
  c Sch Lib - v44 - Ag '96 - p104 [51-250]
  The Mellion Moon Mystery (Illus. by Patrice Aggs)
  c Sch Lib - v45 - F '97 - p23 [51-250]
  The Quasar Quartz Quest (Illus. by Patrice Aggs)
  c Sch Lib - v45 - F '97 - p23 [51-250]

Thief
  c Magpies - v11 - My '96 - p42 [51-250]
Blackman, Sushila - *Graceful Exits*
  PW - v244 - My 12 '97 - p73 [51-250]
Blackmore, Charles - *The Worst Desert on Earth*
  BL - v92 - Ag '96 - p1876+ [51-250]
  GJ - v162 - N '96 - p340 [51-250]
  LJ - v121 - O 15 '96 - p80 [51-250]
Blackmore, Susan J - *In Search of the Light. Rev. and Updated Ed.*
  Choice - v34 - D '96 - p691 [51-250]
  New Sci - v152 - N 16 '96 - p47 [1-50]
  SB - v33 - Mr '97 - p36 [251-500]
  Skeptic - v4 - 3 '96 - p105 [251-500]
Blackstock, Terri - *Never Again Goodbye*
  y BL - v93 - S 1 '96 - p65 [501+]
  When Dreams Cross
  BL - v93 - Ja '97 - p819 [51-250]
  LJ - v122 - F 1 '97 - p66 [51-250]
Blackstone, Stella - *Grandma Went to Market (Illus. by Bernard Lodge)*
  c HB Guide - v7 - Fall '96 - p248 [51-250]
  Where's the Cat? (Illus. by Debbie Harter)
  c HB Guide - v8 - Spr '97 - p10 [51-250]
  Who Are You? (Illus. by Debbie Harter)
  c HB Guide - v8 - Spr '97 - p10 [51-250]
Blackwell, Kenneth - *A Bibliography of Bertrand Russell. Vols. 1-3*
  r Dialogue - v36 - Win '97 - p202+ [251-500]
Blackwill, Robert D - *Damage Limitation or Crisis?*
  NWCR - v50 - Win '97 - p157+ [501+]
Blades, Ann - *Back to the Cabin (Illus. by Ann Blades)*
  c BIC - v26 - Mr '97 - p34 [251-500]
  c Quill & Q - v62 - S '96 - p72 [251-500]
Blaeser, Kimberly - *Gerald Vizenor: Writing in the Oral Tradition*
  Choice - v34 - Ja '97 - p791 [51-250]
Blaikie, Andrew - *Illegitimacy, Sex and Society*
  EHR - v111 - N '96 - p1314+ [251-500]
Blaikie, Piers - *At Risk*
  EG - v72 - O '96 - p460+ [501+]
Blain, Susan A - *Imaging the Word. Vol. 3*
  CC - v113 - D 11 '96 - p1233 [51-250]
Blain, W R - *Hydraulic Engineering Software VI*
  SciTech - v21 - Mr '97 - p81 [51-250]
Blair, Anne E - *Lodge in Vietnam*
  AHR - v102 - F '97 - p224 [501+]
  RAH - v24 - D '96 - p695+ [501+]
Blair, Billie G - *Curriculum: The Strategic Key to Schooling. 2nd Ed.*
  R&R Bk N - v11 - N '96 - p56 [51-250]
Blair, Carol - *Setting the Stage for Strategic Planning for Alberta's Continued Response to HIV/AIDS to the Year 2000*
  J Gov Info - v23 - S '96 - p625 [51-250]
Blair, Clay - *Hitler's U-Boat War*
  BW - v26 - N 3 '96 - p3+ [501+]
  Choice - v34 - Ap '97 - p1402 [51-250]
  KR - v64 - S 15 '96 - p1365 [251-500]
  LJ - v121 - O 15 '96 - p70 [51-250]
  PW - v243 - O 7 '96 - p54+ [51-250]
Blair, John - *Anglo-Saxon Oxfordshire*
  EHR - v111 - N '96 - p1234+ [501+]
  The Cloister and the World
  TLS - Ag 2 '96 - p32 [51-250]
Blair, John P, 1947- - *Local Economic Development*
  EG - v72 - O '96 - p453+ [501+]
Blair, Karen J - *The Torchbearers: Women and Their Amateur Arts Associations in America 1890-1930*
  Am Q - v49 - Mr '97 - p193+ [501+]
Blair, Leona - *Fascination*
  BL - v93 - Ja '97 - p816 [51-250]
  KR - v64 - D 1 '96 - p1686+ [251-500]
  LJ - v121 - N 15 '96 - p87 [51-250]
  PW - v243 - D 16 '96 - p43 [51-250]
Blair, Linda - *Design Sense*
  BL - v93 - S 1 '96 - p49 [51-250]
  LJ - v121 - S 15 '96 - p68 [51-250]
Blair, Malcolm - *Steel Castings Handbook. 6th Ed.*
  r SciTech - v20 - N '96 - p82 [51-250]
Blair, Margaret M - *Ownership and Control*
  ILR - v135 - '96 - p111+ [501+]
  JEL - v34 - D '96 - p1971+ [501+]
  NYRB - v44 - Ap 10 '97 - p38+ [501+]
Blair, Margot - *The Red String*
  c Ch BWatch - v6 - S '96 - p7 [1-50]
Blair, Rob - *The Western San Juan Mountains*
  WHQ - v28 - Spr '97 - p102 [1-50]
Blair, Sara - *Henry James and the Writing of Race and Nation*
  Choice - v34 - D '96 - p611 [51-250]

Blair, Sheila - *The Art and Architecture of Islam 1250-1800*
  MEJ - v51 - Win '97 - p152 [51-250]
  PW - v243 - O 21 '96 - p78 [1-50]
Blair, Tony - *New Britain*
  Obs - S 15 '96 - p1*+ [501+]
  PW - v244 - F 3 '97 - p90 [51-250]
  TLS - O 18 '96 - p13 [501+]
  WSJ-Cent - v99 - Ap 21 '97 - pA16 [501+]
Blais, Jan David - *Flight Path*
  PW - v243 - O 21 '96 - p72 [51-250]
Blais, Madeleine - *In These Girls, Hope Is a Muscle*
  Aethlon - v13 - Spr '96 - p208+ [501+]
  y Emerg Lib - v24 - S '96 - p23 [1-50]
Blais, Marie-Claire - *The Angel of Solitude*
  TranslRevS - v1 - My '95 - p18 [51-250]
Blaise, Clark - *If I Were Me*
  Quill & Q - v63 - Mr '97 - p71 [251-500]
Blaivas, Jerry G - *Evaluation and Treatment of Urinary Incontinence*
  SciTech - v20 - S '96 - p37 [51-250]
Blajan, Daniel - *Foxgloves and Hedgehog Days*
  KR - v65 - Mr 15 '97 - p427 [251-500]
  PW - v244 - F 3 '97 - p84 [51-250]
Blake, Andrew - *The Body Language*
  Obs - S 8 '96 - p18* [51-250]
Blake, Barbara - *A Guide to Children's Books about Asian Americans*
  r Bkbird - v34 - Spr '96 - p56 [51-250]
Blake, Chris - *The Ratpackers*
  y Aust Bk R - N '96 - p60 [501+]
Blake, David - *Researching School-Based Teacher Education*
  R&R Bk N - v11 - N '96 - p55 [51-250]
Blake, David, 1954- - *Pension Schemes and Pension Funds in the United Kingdom*
  ILRR - v50 - Ap '97 - p518+ [501+]
Blake, Gary - *The I Hate Kathie Lee Gifford Book*
  Ent W - F 7 '97 - p64 [51-250]
Blake, Jack - *Comes the Millennium*
  BW - v26 - S 8 '96 - p5 [501+]
Blake, Jennifer - *Garden of Scandal*
  PW - v244 - Mr 10 '97 - p64 [51-250]
  Golden Fancy
  LJ - v122 - Ja '97 - p155 [51-250]
Blake, L L - *The Prince and the Professor*
  CR - v268 - Je '96 - p327+ [501+]
Blake, Lillie Devereux - *Fettered for Life*
  LJ - v122 - F 1 '97 - p112 [1-50]
  PW - v243 - D 2 '96 - p53 [51-250]
Blake, Michael - *Marching to Valhalla*
  y BL - v93 - S 1 '96 - p29 [51-250]
  Esq - v126 - D '96 - p40 [1-50]
  KR - v64 - Ag 15 '96 - p1169 [251-500]
  LJ - v121 - S 15 '96 - p94 [51-250]
  Marching to Valhalla (Blake). Audio Version
  LJ - v122 - Ja '97 - p172 [51-250]
Blake, N F - *A History of the English Language*
  TES - N 15 '96 - p8* [501+]
Blake, Nancy - *Lotions, Potions and Slime*
  c SFR - v21 - Jl '96 - p47 [51-250]
Blake, Naomi - *Enquiry Statistics*
  LR - v45 - 7 '96 - p48+ [51-250]
Blake, Peter - *The Master Builders*
  NYTBR - v101 - S 22 '96 - p40 [1-50]
  No Place like Utopia
  NYTBR - v101 - S 22 '96 - p40 [1-50]
Blake, Philippa - *Waiting for the Sea to Be Blue*
  Books - v10 - Je '96 - p23 [51-250]
  PW - v244 - Mr 31 '97 - p68 [1-50]
Blake, Quentin - *Clown (Illus. by Quentin Blake)*
  c HB Guide - v7 - Fall '96 - p248 [51-250]
  c NYTBR - v101 - S 22 '96 - p28 [501+]
  c NYTLa - v146 - D 9 '96 - pC18 [51-250]
  The Puffin Book of Nonsense Verse (Illus. by Quentin Blake)
  c Bks Keeps - Ja '97 - p23 [51-250]
  Quentin Blake Book of Nonsense Stories (Illus. by Quentin Blake)
  c Bks Keeps - v100 - S '96 - p32 [51-250]
  c Bks Keeps - Ja '97 - p8+ [501+]
  The Quentin Blake Book of Nonsense Stories (Illus. by Quentin Blake)
  c Bks Keeps - Ja '97 - p8+ [501+]
  Quentin Blake Book of Nonsense Stories (Illus. by Quentin Blake)
  c Spec - v277 - D 14 '96 - p77 [51-250]
Blake, Robert J - *Spray (Illus. by Robert J Blake)*
  c HB Guide - v7 - Fall '96 - p248 [51-250]
  c RT - v50 - My '97 - p684 [51-250]

Blakely, Mary Kay - *Red, White, and Oh So Blue*
  BL - v93 - S 1 '96 - p41 [251-500]
  BW - v26 - S 15 '96 - p13 [51-250]
  Ms - v7 - S '96 - p80+ [501+]
  NYTBR - v101 - O 13 '96 - p20 [51-250]
  Wom R Bks - v14 - Ja '97 - p17+ [501+]
Blakely, Mike - *Spanish Blood*
  Roundup M - v4 - D '96 - p24 [51-250]
Blakemore, Michael - *Next Season*
  TLS - D 27 '96 - p22 [51-250]
Blakeslee, Thomas R - *Beyond the Conscious Mind*
  Rapport - v19 - 4 '96 - p34 [251-500]
Blakesley, Lance - *Presidential Leadership from Eisenhower to Clinton*
  SSQ - v78 - Mr '97 - p242+ [501+]
Blalock, Susan E - *Guide to the Secular Poetry of T.S. Eliot*
  r ARBA - v28 - '97 - p443 [51-250]
  r Choice - v34 - Ap '97 - p1306 [51-250]
Blanc, Alan - *Stairs, Steps, and Ramps*
  r SciTech - v20 - S '96 - p52 [51-250]
Blanc, Cecile - *Commentaire Sur S. Jean. Vol. 5*
  Rel St Rev - v22 - O '96 - p301+ [501+]
Blanc, Raymond - *A Blanc Christmas*
  ILN - Christmas '96 - p90 [1-50]
Blancett, Suzanne Smith - *Case Studies in Nursing Case Management*
  SciTech - v21 - Mr '97 - p69 [51-250]
  Reengineering Nursing and Health Care
  AJN - v96 - D '96 - p16N [51-250]
Blanchard, Alice - *The Stuntman's Daughter and Other Stories*
  Choice - v34 - N '96 - p452 [51-250]
  KR - v64 - My 1 '96 - p639 [51-250]
Blanchard, Kenneth H - *Empowerment Takes More than a Minute*
  Per Psy - v50 - Spr '97 - p216+ [501+]
  Managing by Values
  LJ - v122 - F 1 '97 - p92 [51-250]
  Mission Possible
  BL - v93 - S 1 '96 - p2 [51-250]
  Choice - v34 - My '97 - p1543 [51-250]
  LJ - v122 - F 1 '97 - p92 [51-250]
  PW - v243 - S 2 '96 - p102 [51-250]
Blanchard, Olivier Jean - *The Transition in Eastern Europe. Vol. 1*
  Slav R - v55 - Sum '96 - p444+ [501+]
Blanchard, Stephen - *Gargarin and I*
  NS & S - v9 - My 24 '96 - p40 [1-50]
  Wilson's Island
  TLS - F 7 '97 - p22 [501+]
Blanchard, William H - *Neocolonialism American Style 1960-2000*
  Choice - v34 - Ja '97 - p874 [51-250]
  R&R Bk N - v11 - D '96 - p16 [51-250]
Blanchard-Lemee, Michele - *Mosaics of Roman Africa*
  LJ - v122 - F 1 '97 - p76 [51-250]
  PW - v243 - N 18 '96 - p58 [51-250]
Blanchflower, David G - *The Wage Curve*
  BusLR - v21 - 3 '96 - p234 [51-250]
  ILRR - v50 - Ap '97 - p526+ [501+]
Blanchot, Maurice - *Awaiting Oblivion*
  KR - v65 - My 1 '97 - p679 [51-250]
  The Most High
  RCF - v16 - Fall '96 - p184+ [251-500]
  TranslRevS - v2 - D '96 - p21 [51-250]
Bland, Eleanor Taylor - *Keep Still*
  BW - v26 - Ag 18 '96 - p8 [51-250]
Blane, Andrew - *Georges Florovsky: Russian Intellectual and Orthodox Churchman*
  Rel St Rev - v23 - Ap '97 - p192 [51-250]
Blank, G Kim - *Influence and Resistance in Nineteenth-Century English Poetry*
  VS - v39 - Spr '96 - p451+ [501+]
Blank, Martin - *Electromagnetic Fields*
  SciTech - v20 - N '96 - p31 [51-250]
Blank, Robert H - *Encyclopedia of U.S. Biomedical Policy*
  r ARBA - v28 - '97 - p606 [51-250]
  r Choice - v34 - Ja '97 - p766 [51-250]
  r Hast Cen R - v26 - S '96 - p40 [1-50]
  r R&R Bk N - v11 - N '96 - p77 [51-250]
  Human Reproduction, Emerging Technologies, and Conflicting Rights
  Pol Stud J - v24 - Sum '96 - p332 [51-250]
Blank, Stephen - *Responding to Low-Intensity Challenges*
  RSR - v24 - 3 '96 - p46 [51-250]
Blankenthorn, David - *Fatherless America*
  Soc - v33 - S '96 - p89+ [501+]

Blanning, T C W - *The French Revolutionary Wars 1787-1802*
  HT - v47 - Ja '97 - p60+ [501+]
  J Mil H - v61 - Ap '97 - p372+ [501+]
  Joseph II
  EHR - v112 - F '97 - p214+ [251-500]
  The Oxford Illustrated History of Modern Europe
  HRNB - v25 - Fall '96 - p32 [251-500]
  y SLJ - v42 - Ag '96 - p185 [51-250]
  TLS - My 24 '96 - p10 [501+]
Blanpied, Pamela Wharton - *Dragons: The Modern Infestation*
  TLS - Ap 11 '97 - p28 [251-500]
Blanton, Richard E - *Houses and Households*
  AJA - v100 - O '96 - p777+ [501+]
Blase, Joseph - *The Micropolitics of Educational Leadership*
  Choice - v34 - O '96 - p332 [51-250]
Blashford-Snell, John - *Mammoth Hunt*
  New Sci - v151 - S 21 '96 - p54 [51-250]
Blasi, Joseph R - *Kremlin Capitalism*
  Choice - v34 - Ap '97 - p1385 [51-250]
  LJ - v122 - Ja '97 - p114 [51-250]
  NYRB - v44 - Mr 27 '97 - p28+ [501+]
Blasing, Mutlu Konuk - *Politics and Form in Postmodern Poetry*
  VQR - v73 - Win '97 - p14* [51-250]
Blasius, Mark - *Gay and Lesbian Politics*
  J Pol - v58 - Ag '96 - p890+ [501+]
  SSQ - v77 - Je '96 - p457+ [501+]
Blass, Virginia A - *Loaves and Fishes*
  CLW - v67 - D '96 - p46+ [51-250]
Blastenbrei, Peter - *Kriminalitat In Rom 1560-1585*
  J Soc H - v30 - Spr '97 - p752+ [501+]
  Ren Q - v49 - Win '96 - p840+ [501+]
  Six Ct J - v27 - Fall '96 - p885+ [501+]
Blatchford, Claire - *Full Face*
  PW - v244 - Mr 3 '97 - p61 [51-250]
Blatchford, Claire H - *Nick's Mission*
  c SLJ - v42 - O '96 - p120 [51-250]
Blatchford, Roy - *Reflected Values*
  Sch Lib - v44 - Ag '96 - p128 [251-500]
  y TES - D 6 '96 - pR5 [251-500]
Blathwayt, Benedict - *Bella Goes to Sea*
  c Bks Keeps - N '96 - p6+ [51-250]
  Bella's Big Adventure
  c Bks Keeps - N '96 - p6+ [51-250]
  Kip: A Dog's Day (Illus. by Benedict Blathwayt)
  c JB - v60 - O '96 - p181 [51-250]
  c Sch Lib - v44 - Ag '96 - p98 [51-250]
  The Runaway Train (Illus. by Benedict Blathwayt)
  c SLJ - v42 - N '96 - p78 [51-250]
Blatt, Martin Henry - *Work, Recreation, and Culture*
  JEL - v34 - D '96 - p2098 [51-250]
Blatty, William Peter - *Demons Five, Exorcists Nothing*
  Necro - Win '97 - p18+ [501+]
  NYTBR - v102 - Ja 19 '97 - p18 [251-500]
Blatz, Perry K - *Democratic Miners*
  J Am St - v30 - Ap '96 - p142+ [251-500]
Blauer, Ettagale - *Swaziland*
  c HB Guide - v8 - Spr '97 - p171 [51-250]
Blaug, Mark - *The Quantity Theory of Money*
  JEL - v34 - D '96 - p1944+ [501+]
Blaukopf, Kurt - *Musical Life in a Changing Society*
  TranslRevS - v1 - My '95 - p12 [1-50]
Blaumeiser, Hubertus - *Martin Luthers Kreuzestheologie*
  Rel St Rev - v23 - Ap '97 - p191+ [51-250]
  Six Ct J - v27 - Fall '96 - p796+ [501+]
Blauner, Peter - *The Intruder*
  PW - v244 - Ja 27 '97 - p103 [1-50]
  TLS - O 25 '96 - p22 [251-500]
Blaut, James M - *The Colonizer's Model of the World*
  EG - v72 - O '96 - p463+ [501+]
  S&S - v61 - Sum '97 - p272+ [501+]
Blaxter, Loraine - *How to Research*
  R&R Bk N - v11 - N '96 - p76 [51-250]
Blay, Michel - *Les Principia De Newton*
  Isis - v87 - D '96 - p701+ [501+]
Blazek, Jody - *Financial Planning for Nonprofit Organizations*
  ChrPhil - v9 - D 12 '96 - p48 [51-250]
Blazek, Sarah Kirwan - *A Leprechaun's St. Patrick's Day*
  c Ch BWatch - v7 - F '97 - p2 [51-250]
Blazes, Terry Richard - *Goldsmith's Return*
  BWatch - v17 - D '96 - p6 [51-250]
Blazey, Peter - *Love Cries*
  Quill & Q - v62 - Jl '96 - p42 [501+]
Blazin' Auralities
  p Sm Pr R - v28 - O '96 - p14+ [501+]
Blazyca, George - *Monitoring Economic Transition*
  Econ J - v106 - N '96 - p1851+ [51-250]

Bldard-Gibson, Jacqueline - *Ligne Directs*
  TES - Mr 7 '97 - pR8 [51-250]
Blechman, R O - *The Life of Saint Nicholas*
  y BL - v93 - N 15 '96 - p561 [51-250]
  NYTBR - v101 - D 22 '96 - p14 [51-250]
Blecker, Robert A - *U.S. Trade Policy and Global Growth*
  JEL - v35 - Mr '97 - p138+ [501+]
Bledsoe, Jerry - *The Angel Doll*
  NYTBR - v101 - D 8 '96 - p102 [51-250]
Bledsoe, Lucy Jane - *Working Parts*
  BL - v93 - Ap 1 '97 - p1279 [51-250]
  KR - v65 - Mr 1 '97 - p318 [51-250]
  LJ - v122 - Ap 1 '97 - p120+ [51-250]
Bleeding Velvet Octopus
  p Sm Pr R - v28 - D '96 - p13+ [501+]
Blegvad, Lenore - *A Sound of Leaves (Illus. by Erik Blegvad)*
  c HB - v72 - S '96 - p592 [51-250]
  c HB Guide - v7 - Fall '96 - p289+ [51-250]
Bleidt, Barry - *Clinical Research in Pharmaceutical Development*
  SciTech - v20 - D '96 - p54 [51-250]
Bleile, Ken M - *Articulation and Phonological Disorders. 2nd Ed.*
  SciTech - v20 - D '96 - p44 [51-250]
Bleiman, Barbara - *Klondyke Kate and Other Non-Fiction Texts*
  y TES - Mr 7 '97 - p6* [501+]
Blejer, Mario I - *Financial Factors in Economic Stabilization and Growth*
  JEL - v35 - Mr '97 - p270 [51-250]
Blenkinsop, Philip - *The Cars That Ate Bangkok*
  FEER - v160 - Ap 17 '97 - p47 [501+]
Bleser, Carol - *Tokens of Affection*
  Choice - v34 - O '96 - p352 [51-250]
Bless, R C - *Discovering the Cosmos*
  SciTech - v20 - D '96 - p20 [51-250]
Blet, Pierre - *Le Clerge Du Grand Siecle En Ses Assemblees 1615-1717*
  CHR - v83 - Ja '97 - p106+ [501+]
Blevins, Carolyn DeArmond - *Women in Christian History*
  r ARBA - v28 - '97 - p333+ [251-500]
  r CH - v66 - Mr '97 - p214+ [51-250]
Blewett, David - *The Illustration of Robinson Crusoe 1719-1920*
  BC - v45 - Aut '96 - p409+ [501+]
  r Choice - v34 - N '96 - p443 [51-250]
Bliemann, Barbara - *Headless and Other Stories*
  y TES - N 22 '96 - p20* [51-250]
Blinn, James W - *The Aardvark Is Ready for War*
  KR - v65 - Mr 1 '97 - p318+ [51-250]
  LJ - v122 - Ap 1 '97 - p122 [51-250]
  PW - v244 - Ap 28 '97 - p51+ [51-250]
Bliokh, Paval - *Dusty and Self-Gravitational Plasmas in Space*
  Phys Today - v50 - F '97 - p68 [501+]
Blish, James - *A Dusk of Idols and Other Stories*
  LJ - v121 - N 15 '96 - p92 [51-250]
Blishen, Edward - *Oxford Book of Poetry for Children (Illus. by Brian Wildsmith)*
  c Bks Keeps - Ja '97 - p23 [51-250]
  Stand Up, Mr. Dickens (Illus. by Jill Bennett)
  c HB Guide - v7 - Fall '96 - p363 [1-50]
Bliss, Debbie - *Bright Knits for Kids*
  McCall Nee - v42 - D '96 - p13 [51-250]
Bliss, Marilyn - *The Compact Music Dictionary*
  r ARBA - v28 - '97 - p470 [51-250]
Bliss, Michael, 1947- - *What Goes around Comes Around*
  FQ - v50 - Win '96 - p62 [251-500]
  The Word Made Flesh
  Choice - v34 - O '96 - p288+ [251-500]
Blitch, Charles P - *Allyn Young: The Peripatetic Economist*
  JEL - v34 - S '96 - p1403 [51-250]
Blitman, Joe - *Barbie Doll's Cousin Francie and Her Mod, Mod, Mod, Mod World of Fashion*
  r Ant & CM - v101 - S '96 - p27 [1-50]
  r Ant & CM - v101 - N '96 - p31 [1-50]
Blitz, Leo - *Unsolved Problems of the Milky Way*
  SciTech - v20 - D '96 - p22 [51-250]
Blizzard, Richard - *Blizzard's Garden Woodwork*
  BL - v93 - Ap 1 '97 - p1273 [51-250]
Blobaum, Robert E - *Rewolucja: Russian Poland 1904-1907*
  AHR - v101 - D '96 - p1579+ [501+]
Bloch, H Spencer - *Adolescent Development, Psychopathology, and Treatment*
  Soc Ser R - v71 - Mr '97 - p165 [51-250]

Bloch, Konrad - *Blondes in Venetian Paintings, the Nine-Banded Armadillo and Other Essays in Biochemistry*
  Sci - v273 - S 20 '96 - p1672+ [501+]
Bloch, Marc - *Correspondance. Vol. 1*
  JMH - v68 - S '96 - p671+ [501+]
  TLS - D 13 '96 - p10 [501+]
Bloch, Michael - *The Duchess of Windsor*
  BW - v27 - F 16 '97 - p13 [51-250]
  KR - v64 - N 15 '96 - p1643+ [251-500]
  LJ - v122 - Ja '97 - p108 [51-250]
  Mac - v109 - N 11 '96 - p93+ [501+]
  PW - v243 - D 2 '96 - p46 [51-250]
Bloch, R Howard - *Future Libraries*
  CS - v26 - Mr '97 - p241+ [501+]
  LQ - v67 - Ap '97 - p191+ [501+]
Block, David - *Mission Culture on the Upper Amazon*
  CHR - v83 - Ja '97 - p159+ [51-250]
  EHR - v111 - S '96 - p998+ [251-500]
Block, Francesca Lia - *Baby Be-Bop*
  y Emerg Lib - v24 - S '96 - p24 [1-50]
  Girl Goddess #9
  y BL - v93 - O 1 '96 - p340 [51-250]
  y BL - v93 - Ap 1 '97 - p1310 [51-250]
  y CBRS - v25 - Ja '97 - p56 [51-250]
  y CCB-B - v50 - O '96 - p49 [51-250]
  y HB - v72 - N '96 - p742 [251-500]
  y HB Guide - v8 - Spr '97 - p77 [51-250]
  y NYTBR - v102 - Ap 13 '97 - p27 [1-50]
  y SLJ - v42 - S '96 - p224 [51-250]
  y SLJ - v42 - D '96 - p28 [1-50]
  y VOYA - v19 - F '97 - p326 [251-500]
  Missing Angel Juan
  y SLJ - v43 - Ja '97 - p36 [1-50]
  Weetzie Bat (Bresnahan). Audio Version
  y HB - v73 - Ja '97 - p85+ [501+]
  y Kliatt - v31 - Ja '97 - p47 [51-250]
Block, Fred L - *The Vampire State and Other Myths and Fallacies about the U.S. Economy*
  Nat - v264 - Ja 27 '97 - p30+ [501+]
Block, Geoffrey - *Charles Ives and the Classical Tradition*
  Choice - v34 - N '96 - p469 [51-250]
  TLS - O 18 '96 - p18+ [501+]
Block, Lawrence - *The Burglar in the Library*
  PW - v244 - Ap 28 '97 - p53 [51-250]
  Even the Wicked
  BL - v93 - N 15 '96 - p548 [51-250]
  KR - v64 - N 15 '96 - p1633 [51-250]
  LATBR - Ap 20 '97 - p13 [501+]
  NYTBR - v102 - F 16 '97 - p28 [51-250]
  PW - v243 - N 18 '96 - p64 [51-250]
  Trib Bks - F 2 '97 - p4 [51-250]
  Out the Window. Audio Version
  BWatch - v17 - D '96 - p11 [1-50]
  Sometimes They Bite and Other Stories (Weitz). Audio Version
  y Kliatt - v31 - My '97 - p44 [51-250]
Block, Richard N - *Labor Law, Industrial Relations and Employee Choice*
  JEL - v35 - Mr '97 - p240 [51-250]
Block, William M - *Recovery Plan for the Mexican Spotted Owl: Draft*
  J Gov Info - v23 - S '96 - p571 [51-250]
Blockbuster Entertainment Movies and Videos. Electronic Media Version
  r Econ - v339 - My 18 '96 - p16* [501+]
Block De Behar, Lisa - *A Rhetoric of Silence and Other Selected Writings*
  WLT - v70 - Sum '96 - p768 [251-500]
Block's Magazine
  p Sm Pr R - v28 - N '96 - p19 [251-500]
Blodgett, George B - *Record of Deaths in the First Church in Rowley, Massachusetts 1696-1777*
  r EGH - v50 - N '96 - p172 [51-250]
Bloem, Marion - *The Cockatoo's Life*
  BW - v26 - Ag 25 '96 - p12 [51-250]
Bloembergen, N - *Encounters in Magnetic Resonances*
  Sci - v274 - N 15 '96 - p1149 [51-250]
Bloemink, Barbara J - *The Life and Art of Florine Stettheimer*
  Art J - v55 - Sum '96 - p91+ [501+]
Bloesch, Donald - *God the Almighty*
  Rel St Rev - v23 - Ja '97 - p46 [51-250]
Blok, Mark W J - *Dynamic Models of the Firm*
  JEL - v34 - D '96 - p2020 [51-250]
Blom, Frans - *English Catholic Books 1701-1800*
  r ARBA - v28 - '97 - p547 [51-250]
  r R&R Bk N - v12 - F '97 - p11 [1-50]
Blomberg, Craig L - *How Wide the Divide?*
  PW - v244 - Mr 24 '97 - p74 [51-250]

Blomberg, Thomas G - *Punishment and Social Control*
  CS - v25 - N '96 - p796+ [501+]
  Fed Prob - v60 - Je '96 - p86+ [501+]
Blomley, Nicholas K - *Law, Space and the Geographies of Power*
  SSQ - v77 - D '96 - p941+ [501+]
Blomquist, Thomas W - *The Other Tuscany*
  EHR - v112 - F '97 - p174+ [501+]
  Ren Q - v50 - Spr '97 - p264+ [501+]
Blondel, Maurice - *Oeuvres Completes. Vol. 1*
  Dialogue - v35 - Sum '96 - p614+ [501+]
Blonston, Gary - *William Morris: Artifacts/Glass*
  Am Craft - v56 - Ag '96 - p28 [1-50]
Blood, Peter R - *Pakistan: A Country Study*
  MEJ - v50 - Aut '96 - p626 [51-250]
Blood Cell Biochemistry. Vol. 7
  SciTech - v20 - D '96 - p33 [51-250]
Bloom, Adrian - *Summer Garden Glory*
  TES - Ag 23 '96 - p22 [51-250]
Bloom, Alan - *Blooms of Bressingham Garden Plants*
  r Hort - v94 - Mr '97 - p78+ [251-500]
Bloom, Allan David - *Love and Friendship*
  RM - v49 - Je '96 - p913+ [501+]
Bloom, Amy - *Come to Me*
  SFR - v21 - S '96 - p48 [51-250]
  Love Invents Us
  y BL - v93 - D 15 '96 - p708 [51-250]
  BW - v27 - F 23 '97 - p3+ [501+]
  KR - v64 - D 1 '96 - p1687 [251-500]
  LATBR - Ja 12 '97 - p8 [501+]
  LJ - v121 - D '96 - p141 [51-250]
  NYTBR - v102 - Ja 19 '97 - p23 [501+]
  PW - v243 - N 18 '96 - p61 [51-250]
  Trib Bks - Ja 26 '97 - p3 [501+]
Bloom, Carole - *Sugar and Spice*
  BL - v93 - N 15 '96 - p559 [51-250]
  BWatch - v18 - F '97 - p7 [1-50]
  LJ - v121 - D '96 - p135+ [51-250]
  PW - v243 - O 7 '96 - p70 [51-250]
Bloom, Claire - *Leaving a Doll's House*
  Am Theat - v13 - D '96 - p21 [1-50]
  Ant R - v55 - Spr '97 - p237+ [251-500]
  BW - v26 - O 20 '96 - p3 [501+]
  KR - v64 - S 1 '96 - p1286+ [251-500]
  LATBR - O 13 '96 - p3 [501+]
  LJ - v121 - N 15 '96 - p63 [51-250]
  Lon R Bks - v19 - F 20 '97 - p30 [501+]
  NW - v128 - S 30 '96 - p78 [501+]
  NY - v72 - N 4 '96 - p102+ [501+]
  NYTBR - v101 - O 13 '96 - p7 [501+]
  NYTBR - v101 - D 8 '96 - p88 [1-50]
  Obs - N 3 '96 - p16* [501+]
  PW - v243 - S 2 '96 - p104 [51-250]
  Spec - v277 - N 2 '96 - p48+ [501+]
  Spec - v277 - N 23 '96 - p44 [1-50]
  Time - v148 - S 30 '96 - p75 [51-250]
  TLS - O 25 '96 - p31 [501+]
  W&I - v12 - Mr '97 - p257+ [501+]
Bloom, Clive - *Cult Fiction*
  Choice - v34 - My '97 - p1493 [51-250]
  Literature and Culture in Modern Britain. Vol. 1
  RES - v47 - Ag '96 - p446+ [501+]
Bloom, Harold - *Charlotte Bronte's Jane Eyre*
  y BL - v93 - Mr 1 '97 - p828 [51-250]
  Ernest Hemingway's The Sun Also Rises
  y SLJ - v43 - Mr '97 - p197 [51-250]
  Lesbian and Bisexual Fiction Writers
  PW - v244 - F 24 '97 - p80 [1-50]
  Maya Angelou's I Know Why the Caged Bird Sings
  y BL - v93 - Ja '97 - p828 [251-500]
  y SLJ - v43 - Mr '97 - p197 [51-250]
  Omens of Millennium
  BL - v92 - Ag '96 - p1859 [51-250]
  BW - v26 - S 15 '96 - p11 [501+]
  CC - v114 - Ap 9 '97 - p372 [251-500]
  Econ - v341 - D 7 '96 - p9+ [501+]
  LATBR - D 15 '96 - p6 [501+]
  LJ - v121 - O 1 '96 - p83 [51-250]
  Lon R Bks - v18 - O 31 '96 - p10 [501+]
  NS - v125 - N 8 '96 - p44+ [501+]
  NYTBR - v101 - S 8 '96 - p11+ [501+]
  NYTLa - v146 - S 27 '96 - pC32 [501+]
  Utne R - S '96 - p92 [1-50]
  W&I - v12 - Ja '97 - p289+ [501+]
  Ruin the Sacred Truths
  APR - v26 - Ja '97 - p37+ [501+]
  Vergil's Aeneid
  y KR - v64 - D 15 '96 - p1807 [51-250]

  The Western Canon
  Can Lit - Win '96 - p152+ [501+]
  CR - v268 - Je '96 - p331+ [501+]
  Salm - Fall '96 - p216+ [501+]
  Specu - v71 - Jl '96 - p686+ [501+]
  TES - Ja 10 '97 - p6* [501+]
Bloom, James D - *The Literary Bent*
  BW - v27 - Ap 13 '97 - p9 [501+]
  PW - v244 - Mr 10 '97 - p60+ [51-250]
Bloom, John - *A House of Cards*
  KR - v65 - Ja 15 '97 - p107 [251-500]
  LJ - v122 - F 1 '97 - p83 [1-50]
  PW - v244 - F 17 '97 - p206 [51-250]
Bloom, Ken - *American Song. 2nd Ed., Vols. 1-2*
  r ARBA - v28 - '97 - p491 [251-500]
  r BL - v93 - O 1 '96 - p367 [51-250]
  r Choice - v34 - D '96 - p586 [51-250]
Bloom, Lynn - *Composition in the Twenty-First Century*
  Col Comp - v47 - D '96 - p616 [51-250]
Bloom, Paul - *Language and Space*
  R&R Bk N - v12 - F '97 - p75 [51-250]
Bloom, Steven - *No New Jokes*
  KR - v65 - F 1 '97 - p155+ [251-500]
  PW - v244 - F 17 '97 - p211 [51-250]
Bloom, Valerie - *Fruits: A Caribbean Counting Poem (Illus. by David Axtell)*
  c BL - v93 - Mr 15 '97 - p1244+ [51-250]
  c CBRS - v25 - Mr '97 - p92 [51-250]
  c CCB-B - v50 - Ap '97 - p275 [51-250]
  c KR - v65 - F 15 '97 - p297 [51-250]
  c PW - v244 - F 24 '97 - p89+ [51-250]
Bloom, William - *Money, Heart and Mind*
  BL - v93 - O 1 '96 - p310 [51-250]
  LJ - v121 - O 1 '96 - p94 [51-250]
Bloomberg, Michael - *Bloomberg by Bloomberg*
  Bus W - My 5 '97 - p18 [51-250]
Bloomberg Personal
  p LJ - v122 - My 1 '97 - p42+ [51-250]
Bloomfield, Harold H - *How to Be Safe in an Unsafe World*
  PW - v244 - Ap 28 '97 - p63 [251-500]
Bloomfield, Louis A - *How Things Work*
  Choice - v34 - Mr '97 - p1198 [51-250]
  y SB - v33 - Mr '97 - p45 [51-250]
  SciTech - v20 - D '96 - p22 [51-250]
Bloomquist, L Gregory - *The Function of Suffering in Philippians*
  Rel St Rev - v23 - Ja '97 - p74 [51-250]
Bloomquist, Michael L - *Skills Training for Children with Behavior Disorders*
  SB - v32 - N '96 - p231 [51-250]
  SciTech - v20 - S '96 - p41 [51-250]
The Bloomsbury Review
  p Sm Pr R - v28 - S '96 - p13+ [51-250]
Bloor, Edward - *Tangerine*
  y BL - v93 - My 15 '97 - p1573 [51-250]
  y CCB-B - v50 - Mr '97 - p241 [51-250]
  y KR - v65 - F 1 '97 - p219 [51-250]
  y PW - v244 - Mr 24 '97 - p84 [51-250]
Blos, Joan W - *The Days before Now (Illus. by Thomas B Allen)*
  c SLJ - v42 - D '96 - p44+ [51-250]
  Nellie Bly's Monkey (Illus. by Catherine Stock)
  c HB Guide - v7 - Fall '96 - p285 [51-250]
  c SLJ - v42 - D '96 - p45 [51-250]
Blosser, Philip - *Scheler's Critique of Kant's Ethics*
  Ethics - v107 - O '96 - p194+ [51-250]
Blossfeld, Hans-Peter - *The New Role of Women*
  SF - v75 - S '96 - p384+ [251-500]
  Techniques of Event History Modeling
  JEL - v34 - D '96 - p2023 [51-250]
Blot, Jean-Yves - *Underwater Archaeology*
  Nature - v385 - Ja 30 '97 - p407 [51-250]
Blot, Pierre - *Karate for Beginners*
  c BL - v92 - Ag '96 - p1897 [51-250]
Blotner, Joseph - *Robert Penn Warren: A Biography*
  Am - v176 - Mr 22 '97 - p33 [251-500]
  BL - v93 - N 1 '96 - p474 [51-250]
  BW - v27 - F 23 '97 - p5 [501+]
  KR - v64 - N 15 '96 - p1644 [251-500]
  LJ - v121 - D '96 - p92 [51-250]
  NYTBR - v102 - Mr 9 '97 - p11+ [501+]
  PW - v243 - N 11 '96 - p61 [51-250]
  TLS - F 28 '97 - p5+ [501+]
  WSJ-Cent - v99 - F 27 '97 - pA15 [501+]
Blotzer, M A - *Sometimes You Just Want to Feel like a Human Being*
  AJMR - v101 - Jl '96 - p90+ [501+]
Blount, Marcellus - *Representing Black Men*
  Choice - v34 - S '96 - p110 [51-250]

Blow, Christopher J - *Airport Terminals. 2nd Ed.*
R&R Bk N - v11 - D '96 - p58 [51-250]
Blow, J Julian - *Eukaryotic DNA Replication*
Choice - v34 - My '97 - p1522 [51-250]
Blow, Laura - *Financing Regional Government in Britain*
JEL - v34 - D '96 - p2140 [51-250]
Bloyd, Sunni - *Animal Rights*
y SLJ - v42 - O '96 - p45 [1-50]
Bluck, Robert - *Team Management*
LAR - v98 - Je '96 - p317 [51-250]
Blue, Adrianne - *Martina*
y BL - v93 - D 15 '96 - p716 [1-50]
On Kissing
KR - v65 - Ap 1 '97 - p513+ [251-500]
PW - v244 - My 12 '97 - p67 [51-250]
Blue, Rose - *Good Yontif (Illus. by Lynne Feldman)*
c PW - v244 - Ja 13 '97 - p71 [51-250]
c SLJ - v43 - Mr '97 - p171 [51-250]
Blue, Ted - *Delphi Database Development*
SciTech - v20 - N '96 - p11 [51-250]
Blue, William R - *Spanish Comedies and Historical Contexts in the 1620s*
Choice - v34 - Ap '97 - p1343 [51-250]
Blue Jean Magazine: For Girls Who Dare
yp SLJ - v42 - N '96 - p36 [1-50]
Bluegrass Music Festival: 1996 Guide for U.S. and Canada
r LJ - v121 - N 1 '96 - p40 [1-50]
Bluett, Rick - *The Untimely Death of a Nihilist*
TLS - Mr 28 '97 - p22 [501+]
Bluhm, Andreas - *Philipp Otto Runge, Caspar David Friedrich*
BM - v138 - S '96 - p621+ [501+]
Blum, Bill - *The Last Appeal*
PW - v244 - Mr 24 '97 - p81 [51-250]
Blum, Cinzia Sartini - *The Other Modernism*
Choice - v34 - N '96 - p463 [51-250]
Blum, Erhard - *Studien Zur Komposition Des Pentateuch*
Rel St Rev - v23 - Ja '97 - p22+ [501+]
Blum, Joshua - *The United States of Poetry*
y BL - v93 - Ap 1 '97 - p1288 [1-50]
y SLJ - v42 - S '96 - p240 [1-50]
Blum, Karl - *Density Matrix Theory and Applications. 2nd Ed.*
SciTech - v21 - Mr '97 - p21 [51-250]
Blum, Laurie - *Free Money for Small Businesses and Entrepreneurs. 4th Ed.*
r B Ent - v27 - D '96 - p36 [51-250]
Free Money for the Arts. New Expanded, Rev. and Updated Ed.
r TCI - v30 - O '96 - p55 [51-250]
Free Money from the Federal Government for Small Businesses and Entrepreneurs. 2nd Ed.
r ARBA - v28 - '97 - p94 [251-500]
Blum, Raymond - *Math Tricks, Puzzles and Games*
c BL - v93 - Ap 1 '97 - p1341 [1-50]
Blumberg, Rae Lesser - *Engendering Wealth and Well-Being*
NWSA Jnl - v8 - Sum '96 - p134+ [501+]
Blumberg, Rhoda - *Full Steam Ahead*
c BW - v26 - O 6 '96 - p11 [251-500]
c CCB-B - v50 - D '96 - p129 [51-250]
c HB - v72 - S '96 - p607 [51-250]
y HB Guide - v7 - Fall '96 - p385 [51-250]
c NY - v72 - N 18 '96 - p98 [1-50]
c SLJ - v42 - Ag '96 - p150 [51-250]
Blumberg Selinger, Robin L - *Fracture: Instability Dynamics, Scaling, and Ductile/Brittle Behavior*
SciTech - v20 - S '96 - p49 [51-250]
Blume, Judy - *Forever*
y Emerg Lib - v23 - My '96 - p66 [51-250]
Superfudge
c BL - v93 - My 1 '97 - p1506 [1-50]
Tales of a Fourth Grade Nothing (Blume). Audio Version
c BL - v93 - Mr 15 '97 - p1253 [51-250]
c Emerg Lib - v24 - Mr '97 - p24 [1-50]
c PW - v244 - F 3 '97 - p46 [51-250]
Blumenthal, David R - *Facing the Abusing God*
JAAR - v65 - Spr '97 - p206+ [501+]
Blumenthal, Deborah - *The Chocolate-Covered-Cookie Tantrum (Illus. by Harvey Stevenson)*
c CCB-B - v50 - S '96 - p6 [51-250]
c HB Guide - v8 - Spr '97 - p20 [51-250]
c PW - v243 - S 23 '96 - p75 [51-250]
c SLJ - v42 - S '96 - p170+ [51-250]
Blumenthal, Eileen - *Julie Taymor: Playing with Fire*
Am Theat - v13 - D '96 - p21 [1-50]
Blumrosen, Alfred W - *Modern Law*
PSR - v25 - '96 - p310+ [501+]

Blundell, Richard - *The Determinants and Effects of Work-Related Training in Britain*
JEL - v34 - D '96 - p2070 [51-250]
Blundell, Sue - *Women in Ancient Greece*
Rel St Rev - v23 - Ja '97 - p61 [51-250]
Blundell, Tony - *Beware of Boys*
c Par Ch - v20 - N '96 - p3+ [51-250]
Blundell-Jones, Peter - *Hans Scharoun*
TLS - My 24 '96 - p20+ [501+]
Blunden, Edmund - *Overtones of War*
TLS - D 27 '96 - p25 [501+]
Blunkett, David - *On a Clear Day*
TES - O 4 '96 - p7* [51-250]
On a Clear Day (Thorne). Audio Version
c Kliatt - v31 - Mr '97 - p49 [51-250]
Blunt, Alison - *Travel, Gender and Imperialism*
GJ - v162 - Jl '96 - p239 [51-250]
Blunt, Jerry - *Stage Dialects and More Stage Dialects*
Am Theat - v13 - D '96 - p21 [1-50]
Bluth, Christoph - *The Collapse of Soviet Military Power*
JPR - v33 - Ag '96 - p377+ [251-500]
Bluthenthal, Diana Cain - *Matilda the Moocher (Illus. by Diana Cain Bluthenthal)*
c BL - v93 - Mr 15 '97 - p1246 [51-250]
c CCB-B - v50 - Ap '97 - p275 [51-250]
c KR - v65 - Mr 1 '97 - p377 [51-250]
c PW - v244 - Mr 10 '97 - p66 [51-250]
Bly, Carol - *Changing the Bully Who Rules the World*
HMR - Fall '96 - p6+ [501+]
Bly, R D - *Money While You Sleep*
BWatch - v17 - N '96 - p7+ [51-250]
Bly, Robert - *Morning Poems*
PW - v244 - Mr 31 '97 - p71 [51-250]
The Sibling Society
Am - v175 - S 28 '96 - p34+ [501+]
Bks & Cult - v3 - Ja '97 - p24+ [501+]
HMR - Fall '96 - p12+ [501+]
LATBR - S 15 '96 - p4+ [501+]
New R - v215 - S 16 '96 - p31+ [501+]
NS - v125 - N 15 '96 - p47+ [501+]
NYRB - v43 - N 28 '96 - p22+ [501+]
Spec - v277 - D 7 '96 - p42+ [501+]
W&I - v11 - O '96 - p290+ [501+]
The Sibling Society (Bly). Audio Version
BL - v93 - N 15 '96 - p604 [51-250]
The Soul Is Here for Its Own Joy
Bloom Rev - v16 - N '96 - p14 [51-250]
Bly, Robert W - *Why You Should Never Beam Down in a Red Shirt*
SF Chr - v18 - O '96 - p81 [1-50]
Bly, Stephen A, 1944- - *My Foot's in the Stirrup...*
LJ - v121 - N 1 '96 - p52 [51-250]
Stay Away from That City...They Call It Cheyenne
y VOYA - v19 - O '96 - p205 [51-250]
Blyth, Alan - *Opera on Video*
r ON - v61 - O '96 - p65 [251-500]
Blyth, Derek - *Flemish Cities Explored. Rev. Ed.*
TLS - N 1 '96 - p31 [51-250]
Blyth, Eric - *Exclusion from School*
TES - Ag 30 '96 - p32 [51-250]
Blyton, Enid - *Five Fall into Adventure. Book and Audio Version*
c TES - Ag 30 '96 - p28 [51-250]
Five Go Adventuring Again. Book and Audio Version
c TES - Ag 30 '96 - p28 [51-250]
Five Go off to Camp. Book and Audio Version
c TES - Ag 30 '96 - p28 [51-250]
Five Have Plenty of Fun. Book and Audio Version
c TES - Ag 30 '96 - p28 [51-250]
BMA Family Health Encyclopedia. Electronic Media Version
r TES - Mr 14 '97 - p37U [51-250]
Bo, Arno - *I Must Tell You Something*
c Magpies - v11 - S '96 - p31 [51-250]
c Sch Lib - v44 - Ag '96 - p110 [51-250]
Bo, Yang - *Jiang Gang Zhen Dang*
BL - v93 - N 1 '96 - p484 [1-50]
Boa, Elizabeth - *Kafka: Gender, Class, and Race in the Letters and Fictions*
Choice - v34 - N '96 - p462+ [51-250]
Boadt, Lawrence - *Biblical Studies*
Rel Ed - v91 - Fall '96 - p601 [1-50]
Boahen, A Adu - *Mfantsipim and the Making of Ghana*
Choice - v34 - Ap '97 - p1393 [51-250]
Boal, Frederick W - *Shaping a City*
Bks & Cult - v2 - Ja '96 - p11+ [501+]
Boardingham, Robert - *Impressionist Masterpieces in American Museums*
LJ - v122 - F 15 '97 - p130 [51-250]

Boardman, Edna - *All Things Decently and in Order and Other Writing on a Germans from Russia Heritage*
y Kliatt - v31 - My '97 - p20+ [51-250]
Boardman, John - *The Diffusion of Classical Art in Antiquity*
Apo - v144 - Jl '96 - p64+ [501+]
Greek Art. 4th Ed.
LJ - v122 - Ap 15 '97 - p76 [51-250]
Boardman, Peter - *The Boardman Tasker Omnibus*
HM - v293 - Ag '96 - p64+ [501+]
Boardman, Stephen - *The Early Stewart Kings*
TES - D 27 '96 - p16 [1-50]
Boas, Jacob - *We Are Witnesses*
y Emerg Lib - v24 - S '96 - p23 [1-50]
y Kliatt - v31 - Ja '97 - p18 [51-250]
Boas, Ralph P - *A Primer of Real Functions. 4th Ed.*
SciTech - v20 - D '96 - p18 [1-50]
Boateng, Faustine Ama - *Asante*
y SLJ - v43 - Mr '97 - p197+ [51-250]
Boatner, Mark Mayo - *Biographical Dictionary of World War II*
r ARBA - v28 - '97 - p210 [251-500]
r BL - v93 - F 15 '97 - p1040+ [251-500]
r LJ - v122 - Ap 15 '97 - p64 [51-250]
yr SLJ - v43 - F '97 - p136 [51-250]
r TLS - F 7 '97 - p10 [501+]
Boats and Ships (Voyages of Discovery)
c BL - v93 - D 15 '96 - p732 [1-50]
c HB Guide - v7 - Fall '96 - p350 [51-250]
Boaz, David - *The Libertarian Reader*
HE - v53 - F 7 '97 - p17 [51-250]
Nat R - v49 - F 24 '97 - p48+ [501+]
NL - v80 - F 10 '97 - p13+ [501+]
Libertarianism: A Primer
BL - v93 - Ja '97 - p785+ [51-250]
Choice - v34 - My '97 - p1573 [51-250]
HE - v53 - F 7 '97 - p17 [51-250]
KR - v64 - N 15 '96 - p1644+ [251-500]
LATBR - Ja 19 '97 - p6+ [501+]
LJ - v122 - Ja '97 - p123 [51-250]
Nat R - v49 - F 24 '97 - p48+ [501+]
NL - v80 - F 10 '97 - p13+ [501+]
PW - v243 - D 30 '96 - p51+ [51-250]
Reason - v28 - Mr '97 - p56+ [501+]
Trib Bks - Mr 9 '97 - p5 [501+]
WSJ-Cent - v99 - Ja 13 '97 - pA14 [501+]
Bobbio, Norberto - *Ideological Profile of Twentieth-Century Italy*
PSQ - v111 - Win '96 - p710+ [501+]
Thomas Hobbes and the Natural Law Tradition
Sev Cent N - v54 - Fall '96 - p61+ [501+]
Bober, Natalie - *Abigail Adams: Witness to a Revolution*
y BL - v93 - D 15 '96 - p716 [1-50]
y EJ - v85 - N '96 - p132 [251-500]
y Emerg Lib - v24 - S '96 - p23 [1-50]
c RT - v50 - S '96 - p58 [51-250]
Bobkov, Filipp - *KGB I Vlast'*
BL - v93 - O 1 '96 - p327 [1-50]
Bobo, Jacqueline - *Black Women as Cultural Readers*
J Am St - v30 - Ag '96 - p318+ [501+]
NWSA Jnl - v8 - Sum '96 - p130+ [501+]
Bobrowski, Johannes - *Levin's Mill*
PW - v243 - N 4 '96 - p37 [51-250]
Bocchi, F - *Altante Storico Delle Citta Italiane. Vols. 1-9*
r J Urban H - v22 - S '96 - p739+ [501+]
Bock, Carl E - *Credit--Get It!*
ACI - v8 - Fall '96 - p38+ [501+]
Bock, Gregory R - *Olfaction in Mosquito-Host Interactions*
SciTech - v21 - Mr '97 - p46 [51-250]
Bock, Hal - *Steve Young*
c HB Guide - v7 - Fall '96 - p359 [1-50]
Bock, Hans-Hermann - *Data Analysis and Information Systems*
JEL - v34 - D '96 - p2019+ [51-250]
Bock, Philip K - *Psychological Anthropology*
AJPsych - v153 - Ag '96 - p1103 [251-500]
Bockmuehl, Markus - *This Jesus*
BL - v93 - S 1 '96 - p35+ [51-250]
Rel St Rev - v23 - Ap '97 - p178 [51-250]
Bockol, Leslie - *Victorian Majolica*
Ant & CM - v101 - S '96 - p27 [1-50]
Bockoven, Georgia - *An Unspoken Promise*
PW - v243 - D 30 '96 - p63 [51-250]
Bockstoce, John R - *Whales, Ice and Men*
J Am Cult - v19 - Sum '96 - p158 [51-250]
Bockstruck, Lloyd DeWitt - *Revolutionary War Bounty Land Grants Awarded by State Governments*
r Am Geneal - v71 - Ap '96 - p128 [51-250]
r EGH - v50 - N '96 - p159 [51-250]

Bockting, Ineke - *Character and Personality in the Novels of William Faulkner*
AL - v68 - S '96 - p663 [1-50]

Bock-Weiss, Catherine C - *Henri Matisse: A Guide to Research*
r ARBA - v28 - '97 - p370 [251-500]
r Choice - v34 - F '97 - p939 [51-250]
r R&R Bk N - v12 - F '97 - p72 [51-250]

Bodansky, David - *Nuclear Energy*
Choice - v34 - Ja '97 - p834 [51-250]
SciTech - v20 - N '96 - p76 [51-250]

Bodart, Joni Richards - *The Book Talker. Vol. 2*
SLMQ - v25 - Fall '96 - p62+ [51-250]

Boddington, Andy - *Raunds Furnells, Northants*
HT - v46 - O '96 - p55 [1-50]

Bode, Janet - *Food Fight*
c PW - v244 - Ap 14 '97 - p77 [51-250]
Hard Time
y BL - v93 - Ap 1 '97 - p1286 [1-50]
y BL - v93 - Ap 1 '97 - p1306 [1-50]
y HB Guide - v7 - Fall '96 - p316 [51-250]
Trust and Betrayal
y Emerg Lib - v24 - S '96 - p26 [1-50]
y Kliatt - v31 - Mr '97 - p24 [51-250]
y PW - v244 - Ja 20 '97 - p403 [1-50]

Bode, Michael F - *Robotic Observatories*
Robotica - v14 - S '96 - p587 [251-500]

Boden, Deirdre - *The Business of Talk*
Lang Soc - v25 - S '96 - p459+ [501+]

Boden, Margaret A - *Artificial Intelligence*
Choice - v34 - Ja '97 - p832 [51-250]
SciTech - v20 - N '96 - p5 [51-250]
The Philosophy of Artificial Life
Choice - v34 - N '96 - p473 [51-250]

Bodenheimer, Rosemarie - *The Real Life of Mary Ann Evans*
MP - v94 - N '96 - p252+ [501+]

Bodhidharma - *Off the Wall*
Tric - v6 - Fall '96 - p142 [1-50]

Bodie, Zvi - *Securing Employer-Based Pensions*
ILRR - v50 - Ja '97 - p347+ [501+]
JEL - v34 - D '96 - p2072 [51-250]
M Lab R - v119 - O '96 - p85 [501+]

Bodiford, William M - *Soto Zen in Medieval Japan*
Rel St Rev - v22 - O '96 - p313+ [501+]

Bodin, Jean - *On the Demon-Mania of Witches*
Six Ct J - v27 - Fall '96 - p835 [251-500]

Bodine, Walter R - *Discourse Analysis of Biblical Literature*
Rel St Rev - v23 - Ja '97 - p54 [51-250]

Bodkin, Odds - *The Banshee Train (Illus. by Ted Rose)*
c Ch BWatch - v6 - Jl '96 - p4 [51-250]
c PW - v243 - S 16 '96 - p85 [1-50]

Bodnar, John - *Bonds of Affection*
Lon R Bks - v19 - Mr 6 '97 - p22+ [501+]
VQR - v73 - Win '97 - p27* [51-250]

Bodnar, Judit Z - *A Wagonload of Fish (Illus. by Alexi Natchev)*
c HB Guide - v7 - Fall '96 - p319 [1-50]

Bodo, Murray - *A Retreat with Francis and Clare of Assisi*
CLW - v67 - Mr '97 - p37 [51-250]

Bodsworth, Nan - *Mike's Bulldozer and the Big Flood*
c Magpies - v11 - My '96 - p53 [1-50]

Boeckman, Charles - *When the Devil Came to Endless Roundup M - v3 - Ag '96 - p28 [51-250]

Boehler, Jean-Michel - *Une Societe Rurale En Milieu Rhenan. Vols. 1-3*
AHR - v102 - F '97 - p118+ [501+]
EHR - v112 - Ap '97 - p480+ [501+]

Boehling, Rebecca L - *A Question of Priorities*
Choice - v34 - My '97 - p1556 [51-250]

Boehm, Arlene - *A Cheerful Note for Jack (Illus. by Arlene Boehm)*
c Ch BWatch - v7 - Ja '97 - p3 [51-250]

Boehm, Deborah Boliver - *A Zen Romance*
NYRB - v43 - Je 6 '96 - p31+ [501+]
Tric - v6 - Win '96 - p99+ [501+]
Wom R Bks - v14 - N '96 - p26+ [501+]

Boehm, Gottfried - *Canto D'Amore*
BM - v138 - O '96 - p707+ [501+]

Boehmer, Elleke - *Colonial and Postcolonial Literature*
WLT - v70 - Sum '96 - p768+ [501+]

Boehmer, Rainer Michael - *Uruk: Die Graber*
AJA - v101 - Ja '97 - p169+ [501+]

Boehrer, Bruce Thomas - *Monarchy and Incest in Renaissance England*
MP - v94 - Ag '96 - p92+ [501+]

Boelts, Maribeth - *Little Bunny's Preschool Countdown (Illus. by Kathy Parkinson)*
c BL - v93 - S 15 '96 - p245 [51-250]
c HB Guide - v8 - Spr '97 - p10 [51-250]
c SLJ - v42 - N '96 - p78 [51-250]

Boer, Inge - *Orientations 3*
MEJ - v50 - Sum '96 - p456 [51-250]

Boer, J A Den - *Advances in the Neurobiology of Schizophrenia*
AJPsych - v153 - O '96 - p1360+ [501+]

Boer, Johan A Den - *Clinical Management of Anxiety*
SciTech - v21 - Mr '97 - p55 [51-250]

Boesak, Willa - *God's Wrathful Children*
Rel St Rev - v23 - Ja '97 - p51 [51-250]

Boesche, Roger - *Theories of Tyranny*
APSR - v90 - D '96 - p887 [501+]
RM - v50 - D '96 - p388+ [501+]

Boethius - *Institution Arithmetique (Guillaumin)*
Isis - v88 - Mr '97 - p132+ [501+]

Boff, Leonardo - *Ecology and Liberation*
Am - v175 - N 23 '96 - p26+ [501+]
TT - v53 - O '96 - p424 [51-250]

Boga, Steven - *Horseshoes*
y BL - v93 - S 15 '96 - p202 [51-250]
c Ch BWatch - v7 - F '97 - p8 [1-50]

Bogacki, Tomasz - *Cat and Mouse (Illus. by Tomasz Bogacki)*
c CBRS - v24 - Ag '96 - p157 [1-50]
c HB Guide - v8 - Spr '97 - p20 [51-250]
c SLJ - v42 - S '96 - p171 [51-250]
I Hate You! I Like You! (Illus. by Tomasz Bogacki)
c CBRS - v25 - Mr '97 - p85 [1-50]
c KR - v65 - Ja 15 '97 - p138 [51-250]
c SLJ - v43 - Mr '97 - p148 [51-250]

Bogarde, Dirk - *Cleared for Take-Off*
Woman's J - N '96 - p12 [1-50]

Bogart, Greg - *Therapeutic Astrology*
Horoscope - v63 - Ap '97 - p40+ [501+]

Bogart, Jo Ellen - *Gifts (Illus. by Barbara Reid)*
c HB Guide - v7 - Fall '96 - p248+ [51-250]

Bogart, Leo - *Strategy in Advertising. 3rd Ed.*
Choice - v34 - D '96 - p654 [51-250]

Bogart, Stephen Humphrey - *Bogart: In Search of My Father*
Rapport - v19 - 4 '96 - p40 [51-250]
Bogart: In Search of My Father (Whitener). Audio Version
LJ - v121 - O 1 '96 - p142 [51-250]
The Remake: As Time Goes By
BL - v93 - F 1 '97 - p927 [51-250]
KR - v65 - F 1 '97 - p173 [251-500]
PW - v244 - Ja 13 '97 - p58 [51-250]

Bogdanor, Vernon - *The Monarchy and the Constitution*
Choice - v34 - S '96 - p202 [51-250]
PSQ - v111 - Win '96 - p712+ [501+]
Politics and the Constitution
R&R Bk N - v12 - F '97 - p60 [51-250]

Bogdanovich, Peter - *Who the Devil Made It*
BW - v27 - Mr 23 '97 - p13 [51-250]
Ent W - Ap 18 '97 - p60+ [501+]
KR - v65 - F 15 '97 - p263 [251-500]
LATBR - Ap 6 '97 - p4 [501+]
LJ - v122 - Ap 15 '97 - p83 [51-250]
NYTBR - v102 - Ap 20 '97 - p28 [501+]
PW - v244 - Mr 17 '97 - p68 [51-250]

Bogen, Don - *The Known World*
LJ - v122 - F 15 '97 - p137+ [51-250]
PW - v244 - Ja 27 '97 - p94 [51-250]

Boger, John Charles - *Race, Poverty, and American Cities*
JEL - v35 - Mr '97 - p234 [51-250]
LJ - v121 - N 1 '96 - p96 [51-250]

Boggan, Scott - *Developing Online Help for Windows 95*
CBR - v14 - Jl '96 - p19 [51-250]

Bogle, Donald - *Dorothy Dandridge*
BL - v93 - My 15 '97 - p1538 [51-250]

Bogolub, Ellen B - *Helping Families through Divorce*
Readings - v11 - D '96 - p22 [51-250]

Bogue, Ronald - *Violence and Mediation in Contemporary Culture*
R&R Bk N - v12 - F '97 - p12 [51-250]

Bogues, Tyrone - *In the Land of Giants*
Aethlon - v13 - Fall '95 - p159+ [251-500]

Boguraev, Branimir - *Corpus Processing for Lexical Acquisition*
Choice - v34 - Mr '97 - p1195 [51-250]

Bohannan, Paul - *How Culture Works*
CS - v26 - Ja '97 - p105+ [501+]

Bohdal, Susi - *1, 2, 3 What Do You See? (Illus. by Susi Bohdal)*
c KR - v65 - Mr 15 '97 - p458 [51-250]

Bohera, Carme - *Descubre El Colage*
c BL - v93 - F 15 '97 - p1032 [1-50]
Modela Con Barro
c BL - v93 - F 15 '97 - p1032 [1-50]

Bohi, Douglas R - *The Economics of Energy Security*
En Jnl - v18 - 1 '97 - p129+ [501+]
JEL - v34 - S '96 - p1499 [251-500]

Bohjalian, Chris - *Midwives*
y BL - v93 - F 15 '97 - p1001+ [51-250]
KR - v65 - Ja 1 '97 - p5 [251-500]
LJ - v122 - F 1 '97 - p104 [51-250]
PW - v244 - Ja 20 '97 - p390+ [251-500]
Water Witches
Trib Bks - Ap 20 '97 - p8 [1-50]

Bohlender, Sylvia - *Bahamas*
r BL - v93 - S 15 '96 - p210 [1-50]

Bohlman, Philip Vilas - *Central European Folk Music*
r ARBA - v28 - '97 - p489+ [51-250]
r R&R Bk N - v12 - F '97 - p69 [51-250]

Bohlmeijer, Arno - *Something Very Sorry*
y HB Guide - v7 - Fall '96 - p300 [51-250]

Bohman, James - *Public Deliberation*
Choice - v34 - My '97 - p1573 [51-250]

Bohm-Duchen, Monica - *After Auschwitz*
BM - v138 - D '96 - p836 [1-50]

Bohmont, Bert L - *The Standard Pesticide User's Guide. 4th Ed.*
r SciTech - v20 - D '96 - p56 [51-250]

Bohn, William - *Apollinaire and the International Avant-Garde*
LJ - v122 - Ja '97 - p96+ [51-250]

Bohne, Edith - *Die Kunste Und Die Wissenschaften Im Exil 1933-1945*
MLR - v91 - Jl '96 - p800+ [501+]

Bohner, Shaw A - *Software Change Impact Analysis*
SciTech - v20 - N '96 - p10 [51-250]

Bohrer, Karl Heinz - *Suddenness: On the Moment of Aesthetic Appearance*
MLR - v92 - Ja '97 - p142+ [501+]

Boice, James Montgomery - *Here We Stand*
Ch Today - v41 - Ja 6 '97 - p50+ [501+]
Two Loves
Ch Today - v41 - Ja 6 '97 - p50+ [501+]

Boime, Albert - *Art and the French Commune*
AHR - v101 - O '96 - p1221+ [501+]
Historian - v58 - Sum '96 - p893+ [251-500]

Boire, Gary - *Morley Callaghan: Literary Anarchist*
Can Lit - Spr '97 - p222+ [501+]

Boisde, Gilbert - *Chemical and Biochemical Sensing with Optical Fibers and Waveguides*
SciTech - v20 - N '96 - p79 [51-250]

Boishue, Jean De - *Banlieue Mon Amour*
FR - v70 - Mr '97 - p630+ [501+]

Boisot, Max H - *Information Space*
LR - v45 - 7 '96 - p66+ [501+]

Boissery, Beverley - *A Deep Sense of Wrong*
Aust Bk R - O '96 - p18+ [501+]
Beav - v76 - Ag '96 - p46 [251-500]

Boitani, Piero - *The Shadow of Ulysses*
TranslRevS - v1 - My '95 - p6 [51-250]

Boitard, Christian - *B Cells and Autoantibody Production in Autoimmune Diseases*
SciTech - v20 - N '96 - p35 [51-250]

Bojic, Veljko P - *Drame*
WLT - v70 - Sum '96 - p729 [501+]

Bok, Derek - *The State of the Nation*
CC - v114 - Mr 12 '97 - p275 [51-250]
Choice - v34 - Ap '97 - p1417 [51-250]
KR - v64 - D 1 '96 - p1710 [251-500]
LJ - v122 - F 15 '97 - p151 [51-250]
NYTBR - v102 - F 2 '97 - p24 [501+]
PW - v243 - D 16 '96 - p52 [51-250]

Bok, Hannes - *Hannes Bok Drawings and Sketches*
Necro - Fall '96 - p25 [251-500]

Bokovoy, Melissa K - *State-Society Relations in Yugoslavia 1945-1992*
BL - v93 - F 1 '97 - p923+ [51-250]

Bolam, Emily - *The House That Jack Built (Illus. by Emily Bolam)*
c Magpies - v11 - Jl '96 - p45 [1-50]

Boland, C Richard - *Colon, Rectum, and Anus*
r SciTech - v20 - S '96 - p36 [51-250]

Boland, Eavan - *Collected Poems*
Lon R Bks - v18 - Jl 18 '96 - p24+ [501+]
In a Time of Violence
MQR - v36 - Win '97 - p188+ [501+]
Parnassus - v22 - 1 '97 - p223+ [501+]
South HR - v30 - Sum '96 - p304+ [501+]

Object Lessons
    ILS - v16 - Spr '97 - p25 [501+]
    Lon R Bks - v18 - Jl 18 '96 - p24+ [501+]
    MQR - v36 - Win '97 - p188+ [501+]
    Parnassus - v22 - 1 '97 - p223+ [501+]
An Origin like Water
    MQR - v36 - Win '97 - p188+ [501+]
    Parnassus - v22 - 1 '97 - p223+ [501+]
Outside History
    Parnassus - v22 - 1 '97 - p223+ [501+]
Boland, Janice - *Annabel Again (Illus. by Megan Halsey)*
    c RT - v50 - O '96 - p131 [1-50]
A Dog Named Sam (Illus. by G Brian Karas)
    c HB Guide - v7 - Fall '96 - p283 [1-50]
Boland, Vivian - *Ideas in God according to Saint Thomas Aquinas*
    R&R Bk N - v12 - F '97 - p10 [51-250]
Bolden, Tonya - *The Book of African-American Women*
    BW - v27 - Ja 5 '97 - p13 [51-250]
Just Family
    c HB Guide - v7 - Fall '96 - p290 [51-250]
    y VOYA - v19 - O '96 - p205+ [51-250]
Boldrini, Sabrina - *Gravisca: Scavi Nel Santuario Greco 4*
    AJA - v100 - O '96 - p788+ [501+]
Boldyrev, V V - *Reactivity of Solids*
    SciTech - v21 - Mr '97 - p31 [51-250]
Bolen, Dennis E - *Krekshuns*
    Quill & Q - v63 - F '97 - p48 [251-500]
Bolen, Jean Shinoda - *Close to the Bone*
    BL - v93 - O 1 '96 - p313 [51-250]
Close to the Bone (Bolen). Audio Version
    BL - v93 - F 15 '97 - p1038 [51-250]
Boles, Janet K - *Historical Dictionary of Feminism*
    r ARBA - v28 - '97 - p335+ [51-250]
Boles, John B - *Religion in Antebellum Kentucky*
    CAY - v17 - Win '96 - p2 [51-250]
The South through Time. Vols. 1-2
    JSH - v63 - F '97 - p223+ [501+]
Bolesny, Darlene B - *Trail of Darkness*
    y Kliatt - v31 - Ja '97 - p11 [51-250]
Bolger, Daniel P - *The Battle for Hunger Hill*
    BL - v93 - Ap 1 '97 - p1270 [51-250]
    PW - v244 - Mr 17 '97 - p70 [51-250]
Bolick, Clint - *The Affirmative Action Fraud*
    Choice - v34 - S '96 - p209+ [51-250]
Boll, Heinrich - *Der Blasse Hund*
    WLT - v70 - Sum '96 - p681 [501+]
Bollag, Jean-Marc - *Soil Biochemistry. Vol. 9*
    SciTech - v20 - S '96 - p44 [51-250]
Bollas, Christopher - *The New Informants*
    Soc Ser R - v71 - Mr '97 - p153+ [501+]
Bolles, A Lynn - *Sister Jamaica*
    Choice - v34 - O '96 - p322 [51-250]
We Paid Our Dues
    Choice - v34 - Ap '97 - p1400 [51-250]
Bolles, Richard Nelson - *Job-Hunting on the Internet*
    LJ - v121 - D '96 - p108+ [51-250]
Bollet, Alfred J - *Mosby's USMLE Step 2 Reviews-- General Clinical Sciences*
    SciTech - v20 - N '96 - p36 [51-250]
Bollettieri, Nick - *My Aces, My Faults*
    y BL - v92 - Ag '96 - p1850 [251-500]
Bollier, David - *Aiming Higher*
    LJ - v121 - O 1 '96 - p94 [51-250]
    LJ - v122 - Mr 15 '97 - p36 [1-50]
Bologna, Jack - *Corporate Crime Investigation*
    Choice - v34 - F '97 - p1007 [51-250]
    r R&R Bk N - v12 - F '97 - p45 [1-50]
Bolotin, Norman - *For Home and Country*
    c RT - v50 - O '96 - p152 [51-250]
    y RT - v50 - N '96 - p246 [51-250]
Bolozky, Shmuel - *501 Hebrew Verbs*
    r ARBA - v28 - '97 - p392+ [51-250]
Bolster, Richard - *Stendhal: Le Rouge Et Le Noir*
    MLR - v91 - Jl '96 - p731+ [501+]
Bolster, W Jeffrey - *Black Jacks*
    LJ - v122 - Mr 15 '97 - p72 [51-250]
    PW - v244 - Mr 17 '97 - p64 [51-250]
Bolt, Christine - *Feminist Ferment*
    J Am St - v30 - Ag '96 - p339+ [251-500]
Bolton, Brenda - *Innocent III: Studies on Papal Authority and Pastoral Care*
    CH - v65 - D '96 - p679+ [501+]
Bolton, Neal - *The Handbook of Landfill Operations*
    SciTech - v20 - N '96 - p68 [51-250]
Boltzmann, Ludwig - *Hochgeehrter Herr Professor!*
    Isis - v87 - S '96 - p565+ [501+]
Bolus, Jim - *Derby Magic*
    PW - v244 - My 5 '97 - p191 [51-250]

Bolzoni, Lina - *La Stanza Della Memoria*
    MLN - v112 - Ja '97 - p117+ [501+]
    Ren Q - v49 - Aut '96 - p598+ [501+]
    Specu - v71 - Jl '96 - p689+ [501+]
Bomb
    p Sm Pr R - v29 - F '97 - p19 [251-500]
Bombeck, Erma - *Forever, Erma*
    BL - v93 - S 1 '96 - p2 [51-250]
    CSM - v89 - D 12 '96 - p14 [51-250]
    CSM - v89 - Ja 9 '97 - p14 [51-250]
    KR - v64 - S 15 '96 - p1365+ [251-500]
    LJ - v121 - O 15 '96 - p65 [51-250]
    NYTBR - v101 - D 15 '96 - p23 [501+]
    PW - v243 - S 2 '96 - p102+ [51-250]
When You Look Like Your Passport Photo, It's Time to Go Home (Rosenblat). Audio Version
    BWatch - v17 - D '96 - p11 [1-50]
Bomer, Randy - *Time for Meaning*
    JAAL - v40 - D '96 - p322+ [501+]
Bompieri, Franco - *Augusto Di Setteprati*
    BL - v93 - D 1 '96 - p644 [1-50]
Bon, Francois - *C'Etait Toute Une Vie*
    WLT - v70 - Aut '96 - p905 [251-500]
Parking
    WLT - v71 - Win '97 - p101 [501+]
Bona, Damien - *Starring John Wayne as Genghis Khan*
    BW - v26 - D 1 '96 - p12 [51-250]
BonaDea, Artemis - *Conservation Book Repair*
    J Gov Info - v23 - S '96 - p577 [51-250]
Bonadio, Felice A - *A.P. Giannini: Banker of America*
    JEH - v56 - S '96 - p750+ [501+]
Bonanate, Luigi - *Ethics and International Politics*
    JPR - v33 - N '96 - p498 [251-500]
    R&R Bk N - v12 - F '97 - p61 [51-250]
    Theol St - v58 - Mr '97 - p199+ [251-500]
Bonanno, Alessandro - *Caught in the Net*
    AJS - v102 - N '96 - p923+ [501+]
From Columbus to ConAgra
    CS - v25 - S '96 - p599+ [501+]
Bonanno, Margaret Wander - *Preternatural*
    KR - v64 - O 1 '96 - p1433 [51-250]
    LJ - v121 - D '96 - p152 [51-250]
    NYTBR - v102 - Ja 26 '97 - p22 [501+]
    PW - v243 - N 18 '96 - p66 [51-250]
Bonansinga, Jay R - *The Killer's Game*
    KR - v65 - Ja 1 '97 - p5 [251-500]
    LJ - v122 - F 1 '97 - p110 [51-250]
    PW - v244 - F 24 '97 - p65 [51-250]
Bonavia, David - *China's Warlords*
    J Mil H - v61 - Ap '97 - p387+ [501+]
Bonavia, Duccio - *Arte E Historia De Peru Antiguo*
    LA Ant - v7 - Je '96 - p167+ [501+]
Bond, Alyson J - *Understanding Drug Treatment in Mental Health Care*
    SciTech - v20 - D '96 - p45 [51-250]
Bond, Bradley G - *Political Culture in the Nineteenth-Century South*
    JIH - v27 - Spr '97 - p717+ [501+]
Bond, Daniel - *Stage Management. 2nd Ed.*
    TCI - v30 - O '96 - p55 [1-50]
Bond, David J - *Jacques Chessex: Calvinism and the Text*
    MLR - v92 - Ja '97 - p211+ [501+]
Bond, Edward L - *St. James Episcopal Church, Baton Rouge*
    JSH - v62 - N '96 - p862 [51-250]
Bond, Felicia - *Tumble Bumble (Illus. by Felicia Bond)*
    c BL - v93 - N 15 '96 - p593 [51-250]
    c CBRS - v25 - O '96 - p13 [1-50]
    c HB Guide - v8 - Spr '97 - p20 [51-250]
    c KR - v64 - O 1 '96 - p1464 [51-250]
    c LATBR - O 6 '96 - p15 [51-250]
    c NY - v72 - N 18 '96 - p101 [1-50]
    c NYTBR - v102 - Mr 16 '97 - p26 [501+]
    c Par - v71 - D '96 - p252 [1-50]
    c PW - v243 - O 7 '96 - p73 [51-250]
    c SLJ - v42 - O '96 - p85 [51-250]
Bond, Jack W - *How EC and World Bank Policies Are Destroying Agriculture and the Environment*
    Workbook - v21 - Win '96 - p167 [251-500]
Bond, James - *Birds of the West Indies. 5th Ed.*
    Wildbird - v10 - N '96 - p49 [51-250]
Bond, Larry - *The Enemy Within*
    Rapport - v19 - 4 '96 - p33 [251-500]
The Enemy Within (Purdham). Audio Version
    y Kliatt - v31 - Ja '97 - p40 [51-250]
The Enemy Within (Russotto). Audio Version
    LJ - v121 - N '96 - p121 [51-250]
Bond, Mary E - *Canadian Reference Sources*
    r ARBA - v28 - '97 - p11+ [251-500]
    r Choice - v34 - D '96 - p586 [51-250]
    r LJ - v122 - Ap 15 '97 - p37 [51-250]

Bond, Michael - *Bears and Forebears*
    TLS - S 13 '96 - p31 [501+]
Paddington's 1 2 3
    c BL - v93 - Ap 1 '97 - p1340 [1-50]
Bond, Peter - *Reaching for the Stars*
    A & S Sm - v11 - F '97 - p87 [1-50]
Bond, W H - *The Printed Catalogues of the Harvard College Library 1723-1790*
    r ARBA - v28 - '97 - p20 [251-500]
Bondanella, Peter - *Dictionary of Italian Literature. Rev. and Expanded Ed.*
    r ARBA - v28 - '97 - p462 [51-250]
    r Choice - v34 - Ja '97 - p768 [51-250]
Bonde, Sheila - *Fortress-Churches of Languedoc*
    AHR - v101 - D '96 - p1536 [251-500]
    CHR - v82 - Jl '96 - p540+ [501+]
Bonder, Nilton - *The Kabbalah of Envy*
    PW - v244 - My 12 '97 - p72 [51-250]
The Kabbalah of Money
    BL - v93 - O 1 '96 - p296 [51-250]
Bondi, Roberta C - *In Ordinary Time*
    Ch Today - v40 - O 7 '96 - p58 [51-250]
    Comw - v123 - D 6 '96 - p22 [51-250]
Memories of God
    Comw - v123 - D 6 '96 - p22 [51-250]
Bondi, Victor - *American Decades 1980-1989*
    yr ARBA - v28 - '97 - p195+ [51-250]
Bond's Franchise Guide. 1996 Ed.
    r ARBA - v28 - '97 - p90 [251-500]
Bone, Neil - *The Aurora: Sun-Earth Interactions*
    S&T - v93 - Ap '97 - p65 [51-250]
Bonell, Michael Joachim - *UNILEX: International Case Law and Bibliography on the UN Convention on Contracts for the International Sale of Goods*
    r R&R Bk N - v12 - F '97 - p63 [51-250]
Bonfield, Lynn - *Roxanna's Children*
    HRNB - v25 - Fall '96 - p6+ [251-500]
Bonfil, Roberto - *Jewish Life in Renaissance Italy*
    EHR - v111 - N '96 - p1264+ [251-500]
    Ren Q - v49 - Win '96 - p850+ [501+]
Bonfil Batalla, Guillermo - *Mexico Profundo*
    TranslRevS - v2 - D '96 - p12 [501+]
Bong, Jorg - *Die Auflosung Der Disharmonien*
    Ger Q - v69 - Sum '96 - p347+ [501+]
Bonham Carter, Violet - *Lantern Slides*
    Books - v10 - Je '96 - p21 [51-250]
    Choice - v34 - Mr '97 - p1218 [51-250]
    CR - v269 - D '96 - p334+ [51-250]
    LJ - v122 - Mr 15 '97 - p68 [51-250]
    Spec - v276 - My 11 '96 - p36+ [501+]
    TLS - My 24 '96 - p33 [501+]
Bonheim, Jalaja - *Aphrodite's Daughters*
    BL - v93 - My 1 '97 - p1463 [51-250]
Bonhoeffer, Dietrich - *Dietrich Bonhoeffer Works. Vols. 2, 5*
    CC - v114 - Ap 2 '97 - p343+ [501+]
Boniface, Douglas M - *Micro-Electronics: The Structure and Operation of Microprocessor-Based Systems*
    Choice - v34 - Mr '97 - p1190 [51-250]
Boninger, Lorenz - *Die Ritterwurde In Mittelitalien Zwischen Mittelalter Und Fruher Neuzeit*
    Ren Q - v49 - Win '96 - p840+ [501+]
Bonito, Vitaniello - *L'Occhio Del Tiempo*
    Choice - v34 - D '96 - p565 [51-250]
Bonker-Vallon, Angelika - *Metaphysik Und Mathematik Bei Giordano Bruno*
    Isis - v88 - Mr '97 - p137+ [501+]
Bonn, Keith E - *When the Odds Were Even*
    Mar Crp G - v80 - Ag '96 - p76 [501+]
Bonn, Klaus - *Die Idee Der Weiderholung In Peter Handkes Schriften*
    Ger Q - v69 - Fall '96 - p460+ [501+]
Bonnefoy, Yves - *New and Selected Poems*
    TLS - D 20 '96 - p26 [501+]
La Petite Phrase Et La Longue Phrase
    FR - v70 - D '96 - p339+ [501+]
Bonnemaison, Joel - *The Tree and the Canoe*
    Am Ethnol - v23 - N '96 - p916+ [501+]
    Cont Pac - v9 - Spr '97 - p265+ [501+]
Bonnemason, Jean - *Les Langues De France*
    FR - v70 - O '96 - p152+ [501+]
Bonner, Cindy - *The Passion of Dellie O'Barr*
    LJ - v121 - S 15 '96 - p124 [51-250]
    Rapport - v19 - 4 '96 - p24 [251-500]
    Roundup M - v4 - N '96 - p29+ [251-500]
Bonner, Hilary - *The Cruelty of Morning*
    Books - v9 - S '95 - p25 [1-50]
Bonner, John - *Economic Efficiency and Social Justice*
    Econ J - v106 - S '96 - p1475 [51-250]
    JEL - v34 - D '96 - p2014 [51-250]

Bonner, John Tyler - *Sixty Years of Biology*
Nature - v384 - N 14 '96 - p126+ [501+]
SB - v32 - N '96 - p230 [251-500]
Sci - v274 - N 1 '96 - p734 [251-500]
Bonner, Michael - *Aristocratic Violence and Holy War*
MEJ - v50 - Aut '96 - p631 [51-250]
Bonner, Nigel - *Polar Regions*
c Magpies - v11 - Jl '96 - p38 [51-250]
Bonner, Philip - *Apartheid's Genesis 1935-1962*
CS - v25 - S '96 - p624+ [501+]
Bonner, Sherwood - *Like Unto Like*
LJ - v122 - My 1 '97 - p145 [1-50]
PW - v244 - My 12 '97 - p74 [1-50]
Bonner, Thomas Neville - *Becoming a Physician*
AB - v99 - Ap 7 '97 - p1119 [501+]
Isis - v87 - S '96 - p530+ [501+]
Bonnet, Bob - *Science Fair Projects with Electricity and Electronics (Illus. by Karen McKee)*
c BL - v93 - D 1 '96 - p658 [51-250]
y SLJ - v42 - D '96 - p142+ [51-250]
Bonney, Margaret - *Jean-Roland Malet: Premier Historien Des Finances De La Monarchie Francaise*
EHR - v111 - N '96 - p1292+ [501+]
Bonney, Richard - *Origins of the Modern State in Europe 13th-18th Centuries*
Historian - v59 - Win '97 - p458+ [251-500]
Bonnie, Fred - *Food Fights*
PW - v244 - Ap 14 '97 - p57 [51-250]
Bono, James - *The Word of God and the Languages of Man. Vol. 1*
Isis - v87 - S '96 - p543+ [501+]
Bonomini, Angel - *Mas Alla Del Puente*
BL - v93 - Mr 15 '97 - p1232 [1-50]
Bonora, Elena - *Ricerche Su Francesco Sansovino Imprenditore Librario E Letterato*
JMH - v68 - S '96 - p710+ [501+]
Bonsall, Crosby - *El Caso Del Forastero Hambriento (Illus. by Crosby Bonsall)*
c HB Guide - v8 - Spr '97 - p107 [51-250]
c SLJ - v42 - Ag '96 - p178 [51-250]
Mine's the Best
c HB Guide - v7 - Fall '96 - p283 [51-250]
Bonta, Juan Pablo - *American Architects and Texts*
R&R Bk N - v11 - D '96 - p58 [51-250]
Bontempelli, Bruno - *The Traveler's Tree*
TranslRevS - v1 - My '95 - p18 [51-250]
Bontemps, Arna - *Anyplace but Here*
LJ - v122 - My 1 '97 - p145 [1-50]
Bonvillain, Nancy - *The Cheyennes: People of the Plains*
c HB Guide - v8 - Spr '97 - p177 [51-250]
Native American Religion
y BL - v93 - O 1 '96 - p338 [1-50]
The Santee Sioux
y HB Guide - v8 - Spr '97 - p177 [51-250]
Bonvillian, Gary - *The Liberal Arts College Adapting to Change*
Choice - v34 - N '96 - p510 [51-250]
Bonyhady, Tim - *Prehistory to Politics*
Aust Bk R - N '96 - p28+ [501+]
Bonzon, Alfred - *Racine Et Heidegger*
FR - v70 - F '97 - p466+ [501+]
Boobbyer, Philip - *S.L. Frank: The Life and Work of a Russian Philosopher 1877-1950*
Slav R - v55 - Sum '96 - p507+ [501+]
Booch, Grady - *Best of Booch*
SciTech - v21 - Mr '97 - p8 [1-50]
Boockmann, Hartmut - *Kirche Und Gesellschaft Im Heiligen Romischen Reich Des 15. Und 16. Jahrhunderts*
Six Ct J - v27 - Win '96 - p1227+ [501+]
Boohan, Richard - *Energy and Change. Vols. 1-3*
y TES - Ja 3 '97 - pR15 [251-500]
Booher, Dianna - *Get a Life without Sacrificing Your Career*
LJ - v121 - N 15 '96 - p72+ [51-250]
The Book Cupboard
c HB - v72 - N '96 - p720 [251-500]
c HB Guide - v8 - Spr '97 - p20 [51-250]
c PW - v243 - O 7 '96 - p77 [51-250]
Book Industry Trends 1995
r RQ - v36 - Fall '96 - p123 [251-500]
The Book of European Forecasts. 2nd Ed.
r ARBA - v28 - '97 - p112+ [251-500]
Book of Lists for Regulated Hazardous Substances 1996
r ARBA - v28 - '97 - p650 [251-500]
The Book Scene...Especially for Teens. 4th Ed.
yr BL - v93 - S 15 '96 - p252 [51-250]
yr BL - v93 - D 15 '96 - p719 [51-250]
yr SLJ - v43 - Ja '97 - p42 [51-250]
Book Women: A Reader's Community for Those Who Love Women's Words
p Ms - v7 - Mr '97 - p81 [251-500]

Bookbinder, Paul - *Weimar Germany*
Choice - v34 - My '97 - p1556 [51-250]
Booker, Christopher - *The Castle of Lies*
NS - v125 - N 29 '96 - p42+ [501+]
TLS - Ja 3 '97 - p5+ [501+]
Booker, John T - *The Play of Terror in Nineteenth-Century France*
Choice - v34 - My '97 - p1505 [251-500]
Booker, M Keith - *The Dystopian Impulse in Modern Literature*
J Am Cult - v19 - Sum '96 - p136+ [501+]
Joyce, Bakhtin, and the Literary Tradition
ELT - v40 - 2 '97 - p238+ [501+]
Books in Print 1996-97. Vols. 1-9
r ARBA - v28 - '97 - p11 [251-500]
Bookshop. Electronic Media Version
Trib Bks - F 2 '97 - p7 [51-250]
The BookTalker. Book and Electronic Media Version
r Emerg Lib - v23 - My '96 - p42 [1-50]
Booktalking the Award Winners 1993-1994
r Emerg Lib - v23 - My '96 - p39 [251-500]
Boom, Mattie - *A New Art*
BWatch - v17 - S '96 - p3 [1-50]
Boone, Graeme M - *Essays on Medieval Music in Honor of David G. Hughes*
Notes - v53 - S '96 - p61+ [501+]
Boonin-Vail, David - *Thomas Hobbes and the Science of Moral Virtue*
RP - v58 - Sum '96 - p649+ [501+]
Boonstra, Klara - *The ILO and the Netherlands*
ILR - v135 - 5 '96 - p593 [251-500]
Booraem, Hendrik, 1939- - *The Provincial: Calvin Coolidge and His World 1885-1895*
Historian - v58 - Sum '96 - p855+ [251-500]
Pres SQ - v26 - Sum '96 - p906+ [251-500]
Boorer, Suzanne - *The Promise of the Land as Oath*
Rel St Rev - v23 - Ja '97 - p22+ [501+]
Boorstein, Seymour - *Transpersonal Psychotherapy. 2nd Ed.*
SciTech - v20 - N '96 - p44 [251-500]
Boorstein, Sylvia - *That's Funny, You Don't Look Buddhist*
BL - v93 - F 15 '97 - p975 [51-250]
LJ - v122 - F 1 '97 - p86 [51-250]
Tikkun - v12 - Mr '97 - p67+ [501+]
Boorstin, Daniel J - *The Mysterious Science of Law*
Law Q Rev - v113 - Ap '97 - p349+ [501+]
Boorstin, Jon - *Making Movies Work*
Si & So - v6 - N '96 - p38 [1-50]
Pay or Play
Ent W - Ap 4 '97 - p79 [51-250]
KR - v64 - D 15 '96 - p1749 [251-500]
LJ - v122 - Ja '97 - p142 [51-250]
PW - v244 - Ja 13 '97 - p53 [51-250]
Boot, Adrian - *Punk: The Illustrated History of a Music Revolution*
y BL - v93 - D 1 '96 - p636 [51-250]
LJ - v122 - F 1 '97 - p79 [251-500]
Booth, Alan, 1935- - *Family-School Links*
Readings - v11 - D '96 - p30 [51-250]
SB - v32 - O '96 - p199 [251-500]
Stepfamilies: Who Benefits? Who Does Not?
CS - v25 - S '96 - p662+ [501+]
Booth, Alan, Ph.D. - *British Economic Development since 1945*
Choice - v34 - N '96 - p505 [51-250]
JEL - v34 - S '96 - p1464 [251-500]
Booth, Alison - *Famous Last Words*
VS - v39 - Aut '95 - p76+ [501+]
Booth, David - *The Dust Bowl (Illus. by Karen Reczuch)*
c BIC - v25 - D '96 - p36 [251-500]
c Ch Bk News - v20 - Win '97 - p28 [51-250]
c Emerg Lib - v24 - Mr '97 - p27 [1-50]
y JAAL - v40 - Mr '97 - p510 [51-250]
c Quill & Q - v62 - S '96 - p73 [251-500]
c Quill & Q - v63 - F '97 - p51 [251-500]
Images of Nature
c Ch Bk News - v19 - Sum '96 - p32+ [251-500]
Booth, Frank - *The Independent Walker's Guide to France*
r LJ - v122 - Ja '97 - p128 [51-250]
The Independent Walker's Guide to Great Britain
r LJ - v122 - Ja '97 - p128 [51-250]
Booth, Jerry - *You Animal! (Illus. by Nancy King)*
c SB - v32 - N '96 - p241 [51-250]
c SLJ - v42 - N '96 - p96 [51-250]
Booth, Joseph D - *From Xbase to Windows*
SciTech - v20 - D '96 - p9 [1-50]
Booth, Martin - *Opium: A History*
FEER - v160 - Ja 23 '97 - p35 [501+]

War Dog
c JB - v60 - O '96 - p197 [51-250]
y Sch Lib - v44 - N '96 - p168 [51-250]
Booth, Michael R - *Three Tragic Actresses*
Choice - v34 - My '97 - p1510 [51-250]
Booth, Nicholas - *Exploring the Solar System*
y BL - v93 - D 1 '96 - p629 [51-250]
BWatch - v17 - N '96 - p6 [51-250]
Choice - v34 - My '97 - p1521 [51-250]
y SB - v33 - My '97 - p106 [251-500]
SciTech - v21 - Mr '97 - p19 [51-250]
S&T - v93 - Mr '97 - p66 [51-250]
Booth, William James - *Households: On the Moral Architecture of the Economy*
AAPSS-A - v549 - Ja '97 - p209+ [501+]
Politics and Rationality
RP - v58 - Fall '96 - p793+ [501+]
Bootle, Roger - *The Death of Inflation*
Choice - v34 - Ja '97 - p843 [51-250]
NS & S - v9 - Ap 26 '96 - p37 [251-500]
PW - v243 - Jl 22 '96 - p222 [51-250]
WSJ-MW - v78 - N 5 '96 - pA20 [51-250]
Bopp, Richard E - *Reference and Information Services. 2nd Ed.*
r LAR - v98 - Ag '96 - p428 [251-500]
Borasi, Rafaella - *Reconceiving Mathematics Instruction*
Math T - v89 - D '96 - p782 [251-500]
Borba, Michele - *Home Esteem Builders*
BWatch - v17 - N '96 - p5 [51-250]
Borchardt, Alice - *Beguiled*
KR - v64 - N 1 '96 - p1547 [251-500]
PW - v243 - N 25 '96 - p57 [51-250]
Devoted (Page). Audio Version
y Kliatt - v30 - N '96 - p38 [51-250]
Borchardt, Ronald T - *Models for Assessing Drug Absorption and Metabolism*
SciTech - v20 - D '96 - p54 [51-250]
Borcherding, David H - *Romance Writer's Sourcebook. 1st Ed.*
r ARBA - v28 - '97 - p348 [51-250]
Borcherdt, Bill - *Fundamentals of Cognitive-Behavior Therapy*
SciTech - v20 - N '96 - p44 [1-50]
Borch-Jacobsen, Mikkel - *Remembering Anna O.*
Atl - v278 - N '96 - p122 [51-250]
LJ - v121 - O 1 '96 - p107 [51-250]
NYRB - v43 - O 3 '96 - p38+ [501+]
Bord, Janet - *Fairies: Real Encounters with Little People*
Woman's J - Ap '97 - p18 [51-250]
Borden, Iain - *Architecture and the Sites of History*
R&R Bk N - v11 - N '96 - p61 [51-250]
Borden, Louise - *The Little Ships (Illus. by Michael Foreman)*
c BL - v93 - Mr 1 '97 - p1162 [51-250]
c CCB-B - v50 - Ap '97 - p276 [51-250]
c HB - v73 - My '97 - p302+ [251-500]
c KR - v65 - Ap 1 '97 - p549 [51-250]
c PW - v244 - Mr 24 '97 - p83+ [51-250]
Border/Lines
p Utne R - Jl '96 - p118+ [51-250]
Borderes, Yves - *Prelude for a Beginner Trombonist. Vols. 1-2*
Am MT - v46 - D '96 - p62+ [251-500]
Borders, Rebecca - *Beyond the Hill*
r ARBA - v28 - '97 - p270 [51-250]
Bordewich, Fergus M - *Killing the White Man's Indian*
BL - v93 - Ja '97 - p756 [1-50]
Bloom Rev - v16 - S '96 - p20 [501+]
Bordman, Gerald Martin - *American Theatre: A Chronicle of Comedy and Drama 1869-1914*
BL - v93 - F 15 '97 - p1042 [1-50]
J Am Cult - v18 - Win '95 - p103 [51-250]
American Theatre: A Chronicle of Comedy and Drama 1914-1930
r ARBA - v28 - '97 - p523+ [251-500]
J Am Cult - v19 - Sum '96 - p157+ [51-250]
Bordwell, David - *Post-Theory: Reconstructing Film Studies*
AB - v98 - D 9 '96 - p1997 [51-250]
Choice - v34 - O '96 - p290 [51-250]
Film Cr - v21 - Fall '96 - p86+ [501+]
Si & So - v6 - N '96 - p32+ [501+]
Borel, France - *Bacon: Portraits and Self-Portraits*
Obs - D 29 '96 - p27 [501+]
Borer, Alain - *The Essential Joseph Beuys*
Spec - v278 - Ja 11 '97 - p30+ [501+]
Borg, Anders E - *Formynderiets Teori*
JC - v47 - Win '97 - p120+ [501+]
Borg, Marcus J - *The God We Never Knew*
BL - v93 - My 1 '97 - p1463 [51-250]
PW - v244 - F 24 '97 - p81 [51-250]

Jesus at 2000
  Ant R - v55 - Spr '97 - p236+ [251-500]
  BL - v93 - Ja '97 - p784 [51-250]
Jesus in Contemporary Scholarship
  Intpr - v50 - O '96 - p428 [251-500]
Borger, Irene - *From a Burning House. Audio Version*
  Advocate - O 29 '96 - p69+ [251-500]
  LJ - v121 - N 1 '96 - p122 [51-250]
  LJ - v122 - F 15 '97 - p115 [1-50]
  PW - v243 - S 2 '96 - p47 [51-250]
  Quill & Q - v62 - Ag '96 - p37 [1-50]
Borges, Dain - *The Family in Bahia, Brazil 1870-1945*
  J Urban H - v22 - My '96 - p509+ [501+]
Borges, Jorge Luis - *Di Logos Jorge Luis Borges-Ernesto Sabato*
  BL - v93 - Mr 15 '97 - p1232 [1-50]
Labyrinths: Selected Stories and Other Writings
  SFR - v22 - Ja '97 - p48 [51-250]
Borges, Phil - *Tibetan Portraits*
  Bloom Rev - v16 - Jl '96 - p27 [51-250]
  LATBR - S 15 '96 - p10 [251-500]
  Prog - v61 - Ja '97 - p37 [51-250]
  WSJ-MW - v78 - D 5 '96 - pA18 [51-250]
Borgeson, Bet - *Basic Colored Pencil Techniques*
  LJ - v122 - Mr 15 '97 - p63 [51-250]
Borgstedt, Thomas - *Reichsidee Und Liebesethik*
  MLR - v91 - O '96 - p1034+ [251-500]
Boring, John Kadel - *Natural Gardening*
  ı E Mag - v7 - N '96 - p50 [51-250]
  LJ - v121 - D '96 - p66 [1-50]
Boring, M Eugene - *Hellenistic Commentary to the New Testament*
  r ARBA - v28 - '97 - p545+ [51-250]
Boris, Eileen - *Home to Work*
  CS - v25 - S '96 - p617+ [501+]
  CS - v25 - N '96 - p802+ [501+]
Borish, Elaine - *A Legacy of Names*
  LJ - v121 - D '96 - p128 [251-250]
Unpublishable! Rejected Writers from Jane Austen to Zane Grey
  PW - v244 - F 17 '97 - p207 [51-250]
  PW - v244 - F 17 '97 - p207 [51-250]
Borish, Michael S - *On the Road to EU Accession*
  JEL - v35 - Mr '97 - p293 [51-250]
Private Sector Development during Transition
  JEL - v34 - S '96 - p1492 [51-250]
Boritt, Gabor - *Lincoln's Generals*
  RAH - v24 - S '96 - p418+ [501+]
Bork, Robert H - *Slouching towards Gomorrah*
 y BL - v93 - S 1 '96 - p2 [51-250]
  BW - v26 - O 20 '96 - p1+ [51-250]
  CC - v114 - Mr 5 '97 - p252+ [251-500]
  Choice - v34 - Mr '97 - p1238 [51-250]
  Ch Today - v40 - N 11 '96 - p58 [501+]
  CSM - v88 - N 7 '96 - p14 [51-250]
  CSM - v89 - D 12 '96 - p14 [51-250]
  CSM - v89 - Ja 9 '97 - p14 [51-250]
  HE - v52 - O 11 '96 - p10 [501+]
  KR - v64 - Ag 15 '96 - p1199 [251-500]
  LJ - v121 - N 15 '96 - p76+ [51-250]
  Nat - v264 - Ja 27 '97 - p25+ [501+]
  Nat R - v48 - N 11 '96 - p54+ [501+]
  NY - v72 - Ja 13 '97 - p72+ [501+]
  NYTBR - v101 - O 20 '96 - p18 [501+]
  NYTLa - v146 - S 24 '96 - pC16 [501+]
  Pub Int - Win '97 - p89+ [501+]
  Reason - v28 - Ap '97 - p41+ [501+]
  W&I - v12 - Ja '97 - p279+ [501+]
  WSJ-MW - v77 - O 8 '96 - pA20 [501+]
Borkar, Vivek S - *Probability Theory*
  SIAM Rev - v39 - Mr '97 - p149+ [501+]
Borland, Russell - *Running Microsoft Word for Windows 95*
  BL - v92 - Ag '96 - p1868 [501+]
Borman, Jami - *Computer Dictionary for Kids...*
 cr CBR - v15 - Spr '97 - p2 [1-50]
Bormann, Rudiger - *Metastable Phases and Microstructures*
  SciTech - v20 - N '96 - p62 [51-250]
Born, Daniel - *The Birth of Liberal Guilt in the English Novel*
  ELT - v40 - 1 '97 - p69+ [501+]
  Nine-C Lit - v51 - S '96 - p270 [51-250]
Born, Georgina - *Rationalizing Culture*
  AJS - v102 - S '96 - p646+ [501+]
  CS - v26 - Ja '97 - p104+ [501+]
Born, Heidi Von - *En Sida Av Himlen*
  WLT - v70 - Sum '96 - p719+ [51-250]

Borne, Barbara Wood - *100 Research Topic Guides for Students*
 yr ARBA - v28 - '97 - p245 [51-250]
 y CLW - v67 - D '96 - p65 [51-250]
 yr CLW - v67 - Mr '97 - p59 [51-250]
 yr Emerg Lib - v24 - S '96 - p42 [51-250]
 yr SLMQ - v25 - Fall '96 - p63 [51-250]
Bornedal, Peter - *The Interpretations of Art*
  Choice - v34 - Ja '97 - p782 [51-250]
Borneman, John - *Sojourners: The Return of German Jews and the Question of Identity*
  Ger Q - v69 - Fall '96 - p431+ [501+]
Bornet, Vaughn Davis - *An Independent Scholar in Twentieth Century America*
  HER - v66 - Fall '96 - p694+ [251-500]
Bornoff, Nick - *Japan*
 c Sch Lib - v45 - F '97 - p36+ [51-250]
Bornschier, Volker - *Conflicts and New Departures in World Society*
  SF - v75 - Mr '97 - p1126+ [501+]
Western Society in Transition
  Choice - v34 - D '96 - p668 [51-250]
Bornstein, Daniel Ethan - *The Bianchi of 1399*
  Ren Q - v49 - Win '96 - p854+ [501+]
Women and Religion in Medieval and Renaissance Italy
  NYRB - v43 - D 19 '96 - p31+ [501+]
  R&R Bk N - v11 - N '96 - p8 [51-250]
  VQR - v73 - Win '97 - p18* [51-250]
Bornstein, David - *The Price of a Dream*
  Cu H - v95 - N '96 - p394 [501+]
Bornstein, Harry - *Goldilocks and the Three Bears Told in Signed English (Illus. by Annie Lunsford)*
 c PW - v243 - S 9 '96 - p85 [51-250]
Bornstein, Marc H - *Handbook of Parenting. Vol. 2*
  JMF - v58 - N '96 - p1046+ [251-500]
Handbook of Parenting. Vol. 3
 r Fam Relat - v45 - O '96 - p479 [501+]
Handbook of Parenting. Vols. 3-4
  JMF - v58 - N '96 - p1047+ [501+]
Borofka, David - *Hints of His Mortality*
  KR - v64 - O 1 '96 - p1416 [251-500]
  LJ - v122 - Ja '97 - p151 [51-250]
  NYTBR - v102 - Ja 19 '97 - p9 [501+]
  PW - v243 - O 7 '96 - p62 [51-250]
Boron, Atilio A - *State, Capitalism, and Democracy in Latin America*
  APSR - v90 - D '96 - p932+ [501+]
  HAHR - v77 - F '97 - p153+ [251-500]
Boroujerdi, Mehrzad - *Iranian Intellectuals and the West*
  For Aff - v76 - My '97 - p142+ [51-250]
Borowick, Jerome N - *Technical Communication and Its Applications*
  SciTech - v20 - N '96 - p59 [51-250]
Borre, Ole - *The Scope of Government*
  Choice - v34 - S '96 - p201+ [51-250]
Borrelli, Gianfranco - *Ragion Di Stato*
  Lib - v19 - Mr '97 - p99 [51-250]
Borsay, Peter - *The Eighteenth Century Town*
  J Urban H - v22 - My '96 - p516+ [501+]
Borst, Arno - *The Ordering of Time*
  Specu - v71 - Jl '96 - p692+ [51-250]
Borst, Charlotte G - *Catching Babies*
  AAPSS-A - v550 - Mr '97 - p189+ [251-500]
  JIH - v27 - Spr '97 - p720+ [251-500]
  Wom R Bks - v14 - D '96 - p19+ [501+]
Borthwick, J S - *The Garden Plot*
  KR - v65 - F 1 '97 - p173+ [51-250]
Borton, Lady - *Junk Pile! (Illus. by Kimberly Bulcken Root)*
 c CCB-B - v50 - My '97 - p314 [51-250]
 c PW - v244 - F 10 '97 - p83 [51-250]
Borton, D B - *Five Alarm Fire*
  Arm Det - v29 - Fall '96 - p487 [51-250]
Bortz, Fred - *To the Young Scientist*
 y CCB-B - v50 - Ap '97 - p276 [51-250]
Borwein, P - *Polynomials and Polynomial Inequalities*
  SIAM Rev - v38 - D '96 - p705+ [501+]
Borysenko, Joan - *A Woman's Book of Life*
  BL - v93 - Ja '97 - p788 [51-250]
  PW - v243 - D 2 '96 - p48 [51-250]
Bos, M G - *The Inter-Relationship between Irrigation, Drainage, and the Environment in the Aral Sea Basin*
  SciTech - v21 - Mr '97 - p82 [51-250]
Bosc, Patrick - *Fuzziness in Database Management Systems*
  JEL - v34 - D '96 - p2141 [51-250]
Boscagli, Maurizia - *Eye on the Flesh*
  Choice - v34 - D '96 - p598 [51-250]
Bosco, Anna - *Le Edizioni Del XVI Secolo Nella Biblioteca Chelliana Di Grosseto*
 r Lib - v18 - D '96 - p362 [51-250]

Bosco, Henri - *L'Enfant Et La Riviere (Illus. by E Jalabert-Edon)*
 c ChLAQ - v21 - Win '96 - p189+ [501+]
Bosco, Joseph - *A Problem of Evidence*
  LATBR - O 13 '96 - p11 [251-500]
Bose, Bimal K - *Power Electronics and Variable Frequency Drives*
 r SciTech - v20 - D '96 - p79 [51-250]
Bose, Christine E - *Women in the Latin American Development Process*
  APSR - v90 - S '96 - p690+ [501+]
Bose, Sugata - *Credit, Markets, and the Agrarian Economy of Colonial India*
  Historian - v59 - Fall '96 - p169+ [251-500]
Bosher, J F - *Business and Religion in the Age of New France 1600-1760*
  EHR - v112 - Ap '97 - p478+ [501+]
Boskin, Michael J - *Frontiers of Tax Reform*
  JEL - v34 - S '96 - p1438+ [51-250]
Bosley, Deborah - *Let Me Count the Ways*
  Obs - Ap 6 '97 - p18* [51-250]
  Spec - v277 - O 5 '96 - p50 [501+]
  TES - D 27 '96 - p16 [1-50]
Bosnak, Robert - *Christopher's Dream*
  PW - v244 - Mr 31 '97 - p72 [1-50]
Bosq, Denis - *A Course in Stochastic Processes*
  SciTech - v20 - D '96 - p16 [51-250]
Bosquet, Alain - *A Russian Mother*
  BW - v26 - Jl 14 '96 - p6 [51-250]
Boss, Gilbert - *Esquisses De Dialogues Philosophiques*
  Dialogue - v35 - Spr '96 - p396+ [501+]
La Philosophie Et Son Histoire
  RM - v50 - D '96 - p390+ [251-500]
Bosse, Malcolm - *The Examination*
 y Kliatt - v30 - S '96 - p3 [1-50]
 y Kliatt - v30 - S '96 - p6 [51-250]
 y PW - v243 - O 14 '96 - p85 [1-50]
Tusk and Stone
 y Kliatt - v31 - Mr '97 - p6 [1-50]
 c PW - v243 - O 14 '96 - p85 [1-50]
Bost, Hubert - *Un Intellectuel Avant La Lettre*
  Lib - v18 - S '96 - p266+ [501+]
Bostdorff, Denise M - *The Presidency and the Rhetoric of Foreign Crisis*
  JC - v46 - Sum '96 - p176+ [501+]
Bostick, David G - *Prostate Cancer*
  LJ - v122 - Ja '97 - p56 [1-50]
Boston, Kelvin E - *Smart Money Moves for African Americans*
  ACI - v8 - Fall '96 - p37+ [501+]
Boston, Robert - *The Most Dangerous Man in America*
  Hum - v57 - Ja '97 - p42+ [51-250]
The Boston Dog Lover's Companion. 1st Ed.
  Dog Fan - v28 - F '97 - p80 [51-250]
Boston Facts and Figures. 1995 Ed.
 r J Gov Info - v23 - S '96 - p600 [51-250]
Boston Review
 p Sm Pr R - v28 - Jl '96 - p27+ [501+]
Boswell, Jackson Campbell - *Sir Thomas More in the English Renaissance*
 r Ren Q - v49 - Aut '96 - p636+ [501+]
Boswell, James - *James Boswell's Life of Johnson. Vol. 1*
  RES - v48 - F '97 - p114+ [51-250]
A Journey to the Western Islands of Scotland
  SFR - v21 - N '96 - p48 [1-50]
Boswell, John - *Same-Sex Unions in Premodern Europe*
  Specu - v71 - Jl '96 - p693+ [501+]
Boswell, Robert - *American Owned Love*
  KR - v65 - F 15 '97 - p237 [251-500]
  LJ - v122 - Ap 1 '97 - p122 [51-250]
  PW - v244 - F 24 '97 - p63+ [51-250]
  Trib Bks - My 11 '97 - p1+ [501+]
Bosworth, A B - *A Historical Commentary on Arrian's History of Alexander. Vol. 2*
  Rel St Rev - v23 - Ja '97 - p62 [51-250]
Bosworth, Barry - *Reforming Planned Economies in an Integrating World Economy*
  Econ J - v106 - N '96 - p1799+ [501+]
  JEL - v34 - S '96 - p1389+ [501+]
Bosworth, Clifford Edmund - *The Arabs, Byzantium, and Islam*
  R&R Bk N - v11 - D '96 - p10 [51-250]
The New Islamic Dynasties. Enl. and Updated Ed.
 r ARBA - v28 - '97 - p70+ [251-500]
 r MEQ - v4 - Mr '97 - p90 [51-250]
 r R&R Bk N - v12 - F '97 - p18 [51-250]

Bosworth, Patricia - *Anything Your Little Heart Desires*
  KR - v65 - F 1 '97 - p183 [251-500]
  LJ - v122 - Ap 1 '97 - p100 [51-250]
  LJ - v122 - Ap 15 '97 - p90 [501+]
  NYTLa - v146 - My 13 '97 - pC16 [501+]
  PW - v244 - F 10 '97 - p75 [51-250]
  Trib Bks - My 18 '97 - p6+ [501+]
  VV - v42 - Ap 29 '97 - p56 [51-250]
Bosworth, R J B - *Explaining Auschwitz and Hiroshima*
  JMH - v69 - Mr '97 - p119+ [501+]
  Italy and the Wider World 1860-1960
  R&R Bk N - v12 - F '97 - p16 [51-250]
Bosworth, Sheila - *Almost Innocent*
  Bloom Rev - v16 - S '96 - p28 [51-250]
  NYTBR - v101 - S 15 '96 - p44 [1-50]
Botha, W P B - *Wantok*
  WLT - v71 - Win '97 - p209+ [501+]
Botjer, George F - *Sideshow War*
  Choice - v34 - Ap '97 - p1396 [51-250]
  LJ - v121 - S 15 '96 - p78 [51-250]
Botkin, Daniel B - *Our Natural History*
  WAL - v31 - Sum '96 - p175+ [51-250]
Botkin, Gleb - *Lost Tales (Illus. by Gleb Botkin)*
  c NY - v72 - N 18 '96 - p98 [1-50]
Botoman, Rodica - *Discover Romanian*
  MLJ - v80 - Win '96 - p557 [501+]
Botond, Bognar - *Togo Murano: Master Architect of Japan*
  r Choice - v34 - N '96 - p443 [51-250]
Bott, Richard - *Subtilisin Enzymes*
  SciTech - v20 - N '96 - p34 [51-250]
Botta, Mario - *La Cappella Del Monte Tamaro*
  BM - v138 - O '96 - p700 [1-50]
Bottenberg, Joanna - *Shared Creation*
  R&R Bk N - v12 - F '97 - p70 [51-250]
Botterill, Steven - *Dante and the Mystical Tradition*
  MP - v94 - F '97 - p363+ [501+]
Botterweck, G Johannes - *Theological Dictionary of the Old Testament. Vol. 7*
  r ARBA - v28 - '97 - p545 [51-250]
  r Rel St Rev - v23 - Ap '97 - p169 [51-250]
Botti, Timothy J - *Ace in the Hole*
  Choice - v34 - Ja '97 - p861 [51-250]
Botticelli, Sandro - *Michelangelo and Raphael in the Vatican*
  LJ - v122 - Ja '97 - p93+ [251-500]
Bottigheimer, Ruth B - *The Bible for Children*
  Bks & Cult - v3 - Mr '97 - p21+ [501+]
  CC - v113 - O 9 '96 - p937+ [501+]
  Choice - v34 - N '96 - p448 [51-250]
  NYTBR - v101 - D 8 '96 - p66 [501+]
  R&R Bk N - v11 - N '96 - p7 [51-250]
Botting, Fred - *Gothic*
  Choice - v34 - Mr '97 - p1158 [251-500]
Bottner, Barbara - *Bootsie Barker Ballerina (Illus. by G Brian Karas)*
  c BL - v93 - My 1 '97 - p1503 [51-250]
  c CCB-B - v50 - Ap '97 - p276+ [51-250]
  c KR - v65 - Ap 1 '97 - p549 [51-250]
  Nana Hannah's Piano (Illus. by Diana Cain Bluthenthal)
  c BL - v93 - N 15 '96 - p593 [51-250]
  c CBRS - v25 - O '96 - p14 [51-250]
  c HB Guide - v8 - Spr '97 - p20 [51-250]
  c SLJ - v42 - O '96 - p84 [51-250]
Botto, Francis - *PC Multimedia*
  CBR - v14 - Jl '96 - p24 [1-50]
Bottom Line Personal Book of Bests
  LJ - v122 - F 15 '97 - p143+ [51-250]
  PW - v244 - Ja 13 '97 - p68 [1-50]
Bottoms, Bette L - *International Perspectives on Child Abuse and Children's Testimony*
  R&R Bk N - v11 - N '96 - p52 [51-250]
Bottoms, David - *Armored Hearts*
  Poet - v169 - F '97 - p286+ [501+]
  South R - v32 - Aut '96 - p812+ [501+]
Botts, Gregory - *Clouds, Leaves, Waves*
  LJ - v121 - O 1 '96 - p82 [51-250]
Bou, Enric - *Signo Y Memoria*
  Hisp - v79 - S '96 - p440+ [501+]
Bouamama, Said - *Familles Maghrebines De France*
  BL - v93 - F 1 '97 - p930 [1-50]
Boublil, Tsuriel - *Gerushim, Ezrah Rishonah Mishpatit*
  BL - v93 - Mr 1 '97 - p1115 [1-50]
Bouchard, Dave - *Voices from the Wild (Illus. by Ron Parker)*
  c BL - v93 - D 1 '96 - p658 [51-250]
  c Emerg Lib - v24 - Mr '97 - p28 [1-50]
  c HB Guide - v8 - Spr '97 - p151 [51-250]
  c PW - v243 - N 4 '96 - p76 [51-250]
  c Quill & Q - v62 - N '96 - p43+ [251-500]

Bouchard, Denis - *The Semantics of Syntax*
  Choice - v34 - O '96 - p272 [51-250]
Boucher, Denise - *A Coeur De Jour*
  FR - v70 - F '97 - p492+ [501+]
  Les Divines
  FR - v70 - F '97 - p492+ [501+]
Boucher, Sandy - *Opening the Lotus*
  PW - v244 - Ap 14 '97 - p69 [51-250]
Boucher, Virginia - *Interlibrary Loan Practices Handbook. 2nd Ed.*
  R&R Bk N - v12 - F '97 - p102 [51-250]
Boucquey, Eliane - *Un Chasseur Dans L'Image*
  MLR - v91 - Jl '96 - p736+ [501+]
Boudinot, Elias - *Cherokee Editor*
  Bloom Rev - v16 - Jl '96 - p3+ [501+]
Boudjedra, Rachid - *Lettres Algeriennes*
  WLT - v71 - Win '97 - p201+ [501+]
Boue, Juan Carlos - *Venezuela: The Political Economy of Oil*
  HAHR - v76 - Ag '96 - p585+ [251-500]
Boughey, Howard Nathaniel - *Ordinary Social Occasions, Sandcastles, and Structural Reproduction*
  AJS - v102 - My '96 - p272+ [501+]
  CS - v25 - S '96 - p675+ [501+]
Boughton, Doug - *Evaluating and Assessing the Visual Arts in Education*
  Choice - v34 - F '97 - p1014 [251-500]
Bouilhet, Louis - *Louis Bouilhet: Lettres A Gustave Flaubert*
  Lon R Bks - v19 - Ap 3 '97 - p18+ [501+]
Boulad-Ayoub, Josiane - *Mimes Et Parades*
  CPR - v16 - Ap '96 - p84+ [501+]
Boulding, Russell - *EPA Environmental Assessment Sourcebook*
  SciTech - v20 - N '96 - p68 [51-250]
  EPA Environmental Engineering Sourcebook
  SciTech - v20 - D '96 - p70 [51-250]
Boulevard
  p Sm Pr R - v28 - D '96 - p18 [51-250]
  p Sm Pr R - v29 - F '97 - p13+ [51-250]
Boulez, Pierre - *Conversation with Boulez*
  FF - v20 - S '96 - p474+ [251-500]
  Conversations with Boulez
  KR - v64 - My 1 '96 - p679+ [251-500]
Boulle, Pierre - *Bridge on the River Kwai*
  FEER - Anniv '96 - p228 [501+]
Boullosa, Carmen - *They're Cows, We're Pigs*
  BL - v93 - My 1 '97 - p1477 [51-250]
  KR - v65 - Ap 1 '97 - p503 [51-250]
  LJ - v122 - Ap 15 '97 - p116 [51-250]
  PW - v244 - Ap 7 '97 - p71 [51-250]
Bouloux, Pierre-Marc - *Medicine: Self-Assessment Picture Tests. Vols. 1-4*
  SciTech - v21 - Mr '97 - p48 [1-50]
Boultbee, Paul G - *Cayman Islands*
  r ARBA - v28 - '97 - p69 [251-500]
  r R&R Bk N - v11 - D '96 - p18 [1-50]
Boultwood, Jacqueline - *Gene Isolation and Mapping Protocols*
  SciTech - v21 - Mr '97 - p36 [51-250]
Bouma-Prediger, Steven - *The Greening of Theology*
  Rel St Rev - v22 - O '96 - p338 [51-250]
Boundary Element Technology XI
  SciTech - v20 - S '96 - p48 [51-250]
Boundary-Layer Meteorology--25th Anniversary Volume 1970-1995
  SciTech - v21 - Mr '97 - p26 [51-250]
Bounds, J Dennis - *Perry Mason: The Authorship and Reproduction of a Popular Hero*
  R&R Bk N - v12 - F '97 - p89 [51-250]
Boundy, Lynne - *Its Quite an Education*
  TES - S 27 '96 - p8* [51-250]
Bouquet, Simon - *Imitations Et Traduction De Cent Dix-huit Emblemes D'A lciat*
  R&R Bk N - v11 - D '96 - p63 [51-250]
Bour, Laura - *The Wolf*
  c Bks Keeps - Ja '97 - p21 [51-250]
Bouraoui, Hedi - *Nomadaime*
  WLT - v70 - Sum '96 - p663 [51-250]
Bouras, Gillian - *A Stranger Here*
  Aust Bk R - O '96 - p47+ [501+]
Bourcier, Richard J - *L'Humanisme De Georges Duhamel*
  FR - v70 - Mr '97 - p335+ [251-500]
Bourdais, Daniele - *Envol*
  y TES - Ja 24 '97 - p12* [501+]
Bourdeaux, Michael - *The Politics of Religion in Russia and the New States of Eurasia*
  J Ch St - v38 - Sum '96 - p642+ [251-500]
Bourdieu, Pierre - *The Field of Cultural Production*
  Am Q - v49 - Mr '97 - p183+ [501+]

Bourdon, David - *Designing the Earth*
  Art J - v55 - Sum '96 - p95+ [501+]
  Warhol
  NS & S - v9 - My 3 '96 - p40 [1-50]
Boureau, Alain - *Le Droit De Cuissage*
  Specu - v71 - Jl '96 - p696+ [501+]
Bourell, David Lee - *Synthesis and Processing of Nanocrystalline Powder*
  SciTech - v20 - N '96 - p23 [51-250]
Bouret, Claude - *Corot: Le Genie Du Trait, Estampes Et Dessins*
  BM - v138 - Jl '96 - p482+ [501+]
Bourgeau, Vincent - *I'm Sick of It! A Fishy Melodrama (Illus. by Vincent Bourgeau)*
  c PW - v244 - Ap 14 '97 - p77 [1-50]
  I'm Sick of It! A Mouse's Reality Check (Illus. by Vincent Bourgeau)
  c KR - v65 - My 1 '97 - p717 [251-500]
  c PW - v244 - Ap 14 '97 - p77 [1-50]
Bourgeois, Paulette - *Amazing Dirt Book*
  c Inst - v105 - My '96 - p18 [1-50]
  Franklin's Bad Day (Illus. by Brenda Clark)
  c Quill & Q - v62 - D '96 - p38 [51-250]
  Franklin's Halloween (Illus. by Brenda Clark)
  c Quill & Q - v62 - S '96 - p74 [51-250]
  Franklin's School Play
  c Emerg Lib - v24 - Mr '97 - p26 [1-50]
Bourgois, Philippe - *In Search of Respect*
  CS - v25 - N '96 - p793+ [501+]
Bourguignon, Laurence - *A Friend for Tiger (Illus. by Laurence Henno)*
  c HB Guide - v7 - Fall '96 - p249 [51-250]
Bourguignon, Stephane - *Sandman Blues*
  BIC - v25 - S '96 - p24 [501+]
Bourke, Angela - *By Salt Water*
  BL - v93 - Ap 1 '97 - p1280 [51-250]
  ILS - v15 - Fall '96 - p8+ [501+]
  KR - v65 - Mr 1 '97 - p319 [51-250]
  PW - v244 - Ap 28 '97 - p49 [251-500]
Bourke, Joanna - *Dismembering the Male*
  AHR - v102 - F '97 - p111+ [501+]
  Econ - v339 - My 18 '96 - p3*+ [501+]
  HRNB - v25 - Fall '96 - p23 [251-500]
  R&R Bk N - v11 - D '96 - p41 [51-250]
  Husbandry to Housewifery
  VS - v39 - Aut '95 - p107+ [501+]
  Working-Class Cultures in Britain 1890-1960
  HT - v46 - S '96 - p57 [51-250]
Bourke, Paul - *Washington County*
  PHR - v65 - N '96 - p672+ [251-500]
  WHQ - v28 - Spr '97 - p94+ [251-500]
Bourne, Peter G - *Jimmy Carter: A Comprehensive Biography from Plains to Post-Presidency*
  Am - v176 - Mr 22 '97 - p31+ [251-500]
  Bks & Cult - v3 - Mr '97 - p16+ [501+]
  y BL - v93 - F 1 '97 - p923 [51-250]
  LJ - v122 - F 1 '97 - p88 [51-250]
  NYTBR - v102 - Mr 16 '97 - p24+ [501+]
  PW - v244 - Ja 6 '97 - p56 [51-250]
Bourne, Stephen - *Brief Encounters*
  Obs - Mr 16 '97 - p18* [51-250]
Bournique, Jean-Pierre - *Occupation of France and Annexation of Alsace-Lorraine by Germany*
  Phil Lit R - v46 - 1 '97 - p71 [251-500]
Bourque, Bruce J - *Diversity and Complexity in Prehistoric Maritime Societies*
  Am Ant - v61 - Jl '96 - p621+ [501+]
Bourque, Joan - *Dreams of Dolphins Dancing*
  c Ch BWatch - v7 - F '97 - p2 [51-250]
Bourque, Pierre - *Government Online in Canada*
  Quill & Q - v62 - N '96 - p33 [251-500]
Bouteneff, Peter - *Daily Readings in Orthodox Spirituality*
  RR - v55 - N '96 - p661 [1-50]
Boutet, Josiane - *Construire Le Sens*
  Lang Soc - v25 - S '96 - p449+ [501+]
Boutibonnes, Philippe - *Antoni Van Leeuwenhoek 1632-1723*
  Isis - v87 - D '96 - p728+ [251-500]
Bouton, Cynthia A - *The Flour War*
  JIH - v27 - Aut '96 - p315+ [501+]
Bouton, Gary David - *Official Multimedia Publishing for Netscape*
  Quill & Q - v62 - N '96 - p32 [51-250]
Bouton, Jim - *Strike Zone*
  Aethlon - v13 - Fall '95 - p134+ [251-500]
Boutros-Ghali, Boutros - *An Agenda for Development 1995*
  J Gov Info - v23 - S '96 - p676 [51-250]

Egypt's Road to Jerusalem
  KR - v65 - Ap 1 '97 - p542+ [51-250]
  LJ - v122 - My 1 '97 - p124 [51-250]
  PW - v244 - Ap 14 '97 - p66 [51-250]
Boutton, Thomas W - *Mass Spectrometry of Soils*
  SciTech - v20 - S '96 - p44 [51-250]
Boutwell, Jeffrey - *Israeli-Palestinian Security*
  MEJ - v50 - Sum '96 - p453 [51-250]
Bouvard, Marguerite Guzman - *Women Reshaping
  Human Rights*
  Choice - v34 - D '96 - p680 [51-250]
  JPR - v34 - F '97 - p108 [251-500]
  LATBR - Ag 4 '96 - p11 [51-250]
  R&R Bk N - v11 - D '96 - p46 [51-250]
Bouveresse, Jacques - *Wittgenstein Reads Freud*
  MLN - v111 - D '96 - p1034+ [501+]
  NYTBR - v101 - S 22 '96 - p42 [501+]
Bouvier, Nicolas - *Geneva, Zurich, Basel*
  Comp L - v49 - Win '97 - p81+ [501+]
  EHR - v112 - Ap '97 - p548+ [251-500]
Bouza, Tony - *The Decline and Fall of the American
  Empire*
  PW - v243 - S 2 '96 - p107 [51-250]
Bova, Ben - *Brothers*
  Analog - v117 - Ja '97 - p141+ [251-500]
  PW - v243 - N 4 '96 - p71 [1-50]
  PW - v243 - N 18 '96 - p70 [1-50]
Moonrise
  KR - v64 - N 1 '96 - p1569 [51-250]
  LJ - v121 - D '96 - p151+ [51-250]
  LJ - v122 - Ja '97 - p51 [1-50]
Bove, Emmanuel - *Night Departure. No Place*
  TranslRevS - v2 - D '96 - p21 [51-250]
  TranslRevS - v2 - D '96 - p21 [51-250]
Bovens, Mark - *Understanding Policy Fiascoes*
  J Pol - v59 - F '97 - p259+ [501+]
Bowden, Bobby - *Winning's Only Part of the Game*
  y BL - v93 - S 1 '96 - p55 [51-250]
Bowdish, Lynea - *Living with My Stepfather Is Like Living
  with a Moose (Illus. by Blanche Sims)*
  c BL - v93 - Mr 1 '97 - p1162 [51-250]
  c KR - v65 - Ja 15 '97 - p138 [51-250]
This Is Me, Laughing (Illus. by Walter Gaffney-Kessell)
  c HB Guide - v7 - Fall '96 - p249 [1-50]
Bowen, Andy Russell - *A Head Full of Notions (Illus. by
  Lisa Harvey)*
  c SLJ - v43 - Mr '97 - p171+ [51-250]
Bowen, 'Asta - *Hungry for Home*
  y BL - v93 - Ja '97 - p816 [51-250]
  KR - v64 - N 15 '96 - p1617 [251-500]
  PW - v243 - N 25 '96 - p58 [51-250]
  Trib Bks - Mr 9 '97 - p6+ [501+]
Bowen, Charles - *Modem Nation*
  BL - v92 - Ag '96 - p1862+ [501+]
Bowen, Desmond - *History and the Shaping of Irish
  Protestantism*
  Choice - v34 - S '96 - p184 [51-250]
Bowen, Donna Lee - *Everyday Life in the Muslim Middle
  East*
  JTWS - v13 - Fall '96 - p327+ [501+]
Bowen, Elizabeth - *Elizabeth Bowen (Harris). Audio
  Version*
  BL - v93 - S 15 '96 - p264 [51-250]
To the North
  Trib Bks - Mr 2 '97 - p8 [1-50]
Bowen, Gail - *A Killing Spring*
  PW - v244 - Ap 7 '97 - p77 [51-250]
  Quill & Q - v62 - O '96 - p32 [51-250]
Bowen, H V - *Elites, Enterprise and the Making of the
  British Overseas Empire 1688-1775*
  Choice - v34 - Ja '97 - p854 [51-250]
Bowen, Howard R - *Investment in Learning*
  JEL - v35 - Mr '97 - p230 [51-250]
Bowen, J Ray - *Dynamics of Exothermicity*
  SciTech - v20 - N '96 - p23 [51-250]
Bowen, Jan - *Men Talk*
  Aust Bk R - Je '96 - p32+ [501+]
Bowen, Jimmy - *Rough Mix*
  BL - v93 - My 1 '97 - p1472 [51-250]
  KR - v65 - Ap 1 '97 - p514 [251-500]
  LJ - v122 - My 1 '97 - p105 [51-250]
  PW - v244 - Ap 21 '97 - p55 [51-250]
Bowen, John R - *Muslims through Discourse*
  JAAR - v64 - Win '96 - p870+ [501+]
Bowen, Kurt - *Evangelism and Apostasy*
  Choice - v34 - D '96 - p627 [51-250]

Bowen, Michael - *Worst Case Scenario*
  BL - v93 - S 15 '96 - p223 [51-250]
  Ent W - D 20 '96 - p70 [51-250]
  KR - v64 - S 1 '96 - p1272 [51-250]
  LATBR - D 15 '96 - p12 [251-500]
  PW - v243 - S 9 '96 - p67 [51-250]
Bowen, Peter - *Notches*
  BL - v93 - Mr 15 '97 - p1228 [51-250]
  Ent W - F 21 '97 - p121 [51-250]
  KR - v64 - D 15 '96 - p1767+ [51-250]
  NYTBR - v102 - Mr 2 '97 - p20 [51-250]
  PW - v243 - D 2 '96 - p43+ [51-250]
Wolf, No Wolf
  Bloom Rev - v16 - Jl '96 - p16 [251-500]
Bowen, William G - *The Charitable Nonprofits*
  J Hi E - v68 - Mr '97 - p228+ [501+]
Inside the Boardroom
  J Hi E - v68 - Mr '97 - p228+ [501+]
Bower, Anne - *Epistolary Responses*
  Choice - v34 - My '97 - p1493+ [51-250]
Bower, Susan - *Factory Joker*
  Aust Bk R - S '96 - p53+ [501+]
Bower, Tom - *Maxwell: The Final Verdict*
  Obs - D 1 '96 - p17* [1-50]
Bower, Walter - *Scotichronicon. Vol. 4*
  EHR - v112 - Ap '97 - p438+ [501+]
  Specu - v71 - Jl '96 - p698+ [501+]
Bowering, George - *Bowering's B.C.*
  Beav - v76 - O '96 - p47 [51-250]
  Beav - v77 - F '97 - p39 [251-500]
  CF - v75 - D '96 - p36+ [501+]
  Mac - v109 - N 18 '96 - p68 [501+]
  Mac - v109 - D 9 '96 - p64 [1-50]
  Quill & Q - v62 - O '96 - p37 [251-500]
Shoot!
  Can Lit - Win '96 - p148+ [501+]
Bowers, Edgar - *Collected Poems*
  NY - v73 - Ap 7 '97 - p95 [51-250]
  PW - v244 - Ja 27 '97 - p94 [51-250]
Bowers, Fredson - *Principles of Bibliographical
  Description*
  Lib & Cul - v32 - Win '97 - p155+ [501+]
Bowers, Neal - *Words for the Taking*
  BL - v93 - Ja '97 - p806 [51-250]
  KR - v64 - N 1 '96 - p1572+ [251-500]
  LJ - v121 - D '96 - p120 [51-250]
  NY - v72 - Ja 20 '97 - p93+ [501+]
  PW - v243 - N 11 '96 - p65 [51-250]
  Shen - v47 - Spr '97 - p115+ [501+]
  TLS - 1 '97 - p36 [501+]
Bowers, Norman A - *Hidatsa Suprasegmentals*
  R&R Bk N - v11 - D '96 - p60 [51-250]
Bowers, Q David - *American Coin Treasures and Hoards*
  Coin W - v37 - N 11 '96 - p46 [51-250]
  Coin W - v38 - Mr 17 '97 - p10 [251-500]
*A Buyer's and Enthusiast's Guide to Flying Eagle and
  Indian Cents*
  r Coin W - v37 - D 30 '96 - p22 [51-250]
Bowers, Russell H - *Someone or Nothing?*
  R&R Bk N - v12 - F '97 - p9 [51-250]
Bowers, Terrell L - *Ride against the Wind*
  y BL - v93 - D 15 '96 - p708 [51-250]
  Roundup M - v4 - D '96 - p24 [51-250]
Bowers, Toni - *The Politics of Motherhood*
  Choice - v34 - Mr '97 - p1159 [51-250]
  TLS - Mr 21 '97 - p8 [501+]
Bowersock, G W - *Martyrdom and Rome*
  CHR - v82 - Jl '96 - p488+ [501+]
  JR - v77 - Ja '97 - p128+ [501+]
  Theol St - v57 - Mr '96 - p183 [51-250]
Bowersock, William I - *The Christmas Card*
  BWatch - v17 - D '96 - p2 [51-250]
Bowker, Geoffrey C - *Science on the Run*
  Isis - v88 - Mr '97 - p167+ [501+]
  Sci - v274 - N 15 '96 - p1148 [501+]
Bowker, Gordon - *Pursued by Furies*
  NYTBR - v101 - D 8 '96 - p92 [1-50]
  WLT - v70 - Aut '96 - p968 [501+]
Through the Dark Labyrinth
  ILN - Christmas '96 - p90 [501+]
  LJ - v122 - My 1 '97 - p103 [51-250]
  PW - v244 - Ap 14 '97 - p61+ [51-250]
  Spec - v278 - Ja 11 '97 - p37+ [501+]
Bowker, John Westerdale - *The Oxford Dictionary of
  World Religions*
  r LJ - v122 - My 1 '97 - p94 [51-250]
World Religions
  r LJ - v122 - My 1 '97 - p94 [51-250]
Bowker, Robert - *Beyond Peace*
  Choice - v34 - Ap '97 - p1413 [51-250]

**The Bowker Annual Library and Book Trade Almanac
  1996**
  r ARBA - v28 - '97 - p238 [51-250]
Bowler, Gail Hellund - *Artists and Writers Colonies*
  r ARBA - v28 - '97 - p343 [51-250]
Bowler, Peter J - *Biology and Social Thought 1850-1914*
  Isis - v87 - S '96 - p560 [501+]
Life's Splendid Drama
  Am Sci - v85 - Mr '97 - p177+ [501+]
  Choice - v34 - Mr '97 - p1182 [51-250]
  LJ - v121 - N 15 '96 - p85 [51-250]
  Nature - v385 - Ja 9 '97 - p127+ [501+]
  New Sci - v152 - N 9 '96 - p44 [501+]
  SciTech - v20 - D '96 - p30 [51-250]
  TLS - F 21 '97 - p8+ [501+]
The Norton History of the Environmental Sciences
  Isis - v88 - Mr '97 - p126+ [501+]
Bowles, Paul - *Paul Bowles, Music*
  TLS - S 13 '96 - p8 [501+]
Bowles, Rachel - *Maps*
  c Bks Keeps - N '96 - p14 [51-250]
  Sch Lib - v44 - N '96 - p161 [51-250]
Bowles, Stephen E - *The Film Anthologies Index*
  r FQ - v49 - Fall '95 - p62 [51-250]
Bowling, Tim - *Low Water Slack*
  BIC - v26 - F '97 - p25 [51-250]
Bowlt, John E - *Laboratory of Dreams*
  Choice - v34 - Ja '97 - p802 [51-250]
Bowlus, Charles R - *Franks, Moravians, and Magyars*
  Historian - v59 - Win '97 - p459 [51-250]
  Specu - v72 - Ja '97 - p112+ [501+]
Bowman, Alan K - *Literacy and Power in the Ancient
  World*
  HT - v46 - Jl '96 - p55+ [501+]
Bowman, Carl F - *Brethren Society*
  AHR - v101 - O '96 - p1268 [501+]
  CH - v65 - S '96 - p552+ [501+]
Bowman, Carol - *Children's Past Lives*
  PW - v244 - Mr 3 '97 - p60 [51-250]
Bowman, Charles F - *Wisdom of the Gurus*
  SciTech - v21 - Mr '97 - p7 [51-250]
Bowman, Crystal - *Ivan and the Dynamos*
  c KR - v65 - Mr 1 '97 - p378 [51-250]
Bowman, Doug - *The Three Lives of Littleton Blue*
  Roundup M - v4 - O '96 - p30 [51-250]
Bowman, Eric - *Before I Wake*
  KR - v65 - Mr 1 '97 - p319+ [51-250]
  LJ - v122 - Ap 15 '97 - p116 [51-250]
  PW - v244 - Mr 24 '97 - p60 [51-250]
Bowman, Judith S - *The Practical SQL Handbook. 3rd
  Ed.*
  SciTech - v21 - Mr '97 - p8 [51-250]
Bowman, Keith J - *Handbook on Discontinuously
  Reinforced Ceramic Matrix Composites*
  SciTech - v21 - Mr '97 - p77 [51-250]
Bowman, Scott R - *The Modern Corporation and
  American Political Thought*
  BHR - v70 - Aut '96 - p408+ [501+]
  Choice - v34 - O '96 - p360 [51-250]
  JEH - v57 - Mr '97 - p190+ [501+]
  JEL - v34 - S '96 - p1489 [51-250]
Bown, Deni - *The Encyclopedia of Herbs and Their Uses*
  r RQ - v35 - Sum '96 - p559 [501+]
Growing Herbs
  r RQ - v35 - Sum '96 - p558+ [501+]
Bowness, Alan - *Bernard Meadows: Sculpture and
  Drawings*
  BM - v138 - D '96 - p836 [51-250]
Bowser, Benjamin - *Racism and Anti-Racism in World
  Perspective*
  BWatch - v17 - D '96 - p5 [1-50]
Bowsher, Julian - *Biblical Sites*
  c TES - N 8 '96 - p13* [501+]
Bowyer, Kevin - *Advances in Image Understanding*
  SciTech - v20 - N '96 - p116 [51-250]
Box, Su - *You Are Very Special (Illus. by Susie Poole)*
  c Sch Lib - v44 - N '96 - p145 [51-250]
Boxer, Arabella - *The Hamlyn Herb Book*
  Mac - v109 - D 9 '96 - p66 [1-50]
The Herb Book
  BWatch - v17 - N '96 - p7 [51-250]
Boxer, Tim - *Tim Boxer's Jewish Celebrity Anecdotes*
  PW - v243 - S 23 '96 - p70 [51-250]
Boy, Daniel - *L'Ecologie Au Pouvoir*
  Choice - v34 - D '96 - p568 [1-50]
Boyack, Neil - *See Through*
  Aust Bk R - O '96 - p67 [51-250]
Boyarin, Daniel - *Intertexuality and the Reading of
  Midrash*
  TranslRevS - v1 - My '95 - p9 [51-250]

A Radical Jew
 Theol St - v57 - D '96 - p738+ [501+]
Boyarin, Jonathan - *The Ethnology of Reading*
 Can Lit - Spr '97 - p212+ [501+]
Boyarski, Jennie S - *Collection Management in the Electronic Age*
 RQ - v36 - Fall '96 - p88 [1-50]
Boyatzis, Richard E - *Innovation in Professional Education*
 Per Psy - v49 - Aut '96 - p749+ [501+]
Boyce, David George - *The Making of Modern Irish History*
 ILS - v16 - Spr '97 - p31 [501+]
 TLS - S 27 '96 - p5+ [501+]
Boyce, James K - *Economic Policy for Building Peace*
 Choice - v34 - D '96 - p658 [51-250]
 JEL - v34 - D '96 - p2058+ [51-250]
Boyce, William E - *Elementary Differential Equations and Boundary Value Problems. 6th Ed.*
 SciTech - v20 - D '96 - p18 [51-250]
Boyd, Aaron - *Tiger Woods*
 c BL - v93 - My 1 '97 - p1490 [51-250]
 c KR - v65 - My 1 '97 - p717 [51-250]
Boyd, Brian - *Vladimir Nabokov: The American Years*
 Bks & Cult - v1 - N '95 - p26+ [501+]
 Vladimir Nabokov: The Russian Years
 Bks & Cult - v1 - N '95 - p26+ [501+]
Boyd, Candy Dawson - *Daddy, Daddy Be There (Illus. by Floyd Cooper)*
 c RT - v50 - O '96 - p155 [51-250]
 A Different Beat
 c BL - v93 - N 15 '96 - p586 [51-250]
Boyd, Carl - *The Japanese Submarine Force and World War II*
 NWCR - v50 - Win '97 - p166+ [501+]
Boyd, Elza Dinwiddie - *In Our Own Words*
 Bl S - v26 - Sum '96 - p63 [51-250]
Boyd, Gavin - *Structural Competitiveness in the Pacific*
 JEL - v35 - Mr '97 - p212 [51-250]
Boyd, George Elroy - *Two by George*
 Quill & Q - v63 - Mr '97 - p76 [251-500]
Boyd, Gregory A - *Cynic Sage or Son of God?*
 Bks & Cult - v1 - N '95 - p3+ [501+]
Boyd, Herb - *Brotherman*
 y BL - v93 - F 15 '97 - p1014 [1-50]
Boyd, James - *Drums (Illus. by N C Wyeth)*
 y HB Guide - v7 - Fall '96 - p300 [51-250]
Boyd, John - *The Internet Scares Me*
 IRLA - v32 - Ag '96 - p12 [1-50]
Boyd, Julia A - *Embracing the Fire*
 BL - v93 - F 15 '97 - p978 [51-250]
 PW - v243 - D 9 '96 - p54 [51-250]
 In the Company of My Sisters
 y Kliatt - v31 - My '97 - p23 [51-250]
Boyd, Lois A - *Presbyterian Women in America. 2nd Ed.*
 R&R Bk N - v11 - N '96 - p8 [51-250]
Boyd, Loree - *Spirit Moves*
 Choice - v34 - N '96 - p524 [51-250]
Boyd, Malcolm - *Grace Williams*
 TLS - Mr 7 '97 - p32 [51-250]
Boyd, Melba Joyce - *Discarded Legacy*
 Signs - v22 - Win '97 - p462+ [501+]
Boyd, Robert - *People of the Dalles*
 Choice - v34 - N '96 - p524 [51-250]
 WHQ - v27 - Win '96 - p551 [51-250]
Boyd, Susan A - *Ecclesiastical Silver Plate in Sixth Century Byzantium*
 Rel St Rev - v23 - Ja '97 - p79 [51-250]
Boyd, Todd - *Am I Black Enough for You?*
 y BL - v93 - F 15 '97 - p978 [51-250]
Boyd, William - *The Blue Afternoon*
 NYTBR - v102 - Ja 12 '97 - p32 [51-250]
 PW - v243 - D 9 '96 - p66 [1-50]
 The Destiny of Nathalie X and Other Stories
 KR - v65 - F 1 '97 - p178 [1-50]
 LATBR - Ja 19 '97 - p11 [501+]
 NYTBR - v102 - Ja 19 '97 - p9+ [501+]
 PW - v244 - Ja 27 '97 - p80 [51-250]
 Trib Bks - F 2 '97 - p3 [501+]
 An Ice Cream War (Wilby). Audio Version
 Books - v11 - Ap '97 - p19 [1-50]
Boyer, Jay - *Sidney Lumet*
 FQ - v49 - Fall '95 - p62 [51-250]
Boyer, John W - *Culture and Political Crisis in Vienna*
 CHR - v83 - Ja '97 - p121+ [251-500]
 JMH - v69 - Mr '97 - p179+ [501+]
Boyer, M Christine - *The City of Collective Memory*
 CS - v25 - N '96 - p778+ [501+]
 CyberCities: Visual Perception in the Age of Electronic Communication
 Choice - v34 - Ja '97 - p832 [51-250]

Boyer, Mark - *A Month-by-Month Guide to Entertaining Angels*
 RR - v55 - S '96 - p554 [51-250]
Boyer, Pascal - *The Naturalness of Religious Ideas*
 Theol St - v57 - Mr '96 - p160+ [501+]
Boyer, Paul - *When Time Shall Be No More*
 JAAR - v65 - Spr '97 - p226+ [501+]
Boyer, Richard - *Lives of the Bigamists*
 AHR - v101 - D '96 - p1657 [501+]
 JIH - v27 - Win '97 - p556+ [251-500]
 WHQ - v27 - Win '96 - p548 [1-50]
Boyer-Thiollier, Christine - *Francois-Auguste Ravier 1814-1895*
 BM - v138 - S '96 - p614 [251-500]
Boykin, Keith - *One More River to Cross*
 Advocate - S 17 '96 - p83+ [501+]
 BL - v93 - S 15 '96 - p185+ [51-250]
 LJ - v121 - O 15 '96 - p79 [51-250]
 LJ - v121 - N 1 '96 - p86 [1-50]
 SFR - v21 - N '96 - p40 [251-500]
Boyko, Carrie - *Hold Fast Your Dreams (Illus. by Kimberly Colen)*
 y HB Guide - v8 - Spr '97 - p147 [51-250]
 y SLJ - v42 - Ag '96 - p167 [51-250]
 y VOYA - v19 - D '96 - p288 [51-250]
Boyko, John - *Last Steps to Freedom*
 CF - v75 - O '96 - p36+ [501+]
Boylan, Eleanor - *Murder Crossed*
 Arm Det - v29 - Fall '96 - p488 [51-250]
Boylan, Michael A - *The Power to Get In*
 BL - v93 - Ja '97 - p793 [51-250]
 LJ - v122 - Ja '97 - p114 [51-250]
 PW - v243 - N 25 '96 - p62 [51-250]
Boylan, Roger - *Killoyle*
 KR - v65 - Ap 1 '97 - p478+ [251-500]
 LJ - v122 - Ap 1 '97 - p122 [51-250]
 PW - v244 - Ap 14 '97 - p55+ [51-250]
Boylan, Thomas A - *Beyond Rhetoric and Realism in Economics*
 JEL - v34 - D '96 - p1946+ [501+]
Boyle, Alistair - *The Unlucky Seven*
 PW - v244 - F 3 '97 - p98 [51-250]
Boyle, Charles - *Paleface*
 TLS - Jl 7 '96 - p26 [501+]
Boyle, David - *Technology*
 TES - D 13 '96 - p43 [51-250]
Boyle, Deirdre - *Subject to Change*
 Wom R Bks - v14 - Mr '97 - p17+ [501+]
Boyle, Frank A - *A Party of Mad Fellows*
 Choice - v34 - D '96 - p675 [51-250]
Boyle, Frederick R - *Later Families of Sanford-Springvale, Maine*
 Am Geneal - v71 - Ap '96 - p126+ [501+]
Boyle, Gerry - *Lifeline*
 Arm Det - v30 - Win '97 - p90+ [251-500]
 Potshot
 BL - v93 - Mr 1 '97 - p1113 [51-250]
 KR - v65 - F 1 '97 - p174 [251-500]
 LJ - v122 - Mr 15 '97 - p87 [51-250]
 NYTBR - v102 - Mr 16 '97 - p28 [51-250]
 PW - v244 - F 3 '97 - p98 [51-250]
Boyle, Godfrey - *Renewable Energy*
 New Sci - v151 - S 28 '96 - p48 [51-250]
Boyle, James - *Shamans, Software, and Spleens*
 Choice - v34 - Ja '97 - p866 [51-250]
 Cng - v29 - Mr '97 - p54 [51-250]
 NYTBR - v101 - S 22 '96 - p18 [501+]
Boyle, John P - *Church Teaching Authority*
 Theol St - v57 - D '96 - p766+ [501+]
Boyle, Kevin - *The UAW and the Heyday of American Liberalism 1945-1968*
 APSR - v91 - Mr '97 - p181+ [501+]
Boyle, Susan Calafate - *Comerciantes, Arrieros, Y Peones*
 Pub Hist - v19 - Win '97 - p93+ [251-500]
Boyle, T Coraghessan - *East Is East*
 Obs - S 29 '96 - p18* [51-250]
 The Tortilla Curtain
 Books - v10 - Je '96 - p25 [1-50]
 LATBR - S 15 '96 - p11 [51-250]
 NYTBR - v101 - S 15 '96 - p44 [51-250]
 PW - v243 - My 6 '96 - p234 [1-50]
 Reason - v28 - D '96 - p53+ [501+]
 WLT - v70 - Sum '96 - p690 [501+]
 The Tortilla Curtain (Rosenblat). Audio Version
 y Kliatt - v30 - S '96 - p53 [51-250]
 World's End
 Obs - S 29 '96 - p18* [51-250]
Boyles, Denis - *The Lost Lore of a Man's Life*
 PW - v244 - My 12 '97 - p72 [51-250]

A Man's Life
 Esq - v126 - D '96 - p40 [1-50]
 PW - v243 - S 16 '96 - p80 [51-250]
Boylestad, Robert L - *Introductory Circuit Analysis. 8th Ed.*
 SciTech - v20 - D '96 - p74 [51-250]
Boym, Svetlana - *Common Places*
 Cu H - v95 - O '96 - p348 [501+]
Boyne, Philip J - *Osseous Reconstruction of the Maxilla and the Mandible*
 SciTech - v21 - Mr '97 - p66 [51-250]
Boyne, Walter J - *Beyond the Wild Blue*
 KR - v65 - Mr 15 '97 - p427+ [51-250]
 PW - v244 - Ap 28 '97 - p65+ [251-500]
Boyns, Trevor - *British Cost Accounting 1887-1952*
 R&R Bk N - v11 - N '96 - p36 [51-250]
Boynton, G R - *The Art of Campaign Advertising*
 Econ - v341 - O 19 '96 - p7* [51-250]
Boynton, Sandra - *Barnyard Dance*
 c ECEJ - v24 - Win '96 - p110 [51-250]
 Hippos Go Berserk! (Illus. by Sandra Boynton)
 HB Guide - v8 - Spr '97 - p20 [1-50]
 c KR - v64 - S 15 '96 - p1410 [51-250]
 c Par - v71 - D '96 - p251 [1-50]
 c PW - v243 - N 4 '96 - p78 [51-250]
 Horns to Toes and in Between
 c ECEJ - v24 - Win '96 - p109 [51-250]
Boyt, Susie - *The Characters of Love*
 TLS - N 22 '96 - p24 [501+]
 TLS - N 29 '96 - p12 [1-50]
 Woman's J - D '96 - p16 [51-250]
Boyte, Harry C - *Building America*
 Choice - v34 - N '96 - p505 [51-250]
 HMR - Spr '97 - p10+ [501+]
 NCR - v86 - Spr '97 - p93+ [501+]
Bozsoky, Paul G - *De L'Oppression A La Liberte*
 CHR - v83 - Ja '97 - p130+ [251-500]
Braak, Hans Van De - *The Prometheus Complex*
 T&C - v38 - Ja '97 - p235+ [501+]
Braat, J - *Russians and Dutchmen*
 EHR - v112 - F '97 - p195 [251-500]
Braaten, Carl E - *Either/Or: The Gospel or Neopaganism*
 Bks & Cult - v2 - My '96 - p34 [251-500]
Brabec, Barbara - *Handmade for Profit*
 LJ - v121 - O 15 '96 - p56 [51-250]
Bracamonte Y Sosa, Pedro - *La Memoria Enclaustrada*
 HAHR - v76 - Ag '96 - p571+ [251-500]
Bracey, Gerald W - *Final Exam*
 NASSP-B - v80 - S '96 - p113+ [501+]
Bracken, Bruce A - *Handbook of Self-Concept*
 Readings - v11 - D '96 - p25 [51-250]
Bracken, James K - *The British Literacy Book Trade 1700-1820*
 r ARBA - v28 - '97 - p249+ [51-250]
Bracken, Joseph A - *The Divine Matrix*
 Choice - v34 - O '96 - p296 [51-250]
 CLW - v67 - D '96 - p48 [51-250]
 Theol St - v57 - Mr '96 - p189 [251-500]
Brackenbury, Wade - *Yak Butter and Black Tea*
 y BL - v93 - Ja '97 - p810+ [51-250]
 KR - v64 - N 1 '96 - p1573 [251-500]
 LJ - v121 - D '96 - p128 [51-250]
 NYTBR - v101 - D 8 '96 - p31 [251-500]
Brackenridge, J Bruce - *The Key to Newton's Dynamics*
 Choice - v34 - S '96 - p150 [51-250]
 Isis - v87 - D '96 - p701+ [501+]
 Phys Today - v49 - N '96 - p81+ [501+]
Brackett, D W - *Holy Terror*
 BW - v26 - Ag 4 '96 - p3 [501+]
 Choice - v34 - D '96 - p682 [51-250]
 New Sci - v152 - N 9 '96 - p42+ [501+]
Brackett, Ginger Roberts - *Elizabeth Cary: Writer of Conscience*
 y BL - v93 - O 1 '96 - p333 [51-250]
 c Ch BWatch - v7 - Ja '97 - p5 [51-250]
 y HB Guide - v8 - Spr '97 - p155 [51-250]
 y SLJ - v42 - O '96 - p152 [51-250]
Brackett, Michael H - *The Data Warehouse Challenge*
 SciTech - v20 - N '96 - p11 [51-250]
Bradberry, James - *Eakins' Mistress*
 KR - v65 - Mr 15 '97 - p418 [51-250]
 PW - v244 - Ap 7 '97 - p77+ [51-250]
Bradbury, Judy - *One Carton of Oops! (Illus. by Cathy Trachok)*
 c PW - v244 - My 5 '97 - p208 [51-250]
Bradbury, Malcolm - *Dangerous Pilgrimages*
 Choice - v34 - Ja '97 - p791+ [51-250]
 NYTBR - v101 - S 22 '96 - p31 [501+]

Bradbury, Ray - *The Halloween Tree (Illus. by Joseph Mugnaini)*
  y Ch BWatch - v6 - O '96 - p3 [51-250]
  y HB Guide - v8 - Spr '97 - p78 [51-250]
  c LATBR - O 20 '96 - p8 [51-250]
  y PW - v243 - S 30 '96 - p86 [1-50]
  Quicker than the Eye
  y BL - v93 - N 1 '96 - p458 [51-250]
     BW - v26 - D 29 '96 - p6 [51-250]
     KR - v64 - S 15 '96 - p1361 [51-250]
     NYTBR - v102 - F 23 '97 - p20 [51-250]
     PW - v243 - O 7 '96 - p65 [51-250]
Bradby, Marie - *More than Anything Else (Illus. by Chris K Soentpiet)*
  c Inst - v106 - Ag '96 - p42+ [51-250]
  c RT - v50 - N '96 - p243 [51-250]
  c RT - v50 - Mr '97 - p479 [51-250]
Braddick, M J - *The Nerves of State*
     R&R Bk N - v11 - N '96 - p37 [51-250]
  Parliamentary Taxation in Seventeenth-Century England
     AHR - v101 - O '96 - p1203+ [501+]
     Historian - v58 - Sum '96 - p894+ [251-500]
Braddon, Derek - *Privatization: Social Science Themes and Perspectives*
     JEL - v35 - Mr '97 - p245 [51-250]
     R&R Bk N - v11 - N '96 - p32 [51-250]
Braden, John B - *Environmental Policy with Political and Economic Integration*
     Econ J - v107 - Ja '97 - p287 [51-250]
     JEL - v34 - S '96 - p1497 [51-250]
Braden, Maria - *Women Politicians and the Media*
     CJR - v35 - S '96 - p60+ [501+]
Bradfield, Scott - *Animal Planet*
     NS & S - v9 - Ap 26 '96 - p41 [51-250]
Bradford, Barbara Taylor - *Dangerous to Know*
     Books - v9 - S '95 - p22 [1-50]
  Everything to Gain
     Books - v9 - S '95 - p25 [51-250]
  Her Own Rules
     Ent W - Je 28 '96 - p101 [51-250]
     LATBR - S 1 '96 - p10 [51-250]
  y SLJ - v43 - F '97 - p134 [51-250]
  Love in Another Town
     PW - v243 - N 4 '96 - p71 [1-50]
  A Secret Affair
     Spec - v277 - N 16 '96 - p48 [501+]
Bradford, Clare - *Writing the Australian Child*
     Aust Bk R - F '97 - p49+ [501+]
Bradford, David F - *Distributional Analysis of Tax Policy*
     JEL - v34 - D '96 - p2057 [51-250]
Bradford, James C - *Crucible of Empire*
     Parameters - v26 - Aut '96 - p152+ [501+]
  Quarterdeck and Bridge
     LJ - v122 - Ap 15 '97 - p96+ [51-250]
Bradford, Karleen - *More Animal Heroes*
  c Quill & Q - v62 - N '96 - p44 [51-250]
  Shadows on a Sword
  c BIC - v25 - D '96 - p37 [251-500]
  y JAAL - v40 - D '96 - p326+ [251-500]
  y Quill & Q - v62 - Ag '96 - p41 [251-500]
  There Will Be Wolves
  y BL - v92 - Ag '96 - p1894 [51-250]
  y CBRS - v25 - D '96 - p44 [1-50]
  y CCB-B - v50 - O '96 - p50 [51-250]
  y HB Guide - v8 - Spr '97 - p78 [51-250]
  y SLJ - v42 - Ag '96 - p164 [51-250]
Bradford, Sarah - *Elizabeth: A Biography of Britain's Queen*
     Trib Bks - My 18 '97 - p8 [1-50]
     VQR - v73 - Win '97 - p16*+ [51-250]
Bradie, Michael - *The Secret Chain*
     Dialogue - v35 - Fall '96 - p839+ [501+]
Brading, D A - *Church and State in Bourbon Mexico*
     CH - v66 - Mr '97 - p136+ [501+]
     JIH - v27 - Aut '96 - p361+ [501+]
Bradlee, Benjamin C - *A Good Life*
     NYTBR - v101 - O 13 '96 - p32 [51-250]
     Parameters - v26 - Win '96 - p148+ [501+]
     PW - v243 - Jl 22 '96 - p235 [1-50]
     Sew R - v104 - O '96 - p673+ [501+]
Bradley, Bill - *Time Present, Time Past*
     Bks & Cult - v3 - Ja '97 - p37+ [251-500]
     NYTBR - v102 - Mr 30 '97 - p24 [51-250]
     PSQ - v111 - Win '96 - p695+ [501+]
     PW - v243 - N 25 '96 - p70 [1-50]
Bradley, Edwin M - *The First Hollywood Musicals*
  r ARBA - v28 - '97 - p509+ [251-500]
  r Choice - v34 - D '96 - p586 [51-250]
  r R&R Bk N - v11 - N '96 - p67 [51-250]

Bradley, Elizabeth - *Needlework Animals*
     BL - v93 - D 1 '96 - p638 [51-250]
     LJ - v122 - F 15 '97 - p133 [51-250]
Bradley, Fern Marshall - *Rodale's Garden Answers*
     Hort - v94 - Ja '97 - p78 [251-500]
Bradley, George - *The Fire Fetched Down*
     NY - v72 - Ja 20 '97 - p97 [51-250]
Bradley, James E - *Church History*
     CC - v113 - D 4 '96 - p1209 [51-250]
  r Choice - v34 - O '96 - p248+ [51-250]
     CLW - v67 - Mr '97 - p30+ [51-250]
     Six Ct J - v27 - Fall '96 - p843+ [501+]
Bradley, John - *Russia: Building Democracy*
  c HB Guide - v7 - Fall '96 - p380 [51-250]
Bradley, Ken - *Worldviews: The Challenge of Choice*
  y Quill & Q - v62 - D '96 - p40 [51-250]
Bradley, Marion Zimmer - *Exile's Song*
     BWatch - v17 - S '96 - p8 [51-250]
  y VOYA - v19 - D '96 - p276 [251-500]
  Ghostlight
     BWatch - v17 - N '96 - p8 [1-50]
  y Kliatt - v31 - Ja '97 - p11 [51-250]
  Lady of Avalon
  y BL - v93 - Ap 1 '97 - p1268 [51-250]
     KR - v65 - Ap 1 '97 - p479 [251-500]
  Lady of the Trillium
  y Kliatt - v30 - N '96 - p12 [51-250]
  Witchlight
  y BL - v93 - S 1 '96 - p60 [51-250]
     Rapport - v19 - 6 '96 - p19 [251-500]
Bradley, Mark L - *Last Stand in the Carolinas*
     JSH - v63 - F '97 - p187+ [251-500]
Bradley, Martha - *The British Housewife. Vol. 1*
     TLS - D 6 '96 - p29 [501+]
Bradley, Phil - *Ukolug Quick Guide to CD-Rom Networking*
  r LAR - v98 - D '96 - p651 [51-250]
  Ukolug Quick Guide to the Internet
     LAR - v98 - Ag '96 - p427 [251-500]
Bradley, R S - *Climate since A.D. 1500*
     EG - v73 - Ja '97 - p133+ [501+]
     GJ - v162 - Jl '96 - p239+ [251-500]
Bradley, Robert L - *Oil, Gas, and Government. Vols. 1-2*
     En Jnl - v17 - 4 '96 - p168+ [501+]
     JEL - v34 - S '96 - p1470 [251-500]
Bradley, Steve - *The Pruning Handbook*
     BL - v93 - Ap 1 '97 - p1274 [51-250]
Bradley-Cromey, Nancy - *Authority and Autonomy in L'Entree D'Espagne*
     Specu - v71 - Jl '96 - p699+ [501+]
Bradman, T - *Incredibly Creepy Stories (Illus. by P Dennis)*
  c JB - v60 - D '96 - p264 [51-250]
Bradman, Tony - *Dear Mum, Don't Panic (Illus. by Stephen Lewis)*
  c Bks Keeps - Jl '96 - p9 [51-250]
  Dilly and the Goody-Goody (Illus. by Susan Hellard)
  c Bks Keeps - Jl '96 - p8 [51-250]
  c TES - S 20 '96 - p16* [501+]
  Dilly and the Vampire (Illus. by Susan Hellard)
  c TES - S 20 '96 - p16* [501+]
  Help! I'm a Hamster
  c Books - v10 - Je '96 - p25 [51-250]
  It Came from Outer Space (Illus. by Carol Wright)
  c CLW - v67 - Mr '97 - p15 [1-50]
  Through My Window (Illus. by Eileen Browne)
  c Bks Keeps - Mr '97 - p7 [51-250]
  Wow! I'm a Whale (Illus. by Clive Scruton)
  c Bks Keeps - Ja '97 - p22 [51-250]
Bradner, Jeanne H - *The Board Member's Guide*
     ChrPhil - v8 - Je 13 '96 - p38 [51-250]
Bradshaw, Brendan - *Representing Ireland*
     Ren Q - v49 - Win '96 - p884+ [501+]
     Ren Q - v49 - Win '96 - p885+ [501+]
Bradshaw, Graham - *Misrepresentations: Shakespeare and the Materialists*
     RES - v47 - N '96 - p582+ [501+]
Bradshaw, John - *Bradshaw on the Family*
     LJ - v121 - D '96 - p124 [51-250]
  The Future of the Family (Bradshaw). Audio Version
     LJ - v122 - My 1 '97 - p156 [51-250]
Bradshaw, Paul F - *The Changing Face of Jewish and Christian Worship in North America*
     Rel Ed - v91 - Fall '96 - p616 [1-50]
Brady, April A - *Kwanzaa Karamu (Illus. by Barbara Knutson)*
  c RT - v50 - N '96 - p259 [51-250]
Brady, Ciaran - *The Chief Governors*
     AHR - v101 - D '96 - p1547+ [501+]
     EHR - v112 - Ap '97 - p460+ [501+]
     ILS - v15 - Fall '96 - p29 [501+]

Brady, Clark A - *The Burroughs Cyclopaedia*
  r ARBA - v28 - '97 - p442+ [251-500]
  r Choice - v34 - My '97 - p1472 [251-500]
  r LJ - v122 - Ja '97 - p84 [51-250]
Brady, James - *Further Lane*
     PW - v244 - Ap 28 '97 - p51 [251-500]
Brady, James E - *Chemistry: The Study of Matter and Its Changes. 2nd Ed.*
     J Chem Ed - v73 - O '96 - pA241 [251-500]
Brady, Jennifer - *Literary Transmission and Authority*
     CLS - v33 - 3 '96 - p322+ [501+]
Brady, Joan - *Death Comes for Peter Pan*
     TLS - Jl 7 '96 - p24 [501+]
Brady, John - *Bad Boy*
     BL - v93 - Ja '97 - p788 [51-250]
     BW - v27 - Ja 19 '97 - p3 [501+]
     KR - v64 - D 1 '96 - p1710+ [251-500]
     LATBR - Ja 19 '97 - p4+ [501+]
     LJ - v122 - Ja '97 - p123 [51-250]
     NYTBR - v102 - F 16 '97 - p20 [501+]
     PW - v243 - D 16 '96 - p51 [251-500]
     Trib Bks - F 23 '97 - p3+ [501+]
Brady, Kimberley Smith - *Keeper for the Sea (Illus. by Peter M Fiore)*
  c CBRS - v25 - F '97 - p73 [51-250]
  c HB Guide - v8 - Spr '97 - p20+ [51-250]
  c KR - v64 - S 15 '96 - p1396 [51-250]
  c SLJ - v42 - D '96 - p84 [51-250]
Brady, Lois Smith - *Vows: Weddings of the Nineties from the New York Times*
     NYTBR - v102 - F 23 '97 - p17 [51-250]
Brady, Patrick V - *Physics and Chemistry of Mineral Surfaces*
     Choice - v34 - Mr '97 - p1189+ [51-250]
Brady, Philip - *Forged Correspondences*
     Choice - v34 - Ja '97 - p792 [51-250]
Brady, Thomas A - *The Politics of the Reformation in Germany*
     Choice - v34 - Ap '97 - p1354+ [51-250]
  Protestant Politics
     CHR - v82 - O '96 - p708 [251-500]
Braestrup, Peter - *Big Story*
     Parameters - v26 - Win '96 - p148+ [501+]
Bragdon, Kathleen J - *Native People of Southern New England 1500-1650*
     Choice - v34 - O '96 - p345 [51-250]
     W&M Q - v54 - Ja '97 - p263+ [501+]
Bragg, Ginna Bell - *A Simple Celebration*
     BL - v93 - F 15 '97 - p987+ [51-250]
     LJ - v122 - Mr 15 '97 - p84 [51-250]
     PW - v244 - Ja 27 '97 - p99 [51-250]
Bragg, Janet Harmon - *Soaring above Setbacks*
     Choice - v34 - O '96 - p300 [51-250]
  y SLJ - v42 - S '96 - p240 [51-250]
Bragg, Melvyn - *Credo*
     NS & S - v9 - Ap 26 '96 - p39+ [251-500]
     TLS - My 24 '96 - p24 [501+]
Bragg, Steven M - *Just-in-Time Accounting*
     Choice - v34 - F '97 - p1007 [51-250]
Braham, Jeanne - *Crucial Conversations*
     Biography - v19 - Fall '96 - p434+ [501+]
Brahmananda, P R - *Planning for a Wage-Goods Economy*
     JEL - v34 - S '96 - p1476 [51-250]
Brahms, Johannes - *The Brahms-Keller Correspondence*
     TLS - Ap 11 '97 - p18 [501+]
Braid, Helen - *A Stranger at My Table*
     Books - v11 - Ap '97 - p21 [51-250]
Braidotti, Rosi - *Women, the Environment and Sustainable Development*
     Signs - v22 - Win '97 - p496+ [501+]
Braithwaite, Roderick - *Palmerston and Africa*
     Choice - v34 - Ja '97 - p852 [51-250]
     TLS - D 27 '96 - p29 [501+]
Braithwaite, Ronald L - *Prisons and AIDS*
     SciTech - v20 - D '96 - p39 [51-250]
Brake, Laurel - *The Ending of Epochs*
     ELT - v40 - 2 '97 - p210+ [51-250]
Brakefield, Tom - *Kingdom of Might*
     New Sci - v151 - S 21 '96 - p55 [51-250]
Brakeman, Lynne - *Chronology of Women Worldwide*
  r BL - v93 - F 1 '97 - p962 [251-500]
  r LJ - v122 - F 1 '97 - p94 [51-250]
  Spiritual Lemons
     PW - v243 - D 2 '96 - p52 [51-250]
Brakhage, Stan - *Brakhage Scrapbook*
     Parnassus - v22 - 1 '97 - p203+ [501+]
  Film at Wit's End
     Parnassus - v22 - 1 '97 - p203+ [501+]
  Film Biographies
     Parnassus - v22 - 1 '97 - p203+ [501+]

Brakke, David - *Athanasius and the Politics of Asceticism*
  JR - v77 - Ap '97 - p292+ [501+]
  Rel St Rev - v23 - Ap '97 - p152 [51-250]
Brakman, Willem - *Interieur*
  WLT - v71 - Win '97 - p167 [251-500]
  Een Voortreffelijke Ridder
  WLT - v70 - Sum '96 - p707+ [501+]
Brallier, Jess M - *Cocktail Hour*
  BL - v93 - S 1 '96 - p176 [251-500]
Bram, Christopher - *Gossip*
  BL - v93 - Mr 1 '97 - p1109 [51-250]
  KR - v65 - F 1 '97 - p156 [251-500]
  PW - v244 - F 10 '97 - p66 [51-250]
Bramkamp, Maura Alia - *Resculpting*
  Sm Pr R - v28 - S '96 - p12 [251-500]
Bramlett, Jim - *Ride for the High Points*
  BWatch - v17 - S '96 - p4 [1-50]
Brams, Steven J - *Fair Division*
  JEL - v34 - D '96 - p2027+ [51-250]
  Theory of Moves
  Econ J - v107 - Ja '97 - p216+ [501+]
Bramwell, Vicky - *Feeling Great*
  y Sch Lib - v44 - N '96 - p173 [51-250]
Branagh, Kenneth - *Hamlet*
  Ent W - Mr 28 '97 - p61 [51-250]
  TLS - N '96 - p16 [501+]
  Trib Bks - Ja 19 '97 - p8 [1-50]
Brancato, Carolyn Kay - *Institutional Investors and Corporate Governance*
  R&R Bk N - v12 - F '97 - p48 [51-250]
Branch, Michael - *The Uses of Tradition*
  Slav R - v55 - Fall '96 - p665 [501+]
Brand, Alice Garden - *Presence of Mind*
  Col Comp - v47 - O '96 - p437 [51-250]
Brand, Christianna - *Death in High Heels*
  Arm Det - v29 - Sum '96 - p308 [51-250]
Brand, Dionne - *In Another Place, Not Here*
  BIC - v25 - S '96 - p36+ [501+]
  Quill & Q - v62 - My '96 - p26 [501+]
  Land to Light On
  Quill & Q - v63 - Mr '97 - p76 [251-500]
Brand, Irene - *In This Sign Conquer*
  LJ - v121 - N 1 '96 - p52 [51-250]
Brand, Max - *The Bells of San Carlos and Other Stories*
  PW - v243 - Jl 22 '96 - p232 [51-250]
  Farewell, Thunder Moon
  LJ - v121 - S 15 '96 - p102 [1-50]
  The Legend of Thunder Moon
  LJ - v121 - S 15 '96 - p102 [1-50]
  The Mustang Herder (Osborne). Audio Version
  y Kliatt - v31 - My '97 - p42 [51-250]
  Red Wind and Thunder Moon
  LJ - v121 - S 15 '96 - p102 [1-50]
  The Stone That Shines
  BL - v93 - F 1 '97 - p925 [51-250]
  PW - v244 - Ja 27 '97 - p82 [1-50]
  Thunder Moon and the Sky People
  LJ - v121 - S 15 '96 - p102 [1-50]
  The Wolf Strain
  BL - v93 - N 1 '96 - p481 [51-250]
  Roundup M - v4 - D '96 - p24 [51-250]
Brand, Michael - *The Vision of Kings*
  Choice - v34 - O '96 - p264 [51-250]
  LATBR - v263 - S 29 '96 - p15 [51-250]
Brand, Peggy Zeglin - *Feminism and Tradition in Aesthetics*
  JAAC - v54 - Fall '96 - p404+ [501+]
Brand, Salli - *Decorative Walls*
  Books - v10 - Je '96 - p24 [51-250]
Branden, Nathaniel - *The Art of Living Consciously*
  PW - v244 - Mr 17 '97 - p71 [51-250]
Brandenberg, Alexa - *Chop, Simmer, Season (Illus. by Alexa Brandenberg)*
  c KR - v65 - Ap 1 '97 - p549+ [51-250]
  I Am Me! (Illus. by Alexa Brandenberg)
  c HB Guide - v8 - Spr '97 - p10 [51-250]
  c SLJ - v42 - D '96 - p84+ [51-250]
Brandenburg, Jim - *An American Safari (Illus. by Jim Brandenburg)*
  y Emerg Lib - v24 - S '96 - p23 [1-50]
  y Emerg Lib - v24 - S '96 - p26 [1-50]
  c PW - v244 - Ap 21 '97 - p74 [1-50]
  Sand and Fog
  y Kliatt - v30 - N '96 - p28 [51-250]

Scruffy: A Wolf Finds His Place in the Pack (Illus. by Jim Brandenburg)
  c BL - v93 - S 1 '96 - p133 [51-250]
  c CCB-B - v50 - O '96 - p50 [51-250]
  c HB Guide - v8 - Spr '97 - p126 [51-250]
  c Inst - v106 - Mr '97 - p28+ [51-250]
  c SLJ - v42 - D '96 - p111 [51-250]
  c VLS - Win '96 - p21 [51-250]
Brandenburger, Adam M - *Co-Opetition*
  Bus Bk R - v13 - 4 '96 - p44+ [501+]
  LJ - v122 - Mr 15 '97 - p36 [1-50]
Brandes, Francesca - *Jewish Itineraries*
  LJ - v122 - Ja '97 - p128 [51-250]
Brandes, Stuart D - *Warhogs: A History of War Profits in America*
  LJ - v122 - My 1 '97 - p118+ [51-250]
Brandewyne, Rebecca - *Desperado*
  LJ - v121 - N 1 '96 - p112 [1-50]
  Glory Seekers
  PW - v244 - Ap 21 '97 - p68+ [51-250]
Brandis, Marianne - *Rebellion: A Novel of Upper Canada (Illus. by G Brender A Brandis)*
  y Beav - v77 - F '97 - p47 [51-250]
  c BIC - v25 - N '96 - p31 [251-500]
  y Ch Bk News - v20 - Win '97 - p27 [51-250]
  y Emerg Lib - v24 - Mr '97 - p28 [1-50]
  y Quill & Q - v62 - S '96 - p74 [251-500]
Brandist, Craig - *Carnival Culture and the Soviet Modernist Novel*
  Choice - v34 - My '97 - p1505 [51-250]
Brandmuller, Walter - *Copernico, Galilei E La Chiesa*
  Isis - v87 - S '96 - p556+ [501+]
Brandon, Jay - *Defiance County*
  Arm Det - v29 - Fall '96 - p467 [51-250]
  KR - v64 - My 1 '96 - p641 [51-250]
  Local Rules
  Arm Det - v29 - Sum '96 - p280 [51-250]
Brandon, Robert N - *Concepts and Methods in Evolutionary Biology*
  Choice - v34 - D '96 - p635 [51-250]
Brandon, Ruth - *Tickling the Dragon*
  Books - v9 - S '95 - p22 [1-50]
  The Uncertainty Principle
  NS - v125 - N 1 '96 - p47 [251-500]
  TLS - D 20 '96 - p22 [501+]
Brands, H W - *The Wages of Globalism*
  JSH - v63 - F '97 - p208+ [501+]
  RAH - v24 - D '96 - p695+ [501+]
Brandt, Alan - *Double-Diffusive Convection*
  SciTech - v20 - S '96 - p1 [51-250]
Brandt, Brian - *Microsoft Windows NT Server One Step at a Time*
  CBR - v14 - Jl '96 - p23 [1-50]
Brandt, Di - *Dancing Naked*
  Quill & Q - v63 - Ja '97 - p33 [251-500]
Brandt, Nat - *Harlem at War*
  AB - v99 - F 17 '97 - p526+ [501+]
  Bl S - v26 - Sum '96 - p63 [1-50]
  Mr. Tubbs' Civil War
  LJ - v122 - F 1 '97 - p94 [51-250]
Brandt, Steven C - *Focus Your Business*
  BL - v93 - Mr 1 '97 - p1096 [51-250]
Brandt, Thomas - *Neurological Disorders*
  SciTech - v20 - N '96 - p41 [51-250]
Branford, Henrietta - *The Fated Sky*
  c Bks Keeps - N '96 - p10 [51-250]
  y Sch Lib - v45 - F '97 - p44 [51-250]
  y TES - Ja 3 '97 - p22 [51-250]
  Spacebaby (Illus. by Ellis Nadler)
  c Sch Lib - v45 - F '97 - p23 [51-250]
Branham, H A - *Sampras: A Legend in the Works*
  PW - v243 - S 30 '96 - p71 [51-250]
Branham, Mary - *Little Green Man in Ireland*
  PW - v244 - Mr 17 '97 - p80 [51-250]
Branin, Joseph - *Managing Change in Academic Libraries*
  CLW - v67 - Mr '97 - p45+ [251-500]
Branley, Franklyn Mansfield - *Sun and the Solar System*
  c BL - v93 - D 15 '96 - p722 [51-250]
  c Ch BWatch - v6 - D '96 - p6 [1-50]
  c SLJ - v43 - Ja '97 - p118 [51-250]
  What Makes a Magnet? (Illus. by True Kelley)
  c BL - v93 - N 1 '96 - p502 [51-250]
  c HB - v72 - N '96 - p756+ [51-250]
  c HB Guide - v8 - Spr '97 - p112 [51-250]
  c SLJ - v42 - D '96 - p111 [51-250]
Bransby, Lawrence - *Homeward Bound*
  y VOYA - v19 - O '96 - p199+ [501+]
  Outside the Walls
  y JB - v60 - D '96 - p277 [51-250]
  y Sch Lib - v45 - F '97 - p44 [51-250]

Branscomb, Lewis M - *Converging Infrastructures*
  JEL - v35 - Mr '97 - p251 [51-250]
  LJ - v121 - O 1 '96 - p120 [51-250]
Bransford, Helen - *Welcome to Your Facelift*
  Trib Bks - My 25 '97 - p6 [51-250]
Branston, Gill - *The Media Student's Book*
  Si & So - v6 - N '96 - p35 [51-250]
Brantenberg, Gerd - *Egalia's Daughters*
  Bloom Rev - v16 - Jl '96 - p21 [51-250]
Brantley, C L - *The Princeton Review Word Smart Junior*
  y Learning - v25 - N '96 - p82 [51-250]
  The Princeton Review Writing Smart Junior
  y Learning - v25 - N '96 - p82 [51-250]
Brantlinger, Patrick - *Fictions of State*
  Choice - v34 - N '96 - p452+ [51-250]
Branzei, Sylvia - *Animal Grossology (Illus. by Jack Keely)*
  c Learning - v25 - Mr '97 - p38 [51-250]
  c PW - v243 - N 25 '96 - p78 [51-250]
  Grossology: The Science of Really Gross Things (Illus. by Jack Keely)
  y BL - v93 - Ap 1 '97 - p1306 [1-50]
Braschi, Giannina - *Empire of Dreams*
  TranslRevS - v1 - My '95 - p29 [51-250]
Brash, John L - *Interfacial Phenomena and Bioproducts*
  SciTech - v20 - D '96 - p35 [51-250]
Brasher, J Lawrence - *The Sanctified South*
  CH - v65 - S '96 - p535+ [501+]
Brashinsky, Michael - *Russian Critics on the Cinema of Glasnost*
  FQ - v49 - Sum '96 - p58+ [501+]
Brassai - *Henry Miller: The Paris Years*
  NYTBR - v101 - D 8 '96 - p88 [1-50]
  NYTBR - v102 - F 16 '97 - p32 [1-50]
Brasseaux, Carl A - *Creoles of Color in the Bayou Country*
  AHR - v102 - F '97 - p190+ [251-500]
Brasseur, Isabelle - *Brasseur and Eisler*
  Quill & Q - v62 - O '96 - p36 [251-500]
Brassey, Richard - *How to Speak Chimpanzee*
  c Bks Keeps - Jl '96 - p11 [51-250]
  c LA - v73 - D '96 - p625 [51-250]
Brassey's Encyclopedia of Military History and Biography
  r A & S Sm - v11 - D '96 - p96 [251-500]
Braswell, George W, Jr. - *Islam: Its Prophets, Peoples, Politics and Power*
  MEJ - v51 - Win '97 - p154 [51-250]
Bratchel, M E - *Lucca 1430-1494*
  JIH - v27 - Win '97 - p524+ [501+]
  Six Ct J - v27 - Win '96 - p1176+ [501+]
  Specu - v72 - Ja '97 - p114+ [501+]
Bratic, Radoslav - *Zima U Hercegovini*
  WLT - v70 - Sum '96 - p730 [501+]
Bratt, Guy - *The Bisses of Valais*
  GJ - v162 - Jl '96 - p240 [1-50]
Bratt, John - *Trails of Yesterday*
  VQR - v72 - Aut '96 - p141* [1-50]
Bratton, Jacky - *Melodrama: Stage, Picture, Screen*
  FQ - v49 - Sum '96 - p48+ [501+]
Braude, Stephen E - *First Person Plural. Rev. Ed.*
  JP - v60 - S '96 - p257+ [501+]
Brauer, Erich - *The Jews of Kurdistan*
  J Ch St - v38 - Sum '96 - p650+ [501+]
Brault, Jacques - *Il N'y A Plus De Chemin*
  Can Lit - Spr '97 - p231+ [501+]
Braun, Christoph-Friedrich Von - *The Innovation War*
  SciTech - v20 - D '96 - p59 [1-50]
Braun, Dietrich - *Simple Methods for Identification of Plastics. 3rd, Rev. Ed.*
  SciTech - v20 - S '96 - p61 [51-250]
Braun, Edward - *Meyerhold: A Revolution in Theatre*
  Russ Rev - v55 - O '96 - p707+ [501+]
  Theat J - v48 - D '96 - p529+ [501+]
Braun, Herbert - *Our Guerrilas, Our Sidewalks*
  HAHR - v77 - F '97 - p148+ [501+]
Braun, Lilian Jackson - *The Cat Who Said Cheese (Adams). Audio Version*
  Arm Det - v29 - Sum '96 - p354 [51-250]
  The Cat Who Tailed a Thief
  y BL - v93 - D 1 '96 - p619 [51-250]
  CSM - v89 - F 20 '97 - p10 [51-250]
  CSM - v89 - Mr 20 '97 - p14 [51-250]
  KR - v64 - D 1 '96 - p1705 [51-250]
  NYTBR - v102 - Mr 9 '97 - p19 [51-250]
  PW - N 25 '96 - p59 [51-250]
Braun, Matt - *Cimarron Jordan*
  Roundup M - v4 - O '96 - p30 [251-500]
  Noble Outlaw
  Roundup M - v4 - D '96 - p24 [51-250]
  Texas Empire
  Roundup M - v4 - F '97 - p26+ [51-250]

Braun, Michael - *Exil Und Engagement*
  Ger Q - v70 - Win '97 - p89+ [501+]
Braun, Ralph - *Cyprus. 1st Ed.*
  r BL - v93 - S 15 '96 - p210 [1-50]
Braun, Siegmar - *100 and More Basic NMR Experiments*
  SciTech - v20 - N '96 - p21 [51-250]
Braun, Stephen - *Buzz: The Science and Lore of Alcohol and Caffeine*
  y BL - v92 - Ag '96 - p1867+ [51-250]
  y BL - v92 - Ag '96 - p1890 [1-50]
     Choice - v34 - Mr '97 - p1192 [51-250]
     VV - v41 - D 17 '96 - p51+ [501+]
Brauner, Sigrid - *Fearless Wives and Frightened Shrews*
  Ger Q - v70 - Win '97 - p76+ [501+]
Braunger, Manfred - *Burgundy*
  r BL - v93 - S 15 '96 - p210 [1-50]
Brautigan, Richard - *Trout Fishing in America*
  SFR - v22 - Ja '97 - p48 [1-50]
Braverman, Lewis E - *Werner and Ingbar's The Thyroid. 7th Ed.*
  r SciTech - v20 - S '96 - p35 [51-250]
Braverman, Melanie - *East Justice*
  KR - v64 - My 1 '96 - p619 [251-500]
Bravin, Jess - *Squeaky: An American Runaway*
  BL - v93 - My 1 '97 - p1475+ [51-250]
  LJ - v122 - My 1 '97 - p122 [51-250]
  PW - v244 - Ap 7 '97 - p78+ [51-250]
Brawley, Robert L - *Biblical Ethics and Homosexuality*
  Am - v176 - Mr 8 '97 - p31+ [51-250]
  Intpr - v51 - Ap '97 - p197+ [501+]
  Rel St Rev - v23 - Ja '97 - p51+ [51-250]
  TT - v53 - Ja '97 - p508+ [501+]
Brawley, Sean - *The White Peril*
  R&R Bk N - v11 - D '96 - p48 [51-250]
Brawner, Lee B - *Determining Your Public Library's Future Size*
  LAR - v98 - O '96 - p538 [251-500]
Bray, Bernard - *Art De La Lettre*
  MLR - v91 - O '96 - p1005+ [501+]
Bray, Charles - *Dictionary of Glass*
  r ARBA - v28 - '97 - p361+ [51-250]
Bray, George A - *Molecular and Genetic Aspects of Obesity*
  SciTech - v20 - S '96 - p35 [51-250]
Bray, Gerald - *Documents of the English Reformation*
  CH - v65 - S '96 - p502+ [501+]
  Rel St Rev - v23 - Ap '97 - p191 [51-250]
Bray, John - *Burma: The Politics of Constructive Engagement*
  WorldV - v12 - Jl '96 - p17 [51-250]
Bray, Tamara L - *Reckoning with the Dead*
  Pub Hist - v18 - Sum '96 - p43+ [501+]
Bray, Warwick - *The Meeting of Two Worlds*
  EHR - v111 - S '96 - p968+ [501+]
Braybrooke, David - *Logic on the Track of Social Change*
  AJS - v102 - N '96 - p865+ [501+]
  CPR - v16 - O '96 - p315+ [501+]
  Social Rules
  Choice - v34 - S '96 - p168+ [51-250]
Brayer, Elizabeth - *George Eastman: A Biography*
  AB - v99 - F 24 '97 - p619+ [501+]
  BWatch - v17 - S '96 - p8 [51-250]
  Choice - v34 - D '96 - p632 [51-250]
  Pet PM - v25 - N '96 - p12 [51-250]
  TLS - My 24 '96 - p32+ [501+]
Brayshaw, T Christopher - *Trees and Shrubs of British Columbia*
  r SciTech - v20 - D '96 - p31 [1-50]
Brayton, John A - *The Five Thomas Harrises of Isle of Wight County, Virginia*
  r Am Geneal - v71 - O '96 - p254+ [51-250]
  r EGH - v50 - N '96 - p194 [51-250]
  NGSQ - v85 - Mr '97 - p63+ [251-500]
Brazelton, T Berry - *Going to the Doctor (Illus. by Sam Ogden)*
  c BL - v93 - N 15 '96 - p589 [51-250]
  c PW - v243 - S 9 '96 - p84 [51-250]
Bready, Richard - *Thorndike-Barnhart Junior Dictionary*
  yr BL - v93 - O 1 '96 - p373 [501+]
Breakey, William R - *Integrated Mental Health Services*
  Readings - v11 - D '96 - p30 [51-250]
Brear, Holly Beachley - *Inherit the Alamo*
  HAHR - v76 - Ag '96 - p544+ [251-500]
  r Pub Hist - v18 - Fall '96 - p167+ [501+]
  South HR - v31 - Win '97 - p68+ [501+]
Breatnach, Mary - *Boulez and Mallarme*
  R&R Bk N - v11 - D '96 - p56 [51-250]
Brebbia, C A - *Boundary Elements XVIII*
  SciTech - v21 - Mr '97 - p74 [51-250]

The Kobe Earthquake
  Am Sci - v85 - Ja '97 - p78+ [501+]
  Choice - v34 - S '96 - p159 [51-250]
Brecher, Erwin - *Surprising Science Puzzles*
  c Ch BWatch - v6 - My '96 - p1 [1-50]
Brecht, Richard D - *Russian in the United States*
  MLJ - v81 - Spr '97 - p136+ [501+]
Brechtefeld, Jorg - *Mitteleuropa and German Politics 1848 to the Present*
  Choice - v34 - Ap '97 - p1396 [51-250]
Breck, John - *The Shape of Biblical Language*
  Rel St Rev - v23 - Ap '97 - p174 [51-250]
Breckenridge, Carol A - *Orientalism and the Postcolonial Predicament*
  Am Ethnol - v24 - F '97 - p212+ [501+]
Breckler, Rosemary - *Sweet Dried Apples (Illus. by Deborah Kogan Ray)*
  c BL - v93 - S 1 '96 - p124 [51-250]
  c CBRS - v25 - D '96 - p37 [51-250]
  c HB Guide - v8 - Spr '97 - p21 [51-250]
  c KR - v64 - S 1 '96 - p1319 [51-250]
  c PW - v243 - S 9 '96 - p83 [51-250]
  c SLJ - v43 - Mr '97 - p148+ [51-250]
Bredahl, Maury E - *Agriculture, Trade, and the Environment*
  Choice - v34 - O '96 - p328 [51-250]
  JEL - v34 - D '96 - p2128+ [51-250]
Bredero, Adriaan Hendrik - *Bernard of Clairvaux: Between Cult and History*
  Choice - v34 - My '97 - p1514+ [51-250]
  Comw - v124 - Ap 11 '97 - p28 [251-500]
Bredeson, Carmen - *American Writers of the 20th Century*
  c HB Guide - v7 - Fall '96 - p376 [1-50]
  y SLJ - v42 - S '96 - p230 [51-250]
  The Battle of the Alamo
  c HB Guide - v8 - Spr '97 - p172 [51-250]
  Presidential Medal of Freedom Winners
  c CLW - v67 - Mr '97 - p54 [51-250]
  c HB Guide - v8 - Spr '97 - p161 [51-250]
  The Spindletop Gusher
  c HB Guide - v7 - Fall '96 - p313 [51-250]
  Texas
  c Ch BWatch - v6 - D '96 - p6 [1-50]
  c HB Guide - v8 - Spr '97 - p172 [51-250]
Bredin, Alice - *The Virtual Office Survival Handbook*
  LJ - v122 - My 1 '97 - p52 [1-50]
Bree, Linda - *Sarah Fielding*
  Choice - v34 - F '97 - p963 [51-250]
Breece, Hannah - *A School Teacher in Old Alaska*
  VQR - v72 - Aut '96 - p126* [51-250]
  A Schoolteacher in Old Alaska
  NYTBR - v102 - Mr 23 '97 - p28 [51-250]
Breen, David H - *Alberta's Petroleum Industry and the Conservation Board*
  Can Hist R - v78 - Mr '97 - p94+ [501+]
Breer, William - *The Adolescent Molester. 2nd Ed.*
  SciTech - v20 - S '96 - p41 [51-250]
Brefeld, Josephine - *A Guidebook for the Jerusalem Pilgrimage in the Late Middle Ages*
  Specu - v72 - Ja '97 - p116+ [501+]
Breggin, Peter R - *Psychosocial Approaches to Deeply Disturbed Persons*
  SciTech - v20 - N '96 - p45 [51-250]
Bregin, Elana - *The Red-Haired Khumalo*
  y VOYA - v19 - O '96 - p199+ [501+]
Bregman, Jacob I - *Environmental Compliance Handbook*
  SciTech - v21 - Mr '97 - p2 [51-250]
Brehony, Kathleen - *Awakening at Midlife*
  LJ - v121 - O 1 '96 - p107 [51-250]
Breig, James - *The Emotional Jesus*
  CLW - v67 - D '96 - p41+ [51-250]
Breihan, John R - *Martin Aircraft 1909-1960*
  A & S Sm - v11 - O '96 - p91+ [251-500]
Breisch, Agneta - *Frid Och Fredloshet*
  EHR - v111 - N '96 - p1246+ [501+]
Breitenberg, Mark - *Anxious Masculinity in Early Modern England*
  Choice - v34 - Mr '97 - p1159 [51-250]
Breithaupt, Don - *Precious and Few*
  y BL - v93 - N 15 '96 - p561 [51-250]
  LJ - v121 - D '96 - p95 [51-250]
  PW - v243 - O 14 '96 - p79 [51-250]
Breitstein, Ron - *Wine and Dine*
  LJ - v122 - Ap 1 '97 - p62 [1-50]
Brelin, Christa - *Strength in Numbers*
  r ARBA - v28 - '97 - p318 [51-250]
Brem, Caroline - *Returning to Learning*
  TES - O 4 '96 - p7* [51-250]
Breman, Jan - *Wage Hunters and Gatherers*
  CS - v26 - Mr '97 - p194+ [501+]

Bremen, Riet Van - *The Limits of Participation*
  Choice - v34 - Mr '97 - p1215 [51-250]
  TLS - O 4 '96 - p40 [51-250]
Bremer, M N - *Cold Gas at High Redshift*
  SciTech - v20 - D '96 - p22 [51-250]
Bremmer, Ian - *New States, New Politics*
  Choice - v34 - My '97 - p1569+ [51-250]
Bremner, Robert H - *Giving: Charity and Philanthropy in History*
  Soc Ser R - v70 - S '96 - p499 [1-50]
Brenchley, Chaz - *Dispossession*
  PW - v244 - Ap 28 '97 - p55 [51-250]
Brendel, Otto J - *Etruscan Art*
  NYRB - v43 - S 19 '96 - p44+ [501+]
  Rel St Rev - v23 - Ap '97 - p173 [51-250]
Brener, Milton - *Opera Offstage*
  ON - v61 - Ja 11 '97 - p59 [51-250]
Brenna, Duff - *The Holy Book of the Beard*
  Rapport - v19 - 4 '96 - p30 [251-500]
Brennan, Bill - *Irish, Scottish and Border Melodies for Flatpicking Guitar*
  CAY - v17 - Win '96 - p10 [51-250]
Brennan, Christine - *Inside Edge*
  Trib Bks - F 2 '97 - p8 [1-50]
Brennan, Eilis - *Nationalism and Unionism*
  y Sch Lib - v45 - F '97 - p50 [51-250]
Brennan, Georgeanne - *The Children's Kitchen Garden*
  BL - v93 - Mr 15 '97 - p1207+ [51-250]
  PW - v244 - Mr 24 '97 - p79 [51-250]
  Down to Earth
  BL - v93 - N 15 '96 - p559 [51-250]
  BWatch - v18 - F '97 - p7 [51-250]
Brennan, Gregory - *Successfully Self-Employed*
  LJ - v122 - My 1 '97 - p52 [1-50]
Brennan, Herbie - *Mario Scumbini and the Big Pig Swipe (Illus. by David Simonds)*
  c Sch Lib - v44 - Ag '96 - p104 [51-250]
Brennan, James P - *The Labor Wars in Cordoba 1955-1976*
  AHR - v101 - O '96 - p1321+ [501+]
Brennan, Mary C - *Turning Right in the Sixties*
  APSR - v90 - S '96 - p643+ [501+]
  Historian - v59 - Win '97 - p421+ [501+]
  JSH - v63 - F '97 - p211+ [251-500]
  Rapport - v19 - 5 '96 - p44 [251-500]
  RP - v58 - Fall '96 - p859+ [501+]
Brennan, Michael J - *The Theory of Corporate Finance. Vols. 1-2*
  JEL - v35 - Mr '97 - p223+ [51-250]
Brennan, Patrick - *Full-Cycle Youth Evangelization*
  CLW - v67 - Mr '97 - p37 [51-250]
Brennan, Richard P - *Heisenberg Probably Slept Here*
  BL - v93 - D 1 '96 - p629 [51-250]
  Choice - v34 - My '97 - p1519 [51-250]
  LJ - v122 - F 1 '97 - p100 [51-250]
  New Sci - v153 - F 8 '97 - p45 [501+]
  PW - v243 - N 18 '96 - p57 [51-250]
Brennan, Timothy J - *A Shock to the System*
  JEL - v35 - Mr '97 - p251 [51-250]
Brennan, William - *Dehumanizing the Vulnerable*
  Am - v175 - N 9 '96 - p26+ [501+]
Brenneman, Walter L, Jr. - *Crossing the Circle at the Holy Wells of Ireland*
  CH - v66 - Mr '97 - p212+ [51-250]
Brenner, Barbara - *Chibi: A True Story from Japan (Illus. by June Otani)*
  c HB Guide - v7 - Fall '96 - p343 [51-250]
  c Inst - v106 - Mr '97 - p30 [1-50]
Brenner, David J - *Making the Radiation Therapy Decision*
  LJ - v122 - Ja '97 - p57 [1-50]
Brenner, Frederic - *Jews, America*
  CSM - v89 - D 5 '96 - pB1 [1-50]
  LATBR - D 8 '96 - p26 [51-250]
  NYTBR - v101 - S 29 '96 - p21 [51-250]
  NYTLa - v146 - D 2 '96 - pC16 [51-250]
  Pet PM - v25 - F '97 - p60 [51-250]
Brenner, Hans D - *Integrated Psychological Therapy for Schizophrenic Patients (IPT)*
  J ClinPsyc - v57 - N '96 - p553 [501+]
Brenner, Leslie - *Fear of Wine*
  LJ - v122 - Ap 1 '97 - p62 [1-50]
Brenner, Malcolm K - *Gene Therapy in Cancer*
  SciTech - v20 - D '96 - p42 [51-250]
Brenner, Michael - *Nach Dem Holocaust*
  Choice - v34 - D '96 - p567+ [1-50]
  The Renaissance of Jewish Culture in Weimar Germany
  AHR - v102 - F '97 - p127+ [501+]
  AS - v66 - Win '97 - p154+ [501+]
  Rel St Rev - v23 - Ap '97 - p198 [51-250]
  TES - D 27 '96 - p16 [51-250]

Brenner, Peter J - *Der Reisebericht: Die Entwicklung Einer Gattung In Der Deutschen Literatur*
    JMH - v68 - S '96 - p617+ [501+]
   Reisen In Die Neue Welt
    JMH - v68 - S '96 - p617+ [501+]
Brenner, Robert - *Valentine Treasury*
    LJ - v122 - My 1 '97 - p100 [51-250]
Brenner, Walter - *The Information Superhighway and Private Households*
    JEL - v34 - D '96 - p2087 [51-250]
Brenner, Wendy - *Large Animals in Everyday Life*
    Choice - v34 - O '96 - p275 [51-250]
Brenner, Y S - *A Theory of Full Employment*
    JEL - v34 - D '96 - p2033 [51-250]
Brent, Allen - *Hippolytus and the Roman Church in the Third Century*
    CH - v65 - D '96 - p660+ [501+]
    Rel St Rev - v23 - Ap '97 - p189 [51-250]
Brent, Bill - *Make a Zine!*
    BL - v93 - My 15 '97 - p1543 [51-250]
Brent, Isabelle - *Cats Love Christmas Too (Illus. by Isabelle Brent)*
  c HB Guide - v8 - Spr '97 - p152 [51-250]
  c JB - v60 - D '96 - p247 [1-50]
  c PW - v243 - S 30 '96 - p88 [51-250]
  c SLJ - v42 - O '96 - p34 [51-250]
Brent, Robert J - *Applied Cost-Benefit Analysis*
    JEL - v34 - S '96 - p1414 [51-250]
Brent, Ruth - *Popular American Housing*
  r ARBA - v28 - '97 - p500 [251-500]
Brent, William Lee - *Long Time Gone*
    Bl S - v26 - Fall '96 - p82+ [501+]
    Bl S - v26 - Sum '96 - p63+ [51-250]
Brentano, Franz Clemens - *Descriptive Psychology*
    SciTech - v21 - Mr '97 - p1 [1-50]
Brentano, Robert - *A New World in a Small Place*
    EHR - v111 - N '96 - p1250 [251-500]
Brentlinger, John - *The Best of What We Are*
    Nat - v263 - S 30 '96 - p27+ [501+]
    PSQ - v111 - Fall '96 - p557+ [501+]
Bresard, Luc - *Commentaire Sur Le Cantique Des Cantiques*
    Rel St Rev - v22 - O '96 - p301+ [501+]
Breslauer, S Daniel - *Mordecai Kaplan's Thought in a Postmodern Age*
    JR - v77 - Ja '97 - p189+ [501+]
Breslaw, Elaine G - *Tituba, Reluctant Witch of Salem*
    Bl S - v26 - Sum '96 - p64 [51-250]
Breslin, Jimmy - *I Want to Thank My Brain for Remembering Me*
    LATBR - S 15 '96 - p2 [501+]
    NYTBR - v101 - O 13 '96 - p15 [501+]
    NYTBR - v101 - D 8 '96 - p88 [1-50]
    NYTLa - v145 - S 12 '96 - pC17 [501+]
Breslin, Rosemary - *Not Exactly What I Had in Mind*
    BL - v93 - D 1 '96 - p623 [51-250]
    KR - v64 - N 15 '96 - p1645 [251-500]
    LJ - v121 - D '96 - p102 [51-250]
    NYTBR - v102 - F 9 '97 - p17 [501+]
    PW - v243 - N 18 '96 - p52 [51-250]
Breslin, Shaun - *China in the 1980s*
    R&R Bk N - v11 - N '96 - p50 [51-250]
Breslin, Theresa - *Death or Glory Boys*
  c Bks Keeps - Mr '97 - p27 [51-250]
  y JB - v60 - D '96 - p277 [51-250]
  y Sch Lib - v45 - F '97 - p44 [51-250]
   Whispers in the Graveyard
  c RT - v50 - F '97 - p423+ [51-250]
Bresnick-Perry, Roslyn - *Leaving for America*
  c Learning - v25 - Mr '97 - p54 [1-50]
Bressers, J - *Fatigue under Thermal and Mechanical Loading*
    SciTech - v20 - S '96 - p50 [51-250]
Bressett, Kenneth - *Collectible American Coins*
    Coin W - v37 - D 30 '96 - p22 [51-250]
Bret, David - *The Freddie Mercury Story*
    Spec - v277 - D 7 '96 - p51+ [501+]
Breton, Alain - *Rabinal Achi*
    LA Ant - v7 - Je '96 - p174 [51-250]
Breton, Albert - *Competitive Governments*
    Choice - v34 - D '96 - p656+ [51-250]
    JEL - v35 - Mr '97 - p227 [51-250]
   Nationalism and Rationality
    JEL - v34 - S '96 - p1489 [51-250]
Breton, Andre - *Arcanum 17*
    Can Lit - Win '96 - p123+ [501+]
    TranslRevS - v2 - D '96 - p22 [51-250]
   Free Rein
    Choice - v34 - S '96 - p132 [51-250]
    L'Esprit - v36 - Win '96 - p96 [251-500]
    RCF - v16 - Fall '96 - p199+ [251-500]

   The Lost Steps
    Choice - v34 - My '97 - p1503 [51-250]
    PW - v243 - O 21 '96 - p75+ [51-250]
   Martinique, Charmeuse De Serpents
    L'Esprit - v36 - Win '96 - p64+ [501+]
Brett, C E B - *Buildings of County Antrim*
    TLS - Ja 24 '97 - p20 [501+]
Brett, David - *Tallulah Bankhead: A Scandalous Life*
    Books - v11 - Ap '97 - p20 [51-250]
Brett, Doris - *In the Constellation of the Crab*
    Aust Bk R - O '96 - p56+ [501+]
Brett, Jan - *Berlioz the Bear*
  c PW - v243 - O 14 '96 - p85 [1-50]
   Comet's Nine Lives (Illus. by Jan Brett)
  c CBRS - v25 - N '96 - p25 [51-250]
  c HB Guide - v8 - Spr '97 - p21 [51-250]
  c NYTLa - v146 - D 9 '96 - pC18 [51-250]
  c PW - v243 - O 7 '96 - p74 [51-250]
  c SLJ - v42 - D '96 - p85 [51-250]
   The Mitten: A Ukrainian Folktale (Illus. by Jan Brett)
  c Ch BWatch - v7 - F '97 - p5 [1-50]
  c HB Guide - v8 - Spr '97 - p100 [51-250]
  c PW - v243 - O 21 '96 - p85 [1-50]
   Town Mouse, Country Mouse (Illus. by Jan Brett)
  c Magpies - v11 - My '96 - p39+ [251-500]
   The Wild Christmas Reindeer (Illus. by Jan Brett)
  c CLW - v67 - Mr '97 - p13 [51-250]
Brett, Jane - *Five Lost Chicks (Illus. by Kate Davies)*
  c PW - v244 - F 3 '97 - p108 [1-50]
Brett, Michael - *The Berbers*
    Choice - v34 - N '96 - p523 [51-250]
Brett, Rachel - *Children: The Invisible Soldier*
    WorldV - v13 - Ja '97 - p5 [51-250]
Brett, Simon - *Sicken and So Die*
    BL - v93 - Ja '97 - p823 [51-250]
    KR - v64 - O 15 '96 - p1493 [51-250]
    NYTBR - v102 - Ja 5 '97 - p20 [51-250]
   Sicken and So Die (Brett). Audio Version
    LJ - v121 - D '96 - p170 [51-250]
   Situation Tragedy (Howard). Audio Version
    BL - v93 - N 15 '96 - p604 [51-250]
  y Kliatt - v31 - Mr '97 - p46 [51-250]
Brett, Stephen F - *Slavery and the Catholic Tradition*
    Theol St - v57 - Mr '96 - p186+ [251-500]
Brettler, Marc Zvi - *The Creation of History in Ancient Israel*
    Choice - v34 - N '96 - p474 [51-250]
Brettschneider, Marla - *Cornerstones of Peace*
    AAPSS-A - v549 - Ja '97 - p195+ [501+]
   The Narrow Bridge
    Choice - v34 - F '97 - p1026 [51-250]
Breuer, Christine - *Reliefs Und Epigramme Griechischer Privatgrabmaler*
    AJA - v101 - Ja '97 - p179+ [501+]
Breuer, Mordechai - *German-Jewish History in Modern Times. Vol. 1*
    Choice - v34 - Ap '97 - p1397 [51-250]
Breuer, William B - *Feuding Allies*
    Historian - v59 - Fall '96 - p209+ [251-500]
   MacArthur's Undercover War
    Historian - v59 - Fall '96 - p144+ [501+]
   War and American Women
    LJ - v122 - Ap 15 '97 - p95 [51-250]
    PW - v244 - F 10 '97 - p77 [251-500]
Breuilly, John - *Nationalism and the State. 2nd Ed.*
    Crit R - v10 - Spr '96 - p299+ [501+]
Breunig, L C - *The Cubist Poets in Paris*
    MLR - v91 - Jl '96 - p739 [251-500]
    TranslRevS - v2 - D '96 - p2 [51-250]
Brew, Kwesi - *Return of No Return and Other Poems*
    WLT - v70 - Aut '96 - p1014 [501+]
Brew, Paul - *The Northern Ireland Peace Process 1993-1996*
    HT - v46 - O '96 - p58 [1-50]
Brewer, Daniel - *The Discourse of Enlightenment in Eighteenth-Century France*
    FR - v70 - O '96 - p113+ [501+]
Brewer, Ebenezer Cobham - *Brewer's Dictionary of Phrase and Fable. Centenary Ed.*
  r BW - v26 - D 8 '96 - p4 [51-250]
Brewer, Gay - *Presently a Beast*
    Sm Pr R - v28 - Jl '96 - p13 [51-250]
Brewer, James D - *No Justice*
    BWatch - v18 - F '97 - p6+ [1-50]
    KR - v64 - My 1 '96 - p641+ [51-250]
  y SLJ - v42 - O '96 - p150 [51-250]
   The Raiders of 1862
    LJ - v122 - Mr 15 '97 - p72+ [51-250]
Brewer, Jeannie - *A Crack in Forever*
    Woman's J - O '96 - p12 [1-50]

Brewer, John - *Early Modern Conceptions of Property*
    EHR - v112 - Ap '97 - p487+ [501+]
    TLS - Mr 7 '97 - p12 [501+]
Brewer, Lucy - *Public Works Administration*
    R&R Bk N - v11 - D '96 - p30 [51-250]
Brewer, Maria Minich - *Claude Simon: Narrativities without Narrative*
    MLR - v91 - Jl '96 - p740+ [501+]
Brewer, Neil - *Psychology and Policing*
    Per Psy - v49 - Win '96 - p1011+ [501+]
Brewer, Sarah - *Body Facts*
  yr Kliatt - v30 - N '96 - p31 [51-250]
Brewer, Steve - *Shaky Ground*
    BL - v93 - My 15 '97 - p1566 [51-250]
Brewster, Elizabeth - *Away from Home*
    CF - v75 - Ja '97 - p46+ [51-250]
Brewster, Hugh - *Anastasia's Album*
  c BIC - v25 - D '96 - p34+ [501+]
  c BL - v93 - Ja '97 - p765 [1-50]
  c BL - v93 - O 1 '96 - p349 [51-250]
  c BL - v93 - Ap 1 '97 - p1298 [1-50]
  y BL - v93 - Ap 1 '97 - p1306 [1-50]
  c CCB-B - v50 - Ja '97 - p164 [51-250]
  c HB - v73 - My '97 - p75+ [51-250]
  c HB Guide - v8 - Spr '97 - p168 [51-250]
  c KR - v64 - O 15 '96 - p1529 [51-250]
  c PW - v243 - O 21 '96 - p83+ [51-250]
  c Quill & Q - v62 - N '96 - p43 [251-500]
  y SLJ - v42 - D '96 - p149 [51-250]
Brey, Wallace S - *Magnetic Resonance in Perspective*
    Am Sci - v85 - Mr '97 - p180+ [501+]
    Sci - v274 - O 25 '96 - p523 [1-50]
    SciTech - v20 - S '96 - p16 [51-250]
Breymeyer, A I - *Biodiversity Conservation in Transboundary Protected Areas*
    SciTech - v21 - Mr '97 - p34 [51-250]
Breytenbach, Breyten - *Die Hand Vol Vere*
    WLT - v71 - Win '97 - p210 [251-500]
   The Memory of Birds in Times of Revolution
    WLT - v71 - Win '97 - p210+ [501+]
Brezinski, Horst - *The Economic Impact of New Firms in Post-Socialist Countries*
    JEL - v34 - S '96 - p1492 [51-250]
Brian, Denis - *Einstein: A Life*
    Choice - v34 - Ja '97 - p814 [51-250]
    LATBR - Jl 14 '96 - p3+ [501+]
    NH - v105 - Ag '96 - p14 [51-250]
    Spec - v277 - D 14 '96 - p68+ [501+]
    TLS - Jl 19 '96 - p30 [501+]
Bricke, John - *Mind and Morality*
    Choice - v34 - Mr '97 - p1173+ [51-250]
Brickell, Christopher - *A-Z Encyclopedia of Garden Plants*
  r TLS - D 6 '96 - p36 [501+]
Bricker, Harry M - *Le Paleolithique Superieur De L'Abri Pataud (Dordogne)*
    Am Ant - v62 - Ja '97 - p174 [501+]
Bridgers, Sue Ellen - *All Together Now*
  y JAAL - v40 - D '96 - p318 [51-250]
   All We Know of Heaven
  y BL - v93 - O 1 '96 - p321 [51-250]
    LJ - v121 - D '96 - p141 [51-250]
    NYTBR - v101 - N 10 '96 - p56 [51-250]
    PW - v243 - S 9 '96 - p66 [51-250]
  y SLJ - v43 - Ja '97 - p139 [51-250]
Bridges, Douglas S - *Representations of Preferences Orderings*
    JEL - v34 - D '96 - p2024 [51-250]
Bridges, Marilyn - *Egypt: Antiquities from Above*
    Afterimage - v24 - Ja '97 - p23 [1-50]
    A & S Sm - v11 - F '97 - p88+ [51-250]
  y BL - v93 - D 15 '96 - p706 [51-250]
    CSM - v89 - D 5 '96 - pB2+ [51-250]
   This Land Is Your Land
    KR - v65 - My 1 '97 - p711 [51-250]
Bridges, Thomas - *The Culture of Citizenship*
    RP - v59 - Win '97 - p127+ [501+]
Bridgewater, Alan - *Boxes and Chests*
    BL - v93 - Mr 1 '97 - p1100 [51-250]
   Carving Masks
    BL - v93 - Ja '97 - p805 [51-250]
    LJ - v122 - F 15 '97 - p133 [51-250]
Bridgham, Fred - *The Friendly German-English Dictionary*
  r ARBA - v28 - '97 - p390+ [51-250]
  r Choice - v34 - N '96 - p426 [51-250]
Bridson, Gavin - *The History of Natural History*
  r RQ - v35 - Sum '96 - p485 [51-250]
Bridwell, Norman - *Clifford Barks!*
  c Ch BWatch - v6 - Jl '96 - p4 [1-50]
  c HB Guide - v7 - Fall '96 - p237 [1-50]

Clifford's First Easter (Illus. by Norman Bridwell)
  c   RT - v50 - O '96 - p130 [1-50]
Clifford's First Halloween (Illus. by Norman Bridwell)
  c   RT - v50 - O '96 - p130 [1-50]
Brief, Richard P - *Clean Surplus*
  R&R Bk N - v11 - N '96 - p36 [1-50]
Briere, John - *The APSAC Handbook on Child Maltreatment*
  Readings - v12 - Mr '97 - p23+ [51-250]
Brierley, Anthony - *Explorers of the Ancient World*
  c   Ch BWatch - v7 - Ja '97 - p7 [1-50]
  c   HB Guide - v8 - Spr '97 - p162 [51-250]
  c   Magpies - v11 - Jl '96 - p42+ [51-250]
  c   SLJ - v43 - Ja '97 - p97 [51-250]
Brierley, Barry - *White Horse, Red Rider*
  Roundup M - v4 - Ap '97 - p29 [51-250]
Briesemeister, Dietrich - *Brasilien Heute*
  HAHR - v76 - N '96 - p821+ [501+]
Briggs, Andrew - *Advances in Acoustic Microscopy. Vol. 2*
  SciTech - v21 - Mr '97 - p76 [51-250]
Briggs, Asa - *Fins De Siecle*
  Econ - v341 - D 7 '96 - p6* [51-250]
  For Aff - v76 - Mr '97 - p174 [51-250]
  HT - v46 - O '96 - p59 [51-250]
  KR - v64 - N 1 '96 - p1573+ [251-500]
  Obs - D 15 '96 - p17* [501+]
The History of Broadcasting in the United Kingdom. Vol. 5
  AHR - v101 - D '96 - p1547 [501+]
Briggs, Kelly Paul - *Island Alphabet*
  c   HB Guide - v7 - Fall '96 - p385 [51-250]
Briggs, Mary - *Your Role as a Primary School Subject Coordinator*
  TES - Mr 14 '97 - p16* [251-500]
Briggs, Philip J - *Making Foreign Policy*
  Pres SQ - v26 - Fall '96 - p1182+ [501+]
Briggs, Raymond - *The Bear (Illus. by Raymond Briggs)*
  c   Bks Keeps - Ja '97 - p20 [51-250]
  c   RT - v50 - F '97 - p421+ [51-250]
  c   TES - O 18 '96 - p12* [1-50]
The Man
  c   HB Guide - v7 - Fall '96 - p249 [51-250]
Briggs, Robin - *Witches and Neighbors*
  Skeptic - v4 - 4 '96 - p102+ [251-500]
Witches and Neighbours
  NS & S - v9 - Ap 26 '96 - p37+ [251-500]
Briggs, Vernon M - *Mass Immigration and the National Interest. 2nd Ed.*
  JEL - v35 - Mr '97 - p215 [51-250]
  R&R Bk N - v12 - F '97 - p61 [51-250]
Brigham, Clarence S - *History and Bibliography of American Newspapers 1690-1820. Vols. 1-2*
  r   ASInt - v34 - O '96 - p15+ [1-50]
Bright, Charles - *The Powers That Punish*
  Choice - v34 - F '97 - p1041 [51-250]
Bright, Michael - *Robert Browning's Rondures Brave*
  Nine-C Lit - v51 - S '96 - p270 [1-50]
Bright, Susie - *Nothing but the Girl*
  Wom R Bks - v14 - Mr '97 - p6+ [501+]
Susie Bright's Sexual State of the Union
  Advocate - Mr 4 '97 - p55+ [501+]
  KR - v65 - Ja 15 '97 - p108 [251-500]
  NYTBR - v102 - Mr 23 '97 - p16 [501+]
  PW - v244 - Ja 13 '97 - p61 [51-250]
  VLS - Spr '97 - p10+ [501+]
Bright, William - *Colorado Place Names*
  r   Names - v44 - S '96 - p241+ [501+]
Brighton, Catherine - *My Napoleon (Illus. by Catherine Brighton)*
  c   CBRS - v25 - Ap '97 - p101 [1-50]
  c   CCB-B - v50 - My '97 - p314+ [51-250]
  c   KR - v65 - Mr 15 '97 - p459 [51-250]
  c   Obs - Mr 30 '97 - p17* [51-250]
  c   PW - v244 - Ja 6 '97 - p73 [51-250]
Brill, Alida - *A Rising Public Voice*
  NWSA Jnl - v9 - Spr '97 - p107+ [501+]
Brill, Marlene Targ - *Building the Capital City*
  c   HB Guide - v7 - Fall '96 - p384 [51-250]
  c   SLJ - v42 - Ag '96 - p150 [51-250]
Extraordinary Young People
  y   HB Guide - v8 - Spr '97 - p161 [51-250]
  y   SLJ - v42 - O '96 - p152 [51-250]
Illinois
  c   BL - v93 - F 1 '97 - p937 [51-250]
  c   Ch BWatch - v6 - D '96 - p6 [1-50]
  c   HB Guide - v8 - Spr '97 - p172 [51-250]
  c   SLJ - v43 - Mr '97 - p108 [51-250]
Journey for Peace (Illus. by Ruben De Anda)
  c   BL - v93 - S 1 '96 - p120 [51-250]
  c   HB Guide - v8 - Spr '97 - p155 [51-250]
  c   SLJ - v42 - S '96 - p210 [51-250]

Women for Peace
  y   BL - v93 - My 15 '97 - p1569 [51-250]
Brill, Peter L - *The Four Levers of Corporate Change*
  Choice - v34 - Ap '97 - p1382 [51-250]
  LJ - v122 - Mr 15 '97 - p35 [1-50]
Brill, Thomas B - *Decomposition, Combustion and Detonation Chemistry of Energetic Materials*
  SciTech - v20 - S '96 - p17 [51-250]
Brillat-Savarin, Jean Anthelme - *The Physiology of Taste*
  BW - v26 - D 8 '96 - p4 [51-250]
Brillhart, Julie - *When Daddy Took Us Camping*
  c   BL - v93 - My 1 '97 - p1500 [51-250]
Brilmayer, Lea - *American Hegemony*
  Ethics - v107 - O '96 - p155+ [501+]
  Historian - v59 - Fall '96 - p145+ [251-500]
Brimelow, Peter - *Alien Nation*
  BW - v26 - D 15 '96 - p4 [1-50]
  Rapport - v19 - 6 '96 - p34 [251-500]
Brimmicombe-Wood, Lee - *Aliens: Colonial Marines Technical Manual*
  SF Chr - v18 - O '96 - p82 [1-50]
Brimner, Larry Dane - *Being Different*
  y   LATBR - Mr 17 '96 - p11 [51-250]
Brave Mary (Illus. by Marilyn Mets)
  c   HB Guide - v7 - Fall '96 - p249 [51-250]
Firehouse Sal (Illus. by Ethel Gold)
  c   HB Guide - v8 - Spr '97 - p21 [51-250]
If Dogs Had Wings (Illus. by Chris L Demarest)
  c   CLW - v67 - D '96 - p55 [51-250]
  c   HB Guide - v8 - Spr '97 - p11 [51-250]
  c   SLJ - v42 - D '96 - p85 [51-250]
Brin, David - *Brightness Reef*
  y   Kliatt - v31 - Mr '97 - p16 [51-250]
Infinity's Shore
  Analog - v117 - Mr '97 - p151+ [251-500]
  KR - v64 - O 15 '96 - p1500 [51-250]
  PW - v243 - N 18 '96 - p65 [51-250]
Brin, Gershon - *Studies in Biblical Law*
  Rel St Rev - v23 - Ap '97 - p169 [51-250]
Brinch Hansen, Per - *The Search for Simplicity*
  SciTech - v20 - S '96 - p6 [51-250]
Brinckerhoff, Peter C - *Financial Empowerment*
  ChrPhil - v8 - Je 27 '96 - p34 [51-250]
Brindley, Geoff - *Language Assessment in Action*
  MLJ - v80 - Win '96 - p531+ [501+]
Brindley, Keith - *Word for Windows 95 Clear and Simple*
  CBR - v14 - Jl '96 - p26 [1-50]
Briner, Bob - *The Management Methods of Jesus*
  Rapport - v19 - 4 '96 - p38 [251-500]
Briner, Wendy - *Project Leadership. 2nd Ed.*
  R&R Bk N - v12 - F '97 - p39 [51-250]
Bringa, Tone - *Being Muslim the Bosnian Way*
  Am Ethnol - v23 - Ag '96 - p653+ [501+]
  CS - v25 - N '96 - p739+ [501+]
  Rel St Rev - v23 - Ap '97 - p202 [51-250]
Bringhurst, Robert - *The Elements of Typographic Style. 2nd Ed.*
  LJ - v122 - Ja '97 - p92 [51-250]
Bringing Health Care Online
  J Gov Info - v23 - S '96 - p555 [51-250]
Bringman, Wolfgang - *A Pictorial History of Psychology*
  LJ - v122 - F 1 '97 - p97 [51-250]
Brink, Andre - *Imaginings of Sand*
  BL - v93 - O 1 '96 - p321 [51-250]
  KR - v64 - S 1 '96 - p1253 [251-500]
  LJ - v121 - S 15 '96 - p94 [51-250]
  NYTBR - v101 - D 1 '96 - p24 [501+]
  NYTLa - v146 - D 11 '96 - pC21 [501+]
  WSJ-MW - v78 - N 8 '96 - pA13 [501+]
Brink, Andrew - *Obsession and Culture*
  Choice - v34 - D '96 - p611 [51-250]
Brink, Benjamin - *David's Story (Illus. by Benjamin Brink)*
  c   BL - v93 - D 1 '96 - p647 [51-250]
  c   HB Guide - v8 - Spr '97 - p129 [51-250]
  c   SLJ - v42 - O '96 - p128 [51-250]
Brink, Carol Ryrie - *Caddie Woodlawn*
  c   JOYS - v10 - Fall '96 - p46+ [501+]
Goody O'Grumpity (Illus. by Ashley Wolff)
  c   PW - v243 - O 7 '96 - p78 [1-50]
Brink, Jean R - *Privileging Gender in Early Modern England*
  Rel St Rev - v23 - Ja '97 - p83 [51-250]
  Ren & Ref - v20 - Win '96 - p87+ [501+]
Brink, Sonja - *Italienische Zeichnungen Des 16. Bis 18. Jahrhunderts*
  BM - v138 - O '96 - p695+ [501+]
Brink, T L - *Holocaust Survivors' Mental Health*
  Rel St Rev - v22 - O '96 - p334 [51-250]
Brinker-Gabler, Gisela - *Encountering the Other(s)*
  Ger Q - v69 - Spr '96 - p203+ [51-250]

Brinkley, Alan - *The End of Reform*
  AHR - v102 - F '97 - p210+ [501+]
  BusLR - v21 - 3 '96 - p202+ [501+]
  SE - v60 - S '96 - p302 [51-250]
Brinkley, David - *David Brinkley: 11 Presidents, 4 Wars, 22 Political Conventions, 1 Moon Landing, 3 Assassinations, 2,000 Weeks of News and Other Stuff on Television*
  NYTBR - v101 - D 22 '96 - p20 [501+]
  Sew R - v104 - O '96 - p673+ [501+]
David Brinkley: A Memoir
  y   Kliatt - v31 - Mr '97 - p25 [251-500]
  PW - v243 - S 9 '96 - p81 [1-50]
Everyone Is Entitled to My Opinion
  BL - v93 - S 1 '96 - p2 [51-250]
  CSM - v89 - D 12 '96 - p14 [51-250]
  CSM - v89 - Ja 9 '97 - p14 [51-250]
  KR - v64 - Ag 15 '96 - p1199 [51-250]
  LJ - v121 - S 15 '96 - p84 [51-250]
  NYTBR - v101 - N 24 '96 - p19 [51-250]
Brinkley, Joel - *Defining Vision*
  BL - v93 - D 15 '96 - p695+ [51-250]
  BW - v27 - Ja 19 '97 - p7 [501+]
  KR - v64 - N 15 '96 - p1645+ [251-500]
  NYTBR - v102 - F 2 '97 - p25 [501+]
  NYTLa - v146 - F 19 '97 - pC15 [501+]
  PW - v243 - D 16 '96 - p52 [51-250]
Brinkley, M Kent - *The Gardens of Colonial Williamsburg*
  Hort - v74 - O '96 - p77 [51-250]
Brinkman, Martien E - *Progress in Unity?*
  ER - v49 - Ap '97 - p283+ [501+]
  Theol St - v57 - D '96 - p782+ [251-500]
Briody, Thomas Gately - *Rogue's Justice*
  Arm Det - v30 - Win '97 - p92+ [251-500]
Brisac, Genevieve - *Weekend De Chasse A La Mere*
  Spec - v278 - Ja 4 '97 - p37 [501+]
Brisbin, Richard - *Justice Scalia and the Conservative Revival*
  WSJ-Cent - v99 - F 4 '97 - pA17 [51-250]
Briscoe, Joanna - *Mothers and Other Lovers*
  Books - v9 - S '95 - p25 [51-250]
Skin
  TLS - Mr 28 '97 - p22 [251-500]
  Woman's J - Ap '97 - p18 [51-250]
Briscoe, Mary Louise - *American Autobiography 1945-1980*
  r   ASInt - v34 - O '96 - p14+ [1-50]
Briskin, Alan - *The Stirring of Soul in the Workplace*
  BL - v93 - S 1 '96 - p44 [51-250]
  Choice - v34 - F '97 - p1007 [51-250]
  LJ - v121 - O 1 '96 - p85+ [51-250]
Briskin, Jacqueline - *The Crimson Palace*
  Books - v9 - S '95 - p22 [1-50]
Brislin, Richard W - *Improving Intercultural Interactions*
  MLJ - v80 - Fall '96 - p409+ [501+]
Brisset, Annie - *A Sociocritique of Translation*
  R&R Bk N - v12 - F '97 - p77 [51-250]
Brisson, Pat - *Hot Fudge Hero (Illus. by Diana Cain Bluthenthal)*
  c   BL - v93 - Ap 1 '97 - p1333 [51-250]
  c   KR - v65 - Ap 1 '97 - p550 [51-250]
  c   Par Ch - v21 - Mr '97 - p4 [1-50]
Magic Carpet
  c   Inst - v106 - O '96 - p93 [1-50]
Bristol, Michael D - *Big-Time Shakespeare*
  NS - v125 - O 11 '96 - p46+ [501+]
  Obs - v54 - O 13 '96 - p18* [51-250]
Bristol-Myers Squibb Symposium on Pain Research (6th: 1995: Baltimore, Md.) - *Pain Treatment Centers at a Crossroads*
  SciTech - v20 - S '96 - p29 [51-250]
Bristow, Gwen - *Jubilee Trail*
  Nat R - v48 - D 23 '96 - p54 [51-250]
Bristow, John A - *The Bulgarian Economy in Transition*
  Econ - v106 - N '96 - p1847 [251-500]
  JEL - v34 - D '96 - p2123 [51-250]
  R&R Bk N - v11 - D '96 - p25 [51-250]
Bristow, Joseph - *Effeminate England*
  ELT - v40 - 2 '97 - p228+ [501+]
Victorian Women Poets
  Nine-C Lit - v50 - Mr '96 - p552 [1-50]
Britannica CD 2.0. Electronic Media Version
  r   Choice - v34 - N '96 - p440+ [251-500]
  r   HT - v46 - D '96 - p49 [51-250]
Britannica CD 97.0. Electronic Media Version
  cr   BL - v93 - N 1 '96 - p523+ [501+]
Brite, Poppy Z - *Exquisite Corpse*
  HG&LRev - v3 - Fall '96 - p43 [51-250]
  Necro - Fall '96 - p14+ [501+]

British and Cultural Studies Conference (5th: 1994: Oldenburg, Germany) - *The Past in the Present*
R&R Bk N - v12 - F '97 - p15 [51-250]

British Elections and Parties Yearbook 1995
r   CR - v269 - D '96 - p331+ [251-500]

British Library - *Catalogue of Books Printed in the German-Speaking Countries and of German Books Printed in Other Countries from 1601 to 1700 in the British Library. Vols. 1-5*
r   Ger Q - v70 - Win '97 - p77+ [501+]
r   Six Ct J - v27 - Win '96 - p1093+ [501+]
Short-Title Catalogue of Hungarian Books Printed before 1851 in the British Library
r   ARBA - v28 - '97 - p9+ [251-500]
r   LQ - v66 - O '96 - p490+ [501+]

British Library. Information Sciences Service - *Matter of Fax*
r   LAR - v98 - D '96 - p651 [1-50]

British Museum - *A Catalogue of the Lamps in the British Museum. Vol. 4*
r   Apo - v144 - Jl '96 - p65+ [501+]

The British Philatelic Bulletin
p   Am Phil - v110 - S '96 - p828 [251-500]

British Qualifications. 26th Ed.
r   R&R Bk N - v11 - N '96 - p35 [51-250]
yr TES - S 27 '96 - p8* [51-250]

Britnell, R H - *A Commercialising Economy*
Albion - v28 - Win '96 - p669+ [501+]
JEH - v56 - S '96 - p709+ [501+]
The McFarlane Legacy
Albion - v28 - Win '96 - p676+ [501+]

Britnell, Richard H - *Progress and Problems in Medieval England*
JEL - v35 - Mr '97 - p258+ [51-250]

Briton, Derek - *The Modern Practice of Adult Education*
Choice - v34 - Ap '97 - p1392 [251-500]
R&R Bk N - v11 - N '96 - p58 [51-250]

Britt, Brian - *Walter Benjamin and the Bible*
BL - v93 - O 1 '96 - p296 [51-250]
Choice - v34 - My '97 - p1511+ [51-250]

Brittain, C Dale - *Daughter of Magic*
y   Kliatt - v30 - S '96 - p15 [51-250]
SF Chr - v18 - O '96 - p80 [51-250]

Brittain, Vera - *Testament of Youth (Campbell). Audio Version*
y   Kliatt - v31 - Ja '97 - p51 [51-250]

Brittan, Samuel - *Capitalism with a Human Face*
TES - Ja 31 '97 - p7* [51-250]
Market Capitalism and Moral Values
Ethics - v107 - Ja '97 - p392+ [51-250]
JEL - v34 - D '96 - p1942+ [501+]

Britten, Benjamin - *Letters from a Life. Vols. 1-2*
AJPsych - v153 - D '96 - p1645+ [501+]

Britto, Anthony - *Tattoo*
PW - v244 - Ap 28 '97 - p54 [51-250]

Britton, David - *The Adventures of Meng and Ecker*
Obs - Mr 16 '97 - p16* [51-250]
Motherfuckers: The Auschwitz of Oz
NS - v125 - Ag 30 '96 - p44+ [501+]

Britton, John A - *Revolution and Ideology*
AHR - v102 - F '97 - p204 [251-500]
HAHR - v76 - Ag '96 - p578+ [501+]

Britton, John N H - *Canada and the Global Economy*
Choice - v34 - O '96 - p329 [51-250]
R&R Bk N - v11 - N '96 - p27 [51-250]

Brival, Roland - *Le Dernier Des Aloukous*
BL - v93 - F 1 '97 - p930 [1-50]

Brivati, Brian - *The Contemporary History Handbook*
r   TLS - N 1 '96 - p7 [501+]
Hugh Gaitskell
CR - v270 - F '97 - p104+ [501+]
Lon R Bks - v18 - N 14 '96 - p13+ [501+]
NS - v125 - S 27 '96 - p62+ [501+]
NS - v125 - D 20 '96 - p116 [51-250]
Obs - S 29 '96 - p15* [501+]
Spec - v277 - O 5 '96 - p46+ [501+]
TLS - O 11 '96 - p15 [501+]

Brivic, Sheldon - *Joyce's Waking Women*
Choice - v34 - S '96 - p122 [51-250]

Broad, William J - *The Universe Below*
KR - v65 - F 15 '97 - p264 [251-500]
LJ - v122 - Mar 15 '97 - p88 [51-250]
NYTBR - v102 - Ap 20 '97 - p9 [501+]
PW - v244 - F 24 '97 - p76+ [251-500]
Trib Bks - Ap 20 '97 - p6+ [501+]

Broadbent, Donald E - *Decision and Stress*
A J Psy - v109 - Win '96 - p617+ [501+]

Broadbent, Michael - *The New Great Vintage Wine Book. Rev. Ed.*
LJ - v122 - Ap 1 '97 - p62 [1-50]

Broadman, Harry G - *Policy Options for Reform of Chinese State-Owned Enterprises*
JEL - v35 - Mr '97 - p293+ [51-250]

Broadwell, Richard - *Neuroscience, Memory and Language*
AJMR - v101 - Ja '97 - p435+ [501+]

The Brobdingnagian Times
p   Sm Pr R - v29 - Ja '97 - p14 [51-250]

Brocheux, Pierre - *The Mekong Delta*
AHR - v101 - D '96 - p1599+ [501+]
Pac A - v69 - Sum '96 - p283+ [501+]

Brochier, Jean-Jacques - *Pour Sartre*
FR - v70 - D '96 - p337+ [501+]

Brochu, Andre - *Adele Intime*
WLT - v71 - Win '97 - p101+ [251-500]
Dela
FR - v70 - O '96 - p139+ [251-500]

Brock, Bernard L - *Kenneth Burke and Contemporary European Thought*
QJS - v83 - F '97 - p107+ [501+]

Brock, David - *The Seduction of Hillary Rodham*
BW - v26 - O 13 '96 - p1+ [501+]
Ent W - N 15 '96 - p66 [51-250]
Nat R - v48 - D 31 '96 - p48+ [501+]
NYRB - v43 - N 14 '96 - p12+ [501+]
NYTBR - v101 - O 13 '96 - p9+ [501+]
VV - v41 - O 22 '96 - p57+ [251-500]
WSJ-MW - v78 - O 22 '96 - pA20 [501+]

Brock, Gerald W - *Toward a Competitive Telecommunication Industry*
JEL - v34 - D '96 - p2088 [51-250]

Brock, Henry S - *Your Complete Guide to Money Happiness*
BL - v93 - N 1 '96 - p465 [51-250]

Brock, Stephen E - *Preparing for Crises in the Schools*
Adoles - v31 - Fall '96 - p751 [51-250]

Brock, William H - *Science for All*
Choice - v34 - D '96 - p632 [51-250]

Brock-Broido, Lucie - *The Master Letters*
Parnassus - v22 - 1 '97 - p282+ [501+]
Wom R Bks - v14 - N '96 - p24+ [501+]

Brockenbrough, R L - *Highway Engineering Handbook*
SciTech - v20 - D '96 - p70 [51-250]

Brockman, John - *Digerati: Encounters with the Cyber Elite*
SFR - v21 - N '96 - p38 [501+]
The Third Culture
BioSci - v46 - O '96 - p710+ [501+]
Skeptic - v4 - 2 '96 - p108 [251-500]

Brockman, Terra Castiglia - *A Student's Guide to Italian American Genealogy*
yr ARBA - v28 - '97 - p167+ [251-500]
y   SLJ - v42 - O '96 - p152 [51-250]
y   SLMQ - v25 - Fall '96 - p63 [51-250]

Brockmann, Karl Ludwig - *Certified Tropical Timber and Consumer Behavior*
JEL - v35 - Mr '97 - p297+ [51-250]

Brockway, George P - *Economists Can Be Bad for Your Health*
PW - v243 - S 23 '96 - p73 [1-50]

Brockwell, Peter J - *Introduction to Time Series and Forecasting*
JEL - v35 - Mr '97 - p194 [51-250]

Brode, Douglas - *Once Was Enough*
BL - v93 - D 15 '96 - p702+ [51-250]

Broderick, Damien - *Reading by Starlight*
SFS - v24 - Mr '97 - p150+ [501+]
The White Abacus
KR - v65 - F 1 '97 - p178 [51-250]
PW - v244 - F 3 '97 - p99 [51-250]

Broderick, David - *An Early Toll-Road*
ILS - v16 - Spr '97 - p36 [1-50]

Broderick, Mick - *Hibakusha Cinema*
Choice - v34 - My '97 - p1507 [51-250]
Nuclear Movies
r   FQ - v49 - Fall '95 - p62+ [251-500]

Brodersen, Momme - *Walter Benjamin: A Biography*
KR - v64 - O 1 '96 - p1436+ [251-500]
LJ - v121 - N 1 '96 - p70 [51-250]
NS - v125 - N 29 '96 - p46+ [501+]
PW - v243 - S 23 '96 - p64 [251-500]

Brodeur, Jean-Paul - *Comparisons in Policing*
R&R Bk N - v11 - D '96 - p44 [51-250]

Brodeur, Paul - *Secrets: A Writer in the Cold War*
KR - v65 - F 15 '97 - p264 [251-500]
PW - v244 - F 10 '97 - p73+ [51-250]

Brodhead, Richard H - *Cultures of Letters*
Lib & Cul - v32 - Win '97 - p142+ [501+]

Brodie, Deborah - *Writing Changes Everything*
r   BL - v93 - Mr 1 '97 - p1200 [251-500]

Brodie, Janet Farrell - *Contraception and Abortion in Nineteenth-Century America*
JIH - v27 - Aut '96 - p343+ [501+]

Brodie, Thomas L - *The Gospel according to John*
Rel St Rev - v22 - O '96 - p346+ [501+]

Brodkey, Harold - *This Wild Darkness*
BL - v93 - S 1 '96 - p56 [51-250]
HMR - Win '96 - p15+ [501+]
LATBR - O 20 '96 - p15 [501+]
LJ - v121 - O 1 '96 - p88 [51-250]
Lon R Bks - v19 - F 6 '97 - p3+ [501+]
NS - v125 - N 22 '96 - p47+ [501+]
NYTBR - v101 - O 27 '96 - p9 [501+]
NYTBR - v101 - D 8 '96 - p93 [1-50]
NYTLa - v146 - D 24 '96 - pC18 [501+]
Obs - D 8 '96 - p17* [501+]
Spec - v277 - N 16 '96 - p51+ [501+]
TLS - N 15 '96 - p15 [501+]
VV - v41 - D 31 '96 - p47+ [501+]

Brodsky, Joseph - *Homage to Robert Frost*
LATBR - O 20 '96 - p14 [501+]
LJ - v121 - N 15 '96 - p62 [51-250]
NL - v80 - Ja 13 '97 - p14+ [501+]
Wil Q - v20 - Aut '96 - p97 [251-500]
On Grief and Reason
NL - v79 - S 9 '96 - p14+ [501+]
NS - v125 - D 20 '96 - p119+ [501+]
Obs - O 27 '96 - p15* [501+]
TLS - Ja 10 '97 - p6+ [501+]
So Forth
LJ - v122 - Ja '97 - p48 [51-250]
NL - v79 - S 9 '96 - p14+ [501+]
NS - v125 - D 20 '96 - p119+ [501+]
NY - v72 - D 16 '96 - p107+ [501+]
NYTBR - v101 - S 1 '96 - p6 [501+]
NYTBR - v101 - D 8 '96 - p82 [1-50]
TLS - Ja 10 '97 - p6+ [501+]
VLS - Win '96 - p8 [501+]

Brodsky, Michael - *Southernmost and Other Stories*
NYTBR - v102 - Mr 9 '97 - p19 [51-250]

Brody, J J - *Pueblo Indian Painting*
PW - v244 - Ap 21 '97 - p57 [501+]
To Touch the Past
Choice - v34 - S '96 - p191+ [51-250]

Brody, Jane A - *1,001 Great Gifts*
BWatch - v18 - Mr '97 - p1 [1-50]

Brody, Jane E - *Jane Brody's Allergy Fighter*
PW - v244 - Mr 24 '97 - p79+ [51-250]
The New York Times Book of Health
PW - v244 - Ap 21 '97 - p67 [51-250]

Brody, Jean - *Cleo*
NYTBR - v102 - Mr 16 '97 - p32 [51-250]

Brody, Jules - *Lectures De La Fontaine*
MLR - v91 - Jl '96 - p724+ [501+]

Brody, Seymour - *Jewish Heroes and Heroines of America*
r   BL - v93 - Mr 15 '97 - p1258 [51-250]

Brodzinsky, Anne Braff - *The Mulberry Bird (Illus. by Diana L Stanley)*
c   HB Guide - v7 - Fall '96 - p285+ [51-250]
c   SLJ - v42 - N '96 - p78 [51-250]

Broeck, Julien Van Den - *The Economics of Labour Migration*
JEL - v34 - S '96 - p1449 [51-250]
R&R Bk N - v11 - N '96 - p32 [51-250]

Broeke, P W Van Den - *The Prehistory of the Netherlands*
HT - v46 - O '96 - p55 [1-50]

Broer, H W - *Nonlinear Dynamical Systems and Chaos*
SciTech - v20 - S '96 - p13 [51-250]

Broers, Michael - *Europe under Napoleon 1799-1815*
HT - v46 - O '96 - p57 [1-50]

Breeze, Franklin J A - *Mr. Brooks and the Australian Trade*
VS - v39 - Aut '95 - p90+ [501+]

Brogan, T V F - *The Princeton Handbook of Multicultural Poetries*
r   ARBA - v28 - '97 - p466 [51-250]
r   Nine-C Lit - v51 - S '96 - p271 [51-250]

Broinowski, Alison - *The Yellow Lady*
Aust Bk R - D '96 - p93 [1-50]

Brokaw, Meredith - *The Penny Whistle Any Day Is a Holiday Party Book*
BL - v93 - S 15 '96 - p202 [51-250]

Brokenmouth, Robert - *Nick Cave: The Birthday Party and Other Epic Adventures*
Aust Bk R - O '96 - p31+ [501+]

Broks, Peter - *Media Science before the Great War*
Choice - v34 - Ap '97 - p1358 [51-250]
New Sci - v153 - Mr 1 '97 - p49 [51-250]

Brombert, Beth Archer - *Edouard Manet: Rebel in a Frock Coat*
    AB - v99 - Mr 3 '97 - p697+ [501+]
    BM - v138 - S '96 - p610 [501+]
    CR - v269 - S '96 - p166+ [51-250]
    CSM - v88 - O 16 '96 - p13 [501+]
    New R - v216 - F 3 '97 - p43+ [501+]
    NYTBR - v101 - D 8 '96 - p87 [1-50]
    Obs - Ag 18 '96 - p18* [501+]
    TLS - Ag 30 '96 - p20+ [501+]
Bromley, Karen D'Angelo - *Graphic Organizers*
    Emerg Lib - v24 - S '96 - p42 [1-50]
Webbing with Literature. 2nd Ed.
    New Ad - v9 - Fall '96 - p346 [51-250]
Bromley, Theodore Norbert - *The White Rose*
    BIC - v25 - D '96 - p42 [51-250]
Bronfenbrenner, Urie - *The State of Americans*
    JEL - v35 - Mr '97 - p234 [51-250]
    Soc Ser R - v71 - Mr '97 - p164 [1-50]
Bronfman, Edgar M - *The Making of a Jew*
    BL - v93 - O 1 '96 - p317+ [51-250]
    BW - v26 - N 17 '96 - p4+ [501+]
    KR - v64 - S 1 '96 - p1287 [251-500]
    LJ - v121 - O 15 '96 - p65 [51-250]
    PW - v243 - S 2 '96 - p106 [51-250]
    Quill & Q - v62 - O '96 - p34 [501+]
Bronk, William - *The Cage of Age*
    BWatch - v17 - S '96 - p7 [51-250]
    HMR - Spr '97 - p39+ [501+]
    LJ - v121 - D '96 - p98 [51-250]
Bronner, Felix - *Nutrition and Health*
    BioSci - v47 - F '97 - p125+ [501+]
Bronner, Leila Leah - *From Eve to Esther*
    JR - v76 - O '96 - p669+ [501+]
Bronner, Simon J - *Popularizing Pennsylvania*
    Choice - v34 - O '96 - p345 [51-250]
Bronner, Stephen Eric - *Albert Camus: The Thinker, the Artist, the Man*
    y HB Guide - v8 - Spr '97 - p155 [51-250]
    y SLJ - v43 - F '97 - p110 [51-250]
Bronowski, Jacob - *The Ascent of Man*
    Reason - v28 - D '96 - p43 [51-250]
Bronson, Fred - *Billboard's Hottest Hot 100 Hits. Rev. Ed.*
    r ARBA - v28 - '97 - p492+ [51-250]
Bronson, Po - *The First $20 Million Is Always the Hardest*
    BL - v93 - Ja '97 - p816 [51-250]
    Econ - v342 - Mr 15 '97 - p12* [501+]
    KR - v64 - D 15 '96 - p1749 [251-500]
    PW - v243 - D 2 '96 - p39 [51-250]
    Time - v149 - F 24 '97 - p74 [501+]
    Trib Bks - Mr 23 '97 - p2 [501+]
The First $20 Million Is Always the Hardest (Frye). Audio Version
    LJ - v122 - Ap 15 '97 - p138 [51-250]
Bronte, Charlotte - *The Belgian Essays*
    LJ - v122 - Ap 1 '97 - p91 [51-250]
    Obs - Mr 23 '97 - p15* [501+]
Charlotte Bronte's High Life in Verdopolis
    Nine-C Lit - v51 - S '96 - p271 [1-50]
Jane Eyre
    Nine-C Lit - v51 - S '96 - p271 [51-250]
The Letters of Charlotte Bronte. Vol. 1
    HR - v49 - Sum '96 - p301+ [501+]
Shirley
    Nine-C Lit - v50 - Mr '96 - p464+ [501+]
Bronte, Emily - *The Poems of Emily Bronte*
    Nine-C Lit - v51 - S '96 - p271 [51-250]
Wuthering Heights
    NWSA Jnl - v8 - Sum '96 - p17+ [501+]
Wuthering Heights (McCaddon). Audio Version
    y Kliatt - v30 - S '96 - p55 [51-250]
Wuthering Heights (Scales). Audio Version
    Obs - Ja 12 '97 - p18* [51-250]
Brook, Andrew - *Kant and the Mind*
    RM - v49 - Je '96 - p915+ [501+]
Brook, Charles G D - *Essential Endocrinology. 3rd Ed.*
    SciTech - v20 - N '96 - p31 [51-250]
Brook, Christopher - *Monsters in the Garden (Illus. by Christopher Brook)*
    c Bks Keeps - v100 - S '96 - p32 [51-250]
    c JB - v60 - D '96 - p226 [51-250]
    c Sch Lib - v44 - Ag '96 - p98 [51-250]
    c TES - S 27 '96 - p12* [51-250]
Brook, Elaine - *In Search of Shambhala*
    TLS - D 13 '96 - p30 [501+]
Brook, Leslie C - *Two Late Medieval Love Treatises*
    MLR - v92 - Ap '97 - p460+ [251-500]
Brook, Stephen - *The Club*
    TES - Jl 5 '96 - p7* [51-250]

Brooke, John Hedley - *Thinking about Matter*
    J Chem Ed - v73 - Ag '96 - pA177+ [251-500]
Brooke, John L - *The Refiner's Fire*
    JIH - v27 - Aut '96 - p329+ [501+]
    JR - v76 - O '96 - p647+ [501+]
Brooke, Marcus - *Scotland*
    r BL - v93 - S 15 '96 - p210 [1-50]
Brooke, Stephen - *Reform and Reconstruction*
    HRNB - v25 - Fall '96 - p24 [251-500]
Brooke, Wendy - *European Consumer Market Information. 2nd Ed.*
    r LAR - v98 - O '96 - p534 [1-50]
Brooke, William - *Teller of Tales*
    c Emerg Lib - v24 - S '96 - p46 [51-250]
Brooker, Jewel Spears - *Mastery and Escape*
    ELT - v40 - 1 '97 - p89+ [501+]
    Univ Bkmn - v36 - Win '96 - p21+ [501+]
Brooker, Paul - *Twentieth-Century Dictatorship*
    AHR - v101 - O '96 - p1186+ [501+]
Brooker, Peter - *New York Fictions*
    Choice - v34 - S '96 - p122 [51-250]
Brooke-Rose, Christine - *Thru*
    WHR - v50 - Win '97 - p352+ [501+]
Brookes, Tim - *Signs of Life*
    BL - v93 - F 1 '97 - p911 [51-250]
    KR - v65 - Ja 1 '97 - p30 [251-500]
    LJ - v122 - F 1 '97 - p99 [51-250]
    PW - v244 - Ja 6 '97 - p55 [51-250]
Brookfield, Harold - *In Place of the Forest*
    Cont Pac - v9 - Spr '97 - p263+ [501+]
South-East Asia's Environmental Future
    Pac A - v69 - Sum '96 - p280+ [501+]
Brookhiser, Richard - *Founding Father*
    LATBR - Mr 24 '96 - p10 [51-250]
    NYTBR - v101 - D 8 '96 - p87 [1-50]
    PW - v244 - Ja 13 '97 - p73 [1-50]
    TLS - N 15 '96 - p5+ [501+]
    W&M Q - v53 - O '96 - p826+ [501+]
Brooking, Annie - *Intellectual Capital*
    Choice - v34 - Ap '97 - p1383 [501+]
Brookner, Anita - *Altered States*
    BL - v93 - N 1 '96 - p459 [51-250]
    KR - v64 - N 1 '96 - p1547 [251-500]
    LATBR - F 9 '97 - p4 [501+]
    LJ - v121 - D '96 - p141 [51-250]
    NL - v79 - D 16 '96 - p28+ [501+]
    NYTBR - v102 - Ja 26 '97 - p12 [501+]
    PW - v243 - N 11 '96 - p55+ [51-250]
    TES - Jl 26 '96 - p18 [51-250]
    TES - D 27 '96 - p16+ [51-250]
    WSJ-Cent - v99 - F 25 '97 - pA20 [251-500]
Fraud (Massey). Audio Version
    y Kliatt - v31 - Ja '97 - p41 [51-250]
Incidents in the Rue Laugier
    NYTBR - v102 - Mr 16 '97 - p32 [51-250]
    PW - v243 - D 30 '96 - p64 [1-50]
    WLT - v71 - Win '97 - p150 [501+]
Look at Me
    LJ - v122 - My 1 '97 - p145 [1-50]
    NYTBR - v102 - Mr 16 '97 - p32 [51-250]
A Private View (Whale). Audio Version
    LJ - v122 - Ap 1 '97 - p145+ [51-250]
Brooks, Alan - *Frogs Jump (Illus. by Steven Kellogg)*
    c CBRS - v25 - N '96 - p25 [1-50]
    c Emerg Lib - v24 - Mr '97 - p44 [1-50]
    c HB Guide - v8 - Spr '97 - p21 [51-250]
    c PW - v243 - O 7 '96 - p73 [51-250]
    c SLJ - v42 - O '96 - p85 [51-250]
Brooks, Anathea - *Our Coastal Seas, What Is Their Future?*
    J Gov Info - v23 - S '96 - p585 [51-250]
Brooks, Anna - *Friendly Street New Poets Two*
    Aust Bk R - Jl '96 - p57 [251-500]
Brooks, Barbara - *The Scared Child*
    PW - v243 - S 2 '96 - p124+ [51-250]
Brooks, Bruce - *Asylum for Nightface*
    y Emerg Lib - v23 - My '96 - p43 [1-50]
    y HB - v72 - S '96 - p601+ [51-250]
    y HB Guide - v7 - Fall '96 - p300 [51-250]
    y HMR - Fall '96 - p36+ [501+]
    y JAAL - v40 - S '96 - p72 [51-250]
    c KR - v64 - My 1 '96 - p685 [251-500]
    y VOYA - v19 - O '96 - p206 [251-500]
The Moves Make the Man
    y JAAL - v40 - S '96 - p318 [51-250]
The Moves Make the Man (James). Audio Version
    y BL - v93 - My 15 '97 - p1595 [1-50]
NBA by the Numbers
    c BL - v93 - Mr 1 '97 - p1168+ [51-250]

Brooks, Charles E - *Frontier Settlement and Market Revolution*
    Choice - v34 - S '96 - p192 [51-250]
    JEH - v57 - Mr '97 - p248+ [501+]
Brooks, Cleanth - *Community, Religion, Literature*
    Col Lit - v23 - Je '96 - p192+ [501+]
Brooks, Clifford W - *System for Ophthalmic Dispensing. 2nd Ed.*
    SciTech - v20 - D '96 - p50 [51-250]
Brooks, David - *Backward and Upward*
    Econ - v340 - S 14 '96 - p3*+ [501+]
Brooks, David, 1947- - *The Age of Upheaval*
    Albion - v28 - Fall '96 - p524+ [501+]
    Historian - v59 - Win '97 - p459+ [251-500]
Brooks, David C - *Current Review of Laparoscopy. 2nd Ed.*
    SciTech - v20 - S '96 - p37 [51-250]
Brooks, Guy - *Vietnam: A Kick Start Guide for Business Travellers*
    Quill & Q - v62 - S '96 - p23 [51-250]
Brooks, Gwendolyn - *Report from Part Two*
    BW - v27 - F 16 '97 - p8 [51-250]
Brooks, James A - *A Morphology of New Testament Greek*
    Rel St Rev - v23 - Ap '97 - p173 [51-250]
Brooks, Karen - *Agricultural Reform in Russia*
    JEL - v34 - D '96 - p2125+ [51-250]
Brooks, Martha - *Traveling on into the Light*
    y Kliatt - v30 - S '96 - p22 [51-250]
Brooks, Maureen - *Tassie Terms*
    r Aust Bk R - Ag '96 - p67 [1-50]
Brooks, Peter - *Body Work*
    CLS - v33 - 4 '96 - p427+ [501+]
Law's Stories
    Choice - v34 - N '96 - p535+ [51-250]
    New R - v215 - D 9 '96 - p27+ [501+]
Brooks, Philip - *Steffi Graf: Tennis Champ*
    c HB Guide - v7 - Fall '96 - p359 [1-50]
United States
    c HB Guide - v7 - Fall '96 - p359 [51-250]
    c SLJ - v42 - N '96 - p112 [51-250]
The United States Holocaust Memorial Museum
    c HB Guide - v8 - Spr '97 - p167 [51-250]
Brooks, Roger - *Hebrew Bible or Old Testament*
    Rel Ed - v91 - Fall '96 - p601 [1-50]
Unanswered Questions
    Rel Ed - v91 - Fall '96 - p608 [1-50]
Brooks, Roy L - *Integration or Separation?*
    Choice - v34 - My '97 - p1582 [51-250]
Brooks, Susan - *The Geography of the Earth*
    c HB Guide - v7 - Fall '96 - p377 [51-250]
    c SB - v32 - N '96 - p243 [51-250]
    y SLJ - v42 - Ag '96 - p167 [51-250]
Brooks, Terry - *First King Shannara*
    y VOYA - v19 - O '96 - p216 [251-500]
Witches' Brew
    y Kliatt - v30 - S '96 - p15+ [51-250]
Brooks, Thomas R - *The War North of Rome June 1944-May 1945*
    Choice - v34 - Ja '97 - p854+ [51-250]
Brooks, W S - *The Dramatic Criticism of Elizabeth Charlotte, Duchesse D'Orleans*
    FR - v70 - Mr '97 - p596+ [501+]
Brooks, William - *The Oyster*
    New Sci - v152 - D 14 '96 - p44 [51-250]
Brook-Shepherd, Gordon - *The Austrians: A Thousand-Year Odyssey*
    BL - v93 - Ap 1 '97 - p1277 [51-250]
    KR - v65 - F 15 '97 - p264+ [51-250]
    LJ - v122 - Ap 1 '97 - p105 [51-250]
    PW - v244 - F 17 '97 - p200 [51-250]
    WSJ-Cent - v99 - Ap 16 '97 - pA16 [501+]
Brooman, Josh - *Longman History Project Germany 1918-45*
    y TES - S 6 '96 - pR6 [501+]
Broome, Errol - *Fly with Me (Illus. by Jane Walker)*
    c Magpies - v11 - S '96 - p29 [51-250]
Splashback: A Great Greasy Journey
    c Magpies - v11 - Jl '96 - p29 [51-250]
Broomfield, Andrea - *Prose by Victorian Women*
    Choice - v34 - S '96 - p129 [51-250]
    ELT - v40 - 3 '96 - p406 [51-250]
    Nine-C Lit - v51 - D '96 - p419 [1-50]
Broomhead, Frank - *The Book Illustrations of Orlando Jewitt*
    BC - v45 - Aut '96 - p412+ [501+]
Brooten, Bernadette J - *Love between Women*
    Wom R Bks - v14 - Mr '97 - p15+ [501+]
Brophy, Jere E - *Teaching Problem Students*
    R&R Bk N - v11 - D '96 - p55 [51-250]

Brophy, Peter - *Case Studies in Opportunities for Libraries in Europe*
   LAR - v98 - Ag '96 - p425 [251-500]
Quality Management for Information and Library Managers
   LAR - v98 - Jl '96 - p373 [251-500]
   LR - v45 - 8 '96 - p49+ [501+]
   R&R Bk N - v12 - F '97 - p102 [51-250]
Brophy, Robert - *Robinson Jeffers: Dimensions of a Poet*
   RMR - v50 - 2 '96 - p214+ [501+]
Broquard, Vic - *Programming with MFC for Windows 95*
   SciTech - v20 - N '96 - p10 [51-250]
Brosius, Maria - *Women in Ancient Persia 559-331 BC*
   Choice - v34 - S '96 - p182 [51-250]
   HRNB - v25 - Fall '96 - p40 [251-500]
Brosman, Catharine Savage - *Dictionary of Twentieth Century Culture*
   r FR - v70 - O '96 - p129+ [251-500]
Brosnahan, Tom - *New England: A Lonely Planet Travel Survival Kit*
   r LJ - v122 - F 1 '97 - p98 [51-250]
Brossard, Nicole - *Baroque D'Aube*
   WLT - v70 - Aut '96 - p905+ [501+]
Brosterman, Norman - *Inventing Kindergarten*
   PW - v244 - Mr 31 '97 - p52 [51-250]
Brothers, Barbara, 1937- - *British Travel Writers 1837-1875*
   r ARBA - v28 - '97 - p448+ [251-500]
Brothers, Barbara Jo - *Couples: Building Bridges*
   SciTech - v20 - S '96 - p33 [51-250]
Brothers, Barbara Jo, 1940- - *Couples and Change*
   SciTech - v21 - Mr '97 - p54 [51-250]
Broude, Gwen J - *Growing Up*
   r ARBA - v28 - '97 - p321 [251-500]
   yr SLJ - v42 - Ag '96 - p167 [51-250]
Broude, Norma - *The Power of Feminist Art*
   BM - v139 - Ja '97 - p53 [51-250]
   PW - v243 - O 7 '96 - p69 [1-50]
Brouillet, Chrystine - *The Chinese Puzzle*
   c Quill & Q - v62 - My '96 - p34 [51-250]
No Orchids for Andrea! (Illus. by Nathalie Gagnon)
   c Ch BWatch - v6 - N '96 - p3 [51-250]
   c Quill & Q - v62 - N '96 - p48 [51-250]
Brouillette, Liane - *A Geology of School Reform*
   Choice - v34 - Mr '97 - p1211 [51-250]
Broussard, Cheryl D - *Sister CEO*
   BL - v93 - F 15 '97 - p983 [51-250]
   BWatch - v18 - Mr '97 - p3 [51-250]
   LJ - v122 - Ja '97 - p114 [51-250]
   PW - v243 - D 9 '96 - p57 [51-250]
Broussard, Yves - *La Vie Interpretee*
   WLT - v70 - Aut '96 - p913 [251-500]
Brouwer, Frans - *Ars Et Musica In Liturgia*
   Notes - v53 - S '96 - p68+ [501+]
Brouwer, Sigmund - *Blood Ties*
   y BL - v93 - S 1 '96 - p65 [501+]
Thunderbird Spirit
   c Quill & Q - v62 - My '96 - p34 [51-250]
Brouwers, Jeroen - *Rouge Decante*
   WLT - v70 - Sum '96 - p708 [501+]
Brower, Sidney - *Good Neighborhoods*
   Choice - v34 - My '97 - p1582 [51-250]
Brown, A L - *Vehicle Security Systems*
   SciTech - v20 - S '96 - p58 [51-250]
Brown, A L, 1927- - *The University of Glasgow 1451-1996*
   TLS - N 22 '96 - p31 [251-500]
Brown, Alan - *King of the Dark Tower (Illus. by Peter Melnyczuk)*
   c Sch Lib - v45 - F '97 - p23 [51-250]
Brown, Alan, 1950- - *Audrey Hepburn's Neck*
   LATBR - Mr 24 '96 - p6 [501+]
   LJ - v121 - O 1 '96 - p46+ [1-50]
   PW - v244 - F 3 '97 - p102 [1-50]
   Rapport - v19 - 4 '96 - p27 [251-500]
   y SLJ - v42 - Ag '96 - p184 [51-250]
Brown, Alan W - *Component-Based Software Engineering*
   SciTech - v21 - Mr '97 - p8 [51-250]
Brown, Alexandra R - *The Cross and Human Transformation*
   Rel St Rev - v23 - Ja '97 - p74 [51-250]
Brown, Alice - *Politics and Society in Scotland*
   TLS - S 20 '96 - p12 [501+]
Brown, Andrew D - *Popular Piety in Late Medieval England*
   AHR - v101 - D '96 - p1536+ [501+]
   Albion - v28 - Sum '96 - p291+ [501+]
   CHR - v82 - Jl '96 - p549+ [501+]
   Rel St Rev - v23 - Ap '97 - p190 [51-250]

Brown, Andrew J - *William Tyndale on Priests and Preachers*
   TLS - O 4 '96 - p40 [251-500]
Brown, Anne Gassaway - *A La Decouverte Du Petit Prince*
   FR - v70 - D '96 - p362+ [251-500]
Brown, Anthony - *Willy and Hugh*
   c Par Ch - v20 - N '96 - p8 [51-250]
Brown, Anthony F T - *Accident and Emergency. 3rd Ed.*
   SciTech - v20 - N '96 - p40 [51-250]
Brown, Archie - *The Cambridge Encyclopedia of Russia and the Former Soviet Union. 2nd Ed.*
   r BL - v92 - Ag '96 - p1920 [51-250]
   r GJ - v162 - Jl '96 - p223+ [251-500]
The Gorbachev Factor
   BAS - v53 - Ja '97 - p65+ [501+]
   Econ - v341 - N 16 '96 - p8* [51-250]
   For Aff - v75 - N '96 - p161+ [251-500]
   NYRB - v43 - D 19 '96 - p34+ [501+]
Brown, Arthur I - *The Antievolution Works of Arthur I. Brown*
   Isis - v88 - Mr '97 - p160+ [501+]
Brown, Azby - *Small Spaces*
   LJ - v121 - S 15 '96 - p66 [51-250]
Brown, Barbara J - *The Good Detective's Guide to Library Research*
   r LAR - v98 - Je '96 - p321 [51-250]
Brown, Beverly - *The Travelling Pillow (Illus. by Margot Jane Ott)*
   c Ch BWatch - v6 - Jl '96 - p4 [51-250]
Brown, Brenda Lea - *Bringing It Home*
   CF - v75 - Mr '97 - p38+ [501+]
Brown, Bruce Alan - *W.A. Mozart: Cosi Fan Tutte*
   Choice - v34 - Ja '97 - p804+ [51-250]
Brown, C J - *Cattle on a Thousand Hills*
   Choice - v34 - F '97 - p982 [51-250]
Brown, Canter, Jr. - *Fort Meade 1849-1900*
   JSH - v63 - F '97 - p176+ [501+]
Brown, Charles Brockden - *Edgar Huntly*
   Eight-C St - v29 - Sum '96 - p413+ [501+]
Brown, Charles R - *Coloniality in the Cliff Swallow*
   Choice - v34 - N '96 - p484 [51-250]
   SciTech - v20 - S '96 - p21 [51-250]
Brown, Christopher, 1948- - *Rubens's Landscapes*
   BM - v139 - Ja '97 - p54+ [501+]
   Choice - v34 - My '97 - p1485 [51-250]
Brown, Christopher L T - *Web Site Construction Kit for Windows NT*
   SciTech - v21 - Mr '97 - p89 [51-250]
Brown, Clair - *American Standards of Living 1918-1988*
   JEL - v34 - S '96 - p1376+ [501+]
   NYRB - v44 - Mr 6 '97 - p19+ [501+]
Brown, Clifford M - *Tapestries for the Courts of Federico II Ercole and Ferrante Gonzaga 1522-63*
   Apo - v144 - D '96 - p68+ [501+]
Brown, Clifford W - *Serious Money*
   Choice - v34 - O '96 - p362 [251-500]
   PSQ - v111 - Fall '96 - p529+ [501+]
Brown, Colin - *Fighting Talk*
   Books - v11 - Ap '97 - p20 [51-250]
   NS - v126 - Ja 31 '97 - p44+ [501+]
   Obs - F 2 '97 - p15* [501+]
   Spec - v278 - F 8 '97 - p43 [501+]
   TLS - F 28 '97 - p28 [501+]
Brown, Courtney - *Serpents in the Sand*
   AJS - v102 - Jl '96 - p286+ [501+]
   APSR - v91 - Mr '97 - p165+ [501+]
Brown, Craig McFarland - *Tractor (Illus. by Craig McFarland Brown)*
   c RT - v50 - Mr '97 - p500 [51-250]
Brown, Cynthia J - *Poets, Patrons, and Printers*
   MLR - v91 - O '96 - p988 [251-500]
Brown, Dale - *Fatal Terrain*
   KR - v65 - My 1 '97 - p659 [251-500]
Shadows of Steel (Foxworth). Audio Version
   y Kliatt - v30 - S '96 - p51+ [51-250]
Tiger in a Lion's Den
   Aethlon - v13 - Spr '96 - p209+ [501+]
Brown, Daniel W - *Rethinking Tradition in Modern Islamic Thought*
   Choice - v34 - My '97 - p1515 [51-250]
Brown, David, 1948, July, 7- - *Signs of Grace*
   RR - v55 - N '96 - p660 [51-250]
Brown, David, 1953- - *Whitman Juvenile Books*
   r Ant & CM - v101 - D '96 - p30 [1-50]
Brown, David J - *Electronic Publishing and Libraries*
   LR - v45 - 8 '96 - p54+ [501+]
Brown, David K - *Degrees of Control*
   CS - v26 - Mr '97 - p204+ [501+]
Brown, David Paul - *Sertorius, or, The Roman Patriot*
   J Am Cult - v19 - Spr '96 - p87+ [501+]

Brown, Dee Alexander - *The American West*
   WAL - v31 - Sum '96 - p173+ [251-500]
Best of Dee Brown's West
   LJ - v122 - Mr 15 '97 - p73 [51-250]
   PW - v244 - Ja 20 '97 - p388+ [51-250]
Brown, Don, 1949- - *Ruth Law Thrills a Nation (Illus. by Don Brown)*
   c SLJ - v42 - D '96 - p44 [51-250]
Brown, Dona - *Inventing New England*
   AHR - v101 - D '96 - p1619+ [251-500]
   JIH - v27 - Win '97 - p546+ [251-500]
   J Soc H - v30 - Fall '96 - p269+ [501+]
   NEQ - v69 - D '96 - p678+ [501+]
Brown, Edward Espe - *Tomato Blessings and Radish Teachings*
   LJ - v122 - Ap 15 '97 - p110 [51-250]
Brown, Eleanor - *Maiden Speech*
   y Sch Lib - v44 - N '96 - p167 [51-250]
Brown, Elizabeth A R - *The Lit De Justice*
   EHR - v111 - S '96 - p965+ [251-500]
Brown, Fern G - *Daisy and the Girl Scouts (Illus. by Marie DeJohn)*
   c HB Guide - v7 - Fall '96 - p371 [51-250]
Brown, Francis F - *History of the Roman Catholic Diocese of Steubenville, Ohio. Vol. 1*
   CLW - v67 - D '96 - p35+ [251-500]
Brown, Frederick, 1934- - *Zola: A Life*
   Lon R Bks - v18 - S 5 '96 - p7+ [501+]
   NYTBR - v102 - Ja 12 '97 - p32 [51-250]
   Trib Bks - Ja 12 '97 - p2 [1-50]
Brown, Gene - *Movie Time*
   r CLW - v66 - Je '96 - p43 [51-250]
Brown, George Mackay - *Beside the Ocean of Time*
   Books - v9 - S '95 - p24 [1-50]
Following a Lark
   BL - v93 - N 1 '96 - p475 [51-250]
Selected Poems 1954-1992
   Atl - v278 - D '96 - p125 [51-250]
   BL - v93 - N 1 '96 - p475 [51-250]
   PW - v243 - S 30 '96 - p84 [51-250]
Winter Tales
   Woman's J - N '96 - p12 [1-50]
Brown, Grayson Warren - *Jesusgate*
   BL - v93 - Ja '97 - p819 [51-250]
   LJ - v121 - N 1 '96 - p52 [51-250]
Brown, Harry L - *Energy Analysis of 108 Industrial Processes*
   r SciTech - v20 - D '96 - p72 [51-250]
Brown, Howard G - *War, Revolution, and the Bureaucratic State*
   J Mil H - v61 - Ap '97 - p374+ [251-500]
Brown, Hunter - *Images of the Human*
   CLW - v66 - Je '96 - p41 [51-250]
   IPQ - v37 - Je '97 - p244+ [251-500]
Brown, Iem - *Di Serambi*
   WLT - v70 - Aut '96 - p1032 [501+]
Brown, J Carter - *Rings: Five Passions in World Art*
   AB - v99 - Mr 3 '97 - p698+ [501+]
   BW - v26 - D 8 '96 - p10 [51-250]
Brown, J P S - *The Outfit*
   WAL - v31 - Win '97 - p415+ [251-500]
Brown, James D - *The Elements of Language Curriculum*
   MLJ - v80 - Win '96 - p532+ [501+]
Brown, Jane, 1938- - *Lutyens and the Edwardians*
   CR - v269 - S '96 - p165+ [51-250]
   KR - v64 - O 1 '96 - p1437 [251-500]
   LJ - v121 - N 1 '96 - p63 [51-250]
   Spec - v276 - My 18 '96 - p41 [251-500]
Brown, Jane K, 1943- - *Faust: Theater of the World*
   Ger Q - v69 - Sum '96 - p351+ [501+]
Interpreting Goethe's Faust Today
   Ger Q - v69 - Spr '96 - p210+ [501+]
Brown, Jared - *The Theatre in America during the Revolution*
   AL - v69 - Mr '97 - p255 [51-250]
   Theat J - v49 - Mr '97 - p91+ [501+]
Brown, Jason W - *Time, Will, and Mental Process*
   Choice - v34 - N '96 - p541 [51-250]
Brown, Jean - *Traditional Metalworking in Kenya*
   Choice - v34 - O '96 - p322 [51-250]
Brown, Jean E, 1945- - *Exploring Diversity*
   SLMQ - v24 - Sum '96 - p221 [51-250]
   VOYA - v19 - O '96 - p242 [51-250]
Brown, Jeff - *Invisible Stanley (Illus. by Steve Bjorkman)*
   c Bks Keeps - v100 - S '96 - p10 [51-250]
   c SLJ - v42 - D '96 - p85 [51-250]
Brown, Jeffrey - *Indian Air Mails*
   Phil Lit R - v45 - '96 - p345+ [251-500]
Brown, Jennifer S H - *Reading Beyond Words*
   Choice - v34 - Ap '97 - p1407 [51-250]

Brown, Jeremy Houghton - *Horse and Stable Management. 2nd Ed.*
   SciTech - v20 - D '96 - p57 [51-250]
Brown, Jeremy M - *Explaining the Reagan Years in Central America*
   HAHR - v77 - My '97 - p362 [251-500]
Brown, John Gregory - *The Wrecked, Blessed Body of Shelton Lafleur*
   BW - v26 - Jl 7 '96 - p7 [501+]
 y SLJ - v42 - Ag '96 - p184 [51-250]
   TLS - O 11 '96 - p24 [251-500]
   Trib Bks - Mr 23 '97 - p6 [1-50]
Brown, John K - *The Baldwin Locomotive Works 1831-1915*
   JEH - v57 - Mr '97 - p250+ [501+]
   Pub Hist - v19 - Win '97 - p115+ [501+]
Brown, John Russell - *The Oxford Illustrated History of Theatre*
   R&R Bk N - v11 - D '96 - p62 [51-250]
   Theat J - v48 - O '96 - p394+ [501+]
William Shakespeare: Writing for Performance
   Choice - v34 - My '97 - p467 [51-250]
   R&R Bk N - v11 - N '96 - p69 [51-250]
Brown, Jonathan, 1939- - *Kings and Connoisseurs*
   BM - v138 - Ag '96 - p549 [501+]
   Six Ct J - v27 - Fall '96 - p914+ [501+]
Picasso and the Spanish Tradition
   Choice - v34 - Ap '97 - p1325+ [51-250]
   Lon R Bks - v19 - Mr 6 '97 - p3+ [501+]
Brown, Jonathon, 1955- - *Claude Debussy: An Essential Guide to His Life and Work*
 y BL - v93 - My 1 '97 - p1472 [51-250]
Johannes Brahms: An Essential Guide to His Life and Work
 y BL - v93 - My 1 '97 - p1472 [51-250]
Brown, Joseph E - *Lure of the Sea*
   CSM - v88 - N 21 '96 - pB1 [1-50]
 y Kliatt - v31 - Ja '97 - p29+ [251-500]
 y SB - v33 - Ja '97 - p14 [51-250]
Brown, Judith M - *Migration: The Asian Experience*
   EHR - v112 - Ap '97 - p543+ [251-500]
Brown, Judith R - *The I in Science*
   Choice - v34 - O '96 - p363 [51-250]
Brown, Jules - *Hong Kong and Macau*
 r FEER - v160 - Mr 27 '97 - p51 [501+]
Brown, Karen, 1952, Feb, 2- - *Kids Are Cookin'*
 c PW - v244 - Ap 21 '97 - p74 [501+]
Brown, Karen B - *Taxing America*
   Choice - v34 - My '97 - p1550 [51-250]
Brown, Kathan - *Ink, Paper, Metal, Wood*
   LATBR - D 8 '96 - p29 [1-50]
   LJ - v121 - O 15 '96 - p54 [51-250]
Brown, Katrina - *The Causes of Tropical Deforestation*
   Econ J - v106 - S '96 - p1483 [51-250]
   GJ - v163 - Mr '97 - p107+ [251-500]
Brown, Kenneth A - *Four Corners*
   Bloom Rev - v16 - Jl '96 - p16 [51-250]
 y Kliatt - v31 - Ja '97 - p27 [251-500]
   LATBR - D 22 '96 - p6 [51-250]
Brown, Kurt - *Facing the Lion*
   Bloom Rev - v17 - Ja '97 - p14 [51-250]
Brown, L V - *Applied Principles of Horticultural Science*
   SciTech - v21 - Mr '97 - p70 [1-50]
Brown, Larry - *Facing the Music*
   Trib Bks - Ja 19 '97 - p8 [1-50]
Father and Son
   Am - v176 - Ap 5 '97 - p32+ [501+]
   BWatch - v17 - D '96 - p6 [51-250]
   NY - v72 - Ja 27 '97 - p76 [51-250]
   NYTBR - v101 - S 22 '96 - p11 [501+]
   PW - v243 - N 4 '96 - p37 [51-250]
   S Liv - v31 - N '96 - p48 [51-250]
   VLS - S '96 - p13 [501+]
   W&I - v11 - D '96 - p260+ [501+]
Joe (Brown). Audio Version
   S Liv - v31 - Jl '96 - p80 [51-250]
Joe (Stechschulte). Audio Version
   BWatch - v17 - D '96 - p10+ [1-50]
On Fire (Sala). Audio Version
   LJ - v122 - F 15 '97 - p115 [1-50]
Brown, Laurene Krasny - *Rex and Lilly Schooltime (Illus. by Marc Brown)*
 c BL - v93 - My 1 '97 - p1503 [51-250]
 c KR - v65 - Ap 1 '97 - p562 [51-250]
 c PW - v244 - Mr 17 '97 - p85 [51-250]
When Dinosaurs Die (Illus. by Marc Brown)
 c CLW - v67 - Mr '97 - p57 [51-250]
 c HB - v72 - S '96 - p608 [51-250]
 c HB Guide - v7 - Fall '96 - p307 [51-250]
 c PW - v243 - N 4 '96 - p49 [51-250]

Brown, Laurie M - *The Origin of the Concept of Nuclear Forces*
   Choice - v34 - My '97 - p1538 [51-250]
   SciTech - v21 - Mr '97 - p25 [51-250]
Twentieth Century Physics. Vols. 1-3
   S&T - v92 - N '96 - p57 [51-250]
Brown, Les, 1945- - *It's Not over Until You Win!*
   BL - v93 - N 15 '96 - p546 [51-250]
   PW - v243 - N 11 '96 - p65+ [51-250]
It's Not over Until You Win! (Brown). Audio Version
   BWatch - v18 - Mr '97 - p6 [1-50]
Brown, Lester Russell, 1934- - *Tough Choices*
   Nat - v264 - Mr 3 '97 - p29+ [501+]
   SB - v33 - Ja '97 - p6 [251-500]
Who Will Feed China?
   TLS - O 25 '96 - p3+ [501+]
Brown, Linda Beatrice - *Crossing over Jordan*
   NYTBR - v101 - Ag 25 '96 - p28 [1-50]
Brown, Lloyd L - *The Young Paul Robeson*
   KR - v64 - N 15 '96 - p1646 [251-500]
   PW - v243 - D 2 '96 - p45 [51-250]
Brown, Lyle - *Flynn: Whirlpool. Audio Version*
   BWatch - v17 - D '96 - p11 [1-50]
Brown, Malcolm - *The Imperial War Museum Book of the Somme*
   Spec - v277 - N 23 '96 - p46 [1-50]
   TLS - O 11 '96 - p5 [501+]
Brown, Marc - *Arthur Babysits (Illus. by Marc Brown). Book and Audio Version*
 c SLJ - v42 - Ag '96 - p64 [51-250]
Arthur Babysits (Illus. by Marc Brown)
 c PW - v244 - Mr 24 '97 - p85 [1-50]
Arthur Goes to School (Illus. by Marc Brown)
 c HB Guide - v7 - Fall '96 - p237 [51-250]
Arthur Meets the President (Brown) (Illus. by Marc Brown). Book and Audio Version
 c SLJ - v42 - Ag '96 - p64 [51-250]
Arthur Mini Play Book
 c PW - v244 - Mr 10 '97 - p68 [51-250]
Arthur Writes a Story (Illus. by Marc Brown)
 c BL - v93 - S 15 '96 - p245 [51-250]
 c HB Guide - v8 - Spr '97 - p21 [51-250]
 c Inst - v106 - N '96 - p25 [51-250]
 c SLJ - v42 - S '96 - p171 [51-250]
Arthur's New Puppy
 c PW - v244 - Mr 24 '97 - p85 [1-50]
Arthur's Reading Race (Illus. by Marc Brown)
 c HB Guide - v7 - Fall '96 - p283 [51-250]
Arthur's Reading Race. Electronic Media Version
 c PW - v244 - Ja 27 '97 - p38 [51-250]
Arthur's Teacher Trouble. Electronic Media Version
 c HB - v73 - Mr '97 - p219+ [501+]
Wings on Things
 c Ch BWatch - v6 - O '96 - p1 [51-250]
 c HB Guide - v8 - Spr '97 - p55 [51-250]
Brown, Marcia - *Touch and Tell*
 c Inst - v106 - S '96 - p92 [1-50]
Brown, Margaret Wise - *A Child's Good Morning Book (Illus. by Jean Charlot)*
 c HB Guide - v7 - Fall '96 - p237 [51-250]
 c Par - v71 - S '96 - p209 [51-250]
Goodnight Moon (Illus. by Clement Hurd)
 c HB - v73 - Mr '97 - p186 [1-50]
Goodnight Moon: A 50th Anniversary Retrospective (Illus. by Clement Hurd)
 c PW - v244 - F 3 '97 - p108 [51-250]
El Gran Granero Rojo (Illus. by Felicia Bond)
 c HB Guide - v8 - Spr '97 - p107 [51-250]
 c SLJ - v42 - Ag '96 - p178 [51-250]
On Christmas Eve (Illus. by Nancy Edwards Calder)
 c BL - v93 - S 1 '96 - p135 [51-250]
 c HB Guide - v8 - Spr '97 - p21 [51-250]
 c PW - v243 - S 30 '96 - p90 [51-250]
 c SFR - v21 - N '96 - p47 [51-250]
 c SLJ - v42 - O '96 - p34 [51-250]
A Pussycat's Christmas (Illus. by Anne Mortimer)
 c Bks Keeps - N '96 - p21 [51-250]
The Sleepy Men (Illus. by Robert Rayevsky)
 c BL - v93 - O 1 '96 - p357 [51-250]
 c CCB-B - v50 - Ja '97 - p165 [51-250]
 c HB Guide - v8 - Spr '97 - p21 [51-250]
 c SLJ - v42 - D '96 - p85 [51-250]
Brown, Margot - *Our World, Our Rights*
   WorldV - v13 - Ja '97 - p9+ [251-500]
Brown, Marshall - *The Uses of Literary History*
   VQR - v72 - Aut '96 - p118*+ [501+]
Brown, Martin - *Impacts of National Technology Programmes*
   J Gov Info - v23 - S '96 - p674 [51-250]

Brown, Meg Lota - *Donne and the Politics of Conscience in Early Modern England*
   Six Ct J - v27 - Fall '96 - p804+ [501+]
Brown, Michael - *James I*
   EHR - v112 - F '97 - p177+ [251-500]
Brown, Michael E - *Debating the Democratic Peace*
   For Aff - v75 - N '96 - p144 [51-250]
East Asian Security
   For Aff - v76 - Mr '97 - p198 [51-250]
The International Dimensions of Internal Conflict
   For Aff - v75 - S '96 - p136+ [51-250]
   WorldV - v12 - Jl '96 - p7+ [51-250]
Brown, Michael F - *The Channeling Zone*
   NYTBR - v102 - Mr 23 '97 - p24 [501+]
   Trib Bks - My 11 '97 - p9 [501+]
Brown, Michele - *Edward Bear Esq.*
   Ent W - Mr 7 '97 - p60 [51-250]
Brown, Michelle P - *The Book of Cerne*
   R&R Bk N - v11 - D '96 - p5 [51-250]
Understanding Illuminated Manuscripts
   AB - v99 - Mr 3 '97 - p685+ [501+]
Brown, Mildred L - *True Selves*
   BL - v93 - N 1 '96 - p463 [51-250]
Brown, Montague - *Integrated Health Care Delivery*
   SciTech - v20 - S '96 - p27 [51-250]
Brown, Montague, 1952- - *The Quest for Moral Foundations*
   Choice - v34 - N '96 - p473 [51-250]
   Hast Cen R - v26 - Jl '96 - p41 [51-250]
Brown, Morris - *Comprehensive Postanesthesia Care*
 r SciTech - v21 - Mr '97 - p59 [51-250]
Brown, Nicholas, 1961- - *Governing Prosperity*
   Arena - Ap '96 - p51+ [501+]
   Choice - v34 - O '96 - p336 [51-250]
Brown, Nina W - *Expressive Processes in Group Counseling*
   R&R Bk N - v11 - N '96 - p5 [51-250]
Brown, Oren L - *Discover Your Voice*
   R&R Bk N - v11 - N '96 - p59 [51-250]
Brown, Patricia Fortini - *Venice and Antiquity*
   LJ - v122 - F 15 '97 - p145 [51-250]
   NYTBR - v102 - Ap 20 '97 - p34 [51-250]
   Obs - F 23 '97 - p16* [501+]
Brown, Paul - *Global Warming*
   New Sci - v152 - N 2 '96 - p44 [1-50]
   Obs - Ja 19 '97 - p17* [501+]
   PW - v244 - Mr 17 '97 - p73 [51-250]
Brown, Paul Martin - *Wild Orchids of the Northeastern United States*
   BL - v93 - Mr 1 '97 - p1099 [51-250]
   LJ - v122 - Ap 1 '97 - p114 [51-250]
Brown, Paula, 1925- - *Beyond a Mountain Valley*
   Am Ethnol - v24 - F '97 - p264+ [501+]
Brown, Peter, 1948- - *Chaucer at Work*
   Specu - v72 - Ja '97 - p119+ [501+]
Brown, Peter Harry - *Howard Hughes: The Untold Story*
   PW - v244 - Ap 21 '97 - p69 [1-50]
Brown, Peter Robert Lamont - *Authority and the Sacred*
   JR - v77 - Ja '97 - p129+ [501+]
The Rise of Western Christendom
   HRNB - v25 - Fall '96 - p41 [251-500]
Brown, Philip, 1957- - *Higher Education and Corporate Realities*
   J Hi E - v67 - S '96 - p599+ [501+]
Brown, Raymond Edward - *The Death of the Messiah. Vols. 1-2*
   Bks & Cult - v1 - N '95 - p3+ [501+]
Reading the Gospels with the Church
   RR - v56 - Ja '97 - p105+ [1-50]
Brown, Rebecca - *The Gifts of the Body (Brown). Audio Version*
   LJ - v122 - Ap 1 '97 - p144 [51-250]
What Keeps Me Here
   LATBR - O 13 '96 - p4 [501+]
   Ms - v7 - S '96 - p83 [1-50]
   NYTBR - v102 - Ja 26 '97 - p18 [51-250]
   SFR - v21 - S '96 - p4 [251-500]
Brown, Richard - *Encouraging Reading*
   TES - D 13 '96 - p43 [51-250]
Brown, Richard D - *The Strength of a People*
   HRNB - v25 - Fall '96 - p4 [251-500]
   NEQ - v70 - Mr '97 - p166+ [501+]
Brown, Richard E - *The Rose Engagement*
   LJ - v122 - Ap '97 - p153 [51-250]
Brown, Richard Harvey - *Postmodern Representations*
   CS - v25 - S '96 - p703+ [501+]
Brown, Richard W - *Richard Brown's New England*
   CSM - v89 - D 5 '96 - pB2 [51-250]

Brown, Rita Mae - *Murder, She Meowed*
    BL - v93 - O 1 '96 - p324 [51-250]
    KR - v64 - O 15 '96 - p1494 [51-250]
    NYTBR - v101 - D 8 '96 - p50 [51-250]
    PW - v243 - O 14 '96 - p67+ [51-250]
    y SLJ - v43 - Mr '97 - p214 [51-250]
  Pay Dirt
    PW - v243 - S 23 '96 - p74 [1-50]
  Riding Shotgun
    Advocate - Ja 21 '97 - p94 [1-50]
Brown, Robert A, 1946- - *The Golfing Mind*
    LJ - v121 - O 1 '96 - p53 [1-50]
Brown, Robert Alan, 1934- - *Endeavour Views the Earth*
    c Astron - v25 - My '97 - p114 [1-50]
    c SB - v33 - Mr '97 - p48 [51-250]
Brown, Robert Craig - *The Illustrated History of Canada. 2nd Rev. Ed.*
    Beav - v76 - O '96 - p46 [51-250]
Brown, Robert D - *Microclimatic Landscape Design*
    New Sci - v151 - S 28 '96 - p48 [51-250]
Brown, Rodger Lyle - *Ghost Dancing on the Cracker Circuit*
    LJ - v122 - Ap 1 '97 - p113 [51-250]
Brown, Roger H - *Redeeming the Republic*
    AHR - v102 - F '97 - p170 [251-500]
Brown, Roger Lee - *A History of the Fleet Prison, London*
    Choice - v34 - Ap '97 - p1396 [51-250]
Brown, Royal S - *Overtones and Undertones*
    FQ - v49 - Sum '96 - p51+ [501+]
    J Film & Vid - v48 - Win '96 - p57+ [501+]
Brown, Ruth - *The Ghost of Greyfriar's Bobby (Illus. by Ruth Brown)*
    c CCB-B - v50 - S '96 - p6 [51-250]
    c HB Guide - v7 - Fall '96 - p249 [1-50]
    c RT - v50 - Ap '97 - p594 [51-250]
    c SLJ - v42 - Ag '96 - p133 [51-250]
  Greyfriars Bobby
    c Books - v9 - S '95 - p26 [1-50]
  The Tale of the Monstrous Toad (Illus. by Ruth Brown)
    c JB - v60 - D '96 - p226+ [51-250]
    c Sch Lib - v44 - N '96 - p145 [51-250]
  Toad (Illus. by Ruth Brown)
    c BL - v93 - Ja '97 - p856 [51-250]
    c CCB-B - v50 - Mr '97 - p242 [51-250]
    c KR - v64 - D 1 '96 - p1734 [51-250]
    c SLJ - v43 - Mr '97 - p149 [51-250]
Brown, Ruth, 1928- - *Miss Rhythm*
    CAY - v17 - Win '96 - p2 [51-250]
Brown, Sandra - *Exclusive*
    KR - v64 - My 1 '96 - p619 [251-500]
    y SLJ - v42 - D '96 - p150 [51-250]
  Exclusive (Crosby). Audio Version
    y Kliatt - v30 - N '96 - p40 [51-250]
  Fat Tuesday
    BL - v93 - Ap 1 '97 - p1268 [51-250]
    KR - v65 - Ap 1 '97 - p479 [251-500]
    LJ - v122 - My 1 '97 - p136 [51-250]
    PW - v244 - Mr 31 '97 - p58+ [51-250]
Brown, Stanley A - *Medical Applications of Titanium and Its Alloys*
    SciTech - v20 - D '96 - p37 [51-250]
Brown, Sterling A - *A Son's Return*
    BL - v93 - Ja '97 - p811 [51-250]
    LJ - v121 - S 15 '96 - p68 [51-250]
    PW - v243 - O 7 '96 - p67 [51-250]
Brown, Steven D - *Computer Assisted Analytical Spectroscopy*
    SciTech - v20 - D '96 - p27 [51-250]
Brown, Stewart, 1951- - *The Art of Kamau Brathwaite*
    WLT - v71 - Win '97 - p202+ [501+]
Brown, Stuart - *Biographical Dictionary of Twentieth-Century Philosophers*
    r ARBA - v28 - '97 - p528 [51-250]
    r Choice - v34 - D '96 - p586 [51-250]
    r R&R Bk N - v11 - N '96 - p76 [51-250]
Brown, Sue - *Espanol Iningun*
    TES - Mr 7 '97 - pR10 [251-500]
Brown, Susan E - *Better Bones, Better Body*
    BWatch - v17 - S '96 - p10 [1-50]
Brown, Susan M - *You're Dead, David Borelli*
    y Emerg Lib - v24 - S '96 - p26 [1-50]
Brown, Theodore L - *Chemistry: The Central Science. 7th Ed.*
    J Chem Ed - v74 - Ap '97 - p378+ [501+]
Brown, Tom, 1950- - *Grandfather: A Native American's Lifelong Search for Truth and Harmony with Nature*
    Parabola - v22 - F '97 - p120 [1-50]
Brown, Wendy - *States of Injury*
    Bks & Cult - v2 - S '96 - p38+ [251-500]
    CS - v26 - Ja '97 - p120+ [501+]
    RP - v58 - Fall '96 - p847+ [501+]

Brown, Wesley - *The Teachers and Writers Guide to Frederick Douglass*
    Cont Ed - v67 - Sum '96 - p255+ [501+]
Brown, William Wells - *Clotel or the President's Daughter*
    Bl S - v26 - Fall '96 - p100 [51-250]
Brown, Wm. S - *Organic Voice Disorders*
    SciTech - v21 - Mr '97 - p62 [51-250]
The Brown Journal of World Affairs
    p WorldV - v12 - Jl '96 - p11 [51-250]
Browne, Anthony - *Look What I've Got (Illus. by Anthony Browne)*
    c Bks Keeps - Jl '96 - p7+ [51-250]
  Willy the Wizard (Illus. by Anthony Browne)
    c Bks Keeps - v100 - S '96 - p10 [51-250]
    c HB Guide - v7 - Fall '96 - p249 [51-250]
    c SLJ - v42 - D '96 - p28 [51-250]
Browne, E J - *Charles Darwin: A Biography. Vol. 1*
    CR - v269 - D '96 - p333 [1-50]
    y Kliatt - v30 - S '96 - p25+ [51-250]
    NYTBR - v101 - S 15 '96 - p44 [1-50]
    Skeptic - v4 - '96 - p107 [51-250]
Browne, Eileen - *Handa's Surprise*
    c Bks Keeps - Mr '97 - p7 [51-250]
  Tick-Tock (Illus. by David Parkins)
    c Bks Keeps - v100 - S '96 - p9 [51-250]
Browne, Gerald A - *West 47th*
    BW - v26 - Ag 4 '96 - p8 [51-250]
    Rapport - v19 - 4 '96 - p27 [251-500]
Browne, John - *Building of Faith*
    BM - v138 - Ag '96 - p550+ [501+]
Browne, Marshall - *The Gilded Cage*
    Aust Bk R - N '96 - p66+ [51-250]
Browne, Nick - *Cahiers Du Cinema. Vol. 3*
    TLS - Ja 17 '97 - p4+ [501+]
  New Chinese Cinemas
    FQ - v49 - Fall '95 - p57+ [501+]
    TLS - S 27 '96 - p32 [251-500]
Browne, Philippa-Alys - *African Animals ABC (Illus. by Philippa-Alys Browne)*
    c RT - v50 - Mr '97 - p500 [51-250]
  A Gaggle of Geese
    c HB Guide - v7 - Fall '96 - p249 [51-250]
  Kangaroos Have Joeys (Illus. by Philippa-Alys Browne)
    c BL - v93 - N 1 '96 - p502+ [51-250]
    c HB Guide - v8 - Spr '97 - p116 [51-250]
    c KR - v64 - S 1 '96 - p1319 [51-250]
    c SLJ - v42 - N '96 - p96 [51-250]
Browne, William P - *Cultivating Congress*
    AAPSS-A - v549 - Ja '97 - p187+ [501+]
    J Pol - v58 - N '96 - p1222+ [501+]
    SSQ - v78 - Mr '97 - p244+ [501+]
Brownell, Susan - *Training the Body for China*
    Ch Rev Int - v3 - Fall '96 - p367+ [501+]
    CS - v26 - Mr '97 - p245+ [501+]
    J Am Cult - v19 - Sum '96 - p141 [51-250]
    R&R Bk N - v11 - N '96 - p23 [51-250]
    TDR - v40 - Fall '96 - p203 [51-250]
Browner, Jesse - *Turnaway*
    NYTBR - v101 - Ag 25 '96 - p22 [51-250]
Brown-Guillory, Elizabeth - *Women of Color*
    BWatch - v18 - Mr '97 - p3 [51-250]
Browning, Barbara - *Samba: Resistance in Motion*
    Bl S - v26 - Sum '96 - p64 [1-50]
    TDR - v40 - Win '96 - p164+ [501+]
Browning, Charles H - *How to Partner with Managed Care*
    r SciTech - v20 - D '96 - p45 [51-250]
Browning, Graeme - *Electronic Democracy*
    LJ - v121 - O 1 '96 - p120 [51-250]
Browning, Robert - *The Complete Works of Robert Browning. Vol. 6*
    Nine-C Lit - v51 - D '96 - p419+ [51-250]
  The Complete Works of Robert Browning. Vol.6
    R&R Bk N - v11 - N '96 - p70 [51-250]
  The Poetical Works of Robert Browning. Vol. 5
    Nine-C Lit - v51 - S '96 - p271 [51-250]
Browning, Robert L - *Models of Confirmation and Baptismal Affirmation*
    Rel Ed - v91 - Sum '96 - p407+ [501+]
    Theol St - v57 - Mr '96 - p193+ [251-500]
Browning, W R F - *A Dictionary of the Bible*
    r ARBA - v28 - '97 - p543 [51-250]
    r BL - v93 - F 1 '97 - p966 [251-500]
    r LJ - v122 - F 15 '97 - p127 [51-250]
    r TLS - F 7 '97 - p8 [501+]
Brownjohn, Sandy - *Both Sides of the Catflap (Illus. by Liz Pichou)*
    c Sch Lib - v44 - N '96 - p167 [51-250]
    c TES - Jl 26 '96 - pR8 [51-250]

Brownlee, W Elliot - *Federal Taxation in America*
    Choice - v34 - N '96 - p505+ [51-250]
    JEL - v34 - D '96 - p2102+ [51-250]
  Funding the Modern American State 1941-1995
    Choice - v34 - O '96 - p329 [51-250]
    JEL - v34 - D '96 - p2103 [51-250]
Brownlie, Alison - *Senegal*
    c TES - Mr 21 '97 - p18* [251-500]
Brownlow, Arthur H - *Geochemistry. 2nd Ed.*
    SciTech - v20 - N '96 - p24 [51-250]
Brownlow, Kevin - *David Lean: A Biography*
    BW - v27 - Ja 12 '97 - p13 [51-250]
    Ent W - S 6 '96 - p70 [51-250]
    LATBR - N 24 '96 - p6 [501+]
    NYTBR - v101 - O 20 '96 - p23 [51-250]
    Obs - D 1 '96 - p17* [1-50]
    Spec - v276 - My 18 '96 - p39+ [501+]
Brownworth, Victoria A - *Night Bites*
    Bloom Rev - v16 - Jl '96 - p21 [1-50]
Brox, Jane - *Here and Nowhere Else*
    LATBR - S 1 '96 - p11 [51-250]
Brox, Norbert - *A Concise History of the Early Church*
    Theol St - v57 - S '96 - p564+ [251-500]
Broyard, Anatole - *Intoxicated by My Illness*
    Spec - v277 - N 16 '96 - p44 [1-50]
  Kafka Was the Rage
    PW - v244 - My 5 '97 - p206 [1-50]
Broyles-Gonzalez, Yolanda - *El Teatro Campesino*
    TDR - v41 - Spr '97 - p155+ [501+]
    Theat J - v48 - O '96 - p387+ [501+]
Brualdi, Richard A - *Matrices of Sign-Solvable Linear Systems*
    SIAM Rev - v39 - Mr '97 - p145+ [501+]
Brubaker, Linda T - *The Female Pelvic Floor*
    SciTech - v21 - Mr '97 - p63 [51-250]
Brubaker, Rogers - *Nationalism Reframed*
    Choice - v34 - Ap '97 - p1409 [51-250]
    For Aff - v76 - Mr '97 - p190+ [51-250]
Brubaker, Susan Howell - *Basic Level*
    SciTech - v20 - D '96 - p44 [51-250]
Bruce, Annette J - *Tellable Cracker Tales*
    CAY - v17 - Fall '96 - p2 [51-250]
Bruce, Chris - *Gary Hill*
    Art J - v54 - Win '95 - p93+ [501+]
Bruce, Evangeline - *Napoleon and Josephine*
    Historian - v58 - Sum '96 - p895+ [251-500]
    NYTBR - v101 - S 22 '96 - p40 [1-50]
Bruce, H C - *The New Man*
    LJ - v122 - F 1 '97 - p112 [51-250]
Bruce, James P - *Climate Change 1995: Economic and Social Dimensions of Climate Change*
    For Aff - v76 - Mr '97 - p176+ [51-250]
Bruce, Lisa - *Double Trouble (Illus. by Lesley Harker)*
    c Sch Lib - v45 - F '97 - p23 [51-250]
  Jazeera in the Sun (Illus. by Paul Howard)
    c Bks Keeps - N '96 - p7+ [51-250]
  School Trouble (Illus. by Lesley Harker)
    c Sch Lib - v45 - F '97 - p23 [51-250]
Bruce, Lorne - *Free Books for All*
    Can Hist R - v77 - D '96 - p642+ [251-500]
Bruce, Stephen D - *Million Dollar Mouths*
    HR Mag - v41 - Je '96 - p182+ [51-250]
Bruce, Steve - *The Rapture of Politics*
    CS - v26 - Ja '97 - p30+ [501+]
  Religion in the Modern World
    CR - v269 - D '96 - p329+ [501+]
  The Sociology of Religion. Vols. 1-2
    CS - v25 - S '96 - p709+ [501+]
Bruce, Todd - *Jiggers*
    Can Lit - Win '96 - p189+ [501+]
Bruce-Mitford, Miranda - *The Illustrated Book of Signs and Symbols*
    cr BL - v93 - N 15 '96 - p611+ [51-250]
    yr BL - v93 - D 15 '96 - p696 [51-250]
    yr BL - v93 - Ap 1 '97 - p1306 [1-50]
    yr Choice - v34 - F '97 - p939 [51-250]
    cr LJ - v121 - N 1 '96 - p58 [51-250]
    cr PW - v243 - S 30 '96 - p74 [51-250]
    yr Sch Lib - v45 - F '97 - p50 [51-250]
    y SLJ - v43 - F '97 - p136 [51-250]
Bruchac, Joseph - *Between Earth and Sky (Illus. by Thomas Locker)*
    c Emerg Lib - v24 - Mr '97 - p65 [51-250]
    c HB Guide - v7 - Fall '96 - p319 [51-250]
    c RT - v50 - My '97 - p684 [51-250]
  Children of the Longhouse
    c CBRS - v24 - Ag '96 - p166+ [51-250]
    c HB Guide - v7 - Fall '96 - p290 [51-250]
    c KR - v64 - My 1 '96 - p685 [51-250]
    c Parabola - v21 - N '96 - p120 [1-50]

5

The Circle of Thanks (Illus. by Murv Jacob)
c   BL - v93 - N 15 '96 - p581 [51-250]
c   HB Guide - v8 - Spr '97 - p151 [51-250]
c   KR - v64 - O 15 '96 - p1529 [51-250]
Dog People (Illus. by Murv Jacob)
c   Ch BWatch - v6 - Jl '96 - p1+ [1-50]
Eagle Song (Illus. by Dan Andreasen)
c   BL - v93 - F 1 '97 - p939 [51-250]
c   CCB-B - v50 - Mr '97 - p242 [51-250]
c   KR - v64 - D 1 '96 - p1734 [51-250]
c   PW - v243 - D 30 '96 - p67 [51-250]
c   SLJ - v43 - Mr '97 - p149 [51-250]
The Earth under Sky Bear's Feet (Illus. by Thomas Locker)
c   RT - v50 - S '96 - p55 [51-250]
Four Ancestors (Illus. by S S Burrus)
c   HB Guide - v7 - Fall '96 - p319 [51-250]
Gluskabe and the Four Wishes (Illus. by Christine Nyburg Shrader)
c   RT - v50 - N '96 - p245 [51-250]
Returning the Gift
CAY - v16 - Fall '95 - p2 [51-250]
The Story of the Milky Way (Illus. by Virginia A Stroud)
c   Inst - v106 - O '96 - p68 [1-50]
Tell Me a Tale
c   BL - v93 - Mr 15 '97 - p1236 [51-250]
c   PW - v244 - Mr 10 '97 - p69 [51-250]
Bruck, Bill - *The Essential Book for Microsoft Office*
TES - O 18 '96 - p41U [1-50]
Brucker, Peter - *Scheduling Algorithms*
JEL - v34 - D '96 - p2090 [51-250]
Bruckmuller, Ernst - *996-1996 Ostarrichi-Osterreich*
TLS - D 20 '96 - p6 [501+]
Bruckner, Andrew M - *Real Analysis*
SciTech - v20 - D '96 - p17 [51-250]
Brudner, Alan - *The Unity of the Common Law*
Ethics - v107 - Ja '97 - p394 [51-250]
Brudnoy, David - *Life Is Not a Rehearsal*
Advocate - F 4 '97 - p72+ [501+]
BL - v93 - N 15 '96 - p546 [51-250]
KR - v64 - N 1 '96 - p1574 [251-500]
LJ - v121 - D '96 - p102 [51-250]
Nat R - v49 - Ja 27 '97 - p51+ [501+]
NYTBR - v102 - Ap 6 '97 - p20+ [51-250]
NYTLa - v146 - Ja 2 '97 - pB20 [501+]
Brueggemann, Walter - *The Psalms and the Life of Faith*
TT - v53 - Ja '97 - p572 [51-250]
The Threat of Life
CC - v114 - Ap 9 '97 - p371+ [501+]
Bruen, Ken - *Rilke on Black*
KR - v65 - My 1 '97 - p680 [251-500]
Bruenig, Eberhard F - *Conservation and Management of Tropical Rainforests*
Choice - v34 - Ap '97 - p1365 [51-250]
Brugge, David M - *The Navajo-Hopi Land Dispute*
Workbook - v21 - Fall '96 - p135+ [501+]
Bruhn, John G - *Clinical Sociology*
R&R Bk N - v12 - F '97 - p50 [1-50]
Bruice, Paula Yurkanis - *Organic Chemistry*
J Chem Ed - v73 - Ap '96 - pA92 [251-500]
Bruinsma, Reinder - *Seventh-Day Adventist Attitudes toward Roman Catholicism 1845-1965*
CH - v66 - Mr '97 - p166+ [501+]
Brumfield, William Craft - *Lost Russia*
Slav R - v55 - Sum '96 - p503+ [501+]
Brundage, Anthony - *The People's Historian*
VS - v39 - Spr '96 - p448+ [501+]
Brundage, James A - *Medieval Canon Law*
Historian - v59 - Win '97 - p461 [251-500]
Brundage, W Fitzhugh - *A Socialist Utopia in the New South*
Choice - v34 - F '97 - p1023 [51-250]
Brune, Lester H - *The Korean War*
r   ARBA - v28 - '97 - p198 [51-250]
r   Choice - v34 - D '96 - p590 [51-250]
Brunel, Georges - *Dictionnaire Des Eglises De Paris*
r   Choice - v34 - D '96 - p570 [1-50]
Brunello, N - *Critical Issues in the Treatment of Schizophrenia*
J ClinPsyc - v58 - Mr '97 - p126 [501+]
Bruner, Jerome - *The Culture of Education*
Nature - v382 - Jl 18 '96 - p218+ [501+]
NYRB - v44 - Ap 10 '97 - p22+ [501+]
Bruner, Mike - *Gasoline Treasures*
Ant & CM - v101 - D '96 - p30 [1-50]
Brunet, Francois - *Dictionnaire Bilingue De L'Argot D'Aujourd'hui, Anglais-Francais-Francais-Anglais*
r   TLS - F 7 '97 - p9 [501+]
Brunette, Peter - *Deconstruction and the Visual Arts*
JAAC - v54 - Fall '96 - p405+ [51-250]

Brunhoff, Laurent - *Babar's French and English Word Book*
cr HB Guide - v7 - Fall '96 - p326 [1-50]
Bruni, Franco - *Risk Management in Volatile Financial Markets*
JEL - v34 - D '96 - p2052 [51-250]
Bruning, Jochen - *Augsburg In Der Fruhen Neuzeit*
Ren Q - v49 - Win '96 - p840+ [501+]
Brunk, Gregory G - *Understanding Attitudes about War*
Choice - v34 - Ja '97 - p872 [51-250]
R&R Bk N - v12 - F '97 - p25 [51-250]
Brunk, Juanita - *Brief Landing on the Earth's Surface*
Choice - v34 - Ap '97 - p1333 [51-250]
LJ - v121 - N 1 '96 - p71 [51-250]
PW - v243 - N 25 '96 - p73 [1-50]
Brunk, Samuel - *Emiliano Zapata: Revolution and Betrayal in Mexico*
AHR - v102 - F '97 - p236 [251-500]
HAHR - v76 - N '96 - p795+ [251-500]
Brunner, Ernst - *Mr. Skylight*
WLT - v71 - Win '97 - p171 [501+]
Brunner, Otto - *Land and Lordship*
CEH - v29 - 2 '96 - p227+ [501+]
Bruno, Anthony - *Devil's Food*
BL - v93 - Mr 1 '97 - p1112 [51-250]
KR - v64 - D 1 '96 - p1687 [251-500]
PW - v244 - Ja 13 '97 - p56 [51-250]
Bruno, Leonard C - *Science and Technology Firsts*
r   LJ - v122 - My 1 '97 - p94 [51-250]
The Tradition of Technology
r   Isis - v88 - Mr '97 - p172+ [501+]
r   J Gov Info - v23 - S '96 - p551 [1-50]
Bruno, Michael - *Inflation, Growth and Monetary Control*
JEL - v34 - D '96 - p2034+ [51-250]
Bruno, Vincent J - *Cosa IV*
AJA - v100 - O '96 - p777+ [501+]
Bruns, Gerald L - *Hermeneutics Ancient and Modern*
Comp L - v48 - Sum '96 - p294+ [501+]
Bruns, Jean R - *Abstracts of the Wills and Inventories of Bath County, Virginia 1791-1842*
r   EGH - v50 - N '96 - p190 [51-250]
Bruns, Karin - *Kinomythen 1920-1945*
Ger Q - v69 - Sum '96 - p344+ [501+]
Brunschwig, Jacques - *Papers in Hellenistic Philosophy*
Phil R - v105 - Ja '96 - p108+ [501+]
Brunt, Stephen - *Diamond Dreams*
Quill & Q - v62 - Jl '96 - p48 [251-500]
Bruntrager, Hubert - *Der Ironiker Und Der Ideologe*
Ger Q - v69 - Fall '96 - p448+ [501+]
Brunvand, Jan Harold - *American Folklore*
r   ARBA - v28 - '97 - p497 [51-250]
yr BL - v92 - Ag '96 - p1920+ [251-500]
r   BL - v93 - Ja '97 - p769 [1-50]
r   Choice - v34 - O '96 - p247 [51-250]
r   LJ - v122 - Ja '97 - p82 [51-250]
r   LJ - v122 - Ap 15 '97 - p37 [51-250]
yr VOYA - v19 - D '96 - p298 [51-250]
Brusca, Maria Cristina - *The Blacksmith and Devils*
c   SS - v88 - Ja '97 - p29+ [501+]
Brusco, Elizabeth E - *The Reformation of Machismo*
Am Ethnol - v23 - N '96 - p930+ [501+]
Bruser, Madeline - *The Art of Practicing*
y   BL - v93 - F 15 '97 - p990 [51-250]
LJ - v121 - D '96 - p95 [51-250]
Brush, Craig B - *From the Perspective of the Self*
FR - v70 - D '96 - p324+ [501+]
Brush, Stephen G - *Fruitful Encounters*
Choice - v34 - Mr '97 - p1181 [51-250]
New Sci - v153 - Mr 1 '97 - p42 [51-250]
Phys Today - v50 - Ja '97 - p65+ [501+]
SB - v33 - Mr '97 - p38 [51-250]
SciTech - v20 - D '96 - p21 [51-250]
S&T - v92 - D '96 - p66 [1-50]
A History of Modern Planetary Physics. Vols. 1-3
Nature - v384 - N 21 '96 - p227+ [501+]
Nebulous Earth
Choice - v34 - Mr '97 - p1181 [51-250]
New Sci - v153 - Mr 1 '97 - p42 [51-250]
Phys Today - v50 - Ja '97 - p65+ [501+]
SB - v33 - Mr '97 - p38 [251-500]
SciTech - v20 - D '96 - p21 [51-250]
S&T - v92 - D '96 - p66 [1-50]
Transmuted Past
Choice - v34 - N '96 - p486+ [51-250]
New Sci - v153 - Mr 1 '97 - p42 [51-250]
Phys Today - v50 - Ja '97 - p65+ [501+]
SB - v32 - Ag '96 - p167 [51-250]
Sci - v274 - O 25 '96 - p523 [1-50]
S&T - v92 - D '96 - p66 [1-50]

Brussat, Frederic - *Spiritual Literacy*
BL - v93 - O 1 '96 - p306 [51-250]
PW - v243 - S 30 '96 - p75 [51-250]
Brussig, Thomas - *Helden Wie Wir*
WLT - v70 - Sum '96 - p681+ [501+]
Brust, John C M - *Neurotoxic Side Effects of Prescription Drugs*
r   SciTech - v21 - Mr '97 - p52 [51-250]
Brust, Steven - *Freedom and Necessity*
BL - v93 - Mr 15 '97 - p1231 [51-250]
KR - v65 - Ja 15 '97 - p103 [51-250]
LJ - v122 - Ja '97 - p143 [51-250]
PW - v244 - Ja 27 '97 - p77 [51-250]
The Sun, the Moon, and the Stars
y   VOYA - v19 - F '97 - p334 [251-500]
Brustad, Kristen - *Alif Baa*
MEJ - v50 - Aut '96 - p628 [51-250]
Al-Kitab Fii Taallum Al-Arabiyya. Pt. 1
MEJ - v50 - Sum '96 - p454 [51-250]
Brustein, Robert - *Dumbocracy in America*
Sew R - v104 - Jl '96 - pR74+ [501+]
Brustein, William - *The Logic of Evil*
BL - v93 - S 15 '96 - p213 [51-250]
Choice - v34 - Ja '97 - p855 [51-250]
For Aff - v75 - N '96 - p155+ [251-500]
LJ - v121 - O 1 '96 - p97 [51-250]
NYTBR - v101 - S 15 '96 - p46 [501+]
Bruteau, Beatrice - *The Easter Mysteries*
RR - v56 - Ja '97 - p105 [1 50]
Bruton, Alastair - *A Revolution in Progress*
Econ - v342 - F 15 '97 - p5*+ [501+]
Bruton, Noel - *Effective User Support*
LR - v45 - 4 '96 - p67+ [501+]
Bruun, Erik A - *The Book of American Values and Virtues*
LJ - v122 - Ap 1 '97 - p105 [51-250]
Bruycker, Daniel De - *Scotland*
c   HB Guide - v7 - Fall '96 - p382 [51-250]
Tibet
c   HB Guide - v7 - Fall '96 - p383 [51-250]
Bruyne, Jacques De - *A Comprehensive Spanish Grammar*
r   MLJ - v80 - Win '96 - p560+ [501+]
Bryan, Ashley - *Turtle Knows Your Name (Illus. by Ashley Bryan)*
c   SS - v88 - Ja '97 - p29+ [501+]
Bryan, C D B - *Close Encounters of the Fourth Kind*
NYTBR - v101 - Ag 25 '96 - p28 [1-50]
Bryan, Charles S - *A Most Satisfactory Man*
SciTech - v21 - Mr '97 - p46 [1-50]
Bryan, Jenny - *Your Amazing Brain*
c   BL - v93 - D 15 '96 - p732 [1-50]
c   HB Guide - v7 - Fall '96 - p347 [51-250]
Bryan, John - *Manual of Bulbs*
r   ARBA - v28 - '97 - p580+ [51-250]
Bryan, Jonathan - *Journal of a Visit to the Georgia Islands of St. Catherines, Green, Ossabaw, Sapelo, St. Simons, Jekyll, and Cumberland*
JSH - v62 - N '96 - p863 [51-250]
Bryan, Karen - *Communication Disability and the Psychiatry of Old Age*
SciTech - v20 - D '96 - p44 [51-250]
Bryan, Larry - *Design for the Future of Health Care*
Quill & Q - v62 - D '96 - p26+ [501+]
Bryan, Lowell - *Market Unbound*
Bus Bk R - v13 - 4 '96 - p16+ [501+]
Bryan, Mark - *The Prodigal Father*
PW - v244 - My 12 '97 - p68 [51-250]
Bryan, Mary Lynn McCree - *The Jane Addams Papers*
r   ARBA - v28 - '97 - p319+ [251-500]
Bryan, Mike - *Uneasy Rider*
KR - v65 - F 1 '97 - p183 [251-500]
PW - v244 - F 3 '97 - p89+ [51-250]
Time - v149 - Ap 21 '97 - p117 [251-500]
Bryan, Sharon - *Flying Blind*
LJ - v122 - Ja '97 - p103 [51-250]
Bryan County, Oklahoma Cemeteries. Vols. 1-4
r   EGH - v50 - N '96 - p181+ [51-250]
Bryant, Bonnie - *Corey in the Saddle*
c   Ch BWatch - v6 - My '96 - p7 [1-50]
Jasmine Helps a Foal
c   Ch BWatch - v7 - F '97 - p5 [1-50]
Jasmine Trots Ahead
c   Ch BWatch - v6 - Jl '96 - p5 [1-50]
Bryant, Chris - *Possible Dreams*
Lon R Bks - v18 - O 31 '96 - p28+ [501+]
Bryant, Christopher G A - *Practical Sociology*
AJS - v102 - N '96 - p864+ [501+]
Socio - v44 - N '96 - p761+ [501+]
Bryant, Doris - *Beyond Integration*
AJCH - v39 - Jl '96 - p69+ [501+]
Readings - v11 - D '96 - p22 [51-250]

Bryant, G F - *Multivariable Control System Design Techniques*
    SciTech - v21 - Mr '97 - p84 [51-250]
Bryant, J Daniel - *Aluminum and Magnesium for Automotive Applications*
    SciTech - v20 - N '96 - p76 [1-50]
Bryant, Jennifer Fisher - *Lucretia Mott: A Guiding Light*
    y Kliatt - v30 - S '96 - p28 [51-250]
    y VOYA - v19 - O '96 - p226 [251-500]
    Thomas Merton: Poet, Prophet, Priest
    c KR - v65 - My 1 '97 - p717 [51-250]
Bryant, Jonathan M - *How Curious a Land*
    Choice - v34 - S '96 - p192 [51-250]
    HRNB - v25 - Fall '96 - p9 [251-500]
    VQR - v72 - Aut '96 - p116+* [51-250]
Bryant, Joseph M - *Moral Codes and Social Structure in Ancient Greece*
    R&R Bk N - v11 - N '96 - p5 [51-250]
Bryant, Louella - *The Black Bonnet*
    c BL - v93 - F 1 '97 - p939+ [51-250]
    y SLJ - v43 - F '97 - p100 [51-250]
Bryant, Marsha - *Photo-Textualities: Reading Photographs and Literature*
    Choice - v34 - D '96 - p600 [51-250]
Bryant, Philip - *Title Output in the UK*
    LAR - v98 - O '96 - p534 [251-500]
Bryant-Mole, Karen - *Blue (Illus. by Zul Mukhida)*
    c Bks Keeps - v100 - S '96 - p20 [51-250]
    c HB Guide - v8 - Spr '97 - p11 [51-250]
    c KR - v64 - O 15 '96 - p1540 [51-250]
    c SLJ - v43 - Ja '97 - p97 [51-250]
    Flowers (Illus. by Barrie Watts)
    c HB Guide - v7 - Fall '96 - p340 [51-250]
    Green
    c Bks Keeps - v100 - S '96 - p20 [51-250]
    Homes
    Sch Lib - v45 - F '97 - p37 [51-250]
    Insects (Illus. by Barrie Watts)
    c HB Guide - v7 - Fall '96 - p341 [1-50]
    Machines
    c Bks Keeps - v100 - S '96 - p20 [51-250]
    Materials
    c Bks Keeps - v100 - S '96 - p20 [51-250]
    Myself
    c Sch Lib - v45 - F '97 - p37 [51-250]
    People in the Country
    c Sch Lib - v44 - Ag '96 - p110 [51-250]
    People in the Town
    c Sch Lib - v44 - Ag '96 - p110 [51-250]
    Red
    c Bks Keeps - v100 - S '96 - p20 [51-250]
    Soil (Illus. by Barrie Watts)
    c HB Guide - v7 - Fall '96 - p352 [1-50]
    Texture
    c HB Guide - v8 - Spr '97 - p11 [51-250]
    c SLJ - v43 - Ja '97 - p97 [51-250]
    Textures
    c Bks Keeps - v100 - S '96 - p20 [51-250]
    Tools
    c Bks Keeps - v100 - S '96 - p20 [51-250]
    Toys
    c Sch Lib - v45 - F '97 - p37 [51-250]
    Trees (Illus. by Barrie Watts)
    c HB Guide - v7 - Fall '96 - p340 [51-250]
    Water
    c Sch Lib - v45 - F '97 - p37 [51-250]
    Yellow
    c Bks Keeps - v100 - S '96 - p20 [51-250]
Bryar, Rosamund - *Changing Primary Health Care*
    SciTech - v20 - D '96 - p39 [51-250]
Bryce, Robert M - *Cook and Peary*
    BW - v27 - Mr 2 '97 - p9 [501+]
    LJ - v122 - F 1 '97 - p94 [51-250]
    NYTBR - v102 - Ap 20 '97 - p21 [51-250]
Bryce Echenique, Alfredo - *Cuentos Completos*
    WLT - v70 - Aut '96 - p920+ [501+]
    No Me Esperen En Abril
    WLT - v71 - Win '97 - p117+ [501+]
Bryer, Jackson R - *New Essays on F. Scott Fitzgerald's Neglected Stories*
    AL - v68 - S '96 - p666 [51-250]
    The Playwright's Art
    Theat J - v49 - Mr '97 - p96+ [501+]
Bryers, Paul - *In a Pig's Ear*
    Ent W - N 8 '96 - p62+ [51-250]
    LATBR - Mr 23 '97 - p7 [501+]
    MFSF - v92 - Ja '97 - p17+ [251-500]
Brykczynska, Gosia - *Caring: The Compassion and Wisdom of Nursing*
    SciTech - v21 - Mr '97 - p69 [1-50]

Brylinski, J L - *Lie Theory and Geometry*
    SIAM Rev - v38 - S '96 - p545 [1-50]
Brym, Robert J - *The Jews of Moscow, Kiev and Minsk*
    Slav R - v55 - Sum '96 - p467+ [501+]
Brynen, Rex - *Political Liberalization and Democratization in the Arab World. Vol. 1*
    APSR - v90 - D '96 - p933+ [501+]
    MEP - v4 - 4 '96 - p141+ [501+]
    MEQ - v3 - S '96 - p86 [251-500]
Brynes, Mark E - *Politics and Space*
    T&C - v37 - Ap '96 - p392+ [501+]
Brynie, Faith Hickman - *Six-Minute Science Experiments (Illus. by Kim Whittingham)*
    c HB Guide - v8 - Spr '97 - p109 [51-250]
Brynner, Yul - *Yul Brynner, Photographer*
    CSM - v89 - D 5 '96 - pB2+ [51-250]
    Ent W - O 11 '96 - p86 [51-250]
    LATBR - D 8 '96 - p26 [1-50]
    PW - v243 - S 2 '96 - p107+ [51-250]
Bryson, Arthur E, Jr. - *Control of Spacecraft and Aircraft*
    Am Sci - v84 - My '96 - p305+ [501+]
Bryson, Bill - *Made in America*
    TES - D 27 '96 - p16 [51-250]
    Notes from a Small Island
    Books - v9 - S '95 - p23 [51-250]
    Comw - v123 - D 6 '96 - p29 [251-500]
    NYTBR - v101 - D 8 '96 - p90 [1-50]
    PW - v244 - Ap 14 '97 - p72 [1-50]
    TES - D 27 '96 - p16 [51-250]
    Woman's J - O '96 - p12 [1-50]
Brzezinski, Zbigniew - *Out of Control*
    JTWS - v13 - Spr '96 - p396+ [501+]
Bstan-Dzin-Rgya-Mtsho, Dalai Lama XIV - *Healing Anger*
    PW - v244 - My 12 '97 - p72 [51-250]
    The Joy of Living and Dying in Peace
    BL - v93 - Mr 1 '97 - p1071 [51-250]
    PW - v244 - F 10 '97 - p80 [51-250]
Bubeck, Diemut - *Care, Gender, and Justice*
    APSR - v90 - D '96 - p888 [501+]
Buber, Martin - *Scripture and Translation*
    TranslRevS - v1 - My '95 - p9+ [51-250]
Bubnov, N Iu - *Staroobriadcheskaia Kniga V Rossii Vo Vtoroi Polovine XVII v.*
    Slav R - v55 - Fall '96 - p682+ [501+]
Buc, Philippe - *L'Ambiguite Du Livre*
    EHR - v111 - N '96 - p1246 [251-500]
    Specu - v71 - Jl '96 - p704+ [501+]
Bucciantini, Massimo - *Contro Galileo*
    Isis - v88 - Mr '97 - p141+ [501+]
Bucer, Martin - *Correspondance De Martin Bucer. Vol. 3*
    Six Ct J - v27 - Fall '96 - p801+ [501+]
Buchan, Elizabeth - *Beatrix Potter. Rev. Ed.*
    c RSR - v24 - 3 '96 - p26 [51-250]
Buchan, James - *Heart's Journey in Winter*
    Books - v10 - Je '96 - p25 [1-50]
    High Latitudes
    KR - v64 - O 1 '96 - p1416 [251-500]
    LATBR - N 17 '96 - p2 [501+]
    Nat R - v49 - F 10 '97 - p58 [251-500]
    NY - v72 - D 2 '96 - p113+ [501+]
    NYTBR - v101 - N 17 '96 - p34 [501+]
    NYTBR - v101 - D 8 '96 - p80 [1-50]
    PW - v243 - S 16 '96 - p68 [251-500]
    VV - v41 - D 31 '96 - p48+ [501+]
Buchan, John - *The Complete Short Stories. Vol. 1*
    TLS - O 11 '96 - p28 [501+]
    John Buchan's Collected Poems
    CR - v269 - Ag '96 - p109+ [501+]
    TLS - O 11 '96 - p28 [501+]
    Sick Heart River
    ELT - v39 - 4 '96 - p514+ [501+]
Buchan, Ursula - *Gardening for Pleasure*
    PW - v244 - Ja 27 '97 - p100 [51-250]
    Spec - v277 - D 7 '96 - p55 [51-250]
Buchanan, Bill - *Virus*
    PW - v244 - Ja 27 '97 - p102 [51-250]
Buchanan, Bruce - *Renewing Presidential Politics*
    Choice - v34 - Mr '97 - p1239 [51-250]
Buchanan, Carol - *Brother Crow, Sister Corn*
    BL - v93 - Ja '97 - p800 [51-250]
Buchanan, Christy M - *Adolescents after Divorce*
    Choice - v34 - Ap '97 - p1422+ [51-250]
Buchanan, Constance H - *Choosing to Lead*
    Choice - v34 - D '96 - p650 [51-250]
Buchanan, David - *Different Rules*
    Spec - v277 - D 14 '96 - p75 [51-250]
Buchanan, Edna - *Act of Betrayal*
    Arm Det - v29 - Fall '96 - p477 [251-500]
    Arm Det - v29 - Sum '96 - p357+ [51-250]

    Act of Betrayal (Burr). Audio Version
    LJ - v121 - O 1 '96 - p142 [51-250]
    Margin of Error
    BL - v93 - My 1 '97 - p1460 [51-250]
Buchanan, George - *One Alligator Alone*
    c Sch Lib - v44 - S '96 - p145 [51-250]
Buchanan, George, 1506-1582 - *A Critical Edition of George Buchanan's Baptistes and of Its Anonymous Seventeenth-Century Translation, Tyranicall-Government Anatomized*
    Six Ct J - v27 - Fall '96 - p849+ [501+]
Buchanan, George, 1948- - *The Living Room*
    BL - v93 - Ja '97 - p796 [51-250]
    LJ - v122 - Ja '97 - p96 [51-250]
Buchanan, Gregory McClellan - *Explanatory Style*
    A J Psy - v109 - Win '96 - p624+ [501+]
Buchanan, John - *The Road to Guilford Courthouse*
    BL - v93 - F 15 '97 - p998 [51-250]
    KR - v65 - Ja 15 '97 - p108 [251-500]
Buchanan, Kate - *Music Connections*
    TES - S 13 '96 - pR11 [51-250]
Buchanan, Paul D - *Famous Animals of the States*
    r BL - v93 - D 15 '96 - p747+ [51-250]
Buchanan, Paul G - *State, Labor, Capital*
    APSR - v91 - Mr '97 - p206+ [501+]
    JEL - v34 - S '96 - p1466 [51-250]
Buchanan, R Angus - *Engineers and Engineering*
    Choice - v34 - N '96 - p480 [51-250]
Buchanan, Rita - *The Shaker Herb and Garden Book*
    BL - v93 - S 1 '96 - p51+ [51-250]
Buchanan, W Watson - *Clinical Examination of the Musculoskeletal System*
    SciTech - v20 - D '96 - p48 [51-250]
Buchanan, William - *Mackintosh's Masterwork*
    NYRB - v44 - F 20 '97 - p7+ [501+]
Buchenau, Jurgen - *In the Shadow of the Giant*
    Choice - v34 - F '97 - p1021 [51-250]
Bucher, Bernadette - *Descendants De Chouans*
    Am Ethnol - v24 - F '97 - p245+ [501+]
Bucher, Gerard - *Le Testament Poetique*
    FR - v70 - F '97 - p459+ [501+]
Bucher, Ward - *Dictionary of Building Preservation*
    r ARBA - v28 - '97 - p368 [251-500]
    r BL - v93 - D 1 '96 - p684 [51-250]
    r Choice - v34 - Mr '97 - p1135 [51-250]
    r LJ - v122 - F 1 '97 - p70 [51-250]
    r R&R Bk N - v11 - D '96 - p57 [51-250]
Buchhaupt, Siegfried - *Die Gesellschaft Fur Schwerionenforschung*
    Isis - v87 - S '96 - p569+ [251-500]
Buchmann, Christina - *Out of the Garden*
    OS - v32 - Jl '96 - p43 [51-250]
Buchmann, Stephen L - *The Forgotten Pollinators*
    Am Sci - v85 - Mr '97 - p189+ [501+]
    BL - v93 - D 1 '96 - p630 [1-50]
    Choice - v34 - Ja '97 - p818 [51-250]
    KR - v64 - My 1 '96 - p655 [251-500]
    SciTech - v20 - D '96 - p32 [51-250]
Buchmann-Moller, Frank - *You Just Fight for Your Life*
    CAY - v16 - Fall '95 - p11 [51-250]
Bucholz, Robert W - *Orthopaedic Decision Making. 2nd Ed.*
    SciTech - v20 - S '96 - p39 [51-250]
Buchwald, Art - *I'll Always Have Paris*
    BW - v26 - S 1 '96 - p1+ [501+]
    Ent W - S 20 '96 - p74 [51-250]
    LATBR - S 22 '96 - p11 [51-250]
    NYTBR - v101 - S 8 '96 - p22 [51-250]
    Time - v148 - S 30 '96 - p77 [501+]
Buchwald, Jed Z - *Scientific Practice*
    Isis - v88 - Mr '97 - p121+ [501+]
Buck, Anne - *Clothes and the Child*
    Choice - v34 - Ap '97 - p1396+ [51-250]
    TES - Ja 24 '97 - p8* [51-250]
Buck, Caitlin E - *Bayesian Approach to Interpreting Archaeological Data*
    Choice - v34 - Ap '97 - p1375 [51-250]
Buck, Claire - *The Bloomsbury Guide to Women's Literature*
    r RQ - v36 - Win '96 - p219 [51-250]
Buck, Gisela - *Fuzzy the Duckling*
    c Ch BWatch - v6 - My '96 - p1+ [1-50]
    Pete the Puppy
    c Ch BWatch - v6 - My '96 - p1+ [1-50]
    Sadie the Shrew
    c Ch BWatch - v6 - My '96 - p1+ [1-50]
Buck, Nola - *Morning in the Meadow (Illus. by Holly Keller)*
    c PW - v244 - Mr 24 '97 - p85 [1-50]

Oh, Cats! (Illus. by Nadine Bernard Westcott)
  c BL - v93 - N 15 '96 - p596 [51-250]
  c KR - v64 - D 15 '96 - p1796 [51-250]
  c SLJ - v43 - F '97 - p74 [51-250]
Sid and Sam (Illus. by G Brian Karas)
  c BL - v92 - Ag '96 - p1910 [51-250]
  c HB Guide - v7 - Fall '96 - p283 [51-250]
Buck, Rinker - *Flight of Passage*
  PW - v244 - Ap 7 '97 - p78 [51-250]
Buckel, John - *Free to Love*
  Rel St Rev - v23 - Ja '97 - p74 [51-250]
Buckingham, David - *Moving Images*
  JC - v47 - Win '97 - p176+ [501+]
  NS & S - v9 - My 24 '96 - p40 [1-50]
Buckingham, Peter H - *Rebel against Injustice*
  Choice - v34 - O '96 - p345+ [51-250]
Buckingham, Robert W - *The Handbook of Hospice Care Workbook* - v21 - Win '96 - p173+ [251-500]
I'm Pregnant, Now What Do I Do?
  y BL - v93 - F 15 '97 - p1009+ [51-250]
Buckland, Theresa - *Aspects of British Calendar Customs*
  JPC - v29 - Spr '96 - p231+ [51-250]
Buckland, Wendy - *Armed and Dangerous*
  Quill & Q - v62 - D '96 - p24+ [501+]
Buckles, Mary Parker - *Margins: A Naturalist Meets Long Island Sound*
  PW - v244 - Mr 3 '97 - p54+ [51-250]
Buckley, Anthony D - *Negotiating Identity*
  ILS - v15 - Fall '96 - p32 [501+]
Buckley, Carol - *At the Still Point*
  NYTBR - v101 - D 8 '96 - p84 [1-50]
Buckley, Christopher - *Wry Martinis*
  BL - v93 - Mr 1 '97 - p1104 [51-250]
  BW - v27 - Mr 23 '97 - p13 [51-250]
  Ent W - Mr 28 '97 - p62 [51-250]
  KR - v65 - Ja 1 '97 - p30+ [251-500]
  LATBR - Mr 16 '97 - p8 [51-250]
  NYTBR - v102 - Mr 23 '97 - p9+ [501+]
  PW - v243 - D 30 '96 - p44 [51-250]
Buckley, Helen E - *Grandfather and I (Illus. by Jan Ormerod)*
  c LA - v73 - S '96 - p353 [51-250]
Moonlight Kite (Illus. by Elise Primavera)
  c BL - v93 - Mr 15 '97 - p1247 [51-250]
  c CBRS - v25 - Ap '97 - p97 [51-250]
  c CCB-B - v50 - My '97 - p315 [51-250]
  c KR - v65 - F 1 '97 - p219+ [51-250]
  c PW - v244 - Ja 20 '97 - p402 [51-250]
  c SLJ - v43 - Mr '97 - p149 [51-250]
Buckley, J - *The Biography of Thomas Lang*
  Obs - Mr 16 '97 - p18* [501+]
  TES - F 14 '97 - p8* [51-250]
  TLS - Mr 7 '97 - p22 [501+]
Buckley, John F - *Multistate Payroll Guide*
  r ARBA - v28 - '97 - p120 [51-250]
Buckley, Jonathan - *Rock: The Rough Guide*
  yr Kliatt - v31 - Ja '97 - p30 [251-500]
Buckley, Paul - *Glimpsing Reality*
  Choice - v34 - O '96 - p320 [51-250]
Buckley, Peter J - *Canada--UK Bilateral Trade and Investment Relations*
  Econ J - v107 - Ja '97 - p266+ [251-500]
Foreign Direct Investment and Multinational Enterprises
  Econ J - v106 - N '96 - p1836 [251-500]
Buckley, William F - *Brothers No More*
  PW - v243 - S 9 '96 - p80 [1-50]
Brothers No More (Lawrence). Audio Version
  y Kliatt - v30 - S '96 - p44 [51-250]
Buckley: The Right Word
  BL - v93 - N 15 '96 - p546 [51-250]
  KR - v64 - N 1 '96 - p1574+ [251-500]
  LJ - v121 - D '96 - p108 [51-250]
  Nat R - v48 - D 23 '96 - p48+ [501+]
  PW - v243 - N 4 '96 - p60 [51-250]
Marco Polo, If You Can
  LJ - v121 - D '96 - p154 [1-50]
The Story of Henri Tod
  LJ - v121 - D '96 - p154 [1-50]
Buckman, Elcha Shain - *The Handbook of Humor*
  Adoles - v31 - Win '96 - p991 [51-250]
Buckner, Phillip A - *The Atlantic Region to Confederation*
  Can Hist R - v77 - D '96 - p632+ [501+]
  EHR - v111 - N '96 - p1311+ [251-500]
Buckstone, John Baldwin - *Jack Sheppard*
  SFS - v24 - Mr '97 - p181 [1-50]
Bucuvalas, Tina - *South Florida Folklife*
  J Am Cult - v18 - Win '95 - p111 [51-250]
Bucy, Douglas R - *Help Yourself*
  r LJ - v122 - Ja '97 - p84 [51-250]
Budapest and the Best of Hungary (Frommer's Guides)
  r BL - v93 - S 15 '96 - p206+ [1-50]

Buday, Grant - *Under Glass*
  Can Lit - Spr '97 - p214+ [501+]
Budd, Malcolm - *Values of Art, Pictures, Poetry and Music*
  BM - v139 - Ja '97 - p53 [51-250]
Budd, Timothy - *An Introduction to Object-Oriented Programming. 2nd Ed.*
  SciTech - v20 - D '96 - p8 [51-250]
Budde, Gunilla-Friederike - *Auf Dem Weg Ins Burgerleben*
  EHR - v111 - N '96 - p1326+ [251-500]
Budden, Michael Craig - *Protecting Trade Secrets under the Uniform Trade Secrets Act*
  R&R Bk N - v12 - F '97 - p64 [51-250]
Buderi, Robert - *The Invention That Changed the World*
  BL - v93 - O 1 '96 - p312 [51-250]
  BW - v26 - D 1 '96 - p4 [501+]
  CSM - v89 - Ja 14 '97 - p15 [501+]
  For Aff - v76 - Mr '97 - p179 [51-250]
  KR - v64 - Ag 15 '96 - p1200 [251-500]
  Nature - v384 - D 5 '96 - p424+ [501+]
  New Sci - v152 - N 2 '96 - p46 [501+]
  NY - v72 - F 10 '97 - p83 [51-250]
  Sci - v274 - O 11 '96 - p199 [501+]
Budge, Ian - *The New Challenge of Direct Democracy*
  Choice - v34 - Ap '97 - p1415+ [51-250]
Budget Deficits and Debt
  JEL - v34 - D '96 - p2061 [51-250]
Budiansky, Stephen - *The Nature of Horses*
  y BL - v93 - Mr 1 '97 - p1100 [51-250]
  KR - v65 - F 15 '97 - p265 [251-500]
  LJ - v122 - Mr 15 '97 - p84 [51-250]
  Nature - v386 - Mr 27 '97 - p341+ [501+]
  PW - v244 - Mr 31 '97 - p56 [51-250]
Nature's Keepers
  Econ - v339 - My 18 '96 - p12* [51-250]
Budiardjo, Carmel - *Surviving Indonesia's Gulag*
  Prog - v61 - F '97 - p41+ [501+]
  TLS - My 24 '96 - p30+ [501+]
Budick, Sanford - *The Translatability of Cultures*
  WLT - v70 - Aut '96 - p1040 [51-250]
Budnick, Dean - *The Phishing Manual*
  BWatch - v18 - F '97 - p9 [51-250]
Buechner, Frederick - *The Longing for Home*
  BL - v92 - Ag '96 - p1874 [51-250]
  Parabola - v21 - N '96 - p120 [1-50]
Buehner, Caralyn - *Fanny's Dream (Illus. by Mark Buehner)*
  c BL - v93 - Ja '97 - p767 [1-50]
  c BL - v93 - Ap 1 '97 - p1296 [1-50]
  c CCB-B - v50 - S '96 - p7 [51-250]
  c HB Guide - v7 - Fall '96 - p249 [51-250]
  c LATBR - N 10 '96 - p15 [51-250]
  c NW - v128 - D 2 '96 - p88 [1-50]
  c Par Ch - v20 - O '96 - p11 [1-50]
  c RT - v50 - My '97 - p684 [51-250]
  c SLJ - v42 - D '96 - p28 [1-50]
It's a Spoon, Not a Shovel (Illus. by Mark Buehner)
  c LA - v73 - O '96 - p431 [51-250]
Buell, Duncan A - *Splash 2*
  SciTech - v20 - S '96 - p7 [51-250]
Buell, Frederick - *National Culture and the New Global System*
  Can Lit - Spr '97 - p251+ [501+]
  Col Lit - v23 - Je '96 - p181+ [501+]
Buell, John - *Democracy by Other Means*
  Theol St - v57 - S '96 - p575 [251-500]
Sustainable Democracy
  Choice - v34 - Mr '97 - p1239 [51-250]
  R&R Bk N - v11 - D '96 - p24 [51-250]
Buell, Lawrence - *The Environmental Imagination*
  ABR - v18 - D '96 - p8+ [501+]
  AL - v68 - S '96 - p640+ [251-500]
  Nine-C Lit - v50 - Mr '96 - p525+ [501+]
Bueno, Ana - *Special Olympics*
  Aethlon - v13 - Fall '95 - p162 [251-500]
Bueno De Mesquita, Bruce - *European Community Decision Making*
  J Pol - v58 - Ag '96 - p910+ [501+]
Red Flag Over Hong Kong
  FEER - v159 - D 12 '96 - p52+ [501+]
War and Reason
  RP - v58 - Fall '96 - p793+ [501+]
Buero Vallejo, Antonio - *A Dreamer for the People*
  MLR - v91 - Jl '96 - p770+ [501+]
Bueschel, Richard M - *Encyclopedia of Pinball. Vol. 1*
  r Sci - v275 - Mr 21 '97 - p1749 [51-250]

Buetter, Barbara MacDonald - *Simple Puppets from Everyday Materials (Illus. by Barbara MacDonald Buetter)*
  c HB Guide - v8 - Spr '97 - p135 [51-250]
  c SLJ - v43 - Mr '97 - p172 [51-250]
Buettner, Brigitte - *Boccaccio's Des Cleres Et Nobles Femmes*
  LJ - v122 - My 1 '97 - p100 [51-250]
Buettner, Dan - *Maya Quest*
  Pet PM - v25 - D '96 - p34 [51-250]
Bufalino, Gesualdo - *Tommaso E Il Fotografo Cieco*
  BL - v93 - D 1 '96 - p644 [1-50]
  TLS - Jl 19 '96 - p13 [501+]
Bufe, Charles - *The Heretic's Handbook of Quotatons*
  r Skeptic - v4 - 4 '96 - p106 [251-500]
Buffa, Liz - *The Princeton Review Grammar Smart Junior*
  y Learning - v25 - N '96 - p82 [51-250]
Buffet, Jimmy - *Trouble Dolls (Illus. by Lambert Davis)*
  c PW - v244 - Ap 28 '97 - p77 [1-50]
Buffie, Margaret - *The Dark Garden*
  y Can CL - v22 - Sum '96 - p84+ [251-500]
  y Emerg Lib - v24 - Mr '97 - p27 [1-50]
My Mother's Ghost
  c Quill & Q - v62 - My '96 - p13 [501+]
Buffong, Jean - *Snowflakes in the Sun*
  BL - v93 - Ap 1 '97 - p1279+ [51-250]
  KR - v65 - F 15 '97 - p238 [251-500]
Buford, Bill - *The Granta Book of the Family*
  Obs - D 8 '96 - p18* [51-250]
Buford, Thomas O - *In Search of a Calling*
  RM - v50 - S '96 - p147+ [501+]
Bufwack, Mary A - *Finding Her Voice*
  LJ - v121 - N 1 '96 - p41 [51-250]
Bugeja, Michael J - *Family Values*
  PW - v244 - F 17 '97 - p212 [51-250]
Little Dragons
  Choice - v34 - O '96 - p275+ [51-250]
Bugg, D V - *Hadron Spectroscopy and the Confinement Problem*
  SciTech - v20 - S '96 - p15 [51-250]
Bugialli, Giuliano - *Foods of Sicily and Sardinia and the Smaller Islands*
  BL - v93 - F 15 '97 - p988 [51-250]
  PW - v243 - O 21 '96 - p79 [51-250]
Bugliarello, George - *East-West Technology Transfer*
  JEL - v34 - S '96 - p1484 [51-250]
  SciTech - v20 - N '96 - p60 [51-250]
Bugliosi, Vincent - *Outrage: The Five Reasons Why O.J. Simpson Got Away with Murder*
  Esq - v126 - N '96 - p65 [1-50]
  LATBR - Jl 7 '96 - p4 [501+]
  NYTBR - v101 - Jl 21 '96 - p18 [51-250]
  NYTBR - v102 - Ap 20 '97 - p32 [1-50]
  PW - v244 - F 24 '97 - p88 [1-50]
  Sulfur - Fall '96 - p139+ [501+]
The Phoenix Solution (Campanella). Audio Version
  y Kliatt - v30 - S '96 - p58 [51-250]
Bugos, Glenn E - *Engineering the F-4 Phantom II*
  A & S Sm - v11 - Ag '96 - p82+ [51-250]
  Choice - v34 - N '96 - p488 [51-250]
  For Aff - v75 - N '96 - p151 [51-250]
  SciTech - v20 - S '96 - p58 [51-250]
Buhle, E Loren - *Webmaster's Professional Reference*
  r SciTech - v20 - S '96 - p56 [51-250]
Buhle, Paul M - *William Appleman Williams: The Tragedy of Empire*
  RAH - v25 - Mr '97 - p163+ [501+]
  TCR - v98 - Spr '97 - p537+ [501+]
Buhner, Stephen Harrod - *Sacred Plant Medicine*
  Bloom Rev - v16 - N '96 - p14+ [51-250]
  BWatch - v17 - S '96 - p10 [51-250]
  Workbook - v21 - Win '96 - p178+ [501+]
Bui, Tien Khoi - *Duong Vao Dai Hoc Hoa Ky*
  BL - v93 - My 15 '97 - p1568 [1-50]
Bui, Tin - *Following Ho Chi Minh*
  Historian - v59 - Win '97 - p452+ [251-500]
  Quad - v40 - O '96 - p78+ [501+]
Bui, Vinh Phuc - *O Mot Noi Nao*
  BL - v93 - S 1 '96 - p70 [51-250]
Building on Soft Soils
  SciTech - v20 - D '96 - p65 [51-250]
Building Projects for the Home
  LJ - v122 - F 1 '97 - p52 [1-50]
Builta, Jeffrey A - *Extremist Groups*
  r MEQ - v3 - D '96 - p83 [51-250]
Buisseret, David - *Rural Images*
  R&R Bk N - v11 - N '96 - p21 [51-250]
Buitelaar, Ruud - *Latin America's New Insertion in the World Economy*
  JEL - v35 - Mr '97 - p212 [51-250]

Buitrago, Fanny - *Senora De La Miel*
  BL - v93 - Mr 15 '97 - p1232 [1-50]
  Senora Honeycomb
  TLS - Jl 7 '96 - p25 [251-500]
Bujold, Lois McMaster - *Dreamweaver's Dilemma*
  Ext - v37 - Win '96 - p370+ [501+]
  SF Chr - v18 - O '96 - p79 [51-250]
  Falling Free (Hanson). Audio Version
  y Kliatt - v30 - N '96 - p40 [51-250]
  LJ - v121 - S 15 '96 - p114 [51-250]
  SF Chr - v18 - O '96 - p80+ [1-50]
  Memory
  y BL - v93 - S 1 '96 - p69 [51-250]
  PW - v243 - S 23 '96 - p60 [51-250]
  PW - v243 - N 4 '96 - p42 [1-50]
  Shards of Honor (Cowan). Audio Version
  LJ - v122 - Ap 15 '97 - p138 [51-250]
Bukatman, Scott - *Terminal Identity*
  FQ - v49 - Fall '95 - p60+ [501+]
Bukiet, Melvin Jules - *After*
  Trib Bks - Ja 12 '97 - p7 [501+]
  VV - v41 - S 10 '96 - p65+ [501+]
Bukovskii, Vladimir Konstantinovich - *Jugement A Moscou*
  TLS - N 29 '96 - p11 [51-250]
  TLS - Ja 31 '97 - p7+ [501+]
Bukowski, Charles - *Bone Palace Ballet*
  BL - v93 - My 15 '97 - p1557 [51-250]
Bukowski, William M - *The Company They Keep*
  Adoles - v31 - Fall '96 - p751 [51-250]
  Choice - v34 - O '96 - p364 [51-250]
Bulgakov, Mikhail Afanas'evich - *Black Snow*
  LJ - v122 - Ap 1 '97 - p134 [1-50]
  NYTBR - v102 - Mr 30 '97 - p24 [51-250]
  Trib Bks - Mr 9 '97 - p8 [1-50]
  A Country Doctor's Notebook
  LJ - v122 - Ap 1 '97 - p134 [1-50]
  NYTBR - v102 - Mr 30 '97 - p24 [51-250]
  The Heart of a Dog
  LJ - v122 - Ap 1 '97 - p134 [1-50]
  Trib Bks - Mr 16 '97 - p8 [1-50]
Bulger, William M - *While the Music Lasts*
  LATBR - Mr 24 '96 - p2 [501+]
Bulhoes, Antonio - *Os Deuses Mortos*
  WLT - v70 - Sum '96 - p677+ [501+]
Bulkeley, Kelly - *Among All These Dreamers*
  Choice - v34 - Ja '97 - p878 [51-250]
  Rel St Rev - v23 - Ja '97 - p42 [51-250]
  R&R Bk N - v11 - N '96 - p5 [1-50]
Bull, Angela - *A Patchwork of Ghosts*
  c Obs - v54 - O 13 '96 - p18* [51-250]
  y Sch Lib - v45 - F '97 - p44 [51-250]
Bull, Debby - *Blue Jelly*
  BL - v93 - My 1 '97 - p1474 [51-250]
  Ent W - My 16 '97 - p108 [51-250]
  KR - v65 - Mr 15 '97 - p428 [51-250]
Bull, George - *Michelangelo: A Biography*
  BL - v93 - Ja '97 - p802 [51-250]
  KR - v64 - N 1 '96 - p1575 [251-500]
  LJ - v122 - Ja '97 - p92 [51-250]
  PW - v243 - N 11 '96 - p61+ [51-250]
Bull, Martin J - *Contemporary Italy*
  r Choice - v34 - O '96 - p249 [51-250]
Bull, P D - *Lecture Notes on Diseases of the Ear, Nose, and Throat. 8th Ed.*
  SciTech - v20 - S '96 - p40 [51-250]
Bull, Philip - *Land, Politics and Nationalism*
  Choice - v34 - My '97 - p1556 [51-250]
Bullard, Melissa Meriam - *Lorenzo Il Magnifico*
  CHR - v82 - Jl '96 - p559+ [251-500]
  EHR - v112 - F '97 - p181 [501+]
Bullard, Sara - *Teaching Tolerance*
  BL - v93 - S 15 '96 - p186 [251-500]
Bullen, J B - *The Myth of the Renaissance in Nineteenth-Century Writing*
  RES - v47 - N '96 - p610+ [501+]
Buller, Jon - *Felix and the 400 Frogs*
  c BL - v93 - S 15 '96 - p252 [51-250]
Bullhead
  p Sm Pr R - v28 - D '96 - p13+ [501+]
Bulliet, Richard W - *Islam: The View from the Edge*
  JTWS - v13 - Spr '96 - p233+ [501+]
  MEJ - v50 - Aut '96 - p620+ [501+]
Bullis, Ronald K - *Clinical Social Worker Misconduct*
  Soc Ser R - v70 - S '96 - p504 [51-250]
Bullis, W Murray - *Semiconductor Characterization*
  Phys Today - v50 - F '97 - p68+ [501+]
Bullivant, Keith - *The Future of German Literature*
  MLR - v92 - Ja '97 - p257+ [501+]
Bulloch, Ivan - *I Want to Be a Clown*
  c Magpies - v11 - Jl '96 - p39 [51-250]

I Want to Be a Juggler
  c Magpies - v11 - Jl '96 - p39 [51-250]
I Want to Be a Magician
  c Magpies - v11 - Jl '96 - p39 [51-250]
I Want to Be an Acrobat
  c Magpies - v11 - Jl '96 - p39 [51-250]
Bullock, Steven C - *Revolutionary Brotherhood*
  Choice - v34 - N '96 - p524 [51-250]
Bullough, Bonnie - *Gender Blending*
  PW - v243 - D 16 '96 - p47 [51-250]
Bulman, James C - *Shakespeare, Theory, and Performance*
  Theat J - v48 - D '96 - p527+ [501+]
Bulmer, Martin - *Citizenship Today*
  Socio R - v45 - F 1 '97 - p176+ [501+]
  TLS - Ag 30 '96 - p12 [501+]
Bulmer-Thomas, Victor - *The Economic History of Latin America since Independence*
  r HAHR - v76 - Ag '96 - p607+ [501+]
  JIH - v27 - Spr '97 - p734+ [501+]
  The New Economic Model in Latin America and Its Impact on Income Distribution and Poverty
  Choice - v34 - O '96 - p330 [51-250]
  For Aff - v75 - S '96 - p149+ [51-250]
  JEL - v34 - D '96 - p2026 [51-250]
Bulpitt, Christopher J - *Randomised Controlled Clinical Trials. 2nd Ed.*
  r SciTech - v21 - Mr '97 - p44 [51-250]
Bultman, Bethany - *Redneck Heaven*
  PW - v243 - N 11 '96 - p71 [51-250]
  VV - v41 - D 17 '96 - p51+ [501+]
Bumiller, Elisabeth - *The Secrets of Mariko*
  y Kliatt - v31 - Mr '97 - p25 [51-250]
  NYTBR - v102 - Ja 5 '97 - p28 [1-50]
  PW - v243 - O 21 '96 - p78 [1-50]
  Trib Bks - F 23 '97 - p8 [1-50]
Bumpus, Jerry - *The Civilized Tribes*
  RCF - v16 - Fall '96 - p188+ [251-500]
Bumsted, J M - *The Winnipeg General Strike of 1919*
  Can Hist R - v78 - Mr '97 - p110+ [501+]
Bunce, Nigel - *Introduction to Environmental Chemistry*
  J Chem Ed - v73 - N '96 - pA278+ [251-500]
Bunch, Bryan - *Handbook of Current Science and Technology. 2nd Ed.*
  r ARBA - v28 - '97 - p565 [51-250]
Bunch, Chris - *The Seer King*
  KR - v64 - D 1 '96 - p1706+ [51-250]
  PW - v244 - Ja 20 '97 - p399 [51-250]
Bunche, Ralph J - *Ralph J. Bunche: Selected Speeches and Writings*
  Bl S - v26 - Fall '96 - p100+ [51-250]
  Choice - v34 - N '96 - p527 [51-250]
Bundy, Barbara K - *The Future of the Pacific Rim*
  Ch Rev Int - v4 - Spr '97 - p73+ [501+]
Bunge, Mario - *Finding Philosophy in Social Science*
  Choice - v34 - Ap '97 - p1351 [51-250]
  JEL - v35 - Mr '97 - p193+ [51-250]
Bunin, Sherry - *Dear Great American Writers School*
  y LA - v73 - O '96 - p430 [51-250]
Bunis, Davis M - *Yiddish Linguistics*
  r TranslRevS - v1 - My '95 - p5 [51-250]
Bunker, Barbara Benedict - *Conflict, Cooperation, and Justice*
  Per Psy - v50 - Spr '97 - p197+ [501+]
Bunker, Edward - *Dog Eat Dog*
  BW - v26 - D 1 '96 - p6 [51-250]
  LATBR - Ag 18 '96 - p1+ [501+]
Bunkers, Suzanne L - *Inscribing the Daily*
  AB - v99 - Mr 17 '97 - p875+ [501+]
  r Choice - v34 - N '96 - p449+ [51-250]
  SFR - v21 - N '96 - p35 [51-250]
Bunkley, Anita R - *Balancing Act*
  LJ - v122 - Ap 15 '97 - p116 [51-250]
  Starlight Passage
  BW - v26 - Jl 14 '96 - p6 [251-500]
Bunkley, Crawford B - *The African American Network*
  yr BL - v93 - S 15 '96 - p280 [251-500]
  r Choice - v34 - Ap '97 - p1306 [51-250]
  r LJ - v121 - O 15 '96 - p50 [251-500]
  r LJ - v121 - N 1 '96 - p86 [1-50]
Bunn, T Davis - *The Music Box*
  BL - v93 - N 15 '96 - p571 [501+]
  One False Move
  LJ - v122 - F 1 '97 - p66 [51-250]
Bunnell, Paul J - *The New Loyalist Index. Vol. 2*
  r EGH - v50 - N '96 - p159 [51-250]
Bunnin, Nicholas - *The Blackwell Companion to Philosophy*
  r Choice - v34 - O '96 - p248 [51-250]

Bunning, Timothy J - *Liquid Crystals for Advanced Technologies*
  SciTech - v21 - Mr '97 - p78 [51-250]
Bunson, Margaret - *Encyclopedia of Ancient Mesoamerica*
  r ARBA - v28 - '97 - p206 [51-250]
  r R&R Bk N - v12 - F '97 - p27 [51-250]
Bunson, Matthew - *Angels A to Z*
  r Choice - v34 - O '96 - p249 [51-250]
  r RR - v55 - S '96 - p554 [1-50]
  The Sherlock Holmes Encyclopedia
  r BC - v45 - Sum '96 - p265+ [501+]
Bunt, Gerrit H V - *Alexander the Great in the Literature of Medieval Britain*
  RES - v48 - F '97 - p77+ [501+]
  Specu - v72 - Ja '97 - p120+ [251-500]
Bunting, Eve - *The Blue and the Gray (Illus. by Ned Bittinger)*
  c BL - v93 - N 15 '96 - p586 [51-250]
  c CBRS - v25 - F '97 - p73 [1-50]
  c CCB-B - v50 - F '97 - p200+ [51-250]
  c HB Guide - v8 - Spr '97 - p22 [51-250]
  c KR - v64 - N 15 '96 - p1666 [51-250]
  c PW - v243 - N 18 '96 - p74 [51-250]
  c SLJ - v42 - D '96 - p85 [51-250]
  Dandelions (Illus. by Greg Shed)
  c LA - v73 - O '96 - p430 [51-250]
  c RT - v50 - O '96 - p153 [51-250]
  c RT - v50 - N '96 - p244+ [51-250]
  A Day's Work (Illus. by Ronald Himler)
  c CLW - v67 - Mr '97 - p13 [1-50]
  c PW - v244 - Ap 21 '97 - p74 [1-50]
  Going Home (Illus. by David Diaz)
  c BL - v93 - O 1 '96 - p357 [51-250]
  c CBRS - v25 - S '96 - p1 [51-250]
  c CCB-B - v50 - D '96 - p129+ [51-250]
  c CSM - v88 - N 21 '96 - pB4 [51-250]
  c HB Guide - v8 - Spr '97 - p22 [51-250]
  c KR - v64 - S 1 '96 - p1320 [51-250]
  c LATBR - S 1 '96 - p11 [51-250]
  c Learning - v25 - N '96 - p29 [51-250]
  c PW - v243 - S 23 '96 - p76 [51-250]
  c SFR - v21 - N '96 - p47 [51-250]
  c SLJ - v42 - S '96 - p171 [51-250]
  How Many Days to America?
  c Learning - v25 - Mr '97 - p54 [1-50]
  I Am the Mummy Heb-Nefert (Illus. by David Christiana)
  c BL - v93 - My 15 '97 - p1576 [51-250]
  c CCB-B - v50 - My '97 - p315 [51-250]
  c KR - v65 - Ap 1 '97 - p550 [51-250]
  c PW - v244 - Mr 10 '97 - p66+ [51-250]
  Trib Bks - Mr 9 '97 - p7 [51-250]
  I Don't Want to Go to Camp (Illus. by Maryann Cocca-Leffler)
  c HB Guide - v7 - Fall '96 - p249 [51-250]
  Market Day (Illus. by Holly Berry)
  c CLW - v67 - S '96 - p55 [51-250]
  c HB Guide - v7 - Fall '96 - p249 [51-250]
  c RT - v50 - My '97 - p686 [51-250]
  My Backpack (Illus. by Maryann Cocca-Leffler)
  c BL - v93 - My 1 '97 - p1500+ [51-250]
  c PW - v244 - My 12 '97 - p76 [51-250]
  On Call Back Mountain (Illus. by Barry Moser)
  c CBRS - v25 - Mr '97 - p92 [51-250]
  c KR - v65 - Ja 15 '97 - p138 [51-250]
  c PW - v244 - Ja 13 '97 - p74+ [51-250]
  c SLJ - v43 - Mr '97 - p149 [51-250]
  Red Fox Running (Illus. by Wendell Minor)
  c Par Ch - v20 - N '96 - p3 [1-50]
  Secret Place (Illus. by Ted Rand)
  c BL - v93 - S 1 '96 - p140 [51-250]
  c CBRS - v25 - D '96 - p37 [51-250]
  c HB Guide - v8 - Spr '97 - p22 [51-250]
  c SLJ - v42 - S '96 - p171 [51-250]
  Smoky Night
  c New Ad - v9 - Fall '96 - p267+ [501+]
  SOS Titanic
  y HB Guide - v7 - Fall '96 - p300 [51-250]
  y Kliatt - v30 - S '96 - p6 [51-250]
  c Par - v71 - D '96 - p254 [51-250]
  Sunflower House (Illus. by Kathryn Hewitt)
  c Ch BWatch - v6 - My '96 - p5 [1-50]
  c HB Guide - v7 - Fall '96 - p250 [51-250]
  Sunshine Home (Illus. by Diane De Groat)
  c LA - v73 - S '96 - p356 [51-250]

Train to Somewhere (Illus. by Ronald Himler)
c   BL - v93 - Ja '97 - p765 [1-50]
c   BL - v93 - Ap 1 '97 - p1298 [1-50]
c   HB Guide - v7 - Fall '96 - p250 [51-250]
c   Inst - v106 - Ja '97 - p54 [51-250]
c   LATBR - My 26 '96 - p11 [51-250]
c   Par Ch - v21 - Mr '97 - p8 [1-50]
c   RT - v50 - My '97 - p682 [51-250]
Trouble on the T-Ball Team (Illus. by Irene Trivas)
c   BL - v93 - Mr 1 '97 - p1169 [51-250]
c   CCB-B - v50 - Ap '97 - p277 [51-250]
c   Par Ch - v21 - Mr '97 - p4 [1-50]
The Wednesday Surprise
c   Inst - v42 - Ag '96 - p44 [1-50]
Bunting, Jane - *My First Action Word Book (Illus. by Susanna Price)*
c   HB Guide - v7 - Fall '96 - p237 [51-250]
c   SLJ - v42 - Ag '96 - p133 [51-250]
Bunting, Madeleine - *The Model Occupation*
   Choice - v34 - N '96 - p516 [51-250]
Bunting, Mark - *Mark Bunting's Virtual Power*
   BL - v93 - My 15 '97 - p1550 [51-250]
Bunting, Robert - *The Pacific Raincoast*
   LJ - v122 - Ja '97 - p137 [51-250]
Bunyan, John - *A Pilgrim's Progress (Topping). Audio Version*
   Obs - Ja 12 '97 - p18* [51-250]
Burall, Paul - *Product Development and the Environment*
   SciTech - v20 - S '96 - p62 [51-250]
Burandt, Harriet - *Tales from the Homeplace*
c   HB - v73 - My '97 - p314+ [51-250]
c   KR - v65 - F 15 '97 - p297 [51-250]
c   Par Ch - v21 - Mr '97 - p8 [1-50]
c   PW - v244 - Mr 10 '97 - p67 [51-250]
Burbidge, John W - *Real Process*
   R&R Bk N - v12 - F '97 - p3 [51-250]
Burby, Liza N - *Family Violence*
y   BL - v93 - S 15 '96 - p228 [51-250]
y   HB Guide - v7 - Fall '96 - p316 [51-250]
Burch, Hobart A - *Basic Social Policy and Planning Readings*
   LJ - v12 - Mr '97 - p25 [51-250]
Burch, Jonathan - *Astronauts*
c   Ch BWatch - v6 - Jl '96 - p6 [51-250]
Burchfield, Robert - *The Cambridge History of the English Language. Vol. 5*
   RES - v48 - F '97 - p74+ [501+]
Burchill, Scott - *Theories of International Relations*
   Choice - v34 - Ap '97 - p1413 [51-250]
Burckhardt, Jacqueline - *Meret Oppenheim: Beyond the Teacup*
   LJ - v121 - O 1 '96 - p72 [51-250]
   NYTBR - v101 - D 1 '96 - p22 [51-250]
   TLS - N 8 '96 - p33 [251-500]
Burdea, Grigore C - *Force and Touch Feedback for Virtual Reality*
   Robotica - v15 - Mr '97 - p235 [501+]
Burdekin, Richard C K - *Confidence, Credibility and Macroeconomic Policy*
   JEL - v34 - S '96 - p1347+ [501+]
Burden, Michael - *Purcell Remembered*
   FF - v19 - Jl '96 - p425 [501+]
   Notes - v53 - Mr '97 - p791+ [501+]
Burdett, Anita L P - *The Historical Boundaries between Bosnia, Croatia, Serbia*
   GJ - v163 - Mr '97 - p101 [251-500]
Burdett, John - *The Last Six Million Seconds*
   BL - v93 - Ja '97 - p823 [51-250]
   KR - v64 - N 15 '96 - p1618 [251-500]
   LJ - v122 - F 1 '97 - p104+ [51-250]
   PW - v244 - Ja 6 '97 - p64 [251-500]
   Trib Bks - F 16 '97 - p6 [51-250]
Burdick, Michael A - *For God and Fatherland*
   R&R Bk N - v12 - F '97 - p11 [1-50]
Burditt, Joyce - *Buck Naked*
   Arm Det - v29 - Fall '96 - p495 [51-250]
   Arm Det - v30 - Win '97 - p41 [251-500]
   LATBR - My 12 '96 - p11 [51-250]
Bureaucrats in Business
   J Gov Info - v23 - S '96 - p683+ [51-250]
Burford, E J - *Of Bridles and Burnings*
   HT - v46 - Ag '96 - p60 [51-250]
Burg, B R - *An American Seafarer in the Age of Sail*
   AHR - v101 - O '96 - p1287+ [501+]
Burg, Steven L - *War or Peace?*
   For Aff - v76 - My '97 - p140 [51-250]
Burg, Thomas N - *Sieches Volk Macht Siechen Staat*
   AHR - v101 - O '96 - p1200+ [501+]
Burge, Susan B - *Simple Skin Surgery. 2nd Ed.*
   SciTech - v20 - S '96 - p38 [51-250]

Burgel, Johann Christoph - *Gesellschaftlicher Umbruch Und Historie Im Zeitgenössischen Drama Der Islamischen Welt*
   WLT - v70 - Sum '96 - p753 [501+]
Burgen, Stephen - *Your Mother's Tongue*
   Econ - v341 - D 14 '96 - p87 [51-250]
   Spec - v278 - Ja 11 '97 - p35+ [501+]
Burger, Dolores - *Women Who Changed the Heart of the City*
   PW - v243 - D 16 '96 - p54 [51-250]
Burger, Joanna - *A Naturalist along the Jersey Shore*
   Choice - v34 - D '96 - p635 [51-250]
   Under Nat - v23 - 3 '96 - p29 [51-250]
Burger, Leslie - *Red Cross, Red Crescent*
c   BL - v93 - Ja '97 - p848 [251-500]
c   HB Guide - v8 - Spr '97 - p95 [51-250]
c   SLJ - v43 - Ja '97 - p118+ [51-250]
Sister Cities
c   BL - v93 - S 1 '96 - p120+ [51-250]
c   HB Guide - v8 - Spr '97 - p92 [51-250]
c   SLJ - v42 - S '96 - p210+ [51-250]
United Nations High Commissioner for Refugees
c   BL - v93 - Ja '97 - p848 [251-500]
c   HB Guide - v8 - Spr '97 - p95 [51-250]
c   SLJ - v43 - Ja '97 - p118+ [51-250]
y   VOYA - v19 - F '97 - p343 [251-500]
Burger, Nash K - *The Road to West 43rd Street*
   Sew R - v104 - O '96 - p673+ [501+]
Burger, Warren E - *It Is So Ordered*
   Pres SQ - v26 - Sum '96 - p900+ [501+]
Burgess, Adrienne - *Fatherhood Reclaimed*
   NS - v126 - Ap 25 '97 - p46+ [51-250]
   Obs - F 9 '97 - p18* [501+]
Burgess, Anthony - *Byrne: A Novel*
   Obs - S 15 '96 - p18* [51-250]
   WLT - v70 - Sum '96 - p695+ [501+]
A Clockwork Orange (Burgess). Audio Version
   BWatch - v17 - D '96 - p10 [1-50]
   Quill & Q - v62 - Ag '96 - p37 [1-50]
The Malayan Trilogy
   FEER - Anniv '96 - p230 [251-500]
One Hand Clapping
   Obs - N 3 '96 - p18* [51-250]
Burgess, Glenn - *Absolute Monarchy and the Stuart Constitution*
   Choice - v34 - O '96 - p338 [51-250]
   HRNB - v25 - Fall '96 - p19 [251-500]
Burgess, Graham - *The Complete Guide to Chess*
   Books - v11 - Ap '97 - p20 [1-50]
Burgess, Jay - *The Basics of Java Animation*
   SciTech - v21 - Mr '97 - p4 [51-250]
Burgess, Lauren Cook - *An Uncommon Soldier*
y   Kliatt - v30 - S '96 - p26 [51-250]
Burgess, Lynda - *Decorating in Blue and White*
   BL - v92 - Ag '96 - p1873+ [51-250]
Burgess, Lynne - *Clay and Dough*
   TES - F 14 '97 - p16* [251-500]
Pets
   TES - D 13 '96 - p43 [51-250]
Burgess, Melvin - *The Baby and Fly Pie*
y   HB Guide - v7 - Fall '96 - p300 [51-250]
Burning Issy
c   TES - Ap 4 '97 - p8* [501+]
The Earth Giant (Illus. by K Brown)
c   JB - v60 - Ag '96 - p146 [51-250]
Junk
y   Obs - Mr 30 '97 - p17* [251-500]
y   TES - F 7 '97 - p9* [251-500]
Loving April
y   Bks Keeps - Ja '97 - p27 [51-250]
Tiger Tiger
c   JB - v60 - Ag '96 - p153+ [251-500]
y   Sch Lib - v44 - Ag '96 - p117 [51-250]
Burgess, Philip M - *Profile of Western North America*
r   ARBA - v28 - '97 - p116+ [51-250]
Burgess, Thornton W - *The Dear Old Briar-Patch (Norgang). Audio Version*
c   SLJ - v42 - D '96 - p72 [51-250]
Listen and Read the Adventures of Peter Cottontail (Seldes). Book and Audio Version
c   BL - v93 - Mr 15 '97 - p1253 [51-250]
c   Ch BWatch - v6 - Jl '96 - p7 [1-50]
Burgess, W A - *Cowards*
   KR - v65 - Ap 1 '97 - p480 [251-500]
   LJ - v122 - Ap 1 '97 - p122 [51-250]
   PW - v244 - Mr 17 '97 - p76 [51-250]
Burgess-Jackson, Keith - *Rape: A Philosophical Investigation*
   R&R Bk N - v12 - F '97 - p63 [51-250]

Burggraf, Shirley P - *The Feminine Economy and Economic Man*
   Choice - v34 - My '97 - p1546 [51-250]
   NYTBR - v102 - Ja 26 '97 - p21 [501+]
Burghardt, Uwe - *Die Mechanisierung Des Ruhrbergbaus 1890-1930*
   JEH - v56 - S '96 - p719+ [501+]
Burghardt, Walter J - *Preaching the Just Word*
   BL - v93 - N 1 '96 - p463 [51-250]
   CC - v114 - Ap 9 '97 - p371+ [501+]
Burghes, David - *Mathematical Modelling*
y   Math T - v89 - O '96 - p608 [51-250]
Burgos, Julia De - *Song of the Simple Truth*
   BL - v93 - F 15 '97 - p996 [51-250]
   Choice - v34 - My '97 - p1503+ [51-250]
   PW - v244 - F 24 '97 - p85 [51-250]
Burguiere, Andre - *A History of the Family. Vols. 1-2*
   Choice - v34 - D '96 - p662+ [51-250]
Burgunder, Anne - *Zoolutions: A Mathematical Expedition*
   VOYA - v19 - F '97 - p355+ [251-500]
Burkan, Wayne - *Wide-Angle Vision*
   BL - v93 - S 1 '96 - p44 [51-250]
Burke, Andrew E - *Enterprise and the Irish Economy*
   JEL - v34 - D '96 - p2084+ [51-250]
Burke, Bernard F - *An Introduction to Radio Astronomy*
   New Sci - v153 - Mr 1 '97 - p43 [51-250]
Burke, Bernard V - *Ambassador Frederic Sackett and the Collapse of the Weimar Republic 1930 1933*
   AHR - v101 - O '96 - p1306 [501+]
   JMH - v68 - D '96 - p1027+ [501+]
Burke, Carolyn - *Becoming Modern*
   ABR - v18 - O '96 - p16+ [501+]
   Atl - v278 - Ag '96 - p93+ [51-250]
   BL - v93 - Ja '97 - p759 [1-50]
   Choice - v34 - N '96 - p453 [51-250]
   Nat - v264 - F 10 '97 - p29+ [501+]
   NL - v79 - Ag 12 '96 - p24+ [501+]
   NYRB - v43 - S 19 '96 - p57+ [501+]
   TLS - Ag 30 '96 - p3+ [501+]
   Wom R Bks - v14 - O '96 - p1+ [501+]
Burke, David - *Mediterranean France Insider's Guide*
r   BWatch - v17 - S '96 - p5 [51-250]
Burke, David, 1956- - *Street Talk 3*
   CAY - v16 - Fall '95 - p3 [51-250]
Burke, Derek - *Self-Assessment in Accident and Emergency Medicine*
   SciTech - v20 - D '96 - p42 [1-50]
Burke, Frank - *Fellini's Films*
   Choice - v34 - My '97 - p1506 [51-250]
Burke, James - *The Pinball Effect*
   Choice - v34 - F '97 - p981 [51-250]
   NYTBR - v101 - S 15 '96 - p9 [501+]
   Reason - v28 - D '96 - p38+ [51-250]
   Reason - v28 - Ap '97 - p57+ [501+]
The Pinball Effect (Burke). Audio Version
y   Kliatt - v31 - My '97 - p48 [51-250]
   LJ - v121 - N 15 '96 - p107 [51-250]
   LJ - v122 - F 15 '97 - p115 [1-50]
Burke, James Lee - *Burning Angels*
   EJ - v85 - D '96 - p96+ [501+]
Cadillac Jukebox
   LATBR - Ag 25 '96 - p3 [501+]
Cadillac Jukebox (Patton). Audio Version
   Arm Det - v30 - Win '97 - p80 [51-250]
y   Kliatt - v30 - N '96 - p38 [51-250]
Heaven's Prisoners (Hammer). Audio Version
   BL - v93 - My 15 '97 - p1596 [51-250]
In the Electric Mists of the Confederate Dead
   EJ - v85 - D '96 - p96+ [501+]
A Stained White Radiance (Patton). Audio Version
y   Kliatt - v31 - Mr '97 - p46 [51-250]
Burke, Jan - *Hocus*
   BL - v93 - My 1 '97 - p1482 [51-250]
   KR - v65 - F 15 '97 - p256 [51-250]
   LJ - v122 - My 1 '97 - p144 [1-50]
   PW - v244 - Mr 3 '97 - p67 [51-250]
   Trib Bks - My 4 '97 - p6 [51-250]
Burke, John J - *From Home and Abroad*
   Nine-C Lit - v50 - Mr '96 - p552 [1-50]
Burke, Juliet Sharman - *Stories from the Stars (Illus. by Jackie Morris)*
c   HB Guide - v8 - Spr '97 - p100 [51-250]
c   TES - D 6 '96 - p16* [501+]
Burke, Martin J - *The Conundrum of Class*
   CS - v25 - N '96 - p752+ [501+]
   RP - v58 - Sum '96 - p623+ [501+]
Burke, Patrick - *Revolution in Europe 1989*
c   TES - O 4 '96 - p17* [501+]
Burke, Peter - *The Fortunes of the Courtier*
   Lon R Bks - v18 - Ag 22 '96 - p30+ [501+]

Burke, Philip G - *Theory of Electron-Atom Collisions. Pt. 1*
  Phys Today - v49 - N '96 - p84 [501+]
Burke, Phyllis - *Gender Shock*
  LATBR - Ag 18 '96 - p10+ [501+]
  Ms - v7 - S '96 - p83 [1-50]
  Ms - v7 - N '96 - p83 [501+]
Burke, Ruth - *The Games of Poetics*
  Humor - v9 - 3 '96 - p412+ [501+]
Burke, S M - *The British Raj in India*
  HRNB - v25 - Fall '96 - p39 [251-500]
Burke, Sara Z - *Seeking the Highest Good*
  R&R Bk N - v11 - S '96 - p58 [51-250]
Burke, Tom - *Dewey's New Logic*
  ES - v27 - Sum '96 - p173+ [501+]
Burke, Victor Lee - *The Clash of Civilizations*
  HT - v46 - O '96 - p56 [1-50]
Burkert, Walter - *Creation of the Sacred*
  Am - v176 - Mr 8 '97 - p26 [51-250]
  BW - v27 - Mr 2 '97 - p8 [251-500]
  Choice - v34 - My '97 - p1515 [51-250]
  Sew R - v104 - O '96 - p665+ [501+]
  Spec - v277 - N 16 '96 - p46 [1-50]
  TLS - N 29 '96 - p14 [51-250]
  TLS - N 29 '96 - p16 [1-50]
  TLS - D 13 '96 - p26 [501+]
Burkett, Larry - *The Thor Conspiracy*
  HM - v293 - S '96 - p64+ [501+]
Burkhart, James A - *Mules, Jackasses, and Other Misconceptions*
  CAY - v17 - Win '96 - p2 [51-250]
Burkholder, J Peter - *All Made of Tunes*
  TLS - O 18 '96 - p18+ [501+]
  Charles Ives and His World
  Choice - v34 - Ja '97 - p805 [51-250]
  Obs - F 16 '97 - p17* [501+]
Burkholz, Herbert - *The FDA Follies*
  ACI - v7 - Fall '95 - p28+ [501+]
Burkinshaw, Robert K - *Pilgrims in Lotus Land*
  Can Hist R - v78 - Mr '97 - p155+ [501+]
Burkitt, George - *Wheater's Basic Histopathology. 3rd Ed.*
  r SciTech - v21 - Mr '97 - p47 [51-250]
Burks, Brian - *Runs with Horses*
  y Emerg Lib - v24 - S '96 - p26 [1-50]
  Soldier Boy
  y BL - v93 - My 15 '97 - p1573 [51-250]
  y CCB-B - v50 - Ap '97 - p277+ [51-250]
  y KR - v65 - Ap 1 '97 - p550+ [51-250]
Burlaga, Leonard F - *Interplanetary Magnetohydrodynamics*
  Phys Today - v49 - S '96 - p83+ [501+]
Burleigh, Michael - *Death and Deliverance*
  EHR - v112 - Ap '97 - p533+ [501+]
  Historian - v59 - Fall '96 - p179+ [501+]
  HT - v47 - Ja '97 - p51 [501+]
  JIH - v27 - Aut '96 - p324+ [251-500]
  JMH - v68 - D '96 - p1028+ [501+]
Burleigh, Robert - *Flight*
  c PW - v244 - F 3 '97 - p108 [1-50]
  Who Said That? (Illus. by David Catrow)
  c BL - v93 - Mr 1 '97 - p1166 [51-250]
Burleson, Donald R - *Spiders and Milk*
  SF Chr - v18 - O '96 - p76 [51-250]
Burlew, A Kathleen Hoard - *African American Psychology*
  JMSW - v4 - 3 '96 - p99+ [501+]
Burley, David G - *A Particular Condition in Life*
  JIH - v27 - Aut '96 - p358+ [501+]
Burlingame, Dwight F - *Alternative Revenue Sources*
  ChrPhil - v9 - O 31 '96 - p67 [501+]
  Corporate Philanthropy
  ChrPhil - v9 - Ja 9 '97 - p36 [501+]
Burlingame, Jon - *TV's Biggest Hits*
  Emmy - v18 - O '96 - p51 [1-50]
  Ent W - Je 28 '96 - p97 [51-250]
Burlingame, Michael - *The Inner World of Abraham Lincoln*
  Historian - v59 - Fall '96 - p146+ [501+]
  JSH - v62 - N '96 - p811+ [251-500]
Burlingame, Roger - *Of Making Many Books*
  PW - v243 - O 7 '96 - p69 [1-50]
Burma, Ian - *The Missionary and the Libertine*
  NS & S - v9 - My 17 '96 - p39+ [251-500]
Burman, Edward - *Supremely Abominable Crimes*
  Obs - D 29 '96 - p28 [51-250]
Burman, Stephen - *The Black Progress Question*
  APSR - v90 - D '96 - p867+ [501+]
  J Am St - v30 - D '96 - p466+ [251-500]
Burmeister, Joachim - *Musical Poetics*
  Ren Q - v49 - Aut '96 - p684+ [1-50]

Burn, Gordon - *Fullalove*
  Books - v9 - S '95 - p22 [1-50]
  Obs - S 29 '96 - p18* [51-250]
Burnard, Bonnie - *Casino and Other Stories*
  Can Lit - Spr '97 - p236+ [501+]
Burnard, Damon - *Ivana the Inventor*
  c Magpies - v11 - Jl '96 - p28 [1-50]
Burnard, Philip - *Nurses Counselling*
  SciTech - v21 - Mr '97 - p69 [51-250]
Burner, David - *Making Peace with the 60s*
  BL - v93 - S 1 '96 - p58 [51-250]
  BW - v26 - N 24 '96 - p8 [501+]
  Choice - v34 - F '97 - p1023 [501+]
  Econ - v341 - O 19 '96 - p3*+ [501+]
  LJ - v121 - O 1 '96 - p97+ [501+]
  PW - v243 - S 9 '96 - p76 [51-250]
Burnett, Amy Nelson - *The Yoke of Christ*
  CH - v66 - Mr '97 - p113+ [501+]
  EHR - v112 - F '97 - p188+ [501+]
  Historian - v59 - Fall '96 - p180+ [251-500]
Burnett, Chris - *The United Kingdom*
  y Sch Lib - v44 - Ag '96 - p123 [51-250]
Burnett, Frances Hodgson - *A Little Princess (Leishman). Audio Version*
  c BL - v93 - Ap 1 '97 - p1313+ [1-50]
  c CSM - v89 - Mr 27 '97 - pB6 [1-50]
  y HB - v73 - Ja '97 - p85+ [501+]
  y Kliatt - v31 - Mr '97 - p43+ [51-250]
  The Secret Garden
  c HMR - Win '96 - p45 [1-50]
  The Secret Garden. Audio Version
  c TES - Ag 30 '96 - p28 [51-250]
  The Secret Garden (Illus. by Kathy Mitchell)
  c Ch BWatch - v6 - D '96 - p5 [1-50]
Burnett, Jim - *Tee Times*
  PW - v244 - My 12 '97 - p66 [51-250]
Burnett, John - *Biological Recording in the United Kingdom. Vols. 1-2*
  J Gov Info - v23 - S '96 - p643+ [51-250]
Burnett, John, 1925- - *Idle Hands*
  EHR - v111 - N '96 - p1332+ [251-500]
  Useful Toil
  HT - v46 - S '96 - p57 [51-250]
Burney, Fanny - *The Early Journals and Letters of Fanny Burney. Vol. 3, Pt. 1*
  RES - v47 - N '96 - p596+ [501+]
Burnham, David - *Above the Law*
  Dis - v44 - Win '97 - p128+ [501+]
Burnham, Patricia M - *Redefining American History Painting*
  r Choice - v34 - N '96 - p446 [51-250]
Burnham, Robert - *Burnham's Celestial Handbook. Vols. 1-3*
  r S&T - v92 - S '96 - p55 [51-250]
  See and Enjoy the Great Comet
  r S&T - v93 - F '97 - p58 [51-250]
Burnham, Scott - *Beethoven Hero*
  AS - v66 - Spr '97 - p301+ [501+]
  NYRB - v43 - O 3 '96 - p23+ [501+]
  TLS - D 20 '96 - p20 [501+]
Burnie, David - *Everyday Machines (Illus. by John Kelly)*
  c HB Guide - v7 - Fall '96 - p350 [51-250]
Burningham, John - *The Baby*
  c Books - v9 - S '95 - p26 [1-50]
  The Blanket
  c Books - v9 - S '95 - p26 [1-50]
  Cloudland (Illus. by John Burningham)
  c Bks Keeps - Mr '97 - p20 [1-50]
  c BL - v93 - D 15 '96 - p731 [51-250]
  c HB Guide - v8 - Spr '97 - p22 [51-250]
  c JB - v60 - O '96 - p182 [51-250]
  c KR - v64 - O 15 '96 - p1529 [51-250]
  c NYTBR - v102 - Mr 16 '97 - p26 [1-50]
  c PW - v243 - O 14 '96 - p83 [51-250]
  c Sch Lib - v45 - F '97 - p17 [251-500]
  c SLJ - v42 - O '96 - p85 [51-250]
  c TES - S 6 '96 - p7* [501+]
  Courtney
  c Bks Keeps - N '96 - p7 [1-50]
  c TES - O 18 '96 - p12* [1-50]
  The Dog
  c Books - v9 - S '95 - p26 [1-50]
  The Friend
  c Books - v9 - S '95 - p26 [1-50]
  Mr. Gumpy's Outing
  c Bks Keeps - Mr '97 - p7 [1-50]
  The Shopping Basket
  c HB Guide - v7 - Fall '96 - p250 [1-50]
Burnisky, David L - *The Personalities of Melvin Hill Cemetery, Phelps, Ontario County, New York*
  r EGH - v50 - N '96 - p175 [51-250]

Burnley, J D - *The Language of Middle English Literature*
  r MLR - v92 - Ja '97 - p166 [251-500]
  r RES - v47 - Ag '96 - p398+ [501+]
Burns, Alistair - *Dementia*
  r AJPsych - v153 - O '96 - p1362+ [251-500]
Burns, Allan F - *Maya in Exile*
  HAHR - v77 - F '97 - p173+ [251-500]
Burns, Ben - *Nitty Gritty*
  Nat - v262 - Je 17 '96 - p30+ [501+]
Burns, Bryan - *World Cinema: Hungary*
  Choice - v34 - F '97 - p972 [51-250]
Burns, Diane L - *Berries, Nuts and Seeds (Illus. by John F McGee)*
  c BL - v93 - F 15 '97 - p1017 [51-250]
  Snakes, Salamanders, and Lizards (Illus. by Linda Garrow)
  c HB Guide - v7 - Fall '96 - p342 [51-250]
  Trees, Leaves, and Bark (Illus. by Linda Garrow)
  c HB Guide - v7 - Fall '96 - p340 [1-50]
Burns, E Bradford - *Kinship with the Land*
  Utne R - S '96 - p93 [1-50]
  WHQ - v28 - Spr '97 - p103 [1-50]
Burns, Grant - *Sports Pages*
  r RQ - v36 - Win '96 - p218+ [1-50]
Burns, J H - *The True Law of Kingship*
  Choice - v34 - S '96 - p184 [51-250]
Burns, Janice A - *Sarah's Song*
  y Kliatt - v30 - N '96 - p21 [51-250]
Burns, Jimmy - *Hand of God*
  Econ - v341 - N 23 '96 - p102 [501+]
  TLS - D 6 '96 - p30 [501+]
Burns, Kate - *Hide and Seek (Illus. by Dawn Apperley)*
  c BL - v93 - D 15 '96 - p732 [1-50]
  In the Jungle (Illus. by Dawn Apperley)
  c KR - v64 - S 1 '96 - p1331 [51-250]
  In the Ocean (Illus. by Dawn Apperley)
  c HB Guide - v7 - Fall '96 - p237 [1-50]
  In the Sand (Illus. by Dawn Apperley)
  c HB Guide - v7 - Fall '96 - p237 [1-50]
  In the Snow (Illus. by Dawn Apperley)
  c SLJ - v43 - Ja '97 - p76 [1-50]
Burns, Ken - *The Civil War*
  WHQ - v27 - Win '96 - p548+ [51-250]
Burns, Khephra - *Confirmation: The Spiritual Wisdom That Has Shaped Our Lives*
  LJ - v121 - N 1 '96 - p86 [1-50]
Burns, Landon C - *Pat Conroy: A Critical Companion*
  Choice - v34 - N '96 - p453 [51-250]
  R&R Bk N - v11 - N '96 - p73 [51-250]
  y SLJ - v42 - O '96 - p152+ [51-250]
  SLMQ - v25 - Fall '96 - p63 [1-50]
Burns, Marilyn - *How Many Feet? How Many Tails? (Illus. by Lynn Adams)*
  c BL - v93 - F 1 '97 - p949 [51-250]
Burns, Olive Ann - *Cold Sassy Tree*
  y BL - v93 - Ja '97 - p832 [1-50]
Burns, Peggy - *Explorers*
  c Sch Lib - v45 - F '97 - p37 [51-250]
  Inventors
  c Sch Lib - v45 - F '97 - p37 [51-250]
Burns, Ralph A - *Essentials of Chemistry. 2nd Ed.*
  J Chem Ed - v73 - O '96 - pA245 [501+]
  Fundamentals of Chemistry. 2nd Ed.
  J Chem Ed - v73 - O '96 - pA245 [501+]
Burns, Robert I - *Jews in the Notarial Culture*
  MEJ - v51 - Spr '97 - p313+ [51-250]
Burns, Robin J - *Three Decades of Peace Education around the World*
  R&R Bk N - v11 - N '96 - p51 [51-250]
Burns, Sarah - *Inventing the Modern Artist*
  Choice - v34 - My '97 - p1485 [51-250]
  LJ - v122 - F 1 '97 - p76 [51-250]
  PW - v243 - N 18 '96 - p58 [51-250]
Burnside, Madeleine - *Spirits of the Passage*
  y BL - v93 - F 15 '97 - p978 [51-250]
  BW - v27 - Ap 6 '97 - p8 [501+]
Burnside, Tom - *American Racing*
  BWatch - v18 - F '97 - p1 [51-250]
Buron, Nicole De - *Mais T'As Tout Pour Etre Heureuse!*
  BL - v93 - Ja '97 - p827 [1-50]
Burr, Chandler - *Homosexuality and Biology*
  Books - v10 - Je '96 - p21 [1-50]
  A Separate Creation
  BL - v93 - Ja '97 - p758 [1-50]
  BW - v26 - S 1 '96 - p9 [501+]
  Choice - v34 - N '96 - p481 [51-250]
  KR - v64 - My 1 '96 - p655+ [251-500]
  TLS - N 1 '96 - p14 [501+]
Burr, David - *Olivi and Franciscan Poverty*
  CHR - v82 - O '96 - p692+ [501+]

Olivi's Peaceable Kingdom
CH - v65 - S '96 - p462+ [501+]
Burr, J Millard - *Requiem for the Sudan*
For Aff - v75 - S '96 - p159+ [51-250]
Burrell, Brian - *The Words We Live By*
KR - v65 - My 1 '97 - p688 [251-500]
Burrell, C Colston - *The Natural Water Garden*
LJ - v122 - My 1 '97 - p130 [51-250]
PW - v244 - My 5 '97 - p204 [51-250]
Burrell, David B - *Freedom and Creation in Three Traditions*
Rel St - v33 - Mr '97 - p121+ [501+]
Voices from Jerusalem
Rel Ed - v91 - Fall '96 - p611 [1-50]
Burrell, Roy - *Oxford First Ancient History (Illus. by Peter Connolly)*
c SLJ - v42 - N '96 - p39 [51-250]
Burrelle's Media Directory. Vols. 1-5
r LJ - v122 - Ap 15 '97 - p64 [51-250]
Burrill, William - *Hemingway: The Toronto Years 1920-1924*
Can Lit - Spr '97 - p222+ [501+]
Burrin, Philippe - *La France A L'Heure Allemande 1940-1944*
Choice - v34 - D '96 - p568 [1-50]
EHR - v112 - Ap '97 - p535+ [501+]
France under the Germans
BL - v93 - F 1 '97 - p923 [51-250]
For Aff - v76 - Mr '97 - p186 [51-250]
KR - v64 - D 1 '96 - p1711 [251-500]
LJ - v122 - Ja '97 - p118 [51-250]
NYTLa - v146 - Mr 26 '97 - pC17 [501+]
PW - v243 - D 9 '96 - p51+ [51-250]
Living with Defeat
Spec - v278 - Ja 25 '97 - p39 [501+]
Burroughs, Catherine B - *Reading the Social Body*
JPC - v29 - Spr '96 - p232 [51-250]
Burroughs, Jeff - *The Little Team That Could*
Aethlon - v13 - Fall '95 - p180 [251-500]
Burroughs, William James - *Weather*
yr BL - v92 - Ag '96 - p1924 [251-500]
r BW - v27 - Mr 2 '97 - p8 [251-500]
r E Mag - v7 - N '96 - p50 [51-250]
r Nature - v381 - My 16 '96 - p206 [1-50]
Burrow, Colin - *Epic Romance*
Comp L - v48 - Fall '96 - p371+ [501+]
Burrows, Elaine - *The British Cinema Source Book*
r ARBA - v28 - '97 - p506+ [251-500]
Burrows, Jack - *John Ringo: The Gunfighter Who Never Was*
Roundup M - v4 - D '96 - p19 [251-500]
Burrows, Malcolm - *The Neurobiology of an Insect Brain*
r Nature - v385 - F 27 '97 - p785+ [501+]
Burrus, Virginia - *The Making of a Heretic*
Rel St Rev - v23 - Ja '97 - p79 [51-250]
Burschel, Peter - *Soldner Im Nordwestdeutschland Des 16. Und 17. Jahrhunderts*
EHR - v112 - F '97 - p192+ [501+]
Six Ct J - v27 - Win '96 - p1229 [251-500]
Burstall, Terry - *Vietnam: The Australian Dilemma*
Pac A - v69 - Sum '96 - p296 [251-500]
Burstein, Andrew - *The Inner Jefferson*
Historian - v59 - Win '97 - p422+ [251-500]
JSH - v63 - F '97 - p153+ [501+]
RAH - v24 - S '96 - p401+ [501+]
Burstein, Daniel - *Road Warriors*
J Gov Info - v23 - Jl '96 - p521+ [501+]
Nat R - v48 - O 14 '96 - p81+ [501+]
Trib Bks - Ja 12 '97 - p2 [1-50]
Burstein, Janet Handler - *Writing Mothers, Writing Daughters*
Choice - v34 - Mr '97 - p1159 [51-250]
Burston, Daniel - *The Wing of Madness*
Econ - v341 - O 19 '96 - p15* [501+]
New Sci - v152 - N 16 '96 - p48 [51-250]
NYRB - v43 - N 14 '96 - p30+ [501+]
NYTBR - v101 - S 8 '96 - p13 [501+]
SciTech - v20 - N '96 - p42 [1-50]
TLS - S 27 '96 - p27 [501+]
Burstyn, Joan N - *Educating Tomorrow's Valuable Citizen*
Choice - v34 - D '96 - p661 [51-250]
Bursztynski, Sue - *Potions to Pulsars*
c New Sci - v152 - D 14 '96 - p45 [1-50]
Burt, Donald X - *Augustine's World*
Choice - v34 - Ja '97 - p808 [51-250]
Burt, George - *The Art of Film Music*
FQ - v49 - Fall '95 - p39+ [501+]

Burt, James E - *Elementary Statistics for Geographers. 2nd Ed.*
R&R Bk N - v11 - D '96 - p18 [51-250]
SB - v33 - Ja '97 - p10+ [51-250]
Burt, John - *Work without Hope*
VQR - v73 - Win '97 - p29*+ [51-250]
Burt, Mala S - *Stepfamilies: The Step by Step Model of Brief Therapy*
Readings - v12 - Mr '97 - p26+ [51-250]
SciTech - v21 - Mr '97 - p54 [1-50]
Burt, Ramsay - *The Male Dancer*
TDR - v40 - Win '96 - p170+ [501+]
Burt, Richard - *Enclosure Acts*
MLR - v92 - Ja '97 - p174+ [501+]
Licensed by Authority
Shakes Q - v47 - Sum '96 - p207+ [501+]
Burt, Richard K - *On Call in Bone Marrow Transplantation*
SciTech - v21 - Mr '97 - p60 [51-250]
Burt, Sandra - *Changing Methods*
CPR - v16 - O '96 - p317+ [501+]
Burton, Anthony - *Children's Pleasures*
Mag Antiq - v151 - Ap '97 - p518 [251-500]
TES - D 6 '96 - p7* [501+]
Burton, Antoinette - *Burdens of History*
Albion - v28 - Fall '96 - p555+ [501+]
JMH - v69 - Mr '97 - p144+ [501+]
VS - v39 - Win '96 - p239+ [501+]
Burton, Bob - *Endangered Birds!*
c Ch BWatch - v6 - My '96 - p2 [51-250]
Endangered Environments!
c Ch BWatch - v6 - My '96 - p2 [51-250]
Endangered Mammals!
c Ch BWatch - v6 - My '96 - p2 [51-250]
Endangered Sea Life!
c Ch BWatch - v6 - My '96 - p2 [51-250]
Burton, Dennis - *Nature Walks of Central Park*
PW - v244 - Mr 24 '97 - p73 [51-250]
Burton, Fred - *International Business and Europe in Transition*
JEL - v34 - D '96 - p2045 [51-250]
Burton, Jeffrey - *Indian Territory and the United States 1866-1906*
AHR - v102 - F '97 - p182 [251-500]
PHR - v66 - F '97 - p107+ [251-500]
Burton, Jennifer - *Zora Neale Hurston, Eulalie Spence, Marita Bonner, and Others*
Choice - v34 - Mr '97 - p1168 [51-250]
Burton, Joan B - *Theocritus's Urban Mimes*
Rel St Rev - v23 - Ap '97 - p172 [51-250]
TLS - Ja 3 '97 - p13 [501+]
Burton, Katherine - *One Grey Mouse (Illus. by Kim Fernandes)*
c Ch Bk News - v19 - Sum '96 - p29 [51-250]
c Ch BWatch - v6 - My '96 - p3 [51-250]
Burton, LeVar - *Aftermath*
y BL - v93 - N 1 '96 - p459 [51-250]
KR - v64 - D 1 '96 - p1707 [51-250]
LJ - v121 - D '96 - p152 [51-250]
PW - v243 - D 9 '96 - p64 [51-250]
Aftermath (Burton). Audio Version
BWatch - v18 - Mr '97 - p8 [1-50]
Burton, Robert - *The Anatomy of Melancholy*
HR - v49 - Sum '96 - p323+ [501+]
Ren Q - v49 - Win '96 - p892+ [501+]
Burton, Thomas - *Serpent-Handling Believers*
JAAR - v64 - Sum '96 - p449+ [501+]
Burton, Virginia Lee - *Maybelle the Cable Car (Illus. by Virginia Lee Burton)*
c PW - v244 - F 24 '97 - p93 [1-50]
Mike Mulligan and His Steam Shovel. Electronic Media Version
c HB - v73 - Mr '97 - p219+ [501+]
Burton Goldberg Group - *Alternative Medicine*
r BL - v93 - F 1 '97 - p958 [1-50]
Burwell, Rose Marie - *Hemingway: The Postwar Years and the Posthumous Novels*
AL - v69 - Mr '97 - p234+ [251-500]
Burwick, Frederick - *Poetic Madness and the Romantic Imagination*
r Choice - v34 - N '96 - p448 [51-250]
VQR - v72 - Aut '96 - p120* [51-250]
Bury, Stephen, 1954- - *Artists' Books*
Lib - v18 - D '96 - p358+ [501+]
LR - v45 - 6 '96 - p63+ [501+]
Bury, Stephen, 1959- - *The Cobweb*
y Kliatt - v30 - N '96 - p6 [51-250]
Burz, Helen L - *Performance-Based Curriculum for Science*
H Sch M - v4 - Mr '97 - p56 [51-250]

Busbey, Arthur Bresnahan - *Rocks and Fossils*
y BL - v93 - S 1 '96 - p47 [251-500]
r E Mag - v7 - N '96 - p50 [51-250]
Nature - v383 - O 24 '96 - p684 [1-50]
y SB - v32 - Ag '96 - p174 [51-250]
yr SLJ - v42 - Ag '96 - p180 [51-250]
Busby, F M - *The Triad Worlds*
y Kliatt - v30 - N '96 - p12 [51-250]
Busby, Keith - *Word and Image in Arthurian Literature*
R&R Bk N - v12 - F '97 - p72 [51-250]
Busch, Briton Cooper - *Whaling Will Never Do for Me*
CAY - v16 - Fall '95 - p3 [51-250]
Busch, Frederick - *Girls*
BL - v93 - Ja '97 - p816 [51-250]
KR - v65 - Ja 1 '97 - p5+ [251-500]
LATBR - Mr 16 '97 - p2 [501+]
LJ - v122 - F '97 - p105 [51-250]
NYTBR - v102 - Mr 16 '97 - p12 [501+]
PW - v243 - N 25 '96 - p54 [51-250]
Trib Bks - Mr 16 '97 - p5+ [501+]
WSJ-Cent - v99 - Mr 20 '97 - pA14 [51-250]
Busch, Lawrence - *Making Nature, Shaping Culture*
CS - v26 - Mr '97 - p202+ [501+]
Nature - v382 - Ag 1 '96 - p412+ [501+]
SciTech - v20 - N '96 - p57 [51-250]
Busch, Robert H - *The Cougar Almanac*
r Choice - v34 - My '97 - p1525+ [51-250]
Buschman, R G - *Integral Transformations, Operational Calculus, and Generalized Functions*
SciTech - v20 - D '96 - p19 [51-250]
Buschmann, Frank - *Pattern-Oriented Software Architecture*
SciTech - v21 - Mr '97 - p5 [1-50]
Busco, Marie - *Sir Richard Westmacott, Sculptor*
Albion - v28 - Fall '96 - p503+ [501+]
Art Bull - v78 - S '96 - p565+ [501+]
VS - v39 - Win '96 - p262+ [501+]
Busfield, Joan - *Men, Women, and Madness*
SciTech - v20 - S '96 - p32 [51-250]
Wom R Bks - v14 - F '97 - p11 [501+]
Bush, Brian - *A Guide to the Reptiles and Frogs of the Perth Region*
r Choice - v34 - O '96 - p307 [51-250]
Bush, Clifton H - *The Incumbent*
BWatch - v17 - N '96 - p10+ [51-250]
Bush, Michael - *The Pilgrimage of Grace*
Choice - v34 - S '96 - p184 [51-250]
Bush, Ronald - *T.S. Eliot: The Modernist in History*
ASInt - v34 - O '96 - p102+ [501+]
Bushart, Bruno - *Die Fuggerkapelle Bei St. Anna In Augsburg*
Ren Q - v50 - Spr '97 - p324+ [501+]
Ren Q - v50 - Spr '97 - p326+ [501+]
Bush-Brown, Louise - *America's Garden Book. Rev. Ed.*
r LJ - v122 - Ja '97 - p84 [51-250]
r PW - v243 - N 18 '96 - p72 [51-250]
Bushnell, Amy Turner - *Establishing Exceptionalism*
HAHR - v77 - My '97 - p303+ [251-500]
Situado and Sabana
HAHR - v76 - N '96 - p782+ [251-500]
Bushnell, Candace - *Sex and the City*
Ent W - Ag 23 '96 - p116 [51-250]
Spec - v278 - Ap 5 '97 - p34+ [501+]
Bushnell, Dana E - *Nagging Questions*
CPR - v16 - Ag '96 - p247+ [501+]
Ethics - v107 - Ja '97 - p397 [51-250]
Bushnell, Jack - *Sky Dancer (Illus. by Jan Ormerod)*
c BL - v93 - S 15 '96 - p245 [51-250]
c CBRS - v25 - S '96 - p1 [51-250]
c HB Guide - v8 - Spr '97 - p22 [51-250]
c KR - v64 - Ag 15 '96 - p1232 [51-250]
c SLJ - v42 - S '96 - p171 [51-250]
Bushnell, Rebecca W - *A Culture of Teaching*
Choice - v34 - Ja '97 - p848 [51-250]
Bushong, Carolyn N - *The Seven Dumbest Relationship Mistakes Smart People Make*
PW - v244 - My 12 '97 - p70+ [51-250]
Busi, Aldo - *Uses and Abuses*
Obs - F 16 '97 - p18* [51-250]
Busia, Akosua - *The Seasons of Beento Blackbird*
BL - v93 - O 1 '96 - p321 [51-250]
Bloom Rev - v17 - Ja '97 - p19 [1-50]
BW - v26 - S 29 '96 - p4 [501+]
LATBR - Ap 13 '97 - pF+ [51-250]
LJ - v121 - S 15 '96 - p94 [51-250]
LJ - v121 - N 1 '96 - p82 [1-50]
LJ - v122 - Mr 15 '97 - p41 [1-50]
PW - v243 - S 2 '96 - p110 [51-250]
Busiek, Kurt - *Marvels*
VOYA - v19 - F '97 - p323+ [251-500]

Business and Economics Research Directory
  r ARBA - v28 - '97 - p80 [51-250]
  r LJ - v122 - Mr 15 '97 - p54 [51-250]
  r R&R Bk N - v12 - F '97 - p33 [51-250]
Business Consumer Guide - *The Essential Business Buyer's Guide*
  r BL - v93 - Mr 1 '97 - p1097 [51-250]
  r LJ - v122 - F 15 '97 - p144 [51-250]
Business in British Columbia
  J Gov Info - v23 - S '96 - p626 [51-250]
Business Organizations, Agencies, and Publications Directory. 8th Ed.
  r ARBA - v28 - '97 - p80+ [51-250]
Business Phone Book USA 1997
  r BL - v93 - D 15 '96 - p743 [1-50]
  r R&R Bk N - v12 - F '97 - p46 [51-250]
Business Publication Advertising Source
  p Utne R - Mr '97 - p88+ [251-500]
Business Statistics of the United States. 1995 Ed.
  r ARBA - v28 - '97 - p88 [51-250]
  r J Gov Info - v24 - Ja '97 - p74+ [501+]
Buskirk, Martha - *The Duchamp Effect*
  Afterimage - v24 - Ja '97 - p23 [1-50]
  Bloom Rev - v17 - Ja '97 - p23 [51-250]
Buss, Louis - *The Luxury of Exile*
  Obs - Mr 23 '97 - p18* [51-250]
Busse, Ewald W - *The American Psychiatric Press Textbook of Geriatric Psychiatry. 2nd Ed.*
  SciTech - v20 - S '96 - p31 [51-250]
Busser, Marianne - *King Bobble (Illus. by Hans De Beer)*
  c HB Guide - v7 - Fall '96 - p286 [51-250]
Bussiere, Eric - *Paribas 1872-1992*
  Archiv - Fall '94 - p185+ [501+]
Bussmann, Hadumod - *Routledge Dictionary of Language and Linguistics*
  r ARBA - v28 - '97 - p374+ [251-500]
  r Choice - v34 - D '96 - p587 [51-250]
  r R&R Bk N - v11 - N '96 - p62 [51-250]
Buszynski, Leszek - *Russian Foreign Policy after the Cold War*
  Choice - v34 - F '97 - p1030 [51-250]
  R&R Bk N - v12 - F '97 - p17 [51-250]
Butala, Sharon - *Perfection of the Morning*
  PW - v244 - Ap 14 '97 - p72 [1-50]
  Upstream
  KR - v65 - Ja 15 '97 - p76+ [251-500]
Buthelezi, Sipho - *South Africa: The Dynamics and Prospects of Transformation*
  Choice - v34 - Ja '97 - p852 [51-250]
Butin, Philip Walker - *Revelation, Redemption, and Response*
  Six Ct J - v27 - Fall '96 - p906+ [501+]
  Theol St - v57 - Je '96 - p381 [251-500]
Butler, Ann B - *Comparative Vertebrate Neuroanatomy*
  Choice - v34 - O '96 - p306 [51-250]
  Sci - v274 - O 25 '96 - p521+ [501+]
Butler, Anne M, 1938- - *Uncommon Common Women*
  Choice - v34 - Ap '97 - p1402 [51-250]
  Roundup M - v4 - Ap '97 - p21 [251-500]
  United States Senate Election, Expulsion and Censure Cases 1793-1990
  r JSH - v62 - N '96 - p857 [51-250]
Butler, Ava S - *Team Think*
  HR Mag - v41 - O '96 - p148+ [51-250]
Butler, Brett - *Knee Deep in Paradise*
  Ent W - Mr 28 '97 - p63 [51-250]
  PW - v244 - Mr 17 '97 - p81 [1-50]
Butler, Daniel - *America's Dumbest Criminals*
  SEP - v268 - S '96 - p30+ [501+]
Butler, Daphne - *Caring for Young*
  c HB Guide - v7 - Fall '96 - p334 [51-250]
  Finding Shelter
  c HB Guide - v7 - Fall '96 - p334 [51-250]
  Gathering Food
  c HB Guide - v7 - Fall '96 - p334 [51-250]
  Getting Around
  c HB Guide - v7 - Fall '96 - p334 [51-250]
  Pieter Bruegel
  c Sch Lib - v44 - N '96 - p161 [51-250]
  What Happens When Fire Burns?
  c HB Guide - v7 - Fall '96 - p350 [51-250]
  c Learning - v25 - Ag '96 - p96 [51-250]
  What Happens When Flowers Grow?
  c HB Guide - v7 - Fall '96 - p340 [51-250]
  What Happens When Food Cooks?
  c HB Guide - v7 - Fall '96 - p353 [1-50]
  c Learning - v25 - Ag '96 - p96 [51-250]
  What Happens When People Talk?
  c HB Guide - v7 - Fall '96 - p347 [51-250]
  What Happens When Rain Falls?
  c HB Guide - v7 - Fall '96 - p331+ [51-250]

What Happens When Volcanoes Erupt?
  c HB Guide - v7 - Fall '96 - p331+ [51-250]
  c Learning - v25 - Ag '96 - p96 [51-250]
What Happens When Wheels Turn?
  c HB Guide - v7 - Fall '96 - p350 [51-250]
  c Learning - v25 - Ag '96 - p96 [51-250]
What Happens When Wind Blows?
  c HB Guide - v7 - Fall '96 - p332 [51-250]
Butler, David - *British Politics and European Elections 1994*
  PSQ - v111 - Win '96 - p713+ [501+]
Butler, David R - *Zoogeomorphology: Animals as Geomorphic Agents*
  GJ - v163 - Mr '97 - p100 [251-500]
Butler, Diana Hochstedt - *Standing against the Whirlwind*
  CH - v65 - D '96 - p744+ [501+]
Butler, Gwendoline - *Butterfly*
  BL - v93 - Ap 1 '97 - p1280 [51-250]
  PW - v244 - Mr 17 '97 - p79 [51-250]
  The Coffin Tree
  Arm Det - v29 - Sum '96 - p372 [51-250]
  A Dark Coffin
  Arm Det - v30 - Win '97 - p106+ [251-500]
  BL - v93 - D 1 '96 - p642 [51-250]
  KR - v64 - O 15 '96 - p1494 [51-250]
Butler, Heather - *The Grumpy Shepherd and Other Christmas Plays*
  c Bks Keeps - N '96 - p20 [1-50]
Butler, Hubert - *In the Land of Nod*
  ILS - v16 - Spr '97 - p3 [501+]
  TLS - N 29 '96 - p13 [1-50]
  Independent Spirit
  BL - v93 - N 1 '96 - p474 [51-250]
  BW - v26 - N 10 '96 - p8+ [501+]
  KR - v64 - S 15 '96 - p1366+ [251-500]
  LATBR - D 1 '96 - p2 [501+]
  LJ - v121 - O 1 '96 - p76 [51-250]
  New R - v216 - F 3 '97 - p32+ [501+]
  NY - v72 - D 9 '96 - p118 [51-250]
  NYTBR - v101 - D 1 '96 - p6 [501+]
  NYTBR - v101 - D 8 '96 - p88 [1-50]
Butler, J George - *Simpler Times*
  BWatch - v18 - F '97 - p2 [51-250]
  LJ - v121 - D '96 - p114 [51-250]
Butler, Janet G - *Mainframe to Client/Server Migration*
  SciTech - v20 - D '96 - p13 [51-250]
Butler, John - *The Quest for Becket's Bones*
  CR - v270 - F '97 - p110 [51-250]
  Specu - v71 - O '96 - p930+ [501+]
Butler, Josephine - *Cyanide in My Shoe (Bishop). Audio Version*
  BL - v93 - Mr 15 '97 - p1253 [51-250]
Butler, Kathleen Mary - *The Economics of Emancipation*
  AHR - v101 - D '96 - p1655+ [501+]
  HAHR - v76 - N '96 - p825+ [251-500]
Butler, Michael - *The Narrative Fiction of Heinrich Boll*
  Ger Q - v70 - Win '97 - p91+ [501+]
Butler, Octavia E - *Bloodchild and Other Stories*
  NYTBR - v102 - F 23 '97 - p24 [51-250]
  PW - v243 - N 11 '96 - p72 [1-50]
  y SLJ - v42 - D '96 - p33 [1-50]
  Clay's Ark
  NYTBR - v101 - D 29 '96 - p16 [51-250]
Butler, Rex - *What Is Appropriation?*
  Aust Bk R - F '97 - p32+ [501+]
Butler, Robert Olen - *Tabloid Dreams*
  Ant R - v55 - Spr '97 - p242+ [251-500]
  BL - v93 - O 1 '96 - p321 [251-500]
  BW - v26 - N 10 '96 - p1+ [501+]
  LATBR - N 3 '96 - p2 [501+]
  NYTBR - v101 - N 3 '96 - p17 [501+]
  NYTBR - v101 - D 8 '96 - p82 [1-50]
  PW - v243 - S 2 '96 - p110+ [51-250]
  VV - v41 - D 3 '96 - p57 [501+]
Butler, Sandra - *Cancer in Two Voices*
  Ms - v7 - Ja '97 - p82 [1-50]
Butler, Tim, 1949- - *Social Change and the Middle Classes*
  SF - v75 - D '96 - p750+ [501+]
  Socio R - v44 - N '96 - p759+ [501+]
Butler, Timothy - *Discovering Your Career in Business*
  BL - v93 - F 15 '97 - p983 [51-250]
  J Car P&E - v57 - Win '97 - p19 [51-250]
Butlin, N G - *Forming a Colonial Economy*
  AHR - v101 - O '96 - p1263+ [501+]
  JEH - v56 - S '96 - p733+ [501+]
Butlin, Robin A - *Ecological Relations in Historical Times*
  Choice - v34 - S '96 - p181 [51-250]
  Historical Geography
  AAAGA - v86 - S '96 - p611+ [501+]

Butlin, Ron - *The Sound of My Voice*
  VLS - Spr '97 - p23 [501+]
Butt, Gerald - *Life at the Crossroads*
  MEJ - v51 - Win '97 - p131+ [501+]
Butt, Howard E, Jr. - *Renewing America's Soul*
  Ch Today - v40 - O 7 '96 - p59+ [501+]
Butterfield, D Allan - *Biofunctional Membranes*
  SciTech - v20 - S '96 - p59 [51-250]
Butterfield, Fox - *All God's Children*
  AS - v65 - Aut '96 - p602+ [501+]
  y Kliatt - v31 - Mr '97 - p25 [51-250]
  NYTBR - v101 - D 22 '96 - p20 [51-250]
  PW - v243 - O 21 '96 - p78 [1-50]
Butterfield, Jim - *Driving the Amish*
  LJ - v122 - Mr 15 '97 - p78 [51-250]
Butterfield, Moira - *Creative Crafts*
  c Magpies - v11 - Jl '96 - p41 [51-250]
Butterworth, Annette - *Jake Again (Illus. by Nick Butterworth)*
  c JB - v60 - D '96 - p246+ [51-250]
  c Sch Lib - v44 - N '96 - p145 [51-250]
  Jake--The Adventures of an Unusual Dog (Illus. by Nick Butterworth)
  c Bks Keeps - Jl '96 - p9 [51-250]
Butterworth, Nick - *The Badger's Bath (Illus. by Mocl Butterworth)*
  c JB - v60 - Ag '96 - p140+ [51-250]
  Making Faces
  c Bks Keeps - v100 - S '96 - p10 [51-250]
  The Treasure Hunt (Illus. by Nick Butterworth)
  c Bks Keeps - Mr '97 - p18 [51-250]
  c Books - v11 - Ap '97 - p24 [51-250]
  c JB - v60 - D '96 - p227 [51-250]
  c Sch Lib - v45 - F '97 - p17 [51-250]
Buttimer, Anne - *Geography and the Human Spirit*
  AAAGA - v86 - D '96 - p792+ [501+]
Buttlar, Lois J - *Guide to Information Resources in Ethnic Museum, Library, and Archival Collections in the United States*
  r ARBA - v28 - '97 - p235+ [51-250]
  r RQ - v36 - Fall '96 - p130+ [251-500]
Buttler, Friedrich - *Institutional Frameworks and Labor Market Performance*
  JEL - v34 - S '96 - p1443 [51-250]
  JEL - v35 - Mr '97 - p155+ [501+]
Button, John - *On the Loose*
  Aust Bk R - F '97 - p11+ [501+]
Butts, Nancy - *Cheshire Moon*
  c CBRS - v25 - S '96 - p10 [51-250]
  c Ch BWatch - v6 - O '96 - p3 [51-250]
  c HB Guide - v8 - Spr '97 - p62 [51-250]
  c KR - v64 - S 1 '96 - p1320 [51-250]
  c PW - v243 - S 2 '96 - p132 [51-250]
  c SLJ - v42 - N '96 - p103 [51-250]
Butz, Michael R - *Strange Attractors*
  Choice - v34 - My '97 - p1579 [51-250]
Butz, Rick - *How to Sharpen Carving Tools*
  BL - v93 - Mr 1 '97 - p1100 [51-250]
Buu, Sao - *Long Van Tu Cua Thien Day Song*
  BL - v93 - S 1 '96 - p70 [51-250]
Buxton, Richard - *Imaginary Greece*
  CW - v89 - Jl '96 - p512 [251-500]
Buzan, Tony - *The Age of Heresy*
  Spec - v277 - O 26 '96 - p51 [501+]
Buzard, James - *The Beaten Track*
  JMH - v68 - S '96 - p617+ [501+]
Buzzanco, Robert - *Masters of War*
  J Mil H - v60 - O '96 - p803+ [251-500]
  RAH - v25 - Mr '97 - p151+ [501+]
Buzzati, Dino - *The Tartar Step*
  Obs - O 6 '96 - p18* [51-250]
Buzzi, Aldo - *Journey to the Land of the Flies and Other Travels*
  NYTBR - v101 - D 8 '96 - p88 [1-50]
  VQR - v72 - Aut '96 - p139* [51-250]
Byalick, Marcia - *It's a Matter of Trust*
  y New Ad - v9 - Fall '96 - p327+ [501+]
Byars, Betsy - *The Cartoonist*
  c PW - v244 - Mr 17 '97 - p85 [1-50]
  The Computer Nut
  c PW - v244 - Mr 17 '97 - p85 [1-50]
  The Dark Stairs (Fairman). Audio Version
  c BL - v93 - S 15 '96 - p264 [51-250]
  c Emerg Lib - v24 - Mr '97 - p24 [51-250]
  c HB - v72 - S '96 - p566+ [501+]
  Dead Letter
  c HB Guide - v8 - Spr '97 - p62 [51-250]
  Death's Door
  c BL - v93 - Mr 1 '97 - p1162 [51-250]
  The Joy Boys (Illus. by Frank Remkiewicz)
  c HB Guide - v7 - Fall '96 - p283 [51-250]

My Brother, Ant (Illus. by Marc Simont)
  c BL - v93 - Ja '97 - p765 [1-50]
  c BL - v93 - Ap 1 '97 - p1296 [1-50]
  c HB Guide - v7 - Fall '96 - p284 [51-250]
  c RT - v50 - Ap '97 - p590 [51-250]
The Pinballs
  c HMR - Win '96 - p45 [1-50]
Real-Life Stories
  c TES - O 18 '96 - p12* [51-250]
The Summer of the Swans (Moore). Audio Version
  c HB - v72 - S '96 - p566+ [501+]
Tornado (Illus. by Doron Ben-Ami)
  c BL - v93 - S 15 '96 - p238 [51-250]
  c CCB-B - v50 - N '96 - p91 [51-250]
  c HB - v72 - N '96 - p732 [51-250]
  c HB Guide - v8 - Spr '97 - p62 [51-250]
  c SLJ - v42 - N '96 - p78 [51-250]
Wanted...Mud Blossom (Illus. by Jacqueline Rogers)
  c SLJ - v43 - Ja '97 - p36 [1-50]
Byatt, A S - *Angels and Insects (May). Audio Version*
    BL - v93 - N 1 '96 - p522 [51-250]
Babel Tower
    Books - v10 - Je '96 - p23 [51-250]
    NS & S - v9 - My 3 '96 - p40 [501+]
    NYRB - v43 - Je 6 '96 - p17+ [501+]
    NYTBR - v101 - D 8 '96 - p76 [1-50]
    Spec - v276 - My 11 '96 - p34+ [501+]
Babel Tower (Atkins). Audio Version
    BL - v93 - N 1 '96 - p522 [51-250]
  y Kliatt - v30 - S '96 - p42 [51-250]
Imagining Characters
    Obs - N 24 '96 - p18* [51-250]
Sugar and Other Stories
    Critiq - v38 - Win '97 - p105+ [501+]
    Obs - N 24 '96 - p18* [51-250]
Bydlinski, Georg - *Wintergras*
    WLT - v70 - Aut '96 - p952+ [251-500]
Byer, Doris - *Die Grosse Insel*
    Cont Pac - v9 - Spr '97 - p277+ [501+]
Byers, Ann - *Jaime Escalante: Sensational Teacher*
  y BL - v93 - O 1 '96 - p328 [51-250]
  y HB Guide - v8 - Spr '97 - p155 [51-250]
  y SLJ - v42 - S '96 - p230 [51-250]
  y VOYA - v19 - D '96 - p285 [251-500]
Byers, Clive - *Sparrows and Buntings*
  r ARBA - v28 - '97 - p586+ [51-250]
Byers, E Sandra - *Sexual Coercion in Dating Relationships*
    SB - v33 - Ja '97 - p7 [251-500]
Byers, Paula K - *Asian American Genealogical Sourcebook*
  r RQ - v35 - Sum '96 - p546 [251-500]
Hispanic American Genealogical Sourcebook
  r NGSQ - v85 - Mr '97 - p60+ [501+]
Native American Genealogical Sourcebook
  r NGSQ - v84 - D '96 - p308+ [251-500]
Byg, Barton - *Landscapes of Resistance*
    Choice - v34 - O '96 - p289 [51-250]
Bygott, David W - *Black and British*
  c Bks Keeps - Jl '96 - p23 [1-50]
Byham, William - *Zapp! The Lightning of Empowerment*
    Kiplinger - v51 - F '97 - p112 [51-250]
Bykerk, Loree - *U.S. Consumer Interest Groups*
  r J Con A - v30 - Win '96 - p476+ [501+]
Byles, Monica - *Experiments with Senses*
  c Inst - v106 - S '96 - p92 [1-50]
Byng-Hall, John - *Rewriting Family Scripts*
    Fam in Soc - v77 - D '96 - p640+ [501+]
Bynum, Caroline Walker - *The Resurrection of the Body in Western Christianity 200-1336*
    Bks & Cult - v2 - My '96 - p26+ [501+]
    Comw - v124 - D 14 '97 - p23+ [501+]
    JR - v76 - O '96 - p634+ [501+]
    Rel St Rev - v22 - O '96 - p348 [51-250]
    Theol St - v57 - Je '96 - p350+ [501+]
Bynum, W F - *Science and the Practice of Medicine in the Nineteenth Century*
    EHR - v111 - N '96 - p1318+ [251-500]
    T&C - v37 - Ap '96 - p351+ [251-500]
    VS - v39 - Spr '96 - p437+ [501+]
Byock, Ira - *Dying Well*
    BL - v93 - D 15 '96 - p696 [51-250]
    KR - v64 - N 15 '96 - p1646 [251-500]
    LJ - v122 - Ja '97 - p132 [51-250]
    PW - v243 - D 30 '96 - p47 [251-500]
Byrd, Bobby - *The Late Great Mexican Border*
    BL - v93 - Ja '97 - p808 [1-50]
    Workbook - v21 - Win '96 - p183+ [251-500]

Byrd, James - *The Descendants of Richard Byrd (1818-189?) and (1) Rebecca Norman, and (2) Mary Jane Vinson*
    EGH - v50 - N '96 - p192+ [51-250]
Byrd, Max - *Jackson: A Novel*
  y BL - v93 - Mr 15 '97 - p1224 [51-250]
    KR - v65 - Ja 1 '97 - p6 [251-500]
    LJ - v122 - Ja '97 - p143 [51-250]
    PW - v243 - D 2 '96 - p40 [51-250]
    Trib Bks - Ap 13 '97 - p6+ [501+]
    WSJ-Cent - v99 - My 14 '97 - pA20 [501+]
Byrhtferth - *Byrhtferth's Enchiridion (Baker)*
    Isis - v88 - Mr '97 - p134+ [501+]
Byrn, R M F - *Anglo-German Studies*
    MLR - v91 - Jl '96 - p808+ [501+]
Byrne, Brendan - *Romans*
    Am - v176 - Mr 8 '97 - p28 [51-250]
Byrne, David - *Physical Processes*
    TES - D 13 '96 - p43 [51-250]
Byrne, Hugh - *El Salvador's Civil War*
    Choice - v34 - My '97 - p1567+ [51-250]
Byrne, Peter - *Companion Encyclopedia of Theology*
  r Choice - v34 - N '96 - p426 [51-250]
  r LAR - v98 - Jl '96 - p373 [51-250]
  r Rel St - v33 - Mr '97 - p131 [51-250]
Prolegomena to Religious Pluralism
    JR - v77 - Ap '97 - p332+ [501+]
Byrne, Robert - *Byrne's Wonderful World of Pool and Billiards*
    LJ - v121 - O 15 '96 - p64 [51-250]
Byrnes, Robert F - *V.O. Kliuchevskii, Historian of Russia*
    Choice - v34 - S '96 - p185 [51-250]
Byron, Janet - *The Country Music Lover's Guide to the U.S.A.*
  r LJ - v121 - N 1 '96 - p40 [1-50]
Byron, William J - *The 365 Days of Christmas*
    CLW - v67 - Mr '97 - p37 [51-250]
    RR - v55 - N '96 - p659 [1-50]
Byrum, Oliver E - *Old Problems in New Times*
    PAR - v57 - Ja '97 - p83+ [501+]

C

C.R.I.S.: The Combined Retrospective Index Set to Journals in History 1838-1974. Vols. 1-11
r ASInt - v34 - O '96 - p18+ [51-250]
C.R.I.S.: The Combined Retrospective Index Set to Journals in Political Science 1886-1974. Vols. 1-8
r ASInt - v34 - O '96 - p18+ [51-250]
C.R.I.S.: The Combined Retrospective Index Set to Journals in Sociology 1895-1974. Vols. 1-6
r ASInt - v34 - O '96 - p18+ [51-250]
C++ Report: The International Authority on C++ Development 1991-1995. Electronic Media Version
SciTech - v20 - N '96 - p8 [1-50]
Caarceles, Beatriz - *Reforma Y Fraude Fiscal En El Reinado De Carlos II*
JEH - v57 - Mr '97 - p211+ [501+]
Cabaj, Robert P - *Textbook of Homosexuality and Mental Health*
Readings - v12 - Mr '97 - p26 [51-250]
Caballero Bonald, Jose Manuel - *Tiempo De Guerras Perdidas*
WLT - v70 - Sum '96 - p670 [251-500]
Cabestan, Jean-Pierre - *Le Systeme Politique De La Chine Populaire*
Ch Rev Int - v4 - Spr '97 - p79+ [501+]
Cable, Lana - *Carnal Rhetoric*
Col Lit - v23 - O '96 - p193+ [501+]
Cable, Mary - *The Blizzard of '88*
y Kliatt - v31 - Mr '97 - p4 [51-250]
Cabraal, Anil - *Best Practices for Photovoltaic Household Electrification Programs*
JEL - v35 - Mr '97 - p300+ [51-250]
Cabrera, Edgar - *El Calendario Maya*
BL - v93 - S 15 '96 - p227 [1-50]
Cabrera, Jane - *Cat's Colors (Illus. by Jane Cabrera)*
c KR - v65 - Ja 15 '97 - p138 [51-250]
c PW - v244 - Ap 21 '97 - p70 [51-250]
Cabrera Infante, G - *El Delito Por Bailar El Chachacha*
LJ - v122 - Ja '97 - p78 [51-250]
WLT - v70 - Aut '96 - p921+ [501+]
Ella Cantaba Boleros
BL - v93 - Mr 15 '97 - p1232 [1-50]
Holy Smoke
Biography - v19 - Fall '96 - p394+ [501+]
Mi Musica Extremada
BL - v93 - Ap 1 '97 - p1284 [1-50]
Cacace, Filippo - *Advanced Relational Programming*
SciTech - v20 - D '96 - p12 [51-250]
Cacciaglia, Norberto - *Italo Svevo Scrittore Europeo*
MLR - v91 - Jl '96 - p760+ [501+]
Cachey, T J - *Dante Now*
MLR - v92 - Ja '97 - p214+ [501+]
Le Isole Fortunate
MLN - v112 - Ja '97 - p119+ [501+]
Six Ct J - v27 - Win '96 - p1139 [501+]
Cackett, Alan - *The Harmony Illustrated Encyclopedia of Country Music. 3rd Completely Rev. and Updated Ed.*
r LJ - v121 - N 1 '96 - p41 [1-50]
Caddy, Caroline - *Antarctica*
Aust Bk R - S '96 - p52 [501+]
Quad - v40 - N '96 - p84+ [501+]
Caddy, Joyce - *Cocker Spaniels Today*
Dog Fan - v27 - N '96 - p24 [1-50]
Cadigan, Sean T - *Hope and Deception in Conception Bay*
AHR - v101 - D '96 - p1652+ [251-500]
Can Hist R - v78 - Mr '97 - p111+ [501+]
W&M Q - v53 - O '96 - p843+ [501+]
Cadnum, Michael - *Breaking the Fall*
y JB - v60 - O '96 - p198 [51-250]
y Sch Lib - v44 - N '96 - p168 [51-250]
The Judas Glass
y VOYA - v19 - D '96 - p276 [51-250]

Taking It
y TES - F 7 '97 - p9* [51-250]
Zero at the Bone
y BL - v92 - Ag '96 - p1904 [51-250]
y BW - v27 - Ja 12 '97 - p9 [251-500]
y CBRS - v25 - S '96 - p10 [51-250]
y CCB-B - v50 - S '96 - p7 [51-250]
y Ch BWatch - v6 - S '96 - p5 [51-250]
y HB - v72 - S '96 - p602 [251-500]
y HB Guide - v8 - Spr '97 - p78 [51-250]
y JAAL - v40 - S '96 - p72 [51-250]
y VOYA - v19 - F '97 - p326 [251-500]
CADS
p Arm Det - v29 - Sum '96 - p322 [1-50]
Caduto, Michael J - *Native American Gardening*
Nat Peop - v10 - '97 - p78+ [501+]
Cady, Glee - *Mastering the Internet. 2nd Ed.*
r CBR - v14 - S '96 - p29 [1-50]
Cady, Jack - *The Off Season*
NYTBR - v102 - Ja 19 '97 - p28 [1-50]
Cady, John Henry - *Arizona's Yesterdays*
Roundup M - v4 - O '96 - p25 [51-250]
Caesar, Adrian - *Hunger Games*
Aust Bk R - Ag '96 - p59+ [501+]
Caesar, Terry - *Forgiving the Boundaries*
AL - v68 - S '96 - p659+ [251-500]
Caferro, William - *The Unbounded Community*
R&R Bk N - v12 - F '97 - p11 [51-250]
Caffarella, Rosemary - *Planning Programs for Adult Learners*
AE - v46 - Sum '96 - p240+ [501+]
Cafferky, Michael E - *Let Your Customers Do the Talking*
Bus Bk R - v13 - 3 '96 - p96+ [501+]
Cahan, Richard - *The Game That Was*
Econ - v340 - S 14 '96 - p4*+ [501+]
NYTBR - v101 - Ap 7 '96 - p16 [51-250]
Cahen, Paul-Jean - *Commutative Ring Theory*
SciTech - v21 - Mr '97 - p13 [51-250]
Integer-Valued Polynomials
SciTech - v21 - Mr '97 - p12 [51-250]
Cahier, Gabriella - *Registres De La Compagnie Des Pasteurs De Geneve. Vol. 12*
CH - v66 - Mr '97 - p201 [51-250]
Six Ct J - v27 - Win '96 - p1128+ [501+]
Registres De La Compagnie Des Pasteurs De Geneve. Vols. 10-11
CH - v66 - Mr '97 - p200+ [51-250]
Cahill, Dennis J - *Internal Marketing*
JEL - v34 - S '96 - p1462 [51-250]
Cahill, James - *The Lyric Journey*
Choice - v34 - Mr '97 - p1150 [51-250]
Cahill, Kathleen - *EveryWoman's Guide to Prescription and Nonprescription Drugs*
r BL - v93 - Mr 1 '97 - p1188+ [251-500]
Cahill, Kevin M - *Preventive Diplomacy*
NYTBR - v102 - F 9 '97 - p24 [501+]
Cahill, Lisa Sowle - *Sex, Gender, and Christian Ethics*
Choice - v34 - Mr '97 - p1177 [51-250]
Cahill, Susan - *Desiring Italy*
PW - v244 - Mr 17 '97 - p73 [51-250]
Wise Women
Am - v175 - S 21 '96 - p34 [1-50]
y BL - v93 - Ja '97 - p763 [1-50]
BL - v93 - Ja '97 - p808 [1-50]
Bloom Rev - v16 - N '96 - p13 [501+]
Cahill, Thomas - *How the Irish Saved Civilization*
Rapport - v19 - 4 '96 - p40 [251-500]
How the Irish Saved Civilization (Donnelly). Audio Version
BWatch - v18 - Mr '97 - p7 [1-50]

Cahill, Tim - *Pass the Butterworms*
y BL - v93 - F 1 '97 - p920 [51-250]
Ent W - Mr 28 '97 - p62 [51-250]
KR - v64 - D 15 '96 - p1776 [251-500]
LJ - v122 - Ja '97 - p128 [51-250]
NYTBR - v102 - Mr 23 '97 - p17 [501+]
PW - v243 - D 30 '96 - p44 [51-250]
Cahm, Eric - *The Dreyfus Affair in French Society and Politics*
HRNB - v25 - Win '97 - p77 [251-500]
Cahn, Isabelle - *Paul Cezanne: A Life in Art*
BM - v138 - S '96 - p612+ [501+]
Cahn, Matthew Alan - *Thinking about the Environment*
R&R Bk N - v11 - D '96 - p19 [51-250]
Cahn, Robert W - *Physical Metallurgy. 4th Ed., Vols. 1-3*
SciTech - v20 - N '96 - p78 [51-250]
Cahn, Walter - *Romanesque Manuscripts. Vols. 1-2*
TLS - Ja 10 '97 - p30 [501+]
Cahoone, Lawrence E - *The Ends of Philosophy*
RM - v49 - Je '96 - p917+ [251-500]
Cail, Carol - *If Two of Them Are Dead*
Rapport - v19 - 5 '96 - p36 [251-500]
Caimi, Lodovico Caumont - *L'Ebanisteria Genovese Del Settecento*
BM - v138 - O '96 - p693+ [501+]
Cain, Chelsea - *Dharma Girl*
BL - v93 - N 1 '96 - p477 [51-250]
LJ - v121 - O 15 '96 - p80 [51-250]
Ms - v7 - Ja '97 - p82 [251-500]
NYTBR - v101 - N 17 '96 - p18 [501+]
PW - v243 - O 21 '96 - p76+ [51-250]
Cain, P J - *British Imperialism*
Econ J - v106 - S '96 - p1418+ [501+]
Cain, Seymour - *Gabriel Marcel's Theory of Religious Experience*
CC - v113 - O 16 '96 - p983 [51-250]
Cain, William E - *Reconceptualizing American Literary/Cultural Studies*
Choice - v34 - D '96 - p608 [51-250]
R&R Bk N - v11 - D '96 - p64 [51-250]
Caine, Dennis J - *Epidemiology of Sports Injuries*
Choice - v34 - O '96 - p321 [51-250]
SciTech - v20 - S '96 - p28 [1-50]
Caine, K Winston - *The Male Body*
PW - v243 - O 21 '96 - p81 [51-250]
Caines, A J - *Automotive Lubricants Reference Book*
r SciTech - v21 - Mr '97 - p93 [51-250]
Caipora (Organization) - *Women in Brazil*
JTWS - v13 - Spr '96 - p362+ [501+]
Cairncross, Alec - *The British Economy since 1945*
JEL - v34 - D '96 - p2094+ [51-250]
Economic Ideas and Government Policy
Econ J - v106 - N '96 - p1847 [251-500]
JEL - v34 - D '96 - p2093 [51-250]
R&R Bk N - v11 - N '96 - p25 [51-250]
Managing the British Economy in the 1960s
TLS - S 20 '96 - p6+ [501+]
Cairncross, Frances - *Green, Inc.*
JEL - v35 - Mr '97 - p184+ [501+]
Cairncross, John - *An Agent for the Duration*
Books - v10 - Je '96 - p21 [1-50]
Cairney, Trevor H - *Pathways to Literacy*
Sch Lib - v44 - Ag '96 - p128 [51-250]
Cairns, Adrian - *The Making of the Professional Actor*
Choice - v34 - My '97 - p1510 [51-250]
Obs - S 13 '96 - p18* [51-250]
Cairns, Ed - *Children and Political Violence*
Choice - v34 - S '96 - p218 [51-250]
Cairns, John - *Matters of Life and Death*
BL - v93 - F 15 '97 - p984 [51-250]

Cairns, Robert B - *Lifelines and Risks*
 AJS - v102 - Jl '96 - p314+ [501+]
Cairns-Smith, A G - *Evolving the Mind*
 Choice - v34 - O '96 - p363+ [51-250]
Cairo, Shelley - *Our Brother Has Down's Syndrome*
 c Sch Lib - v44 - Ag '96 - p104 [51-250]
Calabrese, Michael A - *Chaucer's Ovidian Arts of Love*
 Specu - v71 - O '96 - p931+ [501+]
Calabrese, Omar - *A Sign of the Times*
 TranslRevS - v1 - My '95 - p6 [51-250]
Calabro, Marian - *Great Courtroom Lawyers*
 y HB Guide - v8 - Spr '97 - p92 [51-250]
Calambokidis, John - *Blue Whales*
 c PW - v244 - My 5 '97 - p192 [51-250]
Calame, Claude - *The Craft of Poetic Speech in Ancient Greece*
 Rel St Rev - v23 - Ap '97 - p171 [51-250]
 TranslRevS - v2 - D '96 - p11 [51-250]
Calasso, Roberto - *KA*
 TLS - N 29 '96 - p11 [51-250]
 The Ruin of Kasch
 TranslRevS - v1 - My '95 - p24 [51-250]
Calder, Judith - *A Study of National Vocational Qualification Achievement through Open and Flexible Routes*
 JEL - v34 - S '96 - p1446 [51-250]
Calder, Kent E - *Asia's Deadly Triangle*
 Econ - v341 - O 19 '96 - p8* [51-250]
 Quad - v40 - N '96 - p80+ [501+]
 Pacific Defense
 Econ - v341 - O 19 '96 - p8* [51-250]
Calder, Norman - *Studies in Early Muslim Jurisprudence*
 Rel St Rev - v23 - Ja '97 - p11+ [501+]
Calder, Richard - *Dead Things*
 KR - v64 - D 15 '96 - p1772 [51-250]
 LJ - v122 - F 15 '97 - p165 [51-250]
 PW - v244 - Ja 27 '97 - p81 [51-250]
Calder, William - *Size, Function and Life History*
 New Sci - v153 - F 1 '97 - p40 [1-50]
Calderon De La Barca, Pedro - *Pedro Calderon De La Barca's The Fake Astrologer*
 TranslRevS - v1 - My '95 - p29 [51-250]
Caldicott, Helen - *A Desperate Passion*
 BL - v93 - S 15 '96 - p186 [51-250]
 Bloom Rev - v16 - N '96 - p17+ [501+]
 BW - v26 - S 1 '96 - p8 [501+]
 LJ - v121 - N 1 '96 - p73 [51-250]
 NYTBR - v101 - S 29 '96 - p22 [501+]
 Prog - v60 - S '96 - p41+ [501+]
 PW - v243 - Jl 22 '96 - p221 [51-250]
 Workbook - v21 - Win '96 - p186+ [501+]
 A Passionate Life
 Aust Bk R - N '96 - p18+ [501+]
Caldwell, D R - *Microbial Physiology and Metabolism*
 BioSci - v46 - O '96 - p704 [501+]
Caldwell, E K - *Bear (Illus. by Diana Magnuson)*
 c SLJ - v42 - Ag '96 - p132+ [51-250]
Caldwell, Erskine - *God's Little Acre (Hammer). Audio Version*
 BWatch - v17 - D '96 - p11 [1-50]
 y Kliatt - v31 - My '97 - p38 [51-250]
 Tobacco Road (MacDonald). Audio Version
 y Kliatt - v30 - S '96 - p53 [51-250]
 Tobacco Road (Schirner). Audio Version
 y Kliatt - v30 - S '96 - p53 [51-250]
Caldwell, Hansonia L - *African American Music: A Chronology 1619-1995*
 r Bl S - v26 - Fall '96 - p101 [1-50]
Caldwell, Ian - *Sumatra: Island of Adventure. 2nd Ed.*
 r BL - v93 - S 15 '96 - p212 [1-50]
Caldwell, Ronald J - *A History of Saint Luke's Episcopal Church Jacksonville, Alabama 1844-1994*
 JSH - v62 - N '96 - p862 [51-250]
Calhoun, Craig - *Critical Social Theory*
 CS - v26 - Ja '97 - p119+ [501+]
 Neither Gods nor Emperors
 AHR - v102 - F '97 - p154+ [501+]
 CS - v25 - S '96 - p631+ [501+]
 TLS - O 25 '96 - p8+ [501+]
Calhoun, John C - *The Papers of John C. Calhoun. Vol. 23*
 R&R Bk N - v12 - F '97 - p24 [51-250]
Calhoun, Mary - *Flood (Illus. by Erick Ingraham)*
 c BL - v93 - Mr 15 '97 - p1238 [51-250]
 c CBRS - v25 - Mr '97 - p92+ [51-250]
 c CCB-B - v50 - Ap '97 - p278 [51-250]
 c KR - v65 - F 1 '97 - p220 [51-250]
 c PW - v244 - Ja 27 '97 - p106 [51-250]
 High-Wire Henry (Illus. by Erick Ingraham)
 c SLJ - v43 - Ja '97 - p36 [1-50]

Tonio's Cat (Illus. by Edward Martinez)
 c BL - v93 - S 15 '96 - p245 [51-250]
 c CBRS - v24 - Ag '96 - p163 [1-50]
 c Ch BWatch - v6 - S '96 - p7 [1-50]
 c HB Guide - v8 - Spr '97 - p22 [51-250]
 c SLJ - v42 - S '96 - p171 [51-250]
 c Smith - v27 - N '96 - p167+ [1-50]
Calhoun, Susan - *Nutrition, Cancer and You*
 LJ - v122 - Ja '97 - p57 [51-250]
Calic, Marie-Janine - *Sozialgeschichte Serbiens 1815-1941*
 EHR - v112 - Ap '97 - p511+ [501+]
 Slav R - v55 - Sum '96 - p458+ [501+]
The California Locator. 1996 Ed.
 r EGH - v50 - N '96 - p163+ [51-250]
California Public Education Partnership - *Priority One*
 EL - v54 - D '96 - p90+ [51-250]
Caligiuri, Paul - *High-Performance Soccer*
 y BL - v93 - S 15 '96 - p202 [51-250]
Calin, William - *The French Tradition and the Literature of Medieval England*
 MLR - v91 - O '96 - p942+ [501+]
 Specu - v71 - Jl '96 - p705+ [501+]
Calinescu, Adriana - *Ancient Jewelry and Archaeology*
 Choice - v34 - Ap '97 - p1379+ [51-250]
Calinescu, Matei - *Rereading*
 MLR - v91 - O '96 - p950+ [501+]
 Poetics T - v17 - Sum '96 - p253+ [501+]
Calingaert, Michael - *European Integration*
 For Aff - v75 - N '96 - p158 [51-250]
Calinger, Ronald - *Classics of Mathematics*
 Math T - v89 - S '96 - p514 [501+]
 Vita Mathematica
 Math T - v90 - Mr '97 - p249+ [51-250]
 SciTech - v20 - S '96 - p3 [1-50]
Calino - *1-2-3 Caterpillar*
 c PW - v244 - Mr 3 '97 - p77 [51-250]
 ABC Snake
 c PW - v244 - Mr 3 '97 - p77 [51-250]
Calipari, John - *Refuse to Lose*
 y BL - v93 - N 1 '96 - p473 [51-250]
 LJ - v121 - O 1 '96 - p87 [51-250]
 PW - v243 - S 9 '96 - p72 [51-250]
Calisher, Hortense - *Age: A Novel*
 NYTBR - v101 - O 20 '96 - p36 [1-50]
 Spec - v276 - My 25 '96 - p32+ [501+]
 In the Slammer with Carol Smith
 KR - v65 - Mr 1 '97 - p320 [51-250]
 LJ - v122 - Ap 1 '97 - p122 [51-250]
 PW - v244 - Mr 17 '97 - p74 [51-250]
Calkins, Robert - *Illuminated Books of the Middle Ages*
 AB - v99 - Mr 3 '97 - p685+ [501+]
Call It Courage
 r SLJ - v42 - Ag '96 - p38 [51-250]
The Call of Silent Love
 RR - v56 - Mr '97 - p220 [1-50]
Callaghan, John - *Rajani Palme Dutt: A Study of British Stalinism*
 S&S - v61 - Spr '97 - p147+ [501+]
Callaghan, Mary Rose - *I Met a Man Who Wasn't There*
 KR - v64 - Ag 15 '96 - p1169 [251-500]
 LJ - v121 - O 1 '96 - p124 [51-250]
 PW - v243 - S 9 '96 - p63 [51-250]
Callaghy, Thomas M - *Hemmed In*
 WP - v49 - O '96 - p92+ [501+]
Callaham, Ludmilla Ignatiev - *Callaham's Russian-English Dictionary of Science and Technology. 4th Ed.*
 r ARBA - v28 - '97 - p563 [51-250]
Callahan, Daniel - *Abortion: Law, Choice and Morality*
 Cons - v17 - Aut '96 - p35+ [501+]
 A World Growing Old
 Hast Cen R - v26 - Mr '96 - p48 [1-50]
 MHR - v10 - Fall '96 - p104+ [501+]
Callahan, David - *State of the Union*
 BL - v93 - My 1 '97 - p1481 [51-250]
 KR - v65 - My 1 '97 - p659 [251-500]
 LJ - v122 - My 1 '97 - p136+ [51-250]
 PW - v244 - My 5 '97 - p198 [51-250]
Callahan, Joan C - *Reproduction, Ethics and the Law*
 SciTech - v20 - N '96 - p51 [51-250]
Callahan, Steven - *Adrift: Seventy-Six Days Lost at Sea*
 y BL - v93 - Ja '97 - p832 [1-50]
 y JAAL - v40 - D '96 - p318 [1-50]
Callan, Ginny - *Beyond the Moon Cookbook*
 LJ - v121 - N 15 '96 - p84 [51-250]
 PW - v243 - S 16 '96 - p79 [51-250]
Callanan, Frank - *T.M. Healy*
 Obs - N 24 '96 - p16* [501+]
Callaway, Barbara - *The Heritage of Islam*
 Africa T - v43 - 3 '96 - p331+ [501+]

Callen, Anna Teresa - *Italian Classics in One Pot*
 BL - v93 - Mr 15 '97 - p1215 [51-250]
 PW - v243 - D 16 '96 - p56 [51-250]
Callen, Anthea - *The Spectacular Body*
 AHR - v101 - D '96 - p1521+ [501+]
 Apo - v145 - Ja '97 - p62+ [501+]
 Art J - v55 - Win '96 - p88+ [501+]
Callen, Paulette - *Charity*
 KR - v65 - Mr 15 '97 - p397+ [251-500]
 LJ - v122 - My 1 '97 - p138 [51-250]
 PW - v244 - Ap 14 '97 - p57+ [51-250]
Callicott, J Baird - *Earth Summit Ethics*
 Choice - v34 - Ja '97 - p813 [51-250]
 R&R Bk N - v11 - D '96 - p19 [51-250]
Callies, David L - *Takings: Land-Development Conditions and Regulatory Takings after Dolan and Lucas*
 ABA Jour - v83 - Ja '97 - p97 [51-250]
Callinan, Paul - *Family Homeopathy*
 r ARBA - v28 - '97 - p610 [51-250]
 r RQ - v35 - Sum '96 - p557+ [251-500]
Callinicos, Alex - *Theories and Narratives*
 AHR - v102 - F '97 - p92+ [501+]
Callon, Scott - *Divided Sun*
 APSR - v91 - Mr '97 - p207+ [501+]
 JEL - v34 - S '96 - p1454+ [51-250]
Callow, Philip - *From Noon to Starry Night*
 AL - v68 - D '96 - p854+ [501+]
 Lost Earth
 BM - v138 - S '96 - p612+ [501+]
 Vincent Van Gogh: A Life
 y Kliatt - v31 - Ja '97 - p18 [251-500]
Callow, Simon - *Orson Welles. Vol. 1*
 Choice - v34 - N '96 - p467+ [51-250]
 CR - v268 - Je '96 - p333 [51-250]
 Ent W - D 27 '96 - p142 [51-250]
 Ent W - F 7 '97 - p65 [1-50]
 Lon R Bks - v18 - O 3 '96 - p23+ [501+]
 NYTBR - v101 - D 8 '96 - p90 [1-50]
 PW - v243 - N 4 '96 - p42 [51-250]
 PW - v244 - Ja 13 '97 - p73 [1-50]
 TES - Ag 2 '96 - pR6 [1-50]
 Trib Bks - F 2 '97 - p8 [1-50]
 W&I - v11 - O '96 - p280+ [501+]
Calloway, Colin G - *The American Revolution in Indian Country*
 AHR - v101 - D '96 - p1617 [501+]
 J Am St - v30 - Ag '96 - p315+ [501+]
 RAH - v24 - D '96 - p579+ [501+]
 W&M Q - v53 - Jl '96 - p637+ [501+]
 New Worlds for All
 KR - v65 - Ja 15 '97 - p109 [251-500]
Calloway, Stephen - *The Elements of Style. Rev. Ed.*
 r BL - v93 - Mr 15 '97 - p1256 [51-250]
Callwell, C E - *Small Wars. 3rd Ed.*
 For Aff - v75 - S '96 - p143 [51-250]
 J Mil H - v61 - Ap '97 - p381+ [501+]
Calmenson, Stephanie - *Engine, Engine, Number Nine (Illus. by Paul Meisel)*
 c PW - v244 - F 24 '97 - p89 [51-250]
 Rockin' Reptiles (Illus. by Lynn Munsinger)
 c BL - v93 - Mr 1 '97 - p1162 [51-250]
 c PW - v244 - Ap 7 '97 - p94 [51-250]
Calne, Roy Yorke - *Art, Surgery and Transplantation*
 Nature - v386 - Mr 27 '97 - p342 [1-50]
Calof, David L - *The Couple Who Became Each Other and Other Tales of a Master Hypnotherapist*
 KR - v64 - S 1 '96 - p1287+ [251-500]
 LJ - v121 - N 15 '96 - p76 [51-250]
 PW - v243 - S 30 '96 - p73 [51-250]
Calo Mariani, Maria Stella - *Federico II: Immagine E Potere*
 Choice - v34 - D '96 - p567 [1-50]
Calvert, Patricia - *Glennis, Before and After*
 y BL - v93 - S 1 '96 - p118 [51-250]
 c CBRS - v25 - N '96 - p33 [51-250]
 c CCB-B - v50 - O '96 - p50+ [51-250]
 c HB Guide - v8 - Spr '97 - p62 [51-250]
 c SLJ - v42 - S '96 - p201 [51-250]
Calvesi, Maurizio - *Guttuso*
 BM - v138 - Ag '96 - p554+ [501+]
Calvi, Gabriele - *L'Elettore Sconosciuto*
 Choice - v34 - D '96 - p568 [1-50]
Calvin, Jean - *Calvin's Ecclesiastical Advice*
 CH - v66 - Mr '97 - p195+ [51-250]
Calvin, William H - *The Cerebral Code*
 Choice - v34 - Ja '97 - p878 [51-250]
 Nature - v384 - N 21 '96 - p228+ [501+]
 New Sci - v152 - N 23 '96 - p46 [501+]
 SB - v33 - Mr '97 - p40 [51-250]

How Brains Think
  BL - v93 - S 1 '96 - p50 [51-250]
  New Sci - v153 - Mr 8 '97 - p44 [251-500]
  NYTBR - v101 - N 17 '96 - p12 [501+]
  SB - v33 - Ja '97 - p5 [251-500]
  Skeptic - v4 - 3 '96 - p107 [251-500]
Calvino, Italo - *Enciclopedia: Arte, Scienza E Letteratura*
  r TLS - O 4 '96 - p39 [501+]
Numbers in the Dark and Other Stories
  NYTBR - v101 - D 1 '96 - p36 [1-50]
  PW - v243 - S 2 '96 - p122 [1-50]
  TLS - O 4 '96 - p39 [501+]
  TLS - N 29 '96 - p12 [51-250]
Saggi. Vols. 1-2
  TLS - O 4 '96 - p39 [501+]
Calvo, Guillermo A - *Money, Exchange Rates, and Output*
  JEL - v35 - Mr '97 - p217+ [51-250]
Calvocoressi, Peter - *World Politics since 1945. 7th Ed.*
  Choice - v34 - Mr '97 - p1234 [51-250]
Calvo Ospina, Hernando - *Salsa! Havana Heat, Bronx Beat*
  HAHR - v76 - Ag '96 - p543+ [501+]
Calvo Serraller, Francisco - *La Imagen Romantica De Espana*
  Choice - v34 - D '96 - p569 [1-50]
Camacho, A - *Division of Labor, Variability, Coordination, and the Theory of Firms and Markets*
  JEL - v34 - S '96 - p1411 [51-250]
  R&R Bk N - v11 - D '96 - p23 [51-250]
Camarca, Claudio - *Ordine Pubblico*
  BL - v93 - D 1 '96 - p644 [1-50]
Camargo Espriu, Rosario - *Mexico: Paso A Paso Guia Turistica*
  LJ - v122 - Ja '97 - p78 [51-250]
Camargo Perez, Gabriel - *Pueblos Y Jornadas Boyacenses*
  HAHR - v77 - F '97 - p147+ [251-500]
Cambitoglou, Alexander - *Classical Art in the Nicholson Museum, Sydney*
  AJA - v101 - Ja '97 - p193+ [251-500]
Camboni, Marina - *Utopia in the Present Tense*
  AL - v68 - S '96 - p665 [51-250]
Cambor, Kathleen - *The Book of Mercy*
  CC - v113 - N 20 '96 - p1169 [51-250]
  CSM - v88 - S 9 '96 - p14 [251-500]
  LATBR - Ag 25 '96 - p6 [501+]
  NYTBR - v101 - D 8 '96 - p79 [1-50]
The Cambridge Ancient History. 2nd Ed., Vol. 6
  HT - v46 - D '96 - p58+ [501+]
The Cambridge Ancient History. 2nd Ed., Vol. 10
  TLS - D 20 '96 - p13 [501+]
Cambridge Astronomy Dictionary
  r ARBA - v28 - '97 - p632 [51-250]
  r Choice - v34 - Ap '97 - p1306 [51-250]
The Cambridge History of American Literature. Vol. 2
  J Am St - v30 - Ap '96 - p162+ [251-500]
The Cambridge History of American Literature. Vol. 8
  r AL - v68 - D '96 - p884+ [51-250]
  Choice - v34 - O '96 - p276 [251-500]
The Cambridge History of China. Vol. 6
  Ch Rev Int - v3 - Fall '96 - p403+ [501+]
  Historian - v58 - Sum '96 - p880+ [501+]
  HJAS - v56 - 2 '96 - p493+ [501+]
Cambridge Reading
  Sch Lib - v44 - Ag '96 - p102 [251-500]
Cambrosio, Alberto - *Exquisite Specificity*
  Nature - v383 - O 31 '96 - p777 [501+]
  Sci - v274 - N 8 '96 - p934+ [501+]
Cameli, A P - *The Information Superhighway*
  Choice - v34 - N '96 - p495 [51-250]
Camenson, Blythe - *Careers for Health Nuts*
  BWatch - v17 - S '96 - p8 [51-250]
Careers for Mystery Buffs and Other Snoops and Sleuths
  y Kliatt - v31 - Ja '97 - p21 [51-250]
Real People Working in Health Care
  yr Kliatt - v31 - Mr '97 - p27+ [51-250]
Real People Working in Sales and Marketing
  yr Kliatt - v31 - Mr '97 - p27+ [51-250]
Real People Working in Service Businesses
  yr Kliatt - v31 - Mr '97 - p27+ [51-250]
Cameron, Alan D - *Thailand: The Post Offices and Their Postmarks since the Introduction of the Postcode System in 1982*
  r Am Phil - v110 - N '96 - p1039 [51-250]
  Phil Lit R - v45 - 3 '96 - p257 [251-500]
Cameron, Ann - *More Stories Huey Tells (Illus. by Lis Toft)*
  c KR - v65 - Mr 15 '97 - p459 [51-250]
  c PW - v244 - Mr 17 '97 - p85 [1-50]

The Stories Huey Tells (Illus. by Lis Toft)
  c JB - v60 - O '96 - p190 [51-250]
  c Sch Lib - v44 - Ag '96 - p98 [51-250]
Cameron, Averil - *The Byzantine and Early Islamic Near East. Vol. 3*
  MEJ - v50 - Aut '96 - p631 [51-250]
Cameron, Catherine M - *Abandonment of Settlements and Regions*
  AJA - v100 - Jl '96 - p605+ [501+]
Dialectics in the Arts
  Choice - v34 - Mr '97 - p1171 [51-250]
  R&R Bk N - v12 - F '97 - p71 [51-250]
Cameron, Debra - *Learning GNU Emacs. 2nd Ed.*
  SciTech - v20 - D '96 - p11 [1-50]
Security Issues for the Internet and the World Wide Web
  SciTech - v20 - D '96 - p14 [51-250]
Cameron, Elspeth - *No Previous Experience*
  Mac - v110 - My 19 '97 - p61 [501+]
Cameron, Fraser - *The European Union's Common Foreign and Security Policy*
  J Gov Info - v23 - S '96 - p566+ [51-250]
Cameron, Ian - *The Book of Film Noir*
  FQ - v49 - Fall '95 - p63 [51-250]
The Book of Westerns
  Choice - v34 - O '96 - p289 [51-250]
The Movie Book of the Western
  TES - Ag 2 '96 - pR6 [1-50]
Cameron, John - *Poverty and Power*
  JEL - v35 - Mr '97 - p148+ [501+]
Cameron, Julia - *The Vein of Gold*
  LJ - v121 - N 1 '96 - p94 [51-250]
  Utne R - S '96 - p91+ [501+]
The Vein of Gold (Cameron). Audio Version
  CSM - v89 - Ja 30 '97 - pB4 [51-250]
  PW - v244 - Ap 7 '97 - p34 [51-250]
Cameron, Julia Margaret Pattle - *Julia Margaret Cameron: Photographs from the J. Paul Getty Museum*
  AB - v99 - F 24 '97 - p622+ [501+]
  Bloom Rev - v16 - N '96 - p23 [51-250]
Cameron, Kenneth M - *Africa on Film*
  JC - v46 - Sum '96 - p202+ [501+]
Cameron, Loren - *Body Alchemy*
  Advocate - S 17 '96 - p60 [1-50]
  Advocate - N 12 '96 - p77+ [501+]
Cameron, M L - *Anglo-Saxon Medicine*
  Specu - v72 - Ja '97 - p121+ [501+]
Cameron, Peter - *Andorra*
  Atl - v279 - F '97 - p109+ [51-250]
  BL - v93 - Ja '97 - p817 [51-250]
  BW - v27 - Ja 26 '97 - p7 [501+]
  KR - v64 - O 15 '96 - p1482 [251-500]
  LJ - v121 - N 15 '96 - p87 [51-250]
  NY - v72 - Ja 27 '97 - p76 [51-250]
  NYTBR - v101 - D 29 '96 - p8 [501+]
  PW - v243 - N 11 '96 - p55 [51-250]
  TLS - F 14 '97 - p21 [501+]
  VV - v42 - Ja 21 '97 - p52+ [501+]
  WSJ-Cent - v99 - Ja 10 '97 - pA9 [251-500]
The Half You Don't Know
  KR - v64 - N 1 '96 - p1564 [51-250]
  LJ - v121 - N 1 '96 - p109 [51-250]
Cameron, Peter John - *The Classics of Catholic Spirituality*
  RR - v55 - N '96 - p661 [1-50]
Cameron, Stella - *Dear Stranger*
  PW - v244 - Mr 31 '97 - p71+ [51-250]
Guilty Pleasures
  PW - v244 - Mr 10 '97 - p64 [51-250]
Cameron, Sue - *Love, Sex, and Murder*
  Rapport - v19 - 5 '96 - p36 [501+]
Camfield, Gregg - *Sentimental Twain*
  MLR - v91 - Jl '96 - p707+ [501+]
  RES - v48 - F '97 - p138+ [501+]
Camille, Michael - *Gothic Art*
  Choice - v34 - F '97 - p955 [51-250]
  LJ - v121 - N 1 '96 - p63 [51-250]
Master of Death
  Choice - v34 - O '96 - p264 [51-250]
  Comw - v123 - O 25 '96 - p25+ [501+]
Camilleri, Andrea - *Il Birraio Di Preston*
  TLS - Jl 19 '96 - p13 [501+]
Camilleri, Carmel - *Difference and Cultures in Europe*
  J Gov Info - v23 - S '96 - p664 [51-250]
Caminer, David - *User-Driven Innovation*
  New Sci - v153 - F 1 '97 - p43 [51-250]
  Obs - Ag 25 '96 - p18* [501+]
Cammarata, John - *A Physician's Guide to Herbal Wellness*
  y SLJ - v43 - Ja '97 - p142 [51-250]
Camp, Anthony - *Everyone Has Roots*
  TES - Jl 26 '96 - pR6 [1-50]

Camp, Carole Ann - *American Astronomers*
  c HB Guide - v7 - Fall '96 - p376 [1-50]
Invitations to Cells
  c SB - v32 - Ag '96 - p179 [251-500]
Invitations to Evolving
  c SB - v32 - Ag '96 - p179 [251-500]
Invitations to Heredity
  c SB - v32 - Ag '96 - p179 [251-500]
Invitations to Interdependence
  c SB - v32 - Ag '96 - p179 [251-500]
Invitations to Life's Diversity
  c SB - v32 - Ag '96 - p179 [251-500]
Invitations to the Matter-Energy Cycle
  c SB - v32 - Ag '96 - p179 [251-500]
Camp, Jeffery - *Paint: A Manual of Pictorial Thought and Practical Advice*
  y CLW - v67 - D '96 - p60 [51-250]
  LJ - v121 - N 15 '96 - p60 [51-250]
  Obs - D 1 '96 - p16* [51-250]
  y SLJ - v42 - S '96 - p240 [51-250]
  TLS - S 13 '96 - p32 [1-50]
  y VOYA - v19 - F '97 - p343+ [251-500]
Camp, Lindsay - *Billy and the Barglebogle (Illus. by Peter Utton)*
  c Sch Lib - v44 - Ag '96 - p98 [51-250]
The Midnight Feast (Illus. by Tony Ross)
  c JB - v60 - D '96 - p227 [51-250]
  c Sch Lib - v45 - F '97 - p17 [51-250]
  c TES - Ja 31 '97 - pR7 [51-250]
Camp, Martin - *Life on the High Wire*
  PW - v243 - D 16 '96 - p53 [51-250]
Camp, Roderic Ai - *Democracy in Latin America*
  HAHR - v76 - N '96 - p833+ [51-250]
Political Recruitment across Two Centuries
  AHR - v102 - F '97 - p234+ [501+]
Polling for Democracy
  Choice - v34 - Mr '97 - p1234 [51-250]
Campagna, Anthony S - *Economic Policy in the Carter Administration*
  JEH - v56 - D '96 - p960+ [501+]
  Pol Stud J - v24 - Sum '96 - p332 [51-250]
  Pres SQ - v26 - Sum '96 - p892 [501+]
Campanella, Thomas - *A Defense of Galileo, the Mathematician from Florence*
  CHR - v82 - O '96 - p726+ [501+]
Campbell, Alan - *Miners, Unions, and Politics 1910-47*
  R&R Bk N - v12 - F '97 - p40 [51-250]
Campbell, Ann - *The New York Public Library Amazing Space (Illus. by Jessica Wolk-Stanley)*
  yr KR - v65 - Ap 1 '97 - p551 [51-250]
  cr PW - v244 - Mr 31 '97 - p77 [51-250]
The New York Public Library Incredible Earth (Illus. by Jessica Wolk-Stanley)
  c BL - v93 - S 15 '96 - p234 [51-250]
  c KR - v64 - S 1 '96 - p1320 [51-250]
  cr SB - v33 - Mr '97 - p48+ [51-250]
  y SLJ - v43 - Ja '97 - p120 [51-250]
Campbell, Antony F - *Sources of the Pentateuch*
  Rel St Rev - v23 - Ja '97 - p22+ [501+]
Campbell, Ballard C - *The Growth of American Government*
  APSR - v90 - S '96 - p644+ [501+]
  Historian - v59 - Win '97 - p423+ [251-500]
  JEH - v56 - S '96 - p752+ [501+]
Campbell, Bethany - *Don't Talk to Strangers*
  PW - v243 - N 11 '96 - p72 [51-250]
  PW - v243 - N 18 '96 - p70 [51-250]
Campbell, Bruce - *Complications in Arterial Surgery*
  SciTech - v20 - S '96 - p39 [51-250]
Campbell, Bruce A - *Introduction to Space Sciences and Spacecraft Applications*
  Choice - v34 - Ap '97 - p1361 [51-250]
  New Sci - v153 - Mr 1 '97 - p45 [251-500]
Campbell, Christian X - *Databook on Mechanical and Thermophysical Properties of Particulate-Reinforced Ceramic Matrix Composites*
  SciTech - v21 - Mr '97 - p77 [51-250]
Databook on Mechanical and Thermophysical Properties of Whisker-Reinforced Ceramic Matrix Composites
  SciTech - v21 - Mr '97 - p77 [51-250]
Campbell, Christopher P - *Race, Myth and the News*
  SSQ - v77 - S '96 - p713+ [501+]
Campbell, Colin - *The Clinton Presidency*
  APSR - v90 - S '96 - p645+ [501+]
  Pres SQ - v27 - Win '97 - p167+ [501+]
Campbell, Colm - *Emergency Law in Ireland 1918-1925*
  Albion - v28 - Sum '96 - p372+ [501+]
  EHR - v111 - N '96 - p1225+ [501+]
Campbell, David - *Contract and Economic Organisation*
  JEL - v34 - D '96 - p2079 [51-250]
  R&R Bk N - v11 - D '96 - p51 [51-250]

The Failure of Marxism
  R&R Bk N - v12 - F '97 - p58 [51-250]
Campbell, David G - *Islands in Space and Time*
  KR - v64 - O 15 '96 - p1503 [251-500]
  LJ - v121 - D '96 - p137 [51-250]
  Nature - v385 - F 13 '97 - p591 [1-50]
  PW - v243 - N 11 '96 - p67 [51-250]
Campbell, Denele Pitts - *Notes of a Piano Tuner*
  PW - v244 - F 17 '97 - p201 [51-250]
Campbell, Don - *The Power of Music (Campbell). Audio Version*
  Quill & Q - v62 - Ag '96 - p37 [1-50]
Campbell, Donald - *Playing for Scotland*
  TLS - D 13 '96 - p20 [501+]
Campbell, Donald E - *Incentives: Motivation and the Economics of Information*
  JEL - v34 - S '96 - p1416 [51-250]
Campbell, Duane - *Choosing Democracy*
  Workbook - v21 - Fall '96 - p124+ [501+]
Campbell, Fiona - *I Can Make Models (Illus. by Michael Evans)*
  c Sch Lib - v44 - N '96 - p161 [51-250]
  c TES - Jl 19 '96 - pR8 [1-50]
Campbell, George L - *Concise Compendium of the World's Languages*
  r ARBA - v28 - '97 - p375 [51-250]
Campbell, James, 1948- - *Understanding John Dewey*
  Ethics - v107 - O '96 - p166+ [501+]
Campbell, James B - *Introduction to Remote Sensing. 2nd Ed.*
  Choice - v34 - Mr '97 - p1188+ [51-250]
  SB - v33 - Mr '97 - p41 [51-250]
  SciTech - v21 - Mr '97 - p1 [51-250]
Campbell, James E - *Cheap Seats*
  Choice - v34 - My '97 - p1575 [51-250]
Campbell, James T - *Songs of Zion*
  AHR - v101 - O '96 - p1122+ [501+]
  Bl S - v26 - Sum '96 - p64 [1-50]
  CC - v113 - O 16 '96 - p980+ [251-500]
  CH - v66 - Mr '97 - p159+ [501+]
  Historian - v59 - Win '97 - p404 [51-250]
Campbell, Jill - *Natural Masques*
  Eight-C St - v29 - Sum '96 - p435+ [501+]
Campbell, John, 1946- - *In Darwin's Wake*
  New Sci - v153 - Mr 8 '97 - p43 [51-250]
  PW - v244 - F 3 '97 - p87 [51-250]
Campbell, John, 1956- - *Past, Space, and Self*
  Phil R - v105 - Ja '96 - p102+ [501+]
  Rel St Rev - v22 - O '96 - p334 [51-250]
Campbell, John L - *Legacies of Change*
  Choice - v34 - Ja '97 - p845 [51-250]
Campbell, John Martin, 1927- - *The Prairie Schoolhouse*
  Bloom Rev - v16 - Jl '96 - p12+ [51-250]
Campbell, Jonathan - *The Use of Scripture in the Damascus Document 1-8, 19-20*
  Rel St Rev - v23 - Ja '97 - p85+ [51-250]
Campbell, Kim - *Time and Chance*
  Quill & Q - v62 - My '96 - p28 [501+]
Campbell, Kumari - *Prince Edward Island*
  c HB Guide - v7 - Fall '96 - p385 [51-250]
Campbell, Louisa - *Phoebe's Fabulous Father (Illus. by Bridget Starr Taylor)*
  c CCB-B - v50 - N '96 - p92 [51-250]
  c HB Guide - v8 - Spr '97 - p22 [51-250]
  c KR - v64 - Ag 15 '96 - p1233 [51-250]
  c PW - v243 - S 23 '96 - p75 [51-250]
  c SLJ - v42 - D '96 - p85+ [51-250]
Campbell, Louise - *Coventry Cathedral*
  r Choice - v34 - N '96 - p443 [51-250]
  TLS - N 8 '96 - p6 [501+]
Campbell, Malcolm - *Ultimate Golf Techniques*
  LJ - v121 - O 1 '96 - p52 [1-50]
Campbell, Mary - *Microsoft Word for Windows 95*
  r CBR - v14 - Jl '96 - p26 [51-250]
World Wide Web Pocket Dictionary
  r CBR - v14 - Jl '96 - p22 [51-250]
Campbell, Murray - *Selected Topics on Electron Physics*
  SciTech - v21 - Mr '97 - p25 [51-250]
Campbell, Naomi - *Naomi*
  Esq - v126 - D '96 - p40 [1-50]
Campbell, Patricia Shehan - *Roots and Branches*
  CAY - v16 - Fall '95 - p1 [51-250]
Campbell, Paul D Q - *Plastic Component Design*
  SciTech - v20 - N '96 - p80 [51-250]
Campbell, Peter R - *Power and Politics in Old Regime France 1720-1745*
  TLS - O 11 '96 - p31+ [501+]
Campbell, R Alastair - *The Elders: Seniority within Earliest Christianity*
  Rel St Rev - v23 - Ap '97 - p188 [51-250]

Campbell, R Thomas - *Southern Thunder*
  PW - v244 - Mr 24 '97 - p71 [51-250]
Campbell, Ramsey - *Far Away and Never*
  Necro - Fall '96 - p7+ [501+]
The House on Nazareth Hill
  Necro - Win '97 - p3+ [501+]
The One Safe Place
  Necro - Win '97 - p3+ [501+]
Campbell, Robert - *The Lion's Share*
  Arm Det - v29 - Fall '96 - p482 [51-250]
Campbell, Robert W - *Soviet and Post-Soviet Telecommunications*
  Slav R - v55 - Sum '96 - p500+ [501+]
Campbell, Rod - *Buster Gets Dressed*
  c Bks Keeps - N '96 - p7 [51-250]
Henry's Ball
  c Bks Keeps - N '96 - p7 [51-250]
Campbell, Scott - *Widower: When Men Are Left Alone*
  BL - v92 - Ag '96 - p1860+ [51-250]
  Readings - v12 - Mr '97 - p22 [51-250]
Campbell, Stanislaus - *From Breviary to Liturgy of the Hours*
  CH - v65 - D '96 - p767+ [501+]
Campbell, Stephen A - *The Science and Engineering of Microelectronic Fabrication*
  Choice - v34 - D '96 - p641 [51-250]
Campbell, Stuart - *The Archaeology of Death in the Ancient Near East*
  AJA - v101 - Ja '97 - p169 [501+]
Campbell, Stueart - *The Loch Ness Monster*
  New Sci - v153 - Ja 18 '97 - p38 [1-50]
Campbell, SueEllen - *Bringing the Mountain Home*
  KR - v64 - S 1 '96 - p1288 [251-500]
  LJ - v121 - O 15 '96 - p86+ [51-250]
Campbell, Susan - *Charleston Kedding: A History of Kitchen Gardening*
  BL - v93 - Mr 15 '97 - p1214+ [51-250]
  Obs - S 1 '96 - p15* [501+]
  PW - v244 - Mr 3 '97 - p70 [51-250]
  TLS - N 22 '96 - p15 [501+]
Campbell, Susie - *Characters from Pre-20th Century Novels*
  y TES - S 20 '96 - pR6 [251-500]
Campbell, Ted A - *Christian Confessions*
  Choice - v34 - O '96 - p296 [51-250]
  Intpr - v51 - Ap '97 - p212+ [501+]
Campbell, Tom D - *The Legal Theory of Ethical Positivism*
  R&R Bk N - v12 - F '97 - p62 [51-250]
Campbell, Walter E - *Across Fortune's Tracks*
  Choice - v34 - O '96 - p346 [51-250]
  JEL - v34 - S '96 - p1466+ [51-250]
Campbell-Kelly, Martin - *Computer: A History of the Information Machine*
  y BL - v92 - Ag '96 - p1858 [51-250]
  y BL - v92 - Ag '96 - p1890 [1-50]
  Choice - v34 - Ja '97 - p832 [51-250]
  Nature - v383 - O 3 '96 - p405 [501+]
  New Sci - v152 - N 30 '96 - p48 [51-250]
  NYTBR - v101 - N 17 '96 - p29 [501+]
Campillo, Antonio - *Algebraic Geometry and Singularities*
  SciTech - v20 - S '96 - p11 [51-250]
Campilonga, Margaret S - *Blue Frogs*
  c Ch BWatch - v7 - F '97 - p2 [1-50]
Campion, Dan - *Peter De Vries and Surrealism*
  CC - v113 - S 11 '96 - p871+ [501+]
Campion, Ed - *Catholic Voices*
  Aust Bk R - D '96 - p51+ [501+]
Campion, Isaac - *The Nature of the Beast*
  y Magpies - v11 - S '96 - p45 [1-50]
Campion, Nicholas - *The Book of World Horoscopes. Rev. and Expanded Ed.*
  r Horoscope - v62 - Ag '96 - p38+ [501+]
Campion, Pierre - *Mallarme: Poesie Et Philosophie*
  FR - v70 - O '96 - p119+ [501+]
Campo, Rafael - *The Poetry of Healing*
  BL - v93 - D 1 '96 - p628 [51-250]
  BW - v27 - F 9 '97 - p7 [501+]
  KR - v64 - N 1 '96 - p1575 [51-250]
  LJ - v121 - D '96 - p131 [51-250]
  Nat - v264 - F 24 '97 - p30+ [501+]
  PW - v243 - N 18 '96 - p55 [51-250]
What the Body Told
  Choice - v34 - O '96 - p276 [51-250]
Campo, Victoria - *Catalogo De Los Pliegos Sueltos Poeticos Del Siglo XVII De La Biblioteca De Antonio Rodriguez Monino*
  r Lib - v18 - S '96 - p273+ [1-50]
Campolo, Anthony - *Ideas for Social Action*
  VOYA - v19 - F '97 - p316 [251-500]

Camporesi, Piero - *Exotic Brew*
  Lon R Bks - v18 - O 31 '96 - p26+ [501+]
The Land of Hunger
  Lon R Bks - v18 - O 31 '96 - p26+ [501+]
The Magic Harvest
  Lon R Bks - v18 - O 31 '96 - p26 [501+]
Campos, Anthony Hohn - *Mexican Folk Tales*
  CAY - v17 - Win '96 - p10 [51-250]
Campos, Jose Edgardo - *The Key to the Asian Miracle*
  For Aff - v75 - N '96 - p147+ [51-250]
  JEL - v34 - D '96 - p2028 [51-250]
Campos, Julieta - *She Has Reddish Hair and Her Name Is Sabina*
  TranslRevS - v1 - My '95 - p29 [251-500]
Camps, A - *Missiology: An Ecumenical Introduction*
  CH - v65 - D '96 - p785+ [501+]
Campus-Free College Degrees. 7th Ed.
  r ARBA - v28 - '97 - p135 [51-250]
Camus, Albert - *The First Man*
  Ant R - v54 - Sum '96 - p361 [251-500]
  Bks & Cult - v2 - My '96 - p19+ [501+]
  CR - v270 - F '97 - p111 [1-50]
  LATBR - O 20 '96 - p15 [51-250]
  NYTBR - v101 - Ag 25 '96 - p28 [51-250]
  Obs - Ja 5 '97 - p18* [51-250]
  Sew R - v104 - Jl '96 - pR66+ [501+]
Camus, Jean-Pierre - *Road Transport Informatics*
  J Gov Info - v23 - S '96 - p666 [501+]
Camus, Renaud - *L'Epuisant Desir De Ces Choses*
  WLT - v70 - Aut '96 - p906 [501+]
Tricks
  TLS - Ag 30 '96 - p22+ [501+]
Canada - *Towards a Rapid Reaction Capability for the United Nations*
  J Gov Info - v23 - S '96 - p621 [51-250]
Canada, Geoffrey - *Fist Stick Knife Gun*
  Ant R - v54 - Sum '96 - p366+ [251-500]
Canada. Information Highway Advisory Council - *Connection Community Content*
  J Gov Info - v23 - S '96 - p611+ [51-250]
Canada. Parliament. Senate. Special Committee on Euthanasia and Assisted Suicide - *Of Life and Death*
  J Gov Info - v23 - S '96 - p617+ [51-250]
Canada. Royal Commission on Aboriginal Peoples - *Treaty Making in the Spirit of Co-Existence*
  J Gov Info - v23 - S '96 - p622 [51-250]
Canada Year Book 1997 on CD-ROM. Electronic Media Version
  r Quill & Q - v63 - Ja '97 - p35 [251-500]
Canadian Archives in 1992
  Archiv - Fall '94 - p175+ [501+]
The Canadian Encyclopedia Plus 1997. Electronic Media Version
  r ARBA - v28 - '97 - p22 [251-500]
  r Quill & Q - v62 - D '96 - p31 [501+]
Canadian Energy Research Institute - *Planning for the Indian Power Sector*
  JEL - v34 - S '96 - p1457 [51-250]
Canadian Environmental Assessment Agency - *Military Flying Activities in Labrador and Quebec*
  J Gov Info - v23 - S '96 - p617 [51-250]
Canadian Geographical Information Systems Source Book
  r J Gov Info - v23 - Jl '96 - p529+ [251-500]
Canadian History: A Reader's Guide. Vols. 1-2
  Can Hist R - v77 - D '96 - p635+ [501+]
Canadian Internet Directory 1997
  r Quill & Q - v63 - F '97 - p28 [501+]
Canadian Internet Handbook 1997
  r Quill & Q - v63 - F '97 - p28 [501+]
Canadian Journal of Development Studies
  p WorldV - v12 - O '96 - p11 [51-250]
Canadian Sourcebook 1997
  r ARBA - v28 - '97 - p4 [251-500]
Canadian Who's Who 1996
  r ARBA - v28 - '97 - p19 [51-250]
Canas, Dionisio - *El Poeta Y La Ciudad*
  Hisp - v79 - D '96 - p782+ [501+]
Canavan, Francis - *The Pluralist Game*
  IPQ - v37 - Mr '97 - p122+ [501+]
Cancer Chemotherapy and Biological Response Modifiers Annual 16
  SciTech - v20 - S '96 - p31 [51-250]
Candaele, Kerry - *Bound for Glory*
  c Ch BWatch - v6 - O '96 - p5 [51-250]
  y HB Guide - v8 - Spr '97 - p173 [51-250]
  y SLJ - v43 - F '97 - p110 [51-250]
Candau, Antonio - *La Obra Narrativa De Jose Maria Merino*
  Hisp - v79 - D '96 - p783+ [501+]

Candib, Lucy M - *Medicine and the Family*
  JMF - v58 - Ag '96 - p801+ [501+]
Candido, Antonio - *On Literature and Society*
  CS - v25 - N '96 - p824+ [501+]
Candido, Joseph - *King John*
  Choice - v34 - Ap '97 - p1337 [51-250]
The Candlewick Book of Animal Tales
  c BL - v93 - O 1 '96 - p353 [51-250]
  c HB Guide - v8 - Spr '97 - p147 [51-250]
  c PW - v243 - O 21 '96 - p85 [51-250]
  c SLJ - v43 - Ja '97 - p98 [51-250]
The Candlewick Book of First Rhymes
  c BL - v93 - N 15 '96 - p589 [51-250]
  c HB Guide - v8 - Spr '97 - p106 [51-250]
  c SLJ - v43 - Ja '97 - p98 [251-500]
Candy, Catherine - *Priestly Fictions*
  ILS - v16 - Spr '97 - p10 [501+]
  Rel St Rev - v23 - Ja '97 - p53 [51-250]
Canemaker, John - *Before the Animation Begins*
  Ent W - N 22 '96 - p130 [51-250]
  LJ - v121 - N 15 '96 - p63 [51-250]
  PW - v243 - S 9 '96 - p77+ [51-250]
  Felix: The Twisted Tale of the World's Most Famous Cat
  LATBR - O 27 '96 - p11 [51-250]
  Tex Avery: The MGM Years 1942-1955
  y BL - v93 - N 15 '96 - p562 [51-250]
Canet, Daniel - *Nuclear Magnetic Resonance*
  Choice - v34 - Ja '97 - p834 [51-250]
  SciTech - v20 - S '96 - p15 [51-250]
Caney, Simon - *National Rights, International Obligations*
  JPR - v34 - F '97 - p108+ [51-250]
Canfield, Cass, Jr. - *Masterworks of Latin American Short Fiction*
  KR - v64 - S 1 '96 - p1268 [51-250]
  LJ - v121 - O 1 '96 - p129+ [51-250]
  PW - v243 - S 9 '96 - p64 [251-500]
Canfield, Clarke - *Now Hiring!*
  BL - v93 - S 15 '96 - p206 [1-50]
  r J Car P&E - v57 - Fall '96 - p19 [251-500]
Canfield, Jack - *The 4th Course of Chicken Soup for the Soul*
  PW - v244 - Mr 3 '97 - p58 [51-250]
Canham, Marsha - *The Last Arrow*
  PW - v244 - Mr 17 '97 - p80 [51-250]
Cann, Kate - *Diving In*
  y Bks Keeps - Ja '97 - p27 [51-250]
  c TES - N 29 '96 - p10* [51-250]
Cannat, Guillaume - *Be Your Own Astronomy Expert (Illus. by Nathalie Locoste)*
  c HB Guide - v8 - Spr '97 - p111 [51-250]
  c S&T - v93 - Ap '97 - p65 [1-50]
Cannell, Dorothy - *God Save the Queen!*
  BL - v93 - Ja '97 - p823+ [51-250]
  KR - v64 - D 15 '96 - p1768 [51-250]
  PW - v243 - N 4 '96 - p66 [51-250]
Cannell, Stephen J - *Final Victim*
  Rapport - v19 - 5 '96 - p34 [251-500]
  King Con
  LJ - v122 - My 1 '97 - p138 [51-250]
  PW - v244 - Ap 28 '97 - p46 [51-250]
Canney, Donald L - *U.S. Coast Guard and Revenue Cutters 1790-1935*
  r R&R Bk N - v11 - D '96 - p72 [1-50]
Canning, Charlotte - *Feminist Theaters in the U.S.A.*
  Choice - v34 - S '96 - p138 [51-250]
Canning, Joseph - *A History of Medieval Political Thought*
  HT - v46 - O '96 - p56 [1-50]
Canning, Kathleen - *Languages of Labor and Gender*
  Choice - v34 - Mr '97 - p1218 [51-250]
  JEL - v35 - Mr '97 - p262 [51-250]
Canning, Peter - *American Dreamers*
  AJR - v19 - Ja '97 - p49 [501+]
  BL - v93 - N 15 '96 - p551 [51-250]
  BW - v27 - F 23 '97 - p7 [501+]
  Econ - v341 - D 7 '96 - p10*+ [501+]
  KR - v64 - S 15 '96 - p1367 [251-500]
  LJ - v121 - D '96 - p110 [51-250]
  NYTBR - v101 - N 24 '96 - p7 [501+]
  NYTLa - v146 - N 21 '96 - pC20 [501+]
  PW - v243 - O 7 '96 - p51 [251-500]
  PW - v243 - N 4 '96 - p42 [51-250]
  VLS - Win '96 - p13+ [501+]
Canning, Shelagh - *Compassion: Zach Lends a Hand (Illus. by Davis Henry)*
  c PW - v243 - N 18 '96 - p78 [51-250]
  Courage: Annie's Race (Illus. by Davis Henry)
  c PW - v243 - N 18 '96 - p78 [51-250]
  Honesty: Zach's Tall Tale (Illus. by Davis Henry)
  c PW - v243 - N 18 '96 - p78 [51-250]

Responsibility: Annie Shows Off
  c PW - v243 - N 18 '96 - p78 [51-250]
Cannings, Richard - *British Columbia: A Natural History*
  CG - v117 - Ja '97 - p76 [251-500]
Cannizzaro, Stanislao - *Lettere A Stanislao Cannizzaro 1868-1872. Vols. 3-4*
  J Chem Ed - v73 - Ag '96 - pA178 [251-500]
Cannon, A E - *I Know What You Do When I Go to School (Illus. by Jennifer Mazzucco)*
  c SLJ - v42 - D '96 - p91 [51-250]
Cannon, Annie - *The Bat in the Boot (Illus. by Annie Cannon)*
  c Emerg Lib - v24 - S '96 - p43 [1-50]
  c HB Guide - v7 - Fall '96 - p250 [51-250]
Cannon, Brian Q - *Remaking the Agrarian Dream*
  R&R Bk N - v12 - F '97 - p34 [51-250]
Cannon, Casey - *Simply AIX*
  SciTech - v21 - Mr '97 - p9 [51-250]
Cannon, Garland - *Objects of Enquiry*
  TLS - Mr 21 '97 - p25 [501+]
Cannon, Janell - *Stellaluna*
  c CLW - v67 - Mr '97 - p13 [1-50]
  Stellaluna. Electronic Media Version
  c BW - v26 - D 15 '96 - p11 [51-250]
  c PW - v243 - N 25 '96 - p33 [51-250]
  Stellaluna (Holt). Audio Version
  c BL - v93 - Ap 1 '97 - p1314 [1-50]
  c Ch BWatch - v6 - Jl '96 - p7 [1-50]
  c CSM - v89 - Ja 30 '97 - pB4 [51-250]
  c Emerg Lib - v24 - Mr '97 - p21 [51-250]
  c SLJ - v43 - F '97 - p71 [51-250]
  Verdi (Illus. by Janell Cannon)
  c KR - v65 - Ap 1 '97 - p551 [51-250]
  c PW - v244 - F 17 '97 - p219 [51-250]
  c Trib Bks - Mr 9 '97 - p7 [51-250]
Cannon, Katie Geneva - *Katie's Canon*
  CLW - v66 - Je '96 - p31 [251-500]
Cannon, Makeda - *Under the Spell of God*
  Bl S - v26 - Fall '96 - p101 [1-50]
Cannon, Michael - *The Borough*
  KR - v65 - Ap 1 '97 - p480 [251-500]
Cannon, Taffy - *Mississippi Treasure Hunt*
  y Kliatt - v30 - S '96 - p6 [51-250]
Cannon, Tom - *Welcome to the Revolution*
  BL - v93 - Mr 15 '97 - p1210 [51-250]
Canny, Nicholas - *Europeans on the Move*
  EHR - v112 - F '97 - p200+ [501+]
  JIH - v27 - Aut '96 - p290+ [501+]
Canon, Rachel - *The Anniversary*
  VQR - v73 - Win '97 - p23* [51-250]
Canovan, Margaret - *Nationhood and Political Theory*
  Choice - v34 - D '96 - p688 [51-250]
  RP - v59 - Spr '97 - p384+ [501+]
  R&R Bk N - v11 - N '96 - p47 [51-250]
Canter, David V - *Psychology in Action*
  R&R Bk N - v11 - D '96 - p2 [51-250]
Canter, Larry W - *Nitrates in Groundwater*
  SciTech - v20 - D '96 - p69 [51-250]
Canter, Mark - *Ember from the Sun*
  y BL - v92 - Ag '96 - p1853 [251-500]
  Ent W - S 27 '96 - p74 [51-250]
  LJ - v122 - Mr 15 '97 - p41 [1-50]
  Ember from the Sun (Bedard). Audio Version
  BWatch - v17 - D '96 - p11 [51-250]
Cantini, Andrea - *Logical Frameworks for Truth and Abstraction*
  SciTech - v20 - N '96 - p5 [51-250]
Canton, Maria P - *The McGraw-Hill PC Programmer's Desk Reference*
  r CBR - v14 - S '96 - p32 [1-50]
  r Choice - v34 - D '96 - p646 [51-250]
  yr SB - v32 - N '96 - p235 [251-500]
  r SciTech - v20 - N '96 - p7 [51-250]
Cantor, Geoffrey - *Michael Faraday*
  Choice - v34 - Ap '97 - p1360 [51-250]
  New Sci - v153 - Ja 18 '97 - p40 [51-250]
Cantor, George - *Historic Festivals*
  r ARBA - v27 - '96 - p177 [51-250]
  r RQ - v35 - Sum '96 - p560+ [251-500]
  Inside Sports World Series Factbook
  r ARBA - v28 - '97 - p294+ [51-250]
  Pop Culture Landmarks
  r ARBA - v28 - '97 - p177+ [51-250]
  The Tigers of '68
  BL - v93 - My 1 '97 - p1474 [51-250]
  LJ - v122 - Ap 15 '97 - p87 [51-250]
  PW - v244 - F 24 '97 - p74 [51-250]
Cantor, Norman F - *The American Century*
  BL - v93 - Mr 1 '97 - p1107+ [51-250]
  PW - v244 - Ja 27 '97 - p84 [51-250]

The Jewish Experience
  BL - v93 - Ja '97 - p813 [51-250]
  PW - v243 - D 2 '96 - p51+ [51-250]
  Medieval Lives
  Specu - v72 - Ja '97 - p122+ [501+]
  The Sacred Chain
  Books - v9 - S '95 - p23 [51-250]
  HT - v46 - D '96 - p53+ [501+]
  TES - O 11 '96 - p8* [51-250]
Cantor, Ruth F - *Parents' Guide to Special Needs Schooling*
  Readings - v11 - S '96 - p24 [51-250]
Cantrill, James G - *The Symbolic Earth*
  Choice - v34 - My '97 - p1483+ [51-250]
Cantwell, Mary - *Manhattan, When I Was Young*
  NYTBR - v101 - S 8 '96 - p28 [51-250]
  PW - v243 - S 9 '96 - p81 [1-50]
Cantwell, Robert - *Bluegrass Breakdown*
  LJ - v121 - N 1 '96 - p41 [1-50]
  Ethnomimesis
  JPC - v29 - Spr '96 - p232 [51-250]
  When We Were Good
  Choice - v34 - S '96 - p137 [51-250]
  Nat - v262 - Je 17 '96 - p25+ [501+]
  Prog - v61 - Ja '97 - p37 [51-250]
Canty, Kevin - *Into the Great Wide Open*
  BW - v26 - D 1 '96 - p6 [51-250]
  LATBR - O 6 '96 - p14+ [51-250]
  NY - v72 - D 23 '96 - p146 [51-250]
  NYTBR - v101 - S 8 '96 - p11 [501+]
  NYTBR - v101 - D 8 '96 - p80 [1-50]
  SFR - v21 - S '96 - p6 [251-500]
Cao, Ky - *The Changing Capital Markets of East Asia*
  Choice - v34 - D '96 - p657 [51-250]
  JEL - v34 - D '96 - p2052+ [51-250]
Cao, Lan - *Everything You Need to Know about Asian American History*
  y Kliatt - v30 - N '96 - p27 [51-250]
Cao, X H - *Rings, Groups, and Algebras*
  SciTech - v20 - N '96 - p13 [51-250]
Cao, Youfang - *Ai Qing Nu Zi Lian Meng*
  BL - v93 - N 1 '96 - p484 [1-50]
Capa, Robert - *Robert Capa: Photographs*
  LATBR - S 1 '96 - p10 [251-500]
  LJ - v121 - O 1 '96 - p74+ [51-250]
  NYTBR - v101 - O 13 '96 - p20 [251-500]
  Pet PM - v25 - D '96 - p20 [51-250]
  WSJ-MW - v78 - D 5 '96 - pA18 [51-250]
Capaldi, Elizabeth D - *Why We Eat What We Eat*
  Choice - v34 - My '97 - p1580 [51-250]
  LJ - v122 - F 1 '97 - p97 [51-250]
Capaldi, Nicholas - *The Art of Deception (Capaldi). Audio Version*
  Quill & Q - v62 - Ag '96 - p37 [251-500]
Capecia, Mayotte - *Je Suis Martiniquaise*
  FR - v70 - Mr '97 - p575+ [501+]
Capek, Karel - *Apocryphal Tales*
  LJ - v122 - My 1 '97 - p142 [51-250]
  Spisy: O Umeni A Kulture/Od Cloveka K Cloveku
  WLT - v70 - Aut '96 - p992 [51-250]
  Tales from Two Pockets
  TranslRevS - v1 - My '95 - p17 [51-250]
Capek, Michael - *Artistic Trickery*
  c RT - v50 - O '96 - p139 [1-50]
  c RT - v50 - D '96 - p347 [51-250]
  Murals: Cave, Cathedral, to Street
  c HB Guide - v8 - Spr '97 - p136 [1-50]
  y SLJ - v42 - O '96 - p154 [51-250]
  y VOYA - v19 - O '96 - p226+ [51-250]
Capel, Anne K - *Mistress of the House, Mistress of Heaven*
  LJ - v122 - My 1 '97 - p101 [51-250]
  PW - v244 - F 3 '97 - p91 [51-250]
Capela, John J - *Dictionary of International Business Terms*
  r ARBA - v28 - '97 - p99 [51-250]
  r CBR - v14 - S '96 - p28 [1-50]
Capen, Richard G, Jr. - *Finish Strong*
  LJ - v121 - S 15 '96 - p82+ [51-250]
Capie, Forrest - *The Future of Central Banking*
  JEL - v34 - D '96 - p1963+ [501+]
Capilano Computing Systems, Ltd. - *Logic Works Verilog Modeler*
  SciTech - v20 - D '96 - p80 [51-250]
Capital Planning Information - *The Value to Libraries of Special Services Provided by Library Suppliers*
  LAR - v98 - O '96 - p537 [251-500]
Capital Update
  p AJN - v97 - F '97 - p62 [51-250]
A Capitol Idea?
  H Sch M - v4 - D '96 - p54 [51-250]

Caplan, Gayle - *Survivors: How to Keep Your Best People on Board after Downsizing*
BWatch - v18 - Mr '97 - p5 [51-250]
HR Mag - v41 - D '96 - p127 [51-250]
LJ - v121 - D '96 - p110 [51-250]
Caplan, Louis R - *Posterior Circulation Disease*
SciTech - v20 - N '96 - p42 [51-250]
Caplan, Mariana - *When Sons and Daughters Choose Alternative Lifestyles*
LJ - v121 - O 1 '96 - p107 [51-250]
Caplan, Paula J - *They Say You're Crazy*
Skeptic - v4 - 2 '96 - p110 [51-250]
Caplin, Elliot - *Al Capp Remembered*
JPC - v29 - Spr '96 - p233 [51-250]
Caplow, Theodore - *Systems of War and Peace*
JPR - v33 - Ag '96 - p378 [251-500]
Capon, Brian - *Plant Survival*
y SB - v32 - N '96 - p236 [51-250]
Capon, Robert Farrar - *The Astonished Heart*
CLW - v67 - D '96 - p35 [251-500]
Capote, Truman - *A Christmas Memory (Illus. by Beth Peck)*
c HB Guide - v8 - Spr '97 - p57 [51-250]
c NYTBR - v101 - D 22 '96 - p16 [1-50]
The Grass Harp
Ent W - N 8 '96 - p59 [51-250]
The Thanksgiving Visitor (Illus. by Beth Peck)
c HB Guide - v8 - Spr '97 - p62 [51-250]
c PW - v243 - S 30 '96 - p86 [51-250]
c SLJ - v42 - D '96 - p91 [51-250]
Capp, Bernard - *The World of John Taylor the Water Poet 1578-1653*
Ren Q - v49 - Aut '96 - p651+ [501+]
Capp, Fiona - *Night Surfing*
TLS - D 20 '96 - p24 [51-250]
Cappelli, Peter - *Change at Work*
HR Mag - v42 - Mr '97 - p134 [51-250]
Capper, Lizanne - *That's My Child*
Readings - v12 - Mr '97 - p23 [51-250]
Cappetti, Carla - *Writing Chicago*
MP - v94 - Ag '96 - p129+ [501+]
Capponi, Pat - *Dispatches from the Poverty Line*
Quill & Q - v63 - Ja '97 - p13 [51-250]
Quill & Q - v63 - F '97 - p43 [501+]
Capps, Donald - *Agents of Hope*
Rel St Rev - v22 - O '96 - p336 [51-250]
The Child's Song
Fam Relat - v45 - Jl '96 - p351 [251-500]
The Depleted Self
Bks & Cult - v2 - Mr '96 - p3+ [501+]
Capps, Lisa - *Constructing Panic*
Readings - v11 - S '96 - p23 [51-250]
Capps, Walter H - *Religious Studies*
TT - v53 - Ja '97 - p534+ [501+]
Cappuccino, Naomi - *Population Dynamics*
Am Sci - v85 - Ja '97 - p82+ [501+]
Capra, Fritjof - *The Web of Life*
y BL - v93 - S 15 '96 - p192 [51-250]
BL - v93 - D 1 '96 - p630 [1-50]
KR - v64 - Ag 15 '96 - p1200 [251-500]
LJ - v121 - O 15 '96 - p87 [51-250]
New Sci - v152 - D 7 '96 - p46+ [501+]
NS - v125 - N 22 '96 - p46+ [501+]
Utne R - Ja '97 - p97 [1-50]
The Web of Life (Prichard). Audio Version
Trib Bks - F 2 '97 - p6 [51-250]
Capriolo, Paola - *La Spettatrice*
TLS - O 4 '96 - p28 [501+]
Un Uomo Di Carattere
TLS - O 4 '96 - p28 [501+]
Capucilli, Alyssa Satin - *Biscuit (Illus. by Pat Schories)*
c BL - v92 - Ag '96 - p1910 [51-250]
c HB Guide - v7 - Fall '96 - p284 [1-50]
Biscuit Finds a Friend (Illus. by Pat Schories)
c BL - v93 - My 1 '97 - p1503 [51-250]
c KR - v65 - Mr 15 '97 - p470 [51-250]
Wee Mouse Christmas (Illus. by Linda Birkinshaw)
c HB Guide - v7 - Fall '96 - p237 [1-50]
Caputo, John D - *Deconstruction in a Nutshell*
LJ - v122 - F 1 '97 - p81 [51-250]
Wil Q - v21 - Win '97 - p100 [251-500]
Caputo, Philip - *Equation for Evil*
NYTBR - v102 - F 23 '97 - p24 [51-250]
PW - v244 - Ja 13 '97 - p73 [1-50]
Exiles
PW - v244 - Ap 28 '97 - p47 [251-500]
A Rumor of War
NYTBR - v102 - F 23 '97 - p24 [1-50]
PW - v243 - O 21 '96 - p78 [1-50]
La Cara Oculta De La Luna
BL - v93 - Mr 15 '97 - p1232 [1-50]

Carabine, Sue - *A Dog's Night before Christmas (Illus. by Shauna Mooney Kawasaki)*
c Dog Fan - v27 - N '96 - p30 [1-50]
Caraion, Ion - *The Error of Being*
TranslRevS - v1 - My '95 - p27 [1-50]
Caramello, Charles - *Henry James, Gertrude Stein, and the Biographical Act*
Choice - v34 - N '96 - p453+ [251-500]
Caras, Roger A - *A Perfect Harmony*
LJ - v121 - N 15 '96 - p85 [51-250]
Nature - v383 - O 31 '96 - p786 [51-250]
Perfect Harmony
New Sci - v153 - Ja 18 '97 - p40 [51-250]
Carbajal, Xavier Joseph - *Captain Nemo*
PW - v243 - D 30 '96 - p59 [51-250]
Carbaugh, Donal A - *Situating Selves*
Choice - v34 - O '96 - p366 [51-250]
CS - v26 - Mr '97 - p232+ [501+]
JC - v47 - Win '97 - p181+ [501+]
R&R Bk N - v12 - F '97 - p51 [51-250]
Carber, Kristine - *Museums and Galleries of San Francisco and the Bay Area*
r BWatch - v17 - S '96 - p6 [51-250]
Carbet, Marie-Magdeleine - *D'Une Rive A L'Autre*
FR - v70 - Mr '97 - p575+ [501+]
Carbo, Nick - *Returning a Borrowed Tongue*
WLT - v70 - Aut '96 - p1035 [501+]
Carbone, Rocco - *Il Comando*
WLT - v70 - Aut '96 - p930 [501+]
Carbone, Sandro Paolo - *Le Scritture Ai Tempi Di Gesu'*
Rel St Rev - v22 - O '96 - p352 [51-250]
Carbonell Cortina, Nestor - *Por La Libertad De Cuba*
BL - v93 - Mr 15 '97 - p1232 [1-50]
BL - v93 - Ap 1 '97 - p1284 [1-50]
Card, Claudia - *Lesbian Choices*
J Homosex - v32 - 1 '96 - p7+ [501+]
J Homosex - v32 - 1 '96 - p21+ [501+]
The Unnatural Lottery
Hast Cen R - v27 - Ja '97 - p38+ [501+]
Card, Emily W - *Managing Your Inheritance*
PW - v243 - D 9 '96 - p54 [51-250]
Card, Orson Scott - *Alvin Journeyman*
y Kliatt - v31 - Ja '97 - p11 [51-250]
Children of the Mind
Analog - v117 - Ja '97 - p141+ [251-500]
PW - v243 - Jl 22 '96 - p230+ [51-250]
y SLJ - v43 - Ja '97 - p139 [51-250]
y VOYA - v19 - F '97 - p334 [251-500]
Children of the Mind (Whitener). Audio Version
y Kliatt - v31 - My '97 - p35+ [51-250]
Ender's Game
y BL - v93 - Ja '97 - p832 [1-50]
The Memory of Earth
y Kliatt - v30 - S '96 - p4 [1-50]
Pastwatch: The Redemption of Christopher Columbus
y BL - v93 - Ap 1 '97 - p1292 [1-50]
Treasure Box
MFSF - v92 - Ja '97 - p21 [51-250]
Cardarelli, Francois - *Scientific Unit Conversion*
New Sci - v153 - Ja 25 '97 - p43 [51-250]
Cardenal, Ernesto - *The Doubtful Strait*
HAHR - v77 - F '97 - p121+ [251-500]
Cardenas, Enrique - *La Hacienda Publica Y La Politica Economica 1929-1958*
AHR - v101 - D '96 - p1659+ [501+]
JEH - v56 - D '96 - p942+ [501+]
Cardillo, Joe - *Pulse*
y BL - v93 - N 15 '96 - p579 [51-250]
y CBRS - v25 - Win '97 - p68+ [51-250]
y HB Guide - v8 - Spr '97 - p78 [51-250]
y KR - v64 - O 1 '96 - p1464 [51-250]
Cardinal, Marie - *In Other Words*
TLS - My 24 '96 - p36 [51-250]
Cardon, Albert H - *Durability Analysis of Structural Composite Systems*
SciTech - v20 - D '96 - p65 [51-250]
Carducci, Giosue - *Selected Verse*
MLR - v91 - O '96 - p1011+ [251-500]
Cardwell, Donald - *The Norton History of Technology*
Isis - v87 - D '96 - p707 [501+]
Cardy, John - *Scaling and Renormalization in Statistical Physics*
New Sci - v153 - F 1 '97 - p42+ [501+]
SciTech - v20 - N '96 - p18 [51-250]
Care, Norman S - *Living with One's Past*
Choice - v34 - My '97 - p1512 [51-250]
The Care and Keeping of Friends (Illus. by Nadine Bernard Westcott)
c PW - v243 - S 9 '96 - p85 [51-250]

CareerXroads: The 1996 Directory to Jobs, Resumes and Career Management on the World Wide Web
J Car P&E - v57 - Fall '96 - p20 [251-500]
r J Car P&E - v57 - Win '97 - p21 [251-500]
Caret, Robert L - *Principles and Applications of Inorganic, Organic, and Biological Chemistry. 2nd Ed.*
SciTech - v21 - Mr '97 - p28 [51-250]
Carew, Edna - *The Language of Money 3. Expanded, Rev., Updated Ed.*
r Choice - v34 - Ja '97 - p766 [51-250]
Carey, Cynthia - *Avian Energetics and Nutritional Ecology*
SciTech - v20 - S '96 - p21 [51-250]
Carey, Diane - *Buried Alive*
y Kliatt - v30 - N '96 - p6 [51-250]
First Strike
y Kliatt - v30 - N '96 - p12 [51-250]
Carey, Francis A - *Organic Chemistry. 3rd Ed.*
J Chem Ed - v73 - D '96 - pA312 [501+]
Carey, G F - *Circuit, Device, and Process Simulation*
Choice - v34 - Mr '97 - p1190 [51-250]
SciTech - v20 - N '96 - p75 [51-250]
Carey, Hilary M - *Believing in Australia*
Aust Bk R - Ag '96 - p16+ [501+]
Carey, Jacqueline - *The Other Family*
y BL - v92 - Ag '96 - p1880 [51-250]
y BL - v92 - Ag '96 - p1891 [1-50]
CSM - v88 - S 9 '96 - p14 [251-500]
LATBR - N 17 '96 - p14 [51-250]
NY - v72 - D 23 '96 - p146 [51-250]
NYTBR - v101 - S 8 '96 - p8+ [501+]
NYTBR - v101 - D 8 '96 - p82 [1-50]
y SLJ - v42 - D '96 - p150 [51-250]
Carey, John - *The Faber Book of Science*
Bloom Rev - v16 - N '96 - p28 [1-50]
Nature - v385 - Ja 2 '97 - p36 [1-50]
New Sci - v152 - N 9 '96 - p42 [51-250]
TES - v12 '96 - p8* [51-250]
Carey, John M - *Term Limits and Legislative Representation*
Choice - v34 - N '96 - p536+ [51-250]
Carey, Larry - *1003 Salt and Pepper Shakers*
Ant & CM - v102 - Ap '97 - p66 [51-250]
Carey, Paul R - *Protein Engineering and Design*
SciTech - v20 - N '96 - p80 [51-250]
Carey, Peter - *The Big Bazoohley*
c Bks Keeps - v Ja '97 - p25 [51-250]
c PW - v243 - O 14 '96 - p85 [1-50]
Collected Short Stories
Books - v9 - S '95 - p22 [1-50]
Obs - Ag 25 '96 - p18* [51-250]
Collected Stories
WLT - v70 - Sum '96 - p757 [501+]
Illywhacker: A Novel
NYTBR - v101 - N 10 '96 - p68 [51-250]
The Unusual Life of Tristan Smith
WLT - v70 - Sum '96 - p757+ [501+]
Carey-Webb, Allen - *Teaching and Testimony*
Choice - v34 - F '97 - p1015 [51-250]
R&R Bk N - v11 - N '96 - p54 [51-250]
Cargill, Carl F - *Open Systems Standardization*
SciTech - v21 - Mr '97 - p12 [51-250]
Cargill, Jack - *Athenian Settlements of the Fourth Century B.C.*
Rel St Rev - v23 - Ap '97 - p170 [51-250]
Cargill, Linda - *Hang Loose*
y Kliatt - v30 - N '96 - p6 [51-250]
y SLJ - v42 - D '96 - p136 [51-250]
Pool Party
y Kliatt - v30 - N '96 - p6 [51-250]
y SLJ - v43 - Ja '97 - p112 [51-250]
Caring for Your Adolescent Ages 12 to 21
r BL - v93 - F 1 '97 - p958+ [1-50]
Caring for Your Baby and Young Child Birth to Age 5
r BL - v93 - F 1 '97 - p958+ [1-50]
Caring for Your School-Age Child Ages 5 to 12
r BL - v93 - F 1 '97 - p958+ [1-50]
Caringer, Denise L - *Additions: Your Guide to Planning and Remodeling*
LJ - v122 - Ja '97 - p140 [51-250]
The New Decorating Book. 7th Ed.
PW - v244 - Mr 3 '97 - p68 [51-250]
Carino, Theresa C - *Perspectives on Philippine Policy towards China*
Ch Rev Int - v3 - Fall '96 - p370+ [501+]

Carkeet, David - *The Error of Our Ways*
  BL - v93 - D 15 '96 - p708 [51-250]
  BW - v27 - F 23 '97 - p3 [501+]
  KR - v64 - O 15 '96 - p1482 [251-500]
  LJ - v121 - N 15 '96 - p87 [51-250]
  NYTBR - v102 - Ja 5 '97 - p10 [251-500]
  PW - v243 - O 14 '96 - p61+ [51-250]
Carl, Leo D - *The CIA Insider's Dictionary of U.S. and Foreign Intelligence, Counterintelligence and Tradecraft*
  r BL - v93 - O 1 '96 - p367+ [51-250]
  r Choice - v34 - N '96 - p426 [51-250]
Carle, Eric - *1, 2, 3 to the Zoo (Illus. by Eric Carle)*
  c Ch BWatch - v6 - O '96 - p6 [1-50]
  c HB Guide - v8 - Spr '97 - p11 [51-250]
  The Art of Eric Carle
  BL - v93 - S 15 '96 - p253 [51-250]
  BW - v27 - Ja 12 '97 - p8 [501+]
  CCB-B - v50 - O '96 - p82 [51-250]
  CSM - v88 - N 21 '96 - pB4 [51-250]
  HB - v73 - Mr '97 - p215+ [51-250]
  SLJ - v42 - D '96 - p46 [51-250]
  From Head to Toe (Illus. by Eric Carle)
  c CBRS - v25 - Ap '97 - p97 [51-250]
  c KR - v65 - Ap 1 '97 - p551 [51-250]
  c PW - v244 - F 17 '97 - p219 [51-250]
  A House for Hermit Crab (Illus. by Mike Terry)
  c Obs - Mr 30 '97 - p17* [51-250]
  Little Cloud (Illus. by Eric Carle)
  c Emerg Lib - v24 - S '96 - p43 [1-50]
  c HB Guide - v7 - Fall '96 - p250 [1-50]
  Papa, Please Get the Moon for Me
  c Bks Keeps - Mr '97 - p18 [51-250]
  The Tiny Seed (Illus. by Eric Carle)
  c Magpies - v11 - Jl '96 - p26 [51-250]
  Today Is Monday (Illus. by Eric Carle)
  c Magpies - v11 - My '96 - p53 [1-50]
  The Very Busy Spider (Illus. by Eric Carle)
  c Bks Keeps - Ja '97 - p18 [51-250]
  The Very Hungry Caterpillar (Illus. by Eric Carle)
  c Bks Keeps - Mr '97 - p7 [51-250]
  c HB - v73 - Mr '97 - p186 [1-50]
  The Very Lonely Firefly (Illus. by Eric Carle)
  c ECEJ - v23 - Sum '96 - p222 [51-250]
  c RT - v50 - O '96 - p135+ [1-50]
  The Very Quiet Cricket
  c PW - v244 - Ap 28 '97 - p77 [1-50]
  Walter the Baker (Illus. by Eric Carle)
  c RT - v50 - O '96 - p136 [1-50]
Carley, James E - *Whittington's Dictionary of Plastics. 3rd Ed. Electronic Media Version*
  r Choice - v34 - S '96 - p108+ [251-500]
Carlier, Omar - *Entre Nation Et Jihad*
  MEJ - v50 - Sum '96 - p429+ [501+]
Carlin, George - *Brain Droppings*
  BL - v93 - Mr 15 '97 - p1202 [51-250]
  KR - v65 - Mr 15 '97 - p428 [251-500]
  PW - v244 - Mr 24 '97 - p72 [51-250]
Carlin, Martha - *Medieval Southwark*
  Choice - v34 - O '96 - p338 [51-250]
Carlin, Richard - *The Big Book of Country Music*
  r LJ - v121 - N 1 '96 - p40 [1-50]
Carline, Jan D - *Mountaineering First Aid. 4th Ed.*
  r BL - v93 - S 15 '96 - p212 [1-50]
  SciTech - v20 - D '96 - p42 [1-50]
Carling, Finn - *Matadorens Hand*
  WLT - v70 - Sum '96 - p713 [501+]
Carlino, Andrea - *La Fabbrica Del Corpo*
  Isis - v88 - Mr '97 - p138+ [501+]
  Ren Q - v49 - Aut '96 - p598+ [501+]
Carlip, Hillary - *Girl Power*
  OOB - v26 - Ag '96 - p18+ [501+]
Carlisi, Karen - *Looking at Our Lives*
  c SLJ - v43 - Ja '97 - p98 [51-250]
Carlisle, Rodney P - *Supplying the Nuclear Arsenal*
  Choice - v34 - F '97 - p993 [51-250]
  SciTech - v20 - D '96 - p80 [51-250]
Carlo, Philip - *The Night Stalker (Aiello). Audio Version*
  LJ - v121 - D '96 - p169 [51-250]
Carlon, Patricia - *The Souvenir*
  PW - v243 - S 2 '96 - p122 [1-50]
  The Whispering Wall
  BL - v93 - S 15 '96 - p223 [51-250]
  KR - v64 - Ag 15 '96 - p1188 [51-250]
  NYTBR - v101 - N 10 '96 - p62 [51-250]
Carlotto, Natascia - *La Citta Custodita*
  EHR - v111 - N '96 - p1248+ [501+]
Carls, Stephen D - *Louis Loucheur and the Shaping of Modern France 1916-1931*
  EHR - v111 - S '96 - p1019+ [501+]
Carlsberg, Kim - *Contact Cards*
  BWatch - v17 - S '96 - p12 [51-250]

Carlson, A Bruce - *Circuits: Engineering Concepts and Analysis of Linear Electric Circuits*
  SciTech - v20 - D '96 - p74 [51-250]
Carlson, Benny - *The State as a Monster*
  Econ J - v107 - Ja '97 - p261 [51-250]
Carlson, David R - *English Humanist Books*
  Lib - v18 - D '96 - p349+ [501+]
Carlson, Eric Stener - *I Remember Julia*
  Bloom Rev - v16 - N '96 - p7 [251-500]
Carlson, Eric W - *A Companion to Poe Studies*
  Choice - v34 - Ap '97 - p1334 [251-500]
  r R&R Bk N - v12 - F '97 - p89 [51-250]
Carlson, Eve B - *Trauma Research Methodology*
  Readings - v11 - D '96 - p24 [51-250]
Carlson, Harry G - *Out of Inferno*
  Am Theat - v13 - D '96 - p21 [1-50]
  Choice - v34 - My '97 - p1502 [51-250]
  LJ - v121 - D '96 - p92+ [51-250]
Carlson, J F - *Modules and Group Algebras*
  SciTech - v20 - S '96 - p9 [51-250]
Carlson, Jon - *Family Therapy*
  SciTech - v21 - Mr '97 - p54 [51-250]
Carlson, Julie A - *In the Theatre of Romanticism*
  RES - v47 - N '96 - p599+ [501+]
Carlson, Karen J - *The Harvard Guide to Women's Health*
  r LJ - v122 - Ap 15 '97 - p37 [51-250]
  PW - v243 - N 4 '96 - p47 [1-50]
  The Harvard Guide to Women's Health. Electronic Media Version
  r BL - v93 - F 1 '97 - p959 [1-50]
  yr LJ - v122 - Ap 1 '97 - p136 [51-250]
Carlson, Kurt - *The Family PC Software Buyer's Guide*
  r LJ - v122 - F 1 '97 - p102 [51-250]
Carlson, Laura - *Literary Laurels. Kids' Ed.*
  r BL - v92 - Ag '96 - p1922 [1-50]
  r PW - v243 - S 2 '96 - p133 [51-250]
  r SLJ - v42 - N '96 - p136 [51-250]
Carlson, Laurie M - *Green Thumbs*
  c Cur R - v36 - D '96 - p13 [51-250]
  Huzzah Means Hooray
  c Cur R - v36 - D '96 - p13 [51-250]
  Kids Camp!
  c Cur R - v36 - D '96 - p13 [51-250]
  More than Moccasins
  c Cur R - v36 - D '96 - p13 [51-250]
  Westward Ho!
  c BL - v93 - O 1 '96 - p344 [51-250]
  c Ch BWatch - v7 - F '97 - p6 [51-250]
  c Cur R - v36 - D '96 - p12+ [51-250]
  c SLJ - v42 - D '96 - p126 [51-250]
Carlson, Lewis H - *We Were Each Other's Prisoners*
  KR - v65 - Mr 1 '97 - p344 [51-250]
  PW - v244 - Mr 24 '97 - p70+ [51-250]
Carlson, Linda - *989 Great Part-Time Jobs in Seattle*
  r J Car P&E - v57 - Win '97 - p16 [51-250]
Carlson, Lori M - *American Eyes*
  y Emerg Lib - v24 - S '96 - p24 [1-50]
  Barrio Streets Carnival Dreams
  y AB - v98 - N 18 '96 - p1729 [51-250]
  y CCB-B - v50 - S '96 - p7+ [51-250]
  y HB - v72 - S '96 - p608+ [51-250]
  y HB Guide - v8 - Spr '97 - p147 [51-250]
  y SLJ - v42 - Ag '96 - p164 [51-250]
  y VOYA - v19 - D '96 - p284 [251-500]
Carlson, Marvin - *Performance: A Critical Introduction*
  Am Theat - v13 - D '96 - p20 [1-50]
  Am Theat - v14 - Ja '97 - p74 [51-250]
Carlson, Maureen - *How to Make Clay Characters*
  BL - v93 - Mr 15 '97 - p1218 [51-250]
Carlson, Nancy - *ABC I Like Me! (Illus. by Nancy Carlson)*
  c BL - v93 - Ap 1 '97 - p1337 [51-250]
  c KR - v65 - My 1 '97 - p717+ [51-250]
  Arnie and the Skateboard Gang (Illus. by Nancy Carlson)
  c RT - v50 - O '96 - p132 [1-50]
  Sit Still!
  c HB Guide - v7 - Fall '96 - p250 [51-250]
Carlson, Paul H - *Empire Builder in the Texas Panhandle*
  Choice - v34 - F '97 - p1023 [51-250]
  JEL - v35 - Mr '97 - p266 [51-250]
  Roundup M - v4 - F '97 - p23 [51-250]
Carlson, Paula J - *Listening for God*
  Intpr - v51 - Ap '97 - p224 [51-250]
Carlson, Richard - *Handbook for the Heart*
  PW - v243 - S 2 '96 - p105 [51-250]
Carlson, Robert V - *Reframing and Reform*
  Choice - v34 - S '96 - p179 [51-250]

Carlson, Ron - *The Hotel Eden*
  KR - v65 - Ap 1 '97 - p480+ [251-500]
  PW - v244 - Ap 7 '97 - p72 [51-250]
Carlstrom, Nancy White - *Better Not Get Wet, Jesse Bear (Illus. by Bruce Degen)*
  c PW - v244 - Mr 17 '97 - p85 [1-50]
  I Love You, Mama, Any Time of Year (Illus. by Bruce Degen)
  c PW - v244 - Mr 24 '97 - p85 [1-50]
  I Love You, Papa, in All Kinds of Weather (Illus. by Bruce Degen)
  c PW - v244 - Mr 24 '97 - p85 [1-50]
  Let's Count It Out, Jesse Bear (Illus. by Bruce Degen)
  c BL - v93 - S 15 '96 - p245 [51-250]
  c CCB-B - v50 - O '96 - p51 [51-250]
  c HB Guide - v8 - Spr '97 - p11 [51-250]
  c NYTBR - v102 - Mr 16 '97 - p26 [1-50]
  c SLJ - v42 - S '96 - p171+ [51-250]
  Raven and River (Illus. by Jon Van Zyle)
  c BL - v93 - My 15 '97 - p1578 [51-250]
  c CBRS - v25 - Ap '97 - p97+ [51-250]
  Ten Christmas Sheep (Illus. by Cynthia Fisher)
  c PW - v243 - S 30 '96 - p93 [1-50]
Carlton, David - *Rising Tension in Eastern Europe and the Former Soviet Union*
  R&R Bk N - v11 - N '96 - p13 [51-250]
Carlton, David L - *Confronting Southern Poverty in the Great Depression*
  JEL - v35 - Mr '97 - p257+ [51-250]
Carlton, Eric - *The Few and the Many*
  Choice - v34 - Ja '97 - p882 [51-250]
  R&R Bk N - v11 - N '96 - p39 [51-250]
Carlton, R Scott - *The International Encyclopaedic Dictionary of Numismatics*
  r Ant & CM - v101 - D '96 - p33 [1-50]
  r BL - v93 - My 15 '97 - p1613+ [501+]
  r Coin W - v37 - O 14 '96 - p80 [51-250]
Carlyon, Les - *True Grit*
  Aust Bk R - D '96 - p74 [51-250]
Carmack, Robert M - *Rebels of Highland Guatemala*
  JIH - v27 - Spr '97 - p740+ [251-500]
Carmagnani, Marcello - *Estado Y Mercado*
  JEH - v56 - D '96 - p942+ [501+]
Carmel, Michael - *Health Care Librarianship and Information Work*
  LQ - v67 - Ja '97 - p81+ [501+]
Carmel, Simon - *Directory of Health and Social Services Databases*
  r LAR - v98 - Jl '96 - p373 [51-250]
Carmelites of Indianapolis - *Hidden Friends*
  RR - v55 - N '96 - p661 [1-50]
  People's Companion to the Breviary. Vols. 1-2
  RR - v56 - Mr '97 - p222 [51-250]
Carmer, Carl - *The Tavern Lamps Are Burning*
  Nine-C Lit - v51 - Mr '97 - p554 [1-50]
Carmesin, Hans-Otto - *Neuronal Adaptation Theory*
  SciTech - v20 - D '96 - p34 [51-250]
Carmichael, Calum M - *The Story of Creation*
  Choice - v34 - Ap '97 - p1355 [51-250]
Carmichael, Cathie - *Slovenia*
  r ARBA - v28 - '97 - p64 [51-250]
  r Choice - v34 - Ja '97 - p766 [51-250]
  R&R Bk N - v11 - N '96 - p13 [51-250]
Carmichael, Clay - *Bear at the Beach (Illus. by Clay Carmichael)*
  c HB Guide - v7 - Fall '96 - p286 [51-250]
Carmichael, Joel - *The Unriddling of Christian Origins*
  Rapport - v19 - 6 '96 - p27 [251-500]
Carmichael, Peter S - *Lee's Young Artillerist*
  JSH - v63 - F '97 - p184+ [251-500]
Carmichael, Virginia - *Framing History*
  Am Q - v49 - Mr '97 - p210+ [501+]
Carmody, Denise Lardner - *Mysticism: Holiness East and West*
  TT - v53 - Ja '97 - p572 [51-250]
  Organizing a Christian Mind
  Rel St Rev - v23 - Ap '97 - p156 [51-250]
  Serene Compassion
  Comw - v123 - S 27 '96 - p27+ [251-500]
Carmody, Isobelle - *The Gathering*
  y PW - v243 - D 2 '96 - p62 [1-50]
  y Sch Lib - v44 - Ag '96 - p117 [51-250]
  Green Monkey Dreams
  y Magpies - v11 - My '96 - p50 [51-250]
Carmody, John - *Cancer and Faith*
  CLW - v66 - Je '96 - p35+ [251-500]
Carmody, John, 1939- - *God Is No Illusion*
  BL - v93 - Ja '97 - p783 [51-250]
  PW - v243 - D 2 '96 - p52+ [51-250]

Living with God...in Good Times and Bad
　Am - v175 - N 2 '96 - p32 [51-250]
　CC - v113 - S 25 '96 - p911 [51-250]
Carnaby, Ann J - *A Guidebook for Creating Three-Dimensional Theatre Art*
　TCI - v30 - O '96 - p57 [51-250]
Carnahan, Sumner - *In the Presence of My Enemies*
　Tric - v6 - Fall '96 - p132+ [501+]
Carne, Marcel - *Ma Vie A Belles Dents*
　BL - v93 - Ja '97 - p827 [1-50]
Carnegie, Garry D - *Accounting History Newsletter 1980-1989 and Accounting History 1989-1994*
　R&R Bk N - v11 - N '96 - p35 [51-250]
Carnegie Task Force on Learning in the Primary Grades - *Years of Promise*
　EL - v54 - D '96 - p88+ [51-250]
Carnes, Jim - *Us and Them (Illus. by Herbert Tauss)*
　y HB Guide - v7 - Fall '96 - p316 [51-250]
Carnes, Mark C - *Mapping America's Past*
　yr ARBA - v28 - '97 - p186 [251-500]
　r BL - v93 - My 1 '97 - p1475 [51-250]
Past Imperfect
　TLS - Ja 3 '97 - p19 [501+]
Carnevale, Anthony Patrick - *The American Mosaic*
　BusLR - v21 - 3 '96 - p235+ [51-250]
Carney, George O - *The Sounds of People and Places*
　AAAGA - v86 - D '96 - p796+ [501+]
Carney, Margaret - *At Grandpa's Sugar Bush (Illus. by Janet Wilson)*
　c Quill & Q - v63 - Ja '97 - p38 [51-250]
Carney, Michael - *Britain in Pictures*
　r BC - v44 - Win '95 - p579+ [501+]
Carney, Ray - *The Films of John Cassavetes*
　J Film & Vid - v48 - Spr '96 - p88+ [501+]
Carnoy, Martin - *Faded Dreams*
　AAPSS-A - v546 - Jl '96 - p167+ [501+]
　APSR - v90 - D '96 - p867+ [501+]
Carol, Anne - *Histoire De L'Eugenisme En France*
　Choice - v34 - D '96 - p568 [1-50]
Caroli, Betty Boyd - *First Ladies. Expanded Ed.*
　CR - v268 - Je '96 - p334 [51-250]
Caroli, Sergio - *Element Speciation in Bioinorganic Chemistry*
　Choice - v34 - N '96 - p486 [51-250]
　r SciTech - v20 - S '96 - p23 [51-250]
The Carolina Quarterly
　p Sm Pr R - v28 - S '96 - p13 [51-250]
Carolus-Barre, Louis - *Le Proces De Canonisation De Saint Louis 1272-1297*
　Specu - v72 - Ja '97 - p124+ [251-500]
Caron, Ann F - *Strong Mothers, Strong Sons*
　VOYA - v19 - D '96 - p256 [1-50]
Caron, George R - *Fire of a Thousand Suns*
　Historian - v58 - Sum '96 - p856+ [251-500]
Caron, James E - *Sut Lovingood's Nat'ral Born Yarnspinner*
　CAY - v17 - Win '96 - p3 [51-250]
　R&R Bk N - v12 - F '97 - p88 [51-250]
Caron, Marie-Therese - *Noblesse Et Pouvoir Royal En France XIIIe-XVIe Siecle*
　Specu - v71 - O '96 - p933+ [501+]
Caroso, Fabritio - *Courtly Dance of the Renaissance*
　Notes - v53 - Mr '97 - p789+ [501+]
Carothers, Thomas - *Assessing Democracy Assistance*
　Cu H - v96 - Mr '97 - p140 [501+]
　For Aff - v75 - N '96 - p162+ [51-250]
　JEL - v34 - D '96 - p2048 [51-250]
Caroti, Stefano - *Nel Segno Di Galileo*
　Isis - v88 - Mr '97 - p142+ [501+]
Carpelan, Bo - *I Det Sedda*
　WLT - v70 - Aut '96 - p978 [251-500]
Urwind
　TLS - D 20 '96 - p23 [251-500]
Carpenter, C Tyler - *Stars without Garters*
　HG&LRev - v3 - Fall '96 - p43 [51-250]
Carpenter, David - *Courting Saskatchewan*
　CG - v117 - Ja '97 - p74+ [501+]
Carpenter, Humphrey - *The Puffin Book of Classic Children's Stories (Illus. by Diz Wallis)*
　c Bks Keeps - Ja '97 - p8+ [501+]
　c JB - v60 - D '96 - p247 [51-250]
　c Sch Lib - v45 - F '97 - p23 [51-250]
Carpenter, Humphrey, 1946- - *The Envy of the World*
　Econ - v340 - S 28 '96 - p102+ [251-500]
　Lon R Bks - v19 - F 6 '97 - p15+ [501+]
　Obs - Ag 25 '96 - p15* [501+]
　Obs - D 1 '96 - p16* [1-50]
　TLS - S 13 '96 - p20+ [501+]

Robert Runcie: The Reluctant Archbishop
　CC - v113 - N 20 '96 - p1171+ [501+]
　Lon R Bks - v18 - O 3 '96 - p3+ [501+]
　NS - v125 - D 20 '96 - p116 [51-250]
　Obs - O 6 '96 - p15* [501+]
　Spec - v277 - S 28 '96 - p44+ [501+]
　Spec - v277 - N 16 '96 - p44 [1-50]
　TLS - O 4 '96 - p29 [501+]
Carpenter, Mary-Chapin - *Dreamland: A Lullaby (Illus. by Julia Noonan)*
　c BL - v93 - N 1 '96 - p506 [51-250]
　c CBRS - v25 - S '96 - p1+ [51-250]
　c HB Guide - v8 - Spr '97 - p22 [1-50]
　c SLJ - v42 - N '96 - p96 [51-250]
Carpenter, Ronald H - *History as Rhetoric*
　AHR - v102 - F '97 - p94 [501+]
　QJS - v83 - F '97 - p123+ [501+]
Carpenter, Scott - *Acts of Fiction*
　MLR - v92 - Ap '97 - p471+ [501+]
Carpenter, William M - *Asian Security Handbook*
　R&R Bk N - v11 - N '96 - p79 [51-250]
Carpentieri, Tony - *Frank and Joe Turn Blue. 3rd Ed.*
　r AB - v98 - N 18 '96 - p1732 [51-250]
Carper, Thomas - *From Nature*
　HR - v49 - Sum '96 - p341+ [501+]
Carr, A D - *Medieval Wales*
　Albion - v28 - Fall '96 - p545+ [501+]
Carr, Archie - *A Naturalist in Florida*
　PW - v243 - N 11 '96 - p72 [1-50]
Carr, Brian - *Companion Encyclopedia of Asian Philosophy*
　r LAR - v99 - Mr '97 - p164 [1-50]
Carr, Christopher - *Style, Society, and Person*
　Am Ant - v61 - Jl '96 - p609+ [501+]
Carr, David K - *Managing the Change Process*
　LJ - v122 - Mr 15 '97 - p35 [1-50]
Carr, David M - *Reading the Fractures of Genesis*
　Choice - v34 - F '97 - p979 [51-250]
　Rel St Rev - v23 - Ja '97 - p57 [51-250]
Carr, Fergus - *NATO in the New European Order*
　R&R Bk N - v12 - F '97 - p100 [51-250]
Carr, Gerry - *Mechanics of Sport*
　SciTech - v20 - N '96 - p32 [51-250]
Carr, Helen - *Inventing the American Primitive*
　R&R Bk N - v11 - D '96 - p65 [51-250]
Carr, Ian - *Jazz: The Rough Guide*
　r ARBA - v28 - '97 - p491 [51-250]
　yr SLJ - v42 - Ag '96 - p185 [51-250]
Carr, J L - *A Month in the Country (Williams). Audio Version*
　Spec - v277 - N 30 '96 - p55 [51-250]
Carr, Jan - *Dark Day, Light Night (Illus. by James Ransome)*
　c HB Guide - v7 - Fall '96 - p250 [51-250]
　c New Ad - v9 - Fall '96 - p327+ [501+]
　c Smith - v27 - N '96 - p165 [1-50]
The Nature of the Beast (Illus. by G Brian Karas)
　c HB Guide - v7 - Fall '96 - p250 [51-250]
Carr, Joe - *Prairie Nights to Neon Lights*
　J Am Cult - v18 - Win '95 - p106 [51-250]
　J Am Cult - v19 - Sum '96 - p133 [501+]
　WHQ - v28 - Spr '97 - p97+ [251-500]
Carr, Kay J - *Belleville, Ottawa, and Galesburg*
　Choice - v34 - Ja '97 - p861 [51-250]
　R&R Bk N - v11 - D '96 - p17 [51-250]
Carr, Michael H - *Water on Mars*
　New Sci - v153 - Mr 1 '97 - p42+ [51-250]
　SB - v32 - Ag '96 - p167 [51-250]
　Sci - v275 - Ja 17 '97 - p321 [501+]
Carr, Patrick - *The Illustrated History of Country Music*
　r LJ - v121 - N 1 '96 - p41 [1-50]
Carr, Philippa - *Miracle at St. Bruno's (White). Audio Version*
　LJ - v122 - Ap 1 '97 - p145 [51-250]
Saraband for Two Sisters (Sandison). Audio Version
　BL - v93 - Mr 15 '97 - p1253 [51-250]
Carr, Roger Vaughan - *The Butterfly (Illus. by Ann James)*
　c Magpies - v11 - S '96 - p26 [51-250]
Carraher, Charles E, Jr. - *Seymour/Carraher's Polymer Chemistry. 4th Ed.*
　SciTech - v20 - D '96 - p27 [51-250]
Carraro, Carlo - *Environmental Policy and Market Structure*
　JEL - v34 - D '96 - p2132 [51-250]
　R&R Bk N - v12 - F '97 - p35 [51-250]
Operations Research and Environmental Management
　R&R Bk N - v12 - F '97 - p42 [51-250]
Carrasco, Juan - *Los Judios Del Reino De Navarra. Vol. 1*
　EHR - v112 - F '97 - p168 [51-250]

Carrasquillo, Angela L - *Language Minority Students in the Mainstream Classroom*
　JAAL - v40 - F '97 - p413+ [501+]
Carr-Brion, K G - *Sampling Systems for Process Analysers. 2nd Ed.*
　r SciTech - v20 - S '96 - p59 [51-250]
Carre, Jacques - *The Crisis of Courtesy*
　Lib - v18 - S '96 - p262+ [501+]
　RES - v47 - Ag '96 - p453+ [501+]
Lord Burlington 1694-1753. Vols. 1-2
　RES - v47 - Ag '96 - p423+ [501+]
Carre, M B - *Recueil De Timbres Sur Amphores Romaines 1987-1988*
　AJA - v100 - Jl '96 - p638 [51-250]
Carrel-Billiard, Marc - *Object-Oriented Application Development with Visual Age for C++ for OS/2*
　SciTech - v20 - S '96 - p8 [51-250]
Carrere, Emmanuel - *Class Trip*
　KR - v64 - D 1 '96 - p1703 [51-250]
　LJ - v122 - Ja '97 - p143+ [51-250]
　NY - v73 - Ap 28 '97 - p227 [51-250]
　NYTBR - v102 - F 2 '97 - p12 [501+]
　PW - v243 - D 9 '96 - p62 [51-250]
La Classe De Neige
　FR - v70 - Mr '97 - p609+ [501+]
Carrere, Ricardo - *Pulping the South*
　New Sci - v151 - S 21 '96 - p54 [1-50]
Carretta, Vincent - *Unchained Voices*
　Bloom Rev - v17 - Ja '97 - p20 [51-250]
　Choice - v34 - Ap '97 - p1341 [51-250]
　PW - v243 - S 9 '96 - p80 [51-250]
　TLS - Mr 7 '97 - p32 [51-250]
Carrick, Carol - *Melanie (Illus. by Alisher Dianov)*
　c BL - v93 - S 15 '96 - p245 [51-250]
　c CCB-B - v50 - N '96 - p92 [51-250]
　c HB Guide - v8 - Spr '97 - p23 [51-250]
　c SLJ - v42 - N '96 - p79 [51-250]
Carrier, David - *The Aesthete in the City*
　JAAC - v55 - Win '97 - p82+ [501+]
Carrier, James G - *Occidentalism: Images of the West*
　CS - v25 - S '96 - p612+ [501+]
Carrier, Joseph - *De Los Otros*
　Am Ethnol - v24 - F '97 - p193+ [501+]
　CS - v26 - Ja '97 - p74+ [501+]
Carrier, Lark - *A Tree's Tale (Illus. by Lark Carrier)*
　c HB Guide - v7 - Fall '96 - p250+ [501+]
　c New Ad - v9 - Fall '96 - p327+ [501+]
　c RT - v50 - Ap '97 - p591 [501+]
Carrier, Roch - *The Basketball Player (Illus. by Sheldon Cohen)*
　c Emerg Lib - v24 - Mr '97 - p26+ [1-50]
　c HB Guide - v8 - Spr '97 - p57 [51-250]
　c Quill & Q - v62 - D '96 - p36 [251-500]
Carriker, Robert C - *Father Peter John De Smet: Jesuit in the West*
　Am - v175 - O 5 '96 - p31 [251-500]
　PHR - v65 - Ag '96 - p479+ [251-500]
　WHQ - v27 - Win '96 - p519+ [501+]
Carril, Pete - *The Smart Take from the Strong*
　PW - v244 - Ja 13 '97 - p61 [51-250]
Carringer, Robert L - *The Making of Citizen Kane*
　LJ - v121 - N 15 '96 - p93 [51-250]
Carrington, Dorothy - *The Dreamhunters of Corsica*
　BL - v93 - N 1 '96 - p477 [51-250]
　PW - v243 - O 21 '96 - p65+ [51-250]
Carrington, Jackie - *Romantic Wedding Destinations. 2nd Ed.*
　BL - v93 - S 15 '96 - p206 [1-50]
Carrington, Leonora - *The Hearing Trumpet*
　LJ - v122 - Ap 15 '97 - p148 [51-250]
Carrithers, Gale H, Jr. - *Milton and the Hermeneutic Journey*
　RES - v48 - F '97 - p106+ [501+]
Carrithers, Michael - *The Assembly of Listeners*
　Rel St Rev - v23 - Ap '97 - p103+ [501+]
Carroll, Bob - *Pancho Villa*
　c HB Guide - v7 - Fall '96 - p371 [51-250]
Carroll, Charles R - *Drugs in Modern Society. 4th Ed.*
　SciTech - v20 - D '96 - p55 [51-250]
Carroll, Colleen - *How Artists See Animals*
　c HB Guide - v8 - Spr '97 - p136 [51-250]
How Artists See People
　c HB Guide - v8 - Spr '97 - p136 [51-250]
How Artists See the Elements
　c HB Guide - v8 - Spr '97 - p136 [51-250]
How the Artists See the Weather
　c HB Guide - v8 - Spr '97 - p136 [51-250]
Carroll, David - *French Literary Fascism*
　AHR - v101 - O '96 - p1223+ [501+]
　FR - v70 - D '96 - p315+ [501+]

Carroll, Denis - *The Man from God Knows Where*
Bks & Cult - v2 - Ja '96 - p11+ [501+]
Carroll, Frances L - *International Biographical Directory of National Archivists, Documentalists, and Librarians*
r LJ - v122 - Ap 15 '97 - p126 [51-250]
Carroll, Gerry - *No Place to Hide*
PW - v243 - D 2 '96 - p56 [1-50]
Carroll, J Frank - *Confederate Treasure in Danville*
Coin W - v37 - D 16 '96 - p24 [51-250]
Carroll, J H - *A Killer in the House*
y VOYA - v19 - O '96 - p202 [501+]
Carroll, J M - *Computer Security. 3rd Ed.*
New Sci - v153 - Mr 1 '97 - p46+ [501+]
Carroll, J R - *The Clan*
Aust Bk R - N '96 - p65 [501+]
Carroll, Jack - *Glenn Gould: Some Portraits of the Artist as a Young Man*
LATBR - Ag 18 '96 - p14+ [51-250]
Carroll, James - *An American Requiem*
BL - v93 - Ja '97 - p759 [1-50]
CSM - v88 - N 12 '96 - p14 [51-250]
Ent W - N 29 '96 - p82 [51-250]
LJ - v122 - Ja '97 - p48 [1-50]
NY - v72 - Ag 12 '96 - p73 [51-250]
NYTBR - v102 - Ap 6 '97 - p32 [1-50]
Trib Bks - My 4 '97 - p8 [1-50]
The City Below
NYTBR - v102 - Ap 6 '97 - p32 [51-250]
Carroll, Jane - *Front Runner*
c Magpies - v11 - Jl '96 - p29 [51-250]
Carroll, Jerry Jay - *Top Dog*
Ent W - S 20 '96 - p74+ [51-250]
Carroll, Joanne - *In the Quietness of My Aunt's House.*
Bad Blood
Aust Bk R - O '96 - p67 [51-250]
Carroll, Jock - *Falling for Marilyn Monroe*
Obs - D 22 '96 - p16* [501+]
Marilyn: The Niagara Photographs
Mac - v109 - D 9 '96 - p66 [1-50]
Carroll, John E - *The Greening of Faith*
BL - v93 - Ja '97 - p783 [51-250]
LJ - v122 - Ja '97 - p105 [51-250]
Carroll, John T - *Preaching the Hard Sayings of Jesus*
LJ - v122 - Ja '97 - p106 [51-250]
Carroll, Jonathan - *The Panic Hand*
BW - v26 - D 29 '96 - p7 [501+]
KR - v64 - S 15 '96 - p1339 [251-500]
LJ - v121 - D '96 - p149 [51-250]
PW - v243 - O 7 '96 - p60 [51-250]
Carroll, Joseph - *Evolution and Literary Theory*
MP - v94 - F '97 - p350+ [501+]
Skeptic - v4 - 4 '96 - p94+ [501+]
VS - v39 - Win '96 - p270+ [501+]
Carroll, Lewis - *Alice in Wonderland. Electronic Media Version*
LR - v45 - 7 '96 - p64 [51-250]
Alice in Wonderland (Jameson). Audio Version
c TES - Jl 19 '96 - pR8 [51-250]
Alice's Adventures in Wonderland (Illus. by Angel Dominguez)
c Ch BWatch - v7 - Ja '97 - p3 [51-250]
c NW - v128 - D 2 '96 - p86 [1-50]
c PW - v243 - N 18 '96 - p78 [51-250]
Alice's Adventures in Wonderland. Electronic Media Version
LAR - v98 - Mr '96 - p162 [51-250]
Lewis Carroll's Jabberwocky (Illus. by Graeme Base)
c BL - v93 - D 15 '96 - p732 [1-50]
c HB Guide - v7 - Fall '96 - p366 [51-250]
The Selected Letters of Lewis Carroll
CR - v270 - F '97 - p110 [1-50]
Obs - Ja 5 '97 - p18* [51-250]
Carroll, Lucy - *Talaq-I-Tafwid: The Muslim Woman's Contractual Access to Divorce*
MEJ - v51 - Spr '97 - p314 [51-250]
Carroll, Michael M - *Nonlinear Effects in Fluids and Solids*
SciTech - v20 - S '96 - p12 [1-50]
Carroll, Michael P - *Veiled Threats*
R&R Bk N - v12 - F '97 - p11 [51-250]
TLS - Mr 28 '97 - p7 [501+]
Carroll, Noel - *Theorizing the Moving Image*
Si & So - v6 - N '96 - p34 [51-250]
Carroll, Rebecca - *Sugar in the Raw*
y BL - v93 - D 15 '96 - p696 [51-250]
y BW - v27 - Ja 12 '97 - p12 [51-250]
y Kliatt - v31 - My '97 - p21 [51-250]
KR - v64 - O 15 '96 - p1503+ [251-500]
Ms - v7 - Ja '97 - p80+ [251-500]
PW - v243 - N 25 '96 - p69 [51-250]

Swing Low
Bloom Rev - v17 - Ja '97 - p18+ [501+]
Carroll, Richard J - *An Economic Record of Presidential Performance*
BusLR - v21 - 3 '96 - p183+ [501+]
Pol Stud J - v24 - Sum '96 - p332 [51-250]
Carroll, Stephen, Dr. - *The Complete Family Guide to Healthy Living*
r ARBA - v28 - '97 - p604 [51-250]
Carroll, Stephen J, 1930- - *Ethical Dimensions of International Management*
Choice - v34 - Mr '97 - p1203 [51-250]
R&R Bk N - v12 - F '97 - p39 [51-250]
Carroll, William C - *Fat King, Lean Beggar*
Choice - v34 - S '96 - p122 [51-250]
Carron, Jean-Claude - *Francois Rabelais: Critical Assessments*
MLR - v92 - Ja '97 - p188+ [501+]
Six Ct J - v27 - Fall '96 - p865 [251-500]
Carrow, Robert - *Turn on the Lights from Bed! (Illus. by Rick Brown)*
y SB - v33 - My '97 - p107 [51-250]
Carruth, Hayden - *Collected Longer Poems*
Parnassus - v22 - 1 '97 - p250+ [501+]
Collected Shorter Poems 1946-1991
BW - v26 - D 1 '96 - p12 [51-250]
LJ - v122 - Ap 1 '97 - p94 [1-50]
Parnassus - v22 - 1 '97 - p250+ [501+]
Scrambled Eggs and Whiskey
BW - v27 - Ja 26 '97 - p8 [51-250]
CSM - v88 - N 12 '96 - p14 [51-250]
Parnassus - v22 - 1 '97 - p250+ [501+]
Selected Essays and Reviews
BW - v26 - D 1 '96 - p12 [51-250]
Parnassus - v22 - 1 '97 - p250+ [501+]
Sitting In. Expanded Ed.
Parnassus - v22 - 1 '97 - p250+ [501+]
Carruthers, Bruce G - *City of Capital*
Choice - v34 - N '96 - p506 [51-250]
JEL - v34 - D '96 - p2097 [51-250]
Carruthers, Leo - *Heroes and Heroines in Medieval English Literature*
MLR - v91 - O '96 - p957+ [501+]
Carruthers, Malcolm - *Male Menopause*
New Sci - v153 - F 22 '97 - p46 [51-250]
Carruthers, Peter - *Language, Thought, and Consciousness*
Choice - v34 - D '96 - p625 [51-250]
RM - v50 - D '96 - p391+ [501+]
TLS - D 27 '96 - p26 [501+]
Theories of Theories of Mind
CPR - v16 - O '96 - p319+ [501+]
Carruthers, Susan L - *Winning Hearts and Minds*
J Mil H - v61 - Ap '97 - p410+ [501+]
Carson, Anne - *Glass, Irony and God*
Ant R - v55 - Spr '97 - p247 [251-500]
Wom R Bks - v14 - N '96 - p24+ [501+]
Carson, Ciaran - *Last Night's Fun*
BL - v93 - Mr 1 '97 - p1102+ [51-250]
LJ - v122 - F 15 '97 - p136 [51-250]
PW - v244 - Ja 27 '97 - p88 [51-250]
Trib Bks - Mr 16 '97 - p7 [501+]
Opera Et Cetera
ILS - v15 - Fall '96 - p10 [501+]
y Sch Lib - v44 - N '96 - p167 [51-250]
TLS - S 27 '96 - p12 [501+]
Carson, Dale - *New Native American Cooking*
y Kliatt - v30 - S '96 - p38 [51-250]
Carson, Diane - *Multiple Voices in Feminist Film Criticism*
J Film & Vid - v48 - Spr '96 - p80+ [501+]
Shared Differences
Afterimage - v24 - Ja '97 - p23 [1-50]
Carson, Glenn Thomas - *Calling Out the Called*
CH - v66 - Mr '97 - p208 [51-250]
Carson, H Glenn - *Get Your Share of Hidden Riches*
Coin W - v38 - Mr 24 '97 - p80 [51-250]
Carson, Jo - *Stories I Ain't Told Nobody Yet*
y JAAL - v40 - D '96 - p320 [51-250]
Carson, Rob - *Mount St. Helens (Illus. by Geff Hinds)*
y Kliatt - v31 - Mr '97 - p4 [51-250]
Carspecken, Phil Francis - *Critical Ethnography in Educational Research*
Choice - v34 - O '96 - p332 [51-250]
Carsten, F L - *The German Workers and the Nazis*
CEH - v29 - 2 '96 - p276+ [501+]
EHR - v112 - Ap '97 - p529+ [501+]
Carstensen, Broder - *Anglizismen-Worterbuch. Vol. 1*
MLR - v91 - O '96 - p1028+ [501+]

Carstensen, Laura L - *The Practical Handbook of Clinical Gerontology*
R&R Bk N - v11 - N '96 - p36 [51-250]
Cart, Michael - *From Romance to Realism*
HB - v72 - S '96 - p625 [51-250]
JAAL - v40 - N '96 - p234+ [501+]
JOYS - v10 - Fall '96 - p97+ [251-500]
LQ - v67 - Ja '97 - p79+ [501+]
My Father's Scar
y BL - v93 - Ap 1 '97 - p1292 [1-50]
y Ch BWatch - v6 - S '96 - p5 [51-250]
y HB Guide - v7 - Fall '96 - p300+ [51-250]
What's So Funny?
New Ad - v9 - Fall '96 - p348+ [51-250]
Carter, Alden R - *Between a Rock and a Hard Place*
y Emerg Lib - v23 - My '96 - p57+ [51-250]
y Emerg Lib - v24 - S '96 - p24 [1-50]
y Kliatt - v30 - S '96 - p3 [1-50]
Big Brother Dustin (Illus. by Dan Young)
c HB - v73 - My '97 - p303+ [51-250]
Bull Catcher
y CCB-B - v50 - Mr '97 - p242+ [51-250]
y KR - v65 - Ja 15 '97 - p138+ [51-250]
Dogwolf
y Kliatt - v30 - N '96 - p6 [51-250]
I'm Tougher than Asthma! (Illus. by Dan Young)
c HB Guide - v7 - Fall '96 - p347 [51-250]
c SB - v32 - O '96 - p212 [51-250]
c SLJ - v42 - Ag '96 - p133 [51-250]
Sheila's Dying
y JAAL - v40 - D '96 - p318+ [51-250]
Carter, Angela - *Burning Your Boats*
LJ - v122 - Ja '97 - p49 [1-50]
Necro - Sum '96 - p1+ [501+]
NYTBR - v101 - D 8 '96 - p79 [1-50]
VLS - Win '96 - p9 [51-250]
The Curious Room
TLS - N 8 '96 - p34 [501+]
Shadow Dance
Books - v9 - S '95 - p24 [1-50]
Carter, Annee - *The Promise of Your Touch*
PW - v244 - Mr 3 '97 - p71 [51-250]
Carter, Betty Smartt - *I Read It in the Wordless Book*
Bks & Cult - v2 - N '96 - p15 [501+]
LJ - v121 - N 1 '96 - p52 [51-250]
Carter, C Allen - *Kenneth Burke and the Scapegoat Process*
Choice - v34 - O '96 - p276 [51-250]
Carter, Charlotte - *Rhode Island Red*
PW - v244 - My 12 '97 - p62 [51-250]
Carter, Dan T - *From George Wallace to Newt Gingrich*
Choice - v34 - My '97 - p1576 [51-250]
PW - v243 - O 14 '96 - p70+ [51-250]
The Politics of Rage
AAPSS-A - v548 - N '96 - p227+ [251-500]
Am - v175 - O 5 '96 - p27+ [501+]
Ant R - v54 - Sum '96 - p370+ [251-500]
APSR - v91 - Mr '97 - p183+ [501+]
CS - v26 - Ja '97 - p26+ [501+]
Historian - v59 - Win '97 - p424+ [501+]
JSH - v62 - N '96 - p852+ [501+]
NYTBR - v102 - Mr 16 '97 - p32 [51-250]
PSQ - v111 - Fall '96 - p562+ [501+]
Carter, Darryl - *Interpretation of Breast Biopsies. 3rd Ed.*
SciTech - v20 - S '96 - p31 [51-250]
Carter, David - *Atlas of General Surgery. 3rd Ed.*
r SciTech - v21 - Mr '97 - p59 [51-250]
Hepatobiliary and Pancreatic Surgery. 5th Ed.
SciTech - v21 - Mr '97 - p51 [51-250]
Carter, David, 1965- - *3D Studio Hollywood and Gaming Effects*
SciTech - v20 - S '96 - p62 [51-250]
Carter, David A - *Bugs at Play*
c PW - v244 - Mr 10 '97 - p68 [51-250]
Bugs at Work
c PW - v244 - Mr 10 '97 - p68 [51-250]
Bugs on the Go
c PW - v244 - Mr 10 '97 - p68 [51-250]
Bugs That Go Bump in the Night
c Ch BWatch - v6 - N '96 - p6 [1-50]
c PW - v243 - S 30 '96 - p85 [51-250]
Busy Bugs, Lazy Bugs
c PW - v244 - Mr 10 '97 - p68 [51-250]
If You're Happy and You Know It
c PW - v244 - Mr 10 '97 - p68 [51-250]
Carter, Elliott - *Elliott Carter: Collected Essays and Lectures 1937-1995*
Choice - v34 - Ap '97 - p1347 [51-250]
Carter, F W - *Trade and Urban Development in Poland*
EHR - v112 - Ap '97 - p457 [501+]

Carter, Harold - *The Study of Urban Geography. 4th Ed.*
GJ - v163 - Mr '97 - p108 [51-250]
Carter, Harold O - *The Measure of California Agriculture*
J Gov Info - v23 - S '96 - p578+ [51-250]
Carter, Jimmy - *Living Faith*
Am - v176 - Mr 22 '97 - p31+ [51-250]
Bks & Cult - v3 - Mr '97 - p16+ [501+]
BL - v93 - S 15 '96 - p178 [51-250]
CC - v114 - Mr 19 '97 - p296+ [501+]
CSM - v89 - Ja 9 '97 - p14 [51-250]
CSM - v89 - Ja 23 '97 - p12 [51-250]
CSM - v89 - F 6 '97 - p14 [51-250]
KR - v64 - S 15 '96 - p1367+ [251-500]
LJ - v121 - O 15 '96 - p63 [51-250]
NYTBR - v102 - Ja 12 '97 - p20 [251-500]
PW - v243 - O 14 '96 - p76 [51-250]
SEP - v269 - Mr '97 - p44+ [501+]
Why Not the Best?
Bks & Cult - v3 - Mr '97 - p16+ [501+]
Carter, John - *ABC for Book Collectors. 7th Ed.*
r Bloom Rev - v16 - N '96 - p22 [1-50]
Carter, John W - *Digital Designing with Programmable Logic Devices*
SciTech - v20 - D '96 - p78 [51-250]
Carter, Keith - *Bones*
SFR - v22 - Ja '97 - p44 [51-250]
Heaven of Animals
Bloom Rev - v16 - N '96 - p23 [51-250]
Carter, Laurence - *Financing Private Infrastructure*
JEL - v35 - Mr '97 - p277 [51-250]
Investment Funds in Emerging Markets
JEL - v35 - Mr '97 - p270 [51-250]
Leasing in Emerging Markets
JEL - v35 - Mr '97 - p270+ [51-250]
Carter, Marina - *Voices from Indenture*
Choice - v34 - F '97 - p1018 [51-250]
Carter, Marshall N - *Promises to Keep*
LJ - v121 - O 15 '96 - p68 [51-250]
PW - v243 - S 9 '96 - p77 [51-250]
Carter, Mary E - *Electronic Highway Robbery*
CBR - v15 - Spr '97 - p2+ [51-250]
LJ - v121 - O 1 '96 - p120 [51-250]
Carter, Pam - *Feminism, Breasts and Breast-Feeding*
AJS - v102 - S '96 - p637+ [501+]
CS - v26 - Ja '97 - p77+ [501+]
Wom R Bks - v14 - O '96 - p25+ [501+]
Carter, Paul - *The Lie of the Land*
Meanjin - v55 - '96 - p651+ [501+]
TLS - S 27 '96 - p32 [51-250]
Carter, Peter - *The Hunted*
y Magpies - v11 - My '96 - p53 [1-50]
Carter, Philip - *Challenging IQ Puzzles*
y Ch BWatch - v7 - F '97 - p8 [1-50]
Carter, Raphael - *The Fortunate Fall*
BWatch - v17 - S '96 - p7 [51-250]
KR - v64 - My 1 '96 - p649 [251-500]
LJ - v121 - O 1 '96 - p47 [1-50]
NYTBR - v101 - S 22 '96 - p25 [51-250]
Rapport - v19 - 6 '96 - p26 [251-500]
Carter, Robert - *Courage*
Books - v10 - Je '96 - p24 [51-250]
Carter, Robert T - *The Influence of Race and Racial Identity in Psychotherapy*
TCR - v98 - Spr '97 - p563+ [501+]
Carter, Ronald - *Introducing Applied Linguistics*
r MLJ - v80 - Win '96 - p533+ [501+]
Carter, Sebastian - *Twentieth Century Type Designers. New Ed.*
Lib - v18 - Je '96 - p167+ [251-500]
Carter, Stephen L - *Integrity*
Comw - v123 - My 17 '96 - p22+ [501+]
y Kliatt - v31 - My '97 - p26+ [51-250]
LATBR - Mr 17 '96 - p4+ [501+]
Rapport - v19 - 4 '96 - p38 [51-250]
Trib Bks - F 16 '97 - p8 [251-500]
W&I - v11 - Jl '96 - p268+ [501+]
Carter, Warren - *Matthew: Storyteller, Interpreter, Evangelist*
Rel St Rev - v23 - Ap '97 - p180+ [51-250]
Carthage: L'Histoire, Sa Trace Et Son Echo
Choice - v34 - D '96 - p569+ [1-50]
Cartier-Bresson, Henri - *America in Passing*
BW - v27 - F 16 '97 - p12 [51-250]
LATBR - D 8 '96 - p26 [51-250]
Cartledge, Bryan - *Population and the Environment*
SB - v32 - Ag '96 - p165 [51-250]
Cartlidge, David R - *Documents for the Study of the Gospels. Rev. and Enlarged Ed.*
Rel St Rev - v23 - Ja '97 - p76 [51-250]
Cartlidge, Michelle - *The Mice of Mousehole*
c PW - v244 - Mr 24 '97 - p85 [51-250]

Cartmill, Matt - *A View to a Death in the Morning*
Nature - v384 - D 5 '96 - p426 [1-50]
Carton, Evan - *Situating College English*
R&R Bk N - v11 - N '96 - p64 [51-250]
Cartoon Bank, Inc. - *E-Mail.This.Book.!*
NY - v72 - D 16 '96 - p109 [1-50]
Cartopedia: The Ultimate World Reference Atlas. Electronic Media Version
cr BL - v92 - Ag '96 - p1918 [51-250]
cr BL - v93 - Ja '97 - p771 [1-50]
Cartwright, Justin - *Not Yet Home*
Obs - N 3 '96 - p17* [501+]
Spec - v277 - S 21 '96 - p47 [501+]
TLS - O 11 '96 - p36 [501+]
Cartwright, Nancy - *Otto Neurath: Philosophy between Science and Politics*
CPR - v16 - O '96 - p322+ [501+]
JEL - v34 - D '96 - p2014 [51-250]
Caruso, Laura - *The Insiders' Guide to Greater Denver. 2nd Ed.*
r Bloom Rev - v16 - Jl '96 - p16 [51-250]
Caruso, Raymond - *Power Programming in HP Openview*
SciTech - v21 - Mr '97 - p9 [51-250]
Caruth, Cathy - *Unclaimed Experience*
Choice - v34 - Mr '97 - p1160 [51-250]
Carvalho, Soniya - *Implementing Projects for the Poor*
JEL - v34 - D '96 - p2114 [51-250]
Carver, Jeffrey A - *The Infinite Sea*
Analog - v117 - Ja '97 - p141+ [251-500]
BL - v92 - Ag '96 - p1888 [51-250]
PW - v243 - Jl 22 '96 - p231 [51-250]
Carver, Jonathan - *Jonathan Carver's Travels through America 1766-1768*
GJ - v162 - N '96 - p342 [51-250]
Carver, Lisa - *Dancing Queen*
PW - v243 - S 9 '96 - p79+ [51-250]
Rollerderby: The Book
Utne R - N '96 - p88+ [1-50]
Carver, Peter - *Notes across the Aisle*
y Ch Bk News - v19 - Sum '96 - p30 [51-250]
Carver, Raymond - *All of Us*
TLS - Ja 24 '97 - p18 [501+]
Great American Writers (Asner). Audio Version
BL - v93 - My 15 '97 - p1596 [51-250]
What We Talk about When We Talk about Love
Obs - Ja 5 '97 - p18* [501+]
TLS - F 21 '97 - p23 [251-500]
Carver, Terrell - *Gender Is Not a Synonym for Women*
APSR - v91 - Mr '97 - p166+ [501+]
Carville, James - *We're Right, They're Wrong*
LATBR - Mr 17 '96 - p3 [501+]
VQR - v72 - Aut '96 - p132* [51-250]
Carwardine, Richard J - *Evangelicals and Politics in Antebellum America*
JR - v77 - Ap '97 - p268+ [501+]
RAH - v24 - D '96 - p601+ [501+]
Cary, Alice - *Jean Craighead George*
c BL - v93 - N 15 '96 - p581 [51-250]
c SLJ - v42 - S '96 - p211 [51-250]
Katherine Paterson
c BL - v93 - My 1 '97 - p1490 [51-250]
Cary, Diana Serra - *The Hollywood Posse*
PHR - v65 - N '96 - p685+ [251-500]
Roundup M - v3 - Ag '96 - p23 [251-500]
What Ever Happened to Baby Peggy?
BL - v93 - O 1 '96 - p314 [51-250]
KR - v64 - Ag 15 '96 - p1201 [251-500]
LJ - v121 - O 1 '96 - p78 [51-250]
PW - v243 - S 9 '96 - p73 [51-250]
Cary, Elizabeth - *The Tragedy of Mariam, the Fair Queen of Jewry*
Shakes Q - v47 - Win '96 - p451+ [501+]
TLS - D 6 '96 - p24 [51-250]
Cary, Francine Curro - *Urban Odyssey*
Choice - v34 - S '96 - p200 [51-250]
Cary, Kate - *Jump Rope (Illus. by David Mostyn)*
c PW - v243 - S 9 '96 - p85 [51-250]
Cary, Lorene - *The Price of a Child*
Bloom Rev - v16 - S '96 - p28 [51-250]
Cary, Noel D - *The Path to Christian Democracy*
Choice - v34 - Ja '97 - p867 [51-250]
Casanova, Carlamaria - *Tebaldi: The Voice of an Angel*
TranslRevS - v2 - D '96 - p7 [51-250]
Casanova, Jose - *Public Religions in the Modern World*
Bks & Cult - v1 - N '95 - p15+ [501+]

Casanova, Mary - *Riot*
c BL - v93 - N 1 '96 - p497 [51-250]
c CBRS - v25 - Win '97 - p69 [51-250]
c CCB-B - v50 - Ja '97 - p165 [51-250]
c HB Guide - v8 - Spr '97 - p63 [51-250]
c LATBR - N 24 '96 - p10 [51-250]
c SLJ - v42 - O '96 - p120 [51-250]
Casanova, Ron - *Each One Teach One*
BL - v93 - S 1 '96 - p42 [51-250]
Casas, Bartolome De Las - *Indian Freedom*
HAHR - v76 - N '96 - p774 [251-500]
Theol St - v57 - Mr '96 - p187 [251-500]
Casas, Edward - *Control of Partial Differential Equations and Applications*
SIAM Rev - v39 - Mr '97 - p174 [51-250]
Casas, Penelope - *Discovering Spain. 2nd Ed.*
r BL - v93 - S 15 '96 - p206 [51-250]
Casati, Roberto - *Holes and Other Superficialities*
J Phil - v93 - N '96 - p585+ [501+]
Phil R - v105 - Ja '96 - p77+ [501+]
Casati Modignani, Sveva - *Il Corsaro E La Rosa*
BL - v93 - D 1 '96 - p644 [1-50]
Caschetta, Mary Beth - *Lucy on the West Coast and Other Lesbian Short Fiction*
BL - v93 - O 1 '96 - p321+ [51-250]
Ms - v7 - N '96 - p80 [501+]
PW - v243 - S 23 '96 - p58 [51-250]
Casciati, Fabio - *Mathematical Models for Structural Reliability Analysis*
SciTech - v20 - N '96 - p65 [51-250]
Cascio, Joseph - *ISO 14000 Guide*
SciTech - v20 - N '96 - p81 [51-250]
Cascone, A G - *Ghost Knight*
c Ch BWatch - v6 - D '96 - p5 [51-250]
Little Magic Shop of Horrors
c Ch BWatch - v7 - F '97 - p4 [51-250]
Casdorph, Paul D - *Prince John Magruder: His Life and Campaigns*
Atl - v278 - D '96 - p126 [51-250]
BL - v93 - N 1 '96 - p477 [51-250]
Choice - v34 - Mr '97 - p1226 [51-250]
LJ - v121 - N 1 '96 - p73 [51-250]
PW - v243 - O 7 '96 - p54 [51-250]
Case, Christopher - *The Ultimate Movie Thesaurus*
r BL - v92 - Ag '96 - p1926 [251-500]
Case, Dianne - *92 Queen's Road*
c Bkbird - v34 - Spr '96 - p26+ [501+]
Love, David (Illus. by Dan Andreasen)
c Bkbird - v34 - Spr '96 - p26+ [501+]
Case, John - *The Genesis Code*
KR - v65 - F 15 '97 - p238 [251-500]
PW - v244 - Mr '97 - p78 [51-250]
Trib Bks - My 18 '97 - p6 [51-250]
Case, LeAnne - *Fitness Aquatics*
LJ - v121 - O 1 '96 - p87 [51-250]
Case, Samuel - *The Socially Responsible Guide to Smart Investing*
Kiplinger - v50 - O '96 - p32+ [501+]
Case, Sue-Ellen - *Cruising the Performative*
Notes - v53 - D '96 - p491+ [501+]
TDR - v41 - Spr '97 - p159 [51-250]
Caseley, Judith - *Jorah's Journal (Illus. by Judith Caseley)*
c BL - v93 - My 1 '97 - p1493 [51-250]
c KR - v65 - My 1 '97 - p718 [51-250]
Priscilla Twice (Illus. by Judith Caseley)
c NYTBR - v101 - S 8 '96 - p28 [51-250]
c RT - v50 - N '96 - p256 [51-250]
Slumber Party! (Illus. by Judith Caseley)
c HB Guide - v7 - Fall '96 - p251 [51-250]
Witch Mama (Illus. by Judith Caseley)
c BL - v93 - S 1 '96 - p135 [51-250]
c HB Guide - v8 - Spr '97 - p23 [51-250]
c PW - v243 - S 30 '96 - p85 [51-250]
c SLJ - v42 - Ag '96 - p121 [51-250]
Caselton, Margaret - *The Gracious Table*
LJ - v122 - Ja '97 - p96 [51-250]
Casement, William - *The Battle of the Books in Higher Education*
TES - Ja 10 '97 - p6* [501+]
The Great Canon Controversy
Cng - v28 - S '96 - p63 [51-250]
VQR - v73 - Win '97 - p24+* [51-250]
Caserta, Thomas G - *Tablets of Stone, Hearts of Flesh*
CLW - v67 - D '96 - p44 [51-250]
Casey, Al - *Casey's Law*
KR - v65 - F 1 '97 - p184 [251-500]
LJ - v122 - Ap 15 '97 - p91 [51-250]
PW - v244 - F 3 '97 - p86 [51-250]
Casey, Edward S - *The Fate of Place*
LJ - v122 - F 1 '97 - p81+ [51-250]

Casey, Maude - *Over the Water*
  y SLJ - v43 - Mr '97 - p112 [1-50]
Casey, Michael - *Millrat*
      Sm Pr R - v28 - D '96 - p4 [51-250]
      VQR - v72 - Aut '96 - p135*+ [51-250]
Casey, Michael, Monk of Tarrawarra - *Sacred Reading*
      Am - v175 - N 2 '96 - p31+ [51-250]
  Toward God
      Am - v175 - N 2 '96 - p31 [51-250]
Casey, Robert P - *Fighting for Life*
      Nat R - v48 - N 11 '96 - p62 [251-500]
Casey, Tom - *Human Error*
      A & S Sm - v11 - D '96 - p94+ [51-250]
      KR - v64 - O 1 '96 - p1417 [251-500]
      PW - v243 - O 21 '96 - p70 [51-250]
Cash, Angela - *Dreamskate*
  y Books - v9 - S '95 - p26 [1-50]
Cash, John Daniel - *Identity, Ideology and Conflict*
      Choice - v34 - F '97 - p1030 [51-250]
Cash, Rosanne - *Bodies of Water*
      Ent W - Ap 4 '97 - p79 [1-50]
      NYTBR - v102 - Ap 6 '97 - p32 [1-50]
      PW - v244 - Mr 17 '97 - p81 [1-50]
      Trib Bks - Ap 6 '97 - p8 [1-50]
Cashin, Jerry - *Developing Second Generation Client/
  Server Applications*
      SciTech - v20 - D '96 - p13 [51-250]
  Implementing and Managing Client/Server Systems
      SciTech - v20 - N '96 - p12 [51-250]
Cashin, Joan E - *Our Common Affairs*
      Choice - v34 - My '97 - p1564 [51-250]
Cashman, John R - *Hazardous Materials Emergencies.
  3rd Ed.*
      SciTech - v20 - N '96 - p59 [51-250]
Cashman, Richard - *The Oxford Companion to Australian
  Cricket*
      Aust Bk R - D '96 - p31+ [501+]
Casimir, Jon - *Postcards from the Net*
      Books - v11 - Ap '97 - p21 [51-250]
Casino Lighting
      TCI - v30 - O '96 - p57 [1-50]
Casmir, Fred L - *Communication in Eastern Europe*
      JMCQ - v73 - Aut '96 - p757+ [501+]
Casper, Claudia - *The Reconstruction*
      BL - v93 - Ja '97 - p817 [51-250]
      KR - v64 - N 1 '96 - p1548 [251-500]
      LJ - v122 - Ja '97 - p144 [51-250]
      NYTBR - v102 - Mr 2 '97 - p18 [51-250]
      PW - v243 - N 11 '96 - p56+ [51-250]
Casper, Gretchen - *Fragile Democracies*
      APSR - v90 - S '96 - p667+ [501+]
  Negotiating Democracy
      Choice - v34 - Mr '97 - p1232 [51-250]
Caspi, Mishael M - *Oral Tradition and Hispanic
  Literature*
      HAHR - v77 - My '97 - p287+ [251-500]
Cass and Birnbaum's Guide to American Colleges. 17th
  Ed.
  yr Kliatt - v30 - S '96 - p28 [51-250]
Cassab, Judy - *Judy Cassab Diaries*
      Aust Bk R - Jl '96 - p32+ [501+]
Cassan, Michel - *Les Imprimes Limousins 1788-1799*
      Lib & Cul - v32 - Win '97 - p140+ [501+]
Cassar, George H - *Asquith as War Leader*
      Historian - v58 - Sum '96 - p896+ [251-500]
Cassatella, Marco A - *Cytokines Produced by
  Polymorphonuclear Neutrophils*
      SciTech - v20 - D '96 - p36 [51-250]
Cass-Beggs, Barbara - *Folk Lullabies of the World*
      CAY - v17 - Win '96 - p1 [51-250]
Cassell, Jay - *The Best of Sports Afield*
      LJ - v121 - S 15 '96 - p74 [51-250]
Cassels, J W S - *Prolegomena to a Middlebrow Arithmetic
  of Curves of Genus 2*
      SciTech - v20 - D '96 - p20 [1-50]
Cassese, Antonio - *Self-Determination of Peoples*
  r HLR - v110 - D '96 - p562 [51-250]
Cassidy, Anne - *Accidental Death*
  y Sch Lib - v45 - F '97 - p44+ [51-250]
Cassidy, Frederic G - *Dictionary of American Regional
  English. Vol. 3*
  r ARBA - v28 - '97 - p383+ [51-250]
Cassieri, Giuseppe - *La Campana Di Mezzanotte*
      WLT - v70 - Sum '96 - p676 [251-500]
Cassingham, Randy - *This Is True*
      Skeptic - v4 - 4 '96 - p106 [251-500]
Cassis, Youssef - *City Bankers 1890-1914*
      EHR - v112 - F '97 - p250+ [501+]
      VS - v39 - Spr '96 - p424+ [501+]

Casson, Mark - *Entrepreneurship and Business Culture*
      Econ J - v107 - Ja '97 - p202+ [501+]
      JEL - v34 - S '96 - p1459+ [51-250]
  Industrial Concentration and Economic Inequality
      Econ J - v107 - Ja '97 - p263+ [251-500]
  The Organization of International Business
      Econ J - v107 - Ja '97 - p202+ [501+]
      JEL - v34 - S '96 - p1430+ [51-250]
Cassuto, Leonard - *The Inhuman Race*
      LJ - v122 - F 15 '97 - p135 [51-250]
  Rereading Jack London
      Choice - v34 - F '97 - p968 [51-250]
Castagnetta, Luigi - *Basis for Cancer Management*
      SciTech - v20 - S '96 - p30 [51-250]
Castagno, John - *Old Masters*
  r R&R Bk N - v12 - F '97 - p71 [51-250]
Castaldo, Nancy Fusco - *Rainy Day Play! (Illus. by
  Loretta Trezzo Braren)*
  c SLJ - v43 - F '97 - p86+ [51-250]
  *Sunny Days and Starry Nights (Illus. by Loretta Trezzo
  Braren)*
  c SB - v33 - Ja '97 - p15 [51-250]
Castaneda, Christopher J - *Gas Pipelines and the
  Emergence of America's Regulatory State*
      Choice - v34 - O '96 - p324 [51-250]
      JEH - v57 - Mr '97 - p256+ [501+]
      JEL - v34 - D '96 - p2088+ [51-250]
Castaneda, Jorge G - *The Mexican Shock*
      NYRB - v43 - O 3 '96 - p31+ [501+]
Castaneda, Omar S - *Abuela's Weave*
  c Learning - v25 - Mr '97 - p54 [1-50]
  Naranjo the Muse
      KR - v65 - My 1 '97 - p677 [51-250]
Castaneda-Zuniga, Wilfrido R - *Interventional Radiology.
  3rd Ed., Vols. 1-2*
      SciTech - v21 - Mr '97 - p59 [51-250]
Castarede, Jean - *Henri IV, Le Roi Venge*
      BL - v93 - Ja '97 - p827 [1-50]
Castellana, Giuseppe - *La Necropoli Protoeneolitica Di
  Piano Vento Nel Territorio Di Palma Di Montechiaro*
      AJA - v100 - O '96 - p773+ [501+]
Castellaneta, Carlo - *La Citta E Gli Inganni*
      BL - v93 - D 1 '96 - p644 [1-50]
Castellani, Francesco Di Matteo - *Ricordanze II*
      Six Ct J - v27 - Win '96 - p1167+ [251-500]
Castellanos, Rosario - *The Book of Lamentations*
      BL - v93 - Ja '97 - p760 [1-50]
      BL - v93 - D 1 '96 - p641 [51-250]
      BW - v27 - Ja 12 '97 - p6+ [501+]
      KR - v64 - O 15 '96 - p1483 [251-500]
      LJ - v121 - O 1 '96 - p124 [51-250]
      NY - v72 - F 10 '97 - p82+ [501+]
      NYTBR - v102 - F 23 '97 - p16 [51-250]
      PW - v243 - O 21 '96 - p69 [51-250]
  Cartas A Ricardo
      Hisp - v79 - S '96 - p454+ [501+]
Castellanos Moya, Horacio - *Recuento De Incertidumbres*
      BL - v93 - S 15 '96 - p227 [1-50]
Castellon, Blanca - *Ama Del Espiritu*
      WLT - v71 - Win '97 - p121+ [501+]
Castells, Manuel - *The Rise of the Network Society*
      Choice - v34 - F '97 - p1010 [51-250]
Castelnuovo, Guido - *Ufficiali E Gentiluomini*
      EHR - v111 - S '96 - p963+ [251-500]
Casteras, Susan P - *The Grosvenor Gallery*
      BM - v138 - O '96 - p701+ [501+]
  r Choice - v34 - N '96 - p444 [51-250]
  *James Smetham: Artist, Author, Pre-Raphaelite
  Associate*
      Albion - v28 - Sum '96 - p337+ [501+]
      VS - v39 - Spr '96 - p464+ [501+]
  A Struggle for Fame
      VS - v39 - Win '96 - p243+ [501+]
Casti, John L - *Would-Be Worlds*
      Choice - v34 - F '97 - p998 [51-250]
      KR - v64 - Ag 15 '96 - p1201 [251-500]
      Nature - v385 - Ja 2 '97 - p33 [501+]
      New Sci - v152 - O 26 '96 - p43 [501+]
      SciTech - v20 - D '96 - p14 [1-50]
Castiglia, Christopher - *Bound and Determined*
      AL - v69 - Mr '97 - p207+ [251-500]
      Choice - v34 - S '96 - p123 [51-250]
      R&R Bk N - v11 - N '96 - p71 [51-250]
Castillo, Amelia Del - *Geminio Deshabitado*
      BL - v93 - Ap 1 '97 - p1284 [1-50]
Castillo, Ana - *Goddess of the Americas*
      BL - v93 - Ja '97 - p808 [1-50]
      Comw - v124 - Mr 14 '97 - p24+ [501+]
      PW - v243 - O 14 '96 - p77 [251-250]

Loverboys: Stories
      BL - v92 - Ag '96 - p1881 [51-250]
      BL - v93 - Ja '97 - p760 [1-50]
      Bloom Rev - v16 - S '96 - p7 [501+]
      BW - v26 - S 1 '96 - p6 [501+]
      LATBR - Ag 25 '96 - p8 [501+]
      NYTBR - v101 - S 8 '96 - p20 [501+]
Castle, Jayne - *Amaryllis*
      Quill & Q - v62 - Jl '96 - p44 [501+]
Castle, John - *Hunting for Treasure*
      Coin W - v37 - S 23 '96 - p16 [51-250]
Castle, Kate - *Ballet*
  c HB Guide - v8 - Spr '97 - p141 [51-250]
  cr PW - v243 - S 16 '96 - p85 [51-250]
  c SLJ - v42 - D '96 - p127 [51-250]
  The Best Ever Book of Ballet
  y Sch Lib - v45 - F '97 - p50 [51-250]
Castle, Kathryn - *Britannia's Children*
      Choice - v34 - N '96 - p454 [51-250]
      TES - Jl 5 '96 - pR3 [501+]
Castle, Roy - *Now and Then*
      Books - v9 - S '95 - p27 [1-50]
Castle, Terry - *The Female Thermometer*
      Col Lit - v23 - O '96 - p199+ [501+]
  Noel Coward and Radclyffe Hall
      Choice - v34 - Ap '97 - p1333 [51-250]
      KR - v64 - O 1 '96 - p1437+ [251-500]
      LATBR - N 17 '96 - p8 [501+]
      LJ - v122 - F 15 '97 - p135 [51-250]
      Nat - v263 - D 9 '96 - p27+ [501+]
      TLS - Mr 21 '97 - p3+ [501+]
Castle, Timothy N - *At War in the Shadow of Vietnam*
      Arm F&S - v22 - Sum '96 - p643+ [501+]
Castleberry, May - *Perpetual Mirage*
      Choice - v34 - D '96 - p601 [51-250]
      LJ - v121 - N 1 '96 - p63 [51-250]
Castleden, Rodney - *The Cerne Giant*
      TLS - Ja 24 '97 - p32 [251-500]
Castleman, Michael - *Nature's Cures*
  r BL - v93 - F 1 '97 - p958 [1-50]
Castleman, Virginia - *Mommi Watta (Illus. by Theodocia
  Swecker)*
  c Ch BWatch - v6 - S '96 - p3 [51-250]
  c SLJ - v43 - Ja '97 - p98 [51-250]
Castles, Stephen - *The Age of Migration*
      AAAGA - v86 - S '96 - p602+ [501+]
      WP - v49 - O '96 - p130+ [501+]
Castner, Henry W - *Discerning New Horizons*
      BioSci - v46 - S '96 - p630 [51-250]
Casto, William R - *The Supreme Court in the Early
  Republic*
      AHR - v101 - D '96 - p1615+ [501+]
      Bks & Cult - v2 - N '96 - p27+ [501+]
      Historian - v59 - Win '97 - p425+ [251-500]
Caston, Anne - *Flying Out with the Wounded*
      PW - v244 - Ap 28 '97 - p71 [51-250]
Castor, Harriet - *Anne Frank (Illus. by Helena Owen)*
  c Bks Keeps - Ja '97 - p24 [251-500]
  c Sch Lib - v45 - F '97 - p37 [51-250]
  Elizabeth I (Illus. by Peter Kent)
  c Bks Keeps - Ja '97 - p24 [251-500]
  c Sch Lib - v45 - F '97 - p39 [51-250]
  Milly of the Rovers (Illus. by Christyan Fox)
  c Sch Lib - v45 - F '97 - p23 [51-250]
Castorina, Jan - *A Taste of Indochina*
      BWatch - v17 - N '96 - p1 [51-250]
Castriota, David - *The Ara Pacis Augustae and the
  Imagery of Abundance in Later Greek and Early Roman
  Imperial Art*
      AJA - v100 - O '96 - p799+ [501+]
      Apo - v144 - N '96 - p58+ [501+]
      TLS - O 18 '96 - p6+ [501+]
Castro, Eduardo Batalha Viveiros De - *From the
  Enemy's Point of View*
      Am Ethnol - v24 - F '97 - p225+ [501+]
Castro, Elizabeth - *HTML for the World Wide Web*
  r CBR - v15 - Spr '97 - p4 [1-50]
      Quill & Q - v62 - My '96 - p22+ [501+]
  HTML for the World Wide Web. 2nd Ed.
      LJ - v122 - My 1 '97 - p132 [1-50]
  Netscape 3 for Windows
      CBR - v14 - N '96 - p36 [1-50]
      LJ - v122 - Ja '97 - p138 [1-50]
Castro, Hebe Maria Mattos De - *Das Cores Do Silencio*
      HAHR - v77 - My '97 - p348+ [251-500]
Castro, Isabel - *A Guide to the Birds of the Galapagos
  Islands*
  r New Sci - v153 - Mr 8 '97 - p45 [51-250]
Castro, Juana - *Alada Mia*
      WLT - v71 - Win '97 - p122 [501+]

Castronovo, Russ - *Fathering the Nation*
  AL - v69 - Mr '97 - p222+ [251-500]
  Ken R - v19 - Win '97 - p162+ [501+]
Caswell, Brian - *Asturias*
  y Aust Bk R - Ag '96 - p62+ [501+]
  y Magpies - v11 - S '96 - p36 [51-250]
Cat (Eyewitness Virtual Reality Series). Electronic Media Version
  y SB - v33 - Mr '97 - p56 [51-250]
Cat, Ivan - *The Eyes of Light and Darkness*
  y Kliatt - v30 - N '96 - p14 [51-250]
Catalani, Mario S - *Decision Making Structures*
  JEL - v34 - D '96 - p2030+ [51-250]
Catalano, Lawrence F - *Pipeline Crossings 1996*
  SciTech - v20 - D '96 - p64 [51-250]
Catala Sanz, Jorge Antonio - *Rentas Y Patrimonios De La Nobleza Valenciana En El Siglo XVIII*
  AHR - v101 - D '96 - p1576+ [501+]
Catalfo, Phil - *Raising Spiritual Children in a Material World*
  PW - v244 - Ap 14 '97 - p70 [51-250]
Cataliotti, Robert H - *The Music in African American Fiction*
  Choice - v34 - S '96 - p123 [51-250]
Catalogazione, Cooperazione, Servizi, Strumenti
  Lib - v18 - D '96 - p361+ [51-250]
Catalogo Della Biblioteca Di Scienze Carlo Vigano
  r Lib - v19 - Mr '97 - p101 [51-250]
Catalogue Switzerland/Liechtenstein, Campione and United Nations, Geneva 1996
  r Am Phil - v110 - Jl '96 - p636 [501+]
Cataneo, David - *Hornsby Hit One Over My Head*
  PW - v244 - Ap 28 '97 - p56 [51-250]
Catapult, Inc. - *Microsoft Access for Windows 95 Step by Step*
  CBR - v14 - Jl '96 - p19 [1-50]
  Microsoft Project for Windows 95 Step by Step
  CBR - v14 - Jl '96 - p22 [1-50]
  Microsoft Word for Windows 95 Step by Step
  CBR - v14 - Jl '96 - p26 [1-50]
  More Microsoft Windows 95 Step by Step
  CBR - v14 - Jl '96 - p23 [1-50]
Catchpole, C K - *Bird Song*
  Nature - v382 - Ag 15 '96 - p592 [501+]
Cate, Curtis - *Andre Malraux: A Biography*
  BL - v93 - Ap 1 '97 - p1276 [51-250]
  KR - v65 - F 1 '97 - p184 [251-500]
  LJ - v122 - F 15 '97 - p135 [51-250]
  PW - v244 - Ja 27 '97 - p84 [51-250]
  WLT - v70 - Sum '96 - p658+ [501+]
  WSJ-Cent - v99 - My 5 '97 - pA16 [501+]
Cate, Dick - *Bernard's Prize (Illus. by Scoular Anderson)*
  c Sch Lib - v44 - Ag '96 - p105 [51-250]
Cate, Phillip Dennis - *The Spirit of Montmartre*
  AB - v98 - Ag 19 '96 - p574+ [501+]
  r Choice - v34 - N '96 - p446 [51-250]
Catfantastic IV
  y Kliatt - v30 - N '96 - p14+ [51-250]
  VOYA - v19 - D '96 - p276+ [51-250]
Cather, Willa - *The Autobiography of S.S. McClure*
  PW - v244 - F 3 '97 - p100 [1-50]
  O Pioneers!
  PW - v244 - F 3 '97 - p100 [1-50]
  Reason - v28 - D '96 - p37 [51-250]
  Stories (Hughes). Audio Version
  BL - v93 - My 15 '97 - p1596 [51-250]
  Willa Cather (Seldes). Audio Version
  BL - v93 - S 15 '96 - p264 [51-250]
Catholic Church. Diocese of Carlisle (England) - *The Register of John Kirkby, Bishop of Carlisle 1332-1352 and the Register of John Ross, Bishop of Carlisle 1325-1332. Vol. 2*
  CH - v66 - Mr '97 - p190 [51-250]
  The Register of John Kirkby, Bishop of Carlisle 1332-1352 and the Register of John Ross, Bishop of Carlisle 1325-1332. Vols. 1-2
  Albion - v28 - Fall '96 - p470+ [501+]
  CHR - v83 - Ja '97 - p89+ [251-500]
Catholic Church. Diocese of Exeter (England). Bishop (1257-1280: Bronescombe) - *The Register of Walter Bronescombe, Bishop of Exeter 1258-1280. Vol. 1*
  Albion - v28 - Fall '96 - p1280+ [501+]
  CH - v66 - Mr '97 - p190 [51-250]
Catholic Church. National Conference of Catholic Bishops. Bishops' Committee on the Liturgy - *God's Mercy Endures Forever*
  Rel Ed - v91 - Fall '96 - p608 [51-250]
Catlett, Estelle - *Track Down Your Ancestors*
  TES - Jl 26 '96 - pR6 [1-50]
Catlin, Alan - *Shelley and the Romantics*
  Sm Pr R - v28 - N '96 - p4 [51-250]

CATO Review of Business and Government
  p JEL - v35 - Mr '97 - p307 [51-250]
Caton, Patrick - *The Passion of Chocolate*
  BWatch - v18 - F '97 - p7 [51-250]
Cattermole, Peter - *Planetary Volcanism. 2nd Ed.*
  Choice - v34 - Ap '97 - p1361 [51-250]
  Phys Today - v50 - Mr '97 - p77 [501+]
Catton, Bruce - *The American Heritage New History of the Civil War*
  Esq - v126 - D '96 - p40 [1-50]
  Obs - F 2 '97 - p17* [51-250]
  PW - v243 - S 23 '96 - p70 [51-250]
Catton, Theodore - *Land Reborn*
  Pub Hist - v19 - Win '97 - p90+ [501+]
Caudwell, Sarah - *Thus Was Adonis Murdered*
  Arm Det - v29 - Fall '96 - p436 [51-250]
Caufield, Catherine - *Masters of Illusion*
  Barron's - v77 - Ja 27 '97 - p49 [501+]
  BL - v93 - D 1 '96 - p626 [51-250]
  BW - v27 - F 16 '97 - p6 [251-500]
  Econ - v342 - Mr 15 '97 - p9* [501+]
  KR - v64 - O 15 '96 - p1504 [251-500]
  LATBR - Ja 19 '97 - p5 [501+]
  LJ - v122 - Mr 15 '97 - p70+ [51-250]
  Nat - v264 - Mr 17 '97 - p38+ [501+]
  NYTBR - v102 - Mr 23 '97 - p19 [51-250]
  PW - v243 - N 25 '96 - p62 [51-250]
Caughie, John - *The Companion to British and Irish Cinema*
  r Si & So - v6 - N '96 - p36 [51-250]
Cauldwell, Rex - *Wiring a House*
  BL - v93 - S 1 '96 - p49 [51-250]
Caulfield, Jon - *City Lives and City Forms*
  Choice - v34 - My '97 - p1561 [51-250]
Caumartin, Francois - *Now You See Them, Now You Don't (Illus. by Francois Caumartin)*
  c SLJ - v43 - Ja '97 - p76 [51-250]
Caumery - *Becassine Aux Ameriques*
  c BL - v93 - N 1 '96 - p500 [1-50]
  Becassine--Quand La Mer Monte
  c BL - v93 - N 1 '96 - p500 [1-50]
Caunitz, William J - *Pigtown*
  NYTBR - v101 - N 10 '96 - p68 [51-250]
Causley, Charles - *Bring in the Holly (Illus. by Lisa Kopper)*
  c Bks Keeps - N '96 - p24 [51-250]
  Collected Poems for Children (Illus. by John Lawrence)
  c Sch Lib - v44 - Ag '96 - p115 [51-250]
  Going to the Fair
  c Obs - S 29 '96 - p18* [51-250]
Caute, David - *Joseph Losey: A Revenge on Life*
  TES - N 22 '96 - p8* [51-250]
Cautela, Joseph R - *Contemporary Issues in Behavior Therapy*
  SciTech - v20 - N '96 - p44 [51-250]
Cauwelaert, Didier Van - *Noces De Sable*
  WLT - v70 - Sum '96 - p655 [251-500]
Cavaiani, Mabel - *The New Diabetic Cookbook. 4th Ed.*
  BWatch - v18 - Mr '97 - p6 [51-250]
Cavalli-Sforza, L L - *The Great Human Diasporas*
  Am Sci - v84 - N '96 - p604 [501+]
  y Kliatt - v31 - My '97 - p30 [51-250]
  NGSQ - v84 - D '96 - p313+ [251-500]
  The History and Geography of Human Genes
  NYTBR - v101 - N 24 '96 - p32 [51-250]
Cavallo, Alberto - *Using MATLAB, SIMULINK and Control System Toolbox*
  SciTech - v20 - D '96 - p72 [51-250]
Cavallo, Jo Ann - *Boiardo's Orlando Innamorato*
  MP - v94 - Ag '96 - p73+ [501+]
Cavanagh, Helen - *The Last Piper*
  c HB Guide - v7 - Fall '96 - p290 [51-250]
  y VOYA - v19 - O '96 - p206 [51-250]
Cavanaugh, Cecelia J - *Lorca's Drawings and Poems*
  Choice - v34 - S '96 - p132 [51-250]
Cavanaugh, Francis X - *The Truth about the National Debt*
  BL - v93 - S 1 '96 - p44 [51-250]
  Bus W - O 28 '96 - p22 [501+]
  JEL - v35 - Mr '97 - p226 [51-250]
  WSJ-MW - v77 - S 24 '96 - pA16 [501+]
Cavanaugh, John William - *Media Effects on Voters*
  AAPSS-A - v550 - Mr '97 - p190 [251-500]
Cave, Alfred A - *The Pequot War*
  Choice - v34 - D '96 - p675 [51-250]
  HRNB - v25 - Win '97 - p64 [251-500]
  NEQ - v70 - Mr '97 - p139+ [501+]
Cave, Emma - *The Lair*
  Spec - v278 - Ap 5 '97 - p38 [251-500]

Cave, Kathryn - *Best Friends For Ever (Illus. by Derek Brazell)*
  c TES - Jl 5 '96 - pR8 [1-50]
  The Emperor's Gruckle Hound (Illus. by Chris Riddell)
  c Bks Keeps - Jl '96 - p12 [51-250]
  c Sch Lib - v44 - Ag '96 - p105 [51-250]
  Similon
  c Bks Keeps - Mr '97 - p25 [51-250]
  Something Else (Illus. by Chris Riddell)
  c Obs - Mr 30 '97 - p17* [51-250]
Cave, Yvonne - *The Succulent Garden*
  BL - v93 - Ap 1 '97 - p1274 [51-250]
Cavell, Stanley - *The Cavell Reader*
  LJ - v122 - F 1 '97 - p84 [51-250]
  Contesting Tears
  Trib Bks - Ap 13 '97 - p3 [501+]
Cavendish, Jane - *The Concealed Fancies*
  Shakes Q - v47 - Win '96 - p396+ [501+]
Cavendish, Margret - *The Convent of Pleasure*
  Shakes Q - v47 - Win '96 - p387+ [501+]
Caves, Richard E - *Multinational Enterprise and Economic Analysis. 2nd Ed.*
  Choice - v34 - S '96 - p174 [51-250]
  JEL - v34 - D '96 - p2045 [51-250]
Cavoukian, Ann - *Who Knows*
  ACI - v9 - Spr '97 - p38+ [501+]
Cavour, Camillo - *Epistolario. Vol. 14, Pts. 1-2*
  EHR - v112 - Ap '97 - p507+ [251-500]
Cawelti, G - *Handbook of Research on Improving Student Achievement*
  Emerg Lib - v24 - S '96 - p42 [51-250]
Caws, Mary Ann - *Robert Motherwell: What Art Holds*
  Choice - v34 - S '96 - p111 [51-250]
  R&R Bk N - v11 - N '96 - p60 [51-250]
Cawthon, Juanita Davis - *Some Early Citizens of Marion County, Texas*
  r EGH - v50 - N '96 - p188 [51-250]
Cawthorn, R Grant - *Layered Intrusions*
  SciTech - v21 - Mr '97 - p33 [51-250]
Cayleff, Susan E - *Babe: The Life and Legend of Babe Didrikson Zaharias*
  AHR - v102 - F '97 - p217 [501+]
  J Am Cult - v19 - Spr '97 - p109+ [501+]
  JSH - v62 - N '96 - p836+ [251-500]
Cayton, Andrew R L - *Frontier Indiana*
  Choice - v34 - F '97 - p1023 [51-250]
  LJ - v121 - O 15 '96 - p70+ [51-250]
Cazauran, Nicole - *Discours Merveilleux De La Vie, Actions Et Deportements De Catherine De Medicis, Royne Mere*
  Ren Q - v50 - Spr '97 - p251+ [501+]
  Six Ct J - v27 - Win '96 - p1135+ [501+]
Cazet, Denys - *Night Lights (Illus. by Denys Cazet)*
  c KR - v65 - F 15 '97 - p297 [51-250]
CD Estimator 1996. Electronic Media Version
  r FHB - Ag '96 - p138 [51-250]
The CD-ROM Directory 1996
  r SLMQ - v25 - Fall '96 - p61 [51-250]
CD-ROMs in Print 1995. Electronic Media Version
  r ARBA - v28 - '97 - p10+ [251-500]
CD-ROMs in Print 1996
  r ARBA - v28 - '97 - p10+ [251-500]
Cea, Jean - *Partial Differential Equations and Functional Analysis*
  SciTech - v20 - S '96 - p10 [51-250]
Ceadel, Martin - *The Origins of War Prevention*
  r Choice - v34 - Ja '97 - p766 [51-250]
Ceard, Jean - *Langage Et Verite*
  Ren & Ref - v19 - Fall '96 - p87 [501+]
Ceballos Gomez, Diana Luz - *Hechiceria, Brujeria, E Inquisicion En El Nuevo Reino De Granada*
  HAHR - v76 - Ag '96 - p562+ [501+]
Cecala, Kathy - *Secret Vow*
  KR - v65 - Mr 1 '97 - p320 [51-250]
  LJ - v122 - Mr 15 '97 - p87 [51-250]
  PW - v244 - Ap 7 '97 - p75 [51-250]
Cech, John - *Angels and Wild Things*
  HB - v73 - Mr '97 - p216 [51-250]
  The Southernmost Cat (Illus. by Kathy Osborn)
  c Ch BWatch - v6 - My '96 - p4 [1-50]
  c HB Guide - v7 - Fall '96 - p286 [51-250]
  c NYTBR - v101 - Ag 25 '96 - p23 [1-50]
Cecil, David, Lord - *The English Poets*
  PW - v244 - Mr 24 '97 - p72 [1-50]
  TLS - D 27 '96 - p32 [251-500]
Cecil, Hugh - *Facing Armageddon*
  Spec - v277 - N 16 '96 - p46 [1-50]
  TLS - O 11 '96 - p6 [501+]
  The Flower of Battle
  Choice - v34 - N '96 - p454 [51-250]

Cecil, Lamar - *Wilhelm II. Vol. 2*
Choice - v34 - Mr '97 - p1218 [51-250]
J Mil H - v61 - Ap '97 - p385+ [501+]

Cecil, Laura - *Preposterous Pete (Illus. by Emma Chichester Clark)*
c JB - v60 - O '96 - p190+ [51-250]

Cela, Camilo Jose - *Mazurka for Two Dead Men*
TranslRevS - v1 - My '95 - p29 [51-250]

Celan, Paul - *Breathturn*
Lon R Bks - v18 - My 23 '96 - p10+ [501+]
Correspondence: Paul Celan and Nelly Sachs
HMR - Win '96 - p8+ [501+]
Selected Poems
TES - D 27 '96 - p16 [51-250]

Celant, Germano - *Tony Cragg*
BL - v93 - D 1 '96 - p636+ [51-250]
LJ - v121 - S 15 '96 - p63 [51-250]

A Celebration of Marine Art
Sea H - Win '96 - p44 [51-250]

Celente, Gerald - *Trends 2000*
BL - v93 - Ja '97 - p788 [51-250]
LJ - v122 - Ja '97 - p114 [51-250]
PW - v243 - D 9 '96 - p57 [51-250]

Celestin, Roger - *From Cannibals to Radicals*
Choice - v34 - N '96 - p463+ [51-250]

Celine, Louis-Ferdinand - *Castle to Castle*
LJ - v122 - My 1 '97 - p145 [1-50]
PW - v244 - F 3 '97 - p102 [1-50]
North
LJ - v121 - N 1 '96 - p112 [1-50]

CEMS Business Review
p JEL - v35 - Mr '97 - p307 [51-250]

Cencini, Alvaro - *Inflation and Unemployment*
JEL - v35 - Mr '97 - p206 [51-250]

Cendrars, Blaise - *Hollywood, Mecca of the Movies*
FIR - v48 - Ja '97 - p103+ [501+]

Cengel, Yunus A - *Introduction to Thermodynamics and Heat Transfer*
SciTech - v21 - Mr '97 - p22 [51-250]

Censer, Jack R - *The French Press in the Age of Enlightenment*
AHR - v101 - D '96 - p1552+ [501+]
JMH - v69 - Mr '97 - p153+ [501+]
Lib & Cul - v32 - Win '97 - p139+ [501+]

Censored: The News That Didn't Make the News--and Why 1996
LATBR - My 12 '96 - p11 [51-250]
SFR - v21 - Jl '96 - p37+ [501+]
Workbook - v21 - Win '96 - p181+ [501+]

Centi, Beatrice - *L'Armonia Impossibile*
Isis - v87 - D '96 - p742+ [501+]

Central Computer and Telecommunications Agency - *Legal Issues and the Internet. Vols. 1-2*
LAR - v98 - N '96 - p595 [51-250]

Central Office of Information - *At Work*
y Sch Lib - v44 - N '96 - p172+ [51-250]
On Holiday
y Sch Lib - v44 - N '96 - p172+ [51-250]

Central to Excellence
TES - F 14 '97 - p23* [1-50]

Centrodi, Giuliano - *Gio Pomodoro: Ornamenti 1954-1996*
Am Craft - v57 - Ap '97 - p28 [1-50]

Cerasano, S P - *Renaissance Drama by Women*
Choice - v34 - D '96 - p616 [51-250]
Ren Q - v50 - Spr '97 - p273+ [501+]

Cerati, Carla - *L'Amica Della Modellista*
BL - v93 - D 1 '96 - p644 [1-50]

Cerda, Martha - *Senora Rodriguez and Other Worlds*
Nat - v264 - Ap 7 '97 - p39+ [501+]
PW - v244 - Mr 10 '97 - p51 [51-250]

Cerny, Charlene - *Recycled, Re-Seen*
Am Craft - v56 - D '96 - p28+ [501+]
Aud - v98 - N '96 - p137 [51-250]
y BL - v92 - Ag '96 - p1872+ [51-250]
y BL - v92 - Ag '96 - p1890 [1-50]
E Mag - v8 - Mr '97 - p48 [51-250]
LJ - v121 - S 15 '96 - p64+ [51-250]

Ceronetti, Guido - *The Silence of the Body*
TranslRevS - v1 - My '95 - p7 [51-250]

Cerreti, Claudio - *Colonie Africane E Cultura Italiana Fra Ottocento E Novecento*
MEJ - v51 - Win '97 - p153 [51-250]

Cerrito, Joann - *Contemporary Artists. 4th Ed.*
r ARBA - v28 - '97 - p365 [51-250]
r R&R Bk N - v11 - N '96 - p59 [51-250]

Cerrolaza, M - *Simulation Modelling in Bioengineering*
SciTech - v21 - Mr '97 - p45 [51-250]

Certification and Accreditation Programs Directory. 1st Ed.
r BL - v93 - Ja '97 - p769 [1-50]
r RQ - v35 - Sum '96 - p547+ [501+]

Cerullo, Mary M - *Coral Reef*
c HB Guide - v7 - Fall '96 - p334 [51-250]
The Octopus: Phantom of the Sea (Illus. by Jeffrey L Rotman)
c BL - v93 - F 1 '97 - p936 [51-250]
c CCB-B - v50 - F '97 - p201 [51-250]
c KR - v64 - N 15 '96 - p1667 [51-250]

Cerulo, Karen A - *Identity Designs*
AJS - v102 - S '96 - p603+ [501+]
CS - v26 - Mr '97 - p244+ [501+]

Cervantes, Fernando - *The Devil in the New World*
HAHR - v76 - N '96 - p789+ [501+]
JR - v77 - Ap '97 - p348+ [501+]

Cervantes Saavedra, Miguel De - *The History of That Ingenious Gentleman Don Quijote De La Mancha*
Sew R - v104 - Jl '96 - pR68+ [501+]

Cervini, Fulvio - *I Portali Della Cattedrale Di Genova E Il Gotico Europeo*
Specu - v71 - O '96 - p935+ [251-500]

Cervo, Amado Luis - *Historia Da Politicia Exterior Do Brasil*
HAHR - v76 - N '96 - p823+ [501+]

Cesaire, Aime - *Cahier D'Un Retour Au Pays Natal*
MLR - v92 - Ja '97 - p212+ [501+]
Notebook of a Return to My Native Land
MLR - v92 - Ja '97 - p212+ [501+]

Cesarani, David - *The Jewish Chronicle and Anglo-Jewry 1841-1991*
HT - v46 - Ag '96 - p57+ [501+]

Cessario, Romanus - *Christian Faith and the Theological Life*
BL - v93 - N 1 '96 - p460 [51-250]

Cezanne, Paul - *Cezanne*
Art J - v55 - Win '96 - p95+ [501+]
BL - v92 - Ag '96 - p1871 [51-250]
BW - v26 - D 8 '96 - p10 [51-250]
Choice - v34 - D '96 - p601 [51-250]

Cha, Dia - *Dia's Story Cloth (Illus. by Chue Cha)*
c CBRS - v24 - Ag '96 - p163 [51-250]
c HB Guide - v7 - Fall '96 - p311+ [51-250]
c RT - v50 - My '97 - p684 [51-250]

Cha, Theresa Hak Kyung - *Dictee*
Col Lit - v23 - O '96 - p23+ [501+]

Chabal, Patrick - *The Post-Colonial Literature of Lusophone Africa*
R&R Bk N - v11 - N '96 - p69 [1-50]

Chabod, Federico - *Italian Foreign Policy*
Choice - v34 - F '97 - p1030 [51-250]
For Aff - v75 - S '96 - p147 [51-250]

Chabran, Richard - *The Latino Encyclopedia. Vols. 1-6*
r ARBA - v28 - '97 - p156+ [251-500]
yr Ch BWatch - v6 - O '96 - p5 [51-250]
r Choice - v34 - S '96 - p100 [51-250]
r RQ - v36 - Win '96 - p298+ [501+]
yr SLJ - v42 - N '96 - p136 [51-250]

Chabrier, Emmanuel - *Works for Piano*
Am MT - v46 - D '96 - p60+ [501+]

Chadam, John - *Pattern Formation*
SIAM Rev - v38 - S '96 - p545 [1-50]

Chadbourn, Mark - *The Eternal*
Necro - Fall '96 - p25+ [51-250]

Chadour, Anna Beatriz - *Rings: The Alice and Louis Koch Collection. Vols. 1-2*
Apo - v145 - Ja '97 - p60 [501+]

Chadwick, Bruce - *Deion Sanders*
c HB Guide - v7 - Fall '96 - p359 [1-50]
When the Game Was Black and White
Aethlon - v13 - Fall '95 - p1171+ [251-500]

Chadwick, Bruce A - *Statistical Handbook on Adolescents in America*
r ARBA - v28 - '97 - p326 [51-250]
r Choice - v34 - F '97 - p950 [51-250]

Chadwick, Douglas H - *The Company We Keep*
y BL - v93 - F 15 '97 - p984+ [51-250]
Choice - v34 - Ap '97 - p1366 [51-250]
CSM - v89 - D 5 '96 - pB3 [51-250]
LATBR - D 8 '96 - p3 [51-250]
LJ - v122 - Ja '97 - p137 [51-250]
VLS - Win '96 - p20 [51-250]

Chadwick, Elizabeth - *Self-Determination, Terrorism, and the International Humanitarian Law of Armed Conflict*
R&R Bk N - v11 - D '96 - p50 [51-250]

Chadwick, Irene - *Dawn Pearl*
WAL - v31 - Fall '96 - p287 [51-250]

Chadwick, John - *Lexicographica Graeca*
r TLS - N 1 '96 - p9+ [501+]

Chadwick, Owen - *A History of Christianity*
R&R Bk N - v11 - N '96 - p7 [51-250]
VQR - v72 - Aut '96 - p117*+ [51-250]

Chadwick, Paul - *Like a Mountain Series*
cp Par Ch - v20 - N '96 - p11 [51-250]

Chadwick, Paxton - *The Life History of Life Histories (Illus. by Paxton Chadwick)*
c BC - v45 - Aut '96 - p382 [51-250]

Chadwick, Vernon - *In Search of Elvis*
BL - v93 - Ja '97 - p803 [51-250]

Chadwick, Whitney - *Significant Others*
CR - v269 - Ag '96 - p112 [51-250]
Women, Art and Society
TES - Ja 3 '97 - p23 [51-250]

Chafe, Wallace - *Discourse, Consciousness and Time*
A J Psy - v109 - Fall '96 - p486+ [501+]

Chafets, Zev - *The Project*
BL - v93 - Mr 1 '97 - p1109 [51-250]
KR - v65 - F 15 '97 - p238+ [251-500]
LJ - v122 - Mr 15 '97 - p87+ [51-250]
PW - v244 - Mr 3 '97 - p65 [51-250]

Chaffee, Wilber A, Jr. - *The Economics of Violence in Latin America*
Parameters - v26 - Win '96 - p155 [1-50]

Chaffey, John - *Managing Wilderness Regions*
TES - Mr 28 '97 - pR5+ [251-500]

Chaffin, Tom - *Fatal Glory*
Choice - v34 - Ap '97 - p1400 [51-250]

Chai, Alan - *Cyberstocks: An Investor's Guide to Internet Companies*
r ARBA - v28 - '97 - p91 [51-250]
BL - v93 - D 15 '96 - p698 [51-250]
r LJ - v122 - F 15 '97 - p144 [51-250]

Chai, Arlene J - *Eating Fire and Drinking Water*
Aust Bk R - O '96 - p50 [501+]
The Last Time I Saw Mother
Bloom Rev - v17 - Ja '97 - p14 [51-250]
NYTBR - v101 - N 10 '96 - p56 [51-250]
Rapport - v19 - 6 '96 - p25 [51-250]

Chaiet, Donna - *Staying Safe on Dates*
y Emerg Lib - v24 - S '96 - p26 [1-50]

Chaiken, Irwin M - *Molecular Diversity and Combinatorial Chemistry*
SciTech - v21 - Mr '97 - p68 [51-250]

Chaikin, Linda - *Golden Palaces*
LJ - v121 - N 1 '96 - p52 [51-250]

Chaikin, P M - *Principles of Condensed Matter Physics*
Sci - v273 - S 6 '96 - p1348 [501+]

Chainey, Graham - *A Literary History of Cambridge. Rev. Ed.*
CR - v269 - O '96 - p224 [51-250]

Chaison, Gary N - *Union Mergers in Hard Times*
Choice - v34 - My '97 - p1543 [51-250]

Chaitin-Chatelin, Francoise - *Lectures on Finite Precision Computations*
Choice - v34 - Mr '97 - p1196+ [51-250]

Chakalov, G - *Elsevier's Dictionary of Science and Technology, English-Russian*
r SciTech - v21 - Mr '97 - p2 [51-250]

Chakravarthy, Srinivas R - *Matrix-Analytic Methods in Stochastic Models*
SciTech - v20 - D '96 - p16 [51-250]

Chakravorty, Swapan - *Society and Politics in the Plays of Thomas Middleton*
TLS - Ag 30 '96 - p32 [251-500]

Chalassery, Joseph - *The Holy Spirit and Christian Initiation in the East Syrian Tradition*
Theol St - v57 - D '96 - p776 [251-500]

Chaleff, Ira - *The Courageous Followers*
NASSP-B - v81 - F '97 - p119 [251-500]
NASSP-B - v81 - F '97 - p119 [251-500]

Chalfonte, Jessica - *I Am Muslim*
c SLJ - v43 - F '97 - p88 [51-250]

Chalip, Laurence - *National Sports Policies*
Choice - v34 - Ja '97 - p836 [51-250]
R&R Bk N - v11 - N '96 - p23 [51-250]

Chalker, Jack L - *The Hot Wired Dodo*
LJ - v122 - F 15 '97 - p165 [51-250]

Challenger, Douglas F - *Durkheim through the Lens of Aristotle*
AJS - v102 - Jl '96 - p269+ [501+]
Ethics - v107 - O '96 - p193 [51-250]
SF - v75 - S '96 - p349+ [251-500]

Challoner, Jack - *Big and Small*
c HB Guide - v8 - Spr '97 - p109 [51-250]
c SB - v33 - Ja '97 - p16 [251-500]
c SLJ - v43 - F '97 - p88 [51-250]
Fast and Slow
c HB Guide - v8 - Spr '97 - p109 [51-250]

Floating and Sinking
  c HB Guide - v8 - Spr '97 - p109 [51-250]
  c SB - v33 - Ja '97 - p16 [251-500]
  c SLJ - v43 - F '97 - p88 [51-250]
Hot and Cold
  c HB Guide - v8 - Spr '97 - p109 [51-250]
  c SB - v33 - Ja '97 - p16 [251-500]
Light and Dark
  c HB Guide - v8 - Spr '97 - p109 [51-250]
Loud and Quiet
  c HB Guide - v8 - Spr '97 - p109 [51-250]
Push and Pull
  c HB Guide - v8 - Spr '97 - p109 [51-250]
The Visual Dictionary of Chemistry
  cr Ch BWatch - v6 - S '96 - p5+ [1-50]
  yr Emerg Lib - v23 - My '96 - p43 [1-50]
  yr HB Guide - v7 - Fall '96 - p331 [51-250]
  yr SB - v32 - Ag '96 - p173 [51-250]
  yr SLJ - v42 - O '96 - p154 [51-250]
  yr VOYA - v19 - F '97 - p364 [251-500]
Wet and Dry
  c HB Guide - v8 - Spr '97 - p109 [51-250]
  c SB - v33 - Ja '97 - p16 [251-500]
  c SLJ - v43 - F '97 - p88 [51-250]
Chalmers, David J - *The Conscious Mind*
  Choice - v34 - D '96 - p625 [51-250]
  NYRB - v44 - Mr 6 '97 - p43+ [501+]
  NYTBR - v101 - D 29 '96 - p22 [501+]
Chalmers, Kenneth - *Bela Bartok*
  M Ed J - v83 - N '96 - p54 [1-50]
  TLS - Jl 7 '96 - p19 [501+]
Chalmers, Malcolm - *Developing the UN Register of Conventional Arms*
  JPR - v33 - Ag '96 - p378+ [501+]
Taking Stock
  JPR - v33 - Ag '96 - p378+ [501+]
Chalmers, William - *No More Worthy*
  BIC - v25 - D '96 - p41 [51-250]
Chamberlain, Austen, Sir - *The Austen Chamberlain Diary Letters*
  Albion - v28 - Sum '96 - p350+ [501+]
Chamberlain, David - *The Creative Monochrome Image*
  LJ - v121 - S 15 '96 - p63 [51-250]
Chamberlain, Diane - *The Escape Artist*
  BL - v93 - Mr 1 '97 - p1109 [51-250]
  KR - v65 - Ja 15 '97 - p77 [251-500]
  LJ - v122 - Ja '97 - p144 [51-250]
  PW - v244 - Ja 20 '97 - p393 [51-250]
  Trib Bks - My 25 '97 - p11 [51-250]
Chamberlain, Geoffrey - *Lecture Notes on Obstetrics. 7th Ed.*
  SciTech - v21 - Mr '97 - p63 [1-50]
Chamberlain, Joseph W - *Physics of the Aurora and Airglow*
  SciTech - v20 - N '96 - p20 [51-250]
Chamberlain, Lesley - *Nietzsche in Turin*
  NS - v125 - D 6 '96 - p56 [501+]
  TLS - F 14 '97 - p31 [501+]
Chamberlain, Michael - *Knowledge and Social Practice in Medieval Damascus 1190-1350*
  AHR - v101 - O '96 - p1254+ [501+]
  JIH - v27 - Aut '96 - p370+ [251-500]
  Rel St Rev - v23 - Ja '97 - p11+ [501+]
Chamberlain, Neil W - *Intellectual Odyssey*
  JEL - v35 - Mr '97 - p240 [51-250]
Chamberlin, Ann - *The Sultan's Daughter*
  LJ - v122 - Ap 15 '97 - p116+ [51-250]
  PW - v244 - Mr 17 '97 - p77 [251-500]
Chambers, Aidan - *The Reading Environment*
  CCB-B - v50 - D '96 - p156 [51-250]
  New Ad - v9 - Fall '96 - p345+ [51-250]
Tell Me
  CCB-B - v50 - D '96 - p156 [51-250]
  New Ad - v9 - Fall '96 - p345+ [51-250]
Chambers, Catherine - *All Saints, All Souls, and Halloween*
  c TES - F 14 '97 - p16* [51-250]
Bark
  c Cur R - v35 - S '96 - p12 [51-250]
  c HB Guide - v7 - Fall '96 - p340 [51-250]
Grasses
  c Bks Keeps - Jl '96 - p22 [51-250]
  c Cur R - v35 - S '96 - p12 [51-250]
  c HB Guide - v7 - Fall '96 - p340 [51-250]
Nuts
  c Cur R - v35 - S '96 - p12 [51-250]
  c HB Guide - v7 - Fall '96 - p353 [51-250]
Shells
  c Cur R - v35 - S '96 - p12 [51-250]
  c HB Guide - v7 - Fall '96 - p334+ [51-250]

Sikh
  c HB Guide - v7 - Fall '96 - p308 [51-250]
Stones
  c Cur R - v35 - S '96 - p12 [51-250]
  c HB Guide - v7 - Fall '96 - p332 [1-50]
Wood
  c Cur R - v35 - S '96 - p12 [51-250]
  c HB Guide - v7 - Fall '96 - p340 [51-250]
Chambers, Douglas - *The Reinvention of the World*
  Choice - v34 - N '96 - p454 [51-250]
Stony Ground
  CF - v75 - N '96 - p39+ [501+]
Chambers, E K - *The Medieval Stage*
  LJ - v122 - F 15 '97 - p166 [51-250]
Chambers, Iain - *Migrancy, Culture, Identity*
  HER - v67 - Spr '97 - p157+ [251-500]
Chambers, John Whiteclay - *World War II, Film, and History*
  Choice - v34 - Ap '97 - p1346 [51-250]
Chambers, Julie - *Baby Bunny's Busy Day (Illus. by Carol Wood)*
  c HB Guide - v7 - Fall '96 - p237 [51-250]
Santa's Busy Christmas (Illus. by Delana Bettoli)
  c PW - v243 - S 30 '96 - p93 [1-50]
Chambers, Lance - *Practical Handbook of Genetic Algorithms. Vols. 1-2*
  SciTech - v20 - S '96 - p11 [51-250]
Chambers, Oswald - *In the Presence of His Majesty*
  Ch Today - v41 - Ap 7 '97 - p43 [51-250]
Studies in the Sermon on the Mount
  BL - v93 - O 1 '96 - p308 [1-50]
Chambers, Simone - *Reasonable Democracy*
  CPR - v16 - O '96 - p325+ [501+]
Chambers, Steven D - *Political Leaders and Military Figures of the Second World War*
  r Choice - v34 - D '96 - p587 [51-250]
  r R&R Bk N - v11 - N '96 - p10 [51-250]
Chambers, Veronica - *Mama's Girl*
  y BL - v93 - Ja '97 - p762 [1-50]
  y BL - v93 - Ap 1 '97 - p1286 [1-50]
  KR - v64 - My 1 '96 - p656 [251-500]
  NY - v72 - S 30 '96 - p87 [51-250]
  Trib Bks - My 18 '97 - p8 [1-50]
  Woman's J - F '97 - p16 [1-50]
Chambers 21st Century Dictionary
  r Obs - F 2 '97 - p15* [501+]
  r TES - S 20 '96 - p7* [501+]
Chambers Biographical Dictionary of Women
  r Obs - Ag 18 '96 - p16* [251-500]
Chambers Children's Illustrated Dictionary
  cr Bks Keeps - v100 - S '96 - p22+ [501+]
Chambers Children's Pocket Dictionary
  cr Sch Lib - v44 - N '96 - p161 [51-250]
Chambers First Dictionary
  cr Bks Keeps - v100 - S '96 - p22+ [501+]
Chambers Super-Mini Dictionary
  cr Bks Keeps - v100 - S '96 - p22+ [501+]
Chambliss, Daniel F - *Beyond Caring*
  SciTech - v20 - N '96 - p57 [51-250]
Chambliss, J J - *Philosophy of Education*
  r ARBA - v28 - '97 - p132+ [51-250]
  r BL - v93 - N 1 '96 - p539+ [251-500]
  r Choice - v34 - Ja '97 - p773+ [51-250]
  r R&R Bk N - v11 - D '96 - p52 [51-250]
Chamieh, Jebran - *Traditionalists, Militants and Liberals in Present Islam*
  MEJ - v50 - Aut '96 - p616+ [501+]
Chamizo, Jose Antonio - *El Cientifico De Sonrisa Contagiosa*
  y JAAL - v40 - S '96 - p77 [51-250]
Chamlee, Paula - *Natural Connections*
  Afterimage - v24 - Ja '97 - p23 [1-50]
Chamoiseau, Patrick - *Chemin D'Ecole*
  FR - v70 - D '96 - p344+ [251-500]
Creole Folktales
  CAY - v16 - Fall '95 - p3 [51-250]
School Days
  KR - v65 - F 1 '97 - p185 [251-500]
  LJ - v122 - My 1 '97 - p103 [51-250]
  NYTBR - v102 - Mr 30 '97 - p14 [51-250]
  PW - v244 - F 10 '97 - p75+ [51-250]

Texaco
  BL - v93 - Ja '97 - p817 [51-250]
  KR - v65 - Ja 1 '97 - p6 [251-500]
  New R - v216 - Ap 28 '97 - p45+ [501+]
  NY - v73 - Mr 24 '97 - p82+ [501+]
  NYTBR - v102 - Mr 30 '97 - p13+ [501+]
  NYTLa - v146 - Mr 31 '97 - pC15 [501+]
  Obs - Mr 9 '97 - p16* [501+]
  PW - v243 - D 9 '96 - p61 [251-500]
  TLS - Mr 21 '97 - p22 [501+]
  Trib Bks - Mr 23 '97 - p4+ [501+]
Chamorro, Violeta - *Dreams of the Heart*
  BL - v92 - Ag '96 - p1850 [251-500]
  BW - v26 - S 8 '96 - p9 [501+]
  LATBR - O 6 '96 - p8+ [501+]
  Nat - v263 - S 30 '96 - p27+ [501+]
  New R - v215 - O 21 '96 - p36+ [501+]
  NYTBR - v101 - S 15 '96 - p19 [501+]
  WSJ-MW - v77 - S 11 '96 - pA16 [501+]
Champe, Gertrud Graubart - *To Set before the King*
  TranslRevS - v2 - D '96 - p17 [51-250]
Champeau, Serge - *Ontologie Et Poesie*
  Choice - v34 - D '96 - p565 [1-50]
Champion, David - *The Mountain Massacres*
  Arm Det - v29 - Fall '96 - p467 [51-250]
Nobody Roots for Goliath
  Arm Det - v29 - Fall '96 - p467 [51-250]
Champion, J A I - *London's Dreaded Visitation*
  Albion - v28 - Fall '96 - p485+ [501+]
Champion, Joyce - *Emily and Alice (Illus. by Sucie Stevenson)*
  c PW - v243 - S 23 '96 - p78 [51-250]
Champion, Malcolm C - *Evolving Concepts in Gastrointestinal Motility*
  SciTech - v20 - D '96 - p48 [1-50]
Champion, Sarah - *Disco Biscuits*
  NS - v126 - F 7 '97 - p48 [501+]
  Obs - F 16 '97 - p18* [51-250]
Champlin, Tim - *The Survivor*
  BL - v93 - N 15 '96 - p569 [51-250]
  Roundup M - v4 - D '96 - p24+ [51-250]
Chan, Anthony B - *Li-Ka-Shing: The Biography*
  Quill & Q - v62 - Jl '96 - p51 [251-500]
Chan, Charis - *China. 3rd Ed.*
  r BL - v93 - S 15 '96 - p212 [1-50]
Chan, Daniel W - *Immunoassay Automation: An Updated Guide to Systems*
  SciTech - v20 - N '96 - p33 [51-250]
Chan, Gillian - *Glory Days and Other Stories*
  y Ch Bk News - v20 - Win '97 - p27 [51-250]
  y Quill & Q - v62 - O '96 - p51 [251-500]
Chan, James L - *Research in Governmental and Nonprofit Accounting. Vol. 9*
  JEL - v35 - Mr '97 - p226+ [51-250]
Chan, Janis Fisher - *Inventing Ourselves Again*
  BWatch - v17 - N '96 - p6 [51-250]
Chan, Kam Wing - *Cities with Invisible Walls*
  Ch Rev Int - v3 - Fall '96 - p375+ [501+]
Chan, Lois Mai - *Dewey Decimal Classification. 2nd Ed., Rev. for DDC21*
  r LAR - v98 - N '96 - p593 [251-500]
Library of Congress Subject Headings. 3rd Ed.
  LQ - v67 - Ap '97 - p201+ [501+]
Chan, Terrence - *UNIX System Programming Using C++*
  SciTech - v20 - D '96 - p10 [51-250]
Chan, Wen S - *ASME Aerospace and Materials Divisions*
  SciTech - v21 - Mr '97 - p94 [51-250]
Chance, Jane - *Medieval Mythography*
  Specu - v72 - Ja '97 - p125+ [501+]
Chand, Meira - *A Choice of Evils*
  KR - v64 - S 1 '96 - p1253+ [251-500]
  PW - v243 - S 30 '96 - p62 [51-250]
Chandavarkar, Rajnarayan - *The Origins of Industrial Capitalism in India*
  EHR - v112 - F '97 - p257+ [251-500]
  JIH - v27 - Win '97 - p573+ [501+]
Chandhuri, Brahma - *Victorian Database on CD-ROM 1970-1995. Electronic Media Version*
  r Choice - v34 - Ap '97 - p1321 [251-500]
Chandler, Adam - *Autumn Dancing*
  Quill & Q - v62 - Jl '96 - p42 [501+]
Chandler, Charlotte - *I, Fellini*
  Obs - Ap 13 '97 - p18* [51-250]
Chandler, David - *The Oxford Illustrated History of the British Army*
  HT - v46 - S '96 - p54+ [501+]
Chandler, Gary - *Alternative Energy Sources*
  c Ch BWatch - v6 - D '96 - p6 [1-50]
  c SLJ - v43 - Ja '97 - p120 [51-250]

Guardians of Wildlife
 c Ch BWatch - v6 - D '96 - p6 [1-50]
 y VOYA - v19 - F '97 - p344 [251-500]
Kids Who Make a Difference
 c BL - v93 - D 1 '96 - p655 [51-250]
 c Ch BWatch - v6 - D '96 - p6 [1-50]
 y VOYA - v19 - F '97 - p344 [251-500]
Natural Foods and Products
 c Ch BWatch - v6 - D '96 - p6 [1-50]
 c SLJ - v43 - Ja '97 - p120 [51-250]
Protecting Our Air, Land, and Water
 c Ch BWatch - v6 - D '96 - p6 [1-50]
 c SLJ - v43 - Ja '97 - p120 [51-250]
 y VOYA - v19 - F '97 - p344 [251-500]
Recycling
 c BL - v93 - D 1 '96 - p655 [51-250]
 c Ch BWatch - v6 - D '96 - p6 [1-50]
Chandler, Harry - *Heat Treater's Guide*
    SciTech - v20 - N '96 - p78 [51-250]
Chandler, Lynette S - *Children with Prenatal Drug Exposure*
    SciTech - v20 - D '96 - p53 [51-250]
Chandler, Raymond - *The Big Sleep (Gould). Audio Version*
    Books - v9 - S '95 - p27 [1-50]
The Little Sister
    KR - v65 - Mr 15 '97 - p421+ [51-250]
    WSJ-MW - v78 - D 9 '96 - pA12 [51-250]
Raymond Chandler Speaking
    LJ - v122 - Ap 15 '97 - p125 [51-250]
Chandler, Steve - *100 Ways to Motivate Yourself (Chandler). Audio Version*
    BWatch - v18 - Mr '97 - p6 [51-250]
Chandmal, Asit - *One Thousand Suns*
    R&R Bk N - v12 - F '97 - p3 [51-250]
Chandra, Anjani - *Health Aspects of Pregnancy and Childbirth*
    J Gov Info - v23 - S '96 - p548 [51-250]
Chandra, Deborah - *Rich Lizard and Other Poems*
 c Ch BWatch - v6 - Jl '96 - p6 [1-50]
Chandra, Vikram - *Love and Longing in Bombay*
    BL - v93 - Mr 1 '97 - p1109 [51-250]
    BW - v27 - Ap 6 '97 - p9 [501+]
    KR - v65 - Ja 1 '97 - p7 [251-500]
    LATBR - Mr 16 '97 - p8 [501+]
    LJ - v122 - Ap 1 '97 - p132 [51-250]
    Obs - Ap 6 '97 - p16* [251-500]
    PW - v244 - Ja 20 '97 - p392 [51-250]
    Spec - v278 - Mr 22 '97 - p41 [501+]
    TLS - Mr 28 '97 - p21 [501+]
    Trib Bks - My 25 '97 - p1+ [501+]
    VLS - Spr '97 - p26 [501+]
Red Earth and Pouring Rain
    Comw - v123 - D 6 '96 - p20+ [51-250]
    PW - v244 - F 3 '97 - p100+ [1-50]
    Trib Bks - Mr 2 '97 - p8 [1-50]
    VLS - Spr '97 - p26 [501+]
Chandrasekhar, Subrahmanyan - *Newton's Principia for the Common Reader*
    Isis - v87 - D '96 - p701+ [501+]
    Phys Today - v49 - N '96 - p81+ [501+]
Chandrupatla, Tirupathi R - *Introduction to Finite Elements in Engineering. 2nd Ed.*
    SciTech - v20 - D '96 - p60 [51-250]
Chaney, Otto Preston - *Zhukov. Rev. Ed.*
    R&R Bk N - v11 - F '97 - p10 [51-250]
Chang, Chan Sup - *The Korean Management System*
    JTWS - v13 - Fall '96 - p213+ [501+]
Chang, Cindy - *What's for Lunch? (Illus. by Jill Dubin)*
 c HB Guide - v7 - Fall '96 - p237 [1-50]
Where's the Mouse? (Illus. by Jill Dubin)
 c HB Guide - v7 - Fall '96 - p237 [1-50]
Chang, Eugene B - *Gastrointestinal, Hepatobiliary, and Nutritional Physiology*
    SciTech - v20 - S '96 - p22 [1-50]
Chang, Ha-Joon - *The Role of the State in Economic Change*
    APSR - v91 - Mr '97 - p208+ [501+]
    JEL - v34 - S '96 - p1489 [51-250]
Chang, Ina - *A Separate Battle*
 y Kliatt - v31 - Ja '97 - p26 [251-500]
Chang, Iris - *Thread of the Silkworm*
    FEER - v159 - S 5 '96 - p47 [501+]
    LATBR - Mr 24 '96 - p10 [51-250]
Chang, J C I - *ASME Aerospace Division*
    SciTech - v21 - Mr '97 - p94 [51-250]
Chang, Jung - *Wild Swans*
    SFR - v21 - Jl '96 - p48 [1-50]
    Spec - v277 - N 16 '96 - p44 [1-50]
Chang, Louis W - *Toxicology of Metals*
    SciTech - v20 - D '96 - p40 [51-250]

Chang, Lynn - *Costumes for Your Cat*
    LATBR - Mr 17 '96 - p10 [51-250]
Chang, Pang-Mei Natasha - *Bound Feet and Western Dress*
    Atl - v278 - O '96 - p122 [51-250]
    BW - v26 - D 22 '96 - p6 [501+]
    NYTLa - v146 - O 14 '96 - pC18 [501+]
Chang, Po-Shu - *Marxism and Human Sociobiology*
    Ch Rev Int - v4 - Spr '97 - p296+ [501+]
Chang, Raymond - *Essential Chemistry*
    J Chem Ed - v73 - O '96 - pA240+ [251-500]
Chang, Shan-Chieh - *Computation of Special Functions*
    SciTech - v20 - D '96 - p18 [51-250]
Changing Childhoods
 c JB - v60 - D '96 - p247+ [51-250]
    Sch Lib - v45 - F '97 - p53 [51-250]
Changnon, Stanley A - *The Great Flood of 1993*
    Choice - v34 - S '96 - p158 [51-250]
Chanoff, David - *Vietnam: A Portrait of Its People at War*
    LJ - v121 - S 15 '96 - p78 [51-250]
    PW - v243 - S 2 '96 - p106 [51-250]
Chansky, Art - *The Dean's List*
    BL - v92 - Ag '96 - p1850 [251-500]
Chantal, Jeanne-Francoise De, Saint - *Sainte Jeanne De Chantal: Correspondance. Vols. 1-5*
    CH - v66 - Mr '97 - p124+ [501+]
Chanter, Barrie - *Building Maintenance Management*
    SciTech - v20 - S '96 - p52 [51-250]
Chao - *Fate of a Grasshopper*
    Aust Bk R - F '97 - p46+ [501+]
Chao, Patricia - *Monkey King*
    BL - v93 - Ja '97 - p817 [51-250]
    BW - v27 - F 23 '97 - p8 [501+]
    KR - v64 - N 15 '96 - p1618 [251-500]
    LATBR - Mr 30 '97 - p10 [501+]
    LJ - v121 - D '96 - p142 [51-250]
    NYTBR - v102 - Mr 16 '97 - p21 [51-250]
    PW - v243 - N 18 '96 - p62 [51-250]
    Time - v149 - My 5 '97 - p101+ [501+]
    Trib Bks - Mr 23 '97 - p3 [501+]
Chao, Sheng - *Paper Boat*
    Aust Bk R - Je '96 - p54 [501+]
Chaon, Dan - *Fitting Ends and Other Stories*
    PS - v70 - Fall '96 - p182+ [501+]
Chapanis, Alphonse - *Human Factors in Systems Engineering*
    Choice - v34 - N '96 - p488 [51-250]
Chapkis, Wendy - *Live Sex Acts*
    PW - v243 - D 9 '96 - p57 [51-250]
Chaplais, Pierre - *Piers Gaveston: Edward II's Adoptive Brother*
    EHR - v111 - N '96 - p1250+ [501+]
Chaplin, Patrice - *Hidden Star*
    KR - v64 - D 15 '96 - p1776+ [251-500]
    PW - v243 - N '96 - p48 [51-250]
Chapman, Allan - *Astronomical Instruments and Their Users*
    SciTech - v20 - D '96 - p20 [51-250]
Chapman, G P - *Water and the Quest for Sustainable Development in the Ganges Valley*
    GJ - v162 - Jl '96 - p224 [51-250]
Chapman, H Perry - *Jan Steen, Painter and Storyteller*
    BM - v138 - D '96 - p844+ [51-250]
    Choice - v34 - O '96 - p266 [51-250]
    LJ - v121 - S 15 '96 - p63 [51-250]
    NYRB - v44 - Ja 9 '97 - p8+ [501+]
    TLS - Ja 24 '97 - p20 [501+]
Chapman, Jean - *Favourite Live Thing*
 c Aust Bk R - S '96 - p60+ [501+]
 c Magpies - v11 - S '96 - p31+ [51-250]
Chapman, John R - *Protein and Peptide Analysis by Mass Spectrometry*
    SciTech - v20 - N '96 - p33 [51-250]
Chapman, K - *Extracellular Regulators of Differentiation and Development*
    SciTech - v20 - N '96 - p27 [51-250]
Chapman, Mark L - *Christianity on Trial*
    Bl S - v26 - Fall '96 - p101 [51-250]
    Bl S - v26 - Sum '96 - p64 [1-50]
Chapman, Michael - *Southern African Literatures*
    Choice - v34 - O '96 - p273 [51-250]
Chapman, Paul H - *Discovering Columbus*
    GJ - v162 - Jl '96 - p238 [51-250]
Chapman, Raymond - *Forms of Speech in Victorian Fiction*
    VS - v39 - Spr '96 - p410+ [501+]
Chapman, Robert L - *Roget's International Thesaurus*
    Obs - D 29 '96 - p27 [501+]
Chapman, Sally - *Hardwired*
    KR - v65 - Mr 15 '97 - p419 [51-250]
    PW - v244 - Mr 17 '97 - p79 [51-250]

Chapman, Stanley - *Merchant Enterprise in Britain*
    JMH - v68 - S '96 - p689+ [501+]
Chapman, Tom - *Growing Old and Needing Care*
    R&R Bk N - v11 - D '96 - p43 [51-250]
Chapman, Victoria L - *Latin American History on File*
 yr SLJ - v42 - N '96 - p136 [51-250]
Chappell, David - *Contractual Correspondence for Architects and Project Managers. 3rd Ed.*
 r SciTech - v20 - N '96 - p3 [51-250]
Report Writing for Architects and Project Managers. 3rd Ed.
    SciTech - v20 - D '96 - p3 [1-50]
Understanding ActiveX and OLE
    SciTech - v20 - D '96 - p8 [51-250]
Chappell, Fred - *Farewell, I'm Bound to Leave You*
 y BL - v93 - Ja '97 - p763 [1-50]
 y BL - v93 - S 1 '96 - p60 [1-50]
    BW - v26 - O 13 '96 - p5 [501+]
    Comw - v123 - D 6 '96 - p24 [51-250]
    Ent W - S 6 '96 - p70 [51-250]
    LATBR - N 10 '96 - p14 [51-250]
    NYTBR - v101 - D 15 '96 - p18 [501+]
    W&I - v12 - Ja '97 - p303+ [501+]
Chappell, Helen - *Slow Dancing with the Angel of Death*
    Arm Det - v29 - Fall '96 - p485 [251-500]
Chappell, John D - *Before the Bomb*
    LJ - v121 - D '96 - p114 [51-250]
Chappell, T D J - *Aristotle and Augustine on Freedom*
    Rel St - v33 - Mr '97 - p129+ [501+]
Chappell, Vere - *The Cambridge Companion to Locke*
    Phil R - v105 - Ja '96 - p120+ [501+]
Chapple, Christopher Key - *Ecological Prospects*
    JAAR - v64 - Fall '96 - p656+ [501+]
Non-Violence to Animals, Earth, and Self in Asian Traditions
    Rel St Rev - v23 - Ap '97 - p113+ [501+]
Chapple, Richard L - *Social and Political Change in Literature and Film*
    J Pop F&TV - v24 - Spr '96 - p44+ [501+]
Chapsal, Madeleine - *Une Femme Heureuse*
    FR - v70 - O '96 - p140+ [501+]
Le Foulard Bleu
    WLT - v71 - Win '97 - p102 [251-500]
Une Soudaine Solitude
    WLT - v70 - Sum '96 - p649 [251-500]
Chaput, Donald - *Virgil Earp: Western Peace Officer*
    Roundup M - v4 - F '97 - p23 [51-250]
Chaqueri, Cosroe - *The Soviet Socialist Republic of Iran 1920-1921*
    AHR - v102 - F '97 - p147+ [501+]
Characters in 19th-Century Literature
 r RQ - v36 - Win '96 - p213+ [51-250]
Characters in 20th-Century Literature. Bks. 1-2
 r RQ - v36 - Win '96 - p207+ [51-250]
Charbonneau, Eileen - *Honor to the Hills*
 y HB Guide - v7 - Fall '96 - p301 [51-250]
Waltzing in Ragtime
    BW - v26 - O 6 '96 - p8 [251-500]
Charbonnet, Gabrielle - *Balancing Act*
 y Ch BWatch - v6 - S '96 - p3 [1-50]
The Bully Coach
 y Ch BWatch - v6 - S '96 - p3 [1-50]
Competition Fever
 c BL - v93 - S 1 '96 - p124+ [51-250]
 y Ch BWatch - v6 - S '96 - p3 [1-50]
Split Decision
 y Ch BWatch - v6 - S '96 - p3 [1-50]
Chard, Chloe - *Transports: Travel, Pleasure and Imaginative Geography 1600-1830*
    TLS - N 22 '96 - p18+ [501+]
Chardiet, Bernice - *Book of Colors*
 c Ch BWatch - v6 - Jl '96 - p4 [1-50]
Chardin, Jean-Jacques - *Ernest Dowson 1867-1900 Et La Crise Fin De Siecle Anglaise*
    ELT - v39 - 3 '96 - p369+ [501+]
Chariton - *Le Roman De Chaireas Et Callirhoe*
    AJP - v117 - Fall '96 - p473+ [501+]
Charkham, Jonathan - *Keeping Good Company*
    JIB - v27 - 4 '96 - p807+ [501+]
Charles, Donald - *Chancay and the Secret of Fire*
 c SS - v88 - Ja '97 - p29+ [501+]
Charles, Faustin - *A Caribbean Counting Book (Illus. by Roberta Arenson)*
 c HB Guide - v7 - Fall '96 - p325 [51-250]
Charles, Jill - *Directory of Theatre Training Programs. 5th Ed.*
 r TCI - v30 - O '96 - p59 [1-50]
Charles, Kate - *A Dead Man out of Mind*
    LJ - v121 - O 15 '96 - p112 [51-250]

Evil Angels among Them
    BL - v93 - O 1 '96 - p324 [51-250]
    NYTBR - v101 - N 24 '96 - p26 [51-250]
Charles, N N - *What Am I? (Illus. by Leo Dillon)*
    c Emerg Lib - v23 - My '96 - p45 [51-250]
Charles, Philip A - *Exploring the X-Ray Universe*
    Am Sci - v85 - Ja '97 - p75+ [501+]
    Choice - v34 - S '96 - p150 [51-250]
Charles, Veronica Martenova - *Necklace of Stars (Illus.
by Veronica Martenova Charles)*
    c Quill & Q - v62 - Ag '96 - p42+ [251-500]
Charles English: Macbeth
    TES - D 6 '96 - p9* [251-500]
**The Charleston Report: Business Insights into the
Library Market**
    p LJ - v122 - My 1 '97 - p146 [51-250]
Charlesworth, Andrew - *An Atlas of Industrial Protest in
Britain 1750-1990*
    r ARBA - v28 - '97 - p75 [251-500]
    r R&R Bk N - v11 - N '96 - p21 [51-250]
Charlesworth, James H - *The Beloved Disciple*
    Theol St - v57 - Je '96 - p377+ [251-500]
Jesus and the Dead Sea Scrolls
    Rel Ed - v91 - Fall '96 - p602 [1-50]
Jesus' Jewishness
    Rel Ed - v91 - Fall '96 - p602 [1-50]
    Rel St Rev - v23 - Ap '97 - p177 [51-250]
Jesus within Judaism
    Rel Ed - v91 - Fall '96 - p601+ [1-50]
*The Messiah: Developments in Earliest Judaism and
Christianity*
    Rel Ed - v91 - Fall '96 - p602 [1-50]
Overcoming Fear between Christians and Jews
    Rel Ed - v91 - Fall '96 - p602 [1-50]
The Pseudepigrapha and Early Biblical Interpretation
    Rel St Rev - v22 - O '96 - p352 [51-250]
Charlesworth, Michael - *J.B. Oldham of Oldham's Hall
1882-1962*
    TLS - Ag 2 '96 - p32 [251-500]
Charlesworth, Sue - *Microsoft Office 95 Unleashed*
    BL - v92 - Ag '96 - p1868 [501+]
Charlet, David Alan - *Atlas of Nevada Conifers*
    r SciTech - v21 - Mr '97 - p37 [51-250]
Charlip, Remy - *Hooray for Me! (Illus. by Vera B
Williams)*
    c BL - v93 - N 15 '96 - p589 [51-250]
    c HB Guide - v8 - Spr '97 - p23 [51-250]
    c PW - v243 - O 14 '96 - p85 [51-250]
Charlton, Nancy Lee - *Derek's Dog Days (Illus. by Chris
L Demarest)*
    c HB Guide - v7 - Fall '96 - p251 [1-50]
Charlton, Randolph S - *Treating Sexual Disorders*
    SciTech - v21 - Mr '97 - p55 [51-250]
Charman, Andrew - *I Wonder Why the Dodo Is Dead and
Other Questions about Extinct and Endangered Animals*
    c HB Guide - v8 - Spr '97 - p116 [51-250]
    c JB - v60 - O '96 - p191 [51-250]
    c Sch Lib - v44 - N '96 - p161+ [51-250]
**Charming Small Hotel Guide: Britain including Ireland.
6th. Ed.**
    r BL - v93 - S 15 '96 - p210 [1-50]
Charmley, John - *Churchill's Grand Alliance*
    NYTBR - v101 - D 29 '96 - p20 [51-250]
A History of Conservative Politics 1900-1996
    Choice - v34 - Mr '97 - p1218 [51-250]
    HT - v46 - O '96 - p58 [1-50]
    Spec - v277 - S 21 '96 - p46+ [501+]
    TLS - S 20 '96 - p9+ [501+]
Charner, Kathy - *The Giant Encyclopedia of Circle Time
and Group Activities for Children 3 to 6*
    r Ch BWatch - v6 - S '96 - p8 [1-50]
Charnitzky, Jurgen - *Die Schulpolitik Des Faschistischen
Regimes In Italien 1922-1943*
    EHR - v112 - F '97 - p260+ [501+]
Charnon-Deutsch, Lou - *An Annotated Bibliography of
Hispanic Feminist Criticism*
    r NWSA Jnl - v9 - Spr '97 - p126+ [501+]
Culture and Gender in Nineteenth-Century Spain
    Choice - v34 - Ja '97 - p801+ [51-250]
Charnwood, Godfrey Rathbone Benson, Baron -
Abraham Lincoln
    LJ - v122 - F 15 '97 - p166 [51-250]
Charpak, Georges - *Feux Follets Et Champignons
Nucleaires*
    Nature - v386 - Mr 27 '97 - p348+ [501+]
Charriere, Henri - *Papillon (Guidall). Audio Version*
    y Kliatt - v31 - Mr '97 - p49 [51-250]
Charskaia, Lidiia - *Gazavat. Tsarskii Gnev*
    BL - v93 - O 1 '96 - p327 [1-50]

Charteris, Richard - *Giovanni Gabrieli ca.1555-1612*
    r ARBA - v28 - '97 - p473 [51-250]
    r R&R Bk N - v11 - D '96 - p56 [51-250]
**Charters and Custumals of the Abbey of Holy Trinity,
Caen. Pt. 2**
    EHR - v112 - F '97 - p161 [251-500]
Chartier, Roger - *Forms and Meanings*
    ABR - v17 - Ag '96 - p11+ [501+]
    CS - v26 - Mr '97 - p241+ [501+]
    NYRB - v43 - Je 6 '96 - p52+ [501+]
Chartrand, Rene - *Napoleonic Wars: Napoleon's Army*
    HT - v46 - O '96 - p57 [1-50]
Charvet, John - *The Idea of an Ethical Community*
    APSR - v91 - Mr '97 - p167+ [501+]
    Ethics - v107 - O '96 - p177 [251-500]
    Theol St - v57 - D '96 - p770+ [501+]
Chary, M Srinivas - *The Eagle and the Peacock*
    JTWS - v13 - Fall '96 - p225+ [501+]
    Pac A - v69 - Fall '96 - p434+ [501+]
    PHR - v65 - Fall '96 - p508+ [251-500]
Charykova, Svitlana - *Smachnoho! Starovynni Ta
Suchasni Retsepty Strav*
    BL - v93 - N 15 '96 - p577 [1-50]
Charyn, Jerome - *El Bronx*
    BL - v93 - D 15 '96 - p710 [51-250]
    KR - v65 - Ja 1 '97 - p21 [51-250]
    LJ - v122 - F 1 '97 - p111 [1-50]
    PW - v243 - D 2 '96 - p43 [51-250]
    Trib Bks - Mr 2 '97 - p5 [51-250]
*Movieland: Hollywood and the Great American Dream
Culture*
    BW - v26 - N 3 '96 - p12 [51-250]
Chase, Agnes - *First Book of Grasses*
    New Sci - v152 - D 7 '96 - p46 [1-50]
Chase, Christopher H - *Developmental Dyslexia*
    SciTech - v20 - D '96 - p53 [51-250]
Chase, Edith Newlin - *Secret Dawn (Illus. by Yolaine
Lefebvre)*
    c SLJ - v42 - N '96 - p79 [51-250]
Chase, Malcolm - *Living and Learning*
    R&R Bk N - v11 - N '96 - p11 [51-250]
Chase, Susan E - *Ambiguous Empowerment*
    ES - v27 - Sum '96 - p134+ [501+]
    TCR - v97 - Sum '96 - p656+ [501+]
Chase, Warren - *General Statistics. 3rd Ed.*
    SciTech - v20 - N '96 - p14 [51-250]
Chasemore, Richard - *Tanks (Illus. by Richard
Chasemore)*
    c Ch BWatch - v6 - S '96 - p5 [1-50]
    c Par Ch - v20 - N '96 - p8 [51-250]
    c SLJ - v43 - Mr '97 - p198 [51-250]
Chase's 1997 Calendar of Events
    r ARBA - v28 - '97 - p4+ [251-500]
    r BL - v93 - D 15 '96 - p743 [1-50]
Chase's Sports Calendar of Events 1997
    r ARBA - v28 - '97 - p291 [51-250]
Chasin, Marshall - *Musicians and the Prevention of
Hearing Loss*
    SciTech - v20 - S '96 - p40 [51-250]
Chasteen, John Charles - *Heroes on Horseback*
    AHR - v102 - F '97 - p244+ [251-500]
    HAHR - v77 - My '97 - p351+ [501+]
Chastel, Andre - *French Art: The Ancient Regime
1620-1775*
    CSM - v88 - N 21 '96 - pB2+ [51-250]
    LATBR - D 8 '96 - p14 [1-50]
    LJ - v122 - F 15 '97 - p130 [51-250]
Chater, Gordon - *The Almost Late Gordon Chater*
    Aust Bk R - Je '96 - p33+ [51-250]
Chatfield, June - *Reptiles (Illus. by James Field)*
    c HB Guide - v7 - Fall '96 - p342 [1-50]
Chatfield, Michael - *The History of Accounting*
    AR - v71 - O '96 - p591+ [501+]
    r ARBA - v28 - '97 - p89 [51-250]
    r Choice - v34 - O '96 - p253 [51-250]
    r RQ - v36 - Win '96 - p296+ [251-500]
Chatgilialoglu, Chryssostomos - *Chemical Synthesis*
    SciTech - v20 - N '96 - p22 [51-250]
Chatham, Anne Bassett Stanley - *Tidewater Families of
the New World and Their Westward Migrations*
    NGSQ - v85 - Mr '97 - p64+ [501+]
Chatham, John C - *The Heart in Diabetes*
    SciTech - v20 - D '96 - p47 [51-250]
Chats Peles (Group of Artists) - *Long Live Music! (Illus.
by Chats Peles (Group of Artists))*
    c CBRS - v25 - Win '97 - p68 [51-250]
    c HB Guide - v8 - Spr '97 - p140 [51-250]
    c KR - v64 - S 15 '96 - p1396+ [51-250]
    c PW - v243 - O 14 '96 - p82 [51-250]
    c SLJ - v42 - D '96 - p133+ [51-250]

Chatterjee, Kalyan - *International Joint Ventures*
    JEL - v34 - S '96 - p1431 [51-250]
Chatterjee, Pranab - *Approaches to the Welfare State*
    Readings - v11 - D '96 - p4+ [501+]
Chatterjee, Pratap - *The Earth Brokers*
    CS - v25 - S '96 - p650+ [501+]
Chatterji, Joya - *Bengal Divided*
    JIH - v27 - Win '97 - p574+ [501+]
Chatterji, Manas - *The Economics of International
Security*
    Econ J - v106 - N '96 - p1844+ [51-250]
Chatterton, Lynne - *Sustainable Dryland Farming*
    Choice - v34 - F '97 - p989 [51-250]
    JEL - v35 - Mr '97 - p295 [51-250]
Chattopadhyay, Arun K - *Surfactants in Solution*
    SciTech - v20 - D '96 - p83 [51-250]
Chattopadhyaya, Brajadulal - *The Making of Early
Medieval India*
    JIH - v27 - Aut '96 - p372+ [251-500]
Chatty, Dawn - *Mobile Pastoralists*
    Choice - v34 - O '96 - p322 [51-250]
    MEJ - v51 - Win '97 - p130+ [501+]
Chatwin, Bruce - *Anatomy of Restlessness*
    Atl - v278 - S '96 - p112 [51-250]
    BL - v92 - Ag '96 - p1874 [51-250]
    BW - v26 - O 27 '96 - p13 [51-250]
    LATBR - Ag 18 '96 - p3+ [501+]
    NYTBR - v101 - S 1 '96 - p17 [51-250]
    TLS - F 14 '97 - p13 [501+]
    VV - v41 - D 3 '96 - p58+ [501+]
In Patagonia
    Critiq - v37 - Sum '96 - p301+ [501+]
Photographs and Notebooks
    NS - v126 - Mr 7 '97 - p44+ [501+]
    Spec - v278 - Ja 25 '97 - p38 [501+]
Chatwin, C R - *Frequency Domain Filtering Strategies for
Hybrid Optical Information Processing*
    SciTech - v20 - S '96 - p51 [51-250]
Chau, Wai-Shing - *The Letter and the Spirit*
    Rel St Rev - v23 - Ja '97 - p82 [51-250]
Chaucer, Geoffrey - *Franklin's Tale*
    MP - v94 - N '96 - p141+ [501+]
The General Prologue. Vol. 2, Pts. A-B
    Specu - v72 - Ja '97 - p127+ [501+]
The House of Fame
    RES - v47 - N '96 - p562+ [501+]
Troilus and Criseyde
    MP - v94 - F '97 - p291+ [501+]
Chaucer Yearbook. Vol. 2
    MLR - v91 - O '96 - p961+ [501+]
Chauncey, George - *Gay New York*
    Am Q - v48 - S '96 - p500+ [501+]
    Historian - v59 - Win '97 - p404 [51-250]
    J Soc H - v30 - Win '96 - p497+ [501+]
Chausse, Sylvie - *The Egg and I (Illus. by Francois
Crozat)*
    c CBRS - v25 - F '97 - p73+ [51-250]
    c KR - v64 - D 1 '96 - p1734 [51-250]
    c SLJ - v43 - F '97 - p74 [51-250]
Chauvet, Jean-Marie - *Dawn of Art*
    NYRB - v43 - N 14 '96 - p8+ [501+]
Chauvet, Louis-Marie - *Symbol and Sacrament*
    Theol St - v57 - S '96 - p550+ [501+]
Chauvire, Christiane - *Peirce Et La Signification*
    Dialogue - v36 - Win '97 - p200+ [501+]
Chavance, Bernard - *The Transformation of Communist
Systems*
    Econ J - v106 - S '96 - p1426+ [501+]
    Slav R - v55 - Sum '96 - p447 [251-500]
Chaves, Jonathan - *Singing of the Source*
    TranslRevS - v1 - My '95 - p15 [51-250]
Chavez Carbajal, Guadalupe - *Propietarios Y Esclavos
Negros En Valladolid De Michoacan 1600-1650*
    HAHR - v77 - My '97 - p311+ [501+]
Chavez-Vasquez, Gloria - *Akum: The Magic of Dreams*
    BWatch - v17 - N '96 - p8 [51-250]
Chavis, Melody Ermachild - *Altars in the Street*
    y BL - v93 - Ap 1 '97 - p1270 [51-250]
    KR - v65 - F 1 '97 - p185 [251-500]
    PW - v244 - Ja 27 '97 - p85 [51-250]
Chavis, William Muse - *Design Lines*
    Bl S - v26 - Sum '96 - p64 [1-50]
Chawla, Navin - *La Madre Teresa*
    LJ - v122 - Ja '97 - p78 [51-250]
Mother Teresa: The Authorized Biography
    y BL - v93 - S 1 '96 - p36 [51-250]
    Parabola - v22 - F '97 - p120 [1-50]
Chayes, Abram - *The New Sovereignty*
    J Pol - v59 - F '97 - p310+ [501+]
Preventing Conflict in the Post-Communist World
    JEL - v34 - D '96 - p2028 [51-250]

Chazan, Robert - *In the Year 1096*
Choice - v34 - O '96 - p338 [51-250]
Chazan, Saralea E - *The Simultaneous Treatment of Parent and Child*
Readings - v11 - S '96 - p27 [51-250]
Cheah, Pheng - *Thinking through the Body of the Law*
R&R Bk N - v11 - D '96 - p50 [51-250]
Cheal, David J - *New Poverty*
Choice - v34 - F '97 - p1042 [51-250]
R&R Bk N - v11 - N '96 - p26 [51-250]
Cheape, Charles W - *Strictly Business*
AHR - v102 - F '97 - p206 [251-500]
JEH - v57 - Mr '97 - p247+ [501+]
Checa, Fernando - *Tiziano Y La Monarquia Hispanica*
BM - v138 - Ag '96 - p552 [251-500]
Six Ct J - v27 - Win '96 - p1164 [501+]
Checkoway, Julie - *Little Sister*
BL - v92 - Ag '96 - p1861 [51-250]
LATBR - N 17 '96 - p4 [501+]
Chedgzoy, Kate - *Voicing Women*
TLS - Ag 2 '96 - p32 [51-250]
Chedid, Andree - *Les Saisons De Passage*
BL - v93 - F 1 '97 - p930 [1-50]
FR - v70 - F '97 - p493+ [501+]
Cheek, Roland - *Learning to Talk Bear*
y BL - v93 - My 1 '97 - p1469 [51-250]
Cheers, Gordon - *Killer Plants and How to Grow Them* (*Illus. by Marjorie Crosby-Fairall*)
c Magpies - v11 - S '96 - p43 [51-250]
Cheesman, Tom - *The Shocking Ballad Picture Show*
Folkl - v107 - '96 - p124 [501+]
Chehak, Susan Taylor - *Smithereens*
y Kliatt - v30 - N '96 - p6 [51-250]
Chekhov, Anton - *Chekhov: A Life in Letters*
Slav R - v55 - Sum '96 - p512+ [501+]
Chekhov: Four Plays
LJ - v122 - Ap 15 '97 - p80 [51-250]
Chekhov, the Complete Plays
LJ - v122 - Ap 15 '97 - p80 [51-250]
PW - v244 - Mr 31 '97 - p68 [1-50]
Kashtanka (Illus. by Gennady Spirin)
c RT - v50 - S '96 - p52 [51-250]
c RT - v50 - O '96 - p133 [1-50]
Chekhov, Anton Pavlovich - *Dear Writer, Dear Actress*
Lon R Bks - v19 - F 20 '97 - p31+ [501+]
Spec - v277 - D 14 '96 - p62+ [251-500]
TLS - D 20 '96 - p36 [501+]
Chemical Intelligence
p J Chem Ed - v74 - Mr '97 - p345+ [501+]
The Chemical Intelligencer
p Nature - v383 - S 5 '96 - p41 [251-500]
Chemical Research Faculties
r ARBA - v28 - '97 - p628 [51-250]
r SciTech - v21 - Mr '97 - p28 [51-250]
Chemical Sciences Graduate School Finder 1995-1996
SciTech - v20 - N '96 - p20 [51-250]
Chemistry and Physics of Carbon. Vol. 25
SciTech - v21 - Mr '97 - p29 [51-250]
Chemistry Citation Index. Electronic Media Version
r ARBA - v28 - '97 - p631 [51-250]
Chen, Ching-Chih - *Planning Global Information Infrastructure*
LRTS - v40 - Jl '96 - p287+ [501+]
SL - v87 - Sum '96 - p235+ [251-500]
Chen, Constance M - *The Sex Side of Life*
Atl - v278 - O '96 - p116+ [501+]
New R - v215 - N 11 '96 - p56+ [501+]
New Sci - v152 - D 7 '96 - p48 [51-250]
Ch'en, Feng - *Economic Transition and Political Legitimacy in Post-Mao China*
APSR - v91 - Mr '97 - p209+ [501+]
Ch Rev Int - v4 - Spr '97 - p82+ [501+]
Chen, Guolin - *Hua Ren Bang Pai*
BL - v93 - N 1 '96 - p484 [1-50]
Chen, Jian - *China's Road to the Korean War*
AHR - v102 - F '97 - p153 [501+]
Ch Rev Int - v4 - Spr '97 - p86+ [501+]
Chen, Jie - *China since the Cultural Revolution*
Ch Rev Int - v4 - Spr '97 - p88+ [501+]
Chen, John S M - *Architectural Perspective Grids*
SciTech - v20 - S '96 - p2 [51-250]
Chen, Lin - *Interest Rate Dynamics, Derivatives Pricing, and Risk Management*
JEL - v34 - D '96 - p2035 [51-250]
Chen, Long-Qing - *Mathematics of Microstructure Evolution*
SciTech - v21 - Mr '97 - p91 [1-50]
Chen, N Y - *Shape Selective Catalysis in Industrial Applications. 2nd Ed.*
SciTech - v20 - N '96 - p79 [51-250]

Chen, Shao Ping - *Modeling of Composites*
SciTech - v20 - N '96 - p63 [51-250]
Chen, Xiao-Mei - *Occidentalism: A Theory of Counter-Discourse in Post-Mao China*
Ch Rev Int - v4 - Spr '97 - p90+ [501+]
Chenetier, Marc - *Beyond Suspicion*
ABR - v17 - Ag '96 - p14 [501+]
Choice - v34 - S '96 - p124 [51-250]
Cheneviere, Alain - *Aru in the Solomon Islands (Illus. by Alain Cheneviere)*
c Ch BWatch - v6 - S '96 - p5 [51-250]
c Cur R - v36 - D '96 - p12 [51-250]
c HB Guide - v8 - Spr '97 - p179 [51-250]
c SLJ - v42 - S '96 - p211+ [51-250]
Maud in France (Illus. by Alain Cheneviere)
c Ch BWatch - v6 - S '96 - p5 [51-250]
c Cur R - v36 - D '96 - p12 [51-250]
c HB Guide - v8 - Spr '97 - p141 [51-250]
c SLJ - v42 - S '96 - p211+ [51-250]
Pak in Indonesia (Illus. by Alain Cheneviere)
c Ch BWatch - v6 - S '96 - p5 [51-250]
c Cur R - v36 - D '96 - p12 [51-250]
c HB Guide - v8 - Spr '97 - p169 [51-250]
c SLJ - v42 - O '96 - p128+ [51-250]
Ramachandra in India
c Ch BWatch - v6 - S '96 - p5 [51-250]
c Cur R - v36 - D '96 - p12 [51-250]
c HB Guide - v8 - Spr '97 - p169 [51-250]
c SLJ - v42 - O '96 - p128+ [51-250]
Cheney, Elyse - *The Literary Insomniac*
BL - v93 - D 15 '96 - p705 [51-250]
KR - v64 - N 1 '96 - p1576 [251-500]
PW - v243 - N 4 '96 - p64 [51-250]
Cheney, Glenn Alan - *Teens with Physical Disabilities*
y Emerg Lib - v24 - S '96 - p26 [1-50]
They Never Knew
y BL - v93 - Ja '97 - p828+ [251-500]
y HB Guide - v8 - Spr '97 - p95 [51-250]
SB - v33 - Mr '97 - p37 [51-250]
Cheney, Lynne V - *Telling the Truth*
Am - v175 - O 12 '96 - p26+ [501+]
PW - v243 - Jl 22 '96 - p235 [1-50]
Cheney, Patrick - *Spenser's Famous Flight*
MLR - v91 - Jl '96 - p700+ [501+]
MP - v94 - Ag '96 - p76+ [501+]
Ren Q - v49 - Aut '96 - p635+ [501+]
RES - v47 - Ag '96 - p407+ [501+]
Chenfeld, Mimi Brodsky - *Creative Experiences for Young Children. 2nd Ed.*
ECEJ - v24 - Win '96 - p113+ [251-500]
Cheng, Cliff - *Masculinities in Organizations*
Choice - v34 - F '97 - p1044 [51-250]
R&R Bk N - v11 - D '96 - p28 [51-250]
Cheng, Franklin Y - *Analysis and Computation*
SciTech - v20 - D '96 - p60 [51-250]
Cheng, I - *Scarlet Memorial*
BW - v26 - Jl 7 '96 - p10 [501+]
Cu H - v95 - S '96 - p290+ [251-500]
Econ - v341 - D 7 '96 - p7* [501+]
FEER - v159 - Ag 15 '96 - p54 [501+]
R&R Bk N - v11 - N '96 - p15 [1-50]
Cheng, Nai-Shan - *The Banker*
TranslRevS - v1 - My '95 - p15 [51-250]
Cheng, Tun-Jen - *Inherited Rivalry*
Ch Rev Int - v4 - Spr '97 - p99+ [501+]
Cheng, Vincent J - *Joyce, Race, and Empire*
ELT - v40 - 1 '97 - p102+ [501+]
TLS - D 20 '96 - p12 [501+]
Chenieux-Gendron, Jacqueline - *Lire Le Regard*
Poetics T - v17 - Sum '96 - p274+ [501+]
Nouveau Monde, Autres Mondes, Surrealisme Et Ameriques
FR - v70 - O '96 - p105+ [501+]
Le Surrealisme Autour Du Monde 1929-1947
FR - v70 - O '96 - p105+ [501+]
Chenoweth, James - *Oddity Odyssey*
BL - v92 - Ag '96 - p1877 [51-250]
LATBR - S 22 '96 - p14 [51-250]
NYTBR - v102 - F 16 '97 - p19 [51-250]
Chentsov, A G - *Finitely Additive Measures and Relaxations of Extremal Problems*
SciTech - v20 - D '96 - p15 [51-250]
Chepesuik, Ron - *Sixties Radicals, Then and Now*
J Am St - v30 - Ap '96 - p174+ [251-500]
Cherchi, Paolo - *Andreas and the Ambiguity of Courtly Love*
Specu - v72 - Ja '97 - p130+ [501+]
Cheremensky, A - *Operator Approach to Linear Control Systems*
SciTech - v20 - D '96 - p72 [51-250]

Cheremisinoff, Nicholas P - *Multiphase Reactor and Polymerization System Hydrodynamics*
SciTech - v20 - D '96 - p84 [51-250]
Cheremisinoff, Paul N - *Advances in Environmental Control Technology*
SciTech - v20 - N '96 - p65 [51-250]
Cheripko, Jan - *Imitate the Tiger*
y HB Guide - v7 - Fall '96 - p301 [51-250]
y JAAL - v40 - N '96 - p232 [51-250]
Cherkas, Michael - *Silent Invasion, Bk. 3: The Tarnished Dreams*
p Quill & Q - v62 - Ag '96 - p26 [51-250]
Silent Invasion, Bk. 4: The Great Fear
p Quill & Q - v62 - Ag '96 - p26 [51-250]
Chern, Kenneth C - *Review of Ophthalmology*
SciTech - v21 - Mr '97 - p61 [51-250]
Chernaik, Warren - *The Politics of the Electronic Text*
Compt & H - v30 - 1 '96 - p98+ [501+]
Sexual Freedom in Restoration Literature
Sev Cent N - v54 - Spr '96 - p19 [251-500]
Six Ct J - v27 - Fall '96 - p809+ [501+]
Cherniack, Reuben M - *Review of Pulmonary and Critical Care Medicine*
SciTech - v20 - S '96 - p36 [51-250]
Chernin, Kim - *Cecilia Bartoli: The Passion of Song*
BL - v93 - F 15 '97 - p990 [51-250]
KR - v65 - Ja 15 '97 - p109 [251-500]
NYTBR - v102 - Mr 16 '97 - p16 [501+]
PW - v243 - D 16 '96 - p47 [51-250]
In My Father's Garden
BWatch - v17 - S '96 - p9 [1-50]
KR - v64 - My 1 '96 - p656+ [251-500]
My Life as a Boy
BL - v93 - My 15 '97 - p1556 [51-250]
PW - v244 - Ap 21 '97 - p54+ [51-250]
Cherniss, Cary - *Beyond Burnout*
TCR - v98 - Win '96 - p352+ [501+]
Chernoff, Maxine - *American Heaven*
A Lib - v27 - Ag '96 - p71 [51-250]
Chernow, Ron - *The Death of the Banker*
PW - v244 - My 12 '97 - p64 [51-250]
Cherny, Lynn - *Wired Women*
OOB - v26 - N '96 - p17 [501+]
Chernyshev, Igor - *Labour Statistics for a Market Economy*
Slav R - v55 - Sum '96 - p441+ [501+]
Cherrill, Paul - *Ten Tiny Turtles (Illus. by Paul Cherrill)*
c RT - v50 - O '96 - p131 [1-50]
c RT - v50 - Mr '97 - p500 [51-250]
Cherrington, Clare - *Calling Tracy*
c LAR - v98 - Mr '96 - p129 [51-250]
Cherry, Conrad - *Hurrying toward Zion*
AJE - v105 - N '96 - p113+ [501+]
Bks & Cult - v2 - S '96 - p28+ [501+]
Cng - v28 - S '96 - p62 [51-250]
Rel St Rev - v23 - Ja '97 - p35+ [501+]
TT - v53 - Ja '97 - p531+ [501+]
Cherry, Deborah - *Painting Women*
Art Bull - v78 - S '96 - p568+ [501+]
Signs - v22 - Win '97 - p469+ [501+]
Cherry, Lynne - *Flute's Journey (Illus. by Lynne Cherry)*
c BL - v93 - Ap 1 '97 - p1334 [51-250]
c CCB-B - v50 - My '97 - p316 [51-250]
c KR - v65 - Ap 1 '97 - p551+ [51-250]
Cherryh, C J - *Cloud's Rider*
BL - v93 - S 15 '96 - p226 [51-250]
LJ - v122 - Ja '97 - p51 [1-50]
NYTBR - v101 - S 15 '96 - p40 [251-500]
y VOYA - v19 - D '96 - p277 [251-500]
Inheritor
y Kliatt - v31 - My '97 - p12 [51-250]
Rider at the Gate
y Kliatt - v31 - Ja '97 - p11+ [51-250]
NYTBR - v101 - S 15 '96 - p40 [251-500]
Cherrypickers' News
p Coin W - v38 - Ja 13 '97 - p56 [51-250]
Chervenak, Frank A - *Current Perspectives on the Fetus as a Patient*
SciTech - v21 - Mr '97 - p63 [51-250]
Chesanow, Neil - *Where Do I Live? (Illus. by Ann Iosa)*
c HB Guide - v7 - Fall '96 - p377 [51-250]
Chesbro, George C - *Dream of a Falling Eagle*
BL - v93 - S 1 '96 - p66 [51-250]
KR - v64 - Ag 15 '96 - p1194 [51-250]
LATBR - O 13 '96 - p8 [51-250]
PW - v243 - S 2 '96 - p117 [51-250]
Chesebrough, David B - *No Sorrow like Our Sorrow*
J Ch St - v38 - Sum '96 - p655+ [251-500]
Cheshire, Paul C - *Territorial Competition in an Integrating Europe*
R&R Bk N - v11 - N '96 - p27 [51-250]

Chesler, Mark A - *Cancer and Self-Help*
  Readings - v11 - D '96 - p27+ [51-250]
  Soc Ser R - v70 - D '96 - p668 [51-250]
Chesman, Andrea - *Church Suppers and Potluck Dinners*
  BWatch - v17 - N '96 - p1 [51-250]
  Salad Suppers
  PW - v244 - Ap 21 '97 - p68 [51-250]
Chesney, Marion - *The Folly*
  BL - v93 - S 1 '96 - p60 [51-250]
Chesnutt, Randall D - *From Death to Life*
  Rel St Rev - v22 - O '96 - p354 [51-250]
Chess, Stella - *Temperament: Theory and Practice*
  Choice - v34 - Mr '97 - p1242 [51-250]
  Readings - v12 - Mr '97 - p29 [51-250]
  SciTech - v21 - Mr '97 - p1 [51-250]
Chessex, Jacques - *La Mort D'Un Juste*
  BL - v93 - Ja '97 - p827 [1-50]
Chester, Deborah - *Reign of Shadows*
 y Kliatt - v30 - S '96 - p16 [51-250]
  Shadow War
 y Kliatt - v31 - My '97 - p12 [51-250]
Chester, Jonathan - *The World of the Penguin*
 y BL - v93 - D 1 '96 - p632 [51-250]
  PW - v243 - O 21 '96 - p68 [1-50]
 y SLJ - v43 - Mr '97 - p218 [51-250]
Chester, Kate - *Death in the Afternoon*
 y Kliatt - v30 - S '96 - p6 [51-250]
Chester, Pamela - *Engendering Slavic Literatures*
  Choice - v34 - N '96 - p466 [51-250]
Chesterman, Ross - *Golden Sunrise*
  TES - Mr 28 '97 - p7* [51-250]
Chesterton, G K - *Collected Works. Vols. 10, 14*
  TLS - D 20 '96 - p9 [501+]
  Father Brown of the Church of Rome
  WSJ-MW - v78 - D 9 '96 - pA12 [1-50]
Chesterton, Gilbert T - *The Man Who Was Thursday*
  BW - v26 - D 8 '96 - p4 [51-250]
Chesworth, Jennifer - *The Ecology of Health*
  Choice - v34 - Ja '97 - p827 [51-250]
  SciTech - v20 - S '96 - p27 [51-250]
Cheung, F B - *ASME Heat Transfer Division. Vol. 3*
  SciTech - v21 - Mr '97 - p22 [51-250]
Cheung, Jeff - *Advanced Laser Processing of Materials*
  SciTech - v20 - D '96 - p66 [51-250]
Cheuse, Alan - *Talking Horse*
  BW - v26 - Jl 7 '96 - p13 [51-250]
Chevalier, Jean - *The Penguin Dictionary of Symbols*
 r CR - v269 - N '96 - p278 [51-250]
Chevalier, Tracy - *The Virgin Blue*
  Books - v11 - Ap '97 - p8 [51-250]
Chevallier, Andrew - *The Encyclopedia of Medicinal Plants*
 r ARBA - v28 - '97 - p610+ [51-250]
 r BL - v93 - D 1 '96 - p629 [51-250]
 r BL - v93 - F 1 '97 - p958 [1-50]
 r Choice - v34 - Mr '97 - p1134 [51-250]
 r LJ - v121 - D '96 - p82 [51-250]
 r LJ - v122 - Ap 15 '97 - p37 [51-250]
 r SciTech - v21 - Mr '97 - p68 [51-250]
Chevannes, Barry - *Rastafari: Roots and Ideology*
  JR - v76 - O '96 - p678+ [501+]
Chevigny, Paul - *Edge of the Knife*
  CS - v26 - Mr '97 - p217+ [501+]
Chevillard, Eric - *The Crab Nebula*
  KR - v65 - Ja 1 '97 - p20 [51-250]
  LJ - v122 - Ja '97 - p144 [51-250]
  NYTBR - v102 - Mr 30 '97 - p16 [51-250]
  PW - v244 - Ja 13 '97 - p57 [51-250]
Chevrier, Jacques - *Williams Sassine Ecrivain De La Marginalite*
  WLT - v70 - Sum '96 - p748+ [501+]
Chevrillon, Claire - *Code Name Christiane Clouet*
  TranslRevS - v2 - D '96 - p7 [51-250]
Chew, Felix S - *Skeletal Radiology. 2nd Ed.*
  SciTech - v21 - Mr '97 - p59 [51-250]
Chew, Lillian - *Managing Derivative Risks*
  TLS - F 21 '97 - p4+ [501+]
Chew, Sing C - *The Underdevelopment of Development*
  CS - v25 - S '96 - p585+ [501+]
Cheyette, Bryan - *Between Race and Culture*
  Choice - v34 - Mr '97 - p1158 [51-250]
Chhabra, Ranbir - *Soil Salinity and Water Quality*
  SciTech - v20 - N '96 - p68 [51-250]
Chiaberto, Silvio - *La Certosa Di Casotto. Vols. 1-2*
  CH - v65 - S '96 - p472+ [251-500]
Chiang, Yet-Ming - *Physical Ceramics*
  Choice - v34 - N '96 - p488 [51-250]
  SciTech - v20 - S '96 - p49 [1-50]

Chiaventone, Frederick J - *A Road We Do Not Know*
 y BL - v93 - S 15 '96 - p218 [51-250]
  Esq - v126 - D '96 - p40 [1-50]
  PW - v243 - Jl 22 '96 - p227+ [51-250]
Chibnik, Michael - *Risky Rivers*
  Am Ethnol - v24 - F '97 - p226+ [501+]
  HAHR - v76 - N '96 - p846+ [251-500]
Chicago, Judy - *Beyond the Flower*
  Bloom Rev - v17 - Ja '97 - p23 [501+]
  Trib Bks - F 23 '97 - p8 [1-50]
  The Dinner Party
  Am Craft - v56 - Ag '96 - p27 [1-50]
  Bloom Rev - v17 - Ja '97 - p23 [501+]
Chicago Hispanic Health Coalition
  J Gov Info - v23 - S '96 - p600 [51-250]
Chick, Sandra - *On the Rocks*
 y Bks Keeps - Ja '97 - p27 [51-250]
 c TES - N 29 '96 - p10* [51-250]
Chickering, Roger - *Imperial Germany*
 r Choice - v34 - D '96 - p590 [51-250]
Chidester, David - *American Sacred Space*
  CC - v114 - Ja 22 '97 - p84* [501+]
Chieco, Kate - *Mission Possible: 200 Ways to Strengthen the Nonprofit Sector's Infrastructure*
  ChrPhil - v9 - N 14 '96 - p39 [51-250]
Chiellino, Gino - *Fremde: A Discourse*
  TranslRevS - v2 - D '96 - p24+ [51-250]
Chiflet, Jean-Loup - *Victoria and Her Times*
 y SLJ - v43 - Mr '97 - p198 [51-250]
Child, Abigail - *Scatter Matrix*
  PW - v243 - Jl 22 '96 - p238 [1-50]
Child, C Allan - *Antarctic and Subantarctic Pycnogonida*
  SciTech - v20 - N '96 - p25 [1-50]
Child, Greg - *Climbing: The Complete Reference*
 r RQ - v35 - Sum '96 - p549+ [251-500]
Child, John - *The Crusades*
 c HB Guide - v8 - Spr '97 - p165 [1-50]
 c SLJ - v42 - S '96 - p212 [51-250]
 y VOYA - v19 - D '96 - p285 [251-500]
Child, Julia - *In Julia's Kitchen with Master Chefs*
  BWatch - v17 - D '96 - p9 [51-250]
Child, Lee - *Killing Floor*
  BL - v93 - Mr 15 '97 - p1228 [51-250]
  KR - v65 - Ja 1 '97 - p7+ [251-500]
  LJ - v122 - F 15 '97 - p161 [51-250]
  PW - v244 - Ja 20 '97 - p393 [251-500]
  Trib Bks - My 18 '97 - p6 [51-250]
  Killing Floor (Hill). Audio Version
 y Kliatt - v31 - My '97 - p41 [51-250]
Child, Lydia Maria Francis - *An Appeal in Favor of That Class of Americans Called Africans*
  AL - v68 - S '96 - p661 [51-250]
  Bl S - v26 - Sum '96 - p64 [1-50]
  Legacy - v14 - 1 '97 - p74 [51-250]
  Over the River and through the Wood (Illus. by David Catrow)
 c BL - v93 - S 1 '96 - p135 [51-250]
 c CBRS - v25 - O '96 - p14 [51-250]
 c CCB-B - v50 - N '96 - p89+ [501+]
 c HB Guide - v8 - Spr '97 - p151 [51-250]
 c PW - v243 - S 30 '96 - p86+ [51-250]
 c SLJ - v42 - O '96 - p111 [51-250]
Childers, Joseph W - *Novel Possibilities*
  Nine-C Lit - v51 - D '96 - p420 [51-250]
Childers, Thomas - *Wings of Morning*
 y Emerg Lib - v24 - S '96 - p23 [1-50]
Childhood (Bygone Britian 1900-1970)
 y Sch Lib - v44 - N '96 - p172+ [51-250]
Childre, Doc Lew - *Teaching Children to Love*
  LJ - v122 - F 15 '97 - p156 [51-250]
Children, Churches and Daddies
 p Sm Pr R - v28 - N '96 - p13 [51-250]
Children's Books: Awards and Prizes. 1996 Ed.
 r ARBA - v28 - '97 - p426 [51-250]
 r BL - v93 - N 15 '96 - p608 [1-50]
 r CCB-B - v50 - D '96 - p156 [51-250]
 r Choice - v34 - My '97 - p1472+ [51-250]
 r R&R Bk N - v12 - F '97 - p103 [51-250]
Children's Books of the Year 1996
 r Inst - v105 - My '96 - p17 [51-250]
Children's Hospital at Yale-New Haven. Pediatric Emergency Dept. - *Now I Know Better*
 c CCB-B - v50 - N '96 - p93 [51-250]
 c HB Guide - v8 - Spr '97 - p130 [51-250]
 c SLJ - v43 - F '97 - p110+ [51-250]
Children's School of Science (Woods Hole, Mass.) - *The Big Book of Nature Projects*
 c PW - v244 - Ap 14 '97 - p77 [51-250]

Childress, Diana - *Prehistoric People of North America*
 c Ch BWatch - v6 - D '96 - p2 [1-50]
 c HB Guide - v8 - Spr '97 - p177 [51-250]
 c SLJ - v42 - D '96 - p127 [51-250]
Childress, Mark - *Henry Bobbity Is Missing (Illus. by Ernie Eldredge)*
 c S Liv - v31 - D '96 - p58 [51-250]
  Joshua and the Big Bad Blue Crabs (Illus. by Mary Barrett Brown)
 c HB Guide - v7 - Fall '96 - p251 [51-250]
Childs, David - *Britain since 1939*
  Albion - v28 - Fall '96 - p537+ [501+]
  Historian - v59 - Win '97 - p462 [251-500]
  HRNB - v25 - Fall '96 - p23+ [251-500]
Childs, James M, Jr. - *Ethics in Business*
  Theol St - v57 - D '96 - p786+ [251-500]
  TT - v53 - Ja '97 - p563+ [51-250]
Childs, Rob - *Soccer Mad (Illus. by Aiden Potts)*
 c Bks Keeps - Jl '96 - p11 [51-250]
 c Sch Lib - v44 - Ag '96 - p105 [51-250]
Childs, S Terry - *Society, Culture and Technology in Africa*
  Am Ant - v62 - Ja '97 - p169 [501+]
Chilson, Richard - *All Will Be Well*
  RR - v55 - N '96 - p661 [1-50]
  God Awaits You
  RR - v55 - N '96 - p661 [1-50]
  You Shall Not Want
  RR - v55 - N '96 - p661 [1-50]
Chilton, Bruce - *Judaism in the New Testament*
  Rel St Rev - v23 - Ap '97 - p195 [51-250]
  Pure Kingdom
  BL - v93 - S 1 '96 - p36 [51-250]
  Choice - v34 - My '97 - p1515 [51-250]
  Trading Places
  LJ - v122 - Ja '97 - p104 [51-250]
Chilton, Paul A - *Security Metaphors*
  JPR - v34 - F '97 - p109 [251-500]
Chin, Frank - *Gunga Din Highway*
  Amerasia J - v22 - 2 '96 - p158+ [501+]
Chin, Steven A - *The Success of Gordon H. Chong and Associates (Illus. by Kim Komenich)*
 y HB Guide - v7 - Fall '96 - p313 [1-50]
 y SLJ - v42 - S '96 - p232 [51-250]
China: Macroeconomic Stability in a Decentralized Economy
  J Gov Info - v23 - S '96 - p684 [51-250]
China Review 1995
  Ch Rev Int - v4 - Spr '97 - p186+ [501+]
Chinas, Beverly - *La Zandunga: Of Fieldwork and Friendship in Southern Mexico*
  RA - v25 - 4 '96 - p241+ [501+]
Chinca, Mark - *History, Fiction, Verisimilitude*
  Ger Q - v69 - Sum '96 - p346+ [501+]
Chinen, Allan B - *Waking the World*
  Parabola - v22 - F '97 - p104+ [251-500]
Chinery, Michael - *How Bees Make Honey*
 c Ch BWatch - v7 - Ja '97 - p3 [1-50]
 c HB Guide - v8 - Spr '97 - p121 [51-250]
 c SB - v33 - My '97 - p112+ [51-250]
 c SLJ - v43 - F '97 - p86 [51-250]
The Chinese Economy
  JEL - v34 - D '96 - p2125 [51-250]
Chinese Stamp Catalog Illustrated in Colors. 1996 Ed.
 r Phil Lit R - v45 - 3 '96 - p251 [51-250]
Ching, Frank D K - *Architecture, Form, Space and Order. 2nd Ed.*
  R&R Bk N - v11 - N '96 - p61 [1-50]
Chin-Lee, Cynthia - *A Is for Asia (Illus. by Yumi Heo)*
 c BL - v93 - Mr 1 '97 - p1165 [51-250]
 c CBRS - v25 - Ap '97 - p102+ [51-250]
 c CCB-B - v50 - My '97 - p316 [51-250]
 c KR - v65 - Mr 15 '97 - p459 [51-250]
 c PW - v244 - F 3 '97 - p106 [51-250]
Chinn, Jeff - *Russians as the New Minority*
  Choice - v34 - N '96 - p529 [51-250]
Chinn, Karen - *Sam and the Lucky Money (Illus. by Cornelius Van Wright)*
 c RT - v50 - N '96 - p258 [51-250]
 c RT - v50 - N '96 - p477+ [51-250]
Chinoy, Mike - *China Live*
  KR - v65 - Mr 1 '97 - p345 [51-250]
  PW - v244 - Mr 3 '97 - p56 [51-250]
Chioles, John - *Aeschylus: Mythic Theatre, Political Voice*
  Theat J - v49 - Mr '97 - p94 [501+]
Chipot, M - *Progress in Partial Differential Equations*
  SIAM Rev - v39 - Mr '97 - p176 [51-250]
Chirban, John T - *Ethical Dilemmas*
  Rel St Rev - v22 - O '96 - p341 [51-250]
  Interviewing in Depth
  R&R Bk N - v11 - N '96 - p5 [51-250]

Personhood: Orthodox Christianity and the Connection Between Body, Mind, and Soul
R&R Bk N - v11 - N '96 - p8 [51-250]
Chirot, Daniel - *How Societies Change*
SF - v75 - S '96 - p357+ [501+]
Modern Tyrants
y Kliatt - v30 - N '96 - p27 [51-250]
Chisholm, James - *South Pass 1868*
Roundup M - v4 - D '96 - p19+ [51-250]
Chisholm, Lynne - *Growing Up in Europe*
Bkbird - v34 - Spr '96 - p55 [51-250]
Chisholm, Margo - *To the Summit*
BL - v93 - Mr 15 '97 - p1219+ [51-250]
KR - v65 - Ja 15 '97 - p110 [251-500]
LJ - v122 - F 15 '97 - p139 [51-250]
NYTBR - v102 - Mr 30 '97 - p17 [51-250]
PW - v244 - F 3 '97 - p87 [51-250]
Chisholm, Michael - *Britain on the Edge of Europe*
Econ J - v106 - N '96 - p1804+ [501+]
Chisholm, P F - *A Season of Knives*
Arm Det - v29 - Sum '96 - p370 [51-250]
BWatch - v17 - S '96 - p1 [51-250]
A Surfeit of Guns
BL - v93 - My 1 '97 - p1481 [51-250]
Chisholm, Roderick M - *A Realistic Theory of Categories*
Choice - v34 - Ap '97 - p1351 [51-250]
Chittenden, Margaret - *Dead Men Don't Dance*
BL - v93 - My 15 '97 - p1566 [51-250]
Chittick, William C - *Imaginal Worlds*
MEJ - v50 - Aut '96 - p618+ [501+]
Chittister, Joan - *Beyond Beijing*
Am - v175 - N 9 '96 - p24 [501+]
The Fire in These Ashes
CLW - v67 - Mr '97 - p29 [251-500]
A Passion for Life
CLW - v67 - Mr '97 - p29 [51-250]
LATBR - v263 - S 29 '96 - p8 [501+]
Psalm Journal for Lent. Vols. 1-2
RR - v56 - Ja '97 - p105 [1-50]
There Is a Season
RR - v55 - N '96 - p659 [1-50]
Chitty, Dennis - *Do Lemmings Commit Suicide?*
Choice - v34 - Ja '97 - p821 [51-250]
Nature - v382 - Jl 25 '96 - p310+ [501+]
Sci - v274 - N 22 '96 - p1321 [1-50]
Chiu, Edmond - *Functional Psychiatric Disorders of the Elderly*
J ClinPsyc - v57 - O '96 - p491 [251-500]
Chiu, Siu-Wai - *Patterns in Fungal Development*
Choice - v34 - Mr '97 - p1185 [51-250]
Chiu, Stephen Wing-Kai - *City-States in the Global Economy*
Choice - v34 - Mr '97 - p1206 [51-250]
R&R Bk N - v12 - F '97 - p37 [51-250]
Chizmar, Richard - *The Earth Strikes Back*
SF Chr - v18 - O '96 - p80 [1-50]
Cho, George - *Trade, Aid and Global Interdependence*
JEL - v35 - Mr '97 - p212 [51-250]
Cho, Yong-Doo - *Financial Factors and Corporate Investment*
JEL - v34 - D '96 - p2055+ [501+]
Choban, Jennie - *Kapusta or Cabbage*
Sm Pr R - v28 - Jl '96 - p8 [501+]
Choca, James P - *Manual for Clinical Psychology Trainees. 3rd Ed.*
SciTech - v20 - N '96 - p43 [51-250]
Chocolate, Deborah M Newton - *Kente Colors (Illus. by John Ward)*
c Emerg Lib - v23 - My '96 - p43 [1-50]
c HB Guide - v7 - Fall '96 - p318 [51-250]
On the Day I Was Born (Illus. by Melodye Rosales)
c RT - v50 - N '96 - p257+ [51-250]
Chocolate Kisses
LJ - v122 - F 15 '97 - p126 [51-250]
Choctaw Census Blue County 1885
r EGH - v50 - N '96 - p183 [51-250]
Choctaw Census Kiamitia County 1885
r EGH - v50 - N '96 - p183 [51-250]
Chodron, Pema - *When Things Fall Apart*
LJ - v122 - Ja '97 - p104 [51-250]
PW - v243 - N 11 '96 - p68 [51-250]
Choe, Jae Y - *Choe Notes. 2nd Ed.*
SciTech - v20 - N '96 - p55 [51-250]
Choi, Sook Nyul - *The Best Older Sister (Illus. by Cornelius Van Wright)*
c BL - v93 - My 1 '97 - p1504 [51-250]
c PW - v244 - F 3 '97 - p107 [51-250]
Choice Ayres, Songs, and Dialogues. Bks. 1-5
Notes - v53 - D '96 - p621+ [251-500]
Chokroverty, Sudhansu - *Management of Epilepsy*
SciTech - v20 - N '96 - p42 [51-250]

Choldenko, Gennifer - *Moonstruck: The True Story of the Cow Who Jumped over the Moon (Illus. by Paul Yalowitz)*
c BL - v93 - Mr 1 '97 - p1169 [51-250]
c KR - v65 - Mr 1 '97 - p378 [51-250]
c PW - v244 - F 10 '97 - p83+ [51-250]
c Trib Bks - My 4 '97 - p6 [51-250]
Chole, Eshetu - *Democratisation Processes in Africa*
Choice - v34 - Mr '97 - p1232 [51-250]
Cholesterol Testing and Treatment in Adults: Final Report
J Gov Info - v23 - S '96 - p639 [51-250]
Cholhan, Ilarion - *Dvanadstat' P'ies Bez Odniel Zibrani Dramatychni Tvory 1945-1989*
BL - v93 - N 15 '96 - p577 [1-50]
Chomsky, Aviva - *West Indian Workers and the United Fruit Company in Costa Rica 1870-1940*
Choice - v34 - S '96 - p189+ [51-250]
PHR - v66 - F '97 - p136+ [251-500]
Chomsky, Noam - *The Cold War and the University*
BL - v93 - F 1 '97 - p911 [51-250]
For Aff - v76 - Mr '97 - p147+ [501+]
KR - v64 - D 15 '96 - p1777 [251-500]
Nat - v264 - Mr 10 '97 - p28+ [501+]
PW - v243 - D 9 '96 - p55 [51-250]
VV - v42 - F 25 '97 - p51 [501+]
Powers and Prospects
BW - v26 - N 24 '96 - p12 [51-250]
Quad - v40 - Jl '96 - p97+ [501+]
RP - v59 - Spr '97 - p395+ [501+]
Syntactic Structures
Nature - v386 - Ap 17 '97 - p670 [501+]
Chomycz, Bob - *Fiber Optic Installations*
SciTech - v20 - N '96 - p73 [51-250]
Chon, Sang-Byong - *Back to Heaven*
WLT - v70 - Sum '96 - p763+ [501+]
Chong, Denise - *The Concubine's Children*
Can Lit - Win '96 - p171+ [501+]
Choo, Andrew L-T - *Hearsay and Confrontation in Criminal Trials*
Law Q Rev - v113 - Ap '97 - p346+ [501+]
Choper, Jesse H - *Securing Religious Liberty*
JR - v77 - Ap '97 - p327+ [501+]
Theol St - v57 - Mr '96 - p192+ [51-250]
Chopin, Kate - *The Awakening*
LATBR - D 8 '96 - p8 [51-250]
LJ - v121 - O 1 '96 - p132 [1-50]
TSWL - v15 - Fall '96 - p289+ [501+]
WHR - v50 - Win '97 - p94*+ [501+]
The Awakening (Ross). Audio Version
Books - v11 - Ap '97 - p19 [1-50]
BWatch - v18 - Mr '97 - p9 [1-50]
The Awakening and Selected Stories (Adler). Audio Version
Books - v11 - Ap '97 - p19 [1-50]
y Kliatt - v30 - S '96 - p42 [51-250]
Chopp, Rebecca S - *Reconstructing Christian Theology*
JR - v76 - O '96 - p657+ [501+]
Saving Work
Bks & Cult - v2 - S '96 - p34 [501+]
Chopra, Deepak - *Creating Health. Audio Version*
Quill & Q - v62 - Ag '96 - p31 [51-250]
The Path to Love
BL - v93 - N 15 '96 - p546 [51-250]
CSM - v89 - F 6 '97 - p14 [51-250]
KR - v64 - N 15 '96 - p1647 [251-500]
LJ - v122 - Ja '97 - p125 [51-250]
PW - v243 - N 25 '96 - p64 [51-250]
Quill & Q - v63 - Ja '97 - p20 [1-50]
Peso Perfecto
LJ - v122 - Ja '97 - p78 [51-250]
Chopra, Gautama - *Child of the Dawn*
LJ - v122 - Ja '97 - p106 [51-250]
PW - v243 - S 9 '96 - p64+ [51-250]
Choquette, Robert - *The Oblate Assault on Canada's Northwest*
Can Hist R - v78 - Mr '97 - p151+ [501+]
CH - v65 - D '96 - p743+ [501+]
Choquette, Sonia - *Your Heart's Desire*
y BL - v93 - Mr 1 '97 - p1071 [51-250]
PW - v244 - F 3 '97 - p87+ [51-250]
Chorafas, Dimitris N - *Financial Models and Simulation*
Econ J - v106 - N '96 - p1838 [251-500]
Chorao, Kay - *The Christmas Story (Illus. by Kay Chorao)*
c BL - v93 - S 1 '96 - p135 [51-250]
c CLW - v67 - D '96 - p53 [51-250]
c CLW - v67 - Mr '97 - p57 [51-250]
c HB Guide - v8 - Spr '97 - p88 [51-250]
c PW - v243 - S 30 '96 - p91 [51-250]
c SLJ - v42 - O '96 - p34 [51-250]

Mother Goose Magic (Illus. by Kay Chorao)
c ECEJ - v24 - Fall '96 - p39 [51-250]
Chorpenning, Joseph F - *Mexican Devotional Retablos from the Peters Collection*
CHR - v83 - Ja '97 - p160 [51-250]
Chotzinoff, Robin - *People with Dirty Hands*
Bloom Rev - v16 - Jl '96 - p12 [51-250]
Hort - v74 - N '96 - p58+ [251-500]
PW - v244 - Ja 13 '97 - p72+ [1-50]
Chou, Eva Shan - *Reconsidering Tu Fu*
Choice - v34 - S '96 - p120 [51-250]
Ch Rev Int - v4 - Spr '97 - p102+ [501+]
Choueiri, Youssef M - *State and Society in Syria and Lebanon*
JTWS - v13 - Spr '96 - p387+ [501+]
Chow, Ben - *Elliptic and Parabolic Methods in Geometry*
SciTech - v21 - Mr '97 - p18 [51-250]
Chow, Kai-Wing - *The Rise of Confucian Ritualism in Late Imperial China*
Ch Rev Int - v3 - Fall '96 - p377+ [501+]
Chowdhury, Subir - *QS-9000 Pioneers*
SciTech - v20 - S '96 - p58 [51-250]
Chown, Marcus - *Afterglow of Creation*
Astron - v24 - D '96 - p102 [251-500]
Choice - v34 - N '96 - p480 [51-250]
SB - v32 - Ag '96 - p166+ [251-500]
Choy, Wayson - *The Jade Peony*
KR - v65 - Mr 1 '97 - p321 [51-250]
LJ - v122 - Ap 1 '97 - p122 [51-250]
PW - v244 - Mr 24 '97 - p59 [51-250]
Choyce, Lesley - *The Coastline of Forgetting*
BIC - v25 - O '96 - p13 [51-250]
Nova Scotia: Shaped by the Sea
Beav - v76 - O '96 - p46+ [51-250]
Beav - v77 - F '97 - p39 [251-500]
CF - v75 - D '96 - p36+ [501+]
Quill & Q - v62 - S '96 - p68 [251-500]
Trap Door to Heaven
Quill & Q - v62 - S '96 - p65 [251-500]
Chraibi, Driss - *L'Homme Du Livre*
FR - v70 - F '97 - p494+ [501+]
Inspector Ali
MEJ - v50 - Sum '96 - p454 [1-50]
Chretien, Jacques - *Environmental Impact on the Airways*
SciTech - v20 - N '96 - p47 [51-250]
Chrisman, Miriam Usher - *Conflicting Visions of Reform*
Six Ct J - v27 - Fall '96 - p860+ [501+]
Chrisp, Peter - *History of Toys and Games*
c Sch Lib - v44 - Ag '96 - p110 [51-250]
c TES - N 8 '96 - p13* [501+]
Mapping the Unknown
c Bks Keeps - Jl '96 - p22 [51-250]
The Norman Conquest
c Bks Keeps - Jl '96 - p23 [51-250]
y Sch Lib - v44 - Ag '96 - p123 [51-250]
The Roman Empire
cr Par Ch - v21 - Mr '97 - p5 [1-50]
Chriss, Neil A - *Black-Scholes and Beyond*
R&R Bk N - v12 - F '97 - p49 [51-250]
Christ, Carl F - *Econometrics, Macroeconomics and Economic Policy*
Econ J - v106 - N '96 - p1833 [51-250]
JEL - v34 - S '96 - p1417 [51-250]
R&R Bk N - v11 - N '96 - p24 [51-250]
Christ, Carol - *Odyssey with the Goddess*
NWSA Jnl - v9 - Spr '97 - p123+ [501+]
Christelow, Eileen - *Five Little Monkeys with Nothing to Do (Illus. by Eileen Christelow)*
c BL - v93 - S 1 '96 - p140+ [51-250]
c CCB-B - v50 - D '96 - p130 [51-250]
c HB Guide - v8 - Spr '97 - p23 [51-250]
c SLJ - v42 - N '96 - p79 [51-250]
What Do Authors Do? (Illus. by Eileen Christelow)
c Inst - v106 - N '96 - p25 [1-50]
c LA - v73 - O '96 - p432 [51-250]
Christensen, Bernhard - *The Inward Pilgrims*
RR - v56 - Ja '97 - p106 [51-250]
Christensen, Bonnie - *Rebus Riot (Illus. by Bonnie Christensen)*
c BL - v93 - My 15 '97 - p1577 [51-250]
c HB - v73 - My '97 - p336 [51-250]
c KR - v65 - Ap 1 '97 - p552 [51-250]
c PW - v244 - Mr 31 '97 - p77 [51-250]
c SLJ - v43 - Mr '97 - p149 [51-250]
Christensen, Carol - *Disability and the Dilemmas of Education and Justice*
TES - F 21 '97 - p8* [501+]
Christensen, F M - *Pornography: The Other Side*
Dialogue - v35 - Spr '96 - p420+ [501+]

Christensen, James - *Voyage of the Basset (Illus. by James Christensen)*
  c PW - v243 - N 11 '96 - p75 [51-250]
  y SLJ - v43 - Ja '97 - p139+ [51-250]
Christensen, Jerome - *Lord Byron's Strength*
  MP - v94 - Ag '96 - p111+ [501+]
  RES - v47 - N '96 - p607+ [501+]
Christensen, Karsten Brejnbjerg - *Violinernes Kemi*
  WLT - v70 - Aut '96 - p971 [501+]
Christensen, Larry B - *Diet-Behavior Relationships*
  SciTech - v20 - N '96 - p45 [51-250]
Christensen, Lis - *A First Glossary of Hiberno-English*
  r ILS - v15 - Fall '96 - p31 [1-50]
Christensen, Lisa - *A Hiker's Guide to Art of the Canadian Rockies*
  Quill & Q - v62 - S '96 - p25 [51-250]
Christensen, Peter - *The Decline of Iranshahr*
  AHR - v101 - O '96 - p1252+ [501+]
Christensen, Thomas J - *Useful Adversaries*
  Choice - v34 - My '97 - p1561 [51-250]
Christian, Deborah - *Mainline*
  SF Chr - v18 - O '96 - p79 [51-250]
Christian, Frank - *Augusta National and The Masters*
  S Liv - v32 - Mr '97 - p62 [51-250]
Christian, Garna L - *Black Soldiers in Jim Crow Texas 1899-1917*
  AHR - v102 - F '97 - p202+ [251-500]
Christian, Glynn - *Edible France*
  LJ - v122 - Ap 1 '97 - p113 [51-250]
Christian, Harry - *The Making of Anti-Sexist Men*
  Socio R - v44 - N '96 - p746+ [501+]
Christian, Peggy - *The Bookstore Mouse (Illus. by Gary Lippincott)*
  c Emerg Lib - v24 - S '96 - p52 [51-250]
Christian, Spencer - *Electing our Government*
  y Kliatt - v31 - Ja '97 - p25 [51-250]
Christian, William - *George Grant: A Biography*
  Archiv - Fall '94 - p199+ [501+]
Christian, William A, 1944- - *Visionaries: The Spanish Republic and the Reign of Christ*
  Am - v175 - O 19 '96 - p27+ [501+]
  Am Ethnol - v24 - F '97 - p242+ [501+]
  BW - v26 - Jl 7 '96 - p4+ [501+]
  Choice - v34 - N '96 - p516 [51-250]
  Comw - v123 - N 22 '96 - p23+ [501+]
  NYRB - v43 - N 28 '96 - p56+ [501+]
  Spec - v277 - N 23 '96 - p44 [51-250]
Christiana, David - *The First Snow (Illus. by David Christiana)*
  c BL - v93 - F 1 '97 - p945 [51-250]
  c CBRS - v25 - D '96 - p37+ [51-250]
  c HB - v73 - Mr '97 - p191+ [51-250]
  c HB Guide - v8 - Spr '97 - p23 [51-250]
  c KR - v64 - O 1 '96 - p1464 [51-250]
  c PW - v243 - N 4 '96 - p75 [51-250]
  c SFR - v21 - N '96 - p47 [1-50]
  c SLJ - v43 - F '97 - p74 [51-250]
Christiano, Thomas - *The Rule of the Many*
  Choice - v34 - Ap '97 - p1416 [51-250]
Christiansen, C B - *I See the Moon*
  y Emerg Lib - v24 - S '96 - p24 [1-50]
  A Snowman on Sycamore Street (Illus. by Melissa Sweet)
  c BL - v93 - O 1 '96 - p348 [51-250]
  c Bloom Rev - v16 - N '96 - p31 [1-50]
  c HB Guide - v8 - Spr '97 - p57 [51-250]
  c SLJ - v42 - N '96 - p79 [51-250]
Christiansen, John B - *Deaf President Now!*
  CS - v26 - Mr '97 - p183 [501+]
Christiansen, Rupert - *Paris Babylon*
  Historian - v58 - Sum '96 - p897+ [251-500]
Christian-Smith, Linda K - *Texts of Desire*
  Ed Theory - v46 - Fall '96 - p525+ [501+]
Christianson, Gale E - *Edwin Hubble: Mariner of the Nebulae*
  Am Sci - v85 - Mr '97 - p181+ [501+]
  Isis - v87 - D '96 - p745+ [501+]
  NYTBR - v102 - Ja 12 '97 - p32 [51-250]
  Isaac Newton and the Scientific Revolution
  c BL - v93 - D 1 '96 - p655 [51-250]
  y HB - v73 - My '97 - p338 [251-500]
  y HB Guide - v8 - Spr '97 - p155 [51-250]
  y SB - v33 - Ja '97 - p14 [51-250]
  y SLJ - v43 - Ja '97 - p120 [51-250]
  y VOYA - v19 - F '97 - p342 [51-250]
Christianson, Paul - *Discourse on History, Law, and Governance in the Public Career of John Selden 1610-1635*
  Choice - v34 - My '97 - p1556 [51-250]
Christianson, Stephen G - *Facts about the Congress*
  r ARBA - v28 - '97 - p270+ [51-250]
  r Choice - v34 - F '97 - p939+ [51-250]

Christie, Agatha - *The Harlequin Tea Set and Other Stories*
  BL - v93 - Mr 15 '97 - p1228 [51-250]
  KR - v65 - Mr 1 '97 - p339 [51-250]
  LJ - v122 - My 1 '97 - p144 [1-50]
  The Murder at Hazelmoor
  BW - v26 - D 15 '96 - p10 [251-500]
  Murder on the Orient Express
  y Kliatt - v30 - S '96 - p2 [1-50]
  The Mysterious Affair at Styles (May). Audio Version
  y Kliatt - v31 - Ja '97 - p42 [51-250]
  The Mysterious Affair at Styles (Suchet). Audio Version
  y Kliatt - v30 - N '96 - p44 [51-250]
Christie, Carl A - *Ocean Bridge*
  Can Hist R - v78 - Mr '97 - p134+ [501+]
  J Mil H - v60 - O '96 - p792+ [251-500]
  Pub Hist - v18 - Sum '96 - p68+ [501+]
Christie, Clive J - *A Modern History of Southeast Asia*
  HRNB - v25 - Fall '96 - p38+ [251-500]
Christie, Ian, 1945- - *The Last Machine*
  Afterimage - v23 - Sum '96 - p24 [501+]
Christie, Ian R - *The Benthams in Russia 1780-1791*
  EHR - v111 - N '96 - p1299+ [251-500]
  British Non-Elite MPS 1715-1820
  Albion - v28 - Fall '96 - p502+ [501+]
  British Non-Elite MPs 1715-1820
  HRNB - v25 - Fall '96 - p21 [51-250]
Christie, Katherine M - *A Bibliography of Oil and Gas Law and Policy 1984 1995*
  r LAR - v99 - F '97 - p104 [51-250]
  A Bibliography of Mineral Law and Policy 1984-1995
  r LAR - v99 - F '97 - p104 [51-250]
Christie, Neil - *Towns in Transition*
  R&R Bk N - v11 - N '96 - p42 [51-250]
Christilian, J D - *Scarlet Women*
  Arm Det - v29 - Sum '96 - p370 [251-500]
Christine, De Pisan - *The Book of the Body Politic*
  MLR - v92 - Ap '97 - p461+ [501+]
  RM - v50 - S '96 - p148+ [501+]
  Le Livre Du Duc Des Vrais Amans
  MLR - v92 - Ap '97 - p461+ [501+]
  The Writings of Christine De Pizan
  JWomHist - v8 - Fall '96 - p228+ [501+]
Christmas (Festival)
  c Bks Keeps - N '96 - p20 [1-50]
Christmas, Joyce - *Mourning Gloria*
  PW - v243 - Jl 22 '96 - p235 [51-250]
Christmas: An Annual Treasury. Vol. 66
  CC - v113 - D 11 '96 - p1233 [1-50]
Christmas and the New Year
  c Bks Keeps - N '96 - p20 [1-50]
Christmas in Colonial and Early America
  c BL - v93 - N 1 '96 - p492 [51-250]
Christmas Kisses
  LJ - v121 - N 15 '96 - p47 [51-250]
A Christmas Miracle
  LJ - v121 - N 15 '96 - p47 [51-250]
Christodoulou, Kyriaki - *Montaigne Et L'Histoire Des Hellenes*
  FR - v70 - D '96 - p325+ [251-500]
Christofides, Louis N - *Aspects of Labour Market Behaviour*
  ILRR - v50 - Ja '97 - p356+ [501+]
Christoph, Peter R - *The Dongan Paper 1683-1688. Pt. 2*
  R&R Bk N - v12 - F '97 - p25 [51-250]
Christoph, Richard T - *Using Microsoft Works 4.0 for Windows 95*
  SciTech - v20 - S '96 - p7 [51-250]
Christophe, Paul - *Les Carnets Du Cardinal Baudrillart 1914-1918*
  CHR - v82 - O '96 - p735+ [501+]
Christopher, Matt - *Challenge at Second Base (Dietz). Audio Version*
  c SLJ - v42 - Ag '96 - p62 [51-250]
  The Comeback Challenge (Illus. by Karen Meyer)
  c HB Guide - v7 - Fall '96 - p290 [51-250]
  Double Play at Short
  c RT - v50 - N '96 - p255 [51-250]
  Fighting Tackle
  c RT - v50 - N '96 - p255 [51-250]
  In the Huddle with...Steve Young
  c BL - v93 - F 15 '97 - p1017+ [51-250]
  c SLJ - v43 - F '97 - p111 [51-250]
  Olympic Dream (Illus. by Karen Meyer)
  c HB Guide - v7 - Fall '96 - p290 [51-250]
  y VOYA - v19 - D '96 - p267 [51-250]
  On the Court with...Grant Hill
  c BL - v93 - F 15 '97 - p1017+ [51-250]
  On the Court with...Michael Jordan
  c BL - v93 - F 15 '97 - p1017+ [51-250]

  On the Ice with...Wayne Gretzky
  c BL - v93 - F 15 '97 - p1017+ [51-250]
  Penalty Shot
  c BL - v93 - Ja '97 - p858 [251-500]
  c KR - v64 - N 1 '96 - p1598 [51-250]
  c SLJ - v43 - F '97 - p74 [51-250]
  Shadow over Second (Illus. by Anna Dewdney)
  c HB Guide - v7 - Fall '96 - p286 [1-50]
  Tough to Tackle. Audio Version
  BL - v93 - S 15 '96 - p264 [51-250]
Christopher, Milbourne - *The Illustrated History of Magic. Rev. Ed.*
  LJ - v121 - O 1 '96 - p78 [51-250]
Christopher, Nicholas - *Somewhere in the Night*
  BL - v93 - Mr 15 '97 - p1218 [51-250]
  KR - v65 - F 1 '97 - p186 [251-500]
  LJ - v122 - Mr 15 '97 - p65 [51-250]
  NYTLa - v146 - Mr 28 '97 - pC30 [501+]
  PW - v244 - F 17 '97 - p204 [51-250]
  VV - v42 - Mr 18 '97 - p58 [501+]
  Veronica
  PW - v244 - F 17 '97 - p217 [1-50]
  Trib Bks - Mr 9 '97 - p8 [1-50]
Christopher, Paul - *The Ethics of War and Peace*
  Rel St Rev - v23 - Ap '97 - p160 [51-250]
Christopher, Peter - *Log Houses*
  Beav - v76 - O '96 - p40 [251-500]
Christopher, Renny - *The Viet Nam War/The American War*
  AL - v69 - Mr '97 - p242+ [251-500]
  Choice - v34 - S '96 - p124 [51-250]
Christopher, Tom - *The 20-Minute Gardener*
  BL - v93 - Ja '97 - p800 [51-250]
  LJ - v122 - Ja '97 - p130 [51-250]
  PW - v244 - Ja 27 '97 - p98 [51-250]
  The 20-Minute Gardener (Christopher). Audio Version
  LJ - v122 - Ap 15 '97 - p139 [51-250]
Christopolous, Christos - *The Transmission-Line Modeling Method TLM*
  SIAM Rev - v38 - D '96 - p711 [501+]
Christou, Paul - *Particle Bombardment for Genetic Engineering of Plants*
  SciTech - v20 - N '96 - p57 [51-250]
Christy, Jim - *Strange Sites*
  BIC - v26 - F '97 - p26+ [501+]
  CG - v116 - S '96 - p82 [51-250]
Chronicle of the 20th Century. Electronic Media Version
  cr BL - v93 - Mr 1 '97 - p1186 [51-250]
  yr Kliatt - v31 - Ja '97 - p33 [51-250]
  r LJ - v122 - Ja '97 - p160 [51-250]
  TES - Ja 10 '97 - p16* [51-250]
  Trib Bks - F 2 '97 - p7 [51-250]
Chronicle of the Olympics 1896-1996
  r ARBA - v28 - '97 - p300 [251-500]
  y SLJ - v42 - Ag '96 - p185 [51-250]
  y VOYA - v19 - O '96 - p227 [251-500]
Chronicle of the World
  r ARBA - v28 - '97 - p211 [251-500]
  r LJ - v122 - Ja '97 - p84 [51-250]
  r PW - v243 - S 30 '96 - p74 [51-250]
Chronicle of the Year 1995
  yr ARBA - v28 - '97 - p211 [51-250]
Chu, Godwin C - *The Great Wall in Ruins*
  RA - v25 - 4 '96 - p257+ [501+]
Chu, Petra Ten-Doesschate - *The Popularization of Images*
  EHR - v112 - F '97 - p228+ [501+]
  FR - v70 - D '96 - p373+ [251-500]
Chu, Quang Minh - *Cam Thong De Voi Dau Kho. Vol. 2*
  BL - v93 - My 15 '97 - p1568 [1-50]
Chu, S N G - *Micromechanics of Advanced Materials*
  SciTech - v21 - Mr '97 - p78 [51-250]
Chu, Yen-An - *Understanding China*
  R&R Bk N - v11 - D '96 - p11 [51-250]
Chua, Daniel K L - *The Galitzin Quartets of Beethoven, Opp. 127, 132, 130*
  TLS - D 20 '96 - p20 [501+]
Chuang-Tzu - *The Book of Chuang Tzu*
  Rel St Rev - v23 - Ap '97 - p203+ [51-250]
Chubyns'kyi, Pavlo - *Mudrist' Vikiv*
  BL - v93 - N 15 '96 - p577 [1-50]
Chudleigh, Mary Lee, Lady - *The Poems and Prose of Mary, Lady Chudleigh*
  Sev Cent N - v54 - Spr '96 - p24 [501+]
Chugh, C P - *Design Criteria for Drill Rigs*
  SciTech - v20 - N '96 - p77 [51-250]
Chukovsky, Kornei - *Telephone (Illus. by Vladimir Radunsky)*
  c PW - v243 - N 18 '96 - p74+ [51-250]
  c SLJ - v42 - D '96 - p91 [51-250]

Chung, Andrew - *The New Specialized Catalogue of Canadian Post Official First Day Covers*
  r Phil Lit R - v45 - '96 - p343+ [251-500]
Chung, Edward K - *Pocket Guide to ECG Diagnosis*
  r SciTech - v20 - S '96 - p35 [51-250]
Chung, Fan R K - *Spectral Graph Theory*
  SciTech - v21 - Mr '97 - p12 [51-250]
Chung, Soon M - *Multimedia Information Storage and Management*
  SciTech - v21 - Mr '97 - p11 [51-250]
Chunovic, Louis - *Bruce Lee: The Tao of the Dragon Warrior*
  y BL - v92 - Ag '96 - p1872 [501+]
  y BL - v92 - Ag '96 - p1890 [51-250]
The Complete Quantum Leap Book
  SF Chr - v18 - O '96 - p82 [1-50]
The Rocky and Bullwinkle Book
  y BL - v93 - S 15 '96 - p199 [51-250]
  Ent W - O 25 '96 - p108 [51-250]
  NYTBR - v102 - Mr 9 '97 - p18 [51-250]
Church, Caroline - *Bouncy Lamb*
  c New Sci - v152 - D 7 '96 - p47 [1-50]
Diver
  c New Sci - v152 - D 7 '96 - p47 [1-50]
Sailor
  c New Sci - v152 - D 7 '96 - p47 [1-50]
Church, F Forrester - *Life Lines*
  BL - v93 - O 1 '96 - p297 [251-500]
  CC - v114 - Mr 19 '97 - p314+ [501+]
  LJ - v121 - O 1 '96 - p86 [51-250]
  PW - v243 - S 2 '96 - p127 [51-250]
Church, James M - *Molecular Genetics and Colorectal Neoplasia*
  SciTech - v20 - N '96 - p41 [51-250]
Church, Robert J - *The 4300 4-8-2s*
  Model R - v64 - Ja '97 - p62 [51-250]
Church, Roy - *The Rise and Decline of the British Motor Industry*
  EHR - v111 - S '96 - p1030 [251-500]
  JEL - v34 - D '96 - p2106 [51-250]
Church, Susan M - *The Future of Whole Language*
  SLJ - v42 - O '96 - p46 [51-250]
Church, Thomas D - *Gardens Are for People. 3rd Ed.*
  Hort - v74 - My '96 - p74+ [501+]
Churchill, Charles B - *Adventurers and Prophets*
  WHQ - v27 - Win '96 - p536+ [501+]
Churchill, Jill - *Silence of the Hams*
  Arm Det - v29 - Fall '96 - p488+ [501+]
War and Peas
  KR - v64 - S 15 '96 - p1356 [51-250]
  LJ - v121 - N 1 '96 - p111 [51-250]
  PW - v243 - S 23 '96 - p59 [51-250]
Churchill, Kevin - *Program-Based Literacy Materials Catalogue. 2nd Ed.*
  r JAAL - v40 - D '96 - p328 [1-50]
Churchill, Robert Paul - *The Ethics of Liberal Democracy*
  Ethics - v107 - O '96 - p178+ [51-250]
Churchill, Ward - *From a Native Son*
  OS - v33 - Mr '97 - p35 [51-250]
Churchill, Winston S - *His Father's Son*
  KR - v65 - My 1 '97 - p688 [251-500]
  PW - v244 - Ap 28 '97 - p56+ [501+]
  TLS - Jl 19 '96 - p14 [501+]
Churchland, Paul M - *The Engine of Reason, the Seat of the Soul*
  Bks & Cult - v2 - Ja '96 - p20+ [501+]
  IPQ - v36 - D '96 - p496+ [501+]
Chute, Marchette - *Stories from Shakespeare*
  Obs - v54 - O 13 '96 - p18* [51-250]
Chutkow, Paul - *Depardieu*
  FR - v70 - O '96 - p162+ [501+]
Depardieu: A Biography
  FR - v70 - O '96 - p162+ [501+]
Chwast, Seymour - *Mr. Merlin and the Turtle (Illus. by Seymour Chwast)*
  c CBRS - v24 - Ag '96 - p158 [51-250]
  c HB Guide - v8 - Spr '97 - p23 [51-250]
  c NYTBR - v102 - F 16 '97 - p25 [1-50]
  c SLJ - v42 - O '96 - p85 [51-250]
The Twelve Circus Rings
  c BL - v93 - Ap 1 '97 - p1340 [1-50]
Chwialkowski, Jerzy - *The Da Capo Catalog of Classical Music Compositions*
  r FF - v20 - S '96 - p472+ [501+]
  r R&R Bk N - v11 - N '96 - p58 [51-250]
Chwin, Stefan - *Hanemann*
  WLT - v71 - Win '97 - p183 [251-500]
Ciappelli, Giovanni - *Una Famiglia E Le Sue Ricordanze*
  Choice - v34 - D '96 - p566 [1-50]
  Six Ct J - v27 - Fall '96 - p889+ [501+]
  Specu - v71 - Jl '96 - p707+ [501+]

Ciardi, John - *The Collected Poems of John Ciardi*
  PW - v244 - F 24 '97 - p84 [51-250]
Ciardi, Marco - *L'Atomo Fantasma*
  Isis - v87 - D '96 - p734+ [501+]
Cicarelli, James - *Joan Robinson: A Bio-Bibliography*
  r ARBA - v28 - '97 - p76+ [51-250]
  r JEL - v35 - Mr '97 - p192 [51-250]
  r R&R Bk N - v11 - D '96 - p22 [1-50]
Cicchetti, Dante - *Adolescence: Opportunities and Challenges*
  SciTech - v21 - Mr '97 - p64 [51-250]
Cicciarella, Charles F - *Research in Physical Education, Exercise Science, and Sport*
  R&R Bk N - v12 - F '97 - p31 [51-250]
Ciccone, F Richard - *Daley: Power and Presidential Politics*
  PW - v243 - S 2 '96 - p107 [51-250]
Cicero, Marcus Tullius - *Cicero: Pro P. Sulla Oratio*
  Choice - v34 - D '96 - p609 [51-250]
De Re Publica
  Rel St Rev - v23 - Ja '97 - p66 [51-250]
M. Tulli Ciceronis De Officiis (Winterbottom)
  CML - v16 - Win '96 - p131+ [501+]
Cicirelli, Victor G - *Sibling Relationships across the Life Span*
  JMF - v58 - Ag '96 - p804 [501+]
  Readings - v11 - S '96 - p22 [51-250]
Cifani, Arabella - *I Piaceri E Le Grazie. Vols. 1-2*
  BM - v138 - Ag '96 - p551 [251-500]
Cifarelli, Megan - *India: One Nation, Many Traditions*
  c HB Guide - v8 - Spr '97 - p169 [51-250]
Cigar, Norman - *Genocide in Bosnia*
  Slav R - v55 - Sum '96 - p461+ [501+]
Cikovsky, Nicolai, Jr. - *Winslow Homer*
  BM - v138 - Jl '96 - p481+ [501+]
Cilurzo, Mary Jeanne - *Health Industry QuickSource*
  r ARBA - v28 - '97 - p599+ [51-250]
Cimbala, Paul - *Historians and Race*
  BWatch - v18 - Mr '97 - p4 [51-250]
Cimbala, Stephen J - *Clinton and Post-Cold War Defense*
  APSR - v90 - D '96 - p953 [501+]
  Pres SQ - v27 - Win '97 - p169+ [501+]
Collective Insecurity
  APSR - v90 - S '96 - p691+ [501+]
The Politics of Warfare
  Choice - v34 - Ap '97 - p1392+ [51-250]
Ciment, James - *Algeria: The Fundamentalist Challenge*
  BL - v93 - Mr 15 '97 - p1222 [51-250]
  LJ - v122 - Mr 15 '97 - p75 [51-250]
Scholastic Encyclopedia of the North American Indian
  cr BL - v93 - N 15 '96 - p614 [501+]
  cr PW - v243 - S 16 '96 - p85 [51-250]
  cr SLJ - v42 - N '96 - p136+ [51-250]
Ciment, Jill - *Half a Life*
  KR - v64 - My 1 '96 - p657 [251-500]
  LATBR - Jl 7 '96 - p10 [51-250]
  Nat - v263 - Ag 26 '96 - p26+ [501+]
Cimet, Adina - *Ashkenazi Jews in Mexico*
  Choice - v34 - My '97 - p1559+ [51-250]
Cinemania 96. Electronic Media Version
  r Econ - v339 - My 18 '96 - p16* [501+]
Cinemania 97. Electronic Media Version
  yr Kliatt - v31 - Mr '97 - p37 [51-250]
  c PW - v244 - Ja 27 '97 - p37 [51-250]
Cingolani, Charles L - *In the Wheat*
  RR - v55 - N '96 - p660 [1-50]
Cioran, E M - *Entretiens*
  WLT - v70 - Sum '96 - p658 [51-250]
History and Utopia
  NS - v125 - D 20 '96 - p117 [51-250]
Tears and Saints
  TranslRevS - v2 - D '96 - p15+ [51-250]
Ciorra, Anthony J - *Everyday Mysticism*
  RR - v55 - S '96 - p540+ [501+]
Cipolla, Frank J - *The Wind Ensemble and Its Repertoire*
  Notes - v53 - S '96 - p84+ [501+]
Cipriani, Arrigo - *Harry's Bar*
  LJ - v121 - S 15 '96 - p85 [51-250]
  NYTBR - v101 - D 22 '96 - p14 [51-250]
Circa Art Magazine
  p ILS - v16 - Spr '97 - p34 [51-250]
Circling the Globe. Electronic Media Version
  cr BL - v92 - Ag '96 - p1918 [51-250]
Ciresi, Rita - *Blue Italian*
  BL - v93 - S 1 '96 - p60+ [51-250]
  Ent W - N 22 '96 - p131 [51-250]
  LJ - v121 - S 15 '96 - p94 [51-250]
  LJ - v122 - Mr 15 '97 - p41 [1-50]
  NYTBR - v101 - S 22 '96 - p34 [501+]
  SFR - v22 - Ja '97 - p30 [501+]

Cirillo, Susan E - *Library Buildings, Equipment, and the ADA*
  LJ - v121 - D '96 - p156 [51-250]
Ciro Fornaro
  Ceram Mo - v45 - Mr '97 - p28 [51-250]
Cisneros, Henry G - *Interwoven Destinies*
  PAR - v57 - Ja '97 - p83+ [501+]
Citino, David - *Broken Symmetry*
  PW - v244 - Ap 28 '97 - p71+ [251-500]
Citra, Becky - *School Campout*
  c Quill & Q - v62 - N '96 - p48 [251-500]
Citro, Constance F - *Measuring Poverty*
  Econ J - v107 - Ja '97 - p223+ [501+]
  JEL - v34 - S '96 - p1368+ [501+]
  Soc Ser R - v70 - D '96 - p670 [51-250]
Citro, Joseph A - *Green Mountain Ghosts, Ghouls and Unsolved Mysteries*
  CAY - v17 - Fall '96 - p10 [51-250]
Passing Strange
  BWatch - v17 - D '96 - p7 [1-50]
Citron, Stephen - *The Musical from the Inside Out*
  TCI - v30 - O '96 - p56 [1-50]
Citroni, Mario - *Poesia E Lettori In Roma Antica*
  Choice - v34 - D '96 - p566 [1-50]
City Profiles USA 1996
  r ARBA - v28 - '97 - p178 [51-250]
City-Smart Guidebook: Denver. 1st Ed.
  r LJ - v122 - F 15 '97 - p153+ [51-250]
Ciufolini, Ignazio - *Gravitation and Inertia*
  Am Sci - v84 - N '96 - p600 [501+]
Ciullo, Jerome V - *Shoulder Injuries in Sport*
  SciTech - v20 - S '96 - p38 [1-50]
Ciullo, Peter A - *Car Keys*
  LJ - v122 - Ap 15 '97 - p114 [51-250]
Civardi, Anne - *The Kingfisher First Encyclopedia*
  cr ARBA - v28 - '97 - p24 [51-250]
  cr BL - v93 - N 1 '96 - p536 [251-500]
  cr Ch BWatch - v6 - N '96 - p1+ [51-250]
  cr CLW - v67 - Mr '97 - p56 [51-250]
  cr PW - v243 - S 16 '96 - p84+ [51-250]
  cr Sch Lib - v45 - F '97 - p41 [51-250]
  cr SLJ - v43 - F '97 - p133 [51-250]
  cr TES - D 6 '96 - p22* [501+]
Civcir, Irfan - *An Economic Approach to the Analysis of the Monetary Sector and Balance of Payments Problems in Turkey*
  JEL - v34 - D '96 - p2051 [51-250]
Civic, Jed - *The Vegetarian Traveler*
  r LJ - v122 - F 15 '97 - p153 [51-250]
Civil Justice Review
  J Gov Info - v23 - S '96 - p632+ [51-250]
The Civil War CD-ROM. Electronic Media Version
  r ARBA - v28 - '97 - p185 [501+]
Civil War Sites Advisory Commission - *Civil War Sites Advisory Commission Report on the Nation's Civil War Battlefields*
  Pub Hist - v18 - Fall '96 - p170+ [501+]
The Civil War Trust's Official Guide to the Civil War Discovery Trail
  r BL - v93 - S 15 '96 - p206+ [1-50]
Civilizations of the Ancient Near East. Vols. 1-4
  AJA - v101 - Ja '97 - p149+ [501+]
  yr RQ - v35 - Sum '96 - p549 [251-500]
Civille, Gail V - *Aroma and Flavor Lexicon for Sensory Evaluation*
  r SciTech - v20 - D '96 - p87 [51-250]
Cixous, Helene - *The Terrible but Unfinished Story of Norodom Sihanouk, King of Cambodia*
  TDR - v40 - Fall '96 - p198+ [501+]
Three Steps on the Ladder of Writing
  TranslRevS - v1 - My '95 - p6+ [501+]
Cizek, Eugen - *Histoire Et Historiens A Rome Dans L'Antiquite*
  Choice - v34 - D '96 - p566 [1-50]
Claghorn, Gene - *Women Composers and Songwriters*
  r AB - v98 - D 9 '96 - p1994 [51-250]
  r ARBA - v28 - '97 - p473+ [251-500]
  r LJ - v122 - F 1 '97 - p79+ [51-250]
Clairmont, Clara Mary Jane - *The Clairmont Correspondence. Vols. 1-2*
  Albion - v28 - Sum '96 - p341+ [501+]
Clairmont, Frederic F - *The Rise and Fall of Economic Liberalism*
  Arena - Je '96 - p51+ [501+]
Clairmont, Patsy - *The Joyful Journey*
  PW - v244 - Ja 27 '97 - p97 [51-250]
Clanchy, M T - *From Memory to Written Record*
  Specu - v72 - Ja '97 - p131+ [501+]
Clancy, Tom - *Acts of War*
  PW - v244 - F 3 '97 - p100 [51-250]

Debt of Honour
Books - v9 - S '95 - p24 [1-50]
Executive Orders
BW - v26 - Ag 18 '96 - p1+ [501+]
CSM - v88 - S 19 '96 - p14 [51-250]
CSM - v88 - N 14 '96 - p14 [51-250]
CSM - v89 - D 19 '96 - p14 [51-250]
CSM - v89 - Ja 16 '97 - p14 [51-250]
CSM - v89 - F 20 '97 - p10 [51-250]
Econ - v341 - D 7 '96 - p3*+ [501+]
Ent W - Ag 23 '96 - p115+ [501+]
LATBR - Ag 25 '96 - p5 [501+]
Nat R - v48 - D 23 '96 - p56 [51-250]
NYRB - v43 - N 14 '96 - p34+ [501+]
NYTBR - v101 - S 22 '96 - p16+ [501+]
Executive Orders (Herrmann). Audio Version
BWatch - v18 - Mr '97 - p6 [1-50]
Marine: A Guided Tour of a Marine Expeditionary Unit
KR - v64 - S 1 '96 - p1288 [251-500]
LJ - v121 - N 1 '96 - p92 [51-250]
Mar Crp G - v81 - F '97 - p75 [501+]
NYRB - v43 - N 14 '96 - p34+ [501+]
SSN: Strategies of Submarine Warfare
BL - v93 - D 15 '96 - p690 [1-50]
Clapham, Christopher - *Africa and the International System*
Choice - v34 - My '97 - p1571+ [51-250]
Clapp, Michael - *Amphibious Assault Falklands*
Spec - v277 - N 30 '96 - p47+ [501+]
Clapp, Rodney - *A Peculiar People*
Bks & Cult - v2 - N '96 - p4 [51-250]
BL - v93 - N 1 '96 - p460 [51-250]
PW - v243 - O 14 '96 - p77 [51-250]
Clapp, Susannah - *With Chatwin*
Lon R Bks - v19 - F 20 '97 - p15+ [501+]
NS - v126 - Mr 7 '97 - p44+ [501+]
Obs - F 9 '97 - p17* [501+]
Spec - v278 - Ja 25 '97 - p38 [501+]
TLS - F 14 '97 - p13 [501+]
Clare, John - *John Clare by Himself*
Obs - S 8 '96 - p18* [51-250]
Poems of the Middle Period 1822-1837. Vols. 1-2
Choice - v34 - F '97 - p963+ [51-250]
Nine-C Lit - v51 - Mr '97 - p555 [51-250]
NYRB - v43 - D 19 '96 - p42+ [501+]
Clare, John D - *Classical Rome*
c SLJ - v42 - N '96 - p39 [1-50]
Clare, Ross - *Income Distribution in Australia*
J Gov Info - v23 - S '96 - p652 [51-250]
Claremont, Chris - *Shadow Dawn (Auberjonois). Audio Version*
y Kliatt - v31 - My '97 - p44 [51-250]
Clark, Al - *Raymond Chandler in Hollywood*
AB - v98 - D 9 '96 - p1997 [51-250]
LATBR - S 22 '96 - p15 [51-250]
LJ - v121 - O 15 '96 - p60 [51-250]
Clark, Alan - *Diaries*
TES - D 27 '96 - p17 [1-50]
Clark, Alison - *About Desire and Other Poems*
Aust Bk R - D '96 - p69+ [501+]
Clark, Andy - *Being There*
New Sci - v153 - Ja 18 '97 - p37 [501+]
SB - v33 - Mr '97 - p36 [51-250]
Clark, Anna - *The Struggle for the Breeches*
EHR - v111 - N '96 - p1220+ [501+]
JIH - v27 - Win '97 - p515+ [501+]
Clark, Anne - *My Jewish Life*
TES - F 14 '97 - p16* [51-250]
Clark, Beverly Lyon - *Regendering the School Story*
Choice - v34 - Ja '97 - p792 [51-250]
Clark, Bryon N - *A List of Pensioners of the War of 1812 (Vermont Claimants)*
r EGH - v50 - N '96 - p196 [51-250]
Clark, Burton R - *Places of Inquiry*
AJS - v102 - Jl '96 - p280+ [501+]
Clark, C M H - *Dear Kathleen, Dear Manning*
Aust Bk R - D '96 - p18+ [501+]
Clark, Christopher, 1953- - *The Communitarian Moment*
AHR - v101 - D '96 - p1622+ [251-500]
CS - v26 - Ja '97 - p61+ [501+]
Clark, Christopher M - *The Politics of Conversion*
AHR - v101 - D '96 - p1564+ [501+]
Clark, Cindy Dell - *Flights of Fancy, Leaps of Faith*
Readings - v11 - D '96 - p16+ [501+]
Clark, Clara Gillow - *Nellie Bishop*
y HB Guide - v7 - Fall '96 - p301 [51-250]
c RT - v50 - Ap '97 - p588 [51-250]
Clark, David - *Schools as Learning Communities*
Choice - v34 - S '96 - p179+ [51-250]
Clark, Dick - *Dick Clark's American Bandstand*
PW - v244 - Mr 31 '97 - p57 [51-250]

Clark, Donald - *Self-Determination: International Perspectives*
Choice - v34 - My '97 - p1572+ [51-250]
TLS - Ap 11 '97 - p12 [501+]
Clark, Edward - *Dictionary Catalog of the Collection of African American Literature in the Mildred F. Sawyer Library of Suffolk University*
r Choice - v34 - S '96 - p93+ [51-250]
Clark, Eliza - *Butterflies and Bottlecaps (Illus. by Vladyana Krykorka)*
c Quill & Q - v62 - My '96 - p34 [251-500]
Clark, Elizabeth - *Country Tales (Illus. by Amanda Harvey)*
c Bks Keeps - Jl '96 - p7 [51-250]
Clark, Elizabeth A - *The Origenist Controversy*
Rel St Rev - v22 - O '96 - p301+ [501+]
Clark, Eve - *The Lexicon in Acquisition*
Lect Y V - v17 - Je '96 - p42+ [501+]
Clark, Forrest D - *Applied Cost Engineering. 3rd Ed.*
SciTech - v21 - Mr '97 - p74 [51-250]
Clark, Geoffrey - *All the Way Home*
KR - v65 - F 15 '97 - p239 [251-500]
PW - v244 - Mr 31 '97 - p64+ [51-250]
Clark, George B - *Their Time in Hell*
Mar Crp G - v81 - F '97 - p77 [501+]
Treading Softly
Mar Crp G - v80 - Ag '96 - p77 [501+]
Clark, Gordon L - *Asian NIEs and the Global Economy*
JEL - v34 - S '96 - p1451+ [51-250]
Clark, Gracia - *Onions Are My Husband*
Am Ethnol - v24 - F '97 - p250+ [501+]
EG - v72 - Jl '96 - p353+ [501+]
Clark, Gregory T - *A Tribute to Robert A. Koch*
Ren Q - v50 - Spr '97 - p321+ [501+]
Clark, Harold Willard - *The Early Writings of Harold W. Clark and Frank Lewis Marsh*
Isis - v88 - Mr '97 - p160+ [501+]
Clark, Henry B - *Serenity, Courage, Wisdom*
Intpr - v51 - Ja '97 - p102+ [251-500]
Clark, Henry C - *La Rochefoucauld and the Language of Unmasking in Seventeenth-Century France*
AHR - v101 - O '96 - p1219 [501+]
Clark, Ian - *Classical Theories of International Relations*
Choice - v34 - Ja '97 - p872 [51-250]
Clark, J C D - *The Language of Liberty 1660-1832*
CH - v66 - Mr '97 - p141+ [501+]
Rel St Rev - v23 - Ap '97 - p202 [51-250]
Samuel Johnson: Literature, Religion and English Cultural Politics from the Restoration to Romanticism
AHR - v102 - F '97 - p103+ [501+]
EHR - v112 - Ap '97 - p491+ [251-500]
Clark, Janie - *Exercise Programming for Older Adults*
SB - v32 - N '96 - p231+ [51-250]
Clark, Jerome - *High Strangeness*
r ARBA - v28 - '97 - p286 [51-250]
Strange and Unexplained Happenings. Vols. 1-3
yr ARBA - v28 - '97 - p288+ [251-500]
y R&R Bk N - v11 - N '96 - p75 [51-250]
Clark, Jon - *James S. Coleman*
R&R Bk N - v11 - N '96 - p38 [51-250]
Clark, Katerina - *Mikhail Bakhtin*
Bks & Cult - v2 - Ja '96 - p26 [1-50]
Petersburg, Crucible of Cultural Revolution
HT - v47 - Ja '97 - p58+ [501+]
Slav R - v55 - Fall '96 - p691+ [501+]
TLS - O 11 '96 - p13+ [501+]
Clark, Kelly James - *Philosophers Who Believe*
JAAR - v64 - Win '96 - p886+ [501+]
Clark, Kenneth - *Looking at Pictures*
TES - Ag 30 '96 - p26 [1-50]
Clark, Leigh - *Evil Incarnate*
SF Chr - v18 - O '96 - p79 [51-250]
Shock Radio
Arm Det - v29 - Fall '96 - p502+ [51-250]
Ent W - S 13 '96 - p127 [51-250]
LJ - v121 - S 15 '96 - p94 [51-250]
Clark, Lynn G - *Agnes Chase's First Book of Grasses. 4th Ed.*
SciTech - v20 - N '96 - p28 [51-250]
Clark, Margaret - *Love on the Net*
y Aust Bk R - S '96 - p59+ [501+]
Pulling the Moves
y Magpies - v11 - S '96 - p36+ [251-500]
The Very Best of Aesop's Fables (Illus. by Charlotte Voake)
c Magpies - v11 - S '96 - p45 [1-50]
Clark, Martin - *Modern Italy 1871-1995*
CR - v269 - D '96 - p328+ [501+]
Clark, Martin P - *ATM Networks*
SciTech - v20 - D '96 - p76 [1-50]

Clark, Mary Higgins - *Moonlight Becomes You*
PW - v244 - Mr 24 '97 - p81 [1-50]
My Gal Sunday
CSM - v88 - N 14 '96 - p14 [51-250]
CSM - v89 - D 19 '96 - p15 [51-250]
KR - v64 - O 1 '96 - p1417+ [251-500]
LATBR - D 15 '96 - p12 [251-500]
NYTBR - v101 - D 15 '96 - p25 [51-250]
PW - v243 - O 7 '96 - p63 [51-250]
My Gal Sunday (Follows). Audio Version
LJ - v121 - D '96 - p170 [51-250]
PW - v243 - N 4 '96 - p30 [51-250]
Pretend You Don't See Her
KR - v65 - Ap 1 '97 - p481 [251-500]
PW - v244 - Mr 31 '97 - p61 [51-250]
Silent Night
PW - v243 - O 14 '96 - p81 [1-50]
Clark, Mary T - *Augustine*
CH - v65 - S '96 - p450+ [251-500]
CHR - v83 - Ja '97 - p161 [51-250]
JR - v76 - O '96 - p624+ [501+]
Specu - v71 - O '96 - p984 [251-500]
Clark, Michael - *Legal Medicine in History*
EHR - v112 - Ap '97 - p552 [251-500]
Clark, Peter - *Small Towns in Early Modern Europe*
JEH - v56 - D '96 - p931+ [501+]
JIH - v27 - Spr '97 - p667+ [251-500]
Clark, R J H - *Biomedical Applications of Spectroscopy*
SciTech - v20 - S '96 - p22 [51-250]
Clark, Ramsey - *The Impact of Sanctions on Iraq*
SFR - v21 - N '96 - p40 [251-500]
Clark, Robert - *In the Deep Midwinter*
CSM - v89 - Ja 13 '97 - p13 [251-500]
KR - v64 - N 1 '96 - p1548 [251-500]
LJ - v121 - D '96 - p142 [51-250]
NYTBR - v102 - F 9 '97 - p20 [251-500]
PW - v243 - N 25 '96 - p57 [51-250]
Time - v149 - F 3 '97 - p71 [251-500]
The Solace of Food
NYTBR - v101 - S 8 '96 - p36 [51-250]
Clark, Robert N - *Control System Dynamics*
Choice - v34 - O '96 - p311 [51-250]
Clark, Roger S - *The Prosecution of International Crimes*
For Aff - v75 - N '96 - p146 [51-250]
R&R Bk N - v11 - D '96 - p50 [51-250]
Clark, Ronald - *Life Drawing*
LJ - v121 - N 15 '96 - p60 [51-250]
Clark, Sam - *The Real Goods Independent Builder*
LJ - v121 - N 15 '96 - p86 [51-250]
Clark, Samuel, 1945- - *State and Status*
AJS - v102 - N '96 - p878+ [501+]
J Soc H - v30 - Fall '96 - p294+ [501+]
Clark, Stephen R L - *How to Live Forever*
Rel St - v32 - D '96 - p529+ [501+]
SFS - v23 - N '96 - p534+ [501+]
Clark, Stuart - *Thinking with Demons*
Obs - Mr 9 '97 - p15* [501+]
Clark, Sylvia - *Organizing Corporate Contributions*
ChrPhil - v8 - O 3 '96 - p44 [501+]
Clark, Thekla - *Wystan and Chester*
LJ - v121 - S 15 '96 - p68 [51-250]
NYTBR - v101 - S 22 '96 - p7 [501+]
PW - v243 - Jl 22 '96 - p222 [51-250]
TES - D 27 '96 - p16 [1-50]
TES - F 21 '97 - p7* [51-250]
Clark, Thomas D - *Pills, Petticoats and Plows*
CAY - v17 - Fall '96 - p10 [51-250]
Clark, Thomas L - *Western Lore and Language*
r ARBA - v28 - '97 - p387 [51-250]
r Bloom Rev - v16 - S '96 - p27 [51-250]
r BW - v26 - Ag 25 '96 - p13 [51-250]
r LJ - v121 - N 1 '96 - p58 [51-250]
r SFR - v21 - N '96 - p28+ [501+]
Clark, Trinkett - *Myth, Magic, and Mystery*
AB - v98 - N 18 '96 - p1733 [251-500]
BL - v93 - S 1 '96 - p52 [51-250]
BW - v26 - S 1 '96 - p7 [251-500]
Ch BWatch - v6 - O '96 - p1 [1-50]
Ch BWatch - v6 - N '96 - p1 [51-250]
HB - v72 - N '96 - p769+ [501+]
SLJ - v42 - N '96 - p142 [51-250]
Clark, Urszula - *An Introduction to Stylistic Text Analysis*
TES - S 20 '96 - pR8 [251-500]
Clark, Veronica - *Music Box (Illus. by Zoe Figg)*
c Sch Lib - v44 - Ag '96 - p110 [51-250]
Clark, VeVe - *Antifeminism in the Academy*
Wom R Bks - v14 - N '96 - p18+ [501+]
Clark, William A V - *Households and Housing*
Choice - v34 - Ap '97 - p1385+ [51-250]

Clark, William R - *Sex and the Origins of Death*
   BL - v93 - N 1 '96 - p467 [51-250]
   BW - v26 - O 20 '96 - p8 [251-500]
   KR - v64 - S 15 '96 - p1368 [251-500]
   Nature - v384 - D 19 '96 - p618 [501+]
   New Sci - v152 - D 14 '96 - p43 [501+]
   NH - v105 - O '96 - p12 [51-250]
   Obs - Mr 2 '97 - p15* [251-500]
   SciTech - v21 - Mr '97 - p37 [51-250]
Clark, William S - *Hawks*
   Wildbird - v10 - Ag '96 - p42 [1-50]
  A Photographic Guide to North American Raptors
   Wildbird - v10 - Ag '96 - p42 [1-50]
Clark County Genealogical Society - *Clark County, Washington Cemeteries. Vols. 7-11*
  r EGH - v50 - N '96 - p191 [51-250]
  Clark County, Washington Marriages. Vols. 11-13
  r EGH - v50 - N '96 - p191 [51-250]
Clarke, Anna - *The Nodland Express (Illus. by Martin Rowson)*
  c JB - v60 - Ag '96 - p141 [51-250]
Clarke, Arthur C - *3001: The Final Odyssey*
  y BL - v93 - Ja '97 - p778 [51-250]
   BW - v27 - Mr 30 '97 - p8 [251-500]
   CSM - v89 - Mr 20 '97 - p14 [51-250]
   Econ - v343 - Ap 12 '97 - p85+ [501+]
   KR - v65 - Ja 1 '97 - p27 [51-250]
   LJ - v122 - F 15 '97 - p164 [51-250]
   NYTBR - v102 - Mr 9 '97 - p7 [501+]
   NYTLa - v146 - Ap 11 '97 - pC29 [501+]
   PW - v244 - F 3 '97 - p99 [51-250]
   TLS - Mr 21 '97 - p22 [501+]
  The City and the Stars
   Reason - v28 - D '96 - p39+ [51-250]
Clarke, Asia Booth - *John Wilkes Booth: A Sister's Memoir*
  y BL - v93 - N 1 '96 - p477+ [51-250]
   BW - v27 - Ja 26 '97 - p13 [51-250]
   LJ - v122 - Ja '97 - p155 [1-50]
Clarke, Austin - *The Origin of Waves*
   Mac - v110 - Ap 21 '97 - p62 [501+]
   Quill & Q - v63 - F '97 - p47 [251-500]
  The Prime Minister
  y Quill & Q - v63 - F '97 - p58 [1-50]
Clarke, Brian W - *Handbook of International Credit Management. 2nd Ed.*
   R&R Bk N - v12 - F '97 - p48 [51-250]
Clarke, Cathy - *Shocking the Web*
   LJ - v122 - Ap 1 '97 - p118 [51-250]
Clarke, Danny - *Scientists and Inventors (Illus. by John Dillow)*
  c Sch Lib - v44 - N '96 - p162 [51-250]
Clarke, David - *Twilight of the Celtic Gods*
   NS & S - v9 - My 24 '96 - p39 [1-50]
Clarke, Donald - *The Rise and Fall of Popular Music*
   Quad - v40 - S '96 - p82+ [501+]
  Wishing on the Moon
   Ant R - v55 - Spr '97 - p249 [51-250]
Clarke, Ernest - *The Siege of Fort Cumberland 1776*
   Can Hist R - v78 - Mr '97 - p127+ [501+]
   W&M Q - v54 - Ap '97 - p436+ [501+]
Clarke, Erskine - *Our Southern Zion*
   Choice - v34 - S '96 - p143 [51-250]
Clarke, Ethne - *Gardening with Foliage Plants*
   PW - v244 - Mr 3 '97 - p70 [51-250]
Clarke, George Elliot - *Eyeing the North Star*
   Quill & Q - v63 - Mr '97 - p70 [251-500]
Clarke, Gillian - *I Can Move the Sea (Illus. by Jenny Fell)*
  c Bks Keeps - N '96 - p10 [51-250]
  c JB - v60 - D '96 - p248 [1-50]
  c Sch Lib - v44 - N '96 - p167 [51-250]
  c TES - O 25 '96 - p7* [251-500]
  The Whispering Room (Illus. by Justin Todd)
  c CCB-B - v50 - Ja '97 - p166 [51-250]
  c HB Guide - v8 - Spr '97 - p150 [51-250]
  c KR - v64 - S 15 '96 - p1397 [51-250]
  c LATBR - O 20 '96 - p8 [51-250]
  c Sch Lib - v45 - F '97 - p41 [51-250]
  c SLJ - v42 - D '96 - p127 [51-250]
Clarke, Graham - *The American Landscape. Vols. 1-3*
   AAAGA - v86 - S '96 - p592+ [501+]
  The Photograph
   LJ - v122 - My 1 '97 - p100 [51-250]
Clarke, Gus - *Michael's Monsters (Illus. by Gus Clarke)*
  c Bks Keeps - Mr '97 - p18 [51-250]
  c JB - v60 - D '96 - p227+ [51-250]
  c Sch Lib - v45 - F '97 - p18 [51-250]
  Scratch 'n' Sniff (Illus. by Gus Clarke)
  c JB - v60 - O '96 - p182 [51-250]
  c Sch Lib - v44 - N '96 - p145 [51-250]

Ten Green Monsters
  c Bks Keeps - N '96 - p6 [51-250]
Clarke, I F - *The Tale of the Next Great War 1871-1914*
   ELT - v39 - 3 '96 - p406 [51-250]
Clarke, Jeanne Nienaber - *Roosevelt's Warrior*
   HRNB - v25 - Fall '96 - p12 [251-500]
   VQR - v72 - Aut '96 - p126* [51-250]
   WHQ - v27 - Win '96 - p529+ [501+]
  Staking out the Terrain. 2nd Ed.
   Choice - v34 - Ja '97 - p874 [51-250]
   Pol Stud J - v24 - Aut '96 - p518 [51-250]
   R&R Bk N - v11 - N '96 - p26 [51-250]
Clarke, Joan - *Artists/Hawaii*
   PW - v243 - N 4 '96 - p70 [51-250]
Clarke, Judith - *The Heroic Life of Al Capsella*
  y Kliatt - v30 - S '96 - p3 [1-50]
  The Lost Day
   Aust Bk R - F '97 - p52 [501+]
Clarke, Micael M - *Thackeray and Women*
   Clio - v25 - Sum '96 - p459+ [501+]
   Nine-C Lit - v50 - Mr '96 - p552 [1-50]
   VS - v39 - Spr '96 - p429+ [501+]
Clarke, Norma - *The Doctor's Daughter (Illus. by Michael Charlton)*
  c JB - v60 - O '96 - p191 [51-250]
  Trouble on the Day
  c Magpies - v11 - My '96 - p53 [1-50]
Clarke, Oz - *Oz Clarke's Wine Atlas*
  r LJ - v122 - Ap 1 '97 - p62 [1-50]
Clarke, Paul A B - *Deep Citizenship*
   TLS - Ag 30 '96 - p12 [501+]
  Dictionary of Ethics, Theology, and Society
  yr ARBA - v28 - '97 - p41 [251-500]
  Dictionary of Ethics, Theology, and Society
  r Choice - v34 - N '96 - p427 [51-250]
Clarke, Penny - *Rain Forest (Illus. by Carolyn Scrace)*
  c HB Guide - v8 - Spr '97 - p116 [51-250]
Clarke, Peter - *Starting from Food*
   TES - F 14 '97 - p16* [51-250]
  Starting from Transport
   TES - F 14 '97 - p16* [51-250]
Clarke, Peter, 1942- - *Capital Cities and Their Hinterlands in Early Modern Europe*
   HT - v46 - O '96 - p56 [1-50]
  Hope and Glory
   BL - v93 - Mr 15 '97 - p1222 [51-250]
   Econ - v341 - D 7 '96 - p7*+ [501+]
   HT - v46 - O '96 - p57 [51-250]
   KR - v65 - F 1 '97 - p186 [251-500]
   LJ - v122 - Ap 1 '97 - p105 [51-250]
   Lon R Bks - v18 - N 28 '96 - p18+ [501+]
   NS - v125 - D 13 '96 - p44+ [501+]
   Spec - v277 - D 21 '96 - p41+ [501+]
   TLS - N 15 '96 - p7+ [501+]
Clarke, Peter A - *The English Nobility under Edward the Confessor*
   EHR - v111 - N '96 - p1237+ [501+]
Clarke, Regina - *Environmental Management*
   R&R Bk N - v12 - F '97 - p97 [51-250]
Clarke, Robert - *Robert Clarke: To B or Not to B*
   FIR - v47 - S '96 - p85+ [251-500]
Clarke, Robin - *Europe's Environment*
   J Gov Info - v23 - S '96 - p668 [51-250]
Clarke, Sally H - *Regulation and the Revolution in United States Farm Productivity*
   AHR - v102 - F '97 - p209 [251-500]
   T&C - v37 - O '96 - p851+ [501+]
Clarke, Sarah - *No Faith in the System*
   NS - v126 - Mr 7 '97 - p48 [501+]
Clarke, Sharon - *Sumner Locke Elliott: Writing Life*
   Aust Bk R - Ag '96 - p12+ [501+]
Clarke, Simon - *Conflict and Change in the Russian Industrial Enterprise*
   JEL - v34 - D '96 - p2126 [51-250]
  Labour Relations in Transition
   JEL - v34 - D '96 - p2074+ [51-250]
  The Workers' Movement in Russia
   APSR - v90 - S '96 - p668+ [501+]
Clarke, Stephen - *R.W. Ketton-Cremer: A Summary Catalogue of His Manuscripts, Notebooks, Correspondence and Related Papers*
  r BC - v46 - Spr '97 - p132 [51-250]
  R.W. Ketton-Cremer: An Annotated Bibliography
  r BC - v45 - Sum '96 - p276+ [251-500]
Clarke, Steve - *Buddhism: A New Approach*
  y Sch Lib - v44 - Ag '96 - p123 [51-250]
  y TES - Mr 21 '97 - p27* [51-250]
Clarke, Thurston - *California Fault*
   NYTBR - v101 - D 8 '96 - p85 [1-50]
   Rapport - v19 - 4 '96 - p34 [251-500]

Clarke, W Norris - *Explorations in Metaphysics*
   RM - v49 - Je '96 - p918+ [501+]
   Theol St - v57 - Mr '96 - p161+ [501+]
Clarke, William - *The Lost Fortune of the Tsars*
   NYTBR - v102 - Ja 12 '97 - p32 [51-250]
Clarke, William C - *The Secret Life of Wilkie Collins*
   CR - v269 - D '96 - p333 [1-50]
Clarke-Evans, Christine - *Diderot's La Religieuse*
   MLR - v92 - Ja '97 - p193+ [251-500]
Clarkin, John F - *Major Theories of Personality Disorder*
   SB - v32 - N '96 - p232 [251-500]
   SciTech - v20 - S '96 - p34 [51-250]
Clark-Lewis, Elizabeth - *Living In, Living Out*
   J Am Cult - v18 - Win '95 - p111+ [251-500]
   Trib Bks - Ja 19 '97 - p8 [1-50]
Clarkson, Wensley - *Quentin Tarantino*
   J Pop F&TV - v24 - Spr '96 - p46+ [501+]
Claro, Christopher - *Comedy Central*
   LJ - v122 - Ap 15 '97 - p83 [51-250]
Clarridge, Duane R - *A Spy for All Seasons*
  y BL - v93 - Ja '97 - p788+ [51-250]
   KR - v64 - N 15 '96 - p1647 [251-500]
   PW - v243 - N 11 '96 - p64 [51-250]
Classic Jump Rope Rhymes (Realworld Guides)
  c PW - v244 - Mr 17 '97 - p85 [51-250]
Classic Outdoor Games (Realworld Guides)
  c PW - v244 - Mr 17 '97 - p85 [51-250]
Classical Women Poets
   BL - v93 - N 1 '96 - p475 [51-250]
  y Sch Lib - v44 - Ag '96 - p114+ [51-250]
   TranslRevS - v2 - D '96 - p1 [51-250]
Classification Plus. Electronic Media Version
  r ARBA - v28 - '97 - p240+ [251-500]
Classroom Connect - *Child Safety on the Internet*
   CBR - v14 - N '96 - p34+ [51-250]
   LJ - v122 - F 1 '97 - p102 [51-250]
  Educator's Internet Companion
   CBR - v15 - Spr '97 - p3 [1-50]
Clatterbaugh, Kenneth C - *Contemporary Perspectives on Masculinity. 2nd Ed.*
   R&R Bk N - v12 - F '97 - p53 [51-250]
Claus, Hugo - *The Swordfish*
   KR - v65 - F 15 '97 - p239+ [51-250]
   PW - v244 - Mr 24 '97 - p60 [51-250]
   TLS - D 13 '96 - p22 [501+]
Clausen, Jan - *Beyond Gay or Straight*
  y HB Guide - v8 - Spr '97 - p89 [51-250]
  y SLJ - v43 - Ja '97 - p120 [51-250]
   Wom R Bks - v14 - Ja '97 - p8 [501+]
Clausen, Soren - *Cultural Encounters*
   Ch Rev Int - v3 - Fall '96 - p380+ [501+]
  The Making of a Chinese City
   Ch Rev Int - v3 - Fall '96 - p384+ [501+]
Clausewitz, Carl Von - *The Campaign of 1812 in Russia*
   Parameters - v26 - Aut '96 - p164+ [501+]
Clauss, James J - *Medea: Essays on Medea in Myth, Literature, Philosophy, and Art*
   TLS - F 14 '97 - p4+ [501+]
Claval, Paul - *La Geographie Culturelle*
   AAAGA - v86 - D '96 - p790+ [501+]
Clavel, Bernard - *Le Carcajou*
   BL - v93 - Ja '97 - p827 [1-50]
Clavel-Leveque, Monique - *Cite Et Territoire*
   AJA - v101 - Ja '97 - p189+ [501+]
  De La Terre Au Ciel
   AJA - v101 - Ja '97 - p189+ [501+]
Clavin, Patricia - *The Failure of Economic Diplomacy*
   Econ J - v106 - N '96 - p1847+ [251-500]
   JEL - v34 - S '96 - p1465+ [51-250]
Clawson, Calvin C - *Mathematical Mysteries*
   BL - v93 - Ja '97 - p758 [1-50]
   Choice - v34 - Ap '97 - p1375 [51-250]
   New Sci - v152 - D 14 '96 - p46 [251-500]
   SB - v33 - Mr '97 - p37 [51-250]
   SciTech - v20 - D '96 - p15 [51-250]
  The Mathematical Traveller
  y BL - v93 - Ap 1 '97 - p1342 [1-50]
Clawson, Patrick L - *The Andean Cocaine Industry*
   Choice - v34 - D '96 - p685 [51-250]
   For Aff - v75 - N '96 - p158+ [51-250]
Clawson, Rudger - *Prisoner for Polygamy*
   CH - v66 - Mr '97 - p152+ [501+]
Clay, Daniel C - *Promoting Food Security in Rwanda through Sustainable Agricultural Productivity*
   JEL - v34 - S '96 - p1476 [51-250]
Clay, John - *R.D. Laing: A Divided Self*
   Econ - v341 - O 19 '96 - p15* [501+]
   PW - v243 - N 18 '96 - p58 [51-250]
   TLS - S 27 '96 - p27 [501+]

Clay, Rebecca - *Ukraine: A New Independence*
c Ch BWatch - v6 - D '96 - p6 [1-50]
c HB Guide - v8 - Spr '97 - p168 [51-250]
Claybourne, Anna - *The World of Shakespeare*
TES - Mr 7 '97 - p7* [501+]
Claydon, Tony - *William III and the Godly Revolution*
Choice - v34 - O '96 - p338 [51-250]
HRNB - v25 - Win '97 - p68 [251-500]
HT - v47 - Mr '97 - p53 [501+]
Clayman, Charles B - *American Medical Association Family Medical Guide. 3rd Ed.*
r BL - v93 - F 1 '97 - p957 [1-50]
Clay-Mendez, Deborah - *Public and Private Roles in Maintaining Military Equipment at the Depot Level*
J Gov Info - v23 - S '96 - p560 [51-250]
Clayton, Anthony - *The Wars of French Decolonization*
EHR - v112 - F '97 - p270 [251-500]
Clayton, Bruce - *Varieties of Southern History*
R&R Bk N - v11 - D '96 - p16 [51-250]
Clayton, Caroline - *Causing a Stink!*
c Sch Lib - v44 - N '96 - p162 [51-250]
Clayton, Cornell W - *Government Lawyers*
R&R Bk N - v11 - D '96 - p51 [51-250]
Clayton, David - *Danny and the Sea of Darkness (Illus. by Stephen Player)*
c Sch Lib - v44 - N '96 - p150 [51-250]
Clayton, Douglas - *Floyd Dell: The Life and Times of an American Rebel*
TLS - Ag 30 '96 - p29 [501+]
Clayton, Elaine - *Ella's Trip to the Museum*
c HB Guide - v7 - Fall '96 - p251 [51-250]
Clayton, Elspeth - *Pakistan*
c TES - Mr 21 '97 - p18* [251-500]
Clayton, Martin - *Leonardo Da Vinci: A Singular Vision*
Choice - v34 - S '96 - p111 [51-250]
WSJ-MW - v78 - D 5 '96 - pA18 [51-250]
Clayton, Mary - *The Old English Lives of St. Margaret*
MLR - v92 - Ja '97 - p162+ [501+]
Clayton, Peter A - *The Valley of the Kings*
c TES - N 8 '96 - p13* [501+]
Clayton, Pomme - *The Orchard Book of Stories from the Seven Seas (Illus. by Sheila Moxley)*
c Bks Keeps - Mr '97 - p21 [51-250]
Clayton, Rubert - *Lotus Notes 4 Plain and Simple*
CBR - v14 - S '96 - p30 [1-50]
Clayton, Sandra - *Old Mr. Bannerjee (Illus. by Vaughan Duck)*
c Magpies - v11 - S '96 - p32 [51-250]
Clean Water, Clean Environment, 21st Century. Vols. 1-3
J Gov Info - v23 - S '96 - p565 [51-250]
Clearman, Deborah - *The Goose's Tale (Illus. by Deborah Clearman)*
c CBRS - v25 - Win '97 - p67 [51-250]
c HB Guide - v8 - Spr '97 - p23 [51-250]
c PW - v243 - S 16 '96 - p84 [51-250]
c SLJ - v42 - O '96 - p85 [51-250]
Clearwater, Scott H - *Market-Based Control*
JEL - v34 - S '96 - p1461+ [51-250]
Cleary, Beverly - *A Girl from Yamhill*
y PW - v243 - O 7 '96 - p78 [51-250]
Henry and Ribsy (Woodman). Audio Version
c BL - v93 - N 15 '96 - p604 [51-250]
Henry Higgins (Illus. by Louis Darling)
c BL - v93 - My 1 '97 - p1506 [1-50]
Janet's Thingamajigs (Illus. by DyAnne DiSalvo-Ryan)
c PW - v244 - My 5 '97 - p211 [1-50]
The Mouse and the Motorcycle (Roberts). Audio Version
c HB - v72 - S '96 - p566+ [501+]
My Own Two Feet
y BL - v93 - D 15 '96 - p716 [1-50]
y Kliatt - v31 - Mr '97 - p25 [51-250]
y PW - v243 - O 7 '96 - p78 [51-250]
y RT - v50 - O '96 - p156 [51-250]
Ralph S. Mouse (Roberts). Audio Version
c HB - v72 - S '96 - p566+ [501+]
Ramona La Chince (Illus. by Louis Darling)
c BL - v93 - My 1 '97 - p1506 [1-50]
Runaway Ralph (Roberts). Audio Version
c HB - v72 - S '96 - p566+ [501+]
Cleary, Brian P - *Give Me Bach My Schubert (Illus. by Rick Dupre)*
c HB Guide - v8 - Spr '97 - p23 [51-250]
c SLJ - v42 - D '96 - p91 [51-250]
It Looks a Lot like Reindeer (Illus. by Rick Dupre)
c HB Guide - v7 - Fall '96 - p251 [51-250]
Jamaica Sandwich? (Illus. by Rick Dupre)
c HB Guide - v7 - Fall '96 - p251 [51-250]
You Never Sausage Love (Illus. by Rick Dupre)
c HB Guide - v8 - Spr '97 - p23 [51-250]
c SLJ - v42 - D '96 - p91 [51-250]

Cleary, Edward L - *Power, Politics, and Pentecostals in Latin America*
Choice - v34 - Ap '97 - p1381 [51-250]
Cons - v17 - Win '96 - p30 [501+]
R&R Bk N - v12 - F '97 - p10 [51-250]
Cleary, John J - *Aristotle and Mathematics*
Isis - v87 - D '96 - p715+ [501+]
RM - v50 - S '96 - p149+ [501+]
Cleary, Jon - *Winter Chill*
Arm Det - v29 - Sum '96 - p373 [251-500]
Cleary, Rita - *Gold Town*
PW - v243 - S 30 '96 - p63 [51-250]
Roundup M - v4 - D '96 - p25 [51-250]
Cleary, Thomas - *The Five Houses of Zen*
LJ - v122 - Mr 15 '97 - p66 [51-250]
Kensho: The Heart of Zen
LJ - v121 - N 15 '96 - p65+ [51-250]
Stopping and Seeing
PW - v244 - Ap 14 '97 - p70 [51-250]
Cleary, William - *Lighten Your Heart*
CLW - v66 - Je '96 - p36+ [51-250]
Prayers to She Who Is
CLW - v67 - Mr '97 - p37+ [51-250]
RR - v55 - N '96 - p661 [1-50]
Cleaver, Richard - *Know My Name*
Intpr - v51 - Ap '97 - p222 [251-500]
Clebsch, Betsy - *A Book of Salvias*
BL - v93 - My 1 '97 - p1471+ [51-250]
Clegg, C J - *Advanced Biology Study Guide*
y TES - Ja 3 '97 - pR15 [251-500]
Clegg, Claude Andrew - *An Original Man*
y BL - v93 - F 15 '97 - p975 [51-250]
BW - v27 - Ap 6 '97 - p5 [501+]
KR - v64 - D 15 '96 - p1777+ [251-500]
LJ - v121 - N 1 '96 - p80 [1-50]
LJ - v122 - F 1 '97 - p88 [51-250]
NYTBR - v102 - F 23 '97 - p19 [501+]
PW - v244 - Mr 24 '97 - p75 [51-250]
Clegg, Holly - *Trim and Terrific One-Dish Favorites*
PW - v244 - Mr 3 '97 - p69 [51-250]
Cleland, John - *Sexual Behaviour and AIDS in the Developing World*
Am Ethnol - v24 - F '97 - p213+ [501+]
CS - v26 - Ja '97 - p110+ [501+]
Clement, Catherine - *Gandhi: Father of a Nation*
HT - v46 - O '96 - p59 [1-50]
y Sch Lib - v45 - F '97 - p50 [51-250]
La Putain Du Diable
BL - v93 - Ja '97 - p827 [1-50]
Clement, Gary - *Just Stay Put (Illus. by Gary Clement)*
c BL - v93 - S 15 '96 - p245 [51-250]
c JB - v60 - O '96 - p182 [51-250]
Clement, Grace - *Care, Autonomy, and Justice*
Choice - v34 - Ja '97 - p808 [51-250]
Clement, Mary - *The Juvenile Justice System*
R&R Bk N - v11 - D '96 - p18 [51-250]
Clement, Olivier - *The Roots of Christian Mysticism*
Theol St - v57 - Je '96 - p366+ [501+]
Clement, Richard W - *The Book in America*
Choice - v34 - Ap '97 - p1322 [51-250]
SFR - v22 - Ja '97 - p5 [251-500]
Clement, Rod - *Just Another Ordinary Day (Illus. by Rod Clement)*
c Magpies - v11 - My '96 - p53 [1-50]
c PW - v244 - Ap 28 '97 - p74 [51-250]
Clement, Russell T - *Four French Symbolists*
r ARBA - v28 - '97 - p370 [51-250]
r Choice - v34 - Mr '97 - p1134 [51-250]
r R&R Bk N - v11 - D '96 - p57 [51-250]
Clements, Alan - *Restless Nation*
NS - v125 - N 29 '96 - p45+ [501+]
Clements, Andrew - *Bright Christmas (Illus. by Kate Kiesler)*
c BL - v93 - S 1 '96 - p136 [51-250]
c CCB-B - v50 - N '96 - p93 [51-250]
c HB Guide - v8 - Spr '97 - p88 [1-50]
c PW - v243 - S 30 '96 - p90 [51-250]
c SLJ - v42 - O '96 - p34 [51-250]
The Christmas Story (Illus. by Tim Wood)
c Ch BWatch - v6 - D '96 - p1 [1-50]
Frindle (Illus. by Brian Selznick)
c BL - v93 - S 1 '96 - p125 [51-250]
c CCB-B - v50 - O '96 - p51+ [51-250]
c HB - v72 - N '96 - p732+ [51-250]
c HB Guide - v8 - Spr '97 - p63 [51-250]
c Par Ch - v21 - Mr '97 - p12 [1-50]
c SLJ - v42 - S '96 - p201 [51-250]

Philipp's Birthday Book (Illus. by Hanne Turk)
c BL - v93 - D 15 '96 - p734 [51-250]
c HB Guide - v8 - Spr '97 - p154 [51-250]
c KR - v64 - O 1 '96 - p1475 [51-250]
c SLJ - v42 - N '96 - p87 [51-250]
Temple Cat (Illus. by Kate Kiesler)
c HB Guide - v7 - Fall '96 - p251 [51-250]
c NYTBR - v102 - Mr 16 '97 - p26 [1-50]
Clements, Cynthia - *George Burns and Gracie Allen*
r R&R Bk N - v12 - F '97 - p82 [51-250]
Clements, Frank A - *The Israeli Secret Services*
r Choice - v34 - Mr '97 - p1134 [51-250]
MEJ - v51 - Win '97 - p150 [51-250]
r R&R Bk N - v11 - D '96 - p48 [51-250]
Kuwait. Rev. Ed.
r ARBA - v28 - '97 - p72 [51-250]
Clements, Keith - *Learning to Speak*
Theol St - v57 - S '96 - p571+ [251-500]
Clements, William M - *Native American Verbal Art*
Choice - v34 - Ap '97 - p1333+ [51-250]
Clements' Encyclopedia of World Governments 1996-1997
r BL - v92 - Ag '96 - p1919 [51-250]
Clemings, Russell Allan - *Mirage: The False Promise of Desert Agriculture*
Econ - v339 - My 18 '96 - p12* [51-250]
Clemoes, Peter - *Interactions of Thought and Language in Old English Poetry*
RES - v48 - F '97 - p76+ [501+]
Clendenin, Daniel B - *Eastern Orthodox Christianity*
Bks & Cult - v2 - Mr '96 - p6+ [501+]
Clephane, Ellen - *Dance of Love*
Books - v10 - Je '96 - p21 [51-250]
Clerc, Philippe - *Tuer Etc.*
WLT - v70 - Aut '96 - p918 [51-250]
Clergeau, Louis - *A Village in France*
LJ - v122 - Ap 1 '97 - p88 [51-250]
PW - v243 - O 7 '96 - p58 [51-250]
Clerici, Luca - *Calvino E Il Comico*
Humor - v10 - 1 '97 - p121+ [501+]
Clessa, J J - *Math and Logic Puzzles for PC Enthusiasts*
y Ch BWatch - v6 - D '96 - p2 [1-50]
Clever Kids Science: Ages 5-7
c SB - v32 - Ag '96 - p178 [251-500]
Clever Kids Science: Ages 8-10
c SB - v32 - Ag '96 - p178 [51-250]
Clevinger, Mary A - *Phase Equilibria Diagrams: 1996 Cumulative Indexes to Annuals '91-'93*
r SciTech - v21 - Mr '97 - p91 [51-250]
Clewlow, Carol - *One for the Money*
Books - v9 - S '95 - p27 [1-50]
Clifford, Eth - *Family for Sale*
c HB Guide - v7 - Fall '96 - p290 [51-250]
Flatfoot Fox and the Case of the Missing Schoolhouse (Illus. by Brian Lies)
c BL - v93 - Mr 15 '97 - p1241 [51-250]
Clifford, James - *Routes: Travel and Translation in the Late Twentieth Century*
BL - v93 - Mr 15 '97 - p1208 [51-250]
KR - v65 - F 15 '97 - p265+ [51-250]
Clifford, Martin - *The New Handbook for Electricians: Based on the 1996 NEC. 2nd Ed.*
SciTech - v20 - S '96 - p53 [51-250]
Clifford, Nick - *Incredible Earth*
c BL - v93 - D 1 '96 - p658 [51-250]
c CBRS - v25 - D '96 - p44 [51-250]
c HB Guide - v8 - Spr '97 - p113 [51-250]
c New Sci - v153 - Ja 25 '97 - p45 [1-50]
c PW - v243 - N 4 '96 - p78 [51-250]
c SLJ - v43 - F '97 - p111 [51-250]
Clift, Eleanor - *War without Bloodshed*
Choice - v34 - D '96 - p689+ [51-250]
Clift, Jean Dalby - *The Archetype of Pilgrimage*
Rel St Rev - v23 - Ja '97 - p43 [51-250]
Clifton, Lucille - *The Book of Light*
LJ - v122 - Ap 1 '97 - p94 [1-50]
Everett Anderson's Nine Month Long (Illus. by Ann Grifalconi)
c Par - v71 - N '96 - p114 [1-50]
El Nino Que No Creia En La Primavera (Illus. by Brinton Turkle)
c BL - v93 - My 1 '97 - p1506 [1-50]
The Terrible Stories
BL - v92 - Ag '96 - p1876 [51-250]
BWatch - v17 - D '96 - p7 [1-50]
LJ - v122 - Ap 1 '97 - p94 [1-50]
PW - v243 - Jl 22 '96 - p236 [51-250]
VQR - v73 - Win '97 - p29* [51-250]
VV - v42 - Ja 7 '97 - p41 [51-250]
Wom R Bks - v14 - Mr '97 - p12+ [501+]

Clifton, R J - *Advances in Failure Mechanism in Brittle Materials*
   SciTech - v21 - Mr '97 - p76 [51-250]
Clifton, Rob - *Perspectives on Quantum Reality*
   SciTech - v20 - N '96 - p18 [51-250]
Climate Research in the Netherlands
   J Gov Info - v23 - S '96 - p660 [1-50]
Climo, Shirley - *The Irish Cinderlad (Illus. by Loretta Krupinski)*
   c ECEJ - v24 - Fall '96 - p41 [51-250]
   c HB Guide - v7 - Fall '96 - p319+ [51-250]
   c RT - v50 - My '97 - p683 [51-250]
   A Treasury of Princesses (Illus. by Ruth Sanderson)
   c HB Guide - v8 - Spr '97 - p100 [51-250]
   c PW - v243 - O 21 '96 - p85 [1-50]
   c SLJ - v42 - O '96 - p111 [51-250]
Cline, David B - *Physical Origin of Homochirality in Life*
   SciTech - v21 - Mr '97 - p41 [51-250]
Cline, Foster - *Parenting Teens with Love and Logic*
   VOYA - v19 - F '97 - p316 [51-250]
Cline, Tony - *Curriculum Related Assessment, Cummins and Bilingual Children*
   MLJ - v81 - Spr '97 - p122+ [251-500]
Cline, William R - *International Debt Reexamined*
   JEL - v34 - S '96 - p1357+ [501+]
Clineaste
   p Sm Pr R - v28 - Jl '96 - p26 [51-250]
Clines, David J A - *Interested Parties*
   Rel St Rev - v23 - Ja '97 - p54+ [51-250]
Clinkscale, Martha Novak - *Makers of the Piano 1700-1820*
   r ARBA - v28 - '97 - p480 [251-500]
Clinton, Bill - *Between Hope and History*
   BW - v26 - Ag 25 '96 - p3 [501+]
   LATBR - S 1 '96 - p4 [251-500]
   LJ - v121 - O 15 '96 - p77 [51-250]
   NYTBR - v101 - S 22 '96 - p24 [51-250]
   Reason - v28 - N '96 - p64+ [501+]
Clinton, Hillary Rodham - *It Takes a Village and Other Lessons Children Teach Us*
   JNE - v65 - Win '96 - p92+ [501+]
   NS - v126 - Mr 27 '97 - p50 [501+]
   NYTBR - v101 - N 3 '96 - p28 [1-50]
   Obs - Mr 23 '97 - p18* [51-250]
   TLS - Jl 19 '96 - p3+ [501+]
   The Unique Voice of Hillary Rodham Clinton
   LJ - v122 - Ja '97 - p123 [51-250]
   PW - v243 - D 30 '96 - p49 [51-250]
Clinton, Susan - *Reading between the Bones*
   y BL - v93 - My 1 '97 - p1485 [51-250]
Cliquet, Robert - *Population and Development*
   R&R Bk N - v12 - F '97 - p34 [51-250]
Clogg, Richard - *Anatolica: Studies in the Greek East in the 18th and 19th Centuries*
   R&R Bk N - v11 - D '96 - p9 [51-250]
Cloke, Kenneth - *Thank God It's Monday!*
   BL - v93 - D 1 '96 - p626+ [51-250]
   LJ - v121 - D '96 - p110 [51-250]
Clopton, Edwin L - *The Mineralogical Record Index: Vols. 1-25*
   r RocksMiner - v71 - S '96 - p358 [501+]
Clor, Harry M - *Public Morality and Liberal Society*
   Choice - v34 - Ja '97 - p836 [51-250]
Clorfene-Casten, Liane - *Breast Cancer*
   LJ - v122 - F 1 '97 - p99 [51-250]
   VV - v41 - O 29 '96 - p63+ [251-500]
Close, Ajay - *Official and Doubtful*
   Obs - Ap 6 '97 - p18* [51-250]
Close, David - *Legislatures and the New Democracies in Latin America*
   JTWS - v13 - Fall '96 - p307+ [501+]
Close, David H - *The Origins of the Greek Civil War*
   AHR - v102 - F '97 - p140+ [501+]
Closing the Circle on the Splitting of the Atom
   J Gov Info - v23 - S '96 - p544 [1-50]
Clot, Andre - *L'Egypte Des Mamelouks*
   MEJ - v50 - Sum '96 - p456+ [51-250]
Clotfelter, Charles T - *Buying the Best*
   Cng - v28 - Jl '96 - p63 [51-250]
   Cng - v28 - S '96 - p58+ [501+]
   JEL - v34 - D '96 - p2063 [51-250]
   Nat R - v48 - N 25 '96 - p74 [51-250]
Clothes (SnapShot)
   c PW - v244 - Ja 6 '97 - p74 [1-50]
Clothier, Paul - *Complete Computer Trainer*
   CBR - v15 - Spr '97 - p2 [1-50]
Clottes, Jean - *The Cave beneath the Sea*
   NYRB - v43 - N 14 '96 - p8+ [501+]
Cloud, Henry - *Safe People*
   y VOYA - v19 - F '97 - p316 [51-250]

Cloud, Stanley - *The Murrow Boys*
   CJR - v35 - N '96 - p61+ [51-250]
   Emmy - v18 - O '96 - p50 [501+]
   Prog - v61 - Ja '97 - p36 [51-250]
   PW - v243 - N 4 '96 - p44 [51-250]
   Rapport - v19 - 5 '96 - p46 [501+]
   Sew R - v104 - O '96 - p673+ [501+]
Cloude, Shane - *An Introduction to Electromagnetic Wave Propagation and Antennas*
   Choice - v34 - S '96 - p159 [51-250]
Clough, Brenda W - *How Like a God*
   KR - v65 - Ja 1 '97 - p27 [51-250]
   LJ - v122 - Mr 15 '97 - p93 [1-50]
   NYTBR - v102 - Ap 6 '97 - p24 [51-250]
   PW - v244 - F 24 '97 - p68 [51-250]
Clough, Cecil H - *The European Outthrust and Encounter*
   EHR - v111 - N '96 - p1269+ [251-500]
Clough, David G - *You Can Be a Philanthropist*
   ChrPhil - v9 - N 14 '96 - p39 [51-250]
Clough, Ronald - *Japanese Business Information*
   LAR - v98 - Jl '96 - p371 [251-500]
Clouting, Ben - *Tickled to Death to Go*
   TLS - S 20 '96 - p32 [251-500]
Clover, Joshua - *Madonna Anno Domini*
   PW - v244 - Mr 31 '97 - p70 [51-250]
Clover Newspaper Index: Clover Magazine Index. Electronic Media Version
   r LAR - v98 - Je '96 - p321 [51-250]
Clower, Jerry - *Stories from Home*
   CAY - v16 - Fall '95 - p11 [51-250]
Clower, Robert W - *Economic Doctrine and Method*
   Econ J - v106 - N '96 - p1830 [251-500]
Clubb, Louise George - *Romance and Aretine Humanism in Sienese Comedy*
   MLR - v92 - Ja '97 - p216+ [501+]
Clum, John M - *Staging Gay Lives*
   Choice - v34 - N '96 - p472+ [51-250]
Clunas, Craig - *Fruitful Sites*
   BM - v138 - D '96 - p829+ [501+]
   TLS - O 25 '96 - p13 [51-250]
Cluny, Claude Michel - *Oeuvre Romanesque*
   WLT - v70 - Aut '96 - p915+ [501+]
Clute, John - *Encyclopedia of Science Fiction*
   r RQ - v36 - Win '96 - p212 [51-250]
   Look at the Evidence
   SFS - v24 - Mr '97 - p139+ [501+]
   Science Fiction: A Visual Encyclopedia
   yr Emerg Lib - v24 - S '96 - p23 [1-50]
   Ext - v37 - Sum '96 - p180+ [501+]
Clyman, Toby W - *Russia through Women's Eyes*
   Choice - v34 - Ap '97 - p1398 [51-250]
   LJ - v122 - Ja '97 - p121 [51-250]
Clymer, Kenton J - *Quest for Freedom*
   AHR - v101 - O '96 - p1314+ [51-250]
   PHR - v65 - Ag '96 - p506+ [501+]
   RAH - v24 - S '96 - p507+ [501+]
Clyne, Michael - *Intercultural Communication at Work*
   Lang Soc - v25 - S '96 - p452+ [501+]
Clyne, T W - *An Introduction to Metal Matrix Composites*
   Am Sci - v84 - My '96 - p304+ [51-250]
Clynes, Michael - *A Brood of Vipers*
   y SLJ - v42 - O '96 - p162 [51-250]
   The Gallows Murders
   y BL - v93 - D 15 '96 - p710 [51-250]
   KR - v64 - O 15 '96 - p1494+ [51-250]
Clynes, Tom - *Music Festivals from Bach to Blues*
   r ARBA - v28 - '97 - p471 [51-250]
Co-Op America's National Green Pages. 1996 Ed.
   r ARBA - v28 - '97 - p648 [51-250]
Co-Op America's National Green Pages. 1997 Ed.
   Workbook - v21 - Win '96 - p176 [251-500]
Coaldrake, William H - *Architecture and Authority in Japan*
   TLS - N 8 '96 - p32 [251-500]
Coalter, Milton J - *The Pluralistic Vision*
   CH - v66 - Mr '97 - p169+ [51-250]
   Vital Signs
   Intpr - v51 - Ap '97 - p217 [251-500]
Coase, R H - *Essays on Economics and Economists*
   JEH - v56 - D '96 - p962+ [501+]
   JEL - v34 - D '96 - p1943+ [501+]
Coate, Malcolm B - *The Economics of the Antitrust Process*
   JEL - v35 - Mr '97 - p247 [51-250]
Coates, David - *Economic and Industrial Performance in Europe*
   Econ J - v106 - S '96 - p1478 [51-250]
   Industrial Policy in Britain
   JEL - v34 - D '96 - p2085 [51-250]
Coates, Isaac - *On the Plains with Custer and Hancock*
   LJ - v122 - Ap 15 '97 - p95 [51-250]

Coates, Jennifer - *Women, Men, and Language*
   NWSA Jnl - v8 - Sum '96 - p117+ [51-250]
Coates, John - *The Claims of Common Sense*
   Choice - v34 - F '97 - p977 [51-250]
Coates, Ken - *Dear Commissioner*
   JEL - v35 - Mr '97 - p241+ [51-250]
   Full Employment for Europe
   JEL - v35 - Mr '97 - p241 [51-250]
Coates, Paul - *Film at the Intersection of High and Mass Culture*
   FQ - v49 - Fall '95 - p44+ [501+]
Cobb, Annie - *Wheels!*
   c BL - v92 - Ag '96 - p1910 [51-250]
Cobb, Cathy - *Creations of Fire*
   y SB - v32 - O '96 - p204 [51-250]
Cobb, Hubbard - *American Battlefields*
   r Parameters - v26 - Aut '96 - p157+ [501+]
Cobb, Jane - *I'm a Little Teapot*
   r Emerg Lib - v24 - Mr '97 - p40 [51-250]
   r SLJ - v42 - Ag '96 - p36 [51-250]
Cobb, John B, Jr. - *Grace and Responsibility*
   TT - v53 - O '96 - p432 [51-250]
   Sustaining the Common Good
   J Ch St - v38 - Aut '96 - p905+ [251-500]
Cobb, Sally Wright - *The Brown Derby Restaurant*
   LATBR - Ja 19 '97 - p9 [51-250]
Cobb, Stephen - *The NCSA Guide to PC and LAN Security*
   SciTech - v20 - D '96 - p13 [51-250]
Cobb, Vicki - *Science Experiments You Can Eat. Rev. and Updated Ed.*
   y Kliatt - v30 - S '96 - p4 [1-50]
Cobbett, William - *The English Gardener*
   Spec - v277 - D 7 '96 - p55 [51-250]
   Surplus Population and the Poor Law Bill
   Folkl - v107 - '96 - p126 [51-250]
Cobblestone
   cp Par Ch - v20 - O '96 - p15 [1-50]
Cobden, Richard - *The European Diaries of Richard Cobden 1846-1849*
   EHR - v112 - Ap '97 - p501+ [501+]
Coburn, Ann - *Web Weaver*
   c TES - Ap 4 '97 - p8* [501+]
   Worm Songs
   c JB - v60 - D '96 - p264 [251-500]
   c TES - Ap 4 '97 - p8* [501+]
Coburn, Broughton - *Aama in America*
   y Kliatt - v30 - S '96 - p34+ [51-250]
Coburn, Jewell Reinhart - *Jouanah: A Hmong Cinderella (Illus. by Anne Sibley O'Brien)*
   c CCB-B - v50 - D '96 - p130 [51-250]
   c SLJ - v43 - Mr '97 - p172 [51-250]
Coburn, Walt - *Stirrup High*
   PW - v244 - Ap 21 '97 - p69 [1-50]
Cocca-Leffler, Maryann - *Clams All Year*
   c HB Guide - v7 - Fall '96 - p251 [51-250]
Cochlaeus, Johannes - *Philippicae I-VII. Vols. 1-2*
   Rel St Rev - v23 - Ap '97 - p192 [51-250]
Cochran, Alastair - *The Search for the Perfect Swing*
   LJ - v121 - O 1 '96 - p52 [1-50]
Cochran, Johnnie L, Jr. - *Journey to Justice*
   ABA Jour - v82 - D '96 - p92+ [501+]
   BW - v26 - N 3 '96 - p5 [501+]
   LATBR - O 13 '96 - p4+ [501+]
   LJ - v121 - N 1 '96 - p80 [1-50]
   New R - v215 - D 9 '96 - p27+ [501+]
   NYTBR - v101 - N 3 '96 - p15+ [501+]
   WSJ-MW - v78 - O 24 '96 - pA16 [51-250]
Cochran, Molly - *The Broken Sword*
   KR - v65 - Mr 1 '97 - p340 [51-250]
   LJ - v122 - Ap 15 '97 - p123 [51-250]
   PW - v244 - Ap 28 '97 - p55 [251-500]
   World without End
   Rapport - v19 - 4 '96 - p26 [251-500]
Cochran, Thomas B - *Making the Russian Bomb*
   NWCR - v50 - Win '97 - p159+ [501+]
Cochran, Tracy - *Transformation: Awakening to the Sacred in Ourselves*
   Parabola - v21 - Ag '96 - p104+ [501+]
Cochrane, Jean - *Down on the Farm*
   Beav - v76 - D '96 - p47 [51-250]
Cochrane, Patricia A - *Purely Rosie Pearl*
   c HB Guide - v7 - Fall '96 - p290 [1-50]
   c Par Ch - v20 - O '96 - p11 [1-50]
Cock-a-Doodle-Doo (Illus. by Maureen Roffey)
   c ECEJ - v24 - Win '96 - p111 [51-250]
Cockburn, Alexander - *Washington Babylon*
   BW - v26 - D 8 '96 - p8 [1-50]
   SFR - v21 - S '96 - p22+ [501+]
Cockburn, Anne - *Teaching under Pressure*
   R&R Bk N - v11 - N '96 - p56 [51-250]

Cockcroft, James D - *Latinos in Beisbol*
  y HB Guide - v8 - Spr '97 - p143 [51-250]
  y SLJ - v43 - Mr '97 - p198 [51-250]
Cockell, Jenny - *Past Lives, Future Lives*
  Books - v10 - Je '96 - p21 [1-50]
Cockerell, Carol - *Subject Index*
  r LAR - v98 - Je '96 - p321 [51-250]
Cockerham, William C - *The Sociology of Medicine*
  CS - v25 - S '96 - p709+ [501+]
Cockett, Abraham T K - *Color Atlas of Urologic Surgery*
  r SciTech - v20 - D '96 - p49 [51-250]
Cockett, Richard - *Thinking the Unthinkable*
  EHR - v112 - F '97 - p270+ [501+]
  HT - v46 - S '96 - p56+ [501+]
Cockrell, Thomas D - *A Mississippi Rebel in the Army of Northern Virginia*
  HRNB - v25 - Win '97 - p91 [251-500]
Cocks, Elijah E - *Who's Who on the Moon*
  r ARBA - v28 - '97 - p632 [51-250]
Cocks, Richard - *The Parliamentary Diary of Sir Richard Cocks 1698-1702*
  TLS - Ja 17 '97 - p30 [501+]
Code, Lorraine - *Rhetorical Spaces*
  QJS - v82 - N '96 - p430+ [501+]
Codex Borgianus - *Codex Borgia*
  LA Ant - v8 - Mr '97 - p63+ [501+]
Codrescu, Andrei - *Alien Candor*
  BW - v26 - D 8 '96 - p8 [51-250]
  LJ v121 O 15 '96 p63 [51 250]
  PW - v243 - N 25 '96 - p73 [51-250]
  The Blood Countess
  SFR - v21 - S '96 - p48 [51-250]
  The Dog with the Chip in His Neck
  NYTBR - v101 - O 20 '96 - p23 [51-250]
Cody, John - *Wings of Paradise*
  Aud - v98 - N '96 - p130 [1-50]
  Choice - v34 - F '97 - p986 [51-250]
  CSM - v88 - S 25 '96 - p15 [501+]
  CSM - v89 - D 12 '96 - p14 [51-250]
  Nature - v384 - D 5 '96 - p423 [1-50]
Cody, Martin L - *Long-Term Studies of Vertebrate Communities*
  SciTech - v21 - Mr '97 - p38 [51-250]
Cody, Tod - *The Cowboy's Handbook*
  c HB Guide - v7 - Fall '96 - p385 [51-250]
  c KR - v64 - My 1 '96 - p685 [51-250]
Coe, David B - *The Children of Amarid*
  KR - v65 - Mr 15 '97 - p422 [51-250]
  LJ - v122 - Ap 15 '97 - p123 [51-250]
  PW - v244 - Ap 28 '97 - p55 [251-500]
Coe, Jonathan - *What a Carve Up!*
  NS - v125 - D 20 '96 - p116 [1-50]
Coe, Lewis - *Wireless Radio*
  Choice - v34 - Ja '97 - p814 [51-250]
  SciTech - v20 - N '96 - p74 [51-250]
Coe, Sophie D - *The True History of Chocolate*
  Atl - v278 - Jl '96 - p109 [51-250]
  LATBR - Ag 25 '96 - p6+ [501+]
  Nature - v382 - Ag 1 '96 - p411+ [501+]
  NYRB - v43 - S 19 '96 - p23+ [501+]
Coel, Margaret - *The Ghost Walker*
  BL - v93 - O 1 '96 - p325 [51-250]
Coelho, Nelly Novaes - *Dicionario Critico Da Literatura Infantil E Juvenil Brasileira Seculos XIXe XX. 4th Rev. and Expanded Ed.*
  r Bkbird - v34 - Spr '96 - p55 [1-50]
Coelho, Paulo - *By the River Piedra I Sat Down and Wept*
  LATBR - O 13 '96 - p14+ [51-250]
  Trib Bks - My 11 '97 - p8 [1-50]
Coen, Ethan - *Fargo*
  Ent W - Mr 28 '97 - p61 [51-250]
Coes, Donald V - *Macroeconomic Crises, Policies, and Growth in Brazil 1964-90*
  HAHR - v76 - Ag '96 - p595+ [251-500]
  J Gov Info - v23 - S '96 - p687 [51-250]
Coetzee, J M - *Giving Offense*
  Bks & Cult - v3 - Mr '97 - p30 [501+]
  Lon R Bks - v19 - F 6 '97 - p14 [501+]
  New R - v215 - N 18 '96 - p30+ [501+]
  NYTBR - v101 - S 22 '96 - p33 [501+]
  WLT - v70 - Aut '96 - p1038+ [501+]
  The Master of Petersburg
  Ant R - v54 - Sum '96 - p374 [251-500]
  The Master of Petersburg (Case). Audio Version
  y Kliatt - v31 - Ja '97 - p42 [51-250]
Coffa, Salvatore - *Rare Earth Doped Semiconductors II*
  SciTech - v21 - Mr '97 - p24 [51-250]
Coffee, John M, Jr. - *The Atwood-Coffee Catalogue of United States and Canadian Transportation Tokens*
  r Coin W - v37 - O 28 '96 - p66 [51-250]

Coffeehouse Magazine
  p Sm Pr R - v28 - N '96 - p19 [51-250]
Coffel, Steve - *Encyclopedia of Garbage*
  yr ARBA - v28 - '97 - p647 [51-250]
Coffelt, Nancy - *The Dog Who Cried Woof (Illus. by Nancy Coffelt)*
  c RT - v50 - O '96 - p157 [51-250]
Coffey, Frank - *America on Wheels*
  Choice - v34 - D '96 - p633 [51-250]
  R&R Bk N - v12 - F '97 - p98 [1-50]
Coffey, Maria - *Three Moons in Vietnam*
  Econ - v340 - S 14 '96 - p7*+ [501+]
  Obs - Mr 2 '97 - p18* [51-250]
Coffey, Peter - *Europe--Toward 2001*
  JEL - v34 - D '96 - p2038 [51-250]
  R&R Bk N - v11 - D '96 - p48 [51-250]
Coffin, Judith G - *The Politics of Women's Work*
  Choice - v34 - D '96 - p668 [51-250]
  TLS - O 11 '96 - p32+ [501+]
  Wom R Bks - v14 - O '96 - p27+ [501+]
Coffman, Elaine - *If You Love Me*
  PW - v244 - Ja 20 '97 - p399 [51-250]
Coffman, Lisa - *Likely*
  PW - v243 - N 25 '96 - p72 [51-250]
Coffman, Taylor - *The Cambria Forest*
  LATBR - My 12 '96 - p11 [1-50]
Cofman, Judita - *Numbers and Shapes Revisited*
  y Math T - v89 - S '96 - p516 [51-250]
Cogan, Priscilla - *Winona's Web*
  BL - v93 - S 15 '96 - p218+ [51-250]
Cogdell, J R - *Foundations of Electrical Engineering. 2nd Ed.*
  SciTech - v20 - D '96 - p74 [51-250]
Coger, Dalvan - *Kenya. Rev. Ed.*
  r ARBA - v28 - '97 - p53 [51-250]
  r R&R Bk N - v11 - D '96 - p12 [51-250]
Coger, Greta M - *New Perspectives on Margaret Laurence*
  Choice - v34 - N '96 - p458 [51-250]
Coggins, James R - *John Smyth's Congregation*
  CH - v65 - S '96 - p492+ [501+]
Coggins, Timothy - *The National Conference on Legal Information Issues*
  IRLA - v32 - D '96 - p12 [51-250]
Coghlan, Frank - *They Still Call Me Junior*
  J Am Cult - v18 - Win '95 - p107 [251-500]
Coghlan, Valerie - *The Big Guide to Irish Children's Books*
  cr Bks Keeps - N '96 - p22 [51-250]
  r LAR - v99 - Mr '97 - p164 [51-250]
  r Sch Lib - v45 - F '97 - p53 [51-250]
Cogliano, Francis D - *No King, No Popery*
  Choice - v34 - S '96 - p143 [51-250]
  Theol St - v58 - Mr '97 - p191+ [251-500]
  W&M Q - v54 - Ap '97 - p434+ [501+]
Cohen, Albert - *Belle Du Seigneur*
  NYTBR - v101 - Ag 25 '96 - p8 [501+]
  NYTBR - v101 - D 8 '96 - p76 [1-50]
  W&I - v11 - N '96 - p235 [251-500]
  W&I - v11 - N '96 - p247+ [501+]
Cohen, Ariel - *Russian Imperialism*
  Choice - v34 - F '97 - p1019 [51-250]
  R&R Bk N - v11 - D '96 - p9 [51-250]
Cohen, Barbara - *The Chocolate Wolf (Illus. by David Ray)*
  c HB Guide - v7 - Fall '96 - p251 [1-50]
  Robin Hood and Little John (Illus. by David Ray)
  c RT - v50 - S '96 - p52+ [51-250]
Cohen, Barbara, 1949- - *Woman's Best Friend*
  Dog Fan - v27 - N '96 - p28 [51-250]
Cohen, Barney - *Preventing and Mitigating AIDS in Sub-Saharan Africa*
  SciTech - v20 - S '96 - p28 [51-250]
Cohen, Barry, 1935, Apr., 4- - *Life with Gough*
  Aust Bk R - O '96 - p66 [51-250]
Cohen, Barry M - *Managing Traumatic Stress through Art*
  AJCH - v38 - Ap '96 - p301+ [501+]
Cohen, Ben - *Ben and Jerry's Double-Dip*
  Fortune - v135 - Ap 28 '97 - p374 [501+]
  PW - v244 - Ap 7 '97 - p85 [51-250]
Cohen, Bernard C - *Democracies and Foreign Policy*
  J Pol - v58 - N '96 - p1253+ [501+]
Cohen, Carl - *Naked Racial Preference*
  Ethics - v107 - Ja '97 - p378+ [501+]
Cohen, Caron Lee - *Where's the Fly? (Illus. by Nancy Barnet)*
  c HB Guide - v7 - Fall '96 - p251 [51-250]
  c New Ad - v9 - Fall '96 - p327+ [501+]
Cohen, Celia - *Smokey O*
  Aethlon - v13 - Fall '95 - p135+ [251-500]

Cohen, Charles Lloyd - *God's Caress*
  Rel St Rev - v23 - Ap '97 - p135+ [501+]
Cohen, Claude - *Guidebook on Molecular Modeling in Drug Design*
  New Sci - v151 - S 28 '96 - p44 [1-50]
Cohen, Colleen Ballerino - *Beauty Queens on the Global Stage*
  Choice - v34 - S '96 - p167 [51-250]
  J Am Cult - v19 - Sum '96 - p137 [51-250]
Cohen, Cynthia B - *New Ways of Making Babies*
  Choice - v34 - Mr '97 - p1193 [51-250]
  Hast Cen R - v27 - Ja '97 - p46 [51-250]
Cohen, Daniel, 1936- - *The Alaska Purchase*
  c HB Guide - v7 - Fall '96 - p385 [51-250]
  Dangerous Ghosts
  c BL - v93 - N 15 '96 - p586 [51-250]
  y BL - v93 - Ap 1 '97 - p1306 [1-50]
  y Ch BWatch - v6 - D '96 - p5 [1-50]
  y HB Guide - v8 - Spr '97 - p78 [51-250]
  Ghostly Warnings (Illus. by David Linn)
  c BL - v93 - S 15 '96 - p238 [51-250]
  c HB Guide - v8 - Spr '97 - p63 [51-250]
  c SLJ - v42 - O '96 - p130 [51-250]
  Joseph McCarthy: The Misuse of Political Power
  y BL - v93 - O 1 '96 - p328 [51-250]
  y HB Guide - v8 - Spr '97 - p155 [51-250]
  y SLJ - v42 - O '96 - p154 [51-250]
  Real Vampires
  c RT - v50 - O '96 - p142 [1-50]
  Southern Fried Rat and Other Gruesome Tales
  y SLJ - v42 - O '96 - p45 [1-50]
  Werewolves
  c BL - v93 - O 1 '96 - p328 [51-250]
  c BW - v26 - S 1 '96 - p7 [251-500]
  c Ch BWatch - v6 - N '96 - p3 [1-50]
  c HB Guide - v8 - Spr '97 - p100 [51-250]
Cohen, Daniel, 1953- - *The Misfortunes of Prosperity*
  Econ J - v106 - S '96 - p1461 [51-250]
Cohen, David - *Law, Violence and Community in Classical Athens*
  TLS - S 20 '96 - p30 [501+]
Cohen, David, 1946- - *Alter Egos*
  Nature - v382 - Ag 29 '96 - p772 [501+]
Cohen, David, 1955- - *A Day in the Life of India*
  Mac - v109 - D 9 '96 - p66 [1-50]
Cohen, David Steven - *Folk Legacies Revisited*
  CAY - v17 - Win '96 - p3 [51-250]
Cohen, David William - *The Combing of History*
  JIH - v27 - Aut '96 - p278+ [501+]
Cohen, E Richard - *The Physics Quick Reference Guide*
  r ARBA - v28 - '97 - p638 [51-250]
Cohen, Eliezer - *Israel's Best Defense*
  NWCR - v49 - Aut '96 - p151+ [501+]
Cohen, Esther - *The Crossroads of Justice*
  Historian - v59 - Fall '96 - p182+ [501+]
Cohen, G A - *Self-Ownership, Freedom and Equality*
  Lon R Bks - v18 - O 31 '96 - p34 [501+]
  TLS - O 25 '96 - p28 [501+]
Cohen, Garnett Kilberg - *Lost Women, Banished Souls*
  BL - v93 - S 15 '96 - p219 [51-250]
  PW - v243 - Jl 22 '96 - p234 [51-250]
Cohen, H F - *The Scientific Revolution*
  Isis - v88 - Mr '97 - p118+ [501+]
  JMH - v68 - S '96 - p662+ [501+]
Cohen, Hennig - *Articles in American Studies 1954-1968. Vols. 1-2*
  r ASInt - v34 - O '96 - p17 [51-250]
  Humor of the Old Southwest. 3rd Ed.
  Humor - v9 - 3 '96 - p414+ [501+]
Cohen, Hubert I - *Ingmar Bergman: The Art of Confession*
  FQ - v49 - Fall '95 - p52+ [501+]
Cohen, I Bernard - *Benjamin Franklin's Science*
  Nature - v383 - O 24 '96 - p682 [1-50]
  Science and the Founding Fathers
  Historian - v58 - Sum '96 - p857 [251-500]
  J Am St - v30 - Ag '96 - p296+ [251-500]
  JSH - v62 - N '96 - p800+ [501+]
  Nature - v385 - F 20 '97 - p693 [1-50]
Cohen, J M - *The Penguin Dictionary of Twentieth-Century Quotations*
  yr Kliatt - v30 - S '96 - p24+ [51-250]
Cohen, Jean - *Theorie De La Poeticite*
  WLT - v70 - Aut '96 - p1038+ [501+]

Cohen, Joel E - *How Many People Can the Earth Support?*
Am Sci - v84 - S '96 - p494+ [501+]
Analog - v117 - F '97 - p145+ [51-250]
Econ - v339 - My 18 '96 - p12* [51-250]
Econ - v339 - My 18 '96 - p12* [51-250]
JEL - v34 - S '96 - p1444 [51-250]
Nature - v385 - Ja 30 '97 - p408 [51-250]
New Sci - v153 - Ja 25 '97 - p42 [1-50]
Cohen, Joshua - *For Love of Country*
W&I - v11 - N '96 - p282+ [501+]
Cohen, Julian - *Sex Matters*
c Bks Keeps - Mr '97 - p27 [51-250]
Cohen, Kate - *The Neppi Modona Diaries*
KR - v64 - N 1 '96 - p1576 [251-500]
PW - v243 - N 4 '96 - p55 [51-250]
Cohen, L Jonathan - *An Essay on Belief and Acceptance*
RM - v50 - D '96 - p392+ [501+]
Cohen, Lawrence B - *Practical Flexible Sigmoidoscopy*
SciTech - v20 - N '96 - p48 [51-250]
Cohen, Leah Hager - *Glass, Paper, Beans*
HMR - Spr '97 - p10 [51-250]
KR - v64 - D 1 '96 - p1711+ [251-500]
LATBR - F 9 '97 - p11 [501+]
LJ - v122 - Ja '97 - p127 [51-250]
NYTBR - v102 - F 9 '97 - p12 [501+]
PW - v243 - N 25 '96 - p60 [251-500]
Trib Bks - F 23 '97 - p9 [501+]
Glass, Paper, Beans. Audio Version
BWatch - v18 - Mr '97 - p7 [1-50]
Heat Lightning
PW - v244 - My 5 '97 - p193 [251-500]
Train Go Sorry
TCR - v98 - Fall '96 - p180+ [501+]
Cohen, Malcolm S - *Labor Shortages as America Approaches the Twenty-First Century*
BusLR - v21 - 3 '96 - p237+ [501+]
Cohen, Marc - *Mecox Road*
BW - v26 - D 8 '96 - p8 [51-250]
Cohen, Margaret - *Spectacles of Realism*
RMR - v50 - 2 '96 - p183+ [501+]
Cohen, Marilyn - *The Warp of Ulster's Past*
PW - v244 - Ja 27 '97 - p92 [51-250]
Cohen, Mark R - *Under Crescent and Cross*
CH - v65 - S '96 - p477+ [251-500]
JIH - v27 - Aut '96 - p286+ [501+]
Specu - v71 - O '96 - p936+ [501+]
Cohen, Martin - *Christian Mission--Jewish Mission*
Rel Ed - v91 - Fall '96 - p611 [1-50]
Cohen, Matt - *The Bookseller*
BL - v92 - Ag '96 - p1880 [51-250]
LATBR - Ag 11 '96 - p10 [51-250]
LATBR - v263 - S 29 '96 - p15 [51-250]
NYTBR - v101 - S 8 '96 - p23 [51-250]
NYTLa - v146 - O 2 '96 - pC17 [501+]
Last Seen
Mac - v109 - N 4 '96 - p70 [501+]
Mac - v109 - D 9 '96 - p64 [1-50]
Cohen, Max - *My Father, My Son*
Choice - v34 - S '96 - p213 [51-250]
Cohen, Michael A - *Preparing for the Urban Future*
JEL - v34 - D '96 - p2137 [51-250]
Cohen, Misha Ruth - *The Chinese Way to Healing*
BWatch - v17 - N '96 - p3 [1-50]
Cohen, Morris L - *A Guide to the Early Reports of the Supreme Court of the United States*
r ARBA - v28 - '97 - p222 [51-250]
LQ - v67 - Ap '97 - p193+ [501+]
Cohen, Morton Norton - *Lewis Carroll: A Biography*
Ant R - v54 - Sum '96 - p368+ [251-500]
Bkbird - v34 - Spr '96 - p56 [1-50]
BW - v27 - Ja 12 '97 - p12 [51-250]
CCB-B - v50 - O '96 - p82 [51-250]
CR - v270 - F '97 - p110 [1-50]
Nature - v385 - Ja 2 '97 - p36 [1-50]
NYTBR - v102 - Mr 9 '97 - p28 [51-250]
Cohen, Naomi G - *Philo Judaeus: His Universe of Discourse*
Rel St Rev - v23 - Ap '97 - p195 [51-250]
Cohen, Norman J - *Self, Struggle, and Change*
PW - v243 - N 11 '96 - p69 [51-250]
Cohen, P T - *The AIDS Knowledge Base. 2nd Ed.*
r BL - v93 - F 1 '97 - p960 [1-50]
Cohen, Paul A - *History in Three Keys*
LJ - v122 - Ja '97 - p118 [51-250]
Cohen, Paul R - *Empirical Methods for Artificial Intelligence*
IEEE Exp - v11 - D '96 - p88 [251-500]
Cohen, Paula Marantz - *Alfred Hitchcock: The Legacy of Victorianism*
AB - v98 - D 9 '96 - p2002+ [251-500]

The Daughter as Reader
Choice - v34 - Ja '97 - p787 [51-250]
Cohen, R A - *Trends in the Health of Older Americans*
J Gov Info - v23 - S '96 - p547 [51-250]
Cohen, Richard A - *Elevations--the Height of the Good in Rosenzweig and Levinas*
Rel St Rev - v23 - Ja '97 - p16+ [501+]
Cohen, Robert, 1941, Apr., 4- - *Understanding Peter Weiss*
Ger Q - v69 - Fall '96 - p462+ [501+]
Cohen, Robert, 1957- - *The Here and Now*
BW - v26 - Jl 14 '96 - p6 [251-500]
NYTBR - v102 - F 2 '97 - p28 [1-50]
PW - v243 - N 11 '96 - p72 [1-50]
Rapport - v19 - 4 '96 - p26 [251-500]
Cohen, Robin - *The Cambridge Survey of World Migration*
r WorldV - v13 - Ja '97 - p5 [51-250]
Cohen, Sharron - *The Mysteries of Research. 2nd Ed.*
CLW - v67 - D '96 - p47+ [51-250]
Cohen, Sheldon M - *Aristotle on Nature and Incomplete Substance*
Choice - v34 - F '97 - p977 [51-250]
Cohen, Sheldon S - *Yankee Sailors in British Gaols*
J Am St - v30 - Ag '96 - p323+ [251-500]
W&M Q - v53 - Jl '96 - p668+ [501+]
Cohen, Sherry Suib - *Looking for the Other Side*
BL - v93 - Mr 15 '97 - p1206 [51-250]
KR - v65 - Ja 15 '97 - p110 [251-500]
LJ - v122 - Ap 15 '97 - p101 [51-250]
PW - v244 - F 17 '97 - p206 [51-250]
Cohen, Smadar - *Microparticulate Systems for the Delivery of Proteins and Vaccines*
SciTech - v20 - D '96 - p55 [51-250]
Cohen, Stephen M - *Operative Laparoscopy and Hysteroscopy*
SciTech - v20 - N '96 - p51 [51-250]
Cohen, Steve - *Adventure Guide to the High Southwest. 2nd Ed.*
r BL - v93 - S 15 '96 - p210 [1-50]
r BWatch - v17 - S '96 - p5 [51-250]
Cohen, Susan D - *Women and Discourse in the Fiction of Marguerite Duras*
FR - v70 - Mr '97 - p605+ [501+]
Cohen, Warren I - *Lyndon Johnson Confronts the World*
MEJ - v50 - Sum '96 - p455 [51-250]
RAH - v24 - D '96 - p695+ [501+]
Pacific Passage
Choice - v34 - S '96 - p183 [51-250]
For Aff - v75 - S '96 - p158+ [251-500]
Cohen, William A - *Sex Scandal*
Choice - v34 - Mr '97 - p1160 [51-250]
TLS - Ja 3 '97 - p36 [51-250]
Cohen, Youssef - *Radicals, Reformers, and Reactionaries*
AAPSS-A - v548 - N '96 - p221+ [501+]
JIH - v27 - Aut '96 - p364+ [501+]
Coherence and Quantum Optics VII
SciTech - v20 - N '96 - p19 [1-50]
Cohl, H Aaron - *Why Are We Scaring Ourselves to Death?*
y BL - v93 - Ap 1 '97 - p1270 [51-250]
Cohn, Bernard S - *Colonialism and Its Forms of Knowledge*
Choice - v34 - Mr '97 - p1216 [51-250]
Cohn, David L - *The Mississippi Delta and the World*
JSH - v62 - N '96 - p834+ [251-500]
Cohn, Jeffrey P - *From Test Tube to Patient. 2nd Ed.*
J Gov Info - v23 - S '96 - p547 [51-250]
Cohn, Lawrence - *Nothing but the Blues*
CSM - v88 - N 21 '96 - p11 [1-50]
Cohn, Michael - *Jewish Bridges*
R&R Bk N - v12 - F '97 - p19 [1-50]
Cohn, Nik - *Need*
BL - v93 - F 1 '97 - p925 [51-250]
KR - v64 - D 15 '96 - p1749+ [251-500]
LATBR - Mr 9 '97 - p8 [501+]
NYTBR - v102 - Mr 9 '97 - p19 [51-250]
PW - v244 - Ja 13 '97 - p54 [51-250]
VV - v42 - F 18 '97 - p55 [501+]
Cohn, Norman Rufus Colin - *Noah's Flood*
Am - v176 - Mr 8 '97 - p22+ [51-250]
Bks & Cult - v3 - Mr '97 - p21+ [501+]
CC - v113 - N 13 '96 - p1123+ [51-250]
Choice - v34 - Ja '97 - p810 [51-250]
LJ - v121 - O 15 '96 - p63 [51-250]
Nature - v385 - Ja 30 '97 - p407+ [501+]
Spec - v277 - N 16 '96 - p43 [1-50]
Cohn, Robert - *Aphasia: A Pathophysiological Key to Memory Function and Volitional Naming*
Choice - v34 - N '96 - p541+ [51-250]

Cohn, Robert M - *Biochemistry and Disease*
SciTech - v20 - N '96 - p39 [51-250]
Cohn, Ruby - *Anglo-American Interplay in Recent Drama*
Clio - v25 - Sum '96 - p472+ [501+]
Cohn, Samuel - *When Strikes Make Sense--And Why*
SF - v75 - S '96 - p377+ [251-500]
Cohn-Sherbok, Dan - *The Crucified Jew*
BL - v93 - Ja '97 - p784 [51-250]
LJ - v122 - Ja '97 - p104+ [51-250]
PW - v244 - Ja 13 '97 - p70 [51-250]
A Dictionary of Judaism and Christianity
r Rel Ed - v91 - Fall '96 - p616 [1-50]
God and the Holocaust
Obs - v54 - O 13 '96 - p15* [501+]
Jewish and Christian Mysticism
Am - v175 - D 7 '96 - p26+ [501+]
Modern Judaism
Choice - v34 - D '96 - p627 [51-250]
Cohn-Sherbok, Lavinia - *A Popular Dictionary of Judaism*
r ARBA - v28 - '97 - p554 [51-250]
Cohodas, Nadine - *The Band Played Dixie*
PW - v244 - Mr 17 '97 - p64 [51-250]
Coignard, Gabrielle De - *Oeuvres Chretiennes*
Six Ct J - v27 - Win '96 - p1134+ [501+]
Coin World Guide to U.S. Coins, Prices and Value Trends 1997
r Coin W - v37 - N 25 '96 - p68 [51-250]
Coincraft's Standard Catalogue of English and United Kingdom Coins 1066 to Date. 2nd Ed.
r Coin W - v37 - N 18 '96 - p88 [51-250]
Coiner, Constance - *Better Red*
AHR - v102 - F '97 - p208+ [251-500]
Cres - v60 - N '96 - p30+ [501+]
S&S - v60 - Win '96 - p509+ [501+]
Cokins, Gary - *Activity-Based Cost Management*
Choice - v34 - N '96 - p502 [51-250]
Colahan, Clark - *The Visions of Sor Maria De Agreda*
CH - v66 - Mr '97 - p202+ [251-500]
Hisp - v79 - D '96 - p785+ [501+]
Colander, David C - *Beyond Microfoundations*
JEL - v34 - D '96 - p2121 [51-250]
The Coming of Keynesianism to America
JEL - v34 - S '96 - p1407 [51-250]
Colas, Santiago - *Postmodernity in Latin America*
HAHR - v77 - F '97 - p88+ [251-500]
Colbert, David - *Eyewitness to America*
y BL - v93 - Ja '97 - p809 [51-250]
Econ - v342 - Mr 8 '97 - p99+ [501+]
PW - v244 - Ja 6 '97 - p52 [51-250]
Trib Bks - Ap 27 '97 - p1+ [501+]
Colbert, Ty C - *Broken Brains or Wounded Hearts*
SciTech - v20 - N '96 - p42 [51-250]
Colborn, Theo - *Our Stolen Future*
Books - v11 - Ap '97 - p20 [51-250]
Env - v39 - Ja '97 - p26 [51-250]
Lon R Bks - v18 - S 5 '96 - p20 [501+]
NYTBR - v101 - Ap 7 '96 - p25 [501+]
NYTBR - v101 - D 8 '96 - p90 [1-50]
y SLJ - v43 - F '97 - p136 [51-250]
Colburn, David R - *The African American Heritage of Florida*
Historian - v59 - Fall '96 - p126 [51-250]
Colburn, Forrest D - *The Vogue of Revolution in Poor Countries*
AHR - v101 - O '96 - p1187+ [501+]
Colby, Robin B - *Some Appointed Work to Do*
VS - v39 - Spr '96 - p427+ [501+]
Colby, Vineta - *World Authors 1985-1990*
yr CLW - v67 - D '96 - p52 [251-500]
Coldsmith, Don - *Tallgrass*
LJ - v122 - Mr 15 '97 - p88 [51-250]
PW - v244 - Mr 3 '97 - p66+ [51-250]
Coldwell, Michael - *Fast Break*
c Quill & Q - v62 - My '96 - p34 [51-250]
Cole, Allan - *Kingdoms of the Night*
y Kliatt - v30 - S '96 - p16 [51-250]
The Warrior Returns
y VOYA - v19 - O '96 - p216 [251-500]
Wizard of the Winds
KR - v65 - Ap 1 '97 - p508 [51-250]
Cole, B - *Physical Rehabilitation Outcome Measures*
J Rehab RD - v34 - Ap '97 - p243+ [251-500]
Cole, Babette - *The Bad Good Manners Book (Illus. by Babette Cole)*
c HB Guide - v7 - Fall '96 - p353 [51-250]
c Magpies - v11 - My '96 - p38 [51-250]
Dr. Dog
c PW - v244 - Mr 17 '97 - p85 [1-50]

Drop Dead (Illus. by Babette Cole)
  c KR - v65 - Mr 1 '97 - p378 [51-250]
  c PW - v244 - Mr 17 '97 - p83 [51-250]
  c Sch Lib - v45 - F '97 - p18 [51-250]
Cole, Brock - *The Goats*
  c HMR - Win '96 - p45 [1-50]
  y JAAL - v40 - D '96 - p318 [51-250]
Cole, Bruce - *The Composer's Handbook*
     TES - Ja 31 '97 - p17* [51-250]
Cole, Carolyn Kozo - *Shades of L.A.*
  y BL - v92 - Ag '96 - p1864 [51-250]
  y BL - v92 - Ag '96 - p1890 [1-50]
     Bl S - v26 - Fall '96 - p104 [51-250]
     LJ - v121 - O 1 '96 - p72+ [51-250]
  y VOYA - v19 - F '97 - p344 [251-500]
Cole, Charles F - *Korea Remembered*
     NWCR - v49 - Aut '96 - p150 [251-500]
Cole, Donna - *Portfolios across the Curriculum and Beyond*
     Emerg Lib - v23 - My '96 - p40+ [51-250]
Cole, James H - *Updating Wilkinson*
  r Ch Rev Int - v3 - Fall '96 - p387+ [51-250]
Cole, Jameson - *A Killing in Quail County*
  y SLJ - v42 - D '96 - p150 [51-250]
Cole, Joanna - *El Autobus Magico En Tiempos De Los Dinosaurios (Illus. by Bruce Degen)*
  c BL - v93 - My 1 '97 - p1506 [1-50]
Bug in a Rug (Illus. by Alan Tiegreen)
  c BL - v93 - S 1 '96 - p133 [51-250]
  c Emerg Lib - v24 - Mr '97 - p44 [1-50]
  c HB Guide - v8 - Spr '97 - p11 [51-250]
  c PW - v243 - S 2 '96 - p132 [51-250]
  c SLJ - v42 - N '96 - p79 [51-250]
Give a Dog a Bone (Illus. by John Speirs)
  c HB Guide - v7 - Fall '96 - p363 [51-250]
I'm a Big Brother (Illus. by Maxie Chambliss)
  c BL - v93 - Mr 1 '97 - p1170 [51-250]
  c PW - v244 - Mr 24 '97 - p85 [1-50]
I'm a Big Sister (Illus. by Maxie Chambliss)
  c BL - v93 - Mr 1 '97 - p1170 [51-250]
  c PW - v244 - Mr 24 '97 - p85 [1-50]
The Magic School Bus Explores Inside the Earth. Electronic Media Version
  c BL - v93 - Ap 1 '97 - p1351 [51-250]
The Magic School Bus in the Time of the Dinosaur
  c CLW - v67 - Mr '97 - p13 [1-50]
The Magic School Bus inside a Beehive (Illus. by Bruce Degen)
  c BL - v93 - S 1 '96 - p121 [51-250]
  c CCB-B - v50 - O '96 - p52 [51-250]
  c CSM - v88 - S 26 '96 - pB4 [51-250]
  c HB - v72 - N '96 - p757 [51-250]
  c HB Guide - v8 - Spr '97 - p121 [51-250]
  c SLJ - v42 - O '96 - p111+ [51-250]
The Magic School Bus Inside a Hurricane (Illus. by Bruce Degen)
  c JB - v60 - D '96 - p248 [51-250]
The Magic Schoolbus Gets Eaten
  c Emerg Lib - v23 - My '96 - p45 [1-50]
On the Bus with Joanna Cole
  c CSM - v88 - S 26 '96 - pB4 [51-250]
  c HB - v72 - S '96 - p609 [51-250]
  c HB Guide - v7 - Fall '96 - p371 [51-250]
  c KR - v64 - My 1 '96 - p686 [51-250]
Riding Silver Star (Illus. by Margaret Miller)
  c HB Guide - v7 - Fall '96 - p359+ [51-250]
You Can't Smell a Flower with Your Ear
  c Inst - v106 - S '96 - p92 [1-50]
Cole, John Y - *On These Walls*
  r J Gov Info - v23 - S '96 - p551 [51-250]
Cole, Jonathan - *The Body and the Self (Vance). Audio Version*
     BL - v93 - F 15 '97 - p1038 [51-250]
Cole, Jonathan R - *The Research University in a Time of Discontent*
     J Hi E - v67 - N '96 - p718+ [501+]
Cole, Kevin N - *Assessment of Communication and Language*
     SciTech - v21 - Mr '97 - p64 [51-250]
Cole, Leonard A - *The Eleventh Plague*
     BW - v26 - N 10 '96 - p4 [501+]
     BWatch - v18 - Mr '97 - p1 [51-250]
     Choice - v34 - My '97 - p1576 [51-250]
     LJ - v121 - N 1 '96 - p92 [51-250]
     Nature - v386 - Mr 27 '97 - p342 [501+]
     New Sci - v152 - N 9 '96 - p42+ [501+]
     SB - v33 - Mr '97 - p37 [251-500]
Cole, Michael, 1938- - *Cultural Psychology*
     LJ - v121 - S 15 '96 - p83 [51-250]
     New Sci - v153 - F 1 '97 - p45 [51-250]

Cole, Michael D - *Apollo 13*
  c RT - v50 - O '96 - p139 [1-50]
John F. Kennedy: President of the New Frontier
  c HB Guide - v7 - Fall '96 - p371 [51-250]
Walt Disney: Creator of Mickey Mouse
  c HB Guide - v7 - Fall '96 - p371 [51-250]
  c SLJ - v42 - Ag '96 - p150+ [51-250]
Cole, Richard R - *Communication in Latin America*
     Choice - v34 - S '96 - p116 [51-250]
     JMCQ - v73 - Win '96 - p995+ [251-500]
Cole, Robert - *Propaganda in Twentieth Century War and Politics*
  r ARBA - v28 - '97 - p279 [251-500]
Cole, Rodney V - *Pacific 2010: Challenging the Future*
     Pac A - v69 - Fall '96 - p455+ [251-500]
Cole, Ronald H - *The History of the Unified Command Plan 1946-1993*
     For Aff - v75 - N '96 - p151 [51-250]
Cole, Sheila - *What Kind of Love?*
  y Emerg Lib - v24 - S '96 - p26 [1-50]
  y Kliatt - v30 - S '96 - p6 [51-250]
Cole, Trish - *Why Do We Wear That?*
  c HB Guide - v8 - Spr '97 - p99 [51-250]
  c SLJ - v43 - Mr '97 - p198 [51-250]
Cole, William - *A Zooful of Animals (Illus. by Lynn Musinger)*
  c Par Ch - v20 - O '96 - p21 [1-50]
Coleman, A D - *Critical Focus*
     Pet PM - v25 - Ag '96 - p10 [51-250]
Coleman, C B - *Three French Comedies*
     Choice - v34 - Ap '97 - p1344+ [51-250]
Coleman, David C - *Fundamentals of Soil Ecology*
     SciTech - v20 - N '96 - p27 [51-250]
Coleman, Debra - *Architecture and Feminism*
     Ms - v7 - N '96 - p81 [251-500]
Coleman, Dorothy Gabe - *Montaigne, Quelques Anciens Et L'Ecriture Des Essais*
     CML - v16 - Spr '96 - p265+ [501+]
Coleman, Eli - *Sex Offender Treatment*
     SciTech - v21 - Mr '97 - p55 [51-250]
Coleman, Evelyn - *White Socks Only (Illus. by Tyrone Geter)*
  c HB Guide - v7 - Fall '96 - p251 [51-250]
  c Smith - v27 - N '96 - p172+ [51-250]
Coleman, Fred - *The Decline and Fall of the Soviet Empire*
     BW - v26 - Ag 25 '96 - p9+ [501+]
     For Aff - v75 - S '96 - p151+ [51-250]
     NL - v79 - Ag 12 '96 - p19+ [501+]
Coleman, Gerald D - *Homosexuality: Catholic Teaching and Pastoral Practice*
     Theol St - v57 - D '96 - p785+ [251-500]
Coleman, Geraldine - *African-American Stories of Triumph over Adversity*
     R&R Bk N - v12 - F '97 - p23 [51-250]
Coleman, Gordon J - *The Addison-Wesley Science Handbook*
  r BL - v93 - D 1 '96 - p683 [251-500]
  r New Sci - v152 - N 2 '96 - p45 [1-50]
Coleman, J A, 1920- - *Cluefinder: A Dictionary of Crossword Clues*
  r ARBA - v28 - '97 - p383 [51-250]
Coleman, James A - *Discourse Variety in Contemporary French*
     MLR - v91 - Jl '96 - p716+ [501+]
Coleman, Jane Candia - *Moving On*
     BL - v93 - F 1 '97 - p925 [51-250]
     PW - v244 - Ja 27 '97 - p82 [51-250]
The Red Drum
     WAL - v31 - Fall '96 - p278+ [251-500]
Coleman, John J - *Party Decline in America*
     Choice - v34 - F '97 - p1035 [51-250]
Coleman, Joyce - *Public Reading and the Reading Public in Late Medieval England and France*
     Choice - v34 - F '97 - p1019 [51-250]
Coleman, Jules L - *In Harm's Way*
     Ethics - v107 - O '96 - p149+ [501+]
Coleman, Lori - *Fundamental Soccer*
  y Emerg Lib - v24 - S '96 - p26 [1-50]
Coleman, Matt - *Trains, Tracks and Tall Timber*
     Model R - v64 - My '97 - p49 [51-250]
Coleman, Michael - *Escape Key*
  y Sch Lib - v44 - N '96 - p168 [51-250]
The Knowledge: Flaming Olympics
  c Books - v10 - Je '96 - p25 [51-250]
Net Bandits
  y Sch Lib - v44 - N '96 - p168 [51-250]
Ridiculous! (Illus. by Gwyneth Williamson)
  c CBRS - v25 - Win '97 - p61 [51-250]
  c SLJ - v43 - F '97 - p74 [51-250]

Weirdo's War
  c Bks Keeps - v100 - S '96 - p13 [51-250]
  y Sch Lib - v45 - F '97 - p46 [51-250]
Coleman, Nick - *The Picador Book of Sports Writing*
     Aethlon - v13 - Spr '96 - p228+ [501+]
Coleman, Peter - *Double Take*
     Quad - v40 - My '96 - p80+ [501+]
Coleman, Ray - *McCartney: Yesterday and Today*
     Books - v9 - S '95 - p22 [1-50]
Coleman, Ronald - *Pre-Law Companion*
     BWatch - v17 - N '96 - p6 [51-250]
     J Car P&E - v57 - Win '97 - p15 [51-250]
Coleman, Sheelagh - *Full Circle*
     TES - D 27 '96 - p16 [1-50]
Coleman, Simon - *Pilgrimage: Past and Present in the World Religions*
     AHR - v102 - F '97 - p86+ [251-500]
Pilgrimage Past and Present in the World Religions
     Rel St Rev - v23 - Ap '97 - p149 [51-250]
Coleman, Val - *Beverly and Marigold*
     KR - v64 - S 15 '96 - p1339 [251-500]
     LJ - v121 - O 1 '96 - p129 [51-250]
     PW - v243 - S 23 '96 - p56 [51-250]
Coleman, Verna - *Adela Pankhurst: The Wayward Suffragette 1885-1961*
     Aust Bk R - v - Ag '96 - p13+ [501+]
     Quad - v40 - D '96 - p83+ [501+]
     TLS - O 4 '96 - p40 [51-250]
Coleman, Wanda - *Native in a Strange Land*
     BW - v26 - D 22 '96 - p12 [51-250]
     HMR - Spr '97 - p7+ [501+]
     LJ - v122 - F 1 '97 - p97 [51-250]
Coleman, William B - *Molecular Diagnostics*
     SciTech - v21 - Mr '97 - p47 [51-250]
Coleman, William D - *Financial Services, Globalization and Domestic Policy Change*
     Choice - v34 - D '96 - p657+ [51-250]
Coleman, William L - *Ten Things Your Teen Will Thank You For...Someday*
     VOYA - v19 - F '97 - p316 [51-250]
Coleridge, Nicholas - *With Friends like These*
     Books - v11 - Ap '97 - p22 [51-250]
     Spec - v278 - F 1 '97 - p33 [501+]
     TLS - F 21 '97 - p23 [251-500]
Coleridge, Samuel Taylor - *Biographia Literaria. Vols. 1-2*
     Biography - v20 - Win '97 - p54+ [501+]
A Choice of Coleridge's Verse
     Agenda - v34 - Spr '96 - p177+ [501+]
Coleridge: Selected Poems
     TLS - N 29 '96 - p11 [1-50]
Coleridge: The Early Family Letters
     Nine-C Lit - v50 - Mr '96 - p552 [1-50]
Shorter Works and Fragments. Vols. 1-2
     Nine-C Lit - v51 - D '96 - p420 [51-250]
Coles, Katharine - *The Measurable World*
     Bloom Rev - v16 - N '96 - p27 [51-250]
Coles, Kim - *I'm Free, but It'll Cost You*
     BL - v93 - Ap 1 '97 - p1266 [51-250]
Coles, Nicholas - *For a Living*
     Per Psy - v49 - Aut '96 - p732+ [501+]
Coles, R T - *From Huntsville to Appomattox*
     Choice - v34 - O '96 - p347 [51-250]
Coles, Robert - *Doing Documentary Work*
     BL - v93 - My 15 '97 - p1543 [51-250]
     KR - v65 - F 15 '97 - p266 [251-500]
In God's House
  c CLW - v67 - D '96 - p58 [51-250]
The Moral Intelligence of Children
     Am - v176 - Ja 4 '97 - p4 [501+]
     BL - v93 - N 15 '96 - p546+ [51-250]
     BW - v26 - D 29 '96 - p1+ [501+]
     KR - v64 - N 15 '96 - p1648 [251-500]
     LATBR - F 2 '97 - p8 [501+]
     LJ - v122 - Ja '97 - p125 [51-250]
     NYTBR - v102 - Mr 2 '97 - p29 [501+]
     NYTLa - v146 - Ja 27 '97 - pC18 [501+]
     PW - v243 - N 18 '96 - p53+ [51-250]
The Moral Intelligence of Children. Audio Version
     Quill & Q - v62 - D '96 - p31 [1-50]
The Story of Ruby Bridges (Illus. by George Ford)
  c SLJ - v42 - D '96 - p45 [51-250]
The Youngest Parents
  y BL - v93 - F 1 '97 - p906 [51-250]
     KR - v65 - Mr 1 '97 - p345 [51-250]
     LJ - v122 - Ap 1 '97 - p112 [51-250]
     PW - v244 - F 10 '97 - p71+ [51-250]
Coles, William E - *Another Kind of Monday*
  y BL - v93 - Ap 1 '97 - p1292 [1-50]
  y HB Guide - v7 - Fall '96 - p301 [51-250]

Coletta, Paolo E - *Allied and American Naval Operations in the European Theater, World War I*
  J Mil H - v61 - Ja '97 - p177+ [501+]
Colford, Paul D - *Howard Stern: King of All Media*
  BW - v26 - Ag 4 '96 - p4 [501+]
  Ent W - Je 28 '96 - p100 [51-250]
  Howard Stern: King of All Media (Gould). Audio Version
  LJ - v121 - N 15 '96 - p104 [51-250]
Colin, Ann - *Willie: Raising and Loving a Child with Attention Deficit Disorder*
  KR - v64 - D 1 '96 - p1712 [251-500]
  PW - v243 - D 16 '96 - p50 [51-250]
  Trib Bks - Mr 16 '97 - p5 [501+]
Colitti, Marcello - *Perspectives of Oil and Gas*
  Nature - v384 - D 12 '96 - p528 [51-250]
Colker, Ruth - *Hybrid: Bisexuals, Multiracials, and Other Misfits under American Law*
  Choice - v34 - N '96 - p537 [51-250]
  Pregnant Men, Practice, Theory and the Law
  Rel St Rev - v22 - O '96 - p341 [51-250]
Colket, Meredith B, Jr. - *Pelot Family Genealogy*
  NGSQ - v84 - S '96 - p229 [51-250]
Coll, Alberto R - *Legal and Moral Constraints on Low-Intensity Conflict*
  J Gov Info - v23 - S '96 - p543 [51-250]
Coll, Blanche D - *Safety Net*
  RAH - v24 - D '96 - p647+ [501+]
Collado-Vides, Julio - *Integrative Approaches to Molecular Biology*
  Choice - v34 - My '97 - p1523 [51-250]
Collar, N J - *Birds to Watch 2*
  r Choice - v34 - O '96 - p307+ [501+]
Collard, Sneed B - *Alien Invaders*
  y BL - v93 - N 1 '96 - p485 [51-250]
  y HB Guide - v8 - Spr '97 - p116 [1-50]
  y SB - v33 - Ja '97 - p12+ [51-250]
  y SLJ - v43 - Ja '97 - p120+ [51-250]
  Animal Dads (Illus. by Steve Jenkins)
  c BL - v93 - My 15 '97 - p1577 [51-250]
  c CCB-B - v50 - My '97 - p316+ [51-250]
  c PW - v244 - Mr 31 '97 - p73 [51-250]
  Our Natural Homes (Illus. by James M Needham)
  c HB Guide - v8 - Spr '97 - p117 [51-250]
  c SLJ - v42 - O '96 - p130 [51-250]
Colle, Ralph Del - *Christ and the Spirit*
  JR - v77 - Ja '97 - p159+ [501+]
College Chemistry Faculties 1996
  r ARBA - v28 - '97 - p140 [51-250]
  SciTech - v20 - N '96 - p20 [51-250]
College Student's Guide to Merit and Other No-Need Funding 1996-1998
  r Choice - v34 - N '96 - p436 [51-250]
  r VOYA - v19 - D '96 - p301 [51-250]
The Collegeville Pastoral Dictionary of Biblical Theology
  r Am - v176 - Mr 8 '97 - p22 [51-250]
  r ARBA - v28 - '97 - p543+ [51-250]
Collen, Lindsey - *The Rape of Sita*
  W&I - v11 - N '96 - p268+ [251-500]
Collenteur, G A - *Economic Decision-Making in a Changing World*
  Econ J - v106 - S '96 - p1462 [51-250]
Colless, Edward - *The Error of My Ways*
  Meanjin - v55 - '96 - p775+ [501+]
Collett, Jonathan - *Greening the College Curriculum*
  Am Sci - v84 - N '96 - p617+ [501+]
  r Choice - v34 - S '96 - p98 [251-500]
Colletta, Nat J - *Case Studies in War-to-Peace Transition*
  JEL - v34 - D '96 - p2059 [51-250]
  The Transition from War to Peace in Sub-Saharan Africa
  JEL - v34 - D '96 - p2059 [51-250]
Colley, Ann C - *Edward Lear and the Critics*
  RES - v48 - F '97 - p133+ [501+]
Collicott, Sharleen - *Seeing Stars*
  c BL - v92 - Ag '96 - p1906 [51-250]
  c HB Guide - v7 - Fall '96 - p251 [51-250]
Collie, Michael - *George Gordon: An Annotated Catalogue of His Scientific Correspondence*
  r SciTech - v21 - Mr '97 - p33 [51-250]
  Murchison in Moray
  Isis - v87 - D '96 - p737+ [51-250]
Collier, George A - *Basta! Land and the Zapatista Rebellion in Chiapas*
  AAAGA - v86 - S '96 - p614+ [501+]
Collier, James - *My Brother Sam Is Dead (Brown). Audio Version*
  y SLJ - v42 - D '96 - p72 [51-250]
Collier, James H - *Scientific and Technical Communication*
  R&R Bk N - v12 - F '97 - p92 [51-250]

Collier, James Lincoln - *Jazz: The American Theme Song*
  MQ - v80 - Fall '96 - p392+ [501+]
  With Every Drop of Blood
  y Kliatt - v31 - My '97 - p5 [251-500]
  c PW - v244 - Ja 20 '97 - p403 [1-50]
Collier, John - *The Backyard*
  c PW - v243 - D 9 '96 - p69 [1-50]
Collier, Mary Jo - *The King's Giraffe (Illus. by Stephan Poulin)*
  c HB Guide - v7 - Fall '96 - p252 [51-250]
Collier, Mel - *Electronic Library and Visual Information Research--ELVIRA 2*
  LR - v45 - 8 '96 - p52+ [501+]
Collier, Michael - *Dams and Rivers*
  BioSci - v47 - Ap '97 - p260 [51-250]
Collier, Peter - *Artistic Relations*
  BM - v138 - S '96 - p614+ [1-50]
  CLS - v33 - 4 '96 - p420+ [501+]
  MLR - v91 - Jl '96 - p729+ [501+]
  The Race Card
  PW - v244 - My 5 '97 - p188 [51-250]
Collier, Richard - *Masculinity, Law, and the Family*
  AJS - v102 - N '96 - p932+ [501+]
Collier, Simon - *A History of Chile 1808-1994*
  Choice - v34 - My '97 - p1560 [51-250]
  TLS - F 7 '97 - p31 [501+]
Collier, Ute - *Energy and Environment in the European Union*
  GJ - v163 - Mr '97 - p107 [1-50]
Collier's Encyclopedia. 1996 Ed., Vols. 1-24
  yr BL - v93 - S 15 '96 - p266+ [501+]
Collier's Encyclopedia 1996. 1996 Ed., Vols. 1-24
  yr SLJ - v43 - F '97 - p128 [51-250]
Collier's Encyclopedia on CD-ROM. Electronic Media Version
  yr BL - v93 - N 1 '96 - p524+ [501+]
  r LJ - v122 - Ja '97 - p160 [51-250]
  r WorldV - v13 - Ja '97 - p23 [51-250]
Colligan, John B - *The Juan Paez Hurtado Expedition of 1695*
  HAHR - v77 - F '97 - p108+ [251-500]
  PHR - v65 - N '96 - p662+ [251-500]
Collignon, Rick - *The Journal of Antonio Montoya*
  Atl - v278 - S '96 - p113 [1-50]
  NYTBR - v101 - Ag 25 '96 - p19 [51-250]
Collin, Matthew - *Altered State*
  New Sci - v154 - My 3 '97 - p46 [1-50]
  PW - v244 - Ap 28 '97 - p59 [251-500]
Collin, Simon - *E-Mail: A Practical Guide*
  CBR - v14 - Jl '96 - p20 [51-250]
  Networking Windows 95
  SciTech - v20 - D '96 - p11 [51-250]
Colling, Herb - *Ninety-Nine Days*
  Beav - v76 - O '96 - p43 [51-250]
Collings, David - *Wordsworthian Errancies*
  RES - v48 - F '97 - p124+ [501+]
Collington, Peter - *On Christmas Eve*
  c TES - D 6 '96 - p16* [1-50]
Collingwood, R G - *Essays in Political Philosophy*
  RM - v50 - D '96 - p395+ [501+]
Collingwood Studies. Vols. 1-2
  Hist & T - v35 - 3 '96 - p412 [251-500]
Collins, Adela Yarbro - *The Beginning of the Gospel*
  JR - v76 - O '96 - p618+ [501+]
Collins, Andrew - *Fodor's Gay Guide to the USA*
  r BL - v93 - S 15 '96 - p206 [1-50]
  r Quill & Q - v62 - S '96 - p24 [51-250]
Collins, Andrew, 1957- - *From the Ashes of Angels*
  NS - v125 - D 20 '96 - p120+ [501+]
Collins, Ardis B - *Hegel on the Modern World*
  Clio - v25 - Spr '96 - p321+ [501+]
Collins, Barbara - *Lethal Ladies*
  Arm Det - v29 - Sum '96 - p347 [51-250]
Collins, Beverly - *The Phonetics of English and Dutch. 3rd Ed.*
  R&R Bk N - v12 - F '97 - p78 [51-250]
Collins, Billy - *The Art of Drowning*
  Bloom Rev - v16 - S '96 - p11 [251-500]
Collins, Bradford R - *12 Views of Manet's Bar*
  BM - v138 - S '96 - p610 [501+]
Collins, Carolyn Strom - *The World of Little House (Illus. by Deborah Maze)*
  c HB Guide - v8 - Spr '97 - p148 [51-250]
Collins, Catherine Fisher - *African-American Women's Health and Social Issues*
  Choice - v34 - Ap '97 - p1371 [51-250]
  SciTech - v21 - Mr '97 - p46 [51-250]
Collins, Christopher - *Authority Figures*
  Choice - v34 - Mr '97 - p1157 [51-250]

Collins, David R - *Casimir Pulaski: Soldier on Horseback (Illus. by Larry Nolte)*
  c HB Guide - v7 - Fall '96 - p371+ [51-250]
  Farmworker's Friend
  c BL - v93 - D 15 '96 - p722 [51-250]
  c HB Guide - v8 - Spr '97 - p156 [51-250]
Collins, Douglas - *Olympic Dreams*
  Pet PM - v25 - Ag '96 - p10 [51-250]
Collins, Hugh - *Autobiography of a Murderer*
  Books - v11 - Ap '97 - p20 [51-250]
  Spec - v278 - F 15 '97 - p28+ [501+]
  TLS - Mr 28 '97 - p12 [501+]
Collins, Irene - *Jane Austen and the Clergy*
  CH - v66 - Mr '97 - p138+ [501+]
Collins, Jackie - *Vendetta: Lucky's Revenge*
  BL - v93 - D 15 '96 - p691+ [51-250]
  CSM - v89 - F 20 '97 - p10 [51-250]
  CSM - v89 - Mr 20 '97 - p14 [51-250]
  Ent W - F 14 '97 - p56 [51-250]
  HMR - Spr '97 - p22+ [501+]
  KR - v64 - D 15 '96 - p1750 [251-500]
  PW - v243 - D 16 '96 - p42 [51-250]
Collins, James B - *Classes, Estates, and Order in Early Modern Brittany*
  EHR - v111 - S '96 - p981+ [501+]
  JMH - v68 - S '96 - p695+ [501+]
  The State in Early Modern France
  Six Ct J - v27 - Fall '96 - p808+ [501+]
Collins, James L - *The Mountain Men*
  c HB Guide - v7 - Fall '96 - p385 [51-250]
Collins, Janet - *The Quiet Child*
  TES - N 29 '96 - p10* [51-250]
Collins, Jeff - *Derrida for Beginners*
  TLS - Mr 21 '97 - p27 [501+]
Collins, Jim - *Architectures of Excess: Cultural Life in the Information Age*
  QJS - v83 - My '97 - p259+ [501+]
Collins, Joan - *Infamous*
  Ent W - Mr 7 '97 - p61 [51-250]
Collins, John J - *Death, Ecstasy, and Other Worldly Journeys*
  JR - v76 - O '96 - p670+ [501+]
  The Scepter and the Star
  Intpr - v50 - O '96 - p426+ [251-500]
  Theol St - v57 - Je '96 - p339+ [501+]
Collins, Joseph - *Chile's Free Market Miracle*
  S&S - v60 - Win '96 - p507+ [501+]
Collins, Mark - *Mister Rogers' Neighborhood*
  JOYS - v10 - Fall '96 - p98+ [251-500]
  R&R Bk N - v12 - F '97 - p81 [51-250]
Collins, Martin J - *Space: Discovery and Exploration*
  Pub Hist - v18 - Fall '96 - p176+ [501+]
Collins, Max Allan - *Damned in Paradise*
  Arm Det - v29 - Fall '96 - p467 [51-250]
  Arm Det - v30 - Win '97 - p18 [51-250]
  BL - v93 - S 15 '96 - p223 [51-250]
  KR - v64 - S 1 '96 - p1272 [51-250]
  Daylight. Audio Version
  LJ - v122 - Ap 1 '97 - p144 [51-250]
  Gil Elvgren: The Wartime Pin-Ups
  BWatch - v18 - Mr '97 - p3 [1-50]
Collins, Michael, 1890-1922 - *In Great Haste*
  BL - v93 - S 15 '96 - p214 [51-250]
  ILS - v15 - Fall '96 - p31 [1-50]
  LJ - v121 - N 15 '96 - p72 [51-250]
  The Path to Freedom
  ILS - v15 - Fall '96 - p31 [1-50]
Collins, Michael, 1946- - *Banks and Industrial Finance in Britain 1800-1939*
  JEL - v34 - D '96 - p2097 [51-250]
Collins, Nancy A - *Dark Love*
  Necro - Fall '96 - p22+ [501+]
  A Dozen Black Roses
  LJ - v122 - Ja '97 - p144 [51-250]
  Forbidden Acts
  Necro - Fall '96 - p22+ [501+]
Collins, Neil - *Politics and Elections in Nineteenth-Century Liverpool*
  EHR - v111 - N '96 - p1316+ [251-500]
Collins, Patricia - *Psychic New York*
  r Horoscope - v63 - Ja '97 - p125 [51-250]
Collins, Paul - *Dream Weavers*
  Aust Bk R - S '96 - p35 [501+]
  y Magpies - v11 - S '96 - p37 [51-250]
Collins, Raymond F - *Preaching the Epistles*
  Am - v176 - Mr 8 '97 - p28 [51-250]
Collins, Ronald K L - *The Death of Discourse*
  Choice - v34 - O '96 - p270 [51-250]
  JC - v47 - Win '97 - p171+ [501+]
Collins, Tess - *The Law of Revenge*
  PW - v244 - My 12 '97 - p74 [51-250]

Collins, Vincent J - *Physiologic and Pharmacologic Bases of Anesthesia*
    SciTech - v20 - S '96 - p38 [51-250]
Collins, Warwick - *Gents*
    KR - v65 - F 1 '97 - p156+ [251-500]
    LJ - v122 - Ap 1 '97 - p122+ [51-250]
    PW - v244 - Mr 17 '97 - p76+ [51-250]
Collins, Wilkie - *Heart and Science*
    BW - v26 - D 15 '96 - p12 [51-250]
No Name
    Spec - v277 - N 23 '96 - p46 [1-50]
The Woman in White (Holm). Audio Version
    TLS - Ag 2 '96 - p24 [51-250]
Collins Children's Encyclopedia
    cr Sch Lib - v45 - F '97 - p37 [51-250]
    cr TES - D 6 '96 - p22* [501+]
Collins COBUILD English Dictionary. New Expanded Ed.
    cr Bks Keeps - v100 - S '96 - p22+ [501+]
    r Choice - v34 - D '96 - p587 [51-250]
Collins Electronic English Dictionary and Thesaurus V2.0. Electronic Media Version
    r TES - Ja 31 '97 - p21* [251-500]
Collins Eyewitness Guides
    c Magpies - v11 - Jl '96 - p39 [1-50]
Collins (Firm: London, England) - *Collins Nations of the World Atlas*
    r ARBA - v28 - '97 - p171+ [51-250]
Collins First Dictionary
    cr Bks Keeps - v100 - S '96 - p22+ [501+]
Collins First Word Book
    cr Bks Keeps - v100 - S '96 - p22+ [501+]
Collins French Dictionary on CD-Rom. Electronic Media Version
    cr TES - Ja 3 '97 - p14U [501+]
Collins Nursery Rhymes. Audio Version
    c TES - Ja 17 '97 - p13* [51-250]
Collins Pocket Primary Dictionary
    cr Bks Keeps - v100 - S '96 - p22+ [501+]
Collins School Dictionary
    cr Bks Keeps - v100 - S '96 - p22+ [501+]
Collins Shorter School Dictionary
    cr Bks Keeps - v100 - S '96 - p22+ [501+]
Collins Songs and Rhymes. Audio Version
    c TES - Ja 17 '97 - p13* [51-250]
Collins Yellow Storybooks
    c Magpies - v11 - Jl '96 - p28 [51-250]
Collins-Lowry, Sharon M - *Black Corporate Executives*
    BL - v93 - N 1 '96 - p465 [51-250]
    LJ - v121 - N 1 '96 - p82 [1-50]
    PW - v243 - N 25 '96 - p67 [51-250]
Collinson, Helen - *Green Guerrillas*
    Choice - v34 - F '97 - p1021+ [51-250]
    TLS - S 6 '96 - p27 [501+]
    WorldV - v13 - Ja '97 - p7+ [251-500]
Collinson, Patrick - *A History of Canterbury Cathedral*
    Albion - v28 - Fall '96 - p456+ [501+]
    Specu - v72 - Ja '97 - p133+ [251-500]
Collinson, Roger - *Sticky Fingers*
    c Sch Lib - v44 - Ag '96 - p105 [51-250]
Collinson, Sarah - *Beyond Borders*
    WP - v49 - O '96 - p130+ [501+]
Collinwood, Dean Walter - *Korea: The High and Beautiful Peninsula*
    c Ch BWatch - v6 - D '96 - p6 [1-50]
    c HB Guide - v8 - Spr '97 - p169 [51-250]
Collis, John - *Mexico*
    r LJ - v121 - O 1 '96 - p112 [51-250]
Collison, Gary Lee - *Shadrach Minkins: From Fugitive Slave to Citizen*
    y BL - v93 - F 15 '97 - p1000 [51-250]
    KR - v65 - Ja 1 '97 - p31 [251-500]
    LJ - v122 - F 15 '97 - p140 [51-250]
    NYTLa - v146 - Mr 12 '97 - pC15 [501+]
Collison, Kerry B - *The Tim-Tim Man*
    Aust Bk R - S '96 - p65 [501+]
Collodi, Carlo - *The Adventures of Pinocchio*
    SFS - v24 - Mr '97 - p181 [1-50]
The Adventures of Pinocchio (Illus. by Fritz Kredel)
    c Ch BWatch - v6 - O '96 - p3 [51-250]
Pinocchio (Illus. by Ed Young)
    c BL - v93 - N 15 '96 - p586+ [51-250]
    c BW - v26 - N 3 '96 - p10 [51-250]
    c CLW - v67 - Mr '97 - p53 [51-250]
    c HB - v72 - N '96 - p720 [51-250]
    c HB Guide - v8 - Spr '97 - p57 [51-250]
    c KR - v64 - Ag 15 '96 - p1233 [51-250]
    c NYTBR - v101 - N 10 '96 - p31 [501+]
    c SLJ - v42 - O '96 - p85 [51-250]

Collon, Dominique - *Ancient Near Eastern Art*
    AJA - v101 - Ja '97 - p167+ [501+]
    r Rel St Rev - v23 - Ap '97 - p164 [51-250]
Collopy, Michael - *Works of Love Are Works of Peace*
    y BL - v93 - S 1 '96 - p36 [51-250]
    Ch Today - v40 - D 9 '96 - p49 [51-250]
    PW - v243 - S 16 '96 - p67 [51-250]
Collver, Michael - *A Catalog of Music for the Cornett*
    r ARBA - v28 - '97 - p480 [51-250]
    r Choice - v34 - F '97 - p940 [51-250]
Collyer, Jaime - *People on the Prowl*
    Choice - v34 - Ap '97 - p1343 [51-250]
    NYTBR - v102 - Ja 19 '97 - p18 [251-500]
    TranslRevS - v2 - D '96 - p32 [51-250]
    TranslRevS - v2 - D '96 - p32 [51-250]
Collymore, George - *Birthpangs of a Nation*
    GJ - v163 - Mr '97 - p100+ [51-250]
Colman, Penny - *Rosie the Riveter*
    y Emerg Lib - v24 - S '96 - p23 [1-50]
    c LA - v73 - O '96 - p437 [251-500]
    y RT - v50 - N '96 - p248 [51-250]
Cologni, Franco - *Platinum by Cartier*
    BL - v93 - S 15 '96 - p199 [51-250]
Colombo, Carlo - *Proceedings of the 3rd International Symposium on Intelligent Robotic Systems '95*
    Robotica - v14 - S '96 - p588+ [251-500]
Colombo, John Robert - *Haunted Toronto*
    Quill & Q - v62 - S '96 - p68 [251-500]
Colombo, Lanfranco - *Italian Portfolio*
    Afterimage - v24 - Ja '97 - p23 [1-50]
Colomer, Josep M - *Political Institutions in Europe*
    Choice - v34 - Ja '97 - p869+ [51-250]
The Colorado Review
    p LMR - v15 - Win '96 - p3+ [501+]
The Colour of Sculpture 1840-1910
    Spec - v277 - D 14 '96 - p76 [51-250]
Colpitt, Frances - *Minimal Art*
    BM - v138 - D '96 - p836 [1-50]
Colson, Charles - *The Body*
    y VOYA - v19 - F '97 - p316+ [51-250]
Evangelicals and Catholics Together
    Cres - v59 - S '96 - p39+ [501+]
Gideon's Torch
    HM - v293 - S '96 - p64+ [501+]
Coltart, Nina - *The Baby and the Bathwater*
    SciTech - v21 - Mr '97 - p55 [51-250]
Colten, Craig E - *The Road to Love Canal*
    T&C - v38 - Ja '97 - p269+ [501+]
Colton, Matthew - *Betrayal of Trust*
    TES - N 1 '96 - p8* [501+]
Colton, Timothy J - *Moscow: Governing the Socialist Metropolis*
    Lon R Bks - v18 - O 3 '96 - p28+ [501+]
    PSQ - v111 - Fall '96 - p554+ [501+]
    VQR - v72 - Aut '96 - p134* [501+]
Coltrane, Scott - *Family Man*
    Choice - v34 - S '96 - p218 [51-250]
    Wom R Bks - v14 - N '96 - p5+ [51-250]
The Columbia Dictionary of Quotations. Electronic Media Version
    r BL - v93 - Ja '97 - p769 [1-50]
The Columbia Encyclopedia on CD-ROM. Electronic Media Version
    yr Kliatt - v31 - My '97 - p32 [51-250]
The Columbia Granger's World of Poetry. Electronic Media Version
    yr ARBA - v28 - '97 - p465 [51-250]
The Columbia World of Quotations. Electronic Media Version
    r ARBA - v28 - '97 - p35+ [251-500]
    r BL - v93 - D 1 '96 - p680 [501+]
Colvin, Clare - *A Fatal Season*
    Spec - v277 - N 23 '96 - p45 [1-50]
Colvin, Gregory L - *Seize the Initiative*
    ChrPhil - v8 - Jl 11 '96 - p44 [51-250]
Colwell, Rita R - *Microbial Diversity in Time and Space*
    SciTech - v21 - Mr '97 - p43 [51-250]
Colwell, Stephen D - *Trouble-Free Travel*
    BL - v93 - S 15 '96 - p206 [1-50]
    LJ - v121 - O 15 '96 - p80+ [51-250]
Coman, Carolyn - *Tell Me Everything*
    y SLJ - v43 - Mr '97 - p112 [1-50]
What Jamie Saw
    y Bks Keeps - Ja '97 - p27 [51-250]
    c JB - v60 - D '96 - p265 [51-250]
    y Kliatt - v31 - My '97 - p5 [51-250]
    c PW - v244 - Mr 3 '97 - p77 [1-50]
    c Sch Lib - v45 - F '97 - p33 [51-250]
    c TES - D 6 '96 - p17* [51-250]
Comanor, Jeffrey - *Fedge Makes a Wish!*
    c HB Guide - v8 - Spr '97 - p23 [51-250]

Comba, Peter - *Molecular Modeling of Inorganic Compounds*
    Choice - v34 - N '96 - p485+ [51-250]
    J Chem Ed - v73 - Je '96 - pA136 [51-250]
Combes, Francoise - *Galaxies and Cosmology*
    Phys Today - v49 - N '96 - p84+ [501+]
Combined Retrospective Index to Book Reviews in Humanities Journals 1802-1974. Vols. 1-10
    r ASInt - v34 - O '96 - p18 [51-250]
Combined Retrospective Index to Book Reviews in Scholarly Journals 1886-1974. Vols. 1-15
    r ASInt - v34 - O '96 - p18 [51-250]
Combrinck-Graham, Lee - *Children in Families at Risk*
    Readings - v11 - S '96 - p22 [51-250]
Combs, Harry - *The Legend of the Painted Horse*
    LJ - v121 - O 15 '96 - p89 [51-250]
    PW - v243 - S 2 '96 - p111 [51-250]
Comden, Betty - *The New York Musicals of Comden and Green*
    CSM - v88 - N 21 '96 - pB3 [51-250]
    LJ - v122 - Ja '97 - p102 [51-250]
Comella, M Angels - *Acuarelas*
    c BL - v93 - F 15 '97 - p1032 [1-50]
Ceras
    c BL - v93 - F 15 '97 - p1032 [1-50]
Temperas
    c BL - v93 - F 15 '97 - p1032 [1-50]
Comer, Douglas E - *Internetworking with TCP/IP. 2nd Ed., Vol. 3*
    SciTech - v20 - S '96 - p55 [51-250]
Comer, James P - *Rallying the Whole Village*
    JNE - v64 - Fall '95 - p488+ [501+]
    Readings - v11 - D '96 - p21 [51-250]
Comer, Tom - *Opportunities for Mathematics in the Primary School*
    TES - O 4 '96 - pR12 [51-250]
Comfort, Bonnie - *Denial*
    PW - v243 - N 18 '96 - p70 [1-50]
Coming Attractions 96
    Quill & Q - v63 - Ja '97 - p34 [501+]
Coming in from the Cold
    Pub Hist - v18 - Sum '96 - p58+ [501+]
Comings, David E - *The Gene Bomb*
    R&R Bk N - v12 - F '97 - p96 [51-250]
Search for the Tourette Syndrome and Human Behavior Genes
    Sci - v274 - N 22 '96 - p1321 [1-50]
Comitae De Consultation Sur L'Administration De La Justice En Milieu Autochtone (Quebec) - *Justice for and by the Aboriginals*
    J Gov Info - v23 - S '96 - p637 [51-250]
Commander, Simon - *Unemployment, Restructuring, and the Labor Market in Eastern Europe and Russia*
    Econ J - v107 - Ja '97 - p286 [251-500]
Commentary
    p Dis - v44 - Win '97 - p101+ [501+]
Commins, David Dean - *Historical Dictionary of Syria*
    r ARBA - v28 - '97 - p73 [51-250]
    r Choice - v34 - F '97 - p940 [51-250]
    r MEQ - v3 - D '96 - p84 [51-250]
    r R&R Bk N - v12 - F '97 - p18 [51-250]
Commission De La Republique Francaise Pour L'Education, La Science Et La Culture - *The Scientific Education of Girls*
    JPR - v33 - Ag '96 - p384 [251-500]
Committee for Economic Development - *Reshaping Government in Metropolitan Areas*
    NCR - v85 - Spr '96 - p66 [51-250]
Committee on Opportunities in Drug Abuse Research - *Pathways of Addiction*
    SciTech - v21 - Mr '97 - p55 [51-250]
Committee on Science, Engineering, and Public Policy (U.S.) - *Careers in Science and Engineering*
    BioSci - v46 - N '96 - p790 [51-250]
Committee on Women's Studies in Asia - *Changing Lives*
    NWSA Jnl - v8 - Sum '96 - p132+ [501+]
Common, Michael - *Sustainability and Policy*
    JEL - v34 - D '96 - p1997+ [501+]
Commons, John R - *Legal Foundations of Capitalism*
    BusLR - v21 - 3 '96 - p28 [51-250]
Commonwealth of Independent States. Statistical Committee - *The Statistical Handbook of Social and Economic Indicators for the Former Soviet Union*
    r ARBA - v28 - '97 - p65+ [251-500]
    r Choice - v34 - D '96 - p587 [51-250]
    r LJ - v121 - S 15 '96 - p58+ [51-250]
The Communicator's Handbook. 3rd Ed.
    r R&R Bk N - v12 - F '97 - p75 [51-250]

Compa, Lance A - *Human Rights, Labor Rights, and International Trade*
  For Aff - v75 - N '96 - p148+ [51-250]
  R&R Bk N - v11 - N '96 - p52 [1-50]
Companies International. Electronic Media Version
  r ARBA - v28 - '97 - p101+ [501+]
  r LJ - v122 - F 15 '97 - p168 [51-250]
Comparative Analysis of Petroleum Exploration Contracts
  SciTech - v20 - D '96 - p81 [51-250]
Compendium of Human Settlements Statistics 1995
  r ARBA - v28 - '97 - p325 [51-250]
Compestine, Ying Chang - *Secrets of Fat-Free Chinese Cooking*
  PW - v244 - My 5 '97 - p203 [51-250]
Competition and Culture on Canada's Information Highway
  J Gov Info - v23 - S '96 - p611 [51-250]
Competitiveness: Forging Ahead
  J Gov Info - v23 - S '96 - p644 [51-250]
The Complete Dog Book for Kids
  cr BL - v93 - Ja '97 - p848+ [251-500]
  c Dog Fan - v28 - F '97 - p78 [51-250]
The Complete Games Trainers Play on CD-ROM. Electronic Media Version
  r LJ - v122 - F 15 '97 - p168 [51-250]
The Complete Hi$panic Media Directory 1996
  r Choice - v34 - Ja '97 - p777 [251-500]
Complete Hostel Vacation Guide to England, Wales and Scotland
  r BL - v93 - S 15 '96 - p206+ [1-50]
Complete List of Reports Published by the British Library 1995
  r LAR - v98 - Mr '96 - p163 [1-50]
The Complete Marquis Who's Who on CD-ROM. Electronic Media Version
  r BL - v93 - Ja '97 - p769 [1-50]
  r BL - v93 - O 1 '96 - p365 [501+]
  r R&R Bk N - v11 - N '96 - p17 [51-250]
The Complete Theory Test for Cars and Motorcycles
  J Gov Info - v23 - S '96 - p644 [51-250]
Complexity
  p Nature - v383 - S 5 '96 - p43 [251-500]
Compound Semiconductors 1995
  SciTech - v20 - S '96 - p57 [51-250]
Comprehensive Dictionary of Measurement and Control. 3rd Ed.
  r ARBA - v28 - '97 - p597 [51-250]
Comprehensive Dissertation Index 1861-1972. Vols. 1-37
  r ASInt - v34 - O '96 - p21 [1-50]
Comprehensive Dissertation Index 1973-1982. Vols. 1-38
  r ASInt - v34 - O '96 - p21 [1-50]
Comprehensive Organometallic Chemistry II. Vols. 1-14
  Choice - v34 - S '96 - p156 [501+]
Comprehensive Supramolecular Chemistry. Vols. 1-11
  Choice - v34 - My '97 - p1527 [51-250]
Compton, David - *The Acolyte*
  BL - v93 - O 1 '96 - p324 [51-250]
  KR - v64 - Ag 15 '96 - p1170 [251-500]
  PW - v243 - S 23 '96 - p57 [51-250]
  The Acolyte (Diamond). Audio Version
  BWatch - v17 - D '96 - p11 [1-50]
  LJ - v122 - F 1 '97 - p126 [51-250]
Compton, Ralph - *The Autumn of the Gun*
  Roundup M - v4 - Ap '97 - p29 [1-50]
  North to the Bitterroot
  Roundup M - v4 - D '96 - p25 [51-250]
Compton's Encyclopedia 1996. Vols. 1-26
  cr BL - v93 - S 15 '96 - p268+ [501+]
Compton's Encyclopedia of American History. Electronic Media Version
  r LJ - v121 - O 1 '96 - p134+ [501+]
  yr SLJ - v42 - Ag '96 - p46 [251-500]
Compton's Interactive Bible: New International Version. Electronic Media Version
  cr BL - v93 - My 15 '97 - p1589 [51-250]
  r LJ - v122 - F 15 '97 - p168+ [51-250]
Compton's Interactive Encyclopedia 1997. Electronic Media Version
  cr BL - v93 - N 1 '96 - p526 [251-500]
  yr Kliatt - v31 - Ja '97 - p33+ [251-500]
Compton's Interactive World Atlas. Electronic Media Version
  yr Kliatt - v31 - Ja '97 - p34 [51-250]
Compton's Reference Collection. Electronic Media Version
  yr Kliatt - v30 - S '96 - p39 [251-500]
Computational Complexity 11
  SciTech - v20 - S '96 - p10 [51-250]
Computer Animation '95
  SciTech - v20 - S '96 - p62 [51-250]

Computer Life
  p TES - O 18 '96 - p43U [51-250]
Computer Security Foundations Workshop - *The Computer Security Foundations Workshop*
  SciTech - v20 - S '96 - p7 [51-250]
Computer Software and Applications Conference 1996
  SciTech - v21 - Mr '97 - p5 [51-250]
Computer Technology 1996
  SciTech - v20 - N '96 - p82 [1-50]
Comrie, Bernard - *The Russian Language in the Twentieth Century. 2nd Ed.*
  Choice - v34 - N '96 - p466 [51-250]
Comsa, Ioan - *Contacte Si Relatii Romano-Americane*
  BL - v93 - D 15 '96 - p714 [1-50]
Comstock, Gary David - *Que(e)rying Religion*
  Choice - v34 - My '97 - p1516 [51-250]
  LJ - v122 - Ap 15 '97 - p103 [51-250]
  Unrepentant, Self-Affirming, Practicing
  Choice - v34 - N '96 - p545 [51-250]
  Rel St Rev - v23 - Ap '97 - p203 [51-250]
  TT - v53 - Ja '97 - p508+ [501+]
Conable, Barbara - *How to Learn the Alexander Technique. 3rd Ed.*
  Am MT - v46 - O '96 - p52 [251-500]
Conacher, D J - *Aeschylus: The Earlier Plays and Related Studies*
  R&R Bk N - v12 - F '97 - p77 [51-250]
Conaghan, Catherine M - *Unsettling Statecraft*
  HAHR - v77 - My '97 - p342+ [501+]
Conant, Susan - *Animal Appetite*
  KR - v65 - F 15 '97 - p256 [51-250]
  PW - v244 - F 3 '97 - p97 [51-250]
  Stud Rites
  LATBR - Jl 14 '96 - p6 [51-250]
Conari Press - *More Random Acts of Kindness (Asner). Audio Version*
  BL - v93 - F 15 '97 - p1038 [51-250]
  Random Acts of Kindness. Audio Version
  y Kliatt - v30 - N '96 - p50+ [51-250]
Conboy, Kenneth - *Shadow War*
  Arm F&S - v22 - Sum '96 - p643+ [501+]
Concise Encyclopedia Biology
  r ARBA - v28 - '97 - p576 [51-250]
  yr BL - v92 - Ag '96 - p1921+ [251-500]
  r Choice - v34 - O '96 - p249 [51-250]
  r New Sci - v154 - My 3 '97 - p49 [51-250]
Concise World Atlas
  r LJ - v122 - Mr 15 '97 - p54 [51-250]
Conde, Maryse - *Conversations with Maryse Conde*
  Choice - v34 - Mr '97 - p1169 [51-250]
  La Migration Des Coeurs
  WLT - v70 - Sum '96 - p747+ [501+]
  Segu
  PW - v243 - Jl 22 '96 - p234 [1-50]
Condee, Nancy - *Soviet Hieroglyphics*
  TLS - N 29 '96 - p21 [501+]
Condon, Matthew - *The Lulu Magnet*
  Aust Bk R - D '96 - p55+ [501+]
  Smashed: Australian Drinking Stories
  Aust Bk R - D '96 - p75 [251-500]
Condon, Richard G - *The Northern Copper Inuit*
  Choice - v34 - Ja '97 - p838 [51-250]
The Condor Token Newsletter
  p Coin W - v37 - O 7 '96 - p18 [51-250]
Condorcet, Jean-Antoine-Nicolas De Caritat, Marquis De - *Condorcet: Foundations of Social Choice and Political Theory*
  Isis - v88 - Mr '97 - p148+ [501+]
  JEL - v34 - S '96 - p1334+ [501+]
Condori Mamani, Gregorio - *Andean Lives*
  Choice - v34 - D '96 - p651 [51-250]
  TranslRevS - v2 - D '96 - p7 [51-250]
Cone, Joseph - *The Northwest Salmon Crisis*
  Choice - v34 - N '96 - p484 [51-250]
  SciTech - v20 - S '96 - p46 [51-250]
  WHQ - v28 - Spr '97 - p95+ [251-500]
Cone, Molly - *Squishy, Misty, Damp and Muddy*
  c AB - v98 - N 18 '96 - p1731 [51-250]
  c HB Guide - v7 - Fall '96 - p335 [51-250]
  c SLJ - v42 - Ag '96 - p133+ [51-250]
Cone, Patrick - *Wildfire (Illus. by Patrick Cone)*
  c BL - v93 - F 15 '97 - p1018 [51-250]
  c Cur R - v36 - D '96 - p13 [51-250]
  c HB Guide - v8 - Spr '97 - p117 [51-250]
  c KR - v64 - N 1 '96 - p1599 [51-250]
  c SB - v33 - Ja '97 - p17+ [51-250]
  c SLJ - v43 - Ja '97 - p99 [51-250]

Conference. Challenging Marketplace Solutions to Problems in the Economics of Information (1995: Washington, D.C.) - *The Economics of Information in the Networked Environment*
  R&R Bk N - v11 - N '96 - p80 [51-250]
Conference in a Series on Modeling Casting and Welding Processes (7th: 1995: London, England) - *Modeling of Casting, Welding and Advanced Solidification Processes VII*
  SciTech - v20 - D '96 - p62 [51-250]
Conference on Actions to Reduce Hunger Worldwide (1993: American University) - *Overcoming Global Hunger*
  J Gov Info - v23 - S '96 - p688 [51-250]
Conference on Chaos and the Changing Nature of Science and Medicine (1995: Mobile, AL) - *Chaos and the Changing Nature of Science and Medicine*
  SciTech - v20 - N '96 - p4 [51-250]
Conference on Emerging Technologies and Applications in Communications (1st: 1996: Portland, Or.) - *Proceedings: The First Conference on Emerging Technologies and Applications in Communications*
  SciTech - v20 - S '96 - p54 [51-250]
Conference on High Velocity Neutron Stars and Gamma-Ray Bursts (1995: La Jolla, CA) - *High Velocity Neutron Stars and Gamma-Ray Bursts*
  SciTech - v20 - S '96 - p13 [51-250]
Conference on Software Engineering Education (9th: 1996: Daytona Beach, Fla.) - *Ninth Conference on Software Engineering Education*
  SciTech - v20 - S '96 - p4 [51-250]
Conference on Superplasticity and Superplastic Forming (1995: Las Vegas, NV) - *Superplasticity and Superplastic Forming 1995*
  SciTech - v20 - N '96 - p63 [51-250]
Conference on the Course of Social and Economic Change in Quebec (1996: Quebec, Quebec) - *A Society Based on Responsibility and Solidarity*
  J Gov Info - v23 - S '96 - p639 [51-250]
Conference on the Editing of Old English Texts (1990: University of Manchester) - *The Editing of Old English*
  RES - v47 - N '96 - p553+ [501+]
Conference on the Fractography of Glasses and Ceramics (3rd: 1995: Alfred University) - *Fractography of Glasses and Ceramics III*
  SciTech - v21 - Mr '97 - p78 [51-250]
Conference on Virginia Woolf (5th: 1995: Otterbein College) - *Virginia Woolf: Texts and Contexts*
  RMR - v50 - 2 '96 - p169+ [501+]
  R&R Bk N - v12 - F '97 - p86 [51-250]
Confiant, Raphael - *Les Maitres De La Parole Creole*
  BL - v93 - F 1 '97 - p930 [1-50]
  La Vierge Du Grand Retour
  Econ - v340 - S 14 '96 - p14*+ [501+]
Conford, Ellen - *The Frog Princess of Pelham*
  c BL - v93 - Mr 15 '97 - p1241+ [51-250]
  c PW - v244 - Mr 24 '97 - p84 [51-250]
Conforti, Joseph A - *Jonathan Edwards, Religious Tradition, and American Culture*
  AL - v68 - D '96 - p849+ [501+]
  CH - v65 - D '96 - p789+ [501+]
  IPQ - v37 - Mr '97 - p120+ [501+]
  W&M Q - v53 - O '96 - p815+ [501+]
Confrontation
  p Sm Pr R - v28 - O '96 - p13+ [501+]
Confucius - *The Analects of Confucius*
  BL - v93 - Ja '97 - p781 [51-250]
  LJ - v122 - F 15 '97 - p138 [51-250]
  NYRB - v44 - Ap 10 '97 - p8+ [501+]
  PW - v244 - Ja 13 '97 - p69+ [51-250]
Conge, Patrick J - *From Revolution to War*
  Choice - v34 - N '96 - p532 [51-250]
Conger, Syndy McMillen - *Mary Wollstonecraft and the Language of Sensibility*
  RES - v48 - F '97 - p122+ [501+]
Congleton, Roger D - *The Political Economy of Environmental Protection*
  JEL - v34 - D '96 - p2132 [51-250]
Congress on Medieval Manuscript Illumination in the Northern Netherlands (1989: Utrecht, Netherlands) - *Masters and Miniatures*
  Lib - v18 - Je '96 - p158+ [501+]
Congressional Quarterly's Politics in America 1996. Book and Electronic Media Version
  r CLW - v66 - Je '96 - p39 [251-500]
Congressional Research Service Index 1916-1994 on CD-ROM. Electronic Media Version
  r J Gov Info - v24 - Ja '97 - p56+ [501+]
The Congressional Yearbook 1994
  R&R Bk N - v11 - D '96 - p47 [51-250]

Conisbee, Philip - *Georges De La Tour and His World*
    BW - v26 - D 8 '96 - p10 [51-250]
    Choice - v34 - F '97 - p955 [51-250]
    Obs - v54 - O 13 '96 - p17* [51-250]
    PW - v243 - N 4 '96 - p61 [51-250]
    Spec - v277 - D 14 '96 - p76 [51-250]
    TLS - D 20 '96 - p18+ [501+]
   In the Light of Italy
    Choice - v34 - D '96 - p601+ [51-250]
    NYRB - v44 - Mr 6 '97 - p10+ [501+]
Conjunctions
   p Am Theat - v13 - D '96 - p20 [1-50]
Conkelton, Sheryl - *Annette Messager*
    Afterimage - v24 - S '96 - p15+ [501+]
Conkin, Paul Keith - *The Uneasy Center*
    AHR - v101 - O '96 - p1274+ [251-500]
    CH - v65 - S '96 - p518+ [501+]
    JIH - v27 - Win '97 - p541+ [501+]
    JR - v76 - O '96 - p644+ [501+]
    JSH - v62 - N '96 - p790+ [501+]
    Theol St - v58 - Mr '97 - p170+ [501+]
Conley, Robert F - *Practical Dispersion*
    SciTech - v20 - S '96 - p59 [51-250]
Conley, Robert J - *The Dark Island*
    Roundup M - v3 - Ag '96 - p28+ [251-500]
Conley, Tom - *The Self-Made Map*
    Choice - v34 - My '97 - p1552 [51-250]
Conlin, Bill - *Batting Cleanup, Bill Conlin*
    LJ - v122 - F 1 '97 - p82 [1-50]
Conlogue, Ray - *Impossible Nation*
    Quill & Q - v62 - N '96 - p36 [251-500]
Conlon-McKenna, Marita - *Fields of Home (Illus. by Donald Teskey)*
   c KR - v65 - Mr 15 '97 - p459 [51-250]
Conly, Jane Leslie - *Crazy Lady!*
   c JOYS - v10 - Fall '96 - p92+ [501+]
   Trout Summer
   y BL - v93 - Ap 1 '97 - p1292 [1-50]
   y Emerg Lib - v23 - My '96 - p57+ [51-250]
   y LA - v73 - O '96 - p432 [51-250]
Conn, Harold O - *TIPS: Transjugular Intrahepatic Portalsystemic Shunts*
    SciTech - v20 - S '96 - p38 [51-250]
Conn, Peter - *Pearl S. Buck: A Cultural Biography*
    Ant R - v55 - Spr '97 - p240 [251-500]
    Choice - v34 - Ja '97 - p792 [51-250]
    FEER - v160 - My 1 '97 - p40 [501+]
    KR - v64 - Ag 15 '96 - p1201+ [251-500]
    LATBR - N 17 '96 - p4+ [501+]
    LJ - v122 - Ja '97 - p49 [1-50]
    Nat - v263 - D 16 '96 - p30+ [501+]
    NYTBR - v101 - N 17 '96 - p13+ [501+]
    NYTBR - v101 - D 8 '96 - p90 [1-50]
    NYTLa - v146 - D 25 '96 - pC26 [501+]
    PW - v243 - Jl 22 '96 - p218+ [51-250]
    PW - v243 - N 4 '96 - p42 [1-50]
Connect: To the Fight against Discrimination and Racism
   p WorldV - v12 - Jl '96 - p11 [51-250]
Connecticut Career Guide
   r J Gov Info - v23 - S '96 - p579+ [51-250]
Connell, Barbara - *Examining the Media*
   y TES - Ap 4 '97 - p15* [51-250]
Connell, Evan S - *The Collected Stories of Evan S. Connell*
    Bks & Cult - v2 - My '96 - p8 [501+]
    HR - v49 - Aut '96 - p483+ [501+]
    PW - v244 - Ap 14 '97 - p72 [1-50]
    WLT - v71 - Win '97 - p150+ [501+]
Connell, James E - *The Charlton Price Guide to Canadian Clocks*
   r ARBA - v28 - '97 - p358 [51-250]
Connell, John - *Pacific 2010: Urbanisation in Polynesia*
    Cont Pac - v9 - Spr '97 - p286+ [501+]
Connell, K H - *Irish Peasant Society*
    ILS - v16 - Spr '97 - p36 [1-50]
Connell, Maria Bryan Harford - *Tokens of Affection*
    AL - v68 - D '96 - p877 [51-250]
    VQR - v73 - Win '97 - p20* [51-250]
Connell, R W - *Masculinities*
    Socio R - v44 - N '96 - p746+ [501+]
Connellan, Tom - *Inside the Magic Kingdom*
    BL - v93 - My 1 '97 - p1467 [51-250]
Connelly, Frances S - *The Sleep of Reason*
    SDA - v4 - Fall '96 - p130+ [501+]
Connelly, Joseph - *Memoirs of Senator Joseph Connelly 1885-1961*
    ILS - v16 - Spr '97 - p36 [51-250]
Connelly, Karen - *The Disorder of Love*
    Quill & Q - v63 - Ja '97 - p18 [1-50]
    Quill & Q - v63 - F '97 - p46 [251-500]

The Small Words in My Body
    BIC - v25 - S '96 - p35 [251-500]
Touch the Dragon
    Obs - S 15 '96 - p18* [51-250]
Connelly, Michael - *The Last Coyote*
    Arm Det - v29 - Sum '96 - p280 [51-250]
The Poet
    LATBR - D 29 '96 - p4 [501+]
The Poet (Schirner). Audio Version
    Arm Det - v29 - Sum '96 - p354 [51-250]
    LJ - v121 - S 15 '96 - p114 [51-250]
Trunk Music
    Arm Det - v30 - Win '97 - p112 [251-500]
    BL - v93 - O 1 '96 - p290+ [51-250]
    BW - v26 - N 17 '96 - p6 [51-250]
    KR - v64 - O 1 '96 - p1418 [251-500]
    LATBR - Ap 20 '97 - p13 [51-250]
    LJ - v121 - O 1 '96 - p130 [51-250]
    NYTBR - v102 - Ja 5 '97 - p20 [51-250]
    PW - v243 - O 21 '96 - p73 [51-250]
    Spec - v278 - Mr 8 '97 - p37 [501+]
    Trib Bks - Ja 5 '97 - p4 [51-250]
    WSJ-Cent - v99 - F 5 '97 - pA16 [51-250]
Trunk Music (Hill). Audio Version
    CSM - v89 - Mr 27 '97 - pB2 [1-50]
    LJ - v122 - F 1 '97 - p127 [51-250]
Conner, Bobbi - *The Parent's Journal Guide to Raising Great Kids*
    PW - v244 - F 17 '97 - p216 [51-250]
Conniff, James - *The Useful Cobbler*
    EHR - v112 - F '97 - p216+ [501+]
Conniff, Richard - *Spineless Wonders*
   y BL - v93 - N 1 '96 - p467 [51-250]
   y BL - v93 - D 1 '96 - p664 [1-50]
    BW - v26 - D 29 '96 - p8 [51-250]
    Choice - v34 - Ap '97 - p1363 [51-250]
    KR - v64 - S 1 '96 - p1289 [251-500]
    LJ - v121 - O 15 '96 - p87 [51-250]
    NH - v105 - N '96 - p16 [1-50]
    PW - v243 - O 21 '96 - p65 [51-250]
Connolly, Colm - *The Illustrated Life of Michael Collins*
   y BL - v93 - Ja '97 - p811 [251-500]
    ILS - v16 - Spr '97 - p36 [1-50]
    PW - v243 - O 14 '96 - p68+ [51-250]
Connolly, Hugh - *The Irish Penitentials and Their Significance for the Sacrament of Penance Today*
    CHR - v82 - Jl '96 - p477+ [251-500]
    Theol St - v57 - Je '96 - p347+ [501+]
Connolly, Joseph - *Stuff*
    Obs - Mr 16 '97 - p16* [501+]
    TLS - F 28 '97 - p22 [501+]
Connolly, Peter - *The Legend of Odysseus (Illus. by Peter Connolly)*
   c SLJ - v42 - N '96 - p39 [1-50]
The Roman Fort
   c SLJ - v42 - N '96 - p39 [1-50]
Connolly, Ray - *In the Sixties*
    Econ - v341 - O 19 '96 - p3*+ [501+]
Connolly, S J - *Religion and Society in 19th-Century Ireland*
    Bks & Cult - v2 - Ja '96 - p11+ [501+]
Connolly, Sean, 1943- - *A Great Place to Die*
    BL - v93 - Mr 15 '97 - p1224 [51-250]
    NYTBR - v102 - Ap 6 '97 - p21 [51-250]
    PW - v244 - F 3 '97 - p96 [51-250]
Connolly, Shane - *Table Flowers*
    BL - v93 - S 15 '96 - p199+ [51-250]
    LJ - v121 - S 15 '96 - p63 [51-250]
Connolly, Thomas - *Mourning into Joy*
    Am - v175 - S 28 '96 - p36+ [501+]
    Notes - v53 - S '96 - p35+ [501+]
Connolly, W Kenneth - *The Indestructible Book*
    LJ - v122 - F 15 '97 - p138 [51-250]
Connolly, William - *The Ethos of Pluralization*
    Tikkun - v11 - S '96 - p86+ [501+]
Connor, Beverly - *A Rumor of Bones*
    PW - v243 - S 23 '96 - p60 [51-250]
Connor, D Russell - *Benny Goodman: Wrappin' It Up*
   r ARBA - v28 - '97 - p488+ [51-250]
Connor, Jerome J - *Introduction to Motion Based Design*
    Am Sci - v85 - Mr '97 - p192+ [501+]
    SciTech - v20 - S '96 - p48 [51-250]
Connor, Kim - *Starting from Houses and Homes*
    TES - F 14 '97 - p16* [51-250]
Connor, Kimberly Rae - *Conversions and Visions in the Writings of African-American Women*
    JAAR - v64 - Fall '96 - p694+ [501+]
    Signs - v22 - Win '97 - p479+ [501+]
Connor, Nikki - *Cardboard Boxes (Illus. by Sarah-Jane Neaves)*
   c HB Guide - v8 - Spr '97 - p135 [51-250]

Plastic Cups (Illus. by Sarah-Jane Neaves)
   c HB Guide - v8 - Spr '97 - p135 [51-250]
Connor, Richard C - *The Lives of Whales and Dolphins*
    LATBR - My 26 '96 - p11 [51-250]
Connor, Sonja L - *The New American Diet Cookbook*
    BL - v93 - F 15 '97 - p988 [51-250]
    LJ - v122 - F 15 '97 - p159 [51-250]
    PW - v244 - Ja 6 '97 - p69 [51-250]
Connor, Tom - *A Parody*
    PW - v243 - S 16 '96 - p78 [51-250]
Conoley, Gillian - *Beckon*
    VQR - v72 - Aut '96 - p137* [51-250]
Conord, Bruce W - *Cesar Chavez*
   y SLJ - v42 - O '96 - p45 [1-50]
Conrad, Barnaby, III - *The Cigar*
    BW - v26 - D 8 '96 - p13 [51-250]
Conrad, Chris - *Hemp for Health*
    PW - v244 - Mr 24 '97 - p80 [51-250]
Conrad, David C - *Status and Identity in West Africa*
    Am Ethnol - v23 - Ag '96 - p647+ [501+]
    JIH - v27 - Spr '97 - p742+ [501+]
Conrad, Doug - *Managed Care Contracting*
    SciTech - v20 - N '96 - p36 [51-250]
Conrad, Hy - *Whodunit--You Decide!*
   y Ch BWatch - v7 - F '97 - p8 [1-50]
Conrad, Joseph - *Heart of Darkness*
    ELT - v40 - 1 '97 - p126 [51-250]
    HM - v294 - Ja '97 - p62+ [501+]
    TLS - My 24 '96 - p5+ [501+]
Lord Jim
    CML - v16 - Win '96 - p131+ [501+]
The Nigger of the Narcissus
    MLR - v92 - Ja '97 - p1+ [501+]
Nostromo (Pennington). Audio Version
   y Ch BWatch - v7 - Ja '97 - p5 [1-50]
    LJ - v122 - F 1 '97 - p126 [51-250]
The Secret Agent (Jennings). Audio Version
   y Ch BWatch - v7 - Ja '97 - p5 [1-50]
The Secret Agent (Howard). Audio Version
    LJ - v122 - Ja '97 - p172+ [51-250]
Under Western Eyes
    Trib Bks - Mr 2 '97 - p8 [1-50]
Victory: An Island Tale
    ELT - v40 - 2 '97 - p251 [51-250]
Conrad, Lawrence I - *The Western Medical Tradition 800 B.C. to A.D. 1800*
    Isis - v87 - S '96 - p528+ [501+]
Conrad, Margaret - *Intimate Relations*
    W&M Q - v53 - O '96 - p842+ [501+]
Conrad, Pam - *Animal Lingo (Illus. by Barbara Bustetter Falk)*
   c RT - v50 - F '97 - p426 [51-250]
Call Me Ahnighito (Illus. by Richard Egielski)
   c LA - v73 - O '96 - p430 [51-250]
Holding Me Here
   y PW - v244 - F 10 '97 - p85 [1-50]
Our House (Illus. by Brian Selznick)
   c RT - v50 - S '96 - p59 [51-250]
Prairie Songs
   y Kliatt - v30 - S '96 - p3 [1-50]
The Rooster's Gift (Illus. by Eric Beddows)
   c BL - v93 - S 15 '96 - p245+ [51-250]
   c BL - v93 - Ap 1 '97 - p1298 [1-50]
   c CBRS - v25 - S '96 - p2 [51-250]
   c Ch BWatch - v6 - N '96 - p6 [1-50]
   c Emerg Lib - v24 - Mr '97 - p27 [1-50]
   c HB - v72 - N '96 - p721+ [251-500]
   c HB Guide - v8 - Spr '97 - p24 [51-250]
   c LATBR - S 1 '96 - p11 [51-250]
   c LATBR - D 8 '96 - p18 [1-50]
   c PW - v243 - S 9 '96 - p82+ [51-250]
   c PW - v243 - N 4 '96 - p48 [1-50]
   c Quill & Q - v62 - Jl '96 - p57 [251-500]
   c SLJ - v42 - S '96 - p177 [51-250]
The Tub Grandfather (Illus. by Richard Egielski)
   c Par Ch - v20 - N '96 - p3 [50-]
Tub People (Sallley) (Illus. by Richard Egielski). Book and Audio Version
   c Ch BWatch - v7 - Ja '97 - p5 [1-50]
The Tub People (Salley) (Illus. by Richard Egielski). Book and Audio Version
   c PW - v244 - F 3 '97 - p46 [51-250]
What I Did for Roman
   y Kliatt - v31 - Ja '97 - p6 [51-250]

Zoe Rising
  c BL - v92 - Ag '96 - p1900 [51-250]
  y CCB-B - v50 - O '96 - p52 [51-250]
  c Ch BWatch - v6 - S '96 - p4 [51-250]
  c HB - v72 - N '96 - p733 [51-250]
  c HB Guide - v8 - Spr '97 - p63 [51-250]
  y JAAL - v40 - F '97 - p409 [51-250]
  c SLJ - v42 - N '96 - p103+ [51-250]
     VOYA - v19 - D '96 - p277+ [51-250]
Conran, Terence - *The Cigar in Art*
  BWatch - v18 - Mr '97 - p1 [1-50]
Terence Conran on Design
  BL - v93 - F 1 '97 - p920 [51-250]
Conrotto, Eugene - *Lost Gold and Silver Mines of the Southwest*
  BWatch - v18 - F '97 - p2 [1-50]
Conroy, David W - *In Public Houses*
  AHR - v101 - D '96 - p1612 [501+]
  Historian - v59 - Win '97 - p426+ [501+]
  J Am Cult - v18 - Win '95 - p107+ [251-500]
  J Am St - v30 - Ag '96 - p314+ [251-500]
  JIH - v27 - Win '97 - p539+ [251-500]
  RAH - v24 - S '96 - p383+ [501+]
  W&M Q - v54 - Ap '97 - p413+ [501+]
Conroy, Maggie Francis - *A World of Love*
  PW - v244 - Mr 31 '97 - p55 [51-250]
Conroy, Pat - *Beach Music. Audio Version*
  EJ - v85 - D '96 - p97 [501+]
Beach Music (Marosz). Audio Version
  y Kliatt - v30 - N '96 - p36 [51-250]
Conroy, Thomas F - *Markets of the U.S. for Business Planners. 2nd Ed., Vols. 1-2*
  r ARBA - v28 - '97 - p126 [251-500]
Consalvi, Peter - *2nd Collector Steiff Values*
  Ant & CM - v101 - O '96 - p55 [51-250]
Considine, Douglas M - *Van Nostrand's Scientific Encyclopedia. 8th Ed., Vols. 1-2*
  r R&R Bk N - v11 - D '96 - p67 [51-250]
  r SciTech - v20 - N '96 - p3 [51-250]
Consortium for Mathematics and Its Applications (U.S.) - *Principles and Practice of Mathematics*
  JEL - v35 - Mr '97 - p194 [51-250]
Constable, George - *The XI, XII, and XIII Olympiads*
  Choice - v34 - F '97 - p1002+ [501+]
Where You Are
  BL - v93 - Ja '97 - p817 [51-250]
  BW - v27 - F 16 '97 - p4 [51-250]
  KR - v64 - N 1 '96 - p1548+ [51-250]
  LJ - v122 - Ja '97 - p144 [51-250]
  NYTBR - v102 - Mr 2 '97 - p18 [51-250]
  PW - v243 - D 2 '96 - p43 [51-250]
  Trib Bks - Mr 2 '97 - p4 [51-250]
Constable, Giles - *Three Studies in Medieval Religious and Social Thought*
  Albion - v28 - Win '96 - p667+ [501+]
  Theol St - v57 - Je '96 - p349+ [251-500]
Constable, Lyn - *Flower Arranging European Styles*
  BL - v93 - Ja '97 - p800 [51-250]
Constable, Nicole - *Christian Souls and Chinese Spirits*
  JAAR - v64 - Sum '96 - p433+ [501+]
Guest People
  Choice - v34 - D '96 - p652 [51-250]
Maid to Order in Hong Kong
  PW - v244 - Ap 28 '97 - p67 [51-250]
Constable, Olivia Remie - *Trade and Traders in Muslim Spain*
  EHR - v112 - F '97 - p168+ [501+]
Constant, Benjamin - *Correspondence Generale 1774-1792*
  MLR - v91 - Jl '96 - p729 [251-500]
Ecrits Litteraires 1800-1813. Vols. 1-2
  MLR - v91 - Jl '96 - p729 [251-500]
Memoires Sur Les Cent-Jours
  MLR - v91 - Jl '96 - p729 [251-500]
Constant, Christine - *The Potter's Palette*
  Ceram Mo - v44 - O '96 - p24 [51-250]
Constante, Lena - *Evadarea Tacuta*
  BL - v93 - D 15 '96 - p714 [1-50]
Constantine, K C - *Family Values*
  BL - v93 - F 15 '97 - p1006 [51-250]
  KR - v65 - Ja 15 '97 - p96 [51-250]
  NYTBR - v102 - Ap 13 '97 - p24 [51-250]
  PW - v244 - F 3 '97 - p98 [51-250]
Good Sons
  Arm Det - v29 - Fall '96 - p493 [251-500]
Constantine, Stephen - *The First World War in British History*
  Albion - v28 - Fall '96 - p531+ [501+]

Constantini, Costanzo - *Conversations with Fellini*
  KR - v64 - D 1 '96 - p1712 [251-500]
  LJ - v122 - F 15 '97 - p136+ [51-250]
  PW - v243 - D 16 '96 - p49 [51-250]
Consultants and Consulting Organizations Directory 1996 Supplement
  r ARBA - v28 - '97 - p81 [51-250]
Consumer Canada 1996
  r ARBA - v28 - '97 - p124+ [501+]
Consumer Mexico 1996
  r ARBA - v28 - '97 - p124+ [501+]
Consumer South Africa 1995
  r ARBA - v28 - '97 - p124+ [501+]
Consumer USA 1996
  r ARBA - v28 - '97 - p124+ [501+]
Consumers Index to Product Evaluations and Information Sources, April-June 1996
  r ARBA - v28 - '97 - p93 [251-500]
Contaminated Soil '95. Vols. 1-2
  SciTech - v20 - N '96 - p68 [51-250]
Conte, Donald J - *Earth Science*
  SciTech - v21 - Mr '97 - p32 [51-250]
Conte, Edouard - *La Quete De La Race*
  JIH - v27 - Spr '97 - p700+ [251-500]
Conte, Paul - *Database Design and Programming for DB2/400*
  SciTech - v21 - Mr '97 - p10 [51-250]
Conte-Helm, Marie - *The Japanese and Europe*
  CR - v269 - O '96 - p215+ [501+]
Contemporary Australian Women 1996/97
  r ARBA - v28 - '97 - p335 [251-500]
  r Choice - v34 - F '97 - p940 [51-250]
Contemporary Authors 1962-. Book and Electronic Media Version
  r ASInt - v34 - O '96 - p14 [51-250]
Contemporary Literary Criticism. Vols. 87-89
  yr ARBA - v28 - '97 - p413+ [251-500]
Contemporary Literary Criticism: Yearbook 1994
  yr ARBA - v28 - '97 - p412+ [51-250]
Contemporary Women's Issues. Electronic Media Version
  r Choice - v34 - My '97 - p1482 [51-250]
  r WorldV - v12 - Jl '96 - p23 [51-250]
Conti, Charles - *Metaphysical Personalism*
  Rel St - v32 - D '96 - p525+ [501+]
  Rel St Rev - v22 - O '96 - p335 [51-250]
  TT - v53 - O '96 - p428 [51-250]
Conti, Fiorenzo - *Excitatory Amino Acids and the Cerebral Cortex*
  SciTech - v20 - D '96 - p34 [51-250]
Conto, Agostino - *L'Antiquario Felice Feliciano, Veronese*
  Lib - v19 - Mr '97 - p99 [251-500]
Contoski, Edmund - *Makers and Takers*
  BL - v93 - F 1 '97 - p914 [51-250]
Contosta, David R - *Villanova University 1842-1992*
  CHR - v83 - Ja '97 - p138+ [501+]
Contratto, Susan - *A Feminist Clinician's Guide to the Memory Debate*
  SciTech - v21 - Mr '97 - p56 [51-250]
Contreras, Don - *We Dance Because We Can*
  Nat Peop - v10 - '97 - p78+ [501+]
Contreras, Manuel E - *Tecnologia Moderna En Los Andes*
  HAHR - v76 - N '96 - p812+ [251-500]
Control and Dynamic Systems. Vol. 79
  SciTech - v20 - N '96 - p70 [51-250]
Convegno Internazionale Di Studi Leopardiani (8th: 1991: Recanari, Italy) - *Lingua E Stile Di Giacomo Leopardi*
  MLR - v91 - Jl '96 - p753+ [501+]
Converse, Florence - *Diana Victrix*
  AL - v69 - Mr '97 - p67+ [501+]
Conversino, Mark J - *Fighting with the Soviets*
  Choice - v34 - Ap '97 - p1402+ [51-250]
Conway, Anne - *The Principles of the Most Ancient and Modern Philosophy*
  TLS - N 1 '96 - p32 [501+]
Conway, David - *Classical Liberalism*
  APSR - v90 - D '96 - p888+ [501+]
  R&R Bk N - v11 - N '96 - p48 [51-250]
Conway, Jill K - *True North (Reading). Audio Version*
  y Kliatt - v30 - N '96 - p51 [51-250]
Written by Herself. Vol. 2
  BW - v26 - O 20 '96 - p12 [51-250]
  y Kliatt - v31 - Mr '97 - p25+ [51-250]
  LJ - v121 - O 1 '96 - p92 [51-250]
  Trib Bks - F 2 '97 - p8 [51-250]
Conway, John H - *The Book of Numbers*
  LJ - v121 - N 1 '96 - p103+ [51-250]
  New Sci - v151 - S 14 '96 - p47 [51-250]

Conway, Kathlyn - *Ordinary Life*
  c Ch BWatch - v7 - F '97 - p6+ [51-250]
  LJ - v122 - Ja '97 - p132 [51-250]
  NYTBR - v102 - Ja 19 '97 - p19 [51-250]
Conway, Ket Tom - *Young Explorer's Guide to Undersea Life (Illus. by Ket Tom Conway)*
  c BL - v93 - S 15 '96 - p233 [51-250]
  c Bloom Rev - v16 - S '96 - p29 [51-250]
  c SB - v32 - O '96 - p210 [51-250]
  c SLJ - v42 - S '96 - p210 [51-250]
Conwell, Kent - *Bumpo, Bill, and the Girls*
  Roundup M - v4 - Ap '97 - p25+ [51-250]
Cony, Carlos Heitor - *Quase Memoria*
  WLT - v70 - Sum '96 - p678 [501+]
Cooey, Paula M - *Family, Freedom and Faith*
  Rel St Rev - v23 - Ja '97 - p50 [51-250]
Coogan, Tim Pat - *Michael Collins: The Man Who Made Ireland*
  Mar Crp G - v81 - Mr '97 - p73+ [501+]
The Troubles: Ireland's Ordeal 1966-1996, and the Search for Peace
  Choice - v34 - D '96 - p668 [51-250]
Cook, Albert - *The Stance of Plato*
  Choice - v34 - Mr '97 - p1174 [51-250]
Cook, Allan R - *Cancer Sourcebook for Women*
  r BL - v93 - F 1 '97 - p959 [1-50]
The New Cancer Sourcebook
  r BL - v93 - F 1 '97 - p958 [1-50]
  r Choice - v34 - Ja '97 - p828 [51-250]
  r SciTech - v20 - N '96 - p40 [51-250]
Cook, Charles - *The Essential Guide to Nature Walking in the United States*
  LJ - v121 - D '96 - p137 [51-250]
Cook, Chris - *The Longman Companion to Britain since 1945*
  CR - v268 - Je '96 - p334 [51-250]
What Happened Where
  r HT - v46 - O '96 - p59 [1-50]
Cook, Christopher D K - *Aquatic and Wetland Plants of India*
  r Choice - v34 - My '97 - p1524 [51-250]
Cook, David - *Launching a Business on the Web. 2nd Ed.*
  CBR - v15 - Spr '97 - p5+ [1-50]
Cook, Diane - *Hot Spots*
  Aud - v98 - N '96 - p136 [1-50]
  LJ - v121 - N 15 '96 - p85 [51-250]
  Nature - v383 - S 26 '96 - p309 [1-50]
  WSJ-MW - v78 - D 5 '96 - pA18 [51-250]
Cook, Don - *The Long Fuse*
  NYTBR - v102 - Ap 20 '97 - p32 [1-50]
Cook, Elizabeth Heckendorn - *Epistolary Bodies*
  Choice - v34 - Ja '97 - p792 [51-250]
Cook, Ferris - *The Garden Trellis*
  LJ - v121 - D '96 - p131 [51-250]
Cook, Harold J - *Trials of an Ordinary Doctor*
  EHR - v112 - F '97 - p204 [251-500]
Cook, J F - *NDE Engineering Codes and Standards and Materials Characterization*
  SciTech - v20 - N '96 - p83 [1-50]
Cook, James H - *Fifty Years on the Old Frontier as Cowboy, Hunter, Guide, Scout and Ranchman*
  CAY - v16 - Fall '95 - p11 [51-250]
Cook, Jeffrey - *Seeking Structure from Nature*
  R&R Bk N - v11 - N '96 - p60 [51-250]
Cook, Jonathan A - *Satirical Apocalypse*
  AL - v69 - Mr '97 - p216+ [251-500]
  Nine-C Lit - v51 - D '96 - p420 [51-250]
Cook, Karin - *What Girls Learn*
  y BL - v93 - F 15 '97 - p1002 [51-250]
  KR - v64 - D 15 '96 - p1750+ [251-500]
  PW - v244 - Ja 6 '97 - p63 [251-500]
Cook, Kevin L - *Dubester's U.S. Census Bibliography with SuDocs Class Numbers and Indexes*
  r A Lib - v27 - Ag '96 - p71 [51-250]
  r ARBA - v28 - '97 - p323 [251-500]
  r Choice - v34 - N '96 - p426+ [51-250]
  r J Gov Info - v24 - Ja '97 - p79+ [501+]
Cook, Lin - *Something like Fire*
  Spec - v277 - N 2 '96 - p42+ [501+]
Cook, Maria Lorena - *The Politics of Economic Restructuring*
  CS - v25 - N '96 - p777+ [501+]
  HAHR - v77 - F '97 - p138+ [501+]
Cook, Mariana Ruth - *Mothers and Sons*
  y Kliatt - v30 - S '96 - p38 [51-250]
  Wom R Bks - v14 - N '96 - p12+ [501+]
Cook, Nick - *Aggressor*
  Books - v10 - Je '96 - p24 [1-50]
Cook, Nigel P - *Practical Electronics*
  SciTech - v20 - D '96 - p77 [51-250]

Cook, Patrick J - *Milton, Spenser, and the Epic Tradition*
r Choice - v34 - N '96 - p448 [51-250]
   R&R Bk N - v11 - N '96 - p66 [51-250]
Cook, Paul, 1944- - *Privatisation Policy and Performance*
r Econ J - v106 - S '96 - p1431+ [501+]
Cook, Philip L - *Zion City, Illinois*
   Choice - v34 - D '96 - p694+ [51-250]
   WHQ - v28 - Spr '97 - p103 [1-50]
Cook, Richard - *The Penguin Guide to Jazz on CD*
r Trib Bks - Ja 12 '97 - p8 [501+]
Cook, Robert - *Baptism of Fire*
   J Am St - v30 - Ap '96 - p137+ [501+]
Cook, Robin - *Chromosome 6*
   BL - v93 - Mr 15 '97 - p1205 [1-50]
   Chromsome 6 (Gaines). Audio Version
   LJ - v122 - My 1 '97 - p153 [51-250]
   Invasion
y BL - v93 - Mr 1 '97 - p1067 [51-250]
   PW - v244 - Mr 3 '97 - p71 [51-250]
Cook, Sarah - *Process Improvement*
   R&R Bk N - v12 - F '97 - p38 [51-250]
Cook, Sharon Anne - *Through Sunshine and Shadow*
   AHR - v102 - F '97 - p227+ [501+]
   Can Hist R - v77 - S '96 - p427+ [501+]
Cook, Stephen L - *Prophecy and Apocalypticism*
   Choice - v34 - N '96 - p474 [51-250]
Cook, Stuart D - *Handbook of Multiple Sclerosis. 2nd Ed.*
   SciTech - v20 - D '96 - p43 [51-250]
Cook, Thomas H - *The Chatham School Affair*
   Arm Det - v29 - Fall '96 - p468 [51-250]
y BL - v92 - Ag '96 - p1885 [51-250]
y BL - v92 - Ag '96 - p1891 [1-50]
y BL - v93 - Ja '97 - p763 [1-50]
   NYTBR - v101 - S 29 '96 - p28 [51-250]
   The Chatham School Affair (Guidall). Audio Version
   BL - v93 - My 15 '97 - p1596 [51-250]
Cook, Wade B - *Wall Street Money Machine (Cook). Audio Version*
   LJ - v122 - Ap 15 '97 - p136 [51-250]
Cook, Will - *The Rain Tree*
   PW - v243 - O 21 '96 - p72 [51-250]
   Roundup M - v4 - D '96 - p25 [51-250]
Cook-Degan, Robert - *The Gene Wars*
   New Sci - v153 - F 1 '97 - p47 [51-250]
Cooke, Andrew - *The Economics of Leisure and Sport*
   Econ J - v106 - S '96 - p1475 [51-250]
Cooke, Bernard - *Why Angels...Are They Real...Really Needed?*
   RR - v55 - S '96 - p554 [51-250]
Cooke, Colin - *An Introduction to Experimental Physics*
y TES - Ja 3 '97 - pR12 [51-250]
Cooke, Dennis - *Persecuting Zeal*
   Spec - v278 - Ja 25 '97 - p37 [501+]
Cooke, Edward S - *Making Furniture in Preindustrial America*
   Choice - v34 - F '97 - p1023 [51-250]
   Mag Antiq - v151 - Ja '97 - p50 [51-250]
   SciTech - v20 - D '96 - p86 [1-50]
Cooke, Elizabeth - *Zeena*
   KR - v64 - Ag 15 '96 - p1170 [251-500]
   LATBR - D 22 '96 - p5 [501+]
   LJ - v121 - S 15 '96 - p94 [51-250]
   PW - v243 - S 2 '96 - p113+ [51-250]
Cooke, James J - *The U.S. Air Service in the Great War 1917-1919*
   Choice - v34 - O '96 - p346 [51-250]
Cooke, Lynne - *Visual Display*
   Afterimage - v24 - N '96 - p14+ [501+]
Cooke, Miriam - *War's Other Voices*
   Choice - v34 - Ja '97 - p788+ [51-250]
   Women and the War Story
   Choice - v34 - Ap '97 - p1330 [51-250]
   LJ - v122 - Ja '97 - p127 [51-250]
Cooke, Paul D - *Hobbes and Christianity*
   Choice - v34 - F '97 - p977 [51-250]
Cooke, Philip - *The Rise of the Rustbelt*
   EG - v73 - Ja '97 - p139+ [501+]
   R&R Bk N - v11 - N '96 - p26 [51-250]
Cooke, Tim - *Looking at Art. Vols. 1-12*
cr SLJ - v43 - F '97 - p130+ [51-250]
Cooke, Trish - *So Much (Illus. by Helen Oxenbury)*
c Bks Keeps - Jl '96 - p6 [51-250]
c Bks Keeps - Mr '97 - p7 [51-250]
c RT - v50 - F '97 - p420 [51-250]

Cook-Lynn, Elizabeth - *Why I Can't Read Wallace Stegner and Other Essays*
   BL - v93 - N 1 '96 - p473+ [51-250]
   CHE - v43 - D 13 '96 - pA18 [51-250]
   Choice - v34 - Ap '97 - p1334 [51-250]
   KR - v64 - O 1 '96 - p1438 [251-500]
   Ms - v7 - Ja '97 - p81 [251-500]
   NYTBR - v102 - Mr 16 '97 - p20 [51-250]
   PW - v243 - N 4 '96 - p68+ [51-250]
   R&R Bk N - v12 - F '97 - p87 [51-250]
Cookson, Catherine - *The Bonny Dawn*
   Spec - v277 - N 16 '96 - p48 [501+]
   The Obsession
   BL - v93 - My 15 '97 - p1539+ [51-250]
   KR - v65 - My 1 '97 - p659+ [251-500]
Cooley, Armanda - *Madam Foreman*
   Esq - v126 - N '96 - p65 [1-50]
Cooley, Nicole - *Resurrection: Poems*
   Choice - v34 - N '96 - p454 [51-250]
Cooley, Thomas F - *Frontiers of Business Cycle Research*
   Econ J - v106 - N '96 - p1834+ [251-500]
   JEL - v34 - S '96 - p1349+ [501+]
Coolidge, Olivia - *The Golden Days of Greece*
c SLJ - v42 - N '96 - p39 [1-50]
Cooling, Benjamin Franklin - *Fort Donelson's Legacy*
   BL - v93 - Mr 15 '97 - p1222 [51-250]
Cooling, Wendy - *Aliens to Earth*
c Books - v11 - Ap '97 - p24 [51-250]
   Bad Dreams
c Books - v11 - Ap '97 - p24 [51-250]
   Books to Enjoy 12-16
   LAR - v99 - F '97 - p101 [51-250]
   On the Run
c Books - v11 - Ap '97 - p24 [51-250]
   The Puffin Book of Stories for Eight-Year-Olds (Illus. by S Cox)
c JB - v60 - D '96 - p248 [51-250]
   The Puffin Book of Stories for Five-Year Olds
c Sch Lib - v44 - Ag '96 - p98 [51-250]
   The Puffin Book of Stories for Seven-Year-Olds (Illus. by S Cox)
c JB - v60 - D '96 - p248+ [51-250]
   Spine Chillers
c Books - v11 - Ap '97 - p24 [51-250]
   Stars in Your Eyes
c Books - v11 - Ap '97 - p24 [51-250]
   Timewatch: Stories of Past and Future
c Books - v11 - Ap '97 - p24 [51-250]
   Top Secret
c Books - v11 - Ap '97 - p24 [51-250]
   Weird and Wonderful
c Books - v11 - Ap '97 - p24 [51-250]
   Wild and Free
c Books - v11 - Ap '97 - p24 [51-250]
Coombe, Tucker - *The Shoresaver's Handbook*
y SB - v32 - N '96 - p235+ [51-250]
r Under Nat - v23 - 3 '96 - p31 [51-250]
Coombes, Annie E - *Reinventing Africa*
   HRNB - v25 - Fall '96 - p36 [251-500]
   VS - v39 - Aut '95 - p116+ [501+]
Coombs, Anne - *Sex and Anarchy*
   Aust Bk R - Je '96 - p7+ [501+]
   Quad - v40 - S '96 - p79+ [501+]
Coombs, Clyde F, Jr. - *Printed Circuits Handbook. 4th Ed.*
r SciTech - v20 - S '96 - p57 [51-250]
Coombs, Karen M - *Sarah on Her Own*
y SLJ - v42 - S '96 - p224 [51-250]
y VOYA - v19 - D '96 - p261 [51-250]
Coombs, Rod - *Technological Collaboration*
   JEL - v34 - S '96 - p1484 [51-250]
Coombs, Ted - *Active X Sourcebook*
   SciTech - v20 - D '96 - p76 [51-250]
   The Netscape LiveWire Sourcebook
   CBR - v15 - Spr '97 - p6 [51-250]
r New Sci - v153 - Ja 18 '97 - p41 [51-250]
Coomer, Joe - *Beachcombing for a Shipwrecked God*
   PW - v244 - Ja 27 '97 - p103 [1-50]
   Sailing in a Spoonful of Water
   KR - v65 - Mr 15 '97 - p429 [251-500]
   LJ - v122 - My 1 '97 - p111 [51-250]
   PW - v244 - My 5 '97 - p185 [51-250]

Cooney, Barbara - *Eleanor (Illus. by Barbara Cooney)*
c BL - v93 - Ja '97 - p767 [1-50]
c BL - v93 - S 15 '96 - p239 [51-250]
c BL - v93 - Ap 1 '97 - p1298 [1-50]
c CCB-B - v50 - N '96 - p93+ [51-250]
c HB - v72 - S '96 - p610+ [51-250]
c HB Guide - v8 - Spr '97 - p156 [51-250]
c Inst - v106 - Ja '97 - p54 [51-250]
c KR - v64 - Ag 15 '96 - p1233 [51-250]
c LATBR - O 6 '96 - p15 [51-250]
c NY - v72 - N 18 '96 - p98 [1-50]
c NYTBR - v101 - D 8 '96 - p78 [501+]
c Par - v72 - F '97 - p149 [51-250]
c PW - v243 - S 23 '96 - p76 [51-250]
c PW - v243 - N 4 '96 - p48 [51-250]
c SLJ - v42 - S '96 - p195+ [51-250]
c SLJ - v42 - D '96 - p28 [1-50]
c Smith - v27 - N '96 - p173+ [1-50]
   Eleanor. Hattie and the Wild Waves (Cooney). Audio Version
   CSM - v89 - Mr 27 '97 - pB8 [51-250]
c PW - v244 - Ap 14 '97 - p32+ [51-250]
   Miss Rumphius
c HB - v73 - Mr '97 - p189 [1-50]
   The Story of Christmas (Illus. by Loretta Krupinski)
c Emerg Lib - v23 - My '96 - p56 [51-250]
Cooney, Caroline B - *Both Sides of Time*
y Ch BWatch - v6 - My '96 - p2? [251-250]
y Kliatt - v31 - My '97 - p12 [51-250]
   Driver's Ed (Guidall). Audio Version
y BL - v93 - N 15 '96 - p604 [51-250]
   The Face on the Milk Carton
y SLJ - v42 - O '96 - p45 [1-50]
   Flash Fire
y Emerg Lib - v24 - S '96 - p26 [1-50]
y Kliatt - v31 - Mr '97 - p6 [51-250]
y Sch Lib - v44 - N '96 - p168 [51-250]
   Flight #116 Is Down
y Kliatt - v30 - S '96 - p3 [1-50]
   Flight #116 Is Down (Guidall). Audio Version
y SLJ - v42 - Ag '96 - p65 [51-250]
   Out of Time
y Ch BWatch - v6 - My '96 - p2 [51-250]
y HB Guide - v7 - Fall '96 - p301 [51-250]
   The Voice on the Radio
y BL - v93 - O 1 '96 - p340 [51-250]
y BL - v93 - Ap 1 '97 - p1292 [1-50]
y CBRS - v25 - O '96 - p20+ [51-250]
y CCB-B - v50 - N '96 - p94 [51-250]
y Ch BWatch - v6 - N '96 - p3 [51-250]
y Emerg Lib - v24 - Mr '97 - p54 [51-250]
y HB Guide - v8 - Spr '97 - p78 [51-250]
y KR - v64 - O 15 '96 - p1529+ [51-250]
y PW - v243 - Jl 22 '96 - p242+ [51-250]
y SLJ - v42 - S '96 - p224 [51-250]
y VOYA - v19 - D '96 - p267+ [251-500]
   Whatever Happened to Janie
y SLJ - v42 - O '96 - p45 [1-50]
Cooney, Eleanor - *Shangri-La*
   Rapport - v19 - 5 '96 - p35 [251-500]
Cooney, Helen - *Underwater Animals*
c HB Guide - v8 - Spr '97 - p117 [1-50]
Cooney, Jerry W - *El Paraguay Bajo Los Lopez*
   HAHR - v76 - N '96 - p824+ [251-500]
Cooney, Linda A - *Samantha Crane on the Run*
y Kliatt - v30 - S '96 - p6 [51-250]
Cooney, Miriam P - *Celebrating Women in Mathematics and Science*
yr JAAL - v40 - D '96 - p327 [51-250]
y LATBR - O 27 '96 - p11 [51-250]
y Learning - v25 - Ja '97 - p57 [1-50]
y SciTech - v20 - D '96 - p6 [51-250]
y SLJ - v42 - O '96 - p154 [51-250]
Coons, Dorothy H - *Quality of Life in Long-Term Care*
   SciTech - v20 - N '96 - p38 [51-250]
Coonts, Stephen - *The Intruders*
   Books - v9 - S '95 - p24 [1-50]
   War in the Air
   KR - v64 - O 15 '96 - p1504+ [251-500]
   PW - v243 - N 11 '96 - p67+ [51-250]
Coontz, Stephanie - *The Way We Really Are*
   KR - v65 - Mr 1 '97 - p345+ [51-250]
   LJ - v122 - Ap 1 '97 - p112 [51-250]
   PW - v244 - F 17 '97 - p200+ [51-250]
Coop, Richard H - *Mind over Golf*
   LJ - v121 - O 1 '96 - p53 [1-50]
Coope, Jessica A - *The Martyrs of Cordoba*
   AHR - v101 - D '96 - p1531+ [251-500]
   Specu - v72 - Ja '97 - p134+ [251-500]

Cooper, Alan - *Philip Roth and the Jews*
Choice - v34 - S '96 - p124 [51-250]
Rel St Rev - v23 - Ja '97 - p90 [51-250]
Cooper, Alan K - *Geology and Seismic Stratigraphy of the Antarctic Margin*
SciTech - v20 - N '96 - p24 [51-250]
Cooper, Andre R - *Cooper's Comprehensive Environmental Desk Reference*
r ARBA - v28 - '97 - p650 [51-250]
r Choice - v34 - O '96 - p249 [51-250]
Cooper, Ann - *Above the Treeline (Illus. by Dorothy Emerling)*
c SB - v33 - Ja '97 - p18 [251-500]
c SLJ - v42 - Ag '96 - p134 [51-250]
Bats: Swift Shadows in the Twilight (Illus. by Gail Kohler Opsahl)
c Inst - v105 - My '96 - p18 [1-50]
In the Forest (Illus. by Dorothy Emerling)
c KR - v64 - My 1 '96 - p686 [51-250]
c SB - v33 - Ja '97 - p18 [51-250]
c SLJ - v42 - Ag '96 - p134 [51-250]
Cooper, B Lee - *Rock Music in American Popular Culture*
r J Am Cult - v19 - Spr '96 - p114+ [501+]
Cooper, Barry - *The Beethoven Compendium*
r CR - v269 - D '96 - p333+ [251-250]
M Ed J - v83 - N '96 - p54 [51-250]
Cooper, Bernard - *Truth Serum*
HG&LRev - v3 - Fall '96 - p50 [51-250]
PW - v244 - My 5 '97 - p206 [1-50]
SFR - v21 - Jl '96 - p6 [501+]
Cooper, Brian - *The Internet*
y Kliatt - v31 - Mr '97 - p34+ [51-250]
Cooper, Carolyn - *Noises in the Blood*
HAHR - v77 - My '97 - p338+ [251-500]
Cooper, Claire - *Marya's Emmets*
c JB - v60 - D '96 - p265 [51-250]
c Sch Lib - v45 - F '97 - p23 [51-250]
Cooper, Clarence, Jr. - *Black!*
PW - v243 - D 16 '96 - p43 [51-250]
Cooper, Cynthia L - *Mockery of Justice*
PW - v244 - Ap 21 '97 - p69 [1-50]
Cooper, D Jason - *Mithras*
BWatch - v17 - S '96 - p11 [1-50]
Cooper, David - *Bartok: Concerto for Orchestra*
TLS - Ap 11 '97 - p19 [501+]
Cooper, David Edward - *Heidegger*
Choice - v34 - D '96 - p625+ [51-250]
World Philosophies
IPQ - v37 - Mr '97 - p124 [51-250]
Cooper, Davina - *Power in Struggle*
APSR - v90 - S '96 - p622+ [501+]
Cooper, Dennis - *Guide*
KR - v65 - Ap 1 '97 - p481+ [251-500]
LJ - v122 - My 1 '97 - p138 [51-250]
PW - v244 - My 5 '97 - p196 [51-250]
Horror Hospital Unplugged
LJ - v122 - Ap 1 '97 - p88 [51-250]
PW - v243 - S 23 '96 - p71+ [51-250]
PW - v243 - N 4 '96 - p37 [1-50]
Cooper, Elisha - *Off the Road*
Ent W - Ja 24 '97 - p52 [51-250]
Cooper, Emmanuel - *The Sexual Perspective. New Ed.*
Art J - v55 - Win '96 - p88+ [501+]
Cooper, Floyd - *Mandela: From the Life of the South African Statesman (Illus. by Floyd Cooper)*
c BL - v93 - S 15 '96 - p243 [51-250]
c CBRS - v25 - S '96 - p7 [51-250]
c HB Guide - v8 - Spr '97 - p156 [51-250]
c NYTBR - v101 - D 8 '96 - p78 [501+]
c SLJ - v42 - N '96 - p96+ [51-250]
Cooper, Frederick - *Decolonization and African Society*
Choice - v34 - Ap '97 - p1393+ [51-250]
Cooper, Gail - *Gopher It!*
Emerg Lib - v24 - Mr '97 - p40+ [501+]
Cooper, Geoffrey - *The Cancer Book*
LJ - v122 - Ja '97 - p56 [1-50]
Cooper, Guy - *Paradise Transformed*
Econ - v341 - D 7 '96 - p15* [51-250]
NYTBR - v101 - D 8 '96 - p41 [51-250]
Cooper, Harlan - *Fade Away*
LATBR - N 10 '96 - p6 [51-250]
Cooper, Helen - *The Baby Who Wouldn't Go to Bed (Illus. by Helen Cooper)*
c Bks Keeps - v100 - S '96 - p32 [51-250]
c JB - v60 - D '96 - p228 [1-50]
c Sch Lib - v44 - N '96 - p145 [51-250]
c TES - Ja 31 '97 - pR7 [51-250]
The Bear under the Stairs (Illus. by Helen Cooper)
c RT - v50 - F '97 - p421 [51-250]

The Boy Who Wouldn't Go to Bed (Illus. by Helen Cooper)
c PW - v244 - My 12 '97 - p75+ [51-250]
Little Monster Did It!
c CBRS - v24 - Ag '96 - p158 [51-250]
c HB Guide - v7 - Fall '96 - p252 [51-250]
Cooper, Helen A - *Thomas Eakins: The Rowing Pictures*
Choice - v34 - N '96 - p443 [51-250]
NYRB - v43 - Ag 8 '96 - p9+ [501+]
Obs - S 1 '96 - p16* [51-250]
Cooper, Ilay - *Arts and Crafts of India*
Am Craft - v56 - Ag '96 - p26 [1-50]
Choice - v34 - S '96 - p111 [51-250]
Cooper, Ilene - *Buddy Love*
c RT - v50 - D '96 - p346 [51-250]
The Dead Sea Scrolls (Illus. by John Thompson)
c BL - v93 - Mr 1 '97 - p1157 [51-250]
c CCB-B - v50 - My '97 - p317 [51-250]
c KR - v65 - Ap 1 '97 - p552 [51-250]
c Trib Bks - My 4 '97 - p7 [51-250]
No-Thanks Thanksgiving
c BL - v93 - S 1 '96 - p134 [1-50]
c HB Guide - v8 - Spr '97 - p63 [51-250]
Star-Spangled Summer
c HB Guide - v7 - Fall '96 - p290 [51-250]
Cooper, J C - *Dictionary of Christianity*
r ARBA - v28 - '97 - p549+ [51-250]
Cooper, J California - *Some Love, Some Pain, Sometime*
BW - v26 - O 13 '96 - p12 [51-250]
NYTBR - v101 - O 20 '96 - p36 [1-50]
PW - v243 - S 2 '96 - p122 [1-50]
Cooper, James W - *Antivirals in the Elderly*
SciTech - v20 - S '96 - p42 [51-250]
Cooper, Jilly - *Appassionata*
TLS - Jl 7 '96 - p25 [251-500]
Cooper, John - *Artists in Crime*
Arm Det - v29 - Sum '96 - p372 [251-500]
Cooper, John Xiros - *T.S. Eliot and the Ideology of Four Quartets*
Choice - v34 - Ja '97 - p792 [51-250]
Cooper, Kate - *The Virgin and the Bride*
Choice - v34 - Ap '97 - p1332 [51-250]
TLS - Ja 10 '97 - p25 [501+]
Cooper, Kathy - *The Complete Book of Floorcloths*
TCI - v30 - O '96 - p55 [1-50]
Cooper, Louise - *Blood Dance*
c Bks Keeps - v100 - S '96 - p16 [51-250]
Daughter of Storms
c Bks Keeps - Jl '96 - p13 [51-250]
y JB - v60 - Ag '96 - p164 [251-500]
y Sch Lib - v44 - Ag '96 - p117 [51-250]
Cooper, Martha - *Anthony Reynoso: Born to Rope*
c CLW - v67 - Mr '97 - p57 [51-250]
c HB Guide - v7 - Fall '96 - p360 [51-250]
Cooper, Melrose - *Life Magic*
c HB Guide - v8 - Spr '97 - p63 [51-250]
c KR - v64 - Ag 15 '96 - p1233+ [51-250]
c SLJ - v43 - F '97 - p100 [51-250]
Cooper, Michael L - *Hell Fighters*
c BL - v93 - F 15 '97 - p1012 [51-250]
c BW - v27 - Ap 6 '97 - p8 [251-500]
c CCB-B - v50 - F '97 - p201 [51-250]
c KR - v64 - N 1 '96 - p1599 [51-250]
y SLJ - v43 - F '97 - p111+ [51-250]
Cooper, Morton - *Stop Committing Voice Suicide*
Adoles - v31 - Fall '96 - p752 [51-250]
Cooper, Natasha - *The Drowning Pool*
BL - v93 - Mr 1 '97 - p1113 [51-250]
KR - v65 - Ja 15 '97 - p102 [51-250]
LJ - v122 - F 1 '97 - p111 [1-50]
PW - v244 - F 24 '97 - p67 [51-250]
Cooper, Paul - *Attention Deficit/Hyperactivity Disorder*
TES - N 1 '96 - pR10 [251-250]
Cooper, Paulette - *277 Secrets Your Dog Wants You to Know*
Dog Fan - v28 - Ja '97 - p36 [51-250]
Cooper, Phillip J - *Battles on the Bench*
AAPSS-A - v547 - S '96 - p183 [251-250]
APSR - v90 - D '96 - p905+ [501+]
HRNB - v25 - Win '97 - p55 [251-250]
Cooper, Rand Richards - *Big as Life*
Obs - O 27 '96 - p18* [51-250]
Cooper, Richard N - *Environment and Resource Policies for the World Economy*
JEL - v34 - S '96 - p1358+ [501+]
Cooper, Robin - *When Lean Enterprises Collide*
AR - v71 - O '96 - p592 [251-500]
Cooper, Susan - *The Boggart*
c Quill & Q - v62 - My '96 - p13 [501+]

The Boggart and the Monster
c BL - v93 - Mr 1 '97 - p1162 [51-250]
c CCB-B - v50 - My '97 - p317 [51-250]
c HB - v73 - My '97 - p315+ [251-500]
c PW - v244 - F 17 '97 - p219+ [51-250]
The Dark Is Rising
y Kliatt - v30 - S '96 - p4 [1-50]
Dreams and Wishes
BW - v26 - Jl 7 '96 - p15 [251-500]
HB - v73 - Ja '97 - p83 [51-250]
SLJ - v42 - S '96 - p136 [51-250]
Cooper, Thomas W - *A Time before Deception*
BL - v93 - D 1 '96 - p623 [51-250]
PW - v243 - O 21 '96 - p61+ [51-250]
Cooper, Wayne F - *Claude McKay: Rebel Sojourner in the Harlem Renaissance*
AL - v68 - D '96 - p886 [1-50]
Cooperstein, Claire - *Johanna*
y SLJ - v42 - D '96 - p33 [1-50]
Cooper-White, Pamela - *The Cry of Tamar*
CC - v113 - Ag 14 '96 - p791+ [251-500]
Coopey, R - *31: Fifty Years Investing in Industry*
Econ J - v106 - N '96 - p1783+ [501+]
Britain in the 1970s
JEL - v34 - D '96 - p2036+ [51-250]
Coote, Belinda - *NAFTA: Poverty and Free Trade in Mexico*
WorldV - v12 - Jl '96 - p18 [51-250]
Coote, Jack H - *Ilford Monochrome Darkroom Practice. 3rd Ed.*
R&R Bk N - v11 - D '96 - p71 [51-250]
Coover, Robert - *Briar Rose*
KR - v64 - D 15 '96 - p1751 [251-500]
LATBR - Ap 13 '97 - pF [51-250]
LJ - v122 - Ja '97 - p144 [51-250]
Nat - v264 - F 10 '97 - p35 [251-500]
NYTBR - v102 - F 16 '97 - p10+ [501+]
PW - v243 - N 25 '96 - p58 [51-250]
Trib Bks - F 9 '97 - p5 [501+]
John's Wife
ABR - v18 - D '96 - p19 [501+]
Ant R - v54 - Sum '96 - p364+ [251-500]
NYRB - v43 - O 17 '96 - p48+ [501+]
NYTBR - v101 - Ap 7 '96 - p7 [501+]
NYTBR - v101 - D 8 '96 - p80 [1-50]
NYTBR - v102 - Ap 13 '97 - p32 [51-250]
PW - v244 - Mr 3 '97 - p72 [1-50]
RCF - v16 - Fall '96 - p183+ [501+]
Pinocchio in Venice
NYTBR - v102 - Ap 13 '97 - p32 [1-50]
Trib Bks - F 16 '97 - p8 [1-50]
Cope, Carol Soret - *Stranger Danger*
PW - v244 - Mr 3 '97 - p70 [51-250]
Cope, David - *Experiments in Musical Intelligence*
R&R Bk N - v11 - N '96 - p59 [51-250]
Cope, Kevin L - *1650-1850: Ideas, Aesthetics, and Inquiries in the Early Modern Era. Vol. 2*
R&R Bk N - v11 - D '96 - p60 [51-250]
Cope, R Douglas - *The Limits of Racial Domination*
JIH - v27 - Aut '96 - p360+ [501+]
Cope, Wendy - *Making Cocoa for Kingsley Amis (Cope). Audio Version*
Obs - F 16 '97 - p18* [51-250]
The Orchard Book of Funny Poems (Illus. by Amanda Vesey)
c Bks Keeps - Ja '97 - p20 [51-250]
Copel, Linda Carman - *Nurse's Clinical Guide to Psychiatric and Mental Health Care*
r ARBA - v28 - '97 - p616 [51-250]
Copeland, Ann - *Season of Apples*
Quill & Q - v62 - O '96 - p40 [251-500]
Copeland, David A - *Colonial American Newspapers*
Choice - v34 - My '97 - p1488 [51-250]
Copeland, Kathy - *Don't Waste Your Time in the North Cascades*
r Bloom Rev - v17 - Ja '97 - p21 [51-250]
Copeland, Lori - *Angelface and Amazing Grace*
PW - v243 - N 18 '96 - p70 [51-250]
Copeland, Warren R - *And the Poor Get Welfare*
Rel St Rev - v22 - O '96 - p341 [51-250]
Copelman, Dina Mira - *London's Women Teachers*
R&R Bk N - v12 - F '97 - p68 [51-250]
Copernicus, Nicolaus - *Documenta Copernicana*
Isis - v87 - D '96 - p723+ [501+]
Copestake, Stephen - *Word of Windows Project Book*
CBR - v14 - Jl '96 - p26 [1-50]
Coping: Living with Cancer
p LJ - v122 - Ja '97 - p58 [1-50]
Copioli, Rosita - *The Blazing Lights of the Sun*
Choice - v34 - D '96 - p619 [51-250]
TranslRevS - v2 - D '96 - p28 [51-250]

Coplan, David B - *In the Time of Cannibals*
Am Ethnol - v23 - Ag '96 - p648 [501+]
Coplans, Peta - *Cat and Dog*
c HB Guide - v7 - Fall '96 - p252 [1-50]
c New Ad - v9 - Fall '96 - p327+ [501+]
Coplien, James O - *Software Patterns*
SciTech - v20 - N '96 - p8 [1-50]
Copp, David - *Morality, Normativity, and Society*
J Ch St - v38 - Sum '96 - p646+ [251-500]
Copp, Terry - *No Price Too High*
Beav - v77 - F '97 - p43+ [501+]
Coppard, Yvonne - *Don't Let It Rain (Illus. by Jim Kavanagh)*
c Sch Lib - v44 - N '96 - p151 [251-500]
Coppedge, Michael - *Strong Parties and Lame Ducks*
HAHR - v77 - F '97 - p146+ [501+]
Coppel, Alfred - *Glory's People*
y VOYA - v19 - D '96 - p278 [251-500]
Coppel, Stephen - *Linocuts of the Machine Age*
Aust Bk R - v - Ag '96 - p29+ [501+]
Coppell, Bill - *Sportspeak: An Encyclopedia of Sport*
r ARBA - v28 - '97 - p293+ [251-500]
Copper, John F - *Taiwan: Nation-State or Province. 2nd Ed.*
Cu H - v95 - S '96 - p291 [51-250]
Words across the Taiwan Strait
Ch Rev Int - v4 - Spr '97 - p111+ [501+]
Copperfield, David - *David Copperfield's Beyond Imagination*
y BL - v93 - Ja '97 - p826 [51-250]
KR - v64 - O 15 '96 - p1483 [251-500]
LJ - v121 - N 1 '96 - p109 [51-250]
PW - v243 - N 18 '96 - p66 [51-250]
David Copperfield's Tales of the Impossible
SF Chr - v18 - O '96 - p80 [1-50]
Coppieters, Bruno - *Contested Borders in the Caucasus*
MEJ - v50 - Sum '96 - p451 [51-250]
Coppola, Vincent - *Dragons of God*
PW - v243 - O 21 '96 - p67 [51-250]
Copus, Julia - *The Shuttered Eye*
Choice - v34 - N '96 - p454 [51-250]
Copy Editor
p Utne R - Ja '97 - p100 [251-500]
Corbalis, Judy - *Tapu: A Novel*
TLS - Jl 19 '96 - p22 [501+]
Corbeil, Jean-Claude - *Visual Dictionary: English-French-German-Spanish*
r LAR - v98 - Ag '96 - p427 [1-50]
Corbeill, Anthony - *Controlling Laughter*
Choice - v34 - Mr '97 - p1215 [51-250]
Econ - v341 - O 5 '96 - p82 [51-250]
Corbett, Elizabeth Burgoyne - *New Amazonia*
ELT - v40 - 1 '97 - p6+ [501+]
Corbett, James - *Through French Windows*
FR - v70 - F '97 - p505+ [501+]
FR - v70 - F '97 - p506+ [501+]
Corbett, Julian S - *Drake and the Tudor Navy*
Sea H - Win '96 - p42 [51-250]
Corbett, Pie - *Custard Pie (Illus. by Jane Eccles)*
c JB - v60 - Ag '96 - p146 [51-250]
It's Raining Cats and Dogs (Illus. by Bee Willey)
c Bks Keeps - v100 - S '96 - p10 [51-250]
Corbett, Sara - *Hold Everything!*
c HB Guide - v8 - Spr '97 - p98 [1-50]
Venus to the Hoop
KR - v65 - My 1 '97 - p688+ [251-500]
What a Doll!
c HB Guide - v7 - Fall '96 - p318 [1-50]
c SLJ - v42 - N '96 - p112 [51-250]
Corbett, Val - *Best of Enemies*
Woman's J - N '96 - p12 [1-50]
Corbett, W J - *The Dragon's Egg and Other Stories (Illus. by Wayne Anderson)*
c JB - v60 - D '96 - p249 [51-250]
Corbett, William - *Furthering My Education*
KR - v65 - F 15 '97 - p266+ [251-500]
LJ - v122 - Ap 15 '97 - p88 [51-250]
PW - v244 - F 10 '97 - p72+ [51-250]
Corbijn, Anton - *Star Trak*
LJ - v122 - Mr 15 '97 - p59 [51-250]
PW - v243 - S 16 '96 - p60 [51-250]
Corbin, Alain - *The Foul and the Fragrant*
Obs - O 6 '96 - p18* [51-250]
Time, Desire and Horror
Choice - v34 - N '96 - p516 [51-250]
The Village of Cannibals
TranslRevS - v1 - My '95 - p18 [51-250]
Women for Hire
J Urban H - v23 - Ja '97 - p231+ [501+]
Corbishley, Mike - *Superstructures*
c Bks Keeps - Mr '97 - p25 [51-250]

What Do We Know about Prehistoric People?
c Bks Keeps - Mr '97 - p24 [51-250]
c HB Guide - v7 - Fall '96 - p378 [51-250]
The Young Oxford History of Britain and Ireland
c Bks Keeps - Ja '97 - p26 [251-500]
c BL - v93 - My 15 '97 - p1569 [51-250]
c JB - v60 - D '96 - p265+ [51-250]
y Sch Lib - v45 - F '97 - p50 [51-250]
c Spec - v277 - D 14 '96 - p77 [1-50]
Corbridge, Stuart - *Development Studies*
GJ - v163 - Mr '97 - p105 [51-250]
Money, Power and Space
GJ - v162 - Jl '96 - p230+ [51-250]
Corby, Paul - *The Invisible God*
CHR - v82 - O '96 - p674+ [501+]
Corby, William - *William Corby, C.S.C.: Memoirs of Chaplain Life*
CH - v65 - S '96 - p521+ [501+]
Corcoran, Lorelei Hilda - *Portrait Mummies from Roman Egypt (I-IV Centuries A.D.)*
AJA - v101 - Ja '97 - p187+ [501+]
Corcoran, Mary P - *Irish Illegals*
SF - v75 - S '96 - p391+ [251-500]
Corcoran, Simon - *The Empire of the Tetrarchs*
Choice - v34 - Ap '97 - p1394 [51-250]
Cordell, Dennis D - *Hoe and Wage*
Choice - v34 - Ja '97 - p852 [51-250]
Cordellier, Dominique - *Pisanello: Le Peintre Aux Sept Vertus*
NYRB - v43 - Ag 8 '96 - p21+ [501+]
Cordes, H O - *The Technique of Pseudodifferential Operators*
SIAM Rev - v38 - S '96 - p540+ [501+]
Cordesman, Anthony H - *The Gulf War*
MEQ - v4 - Mr '97 - p87+ [251-500]
The Lessons of Modern War. Vol. 4
Choice - v34 - O '96 - p346 [51-250]
r MEJ - v51 - Win '97 - p143+ [501+]
Perilous Prospects
Choice - v34 - D '96 - p685 [51-250]
For Aff - v75 - N '96 - p164 [51-250]
MEJ - v51 - Spr '97 - p283+ [501+]
R&R Bk N - v11 - N '96 - p79 [51-250]
Cordingly, David - *Under the Black Flag*
BL - v93 - S 1 '96 - p58 [51-250]
BW - v26 - S 15 '96 - p3 [501+]
CSM - v89 - D 18 '96 - p13 [251-500]
Esq - v126 - D '96 - p40 [1-50]
NY - v72 - O 14 '96 - p100 [51-250]
NYRB - v44 - Mr 6 '97 - p34+ [501+]
NYTBR - v101 - S 15 '96 - p31 [251-500]
y SLJ - v43 - F '97 - p136 [51-250]
Cordner, Michael - *English Comedy*
MLR - v92 - Ap '97 - p453+ [501+]
Four Restoration Marriage Plays
Sev Cent N - v54 - Spr '96 - p18+ [501+]
Cordoba, Carol - *Stowaway*
BW - v26 - D 15 '96 - p1+ [501+]
Cordovez, Diego - *Out of Afghanistan*
JPR - v34 - F '97 - p109+ [251-500]
Mar Crp G - v80 - D '96 - p75 [501+]
Russ Rev - v55 - O '96 - p722+ [251-500]
Cordry, Harold V - *The Multicultural Dictionary of Proverbs*
r BL - v93 - My 15 '97 - p1614 [501+]
Corduneanu, C - *Qualitative Problems for Differential Equations and Control Theory*
SIAM Rev - v38 - D '96 - p714 [1-50]
Corelli, Marie - *The Sorrows of Satan*
ELT - v40 - 1 '97 - p126+ [51-250]
Coren, Michael - *The Man Who Created Narnia*
y BL - v93 - O 1 '96 - p333 [51-250]
c Bloom Rev - v17 - Ja '97 - p12 [51-250]
c CCB-B - v50 - Mr '97 - p243 [51-250]
c Ch Today - v41 - F 3 '97 - p66+ [501+]
Coren, Stanley - *Sleep Thieves*
Choice - v34 - S '96 - p152 [51-250]
Quill & Q - v63 - F '97 - p50 [51-250]
SLJ - v42 - D '96 - p42 [51-250]
Corey, Marianne Schneider - *Groups: Process and Practice. 5th Ed.*
R&R Bk N - v11 - D '96 - p70 [51-250]
Corey, Melinda - *The Encyclopedia of the Victorian World*
r BL - v93 - S 15 '96 - p282+ [51-250]
r BWatch - v17 - D '96 - p8 [51-250]
r RQ - v36 - Win '96 - p293 [251-500]
yr SLJ - v42 - Ag '96 - p180 [51-250]
Corfield, Penelope J - *Power and the Professions in Britain 1700-1850*
JEH - v57 - Mr '97 - p221+ [501+]
J Soc H - v30 - Spr '97 - p779+ [501+]

Work in Towns 850-1850
J Urban H - v22 - S '96 - p720+ [501+]
Cork, David - *The Pig and the Python*
Quill & Q - v63 - Ja '97 - p29 [51-250]
Cork, Richard - *A Bitter Truth*
JMH - v69 - Mr '97 - p127+ [501+]
J Mil H - v61 - Ja '97 - p173+ [501+]
Corkin, Stanley - *Realism and the Birth of the Modern United States*
Choice - v34 - S '96 - p109 [51-250]
Corkran, Charlotte C - *Amphibians of Oregon, Washington, and British Columbia*
r SciTech - v21 - Mr '97 - p38 [1-50]
Corlett, William - *Now and Then*
Books - v9 - S '95 - p8 [251-500]
Books - v9 - S '95 - p24 [1-50]
Corliss, William R - *Science Frontiers and Biological Anomalies*
r Skeptic - v4 - '96 - p1061 [51-250]
Cormack, Margaret - *The Saints in Iceland*
EHR - v112 - Ap '97 - p439+ [251-500]
Specu - v71 - Jl '96 - p708+ [501+]
Corman, Cid - *No Shit*
Sm Pr R - v28 - Jl '96 - p9 [501+]
Cormier, Robert - *In the Middle of the Night*
y Bks Keeps - Ja '97 - p27 [51-250]
y Emerg Lib - v24 - S '96 - p24 [1-50]
y Emerg Lib - v24 - S '96 - p26 [1-50]
y Magpies - v11 - S '96 - p45 [1-50]
y TES - Ap 4 '97 - p8* [51-250]
Tenderness
y BL - v93 - F 1 '97 - p935 [501+]
y CCB-B - v50 - Ap '97 - p278+ [251-500]
y HB - v73 - Mr '97 - p197 [251-500]
y KR - v65 - Ja 1 '97 - p57 [51-250]
y PW - v244 - Ap 13 '97 - p77 [51-250]
y SLJ - v43 - Mr '97 - p184 [51-250]
Corn, A L - *Foundations of Low Vision*
J Rehab RD - v34 - Ap '97 - p241+ [251-500]
Corn, Alfred - *Part of His Story*
Advocate - Mr 18 '97 - p77 [51-250]
KR - v65 - F 1 '97 - p157 [251-500]
LJ - v122 - Mr 15 '97 - p88 [51-250]
PW - v244 - F 10 '97 - p69 [51-250]
The Poem's Heartbeat
LJ - v122 - Ap 1 '97 - p91 [51-250]
PW - v244 - F 24 '97 - p86+ [51-250]
Present
LJ - v122 - Ap 1 '97 - p97 [51-250]
Nat - v264 - Ap 28 '97 - p27+ [501+]
PW - v244 - Mr 31 '97 - p69 [51-250]
Corn, Elaine - *Now You're Cooking for Company*
LJ - v121 - S 15 '96 - p88+ [51-250]
PW - v243 - S 2 '96 - p124 [51-250]
Corn, Joseph J - *Yesterday's Tomorrows*
Analog - v117 - F '97 - p145+ [51-250]
BW - v26 - Ag 25 '96 - p12 [51-250]
SFS - v23 - N '96 - p536 [1-50]
Cornbleth, Catherine - *The Great Speckled Bird*
SE - v61 - F '97 - p112+ [501+]
Cornblit, Oscar - *Power and Violence in the Colonial City*
HAHR - v77 - F '97 - p124+ [251-500]
JEH - v56 - D '96 - p946 [501+]
JIH - v27 - Spr '97 - p736+ [501+]
Cornelius, Randolph R - *The Science of Emotion*
Choice - v34 - O '96 - p364 [51-250]
Cornelius, Wayne A - *Controlling Immigration*
AAAGA - v86 - D '96 - p798+ [501+]
CS - v25 - S '96 - p593+ [501+]
Pol Stud J - v24 - Aut '96 - p518 [51-250]
Cornelius, William J - *Swift and Sure*
PW - v243 - D 30 '96 - p53 [51-250]
Cornell, Gary - *Core Java*
SciTech - v20 - S '96 - p5 [51-250]
Cornell, Jennifer C - *Departures*
ILS - v15 - Fall '96 - p21 [501+]
Cornell, Paul - *The New Trek Program Guide*
r SF Chr - v18 - O '96 - p82 [1-50]
Cornell, T J - *The Beginnings of Rome*
HT - v46 - D '96 - p58+ [501+]
Lon R Bks - v18 - My 23 '96 - p22+ [501+]
Cornell, Tim - *The Second Punic War*
J Mil H - v60 - O '96 - p766+ [251-500]
Corner, James - *Taking Measures across the American Landscape*
KR - v64 - O 1 '96 - p1459 [51-250]
LJ - v121 - D '96 - p87 [51-250]
NH - v105 - N '96 - p16 [1-50]
NW - v128 - N 25 '96 - p79G [251-500]
NY - v72 - Ja 20 '97 - p97 [51-250]

Cornes, Richard - *The Theory of Externalities, Public Goods, and Club Goods. 2nd Ed.*
JEL - v35 - Mr '97 - p201 [51-250]
Corney, Kate - *Vorsprung. Bk. 1*
c Sch Lib - v44 - N '96 - p174 [51-250]
Cornford, Daniel - *Working People of California*
JEH - v57 - Mr '97 - p239+ [501+]
Cornforth, John - *Queen Elizabeth the Queen Mother at Clarence House*
Woman's J - D '96 - p16 [1-50]
Cornia, Giovanni Andrea - *From Adjustment to Development in Africa*
JTWS - v13 - Fall '96 - p289+ [501+]
Cornilliat, Francois - *What Is Literature*
MLR - v92 - Ap '97 - p458+ [501+]
Cornish, Paul - *British Military Planning for the Defense of Germany*
R&R Bk N - v11 - N '96 - p79 [51-250]
Cornog, Martha - *For Sex Education, See Librarian*
r Choice - v34 - F '97 - p940+ [51-250]
r Cur R - v35 - S '96 - p3* [51-250]
r R&R Bk N - v12 - F '97 - p102 [51-250]
Corns, Thomas N - *The Cambridge Companion to English Poetry, Donne to Marvell*
Ren Q - v49 - Aut '96 - p654+ [501+]
Regaining Paradise Lost
MLR - v91 - O '96 - p973+ [501+]
Ren Q - v49 - Win '96 - p887+ [501+]
Cornwall, Marie - *Contemporary Mormonism*
Rel St Rev - v23 - Ja '97 - p94 [51-250]
Cornwall, Robert D - *Visible and Apostolic*
EHR - v111 - S '96 - p988+ [251-500]
Cornwell, Bernard - *The Bloody Ground (Morse). Audio Version*
LJ - v122 - Ap 1 '97 - p144 [51-250]
Rebel (Morse). Audio Version
LJ - v122 - My 1 '97 - p154 [51-250]
Sharpe's Regiment (Davidson). Audio Version
y Kliatt - v31 - Mr '97 - p45 [51-250]
LJ - v121 - S 15 '96 - p114 [51-250]
LJ - v121 - N 15 '96 - p106 [51-250]
Sharpe's Revenge (Davidson). Audio Version
y Kliatt - v31 - Mr '97 - p45 [51-250]
LJ - v122 - F 15 '97 - p175 [51-250]
Sharpe's Siege (Davidson). Audio Version
LJ - v121 - N 1 '96 - p122 [51-250]
Waterloo (Davidson). Audio Version
LJ - v122 - Ap 15 '97 - p139 [51-250]
The Winter King
Books - v9 - S '95 - p10 [501+]
PW - v244 - Ap 21 '97 - p69 [1-50]
Rapport - v19 - 5 '96 - p33 [251-500]
W&I - v11 - Ag '96 - p235 [251-500]
W&I - v11 - Ag '96 - p245+ [501+]
Cornwell, John - *The Power to Harm*
BL - v93 - S 15 '96 - p186 [51-250]
Comw - v124 - Mr 28 '97 - p20+ [501+]
Hast Cen R - v26 - S '96 - p40 [1-50]
LJ - v121 - O 1 '96 - p102 [51-250]
Nat - v264 - Ja 6 '97 - p27+ [501+]
Nature - v383 - O 31 '96 - p783+ [501+]
New Sci - v151 - S 21 '96 - p52+ [501+]
NS - v125 - D 13 '96 - p47 [501+]
Obs - v54 - O 13 '96 - p17* [501+]
Spec - v277 - O 5 '96 - p48 [51-250]
Cornwell, Patricia Daniels - *The Body Farm (Reading). Audio Version*
y Kliatt - v30 - N '96 - p36 [51-250]
Cause of Death
BWatch - v17 - S '96 - p1 [51-250]
CSM - v88 - S 19 '96 - p14 [51-250]
LATBR - Jl 14 '96 - p6 [251-500]
Lon R Bks - v18 - N 14 '96 - p24+ [501+]
Nat R - v48 - D 23 '96 - p56 [51-250]
Spec - v277 - D 14 '96 - p74 [51-250]
TLS - O 11 '96 - p27 [251-500]
Woman's J - O '96 - p12 [1-50]
Cause of Death (Brown). Audio Version
Arm Det - v30 - Win '97 - p80+ [51-250]
y Kliatt - v31 - Mr '97 - p40 [51-250]
LJ - v121 - S 15 '96 - p112 [51-250]
Cause of Death (Reading). Audio Version
LJ - v121 - O 15 '96 - p101 [51-250]
Cause of Death (Brown). Audio Version
Spec - v277 - N 30 '96 - p56 [51-250]
From Potter's Field
y Kliatt - v30 - S '96 - p6+ [1-50]
Lon R Bks - v18 - N 14 '96 - p24+ [501+]

Hornet's Nest
BL - v93 - D 1 '96 - p619 [51-250]
BW - v26 - D 15 '96 - p10 [51-250]
CSM - v89 - F 20 '97 - p10 [51-250]
CSM - v89 - Mr 20 '97 - p14 [51-250]
Ent W - Ja 10 '97 - p50+ [501+]
KR - v64 - D 1 '96 - p1688 [251-500]
LJ - v122 - F 1 '97 - p105 [51-250]
NYTBR - v102 - F 2 '97 - p22 [51-250]
PW - v243 - D 9 '96 - p62 [51-250]
Spec - v278 - Mr 1 '97 - p29+ [501+]
WSJ-Cent - v99 - F 5 '97 - pA16 [51-250]
Hornet's Nest (Sarandon). Audio Version
PW - v244 - Mr 3 '97 - p30 [51-250]
Unnatural Exposure
BL - v93 - My 15 '97 - p1540 [51-250]
PW - v244 - Ap 28 '97 - p53 [251-500]
Coronado, Eugenio - *Molecular Magnetism*
SciTech - v20 - D '96 - p28 [51-250]
Corporate 500. 13th Ed.
r ARBA - v28 - '97 - p310+ [251-500]
Corporate Affiliations PLUS, Spring/Summer 1995. Electronic Media Version
yr ARBA - v28 - '97 - p81 [251-500]
The Corporate Directory of U.S. Public Companies. Electronic Media Version
r ARBA - v28 - '97 - p82 [251-500]
r BL - v93 - My 15 '97 - p1602 [501+]
The Corporate Directory of U.S. Public Companies 1995
r RQ - v35 - Sum '96 - p551+ [251-500]
The Corporate Directory of U.S. Public Companies 1996
r ARBA - v28 - '97 - p82 [251-500]
Corr, Charles A - *Death and Dying, Life and Living. 2nd Ed.*
R&R Bk N - v12 - F '97 - p7 [51-250]
Corr, O Casey - *King: The Bullitts of Seattle and Their Communications Empire*
BL - v93 - N 1 '96 - p463 [51-250]
LJ - v121 - N 1 '96 - p74 [51-250]
Corrain, Lucia - *Giotto and Medieval Art (Illus. by Sergio Ricciardi)*
c CLW - v66 - Je '96 - p47 [51-250]
c RT - v50 - D '96 - p343 [51-250]
Corral, Kimberly - *My Denali (Illus. by Roy Corral)*
c HB Guide - v7 - Fall '96 - p385 [51-250]
Corral Lafuente, Jose Luis - *El Salon Dorado*
BL - v93 - Mr 15 '97 - p1232 [1-50]
Correard, Marie-Helene - *The Oxford-Hachette Concise French Dictionary*
r MLR - v92 - Ja '97 - p181+ [501+]
The Oxford-Hachette French Dictionary
r MLR - v92 - Ja '97 - p181+ [501+]
Corrick, James A - *The Battle of Gettysburg*
y HB Guide - v7 - Fall '96 - p385 [51-250]
Corrigan, Dan - *The Internet University*
r CBR - v15 - Spr '97 - p5 [1-50]
r Choice - v34 - D '96 - p588 [51-250]
Corrington, Robert S - *Ecstatic Naturalism*
Rel St Rev - v23 - Ja '97 - p45 [51-250]
Corris, Peter - *Ringside: A Knockout Collection of Fights and Fighters*
Aust Bk R - D '96 - p30+ [501+]
The Washington Club
Aust Bk R - F '97 - p55+ [501+]
Corry, Dan - *Growth with Stability*
JEL - v34 - S '96 - p1422 [51-250]
Corry, Leo - *Modern Algebra and the Rise of Mathematical Structures*
SciTech - v20 - S '96 - p9 [51-250]
Corry, Matt - *Monolith*
RCF - v16 - Fall '96 - p198 [251-500]
Corsan, W C - *Two Months in the Confederate States*
BL - v93 - S 15 '96 - p213 [51-250]
Corsini, Raymond J - *Concise Encyclopedia of Psychology. 2nd Ed.*
yr ARBA - v28 - '97 - p284+ [251-500]
r Choice - v34 - O '96 - p249 [51-250]
Cortada, James N - *Can Democracy Survive in Western Europe*
R&R Bk N - v12 - F '97 - p60 [251-500]
Cortada, James W - *A Bibliographic Guide to the History of Computer Applications 1950-1990*
r ARBA - v28 - '97 - p620 [251-500]
Information Technology as Business History
Choice - v34 - F '97 - p1007+ [51-250]
JEL - v35 - Mr '97 - p267 [51-250]
R&R Bk N - v11 - D '96 - p34 [1-50]

Second Bibliographic Guide to the History of Computing, Computers, and the Information Processing Industry
r ARBA - v28 - '97 - p619 [51-250]
r Choice - v34 - S '96 - p94 [51-250]
Cortazar, Julio - *Imagen De John Keats*
BL - v93 - Mr 15 '97 - p1232 [1-50]
Cortext
p Sm Pr R - v28 - Jl '96 - p18+ [251-500]
Corti, Eugenio - *Few Returned*
LJ - v122 - My 1 '97 - p119 [51-250]
Cortner, David - *Eight Easy Observing Projects for Amateur Astronomers*
Astron - v25 - Ja '97 - p103 [51-250]
Cortopassi, Joan - *Fat Chance*
BL - v93 - N 15 '96 - p558 [51-250]
Corvi, Roberta - *An Introduction to the Thought of Karl Popper*
New Sci - v152 - N 30 '96 - p46 [51-250]
Corvisier, Andre - *A Dictionary of Military History*
r HT - v46 - S '96 - p54+ [501+]
Corwin, Donna G - *The Time-Out Prescription*
LJ - v121 - N 1 '96 - p102 [51-250]
Corwin, Judith Hoffman - *Christmas Crafts*
c HB Guide - v7 - Fall '96 - p354 [1-50]
c SLJ - v42 - O '96 - p34 [51-250]
Hanukkah Crafts
c HB Guide - v7 - Fall '96 - p354 [1-50]
c SLJ - v42 - O '96 - p34 [51-250]
Corwin, Miles - *The Killing Season*
y BL - v93 - My 1 '97 - p1463 [51-250]
KR - v65 - Mr 1 '97 - p346 [51-250]
LJ - v122 - Ap 15 '97 - p98 [51-250]
PW - v244 - Mr 3 '97 - p54 [51-250]
Corwin, Rebecca B - *Talking Mathematics*
Cur R - v36 - D '96 - p3* [51-250]
Learning - v25 - Ja '97 - p57 [1-50]
Cory, Charlotte - *The Guest*
Spec - v277 - S 21 '96 - p47+ [501+]
TLS - S 6 '96 - p21 [501+]
Cory, Steven - *Pueblo Indian (Illus. by Richard Erickson)*
c HB Guide - v7 - Fall '96 - p390 [51-250]
Corzine, Phyllis - *The Black Death*
y HB Guide - v8 - Spr '97 - p165 [51-250]
c SLJ - v43 - F '97 - p112 [51-250]
Cosculluela, Victor - *The Ethics of Suicide*
Ethics - v107 - O '96 - p175+ [51-250]
Cose, Ellis - *Color-Blind: Seeing beyond Race in a Race-Obsessed World*
y BL - v93 - Ja '97 - p790 [51-250]
KR - v64 - N 1 '96 - p1577 [251-500]
LATBR - Ja 26 '97 - p7 [501+]
LJ - v121 - D '96 - p127 [51-250]
NL - v79 - D 16 '96 - p11+ [501+]
NYTBR - v102 - F 9 '97 - p11+ [501+]
PW - v243 - N 18 '96 - p54 [51-250]
Time - v149 - F 17 '97 - p84+ [501+]
Utne R - Mr '97 - p85 [1-50]
The Darden Dilemma
y BL - v93 - F 15 '97 - p970 [51-250]
KR - v65 - Ja 15 '97 - p111 [251-500]
LJ - v122 - Ap 15 '97 - p102 [51-250]
PW - v244 - Ja 27 '97 - p91 [51-250]
A Man's World
CS - v26 - Mr '97 - p156+ [501+]
Cosey, R Cosey - *Lost in the Alps*
BL - v93 - Mr 15 '97 - p1217+ [51-250]
PW - v244 - F 3 '97 - p97 [51-250]
Cosgrove, Benedict - *Covering the Bases*
BL - v93 - Mr 15 '97 - p1220 [51-250]
LJ - v122 - F 1 '97 - p82 [51-250]
PW - v243 - D 30 '96 - p45+ [251-500]
Cosgrove, Michael H - *The Cost of Winning*
Choice - v34 - S '96 - p175 [51-250]
JEL - v34 - D '96 - p2121+ [51-250]
Cosman, Madeleine Pelner - *Medieval Wordbook*
r ARBA - v28 - '97 - p386 [51-250]
Cosmas, Graham A - *An Army for Empire*
Parameters - v26 - Aut '96 - p152+ [501+]
Cossentino, Francesco - *Local and Regional Response to Global Pressure*
ILR - v135 - 5 '96 - p598+ [251-500]
Cossman, Brenda - *Bad Attitude/s on Trial*
Quill & Q - v62 - D '96 - p29 [251-500]
Costa, D Margaret - *Women and Sport*
Aethlon - v13 - Fall '95 - p150+ [251-500]
Costa, Emilia Viotti Da - *Crowns of Glory, Tears of Blood*
EHR - v112 - F '97 - p228 [251-500]

Costa, Marie - *Abortion: A Reference Handbook. 2nd Ed.*
  r ARBA - v28 - '97 - p303+ [51-250]
  r R&R Bk N - v11 - N '96 - p41 [51-250]
  yr VOYA - v19 - F '97 - p364 [251-500]
Costantino, Mario - *The Italian Way*
  r BL - v93 - S 15 '96 - p212 [1-50]
Costanza, Robert - *Getting Down to Earth*
  Choice - v34 - Ap '97 - p1386+ [51-250]
Costello, Darby - *Astrology*
  yr Kliatt - v30 - N '96 - p31 [51-250]
Costello, Francis J - *Enduring the Most*
  TLS - S 27 '96 - p7 [501+]
Costin, Carolyn - *Your Dieting Daughter*
  LJ - v121 - N 15 '96 - p75 [251-500]
  SciTech - v21 - Mr '97 - p65 [1-50]
Costin, Lela B - *The Politics of Child Abuse in America*
  APSR - v91 - Mr '97 - p184+ [501+]
  Soc Ser R - v71 - Mr '97 - p135+ [501+]
Costs and Effectiveness of Prostate Cancer Screening in Elderly Men
  J Gov Info - v23 - S '96 - p554+ [51-250]
Cote, James E - *Generation on Hold*
  CS - v25 - N '96 - p792+ [501+]
  SF - v75 - S '96 - p361+ [251-500]
Cotell, Catherine M - *Thin Films and Surfaces for Bioactivity and Biomedical Applications*
  SciTech - v20 - D '96 - p38 [51-250]
Cotler, Amy - *My Little House Cookbook (Illus. by Holly Jones)*
  c HB Guide - v7 - Fall '96 - p353 [51-250]
Cotran, Eugene - *The Arab-Israeli Accords*
  R&R Bk N - v12 - F '97 - p62 [51-250]
Cotroneo, Roberto - *Presto Con Fuoco*
  WLT - v71 - Win '97 - p128 [251-500]
Cotsonis, John A - *Byzantine Figural Processional Crosses*
  Specu - v71 - O '96 - p938+ [501+]
Cott, Jonathan - *Thirteen: A Journey into the Number*
  LATBR - Ap 13 '97 - pF [51-250]
  NYTBR - v101 - D 1 '96 - p22 [51-250]
  PW - v243 - O 14 '96 - p75 [51-250]
Cott, Nancy F - *Roots of Bitterness. 2nd Ed.*
  Legacy - v14 - 1 '97 - p73 [51-250]
Cotter, Finbarr E - *Molecular Diagnosis of Cancer*
  SciTech - v20 - N '96 - p40 [51-250]
Cotter, T G - *Techniques in Apoptosis*
  SciTech - v20 - N '96 - p28 [51-250]
Cotter, Theresa - *Christ Is Risen*
  CLW - v66 - Je '96 - p29 [51-250]
Cotterell, Arthur - *The Encyclopedia of Mythology*
  r BL - v93 - S 15 '96 - p282 [51-250]
  The Penguin Encyclopedia of Classical Civilizations
  yr Kliatt - v30 - S '96 - p34 [51-250]
Cotterell, John - *Social Networks and Social Influences in Adolescence*
  Choice - v34 - D '96 - p695 [51-250]
Cotterrell, Roger - *Law's Community*
  AJS - v102 - N '96 - p930+ [501+]
Cottingham, John - *Western Philosophy*
  LJ - v121 - O 1 '96 - p81+ [51-250]
  TES - O 4 '96 - p7* [251-500]
Cottle, Charles M - *Options, Perception and Deception*
  Barron's - v76 - S 2 '96 - p43 [51-250]
  R&R Bk N - v11 - N '96 - p37 [51-250]
Cottman, Michael H - *The Family of Black America*
  y Kliatt - v31 - Ja '97 - p30 [51-250]
  y SLJ - v43 - F '97 - p137 [51-250]
Cotton, Bob - *The Cyberspace Lexicon*
  r Quill & Q - v63 - F '97 - p30 [51-250]
Cotton, C M - *Ethnobotany: Principles and Applications*
  Choice - v34 - My '97 - p1524 [51-250]
  Nature - v382 - Ag 1 '96 - p413 [1-50]
  Sci - v275 - F 28 '97 - p1276 [1-50]
Cotton, Maggie - *Agogo Bells to Xylophone*
  TES - D 6 '96 - p12* [51-250]
Cotton, Peter B - *Practical Gastrointestinal Endoscopy. 4th Ed.*
  SciTech - v20 - N '96 - p48 [51-250]
Cotton, Ralph - *The Price of a Horse*
  Roundup M - v3 - Ag '96 - p29 [51-250]
Cottonwood, Joe - *Babcock*
  c CCB-B - v50 - D '96 - p130+ [51-250]
  c HB Guide - v8 - Spr '97 - p63 [51-250]
  y KR - v64 - O 1 '96 - p1465 [51-250]
  y SLJ - v42 - N '96 - p120 [51-250]

Cottringer, Anne - *Ella and the Naughty Lion (Illus. by Russell Ayto)*
  c BL - v93 - S 1 '96 - p141 [51-250]
  c CBRS - v25 - Ja '97 - p49 [51-250]
  c CCB-B - v50 - O '96 - p52+ [51-250]
  c HB Guide - v8 - Spr '97 - p24 [51-250]
  c PW - v243 - S 2 '96 - p130 [51-250]
  c Sch Lib - v44 - N '96 - p145 [51-250]
  c SLJ - v42 - D '96 - p91 [51-250]
Couch, Carl J - *Information Technologies and Social Orders*
  Choice - v34 - Ja '97 - p882 [51-250]
Couch, Leon W - *Digital and Analog Communication Systems. 5th Ed.*
  SciTech - v21 - Mr '97 - p86 [51-250]
Couderc, Philippe - *Les Plats Qui Ont Fait La France*
  FR - v70 - F '97 - p512 [251-500]
Coudert, Jo - *Seven Cats and the Art of Living*
  KR - v64 - S 1 '96 - p1289 [251-500]
Coughlin, Jack - *The Irish Colony of Saskatchewan*
  Sm Pr R - v28 - Jl '96 - p8 [501+]
Coughlin, Patricia - *Lord Savage*
  PW - v243 - O 14 '96 - p80+ [51-250]
  PW - v243 - N 4 '96 - p40 [1-50]
Coughlin, Sean T - *Storming the Desert*
  LJ - v121 - D '96 - p114 [51-250]
Coughlin, Steven S - *Ethics and Epidemiology*
  Hast Cen R - v26 - Jl '96 - p41 [1-50]
  MHR - v10 - Fall '96 - p85+ [501+]
Cougias, Dorian J - *AppleTalk Network Services*
  SciTech - v20 - D '96 - p7 [51-250]
Coulmas, Florian - *The Blackwell Encyclopedia of Writing Systems*
  r ARBA - v28 - '97 - p374 [51-250]
  r Choice - v34 - F '97 - p942 [51-250]
Coulson, Mark - *Language Understanding. 2nd Ed.*
  MLJ - v80 - Win '96 - p534 [501+]
Coulstock, Patricia H - *The Collegiate Church of Wimborne Minster*
  CH - v66 - Mr '97 - p111+ [501+]
Coultas, Charles L - *Ecology and Management of Tidal Marshes*
  Choice - v34 - Ap '97 - p1363 [51-250]
  SciTech - v20 - N '96 - p27 [51-250]
Coultate, T P - *Food: The Chemistry of its Components. 3rd Ed.*
  SciTech - v20 - D '96 - p87 [51-250]
Coulter, Catherine - *The Aristocrat (Strassman). Audio Version*
  Quill & Q - v62 - Jl '96 - p52 [251-500]
  The Maze
  BL - v93 - My 15 '97 - p1540 [251-500]
  The Wild Baron
  PW - v244 - Mr 3 '97 - p71 [51-250]
Coulter, Lane - *New Mexican Tinwork 1840-1940*
  r CAY - v16 - Fall '95 - p11 [51-250]
Coulter, William - *Simple Gifts*
  CAY - v17 - Win '96 - p10 [51-250]
Council of the European Union - *Report of the Council on the Functioning of the Treaty on European Union*
  J Gov Info - v23 - S '96 - p669 [51-250]
Council on Library Resources - *Public Libraries, Communities, and Technology*
  IRLA - v32 - D '96 - p11+ [51-250]
Counsell, Christine - *Life in Tudor Times*
  c TES - Ap 4 '97 - p12* [501+]
Counsell, Colin - *Signs of Performance*
  Am Theat - v14 - Ja '97 - p74 [51-250]
  TCI - v30 - O '96 - p59 [51-250]
Countermeasures
  p Sm Pr R - v28 - Je '96 - p17+ [51-250]
Counterpoise
  p LJ - v122 - Mr 15 '97 - p95 [51-250]
Countries in Crisis: Hunger 1996
  Soc Ser R - v70 - S '96 - p504 [51-250]
Countries of the World and Their Leaders Yearbook 1996. Vols. 1-2
  r BL - v92 - Ag '96 - p1919 [51-250]
Country Connections: The Magazine of Alternatives
  p Sm Pr R - v28 - N '96 - p14 [501+]
  p Utne R - S '96 - p99+ [251-500]
Country Music Foundation - *Country: The Music and the Musicians from the Beginnings to the '90s. Rev. Ed.*
  r LJ - v121 - N 1 '96 - p40 [1-50]
Country Music (New York, N.Y.) - *The Comprehensive Country Music Encyclopedia*
  r JSH - v62 - N '96 - p851+ [251-500]
  r LJ - v121 - N 1 '96 - p40+ [1-50]
Country Walking
  r Books - v11 - Ap '97 - p21 [1-50]

Countryman, Edward - *Americans: A Collision of Histories*
  Choice - v34 - O '96 - p346 [51-250]
  Americans, A Collision of Histories
  RAH - v25 - Mr '97 - p13+ [501+]
  SE - v61 - Mr '97 - p173+ [501+]
Countryside Commission - *Climate Change, Acidification and Ozone*
  J Gov Info - v23 - S '96 - p644 [51-250]
Counts, Dorothy Ayers - *Over the Next Hill*
  BIC - v26 - Mr '97 - p24 [501+]
  Choice - v34 - Ap '97 - p1423 [51-250]
County and City Extra 1995
  r ARBA - v28 - '97 - p323+ [51-250]
County and City Extra 1996
  r R&R Bk N - v11 - N '96 - p24 [51-250]
Coupe, W A - *German Political Satires from the Reformation to the Second World War. Pt. 1, Vols. 1-2*
  MLR - v92 - Ap '97 - p536+ [501+]
Couper, Heather - *Black Holes (Illus. by Luciano Corbella)*
  y BL - v92 - Ag '96 - p1892 [51-250]
  c BW - v26 - Jl 7 '96 - p15 [251-500]
  c CBRS - v24 - Ag '96 - p163+ [51-250]
  c CLW - v67 - D '96 - p59 [51-250]
  y HB Guide - v7 - Fall '96 - p330 [51-250]
  c JB - v60 - Ag '96 - p154 [51-250]
  c Magpies - v11 - S '96 - p42+ [51-250]
  cr Par Ch - v21 - Mr '97 - p5 [1-50]
  y Sch Lib - v44 - Ag '96 - p123 [51-250]
  c S&T - v92 - N '96 - p57 [51-250]
  c TES - N 8 '96 - p13* [251-500]
Coupland, Douglas - *Generation X*
  Essays CW - Spr '96 - p229+ [501+]
  Polaroids from the Dead
  BW - v26 - S 1 '96 - p13 [51-250]
  NYTBR - v101 - Jl 21 '96 - p8 [501+]
  Quill & Q - v62 - My '96 - p32 [501+]
Coupland, Gary - *People Who Lived in Big Houses*
  R&R Bk N - v11 - N '96 - p17 [51-250]
Couraud, Pierre-Oliver - *Biology and Physiology of the Blood-Brain Barrier*
  SciTech - v21 - Mr '97 - p41 [51-250]
Courmel, Katie - *A Companion Volume to Dr. Jay A. Goldstein's Betrayal by the Brain*
  SB - v33 - My '97 - p103+ [51-250]
Cournos, Francine - *AIDS and People with Severe Mental Illness*
  Readings - v12 - Mr '97 - p28+ [51-250]
Coursey, Don - *Environmental Racism in the City of Chicago*
  J Gov Info - v23 - S '96 - p602 [51-250]
Courtauld, Simon - *Spanish Hours*
  TLS - S 13 '96 - p32 [251-500]
Courtenay, Bryce - *The Potato Factory*
  Books - v11 - Ap '97 - p22 [1-50]
Courtenay, William J - *Capacity and Volition*
  CH - v65 - D '96 - p685+ [501+]
Courtier, Jane - *Indoor Plants*
  PW - v244 - Mr 24 '97 - p79 [51-250]
Courtine, Jean-Francois - *Of the Sublime*
  TranslRevS - v1 - My '95 - p3 [251-500]
Courtney, Cathy - *City Lives*
  NS - v125 - D 13 '96 - p48 [251-500]
  TLS - Ja 24 '97 - p32 [251-500]
Courtney, E - *Musa Lapidaria*
  Class Out - v74 - Win '97 - p82+ [501+]
Courtney-Clarke, Margaret - *Imazighen: The Vanishing Traditions of Berber Women*
  CSM - v89 - D 5 '96 - pB2+ [51-250]
  KR - v64 - Ag 15 '96 - p1228 [51-250]
  LATBR - D 8 '96 - p11 [51-250]
Courtwright, David T - *Violent Land*
  BL - v93 - N 15 '96 - p553 [51-250]
  CSM - v89 - D 16 '96 - p13 [501+]
  CSM - v89 - Ja 9 '97 - p14 [51-250]
  KR - v64 - O 1 '96 - p1438 [251-500]
  LJ - v121 - N 1 '96 - p96 [51-250]
  Nature - v384 - N 7 '96 - p36 [1-50]
  Pub Int - Spr '97 - p108+ [501+]
  SFR - v21 - N '96 - p28+ [501+]
  TLS - F 28 '97 - p9 [501+]
  VV - v41 - D 24 '96 - p59+ [501+]
  WSJ-MW - v78 - D 11 '96 - pA20 [501+]
Cousens, Roger - *Dynamics of Weed Populations*
  Am Sci - v85 - Mr '97 - p186+ [251-500]
  Choice - v34 - O '96 - p306 [51-250]
Cousin, Geraldine - *Shakespeare in Performance*
  Shakes Q - v47 - Sum '96 - p226+ [501+]

Cousins, A D - *More's Utopia and the Utopian Inheritance*
   Six Ct J - v27 - Fall '96 - p947+ [501+]
Cousins, Emily - *Fieldwork: An Expeditionary Learning Outward Bound Reader. Vol. 1*
   HER - v66 - Fall '96 - p696+ [251-500]
Cousins, Julia - *The Pitt Rivers Museum*
   Folkl - v107 - '96 - p115 [51-250]
Cousins, Lucy - *Count with Maisy (Illus. by Lucy Cousins)*
  c PW - v244 - Ap 14 '97 - p74 [51-250]
Humpty Dumpty and Other Nursery Rhymes (Illus. by Lucy Cousins)
  c BL - v93 - S 15 '96 - p246 [51-250]
  c CCB-B - v50 - O '96 - p70 [51-250]
  c HB Guide - v8 - Spr '97 - p106 [51-250]
  c SLJ - v43 - Ja '97 - p83+ [51-250]
Jack and Jill and Other Nursery Rhymes (Illus. by Lucy Cousins)
  c BL - v93 - S 15 '96 - p246 [51-250]
  c CCB-B - v50 - O '96 - p70 [51-250]
  c HB Guide - v8 - Spr '97 - p106 [51-250]
  c SLJ - v43 - Ja '97 - p83+ [51-250]
Katy Cat and Beaky Boo (Illus. by Lucy Cousins)
  c HB Guide - v8 - Spr '97 - p11 [51-250]
  c KR - v64 - S 1 '96 - p1331 [51-250]
  c PW - v243 - O 7 '96 - p77 [51-250]
  c SLJ - v43 - Ja '97 - p76 [51-250]
Maisy's Colors (Illus. by Lucy Cousins)
  c PW - v244 - Ap 14 '97 - p74 [51-250]
Noah's Ark (Illus. by Lucy Cousins)
  c PW - v244 - Ja 27 '97 - p108 [1-50]
Couton, Georges - *La Chair Et L'Ame*
   Rel St Rev - v23 - Ja '97 - p85 [51-250]
Coutts, Cecil C - *Slogan Postmarks of Canada*
   Phil Lit R - v45 - '96 - p343 [251-500]
Coutts, Russell - *Course to Victory*
   Yacht - v181 - Ap '97 - p14 [1-50]
Couture, Susan Arkin - *The Biggest Horse I Ever Did See (Illus. by Claire Ewart)*
  c KR - v65 - My 1 '97 - p718 [51-250]
Melanie Jane (Illus. by Isabelle Dervaux)
  c HB Guide - v7 - Fall '96 - p252 [51-250]
  c KR - v64 - My 1 '96 - p686 [51-250]
  c NYTBR - v101 - S 22 '96 - p28 [1-50]
Couvares, Francis G - *Movie Censorship and American Culture*
   Choice - v34 - Ja '97 - p864 [51-250]
Covarrubias, Alvaro J - *Lending for Electric Power in Sub-Saharan Africa*
   JEL - v35 - Mr '97 - p276 [51-250]
Coveney, Michael - *The World according to Mike Leigh*
   Obs - Ap 13 '97 - p18* [51-250]
The World According to Mike Leigh
   PW - v243 - S 2 '96 - p104 [51-250]
   TES - Ag 2 '96 - pR6 [1-50]
Coveney, Peter - *Frontiers of Complexity*
   BW - v26 - N 24 '96 - p12 [51-250]
   NYTBR - v101 - O 13 '96 - p32 [1-50]
Covey, Stephen R - *The 7 Habits of Highly Effective People*
   Rapport - v19 - 4 '96 - p18+ [501+]
Coville, Bruce - *Aliens Stole My Dad*
  c Bks Keeps - Jl '96 - p12 [51-250]
Bruce Coville's Book of Monsters (Coville). Audio Version
  c BL - v93 - Mr 15 '97 - p1253 [51-250]
The Ghost in the Big Brass Bed (Moore). Audio Version
  c BL - v93 - My 15 '97 - p1595 [1-50]
Goblins in the Castle (Illus. by Katherine Coville)
  c JB - v60 - Ag '96 - p147 [51-250]
  c Sch Lib - v44 - Ag '96 - p105 [51-250]
Into the Land of the Unicorns
  y Emerg Lib - v24 - S '96 - p26 [1-50]
Jennifer Murdley's Toad (Coville). Audio Version
  c BL - v93 - D 15 '96 - p740 [51-250]
  c Emerg Lib - v24 - Mar '97 - p24 [51-250]
  c SLJ - v42 - O '96 - p77+ [51-250]
Jeremy Thatcher, Dragon Hatcher (Coville). Audio Version
  c Ch BWatch - v6 - N '96 - p7 [51-250]
  c HB - v72 - S '96 - p566+ [501+]
The Lapsnatcher (Illus. by Marissa Moss)
  c KR - v65 - Ja 1 '97 - p57 [51-250]
My Grandfather's House (Illus. by Henri Sorensen)
  c HB Guide - v7 - Fall '96 - p252 [51-250]
  c SLJ - v42 - Ag '96 - p121 [51-250]
Oddly Enough
  y Kliatt - v31 - Mr '97 - p16 [51-250]

William Shakespeare's A Midsummer Night's Dream (Illus. by Dennis Nolan)
  c BL - v93 - S 1 '96 - p133 [51-250]
  y BL - v93 - Ap 1 '97 - p1306 [1-50]
  c HB Guide - v8 - Spr '97 - p148 [51-250]
  c KR - v64 - Ag 15 '96 - p1246 [51-250]
  c SLJ - v42 - O '96 - p112 [51-250]
The World's Worst Fairy Godmother (Illus. by Katherine Coville)
  c BL - v93 - Ja '97 - p858 [251-500]
  c PW - v243 - D 2 '96 - p61 [51-250]
Covington, Dennis - *Lasso the Moon*
  y Kliatt - v30 - N '96 - p6 [51-250]
  y PW - v243 - S 16 '96 - p85 [51-250]
Lizard
  y Magpies - v11 - Jl '96 - p33 [51-250]
Salvation on Sand Mountain
   AJPsych - v153 - D '96 - p1647+ [501+]
   LATBR - Mr 17 '96 - p11 [51-250]
Covington, Mary Hamilton - *A Trip East in 1888*
  r EGH - v50 - N '96 - p193 [51-250]
Covington, Michael A - *Prolog Programming in Depth*
   SciTech - v20 - D '96 - p10 [51-250]
Covington, Vicki - *The Last Hotel for Women*
   NYTBR - v101 - Ap 7 '96 - p9 [501+]
   Wom R Bks - v14 - O '96 - p21+ [501+]
Cowan, Andrew - *Common Ground*
   Books - v10 - Je '96 - p23 [1-50]
   NS & S - v9 - My 17 '96 - p40+ [251-500]
Pig
  y BL - v93 - S 15 '96 - p219 [51-250]
   Books - v9 - S '95 - p27 [1-50]
   LATBR - D 22 '96 - p5 [501+]
   LJ - v122 - Mr 15 '97 - p41 [1-50]
   LJ - v122 - Mr 15 '97 - p112 [51-250]
   NY - v72 - D 23 '96 - p146 [51-250]
   NYTBR - v101 - D 15 '96 - p9 [501+]
Cowan, James - *A Mapmaker's Dream*
   Aust Bk R - F '97 - p24 [501+]
   BL - v93 - S 15 '96 - p219 [51-250]
   LATBR - O 27 '96 - p3+ [501+]
   LATBR - D 29 '96 - p8 [51-250]
   LJ - v121 - S 15 '96 - p94+ [51-250]
   NYTBR - v101 - N 24 '96 - p18 [251-500]
Cowan, Mary Morton - *Ice Country*
  c Sea H - Aut '96 - p47 [51-250]
Cowan, Robin - *Profits and Morality*
   Econ J - v107 - Ja '97 - p221+ [501+]
   Ethics - v107 - Ja '97 - p392 [51-250]
Cowan, Tom - *Pocket Guide to Shamanism*
   LJ - v122 - My 1 '97 - p109 [51-250]
Shamanism as a Spiritual Practice for Daily Life
   BL - v93 - O 1 '96 - p296 [51-250]
Coward, Barry - *The Stuart Age. 2nd Ed.*
   HT - v46 - D '96 - p56 [501+]
Coward, Harold - *Ethics and Climate Change*
   Dialogue - v35 - Fall '96 - p829+ [501+]
Cowart, David - *Literary Symbiosis*
   ASInt - v34 - O '96 - p105+ [501+]
Cowasjee, Saros - *Orphans of the Storm*
   WLT - v70 - Aut '96 - p1031+ [501+]
Cowdell, Scott - *Is Jesus Unique?*
   CLW - v67 - D '96 - p35 [51-250]
Cowden, Robert H - *Classical Singers of the Opera and Recital Stages*
  r CLW - v66 - Je '96 - p38+ [251-500]
Cowell, Frank A - *Measuring Inequality. 2nd Ed.*
   JEL - v34 - S '96 - p1412+ [51-250]
Cowell, Ian G - *cDNA Library Protocols*
   SciTech - v21 - Mr '97 - p35 [51-250]
Cowell, Noel M - *Human Resource Management*
   JEL - v34 - D '96 - p2108 [51-250]
Cowell, Stephanie - *The Physician of London*
   Sew R - v104 - Jl '96 - p456+ [501+]
The Players: A Novel of the Young Shakespeare
   KR - v65 - F 15 '97 - p240 [51-250]
   LJ - v122 - Ap 1 '97 - p124 [51-250]
   PW - v244 - F 24 '97 - p63 [51-250]
Cowen, Emory L - *School-Based Prevention for Children at Risk*
   Readings - v12 - Mr '97 - p30 [51-250]
Cowen, Lauren - *Daughters and Mothers (Illus. by Jayne Wexler)*
   PW - v244 - Ap 28 '97 - p66+ [1-50]
Cowen, M P - *Doctrines of Development*
   Choice - v34 - N '96 - p506 [51-250]
Cowen, William W - *A Central African Odyssey*
   Bl S - v26 - Sum '96 - p64 [1-50]
Cowen-Fletcher, Jane - *Baby Angels*
  c HB Guide - v7 - Fall '96 - p237 [51-250]
  c LA - v73 - D '96 - p621 [51-250]

Cowhey, Peter F - *Structure and Policy in Japan and the United States*
   Pac A - v69 - Fall '96 - p412+ [501+]
Cowie, Leonard W - *Sir Robert Peel 1788-1850*
  r ARBA - v28 - '97 - p201 [51-250]
Cowing, Cedric B - *The Saving Remnant*
   CH - v66 - Mr '97 - p129+ [501+]
   JIH - v27 - Spr '97 - p707+ [501+]
   NEQ - v69 - D '96 - p687+ [501+]
   W&M Q - v54 - Ap '97 - p420+ [501+]
Cowles, David - *Living with Miracles*
   KR - v65 - F 1 '97 - p187 [251-500]
   PW - v244 - Mr 17 '97 - p70 [51-250]
Cowles, Fleur - *The Best of Flair*
   LATBR - D 8 '96 - p28+ [51-250]
   LATBR - D 22 '96 - p3+ [501+]
She Made Friends and Kept Them
   KR - v64 - S 15 '96 - p1368 [251-500]
   LATBR - D 22 '96 - p3+ [501+]
   LJ - v121 - O 15 '96 - p65+ [51-250]
   PW - v243 - S 9 '96 - p75 [51-250]
Cowles, Jane - *Pain Relief!*
   LJ - v122 - Ja '97 - p57 [1-50]
Cowley, Abraham - *The Collected Works of Abraham Cowley. Vol. 2, Pt. 1*
   Ren Q - v49 - Win '96 - p882+ [501+]
Cowley, Fraser - *Metaphysical Delusion*
   Dialogue - v35 - Fall '96 - p852+ [501+]
Cowley, John - *Carnival, Canboulay and Calypso*
   Choice - v34 - F '97 - p974 [51-250]
The New Blackwell Guide to Recorded Blues
  r LJ - v121 - N 15 '96 - p54 [51-250]
  r Spec - v278 - Mr 22 '97 - p42+ [501+]
Cowley, Joy - *Gracias, The Thanksgiving Turkey (Illus. by Joe Cepeda)*
  c BL - v93 - S 1 '96 - p136 [51-250]
  c CBRS - v25 - O '96 - p14 [51-250]
  c CCB-B - v50 - N '96 - p89+ [501+]
Gracias: The Thanksgiving Turkey (Illus. by Joe Cepeda)
  c HB Guide - v8 - Spr '97 - p24 [51-250]
Gracias, The Thanksgiving Turkey (Illus. by Joe Cepeda)
  c PW - v243 - S 30 '96 - p86 [51-250]
  c SLJ - v42 - D '96 - p91 [51-250]
The Mouse Bride (Illus. by David Christiana)
  c RT - v50 - D '96 - p345 [51-250]
Cowley, Robert - *The Reader's Companion to Military History*
  yr BL - v93 - F 1 '97 - p966 [251-500]
  r Choice - v34 - My '97 - p1480 [51-250]
  r For Aff - v76 - My '97 - p129+ [51-250]
   LJ - v121 - O 15 '96 - p73 [51-250]
  r NYTLa - v146 - D 18 '96 - pC21 [501+]
Cowper, David S - *Northwest Passage Solo*
   Aethlon - v13 - Fall '95 - p167 [251-500]
Cowx, I G - *Stock Assessment in Inland Fisheries*
   SciTech - v20 - S '96 - p45 [51-250]
Cox, Alan - *Docklands in the Making*
   J Gov Info - v23 - S '96 - p644+ [51-250]
Cox, Andy - *Last Rites and Resurrections. Vol. 1*
   Sm Pr R - v28 - Je '96 - p7 [51-250]
Cox, Bette Yarbrough - *Central Avenue--Its Rise and Fall 1890-C. 1955*
   M Ed J - v83 - N '96 - p55 [51-250]
Cox, Beverly - *Spirit of the West*
   BL - v93 - N 15 '96 - p559 [51-250]
   LJ - v121 - D '96 - p136 [51-250]
   PW - v243 - O 21 '96 - p80 [51-250]
Cox, Brad J - *Superdistribution*
   SciTech - v20 - N '96 - p9 [1-50]
Cox, C Brian - *African Writers. Vols. 1-2*
  r LJ - v122 - My 1 '97 - p94 [51-250]
Cox, Christopher R - *Chasing the Dragon*
   BL - v93 - S 15 '96 - p213 [51-250]
   FEER - v160 - Mr 6 '97 - p45 [251-500]
   NYTBR - v101 - O 13 '96 - p31 [501+]
   PW - v243 - S 9 '96 - p76 [51-250]
Cox, Clinton - *Fiery Vision*
  y BL - v93 - F 15 '97 - p1012 [51-250]
Cox, David - *Retreating from the Cold War*
   Choice - v34 - N '96 - p532 [51-250]
   R&R Bk N - v11 - N '96 - p13 [51-250]
   TLS - D 27 '96 - p6 [501+]
Cox, Donald W - *Doomsday Asteroid*
   Choice - v34 - My '97 - p1521 [51-250]
   SciTech - v21 - Mr '97 - p19 [51-250]
Cox, Earl D - *Fuzzy Logic for Business and Industry*
   SIAM Rev - v39 - Mr '97 - p166+ [501+]
Cox, Elizabeth M - *Women in Modern American Politics*
  r LJ - v122 - My 1 '97 - p96 [51-250]

Women State and Territorial Legislators 1895-1995
  r ARBA - v28 - '97 - p271 [51-250]
  r WHQ - v27 - Win '96 - p550 [1-50]
Cox, Eva - *Leading Women*
    Arena - Ag '96 - p46+ [501+]
Cox, F E G - *The Wellcome Trust History of Tropical Diseases*
  r New Sci - v154 - My 3 '97 - p49 [251-500]
The Wellcome Trust Illustrated History of Tropical Diseases
    Nature - v383 - O 31 '96 - p782 [51-250]
Cox, Fran - *A Conscious Life*
    Choice - v34 - Mr '97 - p1242 [51-250]
Cox, Harvey - *Fire from Heaven*
    Theol St - v57 - Mr '96 - p153+ [501+]
Cox, Jane - *Tracing Your Ancestors in the Public Record Office*
    TES - Jl 26 '96 - pR6 [51-250]
Cox, Janice - *Natural Beauty for All Seasons*
    PW - v243 - O 7 '96 - p72 [51-250]
Cox, Joseph T - *The Written Wars*
    BL - v93 - S 1 '96 - p58 [51-250]
    R&R Bk N - v12 - F '97 - p23 [51-250]
Cox, Josephine - *Vagabonds (Ollerenshaw). Audio Version*
    BWatch - v18 - Mr '97 - p8 [1-50]
Cox, Kath - *Clothes and Uniforms*
  c Bks Keeps - Mr '97 - p22 [51-250]
Food
  c Bks Keeps - Mr '97 - p22 [51-250]
Cox, Margaret - *Wetlands: Archaeology and Nature Conservation*
    J Gov Info - v23 - S '96 - p648+ [51-250]
Cox, Michael - *The Oxford Book of Spy Stories*
  y Magpies - v11 - S '96 - p38+ [251-500]
The Oxford Book of Twentieth-Century Ghost Stories
  y BL - v93 - N 1 '96 - p480 [51-250]
    BW - v26 - O 27 '96 - p13 [51-250]
    Comw - v123 - D 20 '96 - p20+ [501+]
    TLS - D 6 '96 - p25 [501+]
Cox, P A - *The Elements on Earth*
    J Chem Ed - v73 - Ag '96 - pA178 [51-250]
Cox, Philip - *Gender, Genre, and the Romantic Poets*
    R&R Bk N - v11 - N '96 - p69 [51-250]
Cox, Randall - *Birder's Dictionary*
  r Wildbird - v10 - O '96 - p24 [51-250]
Cox, Richard J - *The First Generation of Electronic Records Archivists in the United States*
    Archiv - Spr '96 - p244+ [501+]
Cox, Robert W - *International Political Economy*
    JEL - v35 - Mr '97 - p210+ [51-250]
Cox, Ronald L - *Business and the State in International Relations*
    R&R Bk N - v11 - D '96 - p16 [51-250]
Cox, Stephen - *The Munchkins of Oz*
  y BL - v93 - N 15 '96 - p562 [51-250]
Cox, Steven L - *Essentials of New Testament Greek: A Student's Guide. Rev. Ed.*
    Rel St Rev - v23 - Ja '97 - p66+ [251-500]
Cox, Sue - *Safety, Systems and People*
    SciTech - v20 - N '96 - p59 [51-250]
Cox, Ted - *Reggie Miller: Basketball Sharpshooter*
  y SLJ - v42 - O '96 - p45 [1-50]
Cox, Vic - *The Challenge of Immigration*
  y JOYS - v9 - Sum '96 - p415 [51-250]
Cox, William Price - *South Carolina, off the Beaten Path*
  r Bloom Rev - v16 - Jl '96 - p25 [51-250]
Coxe, Molly - *Big Egg*
  c BL - v93 - My 1 '97 - p1503 [51-250]
Coxon, Michele - *The Cat Who Found His Way Home (Illus. by Michele Coxon)*
  c Sch Lib - v45 - F '97 - p18 [51-250]
Where's My Kitten? (Illus. by Michele Coxon)
  c Bks Keeps - v100 - S '96 - p8+ [51-250]
Where's My Kitten (Illus. by Michele Coxon)
  c Sch Lib - v44 - Ag '96 - p98 [51-250]
Coxon, Terry - *Keep What You Earn*
    BL - v93 - O 1 '96 - p294 [51-250]
Cox-Rearick, Janet - *The Collection of Francis I*
    Obs - Ja 5 '97 - p17* [51-250]
  r Ren Q - v50 - Spr '97 - p310+ [501+]
  r Six Ct J - v27 - Win '96 - p1080+ [501+]

Coy, John - *Night Driving (Illus. by Peter McCarty)*
  c BL - v93 - S 1 '96 - p141 [51-250]
  c CBRS - v25 - O '96 - p14 [51-250]
  c CCB-B - v50 - D '96 - p131 [51-250]
  c HB - v72 - S '96 - p574+ [51-250]
  c HB Guide - v8 - Spr '97 - p24 [51-250]
  c HMR - Win '96 - p40+ [501+]
  c KR - v64 - S 1 '96 - p1320+ [51-250]
  c LATBR - D 8 '96 - p18+ [51-250]
  c NYTBR - v101 - D 22 '96 - p16 [501+]
  c NYTLa - v146 - D 9 '96 - pC18 [51-250]
  c SLJ - v42 - O '96 - p91 [51-250]
Coyle, Harold - *Until the End*
    BL - v92 - Ag '96 - p1880 [51-250]
    PW - v244 - Mr 24 '97 - p81 [1-50]
Until the End (Lewis). Audio Version
    LJ - v122 - Ap 15 '97 - p138 [51-250]
Coyle, Karen - *Format Integration and Its Effect on Cataloging, Training, and Systems*
    LRTS - v40 - Ap '96 - p193+ [501+]
Coyle, Michael - *Ezra Pound, Popular Genres, and the Discourse of Culture*
    ELT - v39 - 3 '96 - p393+ [501+]
Coyle, Neva - *Inside the Privet Hedge*
  y VOYA - v19 - O '96 - p206 [251-500]
Coyne, Richard - *Designing Information Technology in the Postmodern Age*
    ABR - v17 - Ag '96 - p10 [501+]
Cozens, Dominic - *Wings Guide to British Birds*
    New Sci - v153 - Mr 8 '97 - p45 [1-50]
Cozic, Charles P - *An Aging Population*
  y Ch BWatch - v6 - Jl '96 - p2 [1-50]
  y SLJ - v42 - Ag '96 - p167 [51-250]
  y VOYA - v19 - O '96 - p222+ [251-500]
Illegal Immigration
  y BL - v93 - Ja '97 - p828 [251-500]
  y Kliatt - v31 - Mr '97 - p30 [51-250]
  y SLJ - v43 - Ja '97 - p122 [51-250]
The Militia Movement
  y BL - v93 - Mr 1 '97 - p1154 [51-250]
  y Kliatt - v31 - Mr '97 - p29 [51-250]
Politicians and Ethics
  y Ch BWatch - v6 - Jl '96 - p2 [1-50]
Welfare
  y Kliatt - v31 - Mr '97 - p30 [51-250]
  y SLJ - v43 - F '97 - p112 [51-250]
Welfare Reform
  y Kliatt - v31 - Mr '97 - p29 [51-250]
Cozzens, Peter - *The Darkest Days of the War*
    BL - v93 - Mr 15 '97 - p1222 [51-250]
    KR - v65 - F 15 '97 - p267 [251-500]
The Shipwreck of Their Hopes
    RAH - v24 - S '96 - p418+ [501+]
CPB Teacher's Digest
  p SLJ - v42 - D '96 - p48 [1-50]
Crab Orchard Review
  p LMR - v15 - Win '96 - p42+ [51-250]
Crabb, Larry - *Hope When You're Hurting*
    BL - v93 - O 1 '96 - p297 [251-500]
Crace, Jim - *Continent*
    NYTBR - v102 - F 9 '97 - p32 [1-50]
Signals of Distress
    NYTBR - v102 - F 9 '97 - p32 [1-50]
    Trib Bks - Mr 9 '97 - p8 [51-250]
Craddock, Paul T - *Early Metal Mining and Production*
  r Am Ant - v62 - Ja '97 - p153+ [501+]
Craddock, Peter - *Project Libra*
    LAR - v98 - O '96 - p538 [251-500]
Craft, M Charlotte - *Cupid and Psyche (Illus. by K Y Craft)*
  c CCB-B - v50 - S '96 - p8 [51-250]
  c HB Guide - v7 - Fall '96 - p320 [51-250]
  c NY - v72 - N 18 '96 - p1011 [51-250]
Craft, Michael - *Alien Impact*
    NYTBR - v101 - S 22 '96 - p24 [51-250]
Crafton, Barbara Cawthorne - *Meditations on the Book of Psalms*
    LJ - v121 - O 1 '96 - p86 [51-250]
Crafts, Nicholas - *Economic Growth in Europe since 1945*
    Choice - v34 - F '97 - p1011 [51-250]
    Econ - v341 - D 7 '96 - p9* [51-250]
    JEL - v35 - Mr '97 - p258 [51-250]
Cragg, Dan - *Generals in Muddy Boots*
  yr ARBA - v28 - '97 - p253+ [51-250]
Craggs, Stewart R - *Arthur Bliss: A Source Book*
  r Choice - v34 - O '96 - p249 [51-250]
  r R&R Bk N - v11 - N '96 - p58 [51-250]
Craia, Sultana - *Francofonie Si Francofilie*
    BL - v93 - D 15 '96 - p714 [1-50]

Craig, Alan K - *In Quest of Mineral Wealth*
    Am Ant - v61 - Jl '96 - p631 [251-500]
    HAHR - v77 - F '97 - p101+ [501+]
Craig, Amanda - *A Vicious Circle*
    Obs - D 8 '96 - p18* [501+]
    Spec - v277 - D 14 '96 - p67+ [251-500]
    TLS - D 13 '96 - p23 [251-500]
Craig, Bruce D - *Handbook of Corrosion Data. 2nd Ed.*
    SciTech - v20 - D '96 - p63 [51-250]
Craig, Claire - *Animal Babies*
  c BL - v93 - D 15 '96 - p728 [51-250]
  c HB Guide - v8 - Spr '97 - p117 [1-50]
  cr SB - v33 - Ja '97 - p181 [51-250]
Incredible Creatures
  c HB Guide - v8 - Spr '97 - p117 [1-50]
  c KR - v64 - N 15 '96 - p1667 [51-250]
Craig, David - *Landmarks: An Exploration of Great Rocks*
    LJ - v121 - N 15 '96 - p78 [51-250]
Craig, Edward Gordon - *The Correspondence of Edward Gordon Craig and Count Harry Kessler 1903-1937*
    BC - v45 - Win '96 - p576+ [501+]
Craig, Gordon A - *The Politics of the Unpolitical*
    AHR - v101 - D '96 - p1565 [251-500]
    Lon R Bks - v19 - Ja 2 '97 - p26+ [501+]
Craig, John Clark - *Microsoft Visual Basic Workshop*
    CBR - v14 - Jl '96 - p23 [1-50]
Craig, Kenneth M - *Reading Esther*
    Intpr - v51 - Ja '97 - p83 [251-500]
    Theol St - v57 - S '96 - p564 [251-500]
Craig, Lee A - *The Integration of the European Economy 1850-1913*
    Choice - v34 - My '97 - p1546 [51-250]
Craig, Leon Harold - *The War Lover*
    RM - v49 - Je '96 - p919+ [251-500]
Craig, Patricia - *The Oxford Book of Travel Stories*
    BL - v93 - S 1 '96 - p63 [51-250]
Craig, Philip R - *A Deadly Vineyard Holiday*
    LJ - v122 - My 1 '97 - p144 [1-50]
    PW - v244 - Ap 14 '97 - p59 [51-250]
Death on a Vineyard Beach
    BWatch - v17 - S '96 - p1 [1-50]
    KR - v64 - My 1 '96 - p642 [51-250]
Craig, Roy R - *Mechanics of Materials*
    Choice - v34 - F '97 - p993 [51-250]
    Phys Today - v49 - D '96 - p56 [501+]
Craig, Ruth - *Malu's Wolf*
  y Emerg Lib - v23 - My '96 - p58 [51-250]
Craige, Betty Jean - *American Patriotism in a Global Society*
    Choice - v34 - F '97 - p1035 [51-250]
    R&R Bk N - v11 - N '96 - p65 [51-250]
Craighead, John J - *The Grizzly Bears of Yellowstone*
    Am Sci - v85 - Ja '97 - p72+ [51-250]
Craik, Dinah Mulock - *The Little Lame Prince and His Travelling Cloak*
  c ChLAQ - v21 - Fall '96 - p133+ [501+]
Craik, Jennifer - *The Face of Fashion*
    Signs - v22 - Win '97 - p475+ [501+]
Craik, Robert J M - *Sound Transmission through Buildings*
    R&R Bk N - v12 - F '97 - p73 [51-250]
Crain, Edward E - *Historic Architecture in the Caribbean Islands*
    HAHR - v76 - Ag '96 - p540+ [501+]
Crais, Robert - *Indigo Slam*
    BL - v93 - My 1 '97 - p1460 [51-250]
    PW - v244 - Ap 14 '97 - p59 [51-250]
Sunset Express
    Arm Det - v29 - Sum '96 - p374+ [51-250]
    PW - v243 - N 4 '96 - p40 [1-50]
Sunset Express (Stuart). Audio Version
  y Kliatt - v31 - Ja '97 - p46 [51-250]
Crama, Yves - *Production Planning in Automated Manufacturing. 2nd Ed.*
    JEL - v35 - Mr '97 - p253 [51-250]
Cramer, John - *Einstein's Bridge*
    KR - v65 - My 1 '97 - p686 [51-250]
Cramer, Phebe - *Storytelling, Narrative, and the Thematic Apperception Test*
    SciTech - v20 - S '96 - p33 [51-250]
Crandall, B C - *Nanotechnology: Molecular Speculations on Global Abundance*
    Bloom Rev - v16 - N '96 - p28 [51-250]
    Choice - v34 - F '97 - p994 [51-250]
    Fut - v30 - N '96 - p57+ [501+]
Crandall, Chuck - *Flowering, Fruiting and Foliage Vines*
  r Fine Gard - Mr '97 - p78 [51-250]
Planters, Containers, and Raised Beds
    BL - v93 - N 1 '96 - p470 [51-250]
    LJ - v121 - N 1 '96 - p99 [51-250]

Crandell, George W - *The Critical Response to Tennessee Williams*
  r AL - v69 - Mr '97 - p256 [51-250]
    R&R Bk N - v12 - F '97 - p89 [51-250]
  Tennessee Williams: A Descriptive Bibliography
  r AL - v68 - S '96 - p668 [1-50]
Crane, Andy - *Kidnap at Denton Farm. Audio Version*
  c Ch BWatch - v6 - O '96 - p2 [1-50]
Crane, Arnold - *On the Other Side of the Camera*
  PW - v244 - Mr 3 '97 - p61 [51-250]
Crane, D Russell - *Fundamentals of Marital Therapy*
  SciTech - v21 - Mr '97 - p54 [51-250]
Crane, Hamilton - *Sweet Miss Seeton*
  Arm Det - v30 - Win '97 - p97 [251-500]
  BL - v93 - D 15 '96 - p710 [51-250]
  BWatch - v18 - F '97 - p7 [1-50]
  KR - v64 - O 1 '96 - p1426+ [251-500]
  LJ - v121 - D '96 - p151 [51-250]
  PW - v243 - S 30 '96 - p64 [51-250]
Crane, Joan - *Guy Davenport: A Descriptive Bibliography 1947-1995*
  r BC - v45 - Win '96 - p559+ [251-500]
Crane, Nicholas - *Clear Waters Rising*
  Spec - v277 - N 30 '96 - p58 [1-50]
  TLS - O 4 '96 - p44 [501+]
Crane, Peter - *Mutual Fund Investing on the Internet*
  CBR - v15 - Spr '97 - p6 [51-250]
Crane, Randy - *A Simplified Approach to Image Processing*
  SciTech - v20 - N '96 - p66 [51-250]
Crane, Stephen - *Campaign Chronicles*
  c Ch BWatch - v6 - D '96 - p7 [51-250]
  Maggie: A Girl of the Streets
  J Am Cult - v19 - Spr '96 - p43+ [501+]
  Maggie: A Girl of the Streets and Other New York Stories (Bregy). Audio Version
  BL - v93 - My 15 '97 - p1596 [51-250]
Crane, Susan - *Gender and Romance in Chaucer's Canterbury Tales*
  MLR - v92 - Ja '97 - p168+ [501+]
  RES - v47 - N '96 - p564+ [501+]
  Specu - v71 - Jl '96 - p709+ [501+]
Cranfield, Ingrid - *100 Greatest Natural Wonders*
  c JB - v60 - Ag '96 - p154+ [51-250]
Crangle, Colleen - *Language and Learning for Robots*
  Robotica - v14 - S '96 - p588 [251-500]
Crankshaw, Edward - *Maria Theresa*
  CR - v270 - F '97 - p109 [1-50]
Cranor, Carl F - *Are Genes Us?*
  Rel St Rev - v22 - O '96 - p343 [51-250]
Cranston, Maurice - *Jean-Jacques: The Early Life and Work of Jean-Jacques Rousseau 1712-1754*
  New R - v216 - Mr 17 '97 - p40+ [501+]
  The Noble Savage
  New R - v216 - Mr 17 '97 - p40+ [501+]
  The Solitary Self
  BL - v93 - N 15 '96 - p566 [51-250]
  KR - v64 - O 1 '96 - p1439 [251-500]
  New R - v216 - Mr 17 '97 - p40+ [501+]
  WSJ-Cent - v99 - F 18 '97 - pA16 [501+]
Cranston, P - *Superstars on Ice*
  c Emerg Lib - v24 - Mr '97 - p26 [1-50]
Crary, Elizabeth - *Feelings for Little Children (Illus. by Mits Katayama)*
  c PW - v243 - N 25 '96 - p77 [51-250]
  When You're Happy and You Know It (Illus. by Mits Katayama)
  c Ch BWatch - v6 - D '96 - p3 [1-50]
  c Ch BWatch - v6 - D '96 - p8 [1-50]
  When You're Mad and You Know It (Illus. by Mits Katayama)
  c Ch BWatch - v6 - D '96 - p3 [1-50]
  c Ch BWatch - v6 - D '96 - p8 [1-50]
  When You're Shy and You Know It (Illus. by Mits Katayama)
  c Ch BWatch - v6 - D '96 - p3 [1-50]
  c Ch BWatch - v6 - D '96 - p8 [1-50]
  When You're Silly and You Know It (Illus. by Mits Katayama)
  c Ch BWatch - v6 - D '96 - p3 [1-50]
  c Ch BWatch - v6 - D '96 - p8 [1-50]
Crary, Jonathan - *Incorporations*
  ABR - v17 - Ag '96 - p9 [501+]
  Jurassic Technolgies Revenant
  BM - v138 - O '96 - p714+ [501+]
Cravens, Hamilton - *Technical Knowledge in American Culture*
  Choice - v34 - Ja '97 - p816 [51-250]
Crawford, Anne - *Letters of the Queens of England 1100-1547*
  EHR - v111 - S '96 - p959+ [251-500]

Crawford, Barbara - *Rockbridge County Artists and Artisans*
  JSH - v63 - F '97 - p146+ [501+]
Crawford, Cindy - *Cindy Crawford's Basic Face*
  CSM - v88 - N 7 '96 - p14 [51-250]
Crawford, Colin - *Uproar at Dancing Rabbit Creek*
  Aud - v98 - N '96 - p132+ [501+]
  Choice - v34 - F '97 - p982+ [51-250]
  NH - v105 - S '96 - p11 [51-250]
  NYTBR - v101 - O 27 '96 - p20 [501+]
  Trib Bks - F 9 '97 - p3+ [501+]
Crawford, Dorothy Lamb - *Evenings on and off the Roof*
  TLS - Jl 19 '96 - p19 [501+]
Crawford, E David - *Current Genitourinary Cancer Surgery. 2nd Ed.*
  SciTech - v21 - Mr '97 - p61 [51-250]
Crawford, Elisabeth - *Arrhenius: From Ionic Theory to the Greenhouse Effect*
  Choice - v34 - Mr '97 - p1180 [51-250]
  Nature - v384 - N 7 '96 - p36+ [501+]
  Sci - v273 - S 13 '96 - p1512+ [501+]
Crawford, F Marion - *For the Blood Is the Life*
  BW - v27 - F 23 '97 - p11 [251-500]
Crawford, Gary William - *J. Sheridan DeFanu: A Bio-Bibliography*
  r Ext - v37 - Fall '96 - p277+ [501+]
Crawford, Isaiah - *Psychosocial Interventions in HIV Disease*
  Readings - v12 - Mr '97 - p26 [51-250]
Crawford, John - *St. Catherine's Parish Dublin 1840-1900*
  ILS - v16 - Spr '97 - p36 [1-50]
Crawford, Mary - *Talking Difference*
  NWSA Jnl - v8 - Sum '96 - p117+ [501+]
  Per Psy - v50 - Spr '97 - p234+ [501+]
Crawford, Michael J - *Seasons of Grace*
  JR - v77 - Ap '97 - p268+ [501+]
Crawford, R J - *Rotational Moulding of Plastics. 2nd Ed.*
  r SciTech - v20 - D '96 - p84 [51-250]
Crawford, Stanley - *Some Instructions to My Wife Concerning the Upkeep of the House and Marriage and to My Son and Daughter Concerning the Conduct of Their Childhood*
  VLS - S '96 - p8 [501+]
Crawford, Tad - *The Secret Life of Money*
  BWatch - v17 - N '96 - p7 [51-250]
Crawford, Vicki L - *Women in the Civil Rights Movement*
  Signs - v22 - Aut '96 - p237+ [501+]
Crawford, Walt - *Future Libraries*
  LR - v45 - 8 '96 - p48+ [251-500]
Crawford, Walter B - *Samuel Taylor Coleridge: An Annotated Bibliography of Criticism and Scholarship. Vol. 3, Pts. 1-2*
  r ARBA - v28 - '97 - p453 [251-500]
  r Choice - v34 - My '97 - p1480 [51-250]
Crawley, Jacqueline N - *Neuropeptides: Basic and Clinical Advances*
  SciTech - v20 - S '96 - p23 [51-250]
Cray, Ed - *Chief Justice*
  y BL - v93 - My 1 '97 - p1458 [51-250]
  PW - v244 - Ap 21 '97 - p49+ [51-250]
Crayola Kids
  cp Par Ch - v20 - O '96 - p15 [1-50]
CRC Standard Mathematical Tables and Formulae. 30th Ed.
  r ARBA - v28 - '97 - p640+ [51-250]
  yr Choice - v34 - O '96 - p316+ [51-250]
CRC Standard Mathematical Tables and Formulae. 31st Ed.
  SIAM Rev - v38 - D '96 - p691+ [501+]
Creagh, Carson - *Mammals*
  c HB Guide - v8 - Spr '97 - p127 [51-250]
  c SB - v32 - N '96 - p243 [51-250]
  Reptiles
  c HB Guide - v7 - Fall '96 - p342 [1-50]
  c SB - v32 - Ag '96 - p181 [251-500]
  Things with Wings
  cr BL - v93 - D 15 '96 - p728 [51-250]
  c Emerg Lib - v24 - Mr '97 - p45 [1-50]
  c HB Guide - v8 - Spr '97 - p117 [1-50]
  cr SB - v33 - Ja '97 - p19 [51-250]
  c SLJ - v42 - D '96 - p111 [51-250]
Cream, Penelope - *The Complete Book of Sewing*
  y SLJ - v42 - O '96 - p164 [51-250]
Creamer, Robert W - *Babe (Parker). Audio Version*
  BL - v93 - N 15 '96 - p604 [51-250]
  Mantle Remembered
  NYTBR - v101 - Ap 7 '96 - p12+ [501+]
  Stengel: His Life and Times
  NYTBR - v101 - Ap 7 '96 - p24 [51-250]

Crean, Kevin - *Fisheries Management in Crisis*
  SciTech - v20 - S '96 - p45 [51-250]
Creanor, L - *A Hypertext Approach to Information Skills*
  LAR - v98 - S '96 - p479 [51-250]
Crease, Robert P - *The Second Creation. Rev. Ed.*
  SciTech - v20 - N '96 - p17 [51-250]
Creasia, Joan L - *Conceptual Foundations of Professional Nursing Practice. 2nd Ed.*
  SciTech - v20 - S '96 - p43 [51-250]
Creationism in Twentieth Century America. Vols. 1-10
  Zygon - v32 - Mr '97 - p105+ [501+]
Creative Kids
  cp Par Ch - v20 - O '96 - p26 [1-50]
Creative Living Room Decorating
  LJ - v121 - S 15 '96 - p66 [51-250]
Creative Window Treatments
  LJ - v121 - S 15 '96 - p66 [51-250]
Creaton, Heather - *Bibliography of Printed Works on London History to 1939*
  r Albion - v28 - Sum '96 - p279 [501+]
  London
  r ARBA - v28 - '97 - p61 [51-250]
  r Choice - v34 - Ap '97 - p1306 [51-250]
  r R&R Bk N - v12 - F '97 - p15 [51-250]
Crebbin, June - *Cows Moo, Cars Toot (Illus. by Anthony Lewis)*
  c Bks Keeps - N '96 - p9 [51-250]
  Danny's Duck (Illus. by Clara Vulliamy)
  c Bks Keeps - Jl '96 - p6 [51-250]
  Into the Castle (Illus. by John Bendall-Brunello)
  c BL - v92 - Ag '96 - p1906+ [51-250]
  c HB Guide - v7 - Fall '96 - p237+ [51-250]
  c LA - v73 - D '96 - p622 [51-250]
  The Train Ride (Illus. by Stephen Lambert)
  c Bks Keeps - v100 - S '96 - p8 [51-250]
Cree, Laura Murray - *Wendy Stavrianos*
  Aust Bk R - D '96 - p25+ [501+]
Creech, Sharon - *Absolutely Normal Chaos*
  y Kliatt - v31 - Mr '97 - p6 [51-250]
  c PW - v244 - F 3 '97 - p108 [1-50]
  Chasing Redbird
  y BL - v93 - Mr 15 '97 - p1235 [51-250]
  c CBRS - v25 - Mr '97 - p94 [51-250]
  y CCB-B - v50 - Mr '97 - p243 [51-250]
  c HB - v73 - My '97 - p316+ [51-250]
  c KR - v65 - F 1 '97 - p220 [51-250]
  y Obs - Mr 30 '97 - p17* [251-500]
  c PW - v244 - Ja 20 '97 - p403 [51-250]
  y TES - Mr 21 '97 - p14* [251-500]
  The Ghost of Uncle Arvie (Illus. by Simon Cooper)
  c Sch Lib - v45 - F '97 - p23 [51-250]
  Pleasing the Ghost (Illus. by Stacey Schuett)
  c BL - v93 - S 1 '96 - p125 [51-250]
  c CBRS - v25 - S '96 - p10+ [51-250]
  c CCB-B - v50 - O '96 - p53 [51-250]
  c HB Guide - v8 - Spr '97 - p63 [51-250]
  c NYTBR - v102 - F 16 '97 - p25 [1-50]
  c Par Ch - v20 - O '96 - p11 [1-50]
  c PW - v243 - Jl 22 '96 - p242 [51-250]
  c SLJ - v42 - N '96 - p104 [51-250]
  Walk Two Moons
  c JOYS - v10 - Fall '96 - p92+ [501+]
  y Kliatt - v30 - N '96 - p6 [51-250]
Creedy, John - *The Economics of Ageing*
  Econ J - v106 - N '96 - p1841 [51-250]
  Fiscal Policy and Social Welfare
  Econ J - v107 - Ja '97 - p274 [51-250]
  JEL - v34 - D '96 - p2057 [51-250]
  R&R Bk N - v11 - N '96 - p37 [51-250]
  General Equilibrium and Welfare
  JEL - v34 - D '96 - p2027 [51-250]
Creegan, Patrick J - *Asphalt-Concrete Water Barriers for Embankment Dams*
  SciTech - v20 - D '96 - p68 [51-250]
Creel, Catherine - *Wildsong*
  PW - v243 - S 23 '96 - p74 [51-250]
Creeley, Robert - *Memory Gardens*
  LJ - v122 - Ap 1 '97 - p94 [1-50]
  Selected Poems
  LJ - v122 - Ap 1 '97 - p94 [1-50]
Creffield, J W - *Wood Destroying Insects*
  SciTech - v21 - Mr '97 - p70 [51-250]
Creighton, Jill - *The Great Blue Grump (Illus. by Kitty Macaulay)*
  c Quill & Q - v63 - F '97 - p57 [251-500]
Creighton, Margaret S - *Iron Men, Wooden Women*
  AL - v68 - D '96 - p881 [51-250]
  R&R Bk N - v11 - N '96 - p20 [51-250]
  W&M Q - v54 - Ap '97 - p426+ [501+]
Crellin, John K - *Home Medicine*
  Can Hist R - v78 - Mr '97 - p114+ [501+]

Cremieux-Brilhac, Jean-Louis - *La France Libre*
  Spec - v278 - Ja 25 '97 - p39 [501+]
Henri Laugier En Son Siecle
  Isis - v87 - D '96 - p752+ [501+]
Cremmins, Edward T - *The Art of Abstracting. 2nd Ed.*
  LAR - v98 - Ag '96 - p427 [51-250]
Cremo, Michael A - *The Hidden History of the Human Race*
  BWatch - v18 - Mr '97 - p11 [51-250]
  Skeptic - v4 - '96 - p98+ [501+]
Crenne, Helisenne De - *Epistres Familieres Et Invectives*
  Ren Q - v50 - Spr '97 - p251+ [501+]
The Torments of Love
  TranslRevS - v2 - D '96 - p22 [51-250]
Crenshaw, Kimberle - *Critical Race Theory*
  Bl S - v26 - Sum '96 - p64 [1-50]
  New R - v215 - D 9 '96 - p27+ [501+]
Crenshaw, Nadine - *Balor of the Evil Eye*
  SF Chr - v18 - O '96 - p77 [51-250]
Crenshaw, Russell - *The Battle of Tassafaronga*
  NWCR - v49 - Aut '96 - p153+ [501+]
Crepin-Leblond, Thierry - *Le Dressoir Du Prince*
  BM - v139 - Ja '97 - p51+ [251-500]
Cressey, Peter - *Work and Employment in Europe*
  JEL - v34 - S '96 - p1448 [51-250]
Cresswell, Helen - *The Bagthorpe Triangle*
  c Bks Keeps - v100 - S '96 - p10 [51-250]
Bagthorpes Besieged
  c JB - v60 - Ag '96 - p155 [51-250]
Mystery at Winklesea (Illus. by Susan Winter)
  c Bks Keeps - Jl '96 - p9 [51-250]
Mystery Stories (Illus. by Adrian Reynolds)
  c CLW - v67 - D '96 - p56 [51-250]
  y SLJ - v43 - F '97 - p100+ [51-250]
Stonestruck
  c Bks Keeps - N '96 - p10+ [51-250]
  c TES - Ap 4 '97 - p8* [51-250]
The Watchers: A Mystery at Alton Towers (Rodska). Audio Version
  c BL - v93 - S 15 '96 - p264 [51-250]
  c HB - v72 - S '96 - p566+ [501+]
Cresswell, Jasmine - *Secret Sins*
  PW - v243 - D 30 '96 - p63 [51-250]
Cresswell, Joseph - *English Polemics at the Spanish Court*
  EHR - v111 - S '96 - p980+ [51-250]
Cresswell, M J - *Language in the World*
  Phil R - v105 - Ap '96 - p262+ [501+]
Semantic Indexicality
  R&R Bk N - v11 - D '96 - p59 [51-250]
Cresswell, Stephen - *Multiparty Politics in Mississippi 1877-1902*
  JSH - v62 - N '96 - p825+ [251-500]
Cressy, D - *Religion and Society in Early Modern England*
  r CLW - v67 - Mr '97 - p30 [51-250]
Cressy, David - *Birth, Marriage and Death*
  LJ - v122 - My 1 '97 - p119 [51-250]
Creswell, John W - *Research Design*
  HER - v66 - Win '96 - p885+ [501+]
Creswell, Sophia - *Sam Golod: A Novel of St. Petersburg*
  Obs - O 6 '96 - p16* [501+]
Crew, Gary - *Caleb (Illus. by Steven Woolman)*
  y JB - v60 - O '96 - p198+ [51-250]
  c Sch Lib - v44 - N '96 - p150 [251-500]
  c TES - N 22 '96 - p10* [51-250]
The Figures of Julian Ashcraft (Illus. by Hans De Haas)
  c Aust Bk R - N '96 - p63+ [501+]
The Watertower (Illus. by Steven Woolman)
  c Bkbird - v34 - Spr '96 - p51 [51-250]
Crew, Linda - *Children of the River*
  y Kliatt - v30 - S '96 - p3 [1-50]
Crew, Randolph E - *A Killing Shadow*
  Mar Crp G - v80 - N '96 - p78+ [501+]
Crewdson, Joan - *Christian Doctrine in the Light of Michael Polanyi's Theory of Personal Knowledge*
  JR - v77 - Ja '97 - p162+ [501+]
Crewe, Candida - *Falling Away*
  TLS - My 24 '96 - p27 [251-500]
Crewe, Ivor - *The British Electorate 1963-1992*
  r Choice - v34 - D '96 - p588 [51-250]
SDP: The Birth, Life and Death of the Social Democratic Party
  Albion - v28 - '96 - p735+ [501+]
  APSR - v90 - D '96 - p934+ [501+]
Crewe, Sabrina - *The Bear*
  c HB Guide - v8 - Spr '97 - p126 [51-250]
The Bee
  c HB Guide - v8 - Spr '97 - p121 [51-250]
The Butterfly
  c HB Guide - v8 - Spr '97 - p121 [51-250]
The Chimpanzee
  c HB Guide - v8 - Spr '97 - p126 [51-250]

The Frog
  c HB Guide - v8 - Spr '97 - p123 [51-250]
The Kangaroo
  c HB Guide - v8 - Spr '97 - p126 [51-250]
The Ladybug
  HB Guide - v8 - Spr '97 - p121 [51-250]
The Prairie Dog (Illus. by Graham Allen)
  c HB Guide - v8 - Spr '97 - p126 [51-250]
  c SLJ - v43 - Mr '97 - p172 [51-250]
The Salmon (Illus. by Colin Newman)
  c HB Guide - v8 - Spr '97 - p124 [51-250]
  c SLJ - v43 - Mr '97 - p172 [51-250]
The Snake
  c HB Guide - v8 - Spr '97 - p123 [51-250]
The Swallow
  c HB Guide - v8 - Spr '97 - p124 [51-250]
The Whale
  c HB Guide - v8 - Spr '97 - p126 [51-250]
Crews, Clyde F - *American and Catholic*
  CHR - v83 - Ja '97 - p161+ [51-250]
Crews, Donald - *Freight Train*
  c HB Guide - v8 - Spr '97 - p11 [51-250]
Short Cut (Illus. by Donald Crews)
  c Par Ch - v20 - N '96 - p3 [51-250]
Ten Black Dots
  c BL - v93 - Ap 1 '97 - p1340 [1-50]
Crews, Harry - *A Childhood: The Biography of a Place*
  Bloom Rev - v16 - Jl '96 - p24+ [51-250]
The Mulching of America
  NYTBR - v101 - N 10 '96 - p68 [51-250]
  PW - v243 - S 2 '96 - p122 [1-50]
  Trib Bks - Ja 19 '97 - p8 [1-50]
Crews, Nina - *I'll Catch the Moon (Illus. by Nina Crews)*
  c HB Guide - v7 - Fall '96 - p252 [51-250]
  c Inst - v106 - O '96 - p68 [1-50]
Cribb, Julian - *The White Death*
  Aust Bk R - N '96 - p67 [51-250]
Cribb, Robert - *Modern Indonesia*
  AHR - v101 - D '96 - p1600+ [501+]
  Historian - v59 - Fall '96 - p170+ [251-500]
Crichton, Michael - *Airframe*
  y BL - v93 - Ja '97 - p763 [1-50]
  y BL - v93 - N 15 '96 - p548+ [51-250]
  Bus W - D 23 '96 - p18 [51-250]
  CJR - v35 - Mr '97 - p59 [501+]
  CSM - v89 - D 19 '96 - p14 [51-250]
  CSM - v89 - Ja 16 '97 - p14 [51-250]
  CSM - v89 - F 20 '97 - p10 [51-250]
  CSM - v89 - Mr 20 '97 - p14 [51-250]
  Ent W - D 13 '96 - p69+ [501+]
  Fortune - v134 - D 23 '96 - p241 [501+]
  LATBR - D 15 '96 - p3 [501+]
  NS - v125 - D 20 '96 - p121 [501+]
  NY - v72 - D 16 '96 - p103+ [501+]
  NYRB - v44 - Ja 9 '97 - p16+ [501+]
  NYTBR - v101 - D 15 '96 - p12+ [501+]
  NYTLa - v146 - D 5 '96 - pC20 [501+]
  PW - v243 - N 11 '96 - p58 [51-250]
  y SLJ - v43 - Mr '97 - p214 [51-250]
  Time - v148 - D 9 '96 - p88 [251-500]
  WSJ-MW - v78 - D 9 '96 - pA12 [51-250]
Airframe (Cassidy). Audio Version
  y Kliatt - v31 - Mr '97 - p39 [51-250]
Airframe (Brown). Audio Version
  LJ - v122 - Ja '97 - p172 [51-250]
  PW - v243 - D 2 '96 - p30 [51-250]
Jurassic Park
  y BL - v93 - Ja '97 - p832 [1-50]
The Lost World
  Ent W - O 25 '96 - p109 [1-50]
Twister: The Original Screenplay
  New Sci - v151 - S 14 '96 - p44 [1-50]
Crick, Martin - *The History of the Social-Democratic Federation*
  EHR - v112 - Ap '97 - p515 [251-500]
Crick, Michael - *Jeffrey Archer: Stranger than Fiction*
  Books - v10 - Je '96 - p21 [1-50]
Michael Heseltine: A Biography
  Lon R Bks - v19 - Ap 24 '97 - p25+ [501+]
  NS - v126 - Mr 27 '97 - p52 [501+]
  Obs - F 23 '97 - p15* [501+]
  Spec - v278 - Mr 1 '97 - p36 [501+]
  TLS - F 28 '97 - p28 [501+]
Cricket
  cp Par Ch - v20 - O '96 - p15 [1-50]
Crider, Bill - *The Prairie Chicken Kill*
  Arm Det - v29 - Fall '96 - p498 [51-250]
  y BL - v92 - Ag '96 - p1885 [51-250]
  y BL - v92 - Ag '96 - p1891 [1-50]
Winning Can Be Murder
  Arm Det - v29 - Fall '96 - p495 [51-250]

Crihan, Anton - *Drepturile Romanilor Asupra Basarabiei*
  BL - v93 - D 15 '96 - p714 [1-50]
Crime and Economy
  J Gov Info - v23 - S '96 - p664 [51-250]
Crime and Justice in Nevada 1994
  J Gov Info - v23 - S '96 - p588 [51-250]
Crime and the Criminal Justice System in Arizona
  J Gov Info - v23 - S '96 - p578 [51-250]
Crimi, Carolyn - *Outside, Inside (Illus. by Linnea Asplind Riley)*
  c ECEJ - v23 - Sum '96 - p222 [51-250]
Crimmins, Cathy - *Beyond Star Trek*
  PW - v244 - Mr 17 '97 - p72 [51-250]
Revenge of the Christmas Box
  NYTBR - v101 - D 8 '96 - p102 [1-50]
  PW - v243 - O 7 '96 - p61+ [51-250]
Criscuolo, Claire - *Claire's Classic American Vegetarian Cooking*
  LJ - v122 - Ap 15 '97 - p110 [51-250]
  PW - v244 - F 17 '97 - p214 [51-250]
Crisostomi, Paolo - *Amor Di Libro*
  Lib - v18 - D '96 - p361 [51-250]
Crisostomo, Isobelo T - *Filipino Achievers in the USA and Canada*
  r ARBA - v28 - '97 - p154 [251-500]
Crisp, Colin - *The Classic French Cinema 1930-1960*
  FQ - v49 - Fall '95 - p40+ [501+]
Crisp, George R - *Miles Davis*
  y DL - v93 - My 15 '97 - p1569+ [51-250]
Crisp, John - *Introduction to Fiber Optics*
  SciTech - v21 - Mr '97 - p80 [51-250]
Crisp, Mike - *The Practical Director. 2nd Ed.*
  SciTech - v21 - Mr '97 - p98 [51-250]
Crisp, Quentin - *Resident Alien*
  BW - v27 - Ap 13 '97 - p3 [501+]
  KR - v65 - F 1 '97 - p187 [251-500]
  LJ - v122 - Ap 1 '97 - p100 [51-250]
  PW - v244 - F 3 '97 - p83 [51-250]
Crisp, Roger - *How Should We Live?*
  Choice - v34 - Ja '97 - p808+ [51-250]
Crispen, Patrick Douglas - *Atlas for the Information Superhighway*
  r R&R Bk N - v12 - F '97 - p98 [51-250]
Crispin, A C - *The Paradise Snare*
  LJ - v122 - Ap 15 '97 - p123 [51-250]
Crispino, Enrica - *Van Gogh*
  c Sch Lib - v44 - N '96 - p174 [51-250]
  c TES - Ag 23 '96 - p24 [51-250]
Critcher, C - *Regeneration of the Coalfield Areas*
  R&R Bk N - v11 - D '96 - p32 [51-250]
Critchlow, Donald T - *Studebaker: The Life and Death of an American Corporation*
  Nat - v264 - Mr 3 '97 - p32+ [501+]
Critchlow, James - *Radio Hole-in-the-Head/Radio Liberty*
  JMCQ - v73 - Win '96 - p1014+ [251-500]
Critical Arts Ensemble - *The Electronic Disturbance*
  QJS - v83 - My '97 - p230+ [501+]
Crittenden, Jack - *Beyond Individualism*
  Ethics - v107 - Ja '97 - p389 [251-500]
Crnobrnja, Mihailo - *The Yugoslav Drama. 2nd Ed.*
  BIC - v25 - N '96 - p25+ [501+]
Croally, N T - *Euripidean Polemic*
  Rel St Rev - v23 - Ja '97 - p62 [51-250]
Croce, Benedetto - *History of Europe in the Nineteenth Century*
  Wil Q - v21 - Win '97 - p37 [51-250]
Croce, Paul Jerome - *Science and Religion in the Era of William James. Vol. 1*
  AHR - v101 - D '96 - p1631+ [501+]
  Bks & Cult - v2 - Ja '96 - p5 [501+]
  J Am St - v30 - Ap '96 - p163+ [251-500]
  Rel St Rev - v23 - Ja '97 - p92 [51-250]
Crockatt, Richard - *The Fifty Years War*
  AHR - v101 - D '96 - p1649+ [501+]
  RAH - v24 - S '96 - p513+ [501+]
Crocker, Betty - *Betty Crocker's Good and Easy Cookbook*
  LJ - v121 - O 15 '96 - p86 [51-250]
Crocker, Chester A - *Managing Global Chaos*
  For Aff - v76 - Mr '97 - p175 [51-250]
Crockett, Bryan - *The Play of Paradox*
  Six Ct J - v27 - Win '96 - p1218+ [501+]
Crockett, Paul Hampton - *HIV Law*
  Advocate - My 13 '97 - p72 [51-250]
  LJ - v122 - Ap 15 '97 - p98+ [51-250]
  PW - v244 - Mr 10 '97 - p58 [51-250]
Crocombe, Ron - *Educational Development in the Small States of the Commonwealth*
  Cont Pac - v8 - Fall '96 - p465+ [501+]

Croes, Dale R - *The Hoko River Archaeological Site Complex*
  Choice - v34 - D '96 - p651 [51-250]
Croft, Priscilla - *Dealing with Jealousy*
  c BL - v93 - D 1 '96 - p666 [51-250]
  c Ch BWatch - v7 - F '97 - p6 [1-50]
  c SLJ - v42 - N '96 - p97 [51-250]
Croft, Stuart - *Strategies of Arms Control*
  Choice - v34 - My '97 - p1572 [51-250]
Crofton, Eileen - *The Women of Royaumont*
  TLS - Mr 21 '97 - p9 [501+]
Croggon, Alison - *Navigatio*
  Aust Bk R - N '96 - p66 [51-250]
Croke, Vicki - *The Modern Ark*
  BL - v93 - Mr 1 '97 - p1099 [51-250]
  KR - v65 - Ja 15 '97 - p111 [51-250]
  NYTBR - v102 - Mr 23 '97 - p19 [51-250]
  PW - v244 - Ja 20 '97 - p384 [51-250]
  Trib Bks - My 4 '97 - p3 [51-250]
Croll, Carolyn - *Redoute: The Man Who Painted Flowers (Illus. by Carolyn Croll)*
  c CCB-B - v50 - S '96 - p8+ [51-250]
  c HB Guide - v7 - Fall '96 - p355 [51-250]
Croll, Paul - *Teachers, Pupils and Primary Schooling*
  TES - Ja 24 '97 - p10* [251-500]
Croll, Su - *Worlda Mirth*
  Can Lit - Win '96 - p167+ [501+]
Cromartie, Alan - *Sir Matthew Hale 1609-1676*
  AHR - v102 - F '97 - p101+ [501+]
  Albion - v28 - Fall '96 - p484+ [501+]
  Sev Cent N - v54 - Fall '96 - p64+ [501+]
  Six Ct J - v27 - Fall '96 - p825+ [501+]
Cromartie, Michael - *Caesar's Coin Revisited*
  CC - v113 - N 6 '96 - p1089 [51-250]
  Disciples and Democracy
  J Ch St - v38 - Sum '96 - p658+ [251-500]
  A Preserving Grace
  BL - v93 - F 1 '97 - p908 [51-250]
Cromarty, D - *The Wealth of Shrewsbury in the Early Fourteenth Century*
  EHR - v111 - N '96 - p1252+ [251-500]
Crombie, David - *Piano: A Photographic History of the World's Most Celebrated Instrument*
  Am MT - v46 - O '96 - p48+ [501+]
Crombie, Deborah - *Mourn Not Your Dead*
  BWatch - v17 - S '96 - p1 [1-50]
  KR - v64 - My 1 '96 - p648 [51-250]
Cromer, Alan - *Connected Knowledge*
  Wil Q - v21 - Spr '97 - p102 [501+]
Cromley, Elizabeth C - *Gender, Class, and Shelter*
  J Am Cult - v18 - Win '95 - p108 [501+]
Crompton, Anne Eliot - *Gawain and Lady Green*
  KR - v65 - Ja 15 '97 - p77+ [251-500]
  LJ - v122 - Mr 15 '97 - p93 [1-50]
  PW - v244 - Mr 31 '97 - p67+ [51-250]
  The Wildflower Pony
  c Ch BWatch - v6 - O '96 - p3 [51-250]
Crompton, Richmal - *Jimmy (Jarvis). Audio Version*
  c Sch Lib - v44 - N '96 - p150 [51-250]
Crompton, Rob - *IT across the Primary Curriculum*
  TES - Ja 10 '97 - p14* [1-50]
  TES - F 21 '97 - p13* [501+]
Cromwell, Jerry - *Hospital and Physician Rate-Setting Systems*
  r SciTech - v21 - Mr '97 - p47 [51-250]
Cronenberg, David - *Crash*
  Obs - N 24 '96 - p15* [501+]
Croner, Helga - *More Stepping Stones to Jewish-Christian Relations*
  Rel Ed - v91 - Fall '96 - p608+ [1-50]
  Stepping Stones to Further Jewish-Christian Relations
  Rel Ed - v91 - Fall '96 - p608+ [1-50]
Cronin, Anthony - *No Laughing Matter*
  TES - Ag 30 '96 - p25 [51-250]
  Samuel Beckett: The Last Modernist
  Lon R Bks - v18 - N 14 '96 - p8+ [501+]
  NS - v125 - S 27 '96 - p58+ [501+]
  NYRB - v43 - N 14 '96 - p24+ [501+]
  Spec - v277 - S 21 '96 - p45+ [501+]
  TES - O 18 '96 - p7* [501+]
  TLS - S 27 '96 - p3+ [501+]
  TLS - N 29 '96 - p13 [51-250]
Cronin, Blaise - *The Scholar's Courtesy*
  LAR - v98 - N '96 - p594 [51-250]
  LR - v45 - 6 '96 - p71+ [251-500]
  R&R Bk N - v11 - N '96 - p5 [51-250]
Cronin, James E - *The World the Cold War Made*
  For Aff - v76 - Mr '97 - p183 [51-250]
Cronin, Kevin M - *A Friar's Joy*
  Am - v176 - F 15 '97 - p31 [51-250]

Cronin, Leonard - *The Australian Animal Atlas (Illus. by Marion Westmacott)*
  cr Magpies - v11 - Jl '96 - p40 [251-500]
Cronin, Maura - *Country, Class or Craft?*
  EHR - v112 - Ap '97 - p509 [251-500]
Cronin, Michael - *Translating Ireland*
  ILS - v15 - Fall '96 - p7 [501+]
  TLS - S 6 '96 - p9+ [501+]
Cronin, Patrick M - *From Globalism to Regionalism*
  RSR - v24 - 3 '96 - p46 [51-250]
Cronin, Xavier A - *Grave Exodus*
  PW - v243 - O 7 '96 - p56 [51-250]
Cronkite, Walter - *A Reporter's Life*
  AJR - v19 - Mr '97 - p47 [501+]
  Ant R - v55 - Spr '97 - p248+ [51-250]
  y BL - v93 - N 1 '96 - p458 [51-250]
  BW - v26 - D 15 '96 - p3 [501+]
  CSM - v89 - Ja 9 '97 - p14 [51-250]
  CSM - v89 - F 6 '97 - p14 [51-250]
  CSM - v89 - Mr 6 '97 - p14 [51-250]
  Econ - v342 - F 15 '97 - p8*+ [501+]
  Ent W - D 20 '96 - p67+ [501+]
  KR - v64 - O 15 '96 - p1505 [251-500]
  LATBR - Ja 12 '97 - p3 [501+]
  LJ - v121 - D '96 - p102+ [51-250]
  LJ - v121 - D '96 - p106 [501+]
  NL - v79 - D 16 '96 - p18+ [501+]
  NYTBR - v102 - Ja 26 '97 - p7 [501+]
  NYTLa - v146 - D 30 '96 - pC14 [501+]
  PW - v243 - N 4 '96 - p60 [51-250]
  WSJ-MW - v78 - D 6 '96 - pA16 [501+]
  A Reporter's Life (Cronkite). Audio Version
  LJ - v122 - F 1 '97 - p125 [51-250]
  LJ - v122 - F 15 '97 - p115 [1-50]
Cronley, Jay - *Shoot!*
  LJ - v122 - My 1 '97 - p138 [51-250]
  PW - v244 - Ap 14 '97 - p53 [51-250]
Cronon, William - *Uncommon Ground*
  Econ - v339 - My 18 '96 - p12* [51-250]
  NEQ - v69 - D '96 - p680+ [501+]
  PHR - v65 - N '96 - p678+ [251-500]
  Utne R - My '96 - p107 [251-500]
Crook, David - *Orlando Di Lasso's Imitation Magnificats for Counter-Reformation Munich*
  Six Ct J - v27 - Win '96 - p1181+ [501+]
Crook, J A - *Legal Advocacy in the Roman World*
  AHR - v101 - D '96 - p1526 [501+]
Crook, Lorianne - *Crook and Chase*
  LJ - v121 - N 1 '96 - p42 [1-50]
Crook, Malcolm - *Elections in the French Revolution*
  Choice - v34 - F '97 - p1030 [51-250]
  HRNB - v25 - Win '97 - p79 [501+]
  TLS - F 28 '97 - p30 [501+]
Crook, Paul - *Darwinism, War and History*
  EHR - v111 - N '96 - p1329+ [251-500]
Croome, John - *Reshaping the World Trading System*
  JEL - v35 - Mr '97 - p212+ [51-250]
  J Gov Info - v23 - S '96 - p690+ [501+]
Cropley, Arthur J - *Fostering the Growth of High Ability*
  R&R Bk N - v12 - F '97 - p7 [51-250]
Cropper, Elizabeth - *Nicolas Poussin: Friendship and the Love of Painting*
  Ren Q - v50 - Spr '97 - p312+ [501+]
  TLS - N 8 '96 - p12+ [501+]
Cropsey, Joseph - *Plato's World*
  APSR - v90 - S '96 - p623+ [501+]
  Ethics - v107 - O '96 - p197+ [51-250]
  RM - v49 - Je '96 - p920+ [501+]
Crosbie, Lynn - *The Girl Wants To*
  Quill & Q - v62 - Jl '96 - p42 [501+]
  Pearl
  BIC - v26 - F '97 - p19+ [501+]
Crosbie, Michael J - *Architecture Animals (Illus. by Steve Rosenthal)*
  c HB Guide - v7 - Fall '96 - p355 [1-50]
Crosby, Alfred W - *The Measure of Reality*
  BL - v93 - Ja '97 - p811 [51-250]
  Choice - v34 - My '97 - p1556+ [51-250]
  LATBR - Ja 26 '97 - p4 [501+]
  LJ - v122 - Ja '97 - p118 [51-250]
  NYTBR - v102 - Ja 26 '97 - p24 [501+]
  PW - v243 - N 25 '96 - p62+ [51-250]
Crosby, Anthony E, Jr. - *Commemorating Frostburg's Percy Cemetery*
  r EGH - v50 - N '96 - p169+ [51-250]
Crosby, Cathy Lee - *Let the Magic Begin*
  LJ - v122 - F 1 '97 - p88 [51-250]
  PW - v243 - D 30 '96 - p52+ [51-250]

Crosby, Everett U - *Bishop and Chapter in Twelfth-Century England*
  CH - v65 - S '96 - p460+ [501+]
  EHR - v111 - N '96 - p1241+ [251-500]
Crosby, Michael H - *Celibacy: Means of Control or Mandate of the Heart?*
  RR - v55 - S '96 - p545+ [501+]
Crosby, Travis L - *The Two Mr. Gladstones*
  CHE - v43 - Mr 21 '97 - pA22 [51-250]
  NYTLa - v146 - Ja 10 '97 - pC34 [501+]
Crosby, Virginia - *Deadly Prospects*
  KR - v64 - S 1 '96 - p1273 [51-250]
  LJ - v121 - O 1 '96 - p130 [51-250]
Crosland, Margaret - *Sade's Wife*
  NYTBR - v101 - Jl 21 '96 - p18 [51-250]
Crosland, Maurice - *In the Shadow of Lavoisier*
  Isis - v87 - S '96 - p557 [251-500]
Crosland, Susan - *The Magnates*
  Books - v9 - S '95 - p27 [1-50]
Cross, Amanda - *The Collected Stories*
  y BL - v93 - D 15 '96 - p710 [51-250]
  KR - v64 - N 15 '96 - p1638 [51-250]
  PW - v243 - D 9 '96 - p64 [51-250]
  An Imperfect Spy (Mangan). Audio Version
  LJ - v122 - Mr 15 '97 - p102 [51-250]
Cross, Anthony - *By the Banks of the Neva*
  TLS - F 7 '97 - p36 [501+]
Cross, Brian - *It's Not about a Salary...*
  Col Lit - v23 - Je '96 - p177+ [501+]
Cross, Donna Woolfolk - *Pope Joan*
  y BL - v92 - Ag '96 - p1880 [51-250]
  y BL - v92 - Ag '96 - p1891 [1-50]
  LATBR - Ag 4 '96 - p10+ [51-250]
  LJ - v122 - Mr 15 '97 - p41 [1-50]
  y SLJ - v42 - D '96 - p33 [1-50]
  y SLJ - v42 - D '96 - p150 [51-250]
Cross, Elsie Y - *The Diversity Factor*
  Choice - v34 - O '96 - p324+ [51-250]
Cross, Gillian - *The Crazy Shoe Shuffle (Illus. by Nick Sharratt)*
  c Bks Keeps - N '96 - p9 [51-250]
  c ILN - Christmas '96 - p88 [1-50]
  c JB - v60 - D '96 - p249 [51-250]
  The Demon Headmaster Strikes Again
  c Bks Keeps - Ja '97 - p25 [51-250]
  The Great American Elephant Chase
  c SLJ - v42 - N '96 - p40 [1-50]
  New World
  y Bks Keeps - N '96 - p11 [51-250]
  y Kliatt - v31 - Mr '97 - p16 [51-250]
  c PW - v243 - N 18 '96 - p78 [51-250]
  Pictures in the Dark
  c Bks Keeps - Mr '97 - p26 [51-250]
  c BL - v93 - Ja '97 - p858 [251-500]
  y CCB-B - v50 - Ja '97 - p161+ [51-250]
  y Emerg Lib - v24 - Mr '97 - p54 [51-250]
  y HB - v73 - Ja '97 - p54 [51-250]
  y HB Guide - v8 - Spr '97 - p78 [51-250]
  y KR - v64 - O 15 '96 - p1530 [51-250]
  y PW - v243 - S 23 '96 - p77 [51-250]
  y Sch Lib - v45 - F '97 - p46 [51-250]
  Posh Watson
  c Magpies - v11 - S '96 - p45 [1-50]
Cross, Mary - *Advertising and Culture*
  Choice - v34 - Ja '97 - p786 [51-250]
  R&R Bk N - v11 - D '96 - p35 [51-250]
Cross, Peter - *So's Your Old Man*
  KR - v65 - F 15 '97 - p267 [51-250]
  LJ - v122 - Mr 15 '97 - p68 [51-250]
  PW - v244 - F 3 '97 - p84 [51-250]
Cross, Robert - *Elspeth Huxley: A Bibliography*
  r LAR - v98 - S '96 - p480 [251-500]
Cross, Robert G - *Revenue Management*
  BL - v93 - F 1 '97 - p914 [51-250]
  Revenue Management (Cross). Audio Version
  LJ - v122 - My 1 '97 - p153 [51-250]
Cross, Robin - *Movie Magic*
  c PW - v243 - N 25 '96 - p77 [51-250]
Cross, Rod - *The Natural Rate of Unemployment*
  Econ J - v107 - Ja '97 - p209+ [501+]
Crossan, John Dominic - *The Historical Jesus*
  Bks & Cult - v1 - N '95 - p3+ [501+]
Crossette, Barbara - *So Close to Heaven*
  NYTBR - v101 - O 13 '96 - p32 [51-250]
Crossgrove, William - *Die Deutsche Sachliteratur Des Mittelalters*
  Isis - v87 - S '96 - p539+ [501+]
Crossick, Geoffrey - *The Petite Bourgeoisie in Europe 1780-1914*
  Choice - v34 - N '96 - p516 [51-250]
  HRNB - v25 - Win '97 - p78 [501+]

Crossley, Michael - *Qualitative Educational Research in Developing Countries*
  R&R Bk N - v12 - F '97 - p66 [51-250]
Crossley, Rosemary - *Speechless: Facilitating Communication for People without Voices*
  LJ - v122 - F 15 '97 - p155 [51-250]
Crossley-Holland, Nicolle - *Living and Dining in Medieval Paris*
  HT - v46 - O '96 - p55+ [1-50]
Crossman, Virginia - *Politics, Law and Order in Nineteenth-Century Ireland*
  Choice - v34 - My '97 - p1557 [51-250]
Croswell, Ken - *The Alchemy of the Heavens*
  NYTBR - v101 - Ag 25 '96 - p28 [1-50]
  S&T - v92 - S '96 - p53 [51-250]
Croteau, David - *Politics and the Class Divide*
  SF - v75 - S '96 - p369+ [501+]
Croteau, Jean-Yves - *Repertoire Des Series, Feuilletons Et Teleromans Quebecois*
  Archiv - Fall '94 - p187+ [501+]
Crotty, Patrick - *Modern Irish Poetry*
  PW - v243 - N 4 '96 - p47 [1-50]
  WLT - v71 - Win '97 - p196+ [501+]
Crouch, Harold - *Government and Society in Malaysia*
  Choice - v34 - S '96 - p202+ [51-250]
  JEL - v34 - S '96 - p1490 [51-250]
Crouch, Holmes F - *Going into Tax Court*
  BWatch - v18 - F '97 - p10 [51-250]
Crouch, Stanley - *The All-American Skin Game*
  BW - v27 - Mr 30 '97 - p12 [51-250]
  NYTBR - v102 - Mr 2 '97 - p28 [1-50]
  PW - v244 - Ja 13 '97 - p73 [1-50]
Croucher, Phil - *The BIOS Companion*
  BYTE - v21 - O '96 - p167 [51-250]
  The Hard Disk Data Base
  BYTE - v21 - O '96 - p167 [51-250]
Croucher, Trever - *Boots and Books*
  BC - v44 - Win '95 - p492 [51-250]
Crouzel, Henri - *Les Fins Dernieres Selon Origene*
  Rel St Rev - v22 - O '96 - p301+ [501+]
  Origene Et Plotin
  Rel St Rev - v22 - O '96 - p301+ [501+]
Crouzet, Denis - *La Nuit De La Saint-Barthelemy*
  EHR - v111 - N '96 - p1218+ [501+]
Crouzet, Michel - *Le Rouge Et Le Noir*
  FR - v70 - F '97 - p468+ [501+]
Crouzet-Pavan, Elisabeth - *La Mort Lente De Torcello*
  JIH - v27 - Spr '97 - p694+ [251-500]
Crovi, Raffaele - *Il Santo Peccatore*
  BL - v93 - D 1 '96 - p644 [1-50]
Crow, Ben - *Sharing the Ganges*
  CS - v25 - S '96 - p649+ [501+]
Crow, Brian - *An Introduction to Post-Colonial Theatre*
  Am Theat - v14 - Ja '97 - p74 [51-250]
Crow, Loren D - *The Songs of Ascents (Psalms 120-134)*
  Rel St Rev - v23 - Ap '97 - p167 [51-250]
Crow, Mary - *I Have Tasted the Apple*
  Chel - 61 '96 - p137+ [501+]
  MQR - v36 - Spr '97 - p368+ [501+]
  Sm Pr R - v28 - N '96 - p5 [51-250]
Crow, Thomas - *18th Century France to Art of the Sixties*
  TES - Ag 30 '96 - p26 [1-50]
  Emulation: Making Artists for Revolutionary France
  AHR - v101 - D '96 - p1556 [501+]
  Modern Art in the Common Culture
  Choice - v34 - S '96 - p111 [51-250]
  Nat - v263 - O 14 '96 - p33+ [501+]
  TLS - N 8 '96 - p14+ [501+]
  The Rise of the Sixties
  Nat - v263 - O 14 '96 - p33+ [501+]
Crowder, Richard M - *Electric Drives and Their Controls*
  Robotica - v14 - S '96 - p588 [251-500]
Crowdus, Gary - *A Political Companion to American Film*
  Film Cr - v21 - Fall '96 - p71+ [501+]
Crowe, David M - *A History of the Gypsies of Eastern Europe and Russia*
  AHR - v101 - O '96 - p1243 [501+]
Crowe, Elizabeth Powell - *Genealogy Online. 2nd Ed.*
  r CBR - v15 - Spr '97 - p4 [1-50]
  r SB - v33 - Ja '97 - p11 [51-250]
Crowe, Thomas A - *Applications of Counseling in Speech-Language Pathology and Audiology*
  SciTech - v21 - Mr '97 - p52 [51-250]
Crowell, Douglas L - *History of the Coal-Mining Industry in Ohio*
  J Gov Info - v23 - S '96 - p591 [1-50]

Crowell, Jenn - *Necessary Madness*
  BL - v93 - Ja '97 - p778 [51-250]
  KR - v64 - D 1 '96 - p1688 [251-500]
  LJ - v122 - Ja '97 - p144+ [51-250]
  NYTBR - v102 - Mr 23 '97 - p9 [501+]
  PW - v243 - D 9 '96 - p58 [51-250]
  Time - v149 - Mr 3 '97 - p78 [251-500]
Crowell, Nancy A - *Understanding Violence against Women*
  Choice - v34 - Ja '97 - p885 [51-250]
Crowhurst, Norman - *Audio Measurements*
  TCI - v30 - O '96 - p55 [1-50]
Crowley, Elaine - *Cowslips and Chainies*
  PW - v244 - Mr 31 '97 - p54 [51-250]
Crowley, Leonard V - *Introduction to Human Disease. 4th Ed.*
  SciTech - v21 - Mr '97 - p48 [51-250]
Crowley, Mart - *3 Plays*
  Advocate - Je 11 '96 - p55+ [501+]
Crowley, Monica - *Nixon off the Record*
  BW - v26 - Ag 4 '96 - p5 [501+]
  CC - v113 - D 18 '96 - p1258+ [501+]
  For Aff - v75 - My '96 - p152+ [51-250]
  LATBR - Ag 11 '96 - p4 [501+]
  LJ - v121 - O '96 - p104 [51-250]
  NYTBR - v101 - Ag 25 '96 - p5+ [501+]
  y SLJ - v42 - D '96 - p152+ [51-250]
Crowley, Sharon - *Ancient Rhetorics for Contemporary Students*
  Col Comp - v47 - O '96 - p438 [51-250]
Crowley, Walt - *Rites of Passage*
  WHQ - v27 - Win '96 - p540 [251-500]
Crowley, William R - *Oil and Gas on the Internet*
  r ARBA - v28 - '97 - p643 [51-250]
  r Choice - v34 - S '96 - p94 [51-250]
Crown, Judith - *No Hands*
  BL - v93 - O 1 '96 - p310+ [51-250]
  Bus W - D 30 '96 - p34 [251-500]
  KR - v64 - Ag 15 '96 - p1202 [251-500]
  LJ - v121 - N 1 '96 - p74 [51-250]
  NYTBR - v101 - D 1 '96 - p25 [501+]
  PW - v243 - S 23 '96 - p69 [51-250]
  Trib Bks - Ja 5 '97 - p1+ [501+]
Crown, William H - *Handbook on Employment and the Elderly*
  Choice - v34 - Mr '97 - p1203+ [51-250]
  R&R Bk N - v12 - F '97 - p40 [51-250]
Crowther, Peter - *Dante's Disciples*
  SF Chr - v18 - O '96 - p80 [1-50]
  Sm Pr R - v28 - O '96 - p4 [51-250]
  Escardy Gap
  Rapport - v19 - 6 '96 - p19 [51-250]
Crowther, Robert - *Dump Trucks and Diggers*
  c BL - v93 - D 15 '96 - p732 [1-50]
  c Ch BWatch - v6 - O '96 - p6 [1-50]
  My Oxford Pop-Up Surprise 123 (Illus. by Robert Crowther)
  c Bks Keeps - Ja '97 - p19 [51-250]
  My Oxford Pop-up Surprise ABC (Illus. by Robert Crowther)
  c Bks Keeps - Ja '97 - p19 [51-250]
  My Oxford Surprise Pop-Up 123
  c Bks Keeps - Ja '97 - p19 [51-250]
  My Oxford Surprise Pop-Up 123 (Illus. by Robert Crowther)
  c Sch Lib - v44 - N '96 - p145 [51-250]
  c TES - N 29 '96 - p13* [51-250]
  My Oxford Surprise Pop-up ABC
  c Bks Keeps - Ja '97 - p19 [51-250]
  My Oxford Surprise Pop-Up ABC (Illus. by Robert Crowther)
  c Sch Lib - v44 - N '96 - p145 [51-250]
  c TES - N 29 '96 - p13* [51-250]
  Robert Crowther's Pop-Up Olympics
  y BL - v93 - Ap 1 '97 - p1306 [1-50]
  c HB Guide - v7 - Fall '96 - p360 [51-250]
  Tractors and Trucks
  c Ch BWatch - v6 - O '96 - p6 [1-50]
  c PW - v243 - S 23 '96 - p77 [51-250]
Croy, Homer - *Jesse James Was My Neighbor*
  PW - v244 - Ap 21 '97 - p69 [1-50]
Crozat, Francois - *I Am a Little Hedgehog*
  c HB Guide - v7 - Fall '96 - p238 [51-250]
Crozier, Lorna - *A Saving Grace*
  BIC - v26 - Mr '97 - p12+ [501+]
  Quill & Q - v62 - S '96 - p66 [251-500]
Crozier, Michael - *The Left in Search of a Center*
  Choice - v34 - S '96 - p208 [51-250]
Crozier, Ross H - *Evolution of Social Insect Colonies*
  Sci - v274 - N 29 '96 - p1477+ [501+]

The Crucible CD-Rom. Electronic Media Version
  Theat J - v48 - D '96 - p529+ [501+]
Cruickshanks, Eveline - *The Stuart Court in Exile and the Jacobites*
  Albion - v28 - Win '96 - p694+ [501+]
Cruikshank, Dale P - *Neptune and Triton*
  R&R Bk N - v11 - N '96 - p76 [51-250]
  S&T - v92 - S '96 - p53 [1-50]
Cruikshank, Ken - *Close Ties*
  Can Hist R - v78 - Mr '97 - p97+ [501+]
Cruise, David - *The Great Adventure*
  Beav - v76 - O '96 - p46 [51-250]
  BL - v93 - My 15 '97 - p1558 [51-250]
  CG - v117 - Mr '97 - p82+ [501+]
  KR - v65 - Ap 1 '97 - p514+ [251-500]
  Mac - v110 - Mr 24 '97 - p67 [251-500]
  PW - v244 - Ap 7 '97 - p83 [51-250]
  Quill & Q - v62 - N '96 - p42 [251-500]
Crum, Laura - *Hoofprints*
  Arm Det - v29 - Sum '96 - p362 [51-250]
Crum, Robert - *Let's Rodeo! (Illus. by Robert Crum)*
  c CCB-B - v50 - D '96 - p131+ [51-250]
  c HB Guide - v8 - Spr '97 - p143 [51-250]
  c NYTBR - v101 - N 10 '96 - p42 [501+]
  A Season in the Rodeo (Illus. by Robert Crum)
  c BL - v93 - N 1 '96 - p492 [51-250]
  c SLJ - v42 - S '96 - p212 [51-250]
Crumb, R - *The Complete Crumb. Vol. 12*
  BL - v93 - F 15 '97 - p990 [51-250]
Crumey, Andrew - *D'Alembert's Principle*
  NS & S - v9 - Ap 26 '96 - p41 [51-250]
  Obs - Ag 18 '96 - p19 [51-250]
  Music, in a Foreign Language
  KR - v64 - S 15 '96 - p1340 [251-500]
  LJ - v121 - O 1 '96 - p124+ [51-250]
  NYTBR - v102 - Ja 5 '97 - p18 [51-250]
  PW - v243 - S 30 '96 - p59+ [51-250]
Crumley, James - *Bordersnakes*
  KR - v64 - S 1 '96 - p1273 [51-250]
  LJ - v121 - N 1 '96 - p110 [51-250]
  NYTBR - v101 - N 24 '96 - p26 [51-250]
  NYTBR - v101 - D 8 '96 - p94 [1-50]
  PW - v243 - S 30 '96 - p64 [51-250]
Crumlish, Christian - *ABCs of the Internet*
  CBR - v14 - N '96 - p34 [51-250]
  The Internet for Busy People. 1st Ed.
  CBR - v15 - Spr '97 - p4+ [1-50]
  The Internet for Busy People. 2nd Ed.
  LJ - v122 - Ap 1 '97 - p118 [51-250]
  Web Publishing with Netscape for Busy People
  CBR - v15 - Spr '97 - p7 [1-50]
  Word for Windows 95 for Busy People
  CBR - v14 - Jl '96 - p26 [1-50]
Crummell, Alexander - *Civilization and Black Progress*
  HRNB - v25 - Fall '96 - p9 [251-500]
  J Am St - v30 - D '96 - p476+ [501+]
Crummey, Michael - *Arguments with Gravity*
  Quill & Q - v62 - D '96 - p33 [251-500]
Crump, Kenny - *The Use of Benchmark Dose Approach in Health Risk Assessment*
  J Gov Info - v23 - S '96 - p545+ [1-50]
Crump, Leon - *Drive for Show, Putt for Dough*
  PW - v244 - Mr 31 '97 - p51 [51-250]
Crunk, Tony - *Living in the Resurrection*
  Choice - v34 - D '96 - p612 [51-250]
Cruse, Howard - *Stuck Rubber Baby*
  VV - v42 - Ja 7 '97 - p43 [1-50]
Crusemann, Frank - *Die Tora: Theologie Und Sozialgeschichte Des Alttestamentlichen Gesetzes*
  Rel St Rev - v23 - Ja '97 - p22+ [501+]
Crusie, Jennifer - *Anyone but You*
  LJ - v122 - Ja '97 - p51 [1-50]
  LJ - v122 - F 15 '97 - p184 [51-250]
Crusz, Rienzi - *Beatitudes of Ice*
  WLT - v70 - Sum '96 - p696 [501+]
Crutcher, Chris - *Ironman*
  y EJ - v85 - N '96 - p134 [251-500]
  y Emerg Lib - v24 - S '96 - p24 [1-50]
  y Emerg Lib - v24 - S '96 - p26+ [1-50]
  y Kliatt - v30 - S '96 - p8 [51-250]
  Ironman (Guidall). Audio Version
  c BL - v93 - Ap 1 '97 - p1313 [1-50]
  y CSM - v89 - Mr 27 '97 - pB6 [1-50]
  y SLJ - v42 - O '96 - p78+ [51-250]
  The Secrets of Sarah Byrnes
  y Sch Lib - v44 - Ag '96 - p117 [51-250]
  Staying Fat for Sarah Byrnes
  y SLJ - v43 - Ja '97 - p36 [1-50]
Crutcher, Mark - *Lime 5*
  Nat R - v48 - Je 3 '96 - p58 [51-250]
  Rapport - v19 - 5 '96 - p40 [51-250]

Crutchfield, James A - *Eyewitness to American History*
Roundup M - v4 - O '96 - p25 [51-250]
The Santa Fe Trail
Roundup M - v3 - Ag '96 - p23+ [251-500]
Cruysse, Dirk Van Der - *L'Abbe De Choisy, Androgyne Et Mandarin*
Choice - v34 - D '96 - p567 [1-50]
Cruz, Barbara C - *Frida Kahlo: Portrait of a Mexican Painter*
y BL - v93 - N 1 '96 - p485 [51-250]
y HB Guide - v8 - Spr '97 - p137 [51-250]
y SLJ - v42 - O '96 - p154 [51-250]
Cruz, Jesus - *Gentlemen Bourgeois and Revolutionaries*
J Soc H - v30 - Spr '97 - p765+ [501+]
Cruz, Ricardo Cortez - *Five Days of Bleeding*
Chel - 61 '96 - p154+ [501+]
Cruz, Victor De La - *El General Charis Y La Pacificacion Del Mexico Postrevolucionario*
HAHR - v77 - F '97 - p133+ [251-500]
Cruz Martinez, Alejandro - *The Woman Who Outshone the Sun (Illus. by F Olivera)*
c SS - v88 - Ja '97 - p29+ [501+]
Cruz-Saenz, Michele S De - *Spanish Traditional Ballads from Aragon*
Hisp - v79 - D '96 - p786+ [501+]
MLR - v92 - Ja '97 - p223+ [501+]
Crystal, David - *The Cambridge Biographical Dictionary*
r ARBA - v28 - '97 - p12 [51-250]
r BL - v93 - D 15 '96 - p743 [1-50]
r Choice - v34 - D '96 - p587 [51-250]
yr Kliatt - v30 - N '96 - p21 [51-250]
The Cambridge Encyclopedia of Language. 2nd Ed.
New Sci - v153 - Mr 15 '97 - p43 [1-50]
Csaba, Laszlo - *The Capitalist Revolution in Eastern Europe*
Slav R - v55 - Sum '96 - p446+ [501+]
Csampai, Attila - *Callas: Images of a Legend*
BIC - v26 - F '97 - p35+ [251-500]
BL - v93 - N 1 '96 - p471 [51-250]
BW - v26 - D 8 '96 - p13 [51-250]
LATBR - O 20 '96 - p14 [51-250]
PW - v243 - O 21 '96 - p68 [51-250]
Csikszentmihalyi, Mihaly - *Creativity: Flow and the Psychology of Discovery and Invention*
SLJ - v42 - D '96 - p40 [51-250]
Utne R - S '96 - p93+ [501+]
The Evolving Self
A J Psy - v109 - Fall '96 - p465+ [501+]
Finding Flow
PW - v244 - Ap 28 '97 - p61+ [51-250]
CSIS U.S. China Policy Task Force - *Developing a Consensus for the Future*
JEL - v34 - D '96 - p2041 [51-250]
Csorba, Geza - *Nagybanya Muveszete*
BM - v138 - O '96 - p713+ [501+]
Csordas, Thomas J - *Language, Charisma, and Creativity*
Choice - v34 - My '97 - p1515 [51-250]
The CTD Pocket Guide. 1997 Ed.
r Coin W - v38 - My 12 '97 - p34 [51-250]
Cuadra, Angel - *The Poet in Socialist Cuba*
Hisp - v79 - S '96 - p455+ [501+]
Cubberley, Carol W - *Tenure and Promotion for Academic Librarians*
LJ - v121 - S 15 '96 - p104 [51-250]
Cubberley, Paul - *Handbook of Russian Affixes*
MLR - v91 - Jl '96 - p809+ [501+]
Cubitt, Catherine - *Anglo-Saxon Church Councils c.650-c.850*
Albion - v28 - Sum '96 - p280+ [501+]
Cubitt, Sean - *Timeshift: On Video Culture*
Afterimage - v24 - N '96 - p4 [1-50]
Videography: Video Medium as Art and Culture
Afterimage - v24 - N '96 - p4 [1-50]
Cuccio, Joan Fay - *The Geometry of Love*
KR - v65 - F 1 '97 - p157+ [251-500]
PW - v244 - Mr 3 '97 - p66 [51-250]
Cudahy, Brian J - *Around Manhattan Island and Other Maritime Tales of New York*
PW - v244 - Mr 24 '97 - p73 [51-250]
Cuddon, J A - *Horror Stories (Davenport). Audio Version*
y Kliatt - v31 - My '97 - p40 [51-250]
Cue, Kerry - *Australia Unbuttoned*
Aust Bk R - Je '96 - p66 [251-500]
Cuellar, Fred - *How to Buy a Diamond*
LJ - v122 - Mr 15 '97 - p59 [51-250]
Cueto, Ronald - *Souls in Anguish*
MLR - v91 - O '96 - p1021+ [501+]
Cuff, Yvonne Hutchinson - *Ceramic Technology for Potters and Sculptors*
Ceram Mo - v44 - N '96 - p28 [251-500]

Cuffe, Paul - *Captain Paul Cuffe's Logs and Letters 1808-1817*
Bl S - v26 - Fall '96 - p107 [1-50]
Choice - v34 - Ap '97 - p1403 [51-250]
R&R Bk N - v11 - N '96 - p18 [51-250]
Cukier, Daniel - *Coping with Radiation Therapy*
LJ - v122 - Ja '97 - p57 [1-50]
Cuklanz, Lisa M - *Rape on Trial*
Wom R Bks - v14 - Mr '97 - p23+ [501+]
Culbertson, Judi - *The Nursery*
KR - v64 - S 15 '96 - p1356 [51-250]
PW - v243 - O 7 '96 - p65 [51-250]
Culbertson, Margaret - *American House Designs*
r J Am Cult - v19 - Sum '96 - p133+ [51-250]
Culbertson, Roger - *3-D Kid*
c HB Guide - v7 - Fall '96 - p347 [51-250]
Culhane, Terry - *Russian Language and People. New Ed.*
y TES - Mr 7 '97 - pR10 [51-250]
Cull, Nicholas John - *Selling War*
JMH - v69 - Mr '97 - p148+ [501+]
Cullen, Christopher - *Astronomy and Mathematics in Ancient China*
Rel St Rev - v23 - Ap '97 - p204 [51-250]
Cullen, Daniel E - *Freedom in Rousseau's Political Philosophy*
RP - v59 - Win '97 - p169+ [501+]
Cullen, Jim - *Born in the U.S.A.*
KR - v65 - My 1 '97 - p689 [251-500]
PW - v244 - Ap 21 '97 - p50 [51-250]
The Civil War in Popular Culture
AHR - v102 - F '97 - p193+ [501+]
J Am Cult - v19 - Sum '96 - p137+ [501+]
J Am St - v30 - Ap '96 - p148+ [251-500]
Pub Hist - v19 - Win '97 - p112+ [501+]
Cullen, Lynn - *The Three Lives of Harris Harper*
c CLW - v67 - Mr '97 - p59 [51-250]
y Emerg Lib - v24 - S '96 - p54 [51-250]
c HB Guide - v7 - Fall '96 - p290 [51-250]
Cullen, Mary - *Women, Power and Consciousness in Nineteenth Century Ireland*
TLS - O 18 '96 - p31 [251-500]
Cullen, Robert - *Dispatch from a Cold Country*
LJ - v121 - D '96 - p180 [51-250]
NYTBR - v101 - Jl 21 '96 - p19 [51-250]
Rapport - v19 - 5 '96 - p27 [251-500]
y SLJ - v43 - Mr '97 - p214 [51-250]
Cullen-DuPont, Kathryn - *The Encyclopedia of Women's History in America*
r ARBA - v28 - '97 - p336 [51-250]
r Choice - v34 - S '96 - p94 [51-250]
r RQ - v36 - Fall '96 - p127+ [501+]
yr SLJ - v42 - Ag '96 - p180 [51-250]
Cullimore, Stan - *George's Gang in Trouble (Illus. by S Hellard)*
c JB - v60 - Ag '96 - p147 [51-250]
c TES - Jl 5 '96 - pR6 [1-50]
Henrietta and the Big Sale (Illus. by John Farman)
c Books - v10 - Je '96 - p25 [51-250]
Cullinan, Bernice E - *A Jar of Tiny Stars (Illus. by Andi MacLeod)*
c HB Guide - v7 - Fall '96 - p364 [51-250]
c RT - v50 - O '96 - p156 [51-250]
Cullmann, Oscar - *Prayer in the New Testament*
Comw - v124 - Ja 17 '97 - p28 [251-500]
Intpr - v51 - Ja '97 - p80+ [501+]
Theol St - v58 - Mr '97 - p186 [251-500]
Culot, Paul - *Quatre Siecles De Reliure Belgique 1500-1900. Vol. 2*
BC - v45 - Sum '96 - p275+ [251-500]
Culpepper, R Alan - *Exploring the Gospel of John*
Am - v176 - Mr 8 '97 - p27+ [51-250]
Rel St Rev - v23 - Ja '97 - p72 [51-250]
John, the Son of Zebedee
Intpr - v50 - O '96 - p410+ [501+]
Culpin, Christopher - *Making History*
y TES - S 6 '96 - pR7 [501+]
Culshaw, Brian - *Optical Fiber Sensors. Vol. 3*
SciTech - v21 - Mr '97 - p80 [51-250]
Cultural Contributions of Black Americans. Electronic Media Version
Teach Mus - v4 - F '97 - p52 [51-250]
Culture Briefings
r BL - v93 - Ap 1 '97 - p1352+ [251-500]
Culver, Charles M - *Ethics at the Bedside*
Rel St Rev - v22 - O '96 - p342+ [51-250]
Culyer, A J - *Reforming Health Care Systems*
JEL - v35 - Mr '97 - p228 [51-250]
SciTech - v20 - D '96 - p38 [51-250]

Cumings, Bruce - *Korea's Place in the Sun*
Bus W - Mr 10 '97 - p14 [501+]
Econ - v342 - F 15 '97 - p12*+ [501+]
For Aff - v76 - My '97 - p106+ [501+]
KR - v64 - D 15 '96 - p1778 [251-500]
LATBR - Mr 23 '97 - p8 [501+]
LJ - v122 - F 15 '97 - p145 [51-250]
NL - v80 - Mr 10 '97 - p16+ [501+]
PW - v243 - D 16 '96 - p49 [51-250]
Trib Bks - Ap 13 '97 - p11 [501+]
Cumming, David - *Coasts*
c Magpies - v11 - Jl '96 - p38 [51-250]
Cumming, Robert - *Annotated Art*
y Emerg Lib - v24 - S '96 - p26 [1-50]
Cummings, A J G - *Industry, Business and Society in Scotland since 1700*
EHR - v111 - N '96 - p1305+ [251-500]
Cummings, Hugh C, Jr. - *Regulatory Proteins*
SciTech - v21 - Mr '97 - p42 [51-250]
Cummings, Jeffrey L - *Concise Guide to Neuropsychiatry and Behavioral Neurology*
AJPsych - v153 - S '96 - p1226 [251-500]
Cummings, Joe - *Mexico Handbook*
r BL - v93 - S 15 '96 - p212 [1-50]
r BWatch - v17 - S '96 - p5 [51-250]
Myanmar (Burma). 6th Ed.
r Quill & Q - v62 - S '96 - p22 [51-250]
South-East Asia. 8th Ed.
r Quill & Q - v62 - S '96 - p22 [51-250]
Cummings, Pat - *Talking with Artists. Vol. 2*
c RT - v50 - O '96 - p143 [1-50]
Cummings, Priscilla - *Toulouse: The Story of a Canada Goose (Illus. by A R Cohen)*
c HB Guide - v7 - Fall '96 - p286 [51-250]
Cummings, Terrance - *Too Hot to Cool Down*
BW - v26 - D 15 '96 - p13 [51-250]
Cummins, Herman Z - *Disordered Materials and Interfaces*
SciTech - v20 - S '96 - p13 [51-250]
Cummins, John - *Francis Drake: The Lives of a Hero*
HRNB - v25 - Fall '96 - p18 [251-500]
Sea H - Win '96 - p42 [51-250]
Six Ct J - v27 - Fall '96 - p923+ [501+]
Cumpian, Carlos - *Armadillo Charm*
A Lib - v27 - Ag '96 - p71 [51-250]
Trib Bks - Ap 20 '97 - p1+ [501+]
Cumyn, Alan - *Between Families and the Sky*
BIC - v26 - Mr '97 - p11 [501+]
Cunard, Nancy - *Negro: An Anthology*
Bl S - v26 - Fall '96 - p101 [1-50]
BW - v26 - O 20 '96 - p12 [51-250]
LJ - v121 - N 15 '96 - p93 [51-250]
Cunchillos, Jesus-Luis - *Banco De Datos Filologicos Semiticos Noroccidentales. Pt. 1*
r Rel St Rev - v23 - Ja '97 - p56 [51-250]
Cuneo, Michael W - *The Smoke of Satan*
KR - v65 - Mr 15 '97 - p429 [251-500]
Cuney Hare, Maud - *Negro Musicians and Their Music*
Choice - v34 - My '97 - p1508 [51-250]
Cunha, Euclides Da - *Os Sertoes*
Econ - v342 - Mr 1 '97 - p83+ [501+]
Cuninggim, Merrimon - *Uneasy Partners*
Rel St Rev - v23 - Ja '97 - p35+ [501+]
Cunkle, James R - *Stone Magic of the Ancients*
Bloom Rev - v16 - Jl '96 - p16 [51-250]
Cunliffe, Barry - *Iron Age Communities in Britain. 3rd Ed.*
CW - v89 - Jl '96 - p496+ [51-250]
Social Complexity and the Development of Towns in Iberia
Rel St Rev - v23 - Ja '97 - p65 [51-250]
Cunliffe, John - *Postman Pat's Holiday Packing (Illus. by J Hickson)*
c JB - v60 - D '96 - p228 [51-250]
Cunneen, Sally - *In Search of Mary*
BL - v92 - Ag '96 - p1859 [51-250]
CC - v114 - Mr 5 '97 - p242+ [501+]
CLW - v67 - Mr '97 - p31+ [501+]
Comw - v123 - N 22 '96 - p30 [251-500]
LJ - v121 - O 15 '96 - p64 [51-250]
Time - v148 - D 23 '96 - p66+ [501+]
Cunningham, Carol - *Horn of Darkness*
KR - v65 - Ja 15 '97 - p112 [251-500]
LJ - v122 - Ap 1 '97 - p117 [51-250]
NYTLa - v146 - Mr 19 '97 - pC17 [501+]
PW - v244 - F 10 '97 - p78+ [51-250]
Cunningham, David - *A Crow's Journey (Illus. by David Cunningham)*
c CLW - v66 - Je '96 - p46 [51-250]
c HB Guide - v7 - Fall '96 - p252 [51-250]

Cunningham, Donna - *The Moon in Your Life*
  Horoscope - v62 - S '96 - p15+ [501+]
Cunningham, Hilary - *God and Caesar at the Rio Grande*
  Rel St Rev - v23 - Ja '97 - p94 [51-250]
Cunningham, Hillary - *Canada. 5th Ed., Rev.*
  r Quill & Q - v63 - F '97 - p41 [51-250]
Cunningham, Hugh - *Children and Childhood in Western Society since 1500*
  AHR - v102 - F '97 - p85 [501+]
  Bkbird - v34 - Spr '96 - p56 [51-250]
Cunningham, Michael - *Flesh and Blood*
  Obs - S 15 '96 - p18* [51-250]
  VV - v42 - Ja 7 '97 - p41 [51-250]
Cunningham, Noble E, Jr. - *The Presidency of James Monroe*
  Choice - v34 - S '96 - p192 [51-250]
  HRNB - v25 - Fall '96 - p5+ [501+]
  TLS - My 24 '96 - p11+ [501+]
  VQR - v72 - Aut '96 - p115* [51-250]
  W&M Q - v54 - Ap '97 - p458+ [501+]
Cunningham, Patricia - *Pisces Guide to Venomous and Toxic Marine Life of the World*
  yr SB - v32 - O '96 - p206 [51-250]
Cunningham, Philip A - *Education for Shalom*
  Rel Ed - v91 - Fall '96 - p616 [1-50]
  Proclaiming Shalom
  Rel Ed - v91 - Fall '96 - p616 [1-50]
Cunningham, Steve - *Electronic Publishing on CD-ROM*
  LJ - v121 - O 1 '96 - p120 [51-250]
Cunningham, William P - *Environmental Science. 4th Ed.*
  R&R Bk N - v11 - D '96 - p19 [51-250]
Cunqueiro, Alvaro - *Papeles Que Fueron Vidas*
  Hisp - v79 - D '96 - p787+ [501+]
Cuomo, Mario - *Reason to Believe*
  NYTBR - v101 - N 10 '96 - p68 [51-250]
  PW - v243 - S 2 '96 - p121 [1-50]
Cuozzo, Steven - *It's Alive!*
  NYTBR - v101 - N 17 '96 - p35 [501+]
Cupitt, Don - *After God*
  KR - v65 - Ap 1 '97 - p515 [251-500]
  LJ - v122 - Ap 1 '97 - p98 [51-250]
Curious George ABC Adventure. Electronic Media Version
  c Ch BWatch - v7 - Ja '97 - p8 [51-250]
  c HB - v73 - Mr '97 - p219+ [501+]
Curl, James Steven - *Egyptomania: The Egyptian Revival*
  AJA - v101 - Ja '97 - p158+ [501+]
Curl, James Stevens - *Victorian Churches*
  BM - v138 - Ag '96 - p550+ [501+]
Curlee, Lynn - *Ships of the Air (Illus. by Lynn Curlee)*
  c BL - v93 - S 1 '96 - p121 [51-250]
  c CCB-B - v50 - O '96 - p53+ [51-250]
  c HB - v72 - N '96 - p757 [51-250]
  c HB Guide - v8 - Spr '97 - p131 [51-250]
  c SLJ - v42 - S '96 - p212 [51-250]
Curlee, Richard F - *Nature and Treatment of Stuttering. 2nd Ed.*
  SciTech - v20 - D '96 - p44 [51-250]
Curran, Joan Ferris - *Descendants of Salomon Bloch of Janowitz, Bohemia, and Baruch Wollman of Kempenin-Posen, Prussia*
  NGSQ - v85 - Mr '97 - p62+ [251-500]
Curran, William - *Strikeout: A Celebration of the Art of Pitching*
  Aethlon - v13 - Spr '96 - p227 [251-500]
Current, Dean - *Costs, Benefits, and Farmer Adoption of Agro-Forestry*
  JEL - v34 - S '96 - p1497 [51-250]
Current, Richard Nelson - *Loie Fuller: Goddess of Light*
  KR - v65 - Mr 15 '97 - p429+ [251-500]
  PW - v244 - Mr 31 '97 - p51 [51-250]
Current Biography 1940-
  r ASInt - v34 - O '96 - p13+ [51-250]
Current Biography on CD-ROM. Electronic Media Version
  r Choice - v34 - Mr '97 - p1147 [51-250]
  r LJ - v122 - Ap 15 '97 - p40 [1-50]
  yr SLJ - v42 - S '96 - p146 [51-250]
Current Issues in Public Health
  p Nature - v383 - S 5 '96 - p38 [51-250]
Current Issues SourceFile. Electronic Media Version
  r ARBA - v28 - '97 - p31 [251-500]
  r BL - v93 - Ja '97 - p880 [51-250]
  yr LJ - v122 - Ap 1 '97 - p136 [51-250]
Current Opinion in Colloid and Interface Science
  p Nature - v383 - S 5 '96 - p41 [251-500]
Current Practice of Medicine 1996. Vols. 1-4
  SciTech - v21 - Mr '97 - p50 [51-250]
Currey, Anna - *Tickling Tigers*
  c Bks Keeps - Jl '96 - p6 [1-50]
  c Ch BWatch - v6 - S '96 - p7 [51-250]

Currey, Cecil B - *Victory at Any Cost*
  BW - v26 - D 22 '96 - p7 [501+]
  KR - v64 - S 15 '96 - p1369 [251-500]
  Mar Crp G - v81 - F '97 - p78 [501+]
  NYTBR - v102 - F 2 '97 - p20 [51-250]
Currey, Richard - *Lost Highway*
  BL - v93 - My 15 '97 - p1560 [51-250]
  PW - v244 - Mr 31 '97 - p60 [51-250]
Currie, David - *EMU after Maastricht*
  Econ J - v106 - S '96 - p1471 [51-250]
Currie, Gregory - *Image and Mind*
  Choice - v34 - S '96 - p135 [51-250]
Currie, Ian - *Frosts, Freezes and Fairs*
  Nature - v386 - Ap 17 '97 - p667 [1-50]
Currie, Mark - *Metafiction*
  WLT - v70 - Aut '96 - p1039 [501+]
Currie, Pamela - *Literature as Social Action*
  MLR - v92 - Ja '97 - p238+ [501+]
Currie, Sheldon - *The Glace Bay Miners' Museum*
  Beav - v77 - F '97 - p38+ [501+]
Currie, Stephen - *We Have Marched Together*
  y BL - v93 - My 1 '97 - p1485+ [51-250]
Curry, Ann, 1948- - *The Limits of Tolerance*
  LJ - v122 - F 1 '97 - p114 [51-250]
Curry, Anne, 1948- - *Arms, Armies and Fortifications in the Hundred Years War*
  EHR - v112 - Ap '97 - p447 [501+]
  Arms, Armies and Fortifications in the Hundred Years' War
  Historian - v59 - Fall '96 - p183+ [501+]
Curry, Barbara K - *Sweet Words So Brave (Illus. by Jerry Butler)*
  cr BL - v93 - F 15 '97 - p1020 [251-500]
  c Bloom Rev - v16 - N '96 - p29 [51-250]
  cr BW - v26 - D 8 '96 - p21+ [501+]
  c Ch BWatch - v7 - F '97 - p1 [51-250]
  c Cur R - v36 - Ja '97 - p12 [51-250]
  c HB Guide - v8 - Spr '97 - p148 [51-250]
  c KR - v64 - D 1 '96 - p1734 [51-250]
  c PW - v243 - D 2 '96 - p60 [51-250]
Curry, Constance - *Silver Rights*
  Bloom Rev - v17 - Ja '97 - p18 [501+]
  BWatch - v17 - D '96 - p4 [1-50]
  y Kliatt - v31 - Mr '97 - p26 [51-250]
  NYTBR - v101 - N 17 '96 - p40 [51-250]
  NYTBR - v101 - D 8 '96 - p92 [1-50]
  PW - v243 - S 23 '96 - p73 [1-50]
Curry, David A - *UNIX Systems Programming for SVR4*
  SciTech - v20 - N '96 - p10 [51-250]
Curry, David P - *The Constitution of the Federal Republic of Germany*
  AAPSS-A - v546 - Jl '96 - p163+ [501+]
Curry, George E - *The Affirmative Action Debate*
  Bl S - v26 - Fall '96 - p101 [51-250]
Curry, Jane Leftwich - *Poland's Permanent Revolution*
  APSR - v90 - D '96 - p935+ [501+]
  JEL - v34 - S '96 - p1491 [51-250]
Curry, Jane Louise - *Moon Window*
  c CCB-B - v50 - N '96 - p94+ [51-250]
  c Ch BWatch - v7 - Ja '97 - p4 [51-250]
  c HB Guide - v8 - Spr '97 - p64 [51-250]
  c LATBR - S 15 '96 - p11 [51-250]
  c SLJ - v42 - D '96 - p120 [51-250]
Curry, Jennifer - *A Noisy Noise Annoys*
  c TES - Jl 26 '96 - pR8 [51-250]
  Wondercrump Poetry
  c Bks Keeps - N '96 - p10 [51-250]
  c TES - O 25 '96 - p7* [251-500]
Curry, Ramona - *Too Much a Good Thing*
  ABR - v18 - O '96 - p23+ [501+]
Curson, Jon - *Warblers of the Americas*
  r AB - v97 - Je 17 '96 - p2402 [51-250]
Curtain, R F - *An Introduction to Infinite-Dimensional Linear System Theory*
  SIAM Rev - v38 - S '96 - p536+ [501+]
Curti, Anna - *My Very First Nature Craft Book (Illus. by Anna Curti)*
  c BL - v93 - F 1 '97 - p942 [51-250]
  c PW - v243 - D 16 '96 - p61 [51-250]
  c SLJ - v43 - Mr '97 - p172 [51-250]
Curti, Danilo - *Musica E Liturgia Nella Riforma Tridentina*
  Lib - v18 - D '96 - p361 [1-50]
Curtin, Chris - *Irish Urban Cultures*
  Am Ethnol - v24 - F '97 - p246+ [251-500]
Curtin, Michael - *The Cove Shivering Club*
  Obs - D 15 '96 - p18* [51-250]
  TES - Ag 23 '96 - p27 [51-250]

  Redeeming the Wasteland
  CS - v26 - Ja '97 - p99+ [501+]
  J Am St - v30 - D '96 - p467+ [251-500]
  QJS - v83 - F '97 - p115+ [501+]
Curtin, Nancy J - *The United Irishmen*
  Bks & Cult - v2 - Ja '96 - p11+ [501+]
  EHR - v111 - S '96 - p1000 [251-500]
  JIH - v27 - Win '97 - p518+ [251-500]
Curtin, Sharon - *Mustang*
  BWatch - v17 - D '96 - p4 [1-50]
  LJ - v122 - Ja '97 - p137 [51-250]
Curtis, Chara M - *No One Walks on My Father's Moon (Illus. by Rebecca Hyland)*
  c BL - v93 - N 15 '96 - p587 [51-250]
  c Ch BWatch - v7 - Ja '97 - p3 [51-250]
  c PW - v243 - N 11 '96 - p75+ [51-250]
Curtis, Christopher Paul - *The Watsons Go to Birmingham--1963*
  y Emerg Lib - v24 - S '96 - p24 [1-50]
  y Kliatt - v30 - S '96 - p2 [1-50]
  c New Ad - v9 - Fall '96 - p327+ [501+]
  c RT - v50 - N '96 - p257 [51-250]
  c RT - v50 - Mr '97 - p479 [51-250]
  The Watsons Go to Birmingham--1963 (Burton). Audio Version
  y Kliatt - v31 - My '97 - p45+ [51-250]
  LJ - v122 - F 1 '97 - p127 [51-250]
  c Trib Bks - F 2 '97 - p7 [1-50]
Curtis, Elizabeth - *Touching the Past*
  TES - Ap 4 '97 - p12* [51-250]
Curtis, Jack - *Christmas in Calico*
  Roundup M - v4 - F '97 - p27 [51-250]
Curtis, James E - *Physical Activity in Human Experience*
  r Choice - v34 - My '97 - p1538 [51-250]
Curtis, Jamie Lee - *Tell Me Again about the Night I Was Born (Illus. by Laura Cornell)*
  c CBRS - v25 - S '96 - p2 [51-250]
  c CCB-B - v50 - Ja '97 - p166 [51-250]
  c HB - v73 - Ja '97 - p50+ [51-250]
  c HB Guide - v8 - Spr '97 - p11 [51-250]
  c Inst - v106 - Ja '97 - p52 [51-250]
  c SLJ - v42 - O '96 - p91 [51-250]
  c SLJ - v42 - D '96 - p28 [1-50]
Curtis, Jean-Louis - *Andromede*
  BL - v93 - Ja '97 - p827 [1-50]
Curtis, Lynn A - *The State of Families. Vol. 4*
  Fam in Soc - v77 - S '96 - p450+ [501+]
Curtis, Matt - *Elliot Drives Away (Illus. by Jenny Williams)*
  c HB Guide - v7 - Fall '96 - p249 [51-250]
Curtis, Munzee - *When the Big Dog Barks (Illus. by Susan Avishai)*
  c BL - v93 - Mr 1 '97 - p1170 [51-250]
  c CBRS - v25 - Ap '97 - p98 [1-50]
  c PW - v244 - Mr 17 '97 - p82 [51-250]
  c Trib Bks - My 4 '97 - p7 [51-250]
Curtis, Nancy C - *Black Heritage Sites*
  r ARBA - v28 - '97 - p153 [251-500]
  r BL - v93 - O 1 '96 - p367 [51-250]
  r Choice - v34 - D '96 - p588 [51-250]
  r R&R Bk N - v11 - N '96 - p17 [51-250]
Curtis, Sarah - *Health and Societies*
  Choice - v34 - O '96 - p312 [51-250]
Curtis, Susan - *Dancing to a Black Man's Tune*
  AHR - v101 - O '96 - p1287 [501+]
Curtis, Tony - *War Voices*
  WLT - v70 - Aut '96 - p961+ [501+]
Curtis, Tracy - *Creepy Cookies (Illus. by Jean Pidgeon)*
  c LATBR - O 20 '96 - p8 [51-250]
Curtis, William J R - *Modern Architecture since 1900. 3rd Ed.*
  LJ - v121 - O 1 '96 - p132 [1-50]
Curwen, Eliot - *Labrador Odyssey*
  Beav - v76 - D '96 - p43 [501+]
Curzon, Clare - *Close Quarters*
  BL - v93 - F 1 '97 - p927+ [51-250]
  KR - v65 - Ja 1 '97 - p22 [251-500]
  PW - v243 - D 16 '96 - p46 [51-250]
Curzon, M E J - *Kennedy's Paediatric Operative Dentistry. 4th Ed.*
  SciTech - v20 - S '96 - p42 [51-250]
Curzon, Susan Carol - *Managing the Interview*
  LAR - v98 - Je '96 - p318 [51-250]
Cuschieri, Alfred - *Clinical Surgery*
  SciTech - v21 - Mr '97 - p59 [1-50]
Cushing, James T - *Bohmian Mechanics and Quantum Theory*
  SciTech - v21 - Mr '97 - p21 [51-250]
Cushman, Clare - *The Supreme Court Justices. 2nd Ed.*
  yr CLW - v66 - Je '96 - p44 [51-250]

Cushman, Dan - *Cow Country Cookbook*
    CAY - v17 - Win '96 - p10 [51-250]
Valley of the Thousand Smokes
    PW - v243 - O 21 '96 - p72 [51-250]
Cushman, Doug - *Aunt Eater's Mystery Christmas*
  c Emerg Lib - v23 - My '96 - p54+ [51-250]
The Mystery of King Karfu (Illus. by Doug Cushman)
  c BL - v93 - Ja '97 - p866 [251-500]
  c CBRS - v25 - N '96 - p25 [51-250]
  c HB Guide - v8 - Spr '97 - p24 [51-250]
  c PW - v243 - O 21 '96 - p82 [51-250]
  c SLJ - v43 - F '97 - p74+ [51-250]
Cushman, Jean - *Do You Want to Bet?*
  c BL - v93 - Ap 1 '97 - p1341 [1-50]
Cushman, Karen - *The Ballad of Lucy Whipple*
  c BL - v92 - Ag '96 - p1904 [51-250]
  c BL - v93 - Ja '97 - p765 [1-50]
  c CBRS - v25 - S '96 - p11 [51-250]
  c CCB-B - v50 - S '96 - p9 [51-250]
  c CSM - v88 - S 26 '96 - pB3 [51-250]
  c HB - v72 - S '96 - p593 [251-500]
  c HB Guide - v8 - Spr '97 - p64 [51-250]
  c NYTBR - v102 - F 16 '97 - p25 [501+]
  c SLJ - v42 - Ag '96 - p142 [51-250]
  c SLJ - v42 - D '96 - p28 [1-50]
  y VOYA - v19 - D '96 - p268 [251-500]
Catherine, Called Birdy
  c JOYS - v10 - Fall '96 - p92+ [501+]
  y Kliatt - v30 - S '96 - p3 [1-50]
  y Sch Lib - v44 - N '96 - p168 [51-250]
Catherine, Called Birdy (Maberly). Audio Version
  y HB - v73 - Ja '97 - p85+ [501+]
The Midwife's Apprentice
  c Bkbird - v34 - Spr '96 - p52 [51-250]
  y EJ - v85 - N '96 - p131+ [251-500]
  c Emerg Lib - v23 - My '96 - p65 [51-250]
  y Emerg Lib - v24 - S '96 - p24 [1-50]
  c JOYS - v10 - Fall '96 - p92+ [501+]
  y Kliatt - v30 - N '96 - p6+ [51-250]
  y LA - v73 - O '96 - p431 [51-250]
The Midwife's Apprentice (Sterlin). Audio Version
  y HB - v73 - Ja '97 - p85+ [501+]
  y Kliatt - v31 - Mr '97 - p44 [51-250]
The Midwife's Apprentice (Coleman). Audio Version
  c PW - v244 - Ja 13 '97 - p36 [51-250]
Cushman, Thomas - *Notes from Underground*
    CS - v25 - S '96 - p685+ [501+]
    Russ Rev - v55 - O '96 - p727+ [501+]
This Time We Knew
    Choice - v34 - My '97 - p1573 [51-250]
    LJ - v121 - O 1 '96 - p106 [51-250]
Cusic, Don - *Cowboys and the Wild West*
  r J Am Cult - v18 - Win '95 - p108+ [51-250]
Cusick, Dawn - *The Lamp Shade Book*
    LJ - v122 - Ja '97 - p96 [51-250]
Paper and Fabric Mache
  c CAY - v17 - Fall '96 - p10 [51-250]
Cusick, Richie Tankersley - *Starstruck*
  y Kliatt - v31 - Ja '97 - p6 [51-250]
Summer of Secrets
  y Kliatt - v30 - N '96 - p8 [51-250]
Cusk, Rachel - *The Temporary*
    Books - v9 - S '95 - p22 [51-250]
    Woman's J - Ag '96 - p11 [1-50]
Cussler, Clive - *Iceberg (Greenwood). Audio Version*
  y Kliatt - v31 - Ja '97 - p42 [51-250]
The Mediterranean Caper (Greenwood). Audio Version
  y Kliatt - v31 - Ja '97 - p42 [51-250]
The Sea Hunters
    CSM - v88 - O 10 '96 - p10 [501+]
    KR - v64 - Ag 15 '96 - p1202+ [251-500]
  y SLJ - v43 - Mr '97 - p217 [51-250]
The Sea Hunters (Naughton). Audio Version
    BWatch - v18 - Mr '97 - p6 [1-50]
Shock Wave
    HMR - Spr '97 - p22+ [501+]
    PW - v243 - N 4 '96 - p71 [1-50]
Shock Wave (Prichard). Audio Version
  y Kliatt - v31 - Mr '97 - p45+ [51-250]
Cusumano, Michael A - *Microsoft Secrets*
    Obs - Ag 25 '96 - p18* [501+]
Cutler, Colleen D - *Nonlinear Dynamics and Time Series*
    SciTech - v21 - Mr '97 - p15 [51-250]
Cutler, Irving - *The Jews of Chicago*
    Choice - v34 - O '96 - p346 [51-250]
Cutler, Ivor - *Herbert--Five Stories (Illus. by Patrick Benson)*
  c Bks Keeps - v100 - S '96 - p9 [51-250]
Cutler, Jane - *Mr. Carey's Garden (Illus. by G Brian Karas)*
  c HB Guide - v7 - Fall '96 - p252 [51-250]

My Wartime Summers
  c PW - v244 - Mr 10 '97 - p69 [1-50]
Rats! (Illus. by Tracey Campbell Pearson)
  c HB Guide - v7 - Fall '96 - p290 [51-250]
Spaceman
  c BL - v93 - Mr 15 '97 - p1242 [51-250]
  c CCB-B - v50 - My '97 - p318 [51-250]
  c KR - v65 - F 15 '97 - p298 [51-250]
  c PW - v244 - F 24 '97 - p92 [51-250]
Cutler, Karan D - *Tantalizing Tomatoes*
    LJ - v122 - Ap 1 '97 - p114 [51-250]
Cutler, Neal R - *Understanding Alzheimer's Disease*
    BL - v93 - N 15 '96 - p554 [51-250]
    LJ - v121 - N 15 '96 - p82 [51-250]
    SB - v33 - My '97 - p104 [251-500]
Cutler, Thomas J - *The Battle of Leyte Gulf 23-26 October, 1944*
    Amerasia J - v22 - 2 '96 - p177+ [501+]
Cutrer, Thomas W - *Longstreet's Aide*
    JSH - v63 - F '97 - p182+ [51-250]
Cutrofello, Andrew - *The Owl at Dawn*
    Ethics - v107 - O '96 - p191+ [51-250]
Cutrona, Carolyn E - *Social Support in Couples*
    Readings - v12 - Mr '97 - p30 [51-250]
Cutter, Charles R - *The Legal Culture of Northern New Spain 1700-1810*
    AHR - v102 - F '97 - p134+ [251-500]
    PHR - v65 - N '96 - p663+ [501+]
    WHQ - v28 - Spr '97 - p72+ [251-500]
Cutter, Donald C - *California in 1792*
    CHR - v83 - Ja '97 - p162+ [51-250]
Cutting, Linda Katherine - *Memory Slips*
    BL - v93 - D 15 '96 - p703 [51-250]
    BW - v27 - F 2 '97 - p5 [501+]
    KR - v64 - N 15 '96 - p1648 [51-250]
    LJ - v122 - Ja '97 - p125 [51-250]
    NY - v72 - Ja 6 '97 - p73 [51-250]
    NYTBR - v102 - F 9 '97 - p18 [501+]
    PW - v243 - N 18 '96 - p57+ [51-250]
    Trib Bks - Ap 6 '97 - p3 [501+]
Cutts, Robert L - *An Empire of Schools*
    NYTBR - v102 - Mr 16 '97 - p31 [501+]
    PW - v244 - Ja 13 '97 - p65 [51-250]
Cuyler, Margery - *That's Good! That's Bad! (Illus. by David Catrow). Book and Audio Version*
  c SLJ - v43 - Mr '97 - p143 [51-250]
Cwiakala, Charles E - *Bermuda by Air*
  r Am Phil - v110 - N '96 - p1036 [251-500]
CyberHound's Guide to Internet Databases
  r BL - v93 - F 1 '97 - p963+ [251-500]
CyberHound's Guide to Internet Libraries
  r BL - v93 - F 1 '97 - p963+ [251-500]
CyberHound's Internet Guide to the Coolest Stuff Out There
  r ARBA - v28 - '97 - p624 [251-500]
Cymbala, Jim - *Fresh Wind, Fresh Fire*
    BL - v93 - Mr 1 '97 - p1066 [51-250]
Cyr, Dianne J - *The Human Resource Challenge of International Joint Ventures*
    Per Psy - v49 - Aut '96 - p717+ [501+]
Scaling the Ivory Tower
    R&R Bk N - v11 - D '96 - p33 [51-250]
Cyr, Gilles - *Songe Que Je Bouge*
    Can Lit - Win '96 - p180+ [501+]
Cyriax, J H - *Cyriax's Illustrated Manual of Orthopaedic Medicine. 2nd Ed.*
    SciTech - v21 - Mr '97 - p61 [51-250]
Cyriax, Oliver - *Crime: An Encyclopedia*
  r Arm Det - v30 - Win '97 - p117+ [251-500]
Cyrus, Kurt - *Tangle Town (Illus. by Kurt Cyrus)*
  c BL - v93 - My 1 '97 - p1500 [51-250]
  c CCB-B - v50 - Mr '97 - p244 [51-250]
  c KR - v65 - Ja 15 '97 - p139 [51-250]
  c PW - v244 - F 24 '97 - p90 [51-250]
  c SLJ - v43 - Mr '97 - p149+ [51-250]
Cytokine Yearbook. Vol. 1
    SciTech - v20 - N '96 - p35 [51-250]
Cytokines and Molecular Therapy
  p Nature - v383 - S 5 '96 - p36 [251-500]
Cytryn, Leon - *Growing Up Sad*
    Adoles - v31 - Win '96 - p991+ [51-250]
    AJPsych - v154 - F '97 - p279+ [501+]
    Choice - v34 - S '96 - p213+ [51-250]
    Readings - v11 - D '96 - p27 [51-250]
    TES - O 18 '96 - p8* [501+]
Czaj, Kathleen C - *I Hate Goodbyes! (Illus. by Mark Hick)*
  c Ch BWatch - v6 - D '96 - p2 [51-250]
Czajkowski, Chris - *Diary of a Wilderness Dweller*
    CG - v117 - Mr '97 - p79 [251-500]

Czarnecki, Jack - *The Portobello Cookbook*
    BL - v93 - Mr 15 '97 - p1215 [51-250]
    PW - v244 - My 5 '97 - p205 [51-250]
Czech, Kenneth P - *Snapshot: America Discovers the Camera*
  y BL - v93 - F 15 '97 - p1012 [51-250]
  c Cur R - v36 - Ja '97 - p13 [51-250]
  c HB Guide - v8 - Spr '97 - p137 [51-250]
  c KR - v64 - O 15 '96 - p1530 [51-250]
  c SLJ - v42 - D '96 - p127+ [51-250]
Czernecki, Stefan - *The Cricket's Cage (Illus. by Stefan Czernecki)*
  c PW - v244 - Mr 10 '97 - p65+ [51-250]
Zorah's Magic Carpet
  c HB Guide - v7 - Fall '96 - p252 [51-250]
Czerneda, Julie - *Great Careers for People Interested in Communications Technology*
  y SLJ - v42 - N '96 - p129 [51-250]
Cziko, Gary - *Without Miracles*
    BioSci - v46 - D '96 - p872+ [501+]

D

Daalen, Maria Van - *Het Geschenk, De Maker*
WLT - v71 - Win '97 - p168+ [251-500]
Dabrowski, Magdalena - *Kandinsky: Compositions*
Art J - v55 - Fall '96 - p84+ [501+]
Dabscheck, Braham - *The Struggle for Australian Industrial Relations*
JEL - v34 - D '96 - p2075 [51-250]
Dabydeen, Cyril - *Berbice Crossing*
Quill & Q - v63 - Ja '97 - p34 [51-250]
Born in Amazonia
WLT - v70 - Aut '96 - p1015 [501+]
Dabydeen, David - *The Counting House*
Obs - Ag 25 '96 - p16* [501+]
TLS - Ag 2 '96 - p23 [501+]
D'Acci, Julie - *Defining Women*
QJS - v83 - F '97 - p90+ [501+]
Dacey, John S - *Human Development. 3rd Ed.*
R&R Bk N - v11 - N '96 - p5 [51-250]
DaCosta Nunez, Ralph - *The New Poverty*
ChrPhil - v8 - O 3 '96 - p44 [51-250]
Nat - v263 - O 14 '96 - p27+ [501+]
Da Cunha, Derek - *The Evolving Pacific Power Structure*
WorldV - v13 - Ja '97 - p6 [51-250]
Dacyczyn, Amy - *The Tightwad Gazette III*
PW - v243 - D 2 '96 - p55 [51-250]
D'Adamo, Peter J - *Eat Right 4 Your Type*
y BL - v93 - D 1 '96 - p618 [51-250]
LJ - v122 - F 1 '97 - p99 [51-250]
PW - v243 - D 2 '96 - p58 [51-250]
Dadey, Debbie - *Shooting Star (Illus. by Scott Goto)*
c BL - v93 - Mr 15 '97 - p1245 [51-250]
c KR - v65 - Ap 1 '97 - p552 [51-250]
c PW - v244 - Mr 24 '97 - p83 [51-250]
Dadie, Bernard Binlin - *An African in Paris*
TranslRevS - v2 - D '96 - p10+ [51-250]
One Way
TranslRevS - v2 - D '96 - p11 [51-250]
Dadrian, Vahakn N - *The History of the Armenian Genocide*
MEJ - v50 - Aut '96 - p596+ [501+]
Slav R - v55 - Fall '96 - p676+ [501+]
Daduna, Joachim R - *Computer-Aided Transit Scheduling*
JEL - v34 - D '96 - p2140 [51-250]
Daemmrich, Ingrid G - *The Changing Seasons of Humor in Literature. 2nd Ed.*
Humor - v9 - 3 '96 - p406+ [501+]
Daeninckx, Didier - *Les Figurants*
WLT - v70 - Sum '96 - p649+ [501+]
D'Afflitto, Chiara - *L'Eta Di Savonarola*
BM - v138 - S '96 - p628+ [501+]
Daftary, Farhad - *The Assassin Legends*
Historian - v59 - Win '97 - p411+ [251-500]
Mediaeval Isma'ili History and Thought
Choice - v34 - Ja '97 - p812 [51-250]
MEJ - v51 - Win '97 - p154+ [51-250]
Parabola - v21 - N '96 - p121 [1-50]
Dag Hammarskjold Library - *UNBIS Thesaurus. English Ed.*
r J Gov Info - v23 - S '96 - p680 [51-250]
Daga Info
p WorldV - v13 - Ja '97 - p13 [51-250]
Daganzo, Carlos F - *Logistics Systems Analysis. 2nd Ed.*
JEL - v34 - D '96 - p2089 [51-250]
Dagenais, John - *The Ethics of Reading in Manuscript Culture*
CLS - v33 - 2 '96 - p187+ [501+]
Comp L - v48 - Fall '96 - p374+ [501+]
Dagg, Mel - *The Women on the Bridge*
y Can CL - v22 - Fall '96 - p117+ [501+]

Daglish, Neil D - *Education Policy-Making in England and Wales 1895-1911*
R&R Bk N - v12 - F '97 - p68 [51-250]
D'Agostino, Annette M - *Harold Lloyd: A Bio-Bibliography*
r FQ - v49 - Fall '95 - p63+ [51-250]
An Index to Short and Feature Film Reviews in the Moving Picture World
r J Pop F&TV - v24 - Win '97 - p185 [501+]
D'Agostino, Peter - *Transmissions: Theory and Practice for a New Video Aesthetics*
Afterimage - v24 - N '96 - p4 [1-50]
D'Aguiar, Fred - *Dear Future*
BL - v92 - Ag '96 - p1880+ [51-250]
Nat - v264 - Ja 13 '97 - p32+ [501+]
NYTBR - v101 - N 10 '96 - p56 [51-250]
WLT - v71 - Win '97 - p206 [501+]
The Longest Memory
y Emerg Lib - v24 - S '96 - p24 [1-50]
Daheim, Mary - *Nutty as a Fruitcake*
PW - v243 - S 30 '96 - p80 [51-250]
WSJ-MW - v78 - D 9 '96 - pA12 [1-50]
Dahl, Henry S - *Dahl's Law Dictionary: Spanish to English/English to Spanish. 2nd Ed.*
r ARBA - v28 - '97 - p219 [51-250]
Dahl, Per - *Svensk Ingenjorskonst Under Stormaktstiden*
T&C - v38 - Ja '97 - p246+ [501+]
Dahl, Roald - *Boy*
y Kliatt - v30 - S '96 - p4 [1-50]
Charlie and the Chocolate Factory
c New Ad - v9 - Fall '96 - p309+ [501+]
The Great Automatic Grammatizator and Other Stories
y JB - v60 - O '96 - p209 [51-250]
James and the Giant Peach (Illus. by Quentin Blake)
c Books - v10 - Je '96 - p25 [51-250]
James and the Giant Peach (Illus. by Lane Smith)
c HB Guide - v7 - Fall '96 - p290+ [51-250]
Dahlem Workshop on Regulation of Body Weight: Biological and Behavioral Mechanisms (1995: Berlin) - *Regulation of Body Weight*
SciTech - v20 - S '96 - p35 [51-250]
Dahlgren, Peter - *Television and the Public Sphere*
JMCQ - v73 - Aut '96 - p769+ [501+]
QJS - v83 - F '97 - p112+ [501+]
Dahlitz, Julie - *Future Legal Restraints on Arms Proliferation*
R&R Bk N - v12 - F '97 - p100 [51-250]
Dahlstrom, Carol Field - *Great Patchwork Collection*
LJ - v122 - Ap 15 '97 - p80 [1-50]
Dahotre, Narendra B - *Elevated Temperature Coatings*
SciTech - v20 - N '96 - p64 [51-250]
Dahrendorf, Ralf - *LSE: A History of the London School of Economics and Political Science 1895-1995*
AHR - v102 - F '97 - p110+ [501+]
Albion - v28 - Sum '96 - p359+ [501+]
EHR - v111 - S '96 - p947+ [501+]
Daiber, Hans - *The Islamic Concept of Belief in the 4th/10th Century*
MEJ - v50 - Aut '96 - p630 [51-250]
Daigle, France - *Real Life*
TranslRevS - v2 - D '96 - p22 [51-250]
Daigneault, Sylvie - *Bruno Springs Up*
c Quill & Q - v63 - Ja '97 - p38+ [251-500]
Dailey, Franklyn E - *Electronic Imaging Applications and Markets*
R&R Bk N - v11 - D '96 - p32 [51-250]
Dailey, Janet - *Illusions*
BL - v93 - Mr 1 '97 - p1067 [51-250]
KR - v65 - F 1 '97 - p158 [251-500]
PW - v244 - F 3 '97 - p92 [51-250]

Notorious (Larson). Audio Version
y Kliatt - v31 - Ja '97 - p43 [51-250]
Daily, Robert - *Elvis Presley: The King of Rock 'n' Roll*
y BL - v93 - Ap 1 '97 - p1321 [51-250]
c SLJ - v43 - F '97 - p112+ [51-250]
The Daily Mail Centenary CD-ROM. Electronic Media Version
HT - v46 - F 12 '97 - p48 [51-250]
Daitch, Richard W - *Northwest Territories*
c HB Guide - v7 - Fall '96 - p385 [1-50]
Daix, Pierre - *Braudel*
Choice - v34 - D '96 - p568 [1-50]
Dakers, Caroline - *Clouds: The Biography of a Country House*
VS - v39 - Spr '96 - p446+ [501+]
Dakolias, Maria - *The Judicial Sector in Latin America and the Caribbean*
JEL - v34 - D '96 - p2080 [51-250]
Dakos, Kalli - *The Goof Who Invented Homework and Other School Poems (Illus. by Denise Brunkus)*
c BL - v93 - S 15 '96 - p234+ [51-250]
c HB Guide - v8 - Spr '97 - p151 [51-250]
c SLJ - v42 - S '96 - p213 [51-250]
Dalby, Liza C - *Kimono: Fashioning Culture*
Historian - v59 - Win '97 - p404 [51-250]
Dalby, Richard - *Shivers for Christmas*
Arm Det - v30 - Win '97 - p118+ [251-500]
Dalcher, Katharina - *Studia Ietina IV*
AJA - v100 - O '96 - p777+ [501+]
Dal Co, Francesco - *Tadao Ando: Complete Works*
NYTBR - v101 - D 8 '96 - p59 [51-250]
Dale, Ann - *Achieving Sustainable Development*
JEL - v35 - Mr '97 - p298 [51-250]
R&R Bk N - v11 - D '96 - p24 [51-250]
Dale, David - *The 100 Things Everyone Needs to Know about Australia*
Aust Bk R - Je '96 - p65 [251-500]
Dale, Elizabeth - *Maxie's Music*
c TES - Jl 5 '96 - pR6 [1-50]
Dale, Frank - *Delaware Diary*
KR - v64 - My 1 '96 - p657+ [251-500]
Dale, John - *Out West*
TLS - Ja 17 '97 - p20 [501+]
Dale, Mitzi - *What's Tuesday?*
y Quill & Q - v63 - Mr '97 - p79+ [251-500]
Dale, Penny - *Daisy Rabbit's Tree House*
c ECEJ - v23 - Sum '96 - p224 [51-250]
Ten out of Bed (Illus. by Penny Dale)
c Bks Keeps - Jl '96 - p6 [51-250]
c JB - v60 - Ag '96 - p141 [51-250]
c Magpies - v11 - S '96 - p45 [1-50]
Dale, Ruth Jean - *Runaway Wedding*
Quill & Q - v62 - Jl '96 - p44 [501+]
Dale, Stephen - *McLuhan's Children*
BIC - v25 - N '96 - p17+ [501+]
CF - v75 - N '96 - p36+ [501+]
Quill & Q - v62 - Ag '96 - p38 [251-500]
Dale, Virginia - *Never Marry in Morocco*
BL - v93 - S 1 '96 - p61 [51-250]
Daleiden, Joseph L - *The Final Superstition*
Skeptic - v4 - '96 - p102+ [501+]
Daleo, Morgan Simone - *Curriculum of Love (Illus. by Frank Riccio)*
c Bloom Rev - v17 - Ja '97 - p21 [51-250]
Dales, Richard C - *The Problem of the Rational Soul in the Thirteenth Century*
Isis - v88 - Mr '97 - p136+ [501+]
Daley, Anthony - *Steel, State, and Labor*
Choice - v34 - S '96 - p175 [51-250]
Daley, Brian - *Return of the Jedi*
LJ - v121 - N 15 '96 - p92 [51-250]

131

Daley, Robert - *Nowhere to Run*
BL - v92 - Ag '96 - p1853 [251-500]
Daley, Todd M - *Apples and Oranges*
Math T - v89 - S '96 - p512 [51-250]
Dalgish, Gerard M - *Random House Webster's Dictionary of American English*
r Choice - v34 - Ap '97 - p1314 [51-250]
Dalhouse, Mark Taylor - *An Island in the Lake of Fire*
BL - v93 - S 15 '96 - p187 [51-250]
LJ - v121 - O 1 '96 - p83 [51-250]
Dalibard, Jill - *Deed of Gift*
BIC - v25 - N '96 - p6+ [501+]
Dalit International Newsletter
p WorldV - v12 - Jl '96 - p11 [51-250]
Dalkey, Kara - *Bijapur*
y BL - v93 - Ap 1 '97 - p1283 [51-250]
KR - v65 - Mr 1 '97 - p340 [51-250]
LJ - v122 - Ap 15 '97 - p123 [51-250]
PW - v244 - Ap 28 '97 - p54 [51-250]
Goa
y BL - v92 - Ag '96 - p1888 [51-250]
y BL - v92 - Ag '96 - p1891 [1-50]
MFSF - v91 - D '96 - p91+ [501+]
PW - v243 - Jl 22 '96 - p231 [51-250]
Little Sister
y BL - v93 - O 1 '96 - p340+ [51-250]
y CBRS - v25 - S '96 - p11 [1-50]
y CCB-B - v50 - D '96 - p132 [51-250]
c HB Guide - v8 - Spr '97 - p64 [51-250]
c SLJ - v42 - D '96 - p120 [51-250]
y VOYA - v19 - F '97 - p334+ [251-500]
Dalla, Ismail - *The Emerging Asian Bond Market*
JEL - v34 - S '96 - p1435 [51-250]
Dallago, Bruno - *Economic Institutions, Markets and Competition*
JEL - v35 - Mr '97 - p290 [51-250]
Dallas, Gregor - *1815: The Roads to Waterloo*
Spec - v278 - F 1 '97 - p32+ [501+]
TLS - Ja 24 '97 - p29 [501+]
Dallas, Sandra - *The Diary of Mattie Spenser*
BL - v93 - My 15 '97 - p1560 [51-250]
KR - v65 - Ap 1 '97 - p482 [251-500]
PW - v244 - My 5 '97 - p200 [51-250]
The Persian Pickle Club
LJ - v121 - D '96 - p180 [51-250]
The Persian Pickle Club (Kelly). Audio Version
y Kliatt - v31 - Ja '97 - p44+ [51-250]
Dallek, Robert - *Hail to the Chief*
y BL - v92 - Ag '96 - p1862+ [501+]
y BL - v92 - Ag '96 - p1890 [1-50]
BW - v26 - Ag 25 '96 - p3+ [501+]
NYTBR - v101 - S 29 '96 - p21 [51-250]
Wil Q - v20 - Aut '96 - p93 [251-500]
Dalley, Robert J - *Surfin' Guitars. 2nd Ed.*
r R&R Bk N - v11 - D '96 - p56 [51-250]
Dally, Judy - *Friendly Street Reader. No. 20*
Aust Bk R - Ag '96 - p61 [501+]
D'Almeida, Irene Assiba - *Francophone African Women Writers*
FR - v70 - D '96 - p317+ [251-500]
Dalmia, Vasudha - *Representing Hinduism*
Rel St Rev - v23 - Ja '97 - p96 [51-250]
Dalokay, Vedat - *Sister Shako and Kolo the Goat*
c RT - v50 - F '97 - p424+ [51-250]
Dalos, Gyorgy - *A Kulcsfigura*
WLT - v70 - Aut '96 - p997+ [501+]
Daloz, Laurent A - *Common Fire*
Choice - v34 - D '96 - p694 [51-250]
ChrPhil - v8 - Ag 8 '96 - p50 [51-250]
Dalrymple, T A - *Fishing for Trouble*
c Ch BWatch - v7 - Ja '97 - p4 [51-250]
Dalrymple, Theodore - *If Symptoms Still Persist*
Spec - v277 - D 7 '96 - p54 [51-250]
So Little Done
Books - v9 - S '95 - p8+ [251-500]
Dalrymple, William - *From the Holy Mountain*
Obs - Ap 6 '97 - p15* [501+]
Dalsass, Diana - *The New Good Cake Book*
LJ - v121 - N 15 '96 - p84 [51-250]
PW - v243 - O 7 '96 - p71 [51-250]
Dalsimer, Adele M - *America's Eye*
ILS - v16 - Spr '97 - p26+ [501+]
Dalton, Greg - *My Own Backyard*
ILS - v15 - Fall '96 - p31 [51-250]
Dalton, Margot - *First Impression*
PW - v244 - F 17 '97 - p216 [51-250]
Dalton, Mary - *Allowing the Light*
Can Lit - Win '96 - p142+ [501+]
Wild on the Crest
BIC - v25 - O '96 - p25 [501+]

Dalton, Paul - *Conquest, Anarchy and Lordship*
Specu - v72 - Ja '97 - p135+ [501+]
Dalton, Roque - *Small Hours of the Night*
BW - v27 - Ja 26 '97 - p12 [51-250]
BWatch - v17 - N '96 - p9 [51-250]
Nat - v263 - S 30 '96 - p32+ [501+]
PW - v243 - Jl 22 '96 - p236 [51-250]
TranslRevS - v2 - D '96 - p33 [51-250]
Dalton, Russell J - *The Green Rainbow*
AAPSS-A - v549 - Ja '97 - p193+ [501+]
D'Aluisio, Faith - *Women in the Material World*
y BL - v93 - S 15 '96 - p186 [51-250]
Bloom Rev - v16 - S '96 - p31 [501+]
CC - v114 - Ja 1 '97 - p22+ [251-500]
E Mag - v7 - N '96 - p50 [51-250]
LATBR - D 8 '96 - p11 [251-500]
LJ - v121 - S 15 '96 - p75 [51-250]
Pet PM - v25 - O '96 - p11 [51-250]
Daly, Ann - *Done into Dance*
Choice - v34 - S '96 - p139 [501+]
TDR - v40 - Win '96 - p173 [51-250]
Daly, Brenda - *Lavish Self-Divisions*
Choice - v34 - Mr '97 - p1160 [51-250]
Daly, Charles P - *The Magazine Publishing Industry*
JEL - v35 - Mr '97 - p250 [51-250]
Daly, Conor - *Outside Agency*
BL - v93 - Mr 15 '97 - p1228+ [51-250]
KR - v65 - Ap 1 '97 - p504+ [51-250]
LJ - v122 - Ap 1 '97 - p133 [51-250]
PW - v244 - F 24 '97 - p66 [51-250]
Daly, Herman E - *Beyond Growth*
Choice - v34 - F '97 - p1010 [51-250]
JEL - v35 - Mr '97 - p271 [51-250]
Daly, Kerry J - *Families and Time*
R&R Bk N - v12 - F '97 - p52 [51-250]
Daly, M W - *The Sudan*
TLS - Ag 2 '96 - p31 [501+]
Daly, Margo - *Australia: The Rough Guide*
r FEER - v160 - Mr 27 '97 - p52+ [501+]
Daly, Niki - *Why the Sun and Moon Live in the Sky (Illus. by Niki Daly)*
c RT - v50 - S '96 - p52 [51-250]
Daly, Patricia Ellen Martin - *Envisioning the New Adam*
AL - v68 - S '96 - p670 [51-250]
Dalzell, Alexander - *The Criticism of Didactic Poetry*
Choice - v34 - My '97 - p1492+ [51-250]
Dalzell, Tom - *Flappers 2 Rappers*
yr ARBA - v28 - ' 97 - p387 [51-250]
Dalziel, Pamela - *An Indiscretion in the Life of an Heiress and Other Stories*
ELT - v40 - 2 '97 - p196+ [501+]
Dalziel, Paul - *The New Zealand Macroeconomy. 2nd Ed.*
JEL - v35 - Mr '97 - p209 [51-250]
Dam, Kenneth W - *Cryptography's Role in Securing the Information Society*
For Aff - v76 - Mr '97 - p177 [51-250]
Dam, Nikolaos Van - *The Struggle for Power in Syria*
Choice - v34 - N '96 - p529 [51-250]
For Aff - v75 - N '96 - p165 [51-250]
MEJ - v51 - Win '97 - p152 [51-250]
Damas, David - *Bountiful Island*
GJ - v162 - Jl '96 - p236 [51-250]
Damasceno, Leslie Hawkins - *Cultural Space and Theatrical Conventions in the Works of Oduvaldo Vianna Filho*
R&R Bk N - v12 - F '97 - p83 [51-250]
D'Amato, Alfonse - *Power, Pasta, and Politics*
PSQ - v111 - Win '96 - p695+ [501+]
D'Amato, Antoinette - *Cooking and Canning with Mamma D'Amato*
PW - v244 - Ap 21 '97 - p68 [51-250]
D'Amato, Barbara - *The Doctor, the Murder, the Mystery*
y Kliatt - v31 - My '97 - p28 [51-250]
Killer
y BL - v93 - Ja '97 - p763 [1-50]
D'Ambrosio, Charles - *The Point: Stories*
NYTBR - v101 - D 22 '96 - p20 [51-250]
PW - v243 - S 2 '96 - p122 [1-50]
Dame, Frederick William - *Jean-Jacques Rousseau in American Literature*
R&R Bk N - v12 - F '97 - p87 [51-250]
Damian, Carol - *The Virgin of the Andes*
HAHR - v76 - My '96 - p790+ [251-500]
D'Amico, Francine - *Women in World Politics*
NWSA Jnl - v9 - Spr '97 - p107+ [501+]
D'Amico, Joan - *The Math Chef (Illus. by Tina Cash-Walsh)*
c PW - v244 - Ja 20 '97 - p403 [51-250]
c SLJ - v43 - Mr '97 - p198 [51-250]
The Science Chef (Illus. by Tina Cash-Walsh)
c Emerg Lib - v23 - My '96 - p45 [51-250]

The Science Chef Travels around the World (Illus. by Tina Cash-Walsh)
c SB - v32 - Ag '96 - p177+ [51-250]
Damien, Robert - *Bibliotheque Et Etat*
Choice - v34 - D '96 - p566 [1-50]
r CPR - v16 - Ap '96 - p86+ [501+]
Damien Hirst: No Sense of Absolute Corruption
BM - v138 - Ag '96 - p565+ [501+]
D'Amiens, Girart - *Escanor: Roman Arthurien En Vers De La Fin Du XIIIe Siecle. Vols. 1-2*
Specu - v72 - Ja '97 - p110+ [501+]
Damisch, Hubert - *The Judgment of Paris*
Choice - v34 - O '96 - p266 [51-250]
R&R Bk N - v11 - N '96 - p60 [51-250]
The Origin of Perspective
JAAC - v55 - Win '97 - p84+ [501+]
Damjanov, Ivan - *Histopathology: A Color Atlas and Textbook*
SciTech - v20 - N '96 - p38 [51-250]
Dammaj, Zayd Muti - *The Hostage*
TranslRevS - v1 - My '95 - p14 [51-250]
Damon, Duane - *When This Cruel War Is Over*
c BL - v92 - Ag '96 - p1897 [51-250]
c HB Guide - v8 - Spr '97 - p173 [51-250]
y SLJ - v42 - Ag '96 - p167 [51-250]
y VOYA - v19 - O '96 - p227 [51-250]
Damon-Moore, Helen - *Magazines for the Millions*
J Am Cult - v18 - Win '95 - p109+ [501+]
Damousi, Joy - *Gender and War*
J Mil H - v61 - Ap '97 - p386+ [501+]
Damp, Dennis V - *Post Office Jobs*
JEL - v34 - S '96 - p1448 [51-250]
Damrosch, David - *We Scholars*
AS - v66 - Win '97 - p148+ [501+]
Bks & Cult - v2 - S '96 - p26+ [501+]
RP - v59 - Win '97 - p155+ [501+]
TCR - v98 - Spr '97 - p537+ [501+]
Damrosch, Leo - *The Sorrows of the Quaker Jesus*
Choice - v34 - F '97 - p979 [51-250]
Dams, Jeanne M - *The Body in the Transept*
Arm Det - v29 - Sum '96 - p280 [51-250]
Trouble in the Town Hall
BL - v93 - N 1 '96 - p482+ [51-250]
KR - v64 - S 1 '96 - p1273+ [51-250]
LJ - v121 - O 1 '96 - p130 [51-250]
NYTBR - v102 - F 2 '97 - p22 [51-250]
Dana, Barbara - *Young Joan*
y Kliatt - v31 - My '97 - p5 [51-250]
c PW - v244 - F 10 '97 - p85 [1-50]
Danahay, Martin A - *A Community of One*
VS - v39 - Aut '95 - p70+ [501+]
Danaher, Kevin - *50 Years Is Enough*
CS - v26 - Mr '97 - p184+ [501+]
Corporations Are Gonna Get Your Mama
Prog - v61 - Ja '97 - p38 [501+]
Fighting for the Soul of Brazil
HAHR - v77 - My '97 - p350+ [251-500]
Danai, Kourosh - *ASME Dynamic Systems and Control Division*
SciTech - v21 - Mr '97 - p84 [51-250]
Danbom, David B - *Born in the Country*
AHR - v102 - F '97 - p167+ [251-500]
Historian - v58 - Sum '96 - p844+ [501+]
JSH - v63 - F '97 - p220+ [501+]
Danchev, Alex - *International Perspectives on the Yugoslav Conflict*
Choice - v34 - N '96 - p530 [51-250]
Danchin, Pierre - *The Prologues and Epilogues of the Eighteenth Century. Pt. 2*
RES - v47 - Ag '96 - p420+ [501+]
Dancyger, Ken - *The Technique of Film and Video Editing. 2nd Ed.*
SciTech - v21 - Mr '97 - p98 [51-250]
Dandaneau, Steven P - *A Town Abandoned*
AJS - v102 - Ja '97 - p1204+ [501+]
Choice - v34 - O '96 - p366 [51-250]
D'Andrade, Roy - *The Development of Cognitive Anthropology*
Am Ethnol - v23 - N '96 - p934+ [501+]
Dandrey, Patrick - *Actes Du Colloque La Fontaine, De Chateau-Thierry A Vaux-Le-Vicomte. Pt. 2*
MLR - v91 - Jl '96 - p723 [251-500]
Dandy, Evelyn B - *Black Communications*
BWatch - v17 - D '96 - p5 [51-250]
Danforth, Loring M - *The Macedonian Conflict*
Am Ethnol - v24 - F '97 - p240+ [501+]
APSR - v90 - D '96 - p953+ [501+]
TLS - Ja 31 '97 - p24 [501+]
Dang, Duc - *Con Manh Ao Trang*
BL - v93 - My 15 '97 - p1568 [1-50]

Dang, Tran Huan - *Hanh Trinh Mot Hat O*
   BL - v93 - My 15 '97 - p1568 [1-50]
Dangarembga, Tsitsi - *Nervous*
   TSWL - v15 - Fall '96 - p231+ [501+]
Danger, Pierre - *Pulsion Et Desir Dans Les Romans Et Nouvelles De Guy De Maupassant*
   MLR - v92 - Ja '97 - p201 [251-500]
Dangerous Bedfellows - *Policing Public Sex*
   LJ - v122 - Mr 15 '97 - p79 [51-250]
Dangerous Liaisons. Audio Version
   TES - D 27 '96 - p27 [51-250]
Dangler, Jamie Faricellia - *Hidden in the Home*
   CS - v25 - S '96 - p639+ [501+]
Dani, A H - *History of Humanity. Vol. 2*
   r ARBA - v28 - '97 - p216 [51-250]
   R&R Bk N - v11 - N '96 - p8 [51-250]
Danica, Elly - *Beyond Don't*
   Quill & Q - v63 - F '97 - p50 [51-250]
Daniel, Clay - *Death in Milton's Poetry*
   Sev Cent N - v54 - Spr '96 - p2+ [501+]
Daniel, Clifton Truman - *Growing Up with My Grandfather*
   Pres SQ - v26 - Sum '96 - p905 [51-250]
Daniel, Douglass K - *Lou Grant*
   JMCQ - v73 - Aut '96 - p759+ [501+]
Daniel, John - *Looking After*
   BW - v27 - Ja 5 '97 - p13 [51-250]
   KR - v64 - Ag 15 '96 - p1203 [251-500]
   LJ - v121 - O 1 '96 - p88+ [51-250]
   PW - v243 - S 9 '96 - p71 [51-250]
Daniel, LaNelle - *American Drama Criticism: Supplement IV to the Second Edition*
   r ARBA - v28 - '97 - p522 [51-250]
   R&R Bk N - v11 - D '96 - p74 [51-250]
Daniel, Larry J - *Shiloh: The Battle That Changed the Civil War*
   y BL - v93 - F 1 '97 - p923 [51-250]
   KR - v65 - F 1 '97 - p188 [251-500]
   LJ - v122 - Mr 15 '97 - p73 [51-250]
   PW - v244 - Mr 3 '97 - p58+ [51-250]
Daniel, Ruby - *Ruby of Cochin: An Indian Jewish Woman Remembers*
   Rel St Rev - v22 - O '96 - p355 [51-250]
Daniel, Stephen H - *The Philosophy of Jonathan Edwards*
   CH - v65 - S '96 - p506+ [501+]
   RM - v50 - D '96 - p396+ [501+]
   W&M Q - v53 - Jl '96 - p658+ [501+]
Daniel, Yvonne - *Rumba: Dance and Social Change in Contemporary Cuba*
   HAHR - v77 - F '97 - p97 [251-500]
   TDR - v40 - Win '96 - p164+ [501+]
Danieli, Yael - *International Responses to Traumatic Stress*
   R&R Bk N - v12 - F '97 - p55 [51-250]
Daniell, Christopher - *Death and Burial in Medieval England*
   HT - v46 - O '96 - p55 [51-250]
Daniell, David - *William Tyndale: A Biography*
   CHR - v82 - O '96 - p704+ [501+]
   EHR - v112 - Ap '97 - p417+ [501+]
   Rel St Rev - v23 - Ap '97 - p191 [51-250]
Daniell, Rosemary - *The Woman Who Spilled Words All over Herself*
   KR - v65 - Mr 1 '97 - p346+ [51-250]
   PW - v244 - Mr 24 '97 - p69 [51-250]
D'Aniello, Charles A - *Teaching Bibliographic Skills in History*
   Lib & Cul - v32 - Win '97 - p154+ [501+]
Danielou, Jean - *Prayer: The Mission of the Church*
   BL - v93 - S 1 '96 - p36+ [51-250]
Daniels, Bruce C - *Puritans at Play*
   JIH - v27 - Spr '97 - p705+ [501+]
   NEQ - v69 - D '96 - p689+ [501+]
   Rel St Rev - v22 - O '96 - p357 [51-250]
Daniels, Cynthia R - *At Women's Expense*
   Signs - v22 - Aut '96 - p231+ [501+]
Daniels, David - *Murder at the Baseball Hall of Fame*
   Arm Det - v29 - Fall '96 - p498 [251-500]
Daniels, Harry - *An Introduction to Vygotsky*
   Choice - v34 - Mr '97 - p1243 [51-250]
Daniels, Jeremy - *Anfernee Hardaway*
   c Ch BWatch - v6 - Jl '96 - p3 [1-50]
   c HB Guide - v7 - Fall '96 - p360 [51-250]
Daniels, Jim - *Letters to America*
   ABR - v17 - Ag '96 - p17+ [501+]
   Bl S - v26 - Fall '96 - p101 [1-50]
Daniels, Lucy - *Kitten in the Cold*
   c Bks Keeps - N '96 - p21 [1-50]
Daniels, Martha - *Missouri Nature Viewing Guide*
   r J Gov Info - v23 - S '96 - p587 [51-250]

Daniels, Morna - *Cote D'Ivoire*
   r ARBA - v28 - '97 - p52+ [51-250]
   r R&R Bk N - v12 - F '97 - p21 [1-50]
Daniels, Norman - *Benchmarks of Fairness for Health Care Reform*
   Hast Cen R - v26 - S '96 - p40 [1-50]
Daniels, P W - *Service Industries in the World Economy*
   GJ - v162 - Jl '96 - p229 [251-500]
Daniels, Patricia - *The First Christmas (Illus. by Sue Ellen Brown)*
   c HB Guide - v7 - Fall '96 - p310 [1-50]
   Noah's Ark (Illus. by Kathy Rusynyk)
   c HB Guide - v7 - Fall '96 - p308 [1-50]
Daniels, Peter T - *The World's Writing Systems*
   r ARBA - v28 - '97 - p376 [51-250]
Daniels, Ray - *Designing Great Beers*
   BWatch - v18 - F '97 - p1+ [51-250]
Daniels, Rebecca - *Women Stage Directors Speak*
   Am Theat - v14 - Ja '97 - p74 [51-250]
   Choice - v34 - F '97 - p976 [51-250]
   LJ - v122 - Ja '97 - p100+ [51-250]
Daniels, Roger - *Coming to America*
   BW - v26 - D 15 '96 - p1 [1-50]
Daniels, Ronald J - *Corporate Decision-Making in Canada*
   J Gov Info - v23 - S '96 - p612 [51-250]
Danielson, Charlotte - *Enhancing Professional Practice*
   EL - v54 - D '96 - p94 [51-250]
Danielson, Michael N - *Home Team*
   PW - v244 - Mr 3 '97 - p61 [51-250]
   Trib Bks - Mr 30 '97 - p1+ [501+]
Daniken, Erich Von - *The Return of the Gods*
   PW - v244 - Ja 13 '97 - p66+ [501+]
Danilkin, A - *Behavioural Ecology of Siberian and European Roe Deer*
   Choice - v34 - O '96 - p306 [51-250]
Danilov, Victor J - *University and College Museums, Galleries, and Related Facilities*
   r ARBA - v28 - '97 - p33 [51-250]
   r Choice - v34 - D '96 - p588 [51-250]
   r R&R Bk N - v11 - N '96 - p12 [51-250]
Danish Council of Ethics - *Extreme Prematurity*
   Hast Cen R - v26 - Mr '96 - p48 [1-50]
D'Anjou, Leo - *Social Movements and Cultural Change*
   Choice - v34 - D '96 - p695 [51-250]
Dankner, Amnon - *Ha-Kayits Shel Rina Oster*
   BL - v93 - Mr 1 '97 - p1115 [1-50]
Dann, Jack - *The Memory Cathedral*
   PW - v243 - O 7 '96 - p68 [1-50]
Dannenberg, Linda - *French Tarts*
   LJ - v122 - Ap 15 '97 - p110 [51-250]
   PW - v244 - Ap 7 '97 - p88 [51-250]
Dannenberg, Matthias - *Schonheit Des Lebens*
   Ger Q - v69 - Spr '96 - p212+ [501+]
Dannhaeuser, Norbert - *Two Towns in Germany*
   AJS - v102 - Ja '97 - p1183+ [501+]
Danopoulos, Constantine P - *The Political Role of the Military*
   Choice - v34 - My '97 - p1572 [51-250]
Dansk-Norsk Myntpris-Arbok 1995/6
   Coin W - v37 - N 18 '96 - p88 [51-250]
Danson, F M - *Advances in Environmental Remote Sensing*
   GJ - v162 - Jl '96 - p219+ [501+]
Danson, Michael W - *Small Firm Formation and Regional Economic Development*
   Econ J - v107 - Ja '97 - p289 [51-250]
Danspeckgruber, Wolfgang F - *The Iraqi Aggression against Kuwait*
   Choice - v34 - D '96 - p686 [51-250]
   MEJ - v50 - Aut '96 - p629+ [501+]
   R&R Bk N - v11 - N '96 - p14 [51-250]
Dante Alighieri - *Dante Alighieri's Divine Comedy. Vols. 1-2*
   LJ - v122 - Mr 15 '97 - p64 [51-250]
   Dante, Monarchia
   Choice - v34 - O '96 - p284 [51-250]
   TLS - O 25 '96 - p27 [501+]
   Dante's Hell (Ellis)
   Lon R Bks - v18 - Ag 22 '96 - p27+ [501+]
   Dante's Inferno (Musa)
   TLS - O 25 '96 - p27 [501+]
   De Vulgari Eloquentia (Botterill)
   Choice - v34 - Ap '97 - p1343+ [51-250]
   The Divine Comedy
   CLS - v33 - 1 '96 - p35+ [501+]
   The Divine Comedy (Mandelbaum)
   Lon R Bks - v18 - Ag 22 '96 - p27+ [501+]
   The Divine Comedy of Dante Alighieri (Durling). Vol. 1
   Choice - v34 - O '96 - p284+ [51-250]
   TranslRevS - v2 - D '96 - p28 [51-250]

   The Inferno of Dante (Pinsky)
   Lon R Bks - v18 - Ag 22 '96 - p27+ [501+]
   TLS - S 6 '96 - p3+ [501+]
Danticat, Edwidge - *Breath, Eyes and Memory*
   Books - v10 - Je '96 - p24 [51-250]
   Krik? Krak!
   Bks & Cult - v3 - Ja '97 - p8+ [501+]
   BW - v26 - D 15 '96 - p4 [1-50]
   Prog - v61 - Ja '97 - p39 [251-500]
Danto, Arthur C - *After the End of Art*
   AB - v99 - Mr 3 '97 - p694 [51-250]
   LJ - v122 - Ap 1 '97 - p88+ [51-250]
   NYTBR - v102 - F 16 '97 - p21 [501+]
   PW - v243 - D 2 '96 - p47 [51-250]
   Wil Q - v21 - Win '97 - p90+ [501+]
   Encounters and Reflections
   PW - v244 - F 17 '97 - p217 [1-50]
   Playing with the Edge
   Art J - v55 - Fall '96 - p99 [501+]
   JAAC - v55 - Win '97 - p74+ [501+]
D'Antonio, Nancy - *Our Baby from China (Illus. by Nancy D'Antonio)*
   c BL - v93 - Mr 1 '97 - p1165 [51-250]
   c KR - v65 - F 1 '97 - p220 [51-250]
Dantwala, M L - *Dilemmas of Growth*
   JEL - v35 - Mr '97 - p284 [51-250]
   R&R Bk N - v11 - D '96 - p26 [51-250]
Danysk, Cecilia - *Hired Hands*
   CF - v75 - S '96 - p46 [501+]
Danziger, Paula - *Ambar En Cuarto Y Sin Su Amigo (Illus. by Tony Ross)*
   c BL - v93 - F 15 '97 - p1032 [1-50]
   Amber Brown Goes Fourth
   c RT - v50 - D '96 - p343 [51-250]
   Amber Brown Sees Red (Illus. by Tony Ross)
   c BL - v93 - My 15 '97 - p1575 [51-250]
   c PW - v244 - Mr 17 '97 - p85 [1-50]
   Amber Brown Wants Extra Credit (Illus. by Tony Ross)
   c CCB-B - v50 - O '96 - p54 [51-250]
   c HB Guide - v7 - Fall '96 - p291 [51-250]
   c JB - v60 - O '96 - p199 [51-250]
   c LATBR - O 13 '96 - p15 [51-250]
   c Par Ch - v20 - O '96 - p11 [1-50]
   c SLJ - v42 - Ag '96 - p142 [51-250]
   Can You Sue Your Parents for Malpractice? (Danziger). Audio Version
   c Bks Keeps - Mr '97 - p25 [51-250]
   Forever Amber Brown (Illus. by Tony Ross)
   c BL - v93 - N 15 '96 - p587 [51-250]
   c HB - v73 - Ja '97 - p54+ [51-250]
   c HB Guide - v8 - Spr '97 - p57 [51-250]
   c SLJ - v43 - F '97 - p75 [51-250]
   You Can't Eat Your Chicken Pox, Amber Brown (Illus. by Tony Ross)
   c RT - v50 - O '96 - p138 [1-50]
   c RT - v50 - N '96 - p256 [51-250]
Danziger, Sheldon - *America Unequal*
   AAPSS-A - v547 - S '96 - p188 [251-500]
   CS - v25 - N '96 - p754+ [501+]
   ILRR - v50 - Ja '97 - p348+ [501+]
   JEH - v57 - Mr '97 - p242+ [501+]
   JEL - v35 - Mr '97 - p149+ [501+]
   PSQ - v111 - Fall '96 - p523+ [501+]
   RP - v59 - Spr '97 - p410+ [501+]
   Confronting Poverty
   Fam Relat - v45 - Jl '96 - p354+ [251-500]
D'Aprano, Charles - *From Goldrush to Federation*
   Aust Bk R - Je '96 - p67 [1-50]
Da Prato, Giuseppe - *Ergodicity for Infinite Dimensional Systems*
   SciTech - v21 - Mr '97 - p14 [51-250]
D'Aprix, Roger - *Communicating for Change*
   HR Mag - v41 - Je '96 - p182 [51-250]
Dara, Evan - *The Lost Scrapbook*
   Chel - 61 '96 - p154+ [501+]
D'Aragona, Tullia - *Dialogue on the Infinity of Love*
   LJ - v122 - Ap 15 '97 - p80 [51-250]
Darby, Michael R - *Reducing Poverty in America*
   JEL - v34 - S '96 - p1442 [51-250]
Darby, William - *John Ford's Westerns*
   Choice - v34 - O '96 - p289 [51-250]
Darch, Colin - *Tanzania. Rev. Ed.*
   r ARBA - v28 - '97 - p55 [51-250]
   r R&R Bk N - v12 - F '97 - p21 [1-50]
Darcy, Catherine C - *The Institute of the Sisters of Mercy of the Americas*
   RR - v55 - S '96 - p544+ [251-500]
D'Arcy, Paula - *Gift of the Red Bird*
   BL - v93 - S 1 '96 - p36 [51-250]

D'Arcy, William G - *The Anther: Form, Function and Phylogeny*
    Choice - v34 - Mr '97 - p1184 [51-250]
Darcy-Berube, Francoise - *Religious Education at a Crossroads*
    Am - v176 - Ja 18 '97 - p26+ [501+]
Darden, Christopher A - *In Contempt*
    ABA Jour - v82 - D '96 - p92+ [501+]
    Ent W - F 14 '97 - p57 [51-250]
    Esq - v126 - N '96 - p65 [1-50]
    New R - v215 - D 9 '96 - p27+ [501+]
    NYRB - v43 - Je 6 '96 - p7+ [501+]
    NYTBR - v102 - F 9 '97 - p32 [51-250]
    PW - v244 - Ja 13 '97 - p73 [1-50]
    PW - v244 - Ja 27 '97 - p102 [1-50]
    TLS - Jl 19 '96 - p28 [501+]
    In Contempt (Darden). Audio Version
  y Kliatt - v31 - Ja '97 - p49 [51-250]
Darden, Robert - *The Way of an Eagle*
    LJ - v121 - O 1 '96 - p53 [1-50]
Dardick, Irving - *Color Atlas/Text of Salivary Gland Tumor Pathology*
  r SciTech - v21 - Mr '97 - p51 [51-250]
Daremblum, Jaime - *De Yalta A Vancouver*
    BL - v93 - S 15 '96 - p227 [1-50]
Dargie, Henry - *Managing Heart Failure in Primary Care*
    SciTech - v21 - Mr '97 - p57 [51-250]
Dargie, Richard - *The Vikings in Scotland*
  c Sch Lib - v44 - N '96 - p175 [251-500]
Darian, Shea - *Grandpa's Garden (Illus. by Karlyn Holman)*
  c CLW - v67 - D '96 - p56+ [51-250]
  c HB Guide - v7 - Fall '96 - p252+ [51-250]
Darian-Smith, Kate - *Exploration into Australia*
  c BL - v92 - Ag '96 - p1897 [51-250]
  c HB Guide - v8 - Spr '97 - p179 [51-250]
  c SLJ - v42 - S '96 - p210 [51-250]
    Text, Theory, Space
    TLS - Ja 24 '97 - p32 [251-500]
D'Arista, Jane W - *The Evolution of U.S. Finance. Vols. 1-2*
    Econ J - v106 - N '96 - p1838+ [251-500]
Darity, William A, Jr., 1953- - *The Black Underclass*
    SF - v75 - S '96 - p374+ [251-500]
    Economics and Discrimination. Vols. 1-2
    Econ J - v107 - Ja '97 - p277 [251-500]
    JEL - v35 - Mr '97 - p243 [51-250]
D'Arjuzon, Antoine - *Castlereagh 1769-1822, Ou Le Defi A L'Europe De Napoleon*
    TLS - Ja 17 '97 - p19 [501+]
Darko, Amma - *Beyond the Horizon*
    W&I - v11 - N '96 - p267+ [501+]
Darling, Christina - *Mirror (Illus. by Alexandra Day)*
  c BL - v93 - Mr 1 '97 - p1170+ [51-250]
  c KR - v65 - Ja 1 '97 - p57 [51-250]
  c PW - v244 - Ja 13 '97 - p75 [51-250]
  c SLJ - v43 - Mr '97 - p150 [51-250]
Darling, David - *Computers of the Future*
  c HB Guide - v7 - Fall '96 - p350 [51-250]
    The Health Revolution
  c HB Guide - v7 - Fall '96 - p347 [51-250]
  y VOYA - v19 - O '96 - p228 [251-500]
Darling, Jay N - *As Ding Saw Herbert Hoover*
    WHQ - v27 - Win '96 - p550 [51-250]
Darling, John - *Gender Matters in Schools*
    Choice - v34 - O '96 - p332 [51-250]
Darling, Kathy - *Amazon ABC (Illus. by Tara Darling)*
  c Emerg Lib - v23 - My '96 - p43 [1-50]
  c HB Guide - v7 - Fall '96 - p335 [51-250]
  c RT - v50 - Ap '97 - p591 [51-250]
    Arctic Babies (Illus. by Tara Darling)
  c HB Guide - v7 - Fall '96 - p335 [51-250]
  c SB - v33 - Mr '97 - p51 [51-250]
    Chameleon, on Location (Illus. by Tara Darling)
  c BL - v93 - Ap 1 '97 - p1326 [51-250]
  c CCB-B - v50 - My '97 - p318 [51-250]
    Desert Babies (Illus. by Tara Darling)
  c BL - v93 - Ap 1 '97 - p1326 [51-250]
  c CCB-B - v50 - My '97 - p244 [51-250]
  c KR - v65 - Ja 15 '97 - p139 [51-250]
  c SLJ - v43 - Mr '97 - p172 [51-250]
    Komodo Dragon (Illus. by Tara Darling)
  c BL - v93 - F 15 '97 - p1018 [51-250]
  c CCB-B - v50 - My '97 - p318+ [51-250]
  c Trib Bks - Ap 13 '97 - p7 [51-250]
    Rain Forest Babies (Illus. by Tara Darling)
  c HB Guide - v7 - Fall '96 - p335 [51-250]
  c SB - v33 - Mr '97 - p51 [51-250]

    Seashore Babies (Illus. by Tara Darling)
  c BL - v93 - Ap 1 '97 - p1326 [51-250]
  c CCB-B - v50 - Mr '97 - p244 [51-250]
  c SLJ - v43 - Mr '97 - p172 [51-250]
Darling, Tara - *How to Babysit an Orangutan (Illus. by Tara Darling)*
  c BL - v93 - D 15 '96 - p728+ [51-250]
  c HB - v72 - N '96 - p757+ [251-500]
  c HB Guide - v8 - Spr '97 - p126 [51-250]
  c KR - v64 - S 15 '96 - p1397 [51-250]
    PW - v243 - N 11 '96 - p74 [51-250]
  c SLJ - v42 - O '96 - p112 [51-250]
Darling-Hammond, Linda - *Authentic Assessment in Action*
    TCR - v98 - Win '96 - p328+ [501+]
Darlington, David - *The Mojave: A Portrait of the Definitive American Desert*
    NYTBR - v101 - S 1 '96 - p14+ [501+]
Darman, Richard - *Who's in Control?*
    BL - v93 - S 15 '96 - p187 [251-500]
    Bus W - O 14 '96 - p19+ [501+]
    BW - v26 - S 8 '96 - p4 [251-500]
    LJ - v121 - O 15 '96 - p77 [51-250]
    NYTBR - v101 - S 8 '96 - p7 [501+]
    WSJ-MW - v77 - S 6 '96 - pA12 [501+]
Darnton, John - *Neanderthal*
    LJ - v121 - O 1 '96 - p47 [1-50]
    Rapport - v19 - 5 '96 - p29 [501+]
Darnton, Robert - *The Corpus of Clandestine Literature in France 1769-1789*
    JMH - v69 - Mr '97 - p154+ [501+]
    MLR - v92 - Ja '97 - p190+ [501+]
    The Forbidden Best-Sellers of Pre-Revolutionary France
    AHR - v101 - O '96 - p1220+ [501+]
    Ant R - v54 - Fall '96 - p489+ [251-500]
    CR - v270 - Ja '97 - p49+ [501+]
    JMH - v69 - Mr '97 - p154+ [501+]
    MLR - v92 - Ja '97 - p190+ [501+]
D'Arnuk, Nanisi Barrett - *Outside In*
    KR - v64 - Ag 15 '96 - p1188 [51-250]
    LJ - v121 - O 1 '96 - p131 [51-250]
Darr, Katheryn Pfisterer - *Isaiah's Vision and the Family of God*
    Intpr - v50 - O '96 - p423+ [251-500]
Darrah, John - *Paganism in Arthurian Romance*
    MLR - v92 - Ap '97 - p425+ [501+]
    RES - v47 - Ag '96 - p403+ [501+]
    Specu - v71 - Jl '96 - p711+ [501+]
Darrell - *Plainsongs*
    TranslRevS - v2 - D '96 - p19 [51-250]
    TranslRevS - v2 - D '96 - p19 [51-250]
Darrieussecq, Marie - *Pig Tales*
    BL - v93 - Ap 1 '97 - p1280 [51-250]
    KR - v65 - Ap 1 '97 - p504 [51-250]
    LJ - v122 - Mr 15 '97 - p88 [51-250]
    PW - v244 - Mr 3 '97 - p64 [51-250]
Darroch, Gordon - *Property and Inequality in Victorian Ontario*
    Can Hist R - v77 - S '96 - p456+ [501+]
Darrow, Clarence - *The Story of My Life*
    BW - v26 - O 20 '96 - p12 [51-250]
Dart, R K - *Microbiology for the Analytical Chemist*
    SciTech - v20 - S '96 - p16 [51-250]
The Dartmouth Atlas of Health Care
  r R&R Bk N - v11 - N '96 - p21 [51-250]
Dartnell, Michael Y - *Action Directe*
    TLS - Ag 2 '96 - p29 [501+]
Darton, Eric - *Free City*
    Atl - v278 - O '96 - p122 [51-250]
    BL - v93 - S 15 '96 - p219 [51-250]
    LJ - v122 - Ap 15 '97 - p148 [51-250]
    NYTBR - v101 - S 22 '96 - p25 [51-250]
    SFR - v22 - Ja '97 - p20 [501+]
Daruwalla, Keki N - *A Summer of Tigers*
    WLT - v70 - Aut '96 - p1030+ [251-500]
Darvill, Timothy - *Prehistoric Britain from the Air*
    Choice - v34 - F '97 - p1019 [51-250]
Darwall, Stephen - *Equal Freedom*
    Ethics - v107 - Ja '97 - p353+ [501+]
Darwin, Charles - *Charles Darwin's Letters*
    SB - v32 - O '96 - p202 [51-250]
    The Correspondence of Charles Darwin. Vol. 9
    EHR - v112 - F '97 - p238 [251-500]
    Isis - v87 - S '96 - p559+ [251-500]
    On Evolution
  r Choice - v34 - Ap '97 - p1364 [51-250]
Darwin, Roy - *World Agriculture and Climate Change*
    JEL - v34 - S '96 - p1497 [51-250]
Darwin, Tess - *The Scots Herbal*
  r TLS - F 7 '97 - p9 [501+]

Das, Dilip K - *The Asia-Pacific Economy*
    Choice - v34 - Ja '97 - p843 [51-250]
    JEL - v35 - Mr '97 - p284+ [51-250]
    R&R Bk N - v11 - D '96 - p25 [51-250]
Das, Indraneil - *Biogeography of the Reptiles of South Asia*
    Choice - v34 - D '96 - p638 [51-250]
Das, J P - *Cognitive Planning*
    Choice - v34 - My '97 - p1579 [51-250]
Das, Prodeepta - *I is for India (Illus. by Prodeepta Das)*
  c Bks Keeps - v100 - S '96 - p33 [51-250]
  c Emerg Lib - v24 - Mr '97 - p47 [51-250]
  c HB Guide - v8 - Spr '97 - p169 [51-250]
    I Is for India (Illus. by Prodeepta Das)
  c JB - v60 - D '96 - p228 [51-250]
    I is for India (Illus. by Prodeepta Das)
  c Sch Lib - v45 - F '97 - p18 [51-250]
  c SLJ - v42 - N '96 - p97 [51-250]
Das, Veena - *Critical Events*
    CS - v25 - S '96 - p645+ [501+]
    JPR - v34 - F '97 - p110 [51-250]
Dasch, E Julius - *Macmillan Encyclopedia of Earth Sciences. Vols. 1-2*
  r ARBA - v28 - '97 - p631 [51-250]
  r BL - v93 - N 1 '96 - p538 [251-500]
  r LJ - v121 - O 15 '96 - p52 [51-250]
Dasenbrock, Reed Way - *Literary Theory after Davidson*
    JAAR - v64 - Fall '96 - p712+ [501+]
Dasgupta, Subrata - *Technology and Creativity*
    Choice - v34 - S '96 - p148 [51-250]
    SB - v32 - O '96 - p201 [51-250]
Dash, Joan - *We Shall Not Be Moved*
  y BL - v93 - Ap 1 '97 - p1286 [1-50]
  y HB Guide - v7 - Fall '96 - p313+ [51-250]
  c NY - v72 - N 18 '96 - p98 [51-250]
  c NYTBR - v101 - Ag 25 '96 - p23 [501+]
Dash, Leon - *Rosa Lee: A Mother and Her Family in Urban America*
    Bl S - v26 - Fall '96 - p101 [51-250]
    BW - v26 - O 13 '96 - p3+ [501+]
    Choice - v34 - F '97 - p1024 [51-250]
    LATBR - S 22 '96 - p4+ [501+]
    NY - v72 - O 14 '96 - p100 [51-250]
    NYRB - v43 - D 19 '96 - p19+ [501+]
    NYTBR - v101 - N 24 '96 - p28+ [501+]
    PW - v243 - Jl 22 '96 - p219 [51-250]
    Time - v148 - S 30 '96 - p75 [251-500]
    TLS - Ja 10 '97 - p9+ [501+]
    Trib Bks - Ja 5 '97 - p4+ [501+]
    When Children Want Children
    LATBR - S 8 '96 - p11 [51-250]
Dash, Michael I N - *Hidden Wholeness*
    PW - v244 - Mr 10 '97 - p63 [51-250]
Dashwood, Henry - *Rural Rides*
    Books - v9 - S '95 - p25 [1-50]
Daskalova-Perkovska, L - *Bulgarski Folklorni Prikazki*
  r Slav R - v55 - Fall '96 - p675 [501+]
Database and Expert Systems Applications Conference (7th: 1996: Zurich, Switzerland) - *Database and Expert Systems Applications*
    SciTech - v21 - Mr '97 - p8 [51-250]
Dathorne, O R - *Asian Voyages*
    R&R Bk N - v11 - D '96 - p19 [51-250]
Datlow, Ellen - *Black Swan, White Raven*
    KR - v65 - Ap 1 '97 - p510 [51-250]
    Black Thorn, White Rose
  y VOYA - v19 - D '96 - p265 [1-50]
    Off Limits
    SF Chr - v18 - O '96 - p80 [1-50]
    Ruby Slippers, Golden Tears
  y VOYA - v19 - D '96 - p265 [51-250]
    Snow White, Blood Red
  y VOYA - v19 - D '96 - p265 [1-50]
Datta, Sudhin - *Polymeric Compatibilizers*
    SciTech - v20 - N '96 - p81 [51-250]
Daub, G William - *Basic Chemistry. 7th Ed.*
    J Chem Ed - v73 - O '96 - pA241+ [501+]
Dauber, Nicky - *The Vest-Pocket CPA. 2nd Ed.*
    BWatch - v18 - Mr '97 - p4 [51-250]
Dauber, Philip M - *The Three Big Bangs*
    Rapport - v19 - 5 '96 - p39 [251-500]
    S&T - v92 - O '96 - p57 [51-250]
D'Aubigne, Agrippa - *Les Tragiques. Vols. 1-2*
    Ren Q - v50 - Spr '97 - p251+ [501+]
Dauenhauer, Bernard P - *Citizenship in a Fragile World*
    Choice - v34 - F '97 - p1029 [51-250]
Daugharty, Janice - *Earl in the Yellow Shirt*
    KR - v65 - Mr 1 '97 - p321 [51-250]
    PW - v244 - Mr 17 '97 - p77 [51-250]
Daugherty, Franklin - *The Isle of Joy*
    PW - v243 - O 21 '96 - p71+ [51-250]

Daugherty, Jack E - *Industrial Environmental Management*
   R&R Bk N - v11 - N '96 - p28 [51-250]
Daugherty, Tracy - *The Woman in the Oil Field*
   NYTBR - v101 - D 15 '96 - p22 [501+]
   PW - v243 - N 11 '96 - p71 [51-250]
Daughters of the American Revolution: Lineage of Namaqua Chapter Members, Loveland, Colorado, January 8, 1914-October 31, 1994
   r EGH - v50 - N '96 - p165 [51-250]
D'Aulaire, Ingri - *D'Aulaires' Book of Greek Myths. Audio Version*
   c PW - v244 - Ja 13 '97 - p36 [51-250]
   c Smith - v27 - N '96 - p175 [1-50]
Daum, Pierre - *Les Plaisirs Et Les Jours, De Marcel Proust*
   MLR - v92 - Ja '97 - p203+ [251-500]
Daumal, Rene - *You've Always Been Wrong*
   TLS - O 25 '96 - p26 [501+]
Daun, Ake - *Swedish Mentality*
   AB - v98 - Ag 19 '96 - p580+ [501+]
D'Aunet, Leonie - *Jane Osborn*
   MLR - v92 - Ja '97 - p196 [51-250]
Daunton, M J - *Progress and Poverty*
   Albion - v28 - '96 - p707+ [501+]
Daveluy, Paule - *Sylvette Sous La Tente Bleue*
   c Can CL - v22 - Fall '96 - p137+ [501+]
Davenport, Guy - *The Cardiff Team*
   KR - v64 - Ag 15 '96 - p1170+ [251-500]
   Nat - v264 - Ap 7 '97 - p41+ [501+]
   NYTBR - v101 - N 24 '96 - p18 [51-250]
   PW - v243 - S 2 '96 - p113 [51-250]
   Da Vinci's Bicycle
   LJ - v122 - My 1 '97 - p145 [1-50]
   PW - v244 - Ap 14 '97 - p72 [1-50]
   The Hunter Gracchus and Other Papers on Literature and Art
   BL - v93 - D 1 '96 - p637 [51-250]
   KR - v64 - N 1 '96 - p1577 [251-500]
   LJ - v121 - D '96 - p93 [51-250]
   Nat - v264 - Ap 7 '97 - p41+ [501+]
   PW - v243 - N 18 '96 - p58+ [51-250]
Davenport, Marcia - *The Valley of Decision*
   Nat R - v48 - D 23 '96 - p54 [51-250]
Davenport, Roger - *They've Escaped out of His Mind!*
   c TES - F 21 '97 - p8* [51-250]
Davenport-Hines, Richard - *Auden*
   Bks & Cult - v2 - Jl '96 - p30+ [251-500]
   Comw - v123 - O 11 '96 - p23+ [501+]
   NYTBR - v101 - D 8 '96 - p84+ [1-50]
   WLT - v70 - Aut '96 - p968+ [501+]
Daverio, John - *Robert Schumann: Herald of a New Poetic Age*
   BL - v93 - My 1 '97 - p1472+ [51-250]
   Wil Q - v21 - Win '97 - p103 [251-500]
Davey, B J - *Rural Crime in the Eighteenth Century*
   EHR - v111 - N '96 - p1297+ [251-500]
David, Andrew - *The Voyage of HMS Herald to Australia and the South-West Pacific 1852-1861 under the Command of Captain Henry Mangles Denham*
   Sea H - Win '96 - p43+ [251-500]
David, Deirdre - *Rule Britannia*
   ELT - v39 - 3 '96 - p404 [51-250]
   Nine-C Lit - v51 - Mr '97 - p541+ [501+]
David, Elizabeth - *I'll Be with You in the Squeezing of a Lemon*
   TES - Jl 26 '96 - pR5 [51-250]
   An Omelette and a Glass of Wine
   TES - Jl 26 '96 - pR5 [51-250]
   Summer Cooking
   TES - Jl 26 '96 - pR5 [51-250]
David, Fred - *Fashion, Culture, and Identity*
   JPC - v30 - Fall '96 - p199+ [51-250]
David, Jay - *Growing Up Black. Rev. Ed.*
   y BL - v93 - F 15 '97 - p1014 [1-50]
David, Marian - *Correspondence and Disquotation*
   Phil R - v105 - Ja '96 - p82+ [501+]
David, Ron - *Opera for Beginners*
   TES - Ja 10 '97 - p7* [501+]
David Haynes Associates - *Sprig Directory of Periodicals in Sport and Recreation. 3rd Ed.*
   r LAR - v99 - F '97 - p102 [51-250]
David Livingstone and the Victorian Encounter with Africa
   BL - v93 - N 15 '96 - p567+ [51-250]
   LJ - v121 - O 15 '96 - p66 [51-250]
Davidman, Leonard - *Teaching with a Multicultural Perspective*
   ES - v27 - Sum '96 - p154+ [501+]
Davidoff, Leonore - *Worlds Between*
   HT - v46 - S '96 - p57 [51-250]

Davids, Karel - *A Miracle Mirrored*
   JIH - v27 - Spr '97 - p701+ [501+]
David's Flock of Sheep
   c HB Guide - v7 - Fall '96 - p308 [1-50]
Davidson, Abraham A - *Ralph Albert Blakelock*
   AB - v99 - Mr 3 '97 - p693 [51-250]
   Choice - v34 - Ap '97 - p1324 [51-250]
Davidson, Alistair - *Riding the Tiger*
   Quill & Q - v63 - Ja '97 - p31 [51-250]
Davidson, Andrew P - *In the Shadow of History*
   Choice - v34 - D '96 - p651 [51-250]
Davidson, Ann - *Alzheimer's, a Love Story*
   PW - v244 - Ap 7 '97 - p81 [51-250]
Davidson, Ann Locke - *Making and Molding Identity in Schools*
   R&R Bk N - v11 - D '96 - p54 [51-250]
Davidson, Cathy N - *Oxford Companion to Women's Writing in the United States*
   r RQ - v36 - Win '96 - p219 [51-250]
Davidson, D Kirk - *Selling Sin*
   R&R Bk N - v12 - F '97 - p44 [51-250]
Davidson, Diane Mott - *Catering to Nobody (Rosenblat). Audio Version*
   BWatch - v18 - Mr '97 - p7 [1-50]
   Dying for Chocolate (Rosenblat). Audio Version
   BL - v93 - My 15 '97 - p1596 [51-250]
   The Main Corpse
   Arm Det - v30 - Win '97 - p96 [251-500]
   BL - v93 - S 1 '96 - p66 [51-250]
   PW - v243 - Jl 22 '96 - p228+ [51-250]
   The Main Corpse (Rosenblat). Audio Version
   BWatch - v18 - Mr '97 - p7 [1-50]
Davidson, Donald - *The Big Ballad Jamboree*
   BL - v93 - Ja '97 - p760 [1-50]
   Sew R - v104 - Jl '96 - p468+ [501+]
   Sew R - v104 - Jl '96 - p476+ [501+]
Davidson, Eugene - *The Unmaking of Adolf Hitler*
   AB - v98 - Ag 19 '96 - p582+ [501+]
   Choice - v34 - N '96 - p516 [51-250]
   HRNB - v25 - Win '97 - p73 [51-250]
Davidson, Greg - *Economics for a Civilized Society. Rev. Ed.*
   Choice - v34 - F '97 - p1010+ [51-250]
   JEL - v35 - Mr '97 - p209+ [51-250]
   R&R Bk N - v12 - F '97 - p34 [51-250]
Davidson, Homer L - *Troubleshooting and Repairing Compact Disc Players. 3rd Ed.*
   SciTech - v21 - Mr '97 - p92 [51-250]
Davidson, Ian D - *European Monetary Union*
   Choice - v34 - Ja '97 - p844 [51-250]
Davidson, James Dale - *The Sovereign Individual*
   BL - v93 - F 15 '97 - p983 [51-250]
   KR - v64 - D 15 '96 - p1778+ [251-500]
   PW - v243 - D 9 '96 - p53+ [51-250]
   WSJ-Cent - v99 - Mr 31 '97 - pA12 [501+]
Davidson, Jim - *Lyrebird Rising*
   Notes - v53 - D '96 - p440+ [501+]
Davidson, John - *Selected Poems and Prose of John Davidson*
   Choice - v34 - S '96 - p129 [51-250]
   Nine-C Lit - v51 - S '96 - p271+ [1-50]
Davidson, Judith A - *Sport on Film and Video*
   J Am Cult - v18 - Win '95 - p103 [51-250]
Davidson, Keay - *Twister: The Science of Tornadoes and the Making of an Adventure Movie*
   y Kliatt - v30 - S '96 - p35 [51-250]
Davidson, Kenneth R - *C*-Algebras by Example*
   SciTech - v20 - N '96 - p14 [51-250]
Davidson, Miles H - *Columbus Then and Now*
   BL - v93 - My 15 '97 - p1558+ [51-250]
Davidson, Nicole - *Crash Landing*
   y Kliatt - v31 - Ja '97 - p6 [51-250]
   Dying to Dance
   y Kliatt - v30 - S '96 - p8 [51-250]
Davidson, Osha Gray - *Broken Heartland*
   Nat - v263 - N 4 '96 - p27+ [501+]
   VQR - v73 - Win '97 - p33* [1-50]
Davidson, Pamela - *Viacheslav Ivanov: A Reference Guide*
   r Choice - v34 - F '97 - p942 [51-250]
Davidson, Paul - *Can the Free Market Pick Winners?*
   Econ J - v106 - S '96 - p1468 [251-500]
Davidson, Robyn - *Desert Places*
   BL - v93 - Ja '97 - p759 [1-50]
   y BL - v93 - O 1 '96 - p318 [51-250]
   CSM - v89 - Mr 12 '97 - p13 [251-500]
   FEER - v160 - Mr 6 '97 - p45 [251-500]
   KR - v64 - S 1 '96 - p1289+ [251-500]
   LJ - v121 - D '96 - p128+ [51-250]
   NYTBR - v102 - F 16 '97 - p26 [501+]
   Spec - v277 - N 16 '96 - p46 [1-50]
   VV - v41 - D 3 '96 - p57+ [501+]

Davidson, Stephen M - *The Physician-Manager Alliance*
   SciTech - v20 - N '96 - p37 [51-250]
Davidson, Todd - *Trust the Force*
   J ClinPsyc - v58 - F '97 - p90+ [501+]
Davie, Donald - *The Eighteenth-Century Hymn in England*
   JAAR - v64 - Fall '96 - p708+ [501+]
Davie, Jody Shapiro - *Women in the Presence*
   TT - v53 - Ja '97 - p570 [51-250]
Davie, Ronald - *The Voice of the Child*
   R&R Bk N - v11 - N '96 - p43 [51-250]
   TES - S 6 '96 - p8* [51-250]
Davies, Alan - *Introducing Comparative Government*
   y TES - F 21 '97 - p20* [501+]
Davies, Catherine - *Contemporary Feminist Fiction in Spain*
   MLR - v91 - O '96 - p1025 [501+]
   Women Writers in Twentieth-Century Spain and Spanish America
   MLR - v92 - Ja '97 - p232+ [251-500]
Davies, Cecil - *The Plays of Ernst Toller*
   Choice - v34 - D '96 - p618 [51-250]
Davies, Dave - *Kink: An Autobiography*
   BL - v93 - D 15 '96 - p703 [51-250]
   KR - v64 - D 1 '96 - p1713 [251-500]
   LJ - v122 - F 1 '97 - p80 [51-250]
   PW - v243 - D 9 '96 - p52 [51-250]
Davies, David, 1937- - *Velazquez in Seville*
   BM - v138 - D '96 - p839+ [501+]
Davies, David Twiston - *Canada from Afar*
   BIC - v25 - S '96 - p38+ [501+]
   Spec - v278 - F 22 '97 - p32+ [501+]
Davies, Dominic - *Pink Therapy*
   SciTech - v20 - S '96 - p32 [51-250]
Davies, Douglas - *Reusing Old Graves*
   Folkl - v107 - '96 - p125 [251-500]
Davies, Eryl W - *Numbers: Based on the Revised Standard Version*
   Rel St Rev - v23 - Ap '97 - p164 [51-250]
Davies, Gareth - *From Opportunity to Entitlement*
   Choice - v34 - Ja '97 - p861 [51-250]
   R&R Bk N - v11 - D '96 - p42 [51-250]
Davies, Glyn - *A History of Money*
   EHR - v112 - Ap '97 - p553+ [51-250]
Davies, Horton - *The Vigilant God*
   Six Ct J - v27 - Fall '96 - p872+ [501+]
   Worship and Theology in England. Vols. 1-3
   CLW - v67 - D '96 - p34+ [501+]
Davies, Hunter - *The Beatles. 2nd Rev. Ed.*
   LJ - v121 - D '96 - p154 [51-250]
   PW - v243 - S 2 '96 - p121 [1-50]
   Beatrix Potter's Lakeland
   RSR - v24 - 3 '96 - p22 [51-250]
   Living on the Lottery
   Spec - v277 - N 2 '96 - p47+ [501+]
   TLS - N 29 '96 - p32 [251-500]
   The Teller of Tales
   LJ - v121 - N 15 '96 - p62 [51-250]
   PW - v243 - S 23 '96 - p72 [51-250]
Davies, J Clarence - *Comparing Environmental Risks*
   Choice - v34 - S '96 - p147 [51-250]
   Env - v38 - N '96 - p30 [51-250]
   JEL - v34 - S '96 - p1497 [51-250]
   SB - v32 - O '96 - p198+ [251-500]
Davies, J L - *Cardiganshire County History*
   EHR - v111 - S '96 - p949 [251-500]
Davies, John - *Educating Students in a Media-Saturated Culture*
   Choice - v34 - N '96 - p510 [51-250]
Davies, Jonathan - *Given in Evidence*
   Books - v9 - S '95 - p18 [51-250]
Davies, Julian - *The Beholder*
   Aust Bk R - O '96 - p43 [501+]
Davies, Kath - *Egyptians*
   c TES - Jl 5 '96 - pR5 [251-500]
   Greeks
   c TES - Jl 5 '96 - pR5 [251-500]
   The U.S.A.
   c Sch Lib - v44 - Ag '96 - p112 [51-250]
   Vikings
   c TES - Jl 5 '96 - pR5 [251-500]
Davies, Lawrence - *Genetic Algorithms and Simulated Annealing*
   Robotica - v15 - Mr '97 - p234 [251-500]
Davies, Linda - *Wilderness of Mirrors*
   Ent W - O 25 '96 - p109 [1-50]
   PW - v243 - O 14 '96 - p81 [1-50]
Davies, Malcolm - *Penological Esperanto and Sentencing Parochialism*
   R&R Bk N - v11 - N '96 - p46 [51-250]
Davies, Margaret - *The Pastoral Epistles*
   Rel St Rev - v23 - Ja '97 - p74+ [51-250]

Davies, Martin - *Aldus Manutius: Printer and Publisher of Renaissance Venice*
  BC - v45 - Sum '96 - p255+ [51-250]
  LR - v45 - 7 '96 - p79+ [251-500]
The Gutenburg Bible
  HT - v46 - O '96 - p56 [51-250]
Davies, Mike - *Canine and Feline Geriatrics*
  SciTech - v20 - D '96 - p57 [51-250]
Davies, Nicholas - *Diana: The Lonely Princess*
  LATBR - Ag 18 '96 - p3 [501+]
Davies, Nicola - *Big Blue Whale (Illus. by Nick Maland)*
  c HB - v73 - My '97 - p338+ [51-250]
Everything Happens on Mondays
  c TES - Jl 5 '96 - pR8 [51-250]
Davies, Norman - *Europe: A History*
  BL - v93 - S 15 '96 - p214 [251-500]
  BW - v27 - Ja 26 '97 - p13 [51-250]
  CSM - v89 - Ja 30 '97 - pB1+ [501+]
  Econ - v341 - N 16 '96 - p3*+ [501+]
  LJ - v122 - Mr 15 '97 - p73 [51-250]
  Lon R Bks - v19 - F 20 '97 - p7+ [501+]
  NS - v125 - N 1 '96 - p46+ [501+]
  NS - v125 - D 20 '96 - p117 [51-250]
  NYTBR - v101 - D 1 '96 - p15+ [501+]
  NYTBR - v101 - D 8 '96 - p87 [1-50]
  Obs - v54 - O 13 '96 - p15* [501+]
  Spec - v278 - Ja 4 '97 - p33+ [501+]
  TES - N 1 '96 - p7* [501+]
  TES - D 27 '96 - p16+ [1-50]
  TLS - D 20 '96 - p3+ [501+]
  WSJ-MW - v78 - N 18 '96 - pA10 [501+]
Davies, Oliver - *Celtic Christian Spirituality*
  Rel St Rev - v23 - Ja '97 - p82 [51-250]
  RR - v55 - S '96 - p552 [51-250]
Davies, P C W - *Are We Alone?*
  NYTBR - v101 - Ag 25 '96 - p28 [51-250]
Davies, Paul - *Gelignite Jack*
  BIC - v25 - O '96 - p41 [251-500]
  Quill & Q - v62 - Ag '96 - p36 [251-500]
The Ideal Real
  RES - v48 - F '97 - p136+ [501+]
Davies, Philip H J - *The British Secret Services*
  r Choice - v34 - Mr '97 - p1134 [51-250]
  R&R Bk N - v11 - D '96 - p48 [51-250]
Davies, Philip John - *An American Quarter Century*
  HRNB - v25 - Fall '96 - p15 [251-500]
Political Issues in America Today
  R&R Bk N - v11 - N '96 - p48 [51-250]
Davies, Philip R - *Sects and Scrolls*
  R&R Bk N - v11 - N '96 - p6 [51-250]
Whose Bible Is It Anyway?
  Rel St Rev - v23 - Ja '97 - p54 [51-250]
Davies, R R - *The Revolt of Owain Glyn Dwr*
  EHR - v112 - F '97 - p142+ [501+]
  HRNB - v25 - Win '97 - p70+ [251-500]
Davies, Rhys - *Ram with Red Horns*
  BL - v93 - Ja '97 - p817 [51-250]
  KR - v64 - D 15 '96 - p1751 [251-500]
  NYTBR - v102 - Ap 13 '97 - p20 [51-250]
  Spec - v278 - Mr 15 '97 - p37+ [501+]
Davies, Robertson - *The Cornish Trilogy*
  EJ - v85 - D '96 - p95 [501+]
The Cunning Man
  Can Lit - Spr '97 - p224+ [501+]
  MA - v38 - Fall '96 - p403+ [501+]
The Merry Heart
  KR - v65 - My 1 '97 - p689+ [251-500]
  Quill & Q - v62 - S '96 - p69 [251-500]
What's Bred in the Bone (Davidson). Audio Version
  BL - v93 - N 15 '96 - p604 [51-250]
  LJ - v121 - N 15 '96 - p107 [51-250]
Davies, Russell - *Foreign Body*
  CR - v269 - Ag '96 - p107+ [251-500]
Davies, Stevan L - *Jesus the Healer*
  Ant R - v55 - Spr '97 - p236+ [251-500]
  BTB - v27 - Sum '97 - p71+ [501+]
  Rel St Rev - v23 - Ja '97 - p70 [51-250]
  Theol St - v57 - Mr '96 - p182 [251-500]
Davies, Stevie - *Four Dreamers and Emily*
  TLS - Jl 7 '96 - p25 [251-500]
Henry Vaughan
  RES - v48 - F '97 - p103+ [501+]
Davies, Susanna - *Adaptable Livelihoods*
  JEL - v34 - S '96 - p1476+ [51-250]
Davies, W K - *Lifelong Learning*
  TES - N 22 '96 - p29 [251-500]
Davies, Winifred V - *The Changing Voices of Europe*
  MLR - v91 - O '96 - p939+ [501+]
Davignon, Keith R - *Contemporary Counterfeit Capped Bust Half Dollars*
  r Coin W - v38 - Mr 24 '97 - p80 [51-250]

D'Avila-Latourrette, Victor-Antoine - *A Monastic Year*
  Am - v176 - F 15 '97 - p31 [51-250]
Davin, Anna - *Growing Up Poor*
  Choice - v34 - S '96 - p185 [51-250]
  HT - v46 - D '96 - p54 [501+]
  Lon R Bks - v18 - S 5 '96 - p21 [51-250]
Davis, A Brent - *Teaching Mathematics*
  SciTech - v20 - S '96 - p3 [1-50]
Davis, Andrew N - *The Home Environmental Checklist*
  BL - v93 - O 1 '96 - p312+ [51-250]
Davis, Aubrey - *Bone Button Borscht*
  c Emerg Lib - v24 - S '96 - p45 [51-250]
Sody Salleratus (Illus. by Alan Daniel)
  c Quill & Q - v62 - S '96 - p73 [251-500]
Davis, Barbara Kerr - *Read All Your Life*
  r RQ - v36 - Win '96 - p221 [51-250]
Davis, Brent - *The Spelling Bee*
  PW - v243 - S 30 '96 - p62 [51-250]
Davis, Brett - *Hair of the Dog*
  y Kliatt - v31 - My '97 - p12 [51-250]
Davis, Bruce E - *GIS: A Visual Approach*
  R&R Bk N - v11 - D '96 - p18 [51-250]
Davis, Carolyn O'Bagy - *Treasured Earth*
  Am Ant - v61 - Jl '96 - p632+ [251-500]
Davis, Charles R - *Organization Theories and Public Administration*
  Choice - v34 - My '97 - p1573+ [51-250]
Davis, Christopher A - *The Structure of Paul's Theology*
  Rel St Rev - v23 - Ja '97 - p73 [51-250]
Davis, Christopher C - *Lasers and Electro-Optics*
  Nature - v381 - My 16 '96 - p206 [51-250]
  Phys Today - v49 - D '96 - p56+ [501+]
Davis, Cinda-Sue - *The Equity Equation*
  Sci - v273 - Jl 26 '96 - p443+ [501+]
Davis, Cynthia J - *Women Writers in the United States*
  r AL - v69 - Mr '97 - p244+ [251-500]
  r ARBA - v28 - '97 - p337 [251-500]
  r BL - v93 - S 1 '96 - p173 [251-500]
  r Choice - v34 - N '96 - p427 [51-250]
  r Legacy - v14 - 1 '97 - p73 [51-250]
  r Nine-C Lit - v51 - Mr '97 - p555 [51-250]
Davis, Daniel J - *Hazardous Materials Reference Book Cross-Index*
  r SciTech - v20 - D '96 - p71 [51-250]
Davis, Deborah - *Chinese Families in the Post-Mao Era*
  Ch Rev Int - v4 - Spr '97 - p112+ [501+]
  RA - v25 - 4 '96 - p257+ [501+]
Urban Spaces in Contemporary China
  JIH - v27 - Spr '97 - p751+ [501+]
Davis, Diane E - *Urban Leviathan*
  HAHR - v77 - F '97 - p140+ [251-500]
  PSQ - v111 - Win '96 - p737+ [501+]
Davis, Don - *The Gris-Gris Man*
  KR - v65 - Mr 1 '97 - p336 [51-250]
  PW - v244 - Mr 3 '97 - p65 [51-250]
Davis, Donald - *See Rock City*
  y SLJ - v42 - S '96 - p240 [51-250]
Thirteen Miles from Suncrest
  y Kliatt - v31 - Mr '97 - p6 [51-250]
Davis, Douglas - *The New Television*
  Afterimage - v24 - N '96 - p4 [1-50]
Davis, E A - *Science in the Making. Vol. 1*
  Isis - v87 - D '96 - p736+ [501+]
Davis, Edmond - *Mind-Boggling Machines and Amazing Mazes*
  c HB Guide - v7 - Fall '96 - p358 [51-250]
Davis, Elisabeth B - *Guide to Information Sources in the Botanical Sciences. 2nd Ed.*
  r ARBA - v28 - '97 - p579 [51-250]
Using the Biological Literature. 2nd Ed.
  r ARBA - v28 - '97 - p575 [51-250]
Davis, Frances A - *Frank Lloyd Wright: Maverick Architect*
  c BL - v93 - Ja '97 - p833 [51-250]
  c Cur R - v36 - Ja '97 - p12 [51-250]
  y HB Guide - v8 - Spr '97 - p137 [51-250]
  c KR - v64 - O 15 '96 - p1530 [51-250]
  y SLJ - v43 - Ja '97 - p122 [51-250]
Davis, Francis - *Bebop and Nothingness*
  Choice - v34 - N '96 - p469 [51-250]
Davis, Frederic E - *The Windows 95 Bible*
  BL - v92 - Ag '96 - p1868 [501+]
  CBR - v14 - Jl '96 - p24 [1-50]
Davis, Gabriel - *The Moving Book (Illus. by Sue Dennen)*
  c PW - v243 - Mr 31 '97 - p77 [51-250]
Davis, George H - *Structural Geology of Rocks and Regions. 2nd Ed.*
  r New Sci - v151 - S 28 '96 - p46 [501+]
Davis, Gibbs - *Money Madness*
  c PW - v243 - N 25 '96 - p76 [51-250]

Davis, Greg - *Collector's Guide to TV Memorabilia 1960s and 1970s*
  r Ant & CM - v101 - D '96 - p33 [51-250]
Davis, H Leigh - *Totally Unauthorized the 11th Hour*
  Quill & Q - v62 - Ag '96 - p22 [501+]
Davis, Hank - *Small-Town Heroes*
  LJ - v122 - F 1 '97 - p82 [51-250]
  PW - v244 - Ja 13 '97 - p62 [51-250]
Davis, J David - *Finding the God of Noah*
  KR - v64 - My 1 '96 - p658 [251-500]
Davis, J R - *Carbon and Alloy Steels*
  Choice - v34 - O '96 - p311 [51-250]
  SciTech - v20 - N '96 - p64 [51-250]
Cast Irons
  Choice - v34 - Mr '97 - p1190 [51-250]
Davis, James Kirkpatrick - *Assault on the Left*
  KR - v65 - My 1 '97 - p690 [251-500]
Davis, John Bryan - *Keynes's Philosophical Development*
  JEL - v34 - S '96 - p1335+ [501+]
Davis, John H - *Jacqueline Bouvier: An Intimate Memoir*
  BL - v92 - Ag '96 - p1850 [251-500]
  BW - v26 - S 22 '96 - p6 [501+]
  LATBR - S 8 '96 - p4+ [501+]
  Lon R Bks - v18 - N 14 '96 - p19+ [501+]
  NYTBR - v101 - S 1 '96 - p5 [501+]
  Obs - N 10 '96 - p16* [501+]
  PW - v243 - Jl 22 '96 - p219 [51-250]
  Spec - v277 - S 28 '96 - p45+ [501+]
Davis, John H, 1961- - *The Landscape of Belief*
  CC - v113 - N 13 '96 - p1124 [51-250]
  Rel St Rev - v23 - Ja '97 - p92 [51-250]
Davis, Karen - *Prisoned Chickens, Poisoned Eggs*
  BL - v93 - Ap 1 '97 - p1272 [51-250]
  PW - v244 - Mr 17 '97 - p74 [51-250]
Davis, Keith F - *The Photographs of Dorothea Lange*
  Pet PM - v25 - N '96 - p12 [51-250]
Davis, Kenneth C - *Don't Know Much about the Civil War*
  BW - v26 - Jl 7 '96 - p13 [51-250]
  NYTBR - v101 - Jl 21 '96 - p18 [51-250]
Don't Know Much about the Civil War. Audio Version
  LJ - v121 - O 1 '96 - p145 [51-250]
Davis, Kevin - *Getting Into Your Customer's Head*
  Bus Bk R - v13 - 4 '96 - p86+ [501+]
Davis, Kristin - *Financing College*
  y BL - v93 - O 1 '96 - p311 [51-250]
  LJ - v121 - O 15 '96 - p68 [51-250]
Davis, Lance E - *International Capital Markets and American Economic Growth 1820-1914*
  Econ J - v106 - S '96 - p1478+ [51-250]
  JEH - v56 - S '96 - p735+ [501+]
  JEH - v56 - S '96 - p737+ [501+]
Davis, Larry - *Walk Around P-51D*
  A & S Sm - v11 - O '96 - p88 [1-50]
Davis, Laura - *Becoming the Parent You Want to Be*
  BL - v93 - Mr 15 '97 - p1213 [51-250]
  PW - v244 - Ja 27 '97 - p98+ [51-250]
Davis, Lennard J - *Enforcing Normalcy*
  MHR - v10 - Fall '96 - p73+ [501+]
Davis, Lindsey - *Time to Depart*
  y BL - v93 - Ja '97 - p824 [51-250]
  KR - v64 - N 15 '96 - p1634 [51-250]
  LJ - v121 - D '96 - p151 [1-50]
  PW - v243 - D 9 '96 - p64 [51-250]
Davis, Lydia - *Almost No Memory*
  BL - v93 - My 1 '97 - p1479 [251-500]
  KR - v65 - Ap 1 '97 - p482+ [251-500]
  LJ - v122 - Ap 1 '97 - p132 [51-250]
  PW - v244 - Ap 14 '97 - p52 [51-250]
Break It Down
  Lon R Bks - v18 - O 31 '96 - p6 [501+]
  TLS - N 8 '96 - p28 [501+]
The End of the Story
  Lon R Bks - v18 - O 31 '96 - p6 [501+]
  Obs - N 10 '96 - p18* [51-250]
  TLS - N 8 '96 - p28 [501+]
Davis, M Jane - *Security Issues in the Post-Cold War World*
  R&R Bk N - v11 - N '96 - p51 [51-250]
Davis, Mark H - *Empathy: A Social Psychological Approach*
  Choice - v34 - D '96 - p691 [51-250]
Davis, Mary B - *Native America in the 20th Century*
  yr BWatch - v17 - N '96 - p2 [51-250]
Davis, Mary Byrd - *Eastern Old-Growth Forests*
  Choice - v34 - D '96 - p637 [51-250]
Davis, Michael - *The Politics of Philosophy*
  Choice - v34 - N '96 - p533 [51-250]
Davis, Michael G - *Ecology, Sociopolitical Organization, and Cultural Change on the Southern Plains*
  R&R Bk N - v12 - F '97 - p22 [51-250]

Davis, Natalie Zemon - *Women on the Margins*
  Biography - v19 - Fall '96 - p429 [1-50]
  Biography - v19 - Sum '96 - p302+ [501+]
  CH - v65 - D '96 - p714+ [501+]
  HT - v47 - Ja '97 - p52 [501+]
  J Soc H - v30 - Win '96 - p541+ [501+]
  NAR - v281 - S '96 - p45+ [501+]
  Ren Q - v50 - Spr '97 - p347+ [501+]
  Six Ct J - v27 - Win '96 - p1145+ [501+]
  TLS - Jl 19 '96 - p4+ [501+]
Davis, Nathaniel - *A Long Walk to Church*
  AHR - v101 - D '96 - p1587+ [501+]
  Bks & Cult - v2 - Mr '96 - p6+ [501+]
  Historian v58 Sum '96 - p898+ [501+]
  JR - v76 - O '96 - p654+ [501+]
  Russ Rev - v56 - Ja '97 - p144+ [501+]
Davis, Pamela J - *Vocal Fold Physiology*
  SciTech - v20 - N '96 - p32 [51-250]
Davis, Paul K - *Encyclopedia of Invasions and Conquests from Ancient Times to the Present*
  r ARBA - v28 - '97 - p254 [51-250]
  r LJ - v122 - Ja '97 - p84+ [51-250]
Davis, Peter, 1933- - *In Darkest Hollywood*
  Choice - v34 - My '97 - p1506 [51-250]
  PW - v243 - O 21 '96 - p77 [51-250]
Davis, Peter T - *Securing Client/Server Computer Networks*
  CBR - v14 - N '96 - p39 [1-50]
  SciTech - v20 - S '96 - p8 [51-250]
Davis, Philip - *Sudden Shakespeare*
  R&R Bk N - v11 - N '96 - p69 [1-50]
Davis, Philip J - *Mathematical Encounters of the Second Kind*
  SciTech - v21 - Mr '97 - p4 [1-50]
Davis, Phyllis - *CorelDraw 7 for Windows 95/NT*
  LJ - v122 - My 1 '97 - p132 [1-50]
Davis, R O - *Elasticity and Geomechanics*
  Choice - v34 - N '96 - p488 [51-250]
Davis, R W - *Lords of Parliament*
  Historian - v59 - Fall '96 - p184+ [501+]
Davis, Rebecca Harding - *Life in the Iron Mills and Other Stories*
  Am Q - v49 - Mr '97 - p113+ [501+]
Davis, Richard A, Jr. - *The Evolving Coast*
  New Sci - v153 - Mr 15 '97 - p43 [1-50]
Davis, Richard L - *Textbook of Neuropathology. 3rd Ed.*
  SciTech - v21 - Mr '97 - p52 [51-250]
Davis, Richard L, 1951- - *Wind against the Mountain*
  Choice - v34 - Ap '97 - p1394 [51-250]
Davis, Robert - *Tertulia: Advanced Oral Skills in Spanish*
  Hisp - v79 - D '96 - p821+ [501+]
Davis, Robert C - *The War of the Fists*
  EHR - v112 - F '97 - p191+ [501+]
  Ren Q - v49 - Aut '96 - p617+ [501+]
  Six Ct J - v27 - Fall '96 - p903+ [501+]
Davis, Robert H, Jr. - *Slavic and Baltic Library Resources at the New York Public Library*
  Lib & Cul - v32 - Win '97 - p152+ [501+]
Davis, Ronald L - *John Ford: Hollywood's Old Master*
  FQ - v50 - Win '96 - p62 [51-250]
Davis, Scott - *Religion and Justice in the War over Bosnia*
  LJ - v121 - N 15 '96 - p75 [51-250]
Davis, Shelley L - *Unbridled Power*
  BL - v93 - Mr 15 '97 - p1210 [51-250]
  Fortune - v135 - Mr 3 '97 - p174 [501+]
  LJ - v122 - Ap 15 '97 - p91 [51-250]
  PW - v244 - F 17 '97 - p203 [51-250]
Davis, Skeeter - *Bus Fare to Kentucky*
  CAY - v16 - Fall '95 - p11 [51-250]
Davis, Sonny B - *A Brotherhood of Arms*
  Choice - v34 - D '96 - p673 [51-250]
  R&R Bk N - v11 - N '96 - p79 [51-250]
Davis, Steven J - *Job Creation and Destruction*
  Choice - v34 - N '96 - p506 [51-250]
  Econ - v341 - O 19 '96 - p10*+ [501+]
  JEL - v34 - D '96 - p2070 [501+]
Davis, Steven M - *Everglades: The Ecosystem and Its Restoration*
  GJ - v162 - N '96 - p334 [251-500]
Davis, Susan - *The Healthy Woman*
  SB - v32 - O '96 - p201 [51-250]
Davis, Susan Bluestein - *After Midnight*
  Ent W - Ap 4 '97 - p78 [51-250]
Davis, Thomas J - *The Clearest Promises of God*
  Six Ct J - v27 - Fall '96 - p793+ [501+]
  TT - v53 - Ja '97 - p573 [51-250]
Davis, Thulani - *Maker of Saints*
  BL - v93 - S 15 '96 - p219+ [51-250]
  HMR - Win '96 - p24 [501+]
  KR - v64 - Ag 15 '96 - p1171 [251-500]
  NYTBR - v101 - N 17 '96 - p25 [51-250]

Davis, Tracey - *Sammy Davis Jr., My Father*
  KR - v64 - My 1 '96 - p658 [251-500]
Davis, Virginia - *William Waynflete: Bishop and Educationalist*
  Specu - v72 - Ja '97 - p137+ [251-500]
Davis, W E - *The Gathering Storm*
  y VOYA - v19 - O '96 - p206+ [251-500]
  The Proving Ground
  y VOYA - v19 - O '96 - p206+ [51-250]
  The Refining Fire
  LJ - v122 - Ap 1 '97 - p78 [51-250]
Davis, Wade - *One River*
  Aud - v98 - S '96 - p114+ [501+]
  BL - v92 - Ag '96 - p1869 [51-250]
  BL - v93 - Ja '97 - p758 [1-50]
  BW - v27 - F 2 '97 - p6 [501+]
  Mac - v109 - N 4 '96 - p64+ [501+]
  Nature - v384 - N 21 '96 - p229+ [501+]
  NH - v105 - S '96 - p11 [51-250]
  NYTBR - v101 - S 1 '96 - p26 [501+]
Davis, Walter A - *Get the Guests*
  MLR - v91 - O '96 - p985+ [501+]
Davis, Walter Goodwin - *Massachusetts and Maine Families in the Ancestry of Walter Goodwin Davis 1885-1966. Vols. 1-3*
  r Am Geneal - v71 - Ap '96 - p122+ [501+]
Davis, Whitney - *Replications: Archaeology, Art History, Psychoanalysis*
  AB - v99 - Mr 3 '97 - p692 [51-250]
Davis, Will - *Start Your Own Business for $1,000 or Less*
  LJ - v122 - My 1 '97 - p52 [1-50]
Davis, William C - *The Cause Lost*
  Choice - v34 - Ap '97 - p1403 [51-250]
  KR - v64 - S 1 '96 - p1290 [251-500]
  LJ - v121 - N 1 '96 - p78 [51-250]
  WSJ-Cent - v99 - F 26 '97 - pA16 [501+]
  Jefferson Davis: The Man and His Hour
  VQR - v72 - Aut '96 - p141*+ [1-50]
  A Way through the Wilderness
  AHR - v102 - F '97 - p177 [251-500]
Davis-Goff, Annabel - *The Literary Companion to Gambling*
  TLS - D 27 '96 - p36 [501+]
Davison, Jean - *Gender, Lineage, and Ethnicity in Southern Africa*
  R&R Bk N - v12 - F '97 - p30 [51-250]
Davison, Neil R - *James Joyce, Ulysses, and the Construction of Jewish Identity*
  Choice - v34 - N '96 - p455 [51-250]
  TLS - O 11 '96 - p29 [501+]
Davison, Peter Hobley - *George Orwell: A Literary Life*
  Choice - v34 - N '96 - p455 [51-250]
  SFS - v23 - N '96 - p536 [251-500]
Davison, Philip - *The Crooked Man*
  TLS - Ja 17 '97 - p21 [251-500]
Davison, Sydney G - *Basic Theory of Surface States*
  New Sci - v151 - S 28 '96 - p54+ [501+]
Davka
  p Utne R - Jl '96 - p112 [251-500]
Davol, Marguerite W - *Batwings and the Curtain of Night (Illus. by Mary GrandPre)*
  c CCB-B - v50 - Ap '97 - p279 [51-250]
  c KR - v65 - Mr 1 '97 - p379 [51-250]
  c PW - v244 - Mr 3 '97 - p75 [51-250]
  How Snake Got His Hiss (Illus. by Mercedes McDonald)
  c HB Guide - v7 - Fall '96 - p253 [51-250]
D'Avray, D L - *Death and the Prince*
  AHR - v101 - O '96 - p1192+ [501+]
  EHR - v112 - F '97 - p170+ [501+]
Davril, Anselme - *The Winchcombe Sacramentary*
  CH - v65 - D '96 - p675+ [501+]
  Specu - v72 - Ja '97 - p138+ [501+]
Dawe, Donald G - *Christians and Jews Together*
  Rel Ed - v91 - Fall '96 - p609 [1-50]
Dawe, Gerald - *Heart of Hearts*
  ILS - v15 - Fall '96 - p10 [501+]
Dawe, R D - *Sophocles: The Classical Heritage*
  R&R Bk N - v11 - N '96 - p63 [51-250]
Dawes, Kwame - *Prophets*
  WLT - v70 - Aut '96 - p1016+ [501+]
Dawidoff, Nicholas - *The Catcher Was a Spy*
  Aethlon - v13 - Fall '95 - p175+ [501+]
  In the Country of Country
  y BL - v93 - F 15 '97 - p990 [51-250]
  Ent W - My 16 '97 - p108 [51-250]
  KR - v65 - Ja 15 '97 - p112 [251-500]
  LATBR - Mr 30 '97 - p2 [501+]
  NY - v73 - Ap 14 '97 - p85 [51-250]
  PW - v243 - D 16 '96 - p47 [51-250]
  Trib Bks - Ap 6 '97 - p1+ [501+]

Dawisha, Adeed - *The Making of Foreign Policy in Russia and the New States of Eurasia*
  APSR - v90 - S '96 - p692+ [501+]
Dawkins, Richard - *The Blind Watchmaker*
  Bks & Cult - v2 - Ja '96 - p16+ [501+]
  Climbing Mount Improbable
  Aud - v99 - Ja '97 - p108+ [501+]
  y BL - v93 - S 15 '96 - p192 [51-250]
  BL - v93 - D 1 '96 - p630 [1-50]
  Books - v10 - Je '96 - p21 [1-50]
  Books - v11 - Ap '97 - p21 [51-250]
  Choice - v34 - Ap '97 - p1363 [51-250]
  Comw - v123 - D 6 '96 - p29+ [501+]
  LJ - v122 - Ja '97 - p49 [51-250]
  LJ - v121 - N 1 '96 - p105 [51-250]
  Nat R - v48 - O 14 '96 - p83+ [501+]
  Nature - v382 - Jl 25 '96 - p309+ [501+]
  NS & S - v9 - Ap 26 '96 - p35 [251-500]
  NYTBR - v101 - S 29 '96 - p34 [501+]
  PW - v243 - Jl 22 '96 - p222 [51-250]
  Skeptic - v4 - 4 '96 - p103 [501+]
  TLS - S 6 '96 - p24+ [501+]
  The Pocket Watchmaker
  New Sci - v152 - D 7 '96 - p46 [1-50]
  River out of Eden
  Bks & Cult - v2 - Ja '97 - p16+ [501+]
  NYTBR - v101 - S 15 '96 - p44 [51-250]
Dawn, Marva J - *Reaching Out without Dumbing Down*
  TT - v53 - O '96 - p386+ [501+]
Daws, Gavan - *Prisoners of the Japanese*
  NWCR - v49 - Aut '96 - p163 [51-250]
Dawsey, Cyrus B - *The Confederados: Old South Immigrants in Brazil*
  HAHR - v76 - N '96 - p820+ [501+]
Dawson, Anthony Dalston - *The Two Faces of Economics*
  Choice - v34 - F '97 - p1011 [51-250]
Dawson, Carol - *Meeting the Minotaur*
  PW - v244 - My 12 '97 - p56+ [51-250]
Dawson, Doyne - *The Origins of Western Warfare*
  Choice - v34 - Ap '97 - p1394 [51-250]
  J Mil H - v61 - Ap '97 - p356+ [501+]
  PW - v243 - S 16 '96 - p62 [51-250]
Dawson, Geralyn - *The Wedding Raffle*
  PW - v243 - O 7 '96 - p69 [51-250]
Dawson, Imogen - *Food and Feasts in Ancient Greece*
  c HB Guide - v7 - Fall '96 - p378 [51-250]
Dawson, J L - *A Concordance to the Complete Poems and Plays of T.S. Eliot*
  r ARBA - v28 - '97 - p443+ [51-250]
Dawson, Janet - *A Credible Threat*
  y BL - v93 - N 1 '96 - p483 [51-250]
  KR - v64 - S 1 '96 - p1274 [51-250]
  PW - v243 - S 9 '96 - p67+ [51-250]
Dawson, Jeff - *Gay and Lesbian Online*
  r ARBA - v28 - '97 - p307 [51-250]
  HG&LRev - v3 - Fall '96 - p50 [51-250]
  LJ - v122 - Ja '97 - p132 [51-250]
  Quill & Q - v62 - My '96 - p21 [51-250]
Dawson, Jill - *Trick of the Light*
  TLS - Jl 19 '96 - p23 [251-500]
Dawson, John C - *Flow-of-Funds Analysis*
  JEL - v35 - Mr '97 - p207 [51-250]
  R&R Bk N - v11 - D '96 - p24 [51-250]
Dawson, Joseph G, III - *The Texas Military Experience*
  JSH - v62 - N '96 - p847+ [251-500]
Dawson, Kenneth M - *Job Search. 2nd Ed.*
  BWatch - v17 - S '96 - p8 [51-250]
Dawson, Mark - *Nantucket Recipes*
  BL - v93 - Mr 15 '97 - p1215+ [51-250]
Dawson, Mildred L - *Beauty Lab*
  c SLJ - v43 - Mr '97 - p198 [51-250]
Dawson, Wayne E - *The History, Ancestry and Descendants of Davis Billings 1826-1888 and His Wife Adelia Caroline Nichols 1830-1904*
  r EGH - v50 - N '96 - p192 [51-250]
Dawtrey, Liz - *Investigating Modern Art*
  Choice - v34 - F '97 - p956 [51-250]
  VQR - v73 - Win '97 - p32* [51-250]
Day, Aidan - *Romanticism*
  Choice - v34 - Mr '97 - p1158 [251-500]
Day, Alan - *The Falkland Islands, South Georgia, and the South Sandwich Islands*
  r ARBA - v28 - '97 - p69+ [251-500]
  The Falkland Islands, South Georgia and the South Sandwich Islands
  R&R Bk N - v12 - F '97 - p93 [51-250]
Day, David, 1949- - *Claiming a Continent*
  Aust Bk R - N '96 - p34+ [501+]
Day, Dianne - *Fire and Fog*
  BWatch - v17 - S '96 - p1 [51-250]
  y Kliatt - v31 - My '97 - p5+ [51-250]

Day, Dorothy - *Dorothy Day: Arranged for Daily Reading*
RR - v55 - N '96 - p661+ [1-50]
Day, Elaine M - *Studies in Immersion Education*
R&R Bk N - v11 - D '96 - p59 [51-250]
Day, F Holland - *F. Holland Day: Selected Texts and Bibliography*
Choice - v34 - O '96 - p266 [51-250]
Day, Frances Ann - *Multicultural Voices in a Contemporary Literature*
r ES - v27 - Sum '96 - p154+ [501+]
Day, Gary - *British Poetry 1900-50*
ELT - v40 - 1 '97 - p111+ [501+]
Re-Reading Leavis
Choice - v34 - My '97 - p1494 [51-250]
Day, James - *The Vanishing Vision*
J Am Cult - v19 - Sum '96 - p158 [51-250]
Day, Lance - *Biographical Dictionary of the History of Technology*
r ARBA - v28 - '97 - p563 [51-250]
r Choice - v34 - N '96 - p426 [251-500]
Day, Laura - *Practical Intuition*
Books - v11 - Ap '97 - p21 [1-50]
LJ - v121 - O 15 '96 - p78 [51-250]
Day, Malcolm - *The Reader's Digest Children's World Atlas*
cr LATBR - Ag 25 '96 - p11 [51-250]
The World of Castles and Forts
c BL - v93 - Mr 1 '97 - p1157 [51-250]
c SLJ - v43 - F '97 - p113 [51-250]
Day, Marele - *The Disappearances of Madalena Grimaldi*
y SLJ - v42 - N '96 - p140 [51-250]
How to Write Crime
Arm Det - v29 - Fall '96 - p490+ [501+]
Day, Nancy - *Sensational TV*
y HB Guide - v7 - Fall '96 - p307 [51-250]
y SB - v32 - Ag '96 - p172+ [51-250]
Violence in Schools
y HB Guide - v7 - Fall '96 - p316 [51-250]
Day, Noreha Yussof - *Kancil and the Crocodiles (Illus. by Britta Teckentrup)*
c BL - v93 - D 15 '96 - p729 [51-250]
c CBRS - v25 - F '97 - p74 [51-250]
c CCB-B - v50 - Ja '97 - p166+ [51-250]
c HB Guide - v8 - Spr '97 - p100 [51-250]
c KR - v64 - N 1 '96 - p1599+ [51-250]
c PW - v243 - N 4 '96 - p74+ [51-250]
c SLJ - v42 - D '96 - p111 [51-250]
Day, Peter - *Bicycling to Utopia*
SB - v32 - Ag '96 - p168 [51-250]
Day, Robert A - *How to Write and Publish a Scientific Paper*
LR - v45 - 6 '96 - p58+ [251-500]
Day, Trevor - *Math on File*
r Math T - v89 - S '96 - p519+ [251-500]
A Day in the Life of the National Hockey League
Mac - v109 - D 16 '96 - p73 [1-50]
Quill & Q - v62 - N '96 - p38 [51-250]
Dayan, Joan - *Haiti, History, and the Gods*
AHR - v102 - F '97 - p231+ [251-500]
Ant R - v54 - Sum '96 - p362+ [251-500]
Bks & Cult - v3 - Ja '97 - p8+ [501+]
Comw - v123 - O 25 '96 - p27+ [501+]
Daydreams and Nightmares
TranslRevS - v2 - D '96 - p2 [1-50]
WLT - v71 - Win '97 - p181 [501+]
Daymond, M J - *South African Feminisms*
R&R Bk N - v11 - N '96 - p71 [51-250]
Daynard, Jodi - *The Place Within*
BL - v93 - Ja '97 - p808 [1-50]
y BL - v93 - N 15 '96 - p566 [51-250]
LJ - v121 - N 15 '96 - p63 [51-250]
PW - v243 - S 30 '96 - p70 [51-250]
Dayton, Cornelia Hughes - *Women before the Bar*
NYRB - v43 - O 31 '96 - p66+ [501+]
RAH - v25 - Mr '97 - p37+ [501+]
W&M Q - v53 - O '96 - p807+ [501+]
Dazai, Osamu - *Blue Bamboo*
TranslRevS - v1 - My '95 - p25 [1-50]
Deacon, Desley - *Elsie Clews Parsons: Inventing Modern Life*
KR - v65 - Mr 15 '97 - p430 [251-500]
LJ - v122 - Mr 15 '97 - p68+ [51-250]
PW - v244 - Mr 31 '97 - p56 [51-250]
Dead Sea Scrolls. 4Q. Selections - *A Preliminary Edition of the Unpublished Dead Sea Scrolls. Vols. 1-4*
Rel St Rev - v23 - Ap '97 - p194 [51-250]
Quamran Cave 4. Vol. 5
r Rel St Rev - v22 - O '96 - p351+ [51-250]
Dead Sea Scrolls. English - *The Dead Sea Scrolls in English. 4th Ed., Rev. and Extended*
Rel St Rev - v23 - Ja '97 - p86 [51-250]

The Dead Sea Scrolls (Wise)
BL - v93 - N 15 '96 - p553 [51-250]
PW - v243 - O 14 '96 - p78 [51-250]
Theol St - v58 - Mr '97 - p186+ [251-500]
The Dead Sea Scrolls on Microfiche
Rel St Rev - v23 - Ap '97 - p194 [51-250]
Deagan, Kathleen - *Puerto Real*
Am Ant - v61 - Jl '96 - p622+ [501+]
Deakin, B M - *The Youth Labour Market in Britain*
ILR - v135 - 5 '96 - p589+ [501+]
ILRR - v50 - Ap '97 - p527+ [501+]
JEL - v34 - S '96 - p1446 [51-250]
Deakin, John - *John Deakin: Photographs*
VV - v52 - Ja 28 '97 - p48+ [501+]
John Deakin (Schirmer/Mosel)
VLS - Win '96 - p31 [51-250]
Dealer, Stephen - *Lethal Legacy*
Lon R Bks - v18 - S 5 '96 - p17+ [501+]
Dean, Amy E - *Caring for the Family Soul*
BL - v93 - S 1 '96 - p40 [51-250]
Dean, Carolyn J - *Sexuality and Modern Western Culture*
Choice - v34 - D '96 - p695 [51-250]
Dean, David - *Law-Making and Society in Late Elizabethan England*
Choice - v34 - My '97 - p1557 [51-250]
Dean, Hartley - *Welfare, Law and Citizenship*
Readings - v11 - D '96 - p4+ [501+]
Dean, Hazel - *NVQs and How to Get Them*
TES - F 28 '97 - p32 [51-250]
Dean, Joan - *Beginning Teaching in the Secondary School*
TES - O 25 '96 - p2* [501+]
Dean, Jodi - *Solidarity of Strangers*
Wom R Bks - v14 - F '97 - p9 [501+]
Dean, John - *American Popular Culture*
J Am Cult - v19 - Sum '96 - p162 [501+]
European Readings of American Popular Culture
AL - v68 - D '96 - p884 [1-50]
Dean, Pamela - *Tam Lin*
y VOYA - v19 - D '96 - p265 [1-50]
Dean, Philip - *Long Gone Lonesome Cowgirls*
Aust Bk R - D '96 - p76+ [501+]
Dean, Thomas - *Religious Pluralism and Truth*
CPR - v16 - Ag '96 - p249+ [501+]
Dean, Thomas J - *New Venture Formations in United States Manufacturing*
JEL - v34 - S '96 - p1452 [51-250]
Dean, Trevor - *Crime, Society and Law in Renaissance Italy*
EHR - v111 - S '96 - p967+ [251-500]
Dean, Warren - *With Broadax and Firebrand*
HAHR - v76 - Ag '96 - p600+ [501+]
De Anda, Roberto Moreno - *Chicanos and Chicanas in Contemporary Society*
SSQ - v77 - S '96 - p717+ [501+]
DeAndrea, William L - *Fatal Elixir*
KR - v65 - Mr 15 '97 - p419 [51-250]
LJ - v122 - Ap 1 '97 - p133 [51-250]
PW - v244 - F 3 '97 - p98 [51-250]
Killed in the Fog
KR - v64 - S 1 '96 - p1280 [51-250]
LJ - v121 - O 1 '96 - p131 [51-250]
PW - v243 - S 16 '96 - p73 [51-250]
Deane, Bill - *Following the Fugitive*
r ARBA - v28 - '97 - p514 [51-250]
Deane, Seamus - *Reading in the Dark*
y BL - v93 - Ap 1 '97 - p1280 [51-250]
ILS - v16 - Spr '97 - p19 [501+]
KR - v65 - Mr 1 '97 - p321+ [51-250]
LJ - v122 - Mr 15 '97 - p88 [51-250]
Lon R Bks - v18 - S 5 '96 - p15 [251-500]
NS - v125 - Ag 30 '96 - p46 [501+]
NYTLa - v146 - Ap 4 '97 - pC35 [501+]
Obs - Ag 25 '96 - p17* [501+]
PW - v244 - Mr 3 '97 - p64+ [51-250]
TES - D 27 '96 - p16+ [51-250]
TLS - S 27 '96 - p22 [501+]
De Angelis, Barbara - *Ask Barbara*
LJ - v122 - Ja '97 - p125 [51-250]
DeAngelis, James - *The Grantseeker's Handbook of Essential Internet Sites*
r ChrPhil - v9 - O 31 '96 - p67 [51-250]
Dean-Jones, Lesley - *Women's Bodies in Classical Greek Science*
Rel St Rev - v23 - Ap '97 - p171 [51-250]
Deans, Candace - *The Thunderbird Guide to International Business Resources on the World Wide Web*
r Choice - v34 - Ja '97 - p766 [51-250]
De Antonio, Emile - *Painters Painting. Electronic Media Version*
y Kliatt - v31 - Ja '97 - p35 [51-250]

Dear, C B - *The Oxford Companion to World War II*
r ARBA - v28 - '97 - p257 [51-250]
Dear, John - *The God of Peace*
Intpr - v50 - O '96 - p440 [251-500]
Dear, Michael J - *Rethinking Los Angeles*
Choice - v34 - F '97 - p1026+ [51-250]
R&R Bk N - v11 - D '96 - p39 [51-250]
Dear, Peter - *Discipline and Experience*
Albion - v28 - Fall '96 - p486+ [501+]
Isis - v88 - Mr '97 - p122+ [501+]
TLS - S 13 '96 - p27 [501+]
Dear Laura: Letters from Children to Laura Ingalls Wilder
c HB Guide - v7 - Fall '96 - p363+ [51-250]
c RT - v50 - Ap '97 - p595 [51-250]
Dearen, Patrick - *Crossing Rio Pecos*
Roundup M - v4 - O '96 - p25+ [51-250]
Dearing, James W - *Growing a Japanese Science City*
SciTech - v20 - N '96 - p4 [51-250]
Dearling, Robert - *The Illustrated Encyclopedia of Musical Instruments*
r AB - v98 - D 9 '96 - p2000+ [501+]
r ARBA - v28 - '97 - p481 [251-500]
yr BL - v93 - Ja '97 - p892+ [251-500]
r Choice - v34 - Ap '97 - p1310 [51-250]
r LJ - v122 - F 1 '97 - p72 [51-250]
r R&R Bk N - v12 - F '97 - p69 [51-250]
Dearment, Robert K - *Alias Frank Canton*
BL - v92 - Ag '96 - p1877 [51-250]
Roundup M - v4 - F '97 - p23+ [251-500]
Deary, Terry - *The 20th Century*
c Bks Keeps - Mr '97 - p26 [51-250]
True Ghost Stories (Illus. by David Wyatt)
y Kliatt - v31 - Mr '97 - p16 [51-250]
c SLJ - v43 - Ja '97 - p122 [51-250]
True Horror Stories
y Kliatt - v31 - Mr '97 - p16 [51-250]
c SLJ - v43 - Ja '97 - p122 [51-250]
Wicked Words
c Books - v10 - Je '96 - p25 [51-250]
Deas, Malcolm - *El Gobierno Barco*
HAHR - v76 - Ag '96 - p590+ [501+]
Deaton, Angus S - *International Commodity Prices, Macroeconomic Performance, and Politics in Sub-Saharan Africa*
JEL - v34 - D '96 - p2114 [51-250]
Deaver, Jeff - *The Bone Collector*
BL - v93 - D 15 '96 - p692 [51-250]
KR - v64 - D 15 '96 - p1752 [251-500]
LJ - v122 - F 1 '97 - p105 [51-250]
NYTBR - v102 - Mr 16 '97 - p28 [51-250]
PW - v243 - D 16 '96 - p40 [51-250]
WSJ-Cent - v99 - Mr 28 '97 - pA14 [51-250]
The Bone Collector (McCallum). Audio Version
LJ - v122 - Mr 15 '97 - p101+ [51-250]
Deaver, Jeffrey - *Praying for Sleep*
Books - v9 - S '95 - p24 [1-50]
Deaver, Julie Reece - *Chicago Blues*
y Emerg Lib - v24 - S '96 - p27 [1-50]
Say Goodnight, Gracie
y JAAL - v40 - D '96 - p318 [1-50]
Deayton, Angus - *In Search of Happiness*
Books - v9 - S '95 - p23 [1-50]
DeBaggio, Thomas - *Basil: An Herb Lover's Guide*
BL - v93 - S 15 '96 - p195+ [51-250]
BW - v26 - D 29 '96 - p12 [51-250]
BWatch - v17 - D '96 - p9 [51-250]
DeBakey, Michael E - *The New Living Heart*
LJ - v122 - My 1 '97 - p133 [51-250]
De Bartolomeis, Paolo - *Manifolds and Geometry*
SciTech - v20 - D '96 - p20 [1-50]
De Beauport, Elaine - *The Three Faces of Mind*
y BL - v93 - D 15 '96 - p700 [51-250]
PW - v243 - N 4 '96 - p60 [51-250]
De Beck, Billy - *Barney Google and Snuffy Smith*
J Am Cult - v18 - Win '95 - p106+ [51-250]
De Becker, Gavin - *The Gift of Fear*
KR - v65 - My 1 '97 - p711 [51-250]
De Beer, Arrie S - *Mass Media for the Nineties*
JC - v46 - Aut '96 - p162+ [501+]
De Beer, Gabriella - *Contemporary Mexican Women Writers*
Choice - v34 - My '97 - p1504 [51-250]
De Beer, Hans - *Little Polar Bear, Take Me Home! (Illus. by Hans De Beer)*
c BL - v93 - N 1 '96 - p506+ [51-250]
Little Polar Bear, Take Me Home (Illus. by Hans De Beer)
c HB Guide - v8 - Spr '97 - p24 [51-250]
c KR - v64 - S 15 '96 - p1410 [51-250]

Little Polar Bear, Take Me Home! (Illus. by Hans De Beer)
  c SLJ - v42 - N '96 - p79 [51-250]
El Osito Polar Y Su Nueva Amiga
  c BL - v93 - My 1 '97 - p1506 [1-50]
DeBenedette, Valerie - *Caffeine*
  y CLW - v67 - Mr '97 - p55+ [51-250]
  y HB Guide - v8 - Spr '97 - p98 [51-250]
  y SLJ - v42 - S '96 - p232 [51-250]
De Bernieres, Louis - *Captain Corelli's Mandolin*
  NS - v125 - D 20 '96 - p116 [1-50]
  TES - D 27 '96 - p17 [1-50]
  TLS - N 29 '96 - p13 [51-250]
DeBerry, Virginia - *Tryin' to Sleep in the Bed You Made*
  BL - v93 - N 1 '96 - p459 [51-250]
  KR - v64 - N 15 '96 - p1619 [251-500]
  PW - v243 - N 18 '96 - p62 [51-250]
De Bevoise, Ken - *Agents of Apocalypse*
  Historian - v59 - Fall '96 - p171+ [501+]
De Blij, Harm J - *Geography: Realms, Regions, and Concepts. 8th Ed.*
  R&R Bk N - v12 - F '97 - p28 [51-250]
Harm De Blij's Geography Book
  GJ - v162 - N '96 - p343 [1-50]
Deblinger, Esther - *Treating Sexually Abused Children and Their Nonoffending Parents*
  SciTech - v20 - D '96 - p53 [51-250]
DeBlois, Jean - *A Primer for Health Care Ethics*
  Theol St - v57 - Mr '96 - p192 [51-250]
Deboer, Warren R - *Traces behind the Esmeraldas Shore*
  LA Ant - v7 - D '96 - p373+ [501+]
De Botton, Alain - *How Proust Can Change Your Life*
  KR - v65 - Mr 15 '97 - p430+ [251-500]
  Obs - Ap 13 '97 - p16* [501+]
  PW - v244 - Mr 3 '97 - p53 [51-250]
Kiss and Tell
  Books - v9 - S '95 - p22 [1-50]
  NY - v72 - S 23 '96 - p95 [51-250]
DeBresson, Christian - *Economic Interdependence and Innovative Activity*
  JEL - v35 - Mr '97 - p279+ [51-250]
  R&R Bk N - v11 - D '96 - p24 [51-250]
Debrett's Tracing Your Ancestors
  TES - Jl 26 '96 - pR6 [51-250]
Debreu, Gerard - *General Equilibrium Theory. Vols. 1-3*
  JEL - v35 - Mr '97 - p200 [1-50]
Debreuille, Jean-Yves - *Lectures D'Andre Gide*
  FR - v70 - O '96 - p120+ [501+]
De Bruyn, Frans - *The Literary Genres of Edmund Burke*
  Choice - v34 - My '97 - p1494 [51-250]
Decalo, Samuel - *Historical Dictionary of Congo. 3rd Ed.*
  r ARBA - v28 - '97 - p52 [251-500]
  r ARBA - v28 - '97 - p55 [251-500]
  r Choice - v34 - Mr '97 - p1134+ [51-250]
  r R&R Bk N - v12 - F '97 - p21 [51-250]
DeCarava, Roy - *Roy DeCarava: A Retrospective*
  Afterimage - v24 - Ja '97 - p15+ [501+]
  BL - v93 - Ja '97 - p758 [1-50]
  VV - v52 - Ja 28 '97 - p48+ [501+]
De Carlo, Andrea - *Uto*
  Econ - v339 - My 18 '96 - p16*+ [501+]
DeCaro, Louis A, Jr. - *On the Side of My People*
  CC - v113 - S 25 '96 - p902+ [501+]
De Cataldo Neuburger, Luisella - *Women and Terrorism*
  R&R Bk N - v12 - F '97 - p57 [51-250]
DeCesare, Angelo - *Anthony, the Perfect Monster (Illus. by Angelo DeCesare)*
  c HB Guide - v7 - Fall '96 - p284 [1-50]
  c SLJ - v42 - S '96 - p177 [51-250]
De Champeaux, Dennis - *Object-Oriented Development Process and Metrics*
  SciTech - v20 - D '96 - p8 [1-50]
DeChancie, John - *Castle Fantastic*
  SF Chr - v18 - O '96 - p80 [1-50]
From Prussia with Love
  SF Chr - v18 - O '96 - p77 [1-50]
DeChant, Betsy - *Women and Group Psychotherapy*
  SciTech - v20 - N '96 - p44 [51-250]
Dechert, W Davis - *Chaos Theory in Economics*
  JEL - v35 - Mr '97 - p196 [51-250]
De Chirico, Giorgio - *L'Art Metaphysique*
  JAAC - v54 - Fall '96 - p406+ [501+]
DeCicco, Lynne Marie - *Women and Lawyers in the Mid-Nineteenth Century English Novel*
  Nine-C Lit - v51 - Mr '97 - p555 [1-50]
Deck, Allan Figueroa - *Perspectivas: Hispanic Ministry*
  Rel St Rev - v23 - Ap '97 - p156 [51-250]
Deck the Halls (Illus. by Iris Van Rynbach)
  c HB Guide - v8 - Spr '97 - p140 [51-250]
  c PW - v243 - S 30 '96 - p92 [1-50]
  c SLJ - v42 - O '96 - p42 [51-250]

Decker, Ronald - *A Wicked Pack of Cards*
  BW - v27 - Mr 30 '97 - p9 [501+]
  LJ - v122 - Ap 1 '97 - p109 [51-250]
  TLS - Ja 24 '97 - p36 [501+]
Decker, Scott H - *Life in the Gang*
  Choice - v34 - F '97 - p1042 [51-250]
Decker, Therese - *Mariken Van Nieumghen*
  TranslRevS - v1 - My '95 - p17 [51-250]
DeClements, Barthe - *Tough Loser*
  c PW - v243 - N 25 '96 - p78 [1-50]
Decoin, Didier - *La Promeneuse D'Oiseaux*
  WLT - v71 - Win '97 - p102+ [251-500]
De Coteau Orie, Sandra - *Did You Hear Wind Sing Your Name? (Illus. by Christopher Canyon)*
  c LA - v73 - D '96 - p624 [51-250]
Decraemer, W - *The Family Trichodoridae*
  SciTech - v20 - N '96 - p58 [51-250]
De Cristoforo, Violet Kazue - *May Sky*
  y BL - v93 - F 1 '97 - p922 [51-250]
Decter, Ann - *Honour*
  Quill & Q - v62 - My '96 - p25 [251-500]
Dedera, Don - *Navajo Rugs. 2nd Rev. Ed.*
  Nat Peop - v10 - '97 - p78+ [501+]
Dedieu, Thierry - *The Boy Who Ate Words (Illus. by Thierry Dedieu)*
  c PW - v244 - Ap 28 '97 - p75+ [51-250]
De Dios, Emmanuel S - *Choice, Growth and Development*
  JEL - v35 - Mr '97 - p271+ [51-250]
De Domhal, F T - *Medical Informatics*
  SciTech - v20 - N '96 - p36 [51-250]
De Duve, Christian - *Vital Dust*
  BIC - v25 - O '96 - p35+ [501+]
Dee, Arthur - *Fasciculus Chemicus*
  r SciTech - v21 - Mr '97 - p28 [51-250]
Dee, Catherine - *The Girls' Guide to Life (Illus. by Cynthia Jabar)*
  c CBRS - v25 - Ap '97 - p105 [51-250]
  c PW - v244 - Mr 31 '97 - p77 [51-250]
Dee, Ed - *Little Boy Blue*
  BL - v93 - D 1 '96 - p619 [51-250]
  KR - v64 - N 1 '96 - p1549 [251-500]
  PW - v243 - N 11 '96 - p54 [51-250]
Dee, Jonathan - *The Liberty Campaign (Longe). Audio Version*
  y Kliatt - v30 - S '96 - p49 [51-250]
St. Famous
  LATBR - Mr 24 '96 - p10 [51-250]
Deedy, Carmen Agra - *La Cama De Plumas De Agata (Illus. by Laura L Seeley)*
  c BL - v93 - My 1 '97 - p1506 [51-250]
Deem, James M - *3 NBs of Julian Drew*
  y Kliatt - v30 - N '96 - p8 [51-250]
The Very Real Ghost Book of Christina Rose
  c HB Guide - v7 - Fall '96 - p291 [51-250]
  y VOYA - v19 - O '96 - p208 [251-500]
Deems, Edward M - *Holy Days and Holidays*
  JPC - v29 - Spr '96 - p233+ [51-250]
Deen, Rosemary - *Naming the Light*
  LJ - v121 - D '96 - p137 [51-250]
  PW - v243 - N 18 '96 - p69 [51-250]
Deense Keramiek
  Am Craft - v56 - O '96 - p51+ [51-250]
Deep, John - *Developing CGI Applications with Perl*
  CBR - v14 - N '96 - p35 [1-50]
Deery, June - *Aldous Huxley and the Mysticism of Science*
  New Sci - v151 - S 14 '96 - p45 [51-250]
  Obs - N 10 '96 - p15* [501+]
Dees, Morris - *Gathering Storm*
  Bks & Cult - v2 - N '96 - p18+ [501+]
  Nat - v263 - O 28 '96 - p20+ [501+]
Deetz, James - *In Small Things Forgotten. Rev. and Expanded Ed.*
  LATBR - O 6 '96 - p15 [51-250]
  y SB - v33 - Mr '97 - p47 [51-250]
Defect Recognition and Image Processing in Semiconductors 1995
  SciTech - v20 - S '96 - p57 [51-250]
DeFelice, Cynthia C - *The Apprenticeship of Lucas Whitaker*
  c BL - v93 - O 1 '96 - p348 [51-250]
  c BL - v93 - Ap 1 '97 - p1298 [1-50]
  c CCB-B - v50 - O '96 - p54+ [51-250]
  c HB - v73 - Ja '97 - p55 [51-250]
  c HB Guide - v8 - Spr '97 - p64 [51-250]
  y Par Ch - v21 - Mr '97 - p12 [1-50]
  c SLJ - v42 - Ag '96 - p142 [51-250]
  c SLJ - v42 - D '96 - p28 [1-50]
Casey in the Bath (Illus. by Chris L Demarest)
  c HB Guide - v8 - Fall '96 - p253 [1-50]
The Dancing Skeleton (Illus. by Robert Andrew Parker)
  c PW - v243 - S 16 '96 - p85 [1-50]

Three Perfect Peaches (Illus. by Irene Trivas)
  c Ch BWatch - v6 - Jl '96 - p7 [51-250]
  c RT - v50 - Mr '97 - p503 [51-250]
Weasel
  c SLJ - v42 - N '96 - p40 [1-50]
Willy's Silly Grandma (Illus. by Shelley Jackson)
  c CBRS - v25 - Mr '97 - p86 [51-250]
  c HB - v73 - My '97 - p304+ [251-500]
  c KR - v65 - Mr 1 '97 - p379 [51-250]
  c PW - v244 - F 24 '97 - p89 [51-250]
Deffaa, Chip - *Blue Rhythms*
  Choice - v34 - F '97 - p974 [51-250]
Jazz Veterans
  Bloom Rev - v16 - N '96 - p24 [51-250]
  LJ - v121 - O 15 '96 - p59+ [51-250]
Defoe, Daniel - *Jure Divino*
  PQ - v75 - Win '96 - p43+ [501+]
Moll Flanders (Leishman). Audio Version
  BL - v93 - My 15 '97 - p1596 [51-250]
  y Kliatt - v31 - My '97 - p42 [51-250]
Robinson Crusoe
  Reason - v28 - D '96 - p39 [51-250]
Robinson Crusoe (Baker). Audio Version
  c Ch BWatch - v7 - Ja '97 - p5 [1-50]
A Tour through the Whole Island of Great Britain
  PQ - v74 - Fall '95 - p395+ [501+]
Defoort, Carine - *The Pheasant Cap Master*
  R&R Bk N - v12 - F '97 - p1 [51-250]
DeFranca, George G - *Pelvic Locomotor Dysfunction*
  SciTech - v20 - N '96 - p57 [51-250]
DeFrancis, Beth - *The Parents' Resource Almanac*
  r BL - v93 - F 1 '97 - p959 [51-250]
DeFrancis, John - *ABC Chinese-English Dictionary*
  r Choice - v34 - Ap '97 - p1305 [51-250]
Degaetano, Gloria - *Screen Smarts*
  SLJ - v42 - O '96 - p46 [51-250]
Degarmo, E Paul - *Engineering Economy. 10th Ed.*
  SciTech - v20 - D '96 - p60 [51-250]
Degas, Edgar - *Degas by Himself*
  TES - Ag 30 '96 - p26 [1-50]
Degen, Bruce - *Sailaway Home (Illus. by Bruce Degen)*
  c BL - v92 - Ag '96 - p1907 [51-250]
  c HB Guide - v7 - Fall '96 - p238 [51-250]
Degenaar, Marjolein - *Molyneux's Problem*
  R&R Bk N - v11 - D '96 - p3 [51-250]
Degenhardt, William G - *The Amphibians and Reptiles of New Mexico*
  SciTech - v21 - Mr '97 - p38 [1-50]
Degens, T - *Freya on the Wall*
  y CCB-B - v50 - Ap '97 - p279+ [51-250]
  y KR - v65 - F 1 '97 - p221 [51-250]
  y PW - v244 - F 10 '97 - p84 [51-250]
Degeorge, Gail - *The Making of a Blockbuster*
  Trib Bks - Mr 9 '97 - p8 [1-50]
Degh, Linda - *American Folklore and the Mass Media*
  J Am Cult - v18 - Win '95 - p112 [51-250]
  Signs - v22 - Win '97 - p491+ [501+]
Degler, Teri - *The Fiery Muse*
  Quill & Q - v62 - Je '96 - p19 [501+]
Deglin, Judith Hopfer - *Davis's Drug Guide for Nurses. 5th Ed.*
  r SciTech - v20 - N '96 - p55 [51-250]
DeGlopper, Donald R - *Lukang: Commerce and Community in a Chinese City*
  Am Ethnol - v24 - F '97 - p260+ [501+]
Degnon, Dom - *Sails Full and By*
  Aethlon - v13 - Spr '96 - p215 [251-500]
De Goldi, Kate - *Sanctuary*
  y Magpies - v11 - S '96 - p37 [51-250]
DeGraaf, Richard M - *Neotropical Migratory Birds*
  r ARBA - v28 - '97 - p587 [51-250]
De Grauwe, Jan - *Capitula Generalia Cartusiae 1416-1442*
  CH - v66 - Mr '97 - p191+ [51-250]
De Grave, Kathleen - *Swindler, Spy, Rebel*
  AHR - v102 - F '97 - p183 [251-500]
  Legacy - v14 - 1 '97 - p67+ [501+]
DeGrazia, David - *Taking Animals Seriously*
  Choice - v34 - F '97 - p981 [51-250]
De Grazia, Sebastian - *A Country with No Name*
  y BL - v93 - F 15 '97 - p994 [51-250]
  KR - v65 - Ja 15 '97 - p113 [251-500]
  LATBR - Mr 23 '97 - p6 [501+]
  PW - v243 - D 30 '96 - p46 [51-250]
Machiavelli in Hell
  CR - v268 - Je '96 - p333 [51-250]
De Groat, Diane - *Roses Are Pink, Your Feet Really Stink*
  c HB Guide - v7 - Fall '96 - p253 [51-250]

De Groot, Gerard J - *Blighty: British Society in the Era of the Great War*
Choice - v34 - Ja '97 - p855 [51-250]
TLS - O 18 '96 - p32 [501+]
DeGrove, John - *Land, Growth, and Politics*
NCR - v85 - Spr '96 - p64 [51-250]
De Gruchy, John W - *Christianity and Democracy*
Bks & Cult - v2 - My '96 - p24+ [501+]
RP - v58 - Fall '96 - p834+ [501+]
TT - v53 - Ja '97 - p568+ [51-250]
De Grummond, Nancy Thomson - *An Encyclopedia of the History of Classical Archaeology. Vols. 1-2*
r ARBA - v28 - '97 - p183 [51-250]
r BL - v93 - F 1 '97 - p964+ [501+]
r Choice - v34 - My '97 - p1474+ [51-250]
DeHaan, Vici - *State Parks of the South*
r BL - v93 - S 15 '96 - p206 [1-50]
De Hamel, Christopher - *Glossed Books of the Bible and the Origins of the Parisian Booktrade*
AB - v99 - Mr 3 '97 - p685+ [501+]
A History of Illuminated Manuscripts. 2nd Ed.
AB - v99 - Mr 3 '97 - p685+ [501+]
Scribes and Illuminators
AB - v99 - Mr 3 '97 - p685+ [501+]
DeHart, Roy L - *Fundamentals of Aerospace Medicine. 2nd Ed.*
r SciTech - v20 - D '96 - p48 [51-250]
De Haven, Tom - *Derby Dugan's Depression Funnies*
LATBR - Ag 18 '96 - p11 [501+]
NYTBR - v101 - D 8 '96 - p79 [1-50]
y SLJ - v42 - D '96 - p150+ [51-250]
The Orphan's Tent
y CBRS - v25 - S '96 - p11 [51-250]
y HB Guide - v8 - Spr '97 - p78 [51-250]
y SLJ - v42 - O '96 - p144 [51-250]
y VOYA - v19 - D '96 - p268 [251-500]
De Heer, Rolf - *Bad Boy Bubby*
Aust Bk R - Jl '96 - p42+ [501+]
Dehlin, Joel - *Object Programming with Visual Basic 4*
CBR - v14 - S '96 - p32 [1-50]
De Hoop, Adrianus T - *Handbook of Radiation and Scattering of Waves*
SIAM Rev - v39 - Mr '97 - p163+ [501+]
Dehouve, Daniele - *Hacia Una Historia Del Espacio En La Montana De Guerrero*
HAHR - v77 - F '97 - p117+ [251-500]
Dehue, Trudy - *Changing the Rules*
Isis - v87 - D '96 - p760 [501+]
Deichmann, Ute - *Biologists under Hitler*
Choice - v34 - S '96 - p149 [51-250]
HRNB - v25 - Win '97 - p74 [501+]
SciTech - v20 - S '96 - p18 [51-250]
TLS - N 22 '96 - p28 [501+]
Deidier, Roberto - *Il Passo Del Giorno*
WLT - v71 - Win '97 - p129 [501+]
Deift, Percy - *Dynamical Systems and Probabilistic Methods in Partial Differential Equations*
SIAM Rev - v38 - S '96 - p545 [1-50]
Deigh, John - *The Sources of Moral Agency*
Choice - v34 - F '97 - p977+ [51-250]
Hast Cen R - v27 - Ja '97 - p46 [1-50]
Deighton, Len - *Charity*
KR - v64 - O 1 '96 - p1418+ [251-500]
Nat R - v48 - D 23 '96 - p56 [51-250]
NYTBR - v102 - Ja 12 '97 - p21 [251-500]
PW - v243 - N 4 '96 - p64 [51-250]
TLS - S 20 '96 - p23 [251-500]
Trib Bks - Ja 19 '97 - p6 [251-500]
Deines-Jones, Courtney - *Preparing Staff to Serve Patrons with Disabilities*
LAR - v98 - S '96 - p479 [51-250]
Deininger, Klaus W - *Technical Change, Human Capital, and Spillovers in United States Agriculture 1949-1985*
JEH - v56 - S '96 - p746+ [501+]
Deitz, Tom - *Dreamseeker's Road*
y Kliatt - v30 - S '96 - p16 [51-250]
Deivert, Bert - *Film and Video on the Internet*
r BL - v92 - Ag '96 - p1922 [51-250]
r Choice - v34 - D '96 - p588 [51-250]
r Film Cr - v21 - Win '96 - p63+ [501+]
De Janvry, Alain - *State, Market and Civil Organizations*
Econ J - v107 - Ja '97 - p280 [251-500]
DeJesus, Joy L - *Growing Up Puerto Rican*
y BL - v93 - My 15 '97 - p1556 [51-250]
PW - v244 - My 5 '97 - p186 [51-250]
De Jong, Dola - *The Tree and the Vine*
TranslRevS - v2 - D '96 - p20 [51-250]
De Jong, Nicolas J - *Shipbuilding on Prince Edward Island*
Sea H - Sum '96 - p30 [51-250]

De Kay, James Tertius - *Chronicles of the Frigate Macedonian 1809-1922*
Beav - v76 - D '96 - p44 [501+]
DeKieffer, Donald E - *The Citizen's Guide to Lobbying Congress*
BL - v93 - D 15 '96 - p696 [51-250]
Dekmejian, R Hrair - *Islam in Revolution. 2nd Ed.*
Rel St Rev - v23 - Ap '97 - p200 [51-250]
De Knop, Paul - *Worldwide Trends in Youth Sport*
Choice - v34 - N '96 - p498 [51-250]
De Koster, Katie - *Readings on Mark Twain*
y Ch BWatch - v6 - Jl '96 - p2 [1-50]
y Kliatt - v30 - N '96 - p18 [51-250]
y SLJ - v42 - Ag '96 - p167+ [51-250]
De La Billiere, Peter, Sir - *Looking for Trouble*
Books - v9 - S '95 - p24 [1-50]
De La Campa, Roman - *Late Imperial Culture*
WLT - v71 - Win '97 - p235 [501+]
Delacorta - *The Rap Factor*
TranslRevS - v1 - My '95 - p18 [51-250]
Delacorte, Peter - *Time on My Hands*
PW - v244 - Ap 21 '97 - p58 [51-250]
Delacre, Lulu - *De Oro Y Esmeraldas (Illus. by Lulu Delacre)*
c BL - v93 - My 1 '97 - p1506 [1-50]
c SLJ - v42 - N '96 - p132 [51-250]
Golden Tales (Illus. by Lulu Delacre)
c BL - v93 - D 15 '96 - p722 [51-250]
c CCB-B - v50 - Ja '97 - p167 [51-250]
c HB Guide - v8 - Spr '97 - p100 [1-50]
c PW - v243 - S 9 '96 - p85 [51-250]
c SLJ - v42 - S '96 - p213 [51-250]
Delafosse, Claude - *Atlas of Animals*
cr Ch BWatch - v7 - Ja '97 - p2 [1-50]
Atlas of People (Illus. by Denise Millet)
cr SLJ - v43 - F '97 - p88+ [51-250]
Atlas of Plants (Illus. by Sylvaine Perols)
cr HB Guide - v7 - Fall '96 - p340 [51-250]
cr SLJ - v42 - S '96 - p195 [51-250]
Bees (Illus. by Ute Fuhr)
c KR - v65 - Ja 15 '97 - p139 [51-250]
The Butterfly (Illus. by Helliadore)
c Bks Keeps - Ja '97 - p21 [51-250]
Cars and Trucks and Other Vehicles (Illus. by Sophie Kniffke)
c HB Guide - v7 - Fall '96 - p350 [51-250]
Landscapes
c HB Guide - v7 - Fall '96 - p355 [51-250]
Paintings (Illus. by Tony Ross)
c HB Guide - v7 - Fall '96 - p355 [51-250]
The Telephone (Illus. by J-M Poissenot)
c JB - v60 - D '96 - p249 [51-250]
De La Garza, Rodolfo O - *Ethnic Ironies*
APSR - v90 - D '96 - p906+ [501+]
De Laguna, Frederica - *Tales from the Dena*
WLT - v70 - Aut '96 - p1007+ [501+]
De La Haye, Amy - *Surfers, Soulies, Skinheads, and Skaters*
Esq - v126 - D '96 - p40 [1-50]
KR - v64 - D 1 '96 - p1728 [51-250]
LATBR - D 8 '96 - p30 [51-250]
Delahaye, Gilbert - *Martine Chez Tante Lucie*
c BL - v93 - N 1 '96 - p500 [1-50]
Delamare, David - *The Man in the Moon and the Hot Air Balloon*
c HB Guide - v7 - Fall '96 - p253 [1-50]
De La Mare, Walter - *Short Stories 1895-1926*
Obs - D 22 '96 - p15* [501+]
Delaney, A - *Pearl's First Prize Plant (Illus. by A Delaney)*
c KR - v65 - My 1 '97 - p718 [51-250]
c PW - v244 - Ap 21 '97 - p71 [51-250]
Delaney, Gayle - *In Your Dream*
PW - v244 - My 12 '97 - p71+ [51-250]
Delaney, John - *The House of Scribner 1846-1904*
r ARBA - v28 - '97 - p439+ [51-250]
Delaney, Michael - *Deep Doo-Doo*
c BL - v93 - Ja '97 - p858+ [251-500]
c CBRS - v25 - F '97 - p81 [51-250]
c CCB-B - v50 - F '97 - p202 [51-250]
c HB Guide - v8 - Spr '97 - p64 [51-250]
c KR - v64 - O 15 '96 - p1531 [51-250]
c PW - v243 - N 18 '96 - p75+ [51-250]
c SLJ - v42 - D '96 - p120 [51-250]
Delannoy, Luc - *Pres: The Story of Lester Young*
TranslRevS - v1 - My '95 - p12 [1-50]
De-La-Noy, Michael - *Mervyn Stockwood: A Lonely Life*
Spec - v277 - N 30 '96 - p58 [1-50]
TLS - O 4 '96 - p29 [51-250]
Delanty, Gerard - *Inventing Europe*
CH - v66 - Mr '97 - p214 [51-250]

Delany, Hilary - *Equity and the Law of Trusts in Ireland*
Law Q Rev - v113 - Ja '97 - p177 [51-250]
Delany, Martin R - *Blake; or The Huts of America*
AL - v68 - S '96 - p527+ [501+]
Delany, Samuel R - *The Bridge of Lost Desire*
RCF - v16 - Fall '96 - p148+ [501+]
Dhalgren
RCF - v16 - Fall '96 - p129+ [501+]
RCF - v16 - Fall '96 - p136+ [501+]
Flight from Neveryon
RCF - v16 - Fall '96 - p148+ [501+]
Hogg
RCF - v16 - Fall '96 - p125+ [501+]
Longer Views
Nat - v263 - O 28 '96 - p60+ [501+]
NYTBR - v101 - D 29 '96 - p15 [251-500]
SFS - v24 - Mr '97 - p156+ [501+]
Neveryona
RCF - v16 - Fall '96 - p148+ [501+]
Stars in My Pocket like Grains of Sand
RCF - v16 - Fall '96 - p153+ [501+]
Tales of Neveryon
RCF - v16 - Fall '96 - p148+ [501+]
Triton
RCF - v16 - Fall '96 - p142+ [501+]
Wagner/Artaud
RCF - v16 - Fall '96 - p161+ [501+]
Delany, Sarah Louise - *Having Our Say (Goldberg). Audio Version*
CSM - v89 - Mr 27 '97 - pB1 [1-50]
On My Own at 107
BL - v93 - D 15 '96 - p690 [51-250]
KR - v64 - D 1 '96 - p1713 [251-500]
LJ - v122 - F 1 '97 - p90 [51-250]
PW - v243 - D 9 '96 - p56 [51-250]
De La Paz, Luis - *Un Verano Incesante*
BL - v93 - Ap 1 '97 - p1284 [1-50]
WLT - v71 - Win '97 - p115+ [501+]
De La Roche, Elisa - *Teatro Hispano!*
HAHR - v77 - F '97 - p98 [251-500]
TDR - v41 - Spr '97 - p161 [51-250]
r Theat J - v48 - O '96 - p387+ [501+]
De La Ronciere, Charles M - *Religion Paysanne Et Religion Urbaine En Toscane (c. 1250-c. 1450)*
CHR - v82 - O '96 - p690+ [501+]
Delaunois, Angele - *Kotik: The Baby Seal (Illus. by Fred Bruemmer)*
c SLJ - v42 - Ag '96 - p151 [51-250]
Nanook and Naoya (Illus. by Fred Bruemmer)
c SLJ - v42 - Ag '96 - p151 [51-250]
De La Valdene, Guy - *For a Handful of Feathers*
Bloom Rev - v16 - Jl '96 - p23+ [501+]
Delbanco, Andrew - *The Death of Satan*
AHR - v102 - F '97 - p167 [251-500]
NEQ - v69 - S '96 - p500+ [501+]
NYTBR - v101 - D 15 '96 - p40 [1-50]
Rapport - v19 - 4 '96 - p40 [51-250]
Delbard, Henri - *Diary of a Rose Lover*
PW - v243 - S 23 '96 - p70 [51-250]
Delbo, Charlotte - *Auschwitz and After*
TranslRevS - v2 - D '96 - p7+ [51-250]
Del Boca, Angelo - *I Gas Di Mussolini*
J Mil H - v60 - O '96 - p783 [251-500]
Del Bono, Gianna - *Storia Delle Biblioteche Fra Settecento E Novecento*
r Lib - v18 - D '96 - p364 [51-250]
Del Calzo, Nick - *The Triumphant Spirit*
y BL - v93 - Mr 15 '97 - p1223 [51-250]
PW - v244 - F 3 '97 - p91 [1-50]
Del Carmen, Rolando V - *Community Supervision*
Fed Prob - v60 - D '96 - p65 [51-250]
Delchambre, Alain - *CAD Method for Industrial Assembly*
Robotica - v15 - Mr '97 - p233 [251-500]
Delegue, Yves - *Bonaventure Des Periers: Le Cymbalum Mundi Avec Un Dossier Et Des Textes D'Accompagnement*
MLR - v92 - Ap '97 - p465+ [51-250]
Delehanty, Randolph - *Art in the American South*
Choice - v34 - My '97 - p1485 [51-250]
LJ - v122 - F 15 '97 - p131 [51-250]
S Liv - v32 - Mr '97 - p62 [51-250]
Classic Natchez
Choice - v34 - S '96 - p111+ [51-250]
Deleplace, Ghislain - *Money in Motion*
JEL - v34 - D '96 - p2036 [51-250]
Deletant, Dennis - *Ceausescu and the Securitate*
Choice - v34 - D '96 - p682 [51-250]
Cu H - v96 - Mr '97 - p140 [501+]
R&R Bk N - v11 - N '96 - p45 [51-250]
Deleuze, Gilles - *What Is Philosophy?*
TranslRevS - v2 - D '96 - p5 [51-250]

Delft, Pieter Van - *Creative Puzzles of the World*
  Math T - v89 - S '96 - p514 [51-250]
Delgado, Ana Maria - *The Room In-Between*
  ABR - v17 - Ag '96 - p16+ [501+]
Delgado, James P - *Ghost Fleet*
  Choice - v34 - My '97 - p1561 [51-250]
  LJ - v121 - N 1 '96 - p78 [51-250]
Delgado, Maria Isabel - *Chave's Memories*
  SLJ - v42 - D '96 - p91+ [51-250]
Delgado, Maria M - *In Contact with the Gods?*
  LJ - v121 - O 1 '96 - p79+ [51-250]
  Obs - v54 - O 13 '96 - p18* [51-250]
Delgado, Mariano - *Die Metamorphosen Des Messianismus In Den Iberischen Kulturen*
  HAHR - v77 - F '97 - p81+ [501+]
Delgado, Richard - *The Coming Race War*
  Rapport - v19 - 6 '96 - p35 [251-500]
  The Coming Race War? and Other Apocalyptic Tales of America after Affirmative Action and Welfare
  BW - v26 - N 3 '96 - p4+ [501+]
  Choice - v34 - Ja '97 - p882 [51-250]
  New R - v215 - D 9 '96 - p27+ [501+]
  Rapport - v19 - 6 '96 - p35 [251-500]
Delgado Morales, Manuel - *The Calderonian Stage*
  Choice - v34 - My '97 - p1504 [51-250]
Del Galdo, Elisa M - *International User Interfaces*
  New Sci - v153 - Mr 1 '97 - p46+ [501+]
  SciTech - v20 - S '96 - p8 [51-250]
Del Giudice, Daniele - *Takeoff: The Pilot's Lore*
  BL - v93 - My 15 '97 - p1550 [51-250]
  KR - v65 - Mr 15 '97 - p431 [251-500]
  PW - v244 - Mr 10 '97 - p54 [51-250]
  Spec - v278 - Ja 18 '97 - p31 [501+]
Del Giudice, Lusia - *Studies in Italian American Folklore*
  CAY - v16 - Fall '95 - p12 [51-250]
DeLillo, Don - *White Noise*
  Clio - v25 - Spr '96 - p255+ [501+]
  Col Lit - v23 - Je '96 - p25+ [501+]
Delingpole, James - *Fish Show*
  Spec - v278 - Mr 1 '97 - p30 [251-500]
Delinsky, Barbara - *Shades of Grace*
  PW - v244 - Ja 27 '97 - p103 [1-50]
  A Woman's Place
  BL - v93 - F 1 '97 - p907 [51-250]
  KR - v65 - Ja 1 '97 - p8 [251-500]
  LJ - v122 - F 15 '97 - p161 [51-250]
  PW - v244 - Ja 20 '97 - p393+ [51-250]
  Trib Bks - My 11 '97 - p11 [51-250]
De Lint, Charles - *Jack the Giant Killer*
  y VOYA - v19 - D '96 - p265 [1-50]
  Spiritwalk
  Books - v9 - S '95 - p27 [1-50]
  Trader
  y BL - v93 - Ja '97 - p826 [51-250]
  KR - v64 - N 15 '96 - p1639 [51-250]
  LJ - v121 - D '96 - p152 [51-250]
  PW - v243 - D 9 '96 - p65 [51-250]
  Quill & Q - v63 - Ja '97 - p18 [51-250]
  Quill & Q - v63 - F '97 - p49 [251-500]
DeLio, Thomas - *The Music of Morton Feldman*
  Choice - v34 - S '96 - p137 [51-250]
  M Ed J - v83 - N '96 - p54 [1-50]
De Lisle, Harold F - *The Natural History of Monitor Lizards*
  Choice - v34 - D '96 - p638 [51-250]
  SciTech - v20 - N '96 - p29 [1-50]
Delisle, Jean - *Translators through History*
  TranslRevS - v2 - D '96 - p14 [51-250]
Dell, Edmund - *The Chancellors: A History of the Chancellors of the Exchequer 1945-90*
  NS - v125 - N 1 '96 - p44+ [501+]
  TLS - N 29 '96 - p10 [501+]
Dell, Edward, Jr. - *Power Amp Book*
  TCI - v30 - O '96 - p56 [1-50]
Dell, Katharine - *Shaking a Fist at God*
  BL - v93 - F 15 '97 - p975 [51-250]
  LJ - v122 - Ja '97 - p106 [51-250]
Della Coletta, Cristina - *Plotting the Past*
  Choice - v34 - Ap '97 - p1344 [51-250]
Della Croce, Julia - *The Classic Italian Cookbook*
  BWatch - v18 - F '97 - p7 [51-250]
  Salse Di Pomodoro
  BWatch - v17 - N '96 - p1 [51-250]
Dellamora, Richard - *Apocalyptic Overtures*
  VS - v39 - Win '96 - p241+ [501+]
Della Porta, Donatella - *Social Movements, Political Violence, and the State*
  PSQ - v111 - Win '96 - p709+ [501+]
Della Torre, Stefano - *Pellegrino Tibaldi E Il S Fedele Di Milano*
  Apo - v145 - F '97 - p61+ [501+]

Dellepiane, Angela B - *Concordancias Del Poema Martin Fierro. Vols. 1-2*
  Hisp - v79 - D '96 - p801+ [501+]
Dellheim, Charles - *The Disenchanted Isle*
  CS - v26 - Ja '97 - p30+ [501+]
  Rapport - v19 - 4 '96 - p41 [251-500]
Delli Carpini, Michael X - *What Americans Know about Politics and Why It Matters*
  Choice - v34 - S '96 - p210 [51-250]
  R&R Bk N - v11 - N '96 - p49 [51-250]
Dell Orto, Arthur E - *Encyclopedia of Disability and Rehabilitation*
  r ARBA - v28 - '97 - p305 [251-500]
  r BL - v93 - F 1 '97 - p957 [51-250]
  r Choice - v34 - S '96 - p96 [51-250]
Delmaire, Bernard - *Le Diocese D'Arras De 1093 Au Milieu Du XIVe Siecle. Vols. 1-2*
  CHR - v82 - Jl '96 - p531+ [501+]
Delmas, Philippe - *The Rosy Future of War*
  For Aff - v76 - My '97 - p113+ [501+]
  KR - v65 - Mr 15 '97 - p431 [251-500]
  PW - v244 - Ap 28 '97 - p62 [251-500]
DeLoach, Cartha D - *Hoover's FBI. Audio Version*
  LJ - v122 - F 15 '97 - p175+ [51-250]
DeLoach, Charles - *Giants: A Reference Guide from History, the Bible, and Recorded Legend*
  r LAR - v98 - S '96 - p480 [51-250]
DeLong, James V - *Property Matters*
  BL - v93 - F 15 '97 - p978 [51-250]
  KR - v65 - Ja 1 '97 - p31+ [251-500]
  LJ - v122 - F 15 '97 - p147 [51-250]
  PW - v243 - D 30 '96 - p45 [51-250]
  WSJ-Cent - v99 - Ap 2 '97 - pA12 [501+]
DeLong, Thomas A - *Radio Stars*
  r ARBA - v28 - '97 - p351 [251-500]
  r Choice - v34 - My '97 - p1473 [51-250]
Deloria, Vine, Jr. - *Indians and Anthropologists*
  CHE - v43 - My 9 '97 - pA17 [51-250]
DeLorme, Eleanor - *Garden Pavilions and the 18th Century French Court*
  LJ - v121 - O 15 '96 - p54 [51-250]
Delorme, Robert - *The Political Economy of Diversity*
  Econ J - v106 - N '96 - p1830+ [251-500]
Delost, Maria Dannessa - *Introduction to Diagnostic Microbiology*
  SciTech - v21 - Mr '97 - p43 [51-250]
Deloze, Valerie - *Le Paleolithique Moyen Dans Le Nord Du Senonais (Yonne)*
  Am Ant - v62 - Ja '97 - p171 [251-500]
Del Prado, Dana - *Really Weird News Stories (Illus. by Granger Davis)*
  c LATBR - Jl 14 '96 - p11 [51-250]
Delsen, Lei - *Atypical Employment*
  Econ J - v106 - N '96 - p1842 [51-250]
  Gradual Retirement in the OECD Countries
  JEL - v34 - D '96 - p2070+ [51-250]
Delton, Judy - *Camp Ghost-Away (Moore). Audio Version*
  c HB - v73 - My '97 - p357+ [501+]
  Cookies and Crutches (Moore). Audio Version
  c HB - v73 - My '97 - p357+ [501+]
DeLuca, Tom - *The Two Faces of Political Apathy*
  APSR - v90 - D '96 - p890+ [501+]
  PSQ - v111 - Fall '96 - p546 [501+]
DeLuise, Dom - *King Bob's New Clothes (Illus. by Christopher Santoro)*
  c CBRS - v25 - D '96 - p38 [1-50]
  c HB Guide - v8 - Spr '97 - p24 [51-250]
  c PW - v243 - O 7 '96 - p74 [51-250]
  c SLJ - v42 - N '96 - p79+ [51-250]
Delumeau, Jean - *History of Paradise*
  JR - v77 - Ja '97 - p126+ [501+]
Delury, George E - *But What If She Wants to Die?*
  KR - v65 - My 1 '97 - p690+ [251-500]
Deluy, Henri - *Carnal Love*
  TranslRevS - v2 - D '96 - p22 [51-250]
Delval, Marie-Helene - *Reader's Digest Bible for Children (Illus. by Ulises Wensell)*
  c HB Guide - v7 - Fall '96 - p308 [51-250]
Delvaux, Peter - *Leid Soll Lehren*
  MLR - v91 - O '96 - p1045+ [501+]
Del Vecchio, John M - *Carry Me Home*
  NYTBR - v101 - S 29 '96 - p32 [51-250]
Delza, Sophia - *The T'ai-Chi Ch'uan Experience*
  Ch Rev Int - v4 - Spr '97 - p114+ [501+]

Dem Bones (Illus. by Bob Barner)
  c Bks Keeps - Mr '97 - p19 [51-250]
  c BL - v93 - D 1 '96 - p662 [51-250]
  c CBRS - v25 - O '96 - p13 [51-250]
  c HB Guide - v8 - Spr '97 - p129 [51-250]
  c Par Ch - v20 - O '96 - p28 [1-50]
  c PW - v243 - S 16 '96 - p81 [51-250]
  c SLJ - v42 - N '96 - p95+ [51-250]
De Man, Paul - *Aesthetic Ideology*
  LJ - v121 - D '96 - p93 [51-250]
  NYTBR - v101 - N 10 '96 - p18 [501+]
  PW - v243 - D 2 '96 - p50 [51-250]
  Romanticism and Contemporary Criticism
  CLS - v33 - 3 '96 - p312+ [501+]
DeMarco, Neil - *The Twentieth Century*
  y TES - Mr 28 '97 - p13* [501+]
Demarest, Chris L - *Bus (Illus. by Chris L Demarest)*
  c HB Guide - v7 - Fall '96 - p238 [51-250]
  c SLJ - v42 - Ag '96 - p121 [51-250]
  Plane (Illus. by Chris L Demarest)
  c HB Guide - v7 - Fall '96 - p238 [51-250]
  Ship (Illus. by Chris L Demarest)
  c HB Guide - v7 - Fall '96 - p238 [51-250]
  Train (Illus. by Chris L Demarest)
  c HB Guide - v7 - Fall '96 - p238 [51-250]
  c SLJ - v42 - Ag '96 - p121 [51-250]
DeMarr, Mary Jean - *Colleen McCullough: A Critical Companion*
  y Ch BWatch - v6 - S '96 - p7 [51-250]
  SLMQ - v25 - Fall '96 - p63 [1-50]
Demastes, William W - *British Playwrights 1880-1956*
  r ARBA - v28 - '97 - p450+ [51-250]
  r Choice - v34 - My '97 - p1472 [51-250]
  r LJ - v121 - D '96 - p82 [51-250]
  British Playwrights 1956-1995
  r ARBA - v28 - '97 - p451 [251-500]
  r BL - v93 - Ja '97 - p884+ [251-500]
  r Choice - v34 - My '97 - p1472 [51-250]
  r R&R Bk N - v12 - F '97 - p84 [51-250]
  Realism and the American Dramatic Tradition
  Choice - v34 - Ja '97 - p797 [51-250]
Dematons, Charlotte - *Looking for Cinderella (Illus. by Charlotte Dematons)*
  c BL - v93 - S 15 '96 - p246 [51-250]
  c CBRS - v25 - S '96 - p2 [51-250]
  c CCB-B - v50 - O '96 - p55 [51-250]
  c Ch BWatch - v6 - O '96 - p4 [51-250]
  c Ch BWatch - v6 - N '96 - p6 [51-250]
  c HB Guide - v8 - Spr '97 - p24 [51-250]
  c PW - v243 - S 9 '96 - p82 [51-250]
  c SLJ - v43 - Ja '97 - p76 [51-250]
DeMay, Richard M - *The Art and Science of Cytopathology*
  SciTech - v20 - N '96 - p39 [51-250]
Demaziere, Christophe - *Local Economic Development in Europe and the Americas*
  Choice - v34 - S '96 - p176 [51-250]
Dembe, Allard E - *Occupation and Disease*
  Sci - v273 - S 13 '96 - p1513 [501+]
  SciTech - v20 - D '96 - p48 [51-250]
De' Medici Stucchi, Lorenza - *Italy Today the Beautiful Cookbook*
  PW - v244 - Ap 21 '97 - p68 [51-250]
  Lorenza's Pasta
  BWatch - v18 - F '97 - p7 [51-250]
De Mente, Boye - *Chinese in Plain English*
  MLJ - v80 - Fall '96 - p408+ [501+]
  Japan Encyclopedia
  r ARBA - v28 - '97 - p58 [251-500]
  NTC's Dictionary of China's Cultural Code Words
  r ARBA - v28 - '97 - p57 [251-500]
  NTC's Dictionary of Mexican Cultural Code Words
  r ARBA - v28 - '97 - p70 [51-250]
  r Choice - v34 - Ja '97 - p781 [51-250]
Demers, David Pearce - *The Menace of the Corporate Newspaper*
  JMCQ - v73 - Aut '96 - p760+ [501+]
DeMers, John - *Caribbean Cooking*
  PW - v244 - My 5 '97 - p205 [51-250]
Demers, Patricia - *The World of Hannah More*
  Choice - v34 - Mr '97 - p1160 [51-250]
Demerson, Guy - *L'Esthetique De Rabelais*
  FR - v70 - Mr '97 - p594+ [501+]
Demeter, Stephen L - *Disability Evaluation*
  r SciTech - v20 - S '96 - p37 [51-250]
Demetz, Peter - *Prague in Black and Gold*
  KR - v65 - My 1 '97 - p691 [251-500]
Demeude, Hugues - *The Animated Alphabet*
  Spec - v277 - D 14 '96 - p76 [51-250]

Demeulenaere-Douyere, Christiane - *Il Y A 200 Ans Lavoisier*
  Isis - v87 - D '96 - p688+ [501+]
Demi - *Buddha (Illus. by Demi)*
  c BL - v93 - O 1 '96 - p338 [1-50]
  c HB - v72 - S '96 - p611 [51-250]
  c HB Guide - v7 - Fall '96 - p308 [1-50]
  Buddha Stories (Illus. by Demi)
  c BL - v93 - F 15 '97 - p1017 [51-250]
  c CBRS - v25 - Mr '97 - p93 [1-50]
  c CCB-B - v50 - Ap '97 - p280 [51-250]
  c PW - v244 - Ja 27 '97 - p108 [51-250]
  The Dragon's Tale and Other Animal Fables of the Chinese Zodiac (Illus. by Demi)
  c BL - v93 - S 15 '96 - p235 [51-250]
  c CCB-B - v50 - Ja '97 - p167 [51-250]
  c Emerg Lib - v24 - Mr '97 - p44 [1-50]
  c HB Guide - v8 - Spr '97 - p100 [51-250]
  c SLJ - v42 - O '96 - p112 [51-250]
  One Grain of Rice (Illus. by Demi)
  c BL - v93 - Mr 1 '97 - p1166 [51-250]
  c BL - v93 - Ap 1 '97 - p1341 [1-50]
  c CCB-B - v50 - F '97 - p202 [51-250]
  c KR - v65 - Ja 15 '97 - p140 [51-250]
  c PW - v244 - Ja 27 '97 - p106 [51-250]
  c SLJ - v43 - Mr '97 - p172+ [51-250]
Demians D'Archimbaud, Gabrielle - *L'Oppidum De Saint-Blaise Du Ve Au VIIe S. (Bouches-Du-Rhone)*
  AJA - v100 - Jl '96 - p630+ [501+]
  Specu - v71 - O '96 - p939+ [501+]
DeMille, Nelson - *Plum Island*
  PW - v244 - Ap 21 '97 - p60 [51-250]
  Trib Bks - My 18 '97 - p6 [51-250]
Deming, Alison Hawthorne - *The Columbia Anthology of Poetry of the American West*
  Bloom Rev - v16 - Jl '96 - p13+ [501+]
  Poetry of the American West
  LATBR - D 8 '96 - p5 [51-250]
  SFR - v21 - N '96 - p31 [501+]
  Temporary Home Lands
  y Kliatt - v31 - Ja '97 - p27+ [51-250]
Deming, W Edward - *Out of the Crisis*
  Inc. - v18 - D '96 - p60 [251-500]
Deming, Will - *Paul on Marriage and Celibacy*
  JR - v77 - Ap '97 - p289+ [501+]
  Rel St Rev - v23 - Ja '97 - p73 [51-250]
Demirag, Fikret - *Siirin Vaktine Mezmur*
  WLT - v70 - Aut '96 - p1023+ [251-500]
Demitrack, Mark A - *Chronic Fatigue Syndrome*
  Choice - v34 - N '96 - p492 [51-250]
  SB - v32 - N '96 - p232 [51-250]
  SciTech - v20 - S '96 - p29 [51-250]
Demographic Yearbook 1994
  r R&R Bk N - v12 - F '97 - p32 [51-250]
DeMolen, Richard L - *Religious Orders of the Catholic Reformation*
  CHR - v82 - O '96 - p710+ [501+]
De Montmollin, Olivier - *Settlement and Politics in Three Classic Maya Polities*
  LA Ant - v7 - D '96 - p377+ [501+]
De Moor, Johannes C - *Synchronic or Diachronic?*
  Rel St Rev - v23 - Ap '97 - p168 [51-250]
De Mora, S J - *Tributyltin: Case Study of an Environmental Contaminant*
  Choice - v34 - Ap '97 - p1367 [51-250]
Demos
  p New Sci - v152 - D 21 '96 - p71 [1-50]
Demos, John - *The Unredeemed Captive*
  Beav - v77 - F '97 - p46 [51-250]
  Beav - v77 - F '97 - p46 [51-250]
  TLS - Ag 30 '96 - p30 [501+]
De Moss, Geri Crenshaw - *Robert Morris Crenshaw and Blanche Rowe Crenshaw*
  r EGH - v50 - N '96 - p194 [51-250]
DeMott, Benjamin - *The Trouble with Friendship*
  Atl - v279 - F '97 - p102+ [501+]
  BL - v93 - Ja '97 - p756 [1-50]
  Nat - v262 - Je 17 '96 - p33+ [501+]
DeMott, Robert - *Steinbeck's Typewriter*
  AL - v69 - Mr '97 - p249 [1-50]
  Choice - v34 - D '96 - p612 [51-250]
Dempcy, Mary - *Dear Job Stressed*
  LJ - v121 - O 1 '96 - p96 [51-250]
  PW - v243 - S 9 '96 - p80 [51-250]
Dempsey, Charles - *Quattrocento Adriatico*
  R&R Bk N - v12 - F '97 - p71 [51-250]
Demsetz, Harold - *The Economics of the Business Firm*
  JEL - v34 - S '96 - p1411 [51-250]
  JEL - v35 - Mr '97 - p129+ [501+]

Demuth, Patricia Brennan - *Busy at Day Care Head to Toe (Illus. by Jack Demuth)*
  c HB Guide - v7 - Fall '96 - p238 [51-250]
  c KR - v64 - My 1 '96 - p686 [51-250]
Dem'yanov, Vladimir F - *Quasidifferentiability and Nonsmooth Modelling in Mechanics, Engineering and Economics*
  SciTech - v20 - D '96 - p60 [51-250]
DeNale, Robert - *Welding and Weld Automation in Shipbuilding*
  SciTech - v20 - N '96 - p82 [51-250]
DenBoer, Gordon - *Atlas of Historical County Boundaries: Kentucky*
  r ARBA - v28 - '97 - p171 [51-250]
Denby, David - *Great Books*
  AS - v66 - Spr '97 - p290+ [501+]
  BL - v92 - Ag '96 - p1878 [51-250]
  BL - v93 - Ja '97 - p759 [1-50]
  BL - v93 - Ap 1 '97 - p1285 [51-250]
  BW - v26 - S 29 '96 - p3+ [501+]
  CC - v114 - Ap 9 '97 - p368+ [501+]
  Dis - v44 - Spr '97 - p107+ [501+]
  Econ - v341 - O 19 '96 - p4*+ [501+]
  HM - v294 - Ja '97 - p62+ [501+]
  LATBR - O 13 '96 - p8+ [501+]
  New R - v215 - O 7 '96 - p34+ [501+]
  NY - v72 - D 16 '96 - p109 [51-250]
  NYRB - v43 - S 19 '96 - p31+ [501+]
  NYTBR - v101 - S 1 '96 - p10+ [501+]
  NYTBR - v101 - D 8 '96 - p87 [1-50]
  NYTLa - v145 - S 16 '96 - pC14 [501+]
  PW - v243 - Jl 22 '96 - p219 [51-250]
  PW - v243 - N 4 '96 - p42+ [51-250]
  Rapport - v19 - 6 '96 - p32 [251-500]
  TES - Ja 10 '97 - p6* [501+]
  Time - v148 - S 9 '96 - p68 [51-250]
  Utne R - N '96 - p88 [1-50]
  W&I - v12 - Ja '97 - p297+ [501+]
  YR - v85 - Ap '97 - p145+ [501+]
  Sentimental Narrative and the Social Order in France 1760-1820
  FR - v70 - F '97 - p467+ [501+]
Dence, Carlton W - *Pulp Bleaching*
  SciTech - v20 - D '96 - p86 [51-250]
Dench, Emma - *From Barbarians to New Men*
  Choice - v34 - S '96 - p183 [51-250]
Dench, Geoff - *The Frog, the Prince, and the Problem of Men*
  Urban Ed - v31 - S '96 - p346+ [51-250]
  Transforming Men
  W&I - v11 - Ag '96 - p271+ [501+]
Denchfield, Nick - *Charlie the Chicken*
  c PW - v244 - Mr 24 '97 - p85 [51-250]
  The Complete Castle
  c TES - N 22 '96 - p12* [51-250]
  The Great Castle Mystery (Illus. by Steve Cox)
  c PW - v243 - S 23 '96 - p78 [51-250]
Dendel, Esther W - *You Cannot Unsneeze a Sneeze and Other Tales from Liberia*
  CAY - v17 - Fall '96 - p3 [51-250]
Dendle, Brian J - *Spain's Forgotten Novelist*
  MLR - v92 - Ap '97 - p492+ [501+]
Dendy, Leslie - *Tracks, Scats, and Signs (Illus. by Linda Garrow)*
  c HB Guide - v7 - Fall '96 - p335 [51-250]
Deneef, A Leigh - *The Academic's Handbook. 2nd Ed.*
  TCR - v98 - Spr '97 - p537+ [501+]
Denegri, Francesca - *El Abanico Y La Cigarrera*
  BL - v93 - Mr 15 '97 - p1232 [1-50]
Denegri Luna, Felix - *Peru Y Ecuador*
  BL - v93 - Mr 15 '97 - p1232 [1-50]
Denenberg, Barry - *An American Hero*
  y BL - v93 - Ap 1 '97 - p1286 [51-250]
  c HB - v72 - S '96 - p612+ [51-250]
  c HB Guide - v7 - Fall '96 - p372 [51-250]
  y JAAL - v40 - N '96 - p232 [51-250]
  c NYTBR - v102 - Ja 5 '97 - p22 [1-50]
  Voices from Vietnam
  y Emerg Lib - v24 - S '96 - p23 [1-50]
  When Will This Cruel War Be Over?
  c CBRS - v25 - S '96 - p11 [51-250]
  c CCB-B - v50 - O '96 - p55+ [51-250]
  c Ch BWatch - v6 - S '96 - p5 [1-50]
  c HB Guide - v8 - Spr '97 - p64 [51-250]
  c Par - v71 - D '96 - p254 [51-250]
  c PW - v243 - S 2 '96 - p131 [51-250]
  c SLJ - v42 - S '96 - p201 [51-250]
  c Trib Bks - My 4 '97 - p1+ [501+]
  y VOYA - v19 - O '96 - p208 [251-500]

Denes, Magda - *Castles Burning*
  Books - v11 - Ap '97 - p20 [1-50]
  BW - v26 - D 22 '96 - p6+ [501+]
  KR - v64 - O 15 '96 - p1505+ [251-500]
  LATBR - Ja 5 '97 - p6 [501+]
  LJ - v121 - N 1 '96 - p78 [51-250]
  NYTBR - v102 - Ja 26 '97 - p13+ [501+]
  PW - v243 - O 14 '96 - p68 [51-250]
Denevi, Marco - *The Redemption of the Cannibal Woman*
  TranslRevS - v1 - My '95 - p30 [1-50]
Denfeld, Rene - *Kill the Body, the Head Will Fall*
  BL - v93 - Ja '97 - p790 [51-250]
  KR - v64 - D 15 '96 - p1779 [251-500]
  PW - v243 - N 18 '96 - p52 [51-250]
  Trib Bks - F 9 '97 - p6 [501+]
  The New Victorians
  y Kliatt - v31 - Ja '97 - p24 [51-250]
  NYTBR - v102 - Ja 5 '97 - p28 [51-250]
  PW - v243 - S 30 '96 - p79 [1-50]
Deng, Francis M - *Sovereignty as Responsibility*
  Choice - v34 - My '97 - p1573 [51-250]
  For Aff - v76 - My '97 - p147 [51-250]
  JEL - v35 - Mr '97 - p201+ [51-250]
Deng, Z - *Differential Equations and Control Theory*
  SIAM Rev - v39 - Mr '97 - p174 [1-50]
Dengler, Marianna - *The Worry Stone (Illus. by Sibyl Graber Gerig)*
  c BL - v93 - D 15 '96 - p724 [51-250]
  c CBRS - v25 - F '97 - p74 [51-250]
  c HB Guide - v8 - Spr '97 - p24 [51-250]
  c KR - v64 - N 1 '96 - p1600 [51-250]
  c SLJ - v43 - Ja '97 - p76+ [51-250]
Denhart, Jeffrey - *Just Bones*
  PW - v244 - Mr 3 '97 - p72 [1-50]
Deniau, Jean-Francois - *Un Heros Tres Discrete*
  BL - v93 - Ja '97 - p827 [1-50]
Denim, Sue - *The Dumb Bunnies (Illus. by Dav Pilkey)*
  c PW - v244 - F 3 '97 - p108 [51-250]
  The Dumb Bunnies' Easter (Illus. by Dav Pilkey)
  c RT - v50 - O '96 - p132 [1-50]
  The Dumb Bunnies Go to the Zoo (Illus. by Dav Pilkey)
  c BL - v93 - Ap 1 '97 - p1337 [51-250]
  c PW - v243 - D 16 '96 - p61 [1-50]
  c SLJ - v43 - Mr '97 - p150 [51-250]
  Make Way for Dumb Bunnies (Illus. by Dav Pilkey)
  c Ch BWatch - v6 - My '96 - p4 [51-250]
  c HB Guide - v7 - Fall '96 - p253 [51-250]
  c LATBR - Mr 24 '96 - p11 [51-250]
Dening, Greg - *Mr. Bligh's Bad Language*
  JMH - v68 - S '96 - p617+ [501+]
  Performances
  Aust Bk R - Jl '96 - p13+ [501+]
  New Sci - v152 - N 16 '96 - p49 [51-250]
Dening, Sarah - *The Mythology of Sex*
  Obs - D 22 '96 - p17* [51-250]
Denis, A-M - *Concordance Latine Des Pseudepigraphes D'Ancien Testament*
  r Rel St Rev - v23 - Ja '97 - p85 [51-250]
Denker, Henry - *A Place for Kathy*
  KR - v65 - Mr 1 '97 - p322 [51-250]
  LJ - v122 - Ap 1 '97 - p124 [51-250]
  PW - v244 - Ap 14 '97 - p58 [51-250]
Denman, Cherry - *The History Puzzle*
  c HB Guide - v7 - Fall '96 - p377 [51-250]
Denman, Roy - *Missed Chances*
  Econ - v339 - My 18 '96 - p6*+ [251-500]
  TLS - Jl 19 '96 - p31 [51-250]
Dennard, Deborah - *Travis and the Better Mousetrap (Illus. by Theresa Burns)*
  c HB Guide - v7 - Fall '96 - p253 [51-250]
Dennett, Daniel C - *Darwin's Dangerous Idea*
  Am Sci - v84 - My '96 - p289+ [501+]
  Bks & Cult - v2 - My '96 - p16+ [501+]
  Ethics - v107 - O '96 - p170+ [501+]
  IPQ - v36 - D '96 - p487+ [501+]
  Nature - v385 - Ja 2 '97 - p36 [1-50]
  New Sci - v152 - N 9 '96 - p43 [1-50]
  Skeptic - v4 - '96 - p96+ [501+]
  TES - N 22 '96 - p8* [51-250]
  Kinds of Minds
  BW - v26 - S 1 '96 - p4 [251-500]
  Choice - v34 - D '96 - p691+ [51-250]
  J Phil - v94 - F '97 - p97+ [501+]
  KR - v64 - My 1 '96 - p659 [251-500]
  Nature - v384 - N 21 '96 - p228+ [501+]
  NYTBR - v101 - D 29 '96 - p22 [501+]
  Sci - v274 - N 22 '96 - p1321 [1-50]
  Skeptic - v4 - 3 '96 - p107 [1-50]
  VLS - S '96 - p16+ [501+]

Denning, Michael - *The Cultural Front*
    HT - v46 - O '96 - p59 [1-50]
    LJ - v122 - F 15 '97 - p151 [51-250]
    Nat - v264 - Mr 10 '97 - p25+ [501+]
    PW - v244 - Ja 13 '97 - p64 [51-250]
Denning, Peter - *Beyond Calculation*
    LJ - v122 - Mr 15 '97 - p80 [51-250]
Dennis, Anthony J - *The Rise of the Islamic Empire and the Threat to the West*
    BL - v93 - D 1 '96 - p623 [51-250]
Dennis, Barbara - *Elizabeth Barrett Browning: The Hope End Years*
    LJ - v121 - D '96 - p93 [51-250]
    PW - v243 - S 2 '96 - p118 [51-250]
Dennis, David B - *Beethoven in German Politics 1870-1989*
    Choice - v34 - S '96 - p137 [51-250]
    ON - v61 - O '96 - p65 [501+]
Dennis, Everette E - *American Communication Research*
    JC - v47 - Win '97 - p183+ [501+]
Dennis, Jerry - *The Bird in the Waterfall*
    y BL - v93 - S 1 '96 - p47 [51-250]
    BL - v93 - D 1 '96 - p630 [1-50]
Dennis, John V - *A Complete Guide to Bird Feeding*
    LJ - v121 - D '96 - p67 [1-50]
    A Guide to Western Bird Feeding
    LJ - v121 - D '96 - p67 [1-50]
    How to Attract Birds. Rev. Ed.
    LJ - v121 - D '96 - p66 [1-50]
    How to Attract Hummingbirds and Butterflies
    LJ - v121 - D '96 - p66 [1-50]
    Summer Bird Feeding
    LJ - v121 - D '96 - p67 [1-50]
Dennis, Lloyd B - *Practical Public Affairs in an Era of Change*
    Choice - v34 - N '96 - p538+ [51-250]
Dennis, Peter - *Emergency and Confrontation*
    Aust Bk R - Je '96 - p21 [501+]
    Choice - v34 - Ja '97 - p853 [51-250]
    The Oxford Companion to Australian Military History
    r ARBA - v28 - '97 - p254+ [51-250]
    r Choice - v34 - O '96 - p256 [51-250]
Dennis, Rutledge M - *The Black Middle Class*
    CS - v25 - S '96 - p622 [501+]
Dennis, Sandy - *Sandy Dennis: A Personal Memoir*
    KR - v65 - F 15 '97 - p268 [251-500]
    PW - v244 - Mr 3 '97 - p59 [51-250]
Dennison, Robin - *Pass CCRN!*
    SciTech - v20 - S '96 - p44 [51-250]
Denniston, Dorothy Hamer - *The Fiction of Paule Marshall*
    AL - v69 - Mr '97 - p237+ [251-500]
Denniston, Robin - *Churchill's Secret War*
    Spec - v278 - Mr 1 '97 - p31+ [501+]
Denny, Roz - *The Rice Cookbook*
    PW - v244 - Mr 3 '97 - p70 [51-250]
Denny, Sidney - *The Ancient Splendor of Prehistoric Cahokia*
    c BL - v93 - My 1 '97 - p1490 [51-250]
Denoeu, Francois - *2001 French and English Idioms. 2nd Ed.*
    r ARBA - v28 - '97 - p389+ [51-250]
Denoon, David B H - *Ballistic Missile Defense in the Post-Cold War Era*
    NWCR - v49 - Aut '96 - p138+ [251-500]
DeNora, Tia - *Beethoven and the Construction of Genius*
    AJS - v102 - Ja '97 - p1194+ [501+]
    CS - v26 - Ja '97 - p102+ [501+]
    Notes - v53 - Mr '97 - p798+ [501+]
    NYRB - v43 - N 14 '96 - p57+ [501+]
Denou, Violeta - *Mira Las Flores, Teo (Illus. by Violeta Denou)*
    c BL - v93 - F 15 '97 - p1033 [1-50]
    Teo Descubre Las Formas (Illus. by Violeta Denou)
    c BL - v93 - F 15 '97 - p1033 [1-50]
    Teo Descubre Los Colores (Illus. by Violeta Denou)
    c BL - v93 - F 15 '97 - p1033 [1-50]
Dent, David W - *U.S.-Latin American Policymaking*
    Parameters - v26 - Win '96 - p155 [1-50]
Dent, Edward E - *Betrayal: Employee Relations at DuPont 1981-1994*
    r JSH - v62 - N '96 - p863 [1-50]
Dent, Richard J - *Chesapeake Prehistory*
    Am Ant - v62 - Ja '97 - p155+ [501+]

Dent, Tom - *Southern Journey*
    y BL - v93 - Ja '97 - p811 [51-250]
    CSM - v89 - F 10 '97 - p14 [501+]
    CSM - v89 - Mr 6 '97 - p14 [51-250]
    KR - v64 - O 15 '96 - p1506 [251-500]
    LJ - v121 - D '96 - p114 [51-250]
    NYTBR - v102 - F 23 '97 - p17 [51-250]
    PW - v243 - N 4 '96 - p55 [51-250]
Dentin/Pulp Complex
    SciTech - v21 - Mr '97 - p66 [51-250]
Denton, Bradley - *Lunatics*
    BW - v26 - Jl 14 '96 - p3 [501+]
    MFSF - v91 - Ag '96 - p22+ [501+]
    MFSF - v91 - D '96 - p40+ [251-500]
Denton, Kirk A - *Modern Chinese Literary Thought*
    Choice - v34 - S '96 - p121 [51-250]
Denton, Robert E, Jr. - *The Clinton Presidency*
    Choice - v34 - S '96 - p210 [51-250]
    The Media and the Persian Gulf War
    JPC - v30 - Fall '96 - p200+ [501+]
Denton, Terry - *Gasp! (Illus. by Terry Denton)*
    c SLJ - v43 - Mr '97 - p150 [51-250]
Denver (Colo.). Water Dept. - *Xeriscape Plant Guide*
    Bloom Rev - v16 - Jl '96 - p12 [51-250]
    Hort - v74 - D '96 - p59+ [501+]
Denvir, Gearoid - *Amhrain Choilm De Bhailis*
    ILS - v16 - Spr '97 - p28 [501+]
Denvir, John - *Legal Reelism*
    ABA Jour - v83 - F '97 - p90 [501+]
    CHE - v43 - N 8 '96 - pA18 [51-250]
    Choice - v34 - Ja '97 - p804 [51-250]
Denzin, Norman K - *Handbook of Qualitative Research*
    HER - v66 - Win '96 - p890+ [251-500]
De Oliveira, Nicolas - *Installation Art*
    Econ - v341 - D 7 '96 - p15*+ [51-250]
DePamphilis, Melvin L - *DNA Replication in Eukaryotic Cells*
    Choice - v34 - F '97 - p986 [51-250]
    SciTech - v20 - D '96 - p36 [51-250]
De Paola, Tomie - *The Baby Sister (Illus. by Tomie De Paola)*
    c HB Guide - v7 - Fall '96 - p253 [51-250]
    c Par - v71 - N '96 - p114 [1-50]
    Christopher the Holy Giant (Illus. by Tomie De Paola)
    c CLW - v67 - Mr '97 - p13 [1-50]
    c JB - v60 - D '96 - p228 [51-250]
    Days of the Blackbird (Illus. by Tomie De Paola)
    c BL - v93 - Mr 15 '97 - p1247 [51-250]
    c CBRS - v25 - Ap '97 - p98 [51-250]
    c HB - v73 - Mr '97 - p205 [51-250]
    c KR - v64 - D 15 '96 - p1796 [51-250]
    c Par Ch - v21 - Mr '97 - p4 [1-50]
    c PW - v243 - D 16 '96 - p59 [51-250]
    c SLJ - v43 - Mr '97 - p150 [51-250]
    Get Dressed, Santa! (Illus. by Tomie De Paola)
    c PW - v243 - S 30 '96 - p93 [1-50]
    c SLJ - v42 - O '96 - p34 [51-250]
    Mary: The Mother of Jesus (Illus. by Tomie De Paola)
    c BL - v93 - O 1 '96 - p338 [1-50]
    c Emerg Lib - v23 - My '96 - p55+ [51-250]
    c RT - v50 - N '96 - p259 [51-250]
    Strega Nona (Illus. by Tomie De Paola)
    c BL - v93 - S 15 '96 - p246 [51-250]
    c CBRS - v25 - N '96 - p30 [51-250]
    c Emerg Lib - v24 - Mr '97 - p45 [1-50]
    c HB - v72 - N '96 - p722+ [51-250]
    c HB - v73 - Mr '97 - p188 [1-50]
    c HB Guide - v8 - Spr '97 - p24 [51-250]
    c PW - v243 - Jl 22 '96 - p241 [51-250]
    c SLJ - v42 - O '96 - p91 [51-250]
    Tomie's Little Mother Goose (Illus. by Tomie De Paola)
    c HB - v73 - Mr '97 - p186 [1-50]
    c PW - v244 - My 12 '97 - p77 [51-250]
De Paoli, Carlo - *Sexual Healing*
    Quill & Q - v62 - Ag '96 - p32 [51-250]
De Paor, Louis - *Sentences of Earth and Stone*
    Aust Bk R - Ag '96 - p60+ [501+]
De Pauw, Linda Grant - *Documentary History of the First Federal Congress of the United States of America. Vol. 14*
    R&R Bk N - v11 - N '96 - p52 [1-50]
Depestre, Rene - *The Festival of the Greasy Pole*
    TranslRevS - v1 - My '95 - p16+ [51-250]
Depew, David J - *Darwinism Evolving*
    Isis - v88 - Mr '97 - p111+ [501+]
Depoe, Stephen P - *Arthur M. Schlesinger, Jr. and the Ideological History of American Liberalism*
    NEQ - v69 - D '96 - p660+ [501+]
DePorter, Bobbi - *Quantum Business*
    BL - v93 - My 1 '97 - p1467 [51-250]

De Pree, Max - *Dear Zoe*
    Ch Today - v40 - O 7 '96 - p58 [251-500]
DePrince, Elaine - *Cry Bloody Murder*
    y BL - v93 - My 15 '97 - p1538 [51-250]
Depue, Anne - *Climb Your Family Tree (Illus. by Doug Keith)*
    c LATBR - v263 - S 29 '96 - p15 [51-250]
    c PW - v243 - O 7 '96 - p78 [51-250]
De Pury, Albert - *Israel Construit Son Histoire*
    Rel St Rev - v23 - Ap '97 - p165 [51-250]
De Puy, Candace - *The Healing Choice*
    BL - v93 - F 1 '97 - p911+ [51-250]
    LJ - v122 - F 1 '97 - p96 [51-250]
D'Eramo, Luce - *Si Prega Di Non Disturbare*
    WLT - v70 - Sum '96 - p673 [251-500]
Derby, Pat - *Grams, Her Boyfriend, My Family, and Me*
    c PW - v244 - Mr 17 '97 - p85 [1-50]
    y SLJ - v43 - Mr '97 - p112 [1-50]
Derby, Sally - *My Steps (Illus. by Adjoa J Burrowes)*
    c CBRS - v25 - F '97 - p74 [51-250]
    c HB Guide - v8 - Spr '97 - p24+ [51-250]
    c KR - v64 - S 1 '96 - p1321 [51-250]
    c SLJ - v42 - O '96 - p91 [51-250]
Derbyshire, J Denis - *Political Systems of the World. 2nd Ed.*
    r ARBA - v28 - '97 - p263 [51-250]
    r Choice - v34 - O '96 - p249+ [51-250]
Derbyshire, John - *Seeing Calvin Coolidge in a Dream*
    NYTBR - v101 - D 8 '96 - p82 [1-50]
    VQR - v72 - Aut '96 - p130* [51-250]
    VV - v42 - Ja 7 '97 - p41+ [251-500]
Derderian, Tom - *Boston Marathon*
    Aethlon - v13 - Fall '95 - p163 [251-500]
De Regniers, Beatrice Schenk - *David and Goliath (Illus. by Scott Cameron)*
    c BL - v93 - O 1 '96 - p338 [1-50]
    c HB Guide - v7 - Fall '96 - p308 [51-250]
Dereniak, Eustace L - *Infrared Detectors and Systems*
    SciTech - v20 - S '96 - p50 [51-250]
Derenne, Jean-Philippe - *Acute Respiratory Failure in Chronic Obstructive Pulmonary Disease*
    SciTech - v20 - S '96 - p36 [51-250]
Dereske, Jo - *Miss Zukas and the Raven's Dance*
    PW - v243 - N 25 '96 - p70+ [51-250]
    Savage Cut
    PW - v243 - O 14 '96 - p81 [51-250]
Der-Hovanessian, Diana - *The Circle Dancers*
    LJ - v122 - Ap 15 '97 - p84+ [51-250]
    PW - v244 - Mr 31 '97 - p70 [51-250]
De Rico, Ul - *The White Goblin*
    c Bloom Rev - v16 - N '96 - p31 [51-250]
    c HB Guide - v8 - Spr '97 - p64 [51-250]
DeRitter, Jones - *The Embodiment of Characters*
    Eight-C St - v30 - Fall '96 - p99+ [501+]
    RES - v47 - N '96 - p591+ [501+]
Dermenjian, Artin A - *Pressure Vessels and Piping Design, Analysis, and Severe Accidents*
    SciTech - v20 - N '96 - p83 [51-250]
DeRogatis, Jim - *Kaleidoscope Eyes*
    TES - Ja 10 '97 - p7* [501+]
De Rooy, Jacob - *Economic Literacy*
    y Kliatt - v31 - Ja '97 - p24 [51-250]
DeRosa, Marshall L - *The Ninth Amendment and the Politics of Creative Jurisprudence*
    PSQ - v111 - Fall '96 - p547 [501+]
    Univ Bkmn - v36 - Win '96 - p12+ [501+]
De Rosa, Peter - *Pope Patrick*
    BL - v93 - F 15 '97 - p1002 [51-250]
    KR - v65 - Ja 15 '97 - p78 [251-500]
    LJ - v122 - F 15 '97 - p161 [51-250]
    PW - v244 - F 3 '97 - p96 [51-250]
De Rosa, Tina - *Paper Fish*
    Choice - v34 - Ja '97 - p793 [51-250]
    CLW - v67 - Mr '97 - p50 [51-250]
    Comw - v123 - D 6 '96 - p25 [51-250]
    LJ - v122 - Ja '97 - p155 [1-50]
    LJ - v121 - N 1 '96 - p106 [51-250]
    Ms - v7 - Ja '97 - p80 [251-500]
    PW - v243 - S 9 '96 - p81 [1-50]
DeRose, David J - *Sam Shepard*
    JPC - v30 - Fall '96 - p202 [251-500]
DeRose, Steven J - *Making Hypermedia Work*
    Compt & H - v30 - 1 '96 - p93+ [501+]
De'Rossi, Giovangirolamo - *Vita Di Federico Di Montefeltro*
    Six Ct J - v27 - Fall '96 - p886+ [501+]
Derosso, H A - *Under the Burning Sun*
    Roundup M - v4 - F '97 - p27 [51-250]

Derr, Mark - *Dog's Best Friend*
  y BL - v93 - Mr 15 '97 - p1213 [51-250]
     KR - v65 - Ap 1 '97 - p515+ [251-500]
     LJ - v122 - My 1 '97 - p130 [51-250]
Derrett, J D M - *Prophecy in the Cotswolds 1803-1947*
     EHR - v111 - N '96 - p1311 [51-250]
Derricourt, Robin - *An Author's Guide to Scholarly Publishing*
     New Sci - v153 - Mr 1 '97 - p44 [51-250]
  Ideas into Books
     Aust Bk R - Je '96 - p65 [251-500]
Derrida, Jacques - *Archive Fever*
     LJ - v121 - N 1 '96 - p66 [51-250]
  The Gift of Death
     JR - v77 - Ap '97 - p330+ [501+]
     TranslRevS - v2 - D '96 - p17 [51-250]
  Moscou Aller-Retour
     Choice - v34 - D '96 - p565 [1-50]
  On the Name
     Names - v45 - Mr '97 - p67+ [501+]
  Specters of Marx
     CPR - v16 - O '96 - p329+ [501+]
Dershaw, D David - *Interventional Breast Procedures*
     SciTech - v20 - N '96 - p51 [51-250]
Dershowitz, Alan M - *The Abuse Excuse and Other Cop-Outs, Sob Stories, and Evasions of Responsibility*
     QJS - v82 - Ag '96 - p316+ [501+]
  The Advocate's Devil
     Books - v9 - S '95 - p24 [1-50]
  Reasonable Doubts
     ABA Jour - v82 - D '96 - p92+ [501+]
     Ant R - v54 - Fall '96 - p494+ [251-500]
     Esq - v126 - N '96 - p65 [1-50]
     LATBR - Jl 7 '96 - p4 [251-500]
     NYRB - v43 - Je 6 '96 - p7+ [501+]
     NYTBR - v102 - F 9 '97 - p32 [51-250]
     PW - v244 - Ja 13 '97 - p73 [1-50]
     TLS - Jl 19 '96 - p28 [501+]
  The Vanishing American Jew
  y BL - v93 - Ja '97 - p777 [51-250]
     KR - v65 - F 15 '97 - p268 [251-500]
     LATBR - Mr 23 '97 - p3 [501+]
     NYTBR - v102 - Mr 30 '97 - p7 [501+]
     PW - v244 - F 3 '97 - p88 [51-250]
Dertouzos, Michael L - *What Will Be*
     LJ - v122 - My 1 '97 - p135 [51-250]
     NW - v129 - Mr 24 '97 - p12 [51-250]
     NYTBR - v102 - Mr 30 '97 - p26 [501+]
     PW - v244 - Ja 13 '97 - p62 [51-250]
     Quill & Q - v63 - Ja '97 - p20 [1-50]
DeRubertis, Barbara - *Bitty Fish. Book and Audio Version*
  c SLJ - v43 - Mr '97 - p142 [51-250]
  Foxy Fox. Book and Audio Version
  c SLJ - v43 - Mr '97 - p142 [51-250]
  Lucky Duck. Book and Audio Version
  c SLJ - v43 - Mr '97 - p142 [51-250]
  Patty Cat. Book and Audio Version
  c SLJ - v43 - Mr '97 - p142 [51-250]
  Penny Hen. Book and Audio Version
  c SLJ - v43 - Mr '97 - p142 [51-250]
Dervaes, Claudine - *The Travel Dictionary. New Ed.*
  r ARBA - v28 - '97 - p176 [51-250]
Dervin, Daniel - *Enactments: American Modes and Psychohistorical Models*
     Choice - v34 - N '96 - p524 [51-250]
Dery, Mark - *Escape Velocity*
     ABR - v18 - D '96 - p22 [501+]
     Nat - v262 - Je 3 '96 - p36+ [501+]
     Nat R - v48 - O 14 '96 - p81+ [501+]
     SFS - v24 - Mr '97 - p124+ [501+]
  Flame Wars
     QJS - v83 - My '97 - p230+ [501+]
Dery, Robert - *Business Welsh*
  r BusLR - v21 - 3 '96 - p239 [51-250]
Desai, Anita - *Journey to Ithaca*
     NYTBR - v102 - Ja 12 '97 - p32 [51-250]
     Obs - N 3 '96 - p18* [51-250]
     WLT - v71 - Win '97 - p221 [501+]
Desai, Meghnad - *Destiny Not Defeat*
     NS - v126 - Ja 31 '97 - p11 [1-50]
  Macroeconomics and Monetary Theory
     Econ J - v106 - N '96 - p1835 [51-250]
DeSaix, Frank - *Hilary and the Lions (Illus. by Deborah Durland DeSaix)*
  c PW - v243 - S 2 '96 - p133 [51-250]

DeSalle, Rob - *The Science of Jurassic Park and the Lost World*
  y BL - v93 - Ap 1 '97 - p1266 [51-250]
     KR - v65 - Ap 1 '97 - p516 [251-500]
     LJ - v122 - My 1 '97 - p134 [51-250]
     PW - v244 - My 12 '97 - p69 [51-250]
DeSalvo, Louise A - *Breathless: An Asthma Journal*
     BL - v93 - Ap 1 '97 - p1270+ [51-250]
     KR - v65 - F 1 '97 - p188 [251-500]
     LJ - v122 - Ap 1 '97 - p115 [51-250]
  Conceived with Malice
     Biography - v19 - Fall '96 - p429 [1-50]
  Vertigo: A Memoir
     LATBR - Ag 4 '96 - p4 [501+]
De Santis, Hugh - *Beyond Progress*
     For Aff - v75 - S '96 - p135+ [51-250]
     R&R Bk N - v11 - N '96 - p11 [51-250]
Desaulniers, Maurice - *An Alphabet of Sweets*
     PW - v243 - O 7 '96 - p72 [51-250]
De Sauza, James - *Brother Anansi and the Cattle Ranch (Illus. by S Von Mason)*
  c SS - v88 - Ja '97 - p29+ [501+]
Des Barres, Pamela - *Rock Bottom*
     Ent W - N 1 '96 - p61+ [251-500]
     KR - v64 - Ag 15 '96 - p1203 [251-500]
     NYTBR - v102 - Ja 5 '97 - p19 [51-250]
     PW - v243 - S 16 '96 - p64 [51-250]
Descartes Et L'Argumentation Philosophique
     CPR - v16 - O '96 - p327+ [501+]
Desch, H E - *Timber. 7th Ed.*
     SciTech - v20 - N '96 - p63 [51-250]
Des Chene, Dennis - *Physiologia: Natural Philosophy in Late Aristotelian and Cartesian Thought*
     Choice - v34 - O '96 - p320 [51-250]
     IPQ - v37 - Je '97 - p231+ [501+]
     Isis - v88 - Mr '97 - p124 [501+]
     Six Ct J - v27 - Win '96 - p1124+ [501+]
Descola, Philippe - *The Spears of Twilight*
     BL - v92 - Ag '96 - p1877 [51-250]
     BW - v27 - F 2 '97 - p6 [501+]
     Choice - v34 - F '97 - p1005 [51-250]
     NYTBR - v102 - Ja 12 '97 - p13 [501+]
     NYTLa - v146 - N 13 '96 - pC21 [501+]
     TES - Mr 14 '97 - p8* [51-250]
Desens, Marliss C - *The Bed-Trick in English Renaissance Drama*
     Ren Q - v49 - Win '96 - p897+ [501+]
Desetta, Al - *The Heart Knows Something Different*
  y JAAL - v40 - S '96 - p71 [51-250]
  y Kliatt - v30 - N '96 - p26 [51-250]
     Ms - v7 - N '96 - p78+ [501+]
Desgraves, Louis - *Inventaire Des Fonds Montaigne Conserves A Bordeaux*
     Ren Q - v50 - Spr '97 - p251+ [501+]
Deshimaru, Taisen - *Sit: Zen Teachings of Master Taisen Deshimaru*
     Tric - v6 - Win '96 - p108+ [501+]
Deshman, Robert - *The Benedictional of Aethelwold*
     BM - v138 - Ag '96 - p547+ [501+]
     Theol St - v57 - Je '96 - p379+ [251-500]
Design Criteria for Lighting Interior Living Spaces
     TCI - v30 - O '96 - p57 [1-50]
Design, Monitoring and Evaluation of Technical Cooperation Programmes and Projects
     J Gov Info - v23 - S '96 - p671 [51-250]
Design Museum Vitra - *100 Masterpieces from the Vitra Design Museum Collection*
  r Am Craft - v57 - Ap '97 - p28 [51-250]
Design of Sheet Pile Walls
     SciTech - v20 - N '96 - p65 [51-250]
DeSilva, Cara - *In Memory's Kitchen*
     CSM - v89 - Ja 23 '97 - p12 [51-250]
     LJ - v121 - S 15 '96 - p80 [51-250]
     NW - v128 - S 9 '96 - p73 [501+]
     NYTBR - v101 - N 17 '96 - p7 [501+]
     NYTBR - v101 - D 8 '96 - p88 [1-50]
De Silva, K M - *The Traditional Homelands of the Tamils. Rev. 2nd Ed.*
     Pac A - v69 - Sum '96 - p275+ [501+]
DeSimoni, Guido - *CICS Clients Unmasked*
     SciTech - v20 - N '96 - p9 [51-250]
DeSipio, Louis - *Counting on the Latino Vote*
     R&R Bk N - v11 - N '96 - p18 [51-250]
Desiraju, Gautam R - *The Crystal as a Supramolecular Entity*
     SciTech - v20 - S '96 - p17 [51-250]
Deskis, Susan E - *Beowulf and the Medieval Proverb Tradition*
     Choice - v34 - My '97 - p1494 [51-250]

Desmond, Adrian J - *Huxley: From Devil's Disciple to Evolution's High Priest*
     Lon R Bks - v19 - Ap 24 '97 - p17+ [501+]
     Nature - v386 - Mr 27 '97 - p349+ [501+]
     New Sci - v153 - Mr 22 '97 - p43 [501+]
  Huxley: The Devil's Disciple
     EHR - v112 - F '97 - p239 [501+]
Desmond, Cheryl Taylor - *Shaping the Culture of Schooling*
     R&R Bk N - v11 - N '96 - p57 [51-250]
Desmond, Gregory - *Napoleon's Jailer*
     LJ - v121 - N 15 '96 - p72 [51-250]
Desmond, Ray - *Kew: The History of the Royal Botanic Gardens*
     Hort - v74 - O '96 - p71+ [251-500]
     Lon R Bks - v18 - S 19 '96 - p18 [501+]
Desmond, William - *Being and the Between*
     CPR - v16 - O '96 - p331+ [501+]
Desmurs, Jean-Roger - *The Roots of Organic Development*
     SciTech - v20 - D '96 - p82 [51-250]
Desowitz, Robert S - *Who Gave Pinta to the Santa Maria?*
     KR - v65 - Ap 1 '97 - p516 [251-500]
     PW - v244 - Ap 14 '97 - p65 [51-250]
DeSpain, Pleasant - *Eleven Nature Tales (Illus. by Joe Shlichta)*
  c BL - v92 - Ag '96 - p1897+ [51-250]
  c HB Guide - v7 - Fall '96 - p320 [1-50]
  Strongheart Jack and the Beanstalk (Illus. by Joe Shlichta)
  c RT - v50 - D '96 - p347 [51-250]
Despland, Michel - *Reading an Erased Code*
     JR - v77 - Ja '97 - p192+ [501+]
     MLR - v91 - O '96 - p996 [251-500]
Desrosiers, Sylvie - *Faut-Il Croire A La Magie? (Illus. by Daniel Sylvestre)*
  c Can CL - v22 - Sum '96 - p96+ [501+]
Desrosiers-Bonin, Diane - *Rabelais Et L'Humanisme Civil*
     Ren & Ref - v19 - Fall '96 - p92+ [501+]
Dessaix, Robert - *Night Letters*
     Aust Bk R - Ag '96 - p7+ [501+]
     Obs - D 1 '96 - p16* [51-250]
Dessalles, Pierre - *Sugar and Slavery, Family and Race*
     Choice - v34 - O '96 - p342 [51-250]
     VQR - v72 - Aut '96 - p128* [51-250]
Dessen, Alan C - *Recovering Shakespeare's Theatrical Vocabulary*
     Theat J - v48 - D '96 - p527+ [501+]
Dessen, Sarah - *That Summer*
  y BL - v93 - Ja '97 - p764 [1-50]
  y BL - v93 - Ap 1 '97 - p1292 [1-50]
  y CBRS - v25 - F '97 - p81 [51-250]
  y CCB-B - v50 - N '96 - p95 [51-250]
  y Emerg Lib - v24 - Mr '97 - p55 [51-250]
  y HB - v72 - N '96 - p742+ [51-250]
  y HB Guide - v8 - Spr '97 - p79 [51-250]
  y PW - v243 - S 2 '96 - p132 [51-250]
  y SLJ - v42 - O '96 - p144 [51-250]
  y VOYA - v19 - D '96 - p268 [51-250]
D'Este, Carlo - *Patton: A Genius for War*
     AJPsych - v153 - D '96 - p1644 [501+]
     J Mil H - v60 - O '96 - p785+ [501+]
     NYTBR - v101 - D 8 '96 - p90 [1-50]
     NYTBR - v102 - F 23 '97 - p24 [51-250]
     Pres SQ - v26 - Fall '96 - p1186+ [251-500]
Desu, Seshu B - *Ferroelectric Thin Films V*
     SciTech - v21 - Mr '97 - p77 [51-250]
Detambel, Regine - *Le Ventilateur*
     WLT - v70 - Aut '96 - p906+ [501+]
Detecting Women 2
  r ARBA - v28 - '97 - p433 [51-250]
Deth, Jan W Van - *The Impact of Values*
     Choice - v34 - O '96 - p353 [51-250]
Detienne, Marcel - *The Masters of Truth in Archaic Greece*
     Choice - v34 - Ja '97 - p808 [51-250]
De Toth, Andre - *De Toth on De Toth*
     Books - v11 - Ap '97 - p21 [51-250]
  Fragments: Portraits from the Inside
     TES - N 22 '96 - p8* [51-250]
Detroit Cancer Symposium (24th: 1992) - *Basic and Clinical Applications of Flow Cytometry*
     SciTech - v20 - N '96 - p40 [51-250]
Detroit Institute of Arts - *Art of the American Indian Frontier*
  c RT - v50 - O '96 - p139 [1-50]
  The Dodge Collection of Eighteenth-Century French and English Art in the Detroit Institute of Arts
     LJ - v122 - Mr 15 '97 - p59+ [51-250]

Detry, Robert - *Adrienne Ou La Liberte*
  FR - v70 - Mr '97 - p611 [501+]
Detter, Thomas - *Nellie Brown or, the Jealous Wife*
  AL - v68 - D '96 - p878 [51-250]
  Choice - v34 - N '96 - p455 [51-250]
  Nine-C Lit - v51 - D '96 - p420+ [51-250]
Dettke, Barbara - *Die Asiatische Hydra*
  JIH - v27 - Spr '97 - p697+ [501+]
Dettmar, Kevin J H - *The Illicit Joyce of Postmodernism*
  Choice - v34 - Mr '97 - p1160 [51-250]
  R&R Bk N - v12 - F '97 - p86 [51-250]
Dettmer, H William - *Goldratt's Theory of Constraints*
  R&R Bk N - v12 - F '97 - p45 [51-250]
Dettoni, John M - *Introduction to Youth Ministry*
  VOYA - v19 - F '97 - p317 [51-250]
Detweiler, Robert - *Uncivil Rites*
  Choice - v34 - F '97 - p964 [51-250]
Deubner, Christian - *Deutsche Europapolitik*
  JPR - v33 - Ag '96 - p379 [251-500]
Deuker, Carl - *Painting the Black*
  y HB - v73 - My '97 - p317+ [51-250]
  y KR - v65 - Ap 1 '97 - p553 [51-250]
Deursen, W P A Van - *Geographical Information Systems and Dynamic Models*
  GJ - v162 - Jl '96 - p219+ [501+]
Deutsch, David - *The Fabric of Reality*
  New Sci - v153 - Mr 22 '97 - p44+ [501+]
Deutsch, Eliot - *Essays on the Nature of Art*
  R&R Bk N - v12 - F '97 - p7 [51-250]
Deutsch, Nathaniel - *The Gnostic Imagination*
  Rel St Rev - v23 - Ja '97 - p87 [51-250]
Deutsch, R - *Forty New Ancient West Semitic Inscriptions*
  Rel St Rev - v23 - Ap '97 - p164 [51-250]
  New Epigraphic Evidence from the Biblical Period
  Rel St Rev - v23 - Ap '97 - p164 [51-250]
Deutsche, Rosalyn - *Evictions: Art and Spatial Politics*
  Choice - v34 - My '97 - p1485 [51-250]
Deutschland Und Der Westen Im 19. Und 20. Jahrhundert. Vols. 1-2
  EHR - v112 - Ap '97 - p519+ [501+]
DeValeria, Dennis - *Honus Wagner: A Biography*
  Choice - v34 - Ja '97 - p835+ [251-500]
  Honus Wagner: A Biography (Esmo). Audio Version
  y Kliatt - v31 - Mr '97 - p48 [51-250]
  LJ - v121 - D '96 - p169 [51-250]
De Vany, Arthur S - *The Emerging New Order in Natural Gas*
  En Jnl - v18 - 1 '97 - p125+ [501+]
De Varona, Frank - *Latino Literacy*
  KR - v64 - O 1 '96 - p1439 [251-500]
  LJ - v121 - O 15 '96 - p72 [51-250]
  PW - v243 - N 4 '96 - p68 [51-250]
Devauchelle, Roger - *La Reliure: Recherches Historiques, Techniques Et Biographiques Sur La Reliure Francaise*
  Lib - v18 - S '96 - p255+ [501+]
Devaux, Dom Augustin - *Les Origines Du Missel Des Chartreux*
  CH - v66 - Mr '97 - p189 [51-250]
De Vecchi, Nicolo - *Entrepreneurs, Institutions and Economic Change*
  Econ J - v106 - N '96 - p1789+ [501+]
De Vecchi, Pierluigi - *Michelangelo: The Vatican Frescoes*
  Choice - v34 - My '97 - p1485 [51-250]
  LJ - v122 - Mr 15 '97 - p59 [51-250]
  PW - v244 - Ja 13 '97 - p68+ [1-50]
De Vega, Manuel - *Models of Visual Spatial Cognition*
  Choice - v34 - N '96 - p543 [51-250]
Developing English
  TES - Ja 3 '97 - p47U [1-50]
Development
  p JEL - v35 - Mr '97 - p307 [51-250]
Development and Application of Computer Techniques in Environmental Studies V
  SciTech - v21 - Mr '97 - p82 [51-250]
Development in Practice
  p WorldV - v13 - Ja '97 - p13 [51-250]
Development of Education in the Kingdom of Saudi Arabia 1992-1994
  J Gov Info - v23 - S '96 - p660 [1-50]
Devendorf, John F - *Great Lakes Bulk Carriers*
  Sea H - v79 - Win '96 - p47 [1-50]
Deveney, John Patrick - *Paschal Beverly Randolph: A Nineteenth-Century Black American Spiritualist, Rosicrucian, and Sex Magician*
  Choice - v34 - Ap '97 - p1351 [501+]
  R&R Bk N - v12 - F '97 - p7 [51-250]
DeVenney, David P - *Source Readings in American Choral Music*
  M Ed J - v83 - S '96 - p58 [51-250]

Deventer, M Oskar Van - *Fundamentals of Bidirectional Transmission over a Single Optical Fibre*
  SciTech - v20 - S '96 - p55 [51-250]
Dever, Edie - *Goodbye Again*
  PW - v244 - Mr 17 '97 - p72 [1-50]
Deveraux, Robert - *Walking Wounded*
  Necro - Win '97 - p23+ [501+]
Devereaux, Leslie - *Fields of Vision*
  Afterimage - v24 - S '96 - p14 [501+]
Deverell, William - *Railroad Crossing*
  JEL - v34 - S '96 - p1472 [51-250]
Devereux, Paul - *Re-Visioning the Earth*
  PW - v243 - S 9 '96 - p80 [51-250]
Devettere, Raymond J - *Practical Decision Making in Health Care Ethics*
  Theol St - v57 - S '96 - p560+ [501+]
Devi, Yamuna - *The Vegetarian Table: India*
  PW - v244 - Ap 21 '97 - p66 [51-250]
De Vignere, Blaise - *Les Images Ou Tableaux De Platte-Peinture. Vols. 1-2*
  Ren Q - v50 - Spr '97 - p252+ [501+]
Deville, Raymond - *The French School of Spirituality*
  Rel St Rev - v22 - O '96 - p349 [51-250]
Devine, A M - *The Prosody of Greek Speech*
  Rel St Rev - v23 - Ja '97 - p63 [51-250]
Devine, George - *Responses to 101 Questions on Business Ethics*
  CLW - v67 - Mr '97 - p49+ [251-500]
  Hast Cen R - v27 - Ja '97 - p46 [1-50]
Devine, John - *Maximum Security*
  LJ - v121 - O 15 '96 - p70 [51-250]
Devine, Pat - *Competitiveness, Subsidiarity, and Industrial Policy*
  JEL - v34 - D '96 - p2085 [51-250]
  R&R Bk N - v11 - D '96 - p25 [51-250]
Devine, T M - *Clanship to Crofters' War*
  EHR - v111 - N '96 - p1302+ [501+]
  VS - v39 - Aut '95 - p103+ [501+]
  Glasgow. Vol. 1
  Albion - v28 - Sum '96 - p369+ [501+]
  Scottish Elites
  EHR - v112 - Ap '97 - p500+ [501+]
  The Transformation of Rural Scotland
  EHR - v111 - N '96 - p1302+ [501+]
Devins, Neal E - *Shaping Constitutional Values*
  Choice - v34 - F '97 - p1035 [51-250]
  R&R Bk N - v11 - D '96 - p51 [51-250]
Devisch, Rene - *Alimentations, Traditions Et Developpements En Afrique Intertropicale*
  Am Ethnol - v24 - F '97 - p254 [501+]
DeVitis, Joseph L - *The Success Ethic, Education, and the American Dream*
  Choice - v34 - N '96 - p498 [51-250]
  R&R Bk N - v11 - N '96 - p6 [51-250]
Devlin, Judith - *The Rise of the Russian Democrats*
  JPR - v33 - Ag '96 - p379 [251-500]
Devlin, Keith - *Goodbye, Descartes*
  BL - v93 - Ja '97 - p781 [51-250]
  BW - v27 - Mr 2 '97 - p8 [251-500]
  Choice - v34 - My '97 - p1512 [51-250]
  LJ - v121 - D '96 - p137 [51-250]
  PW - v243 - N 4 '96 - p54 [51-250]
  Wil Q - v21 - Win '97 - p92+ [501+]
  WSJ-Cent - v99 - Mr 18 '97 - pA20 [501+]
  Logic and Information
  CPR - v16 - Ap '96 - p91+ [501+]
Devon, Gary - *Wedding Night*
  BW - v27 - F 9 '97 - p12 [51-250]
Devon, Marian - *Miss Kendall Sets Her Cap*
  LJ - v121 - N 15 '96 - p47 [51-250]
De Vos, Gail - *Tales, Rumors, and Gossip*
  CAY - v17 - Fall '96 - p3 [51-250]
  JOYS - v10 - Fall '96 - p99+ [251-500]
  SLJ - v42 - O '96 - p46 [51-250]
  SLMQ - v24 - Sum '96 - p221 [51-250]
  VOYA - v19 - O '96 - p242 [51-250]
  Telling Tales
  Ch Bk News - v19 - Spr '96 - p23 [251-500]
De Vos, Susan - *Household Composition in Latin America*
  CS - v26 - Mr '97 - p200+ [501+]
DeVoto, Bernard - *Mark Twain's America*
  PW - v244 - Mr 17 '97 - p81 [1-50]
DeVries, Dawn - *Jesus Christ in the Preaching of Calvin and Schleiermacher*
  Rel St Rev - v23 - Ja '97 - p46 [51-250]
De Vries, Mary Ann - *Business Thesaurus*
  r ARBA - v28 - '97 - p89 [251-500]
  r CBR - v14 - S '96 - p27 [1-50]
  The Professional Secretary's Book of Lists and Tips
  r Bus Bk R - v13 - 3 '96 - p122 [51-250]

De Waard, Nancy - *Suprising Science*
  c SB - v32 - N '96 - p238 [51-250]
Dewald, Jonathan - *The European Nobility 1400-1800*
  CR - v269 - N '96 - p279 [51-250]
DeWalt, Suzanne - *Home-Based Interior Design Business*
  BWatch - v18 - F '97 - p3 [51-250]
Dewan, Ted - *Top Secret (Illus. by Ted Dewan)*
  c BL - v93 - Ap 1 '97 - p1337 [51-250]
  c KR - v65 - Ja 15 '97 - p140 [51-250]
  c PW - v244 - F 24 '97 - p90 [51-250]
  c SLJ - v43 - Mr '97 - p150 [51-250]
  c TES - O 25 '96 - p12* [51-250]
Dewatripont, Mathias - *The Prudential Regulation of Banks*
  JEL - v34 - S '96 - p1365+ [501+]
Dewdney, A K - *Introductory Computer Science*
  CBR - v14 - N '96 - p33 [51-250]
  Yes, We Have No Neutrons
  y BL - v93 - Ap 1 '97 - p1273 [51-250]
  KR - v65 - Mr 1 '97 - p347+ [51-250]
  PW - v244 - Mr 10 '97 - p59 [51-250]
Dewe, Michael - *Planning and Designing Libraries for Children and Young People*
  LR - v45 - 7 '96 - p43+ [251-500]
Dewees, Don - *Exploring the Domain of Accident Law*
  JEL - v34 - S '96 - p1449+ [51-250]
DeWeese, Gene - *King of the Dead*
  SF Chr - v18 - O '96 - p79 [51-250]
Dewey, Ariane - *Naming Colors*
  c Inst - v106 - Ja '97 - p4* [1-50]
  c LA - v73 - O '96 - p431 [51-250]
Dewey, Donald - *The Biographical History of Baseball*
  r Aethlon - v13 - Spr '96 - p227+ [251-500]
  James Stewart: A Biography
  Ent W - S 27 '96 - p74 [51-250]
  LATBR - O 6 '96 - p3+ [501+]
  NL - v79 - N 4 '96 - p17+ [501+]
  NYTBR - v101 - S 15 '96 - p20 [501+]
  Obs - Ja 12 '97 - p17* [501+]
  Spec - v278 - F 22 '97 - p30+ [501+]
Dewey, Jennifer Owings - *Faces Only a Mother Could Love*
  c HB Guide - v7 - Fall '96 - p335 [51-250]
  Rattlesnake Dance (Illus. by Jennifer Owings Dewey)
  c BL - v93 - Mr 15 '97 - p1236 [51-250]
  c CCB-B - v50 - Mr '97 - p244+ [51-250]
  c HB - v73 - Mr '97 - p211 [51-250]
  c KR - v65 - Ja 15 '97 - p140 [51-250]
  Stories on Stone (Illus. by Jennifer Owings Dewey)
  c HB Guide - v7 - Fall '96 - p390 [51-250]
  c RT - v50 - My '97 - p680 [51-250]
  c Smith - v27 - N '96 - p167 [1-50]
Dewey, Melvil - *Dewey Decimal Classification and Relative Index. 21st Ed., Vols. 1-4*
  r ARBA - v28 - '97 - p241 [251-500]
  r LAR - v99 - Ja '97 - p48 [501+]
  LJ - v121 - N 1 '96 - p113 [51-250]
Dewey, Partick R - *303 CD-ROMs to Use in Your Library*
  r RQ - v35 - Sum '96 - p576+ [251-500]
Dewey for Windows. Electronic Media Version
  r ARBA - v28 - '97 - p241 [501+]
Dews, C L Barney - *This Fine Place So Far from Home*
  TCR - v98 - Spr '97 - p537+ [501+]
Dexter, Catherine - *A Is for Apple, W Is for Witch (Illus. by Capucine Mazille)*
  c BL - v93 - S 15 '96 - p238 [51-250]
  c HB Guide - v8 - Spr '97 - p65 [51-250]
  c KR - v64 - My 1 '96 - p687 [51-250]
  Alien Game
  y Emerg Lib - v24 - S '96 - p27 [1-50]
  I Dream of Murder
  c CCB-B - v50 - Mr '97 - p245 [51-250]
  Safe Return
  c CBRS - v25 - Ja '97 - p56 [51-250]
  c CCB-B - v50 - N '96 - p95 [51-250]
  c HB - v72 - N '96 - p733+ [51-250]
  c HB Guide - v8 - Spr '97 - p65 [51-250]
  c KR - v64 - S 15 '96 - p1397 [51-250]
  c SLJ - v42 - D '96 - p120 [51-250]
Dexter, Colin - *Death Is Now My Neighbor*
  BL - v93 - D 1 '96 - p619+ [51-250]
  Ent W - Ap 4 '97 - p79 [51-250]
  KR - v65 - F 1 '97 - p174 [51-250]
  NYTBR - v102 - Mr 2 '97 - p20 [51-250]
  PW - v243 - D 30 '96 - p57 [51-250]
  WSJ-Cent - v99 - Mr 28 '97 - pA14 [51-250]
  Death Is Now My Neighbor (Whately). Audio Version
  LJ - v122 - My 1 '97 - p153+ [51-250]
  Death Is Now My Neighbour
  ILN - Christmas '96 - p90 [51-250]
  NS - v125 - S 20 '96 - p45 [501+]

Morse's Greatest Mystery and Other Stories (Davidson). Audio Version
  BL - v93 - N 1 '96 - p522 [51-250]
y Kliatt - v30 - N '96 - p42 [51-250]
Morse's Greatest Mystery and Other Stories (Nelson). Audio Version
  Arm Det - v29 - Fall '96 - p472 [51-250]
y Kliatt - v30 - N '96 - p42 [51-250]
Morse's Greatest Mystery and Other Stories (Tull). Audio Version
  BL - v92 - Ag '96 - p1917 [51-250]
y Kliatt - v30 - N '96 - p42 [51-250]
Deych, Genrich M - *Putevoditel': Arkhivnye Dokumenty Po Istorii Evreev V Rossii V XIX-Nachale XX vv.*
  Russ Rev - v55 - O '96 - p692+ [501+]
Deyermond, A D - *La Literatura Perdida De La Edad Media Castellana. Vol. 1*
  MLR - v91 - Jl '96 - p764+ [501+]
Deyermond, Alan - *Letters and Society in Fifteenth-Century Spain*
  MLR - v92 - Ap '97 - p489+ [501+]
Deyo, Frederic C - *Social Reconstructions of the World Automobile Industry*
  R&R Bk N - v12 - F '97 - p42 [51-250]
DeYoung, Alan J - *The Life and Death of a Rural American High School*
  ES - v27 - Sum '96 - p190+ [501+]
D'Haen, Christine - *Morgane*
  WLT - v70 - Sum '96 - p709 [501+]
D'Haene, Elise - *Licking Our Wounds*
  BL - v93 - Mr 1 '97 - p1109 [51-250]
  KR - v65 - Ja 1 '97 - p8 [251-500]
  LJ - v122 - F 15 '97 - p161 [51-250]
  PW - v244 - Ja 20 '97 - p392+ [51-250]
Dhami, Narinder - *Starring Alice MacKenzie*
c Sch Lib - v44 - Ag '96 - p105 [51-250]
Dhanjal, Beryl - *What Do We Know about Sikhism?*
c KR - v64 - D 1 '96 - p1735 [51-250]
c SLJ - v43 - Mr '97 - p173 [51-250]
Dharmadasa, K N O - *Language, Religion, and Ethnic Assertiveness*
  AHR - v101 - O '96 - p1262+ [501+]
Dheensaw, Cleve - *Celebrate the Spirit*
c Quill & Q - v62 - My '96 - p36 [251-500]
Dhimitrakopoulos, Fotis - *Yorghos Seferis-Kypros Hrysanthis Ke I Ghates T'Ai Nikola*
  WLT - v70 - Sum '96 - p742 [251-500]
Dhont, Jan K G - *An Introduction to Dynamics of Colloids*
  SciTech - v21 - Mr '97 - p31 [51-250]
Dia, Mamadou - *Africa's Management in the 1990s and Beyond*
  JEL - v34 - S '96 - p1477 [51-250]
  TLS - Ja 3 '97 - p14+ [501+]
Diabetes A to Z. New Completely Rev. Ed.
r BL - v93 - O 1 '96 - p367 [1-50]
The Diabetes Annual. Vol. 10
  SciTech - v20 - D '96 - p47 [51-250]
Diacu, Florin - *Celestial Encounters*
  New Sci - v153 - Ja 25 '97 - p42+ [51-250]
  Sci - v274 - D 20 '96 - p2032+ [251-500]
Diagnostic and Statistical Manual of Mental Disorders. 4th Ed.
r HM - v294 - F '97 - p61+ [501+]
Diagram Group - *Human Body on File: Physiology*
  SciTech - v20 - D '96 - p33 [51-250]
The Little Giant Encyclopedia of Puzzles
c Ch BWatch - v6 - My '96 - p1 [1-50]
c Math T - v89 - O '96 - p608 [51-250]
Diakite, Baba Wague - *The Hunterman and the Crocodile (Illus. by Baba Wague Diakite)*
c BL - v93 - Mr 15 '97 - p1245 [51-250]
c CBRS - v25 - Mr '97 - p86 [51-250]
c CCB-B - v50 - F '97 - p202+ [51-250]
c KR - v64 - D 15 '96 - p1797 [51-250]
c PW - v243 - D 9 '96 - p67 [51-250]
c SLJ - v43 - Mr '97 - p173 [51-250]
D'iakonov, I M - *Puti Istorii*
  AHR - v101 - O '96 - p1516 [501+]
Dial Up!. 1st Ed.
r ARBA - v28 - '97 - p625 [51-250]
r Choice - v34 - O '96 - p254 [51-250]
Diamandis, Eleftherios P - *Immunoassay*
  SciTech - v20 - N '96 - p33 [51-250]
Diamant, Anita - *Bible Baby Names*
r ARBA - v28 - '97 - p169 [51-250]
r BL - v93 - F 15 '97 - p1040 [51-250]
Diamant, Lincoln - *Yankee Doodle Days*
  LJ - v122 - F 1 '97 - p94 [51-250]
Diamond, Beverley - *Visions of Sound*
  Can Hist R - v78 - Mr '97 - p161+ [501+]

Diamond, Dan - *The Spirit of the Game*
y BL - v93 - S 15 '96 - p203 [51-250]
Diamond, Edwin - *White House to Your House*
  PSQ - v111 - Win '96 - p708+ [501+]
Diamond, Elin - *Performance and Cultural Politics*
  Am Theat - v13 - D '96 - p20 [1-50]
Diamond, Janet - *Exercises for Airplanes and Other Confined Spaces*
  BL - v93 - Ja '97 - p797 [51-250]
Diamond, Jared - *Guns, Germs, and Steel*
  KR - v65 - Ja 15 '97 - p113 [251-500]
  LATBR - Mr 9 '97 - p4 [501+]
  LJ - v122 - F 15 '97 - p159 [51-250]
  Nature - v386 - Mr 27 '97 - p339+ [501+]
  NL - v80 - Mr 10 '97 - p19+ [501+]
  Obs - Ap 13 '97 - p17* [501+]
  PW - v244 - Ja 13 '97 - p60 [51-250]
Why Is Sex Fun?
  LJ - v122 - My 1 '97 - p135 [51-250]
Diamond, Jay - *The World of Fashion. 2nd Ed.*
  TCI - v30 - O '96 - p56 [1-50]
Diamond, Louise - *Multi-Track Diplomacy*
  Bloom Rev - v16 - S '96 - p25 [51-250]
Diamond, Michael - *If You Can Keep It*
  Choice - v34 - Ja '97 - p813 [51-250]
Diamond, Nina L - *Purify Your Body*
  BL - v93 - D 15 '96 - p700 [51-250]
  PW - v243 - N 18 '96 - p73 [51-250]
Diamond, Peter A - *Social Security*
  JEL - v34 - D '96 - p2059 [51-250]
Diamond, Sara - *Facing the Wrath*
  Wom R Bks - v14 - Mr '97 - p21+ [501+]
Roads to Dominion
  APSR - v91 - Mr '97 - p185+ [501+]
  CS - v26 - Ja '97 - p33+ [501+]
  Wom R Bks - v14 - Mr '97 - p21+ [501+]
Diamond, Susan L - *Hard Labor*
  KR - v64 - Ag 15 '96 - p1204 [251-500]
  LJ - v121 - S 15 '96 - p86 [51-250]
Diamonstein, Barbaralee - *Singular Voices*
  KR - v65 - Ap 1 '97 - p542+ [51-250]
  PW - v244 - Ap 28 '97 - p67 [51-250]
Diani, Mario - *Green Networks*
  AJS - v102 - Jl '96 - p293+ [501+]
Dias, Dexter - *Error of Judgement*
  Books - v10 - Je '96 - p12+ [51-250]
Error of Judgment
  BL - v93 - N 15 '96 - p574 [51-250]
  KR - v64 - S 1 '96 - p1274 [51-250]
  LJ - v121 - O 1 '96 - p126 [51-250]
  PW - v243 - S 9 '96 - p68 [51-250]
False Witness
  Rapport - v19 - 4 '96 - p32 [251-500]
Dias, F - *Mathematical Problems in the Theory of Water Waves*
  SciTech - v20 - D '96 - p20 [51-250]
Diaz, Debra - *The Red Camp*
  KR - v64 - S 1 '96 - p1266 [51-250]
Diaz, Jesus - *La Piel Y La Mascara*
  BL - v93 - Ap 1 '97 - p1284 [1-50]
  WLT - v71 - Win '97 - p116 [501+]
Diaz, Junot - *Drown*
  BL - v93 - S 15 '96 - p220 [51-250]
  BL - v93 - Ap 1 '97 - p1285 [1-50]
  BW - v26 - N 3 '96 - p8 [51-250]
  Ent W - O 4 '96 - p56 [51-250]
  HMR - Fall '96 - p18+ [501+]
  LATBR - S 1 '96 - p2 [501+]
  New R - v215 - D 16 '96 - p39+ [501+]
  NS - v125 - N 29 '96 - p48 [251-500]
  NYTBR - v101 - S 29 '96 - p9 [501+]
  NYTBR - v101 - D 8 '96 - p79 [1-50]
  Obs - N 3 '96 - p18* [501+]
  Obs - D 1 '96 - p16* [1-50]
  Obs - D 1 '96 - p17* [1-50]
  SFR - v22 - Ja '97 - p26+ [501+]
  TLS - O 25 '96 - p22 [501+]
  VLS - Win '96 - p9 [501+]
  VV - v41 - S 10 '96 - p65+ [501+]
Diaz, Leo - *Antenna Engineering Using Physical Optics*
  SciTech - v20 - D '96 - p77 [51-250]
Diaz, Luciano - *Symbiosis: An Intercultural Anthology of Poetry*
  Can Lit - Win '96 - p140+ [501+]
Diaz-Cotto, Juanita - *Gender, Ethnicity, and the State*
  Choice - v34 - O '96 - p366 [51-250]
  Wom R Bks - v14 - O '96 - p19+ [501+]
Diaz Del Castillo, Bernal - *The Discovery and Conquest of Mexico 1517-1521*
  For Aff - v75 - N '96 - p160 [251-500]

Diaz-Stevens, Ana Maria - *Oxcart Catholicism on Fifth Avenue*
  Rel St Rev - v23 - Ja '97 - p94+ [51-250]
Dib, Mohammed - *La Nuit Sauvage*
  WLT - v70 - Aut '96 - p1009+ [501+]
DiBattista, Maria - *High and Low Moderns*
  Choice - v34 - Ap '97 - p1336 [51-250]
Dibble, Harold - *The Middle Paleolithic Site of Combe-Capelle Bas*
  Am Ant - v62 - Ja '97 - p164+ [501+]
Dibdin, Michael - *Cosi Fan Tutti*
  KR - v65 - My 1 '97 - p680+ [251-500]
  LJ - v122 - My 1 '97 - p144 [1-50]
  NS - v125 - S 20 '96 - p45 [501+]
  PW - v244 - Ap 7 '97 - p77 [51-250]
  TLS - Ag 30 '96 - p24 [251-500]
The Vintage Book of Classic Crime
  KR - v65 - F 1 '97 - p176 [51-250]
Di Blasi, Debra - *Drought. Say What You Like*
  KR - v64 - D 15 '96 - p1752 [251-500]
  PW - v244 - Ja 6 '97 - p66 [51-250]
Dibrova, Volodymyr - *Peltse and Pentameron*
  KR - v64 - D 1 '96 - p1703 [51-250]
  PW - v243 - N 4 '96 - p67 [51-250]
Di Cagno, Gabriella - *Michelangelo (Illus. by Simone Boni)*
c Sch Lib - v44 - N '96 - p174 [51-250]
c TES - Ag 23 '96 - p24 [51-250]
Michelangelo: Master of the Italian Renaissance (Illus. by Sergio)
y SLJ - v42 - D '96 - p144 [51-250]
Diccionario Didactico De Espanol
cr BL - v93 - Mr 1 '97 - p1196 [51-250]
Diccionario Enciclopedico Salvat Cuatro. Vols. 1-4
yr BL - v93 - Mr 1 '97 - p1196 [51-250]
Diccionario Griego-Espanol. Vol. 4
r Rel St Rev - v23 - Ap '97 - p170 [51-250]
Dick, Bernard F - *Billy Wilder*
  BW - v26 - O 13 '96 - p12 [51-250]
City of Dreams
  KR - v65 - Ap 1 '97 - p517 [251-500]
  PW - v244 - Ap 7 '97 - p81 [51-250]
Dick, Ignace - *Les Melkites: Grecs-Orthodoxes Et Grecs-Catholiques Des Patriarcats D'Antioche, D'Alexandrie Et De Jerusalem*
  MEJ - v51 - Spr '97 - p306+ [501+]
Dick, John A R - *William Tyndale and the Law*
  Albion - v28 - Win '96 - p687+ [501+]
  CH - v65 - S '96 - p478+ [251-500]
  Ren Q - v49 - Win '96 - p871+ [501+]
Dick, Philip K - *Flow My Tears, the Policeman Said*
  Obs - Ag 25 '96 - p18* [501+]
The Man in the High Castle
  Obs - Ag 25 '96 - p18* [501+]
The Shifting Realities of Philip K. Dick
  Ext - v38 - Spr '97 - p82+ [501+]
  SFS - v24 - Mr '97 - p172+ [501+]
The Three Stigmata of Palmer Eldritch
  Obs - Ag 25 '96 - p18* [501+]
Dick, Steven J - *The Biological Universe*
r Astron - v25 - Mr '97 - p102 [251-500]
  Nature - v385 - F 13 '97 - p592+ [501+]
  New Sci - v151 - S 14 '96 - p43 [501+]
  Sci - v275 - Mr 21 '97 - p1748+ [501+]
Dickason, Vance - *The Loudspeaker Design Cookbook. 5th Ed.*
  TCI - v30 - O '96 - p55 [1-50]
Dickens, A G - *Erasmus the Reformer*
  TLS - Ja 10 '97 - p28 [251-500]
Dickens, Charles - *The Amusements of the People and Other Papers*
  Choice - v34 - Mr '97 - p1160+ [51-250]
  LJ - v122 - Ap 1 '97 - p134 [1-50]
  Nine-C Lit - v51 - Mr '97 - p555 [51-250]
  Spec - v277 - D 14 '96 - p61 [501+]
  TLS - Ja 17 '97 - p18 [501+]
A Christmas Carol
c BIC - v25 - D '96 - p32+ [501+]
  SN - v111 - D '96 - p115+ [501+]
A Christmas Carol (Illus. by Patrick Benson)
c Bks Keeps - N '96 - p20 [1-50]
A Christmas Carol (Illus. by Quentin Blake)
c Par Ch - v20 - O '96 - p28 [51-250]
A Christmas Carol (Illus. by Gustave Dore)
  Atl - v278 - D '96 - p126 [51-250]
  LJ - v121 - O 1 '96 - p132 [1-50]
c PW - v243 - S 23 '96 - p62 [51-250]

A Christmas Carol (Illus. by Carter Goodrich)
c BL - v93 - S 1 '96 - p134 [51-250]
c BW - v26 - N 3 '96 - p10 [251-500]
c HB Guide - v8 - Spr '97 - p65 [51-250]
c PW - v243 - S 30 '96 - p92 [51-250]
c SLJ - v42 - O '96 - p34+ [51-250]
A Christmas Carol (Olivier). Audio Version
c BWatch - v17 - D '96 - p11 [1-50]
A Christmas Carol (Palmer). Audio Version
c TES - D 27 '96 - p27 [51-250]
Dicken's Journalism. Vol. 1
RES - v47 - Ag '96 - p434+ [501+]
Dickens' Journalism. Vol. 2
Econ - v342 - F 15 '97 - p14* [501+]
Dombey and Son (Davidson). Vols. 1-2. Audio Version
y Kliatt - v31 - My '97 - p36 [51-250]
LJ - v122 - F 15 '97 - p174 [51-250]
Fun with the Classics: A Christmas Carol (Porter). Audio Version
c SLJ - v43 - F '97 - p70 [51-250]
Great Expectations. Audio Version
Spec - v277 - N 30 '96 - p55 [51-250]
Listen and Read Charles Dickens' A Christmas Carol (Hammond). Book and Audio Version
c BL - v93 - Mr 15 '97 - p1253 [51-250]
c Ch BWatch - v6 - Jl '96 - p7 [1-50]
Oliver Twist (Illus. by Chris Mould)
c JB - v60 - D '96 - p250 [51-250]
Oliver Twist (Margolyes). Audio Version
TLS - Ag 2 '96 - p24 [51-250]
Dickens, Monica - *Befriending: The American Samaritans*
R&R Bk N - v11 - N '96 - p45 [51-250]
Dickens, Ross N - *Contestable Markets Theory, Competition, and the United States Commercial Banking Industry*
JEL - v34 - S '96 - p1436 [51-250]
Dickens Studies Annual. Vol. 22
VS - v39 - Spr '96 - p433+ [501+]
Dickens Studies Annual. Vol. 24
Nine-C Lit - v51 - Mr '97 - p567 [51-250]
Dickerman, Leah - *Building the Collective*
Choice - v34 - D '96 - p600+ [51-250]
LATBR - v263 - S 29 '96 - p14 [51-250]
Dickerson, James - *Goin' Back to Memphis*
y BL - v93 - S 15 '96 - p200 [51-250]
Choice - v34 - My '97 - p1508 [51-250]
Dickey, Christopher - *Innocent Blood*
y BL - v93 - My 1 '97 - p1477 [51-250]
KR - v65 - My 1 '97 - p660 [251-500]
LJ - v122 - My 1 '97 - p138 [51-250]
PW - v244 - My 5 '97 - p199 [51-250]
Dickey, Eric Jerome - *Sister, Sister*
BL - v93 - S 15 '96 - p220 [51-250]
Bloom Rev - v17 - Ja '97 - p19 [1-50]
KR - v64 - Ag 15 '96 - p1171+ [251-500]
LJ - v121 - N 1 '96 - p82 [1-50]
Dickey, James - *Striking In*
Choice - v34 - N '96 - p455 [51-250]
To the White Sea
South R - v33 - Win '97 - p164+ [501+]
Dickey, John S - *On the Rocks*
SciTech - v20 - N '96 - p24 [1-50]
Dickie, Margaret - *Gendered Modernisms*
AL - v68 - D '96 - p882 [51-250]
Dickinson, Donald C - *Henry E. Huntington's Library of Libraries*
Choice - v34 - O '96 - p263 [51-250]
Dickinson, Duo - *Expressive Details*
R&R Bk N - v12 - F '97 - p73 [51-250]
Dickinson, Edward Ross - *The Politics of German Child Welfare from the Empire to the Federal Republic*
Choice - v34 - D '96 - p668 [51-250]
JEL - v34 - S '96 - p1467 [51-250]
Dickinson, Emily - *Emily Dickinson: Selected Poems*
Bloom Rev - v16 - Jl '96 - p27 [1-50]
Emily Dickinson: Selected Poems (Clark). Audio Version
y BL - v93 - Ja '97 - p877 [51-250]
Emily Dickinson's Open Folios
AL - v68 - D '96 - p853+ [501+]
Nine-C Lit - v51 - S '96 - p279 [51-250]
Listen and Read Emily Dickinson's Selected Poems (Seldes). Book and Audio Version
c BL - v93 - Mr 15 '97 - p1253 [51-250]
Poems for Youth (Illus. by Thomas B Allen)
c HB Guide - v7 - Fall '96 - p367 [51-250]
c SLJ - v42 - S '96 - p213+ [51-250]
y VOYA - v19 - O '96 - p228 [51-250]
Dickinson, H T - *The Politics of the People in Eighteenth-Century Britain*
Albion - v28 - Sum '96 - p310+ [501+]
JMH - v69 - Mr '97 - p138+ [501+]

Dickinson, Peter - *Chuck and Danielle (Illus. by Kees De Kiefte)*
c PW - v244 - F 17 '97 - p220 [1-50]
c BL - v93 - Ja '97 - p765 [1-50]
c HB - v72 - S '96 - p593 [51-250]
c HB Guide - v7 - Fall '96 - p291 [51-250]
Chuck and Danielle (Illus. by Robin Lawrie)
c Bks Keeps - N '96 - p23 [51-250]
c JB - v60 - D '96 - p250 [51-250]
c Sch Lib - v45 - F '97 - p23+ [51-250]
Eva
y SLJ - v42 - N '96 - p40 [1-50]
The Gift
y Ch BWatch - v7 - F '97 - p6 [1-50]
The Lion Tamer's Daughter and Other Stories
y BL - v93 - Ap 1 '97 - p1321 [51-250]
y CCB-B - v50 - Mr '97 - p245+ [51-250]
c HB - v73 - Mr '97 - p197+ [251-500]
y KR - v65 - Ja 1 '97 - p58 [51-250]
c PW - v244 - F 24 '97 - p92 [51-250]
y SLJ - v43 - Mr '97 - p184 [51-250]
Dickinson, Robert H - *Selling the Sea*
BL - v93 - N 15 '96 - p556 [51-250]
LJ - v121 - O 15 '96 - p68 [51-250]
Dickinson, Susan - *The Sea Baby (Illus. by Peter Bailey)*
c JB - v60 - D '96 - p250 [51-250]
c Sch Lib - v45 - F '97 - p24 [51-250]
Dickinson, Terence - *Summer Stargazing*
yr SB - v32 - N '96 - p236 [51-250]
S&T - v93 - F '97 - p60 [1-50]
Dickinson, W Calvin - *The War of the Spanish Succession 1702-1713*
r ARBA - v28 - '97 - p200 [51-250]
r Choice - v34 - S '96 - p94 [51-250]
Dicks, Terrance - *Cyberspace Adventure*
c Bks Keeps - N '96 - p11 [51-250]
Harvey and the Beast of Bodmin (Illus. by S Hellard)
c JB - v60 - D '96 - p250+ [51-250]
The Ultimate Game
c Bks Keeps - N '96 - p11 [51-250]
Who Wrote That?
y Bks Keeps - v100 - S '96 - p21 [51-250]
Dickson, Athol - *Whom Shall I Fear?*
BL - v93 - N 15 '96 - p571 [501+]
LJ - v121 - N 1 '96 - p52+ [51-250]
Dickson, David - *The United Irishmen*
Bks & Cult - v2 - Ja '96 - p11+ [501+]
Dickson, Gordon R - *The Dragon and the Djinn*
y SLJ - v42 - O '96 - p162 [51-250]
The Magnificent Wilf
y Kliatt - v30 - S '96 - p16 [51-250]
Dickson, Paul - *The Joy of Keeping Score*
y BL - v93 - Ap 1 '97 - p1342 [1-50]
The Official Rules at Home
BL - v93 - O 1 '96 - p376 [51-250]
What's in a Name?
r ARBA - v28 - '97 - p169+ [51-250]
The Worth Book of Softball
Aethlon - v13 - Fall '95 - p169+ [251-500]
Dickson, T R - *Introduction to Chemistry. 7th Ed.*
J Chem Ed - v73 - Ag '96 - pA174 [251-500]
Dickstein, Morris - *Double Agent*
NYTBR - v102 - Mr 30 '97 - p24 [251-500]
DiConti, Veronica Donahue - *Interest Groups and Education Reform*
Choice - v34 - Ap '97 - p1390 [51-250]
Dicou, Bert - *Edom, Israel's Brother and Antagonist*
Rel St Rev - v23 - Ja '97 - p58 [51-250]
Di Cristina, George R - *A Simplified Guide to Custom Stairbuilding and Tangent Handrailing*
FHB - O '96 - p144+ [501+]
Dictionarul Personalitatilor Publice Si Politice 1992-1994
r BL - v93 - D 15 '96 - p714 [1-50]
Dictionary of American Biography. 1st Suppl.-
r ASInt - v34 - O '96 - p12+ [51-250]
Dictionary of American Biography. Vols. 1-21
r ASInt - v34 - O '96 - p12+ [51-250]
Dictionary of American Biography. Comprehensive Index: Complete through Supplement Ten
r ARBA - v28 - '97 - p17 [251-500]
r BL - v93 - F 15 '97 - p1042 [1-50]
Dictionary of American Literary Characters
r RQ - v36 - Win '96 - p214 [51-250]
Dictionary of International Biography 1996
r ARBA - v28 - '97 - p12+ [51-250]
Dictionary of Irish Literature. Rev. and Expanded Ed., Vols. 1-2
r ARBA - v28 - '97 - p460+ [251-500]
r Choice - v34 - Ap '97 - p1306 [51-250]
r ILS - v16 - Spr '97 - p35 [51-250]
r R&R Bk N - v12 - F '97 - p87 [51-250]

Dictionary of Literary Biography. Vol. 1-
r ASInt - v34 - O '96 - p14 [51-250]
Dictionary of Literary Biography Yearbook 1995
r ARBA - v28 - '97 - p414 [51-250]
The Dictionary of National Biography on CD-ROM. Electronic Media Version
r BL - v93 - D 15 '96 - p744 [51-250]
The Dictionary of Substances and Their Effects (DOSE). Electronic Media Version
r IRLA - v32 - Ag '96 - p6 [51-250]
Dictionnaire Hachette Multimedia. Electronic Media Version
r FR - v70 - Mr '97 - p635+ [501+]
Diderot, Denis - *Diderot on Art. Vols. 1-2*
BM - v138 - S '96 - p614 [251-500]
Le Fils Naturel
Eight-C St - v30 - Spr '97 - p271+ [501+]
Didion, Joan - *The Last Thing He Wanted*
Am - v176 - Ap 5 '97 - p28+ [501+]
BL - v93 - Ja '97 - p760 [1-50]
BW - v26 - S 8 '96 - p1+ [501+]
CSM - v88 - S 19 '96 - p14 [501+]
Ent W - S 20 '96 - p75 [51-250]
HMR - Fall '96 - p19 [501+]
LATBR - Ag 25 '96 - p2 [501+]
LATBR - D 29 '96 - p1 [1-50]
Lon R Bks - v19 - Ap 3 '97 - p20+ [501+]
Ms - v7 - S '96 - p83 [1-50]
Nat R - v48 - N 11 '96 - p57+ [501+]
New R - v215 - O 14 '96 - p44+ [501+]
NW - v128 - S 9 '96 - p68 [251-500]
NY - v72 - S 16 '96 - p95+ [501+]
NYRB - v43 - O 31 '96 - p4+ [501+]
NYTBR - v101 - S 8 '96 - p10 [501+]
NYTBR - v101 - D 8 '96 - p80 [1-50]
NYTLa - v145 - S 3 '96 - pC9+ [501+]
Obs - Ja '97 - p16* [501+]
Rapport - v19 - 6 '96 - p23 [251-500]
Spec - v278 - F 1 '97 - p34 [501+]
TES - Ja 17 '97 - p9* [51-250]
Time - v148 - S 9 '96 - p69 [501+]
TLS - F 14 '97 - p22 [501+]
Wom R Bks - v14 - D '96 - p6+ [501+]
Diefendorf, Barbara B - *Beneath the Cross*
CH - v65 - D '96 - p704+ [501+]
Diefendorf, Elizabeth - *The New York Public Library's Books of the Century*
r ARBA - v28 - '97 - p406 [251-500]
r Ch Today - v40 - D 9 '96 - p49 [501+]
Diefendorf, Jeffrey M - *American Policy and the Reconstruction of West Germany 1945-1955*
EHR - v111 - N '96 - p1353+ [501+]
Diehl, Digby - *Tales from the Crypt*
y BL - v93 - S 1 '96 - p52+ [51-250]
BW - v26 - D 8 '96 - p13 [51-250]
Diehn, Gwen - *Nature Crafts for Kids*
c LATBR - Ag 25 '96 - p11 [51-250]
Diels, Hermann - *Philology and Philosophy*
Rel St Rev - v23 - Ja '97 - p64 [51-250]
Dienst, Richard - *Still Life in Real Time*
Art J - v54 - Win '95 - p102+ [501+]
Dienstfrey, Patricia - *The Woman Without Experiences*
ABR - v17 - Ag '96 - p22 [501+]
Dierikx, Marc - *Fokker: A Transatlantic Biography*
PW - v244 - Ap 28 '97 - p65 [251-500]
Dierks, Leslie - *A Crafter's Book of Santas*
BL - v93 - N 1 '96 - p473 [51-250]
LJ - v121 - O 15 '96 - p56 [51-250]
Making Mosaics
y BL - v93 - Mr 15 '97 - p1218 [51-250]
Ceram Mo - v45 - Ap '97 - p30+ [51-250]
Wreath Magic
LJ - v121 - O 15 '96 - p56 [51-250]
Dierolf, Susanne - *Functional Analysis*
SciTech - v21 - Mr '97 - p16 [51-250]
Diesel Engine Combustion Processes
SciTech - v20 - D '96 - p73 [51-250]
Diesel Era - *EMD's SD60 Series*
Model R - v63 - D '96 - p74 [51-250]
Diesel Modeler's Guide. Vol. 1
Model R - v64 - Ap '97 - p52+ [51-250]
Dietary Phytochemicals in Cancer Prevention and Treatment
SciTech - v20 - D '96 - p42 [51-250]
Dieterle, Diane - *William Booton (1712-1787) of Culpeper County, Virginia and His Descendants*
r EGH - v50 - N '96 - p192 [51-250]
Dietrich, Donald J - *God and Humanity in Auschwitz*
AHR - v101 - O '96 - p1183+ [501+]
J Ch St - v38 - Sum '96 - p667+ [251-500]

Dietrich, Julia - *The Old Left in History and Literature*
 AL - v68 - D '96 - p867+ [501+]
 J Am St - v30 - Ag '96 - p341+ [251-500]
Dietrich, Richard Farr - *Bernard Shaw's Novels*
 Choice - v34 - O '96 - p276+ [51-250]
Dietrich, William - *Northwest Passage*
 y Kliatt - v31 - Ja '97 - p28 [51-250]
Dietz, Ulysses Grant - *Paul J. Stankard: Homage to Nature*
 Am Craft - v57 - Ap '97 - p22+ [501+]
Dietzer, M'Lou - *First Impressions. Vols. 5-6*
 Am MT - v46 - D '96 - p64 [51-250]
Diez De Revenga, Francisco Javier - *Poesia Espanola De Vanguardia 1918-1936*
 MLR - v92 - Ap '97 - p494 [501+]
 WLT - v70 - Sum '96 - p666+ [501+]
Diez Medrano, Juan - *Divided Nations*
 JMH - v69 - Mr '97 - p172+ [501+]
Diez Sanz, Enrique - *La Tierra De Soria*
 Choice - v34 - D '96 - p566 [1-50]
 Choice - v34 - D '96 - p566 [1-50]
Digby, Anne - *Making a Medical Living*
 EHR - v112 - Ap '97 - p499+ [251-500]
 J Soc H - v30 - Fall '96 - p276+ [501+]
Digby-Junger, Richard - *The Journalist as Reformer*
 Choice - v34 - F '97 - p959 [51-250]
 R&R Bk N - v11 - D '96 - p62 [51-250]
Digeser, Peter - *Our Politics, Our Selves?*
 AAPSS-A - v550 - Mr '97 - p168+ [501+]
 J Pol - v58 - Ag '96 - p900+ [501+]
Diggers and Dumpers (Snapshot Books)
 c Ch BWatch - v6 - D '96 - p8 [1-50]
Digges, Deborah - *Rough Music*
 Ken R - v18 - Sum '96 - p191+ [501+]
Diggins, John Patrick - *Max Weber: Politics and the Spirit of Tragedy*
 BW - v26 - O 13 '96 - p6+ [501+]
 Choice - v34 - Ja '97 - p836+ [51-250]
 JEL - v35 - Mr '97 - p192 [51-250]
 RP - v59 - Spr '97 - p389+ [501+]
 Soc - v34 - Mr '97 - p83+ [501+]
 WSJ-MW - v77 - Ag 19 '96 - pA10 [501+]
Digital Libraries '94
 LRTS - v40 - Ap '96 - p192+ [501+]
Dihle, Albrecht - *Greek and Latin Literature of the Roman Empire*
 TranslRevS - v1 - My '95 - p7 [51-250]
Dijk, Lutz Van - *Damned Strong Love*
 y Emerg Lib - v24 - S '96 - p24 [1-50]
 TranslRevS - v2 - D '96 - p25 [51-250]
Dijkstra, Bram - *Evil Sisters*
 BL - v93 - Ja '97 - p756 [1-50]
 BL - v93 - O 1 '96 - p294 [51-250]
 BW - v27 - Ja 26 '97 - p3+ [501+]
 Choice - v34 - My '97 - p1484 [51-250]
 LATBR - N 24 '96 - p8 [501+]
 LJ - v121 - O 1 '96 - p98 [51-250]
 Nat - v264 - F 3 '97 - p34+ [501+]
 NYTBR - v101 - D 8 '96 - p64 [501+]
 PW - v243 - N 4 '96 - p44 [51-250]
Dijs, Carla - *Daddy, Would You Love Me*
 c Ch BWatch - v6 - Jl '96 - p4 [1-50]
 Mommy, Would You Love Me
 c Ch BWatch - v6 - Jl '96 - p4 [1-50]
 Up Pop the Monsters 1,2,3! (Illus. by Carla Dijs)
 c LATBR - O 20 '96 - p8 [1-50]
 c PW - v243 - S 30 '96 - p85 [51-250]
 Who's Afraid? (Illus. by Carla Dijs)
 c HB Guide - v8 - Spr '97 - p12 [51-250]
 c PW - v243 - O 7 '96 - p77 [51-250]
Dikotter, Frank - *Sex, Culture, and Modernity in China*
 Ch Rev Int - v3 - Fall '96 - p388+ [501+]
 Cu H - v95 - S '96 - p291+ [51-250]
 TLS - O 25 '96 - p9+ [501+]
Dilenschneider, Robert L - *The Critical 14 Years of Your Professional Life*
 BL - v93 - My 15 '97 - p1548 [51-250]
Dillard, Philip H - *Sir Arthur Sullivan: A Resource Book*
 r AB - v98 - D 9 '96 - p2000 [251-500]
 r Choice - v34 - My '97 - p1473 [51-250]
Dillehay, Tom D - *Monte Verde*
 Arch - v50 - Mr '97 - p60+ [501+]
 Tombs for the Living
 LA Ant - v7 - Je '96 - p166+ [501+]
Diller, Ann - *The Gender Question in Education*
 Choice - v34 - N '96 - p510 [51-250]
Diller, Daniel C - *The Presidents, First Ladies and Vice Presidents*
 yr Kliatt - v31 - My '97 - p21 [51-250]
Diller, Harriet - *Big Band Sound (Illus. by Andrea Shine)*
 c HB Guide - v7 - Fall '96 - p253 [51-250]

The Faraway Drawer (Illus. by Andrea Shine)
 c HB Guide - v8 - Spr '97 - p25 [51-250]
 c SLJ - v42 - N '96 - p80 [51-250]
Dillery, John - *Xenophon and the History of His Times*
 Choice - v34 - Ap '97 - p1394 [51-250]
Dilley, David D - *Haeger Potteries--Through the Years*
 r Ant & CM - v102 - Ap '97 - p66 [51-250]
Dillingham, William B - *Melville and His Circle*
 LJ - v121 - D '96 - p93 [51-250]
 PW - v243 - O 14 '96 - p70 [51-250]
Dillman, Bradford - *Are You Anybody?*
 BL - v93 - F 1 '97 - p918 [51-250]
 PW - v244 - F 17 '97 - p206 [51-250]
Dillon, Patrick - *The Last Best Thing*
 KR - v64 - S 1 '96 - p1254 [251-500]
 LJ - v121 - O 15 '96 - p89 [51-250]
 NYTBR - v101 - D 1 '96 - p11 [501+]
 PW - v243 - S 16 '96 - p70+ [51-250]
DiLorenzo, Thomas J - *Frightening America's Elderly*
 NYRB - v43 - D 19 '96 - p68+ [501+]
Dilthey, Wilhelm - *Hermeneutics and the Study of History*
 Rel St Rev - v23 - Ja '97 - p45 [51-250]
Dilts, David A - *Assessing What Professors Do*
 J Hi E - v68 - Ja '97 - p112+ [501+]
Dilworth, Leah - *Imagining Indians in the Southwest*
 Choice - v34 - My '97 - p1562 [51-250]
 LJ - v121 - D '96 - p114+ [51-250]
Dilworth, Rankin - *The March to Monterrey*
 Roundup M - v4 - D '96 - p20 [251-500]
 WHQ - v28 - Spr '97 - p102 [1-50]
DIMACS Workshop on DNA Based Computers (1995: Princeton University) - *DNA Based Computers*
 SciTech - v20 - N '96 - p11 [51-250]
Dimand, Mary Ann - *A History of Game Theory. Vol. 1*
 JEL - v35 - Mr '97 - p191 [51-250]
 Women of Value
 Econ J - v106 - N '96 - p1817+ [501+]
Dimes, Francis - *The Building Stone Heritage of Leeds*
 New Sci - v153 - Mr 22 '97 - p47 [51-250]
Dimijian, Greg - *Animalwatch*
 y BL - v93 - N 15 '96 - p557 [51-250]
Dimitri Hadzi
 BL - v93 - D 1 '96 - p636+ [51-250]
Din, Gilbert C - *The New Orleans Cabildo*
 Choice - v34 - Ja '97 - p861+ [51-250]
 R&R Bk N - v11 - D '96 - p17 [51-250]
Dinar, Ariel - *Modeling Economic Management and Policy Issues of Water in Irrigated Agriculture*
 R&R Bk N - v11 - D '96 - p29 [51-250]
Dine, Philip - *Images of the Algerian War*
 J Mil H - v60 - O '96 - p800+ [501+]
Dineen, Jacqueline - *Frederic Chopin*
 c Bks Keeps - Mr '97 - p24 [51-250]
 The Greeks
 c SLJ - v42 - N '96 - p39 [51-250]
 The Romans
 c SLJ - v42 - N '96 - p39 [51-250]
Dineen, Sean - *Functions of Two Variables*
 JEL - v34 - D '96 - p2017 [51-250]
Dines, Carol - *Talk to Me*
 y HB - v73 - My '97 - p318 [251-500]
 y PW - v244 - My 12 '97 - p77 [51-250]
Ding, Wang - *Chu Ye Quan*
 BL - v93 - N 1 '96 - p484 [1-50]
Dingus, Lowell - *Next of Kin*
 LJ - v121 - O 15 '96 - p87+ [51-250]
 Searching for Velociraptor
 c BL - v93 - S 1 '96 - p121 [51-250]
 c HB Guide - v8 - Spr '97 - p114 [51-250]
 c SB - v33 - Ja '97 - p17 [51-250]
 c SLJ - v43 - F '97 - p113 [51-250]
Dingwall, Helen M - *Late Seventeenth-Century Edinburgh*
 EHR - v111 - N '96 - p1289+ [251-500]
Dingwall, Robert - *The Protection of Children. 2nd Ed.*
 r R&R Bk N - v12 - F '97 - p56 [51-250]
Dingwaney, Anuradha - *Between Languages and Cultures*
 Choice - v34 - O '96 - p272 [51-250]
 TLS - S 6 '96 - p9+ [501+]
Dinh, Linh - *Night, Again*
 BWatch - v17 - N '96 - p10 [51-250]
 Choice - v34 - Ja '97 - p790 [251-500]
 TLS - S 6 '96 - p23 [251-500]
 WLT - v71 - Win '97 - p233+ [501+]
DiNitto, Diana M - *Social Welfare. 4th Ed.*
 Soc Ser R - v70 - D '96 - p671 [51-250]
Dinn, Sheila - *Hearts of Gold*
 c Ch BWatch - v6 - N '96 - p8 [51-250]
Dinosaurs Series (Child's World)
 c Ch BWatch - v6 - N '96 - p8 [51-250]
Dintaman, Stephen F - *Creative Grace*
 Rel St Rev - v23 - Ap '97 - p176 [251-500]

Dintrone, Charles V - *Television Program Master Index*
 r ARBA - v28 - '97 - p521 [51-250]
 r BL - v93 - S 1 '96 - p171 [251-500]
 r Choice - v34 - N '96 - p427 [51-250]
DiNucci, Darcy - *Elements of Web Design*
 LJ - v122 - Ap 1 '97 - p118 [51-250]
Dinwiddy, Caroline - *Principles of Cost-Benefit Analysis for Developing Countries*
 JEL - v34 - S '96 - p1481+ [51-250]
Dionetti, Michelle - *Painting the Wind (Illus. by Kevin Hawkes)*
 c BL - v93 - O 1 '96 - p357 [51-250]
 c CBRS - v25 - N '96 - p30 [51-250]
 c HB Guide - v8 - Spr '97 - p25 [51-250]
 c KR - v64 - S 1 '96 - p1321 [51-250]
 c NYTBR - v101 - D 8 '96 - p78 [501+]
 c SLJ - v42 - O '96 - p91 [51-250]
Dionne, E J - *They Only Look Dead*
 Obs - D 1 '96 - p17* [51-250]
 PSQ - v111 - Fall '96 - p548+ [501+]
 Rapport - v19 - 5 '96 - p41 [251-500]
 Trib Bks - Mr 9 '97 - p8 [1-50]
Diouf, Mamadou - *Academic Freedom in Africa*
 JTWS - v13 - Fall '96 - p258+ [501+]
DiPasquale, Denise - *Urban Economics and Real Estate Markets*
 JEL - v34 - S '96 - p1501 [51-250]
DiPego, Gerald - *Cheevey: A Novel*
 Books - v10 - Je '96 - p13 [1-50]
 Cheevey: A Novel (Hall). Audio Version
 y Kliatt - v30 - N '96 - p38 [51-250]
Dippel, John V H - *Bound upon a Wheel of Fire*
 Choice - v34 - S '96 - p185 [51-250]
Dippel, Raye - *Caring for the Alzheimer Patient. 3rd Ed.*
 BWatch - v18 - Mr '97 - p2 [1-50]
Dipper, Frances - *Mysteries of the Ocean Deep*
 c HB Guide - v7 - Fall '96 - p332 [1-50]
 Oceans and Rivers
 c JB - v60 - D '96 - p266 [51-250]
Dipple, Geoffrey - *Antifraternalism and Anticlericalism in the German Reformation*
 Choice - v34 - F '97 - p979 [51-250]
Dirac, P A M - *The Collected Works of P.A.M. Dirac 1924-1948*
 Am Sci - v85 - Ja '97 - p76 [501+]
 Isis - v87 - D '96 - p747 [51-250]
 Phys Today - v49 - S '96 - p84+ [501+]
 Sci - v274 - N 15 '96 - p1149 [1-50]
 General Theory of Relativity
 Phys Today - v49 - S '96 - p84+ [501+]
Directors' and Officers' Liability 1995-
 r RQ - v35 - Sum '96 - p553+ [251-500]
Directory of American Firms Operating in Foreign Countries. 14th Ed., Vols. 1-3
 r ARBA - v28 - '97 - p102 [251-500]
A Directory of American Poets and Fiction Writers. 1995-1996 Ed.
 r ARBA - v28 - '97 - p346 [51-250]
Directory of Chemical Producers and Products. 2nd Ed., Vol. 1, Pt. 1
 r ARBA - v28 - '97 - p628 [51-250]
The Directory of Corporate and Foundation Givers 1996. Vols. 1-2
 r ARBA - v28 - '97 - p311 [251-500]
Directory of Electronic Journals, Newsletters, and Academic Discussion Lists. 6th Ed.
 r ARBA - v28 - '97 - p624+ [51-250]
 r LJ - v121 - S 15 '96 - p104 [51-250]
A Directory of Environmental Electronic Mail Users in Eurasia. 4th Ed.
 r ARBA - v28 - '97 - p648 [51-250]
The Directory of EU Information Sources 1995-1996
 r ARBA - v28 - '97 - p273 [51-250]
 r Choice - v34 - O '96 - p250 [51-250]
Directory of European Research and Development 1997. Vols. 1-2
 r SciTech - v21 - Mr '97 - p2 [51-250]
Directory of Health Grants
 r ARBA - v28 - '97 - p602 [51-250]
Directory of Japan Specialists and Japanese Studies Institutions in the United States and Canada. Vols. 1-3
 r Choice - v34 - Mr '97 - p1135+ [501+]
Directory of Japanese-Affiliated Companies in the EU 1996-97
 r ARBA - v28 - '97 - p102+ [251-500]
Directory of Labor Unions in the United States 1947-1953
 r RQ - v36 - Fall '96 - p49+ [51-250]
Directory of Library Automation. 1996 Ed.
 r R&R Bk N - v11 - D '96 - p73 [51-250]

The Directory of MBAs: 1996/97 Academic Year
  r Choice - v34 - Ja '97 - p768 [51-250]
Directory of National and International Law. 1955-1970 Eds.
  r RQ - v36 - Fall '96 - p49+ [51-250]
Directory of National Helplines 1996
  r BL - v92 - Ag '96 - p1922 [1-50]
  r Choice - v34 - D '96 - p588+ [51-250]
Directory of National Unions and Employee Associations. 1971-1979 Eds.
  r RQ - v36 - Fall '96 - p49+ [51-250]
Directory of Official Information. 1995/1997 Ed.
  r J Gov Info - v23 - S '96 - p653 [1-50]
The Directory of Overseas Catalogs 1997
  r ARBA - v28 - '97 - p103 [251-500]
  r BL - v93 - F 1 '97 - p964 [51-250]
  r R&R Bk N - v12 - F '97 - p44 [51-250]
Directory of Power Plant Equipment and Processes 1996
  r ARBA - v28 - '97 - p643 [51-250]
Directory of Research Grants 1996
  r ARBA - v28 - '97 - p311+ [251-500]
Directory of Research Grants 1997
  r JAAL - v40 - F '97 - p415 [51-250]
Directory of Texas Manufacturers. 1996 Ed., Vols. 1-2
  r JEL - v34 - D '96 - p2087 [51-250]
Directory of the Association for Library and Information Science Education 1995-96
  r LQ - v67 - Ap '97 - p184+ [501+]
Directory of the World's Banks. 11th Ed.
  r R&R Bk N - v12 - F '97 - p48 [51-250]
Directory of Trade and Investment Related Organizations of Developing Countries and Areas in Asia and the Pacific. 7th Ed.
  r ARBA - v28 - '97 - p111 [251-500]
Directory of U.S. Labor Organizations 1982-
  r RQ - v36 - Fall '96 - p50 [251-500]
Di Rienzo, Eugenio - *Alle Origini Della Francia Contemporanea*
  JMH - v68 - S '96 - p696+ [501+]
Diringer, David - *The Illuminated Book. Rev. Ed.*
  AB - v99 - Mr 3 '97 - p685+ [501+]
Dirlik, Arif - *After the Fall*
  S&S - v61 - Sum '97 - p278+ [501+]
Dis, Adriaan Van - *My Father's War*
  NYTBR - v101 - D 15 '96 - p19 [501+]
  TranslRevS - v2 - D '96 - p20 [51-250]
Di Scala, Spencer - *Italian Socialism*
  Choice - v34 - Ja '97 - p868 [51-250]
Disch, Estelle - *Reconstructing Gender*
  Bl S - v26 - Fall '96 - p101 [1-50]
Disch, Thomas M - *The Castle of Indolence*
  NYTBR - v101 - D 1 '96 - p36 [1-50]
Dischell, Stuart - *Evenings and Avenues*
  LJ - v121 - D '96 - p98 [51-250]
Discover the Universe. Book and Electronic Media Version
  Astron - v25 - Ap '97 - p96 [51-250]
Discover the World Picture Atlas
  cr TES - O 4 '96 - p16* [1-50]
Discoveries Series
  c Magpies - v11 - Jl '96 - p38 [51-250]
DISCovering Authors. Electronic Media Version
  yr ARBA - v28 - '97 - p414+ [51-250]
  yr VOYA - v19 - D '96 - p296 [251-500]
DISCovering Biography. Electronic Media Version
  yr BL - v93 - My 15 '97 - p1602+ [251-500]
  r LJ - v122 - Mr 15 '97 - p96+ [51-250]
DISCovering Careers and Jobs Plus. Electronic Media Version
  yr RQ - v35 - Sum '96 - p539+ [501+]
DISCovering Multicultural America. Electronic Media Version
  r ARBA - v28 - '97 - p150 [51-250]
  r BL - v93 - Ja '97 - p769 [1-50]
  r RQ - v36 - Win '96 - p282+ [501+]
DISCovering Science. Electronic Media Version
  yr BL - v93 - My 15 '97 - p1604 [501+]
DISCovering U.S. History. Electronic Media Version
  yr BL - v93 - My 15 '97 - p1606+ [501+]
DISCovering World History. Electronic Media Version
  yr BL - v93 - My 15 '97 - p1606+ [501+]
Discovery Channel (Firm) - *The Leopard Son*
  c BL - v93 - N 1 '96 - p491+ [51-250]
  c CBRS - v25 - Win '97 - p67 [1-50]
  c Ch BWatch - v6 - O '96 - p1 [51-250]
  c Ch BWatch - v6 - N '96 - p7 [51-250]
  c HB Guide - v8 - Spr '97 - p126 [51-250]
  c KR - v64 - O 15 '96 - p1540 [51-250]
  c PW - v243 - N 4 '96 - p76 [51-250]
  c SLJ - v43 - Ja '97 - p96 [51-250]

Disfarmer, Mike - *Disfarmer: 1939-1946 Heber Springs Portraits*
  BL - v93 - F 1 '97 - p918 [51-250]
  LJ - v122 - Ap 1 '97 - p88 [51-250]
  NYTBR - v101 - D 8 '96 - p72+ [251-500]
  VLS - Win '96 - p31 [51-250]
  VV - v52 - Ja 28 '97 - p48+ [501+]
Disher, Garry - *The Sunken Road*
  Woman's J - Ag '96 - p11 [1-50]
  Walk Twenty, Run Twenty
  c Magpies - v11 - S '96 - p31 [51-250]
Di Simplicio, Oscar - *Peccato, Penitenza, Perdono*
  J Soc H - v30 - Win '96 - p503+ [501+]
Disney, Anthony - *Historiography of Europeans in Africa and Asia 1450-1800*
  HAHR - v77 - My '97 - p302+ [251-500]
  R&R Bk N - v12 - F '97 - p18 [51-250]
Disney, Richard - *Can We Afford to Grow Older?*
  Choice - v34 - Mr '97 - p1207 [51-250]
  JEL - v35 - Mr '97 - p234 [51-250]
Dispenza, Joseph - *Live Better Longer*
  PW - v244 - Ap 7 '97 - p89 [51-250]
Disraeli, Benjamin, Earl of Beaconsfield - *Benjamin Disraeli Letters. Vol. 5*
  EHR - v112 - F '97 - p232+ [251-500]
Dissertation Abstracts. Electronic Media Version
  r ARBA - v28 - '97 - p31+ [501+]
Dissertation Abstracts International 1938-
  r ASInt - v34 - O '96 - p21 [51-250]
The Distance Learning Funding Sourcebook. 1996 Ed.
  r ChrPhil - v9 - D 12 '96 - p48 [51-250]
Disturbed Guillotine
  p LMR - v15 - Fall '96 - p40+ [51-250]
Di Tella, Torcuato S - *National Popular Politics in Early Independent Mexico 1820-1847*
  AHR - v102 - F '97 - p233+ [501+]
  Choice - v34 - O '96 - p342+ [51-250]
Dith Pran - *Children of Cambodia's Killing Fields*
  BL - v93 - F 1 '97 - p923 [51-250]
  KR - v65 - Mr 1 '97 - p363 [51-250]
  LJ - v122 - F 15 '97 - p145 [51-250]
  PW - v244 - Mr 17 '97 - p63 [51-250]
Ditmanson, Harold H - *Stepping Stones to Further Jewish-Lutheran Relationships*
  Rel Ed - v91 - Fall '96 - p609 [1-50]
Dittmer, John - *Local People*
  VQR - v72 - Aut '96 - p748+ [501+]
Ditzinger, Thomas - *Vision Magica*
  y JAAL - v40 - S '96 - p77 [1-50]
Divakaruni, Chitra Banerjee - *Arranged Marriage*
  BW - v26 - D 15 '96 - p4 [1-50]
  The Mistress of Spices
  BL - v93 - D 15 '96 - p692 [51-250]
  Ent W - Mr 21 '97 - p69 [51-250]
  KR - v64 - D 15 '96 - p1753 [251-500]
  LATBR - Mr 9 '97 - p10 [501+]
  LJ - v122 - F 1 '97 - p105 [51-250]
  NYTBR - v102 - Ap 13 '97 - p20 [51-250]
  PW - v244 - Ja 13 '97 - p51+ [251-500]
  TLS - Mr 21 '97 - p24 [501+]
  Trib Bks - My 25 '97 - p1+ [501+]
  Woman's J - F '97 - p16 [51-250]
DiVecchio, Jerry Anne - *New Easy Basics Cookbook*
  PW - v244 - Mr 24 '97 - p80 [51-250]
Diver-Stamnes, Ann C - *Prevent, Repent, Reform, Revenge*
  CS - v26 - Mr '97 - p212+ [501+]
Dix, Mark - *Discovering AutoCAD, Release 13*
  SciTech - v21 - Mr '97 - p72 [51-250]
Dixit, Avinash K - *The Making of Economic Policy*
  JEL - v35 - Mr '97 - p202 [51-250]
Dixmier, Jacques - *Enveloping Algebras*
  r SciTech - v20 - S '96 - p9 [51-250]
Dixon, Ann - *Merry Birthday, Nora Noel (Illus. by Mark Graham)*
  c Bloom Rev - v16 - N '96 - p31 [1-50]
  c HB Guide - v8 - Spr '97 - p25 [51-250]
  c PW - v243 - S 30 '96 - p89 [51-250]
  c SLJ - v42 - O '96 - p35 [51-250]
Dixon, Bernard - *Power Unseen*
  y Kliatt - v30 - S '96 - p35 [51-250]
Dixon, C Scott - *The Reformation and Rural Society*
  Choice - v34 - N '96 - p516+ [51-250]
Dixon, Chuck - *Batman: The Joker's Apprentice (Illus. by John Calmette)*
  c HB Guide - v7 - Fall '96 - p253+ [51-250]
  c SF Chr - v18 - O '96 - p80 [1-50]
Dixon, Dougal - *Prehistoric Life*
  c Ch BWatch - v6 - S '96 - p6 [51-250]
  c Cur R - v36 - D '96 - p12 [51-250]
  c HB Guide - v8 - Spr '97 - p114 [51-250]

The Search for Dinosaurs
  c TES - N 8 '96 - p13* [501+]
Dixon, Huw David - *The New Macroeconomics*
  JEL - v34 - S '96 - p1418 [51-250]
Dixon, Joan M - *National Intelligencer and Washington Advertiser Newspaper Abstracts 1800-1805*
  EGH - v50 - N '96 - p165 [51-250]
Dixon, John - *Social Security Programs*
  Soc Ser R - v70 - D '96 - p671 [251-250]
Dixon, Michael Bigelow - *Anne Bogart: Viewpoints*
  TDR - v41 - Spr '97 - p159 [1-50]
  By Southern Playwrights
  R&R Bk N - v11 - N '96 - p72 [1-50]
Dixon, Michael F N - *The Polliticke Courtier*
  Choice - v34 - Mr '97 - p1161 [51-250]
  R&R Bk N - v12 - F '97 - p85 [51-250]
Dixon, Norma - *Kites: Twelve Easy-to-Make Fliers (Illus. by Linda Hendry)*
  c HB Guide - v8 - Spr '97 - p135 [51-250]
Dixon, Phil - *The Negro Baseball Leagues*
  Aethlon - v13 - Fall '95 - p171+ [251-500]
Dixon, Ramon - *How Far Do You Wanna Go?*
  y BL - v93 - F 15 '97 - p993 [51-250]
  KR - v65 - Mr 15 '97 - p432 [251-500]
  PW - v244 - F 17 '97 - p200 [51-250]
Dixon, Stephen - *Frog: A Novel*
  NYTBR - v102 - Mr 23 '97 - p28 [1-50]
  PW - v244 - Ja 13 '97 - p73 [1-50]
  Trib Bks - Mr 16 '97 - p8 [1-50]
  Gould: A Novel in Two Novels
  BL - v93 - F 15 '97 - p1002 [51-250]
  KR - v64 - N 15 '96 - p1619 [251-500]
  LATBR - F 23 '97 - p2 [501+]
  LJ - v122 - Ja '97 - p145 [51-250]
  NYTBR - v102 - Ap 20 '97 - p12 [501+]
  PW - v244 - Ja 6 '97 - p64+ [51-250]
  Trib Bks - F 16 '97 - p6+ [501+]
  Interstate
  NYTBR - v102 - Mr 23 '97 - p28 [51-250]
  PW - v244 - Ja 13 '97 - p73 [1-50]
  Trib Bks - Mr 16 '97 - p8 [1-50]
  VV - v42 - Ja 7 '97 - p41 [51-250]
Dixon, Wheeler Winston - *It Looks at You*
  FQ - v50 - Win '96 - p54+ [501+]
Dizard, Wilson, Jr. - *Old Media/New Media. 2nd Ed.*
  JMCQ - v73 - Win '96 - p1009+ [251-500]
DiZazzo, Raymond - *Saying the Right Thing*
  BL - v93 - Mr 15 '97 - p1210 [51-250]
Dizikes, John - *Opera in America*
  AB - v98 - D 9 '96 - p1994 [51-250]
Djaout, Tahar - *Les Chercheurs D'Os*
  FR - v70 - D '96 - p271+ [501+]
Djebar, Assia - *Vaste Est La Prison*
  FR - v70 - F '97 - p495+ [251-500]
  TLS - D 13 '96 - p12 [501+]
Djerassi, Carl - *The Bourbaki Gambit*
  PW - v243 - S 9 '96 - p80 [1-50]
  Marx, Deceased
  BW - v26 - S 8 '96 - p6 [501+]
  NYTBR - v101 - N 17 '96 - p25 [51-250]
  Sci - v273 - Ag 30 '96 - p1180 [51-250]
Djobadze, Wachtang - *Early Medieval Georgian Monasteries in Historic Tao, Klarjet'i, and Savset'i*
  Specu - v72 - Ja '97 - p139+ [501+]
The DK Geography of the World
  cr ARBA - v28 - '97 - p174 [51-250]
  yr BL - v93 - N 1 '96 - p534 [251-500]
  cr Ch BWatch - v6 - N '96 - p2 [51-250]
  cr JB - v60 - D '96 - p262+ [251-500]
  cr Sch Lib - v44 - N '96 - p162 [51-250]
  cr SLJ - v43 - F '97 - p128 [51-250]
The DLA Financial
  p LJ - v122 - Ja '97 - p158 [51-250]
D'Lacey, Chris - *Juggling with Jeremy (Illus. by Gus Clarke)*
  c Bks Keeps - Jl '96 - p8 [51-250]
Dlugos, Tim - *Powerless: Selected Poems 1973-1990*
  BL - v93 - D 1 '96 - p639+ [51-250]
  BW - v26 - D 8 '96 - p8 [51-250]
Dluhosch, Barbara - *International Competitiveness and the Balance of Payments*
  Choice - v34 - S '96 - p175 [251-250]
  JEL - v34 - S '96 - p1431+ [51-250]
Dmytryk, Edward - *Odd Man Out*
  Choice - v34 - O '96 - p289 [51-250]
  LATBR - N 3 '96 - p8 [501+]
Do, Thong Minh - *Tu Then Tin Hoc Tong Hop*
  r BL - v93 - S 1 '96 - p70 [51-250]
Doak, Cecilia Conrath - *Teaching Patients with Low Literacy Skills. 2nd Ed.*
  AJN - v96 - D '96 - p16M [51-250]

Doan, Daniel - *Indian Stream Republic*
PW - v243 - D 9 '96 - p57 [51-250]
Doan, Van Hai - *Bach Khoa Meo Vat Can Biet*
BL - v93 - My 15 '97 - p1568 [1-50]
Doane, Doris Chase - *Time Changes in the World*
Horoscope - v63 - Mr '97 - p10 [251-500]
Doane, Janice - *From Klein to Kristeva*
Signs - v22 - Aut '96 - p254+ [501+]
Dobash, R Emerson - *Gender and Crime*
CS - v25 - N '96 - p797+ [501+]
Dobbin, Frank - *Forging Industrial Policy*
EHR - v112 - F '97 - p243 [251-500]
Dobbins, Frank - *Music in Renaissance Lyons*
Ren Q - v49 - Win '96 - p914+ [501+]
Dobbs, Michael - *Down with Big Brother*
BL - v93 - Ja '97 - p812 [51-250]
BW - v27 - Ja 5 '97 - p1+ [501+]
For Aff - v76 - My '97 - p139 [51-250]
KR - v64 - N 15 '96 - p1649 [251-500]
LATBR - Ja 26 '97 - p10 [501+]
LJ - v122 - Ja '97 - p123+ [51-250]
NL - v80 - F 10 '97 - p19+ [501+]
NYTBR - v102 - F 9 '97 - p31 [501+]
PW - v243 - N 18 '96 - p54 [51-250]
Time - v149 - Mr 31 '97 - p82+ [251-500]
Goodfellowe MP
NS - v126 - Ja 24 '97 - p45+ [251-500]
Dobbs-Weinstein, Idit - *Maimonides and St. Thomas on the Limits of Reason*
Theol St - v57 - Mr '96 - p185 [251-500]
Dober, Richard P - *Campus Architecture*
R&R Bk N - v11 - N '96 - p56 [51-250]
Doble, John - *Introduction to Radio Propagation for Fixed and Mobile Communications*
SciTech - v20 - D '96 - p76 [51-250]
Dobles, Fabian - *Years Like Brief Days*
TranslRevS - v2 - D '96 - p32 [51-250]
Dobrin, Adam - *Statistical Handbook on Violence in America*
r ARBA - v28 - '97 - p228 [51-250]
r J Gov Info - v24 - Ja '97 - p81+ [501+]
r LJ - v122 - Ap 15 '97 - p40 [51-250]
r RQ - v36 - Fall '96 - p138+ [501+]
Dobroszycki, Lucjan - *Reptile Journalism*
AHR - v102 - F '97 - p139 [501+]
EHR - v112 - Ap '97 - p537+ [251-500]
Dobrushin, R L - *Contemporary Mathematical Physics*
SciTech - v20 - N '96 - p17 [51-250]
Topics in Statistical and Theoretical Physics
SciTech - v20 - D '96 - p24 [51-250]
Dobrynin, Anatoly - *In Confidence*
NYTBR - v102 - F 9 '97 - p32 [51-250]
TLS - D 27 '96 - p7 [501+]
Dobson, Alan P - *Anglo-American Relations in the Twentieth Century*
J Am St - v30 - Ag '96 - p312 [251-500]
Dobson, Andrew - *Jean-Paul Sartre and the Politics of Reason*
CPR - v16 - D '96 - p394+ [501+]
Dobson, Andrew P - *Conservation and Biodiversity*
Nature - v382 - Ag 15 '96 - p594 [501+]
Dobson, David - *Can We Save Them? (Illus. by James M Needham)*
c BL - v93 - Ap 1 '97 - p1326+ [51-250]
c CBRS - v25 - Ap '97 - p102 [51-250]
c KR - v65 - Ja 15 '97 - p140+ [51-250]
c PW - v244 - Mr 10 '97 - p68 [51-250]
Dobson, James C - *Life on the Edge*
y VOYA - v19 - D '96 - p256 [1-50]
y VOYA - v19 - F '97 - p319 [51-250]
Preparing for Adolescence
y VOYA - v19 - F '97 - p318 [51-250]
When God Doesn't Make Sense
y VOYA - v19 - F '97 - p317 [51-250]
Dobson, Keith S - *Advances in Cognitive-Behavioral Therapy*
SciTech - v20 - S '96 - p33 [51-250]
Dobson, Mary - *Smelly Old History: Roman Aromas*
c TES - Mr 21 '97 - p10* [251-500]
Smelly Old History: Tudor Odours
c TES - Mr 21 '97 - p10* [251-500]
Smelly Old History: Victorian Vapours
c TES - Mr 21 '97 - p10* [251-500]
Dobuzinskis, Laurent - *Policy Studies in Canada*
JEL - v34 - D '96 - p2028+ [251-500]
R&R Bk N - v11 - N '96 - p49 [51-250]
Dobyns, Stephen - *The Church of Dead Girls*
KR - v65 - Ap 1 '97 - p483 [251-500]
LJ - v122 - My 1 '97 - p138 [51-250]
PW - v244 - Ap 28 '97 - p48 [251-500]

Common Carnage
HR - v49 - Aut '96 - p503+ [501+]
Velocities: New and Selected Poems
TLS - N 29 '96 - p27 [501+]
Docherty, James C - *Historical Dictionary of Organized Labor*
r ARBA - v28 - '97 - p118 [251-500]
r Choice - v34 - My '97 - p1473 [51-250]
Docherty, Thomas - *Alterities: Criticism, History, Representation*
Choice - v34 - D '96 - p606+ [51-250]
Docker, Julie - *Parliamo Insieme*
MLJ - v80 - Fall '96 - p421+ [501+]
Docking, Jim - *National School Policy*
TES - Jl 5 '96 - p8* [501+]
Dockrill, M L - *The Strategy of the Lloyd George Coalition 1916-1918*
Albion - v28 - Fall '96 - p530+ [501+]
Dockrill, Saki - *Eisenhower's New-Look National Security Policy 1953-61*
Choice - v34 - D '96 - p675 [51-250]
TLS - D 27 '96 - p6 [501+]
Dockter, Albert W - *Estate Settlements in Blount County, Tennessee, Naming Heirs*
r EGH - v50 - N '96 - p186 [51-250]
Documents on British Policy Overseas. 1st Ser., Vol. 7
EHR - v112 - Ap '97 - p540+ [501+]
Dodd, Brian J - *Praying Jesus' Way*
LJ - v122 - My 1 '97 - p109+ [51-250]
Dodd, Christina - *A Knight to Remember*
LJ - v121 - N 15 '96 - p50 [51-250]
Dodd, Lynley - *Schnitzel Von Krumm Forget-Me-Not (Illus. by Lynley Dodd)*
c JB - v60 - O '96 - p182+ [51-250]
Dodd, Mary Ann - *Gardner Read: A Bio-Bibliography*
r ARBA - v28 - '97 - p474 [51-250]
r R&R Bk N - v11 - N '96 - p58 [51-250]
Dodds, Dayle Ann - *Sing, Sophie! (Illus. by Rosanne Litzinger)*
c BL - v93 - My 15 '97 - p1578 [51-250]
c Obs - Mr 30 '97 - p17* [51-250]
c PW - v244 - Ap 14 '97 - p75 [51-250]
Dodds, Dinah - *The Wall in My Backyard*
Ger Q - v69 - Spr '96 - p208+ [501+]
Doderer, Klaus - *Geschichte Des Kinderund Jugendtheaters Zwischen 1945 Und 1970*
Bkbird - v34 - Spr '96 - p55+ [1-50]
Dodge, Bill - *Regional Excellence*
NCR - v85 - Spr '96 - p66 [51-250]
Dodge, Chris - *Everything You Always Wanted to Know about Sandy Berman but Were Afraid to Ask*
LR - v45 - 4 '96 - p64+ [51-250]
Dodge, David - *Nice Work*
SFR - v21 - Jl '96 - p48 [1-50]
Dodge, Mark - *Running Microsoft Excel for Windows 95*
BL - v92 - Ag '96 - p1868 [501+]
Dodge, Pryor - *The Bicycle*
Choice - v34 - N '96 - p479 [51-250]
Lon R Bks - v19 - Ap 24 '97 - p30+ [501+]
Dodge, Theodore Ayrault - *Alexander*
TLS - D 6 '96 - p26 [51-250]
Dodgson, Charles Lutwidge - *The Pamphlets of Lewis Carroll. Vol. 2*
Isis - v87 - S '96 - p565 [251-500]
Dodman, Nicholas - *The Dog Who Loved Too Much*
Books - v10 - Je '96 - p22 [1-50]
The Dog Who Loved Too Much (Dodman). Audio Version
y Kliatt - v30 - N '96 - p48 [51-250]
Dod's Parliamentary Companion 1996
r R&R Bk N - v12 - F '97 - p59 [51-250]
Dodson, DeAnna Julie - *In Honor Bound*
LJ - v122 - F 1 '97 - p66 [51-250]
Dodson, James - *Final Rounds*
BL - v93 - N 1 '96 - p473 [251-500]
KR - v64 - O 15 '96 - p1506 [251-500]
LATBR - Ag 25 '96 - p10 [51-250]
Dodson, Peter - *The Horned Dinosaurs*
BW - v27 - F 9 '97 - p13 [51-250]
Choice - v34 - Mr '97 - p1189 [51-250]
LJ - v121 - S 15 '96 - p90 [51-250]
Nature - v384 - D 5 '96 - p426 [501+]
New Sci - v152 - D 14 '96 - p44+ [501+]
Sci - v274 - O 18 '96 - p367 [501+]
Dodson, Shireen - *The Mother-Daughter Book Club*
KR - v65 - Ap 1 '97 - p543 [51-250]
PW - v244 - Ap 7 '97 - p89 [51-250]
Dodziuk, Helena - *Methods in Stereochemical Analysis*
J Chem Ed - v73 - Ag '96 - pA179 [51-250]

Doebler, Bettie Anne - *Rooted Sorrow*
MLR - v91 - O '96 - p963+ [501+]
Ren Q - v50 - Spr '97 - p268+ [501+]
Doehring, Donald G - *Research Strategies in Human Communication Disorders. 2nd Ed.*
SciTech - v20 - S '96 - p31 [51-250]
Doek, Jaap - *Children on the Move*
R&R Bk N - v11 - D '96 - p40 [51-250]
Doel, Ronald E - *Solar System Astronomy in America*
Phys Today - v50 - Ja '97 - p71+ [501+]
Doelman, A - *Nonlinear Dynamics and Pattern Formation in the Natural Environment*
SIAM Rev - v39 - Mr '97 - p176 [51-250]
Doering, Anita Tylor - *Guide to Local History and Genealogy Resources 1995*
EGH - v50 - N '96 - p192 [51-250]
Doerr, Harriet - *The Tiger in the Grass*
NYTBR - v101 - O 20 '96 - p36 [1-50]
PW - v243 - S 9 '96 - p80 [1-50]
The Tiger in the Grass (Schraf). Audio Version
y Kliatt - v31 - Ja '97 - p46+ [51-250]
Dogen - *Master Dogen's Shobogenzo. Vol. 2*
Tric - v6 - Win '96 - p116 [1-50]
Dogniez, Cecile - *Bibliography of the Septuagint*
r Rel St Rev - v22 - O '96 - p350 [51-250]
Dogra, Ramesh Chander - *Encyclopaedia of Sikh Religion and Culture*
r ARBA - v28 - '97 - p555+ [51-250]
Dohar, William J - *The Black Death and Pastoral Leadership*
CH - v65 - S '96 - p469+ [501+]
CHR - v83 - Ja '97 - p90+ [251-500]
JR - v77 - Ja '97 - p135+ [501+]
Specu - v71 - O '96 - p940+ [501+]
Doheny-Farina, Stephen - *The Wired Neighborhood*
BL - v93 - O 1 '96 - p294 [51-250]
Choice - v34 - Ap '97 - p1379 [51-250]
KR - v64 - Ag 15 '96 - p1204 [251-500]
LJ - v121 - O 1 '96 - p114 [51-250]
New Sci - v152 - D 21 '96 - p72 [251-500]
PW - v243 - S 23 '96 - p69 [51-250]
Utne R - N '96 - p88 [51-250]
Doherty, Berlie - *Daughter of the Sea*
c Bks Keeps - Mr '97 - p25 [51-250]
c TES - Ja 17 '97 - p9* [251-500]
Our Field (Illus. by Robin Bell Corfield)
c Bks Keeps - v100 - S '96 - p32 [51-250]
c JB - v60 - D '96 - p229 [51-250]
c Sch Lib - v45 - F '97 - p18 [51-250]
c Spec - v277 - D 14 '96 - p76+ [51-250]
The Snake-Stone
y Emerg Lib - v24 - S '96 - p53 [51-250]
y HB Guide - v7 - Fall '96 - p301 [51-250]
y NYTBR - v101 - O 27 '96 - p44 [1-50]
The Snake-Stone (Crowley). Audio Version
c BL - v93 - N 1 '96 - p522 [51-250]
Street Child
y Kliatt - v30 - S '96 - p8 [51-250]
c Sch Lib - v44 - Ag '96 - p96+ [501+]
The Vinegar Jar
Rapport - v19 - 6 '96 - p26 [251-500]
White Peak Farm
y SLJ - v43 - Mr '97 - p112 [1-50]
Doherty, Brian - *Democracy and Green Political Thought*
Choice - v34 - Ja '97 - p866 [51-250]
Doherty, Craig A - *The Erie Canal*
c BL - v93 - F 15 '97 - p1018 [51-250]
c HB Guide - v8 - Spr '97 - p137 [51-250]
c SLJ - v43 - F '97 - p89 [51-250]
The Houston Astrodome
c BL - v93 - F 15 '97 - p1018 [51-250]
c HB Guide - v8 - Spr '97 - p137 [51-250]
c SLJ - v43 - F '97 - p113+ [51-250]
The Seattle Space Needle
c HB Guide - v8 - Spr '97 - p137 [51-250]
The Statue of Liberty
c HB Guide - v8 - Spr '97 - p137 [51-250]
c SLJ - v43 - Ja '97 - p99 [51-250]
Doherty, Frank J - *Settlers of the Beekman Patent, Dutchess County, New York. Vol. 3*
NGSQ - v84 - S '96 - p234 [51-250]
Doherty, Justin - *The Acmeist Movement in Russian Poetry*
Russ Rev - v55 - O '96 - p704+ [501+]
Doherty, P C - *The Devil's Hunt*
Quill & Q - v62 - O '96 - p30 [51-250]
Satan's Fire
BL - v93 - N 15 '96 - p574 [51-250]
KR - v64 - O 1 '96 - p1427 [251-500]
A Tapestry of Murders
Arm Det - v29 - Sum '96 - p371 [51-250]

Doherty, Paul - *The Cool Hot Rod and Other Electrifying Experiments on Energy and Matter*
   c SB - v32 - Ag '96 - p178+ [51-250]
The Spinning Blackboard and Other Dynamic Experiments on Force and Motion
   c SB - v32 - Ag '96 - p179 [51-250]
Doherty, William J - *The Intentional Family*
   PW - v244 - Ap 21 '97 - p67 [51-250]
Dohrn-Van Rossum, Gerhard - *History of the Hour*
   BW - v26 - S 8 '96 - p13 [51-250]
   Choice - v34 - D '96 - p633 [51-250]
   Nature - v383 - S 19 '96 - p229+ [501+]
   SciTech - v20 - N '96 - p16 [51-250]
   VQR - v73 - Win '97 - p8* [51-250]
Doig, Ivan - *Bucking the Sun*
   LATBR - My 12 '96 - p3+ [501+]
   VQR - v72 - Aut '96 - p128* [51-250]
   WAL - v31 - Win '97 - p416+ [501+]
Dancing at the Rascal Fair
   BW - v26 - O 6 '96 - p12 [51-250]
   PW - v243 - Jl 22 '96 - p234 [1-50]
English Creek
   y BL - v93 - Ja '97 - p832 [1-50]
Dokey, Cameron - *Be Mine*
   y Kliatt - v31 - My '97 - p17 [51-250]
   y PW - v244 - F 3 '97 - p107+ [51-250]
Dolan, Edward F - *America in World War I*
   c HB Guide - v7 - Fall '96 - p380 [51-250]
In Sports, Money Talks
   y BWatch - v6 - O '96 - p5 [51-250]
   y SLJ - v43 - Ja '97 - p122 [51-250]
Our Poisoned Waters
   y BL - v93 - Mr 1 '97 - p1154 [51-250]
   y CCB-B - v50 - Ap '97 - p280 [51-250]
   y KR - v65 - Ap 1 '97 - p553 [51-250]
   y SLJ - v43 - Mr '97 - p198+ [51-250]
Shaping U.S. Foreign Policy
   y HB Guide - v7 - Fall '96 - p314 [51-250]
Dolan, Ellen M - *Susan Butcher and the Iditarod Trail*
   y Kliatt - v30 - N '96 - p30+ [51-250]
Dolan, Frances E - *Dangerous Familiars*
   EHR - v111 - N '96 - p1278+ [251-500]
   JMH - v68 - S '96 - p678+ [501+]
   MP - v94 - N '96 - p226+ [501+]
The Taming of the Shrew
   Choice - v34 - O '96 - p281+ [51-250]
Dolan, Frederick M - *Allegories of America*
   QJS - v83 - F '97 - p117+ [501+]
Dolan, Jay P - *Hispanic Catholic Culture in the U.S.*
   CH - v66 - Mr '97 - p172+ [501+]
   HAHR - v76 - N '96 - p756+ [501+]
   WHQ - v28 - Spr '97 - p70+ [251-500]
Mexican Americans and the Catholic Church 1900-1965
   CHR - v83 - Ja '97 - p141+ [501+]
   HAHR - v76 - N '96 - p755+ [251-500]
Puerto Rican and Cuban Catholics in the U.S. 1900-1965
   CH - v65 - S '96 - p542+ [501+]
   HAHR - v76 - N '96 - p756+ [501+]
   JR - v77 - Ja '97 - p151+ [501+]
Dolan, Marc - *Modern Lives*
   AL - v68 - D '96 - p879 [51-250]
   Choice - v34 - D '96 - p612 [51-250]
Dolan, Robert J - *Power Pricing*
   BL - v93 - F 1 '97 - p914 [51-250]
Dolan, Sean - *Bob Marley*
   c Ch BWatch - v6 - S '96 - p6 [51-250]
   c HB Guide - v8 - Spr '97 - p156 [51-250]
   y SLJ - v42 - N '96 - p127+ [51-250]
Charles Barkley
   c HB Guide - v7 - Fall '96 - p360 [51-250]
Dolan, Sean B - *Telling the Story*
   Pub Hist - v18 - Sum '96 - p54+ [501+]
Dolan, Terrance - *The Shawnee Indians*
   c HB Guide - v8 - Spr '97 - p177 [51-250]
Dolan, Therese - *Inventing Reality*
   Choice - v34 - Ap '97 - p1324 [51-250]
   PW - v243 - N 11 '96 - p67 [51-250]
Dolan, Timothy Michael - *Some Seed Fell on Good Ground*
   CH - v65 - D '96 - p764+ [501+]
Dolby, R G A - *Uncertain Knowledge*
   New Sci - v153 - F 1 '97 - p44 [501+]
Dolcini, Donatella - *India in the Islamic Era and Southeast Asia 8th to 19th Century (Illus. by Giorgio Bacchin)*
   c HB Guide - v8 - Spr '97 - p170 [51-250]
   y SLJ - v43 - F '97 - p114 [51-250]
Dold, Gaylord - *Schedule Two*
   BL - v93 - S 15 '96 - p224 [51-250]
   NYTBR - v101 - O 13 '96 - p29 [51-250]

The Wichita Mysteries
   PW - v243 - D 30 '96 - p64 [1-50]
Dole, Bob - *The Doles: Unlimited Partners*
   BW - v26 - S 8 '96 - p4 [251-500]
Trusting the People
   NYTBR - v101 - N 3 '96 - p18 [51-250]
D'Olivo, Juan C - *Workshops on Particles and Fields and Phenomenology of Fundamental Interactions*
   SciTech - v21 - Mr '97 - p25 [51-250]
Doll, Don - *Vision Quest. Electronic Media Version*
   AB - v99 - F 24 '97 - p624 [501+]
Dollars for College Series
   Teach Mus - v3 - Ap '96 - p69+ [51-250]
Dollen, B L - *Red Wing Art Pottery 1920s-1960s*
   Ant & CM - v101 - D '96 - p33 [1-50]
Dollerup, Cay - *Teaching Translation and Interpreting 2*
   MLR - v91 - O '96 - p941+ [501+]
Dollinger, Malin - *Everyone's Guide to Cancer Therapy. 2nd Ed.*
   r BL - v93 - F 1 '97 - p958 [1-50]
   LJ - v122 - Ja '97 - p56 [1-50]
Dolman, Sue - *Sue Dolman's Book of Animal Toys*
   LJ - v122 - F 15 '97 - p134 [51-250]
Dolnick, Barrie - *Simple Spells for Success*
   Rapport - v19 - 4 '96 - p18+ [501+]
Dolnikowski, Edith Wilks - *Thomas Bradwardine: A View of Time and a Vision of Eternity in Fourteenth-Century Thought*
   Isis - v87 - D '96 - p717+ [501+]
   Specu - v72 - Ja '97 - p140+ [501+]
Dolphin Log
   cp Par Ch - v20 - O '96 - p15 [1-50]
Dolson, Hildegarde - *Disaster at Johnstown*
   y Kliatt - v31 - Mr '97 - p4 [51-250]
Domainguez, Jorge I - *Technopols: Freeing Politics and Markets in Latin America in the 1990s*
   Choice - v34 - My '97 - p1546 [51-250]
Domb, Risa - *New Women's Writing from Israel*
   Choice - v34 - Ap '97 - p1331 [51-250]
Dombroski, Robert S - *Properties of Writing*
   MLR - v92 - Ap '97 - p480+ [501+]
Dombrovsky, Yury - *The Faculty of Useless Knowledge*
   BW - v27 - Ja 12 '97 - p6 [501+]
   KR - v64 - S 15 '96 - p1340 [251-500]
   LJ - v121 - S 15 '96 - p95 [51-250]
   NYTBR - v101 - N 17 '96 - p15+ [501+]
   NYTBR - v101 - D 8 '96 - p79 [1-50]
   PW - v243 - S 2 '96 - p112 [51-250]
Dombrowski, Daniel A - *Analytic Theism, Hartshorne, and the Concept of God*
   Choice - v34 - F '97 - p978 [51-250]
   R&R Bk N - v12 - F '97 - p10 [51-250]
Dombrowski, Peter - *Policy Responses to the Globalization of American Banking*
   Choice - v34 - D '96 - p658 [51-250]
   JEL - v34 - S '96 - p1436+ [51-250]
   Pol Stud J - v24 - Sum '96 - p332 [51-250]
Domel, August - *Legal Manual for Residential Construction*
   FHB - Ag '96 - p136+ [251-500]
Domenach, Jean-Luc - *The Origins of the Great Leap Forward*
   AHR - v102 - F '97 - p153+ [501+]
   Ch Rev Int - v3 - Fall '96 - p390+ [501+]
   Historian - v59 - Fall '96 - p172+ [501+]
Domhoff, G William - *Finding Meaning in Dreams*
   R&R Bk N - v11 - N '96 - p5 [1-50]
State Autonomy or Class Dominance?
   AJS - v102 - Ja '97 - p1177+ [501+]
   Choice - v34 - S '96 - p210 [51-250]
Dominguez, Angel - *The Twelve Days of Christmas (Illus. by Angel Dominguez)*
   c JB - v60 - D '96 - p229 [51-250]
Dominguez, Jorge I - *Democratic Transitions in Central America*
   For Aff - v76 - My '97 - p138 [51-250]
Democratizing Mexico
   Choice - v34 - O '96 - p353 [51-250]
   JEL - v34 - S '96 - p1415 [51-250]
   Pub Op Q - v60 - Win '96 - p657+ [501+]
   RP - v59 - Win '97 - p201+ [501+]
Dominguez, Maria - *Sobre Literatura Y Otras Complejidades*
   BL - v93 - S 15 '96 - p227 [1-50]
Dominguez, Pablo - *Claves Del Espanol*
   Hisp - v79 - S '96 - p462+ [501+]
Dominic, Gloria - *Brave Bear and the Ghosts (Illus. by Charles Reasoner)*
   c SLJ - v43 - Mr '97 - p173 [51-250]

Coyote and the Grasshoppers (Illus. by Charles Reasoner)
   c SLJ - v43 - Mr '97 - p173 [51-250]
Song of the Hermit Thrush (Illus. by Charles Reasoner)
   c SLJ - v43 - Mr '97 - p173 [51-250]
Dominik, William J - *Speech and Rhetoric in Statius' Thebaid*
   CW - v89 - Jl '96 - p514 [251-500]
Dominion Review
   p LMR - v15 - Fall '96 - p3+ [501+]
Dommel, Darlene Hurst - *Collector's Encyclopedia of the Dakota Potteries*
   r Ant & CM - v101 - S '96 - p27 [51-250]
Domning, Denise - *A Love for All Seasons*
   LJ - v121 - N 15 '96 - p52 [51-250]
Domosh, Mona - *Invented Cities*
   ABR - v18 - D '96 - p4+ [501+]
   Choice - v34 - S '96 - p192 [51-250]
   NL - v79 - Ag 12 '96 - p28+ [501+]
Donagan, Alan - *The Philosophical Papers of Alan Donagan. Vols. 1-2*
   CPR - v16 - Ap '96 - p93+ [501+]
Donaghy, Bronwyn - *Anna's Story*
   Aust Bk R - Jl '96 - p66+ [251-500]
Donahue, Charles, Jr. - *The Records of the Medieval Ecclesiastical Courts. Pt. 2*
   EHR - v112 - F '97 - p170 [251-500]
Donahue, James C - *Mobile Guerrilla Force*
   NWCR - v50 - Win '97 - p152+ [501+]
Donahue, Neil H - *Forms of Disruption*
   Ger Q - v69 - Spr '96 - p218+ [501+]
Donald, David Herbert - *Charles Sumner*
   PW - v243 - S 30 '96 - p79 [1-50]
Lincoln
   Bks & Cult - v2 - N '96 - p25+ [501+]
   CR - v268 - Je '96 - p335 [51-250]
   NEQ - v69 - D '96 - p658+ [501+]
   NYTBR - v101 - N 17 '96 - p40 [51-250]
   RP - v58 - Sum '96 - p620+ [501+]
   TES - N 22 '96 - p8* [51-250]
Donald, Diana - *The Age of Caricature*
   Choice - v34 - D '96 - p668 [51-250]
   TLS - S 20 '96 - p18+ [501+]
Donald, Merlin - *Origins of the Modern Mind*
   Reason - v28 - D '96 - p37 [51-250]
Donald G. Hagman Commemorative Conference (6th) - *Confronting Regional Challenges*
   NCR - v85 - Spr '96 - p64 [51-250]
Donaldson, D J - *Louisiana Fever*
   Arm Det - v29 - Fall '96 - p502 [251-500]
Donaldson, Enid - *The Real Taste of Jamaica*
   BWatch - v17 - D '96 - p9 [51-250]
   y Kliatt - v31 - Ja '97 - p32 [51-250]
Donaldson, Gary A - *America at War since 1945*
   Choice - v34 - My '97 - p1562 [51-250]
   R&R Bk N - v12 - F '97 - p25 [51-250]
Donaldson, Gordon - *The Prime Ministers of Canada*
   y Can CL - v22 - Fall '96 - p109+ [251-500]
Donaldson, Karen B McLean - *Through Students' Eyes*
   Cur R - v36 - Ja '97 - p3* [51-250]
Donaldson, Mike - *Taking Our Time*
   Aust Bk R - N '96 - p44 [501+]
Donaldson, Molla S - *Primary Care*
   SciTech - v20 - D '96 - p39 [51-250]
Donaldson, Scott - *The Cambridge Companion to Ernest Hemingway*
   AL - v68 - D '96 - p880 [1-50]
Donaldson, Stephanie - *Scented Treasures*
   BL - v93 - S 1 '96 - p54 [51-250]
Donaldson, Stephen R - *The Gap into Ruin*
   y VOYA - v19 - O '96 - p216 [251-500]
Donaldson-Evans, Mary - *Autobiography, Historiography, Rhetoric*
   FR - v70 - D '96 - p319+ [501+]
Donati, William - *Ida Lupino: A Biography*
   VQR - v72 - Aut '96 - p125* [1-50]
Donato, Eugenio - *The Script of Decadence*
   CLS - v33 - 4 '96 - p417+ [501+]
Donato, Richard - *Foreign Language Learning*
   MLJ - v81 - Spr '97 - p113+ [501+]
The Doncaster Borough Courtier. Vol. 1
   r EHR - v112 - Ap '97 - p469+ [251-500]
Dondeyne, Desire - *Terre*
   Am MT - v46 - D '96 - p63+ [251-500]
Uranus
   Am MT - v46 - D '96 - p63+ [251-500]
Vega
   Am MT - v46 - D '96 - p63+ [251-500]
Donelson, Kenneth L - *Literature for Today's Young Adults. 5th Ed.*
   r BL - v93 - Mr 1 '97 - p1177 [51-250]

Donesky, Finlay - *David Hare: Moral and Historical Perspectives*
    Choice - v34 - Ap '97 - p1334 [51-250]
Doney, Meryl - *Ears and the Secret Song (Illus. by William Geldart)*
    c CLW - v66 - Je '96 - p46 [51-250]
    Games
    c HB Guide - v8 - Spr '97 - p135 [51-250]
    c SLJ - v43 - Ja '97 - p122 [51-250]
    Jewelry
    c HB Guide - v8 - Spr '97 - p135 [51-250]
    c SLJ - v43 - Ja '97 - p122 [51-250]
    Masks
    c HB Guide - v7 - Fall '96 - p354 [51-250]
    Musical Instruments
    c HB Guide - v7 - Fall '96 - p354 [51-250]
    Puppets
    c HB Guide - v7 - Fall '96 - p354 [51-250]
    Toys
    c HB Guide - v7 - Fall '96 - p354 [51-250]
    Whisker's Great Adventure (Illus. by William Geldart)
    c HB Guide - v7 - Fall '96 - p254 [51-250]
Dong, Yao - *Bei Yang Xiao Xiong Zhang Zuo Lin*
    BL - v93 - N 1 '96 - p484 [1-50]
Dongen, Mirjam Van - *Changing Fatherhood*
    JMF - v58 - Ag '96 - p802+ [501+]
Donhauser, Michael - *Livia Oder Die Reise*
    WLT - v71 - Win '97 - p135+ [501+]
Doniger, Wendy - *Purana Perennis*
    JAAR - v64 - Win '96 - p866+ [501+]
Donkin, Andrew - *Colour Me Crazy*
    c Sch Lib - v44 - N '96 - p151 [51-250]
Donkin, Ellen - *Getting into the Act*
    Theat J - v48 - D '96 - p531+ [501+]
Donleavy, J P - *The Lady Who Liked Clean Rest Rooms*
    PW - v244 - Ap 7 '97 - p71 [51-250]
    TLS - Mr 21 '97 - p23 [251-500]
Donley, Carol - *The Tyranny of the Normal*
    MHR - v10 - Fall '96 - p73+ [501+]
Donne, John - *Pseudo-Martyr*
    Ren Q - v49 - Aut '96 - p657+ [501+]
    The Variorum Edition of the Poetry of John Donne. Vol. 8
    Sev Cent N - v54 - Spr '96 - p1+ [501+]
Donnell, Alison - *The Routledge Reader in Caribbean Literature*
    Choice - v34 - Ja '97 - p788 [51-250]
    Obs - Ja 5 '97 - p16* [501+]
Donnell, Courtney Graham - *Ivan Albright*
    BL - v93 - My 15 '97 - p1554 [51-250]
Donnell, David - *Dancing in the Dark*
    BIC - v25 - S '96 - p22+ [501+]
Donnellon, Anne - *Team Talk*
    Per Psy - v49 - Win '96 - p1007+ [501+]
Donnelly, Jane - *Fearsome Hunters of the Wild*
    c SLJ - v43 - Ja '97 - p99 [51-250]
    Mighty Giants of the Wild
    HB Guide - v8 - Spr '97 - p127 [1-50]
    c SLJ - v43 - Ja '97 - p99 [51-250]
Donnelly, J - *Investigations by Order*
    TES - Ja 3 '97 - pR14 [51-250]
Donner, Joakim - *The Quaternary History of Scandinavia*
    Am Sci - v85 - Ja '97 - p79 [251-500]
Donner, Wendy - *The Liberal Self*
    Dialogue - v35 - Fall '96 - p791+ [501+]
D'Onofrio, Giulio - *Lanfranco Di Pavia E L'Europa Del Secolo XI*
    CHR - v82 - Jl '96 - p526+ [501+]
Donoghue, Denis - *Walter Pater: Lover of Strange Souls*
    ELT - v39 - 4 '96 - p470+ [501+]
    Nine-C Lit - v51 - D '96 - p410+ [501+]
    RMR - v50 - 2 '96 - p185+ [501+]
Donoghue, Emma - *Hood*
    LJ - v121 - O 1 '96 - p156 [51-250]
    TES - D 27 '96 - p17 [51-250]
    Kissing the Witch
    y CCB-B - v50 - Ap '97 - p280+ [51-250]
    y KR - v65 - F 1 '97 - p221 [51-250]
    y PW - v244 - Ap 28 '97 - p76 [51-250]
    Passions between Women
    Eight-C St - v30 - Spr '97 - p321+ [501+]
Donoghue, Frank - *The Fame Machine*
    Choice - v34 - O '96 - p277 [51-250]
    TLS - O 18 '96 - p27 [501+]
Donohue, Joseph - *Oscar Wilde's The Importance of Being Earnest*
    ELT - v39 - 3 '96 - p373+ [501+]
    ILS - v16 - Spr '97 - p14 [501+]

Donohue, Timothy E - *In the Open*
    BL - v93 - S 15 '96 - p187 [51-250]
    LATBR - O 6 '96 - p1+ [501+]
    LATBR - D 29 '96 - p10 [51-250]
    Nat - v263 - O 14 '96 - p27+ [501+]
Donoso, Jose - *Conjesturas Sobre La Memoria De Mi Tribu*
    BL - v93 - Mr 15 '97 - p1232 [1-50]
    Donde Van A Morir Los Elefantes
    Hisp - v79 - D '96 - p824+ [501+]
Donovan, Arthur - *Antoine Lavoisier: Science, Administration, and Revolution*
    Isis - v87 - D '96 - p688+ [501+]
Donovan, Claire - *John Everett Millais 1829-1896*
    BM - v138 - Ag '96 - p557+ [501+]
Donovan, Josephine - *Beyond Animal Rights*
    NWSA Jnl - v9 - Spr '97 - p131+ [501+]
Donovan, Katie - *Dublines*
    ILS - v15 - Fall '96 - p31 [51-250]
    y Sch Lib - v44 - Ag '96 - p115 [51-250]
    Ireland's Women
    TLS - S 27 '96 - p32 [51-250]
Donovan, Stacey - *Dive*
    y Kliatt - v30 - S '96 - p8 [51-250]
Donowitz, Leigh G - *Infection Control in the Child Care Center and Preschool. 3rd Ed.*
    r SciTech - v21 - Mr '97 - p64 [51-250]
Donziger, Steven R - *The Real War on Crime*
    Fed Prob - v60 - Je '96 - p82+ [501+]
Doody, Margaret Anne - *The True Story of the Novel*
    r Choice - v34 - N '96 - p448+ [51-250]
    NS - v126 - F 14 '97 - p48 [501+]
    Obs - F 9 '97 - p16* [501+]
    Spec - v278 - Ja 25 '97 - p36+ [501+]
Doody's Rating Service 1996
    r LJ - v121 - N 15 '96 - p54 [251-500]
Doohan, James - *Beam Me Up, Scotty*
    BL - v93 - N 15 '96 - p547 [51-250]
    PW - v243 - N 11 '96 - p70 [51-250]
Dookeran, Winston C - *Choices and Change*
    JEL - v35 - Mr '97 - p285 [51-250]
Dooley, Anne M - *Plane Death*
    Quill & Q - v62 - O '96 - p32 [51-250]
Dooley, Brian - *Robert Kennedy: The Final Years*
    Choice - v34 - D '96 - p675 [51-250]
Dooley, Dolores - *Equality in Community*
    ILS - v15 - Fall '96 - p15 [501+]
Dooley, Edward - *The Culture of Possibility*
    J Gov Info - v23 - S '96 - p601 [51-250]
Dooley, Maura - *Kissing a Bone*
    Obs - Ja 5 '97 - p17* [51-250]
    y Sch Lib - v45 - F '97 - p41+ [51-250]
Dooley, Norah - *Everybody Bakes Bread (Illus. by Peter J Thornton)*
    c HB Guide - v7 - Fall '96 - p254 [51-250]
Dooley, Patrick K - *The Pluralistic Philosophy of Stephen Crane*
    ASInt - v34 - O '96 - p105 [51-250]
Dooling, Richard - *Blue Streak*
    BL - v92 - Ag '96 - p1861 [51-250]
    Ent W - S 20 '96 - p74 [51-250]
    LATBR - Ag 18 '96 - p6 [501+]
    Critical Care
    NYTBR - v101 - Jl 21 '96 - p28 [51-250]
    Trib Bks - Ja 12 '97 - p2 [1-50]
    White Man's Grave
    SFR - v21 - Jl '96 - p48 [1-50]
Doolittle, James H - *I Could Never Be So Lucky Again*
    y BL - v93 - D 15 '96 - p716 [1-50]
Doonesbury Flashbacks. Electronic Media Version
    LJ - v121 - N 1 '96 - p114+ [501+]
Doorly, Gerald S - *The Voyages of the Morning*
    GJ - v163 - Mr '97 - p108 [51-250]
Doorn-Harder, Pieternella Van - *Contemporary Coptic Nuns*
    MEJ - v50 - Aut '96 - p617+ [501+]
Dopfer, Kurt - *The Global Dimension of Economic Evolution*
    JEL - v34 - D '96 - p2118+ [501+]
Dor, Moshe - *Gehalim Ba-Peh*
    BL - v93 - Mr 1 '97 - p1115 [1-50]
Doran, Charles F - *A New North America*
    For Aff - v75 - N '96 - p154 [51-250]
Doran, Robert - *Birth of a Worldview*
    Theol St - v57 - S '96 - p565 [251-500]
Doran, Susan - *Elizabeth and Religion 1558-1603*
    HT - v46 - Jl '96 - p53 [51-250]
Dore, Ronald - *The Return to Incomes Policy*
    Econ J - v106 - S '96 - p1468 [251-500]
Doreski, William - *The Modern Voice in American Poetry*
    AL - v68 - S '96 - p653+ [251-500]

Dorfman, Ariel - *Konfidenz*
    WLT - v70 - Aut '96 - p922 [251-500]
    Traverse Theatre Presents the World Premiere of Reader
    WLT - v71 - Win '97 - p153+ [501+]
Dorfman, Len - *Beyond Memory*
    New Sci - v152 - O 19 '96 - p49 [51-250]
Dorfman, Merlin - *Software Engineering*
    SciTech - v21 - Mr '97 - p8 [51-250]
Dorfman, Rachelle A - *Clinical Social Work*
    SB - v32 - N '96 - p228 [251-500]
Doriani, Beth Maclay - *Emily Dickinson: Daughter of Prophecy*
    AL - v69 - Mr '97 - p219+ [251-500]
    Nine-C Lit - v51 - D '96 - p421 [51-250]
Doris, Ellen - *Kids and Science. Vols. 1-6 (Illus. by Len Rubenstein)*
    cr SLJ - v42 - N '96 - p137 [51-250]
    Meet the Arthropods (Illus. by Len Rubenstein)
    c Ch BWatch - v6 - S '96 - p6 [51-250]
    c HB Guide - v8 - Spr '97 - p122 [51-250]
Dority, G Kim - *A Guide to Reference Books for Small and Medium-Sized Libraries 1984-1994*
    r LAR - v98 - Ag '96 - p428 [501+]
Dorling, Daniel - *A New Social Atlas of Britain*
    r GJ - v162 - N '96 - p335 [251-500]
Dorling, Philip - *Diplomasi: Australia and Indonesia's Independence*
    J Gov Info - v23 - S '96 - p651+ [51-250]
Dorling Kindersley Children's Illustrated Encyclopedia. 4th Rev. Ed.
    cr JB - v60 - D '96 - p254+ [501+]
Dorling Kindersley, Inc. - *The Eyewitness Atlas of the World. Rev. Ed.*
    yr Books - v10 - Je '96 - p25 [51-250]
Dorling Kindersley Publishing, Inc. - *The Dorling Kindersley World Reference Atlas. 2nd American Ed.*
    r ARBA - v28 - '97 - p172 [51-250]
    r LJ - v122 - F 1 '97 - p70 [51-250]
Dorman, John Frederick - *Claiborne of Virginia*
    NGSQ - v84 - S '96 - p228+ [501+]
Dorman, Peter - *Markets and Mortality*
    ILRR - v50 - Ap '97 - p519+ [501+]
    JEL - v34 - D '96 - p2066+ [51-250]
Dorman, Robert L - *Revolt of the Provinces*
    Am Q - v49 - Mr '97 - p171+ [501+]
Dormand, John R - *Numerical Methods for Differential Equations*
    Choice - v34 - O '96 - p318 [51-250]
Dormann, Genevieve - *La Gourmandise De Guillaume Apollinaire*
    TLS - N 29 '96 - p12+ [51-250]
Dorment, Richard - *James McNeill Whistler*
    Art J - v55 - Win '96 - p99+ [501+]
Dormeyer, Detlev - *Das Neue Testament Im Rahmen Der Antiken Literatur-Geschichte*
    Rel St Rev - v23 - Ap '97 - p177 [51-250]
Dorn, James A - *Money and Markets in the Americas*
    JEL - v34 - S '96 - p1432 [51-250]
Dornberg, John - *Western Europe*
    y SLJ - v42 - S '96 - p232 [51-250]
Dorner, Isaak August - *Divine Immutability*
    Intpr - v50 - O '96 - p436+ [251-500]
Dornstein, Ken - *Accidentally, on Purpose*
    BW - v27 - F 16 '97 - p6 [251-500]
    KR - v64 - O 15 '96 - p1507 [251-500]
    LJ - v121 - N 15 '96 - p74 [51-250]
    PW - v243 - O 14 '96 - p68 [51-250]
    Spec - v278 - Mr 22 '97 - p38 [501+]
    WSJ-MW - v78 - D 20 '96 - pA14
Doro, Ann - *Twin Pickle (Illus. by Clare Mackie)*
    c HB Guide - v7 - Fall '96 - p254 [51-250]
Dorr, Donal - *Divine Energy*
    BL - v93 - S 15 '96 - p182 [51-250]
Dorraj, Manochehr - *The Changing Political Economy of the Third World*
    HAHR - v76 - N '96 - p830+ [251-500]
Dorrien, Gary - *Soul in Society*
    CH - v65 - D '96 - p768+ [501+]
    J Ch St - v38 - Aut '96 - p926+ [501+]
Dorris, Michael - *Cloud Chamber*
    BW - v27 - Ja 12 '97 - p1+ [501+]
    KR - v64 - N 1 '96 - p1549+ [251-500]
    LATBR - F 16 '97 - p13 [501+]
    LJ - v121 - N 15 '96 - p87 [51-250]
    NYTBR - v102 - F 9 '97 - p11 [501+]
    PW - v243 - N 11 '96 - p55 [51-250]
    Time - v149 - F 17 '97 - p88 [251-500]
    Trib Bks - Mr 2 '97 - p6 [501+]

Sees behind Trees
  c BL - v93 - Ja '97 - p765+ [1-50]
  c BL - v93 - S 15 '96 - p239 [51-250]
  c CBRS - v25 - N '96 - p33+ [1-50]
  c CCB-B - v50 - Ja '97 - p168 [51-250]
  c HB - v72 - S '96 - p594+ [51-250]
  c HB Guide - v8 - Spr '97 - p65 [51-250]
  c KR - v64 - S 15 '96 - p1398 [51-250]
     LATBR - N 24 '96 - p10 [51-250]
  c Learning - v25 - N '96 - p30 [51-250]
  c NYTBR - v102 - Ja 19 '97 - p24 [251-500]
  c Par Ch - v21 - Mr '97 - p8 [1-50]
  c PW - v243 - O 7 '96 - p76 [51-250]
  c PW - v243 - N 4 '96 - p48 [1-50]
  c SLJ - v42 - O '96 - p120 [51-250]
  c SLJ - v42 - D '96 - p28 [1-50]
A Yellow Raft in Blue Water
  y BL - v93 - Ja '97 - p832 [1-50]
Dorros, Arthur - *Abuela (Illus. by Elisa Kleven)*
  c PW - v244 - My 5 '97 - p211 [1-50]
Isla (Illus. by Elisa Kleven)
  c HB Guide - v7 - Fall '96 - p327 [51-250]
  c LA - v73 - O '96 - p431 [51-250]
  c RT - v50 - F '97 - p426 [51-250]
A Tree Is Growing (Illus. by S D Schindler)
  c BL - v93 - F 1 '97 - p942 [51-250]
  c KR - v65 - Ja 15 '97 - p141 [51-250]
  c SLJ - v43 - Mr '97 - p173 [51-250]
Dorsey, Candas Jane - *Black Wine*
     KR - v64 - N 15 '96 - p1639 [51-250]
     LJ - v121 - D '96 - p152 [1-50]
     PW - v243 - D 9 '96 - p64 [51-250]
Dorsey, Gary - *Congregation: The Journey Back to Church*
     Bks & Cult - v1 - N '95 - p22+ [501+]
Dorsinville, Max - *James Wait Et Les Lunettes Noires*
     BL - v93 - F 1 '97 - p930 [1-50]
     WLT - v70 - Sum '96 - p749 [251-500]
D'Orso, Michael - *Like Judgment Day*
     Am Vis - v12 - F '97 - p28 [51-250]
     BL - v93 - Ap 1 '97 - p1285 [1-50]
  y Kliatt - v31 - My '97 - p28 [51-250]
Like Judgment Day (Davidson). Audio Version
  y Kliatt - v31 - My '97 - p47 [51-250]
Dosal, Paul J - *Power in Transition*
     HAHR - v77 - F '97 - p145+ [251-500]
     JEH - v56 - S '96 - p728+ [501+]
Dosick, Wayne - *Dancing with God*
     PW - v244 - Mr 24 '97 - p73 [51-250]
Dos Passos, John - *U.S.A.*
     AL - v69 - Mr '97 - p248 [51-250]
     BW - v26 - S 1 '96 - p3 [501+]
     Comw - v124 - Ap 11 '97 - p24+ [501+]
Doss, Erika - *Spirit Poles and Flying Pigs*
     CS - v25 - S '96 - p683+ [501+]
     J Am Cult - v18 - Win '95 - p97 [251-500]
Doss, James D - *The Shaman Laughs*
     PW - v244 - Mr 24 '97 - p81 [1-50]
Dosse, Francois - *New History in France*
     AHR - v101 - O '96 - p1228 [501+]
     JIH - v27 - Aut '96 - p318+ [501+]
Dossey, Larry - *Prayer Is Good Medicine*
     Bloom Rev - v16 - N '96 - p13 [501+]
Doss-Quinby, Eglal - *The Lyrics of the Trouveres*
  r Specu - v72 - Ja '97 - p142+ [501+]
Doster, Paul W - *Mind Set*
     PW - v244 - Ja 13 '97 - p72 [51-250]
Dostoyevsky, Fyodor - *The Double*
     Slav R - v55 - Sum '96 - p399+ [501+]
The Gambler
     Obs - D 1 '96 - p18* [51-250]
Doti, Lynne Pierson - *Banking in an Unregulated Environment*
     JEH - v56 - S '96 - p747+ [501+]
Dotlich, Rebecca Kai - *Sweet Dreams of the Wild (Illus. by Katharine Dodge)*
  c HB Guide - v7 - Fall '96 - p367 [51-250]
Dotoli, Giovanni - *Perspectives De La Recherche Sur Le XVIIe Siecle Francais Aujourd'hui*
     MLR - v91 - Jl '96 - p721+ [51-250]
Stendhal Tra Letteratura E Musica
     MLR - v91 - Jl '96 - p731+ [501+]
Dotsiak, Vira - *Urkrains'ka Kukhnia*
     BL - v93 - N 15 '96 - p577 [1-50]
Doty, Alexander - *Making Things Perfectly Queer*
     J Pop F&TV - v24 - Win '97 - p188+ [501+]
Doty, Leonard A - *Statistical Process Control. 2nd Ed.*
     SciTech - v20 - N '96 - p81 [51-250]

Doty, Mark - *Atlantis*
     LJ - v122 - Ap 1 '97 - p94 [1-50]
     Lon R Bks - v19 - F 6 '97 - p3+ [501+]
     TLS - N 29 '96 - p27 [501+]
Heaven's Coast
     Lon R Bks - v19 - F 6 '97 - p3+ [501+]
     NS - v125 - N 22 '96 - p47+ [501+]
     NYTBR - v101 - D 8 '96 - p88 [1-50]
     Obs - O 20 '96 - p16* [501+]
     PW - v244 - F 3 '97 - p100 [1-50]
     TLS - N 15 '96 - p15 [501+]
My Alexandria
     LJ - v122 - Ap 1 '97 - p94 [1-50]
Doty, Roxanne Lynn - *Imperial Encounters*
     WorldV - v12 - O '96 - p6+ [251-500]
Double, Richard - *Metaphilosophy and Free Will*
     Choice - v34 - Mr '97 - p1174 [51-250]
Double Bassist
  p Notes - v53 - D '96 - p534+ [501+]
Doubler, Michael D - *Closing with the Enemy*
     APH - v43 - Fall '96 - p66 [501+]
DoubleTake
  p Utne R - Jl '96 - p118+ [51-250]
Doubt, Keith - *Towards a Sociology of Schizophrenia*
     SciTech - v20 - S '96 - p33 [51-250]
Doucet, Clive - *The Debris of Planets*
     Can Lit - Win '96 - p189+ [501+]
Dougan, Andy - *Untouchable: A Biography of Robert De Niro*
     PW - v244 - Ja 13 '97 - p68 [51-250]
     Si & So - v6 - N '96 - p36 [51-250]
Dougan, Michael B - *Arkansas History*
  r RQ - v35 - Sum '96 - p485 [51-250]
Arkansas Odyssey
     JSH - v63 - F '97 - p140+ [501+]
Dougherty, Rose Mary - *Group Spiritual Direction*
     RR - v55 - N '96 - p652+ [251-500]
Doughty, Andrew - *Hawaii: The Big Island Revealed*
  r LJ - v121 - D '96 - p130 [51-250]
Doughty, Dick - *Gaza: Legacy of Occupation--A Photographer's Journey*
     MEP - v4 - 4 '96 - p139+ [501+]
     SSQ - v77 - Je '96 - p466+ [251-500]
Doughty, Robert A - *Warfare in the Western World. Vols. 1-2*
     For Aff - v76 - My '97 - p128 [51-250]
Douglas, Aileen - *Uneasy Sensations*
     Albion - v28 - Fall '96 - p493+ [501+]
     Eight-C St - v30 - Spr '97 - p329+ [501+]
Douglas, Ann - *Terrible Honesty*
     Clio - v25 - Spr '96 - p313+ [501+]
     Critm - v38 - Sum '96 - p493+ [501+]
     RAH - v25 - Mr '97 - p113+ [501+]
     RMR - v50 - 2 '96 - p187+ [501+]
     Spec - v277 - N 16 '96 - p44 [1-50]
Douglas, Blaise - *When I Grow Up I Want to Be... (Illus. by Tania Hurt-Newton)*
  c HB Guide - v7 - Fall '96 - p254 [51-250]
  c JB - v60 - O '96 - p191 [51-250]
Douglas, Carole Nelson - *Cat in a Flamingo Fedora*
     PW - v244 - Ap 21 '97 - p64 [51-250]
Cat with an Emerald Eye
     KR - v64 - O 1 '96 - p1427 [251-500]
     PW - v243 - S 16 '96 - p74 [51-250]
Douglas, Davison M - *Reading, Writing, and Race*
     AHR - v102 - F '97 - p219+ [251-500]
     JSH - v62 - N '96 - p845+ [251-500]
Douglas, Diane L - *The Historical Archaeology of Dam Construction Camps in Central Arizona. Vol. 2C*
     Pub Hist - v18 - Fall '96 - p162+ [501+]
Douglas, Geoffrey - *The Game of Their Lives*
     CSM - v89 - D 23 '96 - p15 [51-250]
Douglas, Ian - *Companion Encyclopedia of Geography*
  r Choice - v34 - F '97 - p940 [51-250]
  r R&R Bk N - v12 - F '97 - p28 [51-250]
Douglas, J D - *Twentieth-Century Dictionary of Christian Biography*
  r Bks & Cult - v2 - Jl '96 - p30 [251-500]
Douglas, John - *Journey into Darkness*
     Ent W - F 7 '97 - p61+ [501+]
Douglas, Krystan V - *Guide to British Drama Explication. Vol. 1*
  r AB - v98 - D 9 '96 - p2006 [251-500]
  r ARBA - v28 - '97 - p451 [51-250]
  r Choice - v34 - Mr '97 - p1136 [51-250]
  r R&R Bk N - v12 - F '97 - p84 [51-250]
Douglas, L Warren - *Glaice: An Arbiter Tale*
  y BL - v93 - D 15 '96 - p713 [51-250]
Douglas, Nigel - *The Joy of Opera*
     Obs - D 22 '96 - p16* [501+]

Douglas, Susan - *Where the Girls Are*
     QJS - v83 - F '97 - p90+ [501+]
Douglas-Home, Jessica - *Violet: Life and Loves of Violet Gordon Woodhouse*
     Spec - v277 - N 23 '96 - p43 [51-250]
     Spec - v277 - N 23 '96 - p44 [1-50]
     Spec - v277 - N 30 '96 - p52 [501+]
     TLS - N 15 '96 - p16 [501+]
Douglass, R Bruce - *Catholicism and Liberalism*
     J Ch St - v38 - Aut '96 - p916+ [251-500]
Douglass, Sara - *Battleaxe*
     Aust Bk R - S '96 - p63+ [501+]
Beyond the Hanging Wall
  y Aust Bk R - D '96 - p89+ [501+]
Enchanter
     Aust Bk R - S '96 - p63+ [501+]
Doukas, John - *Research in International Business and Finance*
     JEL - v35 - Mr '97 - p221 [51-250]
Doukellis, P N - *Structures Rurales Et Societes Antiques*
     AJA - v100 - Jl '96 - p607+ [501+]
Doumani, Beshara - *Rediscovering Palestine*
     JIH - v27 - Spr '97 - p744+ [251-500]
Doumani, Carol - *Chinese Checkers (Cassidy). Audio Version*
     LJ - v121 - N 1 '96 - p120 [51-250]
Douthitt, Chris - *Putting Your Mouth Where the Money Is*
     BWatch - v18 - F '97 - p3 [51-250]
Doutriaux, Jerome - *The University Industry Relationship in Science and Technology*
     J Gov Info - v23 - S '96 - p622+ [51-250]
Douzinas, Costas - *Politics, Postmodernity and Critical Legal Studies*
     JC - v47 - Win '97 - p128+ [501+]
Douzou, Laurent - *La Desobeissance: Histoire D'Un Mouvement Et D'Un Journal Clandestins*
     AHR - v101 - O '96 - p1227+ [501+]
Dove, Rita - *Selected Poems of Rita Dove*
     LJ - v122 - Ap 1 '97 - p94 [1-50]
Thomas and Beulah
     WHR - v50 - Win '97 - p359+ [501+]
Dovring, Folke - *Leninism: Political Economy as Pseudoscience*
     JEL - v34 - D '96 - p2014 [51-250]
Dow, Bonnie J - *Prime-Time Feminism*
     Choice - v34 - Ja '97 - p786+ [51-250]
     R&R Bk N - v11 - N '96 - p66 [51-250]
Dow, James R - *The Nazification of an Academic Discipline*
     JMH - v68 - D '96 - p1031+ [501+]
Dow, Karen Hassey - *Contemporary Issues in Breast Cancer*
     SciTech - v20 - D '96 - p42 [51-250]
Dow, Lesley - *Incredible Plants (Illus. by Susanna Addario)*
  c KR - v65 - Mr 15 '97 - p460 [51-250]
Dow, Martin - *The Islamic Baths of Palestine*
     Choice - v34 - My '97 - p1553 [51-250]
Dow, Roger - *Turned On*
     HR Mag - v41 - O '96 - p148 [51-250]
Dow, Sheila C - *Keynes, Knowledge and Uncertainty*
     Econ J - v106 - S '96 - p1466 [51-250]
The Methodology of Macroeconomic Thought. 2nd Ed.
     Choice - v34 - D '96 - p658 [51-250]
     JEL - v34 - D '96 - p2031+ [51-250]
Dowd, Douglas E - *Blues for America*
     PW - v244 - F 3 '97 - p85 [51-250]
Dowd, Kevin - *Competition and Finance*
     Choice - v34 - F '97 - p1011 [51-250]
Dowd, Nancy E - *In Defense of Single-Parent Families*
     LJ - v122 - Ja '97 - p127 [51-250]
Dowdall, George W - *The Eclipse of the State Mental Hospital*
     Choice - v34 - N '96 - p542 [51-250]
Doweiko, Harold - *Concepts of Chemical Dependency. 3rd Ed.*
     Soc Ser R - v70 - S '96 - p503+ [51-250]
Dowie, Mark - *Losing Ground*
     Am Sci - v84 - N '96 - p617+ [501+]
  y Kliatt - v31 - Ja '97 - p28 [51-250]
     NYRB - v44 - F 20 '97 - p30+ [501+]
Dowla, Farid U - *Solving Problems in Environmental Engineering and Geosciences with Artificial Neural Networks*
     Choice - v34 - S '96 - p158 [51-250]
Dowler, Wayne - *An Unnecessary Man*
     BIC - v26 - Mr '97 - p26 [251-500]
     R&R Bk N - v11 - N '96 - p64 [51-250]
     Russ Rev - v55 - O '96 - p701+ [251-500]
Dowley, Ruth - *Creep and Chase*
  c Bks Keeps - Mr '97 - p23 [51-250]

Hiding Places (Illus. by Peter Melnyczuk)
  c Bks Keeps - Ja '97 - p22 [51-250]
  c JB - v60 - Ag '96 - p155 [51-250]
  c Sch Lib - v44 - Ag '96 - p105 [51-250]
Dowling, Claudia Glenn - *Explorers of Light*
     Pet PM - v25 - F '97 - p60 [51-250]
Dowling, Colette - *Red Hot Mamas*
     Wom R Bks - v13 - S '96 - p1+ [501+]
Dowling, Eric - *Love Passion Action*
     Quad - v40 - Jl '96 - p90+ [501+]
Dowling, Linda - *Hellenism and Homosexuality in Victorian Oxford*
     RES - v47 - N '96 - p613+ [501+]
  The Vulgarization of Art
     ELT - v39 - 3 '96 - p405 [51-250]
     Nine-C Lit - v51 - Mr '97 - p546+ [501+]
Dowling, Paul - *Hide and Shriek!*
  c Bks Keeps - Ja '97 - p22 [51-250]
  The Night Journey (Illus. by Paul Dowling)
  c BL - v93 - D 15 '96 - p732 [1-50]
  c JB - v60 - D '96 - p229 [51-250]
  c KR - v64 - N 15 '96 - p1667 [51-250]
  c PW - v243 - D 16 '96 - p58 [51-250]
  c SLJ - v43 - F '97 - p75 [51-250]
  c TES - N 29 '96 - p13* [51-250]
Dowling, Paul, 1945- - *Elvis: The Ultimate Album Cover Book*
     BL - v93 - O 1 '96 - p314 [51-250]
     Esq - v126 - D '96 - p40 [1-50]
  r NYTBR - v101 - N 17 '96 - p24 [51-250]
     PW - v243 - O 14 '96 - p75 [51-250]
Downes, Belinda - *A Stitch in Rhyme (Illus. by Belinda Downes)*
  c BL - v93 - N 1 '96 - p503 [51-250]
  c HB Guide - v8 - Spr '97 - p106+ [51-250]
  c SLJ - v42 - D '96 - p112 [51-250]
Downes, Jim - *The Ghan: From Adelaide to Alice*
     Aust Bk R - O '96 - p69 [1-50]
Downes, Peggy - *The New Older Woman*
     Wom R Bks - v13 - S '96 - p1+ [501+]
Downey, Michael - *Understanding Christian Spirituality*
     Am - v176 - Mr 22 '97 - p28 [51-250]
Downie, J A - *To Settle the Succession of the State*
     RES - v47 - N '96 - p589+ [501+]
Downie, Jill - *A Passionate Pen*
     CF - v75 - O '96 - p41+ [501+]
Downie, Mary Alice - *Snowpaws (Illus. by Kathryn Naylor)*
  c Quill & Q - v62 - Ag '96 - p43 [251-500]
Downing, David C - *Planets in Peril*
     Bks & Cult - v2 - My '96 - p34 [251-500]
Downing, Sybil - *Fire in the Hole*
     Roundup M - v4 - D '96 - p25 [51-250]
Downs, Alan - *Beyond the Looking Glass*
     LJ - v122 - My 1 '97 - p116 [51-250]
     PW - v244 - Mr 24 '97 - p68 [51-250]
  Corporate Executions
     Per Psy - v49 - Win '96 - p998+ [501+]
Downs, Anthony - *New Visions for Metropolitan America*
     NCR - v85 - Spr '96 - p64 [51-250]
     PAR - v57 - Ja '97 - p83+ [501+]
Downs, Donald Alexander - *More than Victims*
     CHE - v43 - D 6 '96 - pA26 [51-250]
     Nat - v264 - Mr 24 '97 - p25+ [501+]
     PW - v243 - O 7 '96 - p55 [51-250]
Downs, George W - *Optimal Imperfection?*
     APSR - v90 - S '96 - p693+ [501+]
     PSQ - v111 - Fall '96 - p549+ [501+]
Downs, Laura Lee - *Manufacturing Inequality*
     JEL - v35 - Mr '97 - p173+ [501+]
     JIH - v27 - Win '97 - p522+ [501+]
Downs, Robert Bingham - *American Library Resources*
  r ASInt - v34 - O '96 - p12 [1-50]
  American Library Resources: Supplement 1950-1961
  r ASInt - v34 - O '96 - p12 [1-50]
  American Library Resources: Supplement 1961-1970
  r ASInt - v34 - O '96 - p12 [1-50]
  American Library Resources: Supplement 1971-1980
  r ASInt - v34 - O '96 - p12 [1-50]
Dowse, Sara - *Digging*
     Aust Bk R - S '96 - p26 [501+]
Dowswell, Paul - *Tales of Real Adventure*
  c Books - v10 - Je '96 - p25 [1-50]
  Tales of Real Heroism
  c Bks Keeps - Ja '97 - p26 [51-250]
Doxiadis, Euphrosyne - *The Mysterious Fayum Portraits*
     TLS - S 27 '96 - p36 [501+]
Doyal, Lesley - *What Makes Women Sick*
     NWSA Jnl - v9 - Spr '97 - p89+ [501+]
D'Oyen, F M - *The Miracle of Life*
  y JB - v60 - D '96 - p278 [51-250]

Doyle, Arthur Conan, Sir - *The Adventure of the Dancing Men (Raleigh). Audio Version*
     Quill & Q - v62 - Jl '96 - p52 [1-50]
  The Annotated Lost World
     Analog - v117 - F '97 - p145+ [51-250]
     SFS - v23 - N '96 - p355+ [501+]
  The Hound of the Baskervilles (Jones). Audio Version
  c TES - D 27 '96 - p27 [1-50]
  The Lost World. Audio Version
     PW - v244 - Ja 6 '97 - p29 [51-250]
  Mysteries of Sherlock Holmes (Illus. by Paul Bachem)
  c Ch BWatch - v6 - D '96 - p5 [1-50]
  Sherlock Holmes
     Bloom Rev - v17 - Ja '97 - p17 [1-50]
  Sherlock Holmes: Tales of Avarice (Hardwicke). Audio Version
     BWatch - v18 - Mr '97 - p9 [1-50]
  y SLJ - v43 - F '97 - p71 [51-250]
  Sherlock Holmes: Tales of Betrayal (Hardwicke). Audio Version
     BWatch - v18 - Mr '97 - p9 [1-50]
  Sherlock Holmes: Tales of Intrigue (Hardwicke). Audio Version
     BWatch - v18 - Mr '97 - p9 [1-50]
  Sherlock Holmes: Tales of Suspense (Hardwicke). Audio Version
     BWatch - v18 - Mr '97 - p9 [1-50]
  y SLJ - v42 - N '96 - p70+ [51-250]
  The Sign of Four
     Signs - v22 - Aut '96 - p52+ [501+]
Doyle, Brian - *Spud in Winter*
  y SLJ - v42 - S '96 - p224 [51-250]
  Spud Sweetgrass
  y SLJ - v42 - S '96 - p224 [51-250]
  Uncle Ronald
  y CCB-B - v50 - F '97 - p203 [51-250]
  y Ch Bk News - v20 - Win '97 - p30 [51-250]
  y Emerg Lib - v24 - Mr '97 - p28 [1-50]
  y HB - v73 - My '97 - p318+ [251-500]
  c KR - v65 - F 1 '97 - p221 [51-250]
  c Quill & Q - v62 - O '96 - p49 [251-500]
  c Quill & Q - v63 - F '97 - p51 [51-250]
Doyle, Chris - *Sailors Guide to the Windward Islands. 8th Ed.*
     Yacht - v181 - F '97 - p16 [1-50]
Doyle, Debra - *Groogleman*
  y CCB-B - v50 - D '96 - p132 [51-250]
  y HB Guide - v8 - Spr '97 - p79 [51-250]
  c SLJ - v42 - D '96 - p120+ [51-250]
Doyle, James - *The Fin De Siecle Spirit*
     Can Lit - Spr '97 - p218+ [501+]
Doyle, Jennifer - *Pop Out*
     LATBR - My 26 '96 - p4 [501+]
Doyle, Jim - *Two Voices*
     LJ - v121 - O 1 '96 - p86 [51-250]
Doyle, John J - *Enabling the Safe Use of Biotechnology*
     Choice - v34 - Mr '97 - p1182 [51-250]
     JEL - v35 - Mr '97 - p280 [51-250]
Doyle, Larry - *Huh Huh for Hollywood*
  y BL - v93 - Ap 1 '97 - p1306 [1-50]
Doyle, Laurence R - *Circumstellar Habitable Zones*
     S&T - v93 - Mr '97 - p66 [51-250]
Doyle, Michael W - *UN Peacekeeping in Cambodia*
     Pac A - v69 - Fall '96 - p450+ [501+]
  Ways of War and Peace
     KR - v65 - Ap 1 '97 - p517 [251-500]
Doyle, Peter - *Understanding Fossils*
     Choice - v34 - Mr '97 - p1189 [51-250]
     Nature - v384 - N 14 '96 - p128 [51-250]
     New Sci - v151 - S 28 '96 - p55 [1-50]
Doyle, Roddy - *The Woman Who Walked into Doors*
     BIC - v25 - O '96 - p17 [501+]
     BL - v93 - Ap 1 '97 - p1285 [1-50]
     Comw - v123 - O 11 '96 - p21+ [501+]
     HR - v49 - Aut '96 - p483+ [501+]
     ILS - v15 - Fall '96 - p14 [501+]
     LATBR - D 29 '96 - p8 [51-250]
     LJ - v122 - Ja '97 - p49 [1-50]
     NS & S - v9 - My 3 '96 - p41 [251-500]
     NYTBR - v101 - D 8 '96 - p84 [1-50]
     NYTBR - v102 - F 23 '97 - p24 [51-250]
     Obs - D 1 '96 - p17* [1-50]
     PW - v243 - N 4 '96 - p37 [1-50]
     PW - v243 - D 9 '96 - p66 [51-250]
     Rapport - v19 - 4 '96 - p30 [251-500]
     SFR - v21 - 3 '96 - p6 [251-500]
     Trib Bks - F 2 '97 - p8 [51-250]
  The Woman Who Walked into Doors (Ryan). Audio Version
     Spec - v277 - N 30 '96 - p55 [1-50]

Dozois, Gardner - *Isaac Asimov's Vampires*
  y Kliatt - v31 - Mr '97 - p18 [51-250]
  Modern Classics of Fantasy
  y BL - v93 - D 1 '96 - p643 [51-250]
     BW - v27 - Ja 26 '97 - p6 [501+]
     LJ - v121 - D '96 - p152 [51-250]
     PW - v243 - D 30 '96 - p59+ [51-250]
Draanen, Wendelin Van - *How I Survived Being a Girl*
  c CBRS - v25 - Mr '97 - p96 [51-250]
  c CCB-B - v50 - Ap '97 - p298+ [51-250]
  c KR - v64 - D 1 '96 - p1741+ [51-250]
  c PW - v244 - Ja 6 '97 - p73+ [51-250]
  c SLJ - v43 - F '97 - p106 [51-250]
Drabble, Margaret - *Angus Wilson: A Biography*
     Choice - v34 - Ap '97 - p1334 [51-250]
     NYTBR - v101 - D 8 '96 - p84 [1-50]
  The Concise Oxford Companion to English Literature. Rev. Ed.
  yr Kliatt - v31 - Mr '97 - p22 [51-250]
  The Oxford Companion to English Literature. Rev. Ed.
     Books - v9 - S '95 - p22 [51-250]
  The Witch of Exmoor
     BL - v93 - My 15 '97 - p1539 [51-250]
     NS - v125 - N 1 '96 - p48 [501+]
     Obs - O 20 '96 - p17* [501+]
     Spec - v277 - O 19 '96 - p46+ [501+]
     TLS - O 11 '96 - p26 [501+]
     Woman's J - D '96 - p16 [51-250]
Drabenstott, Karen Markey - *Enhancing a New Design for Subject Access to Online Catalogs*
     LRTS - v41 - Ja '97 - p60+ [501+]
  Testing a New Design for Subject Access to Online Catalogs
     LQ - v67 - Ap '97 - p201+ [501+]
     LRTS - v41 - Ja '97 - p60+ [501+]
  Using Subject Headings for Online Retrieval
     LRTS - v41 - Ja '97 - p60+ [501+]
Dracos, Th. A - *Three-Dimensional Velocity and Vorticity Measuring and Image Analysis Techniques*
     SciTech - v21 - Mr '97 - p76 [51-250]
Draenger, Gusta Davidson - *Justyna's Narrative*
     AB - v99 - Ap 7 '97 - p1119+ [501+]
  y Kliatt - v31 - My '97 - p21 [251-500]
     Wom R Bks - v14 - O '96 - p12+ [501+]
Draffan, George - *Activist Research Manual of Sources of Information on Corporations*
     Workbook - v21 - Win '96 - p168+ [251-500]
Draft High Peaks Wilderness Complex Unit Management Plan
     J Gov Info - v23 - S '96 - p589 [51-250]
Drager, Olaf - *Religionem Significare*
     AJA - v100 - O '96 - p801+ [501+]
Drago, Gail - *Etta Place: Her Life and Times with Butch Cassidy and the Sundance Kid*
     Roundup M - v3 - Ag '96 - p24 [251-500]
Dragonfly: A Magazine for Young Investigators
  cp Learning - v25 - Mr '97 - p7 [51-250]
Dragonwagon, Crescent - *Brass Button (Illus. by Susan Paradise)*
  c PW - v244 - My 5 '97 - p209 [51-250]
Drainie, Bronwyn - *My Jerusalem*
     Can Lit - Win '96 - p191+ [501+]
Draitser, Emil - *Techniques of Satire*
     Humor - v10 - 1 '97 - p125+ [501+]
Drake, David - *The Fourth Rome*
  y VOYA - v19 - D '96 - p278 [251-500]
  Patriots
     KR - v64 - S 1 '96 - p1280+ [51-250]
     LJ - v121 - O 15 '96 - p93 [51-250]
     PW - v243 - O 21 '96 - p75 [51-250]
  Redliners
     BL - v92 - Ag '96 - p1888+ [51-250]
Drake, Gordon W F - *Atomic, Molecular, and Optical Physics Handbook*
     Choice - v34 - D '96 - p648 [51-250]
     SciTech - v20 - N '96 - p17 [51-250]
Drake, James A - *Rosa Ponselle: A Centenary Biography*
     KR - v65 - F 1 '97 - p189 [51-250]
     PW - v244 - F 3 '97 - p84+ [51-250]
Drake, Jane - *Farming (Illus. by Pat Cupples)*
  c Quill & Q - v62 - Jl '96 - p58 [251-500]
  Forestry (Illus. by Pat Cupples)
  c Quill & Q - v62 - Jl '96 - p58 [251-500]
  Kids Campfire Book
  c Emerg Lib - v24 - Mr '97 - p26 [1-50]
Drake, Paul W - *Labor Movements and Dictatorships*
     Choice - v34 - F '97 - p1011 [51-250]
     R&R Bk N - v12 - F '97 - p41 [51-250]
Drake, Richard - *The Aldo Moro Murder Case*
     TLS - Jl 19 '96 - p6 [501+]

Drake, Robert - *His*
Quill & Q - v62 - Jl '96 - p42 [501+]

Drake, W Avon - *Affirmative Action and the Stalled Quest for Black Progress*
Choice - v34 - F '97 - p1042 [51-250]

Drake Manuscript - *The Drake Manuscript in the Pierpoint Morgan Library*
Spec - v277 - D 14 '96 - p69+ [51-250]

Drakulic, Slavenka - *Cafe Europa*
BL - v93 - F 1 '97 - p912 [51-250]
BW - v27 - Mr 23 '97 - p8 [501+]
KR - v64 - D 15 '96 - p1779+ [251-500]
LATBR - F 16 '97 - p11 [501+]
LJ - v122 - Mr 15 '97 - p76 [51-250]
NY - v73 - Ap 28 '97 - p227 [51-250]
NYTLa - v146 - F 21 '97 - pC34 [501+]
Obs - D 1 '96 - p18* [51-250]
PW - v243 - D 16 '96 - p51+ [51-250]
Spec - v277 - O 19 '96 - p52+ [501+]
TLS - N 29 '96 - p12 [51-250]
VV - v42 - Mr 11 '97 - p55 [501+]

Dramstad, Wenche E - *Landscape Ecology Principles in Landscape Architecture and Land-Use Planning*
Choice - v34 - Mr '97 - p1182 [51-250]

Drane, James F - *Clinical Bioethics*
Rel St Rev - v22 - O '96 - p342 [51-250]

Dranoff, Linda Silver - *Everyone's Guide to the Law*
Quill & Q - v63 - Mr '97 - p73 [251-500]

Draper, Sharon M - *Forged by Fire*
y BL - v93 - F 15 '97 - p1016 [51-250]
y CBRS - v25 - F '97 - p82 [51-250]
y KR - v64 - D 1 '96 - p1735 [51-250]
y PW - v243 - D 16 '96 - p61 [51-250]
y SLJ - v43 - Mr '97 - p184 [51-250]
Lost in the Tunnel of Time (Illus. by Michael Bryant)
c SLJ - v42 - Ag '96 - p142 [51-250]
Tears of a Tiger
y Emerg Lib - v24 - S '96 - p24 [1-50]

Draper, Theodore - *A Struggle for Power*
IndRev - v1 - Spr '97 - p609+ [501+]
LATBR - Ap 20 '97 - p14 [501+]
NYTBR - v101 - D 8 '96 - p93 [1-50]
NYTBR - v102 - Ap 20 '97 - p32 [51-250]

Dratfield, Jim - *The Quotable Feline*
PW - v243 - Jl 22 '96 - p224 [51-250]

Drawert, Kurt - *Wo Es War*
WLT - v71 - Win '97 - p143 [501+]

Drawson, Blair - *Mary Margaret's Tree (Illus. by Blair Drawson)*
c BL - v93 - O 1 '96 - p358 [51-250]
c CBRS - v25 - Ja '97 - p49+ [51-250]
c HB Guide - v8 - Spr '97 - p25 [51-250]
c Quill & Q - v62 - O '96 - p45 [251-500]
c SLJ - v42 - O '96 - p91 [51-250]

Draycott, Pamela - *Sikhism: A New Approach*
y TES - Mr 21 '97 - p27* [51-250]

Dreachslin, Janice L - *Diversity Leadership*
SciTech - v20 - S '96 - p28 [51-250]

Dreams of Decadence
p SF Chr - v18 - O '96 - p82+ [1-50]

Drechsel, Edwin - *Norddeutscher Lloyd Bremen 1857-1970. Vol. 2*
Am Phil - v110 - O '96 - p910 [251-500]

Drees, Willem B - *Religion, Science and Naturalism*
CC - v113 - S 25 '96 - p911+ [51-250]
Choice - v34 - N '96 - p474+ [51-250]
Rel St - v33 - Mr '97 - p125+ [501+]
TLS - F 7 '97 - p27 [501+]

Dregni, Eric - *Ads That Put America on Wheels*
HMR - Spr '97 - p11 [51-250]

Dreifelds, Juris - *Latvia in Transition*
Choice - v34 - D '96 - p668+ [51-250]
For Aff - v75 - S '96 - p152+ [51-250]

Dreisbach, Daniel L - *Religion and Politics in the Early Republic*
Choice - v34 - O '96 - p298 [51-250]
Univ Bkmn - v36 - Win '96 - p16+ [501+]

Dreiser, Theodore - *Dreiser's Russian Diary*
Choice - v34 - Ap '97 - p1334 [51-250]
KR - v64 - Ag 15 '96 - p1221 [251-500]
LJ - v121 - N 1 '96 - p66+ [51-250]
Nat - v264 - F 10 '97 - p32+ [501+]
PW - v243 - S 9 '96 - p72 [51-250]
R&R Bk N - v12 - F '97 - p17 [51-250]
A Hoosier Holiday
PW - v244 - F 10 '97 - p73 [51-250]
Theodore Dreiser's Ev'ry Month
Choice - v34 - Ja '97 - p799 [51-250]

Dreismann, C A C - *New Frontiers in Theoretical Biology*
SciTech - v21 - Mr '97 - p34 [51-250]

Drescher, Fran - *Enter Whining*
Ent W - Mr 14 '97 - p75 [51-250]

Drescher, Henrik - *The Boy Who Ate Around*
c Par Ch - v20 - N '96 - p3 [1-50]
Klutz (Illus. by Henrik Drescher)
c CBRS - v25 - Win '97 - p61+ [51-250]
c HB Guide - v8 - Spr '97 - p25 [51-250]
c NYTBR - v102 - Ap 13 '97 - p27 [1-50]
c SLJ - v42 - D '96 - p92 [51-250]

Dresser, Marianne - *Buddhist Woman on the Edge*
Tric - v6 - Win '96 - p116 [1-50]

Dresser, Norine - *Multicultural Manners*
Nat R - v48 - Je 3 '96 - p55+ [501+]

Dresslar, Jim - *The Engraved Powder Horn*
Roundup M - v4 - O '96 - p26 [51-250]

Dressler, Alan - *Voyage to the Great Attractor*
S&T - v92 - S '96 - p54 [51-250]

Dressler, Mylene - *The Medusa Tree*
BL - v93 - My 1 '97 - p1477 [51-250]
KR - v65 - Mr 15 '97 - p398 [251-500]
LJ - v122 - Ap 1 '97 - p124 [51-250]
PW - v244 - Mr 10 '97 - p48 [51-250]

Dretske, Fred - *Naturalizing the Mind*
TLS - F 7 '97 - p25+ [501+]

Drevet, Patrick - *My Micheline*
TranslRevS - v1 - My '95 - p18+ [51-250]

Drew, Bernard A - *The 100 Most Popular Young Adult Authors*
yr ARBA - v28 - '97 - p430 [51-250]
yr BL - v93 - O 1 '96 - p371+ [51-250]
yr Bloom Rev - v17 - Ja '97 - p21 [51-250]
yr JAAL - v40 - D '96 - p320+ [501+]
yr RQ - v36 - Win '96 - p286+ [251-500]
yr SLMQ - v25 - Fall '96 - p63 [51-250]
r VOYA - v19 - D '96 - p298+ [251-500]
Action Series and Sequels
r RQ - v36 - Win '96 - p225 [51-250]
Heroines: A Bibliography of Women Series Characters in Mystery, Espionage, Action, Science Fiction, Fantasy, Horror, Western, Romance...
r RQ - v36 - Win '96 - p226 [51-250]
Western Series and Sequels. 2nd Ed.
r RQ - v36 - Win '96 - p212+ [51-250]

Drew, David E - *Aptitude Revisited*
Choice - v34 - Ja '97 - p848 [51-250]
Math T - v89 - D '96 - p780 [251-500]
R&R Bk N - v11 - N '96 - p76 [51-250]

Drew, Eileen, 1957- - *The Ivory Crocodile*
Choice - v34 - N '96 - p455 [51-250]
LJ - v121 - O 1 '96 - p47 [1-50]
y SLJ - v43 - Mr '97 - p214 [51-250]

Drew, Eileen P - *Families, Labour Markets, and Gender Roles*
J Gov Info - v23 - S '96 - p667 [51-250]

Drew, Elizabeth - *Showdown: The Struggle between the Gingrich Congress and the Clinton White House*
Choice - v34 - O '96 - p360 [51-250]
NYRB - v43 - Je 6 '96 - p11+ [501+]
NYTBR - v102 - F 23 '97 - p24 [51-250]
TLS - S 20 '96 - p14+ [501+]
Trib Bks - Mr 2 '97 - p8 [1-50]
Whatever It Takes
WSJ-Cent - v99 - My 28 '97 - pA16 [501+]

Drew, Paul - *Talk at Work*
Lang Soc - v25 - D '96 - p616+ [501+]

Drew-Bear, Annette - *Painted Faces on the Renaissance Stage*
Ren Q - v50 - Spr '97 - p275+ [501+]
Shakes Q - v47 - Sum '96 - p219+ [501+]

Drewe, Robert - *The Drowner*
Aust Bk R - O '96 - p9+ [501+]

Drexler, Rosalyn - *Art Does (Not!) Exist*
ABR - v18 - D '96 - p18+ [501+]

Drey, Johann Sebastian - *Brief Introduction to the Study of Theology with Reference to the Scientific Standpoint and the Catholic System*
Theol St - v57 - Mr '96 - p187+ [251-500]

Dreyer, Edward L - *China at War 1901-1949*
TLS - O 25 '96 - p12 [501+]

Dreyfuss, Richard - *The Two Georges*
Rapport - v19 - 5 '96 - p32 [251-500]
y VOYA - v19 - O '96 - p278 [51-250]

Drez, Ronald J - *Voices of D-Day*
y Kliatt - v30 - S '96 - p32+ [51-250]
VQR - v72 - Aut '96 - p142* [1-50]

Dreze, Jean - *India: Economic Development and Opportunity*
New R - v215 - S 30 '96 - p38+ [501+]
The Political Economy of Hunger
JEH - v56 - D '96 - p950+ [501+]

Driffield, Nigel L - *Global Competition and the Labour Market*
JEL - v34 - D '96 - p2072 [51-250]

Drifte, Reinhard - *Japan's Foreign Policy in the 1990s*
Choice - v34 - D '96 - p685 [51-250]

Drimmer, Frederick - *Incredible People*
c KR - v65 - My 1 '97 - p719 [51-250]

Drinkard, Michael - *Disobedience*
SFR - v21 - N '96 - p20+ [501+]

Drinker, Sophie - *Music and Women*
Am MT - v46 - F '97 - p64+ [501+]

Drinkwater, Carol - *Molly*
c Bks Keeps - v100 - S '96 - p16 [51-250]

Driscoll, Jerry A - *Introduction to College Chemistry. 1st Ed.*
J Chem Ed - v73 - O '96 - pA242+ [251-500]

Driskell, David C - *African American Visual Aesthetics*
Bl S - v26 - Fall '96 - p101 [1-50]

Driskell, James E - *Stress and Human Performance*
SB - v33 - Ja '97 - p5 [51-250]

Driver, Felix - *Power and Pauperism*
J Urban H - v23 - N '96 - p94+ [501+]

Driver, Paul - *Manchester Pieces*
Spec - v277 - N 16 '96 - p44 [1-50]
TLS - Ja 10 '97 - p17 [501+]
Penguin English Verse. Vol. 1. Audio Version
LJ - v121 - N 1 '96 - p122 [51-250]
Penguin English Verse. Vols. 1-6. Audio Version
PW - v243 - S 2 '96 - p47 [51-250]

Drlica, Karl - *Double-Edged Sword*
Sci - v274 - N 15 '96 - p1147+ [501+]
Understanding DNA and Gene Cloning. 3rd Ed.
Choice - v34 - Ap '97 - p1363 [51-250]
SB - v33 - Mr '97 - p39 [51-250]
SciTech - v21 - Mr '97 - p36 [51-250]

Drobizheva, Leokadia - *Ethnic Conflict in the Post-Soviet World*
Choice - v34 - Mr '97 - p1232 [51-250]
R&R Bk N - v12 - F '97 - p16 [51-250]

Dronke, Peter - *Nine Medieval Latin Plays*
RES - v47 - Ag '96 - p401+ [51-250]
Specu - v72 - Ja '97 - p144+ [501+]
Verse with Prose from Petronius to Dante
Comp L - v49 - Win '97 - p84+ [501+]

Dronke, Ursula - *Myth and Fiction in Early Norse Lands*
R&R Bk N - v11 - N '96 - p75 [51-250]

Droskowski, Gunther - *Duden: Das Grosse Worterbuch Der Deutschen Sprache. 2nd Ed., Vols. 1-8*
Ger Q - v69 - Spr '96 - p209 [51-250]

Droste, Ronald L - *Theory and Practice of Water and Wastewater Treatment*
Choice - v34 - Ap '97 - p1368 [51-250]
SciTech - v21 - Mr '97 - p82 [51-250]

Drouin, Michel - *L'Affaire Dreyfus De A a Z*
r FR - v70 - D '96 - p376+ [501+]

Drowatzky, John N - *Ethical Decision Making in Physical Activity Research*
Choice - v34 - N '96 - p492 [51-250]

Drozdek, Adam - *The Moral Dimension of Man in the Age of Computers*
CPR - v16 - Ap '96 - p97+ [251-500]

Drozdetskii, Aleks - *Sonlka Zolotaia Ruchka*
BL - v93 - O 1 '96 - p327 [1-50]

Dru, Jean-Marie - *Disruption: Overturning Conventions and Shaking Up the Marketplace*
Choice - v34 - My '97 - p1543 [51-250]
LJ - v121 - N 15 '96 - p69 [51-250]

Drucker, Peter Ferdinand - *Drucker on Asia*
BL - v93 - Ap 1 '97 - p1272+ [51-250]
For Aff - v76 - My '97 - p127+ [51-250]
PW - v243 - N 25 '96 - p66 [51-250]
The Practice of Management
Inc. - v18 - D '96 - p56 [251-500]
A Report on the New Post-Modern World
JEL - v34 - D '96 - p2122 [51-250]

Druckery, Timothy - *Electronic Culture*
BWatch - v18 - F '97 - p9 [51-250]

Drugs in Ontario
J Gov Info - v23 - S '96 - p633 [1-50]

Druick, Douglas - *Paul Gauguin: Pages from the Pacific*
BM - v138 - S '96 - p615 [1-50]

Druitt, Liz - *The Organic Rose Garden*
Fine Gard - N '96 - p72 [51-250]
Hort - v74 - D '96 - p58+ [51-250]

Drukier, Manny - *Carved in Stone*
BIC - v26 - Mr '97 - p15 [501+]
Quill & Q - v62 - O '96 - p34 [501+]

Drukteinis, Albert M - *The Psychology of Back Pain*
SciTech - v20 - N '96 - p50 [51-250]

Drummond, Robert J - *Appraisal Procedures for Counselors and Helping Professionals. 3rd Ed.*
SciTech - v20 - N '96 - p1 [51-250]

Drury, Joan M - *Silent Words*
y BL - v93 - S 1 '96 - p66+ [51-250]
LJ - v121 - O 1 '96 - p130+ [51-250]
NYTBR - v102 - Mr 30 '97 - p23 [51-250]

Druse, Ken - *The Collector's Garden*
Fine Gard - S '96 - p68+ [501+]
Hort - v74 - My '96 - p75+ [501+]

Druxes, Helga - *The Feminization of Dr. Faustus*
CLS - v33 - 3 '96 - p297+ [501+]
MLR - v91 - Jl '96 - p804+ [501+]

Druzhnikov, Yuri - *Informer 001*
Lon R Bks - v19 - Mr 6 '97 - p18+ [501+]
PW - v243 - O 7 '96 - p56 [51-250]
Russkie Mify
BL - v93 - O 1 '96 - p327 [1-50]

Dryden, Charles W - *A-Train: Memoirs of a Tuskegee Airman*
LJ - v122 - Ja '97 - p119 [51-250]

Dryden, John - *The Poems of John Dryden. Vols. 1-2*
RES - v47 - Ag '96 - p417+ [501+]

Dryden, Steve - *Trade Warriors*
AHR - v102 - F '97 - p224+ [251-500]

Dryden, Windy - *Developments in Psychotherapy*
SciTech - v21 - Mr '97 - p53 [51-250]
Handbook of Individual Therapy
SciTech - v21 - Mr '97 - p53 [51-250]

Drysdale, Helena - *Looking for George, Love and Death in Romania*
Obs - O 6 '96 - p18* [51-250]

D'Souza, Dinesh - *The End of Racism*
PW - v243 - Jl 22 '96 - p235 [1-50]

D'Souza, Giles - *Advances in the Use of NOAA AVHRR Data for Land Applications*
SciTech - v20 - S '96 - p1 [51-250]

Duane, Daniel - *Caught Inside*
Ent W - Ap 4 '97 - p78 [51-250]
LATBR - Jl 14 '96 - p4 [501+]
NY - v72 - D 9 '96 - p118 [51-250]
VV - v42 - Ja 7 '97 - p41 [1-50]

Duane, Michael J - *Customized Human Resource Planning*
J Car P&E - v57 - Fall '96 - p20 [51-250]
J Car P&E - v57 - Win '97 - p19+ [251-500]

Duara, Prasenjit - *Rescuing History from the Nation*
CS - v25 - N '96 - p814+ [501+]

Dubber, Geoff - *Organising Voluntary Help in the School Library*
LAR - v98 - Ag '96 - p428 [1-50]
Sch Lib - v44 - Ag '96 - p128 [51-250]

Dube, Richard - *Landscaping Makes Cents*
BL - v93 - F 15 '97 - p991 [51-250]

Dubeck, Paula J - *Women and Work*
r Choice - v34 - O '96 - p327+ [51-250]

Duberman, Martin - *Black Mountain*
HMR - Win '96 - p16+ [501+]

Dubey, Madhu - *Black Women Novelists and the Nationalist Aesthetic*
Signs - v22 - Win '97 - p462+ [501+]

Dubin, Marc S - *Cyprus. 2nd Ed.*
r BL - v93 - S 15 '96 - p210 [1-50]
Rhodes and the Dodecanese plus the East Aegean
r BL - v93 - S 15 '96 - p212 [1-50]

Duble, Richard L - *Turfgrasses: Their Management and Use in the Southern Zone. 2nd Ed.*
SciTech - v20 - S '96 - p44 [51-250]

Dublin, Thomas, 1946- - *Immigrant Voices*
CAY - v16 - Fall '95 - p12 [51-250]
Transforming Women's Work
T&C - v37 - Ap '96 - p354+ [501+]

Dubois, Page - *Sappho Is Burning*
Class Out - v74 - Fall '96 - p40 [251-500]

DuBois, Paul - *Software Portability with Imake. 2nd Ed.*
SciTech - v20 - D '96 - p11 [51-250]

DuBois, W E B - *The Souls of Black Folk*
BW - v26 - D 15 '96 - p12 [51-250]
TES - N 22 '96 - p8* [51-250]
TLS - O 18 '96 - p31 [251-500]

Du Bois, William Pene - *The Twenty-One Balloons (Illus. by William Pene Du Bois)*
c JOYS - v10 - Fall '96 - p35+ [501+]

Dubosarsky, Ursula - *Black Sails, White Sails*
y Aust Bk R - F '97 - p50+ [501+]
Bruno and the Crumhorn
y Bks Keeps - v100 - S '96 - p16 [51-250]
c JB - v60 - D '96 - p278 [51-250]
c Magpies - v11 - My '96 - p42 [251-500]
y Sch Lib - v44 - N '96 - p170 [51-250]

DuBose, Edwin R - *The Illusion of Trust*
Theol St - v57 - S '96 - p576+ [251-500]

DuBosque, D C - *Draw Desert Animals (Illus. by D C DuBosque)*
c BL - v93 - D 15 '96 - p722+ [51-250]
c Par Ch - v20 - N '96 - p8 [51-250]
c SLJ - v43 - Mr '97 - p199 [51-250]

Dubosque, D C - *Draw! Grassland Animals (Illus. by D C Dubosque)*
c SLJ - v42 - S '96 - p214 [51-250]

Dubost, Thierry - *Struggle, Defeat or Rebirth*
Choice - v34 - My '97 - p1494+ [51-250]

Dubovsky, Steven L - *Mind-Body Deceptions*
KR - v65 - Ja 15 '97 - p114 [251-500]
LJ - v122 - Mr 15 '97 - p77 [51-250]
PW - v244 - Ja 20 '97 - p385+ [51-250]

Dubow, Saul - *Scientific Racism in Modern South Africa*
CS - v25 - N '96 - p750+ [501+]

Dubrovin, Vivian - *Storytelling Adventures*
c Ch BWatch - v7 - F '97 - p1 [51-250]

Dubrow, Heather - *Echoes of Desire*
Six Ct J - v27 - Fall '96 - p832+ [501+]

Dubuis, Pierre - *Le Jeu De La Vie Et De La Mort*
Specu - v71 - O '96 - p942+ [501+]

Dubus, Andre - *Dancing after Hours*
Ant R - v54 - Sum '96 - p380 [51-250]
BL - v93 - Ja '97 - p761 [1-50]
Comw - v123 - My 17 '96 - p24+ [501+]
HR - v49 - Aut '96 - p483+ [501+]
NYTBR - v101 - D 8 '96 - p79 [1-50]
PW - v244 - Ja 27 '97 - p103 [1-50]
Sew R - v104 - Jl '96 - pR55+ [51-250]
The Last Worthless Evening
Trib Bks - F 23 '97 - p8 [1-50]
Selected Stories
Sew R - v104 - Jl '96 - pR55+ [51-250]

Duby, Georges - *An 1000, An 2000, Sur Les Traces De Nos Peurs*
Choice - v34 - D '96 - p566 [1-50]
Dames Du XIIe Siecle. Vol. 1
Choice - v34 - D '96 - p566+ [1-50]

Ducatel, Ken - *Employment and Technical Change in Europe*
Econ J - v106 - N '96 - p1842 [51-250]

Duchamp, Marcel - *Duchamp (Faerna)*
y BL - v93 - O 1 '96 - p314+ [51-250]

Ducharme, Rejean - *Va Savoir*
FR - v70 - Mr '97 - p612+ [501+]

Duchemin, Jacqueline - *Mythes Grecs Et Sources Orientales*
Choice - v34 - D '96 - p566 [1-50]

Duchen, Jessica - *Erich Wolfgang Korngold*
FF - v20 - Ja '97 - p378+ [501+]

Duchene, Jacqueline - *Henriette D'Angleterre, Duchesse D'Orleans*
FR - v70 - O '96 - p111+ [501+]
TLS - Ja 3 '97 - p31 [501+]

Duchene, Roger - *L'Impossible Marcel Proust*
FR - v70 - D '96 - p334+ [501+]

Duchesne, Christiane - *La 42e Soeur De Bebert*
c Can CL - v22 - Sum '96 - p108+ [251-500]
Les Peripeties De P. Le Prophete
y Can CL - v22 - Sum '96 - p106+ [251-500]
Who's Afraid of the Dark? (Illus. by Doris Barrette)
c BIC - v25 - D '96 - p36 [251-500]
c Quill & Q - v62 - N '96 - p47 [251-500]

Duchet, Claude - *Balzac, Oeuvres Completes*
FR - v70 - O '96 - p116+ [501+]

Duchin, Peter - *Ghost of a Chance*
LATBR - Ag 4 '96 - p4 [501+]
NYTBR - v101 - D 8 '96 - p87 [1-50]
VQR - v72 - Aut '96 - p124* [51-250]

DuCille, Ann - *The Coupling Convention*
TSWL - v15 - Fall '96 - p355+ [501+]
Skin Trade
CHE - v43 - N 22 '96 - pA16 [51-250]
Choice - v34 - My '97 - p1582 [51-250]
PW - v243 - S 2 '96 - p118 [51-250]

Ducker, Bruce - *Lead Us Not into Penn Station*
Aethlon - v13 - Fall '95 - p133+ [251-500]

Duckworth, Eleanor - *The Having of Wonderful Ideas and Other Essays on Teaching and Learning*
Nat - v263 - O 28 '96 - p32+ [501+]

Duckworth, Marilyn - *Leather Wings*
WLT - v71 - Win '97 - p232 [251-500]

Ducloy, Martial - *Quantum Optics of Confined Systems*
SciTech - v20 - D '96 - p24 [51-250]

Ducrey, Pierre - *Eretria, Fouilles Et Recherches VIII*
AJA - v100 - O '96 - p777+ [501+]

Dudbridge, Glen - *Religious Experience and Lay Society in T'ang China*
Rel St Rev - v23 - Ap '97 - p205 [51-250]

Dudden, Faye E - *Women in the American Theatre*
J Am Cult - v19 - Spr '96 - p99 [251-500]

Dudek, Isabella - *Farm Animals (Illus. by Heinrich Kita)*
c Ch BWatch - v6 - My '96 - p1 [51-250]
House Pets (Illus. by Heinrich Kita)
c Ch BWatch - v6 - My '96 - p1 [51-250]

Dudek, Louis - *Notebooks 1960-1994*
Can Lit - Spr '97 - p249+ [501+]

Dudek, Peter - *Der Ruckblick Auf Die Vergangenheit Wird Sich Nicht Vermeiden Lassen*
Choice - v34 - D '96 - p568 [1-50]

Duder, Tessa - *Falling in Love*
y Magpies - v11 - Jl '96 - p33 [51-250]
In Lane Three, Alex Archer
y Kliatt - v30 - S '96 - p5 [1-50]

Dudley, Ellen - *American Discoveries*
BW - v26 - D 29 '96 - p13 [51-250]
LJ - v121 - O 15 '96 - p81 [51-250]

Dudley, Steve - *Rare Birds Day by Day*
r New Sci - v152 - N 2 '96 - p48 [51-250]

Dudley, William - *African Americans*
y SLJ - v43 - Mr '97 - p199 [51-250]
Asian Americans
y BL - v93 - D 15 '96 - p715 [51-250]
The Civil Rights Movement
y Ch BWatch - v6 - My '96 - p5 [51-250]
y SLJ - v42 - Ag '96 - p168 [51-250]
World War II
y SLJ - v43 - Mr '97 - p199 [51-250]

Due, Tananarive - *The Between, a Novel*
y Kliatt - v30 - S '96 - p8 [51-250]

Dueck, Adele - *Anywhere but Here*
y Quill & Q - v62 - My '96 - p33+ [501+]
c SLJ - v43 - Mr '97 - p184+ [51-250]

Duellman, Elmer - *Elmer's Price Guide to Toys. Vol. 2*
r Ant & CM - v101 - D '96 - p32 [1-50]

Duemer, Joseph - *Dog Music*
CHE - v43 - Ja 24 '97 - pA6 [51-250]

Duerst-Lahti, Georgia - *Gender Power, Leadership, and Governance*
Choice - v34 - S '96 - p201 [51-250]

Dues, Greg - *Called to Parish Ministry*
CLW - v67 - Mr '97 - p38 [51-250]

Duesberg, Peter - *Inventing the AIDS Virus*
New Sci - v152 - D 7 '96 - p50 [51-250]
NYTBR - v101 - Ap 7 '96 - p8+ [501+]

Duey, Kathleen - *Anisett Lundberg*
c SLJ - v42 - D '96 - p122 [51-250]
Mary Alice Peale, Philadelphia 1777
c SLJ - v42 - D '96 - p122 [51-250]
Willow Chase
c BL - v93 - Mr 1 '97 - p1164 [51-250]

Duff, David - *Romance and Revolution*
MP - v94 - F '97 - p402+ [501+]

Duffett-Smith, Peter - *Easy PC Astronomy*
SciTech - v21 - Mr '97 - p19 [51-250]

Duffey, Betsy - *Buster and the Black Hole*
c Sch Lib - v45 - F '97 - p24 [51-250]
c TES - F 21 '97 - p8* [51-250]
Coaster
y Kliatt - v31 - Mr '97 - p6+ [51-250]
Hey, New Kid! (Illus. by Ellen Thompson)
c Emerg Lib - v24 - S '96 - p51 [51-250]
c HB Guide - v7 - Fall '96 - p291 [1-50]
c RT - v50 - Ap '97 - p590 [51-250]
How to Be Cool in Junior School (Illus. by J Douglas)
c JB - v60 - D '96 - p251 [251-500]

Duffie, Darrell - *Dynamic Asset Pricing Theory*
JEL - v34 - S '96 - p1435 [51-250]

Duffield, Jill - *Policy, Practice, and Provision for Children with Specific Learning Difficulties*
R&R Bk N - v11 - N '96 - p57 [51-250]

Duffield, John S - *Power Rules*
J Pol - v58 - N '96 - p1258+ [501+]

Duffin, Jacalyn - *Langstaff: A Nineteenth-Century Medical Life*
Archiv - Fall '94 - p194+ [501+]

Duffus, John H - *Fundamental Toxicology for Chemists*
New Sci - v153 - Mr 1 '97 - p39 [51-250]

Duffy, Bruce - *Last Comes the Egg*
y BL - v93 - Ja '97 - p817+ [51-250]
BW - v27 - F 16 '97 - p9 [501+]
KR - v64 - N 15 '96 - p1619+ [251-500]
LJ - v121 - D '96 - p142 [51-250]
Nat - v264 - Mr 24 '97 - p32+ [501+]
NYTBR - v102 - Mr 9 '97 - p13 [501+]
PW - v243 - D 2 '96 - p42 [51-250]
Trib Bks - Mr 2 '97 - p4 [51-250]

Duffy, Carol Ann - *Stopping for Death (Illus. by Trisha Rafferty)*
  y BL - v92 - Ag '96 - p1893+ [51-250]
  y CCB-B - v50 - S '96 - p9+ [51-250]
  c HB Guide - v7 - Fall '96 - p364 [51-250]
  y JAAL - v40 - F '97 - p409 [51-250]
  c Sch Lib - v44 - Ag '96 - p115 [51-250]
  y SLJ - v42 - Ag '96 - p168 [51-250]
  y VOYA - v19 - O '96 - p238+ [51-250]
Duffy, Dee Dee - *Forest Tracks (Illus. by Janet Marshall)*
  c HB Guide - v7 - Fall '96 - p238 [51-250]
  c Inst - v106 - Mr '97 - p30 [1-50]
  c New Ad - v9 - Fall '96 - p327+ [501+]
Duffy, Godfrey F - *A Guide to Tracing Your Donegal Ancestors*
  r EGH - v50 - N '96 - p156 [51-250]
Duffy, James P - *Lincoln's Admiral*
  BL - v93 - F 15 '97 - p998 [51-250]
  KR - v65 - Ja 15 '97 - p114 [51-250]
  PW - v244 - F 10 '97 - p78 [51-250]
Duffy, Joseph - *Statics and Kinematics with Applications to Robotics*
  Choice - v34 - D '96 - p641 [51-250]
Duffy, Margaret - *Prospect of Death*
  Arm Det - v29 - Fall '96 - p494 [51-250]
  KR - v64 - My 1 '96 - p642 [251-500]
Duffy, Michael - *The New Maritime History of Devon. Vol. 2*
  EHR - v112 - F '97 - p242+ [501+]
Duffy, P J - *Landscapes of South Ulster*
  r ILS - v16 - Spr '97 - p30 [501+]
Duffy, Regis A - *An American Emmaus*
  CLW - v67 - D '96 - p43 [501+]
  RR - v56 - Ja '97 - p100+ [501+]
  Theol St - v57 - Je '96 - p384+ [251-500]
Duffy, Stella - *Wavewalker*
  KR - v64 - S 1 '96 - p1274+ [51-250]
  PW - v243 - O 7 '96 - p67 [51-250]
Duffy, Susan - *American Labor on Stage*
  Choice - v34 - F '97 - p976 [51-250]
  R&R Bk N - v12 - F '97 - p88 [51-250]
Dufournet, Jean - *Philippe De Commynes: Un Historien A L'Aube Des Temps Modernes*
  EHR - v112 - Ap '97 - p452+ [501+]
Dufresne, John - *Love Warps the Mind a Little*
  BL - v93 - D 15 '96 - p708 [51-250]
  BW - v27 - F 9 '97 - p6+ [501+]
  KR - v64 - N 15 '96 - p1620 [251-500]
  NY - v72 - Ja 27 '97 - p76 [51-250]
  NYTBR - v102 - F 16 '97 - p11 [501+]
  NYTLa - v146 - F 7 '97 - pC33 [501+]
  PW - v243 - D 2 '96 - p41 [51-250]
  Trib Bks - Ja 19 '97 - p3 [501+]
The Way That Water Enters Stone
  NYTBR - v102 - Ja 19 '97 - p28 [1-50]
  PW - v243 - N 11 '96 - p71 [1-50]
  Trib Bks - F 16 '97 - p8 [1-50]
Dugan, Ellen - *Picturing the South 1860 to the Present*
  Bloom Rev - v16 - S '96 - p28 [501+]
  LATBR - Ag 4 '96 - p11 [51-250]
Dugan, Roger C - *Electrical Power Systems Quality*
  Choice - v34 - S '96 - p159 [51-250]
Du Gay, Paul - *Consumption and Identity at Work*
  CS - v26 - Mr '97 - p228+ [501+]
  Socio R - v45 - F 1 '97 - p169+ [501+]
Dugdale, Joan - *The Descendant*
  Aust Bk R - Je '96 - p42+ [501+]
Dugdale, John - *Thomas Pynchon: Allusive Parables of Power*
  Poetics T - v18 - Spr '97 - p95+ [501+]
Duggal, Krishan L - *Lightlike Submanifolds of Semi-Riemannian Manifolds and Applications*
  SciTech - v20 - N '96 - p17 [51-250]
Duggan, Anne J - *Kings and Kingship in Medieval Europe*
  EHR - v112 - F '97 - p165+ [251-500]
Duggan, Laurie - *New and Selected Poems 1971-1993*
  Aust Bk R - S '96 - p48+ [501+]
Duggan, Robert D - *Parish Liturgy*
  CLW - v67 - Mr '97 - p39+ [251-500]
Dugger, Mary - *The History of Lesbian Hair and Other Tales of Bent Life in a Straight World*
  Advocate - S 17 '96 - p60 [1-50]
  Prog - v61 - Ja '97 - p31 [251-500]
  Wom R Bks - v14 - Mr '97 - p6+ [501+]
Dugger, William M - *Inequality: Radical Institutionalist Views on Race, Gender, Class, and Nation*
  R&R Bk N - v12 - F '97 - p33 [51-250]
Duggleby, John - *Artist in Overalls*
  c CLW - v67 - D '96 - p61 [51-250]
  c HB Guide - v7 - Fall '96 - p355 [51-250]

Duhamel, Alain - *La Politique Imaginaire*
  FR - v70 - O '96 - p135+ [251-500]
Duhem, Pierre - *Essays in the History and Philosophy of Science*
  Choice - v34 - Ja '97 - p814+ [51-250]
Duignan, Peter - *The Rebirth of the West*
  JPR - v34 - F '97 - p111 [251-500]
The USA and the New Europe 1945-1993
  EHR - v111 - S '96 - p1036+ [251-500]
Duijker, Hubrecht - *Touring in Wine Country: Loire*
  r LJ - v122 - Ap 1 '97 - p113 [51-250]
Duiker, William J - *The Communist Road to Power in Vietnam. 2nd Ed.*
  Choice - v34 - O '96 - p353+ [51-250]
Vietnam: Revolution in Transition
  Pac A - v69 - Fall '96 - p446+ [501+]
Duistermaat, J J - *Fourier Integral Operators*
  SIAM Rev - v39 - Mr '97 - p169+ [501+]
Dujon, Diane - *For Crying Out Loud*
  Ms - v7 - Ja '97 - p82 [1-50]
Dujovne Ortiz, Alicia - *Eva Peron*
  KR - v64 - S 15 '96 - p1381 [251-500]
  LATBR - D 22 '96 - p3 [501+]
  LJ - v121 - O 15 '96 - p66+ [51-250]
  New R - v216 - F 10 '97 - p31+ [501+]
  NL - v80 - F 10 '97 - p17+ [501+]
  NYRB - v44 - F 20 '97 - p27+ [501+]
  NYTBR - v101 - N 24 '96 - p27 [501+]
  Obs - F 9 '97 - p18* [51-250]
  PW - v243 - S 23 '96 - p66 [51-250]
  WSJ-MW - v78 - N 14 '96 - pA18 [251-500]
Duke, Kate - *Archaeologists Dig for Clues (Illus. by Kate Duke)*
  c BL - v93 - D 1 '96 - p662 [51-250]
  c KR - v64 - D 15 '96 - p1797 [51-250]
  c SLJ - v43 - F '97 - p89 [51-250]
Aunt Isabel Makes Trouble (Illus. by Kate Duke)
  c HB Guide - v8 - Spr '97 - p25 [51-250]
  c Inst - v106 - N '96 - p25+ [51-250]
  c KR - v64 - S 15 '96 - p1398 [51-250]
  c PW - v243 - O 14 '96 - p83 [51-250]
  c SLJ - v42 - O '96 - p91+ [51-250]
Duke, Philip - *Beyond Subsistence*
  Am Ant - v62 - Ja '97 - p159+ [501+]
Duke, Simon - *The New European Security Disorder*
  Parameters - v27 - Spr '97 - p169+ [501+]
Duke Dos Santos, Maria I - *Sabine R. Ulibarri: Critical Essays*
  Hisp - v79 - D '96 - p802+ [501+]
Dukelow, W Richard - *The Alpha Males*
  Isis - v87 - D '96 - p756+ [501+]
  SciTech - v20 - S '96 - p21 [51-250]
Dukthas, Ann - *The Time of Murder at Mayerling*
  Arm Det - v30 - Win '97 - p103 [251-500]
  y BL - v93 - D 15 '96 - p710+ [51-250]
  KR - v64 - O 15 '96 - p1495 [51-250]
  PW - v243 - N 4 '96 - p67 [51-250]
Dulberger, Judith A - *Mother Donit Fore the Best*
  Choice - v34 - O '96 - p346+ [51-250]
Duleep, Harriet Orcutt - *Immigrants and Immigration Policy*
  JEL - v34 - D '96 - p2077 [51-250]
Duley, W W - *UV Lasers*
  Choice - v34 - My '97 - p1529 [51-250]
Dulffer, Jost - *Nazi Germany 1933-1945*
  HRNB - v25 - Win '97 - p73+ [501+]
Duliani, Mario - *The City without Women*
  TranslRevS - v1 - My '95 - p7+ [251-500]
Dull, Olga Anna - *Folie Et Rhetorique Dans La Sottie*
  Specu - v71 - Jl '96 - p713+ [501+]
Dulles, Allen Welsh - *From Hitler's Doorstep*
  Choice - v34 - F '97 - p1024 [51-250]
  VQR - v73 - Win '97 - p16* [51-250]
Dulles, John W F - *Carlos Lacerda, Brazilian Crusader. Vol. 2*
  Choice - v34 - D '96 - p674 [51-250]
Dulude, Louise - *Seniority and Employment Equity for Women*
  ILRR - v50 - Ja '97 - p350+ [501+]
Dumais, Marcel - *Le Sermon Sur La Montagne*
  Rel St Rev - v23 - Ja '97 - p72 [51-250]
Dumas, Alexandre - *The Man in the Iron Mask. Audio Version*
  c TES - D 27 '96 - p27 [1-50]
The Three Musketeers (Homewood). Audio Version
  c TES - D 27 '96 - p27 [1-50]
The Three Musketeers (Ward). Audio Version
  c Ch BWatch - v7 - Ja '97 - p5 [1-50]
  c TES - D 27 '96 - p27 [1-50]

Dumas, Ann - *Degas as a Collector*
  BM - v138 - Ag '96 - p553+ [501+]
  NYRB - v43 - O 3 '96 - p48+ [501+]
Du Maurier, Daphne - *Rebecca (Stevenson). Audio Version*
  Obs - F 16 '97 - p18* [51-250]
Dumbleton, Mike - *Mr. Knuckles (Illus. by Leigh Hobbs)*
  c Bks Keeps - N '96 - p9 [51-250]
Dumenil, Lynn - *The Modern Temper*
  J Am St - v30 - Ag '96 - p285 [251-500]
Dumitriu, Severian - *Polysaccharides in Medicinal Applications*
  SciTech - v20 - N '96 - p34 [51-250]
Dumm, Demetrius - *Cherish Christ above All*
  RR - v56 - Mr '97 - p220 [1-50]
Dumm, Thomas L - *United States*
  Am Q - v48 - S '96 - p535+ [51-250]
Dumond, Don E - *Paugvik: A Nineteenth-Century Native Village on Bristol Bay, Alaska*
  Am Ant - v61 - Jl '96 - p633 [251-500]
Dumont, Bruno - *Aux Origines Des Communes*
  JMH - v69 - Mr '97 - p150+ [501+]
Les Communautes Villageoises Dans Les Pays De Dalhem Et De Limbourg XVIe-XVIIe Siecle
  AHR - v101 - O '96 - p1229 [501+]
Dumont, Fernand - *La Part De L'Ombre*
  WLT - v71 - Win '97 - p107+ [501+]
Dumont, Francois - *Usages De La Poesie*
  Can Lit - Win '96 - p163+ [501+]
Dumper, Michael - *The Politics of Jerusalem since 1967*
  MEQ - v4 - Mr '97 - p75+ [501+]
Dumville, David N - *Liturgy and the Ecclesiastical History of Late Anglo-Saxon England*
  CHR - v82 - Jl '96 - p521+ [501+]
  Lib - v18 - Je '96 - p154+ [501+]
The Dun and Bradstreet Regional Business Directory Disc. Electronic Media Version
  r IRLA - v32 - O '96 - p7 [1-50]
Dunant, Sarah - *The Age of Anxiety*
  New Sci - v152 - N 2 '96 - p47 [51-250]
  NS - v125 - N 8 '96 - p44+ [501+]
  Obs - N 10 '96 - p16* [501+]
  TLS - D 6 '96 - p7+ [501+]
Under My Skin
  TES - D 27 '96 - p17 [1-50]
Dunaway, David King - *Writing the Southwest*
  Bloom Rev - v16 - Jl '96 - p15 [251-500]
  WAL - v31 - Win '97 - p393+ [501+]
Dunaway, Wilma A - *The First American Frontier*
  CS - v26 - Mr '97 - p197+ [501+]
  JEH - v56 - S '96 - p738+ [501+]
  JEL - v34 - S '96 - p1473 [51-250]
  PHR - v65 - N '96 - p665+ [501+]
  VQR - v72 - Aut '96 - p116* [51-250]
Dunbar, James - *Tick Tock*
  c Bks Keeps - v100 - S '96 - p20 [51-250]
Dunbar, Joyce - *Indigo and the Whale (Illus. by Geoffrey Patterson)*
  c HB Guide - v7 - Fall '96 - p254 [51-250]
  c Sch Lib - v44 - Ag '96 - p98+ [51-250]
  c SLJ - v42 - Ag '96 - p121 [51-250]
Oops-a-Daisy! and Other Tales for Toddlers (Illus. by Carol Thompson)
  c Bks Keeps - v100 - S '96 - p8 [51-250]
This Is the Star (Illus. by Gary Blythe)
  c Bks Keeps - N '96 - p19 [1-50]
  c BL - v93 - S 1 '96 - p136 [51-250]
  c CBRS - v25 - N '96 - p25 [1-50]
  c HB Guide - v8 - Spr '97 - p89 [1-50]
  c JB - v60 - D '96 - p229 [51-250]
  c KR - v64 - O 1 '96 - p1476 [51-250]
  c PW - v243 - S 30 '96 - p88 [51-250]
  c PW - v243 - N 4 '96 - p48 [1-50]
  c Sch Lib - v44 - N '96 - p146 [51-250]
  c SLJ - v42 - O '96 - p35 [51-250]
  c TES - D 6 '96 - p17* [51-250]
Dunbar, Leila - *Motorcycle Collectibles*
  Ant & CM - v101 - D '96 - p30 [1-50]
Dunbar, Robin - *Grooming, Gossip, and the Evolution of Language*
  BL - v93 - F 15 '97 - p985 [51-250]
  KR - v65 - Ja 15 '97 - p115 [251-500]
  LJ - v122 - Ap 1 '97 - p91 [51-250]
  Nat - v264 - Ap 14 '97 - p33+ [501+]
  NS - v125 - D 20 '96 - p116+ [51-250]
  NYTBR - v102 - Mr 9 '97 - p10 [501+]
  PW - v244 - F 10 '97 - p77 [51-250]
  TLS - S 6 '96 - p25+ [501+]
Dunbar, Sophie - *A Bad Hair Day*
  LATBR - My 12 '96 - p11 [51-250]
  Rapport - v19 - 4 '96 - p31 [51-250]

Dunbar, Tony - *Trick Question*
    BL - v93 - Ja '97 - p824 [51-250]
    KR - v64 - N 15 '96 - p1634 [51-250]
    NYTBR - v102 - Ja 19 '97 - p22 [51-250]
    PW - v243 - D 2 '96 - p44 [51-250]
Dunbar, Wylene - *Margaret Cape*
    KR - v65 - Mr 1 '97 - p322+ [51-250]
    PW - v244 - Mr 24 '97 - p59 [51-250]
Duncan, A B - *Proceedings of the ASME Advanced Energy Systems Division*
    SciTech - v21 - Mr '97 - p74 [51-250]
Duncan, Alistair - *Laws and Order in Eighteenth-Century Chemistry*
    Choice - v34 - My '97 - p1527 [51-250]
    Isis - v88 - Mr '97 - p147 [501+]
    Nature - v386 - Mr 6 '97 - p34 [501+]
    New Sci - v153 - Mr 8 '97 - p43 [51-250]
Duncan, Barry - *Mass Media and Popular Culture, Version 2*
    Emerg Lib - v24 - Mr '97 - p41+ [51-250]
Duncan, Ben - *High Performance Audio Power Amplifiers for Music Performance and Reproduction*
    SciTech - v21 - Mr '97 - p92 [51-250]
Duncan, Beverly - *Explore the Wild*
    c CLW - v67 - Mr '97 - p56 [51-250]
    c Emerg Lib - v23 - My '96 - p43 [1-50]
    c HB Guide - v7 - Fall '96 - p335 [51-250]
Duncan, Carol - *Civilizing Rituals*
    Afterimage - v24 - N '96 - p14+ [501+]
    AJA - v100 - O '96 - p769+ [501+]
    Art J - v55 - Fall '96 - p95+ [501+]
Duncan, Colin A M - *The Centrality of Agriculture*
    Choice - v34 - N '96 - p478 [51-250]
Duncan, Dave - *Cursed*
    BIC - v25 - S '96 - p36 [251-500]
    Present Tense
    PW - v243 - S 30 '96 - p65+ [51-250]
Duncan, David Ewing - *Residents: The Perils and Promise of Educating Young Doctors*
    Choice - v34 - F '97 - p996 [51-250]
Duncan, Dayton - *People of the West*
    c BL - v92 - Ag '96 - p1897 [51-250]
    c CBRS - v25 - S '96 - p12 [51-250]
    c Ch BWatch - v7 - Ja '97 - p7 [1-50]
    c HB Guide - v8 - Spr '97 - p173 [51-250]
    c PW - v243 - S 2 '96 - p132+ [51-250]
    y SLJ - v42 - O '96 - p154+ [51-250]
    The West: An Illustrated History for Children
    c BL - v92 - Ag '96 - p1897 [51-250]
    c CBRS - v25 - S '96 - p12 [51-250]
    c Ch BWatch - v7 - Ja '97 - p7 [1-50]
    c HB Guide - v8 - Spr '97 - p173 [51-250]
    c NY - v72 - N 18 '96 - p101 [51-250]
    c PW - v243 - S 2 '96 - p132+ [51-250]
    y SLJ - v42 - O '96 - p154+ [51-250]
Duncan, Doree - *Life into Art*
    Dance - v70 - N '96 - p78+ [501+]
Duncan, Gallie - *Trade Unionism in Recession*
    ILR - v135 - 5 '96 - p593+ [501+]
Duncan, Garry R - *Canadian Resident Abroad*
    r Quill & Q - v63 - F '97 - p38 [501+]
Duncan, Isadora - *My Life*
    CR - v269 - N '96 - p279 [51-250]
    Dance - v70 - N '96 - p78+ [501+]
    TES - S 6 '96 - p8* [51-250]
Duncan, Lois - *Gallows Hill*
    y CCB-B - v50 - Mr '97 - p246 [51-250]
    y KR - v65 - Ja 1 '97 - p58 [51-250]
    y PW - v244 - Mr 17 '97 - p84 [51-250]
    Killing Mr. Griffin
    y JAAL - v40 - D '96 - p316+ [51-250]
    Locked in Time
    y Kliatt - v30 - S '96 - p2 [1-50]
    The Magic of Spider Woman (Illus. by Shonto Begay)
    c Emerg Lib - v24 - Mr '97 - p65 [51-250]
    c HB Guide - v7 - Fall '96 - p320 [51-250]
    Night Terrors
    y Emerg Lib - v23 - My '96 - p43 [1-50]
    y HB Guide - v7 - Fall '96 - p364 [51-250]
    c KR - v64 - My 1 '96 - p687 [51-250]
    Ransom
    y Magpies - v11 - My '96 - p53 [1-50]
Duncan, Martha Grace - *Romantic Outlaws, Beloved Prisons*
    NYTBR - v102 - Ja 26 '97 - p17 [501+]
Duncan, Patrick Sheane - *Courage under Fire*
    LJ - v121 - O 1 '96 - p47 [1-50]
Duncan, Robert - *Selected Poems. Rev. Ed.*
    LJ - v122 - Ap 1 '97 - p97 [51-250]
Duncan, Sara Jeannette - *Set in Authority*
    Choice - v34 - Ap '97 - p1335 [51-250]

Duncan, Stephen M - *Citizen Warriors*
    BL - v93 - Ja '97 - p790 [51-250]
    KR - v64 - N 15 '96 - p1649 [251-500]
    PW - v243 - N 18 '96 - p56 [51-250]
Duncker, Patricia - *Hallucinating Foucault*
    BL - v93 - F 1 '97 - p925 [51-250]
    BW - v27 - F 9 '97 - p8 [501+]
    Choice - v34 - My '97 - p1495 [51-250]
    LJ - v121 - D '96 - p142 [51-250]
    NY - v73 - Ap 14 '97 - p85 [51-250]
    NYTBR - v102 - F 16 '97 - p15 [501+]
    PW - v243 - O 21 '96 - p68+ [51-250]
    SFR - v22 - Ja '97 - p31 [501+]
    Spec - v277 - N 16 '96 - p43 [1-50]
    Time - v149 - Mr 3 '97 - p76 [251-500]
    Trib Bks - Mr 2 '97 - p3+ [501+]
    VV - v42 - F 11 '97 - p53 [251-500]
Duncklee, John - *Coyotes I Have Known*
    Roundup M - v4 - D '96 - p28 [1-50]
Dundas, James L - *Cap Guns*
    r Ant & CM - v101 - Ag '96 - p18 [1-50]
Dundes, Alan - *The Walled-Up Wife*
    R&R Bk N - v12 - F '97 - p80 [51-250]
Dundes Renteln, Alison - *Folk Law*
    JPC - v30 - Sum '96 - p277 [51-250]
Dundy, Elaine - *The Dud Avocado*
    Nat R - v48 - D 23 '96 - p55 [51-250]
Dungan, Myles - *Irish Voices from the Great War*
    Choice - v34 - S '96 - p185+ [51-250]
Dungworth, Richard - *Windows for Beginners*
    c Ch BWatch - v6 - N '96 - p8 [51-250]
Dunham, Tracy - *The Long Trail Home*
    Roundup M - v4 - Ap '97 - p26 [251-500]
Dunitz, Robin J - *Street Gallery*
    J Am Cult - v19 - Sum '96 - p161 [51-250]
Dunker, Axel - *Den Pessimismus Organisieren*
    Ger Q - v69 - Sum '96 - p358+ [501+]
Dunkerley, Charlotte - *Working with Soft Furnishings*
    BWatch - v18 - F '97 - p2 [1-50]
    LJ - v122 - Ja '97 - p96 [51-250]
Dunkling, Leslie - *The Guinness Book of Names. 7th Ed.*
    r Names - v44 - Je '96 - p+ [501+]
Dunlap, Albert J - *Mean Business*
    BL - v93 - O 1 '96 - p311 [51-250]
    Bus W - O 28 '96 - p26 [51-250]
    BW - v26 - S 22 '96 - p11 [501+]
    Fortune - v134 - S 30 '96 - p200+ [501+]
    LATBR - O 13 '96 - p10 [501+]
    PW - v243 - S 2 '96 - p104 [51-250]
    Quad - v40 - D '96 - p72+ [501+]
    WSJ-MW - v77 - O 7 '96 - pA16 [501+]
Dunlap, Julie - *Birds in the Bushes (Illus. by Ralph L Ramstad)*
    c HB Guide - v8 - Spr '97 - p156 [51-250]
    c SLJ - v42 - O '96 - p130 [51-250]
Dunlap, Lauren - *And I, Francis*
    PW - v243 - S 2 '96 - p127 [51-250]
Dunlap, Patricia Riley - *Riding Astride*
    Choice - v34 - O '96 - p347 [51-250]
Dunlap, Susan - *Cop Out*
    BL - v93 - My 1 '97 - p1481 [51-250]
    KR - v65 - Mr 1 '97 - p336 [51-250]
    PW - v244 - F 17 '97 - p213 [51-250]
Dunlavy, Colleen A - *Politics and Industrialization*
    CEH - v29 - 2 '96 - p243+ [501+]
Dunlop, Beth - *Building a Dream*
    PW - v243 - S 2 '96 - p108 [51-250]
    Miami: Trends and Traditions
    PW - v244 - Ja 20 '97 - p390 [51-250]
Dunlop, Eileen - *The Ghost by the Sea*
    c BL - v93 - Ja '97 - p859 [251-500]
    c CCB-B - v50 - Mr '97 - p246 [51-250]
    c KR - v64 - D 1 '96 - p1735 [51-250]
    c SLJ - v43 - Mr '97 - p187 [51-250]
    Saints of Scotland (Illus. by Adrienne Salgado)
    c Sch Lib - v44 - Ag '96 - p110+ [51-250]
    Tales of St. Patrick
    c HB Guide - v7 - Fall '96 - p291 [1-50]
    Webster's Leap
    c RT - v50 - Mr '97 - p499 [51-250]
Dunlop, M H - *Sixty Miles from Contentment*
    AHR - v101 - D '96 - p1621+ [251-500]
Dunmore, Helen - *Fatal Error*
    y JB - v60 - D '96 - p278 [51-250]
    y Sch Lib - v44 - N '96 - p170 [51-250]
    A Spell of Winter
    Obs - S 15 '96 - p18* [51-250]
    Woman's J - O '96 - p12 [1-50]

    Talking to the Dead
    BL - v93 - My 1 '97 - p1477+ [51-250]
    KR - v65 - Ap 1 '97 - p483 [251-500]
    PW - v244 - My 5 '97 - p194 [51-250]
    Woman's J - Ag '96 - p11 [51-250]
Dunmore, Spencer - *Wings for Victory*
    Can Hist R - v77 - S '96 - p432+ [501+]
Dunn, Carola - *Murder on the Flying Scotsman*
    LJ - v122 - Ja '97 - p153 [1-50]
Dunn, Charles W - *The Conservative Tradition in America*
    Choice - v34 - F '97 - p1033 [51-250]
Dunn, Chris - *Drawing*
    y TES - S 13 '96 - pR10 [251-500]
    Drawing and Painting
    y TES - S 13 '96 - pR10 [251-500]
    Graphics
    y TES - S 13 '96 - pR10 [251-500]
    Photography
    y TES - S 13 '96 - pR10 [251-500]
    Sculpture and Ceramics
    y TES - S 13 '96 - pR10 [251-500]
    Textiles
    y TES - S 13 '96 - pR10 [251-500]
Dunn, David H - *Diplomacy at the Highest Level*
    Choice - v34 - Mr '97 - p1234 [51-250]
Dunn, Douglas - *The Oxford Book of Scottish Short Stories*
    Books - v10 - Je '96 - p24 [1-50]
Dunn, Francis M - *Tragedy's End*
    Choice - v34 - Ja '97 - p790 [51-250]
Dunn, James D G - *The Epistles to the Colossians and to Philemon*
    Am - v176 - Mr 8 '97 - p28+ [51-250]
    Jesus, Paul and the Law
    Rel Ed - v91 - Fall '96 - p602 [1-50]
    The Partings of the Ways between Christianity and Judaism and Their Significance for the Character of Christianity
    Rel Ed - v91 - Fall '96 - p603 [1-50]
Dunn, James R - *Conservative Environmentalism*
    LJ - v121 - D '96 - p137 [51-250]
Dunn, Jerry - *Idiom Savant*
    r PW - v244 - My 12 '97 - p72 [51-250]
Dunn, John, 1940- - *The History of Political Theory and Other Essays*
    APSR - v91 - Mr '97 - p168+ [501+]
    Choice - v34 - O '96 - p358 [51-250]
    TLS - Ag 30 '96 - p14+ [501+]
Dunn, John, 1949- - *The Spread of Islam*
    y HB Guide - v8 - Spr '97 - p164 [51-250]
Dunn, John M - *The Relocation of the North American Indian*
    Ch BWatch - v7 - Ja '97 - p6 [51-250]
Dunn, Kevin - *Pretexts of Authority*
    RES - v47 - N '96 - p570+ [501+]
Dunn, Michael - *Contemporary Painting in New Zealand*
    BWatch - v18 - F '97 - p5 [51-250]
Dunn, Nell - *My Silver Shoes*
    Obs - D 1 '96 - p16* [51-250]
    TLS - Jl 19 '96 - p23 [501+]
    Woman's J - Ag '96 - p11 [51-250]
Dunn, Pete J - *Franklin and Sterling Hill, New Jersey. Vols. 1-5, 1st-2nd Suppls.*
    RocksMiner - v72 - Ja '97 - p67 [501+]
Dunn, Stephen - *The Light of the Body*
    Obs - O 27 '96 - p16* [51-250]
    TLS - O 11 '96 - p27 [51-250]
Dunn, Stephen, 1939- - *Loosestrife*
    BL - v93 - S 1 '96 - p57 [51-250]
    PW - v243 - Jl 22 '96 - p236 [51-250]
Dunn, Timothy J - *The Militarization of the U.S.-Mexico Border 1978-1992*
    Choice - v34 - N '96 - p537 [51-250]
    Parameters - v26 - Win '96 - p157 [1-50]
Dunn, Walter S, Jr. - *The Soviet Economy and the Red Army 1930-1945*
    J Mil H - v60 - O '96 - p784+ [251-500]
    Russ Rev - v55 - O '96 - p719+ [251-500]
Dunn, William - *Boot: An L.A.P.D. Officer's Rookie Year*
    LJ - v121 - S 15 '96 - p81 [51-250]
    PW - v243 - S 2 '96 - p101 [51-250]
Dunnam, Maxie - *The Devil at Noonday*
    Ch Today - v40 - N 11 '96 - p56 [51-250]
Dunnavant, Keith - *Coach: The Life of Paul Bear Bryant*
    BL - v93 - S 15 '96 - p202 [51-250]
    CSM - v88 - N 20 '96 - p15 [251-500]
    y LJ - v121 - O 1 '96 - p87 [51-250]
Dunne, Catherine - *In the Beginning*
    Obs - Mr 23 '97 - p18* [51-250]

Dunne, John Gregory - *Monster: Living Off the Big Screen*
BL - v93 - N 15 '96 - p547 [51-250]
Econ - v342 - Mr 15 '97 - p12* [251-500]
Ent W - Mr 7 '97 - p58+ [501+]
KR - v64 - N 15 '96 - p1649+ [251-500]
LATBR - F 16 '97 - p4 [501+]
LJ - v122 - F 1 '97 - p80 [51-250]
NYRB - v44 - Mr 6 '97 - p38+ [501+]
NYTBR - v102 - Mr 2 '97 - p8+ [501+]
NYTLa - v146 - Mr 5 '97 - pC19 [501+]
PW - v243 - N 11 '96 - p61 [51-250]
Time - v149 - F 24 '97 - p73 [251-500]
Trib Bks - Ap 13 '97 - p3 [501+]
Dunne, Sean - *Time and the Island*
TLS - S 27 '96 - p12 [501+]
Dunnett, Dorothy - *To Lie with Lions*
CSM - v89 - D 18 '96 - p13 [251-500]
KR - v64 - My 1 '96 - p620 [251-500]
Woman's J - Ja '97 - p13 [1-50]
Dunnick, N Reed - *Textbook of Uroradiology. 2nd Ed.*
SciTech - v21 - Mr '97 - p58 [51-250]
Dunnigan, James F - *Digital Soldiers*
CSM - v89 - F 3 '97 - p12 [251-500]
KR - v64 - S 1 '96 - p1290+ [251-500]
LJ - v121 - O 1 '96 - p122 [51-250]
PW - v243 - S 2 '96 - p105 [51-250]
Dunning, Albert - *Intorno A Locatelli. Vols. 1-2*
Notes - v53 - Mr '97 - p796+ [501+]
Dunning, Jennifer - *Alvin Ailey: A Life in Dance*
Advocate - D 10 '96 - p76+ [501+]
y BL - v93 - S 15 '96 - p199 [251-500]
BW - v26 - N 3 '96 - p1+ [501+]
Choice - v34 - My '97 - p1510+ [51-250]
Dance - v71 - Ja '97 - p98 [51-250]
Econ - v342 - Mr 15 '97 - p14*+ [501+]
LATBR - N 17 '96 - p8+ [501+]
LJ - v121 - O 15 '96 - p60 [51-250]
Nat - v264 - F 24 '97 - p32+ [501+]
NY - v72 - N 25 '96 - p117 [51-250]
NYTBR - v101 - N 3 '96 - p13+ [501+]
NYTBR - v101 - D 8 '96 - p84 [1-50]
NYTLa - v146 - O 23 '96 - pC17 [501+]
Dunning-Davies, Jeremy - *Concise Thermodynamics*
Choice - v34 - Ap '97 - p1377 [51-250]
Nature - v386 - Ap 10 '97 - p568 [51-250]
Dunphy, Catherine - *Morgentaler: A Difficult Hero*
Mac - v110 - Ja 13 '97 - p67 [501+]
Quill & Q - v62 - N '96 - p34 [251-500]
Dunphy, Madeleine - *Here Is the Wetland (Illus. by Wayne McLoughlin)*
c Ch BWatch - v7 - Ja '97 - p2 [51-250]
c HB Guide - v8 - Spr '97 - p117 [51-250]
c SLJ - v42 - D '96 - p112 [51-250]
Dunphy, Richard - *The Making of Fianna Fail Power in Ireland 1923-1948*
Albion - v28 - '96 - p741+ [501+]
Dunrea, Olivier - *The Tale of Hilda Louise (Illus. by Olivier Dunrea)*
c CBRS - v25 - Ja '97 - p50 [51-250]
c HB Guide - v8 - Spr '97 - p25 [51-250]
c PW - v243 - S 2 '96 - p130 [51-250]
c SLJ - v42 - S '96 - p177 [51-250]
Dunsby, Jonathan - *Performing Music*
Notes - v53 - S '96 - p94+ [501+]
Dunstan, David - *Victorian Icon*
Aust Bk R - Jl '96 - p11+ [501+]
Dunster, Julian - *Dictionary of Natural Resource Management*
r Choice - v34 - N '96 - p427 [51-250]
Duntze, Dorothee - *The Twelve Days of Christmas*
c Bks Keeps - N '96 - p20 [1-50]
Dupasquier, Philippe - *My Busy Day (Illus. by Philippe Dupasquier)*
c Bks Keeps - Ja '97 - p18 [51-250]
c PW - v244 - Mr 24 '97 - p85 [251-500]
c TES - N 29 '96 - p13* [51-250]
Duper, Linda Leeb - *160 Ways to Help the World*
y VOYA - v19 - O '96 - p228 [51-250]
Duplacey, James - *Hockey Superstars: Amazing Forwards*
c Emerg Lib - v24 - Mr '97 - p26 [1-50]
c HB Guide - v8 - Spr '97 - p143 [251-250]
c PW - v243 - O 14 '96 - p85 [1-50]
Hockey Superstars: Great Goalies
c HB Guide - v8 - Spr '97 - p143 [251-250]
c PW - v243 - O 14 '96 - p85 [1-50]
Hockey Superstars: Top Rookies
c HB Guide - v8 - Spr '97 - p143 [251-250]
c PW - v243 - O 14 '96 - p85 [1-50]
Leafs vs. Canadiens
c Emerg Lib - v24 - Mr '97 - p26 [1-50]

Dupont, Elaine - *Guide Des Aines. 3rd Ed.*
J Gov Info - v23 - S '96 - p637 [51-250]
Dupont, Louis - *Development Planning*
JEL - v35 - Mr '97 - p276+ [51-250]
DuPont, Robert L - *The Selfish Brain*
Choice - v34 - Mr '97 - p1192+ [51-250]
Dupre, Louis - *Passage to Modernity*
CPR - v16 - Ag '96 - p253+ [51-250]
JAAR - v65 - Spr '97 - p218+ [501+]
Dupree, Marguerite W - *Family Structure in the Staffordshire Potteries 1840-1880*
AHR - v101 - D '96 - p1540+ [501+]
Albion - v28 - Fall '96 - p511+ [501+]
JIH - v27 - Win '97 - p513+ [501+]
J Soc H - v30 - Spr '97 - p776+ [501+]
DuPuis, E Melanie - *Creating the Countryside*
AJS - v102 - N '96 - p925+ [501+]
Dupuy, Edward J - *Autobiography of Walker Percy*
Biography - v19 - Fall '96 - p429 [1-50]
Duque Miyar, Evelio - *Mis Memorias*
BL - v93 - Ap 1 '97 - p1284 [1-50]
Duquennoy, Jacques - *The Ghosts' Trip to Loch Ness (Illus. by Jacques Duquennoy)*
c CCB-B - v50 - O '96 - p56 [51-250]
c HB Guide - v8 - Spr '97 - p25 [51-250]
c SLJ - v42 - O '96 - p92 [51-250]
Duquesne, Jacques - *Jesus: An Unconventional Biography*
BL - v93 - F 15 '97 - p975 [51-250]
LJ - v122 - F 1 '97 - p86 [51-250]
Duquette, Georges - *Second Language Practice*
MLJ - v80 - Fall '96 - p398 [251-500]
Duquin, Lorene Hanley - *They Called Her the Baroness*
RR - v56 - Ja '97 - p107 [51-250]
Dural, Teoman - *A New System of Philosophy-Science from the Biological Standpoint*
SciTech - v20 - D '96 - p30 [51-250]
Duran, Eduardo - *Native American Postcolonial Psychology*
Cont Ed - v68 - Fall '96 - p84+ [501+]
Duran, Victor Manuel - *A Marxist Reading of Fuentes, Vargas Llosa and Puig*
MLR - v91 - Jl '96 - p772+ [251-500]
Durand, Jorge - *Miracles on the Border*
HAHR - v77 - F '97 - p94+ [251-500]
Durano, Leopoldo - *Graham Greene: Friend and Brother*
AS - v66 - Win '97 - p128+ [501+]
Durant, Alan - *Angus Rides the Goods Train (Illus. by Chris Riddell)*
c Bks Keeps - Ja '97 - p20 [51-250]
c JB - v60 - D '96 - p230 [251-500]
c Sch Lib - v45 - F '97 - p18 [51-250]
Big Fish, Little Fish
c Bks Keeps - Jl '96 - p6 [51-250]
Creepe Hall
c Magpies - v11 - My '96 - p53 [1-50]
The Good Book
c Bks Keeps - v100 - S '96 - p13 [51-250]
Mouse Party (Illus. by Sue Heap)
c Magpies - v11 - Jl '96 - p45 [1-50]
c RT - v50 - N '96 - p252 [51-250]
Spider McDrew (Illus. by Martin Chatterton)
c Sch Lib - v44 - Ag '96 - p105 [51-250]
Durant, David N - *Life in the Country House*
r CR - v269 - D '96 - p335 [51-250]
r Obs - S 1 '96 - p15* [501+]
Duras, Marguerite - *C'Est Tout*
FR - v70 - F '97 - p496+ [501+]
Durban Women's Bibliography Group - *South African Women*
r Choice - v34 - N '96 - p436 [51-250]
Durbin, Kathie - *Tree Huggers*
Choice - v34 - Ap '97 - p1365 [51-250]
PW - v243 - S 16 '96 - p64 [51-250]
Durbin, William - *The Broken Blade*
c BL - v93 - Mr 1 '97 - p1164 [51-250]
c CCB-B - v50 - F '97 - p203+ [51-250]
c KR - v64 - N 15 '96 - p1668 [51-250]
c PW - v243 - O 30 '96 - p68 [51-250]
c SLJ - v43 - F '97 - p103 [51-250]
Durcan, Paul - *Christmas Day*
PW - v243 - N 25 '96 - p71 [51-250]
Durch, William J - *UN Peacekeeping, American Politics, and the Uncivil Wars of the 1990s*
For Aff - v76 - My '97 - p125 [51-250]
LJ - v122 - Ag 15 '97 - p101 [51-250]
Durczak, Joanna - *Treading Softly, Speaking Low*
ASInt - v34 - O '96 - p101+ [501+]
Durham, Charles W - *Spokesperson Milton*
MLR - v91 - O '96 - p973+ [501+]
Ren Q - v49 - Win '96 - p888+ [501+]

Durham, Jennifer L - *Crime in America*
r ARBA - v28 - '97 - p228 [51-250]
r Choice - v34 - My '97 - p1474 [51-250]
Durier, Roland - *Recent Developments in Optimization*
JEL - v34 - D '96 - p2020+ [51-250]
Durig, Alexander - *Autism and the Crisis of Meaning*
CS - v26 - Mr '97 - p233+ [501+]
R&R Bk N - v12 - F '97 - p96 [51-250]
During, Simon - *The Cultural Studies Reader*
JPC - v29 - Spr '96 - p234 [251-500]
Foucault and Literature
MLR - v91 - O '96 - p946+ [501+]
Patrick White
Quad - v40 - Jl '96 - p88+ [501+]
WLT - v70 - Aut '96 - p1025 [501+]
Durkan, Michael J - *Seamus Heaney: A Reference Guide*
r ARBA - v28 - '97 - p461 [51-250]
r Choice - v34 - My '97 - p1474 [51-250]
Durkee, Noura - *The Animals of Paradise (Illus. by Simon Trethewey)*
c Bks Keeps - Mr '97 - p21 [51-250]
c TES - D 6 '96 - p16* [501+]
Durkheim, Emile - *The Elementary Forms of Religious Life*
AJS - v102 - S '96 - p585+ [501+]
Durnbaugh, Donald F - *Fruit of the Vine*
BL - v93 - S 1 '96 - p38 [51-250]
Durney, Lawrence J - *Trouble in Your Tank?. 3rd Ed.*
SciTech - v20 - D '96 - p86 [1-50]
Durnil, Gordon K - *The Making of a Conservative Environmentalist*
Env - v38 - N '96 - p30 [51-250]
Workbook - v21 - Fall '96 - p141+ [501+]
Durning, Alan Thein - *This Place on Earth*
BL - v93 - O 1 '96 - p294 [51-250]
Choice - v34 - My '97 - p1583 [51-250]
KR - v64 - Ag 15 '96 - p1204+ [251-500]
LJ - v121 - O 15 '96 - p88 [51-250]
Utne R - N '96 - p89 [51-250]
Durrant, A V - *Vectors in Physics and Engineering*
Choice - v34 - My '97 - p1529 [51-250]
Durrant, Lynda - *Echohawk*
c BL - v93 - S 1 '96 - p118 [51-250]
y CCB-B - v50 - O '96 - p56 [51-250]
c HB Guide - v8 - Spr '97 - p65 [51-250]
c PW - v243 - S 9 '96 - p84 [51-250]
c SLJ - v42 - S '96 - p201 [51-250]
Durrant, Michael - *Creative Strategies for School Problems*
Soc Ser R - v70 - S '96 - p502 [51-250]
Durrell, Gerald - *The Best of Gerald Durrell*
New Sci - v152 - N 16 '96 - p56 [51-250]
Keeper (Illus. by Keith West)
c SB - v33 - Mr '97 - p57 [51-250]
Rosy Is My Relative (Glover). Audio Version
y Kliatt - v30 - N '96 - p51 [51-250]
A Zoo in My Luggage (Davenport). Audio Version
y Kliatt - v31 - My '97 - p49 [51-250]
Durrell, Lawrence - *Prospero's Cell*
LJ - v121 - D '96 - p154 [51-250]
Durrenberger, E Paul - *It's All Politics*
Am Ethnol - v23 - Ag '96 - p643+ [501+]
Durrett, Deanne - *Norman Rockwell*
c HB Guide - v8 - Spr '97 - p137 [51-250]
y SLJ - v43 - Mr '97 - p199 [51-250]
Durrett, Richard - *Stochastic Calculus*
SciTech - v20 - N '96 - p13 [51-250]
Durst, Douglas - *Aboriginal Self-Government and Social Services: Final Report*
J Gov Info - v23 - S '96 - p610 [51-250]
Durstin, Larry - *Still Looking*
PW - v244 - Mr 10 '97 - p52 [51-250]
Durston, Christopher - *The Culture of English Puritanism 1560-1700*
HRNB - v25 - Fall '96 - p19 [251-500]
James I
HT - v46 - D '96 - p56 [251-500]
Dusenbery, David B - *Life at Small Scale*
Choice - v34 - F '97 - p986 [51-250]
Nature - v386 - Mr 6 '97 - p36 [501+]
New Sci - v152 - N 30 '96 - p46 [251-500]
y SB - v32 - N '96 - p236 [51-250]
y SciTech - v20 - N '96 - p34 [51-250]
Dusinberre, Juliet - *Shakespeare and the Nature of Women. 2nd Ed.*
R&R Bk N - v11 - N '96 - p69 [51-250]
Dusinberre, William - *Them Dark Days*
Choice - v34 - S '96 - p192 [51-250]
HRNB - v25 - Fall '96 - p7 [251-500]
JEH - v56 - S '96 - p739+ [501+]

Dusky, Lorraine - *Still Unequal*
y BL - v93 - N 1 '96 - p463+ [51-250]
   BW - v26 - N 24 '96 - p4+ [501+]
   KR - v64 - S 15 '96 - p1369 [251-500]
   LJ - v121 - N 1 '96 - p91 [51-250]
   Ms - v7 - N '96 - p80 [501+]
   Nat - v264 - Ja 6 '97 - p31+ [501+]
   PW - v243 - S 16 '96 - p60 [51-250]

Dussling, Jennifer - *Creep Show (Illus. by Jeff Spackman)*
c SLJ - v42 - Ag '96 - p121 [51-250]
Stars (Illus. by Mavis Smith)
c SLJ - v42 - Ag '96 - p134 [51-250]

Dusty, Slim - *Another Day, Another Town*
   Aust Bk R - D '96 - p29 [501+]

Dusty Dog Reviews
p Sm Pr R - v28 - N '96 - p13 [51-250]

Dutcher, Jim - *The Sawtooth Wolves (Illus. by Jim Dutcher)*
y BL - v93 - N 15 '96 - p557 [251-500]
   BWatch - v17 - N '96 - p7 [51-250]
   LJ - v121 - D '96 - p137+ [51-250]
y SB - v33 - Mr '97 - p45+ [51-250]

Dutcher-Walls, Patricia - *Narrative Art, Political Rhetoric*
   Rel St Rev - v23 - Ap '97 - p165 [51-250]

DuTemple, Lesley A - *Tigers (Illus. by Lynn M Stone)*
c HB Guide - v7 - Fall '96 - p344 [51-250]
c SLJ - v42 - S '96 - p196 [51-250]
Whales
c BL - v92 - Ag '96 - p1902 [51-250]
c HB Guide - v7 - Fall '96 - p344 [51-250]

Duteurtre, Benoit - *Gaite Parisienne*
   WLT - v71 - Win '97 - p103 [501+]
Requiem Pour Une Avant-Garde
   WLT - v70 - Sum '96 - p659+ [501+]

Du Toit, P Van Der P - *State Building and Democracy in Southern Africa*
   APSR - v90 - D '96 - p936 [501+]

Dutta, M - *Asia-Pacific Economic Community?*
   JEL - v34 - S '96 - p1426 [51-250]
Asia-Pacific Economies
   JEL - v34 - S '96 - p1426 [51-250]
Asian Economic Regimes. Pts. A-B
   JEL - v35 - Mr '97 - p271 [51-250]

Dutton, David - *Anthony Eden: A Life and Reputation*
   BL - v93 - Ja '97 - p812 [51-250]
   HT - v46 - O '96 - p57+ [1-50]
   Obs - D 15 '96 - p17* [501+]
   PW - v243 - N 18 '96 - p53 [51-250]
   Spec - v277 - D 14 '96 - p71+ [501+]
   TLS - N 8 '96 - p23 [501+]

Dutton, G F - *Harvesting the Edge*
   Spec - v277 - D 7 '96 - p55 [51-250]

Dutton, Geoffrey - *A Rare Bird*
   Aust Bk R - Ag '96 - p20+ [501+]

Dutton, Harlon L - *Racial Healing*
   PW - v243 - S 9 '96 - p81 [1-50]

Dutton, Kenneth R - *The Perfectible Body*
   Art J - v55 - Win '96 - p88+ [501+]

Dutton, Paul Edward - *The Politics of Dreaming in the Carolingian Empire*
   EHR - v112 - F '97 - p156+ [501+]
   Specu - v71 - O '96 - p943+ [501+]

Dutton, Richard - *Ben Jonson, Authority, Criticism*
   Choice - v34 - O '96 - p277 [51-250]
   TLS - Ag 2 '96 - p32 [51-250]

Dutton, Thomas A - *Reconstructing Architecture*
   Choice - v34 - Mr '97 - p1153 [51-250]
   LJ - v121 - S 15 '96 - p64 [51-250]

Dutu, Alexandra - *Sud-Estul European In Vremea*
   EHR - v111 - N '96 - p1307+ [251-500]

Duus, Peter - *The Abacus and the Sword*
   AAPSS-A - v548 - N '96 - p219+ [501+]
   CS - v25 - N '96 - p772+ [501+]
   J Mil H - v61 - Ja '97 - p172+ [251-500]
   TLS - O 25 '96 - p12 [501+]
The Japanese Wartime Empire 1931-1945
   Choice - v34 - D '96 - p665 [51-250]
   JEL - v34 - D '96 - p2103 [51-250]

Duval, Anjela - *Gant Ar Mareou-Bloaz*
   FR - v70 - D '96 - p345+ [501+]

Duve, Thierry De - *Jeff Wall*
   LJ - v121 - O 15 '96 - p55 [51-250]
Kant after Duchamp
   TLS - O 25 '96 - p21 [501+]

Duvignaud, Jean - *Perec Ou La Cicatrice*
   FR - v70 - F '97 - p478+ [501+]

Duxbury, Alyn C - *An Introduction to the World's Oceans. 5th Ed.*
   R&R Bk N - v12 - F '97 - p29 [51-250]

Duy, Lam - *Chuyen Moi Chon Loc*
   BL - v93 - S 1 '96 - p70 [51-250]

Duyen Anh - *Nhung Dua Tre Con My Ham Hiu*
   BL - v93 - S 1 '96 - p70 [51-250]

Duyff, Roberta Larson - *American Dietetic Association's Complete Food and Nutrition Guide*
r BL - v93 - F 1 '97 - p959 [1-50]
The American Dietetic Association's Complete Food and Nutrition Guide
r LJ - v121 - O 15 '96 - p50 [51-250]

Duysters, Geert - *The Dynamics of Technical Innovation*
   Choice - v34 - D '96 - p654 [51-250]
   JEL - v34 - D '96 - p2085+ [51-250]
   R&R Bk N - v11 - N '96 - p25 [51-250]

Duyvendak, Jan Willem - *The Power of Politics*
   CS - v25 - N '96 - p764+ [501+]
   J Pol - v58 - Ag '96 - p922+ [501+]

Dwelle, Jacqueline - *Your First Horse*
y BL - v93 - Mr 1 '97 - p1100 [51-250]
   LJ - v122 - Mr 15 '97 - p80 [51-250]

Dwivedi, O P - *Environmental Policies in the Third World*
   Env - v38 - O '96 - p26 [51-250]

Dworin, Lawrence - *Renovating and Restyling Vintage Homes*
   BL - v93 - S 15 '96 - p194 [51-250]

Dwork, Deborah - *Auschwitz 1270 to the Present*
   BW - v26 - Ag 4 '96 - p3+ [501+]
   Choice - v34 - Mr '97 - p1219 [51-250]
   KR - v64 - My 1 '96 - p659 [251-500]
   Skeptic - v4 - 4 '96 - p100+ [501+]
Auschwitz: 1270 to the Present
   Spec - v277 - N 16 '96 - p46 [1-50]
Auschwitz 1270 to the Present
   TLS - Ja 31 '97 - p4+ [501+]
   WSJ-MW - v78 - D 31 '96 - p5 [501+]

Dworkin, Andrea - *Life and Death*
   BL - v93 - F 15 '97 - p978+ [51-250]
   KR - v65 - Ja 1 '97 - p32 [251-500]
   LATBR - Mr 16 '97 - p9 [501+]
   LJ - v122 - Ja '97 - p127 [51-250]
   Ms - v7 - Mr '97 - p82 [251-500]
   PW - v243 - D 30 '96 - p46 [51-250]

Dworkin, James Paul - *Vocal Pathologies*
   SciTech - v21 - Mr '97 - p62 [51-250]

Dworkin, R M - *Freedom's Law*
   Choice - v34 - O '96 - p358 [51-250]
   CLR - v97 - Ja '97 - p133+ [51-250]
   IPQ - v37 - Je '97 - p232+ [501+]
   JMCQ - v73 - Win '96 - p999+ [501+]
   PW - v243 - N 4 '96 - p44 [51-250]
   TLS - D 6 '96 - p8 [501+]
Life's Dominion
   Cons - v17 - Aut '96 - p35+ [501+]

Dworkin, Ronald William - *The Rise of the Imperial Self*
   Comw - v123 - S 13 '96 - p38+ [501+]

Dworkin, Susan - *The Book of Candy*
   BW - v27 - Ja 19 '97 - p8 [251-500]
   Ent W - O 25 '96 - p109 [51-250]
   LJ - v121 - S 15 '96 - p95 [51-250]
   Ms - v7 - N '96 - p82 [1-50]
   PW - v243 - S 2 '96 - p112 [51-250]

Dwyer, Jim - *Earth Works*
yr ARBA - v28 - '97 - p646 [51-250]
r BL - v93 - Ja '97 - p769 [1-50]
r Choice - v34 - S '96 - p95 [51-250]
r Emerg Lib - v23 - My '96 - p42 [1-50]
r JOYS - v10 - Fall '96 - p100 [251-500]
r SLMQ - v24 - Sum '96 - p221 [51-250]

Dwyer, Kathleen M - *What Do You Mean I Have Attention Deficit Disorder? (Illus. by Gregg A Flory)*
c BL - v92 - Ag '96 - p1898 [51-250]
c CCB-B - v50 - S '96 - p10 [51-250]
c HB Guide - v7 - Fall '96 - p347 [51-250]
c SLJ - v42 - Ag '96 - p151 [51-250]

Dwyer, Mindy - *Coyote in Love (Illus. by Mindy Dwyer)*
c PW - v244 - Ap 21 '97 - p70 [51-250]

Dwyer, Philip G - *Charles-Maurice De Talleyrand 1754-1838*
r ARBA - v28 - '97 - p204 [51-250]

Dyal, Donald H - *Historical Dictionary of the Spanish American War*
r Choice - v34 - D '96 - p589 [51-250]
r J Mil H - v61 - Ja '97 - p171+ [251-500]
r Parameters - v26 - Aut '96 - p152+ [501+]

Dybikowski, James - *On Burning Ground*
   Dialogue - v35 - Sum '96 - p639+ [501+]

Dyck, Cornelius J - *Spiritual Life in Anabaptism*
   Six Ct J - v27 - Win '96 - p1148+ [501+]

Dyck, Elmer - *The Act of Bible Reading*
   Rel St Rev - v23 - Ap '97 - p177 [51-250]

Dyck, Harvey L - *The Pacifist Impulse in Historical Perspective*
   Choice - v34 - D '96 - p664 [51-250]
   R&R Bk N - v11 - N '96 - p51 [51-250]
   TLS - Mr 28 '97 - p26 [501+]

Dyck, Ian - *The Sjovold Site*
   Am Ant - v61 - O '96 - p809+ [501+]

Dycus, Stephen - *National Defense and the Environment*
   Choice - v34 - O '96 - p360 [51-250]

Dye, Daniel - *Short Tails and Treats from Three Dog Bakery*
   BL - v93 - N 15 '96 - p553 [51-250]

Dye, Ira - *The Fatal Cruise of the Argus*
   Beav - v76 - D '96 - p44 [501+]

Dyer, Alan - *Decline and Growth in English Towns 1400-1640*
   JEL - v34 - D '96 - p2095 [51-250]

Dyer, Carolyn Stewart - *Rediscovering Nancy Drew*
   NWSA Jnl - v8 - Fall '96 - p144+ [501+]

Dyer, Christopher - *Everyday Life in Medieval England*
   Historian - v59 - Fall '96 - p185+ [251-500]

Dyer, Geoff - *But Beautiful*
   NY - v72 - S 23 '96 - p95 [51-250]
Out of Sheer Rage
   TLS - Mr 28 '97 - p32 [501+]

Dyer, Jane - *Animal Crackers (Illus. by Jane Dyer)*
c BL - v93 - Ap 1 '97 - p1296 [1-50]
c Ch BWatch - v6 - My '96 - p2 [1-50]
c HB Guide - v7 - Fall '96 - p364+ [1-50]
c LA - v73 - D '96 - p618+ [51-250]
c PW - v243 - N 4 '96 - p48 [1-50]
c RT - v50 - Ap '97 - p592 [51-250]

Dyer, Wayne W - *Manifest Your Destiny*
   BL - v93 - Mr 1 '97 - p1066 [51-250]
   LJ - v122 - My 1 '97 - p109 [51-250]
   PW - v244 - Mr 24 '97 - p71 [51-250]

Dygard, Thomas J - *Infield Hit*
c RT - v50 - N '96 - p253 [51-250]
Running Wild
y BL - v92 - Ag '96 - p1894 [51-250]
y HB Guide - v8 - Spr '97 - p79 [51-250]
c KR - v64 - S 15 '96 - p1398 [51-250]
y SLJ - v42 - S '96 - p224+ [51-250]

Dyhouse, Carol - *No Distinction of Sex?*
   Albion - v28 - '96 - p720+ [501+]

Dyke, Phil - *Modelling Marine Processes*
   SciTech - v20 - S '96 - p19 [51-250]

Dyker, David A - *Investment Opportunities in Russia and the CIS*
   JEL - v34 - S '96 - p1492+ [51-250]

Dykewomon, Elana - *Beyond the Pale*
   PW - v244 - Ap 21 '97 - p63 [51-250]

Dyman, Jenni - *Lurking Feminism*
   R&R Bk N - v11 - N '96 - p73 [51-250]

The Dynamic Human. Electronic Media Version
   Choice - v34 - O '96 - p313 [51-250]
r SciTech - v20 - N '96 - p30 [51-250]

Dysart, Norman - *Like Whispers in the Wind*
   Roundup M - v4 - D '96 - p25+ [501+]

Dyson, Freeman - *From Eros to Gaia*
   Reason - v28 - D '96 - p43 [51-250]
Imagined Worlds
   BL - v93 - Mr 15 '97 - p1212 [51-250]
   BW - v27 - Ap 13 '97 - p5 [501+]
   KR - v65 - F 1 '97 - p189 [251-500]
   LJ - v122 - Ap 15 '97 - p112 [51-250]
   PW - v244 - F 24 '97 - p73 [51-250]
Infinite in All Directions
   PSR - v25 - '96 - p273+ [501+]
Selected Papers of Freeman Dyson. Vol. 5
   Sci - v274 - O 25 '96 - p523 [1-50]

Dyson, George B - *Darwin among the Machines*
   LJ - v122 - My 1 '97 - p130+ [51-250]

Dyson, Michael Eric - *Making Malcolm*
   Bl S - v26 - Fall '96 - p84+ [501+]
   J Bl St - v27 - S '96 - p118+ [501+]
Race Rules
   BW - v26 - N 24 '96 - p8+ [501+]
   BWatch - v17 - D '96 - p5 [51-250]
   KR - v64 - S 1 '96 - p1291 [251-500]
   LJ - v121 - O 1 '96 - p108 [51-250]
   NYTBR - v101 - N 10 '96 - p56+ [51-250]
Race Rules (Dyson). Audio Version
   BL - v93 - My 15 '97 - p1596 [51-250]

Dyzenhaus, David - *Law and Morality*
   R&R Bk N - v12 - F '97 - p62 [51-250]

Dzielska, Maria - *Hypatia of Alexandria*
   Isis - v87 - S '96 - p534+ [501+]
   Rel St Rev - v23 - Ap '97 - p189+ [51-250]

E

Eade, Deborah - *The Oxfam Handbook of Development and Relief. Vols. 1-2*
  r Choice - v34 - S '96 - p95 [51-250]
Eager, Bill - *Using the World Wide Web*
  TES - O 18 '96 - p41U [51-250]
Eagle, Chester - *House of Music*
  Aust Bk R - O '96 - p66 [51-250]
Eagle, Dawn - *Growing Miniature and Patio Roses*
  BL - v93 - O 1 '96 - p314 [51-250]
Eagle, Kathleen - *The Night Remembers*
  KR - v65 - My 1 '97 - p660+ [251-500]
  PW - v244 - My 12 '97 - p60 [51-250]
  Sunrise Song
  LJ - v122 - Ja '97 - p51 [1-50]
Eagle, Selwyn - *Information Sources in Environmental Protection*
  r Choice - v34 - My '97 - p1475+ [51-250]
Eagles, Munroe - *The Almanac of Canadian Politics. 2nd Ed.*
  r Choice - v34 - O '96 - p247 [51-250]
Eagleton, Terry - *Heathcliff and the Great Hunger*
  Col Lit - v23 - O '96 - p178+ [501+]
  The Illusions of Postmodernism
  Choice - v34 - Mr '97 - p1174 [51-250]
  TLS - Mr 28 '97 - p25 [501+]
Eagle Walking Turtle - *Full Moon Stories (Illus. by Eagle Walking Turtle)*
  c KR - v65 - My 1 '97 - p719 [51-250]
Eaker-Rich, Deborah - *Caring in an Unjust World*
  R&R Bk N - v12 - F '97 - p66 [51-250]
Eakin, Paul John - *Touching the World*
  CLS - v33 - 1 '96 - p132+ [501+]
Eales, Anne Bruner - *Army Wives on the American Frontier*
  LJ - v122 - Ja '97 - p119 [51-250]
Eames, Anne - *Christmas Elopement*
  LJ - v121 - N 15 '96 - p48 [51-250]
Eamon, William - *Science and the Secrets of Nature*
  AHR - v101 - D '96 - p1516+ [501+]
  Bks & Cult - v2 - Mr '96 - p30+ [251-500]
  EHR - v112 - F '97 - p193+ [501+]
  JMH - v69 - Mr '97 - p121+ [501+]
  Nature - v385 - Ja 30 '97 - p408 [51-250]
Earl, James W - *Thinking about Beowulf*
  MLR - v92 - Ja '97 - p160+ [501+]
  MP - v94 - N '96 - p207+ [501+]
Earle, Carville - *Concepts in Human Geography*
  Choice - v34 - O '96 - p334 [51-250]
Earle, Robert L - *Identities in North America*
  HAHR - v77 - F '97 - p162+ [251-500]
Earle, Sylvia - *Sea Change*
  Bloom Rev - v16 - N '96 - p28 [251-500]
  Obs - D 1 '96 - p17* [1-50]
Earley, Pete - *Circumstantial Evidence*
  y Kliatt - v30 - N '96 - p26 [51-250]
  Confessions of a Spy
  NS - v126 - Mr 14 '97 - p48 [501+]
  NYTLa - v146 - F 24 '97 - pC16 [501+]
  Spec - v278 - Mr 1 '97 - p34+ [501+]
Earley, Tony - *Here We Are in Paradise*
  SFR - v22 - Ja '97 - p48 [1-50]
  Trib Bks - Ap 27 '97 - p8 [1-50]
Earls, Irene - *Baroque Art*
  r ARBA - v27 - '96 - p366+ [251-500]
  r BL - v93 - D 15 '96 - p745+ [251-500]
  r Choice - v34 - My '97 - p1474 [51-250]
  r LJ - v121 - S 15 '96 - p54 [51-250]
  r R&R Bk N - v12 - F '97 - p71 [51-250]
Earls, Nick - *After January*
  y Kliatt - v31 - Mr '97 - p8 [51-250]
  y Magpies - v11 - My '96 - p47 [251-500]

Zigzag Street
  Aust Bk R - N '96 - p52+ [501+]
Early, Kevin E - *Drug Treatment behind Bars*
  R&R Bk N - v11 - D '96 - p45 [51-250]
Early, Margaret - *Robin Hood (Illus. by Margaret Early)*
  c AB - v98 - N 18 '96 - p1726 [51-250]
  c HB Guide - v8 - Spr '97 - p101 [51-250]
  c KR - v64 - My 1 '96 - p687 [51-250]
  c Magpies - v11 - Jl '96 - p29+ [51-250]
  c SLJ - v42 - Ag '96 - p134 [51-250]
Early, William F - *Contractor and Client Relations to Assure Process Safety*
  SciTech - v21 - Mr '97 - p95 [51-250]
Early Imprints in New Zealand Libraries
  r BC - v45 - Win '96 - p573+ [501+]
  r Lib - v19 - Mr '97 - p88+ [501+]
Earman, John - *Bangs, Crunches, Whimpers and Shrieks*
  IPQ - v36 - D '96 - p494+ [501+]
Earnshaw, Rae - *Digital Media and Electronic Publishing*
  New Sci - v152 - N 30 '96 - p48 [51-250]
Earp, Lawrence - *Guillaume De Machaut: A Guide to Research*
  r Notes - v53 - Mr '97 - p785+ [501+]
EARSeL Symposium on Progress in Environmental Remote Sensing Research and Applications (15th: 1995: Basel, Switzerland) - *Progress in Environmental Remote Sensing Research and Applications*
  SciTech - v20 - D '96 - p2 [51-250]
Earth Summit: The NGO Archives. Electronic Media Version
  WorldV - v12 - O '96 - p23 [251-500]
Earthquakes and the Built Environment Index: 1984-July 1995. Electronic Media Version
  r ARBA - v28 - '97 - p634+ [51-250]
Earthquakes and Volcanoes
  c New Sci - v153 - Ja 25 '97 - p45 [51-250]
Easley, Barbara P - *Obituaries of Benton County, Arkansas. Vol. 6*
  r EGH - v50 - N '96 - p162 [51-250]
Easley, Maryann - *I Am the Ice Worm*
  c CBRS - v25 - D '96 - p44+ [51-250]
  c Ch BWatch - v6 - S '96 - p4 [51-250]
  c HB Guide - v8 - Spr '97 - p65 [51-250]
  c SLJ - v42 - N '96 - p104 [51-250]
Easson, William M - *The Management of the Severely Disturbed Adolescent*
  SciTech - v20 - N '96 - p54 [51-250]
East, Charles - *Distant Friends and Intimate Strangers*
  NYTBR - v101 - O 27 '96 - p39 [51-250]
  PW - v243 - S 2 '96 - p118 [51-250]
East, Harry - *The Liberated Enduser*
  LR - v45 - 7 '96 - p59+ [251-500]
East Asia Analytical Unit - *Overseas Chinese Business Networks in Asia*
  JIB - v27 - 4 '96 - p811+ [501+]
Easterbrook, Gregg - *A Moment on the Earth*
  New Sci - v153 - F 15 '97 - p44 [51-250]
  NS - v125 - S 6 '96 - p45 [501+]
  TLS - F 21 '97 - p11 [501+]
Easterlin, Nancy - *Wordsworth and the Question of Romantic Religion*
  Choice - v34 - Ja '97 - p793 [51-250]
Easterlin, Richard A - *Growth Triumphant*
  Choice - v34 - Ap '97 - p1386 [51-250]
  JEL - v35 - Mr '97 - p282 [51-250]
Easterly, William - *Public Sector Deficits and Macroeconomic Performance*
  JEL - v35 - Mr '97 - p175+ [501+]

Easterman, Daniel - *The Final Judgement*
  KR - v64 - S 1 '96 - p1254+ [251-500]
  LJ - v121 - S 15 '96 - p95 [51-250]
  PW - v243 - O 7 '96 - p60 [51-250]
Eastern Europe and the Commonwealth of Independent States 1997
  r R&R Bk N - v12 - F '97 - p16 [51-250]
Eastlake, William - *Lyric of the Circle Heart*
  PW - v243 - O 7 '96 - p68 [1-50]
Eastland, Terry - *Benchmarks: Great Constitutional Controversies in the Supreme Court*
  Am - v175 - Ag 17 '96 - p28+ [501+]
  Bks & Cult - v2 - N '96 - p27+ [501+]
  Ending Affirmative Action
  y Kliatt - v31 - My '97 - p28 [51-250]
  NY - v72 - N 25 '96 - p106+ [501+]
  NYTBR - v102 - Ap 13 '97 - p32 [1-50]
Eastman, Jacqueline Fisher - *Ludwig Bemelmans*
  Choice - v34 - Mr '97 - p1161 [51-250]
Eastman, John - *Birds of Forest, Yard, and Thicket*
  y BL - v93 - Mr 1 '97 - p1099 [51-250]
Eastman, Richard - *Tangled Tassels*
  PW - v243 - D 30 '96 - p60 [1-50]
Eastman, Yvette - *Dearest Wilding*
  Sew R - v104 - O '96 - pR86+ [501+]
Easton, Alison - *The Making of the Hawthorne Subject*
  AL - v69 - Mr '97 - p214+ [251-500]
Easton, Carol - *No Intermissions*
  Choice - v34 - O '96 - p291 [51-250]
  NYTBR - v101 - D 8 '96 - p89+ [1-50]
Easton, Susan M - *The Problem with Pornography*
  Dialogue - v35 - Spr '96 - p424+ [501+]
Easton, Thomas A - *Taking Sides. 2nd Ed.*
  y SB - v33 - Mr '97 - p42 [51-250]
Eastwood, David - *Governing Rural England*
  EHR - v111 - N '96 - p1306+ [251-500]
Easwaran, Eknath - *The Monkey and the Mango (Illus. by Ilka Jerabek)*
  c HB Guide - v7 - Fall '96 - p254 [51-250]
  c SLJ - v42 - Ag '96 - p134 [51-250]
Eaton, Deborah - *No One Told the Aardvark (Illus. by Jim Spence)*
  c KR - v65 - F 1 '97 - p221 [51-250]
Eaton, Jill - *MinnowKnits: Uncommon Clothes to Knit for Kids*
  LJ - v121 - D '96 - p91 [51-250]
Eaton, Richard M - *The Rise of Islam and the Bengal Frontier 1204-1760*
  JAAR - v64 - Fall '96 - p674+ [501+]
Eatwell, John - *Global Unemployment*
  JEL - v35 - Mr '97 - p135+ [501+]
Eatwell, Roger - *Fascism: A History*
  BL - v92 - Ag '96 - p1861 [51-250]
  Choice - v34 - F '97 - p1016 [51-250]
  CR - v269 - N '96 - p277 [1-50]
  y LJ - v121 - S 15 '96 - p78+ [51-250]
Ebbesen, Thomas W - *Carbon Nanotubes*
  Sci - v275 - Ja 3 '97 - p37 [1-50]
  SciTech - v21 - Mr '97 - p78 [51-250]
Ebbutt, Sheila - *Exploring Shape and Space*
  TES - F 21 '97 - p13* [51-250]
Eber, Christine - *Women and Alcohol in a Highland Maya Town*
  HAHR - v77 - My '97 - p329+ [251-500]
Eberhard, William G - *Female Control*
  Choice - v34 - D '96 - p635+ [51-250]
  Nature - v382 - Ag 29 '96 - p772 [501+]
  Sci - v275 - F 21 '97 - p1075+ [501+]
  TLS - N 29 '96 - p5 [501+]
Eberhardt, Isabelle - *In the Shadow of Islam*
  MEJ - v50 - Aut '96 - p628 [51-250]

Prisoner of Dunes
  MEJ - v50 - Aut '96 - p629 [51-250]
Eberhart, Helmut - *Albanien: Stammesleben Zwischen Tradition Und Moderne*
  Slav R - v55 - Fall '96 - p678+ [501+]
Eberhart, Russell C - *Computational Intelligence PC Tools*
  New Sci - v152 - D 14 '96 - p44 [1-50]
  SciTech - v20 - D '96 - p12 [51-250]
Eberly, Don E - *The Content of America's Character*
  Bks & Cult - v2 - My '96 - p34 [251-500]
Ebersole, Gary L - *Captured by Texts*
  J Am St - v30 - Ag '96 - p330+ [501+]
Ebersole, Lucinda - *Death in Equality*
  KR - v65 - Ja 1 '97 - p9 [251-500]
  LJ - v122 - Mr 15 '97 - p88 [51-250]
  NYTBR - v102 - Ap 20 '97 - p20 [51-250]
  PW - v244 - Ja 27 '97 - p78 [51-250]
Eberstadt, Fernanda - *When the Sons of Heaven Meet the Daughters of the Earth*
  BL - v93 - Mr 1 '97 - p1109 [51-250]
  Ent W - Mr 28 '97 - p62+ [51-250]
  KR - v65 - Ja 15 '97 - p78 [251-500]
  NYTBR - v102 - Mr 30 '97 - p8 [501+]
  PW - v244 - Ja 20 '97 - p391+ [251-500]
  WSJ-Cent - v99 - Mr 10 '97 - pA16 [501+]
Ebert, Myrtle V - *We Are Free*
  Sm Pr R - v28 - Je '96 - p10 [501+]
Ebert, Roger - *Roger Ebert's Book of Film*
  y BL - v93 - N 1 '96 - p472 [51-250]
  BW - v27 - F 16 '97 - p13 [51-250]
  Ent W - F 21 '97 - p120 [51-250]
  KR - v64 - S 15 '96 - p1369+ [251-500]
  LJ - v121 - O 15 '96 - p62 [51-250]
  PW - v243 - O 14 '96 - p71 [51-250]
Eble, Connie - *Slang and Sociability*
  CAY - v17 - Fall '96 - p3 [51-250]
  r Choice - v34 - N '96 - p427 [51-250]
Ebner-Eschenbach, Marie Von - *Their Pavel*
  Choice - v34 - O '96 - p283 [51-250]
  TranslRevS - v2 - D '96 - p25 [51-250]
Ebrey, Patricia Buckley - *The Cambridge Illustrated History of China*
  y Cur R - v36 - Ja '97 - p12 [51-250]
  r FEER - v160 - Mr 13 '97 - p47+ [501+]
  HT - v46 - O '96 - p59 [1-50]
  NH - v105 - S '96 - p11 [1-50]
The Inner Quarters
  Ch Rev Int - v3 - Fall '96 - p393+ [501+]
Eccles, Marjorie - *An Accidental Shroud*
  KR - v64 - N 1 '96 - p1565 [51-250]
  PW - v243 - N 25 '96 - p60 [51-250]
The Company She Kept
  Arm Det - v29 - Fall '96 - p492 [251-500]
Eccleshare, Julia - *Stories to Share (Illus. by Caroline Jayne Church)*
  c Sch Lib - v44 - N '96 - p146 [51-250]
Echegoyen, Luis - *Physical Supramolecular Chemistry*
  SciTech - v21 - Mr '97 - p30 [51-250]
Echenoz, Jean - *Big Blondes*
  KR - v65 - My 1 '97 - p679 [51-250]
  LJ - v122 - Ap 1 '97 - p124 [51-250]
  PW - v244 - Ap 7 '97 - p70+ [51-250]
Les Grandes Blondes
  WLT - v70 - Sum '96 - p650 [501+]
Echevarria Bacigalupe, Miguel Angel - *Alberto Struzzi: Un Precursor Barroco Del Capitalismo Liberal*
  AHR - v101 - D '96 - p1575+ [501+]
Echlin, Kim - *Elephant Winter*
  Quill & Q - v63 - Ja '97 - p35 [251-500]
  SN - v112 - Mr '97 - p14 [51-250]
Eck, Caroline Van - *The Question of Style in Philosophy and the Arts*
  CPR - v16 - Je '96 - p215+ [501+]
Eck, Joe - *Elements of Garden Design (Illus. by Lisa Brooks)*
  Fine Gard - N '96 - p68+ [51-250]
A Year at North Hill (Illus. by Joe Eck)
  AJPsych - v153 - D '96 - p1650+ [501+]
Eckardt, A Roy - *Reclaiming the Jesus of History*
  Rel Ed - v91 - Fall '96 - p612 [1-50]
Eckart, Wolfgang U - *Arztelexikon: Von Der Antike Bis Zum 20. Jahrhundert*
  Isis - v87 - S '96 - p531 [251-500]
Eckbreth, Alan C - *Laser Diagnostics for Combustion Temperature and Species. 2nd Ed.*
  SciTech - v20 - D '96 - p73 [51-250]
Eckes, Alfred E, Jr. - *Opening America's Market*
  Reason - v28 - Ja '97 - p58+ [501+]
Eckett, Stephen - *Investing On-Line*
  BL - v93 - My 15 '97 - p1548 [51-250]

Eckhart, Meister - *Everything as Divine*
  RR - v55 - N '96 - p661 [1-50]
Eckstein, Fritz - *Catalytic RNA*
  Nature - v386 - Mr 13 '97 - p141+ [501+]
Eckstein, Nicholas A - *The District of the Green Dragon*
  CH - v65 - D '96 - p691+ [501+]
  JIH - v27 - Win '97 - p525+ [251-500]
  Six Ct J - v27 - Fall '96 - p887+ [501+]
Eckstein, Richard M - *Directory of Social Service Grants*
  r ARBA - v28 - '97 - p312 [251-500]
Eco, Umberto - *The Island of the Day Before*
  HR - v49 - Sum '96 - p316+ [501+]
  NYTBR - v101 - N 24 '96 - p32 [51-250]
  Obs - D 1 '96 - p18* [51-250]
  PW - v243 - S 30 '96 - p79 [1-50]
  WLT - v70 - Aut '96 - p938 [501+]
The Search for the Perfect Language
  BIC - v25 - O '96 - p26+ [501+]
Sign, Symbol, Code (Lopez-Morillas). Audio Version
  BL - v93 - F 15 '97 - p1038 [51-250]
Econoguide '97: Washington, D.C., Williamsburg, Busch Gardens, Richmond, and Other Area Attractions
  r LJ - v121 - N 15 '96 - p79 [51-250]
Economic and Financial Review
  p JEL - v34 - S '96 - p1505 [51-250]
Economic and Social Progress in Latin America 1995 Report
  r ARBA - v28 - '97 - p66+ [251-500]
Economic and Social Survey of Africa 1994-1995
  r ARBA - v28 - '97 - p109+ [51-250]
Economic Commission for Africa 1994-1995
  r R&R Bk N - v12 - F '97 - p34 [51-250]
Economic Design
  p JEL - v35 - Mr '97 - p307+ [51-250]
Economic Impact Report: National Football League Franchise Opportunities
  J Gov Info - v23 - S '96 - p602 [1-50]
The Economic Journal
  p TLS - Mr 7 '97 - p27+ [501+]
Economic Policy, Technology and Growth
  JEL - v34 - S '96 - p1483 [51-250]
Economic Survey of Europe in 1995-1996
  r ARBA - v28 - '97 - p113 [251-500]
  R&R Bk N - v12 - F '97 - p14 [51-250]
Economic Survey of Latin America and the Caribbean 1993. Vol. 2
  R&R Bk N - v11 - D '96 - p25 [1-50]
The Economics Institute Guide to Graduate Study in Economics and Agricultural Economics in the United States of America and Canada. 9th Ed.
  r JEL - v34 - S '96 - p1404+ [51-250]
Economics, Trade, and Development
  r ARBA - v28 - '97 - p125 [51-250]
Economides, Richard - *Acropolis Restoration*
  AJA - v100 - Jl '96 - p601+ [501+]
Edbury, Peter W - *The Conquest of Jerusalem and the Third Crusade*
  R&R Bk N - v11 - N '96 - p9 [51-250]
Eddenden, A E - *Murder at the Movies*
  BL - v92 - Ag '96 - p1885 [51-250]
  NYTBR - v101 - N 10 '96 - p62 [51-250]
  Quill & Q - v62 - Ag '96 - p35 [251-500]
Eddie, David - *Chump Change*
  BIC - v25 - N '96 - p35 [251-500]
  Quill & Q - v62 - S '96 - p64 [251-500]
Eddison, Sydney - *The Self-Taught Gardener*
  BL - v93 - F 1 '97 - p917 [51-250]
  LJ - v122 - F 1 '97 - p99 [51-250]
  PW - v244 - Ja 27 '97 - p98 [51-250]
Eddlemon, Sherida K - *Records of Randolph County, Missouri 1833-1964*
  r EGH - v50 - N '96 - p173 [51-250]
Eddy, Sue - *Jackson County, Wisconsin Cemeteries. Vol. 1*
  r EGH - v50 - N '96 - p192 [51-250]
Edel, Theodore - *Piano Music for One Hand*
  Teach Mus - v3 - Ap '96 - p69 [51-250]
Edelheit, Abraham J - *The Yishuv in the Shadow of the Holocaust*
  Choice - v34 - D '96 - p674 [51-250]
  R&R Bk N - v11 - N '96 - p15 [51-250]
Edelman, Diana Viklander - *You Shall Not Abhor an Edomite for He Is Your Brother*
  Rel St Rev - v23 - Ja '97 - p58 [51-250]
Edelman, Eva - *Natural Healing for Schizophrenia*
  SciTech - v20 - N '96 - p44 [51-250]
Edelman, Murray - *From Art to Politics*
  JPC - v30 - Fall '96 - p203+ [501+]
Edelman, Ric - *The Truth about Money*
  LJ - v121 - N 15 '96 - p69 [51-250]

Edelstein, A S - *Nanomaterials: Synthesis, Properties, and Applications*
  SciTech - v20 - D '96 - p63 [51-250]
Edelstein, Alan - *Everybody Is Sitting on the Curb*
  R&R Bk N - v11 - N '96 - p17 [51-250]
Eden, Lorraine - *Multinationals in North America*
  R&R Bk N - v11 - D '96 - p29 [51-250]
Edens, John A - *Eleanor Roosevelt: A Comprehensive Bibliography*
  r RQ - v35 - Sum '96 - p485+ [51-250]
Eder, Donna - *School Talk*
  AJS - v102 - S '96 - p640+ [501+]
  CS - v25 - S '96 - p614+ [501+]
Eder, Klaus - *The Social Construction of Nature*
  SciTech - v21 - Mr '97 - p35 [51-250]
Edeskuty, Frederick J - *Safety in the Handling of Cryogenic Fluids*
  SciTech - v20 - S '96 - p61 [51-250]
Edgar, Christopher - *The Nearness of You*
  Cur R - v36 - N '96 - p3* [51-250]
  y Kliatt - v31 - Ja '97 - p22+ [251-500]
Edge, Martin - *The Underwater Photographer*
  R&R Bk N - v12 - F '97 - p99 [51-250]
Edgers, Geoff - *The Midnight Hour*
  c PW - v244 - Ap 21 '97 - p74 [51-250]
Edgerton, Clyde - *Redeye: A Western*
  NYTBR - v101 - S 29 '96 - p32 [51-250]
Edgerton, David - *Science, Technology and the British Industrial Decline 1870-1970*
  Nature - v383 - O 24 '96 - p681 [501+]
Edgerton, Leslie - *The Death of Tarpons*
  LJ - v121 - O 1 '96 - p47 [1-50]
  WAL - v31 - Win '97 - p412+ [251-500]
Edgerton, Robert B - *The Fall of the Asante Empire*
  Historian - v59 - Fall '96 - p135+ [501+]
Edgeworth, Francis Ysidro - *F.Y. Edgeworth: Writings in Probability, Statistics, and Economics. Vols. 1-3*
  JEL - v34 - S '96 - p1406 [51-250]
  R&R Bk N - v11 - D '96 - p68 [51-250]
Edgeworth, Maria - *Practical Education. Vols. 1-3*
  Nine-C Lit - v51 - Mr '97 - p556 [1-50]
Edghill, Rosemary - *Book of Moons*
  MFSF - v91 - S '96 - p43 [51-250]
The Bowl of Night
  KR - v64 - Ag 15 '96 - p1194 [51-250]
  PW - v243 - S 9 '96 - p69 [51-250]
Edidin, Ben M - *Jewish Holidays and Festivals*
  r JPC - v29 - Spr '96 - p258+ [51-250]
The Edifactory Prose of Kievan Rus'
  Slav R - v55 - Sum '96 - p475+ [501+]
Edin, Kathryn - *Making Ends Meet*
  LJ - v122 - My 1 '97 - p127+ [51-250]
Edinger, Monica - *Fantasy Literature in the Elementary Classroom*
  New Ad - v9 - Fall '96 - p348 [51-250]
Edison, Thomas A - *The Papers of Thomas A. Edison. Vol. 3*
  Pub Hist - v18 - Sum '96 - p78+ [501+]
Edleson, Jeffrey L - *Future Interventions with Battered Women and Their Families*
  R&R Bk N - v11 - D '96 - p43 [51-250]
Edley, Christopher F - *Not All Black and White*
  BL - v93 - S 15 '96 - p187+ [51-250]
  Bl S - v26 - Fall '96 - p101 [1-50]
  Choice - v34 - Mr '97 - p1239 [51-250]
  NY - v72 - N 25 '96 - p106+ [501+]
Edmonds, Alex - *Acid Rain*
  c Sch Lib - v45 - F '97 - p37 [51-250]
The Knowledge Factory
  cr PW - v243 - S 16 '96 - p85 [51-250]
Edmonds, Beverly C - *Children's Rights*
  r ARBA - v28 - '97 - p231 [51-250]
  r Choice - v34 - Mr '97 - p1136 [51-250]
Edmonds, Lucinda - *Aria*
  Woman's J - S '96 - p10 [1-50]
Enchanted
  Books - v9 - S '95 - p27 [1-50]
Not Quite an Angel
  Books - v9 - S '95 - p22 [51-250]
Edmondson, Adrian - *The Gobbler*
  Books - v9 - S '95 - p22 [1-50]
Edmonston, Phil - *Lemon-Aid: How to Buy a New Car (Edmonston). Audio Version*
  Quill & Q - v63 - F '97 - p50 [51-250]
Edmunds, Lowell - *Oedipus: A Folklore Casebook*
  Rel St Rev - v23 - Ap '97 - p171 [51-250]
Edmundson, Andrew - *Advanced Biology Statistics*
  y TES - Ja 3 '97 - pR15 [251-500]
Edmundson, Helen - *The Mill on the Floss*
  y Sch Lib - v44 - N '96 - p176 [51-250]

Edmundson, Mark - *Literature against Philosophy, Plato to Derrida*
    Bks & Cult - v3 - Ja '97 - p35+ [501+]
    JAAC - v55 - Win '97 - p68+ [501+]
    TLS - Ag 2 '96 - p26 [501+]
Educational Computing and Technology
    p TES - O 18 '96 - p43U [51-250]
Educational Grants Directory 1996/7
    yr TES - S 27 '96 - p8* [51-250]
Educational Media and Technology Yearbook 1995-1996
    r ARBA - v28 - '97 - p144 [51-250]
    Emerg Lib - v23 - My '96 - p42 [1-50]
    r SLMQ - v24 - Sum '96 - p219 [1-50]
Educators Index of Free Materials 1995
    r ARBA - v28 - '97 - p136 [51-250]
Edvinsson, Leif - *Intellectual Capital*
    BL - v93 - Mr 15 '97 - p1210 [51-250]
    LJ - v122 - Ap 1 '97 - p104 [51-250]
Edward, Alfred W - *Art Deco Sculpture and Metalware*
    Ant & CM - v101 - Ja '97 - p44 [1-50]
Edwards, Adrian - *San Marino*
    r ARBA - v28 - '97 - p63+ [51-250]
    r R&R Bk N - v12 - F '97 - p16 [1-50]
Edwards, Alan F - *Interdisciplinary Undergraduate Programs. 2nd Ed.*
    r Choice - v34 - My '97 - p1474 [51-250]
Edwards, Alistair D N - *Extra-Ordinary Human-Computer Interaction*
    SocSciComR - v14 - Fall '96 - p360+ [501+]
Edwards, Anne - *Streisand: A Biography*
    Advocate - My 13 '97 - p70+ [251-500]
    BL - v93 - F 1 '97 - p906 [51-250]
    KR - v65 - F 15 '97 - p268+ [251-500]
    PW - v244 - Mr 3 '97 - p59+ [51-250]
    Streisand: It Only Happens Once
    TLS - N 22 '96 - p10 [501+]
    Throne of Gold
    NYTBR - v101 - D 8 '96 - p96 [501+]
Edwards, Betty - *Drawing on the Right Side of the Brain*
    BW - v26 - D 8 '96 - p3 [51-250]
Edwards, Bill - *The Standard Carnival Glass Price Guide*
    r ARBA - v28 - '97 - p360+ [251-500]
    Standard Encyclopedia of Carnival Glass. 5th Ed.
    r ARBA - v28 - '97 - p360+ [251-500]
Edwards, Brian - *Towards Sustainable Architecture*
    New Sci - v151 - S 28 '96 - p48 [51-250]
Edwards, Carolyn McVickar - *Sun Stories*
    CAY - v17 - Win '96 - p3 [51-250]
Edwards, Cassie - *White Fire*
    PW - v244 - My 12 '97 - p74 [51-250]
Edwards, Catharine - *Writing Rome*
    TLS - F 14 '97 - p12 [501+]
Edwards, Chris - *The Young Inline Skater*
    c BL - v93 - N 15 '96 - p581+ [51-250]
    c CCB-B - v50 - D '96 - p132+ [51-250]
    c HB Guide - v8 - Spr '97 - p144 [51-250]
    c KR - v64 - O 1 '96 - p1476 [51-250]
    c Sch Lib - v45 - F '97 - p39 [51-250]
    c SLJ - v42 - N '96 - p112 [51-250]
Edwards, Clive D - *Eighteenth-Century Furniture*
    Choice - v34 - Mr '97 - p1150 [51-250]
Edwards, D J - *Nuff Respect*
    Books - v9 - S '95 - p25 [1-50]
Edwards, D S - *Tropical Rainforest Research*
    SciTech - v21 - Mr '97 - p34 [51-250]
Edwards, David B - *Heroes of the Age*
    Choice - v34 - Ap '97 - p1401 [51-250]
Edwards, David T - *Small Farmers and the Protection of the Watersheds*
    JEL - v34 - D '96 - p2108 [51-250]
Edwards, Denis - *Jesus the Wisdom of God*
    TT - v53 - O '96 - p430 [51-250]
Edwards, Douglas R - *Religion and Power*
    Choice - v34 - Mr '97 - p1177 [51-250]
Edwards, Francis - *Robert Persons: The Biography of an Elizabethan Jesuit 1546-1610*
    CHR - v82 - O '96 - p723+ [501+]
Edwards, Frank B - *Melody Mooner Takes Lessons (Illus. by John Bianchi)*
    c Quill & Q - v62 - O '96 - p47 [51-250]
Edwards, Frank S - *A Campaign in New Mexico with Colonel Doniphan*
    WHQ - v27 - Win '96 - p549 [51-250]
Edwards, Franklin R - *The New Finance*
    Choice - v34 - Ap '97 - p1386 [51-250]
Edwards, Fred - *Making Money with Boats*
    BWatch - v17 - S '96 - p8 [51-250]
Edwards, Gavin - *He's Got the Whole World in His Pants*
    BWatch - v18 - Mr '97 - p12 [51-250]
Edwards, Geoffrey - *Klaus Moje: Glass*
    Am Craft - v56 - Ag '96 - p28 [1-50]

Edwards, Grace F - *If I Should Die*
    BL - v93 - My 1 '97 - p1481 [51-250]
    KR - v65 - My 1 '97 - p681 [251-500]
    LJ - v122 - Ap 1 '97 - p132 [51-250]
    PW - v244 - Mr 10 '97 - p52+ [51-250]
    Trib Bks - My 4 '97 - p4 [51-250]
Edwards, Harry - *A Skeptic's Guide to the New Age*
    Aust Bk R - Je '96 - p67 [1-50]
Edwards, Jack E - *How to Conduct Organizational Surveys*
    Choice - v34 - Ap '97 - p1384 [51-250]
    R&R Bk N - v12 - F '97 - p45 [51-250]
Edwards, Jaroldeen - *Things I Wish I'd Known Sooner*
    KR - v65 - Mr 15 '97 - p432 [251-500]
Edwards, Jay - *The Challenge*
    c Sch Lib - v44 - Ag '96 - p104 [51-250]
Edwards, Jefferson D, Jr. - *Purging Racism from Christianity*
    LJ - v121 - N 1 '96 - p86 [1-50]
Edwards, John - *Television IC Data Files*
    SciTech - v21 - Mr '97 - p86 [51-250]
Edwards, John, 1947- - *Keating: The Inside Story*
    Aust Bk R - O '96 - p26+ [501+]
    NS - v126 - Mr 27 '97 - p56 [501+]
    TLS - Ap 11 '97 - p9+ [501+]
Edwards, John, 1949- - *Religion and Society in Spain*
    R&R Bk N - v11 - N '96 - p7 [51-250]
Edwards, John Carver - *Airmen without Portfolio*
    PW - v244 - Mr 17 '97 - p73 [51-250]
Edwards, John R - *Multilingualism*
    MLJ - v81 - Spr '97 - p114+ [501+]
    MLR - v91 - O '96 - p940+ [501+]
Edwards, Jonathan - *A Jonathan Edwards Reader*
    CH - v66 - Mr '97 - p134+ [501+]
    Jonathan Edwards: The Miscellanies A-500
    CH - v66 - Mr '97 - p132+ [501+]
    The Works of Jonathan Edwards. Vol. 13
    RM - v50 - D '96 - p396+ [501+]
Edwards, Joyce - *Fostering Healing and Growth*
    Readings - v12 - Mr '97 - p25 [51-250]
Edwards, Kenneth - *The Four-Masted Barque Lawhill*
    Sea H - Aut '96 - p43 [251-500]
Edwards, Kim - *The Secrets of a Fire King*
    KR - v65 - F 15 '97 - p240 [51-250]
    LJ - v122 - Ap 15 '97 - p122 [51-250]
    NYTBR - v102 - Ap 20 '97 - p20 [51-250]
    PW - v244 - F 24 '97 - p64+ [51-250]
Edwards, Larry - *Bela Lugosi*
    BWatch - v18 - Mr '97 - p11 [51-250]
Edwards, Linda - *A History of Cloth Dolls*
    Ant & CM - v102 - Ap '97 - p66 [51-250]
Edwards, Louis - *N: A Romantic Mystery*
    BL - v93 - My 15 '97 - p1566 [51-250]
    KR - v65 - Ap 1 '97 - p484 [251-500]
    LJ - v122 - Ap 1 '97 - p133 [51-250]
    PW - v244 - Mr 3 '97 - p67 [51-250]
Edwards, Madaline Selima - *Madaline: Love and Survival in Antebellum New Orleans*
    Choice - v34 - S '96 - p195 [51-250]
    Nine-C Lit - v51 - D '96 - p427 [1-50]
Edwards, Mark U - *Printing, Propaganda, and Martin Luther*
    EHR - v112 - F '97 - p185 [501+]
Edwards, Martin - *Perfectly Criminal*
    KR - v65 - F 1 '97 - p176+ [51-250]
    PW - v244 - Mr 3 '97 - p68 [51-250]
Edwards, Pamela Duncan - *Barefoot: Escape on the Underground Railroad (Illus. by Henry Cole)*
    c BL - v93 - F 15 '97 - p1025+ [51-250]
    c CBRS - v25 - F '97 - p80 [51-250]
    c KR - v64 - D 1 '96 - p1736 [51-250]
    c PW - v243 - N 25 '96 - p75 [51-250]
    c SLJ - v43 - F '97 - p75 [51-250]
    Four Famished Foxes and Fosdyke (Illus. by Henry Cole)
    c PW - v244 - My 12 '97 - p77 [1-50]
    Livingstone Mouse (Illus. by Henry Cole)
    c BL - v93 - O 1 '96 - p358 [51-250]
    c CBRS - v25 - D '96 - p38 [1-50]
    c Ch BWatch - v6 - O '96 - p4 [1-50]
    c HB Guide - v8 - Spr '97 - p26 [51-250]
    c SLJ - v42 - S '96 - p177 [51-250]
    Some Smug Slug (Illus. by Henry Cole)
    c HB Guide - v7 - Fall '96 - p254 [51-250]
    c SLJ - v42 - D '96 - p28 [1-50]
Edwards, Paul, 1923- - *Reincarnation: A Critical Examination*
    Skeptic - v4 - 3 '96 - p105 [51-250]
Edwards, Paul, 1940- - *The Best Home Businesses for the 90s. 2nd Ed., Rev. and Expanded*
    LJ - v122 - My 1 '97 - p53 [1-50]

    Teaming Up
    PW - v244 - Ja 13 '97 - p61+ [51-250]
Edwards, Paul, 1950- - *Volcanic Heaven*
    Choice - v34 - N '96 - p461 [51-250]
Edwards, Paul M - *The Inchon Landing, Korea 1950*
    r RQ - v35 - Sum '96 - p486 [51-250]
Edwards, Paul N - *The Closed World*
    Choice - v34 - N '96 - p479+ [51-250]
    Isis - v87 - D '96 - p756 [501+]
    Nat - v262 - Je 3 '96 - p33+ [501+]
    NS - v125 - S 13 '96 - p47 [51-250]
Edwards, Philip - *The Story of the Voyage*
    MLR - v91 - O '96 - p977+ [501+]
Edwards, Richard - *Fly with the Birds (Illus. by Satoshi Katamura)*
    c HB Guide - v7 - Fall '96 - p326 [1-50]
    Moon Frog (Illus. by Sarah Fox-Davies)
    c Bks Keeps - N '96 - p6 [51-250]
    Teaching the Parrot (Illus. by John Lawrence)
    c JB - v60 - O '96 - p192 [51-250]
    c Sch Lib - v44 - N '96 - p167 [51-250]
    c TES - S 27 '96 - p7* [51-250]
    You're Safe Now, Waterdog (Illus. by Sophy Williams)
    c JB - v60 - D '96 - p230 [51-250]
    c Sch Lib - v45 - F '97 - p18 [51-250]
Edwards, Robert - *Wharton Esherick 1887-1970*
    Am Craft - v56 - O '96 - p65 [51-250]
Edwards, Robert R - *Art and Context in Late Medieval English Narrative*
    MLR - v92 - Ap '97 - p427+ [501+]
Edwards, Ron - *The Australian Yarn*
    CAY - v17 - Win '96 - p3 [51-250]
Edwards, Ruth Dudley - *Murder in a Cathedral*
    TLS - F 28 '97 - p23 [251-500]
    The Pursuit of Reason
    JEH - v57 - Mr '97 - p222+ [501+]
    Ten Lords-a-Leaping
    Nat R - v48 - D 23 '96 - p57 [501+]
Edwards, Sebastian - *Capital Controls, Exchange Rates, and Monetary Policy in the World Economy*
    Econ J - v107 - Ja '97 - p267 [51-250]
    JEL - v34 - D '96 - p2051+ [51-250]
Edwards, Susan - *Neurological Physiotherapy*
    SciTech - v20 - N '96 - p41 [51-250]
Edwards, Susie - *The Encyclopedia of Flower Arranging*
    r BL - v93 - Ap 1 '97 - p1275 [51-250]
    r LJ - v122 - Ap 1 '97 - p89 [51-250]
Edwards, Ted - *The X-Files Companion. Vol. 2*
    Obs - D 15 '96 - p16* [501+]
    X-Files Confidential
    r New Sci - v152 - N 30 '96 - p44 [51-250]
Eeckhoudt, Louis - *Risk: Evaluation, Management and Sharing*
    Econ J - v106 - N '96 - p1834 [51-250]
    JEL - v34 - S '96 - p1416 [51-250]
Eedy, David J - *Surgical Dermatology*
    SciTech - v20 - D '96 - p49 [51-250]
Efetov, Konstantin - *Supersymmetry in Disorder and Chaos*
    Nature - v386 - Ap 10 '97 - p568 [51-250]
Eff, Elaine - *You Should Have Been Here Yesterday*
    J Gov Info - v23 - S '96 - p585 [51-250]
Effectiveness and Costs of Osteoporosis Screening and Hormone Replacement Therapy. Vols. 1-2
    J Gov Info - v23 - S '96 - p556 [51-250]
Effelsberg, Wolfgang - *High-Speed Networking for Multimedia Applications*
    r SciTech - v20 - S '96 - p4 [51-250]
Efron, Bradley - *An Introduction to the Bootstrap*
    JEL - v34 - S '96 - p1340+ [501+]
Efron, John M - *Defenders of the Race*
    CEH - v29 - 2 '96 - p257+ [501+]
Efroymson, David P - *Within Context*
    Rel Ed - v91 - Fall '96 - p616+ [1-50]
Egan, Bruce L - *Information Superhighways Revisited*
    SciTech - v21 - Mr '97 - p87 [51-250]
Egan, Desmond - *Elegies*
    ILS - v15 - Fall '96 - p11 [501+]
    WLT - v70 - Aut '96 - p962 [251-500]
Egan, Dorothy - *Painting and Decorating Bird Houses*
    BL - v93 - F 1 '97 - p915+ [51-250]
Egan, Eileen - *For Whom There Is No Room*
    Parabola - v21 - Ag '96 - p90+ [501+]
Egan, Greg - *Distress*
    PW - v244 - My 12 '97 - p63 [51-250]
Egan, Jennifer - *Emerald City*
    NYTBR - v102 - Ap 20 '97 - p32 [51-250]
    The Invisible Circus
    LJ - v121 - S 15 '96 - p124 [51-250]
Egan, Ted - *Justice All Their Own*
    Aust Bk R - Jl '96 - p14+ [501+]

Egan, Terry - *The Good Guys of Baseball*
 c KR - v64 - D 15 '96 - p1797 [51-250]
 Heroes of the Game
 c PW - v244 - Mr 10 '97 - p69 [1-50]
Egan, Tim - *Burnt Toast on Davenport Street (Illus. by Tim Egan)*
 c KR - v65 - F 15 '97 - p298 [51-250]
 c PW - v244 - F 24 '97 - p90 [51-250]
 c Trib Bks - My 4 '97 - p6+ [51-250]
 Metropolitan Cow (Illus. by Tim Egan)
 c Ch BWatch - v6 - My '96 - p3 [1-50]
 c ECEJ - v24 - Spr '97 - p176 [51-250]
 c HB Guide - v7 - Fall '96 - p254+ [51-250]
 c NYTLa - v146 - D 9 '96 - pC18 [501+]
 c Par Ch - v20 - O '96 - p3 [51-250]
 c SLJ - v42 - D '96 - p28 [1-50]
Egerton, John - *Speak Now against the Day*
 VQR - v73 - Win '97 - p179+ [501+]
Egerton, Judy - *Turner: The Fighting Temeraire*
 Albion - v28 - '96 - p716+ [501+]
Egerton, R F - *Electron Energy-Loss Spectroscopy in the Electron Microscope. 2nd Ed.*
 SciTech - v20 - S '96 - p15 [51-250]
Eggebrecht, Hans Heinrich - *Terminologie Der Musik Im 20. Jahrhundert*
 r Notes - v53 - Mr '97 - p783+ [501+]
Egger-Bovet, Howard - *Book of the American Colonies (Illus. by D J Simison)*
 c SLJ - v42 - Ag '96 - p151+ [51-250]
 USKids History (Illus. by D J Simison)
 c HB Guide - v7 - Fall '96 - p385 [51-250]
Eggers, Martin - *Das Grossmährische Reich*
 Slav R - v55 - Fall '96 - p666+ [501+]
 Specu - v71 - O '96 - p945+ [501+]
Eggers, William D - *Revolution at the Roots*
 PAR - v56 - Jl '96 - p400+ [501+]
Eggins, Brian R - *Biosensors: An Introduction*
 Choice - v34 - F '97 - p987 [51-250]
Eggleston, Brian - *The New Engineering Contract*
 SciTech - v20 - N '96 - p3 [51-250]
Eggleston, George Cary - *A Rebel's Recollections*
 y Kliatt - v31 - My '97 - p21 [51-250]
Egielski, Richard - *Buz (Illus. by Richard Egielski)*
 c RT - v50 - S '96 - p57 [51-250]
 c RT - v50 - O '96 - p132 [1-50]
Egilsson, Egill - *Sendiboo Ur Djupunum*
 WLT - v70 - Aut '96 - p975 [501+]
Egleton, Clive - *A Lethal Involvement*
 y BL - v92 - Ag '96 - p1885 [51-250]
 y BL - v92 - Ag '96 - p1891 [1-50]
 NYTBR - v101 - S 1 '96 - p16 [251-500]
 Warning Shot
 BL - v93 - My 15 '97 - p1566 [51-250]
 PW - v244 - My 12 '97 - p58 [51-250]
Egmond, Florike - *Underworlds: Organized Crime in the Netherlands 1650-1800*
 JMH - v68 - S '96 - p719+ [501+]
Egnal, Marc - *Divergent Paths*
 Choice - v34 - D '96 - p675 [51-250]
Egoff, Sheila - *The New Republic of Childhood*
 Can CL - v22 - Fall '96 - p8+ [501+]
 Only Connect. 3rd Ed.
 CCB-B - v50 - My '97 - p340 [51-250]
 HB - v73 - Ja '97 - p83+ [51-250]
Egret, Daniel - *Information and On-Line Data in Astronomy*
 Choice - v34 - S '96 - p150 [51-250]
Egypt (Handbooks of the World)
 r BL - v93 - S 15 '96 - p210 [1-50]
An Egyptian Satire about a Condemned Building
 MEJ - v51 - Spr '97 - p310+ [51-250]
Ehlert, Lois - *Color Farm (Illus. by Lois Ehlert)*
 c PW - v244 - Mr 31 '97 - p76 [51-250]
 Color Zoo (Illus. by Lois Ehlert)
 c PW - v244 - Mr 31 '97 - p76 [51-250]
 Cuckoo: A Mexican Folktale (Illus. by Lois Ehlert)
 c BL - v93 - Ap 1 '97 - p1330 [51-250]
 c KR - v65 - Ap 1 '97 - p553 [51-250]
 c PW - v244 - Ja 20 '97 - p401 [51-250]
 c SLJ - v43 - Mr '97 - p174 [51-250]
 c Trib Bks - Mr 9 '97 - p7 [51-250]
 Eating the Alphabet
 c HB Guide - v7 - Fall '96 - p238 [1-50]
 Fish Eyes (Illus. by Lois Ehlert)
 c BL - v93 - Ap 1 '97 - p1340 [1-50]
 Moon Rope (Illus. by Lois Ehlert)
 c SS - v88 - Ja '97 - p29+ [501+]
 Snowballs (Illus. by Lois Ehlert)
 c LATBR - Mr 24 '96 - p11 [51-250]
 c RT - v50 - S '96 - p54+ [51-250]

 Under My Nose (Illus. by Carlo Ontal)
 c BL - v93 - S 1 '96 - p121 [51-250]
 c HB - v72 - S '96 - p613 [51-250]
 c HB Guide - v7 - Fall '96 - p372 [51-250]
 c SLJ - v42 - D '96 - p112 [51-250]
Ehmer, Josef - *Soziale Traditionen In Zieten Des Wandels*
 J Soc H - v30 - Spr '97 - p771+ [501+]
Ehrenhalt, Alan - *The Lost City*
 BW - v26 - D 8 '96 - p9 [51-250]
 Soc Ser R - v70 - S '96 - p500 [51-250]
Ehrenreich, Barbara - *Blood Rites*
 KR - v65 - Mr 15 '97 - p432+ [251-500]
 LJ - v122 - My 1 '97 - p119+ [51-250]
 PW - v244 - Ap 7 '97 - p82+ [51-250]
 Time - v149 - My 19 '97 - p95 [51-250]
Ehret, Christopher - *Reconstructing Proto-Afroasiatic*
 r TLS - N 1 '96 - p10 [501+]
Ehrhardt, Jana U - *Good Girls Go to Heaven, Bad Girls Go Everywhere*
 PW - v244 - Ja 6 '97 - p54 [51-250]
Ehrhart-Morrison, Dorothy - *No Mountain High Enough*
 LJ - v122 - Ja '97 - p114 [51-250]
 PW - v244 - Ja 6 '97 - p60 [51-250]
Ehrlich, Amy - *When I Was Your Age*
 y Ch BWatch - v6 - My '96 - p2 [1-50]
 y HB Guide - v7 - Fall '96 - p364 [51-250]
 c NYTBR - v101 - S 22 '96 - p28 [1-50]
 c RT - v50 - Ap '97 - p588 [51-250]
 c SLJ - v42 - Ag '96 - p152 [51-250]
 y VOYA - v19 - O '96 - p240+ [501+]
 Where It Stops, Nobody Knows
 y Kliatt - v30 - S '96 - p3 [1-50]
Ehrlich, Cyril - *First Philharmonic*
 AHR - v102 - F '97 - p110 [251-500]
 Albion - v28 - '96 - p715+ [501+]
 Notes - v53 - S '96 - p44+ [501+]
Ehrlich, Eugene - *Les Bons Mots*
 PW - v244 - Mr 31 '97 - p57+ [1-50]
Ehrlich, Gretel - *Questions of Heaven*
 BL - v93 - My 1 '97 - p1474 [51-250]
 KR - v65 - Mr 1 '97 - p348 [51-250]
 PW - v244 - Ap 28 '97 - p69 [51-250]
Ehrlich, Howard J - *Reinventing Anarchy Again*
 LJ - v122 - F 15 '97 - p166 [51-250]
Ehrlich, Paul R - *Betrayal of Science and Reason*
 Aud - v98 - N '96 - p130+ [501+]
 BioSci - v47 - Mr '97 - p182+ [501+]
 y BL - v93 - O 1 '96 - p294 [501+]
 BL - v93 - D 1 '96 - p630 [1-50]
 BW - v26 - O 27 '96 - p1+ [501+]
 Choice - v34 - Mr '97 - p1179 [51-250]
 Econ - v342 - F 15 '97 - p7* [51-250]
 KR - v64 - Ag 15 '96 - p1205 [251-500]
 LJ - v121 - O 15 '96 - p88 [51-250]
 Nature - v383 - O 10 '96 - p494 [501+]
 New Sci - v152 - O 5 '96 - p47 [1-50]
 NYTBR - v101 - D 1 '96 - p22 [51-250]
 Sci - v274 - O 11 '96 - p198 [501+]
 The Stork and the Plow
 Am Sci - v85 - Ja '97 - p88+ [501+]
Ehrlich, Robert - *What If You Could Unscramble an Egg?*
 y BL - v93 - D 1 '96 - p664 [1-50]
 SciTech - v20 - N '96 - p4 [51-250]
Ehrman, Bart D - *The Orthodox Corruption of Scripture*
 CH - v66 - Mr '97 - p81+ [501+]
Ehrman, John - *The Younger Pitt: The Consuming Struggle*
 HT - v47 - Ja '97 - p60+ [501+]
 Spec - v276 - My 18 '96 - p40+ [501+]
 Spec - v277 - N 23 '96 - p45 [1-50]
 TLS - My 24 '96 - p13+ [501+]
 TLS - N 29 '96 - p14 [501+]
**Ehrman, John, 1959- ** - *The Rise of Neoconservatism*
 AAPSS-A - v550 - Mr '97 - p169+ [501+]
Ehrman, Madeline Elizabeth - *Understanding Second Language Learning Difficulties*
 R&R Bk N - v12 - F '97 - p76 [51-250]
Eichengreen, Barry - *Europe's Post-War Recovery*
 JEL - v34 - D '96 - p2095 [501+]
 Globalizing Capital
 For Aff - v76 - Mr '97 - p176 [51-250]
 LJ - v121 - O 1 '96 - p94 [51-250]
 The Political Economy of European Monetary Unification
 EG - v72 - O '96 - p458+ [501+]
 The Reconstruction of the International Economy 1945-1960
 JEL - v34 - S '96 - p1473 [51-250]
Eichenwald, Kurt - *Serpent on the Rock*
 NYTBR - v101 - D 1 '96 - p36 [51-250]

Eicher, David J - *The Civil War in Books*
 r PW - v243 - S 23 '96 - p70 [1-50]
Eicher, Joanne B - *Dress and Ethnicity*
 Am Ethnol - v24 - F '97 - p216+ [501+]
Eichler, Jorg - *Relativistic Atomic Collisions*
 Phys Today - v49 - Ag '96 - p66+ [501+]
Eickelman, Dale F - *Muslim Politics*
 Choice - v34 - S '96 - p203 [51-250]
 For Aff - v75 - N '96 - p165+ [51-250]
 TLS - Ja 31 '97 - p24 [501+]
 Russia's Muslim Frontiers
 JTWS - v13 - Fall '96 - p342+ [501+]
 JTWS - v13 - Spr '96 - p408+ [501+]
Eickhoff, Randy Lee - *The Raid*
 KR - v65 - Ja 15 '97 - p103 [251-500]
 PW - v244 - Ja 27 '97 - p78 [51-250]
Eide, Asbjorn - *Conditions for Civilized Politics*
 Choice - v34 - S '96 - p205 [51-250]
Eide, Erling - *Law and Economics of the Environment*
 JEL - v34 - S '96 - p1450 [51-250]
Eidson, Bill - *The Guardian*
 BL - v93 - N 1 '96 - p483 [51-250]
 KR - v64 - S 15 '96 - p1340+ [251-500]
 LJ - v121 - S 15 '96 - p95 [51-250]
 PW - v243 - O 7 '96 - p63 [51-250]
Eidson, Thomas - *All God's Children*
 Books - v10 - Je '96 - p23 [51-250]
 PW - v244 - My 5 '97 - p197 [51-250]
 TLS - Jl 7 '96 - p25 [251-500]
Eidus, Janice - *The Celibacy Club*
 KR - v65 - F 1 '97 - p158 [251-500]
 NYTBR - v102 - Mr 2 '97 - p18 [51-250]
 PW - v244 - Ja 20 '97 - p394 [51-250]
Eiesland, Nancy L - *The Disabled God*
 J Ch St - v38 - Aut '96 - p918 [51-250]
Eigen, Joel Peter - *Witnessing Insanity*
 AHR - v101 - O '96 - p1208+ [501+]
 CS - v26 - Mr '97 - p215+ [501+]
 Eight-C St - v30 - Spr '97 - p329+ [501+]
 JMH - v68 - D '96 - p980+ [501+]
Eighner, Lars - *Travels with Lizbeth*
 SFR - v21 - S '96 - p48 [51-250]
Eijffinger, Sylvester C W - *The Political Economy of Central-Bank Independence*
 JEL - v35 - Mr '97 - p207+ [51-250]
Eilberg-Schwartz, Howard - *God's Phallus and Other Problems for Men and Monotheism*
 JAAR - v65 - Spr '97 - p199+ [501+]
Eilersen, Gillian Stead - *Bessie Head: Thunder behind Her Ears*
 Africa T - v44 - 1 '97 - p97+ [501+]
 WLT - v71 - Win '97 - p211 [501+]
Einarsen, John - *The Sacred Mountains of Asia*
 Rel St Rev - v23 - Ap '97 - p205+ [51-250]
**Einarson, John, 1952- ** - *American Woman*
 BIC - v25 - S '96 - p29+ [501+]
Einarsson, Goran - *Principles of Lightware Communications*
 SciTech - v20 - S '96 - p55 [51-250]
Einaudi, Luigi - *Beyond Cuba*
 Parameters - v26 - Win '96 - p154 [1-50]
Einfelds, Janis - *Cuku Gramata*
 WLT - v70 - Aut '96 - p999+ [501+]
Einhorn, Barbara - *Citizenship and Democratic Control in Contemporary Europe*
 JEL - v34 - S '96 - p1490 [51-250]
Einhorn, Michael - *Electricity Transmission Pricing and Technology*
 JEL - v34 - S '96 - p1457+ [51-250]
Einstein, Albert - *Albert Einstein/Mileva Maric--the Love Letters*
 TranslRevS - v1 - My '95 - p21 [51-250]
 The Collected Papers of Albert Einstein. Vol. 4
 Isis - v87 - S '96 - p568+ [251-500]
 The Quotable Einstein
 Bloom Rev - v16 - N '96 - p28 [51-250]
 Nature - v383 - O 31 '96 - p774 [251-500]
 New Sci - v152 - D 21 '96 - p74 [251-500]
 NYTBR - v102 - Ap 13 '97 - p21 [51-250]
 PW - v243 - O 14 '96 - p75 [51-250]
Einstein, David - *America Online for Busy People*
 LJ - v122 - Ja '97 - p138 [1-50]
 PCs for Busy People
 y BL - v93 - Mr 1 '97 - p1101 [501+]
EIPASCOPE
 p JEL - v35 - Mr '97 - p308 [51-250]

Eire, Carlos M N - *From Madrid to Purgatory*
    AHR - v102 - F '97 - p132+ [501+]
    CHR - v82 - Jl '96 - p563+ [501+]
    HAHR - v77 - My '97 - p299+ [251-500]
    JIH - v27 - Win '97 - p526+ [501+]
    Spec - v277 - N 23 '96 - p43 [51-250]

Eiselein, Gregory - *Literature and Humanitarian Reform in the Civil War Era*
    Choice - v34 - My '97 - p1495 [51-250]

Eiseley, Loren - *How Flowers Changed the World*
    BWatch - v17 - N '96 - p7 [51-250]

Eisen, George - *Ethnicity and Sport in North American History and Culture*
    Aethlon - v13 - Fall '95 - p148+ [251-500]
    J Am Cult - v19 - Spr '96 - p97+ [501+]

Eisenbach, Helen - *Lesbianism Made Easy*
    Advocate - Je 11 '96 - p56+ [501+]
    KR - v64 - My 1 '96 - p659+ [251-500]
    Prog - v61 - Ja '97 - p31 [251-500]
    Wom R Bks - v14 - Mr '97 - p6+ [501+]

Eisenberg, Avigail I - *Reconstructing Political Pluralism*
    APSR - v90 - S '96 - p624+ [501+]
    Ethics - v107 - Ja '97 - p390 [51-250]
    J Pol - v58 - N '96 - p1234+ [501+]

Eisenberg, Carolyn Woods - *Drawing the Line*
    Choice - v34 - N '96 - p517 [51-250]
    Nat - v263 - D 16 '96 - p25+ [501+]
    TLS - D 27 '96 - p6 [501+]

Eisenberg, Deborah - *Air, 24 Hours*
    Choice - v34 - S '96 - p112 [51-250]
    The Stories (So Far) of Deborah Eisenberg
    LJ - v122 - Ja '97 - p151+ [51-250]
    PW - v243 - D 30 '96 - p53 [251-500]
    The Stories (So far) of Deborah Eisenberg
    Trib Bks - Ap 6 '97 - p8 [1-50]

Eisenberg, John - *The Longest Shot*
    AB - v97 - Je 17 '96 - p2408+ [501+]

Eisenberg, Laura Zittrain - *My Enemy's Enemy*
    JIH - v27 - Win '97 - p565+ [501+]

Eisenberg, Lee - *Breaking Eighty*
    PW - v244 - Mr 31 '97 - p49 [51-250]

Eisenberg, Mickey S - *Life in the Balance*
    BL - v93 - My 1 '97 - p1470 [51-250]

Eisenberg, Ronald L - *Clinical Imaging. 3rd Ed.*
    SciTech - v21 - Mr '97 - p49 [51-250]

Eisenberg, Ronni - *The Overwhelmed Person's Guide to Time Management*
    BL - v93 - Ja '97 - p793 [51-250]

Eisendle, Helmut - *Der Egoist*
    WLT - v70 - Aut '96 - p945+ [251-500]

Eisenhower, Susan - *Mrs. Ike: Memories and Reflections on the Life of Mamie Eisenhower*
    BL - v93 - S 1 '96 - p2+ [51-250]
    BW - v26 - N 17 '96 - p3 [501+]
    KR - v64 - S 1 '96 - p1291+ [251-500]
    LATBR - D 1 '96 - p3 [501+]
    LJ - v121 - O 15 '96 - p66 [51-250]
    NYTBR - v102 - Ja 5 '97 - p19 [51-250]
    PW - v243 - S 16 '96 - p59+ [51-250]

Eisenman, Robert - *James, the Brother of Jesus*
    BL - v93 - F 1 '97 - p909 [51-250]
    KR - v64 - O 15 '96 - p1507 [251-500]
    LJ - v122 - Ja '97 - p105 [51-250]

Eisenman, Stephen - *Gauguin's Skirt*
    Obs - Ap 6 '97 - p18* [51-250]
    PW - v244 - Mr 24 '97 - p68 [51-250]

Eisenpreis, Bettijane - *Coping: A Young Woman's Guide to Breast Cancer Prevention*
    y SLJ - v43 - Ja '97 - p123 [51-250]

Eisenschitz, Bernard - *Nicholas Ray: An American Journey*
    TES - N 22 '96 - p8* [51-250]

Eisenstadt, Michael - *Iranian Military Power*
    MEQ - v4 - Mr '97 - p88 [251-500]

Eisenstadt, S N - *Power, Trust, and Meaning*
    AJS - v102 - Jl '96 - p274+ [501+]
    CS - v25 - N '96 - p827+ [501+]

Eisenstein, Hester - *Inside Agitators*
    Aust Bk R - N '96 - p67 [51-250]

Eisenstein, S M - *Selected Works. Vol. 3*
    Choice - v34 - F '97 - p972+ [51-250]

Eisenstein, Sergei - *Beyond the Stars*
    TranslRevS - v2 - D '96 - p7 [51-250]

Eisenstein, Zillah - *Hatreds: Racialized and Sexualized Conflicts in the 21st Century*
    For Aff - v75 - N '96 - p145 [51-250]

Eisler, Colin - *Masterworks in Berlin*
    CSM - v88 - N 21 '96 - pB2 [51-250]
    LATBR - D 8 '96 - p14 [1-50]
    Mag Antiq - v151 - Ja '97 - p50 [51-250]
    NYTBR - v101 - D 8 '96 - p21+ [501+]
    PW - v243 - N 25 '96 - p65+ [51-250]

Eisler, Hans - *Composing for the Films*
    Si & So - v6 - N '96 - p38 [1-50]

Eismann, Volker - *Die Suche: Das Andere Lehrwerk Fur Deutsch Als Fremdsprache*
    MLJ - v80 - Fall '96 - p417+ [501+]

Eisner, Howard - *Essentials of Project and Systems Engineering Management*
    Choice - v34 - Ap '97 - p1368 [51-250]
    SciTech - v21 - Mr '97 - p74 [51-250]

Eisner, Thomas - *Chemical Ecology*
    Choice - v34 - O '96 - p302 [51-250]

Ekedahl, Carolyn M - *The Wars of Eduard Shevardnadze*
    LJ - v122 - My 1 '97 - p124 [51-250]
    PW - v244 - Mr 3 '97 - p59 [51-250]

Ekiert, Grzegorz - *The State against Society*
    Choice - v34 - My '97 - p1568 [51-250]
    For Aff - v76 - Mr '97 - p192 [51-250]

Ekman, Kerstin - *Blackwater*
    NYTBR - v102 - Mr 9 '97 - p28 [51-250]
    TLS - N 29 '96 - p13 [51-250]
    Trib Bks - F 16 '97 - p8 [1-50]

Ekman, Paul - *The Nature of Emotion*
    A J Psy - v109 - Fall '96 - p496+ [501+]

Ekrem, Inger - *Reformation and Latin Literature in Northern Europe*
    R&R Bk N - v12 - F '97 - p77 [51-250]

Ekwall-Uebelhart, Barbara - *Managing Arms in Peace Processes: Croatia and Bosnia-Herzegovina*
    R&R Bk N - v12 - F '97 - p21 [1-50]

El Salvador: Meeting the Challenge of Globalization
    JEL - v35 - Mr '97 - p279 [51-250]

Elam, Diane - *Feminism and Deconstruction*
    TSWL - v15 - Fall '96 - p374+ [501+]
    Feminism Beside Itself
    NWSA Jnl - v8 - Fall '96 - p166+ [501+]

Elam, Harry Justin - *Colored Contradictions*
    LJ - v121 - O 15 '96 - p57+ [51-250]
    LJ - v121 - N 1 '96 - p84 [1-50]

Elaturoti, D F - *Animal Tales for Children*
    c Bkbird - v34 - Spr '96 - p53+ [1-50]

Elaydi, Saber N - *An Introduction to Difference Equations*
    Choice - v34 - O '96 - p318 [51-250]
    JEL - v34 - S '96 - p1410 [51-250]
    Proceedings of the First International Conference on Differential Equations
    SIAM Rev - v38 - S '96 - p545 [1-50]

Elazar, Daniel Judah - *Covenant and Polity in Biblical Israel*
    J Pol - v58 - Ag '96 - p901+ [501+]
    Israel at the Polls 1992
    J Ch St - v38 - Aut '96 - p925 [51-250]

Elberg, Yehuda - *The Empire of Kalman the Cripple*
    PW - v244 - Ap 14 '97 - p58 [51-250]
    Ship of the Hunted
    PW - v244 - Ap 14 '97 - p58 [51-250]

Elbert, Bruce R - *The Satellite Communication Applications Handbook*
    SciTech - v21 - Mr '97 - p87 [51-250]

Elbogen, Ismar - *Jewish Liturgy*
    TranslRevS - v1 - My '95 - p13 [51-250]

Elboz, Stephen - *The Byzantium Bazaar*
    c Bks Keeps - Jl '96 - p13 [51-250]
    c JB - v60 - Ag '96 - p155+ [51-250]
    y Sch Lib - v44 - Ag '96 - p117 [51-250]
    Ghostlands
    c JB - v60 - D '96 - p251 [51-250]
    c Sch Lib - v45 - F '97 - p24 [51-250]

Elcott, David M - *A Sacred Journey*
    Choice - v34 - N '96 - p475 [51-250]

Elder, Donald C - *Out from Behind the Eight-Ball*
    APH - v43 - Fall '96 - p68 [501+]

Elder, Gregory P - *Chronic Vigour*
    Choice - v34 - Ja '97 - p810 [51-250]

Elder, Jane Lenz - *Trading in Santa Fe*
    WHQ - v28 - Spr '97 - p74+ [51-250]

Elder, John - *American Nature Writers. Vols. 1-2*
    r ARBA - v28 - '97 - p440+ [51-250]
    yr BL - v93 - F 1 '97 - p961+ [251-500]
    r Choice - v34 - Ap '97 - p1305 [51-250]
    r R&R Bk N - v12 - F '97 - p87 [51-250]

Elder, Lindsey - *Early Embraces*
    Advocate - S 17 '96 - p60 [1-50]

Elderbrock, David - *Building Successful Internet Businesses*
    BWatch - v17 - N '96 - p11 [51-250]

Elders, Joycelyn - *Joycelyn Elders, M.D.: From Sharecropper's Daughter to Surgeon General of the United States of America*
    y BL - v93 - S 1 '96 - p3 [51-250]
    BW - v26 - O 6 '96 - p1+ [501+]
    KR - v64 - Ag 15 '96 - p1205+ [251-500]
    LJ - v121 - S 15 '96 - p75 [51-250]
    LJ - v121 - N 1 '96 - p80 [1-50]
    NYTBR - v101 - N 17 '96 - p30+ [501+]
    PW - v243 - S 2 '96 - p103 [51-250]

Eldersveld, Samuel J - *Local Elites in Western Democracies*
    J Pol - v58 - Ag '96 - p905+ [501+]
    Party Conflict and Community Development
    J Pol - v58 - Ag '96 - p887+ [501+]

Eldik, Rudi Van - *Chemistry under Extreme and Non-Classical Conditions*
    SciTech - v21 - Mr '97 - p31 [51-250]

Eldin, Peter - *Card Tricks (Illus. by Dave King)*
    c PW - v243 - S 9 '96 - p85 [51-250]
    The Most Excellent Book of How to Be a Magician (Illus. by Rob Shone)
    c HB Guide - v7 - Fall '96 - p358 [51-250]
    The Most Excellent Book of How to Do Card Tricks (Illus. by Rob Shone)
    c HB Guide - v8 - Spr '97 - p142 [51-250]
    c SLJ - v43 - F '97 - p89+ [51-250]

Eldredge, Niles - *Dominion: Can Nature and Culture Co-Exist?*
    PW - v244 - F 17 '97 - p217 [1-50]

Eldridge, Larry D - *A Distant Heritage*
    J Am Cult - v18 - Win '95 - p97 [51-250]

Eldridge, Philip J - *Non-Government Organizations and Democratic Participation in Indonesia*
    Choice - v34 - Ja '97 - p867+ [51-250]

Eldridge, Richard - *Beyond Representation*
    Choice - v34 - Ap '97 - p1330 [51-250]
    TLS - O 18 '96 - p26 [501+]

Eleanor, Lady - *Prophetic Writings of Lady Eleanor Davies*
    Sev Cent N - v54 - Fall '96 - p54+ [501+]
    VQR - v72 - Aut '96 - p119*+ [51-250]

Electric Cooperatives
    En Jnl - v17 - 4 '96 - p161+ [501+]

Electric Full Stops
    c Bks Keeps - Jl '96 - p13 [51-250]

Electric Power in Asia and the Pacific 1991 and 1992
    r ARBA - v28 - '97 - p645 [51-250]

Electric Power Industry Yearbook 1996
    r ARBA - v28 - '97 - p645 [51-250]

Electric Power Statistics Sourcebook. 3rd Ed.
    r ARBA - v28 - '97 - p645+ [51-250]

Electrical, Optical, and Magnetic Properties of Organic Solid State Materials III
    SciTech - v20 - N '96 - p23 [51-250]

Electroanalytical Chemistry. Vol. 19
    SciTech - v20 - N '96 - p22 [1-50]

Electronic Searching of the Health Sciences Literature
    LJ - v121 - N 1 '96 - p113 [51-250]

Electronic Surveillance in a Digital Age
    J Gov Info - v23 - S '96 - p555 [51-250]

Elegant, Robert - *Last Year in Hong Kong*
    BL - v93 - My 15 '97 - p1560+ [51-250]
    KR - v65 - Ap 1 '97 - p484 [251-500]
    PW - v244 - Ap 21 '97 - p60 [51-250]

Elementary Author/Illustrator Profiles
    cr SLMQ - v25 - Fall '96 - p63 [1-50]

The Elementary School Library Collection. 20th Ed.
    r ARBA - v28 - '97 - p245+ [251-500]
    r Emerg Lib - v24 - S '96 - p42 [1-50]
    r SLMQ - v25 - Fall '96 - p64 [1-50]

The Elementary School Library Collection. 20th Ed. Electronic Media Version
    r ARBA - v28 - '97 - p245+ [251-500]

Elements (Grolier). Vols. 1-15
    cr BL - v93 - Ja '97 - p888 [251-500]

Elen, Albert J - *Italian Late-Medieval and Renaissance Drawing-Books from Giovannino De'Grassi to Palma Giovane*
    Apo - v144 - O '96 - p59 [501+]
    BM - v138 - Jl '96 - p469+ [501+]

Elena, Horacio - *Como Llueve, Guille!*
    c BL - v93 - F 15 '97 - p1033 [1-50]
    Feliz Navidad, Guille!
    c BL - v93 - F 15 '97 - p1033 [1-50]
    El Hermano De Guille
    c BL - v93 - F 15 '97 - p1033 [1-50]

Elevator World
    p Utne R - Mr '97 - p87+ [51-250]

Eley, Beverley - *The Book of David*
Aust Bk R - O '96 - p28+ [501+]
Lon R Bks - v19 - Ap 3 '97 - p30+ [501+]
Eley, Geoff - *Becoming National*
For Aff - v76 - Mr '97 - p175+ [51-250]
Society, Culture, and the State in Germany 1870-1930
HRNB - v25 - Win '97 - p77 [251-500]
Elfring, Tom - *Theory-Building in the Business Sciences*
JEL - v35 - Mr '97 - p254+ [51-250]
Elfyn, Menna - *Cell Angel*
Obs - Mr 2 '97 - p18* [51-250]
Elgert, Klaus D - *Immunology: Understanding the Immune System*
BioSci - v46 - N '96 - p788+ [501+]
Elhard, Jay Robert - *Wolf Tourist*
Roundup M - v4 - Ap '97 - p29 [1-50]
Eliade, Mircea - *Encyclopedia of Religion. Electronic Media Version*
r BL - v93 - O 1 '96 - p365+ [501+]
r Choice - v34 - My '97 - p1482 [51-250]
L'Histoire Des Religions A-T-Elle Un Sens?
JR - v76 - O '96 - p682 [51-250]
Elias, Maurice J - *Social Problem Solving*
Readings - v12 - Mr '97 - p29 [51-250]
SB - v33 - Ja '97 - p5 [251-500]
Elias, Norbert - *The Germans: Power Struggles and the Development of Habitus in the Nineteenth and Twentieth Centuries*
CS - v26 - Mr '97 - p148+ [501+]
HRNB - v25 - Win '97 - p76 [501+]
New R - v216 - Ap 21 '97 - p39+ [501+]
Elias, Scott A - *The Ice-Age History of National Parks in the Rocky Mountains*
Choice - v34 - D '96 - p640 [51-250]
Elias, Stephen - *Patent, Copyright, and Trademark*
r ARBA - v28 - '97 - p233 [51-250]
r J Gov Info - v24 - Ja '97 - p63+ [501+]
Eliasson, Gunnar - *Firm Objectives, Controls and Organization*
JEL - v34 - S '96 - p1452 [51-250]
Elie, Lolis Eric - *Smokestack Lightning*
PW - v244 - Ap 21 '97 - p69 [1-50]
Eliel, Ernest L - *Stereochemistry of Organic Compounds*
r J Chem Ed - v73 - Ag '96 - pA174 [501+]
Elikann, Peter T - *The Tough-on-Crime Myth*
Choice - v34 - F '97 - p1042 [51-250]
Eliopoulos, Charlotte - *Manual of Gerontologic Nursing*
AJN - v96 - N '96 - p16D [51-250]
Eliot, George - *The Lifted Veil*
Nine-C Lit - v51 - Mr '97 - p455+ [501+]
Middlemarch
Nine-C Lit - v50 - Mr '96 - p501+ [501+]
The Mill on the Floss
RES - v47 - Ag '96 - p437 [251-500]
Silas Marner
CLS - v33 - 1 '96 - p69+ [501+]
Eliot, Joshua - *Indonesia Handbook*
r FEER - v160 - Mr 27 '97 - p49+ [501+]
r LJ - v122 - F 1 '97 - p98 [51-250]
Malaysia and Singapore Handbook
r FEER - v160 - Mr 27 '97 - p48+ [501+]
Eliot, T S - *Four Quartets*
Cres - v60 - Christmas '96 - p12+ [501+]
Inventions of the March Hare
BW - v27 - Mr 23 '97 - p6 [501+]
HM - v294 - Ja '97 - p62+ [501+]
LATBR - Ap 20 '97 - p10+ [501+]
Lon R Bks - v18 - O 31 '96 - p8+ [501+]
New R - v216 - Ap 28 '97 - p36+ [501+]
NS - v125 - S 27 '96 - p59 [501+]
NYTBR - v102 - Ap 20 '97 - p14+ [501+]
PW - v244 - Ja 27 '97 - p95 [501+]
Spec - v277 - S 7 '96 - p30+ [501+]
The Waste Land
LJ - v122 - My 1 '97 - p145 [1-50]
PW - v244 - F 3 '97 - p102 [1-50]
Elixhauser, A - *Trends in Hospital Diagnoses for Black Patients and White Patients 1980-87*
J Gov Info - v23 - S '96 - p548 [51-250]
Elizabeth, Martha - *The Return of Pleasure*
BL - v92 - Ag '96 - p1876 [51-250]
Elkhafif, Mahmoud A T - *The Egyptian Economy*
R&R Bk N - v11 - D '96 - p26 [51-250]
Elkin, Judith - *Focus on the Child*
LAR - v99 - F '97 - p102 [251-500]
Sch Lib - v45 - F '97 - p53 [51-250]
c TES - N 8 '96 - p11* [251-500]
Elkin, Stanley - *A Bad Man*
NYTBR - v101 - D 15 '96 - p40 [1-50]
George Mills
NYTBR - v101 - D 15 '96 - p40 [1-50]

The Living End
NYTBR - v101 - D 15 '96 - p40 [1-50]
Mrs. Ted Bliss
BW - v26 - D 15 '96 - p12 [51-250]
NYTBR - v101 - D 15 '96 - p40 [51-250]
PW - v243 - N 25 '96 - p70 [1-50]
WLT - v71 - Win '97 - p165 [51-250]
Elkind, David - *Parenting Your Teenager in the 1990s*
VOYA - v19 - D '96 - p256 [1-50]
Elkins, Aaron - *Twenty Blue Devils*
BL - v93 - Ja '97 - p824 [51-250]
Ent W - Ja 17 '97 - p58+ [51-250]
KR - v64 - N 1 '96 - p1565 [51-250]
NYTBR - v102 - Ja 19 '97 - p22 [51-250]
PW - v243 - N 25 '96 - p59 [51-250]
Elkins, David J - *Beyond Sovereignty*
APSR - v91 - Mr '97 - p229+ [501+]
Theol St - v57 - S '96 - p574+ [251-500]
Elkins, Heather Murray - *Pulpit, Table, and Song*
R&R Bk N - v11 - D '96 - p5 [51-250]
Elkins, James - *The Object Stares Back*
A Lib - v27 - Ag '96 - p71 [51-250]
Elkins, Michael - *Forged in Fury*
NS & S - v9 - My 3 '96 - p37 [1-50]
Elkins, Rita - *The Complete Home Health Advisor*
r ARBA - v28 - '97 - p611 [51-250]
Elleh, Nnamdi - *African Architecture*
Choice - v34 - My '97 - p1485+ [51-250]
Ellenbecker, Todd S - *The Elbow in Sport*
SciTech - v21 - Mr '97 - p60 [1-50]
Ellenberger, Francois - *History of Geology. Vol. 1*
SciTech - v20 - N '96 - p24 [51-250]
Ellenbogen, Kenneth A - *Cardiac Pacing. 2nd Ed.*
SciTech - v20 - D '96 - p47 [51-250]
Ellenhorn, Matthew J - *Ellenhorn's Medical Toxicology. 2nd Ed.*
r SciTech - v21 - Mr '97 - p47 [51-250]
Ellens, J P - *Religious Routes to Gladstonian Liberalism*
CH - v65 - S '96 - p517+ [501+]
EHR - v112 - Ap '97 - p508+ [501+]
VS - v39 - Aut '95 - p95+ [501+]
Elles, Rob - *Molecular Diagnosis of Genetic Diseases*
SciTech - v20 - N '96 - p39 [51-250]
Ellet, William - *A Critical Guide to Management Training Videos and Selected Multimedia 1996*
r ARBA - v28 - '97 - p123 [251-500]
r Choice - v34 - S '96 - p94 [51-250]
r R&R Bk N - v11 - N '96 - p28 [51-250]
Ellings, Richard J - *Southeast Asian Security in the New Millennium*
For Aff - v76 - Mr '97 - p198+ [51-250]
R&R Bk N - v12 - F '97 - p100 [1-50]
Ellingsen, Mark - *A Common Sense Theology*
Intpr - v51 - Ap '97 - p218+ [251-500]
Elliot, Carl - *The Rules of Insanity*
Hast Cen R - v26 - S '96 - p40 [51-250]
Elliot, Faith Robertson - *Gender, Family, and Society*
R&R Bk N - v11 - N '96 - p41 [1-50]
Elliot, Ginny - *Race against Time*
c JB - v60 - O '96 - p199 [51-250]
Elliot, Jack - *Bulbs for the Rock Garden*
r ARBA - v28 - '97 - p571 [51-250]
Elliot, Jason - *Religions of the World (Illus. by L R Galante)*
c Sch Lib - v44 - N '96 - p162 [51-250]
Elliot, Matthew - *Independent Iraq*
Choice - v34 - F '97 - p1022 [51-250]
Elliott, Anthony - *Subject to Ourselves*
Choice - v34 - Ja '97 - p878 [51-250]
Elliott, Cecil D - *Technics and Architecture*
r Isis - v87 - D '96 - p738+ [501+]
Elliott, Clark A - *History of Science in the United States*
r ARBA - v28 - '97 - p562 [501+]
r Choice - v34 - N '96 - p427+ [51-250]
r Isis - v87 - D '96 - p769+ [251-500]
Elliott, David J - *Music Matters*
Notes - v53 - Mr '97 - p770+ [501+]
Elliott, Deni - *The Ethics of Asking*
Ethics - v107 - Ja '97 - p398+ [51-250]
LQ - v66 - O '96 - p480+ [501+]
Elliott, Dyan - *Spiritual Marriage*
JWomHist - v8 - Fall '96 - p228+ [501+]
Elliott, Gary E - *Senator Alan Bible and the Politics of the New West*
PHR - v65 - Ag '96 - p503+ [251-500]
Elliott, J K - *The Apocryphal Jesus*
Rel St Rev - v23 - Ja '97 - p77 [251-500]
Elliott, James - *Cold Cold Heart*
Books - v9 - S '95 - p25 [1-50]

Nowhere to Hide
BL - v93 - My 1 '97 - p1481 [51-250]
KR - v65 - My 1 '97 - p661 [251-500]
LJ - v122 - My 1 '97 - p138 [51-250]
PW - v244 - Ap 28 '97 - p46+ [251-500]
Elliott, Kate - *King's Dragon*
y BL - v93 - F 15 '97 - p1008 [51-250]
KR - v64 - D 1 '96 - p1707 [51-250]
PW - v244 - Ja 20 '97 - p398 [251-500]
Elliott, Keith - *Manuscripts and the Text of the New Testament*
Rel St Rev - v23 - Ap '97 - p173 [51-250]
Elliott, Kim S - *Multi-Storey Precast Concrete Framed Structures*
SciTech - v20 - N '96 - p69 [51-250]
Elliott, Marianne - *Partners in Revolution*
Bks & Cult - v2 - Ja '96 - p11+ [501+]
Wolfe Tone: Prophet of Irish Independence
Bks & Cult - v2 - Ja '96 - p11+ [501+]
Elliott, Max - *Ms. Thang, Real Knights Don't Show Up at 3 in the Morning*
BL - v93 - F 15 '97 - p978 [51-250]
PW - v244 - Ja 6 '97 - p56+ [51-250]
Elliott, Melinda - *Great Excavations*
Am Ant - v62 - Ja '97 - p173 [251-500]
Elliott, Michael - *The Day before Yesterday*
BW - v26 - Ag 25 '96 - p5 [501+]
For Aff - v75 - N '96 - p152 [51-250]
KR - v64 - My 1 '96 - p660 [251-500]
NYTBR - v101 - Ag 25 '96 - p30 [501+]
Elliott, Michele - *Female Sexual Abuse of Children*
Fam in Soc - v77 - D '96 - p639+ [501+]
Elliott, Portia C - *Communication in Mathematics, K-12 and Beyond*
SciTech - v20 - N '96 - p5 [51-250]
Elliott, Richard M - *The Bunyaviridae*
SciTech - v20 - S '96 - p26 [51-250]
Ellis, Albert - *Better, Deeper, and More Enduring Brief Therapy*
Readings - v11 - S '96 - p26+ [51-250]
Ellis, Alice Thomas - *Fairy Tales*
TLS - S 13 '96 - p24 [501+]
Woman's J - N '96 - p12 [1-50]
Serpent on the Rock
Bks & Cult - v2 - Ja '96 - p28 [251-500]
A Welsh Childhood
LJ - v122 - Ja '97 - p110 [51-250]
NYTBR - v102 - Ap 20 '97 - p21 [51-250]
PW - v244 - Ja 20 '97 - p382 [51-250]
Ellis, Barbara - *Attracting Birds and Butterflies*
PW - v244 - Ja 27 '97 - p100 [51-250]
Organic Pest and Disease Control
PW - v244 - Ja 27 '97 - p100 [51-250]
Safe and Easy Lawn Care
PW - v244 - Ja 27 '97 - p100 [51-250]
Ellis, Carol - *The Stalker*
y SLJ - v42 - S '96 - p227 [51-250]
Ellis, Clyde - *To Change Them Forever*
Choice - v34 - O '96 - p347 [51-250]
WHQ - v28 - Spr '97 - p80 [251-500]
Ellis, David - *Imitating Art*
Biography - v19 - Sum '96 - p304+ [501+]
Ellis, Desmond - *Mediating and Negotiating Marital Conflicts*
R&R Bk N - v11 - D '96 - p41 [51-250]
Ellis, Edward Robb - *A Diary of the Century*
NYTBR - v101 - N 24 '97 - p32 [51-250]
Ellis, Frank - *Vasiliy Grossman: The Genesis and Evolution of a Russian Heretic*
Russ Rev - v56 - Ja '97 - p134+ [501+]
Ellis, Geoffrey - *Napoleon*
HT - v46 - O '96 - p57 [1-50]
Ellis, George M - *Gold Rush Desert Trails to San Diego and Los Angeles in 1849*
WHQ - v28 - Spr '97 - p85 [251-500]
Ellis, John H - *Yellow Fever and Public Health in the New South*
J Urban H - v22 - My '96 - p531+ [501+]
Ellis, Joseph J - *American Sphinx*
y BL - v93 - Ja '97 - p812 [51-250]
BW - v27 - F 23 '97 - p1+ [501+]
KR - v65 - Ja 1 '97 - p32+ [251-500]
New R - v216 - Mr 10 '97 - p32+ [51-250]
NL - v79 - D 16 '96 - p9+ [501+]
NYTBR - v102 - Mr 23 '97 - p7 [501+]
NYTLa - v146 - F 11 '97 - pC16 [501+]
PW - v243 - D 2 '96 - p47 [51-250]
Trib Bks - F 16 '97 - p1+ [501+]
Ellis, Joyce - *Tiffany*
y VOYA - v19 - D '96 - p261 [51-250]

Ellis, Julie - *Deadly Obsession*
　BL - v93 - D 1 '96 - p642+ [51-250]
Ellis, Marc H - *Ending Auschwitz*
　J Ch St - v38 - Sum '96 - p660 [51-250]
Ellis, Mark - *Teaching Business English*
　MLJ - v80 - Fall '96 - p412 [501+]
Ellis, Markman - *The Politics of Sensibility*
　Choice - v34 - Ja '97 - p793 [51-250]
Ellis, Merle - *The Great American Meat Book*
　BL - v93 - S 15 '96 - p196 [51-250]
　Esq - v126 - D '96 - p40 [1-50]
　LJ - v121 - S 15 '96 - p89+ [51-250]
Ellis, Patty - *Girl Power*
　y　Ch BWatch - v6 - My '96 - p7 [51-250]
Ellis, Peter Berresford - *Celt and Greek*
　HT - v46 - O '96 - p55 [1-50]
　NS - v126 - Mr 14 '97 - p48 [251-500]
Ellis, R John - *The Chaperonins*
　Sci - v274 - D 13 '96 - p1848 [501+]
　SciTech - v20 - S '96 - p23 [51-250]
Ellis, Ralph D - *Eros in a Narcissistic Culture*
　R&R Bk N - v11 - D '96 - p2 [51-250]
Ellis, Richard - *Deep Atlantic*
　BL - v93 - D 1 '96 - p630 [1-50]
　y　BL - v93 - D 1 '96 - p664 [1-50]
　Choice - v34 - My '97 - p1526 [51-250]
　LATBR - Ja 5 '97 - p10 [501+]
　LJ - v121 - O 1 '96 - p118 [51-250]
　NH - v105 - N '96 - p16 [1-50]
　PW - v243 - S 9 '96 - p75 [51-250]
Ellis, Robert B - *See Naples and Die*
　LJ - v121 - O 1 '96 - p98 [51-250]
Ellis, Rosemary - *Selected Writings of Rosemary Ellis*
　Choice - v34 - D '96 - p645 [51-250]
Ellis, S - *Soils and Environment*
　GJ - v162 - N '96 - p338 [251-500]
Ellis, Sarah - *Back of Beyond*
　y　Ch Bk News - v20 - Win '97 - p27 [51-250]
　y　JAAL - v40 - Mr '97 - p509+ [251-500]
　y　Quill & Q - v62 - O '96 - p51 [251-500]
　c　Quill & Q - v63 - F '97 - p51 [251-500]
　Next-Door Neighbors
　c　SLJ - v43 - Ja '97 - p36 [1-50]
　Out of the Blue
　c　PW - v243 - D 9 '96 - p69 [1-50]
Ellis, Stephen, 1953- - *Africa Now*
　JEL - v34 - S '96 - p1487+ [51-250]
　WorldV - v12 - Jl '96 - p5 [51-250]
Ellis, Steven G, 1950- - *Conquest and Union*
　Albion - v28 - Sum '96 - p296+ [501+]
　Tudor Frontiers and Noble Power
　AHR - v102 - F '97 - p99 [501+]
　Albion - v28 - Fall '96 - p474+ [501+]
　HT - v46 - Ag '96 - p58+ [501+]
Ellis, Susan J - *From the Top Down. Rev. Ed.*
　ChrPhil - v8 - Je 27 '96 - p34 [51-250]
Ellis, Wanda M - *Bryan County, Oklahoma Prestatehood Marriages July 1902-November 07*
　r　EGH - v50 - N '96 - p182+ [51-250]
Ellison, Curtis W - *Country Music Culture*
　LJ - v121 - N 1 '96 - p41 [1-50]
Ellison, Emily - *Rocky Bobocky, the Pizza Man (Illus. by Vickey Bolling)*
　c　Smith - v27 - N '96 - p170 [1-50]
Ellison, Harlan - *The City on the Edge of Forever*
　LJ - v121 - D '96 - p154 [51-250]
　Edgeworks. Vol. 1
　SF Chr - v18 - O '96 - p82 [1-50]
　Edgeworks. Vol. 2
　LJ - v122 - Ja '97 - p155 [1-50]
Ellison, James M - *Integrative Treatment of Anxiety Disorders*
　AJPsych - v154 - Ja '97 - p127+ [501+]
Ellison, Julian - *Murder on the Net*
　TES - O 18 '96 - p41U [51-250]
　TLS - O 18 '96 - p22 [251-500]
Ellison, Marvin M - *Erotic Justice*
　Rel St Rev - v23 - Ap '97 - p159 [51-250]
Ellison, Ralph - *The Collected Essays of Ralph Ellison*
　HR - v49 - Aut '96 - p497+ [501+]

Flying Home and Other Stories
　BL - v93 - Ja '97 - p761 [1-50]
　CSM - v89 - F 10 '97 - p14 [501+]
　Ent W - D 13 '96 - p74+ [51-250]
　KR - v64 - O 1 '96 - p1419+ [251-500]
　LJ - v121 - D '96 - p149 [51-250]
　NYTBR - v102 - Ja 19 '97 - p13+ [501+]
　NYTLa - v146 - D 10 '96 - pC19 [501+]
　Time - v149 - Ja 13 '97 - p76 [51-250]
　W&I - v12 - Mr '97 - p235 [251-500]
　W&I - v12 - Mr '97 - p247+ [501+]
　W&I - v12 - Mr '97 - p253+ [501+]
Invisible Man
　AL - v68 - S '96 - p587+ [501+]
　CLS - v33 - 4 '96 - p372+ [501+]
Ellison, Sheila - *365 Foods Kids Love to Eat*
　Ch BWatch - v6 - My '96 - p7 [51-250]
Ellridge, Arthur - *Mucha: The Triumph of Art Nouveau*
　Atl - v278 - Ag '96 - p94 [51-250]
　LATBR - D 22 '96 - p6 [51-250]
Ellroy, James - *My Dark Places*
　BW - v26 - N 24 '96 - p9 [501+]
　Ent W - N 15 '96 - p63+ [251-500]
　KR - v64 - S 15 '96 - p1370 [501+]
　LATBR - D 1 '96 - p10 [501+]
　LJ - v122 - Ja '97 - p49 [1-50]
　LJ - v121 - N 15 '96 - p74 [1-50]
　Nat - v263 - D 2 '96 - p25+ [501+]
　NS - v125 - N 8 '96 - p46+ [501+]
　NW - v128 - N 11 '96 - p79 [251-500]
　NY - v72 - Ja 20 '97 - p97 [51-250]
　NYTBR - v101 - N 24 '96 - p11+ [501+]
　NYTBR - v101 - D 8 '96 - p89 [1-50]
　NYTLa - v146 - N 5 '96 - pC16 [501+]
　Obs - D 1 '96 - p16* [51-250]
　Obs - D 22 '96 - p17* [501+]
　PW - v243 - O 21 '96 - p63+ [51-250]
　Spec - v277 - N 30 '96 - p50+ [501+]
　Time - v148 - N 25 '96 - p115+ [501+]
　Time - v148 - D 23 '96 - p86 [51-250]
　TLS - N 22 '96 - p26 [501+]
　VV - v41 - D 17 '96 - p52+ [501+]
My Dark Places (Ellroy). Audio Version
　LJ - v122 - F 1 '97 - p126 [51-250]
Ellsworth, Jill H - *The New Internet Business Book*
　CBR - v15 - Spr '97 - p6 [1-50]
　Quill & Q - v62 - My '96 - p22+ [501+]
　The Web after Work for Dummies
　BL - v93 - S 15 '96 - p193 [501+]
Ellsworth, Mary Ellen - *Gertrude Chandler Warner and the Boxcar Children (Illus. by Marie De John)*
　c　PW - v244 - Ap 28 '97 - p77 [251-500]
Ellwand, David - *The Big Book of Beautiful Babies*
　c　NYTBR - v102 - Mr 30 '97 - p18 [501+]
　Emma's Elephant
　c　Obs - Mr 30 '97 - p17* [51-250]
Ellwood, Robert S - *The 60s: Spiritual Awakening*
　J Am Cult - v18 - Win '95 - p116 [251-500]
Elm, Kaspar - *Bernhard Von Clairvaux: Rezeption Und Wirkung Im Mittelalter Und In Der Neuzeit*
　CH - v66 - Mr '97 - p93+ [501+]
　EHR - v112 - Ap '97 - p432+ [501+]
Elm, Susanna - *Virgins of God*
　CH - v66 - Mr '97 - p84+ [501+]
Elmendorf, Anthony D - *Rings, Modules, and Algebras in Stable Homotopy Theory*
　SciTech - v21 - Mr '97 - p18 [51-250]
Elmore, Ronn - *How to Love a Black Man*
　Bl S - v26 - Sum '96 - p64 [1-50]
　PW - v244 - Ja 27 '97 - p103 [1-50]
Elms, Alan C - *Uncovering Lives*
　Biography - v19 - Fall '96 - p429 [1-50]
Elmusa, Sharif - *A Harvest of Technology*
　MEJ - v51 - Win '97 - p126+ [501+]
Elofson, W M - *The Rockingham Connection and the Second Founding of the Whig Party 1768-1773*
　Choice - v34 - S '96 - p186 [51-250]
Elon, Amos - *A Blood-Dimmed Tide*
　LJ - v122 - My 1 '97 - p124 [51-250]
　PW - v244 - Ap 14 '97 - p61 [51-250]
　Founder: A Portrait of the First Rothschild and His Time
　BL - v93 - O 1 '96 - p311 [51-250]
　KR - v64 - S 1 '96 - p1292 [251-500]
　LATBR - N 24 '96 - p8 [501+]
　LJ - v121 - O 1 '96 - p90 [51-250]
　NYRB - v44 - Ja 9 '97 - p37+ [501+]
　NYTBR - v101 - O 27 '96 - p50 [501+]
　NYTLa - v146 - N 4 '96 - pA24 [501+]
　PW - v243 - S 2 '96 - p99+ [51-250]

Founder: Meyer Amschel Rothschild and His Time
　TLS - Ja 17 '97 - p19 [501+]
Elon, Ari - *From Jerusalem to the Edge of Heaven*
　LJ - v121 - O 1 '96 - p83+ [51-250]
　MEJ - v51 - Win '97 - p150+ [51-250]
　Tikkun - v12 - Mr '97 - p70+ [501+]
Elrod, P N - *The Time of the Vampires*
　y　Kliatt - v30 - S '96 - p16 [51-250]
Elsayed, Elsayed A - *Reliability Engineering*
　SciTech - v20 - N '96 - p61 [51-250]
Elsener, Willi - *Music and Menus for Christmas*
　ILN - Christmas '96 - p90 [1-50]
Elshami, Ahmed M - *Networking CD-ROMs*
　SL - v87 - Sum '96 - p234+ [251-500]
El-Shamy, Hasan M - *Folk Traditions of the Arab World. Vols. 1-2*
　Folkl - v107 - '96 - p120+ [501+]
　r　MEJ - v50 - Aut '96 - p624+ [51-250]
Elshtain, Jean Bethke - *Augustine and the Limits of Politics*
　Choice - v34 - N '96 - p473 [51-250]
　RP - v59 - Spr '97 - p365+ [501+]
　Women and War
　Bks & Cult - v2 - Ja '96 - p30 [51-250]
Elsner, James B - *Singular Spectrum Analysis*
　SciTech - v21 - Mr '97 - p87 [1-50]
Elsner, Jas. - *Art and the Roman Viewer*
　AJA - v100 - O '96 - p805+ [501+]
　BM - v138 - Ag '96 - p545+ [501+]
Elson Roessler, Shirley - *Out of the Shadows*
　Choice - v34 - Mr '97 - p1223 [51-250]
　R&R Bk N - v12 - F '97 - p15 [51-250]
Elste, Joan - *True Blue (Illus. by DyAnne DiSalvo-Ryan)*
　c　BL - v93 - N 15 '96 - p596 [51-250]
Elsted, Crispin - *Climate and the Affections*
　BIC - v26 - F '97 - p8+ [501+]
Elster, Jon - *Local Justice in America*
　ACI - v8 - Fall '96 - p34+ [501+]
　The Roundtable Talks and the Breakdown of Communism
　Choice - v34 - Ap '97 - p1415 [51-250]
Elston, Tony - *Genial 2*
　y　TES - Mr 7 '97 - pR9 [51-250]
Elteren, Mel Van - *Imagining America*
　JPC - v29 - Spr '96 - p259+ [51-250]
Eltis, David - *The Military Revolution in Sixteenth-Century Europe*
　Six Ct J - v27 - Fall '96 - p932+ [501+]
Eltis, Sos - *Revising Wilde*
　Nine-C Lit - v51 - D '96 - p421 [51-250]
　VQR - v73 - Win '97 - p14* [51-250]
Eltis, Walter - *Classical Economics, Public Expenditure and Growth*
　Econ J - v106 - S '96 - p1464 [51-250]
Eltit, Diamela - *Sacred Cow*
　Books - v9 - S '95 - p25 [1-50]
　Los Vigilantes
　WLT - v70 - Aut '96 - p922+ [251-500]
Elton, G R - *The English*
　HT - v46 - S '96 - p57 [51-250]
Elton, Hugh - *Frontiers of the Roman Empire*
　Choice - v34 - N '96 - p514 [51-250]
　Warfare in Roman Europe AD 350-425
　Choice - v34 - O '96 - p336 [51-250]
　HRNB - v25 - Win '97 - p88 [251-500]
　J Mil H - v60 - O '96 - p769+ [251-500]
Eluard, Paul - *Unbroken Poetry II*
　BL - v93 - N 1 '96 - p475+ [51-250]
　TranslRevS - v2 - D '96 - p22 [51-250]
Elvira - *Elvira: Transylvania 90210*
　PW - v243 - S 30 '96 - p80 [51-250]
Elwell, Walter A - *Evangelical Dictionary of Biblical Theology*
　r　ARBA - v28 - '97 - p544 [51-250]
　r　Choice - v34 - D '96 - p589 [51-250]
　r　Rel St Rev - v23 - Ja '97 - p69 [51-250]
Elwin, Janet B - *Ties-Ties-Ties: Traditional Quilts from Neckties*
　BL - v93 - S 15 '96 - p201+ [51-250]
Elworthy, Scilla - *Weapons Decisions*
　TLS - F 28 '97 - p25+ [501+]
Ely, Donald P - *Classic Writings on Instructional Technology*
　SLMQ - v25 - Fall '96 - p63 [51-250]
Ely, James W, Jr. - *The Chief Justiceship of Melville W. Fuller 1888-1910*
　IndRev - v1 - Spr '97 - p615+ [501+]
　JEH - v56 - D '96 - p957+ [501+]
　JSH - v62 - N '96 - p826+ [51-250]
　Pres SQ - v26 - Sum '96 - p901+ [501+]

Ely, John Hart - *On Constitutional Ground*
　　TLS - D 27 '96 - p9+ [501+]
Elya, Susan Middleton - *Say Hola to Spanish (Illus. by Loretta Lopez)*
　c　Ch BWatch - v6 - Jl '96 - p5 [1-50]
　c　HB Guide - v8 - Spr '97 - p107 [51-250]
　c　Inst - v42 - Ag '96 - p45 [51-250]
Elytis, Odysseas - *Open Papers*
　　TranslRevS - v1 - My '95 - p23 [51-250]
Elze, Winifred - *Here, Kitty, Kitty*
　　KR - v64 - My 1 '96 - p620 [251-500]
　　Rapport - v19 - 5 '96 - p28 [251-500]
Elzinga, Richard J - *Fundamentals of Entomology. 4th Ed.*
　　SciTech - v20 - D '96 - p32 [51-250]
Ember, Ildiko - *Delights for the Senses*
　　Sev Cent N - v54 - Spr '96 - p28+ [501+]
Emberley, Barbara - *Drummer Hoff (Illus. by Edward Emberley)*
　c　PW - v244 - Ap 28 '97 - p77 [51-250]
Emberley, Peter - *Zero Tolerance*
　　BIC - v25 - D '96 - p23+ [501+]
　　Mac - v109 - S 16 '96 - p69 [501+]
Emberley, Rebecca - *Three Cool Kids (Illus. by Rebecca Emberley)*
　c　Emerg Lib - v24 - S '96 - p46 [51-250]
　c　Inst - v105 - My '96 - p69 [51-250]
Emberson-Bain, Atu - *Labour and Gold in Fiji*
　　JIH - v27 - Aut '96 - p384+ [501+]
Sustainable Development or Malignant Growth?
　　Cont Pac - v9 - Spr '97 - p288+ [501+]
Embry, Jessie L - *Black Saints in a White Church*
　　CH - v65 - S '96 - p543+ [501+]
Emerson, Caryl - *Modest Musorgsky and Boris Godunov*
　　MLR - v92 - Ja '97 - p268+ [251-500]
Emerson, Connie - *The Cheapskate's Guide to Paris*
　r　BL - v93 - S 15 '96 - p206 [1-50]
Emerson, D - *Interpreting Astronomical Spectra*
　　New Sci - v153 - Mr 1 '97 - p43 [51-250]
Emerson, Earl - *The Dead Horse Paint Company*
　　PW - v244 - My 12 '97 - p61+ [51-250]
Going Crazy in Public
　　Arm Det - v30 - Win '97 - p88 [251-500]
　　KR - v64 - My 1 '96 - p642+ [51-250]
The Million-Dollar Tattoo
　　Arm Det - v30 - Win '97 - p113+ [501+]
　　BL - v93 - S 15 '96 - p224 [51-250]
　　LATBR - O 13 '96 - p8 [251-500]
Emerson, Isabelle Putnam - *Twentieth-Century American Music for the Dance*
　r　ARBA - v28 - '97 - p503+ [51-250]
　r　R&R Bk N - v11 - D '96 - p55 [51-250]
Emerson, Jane - *City of Diamond*
　　MFSF - v91 - S '96 - p41+ [251-500]
Emerson, Kathy Lynn - *Face Down in the Marrow-Bone Pie*
　　KR - v65 - F 15 '97 - p257 [251-500]
　　LJ - v122 - Ap 1 '97 - p133 [51-250]
The Writer's Guide to Everyday Life in Renaissance England
　　BL - v92 - Ag '96 - p1874 [51-250]
　yr　SLJ - v43 - F '97 - p37 [51-250]
Emerson, Ken - *Doo-Dah! Stephen Foster and the Rise of American Popular Culture*
　　KR - v65 - Mr 15 '97 - p433 [251-500]
　　LJ - v122 - My 1 '97 - p105 [51-250]
　　PW - v244 - Mr 31 '97 - p53+ [251-500]
　　Trib Bks - My 4 '97 - p5 [501+]
Emerson, Ralph Waldo - *Emerson's Antislavery Writings*
　　ASInt - v34 - O '96 - p104+ [251-500]
　　J Am St - v30 - Ap '96 - p164 [251-500]
The Letters of Ralph Waldo Emerson. Vols. 7-10
　　NEQ - v69 - D '96 - p631+ [501+]
Emerson, Robert M - *Writing Ethnographic Fieldnotes*
　　CS - v25 - S '96 - p705+ [501+]
　　JPR - v34 - F '97 - p111 [51-250]
Emerson, William K - *Encyclopedia of United States Army Insignia and Uniforms*
　r　BL - v93 - Mr 1 '97 - p1186+ [251-500]
Emert, Phyllis Raybin - *Top Lawyers and Their Famous Cases*
　y　BL - v93 - S 1 '96 - p71 [51-250]
　c　CLW - v67 - Mr '97 - p54 [51-250]
　y　HB Guide - v8 - Spr '97 - p92 [51-250]
　y　SLJ - v42 - N '96 - p128 [51-250]
Emery, Amy Fass - *The Anthropological Imagination in Latin American Literature*
　　Choice - v34 - My '97 - p1504 [51-250]
Emery, Anthony - *Greater Medieval Houses of England and Wales 1300-1500. Vol. 1*
　　HT - v46 - O '96 - p56 [51-250]

Emery, Dominic - *Sequence Stratigraphy*
　　SciTech - v21 - Mr '97 - p33 [51-250]
Emery, Marcia - *Intuition (Emery). Audio Version*
　　BL - v93 - N 15 '96 - p604 [51-250]
Emery, Robert F - *The Bond Markets of Developing East Asia*
　　R&R Bk N - v12 - F '97 - p49 [51-250]
Emery, S W - *Plato's Euthyphro, Apology and Crito*
　　CPR - v16 - Ag '96 - p245+ [501+]
Emigh, John - *Masked Performance*
　　Choice - v34 - My '97 - p1511 [51-250]
　　R&R Bk N - v12 - F '97 - p82 [51-250]
Emile Zola Centenary Colloquium (1993: London, England) - *Emile Zola Centenary Colloquium 1893-1993*
　　MLR - v92 - Ap '97 - p474+ [251-500]
Emler, Nicholas - *Adolescence and Delinquency*
　　CS - v26 - Ja '97 - p82+ [501+]
Emmanuel, Steven M - *Kierkegaard and the Concept of Revelation*
　　Rel St - v32 - S '96 - p427 [51-250]
　　Rel St Rev - v23 - Ap '97 - p153 [51-250]
Emme - *True Beauty*
　　LJ - v122 - Ja '97 - p126 [51-250]
Emmel, Barbara - *Argument Revisited*
　　R&R Bk N - v11 - N '96 - p64 [51-250]
Emmerling, Mary - *Mary Emmerling's New Country Collecting*
　　Ant & CM - v101 - S '96 - p27 [1-50]
Emmery, Lena - *Wine Country Bike Rides*
　r　LJ - v122 - Ap 1 '97 - p113 [51-250]
Emmet, A Maitland - *The Scientific Names of the British Lepidoptera*
　　BW - v26 - D 8 '96 - p4 [51-250]
Emmet, Alan - *So Fine a Prospect*
　　Choice - v34 - Ja '97 - p819 [51-250]
　　LATBR - D 8 '96 - p4 [51-250]
　　LJ - v121 - O 15 '96 - p82 [51-250]
　　NYTBR - v101 - D 8 '96 - p41+ [51-250]
Emmett, Ayala - *Our Sisters' Promised Land*
　　Choice - v34 - Mr '97 - p1201 [51-250]
Emmett, Chad F - *Beyond the Basilica*
　　Bks & Cult - v2 - Mr '96 - p17 [501+]
Emmett, David - *Understanding Drugs*
　　TES - O 25 '96 - p8* [251-500]
Emmison, F G - *Essex Wills*
　r　EHR - v112 - Ap '97 - p464 [251-500]
Emmons, Bob - *The Book of Tequila*
　r　BL - v93 - My 15 '97 - p1550 [51-250]
Emmons, Didi - *Vegetarian Planet*
　　BL - v93 - My 15 '97 - p1551+ [51-250]
　　PW - v244 - My 5 '97 - p203 [51-250]
Emory, Jerry - *Dirty, Rotten, Dead? (Illus. by T Taylor Bruce)*
　c　SB - v32 - N '96 - p240 [51-250]
　c　SLJ - v42 - Ag '96 - p152+ [51-250]
Empiricus, Sextus - *Outlines of Scepticism (Annas)*
　　CPR - v16 - Ap '96 - p143+ [501+]
Emploi Plus
　p　Sm Pr R - v28 - D '96 - p19 [251-500]
Employee Duty of Loyalty
　r　ARBA - v28 - '97 - p223 [251-500]
Employee Duty of Loyalty. 1996 Suppl.
　r　ARBA - v28 - '97 - p223 [251-500]
Employment Relations Abstracts. 1952-1958 Eds.
　r　RQ - v36 - Fall '96 - p53+ [51-250]
Empson, William - *Essays on Renaissance Literature. Vol. 1*
　　Ren Q - v49 - Win '96 - p879+ [501+]
Emshwiller, Carol - *Ledoyt, a Novel*
　　Wom R Bks - v14 - Ja '97 - p5+ [501+]
Emsley, Clive - *Crime Histories and Histories of Crime*
　　Hist & T - v36 - F '97 - p108 [501+]
Emsley, John - *The Consumer's Good Chemical Guide*
　　E Mag - v7 - S '96 - p48 [51-250]
　y　Kliatt - v30 - S '96 - p35 [51-250]
Enamels of Limoges 1100-1350
　　Choice - v34 - Mr '97 - p1150 [51-250]
　　R&R Bk N - v11 - N '96 - p62 [51-250]
Encarta 97 Encyclopedia. Deluxe Ed. Electronic Media Version
　yr　BL - v93 - N 1 '96 - p526+ [501+]
　yr　Kliatt - v31 - Ja '97 - p33+ [251-500]
　cr　LJ - v122 - Ap 15 '97 - p128 [51-250]
　r　PW - v244 - Ja 27 '97 - p37 [51-250]
　r　Quill & Q - v62 - D '96 - p31 [501+]
Encarta 97 Encyclopedia. World English Ed. Electronic Media Version
　cr　TES - Mr 14 '97 - p33U [501+]
Encarta '97 World Atlas. Electronic Media Version
　r　PW - v244 - Ja 27 '97 - p37 [51-250]

Enciclopedia Visual: Los Seres Vivos
　cr　BL - v93 - Mr 1 '97 - p1196 [51-250]
Enciclopedia Visual: Paises Del Mundo
　cr　BL - v93 - Mr 1 '97 - p1196 [51-250]
Encinar, Angeles - *Cuentos De Este Siglo*
　　WLT - v71 - Win '97 - p124+ [501+]
Enck, John - *An Introduction to Communications for the AS/400. 2nd Ed.*
　　SciTech - v20 - S '96 - p7 [51-250]
Encyclopedia Americana 1996. Electronic Media Version
　r　ARBA - v28 - '97 - p22+ [501+]
　r　BL - v93 - N 1 '96 - p530 [501+]
　r　Choice - v34 - Ja '97 - p778 [251-500]
　r　LJ - v121 - N 15 '96 - p95+ [501+]
　yr　SLJ - v43 - F '97 - p49 [51-250]
Encyclopedia Americana 1996. Vols. 1-30
　yr　BL - v93 - S 15 '96 - p270+ [501+]
Encyclopedia Britannica CD 97. Electronic Media Version
　r　LJ - v122 - Ap 15 '97 - p128 [51-250]
Encyclopedia of Associations: National Organizations of the U.S. Electronic Media Version
　r　ARBA - v28 - '97 - p26 [51-250]
Encyclopedia of Bioethics. Electronic Media Version
　r　Choice - v34 - Ap '97 - p1320 [501+]
　r　LJ - v121 - D '96 - p160+ [501+]
Encyclopedia of Bioethics. Rev. Ed., Vols. 1-5
　r　Rel St Rev - v22 - O '96 - p279+ [501+]
　r　Rel St Rev - v22 - O '96 - p280+ [501+]
　r　Rel St Rev - v22 - O '96 - p282+ [501+]
　r　Rel St Rev - v22 - O '96 - p284+ [501+]
Encyclopedia of Climate and Weather. Vols. 1-2
　r　ARBA - v28 - '97 - p633 [251-500]
　r　BL - v92 - Ag '96 - p1924 [251-500]
　r　BL - v93 - Ja '97 - p769 [1-50]
　r　Choice - v34 - O '96 - p250 [251-500]
　r　SciTech - v20 - S '96 - p15 [51-250]
Encyclopedia of Computer Science and Technology. Vol. 34, 19th Suppl.
　r　ARBA - v28 - '97 - p621 [251-500]
The Encyclopedia of Democracy. Vols. 1-4
　r　ARBA - v28 - '97 - p276 [251-500]
　r　J Gov Info - v23 - Jl '96 - p523+ [501+]
　r　LQ - v67 - Ap '97 - p186+ [501+]
Encyclopedia of Earth Sciences. Vols. 1-2
　yr　BL - v93 - Ja '97 - p770 [1-50]
　r　Choice - v34 - Ja '97 - p768 [251-500]
　r　R&R Bk N - v11 - D '96 - p68 [51-250]
Encyclopedia of Global Industries. 1st Ed.
　r　ARBA - v28 - '97 - p99 [251-500]
　r　BL - v92 - Ag '96 - p1924 [251-500]
　r　Choice - v34 - O '96 - p250 [251-500]
　r　RQ - v36 - Win '96 - p290+ [501+]
Encyclopedia of Library and Information Science. Vol. 58
　r　ARBA - v28 - '97 - p237 [251-500]
Encyclopedia of Life Sciences. Vols. 1-11
　yr　ARBA - v28 - '97 - p577 [251-500]
　yr　SLJ - v42 - Ag '96 - p181 [51-250]
Encyclopedia of Microcomputers. Vol. 18
　r　ARBA - v28 - '97 - p622+ [251-500]
The Encyclopedia of Philosophy. Supplement
　r　ARBA - v28 - '97 - p528+ [51-250]
　r　BL - v93 - O 1 '96 - p368 [251-500]
　r　Choice - v34 - D '96 - p589 [251-500]
　r　LJ - v121 - O 15 '96 - p50 [51-250]
　r　R&R Bk N - v11 - N '96 - p1 [51-250]
The Encyclopedia of Revolutions and Revolutionaries
　r　ARBA - v28 - '97 - p216 [251-500]
Encyclopedia of the American Constitution. Electronic Media Version
　r　BL - v93 - N 15 '96 - p610 [251-500]
　r　Choice - v34 - Ap '97 - p1320 [251-500]
　r　LJ - v122 - Mr 15 '97 - p97 [51-250]
Encyclopedia of World Crime. Electronic Media Version
　r　BL - v93 - S 1 '96 - p165+ [251-500]
Encyclopedia of World Cultures. Vols. 8-10
　r　ARBA - v28 - '97 - p148+ [251-500]
　r　Choice - v34 - N '96 - p428 [251-500]
Ender, Evelyne - *Sexing the Mind*
　　Choice - v34 - S '96 - p124+ [51-250]
　　Critm - v39 - Win '97 - p121+ [501+]
　　ELT - v39 - 3 '96 - p405 [51-250]
Enderle, Judith Ross - *Francis, the Earthquake Dog (Illus. by Brooke Scudder)*
　c　HB Guide - v7 - Fall '96 - p255 [51-250]
Nell Nugget and the Cow Caper (Illus. by Paul Yalowitz)
　c　HB - v72 - S '96 - p575 [51-250]
　c　HB Guide - v7 - Fall '96 - p255 [51-250]

What's the Matter, Kelly Beans? (Illus. by Blanche Sims)
  c BL - v93 - O 1 '96 - p348 [51-250]
  c CBRS - v25 - S '96 - p7 [51-250]
  c HB Guide - v8 - Spr '97 - p57 [51-250]
  c SLJ - v42 - O '96 - p92 [51-250]
Where Are You, Little Zack? (Illus. by Brian Floca)
  c CBRS - v25 - Ap '97 - p98 [1-50]
  c PW - v244 - F 10 '97 - p83 [51-250]
Enders, Walter - *RATS Handbook for Econometric Time Series*
  JEL - v34 - S '96 - p1410 [51-250]
Endo, Shusaku - *Deep River*
  Bks & Cult - v2 - Ja '96 - p6 [51-250]
  LATBR - Jl 14 '96 - p11 [51-250]
  TranslRevS - v2 - D '96 - p5 [51-250]
The Girl I Left Behind
  Bks & Cult - v2 - Ja '96 - p6 [51-250]
The Samurai
  LJ - v122 - Ap 1 '97 - p124 [51-250]
  PW - v244 - Mr 3 '97 - p72 [1-50]
Endres, Gunter - *Jane's Helicopter Markets and Systems*
  r ARBA - v28 - '97 - p655 [51-250]
Endres, Kathleen L - *Women's Periodicals in the United States*
  r ARBA - v28 - '97 - p340 [251-500]
  r Choice - v34 - My '97 - p1501+ [51-250]
Energy Balances for Europe and North America 1992
  SciTech - v20 - D '96 - p72 [1-50]
Energy Statistics Yearbook 1994
  r R&R Bk N - v12 - F '97 - p42 [51-250]
Eng, Maximo V - *Global Finance*
  JEL - v34 - S '96 - p1432 [51-250]
Eng, Pierre Van Der - *Agricultural Growth in Indonesia*
  JEL - v34 - D '96 - p2104 [51-250]
  R&R Bk N - v11 - N '96 - p31 [51-250]
Eng, Steve - *Jimmy Buffett: The Man from Margaritaville Revealed*
  BL - v93 - D 1 '96 - p637 [51-250]
  KR - v64 - O 15 '96 - p1508 [251-500]
  LJ - v121 - D '96 - p95 [51-250]
  PW - v243 - N 18 '96 - p59 [51-250]
Engberg-Pedersen, Troels - *Paul in His Hellenistic Context*
  Rel St Rev - v23 - Ja '97 - p72+ [51-250]
Engel, Barbara Alpern - *Between the Fields and the City*
  JMH - v69 - Mr '97 - p196 [251-500]
  Slav R - v55 - Fall '96 - p687+ [501+]
Engel, Dean - *Ezra Jack Keats: A Biography with Illustrations*
  c RT - v50 - S '96 - p58 [51-250]
Engel, Evamaria - *Kaiser Friedrich Barbarossa: Landesaubau--Aspekte Seiner Politik--Wirkung*
  EHR - v111 - N '96 - p1242+ [251-500]
Engel, Howard - *Lord High Executioner*
  Beav - v76 - D '96 - p46 [51-250]
  BIC - v26 - F '97 - p37+ [501+]
  BW - v26 - N 17 '96 - p12 [51-250]
  LJ - v121 - D '96 - p120 [51-250]
  Quill & Q - v62 - Ag '96 - p38 [251-500]
Engel, June - *The Complete Breast Book*
  Choice - v34 - S '96 - p161 [51-250]
Engel, Matthew - *Tickle the Public*
  Books - v10 - Je '96 - p21 [1-50]
  Lon R Bks - v18 - Jl 18 '96 - p13+ [501+]
  NS & S - v9 - My 3 '96 - p41 [51-250]
  Spec - v276 - My 18 '96 - p38+ [501+]
  TES - D 27 '96 - p16 [51-250]
Engel, Pascal - *Davidson Et La Philosophie Du Langage*
  CPR - v16 - Ap '96 - p99+ [501+]
  Dialogue - v35 - Spr '96 - p402+ [501+]
Engel, Susan - *The Stories Children Tell*
  Readings - v11 - S '96 - p23 [51-250]
Engelbert, Phillis - *Astronomy and Space. Vols. 1-3*
  yr BL - v93 - My 1 '97 - p1518+ [251-500]
Engelen, G B - *Hydrological Systems Analysis*
  SciTech - v21 - Mr '97 - p1 [51-250]
Engelman, Ralph - *Public Radio and Television in America*
  Choice - v34 - O '96 - p270 [51-250]
  Nat - v264 - Ja 6 '97 - p33+ [501+]
Engeln-Mullges, Gisela - *Numerical Algorithms with C*
  Choice - v34 - F '97 - p998+ [51-250]
  JEL - v35 - Mr '97 - p197 [51-250]
Numerical Algorithms with Fortran
  Choice - v34 - My '97 - p1197 [51-250]
Engels, Dagmar - *Contesting Colonial Hegemony*
  JTWS - v13 - Spr '96 - p405+ [501+]
Engels, Mary Tate - *Tales from Wide Ruins*
  y SLJ - v42 - D '96 - p153 [51-250]

Engerman, Stanley L - *The Cambridge Economic History of the United States. Vol. 1*
  Choice - v34 - O '96 - p328 [51-250]
  JEL - v34 - D '96 - p2093+ [51-250]
Trade and the Industrial Revolution 1700-1850. Vols. 1-2
  JEL - v34 - S '96 - p1473 [51-250]
Engineer, Asghar Ali - *The Rights of Women in Islam*
  MEJ - v51 - Spr '97 - p314 [51-250]
Engl, Heinz W - *Inverse Problems in Geophysical Applications*
  SciTech - v21 - Mr '97 - p74 [51-250]
Regularization of Inverse Problems
  SciTech - v20 - D '96 - p4 [51-250]
Englade, Ken - *Hot Blood*
  LATBR - S 1 '96 - p3 [501+]
England, Len - *Public and Specialised Libraries*
  LR - v45 - 7 '96 - p50+ [251-500]
England, Linda - *3 Kids Dreamin' (Illus. by Dena Schutzer)*
  c CBRS - v25 - Ap '97 - p102 [51-250]
  c PW - v244 - Ap 14 '97 - p76 [51-250]
England, Marjorie A - *Life before Birth. 2nd Ed.*
  SciTech - v21 - Mr '97 - p63 [51-250]
England, Nicholas M - *Music among the Zu'Wa-Si and Related Peoples of Namibia, Botswana and Angola*
  Notes - v53 - Mr '97 - p811+ [501+]
Englander, David - *Britain and America*
  Obs - Ja 26 '97 - p15* [501+]
Retrieved Riches
  HT - v46 - D '96 - p54 [501+]
Englander, Irv - *The Architecture of Computer Hardware and Systems Software*
  Choice - v34 - O '96 - p315 [51-250]
  SciTech - v20 - S '96 - p4 [51-250]
Engle, Lars - *Shakespearean Pragmatism*
  RES - v47 - N '96 - p582+ [501+]
Engle, Paul - *A Lucky American Childhood*
  NYTBR - v101 - S 8 '96 - p22 [51-250]
Engle, Ron - *Maxwell Anderson on the European Stage 1929-1992*
  r ARBA - v28 - '97 - p522+ [51-250]
Englebert, Pierre - *Burkina Faso: Unsteady Statehood in West Africa*
  Choice - v34 - D '96 - p682+ [51-250]
  For Aff - v75 - N '96 - p169+ [51-250]
  R&R Bk N - v11 - N '96 - p16 [51-250]
Engleman, Michael J - *Clinical Decision Making and Treatment Planning in Osseointegration*
  SciTech - v20 - D '96 - p54 [51-250]
Engler, Bernd - *Historiographic Metafiction in Modern American and Canadian Literature*
  Can Lit - Win '96 - p161+ [501+]
Engler, Jim - *The Incompleat Angler*
  AB - v97 - Je 17 '96 - p2410+ [501+]
English, Allan D - *The Cream of the Crop*
  APH - v44 - Spr '97 - p55+ [501+]
  Choice - v34 - Ja '97 - p862 [51-250]
  J Mil H - v61 - Ap '97 - p406+ [501+]
  R&R Bk N - v11 - D '96 - p7 [51-250]
English, Donald - *An Evangelical Theology of Preaching*
  Intpr - v51 - Ap '97 - p224 [51-250]
English, Edward D - *Reading and Wisdom*
  CH - v65 - D '96 - p683+ [501+]
English, John F - *Spiritual Freedom. 2nd Ed.*
  RR - v56 - Mr '97 - p214+ [501+]
English, June A - *Mission, Earth*
  c HB Guide - v8 - Spr '97 - p113 [51-250]
  c PW - v243 - S 16 '96 - p84 [51-250]
  c SLJ - v42 - O '96 - p130+ [51-250]
Transportation: Automobiles to Zeppelins
  c CLW - v67 - D '96 - p60 [51-250]
English, Karen - *Big Wind Coming! (Illus. by Cedric Lucas)*
  c CBRS - v25 - Ja '97 - p50 [51-250]
  c CCB-B - v50 - Ja '97 - p168 [51-250]
Big Wind Coming (Illus. by Cedric Lucas)
  c Cur R - v35 - S '96 - p12 [51-250]
Big Wind Coming! (Illus. by Cedric Lucas)
  c HB Guide - v8 - Spr '97 - p26 [51-250]
  c SLJ - v42 - N '96 - p80 [51-250]
Neeny Coming, Neeny Going (Illus. by Synthia Saint James)
  c HB Guide - v7 - Fall '96 - p255 [51-250]
English, Katharine - *Most Popular Web Sites*
  r CBR - v15 - Spr '97 - p6 [1-50]
  r TES - O 18 '96 - p41U [51-250]
English, Todd - *The Olives Table*
  LJ - v122 - Mr 15 '97 - p84 [51-250]
  PW - v244 - F 3 '97 - p103 [51-250]

English Verse (Penguin Classic). Vol. 1. Audio Version
  Obs - Ja 12 '97 - p18* [51-250]
Engstrom, Stephen - *Aristotle, Kant, and the Stoics*
  Choice - v34 - Ja '97 - p807+ [51-250]
Enhancing Communication: Making Your Case
  LJ - v121 - D '96 - p156 [51-250]
Enhancing Communication: Teaching Technology
  LJ - v121 - D '96 - p156 [51-250]
Enhancing External Communication: Managing Conflict
  LJ - v121 - D '96 - p156 [51-250]
Enhancing Internal Communication: Building Effective Relationships
  LJ - v121 - D '96 - p156 [51-250]
Enhancing Internal Communication: Using Negotiation to Resolve Conflict
  LJ - v121 - D '96 - p156 [51-250]
Enhancing the Safety and Soundness of the Canadian Financial System
  J Gov Info - v23 - S '96 - p612+ [51-250]
Enna, S J - *Mosby's USMLE Step 1 Reviews: Pharmacology*
  SciTech - v20 - S '96 - p42 [1-50]
Ennew, Craig - *Reading for Information*
  TES - D 13 '96 - p43 [51-250]
Ennew, Judith - *Exploitation of Children*
  y BL - v93 - F 1 '97 - p931 [51-250]
  y Sch Lib - v44 - Ag '96 - p126 [51-250]
Ennis, Christine A - *Biological Consequences of Global Climate Change*
  y SB - v33 - Mr '97 - p42+ [51-250]
Ennis, Kathy - *Guidelines for College Libraries. 5th Ed.*
  LR - v45 - 8 '96 - p44+ [501+]
Ennos, A R - *Problem Solving in Environmental Biology*
  y New Sci - v151 - S 28 '96 - p50+ [501+]
Eno, Brian - *A Year with Swollen Appendices*
  TES - Ag 2 '96 - p15 [51-250]
Enos, Theresa - *Encyclopedia of Rhetoric and Composition*
  r ARBA - v28 - '97 - p386+ [51-250]
  r Col Comp - v47 - D '96 - p616 [51-250]
  r JC - v47 - Win '97 - p147+ [501+]
  r QJS - v83 - My '97 - p243+ [501+]
Enright, D J - *Interplay: A Kind of Commonplace Book*
  WLT - v71 - Win '97 - p163+ [501+]
The Oxford Book of the Supernatural
  SF Chr - v18 - O '96 - p81 [1-50]
Enright, Michael J - *Venezuela: The Challenge of Competitiveness*
  Choice - v34 - N '96 - p506 [51-250]
  JEL - v34 - D '96 - p2119 [51-250]
  R&R Bk N - v11 - N '96 - p27 [51-250]
Enright, Neal J - *Ecology of the Southern Conifers*
  R&R Bk N - v12 - F '97 - p94 [51-250]
Enright, Nick - *Blackrock*
  Aust Bk R - D '96 - p76+ [501+]
Enriquez, Laura J - *The Question of Food Security in Cuban Socialism*
  CS - v25 - S '96 - p600+ [501+]
Enriquez, Mariana - *Bajar Es Lo Peor*
  WLT - v71 - Win '97 - p117 [501+]
Ens, Adolf - *Subjects or Citizens?*
  CH - v65 - S '96 - p534+ [501+]
Ensign, Georgianne - *Great Beginnings and Endings*
  y Kliatt - v30 - S '96 - p22 [51-250]
Ensmonger, Audrey - *The Concise Encyclopedia of Food and Nutrition*
  r BL - v93 - F 1 '97 - p959 [1-50]
Ensrud, Barbara - *Best Wine Buys for $12 and Under*
  r LJ - v122 - Ap 1 '97 - p64 [1-50]
Entelis, John P - *Culture and Counterculture in Moroccan Politics*
  MEJ - v51 - Win '97 - p151 [51-250]
Enterline, Lynn - *The Tears of Narcissus*
  Six Ct J - v27 - Win '96 - p1206+ [501+]
Envall, Markku - *Kasioraakkeli*
  WLT - v70 - Aut '96 - p993 [251-500]
Environment and Development Economics
  p JEL - v35 - Mr '97 - p308 [51-250]
Environment and History
  p Nature - v383 - S 5 '96 - p40 [251-500]
Environmental and Health Atlas of Russia
  r Nature - v381 - My 16 '96 - p203+ [501+]
Environmental Grantmaking Foundations 1996
  r ARBA - v28 - '97 - p313 [51-250]
Environmental Impact Assessment: Training Resource Manual
  SciTech - v21 - Mr '97 - p81 [51-250]
Environmental Policy Tools
  J Gov Info - v23 - S '96 - p558 [51-250]
Environmental Telephone Directory. 1996 Ed.
  r ARBA - v28 - '97 - p648 [51-250]

Envision
p TES - O 18 '96 - p43U [51-250]
Enzensberger, Hans Magnus - *Selected Poems*
MLR - v91 - O '96 - p1054 [251-500]
Enzinas, Francisco De - *Epistolario*
CH - v65 - D '96 - p698+ [501+]
Six Ct J - v27 - Fall '96 - p840+ [501+]
EPA Office of Compliance Sector Notebook Project
J Gov Info - v23 - S '96 - p546 [51-250]
Ephraem, Syrius, Saint - *Selected Prose Works*
Rel St Rev - v23 - Ja '97 - p79 [51-250]
Ephron, Nora - *Heartburn*
LATBR - Ag 18 '96 - p15 [51-250]
Obs - S 1 '96 - p18* [51-250]
Epler, Doris - *Networking: Breaking Down the Walls of the Learning Environment*
CLW - v67 - D '96 - p48 [251-500]
The EPM Licensing Letter Sourcebook. 1997 Ed.
r ARBA - v28 - '97 - p82 [51-250]
Epperson, S K - *Green Lake*
Arm Det - v29 - Fall '96 - p501 [251-500]
Eppinga, Jane - *Henry Oian Flipper: West Point's First Black Graduate*
Roundup M - v4 - Ap '97 - p21 [251-500]
Epps, Roselyn Payne - *The Women's Complete Healthbook*
r ARBA - v28 - '97 - p609+ [51-250]
r BL - v93 - F 1 '97 - p959 [1-50]
Epstein, Arthur W - *Dreaming and Other Involuntary Mentation*
SciTech - v20 - N '96 - p41 [51-250]
Epstein, Carole - *Perilous Friends*
BL - v93 - N 1 '96 - p483 [51-250]
KR - v64 - S 15 '96 - p1356+ [51-250]
LJ - v121 - O 1 '96 - p130 [51-250]
PW - v243 - S 16 '96 - p73 [51-250]
Epstein, Daniel Mark - *The Boy in the Well*
HR - v49 - Sum '96 - p341+ [501+]
MQR - v36 - Spr '97 - p368+ [501+]
Epstein, David L - *Chandler and Grant's Glaucoma. 4th Ed.*
SciTech - v20 - D '96 - p50 [51-250]
Epstein, Edward Jay - *Dossier: The Secret History of Armand Hammer*
Barron's - v76 - N 18 '96 - p71 [251-500]
BL - v93 - O 1 '96 - p311 [51-250]
Econ - v341 - D 7 '96 - p10* [501+]
Fortune - v134 - N 11 '96 - p207+ [501+]
KR - v64 - Ag 15 '96 - p1206 [251-500]
LATBR - O 27 '96 - p1+ [501+]
LJ - v121 - O 15 '96 - p66 [51-250]
New R - v215 - D 30 '96 - p35+ [501+]
NL - v79 - N 4 '96 - p14+ [501+]
NYRB - v43 - N 14 '96 - p29 [501+]
NYTBR - v101 - O 13 '96 - p14+ [501+]
NYTBR - v101 - D 8 '96 - p87 [1-50]
WSJ-MW - v77 - O 3 '96 - pA12 [501+]
Epstein, Gerald A - *Macroeconomic Policy after the Conservative Era*
JEL - v34 - S '96 - p1422+ [51-250]
JEL - v35 - Mr '97 - p131+ [501+]
Epstein, James A - *Radical Expression*
JMH - v68 - S '96 - p683+ [501+]
VS - v39 - Aut '95 - p65+ [501+]
Epstein, Jonathon S - *Adolescents and Their Music*
Notes - v53 - S '96 - p91+ [501+]
Epstein, Joseph - *The Norton Book of Personal Essays*
BL - v93 - F 15 '97 - p994 [51-250]
BW - v27 - Ap 13 '97 - p13 [51-250]
LJ - v122 - F 15 '97 - p136 [51-250]
PW - v244 - Ja 27 '97 - p92 [51-250]
With My Trousers Rolled
TLS - N 29 '96 - p15 [51-250]
Epstein, Joshua M - *Growing Artificial Societies*
For Aff - v76 - My '97 - p124 [51-250]
Epstein, Lee - *Contemplating Courts*
SSQ - v77 - Je '96 - p461+ [501+]
The Supreme Court Compendium. 2nd Ed.
r ARBA - v28 - '97 - p223+ [51-250]
Epstein, Leslie - *Pandaemonium*
KR - v65 - Ap 1 '97 - p484+ [251-500]
LJ - v122 - Ap 15 '97 - p117 [51-250]
PW - v244 - Mr 24 '97 - p59+ [51-250]
Trib Bks - My 18 '97 - p3 [51-250]
Epstein, Mikhail N - *After the Future*
Russ Rev - v55 - O '96 - p710+ [501+]

Epstein, Mitch - *Vietnam: A Book of Changes*
HMR - Spr '97 - p13+ [501+]
NYTBR - v101 - D 8 '96 - p72 [51-250]
PW - v243 - O 7 '96 - p51 [51-250]
Utne R - N '96 - p88 [1-50]
VV - v52 - Ja 28 '97 - p48+ [501+]
Epstein, Richard Allen - *Forbidden Grounds*
NY - v72 - N 25 '96 - p106+ [501+]
Mortal Peril
KR - v65 - Mr 15 '97 - p433+ [251-500]
PW - v244 - Mr 17 '97 - p67 [51-250]
Simple Rules for a Complex World
Trib Bks - Ap 27 '97 - p8 [1-50]
Epstein, Steven - *Impure Science*
Choice - v34 - Mr '97 - p1193 [51-250]
LJ - v121 - O 15 '96 - p82+ [51-250]
New Sci - v152 - D 7 '96 - p50 [251-500]
NYTBR - v102 - Ja 12 '97 - p16+ [501+]
Sci - v275 - Ja 17 '97 - p320 [501+]
Epstein, Steven A - *Genoa and the Genoese 958-1528*
Choice - v34 - Mr '97 - p1219 [51-250]
Equality State Almanac 1995
r J Gov Info - v23 - S '96 - p597 [51-250]
Eranova-Cruz, Florencio - *El Amor En Los Tiempos De Castro*
BL - v93 - Ap 1 '97 - p1284 [1-50]
Erasmus, Desiderius - *The Correspondence of Erasmus. Vol. 11*
TLS - Ap 11 '97 - p28 [251-500]
Erasmus on Women (Rummel)
CC - v113 - N 20 '96 - p1179 [51-250]
R&R Bk N - v11 - D '96 - p1 [51-250]
Paraphrase on Acts
Ren Q - v50 - Spr '97 - p309+ [501+]
Paraphrase on the Acts of the Apostles
EHR - v111 - S '96 - p971+ [501+]
Paraphrases on the Epistles to Timothy, Titus and Philemon; the Epistles of Peter and Jude; the Epistle of James; the Epistles of John...
Ren Q - v50 - Spr '97 - p307+ [501+]
Erauso, Catalina De - *Lieutenant Nun*
LATBR - My 12 '96 - p11 [51-250]
NYTBR - v101 - D 8 '96 - p88 [1-50]
Erbe, L H - *Oscillation Theory for Functional Differential Equations*
SIAM Rev - v38 - D '96 - p680+ [501+]
Erbe, Michael - *Querdenken: Dissens Und Toleranz Im Wandel Der Geschichte*
Ren Q - v49 - Win '96 - p840+ [501+]
Erdelyi, Matthew Hugh - *The Recovery of Unconscious Memories*
LJ - v121 - S 15 '96 - p83 [51-250]
New Sci - v153 - F 22 '97 - p42 [51-250]
Erdman, Cheri K - *Live Large!*
LJ - v122 - Ja '97 - p126 [51-250]
PW - v243 - D 2 '96 - p58 [51-250]
Erdman, Nikolai - *The Major Plays of Nikolai Erdman*
Choice - v34 - N '96 - p472 [51-250]
A Meeting about Laughter
Choice - v34 - N '96 - p472 [51-250]
Erdman, Paul Emil - *The Set-Up*
BL - v93 - F 15 '97 - p1002 [51-250]
KR - v65 - F 1 '97 - p159 [251-500]
LJ - v122 - F 1 '97 - p105 [51-250]
PW - v244 - F 10 '97 - p66 [51-250]
The Set-Up (Campanella). Audio Version
PW - v244 - Ap 7 '97 - p33 [51-250]
Tug of War
BL - v93 - S 15 '96 - p191 [51-250]
JEL - v35 - Mr '97 - p218 [51-250]
Erdrich, Louise - *Grandmother's Pigeon (Illus. by Jim LaMarche)*
c HB Guide - v7 - Fall '96 - p255 [51-250]
c NYTBR - v101 - N 10 '96 - p49 [51-250]
c Smith - v27 - N '96 - p168 [51-250]
Tales of Burning Love
Bks & Cult - v2 - S '96 - p6+ [501+]
BL - v93 - Ja '97 - p761 [1-50]
LATBR - D 29 '96 - p4+ [51-250]
NYTBR - v101 - D 8 '96 - p84 [1-50]
Obs - Ja 5 '97 - p15* [501+]
Salm - Win '97 - p220+ [501+]
TLS - F 14 '97 - p21 [501+]
VQR - v72 - Aut '96 - p131* [501+]
Erenberg, Lewis A - *The War in American Culture*
R&R Bk N - v11 - N '96 - p17 [51-250]
Erens, Patricia - *Issues in Feminist Film Criticism*
J Film & Vid - v48 - Spr '96 - p80+ [501+]
Eribon, Didier - *Michel Foucault Et Ses Contemporains*
FR - v70 - Mr '97 - p604+ [501+]

ERIC on CD-ROM. Electronic Media Version
r ARBA - v28 - '97 - p135+ [251-500]
Erickson, Barbara - *Tibet: Abode of the Gods, Pearl of the Motherland*
LJ - v122 - Ap 1 '97 - p110 [51-250]
Erickson, Carolly - *Her Little Majesty*
KR - v65 - Ja 1 '97 - p33 [251-500]
LJ - v122 - Ja '97 - p110 [51-250]
PW - v243 - D 30 '96 - p45 [251-500]
Our Tempestuous Day
CR - v269 - O '96 - p224 [251-250]
Erickson, Charlotte - *Leaving England*
EHR - v111 - N '96 - p1328 [51-250]
VS - v39 - Win '96 - p274+ [501+]
Erickson, John - *The Soviet Armed Forces 1918-1992*
r ARBA - v28 - '97 - p252 [51-250]
Erickson, Jon - *Glacial Geology*
Choice - v34 - S '96 - p158 [51-250]
Marine Geology
Choice - v34 - N '96 - p487 [51-250]
Erickson, Lee - *The Economy of Literary Form*
JEL - v34 - S '96 - p1471 [51-250]
Lib - v18 - D '96 - p354+ [501+]
Erickson, Lynn - *Night Whispers*
PW - v243 - N 18 '96 - p70 [51-250]
Erickson, Martin J - *Introduction to Combinatorics*
Choice - v34 - Ap '97 - p1375+ [51-250]
SciTech - v20 - D '96 - p15 [1-50]
Erickson, Millard J - *How Shall They Be Saved?*
Rel St Rev - v23 - Ja '97 - p47 [51-250]
Erickson, Paul A - *Practical Guide to Occupational Health and Safety*
SciTech - v20 - N '96 - p49 [51-250]
Erickson, Steve - *American Nomad*
BL - v93 - My 15 '97 - p1559 [51-250]
KR - v65 - Mr 15 '97 - p434 [251-500]
PW - v244 - Mr 24 '97 - p67 [51-250]
Amnesiascope
ABR - v17 - Ag '96 - p18 [501+]
Arc D'X
NYTBR - v102 - Ja 12 '97 - p32 [51-250]
Erickson, Tyler - *Pay Severance or Die*
PW - v243 - O 21 '96 - p70 [51-250]
Erickson, Wayne - *Mapping the Faerie Queens*
Choice - v34 - S '96 - p125 [51-250]
Ericson, Margaret D - *Women and Music*
r ARBA - v28 - '97 - p467 [51-250]
Ericson, Steven J - *The Sound of the Whistle*
JEL - v35 - Mr '97 - p268 [51-250]
Ericsson, Jennifer A - *The Most Beautiful Kid in the World (Illus. by Susan Meddaugh)*
c BL - v93 - S 15 '96 - p246+ [51-250]
c CBRS - v25 - Ja '97 - p50 [51-250]
c CCB-B - v50 - O '96 - p57 [51-250]
c HB Guide - v8 - Spr '97 - p26 [51-250]
c SLJ - v42 - O '96 - p92 [51-250]
Erigena, Johannes Scotus - *Carmina*
Specu - v72 - Ja '97 - p145+ [501+]
Eriksen, Erik Oddvar - *The Rationality of the Welfare State*
Choice - v34 - My '97 - p1549 [51-250]
Erikson, Erik H - *Childhood and Society*
Rel St Rev - v22 - O '96 - p323+ [501+]
Dimensions of a New Identity
Rel St Rev - v22 - O '96 - p323+ [501+]
Gandhi's Truth
Rel St Rev - v22 - O '96 - p323+ [501+]
Identity and the Life Cycle
Rel St Rev - v22 - O '96 - p323+ [501+]
Identity: Youth and Crisis
Rel St Rev - v22 - O '96 - p323+ [501+]
In Search of Common Ground
Rel St Rev - v22 - O '96 - p323+ [501+]
Insight and Responsibility
Rel St Rev - v22 - O '96 - p323+ [501+]
The Life Cycle Completed
Rel St Rev - v22 - O '96 - p323+ [501+]
Life History and the Historical Moment
Rel St Rev - v22 - O '96 - p323+ [501+]
Toys and Reasons
Rel St Rev - v22 - O '96 - p323+ [501+]
A Way of Looking at Things
Rel St Rev - v22 - O '96 - p323+ [501+]
Young Man Luther
Rel St Rev - v22 - O '96 - p323+ [501+]
Eriksson, Gunnar - *The Atlantic Vision*
T&C - v38 - Ja '97 - p246+ [501+]
Eriksson, Ralf - *Economic Value and Ways of Life*
Econ J - v106 - N '96 - p1831 [51-250]
Eriksson, Ulf - *Paradis*
WLT - v71 - Win '97 - p171+ [501+]

Erkkila, Betsy - *Breaking Bounds*
　　AL - v69 - Mr '97 - p251 [51-250]
　　Nine-C Lit - v51 - D '96 - p421 [51-250]
Erko, A I - *Diffraction X-Ray Optics*
　　SciTech - v20 - S '96 - p15 [51-250]
Erlande-Brandenburg, Alain - *The Cathedral: The Social and Architectural Dynamics of Construction*
　　AHR - v101 - D '96 - p1535+ [501+]
　　CH - v65 - S '96 - p473+ [251-500]
　　CHR - v82 - O '96 - p684+ [501+]
Erlandson, Jon M - *Early Hunter-Gatherers of the California Coast*
　　Am Ant - v62 - Ja '97 - p161+ [501+]
Erlbach, Arlene - *The Best Friends Book*
　　y Adoles - v31 - Win '96 - p992 [51-250]
　　The Families Book (Illus. by Stephen J Carrera)
　　y Kliatt - v30 - N '96 - p21 [51-250]
　　c SLJ - v42 - Ag '96 - p153 [51-250]
　　Sidewalk Games around the World
　　c BL - v93 - My 1 '97 - p1490+ [51-250]
　　Video Games
　　y Emerg Lib - v24 - S '96 - p26 [1-50]
Erlbruch, Wolf - *Mrs. Meyer the Bird (Illus. by Wolf Erlbruch)*
　　c BL - v93 - Ap 1 '97 - p1337 [51-250]
　　c CCB-B - v50 - My '97 - p319 [51-250]
　　c KR - v65 - F 1 '97 - p222 [51-250]
　　c PW - v244 - Ja 13 '97 - p74 [51-250]
Erlebacher, Gordon - *Wavelets, Theory and Applications*
　　SIAM Rev - v39 - Mr '97 - p177 [51-250]
Erlewein, David L - *Instructions for Veterinary Clients. 3rd Ed.*
　　r SciTech - v20 - N '96 - p58 [51-250]
Erlewine, Michael - *All Music Guide. 2nd Ed.*
　　r CAY - v16 - Fall '95 - p4 [51-250]
　　All Music Guide to the Blues
　　r ARBA - v28 - '97 - p489 [51-250]
　　r Choice - v34 - My '97 - p1471 [51-250]
　　r CSM - v88 - N 21 '96 - p11 [1-50]
　　r LJ - v121 - N 15 '96 - p54 [51-250]
　　r PW - v243 - O 7 '96 - p68 [51-250]
Erlmann, Veit - *Nightsong: Performance, Power, and Practice in South Africa*
　　Choice - v34 - N '96 - p469 [51-250]
　　CS - v26 - Ja '97 - p44+ [501+]
　　TDR - v41 - Spr '97 - p160+ [51-250]
Ermath, M - *America and the Shaping of German Society 1945-1955*
　　HT - v46 - Jl '96 - p52+ [501+]
Ernaux, Annie - *Exteriors*
　　BW - v26 - N 10 '96 - p6 [501+]
　　KR - v64 - S 1 '96 - p1292 [251-500]
　　Nat - v263 - D 16 '96 - p31 [251-500]
　　PW - v243 - S 16 '96 - p69+ [51-250]
　　A Frozen Woman
　　BW - v26 - N 10 '96 - p6 [501+]
　　NYTBR - v102 - Ap 13 '97 - p32 [51-250]
　　Simple Passion
　　TranslRevS - v1 - My '95 - p19 [51-250]
Ernest, John - *Resistance and Reformation in Nineteenth-Century African-American Literature*
　　AL - v69 - Mr '97 - p221+ [251-500]
Erni, John Nguyet - *Unstable Frontiers*
　　JC - v47 - Win '97 - p169+ [51-250]
Ernst, Carl H - *Snakes in Question*
　　y BL - v93 - Ja '97 - p795 [51-250]
Ernst, Carl R - *The Sourcebook of Online Public Record Experts*
　　r AJR - v18 - O '96 - p62 [501+]
　　r ARBA - v28 - '97 - p243+ [251-500]
Ernst, Daniel R - *Lawyers against Labor*
　　ILRR - v50 - O '96 - p160+ [501+]
Ernst, Gordon E, Jr. - *Robert Benchley: An Annotated Bibliography*
　　r AL - v68 - S '96 - p668 [51-250]
Ernst, Kathleen - *The Night Riders of Harpers Ferry*
　　y BL - v93 - Ja '97 - p842+ [251-500]
Ernst, Linda L - *Lapsit Services for the Very Young*
　　JOYS - v9 - Sum '96 - p408+ [501+]
Ernst, Lisa Campbell - *Duke the Dairy Delight Dog (Illus. by Lisa Campbell Ernst)*
　　c BL - v93 - S 1 '96 - p142 [51-250]
　　c CBRS - v25 - S '96 - p2 [51-250]
　　c CCB-B - v50 - Ja '97 - p168+ [51-250]
　　c HB Guide - v8 - Spr '97 - p26 [51-250]
　　c SLJ - v42 - S '96 - p177 [51-250]
　　The Letters Are Lost! (Illus. by Lisa Campbell Ernst)
　　c HB Guide - v7 - Fall '96 - p255 [51-250]
　　c Inst - v42 - Ag '96 - p44 [1-50]
　　Little Red Riding Hood (Illus. by Lisa Campbell Ernst)
　　c Emerg Lib - v24 - S '96 - p46 [51-250]

Walter's Tail
　　c PW - v244 - F 10 '97 - p85 [1-50]
Ernst, Maurice - *Transforming the Core*
　　JEL - v34 - S '96 - p1493 [51-250]
　　Russ Rev - v56 - Ja '97 - p150 [251-500]
Ernst, Ruth Shaw - *The Naturalist's Garden. 3rd Ed.*
　　LJ - v121 - D '96 - p66 [1-50]
Ernst, Tim - *Wilderness Reflections*
　　PW - v243 - N 11 '96 - p68 [1-50]
Erofeev, V V - *Russian Beauty*
　　TranslRevS - v1 - My '95 - p27+ [51-250]
Erofeev, Venedikt - *Moscow Stations*
　　Obs - Ja 19 '97 - p17* [501+]
　　Spec - v278 - Ja 18 '97 - p36 [501+]
　　TLS - Ja 31 '97 - p19 [501+]
　　Ostavlte Moiu Dushu V Pokoe
　　BL - v93 - O 1 '96 - p327 [1-50]
Eron, Joseph B - *Narrative Solutions in Brief Therapy*
　　SciTech - v20 - N '96 - p43 [51-250]
Erotica I
　　Quill & Q - v62 - Jl '96 - p42 [501+]
Erotica II
　　Quill & Q - v62 - Jl '96 - p42 [501+]
Erotica III
　　Quill & Q - v62 - Jl '96 - p42 [501+]
Errani, Paola - *La Biblioteca Di Un Neoclassico*
　　Lib - v19 - Mr '97 - p99 [51-250]
Erricker, Clive - *Buddhist Festivals*
　　c Sch Lib - v44 - Ag '96 - p112 [51-250]
Errington, Elizabeth Jane - *Wives and Mothers, Schoolmistresses and Scullery Maids*
　　W&M Q - v54 - Ap '97 - p453+ [501+]
Errington, Frederick K - *Articulating Change in the Last Unknown*
　　CS - v26 - Mr '97 - p192+ [501+]
Erskin, Aleda - *The Imaginative Body*
　　SciTech - v20 - D '96 - p41 [51-250]
Erskine, Barbara - *House of Echoes*
　　BW - v26 - N 10 '96 - p10 [51-250]
　　Woman's J - D '96 - p16 [1-50]
Erskine-Hill, Howard - *Poetry and the Realm of Politics*
　　Choice - v34 - Ja '97 - p793+ [51-250]
　　TLS - Ag 30 '96 - p32 [251-500]
　　Poetry of Opposition and Revolution
　　TLS - D 27 '96 - p11+ [501+]
Ersoy, Okan K - *Fourier-Related Transforms, Fast Algorithms, and Applications*
　　SciTech - v21 - Mr '97 - p17 [51-250]
Ertas, Atila - *The Engineering Design Process. 2nd Ed.*
　　Choice - v34 - Ap '97 - p1368 [51-250]
　　SciTech - v21 - Mr '97 - p74 [51-250]
Esack, Farid - *Qur'an Liberation and Pluralism*
　　PW - v244 - F 24 '97 - p82+ [51-250]
Esaiasson, Peter - *Representation from Above*
　　R&R Bk N - v11 - D '96 - p48 [51-250]
Esarey, Gary - *How Crows Talk and Willows Walk*
　　WAL - v31 - Fall '96 - p276 [51-250]
Esbensen, Barbara Juster - *Dance with Me (Illus. by Megan Lloyd)*
　　c LA - v73 - O '96 - p430 [51-250]
　　c LA - v73 - D '96 - p623 [51-250]
　　c RT - v50 - O '96 - p157 [51-250]
　　Echoes for the Eye (Illus. by Helen K Davie)
　　c Emerg Lib - v23 - My '96 - p43 [1-50]
　　c HB Guide - v7 - Fall '96 - p367 [1-50]
　　c RT - v50 - Ap '97 - p592 [51-250]
　　Swift as the Wind (Illus. by Jean Cassels)
　　c HB Guide - v7 - Fall '96 - p344 [51-250]
Escallier, Robert - *Les Nouvelles Formes De La Mobilite Spatiale Dans Le Monde Arabe. Vol. 2*
　　MEJ - v50 - Aut '96 - p631 [51-250]
Escamilla Torres, Rogelio Javier - *Mariano Matamoros, Segundo De Morelos Y Terror De Los LLamados Gachupines*
　　HAHR - v76 - Ag '96 - p574+ [501+]
Escobal, P R - *Aquatic Systems Engineering*
　　SciTech - v20 - S '96 - p45 [51-250]
Escobar, Arturo - *Encountering Development*
　　AHR - v101 - D '96 - p1523+ [501+]
　　JTWS - v13 - Fall '96 - p337+ [501+]
Escoffier, Auguste - *Memories of My Life*
　　LJ - v121 - N 15 '96 - p68 [51-250]
Escott, Colin - *Hank Williams: The Biography*
　　LJ - v121 - N 1 '96 - p42 [1-50]
　　Tattooed on Their Tongues
　　LJ - v121 - N 1 '96 - p41 [1-50]
Esders, Viviane - *Our Mothers*
　　Pet PM - v25 - Jl '96 - p36 [51-250]
　　Wom R Bks - v14 - N '96 - p12+ [501+]
Esenwein, George - *Spain at War*
　　JMH - v68 - D '96 - p1013+ [501+]

Esiri, Margaret M - *Oppenheimer's Diagnostic Neuropathology. 2nd Ed.*
　　SciTech - v20 - N '96 - p41 [51-250]
Eskeland, Gunnar S - *Taxing Bads by Taxing Goods*
　　JEL - v34 - D '96 - p2132+ [51-250]
Eskenazi, Gerald - *The Lip: A Biography of Leo Durocher*
　　Aethlon - v13 - Spr '96 - p224+ [251-500]
Eskind, Andrew H - *Index to American Photographic Collections. 3rd Ed.*
　　r ARBA - v28 - '97 - p362 [51-250]
　　r Choice - v34 - N '96 - p431+ [251-500]
Eskridge, William N - *The Case for Same-Sex Marriage*
　　Choice - v34 - N '96 - p545 [51-250]
　　NYTBR - v101 - S 8 '96 - p14 [501+]
Esler, Philip F - *The First Christians in Their Social Worlds*
　　Rel St Rev - v23 - Ja '97 - p68 [51-250]
　　Modelling Early Christianity
　　Rel St Rev - v23 - Ja '97 - p68 [51-250]
Esman, Milton J - *International Organizations and Ethnic Conflict*
　　APSR - v90 - S '96 - p694+ [501+]
Espada, Joao Carlos - *Social Citizenship Rights*
　　Choice - v34 - Ap '97 - p1416 [51-250]
　　TLS - Ja 31 '97 - p25 [501+]
Espada, Martin - *Imagine the Angels of Bread*
　　Bloom Rev - v17 - Ja '97 - p7+ [501+]
　　LJ - v122 - Ap 1 '97 - p94 [1-50]
　　Prog - v60 - S '96 - p43+ [251-500]
　　Prog - v61 - Ja '97 - p39 [51-250]
　　Poetry like Bread
　　TranslRevS - v1 - My '95 - p3+ [51-250]
Esparza, Manuel - *Relaciones Geograficas De Oaxaca 1777-1778*
　　HAHR - v77 - My '97 - p312+ [251-500]
Esperantic Studies
　　p LJ - v122 - Ap 15 '97 - p127 [51-250]
Espiritu, Yen Le - *Asian American Women and Men*
　　Choice - v34 - Mr '97 - p1226+ [51-250]
Espmark, Kjell - *Hatet*
　　WLT - v70 - Aut '96 - p978+ [251-500]
Esposito, David M - *The Legacy of Woodrow Wilson*
　　R&R Bk N - v11 - D '96 - p7 [51-250]
Esposito, John L - *Islam and Democracy*
　　Choice - v34 - D '96 - p685 [51-250]
　　For Aff - v75 - S '96 - p154 [51-250]
　　RP - v59 - Win '97 - p197+ [501+]
　　The Islamic Threat
　　JTWS - v13 - Spr '96 - p233+ [501+]
Esquivel, Laura - *The Law of Love*
　　BL - v92 - Ag '96 - p1853 [251-500]
　　BW - v26 - S 22 '96 - p4+ [501+]
　　CSM - v88 - N 14 '96 - p14 [51-250]
　　Ent W - O 11 '96 - p87 [51-250]
　　LATBR - O 13 '96 - p14 [51-250]
　　NYTBR - v101 - N 17 '96 - p11 [501+]
　　PW - v243 - Jl 22 '96 - p225 [51-250]
　　TLS - O 18 '96 - p23 [251-500]
　　The Law of Love (Arizmendi). Audio Version
　　LJ - v122 - F 1 '97 - p126 [51-250]
　　Trib Bks - F 2 '97 - p6 [51-250]
Esrock, Ellen J - *The Reader's Eye*
　　MLR - v92 - Ap '97 - p420+ [501+]
Ess, Charles - *Philosophical Perspectives on Computer-Mediated Communication*
　　R&R Bk N - v12 - F '97 - p98 [51-250]
　　SciTech - v20 - N '96 - p74 [51-250]
Ess, Hans Van - *Politik Und Gelehrsamkeit In Der Zeit Der Han 202 V. Chr.-220 N. Chr.*
　　Ch Rev Int - v3 - Fall '96 - p547+ [501+]
Essay and General Literature Index 1931-
　　r ASInt - v34 - O '96 - p19 [1-50]
Essence of Romance
　　r RQ - v36 - Win '96 - p218 [51-250]
Essential Facts and Figures
　　yr Kliatt - v30 - N '96 - p31 [51-250]
The Essex Genealogist. Vol. 2
　　EGH - v50 - N '96 - p196 [51-250]
EST Marathon 1995
　　y VOYA - v19 - O '96 - p228 [51-250]
Estabrooks, Maurice - *Electronic Technology, Corporate Strategy, and World Transformation*
　　SocSciComR - v14 - Win '96 - p478+ [501+]
The Estates General on Education 1995-1996
　　J Gov Info - v23 - S '96 - p636 [51-250]
Estell, Doug - *Reading Lists for College-Bound Students. 2nd Ed.*
　　y RQ - v36 - Win '96 - p219+ [51-250]

Estep, Maggie - *Diary of an Emotional Idiot*
BL - v93 - Mr 1 '97 - p1109+ [51-250]
BW - v27 - Mr 23 '97 - p11 [501+]
KR - v65 - Ja 15 '97 - p79 [251-500]
LJ - v122 - Ap 15 '97 - p117 [51-250]
PW - v244 - F 10 '97 - p68 [51-250]
Esterberg, Kristin G - *Lesbian and Bisexual Identities*
LJ - v122 - My 1 '97 - p128 [51-250]
Esterhammer, Angela - *Creating States*
MLR - v91 - O '96 - p974+ [501+]
Estes, Clarissa Pinkola - *The Faithful Gardener*
Rapport - v19 - 4 '96 - p32 [251-500]
The Faithful Gardener (Estes). Audio Version
Bloom Rev - v16 - Jl '96 - p19 [1-50]
Estes, James Martin - *Whether Secular Government Has
the Right to Wield the Sword in Matters of Faith*
CH - v66 - Mr '97 - p194+ [251-500]
Six Ct J - v27 - Win '96 - p1121+ [51-250]
Estes, Kathleen - *The Mermaid's Purse*
c Ch BWatch - v6 - D '96 - p8 [51-250]
c Ch BWatch - v7 - F '97 - p2 [1-50]
Estes, Ralph - *Tyranny of the Bottom Line*
Bus Bk R - v13 - 3 '96 - p16+ [51-250]
LJ - v122 - Mr 15 '97 - p36 [1-50]
Estes, Sally - *Popular YA Reading*
yr Kliatt - v30 - N '96 - p17+ [51-250]
Estess, Patricia Schiff - *Work Concepts for the Future*
LJ - v122 - My 1 '97 - p52 [1-50]
Estey, Ralph H - *Essays on the Early History of Plant
Pathology and Mycology in Canada*
Can Hist R - v77 - S '96 - p448+ [501+]
Estleman, Loren D - *Billy Gashade*
BL - v93 - My 1 '97 - p1478 [51-250]
KR - v65 - F 1 '97 - p159 [251-500]
PW - v244 - F 17 '97 - p211 [51-250]
Roundup M - v4 - Ap '97 - p26+ [251-500]
Never Street
BL - v93 - Mr 15 '97 - p1229 [51-250]
KR - v65 - F 15 '97 - p257 [51-250]
PW - v244 - F 10 '97 - p70 [51-250]
Trib Bks - Ap 13 '97 - p5 [51-250]
Stress
NYTBR - v101 - Ap 7 '96 - p23 [51-250]
Estow, Clara - *Pedro the Cruel of Castile 1350-1369*
AHR - v101 - D '96 - p1538 [251-500]
Estrada, Erik - *Erik Estrada: My Road from Harlem to
Hollywood*
PW - v244 - Mr 10 '97 - p55 [51-250]
Estrin, Barbara L - *Laura: Uncovering Gender and
Genre in Wyatt, Donne, and Marvell*
Sev Cent N - v54 - Fall '96 - p51 [501+]
Estrin, Saul - *Privatization in Central and Eastern Europe*
Econ J - v106 - N '96 - p1845 [51-250]
Esty, Daniel C - *Greening the GATT*
Env - v38 - D '96 - p25 [51-250]
Etala, Emilio - *Atlas of Gastrointestinal Surgery. Vols. 1-2*
r SciTech - v21 - Mr '97 - p60 [51-250]
The Etch a Sketch Book
c PW - v243 - O 7 '96 - p77+ [51-250]
Etcherelli, Claire - *A Propos De Clemence*
MLR - v92 - Ja '97 - p60+ [501+]
Un Arbre Voyageur
MLR - v92 - Ja '97 - p60+ [501+]
Elise Ou La Vraie Vie
MLR - v92 - Ja '97 - p60+ [501+]
Etcheson, Nicole - *The Emerging Midwest*
Choice - v34 - S '96 - p192+ [51-250]
W&M Q - v54 - Ap '97 - p451+ [501+]
Etchison, Dennis - *Double Edge*
PW - v243 - N 11 '96 - p72 [51-250]
Ethier, Wilfred J - *Theory, Policy and Dynamics in
International Trade*
Econ J - v106 - S '96 - p1471+ [51-250]
Etkind, Marc - *...Or Not to Be*
PW - v244 - Ja 27 '97 - p94 [51-250]
Trib Bks - Mr 9 '97 - p8 [1-50]
Etlin, Richard A - *In Defense of Humanism*
Choice - v34 - S '96 - p140 [51-250]
Ets, Marie Hall - *Gilberto Y El Viento. Book and Audio
Version*
c SLJ - v43 - Ja '97 - p69+ [51-250]
Etter, Carolyn - *The Denver Zoo*
WHQ - v27 - Win '96 - p552 [1-50]
Etter, Delores M - *Engineering Problem Solving with
Matlab. 2nd Ed.*
SciTech - v20 - D '96 - p60 [51-250]
Etter, Jim Marion - *Ghost-Town Tales of Oklahoma*
Roundup M - v4 - Mar '96 - p20 [51-250]
Etter-Lewis, Gwendolyn - *Unrelated Kin*
Bl S - v26 - Fall '96 - p101+ [51-250]

Ettin, Andrew Vogel - *Speaking Silences*
MLR - v92 - Ap '97 - p416+ [501+]
Ettinger, Elzbieta - *Hannah Arendt/Martin Heidegger*
TPR - v17 - Sum '96 - p8+ [501+]
Ettorre, Elizabeth - *Gendered Moods*
CS - v26 - Mr '97 - p247+ [501+]
Etue, Elizabeth - *On the Edge*
Quill & Q - v62 - N '96 - p38 [501+]
Etulain, Richard W - *The American West in the Twentieth
Century*
r WAL - v31 - Sum '96 - p183+ [251-500]
*A Bibliographical Guide to the Study of Western
American Literature. 2nd Ed.*
r AL - v68 - S '96 - p667 [1-50]
r ARBA - v28 - '97 - p438 [51-250]
r Nine-C Lit - v50 - Mr '96 - p553 [1-50]
Re-Imagining the Modern American West
BL - v93 - S 15 '96 - p213+ [51-250]
BWatch - v17 - D '96 - p8 [51-250]
Roundup M - v4 - Ap '97 - p29 [1-50]
Etzioni, Amitai - *The New Golden Rule*
BW - v27 - F 16 '97 - p7 [501+]
BWatch - v18 - Mr '97 - p1 [51-250]
For Aff - v76 - My '97 - p123 [51-250]
KR - v64 - N 15 '96 - p1650 [251-500]
LATBR - F 16 '97 - p11 [501+]
Nat R - v49 - Mr 10 '97 - p48+ [501+]
NYTBR - v102 - F 23 '97 - p18 [501+]
PW - v243 - N 18 '96 - p54 [51-250]
TLS - F 7 '97 - p3+ [501+]
Rights and the Common Good
CS - v25 - N '96 - p722+ [501+]
The Spirit of Community
HER - v66 - Win '96 - p844+ [501+]
Etzkorn, Girard J - *Iter Vaticanum Franciscanum*
r R&R Bk N - v12 - F '97 - p11 [51-250]
Euchner, Charles C - *Extraordinary Politics*
Choice - v34 - F '97 - p1035 [51-250]
Eulau, Heinz - *Micro-Macro Dilemmas in Political
Science*
Choice - v34 - Ap '97 - p1416 [51-250]
Eun, Hyone-Myong - *Enzymology Primer for
Recombinant DNA Technology*
SciTech - v20 - N '96 - p33 [51-250]
**The Eurail Guide to Train Travel in the New Europe
1996**
r ARBA - v28 - '97 - p655 [51-250]
The Eurail Guide to World Train Travel 1996
r ARBA - v28 - '97 - p655+ [51-250]
Eurich, S Amanda - *The Economics of Power*
EHR - v111 - N '96 - p1270+ [501+]
Euripides - *Alcestis and Other Plays (Davie)*
TranslRevS - v2 - D '96 - p26 [51-250]
Bacchae (Seaford)
Choice - v34 - Mr '97 - p1157 [51-250]
**Euromicro Workshop on Advanced Mobile Robots (1st:
1996: Kaiserslautern, Germany)** - *Proceedings of the
First Euromicro Workshop on Advanced Mobile Robots*
SciTech - v21 - Mr '97 - p84 [51-250]
**Euromicro Workshop on Real-Time Systems (8th: 1996:
L'Aquila, Italy)** - *Euromicro Workshop on Real-Time
Systems*
SciTech - v20 - N '96 - p7 [51-250]
The Europa World Year Book 1996. Vols. 1-2
r BL - v92 - Ag '96 - p1919 [51-250]
Europe Info
r J Gov Info - v23 - S '96 - p667+ [51-250]
**The European Book World. Pt. 2. Electronic Media
Version**
r LAR - v99 - Ja '97 - p50 [501+]
European Commission - *European Consumer Guide to
the Single Market. 1st Ed.*
J Gov Info - v23 - S '96 - p668 [51-250]
**European Design Automation Conference (1995:
Brighton, England)** - *Euro-DAC '95, European Design
Automation Conference with Euro-VHDL*
SciTech - v20 - S '96 - p3 [51-250]
**European Design Automation Conference (1996: Geneva,
Switzerland)** - *Euro-DAC '96 European Design
Automation Conference with Euro-VHDL and Exhibition*
SciTech - v21 - Mr '97 - p3 [51-250]
European Drinks Marketing Directory 1995
r ARBA - v28 - '97 - p113+ [251-500]
**European Joint Conference on Engineering Systems
Design and Analysis (3rd: 1996: Montpellier,
France)** - *ESDA 1996. Vols. 1-9*
SciTech - v21 - Mr '97 - p75 [51-250]
The European Journal of International Relations
p TLS - Mr 7 '97 - p30 [501+]

**European Journal of Neurology: The Official Journal of
the European Federation of Neurological Societies**
p Nature - v383 - S 5 '96 - p33 [501+]
The European Legacy
p LJ - v121 - D '96 - p158 [51-250]
p LJ - v122 - My 1 '97 - p43 [51-250]
European Marketing Data and Statistics 1996
r ARBA - v28 - '97 - p125 [251-500]
r BusLR - v21 - 3 '96 - p240 [51-250]
**European Oilfield Service, Supply, and Manufacturers
Directory 1996**
r ARBA - v28 - '97 - p644 [51-250]
European Private Label Directory
r ARBA - v28 - '97 - p114 [251-500]
European Regional Incentives 1996-97
r ARBA - v28 - '97 - p114+ [251-500]
**European Symposium EUROFLEX (1993: Lisbon,
Portugal)** - *Flexible Pavements*
SciTech - v20 - D '96 - p71 [51-250]
**European Symposium on Comminution (8th: 1994:
Stockholm, Sweden)** - *Comminution 1994*
SciTech - v21 - Mr '97 - p95 [51-250]
European Transport Trends and Infrastructural Needs
J Gov Info - v23 - S '96 - p666 [51-250]
The European Union Encyclopedia and Directory 1996
r ARBA - v28 - '97 - p273 [251-500]
r J Gov Info - v24 - Ja '97 - p80+ [501+]
Europe's Medium-Sized Companies Directory
r ARBA - v28 - '97 - p114 [251-500]
Eustis, Nelson - *Australian Air Mail Catalogue. 6th Ed.*
r Phil Lit R - v46 - 1 '97 - p69 [501+]
Evaluation Results 1994
JEL - v34 - D '96 - p2116+ [51-250]
Evanghelatos, Kostas - *I Othoni Ton Onomaton*
WLT - v70 - Aut '96 - p1004 [51-250]
Evanhoe, Ed - *Dark Moon*
Pac A - v69 - Fall '96 - p429+ [501+]
Evanovich, Janet - *One for the Money (Critt). Audio
Version*
y Kliatt - v31 - Ja '97 - p44 [51-250]
One for the Money (Petty). Audio Version
y Kliatt - v31 - Ja '97 - p44 [251-500]
Three to Get Deadly
Arm Det - v30 - Win '97 - p94+ [251-500]
BL - v93 - D 1 '96 - p620 [51-250]
KR - v64 - N 15 '96 - p1634+ [51-250]
LJ - v121 - D '96 - p151 [51-250]
NYTBR - v102 - F 16 '97 - p28 [51-250]
PW - v243 - N 25 '96 - p59 [51-250]
Two for the Dough
Arm Det - v29 - Sum '96 - p375 [251-500]
Ent W - S 6 '96 - p71 [1-50]
Obs - D 22 '96 - p18* [51-250]
Woman's J - Ja '97 - p13 [51-250]
Two for the Dough (Petty). Audio Version
y Kliatt - v31 - Ja '97 - p44 [251-500]
Evans, Anthony M - *Introduction to Mineral Exploration*
y New Sci - v151 - S 28 '96 - p46 [501+]
Evans, Arthur V - *An Inordinate Fondness for Beetles*
y BL - v93 - Mr 15 '97 - p1211 [51-250]
BW - v27 - Mr 2 '97 - p8 [251-500]
r LJ - v122 - Ap 15 '97 - p39 [51-250]
r LJ - v122 - Ap 15 '97 - p66 [51-250]
r Nature - v385 - Ja 9 '97 - p127 [1-50]
NH - v106 - F '97 - p13 [1-50]
SB - v33 - My '97 - p103 [501+]
Evans, Brendan - *From Salisbury to Major*
Choice - v34 - D '96 - p683 [51-250]
R&R Bk N - v11 - N '96 - p11 [51-250]
Evans, C Stephen - *The Historical Christ and the Jesus of
Faith*
Choice - v34 - Ja '97 - p810 [51-250]
Why Believe?
Ch Today - v40 - N 11 '96 - p53 [51-250]
Evans, Charles - *American Bibliography. Vols. 1-14*
r ASInt - v34 - O '96 - p9 [51-250]
Evans, Chris - *The Labyrinth of Flames*
J Urban H - v23 - S '96 - p108+ [501+]
Evans, Christopher Hodge - *Social Gospel Liberalism
and the Ministry of Ernest Fremont Tittle*
Choice - v34 - Ap '97 - p1356 [51-250]
Evans, Colin - *The Casebook of Forensic Detection*
LJ - v121 - O 1 '96 - p102+ [51-250]
y SB - v33 - Ja '97 - p13 [51-250]
SciTech - v20 - N '96 - p38 [51-250]
Evans, Craig A - *Anti-Semitism and Early Christianity*
Rel Ed - v91 - Fall '96 - p603 [1-50]
The Synoptic Gospels
Rel St Rev - v23 - Ap '97 - p180 [51-250]

Evans, David - *Time Station London*
    BWatch - v17 - N '96 - p8 [51-250]
  y Kliatt - v31 - Ja '97 - p12 [51-250]
Evans, David, 1952, Sep., 9- - *Sherman's Horsemen*
    Choice - v34 - Ap '97 - p1403 [51-250]
Evans, Donald - *Conceiving the Embryo*
    Hast Cen R - v27 - Ja '97 - p46 [1-50]
    SciTech - v21 - Mr '97 - p39 [51-250]
  Creating the Child
    SciTech - v20 - N '96 - p51 [51-250]
  A Decent Proposal
    Choice - v34 - Ja '97 - p827 [51-250]
Evans, Douglas - *The Classroom at the End of the Hall*
  (Illus. by Larry Di Fiori)
  c BL - v92 - Ag '96 - p1900 [51-250]
  c CBRS - v25 - O '96 - p19 [51-250]
  c CCB-B - v50 - S '96 - p10 [51-250]
  c HB Guide - v8 - Spr '97 - p65 [51-250]
  c NYTBR - v102 - Ja 5 '97 - p22 [1-50]
  c SLJ - v42 - O '96 - p120+ [51-250]
Evans, E Estyn - *Ireland and the Atlantic Heritage*
    ILS - v16 - Spr '97 - p29+ [501+]
    TLS - Ja 24 '97 - p20 [501+]
  The Personality of Ireland
    GJ - v162 - Jl '96 - p219 [251-500]
Evans, Eric J - *The Forging of the Modern State*
    Choice - v34 - D '96 - p669 [51-250]
Evans, Fred J - *Psychology and Nihilism*
    JAAR - v64 - Win '96 - p910+ [501+]
Evans, G R - *The Church and the Churches*
    CH - v65 - S '96 - p555+ [251-500]
  Method in Ecumenical Theology
    Choice - v34 - F '97 - p979+ [51-250]
Evans, Gary - *Chromium Picolinate*
    BL - v92 - Ag '96 - p1869 [51-250]
Evans, Gwynne A - *Practical Numerical Analysis*
    Choice - v34 - Mr '97 - p1197 [51-250]
    SciTech - v20 - D '96 - p17 [51-250]
Evans, H T - *Wales and the Wars of the Roses*
    CR - v270 - Ja '97 - p55 [51-250]
Evans, Harriet - *Women and Sexuality in China*
    LJ - v122 - Ap 15 '97 - p102 [51-250]
Evans, Howard Ensign - *The Natural History of the Long
  Expedition to the Rocky Mountains 1819-1820*
    LJ - v122 - My 1 '97 - p135 [51-250]
Evans, J A S - *The Age of Justinian*
    TLS - S 20 '96 - p30 [501+]
Evans, J Martin - *Milton's Imperial Epic*
    Choice - v34 - S '96 - p125 [51-250]
Evans, James - *Law on the Net*
  r CBR - v15 - Spr '97 - p6 [1-50]
Evans, Jean - *Not Bad for a Foreigner*
    TES - F 28 '97 - p7* [51-250]
Evans, Joel R - *Marketing. 7th Ed.*
    R&R Bk N - v12 - F '97 - p44 [51-250]
Evans, John A - *Planning for Library Development*
    LAR - v98 - Je '96 - p317 [251-500]
Evans, Laura - *The Climb of My Life*
    PW - v243 - S 2 '96 - p103 [51-250]
Evans, Leef - *Thrum*
    BIC - v25 - N '96 - p6+ [501+]
Evans, Lynne - *The Northern Region Economy*
    R&R Bk N - v11 - D '96 - p25 [51-250]
Evans, M I - *Important Bird Areas in the Middle East*
  r Choice - v34 - O '96 - p307+ [501+]
Evans, M Stanton - *The Theme Is Freedom*
    J Ch St - v38 - Sum '96 - p654+ [251-500]
Evans, Marc - *Endurance Athlete's Edge*
    PW - v244 - Ja 27 '97 - p100 [51-250]
Evans, Margery A - *Baudelaire and Intertextuality*
    CLS - v33 - 1 '96 - p128+ [501+]
Evans, Max - *This Chosen Place*
    KR - v65 - F 1 '97 - p190 [251-500]
Evans, Nancy Goyne - *American Windsor Chairs*
    Choice - v34 - S '96 - p112 [51-250]
Evans, Nicholas - *The Horse Whisperer*
    BW - v26 - N 10 '96 - p12 [51-250]
    Ent W - v O 11 '96 - p87 [1-50]
    TES - Jl 19 '96 - pR6 [51-250]
  The Horse Whisperer (Coyote). Audio Version
    BWatch - v18 - Mr '97 - p7 [1-50]
Evans, Peter B - *Embedded Autonomy*
    AAPSS-A - v546 - Jl '96 - p179+ [501+]
    Am Ethnol - v23 - Ag '96 - p655+ [501+]
    APSR - v90 - S '96 - p669 [501+]
    HAHR - v77 - My '97 - p365+ [501+]
Evans, Peter William - *The Films of Luis Bunuel*
    MLR - v91 - O '96 - p1022+ [501+]
Evans, Poppy - *The Complete Guide to Eco-Friendly
  Design*
    BL - v93 - Ja '97 - p796 [51-250]

Evans, Richard J - *Rituals of Retribution*
    Choice - v34 - N '96 - p517 [51-250]
    HT - v47 - Ja '97 - p57 [501+]
    TLS - O 11 '96 - p8+ [501+]
Evans, Richard Paul - *The Christmas Box*
    CSM - v89 - D 19 '96 - p14 [51-250]
    CSM - v89 - Ja 16 '97 - p14 [51-250]
  The First Gift of Christmas
    BWatch - v17 - D '96 - p2 [51-250]
Evans, Robert C - *Jonson and the Contexts of His Time*
    Ren Q - v49 - Win '96 - p872+ [501+]
Evans, Robley - *George Bird Grinnell*
    AL - v69 - Mr '97 - p251 [51-250]
Evans, Ron - *Inktomi and the Ducks and Other Assiniboin
  Trickster Stories (Evans). Audio Version*
  c Trib Bks - F 2 '97 - p7 [1-50]
Evans, Ruth - *Feminist Readings in Middle English
  Literature*
    Comp L - v49 - Win '97 - p87+ [501+]
Evans, Steven Ross - *Voice of the Old Wolf*
    Choice - v34 - F '97 - p1024 [51-250]
Evans, Stewart - *Jack the Ripper--First American Serial
  Killer*
    LJ - v121 - O 1 '96 - p104 [51-250]
    PW - v243 - S 2 '96 - p106+ [51-250]
  The Lodger: The Arrest and Escape of Jack the Ripper
    Books - v9 - S '95 - p23 [1-50]
Evasdaughter, Elizabeth N - *Catholic Girlhood
  Narratives*
  r Choice - v34 - N '96 - p449 [51-250]
Evely, Don - *Knossos: A Labyrinth of History*
    AJA - v100 - Jl '96 - p614+ [501+]
Evelyn, John - *The Writings of John Evelyn*
    BC - v44 - Win '95 - p482+ [251-500]
Evensen, Bruce J - *When Dempsey Fought Tunney*
    Choice - v34 - D '96 - p649 [501+]
Evenson, Debra - *Revolution in the Balance*
    S&S - v60 - Win '96 - p512+ [501+]
Evenson, R E - *Rice Research in Asia*
    Choice - v34 - My '97 - p1525 [51-250]
**The Eventful History of Three Blind Mice (Illus. by
  Winslow Homer)**
  c HB Guide - v7 - Fall '96 - p321 [51-250]
Everdell, William R - *The First Moderns*
    LJ - v122 - Ap 15 '97 - p95+ [51-250]
    PW - v244 - Ap 21 '97 - p53 [51-250]
Everett, Felicity - *Letters from the Grave*
  c JB - v60 - D '96 - p266 [251-500]
  c Sch Lib - v44 - N '96 - p150 [51-250]
Everett, Gabriel - *A Story of Scorpions*
  y BL - v93 - N 15 '96 - p569+ [51-250]
    KR - v64 - O 15 '96 - p1483+ [251-500]
    LJ - v121 - O 15 '96 - p89 [51-250]
    PW - v244 - Ja 27 '97 - p79 [51-250]
Everett, Nigel - *The Tory View of Landscape*
    Critm - v39 - Win '97 - p150+ [501+]
Everett, Percival - *Big Picture*
    NYTBR - v101 - S 15 '96 - p30 [51-250]
  Frenzy
    BL - v93 - Ja '97 - p818 [51-250]
    KR - v64 - N 1 '96 - p1550 [251-500]
    LJ - v122 - Ja '97 - p145+ [51-250]
    PW - v243 - N 18 '96 - p67 [51-250]
  Watershed
    NYTBR - v101 - D 1 '96 - p23 [51-250]
Everett, Peter - *Matisse's War*
    Obs - Ag 25 '96 - p17* [501+]
    Spec - v277 - N 23 '96 - p46 [51-250]
    TLS - N 29 '96 - p11 [51-250]
The Everglade Magazine
  p E Mag - v8 - Ja '97 - p48 [51-250]
Evergreen Chronicles
  p Sm Pr R - v28 - Je '96 - p22 [51-250]
Everingham, Mark - *Revolution and the Multiclass
  Coalition in Nicaragua*
    JEL - v34 - S '96 - p1469 [51-250]
Evers, Charles - *Have No Fear*
  y BL - v93 - S 1 '96 - p3 [51-250]
    KR - v64 - N 1 '96 - p1578 [251-500]
    LJ - v121 - Ja '97 - p110 [51-250]
    LJ - v121 - N 1 '96 - p80 [1-50]
    NYTBR - v102 - Ja 5 '97 - p10+ [501+]
    PW - v243 - N 11 '96 - p64 [51-250]
Evers, Connie - *How to Teach Nutrition to Kids*
    Cur R - v35 - S '96 - p3* [51-250]
Evers, Crabbe - *Tigers Burning*
    Aethlon - v13 - Fall '95 - p140+ [251-500]
Eversole, Robyn - *Flood Fish (Illus. by Sheldon
  Greenberg)*
  c HB Guide - v7 - Fall '96 - p255 [51-250]

Everson, Stephen - *Language*
    Phil R - v105 - Ap '96 - p241+ [501+]
Eversz, Robert M - *Gypsy Hearts*
    BL - v93 - My 15 '97 - p1561 [51-250]
    KR - v65 - Mr 15 '97 - p398+ [251-500]
    PW - v244 - Ap 14 '97 - p55 [51-250]
  Shooting Elvis
    LATBR - My 12 '96 - p4 [251-500]
Everts, Tammy - *Dolphins*
  c HB Guide - v7 - Fall '96 - p344 [1-50]
  Horses
  c HB Guide - v7 - Fall '96 - p346 [51-250]
  Really Weird Animals (Illus. by Christopher Hartley)
  c HB Guide - v7 - Fall '96 - p335 [51-250]
Everything You Need to Know about Diseases
  r ARBA - v28 - '97 - p608+ [51-250]
  r BL - v93 - F 1 '97 - p957 [1-50]
Everything You Need to Know about Medical Tests
  r ARBA - v28 - '97 - p608+ [51-250]
  r BL - v93 - F 1 '97 - p957 [1-50]
**Everything You Need to Know about Medical
  Treatments**
  r ARBA - v28 - '97 - p608+ [51-250]
  r BL - v93 - F 1 '97 - p957 [1-50]
Evetts, Julia - *Gender and Career in Science and
  Engineering*
    Choice - v34 - Ja '97 - p815 [51-250]
Evetts-Secker, Josephine - *Mother and Daughter Tales
  (Illus. by Helen Cann)*
  c HB Guide - v8 - Spr '97 - p100 [1-50]
  c TES - D 6 '96 - p16* [501+]
Evieux, Pierre - *Isidore De Peluse*
    Theol St - v57 - S '96 - p530+ [501+]
Evjen, John O - *Scandinavian Immigrants in New York
  1630-1674*
  r EGH - v50 - N '96 - p157 [51-250]
Evolutionary Biology. Vol. 29
    SciTech - v20 - S '96 - p19 [51-250]
Ewald, Wendy - *I Dreamed I Had a Girl in My Pocket*
    LJ - v121 - S 15 '96 - p64 [51-250]
Ewan, Christine - *Teaching Nursing. 2nd Ed.*
    SciTech - v20 - N '96 - p57 [51-250]
Ewart, Gavin - *Selected Poems 1933-1993*
    TLS - Ja 31 '97 - p22 [501+]
Ewell, Judith - *Venezuela and the United States*
    Choice - v34 - N '96 - p522 [51-250]
    For Aff - v75 - N '96 - p158 [51-250]
Ewen, Stuart - *PR! A Social History of Spin*
    BW - v27 - F 23 '97 - p13 [51-250]
    Choice - v34 - Ap '97 - p1328+ [51-250]
    KR - v64 - O 1 '96 - p1440 [251-500]
    LATBR - D 1 '96 - p4+ [501+]
    LJ - v121 - O 15 '96 - p72 [51-250]
    Nat - v263 - N 18 '96 - p30+ [501+]
    NYTBR - v102 - Mr 2 '97 - p19 [51-250]
    Prog - v60 - D '96 - p41+ [501+]
    PW - v243 - S 16 '96 - p61 [51-250]
    Trib Bks - F 23 '97 - p3+ [501+]
    Utne R - N '96 - p88 [1-50]
Ewert, Allan W - *Culture, Conflict, and Communication in
  the Wildland-Urban Interface*
    AAAGA - v86 - S '96 - p587+ [501+]
Ewing, James - *A Treasury of Tennessee Tales*
    CAY - v17 - Fall '96 - p10 [51-250]
Ewing, Kathleen M H - *A. Aubrey Bodine: Baltimore
  Pictorialist 1906-1970*
    BW - v27 - F 23 '97 - p12 [51-250]
Ewing, Lynne - *Drive-By*
  y BL - v93 - Ap 1 '97 - p1310 [1-50]
  c CCB-B - v50 - S '96 - p11 [51-250]
  c CLW - v67 - D '96 - p56 [51-250]
  c HB Guide - v8 - Spr '97 - p65 [51-250]
  c SLJ - v42 - Ag '96 - p142+ [51-250]
Ewing, Marc - *Running Linux Companion CD-ROM. 2nd
  Ed.*
    LJ - v121 - N 1 '96 - p104 [51-250]
Ewing, Preston - *Let My People Go*
    Bloom Rev - v17 - Ja '97 - p20 [51-250]
    BWatch - v18 - Mr '97 - p4 [51-250]
    Choice - v34 - My '97 - p1562 [51-250]
    Trib Bks - F 16 '97 - p3 [251-500]
Ewing, Steve - *Fateful Rendezvous*
    PW - v244 - Mr 17 '97 - p73 [51-250]
Ewing, Susan - *Lucky Hares and Itchy Bears (Illus. by
  Evon Zerbetz)*
  c Bloom Rev - v16 - N '96 - p31 [51-250]
  c HB Guide - v8 - Spr '97 - p152 [1-50]
  c PW - v243 - S 23 '96 - p77 [51-250]
  c SLJ - v43 - Ja '97 - p99 [51-250]

Ewing, William A - *Blumenfeld Photographs*
 LATBR - D 8 '96 - p30 [51-250]
 LJ - v121 - O 15 '96 - p54 [51-250]
 NYTBR - v101 - D 8 '96 - p74 [51-250]
 Pet PM - v25 - D '96 - p34 [51-250]
 PW - v243 - S 2 '96 - p102 [51-250]
 VLS - Win '96 - p31 [51-250]
 VV - v52 - Ja 28 '97 - p48+ [501+]
 VV - v52 - Ja 28 '97 - p48+ [501+]
 The Body: Photographs of the Human Form
 Art J - v55 - Win '96 - p88+ [501+]
 Inside Information
 New Sci - v152 - D 21 '96 - p71 [51-250]
Examiner (England 1808-)
 p EHR - v111 - N '96 - p1159+ [501+]
Excellence in Ecology. Vol. 4
 Am Sci - v84 - My '96 - p298+ [501+]
Exchanging Experiences of Technology Partnership
 SciTech - v21 - Mr '97 - p72 [51-250]
Exner, George R - *An Accompaniment to Higher Mathematics*
 Choice - v34 - S '96 - p165 [51-250]
 JEL - v34 - S '96 - p1408+ [51-250]
Exner, Richard - *Die Zunge Als Lohn*
 WLT - v71 - Win '97 - p143+ [251-500]
Expansion of Trading Opportunities to the Year 2000 for Asia-Pacific Developing Countries
 J Gov Info - v23 - S '96 - p681+ [51-250]
 R&R Bk N - v11 - N '96 - p28 [51-250]
The Experioddicist
 p Sm Pr R - v28 - Je '96 - p13+ [501+]
Exploring Poetry. Electronic Media Version
 r LJ - v122 - Ja '97 - p160 [51-250]
 yr LJ - v122 - Ap 15 '97 - p40 [1-50]
Exporting to the USA and the Dictionary of International Trade. 1996-97 Ed. Electronic Media Version
 r ARBA - v28 - '97 - p99+ [251-500]
Exquisite Corpse
 p Sm Pr R - v28 - D '96 - p19 [51-250]
Eybers, Elisabeth - *Tydverdryf*
 WLT - v70 - Aut '96 - p1020 [51-250]
Eyck, F Gunther - *The Voice of Nations*
 Notes - v53 - S '96 - p85+ [501+]
Eyden, Brian - *Organelles in Tumor Diagnosis*
 r SciTech - v20 - S '96 - p30 [51-250]
Eye Priory - *Eye Priory Cartulary and Charters. Vol. 2*
 CHR - v82 - Jl '96 - p548+ [251-500]
Eyer, Diane - *Motherguilt: How Our Culture Blames Mothers for What's Wrong with Society*
 Choice - v34 - N '96 - p545 [51-250]
Eyewitness Books
 c Learning - v25 - N '96 - p82 [51-250]
Eyewitness Encyclopedia of Nature 2.0 Version. Electronic Media Version
 cr TES - Mr 14 '97 - p37U [51-250]
Eyewitness Encyclopedia of Science 2.0. Electronic Media Version
 yr Kliatt - v31 - My '97 - p32 [51-250]
 c TES - Mr 14 '97 - p37U [51-250]
Eyewitness Encyclopedia of Space and the Universe. Electronic Media Version
 yr Kliatt - v30 - S '96 - p39+ [51-250]
 cr New Sci - v152 - D 14 '96 - p47 [51-250]
 cr SLJ - v42 - S '96 - p146 [51-250]
Eyewitness Virtual Reality Cat. Electronic Media Version
 cr LJ - v122 - Mr 15 '97 - p97 [51-250]
Eyman, Scott - *The Speed of Sound*
 BL - v93 - F 15 '97 - p991 [51-250]
 KR - v64 - D 15 '96 - p1780 [251-500]
 LATBR - Mr 30 '97 - p9 [501+]
 LJ - v122 - F 15 '97 - p137 [51-250]
 NYTBR - v102 - Mr 9 '97 - p20 [501+]
 PW - v244 - Ja 20 '97 - p385 [51-250]
Eynikel, Erik - *The Reform of King Josiah and the Composition of the Deuteronomistic History*
 Rel St Rev - v23 - Ap '97 - p165 [51-250]
Eyre, Deborah - *Able Children in Ordinary Schools*
 TES - F 28 '97 - p7* [51-250]
Eyre, Elizabeth - *Dirge for a Doge*
 y BL - v93 - Mr 15 '97 - p1229 [51-250]
 KR - v65 - Ja 15 '97 - p97 [251-500]
 LJ - v122 - F 1 '97 - p111 [1-50]
Eyre, Linda - *Lifebalance*
 PW - v243 - D 9 '96 - p66 [1-50]
Eyre, Richard - *Spiritual Serendipity*
 PW - v244 - Mr 31 '97 - p57 [51-250]
Eysenck, H J - *Genius: The Natural History of Creativity*
 AJPsych - v154 - Mr '97 - p430 [251-500]

Rebel with a Cause
 Nature - v386 - Ap 3 '97 - p454 [51-250]
Eysturoy, Annie O - *Daughters of Self-Creation*
 Choice - v34 - O '96 - p277 [51-250]
Ezeala-Harrison, Fidelis - *Economic Development*
 Choice - v34 - F '97 - p1011 [51-250]
 R&R Bk N - v12 - F '97 - p39 [51-250]
Ezekowitz, R Alan B - *Collectins and Innate Immunity*
 SciTech - v21 - Mr '97 - p42 [51-250]
Ezell, Jessica - *Reunion: The Extraordinary Story of a Messenger of Love and Healing*
 Dog Fan - v28 - Ja '97 - p38 [51-250]
 PW - v243 - S 2 '96 - p126 [51-250]
Ezell, Margaret J M - *Cultural Artifacts and the Production of Meaning*
 Can Lit - Spr '97 - p239+ [501+]
Ezera, Regina - *Puka Ola*
 WLT - v70 - Aut '96 - p1000+ [251-500]
Ezergailis, Andrew - *The Holocaust in Latvia 1941-1944*
 Choice - v34 - Ja '97 - p855+ [51-250]
Ezhela, V V - *Particle Physics*
 r Choice - v34 - Ja '97 - p835 [51-250]
 r Sci - v274 - O 25 '96 - p522+ [251-500]
 r SciTech - v20 - N '96 - p19 [51-250]
Ezra, Mark - *The Hungry Otter (Illus. by Gavin Rowe)*
 c HB Guide - v8 - Spr '97 - p26 [51-250]
 c Sch Lib - v44 - N '96 - p146 [51-250]
 c TES - F 21 '97 - p16* [51-250]
Ezrahi, Yaron - *Rubber Bullets*
 BL - v93 - F 15 '97 - p998 [51-250]
 BW - v27 - Ap 6 '97 - p1+ [501+]
 LJ - v122 - Ap 15 '97 - p100 [51-250]
 NL - v80 - Ap 7 '97 - p15+ [501+]
 NYTBR - v102 - Mr 2 '97 - p6 [501+]
 NYTLa - v146 - F 26 '97 - pC15 [501+]
 PW - v244 - F 17 '97 - p204 [51-250]
 Technology, Pessimism, and Postmodernism
 Historian - v59 - Win '97 - p488+ [251-500]
 SFS - v24 - Mr '97 - p160+ [501+]

F

The F. John Barlow Mineral Collection
RocksMiner - v71 - N '96 - p418+ [501+]
Fa, John E - *Evolution and Ecology of Macaque Societies*
Choice - v34 - Mr '97 - p1185+ [51-250]
New Sci - v153 - F 1 '97 - p48 [1-50]
Faasse, Patricia - *Between Seasons and Science*
Isis - v87 - S '96 - p561+ [251-500]
Fabbri, Paolo - *Monteverdi*
Ren Q - v49 - Win '96 - p912+ [501+]
La Fabbrica Del Libro
p BC - v45 - Aut '96 - p381+ [51-250]
Faber, Adele - *How to Talk So Kids Can Learn*
PW - v243 - Jl 22 '96 - p235 [1-50]
Faber, Doris - *Printer's Devil to Publisher*
y SLJ - v42 - O '96 - p164 [51-250]
Faber, Malte Michael - *Ecological Economics*
JEL - v34 - D '96 - p2132 [51-250]
R&R Bk N - v11 - N '96 - p26 [51-250]
Faber, T E - *Fluid Dynamics for Physicists*
SIAM Rev - v38 - D '96 - p700+ [501+]
Fabi, Mark - *Wyrm*
KR - v65 - Ap 1 '97 - p509 [51-250]
LJ - v122 - Ap 15 '97 - p123 [51-250]
Fabian, Bernhard - *Das Deutsche Buch*
Six Ct J - v27 - Win '96 - p1182+ [501+]
*Handbuch Der Deutschen Buchbestande In
Deutschland. Vols. 14-15*
Lib - v19 - Mr '97 - p75+ [501+]
*Handbuch Der Deutschen Buchbestande In Osterreich.
Vols. 1-2*
Lib - v19 - Mr '97 - p75+ [501+]
Fabian, Johannes - *Remembering the Present*
Choice - v34 - My '97 - p1552 [51-250]
Fabian, Stephen Michael - *Space-Time of the Bororo of
Brazil*
JTWS - v13 - Spr '96 - p361 [51-250]
Fabio - *Wild*
PW - v244 - My 12 '97 - p73+ [51-250]
Fabozzi, Frank J - *Fixed Income Mathematics. 3rd Ed.*
R&R Bk N - v11 - D '96 - p36 [51-250]
*The Handbook of Commercial Mortgage-Backed
Securities*
R&R Bk N - v12 - F '97 - p49 [51-250]
Measuring and Controlling Interest Rate Risk
R&R Bk N - v11 - D '96 - p37 [51-250]
Fabre, Michel - *The French Critical Reception of African-
American Literature*
r AL - v68 - S '96 - p667 [1-50]
r Nine-C Lit - v50 - Mr '96 - p553 [1-50]
Fabry, Chris - *The 77 Habits of Highly Ineffective
Christians*
PW - v244 - Ap 14 '97 - p70 [51-250]
Away with the Manger
Ch Today - v40 - O 7 '96 - p56+ [251-500]
Fabulous Sports Babe - *The Babe in Boyland*
Ent W - N 15 '96 - p66 [51-250]
Facio, Gonzalo J - *Litigando En Washington*
BL - v93 - S 15 '96 - p227 [1-50]
Fackenheim, Emil L - *The God Within*
Choice - v34 - O '96 - p293 [51-250]
Jewish Philosophers and Jewish Philosophy
LJ - v121 - D '96 - p97 [51-250]
Facklam, Howard - *Alternative Medicine*
y BL - v93 - D 15 '96 - p715 [51-250]
c Ch BWatch - v6 - N '96 - p2 [1-50]
y SB - v33 - Ja '97 - p13 [51-250]
y SLJ - v43 - Mr '97 - p199+ [51-250]
Facklam, Margery - *Creepy, Crawly, Caterpillars (Illus.
by Paul Facklam)*
c Emerg Lib - v24 - S '96 - p43 [1-50]

Creepy, Crawly Caterpillars (Illus. by Paul Facklam)
c HB Guide - v7 - Fall '96 - p341 [51-250]
Only a Star (Illus. by Nancy Carpenter)
c HB Guide - v8 - Spr '97 - p152 [51-250]
c PW - v243 - S 30 '96 - p89+ [51-250]
c SLJ - v42 - O '96 - p35 [51-250]
Fackler, Elizabeth - *Badlands*
BL - v93 - O 1 '96 - p322 [51-250]
PW - v243 - S 2 '96 - p114 [51-250]
Roundup M - v4 - O '96 - p30+ [251-500]
Faden, Ruth R - *HIV, AIDS and Childbearing*
Hast Cen R - v26 - S '96 - p40 [1-50]
Fagan, Brian M - *Eyewitness to Discovery*
BL - v93 - N 15 '96 - p568 [51-250]
y BL - v93 - D 1 '96 - p664 [1-50]
BW - v27 - F 23 '97 - p13 [51-250]
Nature - v386 - Ap 17 '97 - p669+ [501+]
SB - v33 - My '97 - p105 [251-500]
The Oxford Companion to Archaeology
r BL - v93 - Mr 15 '97 - p1260 [51-250]
r LJ - v122 - F 15 '97 - p129 [51-250]
Nature - v386 - Ap 17 '97 - p669+ [501+]
Sci - v275 - F 28 '97 - p1276 [1-50]
Fagan, Cary - *The Doctor's House*
BIC - v25 - O '96 - p16 [501+]
Fagan, Thomas K - *Historical Encyclopedia of School
Psychology*
r ARBA - v28 - '97 - p132 [251-500]
r Choice - v34 - S '96 - p99 [51-250]
Fagerholm, Monika - *Wonderful Women by the Water*
KR - v65 - Mr 1 '97 - p336 [51-250]
Obs - Mr 30 '97 - p17* [51-250]
PW - v244 - Ja 27 '97 - p76 [51-250]
TLS - Ap 11 '97 - p27 [501+]
Fagette, Paul - *Digging for Dollars*
SB - v33 - Ja '97 - p11 [51-250]
Fagge, Roger - *Power, Culture and Conflict in the
Coalfields*
Choice - v34 - N '96 - p512 [51-250]
R&R Bk N - v11 - N '96 - p33 [51-250]
Faggella, Kathy - *Crayons, Crafts, and Concepts*
c Ch BWatch - v7 - F '97 - p6 [51-250]
Open-Ended Art
c Ch BWatch - v7 - F '97 - p6 [51-250]
Fagin, Dan - *Toxic Deception*
y BL - v93 - F 15 '97 - p986 [51-250]
LJ - v122 - F 1 '97 - p103 [51-250]
PW - v243 - D 2 '96 - p49 [51-250]
Fagin, Ronald - *Reasoning about Knowledge*
New Sci - v151 - S 28 '96 - p51 [1-50]
Faherty, Terence - *Come Back Dead*
BL - v93 - F 15 '97 - p1006 [51-250]
BW - v27 - F 16 '97 - p11 [51-250]
KR - v64 - D 1 '96 - p1705 [51-250]
LJ - v122 - Ja '97 - p153 [51-250]
PW - v243 - D 9 '96 - p63 [51-250]
Kill Me Again
Arm Det - v29 - Sum '96 - p369 [251-500]
Prove the Nameless
BW - v26 - S 15 '96 - p6 [251-500]
KR - v64 - Ag 15 '96 - p1188+ [51-250]
Fahey, James J - *Pacific War Diary*
Afterimage - v24 - Ja '97 - p23 [1-50]
Fahlbusch, Erwin - *Evangelisches Kirchenlexikon*
Rel St Rev - v23 - Ap '97 - p151 [51-250]
Fahringer, Thomas - *Automatic Performance Prediction
of Parallel Programs*
SciTech - v20 - S '96 - p6 [51-250]
Fahs, John - *Cigarette Confidential*
y Kliatt - v31 - My '97 - p28 [51-250]

Fahy, Conor - *Printing a Book at Verona in 1622*
BC - v46 - Spr '97 - p148+ [501+]
Faidley, Warren - *Storm Chaser*
y BL - v93 - S 1 '96 - p47+ [51-250]
y Kliatt - v31 - Ja '97 - p28 [51-250]
y Kliatt - v31 - Mr '97 - p4 [51-250]
Failde, Augusto - *Exito Latino*
LJ - v122 - Ja '97 - p78 [51-250]
Fain, Moira - *Snow Day (Illus. by Moira Fain)*
c CBRS - v25 - S '96 - p2+ [51-250]
c CCB-B - v50 - O '96 - p57 [51-250]
c HB Guide - v8 - Spr '97 - p26 [51-250]
c PW - v243 - S 16 '96 - p83 [51-250]
c SLJ - v42 - O '96 - p92+ [51-250]
Fair, Bryan K - *Notes of a Racial Caste Baby*
BL - v93 - F 15 '97 - p979 [51-250]
CHE - v43 - F 28 '97 - pA21 [51-250]
PW - v243 - D 16 '96 - p50+ [51-250]
Fair, David - *The Fabulous Four Skunks (Illus. by Bruce
Koscielniak)*
c Ch BWatch - v6 - My '96 - p3 [1-50]
c HB Guide - v7 - Fall '96 - p255 [51-250]
Fair, Ray C - *Testing Macroeconometric Models*
r JEL - v34 - S '96 - p1342+ [501+]
Fair, Sylvia - *The Bedspread*
y HMR - Win '96 - p45 [1-50]
Fairbairn, John - *Bindi*
c Magpies - v11 - My '96 - p42 [51-250]
Fairbank, John King - *H.B. Morse: Customs
Commissioner and Historian of China*
PHR - v66 - F '97 - p113+ [501+]
TLS - O 25 '96 - p11 [501+]
Fairbanks, Stephanie - *Spotlight*
y BL - v93 - D 1 '96 - p645 [51-250]
y Ch BWatch - v6 - Jl '96 - p2 [1-50]
Fairbrother, Anne - *Noninfectious Diseases of Wildlife.
2nd Ed.*
SciTech - v20 - D '96 - p57 [51-250]
Fairchild, Elizabeth - *The Rakehell's Reform*
LJ - v121 - N 15 '96 - p48 [51-250]
Fairchilde, Lily - *Song of the Phoenix*
PW - v244 - Mr 17 '97 - p72 [51-250]
Fairclough, Adam - *Race and Democracy*
AAPSS-A - v546 - Jl '96 - p168+ [501+]
AHR - v102 - F '97 - p219 [251-500]
Fairclough, Ellen Louks - *Saturday's Child*
Can Hist R - v77 - D '96 - p628+ [501+]
Fairclough, Jon - *Software Engineering Guides*
SciTech - v20 - D '96 - p10 [51-250]
Fairfield, Helen - *The Embroidery Design Sourcebook*
LJ - v121 - O 15 '96 - p57 [51-250]
Fairhurst, Alice M - *Effective Teaching, Effective
Learning*
Learning - v25 - S '96 - p47 [51-250]
Fairlamb, Horace L - *Critical Conditions*
MLR - v92 - Ja '97 - p154+ [501+]
Fairleigh, John - *When the Tunnels Meet*
BL - v93 - N 1 '96 - p476 [51-250]
WLT - v71 - Win '97 - p134 [501+]
Fairstein, Linda - *Final Jeopardy*
LATBR - Jl 14 '96 - p6 [51-250]
Likely to Die
BL - v93 - My 1 '97 - p1460 [51-250]
KR - v65 - Ap 1 '97 - p505 [51-250]
LJ - v122 - My 1 '97 - p138+ [51-250]
PW - v244 - My 12 '97 - p57+ [51-250]
Fairweather, James S - *Faculty Work and Public Trust*
J Hi E - v68 - Mr '97 - p233+ [501+]
Faist, Thomas - *Social Citizenship for Whom?*
CS - v26 - Ja '97 - p65+ [501+]
ILR - v135 - '96 - p113+ [501+]

Faith, Nicolas - *The World the Railways Made*
　　HT - v47 - Mr '97 - p55 [51-250]
Faithfull, Marianne - *Marianne Faithfull's Year One*
　　Woman's J - Ag '96 - p11 [1-50]
Fakhry, Majid - *Ethical Theories in Islam. 2nd Expanded Ed.*
　　Rel St Rev - v23 - Ja '97 - p3+ [501+]
Falco, Edward - *Acid*
　　HR - v49 - Aut '96 - p483+ [501+]
　　RCF - v16 - Fall '96 - p195+ [251-500]
Falco, Maria - *Feminist Interpretations of Mary Wollstonecraft*
　　Nine-C Lit - v51 - S '96 - p272 [1-50]
Falco, Raphael - *Conceived Presences*
　　Sev Cent N - v54 - Fall '96 - p45+ [501+]
　　South HR - v31 - Win '97 - p83+ [501+]
Falcone, Giovanna - *Le Cinquecentine Della Biblioteca Dell'Archivio Di Stato Di Roma*
　　Lib - v19 - Mr '97 - p99+ [51-250]
Falcone, Paul - *96 Great Interview Questions to Ask before You Hire*
　　BWatch - v17 - N '96 - p11 [51-250]
Falconer, Kieran - *Peru*
　　c HB Guide - v7 - Fall '96 - p392 [51-250]
Faldet, Rachel - *Our Stories of Miscarriage*
　　BL - v93 - Mr 15 '97 - p1214 [51-250]
Falick, Melanie D - *Knitting in America*
　　Am Craft - v56 - D '96 - p33 [51-250]
　　y BL - v93 - S 1 '96 - p54+ [51-250]
Falik, Marilyn M - *Women's Health*
　　Choice - v34 - Mr '97 - p1194 [51-250]
　　SciTech - v20 - D '96 - p38 [51-250]
Falk, Avner - *A Psychoanalytic History of the Jews*
　　Choice - v34 - My '97 - p1561 [51-250]
Falk, Donald A - *Restoring Diversity*
　　Choice - v34 - F '97 - p989 [51-250]
Falk, Harvey - *Jesus the Pharisee*
　　Rel Ed - v91 - Fall '96 - p603 [1-50]
Falk, John - *Bubble Monster and Other Science Fun*
　　c PW - v243 - D 2 '96 - p62 [51-250]
Falk, Randall M - *Jews and Christians in Pursuit of Social Justice*
　　CC - v113 - N 6 '96 - p1093 [51-250]
Falk, Richard - *On Humane Governance*
　　Cu H - v95 - N '96 - p392+ [501+]
　　RP - v58 - Fall '96 - p862+ [501+]
Falkenburg, Reindert Leonard - *Beeld En Zelfbeeld In De Nederlandse Kunst 1550-1750*
　　BM - v138 - N '96 - p757+ [501+]
　　The Fruit of Devotion
　　Apo - v144 - Ag '96 - p71 [501+]
Falkenhausen, Lothar Von - *Suspended Music*
　　Rel St Rev - v22 - O '96 - p359 [51-250]
Falkenstein, Lorne - *Kant's Intuitionism*
　　CPR - v16 - O '96 - p333+ [501+]
Falkenstein, Lynda - *Nichecraft*
　　BL - v92 - Ag '96 - p1865 [51-250]
Falkiner, Suzanne - *Ethel: A Love Story*
　　Aust Bk R - N '96 - p46 [501+]
Falkner, David - *Great Time Coming*
　　Aethlon - v13 - Spr '96 - p225+ [251-500]
　　NYTBR - v101 - Ap 7 '96 - p24 [51-250]
　　Great Time Coming (Davidson). Audio Version
　　y Kliatt - v30 - N '96 - p49 [51-250]
　　LJ - v122 - F 15 '97 - p115 [1-50]
　　The Last Hero
　　NYTBR - v101 - Ap 7 '96 - p12+ [501+]
Fall, Cheryl - *Speed Quilting*
　　BL - v93 - S 1 '96 - p55 [51-250]
Falla, Ricardo - *Masacres De La Selva*
　　BL - v93 - S 15 '96 - p227 [1-50]
Fallada, Hans - *Little Man--What Now?*
　　TLS - O 4 '96 - p14 [501+]
Fallon, Peggy - *Chicken Dinners in One Pot*
　　BL - v93 - Mr 15 '97 - p1215 [51-250]
Fallon, Robert Thomas - *Milton in Government*
　　Ren Q - v49 - Aut '96 - p662+ [501+]
Falloon, Ian R H - *Integrated Mental Health Care*
　　J ClinPsyc - v57 - Jl '96 - p314 [501+]
Falloon, Jane - *Thumbelina (Illus. by Emma Chichester Clark)*
　　c PW - v244 - Mr 31 '97 - p74 [51-250]
Fallows, David - *Songs and Musicians in the Fifteenth Century*
　　R&R Bk N - v11 - N '96 - p59 [51-250]

Fallows, James - *Breaking the News*
　　Bks & Cult - v2 - Jl '96 - p29+ [251-500]
　　BL - v93 - Ja '97 - p756 [1-50]
　　Comw - v123 - O 11 '96 - p27+ [501+]
　　NYTBR - v101 - D 8 '96 - p85 [1-50]
　　NYTBR - v102 - Mr 16 '97 - p32 [51-250]
　　Obs - D 1 '96 - p17* [1-50]
　　PSQ - v111 - Win '96 - p689+ [501+]
　　PW - v243 - D 30 '96 - p64 [1-50]
Falls, Cyril - *The History of the 36th (Ulster) Division*
　　CR - v270 - F '97 - p112 [51-250]
Faloutsos, Christos - *Searching Multimedia Databases by Content*
　　SciTech - v21 - Mr '97 - p6 [51-250]
Falsetto, Mario - *Perspectives on Stanley Kubrick*
　　LJ - v121 - D '96 - p96 [51-250]
Falter, Jurgen - *Hitler's Wahler*
　　JMH - v68 - S '96 - p629+ [501+]
Faltum, Andrew - *The Essex Aircraft Carriers*
　　Sea H - Aut '96 - p44 [51-250]
Falwell, Cathryn - *Dragon Tooth (Illus. by Cathryn Falwell)*
　　c HB Guide - v7 - Fall '96 - p255 [51-250]
　　Feast for 10. Book and Audio Version
　　c SLJ - v42 - O '96 - p77 [51-250]
　　P.J. and Puppy (Illus. by Cathryn Falwell)
　　c BL - v93 - F 15 '97 - p1026 [51-250]
　　c SLJ - v43 - Mr '97 - p150 [51-250]
Family Adventures (Fodor Guides)
　　r BL - v93 - S 15 '96 - p206 [1-50]
Family and Future
　　J Gov Info - v23 - S '96 - p682 [51-250]
Family Archive Viewer. Electronic Media Version
　　r ARBA - v28 - '97 - p165 [251-500]
Family: Challenges for the Future
　　Choice - v34 - My '97 - p1583 [51-250]
The Family Handyman
　　p LJ - v122 - F 1 '97 - p53 [1-50]
Family Internet Companion
　　SciTech - v20 - D '96 - p76 [1-50]
The Family of Cats
　　Nature - v386 - Mr 27 '97 - p348 [1-50]
Family Resource Guide
　　J Gov Info - v23 - S '96 - p595 [1-50]
A Family Treasury of Prayers
　　c BL - v93 - O 1 '96 - p335 [51-250]
　　c HB Guide - v8 - Spr '97 - p87 [51-250]
　　c SLJ - v42 - O '96 - p136 [51-250]
Famous Artists Series
　　c Learning - v25 - N '96 - p82 [51-250]
Famous Spaceships of Fact and Fantasy. 2nd Ed.
　　FSM - v15 - Ja '97 - p79 [1-50]
Fancher, Robert T - *Cultures of Healing*
　　AJPsych - v154 - Ja '97 - p124 [501+]
　　Hast Cen R - v26 - Jl '96 - p41 [1-50]
Fane, Diana - *Converging Cultures*
　　Am Q - v49 - Mr '97 - p138+ [501+]
　　Choice - v34 - O '96 - p266 [51-250]
Fanelli, Sara - *My Map Book*
　　c LA - v73 - O '96 - p431 [51-250]
　　c LATBR - Mr 17 '96 - p11 [51-250]
　　c RT - v50 - D '96 - p344 [51-250]
　　Wolf (Illus. by Sara Fanelli)
　　c BL - v93 - My 15 '97 - p1578+ [51-250]
　　c KR - v65 - My 1 '97 - p719 [51-250]
　　c PW - v244 - Ap 7 '97 - p90 [51-250]
Fang, Biao - *Bei Jing Jian Shi*
　　BL - v93 - My 1 '97 - p1484 [1-50]
Fang, Zhaolun - *Flow Injection Atomic Absorption Spectrometry*
　　J Chem Ed - v73 - Ag '96 - pA178 [51-250]
Fang, Zhihua - *Chinese Short Stories of the Twentieth Century*
　　WLT - v70 - Sum '96 - p759 [501+]
Fangfang, Li - *Wo Liang*
　　BL - v93 - N 1 '96 - p484 [1-50]
Fanica, Pierre-Olivier - *Ecole De Barbizon*
　　r BM - v138 - S '96 - p614 [51-250]
Fankhauser, Samuel - *Valuing Climate Change*
　　JEL - v34 - D '96 - p1999+ [501+]
Fannin, Troy E - *Clinical Optics. 2nd Ed.*
　　SciTech - v21 - Mr '97 - p62 [51-250]
Fanning, David - *Shostakovich Studies*
　　Choice - v34 - S '96 - p138 [51-250]
　　TLS - N 22 '96 - p20 [501+]
Fanning, Richard W - *Peace and Disarmament*
　　NWCR - v49 - Aut '96 - p156+ [501+]
Fanshawe, Andy - *Himalaya Alpine-Style*
　　Choice - v34 - D '96 - p649 [51-250]

Fantham, Elaine - *Roman Literary Culture*
　　Choice - v34 - D '96 - p609 [51-250]
　　R&R Bk N - v11 - D '96 - p59 [51-250]
Fantoni, Marcello - *La Corte Del Granduca*
　　Ren Q - v49 - Aut '96 - p598+ [501+]
Faoro, Victoria - *Ohio Star Quilts*
　　BL - v93 - S 15 '97 - p201+ [51-250]
Faqir, Fadia - *Pillars of Salt*
　　KR - v65 - My 1 '97 - p678 [51-250]
　　NS & S - v9 - My 17 '96 - p40 [1-50]
　　PW - v244 - Ap 28 '97 - p51 [251-500]
The Far East and Australasia 1996
　　r Pac A - v69 - Sum '96 - p294+ [501+]
The Far East and Australasia 1997
　　r ARBA - v28 - '97 - p73 [251-500]
Fara, Patricia - *Sympathetic Attractions*
　　NS - v126 - Ja 31 '97 - p46 [251-500]
　　Obs - F 9 '97 - p15* [251-500]
Farace, Joe - *The Digital Imaging Dictionary*
　　r ARBA - v28 - '97 - p621 [51-250]
　　r SciTech - v21 - Mr '97 - p80 [51-250]
　　Photographer's Digital Studio
　　CBR - v15 - Spr '97 - p9 [51-250]
Faragher, Scott - *Making It in Country Music*
　　LJ - v121 - N 1 '96 - p41 [1-50]
Farago, Claire - *Reframing the Renaissance*
　　Art Bull - v78 - D '96 - p736+ [501+]
　　NYRB - v44 - Ap 10 '97 - p57+ [501+]
Farah, David - *Series Books and the Media*
　　r AB - v98 - N 18 '96 - p1733 [51-250]
Farazmand, Ali - *Public Enterprise Management*
　　R&R Bk N - v12 - F '97 - p39 [51-250]
Farber, Erica - *No Howling in the House (Illus. by Mercer Mayer)*
　　c SLJ - v43 - Ja '97 - p77 [51-250]
Farber, Norma - *The Boy Who Longed for a Lift (Illus. by Brian Selznick)*
　　c BL - v93 - My 15 '97 - p1579 [51-250]
　　c HB - v73 - My '97 - p305+ [251-500]
　　c KR - v65 - My 1 '97 - p719 [51-250]
　　c PW - v244 - Ap 21 '97 - p70 [51-250]
　　I Swim an Ocean in My Sleep (Illus. by Elivia Savadier)
　　c KR - v65 - Mr 1 '97 - p379 [51-250]
　　c PW - v244 - F 10 '97 - p82 [51-250]
Farber, Paul Lawrence - *The Temptations of Evolutionary Ethics*
　　Skeptic - v4 - 2 '96 - p107 [51-250]
Farcau, Bruce W - *The Chaco War*
　　Choice - v34 - Ja '97 - p860 [51-250]
　　J Mil H - v60 - O '96 - p781+ [51-250]
　　The Coup: Tactics in the Seizure of Power
　　Arm F&S - v23 - Fall '96 - p123+ [501+]
　　The Transition to Democracy in Latin America
　　Choice - v34 - F '97 - p1030+ [51-250]
　　R&R Bk N - v12 - F '97 - p60 [51-250]
Fare, Rolf - *Intertemporal Production Frontiers*
　　JEL - v34 - D '96 - p2031 [51-250]
　　R&R Bk N - v11 - D '96 - p23 [51-250]
　　Multi-Output Production and Duality
　　JEL - v34 - S '96 - p1343+ [501+]
Farer, Tom - *Beyond Sovereignty*
　　For Aff - v75 - N '96 - p159+ [251-500]
　　R&R Bk N - v11 - N '96 - p51 [51-250]
Fargas, Laura - *An Animal of the Sixth Day*
　　Choice - v34 - O '96 - p277 [51-250]
　　WLT - v71 - Win '97 - p165 [51-250]
Farge, Arlette - *Subversive Words*
　　Historian - v58 - Sum '96 - p899+ [251-500]
　　Pub Op Q - v60 - Win '96 - p660+ [501+]
Farge, James K - *Registre Des Conclusions De La Faculte De Theologie De L'Universite De Paris. Vol. 2*
　　Six Ct J - v27 - Win '96 - p1156+ [501+]
Fargnoli, A Nicholas - *James Joyce A to Z*
　　r ARBA - v28 - '97 - p461 [51-250]
Farhi, Donna - *The Breathing Book*
　　PW - v243 - S 2 '96 - p125 [51-250]
Farina, Richard - *Been Down So Long It Looks like Up to Me*
　　TLS - S 13 '96 - p25 [501+]
Faris, David - *Plantagenet Ancestry of Seventeenth-Century Colonists*
　　Am Geneal - v71 - Jl '96 - p187 [251-500]
Farish, Leah - *Tinker v. Des Moines*
　　y KR - v65 - Ja 15 '97 - p141 [51-250]
Farish, Terry - *Talking in Animal*
　　y CCB-B - v50 - N '96 - p95+ [51-250]
　　c HB - v73 - Ja '97 - p55+ [51-250]
　　c HB Guide - v8 - Spr '97 - p66 [51-250]
　　c PW - v243 - O 7 '96 - p76 [51-250]
　　c SLJ - v42 - N '96 - p104 [51-250]

Farjeon, Eleanor - *Cats Sleep Anywhere (Illus. by Anne Mortimer)*
  c BL - v93 - S 1 '96 - p133+ [51-250]
  c Ch BWatch - v6 - N '96 - p6 [1-50]
  c Emerg Lib - v24 - Mr '97 - p44 [1-50]
  c HB Guide - v8 - Spr '97 - p152 [1-50]
  c JB - v60 - D '96 - p230 [51-250]
  c PW - v243 - S 16 '96 - p81 [51-250]
  c Sch Lib - v45 - F '97 - p18 [51-250]
  c SLJ - v42 - D '96 - p112 [51-250]
Morning Has Broken (Illus. by Tim Ladwig)
  c BL - v93 - O 1 '96 - p337 [51-250]
  c HB Guide - v8 - Spr '97 - p140 [51-250]
  c KR - v64 - O 15 '96 - p1531 [51-250]
  c SLJ - v42 - D '96 - p112 [51-250]
Farkas, George - *Human Capital or Cultural Capital?*
    Choice - v34 - Ap '97 - p1390 [51-250]
    JEL - v35 - Mr '97 - p230 [51-250]
Farley, Blanche Flanders - *Like a Summer Peach*
    BWatch - v17 - N '96 - p1 [51-250]
    PW - v243 - S 16 '96 - p80 [51-250]
Farley, Carol - *Mr. Pak Buys a Story (Illus. by Benrei Huang)*
  c CCB-B - v50 - My '97 - p319 [51-250]
  c KR - v65 - Mr 1 '97 - p379 [51-250]
Farley, Christopher John - *My Favorite War*
    BW - v26 - N 3 '96 - p8 [251-500]
    Ent W - Ag 23 '96 - p119 [51-250]
    LJ - v122 - Mr 15 '97 - p41 [1-50]
    Nat - v263 - S 9 '96 - p53 [501+]
    NYTBR - v101 - O 13 '96 - p21 [51-250]
    Obs - F 16 '97 - p15* [501+]
    TLS - Mr 28 '97 - p22 [251-500]
    VV - v41 - S 10 '96 - p65+ [501+]
Farley, Reynolds - *The New American Reality*
    Choice - v34 - Ap '97 - p1423 [51-250]
    JEL - v35 - Mr '97 - p234+ [51-250]
State of the Union. Vols. 1-2
    Pol Stud J - v24 - Aut '96 - p518 [51-250]
Farley, Steven - *The Black Stallion's Shadow*
  c BL - v93 - S 15 '96 - p238 [51-250]
  c CCB-B - v50 - S '96 - p11 [51-250]
  c HB Guide - v8 - Spr '97 - p66 [51-250]
  c SLJ - v42 - O '96 - p122 [51-250]
Farlow-Schlerf, Sharrye - *Blow the Trumpets, Loudly!*
    Rapport - v19 - 6 '96 - p29 [251-500]
Farman, Irvin - *Standard of the West*
    JEL - v35 - Mr '97 - p249 [51-250]
Farman, John - *A Phenomenally Phrank History of Philosophy*
  y Sch Lib - v44 - Ag '96 - p123+ [51-250]
The Very Bloody History of Britain (Jones). Audio Version
    Books - v9 - S '95 - p27 [1-50]
Farmanfarmaian, Manucher - *Blood and Oil*
    BL - v93 - Ap 1 '97 - p1266 [51-250]
    KR - v65 - F 1 '97 - p190 [251-500]
    PW - v244 - Ja 27 '97 - p83 [51-250]
    Trib Bks - My 4 '97 - p3+ [501+]
Farmer, Bonnie Cashin - *A Nursing Home and Its Organizational Climate*
    Choice - v34 - Ja '97 - p882 [51-250]
    SciTech - v20 - S '96 - p29 [51-250]
Farmer, David John - *The Language of Public Administration*
    PAR - v57 - Mr '97 - p174+ [501+]
Farmer, Lesley S J - *Informing Young Women*
    Sch Lib - v45 - F '97 - p54 [51-250]
    VOYA - v19 - F '97 - p356 [51-250]
Farmer, Nancy - *The Ear, the Eye, and the Arm*
  y JB - v60 - O '96 - p209+ [501+]
  y Kliatt - v30 - S '96 - p4 [1-50]
The Ear, the Eye, and the Arm (Guidall). Audio Version
  c BL - v93 - Ap 1 '97 - p1313 [1-50]
  c CSM - v89 - Mr 27 '97 - pB6 [1-50]
A Girl Named Disaster
  y BL - v93 - S 1 '96 - p118+ [51-250]
  y BL - v93 - Ap 1 '97 - p1292 [1-50]
  y BL - v93 - Ap 1 '97 - p1302 [1-50]
  c CCB-B - v50 - D '96 - p133 [51-250]
  c HB - v72 - N '96 - p734+ [251-500]
  c HB Guide - v8 - Spr '97 - p66 [51-250]
  y KR - v64 - S 15 '96 - p1399 [51-250]
  y NYTBR - v102 - Mr 16 '97 - p26 [1-50]
  y Par Ch - v20 - O '96 - p11+ [1-50]
  c PW - v243 - N 4 '96 - p48 [1-50]
  y SLJ - v42 - O '96 - p144+ [51-250]
  y SLJ - v42 - D '96 - p28+ [1-50]
  y TES - Ap 4 '97 - p8* [251-500]
  y VOYA - v19 - D '96 - p268 [251-500]

Runnery Granary (Illus. by Jos. A Smith)
  c Ch BWatch - v6 - Jl '96 - p4 [1-50]
  c CLW - v67 - D '96 - p56 [51-250]
  c HB - v72 - S '96 - p575 [51-250]
  c HB Guide - v7 - Fall '96 - p255+ [51-250]
  c SLJ - v42 - Ag '96 - p122 [51-250]
  c Smith - v27 - N '96 - p164 [1-50]
The Warm Place
  y JB - v60 - O '96 - p199+ [51-250]
  c Magpies - v11 - Jl '96 - p30 [51-250]
Farmer, Patti - *What's He Doing Now? (Illus. by Janet Wilson)*
  c Quill & Q - v62 - N '96 - p46 [251-500]
Farmer, Penelope - *Penelope*
  c CBRS - v24 - Ag '96 - p167 [51-250]
  y Ch BWatch - v6 - My '96 - p2 [51-250]
  y HB Guide - v7 - Fall '96 - p301 [51-250]
Twin Trouble (Illus. by Liz Roberts)
  c Bks Keeps - Ja '97 - p21 [51-250]
  c JB - v60 - Ag '96 - p147 [51-250]
  c Sch Lib - v44 - Ag '96 - p105 [51-250]
Two, or, The Book of Twins and Doubles
    Nature - v383 - O 10 '96 - p493+ [501+]
Farmer, Richard - *Lecture Notes on Epidemiology and Public Health Medicine. 4th Ed.*
    SciTech - v20 - S '96 - p27 [1-50]
Farmer, William R - *Crisis in Christology*
    Rel St Rev - v22 - O '96 - p338 [51-250]
Farmer's Market
  p LMR - v15 - Fall '96 - p7+ [501+]
Farndon, John - *What Happens When...? (Illus. by Steve Fricker)*
  c HB Guide - v8 - Spr '97 - p131 [51-250]
  c KR - v64 - N 15 '96 - p1668 [51-250]
  c Par - v71 - D '96 - p254 [1-50]
  c PW - v243 - N 25 '96 - p78 [51-250]
Farnen, Russell F - *Nationalism, Ethnicity, and Identity*
    APSR - v90 - S '96 - p670 [501+]
    JIH - v27 - Aut '96 - p297+ [251-500]
Farnham, Dana A - *Plows, Prosperity, and Cooperation at Agbassa*
    Choice - v34 - Ap '97 - p1394 [51-250]
Farnham, Nicholas H - *Rethinking Liberal Education*
    Choice - v34 - Ja '97 - p850 [51-250]
    Cng - v28 - S '96 - p62 [51-250]
    JEL - v34 - D '96 - p2063+ [51-250]
Farnoaga, Georgiana - *The Phantom Church and Other Stories from Romania*
    KR - v65 - Ja 1 '97 - p19+ [51-250]
Farnsworth, Robert M - *From Vagabond to Journalist*
    Choice - v34 - D '96 - p605 [51-250]
Farova, Anna - *Josef Sudek*
    BM - v139 - Ja '97 - p50+ [501+]
Farr, Cheryl - *High-Tech Practice*
    SciTech - v20 - N '96 - p54 [51-250]
Farr, David F - *Fungi on Rhododendron*
  r ARBA - v28 - '97 - p582 [51-250]
Farr, George - *RPG IV by Example*
    SciTech - v20 - S '96 - p6 [51-250]
Farr, James, 1950- - *Political Science in History*
    JIH - v27 - Spr '97 - p730+ [501+]
Farr, James R - *Authority and Sexuality in Early Modern Burgundy 1550-1730*
    AHR - v101 - D '96 - p1551 [251-500]
    JMH - v69 - Mr '97 - p152+ [501+]
    J Soc H - v30 - Win '96 - p503+ [501+]
    Six Ct J - v27 - Fall '96 - p899+ [501+]
    Six Ct J - v27 - Fall '96 - p900+ [501+]
Farr, Judith - *I Never Came to You in White*
    CSM - v88 - N 13 '96 - p15 [251-500]
    Ent W - O 18 '96 - p75 [51-250]
    LATBR - S 8 '96 - p2 [501+]
    LATBR - D 29 '96 - p11 [1-50]
    LJ - v122 - Mr 15 '97 - p112 [51-250]
    NY - v72 - D 23 '96 - p146 [51-250]
    NYTBR - v101 - O 20 '96 - p22 [51-250]
    Rapport - v19 - 6 '96 - p34 [251-500]
  y SLJ - v43 - Ja '97 - p140 [51-250]
Farrant, M A C - *Word of Mouth*
    Quill & Q - v62 - S '96 - p65 [51-250]
Farrar, Janet - *The Pagan Path*
    Folkl - v107 - '96 - p119 [51-250]
Farred, Grant - *Rethinking C.L.R. James*
    AL - v68 - S '96 - p881 [51-250]
    Choice - v34 - S '96 - p190 [51-250]
Farrell, Edith R - *Side by Side French and English Grammar*
    FR - v70 - D '96 - p363+ [251-500]
    MLJ - v81 - Spr '97 - p128 [251-500]
Farrell, Jacqueline - *The Great Depression*
  y HB Guide - v7 - Fall '96 - p386 [51-250]

Farrell, John - *Freud's Paranoid Quest*
    Choice - v34 - F '97 - p1039 [51-250]
    CSM - v89 - F 27 '97 - pB4 [251-500]
    SciTech - v20 - D '96 - p1 [51-250]
    TLS - S 27 '96 - p30 [501+]
Farrell, Joseph - *Leonardo Sciascia*
    Choice - v34 - S '96 - p132+ [51-250]
Farrell, Mame - *Marrying Malcolm Murgatroyd*
  y Emerg Lib - v23 - My '96 - p58 [51-250]
  c HB Guide - v7 - Fall '96 - p291 [51-250]
  c NYTBR - v101 - Ap 7 '96 - p21 [51-250]
Farrell, Ronald A - *The Black Book and the Mob*
    AJS - v102 - S '96 - p656+ [501+]
Farrell, Theo - *Weapons without a Cause*
    Choice - v34 - My '97 - p1576 [51-250]
Farrell, Wallace B - *On the Boulevard of Galleons*
    Rapport - v19 - 5 '96 - p41 [251-500]
Farren, Mick - *The Time of Feasting*
    KR - v64 - O 1 '96 - p1420 [251-500]
    LJ - v121 - O 15 '96 - p89 [51-250]
    PW - v243 - O 21 '96 - p69+ [51-250]
Farrington, Debra K - *Romancing the Holy*
    Am - v176 - F 15 '97 - p33 [51-250]
    PW - v244 - Mr 10 '97 - p62 [51-250]
Farrington, Karen - *Dark Justice*
    LJ - v121 - D '96 - p120 [51-250]
Farrington, Tim - *The California Book of the Dead*
    BL - v93 - My 1 '97 - p1478 [51-250]
    KR - v65 - Mr 1 '97 - p323 [51-250]
    LJ - v122 - Ap 1 '97 - p124 [51-250]
    PW - v244 - Mr 31 '97 - p62 [51-250]
Farris, Katherine - *You Asked?*
  cr Par Ch - v21 - Mr '97 - p5 [1-50]
  c Quill & Q - v62 - S '96 - p75 [251-500]
  c SB - v33 - Ja '97 - p15 [51-250]
Farris, Michael - *Anonymous Tip*
    LJ - v121 - N 1 '96 - p54 [51-250]
Farris, Pamela J - *Young Mouse and Elephant (Illus. by Valeri Gorbachev)*
  c Ch BWatch - v6 - My '96 - p3 [1-50]
  c HB Guide - v7 - Fall '96 - p320 [51-250]
Farrisi, Theresa Rodriguez - *Diaper Changes*
    BL - v93 - My 15 '97 - p1550 [51-250]
Farrow, David A - *The Root of All Evil*
    PW - v244 - Mr 17 '97 - p79+ [51-250]
Farrow, Mia - *What Falls Away*
    BL - v93 - Mr 15 '97 - p1205 [1-50]
    CSM - v89 - Mr 6 '97 - p14 [51-250]
    Econ - v343 - Ap 12 '97 - p86 [501+]
    Ent W - F 21 '97 - p117+ [501+]
    Mac - v110 - Ap 7 '97 - p88 [501+]
    NS - v126 - Mr 7 '97 - p45+ [501+]
    NW - v129 - F 17 '97 - p65 [501+]
    NYTBR - v102 - F 23 '97 - p9 [501+]
    Obs - F 16 '97 - p16* [501+]
    Spec - v278 - Mr 8 '97 - p33+ [501+]
    Time - v149 - F 17 '97 - p91 [501+]
What Falls Away (Farrow). Audio Version
    PW - v244 - Mr 3 '97 - p30+ [51-250]
Farson, Daniel - *Never a Normal Man*
    Spec - v278 - Mr 22 '97 - p45 [501+]
    TLS - Mr 21 '97 - p36 [501+]
Farson, Richard - *Management of the Absurd*
    Per Psy - v50 - Spr '97 - p220+ [501+]
Management of the Absurd (Farson). Audio Version
    LJ - v121 - O 15 '96 - p101 [51-250]
Faruqee, Rashid - *Managing Price Risk in the Pakistan Wheat Market*
    JEL - v35 - Mr '97 - p295+ [51-250]
Faruque, Saleh - *Cellular Mobile Systems Engineering*
    SciTech - v21 - Mr '97 - p89 [1-50]
Farwell, Byron - *Burton (Vance). Audio Version*
  y Kliatt - v30 - S '96 - p56 [51-250]
Farwell, Marilyn R - *Heterosexual Plots and Lesbian Narratives*
    Wom R Bks - v14 - N '96 - p14+ [501+]
Faryna, Stan - *Black and Right*
    PW - v244 - Ap 21 '97 - p52 [51-250]
Farzad, Bahman - *Teach Yourself the Simplified Zone System of Light Measurement*
    Pet PM - v25 - Jl '96 - p36 [51-250]
Fasching, Darrell J - *The Coming of the Millennium*
    Rel St Rev - v23 - Ja '97 - p46 [51-250]
Faschinger, Lilian - *Magdalena Sunderin*
    WLT - v70 - Aut '96 - p946 [501+]
Magdalena the Sinner
    TLS - D 13 '96 - p22 [501+]
    Woman's J - D '96 - p16 [1-50]
Fase, Martin M G - *How to Write the History of a Bank*
    R&R Bk N - v12 - F '97 - p47 [51-250]

Fasel, George - *Modern Europe in the Making*
Wil Q - v21 - Win '97 - p37 [1-50]
Fasman, Gerald D - *Circular Dichroism and the Conformational Analysis of Biomolecules*
SciTech - v20 - S '96 - p23 [51-250]
Fasoli, Gina - *Vitale E Agricola*
CHR - v82 - O '96 - p683+ [251-500]
Fass, Craig - *Six Degrees of Kevin Bacon*
BW - v26 - N 3 '96 - p12 [51-250]
Ent W - O 18 '96 - p72 [251-500]
Fassmann, Heinz - *European Migration in the Late Twentieth Century*
CS - v25 - S '96 - p593+ [501+]
Fast, Howard - *An Independent Woman*
BL - v93 - My 1 '97 - p1460+ [51-250]
Spartacus
BW - v26 - N 17 '96 - p12 [51-250]
LJ - v122 - F 1 '97 - p112 [1-50]
Fast Company
p SFR - v21 - S '96 - p10+ [501+]
Fast Reference Facts. Electronic Media Version
r RQ - v36 - Win '96 - p283+ [501+]
Fastovsky, David E - *The Evolution and Extinction of the Dinosaurs*
y BL - v93 - D 1 '96 - p664 [1-50]
Choice - v34 - O '96 - p310 [51-250]
SB - v32 - O '96 - p200 [251-500]
Sci - v273 - S 27 '96 - p1807+ [501+]
Fatiah - *Algerie: Chronique D'Une Femme Dans La Tourmante*
BL - v93 - F 1 '97 - p930 [1-50]
Fatigue and Fracture 1996. Vols. 1-2
SciTech - v20 - N '96 - p82 [51-250]
Fatigue and Fracture of Ordered Intermetallic Materials II
SciTech - v20 - N '96 - p64 [51-250]
Fattorini, Emma - *Germania E Santa Sede*
CH - v66 - Mr '97 - p160+ [501+]
Fatus, Sophie - *Holes*
c PW - v244 - Mr 10 '97 - p67 [51-250]
Spots
c PW - v244 - Mr 10 '97 - p67 [51-250]
Squares
c PW - v244 - Mr 10 '97 - p67 [51-250]
Stripes
c PW - v244 - Mr 10 '97 - p67 [51-250]
Faucheux, Sylvie - *Models of Sustainable Development*
JEL - v34 - D '96 - p2132+ [51-250]
Fauconnier, Bernard - *L'Incendie De La Sainte-Victoire*
FR - v70 - D '96 - p346+ [251-500]
Fauconnier, Gilles - *Spaces, Worlds, and Grammar*
Choice - v34 - Ap '97 - p1421 [51-250]
Faue, Elizabeth - *Community of Suffering and Struggle*
J Urban H - v23 - N '96 - p120+ [501+]
Faulkenberry, Luces M - *Electrical Power Distribution and Transmission*
SciTech - v20 - N '96 - p72 [51-250]
Faulkner, Howard J - *Dear Dr. Menninger*
LJ - v122 - Ap 15 '97 - p101 [51-250]
Faulkner, Jim - *Talking about William Faulkner*
Choice - v34 - O '96 - p283 [51-250]
Faulkner, John - *Men Working*
LATBR - S 1 '96 - p4 [501+]
Faulkner, Keith - *The Wide-Mouthed Frog (Illus. by Jonathan Lambert)*
c HB Guide - v7 - Fall '96 - p238+ [51-250]
Faulkner, Keith, 1940- - *Jane's Warship Recognition Guide*
yr ARBA - v28 - '97 - p260 [251-500]
r BL - v93 - F 15 '97 - p1042 [51-250]
Faulkner, Quentin - *Wiser Than Despair*
CC - v114 - Ja 29 '97 - p109 [251-500]
Faulkner, William - *Mosquitoes*
BW - v27 - F 23 '97 - p12 [51-250]
NYTBR - v102 - Mr 23 '97 - p28 [1-50]
Trib Bks - Mr 2 '97 - p8 [1-50]
Soldiers' Pay
BW - v27 - F 23 '97 - p12 [51-250]
NYTBR - v102 - Mr 23 '97 - p28 [51-250]
Faulks, Sebastian - *Birdsong*
AJPsych - v153 - D '96 - p1640 [251-500]
LATBR - D 29 '96 - p8 [51-250]
NS - v125 - D 20 '96 - p116 [1-50]
NYTBR - v101 - D 8 '96 - p76+ [1-50]
Spec - v277 - N 16 '96 - p44 [1-50]
The Fatal Englishman
NS & S - v9 - Ap 26 '96 - p30+ [251-500]
Spec - v277 - N 16 '96 - p43 [1-50]
Faull, Katherine M - *Anthropology and the German Enlightenment*
Ger Q - v70 - Win '97 - p68+ [501+]

Faupel, D William - *The Everlasting Gospel*
Choice - v34 - F '97 - p980 [51-250]
Faure, Bernard - *Visions of Power*
Choice - v34 - N '96 - p475 [51-250]
Faure, David - *Down to Earth*
Ch Rev Int - v4 - Spr '97 - p121+ [51-250]
Faure, Olivier - *Histoire Sociale De La Medecine (XVIIIe-XXe Siecles)*
J Soc H - v30 - Spr '97 - p759+ [501+]
Fauss, Richard - *A Bibliography of Labor History in Newsfilm. Vols. 1-4*
r RQ - v36 - Fall '96 - p55 [51-250]
Faust, Drew Gilpin - *Mothers of Invention*
AHR - v102 - F '97 - p191+ [501+]
NYTBR - v101 - D 8 '96 - p89 [1-50]
y SLJ - v42 - N '96 - p141 [51-250]
VQR - v72 - Aut '96 - p115* [51-250]
Wom R Bks - v14 - Mr '97 - p13+ [501+]
Faust, Joe Clifford - *Ferman's Devils*
MFSF - v92 - Mr '97 - p37 [51-250]
Faust, John R - *China in World Politics*
Ch Rev Int - v4 - Spr '97 - p124+ [501+]
Faust, Ron - *Lord of the Dark Lake*
BL - v92 - Ag '96 - p1885 [51-250]
Split Image
BL - v93 - My 15 '97 - p1566 [51-250]
KR - v65 - Ap 1 '97 - p485 [251-500]
LJ - v122 - My 1 '97 - p139 [51-250]
Fauteux, Kevin - *The Recovery of Self*
Rel St Rev - v23 - Ap '97 - p141+ [501+]
Fauth, Wolfgang - *Helios Megistos*
Rel St Rev - v22 - O '96 - p346 [51-250]
Faux, Jeff - *The Party's Not Over*
Choice - v34 - F '97 - p1035+ [51-250]
Nat - v263 - O 28 '96 - p16+ [501+]
NYTBR - v101 - Ag 25 '96 - p12 [501+]
Prog - v60 - O '96 - p40+ [501+]
Favro, Diane - *The Urban Image of Augustan Rome*
Choice - v34 - Mr '97 - p1215+ [51-250]
TLS - F 14 '97 - p12 [501+]
Fawaz, Leila Tarazi - *An Occasion for War*
JTWS - v13 - Spr '96 - p391+ [501+]
Fawcett, Bill - *Hunters and Shooters*
PW - v243 - O 14 '96 - p81 [1-50]
Fawcett, Edgar - *Douglas Duane. Electronic Media Version*
SF Chr - v18 - O '96 - p79 [51-250]
Fawcett, Patricia - *A Family Weekend*
Woman's J - Ja '97 - p13 [51-250]
Faxon, Susan - *Addison Gallery of American Art*
LJ - v122 - Ja '97 - p92+ [51-250]
Fay, Brian - *Contemporary Philosophy of Social Science*
Choice - v34 - D '96 - p626 [51-250]
Fay, Nancy - *Written with a Spoon*
AB - v98 - O 14 '96 - p1236 [51-250]
Fay, Peter Ward - *The Forgotten Army*
EHR - v111 - N '96 - p1350 [251-500]
Fay, Stephen - *The Collapse of Barings*
BL - v93 - F 15 '97 - p983 [51-250]
For Aff - v76 - My '97 - p126 [51-250]
LJ - v122 - Ap 15 '97 - p91 [51-250]
NYTBR - v102 - F 16 '97 - p10 [501+]
PW - v243 - D 2 '96 - p47 [51-250]
Fayyad, Usama M - *Advances in Knowledge Discovery and Data Mining*
JEL - v35 - Mr '97 - p304+ [51-250]
Fazeli, Rafat - *The Economic Impact of the Welfare State and Social Wage*
R&R Bk N - v11 - D '96 - p31 [51-250]
Fazio, Brenda Lena - *Grandfather's Story (Illus. by Brenda Lena Fazio)*
c BL - v93 - N 15 '96 - p593 [51-250]
c CBRS - v25 - D '96 - p38 [51-250]
c Ch BWatch - v6 - O '96 - p4 [1-50]
c Ch BWatch - v7 - Ja '97 - p3 [51-250]
c PW - v243 - S 16 '96 - p82 [51-250]
c SLJ - v43 - Mr '97 - p162 [51-250]
FDR: Franklin Delano Roosevelt. Electronic Media Version
r LJ - v122 - Mr 15 '97 - p97 [51-250]
r LJ - v122 - Ap 15 '97 - p40 [1-50]
Feagin, Joe R - *The Agony of Education*
Bl S - v26 - Fall '96 - p102 [1-50]
Feagin, Susan L - *Reading with Feeling*
r Choice - v34 - N '96 - p449 [51-250]
Feal, Rosemary Geisdorfer - *Painting on the Page*
Hisp - v79 - S '96 - p442+ [501+]
Fear, A T - *Rome and Baetica*
Choice - v34 - F '97 - p1017 [51-250]
Fearn-Banks, Kathleen - *Crisis Communications*
Choice - v34 - N '96 - p502+ [51-250]

Fearrington, Ann - *Christmas Lights (Illus. by Ann Fearrington)*
c BL - v93 - S 1 '96 - p136 [51-250]
c CBRS - v25 - O '96 - p14+ [1-50]
c HB Guide - v8 - Spr '97 - p26 [1-50]
c KR - v64 - O 15 '96 - p1531 [51-250]
c PW - v243 - S 30 '96 - p89 [51-250]
c SLJ - v42 - O '96 - p35 [51-250]
Feather, Jane - *Diamond Slipper*
PW - v243 - D 30 '96 - p63 [51-250]
Feather, John - *International Encyclopedia of Information and Library Science*
r Choice - v34 - My '97 - p1476 [51-250]
Preservation Management
LAR - v98 - Jl '96 - p369 [251-500]
R&R Bk N - v12 - F '97 - p102 [51-250]
Featherston, Elena - *Skin Deep*
Bl S - v26 - Sum '96 - p55 [501+]
Featherstone, Ivy - *McNeil NYPD 2*
Sm Pr R - v28 - O '96 - p7 [51-250]
Featherstone, Kevin - *Greece in a Changing Europe*
R&R Bk N - v11 - N '96 - p12 [51-250]
Featherstone, M - *Images of Aging*
Socio R - v45 - My '97 - p325+ [501+]
Feder, Don - *Who's Afraid of the Religious Right?*
HE - v52 - S 20 '96 - p12+ [501+]
Nat R - v48 - S 2 '96 - p98 [51-250]
Feder, Kenneth L - *Frauds, Myths, and Mysteries*
Skeptic - v4 - 2 '96 - p109 [251-500]
Feder, Paula Kurzband - *The Feather-Bed Journey (Illus. by Stacey Schuett)*
c CLW - v66 - Je '96 - p46+ [251-500]
Federal Employee's Almanac. 43rd Ed.
r J Gov Info - v24 - Ja '97 - p64+ [501+]
Federal Financial Support of Business
J Gov Info - v23 - S '96 - p559 [51-250]
Federman, Raymond - *Critifiction: Postmodern Essays*
ABR - v17 - Ag '96 - p5 [501+]
Federschmidt, Karl H - *Theologie Aus Asiatischen Quellen*
Rel St Rev - v22 - O '96 - p340 [51-250]
Fedorko, Kathy A - *Gender and the Gothic in the Fiction of Edith Wharton*
AL - v69 - Mr '97 - p227+ [501+]
Fedoroff, Sergey - *Protocols for Neural Cell Culture. 2nd Ed.*
SciTech - v21 - Mr '97 - p40 [51-250]
Fedou, Michel - *La Sagesse Et Le Monde*
Theol St - v58 - Mr '97 - p156+ [501+]
Feduccia, Alan - *The Origin and Evolution of Birds*
Am Sci - v85 - Mr '97 - p178+ [501+]
Choice - v34 - F '97 - p990 [51-250]
LJ - v121 - S 15 '96 - p90 [51-250]
Nature - v384 - N 21 '96 - p230 [51-250]
New Sci - v153 - Mr 1 '97 - p44 [501+]
SB - v33 - Ja '97 - p8 [51-250]
Fee, Gordon D - *Paul's Letter to the Philippians*
Ch Today - v40 - N 11 '96 - p54+ [501+]
Feeley-Harnik, Gillian - *A Green Estate*
Am Ethnol - v24 - F '97 - p249+ [501+]
Feelings, Tom - *The Middle Passage (Illus. by Tom Feelings)*
y Emerg Lib - v24 - S '96 - p23 [1-50]
c NYTBR - v101 - Ap 7 '96 - p21 [1-50]
y RT - v50 - N '96 - p246+ [51-250]
y SLJ - v42 - D '96 - p33 [1-50]
Feenberg, Andrew - *Alternative Modernity*
AJS - v102 - Jl '96 - p258+ [501+]
Feeney, Josephine - *My Family and Other Natural Disasters*
c Sch Lib - v44 - Ag '96 - p96+ [501+]
Truth, Lies and Homework
c JB - v60 - Ag '96 - p156 [51-250]
y Sch Lib - v44 - N '96 - p170 [51-250]
Feeney, Judith - *Adult Attachment*
Choice - v34 - D '96 - p692 [51-250]
R&R Bk N - v11 - N '96 - p4 [51-250]
Feess, Susanne - *Provence*
r BL - v93 - S 15 '96 - p210 [1-50]
Fehl, Philipp P - *Decorum and Wit*
JAAR - v65 - Spr '97 - p237+ [501+]
Fehr, Hans - *Welfare Effects of Value-Added Tax Harmonization in Europe*
JEL - v34 - D '96 - p2058 [51-250]
Fehren, Henry - *Good News for Alienated Catholics*
CLW - v67 - D '96 - p43 [251-500]
Fehrenbach, Heide - *Cinema in Democratizing Germany*
AHR - v101 - D '96 - p1571+ [501+]
Fehrenbach, R J - *Private Libraries in Renaissance England. Vols. 1-2*
r Lib & Cul - v32 - Win '97 - p135+ [501+]

Fehrenbacher, Don Edward - *Recollected Words of Abraham Lincoln*
　　Atl - v278 - D '96 - p119+ [501+]
　　New R - v216 - Ja 20 '97 - p26+ [501+]
Feifer, Jane - *Ancient Akamas I*
　　AJA - v100 - O '96 - p812 [251-500]
Feiffer, Jules - *A Barrel of Laughs, a Vale of Tears*
　y Emerg Lib - v23 - My '96 - p58 [51-250]
　c RT - v50 - Mr '97 - p503 [51-250]
Feig, Barry - *Marketing Straight to the Heart*
　　BL - v93 - My 1 '97 - p1467 [51-250]
　　LJ - v122 - My 1 '97 - p116+ [51-250]
Feigelson, Kristian - *L'URSS Et Sa Television*
　　Slav R - v55 - Fall '96 - p701+ [501+]
Feigon, Lee - *Demystifying Tibet*
　　FEER - v159 - O 10 '96 - p58 [251-500]
Fein, Ellen - *The Rules: Time-Tested Secrets for Capturing the Heart of Mr. Right*
　　Nat R - v48 - D 23 '96 - p58 [51-250]
The Rules: Time-Tested Secrets for Capturing the Heart of Mr. Right. Audio Version
　　BWatch - v18 - Mr '97 - p8 [1-50]
Fein, Jessica - *Moving On*
　　BL - v93 - S 1 '96 - p49 [51-250]
Feinberg, Barbara Silberdick - *Constitutional Amendments*
　c Ch BWatch - v6 - O '96 - p5 [51-250]
　y SLJ - v42 - D '96 - p144 [51-250]
Next in Line
　y HB Guide - v8 - Spr '97 - p173 [51-250]
　y SLJ - v43 - F '97 - p114 [51-250]
Term Limits for Congress?
　c Ch BWatch - v6 - My '96 - p5 [1-50]
　c Ch BWatch - v6 - O '96 - p5 [51-250]
　c SLJ - v42 - Ag '96 - p153+ [51-250]
Feinberg, Leslie - *Transgender Warriors*
　　Choice - v34 - N '96 - p545 [51-250]
Feinberg, Neal - *Dylan Programming*
　　SciTech - v20 - D '96 - p9 [51-250]
Feinberg, Richard - *Seafaring in the Contemporary Pacific Islands*
　　Am Ethnol - v24 - F '97 - p262+ [501+]
Feinberg, Sandra - *Serving Families and Children through Partnerships*
　　A Lib - v27 - Ag '96 - p71 [51-250]
　　SLJ - v42 - D '96 - p46 [51-250]
　　SLMQ - v25 - Fall '96 - p61 [51-250]
Feinberg, Todd E - *Behavioral Neurology and Neuropsychology*
　　SciTech - v21 - Mr '97 - p51 [51-250]
Feingold, Henry L - *Lest Memory Cease*
　　Choice - v34 - My '97 - p1562 [51-250]
Feinler-Torriani, Luciana - *Mastering Italian Vocabulary*
　r MLJ - v80 - Win '96 - p552 [501+]
Feinstein, Alvan R - *Multivariable Analysis*
　　SciTech - v20 - D '96 - p17 [51-250]
Feinstein, Charles H - *Banking, Currency, and Finance in Europe between the Wars*
　　Econ J - v106 - S '96 - p1422+ [501+]
　　JEL - v35 - Mr '97 - p174+ [501+]
Feinstein, David - *The Mythic Path*
　　BL - v93 - Mr 15 '97 - p1206 [51-250]
　　PW - v244 - Mr 31 '97 - p57 [51-250]
Feinstein, Elaine - *Daylight*
　　Econ - v342 - Mr 29 '97 - p93 [51-250]
Feinstein, John - *A Civil War*
　　BL - v93 - N 15 '96 - p565 [51-250]
　　KR - v64 - S 15 '96 - p1371 [251-500]
　y LJ - v121 - O 1 '96 - p87 [51-250]
　　NYTBR - v101 - N 3 '96 - p18+ [51-250]
　　PW - v243 - S 16 '96 - p61 [51-250]
Winter Games
　　PW - v244 - F 17 '97 - p217 [1-50]
Feinstein, Sascha - *The Second Set. Vol. 2*
　　LJ - v121 - N 1 '96 - p84 [1-50]
　　PW - v243 - S 30 '96 - p83 [51-250]
Feintuch, David - *Fisherman's Hope*
　　SF Chr - v18 - O '96 - p77 [51-250]
Midshipman's Hope
　y Emerg Lib - v24 - S '96 - p24 [1-50]
The Still
　　KR - v65 - My 1 '97 - p684 [51-250]
Voices of Hope
　　MFSF - v92 - F '97 - p45 [51-250]
　y VOYA - v19 - O '96 - p216+ [251-500]
Feist, Peter H - *French Impressionism*
　　BM - v138 - S '96 - p615 [51-250]
Feist, Raymond E - *Rage of a Demon King*
　y BL - v93 - Mr 1 '97 - p1067+ [51-250]
　　KR - v65 - F 1 '97 - p178 [51-250]
　　PW - v244 - Mr 31 '97 - p67 [51-250]

Feixenet, Anna - *Adorna Con Mosaico*
　c BL - v93 - F 15 '97 - p1032 [1-50]
Fekete, John - *Moral Panic*
　　Dialogue - v35 - Spr '96 - p343+ [501+]
Felber, Lynette - *Gender and Genre in Novels without End*
　　ELT - v40 - 1 '97 - p95+ [501+]
　　Nine-C Lit - v51 - S '96 - p272 [1-50]
Felcone, Joseph J - *New Jersey Books 1801-1860*
　r AB - v98 - N 25 '96 - p1826 [501+]
Feld, Jacob - *Construction Failure. 2nd Ed.*
　　SciTech - v21 - Mr '97 - p83 [51-250]
Feld, Leonard G - *Hypertension in Children*
　　SciTech - v21 - Mr '97 - p64 [51-250]
Feldberg, Georgina D - *Disease and Class*
　　Isis - v87 - S '96 - p576 [501+]
Felden, Tamara - *Frauen Reisen*
　　Ger Q - v69 - Sum '96 - p354+ [501+]
Feldenkirchen, Wilfried - *Werner Von Siemens: Inventor and International Entrepreneur*
　　T&C - v37 - Ap '96 - p381+ [501+]
Felder, Leonard - *The Ten Challenges*
　　PW - v244 - Ja 27 '97 - p96 [51-250]
Feldhaus, Anne - *Water and Womanhood*
　　Wom R Bks - v13 - S '96 - p26+ [501+]
Feldhay, Rivka - *Galileo and the Church*
　　CPR - v16 - Ap '96 - p101+ [501+]
　　Theol St - v57 - Je '96 - p354+ [501+]
Feldman, Andrew J - *The Sierra Club Green Guide*
　r ARBA - v28 - '97 - p649 [51-250]
　r BL - v92 - Ag '96 - p1926 [51-250]
　r Workbook - v21 - Win '96 - p176+ [501+]
Feldman, Anita - *Inside Tap*
　　Choice - v34 - D '96 - p624 [51-250]
Feldman, Christian - *God's Gentle Rebels*
　　RR - v56 - Ja '97 - p106 [1-50]
Feldman, David, 1950- - *How Do Astronauts Scratch an Itch?*
　　PW - v243 - S 9 '96 - p76 [51-250]
What Are Hyenas Laughing At, Anyway? (Illus. by Kassie Schwan)
　y Kliatt - v31 - Ja '97 - p33 [51-250]
Feldman, David, 1957- - *Englishmen and Jews*
　　HT - v46 - Ag '96 - p57+ [501+]
Feldman, David Lewis - *The Energy Crisis*
　　JEL - v35 - Mr '97 - p301 [51-250]
　　R&R Bk N - v12 - F '97 - p41 [51-250]
Feldman, Dorel - *Synthetic Polymers*
　　Choice - v34 - F '97 - p991 [51-250]
Feldman, Ellen - *Rearview Mirror*
　　LJ - v121 - N 1 '96 - p132 [51-250]
　　PW - v243 - N 4 '96 - p71 [1-50]
Feldman, Eve B - *Birthdays! Celebrating Life around the World*
　c HB Guide - v7 - Fall '96 - p318 [51-250]
　c SLJ - v42 - Ag '96 - p134+ [51-250]
Feldman, Gerald D - *The Great Disorder*
　　JEH - v56 - S '96 - p720+ [501+]
Feldman, Glenn - *From Demagogue to Dixiecrat*
　　BusLR - v21 - 3 '96 - p211+ [501+]
　　Choice - v34 - S '96 - p193 [51-250]
　　JSH - v62 - N '96 - p835+ [251-500]
Feldman, Irving - *The Life and Letters*
　　Poet - v169 - F '97 - p288+ [501+]
Feldman, Jamie L - *Plague Doctors*
　　AJS - v102 - S '96 - p648+ [501+]
Feldman, Lawrence H - *Mountains of Fire, Lands That Shake*
　　LA Ant - v7 - Mr '96 - p84+ [501+]
Feldman, Martha - *City Culture and the Madrigal at Venice*
　　TLS - Ag 2 '96 - p20 [501+]
Feldman, Paula R - *Romantic Women Writers*
　　NWSA Jnl - v8 - Sum '96 - p147+ [501+]
Feldman, Robert S - *The Psychology of Adversity*
　　R&R Bk N - v11 - D '96 - p38 [51-250]
Feldman, Shai - *The Future of U.S.-Israel Strategic Cooperation*
　　MEJ - v50 - Aut '96 - p626 [51-250]
　　MEQ - v4 - Mr '97 - p87 [51-250]
Feldman, Stephen M - *Please Don't Wish Me a Merry Christmas*
　　BL - v93 - D 1 '96 - p624 [51-250]
Feldman, Susan - *Something That Happens to Other People*
　　Aust Bk R - F '97 - p25 [501+]
Feldshuh, Muriel - *Flip-Up Bulletin Boards*
　　Cur R - v36 - D '96 - p3* [51-250]
Feldstein, Martin - *American Economic Policy in the 1980s*
　　Econ J - v106 - S '96 - p1469 [251-500]

Empirical Foundations of Household Taxation
　　JEL - v34 - D '96 - p2058 [51-250]
　　R&R Bk N - v11 - N '96 - p38 [51-250]
Feldstein, Paul J - *The Politics of Health Legislation. 2nd Ed.*
　　R&R Bk N - v11 - D '96 - p69 [51-250]
　　SciTech - v20 - D '96 - p38 [51-250]
Feldstein, Richard - *Political Correctness*
　　LJ - v121 - D '96 - p127 [51-250]
Reading Seminars I and II
　　R&R Bk N - v12 - F '97 - p5 [51-250]
Felgner, Philip L - *Artificial Self-Assembling Systems for Gene Delivery*
　　SciTech - v21 - Mr '97 - p48 [51-250]
Felice, Cynthia - *Promised Land*
　　KR - v65 - Ja 1 '97 - p28 [51-250]
　　LJ - v122 - F 15 '97 - p165 [51-250]
　　PW - v244 - Ja 27 '97 - p82 [51-250]
Felice, William F - *Taking Suffering Seriously*
　　Choice - v34 - F '97 - p1029 [51-250]
　　R&R Bk N - v11 - D '96 - p46 [51-250]
Felici, Lucia - *Tra Riforma Ed Eresea, La Giovinezza Di Martin Borrhaus 1499-1528*
　　Six Ct J - v27 - Win '96 - p1168+ [251-500]
Feliciano, Hector - *The Lost Museum*
　　PW - v244 - Ap 28 '97 - p59 [251-500]
Felinto, Marilene - *The Women of Tijucopapo*
　　TranslRevS - v1 - My '95 - p27 [51-250]
Fell, Alison - *The Pillow Boy of the Lady Onogoro*
　　Trib Bks - Mr 9 '97 - p8 [1-50]
Fell, Derek - *Glorious Flowers*
　　BL - v93 - D 15 '96 - p705 [51-250]
　　LJ - v122 - F 1 '97 - p76 [51-250]
Feller, Carline - *Windy Day*
　c Inst - v106 - S '96 - p87 [1-50]
Feller, Daniel - *The Jacksonian Promise*
　　RAH - v25 - Mr '97 - p58+ [501+]
Felli, Ernesto - *The Service Sector*
　　JEL - v34 - D '96 - p2087 [51-250]
Fellman, Michael - *Citizen Sherman*
　　JSH - v63 - F '97 - p172+ [501+]
Fellows, Will - *Farm Boys*
　　Choice - v34 - Ja '97 - p837 [51-250]
　　Esq - v126 - D '96 - p40 [1-50]
　　LJ - v121 - O 1 '96 - p108 [51-250]
Felman, Shoshana - *What Does a Woman Want?*
　　MLR - v91 - O '96 - p951+ [501+]
Felsenstein, Frank - *Anti-Semitic Stereotypes*
　　CH - v65 - D '96 - p726+ [501+]
Felshin, Nina - *But Is It Art?*
　　CS - v25 - S '96 - p681+ [501+]
Felski, Rita - *The Gender of Modernity*
　　South CR - v29 - Fall '96 - p282+ [501+]
Felson-Rubin, Nancy - *Regarding Penelope*
　　Comp L - v48 - Sum '96 - p298+ [501+]
　　CW - v90 - S '96 - p62+ [251-500]
Felstiner, John - *Paul Celan: Poet, Survivor, Jew*
　　Lon R Bks - v18 - My 23 '96 - p10+ [501+]
　　NYRB - v43 - N 14 '96 - p38+ [501+]
　　TLS - N 29 '96 - p12 [51-250]
　　TranslRevS - v2 - D '96 - p8 [51-250]
Felt, James W - *Making Sense of Your Freedom*
　　IPQ - v37 - Mr '97 - p119+ [501+]
Feltham, Colin - *What Is Counseling?*
　　CS - v26 - Ja '97 - p96+ [51-250]
Felton, William - *A Treatise on Carriages*
　　Ant & CM - v101 - Ja '97 - p44 [51-250]
Felver, Christopher - *Angels, Anarchists and Gods*
　　ABR - v18 - D '96 - p10+ [501+]
　　BL - v93 - D 15 '96 - p703 [51-250]
Female Education in the Age of Enlightenment. Vols. 1-6
　　R&R Bk N - v12 - F '97 - p53 [51-250]
Fenchel, Tom - *Ecology and Evolution in Anoxic Worlds*
　　BioSci - v46 - O '96 - p700+ [501+]
Fendel, Dan - *Baker's Choice*
　　Math T - v89 - S '96 - p514 [51-250]
Fendley, Alison - *Saatchi and Saatchi*
　　BL - v93 - N 15 '96 - p556 [51-250]
　　BW - v27 - Ja 5 '97 - p6 [251-500]
　　Econ - v342 - Mr 15 '97 - p13* [501+]
　　LJ - v121 - N 15 '96 - p69+ [51-250]
　　PW - v243 - S 30 '96 - p67 [51-250]
Fenelon, Francois De Salignac De La Mothe - *Fenelon: Meditations on the Heart of God*
　　PW - v244 - Ap 28 '97 - p70 [51-250]
Fenelon: Talking with God
　　LJ - v122 - My 1 '97 - p110 [51-250]
　　PW - v244 - Ap 28 '97 - p70 [1-50]
Feng, Chi-Tsai - *The Three-Inch Golden Lotus*
　　South HR - v31 - Win '97 - p89+ [501+]
　　TranslRevS - v1 - My '95 - p15 [51-250]

Fenichel, Otto M - *The Psychoanalytic Theory of Neurosis*
  AJPsych - v153 - O '96 - p1363+ [501+]
Fenichell, Stephen - *Plastic: The Making of a Synthetic Century*
  Choice - v34 - Ja '97 - p822 [51-250]
  Econ - v341 - O 19 '96 - p13* [251-500]
  Ent W - Ag 23 '96 - p116+ [51-250]
  KR - v64 - My 1 '96 - p660+ [251-500]
  LJ - v121 - O 1 '96 - p94 [51-250]
  New R - v215 - D 2 '96 - p50+ [501+]
  NY - v72 - O 7 '96 - p96 [51-250]
Fenicle, Diane L - *The Historical Archaeology of Dam Construction Camps in Central Arizona. Vol. 2B*
  Pub Hist - v18 - Fall '96 - p162+ [501+]
Feniger, Mani - *Journey from Anxiety to Freedom*
  PW - v244 - Ja 6 '97 - p71 [51-250]
Feniger, Susan - *Cantina: The Best of Casual Mexican Cooking*
  CSM - v89 - D 13 '96 - p11 [1-50]
  PW - v243 - S 2 '96 - p124 [51-250]
Fenkl, Heinz Insu - *Memories of My Ghost Brother*
  BL - v93 - N 1 '96 - p481 [51-250]
  KR - v64 - S 15 '96 - p1341 [251-500]
  LJ - v121 - O 1 '96 - p126 [51-250]
  NY - v72 - D 23 '96 - p146 [51-250]
  PW - v243 - S 23 '96 - p55+ [51-250]
  SFR - v22 - Ja '97 - p24+ [501+]
Fenlon, Iain - *Con Che Soavita*
  TLS - Ag 2 '96 - p20 [501+]
  Music, Print and Culture in Early Sixteenth-Century Italy
  TLS - My 24 '96 - p23 [501+]
Fenn, Richard K - *The Endangered Self*
  Rel St Rev - v23 - Ap '97 - p150 [51-250]
  The Persistence of Purgatory
  AJS - v102 - Ja '97 - p1190+ [501+]
  Choice - v34 - N '96 - p475 [51-250]
Fennelly, Tony - *1-900-Dead*
  KR - v64 - N 1 '96 - p1565+ [51-250]
  PW - v243 - N 11 '96 - p59+ [51-250]
Fenner, Carol - *Yolonda's Genius*
  c PW - v243 - D 30 '96 - p68 [1-50]
Fenno, Richard F - *Senators on the Campaign Trail*
  Choice - v34 - D '96 - p690 [51-250]
Fenton, John Y - *South Asian Religions in the Americas*
  r J Ch St - v38 - Aut '96 - p914+ [251-500]
Fenton, Kate - *Balancing on Air*
  Woman's J - S '96 - p10 [51-250]
Fenton, Peter - *I Forgot to Wear Underwear on a Glass-Bottom Boat*
  PW - v244 - Ap 14 '97 - p68 [51-250]
Fenwick, G R - *Agri-Food Quality*
  SciTech - v20 - N '96 - p80 [51-250]
Fenwick, John R K - *Worship in Transition*
  Theol St - v57 - D '96 - p787 [251-500]
  TT - v53 - O '96 - p426 [51-250]
Fenwick, Peter - *The Truth in the Light*
  JP - v60 - Je '96 - p171+ [501+]
Feofanov, Yuri - *Politics and Justice in Russia*
  Choice - v34 - D '96 - p683 [51-250]
Ferber, Elizabeth - *Diabetes*
  y BL - v93 - D 15 '96 - p715 [51-250]
  y HB Guide - v8 - Spr '97 - p129 [51-250]
  y SLJ - v43 - F '97 - p114 [51-250]
  A Life with Animals
  c Ch BWatch - v7 - F '97 - p7 [1-50]
  c HB Guide - v8 - Spr '97 - p156 [51-250]
  Steven Spielberg
  c Ch BWatch - v6 - N '96 - p2 [1-50]
  c HB Guide - v8 - Spr '97 - p156 [51-250]
  y SLJ - v43 - Ja '97 - p123 [51-250]
  The Walker's Companion (Illus. by Cathy Johnson)
  r E Mag - v7 - N '96 - p50 [51-250]
Ferber, Jane S - *A Woman Doctor's Guide to Depression*
  LJ - v122 - Mr 15 '97 - p77 [51-250]
Ferguson, Adam - *The Correspondence of Adam Ferguson. Vols. 1-2*
  Lon R Bks - v18 - N 14 '96 - p14+ [501+]
Ferguson, Alane - *Secrets*
  c PW - v244 - My 12 '97 - p76 [51-250]
  Tumbleweed Christmas (Illus. by Tom Sully)
  c Bloom Rev - v16 - N '96 - p31 [51-250]
  c CBRS - v25 - O '96 - p15 [51-250]
  c CCB-B - v50 - N '96 - p96 [51-250]
  c HB Guide - v8 - Spr '97 - p26 [51-250]
  c KR - v64 - O 1 '96 - p1465 [51-250]
  c PW - v243 - S 30 '96 - p90 [51-250]
  c SLJ - v42 - O '96 - p35 [51-250]

Ferguson, Andrew - *Fools' Names, Fools' Faces*
  BL - v93 - S 15 '96 - p188 [51-250]
  BW - v26 - S 8 '96 - p13 [51-250]
  KR - v64 - Ag 15 '96 - p1206+ [251-500]
  PW - v243 - S 30 '96 - p73 [51-250]
  WSJ-MW - v77 - O 9 '96 - pA16 [501+]
Ferguson, Everett - *Encyclopedia of Early Christianity. 2nd Ed., Vols. 1-2*
  r LJ - v122 - My 1 '97 - p96 [51-250]
Ferguson, Gail - *Tubu the Friendly Tokolosh*
  c Sch Lib - v44 - N '96 - p150 [51-250]
Ferguson, Gary, 1956- - *Spirits of the Wild*
  y SLJ - v43 - Ja '97 - p142 [51-250]
  The Sylvan Path
  BL - v93 - Mr 1 '97 - p1102 [51-250]
  KR - v65 - Ja 1 '97 - p33 [251-500]
  PW - v244 - F 17 '97 - p206 [51-250]
Ferguson, Gary Lynn - *Song Finder*
  r Notes - v53 - D '96 - p449+ [501+]
  r Teach Mus - v4 - Ag '96 - p52 [51-250]
Ferguson, Kitty - *Prisons of Light*
  Choice - v34 - F '97 - p985 [51-250]
  New Sci - v151 - S 21 '96 - p51 [501+]
  SB - v33 - My '97 - p102 [251-500]
  SciTech - v20 - D '96 - p21 [51-250]
  S&T - v92 - N '96 - p57 [1-50]
  Stephen Hawking: Quest for a Theory of the Universe
  y BL - v93 - D 15 '96 - p716 [1-50]
Ferguson, Maggie - *Fever Rising*
  LJ - v122 - F 15 '97 - p125 [51-250]
Ferguson, Neil - *English Weather*
  NS - v125 - N 22 '96 - p46 [501+]
  Spec - v277 - O 26 '96 - p51+ [251-500]
  TLS - N 8 '96 - p27 [251-500]
Ferguson, Niall - *Paper and Iron*
  Historian - v59 - Fall '96 - p186+ [251-500]
  HT - v46 - Jl '96 - p54+ [501+]
Ferguson, Priscilla Parkhurst - *Paris as Revolution*
  CS - v25 - N '96 - p780+ [501+]
  JMH - v68 - S '96 - p701+ [501+]
Ferguson, R Brian - *War in the Tribal Zone*
  SSQ - v77 - Je '96 - p445+ [501+]
  Yanomami Warfare
  Am Ethnol - v24 - F '97 - p227+ [501+]
Ferguson, Robert - *Henrik Ibsen: A New Biography*
  Econ - v342 - F 15 '97 - p8* [501+]
  Spec - v278 - Ja 4 '97 - p31+ [501+]
  TLS - Ja 17 '97 - p11+ [501+]
Ferguson, Russell - *Sigmar Polke Photoworks*
  BM - v138 - D '96 - p850+ [501+]
Ferguson, Thomas - *Golden Rule*
  IndRev - v1 - Spr '96 - p139+ [501+]
  J Pol - v58 - N '96 - p1214+ [501+]
Ferguson, Tom - *Health Online*
  r ARBA - v28 - '97 - p605 [51-250]
Ferguson, Trevor - *The Fire Line*
  Can Lit - Win '96 - p182+ [501+]
  The Timekeeper
  Quill & Q - v63 - F '97 - p50 [1-50]
Ferguson, V S - *Inanna Hyper-Luminal*
  Mag Bl - Mr '97 - p57 [51-250]
Ferguson, William M - *The Anasazi of Mesa Verde and the Four Corners*
  Bloom Rev - v16 - N '96 - p26 [51-250]
Ferguson, Yale H - *Polities: Authority, Identities, and Change*
  Choice - v34 - D '96 - p686 [51-250]
Ferguson's Off to College
  yp LJ - v122 - F 15 '97 - p167 [51-250]
Ferling, John - *John Adams: A Life*
  y Kliatt - v30 - N '96 - p21+ [51-250]
Ferlinghetti, Lawrence - *City Lights Pocket Poets Anthology*
  Sm Pr R - v28 - Je '96 - p1+ [501+]
  A Far Rockaway of the Heart
  BL - v93 - My 15 '97 - p1557 [51-250]
  PW - v244 - Mr 31 '97 - p69 [51-250]
Ferman, Barbara - *Challenging the Growth Machine*
  Choice - v34 - Ja '97 - p874 [51-250]
  Pol Stud J - v24 - Aut '96 - p519 [51-250]
Ferman, Claudia - *The Postmodern in Latin and Latino American Cultural Narratives*
  R&R Bk N - v12 - F '97 - p27 [51-250]
Fernandes, Maria Da Conceicao - *Portugal, 8 Seculos Em Banda Desenhada (Illus. by Jose Morim)*
  c Bkbird - v34 - Spr '96 - p52 [1-50]
Fernandez, Benedict J - *Protest: Photographs 1963-1995*
  LJ - v122 - F 15 '97 - p131 [51-250]
Fernandez, Charles - *Configuring CDE*
  SciTech - v20 - S '96 - p4 [51-250]

Fernandez, Damian J - *Central America and the Middle East*
  JTWS - v13 - Spr '96 - p347+ [501+]
Fernandez, Eugenie - *Waves in the Bathtub*
  c CBRS - v25 - F '97 - p74 [51-250]
Fernandez, F Anibal - *Microwave and Optical Wageguide Analysis by the Finite Element Method*
  SciTech - v20 - S '96 - p57 [51-250]
Fernandez, Rosa - *Charlemos Un Poco. 3rd Ed.*
  Hisp - v79 - S '96 - p463+ [501+]
Fernandez, Sergio - *Olvidame: Novelas De Amor Para La Monja Portuguesa*
  WLT - v70 - Sum '96 - p664+ [501+]
Fernandez-Armesto, Felipe - *Millennium: A History of the Last Thousand Years*
  Books - v9 - S '95 - p23 [1-50]
  New R - v215 - D 23 '96 - p35+ [501+]
  NYTBR - v102 - Ja 5 '97 - p28 [51-250]
  Sea H - Aut '96 - p42 [51-250]
  Reformation: Christianity and the World 1500-2000
  Spec - v277 - D 7 '96 - p45+ [501+]
  TLS - D 20 '96 - p4+ [501+]
  Reformations: A Radical Interpretation of Christianity and the World 1500-2000
  KR - v65 - F 15 '97 - p269 [251-500]
  LJ - v122 - Ap 1 '97 - p98 [51-250]
  PW - v244 - Mr 24 '97 - p73 [51-250]
Fernandez Jilberto, A E - *Liberalization in the Developing World*
  JEL - v34 - D '96 - p2114+ [51-250]
Fernandez Marcos, Natalio - *Scribes and Translators*
  Rel St Rev - v23 - Ja '97 - p86 [51-250]
Fernandez-Morera, Dario - *American Academia and the Survival of Marxist Ideas*
  R&R Bk N - v12 - F '97 - p66 [51-250]
Fernando, Suman - *Mental Health in a Multi-Ethnic Society*
  Choice - v34 - D '96 - p645 [51-250]
Ferncase, Richard K - *Outsider Features*
  Choice - v34 - D '96 - p621+ [51-250]
  R&R Bk N - v11 - N '96 - p66 [1-50]
Ferner, Jurgen - *Versohnung Und Progression*
  Ger Q - v70 - Win '97 - p79+ [501+]
Ferran, Denise - *William John Leech: An Irish Painter Abroad*
  Spec - v277 - D 14 '96 - p76 [51-250]
Ferrara, James L M - *Graft-vs.-Host Disease. 2nd Ed.*
  r SciTech - v20 - D '96 - p49 [51-250]
Ferrara, Judith M - *Peer Mediation*
  VOYA - v19 - F '97 - p356 [251-500]
Ferrari, Marco - *Deserts*
  New Sci - v151 - S 21 '96 - p55 [51-250]
Ferrari, Mirella - *Medieval and Renaissance Manuscripts at the University of California, Los Angeles. Vol. 2*
  r Lib - v18 - S '96 - p254+ [501+]
Ferrari, Rita - *Innocence, Power, and the Novels of John Hawkes*
  Choice - v34 - F '97 - p964 [51-250]
Ferraris, Joan D - *Molecular Zoology*
  r BioSci - v47 - Mr '97 - p194+ [501+]
  Sci - v275 - Ja 3 '97 - p36+ [501+]
  SciTech - v20 - S '96 - p19 [51-250]
Ferrars, Elizabeth - *Alibi for a Witch (Langford). Audio Version*
  y Kliatt - v31 - Mr '97 - p39 [51-250]
  Milk of Human Kindness (Haddon). Audio Version
  BL - v93 - F 15 '97 - p1038 [51-250]
  Scatter His Ashes (Stafford). Audio Version
  BL - v93 - N 1 '96 - p522 [51-250]
  y Kliatt - v31 - Ja '97 - p45 [51-250]
Ferrarte, Joan - *Papers Sobre Carles Riba*
  MLR - v92 - Ja '97 - p233+ [251-500]
Ferrazzi, Cecilia - *Autobiography of an Aspiring Saint*
  BL - v93 - N 15 '96 - p552 [51-250]
  PW - v243 - N 11 '96 - p68 [51-250]
Ferre, Barbara Meister - *Stability and Change in the Pennsylvania German Dialect of an Old Order Amish Community in Lancaster County*
  Ger Q - v69 - Sum '96 - p345+ [501+]
Ferre, Frederick - *Being and Value*
  Choice - v34 - S '96 - p140 [51-250]
  CPR - v16 - O '96 - p336+ [501+]
  Philosophy of Technology
  New Sci - v153 - F 1 '97 - p43 [51-250]
Ferre, Rosario - *The House on the Lagoon*
  y Kliatt - v31 - Ja '97 - p6 [51-250]
  NYTBR - v101 - N 10 '96 - p68 [51-250]
  WLT - v70 - Sum '96 - p690+ [501+]
  Sweet Diamond Dust
  NYTBR - v101 - N 10 '96 - p68 [1-50]

Ferreiro, E - *Caperucita Roja Aprende A Escribir*
   Lect Y V - v17 - D '96 - p55+ [501+]
Ferrell, Carolyn - *Don't Erase Me*
   BL - v93 - My 1 '97 - p1479 [251-500]
   PW - v244 - Ap 21 '97 - p59 [51-250]
Ferrell, Keith - *Passing Judgment*
   Arm Det - v29 - Sum '96 - p363+ [251-500]
Ferrell, Nancy Warren - *The Battle of the Little Bighorn in American History*
   c   HB Guide - v8 - Spr '97 - p177 [51-250]
   c   SB - v33 - Ja '97 - p21 [251-500]
   c   SLJ - v42 - D '96 - p128 [51-250]
Ferrell, Robert H - *Dictionary of American History Supplement. Vols. 1-2*
   yr ARBA - v28 - '97 - p191 [51-250]
   r   BL - v93 - N 1 '96 - p534 [251-500]
   r   Choice - v34 - Ja '97 - p768 [51-250]
   r   R&R Bk N - v11 - D '96 - p13 [51-250]
   Harry S. Truman (Runger). Audio Version
   y   Kliatt - v30 - N '96 - p49 [51-250]
   Harry S. Truman and the Bomb
   SB - v32 - O '96 - p202 [51-250]
   The Strange Deaths of President Harding
   BL - v93 - N 15 '96 - p568 [251-500]
   CHE - v43 - N 29 '96 - pA18 [251-500]
   LJ - v121 - N 1 '96 - p88 [51-250]
Ferrer, Linda - *Eros*
   PW - v243 - O 21 '96 - p62+ [51-250]
   VLS - Win '96 - p25+ [501+]
Ferrer Bermejo, Jose - *Silvestre Y Los Ladrones De Suenos*
   y   JAAL - v40 - S '96 - p77 [51-250]
Ferrer I Mallol, Maria Teresa - *Miscellania De Textos Medievals. Vol. 7*
   EHR - v112 - Ap '97 - p435+ [501+]
Ferri, Aldo - *Elasto-Impact and Friction in Dynamic Systems*
   SciTech - v21 - Mr '97 - p74 [51-250]
Ferri De Lazara, Leopoldo - *Italians at the Court of Siam*
   FEER - v160 - Ja 9 '97 - p58 [501+]
Ferrier, Carole - *As Good as a Yarn with You*
   Aust Bk R - Ag '96 - p67 [1-50]
Ferrigno, Robert - *Dead Silent*
   BW - v26 - S 15 '96 - p6 [251-500]
   NYTBR - v101 - S 8 '96 - p26 [51-250]
Ferril, Thomas Hornsby - *Thomas Hornsby Ferril and the American West*
   Bloom Rev - v16 - N '96 - p18+ [51-250]
Ferris, Craig F - *Understanding Aggressive Behavior in Children*
   New Sci - v153 - F 1 '97 - p40+ [501+]
   SciTech - v21 - Mr '97 - p65 [51-250]
Ferris, David S - *Walter Benjamin: Theoretical Questions*
   VQR - v73 - Win '97 - p16* [51-250]
Ferris, Jean - *All That Glitters*
   y   HB Guide - v7 - Fall '96 - p301 [51-250]
   Into the Wind
   y   Kliatt - v30 - S '96 - p8 [51-250]
   y   SLJ - v42 - S '96 - p227 [51-250]
   y   VOYA - v19 - D '96 - p261 [51-250]
   Song of the Sea
   y   VOYA - v19 - O '96 - p208 [51-250]
Ferris, Kathleen - *James Joyce and the Burden of Disease*
   TLS - D 20 '96 - p12 [501+]
Ferris, Steve - *The Cub-Hunting Season*
   TLS - Jl 7 '96 - p23 [251-500]
Ferris, Timothy - *The Whole Shebang*
   KR - v65 - Mr 15 '97 - p434+ [251-500]
   LJ - v122 - F 15 '97 - p159 [51-250]
   PW - v244 - F 24 '97 - p70 [51-250]
Ferriss, Susan - *The Fight in the Fields*
   KR - v65 - Mr 1 '97 - p348 [51-250]
   LATBR - Ap 13 '97 - pC [501+]
   LJ - v122 - Ap 1 '97 - p114 [51-250]
   PW - v244 - F 24 '97 - p74 [51-250]
Ferro, Marc - *Colonization: A Global History*
   NS - v126 - Mr 14 '97 - p44+ [501+]
   Obs - F 16 '97 - p17* [501+]
Ferroni, Pietro - *Discorso Storico Della Mia Vita Naturale E Civile Dal 1745 Al 1825*
   Isis - v87 - S '96 - p554+ [251-500]
Ferrucci, Franco - *The Life of God (As Told by Himself)*
   BW - v26 - Ag 25 '96 - p11 [501+]
   NYTBR - v101 - D 8 '96 - p80 [1-50]
   Lontano Da Casa
   WLT - v70 - Aut '96 - p931 [251-500]
Ferry, Anne - *The Title to the Poem*
   r   Choice - v34 - N '96 - p449 [51-250]
   Nine-C Lit - v51 - D '96 - p421 [51-250]
Ferry, Charles - *A Fresh Start*
   y   VOYA - v19 - O '96 - p208 [51-250]

Ferry, David - *Dwelling Places*
   WHR - v50 - Spr '96 - p63+ [501+]
   Gilgamesh: A Rendering in English Verse
   WHR - v50 - Spr '96 - p63+ [501+]
Ferry, Luc - *L'Homme-Dieu Ou Le Sens De La Vie*
   TLS - N 29 '96 - p15 [51-250]
   Homo Aestheticus
   JMH - v69 - Mr '97 - p124+ [501+]
   The New Ecological Order
   Ethics - v107 - O '96 - p189+ [501+]
   Isis - v87 - D '96 - p768+ [501+]
   Why We Are Not Nietzscheans
   LJ - v122 - Ap 1 '97 - p97 [51-250]
Ferry, Steven - *Russian Americans*
   yr Ch BWatch - v6 - O '96 - p5 [51-250]
   c   HB Guide - v7 - Fall '96 - p312 [51-250]
Ferster, Judith - *Fictions of Advice*
   Choice - v34 - D '96 - p612 [51-250]
Fertig, Judith - *Pure Prairie*
   BWatch - v17 - S '96 - p2 [51-250]
Ferziger, Joel H - *Computational Methods for Fluid Dynamics*
   Choice - v34 - N '96 - p488+ [51-250]
   Phys Today - v50 - Mr '97 - p80+ [501+]
Feshbach, Murray - *Ecological Disaster*
   Nature - v381 - My 16 '96 - p203+ [501+]
Feske, Victor - *From Belloc to Churchill*
   Choice - v34 - Mr '97 - p1219 [51-250]
Fest, Joachim - *Plotting Hitler's Death*
   y   BL - v93 - S 15 '96 - p214 [51-250]
   BW - v26 - D 29 '96 - p5 [51-250]
   For Aff - v76 - Mr '97 - p185 [251-500]
   KR - v64 - Ag 15 '96 - p1207 [251-500]
   NS - v125 - N 8 '96 - p46 [501+]
   NYRB - v44 - Ja 9 '97 - p49+ [501+]
   NYTBR - v101 - N 10 '96 - p64 [501+]
   NYTLa - v146 - O 21 '96 - pC16 [501+]
   Obs - D 8 '96 - p15* [501+]
   Spec - v277 - O 19 '96 - p45 [501+]
   TLS - N 22 '96 - p28 [501+]
   WSJ-MW - v78 - N 26 '96 - pA20 [501+]
Festinger, Leon - *A Theory of Cognitive Dissonance*
   A J Psy - v110 - Spr '97 - p127+ [501+]
Festle, Mary Jo - *Playing Nice*
   Choice - v34 - My '97 - p1538+ [51-250]
   Ms - v7 - N '96 - p82 [1-50]
   Wom R Bks - v14 - D '96 - p13 [501+]
Fetherling, Douglas - *Way Down Deep in the Belly of the Beast*
   BIC - v25 - O '96 - p20+ [501+]
   CF - v75 - Mr '97 - p45+ [501+]
   Quill & Q - v62 - S '96 - p70 [251-500]
Fetzer, Philip - *The Ethnic Moment*
   y   BL - v93 - N 1 '96 - p463 [251-500]
Feuchtwang, Stephan - *The Imperial Metaphor*
   Ch Rev Int - v3 - Fall '96 - p397+ [501+]
Feuer, A B - *The Spanish-American War at Sea*
   Parameters - v26 - Aut '96 - p152+ [501+]
Feuer, Arie - *Sampling in Digital Signal Processing and Control*
   SciTech - v20 - N '96 - p72 [51-250]
Feuer, Bryan - *Mycenaean Civilization*
   r   ARBA - v28 - '97 - p204+ [251-500]
Feuer, Elizabeth - *Lost Summer*
   c   RT - v50 - N '96 - p254 [51-250]
   Paper Doll
   y   Kliatt - v30 - S '96 - p4 [1-50]
Feuer, Jane - *Seeing through the Eighties*
   Aust Bk R - N '96 - p48 [501+]
Feuer, Kathryn B - *Tolstoy and the Genesis of War and Peace*
   Choice - v34 - My '97 - p1505+ [51-250]
   LJ - v122 - Ja '97 - p98 [51-250]
Feuerbach, Paul Johann Anselm - *Lost Prince*
   Choice - v34 - S '96 - p214 [51-250]
Feuerbach, Paul Johann Anselm, Ritter Von - *The Wild Child*
   Trib Bks - Mr 16 '97 - p8 [1-50]
Feuerhahn, Ronald R - *Hermann Sasse: A Bibliography*
   r   ARBA - v28 - '97 - p532 [251-500]
Feuerstein, Georg - *The Philosophy of Classical Yoga*
   Parabola - v21 - N '96 - p121 [1-50]
Feuerstein, Giora Z - *Coronary Restenosis*
   SciTech - v21 - Mr '97 - p57 [51-250]
Fey, Michael S - *The Top 100 Morgan Dollar Varieties*
   r   Coin W - v37 - O 14 '96 - p80 [51-250]
Feydeau, Georges - *Five by Feydeau*
   TranslRevS - v1 - My '95 - p19 [51-250]
Feyder, Vera - *Le Fond De L'Etre Est Froid 1966-1992*
   WLT - v70 - Aut '96 - p913+ [501+]

Feyerabend, Paul - *Killing Time*
   Bks & Cult - v2 - Mr '96 - p9 [501+]
   Obs - Ja 26 '97 - p18* [51-250]
   TLS - N 29 '96 - p14 [1-50]
Feyerick, Ada - *Genesis: World of Myths and Patriarchs*
   LJ - v122 - Ap 15 '97 - p86 [51-250]
   PW - v244 - Mr 24 '97 - p75 [51-250]
Feynman, Richard - *Surely You're Joking, Mr. Feynman*
   Trib Bks - S 18 '97 - p8 [1-50]
Fforde, Katie - *Wild Designs*
   Books - v10 - Je '96 - p17 [51-250]
Ffrench, Godwyn Ainsley - *The French Letters of Godwyn Ainsley Ffrench*
   TLS - Ja 3 '97 - p32 [501+]
Ffrench, Patrick - *The Time of Theory*
   Lon R Bks - v18 - D 12 '96 - p5+ [501+]
Ffrench-Davis, Ricardo - *Coping with Capital Surges*
   JEL - v34 - D '96 - p1965+ [501+]
Fi
   p   LJ - v121 - D '96 - p158 [51-250]
Fialka, John J - *War by Other Means*
   BL - v93 - Ja '97 - p793 [51-250]
   Bus W - F 10 '97 - p16+ [501+]
   Bus W - F 10 '97 - p16 [1-50]
   For Aff - v76 - My '97 - p126+ [251-500]
   Fortune - v135 - F 17 '97 - p136 [501+]
   KR - v64 - D 1 '96 - p1714 [251-500]
   NYTBR - v102 - F 16 '97 - p17 [501+]
   PW - v243 - N 25 '96 - p62 [251-500]
   WSJ-Cent - v99 - Ap 3 '97 - pA16 [501+]
Fiallo, Amalio - *Hacia Una Democracia Participativa*
   BL - v93 - Ap 1 '97 - p1284 [1-50]
Fiamengo, Marya - *White Linen Remembered*
   Quill & Q - v62 - D '96 - p33 [251-500]
Fiamminghi A Roma 1508-1608
   r   Choice - v34 - D '96 - p570 [1-50]
Fiand, Barbara - *Wrestling with God*
   Am - v176 - F 15 '97 - p30 [51-250]
Fiarotta, Noel - *Water Science, Water Fun*
   c   HB Guide - v8 - Spr '97 - p110 [51-250]
Fiarotta, Phyllis - *Papercrafts around the World*
   c   HB Guide - v7 - Fall '96 - p354 [1-50]
   c   SLJ - v42 - Ag '96 - p154 [51-250]
Fiberarts Design Book V
   Surface DJ - v20 - Sum '96 - p33 [501+]
Fibkins, William L - *Getting Everyone on Board to Help Teenagers*
   NASSP-B - v80 - S '96 - p118+ [501+]
Ficher, Miguel - *Latin American Classical Composers*
   r   ARBA - v28 - '97 - p476 [51-250]
   r   LJ - v121 - D '96 - p84+ [51-250]
Fichte, Johann Gottlieb - *Nachgelassene Schriften. Vol. 10*
   RM - v50 - S '96 - p151+ [501+]
Ficino, Marsilio - *Meditations on the Soul*
   Parabola - v21 - N '96 - p102+ [501+]
Ficken, Robert E - *Rufus Woods, the Columbia River, and the Building of Modern Washington*
   PHR - v65 - N '96 - p682+ [501+]
   WHQ - v27 - Win '96 - p515 [251-500]
Fiddler, Allyson - *Rewriting Reality*
   Ger Q - v69 - Spr '96 - p228+ [501+]
Fidge, Louis - *Bible Stories: Old Testament*
   c   TES - O 4 '96 - p16* [251-500]
   Essential English: Introductory Book. Bks. 1-4
   TES - Mr 14 '97 - p16* [251-500]
Fido, Martin - *The World's Worst Medical Mistakes*
   New Sci - v152 - N 2 '96 - p46 [51-250]
Fiedler, Leslie - *Tyranny of the Normal*
   BL - v93 - S 15 '96 - p203 [51-250]
   LATBR - O 13 '96 - p14 [51-250]
   LJ - v121 - D '96 - p99 [51-250]
   NY - v72 - D 2 '96 - p115 [51-250]
   NYTBR - v101 - O 20 '96 - p20 [501+]
   NYTLa - v146 - S 30 '96 - pC15 [501+]
   W&I - v11 - N '96 - p272+ [501+]
Fiedler, Lisa - *Curtis Piperfield's Biggest Fan*
   y   PW - v244 - My 5 '97 - p211 [1-50]
Fiedler, Peggy Lee - *Rare Lilies of California*
   Choice - v34 - My '97 - p1524 [51-250]
Field, Alexander J - *Research in Economic History. Vol. 16*
   JEL - v35 - Mr '97 - p257 [51-250]
Field, Carol - *In Nonna's Kitchen*
   BL - v93 - My 15 '97 - p1552 [51-250]
   LJ - v122 - Ap 15 '97 - p109 [51-250]
   PW - v244 - Ap 7 '97 - p88 [51-250]
Field, Eugene - *Poems of Childhood (Illus. by Maxfield Parrish)*
   c   HB Guide - v8 - Spr '97 - p152 [51-250]

Field, J V - *Renaissance and Revolution*
EHR - v111 - N '96 - p1276 [251-500]
Field, John - *A History of English Field-Names*
EHR - v111 - S '96 - p1039 [51-250]
Field, Kate - *Kate Field: Selected Letters*
Choice - v34 - Ap '97 - p1329 [51-250]
R&R Bk N - v12 - F '97 - p88 [51-250]
Field, Mark I - *The Courier Air Travel Handbook. 6th Ed.*
BL - v93 - S 15 '96 - p206 [1-50]
Field, Michael - *Symmetry in Chaos*
SciTech - v21 - Mr '97 - p3 [51-250]
Field, Michael, 1949- - *Inside the Arab World*
PSQ - v111 - Fall '96 - p537+ [501+]
Field, Rachel - *Prayer for a Child (Illus. by Elizabeth Orton Jones)*
c PW - v244 - Mr 24 '97 - p76+ [51-250]
A Field Trip to the Sky. Electronic Media Version
yr Kliatt - v30 - S '96 - p40 [51-250]
Fielder, John - *Photographing the Landscape*
Bloom Rev - v16 - N '96 - p24 [51-250]
Fieldhouse, D K - *Merchant Capital and Economic Decolonization*
EHR - v111 - N '96 - p1226+ [501+]
Fielding, Helen - *Bridget Jones's Diary*
Spec - v277 - N 16 '96 - p43 [1-50]
TLS - N 1 '96 - p26 [501+]
Fielding, Henry - *Joseph Andrews*
Clio - v25 - Sum '96 - p393+ [501+]
Fielding, Joy - *Missing Pieces*
BL - v93 - My 15 '97 - p1540 [51-250]
Tell Me No Secrets
Arm Det - v30 - Win '97 - p70 [51-250]
Fielding, Penny - *Writing and Orality*
Choice - v34 - Ja '97 - p794 [51-250]
Nine-C Lit - v51 - Mr '97 - p556 [1-50]
Fielding, Steven - *England Arise!*
AHR - v102 - F '97 - p115+ [501+]
Albion - v28 - Fall '96 - p539+ [501+]
Fielding's Thailand, Including Cambodia, Laos, Myanmar
r FEER - v160 - Mr 27 '97 - p50 [501+]
Fields, Debbi - *Debbi Fields' Great American Desserts*
BL - v92 - Ag '96 - p1871 [51-250]
Fields, Doug - *Help! I'm a Volunteer Youth Worker!*
VOYA - v19 - F '97 - p317 [51-250]
Fields, Jennie - *Crossing Brooklyn Ferry*
BL - v93 - My 15 '97 - p1561 [51-250]
KR - v65 - Ap 1 '97 - p485+ [251-500]
PW - v244 - Ap 28 '97 - p48 [51-250]
Fields, Wayne - *Union of Words*
Pub Int - Sum '96 - p96+ [501+]
Fiell, Charlotte - *Charles Rennie Mackintosh 1868-1928*
NYRB - v44 - F 20 '97 - p7+ [501+]
TLS - O 18 '96 - p21 [501+]
Fienberg, Anna - *Dead Sailors Don't Bite (Illus. by Ann James)*
c Magpies - v11 - S '96 - p32 [51-250]
c TES - Mr 21 '97 - p11* [51-250]
The Hottest Boy Who Ever Lived (Illus. by Kim Gamble)
c Bks Keeps - N '96 - p8 [51-250]
Pirate Trouble for Wiggy and Boa
c TES - Mr 21 '97 - p11* [51-250]
Tashi and the Ghosts (Illus. by Kim Gamble)
c Magpies - v11 - S '96 - p30 [51-250]
Fienup-Riordan, Ann - *Freeze Frame*
AB - v98 - D 9 '96 - p1996+ [51-250]
Fiery, Dennis - *How to Hide Things in Public Places*
BL - v93 - Ja '97 - p796 [51-250]
Fifer, Sally Jo - *Energy and Environmental Challenges in Central Asia and the Caucasus*
JEL - v34 - D '96 - p2136 [51-250]
Illuminating Video
Afterimage - v24 - N '96 - p4 [1-50]
Art J - v54 - Win '95 - p106+ [501+]
Fiffer, Sharon Sloan - *Family: American Writers Remember Their Own*
BL - v93 - Ja '97 - p808 [1-50]
BL - v93 - N 1 '96 - p474 [251-500]
KR - v64 - O 1 '96 - p1440 [251-500]
LJ - v121 - N '96 - p67 [51-250]
PW - v243 - S 2 '96 - p101 [51-250]
Fifield, Barringer - *Seeing Pittsburgh*
LJ - v121 - N 15 '96 - p78 [51-250]
Figert, Anne E - *Women and the Ownership of PMS*
Choice - v34 - F '97 - p1040 [51-250]
Figes, Kate - *The Penguin Book of International Women's Stories*
Trib Bks - Mr 2 '97 - p8 [1-50]

Figes, Orlando - *A People's Tragedy*
BW - v27 - Ap 6 '97 - p6+ [501+]
KR - v65 - Ja 1 '97 - p34 [251-500]
LATBR - Mr 16 '97 - p6+ [501+]
LJ - v122 - F 1 '97 - p94 [51-250]
Lon R Bks - v18 - O 31 '96 - p3+ [501+]
New R - v216 - Mr 31 '97 - p36+ [501+]
NS - v125 - Ag 30 '96 - p47 [501+]
NYTBR - v102 - Mr 9 '97 - p9 [501+]
Obs - O 6 '96 - p16* [501+]
PW - v243 - D 30 '96 - p43+ [51-250]
Time - v149 - Ap 21 '97 - p118 [501+]
Figley, Charles R - *Compassion Fatigue*
Readings - v11 - S '96 - p23+ [51-250]
Figley, Marty Rhodes - *Mary and Martha (Illus. by Cat Bowman Smith)*
c CLW - v66 - Je '96 - p49 [51-250]
Figueroa, Esther - *Sociolinguistic Metatheory*
Lang Soc - v26 - Mr '97 - p137+ [501+]
Figueroa, Julio C - *The Scientific Survey of Puerto Rico and the Virgin Islands*
SciTech - v20 - N '96 - p25 [51-250]
Fiksel, Joseph - *Design for Environment*
Env - v39 - Mr '97 - p26 [51-250]
Filanci, Franco - *Floreale and C. La Serie Che Non C'e Floral and Co.*
Phil Lit R - v45 - '96 - p346+ [251-500]
Filbee, Marjorie - *Celtic Cornwall*
HT - v46 - O '96 - p55 [1-50]
Files, Lolita - *Scenes from a Sistah*
y BL - v93 - F 15 '97 - p1002 [51-250]
KR - v65 - Ja 1 '97 - p9 [251-500]
PW - v244 - Ja 6 '97 - p62 [51-250]
Files, Meg - *Home Is the Hunter and Other Stories*
NAR - v282 - Mr '97 - p43+ [501+]
Filicori, Marco - *Treatment with GnRH Analogs*
SciTech - v20 - D '96 - p54 [51-250]
Filina, N N - *Cryogenic Two-Phase Flow*
SciTech - v20 - S '96 - p61 [51-250]
Filion, Michel - *Radiodiffusion et Societe Distincte*
Can Hist R - v77 - S '96 - p450+ [501+]
Filipelli, Ronald L - *Labor Conflict in the United States*
r RQ - v36 - Fall '96 - p50 [51-250]
Filippini, Graziella Allegri - *Recent Advances in Tryptophan Research*
SciTech - v21 - Mr '97 - p42 [51-250]
Fillitz, Hermann - *Der Traum Vom Gluck. Vols. 1-2*
BM - v138 - D '96 - p846+ [501+]
Fillmore, Peter A - *Operator Algebras and Their Applications*
SciTech - v21 - Mr '97 - p16 [51-250]
A User's Guide to Operator Algebras
Choice - v34 - Ja '97 - p833 [51-250]
Film Actors Guide 1997
r ARBA - v28 - '97 - p520+ [51-250]
Film Producers, Studios, Agents and Casting Directors Guide. 5th Ed.
r ARBA - v28 - '97 - p353 [51-250]
Film Writers Guide. 6th Ed.
r ARBA - v28 - '97 - p353 [51-250]
Filmer-Davis, Kath - *Fantasy Fiction and Wealth Myth*
SFS - v24 - Mr '97 - p181 [1-50]
Fil'mova Tvorchist' IAroslava Kulynycha
BL - v93 - N 15 '96 - p577 [1-50]
Filreis, Alan - *Modernism from Right to Left*
Poetics T - v18 - Spr '97 - p113+ [501+]
RES - v48 - F '97 - p140+ [501+]
Filteau, Claude - *Poetiques De La Modernite*
Can Lit - Win '96 - p197+ [501+]
Filtzer, Donald - *Soviet Workers and the Collapse of Perestroika*
APSR - v90 - S '96 - p668+ [501+]
Fimmel, Richard O - *Pioneering Venus*
J Gov Info - v23 - N '96 - p552 [51-250]
Finamore, Daniel - *Across the Western Ocean*
Mag Antiq - v150 - Ag '96 - p144+ [501+]
Financial, Economic and Social Trends 1985-1994
J Gov Info - v23 - S '96 - p602+ [51-250]
Finch, Annie - *Eve*
PW - v244 - Mr 31 '97 - p70 [51-250]
Finch, L Boyd - *Confederate Pathway to the Pacific*
Roundup M - v4 - O '96 - p26 [51-250]
WHQ - v28 - Spr '97 - p75+ [251-500]
Finch, Phillip - *F2F*
PW - v243 - D 2 '96 - p56 [1-50]
Finch, Robert - *The Smithsonian Guides to Natural America: Southern New England*
r BL - v93 - S 15 '96 - p212 [1-50]
yr Kliatt - v30 - S '96 - p35 [51-250]

Fincham, Jack E - *Advancing Prescription Medicine Compliance*
SB - v32 - Ag '96 - p169 [51-250]
Fincham, Kenneth - *The Early Stuart Church 1603-1642*
CH - v65 - S '96 - p495+ [501+]
Visitation Articles and Injunctions of the Early Stuart Church. Vol. 1
EHR - v111 - N '96 - p1277 [251-500]
Finchler, Judy - *Miss Malarkey Doesn't Live in Room 10 (Illus. by Kevin O'Malley)*
c ECEJ - v23 - Sum '96 - p224 [51-250]
c RT - v50 - O '96 - p156+ [51-250]
Finckenauer, James O - *Russian Youth*
Russ Rev - v56 - Ja '97 - p142+ [501+]
Finder, Joseph - *The Zero Hour*
LATBR - Ag 4 '96 - p8+ [501+]
PW - v244 - Mr 17 '97 - p81 [1-50]
Rapport - v19 - 5 '96 - p29 [251-500]
The Zero Hour (Charles). Audio Version
LJ - v121 - S 15 '96 - p115 [51-250]
Finders, Margaret J - *Just Girls*
Adoles - v32 - Spr '97 - p245 [51-250]
Findings from the Wildland Firefighters Human Factors Workshop
J Gov Info - v23 - S '96 - p567 [51-250]
Findlay, Alison - *Illegitimate Power*
Shakes Q - v47 - Sum '96 - p214+ [501+]
Findlay, Ronald - *Factor Proportions, Trade, and Growth*
JEL - v34 - D '96 - p1966+ [501+]
Findlay, Trevor - *Cambodia: The Legacy and Lessons of UNTAC*
Pac A - v69 - Fall '96 - p450+ [501+]
Findlen, Barbara - *Listen Up*
OOB - v26 - Ag '96 - p18+ [501+]
Findlen, Paula - *Possessing Nature*
EHR - v112 - F '97 - p193+ [501+]
JHI - v57 - O '96 - p725+ [501+]
JMH - v68 - D '96 - p1006+ [501+]
Six Ct J - v27 - Fall '96 - p937+ [501+]
Findley, Timothy - *Dust to Dust*
Mac - v110 - My 19 '97 - p62 [251-500]
Quill & Q - v63 - Ja '97 - p18 [51-250]
Quill & Q - v63 - Mr '97 - p70 [251-500]
The Piano Man's Daughter
Can Lit - Win '96 - p169+ [501+]
KR - v64 - My 1 '96 - p620+ [251-500]
NYTBR - v101 - S 29 '96 - p26 [501+]
Rapport - v19 - 5 '96 - p28 [251-500]
VQR - v73 - Win '97 - p24* [51-250]
WLT - v70 - Aut '96 - p958+ [251-500]
The Trials of Ezra Pound
Can Lit - Win '96 - p121+ [501+]
You Went Away
BIC - v25 - N '96 - p2 [501+]
Mac - v109 - N 11 '96 - p84 [501+]
Mac - v109 - D 9 '96 - p64 [1-50]
Quill & Q - v62 - O '96 - p42 [251-500]
Findling, John E - *Events That Changed America in the Twentieth Century*
yr BWatch - v17 - S '96 - p6 [51-250]
yr SLJ - v43 - F '97 - p128 [51-250]
yr SLMQ - v25 - Fall '96 - p63 [51-250]
r VOYA - v19 - D '96 - p299+ [251-500]
Historical Dictionary of the Modern Olympic Movement
r ARBA - v28 - '97 - p300+ [251-500]
r Choice - v34 - S '96 - p166 [51-250]
r RQ - v36 - Fall '96 - p131 [51-250]
Fine, Agnes - *Parrains, Marraines*
EHR - v111 - N '96 - p1229+ [251-500]
Fine, Anne - *The Book of the Banshee*
c Sch Lib - v44 - Ag '96 - p115 [51-250]
Care of Henry (Illus. by Paul Howard)
c Bks Keeps - Ja '97 - p21 [51-250]
c Sch Lib - v45 - F '97 - p24 [51-250]
Countdown (Illus. by David Higham)
c JB - v60 - Ag '96 - p147+ [51-250]
Flour Babies
y Kliatt - v30 - S '96 - p3 [1-50]
y SLJ - v43 - Mr '97 - p112 [1-50]
Goggle-Eyes
c Sch Lib - v44 - Ag '96 - p96+ [501+]
How to Write Really Badly (Illus. by Philippe Dupasquier)
c Bks Keeps - Jl '96 - p12 [51-250]
c JB - v60 - Ag '96 - p156 [51-250]
Madame Doubtfire
c Sch Lib - v44 - Ag '96 - p96+ [501+]
Ojos Saltones
y JAAL - v40 - S '96 - p77 [51-250]

Step by Wicked Step
y Ch BWatch - v6 - O '96 - p3 [1-50]
c CLW - v67 - Mr '97 - p51 [251-500]
c HB Guide - v7 - Fall '96 - p291 [51-250]
y JAAL - v40 - N '96 - p233 [51-250]
y JB - v60 - O '96 - p200 [51-250]
c Magpies - v11 - S '96 - p45 [1-50]
c Sch Lib - v44 - Ag '96 - p96+ [501+]
c SLJ - v42 - D '96 - p29 [1-50]
c SLJ - v43 - Mr '97 - p112 [1-50]
The Tulip Touch
c Bks Keeps - v100 - S '96 - p33 [51-250]
c Bks Keeps - Ja '97 - p25 [51-250]
y Obs - Ap 13 '97 - p18* [51-250]
y Sch Lib - v45 - F '97 - p46 [51-250]
c TES - D 6 '96 - p17* [501+]
c TES - D 27 '96 - p16 [1-50]
Fine, Ben - *Consumption in the Age of Affluence*
   JEL - v34 - D '96 - p2024 [51-250]
Fine, Carla - *No Time to Say Goodbye*
   BL - v93 - D 1 '96 - p624 [51-250]
   LJ - v121 - D '96 - p124 [51-250]
   PW - v243 - N 4 '96 - p56 [51-250]
Fine, Deborah - *Star Wars Chronicles*
   Ent W - F 21 '97 - p120 [51-250]
Fine, Doreen - *What Do We Know about Judaism?*
c CLW - v67 - Mr '97 - p56 [51-250]
c HB Guide - v8 - Spr '97 - p87 [51-250]
c Magpies - v11 - Jl '96 - p38+ [51-250]
c SLJ - v43 - F '97 - p114 [51-250]
Fine, Gary Alan - *Kitchens: The Culture of Restaurant Work*
   CS - v26 - Mr '97 - p219+ [501+]
A Second Chicago School?
   AJS - v102 - Jl '96 - p252+ [501+]
Fine, Sara F - *The First Helping Interview*
   R&R Bk N - v11 - D '96 - p3 [51-250]
Fine, Sidney - *Without Blare of Trumpets*
   AHR - v101 - O '96 - p1300+ [501+]
   ILRR - v50 - Ja '97 - p362+ [501+]
Fine, Steven - *Sacred Realm*
   MEJ - v51 - Spr '97 - p310 [51-250]
Fine Homebuilding
p LJ - v122 - F 1 '97 - p53 [1-50]
Fineberg, Jonathan - *Art since 1940*
   Art Bull - v79 - Mr '97 - p164+ [501+]
   Art J - v55 - Sum '96 - p103+ [501+]
Finegold, Kenneth - *Experts and Politicians*
   AHR - v102 - F '97 - p202 [251-500]
   APSR - v90 - S '96 - p646+ [501+]
   J Am St - v30 - Ap '96 - p140+ [251-500]
   J Pol - v58 - Ag '96 - p884+ [501+]
State and Party in America's New Deal
   AJS - v102 - Jl '96 - p292+ [501+]
   CS - v26 - Ja '97 - p35+ [501+]
   JIH - v27 - Spr '97 - p729+ [251-500]
   J Pol - v58 - N '96 - p1217+ [501+]
   PSQ - v111 - Win '96 - p718+ [501+]
Fineman, Martha Albertson - *The Neutered Mother, the Sexual Family and Other Twentieth Century Tragedies*
   Signs - v22 - Aut '96 - p231+ [501+]
Fingar, Peter - *The Blueprint for Business Objects*
   SciTech - v20 - N '96 - p7 [51-250]
Next Generation Computing
   SciTech - v20 - S '96 - p5 [51-250]
Fingarette, Herbert - *Death*
   BWatch - v18 - Mr '97 - p10 [51-250]
Finger, J Michael - *The Uruguay Round*
   JEL - v35 - Mr '97 - p213 [51-250]
Fingerman, Daniel - *Lotus Word Pro 96 for Windows 3.1*
   CBR - v14 - Jl '96 - p26 [1-50]
Lotus Word Pro 96 for Windows 95
   CBR - v14 - Jl '96 - p26 [1-50]
Fingleton, John - *Competition Policy and the Transformation of Central Europe*
   JEL - v35 - Mr '97 - p294 [251-500]
Fink, Arlene - *The Survey Kit. Vols. 1-9*
r Per Psy - v49 - Win '96 - p1019+ [501+]
Fink, Gary M - *Biographical Dictionary of American Labor*
r RQ - v36 - Fall '96 - p54 [51-250]
Labor Unions
r RQ - v36 - Fall '96 - p51 [51-250]
Race, Class, and Community in Southern Labor History
   ILRR - v50 - O '96 - p180+ [501+]
   JSH - v62 - N '96 - p846+ [501+]
State Labor Proceedings
r RQ - v36 - Fall '96 - p52 [51-250]
Fink, Jon Stephen - *If He Lived*
   TLS - F 21 '97 - p22 [501+]

Fink, Leon - *Intellectuals and Public Life*
   CS - v26 - Mr '97 - p234+ [501+]
Fink, Nan - *Stranger in the Midst*
   BL - v93 - F 15 '97 - p975 [51-250]
   KR - v65 - Ja 1 '97 - p34 [51-250]
   PW - v244 - F 24 '97 - p82 [51-250]
   Utne R - Mr '97 - p83 [251-500]
Finkbeiner, Betty Ladley - *Practice Management for the Dental Team. 4th Ed.*
   SciTech - v20 - S '96 - p42 [51-250]
Finke, Michael C - *Metapoesis: The Russian Tradition from Pushkin to Chekhov*
   Slav R - v55 - Fall '96 - p702+ [501+]
Finkel, Alicia - *Romantic Stages*
   Choice - v34 - N '96 - p472 [51-250]
   TCI - v30 - O '96 - p52+ [501+]
Finkelman, Paul - *Slavery and the Founders*
   JIH - v27 - Spr '97 - p715+ [251-500]
   JSH - v63 - F '97 - p157+ [501+]
   W&M Q - v54 - Ja '97 - p271+ [501+]
Finkelstein, Barbara - *The First Year of Nursing*
y BL - v93 - S 15 '96 - p194 [51-250]
   LJ - v121 - N 15 '96 - p82 [51-250]
Finkelstein, Caroline - *Germany*
   PS - v70 - Fall '96 - p175+ [501+]
Finkelstein, Haim - *Salvador Dali's Art and Writing 1927-1942*
   L'Esprit - v36 - Win '96 - p97+ [501+]
Finkelstein, Israel - *Living on the Fringe*
   AJA - v101 - Ja '97 - p170+ [501+]
   Rel St Rev - v23 - Ja '97 - p55 [51-250]
Finkelstein, Jay - *See No Evil*
   PW - v243 - S 9 '96 - p81 [51-250]
Finkelstein, Joanne - *After a Fashion*
   Aust Bk R - Je '96 - p31+ [501+]
Finkelstein, Norman G - *Image and Reality of the Israel-Palestine Conflict*
   Lon R Bks - v18 - O 31 '96 - p16+ [501+]
   MEJ - v51 - Spr '97 - p294+ [501+]
   MEQ - v3 - S '96 - p82 [251-500]
   WorldV - v12 - Jl '96 - p7 [51-250]
The Rise and Fall of Palestine
   KR - v64 - O 1 '96 - p1441 [251-500]
   LJ - v121 - N 15 '96 - p75 [51-250]
   Nat - v264 - Ap 21 '97 - p25+ [501+]
   PW - v243 - N 11 '96 - p70 [51-250]
Finkenstadt, Barbel - *Nonlinear Dynamics in Economics*
   JEL - v34 - D '96 - p2129 [51-250]
Finkielkraut, Alain - *The Defeat of the Mind*
   Lon R Bks - v18 - O 31 '96 - p32+ [501+]
The Imaginary Jew
   Lon R Bks - v18 - O 31 '96 - p32+ [501+]
   PW - v244 - Mr 17 '97 - p81 [1-50]
Finkin, Matthew W - *The Case for Tenure*
   Choice - v34 - My '97 - p1550 [51-250]
Finlayson, Ann - *Naming Rumpelstiltskin*
   Quill & Q - v62 - N '96 - p37 [251-500]
Finlayson, C Max - *Classification and Inventory of the World's Wetlands*
   SciTech - v20 - N '96 - p2 [51-250]
Landscape and Vegetation Ecology of the Kakadu Region, Northern Australia
   SciTech - v20 - N '96 - p28 [1-50]
Finlayson, Geoffrey - *Citizen, State, and Social Welfare in Britain 1830-1990*
   Albion - v28 - Sum '96 - p356+ [501+]
   EHR - v111 - S '96 - p1012+ [501+]
   JMH - v68 - S '96 - p686+ [501+]
   VS - v39 - Spr '96 - p419+ [501+]
Finlayson, Judith - *Against the Current*
   Wom R Bks - v14 - O '96 - p23+ [501+]
Finley, Karen - *Living It Up*
   Ent W - O 18 '96 - p74 [51-250]
   KR - v64 - Ag 15 '96 - p1207 [251-500]
   PW - v243 - S 9 '96 - p74 [51-250]
Finley, Milton - *The Most Monstrous of Wars*
   AHR - v101 - O '96 - p1241+ [501+]
Finley, Mitch - *Season of New Beginnings*
   RR - v56 - Ja '97 - p105 [1-50]
Season of Promises
   RR - v55 - N '96 - p661 [1-50]
The Seeker's Guide to Being Catholic
   PW - v244 - Ap 14 '97 - p70 [51-250]
Finley, Randy - *From Slavery to Uncertain Freedom*
   Bl S - v26 - Fall '96 - p102 [51-250]
   Choice - v34 - D '96 - p675+ [51-250]
Finn, Geraldine - *Why Althusser Killed His Wife*
   Choice - v34 - S '96 - p141 [51-250]
Finn, Margaret L - *Mary Tyler Moore*
y Ch BWatch - v6 - S '96 - p6 [51-250]
y HB Guide - v8 - Spr '97 - p156 [51-250]

Finn, Thomas M - *Early Christian Baptism and the Catechumenate*
   CH - v65 - S '96 - p451+ [501+]
Finnegan, Richard B - *Irish Government Publications*
r LAR - v98 - Ag '96 - p425 [251-500]
Finnegan, Ruth - *South Pacific Oral Traditions*
   Biography - v19 - Fall '96 - p429 [1-50]
   JIH - v27 - Spr '97 - p753+ [251-500]
Finnegan, William - *Crossing the Line*
   Africa T - v44 - 1 '97 - p94+ [501+]
Finnemore, Martha - *National Interests in International Society*
   Choice - v34 - Ap '97 - p1413 [51-250]
Finney, Ben - *Voyage of Rediscovery*
   Cont Pac - v8 - Fall '96 - p456+ [501+]
Finney, Ernest J - *Flights in the Heavenlies*
   Sew R - v104 - Jl '96 - pR52+ [251-500]
Finney, Fred - *Mystery History of a Pirate Galleon (Illus. by Mike Bell)*
c HB Guide - v8 - Spr '97 - p164 [51-250]
c Sch Lib - v45 - F '97 - p37+ [51-250]
Finney, Jack - *From Time to Time (Hecht). Audio Version*
y Kliatt - v30 - S '96 - p53 [51-250]
Time and Again (Hecht). Audio Version
y Kliatt - v30 - S '96 - p53 [51-250]
Finnie, Fleur - *Don't Stand on the Grass*
   Aust Bk R - D '96 - p74 [51-250]
Finnie, Sue - *Ok! Stage 2*
   TES - Mr 14 '97 - p20 [251-500]
Finnigan, Jerome P - *The Manager's Guide to Benchmarking*
   HR Mag - v41 - O '96 - p150 [51-250]
Finnis, A - *Cat-Dogs and Other Tales of Horror*
y Emerg Lib - v24 - S '96 - p26 [1-50]
Fino, Susan P - *The Michigan State Constitution*
r R&R Bk N - v11 - D '96 - p52 [51-250]
Finster, Howard - *The Night before Christmas (Illus. by Howard Finster)*
c S Liv - v31 - D '96 - p58 [51-250]
Finzsch, Norbert - *Different Restorations*
   R&R Bk N - v12 - F '97 - p24 [1-50]
Fiore, Carole D - *Programming for Young Children*
   BL - v93 - S 15 '96 - p253+ [51-250]
   Emerg Lib - v24 - Mr '97 - p42 [1-50]
Fiorentini, Gianluca - *The Economics of Organised Crime*
   JEL - v34 - S '96 - p1450 [51-250]
   JEL - v35 - Mr '97 - p161+ [501+]
Fiorenza, Elisabeth Schussler - *But She Said*
   Rel St Rev - v22 - O '96 - p293+ [501+]
   Rel St Rev - v22 - O '96 - p296+ [501+]
Fire Engine (Snapshot Books)
c Ch BWatch - v6 - D '96 - p8 [1-50]
Fireside, Harvey - *Young People from Bosnia Talk about War*
y CLW - v67 - Mr '97 - p59 [51-250]
y HB Guide - v8 - Spr '97 - p167 [51-250]
y KR - v64 - Ag 15 '96 - p1234 [51-250]
y SLJ - v42 - O '96 - p156 [51-250]
y VOYA - v19 - F '97 - p344 [251-500]
Firestein, Beth A - *Bisexuality: The Psychology and Politics of an Invisible Minority*
   R&R Bk N - v11 - D '96 - p40 [51-250]
Firestien, Roger L - *Leading on the Creative Edge*
   LJ - v122 - F 1 '97 - p92 [51-250]
Firkatian, Mari A - *The Forest Traveler*
   R&R Bk N - v12 - F '97 - p17 [51-250]
Firmage, Richard A - *The Alphabet Abecedarium*
   JC - v46 - Sum '96 - p205+ [251-500]
Firmin, Peter - *Nina's Machines*
c Bks Keeps - v99 - Mr '97 - p16 [51-250]
Firmin-Sellers, Kathryn - *The Transformation of Property Rights in the Gold Coast*
   Choice - v34 - Mr '97 - p1232+ [51-250]
   JEL - v35 - Mr '97 - p296 [51-250]
Firminus Verris - *Dictionarius/Dictionnaire Latin-Francais De Firmin Le Ver (Merrilees)*
r Specu - v71 - O '96 - p948+ [501+]
Firpo, Massimo - *Il Processo Inquisitoriale Del Cardinal Giovanni Morone. Vol. 6*
   CHR - v82 - O '96 - p719+ [501+]
Firshein, Richard N - *Reversing Asthma*
   LJ - v121 - O 15 '96 - p84 [51-250]
First, Michael B - *DSM-IV Handbook of Differential Diagnosis*
   J ClinPsyc - v57 - Ag '96 - p375 [251-500]
First Farm Rhymes (Illus. by Lynn Adams)
c PW - v243 - N 18 '96 - p77 [51-250]
The First International Credit Card Catalog 1997
r Coin W - v38 - Ja 27 '97 - p42 [51-250]
First Things
p TLS - Mr 7 '97 - p26+ [501+]

First Thousand Words
  cr Bks Keeps - v100 - S '96 - p22+ [501+]
Firstenberg, Paul B - *The 21st Century Nonprofit*
  ChrPhil - v8 - Ag 8 '96 - p50 [51-250]
Firth, Alan - *The Discourse of Negotiation*
  Lang Soc - v25 - S '96 - p463+ [501+]
Fisas Armengol, Vincenc - *Blue Geopolitics*
  JPR - v33 - Ag '96 - p379+ [251-500]
Fiscal Management in Russia
  JEL - v34 - D '96 - p2061 [51-250]
Fisch, Robert O - *Light from the Yellow Star*
  c HB Guide - v7 - Fall '96 - p380 [51-250]
Fischel, Daniel - *Payback: The Conspiracy to Destroy
  Michael Milken and His Financial Revolution*
  Pub Int - Sum '96 - p91+ [501+]
Fischel, Emma - *Alexander Graham Bell (Illus. by Lesley
  Bisseker)*
  c Bks Keeps - Ja '97 - p24 [251-500]
  c Sch Lib - v45 - F '97 - p37 [51-250]
  Faces at the Window
  c Sch Lib - v44 - N '96 - p150 [51-250]
  My Teacher the Ghost (Illus. by Antony Lewis)
  c Sch Lib - v44 - N '96 - p150 [51-250]
Fischel, William A - *Regulatory Takings*
  JEL - v34 - D '96 - p1981+ [501+]
Fischer, Clare B - *Of Spirituality*
  r ARBA - v28 - '97 - p532+ [251-500]
  r Choice - v34 - S '96 - p98 [51-250]
Fischer, Claude S - *Inequality by Design*
  Bl S - v26 - Fall '96 - p102 [51-250]
  Choice - v34 - Ja '97 - p879+ [51-250]
  JEL - v35 - Mr '97 - p232 [51-250]
  LJ - v121 - O 15 '96 - p79 [51-250]
  NS - v125 - D 20 '96 - p118+ [501+]
  Pub Int - Win '97 - p113+ [501+]
  Skeptic - v4 - 3 '96 - p108+ [501+]
Fischer, Daniel - *Hubble: A New Window to the Universe*
  Choice - v34 - D '96 - p634 [51-250]
  SciTech - v20 - S '96 - p13 [51-250]
  S&T - v92 - D '96 - p63+ [501+]
  WSJ-MW - v78 - D 5 '96 - pA18 [51-250]
Fischer, David Hackett - *The Great Wave*
  BL - v93 - O 1 '96 - p311 [51-250]
  CHE - v43 - D 20 '96 - pA15 [51-250]
  LJ - v121 - O 1 '96 - p98 [51-250]
  NS - v126 - Mr 14 '97 - p45+ [501+]
  NYTBR - v102 - Ja 5 '97 - p29 [501+]
  WSJ-MW - v78 - D 19 '96 - pA16 [501+]
  Paul Revere's Ride (Estell). Audio Version
  y Kliatt - v31 - Ja '97 - p50 [251-500]
Fischer, Erica - *Aimee and Jaguar*
  OOB - v26 - N '96 - p18 [501+]
  Wom R Bks - v14 - N '96 - p9+ [501+]
Fischer, Frank - *Greening Environmental Policy*
  APSR - v90 - S '96 - p695+ [501+]
  Env - v38 - N '96 - p29 [51-250]
Fischer, Hans - *Pitschi (Illus. by Hans Fischer)*
  c HB Guide - v8 - Spr '97 - p26+ [51-250]
  c JB - v60 - D '96 - p230+ [251-500]
  c PW - v243 - N 4 '96 - p78 [51-250]
  Puss in Boots (Illus. by Hans Fischer)
  c BL - v93 - N 15 '96 - p592 [51-250]
  c HB Guide - v8 - Spr '97 - p104 [51-250]
  c PW - v243 - N 4 '96 - p78 [51-250]
Fischer, Irmtraud - *Tora Fur Israel, Tora Fur Die Volker*
  Rel St Rev - v23 - Ja '97 - p58+ [51-250]
Fischer, John, 1947- - *What On Earth Are We Doing?*
  Bks & Cult - v3 - Ja '97 - p26 [501+]
  What on Earth Are We Doing?
  Ch Today - v41 - Ap 7 '97 - p43 [51-250]
Fischer, John Martin - *The Metaphysics of Free Will*
  CPR - v16 - O '96 - p340+ [501+]
  Ethics - v107 - O '96 - p141+ [501+]
  J Phil - v94 - Mr '97 - p156+ [501+]
Fischer, Kathleen - *Autumn Gospel*
  RR - v55 - N '96 - p655+ [251-500]
Fischer, Kerwin - *Green Places in Small Spaces*
  BL - v93 - My 1 '97 - p1472 [51-250]
Fischer, Klaus P - *Nazi Germany*
  Bks & Cult - v3 - Mr '97 - p38+ [51-250]
  NYTBR - v101 - Ag 25 '96 - p28 [1-50]
Fischer, Lucy - *Cinematernity: Film, Motherhood, Genre*
  Afterimage - v24 - Ja '97 - p22 [1-50]
Fischer, Peter A - *Migration and Economic Integration in
  the Nordic Common Labour Market*
  JEL - v34 - D '96 - p2045+ [51-250]
Fischer, Roger A - *Them Damned Pictures*
  Choice - v34 - S '96 - p193 [51-250]

Fischer, Tibor - *The Collector Collector*
  BL - v93 - My 1 '97 - p1478 [51-250]
  KR - v65 - Mr 15 '97 - p399 [251-500]
  Obs - Mr 9 '97 - p17* [501+]
  PW - v244 - Ap 7 '97 - p72+ [51-250]
  Spec - v278 - Mr 15 '97 - p38 [501+]
  TLS - Mr 7 '97 - p22 [501+]
Fischer-Lichte, Erika - *Arbeitsfelder Der
  Theaterwissenschaft*
  Ger Q - v69 - Fall '96 - p438+ [501+]
Fischer-Rizzi, Susanne - *Medicine of the Earth*
  BL - v93 - D 15 '96 - p700+ [51-250]
  BWatch - v18 - Mr '97 - p2 [51-250]
Fischer-Schreiber, Ingrid - *The Shambhala Dictionary of
  Taoism*
  r ARBA - v28 - '97 - p556 [51-250]
Fisdel, Steven A - *The Dead Sea Scrolls*
  LJ - v122 - My 1 '97 - p109 [51-250]
Fish, M Steven - *Democracy from Scratch*
  Historian - v59 - Fall '96 - p128+ [501+]
  Russ Rev - v55 - O '96 - p724+ [501+]
Fish, Margery - *We Made a Garden*
  NYTBR - v101 - D 8 '96 - p42 [251-500]
Fish, Stanley - *There's No Such Thing as Free Speech,
  and It's a Good Thing, Too*
  JC - v47 - Win '97 - p128+ [501+]
  MLR - v92 - Ap '97 - p412+ [501+]
Fish Stories
  p LMR - v15 - Fall '96 - p41+ [51-250]
Fishbein, Samuel B - *Flight Management Systems*
  T&C - v38 - Ja '97 - p265+ [501+]
Fishel, Edwin C - *The Secret War for the Union*
  APH - v44 - Spr '97 - p55 [501+]
  BL - v92 - Ag '96 - p1879 [251-500]
  BW - v26 - D 22 '96 - p3+ [501+]
  Choice - v34 - Ja '97 - p862 [51-250]
  J Mil H - v61 - Ap '97 - p379+ [501+]
  VQR - v73 - Win '97 - p7* [501+]
Fishelov, David - *Metaphors of Genre*
  CLS - v33 - 2 '96 - p221+ [501+]
Fisher, Abraham - *Muscarinic Agonists and the Treatment
  of Alzheimer's Disease*
  SciTech - v20 - S '96 - p34 [51-250]
Fisher, Aileen - *The Story of Easter (Illus. by Stefano
  Vitale)*
  c BL - v93 - D 15 '96 - p729 [51-250]
  c KR - v64 - D 1 '96 - p1736 [51-250]
  c NYTBR - v102 - Mr 30 '97 - p18 [1-50]
  c PW - v244 - Ja 27 '97 - p97 [51-250]
  c SLJ - v43 - Mr '97 - p174 [51-250]
Fisher, Alan - *The Rage of Angels*
  KR - v65 - Mr 1 '97 - p323+ [51-250]
  PW - v244 - Ap 28 '97 - p52 [251-500]
Fisher, Anne Kinsman - *The Legend of Tommy Morris*
  PW - v243 - S 2 '96 - p110 [51-250]
  The Masters of the Spirit
  PW - v244 - Mr 31 '97 - p62 [51-250]
Fisher, Anthony C - *Environmental and Resource
  Economics*
  Econ J - v106 - S '96 - p1484 [251-500]
Fisher, Catherine - *The Soul Thieves*
  y JB - v60 - O '96 - p200 [251-500]
  y Sch Lib - v44 - N '96 - p170 [51-250]
Fisher, Charles - *Education and Technology*
  Choice - v34 - Mr '97 - p1211 [51-250]
Fisher, David E - *Tube: The Invention of Television*
  Am Sci - v85 - Ja '97 - p87+ [501+]
  y BL - v93 - S 1 '96 - p49 [51-250]
  y BL - v93 - D 1 '96 - p664 [1-50]
  Choice - v34 - Mr '97 - p1190 [51-250]
  New Sci - v152 - N 16 '96 - p50 [251-500]
  VV - v41 - S 24 '96 - p42+ [501+]
Fisher, Dorothy Canfield - *Seasoned Timber*
  AL - v68 - D '96 - p885 [51-250]
Fisher, Eugene J - *Faith without Prejudice*
  Rel Ed - v91 - Fall '96 - p617 [1-50]
  Homework for Christians. 3rd, Rev. Ed.
  Rel Ed - v91 - Fall '96 - p617 [1-50]
  In Our Time
  Rel Ed - v91 - Fall '96 - p609+ [51-250]
  Interwoven Destinies
  Rel Ed - v91 - Fall '96 - p610 [1-50]
  *Seminary Education and Christian Jewish-Relations.
  2nd, Rev. Ed.*
  Rel Ed - v91 - Fall '96 - p617 [1-50]
  Twenty Years of Jewish-Catholic Relations
  Rel Ed - v91 - Fall '96 - p610 [1-50]
  Understanding the Jewish Experience
  Rel Ed - v91 - Fall '96 - p617 [51-250]

Fisher, Gary - *Gary in Your Pocket*
  BW - v26 - N 3 '96 - p8 [251-500]
  LJ - v121 - S 15 '96 - p84 [51-250]
Fisher, Glenn W - *The Worst Tax?*
  Choice - v34 - S '96 - p175 [51-250]
  JEH - v57 - Mr '97 - p254+ [501+]
  Pol Stud J - v24 - Sum '96 - p332 [51-250]
  WHQ - v27 - Win '96 - p550 [51-250]
Fisher, James L - *Presidential Leadership*
  Choice - v34 - Ja '97 - p848 [51-250]
Fisher, James T - *Dr. America*
  KR - v65 - F 1 '97 - p191 [51-250]
Fisher, Jim - *Fall Guys*
  KR - v64 - N 1 '96 - p1578 [251-500]
  PW - v243 - N 4 '96 - p56 [51-250]
Fisher, John H - *The Emergence of Standard English*
  Choice - v34 - S '96 - p118 [51-250]
Fisher, Joseph C - *Killer among Us*
  KR - v65 - Mr 1 '97 - p349 [51-250]
  LJ - v122 - My 1 '97 - p122+ [51-250]
  PW - v244 - Ap 14 '97 - p64 [51-250]
Fisher, Leonard Everett - *The Cabinetmakers*
  c HB Guide - v8 - Spr '97 - p173 [1-50]
  The Doctors
  c HB Guide - v8 - Spr '97 - p173 [1-50]
  The Glassmakers
  c HB Guide - v8 - Spr '97 - p173 [1-50]
  Marie Curie
  c SLJ - v42 - D '96 - p45 [51-250]
  Moses (Illus. by Leonard Everett Fisher)
  c RT - v50 - S '96 - p52 [51-250]
  Niagara Falls
  y BL - v93 - S 1 '96 - p71 [51-250]
  c HB Guide - v7 - Fall '96 - p386 [51-250]
  c SLJ - v42 - O '96 - p132 [51-250]
  The Schoolmasters
  c HB Guide - v8 - Spr '97 - p173 [1-50]
  The Silversmiths
  c HB Guide - v8 - Spr '97 - p173 [1-50]
  Theseus and the Minotaur
  c SLJ - v42 - N '96 - p38 [1-50]
  William Tell (Illus. by Leonard Everett Fisher)
  c Emerg Lib - v24 - S '96 - p44 [1-50]
  c HB Guide - v7 - Fall '96 - p320 [51-250]
  c RT - v50 - Ap '97 - p594 [51-250]
Fisher, Lillian - *Brave Bessie*
  c Ch BWatch - v6 - My '96 - p6 [51-250]
Fisher, Lloyd D - *Biostatistics: A Methodology for the
  Health Sciences*
  SciTech - v20 - N '96 - p26 [51-250]
Fisher, Louis - *Presidential War Power*
  AHR - v101 - D '96 - p1647 [501+]
  RAH - v24 - S '96 - p524+ [501+]
Fisher, M F K - *A Welcoming Life*
  PW - v244 - Ap 7 '97 - p86+ [51-250]
Fisher, Marc - *After the Wall*
  WP - v49 - Ja '97 - p282+ [501+]
Fisher, Mark - *The Millionaire's Secrets*
  Rapport - v19 - 4 '96 - p18+ [501+]
Fisher, Nancy L - *Cultural and Ethnic Diversity*
  Choice - v34 - My '97 - p1533 [51-250]
Fisher, Naomi D - *Changing the Culture*
  Am Sci - v85 - Mr '97 - p191+ [501+]
Fisher, Nick - *A Complete Guide to Kissing*
  Obs - Ja 19 '97 - p16* [501+]
  y TES - F 14 '97 - p7* [251-500]
Fisher, Philip - *Common Stocks and Uncommon Profits*
  Barron's - v76 - S 2 '96 - p43 [51-250]
Fisher, Robert - *Stories for Thinking*
  TES - D 6 '96 - p12* [501+]
Fisher, Robin - *From Maps to Metaphors*
  Can Hist R - v77 - S '96 - p433+ [501+]
Fisher, Ronald C - *State and Local Public Finance. 2nd
  Ed.*
  JEL - v34 - D '96 - p2056 [51-250]
Fisher, Roy - *The Dow Low Drop*
  Lon R Bks - v19 - Ja 2 '97 - p30+ [501+]
  y Sch Lib - v44 - Ag '96 - p115 [51-250]
Fisher, Sally - *The Square Halo and Other Mysteries of
  Western Art*
  CC - v113 - N 13 '96 - p1123 [51-250]
Fisher, Stephen - *Man and the Maritime Environment*
  GJ - v162 - Jl '96 - p238 [51-250]
Fisher, Stephen J, 1940- - *Colon Cancer and the Polyps
  Connection*
  LJ - v122 - Ja '97 - p156 [51-250]
Fisher, Sue - *Gardener's World*
  BL - v92 - Ag '96 - p1870 [51-250]
Fisher, Sue, 1936- - *Nursing Wounds*
  CS - v25 - S '96 - p694+ [501+]
  MHR - v10 - Fall '96 - p119+ [501+]

Fisher, William Scott - *New York City Methodist Marriages 1785-1893. Vols. 1-2*
    Am Geneal - v71 - O '96 - p256 [251-500]
Fishkin, James S - *The Voice of the People*
    APSR - v90 - S '96 - p625+ [501+]
    PSQ - v111 - Fall '96 - p534+ [501+]
Fishkin, Shelley Fisher - *Lighting Out for the Territory*
    Econ - v342 - Mr 15 '97 - p13*+ [501+]
    KR - v64 - N 1 '96 - p1579 [251-500]
    LATBR - Ja 26 '97 - p3+ [501+]
    LJ - v122 - Ja '97 - p98 [51-250]
    NYTBR - v102 - Ja 19 '97 - p19 [51-250]
    PW - v243 - N 18 '96 - p54+ [51-250]
Fishlock, Trevor - *My Foreign Country*
    Obs - Ap 6 '97 - p15* [501+]
Fishman, Alfred P - *Pulmonary Rehabilitation*
    SciTech - v20 - S '96 - p36 [51-250]
Fishman, Cathy Goldberg - *On Passover (Illus. by Melanie W Hall)*
    c BL - v93 - Mr 1 '97 - p1165 [51-250]
    c KR - v65 - Ap 1 '97 - p553+ [51-250]
    c PW - v244 - F 24 '97 - p83 [51-250]
Fishman, David E - *Russia's First Modern Jews*
    Slav R - v55 - Sum '96 - p466+ [501+]
Fishman, Nina - *The British Communist Party and the Trade Unions 1933-45*
    S&S - v61 - Spr '97 - p143+ [501+]
Fishman, Stephen - *Wage Slave No More*
    LJ - v122 - Ap 15 '97 - p99 [51 250]
Fishman, Sylvia Barack - *A Breath of Life*
    Signs - v22 - Aut '96 - p234+ [501+]
Fisk, E K - *Hardly Ever a Dull Moment*
    Pac A - v69 - Sum '96 - p301+ [501+]
Fisk, Josiah - *Composers on Music. 2nd Ed.*
    LJ - v121 - D '96 - p95 [51-250]
    PW - v243 - D 9 '96 - p66 [1-50]
Fisk, William Lyons - *The Scottish High Church Tradition in America*
    CH - v65 - D '96 - p736+ [501+]
    Historian - v58 - Sum '96 - p858 [251-500]
Fiske, Jane Fletcher - *The New England Historical and Genealogical Register: Index of Persons, Volumes 51-148. Vols. 1-4*
    r Am Geneal - v71 - Jl '96 - p188 [51-250]
Fiske, Peter - *To Boldy Go...*
    BioSci - v46 - D '96 - p876 [51-250]
Fiske, Robert Hartwell - *The Writer's Digest Dictionary of Concise Writing*
    r ARBA - v28 - '97 - p350 [51-250]
    r Choice - v34 - Ja '97 - p768+ [51-250]
The Fiske Guide to Colleges 1997
    yr Kliatt - v30 - N '96 - p24 [51-250]
Fiss, Owen M - *The Irony of Free Speech*
    ABA Jour - v82 - O '96 - p100 [501+]
    y BL - v93 - S 1 '96 - p40 [51-250]
    BW - v26 - S 8 '96 - p5 [501+]
    Choice - v34 - Ja '97 - p874 [51-250]
    JMCQ - v73 - Win '96 - p1004+ [501+]
    NYTBR - v101 - S 22 '96 - p32 [501+]
    Pub Int - Win '97 - p119+ [501+]
Liberalism Divided
    Choice - v34 - O '96 - p358+ [501+]
Fissel, Mark Charles - *The Bishops' Wars*
    EHR - v111 - S '96 - p983+ [251-500]
Fist, Stewart - *The Informatics Handbook*
    r Choice - v34 - Ja '97 - p769 [51-250]
Fister, Barbara - *Third World Women's Literature*
    r RQ - v35 - Sum '96 - p565+ [251-500]
Fiszel, Geoffrey L - *How to Start Your Own Private Investment Partnership*
    R&R Bk N - v12 - F '97 - p64 [51-250]
Fitt, Sally Sevey - *Dance Kinesiology. 2nd Ed.*
    Choice - v34 - My '97 - p1511 [51-250]
Fitter, Chris - *Poetry, Space, Landscape*
    MLN - v111 - D '96 - p1054+ [251-500]
Fitterling, Thomas - *Thelonious Monk: His Life and Music*
    PW - v244 - My 5 '97 - p186 [51-250]
Fittipaldi, Teodoro - *Il Museo Di San Martino De Napoli*
    Choice - v34 - D '96 - p570 [1-50]
Fitts, Karen - *Left Margins*
    Col Comp - v47 - O '96 - p424+ [501+]
Fitzball, Edward - *The Inchcape Bell. Did You Ever Send Your Wife to Camberwell? The Game of Speculation. The Lights o' London. The Middleman*
    ELT - v39 - 3 '96 - p404 [51-250]
Fitzgerald, Astrid - *An Artist's Book of Inspiration*
    Parabola - v21 - Ag '96 - p120 [1-50]
Fitzgerald, Bernadette - *The Language of Reading*
    y Sch Lib - v45 - F '97 - p50 [51-250]
    y TES - N 22 '96 - p20* [51-250]

FitzGerald, Eileen - *You're So Beautiful*
    NYTBR - v101 - N 17 '96 - p14 [501+]
    NYTBR - v101 - D 8 '96 - p84 [1-50]
Fitzgerald, F Scott - *F. Scott Fitzgerald on Authorship*
    AB - v99 - Ja 27 '97 - p226+ [501+]
    BL - v93 - S 1 '96 - p33 [1-50]
    Bloom Rev - v17 - Ja '97 - p12 [251-500]
    Choice - v34 - Mr '97 - p1161 [51-250]
    LATBR - Ja 19 '97 - p9 [501+]
F. Scott Fitzgerald: The Princeton Years
    LJ - v121 - N 15 '96 - p62 [51-250]
The Jazz Age
    HMR - Win '96 - p12+ [501+]
    LJ - v121 - S 15 '96 - p102 [51-250]
A Life in Letters
    HMR - Win '96 - p8+ [501+]
The Love of the Last Tycoon
    RES - v47 - Ag '96 - p450+ [501+]
The Short Stories of F. Scott Fitzgerald
    HMR - Win '96 - p12+ [501+]
This Side of Paradise
    AL - v68 - S '96 - p662 [51-250]
    LJ - v121 - N 15 '96 - p93 [51-250]
Fitzgerald, Frank T - *The Cuban Revolution in Crisis*
    Parameters - v26 - Win '96 - p158 [1-50]
    S&S - v61 - Sum '97 - p280+ [501+]
Fitzgerald, John, 1951- - *Awakening China*
    Choice - v34 - My '97 - p1554 [51-250]
    LJ - v121 - D '96 - p116 [51-250]
Fitzgerald, John D - *The Great Brain Is Back (Illus. by Diane DeGroat)*
    c RT - v50 - Mr '97 - p498 [51-250]
Fitzgerald, John F - *African Greenhouse Gas Emission Inventories and Mitigation Options*
    SciTech - v20 - D '96 - p70 [51-250]
Fitzgerald, Judith - *Habit of Blues*
    Can Lit - Win '96 - p167+ [501+]
Fitzgerald, Karen - *The Story of Oxygen*
    c HB Guide - v8 - Spr '97 - p112 [51-250]
    c SLJ - v42 - S '96 - p214 [51-250]
Fitzgerald, Keith - *The Face of the Nation*
    Choice - v34 - D '96 - p688 [51-250]
Fitzgerald, Matthew - *Harvey's Wish (Illus. by Jean Pidgeon)*
    c RT - v50 - O '96 - p136+ [1-50]
Fitzgerald, Oscar P - *Four Centuries of American Furniture*
    r Ant & CM - v101 - Jl '96 - p25 [1-50]
FitzGerald, Patrick - *Managing Sustainable Development in South Africa*
    Choice - v34 - Ja '97 - p845+ [51-250]
    JEL - v34 - D '96 - p2108+ [51-250]
Fitzgerald, Penelope - *The Blue Flower*
    BW - v27 - Ap 6 '97 - p3+ [501+]
    KR - v65 - F 15 '97 - p241 [251-500]
    LATBR - Ap 13 '97 - pB [501+]
    NYTBR - v102 - Ap 13 '97 - p9 [501+]
    Obs - S 8 '96 - p18* [51-250]
    PW - v244 - Mr 10 '97 - p51+ [51-250]
    Woman's J - S '96 - p10 [51-250]
    WSJ-Cent - v99 - Ap 8 '97 - pA20 [501+]
Fitzgerald, Robert - *Rowntree and the Marketing Revolution 1862-1969*
    Albion - v28 - '96 - p725+ [501+]
    EHR - v112 - Ap '97 - p522+ [501+]
Fitzgerald, Thomas E - *The Orthodox Church*
    CH - v65 - D '96 - p781+ [51-250]
Fitz-Gibbon, Sally - *The Patchwork House (Illus. by Dean Griffiths)*
    c BIC - v26 - F '97 - p33 [251-500]
Fitzgibbons, Athol - *Adam Smith's System of Liberty, Wealth, and Virtue*
    APSR - v90 - S '96 - p626+ [501+]
Fitzharris, Tim - *Nature Photography*
    LATBR - My 12 '96 - p11 [51-250]
Fitzhugh, Bill - *Pest Control*
    BW - v27 - Mr 23 '97 - p11 [501+]
    Ent W - Mr 14 '97 - p74 [51-250]
    KR - v65 - Ja 15 '97 - p79 [251-500]
    PW - v244 - F 3 '97 - p95 [51-250]
Fitzhugh, Louise - *Harriet the Spy*
    c HMR - Win '96 - p45 [1-50]
    y SFR - v21 - S '96 - p48 [51-250]
FitzHugh, Terrick - *How to Write a Family History*
    TES - Jl 26 '96 - pR6 [51-250]
Fitzmaurice, Gabriel - *The Village Sings*
    BL - v92 - Ag '96 - p1876 [51-250]
    c Sch Lib - v44 - N '96 - p167 [51-250]
Fitzmaurice, John - *Damming the Danube*
    R&R Bk N - v11 - N '96 - p31 [51-250]

Fitzmaurice, Mick - *Morris Macmillipede (Illus. by Satoshi Kitamura)*
    c Bks Keeps - Jl '96 - p11 [51-250]
Fitzmyer, Joseph A - *Spiritual Exercises Based on Paul's Epistle to the Romans*
    RR - v55 - N '96 - p653+ [51-250]
Fitzpatrick, James E - *Dermatology Secrets*
    SciTech - v20 - D '96 - p54 [51-250]
Fitzpatrick, Mary Anne - *Explaining Family Interactions*
    JMF - v58 - N '96 - p1044+ [251-500]
Fitzpatrick, Sheila - *Stalin's Peasants*
    AHR - v101 - O '96 - p1249+ [501+]
    EHR - v111 - N '96 - p1339+ [501+]
    VQR - v73 - Win '97 - p34* [1-50]
Fitzpatrick, Sonya - *What the Animals Tell Me*
    PW - v244 - Ap 28 '97 - p67 [51-250]
Fitzroy Dearborn Directory of the World's Banks. 11th Ed.
    r ARBA - v28 - '97 - p94 [251-500]
    r Choice - v34 - Ap '97 - p1307 [51-250]
Fitzsimmons, Cecilia - *Animal Habitats (Illus. by Adam Hook)*
    c HB Guide - v7 - Fall '96 - p335+ [51-250]
Creatures of the Past
    c HB Guide - v7 - Fall '96 - p333 [51-250]
Fruit (Illus. by Cecilia Fitzsimmons)
    c Sch Lib - v44 - N '96 - p162 [51-250]
Vegetables and Herbs (Illus. by Cecilia Fitzsimmons)
    c Sch Lib - v44 - N '96 - p162 [51-250]
Water Life (Illus. by Helen Ward)
    c HB Guide - v7 - Fall '96 - p335+ [51-250]
Fitzsimmons, Michael P - *The Remaking of France*
    EHR - v112 - F '97 - p219+ [251-500]
Fitzsimmons, Richard - *Pro-Choice/Pro-Life Issues in the 1990s*
    r R&R Bk N - v11 - D '96 - p40 [1-50]
Fitzsimmons, Thomas - *The New Poetry of Japan--the 70s and 80s*
    TranslRevS - v1 - My '95 - p3 [1-50]
Fitzwater, Marlin - *Call the Briefing!*
    JMCQ - v73 - Aut '96 - p755+ [501+]
    NYTBR - v101 - N 17 '96 - p40 [51-250]
Fivaz, Bill - *The Cherrypickers' Top 150*
    r Coin W - v38 - Ja 6 '97 - p98 [51-250]
Five, Cora Lee - *Bridging the Gap*
    JAAL - v40 - F '97 - p412+ [501+]
Five Little Ducks (Story Web Series). Electronic Media Version
    c SLJ - v43 - F '97 - p49+ [51-250]
Five Points
    p LJ - v121 - D '96 - p158 [51-250]
Fix, Michael - *Setting the Record Straight*
    BW - v26 - D 15 '96 - p4 [1-50]
Fizel, John - *Baseball Economics*
    Choice - v34 - Ap '97 - p1385 [51-250]
Fjardo, Laurie L - *A Comprehensive Approach to Stereotactic Breast Biopsy*
    SciTech - v20 - S '96 - p40 [51-250]
Fjellheim, Freddy O - *Rov: Folkelivsskildring*
    WLT - v70 - Sum '96 - p713+ [501+]
Flachenecker, Helmut - *Schotenkloster: Irische Benediktinerkonvente Im Hochmittelalterlichen Deutschland*
    CHR - v82 - Jl '96 - p530+ [501+]
Flamhaft, Ziva - *Israel on the Road to Peace*
    Choice - v34 - N '96 - p532 [51-250]
    For Aff - v75 - N '96 - p163+ [51-250]
    MEQ - v3 - S '96 - p83 [251-500]
Flamm, Kenneth - *Mismanaged Trade?*
    Choice - v34 - Ap '97 - p1386 [51-250]
    JEL - v35 - Mr '97 - p213 [51-250]
    R&R Bk N - v12 - F '97 - p42 [51-250]
Flamming, Douglas - *Creating the Modern South*
    T&C - v38 - Ja '97 - p253+ [501+]
Flanagan, Alice K - *A Busy Day at Mr. Kang's Grocery Store (Illus. by Christine Osinski)*
    c HB Guide - v8 - Spr '97 - p91 [51-250]
    c SLJ - v42 - D '96 - p112 [51-250]
Call Mr. Vasquez, He'll Fix It! (Illus. by Christine Osinski)
    c HB Guide - v8 - Spr '97 - p91 [51-250]
    c SLJ - v42 - D '96 - p112 [51-250]
Desert Birds
    c HB Guide - v7 - Fall '96 - p343 [51-250]
    c SLJ - v42 - Ag '96 - p136 [51-250]
Masks!
    c HB Guide - v7 - Fall '96 - p318 [1-50]
    c SLJ - v42 - N '96 - p112 [51-250]

Ms. Davison, Our Librarian (Illus. by Christine Osinski)
c BL - v93 - Ja '97 - p863 [251-500]
c HB Guide - v8 - Spr '97 - p91 [51-250]
c SLJ - v43 - F '97 - p90 [51-250]
Night Birds
c HB Guide - v7 - Fall '96 - p343 [51-250]
c SLJ - v42 - Ag '96 - p136 [51-250]
Riding the Ferry with Captain Cruz (Illus. by Christine Osinski)
c BL - v93 - Ja '97 - p863 [251-500]
c HB Guide - v8 - Spr '97 - p91 [51-250]
c SLJ - v43 - F '97 - p90 [51-250]
Seabirds
c HB Guide - v7 - Fall '96 - p343 [51-250]
c SLJ - v42 - Ag '96 - p136 [51-250]
Songbirds
c HB Guide - v7 - Fall '96 - p343 [51-250]
c SLJ - v42 - D '96 - p112+ [51-250]
Talking Birds
c HB Guide - v7 - Fall '96 - p343 [51-250]
c SLJ - v42 - D '96 - p112+ [51-250]
The Wilsons, a House-Painting Team (Illus. by Christine Osinski)
c HB Guide - v8 - Spr '97 - p91 [51-250]
c SLJ - v43 - F '97 - p90 [51-250]
Flanagan, Brenda - *You Alone Are Dancing*
KR - v64 - My 1 '96 - p639 [51-250]
NYTBR - v101 - O 27 '96 - p39 [51-250]
Flanagan, David - *JavaScript: The Definitive Guide. 2nd Ed.*
r LJ - v122 - Ap 1 '97 - p118 [51-250]
Flanagan, Dawn P - *Contemporary Intellectual Assessment*
Adoles - v32 - Spr '97 - p245 [51-250]
Choice - v34 - My '97 - p1579 [51-250]
Flanagan, E M, Jr. - *Rakkasans: The Combat History of the 187th Airborne Infantry*
KR - v65 - F 1 '97 - p191 [251-500]
Flanagan, Geraldine Lux - *Beginning Life*
BW - v26 - O 20 '96 - p8 [51-250]
y VOYA - v19 - F '97 - p344+ [251-500]
Flanagan, Jana Ricketts - *Vision 2001*
SciTech - v20 - S '96 - p48 [51-250]
Flanagan, Kieran - *The Enchantment of Sociology*
Choice - v34 - N '96 - p545 [51-250]
Flanagan, Owen - *Self Expressions*
Choice - v34 - S '96 - p214 [51-250]
Flanagan, Timothy J - *Americans View Crime and Justice*
R&R Bk N - v11 - N '96 - p46 [51-250]
Flandrin, Jean-Louis - *Histoire De L'Alimentation*
TLS - Ja 31 '97 - p9 [501+]
Flannery, Edward H - *The Anguish of the Jews. Rev. Ed.*
Rel Ed - v91 - Fall '96 - p606 [1-50]
Flannery, Kathryn T - *The Emperor's New Clothes*
Col Comp - v47 - O '96 - p424+ [501+]
Flannery, Kent V - *Early Formative Pottery of the Valley of Oaxaca*
LA Ant - v7 - Mr '96 - p86+ [501+]
Flannery, Kevin L - *Ways into the Logic of Alexander of Aphrodisias*
CPR - v16 - O '96 - p345+ [501+]
Flannery, Mary - *Fountain House*
Adoles - v32 - Spr '97 - p245+ [51-250]
Flannery, Sean - *Kilo Option (Griffin). Audio Version*
y Kliatt - v31 - My '97 - p41 [51-250]
Flannery, T F - *Tree Kangaroos*
Nature - v385 - F 20 '97 - p692 [501+]
Flannery, Tim - *The Future Eaters*
New Sci - v152 - N 23 '96 - p47 [51-250]
Flashar, Hellmut - *Altertumswissenschaft In Den 20er Jahren*
Choice - v34 - D '96 - p566 [1-50]
Flaubert, Gustave - *Flaubert in Egypt*
TLS - O 4 '96 - p7 [501+]
Madame Bovary (Pickup). Audio Version
TLS - Ag 2 '96 - p24 [51-250]
Salammbo
MLN - v111 - S '96 - p625+ [501+]
A Simple Heart
TranslRevS - v2 - D '96 - p22+ [51-250]
Flaumenhaft, Mera J - *The Civic Spectacle*
RP - v59 - Win '97 - p127+ [501+]
Flavell, Linda - *Dictionary of Word Origins*
r ARBA - v28 - '97 - p380 [51-250]
Flawia De Fernandez, Nilda Maria - *Miradas, Versiones Y Escrituras*
BL - v93 - Mr 15 '97 - p1232 [1-50]
Fleagle, John G - *Anthropoid Origins*
Am Sci - v84 - S '96 - p502 [251-500]
Fleddermann, Harry T - *Mark and Q*
Rel St Rev - v23 - Ap '97 - p182+ [51-250]

Fleener, Mary - *Life of the Party*
BL - v93 - N 15 '96 - p562 [51-250]
Fleetwood, William C, Jr. - *Tidecraft: The Boats of South Carolina, Georgia and Northeastern Florida 1550-1950. 2nd Ed.*
Sea H - Sum '96 - p30+ [51-250]
Flegg, Columba Graham - *Gathered under Apostles*
CH - v65 - D '96 - p750+ [501+]
Fleisch, Herbert - *Bisphosphonates in Bone Disease. 2nd Ed.*
SciTech - v20 - D '96 - p48 [51-250]
Fleischman, Paul - *Bull Run*
y Kliatt - v30 - S '96 - p3 [1-50]
Bull Run. Audio Version
c HB - v72 - S '96 - p566+ [501+]
c SLJ - v42 - N '96 - p70 [51-250]
Dateline: Troy (Illus. by Gwen Frankfeldt)
y BL - v93 - Ap 1 '97 - p1286 [1-50]
y Emerg Lib - v23 - My '96 - p43 [1-50]
y HB Guide - v7 - Fall '96 - p320 [51-250]
c Magpies - v11 - Jl '96 - p33+ [51-250]
c NYTBR - v101 - O 13 '96 - p26 [251-500]
c RT - v50 - D '96 - p345 [51-250]
y VOYA - v19 - D '96 - p285+ [251-500]
A Fate Totally Worse than Death
y JB - v60 - O '96 - p200+ [51-250]
y RT - v50 - O '96 - p141 [1-50]
y Sch Lib - v44 - Ag '96 - p117 [51-250]
Rear View Mirrors
y JAAL - v40 - D '96 - p318 [51-250]
Seedfolks (Illus. by Judy Pedersen)
c BL - v93 - My 15 '97 - p1573 [51-250]
c HB - v73 - My '97 - p320 [51-250]
c KR - v65 - My 1 '97 - p720 [51-250]
c PW - v244 - Ap 7 '97 - p93 [51-250]
Fleischman, Paul R - *Cultivating Inner Peace*
LJ - v122 - My 1 '97 - p110 [51-250]
Fleischman, Sid - *The 13th Floor (Illus. by Peter Sis)*
c New Ad - v9 - Fall '96 - p327+ [501+]
c RT - v50 - Mr '97 - p499 [51-250]
The 13th Floor (Adamson). Audio Version
c BL - v93 - S 15 '96 - p264 [51-250]
c HB - v72 - S '96 - p566+ [501+]
The Abracadabra Kid
c BL - v93 - Ja '97 - p764 [1-50]
c BL - v93 - S 1 '96 - p126 [51-250]
y BL - v93 - Ap 1 '97 - p1286 [1-50]
y BL - v93 - Ap 1 '97 - p1302 [1-50]
c CBRS - v25 - S '96 - p12 [51-250]
y CCB-B - v50 - S '96 - p11+ [51-250]
c HB - v72 - N '96 - p758 [251-500]
c HB Guide - v8 - Spr '97 - p157 [51-250]
c NYTBR - v101 - N 10 '96 - p46+ [501+]
c PW - v243 - Jl 22 '96 - p243 [51-250]
c SLJ - v42 - Ag '96 - p154+ [51-250]
c SLJ - v42 - D '96 - p29 [1-50]
Jingo Django (Dufris). Audio Version
c BL - v93 - N 1 '96 - p522 [51-250]
The Midnight Horse (Illus. by Peter Sis)
c SLJ - v42 - N '96 - p40 [1-50]
The Whipping Boy (Illus. by Peter Sis)
c JOYS - v10 - Fall '96 - p35+ [501+]
Fleischner, Jennifer - *The Dred Scott Case*
c BL - v93 - My 1 '97 - p1491 [51-250]
Mastering Slavery
Choice - v34 - Ja '97 - p794 [51-250]
Nine-C Lit - v51 - Mr '97 - p556 [51-250]
Fleisher, Mark S - *Beggars and Thieves*
AJS - v102 - S '96 - p626+ [501+]
Fleisher, Paul - *Life Cycles of a Dozen Diverse Creatures*
c BL - v93 - Ja '97 - p766 [1-50]
c BL - v93 - D 1 '96 - p659 [51-250]
c Ch BWatch - v7 - F '97 - p5 [1-50]
c HB Guide - v8 - Spr '97 - p117 [51-250]
c SLJ - v43 - Ja '97 - p123 [51-250]
Fleisser, Marieluise - *Die List: Fruhe Erzahlungen*
WLT - v71 - Win '97 - p136 [251-500]
Fleming, Candace - *Madame LaGrande and Her So High, to the Sky, Uproarious Pompadour (Illus. by S D Schindler)*
c HB Guide - v7 - Fall '96 - p256 [51-250]
c KR - v64 - My 1 '96 - p687 [51-250]
Women of the Lights (Illus. by James Watling)
c HB Guide - v7 - Fall '96 - p376 [51-250]
Fleming, Dan - *Power Play*
TES - D 6 '96 - p7* [501+]
Fleming, Deborah - *A Man Who Does Not Exist*
ELT - v40 - 1 '97 - p127 [51-250]
Fleming, Denise - *Barnyard Banter*
c TES - Mr 28 '97 - p11* [1-50]

Count! (Illus. by Denise Fleming)
c BL - v93 - Ap 1 '97 - p1340+ [1-50]
c PW - v244 - Ja 27 '97 - p108 [51-250]
Where Once There Was a Wood (Illus. by Denise Fleming)
c AB - v98 - N 18 '96 - p1731 [51-250]
c BL - v93 - Ap 1 '97 - p1296 [1-50]
c HB Guide - v7 - Fall '96 - p256 [51-250]
c Inst - v106 - Mr '97 - p27+ [1-50]
Fleming, John V - *Classical Imitation and Interpretation in Chaucer's Troilus*
Comp L - v48 - Fall '96 - p377+ [501+]
Fleming, Lee - *Hot Licks*
Advocate - S 17 '96 - p60 [1-50]
Rock, Rhythm and Reels
Quill & Q - v63 - Mr '97 - p75 [251-500]
Fleming, M C - *Instat: International Statistics Sources. Vols. 1-2*
r ARBA - v28 - '97 - p325 [51-250]
Fleming, Robert - *Rescuing a Neighborhood (Illus. by Porter Gifford)*
c RT - v50 - O '96 - p142 [1-50]
The Success of Caroline Jones Advertising, Inc. (Illus. by Michael Harris)
y HB Guide - v7 - Fall '96 - p313 [1-50]
Fleming, Robert, 1950- - *The Wisdom of the Elders*
Bl S - v26 - Sum '96 - p64 [51-250]
Fleming, Sibley - *How to Rock Your Baby (Illus. by John Amoss)*
c PW - v244 - Mr 3 '97 - p74 [51-250]
Flemmig, Jorg - *Moderne Makrookonomik*
JEL - v34 - D '96 - p2119 [1-50]
Flesch, Rudolf - *The Classic Guide to Better Writing*
LJ - v121 - O 1 '96 - p132 [1-50]
Flesh and the Word 4
PW - v244 - Ap 21 '97 - p62 [51-250]
Fletcher, Anne M - *Eating Thin for Life*
PW - v243 - N 18 '96 - p72 [51-250]
Fletcher, Anthony - *Gender, Sex and Subordination in England 1500-1800*
Albion - v28 - Win '96 - p689+ [501+]
EHR - v112 - Ap '97 - p419+ [501+]
HT - v47 - Ja '97 - p52 [501+]
Six Ct J - v27 - Win '96 - p1233+ [501+]
W&M Q - v54 - Ja '97 - p266+ [501+]
Religion, Culture and Society in Early Modern Britain
EHR - v111 - N '96 - p1271+ [501+]
Fletcher, Banister, Sir - *Sir Banister Fletcher's A History of Architecture. 20th Ed.*
r TLS - N 1 '96 - p8 [501+]
Fletcher, Colin - *River: One Man's Journey Down the Colorado, Source to Sea*
BW - v27 - Ap 13 '97 - p10 [501+]
KR - v65 - F 15 '97 - p269+ [251-500]
LJ - v122 - Ap 1 '97 - p117 [51-250]
PW - v244 - Mr 17 '97 - p69 [51-250]
Fletcher, Ian - *Napoleonic Wars: Wellington's Army*
HT - v46 - O '96 - p57 [1-50]
Fletcher, J M W - *Edward Willis Redfield 1869-1965*
Choice - v34 - Mr '97 - p1150+ [51-250]
Fletcher, John Gould - *Selected Letters of John Gould Fletcher*
Choice - v34 - N '96 - p455+ [51-250]
Fletcher, Marilyn - *Readers Guide to Twentieth-Century Science Fiction*
r RQ - v36 - Win '96 - p224 [51-250]
Fletcher, Ralph - *Buried Alive (Illus. by Andrew Moore)*
y BL - v93 - Ap 1 '97 - p1306 [1-50]
y HB Guide - v7 - Fall '96 - p367 [51-250]
y HMR - Win '96 - p47+ [501+]
y VOYA - v19 - O '96 - p228 [51-250]
Ordinary Things (Illus. by Walter Lyon Krudop)
y KR - v65 - Mr 15 '97 - p460 [51-250]
Spider Boy
c CCB-B - v50 - Ap '97 - p281 [51-250]
c KR - v65 - Mr 15 '97 - p460 [51-250]
What a Writer Needs
Inst - v106 - N '96 - p41 [1-50]
Fletcher, Roland - *The Limits of Settlement Growth*
AJA - v101 - Ja '97 - p162+ [501+]
Am Ant - v61 - O '96 - p799+ [501+]
Fletcher, Sheila - *Victorian Girls*
Spec - v278 - Mr 1 '97 - p35+ [501+]
Fletcher, Susan - *Sign of the Dove*
c Ch BWatch - v6 - O '96 - p3 [51-250]
c HB - v72 - S '96 - p595 [51-250]
c HB Guide - v7 - Fall '96 - p291+ [51-250]
Fletcher, William A - *Rebel Private*
JSH - v62 - N '96 - p816+ [251-500]

Fletcher-Campbell, Felicity - *The Resourcing of Special Educational Needs*
LAR - v98 - S '96 - p480 [1-50]

Fleurant, Gerdes - *Dancing Spirits*
Choice - v34 - My '97 - p1508 [51-250]
R&R Bk N - v12 - F '97 - p70 [51-250]

Fleutiaux, Pierrette - *Allons-Nous Etre Heureux?*
FR - v70 - F '97 - p497+ [251-500]

Flewelling, Lynn - *Luck in the Shadows*
y Kliatt - v31 - Ja '97 - p12 [251-250]
Stalking Darkness
y Kliatt - v31 - My '97 - p12 [51-250]

Flexner, Eleanor - *Century of Struggle. Enl. Ed.*
y Kliatt - v31 - Mr '97 - p30 [51-250]

Flichy, Patrice - *Dynamics of Modern Communication*
JMCQ - v73 - Win '96 - p998+ [501+]

Fliegel, Larry - *The Na+/H+ Exchanger*
SciTech - v20 - S '96 - p23 [51-250]

Flier, Michael S - *Medieval Russian Culture. Vol.2*
MLR - v91 - Jl '96 - p810+ [501+]

Flinn, Denny Martin - *Musical! A Grand Tour*
TCI - v30 - O '96 - p59 [1-50]

Flint, Betty M - *Pathways to Maturity*
R&R Bk N - v11 - D '96 - p43 [51-250]

Flint, David - *Bosnia: Can There Ever Be Peace?*
c HB Guide - v7 - Fall '96 - p380 [51-250]
Geography and Change
y TES - Mr 28 '97 - pR7 [251-500]
Great Britain
c HB Guide - v8 - Spr '97 - p168 [51-250]
South Africa
c HB Guide - v8 - Spr '97 - p171 [51-250]

Flint, Kate - *Victorian Love Stories*
BL - v93 - O 1 '96 - p324 [51-250]
Econ - v341 - N 16 '96 - p17* [251-500]
PW - v243 - O 21 '96 - p69 [51-250]
TLS - D 13 '96 - p25 [501+]
The Woman Reader 1837-1914
ELT - v39 - 3 '96 - p405 [51-250]

Flippo, Hyde - *The German Way*
r BL - v93 - S 15 '96 - p212 [1-50]

Flitter, Marc - *Judith's Pavilion*
BL - v93 - Ap 1 '97 - p1273 [51-250]
BW - v27 - Mr 30 '97 - p13 [51-250]
KR - v65 - F 15 '97 - p270 [251-500]
LJ - v122 - Ap 15 '97 - p106 [51-250]
PW - v244 - F 17 '97 - p201 [51-250]

Floca, Brian - *The Frightful Story of Harry Walfish (Illus. by Brian Floca)*
c BL - v93 - Ap 1 '97 - p1333+ [51-250]
c CBRS - v25 - Ap '97 - p98 [51-250]
c KR - v65 - F 1 '97 - p222 [51-250]
c SLJ - v43 - Mr '97 - p152 [51-250]

Flood, Elizabeth Clair - *Rocky Mountain Home*
R&R Bk N - v12 - F '97 - p74 [51-250]

Flood, Gavin - *An Introduction to Hinduism*
Choice - v34 - Ja '97 - p810+ [51-250]

Flood, John, 1962- - *Bag Men*
BL - v93 - Ja '97 - p824 [51-250]
KR - v64 - N 1 '96 - p1550+ [251-500]
LJ - v121 - D '96 - p142 [51-250]
NYTBR - v102 - F 16 '97 - p18 [251-500]
PW - v243 - N 25 '96 - p56+ [51-250]
Trib Bks - F 16 '97 - p6 [51-250]
WSJ-Cent - v99 - F 5 '97 - pA16 [51-250]

Flood, John L - *The German Book 1450-1750*
BC - v45 - Win '96 - p571+ [501+]
Lib - v19 - Mr '97 - p84+ [501+]
Six Ct J - v27 - Win '96 - p1182+ [501+]

Flood, Lawrence - *Unions and Public Policy*
APSR - v91 - Mr '97 - p186+ [501+]

Flood, Nancy Bohac - *From the Mouth of the Monster Eel (Illus. by Margo Vitarelli)*
c Ch BWatch - v6 - Jl '96 - p1 [1-50]
c HB Guide - v8 - Spr '97 - p101 [51-250]

Flood, Patrick C - *Managing without Traditional Methods*
Per Psy - v50 - Spr '97 - p191+ [501+]

Flood, Robert P - *Speculative Bubbles, Speculative Attacks and Policy Switching*
Econ J - v107 - Ja '97 - p213+ [501+]

Flook, Maria - *You Have the Wrong Man*
LATBR - Mr 17 '96 - p10 [51-250]

Flora, Kate - *Death at the Wheel*
KR - v64 - S 1 '96 - p1275 [51-250]
LJ - v121 - O 1 '96 - p131 [51-250]
PW - v243 - S 23 '96 - p59+ [51-250]

Florack, Ruth - *Wedekinds Lulu*
Ger Q - v70 - Win '97 - p90+ [501+]

Florence, Gene - *Elegant Glassware of the Depression Era. 7th Ed.*
r Ant & CM - v101 - F '97 - p33 [251-500]

Florence (Duchy) - *Provvisioni Concernenti L'Ordinamento Della Repubblica Fiorentina 1494-1512. Vol. 1*
EHR - v112 - F '97 - p184 [251-500]

Florencio Puntas, Antonio - *Empresariado Agricola Y Cambio Economico 1880-1936*
HAHR - v76 - N '96 - p796+ [501+]

Flores, Philip J - *Group Psychotherapy with Addicted Populations. 2nd Ed.*
SciTech - v21 - Mr '97 - p55 [1-50]

Flores, Richard R - *Los Pastores: History and Performance in the Mexican Shepherd's Play of South Texas*
Choice - v34 - N '96 - p467 [51-250]
WHQ - v28 - Spr '97 - p102 [1-50]

Flores D'Arcais, Francesca - *Giotto*
BM - v138 - O '96 - p698+ [501+]

Flori, Monica - *Streams of Silver*
MLR - v92 - Ap '97 - p497+ [501+]

Florian, Douglas - *In the Swim (Illus. by Douglas Florian)*
c BL - v93 - Mr 15 '97 - p1245 [51-250]
c CCB-B - v50 - My '97 - p320 [51-250]
c KR - v65 - F 15 '97 - p298 [51-250]
c PW - v244 - Mr 10 '97 - p68 [51-250]
c Trib Bks - Ap 13 '97 - p7 [51-250]
On the Wing (Illus. by Douglas Florian)
c HB Guide - v7 - Fall '96 - p367 [1-50]
c Inst - v106 - Mr '97 - p30 [51-250]
c RT - v50 - My '97 - p685 [51-250]

Florian, John - *Practical Thermoforming*
SciTech - v20 - D '96 - p84 [51-250]

Florida Cuban Heritage Trail
J Gov Info - v23 - S '96 - p580+ [51-250]

Florida (Insight Compact Guides)
r BL - v93 - S 15 '96 - p210 [1-50]

Florman, Samuel C - *The Existential Pleasures of Engineering*
Reason - v28 - D '96 - p42 [51-250]
The Introspective Engineer
NYTBR - v102 - F 9 '97 - p32 [1-50]
SciTech - v20 - N '96 - p81 [51-250]
Trib Bks - F 16 '97 - p8 [1-50]

Flory, Wayne Seelye - *The Gnostic Concept of Authority and the Nag Hammadi Documents*
Rel St Rev - v23 - Ap '97 - p188 [51-250]

Floud, Roderick - *The Economic History of Britain since 1700. 2nd Ed., Vols. 1-3*
Econ J - v107 - Ja '97 - p204+ [501+]

Floudas, C A - *State of the Art in Global Optimization*
SciTech - v20 - S '96 - p11 [51-250]

Flournoy, Theodore - *From India to the Planet Mars*
Lon R Bks - v18 - My 23 '96 - p3+ [501+]

Flournoy, Valerie - *The Patchwork Quilt (Illus. by Jerry Pinkney)*
c Learning - v25 - Mr '97 - p54 [1-50]
Tanya's Reunion (Illus. by Jerry Pinkney)
c LA - v73 - S '96 - p356 [51-250]
c RT - v50 - S '96 - p55 [51-250]
c RT - v50 - N '96 - p243 [51-250]

Flournoy, Vanessa - *Celie and the Harvest Fiddler (Illus. by James E Ransome)*
c HB Guide - v7 - Fall '96 - p256 [51-250]
c RT - v50 - O '96 - p158 [51-250]

Flow-Induced Vibration 1996
SciTech - v20 - N '96 - p82 [51-250]

Flower, Celeste - *Diaries and Letters*
y TES - S 20 '96 - pR6 [251-500]

Flower, Michael A - *Theopompus of Chios: History and Rhetoric in the Fourth Century B.C.*
AJP - v117 - Fall '96 - p495+ [501+]
Rel St Rev - v22 - O '96 - p345 [51-250]

Flowerdew, Bob - *The Complete Book of Fruit*
BL - v92 - Ag '96 - p1870 [51-250]

Flowers, Robin - *Computing for Site Managers*
SciTech - v20 - S '96 - p52 [51-250]

Flowers, Sandra Hollin - *African American Nationalist Literature of the 1960s*
AL - v69 - Mr '97 - p249+ [51-250]

Flowers, Sarah - *The Reformation*
y HB Guide - v7 - Fall '96 - p382 [51-250]
Sports in America
c BL - v93 - S 1 '96 - p71 [51-250]
y HB Guide - v8 - Spr '97 - p144 [51-250]

Floyd, Elaine - *Advertising from the Desktop*
CBR - v14 - S '96 - p27 [1-50]

Floyd, Maita - *Stolen Years*
SS - v87 - S '96 - p233+ [501+]

Floyd, Malcolm - *World Musics in Education*
R&R Bk N - v11 - N '96 - p59 [51-250]
TES - S 13 '96 - pR11 [251-500]

Floyd, Samuel A, Jr. - *The Power of Black Music*
BW - v26 - D 1 '96 - p12 [51-250]
Notes - v53 - Mr '97 - p812+ [501+]
NYTBR - v101 - D 29 '96 - p20 [1-50]

Floyd, Thomas L - *Digital Fundamentals. 6th Ed.*
SciTech - v20 - D '96 - p77 [51-250]
Electronic Devices. 4th Ed.
SciTech - v20 - S '96 - p57 [1-50]
Principles of Electric Circuits. 5th Ed.
SciTech - v20 - D '96 - p74 [51-250]
SciTech - v21 - Mr '97 - p86 [51-250]

Flueckiger, Gerald E - *Control, Information, and Technological Change*
JEL - v34 - S '96 - p1411 [51-250]

Flueckiger, Joyce Burkhalter - *Gender and Genre in the Folklore of Middle India*
Choice - v34 - Ap '97 - p1322 [51-250]

Flugel, Maria - *Dinosaurs and Other Prehistoric Animals*
c Ch BWatch - v6 - My '96 - p1 [51-250]

Flugge, Manfred - *Le Tourbillon De La Vie*
FR - v70 - F '97 - p484+ [501+]

Fluid Power Systems and Technology 1996
SciTech - v21 - Mr '97 - p85 [51-250]

Fluid-Structure Interaction 1996
SciTech - v20 - D '96 - p85 [1-50]

Flusfeder, David - *Like Plastic*
TLS - S 6 '96 - p22 [501+]

Flusser, Alan - *Style and the Man*
NYTLa - v146 - D 2 '96 - pC16 [51-250]

Flynn, Gerard - *The Aesthetic Code of Don Ramon Del Valle-Inclan*
Hisp - v79 - D '96 - p788+ [501+]

Flynn, James - *One Hundred Centuries of Solitude*
Env - v38 - O '96 - p25 [51-250]

Flynn, Keith - *The Book of Monsters*
Sm Pr R - v28 - O '96 - p12 [251-500]

Flynn, Michael F - *Firestar*
MFSF - v91 - S '96 - p44 [51-250]
New Sci - v152 - O 5 '96 - p50 [51-250]
The Forest of Time and Other Stories
BL - v93 - Mr 15 '97 - p1231 [51-250]
KR - v65 - F 1 '97 - p177 [51-250]
LJ - v122 - Mr 15 '97 - p93 [1-50]
PW - v244 - Mr 24 '97 - p64 [251-500]

Flynn, Peter - *World Wide Web Handbook*
CBR - v14 - Jl '96 - p22 [1-50]

Flynn, T T - *Rawhide: A Western Quintet*
PW - v243 - O 14 '96 - p66 [51-250]

Flynn, Thomas M - *Cryogenic Engineering*
SciTech - v20 - D '96 - p83 [51-250]

Flynn, Warren - *Different Voices*
y Magpies - v11 - My '96 - p47+ [251-500]

Flynt, Larry - *An Unseemly Man*
NYRB - v44 - F 6 '97 - p25+ [501+]
PW - v243 - O 21 '96 - p62 [51-250]

Flyway
p LMR - v15 - Win '96 - p7+ [501+]

Fobel, Jim - *Jim Fobel's Casseroles*
BL - v93 - F 15 '97 - p988 [51-250]
LJ - v122 - Mr 15 '97 - p84 [51-250]
PW - v243 - D 16 '96 - p55 [51-250]

Fodor, James - *Christian Hermeneutics*
Theol St - v57 - D '96 - p758+ [501+]

Fodor's Canada 1997
r Quill & Q - v63 - F '97 - p41 [51-250]

Foege, Alec - *The Empire God Built*
BL - v93 - S 15 '96 - p182 [51-250]
LJ - v121 - S 15 '96 - p72+ [51-250]
PW - v243 - S 30 '96 - p73 [51-250]

Foerstel, Karen - *Climbing the Hill*
Choice - v34 - S '96 - p210 [51-250]

Foerster, Andreas - *Institutional Analysis of Development Administration*
JEL - v34 - D '96 - p2115 [51-250]

Fogel, Joshua A - *The Literature of Travel in the Japanese Rediscovery of China 1862-1945*
AHR - v102 - F '97 - p156+ [501+]
Ch Rev Int - v4 - Spr '97 - p127+ [501+]

Fogelin, Robert J - *Pyrrhonian Reflections on Knowledge and Justification*
IPQ - v37 - Mr '97 - p115+ [501+]

Fogg, Martyn - *Terraforming*
Reason - v28 - D '96 - p45 [51-250]

Fogg Art Museum - *David to Corot*
Choice - v34 - Ja '97 - p784 [51-250]

Fogle, Bruce - *Cocker Spaniel*
y BL - v93 - Ap 1 '97 - p1306 [1-50]
German Shepherd
SB - v32 - N '96 - p234 [51-250]
Golden Retriever
y BL - v93 - Ap 1 '97 - p1306 [1-50]

Labrador Retriever
  y BL - v93 - Ap 1 '97 - p1306 [1-50]
     SB - v32 - N '96 - p234 [51-250]
Fogleman, Aaron Spencer - *Hopeful Journeys*
     Choice - v34 - S '96 - p193+ [51-250]
     NGSQ - v84 - D '96 - p307+ [251-500]
Foglesong, David S - *America's Secret War against*
Bolshevism
     HRNB - v25 - Fall '96 - p11 [251-500]
     Pres SQ - v26 - Fall '96 - p1170+ [501+]
     RAH - v24 - D '96 - p624+ [501+]
Fogo, Rod - *Descendants of John Fogo and Mary Lambie*
  r EGH - v50 - N '96 - p193+ [51-250]
Folan, Ciaran - *Freak Nights*
     BL - v93 - Mr 15 '97 - p1224 [51-250]
Folberg, Neil - *And I Shall Dwell among Them*
     R&R Bk N - v12 - F '97 - p9 [51-250]
Folbre, Nancy - *The Economics of the Family*
     JEL - v34 - D '96 - p2067 [51-250]
     R&R Bk N - v11 - D '96 - p40 [51-250]
The New Field Guide to the U.S. Economy
  y VOYA - v19 - D '96 - p286 [251-500]
Who Pays for the Kids?
     Signs - v22 - Win '97 - p440+ [501+]
Folda, Jaroslav - *The Art of the Crusaders in the Holy*
Land 1098-1187
     BM - v139 - Ja '97 - p45+ [501+]
     Choice - v34 - O '96 - p266+ [51-250]
Folding and Design
  p Nature - v383 - S 5 '96 - p37 [251-500]
Foley, Daniel J - *Christmas in the Good Old Days*
     CAY - v17 - Win '96 - p11 [51-250]
Foley, Douglas E - *The Heartland Chronicles*
     CS - v25 - S '96 - p643+ [501+]
Foley, Edward - *Foundations of Christian Music*
     CH - v66 - Mr '97 - p185+ [51-250]
Foley, Erin - *Costa Rica*
  c Ch BWatch - v7 - Ja '97 - p3 [1-50]
El Salavador
  y JOYS - v9 - Sum '96 - p415 [51-250]
Foley, Helene P - *The Homeric Hymn to Demeter*
     JAAR - v64 - Sum '96 - p439+ [501+]
     Rel St Rev - v23 - Ap '97 - p171 [51-250]
Foley, John Miles - *Immanent Art*
     CAY - v16 - Fall '95 - p12 [51-250]
The Singer of Tales in Performance
     Rel St Rev - v23 - Ap '97 - p161 [51-250]
**Foley, Michael, 1947- ** - *The Road to Notown*
     KR - v65 - F 15 '97 - p241 [251-500]
**Foley, Michael, 1948- ** - *Congress and the Presidency*
     Choice - v34 - O '96 - p360 [51-250]
Foley, Mike - *Fundamental Hockey (Illus. by Andy King)*
  c HB Guide - v7 - Fall '96 - p360 [1-50]
Foley, Robert - *Humans before Humanity*
     Lon R Bks - v18 - O 31 '96 - p36+ [501+]
     New Sci - v153 - Mr 22 '97 - p45 [51-250]
Foley, Timothy P - *Gender and Colonialism*
     ILS - v15 - Fall '96 - p9 [501+]
Foley, Todd - *The Microsoft Exchange Guide*
     SciTech - v21 - Mr '97 - p11 [51-250]
Foley, Tom - *Measuring Lives*
     KR - v64 - N 1 '96 - p1551 [251-500]
     LJ - v121 - D '96 - p142 [51-250]
     PW - v243 - N 4 '96 - p65 [51-250]
Folger, Joseph P - *New Directions in Mediation*
     QJS - v82 - Ag '96 - p310+ [501+]
Folger Collective on Early Women Critics (Scholarly
Group) - *Women Critics 1660-1820*
     Choice - v34 - S '96 - p120 [51-250]
Foliot, Gilbert - *Letters and Charters of Gilbert Foliot*
     EHR - v111 - S '96 - p952+ [501+]
Folkard, Margaret - *Sundials Australia*
     S&T - v92 - D '96 - p66 [51-250]
Folkemer, Donna - *Adult Foster Care for the Elderly.*
Vols. 1-2
     ACI - v9 - Spr '97 - p39+ [501+]
Folkers, Gladys - *Taking Charge of My Mind and Body*
  y PW - v244 - Mr 10 '97 - p69 [51-250]
Folkert, Kendall W - *Scripture and Community*
     Rel St Rev - v23 - Ap '97 - p113+ [501+]
Follett, James - *Sabre*
     Books - v11 - Ap '97 - p22 [1-50]

Follett, Ken - *The Third Twin*
     BL - v93 - S 1 '96 - p29 [51-250]
     CSM - v88 - N 14 '96 - p14 [51-250]
     CSM - v89 - D 19 '96 - p14 [51-250]
     CSM - v89 - Ja 16 '97 - p14 [51-250]
     Ent W - D 6 '96 - p58+ [51-250]
     KR - v64 - S 1 '96 - p1255 [251-500]
     LJ - v121 - S 15 '96 - p95 [51-250]
     PW - v243 - S 2 '96 - p109 [51-250]
  y SLJ - v43 - F '97 - p134 [51-250]
The Third Twin (Venora). Audio Version
     LJ - v122 - Ja '97 - p173 [51-250]
     PW - v243 - N 4 '96 - p30 [51-250]
Follett, Mary Parker - *Prophet of Management*
     BHR - v70 - Aut '96 - p405+ [501+]
Follis, Bryan A - *A State under Siege*
     AHR - v101 - D '96 - p1549+ [501+]
Folse, Keith S - *Discussion Starters*
     MLJ - v81 - Spr '97 - p124+ [501+]
Folsing, Albrecht - *Albert Einstein: A Biography*
     BL - v93 - F 15 '97 - p985 [51-250]
     BW - v27 - Mr 30 '97 - p4 [501+]
     KR - v65 - Ja 1 '97 - p35 [251-500]
     LJ - v122 - F 15 '97 - p159 [51-250]
     NYRB - v44 - Ap 10 '97 - p14+ [501+]
     PW - v244 - F 10 '97 - p76+ [51-250]
Folz, David H - *Survey Research for Public Administration*
     Choice - v34 - O '96 - p353 [51-250]
Fombrun, Charles J - *Reputation: Realizing Value from*
the Corporate Image
     Bus Bk R - v13 - 3 '96 - p72+ [501+]
Fomby, Thomas B - *Bayesian Methods Applied to Time*
Series Data
     JEL - v34 - D '96 - p2018 [51-250]
Fonda, Jane - *Jane Fonda: Cooking for Healthy Living*
     NYTBR - v101 - D 8 '96 - p70+ [251-500]
Foner, Eric - *Freedom's Lawmakers. Rev. Ed.*
  r BL - v93 - F 15 '97 - p1041+ [51-250]
  r BW - v26 - S 15 '96 - p12 [51-250]
Foner, Philip S - *First Facts of American Labor*
  r RQ - v36 - Fall '96 - p50 [1-50]
Fones-Wolf, Elizabeth A - *Selling Free Enterprise*
     ASInt - v34 - O '96 - p95+ [501+]
     CH - v65 - S '96 - p541+ [251-500]
Fong, Glenn Randall - *Export Dependence Versus the*
New Protectionism
     JEL - v34 - S '96 - p1426 [51-250]
Fonseca, Isabel - *Bury Me Standing*
     Choice - v34 - Ap '97 - p1380 [251-500]
  y Kliatt - v31 - Ja '97 - p24 [51-250]
     Lon R Bks - v18 - Ag 22 '96 - p16 [501+]
     NYTBR - v102 - F 9 '97 - p32 [51-250]
     PW - v243 - S 9 '96 - p81 [1-50]
     Tikkun - v11 - S '96 - p92+ [501+]
     Trib Bks - Ja 12 '97 - p2 [1-50]
Fontana, Biancamaria - *The Invention of the Modern*
Republic
     EHR - v112 - F '97 - p222+ [501+]
Fontana, Joseph - *The Distorted Past*
     HAHR - v76 - Ag '96 - p550+ [251-500]
Fontana, Marco - *Prufer Domains*
     SciTech - v20 - D '96 - p16 [51-250]
Fontane, Theodor - *Effi Briest*
     TranslRevS - v2 - D '96 - p25 [51-250]
Fontanel, Beatrice - *Babies: History, Art and Folklore*
     KR - v65 - Mr 15 '97 - p453 [51-250]
     PW - v244 - Ap 14 '97 - p68 [1-50]
Fonte, Moderata - *Tredici Canti Del Floridoro*
     MLN - v112 - Ja '97 - p114+ [501+]
Fontenay, Charles L - *Kipton: Murder on Stage*
  c Cur R - v36 - D '96 - p12 [51-250]
Fontenay, Patrick De - *Western Europe in Transition*
     J Gov Info - v23 - S '96 - p672+ [51-250]
Fontenelle, M. De - *Elements De La Geometrie De*
L'Infini
     Isis - v87 - S '96 - p549+ [501+]
Fontenot, Mary Alice - *Clovis Crawfish and Bidon Box*
Turtle (Illus. by Scott R Blazek)
  c HB Guide - v7 - Fall '96 - p256 [51-250]
Clovis Ecrevisse Et Bidon Tortue Terrestre (Illus. by
Scott R Blazek)
  c HB Guide - v7 - Fall '96 - p327 [51-250]
Clovis Ecrevisse Et L'Oiseau Orphelin (Illus. by Eric
Vincent)
  c HB Guide - v8 - Spr '97 - p108 [51-250]
Fontes, Montserrat - *Dreams of the Centaur*
     PW - v244 - Mr 24 '97 - p81 [1-50]
Food (Snapshot)
  c PW - v244 - Ja 6 '97 - p74 [1-50]
Food and Beverage Market Place 1996
  r ARBA - v28 - '97 - p569 [51-250]

Food Lover's Companion to France
  r BL - v93 - S 15 '96 - p206+ [1-50]
Food Lover's Companion to Italy
  r BL - v93 - S 15 '96 - p206+ [1-50]
Food Processing Automation IV
     Robotica - v15 - Mr '97 - p233 [251-500]
Foon, Dennis - *Mirror Game*
  y Can CL - v22 - Sum '96 - p40+ [501+]
New Candadian Kid. Invisible Kids
  y Can CL - v22 - Sum '96 - p40+ [501+]
Seesaw
  y Can CL - v22 - Sum '96 - p40+ [501+]
Skin. Liars
  y Can CL - v22 - Sum '96 - p40+ [501+]
War
  y Can CL - v22 - Sum '96 - p40+ [501+]
Foos, Laurie - *Ex Utero*
     PW - v243 - S 2 '96 - p122 [1-50]
Portrait of the Walrus by a Young Artist
     BL - v93 - My 1 '97 - p1478 [51-250]
     KR - v65 - F 15 '97 - p242 [251-500]
     LJ - v122 - Ap 1 '97 - p124+ [51-250]
     PW - v244 - Ap 28 '97 - p48 [51-250]
Foot, David - *Wally Hammond: The Reasons Why*
     TLS - D 6 '96 - p31 [501+]
Foot, David K - *Boom, Bust, and Echo*
     BIC - v25 - O '96 - p2+ [501+]
Boom, Bust and Echo
     CF - v75 - D '96 - p39+ [501+]
     Mac - v109 - D 9 '96 - p64 [1-50]
Boom, Bust, and Echo
     Quill & Q - v62 - My '96 - p30 [501+]
Foot, Michael - *H.G.: The History of Mr. Wells*
     ELT - v40 - 1 '97 - p86+ [501+]
     SF Chr - v18 - O '96 - p81 [1-50]
Foot, Paul - *Murder at the Farm*
     Obs - Ap 13 '97 - p18* [251-500]
Foot, Rosemary - *The Practice of Power*
     APSR - v91 - Mr '97 - p230+ [501+]
Foote, Horton - *Collected Plays. Vol. 2*
     BL - v93 - S 15 '96 - p203 [251-500]
     LJ - v121 - S 15 '96 - p68 [51-250]
Foote, Kenneth E - *Re-Reading Cultural Geography*
     SSQ - v77 - Je '96 - p460+ [501+]
Foote, Shelby - *The Correspondence of Shelby Foote and*
Walker Percy
     Choice - v34 - Ap '97 - p1335 [51-250]
     Comw - v124 - F 28 '97 - p24+ [51-250]
     KR - v64 - O 1 '96 - p1456 [251-500]
     LJ - v121 - N 15 '96 - p62 [51-250]
     NYTBR - v101 - D 1 '96 - p27 [51-250]
     NYTBR - v101 - D 8 '96 - p85 [1-50]
     PW - v243 - O 14 '96 - p75 [51-250]
     Trib Bks - My 25 '97 - p5 [501+]
Forabosco, Giovannantonio - *Il Settimo Senso*
     Humor - v9 - 3 '96 - p399+ [501+]
Foran, Charles - *Butterfly Lovers*
     BIC - v25 - D '96 - p21+ [501+]
     Mac - v109 - S 23 '96 - p66 [501+]
     Quill & Q - v62 - Jl '96 - p53 [251-500]
Forbath, Peter - *Lord of the Kongo*
     BL - v93 - N 1 '96 - p481 [51-250]
     KR - v64 - S 15 '96 - p1341+ [251-500]
     NYTBR - v102 - Mr 16 '97 - p21 [51-250]
     PW - v243 - O 14 '96 - p64 [51-250]
Lord of the Kongo (Caulfield). Audio Version
     LJ - v122 - Ap 1 '97 - p145 [51-250]
Forbes, Anna - *Kids with AIDS*
  c SLJ - v43 - Ja '97 - p99+ [51-250]
When Someone You Know Has AIDS
  c SLJ - v42 - D '96 - p128 [51-250]
Where Did AIDS Come From?
  c SLJ - v42 - D '96 - p128 [51-250]
Forbes, Charles D - *Color Atlas and Text of Clinical*
Medicine. 2nd Ed.
  r SciTech - v21 - Mr '97 - p48 [51-250]
Forbes, Edith - *Exit to Reality*
     KR - v65 - Ap 1 '97 - p509 [51-250]
     PW - v244 - Mr 17 '97 - p75 [51-250]
Nowle's Passing
     Bloom Rev - v16 - Jl '96 - p21 [1-50]
Forbes, Gordon - *Too Soon to Panic*
     KR - v65 - Mr 15 '97 - p435 [251-500]
     PW - v244 - Mr 10 '97 - p55 [51-250]
Forbes, Robert Bennet - *Letters from China*
     Sea H - Win '96 - p46+ [51-250]
Forceville, Charles - *Pictorial Metaphor in Advertising*
     R&R Bk N - v11 - N '96 - p36 [51-250]
Forche, Carolyn - *The Angel of History*
     Salm - Sum '96 - p195+ [501+]

Forciea, Mary Ann - *Geriatric Secrets*
  SciTech - v20 - D '96 - p48 [1-50]
Ford, Alan - *As by Law Established*
  CH - v65 - D '96 - p777+ [501+]
Ford, Barbara - *The Most Wonderful Movie in the World*
  c HB Guide - v8 - Spr '97 - p66 [51-250]
  c KR - v64 - My 1 '96 - p688 [51-250]
Ford, Brent A - *Project Earth Science*
  c SB - v32 - Ag '96 - p179 [51-250]
Ford, Brian - *BSE: The Facts*
  Lon R Bks - v18 - S 5 '96 - p17+ [501+]
Ford, Charles Howard - *Hannah More: A Critical Biography*
  Choice - v34 - Mr '97 - p1160 [51-250]
  R&R Bk N - v12 - F '97 - p85 [51-250]
Ford, Charles V - *Lies! Lies!! Lies!!!*
  Readings - v11 - S '96 - p31 [51-250]
Ford, Donna Y - *Reversing Underachievement among Gifted Black Students*
  Choice - v34 - F '97 - p1014 [51-250]
  HER - v67 - Spr '97 - p154+ [501+]
Ford, Ford Madox - *The Good Soldier*
  ELT - v40 - 2 '97 - p133+ [501+]
Ford, G M - *The Bum's Rush*
  PW - v244 - Mr 10 '97 - p53 [51-250]
  Trib Bks - My 4 '97 - p4 [51-250]
Cast in Stone
  Arm Det - v29 - Fall '96 - p495+ [51-250]
  y SLJ - v43 - Ja '97 - p140 [51-250]
Who in Hell Is Wanda Fuca?
  Arm Det - v29 - Sum '96 - p280+ [51-250]
  PW - v243 - S 23 '96 - p74 [1-50]
  Rapport - v19 - 4 '96 - p30 [251-500]
Ford, Glyn - *Changing States*
  TLS - D 20 '96 - p29 [501+]
Ford, J L - *G.L.S. Shackle: The Dissenting Economist's Economist*
  Econ J - v107 - Ja '97 - p243+ [501+]
Ford, John T - *Religious Liberty*
  Rel St Rev - v23 - Ap '97 - p153 [51-250]
Ford, Joseph B - *Sorokin and Civilization*
  R&R Bk N - v11 - N '96 - p38 [51-250]
Ford, Kenneth L - *Aunt Minnie's Atlas and Imaging-Specific Diagnosis*
  r SciTech - v21 - Mr '97 - p49 [51-250]
Ford, Kenneth M - *Android Epistemology*
  Robotica - v14 - N '96 - p697+ [501+]
The Robot's Dilemma Revisited
  BYTE - v21 - N '96 - p38 [251-500]
Ford, Michael Thomas - *Voices of AIDS*
  y Emerg Lib - v24 - S '96 - p23 [1-50]
The World Out There
  y VOYA - v19 - F '97 - p345 [251-500]
Ford, Miela - *Follow the Leader (Illus. by Miela Ford)*
  c HB Guide - v8 - Spr '97 - p12 [1-50]
  c SLJ - v42 - S '96 - p177 [51-250]
What Color Was the Sky Today? (Illus. by Sally Noll)
  c BL - v93 - My 1 '97 - p1501 [51-250]
  c SLJ - v43 - Mr '97 - p152 [51-250]
Ford, R A - *Homemade Lightning. 2nd Ed.*
  y SB - v32 - O '96 - p206 [51-250]
Ford, Richard - *Independence Day*
  Bloom Rev - v16 - Jl '96 - p22 [501+]
  NS - v125 - D 20 '96 - p116 [51-250]
  Reason - v28 - D '96 - p53+ [501+]
  S Liv - v31 - Jl '96 - p80 [51-250]
Wildlife
  Obs - O 20 '96 - p18* [51-250]
Women with Men
  BL - v93 - My 15 '97 - p1540 [51-250]
  PW - v244 - My 12 '97 - p57 [51-250]
Ford, Simon - *The Realization and Suppression of the Situationist International*
  r ARBA - v28 - '97 - p364 [251-500]
Ford, Thomas - *A History of Illinois*
  WHQ - v27 - Win '96 - p544+ [251-500]
Ford, Trowbridge H - *Henry Brougham and His World*
  Albion - v28 - Fall '96 - p508+ [501+]
Fordham, David - *Traditional Hymns*
  BWatch - v17 - D '96 - p1 [51-250]
Fordham, John - *Shooting from the Hip*
  LJ - v121 - O 1 '96 - p79 [51-250]
Fordham, Michael - *Analyst-Patient Interaction*
  SciTech - v20 - N '96 - p43 [1-50]
Fordham, Signithia - *Blacked Out*
  AJE - v105 - My '97 - p351+ [501+]
  Bl S - v26 - Fall '96 - p102 [1-50]
  HER - v66 - Win '96 - p887+ [501+]
Fordham, Walter - *Iliana: A Winter Solstice Tale (Illus. by Tatjana Krizmanic)*
  c Tric - v6 - Win '96 - p117 [1-50]

Forecasting the Future
  E Mag - v8 - Mr '97 - p49 [1-50]
  y SB - v32 - O '96 - p203+ [251-500]
Forehand, Rex - *Parenting the Strong-Willed Child*
  Readings - v11 - D '96 - p29 [51-250]
Foreign Policy in Focus
  p WorldV - v13 - Ja '97 - p13+ [51-250]
Foreman, Freddie - *Respect*
  Books - v10 - Je '96 - p21 [1-50]
Foreman, Gordon P - *PC Buyer's Handbook: Summer 1996*
  LJ - v121 - O 1 '96 - p120 [51-250]
Foreman, Martin - *The Butterfly's Wing*
  LJ - v121 - O 1 '96 - p126 [51-250]
Foreman, Michael - *After the War Was Over (Illus. by Michael Foreman)*
  c BW - v26 - Jl 7 '96 - p15 [51-250]
  c Smith - v27 - N '96 - p167 [1-50]
The Little Reindeer (Illus. by Michael Foreman)
  c Bks Keeps - N '96 - p21 [1-50]
  c JB - v60 - D '96 - p231 [1-50]
Seal Surfer (Illus. by Michael Foreman)
  c BL - v93 - My 1 '97 - p1501 [51-250]
  c Books - v10 - Je '96 - p25 [51-250]
  c CCB-B - v50 - My '97 - p320 [51-250]
  c JB - v60 - O '96 - p183 [51-250]
  c PW - v244 - Mr 24 '97 - p83 [51-250]
  c Sch Lib - v44 - Ag '96 - p105+ [51-250]
  c SLJ - v43 - Mr '97 - p152 [51-250]
Surprise! Surprise! (Illus. by Michael Foreman)
  c HB Guide - v7 - Fall '96 - p256 [51-250]
Foreman, Richard - *No-Body*
  KR - v64 - D 15 '96 - p1753 [251-500]
  LJ - v122 - Mr 15 '97 - p88 [51-250]
  NYTBR - v102 - Ap 6 '97 - p21 [51-250]
  PW - v244 - Ja 27 '97 - p79 [51-250]
Foreman-Peck, James - *The British Motor Industry*
  Econ J - v106 - S '96 - p1476 [51-250]
Public and Private Ownership of British Industry 1820-1990
  EHR - v111 - N '96 - p1335+ [251-500]
Smith and Nephew in the Health Care Industry
  JEH - v56 - S '96 - p717+ [501+]
Forest, Edward - *Interactive Marketing*
  Choice - v34 - N '96 - p503 [51-250]
Forest, Heather - *A Big Quiet House (Illus. by Susan Greenstein)*
  c BL - v93 - O 1 '96 - p353+ [51-250]
  c Bloom Rev - v17 - Ja '97 - p21 [51-250]
  c Ch BWatch - v7 - F '97 - p3 [1-50]
  c HB Guide - v8 - Spr '97 - p101 [51-250]
  c PW - v243 - O 7 '96 - p74 [51-250]
  c SFR - v21 - S '96 - p47 [501+]
  c SLJ - v42 - N '96 - p97 [51-250]
Wisdom Tales from around the World
  c BL - v93 - Mr 1 '97 - p1157 [51-250]
  c CCB-B - v50 - F '97 - p204 [51-250]
  c HB Guide - v8 - Spr '97 - p101 [51-250]
  c KR - v64 - O 15 '96 - p1531 [51-250]
  c PW - v243 - D 2 '96 - p62 [51-250]
Forest, Jim - *Praying with Icons*
  BL - v93 - F 15 '97 - p976 [501+]
Forest, Philippe - *Histoire De Tel Quel 1960-1982*
  Lon R Bks - v18 - D 12 '96 - p5+ [501+]
  WLT - v71 - Win '97 - p113 [501+]
Forest Insect and Disease Conditions in the United States 1994
  J Gov Info - v23 - S '96 - p567 [51-250]
Forest Resources Assessment 1990
  J Gov Info - v23 - S '96 - p670 [51-250]
The Forest Service Program for Forest and Rangeland Resources
  J Gov Info - v23 - S '96 - p567+ [51-250]
Foresta, Merry A - *American Photographs*
  Choice - v34 - My '97 - p1486 [51-250]
  LJ - v122 - Mr 15 '97 - p60 [51-250]
  Mag Antiq - v151 - Ja '97 - p32 [251-500]
Forester, C S - *Rifleman Dodd*
  Mar Crp G - v80 - Ag '96 - p74 [501+]
Forestier, Georges - *Essai De Genetique Theatrale*
  MLR - v92 - Ap '97 - p466+ [501+]
Forey, Alan - *Military Orders and Crusades*
  CHR - v82 - Jl '96 - p536+ [501+]
Forgacs, Eva - *The Bauhaus Idea and Bauhaus Politics*
  CEH - v29 - 2 '96 - p259+ [501+]
Forge, Andrew - *Monet*
  BM - v138 - S '96 - p615 [1-50]
Willem De Kooning: Sculpture
  BM - v138 - Ag '96 - p565+ [501+]

Forget, Evelyn L - *The Peasant in Economic Thought*
  Econ J - v106 - S '96 - p1464 [51-250]
  JEL - v34 - D '96 - p2011 [51-250]
Forkroads: A Journal of Ethnic-American Literature
  p LMR - v15 - Fall '96 - p11+ [501+]
Forman, F N - *Mastering British Politics*
  CR - v269 - S '96 - p160+ [501+]
Forman, Paul - *National Military Establishments and the Advancement of Science and Technology*
  Nature - v383 - S 12 '96 - p136 [501+]
  Sci - v274 - N 29 '96 - p1476 [501+]
  SciTech - v20 - D '96 - p87 [51-250]
Forman, Richard T T - *Land Mosaics*
  GJ - v162 - N '96 - p342 [51-250]
Forman, Werner - *Hieroglyphs and the Afterlife in Ancient Egypt*
  Parabola - v21 - Ag '96 - p120 [1-50]
Formica, Marina - *La Citta E La Rivoluzione*
  EHR - v111 - N '96 - p1304+ [251-500]
Formula I Motor Racing Book
  c BL - v93 - D 15 '96 - p723 [51-250]
Fornberg, Tord - *Texts and Contexts*
  Rel St Rev - v23 - Ja '97 - p68+ [51-250]
Forni, Giovanna Maria - *Monument: Antichi Di Roma Nei Disegni Di Alberto Alberti*
  Ren Q - v50 - Spr '97 - p319+ [501+]
Forni, Pier Massimo - *Adventures in Speech*
  Choice - v34 - N '96 - p464 [51-250]
Forrest, Alan - *The Revolution in Provincial France*
  TLS - F 28 '97 - p30 [501+]
Forrest, Duncan - *A Glimpse of Hell*
  Choice - v34 - My '97 - p1566 [51-250]
Forrest, Elizabeth - *Killjoy*
  y Kliatt - v30 - S '96 - p16 [51-250]
Forrest, Katherine V - *Liberty Square*
  Advocate - S 17 '96 - p60 [1-50]
  Arm Det - v29 - Fall '96 - p494 [51-250]
  BL - v93 - S 1 '96 - p67 [51-250]
Forrest, Martin - *History KS2*
  TES - D 13 '96 - p43 [51-250]
Forrest, Peter - *God without the Supernatural*
  Choice - v34 - F '97 - p978 [51-250]
Forrest, Tim - *The Bulfinch Anatomy of Antique Furniture*
  r LATBR - D 8 '96 - p4 [51-250]
Forrester, James W - *Being Good and Being Logical*
  R&R Bk N - v11 - N '96 - p3 [51-250]
Forrester, John - *Dispatches from the Freud Wars*
  KR - v65 - F 1 '97 - p192 [251-500]
Forrester, Mary Gore - *Persons, Animals, and Fetuses*
  R&R Bk N - v11 - D '96 - p4 [51-250]
Forrester, Susan - *The Educational Funding Guide*
  yr TES - S 27 '96 - p8* [51-250]
Fors, Gunnar - *R&D and Technology Transfer by Multinational Enterprises*
  JEL - v35 - Mr '97 - p280 [51-250]
Forsen, Jeannette - *The Twilight of the Early Helladics*
  AJA - v100 - Jl '96 - p611+ [501+]
Forshaw, James Michael - *Birding*
  r E Mag - v7 - N '96 - p50 [51-250]
Forster, Colin - *France and Botany Bay*
  Aust Bk R - O '96 - p18+ [501+]
Forster, E M - *Maurice (Firth). Audio Version*
  LJ - v121 - N 1 '96 - p121 [51-250]
A Room with a View. Audio Version
  Quill & Q - v62 - Jl '96 - p52 [1-50]
Where Angels Fear to Tread (Fry). Audio Version
  TLS - Ag 2 '96 - p24 [1-50]
Forster, Elke M - *Protection or Liberalization?*
  R&R Bk N - v12 - F '97 - p41 [51-250]
Forster, Marc R - *The Counter-Reformation in the Villages*
  CHR - v82 - O '96 - p720+ [501+]
Forster, Margaret - *Hidden Lives*
  CR - v269 - N '96 - p277 [51-250]
  TES - S 6 '96 - p8* [51-250]
  Woman's J - Ag '96 - p11 [1-50]
Forster, Peter G - *The Tanzanian Peasantry*
  R&R Bk N - v11 - N '96 - p31 [51-250]
Forster, R A - *Character Witness*
  PW - v244 - Mr 3 '97 - p71 [51-250]
Forster, Suzanne - *Innocence*
  PW - v244 - Ja 13 '97 - p72 [51-250]
Forsyth, Ann - *Monster Maze (Illus. by S Holmes)*
  c JB - v60 - Ag '96 - p148 [51-250]
  c TES - Jl 5 '96 - pR6 [1-50]

Forsyth, Frederick - *Icon*
  y BL - v93 - S 1 '96 - p29 [51-250]
    Econ - v341 - D 7 '96 - p3*+ [501+]
    Nat R - v48 - D 23 '96 - p56 [51-250]
    NYTBR - v101 - N 3 '96 - p19 [51-250]
  y SLJ - v43 - Mr '97 - p214+ [51-250]
    TLS - S 6 '96 - p22 [501+]
  Icon (Lang). Audio Version
    BWatch - v18 - Mr '97 - p7 [1-50]
  y Kliatt - v31 - My '97 - p40 [51-250]
Forsyth, Murray - *The Political Classics*
    Choice - v34 - Ap '97 - p1417 [51-250]
Forsyth, William H - *The Pieta in French Late Gothic Sculpture*
    Six Ct J - v27 - Fall '96 - p879+ [501+]
    Specu - v72 - Ja '97 - p147+ [501+]
Fort, Andrew O - *Living Liberation in Hindu Thought*
    Rel St Rev - v23 - Ja '97 - p96 [51-250]
Forta, Arye - *Judaism: A Dictionary*
  yr Sch Lib - v45 - F '97 - p51 [51-250]
Forte, Allen - *The American Popular Ballad of the Golden Era 1924-1950*
    TLS - Jl 19 '96 - p18+ [501+]
Forte, Dieter - *Der Junge Mit Den Blutigen Schuhen*
    WLT - v70 - Sum '96 - p682+ [501+]
Forte, Maurizio - *Virtual Archaeology*
    KR - v65 - Mr 15 '97 - p453 [51-250]
Fortenbaugh, William W - *Peripatetic Rhetoric after Aristotle*
    QJS - v82 - Ag '96 - p321+ [501+]
Fortin, John R - *Clarembald of Arras as a Boethian Commentator*
    CH - v66 - Mr '97 - p188 [51-250]
Fortino, Andres - *Multivendor Networking*
    CBR - v14 - S '96 - p30 [51-250]
  Networking Technologies
    CBR - v15 - Spr '97 - p1 [1-50]
Forum on Research and Technology Advances in Digital Libraries (3rd: 1996: Washington, DC) - *Forum on Research and Technology Advances in Digital Libraries*
    R&R Bk N - v11 - N '96 - p80 [51-250]
Forward, Robert L - *Saturn Rukh*
    KR - v65 - Ja 15 '97 - p103+ [51-250]
    LJ - v122 - F 15 '97 - p165 [51-250]
    PW - v244 - F 24 '97 - p68 [51-250]
Forward, Susan - *Emotional Blackmail*
    PW - v244 - Ap 21 '97 - p54 [51-250]
Forward, Toby - *Ben's Christmas Carol (Illus. by Ruth Brown)*
  c BL - v93 - S 1 '96 - p136 [51-250]
  c CBRS - v25 - D '96 - p38 [51-250]
  c Ch BWatch - v6 - D '96 - p1 [1-50]
  c HB - v72 - N '96 - p723 [51-250]
  c HB Guide - v8 - Spr '97 - p27 [51-250]
  c PW - v243 - S 30 '96 - p89 [51-250]
  c SLJ - v42 - O '96 - p35+ [51-250]
  The Christmas Mouse (Illus. by Ruth Brown)
  c Bks Keeps - N '96 - p20 [51-250]
  c JB - v60 - D '96 - p231 [51-250]
  c Sch Lib - v44 - N '96 - p146 [51-250]
  c TES - D 6 '96 - p17* [501+]
  Making Faces (Illus. by James Marsh)
  c Obs - Mr 30 '97 - p17* [51-250]
  Pie Magic (Illus. by Laura Cornell)
  c HB - v72 - S '96 - p595 [51-250]
  c HB Guide - v8 - Spr '97 - p66 [51-250]
  Wyvern Fall
  c Bks Keeps - v100 - S '96 - p10 [51-250]
Fosdick, Lloyd D - *An Introduction to High-Performance Scientific Computing*
    Phys Today - v49 - D '96 - p55+ [501+]
    SciTech - v20 - N '96 - p6 [51-250]
Foskett, A C - *The Subject Approach to Information. 5th Ed.*
    LAR - v99 - Ja '97 - p49 [51-250]
Foss, Christopher F - *Jane's Tank and Combat Vehicle Recognition Guide*
  r ARBA - v28 - '97 - p259+ [51-250]
  r BL - v93 - F 15 '97 - p1042 [51-250]
Foss, Jason - *Lady in the Lake*
    KR - v65 - Mr 15 '97 - p419+ [51-250]
    LJ - v122 - Ap 1 '97 - p133 [51-250]
    PW - v244 - F 24 '97 - p67 [51-250]
Foss, Maureen - *The Cadillac Kind*
    BIC - v25 - O '96 - p39+ [51-250]
Fossati, Amedeo - *Economic Modelling under the Applied General Equilibrium Approach*
    JEL - v34 - S '96 - p1413+ [51-250]
Fossey, Dian - *Gorillas in the Mist*
  y BL - v93 - Ja '97 - p832 [1-50]

Foster, Alan Dean - *Dinotopia Lost*
    SF Chr - v18 - O '96 - p78+ [51-250]
  Greenthieves
    LJ - v121 - D '96 - p154 [1-50]
  The Howling Stones
    LJ - v122 - F 15 '97 - p164+ [51-250]
    PW - v244 - Ja 27 '97 - p81 [51-250]
  Jed the Dead
    PW - v243 - D 30 '96 - p64 [51-250]
  Mad Amos
    MFSF - v91 - Ag '96 - p29+ [501+]
Foster, Andy - *Radio Comedy 1938-1968*
    Spec - v277 - N 16 '96 - p42 [1-50]
Foster, Buddy - *Foster Child*
    Ent W - My 16 '97 - p105+ [501+]
Foster, Cecil - *A Place Called Heaven*
    Mac - v110 - Ja 13 '97 - p66 [501+]
    Quill & Q - v63 - F '97 - p44 [251-500]
Foster, Christopher - *The State under Stress*
    Spec - v277 - N 23 '96 - p44 [1-50]
Foster, David William - *Violence in Argentine Literature*
    HAHR - v77 - My '97 - p357+ [501+]
Foster, Emily - *The Ohio Frontier*
    Nine-C Lit - v51 - D '96 - p422 [1-50]
Foster, Gerald L - *A Field Guide to Trains of North America*
  r ARBA - v28 - '97 - p656 [51-250]
  r Model R - v63 - O '96 - p52+ [51-250]
Foster, Hal - *Compulsive Beauty*
    Can Lit - Win '96 - p123+ [501+]
  The Return of the Real
    LJ - v122 - F 15 '97 - p131 [51-250]
    PW - v243 - S 2 '96 - p118 [51-250]
Foster, Henry W - *Make a Difference*
  y BL - v93 - My 15 '97 - p1550+ [51-250]
    LJ - v122 - My 1 '97 - p114 [51-250]
Foster, Janet - *British Archives. 3rd Ed.*
  r ARBA - v28 - '97 - p201+ [51-250]
Foster, John - *Action Rhymes (Illus. by Carol Thompson)*
  c Bks Keeps - Mr '97 - p18 [51-250]
  Chanting Rhymes (Illus. by Carol Thompson)
  c Bks Keeps - Mr '97 - p18 [51-250]
  Counting Rhymes (Illus. by Carol Thompson)
  c Bks Keeps - Mr '97 - p18 [51-250]
  Crack Another Yolk
  c Sch Lib - v44 - N '96 - p167 [51-250]
  Finger Rhymes (Illus. by Carol Thompson)
  c Bks Keeps - Mr '97 - p18 [51-250]
  Hot Heads, Warm Hearts, Cold Streets
  y Sch Lib - v44 - My '96 - p115 [51-250]
  y TES - S 20 '96 - pR6 [501+]
  An Orange Poetry Paintbox
  c Sch Lib - v45 - F '97 - p43 [51-250]
  A Purple Poetry Paintbox
  c Sch Lib - v45 - F '97 - p43 [51-250]
  Standing on the Sidelines
  y Magpies - v11 - Jl '96 - p37 [51-250]
  Studywise 1
  y Sch Lib - v44 - Ag '96 - p124 [51-250]
  You Little Monkey! (Illus. by Jan Lewis)
  c Sch Lib - v44 - Ag '96 - p115+ [51-250]
Foster, John E - *Australian Children's Literature*
    Aust Bk R - Jl '96 - p58+ [501+]
    Magpies - v11 - Jl '96 - p14 [501+]
Foster, John L, 1930- - *Hymns, Prayers, and Songs*
    Rel St Rev - v23 - Ap '97 - p164 [51-250]
Foster, John Wilson - *The Idea of the Union*
    ILS - v15 - Fall '96 - p15+ [501+]
Foster, Leila Merrell - *Afghanistan*
  c HB Guide - v8 - Spr '97 - p170 [51-250]
Foster, Maureen - *The Flower Arranger's Encyclopedia of Preserving and Drying*
  r BL - v93 - O 1 '96 - p316 [51-250]
Foster, Michele - *Black Teachers on Teaching*
  y BL - v93 - F 15 '97 - p979 [51-250]
    LJ - v121 - D '96 - p112 [51-250]
    LJ - v121 - N 1 '96 - p82 [1-50]
    PW - v243 - D 30 '96 - p49+ [251-500]
Foster, Nelson - *The Roaring Stream*
    Bloom Rev - v16 - N '96 - p14 [51-250]
    BW - v26 - O 13 '96 - p13 [51-250]
    PW - v243 - N 4 '96 - p46 [51-250]
Foster, Patricia - *Sister to Sister*
  y Kliatt - v31 - Mr '97 - p28 [251-500]
    PW - v243 - D 30 '96 - p64 [1-50]
Foster, R F - *The Oxford Illustrated History of Ireland*
    Bks & Cult - v2 - Ja '96 - p11+ [501+]

  W.B. Yeats: A Life. Vol. 1
    CHE - v43 - Ap 11 '97 - pA19 [51-250]
    ILS - v16 - Spr '97 - p5 [501+]
    KR - v65 - F 1 '97 - p192 [251-500]
    LJ - v122 - Ap 1 '97 - p91 [51-250]
    NS - v126 - Mr 21 '97 - p56 [51-250]
    NYTBR - v102 - Ap 6 '97 - p10+ [501+]
    Obs - Mr 16 '97 - p16* [501+]
    PW - v244 - Mr 3 '97 - p55 [51-250]
    Spec - v278 - Mr 15 '97 - p34+ [501+]
    TES - Mr 28 '97 - p7* [501+]
    TLS - Ap 11 '97 - p1667+ [501+]
    Wil Q - v21 - Spr '97 - p94+ [501+]
    WSJ-Cent - v99 - Ap 23 '97 - pA16 [501+]
Foster, R W - *Basic Pharmacology. 4th Ed.*
    SciTech - v20 - N '96 - p55 [51-250]
Foster, S G - *The Making of the Australian National University 1946-1996*
    Aust Bk R - O '96 - p23+ [501+]
Foster, Sandra - *You Can't Take It with You*
    Quill & Q - v63 - Ja '97 - p26+ [51-250]
Foster, Sesshu - *City Terrace Field Manual*
    SFR - v21 - N '96 - p23 [501+]
Foster, Shirley - *What Katy Read*
    ELT - v39 - 3 '96 - p366+ [501+]
    JPC - v30 - Fall '96 - p204+ [501+]
    NWSA Jnl - v8 - Fall '96 - p144+ [501+]
Foster, Simon - *Okinawa 1945*
    Mar Crp G - v80 - N '96 - p81+ [501+]
Foster, Steven - *Herbs for Your Health*
    BWatch - v17 - D '96 - p3 [1-50]
Foster, Susan Leigh - *Choreographing History*
    TDR - v40 - Win '96 - p161+ [501+]
  Choreography and Narrative
    Choice - v34 - Ap '97 - p1350 [51-250]
    LJ - v121 - O 1 '96 - p79 [51-250]
Foster, William C - *Spanish Expeditions into Texas 1689-1768*
    JSH - v63 - F '97 - p143+ [251-500]
Fostering: A Community Service Strategy for the Year 2000. Vols. 1-2
    J Gov Info - v23 - S '96 - p631 [51-250]
Fostering Continued Excellence in Adult Learning
    J Gov Info - v23 - S '96 - p623 [51-250]
Fostering Technological Dynamism
    R&R Bk N - v12 - F '97 - p35 [51-250]
Fostle, D W - *The Steinway Saga*
    Notes - v53 - S '96 - p81+ [501+]
Foucart, Jacques - *Les Peintures Flamande, Hollandaise Et Allemande XVe, XVIe, XVIIe Siecles*
  r Choice - v34 - D '96 - p570 [1-50]
Foucault, Michel - *Ethics: Subjectivity and Truth*
    LJ - v122 - Mr 15 '97 - p66 [51-250]
    PW - v244 - Mr 17 '97 - p73 [51-250]
  Foucault: Language to Infinity (Lopez-Morillas). Audio Version
    PW - v243 - O 7 '96 - p34 [51-250]
Fouilloux, Etienne - *La Collection Sources Chretiennes*
    CHR - v83 - Ja '97 - p163+ [51-250]
    Theol St - v57 - Je '96 - p382+ [251-500]
Foulcher, John - *The Honeymoon Snaps*
    Quad - v40 - S '96 - p86 [501+]
Foulds, Trevor - *The Thurgarton Cartulary*
  r EHR - v112 - Ap '97 - p443+ [501+]
Fouli, Janet - *Structure and Identity*
    ELT - v40 - 2 '97 - p225+ [501+]
Foulkes, Christopher - *Larousse Encyclopedia of Wine*
  r LJ - v122 - Ap 1 '97 - p62 [1-50]
The Foundation 1,000 1996/1997
  r ChrPhil - v9 - N 14 '96 - p39 [51-250]
The Foundation Directory Supplement
  r ChrPhil - v8 - O 3 '96 - p44 [1-50]
Foundation Reporter 1997
  r ChrPhil - v8 - Je 27 '96 - p34 [1-50]
Foundations for Osteopathic Medicine
    SciTech - v21 - Mr '97 - p69 [51-250]
Foundations for the Future
    J Gov Info - v23 - S '96 - p630 [51-250]
Fount Christian Thinkers
    TES - F 21 '97 - p7* [51-250]
Fountain, Gary - *Remembering Elizabeth Bishop*
    NYTBR - v101 - S 1 '96 - p24 [1-50]
Fountain, Joanna - *Subject Headings for School and Public Libraries. 2nd Ed.*
  r SLMQ - v25 - Fall '96 - p63 [51-250]
Fountas, Steve - *European Integration and Regional Policy*
    Econ J - v106 - S '96 - p1484+ [251-500]
Fouque, Jean-Pierre - *Stochastic Analysis*
    SciTech - v21 - Mr '97 - p14 [51-250]

Fourcade, Dominique - *Xbo*
TranslRevS - v1 - My '95 - p19 [1-50]
Fowke, Edith - *A Family Heritage*
Folkl - v107 - '96 - p120 [501+]
Fowkes, Ben - *The Disintegration of the Soviet Union*
Choice - v34 - Ap '97 - p1409 [51-250]
Fowler, Alastair - *The Country House Poem*
RES - v47 - Ag '96 - p412+ [501+]
Time's Purpled Masquers
TLS - D 13 '96 - p3+ [501+]
Fowler, Allan - *Arctic Tundra*
c HB Guide - v8 - Spr '97 - p117 [51-250]
The Biggest Animal on Land
c HB Guide - v7 - Fall '96 - p345 [1-50]
c SLJ - v42 - Ag '96 - p136 [51-250]
The Dewey Decimal System
c BL - v93 - F 1 '97 - p936 [51-250]
Gator or Croc?
c HB Guide - v8 - Spr '97 - p123 [51-250]
A Good Night's Sleep
c HB Guide - v8 - Spr '97 - p129 [51-250]
It Could Still Be a Lake
c HB Guide - v7 - Fall '96 - p332 [1-50]
It Could Still Be a Worm
c HB Guide - v7 - Fall '96 - p341 [1-50]
It Could Still Be Coral
c HB Guide - v8 - Spr '97 - p117 [51-250]
The Library of Congress
c HB Guide - v8 - Spr '97 - p85 [51-250]
c SLJ - v43 - F '97 - p90 [51-250]
Life in a Pond
c HB Guide - v7 - Fall '96 - p336 [1-50]
Life in a Tide Pool
c HB Guide - v8 - Spr '97 - p117 [51-250]
Save the Rain Forests
c HB Guide - v8 - Spr '97 - p117 [51-250]
Spiders Are Not Insects
c HB Guide - v7 - Fall '96 - p341 [1-50]
c SLJ - v42 - Ag '96 - p136 [51-250]
Stars in the Sky
c HB Guide - v7 - Fall '96 - p330 [1-50]
What Do You See in a Cloud?
c HB Guide - v7 - Fall '96 - p332 [1-50]
c SLJ - v42 - Ag '96 - p136 [51-250]
Fowler, Arlen L - *The Black Infantry in the West 1869-1891*
Bl S - v26 - Fall '96 - p102 [51-250]
Roundup M - v4 - D '96 - p20+ [51-250]
Fowler, Bev - *Everything You Ever Wanted to Know about AIDS, but Were Afraid to Ask*
PW - v244 - F 17 '97 - p216 [51-250]
Fowler, Charles - *Strong Arts, Strong Schools*
BL - v93 - S 15 '96 - p188 [51-250]
M Ed J - v83 - Mr '97 - p43 [51-250]
Fowler, Christopher - *Psychoville*
SF Chr - v18 - O '96 - p76 [51-250]
Fowler, Connie May - *Before Women Had Wings*
NYTBR - v101 - Jl 21 '96 - p15 [501+]
PW - v244 - Ap 14 '97 - p72 [1-50]
Fowler, David - *The First Teenagers*
JEH - v57 - Mr '97 - p223+ [501+]
J Soc H - v30 - Spr '97 - p736+ [501+]
Fowler, David C - *The Life and Times of John Trevisa, Medieval Scholar*
TLS - N 1 '96 - p28 [501+]
Fowler, Earlene - *Goose in the Pond*
KR - v65 - Ap 1 '97 - p505 [51-250]
PW - v244 - Mr 24 '97 - p62 [51-250]
Fowler, Floyd J, Jr. - *Improving Survey Questions*
Pub Op Q - v60 - Sum '96 - p341+ [501+]
Fowler, H W - *The New Fowler's Modern English Usage. 3rd Ed.*
r ARBA - v28 - '97 - p349 [251-500]
r Atl - v278 - D '96 - p112+ [501+]
r BL - v93 - Mr 1 '97 - p1195 [501+]
r Bloom Rev - v17 - Ja '97 - p17 [51-250]
r LJ - v122 - Mr 15 '97 - p57 [51-250]
Lon R Bks - v19 - Ja 2 '97 - p11+ [501+]
r Nat R - v49 - F 10 '97 - p52+ [501+]
r NY - v72 - D 23 '96 - p142+ [501+]
r NYTLa - v146 - D 26 '96 - pC25 [501+]
Obs - Ja 5 '97 - p18* [501+]
Spec - v277 - N 16 '96 - p46 [1-50]
TES - N 15 '96 - p8* [501+]
r TLS - F 7 '97 - p6 [501+]
r WSJ-MW - v78 - D 2 '96 - pA16 [501+]
Fowler, Ian - *African Crossroads*
Choice - v34 - Ja '97 - p851+ [51-250]

Fowler, Karen Joy - *The Sweetheart Season*
LATBR - v263 - S 29 '96 - p2 [501+]
NYTBR - v101 - O 13 '96 - p27 [501+]
NYTBR - v101 - D 8 '96 - p82 [1-50]
PW - v243 - Jl 22 '96 - p226+ [51-250]
Wom R Bks - v14 - Mr '97 - p16+ [501+]
Fowler, Marian - *The Way She Looks Tonight*
BIC - v26 - F '97 - p27 [501+]
KR - v64 - O 1 '96 - p1441 [501+]
LJ - v121 - O 1 '96 - p108 [51-250]
Mac - v109 - N 11 '96 - p93+ [501+]
PW - v243 - S 2 '96 - p100 [51-250]
Fowler, Michael Ross - *Law, Power, and the Sovereign State*
J Pol - v59 - F '97 - p310+ [501+]
Fowler, Patrick W - *An Atlas of Fullerenes*
r Am Sci - v84 - My '96 - p292+ [501+]
Fowler, Richard - *Here We Are! (Illus. by Richard Fowler)*
c JB - v60 - D '96 - p231 [51-250]
Little Chick's Big Adventure
c HB Guide - v7 - Fall '96 - p239 [51-250]
Fowler, Rick - *The Unwelcome Companion*
BWatch - v17 - N '96 - p3 [51-250]
Fowler, Robert Booth, 1940- - *The Greening of Protestant Thought*
CC - v113 - S 11 '96 - p866+ [251-500]
TT - v53 - O '96 - p418+ [501+]
Religion and Politics in America
Cons - v17 - Sum '96 - p38 [501+]
J Ch St - v38 - Aut '96 - p903+ [251-500]
SSQ - v78 - Mr '97 - p236+ [501+]
Theol St - v57 - S '96 - p572 [251-500]
Fowler, Robert H - *Voyage to Honor*
PW - v243 - S 23 '96 - p61 [51-250]
Fowler, Veronica Lorson - *Gardening in Iowa and Surrounding Areas*
PW - v244 - F 3 '97 - p104 [51-250]
Fowler, William M, Jr. - *Silas Talbot: Captain of Old Ironsides*
NWCR - v50 - Win '97 - p169+ [501+]
Fowles, Jib - *Advertising and Popular Culture*
Choice - v34 - S '96 - p170 [51-250]
JMCQ - v73 - Aut '96 - p751+ [501+]
Fowles, John - *The Collector (Wilby). Audio Version*
BL - v93 - Mr 15 '97 - p1253 [51-250]
The Tree. The Nature of Nature
Bloom Rev - v16 - N '96 - p29 [501+]
LATBR - D 8 '96 - p15 [251-500]
Fox, Arnold - *Alternative Healing*
r Quill & Q - v62 - Ag '96 - p31 [51-250]
Fox, Barry - *Foods to Heal By*
r BWatch - v17 - D '96 - p3 [1-50]
Fox, Charles F - *Postmodern Public Administration*
PAR - v57 - Mr '97 - p174+ [501+]
Fox, Christopher - *Inventing Human Science*
JIH - v27 - Spr '97 - p669+ [251-500]
Fox, Claire G - *Benjamin Rush, M.D.: A Bibliographic Guide*
r ARBA - v28 - '97 - p186 [51-250]
r Choice - v34 - D '96 - p589 [51-250]
r Isis - v88 - Mr '97 - p173 [501+]
r R&R Bk N - v11 - D '96 - p74 [51-250]
Fox, Dan - *Go In and Out the Window*
c BW - v26 - D 8 '96 - p2+ [51-250]
Fox, Geoff - *Celebrating Children's Literature in Education*
ChLAQ - v21 - Win '96 - p203+ [501+]
JOYS - v9 - Sum '96 - p409+ [501+]
Fox, Geoffrey E - *Hispanic Nation*
BW - v26 - S 8 '96 - p3+ [501+]
BWatch - v17 - S '96 - p10 [51-250]
Fox, Hugh - *The Point of Points and Other Stories*
Sm Pr R - v29 - F '97 - p8 [51-250]
Fox, James - *Killer on Campus*
Arm Det - v29 - Fall '96 - p505+ [251-500]
y Kliatt - v30 - S '96 - p32 [51-250]
Fox, John, 1863-1919 - *The Heart of the Hills*
LJ - v122 - My 1 '97 - p145 [1-50]
Fox, John, 1955- - *Finding What You Didn't Lose*
Bloom Rev - v16 - N '96 - p14 [51-250]
Fox, John Howard - *The Poetry of Fifteenth-Century France. Vols. 1-2*
MLR - v92 - Ap '97 - p463+ [501+]
Fox, Julian - *Woody: Movies from Manhattan*
y BL - v93 - N 1 '96 - p471 [51-250]
Choice - v34 - Ap '97 - p1345 [51-250]
Ent W - Ja 17 '97 - p58 [51-250]
LJ - v121 - D '96 - p95+ [51-250]
PW - v243 - O 14 '96 - p69 [51-250]
Si & So - v6 - N '96 - p36 [1-50]

Fox, L L - *Preservation Microfilming. 2nd Ed.*
LAR - v98 - D '96 - p652 [501+]
Fox, Louisa - *Every Monday in the Mailbox (Illus. by Jan Naimo Jones)*
c RT - v50 - O '96 - p132 [1-50]
Fox, Mary Virginia - *Lasers*
c HB Guide - v7 - Fall '96 - p349+ [51-250]
Rockets
c HB Guide - v7 - Fall '96 - p352 [51-250]
Satellites
c Ch BWatch - v6 - My '96 - p6 [51-250]
c HB Guide - v7 - Fall '96 - p352 [51-250]
c SB - v32 - Ag '96 - p181 [51-250]
c SLJ - v42 - Ag '96 - p148+ [51-250]
Somalia
c HB Guide - v8 - Spr '97 - p171 [51-250]
Fox, Matthew - *Natural Grace*
Bloom Rev - v16 - N '96 - p13 [251-500]
KR - v64 - My 1 '96 - p661 [251-500]
Rapport - v19 - 5 '96 - p41 [251-500]
The Physics of Angels
BWatch - v17 - N '96 - p2 [51-250]
Fox, Mem - *A Bedtime Story (Illus. by Elivia Savadier)*
c CBRS - v25 - S '96 - p3 [51-250]
c CSM - v88 - S 26 '96 - pB1 [51-250]
c HB Guide - v8 - Spr '97 - p27 [51-250]
c SLJ - v42 - D '96 - p92 [51-250]
Feathers and Fools (Illus. by Nicholas Wilton)
o Emerg Lib - v24 - S '96 - p43 [1-50]
c HB Guide - v7 - Fall '96 - p256 [51-250]
Wombat Divine (Illus. by Kerry Argent)
c Emerg Lib - v24 - Mr '97 - p45 [1-50]
c HB Guide - v8 - Spr '97 - p27 [51-250]
c NYTBR - v101 - D 22 '96 - p16 [1-50]
c PW - v243 - S 30 '96 - p90 [51-250]
c SFR - v21 - N '96 - p45 [51-250]
c SLJ - v42 - O '96 - p36 [51-250]
Zoo-Looking (Illus. by Candace Whitman)
c HB Guide - v7 - Fall '96 - p256 [1-50]
c NW - v128 - D 2 '96 - p84 [51-250]
Fox, Michael W - *Agricide: The Hidden Farm and Food Crisis That Affects Us All. 2nd Ed.*
SciTech - v20 - S '96 - p44 [51-250]
Fox, Paula - *The Eagle Kite*
y Ch BWatch - v6 - N '96 - p7 [1-50]
y EJ - v85 - N '96 - p132+ [251-500]
y Kliatt - v31 - Ja '97 - p6 [51-250]
y PW - v243 - O 14 '96 - p85 [1-50]
y RT - v50 - N '96 - p246 [51-250]
y SLJ - v43 - Mr '97 - p112 [1-50]
The Gathering Darkness
y Bks Keeps - v100 - S '96 - p17 [51-250]
A Likely Place (Illus. by Edward Ardizzone)
c PW - v244 - My 5 '97 - p211 [1-50]
The Slave Dancer (MacNicol). Audio Version
c PW - v244 - Ja 13 '97 - p36 [51-250]
Fox, Richard, 1945- - *Thinking Matters*
c Sch Lib - v44 - Ag '96 - p128 [51-250]
c TES - S 20 '96 - pR6 [251-500]
Fox, Richard Logan - *Gender Dynamics in Congressional Elections*
R&R Bk N - v12 - F '97 - p54 [51-250]
Fox, Richard Wightman - *A Companion to American Thought*
Bks & Cult - v2 - Jl '96 - p19+ [501+]
CR - v269 - S '96 - p168 [51-250]
Fox, Robert - *Science, Industry, and the Social Order in Post-Revolutionary France*
T&C - v37 - O '96 - p836+ [501+]
Technological Change
Choice - v34 - F '97 - p984 [51-250]
Fox, Roy F - *Harvesting Minds*
Choice - v34 - Mr '97 - p1211 [51-250]
PW - v243 - S 30 '96 - p74 [51-250]
Fox, Stephen - *Big Leagues*
Aethlon - v13 - Spr '96 - p203+ [501+]
Fox, Thomas C - *Sexuality and Catholicism*
Theol St - v57 - Je '96 - p387+ [251-500]
Fox, William, 1935- - *Public Administration Dictionary*
r Choice - v34 - S '96 - p98 [51-250]
Fox, William L, 1949- - *TumbleWords: Writers Reading the West*
WAL - v31 - Win '97 - p392+ [251-500]
Fox, William L, 1953- - *Willard L. Sperry: The Quandaries of a Liberal Protestant Mind 1914-1939*
CH - v65 - D '96 - p754+ [501+]
Fox, Zachary Alan - *All Fall Down*
KR - v65 - Ja 15 '97 - p80 [251-500]
PW - v244 - Ja 27 '97 - p77+ [51-250]

Fox-Davies, Sarah - *Little Caribou (Illus. by Sarah Fox-Davies)*
  c BL - v93 - D 1 '96 - p662 [51-250]
  c HB - v73 - Ja '97 - p51 [51-250]
  c HB Guide - v8 - Spr '97 - p27 [51-250]
  c JB - v60 - O '96 - p183 [51-250]
  c Magpies - v11 - S '96 - p28 [51-250]
  c PW - v243 - N 11 '96 - p74 [51-250]
  c Sch Lib - v44 - Ag '96 - p99 [51-250]
  c SLJ - v42 - D '96 - p92 [51-250]
  c TES - F 21 '97 - p16* [51-250]
Foxe-Tyler, Cynthia - *Dream On (Foxe-Tyler). Audio Version*
  PW - v243 - N 4 '96 - p32 [51-250]
Fox-Genovese, Elizabeth - *Feminism Is Not the Story of My Life*
  Nat R - v48 - Je 3 '96 - p54+ [501+]
  NYRB - v43 - N 28 '96 - p22+ [501+]
  Prog - v61 - Ja '97 - p33+ [501+]
  PW - v243 - D 30 '96 - p64 [1-50]
  Wom R Bks - v13 - S '96 - p17+ [501+]
Foxhall, L - *Greek Law in Its Political Setting*
  HRNB - v25 - Fall '96 - p41 [251-500]
  Rel St Rev - v23 - Ja '97 - p60+ [51-250]
Foxton, Rosemary - *Hear the Word of the Lord*
  r Albion - v28 - Sum '96 - p305+ [501+]
  r Lib - v18 - S '96 - p264+ [501+]
Foxworth, Jo - *The Bordello Cookbook*
  PW - v243 - D 2 '96 - p58 [51-250]
Foxxe, Ellen - *Season of Storms*
  y Kliatt - v30 - S '96 - p18 [51-250]
Foy, Chester L - *Pesticide Formulation and Adjuvant Technology*
  SciTech - v20 - D '96 - p56 [51-250]
Foy, George - *Contraband*
  KR - v65 - Mr 1 '97 - p340+ [51-250]
  PW - v244 - Mr 24 '97 - p63 [51-250]
The Shift
  KR - v64 - My 1 '96 - p649 [251-500]
  PW - v244 - Mr 17 '97 - p81 [1-50]
Foy, Jessica H - *The Arts in the American Home 1890-1930*
  T&C - v37 - Ap '96 - p375+ [501+]
Fracture Mechanics of Ceramics. Vols. 11-12
  SciTech - v21 - Mr '97 - p78 [51-250]
Fraden, Jacob - *Adventures of an Inventor*
  Choice - v34 - O '96 - p311 [51-250]
Handbook of Modern Sensors. 2nd Ed.
  SciTech - v21 - Mr '97 - p72 [51-250]
Frader, Laura L - *Gender and Class in Modern Europe*
  JEL - v35 - Mr '97 - p262 [51-250]
  TLS - 1 '97 - p32 [51-250]
Fradin, Dennis Brindell - *Louis Braille: The Blind Boy Who Wanted to Read*
  c BL - v93 - My 1 '97 - p1499 [51-250]
We Have Conquered Pain
  c HB - v72 - S '96 - p613 [51-250]
  y HB Guide - v7 - Fall '96 - p347 [51-250]
  c KR - v64 - My 1 '96 - p688 [51-250]
Fradkin, Efim S - *Conformal Quantum Field Theory in D-Dimensions*
  SciTech - v21 - Mr '97 - p21 [51-250]
Fradkin, Philip L - *A River No More*
  LATBR - S 22 '96 - p15 [51-250]
The Seven States of California
  PW - v244 - F 3 '97 - p100 [1-50]
Fradkin, Robert A - *The Well-Tempered Announcer*
  r ARBA - v28 - '97 - p483 [51-250]
  r Choice - v34 - Ja '97 - p769 [51-250]
  FF - v20 - N '96 - p516+ [251-500]
Frady, Marshall - *Jesse: The Life and Pilgrimage of Jesse Jackson*
  Bl S - v26 - Fall '96 - p102 [51-250]
  Choice - v34 - N '96 - p524 [51-250]
  KR - v64 - My 1 '96 - p661+ [251-500]
  LATBR - D 29 '96 - p10 [51-250]
  NY - v72 - D 16 '96 - p109 [51-250]
  NYRB - v43 - S 19 '96 - p61+ [501+]
  NYTBR - v101 - D 8 '96 - p88 [1-50]
Fraghou-Kikilia, Ritsa - *Katrapakian*
  WLT - v70 - Aut '96 - p1002 [251-500]
Frailey, Fred W - *How to Pick Stocks*
  BL - v93 - Mr 1 '97 - p1097 [51-250]
Fraim, John - *Spirit Catcher*
  AB - v98 - D 9 '96 - p1996 [51-250]
Frame, Donald - *Montaigne: Une Vie, Une Oeuvre 1533-1592*
  Six Ct J - v27 - Win '96 - p1173+ [501+]
Frame, Randall L - *How Right Is the Right?*
  Bks & Cult - v2 - N '96 - p20+ [501+]

Fra-Molinero, Baltasar - *La Imagen De Los Negros En El Teatro Del Siglo De Oro*
  Hisp - v79 - S '96 - p441+ [501+]
Le Francais Langue Commune
  J Gov Info - v23 - S '96 - p636+ [51-250]
Francard, Michel - *L'Insecurite Linguistique Dans Les Communautes Francophones Peripheriques*
  FR - v70 - D '96 - p358+ [501+]
Francaviglia, Richard V - *Essays on the Changing Images of the Southwest*
  AAAGA - v86 - S '96 - p596+ [501+]
  PHR - v65 - Ag '96 - p489+ [251-500]
Main Street Revisited
  Bloom Rev - v16 - S '96 - p28 [51-250]
  Choice - v34 - N '96 - p524+ [51-250]
  R&R Bk N - v12 - F '97 - p55 [51-250]
  WHQ - v28 - Spr '97 - p92+ [251-500]
The Shape of Texas
  GJ - v162 - N '96 - p333+ [251-500]
France, John - *Victory in the East*
  EHR - v111 - N '96 - p1239+ [501+]
  Specu - v72 - Ja '97 - p151+ [501+]
France, L B - *With Rod and Line in Colorado Waters*
  Bloom Rev - v17 - Ja '97 - p17 [51-250]
France, Melissa Dorfman - *Pooh's Little Etiquette Book (Illus. by Ernest H Shepard)*
  c HB Guide - v7 - Fall '96 - p353 [51-250]
France, Peter - *Hermits: The Insights of Solitude*
  CR - v269 - N '96 - p279+ [51-250]
  KR - v65 - My 1 '97 - p691+ [251-500]
  Spec - v277 - N 16 '96 - p46 [1-50]
Francesca, Ersilia - *Introduzione Alle Regole Alimentari Islamiche*
  MEJ - v51 - Win '97 - p154 [51-250]
Franceschina, John - *Sisters of Gore*
  R&R Bk N - v12 - F '97 - p84 [1-50]
Franchini, Silvia - *Elites Ed Educazione Femminile Nell'Italia Dell'Ottocento*
  JMH - v68 - S '96 - p716+ [501+]
Franchot, Jenny - *Roads to Rome*
  JAAR - v64 - Fall '96 - p705+ [501+]
  JR - v77 - Ap '97 - p300+ [501+]
Francione, Gary L - *Animals, Property, and the Law*
  Ethics - v107 - Ja '97 - p395 [51-250]
  HLR - v110 - D '96 - p559+ [51-250]
Rain without Thunder
  Choice - v34 - Mr '97 - p1182 [51-250]
  PW - v243 - Jl 22 '96 - p233 [51-250]
Francis, of Assisi, Saint - *True Joy*
  RR - v55 - N '96 - p661 [1-50]
Francis, Bob - *Discovering Advanced Mathematics: Pure Mathematics*
  y TES - O 4 '96 - pR12 [501+]
Francis, Clare - *Betrayal (Beale). Audio Version*
  LJ - v121 - N 1 '96 - p120 [51-250]
Francis, Daniel - *Copying People*
  CG - v117 - Mr '97 - p85 [51-250]
Francis, Dave - *Just a Thought*
  y Sch Lib - v45 - F '97 - p50 [51-250]
  TES - D 6 '96 - pR6 [51-250]
The New Unblocked Manager. Rev. Ed.
  R&R Bk N - v11 - N '96 - p29 [51-250]
Francis, Diane - *The Fight for Canada*
  Quill & Q - v62 - N '96 - p36 [251-500]
Francis, Dick - *Come to Grief*
  Books - v9 - S '95 - p22 [1-50]
  y Kliatt - v30 - N '96 - p8 [51-250]
Come to Grief (Jones). Audio Version
  y Kliatt - v31 - Ja '97 - p38 [51-250]
Dead Cert (Prebble). Audio Version
  y Kliatt - v30 - S '96 - p46 [51-250]
Enquiry (Howard). Audio Version
  BL - v93 - N 1 '96 - p522 [51-250]
For Kicks (Gaminara). Audio Version
  y Kliatt - v31 - My '97 - p38 [51-250]
Nerve (Britton). Audio Version
  TLS - Ag 2 '96 - p24 [1-50]
To the Hilt
  Arm Det - v30 - Win '97 - p117 [251-500]
  Atl - v278 - N '96 - p122 [51-250]
  BL - v93 - S 1 '96 - p29 [51-250]
  CSM - v88 - N 14 '96 - p14 [51-250]
  KR - v64 - Ag 15 '96 - p1172 [251-500]
  LATBR - N 10 '96 - p6 [51-250]
  LJ - v121 - N 1 '96 - p131 [51-250]
  Nat R - v48 - D 23 '96 - p57 [51-250]
  NYTBR - v101 - O 13 '96 - p29 [51-250]
  y SLJ - v43 - Ja '97 - p140 [51-250]
To the Hilt (Britton). Audio Version
  CSM - v88 - O 31 '96 - pB4 [51-250]

Whip Hand (Ford). Audio Version
  y Kliatt - v31 - My '97 - p46 [51-250]
Francis, Dylan - *The Risk of Being Alive*
  Obs - D 22 '96 - p15* [501+]
Francis, Greta - *Childhood Obsessive Compulsive Disorder*
  SciTech - v20 - D '96 - p53 [51-250]
Francis, John - *Bicycling (Illus. by Art Seiden)*
  c HB Guide - v7 - Fall '96 - p360 [51-250]
Francis, Leslie - *Date Rape*
  Wom R Bks - v14 - Mr '97 - p23+ [501+]
Francis, Mark - *Governors and Settlers*
  VS - v39 - Aut '95 - p83+ [501+]
A History of English Political Thought in the Nineteenth Century
  EHR - v112 - F '97 - p235+ [501+]
  VS - v39 - Win '96 - p256+ [501+]
Francis, Martin - *The Conservatives and British Society 1880-1990*
  HT - v46 - O '96 - p58 [1-50]
  TLS - F 28 '97 - p12 [501+]
Francis, Matthew - *Blizzard*
  Obs - Ja 5 '97 - p17* [51-250]
Francis, Richard - *Negotiating Rapture*
  LJ - v121 - N 15 '96 - p59 [251-500]
  VQR - v73 - Win '97 - p32* [51-250]
Francis, Richard, 1945- - *Transcendental Utopias*
  LJ - v122 - F 15 '97 - p145+ [51-250]
  PW - v244 - F 24 '97 - p77 [51-250]
Francis, Richard P - *Christian Humanism*
  Choice - v34 - S '96 - p143 [51-250]
Francis, Sarah - *Odd Fish and Englishmen*
  TLS - Jl 7 '96 - p24 [501+]
Francisco De Goya Y La Estampa De Su Epoca
  BM - v138 - S '96 - p630+ [501+]
Franck, Dan - *My Russian Love*
  BL - v93 - F 15 '97 - p1002+ [51-250]
  KR - v64 - D 1 '96 - p1688+ [251-500]
  NYTBR - v102 - Mr 9 '97 - p19 [51-250]
  NYTLa - v146 - Mr 21 '97 - pC32 [501+]
  PW - v243 - D 30 '96 - p55+ [51-250]
Tabac
  FR - v70 - D '96 - p347+ [251-500]
Franck, Irene - *Parenting A to Z*
  r LJ - v122 - Mr 15 '97 - p54 [51-250]
Franck, Matthew J - *Against the Imperial Judiciary*
  AHR - v102 - F '97 - p173 [501+]
  Choice - v34 - O '96 - p360+ [51-250]
  RP - v59 - Win '97 - p149+ [501+]
Franck, Thomas M - *Fairness in International Law and Institutions*
  Lon R Bks - v18 - Ag 22 '96 - p14+ [501+]
International Law Decisions in National Courts
  R&R Bk N - v11 - N '96 - p53 [51-250]
Francke, Linda Bird - *Ground Zero*
  KR - v65 - My 1 '97 - p711+ [51-250]
  PW - v244 - My 12 '97 - p70 [51-250]
Francome, John - *Dead Ringer*
  Books - v9 - S '95 - p22 [51-250]
Francovich, Ricardo - *La Storia Dell'Alto Medieovo Italiano (VI-X Secolo) Alla Luce Dell'Archeologia*
  AJA - v100 - O '96 - p807+ [501+]
Franey, Pierre - *Pierre Franey Cooks with His Friends*
  BL - v93 - Mr 15 '97 - p1216 [51-250]
  LJ - v122 - Mr 15 '97 - p82 [51-250]
  PW - v244 - Mr 3 '97 - p70 [51-250]
Frangsmyr, Tore - *Linnaeus: The Man and His Work*
  Isis - v87 - S '96 - p551+ [501+]
Frank, Andrew - *The Birth of Black America*
  y HB Guide - v7 - Fall '96 - p386 [51-250]
  y SLJ - v42 - O '96 - p156 [51-250]
Frank, Anne - *The Diary of a Young Girl: The Definitive Edition*
  y BL - v93 - D 15 '96 - p716 [1-50]
  y Emerg Lib - v24 - S '96 - p23 [1-50]
  y Kliatt - v30 - S '96 - p4 [1-50]
  Lon R Bks - v19 - Mr 6 '97 - p11+ [501+]
  Obs - F 9 '97 - p17* [501+]
  Spec - v278 - F 1 '97 - p30+ [501+]
  y TES - Ja 31 '97 - p7* [501+]
  TranslRevS - v2 - D '96 - p20 [51-250]
Frank, Ben G - *A Travel Guide to Jewish Europe. 2nd Ed.*
  r ARBA - v28 - '97 - p200 [51-250]
Frank, Dana - *Purchasing Power*
  JIH - v27 - Aut '96 - p353+ [501+]
Frank, Daniel H - *History of Jewish Philosophy*
  Choice - v34 - My '97 - p1512 [51-250]
  r LAR - v99 - Mr '97 - p164 [1-50]
A People Apart
  JAAR - v65 - Spr '97 - p201+ [501+]

Frank, Isnard Wilhelm - *A Concise History of the Medieval Church*
   CHR - v83 - Ja '97 - p164+ [51-250]

Frank, Ivan Cecil - *Building Self-Esteem in At-Risk Youth*
   R&R Bk N - v11 - N '96 - p4 [51-250]

Frank, Joachim - *Three-Dimensional Electron Microscopy of Macromolecular Assemblies*
   SciTech - v20 - N '96 - p26 [51-250]

Frank, Joseph - *Dostoevsky: The Miraculous Years 1865-1871*
   Comp L - v48 - Fall '96 - p387+ [501+]

Frank, Larry - *New Kingdom of the Saints*
   HAHR - v76 - N '96 - p758+ [501+]

Frank, Lucy - *I Am an Artichoke*
   y Kliatt - v31 - Mr '97 - p8 [51-250]
   y PW - v243 - N 18 '96 - p78 [51-250]
Will You Be My Brussels Sprout?
   y HB Guide - v7 - Fall '96 - p301 [1-50]
   y VOYA - v19 - O '96 - p208+ [251-500]

Frank, Michael - *Dorfliche Gesellschaft Und Kriminalitat*
   J Soc H - v30 - Spr '97 - p750+ [501+]

Frank, R M - *Al-Ghazali and the Ash'arite School*
   Rel St Rev - v23 - Ja '97 - p90 [51-250]

Frank, Robert H - *The Winner-Take-All Society*
   NYTBR - v101 - S 1 '96 - p24 [51-250]
   Obs - D 1 '96 - p16* [1-50]
   PSQ - v111 - Fall '96 - p523+ [501+]
   PW - v243 - Jl 22 '96 - p235 [1-50]

Frank, Sabine - *Libya Im 20. Jahrhundert*
   MEJ - v51 - Win '97 - p151 [51-250]

Frank, Stephen P - *Cultures in Flux*
   EHR - v111 - N '96 - p1339+ [501+]

Frank, Steven - *The Allisons: America's First Family of Stock-Car Racing*
   c HB Guide - v7 - Fall '96 - p359 [51-250]
   y SLJ - v42 - Ag '96 - p168 [51-250]

Frank, Thaisa - *Finding Your Writer's Voice*
   BWatch - v18 - F '97 - p4 [51-250]

Frank, Vivien - *Masks: From Countries around the World*
   c PW - v243 - S 2 '96 - p133 [51-250]

Frank, William A - *Duns Scotus, Metaphysician*
   CPR - v16 - Ag '96 - p254+ [501+]

Frank, Yitzchak - *Pediatric Behavioral Neurology*
   SciTech - v21 - Mr '97 - p64 [51-250]

The Frank Lloyd Wright Companion. Electronic Media Version
   LJ - v121 - S 15 '96 - p105+ [501+]

Franke, Herman - *The Emancipation of Prisoners*
   J Soc H - v30 - Spr '97 - p748+ [501+]

Franke, William - *Dante's Interpretive Journey*
   Choice - v34 - O '96 - p285 [251-500]
   IPQ - v37 - Je '97 - p253 [51-250]

Frankel, Charles - *Volcanoes of the Solar System*
   Choice - v34 - Ap '97 - p1361+ [51-250]
   Nature - v384 - N 7 '96 - p38 [501+]
   New Sci - v152 - O 12 '96 - p41 [501+]
   Phys Today - v50 - Mr '97 - p77 [501+]
   Sci - v275 - Ja 24 '97 - p496+ [501+]
   SciTech - v20 - D '96 - p21 [51-250]
   S&T - v93 - Ap '97 - p62+ [501+]

Frankel, Ellen - *The Five Books of Miriam*
   y BL - v93 - O 1 '96 - p306 [51-250]
   LJ - v122 - Ja '97 - p105 [51-250]

Frankel, Fred - *Good Friends Are Hard to Find*
   PW - v243 - O 21 '96 - p80 [51-250]

Frankel, Jeffrey A - *The Microstructure of Foreign Exchange Markets*
   JEL - v34 - D '96 - p2048 [51-250]
   JEL - v35 - Mr '97 - p140+ [501+]
   R&R Bk N - v11 - N '96 - p36 [51-250]

Frankel, Jennie Louise - *You'll Never Make Love in This Town Again*
   Ent W - N 1 '96 - p65 [1-50]
   LATBR - Mr 17 '96 - p10 [51-250]

Frankel, Ken - *Off the Wall!*
   CAY - v17 - Win '96 - p4 [51-250]

Frankel, Noralee - *Break Those Chains at Last*
   y Ch BWatch - v6 - My '96 - p5 [51-250]
   y HB Guide - v7 - Fall '96 - p386 [51-250]

Frankel, Rafael - *History and Technology of Olive Oil in the Holy Land*
   AJA - v100 - Jl '96 - p636 [251-500]
   T&C - v38 - Ja '97 - p242+ [501+]

Franken, Al - *Rush Limbaugh Is a Big Fat Idiot and Other Observations*
   Prog - v61 - Ja '97 - p36 [51-250]
   PW - v243 - O 21 '96 - p78 [1-50]

Frankenthaler, Helen - *Valentine for Mr. Wonderful*
   NYTBR - v102 - Ja 19 '97 - p19 [51-250]
   PW - v243 - N 25 '96 - p66 [51-250]

Franketienne - *L'Amerique Saigne*
   BL - v93 - F 1 '97 - p930 [1-50]

Frankl, Ron - *Richard Petty*
   c HB Guide - v7 - Fall '96 - p359 [51-250]

Frankl, Viktor Emil - *Viktor Frankl--Recollections*
   BL - v93 - My 1 '97 - p1470 [51-250]
   PW - v244 - Ap 14 '97 - p64 [51-250]

Franklet, Duane - *Bad Memory*
   LJ - v122 - Ap 15 '97 - p117 [51-250]
   PW - v244 - My 12 '97 - p60 [51-250]

Franklin, Benjamin, 1706-1790 - *Benjamin Franklin's The Art of Virtue*
   LJ - v121 - S 15 '96 - p102 [1-50]

Franklin, Benjamin, 1939- - *Recollections of Anais Nin by Her Contemporaries*
   PW - v243 - D 9 '96 - p58 [51-250]

Franklin, Carl - *Visual Basic 4.0 Internet Programming*
   CBR - v14 - S '96 - p32 [51-250]
   SciTech - v20 - N '96 - p9 [51-250]

Franklin, Cheryl J - *Ghost Shadow*
   y Kliatt - v31 - Mr '97 - p16 [51-250]

Franklin, Colin - *Book Collecting as One of the Fine Arts*
   BC - v45 - Aut '96 - p385 [51-250]
   R&R Bk N - v11 - N '96 - p79 [51-250]

Franklin, David, 1961- - *Rosso in Italy*
   Ren Q - v49 - Win '96 - p905+ [501+]

Franklin, David Byrd - *The Scottish Regency of the Earl of Arran*
   Albion - v28 - Sum '96 - p366+ [501+]
   Six Ct J - v27 - Win '96 - p1166+ [501+]

Franklin, Eric N - *Dynamic Alignment through Imagery*
   SciTech - v20 - S '96 - p38 [51-250]

Franklin, H Bruce - *M.I.A., or, Mythmaking in America*
   S&S - v61 - Sum '97 - p292+ [501+]

Franklin, Jane - *Equality*
   TLS - Ap 11 '97 - p5+ [501+]

Franklin, John Hope - *African Americans and the Living Constitution*
   JSH - v62 - N '96 - p798+ [501+]

Franklin, Judy A - *Recent Advances in Robot Learning*
   SciTech - v21 - Mr '97 - p84 [51-250]

Franklin, Keith B J - *The Mouse Brain in Stereotaxic Coordinates*
   r SciTech - v21 - Mr '97 - p39 [51-250]

Franklin, Kristine L - *Iguana Beach (Illus. by Lori Lohstoeter)*
   c KR - v65 - My 1 '97 - p720 [51-250]
Lone Wolf
   c CCB-B - v50 - My '97 - p320+ [51-250]
   c KR - v65 - Mr 1 '97 - p380 [51-250]
Nerd No More
   c CBRS - v25 - Ja '97 - p54 [1-50]
   c CCB-B - v50 - O '96 - p57+ [51-250]
   c HB - v72 - N '96 - p735+ [51-250]
   c HB Guide - v8 - Spr '97 - p66 [51-250]
   c Par Ch - v21 - Mr '97 - p8 [1-50]
   c SLJ - v42 - O '96 - p122 [51-250]
Out of the Dump
   c BL - v93 - Ja '97 - p766 [1-50]
   c HB Guide - v7 - Fall '96 - p392 [51-250]
   c New Ad - v9 - Fall '96 - p327+ [501+]
The Wolfhound (Illus. by Kris Waldherr)
   c BL - v93 - N 1 '96 - p507 [51-250]
   c CBRS - v25 - N '96 - p30 [51-250]
   c HB Guide - v8 - Spr '97 - p27 [51-250]
   c SLJ - v43 - F '97 - p81 [51-250]

Franklin, M J - *Medieval Ecclesiastical Studies in Honour of Dorothy M. Owen*
   Albion - v28 - Win '96 - p675 [501+]

Franklin, Margery B - *Development and the Arts*
   JAAC - v54 - Fall '96 - p407+ [501+]

Franklin, Michael J, 1949- - *Sir William Jones*
   TLS - Mr 21 '97 - p25 [501+]

Franklin, Peter - *The Taxpayers of Medieval Gloucestershire*
   EHR - v111 - S '96 - p961+ [251-500]

Franklin, Simon - *The Emergence of Rus 750-1200*
   Choice - v34 - N '96 - p517 [51-250]

Franklin, Stan - *Artificial Minds*
   TLS - Ja 10 '97 - p26 [501+]

Franklin, V P - *Living Our Stories, Telling Our Truths*
   AHR - v101 - O '96 - p1270 [501+]
   Biography - v20 - Win '97 - p105+ [501+]
   Bl S - v26 - Fall '96 - p102 [51-250]

Franklin, Wayne - *Mapping American Culture*
   J Am Cult - v19 - Sum '96 - p158 [251-500]
   J Am St - v30 - D '96 - p473+ [251-500]

Franko, Mark - *Dancing Modernism/Performing Politics*
   TDR - v40 - Win '96 - p154+ [501+]

Frankovich, Nicholas - *The Columbia Granger's Index to Poetry in Collected and Selected Works*
   r ARBA - v28 - '97 - p464+ [51-250]
   r BL - v93 - Mr 15 '97 - p1256 [251-500]

Franks, Don - *Entertainment Awards*
   r ARBA - v28 - '97 - p502 [51-250]
   r BL - v93 - Ja '97 - p770 [1-50]
   r BL - v93 - S 15 '96 - p283+ [51-250]
   r Choice - v34 - N '96 - p430 [51-250]
   r RQ - v36 - Win '96 - p293+ [251-500]

Franks, Tim - *Oxford Reading Tree Teacher's Guide 4*
   TES - Ja 10 '97 - p14* [501+]

Frank-Spohrer, Gail C - *Community Nutrition*
   SciTech - v20 - N '96 - p37 [51-250]

Franses, Philip Hans - *Periodicity and Stochastic Trends in Economic Time Series*
   JEL - v35 - Mr '97 - p195+ [51-250]

Fransman, Martin - *Japan's Computer and Communications Industry*
   JEL - v34 - S '96 - p1455 [51-250]

Frantz, Donald G - *Blackfoot Dictionary of Stems, Roots, and Affixes. 2nd Ed.*
   r ARBA - v28 - '97 - p401 [251-500]

Frantzen, Allen J - *The Work of Work*
   Albion - v28 - Sum '96 - p281+ [501+]
   EHR - v111 - N '96 - p1235+ [251-500]

Frantzen, Piet - *China's Economic Evolution*
   Ch Rev Int - v3 - Fall '96 - p413+ [501+]

Frantzich, Stephen - *The C-Span Revolution*
   BL - v93 - S 1 '96 - p40 [51-250]
   Choice - v34 - Mr '97 - p1154 [51-250]

Franz, Erhard - *Population Policy in Turkey*
   MEJ - v50 - Sum '96 - p452 [51-250]

Franz, Jennifer D - *Cleaner Air Partnership*
   J Gov Info - v23 - S '96 - p601 [51-250]

Franz, Marie-Louise Von - *Archetypal Dimensions of the Psyche*
   LJ - v122 - Ap 1 '97 - p111+ [51-250]

Franzen, Jonathan - *The Twenty-Seventh City*
   PW - v244 - Ap 21 '97 - p69 [1-50]
   Time - v149 - Ap 14 '97 - p89+ [501+]
   Trib Bks - My 18 '97 - p8 [1-50]

Franzen, O - *Somesthesis and the Neurobiology of the Somatosensory Cortex*
   SciTech - v20 - S '96 - p22 [51-250]

Franzen, Trisha - *Spinsters and Lesbians*
   Choice - v34 - D '96 - p676 [51-250]
   Wom R Bks - v14 - D '96 - p10+ [501+]

Franzosi, Roberto - *The Puzzle of Strikes*
   ILRR - v50 - Ap '97 - p510+ [501+]
   J Pol - v58 - N '96 - p1249+ [501+]

Frappier-Mazur, Lucienne - *Writing the Orgy*
   Choice - v34 - D '96 - p619 [51-250]
   R&R Bk N - v11 - N '96 - p68 [51-250]

Frary, Dave - *The Pennsy Middle Division in HO Scale*
   Model R - v63 - N '96 - p60 [51-250]

Frary, Michael L - *Flat Tops Fire Management Area Guidebook for Prescribed Natural Fire Planning and Implementation*
   J Gov Info - v23 - S '96 - p567 [51-250]

Frase, H Michael - *Fatal Gift*
   KR - v64 - S 15 '96 - p1342 [251-500]
   LJ - v121 - N 15 '96 - p87 [51-250]
   PW - v243 - O 7 '96 - p62 [51-250]

Fraser, Anthea - *I'll Sing You Two-O*
   Arm Det - v30 - Win '97 - p90 [251-500]
   KR - v64 - O 15 '96 - p1495 [51-250]
Motive for Murder
   KR - v65 - Mr 15 '97 - p420 [51-250]
   LJ - v122 - Ap 1 '97 - p133 [1-50]
   PW - v244 - F 24 '97 - p67 [51-250]

Fraser, Antonia - *Cromwell (Peters). Audio Version*
   y Kliatt - v30 - S '96 - p56 [51-250]
Faith and Treason
   BL - v93 - O 1 '96 - p318 [51-250]
   Comw - v124 - Ja 17 '96 - p18+ [501+]
   CSM - v89 - D 18 '96 - p13 [501+]
   KR - v64 - Ag 15 '96 - p1208 [251-500]
   LJ - v121 - O 1 '96 - p98+ [51-250]
   NY - v72 - N 11 '96 - p119 [51-250]
   NYTBR - v101 - O 27 '96 - p13 [501+]
The Gunpowder Plot
   NS - v125 - Ag 30 '96 - p48 [501+]
   Obs - Ag 25 '96 - p15* [501+]
   Obs - D 1 '96 - p17* [1-50]
   TLS - Ag 30 '96 - p25 [501+]
   TLS - N 29 '96 - p11 [1-50]
The Lives of the Kings and Queens of England
   Six Ct J - v27 - Fall '96 - p935+ [501+]
Political Death (Hodge). Audio Version
   y Kliatt - v31 - Ja '97 - p45 [51-250]

Fraser, Brian J - *Church, College, and Clergy*
Can Hist R - v78 - Mr '97 - p153+ [501+]
The Study of Religion in British Columbia
Rel St Rev - v23 - Ap '97 - p202 [51-250]
Fraser, Christine Marion - *A Rhanna Mystery*
Books - v11 - Ap '97 - p22 [51-250]
Storm Over Rhanna (Heilbron). Audio Version
BWatch - v18 - Mr '97 - p8 [1-50]
Fraser, Flora - *The Unruly Queen*
BL - v93 - Ja '97 - p760 [51-250]
CR - v268 - Je '96 - p330 [51-250]
LATBR - Ag 18 '96 - p3 [501+]
NYTBR - v101 - D 8 '96 - p93+ [1-50]
Obs - Mr 30 '97 - p17* [251-500]
VQR - v73 - Win '97 - p20* [51-250]
Fraser, George - *Success Runs in Our Race*
Bl S - v26 - Fall '96 - p102 [1-50]
Fraser, James - *Japanese Modern*
Choice - v34 - S '96 - p112 [51-250]
Fraser, John - *Stolen China*
BIC - v25 - D '96 - p41 [251-500]
Mac - v109 - D 9 '96 - p70 [251-500]
Fraser, Keath - *As for Me and My Body*
Quill & Q - v63 - F '97 - p44 [501+]
Popular Anatomy
Can Lit - Spr '97 - p242+ [501+]
Telling My True Love Lies
Quill & Q - v63 - Ja '97 - p35 [51-250]
Fraser, Kennedy - *Ornament and Silence*
Ent W - Ja 10 '97 - p52 [51-250]
KR - v64 - S 1 '96 - p1293 [251-500]
Nat - v264 - F 3 '97 - p30+ [501+]
NY - v72 - D 16 '96 - p109 [51-250]
NYTBR - v101 - D 29 '96 - p7 [501+]
PW - v243 - S 2 '96 - p100 [51-250]
Fraser, Laura - *Losing It*
y BL - v93 - D 1 '96 - p628 [51-250]
BW - v26 - D 29 '96 - p3 [501+]
Ent W - Ja 31 '97 - p54 [51-250]
KR - v64 - O 15 '96 - p1508 [51-250]
LJ - v122 - Ja '97 - p132 [51-250]
NYTBR - v102 - Ja 12 '97 - p20 [251-500]
PW - v243 - D 2 '96 - p50 [51-250]
Fraser, Mary Ann - *Forest Fire!*
c HB Guide - v7 - Fall '96 - p336 [51-250]
In Search of the Grand Canyon
c LA - v73 - O '96 - p440 [51-250]
Fraser, Nicholas - *Eva Peron (May). Audio Version*
y Kliatt - v31 - Ja '97 - p48 [251-500]
Evita: The Real Life of Eva Peron
PW - v243 - S 2 '96 - p121 [1-50]
Fraser, P M - *Cities of Alexander the Great*
Choice - v34 - Mr '97 - p1216 [51-250]
Fraser, Steven - *The Bell Curve Wars*
Soc - v34 - Mr '97 - p78+ [501+]
Frasier, David K - *Murder Cases of the Twentieth Century*
r AB - v99 - F 10 '97 - p410+ [501+]
r ARBA - v28 - '97 - p226 [251-500]
r Choice - v34 - F '97 - p943 [51-250]
r LJ - v121 - D '96 - p84 [51-250]
r R&R Bk N - v12 - F '97 - p57 [51-250]
Frasier, Debra - *On the Day You Were Born (Illus. by Debra Frasier)*
c PW - v244 - Mr 24 '97 - p85 [51-250]
Fratzscher, Oliver - *The Political Economy of Trade Integration*
JEL - v35 - Mr '97 - p213 [51-250]
Fraustino, Lisa - *Ash*
y Emerg Lib - v24 - S '96 - p24 [1-50]
Frawley, Maria H - *Anne Bronte*
Choice - v34 - F '97 - p965 [51-250]
Nine-C Lit - v51 - Mr '97 - p556 [51-250]
Fraxedas, J Joaquin - *La Travesia Solitaria De Juan Cabrera*
Hisp - v79 - S '96 - p474+ [501+]
Frayling, Christopher - *Film Classics*
SF Chr - v18 - O '96 - p81 [1-50]
Nightmare: The Birth of Horror
Obs - D 29 '96 - p27 [51-250]
TLS - Ap 11 '97 - p20 [501+]
Frayn, Keith N - *Metabolic Regulation*
Choice - v34 - N '96 - p482 [51-250]
SciTech - v20 - N '96 - p31 [51-250]
Frayne, Trent - *Trent Frayne's All Stars*
Quill & Q - v62 - Jl '96 - p48 [501+]
Fraysse, Olivier - *Lincoln, Land, and Labor 1809-60*
J Am St - v30 - Ap '96 - p137+ [501+]
Frazee, Steve - *Hidden Gold*
PW - v244 - Ap 14 '97 - p60 [51-250]
Frazer, Heather T - *We Have Just Begun to Not Fight*
PSQ - v111 - Fall '96 - p560+ [501+]

Frazer, James George, Sir - *The Golden Bough. New Abridgement from the 2nd and 3rd Eds.*
RES - v47 - N '96 - p627+ [501+]
Frazer, Margaret - *The Murderer's Tale*
Arm Det - v30 - Win '97 - p102 [251-500]
BWatch - v17 - S '96 - p2 [1-50]
Frazer, William - *The Florida Land Boom*
JEH - v56 - S '96 - p748+ [51-250]
Frazeur, Joyce - *Cycles (Moon Poems)*
Sm Pr R - v28 - S '96 - p12 [51-250]
Frazier, Amy - *Waiting at the Altar*
Quill & Q - v62 - Jl '96 - p44 [501+]
Frazier, Charles - *Cold Mountain*
KR - v65 - Ap 1 '97 - p503 [51-250]
PW - v244 - My 5 '97 - p196+ [51-250]
Frazier, Donald S - *Blood and Treasure*
AHR - v101 - D '96 - p1628 [501+]
JSH - v62 - N '96 - p819+ [251-500]
Frazier, Howard S - *Medicine Worth Paying For*
J Con A - v31 - Sum '97 - p168+ [501+]
Frazier, Ian - *Coyote v. Acme*
NYTBR - v101 - D 8 '96 - p79 [1-50]
PW - v244 - Ap 21 '97 - p69 [1-50]
Trib Bks - My 11 '97 - p8 [1-50]
VLS - Win '96 - p9 [51-250]
Dating Your Mom
VQR - v72 - Aut '96 - p143* [1-50]
Frazier, Kendrick - *The UFO Invasion*
y BL - v93 - Mr 15 '97 - p1206 [51-250]
Frechuret, M - *1946, L'Art De La Reconstruction*
BM - v138 - S '96 - p625+ [501+]
Freda, Joseph - *Suburban Guerrillas*
LATBR - N 10 '96 - p15 [51-250]
Frede, Michael - *Rationality in Greek Thought*
Choice - v34 - Ap '97 - p1353 [51-250]
Frederic, Louis - *Borobudur*
NYTBR - v101 - D 8 '96 - p56 [51-250]
Frederick, Joan - *T.C. Cannon: He Stood in the Sun*
Bloom Rev - v16 - Jl '96 - p18 [501+]
Frederick, Judith A - *As Time Goes By...*
J Gov Info - v23 - S '96 - p610 [51-250]
Frederick, William C - *Values, Nature, and Culture in the American Corporation*
JEL - v34 - S '96 - p1460 [51-250]
Rel St Rev - v23 - Ja '97 - p51 [51-250]
Fredericks, Anthony D - *Exploring the Rainforest*
c Ch BWatch - v6 - Jl '96 - p1 [1-50]
E Mag - v8 - Mr '97 - p49 [1-50]
Simple Nature Experiments with Everyday Materials (Illus. by Frances Zweifel)
c HB Guide - v7 - Fall '96 - p328 [51-250]
Fredrickson, George M - *Black Liberation*
Africa T - v44 - 1 '97 - p90+ [501+]
AHR - v101 - O '96 - p1122+ [501+]
Dis - v44 - Spr '97 - p122+ [501+]
NYTBR - v101 - D 29 '96 - p20 [1-50]
Free Materials for Schools and Libraries
p Emerg Lib - v23 - My '96 - p40 [51-250]
Freed, John B - *Noble Bondsmen*
CEH - v29 - 2 '96 - p235+ [501+]
CHR - v82 - Jl '96 - p534 [251-500]
Freed, Les - *The History of Computers*
SciTech - v20 - N '96 - p6 [51-250]
Freedman, Charles E - *The Triumph of Corporate Capitalism in France 1867-1914*
EHR - v112 - F '97 - p248+ [501+]
JMH - v68 - S '96 - p706+ [501+]
Freedman, Alan - *The Computer Desktop Encyclopedia*
r ARBA - v28 - '97 - p622 [51-250]
r CBR - v15 - Spr '97 - p2 [51-250]
r Choice - v34 - F '97 - p943 [51-250]
r R&R Bk N - v12 - F '97 - p92 [1-50]
The Computer Desktop Encyclopedia. Electronic Media Version
r LJ - v121 - N 15 '96 - p95+ [501+]
Freedman, Aviva - *Genre and the New Rhetoric*
Col Comp - v47 - D '96 - p605+ [501+]
Learning and Teaching Genre
Col Comp - v47 - D '96 - p605+ [501+]
Freedman, David H - *At Large*
KR - v65 - My 1 '97 - p692 [251-500]
Freedman, Diane P - *The Intimate Critique*
Can Lit - Win '96 - p137+ [501+]
Freedman, Estelle B - *Maternal Justice*
BW - v26 - Ag 4 '96 - p6 [501+]
Choice - v34 - N '96 - p545+ [51-250]
R&R Bk N - v11 - N '96 - p46 [51-250]
Wom R Bks - v14 - D '96 - p14+ [501+]
Freedman, J F - *Key Witness*
BL - v93 - My 15 '97 - p1540+ [51-250]

Freedman, James O - *Idealism and Liberal Education*
Choice - v34 - Ja '97 - p848 [51-250]
Freedman, Jill - *Narrative Therapy*
SciTech - v20 - D '96 - p45 [1-50]
Freedman, Luba - *Titian's Portraits through Aretino's Lens*
Six Ct J - v27 - Win '96 - p1178+ [501+]
Freedman, Ralph - *Life of a Poet*
Lon R Bks - v18 - Ag 22 '96 - p8+ [501+]
VQR - v73 - Win '97 - p20* [51-250]
Wil Q - v20 - Aut '96 - p96+ [251-500]
Freedman, Robert O - *The Middle East after Iraq's Invasion of Kuwait*
JTWS - v13 - Fall '96 - p325+ [501+]
Freedman, Russell - *Eleanor Roosevelt: A Life of Discovery*
c BL - v93 - D 15 '96 - p716 [1-50]
y Kliatt - v31 - My '97 - p21 [51-250]
Kids at Work
y Kliatt - v30 - S '96 - p3 [1-50]
The Life and Death of Crazy Horse (Illus. by Amos Bad Heart Bull)
y BL - v93 - Ja '97 - p764 [1-50]
y BL - v93 - Ap 1 '97 - p1286 [1-50]
y BL - v93 - Ap 1 '97 - p1302 [1-50]
y BL - v93 - Ap 1 '97 - p1306 [1-50]
c Ch BWatch - v6 - Jl '96 - p4 [51-250]
c CLW - v67 - D '96 - p64 [51-250]
c HB - v72 - S '96 - p614 [51-250]
c HB Guide - v7 - Fall '96 - p372 [51-250]
y SLJ - v42 - D '96 - p29 [1-50]
y VOYA - v19 - O '96 - p228+ [251-500]
Lincoln: A Photobiography
y Kliatt - v30 - S '96 - p4 [1-50]
Out of Darkness (Illus. by Kate Kiesler)
c BL - v93 - Mr 1 '97 - p1157+ [51-250]
c CBRS - v25 - Mr '97 - p94 [51-250]
c CCB-B - v50 - My '97 - p321 [51-250]
c HB - v73 - My '97 - p339+ [251-500]
c KR - v65 - F 1 '97 - p222 [51-250]
c SLJ - v43 - Mr '97 - p200 [51-250]
The Wright Brothers
c BL - v93 - D 15 '96 - p716 [1-50]
Freedman, Samuel G - *The Inheritance: How Three Families and America Moved from Roosevelt to Reagan and Beyond*
Bks & Cult - v2 - N '96 - p4 [51-250]
BL - v93 - S 15 '96 - p188+ [51-250]
Bus W - S 30 '96 - p13 [501+]
BW - v26 - O 20 '96 - p1+ [501+]
BW - v26 - D 8 '96 - p9 [51-250]
LATBR - v263 - S 29 '96 - p6+ [501+]
Nat - v263 - O 28 '96 - p11+ [501+]
NY - v72 - N 25 '96 - p117 [51-250]
NYTBR - v101 - S 22 '96 - p15 [501+]
NYTBR - v101 - D 8 '96 - p88 [1-50]
NYTLa - v146 - O 11 '96 - pC37 [501+]
W&I - v12 - F '97 - p257+ [501+]
Upon This Rock
Intpr - v51 - Ja '97 - p110 [51-250]
Freedman, Suzanne - *Louis Brandeis: The People's Justice*
y HB Guide - v7 - Fall '96 - p372 [51-250]
c SLJ - v42 - N '96 - p112 [51-250]
Freedman, Terry - *Making Time with IT*
TES - Ja 3 '97 - p47U [1-50]
Freeling, Nicolas - *A Dwarf Kingdom*
Arm Det - v30 - Win '97 - p107+ [251-500]
Freely, Maureen - *The Other Rebecca*
TLS - N 15 '96 - p25 [51-250]
What about Us?
VV - v42 - Ja 7 '97 - p42 [1-50]
Freeman, Alan - *Marx and Non-Equilibrium Economics*
JEL - v34 - S '96 - p1407+ [51-250]
Freeman, Anthony - *God in Us*
Lon R Bks - v18 - O 3 '96 - p3+ [501+]
Freeman, Charles - *The Ancient Greeks*
c Ch BWatch - v6 - S '96 - p6 [51-250]
c Cur R - v36 - D '96 - p12 [51-250]
c HB Guide - v8 - Spr '97 - p165 [51-250]
c SLJ - v42 - S '96 - p214 [51-250]
Egypt, Greece, and Rome
y BL - v93 - D 15 '96 - p706 [51-250]
LJ - v122 - Ja '97 - p119+ [51-250]
Freeman, David - *Between Worlds*
MLJ - v80 - Win '96 - p535 [251-500]
Freeman, Derek - *Margaret Mead and the Heretic*
Trib Bks - F 2 '97 - p8 [1-50]
Freeman, Don - *Corduroy*
c HB - v73 - Mr '97 - p187 [1-50]

Freeman, James - *Angels Sing in Me. Audio Version*
    BWatch - v18 - Mr '97 - p8 [1-50]
Freeman, John W - *The Metropolitan Opera Stories of the*
    Great Operas. Vol. 2
    Choice - v34 - My '97 - p1508 [51-250]
    LJ - v121 - N 15 '96 - p63+ [51-250]
    PW - v243 - S 30 '96 - p74 [51-250]
Freeman, Jon C - *Fundamentals of Microwave*
    Transmission Lines
    r SciTech - v20 - S '96 - p58 [51-250]
Freeman, Judith - *A Desert of Pure Feeling*
    PW - v244 - My 12 '97 - p74 [1-50]
    Wom R Bks - v14 - O '96 - p21+ [501+]
Freeman, Judy - *More Books Kids Will Sit Still For*
    Inst - v105 - My '96 - p69 [51-250]
    SLJ - v42 - S '96 - p112 [1-50]
Freeman, Marcia S - *Building a Writing Community*
    Inst - v106 - O '96 - p14 [51-250]
Freeman, Martha - *Stink Bomb Mom*
    c CCB-B - v50 - F '97 - p204 [51-250]
    c HB Guide - v8 - Spr '97 - p66 [51-250]
    c KR - v64 - O 15 '96 - p1532 [51-250]
    c SLJ - v42 - D '96 - p122 [51-250]
    y VOYA - v19 - D '96 - p268 [251-500]
Freeman, Mary Wilkins - *A Mary Wilkins Freeman*
    Reader
    BL - v93 - Mr 1 '97 - p1110 [51-250]
Freeman, Michael - *Children's Rights*
    R&R Bk N - v12 - F '97 - p63 [51-250]
Freeman, Neil B - *The Politics of Power*
    JEL - v34 - D '96 - p2089 [51-250]
Freeman, Pamela - *Victor's Quest (Illus. by Kim Gamble)*
    c Magpies - v11 - Jl '96 - p30 [51-250]
Freeman, Randy A - *Robust Nonlinear Control Design*
    SciTech - v20 - N '96 - p15 [51-250]
Freeman, Richard B - *Differences and Changes in Wage*
    Structures
    Econ J - v106 - N '96 - p1842 [51-250]
    ILRR - v50 - O '96 - p176+ [51-250]
    JEL - v34 - S '96 - p1369+ [501+]
Freeman, Roger L - *Telecommunication System*
    Engineering. 3rd Ed.
    Choice - v34 - D '96 - p642 [51-250]
    SciTech - v20 - N '96 - p73 [51-250]
Freeman, Roland L - *A Communion of the Spirits*
    BL - v93 - F 15 '97 - p992 [51-250]
    BW - v26 - D 8 '96 - p11 [51-250]
    PW - v243 - S 23 '96 - p70 [51-250]
Freeman, Suzanne - *The Cuckoo's Child*
    c BL - v93 - Ja '97 - p766 [1-50]
    y BL - v93 - Ap 1 '97 - p1292 [1-50]
    y Emerg Lib - v24 - S '96 - p43 [1-50]
    c HB Guide - v7 - Fall '96 - p292 [51-250]
    c HMR - Fall '96 - p36+ [501+]
    c NYTBR - v101 - O 13 '96 - p26 [1-50]
    c PW - v243 - N 4 '96 - p48 [51-250]
    c SLJ - v42 - D '96 - p29 [1-50]
    c SLJ - v43 - Mr '97 - p112 [1-50]
Freeman-Bell, Gail - *Management in Engineering. 2nd Ed.*
    SciTech - v20 - S '96 - p48 [51-250]
Freeman-Grenville, G S P - *The Holy Land: A Pilgrim's*
    Guide to Israel, Jordan and the Sinai
    r MEJ - v50 - Sum '96 - p451 [51-250]
    The Holy Land: A Pilgrim's Guide to Israel, Jordan,
    and the Sinai
    Rel St Rev - v23 - Ap '97 - p174 [51-250]
Freemantle, Brian - *Bomb Grade*
    y BL - v93 - Mr 1 '97 - p1113 [51-250]
    KR - v65 - Ja 1 '97 - p9+ [251-500]
    PW - v244 - F 10 '97 - p67 [51-250]
    No Time for Heroes
    PW - v243 - N 18 '96 - p70 [1-50]
    The Octopus: Europe in the Grip of Organized Crime
    PW - v243 - S 30 '96 - p71 [1-50]
Freer, Blaine - *West Coast Seafood Recipes*
    BWatch - v17 - D '96 - p10 [51-250]
Freer, Charles Lang - *With Kindest Regards*
    Art J - v55 - Win '96 - p99+ [501+]
Freethy, Barbara - *Ryan's Return*
    PW - v243 - S 2 '96 - p122 [51-250]
Fregoso, Rosa Linda - *The Bronze Screen*
    Am Q - v48 - S '96 - p516+ [501+]
Frei, Matt - *Getting the Boot*
    Soc - v34 - Ja '97 - p84+ [501+]
    Italy: The Unfinished Revolution
    Obs - Ja 19 '97 - p18* [51-250]
Freiberg, Jack - *The Lateran in 1600*
    CH - v66 - Mr '97 - p199+ [51-250]
    Six Ct J - v27 - Fall '96 - p819+ [501+]

Freiberg, Kevin - *Nuts! Southwest Airlines' Crazy Recipe*
    for Business and Personal Success
    Bus Bk R - v14 - 1 '97 - p68+ [501+]
    Bus W - F 24 '97 - p15 [51-250]
    LJ - v121 - O 1 '96 - p94+ [51-250]
    PW - v243 - S 30 '96 - p70 [51-250]
Freidel, Frank - *Harvard Guide to American History. Rev.*
    Ed., Vols. 1-2
    r ASInt - v34 - O '96 - p7 [51-250]
    The White House
    J Am Cult - v18 - Win '95 - p98 [251-500]
    Pres SQ - v26 - Sum '96 - p887+ [501+]
Freidin, Robert - *Current Issues in Comparative*
    Grammar
    R&R Bk N - v12 - F '97 - p76 [51-250]
Freidlander, Saul - *Probing the Limits of Representation*
    Poetics T - v17 - Sum '96 - p241+ [51-250]
Freidlin, Mark I - *Markov Processes and Differential*
    Equations
    SciTech - v20 - S '96 - p9 [51-250]
Freije, Matthew R - *Legionellae Control in Health Care*
    Facilities
    Choice - v34 - D '96 - p642 [51-250]
    SB - v32 - N '96 - p232 [501+]
    SciTech - v20 - S '96 - p28 [51-250]
Freiman, Marcelle - *Monkey's Wedding*
    Aust Bk R - S '96 - p54+ [501+]
Freire, Paulo - *Letters to Cristina*
    BL - v93 - N 15 '96 - p553 [51-250]
    PW - v243 - Jl 22 '96 - p233 [51-250]
Freireich, Emil J - *Molecular Genetics and Therapy of*
    Leukemia
    SciTech - v20 - N '96 - p46 [51-250]
Freireich, Valerie J - *The Beacon*
    Analog - v117 - Mr '97 - p152+ [251-500]
    y Kliatt - v31 - Mr '97 - p16 [51-250]
    LJ - v121 - S 15 '96 - p101 [51-250]
    NYTBR - v101 - D 29 '96 - p16 [51-250]
Freitag, Burkhard - *Object Orientation with Parallelism*
    and Persistence
    SciTech - v21 - Mr '97 - p12 [51-250]
Freitag, Ruth S - *The Battle of the Centuries*
    r J Gov Info - v23 - S '96 - p552 [1-50]
Freke, Timothy - *The Complete Guide to World Mysticism*
    Books - v11 - Ap '97 - p20 [51-250]
Frelinghuysen, Alice Cooney - *American Art Pottery*
    Am Craft - v56 - Ag '96 - p26 [1-50]
Fremon, Celeste - *Father Greg and the Homeboys*
    y Emerg Lib - v24 - S '96 - p23 [1-50]
Fremon, David K - *Japanese-American Internment in*
    American History
    y BL - v93 - Ja '97 - p833+ [251-500]
    c HB Guide - v8 - Spr '97 - p167 [51-250]
    y VOYA - v19 - D '96 - p286 [251-500]
    Running Away
    y HB Guide - v7 - Fall '96 - p316 [51-250]
Frenaud, Andre - *Gloses A La Sorciere*
    WLT - v70 - Sum '96 - p660+ [501+]
    Rome the Sorceress
    TranslRevS - v2 - D '96 - p23 [51-250]
French, Albert - *Patches of Fire*
    y BL - v93 - D 15 '96 - p695 [51-250]
    KR - v64 - N 15 '96 - p1650+ [251-500]
    LJ - v122 - Ja '97 - p108+ [51-250]
    LJ - v121 - N 1 '96 - p80 [1-50]
    NYTBR - v102 - Ja 26 '97 - p10 [501+]
    PW - v243 - N 25 '96 - p64 [51-250]
French, David - *Contemporary Television*
    Afterimage - v24 - N '96 - p15 [51-250]
French, Fiona - *Lord of the Animals (Illus. by Fiona*
    French)
    c KR - v65 - Ap 1 '97 - p554 [51-250]
    c PW - v244 - Mr 17 '97 - p83 [51-250]
French, Jackie - *Beyond the Boundaries*
    Aust Bk R - S '96 - p60+ [501+]
    Mind's Eye
    c Magpies - v11 - My '96 - p42+ [51-250]
    Summerland
    c Magpies - v11 - S '96 - p32 [51-250]
    A Wombat Named Bosco (Illus. by Bettina Guthridge)
    c Magpies - v11 - S '96 - p32+ [51-250]
French, Karl - *Screen Violence*
    Obs - O 27 '96 - p16* [251-500]
    Si & So - v6 - N '96 - p34 [51-250]
    TLS - N 8 '96 - p35 [501+]
French, Lorely - *German Women as Letter Writers*
    1750-1850
    Choice - v34 - Ja '97 - p800 [51-250]

French, Marilyn - *My Summer with George*
    Ms - v7 - S '96 - p83 [1-50]
    NYTBR - v101 - Ag 25 '96 - p6 [501+]
    Rapport - v19 - 6 '96 - p25 [251-500]
French, Nicci - *The Memory Game*
    Books - v11 - Ap '97 - p22 [51-250]
    NS - v126 - F 21 '97 - p46+ [501+]
    Obs - F 2 '97 - p17* [501+]
    TLS - D 27 '96 - p22 [501+]
French, Philip - *The Faber Book of Movie Verse*
    Parnassus - v22 - 1 '97 - p154+ [501+]
French, R A - *Plans, Pragmatism and People*
    GJ - v163 - Mr '97 - p109 [51-250]
    Slav R - v55 - Fall '96 - p699+ [501+]
French, R K - *Before Science*
    Choice - v34 - My '97 - p1512 [51-250]
    SciTech - v20 - D '96 - p1 [51-250]
    William Harvey's Natural Philosophy
    EHR - v112 - F '97 - p197+ [501+]
    Isis - v87 - D '96 - p724+ [501+]
French, Rebecca Redwood - *The Golden Yoke*
    JR - v77 - Ap '97 - p343+ [501+]
French, Robert M - *The Subtlety of Sameness*
    Choice - v34 - O '96 - p316 [51-250]
French, Sean - *The Dreamer of Dreams*
    Obs - D 22 '96 - p18* [51-250]
French, Thomas - *South of Heaven*
    y Kliatt - v30 - N '96 - p24 [51-250]
    LATBR - My 26 '96 - p11 [51-250]
French, Vivian - *Bob the Dog*
    c Sch Lib - v44 - N '96 - p146 [51-250]
    Lazy Jack (Illus. by Russell Ayto)
    c Bks Keeps - N '96 - p6 [51-250]
    Morris and the Cat Flap
    c Magpies - v11 - Jl '96 - p28 [51-250]
    Oliver's Vegetables (Illus. by Alison Bartlett)
    c RT - v50 - F '97 - p421 [51-250]
    A Song for Little Toad (Illus. by Barbara Firth)
    c Magpies - v11 - My '96 - p38 [51-250]
    Spider Watching
    c CLW - v67 - Mr '97 - p13 [1-50]
    Squeaky Cleaners in a Hole
    c Bks Keeps - Jl '96 - p9 [51-250]
    Squeaky Cleaners in a Muddle
    c Bks Keeps - Jl '96 - p9 [51-250]
French, William E - *A Peaceful and Working People*
    Choice - v34 - O '96 - p343 [51-250]
French-American Foundation - *Parallel Views*
    J Rehab RD - v33 - Jl '96 - p336 [251-500]
French Constitution
    J Gov Info - v23 - S '96 - p658 [1-50]
The French Renaissance in Prints, from the Bibliotheque
Nationale De France
    Ren Q - v49 - Win '96 - p910+ [501+]
Frend, William H C - *The Archaeology of Early*
    Christianity
    Choice - v34 - F '97 - p1017 [51-250]
    CLW - v67 - Mr '97 - p30 [251-500]
    TLS - O 18 '96 - p10+ [501+]
Frendreis, John P - *The Modern Presidency and*
    Economic Policy
    SSQ - v78 - Mr '97 - p243+ [501+]
Frenkel, Daan - *Understanding Molecular Simulation*
    SciTech - v20 - N '96 - p23 [51-250]
Frensch, Peter A - *Complex Problem Solving*
    Math T - v89 - S '96 - p514 [51-250]
Frerck, Robert - *Eternal Mexico*
    BL - v93 - N 15 '96 - p568 [51-250]
Frere, Jane - *Sticky Little Fingers (Illus. by Bettina*
    Paterson)
    c Sch Lib - v45 - F '97 - p19 [51-250]
Frerking, Gary - *Borland Delphi How-To*
    BYTE - v21 - O '96 - p168 [51-250]
Fresco, Louise O - *The Future of Our Land*
    GJ - v162 - Jl '96 - p238 [51-250]
Frese, Dolores Warwick - *An Ars Legendi for Chaucer's*
    Canterbury Tales
    Comp L - v48 - Fall '96 - p377+ [501+]
Fresh and Tasty: Women's Snowboarding
    p Workbook - v21 - Fall '96 - p146 [51-250]
Freshman
    y PW - v243 - D 9 '96 - p69 [51-250]
Freshmen
    y Cur R - v36 - N '96 - p13 [51-250]
Fretwell, Barry - *Clematis as Companion Plants*
    Hort - v74 - D '96 - p59 [51-250]

Freud, Lucian - *Lucian Freud (Bernard)*
    BW - v26 - D 8 '96 - p11 [51-250]
    LATBR - D 8 '96 - p28+ [1-50]
    NYTBR - v101 - D 8 '96 - p21 [501+]
    Obs - S 15 '96 - p17* [51-250]
    Spec - v277 - O 12 '96 - p50 [501+]
    TLS - O 4 '96 - p40 [1-50]
    VLS - Win '96 - p22 [51-250]
Freud, Sigmund - *The Correspondence of Sigmund Freud and Sandor Ferenczi. Vol. 2*
    Choice - v34 - S '96 - p214 [51-250]
    Choice - v34 - Ja '97 - p878 [51-250]
    Isis - v88 - Mr '97 - p155+ [501+]
    VQR - v72 - Aut '96 - p126* [51-250]
    Psychological Writings and Letters
    TranslRevS - v2 - D '96 - p18 [1-50]
    Totem and Taboo
    JAAR - v64 - Fall '96 - p557+ [501+]
Freudberg, Frank - *Gasp! A Novel of Revenge*
    Rapport - v19 - 5 '96 - p36 [51-250]
Freudenheim, Ellen - *Healthspeak: A Complete Dictionary of America's Health Care System*
    r ARBA - v28 - '97 - p600 [51-250]
    r HR Mag - v41 - S '96 - p138 [51-250]
Freudenthal, Gad - *Aristotle's Theory of Material Substance*
    Isis - v87 - S '96 - p533+ [251-500]
    Rel St Rev - v23 - Ap '97 - p172 [51-250]
Freund, Gerald - *Narcissism and Philanthropy*
    AS - v66 - Spr '97 - p298+ [501+]
    CSM - v89 - D 9 '96 - p15 [501+]
    NYTBR - v101 - N 17 '96 - p42 [501+]
    PW - v243 - S 9 '96 - p72 [51-250]
Freund, John E - *Modern Elementary Statistics. 9th Ed.*
    SciTech - v20 - D '96 - p16 [51-250]
Freund, Rudolf J - *Statistical Methods. Rev. Ed.*
    SciTech - v20 - D '96 - p17 [51-250]
Freundlich, Irwin M - *A Radiologic Approach to Diseases of the Chest. 2nd Ed.*
    SciTech - v21 - Mr '97 - p59 [51-250]
Freundlich, Lawrence S - *George Rodrigue: A Cajun Artist*
    BL - v93 - Ja '97 - p802 [51-250]
Frevert, Ute - *Mann Und Weib, Und Weib Und Mann*
    Choice - v34 - D '96 - p569 [1-50]
Frey, Darcy - *The Last Shot*
    y Emerg Lib - v24 - S '96 - p23 [1-50]
Frey, Julia - *Toulouse-Lautrec: A Life (Schraf). Audio Version*
    y Kliatt - v31 - Mr '97 - p50+ [51-250]
Frey, Stephen W - *The Inner Sanctum*
    BL - v93 - My 1 '97 - p1461 [51-250]
    KR - v65 - My 1 '97 - p661+ [251-500]
    LJ - v122 - My 1 '97 - p139 [51-250]
    The Takeover (Stinton). Audio Version
    Books - v9 - S '95 - p27 [1-50]
    The Vulture Fund
    Arm Det - v29 - Fall '96 - p504 [251-500]
    PW - v244 - Mr 31 '97 - p72 [1-50]
    The Vulture Fund (Guidall). Audio Version
    BWatch - v18 - Mr '97 - p7 [1-50]
Freyd, Jennifer J - *Betrayal Trauma*
    Choice - v34 - Ap '97 - p1419 [51-250]
    KR - v64 - N 1 '96 - p1579 [251-500]
    NYTBR - v102 - Ja 26 '97 - p20 [501+]
    SciTech - v21 - Mr '97 - p65 [51-250]
Freyer, Tony A - *Producers versus Capitalists*
    AHR - v101 - O '96 - p1279+ [501+]
Frias Nunez, Marcelo - *Tras El Dorado Vegetal*
    Isis - v87 - D '96 - p733+ [501+]
Friberg, Bo - *The Professional Pastry Chef*
    CSM - v89 - D 13 '96 - p10 [51-250]
Friberg, Gosta - *Krigsvintrar*
    WLT - v70 - Sum '96 - p720 [51-250]
Frick, David - *Meletij Smotryc'kyj*
    Six Ct J - v27 - Fall '96 - p858+ [51-250]
Frick, Devin - *Collectible Kay Finch*
    Ant & CM - v102 - Ap '97 - p66 [51-250]
Frickhinger, Karl Albert - *Fossil Atlas, Fishes*
    r ARBA - v28 - '97 - p637 [51-250]
    r BL - v92 - Ag '96 - p1924+ [251-500]
Friday, Nancy - *The Power of Beauty*
    KR - v64 - My 1 '96 - p662 [251-500]
    Woman's J - Ap '97 - p18 [51-250]
Fried, Hedi - *The Road to Auschwitz*
    y Kliatt - v31 - Mr '97 - p26 [51-250]
    PW - v243 - S 2 '96 - p118 [51-250]
Fried, Johannes - *Der Weg In Die Geschichte*
    AHR - v101 - D '96 - p1530+ [501+]

Fried, Michael - *Manet's Modernism*
    Bloom Rev - v16 - N '96 - p24 [51-250]
    Choice - v34 - O '96 - p267 [51-250]
    New R - v216 - F 3 '97 - p43+ [501+]
    VQR - v72 - Aut '96 - p140* [51-250]
Fried, SuEllen - *Bullies and Victims*
    LJ - v121 - O 15 '96 - p84 [51-250]
Friedeburg, Robert Von - *Sundenzucht Und Sozialer Wandel*
    EHR - v111 - S '96 - p979+ [51-250]
Friedel, Robert - *Zipper*
    NS & S - v9 - My 17 '96 - p39 [1-50]
Friedemann, Marie-Luise - *The Framework of Systemic Organization*
    Fam Relat - v45 - O '96 - p479+ [251-500]
Frieden, Bernard J - *Downtown, Inc.*
    J Urban H - v22 - S '96 - p750+ [501+]
    Metropolitan America
    NCR - v85 - Spr '96 - p63 [51-250]
Frieden, Sarajo - *The Care and Feeding of Fish (Illus. by Sarajo Frieden)*
    c BL - v93 - N 15 '96 - p593 [51-250]
    c CBRS - v25 - Win '97 - p62 [51-250]
    c CCB-B - v50 - O '96 - p58 [51-250]
    c Ch BWatch - v6 - N '96 - p6 [1-50]
    c HB Guide - v8 - Spr '97 - p27 [51-250]
    c SLJ - v42 - O '96 - p94 [51-250]
Friedgut, Theodore H - *Iuzovka and Revolution. Vol. 2*
    Russ Rev - v56 - Ja '97 - p138 [501+]
    Iuzovka and Revolution. Vols. 1-2
    JMH - v68 - S '96 - p742+ [501+]
Friedheim, William - *Freedom's Unfinished Revolution*
    SLMQ - v25 - Fall '96 - p63+ [1-50]
Friedhoffer, Bob - *Physics Lab in a Housewares Store (Illus. by Joe Hosking)*
    c SLJ - v43 - Ja '97 - p124 [51-250]
Friedhoffer, Robert - *Magic and Perception (Illus. by Linda Eisenberg)*
    y HB Guide - v8 - Spr '97 - p142 [51-250]
    c SLJ - v42 - S '96 - p214 [51-250]
    Physics Lab in a Hardware Store (Illus. by Joe Hosking)
    c BL - v93 - D 1 '96 - p656 [51-250]
    c HB Guide - v8 - Spr '97 - p112 [51-250]
    Physics Lab in a Housewares Store (Illus. by Joe Hosking)
    c BL - v93 - D 1 '96 - p656 [51-250]
    c HB Guide - v8 - Spr '97 - p112 [51-250]
Friedl, Vicki L - *Women in the United States Military 1901-1995*
    r ARBA - v28 - '97 - p252 [251-500]
    r BL - v93 - D 15 '96 - p750 [251-500]
    r Choice - v34 - Ap '97 - p1307 [51-250]
    r R&R Bk N - v12 - F '97 - p100 [51-250]
Friedland, Martin L - *A Place Apart*
    J Gov Info - v23 - S '96 - p618 [51-250]
Friedland, Roger - *To Rule Jerusalem*
    CS - v26 - Mr '97 - p141+ [501+]
    LATBR - Jl 14 '96 - p1+ [501+]
    LATBR - D 29 '96 - p3+ [51-250]
    Lon R Bks - v18 - O 31 '96 - p16+ [501+]
    Rel St Rev - v23 - Ap '97 - p198+ [51-250]
Friedlander, Daniel - *Five Years After*
    AAPSS-A - v547 - S '96 - p189 [501+]
    Soc Ser R - v71 - Mr '97 - p144+ [501+]
Friedlander, Henry - *The Origins of Nazi Genocide*
    AHR - v102 - F '97 - p128+ [501+]
    HRNB - v25 - Fall '96 - p31 [501+]
    Rel St Rev - v23 - Ap '97 - p198 [51-250]
Friedlander, Lee - *The Desert Seen*
    NYTBR - v101 - D 8 '96 - p72 [51-250]
    VV - v52 - Ja 28 '97 - p48+ [501+]
Friedlander, Michael W - *At the Fringes of Science*
    Isis - v87 - D '96 - p767+ [501+]
Friedlander, Paul - *Rock and Roll*
    Ant R - v54 - Sum '96 - p366 [251-500]
    PMS - v19 - Win '95 - p118+ [501+]
Friedlander, Saul - *Nazi Germany and the Jews. Vol. 1*
    BL - v93 - Ja '97 - p812 [51-250]
    Choice - v34 - My '97 - p1557 [51-250]
    For Aff - v76 - My '97 - p134+ [251-500]
    KR - v64 - D 1 '96 - p1714+ [51-250]
    LATBR - F 23 '97 - p8 [501+]
    LJ - v122 - F 1 '97 - p94 [51-250]
    NYTBR - v102 - F 23 '97 - p12+ [501+]
    PW - v243 - D 2 '96 - p46 [51-250]
Friedman, Amy - *The Spectacular Gift and Other Tales from Tell Me a Story (Illus. by Jillian Hulme Gilliland)*
    c HB Guide - v7 - Fall '96 - p320 [1-50]
Friedman, Barry D - *Regulation in the Reagan-Bush Era*
    APSR - v90 - S '96 - p647+ [501+]

Friedman, Bruce Jay - *The Collected Short Fiction of Bruce Jay Friedman*
    Trib Bks - Ja 19 '97 - p8 [1-50]
    A Father's Kisses
    BL - v93 - S 1 '96 - p61 [51-250]
    LATBR - N 17 '96 - p14 [51-250]
    NYTBR - v101 - O 27 '96 - p26 [501+]
    NYTBR - v101 - D 8 '96 - p79 [1-50]
Friedman, C S - *Crown of Shadows*
    y Kliatt - v31 - Ja '97 - p12 [51-250]
Friedman, David - *Hidden Order*
    BL - v92 - Ag '96 - p1865 [51-250]
    BYTE - v21 - S '96 - p178 [51-250]
Friedman, Edward - *National Identity and Democratic Prospects in Socialist China*
    Ch Rev Int - v3 - Fall '96 - p415+ [501+]
    The Politics of Democratization
    Ch Rev Int - v4 - Spr '97 - p131+ [501+]
Friedman, Emily - *The Right Thing*
    Hast Cen R - v26 - S '96 - p40 [51-250]
Friedman, Francine - *The Bosnian Muslims*
    APSR - v91 - Mr '97 - p211+ [501+]
    VQR - v72 - Aut '96 - p133*+ [51-250]
Friedman, George - *The Future of War*
    KR - v64 - D 15 '96 - p1780 [251-500]
    LJ - v121 - D '96 - p122 [51-250]
    PW - v243 - D 30 '96 - p47 [51-250]
    WSJ-Cent - v99 - Mr 11 '97 - pA20 [501+]
Friedman, Herman - *Microorganisms and Autoimmune Diseases*
    SciTech - v20 - N '96 - p46 [51-250]
Friedman, J M - *The Effects of Drugs on the Fetus and Nursing Infant*
    r ARBA - v28 - '97 - p617 [51-250]
    r SciTech - v20 - S '96 - p40 [1-50]
Friedman, Jerome - *The Battle of the Frogs and Fairford's Flies*
    Ren Q - v49 - Win '96 - p862+ [501+]
Friedman, John B - *Northern English Books, Owners, and Makers in the Late Middle Ages*
    Albion - v28 - Win '96 - p672+ [501+]
    LQ - v67 - Ja '97 - p92+ [501+]
Friedman, Julian - *Writing Long-Running Television Series*
    Si & So - v6 - N '96 - p36 [51-250]
Friedman, Kinky - *God Bless John Wayne*
    PW - v243 - S 23 '96 - p74 [1-50]
    The Love Song of J. Edgar Hoover
    BL - v92 - Ag '96 - p1885+ [51-250]
    LATBR - O 13 '96 - p8 [51-250]
    The Love Song of J. Edgar Hoover (Whitener). Audio Version
    LJ - v121 - O 1 '96 - p144 [51-250]
    PW - v243 - O 7 '96 - p32 [51-250]
Friedman, Lawrence M - *Legal Culture and the Legal Profession*
    R&R Bk N - v11 - N '96 - p51 [51-250]
Friedman, Lawrence S - *The Cinema of Martin Scorsese*
    LJ - v122 - My 1 '97 - p105 [51-250]
Friedman, Lynn - *A Woman Doctor's Guide to Miscarriage*
    LJ - v121 - S 15 '96 - p86 [51-250]
Friedman, Marilyn - *Feminism and Community*
    Ethics - v107 - Ja '97 - p391 [51-250]
    Political Correctness
    Ethics - v107 - O '96 - p188+ [251-500]
Friedman, Melvin J - *Traditions, Voices, and Dreams*
    ABR - v17 - Ag '96 - p15 [501+]
    Critiq - v37 - Sum '96 - p313+ [501+]
    J Am St - v30 - D '96 - p481+ [251-500]
Friedman, Meyer - *Type A Behavior*
    SciTech - v21 - Mr '97 - p53 [51-250]
Friedman, Michael Jan - *Crossover*
    y Kliatt - v31 - Ja '97 - p12 [51-250]
    Crossover (Frakes). Audio Version
    SF Chr - v18 - O '96 - p82 [1-50]
    Fantastic Four
    PW - v244 - My 12 '97 - p63 [51-250]
    Kahless (Conway). Audio Version
    y Kliatt - v30 - N '96 - p46 [51-250]
    Saratoga
    y Kliatt - v31 - Ja '97 - p12 [51-250]
Friedman, Morton P - *Cognitive Ecology*
    Choice - v34 - S '96 - p213 [51-250]
Friedman, Philip - *Grand Jury*
    Arm Det - v29 - Fall '96 - p500+ [251-500]
    Grand Jury (Rubinstein). Audio Version
    Arm Det - v29 - Fall '96 - p472+ [51-250]
    BL - v93 - F 15 '97 - p1038 [51-250]
    y Kliatt - v31 - Mr '97 - p42 [51-250]
    Quill & Q - v62 - My '96 - p31 [1-50]

Friedman, R Seth - *The Factsheet Five Zine Reader*
   KR - v65 - Ap 1 '97 - p543 [51-250]
   PW - v244 - Ap 14 '97 - p68 [51-250]
Friedman, Raymond A - *Front Stage, Backstage*
   Econ J - v106 - N '96 - p1843 [51-250]
Friedman, Richard Elliott - *The Disappearance of God*
   JR - v77 - Ap '97 - p311+ [501+]
   Skeptic - v4 - 4 '96 - p101+ [251-500]
   Theol St - v57 - D '96 - p735+ [501+]
Friedman, Sally - *Swimming the Channel*
   BL - v93 - S 1 '96 - p55 [51-250]
   LATBR - N 3 '96 - p6 [501+]
   LJ - v121 - S 15 '96 - p83 [51-250]
   NYTBR - v101 - N 3 '96 - p18 [51-250]
Friedman, Stanton T - *Top Secret/MAJIC*
   y BL - v93 - S 15 '96 - p181 [51-250]
   LJ - v121 - O 1 '96 - p118 [51-250]
   PW - v243 - S 23 '96 - p70 [51-250]
Friedman, Steven - *Time-Effective Psychotherapy*
   SciTech - v21 - Mr '97 - p54 [51-250]
Friedman, Susan W - *Marc Bloch, Sociology and Geography*
   Choice - v34 - F '97 - p1016 [51-250]
Friedman-Kasaba, Kathie - *Memories of Migration*
   R&R Bk N - v12 - F '97 - p25 [51-250]
Friedrich, Elizabeth - *Leah's Pony (Illus. by Michael Garland)*
   c HB Guide - v7 - Fall '96 - p256+ [51-250]
   c Par - v71 - D '96 - p254 [51-250]
   c RT - v50 - Mr '97 - p502 [51-250]
Friedrich, Otto - *Blood and Iron*
   NYRB - v43 - Je 6 '96 - p20+ [501+]
   NYTBR - v101 - D 8 '96 - p85 [1-50]
   NYTBR - v102 - Ja 5 '97 - p28 [51-250]
Friedrichs, Christopher R - *The Early Modern City 1450-1750*
   Historian - v58 - Sum '96 - p900+ [501+]
   HT - v47 - Ja '97 - p56+ [501+]
Friedrichs, David O - *Trusted Criminals*
   Choice - v34 - S '96 - p218 [51-250]
Friel, Ian - *The Good Ship*
   Albion - v28 - Win '96 - p673+ [501+]
   Sea H - Win '96 - p42 [51-250]
Friend, Charles E - *All the Proud Ships*
   y Kliatt - v30 - S '96 - p8+ [51-250]
Fries, Kenny - *Body, Remember*
   KR - v64 - O 15 '96 - p1508+ [51-250]
   LJ - v122 - Ja '97 - p110 [51-250]
   Prog - v61 - Mr '97 - p43 [251-500]
   PW - v243 - O 21 '96 - p61 [51-250]
Friesen, Delores - *All Are Witnesses*
   Am - v176 - F 15 '97 - p33 [51-250]
Friesner, Esther - *Blood Muse*
   SF Chr - v18 - O '96 - p80 [1-50]
   Child of the Eagle
   y Kliatt - v30 - S '96 - p18 [51-250]
   SF Chr - v18 - O '96 - p79+ [51-250]
   The Psalms of Herod
   Analog - v117 - F '97 - p145+ [501+]
Frieze
   p SFR - v21 - S '96 - p45 [51-250]
Frigon, Normand L - *Achieving the Competitive Edge*
   R&R Bk N - v11 - D '96 - p27 [51-250]
   Practical Guide to Experimental Design
   Choice - v34 - Ap '97 - p1370 [51-250]
   SciTech - v21 - Mr '97 - p71 [51-250]
Friman, H Richard - *NarcoDiplomacy: Exporting the U.S. War on Drugs*
   Choice - v34 - Ap '97 - p1418 [51-250]
Frisch, U - *Turbulence: The Legacy of A.N. Kolmogorov*
   Nature - v382 - Jl 25 '96 - p311+ [501+]
   Phys Today - v49 - N '96 - p82+ [501+]
Frisch, Walter - *Brahms, the Four Symphonies*
   Choice - v34 - Ap '97 - p1347 [51-250]
Frison, George C - *The Mill Iron Site*
   Choice - v34 - N '96 - p500+ [51-250]
Frison-Roche, Roger - *A History of Mountain Climbing*
   BW - v26 - D 8 '96 - p12 [51-250]
   Choice - v34 - Ap '97 - p1378 [51-250]
   LJ - v122 - Ja '97 - p107 [51-250]
   PW - v243 - S 30 '96 - p74 [51-250]
   VLS - Win '96 - p20 [51-250]
Fristedt, Bert - *A Modern Approach to Probability Theory*
   SciTech - v21 - Mr '97 - p14 [51-250]
Frith, Simon - *Performing Rites*
   y BL - v93 - S 1 '96 - p53 [51-250]
   Choice - v34 - Ja '97 - p805 [51-250]
   LJ - v121 - S 15 '96 - p69+ [51-250]
   NS - v125 - N 8 '96 - p48 [501+]
   PW - v243 - Jl 22 '96 - p223 [51-250]
   TLS - Ja 17 '97 - p11 [501+]

Fritz, Hans - *Kastratengesang: Hormonelle, Konstitutionelle Und Padagogische Aspekte*
   Notes - v53 - S '96 - p52+ [501+]
Fritz, Jean - *Around the World in a Hundred Years*
   c Ch BWatch - v6 - O '96 - p1 [51-250]
   Bully for You, Teddy Roosevelt!
   y Kliatt - v31 - My '97 - p21+ [51-250]
   c PW - v244 - F 3 '97 - p108 [1-50]
Fritz, Stephen G - *Frontsoldaten: The German Soldier in World War II*
   AHR - v102 - F '97 - p129 [501+]
   J Soc H - v30 - Win '96 - p552+ [501+]
   Mar Crp G - v81 - Mr '97 - p75 [501+]
Fritz, Volkmar - *The City in Ancient Israel*
   Rel St Rev - v23 - Ja '97 - p56 [51-250]
   Das Erste Buch Der Konige
   Rel St Rev - v23 - Ap '97 - p165 [51-250]
Fritze, Ronald H - *Historical Dictionary of Stuart England 1603-1689*
   r ARBA - v28 - '97 - p202 [51-250]
   r Choice - v34 - S '96 - p99 [51-250]
   r LJ - v122 - Ap 15 '97 - p39 [51-250]
Fritzsche, Peter - *A Nation of Fliers*
   JMH - v68 - S '96 - p735+ [501+]
   Reading Berlin 1900
   Choice - v34 - O '96 - p283+ [501+]
Froes, F H - *Synthesis/Processing of Lightweight Metallic Materials*
   SciTech - v20 - N '96 - p64 [51-250]
Froese, Deborah L - *The Wise Washerman (Illus. by Wang Kui)*
   c CBRS - v25 - F '97 - p74+ [51-250]
   c CCB-B - v50 - D '96 - p133+ [51-250]
   c HB Guide - v8 - Spr '97 - p101 [51-250]
   c PW - v243 - N 11 '96 - p73 [51-250]
   c SLJ - v43 - Ja '97 - p100 [51-250]
Frohnen, Bruce - *The New Communitarians and the Crisis of Modern Liberalism*
   Choice - v34 - D '96 - p688 [51-250]
   RP - v59 - Spr '97 - p398+ [501+]
   TLS - Ja 17 '97 - p24 [501+]
   WSJ-MW - v77 - S 26 '96 - pA10 [51-250]
Frohock, Fred M - *Healing Powers*
   RA - v25 - 3 '96 - p167+ [501+]
Frolich, Margrit - *Between Affluence and Rebellion*
   R&R Bk N - v11 - N '96 - p75 [1-50]
Frolich, Thomas - *Archaeologie Und Seismologie*
   AJA - v100 - O '96 - p811+ [51-250]
Frolick, Billy - *What I Really Want to Do Is Direct*
   KR - v64 - O 1 '96 - p1442 [251-500]
   LJ - v121 - N 1 '96 - p68 [51-250]
   PW - v243 - S 2 '96 - p101 [51-250]
Fromentin, Eugene - *La Correspondance D'Eugene Fromentin. Vols. 1-2*
   BM - v138 - S '96 - p609 [501+]
Fromkin, David - *In the Time of the Americans*
   VQR - v72 - Aut '96 - p141* [1-50]
Fromm, Pete - *Dry Rain*
   BL - v93 - Mr 15 '97 - p1224 [51-250]
   KR - v65 - F 15 '97 - p242 [251-500]
   LJ - v122 - Ap 15 '97 - p122 [51-250]
   PW - v244 - Mr 17 '97 - p78 [51-250]
   King of the Mountain
   Aethlon - v13 - Fall '95 - p141+ [251-500]
Frommer, Myrna - *It Happened in Brooklyn*
   Ant R - v54 - Sum '96 - p372+ [251-500]
   It Happened in the Catskills
   PW - v243 - S 23 '96 - p73 [1-50]
Frommer, Sara Hoskinson - *Murder and Sullivan*
   KR - v65 - Ap 1 '97 - p505+ [51-250]
   PW - v244 - Mr 10 '97 - p53 [51-250]
Frommer's Best Beach Vacations: The Mid-Atlantic from New York to Washington, D.C.
   r BL - v93 - S 15 '96 - p206+ [1-50]
Frommer's Canada. 9th Ed.
   r Quill & Q - v63 - F '97 - p41 [51-250]
Frommer's Montana and Wyoming
   r BL - v93 - S 15 '96 - p210 [1-50]
Frommer's Nova Scotia, New Brunswick and Prince Edward Island
   r BL - v93 - S 15 '96 - p210 [1-50]
Frommer's San Francisco by Night (Frommer's Guide). 1st Ed.
   r BL - v93 - S 15 '96 - p210 [1-50]
Frontera
   p Utne R - N '96 - p94+ [251-500]
Frontiers '96
   SciTech - v21 - Mr '97 - p4 [51-250]
Frost, Alan - *East Coast Country*
   Aust Bk R - N '96 - p23+ [501+]

Frost, Carol - *Venus and Don Juan*
   LJ - v121 - S 15 '96 - p72 [51-250]
Frost, Dan R - *The LSU College of Engineering. Vol. 1*
   JSH - v63 - F '97 - p188+ [251-500]
Frost, David, Jr. - *Witness to Injustice*
   JSH - v62 - N '96 - p861 [1-50]
   JSH - v63 - F '97 - p194+ [251-500]
Frost, Ginger S - *Promises Broken*
   JIH - v27 - Spr '97 - p679+ [501+]
Frost, Harold J - *Polycrystalline Thin Films*
   SciTech - v21 - Mr '97 - p22 [51-250]
Frost, Jenny - *Creativity in Primary Science*
   TES - F 28 '97 - p16* [251-500]
Frost, Lee - *Taking Pictures for Profit*
   Pet PM - v25 - F '97 - p8+ [51-250]
Frost, Mary Pierce - *The Mexican Revolution*
   y BL - v93 - Ja '97 - p836 [251-500]
   y HB Guide - v8 - Spr '97 - p173 [51-250]
   y SLJ - v43 - Ja '97 - p124 [51-250]
Frost, Mervyn - *Ethics in International Relations*
   Choice - v34 - D '96 - p686 [51-250]
Frost, Peter J - *Rhythms of Academic Life*
   R&R Bk N - v11 - N '96 - p55 [51-250]
Frost, Richard - *Neighbor Blood*
   LJ - v121 - O 1 '96 - p82 [51-250]
Frost, Robert - *Collected Poems, Plays and Prose*
   NYRB - v43 - Ag 8 '96 - p40+ [501+]
   Poet - v168 - Jl '96 - p232+ [501+]
   Robert Frost: Selected Poems
   Bloom Rev - v16 - Jl '96 - p27 [1-50]
   Versed in Country Things
   Bloom Rev - v16 - Jl '96 - p20+ [51-250]
   LATBR - My 12 '96 - p10 [51-250]
Frost, Roger - *IT in Primary Science*
   TES - Ja 3 '97 - p47U [1-50]
Frost, Sue - *Redeem the Time*
   Books - v10 - Je '96 - p17 [51-250]
Frostenson, Katarina - *2 Skadespel*
   WLT - v71 - Win '97 - p172 [251-500]
Froula, Christine - *Modernism's Body*
   Choice - v34 - N '96 - p456 [51-250]
   R&R Bk N - v11 - N '96 - p70 [51-250]
Frow, Mayerlene - *Roots of the Future*
   Sch Lib - v44 - N '96 - p177 [51-250]
Frowen, Stephen F - *Financial Decision-Making and Moral Responsibility*
   Econ J - v106 - N '96 - p1831+ [251-500]
Froyen, Richard T - *Macroeconomics: Theories and Policies. 5th Ed.*
   JEL - v34 - S '96 - p1417+ [51-250]
Frucht, Abby - *Life before Death*
   KR - v65 - My 1 '97 - p662 [251-500]
Fruchtman, Jack, Jr. - *Thomas Paine: Apostle of Freedom*
   EHR - v112 - F '97 - p217+ [251-500]
Frum, David - *Dead Right*
   CS - v26 - Ja '97 - p30+ [501+]
   What's Right
   BIC - v25 - S '96 - p26+ [501+]
   BW - v26 - Ag 18 '96 - p5+ [501+]
   KR - v64 - My 1 '96 - p662 [251-500]
Frum, Linda - *Barbara Frum: A Daughter's Memoir*
   BIC - v26 - F '97 - p24 [501+]
   Mac - v109 - N 4 '96 - p68 [501+]
   Quill & Q - v62 - O '96 - p34 [501+]
Frumkin, Lyn R - *Questions and Answers on AIDS. 3rd Ed.*
   Advocate - Ap 29 '97 - p73 [51-250]
Fruton, Joseph S - *Eighty Years*
   Isis - v87 - S '96 - p507+ [501+]
   A Skeptical Biochemist
   Isis - v87 - S '96 - p507+ [501+]
Fry, Alan - *How a People Die*
   Can Lit - Win '96 - p139+ [501+]
   Wilderness Survival Handbook
   LJ - v121 - S 15 '96 - p74 [51-250]
Fry, Maxwell J - *Central Banking in Developing Countries*
   JEL - v35 - Mr '97 - p208 [51-250]
Fry, Paul H - *A Defense of Poetry*
   Critm - v38 - Fall '96 - p642+ [501+]
Fry, Roger Eliot - *A Roger Fry Reader*
   BW - v26 - Ag 4 '96 - p12 [51-250]
   TLS - Ap 11 '97 - p28 [251-500]
Fry, Ronald W - *Ace Any Test. 3rd Ed.*
   y SLJ - v42 - O '96 - p156 [51-250]
   Get Organized
   y Kliatt - v30 - S '96 - p28 [51-250]
   How to Study. 4th Ed.
   y Ch BWatch - v6 - S '96 - p7 [51-250]
   y SLJ - v42 - O '96 - p156 [51-250]

Last Minute Study Tips
y Ch BWatch - v6 - S '96 - p7 [51-250]
y Kliatt - v30 - S '96 - p28+ [51-250]
Use Your Computer
y Kliatt - v30 - S '96 - p28 [51-250]
Fry, Stephen - *Making History*
NS - v125 - S 27 '96 - p62 [251-500]
Spec - v277 - S 14 '96 - p44 [501+]
TLS - S 27 '96 - p24+ [501+]
Woman's J - N '96 - p12 [1-50]
Fryatt, Evelyn Howe - *Candy Making for Beginners*
BL - v93 - F 15 '97 - p988 [51-250]
Fryde, E B - *Peasants and Landlords in Later Medieval England*
Choice - v34 - Ap '97 - p1397 [51-250]
Frydman, Roman - *Privatization in Eastern Europe*
Econ J - v106 - N '96 - p1845 [51-250]
Slav R - v55 - Sum '96 - p449+ [501+]
Frye, David - *Indians into Mexicans*
Choice - v34 - N '96 - p522 [51-250]
Frye, Fredric L - *Self-Assessment Color Review of Reptiles and Amphibians*
SciTech - v20 - D '96 - p57 [51-250]
Frye, Northrop - *The Correspondence of Northrop Frye and Helen Kemp 1932-1939. Vols. 1-2*
BIC - v25 - D '96 - p18+ [501+]
Choice - v34 - Ap '97 - p1335+ [51-250]
Frye, Richard N - *The Heritage of Central Asia*
Choice - v34 - Ja '97 - p860+ [51-250]
Frye, Susan - *Elizabeth I: The Competition for Representation*
JMH - v68 - S '96 - p675+ [501+]
Frykenberg, Robert Eric - *History and Belief*
CC - v113 - D 4 '96 - p1210 [51-250]
Choice - v34 - F '97 - p1016 [51-250]
Fu, Charles Wei-Hsun - *Buddhist Behavioral Codes and the Modern World*
J Ch St - v38 - Aut '96 - p907+ [251-500]
Fu, Danling - *My Trouble Is My English*
ES - v27 - Sum '96 - p163+ [501+]
Fu, Jianwen - *Da Dao Ge*
BL - v93 - N 1 '96 - p484 [1-50]
Fu, Zhengyuan - *China's Legalists*
Rel St Rev - v23 - Ja '97 - p97 [51-250]
R&R Bk N - v11 - N '96 - p46 [51-250]
Fubini, Enrico - *Music and Culture in Eighteenth-Century Europe*
r JAAC - v54 - Fall '96 - p408+ [501+]
Fubini, Riccardo - *Italia Quattrocentesca*
EHR - v112 - F '97 - p181 [501+]
Ren Q - v49 - Aut '96 - p598+ [501+]
Fuchs, Elinor - *The Death of Character*
Am Theat - v13 - D '96 - p20 [1-50]
Am Theat - v14 - Ja '97 - p70+ [501+]
Choice - v34 - D '96 - p624 [51-250]
TCI - v30 - O '96 - p57 [1-50]
Fuchs, Hans U - *The Dynamics of Heat*
Choice - v34 - O '96 - p320 [51-250]
Fuchs, Joseph S J - *Moral Demands and Personal Obligations*
JR - v77 - Ja '97 - p170+ [501+]
Fuchs, Roland J - *Mega-City Growth and the Future*
J Gov Info - v23 - S '96 - p678 [51-250]
Fuchs, Thomas - *Die Mechanisierung Des Herzens*
Isis - v87 - D '96 - p724+ [501+]
Fuchs, Victor R - *Individual and Social Responsibility*
JEL - v34 - S '96 - p1440+ [51-250]
JEL - v35 - Mr '97 - p150+ [51-250]
Fucito, Salvatore - *Caruso and the Art of Singing*
M Ed J - v83 - Jl '96 - p50 [51-250]
Fuentes, Carlos - *Diana, the Goddess Who Hunts Alone*
Ant R - v54 - Sum '96 - p367+ [251-500]
WLT - v70 - Sum '96 - p671+ [501+]
A New Time for Mexico
Choice - v34 - N '96 - p523 [51-250]
CSM - v88 - O 9 '96 - p13 [501+]
For Aff - v75 - S '96 - p149 [51-250]
LATBR - Ag 18 '96 - p4 [501+]
VQR - v73 - Win '97 - p25*+ [51-250]
Fuery, Patrick - *The Theory of Absence*
CPR - v16 - Je '96 - p160+ [501+]
Fuguet, Alberto - *Bad Vibes*
KR - v65 - Ja 15 '97 - p80 [251-500]
PW - v244 - F 24 '97 - p62 [51-250]
Fuhrer, Karl Christian - *Mieter, Hausbesitzer, Staat Und Wohnungsmarkt*
AHR - v102 - F '97 - p130+ [501+]
Fuhrman, Chris - *The Dangerous Lives of Altar Boys*
LATBR - Mr 24 '96 - p11 [51-250]

Fuhrman, Mark - *Murder in Brentwood*
CSM - v89 - Mr 6 '97 - p14 [51-250]
CSM - v89 - Ap 3 '97 - p14 [51-250]
NYTBR - v102 - Mr 23 '97 - p30 [501+]
Fuhrmann, Ingeburg - *Fortalecer La Familia*
Lect Y V - v17 - S '96 - p45 [501+]
Fuhrmann, Paul Abraham - *A Polynomial Approach to Linear Algebra*
Choice - v34 - My '97 - p1536 [51-250]
JEL - v34 - D '96 - p2021 [51-250]
Fujii, James A - *Complicit Fictions*
MP - v94 - Ag '96 - p132+ [501+]
Fujimura, Joan H - *Crafting Science*
LJ - v122 - F 1 '97 - p103 [51-250]
Nature - v386 - Mr 13 '97 - p139+ [501+]
Fujimura-Fanselow, Kumiko - *Japanese Women*
NWSA Jnl - v9 - Spr '97 - p117+ [501+]
Fujioka, Yasuhiro - *John Coltrane: A Discography and Musical Biography*
r Notes - v53 - Mr '97 - p810+ [501+]
Fujita, Shigeji - *Quantum Statistical Theory of Superconductivity*
SciTech - v21 - Mr '97 - p24 [51-250]
Fujitani, T - *Splendid Monarchy*
Choice - v34 - Mr '97 - p1216 [51-250]
TLS - N 29 '96 - p13 [51-250]
Fukao, Mitsuhiro - *Financial Integration, Corporate Governance, and the Performance of Multinational Companies*
Econ J - v107 - Ja '97 - p273 [251-500]
Fukaya, Michiyo - *A Fire Is Burning, It Is in Me*
BL - v93 - S 1 '96 - p56 [51-250]
Fukuda, Hanaka - *Favorite Songs of Japanese Children*
c CAY - v17 - Fall '96 - p10 [51-250]
Fukuyama, Francis - *Trust: The Social Virtues and the Creation of Prosperity*
CR - v270 - F '97 - p111 [51-250]
RP - v58 - Fall '96 - p829+ [501+]
TES - Ja 31 '97 - p7* [51-250]
Fulbrook, Mary - *Anatomy of a Dictatorship*
APSR - v90 - D '96 - p936+ [501+]
HRNB - v25 - Win '97 - p73 [251-500]
National Histories and European History
EHR - v111 - S '96 - p1041+ [251-500]
Fuld, James J - *The Book of World-Famous Music. 4th Ed., Rev. and Enl.*
CAY - v16 - Fall '95 - p4 [51-250]
Fulford, Margaret - *The Canadian Women's Movement 1960-1990*
Archiv - Fall '94 - p192+ [501+]
Fulford, Robert C - *Dr. Fulford's Touch of Life*
BL - v93 - S 1 '96 - p50 [51-250]
LJ - v121 - O 1 '96 - p116 [51-250]
Dr. Fulford's Touch of Life. Audio Version
Quill & Q - v62 - S '96 - p71 [1-50]
Fulghum, Robert - *True Love*
BL - v93 - D 15 '96 - p690+ [51-250]
PW - v244 - Ja 27 '97 - p91 [51-250]
Fulker, Tina - *Loose Change*
Sm Pr R - v28 - Je '96 - p9 [51-250]
Fulkerson, John P - *Disorders of the Patellofemoral Joint. 3rd Ed.*
SciTech - v21 - Mr '97 - p60 [51-250]
Fuller, Errol - *The Lost Birds of Paradise*
NH - v105 - S '96 - p42+ [501+]
Fuller, Gerald - *Stories for All Seasons*
CLW - v67 - D '96 - p42+ [51-250]
Fuller, Graham E - *Algeria: The Next Fundamentalist State?*
For Aff - v75 - N '96 - p165 [51-250]
Fuller, Henry B - *The Chevalier of Pensieri-Vani*
RMR - v50 - 2 '96 - p147+ [501+]
Fuller, John - *Collected Poems*
TLS - N 29 '96 - p14 [51-250]
TLS - F 28 '97 - p10+ [501+]
Stones and Fires
Spec - v277 - N 16 '96 - p44 [1-50]
Fuller, Kathryn H - *At the Picture Show*
BL - v93 - D 15 '96 - p696 [51-250]
Choice - v34 - Mr '97 - p1170 [51-250]
Fuller, Kimberly - *Home*
y KR - v65 - Ap 1 '97 - p554 [51-250]
Fuller, Kristi - *Eat and Stay Slim*
BL - v93 - F 15 '97 - p987 [51-250]
Low-Fat and Luscious Italian
PW - v244 - Ja 6 '97 - p69 [51-250]
Fuller, Margaret - *The Woman and the Myth. Rev. and Expanded Ed.*
Legacy - v14 - 1 '97 - p69+ [501+]

Fuller, Robert C - *Naming the Antichrist*
AHR - v101 - O '96 - p1267 [501+]
Am - v175 - Jl 20 '96 - p27+ [501+]
Rel St Rev - v23 - Ap '97 - p135+ [501+]
Religion and Wine
Choice - v34 - S '96 - p148 [51-250]
Rel St Rev - v23 - Ja '97 - p93 [51-250]
VQR - v72 - Aut '96 - p139*+ [51-250]
Fuller, Vernella - *Unlike Normal Women*
BL - v93 - Ja '97 - p818 [51-250]
PW - v243 - N 18 '96 - p67 [51-250]
Fullerton, John - *The Monkey House*
BW - v26 - Ag 18 '96 - p9 [501+]
Econ - v341 - D 7 '96 - p3*+ [501+]
LJ - v122 - Mr 15 '97 - p42 [1-50]
NYTBR - v101 - S 1 '96 - p7 [501+]
W&I - v11 - D '96 - p281+ [501+]
The Monkey House (Charles). Audio Version
LJ - v122 - F 1 '97 - p126 [51-250]
Fullilove, Eric James - *Circle of One*
MFSF - v92 - Mr '97 - p36 [51-250]
Fullinwider, Robert K - *Public Education in a Multicultural Society*
CC - v113 - N 20 '96 - p1134+ [501+]
Choice - v34 - N '96 - p511 [51-250]
Fulton, Alice - *Dance Script with Electric Ballerina*
Parnassus - v22 - 1 '97 - p296+ [501+]
Palladium
Parnassus - v22 - 1 '97 - p296+ [501+]
Powers of Congress
Parnassus - v22 - 1 '97 - p296+ [501+]
Sensual Math
Ken R - v18 - Sum '96 - p214+ [501+]
Parnassus - v22 - 1 '97 - p296+ [501+]
Fulton, Bruce - *Wayfarer: New Fiction by Korean Women*
KR - v65 - Mr 1 '97 - p335 [51-250]
PW - v244 - Mr 24 '97 - p61 [51-250]
Fulton, William - *The Reluctant Metropolis*
PW - v244 - Ap 7 '97 - p81 [51-250]
Fulweiler, Howard W - *Here a Captive Heart Busted*
VS - v39 - Win '96 - p272+ [501+]
Fumagalli, Vito - *Scrivere La Storia*
Choice - v34 - D '96 - p567 [1-50]
Fumerton, Patricia - *Cultural Aesthetics*
Clio - v25 - Sum '96 - p421+ [501+]
Fumia, Molly - *Honor Thy Children*
BL - v93 - F 1 '97 - p912 [51-250]
LJ - v122 - Ja '97 - p110 [51-250]
PW - v243 - D 30 '96 - p50 [51-250]
Fund Raiser's Guide to Religious Philanthropy 1996
r ARBA - v28 - '97 - p313 [51-250]
Funder, Lise - *Nordisk Smukkekunst*
BM - v139 - Ja '97 - p52 [51-250]
Funderburg, Anne Cooper - *Chocolate, Strawberry and Vanilla*
BWatch - v17 - S '96 - p2 [51-250]
Funding Sources for Community and Economic Development 1996
r ARBA - v28 - '97 - p313+ [51-250]
r ChrPhil - v8 - Je 13 '96 - p38 [51-250]
The FundLine Advisor. 1997 Ed.
Quill & Q - v63 - Ja '97 - p25 [51-250]
Funiciello, Theresa - *Tyranny of Kindness*
NWSA Jnl - v8 - Sum '96 - p107+ [501+]
Funk, Hermann - *Sowieso: A German Course for Young People*
y MLJ - v80 - Win '96 - p547+ [501+]
Funk, Robert Walter - *Honest to Jesus*
BL - v93 - N 1 '96 - p460 [51-250]
CC - v114 - Mr 19 '97 - p312+ [501+]
NYTBR - v102 - Mr 2 '97 - p19 [501+]
PW - v243 - S 16 '96 - p67 [501+]
Funk, Sandra G - *Key Aspects of Caring for the Acutely Ill*
AJN - v96 - N '96 - p16G [51-250]
Funk and Wagnalls New Encyclopedia 1996. Vols. 1-29
yr BL - v93 - S 15 '96 - p272+ [501+]
Funnell, Barbara E - *The Role of the Bacterial Membrane in Chromosome Replication and Partition*
SciTech - v20 - S '96 - p24 [51-250]
Funston, Sylvia - *Scary Science (Illus. by Dusan Petricic)*
c CLW - v67 - D '96 - p60 [51-250]
c Emerg Lib - v24 - Mr '97 - p26 [1-50]
c LATBR - O 20 '96 - p8 [51-250]
c Quill & Q - v62 - Ag '96 - p44 [251-500]
Furbank, P N - *Defoe De-Attributions*
Lib - v18 - Je '96 - p163+ [501+]
Furbish, David Jon - *Fluid Physics in Geology*
Choice - v34 - Mr '97 - p1189 [51-250]

Furgurson, Ernest B - *Ashes of Glory*
  BL - v93 - S 1 '96 - p58 [51-250]
  BW - v26 - O 6 '96 - p3 [501+]
  NYTBR - v101 - S 29 '96 - p24 [501+]
  S Liv - v31 - N '96 - p48 [51-250]
Furht, Borko - *Multimedia Systems and Techniques*
  SciTech - v20 - D '96 - p7 [51-250]
  Multimedia Tools and Applications
  SciTech - v20 - D '96 - p7 [51-250]
Furia, Philip - *Ira Gershwin: The Art of the Lyricist*
  NYRB - v43 - O 17 '96 - p35+ [501+]
  RAH - v25 - Mr '97 - p113+ [501+]
  TLS - Ja 17 '97 - p13 [501+]
Furino, Steven - *Frames and Resolvable Designs*
  SciTech - v20 - N '96 - p13 [51-250]
Furlong, Monica - *Visions and Longings*
  Bks & Cult - v3 - Mr '97 - p39 [251-500]
  Choice - v34 - N '96 - p475 [51-250]
  Comw - v123 - N 22 '96 - p28 [51-250]
  TLS - Mr 28 '97 - p6 [501+]
Furlong, Nicola - *Teed Off*
  BIC - v26 - F '97 - p36 [51-250]
Furman, Erna - *Preschoolers: Questions and Answers*
  Readings - v11 - S '96 - p29 [51-250]
Furman, Jan - *Toni Morrison's Fiction*
  AL - v69 - Mr '97 - p239 [251-500]
Furman, Laura - *Bookworms: Great Writers and Readers Celebrate Reading*
  y   BL - v93 - N 15 '96 - p566 [51-250]
  Bloom Rev - v17 - Ja '97 - p14 [51-250]
  BW - v26 - N 10 '96 - p12 [51-250]
  LJ - v121 - N 15 '96 - p62 [51-250]
Furomoto, Toshi - *International Aspects of Irish Literature*
  TLS - S 27 '96 - p13 [501+]
Furr, Jo - *Easy Word Games*
  Cur R - v36 - Ap '97 - p3* [51-250]
Furr, Keith A - *CRC Handbook of Laboratory Safety. 4th Ed.*
  r   ARBA - v28 - '97 - p630 [51-250]
Furrer, Roger MacPherson - *He Alo A He Alo*
  Pac A - v69 - Fall '96 - p454+ [501+]
Fursenko, Aleksandr - *One Hell of a Gamble*
  KR - v65 - My 1 '97 - p692 [251-500]
Furst, Alan - *The World at Night*
  Books - v11 - Ap '97 - p21 [51-250]
  NYTBR - v101 - S 8 '96 - p23 [251-500]
  Spec - v278 - F 22 '97 - p30 [501+]
  VQR - v73 - Win '97 - p22* [51-250]
Furst, Lilian R - *All Is True*
  AL - v68 - D '96 - p860+ [501+]
  Rel St Rev - v23 - Ja '97 - p53 [51-250]
Furst, Peter - *Don Quixote in Exile*
  R&R Bk N - v11 - N '96 - p74 [1-50]
Furth, Hans G - *Desire for Society*
  R&R Bk N - v12 - F '97 - p66 [51-250]
Furton, Edward - *A Medieval Semiotic*
  RM - v50 - S '96 - p153+ [501+]
Furtwangler, Albert - *Acts of Discovery*
  VQR - v73 - Win '97 - p183+ [501+]
Furutani, Dale - *Death in Little Tokyo*
  KR - v64 - Ag 15 '96 - p1189 [51-250]
  PW - v243 - S 2 '96 - p117 [51-250]
Fusco, Coco - *English Is Broken Here*
  Art J - v55 - Fall '96 - p91+ [501+]
Fusco, Richard - *Maupassant and the American Short Story*
  MLR - v91 - Jl '96 - p734+ [501+]
Fuss, Charles J - *Joan Baez: A Bio-Bibliography*
  r   ARBA - v28 - '97 - p490 [51-250]
  r   R&R Bk N - v11 - D '96 - p56 [51-250]
Fussel, Stephan - *Artibus: Kulturwissenschaft Und Deutsche Philologie Des Mittelalters Und Der Fruhen Neuzeit*
  Ren Q - v49 - Win '96 - p840+ [501+]
Fussell, Betty - *Home Bistro*
  BL - v93 - Mr 15 '97 - p1216 [51-250]
  LJ - v122 - Ap 15 '97 - p110 [51-250]
  PW - v244 - Ap 7 '97 - p88 [51-250]
Fussell, Paul - *Abroad: British Literary Traveling between the Wars*
  JMH - v68 - S '96 - p617+ [501+]
  The Anti-Egotist: Kingsley Amis, Man of Letters
  Sew R - v104 - Jl '96 - p452+ [501+]

Doing Battle
  BL - v93 - Ja '97 - p759 [1-50]
  BL - v93 - S 1 '96 - p56 [51-250]
  BW - v26 - S 29 '96 - p1+ [501+]
  LATBR - O 20 '96 - p4+ [501+]
  LATBR - D 29 '96 - p10 [51-250]
  Mar Crp G - v81 - F '97 - p71+ [501+]
  Nat R - v49 - F 24 '97 - p50+ [501+]
  NY - v72 - Ja 13 '97 - p79 [51-250]
  NYTBR - v101 - S 29 '96 - p18 [501+]
  NYTLa - v146 - O 9 '96 - pC18 [501+]
  PW - v243 - Jl 22 '96 - p218 [51-250]
  Utne R - N '96 - p88 [1-50]
  WSJ Cent - v99 - Mr 27 '97 - pA20 [501+]
Fuster, Joaquin M - *Memory in the Cerebral Cortex*
  AJPsych - v153 - N '96 - p1496+ [501+]
The Future of Naval Operations in Alameda County
  J Gov Info - v23 - S '96 - p603 [51-250]
The Future of the Canadian Broadcasting Corporation in the Multi-Channel Universe
  J Gov Info - v23 - S '96 - p613 [51-250]
Future Visions
  J Gov Info - v23 - S '96 - p555 [51-250]
Fye, W Bruce - *American Cardiology*
  AB - v99 - Mr 31 '97 - p1043+ [501+]
  Sci - v274 - O 25 '96 - p523 [1-50]
Fyfield, Frances - *Without Consent*
  Spec - v278 - Ap 5 '97 - p38 [51-250]
  TLS - D 20 '96 - p22 [251-500]
  Woman's J - D '96 - p16 [1-50]
Fyle, C Magbaily - *The State and the Provision of Social Services in Sierra Leone since Independence 1961-1991*
  Africa T - v43 - 4 '96 - p436+ [501+]
Fylypchak, Ivan - *Anna IAroslavna-Koroleva Frantsii*
  BL - v93 - N 15 '96 - p577 [1-50]

G

G.F.W.: Golf for Women
p LJ - v121 - O 1 '96 - p52 [1-50]
G7 Ministerial Conference on the Global Information Society (1995: Brussels, Belgium) - *Ministerial Conference Summary*
J Gov Info - v23 - S '96 - p668 [51-250]
Gaard, Greta - *Ecofeminism, Women, Animals, Nature*
Signs - v22 - Win '97 - p496+ [501+]
Gaarder, Jostein - *The Christmas Mystery (Illus. by Rosemary Wells)*
c Bks Keeps - N '96 - p20 [51-250]
y BL - v93 - S 1 '96 - p30 [51-250]
c BW - v26 - D 8 '96 - p12 [51-250]
c BW - v26 - D 15 '96 - p10 [51-250]
c CC - v113 - D 11 '96 - p1234 [51-250]
c ILN - Christmas '96 - p88+ [501+]
KR - v64 - S 1 '96 - p1269 [51-250]
PW - v243 - S 23 '96 - p55 [51-250]
The Solitaire Mystery
KR - v64 - My 1 '96 - p621 [251-500]
NYTBR - v101 - S 1 '96 - p16 [51-250]
y SLJ - v42 - S '96 - p239 [51-250]
y TES - Jl 5 '96 - pR2 [251-500]
y VOYA - v19 - D '96 - p268+ [51-250]
The Solitaire Mystery. Abridged Ed. Audio Version
y Kliatt - v30 - N '96 - p45 [51-250]
The Solitaire Mystery. Unabridged Ed. Audio Version
y Kliatt - v30 - N '96 - p45 [51-250]
Sophie's World
Bks & Cult - v3 - Ja '97 - p6 [501+]
y Bks Keeps - Jl '96 - p25 [501+]
S&T - v92 - S '96 - p53 [51-250]
Sophie's World (Needleman). Audio Version
y Ch BWatch - v6 - My '96 - p7 [51-250]
y Kliatt - v30 - N '96 - p45+ [51-250]
Gabaccia, Donna - *From the Other Side*
JIH - v27 - Win '97 - p547+ [501+]
NWSA Jnl - v9 - Spr '97 - p110+ [501+]
Gabaldon, Diana - *Drums of Autumn*
BL - v93 - N 15 '96 - p549 [51-250]
CSM - v89 - Ja 16 '97 - p14 [51-250]
KR - v64 - N 15 '96 - p1620+ [251-500]
LJ - v121 - N 15 '96 - p87+ [51-250]
PW - v243 - N 18 '96 - p62 [51-250]
Drums of Autumn (James). Audio Version
BWatch - v18 - Mr '97 - p7 [1-50]
y Kliatt - v31 - My '97 - p36 [51-250]
Voyager
Books - v9 - S '95 - p24 [1-50]
Voyager (James). Audio Version
y Kliatt - v30 - N '96 - p46 [51-250]
Gabbard, Krin - *Jammin' at the Margins*
AB - v98 - D 9 '96 - p1996 [51-250]
Choice - v34 - O '96 - p288 [51-250]
Ent W - S 20 '96 - p74 [51-250]
R&R Bk N - v11 - N '96 - p59 [51-250]
TLS - Ja 3 '97 - p19 [501+]
Representing Jazz
J Am St - v30 - Ag '96 - p289+ [501+]
Gabbe, Steven G - *Obstetrics: Normal and Problem Pregnancies. 3rd Ed.*
SciTech - v20 - D '96 - p52 [51-250]
Gabe, Jonathon - *Medicine, Health and Risk*
Socio R - v45 - F 1 '97 - p183+ [501+]
Gabler, Hans Walter - *Contemporary German Editorial Theory*
Ger Q - v69 - Fall '96 - p440+ [501+]
Gabor, Andrea - *Einstein's Wife*
y Kliatt - v30 - N '96 - p22 [51-250]
Sci - v274 - O 25 '96 - p523 [1-50]

Gabor, Don - *Talking with Confidence for the Painfully Shy*
BL - v93 - F 15 '97 - p974 [51-250]
PW - v244 - Ja 27 '97 - p93 [51-250]
Gabriel, H Paul - *Anticipating Adolescence*
VOYA - v19 - D '96 - p256 [1-50]
Gabriel, Kathryn - *Gambler Way*
BL - v93 - S 15 '96 - p189 [51-250]
Gabriele, Edward Francis - *From Many, One*
CLW - v67 - Mr '97 - p36 [51-250]
My Soul Magnifies the Lord
CLW - v67 - Mr '97 - p32 [251-500]
Gacek, Adam - *Arabic Lithographed Books*
r MEJ - v51 - Win '97 - p149 [51-250]
r R&R Bk N - v11 - D '96 - p73 [51-250]
Gach, Gary - *Pocket Guide to the Internet*
New Sci - v152 - N 30 '96 - p48 [51-250]
Gachechiladze, R G - *The New Georgia*
GJ - v163 - Mr '97 - p97 [501+]
JEL - v34 - D '96 - p2137 [51-250]
R&R Bk N - v11 - N '96 - p40 [51-250]
Gachie-Pineda, Maryse - *La Frontiere Mexique-Etats-Unis*
JSH - v62 - N '96 - p808+ [251-500]
Gachot, Theodore - *Mermaids: Nymphs of the Sea*
Mac - v109 - D 9 '96 - p66 [1-50]
MFSF - v92 - Mr '97 - p35 [51-250]
Gackenbach, Dick - *Barker's Crime (Illus. by Dick Gackenbach)*
c HB Guide - v7 - Fall '96 - p257 [51-250]
Gacquin, William - *Roscommon before the Famine*
ILS - v16 - Spr '97 - p36 [1-50]
Gadamer, Hans Georg - *The Enigma of Health*
Hast Cen R - v27 - Ja '97 - p46 [51-250]
R&R Bk N - v11 - D '96 - p69 [51-250]
Literature and Philosophy in Dialogue
Rel St Rev - v23 - Ap '97 - p161 [51-250]
Gaddis, John Lewis - *We Now Know*
Econ - v342 - Mr 15 '97 - p4* [501+]
KR - v65 - Mr 1 '97 - p349 [51-250]
Gaddy, Barbara B - *School Wars*
CC - v113 - N 20 '96 - p1134+ [501+]
Choice - v34 - F '97 - p1014 [51-250]
EL - v54 - F '97 - p84 [251-500]
Gaddy, C Welton - *Adultery and Grace*
PW - v243 - N 11 '96 - p69 [51-250]
Gaddy, Clifford G - *The Price of the Past*
Choice - v34 - F '97 - p1012 [51-250]
For Aff - v75 - N '96 - p162 [51-250]
JEL - v35 - Mr '97 - p225 [51-250]
Gadgil, Madhav - *Ecology and Equity*
GJ - v162 - N '96 - p341 [51-250]
Gadia, Madhu - *Lite and Luscious Cuisine of India*
BL - v93 - Mr 15 '97 - p1216 [51-250]
Gadoffre, Gilbert - *Renaissances Europeennes Et Renaissance Francaise*
Ren Q - v50 - Spr '97 - p251+ [501+]
Gadol, Peter - *The Mystery Roast*
PW - v243 - D 9 '96 - p66 [51-250]
Gadotti, Moacir - *Pedagogy of Praxis*
Choice - v34 - Ja '97 - p849 [51-250]
The Gadsden Times 1867-1871
EGH - v50 - N '96 - p160+ [51-250]
Gadzey, Anthony Tuo-Kofi - *The Political Economy of Power*
Choice - v34 - Mr '97 - p1208 [51-250]
Gaeddert, Louann - *Breaking Free*
y Kliatt - v31 - Mr '97 - p8 [51-250]
c PW - v243 - N 25 '96 - p78 [1-50]

Gaesser, Glenn A - *Big Fat Lies*
BL - v93 - S 1 '96 - p50 [51-250]
PW - v243 - S 2 '96 - p125 [51-250]
Gaff, Alan D - *On Many a Bloody Field*
BWatch - v18 - F '97 - p6 [51-250]
Choice - v34 - My '97 - p1562 [51-250]
KR - v64 - O 15 '96 - p1509 [251-500]
LJ - v121 - D '96 - p116 [51-250]
Gaffington, Urslan Judith - *Silver Berries and Christmas Magic (Illus. by Steven Morris)*
c PW - v243 - S 30 '96 - p91 [51-250]
c SLJ - v42 - O '96 - p36 [51-250]
Gaffney, Jeffrey S - *Humic and Fulvic Acids*
SciTech - v21 - Mr '97 - p30 [51-250]
Gaffney, John, 1950- - *Political Parties and the European Union*
Choice - v34 - D '96 - p687 [51-250]
Gaffney, John E - *Software Measurement Guidebook*
CBR - v14 - Jl '96 - p25 [1-50]
Gaffney, Timothy R - *Grandpa Takes Me to the Moon (Illus. by Barry Root)*
c CBRS - v24 - Ag '96 - p158 [51-250]
c CCB-B - v50 - O '96 - p58 [51-250]
c HB Guide - v8 - Spr '97 - p27 [51-250]
c Inst - v106 - O '96 - p68 [1-50]
c NYTBR - v102 - Ja 5 '97 - p22 [1-50]
c PW - v243 - Jl 22 '96 - p241 [51-250]
c SLJ - v42 - S '96 - p178 [51-250]
Gafoor, A L M Abdul - *Interest-Free Commercial Banking*
JEL - v34 - D '96 - p2127+ [51-250]
Participatory Financing through Investment Banks and Commercial Banks
JEL - v35 - Mr '97 - p295 [51-250]
Gagarin, Michael - *Early Greek Political Thought from Homer to the Sophists*
CPR - v16 - Ap '96 - p103+ [501+]
Ethics - v107 - Ja '97 - p400 [51-250]
Gage, Amy Glaser - *Pascual's Magic Pictures (Illus. by Karen Dugan)*
c HB Guide - v8 - Spr '97 - p27 [51-250]
c SLJ - v42 - D '96 - p92 [51-250]
Gage Canadian Dictionary
r BIC - v26 - Mr '97 - p2+ [501+]
Gagnon, Eric - *What's on the Internet. 3rd Ed.*
CBR - v14 - N '96 - p37 [51-250]
Gagnon, Francois-Marc - *Images Du Castor Canadien XVIe-XVIIIe*
Can Hist R - v77 - D '96 - p638+ [501+]
Gagnon, Madeleine - *Le Vent Majeur*
WLT - v70 - Aut '96 - p907 [501+]
Gaiduk, Ilya V - *The Soviet Union and the Vietnam War*
Choice - v34 - N '96 - p517 [51-250]
For Aff - v75 - S '96 - p152 [51-250]
J Mil H - v61 - Ap '97 - p414+ [501+]
RAH - v25 - Mr '97 - p157+ [501+]
TLS - O 11 '96 - p12 [501+]
VQR - v72 - Aut '96 - p133* [51-250]
Gailey, Harry A - *The War in the Pacific*
Pres SQ - v26 - Fall '96 - p1180+ [501+]
Gaillard, Frye - *If I Were a Carpenter*
ChrPhil - v8 - Ag 8 '96 - p50 [51-250]
y SLJ - v42 - O '96 - p164+ [51-250]
Gaillot, Jacques - *Voice from the Desert*
Am - v176 - F 15 '97 - p30+ [251-500]
BL - v93 - O 1 '96 - p296 [51-250]
Comw - v124 - Ap 11 '97 - p27+ [251-500]
LJ - v121 - O 1 '96 - p86 [51-250]
Gailly, Christian - *Be-Bop*
WLT - v70 - Sum '96 - p650+ [251-500]

Gaiman, Neil - *Neverwhere*
  y BL - v93 - My 15 '97 - p1541 [51-250]
The Sandman: Book of Dreams
     Books - v11 - Ap '97 - p23 [51-250]
     PW - v243 - Jl 22 '96 - p231+ [51-250]
  y VOYA - v19 - F '97 - p340 [251-500]
Gaines, Ernest J - *A Gathering of Old Men*
     South CR - v28 - Spr '96 - p44+ [501+]
A Gathering of Old Men. Audio Version
  y Kliatt - v31 - Mr '97 - p42 [51-250]
Gaines, Kevin K - *Uplifting the Race*
     Bl S - v26 - Sum '96 - p64 [1-50]
     HRNB - v25 - Win '97 - p55 [251-500]
Gaines, Patrice - *Moments of Grace*
     BL - v93 - F 1 '97 - p908 [51-250]
     LJ - v122 - Ja '97 - p106 [51-250]
     PW - v244 - Ja 13 '97 - p66 [51-250]
Gainor, J Ellen - *Imperialism and Theatre*
     Theat J - v48 - D '96 - p533+ [501+]
Gair, Angela - *Acrylics: A Step-by-Step Guide to Acrylics Techniques*
     LJ - v121 - N 15 '96 - p60 [51-250]
Artist's Manual
  y Kliatt - v30 - S '96 - p37+ [51-250]
Drawing: A Step-by-Step Guide to Drawing Techniques
     LJ - v121 - N 15 '96 - p60 [51-250]
Watercolor: A Step-by-Step Guide to Watercolor Techniques
     LJ - v121 - N 15 '96 - p60 [51-250]
Gais, Thomas - *Improper Influence*
     Choice - v34 - O '96 - p361 [51-250]
Gaitano, Nick - *Jaded*
     NYTBR - v101 - Ap 7 '96 - p23 [51-250]
Gaite, Carmen Martin - *Variable Cloud*
     Choice - v34 - D '96 - p620 [51-250]
Gaither, Carl C - *Statistically Speaking*
     New Sci - v153 - Ja 18 '97 - p39 [51-250]
  r SciTech - v21 - Mr '97 - p14 [51-250]
Gaitskill, Mary - *Because They Wanted To*
     Advocate - Mr 4 '97 - p59 [51-250]
     BL - v93 - Ja '97 - p818 [51-250]
     KR - v64 - N 15 '96 - p1621 [251-500]
     LATBR - Ja 19 '97 - p2 [501+]
     LJ - v122 - Ja '97 - p152 [51-250]
     Ms - v7 - Ja '97 - p79+ [251-500]
     NW - v129 - Ja 29 '97 - p57 [501+]
     NYTBR - v102 - F 9 '97 - p8+ [501+]
     PW - v243 - N 25 '96 - p57+ [251-500]
     Trib Bks - Mr 9 '97 - p9 [501+]
     VV - v42 - F 4 '97 - p51 [501+]
Gajek, Konrad - *Das Breslauer Schultheater Im 17. Und 18. Jahrhundert*
     MLR - v92 - Ja '97 - p236+ [501+]
Gajic, Zoran - *Lyapunov Matrix Equation in System Stability and Control*
     SIAM Rev - v38 - D '96 - p691 [501+]
Modern Control Systems Engineering
     SciTech - v21 - Mr '97 - p84 [51-250]
Gajski, Daniel D - *Principles of Digital Design*
     SciTech - v20 - D '96 - p78 [51-250]
Gal, Allon - *Envisioning Israel*
     MEJ - v51 - Spr '97 - p309 [51-250]
Galanaki, Rhea - *The Life of Ismail Ferik Pasha*
     PW - v243 - S 30 '96 - p62 [51-250]
     TranslRevS - v2 - D '96 - p26+ [51-250]
Galang, M Evelina - *Her Wild American Self*
     Choice - v34 - O '96 - p277 [51-250]
     RCF - v16 - Fall '96 - p196 [251-500]
  y SLJ - v42 - N '96 - p141 [51-250]
Galas, Judith C - *Drugs and Sports*
  y HB Guide - v8 - Spr '97 - p98 [51-250]
Gay Rights
  y HB Guide - v7 - Fall '96 - p316 [51-250]
Galassi, Peter - *Before Photography*
     NYRB - v44 - Mr 6 '97 - p10+ [501+]
Corot in Italy
     NYRB - v44 - Mr 6 '97 - p10+ [501+]
Galassi, Susan Grace - *Picasso's Variations on the Masters*
     Choice - v34 - Ja '97 - p783 [51-250]
     LATBR - D 8 '96 - p28 [1-50]
     LJ - v122 - F 1 '97 - p76+ [251-500]
     PW - v243 - O 7 '96 - p50 [51-250]
Galbraith, John Kenneth - *The Good Society*
     TLS - O 11 '96 - p16 [501+]
Galbraith, Judy - *The Gifted Kids' Survival Guide. Rev., Expanded, and Updated Ed.*
  y Ch BWatch - v6 - D '96 - p2 [51-250]
  y SLJ - v43 - F '97 - p114 [51-250]

Galbraith, Stuart - *The Japanese Filmography*
  r ARBA - v28 - '97 - p510 [51-250]
  r Choice - v34 - S '96 - p98 [51-250]
  r RQ - v36 - Win '96 - p298 [251-500]
Galchinsky, Michael - *The Origin of the Modern Jewish Woman Writer*
     Nine-C Lit - v51 - Mr '97 - p556 [51-250]
     R&R Bk N - v11 - N '96 - p69 [51-250]
     TLS - O 11 '96 - p29 [501+]
Galderisi, Claudio - *Le Lexique De Charles D'Orleans Dans Les Rondeaux*
     FR - v70 - O '96 - p154+ [251-500]
Galdikas, Birute Marija Filomena - *Reflections of Eden*
     BW - v26 - S 1 '96 - p12 [51-250]
     New Sci - v152 - O 12 '96 - p42 [1-50]
     NYTBR - v101 - D 1 '96 - p36 [51-250]
Galdone, Paul - *Los Tres Osos (Illus. by Paul Galdone)*
  c BL - v93 - My 1 '97 - p1506+ [1-50]
Gale, Peggy - *Video by Artists*
     Afterimage - v24 - N '96 - p4 [1-50]
Gale, Steven H - *Encyclopedia of British Humorists. Vols. 1-2*
  r ARBA - v28 - '97 - p450 [51-250]
  r BL - v92 - Ag '96 - p1922+ [251-500]
  r Choice - v34 - O '96 - p250 [51-250]
Gale, Vi - *The Prescott Street Reader*
     Bloom Rev - v17 - Ja '97 - p21+ [51-250]
Gale, Xin Lui - *Teachers, Discourses, and Authority in the Postmodern Composition Classroom*
     R&R Bk N - v12 - F '97 - p78 [51-250]
Gale Directory of Publications and Broadcast Media 1990-. Book and Electronic Media Version
  r ASInt - v34 - O '96 - p16 [51-250]
Galeano, Eduardo - *El Futbol A Sol Y Sombra*
     WLT - v70 - Aut '96 - p926 [501+]
Walking Words
     PW - v243 - D 30 '96 - p64 [1-50]
Galef, David - *Tracks (Illus. by Tedd Arnold)*
  c HB Guide - v7 - Fall '96 - p257 [51-250]
Galens, Judy - *Gale Encyclopedia of Multicultural America. Vols. 1-2*
  yr RQ - v35 - Sum '96 - p558 [251-500]
Galenson, Walter - *The American Labor Movement 1955-1995*
     Choice - v34 - S '96 - p170 [51-250]
     M Lab R - v119 - O '96 - p85+ [501+]
Galeotti, Mark - *Afghanistan: The Soviet Union's Last War*
     Slav R - v55 - Fall '96 - p697+ [501+]
The Kremlin's Agenda
     JPR - v33 - Ag '96 - p380 [251-500]
Gale's Career Guidance System. Electronic Media Version
  yr RQ - v36 - Fall '96 - p121+ [501+]
Gale's Ready Reference Shelf. Electronic Media Version
  r ARBA - v28 - '97 - p26+ [501+]
  r BL - v93 - D 15 '96 - p744 [501+]
  r Choice - v34 - Mr '97 - p1147+ [501+]
Galford, Ellen - *The XXIII Olympiad*
     Choice - v34 - F '97 - p1002+ [501+]
Galich, Franz - *Huracan Corazon Del Cielo*
     BL - v93 - S 15 '96 - p227 [1-50]
Galicich, Anne - *The German Americans*
  c HB Guide - v7 - Fall '96 - p312 [1-50]
Galilea, Segundo - *Temptation and Discernment*
     Am - v175 - N 2 '96 - p29+ [51-250]
Galindo, Alberto Flores - *Dos Ensayos Sobre Jose Maria Arguedas*
     HAHR - v76 - N '96 - p810 [251-500]
Galindo, Rudy - *Icebreaker: The Autobiography of Rudy Galindo*
     Advocate - Mr 18 '97 - p77 [51-250]
     KR - v65 - Mr 15 '97 - p454 [251-500]
     LJ - v122 - Ap 15 '97 - p87 [51-250]
     PW - v244 - Mr 3 '97 - p57 [51-250]
Galindo, Sergio - *Otilia's Body*
     TranslRevS - v1 - My '95 - p30 [51-250]
Galinov, Mireille - *London in Paint*
     Obs - D 22 '96 - p18* [501+]
Galinsky, Karl - *Augustan Culture*
     Choice - v34 - D '96 - p665 [51-250]
Galison, Peter - *The Disunity of Science*
     AJS - v102 - Ja '97 - p1238+ [501+]
     Choice - v34 - N '96 - p478 [51-250]
     SciTech - v20 - S '96 - p2 [51-250]
Galizzi, Giovanni - *Economics of Innovation*
     JEL - v34 - D '96 - p2086 [51-250]
Gall, Stanley A - *Multiple Pregnancy and Delivery*
     SciTech - v20 - S '96 - p40 [51-250]

Gall, Susan - *The Gale Encyclopedia of Psychology*
  yr ARBA - v28 - '97 - p285 [51-250]
  yr BL - v93 - D 15 '96 - p748 [51-250]
  r Choice - v34 - Ap '97 - p1307 [51-250]
  yr LJ - v122 - F 1 '97 - p72 [51-250]
Gall, Timothy L - *Junior Worldmark Encyclopedia of the Canadian Provinces*
  cr BL - v93 - N 1 '96 - p538 [1-50]
Junior Worldmark Encyclopedia of the Nations. Vols. 1-9
  cr ARBA - v28 - '97 - p45 [251-500]
  cr BL - v92 - Ag '96 - p1918 [51-250]
  cr SLJ - v42 - Ag '96 - p182 [51-250]
Junior Worldmark Encyclopedia of the States. Vols. 1-4
  cr BL - v92 - Ag '96 - p1925+ [251-500]
  cr SLJ - v42 - N '96 - p137 [51-250]
  yr VOYA - v19 - O '96 - p244 [51-250]
Statistics on Crime and Punishment
  r ARBA - v28 - '97 - p229 [251-500]
  r Choice - v34 - F '97 - p950 [51-250]
  r LJ - v122 - F 1 '97 - p74+ [251-500]
Statistics on Weapons and Violence
  r ARBA - v28 - '97 - p230 [51-250]
  r LJ - v122 - F 1 '97 - p74+ [251-500]
  r RQ - v36 - Fall '96 - p138+ [501+]
Gallagher, Catherine - *Nobody's Story*
     Eight-C St - v29 - Sum '96 - p443+ [501+]
     RES - v48 - F '97 - p112+ [501+]
Gallagher, David M - *Thomas Aquinas and His Legacy*
     RM - v49 - Je '96 - p922+ [501+]
Gallagher, Gary W - *Chancellorsville: The Battle and Its Aftermath*
     HRNB - v25 - Win '97 - p59 [251-500]
Lee the Soldier
     J Mil H - v61 - Ja '97 - p166+ [251-500]
     NYTBR - v101 - S 15 '96 - p32 [501+]
The Third Day at Gettysburg and Beyond
     RAH - v24 - S '96 - p418+ [501+]
Gallagher, John - *Perfect Enemies*
     BW - v26 - O 27 '96 - p3+ [501+]
     Choice - v34 - F '97 - p1036 [51-250]
     Nat - v263 - S 9 '96 - p44+ [501+]
Gallagher, Maggie - *The Abolition of Marriage*
     Comw - v123 - My 17 '96 - p18+ [501+]
     New R - v216 - Ap 14 '97 - p30+ [501+]
Gallagher, Mark - *The Yankee Encyclopedia*
  r NYTBR - v101 - Ap 7 '96 - p16 [51-250]
Gallagher, Michael, 1951- - *The Referendum Experience in Europe*
     TLS - O 18 '96 - p12 [501+]
Gallagher, Michael G - *China Environmental Report*
  r ARBA - v28 - '97 - p106+ [251-500]
     SciTech - v20 - N '96 - p2 [51-250]
Gallagher, Stephen - *Red, Red Robin*
     Rapport - v19 - 6 '96 - p20 [251-500]
Gallagher, Tess - *My Black Horse*
     WLT - v70 - Aut '96 - p962+ [251-500]
Gallagher, Tom - *Romania after Ceausescu*
     Cu H - v96 - Mr '97 - p140 [501+]
Gallagher, William B - *When Dinosaurs Roamed New Jersey*
     LJ - v122 - My 1 '97 - p135 [51-250]
     PW - v244 - Mr 10 '97 - p61 [51-250]
Gallagher, Winifred - *I.D.: How Heredity and Experience Make You Who You Are*
     NYTBR - v101 - D 8 '96 - p88 [1-50]
Galland, Leo - *The Four Pillars of Healing*
     BL - v93 - My 15 '97 - p1551 [51-250]
     PW - v244 - My 5 '97 - p204 [51-250]
Gallant, Christine - *Tabooed Jung*
     Choice - v34 - D '96 - p692 [51-250]
     R&R Bk N - v11 - N '96 - p3 [1-50]
Gallant, Mavis - *The Collected Stories of Mavis Gallant*
     Am - v176 - F 8 '97 - p33+ [501+]
     BL - v93 - S 1 '96 - p62 [51-250]
     CSM - v89 - Ja 15 '97 - p15 [501+]
     Ent W - O 11 '96 - p87 [51-250]
     KR - v64 - S 1 '96 - p1268 [51-250]
     LATBR - O 6 '96 - p1+ [501+]
     LATBR - D 29 '96 - p5 [51-250]
     LJ - v122 - Ja '97 - p49 [1-50]
     New R - v215 - N 25 '96 - p42+ [501+]
     NY - v72 - D 16 '96 - p107 [51-250]
     NYRB - v43 - O 17 '96 - p12+ [501+]
     NYTBR - v101 - O 13 '96 - p11+ [501+]
     NYTBR - v101 - D 8 '96 - p11 [51-250]
     PW - v243 - N 4 '96 - p37 [1-50]
     TLS - N 29 '96 - p13 [51-250]
     VLS - Win '96 - p9 [51-250]
     WSJ-MW - v77 - S 18 '96 - pA16 [501+]

The Selected Stories of Mavis Gallant
  BIC - v25 - D '96 - p4+ [501+]
  Mac - v109 - D 9 '96 - p64 [1-50]
  Quill & Q - v62 - O '96 - p33 [501+]
  TLS - Ap 11 '97 - p25 [501+]
Gallardo, Juan C - *Beam Dynamics and Technology Issues for U+U-Muons Colliders*
  SciTech - v20 - S '96 - p15 [51-250]
Gallarotti, Giulio M - *The Anatomy of an International Monetary Regime*
  AAPSS-A - v546 - Jl '96 - p178+ [501+]
Gallat-Morin, Elisabeth - *Jean Girard: Musicien En Nouvelle-France, Bourges, 1696 - Montreal 1765*
  Can Hist R - v78 - Mr '97 - p145+ [501+]
Gallay, Alan - *Colonial Wars of North America 1512-1763*
  r ARBA - v28 - '97 - p190+ [51-250]
  r J Mil H - v61 - Ap '97 - p367+ [501+]
  r RQ - v36 - Win '96 - p290 [251-500]
  yr SLJ - v43 - F '97 - p128 [51-250]
Gallegos, Sallie - *Stone Horses*
  Choice - v34 - O '96 - p278 [51-250]
Gallhofer, Irmtraud M - *Foreign Policy Decision-Making*
  Choice - v34 - S '96 - p207+ [51-250]
Galli, Barbara Ellen - *Franz Rosenzweig and Jehuda Halevi*
  Rel St Rev - v22 - O '96 - p350 [51-250]
Galli, Letizia - *Mona Lisa: The Secret of a Smile (Illus. by Letizia Galli)*
  c HB Guide - v8 - Spr '97 - p137 [51-250]
Gallichan, Gilles - *Livre Et Politique Au Bas-Canada 1791-1849*
  r Can Hist R - v77 - D '96 - p640+ [501+]
Galliher, John F - *Marginality and Dissent in Twentieth-Century American Sociology*
  CS - v25 - S '96 - p669+ [501+]
Gallimard Jeunesse - *The History of Making Books*
  c BW - v26 - O 13 '96 - p13 [51-250]
  c PW - v243 - N 18 '96 - p78 [51-250]
  c SLJ - v42 - O '96 - p134 [51-250]
Gallina, Jill - *Christmas Pins, Past and Present*
  Ant & CM - v101 - D '96 - p33 [51-250]
Gallison, Kate - *Devil's Workshop*
  Arm Det - v29 - Sum '96 - p367 [51-250]
Unholy Angels
  Arm Det - v30 - Win '97 - p98 [251-500]
  PW - v243 - Jl 22 '96 - p235 [51-250]
Gallo, F Alberto - *Music in the Castle*
  TranslRevS - v2 - D '96 - p14 [51-250]
Gallo, Max - *L'Ambitieuse*
  WLT - v70 - Aut '96 - p907+ [501+]
Gallop, Jane - *Feminist Accused of Sexual Harassment*
  LJ - v122 - Ap 15 '97 - p102+ [51-250]
  PW - v244 - Mr 24 '97 - p69 [51-250]
Galloway, Janice - *Where You Find It*
  Books - v10 - Je '96 - p22 [51-250]
Galloway, Patricia - *Choctaw Genesis 1500-1700*
  Choice - v34 - S '96 - p194 [51-250]
  Roundup M - v3 - Ag '96 - p24 [251-500]
  WHQ - v27 - Win '96 - p551 [1-50]
Galloway, Priscilla - *Aleta and the Queen (Illus. by Normand Cousineau)*
  c Ch Bk News - v19 - Sum '96 - p33 [251-500]
  c JB - v60 - O '96 - p201 [51-250]
Atlanta: The Fastest Runner in the World (Illus. by Normand Cousineau)
  c Ch Bk News - v19 - Sum '96 - p33 [251-500]
Truly Grim Tales
  c Can CL - v22 - Sum '96 - p85+ [501+]
  y Emerg Lib - v24 - S '96 - p24 [1-50]
  y Emerg Lib - v24 - S '96 - p27 [1-50]
  y Emerg Lib - v24 - S '96 - p46 [1-50]
Galouchko, Annouchka G - *Sho and the Demons of the Deep (Illus. by Annouchka G Galouchko)*
  c Ch Bk News - v19 - Spr '96 - p23+ [251-500]
  c JB - v60 - O '96 - p184 [51-250]
Galper, Allan S - *From Bolshoi to Be'er Sheva, Scientists to Streetsweepers*
  Rel St Rev - v22 - O '96 - p355+ [51-250]
Galster, George - *Reality and Research*
  JEL - v34 - S '96 - p1502 [51-250]
Galston, William A - *Rural Development in the United States*
  EG - v72 - O '96 - p453+ [501+]
Galt, Margot Fortunato - *Up to the Plate*
  c Trib Bks - Mr 30 '97 - p4 [51-250]
Galtung, Johan - *Peace by Peaceful Means*
  JPR - v33 - N '96 - p498+ [51-250]
Galvao, Patricia - *Industrial Park*
  TranslRevS - v1 - My '95 - p27 [51-250]
Galvin, Brendan - *Sky and Island Light*
  PW - v243 - D 30 '96 - p61 [51-250]

Galvin, Irene Flum - *The Ancient Maya*
  c Ch BWatch - v7 - Ja '97 - p3 [1-50]
  c HB Guide - v8 - Spr '97 - p165 [51-250]
  y SLJ - v43 - Mr '97 - p200 [51-250]
Brazil: Many Voices, Many Faces
  c HB Guide - v8 - Spr '97 - p179 [51-250]
Japan: A Modern Land with Ancient Roots
  c HB Guide - v7 - Fall '96 - p383 [51-250]
Galvin, James - *Lethal Frequencies*
  WAL - v31 - Fall '96 - p276+ [251-500]
The Meadow
  TPR - v17 - Fall '96 - p3+ [501+]
Resurrection Update
  BL - v93 - Ap 1 '97 - p1277 [51-250]
  LJ - v122 - F 1 '97 - p84 [51-250]
  PW - v244 - F 24 '97 - p87 [1-50]
Galvin, Patrick - *New and Selected Poems*
  ILS - v16 - Spr '97 - p20 [501+]
Gamagami, Parvis - *Atlas of Mammography*
  r SciTech - v21 - Mr '97 - p63 [51-250]
Gambaro, Griselda - *Bad Blood*
  TranslRevS - v1 - My '95 - p30 [1-50]
Information for Foreigners
  TranslRevS - v1 - My '95 - p30 [1-50]
Gambetta, Diego - *Were They Pushed or Did They Jump?*
  CS - v26 - Mr '97 - p205+ [501+]
Gambi, Lucio - *La Galleria Delle Carte Geografiche In Vaticano*
  Art Bull - v79 - Mr '97 - p156+ [501+]
Gambill, Henrietta - *Self-Control (Illus. by Mechelle Ann)*
  c HB Guide - v8 - Spr '97 - p86 [51-250]
Gamble, Andrew - *Hayek: The Iron Cage of Liberty*
  TLS - S 20 '96 - p4+ [501+]
  Wil Q - v20 - Aut '96 - p102+ [251-500]
Regionalism and World Order
  TLS - Mr 21 '97 - p28 [501+]
Gamble, Clive - *Timewalkers: The Prehistory of Global Colonization*
  Am Ant - v61 - O '96 - p798+ [501+]
  Can Lit - Win '96 - p125+ [501+]
Gamble, Harry Y - *Books and Readers in the Early Church*
  CH - v65 - D '96 - p665+ [501+]
  CHR - v82 - Jl '96 - p492+ [251-500]
  JR - v77 - Ap '97 - p295+ [501+]
  Theol St - v57 - Mr '96 - p183+ [251-500]
Gamble, John - *What Your Clients Won't Tell You...and Your Managers Don't Know*
  JEL - v34 - S '96 - p1460 [51-250]
Gamble, Kim - *You Can Do Great Lettering*
  c Cur R - v36 - N '96 - p12 [51-250]
Gambling, Trevor - *Business and Accounting Ethics in Islam*
  Rel St Rev - v23 - Ja '97 - p3+ [501+]
Gamboni, Dario - *The Destruction of Art*
  HT - v46 - O '96 - p57 [1-50]
Gambrell, Jamey - *Telephone (Illus. by Vladimir Radunsky)*
  c BL - v93 - D 15 '96 - p729+ [51-250]
  c Bloom Rev - v16 - N '96 - p31 [51-250]
  c HB Guide - v8 - Spr '97 - p23 [51-250]
  c KR - v64 - N 1 '96 - p1599 [51-250]
  c LATBR - D 8 '96 - p18+ [51-250]
  c Sch Lib - v45 - F '97 - p18 [51-250]
Gameson, Richard - *The Early Medieval Bible*
  CH - v66 - Mr '97 - p98+ [501+]
  EHR - v112 - Ap '97 - p427+ [501+]
  MLR - v92 - Ap '97 - p408+ [501+]
The Role of Art in the Late Anglo-Saxon Church
  CH - v65 - D '96 - p676+ [501+]
Gamma Titanium Aluminides
  SciTech - v20 - D '96 - p28 [51-250]
Gammage, Richard B - *Indoor Air and Human Health. 2nd Ed.*
  Choice - v34 - Ap '97 - p1372 [51-250]
  SciTech - v20 - D '96 - p39 [51-250]
Gammel, Irene - *Sexualizing Power in Naturalism*
  Can Lit - Win '96 - p133+ [501+]
Gammer, Moshe - *Muslim Resistance to the Tsar*
  Historian - v58 - Sum '96 - p902+ [501+]
Gammie, Malcolm - *Striking the Balance*
  Econ J - v107 - Ja '97 - p275 [51-250]
Gamst, Frederick C - *Meanings of Work*
  CS - v26 - Mr '97 - p231+ [51-250]
Gamwell, Franklin I - *The Meaning of Religious Freedom*
  JR - v77 - Ja '97 - p173+ [501+]
Gamwell, Lynn - *Madness in America*
  CS - v25 - S '96 - p695+ [501+]
  Isis - v87 - S '96 - p577+ [251-500]
  LATBR - Mr 30 '97 - p6 [501+]

Gandara, Alejandro - *Nunca Sere Como Te Quiero*
  y JAAL - v40 - S '96 - p77 [51-250]
Gandara, Patricia - *Over the Ivy Walls*
  CS - v25 - S '96 - p654+ [501+]
Gander, Forrest - *Mouth to Mouth*
  TranslRevS - v1 - My '95 - p3 [51-250]
Gandolfi, Simon - *White Sands*
  BL - v93 - F 1 '97 - p928 [51-250]
  KR - v64 - D 15 '96 - p1753+ [251-500]
  LJ - v122 - Ja '97 - p146 [51-250]
  PW - v244 - Ja 6 '97 - p66 [51-250]
Gandolfo, Giancarlo - *Economic Dynamics. 3rd Ed., Completely Rev. and Enlarged*
  JEL - v34 - D '96 - p2021 [51-250]
Gandt, Francois De - *Force and Geometry in Newton's Principia*
  Isis - v87 - D '96 - p701+ [501+]
  Phys Today - v49 - N '96 - p81+ [501+]
Gandt, Robert - *Bogeys and Bandits*
  y BL - v93 - My 15 '97 - p1545 [51-250]
  PW - v244 - My 5 '97 - p188 [51-250]
Gandy, Debrena Jackson - *Sacred Pampering Principles*
  BL - v93 - F 15 '97 - p974 [51-250]
  LJ - v121 - N 15 '96 - p76 [51-250]
Ganeri, Anita - *Animal Hideaways (Illus. by Halli Verrinder)*
  c SLJ - v42 - Ag '96 - p136 [51-250]
Bizarre Beasts and Other Oddities of Nature
  c KR - v64 - O 15 '96 - p1532 [51-250]
  c PW - v243 - N 25 '96 - p77 [51-250]
Buddhist
  c Sch Lib - v44 - N '96 - p166 [51-250]
  c TES - F 14 '97 - p16* [51-250]
Creature Features (Illus. by Steve Fricker)
  c PW - v244 - Ap 28 '97 - p76 [51-250]
Dragons and Monsters (Illus. by Alan Baker)
  c Sch Lib - v45 - F '97 - p24 [51-250]
Forests
  c Magpies - v11 - Jl '96 - p38 [1-50]
From Candle to Quartz Clock
  c Bks Keeps - Ja '97 - p26 [51-250]
From Cubit to Kilogram
  c Bks Keeps - Ja '97 - p26 [51-250]
Funny Bones and Other Body Parts (Illus. by Steve Fricker)
  c PW - v244 - Ap 28 '97 - p76 [51-250]
Hindu
  c HB Guide - v7 - Fall '96 - p308 [51-250]
Inside the Body (Illus. by Giuliano Fornari)
  c BL - v93 - D 15 '96 - p732 [1-50]
  y BL - v93 - Ap 1 '97 - p1306 [1-50]
  c Ch BWatch - v6 - S '96 - p6 [1-50]
  cr CLW - v67 - D '96 - p60 [51-250]
  c HB Guide - v8 - Spr '97 - p129 [51-250]
  c New Sci - v152 - N 16 '96 - p54 [51-250]
  cr Par Ch - v21 - Mr '97 - p5 [51-50]
  c Sch Lib - v44 - N '96 - p162 [51-250]
  c SLJ - v42 - Ag '96 - p155 [51-250]
  c TES - N 22 '96 - p12* [51-250]
Out of the Ark (Illus. by Jackie Morris)
  c HB Guide - v7 - Fall '96 - p308 [51-250]
Prickly and Poisonous
  c HB Guide - v7 - Fall '96 - p336 [51-250]
Religions Explained
  c PW - v244 - F 24 '97 - p83 [51-250]
The Story of Numbers and Counting
  c BL - v93 - F 1 '97 - p936 [51-250]
  c BL - v93 - Ap 1 '97 - p1341 [1-50]
  c Cur R - v36 - Ja '97 - p12 [51-250]
  c SLJ - v43 - F '97 - p90 [51-250]
The Story of Writing and Printing
  c BL - v93 - F 1 '97 - p936 [51-250]
  c KR - v64 - D 1 '96 - p1736 [51-250]
  c SLJ - v43 - F '97 - p90 [51-250]
What Do We Know about Hinduism?
  c CLW - v67 - Mr '97 - p56+ [251-500]
  c HB Guide - v8 - Spr '97 - p87 [51-250]
  c Magpies - v11 - Jl '96 - p38+ [51-250]
  c SLJ - v43 - F '97 - p114 [51-250]
What They Don't Tell You about Shakespeare (Illus. by Alan Rowe)
  c Bks Keeps - Ja '97 - p26 [51-250]
The Young Person's Guide to the Orchestra
  c BL - v93 - O 1 '96 - p345 [51-250]
  c SLJ - v43 - F '97 - p132 [51-250]
The Young Person's Guide to the Orchestra. Book and Electronic Media Version
  c Par - v71 - D '96 - p254 [51-250]
Ganesan, Kumar - *Air Toxics*
  SciTech - v21 - Mr '97 - p82 [1-50]

Gangi, William - *Saving the Constitution from the Courts*
APSR - v90 - S '96 - p648+ [501+]
PSQ - v111 - Win '96 - p720+ [501+]
Univ Bkmn - v36 - Fall '96 - p14+ [501+]

Ganguly, Sumit - *Mending Fences*
For Aff - v75 - N '96 - p168 [51-250]
R&R Bk N - v11 - D '96 - p11 [51-250]

Gani, Michela - *Carte Decorate*
Lib - v19 - Mr '97 - p100 [51-250]

Ganim, John M - *Chaucerian Theatricality*
Comp L - v48 - Fall '96 - p377+ [501+]

Gannett, Lewis - *Magazine Beach*
MFSF - v91 - D '96 - p99 [251-500]

Gannicott, K G - *Pacific 2010: Women's Education and Economic Development in Melanesia*
Cont Pac - v8 - Fall '96 - p465+ [501+]

Gannon, Michael - *Rebel Bishop*
PW - v244 - Mr 17 '97 - p81 [1-50]

Gannon, Steve - *A Song for the Asking*
y BL - v93 - F 1 '97 - p925 [51-250]
KR - v64 - D 1 '96 - p1689 [251-500]
LJ - v121 - D '96 - p142 [51-250]
PW - v243 - N 11 '96 - p54+ [51-250]
A Song for the Asking (Sanders). Audio Version
LJ - v122 - Ap 15 '97 - p138 [51-250]

Gans, Eduard - *Ruckblicke Auf Personen Und Zustande*
MLR - v91 - O '96 - p1044+ [251-500]

Gans, Herbert J - *People, Plans, and Policies*
J Urban II - v22 - S '96 - p750+ [501+]
The War against the Poor
AAPSS-A - v548 - N '96 - p233+ [501+]
AJS - v102 - S '96 - p627+ [501+]
Nat R - v48 - Je 3 '96 - p53+ [501+]
NYTBR - v101 - S '96 - p24 [1-50]
Soc Ser R - v70 - S '96 - p499+ [51-250]

Gans, Roma - *How Do Birds Find Their Way? (Illus. by Paul Mirocha)*
c HB Guide - v7 - Fall '96 - p343 [51-250]
Let's Go Rock Collecting (Illus. by Holly Keller)
c BL - v93 - My 15 '97 - p1577 [51-250]

Gans, Werner - *Fundamental Principles of Molecular Modeling*
SciTech - v20 - S '96 - p17 [51-250]

Gansler, Jacques S - *Defense Conversion*
Econ J - v106 - S '96 - p1476 [251-500]
JEL - v35 - Mr '97 - p165+ [501+]
PSQ - v111 - Win '96 - p721+ [501+]

Gantos, Jack - *Desire Lines*
y CBRS - v25 - Ap '97 - p105 [51-250]
y CCB-B - v50 - Ap '97 - p281+ [51-250]
y KR - v65 - F 15 '97 - p92 [51-250]
y PW - v244 - F 24 '97 - p92 [51-250]
Rotten Ralph's Rotten Romance (Illus. by Nicole Rubel)
c BL - v93 - N 15 '96 - p593 [51-250]
c HB - v72 - N '96 - p723 [51-250]
c KR - v64 - N 1 '96 - p1600 [51-250]
c PW - v243 - N 25 '96 - p75 [51-250]
c SLJ - v43 - F '97 - p81 [51-250]
Zip Six
LATBR - O 6 '96 - p14 [51-250]

Gantschev, Ivan - *El Lago De La Luna*
c BL - v93 - My 1 '97 - p1507 [1-50]
Moon Lake (Illus. by Ivan Gantschev)
c Ch BWatch - v6 - O '96 - p5 [1-50]
c HB Guide - v8 - Spr '97 - p28 [51-250]

Ganz, David - *Corbie in the Carolingian Renaissance*
Lib - v18 - Je '96 - p156+ [501+]

Ganzha, Victor G - *Numerical Solutions for Partial Differential Equations*
Choice - v34 - Mr '97 - p1197 [51-250]
SciTech - v20 - N '96 - p14 [51-250]

The Gap Year Guidebook 1997/98
y TES - S 27 '96 - p8* [51-250]

Gapen, Patrice - *An Introduction to AS/400 System Operations*
SciTech - v20 - D '96 - p12 [51-250]

Gapenski, Louis C - *Understanding Health Care Financial Management. 2nd Ed.*
SciTech - v20 - D '96 - p40 [51-250]

Gaposchkin, Cecilia Helena Payne - *Cecilia Payne-Gaposchkin: An Autobiography and Other Recollections. 2nd Ed.*
Choice - v34 - N '96 - p481 [51-250]
Sci - v273 - Ag 30 '96 - p1180 [251-500]

Gapper, John - *All That Glitters*
Spec - v277 - O 5 '96 - p52 [501+]
TLS - N 22 '96 - p29 [501+]

Garab Dorje - *The Golden Letters*
Tric - v6 - Win '96 - p116 [1-50]

Garaczi, Laszlo - *Mintha Elnel*
WLT - v71 - Win '97 - p192+ [501+]

Garay, Luis - *Pedrito's Day (Illus. by Luis Garay)*
c BL - v93 - Mr 1 '97 - p1171 [51-250]
c CBRS - v25 - Ap '97 - p98+ [51-250]
c PW - v244 - Mr 3 '97 - p75 [51-250]
c Quill & Q - v63 - F '97 - p56+ [251-500]

Garay, Paul N - *Pump Application Desk Book. 3rd Ed.*
SciTech - v20 - D '96 - p73 [51-250]

Garb, Tamar - *Sisters of the Brush*
Signs - v22 - Win '97 - p469+ [501+]

Garbarino, James - *Raising Children in a Socially Toxic Environment*
Fam in Soc - v78 - Mr '97 - p218+ [501+]

Garber, Marjorie - *Dog Love*
Dog Fan - v28 - Ja '97 - p39 [51-250]
KR - v64 - S 1 '96 - p1293 [251-500]
NYTBR - v101 - N 17 '96 - p11+ [501+]
PW - v243 - S 23 '96 - p68 [51-250]
Trib Bks - F 9 '97 - p1+ [501+]

Garber, Zev - *Shoah: The Paradigmatic Genocide*
Rel St Rev - v22 - O '96 - p355 [251-500]

Garboli, Cesare - *Il Gioco Segreto*
BL - v93 - D 1 '96 - p644 [1-50]

Garcia, Carlos Ernesto - *Even Rage Will Rot*
TranslRevS - v1 - My '95 - p30 [51-250]

Garcia, Carmen - *Mejor Dicho*
Hisp - v79 - D '96 - p822+ [501+]

Garcia, Clara Ines - *El Bajo Cauca Antioqueno*
HAHR - v77 - My '97 - p339+ [501+]

Garcia, Connie - *Tecnicas Narrativas De La Novelistica De Sergio Galindo*
Hisp - v79 - D '96 - p804+ [501+]

Garcia, Cristina - *The Aguero Sisters*
BL - v93 - My 1 '97 - p1478 [51-250]
KR - v65 - Mr 1 '97 - p324 [51-250]
LJ - v122 - Mr 15 '97 - p88+ [51-250]
NYTLa - v146 - My 27 '97 - pC16 [501+]
PW - v244 - Mr 10 '97 - p48 [251-500]
Time - My 12 '97 - p88 [251-500]

Garcia, Dionisia - *Tiempos Del Cantar*
WLT - v70 - Sum '96 - p672 [51-250]

Garcia, Guy - *Spirit of the Maya (Illus. by Ted Wood)*
c RT - v50 - Mr '97 - p502 [51-250]

Garcia, Jerry - *The Teddy Bears' Picnic (Illus. by Bruce Whatley)*
c CBRS - v24 - Ag '96 - p158 [51-250]

Garcia, John - *The Success of Hispanic Magazine (Illus. by Ricardo Vargas)*
y HB Guide - v7 - Fall '96 - p313 [1-50]

Garcia, Juan R - *Mexicans in the Midwest 1900-1932*
Choice - v34 - My '97 - p1562 [51-250]

Garcia, Maria Cristina - *Havana USA*
HRNB - v25 - Fall '96 - p16 [251-500]

Garcia, Mario T - *Memories of Chicano History*
Am Q - v49 - Mr '97 - p215+ [501+]

Garcia, Nasario P - *Tata: A Voice from the Rio Puerco*
CAY - v17 - Fall '96 - p10 [51-250]

Garcia, Ofelia - *Policy and Practice in Bilingual Education*
MLJ - v80 - Fall '96 - p406 [501+]

Garcia-Aguilera, Carolina - *Bloody Shame*
BL - v93 - F 15 '97 - p1006 [51-250]
KR - v65 - Ja 1 '97 - p22 [251-500]
LJ - v122 - F 1 '97 - p110 [51-250]
PW - v243 - D 30 '96 - p58 [51-250]
Trib Bks - F 2 '97 - p4 [51-250]
Bloody Waters
y Kliatt - v31 - My '97 - p6 [51-250]

Garcia Bourrellier, Rocio - *Las Cortes De Navarra Desde Su Incorporacion A La Corona De Castilla. Vols. 1-2*
EHR - v111 - S '96 - p980 [251-500]

Garcia De Palacio, Diego - *Nautical Instruction 1587*
Sea H - Win '96 - p42 [51-250]

Garcia Duran, Mauricio - *De La Uribe A Tlaxcala*
HAHR - v76 - N '96 - p806+ [501+]

Garcia Fernandez, Maximo - *Herencia Y Patrimonio Familiar En La Castilla Del Antiguo Regimen 1650-1834*
Choice - v34 - D '96 - p567 [1-50]
Choice - v34 - D '96 - p567 [1-50]

Garcia Lorca, Federico - *Blood Wedding*
ILS - v16 - Spr '97 - p35 [51-250]

Garcia Marquez, Gabriel - *Del Amor Y Otros Demonios*
Hisp - v79 - D '96 - p772+ [501+]
News of a Kidnapping
BL - v93 - My 1 '97 - p1458 [51-250]
KR - v65 - My 1 '97 - p693 [251-500]
PW - v244 - Ap 28 '97 - p58 [251-500]
WSJ-Cent - v99 - Je 3 '97 - pA20 [501+]
Noticia De Un Secuestro
BL - v93 - Mr 15 '97 - p1232 [1-50]
TLS - O 4 '96 - p26 [501+]

Of Love and Other Demons
y Kliatt - v30 - S '96 - p10 [51-250]
LATBR - Jl 7 '96 - p11 [51-250]
The Story of a Shipwrecked Sailor
y Kliatt - v30 - S '96 - p3 [1-50]

Garcia Morales, Adelaida - *La Tia Agueda*
WLT - v70 - Sum '96 - p665+ [251-500]

Garcia Ramis, Magali - *Happy Days, Uncle Sergio*
y JOYS - v9 - Sum '96 - p415+ [51-250]

Garcia-Rivera, Alex - *St. Martin De Porres: The Little Stories and the Semiotics of Culture*
CH - v66 - Mr '97 - p199 [51-250]

Garcia Y Robertson, R - *The Virgin and the Dinosaur*
MFSF - v92 - Ja '97 - p21+ [51-250]

Gardam, Jane - *Tufty Bear (Illus. by Peter Melnyczuk)*
c JB - v60 - O '96 - p192 [51-250]
c Sch Lib - v44 - N '96 - p150 [51-250]

Gardam, Jane, 1928- - *Faith Fox*
Books - v11 - Ap '97 - p22 [51-250]
Going Into a Dark House
Books - v9 - S '95 - p27 [1-50]

Gardaphe, Fred L - *Italian Signs, American Streets*
AL - v69 - Mr '97 - p243+ [251-500]
Choice - v34 - N '96 - p456 [51-250]

Gardell, Mattias - *In the Name of Elijah Muhammad*
Choice - v34 - Ap '97 - p1356 [51-250]
MEQ - v4 - Mr '97 - p91+ [251-500]
NYRB - v43 - S 19 '96 - p61+ [501+]
PW - v243 - S 16 '96 - p66 [51-250]

Gardella, Robert - *Harvesting Mountains*
BHR - v70 - Aut '96 - p431+ [501+]
JIH - v27 - Aut '96 - p378+ [501+]

Gardella, Tricia - *Casey's New Hat (Illus. by Margot Apple)*
c PW - v244 - F 3 '97 - p106 [51-250]

Gardels, Nathan P - *At Century's End*
AB - v98 - S 16 '96 - p837+ [501+]

Garden (Snapshot)
c PW - v244 - Ja 6 '97 - p74 [1-50]

Garden, Nancy - *Good Moon Rising*
y BL - v93 - O 1 '96 - p340 [51-250]
y CBRS - v25 - O '96 - p21 [51-250]
y CCB-B - v50 - D '96 - p134 [51-250]
y Ch BWatch - v7 - F '97 - p4 [51-250]
y HB - v72 - N '96 - p743+ [251-500]
c HB Guide - v8 - Spr '97 - p79 [51-250]
y JAAL - v40 - F '97 - p408 [51-250]
y KR - v64 - Ag 15 '96 - p1234 [51-250]
y SLJ - v42 - O '96 - p147 [51-250]
y VOYA - v19 - D '96 - p269+ [251-500]

Garden Club of America - *Plants That Merit Attention. Vol. 2*
ARBA - v28 - '97 - p585 [51-250]
BL - v93 - S 15 '96 - p195 [51-250]
BWatch - v18 - F '97 - p11 [1-50]
Choice - v34 - Mr '97 - p1185 [51-250]
CSM - v89 - F 27 '97 - pB2 [51-250]
Fine Gard - Mr '97 - p76 [51-250]
r NYTBR - v101 - D 8 '96 - p42 [51-250]
PW - v243 - O 7 '96 - p70 [51-250]

Garden Trees (Eyewitness Handbooks)
r ARBA - v28 - '97 - p583+ [51-250]

Gardener, Sally - *Playtime Rhymes. Audio Version*
c TES - Ja 17 '97 - p13* [51-250]

Gardener, Theodore Roosevelt - *Lotusland: A Photographic Odyssey*
Bloom Rev - v16 - Jl '96 - p17 [51-250]

Gardezi, Hassan N - *The Political Economy of International Labour Migration*
CS - v25 - S '96 - p593+ [501+]

Gardies, Jean-Louis - *Les Fondements Semantiques Du Discours Naturel*
Dialogue - v36 - Win '97 - p197+ [501+]

Gardiner, Alan - *Longman Homework Handbook*
y TES - Ja 10 '97 - p10* [251-500]

Gardiner, James - *Who's a Pretty Boy Then?*
Books - v11 - Ap '97 - p20 [1-50]

Gardiner, Juliet - *The Columbia Companion to British History*
r BL - v93 - Mr 15 '97 - p1254+ [51-250]
Oscar Wilde: A Life in Letters, Writings and Wit
LJ - v121 - N 1 '96 - p67 [51-250]

Gardiner, Robin - *The Riddle of the Titanic*
J Am Cult - v19 - Sum '96 - p141+ [501+]

Gardiner, Tony - *Mathematical Challenge*
y TES - Mr 21 '97 - pR11 [51-250]

Gardlund, Torsten - *The Life of Knut Wicksell*
JEL - v34 - D '96 - p2014+ [51-250]
R&R Bk N - v11 - D '96 - p22 [51-250]

Gardner, B Delworth - *Plowing Ground in Washington*
JEL - v34 - S '96 - p1398+ [501+]

Gardner, Brian - *European Agriculture*
New Sci - v153 - Mr 1 '97 - p42 [51-250]
Gardner, Carol Brooks - *Passing By*
AJS - v102 - Ja '97 - p1214+ [501+]
Gardner, Craig Shaw - *Dragon Burning*
KR - v64 - Ag 15 '96 - p1195 [51-250]
PW - v243 - S 30 '96 - p66 [51-250]
Dragon Circle
LJ - v121 - O 15 '96 - p93 [51-250]
Gardner, David - *The Motley Fool Investment Guide*
PW - v243 - D 9 '96 - p66 [1-50]
Gardner, E Clinton - *Justice and Christian Ethics*
Rel St Rev - v22 - O '96 - p341 [51-250]
Gardner, Helen - *Gardner's Art through the Ages. 10th Ed.*
Art J - v55 - Sum '96 - p99+ [501+]
LATBR - D 8 '96 - p14 [51-250]
LJ - v121 - S 15 '96 - p65 [51-250]
Gardner, Howard - *Leading Minds*
BusLR - v21 - 3 '96 - p241 [251-500]
Per Psy - v50 - Spr '97 - p222+ [501+]
Gardner, James Alan - *Expendable*
PW - v244 - My 5 '97 - p205+ [51-250]
Gardner, James V - *Geology of the United States' Seafloor*
Choice - v34 - F '97 - p992 [51-250]
Gardner, Jo Ann - *Living with Herbs*
BL - v93 - F 15 '97 - p987 [51-250]
LJ - v122 - Mr 15 '97 - p80 [51-250]
PW - v244 - Ja 6 '97 - p70 [51-250]
Gardner, Katy - *Global Migrants, Local Lives*
Am Ethnol - v24 - F '97 - p257 [251-500]
CS - v26 - Mr '97 - p194+ [501+]
Gardner, Laurence - *Bloodline of the Holy Grail*
LJ - v121 - O 15 '96 - p64 [51-250]
PW - v243 - S 30 '96 - p76 [51-250]
Gardner, Leonard - *Fat City*
LATBR - v263 - S 29 '96 - p15 [51-250]
LJ - v121 - N 1 '96 - p112 [1-50]
SFR - v21 - N '96 - p20+ [501+]
Gardner, Lloyd C - *Pay Any Price*
JSH - v63 - F '97 - p205+ [501+]
NWCR - v49 - Aut '96 - p148+ [501+]
PHR - v65 - N '96 - p696+ [501+]
PSQ - v111 - Fall '96 - p536+ [501+]
RAH - v24 - D '96 - p692+ [501+]
Spheres of Influence
EHR - v111 - S '96 - p1028 [251-500]
Gardner, Martin, 1914- - *The Night Is Large*
BW - v26 - Jl 14 '96 - p5 [501+]
KR - v64 - My 1 '96 - p663 [251-500]
New Sci - v152 - N 30 '96 - p46 [251-500]
Skeptic - v4 - 3 '96 - p104 [251-500]
The Universe in a Handkerchief
Am Sci - v85 - Ja '97 - p86+ [501+]
Choice - v34 - D '96 - p647 [51-250]
JEL - v34 - D '96 - p2141 [51-250]
Urantia: The Great Cult Mystery
Skeptic - v3 - '95 - p102 [51-250]
Weird Water and Fuzzy Logic
Choice - v34 - My '97 - p1518 [51-250]
Gardner, Mary - *Boat People*
NYTBR - v102 - F 2 '97 - p28 [1-50]
Gardner, Philip - *Talking to Ghosts*
Can Lit - Win '96 - p144+ [501+]
Gardner, Richard A - *Dream Analysis in Psychotherapy*
SciTech - v20 - D '96 - p45 [51-250]
Gardner, Richard J - *Geometric Tomography*
r SIAM Rev - v39 - Mr '97 - p144+ [501+]
Gardner, Robert, 1929- - *Where on Earth Am I?*
y BL - v93 - F 15 '97 - p1012 [51-250]
y HB Guide - v8 - Spr '97 - p111 [51-250]
y SLJ - v43 - F '97 - p115 [51-250]
Gardner, Robert G - *A Decade of Debate and Division*
CH - v65 - D '96 - p730+ [501+]
Gardner, Theodore Roosevelt - *Lotusland: A Photographic Odyssey*
Hort - v74 - N '96 - p64+ [251-500]
Garelick, May - *Look at the Moon (Illus. by Barbara Garrison)*
c BL - v93 - N 15 '96 - p593 [51-250]
c HB Guide - v8 - Spr '97 - p28 [51-250]
c NYTBR - v102 - Mr 30 '97 - p18 [1-50]
c SLJ - v43 - Ja '97 - p77 [51-250]
What Makes a Bird a Bird? (Illus. by Trish Hill)
c Ch BWatch - v6 - Jl '96 - p6 [51-250]
Garfagnini, Gian Carlo - *Lorenzo Il Magnifico E Il Suo Mondo*
EHR - v111 - N '96 - p1262+ [251-500]

Garfield, Bob - *Waking Up Screaming from the American Dream*
PW - v244 - Ap 21 '97 - p54 [51-250]
Garfield, Charles - *Sometimes My Heart Goes Numb*
PW - v244 - Ap 14 '97 - p72 [1-50]
Garfield, Deborah M - *Harriet Jacobs and Incidents in the Life of a Slave Girl*
AL - v68 - S '96 - p665 [51-250]
Nine-C Lit - v51 - S '96 - p272 [1-50]
Garfield, Leon - *Shakespeare Stories II (Illus. by Michael Foreman)*
c Bks Keeps - N '96 - p10 [51-250]
Garfield, Patricia - *The Dream Messenger*
PW - v244 - Ja 20 '97 - p390 [51-250]
Garfield, Simon - *The Wrestling*
TLS - N 29 '96 - p36 [501+]
Garfinkel, Irwin - *Social Policies for Children*
Pol Stud J - v24 - Aut '96 - p519 [51-250]
Garfinkel, Michelle R - *The Political Economy of Conflict and Appropriation*
JEL - v35 - Mr '97 - p202 [51-250]
Garfinkle, Adam - *Telltale Hearts*
PSQ - v111 - Win '96 - p729+ [501+]
Tikkun - v11 - Jl '96 - p68+ [501+]
Garfinkle, Richard - *Celestial Matters*
MFSF - v91 - Ag '96 - p33 [51-250]
Rapport - v19 - 5 '96 - p32 [251-500]
Garg, Samidha - *Racism*
c Bks Keeps - v100 - S '96 - p21 [51-250]
y BL - v93 - F 1 '97 - p931 [51-250]
Gargola, Daniel J - *Lands, Laws, and Gods*
Rel St Rev - v23 - Ja '97 - p65+ [51-250]
Garigue, Philippe - *De La Condition Humaine*
WLT - v70 - Sum '96 - p656 [251-500]
Garland, Alex - *The Beach*
BL - v93 - D 1 '96 - p620 [51-250]
BW - v27 - F 9 '97 - p9 [501+]
KR - v64 - D 15 '96 - p1754 [251-500]
LATBR - F 2 '97 - p2 [501+]
LJ - v122 - F 1 '97 - p105 [51-250]
NYTBR - v102 - Mr 16 '97 - p27 [501+]
Obs - O 27 '96 - p16* [51-250]
PW - v243 - D 2 '96 - p39 [51-250]
Spec - v277 - O 5 '96 - p54 [501+]
Time - v149 - Mr 3 '97 - p74+ [251-500]
TLS - O 18 '96 - p24 [501+]
VV - v42 - Mr 11 '97 - p56 [501+]
The Beach (Page). Audio Version
PW - v244 - Mr 3 '97 - p30 [51-250]
Garland, David E - *Reading Matthew*
Rel St Rev - v23 - Ap '97 - p182 [51-250]
Garland, Kit - *Embrace the Night*
PW - v243 - S 2 '96 - p122 [51-250]
Garland, Mark A - *Ghost of a Chance*
y Kliatt - v30 - S '96 - p18 [51-250]
Garland, Robert - *The Eye of the Beholder*
AJP - v117 - Win '96 - p667+ [501+]
Garland, Sarah - *Madam Sizzers*
c Bks Keeps - Ja '97 - p22 [51-250]
Seeing Red (Illus. by Tony Ross)
c CBRS - v25 - D '96 - p39 [51-250]
c Ch BWatch - v6 - O '96 - p4 [51-250]
c HB Guide - v8 - Spr '97 - p28 [51-250]
c JB - v60 - O '96 - p184 [51-250]
c Sch Lib - v44 - Ag '96 - p99 [51-250]
c SLJ - v42 - N '96 - p80 [51-250]
c Smith - v27 - N '96 - p165 [1-50]
c TES - Jl 5 '96 - pR2 [501+]
The Survival of Arno Mostyn
c Bks Keeps - N '96 - p9 [51-250]
Tex the Cowboy (Illus. by Sarah Garland)
c RT - v50 - O '96 - p135 [1-50]
What Am I Doing?
c TES - Mr 28 '97 - p11* [1-50]
Who Can I Be?
c TES - Mr 28 '97 - p11* [1-50]
Garland, Sherry - *Cabin 102*
c HB Guide - v7 - Fall '96 - p292 [51-250]
Indio
y Emerg Lib - v24 - S '96 - p24 [1-50]
The Last Rainmaker
y BL - v93 - Ap 1 '97 - p1322 [51-250]
Letters from the Mountain
y BL - v93 - O 1 '96 - p342 [51-250]
y CBRS - v25 - D '96 - p45 [51-250]
y CCB-B - v50 - Ja '97 - p169 [51-250]
y HB Guide - v8 - Spr '97 - p79 [51-250]
y HMR - Fall '96 - p36+ [501+]
y Kliatt - v31 - Mr '97 - p8 [51-250]
y KR - v64 - S 15 '96 - p1399 [51-250]
y SLJ - v42 - N '96 - p120 [51-250]

The Lotus Seed (Illus. by Tatsuro Kiuchi)
c PW - v244 - Mr 3 '97 - p77 [1-50]
Garlicki, Andrzej - *Jozef Pilsudski 1867-1935*
AHR - v102 - F '97 - p138 [251-500]
Garlock, Dorothy - *Larkspur*
PW - v243 - D 30 '96 - p63 [51-250]
Garlock, Kristen L - *Building the Service-Based Library Web Site*
Kliatt - v31 - Ja '97 - p30 [51-250]
RQ - v36 - Fall '96 - p155+ [251-500]
SLJ - v42 - Ag '96 - p36 [51-250]
SLMQ - v24 - Sum '96 - p219 [51-250]
Garment, Leonard - *Crazy Rhythm*
BL - v93 - Mr 1 '97 - p1108 [51-250]
BW - v27 - Mr 2 '97 - p1+ [501+]
KR - v65 - Ja 1 '97 - p35 [251-500]
LJ - v122 - F 1 '97 - p90 [51-250]
NYTBR - v102 - Mr 2 '97 - p10+ [501+]
NYTLa - v146 - Mr 3 '97 - pC18 [501+]
PW - v243 - D 30 '96 - p43 [51-250]
WSJ-Cent - v99 - F 28 '97 - pA12 [501+]
Garmon, John - *Hurting for More Territory*
Sm Pr R - v28 - Je '96 - p8 [251-500]
Garms, J - *Die Mittelalterlichen Grabmaler In Rom Und Latium Vom 13. Bis Zum 15. Jahrhundert. Vol. 2*
BM - v138 - D '96 - p30 [501+]
Garnaut, Ross - *The Third Revolution in the Chinese Countryside*
JEL - v35 - Mr '97 - p296 [51-250]
Garner, Alan - *Elidor (Green). Audio Version*
c PW - v244 - Ap 14 '97 - p32 [51-250]
Little Red Hen (Illus. by Norman Messenger)
c Books - v11 - Ap '97 - p24 [51-250]
Strandloper
Aust Bk R - S '96 - p34 [501+]
NS & S - v9 - My 24 '96 - p38+ [501+]
TLS - My 24 '96 - p24 [501+]
Garner, Bryan - *A Dictionary of Modern Legal Usage. 2nd Ed.*
r RQ - v35 - Sum '96 - p553 [251-500]
Garner, Helen - *The First Stone*
KR - v65 - Mr 1 '97 - p349+ [51-250]
NYTBR - v102 - Ap 20 '97 - p31 [501+]
PW - v244 - Mr 10 '97 - p55+ [51-250]
Garner, James Finn - *Politically Correct Bedtime Stories*
y Emerg Lib - v24 - S '96 - p46 [51-250]
Politically Correct Bedtime Stories (French). Audio Version
Books - v9 - S '95 - p27 [1-50]
Garner, Jerry - *Careers in Horticulture and Botany*
y Kliatt - v31 - Ja '97 - p21+ [51-250]
Garner, Philippe - *Sixties Design*
VLS - Win '96 - p21 [51-250]
Garnett, George - *Law and Government in Medieval England and Normandy*
EHR - v111 - S '96 - p950+ [501+]
Garnett, Mark - *Principles and Politics in Contemporary Britain*
Choice - v34 - N '96 - p529+ [51-250]
TLS - N 22 '96 - p30 [501+]
Garnett, Su - *The Home Corner*
TES - F 14 '97 - p16* [251-500]
Garnett, Tay - *Directing: Learn from the Masters*
LJ - v121 - O 1 '96 - p79 [51-250]
Si & So - v6 - N '96 - p36+ [51-250]
Garnham, Neal - *The Courts, Crime and the Criminal Law in Ireland 1692-1760*
ILS - v16 - Spr '97 - p36 [51-250]
Garnier, Rowan - *100% Mathematical Proof*
Choice - v34 - F '97 - p999 [51-250]
y New Sci - v151 - S 28 '96 - p44+ [501+]
Garnot, Benoit - *Le Diable Au Couvent*
Choice - v34 - D '96 - p567 [1-50]
Garofalo, Robert Joseph - *Instructional Designs for Middle/Junior High School Band. Vols. 1-2*
Teach Mus - v4 - Ag '96 - p51 [1-50]
Garon, Paul - *Blues and the Poetic Spirit. Rev. and Expanded Ed.*
BWatch - v17 - N '96 - p9 [51-250]
Garrard, John - *The Bones of Berdichev*
New R - v216 - F 3 '97 - p34+ [501+]
TLS - D 6 '96 - p13 [501+]
Garraty, John A - *Encyclopedia of American Biography. 2nd Ed.*
r ARBA - v28 - '97 - p17+ [51-250]
r BL - v93 - Ja '97 - p892 [51-250]
r Choice - v34 - Mr '97 - p1136 [51-250]
r LJ - v122 - Ja '97 - p86 [51-250]
r R&R Bk N - v12 - F '97 - p13 [51-250]
Garretson, James D - *The Deadwood Conspiracy*
y SLJ - v42 - S '96 - p239 [51-250]

Garrett, Annie - *Angel Flying Too Close to the Ground*
PW - v244 - F 17 '97 - p217 [1-50]
Because I Wanted You
PW - v244 - My 12 '97 - p55 [51-250]
Garrett, D - *Freedom of Information in Delaware*
J Gov Info - v23 - S '96 - p580 [51-250]
Garrett, Don - *The Cambridge Companion to Spinoza*
r Isis - v88 - Mr '97 - p145+ [501+]
Garrett, Donald E - *Potash: Deposits, Processing, Properties and Uses*
Choice - v34 - Ap '97 - p1368 [51-250]
Garrett, George P, 1929- - *An Evening Performance*
BW - v26 - N 17 '96 - p12 [51-250]
The King of Babylon Shall Not Come Against You
Sew R - v104 - Jl '96 - p476+ [501+]
Garrett, J Howard - *The Dirt Doctor's Guide to Organic Gardening*
Workbook - v21 - Fall '96 - p133 [251-500]
Howard Garrett's Plants for Texas. 1st Ed.
Choice - v34 - My '97 - p1524 [51-250]
Garrett, Mark - *Transportation Planning on Trial*
Choice - v34 - N '96 - p489 [51-250]
Garrett, R - *Biochemistry*
J Chem Ed - v74 - F '97 - p189+ [501+]
Garrett, Stephen A - *Conscience and Power*
Choice - v34 - Ap '97 - p1414 [51-250]
Garrett, Wendell - *American Colonial*
NEQ - v69 - D '96 - p691+ [501+]
Our Changing White House
J Am Cult - v19 - Spr '96 - p112 [51-250]
Garrett, William E - *The U.S. Soccer Sports Medicine Book*
SciTech - v20 - N '96 - p49 [51-250]
Garrido, Margarita - *Reclamos Y Representaciones*
HAHR - v76 - Ag '96 - p564+ [51-250]
Garrioch, David - *The Formation of the Parisian Bourgeoisie 1690-1830*
LJ - v122 - Ap 1 '97 - p105+ [51-250]
Garrison, David - *Gongora and the Pyramus and Thisbe Myth from Ovid to Shakespeare*
Hisp - v79 - S '96 - p442 [501+]
Garrison, Elise P - *Groaning Tears*
Class Out - v74 - Win '97 - p78+ [251-500]
CW - v90 - S '96 - p63+ [251-500]
Garrison, J Gregory - *Heavy Justice*
Aethlon - v13 - Fall '95 - p154+ [251-500]
Garrison, Jennifer - *A Million Visions of Peace*
c RT - v50 - O '96 - p142 [1-50]
Garrison, Robert, Jr. - *The Nutrition Desk Reference. 3rd Ed.*
r RQ - v36 - Fall '96 - p135+ [251-500]
Garrison, Webb - *A Treasury of Pennsylvania Tales*
CAY - v17 - Fall '96 - p3 [51-250]
Garrisson, Janine - *A History of Sixteenth-Century France 1483-1598*
Six Ct J - v27 - Win '96 - p1065+ [501+]
Garritz, Amalia - *Impresos Novohispanos 1808-1821*
r Lib - v18 - S '96 - p274 [1-50]
Garros, Veronique - *Intimacy and Terror*
NYRB - v43 - O 3 '96 - p4+ [501+]
Garrow, David J - *Liberty and Sexuality*
Soc - v33 - S '96 - p81+ [501+]
Soc - v33 - S '96 - p81+ [501+]
Garry, Jim - *This Ol' Drought Ain't Broke Us Yet*
CAY - v17 - Fall '96 - p4 [51-250]
Garry, Patrick M - *A Nation of Adversaries*
BL - v93 - My 15 '97 - p1545 [51-250]
Garson, Eugenia - *The Laura Ingalls Wilder Songbook* (Illus. by Garth Williams)
c HB Guide - v7 - Fall '96 - p357 [51-250]
Garson, G David - *Computer Technology and Social Issues*
SciTech - v20 - S '96 - p8 [51-250]
Garten, Jeffrey E - *The Big Ten*
BL - v93 - My 15 '97 - p1545 [51-250]
KR - v65 - Ap 1 '97 - p518 [251-500]
Garth Turner's 1997 RRSP Guide
Quill & Q - v63 - Ja '97 - p26 [51-250]
Gartman, David - *Auto Opium*
T&C - v37 - Ap '96 - p377+ [501+]
Gartner, Barbara L - *Plant Stems*
r Am Sci - v85 - Mr '97 - p188 [51-250]
Gartner, Heinz - *Constanze Mozart*
TranslRevS - v1 - My '95 - p12 [51-250]
John Christian Bach: Mozart's Friend and Mentor
Notes - v53 - S '96 - p70+ [501+]
TranslRevS - v1 - My '95 - p12 [51-250]
Gartner, Robert - *High Performance through Teamwork*
y Cur R - v36 - N '96 - p13 [51-250]
y SLJ - v42 - Ag '96 - p168 [51-250]

Gartner, William C - *Tourism Development*
R&R Bk N - v12 - F '97 - p28 [51-250]
Garton, Janet - *Contemporary Norwegian Women's Writing*
Choice - v34 - S '96 - p131 [51-250]
Garton, Ray - *Shackled*
PW - v244 - Mr 3 '97 - p72 [51-250]
Garton Ash, Timothy - *In Europe's Name*
Wil Q - v21 - Win '97 - p38 [51-250]
WP - v49 - Ja '97 - p282+ [501+]
Garver, Eugene - *Aristotle's Rhetoric*
AJP - v117 - Win '96 - p651+ [501+]
J Pol - v58 - N '96 - p1238+ [501+]
Rel St Rev - v22 - O '96 - p345 [51-250]
Garver, Newton - *Derrida and Wittgenstein*
MLR - v92 - Ja '97 - p155+ [501+]
Garvey, Ellen Gruber - *The Adman in the Parlor*
r Choice - v34 - N '96 - p447 [51-250]
Legacy - v14 - 1 '97 - p64+ [501+]
Wom R Bks - v13 - S '96 - p13+ [501+]
Garvey, John H - *What Are Freedoms For?*
Choice - v34 - Ap '97 - p1416 [51-250]
Garvin, Tom - *1922: The Birth of Irish Democracy*
Choice - v34 - My '97 - p1557 [51-250]
Garwood, Alfred N - *Weather America*
r ARBA - v28 - '97 - p634 [51-250]
r Choice - v34 - Ja '97 - p776 [51-250]
r LJ - v122 - Ap 15 '97 - p40 [51-250]
Garwood, Julie - *The Wedding (Crossley). Audio Version*
BWatch - v18 - Mr '97 - p7 [1-50]
Garza, Hedda - *African Americans and Jewish Americans*
y Kliatt - v31 - My '97 - p28+ [51-250]
Barred from the Bar
y HB Guide - v7 - Fall '96 - p314 [51-250]
y Kliatt - v31 - Mr '97 - p30 [51-250]
y KR - v64 - My 1 '96 - p688 [51-250]
Women in Medicine
y Kliatt - v31 - Mr '97 - p30 [51-250]
Gasaway, Laura N - *Law Librarianship*
R&R Bk N - v12 - F '97 - p102 [51-250]
Libraries and Copyright
r CLW - v67 - D '96 - p50 [51-250]
Gasche, Rodolphe - *Inventions of Difference*
Can Lit - Win '96 - p195+ [501+]
Gascoigne, David - *Michel Tournier*
TLS - Ja 10 '97 - p22 [501+]
Gascoigne, John - *Joseph Banks and the English Enlightenment*
AHR - v101 - D '96 - p1540 [501+]
EHR - v112 - F '97 - p220+ [251-500]
Isis - v88 - Mr '97 - p149+ [501+]
JMH - v69 - Mr '97 - p137+ [501+]
Gascoigne, Marc - *You Can Surf the Net!*
c BL - v93 - D 15 '96 - p723 [51-250]
c PW - v243 - N 25 '96 - p78 [1-50]
Gascoyne, David - *Selected Verse Translations*
TLS - D 20 '96 - p26 [501+]
Gash, Jonathan - *Different Women Dancing*
KR - v65 - My 1 '97 - p681 [251-500]
PW - v244 - Ap 7 '97 - p76+ [251-500]
The Possessions of a Lady
Arm Det - v30 - Win '97 - p92 [251-500]
BL - v92 - Ag '96 - p1886 [51-250]
Gasiorowicz, Stephen - *Quantum Physics. 2nd Ed.*
New Sci - v151 - S 28 '96 - p54+ [501+]
Gask, Marina - *True Romance*
y Sch Lib - v44 - N '96 - p170 [51-250]
Gaskell, Elizabeth - *The Life of Charlotte Bronte*
VS - v39 - Aut '95 - p1+ [501+]
Mary Barton
Col Lit - v23 - O '96 - p2+ [501+]
Trib Bks - Ap 6 '97 - p8 [1-50]
Private Voices
TLS - O 25 '96 - p36 [501+]
Wives and Daughters (Scales). Audio Version
Spec - v277 - N 30 '96 - p55 [1-50]
Gaskell, Philip - *A New Introduction to Bibliography*
Lib & Cul - v32 - Win '97 - p155+ [501+]
Gaskell, Rosalind M - *Feline and Canine Infectious Diseases*
r SciTech - v20 - D '96 - p57 [51-250]
Gaskill, D Kurt - *III-Nitride, SiC, and Diamond Materials for Electronic Devices*
SciTech - v21 - Mr '97 - p90 [51-250]
Gaskin, James E - *NetWare to Internet Gateways*
SciTech - v20 - S '96 - p56 [51-250]
Gaskins, Richard H - *Burdens of Proof in Modern Discourse*
Soc Ser R - v70 - S '96 - p482+ [501+]

Gaspar, David Barry - *Black Women and Slavery in the Americas*
Bl S - v26 - Fall '96 - p102+ [1-50]
More than Chattel
Am Vis - v12 - F '97 - p29 [51-250]
Bloom Rev - v16 - S '96 - p27 [51-250]
Choice - v34 - O '96 - p334 [51-250]
TLS - N 22 '96 - p31 [251-500]
Gasparini, Leonard - *I Once Had a Pet Praying Mantis* (Illus. by Robert A Dykstra)
c Ch Bk News - v19 - Spr '96 - p22+ [251-500]
Gasparri, Francoise - *Introduction A L'Histoire De L'Ecriture*
Specu - v72 - Ja '97 - p152+ [501+]
Gasparski, Wojciech W - *Human Action in Business*
JEL - v35 - Mr '97 - p253 [51-250]
Gasquet, F A - *Ancestral Prayers*
RR - v55 - N '96 - p661 [1-50]
Gass, Ken - *Claudius*
Can Lit - Spr '97 - p219+ [501+]
Gass, William H - *Finding a Form*
ABR - v18 - D '96 - p21+ [501+]
BW - v26 - S 22 '96 - p13 [51-250]
Choice - v34 - F '97 - p960 [51-250]
LATBR - S 22 '96 - p4+ [501+]
NYTBR - v102 - Mr 9 '97 - p6 [501+]
NYTLa - v146 - D 19 '96 - pC15 [501+]
Omensetter's Luck
Trib Bks - Ap 20 '97 - p8 [1-50]
The Tunnel
Meanjin - v55 - 3 '96 - p510+ [501+]
Quad - v40 - Jl '96 - p87+ [501+]
The Writer in Politics
Rapport - v19 - 5 '96 - p43 [251-500]
Gassenschmidt, Christoph - *Jewish Liberal Politics in Tsarist Russia 1900-1914*
AHR - v102 - F '97 - p141 [251-500]
Gasser, Robert P H - *An Introduction to Statistical Thermodynamics*
Choice - v34 - O '96 - p320 [51-250]
Gaster, Robin - *Bit by Bit*
Choice - v34 - D '96 - p656 [51-250]
R&R Bk N - v11 - D '96 - p32 [51-250]
Gastineau, Gary L - *The Dictionary of Financial Risk Management*
r Choice - v34 - My '97 - p1475 [51-250]
r R&R Bk N - v12 - F '97 - p47 [51-250]
Gaston, Bill - *Bella Combe Journal*
CF - v75 - D '96 - p45+ [501+]
Gaston, James C - *Ethics and National Defense*
NWCR - v49 - Aut '96 - p146+ [501+]
Gaston, Kevin J - *Biodiversity: A Biology of Numbers and Difference*
SciTech - v20 - N '96 - p25 [1-50]
Gastrow, Peter - *Bargaining for Peace*
JTWS - v13 - Spr '96 - p333+ [501+]
Gasvik, Kjell J - *Optical Metrology. 2nd Ed.*
SciTech - v20 - S '96 - p14 [51-250]
Gat, Azar - *The Development of Military Thought*
JMH - v68 - S '96 - p666+ [501+]
The Origins of Military Thought
JMH - v68 - S '96 - p666+ [501+]
Gat, Moshe - *Britain and Italy 1943-1949*
Albion - v28 - '96 - p727+ [501+]
Choice - v34 - S '96 - p186 [51-250]
Gatchel, Robert J - *Psychological Approaches to Pain Management*
Readings - v11 - D '96 - p30 [51-250]
SciTech - v20 - N '96 - p39 [51-250]
Gateley, Edwina - *There Was No Path So I Trod One*
RR - v55 - N '96 - p660 [1-50]
Gates, Beatrix - *The Wild Good*
LJ - v122 - F 1 '97 - p98 [51-250]
Gates, Bill - *The Road Ahead*
Nat R - v48 - O 14 '96 - p81+ [501+]
Tikkun - v11 - S '96 - p90+ [501+]
The Road Ahead. Completely Rev. and Up-to-Date
Ent W - N 15 '96 - p67 [1-50]
y Kliatt - v31 - Ja '97 - p30 [51-250]
LATBR - D 22 '96 - p6 [51-250]
NYTBR - v101 - N 24 '96 - p32 [51-250]
Obs - F 23 '97 - p18* [51-250]
PW - v243 - S 30 '96 - p79 [1-50]
QJS - v83 - My '97 - p230+ [501+]
The Road Ahead (Adamson). Completely Rev. and Up-to-Date. Audio Version
LJ - v122 - F 15 '97 - p174 [51-250]
Gates, Galen - *Trees*
Hort - v94 - Mr '97 - p78 [251-500]
Gates, Grace Hooten - *The Model City of the New South*
JEL - v34 - S '96 - p1471+ [51-250]

Gates, Henry Louis - *The Future of the Race*
JNE - v64 - Fall '95 - p486+ [501+]
NYTBR - v102 - Mr 2 '97 - p28 [1-50]
PW - v243 - D 9 '96 - p65+ [1-50]
Thirteen Ways of Looking at a Black Man
BL - v93 - F 15 '97 - p970 [51-250]
BW - v27 - F 16 '97 - p13 [51-250]
KR - v64 - D 15 '96 - p1781 [251-500]
LJ - v122 - F 15 '97 - p151 [51-250]
NYTBR - v102 - F 9 '97 - p21 [51-250]
NYTLa - v146 - Ja 28 '97 - pC13 [501+]
PW - v243 - D 30 '96 - p46 [51-250]
Trib Bks - Mr 16 '97 - p6+ [501+]
Gates, Hill - *China's Motor*
AJS - v102 - Ja '97 - p1168+ [501+]
Choice - v34 - S '96 - p175 [51-250]
Gates, Joanne E - *Elizabeth Robins 1862-1952*
ELT - v39 - 4 '96 - p487+ [501+]
Gates, Paul W - *The Jeffersonian Dream*
BusLR - v21 - 3 '96 - p241+ [51-250]
JEH - v57 - Mr '97 - p251+ [501+]
Gates, Phil - *Nature Got There First*
c Ch BWatch - v6 - Jl '96 - p6 [51-250]
c CLW - v67 - D '96 - p60+ [51-250]
Gates, Robert M - *From the Shadows*
Rapport - v19 - 6 '96 - p31 [251-500]
Gates, Robert Michael - *From the Shadows*
BW - v26 - Jl 14 '96 - p1+ [501+]
Econ - v341 - N 2 '96 - p85+ [501+]
FEER - v159 - O 3 '96 - p86 [501+]
HRNB - v25 - Fall '96 - p14+ [251-500]
Rapport - v19 - 6 '96 - p31 [251-500]
Spec - v277 - N 16 '96 - p44 [1-50]
TLS - D 27 '96 - p6 [501+]
Gates, Susan - *Firebug*
c JB - v60 - D '96 - p267 [51-250]
y Sch Lib - v45 - F '97 - p46 [51-250]
Gates-Coon, Rebecca - *The Landed Estates of the Esterhazy Princes*
EHR - v112 - Ap '97 - p489+ [501+]
Gath, Isak - *Advances in Processing and Pattern Analysis of Biological Signals*
SciTech - v21 - Mr '97 - p45 [51-250]
Gath, Tracy - *Science Books and Films' Best Books for Children 1992-1995*
r BL - v93 - S 15 '96 - p285 [51-250]
r SLJ - v42 - S '96 - p112 [1-50]
Gathercole, Patricia M - *Animals in Medieval French Manuscript Illumination*
MLR - v92 - Ja '97 - p186+ [251-500]
Gathorne-Hardy, Jonathan - *Particle Theory*
Obs - D 29 '96 - p28 [51-250]
Gatiss, Mark - *James Whale: A Biography*
FIR - v47 - Jl '96 - p116 [501+]
Gatrell, Peter - *Government, Industry and Rearmament in Russia 1900-1914*
EHR - v111 - S '96 - p1013+ [501+]
J Mil H - v61 - Ap '97 - p384+ [251-500]
Gatrell, V A C - *The Hanging Tree*
Albion - v28 - Sum '96 - p327+ [501+]
HT - v47 - Ja '97 - p57 [501+]
JIH - v27 - Aut '96 - p304+ [501+]
JMH - v68 - D '96 - p983+ [501+]
VS - v39 - Win '96 - p286+ [501+]
Gatten, Jeffrey N - *Rock Music Scholarship*
r AB - v98 - D 9 '96 - p2002 [51-250]
r ARBA - v28 - '97 - p493 [51-250]
r PMS - v19 - Win '95 - p105+ [501+]
Gaubatz, Kathryn Taylor - *Crime in the Public Mind*
Soc - v34 - Mr '97 - p88 [501+]
Gaubatz, Piper Rae - *Beyond the Great Wall*
Choice - v34 - N '96 - p515 [51-250]
Pac A - v69 - Sum '96 - p305 [51-250]
Gauch, Patricia Lee - *Christina Katerina and Fats and the Great Neighborhood War (Illus. by Stacey Schuett)*
c BL - v93 - Mr 1 '97 - p1171 [51-250]
c PW - v244 - Mr 10 '97 - p69 [1-50]
c SLJ - v43 - Mr '97 - p152 [51-250]
Tanya Steps Out (Illus. by Satomi Ichikawa)
c BL - v93 - D 15 '96 - p732 [1-50]
c KR - v64 - S 1 '96 - p1331 [51-250]
c SLJ - v42 - D '96 - p92 [51-250]
Uncle Magic
c CLW - v67 - Mr '97 - p13 [1-50]
Gauci, Perry - *Politics and Society in Great Yarmouth 1660-1722*
Choice - v34 - N '96 - p517 [51-250]
Gaughan, Patrick A - *Mergers, Acquisitions, and Corporate Restructurings*
Choice - v34 - O '96 - p329 [51-250]

Gaughen, Barbara - *Book Blitz*
BWatch - v18 - Mr '97 - p12 [51-250]
Gauguin, Paul - *Gauguin's Intimate Journals*
AB - v99 - Mr 3 '97 - p693 [51-250]
The Writings of a Savage
LJ - v121 - D '96 - p154 [51-250]
Gauhari, Farooka - *Searching for Saleem*
LJ - v121 - O 15 '96 - p67 [51-250]
PW - v243 - O 21 '96 - p67+ [51-250]
Gaukroger, Stephen - *Descartes: An Intellectual Biography*
AHR - v102 - F '97 - p116+ [501+]
Isis - v87 - S '96 - p544+ [501+]
Gaul, Wolfgang - *From Data to Knowledge*
JEL - v34 - D '96 - p2023 [51-250]
Gauld, Alan - *A History of Hypnotism*
J ClinPsyc - v57 - O '96 - p491 [501+]
Skeptic - v4 - '96 - p107 [51-250]
Gaulden, Albert Clayton - *Clearing for the Millennium*
LJ - v122 - My 1 '97 - p110 [51-250]
PW - v244 - Ja 13 '97 - p68 [51-250]
Gauldie, Robin - *Walking Amsterdam*
r BL - v93 - S 15 '96 - p212 [1-50]
Gauna, Max - *The Rabelaisian Mythologies*
MLR - v92 - Ap '97 - p464+ [501+]
Gaunt, Peter - *Oliver Cromwell*
Choice - v34 - S '96 - p186 [51-250]
HRNB - v25 - Fall '96 - p20 [251-500]
J Mil H - v61 - Ja '97 - p154+ [251-500]
Gauper, Beth - *Midwest Weekends*
r BWatch - v17 - S '96 - p6 [51-250]
Gaustad, Edwin S - *Neither King nor Prelate*
CH - v66 - Mr '97 - p139+ [501+]
Sworn on the Altar of God
CC - v113 - Ag 28 '96 - p824+ [251-500]
CLW - v67 - D '96 - p37 [51-250]
HRNB - v25 - Fall '96 - p42+ [251-500]
Rel St Rev - v23 - Ap '97 - p202 [51-250]
W&M Q - v53 - O '96 - p823+ [501+]
Gauthier, Isabelle - *Hot Pantz*
OOB - v26 - Jl '96 - p8 [501+]
Gauthier, Anne Helene - *The State and the Family*
Choice - v34 - My '97 - p1583 [51-250]
Gauthier, Gail - *My Life among the Aliens*
c HB Guide - v7 - Fall '96 - p292 [51-250]
Gauthier, Serge - *Clinical Diagnosis and Management of Alzheimer's Disease*
SciTech - v20 - N '96 - p45 [51-250]
Gautreaux, Tim - *Same Place, Same Things*
BL - v93 - S 1 '96 - p61+ [51-250]
Comw - v123 - N 8 '96 - p24+ [501+]
LATBR - O 6 '96 - p14 [51-250]
NAR - v282 - Mr '97 - p43+ [501+]
NYTBR - v101 - S 22 '96 - p16 [501+]
S Liv - v31 - O '96 - p108 [51-250]
Gavenda, Victor - *Mac Bible Goodies Pack. Electronic Media Version*
CBR - v14 - N '96 - p33 [1-50]
Gaventa, Beverly Roberts - *Mary: Glimpses of the Mother of Jesus*
CC - v113 - O 16 '96 - p979+ [501+]
Theol St - v57 - D '96 - p774 [251-500]
TT - v53 - Ja '97 - p528+ [501+]
Gavin, Jamila - *Fine Feathered Friend (Illus. by Carol Walters)*
c Sch Lib - v45 - F '97 - p24 [51-250]
Grandpa's Indian Summer
c TES - Jl 5 '96 - pR8 [51-250]
Our Favorite Stories from around the World (Illus. by Barnabas Kindersley)
c PW - v244 - Ap 28 '97 - p77 [51-250]
The Wormholers
y ILN - Christmas '96 - p88 [1-50]
Gavrilov, G P - *Problems and Exercises in Discrete Mathematics*
SciTech - v20 - N '96 - p5 [51-250]
Gavroglu, Kostas - *Fritz London: A Scientific Biography*
Isis - v87 - D '96 - p748 [501+]
Gawley, Robert E - *Principles of Asymmetric Synthesis*
New Sci - v153 - Mr 1 '97 - p38+ [51-250]
Gawronski, Raymond - *Word and Silence*
Choice - v34 - O '96 - p296 [51-250]
Gay, Douglas - *The Not-So-Minor Leagues*
c HB Guide - v7 - Fall '96 - p360 [51-250]
Gay, Kathlyn - *Emma Goldman*
c HB Guide - v8 - Spr '97 - p157 [1-50]
y SLJ - v42 - D '96 - p146 [51-250]

Encyclopedia of North American Eating and Drinking Traditions, Customs and Rituals
r ARBA - v28 - '97 - p569 [51-250]
r BL - v93 - F 15 '97 - p1041 [51-250]
r Choice - v34 - Ap '97 - p1307+ [51-250]
r R&R Bk N - v12 - F '97 - p31 [51-250]
Heroes of Conscience
r ARBA - v28 - '97 - p13 [51-250]
r BL - v93 - Ap 1 '97 - p1356+ [251-500]
Korean War
y BL - v93 - N 15 '96 - p582 [51-250]
y SLJ - v42 - D '96 - p146 [51-250]
Persian Gulf War
c SLJ - v43 - F '97 - p115 [51-250]
Saving the Environment
y BL - v93 - S 1 '96 - p71 [51-250]
y CCB-B - v50 - O '96 - p59 [51-250]
y HB Guide - v8 - Spr '97 - p97 [51-250]
y SLJ - v42 - O '96 - p156 [51-250]
y VOYA - v19 - O '96 - p229 [51-250]
Vietnam War
y BL - v93 - N 15 '96 - p582 [51-250]
y SLJ - v42 - D '96 - p146 [51-250]
y VOYA - v19 - F '97 - p345+ [251-500]
Gay, Marie-Louise - *Fat Charlie's Circus (Illus. by Marie-Louise Gay)*
c KR - v65 - Mr 15 '97 - p460 [51-250]
Gay, Martin, 1950- - *The Information Superhighway*
y Ch BWatch - v6 - Jl '96 - p7 [1-50]
c SB - v32 - Ag '96 - p176 [51-250]
The New Information Revolution
r ARBA - v28 - '97 - p242+ [501+]
r LJ - v122 - Ap 15 '97 - p68 [51-250]
Gay, Penny - *As She Likes It*
Six Ct J - v27 - Fall '96 - p811+ [501+]
Theat J - v48 - O '96 - p392+ [501+]
Gay, Peter - *The Bourgeois Experience. Vol. 4*
CC - v113 - S 25 '96 - p909+ [251-500]
J Soc H - v30 - Win '96 - p556+ [501+]
NYTBR - v102 - Ja 5 '97 - p28 [51-250]
PW - v243 - S 23 '96 - p73 [1-50]
The Naked Heart
Historian - v59 - Win '97 - p463 [251-500]
Gay, Ruth - *Unfinished People*
Choice - v34 - Ap '97 - p1404 [51-250]
KR - v64 - S 15 '96 - p1371 [501+]
LJ - v121 - N 1 '96 - p88 [51-250]
NL - v80 - Ja 13 '97 - p18+ [501+]
NS - v126 - F 28 '97 - p46+ [501+]
NY - v72 - Ja 6 '97 - p73 [51-250]
NYTBR - v102 - Ja 5 '97 - p11 [501+]
Obs - Ja 19 '97 - p18* [501+]
PW - v243 - S 23 '96 - p64 [51-250]
Gay, William - *Capitalism with a Human Face*
Choice - v34 - N '96 - p530 [51-250]
CPR - v16 - Je '96 - p162+ [501+]
Gayle, Katie - *Snappy Jazzy Jewelery*
c Sch Lib - v44 - Ag '96 - p112 [51-250]
Snappy Jazzy Jewelry
c HB Guide - v7 - Fall '96 - p354 [51-250]
c PW - v244 - Ap 21 '97 - p74 [1-50]
Gaylin, Willard - *The Perversion of Autonomy*
Choice - v34 - N '96 - p534 [51-250]
Cng - v28 - N '96 - p63 [51-250]
Hast Cen R - v26 - Jl '96 - p41 [1-50]
NYTBR - v101 - S 8 '96 - p28 [51-250]
Gaylord, Richard J - *Computer Simulations with Mathematica*
Am Sci - v84 - My '96 - p303+ [501+]
Gaynor, Adam - *Portraits of Recovery*
PW - v244 - Ja 20 '97 - p389 [51-250]
Gaynor, Gerard H - *Handbook of Technology Management*
SciTech - v20 - D '96 - p58 [51-250]
Gayon, Jean - *Darwin Et L'Apres-Darwin*
Isis - v88 - Mr '97 - p111+ [501+]
Gayton, Don - *Landscapes of the Interior*
CG - v116 - N '96 - p86 [251-500]
Gaziaux, Eric - *Morale De La Foi Et Morale Autonome*
Theol St - v57 - Je '96 - p385 [251-500]
Gazzaniga, Michael S - *Consciousness and the Brain (Lopez-Morillas). Audio Version*
BL - v93 - F 15 '97 - p1038 [51-250]
Gear, Kathleen O'Neal - *People of the Silence*
y BL - v93 - Ja '97 - p818 [51-250]
KR - v64 - N 15 '96 - p1621 [251-500]
PW - v243 - D 2 '96 - p42 [51-250]
People of the Silence. Audio Version
BWatch - v18 - Mr '97 - p9 [51-250]

Gear, W Michael - *The Morning River*
    KR - v64 - My 1 '96 - p621+ [251-500]
    Roundup M - v3 - Ag '96 - p29 [251-500]
Gearino, G D - *What the Deaf-Mute Heard (Whitener). Audio Version*
    Arm Det - v29 - Fall '96 - p473 [51-250]
    LJ - v121 - N 1 '96 - p112 [51-250]
Gearty, Conor - *Understanding Human Rights*
    Choice - v34 - S '96 - p209 [51-250]
Geary, David - *Graphic Java*
    CBR - v14 - N '96 - p35 [51-250]
    New Sci - v153 - Ja 18 '97 - p41 [51-250]
Geary, Rick - *Jack the Ripper*
  y Emerg Lib - v24 - S '96 - p27 [1-50]
Geber, Sara Zeff - *How to Manage Stress for Success*
    Per Psy - v50 - Spr '97 - p257+ [501+]
Gebhard, David - *The National Trust Guide to Art Deco in America*
    BWatch - v18 - F '97 - p5 [51-250]
    LJ - v121 - O 15 '96 - p54 [51-250]
    PW - v243 - O 21 '96 - p77 [51-250]
Gebhard, Patricia - *The Reference Realist in Library Academia*
    LJ - v122 - My 1 '97 - p146 [51-250]
Gebhardt, Jurgen - *Americanism: Revolutionary Order and Societal Self-Interpretation in the American Republic*
    TranslRevS - v1 - My '95 - p8 [51-250]
Geddes, Anne - *Down in the Garden*
    CSM - v89 - D 12 '96 - p14 [51-250]
    CSM - v89 - Ja 9 '97 - p14 [51-250]
    LATBR - D 8 '96 - p10 [51-250]
    PW - v243 - S 16 '96 - p65 [51-250]
    Time - v148 - N 18 '96 - p109 [1-50]
  The Twelve Days of Christmas
    Books - v9 - S '95 - p22 [1-50]
Geddes, Barbara - *Politician's Dilemma*
    JEL - v35 - Mr '97 - p287 [51-250]
Geddes, Gary - *Girl by the Water*
    Can Lit - Win '96 - p145+ [501+]
Geddes, Margaret - *Remembering Weary*
    Aust Bk R - F '97 - p15+ [501+]
Geddes, Robert - *Cities in Our Future*
    BL - v93 - F 1 '97 - p911 [51-250]
Gedge, Pauline - *House of Illusions*
    KR - v65 - Mr 15 '97 - p399 [251-500]
    PW - v244 - Ap 21 '97 - p61 [51-250]
Gedicks, Al - *The New Resource Wars*
    SSQ - v77 - Je '96 - p445+ [501+]
Gedicks, Frederick Mark - *The Rhetoric of Church and State*
    APSR - v90 - D '96 - p907+ [501+]
Gedo, John E - *The Artist and the Emotional World*
    Choice - v34 - Ja '97 - p879 [51-250]
    R&R Bk N - v11 - N '96 - p5 [51-250]
  The Languages of Psychoanalysis
    Readings - v11 - D '96 - p27 [51-250]
Gee, Henry - *Before the Backbone*
    Choice - v34 - F '97 - p990 [51-250]
    Nature - v384 - N 28 '96 - p324+ [501+]
    New Sci - v151 - S 28 '96 - p55 [1-50]
    Sci - v274 - D 6 '96 - p1629 [501+]
Geer, Ira W - *Glossary of Weather and Climate*
  r Choice - v34 - My '97 - p1475 [51-250]
Geeraerts, Jef - *Goud*
    WLT - v70 - Aut '96 - p972 [251-500]
Geertz, Clifford - *After the Fact*
    JPR - v33 - N '96 - p499 [51-250]
    JR - v77 - Ap '97 - p336+ [501+]
    Soc - v34 - Mr '97 - p89+ [501+]
Geeslin, Campbell - *In Rosa's Mexico (Illus. by Andrea Arroyo)*
  c BL - v93 - N 15 '96 - p594 [51-250]
  c CCB-B - v50 - Ja '97 - p169+ [51-250]
  c Emerg Lib - v24 - Mr '97 - p45 [1-50]
  c HB Guide - v8 - Spr '97 - p28 [51-250]
  c PW - v243 - N 18 '96 - p74 [51-250]
  c SLJ - v42 - D '96 - p92 [51-250]
Geffcken, Katherine A - *Comedy in the Pro Caelio*
    Class Out - v74 - Spr '97 - p120 [251-500]
Gefou-Madianou, Dimitra - *Alcohol, Gender and Culture*
    Am Ethnol - v23 - Ag '96 - p656+ [501+]
Gegov, Alexander - *Distributed Fuzzy Control of Multivariable Systems*
    SciTech - v20 - N '96 - p70 [51-250]
Gehler, Michael - *Karl Gruber, Reden Und Documente 1945-1953*
    JMH - v68 - S '96 - p737+ [501+]
  Osterreich Und Die Europaische Integration 1945-1993
    JMH - v68 - S '96 - p737+ [501+]

Gehm, Fred - *Quantitative Trading and Money Management*
    Barron's - v76 - S 2 '96 - p43 [51-250]
Gehman, Pleasant - *Princess of Hollywood*
    PW - v243 - Jl 22 '96 - p238 [51-250]
    Sm Pr R - v29 - Ja '97 - p12 [501+]
Gehring, Wes D - *American Dark Comedy*
    Choice - v34 - D '96 - p622 [51-250]
    R&R Bk N - v11 - D '96 - p61 [51-250]
Geier, James T - *Network Reengineering*
    SciTech - v20 - N '96 - p74 [51-250]
Geiger, Brenda - *Family, Justice, and Delinquency*
    Fam Relat - v45 - Jl '96 - p355 [251-500]
  Fathers as Primary Caregivers
    Readings - v11 - D '96 - p30 [251-500]
Geiler Von Kaysersberg, Johann - *Johannes Geiler Von Keysersberg Samtliche Werke. Bks. 1-3*
    Six Ct J - v27 - Win '96 - p1126+ [501+]
Geis, Robert J - *Personal Existence after Death*
    CPR - v16 - D '96 - p396+ [501+]
    RM - v50 - S '96 - p154+ [501+]
Geise, Judie - *The New American Kitchen Cookbook*
    BL - v93 - F 15 '97 - p988 [51-250]
    PW - v244 - Ja 27 '97 - p99 [51-250]
Geisert, Arthur - *The Etcher's Studio (Illus. by Arthur Geisert)*
  c BL - v93 - Ap 1 '97 - p1337 [51-250]
  c HB - v73 - My '97 - p306+ [251-500]
  c KR - v65 - F 15 '97 - p299 [51-250]
  c PW - v244 - Mr 3 '97 - p74 [51-250]
  c Trib Bks - My 4 '97 - p7 [51-250]
  Pigs from 1 to 10
  c CLW - v67 - Mr '97 - p14 [1-50]
  Pigs from A to Z
  c Par Ch - v20 - O '96 - p21 [51-250]
  Roman Numerals I to MM (Illus. by Arthur Geisert)
  c Emerg Lib - v24 - S '96 - p44 [1-50]
  c HB - v72 - S '96 - p575+ [51-250]
  c HB Guide - v7 - Fall '96 - p329 [51-250]
  c LATBR - Jl 14 '96 - p11 [51-250]
  c Learning - v25 - Ja '97 - p56 [1-50]
  c SLJ - v42 - S '96 - p196 [51-250]
Geiskopf-Hadler, Susann - *The Best 125 Meatless Mediterranean Dishes*
    BWatch - v18 - F '97 - p7 [1-50]
Geisler, Norman L - *Roman Catholics and Evagelicals*
    CLW - v66 - Je '96 - p33+ [501+]
Geison, Gerald L - *The Private Science of Louis Pasteur*
    AHR - v101 - D '96 - p1557+ [501+]
    JIH - v27 - Win '97 - p521+ [251-500]
Geissman, Grant - *Mad about the Seventies*
    LATBR - v263 - S 29 '96 - p15 [51-250]
Geist, Valerius - *Buffalo Nation*
  y BL - v93 - F 1 '97 - p915 [51-250]
    Nature - v385 - Ja 9 '97 - p128 [1-50]
Geister, Philip - *Aufhebung Zur Eigentlichkeit*
    Theol St - v58 - Mr '97 - p193+ [251-500]
Gelb, Alvin M - *Clinical Gastroenterology in the Elderly*
    SciTech - v20 - D '96 - p47 [51-250]
Gelb, Eric - *10-Minute Guide to Annual Reports and Prospectuses*
    BWatch - v18 - Mr '97 - p5 [51-250]
Gelb, Joseph - *Tax Accounting for Small Business*
    BL - v93 - F 1 '97 - p914 [51-250]
Gelb, Joyce - *Women of Japan and Korea*
    J Pol - v58 - Ag '96 - p870+ [51-250]
Gelbert, Doug - *So Who the Heck Was Oscar Mayer?*
    LJ - v122 - Ja '97 - p114 [51-250]
  r PW - v243 - S 30 '96 - p80 [51-250]
Gelbspan, Ross - *The Heat Is On*
  y BL - v93 - My 15 '97 - p1545+ [51-250]
    KR - v65 - Mr 15 '97 - p435 [251-500]
    PW - v244 - Ap 28 '97 - p62+ [251-500]
Gelder, Ken - *The Oxford Book of Australian Ghost Stories*
  y Magpies - v11 - Jl '96 - p35 [51-250]
Gelderman, Carol - *All the Presidents' Words*
    BL - v93 - Ja '97 - p790 [51-250]
    KR - v65 - Ja 15 '97 - p115 [251-500]
    LJ - v122 - F 15 '97 - p148 [51-250]
    PW - v244 - Ja 6 '97 - p52+ [51-250]
Geldreich, Edwin E - *Microbial Quality of Water Supply in Distribution Systems*
    SciTech - v20 - D '96 - p68 [51-250]
Geldzahler, Henry - *Making It New*
    NYTBR - v102 - Ja 19 '97 - p28 [1-50]
Gelernter, David - *1939: The Lost World of the Fair*
    T&C - v37 - O '96 - p832+ [501+]
Gelfand, I M - *The Gelfand Mathematical Seminars 1993-1995*
    SciTech - v20 - S '96 - p11 [1-50]

Gelfant, Blanche H - *Cross-Cultural Reckonings*
    Russ Rev - v55 - O '96 - p703+ [501+]
Gelinas, Ayn - *Creative Applications*
    R&R Bk N - v12 - F '97 - p46 [51-250]
Gelissen, Rena Kornreich - *Rena's Promise*
    TLS - Mr 21 '97 - p13 [51-250]
    Wom R Bks - v14 - O '96 - p12+ [501+]
Gellatley, Juliet - *The Livewire Guide to Going, Being and Staying Veggie!*
  y Bks Keeps - Ja '97 - p27 [51-250]
Geller, R - *Electron Cyclotron Resonance Ion Sources and ECR Plasmas*
  r SciTech - v21 - Mr '97 - p25 [51-250]
Geller, Shari - *Fatal Convictions*
    Arm Det - v30 - Win '97 - p70 [51-250]
    Bloom Rev - v17 - Ja '97 - p14 [51-250]
    LJ - v121 - S 15 '96 - p95 [51-250]
    LJ - v122 - Mr 15 '97 - p42 [1-50]
    PW - v243 - S 23 '96 - p58 [51-250]
  Fatal Convictions (Esterman). Audio Version
    BWatch - v17 - D '96 - p10 [1-50]
Geller, William A - *Police Violence*
    Choice - v34 - Ap '97 - p1424 [51-250]
Gelles, Richard J - *The Book of David*
    JMF - v59 - F '97 - p235+ [501+]
    Soc Ser R - v71 - Mr '97 - p135+ [501+]
Gellman, Marc - *God's Mailbox (Illus. by Debbie Tilley)*
  c HB Guide - v7 - Fall '96 - p309 [51-250]
Gellner, Ernest - *Conditions of Liberty*
    AS - v66 - Spr '97 - p303+ [501+]
Gellrich, Jesse M - *Discourse and Dominion in the Fourteenth Century*
    AHR - v101 - O '96 - p1194+ [501+]
Gelm, Richard J - *Politics and Religious Authority*
    J Ch St - v38 - Sum '96 - p651+ [251-500]
Gelman, A - *Bayesian Data Analysis*
    New Sci - v151 - S 28 '96 - p49 [251-500]
Gelman, Juan - *Unthinkable Tenderness*
    PW - v244 - F 24 '97 - p87 [51-250]
Gelpi, Donald L - *The Turn to Experience in Contemporary Theology*
    Theol St - v57 - S '96 - p570+ [251-500]
Geluykens, Ronald - *The Pragmatics of Discourse Anaphora in English*
    Lang Soc - v26 - Mr '97 - p147+ [501+]
Gemelli, Ralph - *Normal Child and Adolescent Development*
    Choice - v34 - Ja '97 - p879 [51-250]
Gemmell, David - *Last Sword of Power*
  y Kliatt - v31 - Ja '97 - p12 [51-250]
Gemmell, Kathy - *Storms and Hurricanes*
  c Sch Lib - v44 - N '96 - p162 [51-250]
Gemmill, Elizabeth - *Changing Values in Medieval Scotland*
    Albion - v28 - Fall '96 - p542+ [501+]
Gen, Mitsuo - *Genetic Algorithms and Manufacturing Design*
    SciTech - v21 - Mr '97 - p71 [51-250]
Gendlin, Eugene T - *Focusing-Oriented Psychotherapy*
    SciTech - v20 - S '96 - p33 [1-50]
Gendzier, Irene L - *Notes from the Minefield*
    For Aff - v76 - My '97 - p143 [51-250]
Genealogical and Local History Books in Print: Family History Volume. 5th Ed.
  r ARBA - v28 - '97 - p163 [51-250]
The Genealogy Annual 1995
  r BL - v93 - Mr 1 '97 - p1195 [51-250]
Geneen, Harold - *The Synergy Myth and Other Ailments of Business Today*
    KR - v65 - F 15 '97 - p270 [251-500]
    LJ - v122 - Mr 15 '97 - p71 [51-250]
    PW - v244 - Ja 27 '97 - p88 [51-250]
Genet, Donna - *Father Junipero Serra: Founder of California Missions*
  y HB Guide - v7 - Fall '96 - p372 [51-250]
  c SLJ - v42 - S '96 - p214+ [51-250]
Genet, Jacqueline - *Irish Writers and Their Creative Process*
    TLS - S 27 '96 - p13 [501+]
  Rural Ireland, Real Ireland?
    TLS - S 27 '96 - p13 [501+]
Genet, Jean - *Splendid's*
    WLT - v70 - Aut '96 - p912+ [501+]
Genetic Engineering. Vol. 18
    SciTech - v20 - S '96 - p19 [51-250]
Genette, Gerard - *Mimologics*
    TranslRevS - v2 - D '96 - p11 [51-250]

Geneva, Ann - *Astrology and the Seventeenth Century Mind*
  Albion - v28 - Fall '96 - p479+ [501+]
  HT - v46 - Jl '96 - p57 [501+]
  Lon R Bks - v18 - My 23 '96 - p31+ [501+]
Genge, Ngaire - *The New Unofficial X-Files Companion II*
  Obs - D 15 '96 - p16* [501+]
  The Unofficial X-Files Companion
  Ent W - Je 28 '96 - p96 [51-250]
Genini, Ronald - *Theda Bara: A Biography of the Silent Screen Vamp*
  Choice - v34 - N '96 - p468 [51-250]
The Genius of Edison. Electronic Media Version
  y Kliatt - v31 - Mr '97 - p37+ [51-250]
Genkin, S A - *Mathematical Circles*
  y SciTech - v20 - N '96 - p12 [1-50]
Genne, Beth - *The Making of a Choreographer*
  Dance - v71 - F '97 - p122+ [501+]
Gennes, Pierre-Gilles De - *Fragile Objects*
  Choice - v34 - F '97 - p1001 [51-250]
  Sci - v274 - N 22 '96 - p1321 [1-50]
Genome Research
  p Nature - v383 - S 5 '96 - p39 [251-500]
Genova, Judith - *Wittgenstein: A Way of Seeing*
  CPR - v16 - Ag '96 - p257+ [501+]
Genova, Pamela Antonia - *Andre Gide Dans Le Labyrinthe De La Mythotextualite*
  MLR - v92 - Ja '97 - p202+ [251-500]
  WLT - v70 - Sum '96 - p663 [51-250]
Genovese, Eugene D - *The Southern Tradition*
  South HR - v31 - Win '97 - p71+ [501+]
Genovese, Peter - *Jersey Diners*
  PW - v243 - N 11 '96 - p68 [51-250]
Genscher, Hans Dietrich - *Erinnerungen*
  Choice - v34 - D '96 - p568 [1-50]
Gensini, Sergio - *Roma Capitale 1447-1527*
  r CHR - v83 - Ja '97 - p93+ [501+]
  EHR - v112 - Ap '97 - p455+ [501+]
Gensler, Harry J - *Formal Ethics*
  Choice - v34 - Ja '97 - p808 [51-250]
Gensler, Howard - *The American Welfare System*
  JEL - v34 - D '96 - p2064 [51-250]
  Soc Ser R - v71 - Mr '97 - p166 [1-50]
  A Guide to China's Tax and Business Laws
  Ch Rev Int - v4 - Spr '97 - p134+ [501+]
Gent, Lucy - *Albion's Classicism*
  Art Bull - v78 - D '96 - p736+ [501+]
  BM - v138 - Ag '96 - p548+ [501+]
  Six Ct J - v27 - Win '96 - p1231 [251-500]
Gentilcore, David - *From Bishop to Witch*
  Rel St Rev - v23 - Ja '97 - p85 [51-250]
Gentile, Emilio - *The Sacralization of Politics in Fascist Italy*
  Choice - v34 - Mr '97 - p1220 [51-250]
Gentle, Victor - *Bladderworts: Trapdoors to Oblivion*
  c SB - v33 - My '97 - p111 [51-250]
  Butterworts: Greasy Cups of Death
  c SB - v33 - My '97 - p111 [51-250]
  Carnivorous Mushrooms
  c SB - v33 - My '97 - p111 [51-250]
  Pitcher Plants
  c SB - v33 - My '97 - p111 [51-250]
  Sundews: A Sweet and Sticky Death
  c SB - v33 - My '97 - p111+ [51-250]
  Venus Flytraps and Waterwheels
  c SB - v33 - My '97 - p112 [51-250]
Gentry, Alwyn H - *A Field Guide to the Families and Genera of Woody Plants of Northwest South America (Colombia, Ecuador, Peru)*
  r AB - v97 - Je 17 '96 - p2397 [51-250]
  r SB - v33 - Ja '97 - p8 [51-250]
Gentry, Anita - *Night Summons*
  KR - v64 - S 1 '96 - p1275 [51-250]
Gentry, Francis G - *German Epic Poetry*
  TranslRevS - v2 - D '96 - p2 [1-50]
Gentry, Peter John - *The Asterisked Materials in the Greek Job*
  Rel St Rev - v23 - Ap '97 - p195 [51-250]
Geoffrion, Bernard - *Boom Boom: The Life and Times of Bernard Geoffrion*
  Mac - v109 - D 16 '96 - p72 [1-50]
  Quill & Q - v62 - N '96 - p38 [501+]
Geoghegan, Adrienne - *Dogs Don't Wear Glasses*
  c HB Guide - v7 - Fall '96 - p257 [51-250]
The Geologist's Directory 1996
  r GJ - v163 - Mr '97 - p105+ [51-250]
Geopedia. Electronic Media Version
  yr BL - v92 - Ag '96 - p1918 [51-250]
George, Alice Rose - *25 and Under: Photographers*
  LJ - v122 - Ap 15 '97 - p78 [51-250]

George, Anne - *Murder Runs in the Family*
  PW - v244 - Ap 14 '97 - p71 [51-250]
George, Diane Hume - *The Lonely Other*
  Wom R Bks - v14 - D '96 - p1+ [51-250]
George, Elizabeth - *Deception on His Mind*
  BL - v93 - My 15 '97 - p1541 [51-250]
  In the Presence of the Enemy
  Arm Det - v29 - Sum '96 - p362+ [251-500]
  Ent W - D 27 '96 - p142 [51-250]
  LATBR - My 12 '96 - p11 [51-250]
  In the Presence of the Enemy (Peters). Audio Version
  CSM - v89 - Mr 27 '97 - pB2 [1-50]
  LJ - v121 - S 15 '96 - p114 [51-250]
George, James - *Asking for the Earth*
  Parabola - v21 - Ag '96 - p98 [501+]
George, Jean Craighead - *The Case of the Missing Cutthroats*
  c CLW - v67 - D '96 - p65 [51-250]
  c HB Guide - v7 - Fall '96 - p292 [1-50]
  Dipper of Copper Creek (Illus. by Jean Craighead George)
  c HB Guide - v7 - Fall '96 - p292 [51-250]
  Everglades (Illus. by Wendell Minor)
  c LA - v73 - O '96 - p439+ [51-250]
  c New Ad - v9 - Fall '96 - p327+ [501+]
  c PW - v244 - Ap 28 '97 - p77 [1-50]
  c RT - v50 - N '96 - p242 [1-50]
  Look to the North (Illus. by Lucia Washburn)
  c CBRS - v25 - Ap '97 - p102 [51-250]
  c KR - v65 - Ap 1 '97 - p554 [51-250]
  c PW - v244 - Ap 7 '97 - p91 [51-250]
  The Tarantula in My Purse and 172 Other Wild Pets (Illus. by Jean Craighead George)
  c BL - v93 - N 15 '96 - p581 [51-250]
  c CCB-B - v50 - D '96 - p134 [51-250]
  c CSM - v88 - S 26 '96 - pB4 [51-250]
  c HB Guide - v8 - Spr '97 - p157 [51-250]
  c KR - v64 - Ag 15 '96 - p1234 [51-250]
  c NYTBR - v101 - N 10 '96 - p46+ [501+]
  c PW - v243 - S 2 '96 - p132 [51-250]
  c SLJ - v42 - O '96 - p132 [51-250]
  There's an Owl in the Shower (Illus. by Christine Herman Merrill)
  c RT - v50 - S '96 - p56+ [51-250]
  Vulpes, the Red Fox (Illus. by Jean Craighead George)
  c HB Guide - v7 - Fall '96 - p292 [51-250]
George, Jill A - *Team Member's Survival Guide*
  HR Mag - v42 - F '97 - p124 [51-250]
George, John - *American Extremists*
  Choice - v34 - Ja '97 - p875 [251-500]
George, Kenneth M - *Showing Signs of Violence*
  Am Ethnol - v24 - F '97 - p257+ [501+]
George, Kristine O'Connell - *The Great Frog Race and Other Poems (Illus. by Kate Kiesler)*
  c BL - v93 - Mr 15 '97 - p1238 [51-250]
  c CBRS - v25 - Mr '97 - p93 [1-50]
  c KR - v65 - F 15 '97 - p299 [51-250]
  c PW - v244 - Ja 27 '97 - p107 [51-250]
George, Leonard - *Alternative Realities*
  r JP - v60 - Mr '96 - p78+ [501+]
  r Skeptic - v4 - '96 - p107 [51-250]
  Crimes of Perception
  r CH - v66 - Mr '97 - p213+ [51-250]
George, Lindsay Barrett - *Around the Pond (Illus. by Lindsay Barrett George)*
  c BL - v93 - S 15 '96 - p247 [51-250]
  c HB Guide - v8 - Spr '97 - p28 [51-250]
  c Inst - v106 - Mr '97 - p30 [51-250]
  c SLJ - v42 - S '96 - p178 [51-250]
  In the Snow (Illus. by Lindsay Barrett George)
  c RT - v50 - Mr '97 - p501 [51-250]
George, Margaret - *The Memoirs of Cleopatra*
  BL - v93 - Mr 15 '97 - p1203+ [51-250]
  Ent W - My 16 '97 - p109 [51-250]
  KR - v65 - Mr 15 '97 - p400 [251-500]
  LJ - v122 - My 1 '97 - p139 [51-250]
  PW - v244 - Mr 24 '97 - p58 [51-250]
George, Nelson - *Seduced*
  BW - v27 - F 16 '97 - p12 [51-250]
George, Robert - *Making Men Moral*
  PSR - v25 - '96 - p354+ [501+]
George, Susan - *Faith and Credit*
  CS - v26 - Mr '97 - p184+ [501+]
George, Timothy - *Baptists and Their Doctrines*
  CH - v66 - Mr '97 - p206+ [51-250]
George, Twig C - *A Dolphin Named Bob (Illus. by Christine Herman Merrill)*
  c HB Guide - v7 - Fall '96 - p292 [51-250]
Georges, Pericles - *Barbarian Asia and the Greek Experience*
  Rel St Rev - v23 - Ja '97 - p60 [51-250]

Georges Duhamel, Medecin-Ecrivain De Guerre
  FR - v70 - F '97 - p474+ [501+]
Georgia Public Education Report Cards 1994-1995. Vols. 1-4
  J Gov Info - v23 - S '96 - p581 [51-250]
Georgia: Reform in the Food and Agriculture Sector
  JEL - v35 - Mr '97 - p294+ [51-250]
Georgiade, Gregory S - *Georgiade Plastic, Maxillofacial and Reconstructive Surgery. 3rd Ed.*
  SciTech - v21 - Mr '97 - p60 [51-250]
Georgi-Findlay, Brigitte - *The Frontiers of Women's Writing*
  Choice - v34 - D '96 - p612+ [51-250]
  Nine-C Lit - v51 - Mr '97 - p557 [51-250]
  WHQ - v28 - Spr '97 - p104 [1-50]
Geppert, Hans Vilmar - *Der Realistische Weg*
  MLR - v91 - O '96 - p944+ [501+]
Ger, Ralph - *Essentials of Clinical Anatomy. 2nd Ed.*
  SciTech - v20 - D '96 - p33 [51-250]
Gera, Deborah Levine - *Xenophon's Cyropaedia*
  CW - v89 - Jl '96 - p517 [501+]
Geraghty, Paul - *The Hunter*
  c Bks Keeps - N '96 - p8 [51-250]
  Solo (Illus. by Paul Geraghty)
  c HB Guide - v7 - Fall '96 - p257 [1-50]
Geraghty, Tony - *Beyond the Front Line*
  Econ - v342 - F 1 '97 - p87+ [501+]
  Spec - v277 - O 19 '96 - p50 [501+]
Gerami, Shahin - *Women and Fundamentalism*
  CS - v26 - Mr '97 - p238 [501+]
Gerard, David - *Brief Transit*
  LAR - v99 - Ja '97 - p48 [51-250]
Gerard, Jessica - *Country House Life*
  EHR - v112 - F '97 - p239+ [251-500]
  J Soc H - v30 - Spr '97 - p787+ [501+]
Gerard-Varet, Louis-Andre - *Le Modele Et L'Enquete*
  JEL - v34 - D '96 - p2012+ [51-250]
Geras, Adele - *Beauty and the Beast and Other Stories (Illus. by Louise Brierley)*
  c Bks Keeps - v100 - S '96 - p32 [51-250]
  c Bks Keeps - Ja '97 - p8+ [501+]
  c BL - v93 - N 15 '96 - p582 [51-250]
  c HB Guide - v8 - Spr '97 - p148 [51-250]
  c JB - v60 - D '96 - p251+ [51-250]
  c KR - v64 - O 15 '96 - p1532 [51-250]
  c PW - v243 - N 25 '96 - p74 [51-250]
  c SLJ - v43 - F '97 - p90+ [51-250]
  Cinderella (Illus. by Gwen Tourret)
  c Sch Lib - v45 - F '97 - p20 [51-250]
  From Lullaby to Lullaby (Illus. by Kathryn Brown)
  c KR - v65 - Ap 1 '97 - p554+ [51-250]
  c PW - v244 - Mr 17 '97 - p82 [51-250]
  A Treasury of Jewish Stories (Illus. by Jane Cope)
  c CLW - v67 - D '96 - p62 [251-500]
Geras, Norman - *Solidarity in the Conversation of Humankind*
  Ethics - v107 - Ja '97 - p388+ [51-250]
Gerber, Haim - *State, Society, and Law in Islam*
  AHR - v101 - O '96 - p1256+ [251-500]
Gerber, Scott Douglas - *To Secure These Rights*
  AHR - v102 - F '97 - p172 [501+]
Gerberg, Mort - *Geographunny: A Book of Global Riddles*
  c Inst - v106 - O '96 - p93 [1-50]
Gerbet, Marie-Claude - *Les Noblesses Espagnoles Au Moyen Age XIe-XV Siecle*
  r AHR - v102 - F '97 - p96+ [501+]
Gerbner, George - *Invisible Crises*
  Choice - v34 - Mr '97 - p1154 [51-250]
Gerdts, William H - *Theodore Clement Steele: An American Master of Light*
  Mag Antiq - v151 - Ja '97 - p28+ [251-500]
  William Glackens
  BL - v93 - S 1 '96 - p53 [51-250]
  Choice - v34 - F '97 - p955 [51-250]
  LATBR - D 8 '96 - p14 [1-50]
Gere, David - *Looking Out*
  TDR - v40 - Fall '96 - p202 [51-250]
Geremek, Bronislaw - *The Common Roots of Europe*
  Choice - v34 - F '97 - p1019 [51-250]
  Poverty: A History
  AHR - v101 - D '96 - p1524 [501+]
Gergen, Kenneth J - *Realities and Relationships*
  CS - v25 - S '96 - p676+ [501+]
Gerhard, Peter - *Sintesis E Indice De Los Mandamientos Virreinales 1548-1553*
  HAHR - v77 - F '97 - p111+ [501+]
Gerhard Richter: 100 Bilder
  ABR - v18 - D '96 - p14 [501+]
Gerhard Richter: Painting in the Nineties
  Art J - v55 - Fall '96 - p89+ [501+]

Gerhardstein, Virginia Brokaw - *Dickinson's American Historical Fiction. 5th Ed.*
  r RQ - v36 - Win '96 - p216 [51-250]

Gerhardt, Lillian - *School Library Journal's Best*
  CCB-B - v50 - My '97 - p340 [51-250]

Gerhardt, Michael J - *The Federal Impeachment Process*
  APSR - v90 - D '96 - p908+ [501+]

Gerhardt, Rosario A - *Electrically Based Microstructural Characterization*
  SciTech - v20 - D '96 - p62 [51-250]

Gerholdt, James - *Beetles*
  c Ch BWatch - v6 - Jl '96 - p6 [51-250]
Butterflies
  c Ch BWatch - v6 - Jl '96 - p6 [51-250]
Grasshoppers
  c Ch BWatch - v6 - Jl '96 - p6 [51-250]

Gerigk, Horst-Jurgen - *Die Russen In Amerika*
  Slav R - v55 - Sum '96 - p519+ [501+]

Geringer, Laura - *The Pomegranate Seeds (Illus. by Leonid Gore)*
  c Ch BWatch - v6 - My '96 - p3 [1-50]

Gerke, Pamela - *Multicultural Plays for Children. Vol. 1*
  c SLJ - v42 - S '96 - p196 [51-250]
Multicultural Plays for Children. Vol. 2
  c SLJ - v43 - Mr '97 - p200 [51-250]
Multicultural Plays for Children. Vols. 1-2
  c BL - v93 - D 1 '96 - p649+ [51-250]

Germain, Carel B - *The Life Model of Social Work Practice. 2nd Ed.*
  R&R Bk N - v11 - N '96 - p43 [51-250]

Germain, Richard N - *Dollars through the Doors*
  R&R Bk N - v11 - N '96 - p36 [51-250]

Germain, Sylvie - *Eclat De Sel*
  Econ - v340 - S 14 '96 - p14*+ [501+]
Immensites
  FR - v70 - O '96 - p141+ [251-500]

German, O V - *Problem Solving*
  SciTech - v20 - N '96 - p5 [51-250]

German, Randall M - *Sintering Technology*
  SciTech - v20 - D '96 - p81 [51-250]

German Monitor 30
  p Ger Q - v69 - Sum '96 - p364+ [501+]

Germany (Insight Guides)
  r BL - v93 - S 15 '96 - p210 [1-50]

Germany (West). Monopolkommission - *German Monopolies Commission 1984-1993*
  JEL - v34 - S '96 - p1453+ [51-250]

Germer, Jerry - *The Complete Guide to Building and Outfitting an Office in Your Home*
  LJ - v122 - F 1 '97 - p53 [1-50]

Gernant, Karen - *Imagining Women*
  CAY - v17 - Fall '96 - p4 [51-250]
  Ch Rev Int - v4 - Spr '97 - p136+ [501+]

Gernet, Jacques - *Buddhism in Chinese Society*
  Ch Rev Int - v3 - Fall '96 - p418+ [501+]
  Historian - v59 - Win '97 - p449+ [251-500]
  JEH - v57 - Mr '97 - p225+ [501+]

Gerrard, Christine - *The Patriot Opposition to Walpole*
  EHR - v112 - Ap '97 - p485+ [501+]
  MP - v94 - F '97 - p393+ [501+]

Gerrard, Michael B - *Whose Backyard, Whose Risk*
  JEL - v35 - Mr '97 - p243+ [51-250]

Gerrard, Roy - *Wagons West! (Illus. by Roy Gerrard)*
  c HB Guide - v7 - Fall '96 - p257 [51-250]
  c JB - v60 - Ag '96 - p141 [51-250]
  c Sch Lib - v44 - Ag '96 - p99 [51-250]
  c SLJ - v42 - D '96 - p29 [1-50]

Gerritsen, Tess - *Harvest (Guidall). Audio Version*
  BWatch - v18 - Mr '97 - p7 [1-50]
  y Kliatt - v31 - Mr '97 - p42 [51-250]

Gerschel, Liz - *Quartet of Stories*
  y Sch Lib - v45 - F '97 - p46 [51-250]
  y TES - F 28 '97 - pR7 [501+]

Gershator, Phillis - *Sweet, Sweet Fig Banana (Illus. by Fritz Millvoix)*
  c CLW - v66 - Je '96 - p51 [51-250]
  c HB Guide - v7 - Fall '96 - p257 [51-250]

Gershman, Suzy - *Born to Shop: Hong Kong. 6th Ed.*
  r BL - v93 - S 15 '96 - p206+ [1-50]
Born to Shop: New York. 6th Ed.
  r BL - v93 - S 15 '96 - p206+ [1-50]

Gershoni, Israel - *Redefining the Egyptian Nation 1930-1945*
  AHR - v102 - F '97 - p146+ [501+]
  JIH - v27 - Win '97 - p567+ [251-500]

Gershwin, M Eric - *Diseases of the Sinuses*
  SciTech - v20 - N '96 - p51 [51-250]

Gersick, Kelin E - *Generation to Generation*
  BL - v93 - Ja '97 - p793+ [51-250]
  Choice - v34 - Ap '97 - p1383 [51-250]

Gersie, Alida - *Dramatic Approaches to Brief Therapy*
  Readings - v11 - S '96 - p26 [51-250]

Gerson, Barbara - *The Therapist as a Person*
  Choice - v34 - Ap '97 - p1421 [51-250]

Gerson, Kathleen - *No Man's Land*
  Signs - v22 - Win '97 - p440+ [501+]

Gerson, Lloyd P - *Plotinus*
  RM - v50 - D '96 - p399+ [501+]

Gerson, Mark - *The Essential Neoconservative Reader*
  ABR - v18 - O '96 - p18+ [501+]
  Bloom Rev - v16 - S '96 - p23 [501+]
  Econ - v340 - S 14 '96 - p3*+ [501+]
  Pub Int - Win '97 - p95+ [501+]
In the Classroom
  Choice - v34 - My '97 - p1550+ [51-250]
  CSM - v89 - F 3 '97 - p12 [251-500]
  KR - v64 - O 15 '96 - p1509+ [251-500]
  LJ - v121 - D '96 - p112 [51-250]
The Neoconservative Vision
  TLS - Ag 30 '96 - p8 [501+]

Gerson, Mary-Joan - *The Embedded Self*
  Readings - v12 - Mr '97 - p30 [51-250]
People of Corn (Illus. by Carla Golembe)
  c RT - v50 - Mr '97 - p502 [51-250]
  c SS - v88 - Ja '97 - p29+ [501+]

Gerson, Sharon J - *Technical Writing. 2nd Ed.*
  R&R Bk N - v11 - D '96 - p60 [51-250]

Gerstein, Mordicai - *Bedtime, Everybody!*
  c HB Guide - v7 - Fall '96 - p257 [51-250]
Behind the Couch (Illus. by Mordicai Gerstein)
  c CCB-B - v50 - S '96 - p12 [51-250]
  c HB Guide - v7 - Fall '96 - p286 [1-50]

Gerstenberger, Erhard - *Leviticus: A Commentary*
  Am - v176 - Mr 8 '97 - p23 [51-250]

Gersting, Judith L - *Visual Basic Programming*
  SciTech - v20 - S '96 - p6 [51-250]

Gerstner, Patsy - *Henry Darwin Rogers 1808-1866*
  AHR - v101 - O '96 - p1277+ [501+]

Gert, Bernard - *Morality and the New Genetics*
  Hast Cen R - v26 - Jl '96 - p41 [1-50]

The Gertrude Stein Awards in Innovative American Poetry 1994-1995
  PW - v243 - D 30 '96 - p60 [251-500]

Gertz, Susan E - *Teaching Physical Science through Children's Literature*
  SB - v32 - O '96 - p200 [501+]

Gervay, Susanne - *Shadows of Olive Trees*
  y Aust Bk R - N '96 - p62+ [501+]
Victoria's a Star (Illus. by Cathy Wilcox)
  c Magpies - v11 - S '96 - p33 [51-250]

Gery, John - *Nuclear Annihilation and Contemporary American Poetry*
  Choice - v34 - S '96 - p125 [51-250]

Gerzina, Gretchen - *Black England*
  Lon R Bks - v19 - F 20 '97 - p23+ [501+]
Black London
  W&M Q - v53 - Jl '96 - p652+ [501+]

Gerzon, Mark - *A House Divided*
  Fut - v30 - S '96 - p56+ [501+]

Gerzon, Robert - *Finding Serenity in the Age of Anxiety*
  PW - v244 - Ap 7 '97 - p84 [51-250]

Gessen, Masha - *Dead Again*
  PW - v244 - Mr 31 '97 - p48 [51-250]
Half a Revolution
  WLT - v70 - Aut '96 - p983+ [501+]

Gessner, David - *A Wild, Rank Place*
  BL - v93 - Mr 15 '97 - p1208 [51-250]
  KR - v65 - F 1 '97 - p193 [251-500]
  PW - v244 - F 24 '97 - p74+ [51-250]

Gestrich, Andreas - *Absolutismus Und Offentlichkeit*
  EHR - v112 - F '97 - p206+ [501+]

Getaways
  p LJ - v122 - My 1 '97 - p43 [51-250]

Gettings, John - *Couples: A Photographic Documentary of Gay and Lesbian Relationships*
  PW - v243 - S 23 '96 - p70 [51-250]

Gettins, Peter G W - *Serpins: Structure, Function and Biology*
  SciTech - v20 - N '96 - p34 [51-250]

Getty, Sarah - *The Land of Milk and Honey*
  PW - v243 - N 25 '96 - p72+ [51-250]

Getz, David - *Floating Home (Illus. by Michael Rex)*
  c BL - v93 - My 1 '97 - p1501 [51-250]
  c CBRS - v25 - Ap '97 - p102+ [51-250]
  c CCB-B - v50 - My '97 - p309+ [501+]
  c KR - v65 - Mr 1 '97 - p380 [51-250]
Life on Mars (Illus. by Peter McCarty)
  c BL - v93 - My 15 '97 - p1574 [51-250]
  c KR - v65 - Mr 15 '97 - p461 [51-250]

Getz, Ken - *Microsoft Access 2.0 How-To CD*
  CBR - v14 - Jl '96 - p19 [51-250]

Microsoft Access 95 How To
  SciTech - v20 - D '96 - p13 [51-250]

Getz, Leslie - *Dancers and Choreographers*
  r ARBA - v28 - '97 - p502+ [51-250]

Getzen, Thomas E - *Health Economics*
  SciTech - v21 - Mr '97 - p46 [51-250]

Getz-Gentle, Pat - *Stone Vessels of the Cyclades in the Early Bronze Age*
  Choice - v34 - My '97 - p1540 [51-250]

Gever, Martha - *Queer Looks*
  FQ - v49 - Sum '96 - p56+ [501+]

Gewanter, David - *In the Belly*
  PW - v244 - Ja 27 '97 - p95 [51-250]

Gewirth, Alan - *The Community of Rights*
  Choice - v34 - N '96 - p534 [51-250]
  JEL - v34 - S '96 - p1414 [51-250]

Geyer, Georgie Anne - *Americans No More*
  BL - v93 - S 1 '96 - p40+ [51-250]
  Bloom Rev - v16 - S '96 - p24 [51-250]
  BW - v26 - D 15 '96 - p5 [501+]
  LATBR - O 27 '96 - p5+ [501+]
  LJ - v121 - S 15 '96 - p84 [51-250]
  Nat R - v48 - O 28 '96 - p71+ [501+]
  NYTBR - v101 - N 17 '96 - p24 [51-250]
  PW - v243 - Jl 22 '96 - p222+ [51-250]

Geyer-Ryan, Helga - *Fables of Desire*
  MLR - v92 - Ja '97 - p140 [251-500]

Geyssen, John W - *Imperial Panegyric in Statius*
  R&R Bk N - v12 - F '97 - p77 [51-250]

Ghafouri-Shiraz, H - *Distributed Feedback Laser Diodes*
  SciTech - v21 - Mr '97 - p87 [51-250]
Fundamentals of Laser Diode Amplifiers
  SciTech - v20 - S '96 - p51 [1-50]

Ghan, S J - *Regional Impacts of Global Climate Change*
  Env - v39 - Ja '97 - p26 [51-250]

Ghana. President (1981-: Rawlings) - *Ghana Vision 2020*
  J Gov Info - v23 - S '96 - p658 [1-50]

Ghatak, Subrata - *The Macroeconomic Environment*
  JEL - v34 - D '96 - p2031 [51-250]

Ghazi, Polly - *Getting a Life*
  NS - v126 - F 21 '97 - p44+ [501+]

Ghazi, Suhaib Hamid - *Ramadan (Illus. by Omar Rayyan)*
  c BL - v93 - O 1 '96 - p337 [51-250]
  c CBRS - v25 - S '96 - p7 [51-250]
  c CCB-B - v50 - D '96 - p134+ [51-250]
  c Ch BWatch - v6 - O '96 - p4 [1-50]
  c HB Guide - v8 - Spr '97 - p89 [51-250]
  c SLJ - v42 - O '96 - p113 [51-250]

Ghebali, Victor-Yves - *European Security in the 1990s*
  J Gov Info - v23 - S '96 - p677 [51-250]
  J Gov Info - v24 - Ja '97 - p60+ [51-250]

Gheissari, Nick - *Russia and Beyond*
  PW - v243 - S 9 '96 - p78 [51-250]

Gherardi, Evaristo - *Le Theatre Italien. Vol. 1*
  MLR - v91 - Jl '96 - p722+ [251-500]

Gherman, Beverly - *Robert Louis Stevenson: Teller of Tales*
  c BL - v93 - O 1 '96 - p328 [51-250]
  y HB Guide - v8 - Spr '97 - p157 [51-250]
  c KR - v64 - S 1 '96 - p1321 [51-250]
  c SLJ - v43 - F '97 - p115 [51-250]

Ghezzi, Bert - *Miracle of the Saints*
  PW - v243 - S 16 '96 - p67 [51-250]

Ghigna, Charles - *Riddle Rhymes (Illus. by Julia Gorton)*
  c NYTBR - v101 - Ap 7 '96 - p21 [501+]

Ghimosoulis, Kostis - *Mia Nihta Me Tin Kokkini*
  WLT - v70 - Aut '96 - p1002 [51-250]

Ghirardo, Diane - *Architecture after Modernism*
  Choice - v34 - Mr '97 - p1152 [51-250]
  LJ - v122 - Mr 15 '97 - p60 [51-250]

Ghorayshi, Parvin - *Women and Work in Developing Countries*
  JTWS - v13 - Spr '96 - p418+ [501+]
Women, Work, and Gender Relations in Developing Countries
  R&R Bk N - v12 - F '97 - p54 [51-250]

Ghosh, A - *Challenges in Ceramic Product Development, Manufacture, and Commercialization*
  SciTech - v21 - Mr '97 - p77 [51-250]

Ghosh, Amitav - *The Calcutta Chromosome*
  NS - v125 - S 6 '96 - p47 [501+]
  Spec - v277 - N 16 '96 - p42 [1-50]
  TLS - Ag 2 '96 - p23 [501+]
  WLT - v71 - Win '97 - p221+ [501+]

Ghosh, Bishnupriya - *Interventions: Feminist Dialogues on Third World Women's Literature and Film*
  Choice - v34 - Ap '97 - p1323 [51-250]

Ghosh, Dilip K - *Managerial Finance in the Corporate Economy*
  Econ J - v106 - N '96 - p1839 [251-500]

New Advances in Financial Economics
  Econ J - v107 - Ja '97 - p273 [51-250]
Ghosh, Malay K - *Polyimides: Fundamentals and Applications*
  r SciTech - v20 - D '96 - p84 [51-250]
Ghosh, Subir - *Statistics of Quality*
  r SciTech - v20 - D '96 - p85 [51-250]
Giacchetti, Claudine - *Maupassant: Espaces Du Roman*
  FR - v70 - F '97 - p470+ [501+]
Giacobino, Margherita - *Casalinghe All'Inferno*
  BL - v93 - D 1 '96 - p644 [1-50]
Giacometti, Alberto - *Alberto Giacometti 1901-1966*
  TLS - N 8 '96 - p17 [501+]
Giambelluca, Thomas W - *Climate Change*
  Choice - v34 - Ap '97 - p1377 [51-250]
Giamei, Anthony F - *Mechanical Properties and Phase Transformation of Multiphase Intermetallic Alloys*
  SciTech - v20 - N '96 - p64 [51-250]
Giamo, Benedict - *The Homeless of Ironweed*
  Choice - v34 - My '97 - p1495+ [51-250]
Gianaris, Nicholas V - *Geopolitical and Economic Changes in the Balkan Countries*
  Choice - v34 - Ja '97 - p844 [51-250]
  JEL - v35 - Mr '97 - p285 [51-250]
  R&R Bk N - v11 - D '96 - p25 [51-250]
Giannetto, Nella - *Il Sudario Delle Caligini*
  MLN - v112 - Ja '97 - p125+ [501+]
Gianturco, Carolyn - *Alessandro Stradella 1639-1682*
  Ren Q - v49 - Aut '96 - p686+ [501+]
Gianturco, Michael - *How to Buy Technology Stocks*
  PW - v243 - S 23 '96 - p73 [1-50]
Giard, Luce - *Les Jesuites A La Renaissance*
  Ren Q - v50 - Spr '97 - p251+ [501+]
Giardino, Vittorio - *A Jew in Communist Prague. Vol. 1*
  BW - v27 - Ap 13 '97 - p12 [51-250]
  KR - v65 - My 1 '97 - p677 [51-250]
  LJ - v122 - My 1 '97 - p140 [51-250]
Giarratano, Susan - *Entering Adulthood*
  Adoles - v31 - Win '96 - p993 [51-250]
Gibb, James G - *The Archaeology of Wealth*
  Choice - v34 - Ja '97 - p862 [51-250]
  R&R Bk N - v11 - N '96 - p35 [51-250]
Gibbal, Jean-Marie - *Genii of the River Niger*
  JTWS - v13 - Spr '96 - p308+ [501+]
Gibbon, Edward - *History of the Decline and Fall of the Roman Empire. Vols. 1-3*
  BW - v26 - D 8 '96 - p15 [51-250]
  BW - v26 - D 15 '96 - p12 [51-250]
  PS - v70 - Win '96 - p174+ [501+]
Gibbon, Peter - *Structural Adjustment and Socio-Economic Change in Sub-Saharan Africa*
  JEL - v35 - Mr '97 - p277 [51-250]
Gibboney, Douglas Lee - *Stonewall Jackson at Gettysburg*
  BWatch - v17 - D '96 - p6 [51-250]
Gibboney, Richard A - *The Stone Trumpet*
  ES - v27 - Sum '96 - p183+ [501+]
Gibbons, Alan - *Ganging Up*
  c Bks Keeps - v100 - S '96 - p10+ [51-250]
  c TES - Jl 5 '96 - pR8 [51-250]
  Street of Tall People
  c Bks Keeps - v100 - S '96 - p10+ [51-250]
Gibbons, B J - *Gender in Mystical and Occult Thought*
  HRNB - v25 - Win '97 - p69+ [251-500]
Gibbons, Brian - *Shakespeare and Multiplicity*
  RES - v47 - Ag '96 - p411+ [501+]
Gibbons, Dave - *World's Finest*
  VOYA - v19 - F '97 - p323 [51-250]
Gibbons, Faye - *Mountain Wedding (Illus. by Ted Rand)*
  c CCB-B - v50 - S '96 - p12 [51-250]
  c HB Guide - v7 - Fall '96 - p257 [51-250]
  c NYTBR - v101 - S 8 '96 - p28 [51-250]
  Night in the Barn (Illus. by Erick Ingraham)
  c RT - v50 - S '96 - p58 [51-250]
Gibbons, Gail - *Cats (Illus. by Gail Gibbons)*
  c HB Guide - v8 - Spr '97 - p128 [1-50]
  c SB - v32 - O '96 - p211 [51-250]
  c SB - v33 - Mr '97 - p57 [51-250]
  c SLJ - v42 - D '96 - p113 [51-250]
  Click! A Book about Cameras and Taking Pictures
  c BL - v93 - Ap 1 '97 - p1334 [51-250]
  Deserts (Illus. by Gail Gibbons)
  c CBRS - v25 - N '96 - p26 [51-250]
  c HB Guide - v8 - Spr '97 - p117 [1-50]
  c SLJ - v43 - Ja '97 - p100 [51-250]
  Dogs (Illus. by Gail Gibbons)
  c HB Guide - v7 - Fall '96 - p346 [51-250]
  c SLJ - v42 - S '96 - p196 [51-250]
  The Honey Makers (Illus. by Gail Gibbons)
  c BL - v93 - Mr 15 '97 - p1245+ [51-250]
  c CCB-B - v50 - Ap '97 - p282 [51-250]
  c KR - v65 - Ja 15 '97 - p141 [51-250]

The Moon Book (Illus. by Gail Gibbons)
  c BL - v93 - My 1 '97 - p1499 [51-250]
  c Par Ch - v21 - Mr '97 - p4 [1-50]
  Planet Earth/Inside Out (Illus. by Gail Gibbons)
  c Inst - v105 - My '96 - p39 [1-50]
  c RT - v50 - S '96 - p56 [51-250]
Gibbons, Jean Dickinson - *Nonparametric Methods for Quantitative Analysis. 3rd Ed.*
  SciTech - v21 - Mr '97 - p71 [51-250]
Gibbons, Kaye - *Ellen Foster (Gibbons). Audio Version*
  y Kliatt - v31 - Ja '97 - p40 [51-250]
  LJ - v121 - N 1 '96 - p120+ [51-250]
  Sights Unseen
  NYTBR - v101 - N 24 '96 - p32 [51-250]
  PW - v243 - O 21 '96 - p79 [1-50]
  A Virtuous Woman
  Obs - S 8 '96 - p18* [51-250]
Gibbons, Luke - *Transformations in Irish Culture*
  ILS - v16 - Spr '97 - p32 [501+]
Gibbons, Mary Weitzel - *Giambologna, Narrator of the Catholic Reformation*
  CHR - v82 - O '96 - p724+ [501+]
  Giambologna: Narrator of the Catholic Reformation
  Ren Q - v49 - Win '96 - p861+ [501+]
Gibbons, Reginald - *Sweetbitter*
  Bloom Rev - v16 - Jl '96 - p22 [501+]
Gibbons, Sarah L - *Kant's Theory of Imagination*
  IPQ - v36 - S '96 - p360+ [501+]
  RM - v49 - Je '96 - p923+ [501+]
Gibbons, William Conrad - *The U.S. Government and the Vietnam War. Pt. 4*
  NWCR - v49 - Aut '96 - p163+ [51-250]
Gibbons Stamp Monthly
  p Am Phil - v110 - S '96 - p827 [51-250]
Gibbs, Adrian J - *Molecular Basis of Virus Evolution*
  Sci - v273 - Ag 30 '96 - p1179+ [501+]
Gibbs, Jack P - *A Theory about Control*
  SF - v75 - S '96 - p346+ [501+]
  SF - v75 - D '96 - p743+ [501+]
Gibbs, Jenny - *A Handbook for Interior Designers*
  LJ - v121 - S 15 '96 - p68 [51-250]
Gibbs, Jewelle Taylor - *Race and Justice*
  BW - v27 - Ja 12 '97 - p4 [501+]
  BWatch - v17 - D '96 - p40+ [51-250]
  BWatch - v18 - Mr '97 - p4 [51-250]
  Choice - v34 - Mr '97 - p1244 [51-250]
  LJ - v121 - O 1 '96 - p104 [51-250]
  PW - v243 - O 14 '96 - p72 [51-250]
Gibbs, Robert - *Correlations in Rosenzweig and Levinas*
  Rel St Rev - v23 - Ja '97 - p16+ [501+]
Gibbs, Scott R - *Mosby's Medical Surfari*
  r BL - v93 - F 1 '97 - p956+ [1-50]
  r SciTech - v21 - Mr '97 - p44 [51-250]
Gibbs, Tyson - *A Guide to Ethnic Health Collections in the United States*
  r ARBA - v28 - '97 - p602+ [51-250]
  r Choice - v34 - Ja '97 - p769 [251-500]
  r R&R Bk N - v11 - N '96 - p72 [51-250]
Giberga, Jane Sughrue - *Friends to Die For*
  y CCB-B - v50 - Mr '97 - p247 [51-250]
Gibilisco, Stan - *McGraw-Hill Encyclopedia of Personal Computing*
  r ARBA - v28 - '97 - p623 [51-250]
  r BL - v93 - Ja '97 - p770 [1-50]
Giblin, James Cross - *The Dwarf, the Giant, and the Unicorn (Illus. by Claire Ewart)*
  c BL - v93 - D 1 '96 - p666+ [51-250]
  c HB Guide - v8 - Spr '97 - p101 [51-250]
  c KR - v64 - O 1 '96 - p1465 [51-250]
  c PW - v243 - N 11 '96 - p75 [51-250]
  c SLJ - v42 - O '96 - p113 [51-250]
  When Plague Strikes (Illus. by David Frampton)
  c BW - v26 - O 6 '96 - p11 [501+]
  y EJ - v85 - N '96 - p133 [251-500]
  y Emerg Lib - v24 - S '96 - p23 [1-50]
  y LA - v73 - O '96 - p441+ [51-250]
Giblin, Nan J - *Finding Help*
  r ARBA - v28 - '97 - p29 [51-250]
Gibney, Frank - *Senso: The Japanese Remember the Pacific War*
  Pac A - v69 - Fall '96 - p423+ [501+]
Gibson, A J S - *Prices, Food, and Wages in Scotland 1550-1780*
  EHR - v112 - Ap '97 - p477+ [501+]
  JIH - v27 - Win '97 - p509+ [501+]
Gibson, Bob - *Stranger to the Game*
  Aethlon - v13 - Fall '95 - p178+ [251-500]
Gibson, Charles Dana - *Assault and Logistics*
  JSH - v62 - N '96 - p817+ [251-500]
Gibson, Donald - *Battling Wall Street*
  J Am St - v30 - Ap '96 - p154 [251-500]

Gibson, Edward L - *Class and Conservative Parties*
  R&R Bk N - v11 - N '96 - p49 [51-250]
Gibson, Greg - *Remodel! An Architect's Advice on Home Remodeling*
  LJ - v122 - F 1 '97 - p52 [1-50]
Gibson, James - *Thomas Hardy: A Literary Life*
  Choice - v34 - S '96 - p125+ [51-250]
  CR - v269 - S '96 - p158+ [501+]
  ELT - v40 - 2 '97 - p194+ [501+]
Gibson, James William - *Warrior Dreams*
  J Am Cult - v19 - Sum '96 - p135+ [251-500]
Gibson, John - *Transformation from Below*
  JEL - v34 - D '96 - p2124 [51-250]
  R&R Bk N - v11 - N '96 - p50 [51-250]
Gibson, John S - *Dictionary of International Human Rights Law*
  r ARBA - v28 - '97 - p231+ [51-250]
  r Choice - v34 - Ap '97 - p1414 [51-250]
Gibson, Joyce M - *Scotland County Emerging 1750-1900*
  EGH - v50 - N '96 - p178+ [51-250]
Gibson, Margaret - *Earth Elegy*
  BL - v93 - Mr 1 '97 - p1106 [51-250]
  LJ - v122 - Mr 15 '97 - p66 [51-250]
Gibson, Mary Ellis - *Epic Reinvented*
  AL - v68 - D '96 - p879 [51-250]
  Choice - v34 - S '96 - p126 [51-250]
  Nine-C Lit - v51 - S '96 - p272 [1-50]
Gibson, Nancy - *Wolves*
  y BL - v93 - N 15 '96 - p557 [251-500]
Gibson, Ray - *Printing*
  c Sch Lib - v44 - N '96 - p162 [51-250]
Gibson, Richard G - *History of Programming Languages*
  Choice - v34 - S '96 - p163+ [51-250]
Gibson, Walter S - *Pieter Bruegel the Elder: Two Studies*
  Ren Q - v49 - Aut '96 - p678+ [51-250]
Gibson, William, 1948- - *Idoru*
  Analog - v117 - Mr '97 - p149+ [51-250]
  BL - v92 - Ag '96 - p1853+ [251-500]
  Books - v11 - Ap '97 - p23 [51-250]
  BW - v26 - O 27 '96 - p11 [501+]
  CSM - v88 - O 31 '96 - pB3 [251-500]
  FEER - v160 - Ja 9 '97 - p59 [501+]
  Mac - v109 - N 25 '96 - p129 [501+]
  MFSF - v92 - F '97 - p40+ [251-500]
  New Sci - v152 - N 23 '96 - p48 [51-250]
  NS - v125 - O 11 '96 - p44+ [501+]
  NS - v125 - D 20 '96 - p117 [51-250]
  NYTBR - v101 - S 8 '96 - p6 [501+]
  Obs - O 27 '96 - p15* [501+]
  PW - v243 - N 4 '96 - p42 [1-50]
  TLS - S 27 '96 - p25 [501+]
  VV - v41 - S 24 '96 - p41 [501+]
  Idoru (Sanders). Audio Version
  y Kliatt - v31 - Ja '97 - p41+ [51-250]
  PW - v243 - D 2 '96 - p30 [51-250]
Gibson, William, 1959- - *Church, State and Society 1760-1850*
  CH - v66 - Mr '97 - p145+ [501+]
Gibson-Graham, J K - *The End of Capitalism (as We Knew It)*
  Choice - v34 - Mr '97 - p1208 [51-250]
Gidal, Tim - *Jerusalem in 3000 Years*
  LJ - v121 - O 1 '96 - p99 [51-250]
  NYTBR - v101 - D 8 '96 - p13+ [501+]
  PW - v243 - Jl 22 '96 - p223 [51-250]
Giddens, Anthony - *Beyond Left and Right*
  Ethics - v107 - Ja '97 - p401+ [51-250]
  Politics, Sociology and Social Theory
  APSR - v90 - S '96 - p619+ [501+]
  TLS - D 13 '96 - p29 [501+]
Giddins, Gary - *Faces in the Crowd*
  PW - v243 - O 21 '96 - p78 [1-50]
Gide, Andre - *Corydon*
  MLR - v91 - Jl '96 - p582+ [501+]
Giele, Janet Zollinger - *Two Paths to Women's Equality*
  AJS - v102 - N '96 - p889+ [501+]
Gielgud, John - *An Actor and His Time*
  Obs - S 15 '96 - p18* [51-250]
Giencke, Patricia - *Portable C++*
  SciTech - v20 - N '96 - p9 [51-250]
Gieras, Jacek F - *Permanent Magnet Motor Technology*
  r SciTech - v21 - Mr '97 - p86 [51-250]
Giersch, Herbert - *Urban Agglomeration and Economic Growth*
  JEL - v34 - D '96 - p2137 [51-250]
Gies, David Thatcher - *The Theatre in Nineteenth-Century Spain*
  Hisp - v79 - D '96 - p790+ [501+]
  MLR - v92 - Ja '97 - p230+ [501+]
Gies, Miep - *Anne Frank Remembered*
  y BL - v93 - Ja '97 - p832 [1-50]

Giesecke, Joan - *The Dynamic Library Organizations in a Changing Environment*
   LR - v45 - 6 '96 - p59+ [501+]
Giesen, Carol A B - *Coal Miners' Wives*
   J Am Cult - v19 - Spr '96 - p99+ [501+]
Giesen, Heinz - *Herrschaft Gottes--Heute Oder Morgen?*
   Rel St Rev - v23 - Ja '97 - p70 [51-250]
Giff, Patricia Reilly - *Dance with Rosie (Illus. by Julie Durrell)*
   c BL - v93 - S 1 '96 - p125+ [51-250]
   c CCB-B - v50 - D '96 - p135 [51-250]
   c HB Guide - v8 - Spr '97 - p66 [51-250]
   c PW - v243 - O 7 '96 - p76 [51-250]
   c SLJ - v43 - Ja '97 - p77 [51-250]
   Good Luck, Ronald Morgan! (Illus. by Susanna Natti)
   c CCB-B - v50 - O '96 - p59 [51-250]
   c HB Guide - v8 - Spr '97 - p55 [51-250]
   c SLJ - v42 - S '96 - p178 [51-250]
   Lily's Crossing
   c BL - v93 - F 1 '97 - p941 [51-250]
   c CCB-B - v50 - Ap '97 - p282+ [251-500]
   c HB - v73 - Mr '97 - p198 [51-250]
   c KR - v64 - N 1 '96 - p1600 [51-250]
   c PW - v244 - Ja 20 '97 - p403 [51-250]
   c SLJ - v43 - F '97 - p103 [51-250]
   Not-So-Perfect Rosie
   c BL - v93 - My 1 '97 - p1493 [51-250]
   Pet Parade (Illus. by Blanche Sims)
   c BL - v93 - S 15 '96 - p238 [51-250]
   c SLJ - v42 - Ag '96 - p122 [51-250]
   Ronald Morgan Goes to Camp (Illus. by Susanna Natti)
   c RT - v50 - N '96 - p252 [51-250]
   Rosie's Nutcracker Dreams (Illus. by Julie Durrell)
   c BL - v93 - S 1 '96 - p125+ [51-250]
   c CCB-B - v50 - D '96 - p135 [51-250]
   c HB Guide - v8 - Spr '97 - p66 [51-250]
   c SLJ - v43 - Ja '97 - p77 [51-250]
   Starring Rosie (Illus. by Julie Durrell)
   c BL - v93 - D 15 '96 - p726 [51-250]
   c SLJ - v43 - Mr '97 - p152 [51-250]
Giffin, Michael - *Arthur's Dream*
   Aust Bk R - Ag '96 - p14+ [501+]
Gifford, Allen - *Living Well with HIV and AIDS*
   BL - v93 - S 1 '96 - p50 [51-250]
Gifford, Barry - *Baby Cat-Face*
   PW - v244 - Ap 14 '97 - p72 [1-50]
   The Phantom Father
   KR - v65 - Mr 15 '97 - p435+ [251-500]
   LJ - v122 - My 1 '97 - p103+ [51-250]
   PW - v244 - Mr 3 '97 - p53+ [51-250]
Gifford, Clive - *Mindmaster*
   c Sch Lib - v45 - F '97 - p24 [1-50]
   The Time Warp Virus
   c New Sci - v152 - D 14 '96 - p46 [1-50]
Gifford, Paul - *Paul Valery: Charmes*
   MLR - v91 - Jl '96 - p735+ [51-250]
Gifford, Thomas - *Saints Rest*
   BL - v93 - S 1 '96 - p67 [51-250]
Giganti, Paul - *Each Orange Had Eight Slices (Illus. by Donald Crews)*
   c BL - v93 - Ap 1 '97 - p1341 [1-50]
Giger, H R - *Film Design*
   BWatch - v18 - F '97 - p4 [1-50]
   Species
   SF Chr - v18 - O '96 - p81 [1-50]
Giggs, Ryan - *Ryan Giggs: My Story*
   Books - v9 - S '95 - p24 [1-50]
Giglio, Virginia - *Southern Cheyenne Women's Songs*
   CAY - v17 - Fall '96 - p11 [51-250]
Gil, Eliana - *Play in Family Therapy*
   Fam in Soc - v77 - S '96 - p453 [501+]
   Systemic Treatment of Families Who Abuse
   Readings - v11 - S '96 - p30 [51-250]
   Treating Abused Adolescents
   Readings - v11 - D '96 - p29 [51-250]
   y SB - v32 - N '96 - p237 [51-250]
Gil, Fernando - *Primeras Doctrinas Del Nuevo Mundo*
   HAHR - v76 - Ag '96 - p557+ [501+]
Gilbar, Steven - *Reading in Bed*
   AB - v98 - N 25 '96 - p1826+ [501+]
Gilberg, Gail Hosking - *Snake's Daughter*
   KR - v65 - Mr 15 '97 - p436 [251-500]
   PW - v244 - Ap 28 '97 - p64 [51-250]
Gilbert, Adrian - *The French Revolution*
   c TES - O 4 '96 - p17* [501+]
   The Russian Revolution
   c TES - O 4 '96 - p17* [501+]
Gilbert, Adrian G - *Magi: Quest for a Secret Tradition*
   NS - v125 - D 20 '96 - p120+ [501+]
Gilbert, Avery N - *Compendium of Olfactory Research*
   SciTech - v21 - Mr '97 - p41 [51-250]

Gilbert, Barbara Snow - *Stone Water*
   c BL - v93 - D 15 '96 - p721 [51-250]
   c CBRS - v25 - N '96 - p34 [51-250]
   y CCB-B - v50 - Ja '97 - p170 [51-250]
   y HB Guide - v8 - Spr '97 - p79 [51-250]
   y KR - v64 - O 15 '96 - p1532 [51-250]
   c PW - v243 - N 18 '96 - p76 [51-250]
   y SLJ - v42 - D '96 - p29 [1-50]
   y SLJ - v42 - D '96 - p136 [51-250]
Gilbert, Daniel R - *Ethics through Corporate Strategy*
   Choice - v34 - Ap '97 - p1383+ [51-250]
Gilbert, Elliot M - *Telecommunications Wiring for Commercial Buildings*
   SciTech - v20 - N '96 - p73 [51-250]
Gilbert, Jack - *The Great Fires*
   APR - v26 - Ja '97 - p37+ [501+]
Gilbert, James - *Redeeming Culture*
   Wil Q - v21 - Spr '97 - p108+ [251-500]
Gilbert, Kevin - *Me and Mary Kangaroo*
   c Magpies - v11 - Jl '96 - p45 [1-50]
Gilbert, Laurel - *SurferGrrrls: Look Ethel! An Internet Guide for Us!*
   Ms - v7 - Ja '97 - p80 [51-250]
   PW - v243 - Jl 22 '96 - p234 [51-250]
Gilbert, Lawrence I - *Metamorphosis: Postembryonic Reprogramming of Gene Expression in Amphibian and Insect Cells*
   SciTech - v20 - S '96 - p20 [51-250]
Gilbert, Marc Jason - *The Tet Offensive*
   Choice - v34 - Ap '97 - p1408 [51-250]
   R&R Bk N - v12 - F '97 - p20 [51-250]
   The Vietnam War
   J Am Cult - v19 - Sum '96 - p134 [251-500]
Gilbert, Mark - *The Italian Revolution*
   APSR - v90 - S '96 - p670+ [501+]
Gilbert, Martin, 1936- - *The Boys: The Untold Story of 732 Young Concentration Camp Survivors*
   KR - v65 - Ja 15 '97 - p116 [251-500]
   LJ - v122 - Mr 15 '97 - p73 [51-250]
   NYTBR - v102 - Ap 20 '97 - p16 [501+]
   PW - v244 - F 3 '97 - p90 [51-250]
   The Boys: Triumph over Adversity
   NS - v125 - D 20 '96 - p122 [501+]
   Spec - v277 - O 26 '96 - p52 [501+]
   TLS - N 22 '96 - p26+ [501+]
   TLS - N 29 '96 - p14 [51-250]
   The Churchill War Papers. Vol. 2
   APH - v43 - Fall '96 - p66+ [501+]
   The First World War
   Books - v9 - S '95 - p24 [1-50]
   In Search of Churchill
   Trib Bks - Mr 9 '97 - p8 [1-50]
   Jerusalem in the Twentieth Century
   CR - v269 - O '96 - p217+ [501+]
   KR - v64 - Ag 15 '96 - p1208 [251-500]
   LJ - v121 - O 1 '96 - p99 [51-250]
   Lon R Bks - v18 - O 31 '96 - p16+ [501+]
   MEQ - v4 - Mr '97 - p75+ [501+]
   NYTBR - v101 - D 8 '96 - p13+ [501+]
   TLS - Mr 7 '97 - p8+ [501+]
   WSJ-MW - v78 - O 14 '96 - pA12 [501+]
   Jerusalem: Rebirth of a City
   MEQ - v4 - Mr '97 - p75+ [501+]
Gilbert, Michael - *Into Battle*
   KR - v64 - N 15 '96 - p1635 [51-250]
   LJ - v122 - Ja '97 - p153 [1-50]
   NYTBR - v102 - Mr 23 '97 - p18 [51-250]
   PW - v243 - N 18 '96 - p64 [51-250]
Gilbert, Neil - *Welfare Justice*
   AAPSS-A - v550 - Mr '97 - p181+ [251-500]
   BusLR - v21 - 3 '96 - p242+ [51-250]
Gilbert, Paul - *La Simplicite Du Principe*
   RM - v50 - D '96 - p400+ [501+]
Gilbert, Richard - *Making Cities Work*
   New Sci - v152 - O 26 '96 - p47 [51-250]
Gilbert, Richard J - *International Comparisons of Electricity Regulation*
   JEL - v34 - D '96 - p2089 [51-250]
Gilbert, Sandra M - *Ghost Volcano*
   NYTBR - v102 - Mr 30 '97 - p24 [1-50]
   Poet - v169 - D '96 - p156+ [501+]
   No Man's Land. Vol. 3
   RES - v47 - N '96 - p632+ [501+]
   Signs - v22 - Win '97 - p458+ [501+]
   Wrongful Death
   Comw - v123 - D 6 '96 - p20 [51-250]
   NYTBR - v102 - Mr 30 '97 - p24 [51-250]
   Obs - S 15 '96 - p15* [501+]
   PW - v244 - F 17 '97 - p217 [1-50]
   Trib Bks - Mr 30 '97 - p2 [1-50]

Gilbert, Sid - *Gender Tracking in University Programs*
   J Gov Info - v23 - S '96 - p613+ [51-250]
Gilbert, Steven E - *The Music of Gershwin*
   TLS - Jl 19 '96 - p18+ [501+]
Gilbert, Suzie - *Hawk Hill (Illus. by Sylvia Long)*
   c BL - v93 - N 1 '96 - p497+ [51-250]
   c CBRS - v25 - Win '97 - p67 [51-250]
   c CCB-B - v50 - D '96 - p135 [51-250]
   c HB Guide - v8 - Spr '97 - p28 [51-250]
   c PW - v243 - O 7 '96 - p74 [51-250]
   c SLJ - v42 - N '96 - p80 [51-250]
   c Smith - v27 - N '96 - p171 [1-50]
Gilbert, Sylvie - *Arousing Sensation*
   Quill & Q - v62 - O '96 - p38 [251-500]
Gilbert, Thomas - *Dead Ball*
   y BL - v93 - S 1 '96 - p71+ [501+]
   y HB Guide - v8 - Spr '97 - p144 [51-250]
   y SLJ - v42 - S '96 - p232 [51-250]
   The Good Old Days
   y HB Guide - v8 - Spr '97 - p144 [51-250]
   y SLJ - v43 - F '97 - p115+ [51-250]
   The Soaring Twenties
   y HB Guide - v8 - Spr '97 - p144 [51-250]
   y SLJ - v43 - Ja '97 - p124 [51-250]
Gilbert, W Stephen - *The Life and Work of Dennis Potter*
   TES - Ag 2 '96 - pR6 [1-50]
Gilbert-Barnes, Enid - *Potter's Pathology of the Fetus and Infant. Vols. 1-2*
   SciTech - v20 - N '96 - p52 [51-250]
Gilbert-Rolfe, Jeremy - *Beyond Piety*
   Art J - v55 - Fall '96 - p97+ [501+]
Gilbreath, Robert D - *Escape from Management Hell*
   Kiplinger - v51 - F '97 - p110+ [51-250]
Gilchrist, Ellen - *Age of Miracles (Peiffer). Audio Version*
   y Kliatt - v30 - S '96 - p42 [51-250]
   The Courts of Love
   BW - v27 - F 16 '97 - p4 [251-500]
   Ent W - Ja 10 '97 - p52+ [51-250]
   KR - v64 - S 1 '96 - p1255+ [251-500]
   LJ - v121 - S 15 '96 - p99 [51-250]
   NY - v72 - N 25 '96 - p117 [51-250]
   NYTBR - v101 - N 17 '96 - p25 [51-250]
Gilchrist, J Brian - *Genealogy and Local History to 1900*
   r ARBA - v28 - '97 - p163+ [51-250]
Gilchrist, Roberta - *Contemplation and Action*
   CHR - v83 - Ja '97 - p165 [51-250]
Gildea, Robert - *Barricades and Borders. 2nd Ed.*
   CR - v269 - O '96 - p223 [51-250]
   France since 1945
   EHR - v112 - F '97 - p149+ [501+]
Gildea, William - *When the Colts Belonged to Baltimore*
   Aethlon - v13 - Spr '96 - p211+ [501+]
Gilder, George - *Life after Television*
   QJS - v83 - My '97 - p230+ [501+]
Giles, Christopher - *Living with the State*
   JEL - v34 - D '96 - p2139 [51-250]
Giles, Fiona - *Dick for a Day*
   BL - v93 - Ja '97 - p806 [51-250]
   Ent W - Ap 18 '97 - p61 [51-250]
   PW - v243 - D 16 '96 - p51 [51-250]
Giles, Gail - *Breath of the Dragon (Illus. by June Otani)*
   c BL - v93 - Ap 1 '97 - p1334 [51-250]
   c CCB-B - v50 - Ap '97 - p283 [51-250]
   c KR - v65 - Ap 1 '97 - p555 [51-250]
Giles, James R - *The Naturalistic Inner-City Novel in America*
   AL - v68 - S '96 - p648+ [251-500]
   J Am St - v30 - D '96 - p474+ [251-500]
Giles, Judy - *Women, Identity and Private Life in Britain 1900-50*
   Albion - v28 - Sum '96 - p354+ [501+]
Giles, Molly - *Creek Walk and Other Stories*
   BL - v93 - Ja '97 - p818 [51-250]
   KR - v64 - D 1 '96 - p1689+ [251-500]
   Ms - v7 - Mr '97 - p83 [1-50]
   NYTBR - v102 - Mr 2 '97 - p10 [501+]
   PW - v243 - D 30 '96 - p54 [51-250]
Giles, Vic - *Creative Newspaper Design. 2nd Ed.*
   R&R Bk N - v11 - D '96 - p73 [51-250]
Gilgamesh - *The Epic of Gilgamesh (Pasco). Audio Version*
   Obs - Ja 12 '97 - p18* [51-250]
Gilham, Bill - *Child Safety*
   TES - Ag 30 '96 - p32 [501+]
Gilheany, Sheila - *A Little Book of Stars*
   S&T - v92 - O '96 - p57 [1-50]
Gilje, Paul A - *Rioting in America*
   Choice - v34 - O '96 - p347 [51-250]
   TLS - Ja 31 '97 - p29 [251-500]

Gill, A A - *Sap Rising*
NS - v125 - S 6 '96 - p46 [251-500]
TLS - O 4 '96 - p27 [251-500]
Woman's J - O '96 - p12 [1-50]

Gill, Bartholomew - *The Death of an Irish Sea Wolf*
KR - v64 - S 1 '96 - p1275+ [51-250]
NYTBR - v101 - D 8 '96 - p50 [51-250]
PW - v243 - S 2 '96 - p116 [51-250]

Gill, Bates - *China's Arms Acquisitions from Abroad*
For Aff - v76 - Mr '97 - p178+ [51-250]

Gill, Brendan - *Late Bloomers*
AS - v66 - Win '97 - p135+ [501+]
LATBR - N 10 '96 - p14 [51-250]
New Sci - v152 - O 19 '96 - p46 [1-50]

Gill, Carolyn Bailey - *Maurice Blanchot: The Demand of Writing*
TLS - D 13 '96 - p32 [251-500]

Gill, Chris - *Where to Ski*
r   LJ - v121 - N 15 '96 - p79 [51-250]

Gill, Christopher - *Personality in Greek Epic, Tragedy, and Philosophy*
Choice - v34 - O '96 - p274 [51-250]

Gill, Graeme - *The Collapse of a Single-Party System*
J Pol - v58 - Ag '96 - p926+ [501+]
Power in the Party
Choice - v34 - Ap '97 - p1409 [51-250]

Gill, James - *Lords of Misrule*
BL - v93 - F 15 '97 - p979 [51-250]
KR - v64 - D 15 '96 - p1781 [251-500]
LJ - v122 - F 1 '97 - p95+ [51-250]

Gill, John - *Queer Noises*
Notes - v53 - S '96 - p55+ [501+]

Gill, LaVerne McCain - *African American Women in Congress*
y   BL - v93 - F 15 '97 - p979 [51-250]
LJ - v121 - D '96 - p122 [51-250]
LJ - v121 - N 1 '96 - p84 [1-50]

Gill, Leslie - *Precarious Dependencies*
HAHR - v76 - Ag '96 - p593+ [251-500]

Gill, Michael - *Fired Up!*
BL - v93 - S 15 '96 - p191 [51-250]

Gill, Pat - *Interpreting Ladies*
RES - v48 - F '97 - p111 [501+]

Gill, Robin - *Readings in Modern Theology*
Comw - v123 - S 27 '96 - p27 [251-500]

Gill, Tepper L - *New Frontiers in Physics. Vols. 1-2*
SciTech - v21 - Mr '97 - p22 [51-250]
New Frontiers in Relativities
SciTech - v21 - Mr '97 - p21 [51-250]

Gillard, Marni - *Storyteller, Story-Teacher*
JOYS - v10 - Win '97 - p219 [51-250]

Gillen, Gerard - *Music and Irish Cultural History*
LR - v45 - 7 '96 - p77+ [501+]

Gillerman, Dorothy - *Enguerran De Marigny and the Church of Notre-Dame at Ecouis*
Specu - v71 - O '96 - p949+ [501+]

Gillespie, David C - *The Twentieth Century Russian Novel*
R&R Bk N - v12 - F '97 - p78 [51-250]

Gillespie, Don C - *The Search for Thomas F. Ward, Teacher of Frederick Delius*
Notes - v53 - Mr '97 - p801+ [501+]

Gillespie, John, 1921- - *Notable Twentieth-Century Pianists. Vols. 1-2*
r   Am MT - v46 - O '96 - p49+ [501+]
r   RQ - v35 - Sum '96 - p562+ [251-500]

Gillespie, John T, 1928- - *Best Books for Senior High Readers*
yr RQ - v36 - Win '96 - p214 [51-250]
The Newbery Companion
r   BL - v93 - Mr 1 '97 - p1177 [51-250]

Gillespie, Marie - *Television, Ethnicity, and Cultural Change*
AJS - v102 - Jl '96 - p308+ [501+]

Gillespie, Michael Allen - *Nihilism before Nietzsche*
JMH - v68 - D '96 - p976+ [501+]
JR - v77 - Ap '97 - p328+ [501+]

Gillespie, Michael Patrick - *Oscar Wilde and the Poetics of Ambiguity*
Choice - v34 - Mr '97 - p1161 [51-250]
Nine-C Lit - v51 - Mr '97 - p557 [1-50]
The Picture of Dorian Gray
ELT - v39 - 3 '96 - p373+ [501+]

Gillespie, Raymond - *Account Roll of the Holy Trinity Priory, Dublin 1337-1346*
ILS - v16 - Spr '97 - p36 [51-250]
Cavan
ILS - v15 - Fall '96 - p31 [1-50]

Gillespie, Richard - *Democratic Spain*
JEL - v34 - D '96 - p2041 [51-250]

Gillett, Charlie - *The Sound of the City. 2nd Ed., Newly Illustrated and Expanded*
CAY - v17 - Fall '96 - p4 [51-250]

Gillett, Mary C - *The Army Medical Department 1865-1917*
WHQ - v27 - Win '96 - p544 [251-500]

Gillett, Stephen L - *World-Building: A Writer's Guide to Constructing Star Systems and Life Supporting Planets*
Astron - v24 - D '96 - p104 [51-250]
MFSF - v91 - S '96 - p44+ [251-500]

Gillette, Douglas - *The Shaman's Secret*
LJ - v122 - Ap 1 '97 - p98 [51-250]
PW - v244 - Ap 28 '97 - p68 [51-250]

Gillette, Howard - *Southern City, National Ambition*
Pub Hist - v18 - Sum '96 - p91+ [501+]

Gillette, J Lynett - *Dinosaur Ghosts (Illus. by Douglas Henderson)*
c   BL - v93 - Ap 1 '97 - p1328 [51-250]
c   KR - v65 - Ja 15 '97 - p142 [51-250]

Gillette, Steve - *Songwriting and the Creative Process*
r   CAY - v16 - Fall '95 - p4 [51-250]

Gilley, Sheridan - *A History of Religion in Britain*
EHR - v112 - F '97 - p152+ [501+]

Gillham, Fred E M - *Cotton Production Prospects for the Next Decade*
JEL - v34 - S '96 - p1494 [51-250]

Gilliam, Bryan - *Music Performance during the Weimar Republic*
CEH - v29 - 1 '96 - p93+ [501+]

Gilliam, Richard - *Phantoms of the Night*
y   Kliatt - v30 - S '96 - p18 [51-250]

Gillies, David - *Between Principle and Practice*
Choice - v34 - Ja '97 - p870 [51-250]

Gillies, Donald - *Artificial Intelligence and Scientific Method*
New Sci - v152 - N 9 '96 - p41 [501+]
SciTech - v21 - Mr '97 - p3 [51-250]

Gillies, John - *Shakespeare and the Geography of Difference*
MP - v94 - F '97 - p382+ [501+]
RES - v47 - N '96 - p584+ [501+]
Shakes Q - v47 - Sum '96 - p212+ [501+]

Gillies, Mary Ann - *Henri Bergson and British Modernism*
Choice - v34 - Mr '97 - p1161+ [51-250]
R&R Bk N - v12 - F '97 - p84 [51-250]

Gillieson, David - *Caves: Processes, Development and Management*
Choice - v34 - My '97 - p1528 [51-250]
New Sci - v153 - F 1 '97 - p40 [51-250]
Sci - v275 - Ja 31 '97 - p625 [1-50]

Gilligan, James - *Violence: Our Deadly Epidemic and Its Causes*
Readings - v11 - S '96 - p18+ [501+]
Violence: Reflections on a National Epidemic
PW - v244 - My 5 '97 - p206 [1-50]

Gilliland, Cazekiel - *Becoming Gods*
BWatch - v17 - N '96 - p4+ [51-250]

Gillingham, John - *Richard Coeur De Lion*
Specu - v71 - Jl '96 - p716+ [501+]

Gillis, Jennifer Storey - *Puddle Jumpers (Illus. by Patti Delmonte)*
c   PW - v243 - S 9 '96 - p84 [51-250]
Tooth Truth (Illus. by Patti Delmonte)
c   PW - v243 - S 9 '96 - p84 [51-250]

Gillis, John R - *Commemorations: The Politics of National Identity*
J Am Cult - v18 - Win '95 - p110+ [251-500]
The European Experience of Declining Fertility 1850-1970
JMH - v68 - S '96 - p664+ [501+]
A World of Their Own Making
Choice - v34 - D '96 - p695 [51-250]

Gillman, Neil - *The Death of Death*
BL - v93 - My 15 '97 - p1545 [51-250]

Gilloch, Graeme - *Myth and Metropolis*
Choice - v34 - S '96 - p186 [51-250]

Gillon, Margaret - *Lesbians in Print*
r   ARBA - v28 - '97 - p308 [51-250]

Gilman, Charlotte Perkins - *The Diaries of Charlotte Perkins Gilman. Vols. 1-2*
NEQ - v70 - Mr '97 - p134+ [501+]
The Later Poetry of Charlotte Perkins Gilman
AL - v69 - Mr '97 - p247 [51-250]
Choice - v34 - Ja '97 - p796 [51-250]
The Yellow Wall Paper and Other Stories
ELT - v39 - 3 '96 - p405 [501+]
The Yellow Wallpaper (Phillips). Audio Version
PW - v244 - Ja 6 '97 - p29 [51-250]
The Yellow Wallpaper. To Build a Fire. Audio Version
BL - v92 - Ag '96 - p1917 [51-250]

Gilman, Dorothy - *The Bells of Freedom*
y   CLW - v66 - Je '96 - p53 [51-250]
Mrs. Pollifax and the Lion Killer
Arm Det - v29 - Sum '96 - p368 [251-500]
PW - v243 - N 4 '96 - p71 [1-50]
Mrs. Pollifax, Innocent Tourist
y   BL - v93 - F 1 '97 - p928 [51-250]
KR - v64 - D 15 '96 - p1772 [51-250]
PW - v243 - D 30 '96 - p57+ [51-250]

Gilman, Laura Anne - *Otherwere: Stories of Transformation*
y   Kliatt - v31 - Ja '97 - p12+ [51-250]
MFSF - v92 - Ja '97 - p23 [51-250]

Gilman, Phoebe - *The Gypsy Princess (Illus. by Phoebe Gilman)*
c   BL - v93 - F 1 '97 - p945 [51-250]
c   CCB-B - v50 - Mr '97 - p247 [51-250]
c   SLJ - v43 - Mr '97 - p152 [51-250]
Something from Nothing
c   CLW - v67 - Mr '97 - p14 [1-50]

Gilman, Richard - *Chekhov's Plays*
Am Theat - v13 - S '96 - p66+ [501+]
Am Theat - v13 - D '96 - p21 [1-50]
TLS - D 6 '96 - p11+ [501+]
VQR - v72 - Aut '96 - p122* [251-500]

Gilman, Sander L - *Franz Kafka, the Jewish Patient*
Rel St Rev - v23 - Ap '97 - p197 [51-250]
Jews in Today's German Culture
Critm - v38 - Sum '96 - p491+ [501+]
Ger Q - v69 - Fall '96 - p429+ [501+]
J Ch St - v38 - Aut '96 - p912+ [251-500]
Picturing Health and Illness
Isis - v87 - D '96 - p711+ [251-500]
Smart Jews
AB - v99 - Mr 24 '97 - p968+ [501+]
BIC - v26 - F '97 - p22+ [501+]
Choice - v34 - Ja '97 - p837 [51-250]
New Sci - v153 - F 1 '97 - p49 [501+]
TLS - Mr 7 '97 - p6+ [501+]

Gilmartin, Christina Kelley - *Engendering the Chinese Revolution*
APSR - v90 - D '96 - p937+ [501+]
Ch Rev Int - v4 - Spr '97 - p1+ [501+]
HRNB - v25 - Fall '96 - p37+ [251-500]

Gilmer, Maureen - *Makeovers from the Budget Gardener*
BL - v93 - My 1 '97 - p1472 [51-250]
LJ - v122 - My 1 '97 - p130 [51-250]
PW - v244 - Ap 7 '97 - p87 [51-250]

Gilmore, Glenda Elizabeth - *Gender and Jim Crow*
Am Vis - v12 - F '97 - p28 [51-250]
BW - v26 - N 10 '96 - p3+ [51-250]
Choice - v34 - Ap '97 - p1404 [51-250]
Nat - v263 - N 4 '96 - p29+ [501+]
Wom R Bks - v14 - F '97 - p6+ [501+]

Gilmore, Rachna - *Lights for Gita*
c   Emerg Lib - v24 - Mr '97 - p47 [51-250]
Roses for Gita (Illus. by Alice Priestley)
c   Ch Bk News - v20 - Win '97 - p29 [51-250]
c   Quill & Q - v62 - N '96 - p45 [251-500]

Gilmore, William C - *Dirty Money*
J Gov Info - v23 - S '96 - p664 [51-250]

Gilmour, David - *Curzon*
Spec - v277 - N 23 '96 - p44 [51-250]

Gilmour, H B - *The Amazing Zoo (Illus. by Nate Evans)*
c   SLJ - v42 - Ag '96 - p122 [51-250]

Gilmour, John B - *Strategic Disagreement*
APSR - v90 - D '96 - p909+ [501+]
J Pol - v59 - F '97 - p264+ [501+]

Gilpin, Alan - *The Dictionary of Environment and Sustainable Development*
r   New Sci - v152 - O 26 '96 - p47 [51-250]

Gilpin, Clark - *A Preface to Theology*
CC - v114 - Mr 19 '97 - p318+ [251-500]

Gilpin, William - *Observations on Cumberland and Westmoreland 1786*
TLS - Ja 24 '97 - p13 [501+]

Gilroy, Beryl - *Gather the Faces*
WLT - v71 - Win '97 - p206+ [501+]

Gilroy, Paul - *The Black Atlantic*
Am Q - v48 - D '96 - p740+ [501+]

Gilsenan, Michael - *Lords of the Lebanese Marches*
Am Ethnol - v24 - F '97 - p203+ [501+]
Choice - v34 - O '96 - p323 [51-250]
MEP - v5 - 1 '97 - p204+ [501+]
MEQ - v3 - S '96 - p84 [251-500]
TLS - N 29 '96 - p13 [51-250]

Gilson, Anne Bathurst - *Eros Breaking Free*
Theol St - v57 - S '96 - p576 [251-500]

Gilson, Jamie - *Wagon Train 911*
  c BL - v93 - S 1 '96 - p130 [51-250]
  c CCB-B - v50 - Ja '97 - p170 [51-250]
  c Cur R - v36 - D '96 - p12 [51-250]
  c HB Guide - v8 - Spr '97 - p67 [51-250]
  c SLJ - v42 - S '96 - p201+ [51-250]
Gilson, Norbert - *Konzepte Von Elektrizitatsversorgung Und Elektrizitatswirtschaft*
    Isis - v87 - S '96 - p572+ [501+]
Gilster, Paul - *Digital Literacy*
  y BL - v93 - F 15 '97 - p985+ [51-250]
    LJ - v122 - F 15 '97 - p155 [51-250]
    New Sci - v153 - Mr 22 '97 - p44 [51-250]
    PW - v244 - Ja 20 '97 - p384 [51-250]
  Finding It on the Internet. 2nd Ed.
    CBR - v14 - N '96 - p35 [1-50]
Gilstrap, John - *Nathan's Run*
  y BL - v93 - Ap 1 '97 - p1292 [1-50]
    LJ - v121 - O 1 '96 - p47 [1-50]
  Nathan's Run (Glover). Audio Version
  y Kliatt - v30 - N '96 - p44 [51-250]
  Nathan's Run (Guidal). Audio Version
  y Kliatt - v31 - Ja '97 - p42+ [251-500]
Gilyard, Keith - *Spirit and Flame*
    PW - v244 - Ja 27 '97 - p95 [51-250]
Gimpel, Charles - *Between Two Cultures*
    Can Lit - Win '96 - p156+ [501+]
Gimpel, Jean - *The End of the Future*
    SocSciComR - v14 - Win '96 - p480+ [501+]
    T&C - v37 - O '96 - p831+ [501+]
Gindikin, Simon - *Functional Analysis on the Eve of the 21st Century. Vol. 1*
    SIAM Rev - v38 - D '96 - p713 [1-50]
  Topics in Geometry
    SciTech - v20 - S '96 - p12 [51-250]
Gindlesperger, James - *Escape from Libby Prison*
  y SLJ - v43 - F '97 - p134 [51-250]
Ginenthal, Charles - *Carl Sagan and Immanuel Velikovsky*
    Skeptic - v4 - 4 '96 - p107 [501+]
The Gingerbread Man. Electronic Media Version
  c LAR - v98 - N '96 - p595 [51-250]
The Gingerbread Man (Illus. by John A Rowe)
  c HB Guide - v7 - Fall '96 - p323+ [51-250]
  c SLJ - v42 - Ag '96 - p136 [51-250]
Gingrich, Candace - *The Accidental Activist*
    BL - v93 - S 1 '96 - p29 [1-50]
    BW - v26 - Ag 18 '96 - p4 [251-500]
    Ent W - S 13 '96 - p126 [51-250]
    Nat - v263 - S 9 '96 - p44+ [501+]
    NYTBR - v101 - S 8 '96 - p9 [501+]
    Wom R Bks - v14 - D '96 - p18+ [501+]
Ginifer, Jeremy - *Managing Arms in Peace Processes*
    For Aff - v75 - S '96 - p160 [51-250]
Ginley, David - *Thin Films for Photovoltaic and Related Device Applications*
    SciTech - v21 - Mr '97 - p91 [51-250]
Ginsberg, Allen - *Howl and Other Poems*
    LJ - v122 - Ap 1 '97 - p94 [1-50]
  Illuminated Poems
    BWatch - v17 - S '96 - p9 [51-250]
  Journals Mid-Fifties 1954-1958
    PS - v70 - Win '96 - p188+ [501+]
  Selected Poems 1947-1995
    Advocate - S 17 '96 - p60 [1-50]
    BL - v92 - Ag '96 - p1876 [51-250]
    Mac - v109 - N 11 '96 - p95+ [501+]
    NY - v72 - N 4 '96 - p98+ [501+]
  White Shroud
    LJ - v122 - Ap 1 '97 - p94 [51-250]
Ginsberg, Art - *Mr. Food*
    PW - v243 - O 21 '96 - p81 [1-50]
Ginsberg, Elaine K - *Passing the Fictions of Identity*
    Choice - v34 - My '97 - p1498 [51-250]
Ginsberg, Rick - *Commissions, Reports, Reforms, and Educational Policy*
    HER - v66 - Win '96 - p891 [501+]
Ginsberg, Susan - *Family Wisdom*
  r ARBA - v28 - '97 - p36 [51-250]
  r BL - v93 - Mr 1 '97 - p1190 [251-500]
Ginsburg, Faye D - *Conceiving the New World Order*
    Am Ethnol - v24 - F '97 - p220+ [501+]
    CS - v25 - S '96 - p591+ [501+]
Ginsburg, Mark B - *The Politics of Educators' Work and Lives*
    ES - v27 - Sum '96 - p177+ [501+]
Ginsburg, Michal Peled - *Economies of Change*
    Choice - v34 - D '96 - p607 [51-250]
    Nine-C Lit - v51 - D '96 - p422 [51-250]

Ginsburg, Mirra - *Clay Boy (Illus. by Jos. A Smith)*
  c HB - v73 - Mr '97 - p206+ [51-250]
  c KR - v65 - My 1 '97 - p720 [51-250]
  c PW - v244 - My 5 '97 - p209 [51-250]
Ginsburgh, Judy Caplan - *Jewish Entertainment Resource Directory*
  r CAY - v16 - Fall '95 - p4 [51-250]
Ginzberg, Eli - *Louis Ginzberg: Keeper of the Law*
    BL - v93 - O 1 '96 - p308 [1-50]
  Tomorrow's Hospital
    Choice - v34 - N '96 - p492 [51-250]
    JEL - v34 - D '96 - p2062 [51-250]
Ginzburg, Lidiia - *Blockade Diary*
    LATBR - D 29 '96 - p11 [1-50]
    WLT - v70 - Sum '96 - p722 [501+]
Gioia, Dana - *Formal Introductions*
    HR - v49 - Aut '96 - p513+ [501+]
Giordano, Emilio - *La Corazza E La Spada*
    MLR - v91 - Jl '96 - p753+ [501+]
Giordano, Gerard - *Literacy: Programs for Adults with Developmental Disabilities*
    JAAL - v40 - Mr '97 - p507+ [501+]
Gioseffi, Daniela - *In Bed with the Exotic Enemy*
    BL - v93 - F 15 '97 - p1003 [51-250]
    PW - v244 - Ja 13 '97 - p57 [51-250]
Giovanni, Nikki - *The Genie in the Jar (Illus. by Chris Raschka)*
  c ECEJ - v24 - Spr '97 - p174 [51-250]
  c HB Guide - v7 - Fall '96 - p367 [51-250]
  c RT - v50 - My '97 - p684 [51-250]
  Grand Mothers
  y PW - v243 - S 16 '96 - p85 [1-50]
  Love Poems
  y BL - v93 - Ja '97 - p809 [51-250]
    LJ - v121 - N 1 '96 - p84 [1-50]
    LJ - v122 - F 1 '97 - p84 [51-250]
    PW - v243 - D 30 '96 - p62 [1-50]
  Shimmy Shimmy Shimmy like My Sister Kate
  y AB - v98 - N 18 '96 - p1728+ [51-250]
  y BL - v93 - F 15 '97 - p1014 [1-50]
  y HB Guide - v8 - Spr '97 - p150 [51-250]
  y RT - v50 - Ap '97 - p593 [51-250]
  y VOYA - v19 - O '96 - p229+ [251-500]
  The Sun Is So Quiet (Illus. by Ashley Bryan)
  c CBRS - v25 - N '96 - p31 [1-50]
  c HB Guide - v8 - Spr '97 - p152 [51-250]
  c Par Ch - v20 - O '96 - p11 [1-50]
  c PW - v243 - O 21 '96 - p83 [51-250]
  c SLJ - v43 - Ja '97 - p100 [51-250]
Giovannini, Alberto - *The Debate on Money in Europe*
    Econ J - v106 - N '96 - p1836 [51-250]
    JEL - v34 - S '96 - p1432 [51-250]
Giovinazzo, Buddy - *Poetry and Purgatory*
    BL - v93 - D 15 '96 - p708 [51-250]
    KR - v64 - N 1 '96 - p1551 [251-500]
    LJ - v121 - D '96 - p145 [51-250]
    PW - v243 - N 11 '96 - p71 [51-250]
Gipson, Carolyn Renee - *The McGraw-Hill Dictionary of International Trade and Finance*
  r R&R Bk N - v11 - N '96 - p34 [51-250]
Giraldo, Javier - *Colombia: The Genocidal Democracy*
    BL - v93 - S 15 '96 - p189 [51-250]
    Prog - v60 - N '96 - p39+ [501+]
Girard, Marc - *La Passion De Charles Bovary*
    MLR - v92 - Ja '97 - p197+ [251-500]
Girard, Paula Tanner - *A Father for Christmas*
    LJ - v121 - N 15 '96 - p48 [51-250]
  A Valentine Bouquet
    LJ - v122 - F 15 '97 - p126 [51-250]
Girard, Rene - *The Girard Reader*
    LJ - v121 - N 15 '96 - p77 [51-250]
  Resurrection from the Underground
    KR - v65 - Ja 15 '97 - p116 [251-500]
    LJ - v122 - Ap 1 '97 - p91 [51-250]
Girardi, Michele - *Giacomo Puccini: L'Arte Internazionale Di Un Musicista Italiano*
    Notes - v53 - Mr '97 - p803+ [501+]
Girardi, Robert - *The Pirate's Daughter*
    Books - v11 - Ap '97 - p22 [51-250]
    KR - v64 - O 15 '96 - p1484 [251-500]
    NYTBR - v102 - F 16 '97 - p18 [51-250]
  The Pirate's Daughter. Audio Version
    BWatch - v18 - Mr '97 - p7 [1-50]
Girardin, G Russell - *Dillinger: The Untold Story*
    J Am Cult - v18 - Win '95 - p98 [51-250]
Giraud, Marcel - *A History of French Louisiana. Vol. 2*
    TranslRevS - v1 - My '95 - p10 [51-250]
Girden, Ellen R - *Evaluating Research Articles from Start to Finish*
    R&R Bk N - v11 - D '96 - p67 [51-250]
    SciTech - v21 - Mr '97 - p3 [1-50]

Girdner, Jaqueline - *Adjusted to Death*
    Arm Det - v29 - Fall '96 - p436+ [251-500]
  A Cry for Self-Help
    KR - v65 - Mr 1 '97 - p337 [51-250]
    PW - v244 - Mr 3 '97 - p67 [51-250]
  Most Likely to Die
    Arm Det - v29 - Fall '96 - p483+ [251-500]
Gire, Ken - *Between Heaven and Earth*
    BL - v93 - O 1 '97 - p909 [51-250]
Girgus, Sam B - *The Films of Woody Allen*
    J Pop F&TV - v24 - Win '97 - p190 [501+]
Girls' Life
  cp Par Ch - v20 - O '96 - p15 [1-50]
Girls to the Rescue
  c Cur R - v36 - D '96 - p12 [51-250]
Girls to the Rescue. No. 2
  c Cur R - v36 - D '96 - p12 [51-250]
  c HB Guide - v8 - Spr '97 - p148 [51-250]
  c SLJ - v43 - F '97 - p82 [51-250]
Girolami, Patrizia - *L'Antiteodicea: Dio, Dei, Religione Nello Zibaldone Di Giacomo Leopardi*
    MLR - v91 - O '96 - p1010+ [501+]
Giroux, Henry A - *Between Borders*
    QJS - v83 - F '97 - p127+ [501+]
  Disturbing Pleasures
    QJS - v83 - F '97 - p127+ [501+]
  Fugitive Cultures
    Nat - v263 - O 21 '96 - p27+ [501+]
Girshick, Lori B - *Soledad Women*
    Fed Prob - v60 - D '96 - p64 [501+]
    R&R Bk N - v11 - N '96 - p45 [51-250]
Girvin, Brian - *The Right in the Twentieth Century*
    EHR - v112 - Ap '97 - p533 [51-250]
Girzone, Joseph - *Joshua*
    CSM - v89 - N 25 '96 - p12 [51-250]
    CSM - v89 - Ja 23 '97 - p12 [51-250]
Gisbert, Joan Manuel - *Los Armarios Negros*
  y BL - v93 - F 15 '97 - p1032 [1-50]
GISDECO Seminar (1991: Utrecht University) - *Possibilities and Constraints of GIS Applications in Developing Countries*
    AAAGA - v86 - D '96 - p802+ [501+]
Gish, Robert - *Beautiful Swift Fox*
    Choice - v34 - Mr '97 - p1162 [51-250]
    Roundup M - v4 - Ap '97 - p22 [251-500]
  Beyond Bounds
    Choice - v34 - Ja '97 - p794 [51-250]
  Nueva Granada
    WAL - v31 - Sum '96 - p187+ [251-500]
  When Coyote Howls
    WAL - v31 - Sum '96 - p174 [51-250]
Gish, Steven - *Ethiopia*
  c HB Guide - v7 - Fall '96 - p384 [51-250]
  y SLJ - v42 - Ag '96 - p168 [51-250]
Giskin, Howard - *Chinese Folktales*
    LJ - v122 - F 15 '97 - p140 [51-250]
Gispen, Kees - *What Made the South Different?*
    CAY - v17 - Fall '96 - p11 [51-250]
Gissing, George - *The Collected Letters of George Gissing. Vol. 5*
    RES - v47 - N '96 - p619+ [501+]
  The Collected Letters of George Gissing. Vol. 7
    ELT - v39 - 3 '96 - p348+ [501+]
    Nine-C Lit - v51 - S '96 - p272 [51-250]
  The Collected Letters of George Gissing. Vol. 8
    ELT - v40 - 2 '97 - p184+ [501+]
    Spec - v277 - N 16 '96 - p46 [1-50]
  The Collected Letters of George Gissing. Vol. 9
    Spec - v278 - Ap 5 '97 - p36 [501+]
  George Gissing's American Notebook
    Nine-C Lit - v50 - Mr '96 - p553 [1-50]
  The Poetry of George Gissing
    Nine-C Lit - v50 - Mr '96 - p553 [1-50]
Gitin, Seymour - *Recent Excavations in Israel*
    AJA - v100 - Jl '96 - p610+ [501+]
Gitlin, Todd - *The Twilight of Common Dreams*
    Bks & Cult - v2 - S '96 - p20 [501+]
    CS - v25 - N '96 - p725+ [501+]
    NYTBR - v102 - F 2 '97 - p28 [1-50]
    PW - v243 - O 21 '96 - p78 [1-50]
    Tikkun - v11 - S '96 - p86+ [501+]
    VQR - v72 - Aut '96 - p755+ [501+]
Gitlitz, David M - *Secrecy and Deceit*
    AB - v99 - Mr 24 '97 - p966+ [501+]
Gittings, John - *Real China*
    FEER - v159 - S 26 '96 - p50+ [501+]
Gittleman, Ann Louise - *Get the Salt Out*
    BL - v93 - Ja '97 - p797 [51-250]
  Get the Sugar Out
    BL - v92 - Ag '96 - p1869 [51-250]

Gittleman, John L - *Carnivore Behavior, Ecology, and Evolution. Vol. 2*
 Choice - v34 - D '96 - p638 [51-250]
Giugale, Marcelo M - *Private Sector Development in Egypt*
 MEJ - v50 - Aut '96 - p625+ [51-250]
 MEQ - v4 - Mr '97 - p91 [251-500]
Giuli, Eraldo - *Categorical Topology*
 SciTech - v20 - N '96 - p13 [51-250]
Giuliano, Geoffrey - *Behind Blue Eyes*
 Advocate - S 17 '96 - p60 [1-50]
 Advocate - N 26 '96 - p67+ [501+]
 KR - v64 - S 15 '96 - p1372 [251-500]
 LJ - v121 - O 15 '96 - p60 [51-250]
Giurgiu, Eugen - *Cu Frunzele In Vant*
 BL - v93 - D 15 '96 - p714 [1-50]
Givens, Peter - *Human Biology and Health Studies*
 TES - Ja 3 '97 - pR11 [51-250]
Given-Wilson, Chris - *An Illustrated History of Late Medieval England*
 HT - v46 - O '96 - p56 [1-50]
 TLS - Ja 3 '97 - p29 [501+]
Givon, Hannah Gelman - *We Shake in a Quake (Illus. by David Uttal)*
 c HB Guide - v8 - Spr '97 - p28 [51-250]
 c KR - v64 - S 1 '96 - p1321 [51-250]
 c LATBR - S 22 '96 - p15 [51-250]
 c PW - v243 - O 7 '96 - p78 [51-250]
 c SLJ - v43 - Ja '97 - p100+ [51-250]
Gjelstad, Jorn - *Nuclear Rivalry and International Order*
 R&R Bk N - v11 - D '96 - p49 [51-250]
Gladden, Scott C - *Marketing and Selling A/E and Other Engineering Services*
 SciTech - v20 - S '96 - p48 [51-250]
Glade, William - *Bigger Economies, Smaller Governments*
 JEL - v34 - D '96 - p2083 [51-250]
 R&R Bk N - v11 - N '96 - p32 [51-250]
Gladieux, Lawrence E - *The College Aid Quandary*
 JEL - v34 - S '96 - p1442 [51-250]
 J Hi E - v68 - Ja '97 - p115+ [501+]
Glading, Gregory T - *64 Intruder*
 Rapport - v19 - 4 '96 - p23 [51-250]
Glaeser, Bernhard - *Environment, Development, Agriculture*
 GJ - v162 - N '96 - p341 [51-250]
Glaister, Geoffrey Ashall - *Encyclopedia of the Book. 2nd Ed.*
 r ARBA - v28 - '97 - p250 [51-250]
 r BC - v45 - Win '96 - p543+ [51-250]
 r BL - v93 - S 1 '96 - p166 [1-50]
 r Bloom Rev - v16 - N '96 - p22 [1-50]
 r LAR - v98 - D '96 - p651 [1-50]
 r R&R Bk N - v11 - D '96 - p73 [51-250]
Glaister, Lesley - *The Private Parts of Women*
 Obs - N 3 '96 - p18* [51-250]
Glamuzina, Julie - *Parker and Hulme*
 OOB - v26 - Ag '96 - p23 [501+]
Glancy, Diane - *The Only Piece of Furniture in the House*
 KR - v64 - S 1 '96 - p1266 [51-250]
 LJ - v121 - N 1 '96 - p106 [51-250]
 NYTBR - v102 - Ja 5 '97 - p18 [51-250]
 PW - v243 - O 7 '96 - p59 [51-250]
Pushing the Bear
 y BL - v92 - Ag '96 - p1881 [51-250]
 y BL - v92 - Ag '96 - p1891 [1-50]
 Bloom Rev - v16 - S '96 - p19 [501+]
 BW - v26 - O 6 '96 - p3 [51-250]
 Comw - v123 - D 6 '96 - p24 [51-250]
 LJ - v122 - Mr 15 '97 - p42 [1-50]
 WLT - v71 - Win '97 - p198+ [501+]
 Wom R Bks - v14 - Ja '97 - p13 [501+]
The West Pole
 KR - v65 - Ja 15 '97 - p117 [251-500]
 LJ - v122 - Mr 15 '97 - p70 [51-250]
 PW - v244 - F 10 '97 - p76 [51-250]
Glancy, Maida - *Harmony in the Kitchen*
 Am MT - v46 - D '96 - p65 [51-250]
Glants, Musya - *Food in Russian History and Culture*
 PW - v244 - My 12 '97 - p72 [51-250]
Glantz, David M - *When Titans Clashed*
 NWCR - v50 - Win '97 - p162+ [501+]
Glantz, Michael H - *Currents of Change*
 Choice - v34 - Mr '97 - p1198 [51-250]
 Nature - v385 - Ja 2 '97 - p35 [501+]
 New Sci - v153 - Ja 25 '97 - p44 [501+]
Glantz, Stanton A - *The Cigarette Papers*
 ABA Jour - v82 - Ag '96 - p104 [501+]
 Choice - v34 - O '96 - p312 [51-250]
 Reason - v28 - D '96 - p46+ [501+]
 Sci - v273 - Ag 9 '96 - p744+ [501+]

Glanville, Philippa - *Silver: History and Design*
 BL - v93 - Ja '97 - p802 [51-250]
 LJ - v121 - D '96 - p90 [51-250]
Glare, P G W - *Greek-English Lexicon: Revised Supplement*
 r Rel St Rev - v23 - Ap '97 - p173 [51-250]
Glasel, Jay A - *Introduction to Biophysical Methods for Protein and Nucleic Acid Research*
 J Chem Ed - v73 - Ag '96 - pA179 [51-250]
Glaser, Chris - *Uncommon Calling*
 Intpr - v51 - Ap '97 - p222 [251-500]
Glaser, Connie - *Swim with the Dolphins. Audio Version*
 BWatch - v18 - Mr '97 - p8 [1-50]
Glaser, Daniel - *Preparing Convicts for Law-Abiding Lives*
 Fed Prob - v60 - Je '96 - p84+ [501+]
Glaser, James M - *Race, Campaign Politics, and the Realignment in the South*
 Choice - v34 - Ja '97 - p875 [51-250]
Glaser, Linda - *Compost! Growing Gardens from Your Garbage (Illus. by Anca Hariton)*
 c HB Guide - v7 - Fall '96 - p352 [51-250]
 c SB - v33 - Mr '97 - p53 [51-250]
Glaser, Sherry - *Family Secrets*
 BL - v93 - D 15 '96 - p705 [51-250]
 KR - v64 - N 15 '96 - p1651 [251-500]
 PW - v243 - N 18 '96 - p68 [51-250]
Glasgow, Karen - *Irises: A Practical Gardening Guide*
 BL - v93 - My 1 '97 - p1472 [51-250]
Glasner, David - *Business Cycles and Depressions*
 BWatch - v18 - Mr '97 - p5 [1-50]
Glaspey, Terry W - *Great Books of the Christian Tradition and Other Books Which Have Shaped Our World*
 VOYA - v19 - O '96 - p242 [51-250]
Not a Tame Lion
 Ch Today - v41 - F 3 '97 - p66+ [501+]
Glass, Andrew - *The Sweetwater Run (Illus. by Andrew Glass)*
 c BL - v93 - D 15 '96 - p731 [51-250]
 c CCB-B - v50 - D '96 - p135+ [51-250]
 c HB Guide - v8 - Spr '97 - p28 [51-250]
 c KR - v64 - S 15 '96 - p1399 [51-250]
 c NYTBR - v101 - N 10 '96 - p42 [501+]
 c Par - v71 - D '96 - p252 [51-250]
 c PW - v243 - O 7 '96 - p75 [51-250]
 c SLJ - v42 - N '96 - p80 [51-250]
The Sweetwater Run (Guidall). Audio Version
 c HB - v73 - My '97 - p357+ [501+]
Glass, Don - *How Can You Tell if a Spider Is Dead? and More Moments of Science*
 Bloom Rev - v16 - N '96 - p27 [51-250]
 y Kliatt - v31 - Ja '97 - p27 [51-250]
 KR - v64 - Ag 15 '96 - p1209 [51-250]
 New Sci - v152 - D 21 '96 - p66 [1-50]
 r PW - v243 - S 2 '96 - p121 [51-250]
 y SB - v33 - Mr '97 - p44 [51-250]
Glass, James M - *Psychosis and Power*
 Ethics - v107 - Ja '97 - p402 [51-250]
Glass, Leslie - *Loving Time*
 BL - v93 - S 15 '96 - p224 [51-250]
 KR - v64 - S 1 '96 - p1276 [51-250]
 PW - v243 - S 9 '96 - p63 [51-250]
Glass, Lillian - *Attracting Terrific People*
 PW - v244 - F 17 '97 - p204+ [51-250]
Glasscock, Sarah - *10 Women Who Helped Shape America*
 Cur R - v36 - F '97 - p3* [51-250]
Glasser, Leah Blatt - *In a Closet Hidden*
 Choice - v34 - D '96 - p613 [51-250]
 Nine-C Lit - v51 - Mr '97 - p557 [51-250]
Glasser, Ronald - *The Light in the Skull*
 KR - v65 - Mr 1 '97 - p350 [51-250]
 PW - v244 - Mr 10 '97 - p60 [51-250]
Glasser, Ruth - *My Music Is My Flag*
 AHR - v101 - O '96 - p1296 [501+]
 HAHR - v76 - N '96 - p761+ [501+]
 J Am St - v30 - Ag '96 - p313+ [251-500]
 Notes - v53 - S '96 - p88+ [501+]
Glasser, Theodore L - *Public Opinion and the Communication of Consent*
 JC - v47 - Win '97 - p160+ [501+]
Glassman, Bernard - *Instructions to the Cook. Audio Version*
 BWatch - v18 - Mr '97 - p6 [51-250]
Glassman, Bruce - *The Crash of '29 and The New Deal*
 c SE - v60 - S '96 - p303 [1-50]
Glater, Ruth Ann Bobrov - *Slam the Door Gently*
 BL - v93 - Ja '97 - p795 [51-250]
Glatt, Lisa - *Monsters and Other Lovers*
 Sm Pr R - v29 - F '97 - p11+ [501+]

Glatthorn, Allan A - *Content of the Curriculum. 2nd Ed.*
 NASSP-B - v80 - S '96 - p115+ [501+]
Glavac, Cynthia - *In the Fullness of Life*
 RR - v56 - Mr '97 - p222 [1-50]
Glavich, Mary Kathleen - *Discipline Made Easy*
 CLW - v67 - Mr '97 - p38 [51-250]
Handbook for Catholic Youth
 y CLW - v66 - Je '96 - p54 [51-250]
Glavin, Terry - *Dead Reckoning*
 CG - v116 - S '96 - p76+ [501+]
This Ragged Place
 Quill & Q - v63 - Ja '97 - p32 [51-250]
Glaze, Dave - *Who Took Henry and Mr. Z?*
 y BIC - v25 - N '96 - p33+ [501+]
 c Quill & Q - v62 - Ag '96 - p43 [51-250]
Glazer, Mary - *The Cup of Wrath*
 Rapport - v19 - 6 '96 - p31 [251-500]
Glazer, Nathan - *Beyond the Melting Pot*
 BW - v26 - D 15 '96 - p1 [1-50]
We Are All Multiculturalists Now
 BL - v93 - Mr 15 '97 - p1208 [51-250]
 For Aff - v76 - My '97 - p123 [51-250]
 KR - v65 - Ja 15 '97 - p117 [251-500]
 NYTLa - v146 - Mr 20 '97 - pC20 [501+]
 PW - v244 - F 10 '97 - p78 [51-250]
 WSJ-Cent - v99 - Mr 24 '97 - pA16 [501+]
Glazner, Greg - *Singularity*
 LJ - v121 - N 15 '96 - p65 [51-250]
 PW - v243 - N 25 '96 - p72 [51-250]
Gleason, Abbott - *Totalitarianism: The Inner History of the Cold War*
 JPR - v34 - F '97 - p111+ [51-250]
Gleason, David K - *Atlanta*
 JSH - v62 - N '96 - p863+ [51-250]
Gleason, Katherine - *Native American Literature*
 c HB Guide - v8 - Spr '97 - p148 [51-250]
 y SLJ - v43 - Mr '97 - p200 [51-250]
Gleason, Philip - *Contending with Modernity*
 Bks & Cult - v2 - S '96 - p31+ [501+]
 CHR - v83 - Ja '97 - p144+ [251-500]
 Cres - v59 - Sum '96 - p39+ [501+]
 HER - v66 - Fall '96 - p684+ [501+]
 Rel St Rev - v23 - Ja '97 - p35+ [501+]
 TT - v53 - O '96 - p424 [51-250]
Gleason, Randall C - *John Calvin and John Owen on Mortification*
 CH - v65 - S '96 - p501+ [501+]
 Six Ct J - v27 - Fall '96 - p870+ [251-500]
Gledhill, Christine - *Nationalising Femininity*
 Si & So - v6 - N '96 - p35 [1-50]
Gleditsch, Nils P - *The Peace Dividend*
 JEL - v35 - Mr '97 - p225 [51-250]
Glees, Anthony - *Reinventing Germany*
 Choice - v34 - Ap '97 - p1410 [51-250]
Gleeson, Brian - *The Savior Is Born (Freeman) (Illus. by Robert Van Nutt). Book and Electronic Media Version*
 c BL - v93 - N 15 '96 - p589 [51-250]
 c PW - v243 - N 11 '96 - p35 [51-250]
Gleeson, Libby - *The Princess and the Perfect Dish (Illus. by Armin Greder)*
 c JB - v60 - D '96 - p252 [51-250]
 c Sch Lib - v44 - N '96 - p146 [51-250]
Skating on Sand (Illus. by Ann James)
 c Bks Keeps - v100 - S '96 - p12 [51-250]
Gleiter, Jan - *Lie Down with Dogs*
 Arm Det - v29 - Fall '96 - p438 [51-250]
Gleitzman, Morris - *Belly Flop*
 c Bks Keeps - Mr '97 - p23+ [51-250]
 c Magpies - v11 - S '96 - p33 [51-250]
 c Sch Lib - v45 - F '97 - p24 [51-250]
 c TES - F 21 '97 - p8* [51-250]
Puppy Fat
 c HB Guide - v7 - Fall '96 - p292 [51-250]
 y Kliatt - v30 - S '96 - p10 [51-250]
 c Par - v71 - S '96 - p209 [51-250]
Gleize, Jean-Marie - *Le Theatre Du Poeme*
 WLT - v70 - Sum '96 - p657+ [501+]
Glenberg, Arthur M - *Learning from Data. 2nd Ed.*
 SB - v32 - O '96 - p196 [251-500]
Glendale Data Book
 r J Gov Info - v23 - S '96 - p600 [51-250]
Glendinning, Matthew - *Sons and Mothers*
 Obs - N 24 '96 - p15* [501+]
 Spec - v277 - N 23 '96 - p49 [501+]
Glendinning, Victoria - *Electricity*
 NYTBR - v102 - Mr 2 '97 - p28 [51-250]
Glendon, Mary Ann - *A Nation under Lawyers*
 NYTBR - v101 - D 15 '96 - p40 [1-50]
Seedbeds of Virtue
 Soc Ser R - v71 - Mr '97 - p164 [51-250]

Glenisson, Jean - *Le Livre D'Enfance Et De Jeunesse En France*
    Bkbird - v34 - Spr '96 - p55 [1-50]
Glenn, Camille - *Camille Glenn's Old-Fashioned Christmas Cookbook*
    LJ - v121 - N 15 '96 - p84 [51-250]
    PW - v243 - S 16 '96 - p78+ [51-250]
Glenn, Charles Leslie - *Educating Immigrant Children*
    Choice - v34 - Mr '97 - p1211+ [51-250]
    R&R Bk N - v11 - D '96 - p55 [51-250]
Glenn, Evelyn Nakano - *Mothering: Ideology, Experience, and Agency*
    JWomHist - v8 - Fall '96 - p219+ [501+]
    Signs - v22 - Win '97 - p440+ [501+]
Glenn, Mel - *The Taking of Room 114*
  y BL - v93 - Mr 1 '97 - p1154 [51-250]
  c CCB-B - v50 - Mr '97 - p247+ [51-250]
  y KR - v65 - F 1 '97 - p222+ [51-250]
  y Trib Bks - Ap 13 '97 - p7 [51-250]
Who Killed Mr. Chippendale?
  y BL - v93 - Ap 1 '97 - p1286 [1-50]
  y BL - v93 - Ap 1 '97 - p1306 [1-50]
  y CBRS - v24 - Ag '96 - p167 [51-250]
  y HB Guide - v7 - Fall '96 - p301 [51-250]
  y JAAL - v40 - N '96 - p232 [51-250]
  y KR - v64 - My 1 '96 - p688+ [51-250]
  y VOYA - v19 - D '96 - p287 [251-500]
Glenn, Myra C - *Thomas K. Beecher: Minister to a Changing America 1824-1900*
    Choice - v34 - My '97 - p1515+ [51-250]
Glenn, Patricia Brown - *Discover America's Favorite Architects (Illus. by Joe Stites)*
  c Ch BWatch - v6 - D '96 - p7 [51-250]
  c KR - v64 - N 1 '96 - p1600+ [51-250]
  c PW - v243 - N 25 '96 - p77 [1-50]
  y SLJ - v43 - Ja '97 - p124+ [51-250]
Glenz, W - *A Glossary of Plastics Terminology in 5 Languages. 3rd Ed.*
  r ARBA - v28 - '97 - p627 [51-250]
Glessmer, Uwe - *Einleitung In Die Targume Zum Pentateuch*
    Rel St Rev - v23 - Ja '97 - p85 [51-250]
Glete, Jan - *Navies and Nations. Vols. 1-2*
    NWCR - v49 - Aut '96 - p159+ [501+]
Glick, Ruth - *Skinny Italian Cooking*
    BWatch - v17 - N '96 - p1 [51-250]
    BWatch - v18 - F '97 - p8 [1-50]
    PW - v243 - O 21 '96 - p80 [51-250]
Glick, Thomas F - *From Muslim Fortress to Christian Castle*
    TLS - Ja 3 '97 - p28 [501+]
Glickman, Marty - *The Fastest Kid on the Block*
    BWatch - v17 - D '96 - p8 [51-250]
    Choice - v34 - My '97 - p1539 [51-250]
    KR - v64 - O 1 '96 - p1442 [251-500]
Glickman, Nora - *Argentine Jewish Theatre*
    Choice - v34 - Ja '97 - p801 [51-250]
    LJ - v121 - D '96 - p92 [51-250]
Glink, Ilyce R - *10 Steps to Home Ownership*
    LJ - v121 - D '96 - p110 [51-250]
Gliori, Debi - *Mr. Bear to the Rescue*
  c Sch Lib - v45 - F '97 - p18 [51-250]
Mr. Bear's Picnic
  c Bks Keeps - v100 - S '96 - p8 [51-250]
The Princess and the Pirate King
  c HB Guide - v8 - Spr '97 - p29 [51-250]
  c PW - v243 - S 9 '96 - p82 [51-250]
  c Sch Lib - v45 - F '97 - p18 [51-250]
The Snow Lambs (Illus. by Debi Gliori)
  c BL - v93 - N 15 '96 - p584 [51-250]
  c CBRS - v25 - D '96 - p39 [1-50]
  c CCB-B - v50 - F '97 - p204+ [51-250]
  c HB Guide - v8 - Spr '97 - p29 [51-250]
  c NYTBR - v102 - F 2 '97 - p18 [1-50]
  c SLJ - v42 - O '96 - p94 [51-250]
Gliserman, Martin - *Psychoanalysis, Language, and the Body of the Text*
    Choice - v34 - D '96 - p613 [51-250]
    ELT - v40 - 1 '97 - p127 [51-250]
Glissant, Edouard - *Malemort*
    MLR - v91 - Jl '96 - p597+ [501+]
Global Biodiversity: An International Forum on the Variety of Life on Earth...Research, Conservation and Wise Use
  p WorldV - v12 - O '96 - p11+ [51-250]
Global Communications
    J Gov Info - v23 - S '96 - p555 [51-250]
Global Economic Prospects and the Developing Countries 1996
    JEL - v35 - Mr '97 - p211 [51-250]

Global Emission Experiences
    SciTech - v20 - D '96 - p80 [51-250]
A Global Marketplace for Consumers
    J Gov Info - v23 - S '96 - p673 [51-250]
Global Population Policy Data Base 1993
  r J Gov Info - v23 - S '96 - p677 [51-250]
Global Warming: Economic Dimensions and Policy Responses
    J Gov Info - v23 - S '96 - p673 [51-250]
Glock, Hans-Johann - *A Wittgenstein Dictionary*
  r ARBA - v28 - '97 - p529+ [51-250]
Gloor, Peter - *Elements of Hypermedia Design*
    BYTE - v22 - Ap '97 - p38 [51-250]
    SciTech - v21 - Mr '97 - p9 [51-250]
Glosove Na Zheni
    WLT - v71 - Win '97 - p126 [51-250]
Gloss, Molly - *The Jump-Off Creek*
    BW - v26 - D 8 '96 - p4 [51-250]
Glossary of HIV/AIDS-Related Terms
  r J Gov Info - v23 - S '96 - p546 [1-50]
Glossary of Insurance and Risk Management Terms. 6th Ed.
  r ARBA - v28 - '97 - p98 [251-500]
Gloster, Peter - *The Way Microsoft Word for Windows 95 Works*
    BL - v92 - Ag '96 - p1868 [501+]
Glotfelty, Cheryll - *The Ecocriticism Reader*
    TLS - F 21 '97 - p12 [501+]
    VQR - v72 - Aut '96 - p120* [51-250]
    WAL - v31 - Win '97 - p401+ [251-500]
Glouberman, Michael - *3rd Rock from the Sun*
    Ent W - N 22 '96 - p130 [51-250]
Glover, David - *Vampires, Mummies, and Liberals*
    Choice - v34 - F '97 - p965 [51-250]
Glover, David, 1953, Sep., 9- - *The Oxford Children's A to Z of Mathematics*
  c JB - v60 - D '96 - p252 [51-250]
  c Sch Lib - v45 - F '97 - p38 [51-250]
Glover, David M - *The Young Oxford Book of the Human Being*
  c Sch Lib - v45 - F '97 - p50 [51-250]
Glover, Derek - *The Management of Mentoring*
    R&R Bk N - v11 - D '96 - p53 [51-250]
Glover, Mike - *Perl 5 How-To*
    SciTech - v20 - D '96 - p9 [51-250]
Gluck, Jay - *Surveyors of Persian Art*
    MEJ - v51 - Win '97 - p150 [51-250]
Zen Combat
    BWatch - v18 - F '97 - p9 [1-50]
Gluck, Louise - *Meadowlands*
    LJ - v122 - Ap 1 '97 - p94 [1-50]
    Poet - v169 - Mr '97 - p339+ [501+]
    WLT - v71 - Win '97 - p156+ [501+]
    Wom R Bks - v14 - N '96 - p24+ [501+]
    YR - v84 - O '96 - p158+ [501+]
Proofs and Theories
    APR - v26 - Ja '97 - p37+ [501+]
The Wild Iris
    APR - v26 - Ja '97 - p37+ [501+]
    LJ - v122 - Ap 1 '97 - p94 [1-50]
Gluckman, Amy - *Homo Economics*
    LJ - v122 - F 15 '97 - p151+ [51-250]
    PW - v243 - D 9 '96 - p58 [51-250]
Gluzman, Michael - *Israel: A Traveler's Literary Companion*
    BL - v93 - S 15 '96 - p210 [1-50]
    KR - v64 - S 1 '96 - p1267 [51-250]
    LJ - v121 - O 15 '96 - p81 [51-250]
    PW - v243 - S 16 '96 - p75 [51-250]
Glyde, Henry R - *Excitations in Liquid and Solid Helium*
    Phys Today - v49 - Ag '96 - p68+ [501+]
Glyde, Tanya - *Clever Girl*
    Books - v9 - S '95 - p8 [251-500]
Glyn, Andrew - *Paying for Inequality*
    JEL - v34 - S '96 - p1413 [51-250]
Glyn-Jones, Anne - *Holding Up a Mirror*
    TLS - D 27 '96 - p28 [501+]
Glynn, Sean - *Modern Britain*
    Choice - v34 - N '96 - p507 [51-250]
    JEL - v34 - D '96 - p2095 [51-250]
Gnedenko, Boris V - *Random Summation*
    SciTech - v20 - S '96 - p3 [51-250]
Gneuss, Helmut - *English Language Scholarship*
  r ARBA - v28 - '97 - p373 [51-250]
Gnocchi, Gene - *Il Signor Leprotti E Sensibile*
    WLT - v70 - Aut '96 - p938+ [251-500]
Go for Goal (Dolphin Quids for Kids)
  c Books - v11 - Ap '97 - p24 [51-250]

Goad, Jim - *The Redneck Manifesto*
    BL - v93 - My 1 '97 - p1463+ [51-250]
    KR - v65 - Ap 1 '97 - p518 [251-500]
    PW - v244 - Ap 14 '97 - p66+ [51-250]
Goald, Robert S - *Behind the Scenes at the Local News*
    J Film & Vid - v48 - Spr '96 - p94+ [501+]
Goatley, David Emmanuel - *Were You There?*
    Bl S - v26 - Fall '96 - p103 [1-50]
Goban-Klas, Tomasz - *The Orchestration of the Media*
    JC - v46 - Aut '96 - p171+ [501+]
Gobetti, Daniela - *2001 Italian and English Idioms. 2nd Ed.*
  r Choice - v34 - O '96 - p247 [51-250]
Goble, Paul - *Remaking the Earth (Illus. by Paul Goble)*
  c BL - v93 - S 15 '96 - p235 [51-250]
  c Emerg Lib - v24 - Mr '97 - p64 [51-250]
  c HB Guide - v8 - Spr '97 - p101 [1-50]
  c SLJ - v42 - O '96 - p113 [51-250]
The Return of the Buffaloes (Illus. by Paul Goble)
  c HB Guide - v7 - Fall '96 - p320+ [51-250]
Gobry-Valle, Armande - *Le Puits D'Exil*
    FR - v70 - D '96 - p348+ [251-500]
Gocek, Fatma Muge - *Rise of the Bourgeoisie, Demise of Empire*
    AJS - v102 - S '96 - p604+ [501+]
    J Soc H - v30 - Spr '97 - p758+ [501+]
    MEJ - v51 - Spr '97 - p307+ [501+]
Godard, Barbara - *Collaboration in the Feminine*
    Can Lit - Win '96 - p173+ [501+]
Goddard, David - *Sacred Magic of the Angels*
    BWatch - v17 - S '96 - p11 [51-250]
Goddard, Hugh - *Christians and Muslims*
    Rel St Rev - v22 - O '96 - p340 [51-250]
Goddard, Jerome - *Physician's Guide to Arthropods of Medical Importance. 2nd Ed.*
  r SciTech - v20 - D '96 - p32 [51-250]
Goddard, John - *John Goddard's Trout-Fishing Techniques*
    BL - v93 - S 15 '96 - p202 [51-250]
Goddard, Peter - *Target Geography. Bks. 1-2*
  y TES - Mr 28 '97 - pR7 [251-500]
Goddard, Robert - *Out of the Sun*
    LJ - v122 - My 1 '97 - p139 [51-250]
    PW - v244 - My 5 '97 - p197 [51-250]
Goddard, Stephen, 1947- - *Feed Management in Intensive Aquaculture*
    SciTech - v20 - D '96 - p57 [51-250]
Goddard, Stephen B - *Getting There*
    JEL - v35 - Mr '97 - p268 [51-250]
Goddard, V - *The Anthropology of Europe*
    Am Ethnol - v23 - Ag '96 - p652+ [501+]
Godden, Malcolm - *From Anglo-Saxon to Early Middle English*
    MLR - v92 - Ja '97 - p165 [251-500]
    RES - v47 - N '96 - p556+ [501+]
Godden, Rumer - *Black Narcissus (Blair). Audio Version*
  y Kliatt - v30 - S '96 - p44 [51-250]
Cockcrow to Starlight (Illus. by Maggie Kneen)
  c TES - S 27 '96 - p7* [51-250]
Cockrow to Starlight (Illus. by Maggie Kneen)
  c JB - v60 - O '96 - p201 [51-250]
Kingfishers Catch Fire (Blair). Audio Version
  y Kliatt - v30 - S '96 - p44 [51-250]
The Little Chair (Illus. by Pauline Baynes)
  c JB - v60 - Ag '96 - p148 [51-250]
  c Sch Lib - v44 - Ag '96 - p102+ [51-250]
A Pocket Book of Spiritual Poems
    Obs - Ja 5 '97 - p17* [51-250]
Premlata and the Festival of Lights (Illus. by Ian Andrew)
  c Bks Keeps - Ja '97 - p23 [51-250]
  c Books - v10 - Je '96 - p25 [1-50]
  c HB - v73 - My '97 - p320+ [51-250]
  c JB - v60 - O '96 - p192 [51-250]
  c KR - v65 - Mr 1 '97 - p380 [51-250]
  c PW - v244 - Ja 27 '97 - p107 [51-250]
  c Sch Lib - v44 - N '96 - p150 [51-250]
Godel, Kurt - *Unpublished Philosophical Essays*
    SciTech - v20 - S '96 - p3 [51-250]
Godfrey, Jenny - *Visual Resources for Design*
    LAR - v98 - Mr '96 - p164 [51-250]
Godfrey, Martyn - *Do You Want Fries with That?*
  c BIC - v25 - O '96 - p31 [51-250]
Godfrey, Neale S - *A Money Adventure (Illus. by Rany Verougstraete)*
  c HB Guide - v7 - Fall '96 - p314 [51-250]
Godfrey, Sheila - *The Principles and Practice of Electrical Epilation. 2nd Ed.*
    SciTech - v21 - Mr '97 - p66 [51-250]

Godfrey, Sheldon J - *Search Out the Land*
  Beav - v76 - Ag '96 - p46 [251-500]
  Beav - v77 - F '97 - p42+ [501+]
Godin, Seth - *Point and Click Investor*
  BL - v93 - S 1 '96 - p45 [51-250]
Godlewska, Anne - *Geography and Empire*
  GJ - v162 - N '96 - p343 [51-250]
Godon, Ingrid - *I Spy--Everything!*
  c Magpies - v11 - Jl '96 - p24 [51-250]
Godoy, Luis A - *Thin-Walled Structures with Structural
Imperfections*
  SciTech - v20 - N '96 - p65 [51-250]
God's Week of Creation
  c HB Guide - v7 - Fall '96 - p308 [1-50]
Godson, Roy - *Dirty Tricks or Trump Cards*
  Soc - v34 - N '96 - p103+ [501+]
  U.S. Intelligence at the Crossroads
  NWCR - v49 - Aut '96 - p141+ [501+]
  PSQ - v111 - Fall '96 - p530+ [501+]
Godson, Susan H - *The College of William and Mary.
Vols. 1-2*
  JSH - v62 - N '96 - p856 [51-250]
Godwin, Francis - *The Man in the Moon*
  Sev Cent N - v54 - Fall '96 - p74 [501+]
  Six Ct J - v27 - Win '96 - p1127+ [501+]
  The Man in the Moone
  New Sci - v153 - Ja 18 '97 - p39 [1-50]
Godwin, Gail - *Dream Children*
  LATBR - S 15 '96 - p11 [51-250]
Godwin, Joscelyn - *Music and the Occult*
  TLS - Ja 24 '97 - p18 [501+]
Godwin, Peter - *Mukiwa: A White Boy in Africa*
  BW - v26 - Jl 7 '96 - p10+ [501+]
  Econ - v339 - My 18 '96 - p9*+ [501+]
  NY - v72 - S 23 '96 - p94+ [501+]
Godwin, Sarah - *Where's Caterpillar? (Illus. by Louise
Batchelor)*
  c HB Guide - v7 - Fall '96 - p239 [51-250]
Godwin, William - *Caleb Williams*
  VV - v42 - Ja 7 '97 - p43 [51-250]
Goehlert, Robert U - *Members of Congress*
  r ARBA - v28 - '97 - p264 [251-500]
  The United States Congress
  r RQ - v35 - Sum '96 - p486 [51-250]
Goellner, Ellen W - *Bodies of the Text*
  Dance RJ - v28 - Fall '96 - p83+ [501+]
  TDR - v40 - Win '96 - p158+ [501+]
Goennel, Heidi - *I Pretend (Illus. by Heidi Goennel)*
  c RT - v50 - D '96 - p346 [51-250]
Goepper, Roger - *Alchi: Ladakh's Hidden Buddhist
Sanctuary*
  BL - v93 - N 15 '96 - p562+ [51-250]
  Tric - v6 - Win '96 - p117 [1-50]
Goergen, Donald J - *Jesus, Son of God, Son of Mary,
Immanuel*
  Theol St - v57 - D '96 - p779 [251-500]
Goering, John - *Mortgage Lending, Racial Discrimination,
and Federal Policy*
  Choice - v34 - Ap '97 - p1389 [51-250]
Goertzel, Ted - *Linus Pauling: A Life in Science and
Politics*
  y Kliatt - v31 - Mr '97 - p26 [51-250]
Goethe, Johann Wolfgang Von - *Correspondence
between Goethe and Schiller 1794-1805*
  TranslRevS - v1 - My '95 - p22 [51-250]
  Faust: Parts 1 and 2
  TranslRevS - v2 - D '96 - p25 [51-250]
Goetschel, Willi - *Constituting Critique*
  Ger Q - v69 - Fall '96 - p427+ [501+]
Goetting, Ann - *Individual Voices, Collective Visions*
  TCR - v98 - Spr '97 - p537+ [501+]
Goetz, Hans - *To Live Is to Think*
  CPR - v16 - Ag '96 - p259+ [501+]
Goetz, Rainer - *Spanish Golden Age Autobiography in Its
Context*
  Hisp - v79 - S '96 - p444+ [501+]
Goetzfridt, Nicholas J - *Indigenous Literature of Oceania*
  Cont Pac - v9 - Spr '97 - p284+ [501+]
Goff, Brian - *Regulation and Macroeconomic Performance*
  JEL - v34 - S '96 - p1455 [51-250]
Goffar, Janine - *C.S. Lewis Index*
  r Bks & Cult - v3 - Mr '97 - p39 [251-500]
  r Ch Today - v41 - F 3 '97 - p66+ [501+]
Goffette, Guy - *Le Pecheur D'Eau*
  FR - v70 - O '96 - p142+ [251-500]
Goffstein, M B - *Goldie the Dollmaker*
  c PW - v244 - Mr 10 '97 - p69 [1-50]
Gogarty, Oliver St. John - *Tumbling in the Hay*
  LJ - v121 - N 1 '96 - p112 [1-50]

Gogerty, Clare - *Conflict in Art*
  c HB Guide - v8 - Spr '97 - p137 [51-250]
  c SLJ - v43 - F '97 - p116 [51-250]
Gogh, Vincent Van - *The Letters of Vincent Van Gogh*
  Atl - v278 - O '96 - p121+ [501+]
  BL - v92 - Ag '96 - p1873 [51-250]
  BW - v26 - O 20 '96 - p13 [51-250]
  NYTBR - v102 - Ja 19 '97 - p19 [51-250]
  Obs - D 1 '96 - p17* [1-50]
  TLS - Ag 30 '96 - p21 [501+]
  TranslRevS - v2 - D '96 - p9 [51-250]
  TranslRevS - v2 - D '96 - p9 [51-250]
Gogol, Nikolai - *Dead Souls*
  TLS - N 29 '96 - p12 [51-250]
  The Government Inspector
  Nature - v385 - Ja 23 '97 - p311 [501+]
  Plays and Petersburg Tales
  TranslRevS - v2 - D '96 - p31 [51-250]
Gogol, Sara - *A Mien Family*
  c Ch BWatch - v6 - O '96 - p5 [51-250]
  c HB Guide - v8 - Spr '97 - p90 [51-250]
  c SLJ - v43 - Ja '97 - p125 [51-250]
Goguen, Joseph A - *Algebraic Semantics of Imperative
Programs*
  SciTech - v20 - N '96 - p8 [1-50]
GoGwilt, Christopher Lloyd - *The Invention of the West*
  Clio - v25 - Sum '96 - p467+ [501+]
  VS - v39 - Spr '96 - p415+ [501+]
Goheen, Miriam - *Men Own the Fields, Women Own the
Crops*
  Choice - v34 - My '97 - p1540 [51-250]
  JEL - v34 - D '96 - p2109 [51-250]
Goin, Peter - *Humanature*
  Bloom Rev - v16 - N '96 - p28 [51-250]
  Nature - v383 - S 12 '96 - p137 [1-50]
  NH - v105 - Ag '96 - p14 [51-250]
Goings, Kenneth W - *Mammy and Uncle Mose*
  Am Q - v48 - D '96 - p746+ [501+]
  The New African American Urban History
  Bl S - v26 - Fall '96 - p103 [51-250]
  BWatch - v17 - D '96 - p5 [1-50]
Goizueta, Roberto S - *Caminemos Con Jesus*
  Theol St - v57 - S '96 - p553+ [501+]
Gokcen, N A - *Thermodynamics. 2nd Ed.*
  SciTech - v20 - N '96 - p18 [51-250]
Gokhale, Vibha Bakshi - *Walking the Tightrope*
  Choice - v34 - Ap '97 - p1342 [51-250]
  R&R Bk N - v11 - D '96 - p67 [51-250]
Golan, Jonathan S - *Foundations of Linear Algebra*
  Choice - v34 - N '96 - p496 [51-250]
Golan, Romy - *Modernity and Nostalgia*
  Art Bull - v78 - D '96 - p745+ [501+]
  BM - v138 - D '96 - p833+ [501+]
Golant, Mitch - *What to Do When Someone You Love Is
Depressed*
  PW - v244 - Ja 27 '97 - p100 [51-250]
Golany, Gideon S - *Geo-Space Urban Design*
  Choice - v34 - F '97 - p1016 [51-250]
  R&R Bk N - v11 - D '96 - p42 [51-250]
Gold, Carolyn J - *Dragonfly Secret*
  c KR - v65 - My 1 '97 - p720+ [51-250]
  c PW - v244 - Ap 21 '97 - p73 [51-250]
Gold, Herbert - *Best Nightmare on Earth*
  Bks & Cult - v3 - Ja '97 - p8+ [501+]
  She Took My Arm as if She Loved Me
  PW - v244 - My 5 '97 - p198+ [51-250]
Gold, Jerold R - *Key Concepts in Psychotherapy
Integration*
  Readings - v11 - S '96 - p30 [51-250]
Gold, Jerome - *Publishing Lives*
  Sm Pr R - v28 - Je '96 - p11 [251-500]
Gold, John R - *Imagining Scotland*
  R&R Bk N - v12 - F '97 - p28 [51-250]
Gold, Mark S - *Tobacco*
  Readings - v11 - S '96 - p24 [51-250]
Gold, Michael - *The Implications of the Evolution of
European Integration for UK Labour Markets*
  JEL - v34 - D '96 - p2077 [51-250]
Gold, Peter - *Navajo and Tibetan Sacred Wisdom*
  Parabola - v21 - N '96 - p91+ [501+]
Gold, Richard - *Running a School*
  TES - F 14 '97 - p19U [251-500]
Gold, Rozanne - *Recipes 1-2-3*
  BWatch - v17 - S '96 - p2 [51-250]
  PW - v243 - N 4 '96 - p47 [1-50]
Gold, Ruth Glasberg - *Ruth's Journey*
  y SLJ - v43 - Ag '96 - p185 [51-250]
Gold, Steven D - *The Fiscal Crisis of the States*
  Pol Stud J - v24 - Sum '96 - p321+ [501+]
Gold, Susan Dudley - *Indian Treaties*
  c BL - v93 - My 15 '97 - p1574 [51-250]

  Land Pacts
  c BL - v93 - My 15 '97 - p1574 [51-250]
Gold, Todd - *Comic Relief*
  y BL - v93 - O 1 '96 - p314 [51-250]
  Ent W - D 13 '96 - p74 [51-250]
Goldammer, Johann Georg - *Fire in Ecosystems of
Boreal Eurasia*
  SciTech - v20 - D '96 - p31 [51-250]
Gol'danskii, Vitalii I - *Essays of a Soviet Scientist*
  Sci - v276 - My 9 '97 - p910 [251-500]
Goldbarth, Albert - *Adventures in Ancient Egypt*
  LJ - v121 - D '96 - p98 [51-250]
  PW - v243 - N 25 '96 - p71 [51-250]
  *A Lineage of Ragpickers, Songpluckers, Elegiasts and
Jewelers*
  ABR - v18 - D '96 - p17+ [501+]
  Sm Pr R - v28 - Jl '96 - p12 [251-500]
Goldberg, Carl - *Speaking with the Devil*
  Rapport - v19 - 6 '96 - p30 [251-500]
Goldberg, Ellis Jay - *The Social History of Labor in the
Middle East*
  MEJ - v50 - Sum '96 - p453+ [51-250]
  WorldV - v12 - Jl '96 - p10 [51-250]
Goldberg, Hank M - *The Prosecution Responds*
  ABA Jour - v82 - D '96 - p92+ [501+]
  Esq - v126 - N '96 - p65 [1-50]
Goldberg, Harvey E - *Sephardi and Middle Eastern
Jewries*
  MEJ - v50 - Sum '96 - p456 [51-250]
  Rel St Rev - v23 - Ap '97 - p197 [51-250]
Goldberg, J J - *Jewish Power*
  BL - v93 - N 15 '96 - p553 [51-250]
  BW - v26 - D 29 '96 - p4+ [501+]
  Comw - v124 - Ja 17 '97 - p21+ [501+]
  KR - v64 - O 1 '96 - p1442+ [251-500]
  LATBR - D 1 '96 - p6+ [501+]
  LJ - v121 - D '96 - p116 [51-250]
  NYTBR - v102 - F 9 '97 - p25 [501+]
  PW - v243 - S 30 '96 - p69 [51-250]
Goldberg, Jake - *Albert Einstein*
  y BL - v93 - S 1 '96 - p71 [51-250]
  y HB Guide - v8 - Spr '97 - p157 [51-250]
  y SLJ - v42 - D '96 - p146 [51-250]
  The Disappearing American Farm
  y HB Guide - v7 - Fall '96 - p314 [1-50]
  y VOYA - v19 - O '96 - p230 [251-500]
Goldberg, Jan - *Real People Working in Communications*
  yr Kliatt - v31 - Mr '97 - p27+ [51-250]
Goldberg, Jim, 1953- - *Hospice: A Photographic Inquiry*
  LATBR - D 8 '96 - p9 [501+]
  Raised by Wolves
  Afterimage - v23 - Sum '96 - p12+ [501+]
Goldberg, Joel S - *USMLE Step 1 Review*
  SciTech - v20 - S '96 - p26 [51-250]
Goldberg, Lee - *Beyond the Beyond*
  KR - v65 - Ja 15 '97 - p80+ [251-500]
  LATBR - Ap 20 '97 - p13 [501+]
  PW - v244 - F 24 '97 - p65 [51-250]
Goldberg, Leonard S - *Deadly Care*
  BWatch - v17 - S '96 - p1 [51-250]
  Deadly Harvest
  BL - v93 - Mr 15 '97 - p1224+ [51-250]
  KR - v65 - Mr 15 '97 - p400 [251-500]
  LJ - v122 - Mr 15 '97 - p90 [51-250]
  PW - v244 - Ap 7 '97 - p75 [51-250]
Goldberg, Marshall - *A Deadly Operation*
  LJ - v121 - O 15 '96 - p94 [1-50]
  Intelligence
  LJ - v121 - O 15 '96 - p94 [1-50]
Goldberg, Michael - *Getting Your Boss's Number and
Many Other Ways to Use the Ennea Program at Work*
  PW - v243 - S 16 '96 - p66 [51-250]
  Why Should Jews Survive?
  MEJ - v51 - Win '97 - p155 [51-250]
Goldberg, Robert Alan - *Barry Goldwater*
  AAPSS-A - v548 - N '96 - p228+ [251-500]
  AHR - v102 - F '97 - p216+ [251-500]
  Historian - v59 - Win '97 - p427+ [501+]
  J Am St - v30 - Ag '96 - p300+ [251-500]
  SSQ - v77 - D '96 - p944+ [501+]
  WHQ - v27 - Win '96 - p534+ [501+]
Goldberg, Stanley A - *Clinical Skills for Speech-Language
Pathologists*
  SciTech - v21 - Mr '97 - p52 [51-250]
Goldberg, Steven - *Culture Clash*
  SSQ - v78 - Mr '97 - p239+ [501+]
  Why Men Rule
  Socio R - v44 - N '96 - p746+ [501+]

Goldberger, Marvin L - *Research-Doctorate Programs in the United States*
  r Choice - v34 - S '96 - p103 [251-500]
  r CS - v25 - N '96 - p729+ [501+]

Goldberger, Nancy Rule - *Knowledge, Difference, and Power*
    BWatch - v18 - F '97 - p9 [51-250]
    PW - v243 - N 18 '96 - p55 [51-250]

Goldberger, Paul - *Richard Meier Houses*
    TLS - Ja 31 '97 - p16 [501+]

Goldbeter, Albert - *Biochemical Oscillations and Cellular Rhythms*
    Nature - v386 - Ap 3 '97 - p454 [1-50]

Gold-Biss, Michael - *The Discourse on Terrorism*
    QJS - v82 - Ag '96 - p315+ [501+]

Goldblatt, David - *Social Theory and the Environment*
    TLS - F 21 '97 - p10+ [501+]

Goldblatt, Howard - *Chairman Mao Would Not Be Amused*
    Ch Rev Int - v4 - Spr '97 - p138+ [501+]
    LATBR - Mr 24 '96 - p11 [51-250]

Goldblatt, Peter - *Gladiolus in Tropical Africa*
    R&R Bk N - v11 - N '96 - p77 [51-250]

Golden, Christopher - *Daredevil: Predator's Smile*
    MFSF - v91 - D '96 - p91+ [501+]

Golden, Eve - *Vamp: The Rise and Fall of Theda Bara*
    FIR - v47 - Jl '96 - p117+ [501+]

Golden, Marita - *Saving Our Sons*
    HER - v66 - Win '96 - p879+ [501+]
  Skin Deep
  y Kliatt - v31 - Ja '97 - p24 [51-250]
    TLS - N 29 '96 - p14 [1-50]

Golden, Susan L - *Secrets of Successful Grantsmanship*
    BL - v93 - F 1 '97 - p914 [51-250]

Golden, William T - *Impacts of the Early Cold War on the Formulation of U.S. Science Policy*
    Isis - v87 - D '96 - p755 [501+]

The Golden Age of Dutch Manuscript Painting
    AB - v99 - Mr 3 '97 - p685+ [501+]

Goldenstern, Joyce - *Lost Cities*
  c HB Guide - v7 - Fall '96 - p378 [51-250]
  c SB - v32 - Ag '96 - p182 [51-250]

Goldfarb, Clifford S - *The Great Shadow*
    Quill & Q - v62 - O '96 - p38 [251-500]

Goldfrank, David M - *The Origins of the Crimean War*
    EHR - v111 - S '96 - p1004 [51-250]

Goldgar, Anne - *Impolite Learning*
    HT - v46 - D '96 - p52+ [501+]
    JHI - v57 - O '96 - p725+ [501+]
    JIH - v27 - Win '97 - p532+ [501+]

Goldhagen, Daniel Jonah - *Hitler's Willing Executioners*
    Ant R - v54 - Sum '96 - p359+ [251-500]
    APSR - v91 - Mr '97 - p212+ [501+]
    BIC - v25 - S '96 - p31+ [501+]
    Books - v11 - Ap '97 - p21 [1-50]
    CC - v113 - O 16 '96 - p974+ [501+]
    CR - v268 - Je '96 - p335 [51-250]
    For Aff - v75 - N '96 - p128+ [501+]
    JMH - v69 - Mr '97 - p187+ [501+]
    LATBR - Mr 24 '96 - p4 [501+]
    LATBR - D 29 '96 - p3 [51-250]
    LJ - v122 - Ja '97 - p49 [51-250]
    Lon R Bks - v19 - Ja 23 '97 - p20+ [501+]
    Mac - v109 - Je 3 '96 - p58+ [501+]
    Meanjin - v55 - 3 '96 - p518+ [501+]
    MQR - v36 - Spr '97 - p361+ [501+]
    NYRB - v43 - N 28 '96 - p18+ [501+]
    NYTBR - v101 - D 8 '96 - p88 [1-50]
    NYTBR - v102 - F 16 '97 - p32 [51-250]
    Obs - D 1 '96 - p16* [51-250]
    Obs - F 23 '97 - p18* [51-250]
    PW - v244 - Ja 13 '97 - p73 [1-50]
    Spec - v277 - N 30 '96 - p58 [51-250]
    Tikkun - v11 - Jl '96 - p62+ [501+]
    Time - v148 - D 23 '96 - p86 [51-250]
    TLS - Jl 7 '96 - p9+ [501+]
    TLS - N 29 '96 - p14 [51-250]
    Trib Bks - Mr 16 '97 - p8 [1-50]
    VQR - v72 - Aut '96 - p738+ [501+]
    VV - v42 - Ja 7 '97 - p42 [251-500]

Goldhill, Simon - *Foucault's Virginity*
    Rel St Rev - v23 - Ja '97 - p64 [51-250]

Goldin, Barbara Diamond - *Bat Mitzvah*
  c BL - v93 - O 1 '96 - p338 [1-50]

Coyote and the Fire Stick (Illus. by Will Hillenbrand)
  c BL - v93 - O 1 '96 - p345 [51-250]
  c CBRS - v25 - N '96 - p31 [51-250]
  c Emerg Lib - v24 - Mr '97 - p64 [51-250]
  c HB - v72 - N '96 - p748 [51-250]
  c HB Guide - v8 - Spr '97 - p101 [51-250]
  c PW - v243 - O 21 '96 - p83 [51-250]
  c SLJ - v42 - O '96 - p113+ [51-250]
The Girl Who Lived with the Bears (Illus. by Andrew Plewes)
  c PW - v244 - Ap 7 '97 - p91+ [51-250]
The Passover Journey (Illus. by Neil Waldman)
  c PW - v244 - F 24 '97 - p84 [1-50]
While the Candles Burn (Illus. by Elaine Greenstein)
  c BL - v93 - S 15 '96 - p238 [51-250]
  c CCB-B - v50 - N '96 - p96+ [51-250]
  c HB Guide - v8 - Spr '97 - p67 [51-250]
  c KR - v64 - O 1 '96 - p1466 [51-250]
  c NYTBR - v101 - D 8 '96 - p78 [1-50]
  c PW - v243 - S 30 '96 - p87 [51-250]
  c SLJ - v42 - O '96 - p36 [51-250]

Goldin, Ian - *The Economics of Sustainable Development*
    Econ J - v106 - N '96 - p1806+ [501+]
    JEL - v34 - D '96 - p1991+ [501+]

Goldin, Nan - *I'll Be Your Mirror*
    LJ - v121 - N 15 '96 - p58 [51-250]

Goldin, Owen - *Explaining an Eclipse*
    Choice - v34 - S '96 - p626 [51-250]

Golding, Alan - *From Outlaw to Classic*
    AL - v68 - S '96 - p652+ [251-500]

Golding, Brian - *Conquest and Colonisation*
    EHR - v112 - Ap '97 - p429+ [501+]
    Specu - v72 - Ja '97 - p154+ [501+]

Golding, John - *Braque: The Late Works*
    NYRB - v44 - Mr 27 '97 - p31+ [501+]
    Obs - Mr 2 '97 - p18* [51-250]
    TLS - F 14 '97 - p18+ [501+]
  Visions of the Modern
    TES - Ag 30 '96 - p26 [51-250]

Golding, Peter - *Black Jack McEwen: Political Gladiator*
    Aust Bk R - F '97 - p13+ [501+]

Golding, William - *The Double Tongue*
    Obs - Ag 18 '96 - p19* [51-250]
    WLT - v70 - Sum '96 - p691+ [501+]

Goldingay, John - *Models for Interpretation of Scripture*
    Bks & Cult - v2 - Mr '96 - p31 [251-500]
    TT - v53 - Ja '97 - p544+ [501+]
  Models for Scripture
    Intpr - v50 - O '96 - p434+ [51-250]
    Theol St - v57 - Mr '96 - p141+ [501+]

Goldman, Alan - *Doing Business with the Japanese*
    Pac A - v69 - Fall '96 - p416+ [501+]
    TLS - O 25 '96 - p13 [251-500]

Goldman, Alan H, 1945- - *Aesthetic Value*
    CPR - v16 - Ap '96 - p106+ [501+]

Goldman, Anne - *Take My Word*
    Biography - v19 - Fall '96 - p429 [1-50]

Goldman, E M - *Getting Lincoln's Goat*
  y Emerg Lib - v24 - S '96 - p24 [1-50]
  Money to Burn
  y Kliatt - v30 - S '96 - p10 [51-250]
  The Night Room
  y Emerg Lib - v24 - S '96 - p27 [1-50]
  Shrinking Pains
  c HB Guide - v8 - Spr '97 - p67 [51-250]
  c KR - v64 - O 1 '96 - p1466 [51-250]
  c SLJ - v42 - S '96 - p202 [51-250]

Goldman, Elizabeth - *Believers: Spiritual Leaders of the World*
  y BL - v93 - O 1 '96 - p338 [1-50]
  y HB Guide - v7 - Fall '96 - p309 [51-250]
  yr SLJ - v42 - N '96 - p137 [51-250]

Goldman, Emma - *Red Emma Speaks*
    Bloom Rev - v16 - N '96 - p18 [51-250]

Goldman, Francisco - *The Long Night of White Chickens*
    SFR - v21 - Jl '96 - p48 [1-50]
  The Ordinary Seaman
    BL - v93 - Ja '97 - p817 [51-250]
    KR - v64 - D 1 '96 - p1690 [251-500]
    LATBR - F 16 '97 - p9 [501+]
    LJ - v122 - Ja '97 - p146 [51-250]
    NY - v73 - Mr 31 '97 - p104+ [251-500]
    NYTBR - v102 - Mr 16 '97 - p17 [501+]
    Obs - Mr 9 '97 - p18* [501+]
    PW - v243 - N 25 '96 - p55 [251-500]
    Trib Bks - F 23 '97 - p7 [501+]
    VV - v42 - Mr 4 '97 - p53 [501+]

Goldman, Glenn - *Architectural Graphics*
    R&R Bk N - v12 - F '97 - p73 [51-250]

Goldman, Harvey - *Politics, Death, and the Devil*
    Ger Q - v69 - Fall '96 - p448+ [501+]

Goldman, Jane - *The X-Files Book of the Unexplained. Vol. 2*
    Obs - D 15 '96 - p16* [501+]

Goldman, Kevin - *Conflicting Accounts*
    BL - v93 - D 1 '96 - p627 [51-250]
    Bus W - F 3 '97 - p15 [51-250]
    BW - v27 - Ja 5 '97 - p6 [251-500]
    Econ - v342 - Mr 15 '97 - p13* [501+]
    Fortune - v135 - Ja 13 '97 - p139 [501+]
    KR - v64 - N 1 '96 - p1580 [251-500]
    LJ - v122 - Ja '97 - p114+ [51-250]
    NYTBR - v102 - F 23 '97 - p17 [51-250]
    PW - v243 - N 4 '96 - p55 [51-250]

Goldman, Lawrence - *Dons and Workers*
    Choice - v34 - O '96 - p332+ [51-250]

Goldman, Martin S - *Crazy Horse: War Chief of the Oglala Sioux*
  y HB Guide - v7 - Fall '96 - p372 [51-250]
  y SLJ - v42 - S '96 - p232+ [51-250]

Goldman, Merle - *Sowing the Seeds of Democracy in China*
    Ch Rev Int - v4 - Spr '97 - p141+ [501+]

Goldman, Nikkie - *Teenage Suicide*
  y BL - v92 - Ag '96 - p1892 [51-250]
  y HB Guide - v7 - Fall '96 - p316 [51-250]
  y SLJ - v42 - Ag '96 - p168+ [51-250]

Goldman, Paul - *Victorian Illustration*
    BC - v46 - Spr '97 - p152+ [501+]
    Choice - v34 - F '97 - p955 [51-250]
    Nine-C Lit - v51 - Mr '97 - p557 [1-50]

Goldman, Robert - *Sign Wars*
    JEL - v34 - D '96 - p2093 [51-250]

Goldman, Shalom - *The Wiles of Women/The Wiles of Men*
    MEJ - v51 - Spr '97 - p301+ [501+]

Goldman, Shifra M - *Dimension of the Americas*
    Bloom Rev - v16 - S '96 - p31 [501+]

Goldman, William - *Absolute Power*
    BL - v93 - F 15 '97 - p991+ [51-250]
  Five Screenplays
    BL - v93 - F 15 '97 - p991+ [51-250]
  The Ghost and the Darkness
    BL - v93 - F 15 '97 - p991+ [51-250]

Goldman Family - *His Name Is Ron*
    CSM - v89 - Mr 6 '97 - p14 [51-250]

Goldreich, Gloria - *Ten Traditional Jewish Children's Stories (Illus. by Jeffrey Allon)*
  c HB Guide - v8 - Spr '97 - p102 [51-250]

Goldscheider, Calvin - *Israel's Changing Society*
    AJS - v102 - Ja '97 - p1185+ [501+]
    Choice - v34 - S '96 - p190 [51-250]
    For Aff - v75 - S '96 - p154+ [51-250]

Goldscheider, Ludwig - *Paintings, Sculpture, Architecture*
    LJ - v121 - N 1 '96 - p112 [1-50]

Goldschmidt, Arthur, Jr. - *A Concise History of the Middle East. 5th Ed.*
    MEJ - v50 - Aut '96 - p629 [51-250]

Goldschmidt, Tijs - *Darwin's Dreampond*
    LJ - v121 - O 1 '96 - p118+ [51-250]
    Nature - v383 - O 17 '96 - p590+ [501+]
    New Sci - v152 - O 12 '96 - p42+ [501+]
    NY - v73 - Ap 28 '97 - p227 [51-250]
    NYTBR - v101 - D 1 '96 - p18+ [501+]
    PW - v243 - S 16 '96 - p64 [51-250]

Goldsmith, Donald - *The Astronomers*
    S&T - v92 - S '96 - p54 [51-250]
  Einstein's Greatest Blunder?
    South HR - v31 - Win '97 - p87+ [501+]
  The Hunt for Life on Mars
  y BL - v93 - F 1 '97 - p915 [51-250]
    KR - v64 - D 15 '96 - p1782 [251-500]
    PW - v244 - Ja 13 '97 - p66 [51-250]

Goldsmith, Evelyn - *My First Oxford Dictionary*
  cr Bks Keeps - v100 - S '96 - p22+ [501+]

Goldsmith, Marlene Herbert - *Political Incorrectness*
    Aust Bk R - Jl '96 - p30+ [501+]

Goldsmith, Oliver - *The Citizen of the World*
    CLS - v33 - 1 '96 - p15+ [501+]
  The Vicar of Wakefield (Tull). Audio Version
  y Kliatt - v30 - S '96 - p54 [51-250]

Goldsmith, Olivia - *Bestseller*
    LATBR - S 22 '96 - p6 [501+]
  The First Wives Club
    Ent W - N 8 '96 - p59+ [51-250]
  Marrying Mom
    BL - v93 - O 1 '96 - p291 [51-250]
    Ent W - N 29 '96 - p108 [51-250]
    KR - v64 - O 1 '96 - p1420 [251-500]
    PW - v243 - O 7 '96 - p61 [51-250]
  Marrying Mom (Goldsmith). Audio Version
    PW - v244 - F 3 '97 - p42 [51-250]

Goldstein, Alice - *China: The Many Facets of Demographic Change*
R&R Bk N - v11 - D '96 - p23 [51-250]
Goldstein, Arnold P - *The Psychology of Vandalism*
Readings - v11 - D '96 - p27 [51-250]
Violence in America
BL - v93 - S 15 '96 - p186 [251-500]
Goldstein, Carl - *Teaching Art*
Choice - v34 - S '96 - p112 [51-250]
TLS - Mr 21 '97 - p20+ [501+]
Goldstein, Catherine - *Un Theoreme De Fermat Et Ses Lecteurs*
Isis - v88 - Mr '97 - p144+ [501+]
Goldstein, Darra - *The Vegetarian Hearth*
BL - v93 - D 15 '96 - p701 [51-250]
BWatch - v18 - F '97 - p7 [51-250]
LJ - v122 - F 15 '97 - p158 [51-250]
PW - v243 - N 4 '96 - p72+ [51-250]
Goldstein, Douglas - *The Online Guide to Healthcare Management and Medicine*
SciTech - v20 - D '96 - p38 [51-250]
Goldstein, Ernest - *The Journey of Diego Rivera*
y HB Guide - v7 - Fall '96 - p355 [51-250]
y VOYA - v19 - O '96 - p230 [251-500]
Goldstein, Jay A - *Betrayal by the Brain*
SB - v33 - My '97 - p104 [51-250]
SciTech - v20 - D '96 - p41 [51-250]
Goldstein, Joseph - *The Best Interests of the Child*
LJ - v121 - N 1 '96 - p91 [51-250]
PW - v243 - O 7 '96 - p58 [51-250]
Goldstein, Joyce - *Kitchen Conversations*
BL - v93 - D 15 '96 - p701 [51-250]
LJ - v122 - F 15 '97 - p158 [51-250]
PW - v243 - N 18 '96 - p71 [51-250]
Taverna
CSM - v89 - D 13 '96 - p11 [1-50]
Goldstein, Kurt - *The Organism: A Holistic Approach to Biology Derived from Pathological Data in Man*
Isis - v87 - S '96 - p578+ [501+]
Goldstein, Larry J - *Brief Calculus and Its Applications. 7th Ed.*
SciTech - v20 - S '96 - p10 [51-250]
Goldstein, Lisa - *Walking the Labyrinth*
BWatch - v17 - N '96 - p8 [1-50]
MFSF - v91 - Ag '96 - p33+ [51-250]
MFSF - v91 - S '96 - p34+ [251-500]
Goldstein, Melvyn C - *The Struggle for Modern Tibet*
LJ - v122 - Mr 15 '97 - p76 [51-250]
PW - v244 - F 3 '97 - p91 [51-250]
Goldstein, Norm - *The Associated Press Stylebook and Libel Manual. 6th Ed.*
r BL - v93 - My 1 '97 - p1514 [1-50]
Goldstein, Rebecca - *Mazel*
y Kliatt - v30 - N '96 - p8 [51-250]
LATBR - S 22 '96 - p15 [51-250]
NYTBR - v101 - S 1 '96 - p24 [1-50]
PW - v243 - Jl 22 '96 - p234 [1-50]
Goldstein, Richard - *Ivy League Autumns*
VQR - v73 - Win '97 - p7* [51-250]
Mine Eyes Have Seen
KR - v65 - My 1 '97 - p693 [251-500]
Goldstein, Robert Justin - *Burning the Flag*
BW - v26 - Ag 25 '96 - p13 [51-250]
Choice - v34 - D '96 - p690 [51-250]
HRNB - v25 - Win '97 - p52 [251-500]
Lon R Bks - v19 - Mr 6 '97 - p22+ [501+]
R&R Bk N - v11 - N '96 - p9 [51-250]
Desecrating the American Flag
Choice - v34 - My '97 - p1576 [51-250]
Saving Old Glory
J Am Cult - v18 - Win '95 - p98+ [51-250]
Goldstein, Ronald E - *Change Your Smile. 3rd Ed.*
SciTech - v21 - Mr '97 - p66 [51-250]
Goldstein, Sam - *Understanding and Managing Children's Classroom Behavior*
Readings - v11 - S '96 - p23 [51-250]
Goldstein, Sanford M - *Adverse Cutaneous Reactions to Medication*
r SciTech - v20 - S '96 - p42 [51-250]
Goldstein, Sidney - *Jews on the Move*
CS - v26 - Ja '97 - p69+ [501+]
R&R Bk N - v12 - F '97 - p23 [51-250]
Goldstone, Lawrence - *Used and Rare*
KR - v65 - Mr 15 '97 - p436+ [251-500]
LJ - v122 - My 1 '97 - p104 [51-250]
PW - v244 - Mr 31 '97 - p54 [51-250]
Goldstone, Nancy - *Mommy and the Money*
BL - v93 - F 1 '97 - p928 [51-250]
KR - v65 - Ja 1 '97 - p22+ [251-500]
PW - v243 - D 16 '96 - p46 [51-250]

Goldsworthy, Andy - *Wood*
NYTBR - v102 - Ja 5 '97 - p19 [251-500]
Goldsworthy, Kerryn - *Australian Love Stories*
Aust Bk R - D '96 - p42+ [501+]
Helen Garner
Aust Bk R - D '96 - p8+ [501+]
Goldsworthy, Peter - *If, Then*
Aust Bk R - N '96 - p50+ [501+]
Keep It Simple, Stupid
Aust Bk R - N '96 - p50+ [501+]
Goldthwaite, John - *The Natural History of Make-Believe*
NS & S - v9 - My 24 '96 - p37+ [251-500]
c NY - v72 - N 18 '96 - p99 [251-500]
TES - Jl 5 '96 - p7* [501+]
TES - D 27 '96 - p16 [1-50]
Gole, Nilufer - *The Forbidden Modern*
Choice - v34 - My '97 - p1540+ [51-250]
Goleman, Daniel - *Emotional Intelligence*
EL - v54 - S '96 - p10 [251-500]
Fam in Soc - v78 - Ja '97 - p104+ [501+]
Per Psy - v49 - Aut '96 - p711+ [501+]
Golembiewski, Robert T - *Global Burnout*
JEL - v35 - Mr '97 - p237 [51-250]
Golenbock, Peter - *Cowboys Have Always Been My Heroes*
y BL - v93 - My 15 '97 - p1538 [51-250]
Teammates (Illus. by Paul Bacon)
c Trib Bks - Mr 30 '97 - p4 [51-250]
Wrigleyville: A Magical History Tour of the Chicago Cubs
Econ - v340 - S 14 '96 - p4*+ [501+]
NYTBR - v101 - Ap 7 '96 - p16 [251-500]
Golf Digest
p LJ - v121 - O 1 '96 - p52 [1-50]
Golf Magazine
p LJ - v121 - O 1 '96 - p52 [1-50]
Golinelli, Paolo - *I Poteri Dei Canossa Da Reggio Emilia All'Europa*
Specu - v72 - Ja '97 - p155+ [501+]
Gollaher, David L - *Voice for the Mad*
Historian - v58 - Sum '96 - p842 [51-250]
RAH - v24 - D '96 - p618+ [501+]
Gollattascheck, James F - *Europe the European Way*
LJ - v121 - N 1 '96 - p98 [51-250]
Golley, John - *Genesis of the Jet*
New Sci - v152 - O 5 '96 - p47 [1-50]
Gollub, Matthew - *The Twenty-Five Mixtec Cats (Illus. by L Martinez)*
c SS - v88 - Ja '97 - p29+ [501+]
Uncle Snake (Illus. by Leovigildo Martinez)
c BL - v93 - O 1 '96 - p355 [51-250]
c CCB-B - v50 - O '96 - p59+ [51-250]
c HB Guide - v8 - Spr '97 - p29 [51-250]
c SLJ - v42 - O '96 - p114 [51-250]
Gollwitzer, Peter M - *The Psychology of Action*
SciTech - v20 - D '96 - p1 [51-250]
Golomb, Solomon W - *Polyominoes: Puzzles, Patterns, Problems, and Packings*
Math T - v90 - Ja '97 - p72 [51-250]
Golopentia, Sanda - *Cartea Plecarii*
WLT - v70 - Aut '96 - p943 [501+]
Golsan, Richard J - *Memory, the Holocaust, and French Justice*
NYRB - v43 - O 3 '96 - p36+ [501+]
Golston, Sydele E - *Changing Woman of the Apache*
y HB Guide - v7 - Fall '96 - p390 [51-250]
y KR - v64 - My 1 '96 - p689 [51-250]
y SLJ - v42 - N '96 - p128 [51-250]
y VOYA - v19 - D '96 - p287 [51-250]
Golub, Gene H - *Matrix Computations. 3rd Ed.*
SciTech - v21 - Mr '97 - p13 [51-250]
Golub, Spencer - *The Recurrence of Fate*
Theat J - v48 - O '96 - p395+ [501+]
Gom, Leona - *After-Image: A Vicky Bauer Mystery*
Arm Det - v30 - Win '97 - p115 [251-500]
KR - v64 - Ag 15 '96 - p1189 [51-250]
Gombar, Christina - *Black Explorers*
y HB Guide - v8 - Spr '97 - p161 [51-250]
Gombrich, E H - *The Essential Gombrich*
BW - v26 - Ag 4 '96 - p12 [51-250]
Choice - v34 - D '96 - p602 [51-250]
NYTBR - v101 - N 24 '96 - p15+ [501+]
NYTBR - v101 - D 8 '96 - p87 [1-50]
Shadows: The Depiction of Cast Shadows in Western Art
Art J - v56 - Spr '97 - p103 [501+]
The Story of Art. 16th Ed.
R&R Bk N - v12 - F '97 - p71 [51-250]
TES - Ag 30 '96 - p26 [51-250]
Gombrowicz, Witold - *Trans-Atlantyk*
TLS - O 4 '96 - p38 [501+]

Gomes, Peter J - *The Good Book*
y BL - v93 - O 1 '96 - p296+ [51-250]
BW - v27 - Mr 23 '97 - p7 [501+]
Ch Today - v41 - Ap 7 '97 - p42+ [501+]
CSM - v89 - Ja 23 '97 - p12 [51-250]
Econ - v342 - Ja 18 '97 - p82 [251-500]
LATBR - Ja 5 '97 - p8 [501+]
LJ - v121 - D '96 - p99+ [51-250]
LJ - v122 - Ja '97 - p49 [1-50]
PW - v243 - S 16 '96 - p66+ [51-250]
Time - v149 - Ja 27 '97 - p77 [51-250]
Gomes-Casseres, Benjamin - *The Alliance Revolution*
Choice - v34 - D '96 - p654 [51-250]
JEL - v34 - D '96 - p2081+ [51-250]
Gomez, Alejandro - *Romulo Betancourt Y El Partido Comunista De Costa Rica*
BL - v93 - S 15 '96 - p227 [1-50]
Gomez, Arthur R - *Quest for the Golden Circle*
PHR - v65 - N '96 - p694+ [251-500]
Gomez, Cesar - *Quantum Groups in Two-Dimensional Physics*
SciTech - v20 - D '96 - p22 [51-250]
Gomez De Avellaneda Y Arteaga, Gertrudis - *Sab. Autobiography*
TranslRevS - v1 - My '95 - p28+ [51-250]
Gomez Lara, Ruben L - *Intertextualidad Generative En El Beso De La Mujer Arana, De Manuel Puig*
BL - v93 - Mr 15 '97 - p1232 [1-50]
Gomez-Lobo, Alfonso - *The Foundations of Socratic Ethics*
Phil R - v105 - Ap '96 - p233+ [501+]
Gomez-Martinez, Jose Luis - *Pensamiento De La Liberacion*
Hisp - v79 - D '96 - p805+ [501+]
Gomez-Pena, Guillermo - *The New World Border*
Nat - v263 - O 28 '96 - p54+ [501+]
Gomez Perez, Maria Del Carmen - *El Sistema Defensivo Americano*
HAHR - v76 - N '96 - p770+ [501+]
Gomez-Quinones, Juan - *Mexican American Labor 1790-1990*
r PHR - v65 - Ag '96 - p477+ [501+]
Gomez Zepeda, Ignacio - *Historia De Las Unidades De Riego*
HAHR - v76 - N '96 - p799 [251-500]
Gomi, Taro - *Santa through the Window*
c Emerg Lib - v23 - My '96 - p54+ [51-250]
Gomori, George - *My Manifold City*
WLT - v71 - Win '97 - p193 [251-500]
Gompert, David C - *America and Europe*
For Aff - v76 - My '97 - p131+ [51-250]
Goncharoff, Nicko - *Hong Kong*
r FEER - v160 - Mr 27 '97 - p51 [501+]
Goncharov, Sergei - *Uncertain Partners*
EHR - v112 - Ap '97 - p542+ [501+]
Gonen, Amiram - *Between City and Suburb*
R&R Bk N - v11 - D '96 - p31 [51-250]
Gong, Alfred - *Israels Letzter Psalm*
WLT - v70 - Sum '96 - p685+ [501+]
Gong, Gerrit W - *Remembering and Forgetting*
For Aff - v75 - N '96 - p167+ [51-250]
Gonick, Larry - *The Cartoon Guide to Genetics. Updated Ed.*
NGSQ - v84 - Je '96 - p152 [51-250]
The Cartoon Guide to the Environment
New Sci - v153 - Ja 4 '97 - p37 [1-50]
y SLJ - v42 - S '96 - p240 [51-250]
Gonnet, Dominique - *La Liberte Religieuse A Vatican II*
Theol St - v57 - Je '96 - p359+ [501+]
Gonzales, Doreen - *AIDS: Ten Stories of Courage*
c HB Guide - v7 - Fall '96 - p376 [1-50]
Cesar Chavez: Leader for Migrant Farm Workers
y BL - v93 - O 1 '96 - p328 [51-250]
y HB Guide - v7 - Fall '96 - p372 [51-250]
y VOYA - v19 - F '97 - p346 [51-250]
Diego Rivera: His Art, His Life
y BL - v93 - N 1 '96 - p485 [51-250]
y HB Guide - v8 - Spr '97 - p137 [51-250]
y SLJ - v42 - O '96 - p154 [51-250]
Gonzales, Ray - *The Heat of Arrivals*
PW - v243 - S 30 '96 - p83 [51-250]
Gonzalez, Alexander G - *Assessing the Achievement of J.M. Synge*
Choice - v34 - My '97 - p1493 [51-250]
ILS - v16 - Spr '97 - p35 [1-50]
Gonzalez, Fernan E - *Violencia En La Region Andina*
HAHR - v76 - Ag '96 - p588+ [251-500]
Gonzalez, Gilbert G - *Labor and Community*
AHR - v102 - F '97 - p237 [251-500]
HAHR - v77 - My '97 - p289+ [251-500]

Gonzalez, Jovita - *Caballero*
  KR - v64 - My 1 '96 - p639 [51-250]
Gonzalez, Lola - *Guardate De Los Idus*
  y JAAL - v40 - S '96 - p77+ [51-250]
Gonzalez, Lucia M - *The Bossy Gallito (Illus. by Lulu Delacre)*
  c SS - v88 - Ja '97 - p29+ [501+]
  Senor Cat's Romance and Other Favorite Stories from Latin America (Illus. by Lulu Delacre)
  c BL - v93 - F 1 '97 - p943 [51-250]
  c CBRS - v25 - Mr '97 - p86 [51-250]
  c CCB-B - v50 - Ap '97 - p283 [51-250]
  c HB - v73 - Mr '97 - p207 [51-250]
  c PW - v244 - Ja 6 '97 - p73 [51-250]
  c SLJ - v43 - F '97 - p91 [51-250]
Gonzalez, Philip - *The Blessing of the Animals*
  Dog Fan - v28 - Ja '97 - p37 [51-250]
  PW - v243 - S 23 '96 - p70 [51-250]
Gonzalez, Ray - *Inheritance of Light*
  WAL - v31 - Fall '96 - p284 [251-500]
  Muy Macho
  BW - v26 - S 15 '96 - p12 [51-250]
  SFR - v21 - S '96 - p34+ [501+]
Gonzalez Echevarria, Roberto - *The Cambridge History of Latin American Literature. Vols. 1-3*
  r Choice - v34 - My '97 - p1504 [51-250]
  r LJ - v122 - Ap 15 '97 - p37 [51-250]
Gonzalez Mandri, Flora - *Jose Donoso's House of Fiction*
  Hisp - v79 - D '96 - p806 [501+]
Gonzalez Vasquez, Fernando - *Colan En Cariay*
  BL - v93 - S 15 '96 - p227 [1-50]
Gonzalez-Vega, Laureano - *Algorithms in Algebraic Geometry and Applications*
  SciTech - v20 - D '96 - p19 [51-250]
Gooch, Brad - *City Poet*
  South CR - v28 - Spr '96 - p288+ [501+]
  The Golden Age of Promiscuity
  Advocate - Je 11 '96 - p57+ [251-500]
Gooch, Paul W - *Reflections on Jesus and Socrates*
  LJ - v122 - Mr 15 '97 - p66+ [51-250]
Good, Jeffrey - *Poison Mind*
  PW - v243 - O 21 '96 - p78 [1-50]
Good, Mary-Jo Delvecchio - *American Medicine*
  CS - v26 - Mr '97 - p250+ [501+]
Good, Merle - *20 Most Asked Questions about the Amish and Mennonites*
  CAY - v17 - Fall '96 - p4 [51-250]
Good, Phyllis Pellman - *Recipes from Central Market*
  PW - v243 - D 2 '96 - p57 [51-250]
Good, Timothy - *Beyond Top Secret*
  Books - v10 - Je '96 - p21 [51-250]
The Good Hotel Guide: France 1997
  r Books - v11 - Ap '97 - p20 [51-250]
Good Housekeeping Cook's Year
  Books - v9 - S '95 - p23 [51-250]
Good Reading. 23rd Ed.
  RQ - v36 - Win '96 - p215 [51-250]
The Good Skiing Guide 1997
  r ARBA - v28 - '97 - p301 [251-500]
Goodale, Jane C - *To Sing with Pigs Is Human*
  Am Ethnol - v23 - N '96 - p918+ [501+]
  CS - v25 - N '96 - p808+ [501+]
  The Two-Party Line
  Choice - v34 - Ap '97 - p1380 [51-250]
Goodall, Dominic - *Hindu Scriptures*
  TranslRevS - v2 - D '96 - p17+ [51-250]
Goodall, Francis - *International Bibliography of Business History*
  r Choice - v34 - Ap '97 - p1310 [51-250]
Goodall, Jane - *Artaud and the Gnostic Drama*
  L'Esprit - v36 - Win '96 - p101+ [251-500]
Goodbourn, Stephen - *Eukaryotic Gene Transcription*
  SciTech - v20 - D '96 - p30 [51-250]
Goodby, James E - *Regional Conflicts*
  J Pol - v59 - F '97 - p318+ [501+]
Goodchild, Michael F - *GIS and Environmental Modeling*
  SciTech - v20 - N '96 - p1 [51-250]
Goodchild, Philip - *Gilles Deleuze and the Question of Philosophy*
  Choice - v34 - S '96 - p141 [51-250]
Goode, Diane - *Mama's Perfect Present (Illus. by Diane Goode)*
  c CCB-B - v50 - D '96 - p136 [51-250]
  c HB - v72 - N '96 - p723+ [51-250]
  c HB Guide - v8 - Spr '97 - p29 [51-250]
  c LATBR - O 6 '96 - p15 [51-250]
  c NYTBR - v102 - Ja 19 '97 - p24 [1-50]
  c PW - v243 - S 2 '96 - p129 [51-250]
  c SLJ - v42 - S '96 - p178 [51-250]
Goode, Erica - *Letters for Our Children*
  LJ - v121 - D '96 - p127 [51-250]

Gooden, Andrea R - *Computers in the Classroom*
  BL - v93 - O 1 '96 - p294 [51-250]
  LJ - v121 - O 15 '96 - p70 [51-250]
Goodenough, Elizabeth - *Infant Tongues*
  ChLAQ - v21 - Fall '96 - p140+ [501+]
Goodfellow, William D - *SongCite: An Index to Popular Songs*
  r Notes - v53 - D '96 - p449+ [501+]
Goodhart, C A E - *The Central Bank and the Financial System*
  Econ J - v107 - Ja '97 - p265 [51-250]
Goodhart, Pippa - *Flow*
  c TES - Jl 5 '96 - pR8 [1-50]
Goodhart, Sandor - *Sacrificing Commentary*
  Choice - v34 - Ja '97 - p787+ [51-250]
  R&R Bk N - v11 - D '96 - p60 [51-250]
Goodheart, Eugene - *The Reign of Ideology*
  Choice - v34 - Ap '97 - p1330 [51-250]
Goodich, Michael E - *Violence and Miracle in the Fourteenth Century*
  CC - v113 - O 16 '96 - p983 [51-250]
  CH - v66 - Mr '97 - p100+ [501+]
  HRNB - v25 - Fall '96 - p26 [251-500]
  JR - v77 - Ap '97 - p299+ [501+]
  Specu - v72 - Ja '97 - p157+ [501+]
Goodin, Robert E - *The Theory of Institutional Design*
  JEL - v35 - Mr '97 - p202 [51-250]
  Utilitarianism as a Public Philosophy
  Hast Cen R - v27 - Ja '97 - p38+ [501+]
  TLS - D 27 '96 - p27 [501+]
Gooding, Janda - *Chasing Shadows*
  Aust Bk R - O '96 - p34+ [51-250]
Goodison, Lorna - *To Us, All Flowers Are Roses*
  WLT - v70 - Sum '96 - p750 [501+]
Goodkind, Terry - *Blood of the Fold*
  y BL - v93 - N 15 '96 - p576 [51-250]
  KR - v64 - O 1 '96 - p1434 [51-250]
  PW - v243 - O 7 '96 - p66 [51-250]
  Stone of Tears
  y Kliatt - v31 - Mr '97 - p16+ [51-250]
Goodman, Al - *The World on a String*
  BL - v93 - My 15 '97 - p1543+ [51-250]
Goodman, Allegra - *The Family Markowitz*
  BL - v93 - S 15 '96 - p203+ [51-250]
  LATBR - F 16 '97 - p10 [501+]
  NY - v72 - D 16 '96 - p109 [51-250]
  NYTBR - v101 - N 3 '96 - p14 [501+]
  NYTBR - v101 - D 8 '96 - p79 [1-50]
  NYTLa - v146 - O 22 '96 - pC19 [501+]
Goodman, Bryna - *Native Place, City, and Nation*
  Ch Rev Int - v4 - Spr '97 - p145+ [501+]
  JEH - v57 - Mr '97 - p227+ [501+]
  JIH - v27 - Spr '97 - p749+ [501+]
Goodman, David - *Gold Seeking*
  AAAGA - v86 - D '96 - p789+ [501+]
Goodman, Dena - *The Republic of Letters*
  JHI - v57 - O '96 - p725+ [501+]
  RM - v50 - D '96 - p402+ [501+]
Goodman, Fred - *The Mansion on the Hill*
  BL - v93 - Ja '97 - p802+ [51-250]
  Ent W - Ja 24 '97 - p49+ [501+]
  KR - v64 - D 1 '96 - p1715 [251-500]
  LATBR - F 2 '97 - p4 [501+]
  LJ - v122 - F 1 '97 - p80 [51-250]
  NY - v73 - Mr 24 '97 - p83 [51-250]
  NYTBR - v102 - Mr 2 '97 - p24 [501+]
  NYTLa - v146 - F 28 '97 - pC36 [501+]
  PW - v244 - Ja 6 '97 - p60 [51-250]
  Trib Bks - Mr 2 '97 - p7 [501+]
Goodman, Jo - *My Steadfast Heart*
  PW - v244 - F 10 '97 - p81 [51-250]
Goodman, Joan Elizabeth - *Bernard's Bath (Illus. by Dominic Catalano)*
  c HB Guide - v7 - Fall '96 - p239 [51-250]
  c RT - v50 - Mr '97 - p503 [51-250]
  The Winter Hare
  c BL - v93 - N 15 '96 - p587+ [51-250]
  c CBRS - v25 - Ja '97 - p56 [51-250]
  y CCB-B - v50 - F '97 - p205 [51-250]
  y HB Guide - v8 - Spr '97 - p79 [51-250]
  c KR - v64 - O 1 '96 - p1466 [51-250]
  y SLJ - v42 - N '96 - p120 [51-250]
  y VOYA - v19 - F '97 - p327 [251-500]
Goodman, Jonathan - *The Passing of Starr Faithfull*
  Arm Det - v29 - Fall '96 - p506 [251-500]
Goodman, Jordan E - *Everyone's Money Book*
  PW - v243 - N 25 '96 - p70 [1-50]
Goodman, Ken - *On Reading*
  Learning - v25 - S '96 - p48 [51-250]
  SLJ - v43 - Mr '97 - p115 [51-250]

Goodman, Paul - *Format and Anxiety*
  ABR - v17 - Ag '96 - p18 [51-250]
Goodman, Susan E - *The Great Antler Auction (Illus. by Michael J Doolittle)*
  c BL - v93 - S 1 '96 - p121+ [51-250]
  c CCB-B - v50 - O '96 - p60 [51-250]
  c HB Guide - v8 - Spr '97 - p127 [51-250]
  c SLJ - v42 - S '96 - p215 [51-250]
Goodman, Susan Tumarkin - *Russian Jewish Artists in a Century of Change 1890-1990*
  New R - v216 - F 3 '97 - p34+ [501+]
Goodman, Yetta - *Notes from a Kidwatcher*
  EL - v54 - O '96 - p89+ [501+]
Goodnick, Paul J - *Predictors of Treatment Response in Mood Disorders*
  AJPsych - v154 - Mr '97 - p432+ [501+]
Goodnough, David - *Jose Marti: Cuban Patriot and Poet*
  y BL - v93 - S 1 '96 - p113 [51-250]
  y HB Guide - v7 - Fall '96 - p372 [51-250]
Goodowens, James B - *A User's Guide to Federal Architect-Engineer Contracts. 2nd Ed.*
  SciTech - v20 - N '96 - p3 [51-250]
Goodrick-Clarke, Nicholas - *The Occult Roots of Nazism*
  NYRB - v43 - O 3 '96 - p38+ [501+]
Goodridge, John - *Rural Life in Eighteenth-Century English Poetry*
  Choice - v34 - Ja '97 - p794 [51-250]
Goodsell, David S - *Our Molecular Nature*
  Choice - v34 - N '96 - p182 [51-250]
  SciTech - v20 - S '96 - p22 [51-250]
Goodsell, Don - *Dictionary of Automotive Engineering. 2nd Ed.*
  r ARBA - v28 - '97 - p594 [51-250]
Goodstein, David L - *Feynman's Lost Lecture*
  Am Sci - v85 - Mr '97 - p184+ [501+]
  Ant R - v54 - Fall '96 - p490 [51-250]
  Astron - v25 - Ja '97 - p103 [51-250]
  y BL - v93 - Ap 1 '97 - p1342 [1-50]
  Choice - v34 - N '96 - p480 [51-250]
  Obs - Ag 18 '96 - p17* [501+]
  Phys Today - v49 - N '96 - p81+ [501+]
  Sci - v273 - Ag 30 '96 - p1180 [51-250]
Goodwin, Alan M - *Principles of Precambrian Geology*
  Nature - v384 - N 7 '96 - p38 [1-50]
Goodwin, Brian - *How the Leopard Changed Its Spots*
  Am Sci - v84 - My '96 - p300+ [501+]
  BIC - v25 - O '96 - p35+ [501+]
Goodwin, Doris Kearns - *No Ordinary Time*
  SE - v60 - S '96 - p302 [1-50]
Goodwin, Greenville - *Myths and Tales of the White Mountain Apache*
  CAY - v16 - Fall '95 - p5 [51-250]
Goodwin, James - *Perspectives on Akira Kurosawa*
  FQ - v49 - Sum '96 - p52+ [501+]
Goodwin, Jan - *The Price of Honor*
  Rel St Rev - v23 - Ap '97 - p201 [51-250]
Goodwin, Janet R - *Alms and Vagabonds*
  Rel St Rev - v22 - O '96 - p313+ [501+]
Goodwin, June - *Heart of Whiteness*
  Bks & Cult - v2 - Jl '96 - p30 [251-500]
Goodwin, Neva R - *As If the Future Mattered*
  JEL - v34 - D '96 - p2133 [51-250]
  The Consumer Society
  Choice - v34 - My '97 - p1546 [51-250]
Goodwin, Sarah Webster - *Death and Representation*
  VS - v39 - Aut '95 - p77+ [501+]
Goodwin, Simon - *Hubble's Universe*
  y BL - v93 - D 1 '96 - p629 [51-250]
  KR - v64 - D 1 '96 - p1728 [51-250]
  Nature - v385 - Ja 2 '97 - p33 [1-50]
  New Sci - v152 - D 14 '96 - p46 [51-250]
  PW - v243 - D 2 '96 - p51 [51-250]
  S&T - v93 - Mr '97 - p66 [1-50]
  WSJ-MW - v78 - D 5 '96 - pA18 [51-250]
Goody, Jack - *The East in the West*
  Choice - v34 - D '96 - p652 [51-250]
  NS & S - v9 - My 17 '96 - p39+ [251-500]
  The Expansive Moment
  Am Ethnol - v24 - F '97 - p211+ [501+]
  Choice - v34 - O '96 - p323 [51-250]
  JIH - v27 - Win '97 - p561+ [501+]
Goodyear, George F - *Society and Museum*
  Isis - v87 - S '96 - p562+ [501+]
Gookin, Dan - *Dan Gookin's Web Wambooli*
  CBR - v15 - Spr '97 - p3 [1-50]
  LJ - v122 - F 1 '97 - p102 [51-250]
Goonan, Kathleen Ann - *The Bones of Time*
  y SLJ - v42 - D '96 - p152 [51-250]
Gooneratne, Yasmine - *The Pleasures of Conquest*
  FEER - v159 - O 10 '96 - p58 [251-500]
  Meanjin - v55 - 2 '96 - p358+ [501+]

Gopinath, Ash - *Heat Transfer in Microgravity*
SciTech - v21 - Mr '97 - p22 [51-250]
Gopnik, Alison - *Words, Thoughts, and Theories*
SB - v33 - My '97 - p100 [251-500]
Goradia, Nayana - *Lord Curzon*
EHR - v111 - S '96 - p1017+ [251-500]
Goralski, Walter - *VRML: Exploring Virtual Words on the Internet*
SciTech - v20 - D '96 - p12 [51-250]
Goran, Lester - *Tales from the Irish Club*
HR - v49 - Aut '96 - p483+ [501+]
NYTBR - v101 - D 8 '96 - p84 [1-50]
Gorbachev, Mikhail Sergeevich - *Memoirs*
BL - v93 - S 15 '96 - p178+ [51-250]
BW - v26 - N 10 '96 - p5 [501+]
Choice - v34 - Ap '97 - p1410 [51-250]
CSM - v89 - Ja 30 '97 - pB1+ [501+]
For Aff - v76 - Mr '97 - p190 [51-250]
KR - v64 - S 1 '96 - p1294 [251-500]
LATBR - N 17 '96 - p1+ [501+]
LJ - v121 - S 15 '96 - p75 [51-250]
Nat - v264 - F 10 '97 - p30+ [501+]
NL - v79 - D 16 '96 - p16+ [501+]
NY - v72 - N 18 '96 - p101+ [501+]
NYRB - v43 - D 19 '96 - p34+ [501+]
NYTBR - v101 - O 20 '96 - p7+ [501+]
NYTBR - v101 - D 8 '96 - p89 [1-50]
NYTLa - v146 - Ja 7 '97 - pC16 [501+]
Obs - D 1 '96 - p16* [501+]
PW - v243 - S 2 '96 - p102 [51-250]
TLS - D 27 '96 - p4+ [501+]
WSJ-MW - v77 - O 11 '96 - pA8 [501+]
Zhiznl I Reformy. Vols. 1-2
BL - v93 - O 1 '96 - p327 [1-50]
Gordeeva, Ekaterina - *My Sergei*
y BL - v93 - O 1 '96 - p290 [51-250]
CSM - v88 - N 7 '96 - p14 [51-250]
CSM - v89 - D 12 '96 - p14 [51-250]
CSM - v89 - Ja 9 '97 - p14 [51-250]
CSM - v89 - F 6 '97 - p14 [51-250]
CSM - v89 - Mr 6 '97 - p14 [51-250]
KR - v64 - S 15 '96 - p1391 [51-250]
LJ - v121 - N 15 '96 - p67 [51-250]
PW - v243 - S 23 '96 - p63+ [51-250]
My Sergei (Gordeeva). Audio Version
BWatch - v18 - Mr '97 - p8 [1-50]
Gordimer, Nadine - *Burger's Daughter*
SFR - v21 - Jl '96 - p48 [1-50]
Writing and Being
BW - v26 - D 22 '96 - p12 [51-250]
Obs - N 24 '96 - p18* [51-250]
Gordon, A David - *Controversies in Media Ethics*
JMCQ - v73 - Aut '96 - p758+ [501+]
Gordon, Avery F - *Mapping Multiculturalism*
Bloom Rev - v16 - S '96 - p23 [501+]
Gordon, Barry H - *Your Father, Your Self*
LJ - v121 - O 15 '96 - p78 [51-250]
PW - v243 - S 16 '96 - p65 [51-250]
Gordon, Bruce - *Protestant History and Identity in Sixteenth-Century Europe. Vols. 1-2*
Choice - v34 - Ap '97 - p1357 [51-250]
Gordon, Bryan C - *People of Sunlight, People of Starlight*
Choice - v34 - F '97 - p1005+ [51-250]
R&R Bk N - v11 - D '96 - p13 [51-250]
Gordon, Caroline - *Aleck Maury, Sportsman*
BW - v27 - Mr 2 '97 - p12 [51-250]
Gordon, Colin - *New Deals*
ILRR - v50 - Ap '97 - p537+ [501+]
Gordon, Dan, 1947- - *Davin*
c KR - v65 - Ja 15 '97 - p142 [51-250]
c PW - v244 - Ap 7 '97 - p92+ [51-250]
c SLJ - v43 - Mr '97 - p152+ [51-250]
Gordon, Daniel, 1961- - *Citizens without Sovereignty*
EHR - v112 - Ap '97 - p493+ [501+]
FR - v70 - O '96 - p112+ [501+]
Historian - v59 - Fall '96 - p187+ [501+]
JHI - v57 - O '96 - p725+ [501+]
Gordon, David George - *The Compleat Cockroach*
New Sci - v152 - O 26 '96 - p44 [51-250]
PW - v243 - O 14 '96 - p80 [51-250]
y SB - v33 - Mr '97 - p46 [51-250]
Gordon, David M - *Fat and Mean*
Bus W - Je 10 '96 - p14 [501+]
Choice - v34 - O '96 - p329 [51-250]
Econ - v341 - O 19 '96 - p10* [501+]
JEL - v34 - D '96 - p2077+ [51-250]
NYRB - v44 - Ap 10 '97 - p38+ [501+]
Gordon, Edythe Mae - *Selected Works of Edythe Mae Gordon*
AL - v69 - Mr '97 - p258 [1-50]

Gordon, Felicia - *Early French Feminisms 1830-1940*
Choice - v34 - D '96 - p669 [51-250]
Gordon, Fon Louise - *Caste and Class*
JSH - v63 - F '97 - p189+ [501+]
Gordon, Fred Jay - *Benjamin Grabbed His Chicken and Ran*
LJ - v122 - Ap 15 '97 - p125 [51-250]
Gordon, G A H - *The Rules of the Game*
Spec - v277 - N 16 '96 - p46 [1-50]
TLS - F 28 '97 - p29 [501+]
Gordon, Haim - *Quicksand: Israel, the Intifada, and the Rise of Political Evil in Democracies*
Am - v175 - N 30 '96 - p27+ [501+]
RP - v59 - Win '97 - p183+ [501+]
Gordon, Herb - *Essential Skiing*
LJ - v121 - N 15 '96 - p67 [51-250]
Gordon, Ian - *Looking for a Rain God and Other Short Stories from Africa*
y TES - S 20 '96 - pR7 [1-50]
Gordon, Jacquie - *Flanders Point*
y BL - v93 - My 15 '97 - p1561 [51-250]
Gordon, James S - *Manifesto for a New Medicine*
Readings - v11 - D '96 - p10+ [501+]
VQR - v73 - Win '97 - p31* [501+]
Gordon, John - *Gilroy's Ghost*
y Magpies - v11 - S '96 - p45 [1-50]
Gordon, John Steele - *Hamilton's Blessing*
BL - v93 - Ja '97 - p794 [51-250]
KR - v65 - Ja 1 '97 - p36 [251-500]
LJ - v122 - Ja '97 - p115 [51-250]
NYTLa - v146 - F 6 '97 - pC20 [501+]
PW - v243 - D 2 '96 - p44+ [51-250]
WSJ-Cent - v99 - F 13 '97 - pA16 [501+]
Gordon, Josh - *Tough Calls*
BL - v93 - D 15 '96 - p699 [51-250]
Gordon, Karen Elizabeth - *The Deluxe Transitive Vampire*
HER - v66 - Fall '96 - p695 [251-500]
Paris out of Hand
Ant R - v55 - Spr '97 - p244+ [251-500]
LATBR - S 22 '96 - p14 [51-250]
Gordon, Katharine - *The Peacock Rider*
BL - v93 - D 15 '96 - p708 [51-250]
Gordon, Lewis R - *Existence in Black*
BWatch - v18 - Mr '97 - p4 [51-250]
Fanon and the Crisis of European Man
CS - v26 - Mr '97 - p161+ [501+]
Gordon, Linda - *Pitied but Not Entitled*
NWSA Jnl - v8 - Sum '96 - p107+ [501+]
Gordon, Lois - *The World of Samuel Beckett 1906-1946*
Am Theat - v14 - F '97 - p56 [51-250]
Econ - v339 - My 18 '96 - p13*+ [251-500]
NYRB - v43 - N 14 '96 - p24+ [501+]
TLS - S 27 '96 - p3+ [501+]
WLT - v71 - Win '97 - p162 [501+]
Gordon, Lyndall - *Charlotte Bronte: A Passionate Life*
Historian - v58 - Sum '96 - p903+ [251-500]
HR - v49 - Sum '96 - p301+ [501+]
Gordon, Lynn - *Adventure in the Witch's House (Illus. by Susan Synarski)*
c PW - v243 - S 30 '96 - p86 [51-250]
Lights Out (Illus. by Susan Synarski)
c LATBR - O 20 '96 - p8 [51-250]
Messipes (Illus. by Susan Synarski)
c PW - v243 - N 18 '96 - p77 [51-250]
Gordon, Maria - *Fun with Materials (Illus. by Mike Gordon)*
c HB Guide - v8 - Spr '97 - p131 [51-250]
Rocks and Soil (Illus. by Mike Gordon)
c HB Guide - v8 - Spr '97 - p113 [51-250]
Gordon, Mary - *The Shadow Man*
Comw - v123 - My 17 '96 - p17+ [501+]
LATBR - My 26 '96 - p3 [501+]
NL - v79 - Ag 12 '96 - p26+ [501+]
NYTBR - v101 - D 8 '96 - p92 [1-50]
PW - v244 - Ap 14 '97 - p72 [1-50]
Woman's J - Ag '96 - p11 [51-250]
Gordon, Michael - *A True Believer*
Aust Bk R - O '96 - p26+ [501+]
Gordon, Myron J - *Finance, Investment and Macroeconomics*
Econ J - v106 - S '96 - p1469 [51-250]
Gordon, Neil - *Sacrifice of Isaac*
Ent W - D 6 '96 - p59 [51-250]
PW - v243 - N 18 '96 - p70 [1-50]
Gordon, Noah - *Matters of Choice*
PW - v244 - Ap 21 '97 - p69 [1-50]
Gordon, Pamela - *Epicurus in Lycia*
Choice - v34 - My '97 - p1512 [51-250]
Gordon, Paul - *The Critical Double*
MLR - v92 - Ap '97 - p417+ [501+]

Gordon, R J F - *Human Rights in the United Kingdom*
TLS - Mr 7 '97 - p14 [501+]
Gordon, R L - *Image and Value in the Graeco-Roman World*
TLS - F 14 '97 - p7 [501+]
Gordon, Richard, 1921- - *An Alarming History of Famous and Difficult! Patients*
y BL - v93 - Mr 15 '97 - p1213 [51-250]
An Alarming History of Famous and Difficult Patients
KR - v65 - Ja 15 '97 - p118 [251-500]
PW - v244 - F 24 '97 - p80 [1-50]
Gordon, Robert, 1961- - *It Came from Memphis*
CAY - v16 - Fall '95 - p5 [51-250]
CAY - v17 - Win '96 - p4 [51-250]
The King on the Road
VQR - v73 - Win '97 - p30* [51-250]
Gordon, Robert B - *American Iron 1607-1900*
Choice - v34 - D '96 - p633 [51-250]
Isis - v88 - Mr '97 - p128+ [501+]
JEL - v34 - D '96 - p2106 [51-250]
SciTech - v20 - N '96 - p78 [51-250]
Gordon, Robert P - *The Place Is Too Small for Us*
Rel St Rev - v23 - Ap '97 - p163 [51-250]
Gordon, Rochelle H - *Climb a Fallen Ladder*
LJ - v122 - Ap 1 '97 - p150 [51-250]
Gordon, Rory - *Primary Behaviour File*
TES - Ja 10 '97 - p14* [1-50]
Gordon, Ruth - *Pierced by a Ray of Sun*
y Emerg Lib - v24 - S '96 - p24 [1-50]
Gordon, Sarah - *Passage to Union*
BW - v26 - D 22 '96 - p3 [501+]
BWatch - v18 - F '97 - p2 [51-250]
Choice - v34 - Ap '97 - p1404 [51-250]
KR - v64 - O 15 '96 - p1510 [51-250]
LJ - v122 - Ja '97 - p120 [51-250]
PW - v243 - N 11 '96 - p64 [51-250]
Gordon, Stewart, 1930- - *A History of Keyboard Literature*
Choice - v34 - O '96 - p290+ [51-250]
M Ed J - v83 - Jl '96 - p52 [51-250]
Gordon, Stewart, 1945- - *Marathas, Marauders, and State Formation in Eighteenth-Century India*
EHR - v111 - N '96 - p1296+ [251-500]
Gordon, Suzanne - *Life Support*
y BL - v93 - F 15 '97 - p986 [51-250]
KR - v65 - Ja 1 '97 - p36 [251-500]
LJ - v122 - F 1 '97 - p99 [51-250]
PW - v244 - Ja 20 '97 - p388 [51-250]
Trib Bks - Mr 23 '97 - p3 [501+]
Gordon, Taylor - *Born to Be*
Bl S - v26 - Sum '96 - p64+ [51-250]
Gordon, Thomas - *Making the Patient Your Partner*
J ClinPsyc - v57 - N '96 - p552+ [501+]
Gordon, William A - *The Ultimate Hollywood Tour Book*
r FIR - v47 - S '96 - p84+ [251-500]
Gordon Pape's 1997 Buyer's Guide to Mutual Funds
r Quill & Q - v63 - Ja '97 - p24 [51-250]
Gordon Pape's 1997 Buyer's Guide to RRSP
r Quill & Q - v63 - Ja '97 - p26 [51-250]
Gordon-Reed, Annette - *Thomas Jefferson and Sally Hemings*
BL - v93 - Ap 1 '97 - p1279 [51-250]
New R - v216 - Mr 10 '97 - p32+ [501+]
NY - v73 - Ap 7 '97 - p95 [51-250]
PW - v244 - F 3 '97 - p84 [51-250]
Gore, Tipper - *Picture This*
Ent W - S 20 '96 - p73 [51-250]
S Liv - v32 - Mr '97 - p62 [51-250]
Gorecki, Jan - *Justifying Ethics*
AJS - v102 - Ja '97 - p1227+ [501+]
Gorecki, Piotr - *Parishes, Tithes and Society in Earlier Medieval Poland c. 1100-c. 1250*
CHR - v82 - Jl '96 - p533 [251-500]
Gorenberg, Gershom - *Seventy Facets*
PW - v244 - Ja 13 '97 - p71 [51-250]
Gorenc, B - *Steel Designer's Handbook. 6th Ed.*
SciTech - v21 - Mr '97 - p79 [51-250]
Gores, Joe - *Contract Null and Void*
LATBR - Ag 11 '96 - p8 [51-250]
PW - v243 - N 4 '96 - p40 [1-50]
Gorgas, Josiah - *The Journals of Josiah Gorgas 1857-1878*
T&C - v37 - O '96 - p845+ [251-500]
Gorham, Deborah - *Vera Brittain: A Feminist Life*
Choice - v34 - O '96 - p278 [51-250]
Gorham, Sarah - *The Tension Zone*
Sm Pr R - v28 - S '96 - p1+ [251-500]
Goring, Rosemary - *Larousse Dictionary of Literary Characters*
r RES - v47 - N '96 - p636+ [501+]

Goring, Ruth - *Dias Festivos Y Celebraciones*
  c SLJ - v42 - Ag '96 - p178 [51-250]
Gorkin, Michael - *Three Mothers, Three Daughters*
  Choice - v34 - D '96 - p652 [51-250]
  MEJ - v51 - Spr '97 - p291+ [501+]
  y SLJ - v42 - D '96 - p153 [51-250]
  Wom R Bks - v14 - Ja '97 - p14+ [501+]
Gorman, Edward - *Cage of Night*
  MFSF - v91 - O '96 - p63+ [251-500]
  MFSF - v91 - D '96 - p98+ [51-250]
  Cold Blue Midnight
  Arm Det - v30 - Win '97 - p86+ [251-500]
  BL - v93 - N 1 '96 - p483 [51-250]
  KR - v64 - S 15 '96 - p1360 [51-250]
  The Fatal Frontier
  BL - v93 - Ja '97 - p824 [51-250]
  PW - v243 - N 25 '96 - p59+ [51-250]
  The Fine Art of Murder
  r RQ - v36 - Win '96 - p223 [51-250]
  Hawk Moon
  Rapport - v19 - 5 '96 - p27 [251-500]
  Love Kills
  y BL - v93 - My 1 '97 - p1482 [51-250]
  LJ - v122 - My 1 '97 - p144 [1-50]
Gorman, Greg - *Inside Life*
  BWatch - v18 - Mr '97 - p10 [1-50]
  LJ - v122 - Mr 15 '97 - p59 [51-250]
Gorman, Jack M - *The New Psychiatry*
  LJ - v121 - N 1 '96 - p94 [51-250]
Gorman, Jacquelin - *The Seeing Glass*
  PW - v244 - My 5 '97 - p185 [51-250]
Gorman, Paul R - *Left Intellectuals and Popular Culture in Twentieth-Century America*
  Cng - v29 - Mr '97 - p54 [51-250]
  HRNB - v25 - Fall '96 - p13+ [251-500]
  RAH - v25 - Mr '97 - p107+ [501+]
Gorman, Robert A - *Michael Harrington: Speaking American*
  RAH - v25 - Mr '97 - p163+ [501+]
Gorman, W M - *Collected Works of W.M. Gorman. Vol. 1*
  JEL - v34 - D '96 - p2024+ [51-250]
Gormley, Beatrice - *First Ladies*
  c BL - v93 - Mr 15 '97 - p1236 [51-250]
  Maria Mitchell: The Soul of an Astronomer
  y Kliatt - v30 - S '96 - p28 [51-250]
Gormley, William T - *Everybody's Children*
  Pol Stud J - v24 - Aut '96 - p519 [51-250]
  Soc Ser R - v70 - D '96 - p658+ [501+]
Gormley, William T, Jr. - *Everybody's Children*
  AAPSS-A - v547 - S '96 - p188+ [251-500]
  APSR - v90 - S '96 - p649+ [501+]
Gorn, Elliott J - *Muhammad Ali, the Peoples Champ*
  Bl S - v26 - Sum '96 - p65 [1-50]
  Muhammad Ali, The People's Champ
  J Soc H - v30 - Win '96 - p532 [251-500]
Gornick, Vivian - *Approaching Eye Level*
  BL - v93 - S 15 '96 - p189 [51-250]
  LATBR - O 27 '96 - p6 [501+]
  Ms - v7 - S '96 - p83 [1-50]
  Nat - v263 - O 21 '96 - p29+ [501+]
  NYTBR - v101 - O 13 '96 - p12 [501+]
  Wom R Bks - v14 - O '96 - p7+ [501+]
Gorodnikov, Sergei - *Russkaia Ruletka*
  BL - v93 - O 1 '96 - p327 [1-50]
Gorog, Judith - *In a Creepy, Creepy Place and Other Scary Stories (Illus. by Kimberly Bulcken Root)*
  c BL - v93 - Ja '97 - p859 [251-500]
  c HB - v73 - Ja '97 - p56 [51-250]
  c HB Guide - v8 - Spr '97 - p58 [51-250]
  c PW - v243 - S 30 '96 - p86 [1-50]
  c SLJ - v43 - F '97 - p81 [51-250]
  When Nobody's Home
  y BL - v93 - Ap 1 '97 - p1310 [1-50]
  y HB Guide - v7 - Fall '96 - p301+ [51-250]
  y VOYA - v19 - D '96 - p278+ [251-500]
  Zilla Sasparilla and the Mud Baby (Illus. by Amanda Harvey)
  c HB Guide - v7 - Fall '96 - p257+ [51-250]
  c Smith - v27 - N '96 - p164 [1-50]
Gorostiza, Carlos - *El Patio De Atras*
  BL - v93 - Mr 15 '97 - p1232 [1-50]
Gorra, Michael - *After Empire*
  LJ - v122 - Ja '97 - p98 [51-250]

Gorrell, Gena K - *North Star to Freedom*
  c BL - v93 - F 15 '97 - p1012 [51-250]
  c CBRS - v25 - Ap '97 - p105 [51-250]
  c CCB-B - v50 - F '97 - p205 [51-250]
  y Ch Bk News - v20 - Win '97 - p31 [51-250]
  c KR - v64 - N 15 '96 - p1668+ [51-250]
  c NYTBR - v102 - F 16 '97 - p25 [1-50]
  c Par Ch - v21 - Mr '97 - p8 [1-50]
  c PW - v243 - D 16 '96 - p61 [51-250]
  y SLJ - v43 - Ja '97 - p125+ [51-250]
Gorski, William T - *Yeats and Alchemy*
  R&R Bk N - v12 - F '97 - p86 [51-250]
Goscilo, Helena - *Dehexing Sex*
  Choice - v34 - O '96 - p287 [51-250]
  TLS - Ja 3 '97 - p23 [501+]
  Wom R Bks - v14 - F '97 - p12+ [501+]
  The Explosive World of Tatyana N. Tolstaya's Fiction
  Choice - v34 - Mr '97 - p1169+ [51-250]
  R&R Bk N - v12 - F '97 - p79 [51-250]
  Russia--Women--Culture
  Choice - v34 - N '96 - p521 [51-250]
Goscinny - *Asterix and Obelix All at Sea*
  c Spec - v277 - D 14 '96 - p77 [1-50]
Gosden, John R - *PRINS and In Situ PCR Protocols*
  SciTech - v20 - D '96 - p30 [51-250]
Gosden, Roger - *Cheating Time*
  KR - v64 - O 1 '96 - p1443 [251-500]
  y SB - v33 - My '97 - p108 [51-250]
Gosden, Roger G - *Transplantation of Ovarian and Testicular Tissues*
  SciTech - v20 - S '96 - p38 [51-250]
Gose, Earl - *Pattern Recognition and Image Analysis*
  SciTech - v20 - N '96 - p66 [51-250]
Goslee, David - *Romanticism and the Anglican Newman*
  Theol St - v57 - D '96 - p754+ [501+]
Gosliner, Terrence - *Coral Reef Animals of the Indo-Pacific*
  r ARBA - v28 - '97 - p590 [51-250]
  r BWatch - v17 - N '96 - p7 [51-250]
Gosling, J A - *Human Anatomy. 3rd Ed.*
  r SciTech - v20 - N '96 - p30 [1-50]
Gosling, James - *The Java Language Specification*
  r SciTech - v20 - D '96 - p9 [51-250]
Gosling, Paula - *The Dead of Winter*
  Arm Det - v29 - Sum '96 - p366+ [251-500]
Goslinga, Marian - *A Bibliography of the Caribbean*
  r ARBA - v28 - '97 - p67 [251-500]
  r Choice - v34 - My '97 - p1475 [51-250]
The Gospel on Campus. 2nd Ed.
  CLW - v67 - D '96 - p44 [51-250]
Gospodarstvo Istre
  p JEL - v34 - S '96 - p1505 [51-250]
Goss, Glenda Dawn - *The Sibelius Companion*
  Choice - v34 - My '97 - p1509+ [51-250]
Goss, Linda - *The Frog Who Wanted to Be a Singer (Illus. by Cynthia Jabar)*
  c HB Guide - v7 - Fall '96 - p258 [51-250]
  It's Kwanzaa Time!
  c RT - v50 - N '96 - p259 [51-250]
  Talk That Talk
  y BL - v93 - F 15 '97 - p1014 [1-50]
Goss-Custard, John D - *The Oystercatcher: From Individuals to Populations*
  Choice - v34 - My '97 - p1526 [51-250]
Gossmann, Wilhelm - *Poetisierung--Politisierung*
  Ger Q - v69 - Spr '96 - p215+ [501+]
  MLR - v92 - Ap '97 - p507+ [501+]
Gostin, Jennifer - *Peregrine's Rest*
  BL - v93 - S 1 '96 - p62 [51-250]
  SFR - v21 - S '96 - p4 [251-500]
Gosudarstvennyi Arkhiv Rossiiskoi Federatsii - *Arkhiv Noveishei Istorii Rossii. Vols. 1-3*
  Russ Rev - v55 - O '96 - p692+ [501+]
Gotelli, Nicholas J - *Null Models in Ecology*
  Choice - v34 - Ap '97 - p1363+ [51-250]
Gotlieb, Marc - *The Plight of Emulation*
  Art Bull - v79 - Mr '97 - p160+ [501+]
  BM - v138 - F '97 - p609+ [501+]
  Choice - v34 - F '97 - p955+ [51-250]
  Lon R Bks - v19 - Ap 3 '97 - p16+ [501+]
Gott, Philip G - *Automotive Air-Conditioning Refrigerant Service Guide. 2nd Ed.*
  SciTech - v20 - D '96 - p80 [51-250]
Gott, Tedd - *Don't Leave Me This Way*
  Art J - v54 - Win '95 - p87+ [501+]
Gottdiener, Mark - *Postmodern Semiotics*
  CS - v25 - S '96 - p701+ [501+]
  The Theming of America
  HMR - Spr '97 - p10+ [501+]
Gottfried, Heidi - *Feminism and Social Change*
  Choice - v34 - S '96 - p167 [51-250]

Gottfried, Robert R - *Economics, Ecology, and the Roots of Western Faith*
  TT - v53 - O '96 - p418+ [501+]
Gottfried, Roy - *Joyce's Iritis and the Irritated Text*
  ABR - v18 - O '96 - p28+ [501+]
Gottfried, Ted - *Alan Turing: The Architect of the Computer Age*
  y CCB-B - v50 - F '97 - p206 [51-250]
  y HB Guide - v8 - Spr '97 - p157 [51-250]
  Capital Punishment
  y BL - v93 - F 1 '97 - p931 [51-250]
  James Baldwin: Voice from Harlem
  y BL - v93 - My 15 '97 - p1569 [51-250]
Gotti, Victoria - *The Senator's Daughter*
  BL - v93 - Mr 15 '97 - p1225 [51-250]
  KR - v65 - Ja 1 '97 - p10 [251-500]
  LJ - v122 - F 15 '97 - p161 [51-250]
  NYTBR - v102 - Mr 16 '97 - p21 [51-250]
  PW - v244 - Ja 27 '97 - p77 [51-250]
  Trib Bks - Ap 6 '97 - p5 [51-250]
Gottleib, Bill - *New Choices in Natural Healing*
  r BL - v93 - F 1 '97 - p958 [1-50]
Gottlieb, Dale - *Bottom of the Ninth*
  c PW - v244 - Mr 24 '97 - p85 [51-250]
  Where Jamaica Go? (Illus. by Dale Gottlieb)
  c BL - v93 - O 1 '96 - p358 [51-250]
  c CBRS - v25 - Win '97 - p62 [1-50]
  c HB Guide - v8 - Spr '97 - p29 [51-250]
  c PW - v243 - S 16 '96 - p81 [51-250]
  c SLJ - v42 - N '96 - p80 [51-250]
Gottlieb, Eli - *The Boy Who Went Away*
  y BL - v93 - D 15 '96 - p708+ [51-250]
  BW - v27 - F 16 '97 - p4 [251-500]
  KR - v64 - N 1 '96 - p1552 [51-250]
  LATBR - F 16 '97 - p13 [501+]
  LJ - v121 - D '96 - p145 [51-250]
  NYTBR - v102 - F 16 '97 - p16 [501+]
  PW - v243 - N 18 '96 - p63 [51-250]
Gottlieb, Robert - *Reading Jazz*
  Comw - v124 - Mr 28 '97 - p23+ [501+]
  Esq - v126 - D '96 - p40 [1-50]
  KR - v64 - S 15 '96 - p1391 [51-250]
  LJ - v121 - N 1 '96 - p70 [51-250]
  NY - v73 - Mr 10 '97 - p93 [51-250]
  NYTBR - v101 - D 22 '96 - p15 [51-250]
  PW - v243 - O 7 '96 - p51 [51-250]
  Trib Bks - Ja 12 '97 - p1+ [501+]
  WSJ-MW - v78 - N 20 '96 - pA20 [501+]
Gottlieb, Roger S - *Radical Philosophy*
  Ethics - v107 - O '96 - p168+ [501+]
Gottman, John - *The Heart of Parenting*
  LJ - v122 - Ja '97 - p136 [51-250]
  PW - v243 - D 16 '96 - p56 [51-250]
Gotto, A M - *Drugs Affecting Lipid Metabolism*
  SciTech - v21 - Mr '97 - p56 [51-250]
Gottschalk, Charles M - *Industrial Energy Conservation*
  Choice - v34 - Ja '97 - p824+ [51-250]
  SciTech - v20 - S '96 - p52 [51-250]
Gottschild, Brenda Dixon - *Digging the Africanist Presence in American Performance*
  Bl S - v26 - Fall '96 - p103 [51-250]
  Choice - v34 - Ap '97 - p1350 [251-500]
  Dance - v71 - Ja '97 - p98 [51-250]
Gotzkowsky, Bodo - *Volksbucher: Prosaromane, Renaissancenovellen, Versdichtungen Und Schwankbucher. Pt. 2*
  MLR - v91 - Jl '96 - p781+ [501+]
Goubert, Pierre - *Le Siecle De Louis XIV*
  TLS - Ja 3 '97 - p31 [501+]
Gouda, Frances - *Poverty and Political Culture*
  AHR - v101 - O '96 - p1229+ [251-500]
Goudge, Eileen - *Trail of Secrets*
  Rapport - v19 - 4 '96 - p24 [251-500]
  Trib Bks - Ap 6 '97 - p5 [51-250]
Goudge, Elizabeth - *The Dean's Watch*
  y Bkbird - v34 - Spr '96 - p29 [1-50]
  Green Dolphin Street
  y Bkbird - v34 - Spr '96 - p28+ [51-250]
  Island Magic
  y Bkbird - v34 - Spr '96 - p28+ [51-250]
  The Little White Horse
  c Bkbird - v34 - Spr '96 - p29 [51-250]
  The Middle Window
  y Bkbird - v34 - Spr '96 - p29 [1-50]
  Towers in the Mist
  y Bkbird - v34 - Spr '96 - p29 [1-50]
Goudie, A S - *The Environment of the British Isles*
  GJ - v162 - Jl '96 - p242 [51-250]
Goudsblom, Johan - *The Course of Human History*
  R&R Bk N - v11 - D '96 - p38 [51-250]

Goudsmit, Jaap - *Viral Sex*
  Advocate - Ap 29 '97 - p73 [51-250]
y BL - v93 - Mr 15 '97 - p1213 [51-250]
  KR - v65 - Mr 1 '97 - p350+ [51-250]
  LJ - v122 - Ap 15 '97 - p112 [51-250]
Goudsmit, Samuel A - *Alsos*
  Choice - v34 - O '96 - p300+ [51-250]
  R&R Bk N - v11 - D '96 - p7 [51-250]
Gough, Bob - *The Smart Gardener's Guide to Growing Vegetables*
r Hort - v94 - Ja '97 - p78+ [251-500]
Gough, Deborah Mathias - *Christ Church, Philadelphia*
  CH - v65 - S '96 - p550+ [501+]
Gough, Hugh - *De Gaulle and Twentieth-Century France*
  EHR - v111 - N '96 - p1352+ [251-500]
Gough, Jeanne - *Education Sourcebook*
r BL - v93 - My 15 '97 - p1611+ [51-250]
r Emerg Lib - v24 - Mr '97 - p42 [1-50]
Gough, Laurence - *Memory Lane*
  Quill & Q - v62 - O '96 - p31 [251-500]
Gough, Robert E - *Blueberries: A Century of Research*
  SB - v32 - O '96 - p202 [51-250]
  SciTech - v20 - S '96 - p44 [51-250]
Gough, William - *Vibrations and Waves. 2nd Ed.*
  Phys Today - v49 - D '96 - p53+ [501+]
Gouk, Penelope - *Wellsprings of Achievement*
  T&C - v38 - Ja '97 - p248+ [251-500]
Gould, Alan - *Mermaid*
  Quad - v40 - O '96 - p77+ [501+]
  The Totem Ship
  Aust Bk R - Jl '96 - p53+ [501+]
  Quad - v40 - O '96 - p77+ [501+]
  TLS - N 29 '96 - p14 [51-250]
Gould, David - *Immigrant Links to the Home Country*
  JEL - v34 - S '96 - p1426+ [51-250]
Gould, Evelyn - *The Fate of Carmen*
  Choice - v34 - Ap '97 - p1322 [51-250]
Gould, Glenn - *Glenn Gould: Selected Letters*
  Can Lit - Win '96 - p135+ [501+]
Gould, Graham - *The Desert Fathers on Monastic Community*
  CH - v66 - Mr '97 - p87+ [501+]
Gould, Harold A - *Grass Roots Politics in India*
  Pac A - v69 - Fall '96 - p437+ [251-500]
Gould, James L - *Sexual Selection*
  Nature - v385 - F 20 '97 - p693 [1-50]
Gould, Jay M - *The Enemy Within*
  Choice - v34 - D '96 - p644 [51-250]
  Nat - v263 - D 9 '96 - p31+ [501+]
Gould, Jean - *Season of Adventure*
  LJ - v121 - N 1 '96 - p98 [51-250]
  PW - v243 - S 16 '96 - p76 [51-250]
Gould, Jennifer - *Vodka, Tears, and Lenin's Angel*
  KR - v65 - F 1 '97 - p193 [251-500]
  LJ - v122 - Mr 15 '97 - p76 [51-250]
  PW - v244 - F 3 '97 - p88 [51-250]
Gould, Kenneth A - *Local Environmental Struggles*
  Choice - v34 - My '97 - p1518 [51-250]
Gould, Laura - *Cats Are Not Peas*
  Choice - v34 - Ap '97 - p987+ [51-250]
  New Sci - v152 - D 7 '96 - p49 [251-500]
Gould, Lewis L - *American First Ladies*
r ARBA - v28 - '97 - p188 [51-250]
yr BL - v92 - Ag '96 - p1920 [251-500]
r BWatch - v17 - D '96 - p12 [51-250]
r Choice - v34 - O '96 - p247 [51-250]
y SLJ - v42 - Ag '96 - p186 [51-250]
r VOYA - v19 - D '96 - p297+ [51-250]
Gould, Lois - *No Brakes*
  BW - v27 - Mr 30 '97 - p11 [501+]
  KR - v65 - Ja 1 '97 - p10+ [251-500]
  LJ - v122 - F 15 '97 - p161 [51-250]
  NYTBR - v102 - Ap 20 '97 - p20 [51-250]
  PW - v244 - F 3 '97 - p94 [51-250]
Gould, Peter L - *Photo Marketing Guidebook '96-'97*
r Pet PM - v25 - N '96 - p12 [51-250]
Gould, Roger V - *Insurgent Identities*
  AJS - v102 - N '96 - p876+ [501+]
  CS - v25 - N '96 - p757+ [501+]
  JIH - v27 - Spr '97 - p689+ [501+]
  J Soc H - v30 - Spr '97 - p745+ [501+]
  SF - v75 - D '96 - p754+ [501+]
Gould, Stephen Jay - *Dinosaur in a Haystack*
y BL - v93 - D 1 '96 - p664 [1-50]
  NYRB - v43 - O 17 '96 - p33+ [501+]
  NYTBR - v101 - D 8 '96 - p87 [1-50]
  NYTBR - v102 - F 16 '97 - p32 [51-250]
  Skeptic - v4 - '96 - p106 [51-250]
  Trib Bks - Ja 19 '97 - p8 [1-50]

Full House
  Aud - v98 - S '96 - p112+ [501+]
  BL - v93 - Ja 15 '97 - p758 [1-50]
  BW - v26 - S 1 '96 - p5 [501+]
  BWatch - v17 - N '96 - p6 [51-250]
  Comw - v123 - D 6 '96 - p29+ [501+]
  LATBR - O 20 '96 - p10 [501+]
  Nature - v383 - O 31 '96 - p771+ [501+]
  New Sci - v152 - O 5 '96 - p46+ [501+]
  NYRB - v43 - O 17 '96 - p33+ [501+]
  NYTBR - v101 - S 22 '96 - p9+ [501+]
  NYTBR - v101 - D 8 '96 - p87 [1-50]
  Pub Int - Spr '97 - p120+ [501+]
  Skeptic - v4 - 3 '96 - p103 [501+]
  WSJ-MW - v77 - S 5 '96 - pA16 [501+]
Life's Grandeur
  Nature - v383 - O 31 '96 - p771+ [501+]
  New Sci - v152 - O 5 '96 - p46+ [501+]
  NS - v125 - N 29 '96 - p48 [501+]
  Spec - v277 - N 30 '96 - p48+ [501+]
  TES - D 13 '96 - p32 [501+]
The Mismeasure of Man. Rev. and Expanded Ed.
  BW - v26 - S 1 '96 - p4 [251-500]
  Choice - v34 - D '96 - p692 [51-250]
  Soc - v34 - Mr '97 - p78+ [501+]
Gould, Steven - *Wildside*
y BL - v93 - Ap 1 '97 - p1292 [1-50]
  Rapport - v19 - 5 '96 - p32 [251-500]
y VOYA - v19 - F '97 - p336 [251-500]
Gould, Tony - *A Summer Plague*
  Isis - v88 - Mr '97 - p165+ [501+]
Gould, W T S - *Population Migration and the Changing World Order*
  GJ - v162 - Jl '96 - p240+ [51-250]
Gould, Wilbur A - *Unit Operations for the Food Industries*
r SciTech - v20 - S '96 - p60 [51-250]
Gould, William - *Ford*
y Sch Lib - v44 - Ag '96 - p124 [51-250]
  McDonald's
c Bks Keeps - v100 - S '96 - p21 [51-250]
y Sch Lib - v44 - Ag '96 - p124 [51-250]
Goulden, R J - *Kent Town Guides 1763-1900*
r BC - v45 - Win '96 - p575+ [51-250]
r LAR - v98 - O '96 - p537 [251-500]
r Lib - v18 - D '96 - p351+ [501+]
Goulder, Michael - *St. Paul versus St. Peter*
  Bks & Cult - v1 - N '95 - p3+ [501+]
Goulding, Edwin - *Fuchsias: The Complete Guide*
r Choice - v34 - S '96 - p154 [51-250]
Goulding, Michael - *Floods of Fortune*
  Choice - v34 - S '96 - p152 [51-250]
Goulding, Phil G - *Ticket to the Opera*
r BL - v93 - Mr 1 '97 - p1198 [251-500]
  LJ - v121 - N 15 '96 - p64 [51-250]
Goulemot, Jean Marie - *Forbidden Texts*
  Eight-C St - v30 - Spr '97 - p323+ [501+]
Goulter, Christina J M - *A Forgotten Offensive*
  APH - v44 - Spr '97 - p58 [251-500]
Gourdeau, Claire - *Les Delices De Nos Coeurs*
  Can Hist R - v78 - Mr '97 - p143+ [501+]
Gourgouris, Stathis - *Dream Nation*
  Choice - v34 - Ap '97 - p1410 [501+]
Gourley, Catherine - *Beryl Markham: Never Look Back*
y BL - v93 - Mr 15 '97 - p1233 [51-250]
y Kliatt - v31 - My '97 - p22 [51-250]
  Sharks! True Stories and Legends
c CCB-B - v50 - Ja '97 - p171 [51-250]
c HB Guide - v8 - Spr '97 - p124 [51-250]
c SLJ - v42 - D '96 - p128+ [51-250]
Gourse, Leslie - *Billie Holiday: The Tragedy and Triumph of Lady Day*
y Kliatt - v31 - Mr '97 - p26 [51-250]
  Dizzy Gillespie and the Birth of Bebop
y BL - v93 - D 15 '96 - p716 [1-50]
  Mahalia Jackson: Queen of Gospel Song
y BL - v92 - Ag '96 - p1893 [51-250]
y HB Guide - v8 - Spr '97 - p157 [51-250]
y SLJ - v42 - Ag '96 - p170 [51-250]
Gouwens, David J - *Kierkegaard as Religious Thinker*
  Theol St - v57 - D '96 - p752+ [501+]
Gouyet, Jean-Francois - *Physics and Fractal Structures*
  Am Sci - v85 - Mr '97 - p183+ [501+]
  Choice - v34 - D '96 - p648 [51-250]
Gove, H E - *Relic, Icon, or Hoax?*
  Nature - v385 - Ja 23 '97 - p310 [501+]
  New Sci - v153 - F 1 '97 - p42 [1-50]
  Sci - v275 - Ja 3 '97 - p37 [1-50]
Gove, Thomas P - *The Best Directory of Recruiters. 4th Ed.*
r ARBA - v28 - '97 - p118+ [251-500]

The Best Directory of Recruiters On-Line
r ARBA - v28 - '97 - p118+ [251-500]
Gove Inquiry into Child Protection (B.C.) - *Report of the Gove Inquiry into Child Protection in British Columbia. Vol. 3*
  J Gov Info - v23 - S '96 - p627 [51-250]
Govea, Wenonah Milton - *Nineteenth- and Twentieth-Century Harpists*
r Notes - v53 - S '96 - p59+ [501+]
Gover, Paula K - *White Boys and River Girls*
  NYTBR - v101 - D 1 '96 - p36 [1-50]
Governance in Transition
  J Gov Info - v23 - S '96 - p673+ [51-250]
Government Assistance Almanac 1996-97
r ARBA - v28 - '97 - p312+ [51-250]
The Government Directory of Addresses and Telephone Numbers. 4th Ed.
r BusLR - v21 - 3 '96 - p243 [1-50]
Government Phone Book USA 1997
r BL - v93 - F 15 '97 - p1042 [1-50]
The Government We Choose
  J Gov Info - v23 - S '96 - p586 [51-250]
Govier, Jacquie - *Create Your Own Stage Costumes*
  TCI - v31 - Mr '97 - p54+ [251-500]
Govier, Katherine - *Angel Walk*
  BIC - v25 - O '96 - p9+ [501+]
  Mac - v109 - D 9 '96 - p64 [1-50]
  Quill & Q - v62 - S '96 - p64 [251-500]
  Without a Guide
  BL - v93 - Ja '97 - p808 [1-50]
Govorchin, Gerald Gilbert - *From Russia to America with Love*
  Slav R - v55 - Sum '96 - p494+ [501+]
Gow, Andrew Colin - *The Red Jews*
  AHR - v101 - D '96 - p1533 [251-500]
  Six Ct J - v27 - Win '96 - p1057+ [501+]
Gowans, Christopher - *Innocence Lost*
  Hast Cen R - v27 - Ja '97 - p38+ [501+]
Gowdy, Barbara - *Mister Sandman*
  BL - v93 - Mr 15 '97 - p1225 [51-250]
  BW - v27 - Mr 30 '97 - p3 [501+]
  Ent W - Ap 18 '97 - p62 [51-250]
  KR - v65 - F 15 '97 - p242+ [51-250]
  LJ - v122 - Ap 1 '97 - p125 [51-250]
  NYRB - v44 - Ap 10 '97 - p54+ [501+]
  PW - v244 - Ja 6 '97 - p61+ [251-500]
  VLS - Spr '97 - p20 [501+]
  We So Seldom Look on Love
  PW - v244 - Mr 31 '97 - p68 [51-250]
  Trib Bks - Ap 27 '97 - p8 [1-50]
Gowdy, Catherine Lutes - *Cemetery Records. Vol. 2*
r EGH - v50 - N '96 - p164 [51-250]
Gowdy, John - *Economic Theory for Environmentalists*
  JEL - v35 - Mr '97 - p298 [51-250]
Gower, Barry - *Scientific Method*
  New Sci - v153 - F 1 '97 - p46 [51-250]
Gowing, Laura - *Domestic Dangers*
  Choice - v34 - Ap '97 - p1397 [51-250]
Goyard-Fabre, Simone - *La Construction De La Paix Ou Le Travail De Sisyphe*
  Dialogue - v35 - Sum '96 - p636+ [501+]
Goyen, William - *William Goyen: Selected Letters from a Writer's Life*
  ASInt - v34 - O '96 - p111 [501+]
Goytisolo, Juan - *The Marx Family Saga*
  TLS - Jl 7 '96 - p22 [501+]
Gozzano, Guido - *Journey toward the Cradle of Mankind*
  R&R Bk N - v11 - D '96 - p63 [51-250]
Gozzi, Marco - *Le Fonti Liturgiche A Stampa Della Biblioteca Musicale L. Feininger Presso Il Castello Del Buonconsiglio Di Trento. Vols. 1-2*
r Notes - v53 - D '96 - p446+ [501+]
Grabar, Oleg - *The Shape of the Holy*
  HT - v46 - O '96 - p55 [1-50]
Graber, Julia A - *Transitions through Adolescence*
  Adoles - v32 - Spr '97 - p246 [51-250]
r Choice - v34 - D '96 - p694 [51-250]
r SB - v33 - Ja '97 - p6 [251-500]
Graber, Mark A - *Rethinking Abortion*
  Choice - v34 - O '96 - p361 [51-250]
  RP - v59 - Spr '97 - p412+ [501+]
Grabowski, John - *Awesome Almanac--New York*
cr ARBA - v28 - '97 - p48 [51-250]
Grabowsky-Hotamanidis, Anja - *Zur Bedeutung Mystischer Denktradition Im Werk Von Hermann Broch*
  Ger Q - v69 - Fall '96 - p452+ [501+]
Grace, C L - *The Book of Shadows*
  Arm Det - v30 - Win '97 - p98 [501+]
  KR - v64 - My 1 '96 - p643 [251-500]

Grace, Eric S - *Biotechnology Unzipped*
   Mac - v110 - Ap 14 '97 - p62+ [501+]
   PW - v244 - Mr 17 '97 - p73 [51-250]
Whale: Giant of the Ocean
   Quill & Q - v62 - Jl '96 - p48 [51-250]
Grace, Patricia - *The Kuia and the Spider*
  c New Ad - v9 - Fall '96 - p309+ [501+]
The Sky People
   Books - v9 - S '95 - p24 [1-50]
Gracheva, A M - *Aleksei Remizov: Issledovaniia I*
Materialy
   Russ Rev - v56 - Ja '97 - p130+ [501+]
Gracia, Jorge J E - *Individuation in Scholasticism*
   Phil R - v105 - Ja '96 - p112+ [501+]
Gracyk, Theodore - *Rhythm and Noise*
   Nat - v263 - D 23 '96 - p32+ [501+]
Gradenwitz, Peter - *The Music of Israel. 2nd Ed., Rev.*
and Expanded
   Choice - v34 - Ap '97 - p1347 [51-250]
   LJ - v122 - Ja '97 - p101 [51-250]
Gradshteyn, I S - *Table of Integrals, Series, and Products.*
5th Ed. Electronic Media Version
   SciTech - v20 - D '96 - p17 [51-250]
Grady, James - *Unusual Suspects*
   Arm Det - v30 - Win '97 - p74 [51-250]
Graedon, Joe - *The People's Guide to Deadly Drug*
Interactions
  r ARBA - v28 - '97 - p617+ [51-250]
  r BL - v93 - F 1 '97 - p959 [1-50]
Graef, Eva - *Martin Salander: Politik Und Poesie In*
Gottfried Kellers Grunderzeitroman
   Ger Q - v69 - Spr '96 - p216+ [501+]
Graef, Renee - *Hello, Laura! (Illus. by Renee Graef)*
  c HB Guide - v8 - Spr '97 - p12 [51-250]
Laura Helps Pa (Illus. by Renee Graef)
  c HB Guide - v8 - Spr '97 - p12 [51-250]
Laura's Garden (Illus. by Renee Graef)
  c HB Guide - v8 - Spr '97 - p12 [51-250]
Graetz, Michael - *The Jews in Nineteenth-Century France*
   Choice - v34 - O '96 - p338+ [51-250]
Graetz, Michael J - *The Decline (and Fall?) of the*
Income Tax
   KR - v65 - Mr 1 '97 - p351 [51-250]
Graf, Christine - *The Cafes of Paris*
   BL - v93 - S 15 '96 - p210 [1-50]
   LJ - v121 - O 1 '96 - p112 [51-250]
Graf, Holger Thomas - *Konfession Und Internationales*
System
   CHR - v82 - O '96 - p715+ [251-500]
Graf, Johannes - *Die Notwendige Reise*
   MLR - v92 - Ap '97 - p528+ [501+]
Graf, Rudolf F - *Encyclopedia of Electronic Circuits. Vol.*
6
  r ARBA - v28 - '97 - p595 [251-500]
Modern Dictionary of Electronics. 6th Ed.
  r SciTech - v21 - Mr '97 - p89 [51-250]
Graf, William L - *Plutonium and the Rio Grande*
   AAAGA - v87 - Mr '97 - p184+ [501+]
Graff, Gary - *MusicHound Rock*
  r ARBA - v28 - '97 - p494+ [251-500]
Graff, Harvey J - *Conflicting Paths*
   JIH - v27 - Aut '96 - p344+ [501+]
   J Soc H - v30 - Spr '97 - p733+ [501+]
The Labyrinths of Literacy
   Col Comp - v47 - D '96 - p616+ [51-250]
Graff, Henry F - *The Presidents: A Reference History.*
2nd Ed.
  r ARBA - v28 - '97 - p266 [251-500]
  r BL - v93 - S 1 '96 - p170 [251-500]
  r Choice - v34 - Ja '97 - p774 [51-250]
  r R&R Bk N - v11 - N '96 - p17 [51-250]
Grafman, Rafi - *Crowning Glory*
   AB - v99 - Mr 24 '97 - p962+ [501+]
Grafstein, Jerry S - *Beyond Imagination*
   PW - v243 - S 16 '96 - p65 [51-250]
Grafton, Anthony - *Joseph Scaliger: A Study in the*
History of Classical Scholarship. Vol. 2
   Ren Q - v49 - Aut '96 - p669+ [501+]
Rome Reborn
   Ren Q - v49 - Aut '96 - p618+ [501+]
Grafton, Sue - *L Is for Lawless*
   Spec - v277 - S 7 '96 - p37 [51-250]
L Is for Lawless (Kaye). Audio Version
   Arm Det - v29 - Sum '96 - p354+ [51-250]

M Is for Malice
  y BL - v93 - S 15 '96 - p180 [51-250]
   BW - v26 - N 17 '96 - p6 [51-250]
   CSM - v88 - N 14 '96 - p14 [51-250]
   CSM - v89 - D 19 '96 - p14 [51-250]
   Ent W - D 6 '96 - p58 [51-250]
   KR - v64 - S 1 '96 - p1276 [51-250]
   LATBR - N 10 '96 - p6 [51-250]
   NYTBR - v101 - N 10 '96 - p62 [51-250]
   PW - v243 - S 30 '96 - p64 [51-250]
  y SLJ - v43 - Mr '97 - p215 [51-250]
   Spec - v278 - Ap 5 '97 - p38 [51-250]
   TLS - F 7 '97 - p23 [51-250]
Graham, Benjamin - *The Memoirs of the Dean of Wall*
Street
   Econ - v341 - O 19 '96 - p12* [251-500]
Graham, Billy - *Just as I Am*
   BL - v93 - My 15 '97 - p1542 [1-50]
Graham, Bob - *Greetings from Sandy Beach (Illus. by Bob*
Graham)
  c Magpies - v11 - Jl '96 - p10+ [501+]
Spirit of Hope (Illus. by Bob Graham)
  c BL - v93 - D 1 '96 - p668 [51-250]
  c CBRS - v25 - Win '97 - p67 [1-50]
  c HB Guide - v8 - Spr '97 - p29 [51-250]
  c SLJ - v43 - Mr '97 - p159 [51-250]
  c Smith - v27 - N '96 - p164 [1-50]
Graham, Brian - *Geography and Air Transport*
   GJ - v162 - N '96 - p336+ [251-500]
Graham, Bruce Desmond - *Choice and Democratic Order*
   EHR - v112 - F '97 - p263+ [501+]
   JMH - v68 - S '96 - p708+ [501+]
Graham, Duncan - *The Education Racket*
   TES - D 27 '96 - p16 [51-250]
Mainstream Mathematics for GCSE
  y TES - O 4 '96 - pR15 [251-500]
Graham, Elizabeth - *The Highlands of the Lowlands*
   LA Ant - v7 - Je '96 - p170+ [501+]
Graham, Harriet - *A Boy and His Bear*
  y CCB-B - v50 - F '97 - p206 [51-250]
  y HB Guide - v8 - Spr '97 - p79 [51-250]
  c KR - v64 - S 1 '96 - p1322 [51-250]
  c SLJ - v42 - N '96 - p104 [51-250]
  c SLJ - v42 - D '96 - p29 [1-50]
Graham, Heather - *A Magical Christmas*
   BL - v93 - N 1 '96 - p481 [51-250]
   LJ - v121 - N 15 '96 - p48 [51-250]
   NYTBR - v101 - D 8 '96 - p102 [51-250]
Rebel
   PW - v244 - F 3 '97 - p100 [51-250]
Graham, Ian, 1953- - *How Things Work*
  c HB Guide - v7 - Fall '96 - p350 [51-250]
  c Magpies - v11 - Jl '96 - p38 [51-250]
Graham, Ian S, 1955- - *HTML Sourcebook. 2nd Ed.*
  r CBR - v14 - S '96 - p29 [1-50]
Graham, John D - *Risk versus Risk*
   JEL - v34 - S '96 - p1416+ [51-250]
   PSQ - v111 - Fall '96 - p543+ [501+]
Graham, John T - *Theory of History in Ortega y Gasset*
   LJ - v121 - N 1 '96 - p70 [51-250]
Graham, Jorie - *The Dream of the Unified Field*
   LJ - v122 - Ap 1 '97 - p95 [1-50]
   Lon R Bks - v18 - Ag 22 '96 - p25+ [501+]
   NYTBR - v101 - D 8 '96 - p79 [1-50]
   NYTBR - v102 - F 16 '97 - p32 [1-50]
   Trib Bks - F 16 '97 - p8 [1-50]
Erosion
   Shen - v46 - Sum '96 - p48+ [501+]
Graham, Katharine - *Personal History*
   AJR - v19 - Ap '97 - p53 [501+]
   BL - v93 - Ja '97 - p777 [51-250]
   Bus W - F 24 '97 - p18+ [501+]
   BW - v27 - Ja 26 '97 - p1+ [501+]
   CSM - v89 - F 18 '97 - p14 [501+]
   CSM - v89 - Mr 6 '97 - p14 [51-250]
   CSM - v89 - Ap 3 '97 - p14 [51-250]
   Econ - v342 - Ja 4 '97 - p82 [251-500]
   Ent W - Mr 7 '97 - p60 [51-250]
   KR - v65 - Ja 1 '97 - p36+ [251-500]
   LATBR - F 16 '97 - p3 [501+]
   LJ - v122 - F 15 '97 - p140+ [51-250]
   NYTBR - v102 - F 9 '97 - p13+ [501+]
   NYTLa - v146 - F 3 '97 - pC14 [501+]
   PW - v244 - Ja 6 '97 - p55+ [251-500]
   Time - v149 - F 3 '97 - p69 [501+]
   Trib Bks - Mr 2 '97 - p1+ [501+]
   WSJ-Cent - v99 - Ja 31 '97 - pA16 [501+]
Personal History (Graham). Audio Version
   CSM - v89 - F 27 '97 - pB4 [51-250]
Graham, Kenneth J E - *The Performance of Conviction*
   Shakes Q - v47 - Sum '96 - p216+ [501+]

Graham, Laurie, 1947- - *The Ten O'Clock Horses*
   Obs - O 27 '96 - p18* [51-250]
   Obs - D 1 '96 - p16* [1-50]
   Woman's J - S '96 - p10 [51-250]
Graham, Laurie, 1949- - *On the Line at Subaru-Isuzu*
   AAPSS-A - v550 - Mr '97 - p196+ [251-500]
   BusLR - v21 - 3 '96 - p187+ [501+]
   ILRR - v50 - Ap '97 - p532+ [501+]
   Per Psy - v49 - Aut '96 - p714+ [501+]
Graham, Lawrence - *Member of the Club*
   BW - v26 - O 13 '96 - p12 [51-250]
   Ent W - O 11 '96 - p87 [1-50]
   LATBR - O 27 '96 - p11 [51-250]
Proversity: Getting Past Face Value and Finding the
Soul of People
   LJ - v121 - N 1 '96 - p82 [1-50]
Graham, Loren - *Mose*
   South R - v32 - Aut '96 - p761+ [501+]
Graham, Margaret - *A Distant Dream*
   Books - v9 - S '95 - p22 [51-250]
Graham, Martha - *Mobile Farmers*
   Am Ant - v61 - Jl '96 - p616+ [501+]
Graham, Michael F - *The Uses of Reform*
   R&R Bk N - v12 - F '97 - p12 [51-250]
Graham, Nigel - *Advances in Slow Sand and Alternative*
Biological Filtration
   SciTech - v20 - D '96 - p69 [51-250]
Graham, Philip, 1951- - *How to Read an Unwritten*
Language
  y Kliatt - v31 - My '97 - p6 [51-250]
   NYTBR - v102 - Ja 12 '97 - p32 [1-50]
Interior Design
   KR - v64 - O 1 '96 - p1421 [251-500]
   LJ - v121 - N 1 '96 - p110 [51-250]
   NYTBR - v101 - D 8 '96 - p38 [501+]
   PW - v243 - O 7 '96 - p58+ [51-250]
Graham, Richard - *Independence in Latin America*
   HAHR - v77 - F '97 - p125+ [501+]
Graham, Richard H - *SR-71 Revealed*
   A & S Sm - v11 - O '96 - p88+ [251-500]
Graham, Robin Lee - *Dove*
  y JAAL - v40 - D '96 - p318 [1-50]
Graham, Sara Hunter - *Woman Suffrage and the New*
Democracy
   LJ - v121 - N 15 '96 - p72 [51-250]
Graham, Stedman - *You Can Make It Happen*
   BL - v93 - F 15 '97 - p983 [51-250]
   PW - v244 - F 3 '97 - p88 [51-250]
Graham, Stephen, 1965- - *Telecommunications and the*
City
   JC - v47 - Win '97 - p136+ [501+]
   New Sci - v152 - N 30 '96 - p46 [51-250]
Graham, Stephen R - *Cosmos in the Chaos*
   AHR - v102 - F '97 - p185+ [501+]
   Bks & Cult - v2 - Ja '96 - p30 [51-250]
   CC - v113 - O 16 '96 - p981+ [251-500]
   CH - v65 - D '96 - p739+ [501+]
   CHR - v82 - O '96 - p740+ [501+]
Graham, Steve - *Dear Old Donegal (Illus. by John*
O'Brien)
  c HB Guide - v7 - Fall '96 - p357 [51-250]
Graham, Terry - *The Guide to Improve Your Credit*
   BWatch - v17 - S '96 - p9 [51-250]
Graham, W Fred - *Later Calvinism*
   CH - v66 - Mr '97 - p135+ [501+]
   JMH - v68 - S '96 - p660+ [501+]
Graham, William C - *Half Finished Heaven*
   CH - v65 - D '96 - p747+ [501+]
Graham, Winston - *Demelza (Britton). Audio Version*
  y Kliatt - v30 - N '96 - p38 [51-250]
Jeremy Poldark (Britton). Audio Version
  y Kliatt - v30 - N '96 - p38 [51-250]
Warleggan (Britton). Audio Version
  y Kliatt - v31 - My '97 - p45 [51-250]
Graham-Brown, Robin - *Lecture Notes on Dermatology.*
7th Ed.
   SciTech - v21 - Mr '97 - p66 [51-250]
Graham-Campbell, James - *The Viking-Age Gold and*
Silver of Scotland A.D. 850-1100
   Specu - v71 - O '96 - p951+ [501+]
Graham-Dixon, Andrew - *Paper Museum*
   TLS - N 8 '96 - p14+ [501+]
Grahame, Kenneth - *The River Bank and Other Stories*
from The Wind in the Willows (Illus. by Inga Moore)
  c Bks Keeps - Ja '97 - p21 [51-250]
  c HB Guide - v8 - Spr '97 - p58 [51-250]
  c PW - v243 - N 25 '96 - p77 [51-250]
  c SLJ - v43 - Ja '97 - p77 [51-250]
The Wind in the Willows
  c ChLAQ - v21 - Fall '96 - p126+ [501+]

The Wind in the Willows. Audio Version
  c TES - D 27 '96 - p27 [1-50]
Graham-White, Anthony - *Punctuation and Its Dramatic Value in Shakespearean Drama*
  MLR - v92 - Ap '97 - p450 [501+]
Grainger, Percy - *The All-Round Man*
  Notes - v53 - S '96 - p75+ [501+]
Grainville, Patrick - *Le Lien*
  BL - v93 - Ja '97 - p827 [1-50]
Gralla, Preston - *Online Kids*
  c LATBR - S 22 '96 - p15 [51-250]
  c SLJ - v42 - S '96 - p215 [51-250]
  c TES - O 18 '96 - p41U [1-50]
Grambling, Lois G - *Can I Have a Stegosaurus, Mom? Can I? Please!? (Illus. by H B Lewis)*
  c RT - v50 - O '96 - p132 [1-50]
Night Sounds (Illus. by Randall F Ray)
  c SLJ - v42 - Ag '96 - p122 [51-250]
Gramling, Robert - *Oil on the Edge*
  CS - v25 - N '96 - p806+ [501+]
Gramsci, Antonio - *Prison Letters*
  Obs - O 20 '96 - p18* [51-250]
Prison Notebooks. Vol. 2
  R&R Bk N - v12 - F '97 - p16 [51-250]
Gran, Peter - *Beyond Eurocentrism*
  Choice - v34 - D '96 - p669 [51-250]
El Gran Libro Ilustrado De Las Labores
  LJ - v122 - Ja '97 - p78+ [51-250]
Granatstein, J L - *Yankee Go Home?*
  Beav - v77 - F '97 - p46 [501+]
  BL - v93 - D 1 '96 - p624 [51-250]
  Mac - v109 - D 16 '96 - p74 [501+]
  Quill & Q - v62 - S '96 - p67 [251-500]
Grand, Mark - *Java Language Reference*
  r LJ - v122 - Ap 1 '97 - p118 [51-250]
Grand Street
  p Utne R - Jl '96 - p118+ [51-250]
Grandin, Temple - *Thinking in Pictures and Other Reports from My Life with Autism*
  Atl - v279 - F '97 - p110 [51-250]
  PW - v243 - O 7 '96 - p69 [1-50]
Grandy, David A - *Leo Szilard: Science as a Mode of Being*
  Choice - v34 - F '97 - p983 [51-250]
Granfield, Linda - *Amazing Grace (Illus. by Janet Wilson)*
  c Quill & Q - v63 - Ja '97 - p37 [1-50]
Cowboy: An Album
  y Kliatt - v30 - S '96 - p3 [1-50]
In Flanders Fields (Illus. by Janet Wilson)
  c BL - v93 - N 1 '96 - p496 [51-250]
  c BW - v26 - D 8 '96 - p20 [51-250]
  c HB Guide - v8 - Spr '97 - p152 [51-250]
  c KR - v64 - N 1 '96 - p1601 [51-250]
  c SLJ - v42 - D '96 - p129 [51-250]
Grange, William - *Comedy in the Weimar Republic*
  r Choice - v34 - Mr '97 - p1172 [51-250]
  r R&R Bk N - v12 - F '97 - p90 [51-250]
Grangeat, Pierre - *Three-Dimensional Image Reconstruction in Radiology and Nuclear Medicine*
  SciTech - v20 - D '96 - p38 [51-250]
Granger, Ann - *A Candle for a Corpse*
  KR - v64 - My 1 '96 - p643 [251-500]
A Touch of Mortality
  KR - v65 - Ja 15 '97 - p97 [51-250]
A Word after Dying
  Books - v11 - Ap '97 - p22 [51-250]
Granger, Bill - *Drover and the Designated Hitter*
  Aethlon - v13 - Spr '96 - p202+ [501+]
Granger, Gilles-Gaston - *Le Probable, Le Possible Et Le Virtuel*
  Choice - v34 - D '96 - p565 [1-50]
Granheim, Else - *Public Library Legislation in Europe*
  LAR - v98 - D '96 - p650 [51-250]
Granin, Daniil - *Begstvo V Rossiiu*
  BL - v93 - O 1 '96 - p327 [1-50]
The Granite Review
  p LMR - v15 - Win '96 - p43+ [51-250]
Grannum, Guy - *Tracing Your West Indian Ancestors*
  r Am Geneal - v71 - Jl '96 - p190 [51-250]
  J Gov Info - v23 - S '96 - p648 [51-250]
Granoff, Phyllis - *The Clever Adulteress and Other Stories*
  Rel St Rev - v23 - Ap '97 - p113+ [501+]
Granovetter, Mark - *Getting a Job. 2nd Ed.*
  AJS - v102 - N '96 - p893+ [501+]
Granqvist, Raoul - *Imitation as Resistance*
  Nine-C Lit - v51 - Mr '97 - p557 [51-250]
Granrose, Cherlyn S - *Work-Family Role Choices for Women in Their 20s and 30s*
  Choice - v34 - My '97 - p1583 [51-250]
  HR Mag - v42 - F '97 - p122 [51-250]
  J Car P&E - v57 - Win '97 - p17 [251-500]

Grant, Alan - *Contemporary American Politics*
  JPR - v34 - F '97 - p112 [251-500]
Grant, Alexander - *Medieval Scotland*
  EHR - v111 - S '96 - p953+ [251-500]
Uniting the Kingdom?
  HRNB - v25 - Win '97 - p66+ [251-500]
  R&R Bk N - v11 - D '96 - p8 [51-250]
Grant, August E - *Communication Technology Update. 5th Ed.*
  SciTech - v20 - N '96 - p74 [51-250]
Grant, Barry Keith - *The Dread of Difference*
  LJ - v122 - F 1 '97 - p80 [51-250]
Film Genre Reader II
  Bloom Rev - v16 - S '96 - p31 [51-250]
  Choice - v34 - S '96 - p135 [51-250]
Grant, Bruce - *The Budd Family*
  Aust Bk R - S '96 - p66+ [501+]
Grant, Bruce, 1964- - *In the Soviet House of Culture*
  AJS - v102 - S '96 - p613+ [501+]
  Am Ethnol - v24 - F '97 - p239+ [501+]
Grant, Carl A - *After the School Bell Rings*
  R&R Bk N - v11 - N '96 - p57 [51-250]
  TES - Ag 30 '96 - p32 [51-250]
Grant, Charles L - *Symphony*
  KR - v64 - D 15 '96 - p1754+ [251-500]
  PW - v244 - Ja 13 '97 - p55 [51-250]
Grant, Cynthia D - *Mary Wolf*
  y Emerg Lib - v24 - S '96 - p24 [1-50]
  y PW - v244 - F 24 '97 - p93 [1-50]
Grant, Daniel - *The Business of Being an Artist*
  Ceram Mo - v44 - S '96 - p30+ [251-500]
Grant, Edward - *Planets, Stars and Orbs*
  New Sci - v153 - F 15 '97 - p43 [51-250]
Grant, Elizabeth - *A Highland Lady in France 1843-1845*
  TLS - Mr 7 '97 - p32 [51-250]
Grant, George, 1954- - *The Patriot's Handbook*
  LJ - v122 - Ja '97 - p120 [51-250]
Grant, George Parkin - *George Grant: Selected Letters*
  BIC - v25 - N '96 - p19+ [501+]
  R&R Bk N - v11 - N '96 - p2 [51-250]
Philosophy in the Mass Age
  CPR - v16 - Je '96 - p165+ [501+]
Time as History
  CPR - v16 - Je '96 - p165+ [501+]
Grant, H Roger - *Erie Lackawanna*
  BusLR - v21 - 3 '96 - p210+ [501+]
Railroad Postcards in the Age of Steam
  J Am Cult - v18 - Win '95 - p99 [51-250]
Grant, J Kerry - *A Companion to The Crying of Lot 49*
  J Am St - v30 - Ap '96 - p182+ [501+]
Grant, James - *The Trouble with Prosperity*
  Barron's - v76 - N 25 '96 - p52 [501+]
  BL - v93 - N 15 '96 - p556 [51-250]
  BW - v26 - N 17 '96 - p11 [51-250]
  Choice - v34 - Ap '97 - p1387 [51-250]
  NYTBR - v101 - N 10 '96 - p70 [501+]
  PW - v243 - O 14 '96 - p72 [51-250]
  WSJ-MW - v78 - N 12 '96 - pA16 [501+]
Grant, Jim, 1942- - *The Looping Handbook*
  Inst - v106 - Mr '97 - p6 [51-250]
  Learning - v25 - Mr '97 - p14+ [51-250]
The Multiage Handbook
  r Learning - v25 - S '96 - p47+ [51-250]
Grant, Johnny - *Very Close to Trouble*
  PW - v243 - N 25 '96 - p68 [51-250]
Grant, Judith Skelton - *Robertson Davies: Man of Myth*
  Bks & Cult - v2 - Jl '96 - p13 [501+]
  WLT - v71 - Win '97 - p163 [251-500]
Grant, Larry - *One In a Million (Illus. by Reggie Byers)*
  c BW - v26 - D 8 '96 - p21+ [501+]
Grant, Linda - *Lethal Genes*
  y BL - v93 - O 1 '96 - p324+ [51-250]
  BWatch - v18 - F '97 - p6 [51-250]
  KR - v64 - Ag 15 '96 - p1189+ [51-250]
  PW - v243 - Jl 22 '96 - p228 [51-250]
Grant, Mariel - *Propaganda and the Role of the State in Inter-War Britain*
  EHR - v112 - Ap '97 - p528+ [501+]
Grant, Michael, 1914- - *Art in the Roman Empire*
  Choice - v34 - O '96 - p267 [51-250]
The Classical Greeks
  y SLJ - v42 - N '96 - p39 [51-250]
Cleopatra (Runger). Audio Version
  BL - v93 - My 15 '97 - p1596 [51-250]
  BWatch - v18 - Mr '97 - p7+ [1-50]
  y Kliatt - v31 - My '97 - p46+ [51-250]
Julius Caesar (Runger). Audio Version
  y Kliatt - v31 - My '97 - p47 [51-250]

Grant, Neil - *The Egyptians*
  c Ch BWatch - v6 - S '96 - p6 [51-250]
  c Cur R - v36 - D '96 - p12 [51-250]
  c HB Guide - v8 - Spr '97 - p165 [51-250]
  c SLJ - v42 - S '96 - p214 [51-250]
Grant, Pamela - *The Lost Mine*
  c Bks Keeps - N '96 - p11 [51-250]
  y Sch Lib - v44 - N '96 - p170 [51-250]
Grant, Patrick - *Personalism and the Politics of Culture*
  Choice - v34 - Mr '97 - p1174 [501+]
Grant, R G - *1848: Year of Revolution*
  c TES - O 4 '96 - p17* [501+]
The American Revolution
  c TES - O 4 '96 - p17* [501+]
Grant, Richard - *Tex and Molly in the Afterlife*
  LJ - v121 - S 15 '96 - p95+ [51-250]
Grant, Rob - *Red Dwarf Backwards*
  Books - v10 - Je '96 - p23 [1-50]
Grant, Robert M - *Heresy and Criticism*
  JAAR - v64 - Win '96 - p878+ [501+]
Grant, Stephanie - *The Passion of Alice*
  y Kliatt - v31 - Ja '97 - p6 [51-250]
  NYTBR - v101 - O 13 '96 - p32 [1-50]
Grant, Tracy - *Shadows of the Heart*
  PW - v243 - O 21 '96 - p78 [51-250]
Grant, Ulysses S - *Personal Memoirs of U.S. Grant*
  VQR - v72 - Aut '96 - p141* [1-50]
Grant, Wyn - *Autos, Smog, and Pollution Control*
  APSR - v90 - D '96 - p910+ [501+]
Granta 54
  p NYRB - v43 - Ag 8 '96 - p16+ [501+]
Granta 55
  p Obs - N 3 '96 - p18* [51-250]
  p TES - O 25 '96 - p7* [501+]
  p VV - v41 - N 19 '96 - p59+ [501+]
Granta 56
  p NS - v126 - Ja 17 '97 - p44+ [501+]
Grantham, Dewey W - *The South in Modern America*
  JSH - v62 - N '96 - p767+ [501+]
Grants and Awards Available to American Writers 1996-97
  r ARBA - v28 - '97 - p314 [51-250]
Grants for Recreation, Sports and Athletics. 1994 Ed.
  Adoles - v31 - Win '96 - p992 [51-250]
Grants on Disc. Electronic Media Version
  r ARBA - v28 - '97 - p314+ [51-250]
The Grants Register 1997
  r R&R Bk N - v12 - F '97 - p68 [51-250]
Grapard, Allan G - *The Protocol of the Gods*
  Rel St Rev - v22 - O '96 - p313+ [501+]
Graph
  p ILS - v16 - Spr '97 - p34 [251-500]
Graphis Press Corp. - *Information Architects*
  LJ - v121 - O 1 '96 - p120 [1-50]
Graser, Marcus - *Der Blockierte Wohlfahrtsstaat*
  AHR - v101 - D '96 - p1567+ [501+]
Grass, Gunter - *Cat and Mouse and Other Writings*
  TranslRevS - v2 - D '96 - p25 [1-50]
Novemberland: Selected Poems 1956-1993
  Am - v175 - O 26 '96 - p26 [251-500]
  TranslRev - 51 '96 - p53+ [501+]
Ein Weites Feld
  Lon R Bks - v18 - O 17 '96 - p3+ [501+]
Grassby, Richard - *The Business Community of Seventeenth-Century England*
  JEL - v34 - S '96 - p1453 [51-250]
  Six Ct J - v27 - Win '96 - p1101+ [501+]
The English Gentleman in Trade
  EHR - v111 - N '96 - p1287+ [251-500]
Grasselli, Gabriella - *British and American Responses to the Soviet Invasion of Afghanistan*
  R&R Bk N - v12 - F '97 - p23 [51-250]
Grasso, Kenneth L - *Catholicism, Liberalism, and Communitarianism*
  APSR - v90 - S '96 - p627+ [501+]
  IPQ - v36 - S '96 - p364+ [501+]
  SSQ - v78 - Mr '97 - p237+ [501+]
Grasso, Silvana - *Ninna Nanna Del Lupo*
  WLT - v70 - Aut '96 - p931+ [251-500]
Grathwol, Robert P - *American Forces in Berlin*
  Pub Hist - v18 - Sum '96 - p58+ [501+]
Gratt, Lawrence B - *Air Toxic Risk Assessment and Management*
  Choice - v34 - F '97 - p996 [51-250]
Graubart, Julian I - *Golf's Greatest Championship*
  BL - v93 - My 15 '97 - p1555 [51-250]
  LJ - v122 - Ap 1 '97 - p99 [51-250]
  PW - v244 - F 24 '97 - p71+ [51-250]
  Trib Bks - My 18 '97 - p7 [501+]
Grauer, Neil A - *Remember Laughter*
  JMCQ - v73 - Win '96 - p1005+ [251-500]

Graumann, Thomas - *Christus Interpres*
   CH - v65 - S '96 - p448+ [501+]
Grauvogel, Gerd Wilhelm - *Theodor Von Wachter: Christ Und Sozialdemokrat*
   CH - v65 - D '96 - p757+ [501+]
Gravel, Francois - *Ostend*
   Quill & Q - v62 - O '96 - p41 [251-500]
Gravel, Geary - *The Shadowsmith*
   y   Kliatt - v31 - Ja '97 - p14 [51-250]
Gravelle, Karen - *The Period Book (Illus. by Debbie Palen)*
   c   HB Guide - v7 - Fall '96 - p348 [51-250]
Graver, David - *The Aesthetics of Disturbance*
   Theat J - v48 - O '96 - p401+ [501+]
Graver, Lawrence - *An Obsession with Anne Frank*
   Biography - v19 - Fall '96 - p429+ [1-50]
Graves, Bonnie - *Mystery of the Tooth Gremlin (Illus. by Paige Billin-Frye)*
   c   BL - v93 - My 15 '97 - p1575 [51-250]
Graves, Donald H - *Writing: Teachers and Children at Work*
   New Ad - v9 - Fall '96 - p309+ [501+]
Graves, Earl G - *How to Succeed in Business without Being White*
   BL - v93 - Ap 1 '97 - p1266 [51-250]
   LJ - v122 - Ap 15 '97 - p91+ [51-250]
   PW - v244 - Ap 7 '97 - p86 [51-250]
Graves, John - *Financial Professional's Internet Guide*
   LJ - v122 - F 15 '97 - p144 [51-250]
Graves, John, 1920- - *A John Graves Reader*
   BW - v26 - O 20 '96 - p12 [51-250]
Graves, Johnathan - *Global Environmental Change*
   y   New Sci - v151 - S 28 '96 - p50+ [501+]
Graves, Michael F - *The First R*
   Choice - v34 - Mr '97 - p1211 [51-250]
Graves, Richard Perceval - *Robert Graves and the White Goddess 1940-85*
   BW - v26 - Ag 25 '96 - p6 [501+]
   LJ - v121 - O 15 '96 - p58 [51-250]
   NYTBR - v101 - N 10 '96 - p22 [501+]
Graves, Robert - *Complete Short Stories*
   LJ - v121 - O 15 '96 - p92 [51-250]
   PW - v243 - N 4 '96 - p64 [51-250]
Gravesteijn, J - *Multilingual Thesaurus of Geosciences. 2nd Ed.*
   r   ARBA - v28 - '97 - p635 [51-250]
Gravett, Christopher - *The Knight's Handbook*
   c   CCB-B - v50 - My '97 - p322 [51-250]
   c   KR - v65 - My 1 '97 - p721 [51-250]
   c   PW - v244 - Ap 21 '97 - p74 [51-250]
   The World of the Medieval Knight (Illus. by Brett Breckon)
   c   Bks Keeps - Mr '97 - p24 [51-250]
   c   BL - v93 - Ja '97 - p850 [51-250]
   c   Sch Lib - v45 - F '97 - p38 [51-250]
   c   SLJ - v43 - Mr '97 - p200 [51-250]
Gray, Adele - *New Game, New Rules*
   JEL - v34 - D '96 - p2090+ [51-250]
   R&R Bk N - v11 - N '96 - p31 [51-250]
Gray, Alasdair - *Lanark: A Life in 4 Books*
   NYTBR - v101 - Ag 25 '96 - p28 [51-250]
   Why Scots Should Rule Scotland
   Obs - Ap 6 '97 - p18* [501+]
Gray, Andrew - *The Arakmbut: Mythology, Spirituality, and History in an Amazonian Community*
   R&R Bk N - v12 - F '97 - p28 [51-250]
Gray, Chris Hables - *Postmodern War*
   PW - v244 - Ap 28 '97 - p62 [251-500]
   Technohistory: Using the History of American Technology in Interdisciplinary Research
   Choice - v34 - Ap '97 - p1361 [51-250]
Gray, Colin S - *Explorations in Strategy*
   Choice - v34 - D '96 - p688 [51-250]
Gray, Donald H - *Biotechnical and Soil Bioengineering Slope Stabilization*
   Choice - v34 - F '97 - p994 [51-250]
   SciTech - v20 - D '96 - p65 [51-250]
Gray, Douglas - *Homebuying Made Easy. 2nd Ed.*
   r   Quill & Q - v63 - Mr '97 - p23 [251-500]
Gray, Ed - *Wings from Cover*
   PW - v243 - O 7 '96 - p50 [51-250]
Gray, Fred - *Bus Ride to Justice*
   BWatch - v18 - Mr '97 - p3 [51-250]
Gray, Gallagher - *A Motive for Murder*
   Arm Det - v29 - Fall '96 - p487+ [51-250]
Gray, Ginna - *No Truer Love*
   PW - v243 - O 14 '96 - p81 [51-250]
Gray, Herman - *Watching Race*
   Afterimage - v24 - Ja '97 - p23 [51-250]
   CS - v25 - S '96 - p688+ [501+]

Gray, John, 1946- - *Lost in North America*
   Can Lit - Win '96 - p160+ [501+]
Gray, John, 1948- - *Endgames: Questions in Late Modern Political Thought*
   NS - v126 - Mr 27 '97 - p54 [501+]
   TLS - Ap 11 '97 - p3+ [501+]
   Enlightenment's Wake
   Dis - v43 - Fall '96 - p132+ [501+]
   RP - v58 - Fall '96 - p807+ [501+]
   Isaiah Berlin
   Choice - v34 - O '96 - p293 [51-250]
   Hast Cen R - v26 - Jl '96 - p41 [1-50]
   JEL - v34 - D '96 - p2141+ [51-250]
   Nat R - v48 - N 25 '96 - p69+ [501+]
   NYTBR - v101 - D 8 '96 - p88 [1-50]
   Reason - v28 - N '96 - p66+ [501+]
   RM - v50 - D '96 - p403+ [501+]
   Liberalism. 2nd Ed.
   JEL - v34 - S '96 - p1414 [51-250]
Gray, John, 1951- - *Lo Que Tu Madre No Te Dijo Y Tu Padre No Sabia*
   LJ - v122 - Ja '97 - p79 [51-250]
   Men Are from Mars, Women Are from Venus
   CSM - v88 - N 7 '96 - p14 [51-250]
   CSM - v89 - D 12 '96 - p14 [51-250]
   CSM - v89 - Ja 9 '97 - p14 [51-250]
   CSM - v89 - F 6 '97 - p14 [51-250]
   CSM - v89 - Mr 6 '97 - p14 [51-250]
   CSM - v89 - Ap 3 '97 - p14 [51-250]
   Men Are from Mars, Women Are from Venus. Electronic Media Version
   LJ - v121 - O 15 '96 - p96+ [501+]
Gray, John Shapley - *Interprocess Communications in UNIX*
   SciTech - v20 - N '96 - p6 [51-250]
Gray, Keith - *Creepers*
   y   Bks Keeps - Jl '96 - p13 [51-250]
   c   Bks Keeps - Mr '97 - p27 [51-250]
   y   JB - v60 - O '96 - p201+ [251-500]
   y   Sch Lib - v44 - N '96 - p170 [51-250]
Gray, Libba Moore - *Is There Room on the Feather Bed? (Illus. by Nadine Bernard Westcott)*
   c   BL - v93 - Mr 1 '97 - p1171+ [51-250]
   c   CBRS - v25 - Mr '97 - p86 [51-250]
   c   KR - v65 - Mr 15 '97 - p461 [51-250]
   c   PW - v244 - Ja 20 '97 - p400 [51-250]
   Little Lil and the Swing-Singing Sax (Illus. by Lisa Cohen)
   c   BL - v93 - S 1 '96 - p142 [51-250]
   c   CBRS - v25 - O '96 - p19 [51-250]
   c   CCB-B - v50 - F '97 - p206+ [51-250]
   c   HB Guide - v8 - Spr '97 - p29 [51-250]
   c   KR - v64 - S 15 '96 - p1400 [51-250]
   c   PW - v243 - O 14 '96 - p83 [51-250]
   c   SLJ - v42 - N '96 - p81 [51-250]
   My Mama Had a Dancing Heart (Illus. by Raul Colon)
   c   LA - v73 - D '96 - p622+ [51-250]
Gray, Lois S - *Under the Stars*
   JEL - v34 - D '96 - p2075 [51-250]
   TCI - v30 - O '96 - p53+ [501+]
Gray, Lyn - *The ABC Collection*
   TES - Jl 5 '96 - pR7 [251-500]
Gray, Marcus - *Last Gang in Town*
   BL - v93 - S 15 '96 - p200 [51-250]
   BWatch - v17 - N '96 - p9 [51-250]
   LJ - v121 - S 15 '96 - p70 [51-250]
Gray, Nigel - *The Dog Show (Illus. by Margaret Wilson)*
   c   Magpies - v11 - Jl '96 - p26 [51-250]
   Running Away from Home (Illus. by Gregory Rogers)
   c   Aust Bk R - Je '96 - p63 [501+]
   c   BL - v92 - Ag '96 - p1907 [51-250]
   c   HB Guide - v7 - Fall '96 - p258 [1-50]
   c   Magpies - v11 - My '96 - p38 [51-250]
Gray, Richard, 1947- - *Cinemas in Britain*
   Si & So - v6 - N '96 - p34 [51-250]
Gray, Richard J - *The Life of William Faulkner*
   J Am St - v30 - Ap '96 - p143+ [501+]
   MLR - v91 - Jl '96 - p710+ [501+]
Gray, Richard Stanley - *World Agriculture in a Post-GATT Environment*
   JEL - v34 - S '96 - p1494+ [51-250]
Gray, Richard T - *Stations of the Divided Subject*
   Ger Q - v70 - Win '97 - p65+ [501+]
Gray, Robert, 1945- - *Lineations*
   Aust Bk R - F '97 - p41 [501+]
Gray, Robert Q - *The Factory Question and Industrial England 1830-1860*
   Choice - v34 - Mr '97 - p1220 [51-250]
Gray, Rose - *The River Cafe Cook Book*
   TES - D 27 '96 - p17 [1-50]

Gray, Sharon A - *Health of Native People of North America*
   r   ARBA - v28 - '97 - p157 [51-250]
   r   R&R Bk N - v12 - F '97 - p95 [51-250]
Gray, Spalding - *Monster in a Box (Gray). Audio Version*
   BL - v93 - F 15 '97 - p1038 [51-250]
Gray, Susan E - *The Yankee West*
   Choice - v34 - Ap '97 - p1404 [51-250]
Gray, W M, 1953- - *Soldiers of the King*
   Beav - v76 - D '96 - p44 [501+]
Gray, Walter D - *Interpreting American Democracy in France*
   FR - v70 - D '96 - p374+ [501+]
Gray, William - *Shares*
   Arm Det - v29 - Sum '96 - p364 [251-500]
Gray, Winifred - *Diagnostic Cytopathology*
   SciTech - v21 - Mr '97 - p47 [51-250]
Grayson, A Kirk - *Assyrian Rulers of the Early First Millennia BC. Vol. 2*
   R&R Bk N - v12 - F '97 - p79 [51-250]
Grayson, Elizabeth - *So Wide the Sky*
   PW - v244 - F 10 '97 - p81 [51-250]
Grayson, Lesley - *Scientific Deception*
   LAR - v98 - Mr '96 - p164 [51-250]
Graziunas, Diana - *Thinning the Predators (Garber). Audio Version*
   y   Kliatt - v30 - S '96 - p52+ [51-250]
Grazzini, Francesca - *Flower, Why Do You Smell So Nice? (Illus. by Chiara Carrer)*
   c   HB Guide - v8 - Spr '97 - p121 [51-250]
   c   PW - v243 - N 18 '96 - p78 [51-250]
   c   SLJ - v43 - Ja '97 - p101 [51-250]
   Rain, Where Do You Come From? (Illus. by Chiara Carrer)
   c   HB Guide - v8 - Spr '97 - p113 [51-250]
   c   PW - v243 - N 18 '96 - p78 [51-250]
   c   SLJ - v43 - Ja '97 - p101 [51-250]
   Sun, Where Do You Go? (Illus. by Chiara Carrer)
   c   HB Guide - v8 - Spr '97 - p112 [51-250]
   c   KR - v64 - O 15 '96 - p1533 [51-250]
   c   PW - v243 - N 18 '96 - p78 [51-250]
   c   SLJ - v43 - Ja '97 - p101 [51-250]
   Wind, What Makes You Move? (Illus. by Chiara Carrer)
   c   HB Guide - v8 - Spr '97 - p113 [51-250]
   c   PW - v243 - N 18 '96 - p78 [51-250]
   c   SLJ - v43 - Ja '97 - p101 [51-250]
Great Britain. Central Office of Information - *Facts about Britain 1945 to 1995. Electronic Media Version*
   r   J Gov Info - v23 - S '96 - p645 [51-250]
   Women in Britain
   LAR - v98 - S '96 - p479 [1-50]
Great Britain. Central Statistical Office - *Fighting with Figures*
   J Gov Info - v23 - S '96 - p645 [51-250]
Great Britain. Dept. for Education and Employment - *Grants for Education Support and Training*
   J Gov Info - v23 - S '96 - p646 [51-250]
Great Britain. Dept. of Transport - *Transport: The Way Forward*
   J Gov Info - v23 - S '96 - p648 [51-250]
Great Britain. Ministry of Defence (Navy) - *War with Japan. Vols. 1-4*
   J Gov Info - v23 - S '96 - p648 [51-250]
Great Britain. Office for National Statistics - *Guide to Official Statistics*
   J Gov Info - v23 - S '96 - p646 [51-250]
Great Britain. Ordinance Survey - *Statlas UK*
   r   J Gov Info - v23 - S '96 - p648 [51-250]
Great Britain. Parliament. House of Commons. Agriculture and Health Committees - *Bovine Spongiform Encephalopathy (BSE) and Creutzfeldt-Jakob Disease (CJD): Recent Developments*
   Lon R Bks - v18 - S 5 '96 - p17+ [501+]
Great Britain. Prime Minister - *The Citizen's Charter*
   J Gov Info - v23 - S '96 - p644 [501+]
Great Britain. Treasury. Central Computer and Telecommunications Agency - *An Introduction to Geographic Information Systems 1994*
   GJ - v162 - Jl '96 - p242 [1-50]
Great Dates in Islamic History
   r   ARBA - v28 - '97 - p71 [51-250]
Great Events. Vols. 1-3
   r   ARBA - v28 - '97 - p216 [51-250]
   r   LJ - v122 - Ap 1 '97 - p82 [51-250]
Great Events. Vols. 11-13
   r   R&R Bk N - v12 - F '97 - p13 [51-250]
Great Girl Food (Illus. by Judy Pelikan)
   c   PW - v243 - S 9 '96 - p85 [51-250]
Greaves, A E - *Stendhal's Italy*
   MLR - v91 - O '96 - p997+ [251-500]

Greaves, David - *Philosophical Problems in Health Care*
Hast Cen R - v26 - Jl '96 - p41 [1-50]

Greco, Albert N - *The Book Publishing Industry*
JEL - v35 - Mr '97 - p250 [51-250]

Greco, Giorgio Del - *Catalogo Delle Edizioni Antiche Possedute Dalla Biblioteca Della Camera Dei Deputati Sec. XV-XVII*
r Lib - v18 - D '96 - p362 [51-250]

Gree, Alain - *Les Farfeluches Autour Du Monde*
c BL - v93 - N 1 '96 - p500 [1-50]
Les Farfeluches Jouent Avec Les Couleurs
c BL - v93 - N 1 '96 - p500 [1-50]

Greed, Clara - *Implementing Town Planning*
GJ - v163 - Mr '97 - p101+ [251-500]

Greeley, Andrew M - *Angel Light (Dukes). Audio Version*
y Kliatt - v30 - S '96 - p42 [51-250]
Happy Are the Oppressed
Arm Det - v30 - Win '97 - p90 [251-500]
BL - v93 - S 1 '96 - p67 [51-250]
Irish Lace
KR - v64 - S 1 '96 - p1256 [251-500]
LJ - v121 - N 1 '96 - p106 [51-250]
PW - v243 - O 14 '96 - p67 [51-250]
Sex: The Catholic Experience
CLW - v66 - Je '96 - p34 [51-250]
Summer at the Lake
BL - v93 - Ap 1 '97 - p1268 [51-250]
KR - v65 - Mr 15 '97 - p401 [251-500]
LJ - v122 - Ap 15 '97 - p117 [51-250]
White Smoke
CLW - v67 - Mr '97 - p50+ [251-500]
White Smoke. Audio Version
BL - v93 - F 15 '97 - p1038 [51-250]
y Kliatt - v31 - Mr '97 - p47 [51-250]

Greeley, Ronald - *The NASA Atlas of the Solar System*
r Nature - v386 - Mr 27 '97 - p340+ [501+]
r New Sci - v153 - Mr 15 '97 - p44 [51-250]
r NH - v106 - Mr '97 - p10+ [501+]

Greeley, Valerie - *The Acorn's Story (Illus. by Valerie Greeley)*
c Bks Keeps - Ja '97 - p19+ [51-250]

Green, Alan, 1931- - *A Company Discovers Its Soul*
Kiplinger - v51 - F '97 - p112 [51-250]

Green, Alan, 1962- - *Allen Sapp: A Bio-Bibliography*
r ARBA - v28 - '97 - p475 [51-250]
r Choice - v34 - F '97 - p943 [51-250]
r R&R Bk N - v11 - D '96 - p55 [51-250]

Green, Anne - *Privileged Anonymity*
TLS - Ja 10 '97 - p23 [501+]

Green, Archie - *Calf's Head and Union Tale*
CAY - v17 - Win '96 - p1 [1-50]
Songs about Work
JPC - v29 - Spr '96 - p235 [51-250]

Green, Bill - *Pink Water Down*
Aust Bk R - Jl '96 - p65 [501+]

Green, Candida Lycett - *England: Travels through an Unwrecked Landscape*
LJ - v121 - N 1 '96 - p98 [51-250]

Green, Charles - *Peripheral Vision*
Aust Bk R - Ag '96 - p32+ [501+]
Meanjin - v55 - 2 '96 - p308+ [501+]

Green, Christine - *Deadly Partners*
BL - v93 - Ja '97 - p824+ [51-250]
KR - v64 - N 15 '96 - p1635 [51-250]
PW - v243 - N '96 - p60 [51-250]

Green, D H - *Medieval Listening and Reading*
MLR - v91 - Jl '96 - p775+ [501+]
MP - v94 - F '97 - p354+ [501+]
Specu - v71 - O '96 - p952+ [501+]

Green, David - *Taking Stock*
Rapport - v19 - 4 '96 - p18+ [501+]

Green, David R, 1954- - *From Artisans to Paupers*
Albion - v28 - '96 - p708+ [501+]
JEH - v57 - Mr '97 - p218+ [501+]
R&R Bk N - v12 - F '97 - p36 [51-250]

Green, Donald P - *Pathologies of Rational Choice Theory*
RP - v58 - Fall '96 - p793+ [501+]

Green, Douglas - *Tender Roses for Tough Climates*
BL - v93 - My 1 '97 - p1472 [51-250]

Green, Duncan - *Silent Revolution*
Cu H - v96 - F '97 - p89+ [501+]
Econ J - v106 - N '96 - p1797+ [501+]
HAHR - v77 - F '97 - p154+ [501+]

Green, E H H - *The Crisis of Conservatism*
HT - v46 - S '96 - p56+ [501+]
TES - Ja 31 '97 - p7* [51-250]

Green, Edward C - *AIDS and STDs in Africa*
JTWS - v13 - Spr '96 - p327+ [501+]

Green, Geoffrey - *The Vineland Papers*
Poetics T - v18 - Spr '97 - p95+ [501+]

Green, J R - *Theatre in Ancient Greek Society*
AJA - v101 - Ja '97 - p154+ [501+]

Green, James H - *The Irwin Handbook of Telecommunications. 3rd Ed.*
Choice - v34 - Mr '97 - p1190 [51-250]
SciTech - v20 - D '96 - p75 [51-250]

Green, Jen - *Volcanoes*
c Sch Lib - v45 - F '97 - p37 [51-250]

Green, Joanta H - *Renewable Energy Systems in Southeast Asia*
SciTech - v20 - N '96 - p70 [51-250]

Green, Joel B - *The Death of Jesus*
Rel St Rev - v23 - Ap '97 - p178 [51-250]
Jesus of Nazareth, Lord and Christ
Rel St Rev - v23 - Ap '97 - p177+ [251-500]
The Theology of the Gospel of Luke
JR - v77 - Ja '97 - p125+ [501+]

Green, Joey - *Paint Your House with Powdered Milk*
Ent W - O 4 '96 - p55 [251-500]
Selling Out (Green). Audio Version
Quill & Q - v62 - My '96 - p31 [1-50]

Green, John - *Counselling in HIV Infection and AIDS. 2nd Ed.*
SciTech - v20 - D '96 - p46 [51-250]

Green, John O, 1945- - *The New Age of Communications*
y Kliatt - v31 - My '97 - p29 [251-500]
PW - v244 - Ja 6 '97 - p61 [1-50]

Green, Jonathan, 1955- - *Gullah Images*
BL - v93 - F 15 '97 - p992 [51-250]
BW - v26 - D 8 '96 - p11 [51-250]
BWatch - v17 - D '96 - p4 [1-50]
B Liv - v32 - F '97 - p80 [51-250]

Green, Jonathon - *Cassell Dictionary of Insulting Quotations*
r Am - v176 - Mr 29 '97 - p2 [501+]
r BL - v93 - My 15 '97 - p1616 [51-250]
r Spec - v278 - Ja 11 '97 - p35+ [501+]
Chasing the Sun
NY - v72 - Ja 20 '97 - p97 [51-250]
NYTBR - v102 - Mr 2 '97 - p19 [51-250]
Words Apart
Econ - v341 - D 14 '96 - p87 [501+]
Spec - v278 - Ja 11 '97 - p35 [501+]

Green, Julien - *L'Avenir N'est A Personne 1990-1992*
FR - v70 - O '96 - p143+ [251-500]
On Est Si Serieux Quand On A Dix-Neuf Ans
FR - v70 - F '97 - p498+ [251-500]
Pourquoi Suis-Je Moi?
TLS - O 4 '96 - p9 [501+]
WLT - v71 - Win '97 - p111+ [501+]
Restless Youth 1922-1929
BW - v26 - Jl 14 '96 - p4 [501+]
The Stars of the South
BL - v93 - S 1 '96 - p62 [51-250]
LJ - v121 - N 1 '96 - p106 [51-250]
TLS - N 8 '96 - p28 [501+]

Green, Karen - *The Woman of Reason*
Ethics - v107 - O '96 - p187 [51-250]

Green, Lila - *Making Sense of Humor (Green). Audio Version*
LJ - v121 - O 15 '96 - p103 [51-250]

Green, Lorne - *Chief Engineer*
Can Hist R - v77 - D '96 - p622+ [501+]

Green, Mark - *The Consumer Bible*
r Workbook - v21 - Fall '96 - p122+ [501+]

Green, Mary - *Phonic Awareness 1 and 2*
TES - D 13 '96 - p43 [51-250]

Green, Mary Jean - *Postcolonial Subjects*
Choice - v34 - Mr '97 - p1169 [51-250]
WLT - v71 - Win '97 - p235+ [501+]

Green, Max - *Epitaph for American Labor*
Choice - v34 - Mr '97 - p1203 [51-250]
Comw - v124 - D 14 '97 - p20+ [501+]
WSJ-MW - v78 - D 4 '96 - pA14 [501+]

Green, Melissa - *Colour Is the Suffering of Light*
Lon R Bks - v18 - Jl 18 '96 - p18+ [501+]

Green, Michael, 1930- - *Who Is This Jesus?*
Quill & Q - v62 - D '96 - p18 [51-250]

Green, Michael J - *Arming Japan*
Arm F&S - v23 - Fall '96 - p115+ [501+]
PSQ - v111 - Win '96 - p703+ [501+]

Green, Miranda J - *The Celtic World*
Am Ant - v61 - Jl '96 - p611+ [501+]

Green, Patricia J - *A Profile of the American High School Senior in 1992*
EL - v54 - O '96 - p92 [51-250]

Green, Paul C - *Get Hired!*
BL - v92 - Ag '96 - p1865 [51-250]

Green, Peter - *The Greco-Persian Wars*
TLS - F 14 '97 - p11+ [501+]

Green, Richard - *Images of the Greek Theatre*
AJA - v101 - Ja '97 - p154+ [501+]

Green, Robert - *Alexander the Great*
c Ch BWatch - v7 - F '97 - p7 [51-250]
c HB Guide - v8 - Spr '97 - p158 [51-250]
y Kliatt - v31 - Ja '97 - p19 [51-250]
c SLJ - v42 - S '96 - p215 [51-250]
Cleopatra
c HB Guide - v8 - Spr '97 - p158 [51-250]
y Kliatt - v31 - Ja '97 - p19 [51-250]
c SLJ - v42 - S '96 - p215 [51-250]
Hannibal
c HB Guide - v8 - Spr '97 - p165 [51-250]
c SLJ - v43 - F '97 - p116 [51-250]
Herod the Great
c Ch BWatch - v7 - F '97 - p7 [51-250]
c HB Guide - v8 - Spr '97 - p158 [51-250]
y Kliatt - v31 - Ja '97 - p19 [51-250]
c SLJ - v42 - S '96 - p215 [51-250]
Julius Caesar
c HB Guide - v8 - Spr '97 - p165 [51-250]
c SLJ - v43 - F '97 - p116 [51-250]
Tutankhamun
c HB Guide - v7 - Fall '96 - p378 [1-50]
y Kliatt - v31 - Ja '97 - p19 [51-250]

Green, Robert A - *The Hurdy-Gurdy in Eighteenth-Century France*
Notes - v53 - Mr '97 - p797+ [501+]

Green, Roger J - *Catherine Booth: A Biography*
LJ - v121 - N 15 '96 - p66 [51-250]

Green, Ruth M - *The Wearing of Costume*
TCI - v30 - O '96 - p52 [251-500]

Green, S J D - *The Boundaries of the State in Modern Britain*
Choice - v34 - Ap '97 - p1409 [51-250]
Lon R Bks - v18 - My 23 '96 - p16+ [501+]
Religion in the Age of Decline
Choice - v34 - Mr '97 - p1220 [51-250]

Green, Scott E - *Isaac Asimov: An Annotated Bibliography of the Asimov Collection at Boston University*
r ARBA - v28 - '97 - p442 [51-250]
r SFS - v23 - N '96 - p533 [51-250]

Green, Septima - *Shannon Miller: American Gymnast*
c SLJ - v42 - Ag '96 - p155 [51-250]

Green, Sharon - *Convergence*
PW - v243 - O 7 '96 - p69 [51-250]

Green, Terence M - *Blue Limbo*
KR - v64 - N 15 '96 - p1639 [51-250]
PW - v243 - D 30 '96 - p59 [51-250]
Quill & Q - v63 - F '97 - p49 [251-500]
Shadow of Ashland
MFSF - v91 - Ag '96 - p28+ [501+]
NYTBR - v101 - S 15 '96 - p30 [51-250]

Green, Tim, 1963- - *The Dark Side of the Game (Green). Audio Version*
y Kliatt - v30 - N '96 - p48 [51-250]
LJ - v121 - O 15 '96 - p103 [51-250]
PW - v243 - O 7 '96 - p34 [51-250]
Quill & Q - v62 - Ag '96 - p37 [1-50]
Marauders
KR - v65 - Mr 1 '97 - p324 [51-250]
LJ - v122 - Ap 1 '97 - p125 [51-250]
PW - v244 - Mr 3 '97 - p63 [51-250]
Outlaws
BW - v26 - Ag 4 '96 - p8 [51-250]
Titans
Aethlon - v13 - Fall '95 - p138 [251-500]

Green, Vivian Hubert Howard - *The Madness of Kings*
EHR - v111 - S '96 - p1039+ [251-500]
A New History of Christianity
Am - v175 - S 21 '96 - p33+ [51-250]
BL - v93 - N 1 '96 - p460+ [51-250]
Econ - v342 - Ja 18 '97 - p82 [251-500]
HT - v46 - O '96 - p55 [1-50]
LJ - v121 - O 1 '96 - p84 [51-250]

Green, William, 1953- - *Oneota Archaeology*
Am Ant - v61 - O '96 - p808+ [501+]

Green, William C - *North American Auto Unions in Crisis*
APSR - v91 - Mr '97 - p181+ [501+]
Choice - v34 - S '96 - p173+ [51-250]
CS - v26 - Mr '97 - p165+ [501+]
R&R Bk N - v12 - F '97 - p40 [51-250]

Green, William Scott - *The Religion Factor*
BL - v93 - N 1 '96 - p462 [51-250]
PW - v243 - S 30 '96 - p75 [51-250]

Green Anarchist
p Sm Pr R - v28 - Je '96 - p22 [251-500]

Green Egg
p Sm Pr R - v28 - O '96 - p17+ [251-500]

Green: Personal Finance for the Unashamed
  p Utne R - Jl '96 - p113+ [251-500]
Greenawalt, Kent - *Fighting Words*
    CPR - v16 - O '96 - p348+ [501+]
  Private Consciences and Public Reasons
    Ethics - v107 - Ja '97 - p358+ [501+]
    Hast Cen R - v26 - Mr '96 - p47+ [501+]
Greenaway, David - *Current Issues in International Trade. 2nd Ed.*
    JEL - v34 - D '96 - p2041 [51-250]
Greenaway, Frank - *Asombrosos Murcielagos*
  c BL - v93 - F 15 '97 - p1032 [1-50]
Greenaway, Theresa - *The Really Fearsome Blood-Loving Vampire Bat and Other Creatures with Strange Eating Habits*
  cr CBRS - v25 - Ja '97 - p54+ [51-250]
  c CLW - v67 - D '96 - p61 [51-250]
  c HB Guide - v8 - Spr '97 - p117 [51-250]
  c PW - v243 - N 11 '96 - p77 [51-250]
  c SB - v33 - Mr '97 - p51 [51-250]
  c Sch Lib - v44 - N '96 - p162 [51-250]
  c SLJ - v43 - Ja '97 - p101 [51-250]
  The Really Hairy Scary Spider and Other Creatures with Lots of Legs (Illus. by F Greenaway)
  cr CBRS - v25 - Ja '97 - p54+ [51-250]
  c CLW - v67 - D '96 - p61 [51-250]
  c HB Guide - v8 - Spr '97 - p122 [51-250]
  c JB - v60 - O '96 - p193 [51-250]
  c PW - v243 - N 11 '96 - p77 [51-250]
  c SB - v33 - Mr '97 - p51 [51-250]
  c Sch Lib - v44 - N '96 - p162 [51-250]
  c SLJ - v43 - Ja '97 - p101 [51-250]
  The Really Horrible Horned Toad and Other Cold, Clammy Creatures
  cr CBRS - v25 - Ja '97 - p54+ [51-250]
  c HB Guide - v8 - Spr '97 - p117 [1-50]
  c PW - v243 - N 11 '96 - p77 [51-250]
  c SB - v33 - Mr '97 - p51 [51-250]
  c Sch Lib - v44 - N '96 - p162 [51-250]
  c SLJ - v43 - Ja '97 - p101 [51-250]
  The Really Wicked Droning Wasp and Other Things That Bite and Sting
  cr CBRS - v25 - Ja '97 - p54+ [51-250]
  c HB Guide - v8 - Spr '97 - p122 [51-250]
  c PW - v243 - N 11 '96 - p77 [51-250]
  c SB - v33 - Mr '97 - p51 [51-250]
  c Sch Lib - v44 - N '96 - p162 [51-250]
  c SLJ - v43 - Ja '97 - p101 [51-250]
Greenbaum, Sidney - *The Longman Guide to English Usage*
  c TES - Jl 5 '96 - p7* [1-50]
  The Oxford English Grammar
    Lon R Bks - v18 - Jl 18 '96 - p16+ [501+]
Greenberg, Dan - *Moses Supposes*
    PW - v244 - Mr 3 '97 - p61 [51-250]
Greenberg, David F - *Criminal Careers. Vols. 1-2*
    R&R Bk N - v12 - F '97 - p57 [51-250]
Greenberg, Gail - *A Comprehensive Guide for Listing a Building in the National Register of Historic Places*
    BL - v92 - Ag '96 - p1861 [51-250]
Greenberg, Gary - *The Moses Mystery*
    LJ - v121 - N 1 '96 - p88 [51-250]
    NYTBR - v102 - Ja 26 '97 - p19 [51-250]
Greenberg, Gerald S - *Tabloid Journalism*
  r ARBA - v28 - '97 - p345 [251-500]
  r Choice - v34 - F '97 - p943+ [51-250]
  r R&R Bk N - v11 - D '96 - p62 [51-250]
Greenberg, Jack - *Crusaders in the Courts*
    JIH - v27 - Win '97 - p551+ [501+]
Greenberg, Jan - *American Eye*
  y Emerg Lib - v24 - S '96 - p23 [1-50]
Greenberg, Judith E - *Getting into the Game*
  y CCB-B - v50 - My '97 - p322 [51-250]
  Journal of a Revolutionary War Woman
  y BL - v93 - S 1 '96 - p113 [51-250]
  y HB Guide - v7 - Fall '96 - p386 [51-250]
  y SLJ - v42 - Ag '96 - p170 [51-250]
  y VOYA - v19 - F '97 - p346 [51-250]
  Newcomers to America
  c HB Guide - v7 - Fall '96 - p312 [51-250]
  y SLJ - v42 - Ag '96 - p170 [51-250]
  y VOYA - v19 - F '97 - p346 [251-500]
Greenberg, Keith Elliot - *Magic Johnson: Champion with a Cause*
  y SLJ - v42 - O '96 - p45 [1-50]
  Rwanda (Illus. by John Isaac)
  c KR - v64 - N 15 '96 - p1669 [51-250]
  Stunt Woman (Illus. by Tim Sanders)
  c BL - v93 - F 1 '97 - p936+ [51-250]
  c HB Guide - v8 - Spr '97 - p91 [51-250]
  c SLJ - v43 - Ja '97 - p101 [51-250]

Test Pilot (Illus. by Pedro E Ybanez)
  c BL - v93 - F 1 '97 - p936+ [51-250]
  c HB Guide - v8 - Spr '97 - p91 [51-250]
Zack's Story (Illus. by Carol Halebian)
  c HB Guide - v8 - Spr '97 - p89 [51-250]
  c SLJ - v43 - Mr '97 - p200+ [51-250]
Greenberg, Kenneth S - *Honor and Slavery*
    Choice - v34 - N '96 - p525 [51-250]
    HRNB - v25 - Win '97 - p60 [251-500]
    Nat R - v48 - S 16 '96 - p66+ [501+]
    RP - v59 - Win '97 - p146+ [501+]
    TLS - F 7 '97 - p32 [251-500]
Greenberg, Mark L - *Speak Silence*
    R&R Bk N - v11 - D '96 - p64 [51-250]
Greenberg, Martin Harry - *Future Net*
  y Kliatt - v31 - Ja '97 - p14 [51-250]
    LJ - v121 - S 15 '96 - p100 [51-250]
  Great Writers and Kids Write Mystery Stories (Illus. by Gahan Wilson)
  c KR - v64 - D 15 '96 - p1798 [51-250]
  Holmes for the Holidays
  y BL - v93 - O 1 '96 - p325 [51-250]
    KR - v64 - S 15 '96 - p1360 [51-250]
    LJ - v121 - O 1 '96 - p131 [1-50]
    PW - v243 - S 16 '96 - p73+ [51-250]
    WSJ-MW - v78 - D 9 '96 - pA12 [1-50]
  Werewolves
    Necro - Sum '96 - p8+ [501+]
  White House Horrors
  y Kliatt - v31 - Ja '97 - p14 [51-250]
Greenberg, Maurice R - *Making Intelligence Smarter*
    NWCR - v49 - Aut '96 - p142+ [501+]
Greenberg, Pam - *Guide to Legislative Information Technology*
  r J Gov Info - v24 - Ja '97 - p61+ [501+]
Greenberg, Richard H - *Pathways: Jews Who Return*
    LJ - v122 - Ja '97 - p105 [51-250]
    PW - v243 - D 16 '96 - p53 [51-250]
Greenberg, Robert M - *Splintered Worlds*
    NEQ - v69 - S '96 - p513+ [501+]
Greenberg, Stanley B - *Middle Class Dreams. Rev. and Updated Ed.*
    JEL - v34 - D '96 - p2029 [51-250]
    NYTBR - v101 - O 27 '96 - p48 [1-50]
Greenblat, Rodney Alan - *Thunder Bunny (Illus. by Rodney Alan Greenblat)*
  c CBRS - v25 - Mr '97 - p86+ [51-250]
  c KR - v64 - D 1 '96 - p1736 [51-250]
  c PW - v243 - D 9 '96 - p67 [51-250]
  c SLJ - v43 - Mr '97 - p159 [51-250]
Greenblatt, Joel - *You Can Be a Stock Market Genius Even if You're Not Too Smart*
    BL - v93 - Mr 1 '97 - p1097 [51-250]
    LJ - v122 - Ap 15 '97 - p92 [51-250]
    WSJ-Cent - v99 - My 12 '97 - pA12 [51-250]
Greenblatt, Stephen - *Redrawing the Boundaries*
    Clio - v25 - Sum '96 - p421+ [501+]
Greenburg, Dan - *Dr. Jekyll, Orthodontist (Illus. by Jack E Davis)*
  c SLJ - v43 - Mr '97 - p159 [51-250]
  A Ghost Named Wanda (Illus. by Jack E Davis)
  c SLJ - v43 - F '97 - p81 [51-250]
  Great-Grandpa's in the Litter Box (Illus. by Jack E Davis)
  c BL - v93 - Ja '97 - p859 [251-500]
  c SLJ - v43 - F '97 - p81 [51-250]
  I'm Out of My Body...Please Leave a Message (Illus. by Jack E Davis)
  c KR - v64 - D 15 '96 - p1798 [51-250]
  c SLJ - v43 - Mr '97 - p159 [51-250]
  Through the Medicine Cabinet (Illus. by Jack E Davis)
  c BL - v93 - Ja '97 - p859 [251-500]
  c SLJ - v43 - F '97 - p81 [51-250]
  Zap! I'm a Mind Reader (Illus. by Jack E Davis)
  c SLJ - v43 - F '97 - p81 [51-250]
Greene, A C - *Christmas Memories*
    BWatch - v17 - D '96 - p1 [1-50]
    Roundup M - v4 - D '96 - p28 [1-50]
Greene, Bob - *The 50-Year Dash*
    BL - v93 - D 15 '96 - p691 [51-250]
    KR - v64 - D 15 '96 - p1783 [251-500]
    NYTBR - v102 - Mr 16 '97 - p20 [51-250]
    PW - v243 - D 2 '96 - p45+ [51-250]
  The 50-Year Dash (Greene). Audio Version
    LJ - v122 - Ap 15 '97 - p139 [51-250]
    PW - v244 - F 3 '97 - p42 [51-250]

Make the Connection
    BL - v93 - O 1 '96 - p292 [1-50]
    CSM - v88 - N 7 '96 - p14 [51-250]
    CSM - v89 - D 12 '96 - p14 [51-250]
    CSM - v89 - Ja 9 '97 - p14 [51-250]
    CSM - v89 - F 6 '97 - p14 [51-250]
    CSM - v89 - Ap 3 '97 - p14 [51-250]
    Ent W - S 20 '96 - p70 [251-500]
Greene, Carol - *Eugene Field: The Children's Poet*
  c CLW - v67 - Mr '97 - p14 [1-50]
  Firefighters Fight Fires
  c HB Guide - v8 - Spr '97 - p91 [51-250]
  Joy to the World (Illus. by Christopher Gray)
  c PW - v243 - S 30 '96 - p90 [51-250]
  c SLJ - v42 - O '96 - p36 [51-250]
  Police Officers Protect People
  c HB Guide - v8 - Spr '97 - p91 [51-250]
  c SLJ - v43 - Mr '97 - p174 [51-250]
  Veterinarians Help Animals
  c HB Guide - v8 - Spr '97 - p91 [51-250]
Greene, Dana - *The Living of Maisie Ward*
    LJ - v122 - Ap 15 '97 - p88 [51-250]
Greene, Ellin - *Ling-Li and the Phoenix Fairy (Illus. by Zong-Zhou Wang)*
  c HB Guide - v7 - Fall '96 - p321 [51-250]
  c RT - v50 - Ap '97 - p594 [51-250]
  Storytelling. Art and Technique. 3rd Ed.
  r CLW - v67 - Mr '97 - p47 [51-250]
  r R&R Bk N - v12 - F '97 - p67 [51-250]
    SLJ - v42 - S '96 - p112+ [1-50]
Greene, Graham - *British Dramatists*
    PW - v244 - Mr 24 '97 - p72 [1-50]
  The Quiet American
    FEER - Anniv '96 - p225 [501+]
    J Am St - v30 - Ap '96 - p65+ [501+]
Greene, Harry W - *Snakes: The Evolution of Mystery in Nature*
    BL - v93 - My 1 '97 - p1469 [251-500]
    KR - v65 - Ap 1 '97 - p519 [251-500]
    LJ - v122 - My 1 '97 - p135 [51-250]
Greene, Jack P - *Interpreting Early America*
    HRNB - v25 - Win '97 - p62+ [251-500]
  Negotiated Authorities
    Can Hist R - v77 - D '96 - p643+ [501+]
    EHR - v112 - F '97 - p210+ [501+]
    JIH - v27 - Aut '96 - p332+ [501+]
  Understanding the American Revolution
    HRNB - v25 - Fall '96 - p4 [251-500]
    JSH - v63 - F '97 - p149+ [501+]
    NEQ - v69 - S '96 - p502+ [501+]
Greene, Jeffrey P - *American Furniture of the 18th Century*
    Choice - v34 - Ja '97 - p783 [51-250]
Greene, John Robert - *The Presidency of Gerald R. Ford*
    AHR - v101 - D '96 - p1650+ [251-500]
Greene, Liz - *Barriers and Boundaries*
    Horoscope - v63 - Ap '97 - p42+ [501+]
  Neptune, and the Quest for Redemption
    Horoscope - v62 - O '96 - p16+ [501+]
Greene, Lorenzo J - *Selling Black History for Carter G. Woodson*
    Choice - v34 - F '97 - p1024 [51-250]
Greene, Maxine - *Releasing the Imagination*
    AJE - v105 - N '96 - p102+ [501+]
    ES - v27 - Fall '96 - p292+ [501+]
Greene, Melissa Fay - *The Temple Bombing*
    Choice - v34 - S '96 - p194 [51-250]
    LATBR - D 29 '96 - p8 [51-250]
    NS & S - v9 - My 17 '96 - p41 [251-500]
    NYRB - v43 - S 19 '96 - p53+ [501+]
    NYTBR - v101 - D 8 '96 - p93 [1-50]
    PW - v244 - Ap 21 '97 - p69 [1-50]
    S Liv - v31 - Jl '96 - p80 [51-250]
  The Temple Bombing (Cioffi). Audio Version
    LJ - v121 - S 15 '96 - p115 [51-250]
Greene, Sandra E - *Gender, Ethnicity, and Social Change on the Upper Slave Coast*
    Choice - v34 - N '96 - p514 [51-250]
Greene, Stephanie - *Owen Foote, Second Grade Strongman (Illus. by Dee DeRosa)*
  c HB Guide - v7 - Fall '96 - p286 [51-250]
Greene, Vivien - *The Vivien Greene Doll's House Collection*
    BM - v139 - Ja '97 - p48+ [251-500]

Greenfield, Eloise - *For the Love of the Game (Illus. by Jan Spivey Gilchrist)*
  c BL - v93 - F 15 '97 - p1024 [51-250]
  c CBRS - v25 - F '97 - p80 [1-50]
  c CCB-B - v50 - Mr '97 - p248 [51-250]
  c Ch BWatch - v7 - F '97 - p2 [51-250]
  c HB - v73 - Mr '97 - p209+ [51-250]
  c PW - v243 - D 30 '96 - p66 [51-250]
  c SLJ - v43 - Mr '97 - p174+ [51-250]
  c Trib Bks - Mr 9 '97 - p7 [51-250]
Kia Tanisha (Illus. by Jan Spivey Gilchrist)
  c PW - v243 - D 16 '96 - p61 [51-250]
Kia Tanisha Drives Her Car (Illus. by Jan Spivey Gilchrist)
  c KR - v64 - D 1 '96 - p1742 [51-250]
  c PW - v243 - D 16 '96 - p61 [51-250]
On My Horse (Illus. by Jan Spivey Gilchrist)
  c LA - v73 - D '96 - p622 [51-250]
Greenfield, Jeanette - *The Return of Cultural Treasures. 2nd Ed.*
  Aust Bk R - O '96 - p69 [1-50]
Greenfield, Jeff - *The People's Choice*
  BW - v26 - D 8 '96 - p6 [51-250]
  y Kliatt - v30 - N '96 - p8 [1-50]
  NYTBR - v101 - N 3 '96 - p28 [51-250]
Greenfield, John R - *British Short-Fiction Writers 1800-1880*
  r ARBA - v28 - '97 - p447 [51-250]
  ELT - v39 - 4 '96 - p526 [51-250]
Greenfield, Lauren - *Fast Forward*
  Ent W - My 16 '97 - p108 [51-250]
  PW - v244 - Ap 28 '97 - p68 [51-250]
Greenfield, Monica - *Waiting for Christmas (Illus. by Jan Spivey Gilchrist)*
  c BL - v93 - S 1 '96 - p136 [51-250]
  c CBRS - v25 - O '96 - p15 [51-250]
  c Ch BWatch - v6 - D '96 - p1 [1-50]
  c HB Guide - v8 - Spr '97 - p29 [51-250]
  c PW - v243 - S 30 '96 - p89 [51-250]
  c SFR - v21 - N '96 - p47 [51-250]
  c SLJ - v42 - O '96 - p36 [51-250]
Greenfield, Patrick M - *Cross-Cultural Roots of Minority Child Development*
  AJMR - v101 - N '96 - p331+ [501+]
Greenfield, Robert - *Dark Star*
  y BL - v92 - Ag '96 - p1871 [51-250]
  y BL - v92 - Ag '96 - p1890 [1-50]
Greenfield, Sumner - *Lorca, Valle-Inclan Y Las Esteticas De La Disidencia*
  Hisp - v79 - S '96 - p445+ [501+]
Greenfield, Susan A - *The Human Mind Explained*
  R&R Bk N - v12 - F '97 - p6 [51-250]
Greengrass, Mark - *Samuel Hartlib and Universal Reformation*
  Albion - v28 - Fall '96 - p491+ [501+]
  Six Ct J - v27 - Win '96 - p1098+ [501+]
Greenhalgh, Liz - *Libraries in a World of Cultural Change*
  LR - v45 - 5 '96 - p63+ [501+]
Greenhill, Basil - *The Schooner Bertha L. Downs*
  Sea H - Aut '96 - p43+ [251-500]
Greenhill, Pauline - *Ethnicity in the Mainstream*
  CAY - v16 - Fall '95 - p5 [51-250]
Greenhous, Brereton - *The Crucible of War 1939-1945*
  Can Hist R - v78 - Mr '97 - p132+ [501+]
Greenhouse, Carol J - *A Moment's Notice*
  Choice - v34 - Mr '97 - p1201 [51-250]
Greenhut, Melvin L - *Location Economics*
  Econ J - v107 - Ja '97 - p289 [251-500]
Spatial Microeconomics
  Econ J - v107 - Ja '97 - p289 [251-500]
Greenleaf, Monika - *Pushkin and Romantic Fashion*
  Russ Rev - v56 - Ja '97 - p127 [501+]
Greenleaf, Robert K - *On Becoming a Servant-Leader*
  LJ - v122 - Mr 15 '97 - p35 [1-50]
Greenleaf, Stephen - *Past Tense*
  BL - v93 - Mr 15 '97 - p1229 [51-250]
  KR - v65 - F 15 '97 - p257+ [51-250]
  PW - v244 - F 17 '97 - p213 [51-250]
Greenlee, J Harold - *Introduction to New Testament Textual Criticism. Rev. Ed.*
  Rel St Rev - v23 - Ja '97 - p67 [51-250]
Greenlees, John - *Maps and the Landscape*
  c TES - Mr 28 '97 - pR6 [51-250]
Greenman, Ben - *NetMusic: Your Guide to Rock and More on the Internet and Online Services*
  r Notes - v53 - Mr '97 - p778+ [501+]
Greenough, Sarah - *Harry Callahan*
  Art J - v55 - Win '96 - p103+ [501+]
  LATBR - Ag 18 '96 - p14 [51-250]

Greenslade, William - *Degeneration, Culture and the Novel 1880-1940*
  RES - v47 - N '96 - p619+ [501+]
Greenspan, Dorie - *Baking with Julia*
  BL - v93 - O 1 '96 - p290 [51-250]
  CSM - v89 - D 13 '96 - p10 [51-250]
  LJ - v121 - D '96 - p135 [51-250]
  Mac - v109 - D 9 '96 - p66 [1-50]
  NYTBR - v101 - D 8 '96 - p70 [251-500]
  PW - v243 - N 4 '96 - p73 [51-250]
Pancakes: From Morning to Midnight
  BL - v93 - D 15 '96 - p701 [51-250]
  LJ - v121 - D '96 - p135 [51-250]
Greenspan, Ezra - *The Cambridge Companion to Walt Whitman*
  J Am St - v30 - Ag '96 - p340+ [501+]
  Nine-C Lit - v50 - Mr '96 - p553 [51-250]
Greenspan, Karen - *The Timetables of Women's History*
  r HER - v67 - Spr '97 - p156+ [51-250]
Greenspan, Patricia - *Practical Guilt*
  Hast Cen R - v27 - Ja '97 - p38+ [501+]
Greenspan, Ralph J - *Fly Pushing*
  Sci - v276 - Ap 4 '97 - p47 [1-50]
Greenspan, Stanley I - *Developmentally Based Psychotherapy*
  BWatch - v18 - F '97 - p12 [51-250]
  Choice - v34 - My '97 - p1579 [51-250]
  SciTech - v21 - Mr '97 - p54 [51-250]
The Growth of the Mind
  y BL - v93 - F 1 '97 - p908 [51-250]
  BW - v27 - Ap 13 '97 - p4+ [501+]
  KR - v64 - D 1 '96 - p1715+ [251-500]
  PW - v244 - Ja 27 '97 - p91+ [51-250]
Greenspon, Edward - *Double Vision*
  CF - v75 - Ja '97 - p42+ [501+]
  Mac - v109 - D 9 '96 - p64 [1-50]
  Quill & Q - v62 - N '96 - p36 [251-500]
Greenstein, Elaine - *Mrs. Rose's Garden (Illus. by Elaine Greenstein)*
  c HB Guide - v7 - Fall '96 - p258 [51-250]
Greenstein, Ran - *Genealogies of Conflict*
  AJS - v102 - N '96 - p880+ [501+]
  CS - v25 - N '96 - p745+ [501+]
  For Aff - v76 - Mr '97 - p201 [51-250]
Greenstone, J David - *The Lincoln Persuasion*
  AS - v66 - Win '97 - p136+ [501+]
  Bks & Cult - v2 - N '96 - p22+ [501+]
Greenwald, Jeff - *Shopping for Buddhas*
  LJ - v121 - D '96 - p130 [51-250]
Greenway, Rosalynne - *A Ladder to the Stars (Illus. by Prue Berthon)*
  c JB - v60 - D '96 - p232 [51-250]
Greenway, Shirley - *Two's Company (Illus. by Oxford Scientific Films)*
  c KR - v65 - Mr 1 '97 - p381 [51-250]
Greenwood, Barbara - *Pioneer Crafts (Illus. by Heather Collins)*
  c Quill & Q - v63 - F '97 - p53+ [251-500]
Greenwood, Janette Thomas - *Bittersweet Legacy*
  AHR - v101 - O '96 - p1284+ [501+]
Greenwood, Kerry - *The Broken Wheel*
  c Magpies - v11 - Jl '96 - p34 [51-250]
Electra: The Delphic Women
  Aust Bk R - Jl '96 - p49+ [501+]
Urn Burial
  Aust Bk R - Je '96 - p64 [1-50]
Whaleroad
  y Aust Bk R - O '96 - p63 [501+]
Greenwood, Pippa - *Gardening Hints and Tips*
  LJ - v121 - O 15 '96 - p82 [51-250]
Greenwood, Sadja - *Menopause, Naturally. 4th Ed.*
  Workbook - v21 - Win '96 - p188+ [501+]
Greenwood, Ted - *What Do We Do with Dawson? (Illus. by Terry Denton)*
  c Aust Bk R - S '96 - p61+ [501+]
  c Magpies - v11 - S '96 - p27 [51-250]
Greer, Allan - *The Pirates and the People*
  Beav - v77 - F '97 - p47 [1-50]
Greer, Germaine - *Slip-Shod Sibyls*
  CR - v269 - N '96 - p277+ [51-250]
  Meanjin - v55 - 2 '96 - p208+ [501+]
Greer, Gery - *Billy the Ghost and Me (Illus. by Roger Roth)*
  c BL - v93 - N 15 '96 - p596 [51-250]
  c SLJ - v43 - Mr '97 - p159 [51-250]
Greer, Jane - *How Could You Do This to Me?*
  LJ - v122 - Ja '97 - p126 [51-250]
  PW - v243 - O 21 '96 - p61 [51-250]

Greer, Robert O - *The Devil's Red Nickel*
  BL - v93 - Mr 1 '97 - p1113 [51-250]
  KR - v65 - Ja 15 '97 - p97+ [51-250]
  LJ - v122 - F 1 '97 - p110 [51-250]
  PW - v244 - Ja 6 '97 - p67 [51-250]
  Trib Bks - Ap 13 '97 - p8 [51-250]
Greeson, Aaron David, III - *The Recovery of Race in America*
  QJS - v83 - My '97 - p251+ [501+]
Greetham, D C - *Scholarly Editing*
  LQ - v67 - Ap '97 - p206+ [501+]
Greger, C Shana - *Cry of the Benu Bird*
  c Ch BWatch - v6 - My '96 - p3 [1-50]
  c HB Guide - v7 - Fall '96 - p321 [51-250]
Greger, Debora - *Desert Fathers, Uranium Daughters*
  BL - v93 - N 15 '96 - p567 [51-250]
  y Kliatt - v31 - Mr '97 - p22+ [251-500]
  NYTBR - v102 - F 2 '97 - p21 [51-250]
  PW - v243 - N 25 '96 - p73 [51-250]
Gregerson, Linda - *The Reformation of the Subject*
  Clio - v25 - Sum '96 - p421+ [501+]
  Six Ct J - v27 - Win '96 - p1105+ [501+]
The Woman Who Died in Her Sleep
  LJ - v121 - O 15 '96 - p63 [51-250]
  Shen - v47 - Spr '97 - p117+ [501+]
Gregg, Gary L - *The Presidential Republic*
  Choice - v34 - My '97 - p1576 [51-250]
Gregg, John - *Maurice Blanchot and the Literature of Transgression*
  MP - v94 - N '96 - p279+ [501+]
Gregg, Noel - *Adults with Learning Disabilities*
  Readings - v11 - S '96 - p30 [51-250]
Gregoire, Henri - *An Enquiry Concerning the Intellectual and Moral Faculties, and Literature of Negroes*
  LJ - v122 - Ja '97 - p155 [1-50]
On the Cultural Achievements of Negroes
  AB - v99 - F 17 '97 - p520+ [501+]
Gregoire, Tanya - *Museum of Science Activities for Kids (Illus. by Julie Fraenkel)*
  c Ch BWatch - v7 - F '97 - p7+ [51-250]
Gregoriadis, Gregory - *Targeting of Drugs 5*
  SciTech - v21 - Mr '97 - p68 [51-250]
Gregory, Lady - *Lady Gregory's Diaries 1892-1902*
  TLS - S 27 '96 - p31 [501+]
  VQR - v73 - Win '97 - p18* [51-250]
Gregory, Adrian - *The Silence of Memory*
  Albion - v28 - Sum '96 - p349+ [501+]
  EHR - v112 - F '97 - p261+ [251-500]
Gregory, Christopher D - *Apoptosis and the Immune Response*
  BioSci - v46 - O '96 - p705 [501+]
Gregory, Derek - *Human Geography*
  GJ - v162 - Jl '96 - p231+ [251-500]
Gregory, Desmond - *Malta, Britain and the European Powers 1793-1815*
  HT - v47 - Ja '97 - p60+ [501+]
Gregory, Donald - *History of the Western Highlands and Isles of Scotland from A.D. 1493 to A.D. 1625*
  EGH - v50 - N '96 - p157+ [51-250]
Gregory, Hugh - *Soul Music A-Z. Rev. Ed.*
  r CAY - v17 - Fall '96 - p5 [51-250]
Gregory, Kristiana - *Across the Wide and Lonesome Prairie*
  c KR - v64 - D 1 '96 - p1737 [51-250]
  c PW - v244 - F 24 '97 - p93 [1-50]
  c SLJ - v43 - Mr '97 - p187 [51-250]
  c Trib Bks - My 4 '97 - p1+ [501+]
The Stowaway: A Tale of California Pirates
  c RT - v50 - Mr '97 - p498+ [51-250]
The Winter of Red Snow
  c CBRS - v25 - S '96 - p11 [51-250]
  c CCB-B - v50 - O '96 - p55+ [51-250]
  c Ch BWatch - v6 - S '96 - p5 [1-50]
  c HB Guide - v8 - Spr '97 - p64 [51-250]
  c Par - v71 - D '96 - p254 [51-250]
  c PW - v243 - S 2 '96 - p131 [51-250]
  c SLJ - v42 - S '96 - p202 [51-250]
  c Trib Bks - My 4 '97 - p1+ [501+]
  y VOYA - v19 - O '96 - p209 [251-500]
Gregory, Nan - *How Smudge Came (Illus. by Ron Lightburn)*
  c BL - v93 - Ja '97 - p767 [1-50]
  y JAAL - v40 - Mr '97 - p511 [51-250]
  c PW - v244 - My 5 '97 - p211 [1-50]
Gregory, Philippa - *Diggory and the Boa Conductor (Illus. by Jacqueline East)*
  c Bks Keeps - Jl '96 - p11 [51-250]

The Little House
  KR - v64 - S 1 '96 - p1256 [251-500]
  LJ - v121 - O 1 '96 - p126 [51-250]
  PW - v243 - S 9 '96 - p66 [51-250]
  Woman's J - Ap '97 - p18 [51-250]
Gregory, Richard - *Mirrors in Mind*
  LJ - v121 - O 1 '96 - p122 [51-250]
  Nature - v385 - F 27 '97 - p785 [501+]
  New Sci - v152 - N 16 '96 - p44+ [501+]
Gregory, Sarah - *Public Trust*
  PW - v244 - Ja 27 '97 - p102 [51-250]
Gregory, Susanna - *An Unholy Alliance*
  KR - v64 - O 15 '96 - p1495+ [51-250]
  LJ - v121 - D '96 - p150 [51-250]
  PW - v243 - N 25 '96 - p60 [51-250]
Gregory, Valiska - *Looking for Angels (Illus. by Leslie Baker)*
  c HB Guide - v7 - Fall '96 - p258 [51-250]
  When Stories Fell like Shooting Stars (Illus. by Stefano Vitale)
  c BL - v93 - Ja '97 - p860 [251-500]
  c CBRS - v25 - N '96 - p26 [1-50]
  c CCB-B - v50 - F '97 - p207 [51-250]
  c HB Guide - v8 - Spr '97 - p29 [51-250]
  c PW - v243 - O 21 '96 - p82 [51-250]
  c SLJ - v42 - O '96 - p94 [51-250]
Gregory, Winifred - *American Newspapers 1821-1936*
  r ASInt - v34 - O '96 - p16 [1-50]
Gregotti, Vittorio - *Inside Architecture*
  Choice - v34 - F '97 - p956 [51-250]
Gregson, Bob - *Rebirth of the Small Family Farm*
  Workbook - v21 - Win '96 - p166 [251-500]
Gregson, Nicky - *Servicing the Middle Classes*
  AAAGA - v86 - S '96 - p607+ [501+]
Greider, Goran - *Nar Fabrikerna Tystnar*
  WLT - v70 - Sum '96 - p716+ [501+]
Greider, William - *One World, Ready or Not*
  BL - v93 - D 15 '96 - p699 [51-250]
  Bus W - Ja 20 '97 - p14 [501+]
  BW - v27 - Ja 19 '97 - p4+ [501+]
  For Aff - v76 - Ja '97 - p146+ [501+]
  Har Bus R - v75 - Ja '97 - p144+ [501+]
  KR - v64 - N 1 '96 - p1580 [251-500]
  LATBR - Ja 12 '97 - p4 [501+]
  LJ - v122 - Ja '97 - p115 [51-250]
  NW - v129 - F 10 '97 - p67 [501+]
  NYTBR - v102 - Ja 19 '97 - p12 [501+]
  Reason - v28 - Ap '97 - p54+ [501+]
  Time - v149 - Mr 24 '97 - p99+ [501+]
  WSJ-Cent - v99 - Ja 17 '97 - pA11 [501+]
Greif, Martin - *200 Intriguing Chess Puzzles*
  y Ch BWatch - v7 - F '97 - p8 [1-50]
Greif, Siegfried - *Handbook for Self-Organized Learning*
  Per Psy - v50 - Spr '97 - p251+ [501+]
Greisch, Jean - *Ontologie Et Temporalite*
  Dialogue - v35 - Spr '96 - p399+ [501+]
Grejniec, Michael - *Good Morning, Good Night*
  c PW - v244 - Ap 28 '97 - p77 [1-50]
Grekova, I - *Svezho Predanie*
  BL - v93 - O 1 '96 - p327 [1-50]
Grell, Ole Peter - *The Scandinavian Reformation*
  Bks & Cult - v1 - N '95 - p30 [51-250]
  CHR - v82 - O '96 - p698+ [501+]
  EHR - v112 - Ap '97 - p462 [501+]
Gremion, Pierre - *Intelligence De L'Anticommunisme*
  JMH - v68 - D '96 - p1002+ [501+]
Grenander, Ulf - *Elements of Pattern Theory*
  Choice - v34 - Ap '97 - p1376 [51-250]
  SciTech - v20 - D '96 - p4 [51-250]
Grendler, Paul F - *Books and Schools in the Italian Renaissance*
  Lib & Cul - v32 - Win '97 - p131+ [501+]
Grene, Marjorie - *A Philosophical Testament*
  CPR - v16 - Ap '96 - p108+ [501+]
Grenfell, Diana - *The Gardener's Guide to Growing Hostas*
  Fine Gard - Ja '97 - p70 [251-500]
Grenfell, Monica - *Five Days to a Flatter Stomach*
  Books - v11 - Ap '97 - p21 [51-250]
Grenfell-Hill, Jeffrey - *Growing Up in Wales 1895-1939*
  TES - F 28 '97 - p7* [501+]
Grenier, Catherine - *Luciano Fabro*
  BM - v139 - Ja '97 - p62+ [501+]
Grennan, Eamon - *So It Goes*
  ILS - v16 - Spr '97 - p24+ [501+]
  WLT - v71 - Win '97 - p165+ [51-250]
Grenville, Anthony - *Cockpit of Ideologies*
  MLR - v92 - Ap '97 - p522+ [501+]
Grenz, Stanley J - *A Primer on Postmodernism*
  CC - v114 - My 7 '97 - p455+ [501+]

Grescoe, Paul - *The Merchants of Venus*
  Mac - v109 - O 21 '96 - p90 [501+]
  Quill & Q - v62 - Ag '96 - p38 [501+]
Gresham, Perry S - *The Sign of the Golden Grasshopper*
  Six Ct J - v27 - Fall '96 - p862+ [501+]
Gretz, Susanna - *The Nut Map*
  c Bks Keeps - Jl '96 - p8 [51-250]
Greve, Michael S - *The Demise of Environmentalism in American Law*
  Reason - v28 - Ja '97 - p56+ [501+]
Greven, Philip - *Spare the Child*
  Rel St Rev - v23 - Ap '97 - p135+ [501+]
Grewal, Inderpal - *Scattered Hegemonies*
  Amerasia J - v22 - 3 '96 - p166+ [501+]
Grey, Alan H - *Aotearoa and New Zealand*
  AHR - v102 - F '97 - p159 [51-250]
Grey, Jane - *She Wields a Pen*
  Obs - F 16 '97 - p15* [501+]
Grey, Johnny - *The Art of Kitchen Design*
  LJ - v122 - Ja '97 - p96 [51-250]
Grey, Rudolph - *Nightmare of Ecstasy*
  TES - Ag 2 '96 - pR6 [51-250]
Grey, Vivian - *Moe Berg: The Spy behind Home Plate*
  c CBRS - v25 - Ap '97 - p105+ [51-250]
  y HB Guide - v8 - Spr '97 - p158 [51-250]
Grey, Zane - *The Last Trail*
  y SLJ - v42 - Ag '96 - p184 [51-250]
Gribbin, John - *Companion to the Cosmos*
  Astron - v25 - Ja '97 - p103 [51-250]
  Choice - v34 - My '97 - p1521 [51-250]
  r LJ - v122 - F 1 '97 - p72 [51-250]
  r Nature - v386 - Mr 13 '97 - p142 [51-250]
  r TES - Ag 23 '96 - p27 [251-500]
  Darwin in 90 Minutes
  y TES - Mr 14 '97 - p8* [51-250]
  Earthquakes and Volcanoes
  y Kliatt - v31 - Mr '97 - p4+ [51-250]
  Einstein in 90 Minutes
  y TES - Mr 14 '97 - p8* [51-250]
  Fire on Earth
  y BL - v93 - D 1 '96 - p664 [1-50]
  BW - v26 - O 20 '96 - p8 [251-500]
  Nat - v263 - O 28 '96 - p38+ [501+]
  New Sci - v152 - O 19 '96 - p47 [1-50]
  Halley in 90 Minutes
  y TES - Mr 14 '97 - p8* [51-250]
  In the Beginning
  Skeptic - v3 - '95 - p101+ [51-250]
  Marie Curie in 90 Minutes
  y TES - Mr 14 '97 - p8* [51-250]
  Schrodinger's Kittens and the Search for Reality
  NYTBR - v101 - O 13 '96 - p32 [1-50]
  Scientists in 90 Minutes
  y TES - Mr 14 '97 - p8* [51-250]
  Watching the Weather
  New Sci - v152 - O 12 '96 - p43 [1-50]
Gribbin, Mary - *Big Bugs (Illus. by Andrew Tewson)*
  c PW - v243 - S 9 '96 - p84 [51-250]
  c SLJ - v43 - Ja '97 - p102 [51-250]
  Big Ocean Creatures (Illus. by Julian Baker)
  c PW - v243 - S 9 '96 - p84 [51-250]
  c SLJ - v43 - Ja '97 - p102 [51-250]
  Big Trucks (Illus. by Julian Baker)
  c PW - v243 - S 9 '96 - p84 [51-250]
Griboyedov, Alexander S - *Distress from Cleverness*
  MLR - v92 - Ja '97 - p263+ [501+]
Grice, Phil - *Weekly Themes for Assemblies*
  TES - D 6 '96 - pR5 [251-500]
Grier, James - *The Critical Editing of Music*
  M Ed J - v83 - Mr '97 - p44 [51-250]
Gries, John Paul - *Roadside Geology of South Dakota*
  SciTech - v20 - N '96 - p24 [51-250]
Grieve, James - *Dictionary of Contemporary French Connectors*
  yr ARBA - v28 - '97 - p390 [251-500]
Grieve Smith, John - *Full Employment*
  NS - v126 - Ap 25 '97 - p53+ [501+]
Grifalconi, Ann - *Not Home*
  c RT - v50 - Mr '97 - p480 [51-250]
Griffin, Adele - *Rainy Season*
  c CBRS - v25 - D '96 - p45 [51-250]
  y CCB-B - v50 - F '97 - p207 [51-250]
  c HB - v73 - Mr '97 - p198+ [251-500]
  y KR - v64 - S 15 '96 - p1400 [51-250]
  c PW - v243 - O 14 '96 - p84 [51-250]
  c SLJ - v42 - N '96 - p104+ [51-250]
  Split Just Right
  y KR - v65 - Ap 1 '97 - p555 [51-250]
  c PW - v244 - Ap 7 '97 - p93 [51-250]
Griffin, Alice - *Understanding Arthur Miller*
  Choice - v34 - N '96 - p456 [51-250]

Griffin, Allan - *Bose-Einstein Condensation*
  New Sci - v151 - S 28 '96 - p54+ [501+]
  Sci - v274 - N 22 '96 - p1321 [1-50]
Griffin, Carolyn Welch - *Beyond Acceptance*
  LJ - v121 - N 1 '96 - p94 [51-250]
Griffin, D D - *Fie! Fie! Fi-Fi!*
  AB - v99 - Ja 27 '97 - p226+ [501+]
  BL - v93 - S 1 '96 - p33 [1-50]
Griffin, David H - *Fungal Physiology. 2nd Ed.*
  SciTech - v20 - S '96 - p20 [51-250]
Griffin, Geoffrey - *The Magic Bat (Illus. by Don Weller)*
  c RT - v50 - O '96 - p137 [1-50]
Griffin, Ginger L - *The TSCA Compliance Handbook. 3rd Ed.*
  r R&R Bk N - v11 - D '96 - p52 [51-250]
Griffin, James - *Value Judgement*
  Choice - v34 - F '97 - p978 [51-250]
Griffin, John R - *Optometric Management of Reading Dysfunction*
  SciTech - v21 - Mr '97 - p63 [1-50]
Griffin, Judy - *Mother Nature's Herbal*
  BL - v93 - Mr 15 '97 - p1213+ [51-250]
Griffin, Kathleen M - *Handbook of Subacute Health Care*
  AJN - v96 - N '96 - p16D [51-250]
Griffin, Keith - *New Approaches to Development Cooperation*
  JEL - v35 - Mr '97 - p272 [51-250]
  Social Policy and Economic Transformation in Uzbekistan
  JEL - v35 - Mr '97 - p290 [51-250]
Griffin, Keith L - *Revolution and Religion*
  JR - v76 - O '96 - p643+ [501+]
Griffin, L L - *Something That a Cowboy Knows*
  Bloom Rev - v16 - Jl '96 - p17 [51-250]
Griffin, Larry J - *The South as an American Problem*
  JSH - v63 - F '97 - p213+ [501+]
Griffin, Leonard - *Taking Tea with Clarice Cliff*
  Ceram Mo - v45 - F '97 - p20 [251-500]
Griffin, Martin I J, Jr. - *Latitudinarianism in the Seventeenth-Century Church of England*
  Historian - v58 - Sum '96 - p904+ [251-500]
Griffin, Nancy - *Hit and Run*
  Bus W - D 16 '96 - p19+ [51-250]
  Ent W - D 27 '96 - p143 [51-250]
  KR - v64 - My 1 '96 - p663 [251-500]
  Hit and Run (McLarty). Audio Version
  y Kliatt - v31 - Ja '97 - p49 [51-250]
Griffin, Peni R - *Margo's House*
  c BL - v93 - S 1 '96 - p130 [51-250]
  c CBRS - v25 - D '96 - p42 [51-250]
  c CCB-B - v50 - N '96 - p97 [51-250]
  c HB Guide - v8 - Spr '97 - p67 [51-250]
  c KR - v64 - S 1 '96 - p1322 [51-250]
  c SLJ - v42 - O '96 - p122 [51-250]
  Switching Well
  c SLJ - v43 - Ja '97 - p36 [1-50]
Griffin, Stephen M - *American Constitutionalism*
  Choice - v34 - Mr '97 - p1239 [51-250]
Griffin, Susan - *A Chorus of Stones*
  SFR - v21 - N '96 - p48 [51-250]
  The Eros of Everyday Life
  NYTBR - v101 - N 17 '96 - p40 [1-50]
Griffin, W E B - *Behind the Lines (Hill). Audio Version*
  y Kliatt - v30 - S '96 - p44 [51-250]
  Blood and Honor
  BL - v93 - N 15 '96 - p549 [51-250]
  CSM - v89 - Ja 16 '97 - p14 [501+]
  KR - v64 - N 1 '96 - p1552 [251-500]
  PW - v243 - D 2 '96 - p41 [51-250]
Griffis, Joan A - *Illiana Ancestors. Vol. 5*
  r EGH - v50 - N '96 - p166 [51-250]
Griffith, Gary K - *The Quality Technician's Handbook. 3rd Ed.*
  SciTech - v20 - N '96 - p81 [51-250]
Griffith, Helen V - *Grandaddy's Stars (Illus. by James Stevenson)*
  c RT - v50 - N '96 - p257 [51-250]
Griffith, Ivelaw Lloyd - *The Quest for Security in the Caribbean*
  JTWS - v13 - Spr '96 - p344+ [501+]
Griffith, J A G - *Judicial Politics since 1920*
  EHR - v111 - S '96 - p1033+ [251-500]
Griffith, John W - *Classics of Children's Literature. 4th Ed.*
  SLJ - v42 - S '96 - p112 [1-50]
Griffith, John W, 1964- - *Joseph Conrad and the Anthropological Dilemma*
  ELT - v39 - 3 '96 - p400+ [501+]
Griffith, Linda - *Cooking under Cover*
  LJ - v121 - N 15 '96 - p84 [51-250]
  PW - v243 - S 2 '96 - p123 [51-250]

Griffith, Nicola - *Bending the Landscape*
KR - v65 - Ja 1 '97 - p27 [51-250]
LJ - v121 - D '96 - p152 [51-250]
MFSF - v92 - Mr '97 - p33+ [501+]
PW - v244 - F 24 '97 - p68 [51-250]
Slow River
Trib Bks - F 2 '97 - p8 [1-50]
y VOYA - v19 - F '97 - p327 [251-500]
Griffith, Paddy - *Battle Tactics of the Western Front*
EHR - v112 - F '97 - p254+ [501+]
British Fighting Methods in the Great War
For Aff - v76 - Mr '97 - p180 [51-250]
Griffith, R Drew - *The Theatre of Apollo*
R&R Bk N - v12 - F '97 - p77 [51-250]
Griffith-Jones, Stephany - *Financial Reform in Central and Eastern Europe*
Slav R - v55 - Sum '96 - p447+ [501+]
Griffiths, Antony - *Prints and Printmaking. 2nd Ed.*
Choice - v34 - D '96 - p602 [51-250]
LJ - v122 - F 15 '97 - p131 [51-250]
Griffiths, Bede - *A Human Search*
LJ - v122 - My 1 '97 - p110+ [51-250]
Griffiths, Bruce - *The Welsh Academy English-Welsh Dictionary*
r MLJ - v81 - Spr '97 - p147+ [501+]
Griffiths, Franklyn - *Strong and Free*
BIC - v25 - N '96 - p29 [501+]
CF - v75 - S '96 - p40 [501+]
Griffiths, Ieuan Ll. - *The African Inheritance*
GJ - v162 - N '96 - p340 [51-250]
Griffiths, John, 1940- - *The Presidential Archive*
NYTBR - v101 - S 29 '96 - p20 [51-250]
Griffiths, John Charles - *Nimbus: Technology Serving the Arts*
Notes - v53 - D '96 - p485+ [501+]
Griffiths, Mark - *Adolescent Gambling*
Adoles - v31 - Win '96 - p993 [51-250]
Griffiths, Mary - *Activities for Public Sector Training*
R&R Bk N - v11 - D '96 - p42 [51-250]
Griffiths, Morwenna - *Antiracism, Culture and Social Justice in Education*
TES - Mr 28 '97 - p7* [51-250]
Feminisms and the Self
CPR - v16 - D '96 - p399+ [501+]
Griffiths, Nicholas - *The Cross and the Serpent*
Choice - v34 - O '96 - p343 [51-250]
Griffiths, Paul - *Modern Music and After*
Choice - v34 - O '96 - p291 [51-250]
Youth and Authority
Choice - v34 - D '96 - p669 [51-250]
Griffiths, Philip Jones - *Dark Odyssey*
BL - v93 - Ja '97 - p758 [1-50]
y BL - v93 - N 15 '96 - p561 [51-250]
Esq - v126 - D '96 - p40 [1-50]
LJ - v122 - Ja '97 - p93 [51-250]
NYTBR - v101 - My '96 - p74 [51-250]
Obs - D 8 '96 - p18* [51-250]
Griffiths, Tom - *Hunters and Collectors*
Choice - v34 - My '97 - p1554 [51-250]
HT - v47 - Ja '97 - p53 [501+]
Meanjin - v55 - '96 - p718+ [501+]
TLS - F 7 '97 - p30 [501+]
Griffiths, Trevor R - *A Midsummer Night's Dream*
Choice - v34 - F '97 - p977 [51-250]
Griffiths, Vivienne - *Adolescent Girls and Their Friends*
TCR - v98 - Spr '97 - p565+ [501+]
Grigely, Joseph - *Textualterity: Art, Theory, and Textual Criticism*
Choice - v34 - S '96 - p110 [51-250]
Grigg, Neil S - *Water Resources Management*
SciTech - v20 - N '96 - p2 [51-250]
Grigg, Richard - *When God Becomes Goddess*
RR - v56 - Ja '97 - p100+ [501+]
Grigoriev, Igor S - *Handbook of Physical Quantities*
r Choice - v34 - My '97 - p1538 [51-250]
Grigsby, Jean - *Sinkler/Sinclair/St. Clair. Update 1996*
r EGH - v50 - N '96 - p195 [51-250]
Griliches, Diane Asseo - *Library: The Drama Within*
BL - v92 - Ag '96 - p1858 [51-250]
LATBR - Jl 14 '96 - p10 [51-250]
NYTBR - v102 - Mr 23 '97 - p19 [251-500]
R&R Bk N - v11 - N '96 - p80 [51-250]
Grillmeier, Aloys - *Christ in Christian Tradition. Vol. 2, Pt. 4*
Rel St Rev - v23 - Ap '97 - p152 [51-250]
Grillo, Peter R - *The Jerusalem Continuations*
MLR - v91 - Jl '96 - p717+ [51-250]
Grimal, Nicolas - *A History of Ancient Egypt*
Class Out - v74 - Spr '97 - p123 [51-250]
Grimaldi, David A - *Amber: Window to the Past*
Nature - v383 - S 19 '96 - p227 [1-50]

Grimes, John - *A Concise Dictionary of Indian Philosophy. Rev. Ed.*
r R&R Bk N - v12 - F '97 - p1 [51-250]
Grimes, Martha - *Hotel Paradise*
Arm Det - v29 - Fall '96 - p479+ [251-500]
y BL - v93 - Ja '97 - p763 [1-50]
Books - v10 - Je '96 - p23 [1-50]
LATBR - My 26 '96 - p6+ [501+]
y SLJ - v42 - O '96 - p162 [51-250]
Hotel Paradise (Jones). Audio Version
BL - v93 - N '96 - p522 [51-250]
Grimes, Nikki - *Come Sunday (Illus. by Michael Bryant)*
c BL - v93 - Ja '97 - p767 [1-50]
c BL - v93 - O 1 '96 - p338 [1-50]
c BL - v93 - Ap 1 '97 - p1305 [1-50]
c CCB-B - v50 - Mr '97 - p248+ [51-250]
c HB Guide - v7 - Fall '96 - p367 [51-250]
c NYTBR - v101 - S 22 '96 - p28 [1-50]
Portrait of Mary
RR - v55 - N '96 - p659 [1-50]
Wild, Wild Hair (Illus. by George Ford)
c BL - v93 - My 1 '97 - p1503 [51-250]
Grimes, Terris McMahan - *Somebody Else's Child*
Arm Det - v29 - Sum '96 - p309+ [51-250]
Grimes, Tom - *Season's End*
NYTBR - v101 - D 29 '96 - p14 [51-250]
Grimm, Jacob - *The Brave Little Tailor (Illus. by Sergei Goloshapov)*
c KR - v65 - Ap 1 '97 - p555 [51-250]
c PW - v244 - Ap 28 '97 - p75 [51-250]
The Bremen Town Musicians (Illus. by Bernadette Watts)
c PW - v244 - Ap 14 '97 - p77 [1-50]
The Brothers Grimm (Illus. by Michael Foreman)
c KR - v65 - F 15 '97 - p299 [51-250]
c PW - v244 - Mr 10 '97 - p69 [51-250]
The Nose Tree and Other Grimms' Fairy Tales (Ringenberg). Audio Version
c BL - v93 - Ag '96 - p1917 [51-250]
Rapunzel (Illus. by Maja Dusikova)
c KR - v65 - My 1 '97 - p721 [51-250]
Rumpelstiltskin (Illus. by Bernadette Watts)
c PW - v243 - D 2 '96 - p62 [1-50]
The Six Servants (Illus. by Sergei Goloshapov)
c HB Guide - v7 - Fall '96 - p321 [1-50]
Snow White and Rose Red (Illus. by Bernadette Watts)
c PW - v244 - Ap 14 '97 - p77 [1-50]
Grimm, Jurgen - *Le Pouvoir Des Fables. Vol. 1*
MLR - v91 - Jl '96 - p724+ [501+]
Grimshaw, Caroline - *Art*
c Sch Lib - v45 - F '97 - p38 [51-250]
Music
c Sch Lib - v45 - F '97 - p38 [51-250]
Grimshaw, David J - *Bringing Geographical Information Systems into Business*
GJ - v163 - Mr '97 - p108 [1-50]
Grimsley, Jim - *My Drowning*
Advocate - Mr 4 '97 - p59 [51-250]
BL - v93 - N 15 '96 - p549 [51-250]
KR - v64 - N 1 '96 - p1552+ [251-500]
LJ - v121 - N 1 '96 - p107 [51-250]
NYTBR - v102 - F 2 '97 - p17 [501+]
PW - v243 - N 4 '96 - p61 [51-250]
Grimsley, Mark - *The Hard Hand of War*
JSH - v63 - F '97 - p180+ [501+]
RAH - v24 - S '96 - p426+ [501+]
Grimson, Todd - *Brand New Cherry Flavor*
KR - v64 - S 1 '96 - p1257 [251-500]
LJ - v121 - S 15 '96 - p96 [51-250]
Necro - Win '97 - p18+ [501+]
NS - v125 - D 6 '96 - p55 [251-500]
Obs - N 10 '96 - p18* [51-250]
PW - v243 - O 7 '96 - p63 [51-250]
TLS - D 20 '96 - p24 [251-500]
Stainless
Necro - Sum '96 - p7 [501+]
Grin, Ts. I - *Sotrudniki Rossiiskoi Natsional'noi Biblioteki*
r LJ - v18 - D '96 - p365 [51-250]
Grinberg, Arkady - *Seamless Networks*
Choice - v34 - Ap '97 - p1370 [51-250]
Grindal, Bruce - *Bridges to Humanity*
Am Ethnol - v24 - F '97 - p220 [501+]
Grindle, Juliet - *Tess of the D'Urbervilles*
ELT - v40 - 2 '97 - p196+ [501+]
Grindle, Merilee S - *Challenging the State*
Choice - v34 - N '96 - p530 [51-250]
TLS - Ja 3 '97 - p14+ [501+]
Grindley, Peter - *Standards Strategy and Policy*
JEL - v35 - Mr '97 - p166+ [501+]
Grindley, Sally - *Christmas Stories for the Very Young (Illus. by Helen Cooper)*
c Bks Keeps - N '96 - p19+ [51-250]

Little Elephant Thunderfoot (Illus. by John Butler)
c Bks Keeps - Mr '97 - p19 [51-250]
Peter's Place (Illus. by Michael Foreman)
c HB Guide - v7 - Fall '96 - p258 [51-250]
c New Ad - v9 - Fall '96 - p327+ [501+]
Toybox Tales (Illus. by Andy Ellis)
c Sch Lib - v45 - F '97 - p19 [51-250]
The Ugly Duckling (Illus. by Bert Kitchen)
c Sch Lib - v45 - F '97 - p20 [51-250]
Why Is the Sky Blue? (Illus. by Susan Varley)
c KR - v65 - My 1 '97 - p721 [51-250]
c Sch Lib - v45 - F '97 - p19 [51-250]
c TES - Ja 10 '97 - p8* [51-250]
Grindon, Leger - *Shadows on the Past*
FQ - v49 - Fall '95 - p59+ [501+]
Griner, Ned H - *The Bethel Pike Pottery*
Am Craft - v56 - D '96 - p30 [51-250]
Ceram Mo - v44 - S '96 - p28 [251-500]
Griner, Paul - *Follow Me*
NYTBR - v101 - S 8 '96 - p21 [501+]
Gringeri, Christina E - *Getting By*
CS - v25 - S '96 - p617+ [501+]
CS - v25 - N '96 - p802+ [501+]
EG - v73 - Ja '97 - p131+ [501+]
Grinnell, George Bird - *Two Great Scouts and Their Pawnee Battalion*
Roundup M - v4 - F '97 - p24 [51-250]
Grinspoon, David Harry - *Venus Revealed*
Astron - v25 - My '97 - p112 [501+]
y BL - v93 - F 1 '97 - p915 [51-250]
KR - v64 - D 1 '96 - p1716 [251-500]
LJ - v122 - F 15 '97 - p159 [51-250]
NH - v106 - Mr '97 - p13 [1-50]
PW - v243 - D 30 '96 - p46+ [251-500]
S&T - v93 - Ap '97 - p65 [51-250]
Grinstein, Alexander - *The Remarkable Beatrix Potter*
AJPsych - v153 - D '96 - p1646+ [501+]
Grint, Keith - *The Gender-Technology Relation*
SocSciComR - v14 - Win '96 - p487+ [501+]
T&C - v38 - Ja '97 - p232+ [501+]
Grippando, James - *The Informant*
BL - v92 - Ag '96 - p1854 [251-500]
NYTBR - v101 - O 13 '96 - p29 [51-250]
PW - v243 - Jl 22 '96 - p227 [51-250]
The Informant (Naughton). Audio Version
BWatch - v17 - D '96 - p10 [51-250]
The Informant (Guidall). Audio Version
LJ - v122 - Ap 1 '97 - p145 [51-250]
Grippo, Alison - *NetLove: The 75 Most Erogenous Zones in Cyberspace*
LJ - v122 - Ap 1 '97 - p118 [51-250]
Grisewood, John - *The Kingfisher First Dictionary*
cr CLW - v66 - Je '96 - p48+ [251-500]
Grisham, John - *The Chamber*
Ent W - N 8 '96 - p59+ [51-250]
The Chamber (Beck). Audio Version
BWatch - v17 - D '96 - p11 [1-50]
BWatch - v18 - Mr '97 - p7 [1-50]
LJ - v122 - F 1 '97 - p126 [51-250]
The Partner
BL - v93 - Mr 15 '97 - p1205 [1-50]
CSM - v89 - Mr 20 '97 - p14 [51-250]
CSM - v89 - Mr 26 '97 - p13 [251-500]
Ent W - Mr 14 '97 - p71+ [251-500]
KR - v65 - F 1 '97 - p160 [251-500]
PW - v244 - F 10 '97 - p69+ [51-250]
The Runaway Jury
Arm Det - v30 - Win '97 - p70+ [51-250]
CSM - v88 - S 19 '96 - p14 [51-250]
Ent W - F 21 '97 - p121 [51-250]
Nat R - v48 - D 23 '96 - p56 [51-250]
New R - v215 - N 4 '96 - p27 [501+]
PW - v244 - F 24 '97 - p88 [1-50]
Spec - v276 - My 18 '96 - p34+ [501+]
The Runaway Jury (Beck). Abridged Version. Audio Version
LJ - v121 - S 15 '96 - p114 [51-250]
The Runaway Jury (Muller). Unabridged Version. Audio Version
BWatch - v18 - Mr '97 - p7 [1-50]
y Kliatt - v31 - Mr '97 - p45 [51-250]
LJ - v122 - F 1 '97 - p127 [51-250]
LJ - v122 - F 15 '97 - p114 [1-50]
Grishaw, Joshua - *My Heart Is Full of Wishes (Illus. by Lane Yerkes)*
c RT - v50 - O '96 - p137 [1-50]
Griskey, Richard G - *Chemical Engineering for Chemists*
SciTech - v21 - Mr '97 - p94 [51-250]
Griswold, Wendy - *Cultures and Societies in a Changing World*
SF - v75 - S '96 - p352+ [251-500]

Griswold Del Castillo, Richard - *North to Aztlan*
Choice - v34 - Mr '97 - p1227 [51-250]
Gritsch, Eric W - *Martin Luther: Faith in Christ and the Gospel*
CLW - v67 - D '96 - p37 [51-250]
Grob, Gerald N - *The Mad Among Us*
J Soc H - v30 - Fall '96 - p272+ [501+]
Grodin, Charles - *We're Ready for You, Mr. Grodin*
FIR - v47 - S '96 - p84 [251-500]
Groell, Anne Lesley - *Anvil of the Sun*
y Kliatt - v31 - Mr '97 - p18 [51-250]
MFSF - v91 - D '96 - p91+ [501+]
Groenewegen, John - *Transaction Cost Economics and Beyond*
JEL - v34 - D '96 - p2025 [51-250]
Groenewegen, Peter - *Economics and Ethics?*
JEL - v35 - Mr '97 - p189 [51-250]
A Soaring Eagle
Albion - v28 - Fall '96 - p523+ [501+]
JEL - v34 - D '96 - p1989+ [501+]
Grof, Christina - *The Stormy Search for the Self*
Rel St Rev - v23 - Ap '97 - p141+ [501+]
Grofman, Bernard - *Legislative Term Limits*
JEL - v34 - D '96 - p2029 [51-250]
R&R Bk N - v11 - D '96 - p47 [51-250]
The Grolier Library of International Biographies. Vols. 1-10
cr ARBA - v28 - '97 - p13 [51-250]
The Grolier Library of Science Biographies. Vols. 1-10
r LJ - v122 - Ap 1 '97 - p82 [51-250]
The Grolier Multimedia Encyclopedia 1996. Electronic Media Version
cr BYTE - v21 - O '96 - p167 [1-50]
cr Choice - v34 - O '96 - p260 [501+]
The Grolier Multimedia Encyclopedia 1997. Electronic Media Version
cr BL - v93 - N 1 '96 - p530+ [501+]
Grolier Science Fiction. Electronic Media Version
r Choice - v34 - O '96 - p260+ [501+]
The Grolier Student Encyclopedia of Science, Technology and the Environment. Vols. 1-11
cr ARBA - v28 - '97 - p564 [51-250]
cr SLJ - v42 - Ag '96 - p181 [51-250]
Grollman, Earl A - *When Someone You Love Has Alzheimer's*
BL - v93 - N 15 '96 - p554 [51-250]
Grondin, Jean - *Introduction to Philosophical Hermeneutics*
Rel St Rev - v23 - Ap '97 - p150+ [51-250]
Groneman, Bill - *Eyewitness to the Alamo*
Roundup M - v4 - D '96 - p21 [251-500]
Groner, Daniel - *Java Language API Super Bible*
LJ - v121 - D '96 - p138 [51-250]
Groom, Winston - *Gone the Sun*
PW - v243 - O 14 '96 - p81 [1-50]
Shrouds of Glory (Whitener). Audio Version
y Kliatt - v30 - S '96 - p59 [51-250]
Grooms, Anthony - *Trouble No More*
Choice - v34 - O '96 - p278 [51-250]
Grooms, Steve - *The Return of the Wolf*
AB - v97 - Je 17 '96 - p2404 [51-250]
Groos, Arthur - *Romancing the Grail*
Ger Q - v70 - Win '97 - p75+ [501+]
Groothuis, Rebecca Merrill - *Good News for Women*
LJ - v122 - F 15 '97 - p138 [51-250]
Groppi, Angela - *I Conservatori Della Virtu*
JMH - v68 - S '96 - p712+ [501+]
Gros, Daniel - *Winds of Change*
Econ J - v106 - N '96 - p1799+ [501+]
r JEL - v34 - D '96 - p1992+ [501+]
Grose, Peter - *Continuing the Inquiry*
For Aff - v76 - Ja '97 - p159+ [501+]
Gentleman Spy
NYTBR - v101 - O 27 '96 - p48 [51-250]
Groseclose, David A - *James A. Michener: A Bibliography*
r AB - v99 - Ja 20 '97 - p156 [501+]
r ARBA - v28 - '97 - p445 [251-500]
r Choice - v34 - O '96 - p252 [51-250]
r R&R Bk N - v11 - N '96 - p73 [51-250]
Grosh, Margaret E - *A Manual for Planning and Implementing the Living Standards Measurement Study Survey*
r JEL - v35 - Mr '97 - p233 [51-250]
Grosholz, Emily - *Telling the Barn Swallow*
PW - v243 - D 30 '96 - p62 [1-50]
PW - v244 - Ja 6 '97 - p58 [51-250]
Gross, Alan G - *The Rhetoric of Science*
Nature - v383 - O 24 '96 - p682 [1-50]
Rhetorical Hermeneutics
R&R Bk N - v12 - F '97 - p76 [51-250]

Gross, Charles J - *The Air National Guard and the American Military Tradition*
APH - v44 - Spr '97 - p60 [251-500]
Parameters - v26 - Aut '96 - p163+ [251-500]
Gross, David C - *Hippocrene Practical English-Yiddish, Yiddish-English Dictionary: Romanized. Expanded Ed.*
r ARBA - v28 - '97 - p404 [251-500]
Gross, Eberhard K U - *Density Functional Theory*
Am Sci - v84 - S '96 - p497 [251-500]
Gross, Edward - *Captain's Log*
Ant R - v54 - Fall '96 - p488+ [251-500]
Gross, Harvey - *Sound and Form in Modern Poetry. 2nd Ed.*
Choice - v34 - D '96 - p607 [51-250]
Gross, James A - *Broken Promise*
APSR - v91 - Mr '97 - p186+ [501+]
ILRR - v50 - Ap '97 - p515+ [501+]
Gross, Jeffrey - *Musculoskeletal Examination*
r SciTech - v20 - D '96 - p48 [51-250]
Gross, Karen - *Failure and Forgiveness*
BL - v93 - Mr 1 '97 - p1098 [51-250]
Gross, Ken - *The Talk Show Defense*
KR - v65 - Ap 1 '97 - p506 [51-250]
LJ - v122 - My 1 '97 - p143 [51-250]
PW - v244 - Mr 31 '97 - p66 [51-250]
Gross, Liza - *Handbook of Leftist Guerrilla Groups in Latin America and the Caribbean*
r ARBA - v28 - '97 - p274 [251-500]
Gross, Michael - *Model. The Ugly Business of Beautiful Women*
Books - v9 - S '95 - p23 [1-50]
Gross, Paul R - *The Flight from Science and Reason*
New Sci - v153 - Mr 1 '97 - p49 [1-50]
R&R Bk N - v11 - N '96 - p75 [51-250]
SB - v33 - My '97 - p101+ [501+]
Higher Superstition
Ant R - v54 - Sum '96 - p373+ [251-500]
Soc - v33 - Jl '96 - p94+ [501+]
Gross, Philip - *Scratch City*
c JB - v60 - Ag '96 - p148+ [51-250]
Transformer
y Sch Lib - v45 - F '97 - p49 [51-250]
Gross, Rita M - *Feminism and Religion*
LJ - v121 - S 15 '96 - p73 [51-250]
PW - v243 - S 30 '96 - p76 [51-250]
Gross, Sabine - *Lese-Zeichen: Kognition, Medium Und Materialitat Im Leseprozess*
Ger Q - v69 - Spr '96 - p200+ [501+]
Poetics T - v18 - Spr '97 - p117+ [501+]
Gross, Samuel - *Hematology: A Problem-Oriented Approach*
SciTech - v20 - D '96 - p47 [51-250]
Gross, Steven E - *Compensation for Teams*
Per Psy - v49 - Win '96 - p1016+ [501+]
Grossfeld, Stan - *Lost Futures*
KR - v65 - Ap 1 '97 - p543 [51-250]
PW - v244 - Mr 31 '97 - p57 [51-250]
Grosshandler-Smith, Janet - *Working Together against Drinking and Driving*
c SLJ - v43 - F '97 - p107+ [51-250]
Grossi, Paolo - *L'Ordine Giuridico Medievale*
Choice - v34 - D '96 - p567 [1-50]
Grossinger, Harvey - *The Quarry: Stories by Harvey Grossinger*
KR - v65 - Mr 15 '97 - p401 [251-500]
PW - v244 - Mr 10 '97 - p48 [51-250]
Grossinger, Richard - *New Moon*
LATBR - Ag 4 '96 - p7 [501+]
Grosskurth, Phyllis - *Byron: The Flawed Angel*
BL - v93 - Ap 1 '97 - p1277 [51-250]
KR - v65 - Mr 1 '97 - p351+ [51-250]
LJ - v122 - Ap 15 '97 - p80+ [51-250]
Mac - v110 - Ap 28 '97 - p61 [501+]
NS - v126 - F 28 '97 - p48 [501+]
NYTBR - v102 - Ap 13 '97 - p13 [501+]
Obs - F 23 '97 - p16* [501+]
PW - v244 - Mr 3 '97 - p57 [501+]
Woman's J - F '97 - p16 [1-50]
Grossman, Bill - *My Little Sister Ate One Hare (Illus. by Kevin Hawkes)*
c CCB-B - v50 - Ja '97 - p171+ [51-250]
c HB Guide - v8 - Spr '97 - p29 [51-250]
c NYTBR - v102 - Mr 16 '97 - p26 [501+]
c SLJ - v42 - D '96 - p29 [1-50]
c SLJ - v42 - D '96 - p92+ [51-250]
Grossman, C Barrie - *Magnetic Resonance Imaging and Computed Tomography of the Head and Spine. 2nd Ed.*
SciTech - v20 - S '96 - p37 [51-250]
Grossman, David - *The Book of Intimate Grammar*
NS & S - v9 - My 17 '96 - p40 [1-50]

Grossman, Elizabeth Greenwell - *The Civic Architecture of Paul Cret*
TLS - F 7 '97 - p19 [501+]
Grossman, Gene M - *Economic Growth. Vols. 1-2*
JEL - v35 - Mr '97 - p282+ [51-250]
Handbook of International Economics. Vol. 3
JEL - v34 - S '96 - p1424 [51-250]
Grossman, Grace Cohen - *New Beginnings*
Choice - v34 - Ja '97 - p784+ [51-250]
Grossman, James R - *A Chance to Make Good*
c Cur R - v36 - Ap '97 - p12 [51-250]
Grossman, Mark - *The ABC-CLIO Companion to the Native American Rights Movement*
r ARBA - v28 - '97 - p158 [51-250]
r BWatch - v18 - Mr '97 - p11+ [51-250]
r LJ - v122 - Ja '97 - p86 [51-250]
Encyclopedia of the Persian Gulf War
r ARBA - v28 - '97 - p207 [51-250]
yr SLJ - v42 - Ag '96 - p181 [51-250]
Grossman, Patricia - *Four Figures in Time*
Bloom Rev - v17 - Ja '97 - p14+ [251-500]
Grossman, Vassily - *Life and Fate*
SFR - v21 - Jl '96 - p48 [51-250]
Grossman, Wendy - *Remembering the Future*
New Sci - v153 - Mr 8 '97 - p43 [51-250]
Grossmann, Atina - *Reforming Sex*
AHR - v102 - F '97 - p126 [501+]
JIH - v27 - Win '97 - p530+ [501+]
Grossmann, Ignacio E - *Global Optimization in Engineering Design*
SciTech - v20 - N '96 - p79 [51-250]
Grossmith, George - *Diary of a Nobody (Hardiman). Audio Version*
Books - v11 - Ap '97 - p19 [1-50]
Grossnick, Roy A - *Dictionary of American Naval Aviation Squadrons. Vol. 1*
r J Gov Info - v23 - S '96 - p543 [51-250]
Grosso, Stephen - *Experiencing Lourdes*
Am - v176 - F 15 '97 - p32 [51-250]
Grosvenor, Theodore P - *Primary Care Optometry. 3rd Ed.*
SciTech - v20 - D '96 - p50 [51-250]
Grosvenor, Vertamae - *Vertamae Cooks in the Americas' Family Kitchen*
BL - v93 - F 15 '97 - p988 [51-250]
Grosz, E A - *Sexy Bodies*
Choice - v34 - S '96 - p110 [51-250]
Space, Time, and Perversion
L'Esprit - v36 - Win '96 - p105+ [251-500]
Volatile Bodies
Dance RJ - v28 - Fall '96 - p92+ [501+]
Grotans, Anna A - *The St. Gall Tractate*
r Specu - v72 - Ja '97 - p158+ [501+]
Grote, Dick - *The Complete Guide to Performance Appraisal*
HR Mag - v42 - F '97 - p124 [51-250]
Groth, Siegfried - *Namibia: The Wall of Silence*
Africa T - v43 - 4 '96 - p417+ [501+]
Grotius, Hugo - *Hugo Grotius, Ordinum Hollandiae Ac Westfrisiae Pietas*
Six Ct J - v27 - Fall '96 - p802+ [501+]
Groton, Anne H - *From Alpha to Omega*
CW - v89 - Jl '96 - p508+ [251-500]
Grotzes, George - *Math into LATEX*
SIAM Rev - v38 - S '96 - p535 [51-250]
Group for the Advancement of Psychiatry. Committee on Therapeutic Care - *Mental Health in Remote Rural Developing Areas*
Readings - v11 - D '96 - p21 [51-250]
Group of Lisbon - *Limits to Competition*
Choice - v34 - D '96 - p659 [51-250]
JEL - v34 - D '96 - p2038+ [51-250]
Grout, Donald Jay - *A History of Western Music*
CR - v269 - Ag '96 - p110+ [51-250]
Grove, Andrew S - *Only the Paranoid Survive*
BL - v93 - S 15 '96 - p191 [51-250]
Bus Bk R - v14 - 1 '97 - p56+ [501+]
Fortune - v134 - O 14 '96 - p216+ [501+]
Har Bus R - v74 - N '96 - p168+ [501+]
LJ - v122 - Mr 15 '97 - p35 [1-50]
New R - v216 - Mr 3 '97 - p43+ [501+]
Reason - v28 - D '96 - p44 [251-500]
Time - v148 - O 21 '96 - p88+ [501+]
WSJ-Cent - v99 - Ja 20 '97 - pA12 [251-500]
Only the Paranoid Survive (Dean). Audio Version
LJ - v122 - F 1 '97 - p125+ [51-250]
Grove, Doris - *One Rainy Night*
c CLW - v67 - Mr '97 - p14 [1-50]
Grove, Nicola - *Odyssey Now*
TES - N 1 '96 - pR10 [251-500]

Grove, Noel - *Birds of North America*
  y BL - v93 - Mr 1 '97 - p1099 [51-250]
      Bloom Rev - v17 - Ja '97 - p23 [51-250]
      CSM - v89 - D 5 '96 - pB3 [1-50]
      LJ - v122 - F 15 '97 - p159 [51-250]
      PW - v243 - O 14 '96 - p71 [51-250]
Grove, Richard H - *Green Imperialism*
      AHR - v101 - O '96 - p1199+ [501+]
      BioSci - v46 - O '96 - p698+ [501+]
      JIH - v27 - Aut '96 - p291+ [501+]
      Nature - v384 - D 5 '96 - p426 [1-50]
Grove, Valerie - *Dear Dodie*
      PW - v244 - Ap 28 '97 - p60 [51-250]
Grove, Vicki - *The Crystal Garden*
  c RT - v50 - N '96 - p253 [51-250]
      Rimwalkers
  y Kliatt - v31 - Ja '97 - p8 [51-250]
Grover, Jan Zita - *North Enough*
      BL - v93 - F 1 '97 - p920 [51-250]
      KR - v64 - D 1 '96 - p1716 [251-500]
      NYTBR - v102 - Ap 6 '97 - p20 [51-250]
      PW - v243 - D 16 '96 - p48+ [51-250]
Grover, Max - *Circles and Squares Everywhere!*
  c HB Guide - v7 - Fall '96 - p239 [51-250]
Grover, Mikell P - *Fundamentals of Modern
      Manufacturing*
      SciTech - v20 - D '96 - p85 [51-250]
Grover, Varun - *Business Process Change*
      R&R Bk N - v11 - N '96 - p29 [51-250]
Grover, Wayne - *Dolphin Treasure (Illus. by Jim Fowler)*
  c BL - v92 - Ag '96 - p1900 [51-250]
  c HB Guide - v7 - Fall '96 - p292 [51-250]
Groves, Dawn - *The Writer's Guide to the Internet*
      BWatch - v18 - F '97 - p4 [51-250]
Groves, Julian McAllister - *Hearts and Minds*
      PW - v244 - Ja 13 '97 - p64+ [51-250]
Groves, Michael J - *Aseptic Pharmaceutical
      Manufacturing II*
      SciTech - v20 - S '96 - p43 [51-250]
Groze, Victor - *Successful Adoptive Families*
      AJS - v102 - N '96 - p885+ [501+]
      Choice - v34 - S '96 - p218 [51-250]
      JMF - v59 - F '97 - p237+ [501+]
      Readings - v12 - Mr '97 - p29 [51-250]
Grubb, Alan - *The Politics of Pessimism*
      Choice - v34 - Ja '97 - p856 [51-250]
Grubb, Andrew - *Justice and Health Care*
      Choice - v34 - D '96 - p681 [51-250]
Grubb, James S - *Provincial Families of the Renaissance*
      Choice - v34 - Mr '97 - p1220 [51-250]
      R&R Bk N - v12 - F '97 - p52 [51-250]
Grubb, W Norton - *Learning to Work*
      JEL - v35 - Mr '97 - p237 [51-250]
Grubbs, Judith Evans - *Law and Family in Late Antiquity*
      Rel St Rev - v23 - Ja '97 - p63 [51-250]
Gruber, Franz - *Diskurs Und Konsens Im Prozess
      Theologischer Wahrheit*
      JR - v77 - Ja '97 - p164+ [501+]
Gruber, Joan M - *Mature Money*
      R&R Bk N - v12 - F '97 - p47 [1-50]
Gruber, Mayer I - *Women in the Biblical World. Vol. 1*
  r ARBA - v28 - '97 - p540 [51-250]
  r Choice - v34 - N '96 - p430 [51-250]
Gruber, Scott A - *Local Immunosuppression of Organ
      Transplants*
      SciTech - v20 - S '96 - p26 [51-250]
Grubrich-Simitis, Ilse - *Back to Freud's Texts*
      Choice - v34 - Ap '97 - p1419+ [51-250]
      NYTBR - v102 - F 16 '97 - p13+ [501+]
Grudermeyer, David - *Sensible Self-Help*
  r BWatch - v17 - S '96 - p10 [51-250]
Grudin, Robert - *On Dialogue*
      HR - v49 - Win '97 - p681+ [501+]
Grue, John - *Waves and Nonlinear Processes in
      Hydrodynamics*
      SciTech - v20 - D '96 - p20 [51-250]
Gruen, Arno - *The Insanity of Normality*
      TranslRevS - v1 - My '95 - p8 [51-250]
Gruen, Erich S - *Culture and National Identity in
      Republican Rome*
      CW - v89 - Jl '96 - p498 [251-500]
      TLS - My 24 '96 - p36 [51-250]
Gruen, John - *Flowers and Fables (Illus. by Rafal
      Olbinski)*
  c HB Guide - v8 - Spr '97 - p67 [51-250]
  y KR - v64 - O 1 '96 - p1466 [51-250]
  c SLJ - v43 - F '97 - p103 [51-250]
Gruenfeld, Lee - *The Halls of Justice*
      Rapport - v19 - 5 '96 - p37 [251-500]
      The Halls of Justice (Whitener). Audio Version
  y Kliatt - v31 - My '97 - p38+ [51-250]

Gruesser, John Cullen - *The Unruly Voice*
      AL - v69 - Mr '97 - p251+ [251-500]
      Choice - v34 - Ja '97 - p799 [51-250]
Grugel, Jean - *Politics and Development in the Caribbean
      Basin*
      HAHR - v76 - N '96 - p842+ [251-500]
Grumbach, Doris - *The Book of Knowledge*
      Am - v175 - Ag 17 '96 - p26+ [501+]
      Life in a Day
      BL - v93 - S 1 '96 - p56 [51-250]
      BW - v26 - O 27 '96 - p10 [501+]
      BW - v26 - D 8 '96 - p6 [51-250]
      KR - v64 - S 1 '96 - p1294 [251-500]
      LATBR - Ap 13 '97 - pF [51-250]
      NYTBR - v101 - D 22 '96 - p14 [51-250]
Grumbine, R Edward - *Environmental Policy and
      Biodiversity*
      BioSci - v46 - O '96 - p695+ [501+]
Grumet, Robert S - *Historic Contact*
  r HRNB - v25 - Win '97 - p63+ [251-500]
      NEQ - v70 - Mr '97 - p141+ [501+]
      Pub Hist - v18 - Fall '96 - p155+ [501+]
      W&M Q - v54 - Ja '97 - p263+ [501+]
      Northeastern Indian Lives 1632-1816
      Choice - v34 - N '96 - p527 [51-250]
Grunbaum, Irene - *Escape through the Balkans*
      TranslRevS - v2 - D '96 - p8 [51-250]
      Wom R Bks - v14 - O '96 - p12+ [501+]
Grunbein, Durs - *Galilei Vermisst Dantes Holle Und
      Bleibt An Den Massen Hangen*
      WLT - v71 - Win '97 - p145 [501+]
Grunberg, Arnon - *Blue Mondays*
  y BL - v93 - Ja '97 - p818+ [51-250]
      CSM - v89 - Ja 15 '97 - p15 [51-250]
      KR - v64 - D 1 '96 - p1690 [251-500]
      LJ - v122 - Ja '97 - p146 [51-250]
      NYTBR - v102 - F 2 '97 - p11 [501+]
      PW - v243 - D 9 '96 - p61 [51-250]
Grunberg, Bernard - *L'Univers Des Conquistadores*
      HAHR - v77 - My '97 - p308+ [501+]
Grunberg, Isabelle - *Rival States, Rival Firms*
      JEL - v35 - Mr '97 - p206 [51-250]
Grundy, Stephan - *Attila's Treasure*
      BL - v92 - Ag '96 - p1881 [51-250]
  y Kliatt - v30 - N '96 - p8 [51-250]
Grunert, Klaus G - *Market Orientation in Food and
      Agriculture*
      JEL - v34 - S '96 - p1462 [51-250]
Grunes, Barbara - *All American Vegetarian*
  y Kliatt - v31 - Ja '97 - p30+ [251-500]
      All-American Waves of Grain
      LJ - v122 - Ap 15 '97 - p110 [51-250]
      PW - v244 - Mr 24 '97 - p78 [51-250]
Grunfeld, A Tom - *The Making of Modern Tibet. Rev. Ed.*
      R&R Bk N - v12 - F '97 - p20 [51-250]
Grunfeld, Frederic V - *Rodin: A Biography (Vance). Pts.
      1-2. Audio Version*
  y Kliatt - v31 - Mr '97 - p50 [51-250]
      LJ - v122 - Ja '97 - p170 [51-250]
Grunfeld, Mihai G - *Antologia De La Poesia
      Latinoamericana De Vanguardia 1916-1935*
      WLT - v70 - Sum '96 - p669 [251-500]
Grunsell, Angela - *Ethiopia*
  c Sch Lib - v44 - Ag '96 - p110 [51-250]
Grunwald, Ernest - *Thermodynamics of Molecular
      Species*
      SciTech - v21 - Mr '97 - p31 [51-250]
Grunwald, Henry - *One Man's America*
      BL - v93 - Ja '97 - p781 [51-250]
      BW - v27 - Ja 26 '97 - p1+ [501+]
      CJR - v35 - Ja '97 - p55+ [501+]
      KR - v64 - O 15 '96 - p1510+ [251-500]
      LJ - v121 - N 15 '96 - p68 [51-250]
      NL - v79 - D 16 '96 - p20+ [501+]
      NYTBR - v102 - Ja 5 '97 - p9 [501+]
      PW - v243 - N 4 '96 - p52 [51-250]
      WSJ-Cent - v99 - Ja 8 '97 - pA14 [501+]
Grunwald, Lisa - *New Year's Eve*
      BL - v93 - N 1 '96 - p481 [51-250]
      KR - v64 - O 15 '96 - p1484+ [251-500]
      LJ - v121 - O 15 '96 - p89 [51-250]
      NYTBR - v102 - F 2 '97 - p21 [51-250]
      PW - v243 - O 14 '96 - p62 [51-250]
      Trib Bks - F 2 '97 - p9 [501+]
      W&I - v12 - Ap '97 - p292+ [501+]
      Now, Soon, Later (Illus. by Jane Johnson)
  c CBRS - v24 - Ag '96 - p158 [1-50]
  c CCB-B - v50 - O '96 - p60+ [51-250]
  c HB Guide - v8 - Spr '97 - p12 [51-250]
  c SLJ - v42 - S '96 - p178 [51-250]

Grupen, Claus - *Particle Detectors*
      Choice - v34 - Mr '97 - p1198 [51-250]
      SciTech - v20 - N '96 - p19 [51-250]
Grygier, Pat Sandiford - *A Long Way from Home*
      Can Hist R - v77 - S '96 - p446+ [501+]
Gu, Weiqun - *Conflicts of Divided Nations*
      APSR - v91 - Mr '97 - p224 [501+]
Guan, Yuqian - *Dao Chu Liu Qing*
      BL - v93 - My 1 '97 - p1484 [1-50]
Guardino, Peter F - *Peasants, Politics, and the Formation
      of Mexico's National State*
      Choice - v34 - N '96 - p523 [51-250]
Guare, John - *John Guare. Vol. 1*
      LJ - v122 - Ja '97 - p98 [51-250]
      The War against the Kitchen Sink
      BL - v93 - S 15 '96 - p203 [251-500]
Guareschi, Giovanni - *Ciao, Don Camillo*
      BL - v93 - D 1 '96 - p644 [1-50]
Guarino-Ghezzi, Susan - *Balancing Juvenile Justice*
      CS - v26 - Ja '97 - p84+ [501+]
Guarnaccia, Steven - *Skeleton Closet (Illus. by Steven
      Guarnaccia)*
  c LATBR - O 20 '96 - p8 [51-250]
  c PW - v243 - S 30 '96 - p85 [51-250]
Guastello, Stephen J - *Chaos, Catastrophe, and Human
      Affairs*
      Per Psy - v50 - Spr '97 - p200+ [501+]
Guazzone, Laura - *The Islamist Dilemma*
      Choice - v34 - O '96 - p357 [51-250]
      For Aff - v75 - N '96 - p166 [51-250]
      MEJ - v50 - Aut '96 - p630 [51-250]
      MEQ - v3 - S '96 - p82+ [251-500]
Gubar, Susan - *Racechanges: White Skin, Black Face in
      American Culture*
      KR - v65 - Ap 1 '97 - p519 [251-500]
Gude, Mary Louise - *Louis Massignon: The Crucible of
      Compassion*
      LJ - v122 - Ja '97 - p110+ [251-500]
Guderjan, Thomas H - *Maya Maritime Trade, Settlement,
      and Populations on Ambergris Caye, Belize*
      LA Ant - v7 - Je '96 - p173+ [501+]
Gudgeon, Chris - *Out of This World*
      Quill & Q - v62 - O '96 - p36 [251-500]
Gudmundson, Donald E - *Research Strategies for Small
      Businesses*
      JEL - v34 - S '96 - p1460 [51-250]
Gudmundson, Lowell - *Central America 1821-1871*
      HAHR - v77 - My '97 - p330+ [251-500]
Gudmundsson, Einar Mar - *Angels of the Universe*
      KR - v65 - F 1 '97 - p172 [51-250]
      PW - v244 - Ja 20 '97 - p392 [251-500]
Gudorf, Christine E - *Body, Sex, and Pleasure*
      Intpr - v51 - Ja '97 - p106+ [251-500]
Gudykunst, William B - *Bridging Japanese/North
      American Differences*
      MLJ - v80 - Win '96 - p554 [501+]
      *Communication in Personal Relationships across
      Cultures*
      R&R Bk N - v11 - D '96 - p38 [51-250]
Guegan, Gerard - *L'ABCdaire Du Cinema Francais*
      FR - v70 - D '96 - p369+ [501+]
      Debord Est Mort, Le Che Aussi, Et Alors?
      TLS - O 4 '96 - p8 [501+]
Guelbenzu, Jose Maria - *El Sentimiento*
      WLT - v71 - Win '97 - p126 [251-500]
Guelke, Adrian - *The Age of Terrorism and the
      International Political System*
      APSR - v91 - Mr '97 - p231+ [501+]
Guelzo, Allen C - *For the Union of Evangelical
      Christendom*
      JR - v77 - Ja '97 - p145+ [501+]
Guenther, Beatrice Martina - *The Poetics of Death*
      R&R Bk N - v11 - N '96 - p75 [51-250]
Guenther, Titus F - *Rahner and Metz*
      Theol St - v57 - Mr '96 - p157+ [501+]
Guerard, Albert J - *The Hotel in the Jungle*
      ABR - v18 - O '96 - p16+ [501+]
Guerin, M Victoria - *The Fall of Kings and Princes*
      Specu - v72 - Ja '97 - p160+ [501+]
Guerin, Philip J - *Working with Relationship Triangles*
      Choice - v34 - My '97 - p1582 [51-250]
      Readings - v12 - Mr '97 - p30 [51-250]
      SciTech - v21 - Mr '97 - p55 [1-50]
Guerin-Gonzales, Camille - *Mexican Workers and
      American Dreams*
      JIH - v27 - Win '97 - p550+ [501+]
Guernsey, Alfred H - *Harper's Pictorial History of the
      Civil War*
      yr SLJ - v42 - D '96 - p153 [51-250]

Guernsey, JoAnn Bren - *Voices of Feminism*
 y   BL - v93 - S 15 '96 - p228 [51-250]
 c   Ch BWatch - v6 - S '96 - p5 [1-50]
 y   HB Guide - v8 - Spr '97 - p95 [51-250]
 Youth Violence
 y   HB Guide - v8 - Spr '97 - p95 [51-250]
 y   SLJ - v43 - Ja '97 - p126 [51-250]
 y   VOYA - v19 - F '97 - p348 [251-500]
Guerrini, M - *La Biblioteca Antica Dell'Osservatorio Ximeniano. Vols. 1-2*
 r   Lib - v18 - D '96 - p347+ [501+]
Guest, Barbara - *Selected Poems*
 Lon R Bks - v18 - Ag 22 '96 - p25+ [501+]
Guest, Judith - *Errands*
 Ent W - F 14 '97 - p57 [51-250]
 KR - v64 - O 1 '96 - p1421 [251-500]
 LJ - v121 - O 15 '96 - p90 [51-250]
 NYTBR - v102 - Ja 12 '97 - p18 [501+]
 Trib Bks - F 2 '97 - p9 [501+]
Guevara, Ernesto - *The Bolivian Diary of Ernesto Che Guevara*
 HAHR - v76 - N '96 - p826+ [501+]
 Parameters - v26 - Win '96 - p158 [1-50]
 Episodes of the Cuban Revolutionary War 1956-58
 Choice - v34 - S '96 - p190 [51-250]
 HAHR - v76 - N '96 - p826+ [501+]
 The Motorcycle Diaries
 BW - v26 - O 27 '96 - p12 [51-250]
 LATBR - D 22 '96 - p6 [51-250]
 PW - v243 - S 23 '96 - p73 [1-50]
Guevara Mann, Carlos - *Panamanian Militarism*
 WorldV - v12 - Jl '96 - p9+ [51-250]
Guggenheim, Joseph - *Tax Credits for Low Income Housing. 9th Ed.*
 R&R Bk N - v11 - D '96 - p37 [51-250]
Guggenheim, K Y - *Basic Issues of the History of Nutrition*
 SB - v33 - Ja '97 - p10 [251-500]
Guggisberg, Hans - *Umgang Mit Jacob Burckhardt*
 Ren Q - v49 - Win '96 - p840+ [501+]
Gugler, Josef - *The Urban Transformation of the Developing World*
 Choice - v34 - Ap '97 - p1393 [51-250]
Gugler, Laurel Dee - *Muddle Cuddle (Illus. by Vlasta Van Kampen)*
 c   Quill & Q - v63 - Mr '97 - p78 [251-500]
Guglielmi, Nilda - *Guia Para Viajeros Medievales (Oriente, Siglos XIII-XV)*
 Specu - v71 - O '96 - p954+ [501+]
Guha-Thakurta, Tapati - *The Making of a New Indian Art*
 Art J - v55 - Fall '96 - p93+ [501+]
Guia De Alojamiento En Casas Rurales De Espana 1996
 r   BL - v93 - Mr 15 '97 - p1232 [1-50]
Guiberson, Brenda Z - *Into the Sea (Illus. by Alix Berenzy)*
 c   BL - v93 - S 15 '96 - p243 [51-250]
 c   CCB-B - v50 - S '96 - p13 [51-250]
 c   HB - v72 - N '96 - p759 [51-250]
 c   HB Guide - v8 - Spr '97 - p123 [51-250]
 c   SLJ - v42 - S '96 - p196+ [51-250]
 c   SLJ - v42 - D '96 - p29 [1-50]
Guibert, Abbot of Nogent-Sous-Coucy - *A Monk's Confession*
 TranslRevS - v2 - D '96 - p9 [51-250]
Guibert, Herve - *Blindsight*
 BW - v26 - D 22 '96 - p9 [51-250]
 PW - v243 - S 2 '96 - p114 [51-250]
 Ghost Image
 BW - v26 - Ag 25 '96 - p12 [51-250]
 TranslRevS - v2 - D '96 - p14+ [51-250]
Guicciardini, Francesco - *Dialogue on the Government of Florence*
 Ren Q - v49 - Win '96 - p856+ [501+]
Guide to Greater Washington D.C. Grantmakers. 2nd Ed.
 r   ChrPhil - v8 - O 3 '96 - p44 [51-250]
A Guide to Helping Students Develop Their IEPs. Audio Version
 EL - v54 - S '96 - p106 [51-250]
Guide to Official Statistics. Electronic Media Version
 r   LAR - v99 - Mr '97 - p160 [51-250]
The Guide to the Federal Budget 1997
 JEL - v34 - S '96 - p1440 [51-250]
A Guide to the Project Management Body of Knowledge. 1995 Ed.
 Choice - v34 - N '96 - p503 [51-250]
Guide to the Top Southern California Companies
 r   BWatch - v17 - S '96 - p3 [51-250]

Guidelines for Writing Effective Operating and Maintenance Procedures
 SciTech - v20 - N '96 - p79 [51-250]
Guider, Margaret Eletta - *Daughters of Rahab*
 JAAR - v65 - Spr '97 - p224+ [501+]
 JR - v77 - Ap '97 - p302+ [501+]
Guido, John F - *The Regla Papers*
 HAHR - v76 - Ag '96 - p559 [251-500]
Guilbert, Cecile - *Pour Guy Debord*
 TLS - O 4 '96 - p8 [501+]
Guild, Nicholas - *Angel*
 PW - v243 - N 4 '96 - p71 [1-50]
Guild, Tricia - *Tricia Guild in Town*
 LJ - v122 - Ja '97 - p95 [51-250]
 PW - v243 - S 16 '96 - p65 [51-250]
Guiley, Rosemary - *Encyclopedia of Angels*
 r   BL - v93 - My 15 '97 - p1612 [51-250]
 r   LJ - v121 - N 15 '96 - p54 [51-250]
 The Encyclopedia of Witches and Witchcraft
 r   CAY - v17 - Win '96 - p11 [51-250]
Guillaume Postel Et Jean Boulaese
 CH - v66 - Mr '97 - p196+ [51-250]
Guillen, Claudio - *The Challenge of Comparative Literature*
 MP - v94 - N '96 - p284+ [501+]
Guillen, Mauro E - *Models of Management*
 JEH - v56 - D '96 - p970+ [501+]
Guillen, Michael - *Five Equations That Changed the World*
 y   BL - v93 - Ap 1 '97 - p1342 [1-50]
 BW - v26 - S 8 '96 - p12 [51-250]
Guillet, Jean-Pierre - *La Fete Est A L'Eau (Illus. by Gilles Tibo)*
 c   Can CL - v22 - Sum '96 - p100+ [501+]
Guillevic, Eugene - *Du Silence*
 WLT - v70 - Aut '96 - p918 [51-250]
 On Silence
 WLT - v70 - Aut '96 - p918 [251-500]
Guilliatt, Richard - *Talk of the Devil*
 Aust Bk R - N '96 - p31+ [501+]
Guillory, John - *Cultural Capital*
 MP - v94 - N '96 - p286+ [501+]
Guilloton, Noelle - *Le Francais Au Bureau*
 J Gov Info - v23 - S '96 - p636 [51-250]
Guilmartin, John F, Jr. - *A Very Short War*
 J Mil H - v60 - O '96 - p805+ [501+]
 NWCR - v50 - Win '97 - p149+ [501+]
 Parameters - v26 - Win '96 - p162+ [501+]
Guinier, Lani - *Becoming Gentlemen*
 KR - v65 - F 1 '97 - p194 [251-500]
 LJ - v122 - Ap 1 '97 - p109 [51-250]
 PW - v244 - Mr 3 '97 - p57 [51-250]
Guinn, Jeff - *Dallas Cowboys*
 BL - v93 - D 1 '96 - p638 [51-250]
Guinness, Alec - *Blessings in Disguise*
 Spec - v277 - N 16 '96 - p42 [1-50]
 TLS - N 15 '96 - p40 [501+]
 My Name Escapes Me
 Am - v176 - Mr 8 '97 - p2 [501+]
 Spec - v277 - O 5 '96 - p50+ [501+]
 Spec - v277 - N 16 '96 - p42 [1-50]
 Spec - v277 - N 16 '96 - p46 [1-50]
 Spec - v277 - N 23 '96 - p44 [1-50]
 Spec - v277 - N 30 '96 - p58 [1-50]
 TLS - N 15 '96 - p40 [501+]
Guinness, Bunny - *Creating a Family Garden*
 CSM - v89 - F 27 '97 - pB1+ [501+]
 CSM - v89 - Mr 20 '97 - p14 [51-250]
 NYTBR - v101 - D 8 '96 - p42 [51-250]
Guinness, Louise - *Fathers: An Anthology*
 NS - v126 - Ap 25 '97 - p46+ [501+]
 Spec - v277 - N 23 '96 - p48 [501+]
 TLS - N 22 '96 - p36 [501+]
 VV - v42 - Ja 7 '97 - p42 [51-250]
The Guinness Book of Records. 1997 Ed.
 yr   Kliatt - v31 - My '97 - p32 [51-250]
The Guinness Book of World Records 1997
 r   BL - v93 - D 15 '96 - p743 [1-50]
The Guinness Encyclopedia. 2nd Ed.
 r   Books - v9 - S '95 - p11 [251-500]
Guinness Multimedia Disc of Records. 1996 Ed. Electronic Media Version
 yr   Kliatt - v30 - S '96 - p40 [51-250]
Guinther, John - *Direction of Cities*
 BL - v93 - N 15 '96 - p553 [51-250]
 KR - v64 - O 1 '96 - p1443+ [251-500]
 LJ - v121 - O 15 '96 - p54+ [51-250]
 PW - v243 - O 7 '96 - p52 [51-250]
Guirao, Olga - *Adversarios Admirables*
 WLT - v71 - Win '97 - p118+ [501+]

Guldin, Gregory Eliyu - *The Saga of Anthropology in China*
 JTWS - v13 - Fall '96 - p227+ [501+]
Gullberg, Jan - *Mathematics: From the Birth of Numbers*
 y   BL - v93 - Ap 1 '97 - p1273 [51-250]
 y   BL - v93 - Ap 1 '97 - p1342 [1-50]
 PW - v244 - Ja 27 '97 - p90 [51-250]
Gullette, Margaret Morganroth - *Cultural Combat*
 LJ - v122 - Ap 15 '97 - p103 [51-250]
Gulley, Philip - *Front Porch Tales*
 BL - v93 - Mr 1 '97 - p1111 [51-250]
Gulliver, P H - *Merchants and Shopkeepers*
 Am Ethnol - v23 - N '96 - p921+ [501+]
 ILS - v16 - Spr '97 - p36 [1-50]
 JIH - v27 - Spr '97 - p683+ [251-500]
 J Soc H - v30 - Fall '96 - p290+ [501+]
Gummelt, Volker - *Lex Et Evangelium*
 CH - v65 - S '96 - p481+ [501+]
Gummett, Philip - *Globalization and Public Policy*
 JEL - v34 - D '96 - p2041+ [51-250]
 Military R&D after the Cold War
 JEL - v35 - Mr '97 - p280+ [251-500]
Gump, James O - *The Dust Rose like Smoke*
 W&M Q - v54 - Ja '97 - p277+ [501+]
Gunawardena, Nalaka - *Felicitation Volume in Honour of Prof. C. Suriyakumaran, Knight Commander of the Most Noble Order of the Crown of Thailand*
 JEL - v34 - D '96 - p2040 [51-250]
Gunce, Ergin - *A Flower Much as Turkey*
 WLT - v71 - Win '97 - p219 [251-500]
Gundavaram, Shishir - *CGI Programming on the World Wide Web*
 LJ - v122 - Ja '97 - p138 [51-250]
Gundersen, Adolf G - *The Environmental Promise of Democratic Deliberation*
 J Pol - v58 - N '96 - p1228+ [501+]
Gunderson, Steve - *House and Home*
 BL - v92 - Ag '96 - p1861 [51-250]
 Nat - v263 - S 9 '96 - p44+ [501+]
Gundle, Stephen - *The New Italian Republic*
 Choice - v34 - O '96 - p354 [51-250]
Gunesekera, Romesh - *Monkfish Moon*
 LATBR - Ag 18 '96 - p15 [51-250]
 NYTBR - v101 - S 1 '96 - p24 [1-50]
Gunew, Sneja - *Framing Marginality*
 Can Lit - Win '96 - p199+ [501+]
Gunn, Janet Varner - *Second Life*
 MEJ - v50 - Aut '96 - p603+ [501+]
Gunn, Kirsty - *The Keepsake*
 BL - v93 - D 15 '96 - p709 [51-250]
 LJ - v121 - N 15 '96 - p88 [51-250]
 Lon R Bks - v19 - Ap 3 '97 - p22+ [501+]
 NYTLa - v146 - Ap 23 '97 - pC14 [501+]
 Obs - Mr 2 '97 - p17* [501+]
 PW - v244 - Ja 6 '97 - p61 [51-250]
 TLS - F 28 '97 - p22 [501+]
Gunn, S J - *Early Tudor Government 1485-1558*
 Albion - v28 - Fall '96 - p473+ [501+]
Gunning, Sandra - *Race, Rape, and Lynching*
 Choice - v34 - My '97 - p1496 [51-250]
Gunson, Christopher - *Over on the Farm (Illus. by Christopher Gunson)*
 c   Bks Keeps - v100 - S '96 - p8 [51-250]
 c   BL - v93 - F 1 '97 - p946 [51-250]
 c   KR - v65 - Ja 15 '97 - p142 [51-250]
 c   Magpies - v11 - S '96 - p45 [1-50]
 c   Par Ch - v21 - Mr '97 - p4 [1-50]
 c   PW - v244 - Ja 27 '97 - p105 [51-250]
 c   SLJ - v43 - Mr '97 - p159 [51-250]
Gunst, Kathy - *The Parenting Cookbook*
 LJ - v121 - N 15 '96 - p84 [51-250]
 PW - v243 - O 21 '96 - p79+ [51-250]
Gunston, Bill - *Jane's Aero-Engines*
 r   ARBA - v28 - '97 - p592 [51-250]
Gunstone, F D - *Fatty Acid and Lipid Chemistry*
 Choice - v34 - O '96 - p308 [51-250]
Gunter, Wagner - *An Exegetical Bibliography of the New Testament. Vol. 4*
 r   ARBA - v28 - '97 - p539 [51-250]
Gunther, John - *Inside U.S.A.: 50th Anniversary Edition*
 Trib Bks - Ap 27 '97 - p1+ [501+]
Gunther, Richard - *The Politics of Democratic Consolidation*
 APSR - v90 - S '96 - p672+ [501+]
 J Pol - v59 - F '97 - p298+ [501+]
Guntlow, Pauline - *Be Your Own Home Decorator*
 LJ - v122 - Ja '97 - p96 [51-250]
Gunton, Colin E - *A Brief Theology of Revelation*
 Theol St - v57 - S '96 - p571 [251-500]
Gunvaldsen Klaassen, Tonja - *Clay Birds*
 BIC - v25 - N '96 - p6+ [501+]

Gunzel, Beate - *Aelfwine's Prayerbook*
Specu - v72 - Ja '97 - p100+ [501+]
Gunzenhauser, Margot - *The Square Dance and Contra Dance Handbook*
r ARBA - v28 - '97 - p503 [51-250]
r RQ - v36 - Fall '96 - p139 [251-500]
Guo, Dajun - *Nonlinear Integral Equations in Abstract Spaces*
SciTech - v21 - Mr '97 - p17 [51-250]
Guppy, Darius - *Roll the Dice*
PW - v244 - Ja 27 '97 - p93 [1-50]
Gupta, Kanhaya L - *Financial Liberalization and Investment*
JEL - v34 - D '96 - p2109 [51-250]
Gupta, R K - *Social Action and Non-Violence*
Ethics - v107 - Ja '97 - p387 [51-250]
Gupta, Sudhir - *Immunology of HIV Infection*
SciTech - v21 - Mr '97 - p56 [51-250]
Mechanisms of Lymphocyte Activation and Immune Regulation VI
SciTech - v21 - Mr '97 - p43 [51-250]
Gupton, Guy W - *HVAC Controls*
r SciTech - v20 - D '96 - p71 [51-250]
Gur, Batya - *Ha-Merhak Ha-Nakhoni*
BL - v93 - Mr 1 '97 - p1115 [1-50]
Gura, Philip F - *The Crossroads of American History and Literature*
AB - v98 - O 7 '96 - p1150+ [501+]
Nine-C Lit - v51 - D '96 - p422 [51-250]
Guralnick, Michael J - *The Effectiveness of Early Intervention*
SciTech - v21 - Mr '97 - p64 [51-250]
Guralnick, Peter - *Feel like Going Home*
CSM - v88 - N 21 '96 - p11 [1-50]
Lost Highway
CSM - v88 - N 21 '96 - p11 [1-50]
Gurdon, Charles - *The Horn of Africa*
JTWS - v13 - Fall '96 - p266+ [501+]
Gurewich, Nathan - *Java Manual of Style*
r CBR - v14 - S '96 - p29 [1-50]
Gurewitch, Morton - *The Ironic Temper and the Comic Imagination*
Humor - v9 - 3 '96 - p417+ [501+]
Gurian, Michael - *The Wonder of Boys*
BL - v93 - O 1 '96 - p313 [51-250]
LATBR - Ag 4 '96 - p11 [51-250]
LJ - v121 - S 15 '96 - p88 [51-250]
PW - v243 - S 2 '96 - p125 [51-250]
Gurkewitz, Rona - *3-D Geometric Origami*
Math T - v89 - D '96 - p782 [251-500]
Gurley, Ted - *Plug In*
Choice - v34 - N '96 - p469+ [251-500]
Gurnah, Abdulrazak - *Admiring Silence*
BL - v93 - O 1 '96 - p322 [51-250]
KR - v64 - Ag 15 '96 - p1172+ [251-500]
LJ - v121 - O 1 '96 - p126 [51-250]
NYTBR - v101 - O 20 '96 - p22 [51-250]
Obs - O 20 '96 - p18* [501+]
PW - v243 - S 16 '96 - p69 [51-250]
Spec - v277 - S 14 '96 - p38 [501+]
TLS - S 20 '96 - p24 [501+]
VV - v41 - D 10 '96 - p59+ [501+]
Essays on African Writing 2
WLT - v70 - Sum '96 - p744+ [501+]
Gurney, Alan - *Below the Convergence*
y BL - v93 - F 1 '97 - p922 [51-250]
KR - v64 - D 15 '96 - p1783 [251-500]
New Sci - v154 - My 3 '97 - p48 [51-250]
NYTBR - v102 - Mr 30 '97 - p10+ [501+]
PW - v243 - D 30 '96 - p50+ [51-250]
Trib Bks - Ap 6 '97 - p6 [501+]
Gurney, David W - *Escriba Con Estilo!*
MLJ - v80 - Fall '96 - p429+ [501+]
Gurney, James - *Dinotopia: Audio Adventure. Audio Version*
CSM - v88 - O 31 '96 - pB4 [51-250]
Dinotopia: The World Beneath. Audio Version
CSM - v88 - O 31 '96 - pB4 [51-250]
y Kliatt - v31 - Ja '97 - p40 [51-250]
Gurney, Stephen - *British Poetry of the Nineteenth Century*
VS - v39 - Spr '96 - p451+ [501+]
Guroian, Vigen - *Life's Living toward Dying*
CC - v114 - F 5 '97 - p164+ [501+]
Gurr, Andrew - *The Shakespearian Playing Companies*
Choice - v34 - D '96 - p624 [51-250]
TLS - D 20 '96 - p21 [501+]
Gurr, Ted Robert - *Ethnic Conflict in World Politics*
SSQ - v77 - Je '96 - p445+ [501+]
Gurrieri, Francesco - *Palaces of Florence*
PW - v243 - N 25 '96 - p66 [51-250]

Gursel, Kadri - *Dagdakiler*
TLS - N 29 '96 - p14 [51-250]
Gursha, James E - *High Performance Cluster Configuration System Management*
SciTech - v21 - Mr '97 - p11 [1-50]
Gurskii, Lev - *Peremena Mest*
BL - v93 - O 1 '96 - p327 [1-50]
Gurstein, Rochelle - *The Repeal of Reticence*
New R - v215 - N 11 '96 - p56+ [501+]
PW - v243 - Jl 22 '96 - p223 [51-250]
WSJ-MW - v78 - D 3 '96 - pA18 [501+]
Gurval, Robert Alan - *Actium and Augustus*
HRNB - v25 - Fall '96 - p42 [251-500]
Gurvis, Sandra - *Way Stations to Heaven*
r CLW - v67 - Mr '97 - p43+ [251-500]
Gusfield, Joseph R - *Contested Meanings*
Choice - v34 - Ja '97 - p882+ [51-250]
R&R Bk N - v11 - N '96 - p44 [51-250]
Gushee, David P - *The Righteous Gentiles of the Holocaust*
J Ch St - v38 - Aut '96 - p909+ [251-500]
Guskey, Thomas R - *Implementing Mastery Learning. 2nd Ed.*
R&R Bk N - v11 - N '96 - p54 [51-250]
Gussow, Mel - *Conversations with and about Beckett*
Am Theat - v13 - D '96 - p21 [1-50]
Am Theat - v14 - F '97 - p56 [51-250]
TLS - O 18 '96 - p31 [51-250]
Gustafson, Jack - *How to Be a Black Belt in the Art of Life*
Sm Pr R - v28 - D '96 - p11 [51-250]
Gustafson, James P - *The Dilemmas of Brief Psychotherapy*
AJPsych - v153 - S '96 - p1229+ [501+]
Gustafson, Ralph - *Collected Poems. Vol. 3*
Can Lit - Win '96 - p187+ [501+]
Gustafsson, Harald - *Political Interaction in the Old Regime*
EHR - v111 - S '96 - p995+ [251-500]
Gustafsson, Lars - *Tjanarinnan*
WLT - v71 - Win '97 - p172+ [251-500]
Gusterson, Hugh - *Nuclear Rites*
Choice - v34 - Mr '97 - p1198+ [51-250]
JEL - v35 - Mr '97 - p281 [51-250]
Nat - v263 - D 30 '96 - p25+ [501+]
R&R Bk N - v12 - F '97 - p99 [51-250]
Gustin, Joseph F - *Disaster and Recovery Planning*
r R&R Bk N - v12 - F '97 - p45 [51-250]
Safety Management
R&R Bk N - v12 - F '97 - p41 [51-250]
Gutcheon, Beth - *The New Girls*
y LATBR - Ag 11 '96 - p11 [51-250]
Saying Grace
Rapport - v19 - 4 '96 - p31 [251-500]
Gutek, Barbara A - *The Dynamics of Service*
CS - v26 - Mr '97 - p227+ [501+]
Per Psy - v49 - Win '96 - p1030+ [501+]
Gutelle, Andrew - *Who Made This Big Mess? (Illus. by Sally Schaedler)*
c HB Guide - v7 - Fall '96 - p258 [1-50]
Guterson, David - *The Country Ahead of Us, the Country Behind*
Lon R Bks - v18 - O 3 '96 - p27+ [501+]
The Country Ahead of Us, the Country Behind (Scott). Audio Version
BL - v93 - N 15 '96 - p604 [51-250]
Snow Falling on Cedars
Lon R Bks - v18 - O 3 '96 - p27+ [501+]
NS - v125 - D 20 '96 - p116 [1-50]
Spec - v277 - N 16 '96 - p46 [1-50]
TES - Jl 19 '96 - pR6 [1-50]
TES - D 27 '96 - p16 [1-50]
TES - D 27 '96 - p17 [51-250]
Snow Falling on Cedars (Guidall). Audio Version
y Kliatt - v31 - Ja '97 - p46 [51-250]
Snow Falling on Cedars (Mariner). Audio Version
BL - v93 - F 15 '97 - p1038 [51-250]
LJ - v122 - F 15 '97 - p114 [1-50]
Guth, Alan - *The Inflationary Universe*
PW - v244 - Ap 28 '97 - p67 [1-50]
Guthke, Karl S - *Schillers Dramen*
MLR - v91 - O '96 - p1037+ [501+]
Guthkelch, A Norman - *The Scientific Foundations of Neurology*
SciTech - v21 - Mr '97 - p51 [51-250]
Guthrie, A B, Jr. - *The Big Sky*
WAL - v31 - Fall '96 - p195+ [501+]
Guthrie, Patricia - *Catching Sense*
Bl S - v26 - Fall '96 - p103 [51-250]
Choice - v34 - O '96 - p347+ [51-250]

Guthrie, Stewart, 1941- - *Faces in the Clouds*
JAAR - v64 - Sum '96 - p457+ [501+]
Rel St - v33 - Mr '97 - p131+ [51-250]
Gutierrez, Andrew Paul - *Applied Population Ecology*
Choice - v34 - O '96 - p302+ [51-250]
Gutierrez, David G - *Walls and Mirrors*
AHR - v101 - D '96 - p1635 [501+]
HAHR - v77 - F '97 - p92+ [501+]
PHR - v65 - Ag '96 - p484+ [501+]
Gutierrez, Donald - *The Holiness of the Real*
Bloom Rev - v17 - Ja '97 - p15+ [51-250]
Choice - v34 - Mr '97 - p1162 [51-250]
Gutierrez, Gustavo - *Las Casas: In Search of the Poor of Jesus Christ*
r JAAR - v64 - Fall '96 - p699+ [501+]
Gutierrez-Jones, Carl - *Rethinking the Borderlands*
QJS - v83 - F '97 - p113+ [501+]
Gutkind, Lee - *Creative Nonfiction*
y Sm Pr R - v28 - O '96 - p13+ [501+]
Gutknecht, Christoph - *Translating by Factors*
R&R Bk N - v11 - N '96 - p63 [51-250]
TranslRevS - v2 - D '96 - p13 [51-250]
Gutman, Bill - *Be Aware of Danger*
c BL - v93 - F 1 '97 - p931 [51-250]
c SLJ - v43 - F '97 - p116 [51-250]
Becoming Your Bird's Best Friend (Illus. by Anne Canevari Green)
c BL - v93 - D 1 '96 - p650 [51-250]
c CBRS - v25 - D '96 - p42 [51-250]
c HB Guide - v8 - Spr '97 - p125 [51-250]
c SLJ - v42 - N '96 - p112+ [51-250]
Becoming Your Dog's Best Friend (Illus. by Anne Canevari Green)
c BL - v93 - D 1 '96 - p650 [51-250]
c CBRS - v25 - D '96 - p42 [51-250]
c HB Guide - v8 - Spr '97 - p128 [51-250]
c SLJ - v42 - N '96 - p112+ [51-250]
Frank Thomas: Power Hitter
c HB Guide - v7 - Fall '96 - p361 [1-50]
Gail Devers
c HB Guide - v7 - Fall '96 - p361 [51-250]
c SLJ - v42 - N '96 - p113 [51-250]
Grant Hill, a Biography
y Kliatt - v31 - Mr '97 - p36+ [51-250]
Grant Hill: Basketball's High Flier
c HB Guide - v8 - Spr '97 - p144 [51-250]
c SLJ - v43 - F '97 - p91 [51-250]
Harmful to Your Health
c BL - v93 - F 1 '97 - p931 [51-250]
c SLJ - v43 - F '97 - p116 [51-250]
Hazards at Home
c Ch BWatch - v6 - Jl '96 - p8 [1-50]
c SLJ - v42 - S '96 - p215+ [51-250]
Jim Eisenreich
c HB Guide - v7 - Fall '96 - p361 [51-250]
Julie Krone
c HB Guide - v7 - Fall '96 - p361 [51-250]
c SLJ - v43 - F '97 - p91 [51-250]
Recreation Can Be Risky
c Ch BWatch - v6 - Jl '96 - p8 [1-50]
c SLJ - v42 - S '96 - p215+ [51-250]
y VOYA - v19 - O '96 - p230 [251-500]
Steve Young: NFL Passing Wizard
c HB Guide - v8 - Spr '97 - p144 [51-250]
c SLJ - v43 - F '97 - p91 [51-250]
Troy Aikman: Super Quarterback
c HB Guide - v7 - Fall '96 - p361 [1-50]
Gutman, Dan - *Gymnastics*
c HB Guide - v7 - Fall '96 - p361 [51-250]
c SLJ - v42 - Ag '96 - p155+ [51-250]
y VOYA - v19 - D '96 - p287 [51-250]
Honus and Me
y KR - v65 - F 1 '97 - p223 [51-250]
c PW - v244 - F 10 '97 - p84 [51-250]
c Trib Bks - Mr 30 '97 - p4+ [51-250]
The Kid Who Ran for President
c BL - v93 - N 1 '96 - p498 [51-250]
c CBRS - v25 - Ja '97 - p57 [51-250]
c CCB-B - v50 - N '96 - p97 [51-250]
c HB Guide - v8 - Spr '97 - p67 [51-250]
c KR - v64 - S 15 '96 - p1400 [51-250]
c PW - v243 - N 11 '96 - p76 [51-250]
c SLJ - v42 - N '96 - p106 [51-250]
Gutmann, Amy - *Democracy and Disagreement*
BW - v26 - S 8 '96 - p5 [501+]
CC - v113 - N 20 '96 - p1134+ [501+]
Choice - v34 - F '97 - p1033 [501+]
LJ - v121 - D '96 - p122 [51-250]
New R - v215 - N 25 '96 - p36+ [501+]
NYTBR - v101 - D 29 '96 - p21 [501+]
TLS - Ja 17 '97 - p25 [501+]

Gutteling, Jan M - *Exploring Risk Communication*
  Nature - v385 - Ja 9 '97 - p129+ [501+]
  SciTech - v20 - D '96 - p58 [51-250]
Gutteridge, William - *South Africa's Defence and Security into the 21st Century*
  R&R Bk N - v12 - F '97 - p100 [51-250]
Guttmann, Allen - *The Erotic in Sports*
  KR - v64 - Ag 15 '96 - p1209 [251-500]
  TLS - F 14 '97 - p27 [501+]
Gutt-Mostowy, Jan - *Highlander Polish-English/English-Highlander Polish Dictionary*
  r   ARBA - v28 - '97 - p397 [51-250]
Gutwirth, Madelyn - *The Twilight of the Goddesses*
  FR - v70 - O '96 - p114+ [501+]
Gutzke, David W - *Alcohol in the British Isles from Roman Times to 1996*
  r   ARBA - v28 - '97 - p202 [51-250]
  r   Choice - v34 - Ja '97 - p769+ [51-250]
  r   HT - v46 - O '96 - p58 [1-50]
  r   R&R Bk N - v11 - N '96 - p44 [51-250]
Guy, David - *Football Dreams*
  y   Kliatt - v30 - S '96 - p5 [1-50]
Guy, Donna J - *Sex and Danger in Buenos Aires*
  Historian - v59 - Win '97 - p428+ [251-500]
Guy, Ginger Foglesong - *Fiesta! (Illus. by Rene King Moreno)*
  c   CBRS - v24 - Ag '96 - p159 [51-250]
  c   SLJ - v42 - S '96 - p178 [51-250]
Guy, J A - *The Reign of Elizabeth I*
  Six Ct J - v27 - Win '96 - p1103+ [501+]
Guy, Jonathan - *Hawkwood*
  c   JB - v60 - O '96 - p202 [51-250]
  Pyne
  c   SLJ - v42 - Ag '96 - p144 [51-250]
Guy, Josephine M - *The Victorian Social-Problem Novel*
  Choice - v34 - Mr '97 - p1162 [51-250]
  TLS - F 14 '97 - p24 [251-500]
Guy, Rosa - *The Sun, the Sea, a Touch of the Wind*
  y   Kliatt - v31 - My '97 - p6 [51-250]
Guyer, Jane I - *Money Matters*
  Historian - v58 - Sum '96 - p849+ [251-500]
Guyotjeannin, Olivier - *Les Cartulaires*
  EHR - v111 - N '96 - p1245 [251-500]
  Diplomatique Medievale
  r   Specu - v71 - Jl '96 - p685+ [501+]
Guze, Samuel B - *Adult Psychiatry*
  SciTech - v21 - Mr '97 - p53 [51-250]
Guzik, Alberto - *Risco Da Vida*
  WLT - v70 - Sum '96 - p678+ [251-500]
Guzzetti, Paula - *The Last Hawaiian Queen*
  c   Ch BWatch - v7 - F '97 - p7 [1-50]
  Last Hawaiian Queen
  c   Ch BWatch - v7 - F '97 - p7 [1-50]
  The Last Hawaiian Queen
  c   HB Guide - v8 - Spr '97 - p156 [51-250]
  c   SLJ - v43 - Mr '97 - p175 [51-250]
Gwartney, James - *Economic Freedom of the World 1975-1995*
  r   Choice - v34 - O '96 - p252 [51-250]
Gwinnutt, Carl L - *Clinical Anaesthesia*
  SciTech - v21 - Mr '97 - p60 [1-50]
Gwynn, Mary - *30-Minute Vegetarian Recipes*
  BWatch - v17 - D '96 - p9 [1-50]
Gwynn-Jones, Terry - *Wild Blue Yonder*
  Aust Bk R - S '96 - p66 [251-500]
Gyekye, Kwame - *An Essay on African Philosophical Thought. Rev. Ed.*
  Choice - v34 - S '96 - p141 [51-250]
Gyimah-Boadi, E - *Ghana under PNDC Rule*
  Africa T - v43 - 4 '96 - p431+ [501+]
Gyorgyey, Clara - *A Mirror to the Cage*
  TranslRevS - v1 - My '95 - p2 [51-250]

H

H2SO4
p Sm Pr R - v28 - N '96 - p13+ [51-250]
Ha, Ky Lam - *Vung Da Ngam*
BL - v93 - S 1 '96 - p70 [51-250]
Ha, Mai Phuong - *Ngon Ngu Van Tu Viet Nam*
BL - v93 - S 1 '96 - p70 [51-250]
Haack, Susan - *Deviant Logic, Fuzzy Logic*
LJ - v121 - O 1 '96 - p81 [51-250]
Haag, Herbert - *Der Gottesknecht Bei Deutero-Jesaja*
Rel St Rev - v23 - Ja '97 - p59 [51-250]
Haak, Bob - *The Golden Age*
LATBR - D 8 '96 - p14 [1-50]
Haakonssen, Knud - *Natural Law and Moral Philosophy*
APSR - v91 - Mr '97 - p169 [501+]
Haar, Charles M - *Suburbs under Siege*
Choice - v34 - N '96 - p498+ [51-250]
Nat - v264 - Mr 31 '97 - p30+ [501+]
Haar, Michel - *Nietzsche and Metaphysics*
JR - v77 - Ap '97 - p328+ [501+]
Haas, Adelaide - *The Woman's Guide to Hysterectomy*
NWSA Jnl - v9 - Spr '97 - p121+ [501+]
Haas, David - *Praying with the Word*
CLW - v67 - Mr '97 - p35 [51-250]
Haas, Elson S - *The Detox Diet*
PW - v243 - N 18 '96 - p73 [51-250]
Haas, Irene - *A Summertime Song (Illus. by Irene Haas)*
c BL - v93 - My 15 '97 - p1579 [51-250]
c HB - v73 - My '97 - p307 [51-250]
c KR - v65 - Ap 1 '97 - p556 [51-250]
c PW - v244 - Mr 24 '97 - p82 [51-250]
Haas, J M - *A Management Odyssey*
EHR - v112 - F '97 - p226+ [251-500]
Haas, Jessie - *Be Well, Beware (Illus. by Jos. A Smith)*
c HB Guide - v7 - Fall '96 - p293 [1-50]
Clean House (Illus. by Yossi Abolafia)
c HB Guide - v7 - Fall '96 - p286 [51-250]
Sugaring (Illus. by Jos. A Smith)
c BL - v93 - N 15 '96 - p594 [51-250]
c Emerg Lib - v24 - Mr '97 - p45 [1-50]
c HB Guide - v8 - Spr '97 - p30 [51-250]
c SLJ - v42 - O '96 - p94+ [51-250]
Westminster West
c CCB-B - v50 - Ap '97 - p284 [51-250]
y HB - v73 - My '97 - p321 [251-500]
c KR - v65 - F 1 '97 - p223 [51-250]
Haas, Lisbeth - *Conquests and Historical Identities in California 1769-1936*
AHR - v101 - D '96 - p1610+ [501+]
PHR - v65 - Ag '96 - p476+ [251-500]
Haas, William J - *China Voyager*
Choice - v34 - O '96 - p301 [51-250]
Haass, Richard N - *Intervention: The Use of American Military Force in the Post-Cold War World*
Arm F&S - v22 - Sum '96 - p651+ [501+]
Haasse, Hella S - *Threshold of Fire*
Spec - v278 - F 1 '97 - p32 [501+]
TLS - F 21 '97 - p23 [251-500]
Haavikko, Paavo - *Prospero: Muistelmat Vuosilta 1967-1995*
WLT - v70 - Aut '96 - p993+ [501+]
Yksityisia Asioita
WLT - v71 - Win '97 - p187+ [501+]
Habakkuk, John - *Marriage, Debt and the Estates System*
J Soc H - v30 - Win '96 - p536+ [501+]
Habens, Alison - *Dreamhouse*
Ent W - Mr 21 '97 - p69 [51-250]
NYTBR - v102 - Mr 9 '97 - p28 [51-250]
Obs - S 1 '96 - p18* [51-250]

Haber, Judith - *Pastoral and the Poetics of Self-Contradiction*
RES - v48 - F '97 - p90+ [501+]
Sev Cent N - v54 - Spr '96 - p6 [501+]
Haber, Karen - *Bless the Beasts*
y Kliatt - v31 - Mr '97 - p18 [51-250]
Haber, Russell - *Dimensions of Psychotherapy Supervision*
SciTech - v20 - D '96 - p45 [51-250]
Haberer, Erich - *Jews and Revolution in Nineteenth-Century Russia*
AHR - v101 - D '96 - p1582+ [501+]
Russ Rev - v56 - Ja '97 - p136+ [501+]
Katalog Der Deutschen Luftpost. Pt. 8
r Am Phil - v111 - F '97 - p163 [51-250]
Haberman, Martin - *Star Teachers of Children in Poverty*
EL - v54 - F '97 - p84+ [251-500]
Habermas, Jurgen - *Between Facts and Norms*
Choice - v34 - Ja '97 - p872 [51-250]
R&R Bk N - v11 - N '96 - p52 [51-250]
Socio R - v45 - My '97 - p343+ [501+]
Debating the Future of Philosophy
R&R Bk N - v12 - F '97 - p2 [51-250]
Faktizitat Und Geltung
Dialogue - v35 - Spr '96 - p307+ [501+]
The Past as Future
South HR - v30 - Fall '96 - p375+ [501+]
WP - v49 - Ja '97 - p282+ [501+]
Haberstroh, Jack - *Ice Cube Sex*
ACI - v7 - Fall '95 - p29+ [501+]
Haberstroh, Patricia Boyle - *Women Creating Women*
ILS - v15 - Fall '96 - p12 [501+]
TLS - N 1 '96 - p22 [251-500]
Habib, Irfan - *Essays in Indian History*
JEH - v56 - D '96 - p949+ [501+]
Habitats Series
c Magpies - v11 - Jl '96 - p38 [51-250]
Hachey, Jean-Marc - *The Canadian Guide to Working and Living Overseas. 2nd Ed.*
r Quill & Q - v63 - F '97 - p38 [501+]
Hachey, Thomas E - *The Irish Experience. Rev. Ed.*
R&R Bk N - v11 - D '96 - p8 [51-250]
Hachtel, Gary D - *Logic Synthesis and Verification Algorithms*
SciTech - v21 - Mr '97 - p92 [51-250]
Hachten, William A - *The World News Prism. 4th Ed.*
Choice - v34 - S '96 - p116 [51-250]
JMCQ - v73 - Win '96 - p1022+ [251-500]
Hackbarth, Steven - *The Educational Technology Handbook*
Choice - v34 - D '96 - p661 [51-250]
Hackenberry, Charles - *I Rode with Jesse James*
Roundup M - v4 - Ap '97 - p27 [251-500]
Hacker, Andrew - *Money: Who Has How Much and Why*
PW - v244 - My 12 '97 - p69 [51-250]
Hacker, Barton C - *Elements of Controversy*
Historian - v59 - Win '97 - p405 [51-250]
T&C - v37 - Ap '96 - p389+ [501+]
Hacker, Edward A - *The I Ching Handbook*
Ch Rev Int - v3 - Fall '96 - p423+ [501+]
Hacker, Jacob S - *The Road to Nowhere*
BL - v93 - Ja '97 - p790 [51-250]
NYTBR - v102 - Mr 23 '97 - p15 [501+]
Hacker, Kenneth L - *Candidate Images in Presidential Elections*
APSR - v90 - S '96 - p650+ [501+]
Hacker, Marilyn - *Selected Poems 1965-1990*
LJ - v122 - Ap 1 '97 - p95 [1-50]
Winter Numbers
LJ - v122 - Ap 1 '97 - p95 [1-50]
Hacker, P M S - *Wittgenstein: Mind and Will*
Lon R Bks - v18 - O 31 '96 - p30+ [501+]

Wittgenstein's Place in Twentieth-Century Analytic Philosophy
Choice - v34 - Mr '97 - p1174 [51-250]
Lon R Bks - v18 - O 31 '96 - p30+ [501+]
TLS - Ja 3 '97 - p9+ [501+]
Hacker, Shyrle Pedlar - *A Gold Miner's Daughter*
LJ - v121 - D '96 - p104 [51-250]
Hackerman, Norman - *Conversations on the Uses of Science and Technology*
Sci - v274 - N 15 '96 - p1149 [1-50]
Hackett, David G - *Religion and American Culture*
Bks & Cult - v2 - N '96 - p38 [251-500]
The Silent Dialogue
BL - v93 - N 1 '96 - p462 [51-250]
LJ - v121 - N 15 '96 - p66 [51-250]
Hackett, Helen - *Virgin Mother, Maiden Queen*
EHR - v112 - F '97 - p190+ [501+]
Rel St Rev - v23 - Ap '97 - p191 [51-250]
RES - v47 - N '96 - p579+ [501+]
Six Ct J - v27 - Win '96 - p1198+ [501+]
Hacking, Ian - *Rewriting the Soul*
AJCH - v38 - Ap '96 - p303+ [501+]
Bks & Cult - v3 - Ja '97 - p17+ [501+]
CPR - v16 - D '96 - p402+ [501+]
Hist & T - v36 - F '97 - p63+ [501+]
Ken R - v19 - Win '97 - p158+ [501+]
Hacking, Sue Muller - *Mount Everest and Beyond*
c Ch BWatch - v7 - F '97 - p7 [1-50]
c HB Guide - v8 - Spr '97 - p156 [51-250]
c SLJ - v43 - F '97 - p91+ [51-250]
Hackler, Micah S - *Coyote Returns*
Arm Det - v29 - Fall '96 - p492+ [51-250]
Legend of the Dead
Arm Det - v29 - Fall '96 - p437+ [251-500]
Hackmann, W D - *Learning, Language and Invention*
T&C - v37 - Ap '96 - p344+ [501+]
Hackworth, David H - *Hazardous Duty*
BL - v93 - S 15 '96 - p189 [51-250]
BW - v26 - O 6 '96 - p3+ [501+]
LJ - v121 - O 1 '96 - p99+ [51-250]
Mar Crp G - v80 - D '96 - p73 [501+]
WSJ-MW - v77 - S 17 '96 - pA14
Hadaller, David - *Gynicide: Women in the Novels of William Styron*
Choice - v34 - O '96 - p278 [51-250]
Hadas, Rachel - *The Empty Bed*
Poet - v169 - F '97 - p298+ [501+]
Hadda, Janet - *Isaac Bashevis Singer: A Life*
BL - v93 - Ap 1 '97 - p1276 [51-250]
KR - v65 - F 1 '97 - p194 [251-500]
LJ - v122 - F 15 '97 - p135 [51-250]
PW - v244 - Mr 10 '97 - p57+ [51-250]
Haddad, Annette - *Travelers' Tales Brazil*
r BL - v93 - S 15 '96 - p212 [1-50]
Haddad, Gabriel G - *Tissue Oxygen Deprivation*
SciTech - v20 - N '96 - p39 [51-250]
Haddad, Yvonne Yasbeck - *Muslim Communities in North America*
Rel St Rev - v23 - Ja '97 - p94 [51-250]
Haddam, Jane - *And One to Die On*
LATBR - Jl 14 '96 - p6 [51-250]
Hadden, John W - *Immunopharmacology Reviews. Vol. 2*
SciTech - v20 - D '96 - p55 [51-250]
Hadden, Richard W - *On the Shoulders of Merchants*
JEH - v56 - D '96 - p930+ [501+]

Haddix, Margaret Peterson - *Don't You Dare Read This, Mrs. Dunphrey*
  y BL - v93 - Ap 1 '97 - p1292 [1-50]
  y BL - v93 - Ap 1 '97 - p1310 [1-50]
  y CBRS - v25 - Ja '97 - p57 [51-250]
  y CCB-B - v50 - Ja '97 - p172 [51-250]
  y HB Guide - v8 - Spr '97 - p79 [51-250]
  y KR - v64 - S 1 '96 - p1322 [51-250]
  y SLJ - v42 - O '96 - p147 [51-250]
  y VOYA - v19 - D '96 - p270 [251-500]
Running Out of Time
  y BL - v93 - Ap 1 '97 - p1292 [1-50]
  y Emerg Lib - v24 - S '96 - p27 [1-50]
Haddock, Patricia - *Teens and Gambling*
  y HB Guide - v7 - Fall '96 - p316+ [51-250]
  y SLJ - v42 - Ag '96 - p170 [51-250]
  y VOYA - v19 - O '96 - p232 [251-500]
Haddon, Mark - *The Sea of Tranquillity (Illus. by Christian Birmingham)*
  c Bks Keeps - Mr '97 - p19+ [51-250]
  c HB Guide - v8 - Spr '97 - p30 [51-250]
  c Inst - v106 - O '96 - p68 [51-250]
  c Magpies - v11 - S '96 - p28 [51-250]
  c PW - v243 - S 16 '96 - p82+ [51-250]
  c Sch Lib - v45 - F '97 - p19 [51-250]
  c SLJ - v42 - S '96 - p178 [51-250]
  c TES - N 22 '96 - p10* [51-250]
Haddow, Robert H - *Pavilions of Plenty*
    PW - v244 - Mr 31 '97 - p51+ [51-250]
Haden-Guest, Anthony - *The Last Party*
    BL - v93 - Ap 1 '97 - p1274+ [51-250]
    KR - v65 - F 15 '97 - p271 [251-500]
    LJ - v122 - Ap 1 '97 - p112 [51-250]
    NYTBR - v102 - Ap 13 '97 - p11 [501+]
    PW - v244 - Mr 17 '97 - p66 [51-250]
    VV - v42 - Ap 22 '97 - p55 [251-500]
    WSJ-Cent - v99 - Ap 10 '97 - pA12 [501+]
True Colors
    BL - v93 - N 15 '96 - p562 [251-500]
    KR - v64 - S 1 '96 - p1294+ [251-500]
    LJ - v121 - O 15 '96 - p55 [51-250]
    NYTBR - v102 - Mr 9 '97 - p18 [51-250]
    PW - v243 - S 23 '96 - p62 [51-250]
Hadfield, Andrew - *Literature, Politics, and National Identity*
    MLR - v92 - Ja '97 - p175+ [251-500]
    MP - v94 - F '97 - p376+ [501+]
    RES - v47 - N '96 - p569+ [501+]
Hadgraft, Nicholas - *Conservation and Preservation in Small Libraries*
    BC - v44 - Win '95 - p498+ [251-500]
Hadithi, Mwenye - *Hot Hippo (Illus. by Adrienne Kennaway)*
  c HB - v73 - Mr '97 - p187 [1-50]
Hadleigh, Boze - *Hollywood Gays*
    Advocate - S 17 '96 - p60 [1-50]
    LJ - v121 - O 1 '96 - p79 [51-250]
    PW - v243 - S 9 '96 - p73 [51-250]
Hadley, Elaine - *Melodramatic Tactics*
    Nine-C Lit - v51 - D '96 - p407+ [501+]
Hadley, Janet - *Abortion: Between Freedom and Necessity*
    Choice - v34 - My '97 - p1583 [51-250]
    NS & S - v9 - Ap 26 '96 - p32+ [251-500]
    PW - v243 - O 21 '96 - p64 [251-500]
Hadley, Joyce - *Guide to Networking*
    BWatch - v18 - F '97 - p3 [1-50]
Hadley, Leila - *A Journey with Elsa Cloud*
    KR - v65 - Ap 1 '97 - p519+ [251-500]
    LJ - v122 - Ap 15 '97 - p104 [51-250]
    PW - v244 - Ap 7 '97 - p62 [51-250]
Hadley, Michael L - *Count Not the Dead*
    Sea H - Aut '96 - p44+ [51-250]
Hadot, Pierre - *Plotinus, or, The Simplicity of Vision*
    TranslRevS - v1 - My '95 - p13 [51-250]
Haeberli, Andre - *Human Protein Data*
    J Chem Ed - v73 - Ag '96 - pA178 [501+]
Haebler, Konrad - *Introduccion Al Estudio De Los Incunables*
    Lib - v18 - S '96 - p275 [51-250]
Haefner, James W - *Modeling Biological Systems*
    Choice - v34 - Ja '97 - p818 [51-250]
Haege, Glenn - *Fix It Fast and Easy!. 2nd Rev. Ed.*
    LJ - v122 - F 1 '97 - p51 [1-50]
Haezewindt, Bernard P R - *Guy De Maupassant: De L'Anecdote Au Conte Litteraire*
    FR - v70 - F '97 - p471+ [251-500]
Hafemeister, Thomas L - *Resolving Disputes over Life-Sustaining Treatment*
    Hast Cen R - v27 - Ja '97 - p46 [51-250]
Hafen, Brent Q - *Mind/Body Health*
    Choice - v34 - My '97 - p1534 [51-250]

Hafen, LeRoy R - *French Fur Traders and Voyaguers in the American West*
    PHR - v65 - N '96 - p666+ [251-500]
Hafiz - *The Green Sea of Heaven*
    Rel St Rev - v22 - O '96 - p356 [51-250]
Hafiz, Reza - *The Poems of Hafez*
    Rel St Rev - v23 - Ap '97 - p199 [51-250]
Hafner, Dorinda - *Dorinda's Taste of the Caribbean*
    BWatch - v17 - N '96 - p1 [51-250]
    LJ - v121 - S 15 '96 - p89 [51-250]
Hafner, Katie - *Where Wizards Stay Up Late*
    Bus W - S 16 '96 - p19 [501+]
    BYTE - v21 - Ag '96 - p34 [251-500]
    BYTE - v21 - N '96 - p132 [1-50]
    NW - v128 - S 9 '96 - p74 [51-250]
    NYTBR - v101 - S 8 '96 - p19 [501+]
    Sci - v274 - D 6 '96 - p1627+ [501+]
Hafner, Marylin - *A Year with Molly and Emmett (Illus. by Marylin Hafner)*
  c PW - v244 - Ap 28 '97 - p75 [51-250]
Hafter, Daryl M - *European Women and Preindustrial Craft*
    BHR - v70 - Sum '96 - p288 [251-500]
    HRNB - v25 - Fall '96 - p29 [251-500]
    T&C - v38 - Ja '97 - p249+ [501+]
Hagan, Jacqueline Maria - *Deciding to Be Legal*
    CS - v25 - S '96 - p648+ [501+]
Hagan, John - *Crime and Disrepute*
    SF - v75 - S '96 - p389+ [501+]
Gender in Practice
    AJS - v102 - Jl '96 - p318+ [501+]
    HLR - v110 - D '96 - p559 [51-250]
    SF - v75 - S '96 - p385+ [251-500]
Hagberg, David - *Assassin*
    BL - v93 - My 1 '97 - p1478 [51-250]
    KR - v65 - My 1 '97 - p662 [251-500]
    LJ - v122 - My 1 '97 - p139+ [51-250]
    PW - v244 - My 12 '97 - p59 [51-250]
Hagberg, G L - *Art as Language*
    JAAC - v54 - Fall '96 - p388+ [501+]
Meaning and Interpretation
    JAAC - v55 - Win '97 - p81+ [501+]
Hage, Jerald - *Formal Theory in Sociology*
    SSQ - v77 - S '96 - p708+ [501+]
Hagedoorn, John - *Technical Change and the World Economy*
    Econ J - v106 - S '96 - p1480 [51-250]
Hagedorn, Dan - *Aircraft of the Chaco War 1928-1935*
    APH - v44 - Spr '97 - p57+ [251-500]
Hagedorn, Jessica - *The Gangster of Love*
    Ms - v7 - S '96 - p81 [251-500]
    Nat - v263 - O 28 '96 - p64+ [501+]
    NYTBR - v101 - S 15 '96 - p14+ [501+]
    Time - v148 - S 16 '96 - p82+ [501+]
    VLS - S '96 - p7 [501+]
Hagedorn, John M - *Forsaking Our Children*
    Soc Ser R - v71 - Mr '97 - p149+ [501+]
Hagee, John - *The Beginning of the End*
    CSM - v89 - N 25 '96 - p12 [51-250]
    CSM - v89 - Ja 23 '97 - p12 [51-250]
Hagel, John - *Net Gain*
    LJ - v122 - Mr 15 '97 - p71 [51-250]
Hagemann, Susanne - *Studies in Scottish Fiction 1945 to the Present*
    R&R Bk N - v12 - F '97 - p87 [51-250]
Hagen, Jon B - *Radio-Frequency Electronics*
    Choice - v34 - Ap '97 - p1370 [51-250]
Hagen, Margaret A - *Whores of the Court*
    BL - v93 - Mr 1 '97 - p1092+ [51-250]
    KR - v65 - Ja 15 '97 - p118 [251-500]
    LJ - v122 - Ap 1 '97 - p109 [51-250]
    PW - v244 - Ja 13 '97 - p61 [51-250]
    WSJ-Cent - v99 - Ap 24 '97 - pA16 [501+]
Hager, George - *Mirage: Why Neither Democrats nor Republicans Can Balance the Budget, End the Deficit, and Satisfy the Public*
    BL - v93 - Ap 1 '97 - p1272 [51-250]
    Bus W - My 12 '97 - p20 [501+]
    KR - v65 - F 1 '97 - p195 [251-500]
    LJ - v122 - F 15 '97 - p148 [51-250]
    PW - v244 - Ja 27 '97 - p84 [51-250]
    Trib Bks - Ap 13 '97 - p5 [501+]
Hager, Jean - *The Spirit Caller*
    KR - v65 - Mr '97 - p337 [51-250]
    LJ - v122 - My 1 '97 - p144 [51-250]
    PW - v244 - Mr 17 '97 - p79 [51-250]
Hager, Thomas - *Force of Nature*
    Am Sci - v84 - My '96 - p291+ [501+]
    Spec - v277 - S 14 '96 - p38+ [501+]
Hagerman, Randi Jenssen - *Fragile X Syndrome. 2nd Ed.*
    SciTech - v20 - D '96 - p53 [51-250]

Hagerty, Donald J - *Beyond the Visible Terrain*
    A Art - v61 - Mr '97 - p100 [251-500]
    Bloom Rev - v16 - N '96 - p23+ [501+]
Canyon De Chelly
    LATBR - Ag 25 '96 - p11 [51-250]
Haggard, Ezra - *Perennials for the Lower Midwest*
    BL - v93 - S 15 '96 - p195 [51-250]
    LJ - v122 - Ja '97 - p130 [51-250]
Haggard, H Rider - *She (Williams). Audio Version*
  y Kliatt - v30 - S '96 - p52 [51-250]
Haggard, Stephan - *The Political Economy of Democratic Transitions*
    RP - v59 - Win '97 - p194+ [501+]
Voting for Reform
    Econ J - v106 - N '96 - p1797+ [501+]
Haggerty, Gary - *A Guide to Popular Music Reference Books*
  r Notes - v53 - D '96 - p482+ [501+]
  r PMS - v19 - Win '95 - p105+ [501+]
Haggerty, George - *Professions of Desire*
    AL - v68 - D '96 - p883 [51-250]
Haggman, Kai - *Perheen Vuosisata*
    AHR - v101 - D '96 - p1574+ [501+]
Haggstrom, Margaret Austin - *The Foreign Language Classroom*
    FR - v70 - D '96 - p364+ [501+]
    MLJ - v80 - Fall '96 - p399 [501+]
Haglund, David G - *Alliance within the Alliance*
    Arm F&S - v23 - Win '96 - p303+ [501+]
NATO's Eastern Dilemmas
    Parameters - v27 - Spr '97 - p169+ [501+]
Hagman, Barry - *The PFA Footballers Factfile*
  r Books - v9 - S '95 - p24 [1-50]
Hagopian, Frances - *Traditional Politics and Regime Change in Brazil*
    Choice - v34 - Ap '97 - p1410 [51-250]
Hagstrum, Jean H - *Esteem Enlivened by Desire*
    MLR - v91 - Jl '96 - p680+ [501+]
Hague, Kathleen - *Calendarbears: A Book of Months (Illus. by Michael Hague)*
  c BL - v93 - Mr 15 '97 - p1247 [51-250]
  c PW - v244 - Mr 17 '97 - p85 [1-50]
Hague, Michael - *The Perfect Present (Illus. by Michael Hague)*
  c BL - v93 - S 1 '96 - p136 [51-250]
  c CBRS - v25 - O '96 - p15 [51-250]
  c HB Guide - v8 - Spr '97 - p30 [51-250]
  c PW - v243 - S 30 '96 - p88 [51-250]
  c SLJ - v42 - O '96 - p36+ [51-250]
Teddy Bear, Teddy Bear (Illus. by Michael Hague)
  c PW - v244 - Ja 27 '97 - p108 [1-50]
Hahl-Koch, Jelena - *Kandinsky*
    Art - v55 - Fall '96 - p84+ [501+]
Hahn, Don - *Animation Magic*
  c BL - v93 - S 1 '96 - p122 [51-250]
  c HB Guide - v8 - Spr '97 - p137 [51-250]
  c LATBR - Ag 18 '96 - p15 [51-250]
  c SLJ - v42 - O '96 - p132 [51-250]
Hahn, Frank - *A Critical Essay on Modern Macroeconomic Theory*
    JEL - v35 - Mr '97 - p132+ [501+]
Hahn, Hans J - *German Thought and Culture*
    HRNB - v25 - Fall '96 - p32 [251-500]
Hahn, Harley - *The Internet Yellow Pages. 3rd Ed.*
  r CBR - v14 - Jl '96 - p21 [1-50]
  r Choice - v34 - Ja '97 - p772 [251-500]
Hahn, Jeffrey W - *Democratization in Russia*
    APSR - v91 - Mr '97 - p213+ [501+]
Hahn, Kurt - *Kurt Hahn's Schools and Legacy*
    TES - Mr 28 '97 - p7* [51-250]
Hahn, Mary Downing - *Following My Own Footsteps*
  c BL - v93 - S 15 '96 - p240 [51-250]
  c CCB-B - v50 - O '96 - p61 [51-250]
  c Ch BWatch - v6 - O '96 - p3 [51-250]
  c HB - v72 - S '96 - p595+ [51-250]
  c HB Guide - v8 - Spr '97 - p67 [51-250]
  c SLJ - v42 - N '96 - p106 [51-250]
The Gentleman Outlaw and Me--Eli
  c HB - v72 - S '96 - p596 [51-250]
  c HB Guide - v7 - Fall '96 - p293 [51-250]
Look for Me by Moonlight
  y Emerg Lib - v24 - S '96 - p27 [1-50]
  y Kliatt - v31 - My '97 - p12+ [51-250]
  y PW - v244 - Mr 17 '97 - p85 [1-50]
Stepping on the Cracks
  c SLJ - v43 - Ja '97 - p36 [1-50]
Hahn, Michael P - *Life Support*
    SciTech - v21 - Mr '97 - p50 [51-250]
Hahn, Robert W - *Risks, Costs, and Lives Saved*
    JEL - v35 - Mr '97 - p247+ [51-250]

Hahn, Stefan L - *Hilbert Transforms in Signal Processing*
SciTech - v21 - Mr '97 - p87 [51-250]
Hahn, Susan - *Confession*
BL - v93 - D 1 '96 - p640 [51-250]
PW - v244 - Ja 27 '97 - p95 [51-250]
Trib Bks - Ap 20 '97 - p1+ [501+]
Hahn, Ulla - *Epikurs Garten*
WLT - v70 - Sum '96 - p686 [501+]
Haidar, Aziz - *On the Margins*
Choice - v34 - S '96 - p175+ [51-250]
JEL - v34 - D '96 - p2067 [51-250]
Haig, Catherine - *Making the Most of Bathrooms*
LJ - v122 - Ja '97 - p96 [51-250]
Haig-Brown, Alan - *The Fraser River*
Mac - v109 - D 9 '96 - p66 [1-50]
Haigh, Christopher - *English Reformations*
JMH - v69 - Mr '97 - p131+ [501+]
Haigh, Gerald - *The TES Guide for Heads and Senior Staff*
TES - Ja 24 '97 - p9* [501+]
The TES Guide to School Management
TES - Ja 24 '97 - p9* [501+]
Haigh, Gideon - *Australian Cricket Anecdotes*
Aust Bk R - D '96 - p31+ [501+]
Haight-Ashbury in the Sixties. Electronic Media Version
LJ - v121 - N 1 '96 - p114+ [501+]
Hailey, Arthur - *Detective*
BL - v93 - My 1 '97 - p1482 [51-250]
Hailey, Christopher - *Franz Schreker 1878-1934*
New R - v216 - Ja 27 '97 - p31+ [501+]
Haill, Catherine - *Fun without Vulgarity*
BW - v27 - Ap 6 '97 - p12 [51-250]
LAR - v99 - Mr '97 - p161 [1-50]
Haillet, Pierre - *Le Conditionnel Dans Le Discours Jouranlistique*
FR - v70 - Mr '97 - p634+ [251-500]
Haine, Malou - *400 Lettres De Musiciens Au Musee Royal De Mariemont*
Notes - v53 - D '96 - p466+ [501+]
Haine, W Scott - *The World of the Paris Cafe*
Choice - v34 - S '96 - p186 [51-250]
HRNB - v25 - Fall '96 - p29 [251-500]
TLS - S 20 '96 - p36 [501+]
VQR - v72 - Aut '96 - p140* [51-250]
Haines, Aubrey L - *Yellowstone Place Names*
BWatch - v17 - S '96 - p6 [51-250]
The Yellowstone Story. Rev. Ed., Vols. 1-2
BWatch - v17 - S '96 - p6 [51-250]
Haines, Carolyn - *Touched*
NYTBR - v101 - S 22 '96 - p25 [51-250]
Haines, David W - *Refugees in America in the 1990s*
r BL - v93 - O 1 '96 - p372 [51-250]
r Choice - v34 - Ja '97 - p876+ [51-250]
r R&R Bk N - v11 - D '96 - p43 [51-250]
Haines, Duane E - *Fundamental Neuroscience*
SciTech - v21 - Mr '97 - p40 [1-50]
Haines, Herbert H - *Against Capital Punishment*
HRNB - v25 - Win '97 - p52+ [251-500]
Haines, John - *Fables and Distances*
Bloom Rev - v16 - Jl '96 - p11+ [501+]
The Owl in the Mask of the Dreamer
y Kliatt - v31 - My '97 - p18 [51-250]
Haines, Max - *Celebrity Murders and Other Nefarious Deeds*
Quill & Q - v62 - O '96 - p39 [251-500]
Haining, Peter - *Ghost Movies II*
LJ - v121 - N 1 '96 - p109+ [51-250]
Murder at the Races
Arm Det - v29 - Fall '96 - p469 [251-500]
Haisken-DeNew, John P - *Migration and the Interindustry Wage Structure in Germany*
JEL - v35 - Mr '97 - p242 [51-250]
Haislop, Neil - *Giants of Country Music*
r LJ - v121 - N 1 '96 - p41 [1-50]
Hajdu, David - *Lush Life*
BL - v93 - Ja '97 - p758 [51-250]
Choice - v34 - N '96 - p470 [51-250]
LATBR - Jl 14 '96 - p3 [501+]
New R - v215 - S 30 '96 - p42+ [501+]
NYTBR - v101 - D 8 '96 - p88 [1-50]
Readings - v12 - Mr '97 - p10+ [501+]
Wil Q - v21 - Win '97 - p102 [251-500]
Hajdusiewicz, Babs Bell - *Mary Carter Smith, African American Storyteller*
c CLW - v66 - Je '96 - p49+ [251-500]
Hajer, Maarten A - *The Politics of Environmental Discourse*
Choice - v34 - N '96 - p478+ [51-250]
SF - v75 - Mr '97 - p1138+ [501+]
Hakanson, Bjorn - *Gora Slut*
WLT - v70 - Aut '96 - p979 [251-500]

Haken, Hermann - *Molecular Physics and Elements of Quantum Chemistry*
Phys Today - v50 - F '97 - p66+ [501+]
Principles of Brain Functioning
Choice - v34 - S '96 - p152 [51-250]
Hakim, Catherine - *Key Issues in Women's Work*
Choice - v34 - N '96 - p503 [51-250]
ILR - v135 - 5 '96 - p591+ [501+]
Hakim, Joy - *War, Terrible War*
y CAY - v16 - Fall '95 - p5 [51-250]
Hakken, David - *Computing Myths, Class Realities*
SocSciComR - v14 - Sum '96 - p241+ [501+]
Hakluyt, Richard - *A Particuler Discourse Concerning the Greate Necessitie and Manifolde Commodyties That Are like to Growe to This Realme of England*
EHR - v111 - N '96 - p1273 [251-500]
A Particuler Discourse Concerning the Greate Necessitie and Manifolde Commodyties That Are like to Growe to This Realme of Englande
GJ - v162 - Jl '96 - p222 [501+]
Hakutani, Yoshinobu - *The City in African American Literature*
J Am St - v30 - Ap '96 - p159+ [251-500]
Richard Wright and Racial Discourse
Choice - v34 - F '97 - p965 [51-250]
R&R Bk N - v11 - N '96 - p73 [51-250]
Halal, William E - *The New Management*
Choice - v34 - D '96 - p654 [51-250]
Halam, Ann - *The Fear Man*
c Bks Keeps - v100 - S '96 - p13 [51-250]
c Magpies - v11 - Jl '96 - p45 [1-50]
Halanay, Aristide - *Time-Varying Discrete Linear Systems*
SIAM Rev - v38 - D '96 - p684+ [501+]
Halberstadt, Hans - *The American Family Farm*
LJ - v121 - N 15 '96 - p80 [51-250]
Halberstam, David - *The Making of a Quagmire*
Parameters - v26 - Win '96 - p148+ [501+]
October 1964
Aethlon - v13 - Fall '95 - p177+ [251-500]
Halberstam, Judith - *Posthuman Bodies*
Bks & Cult - v3 - Ja '97 - p14+ [501+]
Pub Int - Sum '96 - p87+ [501+]
TDR - v40 - Fall '96 - p2 [501+]
Skin Shows
J Am Cult - v19 - Sum '96 - p139+ [501+]
TLS - My 24 '96 - p36 [51-250]
Haldane, Andrew G - *Targeting Inflation*
Econ J - v107 - Ja '97 - p211+ [501+]
Haldane, Suzanne - *Teddies and Machines*
c HB Guide - v7 - Fall '96 - p239 [1-50]
Teddies and Trucks
c HB Guide - v7 - Fall '96 - p239 [1-50]
Halder, Winfrid - *Katholische Vereine In Baden Und Wurttemberg 1848-1914*
CHR - v83 - Ja '97 - p117+ [501+]
Haldon, John - *The State and the Tributary Mode of Production*
S&S - v61 - Sum '97 - p257+ [501+]
Hale, Alan - *Everybody's Comet*
Astron - v24 - D '96 - p102 [51-250]
Choice - v34 - Mr '97 - p1181 [51-250]
NH - v106 - Mr '97 - p13 [1-50]
S&T - v93 - F '97 - p56+ [501+]
Hale, Constance - *Wired Style*
r ARBA - v28 - '97 - p349+ [251-500]
r LJ - v121 - O 1 '96 - p70 [51-250]
Hale, Frederick - *Janet Campbell Hale*
AL - v69 - Mr '97 - p251 [51-250]
Hale, Janet Campbell - *Bloodlines: Odyssey of a Native Daughter*
JWomHist - v8 - Fall '96 - p205+ [501+]
Hale, John - *The Civilization of Europe in the Renaissance*
Six Ct J - v27 - Win '96 - p1087+ [501+]
Hale, Nathan G, Jr. - *The Rise and Crisis of Psychoanalysis in the United States*
RAH - v24 - S '96 - p476+ [501+]
Hale, Sarah Josepha - *Early American Cookery*
LJ - v122 - My 1 '97 - p145 [1-50]
Traits of American Life
Legacy - v14 - 1 '97 - p13+ [501+]
Hale, Sondra - *Gender Politics in Sudan*
Choice - v34 - D '96 - p664 [51-250]
Hale, Thomas - *Spun Yarns and Scuttlebutt*
Sea H - Win '96 - p46 [51-250]
Hale, Thomas A - *The Epic of Askia Mohammed*
Bl S - v26 - Sum '96 - p65 [1-50]
Hale, Wayne - *Light Metals 1996*
SciTech - v21 - Mr '97 - p94 [51-250]
Halebsky, Sandor - *Capital, Power, and Inequality in Latin America*
HAHR - v77 - My '97 - p359+ [251-500]

Hales, Dianne - *Caring for the Mind*
r BL - v93 - F 1 '97 - p959 [1-50]
Hales, Robert E - *The American Psychiatric Press Synopsis of Psychiatry*
AJPsych - v153 - O '96 - p1357+ [251-500]
SciTech - v20 - S '96 - p32 [51-250]
Haley, Gail E - *Two Bad Boys (Illus. by Gail E Haley)*
c CBRS - v25 - S '96 - p7+ [51-250]
c Emerg Lib - v24 - Mr '97 - p64 [51-250]
c HB Guide - v8 - Spr '97 - p102 [51-250]
c LATBR - Ag 4 '96 - p11 [251-500]
c SLJ - v42 - Ag '96 - p136 [51-250]
Haley, Jan - *J. Rooker, Manatee (Illus. by Paul Brent)*
c S Liv - v31 - D '96 - p58 [51-250]
Haley, Jay - *Learning and Teaching Therapy*
Readings - v12 - Mr '97 - p27 [51-250]
SciTech - v20 - N '96 - p43 [51-250]
Halford, Robert G - *The Unknown Navy*
Beav - v76 - O '96 - p44+ [501+]
Haliczer, Stephen - *Sexuality in the Confessional*
Theol St - v58 - Mr '97 - p184+ [501+]
Halikowska, Teresa - *The Eagle and the Crow*
KR - v65 - Mr 1 '97 - p335 [51-250]
Spec - v277 - N 30 '96 - p56+ [501+]
Halivni, David Weiss - *The Book and the Sword*
y BL - v93 - N 1 '96 - p478 [51-250]
KR - v64 - S 15 '96 - p1372 [251-500]
LJ - v121 - N 1 '96 - p88 [51-250]
PW - v243 - O 21 '96 - p65 [51-250]
Hall, A Rupert - *Isaac Newton, Adventurer in Thought*
SciTech - v20 - D '96 - p22 [1-50]
Hall, Austin - *The Blind Spot*
Ext - v37 - Sum '96 - p139+ [501+]
Hall, B Clarence - *The South*
JSH - v62 - N '96 - p850+ [501+]
Hall, Barbara - *Dixie Storms*
y SLJ - v43 - Mr '97 - p113 [1-50]
The House across the Cove
y Emerg Lib - v24 - S '96 - p27 [1-50]
y Sch Lib - v45 - F '97 - p46 [51-250]
Hall, Brian - *The Saskiad*
y BL - v93 - D 1 '96 - p642 [51-250]
BW - v27 - F 9 '97 - p8 [501+]
KR - v64 - N 1 '96 - p1553 [251-500]
LATBR - Ja 26 '97 - p2 [501+]
LJ - v121 - N 1 '96 - p107 [51-250]
NS - v125 - O 18 '96 - p43+ [501+]
NY - v73 - Mr 10 '97 - p92+ [501+]
NYTBR - v102 - Ja 19 '97 - p17 [501+]
Obs - N 24 '96 - p18* [501+]
y SLJ - v43 - Mr '97 - p215 [51-250]
TLS - O 18 '96 - p24 [501+]
Hall, C M - *Polar Tourism*
GJ - v162 - Jl '96 - p232+ [251-500]
Hall, Charles - *Paul Nash: Aerial Creatures*
BM - v139 - Ja '97 - p59+ [501+]
Hall, Charles J - *A Chronicle of American Music 1700-1995*
r ARBA - v28 - '97 - p469 [51-250]
Hall, Christine - *Tales from Other Times*
y TES - N 22 '96 - p20* [51-250]
Hall, Christopher G L - *Steel Phoenix*
BL - v93 - F 15 '97 - p983 [51-250]
LJ - v122 - F 1 '97 - p92 [51-250]
PW - v243 - D 9 '96 - p54 [51-250]
Hall, Colin - *Taking Time Off*
y LJ - v121 - O 1 '96 - p96 [51-250]
Hall, Daniel - *Strange Relation*
NYRB - v43 - S 19 '96 - p49+ [501+]
Hall, Darwin C - *Marginal Cost Rate Design and Wholesale Water Markets*
JEL - v35 - Mr '97 - p298+ [51-250]
Hall, David D - *Cultures of Print*
AB - v98 - N 25 '96 - p1831+ [501+]
LJ - v121 - O 15 '96 - p58 [51-250]
Hall, David E - *African Acronyms and Abbreviations*
r Choice - v34 - O '96 - p252 [51-250]
r LAR - v98 - Je '96 - p321 [51-250]
Hall, David L - *Anticipating China*
Ch Rev Int - v3 - Fall '96 - p425+ [501+]
IPQ - v36 - S '96 - p379 [51-250]
Hall, David W - *The Practice of Confessional Subscription*
TT - v53 - O '96 - p424+ [51-250]
Hall, Donald, 1928- - *Death to the Death of Poetry*
MQR - v35 - Fall '96 - p745+ [501+]
The Farm Summer 1942
c Smith - v27 - N '96 - p162 [51-250]
Life Work
MQR - v35 - Fall '96 - p745+ [501+]
Smith - v27 - N '96 - p161 [51-250]

Lucy's Christmas
  c - Smith - v27 - N '96 - p162 [51-250]
Lucy's Summer
  c - Smith - v27 - N '96 - p162 [51-250]
The Man Who Lived Alone
  c - Smith - v27 - N '96 - p162 [51-250]
Old Home Day (Illus. by Emily Arnold McCully)
  c - BL - v93 - S 1 '96 - p126 [51-250]
  c - CBRS - v25 - D '96 - p39 [1-50]
  c - CCB-B - v50 - O '96 - p61 [51-250]
  c - HB - v72 - N '96 - p724+ [51-250]
  c - HB Guide - v8 - Spr '97 - p58 [51-250]
  c - LATBR - Ag 4 '96 - p11 [251-500]
  c - LATBR - D 8 '96 - p18 [1-50]
  c - SLJ - v42 - O '96 - p96 [51-250]
  c - Smith - v27 - N '96 - p162 [51-250]
The Old Life
  BW - v27 - Ja 26 '97 - p8 [51-250]
The Ox-Cart Man (Illus. by Barbara Cooney)
  c - Smith - v27 - N '96 - p161+ [251-500]
Principal Products of Portugal
  MQR - v35 - Fall '96 - p745+ [501+]
Prose and Poetry (Hall). Audio Version
  BL - v93 - My 15 '97 - p1596 [1-50]
String Too Short to Be Saved
  Smith - v27 - N '96 - p161 [51-250]
When Willard Met Babe Ruth (Illus. by Barry Moser)
  c - HB - v72 - S '96 - p589 [51-250]
  c - HB Guide - v7 - Fall '96 - p286 [51-250]
  c - NYTLa - v146 - D 9 '96 - pC18 [51-250]
  c - Smith - v27 - N '96 - p163 [51-250]
  c - Time - v148 - D 9 '96 - p79 [51-250]
  c - Trib Bks - Mr 30 '97 - p4 [51-250]
Hall, Donald E, 1960- - *Muscular Christianity*
  MLR - v91 - Jl '96 - p704+ [501+]
  VS - v39 - Win '96 - p290+ [501+]
RePresenting Bisexualities
  AL - v69 - Mr '97 - p254 [51-250]
Hall, Doug, 1959- - *The Maverick Mindset*
  BL - v93 - F 15 '97 - p974 [51-250]
  PW - v244 - Ja 20 '97 - p389+ [51-250]
Hall, E Raymond - *Mammals of Nevada*
  r - SciTech - v20 - D '96 - p33 [1-50]
Hall, Eleanor J - *The Lewis and Clark Expedition*
  y - HB Guide - v7 - Fall '96 - p377 [51-250]
Hall, Eliza Calvert - *A Quilter's Wisdom*
  CAY - v17 - Win '96 - p11 [51-250]
Hall, Elizabeth - *Child of the Wolves*
  c - HB Guide - v7 - Fall '96 - p293 [51-250]
Venus among the Fishes
  y - PW - v243 - S 23 '96 - p78 [51-250]
Hall, Fred M - *It's about Time*
  Choice - v34 - O '96 - p291 [51-250]
  Rapport - v19 - 4 '96 - p15+ [501+]
Hall, G S - *General Relativity*
  SciTech - v21 - Mr '97 - p3 [51-250]
Hall, Godfrey - *Outer Space (Illus. by Kuo Kang Chen)*
  c - PW - v243 - N 11 '96 - p77 [51-250]
Hall, Gordon C Nagayama - *Theory-Based Assessment,*
Treatment and Prevention of Sexual Aggression
  New Sci - v153 - F 1 '97 - p40+ [501+]
Hall, Gregory - *A Cement of Blood*
  Books - v11 - Ap '97 - p21 [51-250]
Hall, Gwendolyn Midlo - *Africans in Colonial Louisiana*
  J Am St - v30 - D '96 - p496+ [501+]
Hall, James W, 1948- - *Audiologists' Desk Reference. Vol.*
1
  r - SciTech - v21 - Mr '97 - p62 [51-250]
Hall, Jim, 1947- - *Buzz Cut*
  Arm Det - v29 - Fall '96 - p500 [251-500]
  PW - v244 - Mr 3 '97 - p72 [1-50]
Buzz Cut (Muller). Audio Version
  y - Kliatt - v31 - Ja '97 - p37 [51-250]
  LJ - v122 - F 15 '97 - p114 [1-50]
Buzz Cut (Patton). Audio Version
  y - Kliatt - v31 - Ja '97 - p37 [51-250]
Games for Infants
  TES - N 22 '96 - p16* [251-500]
Gone Wild (Guidall). Audio Version
  y - Kliatt - v30 - S '96 - p50 [51-250]
Gymnastics Activities for Infants
  TES - N 22 '96 - p16* [251-500]
Mean High Tide (Muller). Audio Version
  y - Kliatt - v30 - S '96 - p50 [51-250]
Red Sky at Night
  BL - v93 - My 15 '97 - p1540 [51-250]
Under Cover of Daylight
  PW - v244 - Mr 3 '97 - p72 [1-50]
Hall, John A - *Civil Society*
  CS - v26 - Mr '97 - p171+ [501+]

Hall, Karen - *Dark Debts*
  BW - v26 - S 15 '96 - p7 [501+]
  LJ - v122 - Mr 15 '97 - p42 [1-50]
  NYTBR - v101 - S 29 '96 - p20 [51-250]
  PW - v244 - My 12 '97 - p74 [1-50]
Dark Debts (Heald). Audio Version
  y - Kliatt - v31 - Mr '97 - p40 [51-250]
  LJ - v121 - N 1 '96 - p120 [51-250]
  PW - v243 - S 2 '96 - p47 [51-250]
Hall, Katy - *Bunny Riddles (Illus. by Nicole Rubel)*
  c - BL - v93 - N 15 '96 - p596 [51-250]
  c - SLJ - v43 - F '97 - p92 [51-250]
Chickie Riddles (Illus. by Thor Wickstrom)
  c - BL - v93 - N 15 '96 - p596 [51-250]
  c - SLJ - v43 - F '97 - p92 [51-250]
Easter Yolks (Illus. by R W Alley)
  c - PW - v243 - D 16 '96 - p61 [51-250]
Hearty Har Har (Illus. by R W Alley)
  c - PW - v243 - D 16 '96 - p61 [51-250]
Sheepish Riddles (Illus. by R W Alley)
  c - HB Guide - v7 - Fall '96 - p358 [1-50]
Trick or Eeek! and Other Ha Ha Halloween Riddles
(Illus. by R W Alley)
  c - LATBR - O 20 '96 - p8 [1-50]
Trick or Eeek! And Other Ha Ha Halloween Riddles
(Illus. by R W Alley)
  c - PW - v243 - S 30 '96 - p86 [51-250]
Hall, Kim F - *Things of Darkness*
  Six Ct J - v27 - Win '96 - p1122+ [501+]
Hall, Kira - *Gender Articulated*
  Choice - v34 - S '96 - p118 [51-250]
Hall, Kirsten - *At the Carnival (Illus. by Laura Rader)*
  c - BL - v93 - F 1 '97 - p949 [51-250]
Madame Boskey's Fortune Telling Kit (Illus. by Dana
Cooper)
  c - PW - v243 - N 4 '96 - p78 [51-250]
My Brother, the Brat (Illus. by Joan Holub)
  c - Learning - v25 - Ag '96 - p96 [51-250]
Hall, Laurie - *An Affair of the Mind*
  BL - v93 - O 1 '96 - p297 [51-250]
Hall, Lee - *Athena: A Biography*
  KR - v65 - Mr 1 '97 - p352 [51-250]
  LJ - v122 - Ap 1 '97 - p91+ [51-250]
  PW - v244 - Mr 24 '97 - p67 [51-250]
Hall, Linda, 1950- - *November Veil*
  LJ - v122 - Ap 1 '97 - p78 [51-250]
Hall, Linda B, 1939- - *Oil, Banks, and Politics*
  AHR - v102 - F '97 - p204+ [251-500]
Hall, M Ann - *Feminism and Sporting Bodies*
  Choice - v34 - O '96 - p321 [51-250]
Hall, Marny - *Sexualities*
  BWatch - v18 - Mr '97 - p2 [51-250]
Hall, Martin - *Charlie and Tess (Illus. by Catherine*
Walters)
  c - CBRS - v25 - F '97 - p75 [51-250]
  c - PW - v243 - D 9 '96 - p68 [51-250]
  c - SLJ - v43 - Mr '97 - p159+ [51-250]
Hall, Matthew - *The Art of Breaking Glass*
  BL - v93 - Mr 1 '97 - p1068 [51-250]
  KR - v65 - Mr 15 '97 - p401+ [251-500]
  LJ - v122 - Ap 1 '97 - p125 [51-250]
  PW - v244 - Mr 17 '97 - p76 [251-500]
Hall, Michael - *Leaving Home*
  Obs - O 6 '96 - p17* [501+]
  TES - O 11 '96 - p8* [501+]
  TLS - O 25 '96 - p19 [501+]
Hall, Nigel - *Listening to Children Think*
  TES - O 25 '96 - p12* [251-500]
Hall, Oakley - *Separations*
  PW - v244 - Ap 21 '97 - p61+ [51-250]
Warlock
  LJ - v121 - O 15 '96 - p94 [51-250]
  Roundup M - v4 - D '96 - p26+ [501+]
Hall, Pamela M - *Narrative and the Natural Law*
  Bks & Cult - v1 - N '95 - p31 [51-250]
  Rel St Rev - v23 - Ja '97 - p49+ [51-250]
Hall, Parnell - *Scam*
  BL - v93 - Mr 1 '97 - p1113 [51-250]
  KR - v65 - F 15 '97 - p258 [51-250]
  PW - v244 - Ja 27 '97 - p80 [51-250]
Hall, Patricia - *The Dead of Winter*
  BL - v93 - F 1 '97 - p928 [51-250]
  KR - v65 - Ja 1 '97 - p23 [51-250]
  PW - v244 - Ja 6 '97 - p68 [51-250]
Hall, Pauline - *Fun for Ten Fingers (Illus. by Caroline*
Crossland)
  c - Sch Lib - v44 - Ag '96 - p112 [51-250]
Hall, Peter Dobkin - *Inventing the Nonprofit Sector and*
Other Essays on Philanthropy, Voluntarism, and
Nonprofit Organizations
  BHR - v70 - Sum '96 - p280+ [501+]

Hall, Radclyffe - *The Well of Loneliness*
  Crit Q - v38 - Aut '96 - p3+ [501+]
  TSWL - v15 - Fall '96 - p253+ [501+]
Your John
  KR - v64 - D 15 '96 - p1782 [251-500]
  LJ - v122 - F 15 '97 - p135 [51-250]
  PW - v243 - D 30 '96 - p47+ [251-500]
  TLS - Mr 21 '97 - p3+ [501+]
Hall, Ray - *Europe's Population*
  GJ - v162 - Jl '96 - p225 [251-500]
Hall, Richard L - *Participation in Congress*
  Choice - v34 - F '97 - p1036 [51-250]
Hall, Robert A - *Fighters from the Fringe*
  Aust Bk R - Jl '96 - p66 [251-500]
Hall, Rodney - *The Island in the Mind*
  Aust Bk R - N '96 - p10+ [501+]
Hall, Stephen F - *From Kitchen to Market. 2nd Ed.*
  LJ - v122 - My 1 '97 - p53 [1-50]
Hall, Stephen S - *A Commotion in the Blood*
  BL - v93 - My 15 '97 - p1551 [51-250]
  PW - v244 - My 12 '97 - p70 [51-250]
Hall, Stuart - *Questions of Cultural Identity*
  Afterimage - v24 - Ja '97 - p23 [51-250]
Hall, Timothy D - *Contested Boundaries*
  AHR - v101 - D '96 - p1612+ [501+]
  CH - v65 - S '96 - p511+ [501+]
  J Am Cult - v19 - Spr '96 - p100 [251-500]
  JR - v76 - O '96 - p641+ [501+]
  W&M Q - v53 - Jl '96 - p661+ [501+]
Hall, Tom T - *What a Book!*
  Ent W - Ja 31 '97 - p55 [51-250]
Hall, Wade - *Hell-Bent for Music*
  AB - v98 - D 9 '96 - p1994 [51-250]
  CAY - v17 - Win '96 - p4 [51-250]
  LJ - v121 - N 1 '96 - p42 [1-50]
Hall, Wendy - *Rethinking Hypermedia*
  SciTech - v20 - N '96 - p10 [51-250]
Hall, William M - *From Memories to Mental Illness*
  R&R Bk N - v11 - D '96 - p3 [51-250]
Hall, Zoe - *The Apple Pie Tree (Illus. by Shari Halpern)*
  c - BL - v93 - O 1 '96 - p355 [51-250]
  c - CBRS - v25 - Win '96 - p62 [51-250]
  c - CCB-B - v50 - D '96 - p136+ [51-250]
  c - HB Guide - v8 - Spr '97 - p30 [51-250]
  c - KR - v64 - Ag 15 '96 - p1234 [51-250]
  c - SLJ - v42 - D '96 - p113 [51-250]
Hallback, M - *Turbulence and Transition Modelling*
  SciTech - v20 - D '96 - p61 [51-250]
Hallberg, William - *The Soul of Golf*
  PW - v244 - Ap 21 '97 - p53 [51-250]
Haller, John S, Jr. - *Medical Protestants*
  AAPSS-A - v549 - Ja '97 - p201+ [501+]
Hallett, J P - *Compromising Traditions*
  Lon R Bks - v19 - Ja 23 '97 - p10+ [501+]
Halley, Ned B - *Farm (Illus. by Geoff Brightling)*
  c - Bks Keeps - Jl '96 - p22 [51-250]
  c - Emerg Lib - v23 - My '96 - p43 [1-50]
  c - HB Guide - v7 - Fall '96 - p352 [1-50]
  c - Magpies - v11 - Jl '96 - p39 [1-50]
Halliday, David - *Fundamentals of Physics. 5th Ed.*
  SB - v33 - Ja '97 - p7 [251-500]
  SciTech - v20 - D '96 - p22 [51-250]
  SciTech - v21 - Mr '97 - p20 [1-50]
  SciTech - v21 - Mr '97 - p20 [1-50]
Halliday, Fred - *Islam and the Myth of Confrontation*
  For Aff - v75 - S '96 - p154 [51-250]
  Rel St Rev - v22 - O '96 - p357 [51-250]
Halliday, Jan - *Native Peoples of the Northwest*
  r - Nat Peop - v10 - '97 - p78+ [501+]
Hallinan, P K - *Three Freckles Past a Hair (Illus. by Sally*
Bourgeois)
  c - HB Guide - v8 - Spr '97 - p30 [51-250]
Hallissy, Margaret - *A Companion to Chaucer's*
Canterbury Tales
  y - CLW - v67 - Mr '97 - p50 [51-250]
Halliwell, Jonathan - *The Physical Origins of Time*
Asymmetry
  New Sci - v151 - S 28 '96 - p54+ [501+]
Hallman, David - *Ecotheology: Voices from North and*
South
  JAAR - v64 - Fall '96 - p691+ [501+]
Hallowell, Edward - *When You Worry About the Child*
You Love
  Adoles - v31 - Fall '96 - p752 [51-250]
Hall-Patton, Mark P - *Memories of the Land*
  r - Names - v45 - Mr '97 - p18 [251-500]
Halls, W D - *Politics, Society, and Christianity in Vichy*
France
  AHR - v101 - O '96 - p1225+ [501+]
Hallum, Anne Motley - *Beyond Missionaries*
  Choice - v34 - My '97 - p1516 [51-250]

Hallworth, Grace - *Down by the River (Illus. by Caroline Binch)*
  c BL - v93 - F 15 '97 - p1014 [1-50]
  c CBRS - v25 - F '97 - p75 [51-250]
  c CCB-B - v50 - Ja '97 - p172 [51-250]
  c Ch BWatch - v7 - F '97 - p2 [1-50]
  c HB Guide - v8 - Spr '97 - p107 [51-250]
  c Sch Lib - v45 - F '97 - p19 [51-250]
  c SLJ - v42 - D '96 - p113 [51-250]
  c TES - S 6 '96 - p6* [251-500]

Halm, Heinz - *Shi'a Islam*
     BL - v93 - Mr 15 '97 - p1207 [51-250]
     Choice - v34 - My '97 - p1516 [51-250]
     LJ - v122 - Ap 15 '97 - p86 [51-250]
     MEQ - v4 - Mr '97 - p92+ [51-250]

Halme, Kathleen - *Every Substance Clothed*
  y Kliatt - v30 - S '96 - p23 [51-250]
     MQR - v36 - Spr '97 - p368+ [501+]

Halmo, Joan - *A Triduum Sourcebook. Vols. 1-3*
  r CLW - v67 - D '96 - p54+ [51-250]

Halonen, Jane S - *Psychology: Contexts of Behavior. 2nd Ed.*
     R&R Bk N - v11 - N '96 - p3 [1-50]

Halperin, David J - *Seeking Ezekiel*
     JAAR - v64 - Fall '96 - p678+ [501+]

Halperin, David M - *Saint Foucault*
     FR - v70 - O '96 - p106+ [251-500]

Halperin, James L - *The Truth Machine*
  y CLW - v67 - D '96 - p64+ [251-500]
     PW - v243 - S 30 '96 - p65 [51-250]

Halperin, John - *Eminent Georgians*
     ELT - v40 - 1 '97 - p80+ [501+]
  The Life of Jane Austen
     BW - v27 - Mr 2 '97 - p12 [51-250]

Halperin, Rhoda H - *Cultural Economies Past and Present*
     Am Sci - v84 - My '96 - p301+ [501+]

Halperin, Wendy Anderson - *When Chickens Grow Teeth (Illus. by Wendy Anderson Halperin)*
  c HB Guide - v8 - Spr '97 - p57 [51-250]
  c NYTBR - v102 - Mr 2 '97 - p25 [501+]
  c PW - v243 - S 2 '96 - p129 [51-250]
  c SLJ - v42 - S '96 - p178+ [51-250]

Halpern, David - *Mental Health and the Built Environment*
     Readings - v11 - S '96 - p30 [51-250]
  Options for Britain
     Choice - v34 - N '96 - p531 [51-250]

Halpern, Diane F - *Changing College Classrooms*
     MLJ - v80 - Fall '96 - p400 [251-500]

Halpern, Paul - *The Structure of the Universe*
  y Kliatt - v31 - My '97 - p29 [251-500]

Halpern, Rick - *Meatpackers: An Oral History of Black Packinghouse Workers and Their Struggle for Racial and Economic Equality*
     BL - v93 - D 1 '96 - p627 [51-250]
     LJ - v121 - N 15 '96 - p73 [51-250]

Halpern, Robert - *Rebuilding the Inner City*
     Soc Ser R - v70 - D '96 - p660+ [501+]

Halpern, Stephen C - *On the Limits of the Law*
     AAPSS-A - v546 - Jl '96 - p169+ [501+]
     AHR - v101 - D '96 - p1644+ [501+]
     APSR - v91 - Mr '97 - p187+ [501+]
     J Hi E - v68 - Mr '97 - p235+ [501+]

Halpern, Thomas - *The Limits of Dissent*
     Bloom Rev - v16 - S '96 - p23 [51-250]
     Choice - v34 - Ja '97 - p875 [251-500]

Halpert, Herbert - *Folktales of Newfoundland. Vols. 1-2*
     Choice - v34 - F '97 - p965 [51-250]
     R&R Bk N - v11 - D '96 - p20 [51-250]

Halpert, Sam - *Raymond Carver: An Oral Biography*
     Biography - v19 - Fall '96 - p430 [1-50]

Halpin, Terry - *Conceptual Schema and Relational Database Design. 2nd Ed.*
     SciTech - v20 - S '96 - p8 [51-250]

Halprin, Anna - *Moving toward Life*
     Dance RJ - v28 - Fall '96 - p86+ [501+]
     TDR - v40 - Fall '96 - p202 [51-250]

Halprin, Sara - *Look at My Ugly Face!*
  y Kliatt - v30 - S '96 - p30 [51-250]

Halsall, Guy - *Settlement and Social Organization*
     Choice - v34 - O '96 - p339 [51-250]

Halse, Elizabeth - *The Morton Years*
     LAR - v98 - Jl '96 - p373 [1-50]

Halsell, Grace - *In Their Shoes*
     MEP - v5 - 1 '97 - p213+ [501+]
     PW - v243 - S 2 '96 - p105 [51-250]

Halsey, A H - *Change in British Society. 4th Ed.*
     HT - v46 - S '96 - p57 [51-250]

Halsey, A H, 1923- - *No Discouragement*
     NS - v125 - D 6 '96 - p52+ [501+]
     Spec - v278 - Ja 18 '97 - p30+ [501+]
     TES - Mr 14 '97 - p9* [501+]
     TLS - Ja 24 '97 - p12 [501+]

Halsey, Edmund - *Brother against Brother*
     KR - v65 - Ap 1 '97 - p520 [251-500]
     PW - v244 - Ap 21 '97 - p56 [51-250]

Halsey, Francis Whiting - *The Old New York Frontier*
  r EGH - v50 - N '96 - p174+ [51-250]

Halter, Marilyn - *New Migrants in the Marketplace*
     CS - v25 - S '96 - p673+ [501+]

Halter, Peter - *The Revolution in the Visual Arts and the Poetry of William Carlos Williams*
     RES - v48 - F '97 - p142+ [501+]

Halton, Eugene - *Bereft of Reason*
     CS - v25 - S '96 - p699+ [501+]
     RM - v49 - Je '96 - p925+ [501+]

Halvey, John K - *Information Technology Outsourcing Transactions*
     SciTech - v20 - N '96 - p59 [51-250]

Halvorson, Michael - *Learn Visual Basic Now*
     CBR - v14 - S '96 - p31 [1-50]

Halvorson, William L - *Science and Ecosystem Management in the National Parks*
     Choice - v34 - D '96 - p632 [51-250]
     R&R Bk N - v11 - N '96 - p78 [51-250]

Hama, Noriko - *Disintegrating Europe*
     JEL - v34 - D '96 - p2042 [51-250]

Hamada, Koichi - *Strategic Approaches to the International Economy*
     JEL - v35 - Mr '97 - p218 [51-250]

Hamaker-Zondag, Karen - *Planetary Symbolism in the Horoscope*
     Horoscope - v62 - D '96 - p18 [501+]

Hamalainen, Helvi - *Kadotettu Puutarha*
     WLT - v70 - Sum '96 - p732 [501+]
  Saadyllinen Murhenaytelma
     WLT - v70 - Sum '96 - p732 [501+]

Hamalian, Leo - *D.H. Lawrence and Nine Women Writers*
     Choice - v34 - N '96 - p456 [51-250]
     ELT - v40 - 2 '97 - p251+ [51-250]

Hamamoto, Darrell Y - *Monitored Peril*
     J Pop F&TV - v24 - Spr '96 - p47+ [501+]

Hamanaka, Sheila - *On the Wings of Peace*
  y RT - v50 - N '96 - p247 [51-250]

Hamann, Brigitte - *Bertha Von Suttner: A Life for Peace*
     R&R Bk N - v11 - D '96 - p49 [1-50]
  Hitlers Wien
     TLS - Ja 31 '97 - p3+ [501+]

Hamber, Anthony J - *A Higher Branch of the Art*
  r Choice - v34 - N '96 - p444 [51-250]

Hamblin, Ken - *Pick a Better Country*
     CSM - v89 - D 11 '96 - p15 [51-250]
     KR - v64 - S 1 '96 - p1295 [51-250]
     LJ - v121 - N 1 '96 - p86 [1-50]

Hambly, Barbara - *Children of the Jedi*
  y Kliatt - v30 - N '96 - p14 [51-250]
  A Free Man of Color
     PW - v244 - My 5 '97 - p197 [51-250]
  Mother of Winter
  y BL - v93 - S 1 '96 - p29+ [51-250]
     BWatch - v18 - F '97 - p4 [51-250]
     LJ - v121 - S 15 '96 - p101 [51-250]
     PW - v243 - S 16 '96 - p74 [51-250]
  Planet of Twilight
  y BL - v93 - F 1 '97 - p907 [51-250]
     LJ - v122 - Mr 15 '97 - p93 [1-50]
     PW - v244 - Ap 28 '97 - p54 [51-250]
  Those Who Hunt the Night
  y BL - v93 - Ja '97 - p832 [1-50]

Hambourg, Maria Morris - *Nadar*
     YR - v84 - O '96 - p128+ [501+]

Hambrick-Stowe, Charles E - *Charles G. Finney and the Spirit of American Evangelicalism*
     BL - v92 - Ag '96 - p1859 [51-250]
     Choice - v34 - Mr '97 - p1177 [51-250]

Hamburg, Joseph - *Merriam-Webster's Medical Office Handbook. 2nd Ed.*
     SciTech - v20 - N '96 - p35 [51-250]

Hamby, Alonzo L - *Man of the People*
     RAH - v24 - D '96 - p686+ [501+]

Hamdun, Said - *Ibn Battuta in Black Africa*
     MEJ - v50 - Sum '96 - p457 [51-250]

Hameau, Marie-Anne - *Je Lis Tu Lis*
  c BL - v93 - N 1 '96 - p500 [51-250]

Hamelin, Louis - *Betsi Larousse Ou L'Ineffable Ecceite De La Loutre*
     FR - v70 - D '96 - p349+ [501+]

Hamelink, Cees - *World Communication*
  r R&R Bk N - v11 - N '96 - p63 [51-250]

Hamelink, Jacques - *Boheems Glas*
     WLT - v70 - Aut '96 - p972+ [501+]

Hamer, Andrew - *A Short Guide to the Retention of Documents*
     LAR - v98 - Jl '96 - p369 [1-50]

Hamer, Forrest - *Call and Response*
     Bl S - v26 - Sum '96 - p65 [1-50]
     HR - v49 - Aut '96 - p503+ [501+]

Hamer, Philip M - *A Guide to Archives and Manuscripts in the United States*
  r ASInt - v34 - O '96 - p11 [1-50]

Hameroff, Stuart R - *Toward a Science of Consciousness*
     SciTech - v20 - S '96 - p22 [51-250]

Hamerow, Theodore S - *On the Road to the Wolf's Lair*
     PW - v244 - Mr 24 '97 - p71 [51-250]

Hamesse, Jacqueline - *De L'Homelie Au Sermon*
     EHR - v111 - S '96 - p956+ [251-500]

Hamill, Denis - *House on Fire*
     LJ - v121 - N 1 '96 - p132 [51-250]

Hamill, Pete - *Piecework*
     Trib Bks - My 25 '97 - p8 [1-50]
  Snow in August
     BL - v93 - Mr 1 '97 - p1068 [51-250]
     KR - v65 - Mr 1 '97 - p325 [51-250]
     LJ - v122 - F 15 '97 - p162 [51-250]
     NYTLa - v146 - My 1 '97 - pC20 [501+]
     PW - v244 - Mr 17 '97 - p76 [251-500]
  The Times Square Gym
     LATBR - D 8 '96 - p2 [1-50]

Hamill, Sam - *Destination Zero*
     Parabola - v21 - Ag '96 - p100+ [501+]
  The Gift of Tongues
     LJ - v121 - S 15 '96 - p72 [51-250]
     PW - v243 - S 30 '96 - p81 [51-250]

Hamill, Tony - *Singular Voices*
     Can Lit - Spr '97 - p229+ [501+]

Hamilton, A C - *A New Partnership*
     J Gov Info - v23 - S '96 - p617 [51-250]

Hamilton, Edward Walter, Sir - *The Diary of Sir Edward Walter Hamilton 1885-1906*
     EHR - v112 - F '97 - p245+ [501+]

Hamilton, Geoff - *Geoff Hamilton's Private Paradise*
     Books - v11 - Ap '97 - p20 [51-250]

Hamilton, Heidi E - *Conversations with an Alzheimer's Patient*
     Lang Soc - v25 - S '96 - p468+ [501+]

Hamilton, Hugo - *Headbanger*
     TLS - Mr 21 '97 - p23 [501+]

Hamilton, Ian - *Walking Possession*
     BL - v93 - S 15 '96 - p204 [51-250]
     BW - v26 - O 27 '96 - p13 [51-250]
     LJ - v121 - S 15 '96 - p69 [51-250]

Hamilton, James - *Arthur Rackham: A Life with Illustrations*
     LATBR - Jl 7 '96 - p11 [51-250]

Hamilton, Jane - *The Book of Ruth*
     Ent W - Mr 21 '97 - p65+ [501+]
  The Book of Ruth (Winningham). Audio Version
     LJ - v122 - My 1 '97 - p153 [501+]
  A Map of the World
  y EJ - v85 - S '96 - p109+ [501+]

Hamilton, Janice - *Quebec*
  c HB Guide - v7 - Fall '96 - p385 [1-50]

Hamilton, John Maxwell - *Hold the Press*
     AJR - v18 - S '96 - p53 [51-250]
     Choice - v34 - D '96 - p605 [51-250]
     JMCQ - v73 - Win '96 - p1001 [251-500]

Hamilton, Julia - *A Pillar of Society*
     Spec - v277 - N 23 '96 - p46 [1-50]

Hamilton, Keith - *The Practice of Diplomacy*
     EHR - v112 - Ap '97 - p550 [251-500]

Hamilton, Kenneth - *Liszt: Sonata in B Minor*
     TLS - Ap 11 '97 - p19 [501+]

Hamilton, Martha - *Stories in My Pocket*
     BL - v93 - Ja '97 - p850 [251-500]
     CCB-B - v50 - Mr '97 - p263 [51-250]

Hamilton, Michelle - *Sewing Victorian Doll Clothes*
     Ant & CM - v102 - Mr '97 - p33 [51-250]
     LJ - v122 - Ap 15 '97 - p79 [51-250]
     TCI - v30 - O '96 - p55 [1-50]

Hamilton, Morse - *Belching Hill (Illus. by Forest Rogers)*
  c PW - v244 - Mr 17 '97 - p84 [51-250]

Hamilton, Neil A, 1949- - *Founders of Modern Nations*
  yr SLJ - v42 - Ag '96 - p181 [51-250]
  Militias in America
  r ARBA - v28 - '97 - p276 [51-250]
  r Choice - v34 - My '97 - p1475 [51-250]
  yr SLJ - v43 - Mr '97 - p201 [51-250]

Hamilton, Neil W - *Zealotry and Academic Freedom*
     CS - v25 - S '96 - p659+ [501+]
     ES - v27 - Fall '96 - p261+ [501+]

Hamilton, Peter F - *Mindstar Rising*
  PW - v243 - Jl 22 '96 - p232 [51-250]
The Reality Dysfunction
  Books - v11 - Ap '97 - p20 [51-250]
Hamilton, Richard F - *The Social Misconstruction of Reality*
  Bks & Cult - v3 - Mr '97 - p11 [501+]
  Choice - v34 - F '97 - p1003 [51-250]
  CPR - v16 - D '96 - p406+ [501+]
Hamilton, Victoria - *The Analyst's Preconscious*
  Choice - v34 - Mr '97 - p1243 [51-250]
Hamilton, Virginia - *Her Stories (Illus. by Leo Dillon)*
  c Bkbird - v34 - Spr '96 - p52 [1-50]
  c BL - v93 - F 15 '97 - p1014 [1-50]
  c ECEJ - v24 - Fall '96 - p40 [51-250]
  y Emerg Lib - v24 - S '96 - p23 [1-50]
  y LA - v73 - O '96 - p430 [51-250]
  c RT - v50 - S '96 - p57 [51-250]
  c RT - v50 - Mr '97 - p479 [51-250]
The House of Dies Drear (Thigpen). Audio Version
  y BL - v93 - My 15 '97 - p1595 [1-50]
In the Beginning
  y Kliatt - v30 - S '96 - p3 [1-50]
M.C. Higgins the Great
  c JOYS - v10 - Fall '96 - p46+ [501+]
Plain City
  y JAAL - v40 - S '96 - p78 [51-250]
  y Kliatt - v30 - S '96 - p3 [1-50]
  y SLJ - v43 - Mr '97 - p113 [1-50]
When Birds Could Talk and Bats Could Sing (Illus. by Barry Moser)
  c BL - v93 - Ap 1 '97 - p1305 [1-50]
  c HB - v72 - S '96 - p604+ [51-250]
  c HB Guide - v7 - Fall '96 - p321 [51-250]
  c Inst - v106 - Mr '97 - p30 [51-250]
  c NY - v72 - N 18 '96 - p101 [1-50]
  c NYTBR - v101 - S 22 '96 - p28 [1-50]
  c PW - v243 - N 4 '96 - p48 [1-50]
  c RT - v50 - Ap '97 - p595 [51-250]
  c SLJ - v42 - D '96 - p29 [1-50]
Hamilton, W D - *Narrow Roads of Gene Land. Vol. 1*
  Choice - v34 - O '96 - p303 [51-250]
  NS & S - v9 - My 17 '96 - p39 [1-50]
  SB - v32 - Ag '96 - p167+ [251-500]
  Skeptic - v4 - 2 '96 - p107 [251-500]
Hamilton, William - *A Quest for the Post-Historical Jesus*
  Rel St Rev - v22 - O '96 - p338+ [51-250]
Hamilton, William B - *Place Names of Atlantic Canada*
  Beav - v76 - D '96 - p47 [51-250]
  r BIC - v25 - N '96 - p40 [501+]
  r Quill & Q - v62 - O '96 - p40 [251-500]
  r R&R Bk N - v12 - F '97 - p27 [51-250]
Hamilton-Paterson, James - *The Music: Stories*
  KR - v64 - S 15 '96 - p1342+ [251-500]
  NYTBR - v101 - N 24 '96 - p11 [501+]
  NYTBR - v101 - D 8 '96 - p82 [1-50]
  Obs - D 8 '96 - p18* [51-250]
  PW - v243 - S 23 '96 - p70+ [251-500]
Hamley, Dennis - *Dead Ringer*
  y Sch Lib - v45 - F '97 - p46 [51-250]
Hamlin, Alan P - *Ethics and Economics. Vols. 1-2*
  JEL - v34 - S '96 - p1403+ [51-250]
  R&R Bk N - v11 - D '96 - p22 [51-250]
Hamlin, E John - *Surely There Is a Future*
  Rel St Rev - v23 - Ap '97 - p168 [51-250]
Hamlin, Rick - *Finding God on the A Train*
  BL - v93 - F 15 '97 - p976 [501+]
Hamlin, Roger E - *Economy without Walls*
  JEL - v34 - D '96 - p2140+ [51-250]
  R&R Bk N - v11 - N '96 - p26 [51-250]
Hamlin, William M - *The Image of America in Montaigne, Spenser, and Shakespeare*
  J Am St - v30 - Ag '96 - p320+ [501+]
  Six Ct J - v27 - Win '96 - p1201+ [501+]
  W&M Q - v53 - O '96 - p797+ [501+]
Hamm, Berndt - *Reformationstheorien: Ein Kirchenhistorischer Disput Uber Einheit Und Vielfalt Der Reformation*
  CH - v65 - D '96 - p697+ [501+]
Hamm, Charles - *Irving Berlin: Songs from the Melting Pot*
  BL - v93 - Ap 1 '97 - p1275 [51-250]
  KR - v65 - F 15 '97 - p271 [251-500]
  LJ - v122 - Ap 1 '97 - p93 [51-250]
Putting Popular Music in Its Place
  J Am St - v30 - Ap '96 - p134+ [251-500]
Hamm, Mark S - *Apocalypse in Oklahoma*
  KR - v65 - F 1 '97 - p195 [251-500]
  LJ - v122 - Ap 1 '97 - p110 [51-250]
Hamm, Michael F - *Kiev: A Portrait 1800-1917*
  AB - v98 - S 9 '96 - p750+ [501+]

Hamm, Richard F - *Shaping the Eighteenth Amendment*
  AHR - v101 - O '96 - p1292 [501+]
  JIH - v27 - Aut '96 - p346+ [251-500]
Hamm, Thomas D - *God's Government Begun*
  AHR - v102 - F '97 - p184+ [501+]
  NEQ - v70 - Mr '97 - p172+ [501+]
Hamm, Tricia - *Resources for Learning in College Libraries*
  LR - v45 - 8 '96 - p51+ [251-500]
Hamma, Robert M - *Let's Say Grace*
  CLW - v66 - Je '96 - p36 [51-250]
Hammad, Alam Al-Huda - *Mawsuat Mustalahat Al-Hasub*
  r MEJ - v50 - Sum '96 - p450 [51-250]
Hammer, Carl - *Freak Show*
  Ent W - Ag 23 '96 - p118 [51-250]
Hammer, Michael - *Beyond Reengineering*
  Bus Bk R - v13 - 4 '96 - p30+ [501+]
  HR Mag - v41 - D '96 - p124 [501+]
  LJ - v121 - S 15 '96 - p77 [51-250]
  NS - v126 - Ja 17 '97 - p45+ [501+]
Hammers
  p Sm Pr R - v29 - F '97 - p22 [251-500]
Hammett, A L - *Expanding Export Markets*
  R&R Bk N - v11 - D '96 - p32 [51-250]
Hammick, Georgina - *The Arizona Game*
  Lon R Bks - v18 - O 17 '96 - p17+ [501+]
People for Lunch. Spoilt
  Lon R Bks - v18 - O 17 '96 - p17+ [501+]
Hammond, Elaine Breault - *The Secret under the Whirlpool*
  c BIC - v26 - Mr '97 - p32 [251-500]
  c Can CL - v22 - Fall '96 - p125+ [501+]
  c Quill & Q - v62 - O '96 - p47 [51-250]
Hammond, Emily - *Breathe Something Nice*
  BL - v93 - Ap 1 '97 - p1280 [51-250]
  PW - v244 - Mr 31 '97 - p63+ [51-250]
Hammond, Frederick - *Music and Spectacle in Baroque Rome*
  CHR - v82 - O '96 - p728+ [501+]
  JMH - v68 - S '96 - p714+ [501+]
  Notes - v53 - S '96 - p49+ [501+]
Hammond, Gerald - *Carriage of Justice*
  Arm Det - v29 - Sum '96 - p360 [251-500]
Mad Dogs and Scotsmen
  KR - v64 - S 15 '96 - p1360 [501+]
Sink or Swim
  BL - v93 - My 1 '97 - p1482 [51-250]
  PW - v244 - Mr 17 '97 - p80 [51-250]
Hammond, J Daniel - *Theory and Measurement*
  JEL - v34 - D '96 - p2013 [51-250]
Hammond, Kenneth R - *Human Judgment and Social Policy*
  Choice - v34 - Ap '97 - p1379 [51-250]
Hammond, Lee - *How to Draw Portraits in Colored Pencil from Photographs*
  y BL - v93 - Mr 15 '97 - p1219 [51-250]
  LJ - v122 - Mr 15 '97 - p63 [51-250]
Hammond, N G L - *The Genius of Alexander the Great*
  y BL - v93 - F 15 '97 - p998 [51-250]
  KR - v65 - Ja 1 '97 - p37 [251-500]
  LATBR - Mr 9 '97 - p3 [501+]
  LJ - v122 - Mr 15 '97 - p73 [51-250]
  Obs - F 9 '97 - p16* [501+]
  PW - v244 - F 3 '97 - p87 [51-250]
Hammond, Nicholas - *Playing with Truth*
  Ren Q - v49 - Aut '96 - p634+ [251-500]
Hammond, Paul - *Love between Men in English Literature*
  Choice - v34 - F '97 - p965 [51-250]
  TLS - Mr 28 '97 - p25 [501+]
Hammond, Robert - *Gynaecological Symptoms in Primary Care*
  SciTech - v20 - N '96 - p51 [51-250]
Hammond, Stefan - *Sex and Zen and a Bullet in the Head*
  y BL - v92 - Ag '96 - p1872 [501+]
  BL - v92 - Ag '96 - p1890 [501+]
  Ent W - S 13 '96 - p126 [51-250]
  r FEER - v159 - S 19 '96 - p53+ [501+]
Hammond, William M - *The Military and the Media 1968-1973*
  Wil Q - v21 - Win '97 - p97+ [251-500]
Public Affairs
  Choice - v34 - D '96 - p676 [51-250]
  For Aff - v75 - N '96 - p150+ [501+]
Hammond Incorporated - *Citation World Atlas*
  r ARBA - v28 - '97 - p172 [251-500]
Hammond Atlas of the 20th Century
  yr ARBA - v28 - '97 - p208+ [501+]
  r BL - v93 - D 15 '96 - p748+ [251-500]
  r Choice - v34 - Ap '97 - p1309 [51-250]

Hammond New Century World Atlas
  r ARBA - v28 - '97 - p173 [51-250]
The New Comparative World Atlas
  r BL - v93 - N 15 '96 - p608 [1-50]
  cr SLJ - v43 - F '97 - p132 [51-250]
Hamnett, Brian - *Juarez*
  EHR - v111 - S '96 - p1005+ [251-500]
Hamouda, Omar F - *Probability in Economics*
  JEL - v34 - D '96 - p2017 [51-250]
  R&R Bk N - v11 - D '96 - p22 [51-250]
Hampden-Turner, Charles - *The Seven Cultures of Capitalism*
  Hum - v57 - Ja '97 - p41+ [501+]
Hampe, Barry - *Making Documentary Films and Reality Videos*
  y BL - v93 - Ja '97 - p781 [51-250]
  LJ - v122 - Ja '97 - p101 [51-250]
Hampl, Patricia - *Burning Bright*
  RR - v55 - N '96 - p660 [1-50]
Hampshire, Susan - *Rosie's Ballet Slippers (Illus. by Maria Teresa Meloni)*
  c HB Guide - v7 - Fall '96 - p258 [51-250]
Hampson, Daphne - *After Christianity*
  TLS - Mr 28 '97 - p5 [501+]
Hampson, Fen Osler - *Earthly Goods*
  Choice - v34 - Ap '97 - p1351+ [51-250]
Nurturing Peace
  Choice - v34 - Mr '97 - p1234 [51-250]
Hampton, Bo - *Verdilak*
  SF Chr - v18 - O '96 - p81 [1-50]
Hampton, Bruce - *The Great American Wolf*
  yr BL - v93 - N 15 '96 - p557 [251-500]
  yr BL - v93 - D 1 '96 - p664 [1-50]
  KR - v64 - O 15 '96 - p1511 [251-500]
  LATBR - Ja 26 '97 - p8 [501+]
  LJ - v121 - D '96 - p137+ [51-250]
  PW - v243 - N 4 '96 - p53 [51-250]
  Trib Bks - Mr 9 '97 - p6+ [501+]
Hampton, Mary N - *The Wilsonian Impulse*
  Choice - v34 - D '96 - p686 [51-250]
  For Aff - v76 - Mr '97 - p182+ [51-250]
  R&R Bk N - v11 - N '96 - p18 [51-250]
Hampton, Robert L - *Preventing Violence in America*
  Readings - v11 - S '96 - p28 [51-250]
Hamri, Thorsteinn - *Thao Talar I Trjanum*
  WLT - v70 - Aut '96 - p975+ [501+]
Hamrin, Carol Lee - *Decision Making in Deng's China*
  Ch Rev Int - v3 - Fall '96 - p427+ [501+]
Hamston, Julie - *Integrating Socially*
  SS - v87 - S '96 - p234+ [501+]
Hamstra, Bruce - *How Therapists Diagnose*
  r BL - v93 - F 1 '97 - p959 [1-50]
Hamsun, Knut - *Hunger*
  Obs - Ja 26 '97 - p17* [501+]
  RCF - v16 - Fall '96 - p21+ [501+]
  TLS - D 6 '96 - p24 [51-250]
Mysteries
  RCF - v16 - Fall '96 - p21+ [501+]
Pan
  RCF - v16 - Fall '96 - p21+ [501+]
Victoria
  RCF - v16 - Fall '96 - p21+ [501+]
  TranslRevS - v1 - My '95 - p5 [51-250]
The Women at the Pump
  TranslRevS - v2 - D '96 - p5 [51-250]
Hamvai, Kornel - *Marton Partjelzo Fazik*
  WLT - v70 - Aut '96 - p998 [501+]
Han, Oki S - *Kongi and Potgi (Illus. by Oki S Han)*
  c BL - v93 - N 15 '96 - p589+ [51-250]
  c CCB-B - v50 - F '97 - p207+ [51-250]
  c HB Guide - v8 - Spr '97 - p102 [51-250]
  c KR - v64 - N 15 '96 - p1669 [51-250]
  c SLJ - v42 - D '96 - p113 [51-250]
Han, Suzanne Crowder - *The Rabbit's Escape (Illus. by Yumi Heo)*
  c Inst - v105 - My '96 - p68+ [1-50]
Hanania, Tony - *Homesick*
  Obs - F 23 '97 - p17* [51-250]
  TLS - Mr 7 '97 - p22 [501+]
Hanauer, Cathi - *My Sister's Bones*
  y BL - v93 - Ap 1 '97 - p1292 [1-50]
  y Ch BWatch - v6 - O '96 - p3 [51-250]
Hanawalt, Barbara A - *City and Spectacle in Medieval Europe*
  CH - v65 - S '96 - p476+ [501+]
  CLS - v33 - 4 '96 - p414+ [501+]
Growing Up in Medieval London
  EHR - v111 - N '96 - p1255+ [251-500]
  JWomHist - v8 - Fall '96 - p228+ [501+]
  Specu - v71 - O '96 - p956+ [501+]

Hanaway, Joseph - *McGill Medicine. Vol. 1*
Choice - v34 - O '96 - p313 [51-250]
Hance, Olivier - *Business and Law on the Internet*
New Sci - v151 - S 14 '96 - p46 [51-250]
Hanchar, Peggy - *Lady of the Mist*
PW - v244 - Mr 24 '97 - p81 [51-250]
Hanchard, Michael George - *Orpheus and Power*
JIH - v27 - Aut '96 - p366+ [501+]
Hancock, Barry W - *Cancer Care in the Community*
SciTech - v20 - N '96 - p37 [1-50]
Cancer Care in the Hospital
SciTech - v20 - N '96 - p40 [51-250]
Hancock, David - *Citizens of the World*
BHR - v70 - Sum '96 - p271+ [501+]
Choice - v34 - S '96 - p187 [51-250]
W&M Q - v54 - Ap '97 - p416+ [501+]
Hancock, Jonathan - *Have a Mega Memory (Illus. by Tony Smith)*
y Sch Lib - v44 - N '96 - p174 [51-250]
Hancock, Ralph C - *The Legacy of the French Revolution*
APSR - v91 - Mr '97 - p214+ [501+]
Hancock, Virgil - *Chihuahua: Pictures from the Edge*
BL - v93 - Ja '97 - p812 [51-250]
LATBR - D 8 '96 - p5 [51-250]
Hand, Elizabeth - *Glimmering*
KR - v65 - Ja 15 '97 - p104 [51-250]
LJ - v122 - Mr 15 '97 - p93 [51-250]
PW - v244 - F 3 '97 - p99 [51-250]
Hand, Sean - *Facing the Other*
Choice - v34 - D '96 - p626 [51-250]
Hand, Sergeant George - *The Civil War in Apacheland*
WHQ - v27 - Win '96 - p549 [51-250]
Hand, Susanne C - *New Jersey Architecture*
Pub Hist - v19 - Win '97 - p96+ [501+]
Hand, Vivienne - *Zanzotto*
MLR - v91 - O '96 - p1015+ [501+]
Handberg, Roger - *The Future of the Space Industry*
APSR - v90 - S '96 - p651+ [501+]
The Handbook for No-Load Investors. 1996 Ed.
r WSJ-MW - v77 - S 19 '96 - pA16 [51-250]
Handbook for the 1997 Young Reader's Choice Awards
r SLJ - v42 - D '96 - p48 [51-250]
Handbook for the International Treaties for the Protection of the Ozone Layer. 4th Ed.
SciTech - v21 - Mr '97 - p29 [51-250]
Handbook of Hispanic Cultures in the United States. Vols. 1-4
Hisp - v79 - D '96 - p810+ [501+]
Handbook of International Trade and Development Statistics 1994
r J Gov Info - v23 - Jl '96 - p525+ [501+]
Handbook of International Trade and Development Statistics 1995
R&R Bk N - v11 - D '96 - p32 [51-250]
Handbook of Latin American Studies CD-ROM. Electronic Media Version
r HAHR - v77 - F '97 - p75+ [501+]
r WorldV - v12 - O '96 - p23+ [251-500]
Handbook of United States Coins 1997
r Coin W - v37 - S 30 '96 - p68 [51-250]
Handel, Peter H - *Quantum 1/f Noise and Other Low Frequency Fluctuations in Electronic Devices*
SciTech - v20 - S '96 - p56 [51-250]
Handel-Mazzetti, Heinrich - *A Botanical Pioneer in South West China*
Nature - v386 - Ap 3 '97 - p455+ [501+]
Handelsman, Judith - *Growing Myself*
KR - v64 - My 1 '96 - p664 [251-500]
Handke, Peter - *A Journey to the Rivers*
BL - v93 - Ja '97 - p806+ [51-250]
KR - v64 - N 1 '96 - p1581 [251-500]
LATBR - Ja 12 '97 - p12 [51-250]
LJ - v122 - Ja '97 - p124 [51-250]
New R - v216 - Mr 3 '97 - p34+ [501+]
NYTBR - v102 - Ap 6 '97 - p16+ [501+]
PW - v243 - N 11 '96 - p63 [51-250]
Utne R - Mr '97 - p83+ [51-250]
Voyage to the Sonorous Land. The Hour We Knew Nothing of Each Other
Choice - v34 - Ja '97 - p800 [51-250]
TranslRevS - v2 - D '96 - p25 [51-250]
Eine Winterliche Reise Zu Den Flussen Donau, Save, Morawa Und Drina Oder Gerechtigkeit Fur Serbien
WLT - v71 - Win '97 - p147+ [251-500]
Handleman, Stephen - *Comrade Criminal*
AAPSS-A - v546 - Jl '96 - p164+ [501+]
Handler, Andrew - *A Man for All Connections*
Choice - v34 - O '96 - p339 [51-250]

Handler, David - *The Man Who Loved Women to Death*
BL - v93 - My 1 '97 - p1483 [51-250]
LJ - v122 - Ap 1 '97 - p133 [51-250]
PW - v244 - Mr 24 '97 - p62 [51-250]
Handler, Evan - *Time on Fire*
Spec - v277 - D 7 '96 - p48 [501+]
Trib Bks - My 11 '97 - p8 [1-50]
Handler, Joel F - *Down from Bureaucracy*
JEL - v34 - D '96 - p2083 [51-250]
The Poverty of Welfare Reform
AAPSS-A - v550 - Mr '97 - p182+ [251-500]
Handley, Mark - *The World Wide Web*
LR - v45 - 4 '96 - p61+ [501+]
Handrinos, George - *The Birds of Greece*
r New Sci - v153 - Mr 8 '97 - p45 [51-250]
Hands, Anthony - *Sources for the Poetry of T.S. Eliot*
RES - v47 - N '96 - p627+ [501+]
Hands, Timothy - *Thomas Hardy*
ELT - v39 - 3 '96 - p353+ [501+]
Handy, Charles - *Beyond Certainty*
Books - v9 - S '95 - p23 [1-50]
Handy, Ellen - *Pictorial Effect/Naturalistic Vision*
VS - v39 - Spr '96 - p391+ [501+]
Haneda, Masahi - *Islamic Urban Studies*
GJ - v163 - Mr '97 - p106 [51-250]
Hanel, Wolfram - *Abby (Illus. by Alan Marks)*
c BL - v93 - D 1 '96 - p651 [51-250]
c HB Guide - v8 - Spr '97 - p58 [51-250]
c KR - v64 - O 15 '96 - p1540 [51-250]
c SLJ - v43 - Ja '97 - p77+ [51-250]
The Gold at the End of the Rainbow (Illus. by Loek Koopmans)
c BL - v93 - Ap 1 '97 - p1337 [51-250]
c CCB-B - v50 - My '97 - p322+ [51-250]
Mia the Beach Cat (Illus. by Kirsten Hocker)
c Bks Keeps - Jl '96 - p9 [51-250]
The Other Side of the Bridge (Illus. by Alex De Wolf)
c SLJ - v43 - Ja '97 - p83 [51-250]
c HB Guide - v8 - Spr '97 - p58 [51-250]
Hanes, W Travis - *Imperial Diplomacy in the Era of Decolonization*
MEJ - v51 - Spr '97 - p304+ [501+]
Haney-Lopez, Ian - *White by Law*
Bl S - v26 - Sum '96 - p66 [1-50]
Choice - v34 - O '96 - p361 [51-250]
Hanging Loose
p Sm Pr R - v28 - D '96 - p22 [51-250]
Hango, Angeline - *Truthfully Yours*
Essays CW - Spr '96 - p36+ [501+]
Hanhardt, John G - *Video Culture*
Art J - v54 - Win '95 - p106+ [501+]
Hanioglu, M Sukru - *The Young Turks in Opposition*
AHR - v101 - D '96 - p1589 [501+]
Historian - v59 - Fall '96 - p189+ [501+]
MEJ - v50 - Aut '96 - p606+ [501+]
Hanke, Lewis - *Guide to the Study of United States History Outside the U.S. 1945-1980. Vols. 1-5*
r ASInt - v34 - O '96 - p7+ [51-250]
Hanke, Martin - *Conjugate Gradient Type Methods for Ill-Posed Problems*
SIAM Rev - v38 - D '96 - p682+ [501+]
Hanke, Steve H - *Russian Currency and Finance*
JEL - v34 - D '96 - p1994+ [501+]
Hankins, Barry - *God's Rascal*
BL - v93 - S 15 '96 - p187 [51-250]
Choice - v34 - F '97 - p980 [51-250]
Hankins, Thomas L - *Instruments and the Imagination*
T&C - v38 - Ja '97 - p233+ [501+]
Hanks, William F - *Language and Communicative Practices*
Am Ethnol - v24 - F '97 - p222+ [501+]
Hanley, Alice - *Love across the Color Line*
Choice - v34 - D '96 - p677 [51-250]
VQR - v73 - Win '97 - p18*+ [51-250]
Wom R Bks - v14 - N '96 - p21+ [501+]
Hanley, Mark Y - *Beyond a Christian Commonwealth*
Rel St Rev - v22 - O '96 - p358 [51-250]
Hanlon, Robert T - *Cephalopod Behaviour*
Choice - v34 - F '97 - p990 [51-250]
Hanly, Sheila - *Big Book of Animals*
c PW - v244 - Ap 28 '97 - p77 [51-250]
Hanmer, Trudy J - *The Gender Gap in Schools*
y HB Guide - v7 - Fall '96 - p314 [51-250]
Hann, John H - *A History of the Timucua Indians and Missions*
Choice - v34 - S '96 - p194 [51-250]
Hanna, Gila - *Towards Gender Equity in Mathematics Education*
R&R Bk N - v12 - F '97 - p92 [51-250]
Hanna, Jack - *Jack Hanna's Ultimate Guide to Pets*
LJ - v121 - N 15 '96 - p80 [51-250]

Jungle Jack Hanna's Safari Adventure (Illus. by Rick A Preberg)
c CBRS - v25 - Ja '97 - p55 [51-250]
c HB Guide - v8 - Spr '97 - p117 [51-250]
c SLJ - v42 - N '96 - p97+ [51-250]
Hanna, Martha - *The Mobilization of Intellect*
TLS - O 18 '96 - p28 [501+]
Hanna, Nagy - *The East Asian Miracle and Information Technology*
JEL - v35 - Mr '97 - p281 [51-250]
Hanna, Nelly - *The State and Its Servants*
MEJ - v50 - Aut '96 - p626 [51-250]
Hanna, Susan - *Property Rights and the Environment*
Env - v38 - N '96 - p29+ [51-250]
Hannaford, Carla - *Smart Moves*
LAR - v98 - Jl '96 - p371 [251-500]
Hannaford, Ivan - *Race: The History of an Idea in the West*
NS - v125 - D 13 '96 - p45+ [501+]
Hannah, Barry - *High Lonesome*
BL - v93 - S 15 '96 - p220 [51-250]
KR - v64 - Ag 15 '96 - p1173 [251-500]
LJ - v121 - N 1 '96 - p110 [51-250]
New R - v216 - F 10 '97 - p40+ [501+]
NYTBR - v101 - O 27 '96 - p14 [501+]
PW - v243 - S 2 '96 - p110 [51-250]
Rapport - v19 - 6 '96 - p21 [251-500]
WSJ-MW - v78 - O 25 '96 - pA12 [501+]
Hannah, Karen L - *West Virginia Women*
J Gov Info - v23 - S '96 - p596 [51-250]
Hannah, Kristin - *Home Again*
LJ - v122 - Ja '97 - p51 [1-50]
LJ - v121 - N 15 '96 - p52 [51-250]
PW - v243 - N 4 '96 - p40+ [1-50]
Hannah, Sophie - *Hotels like Houses*
TLS - D 20 '96 - p25 [501+]
Hannam, June - *British Women's History*
r ARBA - v28 - '97 - p331+ [51-250]
Hannan, Kate - *China, Modernisation and the Goal of Prosperity*
Econ J - v106 - N '96 - p1849 [251-500]
Hannant, Larry - *The Infernal Machine*
AHR - v102 - F '97 - p229+ [251-500]
Hannay, Lorraine - *I'm Not Scared*
c Magpies - v11 - My '96 - p53 [1-50]
Hanne, Michael - *The Power of the Story*
MLR - v92 - Ap '97 - p415+ [501+]
Hannegan, Eileen R - *Know Your Truth, Speak Your Truth, Live Your Truth*
Rapport - v19 - 5 '96 - p40 [251-500]
Hanners, LaVerne - *The Lords of the Valley*
WHQ - v27 - Win '96 - p548 [1-50]
Hannes, Matt - *The Container Revolution*
Model R - v64 - Mr '97 - p52 [51-250]
Hannesson, Rognvaldur - *Fisheries Mismanagement*
SciTech - v20 - D '96 - p58 [51-250]
Hannestad, Niels - *Tradition in Late Antique Sculpture*
CW - v90 - S '96 - p66+ [251-500]
Hannigan, John A - *Environmental Sociology*
Env - v39 - Mr '97 - p25+ [51-250]
Socio R - v44 - N '96 - p765+ [501+]
Hannon, Bill - *Agents in My Brain*
PW - v244 - My 5 '97 - p192 [51-250]
Hannon, Howard - *Agony in the Garden*
BL - v93 - S 15 '96 - p182 [51-250]
Hannoosh, Michele - *Painting and the Journal of Eugene Delacroix*
Art Bull - v79 - Mr '97 - p160+ [501+]
BM - v138 - S '96 - p608+ [51-250]
Hannum, Hildegarde - *People, Land, and Community*
KR - v65 - F 1 '97 - p196 [251-500]
Hanotel, Valerie - *Les Cathos*
FR - v70 - O '96 - p136+ [501+]
Hansard, Luke - *The Auto-Biography of Luke Hansard*
Lib - v18 - D '96 - p352+ [501+]
Hansard, Peter - *Jig, Fig and Mrs. Pig (Illus. by Francesca Martin)*
c Bks Keeps - Jl '96 - p9 [51-250]
Hansen, Anne Chaplin - *Den Vilde Jomfru*
WLT - v70 - Sum '96 - p707 [501+]
Hansen, Biruta Akerbergs - *Parading with Piglets*
c BL - v93 - D 15 '96 - p732 [1-50]
c HB Guide - v7 - Fall '96 - p239 [51-250]
Hansen, Brad - *The Dictionary of Multimedia*
yr BL - v93 - My 15 '97 - p1611 [51-250]
Hansen, Brooks - *The Chess Garden*
Bks & Cult - v2 - S '96 - p10 [501+]
y Kliatt - v31 - My '97 - p14 [51-250]
NYTBR - v101 - D 1 '96 - p36 [51-250]
Trib Bks - Ja 12 '97 - p2 [1-50]

Hansen, Chadwick - *Witchcraft at Salem*
   Bks & Cult - v3 - Ja '97 - p17+ [501+]
Hansen, David A - *Materials Selection for Hydrocarbon and Chemical Plants*
   SciTech - v20 - D '96 - p71 [51-250]
Hansen, David T - *The Call to Teach*
   ES - v27 - Sum '96 - p194+ [501+]
Hansen, Derek - *Psycho Cat*
   Aust Bk R - F '97 - p58 [51-250]
Hansen, Erik Fosnes - *Psalm at Journey's End*
   BW - v26 - N 10 '96 - p10 [251-500]
   LATBR - Ag 18 '96 - p2 [501+]
   NYTBR - v101 - Ag 25 '96 - p19 [51-250]
   W&I - v12 - Ja '97 - p271+ [501+]
Hansen, Gladys - *San Francisco Almanac. Rev. Ed.*
   r ARBA - v28 - '97 - p47 [251-500]
Hansen, James R - *Spaceflight Revolution*
   APH - v43 - Win '96 - p64 [251-500]
   Pub Hist - v18 - Sum '96 - p70+ [501+]
Hansen, Keith W - *Tragic Lucidity*
   FR - v70 - O '96 - p123+ [501+]
Hansen, Kurt - *Skibspost Til Og Fra Danmark I Midten Af 1800-Tallet*
   r Phil Lit R - v45 - '96 - p344+ [251-500]
Hansen, Miriam - *Babel and Babylon*
   Signs - v22 - Aut '96 - p248+ [501+]
Hansen, Ole Steen - *Vietnam*
   c BL - v93 - Mr 1 '97 - p1158 [51-250]
   c HB Guide - v8 - Spr '97 - p170 [51-250]
Hansen, Ron - *The Assassination of Jesse James by the Coward Robert Ford*
   NYTBR - v102 - Mr 9 '97 - p28 [51-250]
   Atticus
   Am - v174 - My 25 '96 - p28+ [501+]
   BL - v93 - Ja '97 - p761 [1-50]
   Comw - v123 - D 6 '96 - p25 [51-250]
   Ent W - F 14 '97 - p57 [51-250]
   NYTBR - v101 - D 8 '96 - p76 [1-50]
   NYTBR - v102 - Mr 9 '97 - p28 [51-250]
   PW - v243 - N 4 '96 - p37 [51-250]
   PW - v244 - Ja 13 '97 - p73 [1-50]
   Sew R - v104 - Jl '96 - p461+ [501+]
   Trib Bks - F 23 '97 - p8 [1-50]
   Desperadoes: A Novel
   NYTBR - v102 - Mr 9 '97 - p28 [51-250]
   Trib Bks - My 25 '97 - p8 [1-50]
Hanski, Ilkka - *Metapopulation Biology*
   r Choice - v34 - Ap '97 - p1364 [51-250]
   SciTech - v21 - Mr '97 - p35 [51-250]
Hanson, Clare - *Virginia Woolf*
   RMR - v50 - 2 '96 - p169+ [501+]
Hanson, David R - *C Interfaces and Implementations*
   SciTech - v20 - D '96 - p9 [51-250]
Hanson, Jarice - *New Communication Technologies in Developing Countries*
   JC - v46 - Sum '96 - p183+ [501+]
Hanson, Jeanne K - *The Beastly Book*
   y Kliatt - v30 - S '96 - p4 [1-50]
Hanson, Jim M - *The Next Cold War?*
   Choice - v34 - F '97 - p1031+ [51-250]
   R&R Bk N - v12 - F '97 - p14 [1-50]
Hanson, John H - *Migration, Jihad, and Muslim Authority in West Africa*
   Choice - v34 - Mr '97 - p1214 [51-250]
Hanson, Kenneth - *The Dead Sea Scrolls*
   PW - v244 - Ap 28 '97 - p69 [51-250]
Hanson, Marci J - *Atypical Infant Development. 2nd Ed.*
   SciTech - v20 - S '96 - p41 [51-250]
Hanson, Mark Victor - *Out of the Blue*
   Utne R - Jl '96 - p109 [51-250]
Hanson, Paul D - *Isaiah 40-66*
   Rel St Rev - v23 - Ja '97 - p59 [51-250]
Hanson, Regina - *The Face at the Window (Illus. by Linda Saport)*
   c CCB-B - v50 - My '97 - p323 [51-250]
   c KR - v65 - Ap 1 '97 - p556 [51-250]
Hanson, Rick - *Still Life*
   KR - v64 - My 1 '96 - p648 [51-250]
Hanson, Sandra L - *Lost Talent*
   Choice - v34 - Ja '97 - p813 [51-250]
Hanson, Stephen E - *Can Europe Work?*
   AJS - v102 - Ja '97 - p1173+ [501+]
   APSR - v90 - D '96 - p954+ [501+]
Hanson, Victor Davis - *Fields without Dreams*
   Trib Bks - Mr 16 '97 - p8 [1-50]
   The Other Greeks
   Rel St Rev - v23 - Ja '97 - p60 [51-250]

Hansson, Bobby - *The Fine Art of the Tin Can*
   Am Craft - v56 - Ag '96 - p27 [1-50]
   BL - v93 - O 1 '96 - p316 [51-250]
   BWatch - v18 - F '97 - p5 [51-250]
   LJ - v121 - O 15 '96 - p56 [51-250]
Hanushek, Eric A - *Assessing Knowledge of Retirement Behavior*
   R&R Bk N - v12 - F '97 - p41 [51-250]
   Making Schools Work
   BusLR - v21 - 3 '96 - p197+ [501+]
Hanyan, Craig - *De Witt Clinton and the Rise of the People's Men*
   Choice - v34 - Ap '97 - p1404 [51-250]
   R&R Bk N - v11 - D '96 - p16 [51-250]
Hapke, Laura - *Daughters of the Great Depression*
   AL - v68 - D '96 - p865+ [501+]
   SE - v60 - S '96 - p302 [51-250]
Happy Families
   c Bks Keeps - N '96 - p4+ [501+]
Haq, Mahbub Ul - *Reflections on Human Development*
   JEL - v35 - Mr '97 - p177+ [501+]
   M Lab R - v119 - N '96 - p53 [501+]
   The Tobin Tax
   JEL - v35 - Mr '97 - p227+ [51-250]
   The UN and the Bretton Woods Institutions
   Econ J - v107 - Ja '97 - p272 [51-250]
Harahan, Joseph P - *On-Site Inspections under the INF Treaty*
   Pub Hist - v19 - Win '97 - p120+ [501+]
Harak, G Simon - *Aquinas and Empowerment*
   Rel St Rev - v23 - Ap '97 - p157 [51-250]
Haramundanis, Katherine - *Exploring Workstation Applications with CDE and Motif*
   SciTech - v20 - D '96 - p7 [51-250]
Harasim, Linda - *Learning Networks*
   SocSciComR - v14 - Fall '96 - p352+ [501+]
Harasymowicz, Jerry - *I Live on a Raft*
   c TranslRevS - v1 - My '95 - p10 [51-250]
Harbaugh, Karen - *Cupid's Mistake*
   LJ - v121 - N 15 '96 - p48 [51-250]
Harbeson, John W - *Africa in World Politics. 2nd Ed.*
   JTWS - v13 - Spr '96 - p276+ [501+]
Harbin, Michael A - *To Serve Other Gods*
   CH - v65 - S '96 - p556+ [501+]
Harbison, Elizabeth M - *Loaves of Fun*
   c BL - v93 - My 1 '97 - p1491 [51-250]
Harbison, Robert - *Thirteen Ways*
   PW - v244 - Ap 28 '97 - p64 [251-500]
Harborne, Jeffrey B - *Dictionary of Plant Toxins. Vol. 1*
   r Choice - v34 - Mr '97 - p1184 [51-250]
   r SciTech - v20 - D '96 - p40 [51-250]
Harbour, Elizabeth - *A First Picture Book of Nursery Rhymes (Illus. by Elizabeth Harbour)*
   c HB Guide - v7 - Fall '96 - p325 [51-250]
   c SLJ - v42 - Ag '96 - p136+ [51-250]
Harbury, Jennifer K - *Searching for Everardo*
   BW - v27 - Mr 23 '97 - p1+ [501+]
   KR - v65 - Ja 15 '97 - p119 [251-500]
   PW - v244 - Ja 13 '97 - p63+ [51-250]
Harcourt, Mike - *A Measure of Defiance*
   Mac - v109 - O 28 '96 - p63 [501+]
Hardaway, Roger D - *A Narrative Bibliography of the African American Frontier*
   r ARBA - v28 - '97 - p187 [51-250]
Hardcastle, Michael - *The Fastest Bowler in the World*
   y Sch Lib - v44 - Ag '96 - p117 [51-250]
Hardcastle, Valerie Gray - *How to Build a Theory in Cognitive Science*
   Choice - v34 - O '96 - p364 [51-250]
Hardeman, Hilde - *Coming to Terms with the Soviet Regime*
   AHR - v101 - D '96 - p1584+ [501+]
   EHR - v112 - Ap '97 - p525+ [501+]
Harden, Blaine - *A River Lost*
   Ant R - v55 - Spr '97 - p241 [251-500]
   Choice - v34 - D '96 - p636 [51-250]
   Econ - v341 - O 19 '96 - p6*+ [501+]
   NYTBR - v101 - Jl 21 '96 - p30
   NYTBR - v101 - D 8 '96 - p92 [1-50]
   VV - v42 - Ja 7 '97 - p43 [51-250]
Harden, Edgar F - *A Checklist of Contributions by William Makepeace Thackeray to Newspapers, Periodicals, Books, and Serial Part Issues 1828-1864*
   r Nine-C Lit - v51 - Mr '97 - p558 [51-250]
   Vanity Fair
   Nine-C Lit - v50 - Mr '96 - p554 [1-50]
Hardie, Kerry - *A Furious Place*
   BL - v93 - F 1 '97 - p921 [51-250]
Hardimon, Michael O - *Hegel's Social Philosophy*
   Phil R - v105 - Ja '96 - p128+ [501+]

Hardin, James - *German Baroque Writers 1580-1660*
   r ARBA - v28 - '97 - p460 [51-250]
Hardin, Russell - *One for All*
   Ethics - v107 - Ja '97 - p361+ [501+]
   J Pol - v58 - Ag '96 - p863+ [501+]
Hardin, Stephen L - *Texian Iliad*
   Roundup M - v3 - Ag '96 - p24+ [501+]
Hardin, Wes - *Henry Ford Museum (Illus. by Wes Hardin)*
   c PW - v244 - Mr 3 '97 - p77 [51-250]
Harding, Anthony John - *The Reception of Myth in English Romanticism*
   Nine-C Lit - v51 - D '96 - p400+ [501+]
Harding, Donal - *The Leaving Summer*
   y CCB-B - v50 - S '96 - p13 [51-250]
   y HB Guide - v8 - Spr '97 - p79 [51-250]
Harding, Gunnar - *Stora Scenen*
   WLT - v70 - Sum '96 - p717 [501+]
Harding, Michael P - *New Plays from the Abbey Theatre 1993-1995*
   Choice - v34 - My '97 - p1497 [51-250]
   ILS - v16 - Spr '97 - p36 [1-50]
Harding, Mildred Davis - *Air-Bird in the Water*
   Choice - v34 - D '96 - p613 [51-250]
   Nine-C Lit - v51 - Mr '97 - p558 [1-50]
Harding, Phillip - *Androtion and the Atthis*
   Rel St Rev - v23 - Ja '97 - p61 [51-250]
Harding, Richard - *The Evolution of the Sailing Navy 1509-1815*
   J Mil II - v60 - O '96 - p772+ [251-500]
Hardle, Wolfgang - *Statistical Theory and Computational Aspects of Smoothing*
   JEL - v35 - Mr '97 - p194+ [51-250]
Hardman, John - *French Politics 1774-1789*
   EHR - v112 - Ap '97 - p494+ [501+]
   HT - v47 - Mr '97 - p52+ [501+]
   Louis XVI
   JMH - v69 - Mr '97 - p157+ [51-250]
Hardt, Hanno - *Newsworkers: Toward a History of the Rank and File*
   JEL - v34 - S '96 - p1467 [51-250]
   WHQ - v27 - Win '96 - p550 [51-250]
Hardwick, Gary - *Double Dead*
   BL - v93 - My 15 '97 - p1566+ [51-250]
   LJ - v122 - My 1 '97 - p140 [51-250]
Hardwick, Joan - *The Yeats Sisters*
   Lon R Bks - v18 - Jl 18 '96 - p20+ [501+]
Hardy, Anna Simpson - *History of Hope, Maine*
   Am Geneal - v71 - Ap '96 - p127+ [251-500]
Hardy, Anne - *The Epidemic Streets*
   EHR - v112 - F '97 - p241+ [501+]
   VS - v39 - Aut '95 - p69+ [501+]
Hardy, Charlotte - *Far from Home*
   BL - v93 - Ja '97 - p820 [51-250]
   LJ - v121 - D '96 - p145 [51-250]
   PW - v243 - N 11 '96 - p57 [51-250]
   y SLJ - v43 - F '97 - p134 [51-250]
Hardy, Edward - *Geyser Life*
   BL - v92 - Ag '96 - p1881 [51-250]
   CSM - v88 - S 9 '96 - p14 [251-500]
   NYTBR - v101 - O 20 '96 - p22 [251-500]
Hardy, Emma Lavinia Gifford - *Letters of Emma and Florence Hardy*
   ELT - v40 - 1 '97 - p77+ [501+]
   Lon R Bks - v18 - N 14 '96 - p22 [501+]
   Nine-C Lit - v51 - D '96 - p424 [1-50]
   TLS - N 1 '96 - p3+ [501+]
Hardy, Gayle J - *Subject Guide to U.S. Government Reference Sources. 2nd Ed.*
   r BL - v93 - Ja '97 - p901 [251-500]
   r Choice - v34 - Mr '97 - p1137 [51-250]
   r R&R Bk N - v12 - F '97 - p103 [51-250]
Hardy, James D - *The New York Giants Base Ball Club*
   Choice - v34 - F '97 - p1002 [51-250]
Hardy, James E - *Mercury Free*
   BL - v93 - O 1 '96 - p313 [51-250]
Hardy, James Earl - *2nd Time Around*
   Advocate - S 17 '96 - p59+ [501+]
   Advocate - O 15 '96 - p85+ [251-500]
   Advocate - Ja 21 '97 - p94 [1-50]
   BL - v93 - S 15 '96 - p220 [51-250]
   KR - v64 - Ag 15 '96 - p1173 [251-500]
   PW - v243 - O 7 '96 - p66 [51-250]
   Boyz II Men
   y Ch BWatch - v6 - N '96 - p2 [51-250]
   c HB Guide - v8 - Spr '97 - p161 [51-250]
Hardy, Melissa A - *Ending a Career in the Auto Industry*
   JEL - v35 - Mr '97 - p237+ [51-250]
   R&R Bk N - v12 - F '97 - p41 [51-250]
Hardy, Sian - *A Treasury of Christmas Stories*
   c Bks Keeps - N '96 - p19 [1-50]

Hardy, Tad - *Lost Cat (Illus. by David Goldin)*
  c HB Guide - v7 - Fall '96 - p258 [51-250]
  c NYTBR - v101 - O 13 '96 - p26 [1-50]
Hardy, Thomas - *The Complete Poetical Works of Thomas Hardy. Vols. 4-5*
    ELT - v39 - 3 '96 - p333+ [501+]
    Nine-C Lit - v51 - D '96 - p423 [1-50]
    RES - v47 - N '96 - p617+ [501+]
  Jude the Obscure
    Ent W - N 8 '96 - p59+ [51-250]
    Woman's J - S '96 - p10 [1-50]
  Life's Little Ironies
    ELT - v40 - 2 '97 - p252 [51-250]
  Moments of Vision and Miscellaneous Verses
    RES - v47 - N '96 - p618+ [501+]
  The Return of the Native (Rickman). Audio Version
    TES - D 27 '96 - p27 [51-250]
  Short Stories by Thomas Hardy
  y TES - S 20 '96 - pR6 [251-500]
  Tess of the D'Urbervilles (Firth). Audio Version
    BL - v93 - F 15 '97 - p1038 [51-250]
  The Woodlanders (Rowe). Audio Version
    TES - D 27 '96 - p27 [51-250]
Hardy-Fanta, Carol - *Latina Politics, Latino Politics*
    Signs - v22 - Aut '96 - p237+ [501+]
Hare, Douglas R A - *Mark*
    Am - v176 - Mr 8 '97 - p27 [51-250]
Hare, John E - *The Moral Gap*
    Choice - v34 - Ap '97 - p1352 [51-250]
Hare, Paul - *An Introduction to the UK Economy. 2nd Ed.*
    JEL - v34 - S '96 - p1405 [51-250]
Hare, Ralph - *Geography in the School Grounds*
    Sch Lib - v44 - N '96 - p176+ [51-250]
Hare, Steve - *Penguin Portrait*
    TES - D 27 '96 - p16 [51-250]
Har-El, Shai - *Struggle for Domination in the Middle East*
    Six Ct J - v27 - Win '96 - p1091+ [501+]
Harenberg, Job - *Nonanticoagulant Actions of Glycosaminoglycans*
    SciTech - v20 - D '96 - p55 [51-250]
Hares, Rod - *BD*
  yp TES - Mr 7 '97 - pR9 [51-250]
Hareven, Shulamith - *Otsar Ha-Milim Shel Ha-Shalom*
    BL - v93 - Mr 1 '97 - p1115 [1-50]
  Thirst: The Desert Trilogy
    NYTBR - v101 - D 15 '96 - p37 [501+]
Hargrave, Margaret Packham - *A Woman of Air*
    Aust Bk R - Je '96 - p46+ [501+]
Hargreaves, Alec G - *Immigration, Race and Ethnicity in Contemporary France*
  r Choice - v34 - O '96 - p366+ [51-250]
  Racism, Ethnicity and Politics in Contemporary Europe
    CS - v25 - S '96 - p593+ [501+]
Hargrove, Erwin C - *Prisoners of Myth*
    J Am St - v30 - Ap '96 - p184+ [501+]
Hargrove, Nancy D - *The Journey toward Ariel*
    RES - v47 - Ag '96 - p451+ [501+]
Haricombe, Lorraine J - *Out in the Cold*
    LQ - v66 - O '96 - p486+ [501+]
    LR - v45 - 6 '96 - p66+ [501+]
Harik, Ramsay M - *Women in the Middle East*
  y BL - v93 - D 1 '96 - p645 [51-250]
  y HB Guide - v8 - Spr '97 - p170 [51-250]
  y SLJ - v43 - Ja '97 - p126 [51-250]
Hariman, Robert - *Political Style*
    JC - v47 - Win '97 - p163+ [501+]
Haring, Bernard - *Priesthood Imperiled*
    BL - v93 - O 1 '96 - p297 [51-250]
Haring, Keith - *Keith Haring: Journals*
    BW - v26 - Ag 25 '96 - p13 [51-250]
    KR - v64 - My 1 '96 - p664 [251-500]
Harjo, Joy - *Reinventing the Enemy's Language*
    Ms - v7 - Mr '97 - p83 [1-50]
    PW - v244 - Ap 21 '97 - p57 [51-250]
  The Spiral of Memory
    WLT - v71 - Win '97 - p200 [51-250]
Harkavy, Oscar - *Curbing Population Growth*
    SF - v75 - D '96 - p745+ [501+]
Harker, Lesley - *Carlos and Little Wolf (Illus. by Lesley Harker)*
  c Bks Keeps - Jl '96 - p11 [51-250]
  c KR - v64 - D 1 '96 - p1737 [51-250]
  Wishing Moon (Illus. by Lesley Harker). Book and Audio Version
  c Sch Lib - v44 - N '96 - p146 [51-250]
Harker, Patrick T - *The Service Productivity and Quality Challenge*
    JEL - v35 - Mr '97 - p168+ [51-250]
Harkness, Helen Leslie - *The Career Chase*
    BL - v93 - My 15 '97 - p1548 [51-250]
    HR Mag - v42 - Mr '97 - p134+ [51-250]

Harkness, Jan - *Nelson Canadian Dictionary of the English Language*
  r Quill & Q - v62 - O '96 - p40 [251-500]
Harkness, Sara - *Parents' Cultural Belief Systems*
    JMF - v59 - F '97 - p233 [251-500]
Harl, Kenneth W - *Coinage in the Roman Economy 300 B.C. to A.D. 700*
    Choice - v34 - F '97 - p1017 [251-500]
    JEL - v35 - Mr '97 - p258 [51-250]
    R&R Bk N - v11 - D '96 - p6 [51-250]
Harlan, Judith - *Puerto Rico: Deciding Its Future*
  y BL - v93 - Ja '97 - p836 [251-500]
  c Ch BWatch - v6 - N '96 - p2 [1-50]
Harlan, Louis R - *All at Sea*
    J Mil H - v61 - Ap '97 - p407+ [501+]
Harland, Alan T - *Choosing Correctional Options That Work*
    Fed Prob - v60 - S '96 - p86+ [501+]
Harland, Bryce - *Collision Course*
    Econ - v341 - O 19 '96 - p8* [501+]
Harland, Jackie - *The Easter Chicks (Illus. by Jackie Harland)*
  c Ch BWatch - v6 - S '96 - p1 [1-50]
  c HB Guide - v7 - Fall '96 - p243 [51-250]
Harland, Richard - *Beyond Superstructuralism*
    MLR - v91 - Jl '96 - p677+ [501+]
Harleman, Ann - *Bitter Lake*
    KR - v64 - N 15 '96 - p1622 [251-500]
    LJ - v122 - Ja '97 - p146 [51-250]
    NYTBR - v102 - F 9 '97 - p26 [501+]
    PW - v243 - D 9 '96 - p62 [51-250]
Harlen, Johnathan - *Fireflies*
  y Aust Bk R - N '96 - p61+ [501+]
Harley, Bill - *Sarah's Story (Illus. by Eve Aldridge)*
  c CBRS - v25 - Win '97 - p62 [51-250]
  c CCB-B - v50 - Mr '97 - p249 [51-250]
  c HB Guide - v8 - Spr '97 - p30 [51-250]
  c SLJ - v43 - Ja '97 - p83 [51-250]
  Sitting Down to Eat (Illus. by Kitty Harvill)
  c Ch BWatch - v6 - Jl '96 - p5 [1-50]
  c Ch BWatch - v7 - Ja '97 - p4 [1-50]
  c HB Guide - v8 - Spr '97 - p30 [51-250]
  c KR - v64 - S 15 '96 - p1411 [51-250]
  c NW - v128 - D 2 '96 - p84 [51-250]
  c SLJ - v43 - Ja '97 - p83 [51-250]
Harley, C Knick - *The Integration of the World Economy 1850-1914. Vols. 1-2*
    JEL - v34 - S '96 - p1473+ [51-250]
Harley, J B - *Cartography in the Traditional East and Southeast Asian Societies*
    GJ - v163 - Mr '97 - p107 [51-250]
  The History of Cartography. Vol. 2, Bk. 2
    T&C - v37 - Ap '96 - p340+ [501+]
Harley, Sharon - *The Timetables of African-American History*
    JSH - v62 - N '96 - p857+ [51-250]
Harley, Trevor A - *The Psychology of Language*
    Choice - v34 - S '96 - p124 [51-250]
Harley Hahn's Internet and Web Yellow Pages. 1997 Ed.
  r CBR - v15 - Spr '97 - p4 [1-50]
Harlin, Lindsey - *From the Margins of Hindu Marriage*
    Am Ethnol - v23 - N '96 - p919+ [501+]
Harline, Craig - *The Burdens of Sister Margaret*
    CHR - v82 - O '96 - p727+ [251-500]
    Ren Q - v49 - Win '96 - p896+ [501+]
Harloe, Michael - *The Sociology of Urban Communities. Vols. 1-3*
    R&R Bk N - v11 - D '96 - p42 [51-250]
Harlow, Barbara - *After Lives*
    MEJ - v51 - Spr '97 - p310 [51-250]
Harlow, Daniel C - *The Greek Apocalypse of Baruch (3 Baruch) in Hellenistic Judaism and Early Christianity*
    Rel St Rev - v23 - Ja '97 - p86 [51-250]
    Rel St Rev - v23 - Ap '97 - p196 [51-250]
Harman, Amanda - *Elephants*
  c HB Guide - v7 - Fall '96 - p345 [51-250]
  c SB - v32 - O '96 - p211 [501+]
  c SLJ - v42 - Ag '96 - p156 [51-250]
  Leopards
  c HB Guide - v7 - Fall '96 - p345 [51-250]
  c SB - v32 - O '96 - p211 [501+]
  c SLJ - v42 - Ag '96 - p156 [51-250]
  Lions
  c Ch BWatch - v7 - Ja '97 - p3 [51-250]
  c HB Guide - v8 - Spr '97 - p127 [51-250]
  c SB - v33 - Mr '97 - p51 [51-250]
  Manatees and Dugongs
  c Ch BWatch - v7 - Ja '97 - p3 [51-250]
  c HB Guide - v8 - Spr '97 - p127 [51-250]
  c SB - v33 - Mr '97 - p51 [51-250]
  c SLJ - v43 - F '97 - p92 [51-250]

  Rhinoceroses
  c Ch BWatch - v7 - Ja '97 - p3 [51-250]
  c HB Guide - v8 - Spr '97 - p127 [51-250]
  c SB - v33 - Mr '97 - p51 [51-250]
  c SLJ - v43 - F '97 - p92 [51-250]
  Sharks
  c HB Guide - v7 - Fall '96 - p343 [51-250]
  c SB - v32 - O '96 - p211 [501+]
  c SLJ - v42 - Ag '96 - p156 [51-250]
  South American Monkeys
  c HB Guide - v7 - Fall '96 - p345 [51-250]
  c SB - v32 - O '96 - p211 [501+]
  c SLJ - v42 - Ag '96 - p156 [51-250]
  Tigers
  c HB Guide - v7 - Fall '96 - p345 [51-250]
  Whales
  c HB Guide - v7 - Fall '96 - p345 [51-250]
  c SB - v32 - O '96 - p211 [501+]
  c SLJ - v42 - Ag '96 - p156 [51-250]
Harman, Barbara Leah - *The New Nineteenth Century*
    Choice - v34 - O '96 - p279 [51-250]
    Nine-C Lit - v51 - D '96 - p422+ [51-250]
Harman, Gilbert - *Moral Relativism and Moral Objectivity*
    IPQ - v37 - Mr '97 - p113+ [501+]
Harmening, Denise M - *Clinical Hematology and Fundamentals of Hemostasis. 3rd Ed.*
    SciTech - v21 - Mr '97 - p48 [51-250]
Harmetz, Aljean - *On the Road to Tara*
    Choice - v34 - My '97 - p1506+ [51-250]
    FIR - v48 - Ja '97 - p103 [501+]
    KR - v64 - S 15 '96 - p1391 [51-250]
    LJ - v122 - F 1 '97 - p80 [51-250]
    PW - v243 - S 9 '96 - p78 [51-250]
    Si & So - v6 - N '96 - p35 [51-250]
Harmless, William - *Augustine and the Catechumenate*
    Am - v175 - N 16 '96 - p25+ [501+]
    CHR - v83 - Ja '97 - p166 [51-250]
    Theol St - v58 - Mr '97 - p161+ [501+]
Harmon, Anne N - *Ambergris and Arrowheads*
    CAY - v17 - Win '96 - p4 [51-250]
  ...And I Never Learned to Yodel
    CAY - v17 - Win '96 - p4 [51-250]
Harmon, Charles - *Using the Internet, Online Services and CD-ROMs for Writing Research and Term Papers*
    Emerg Lib - v24 - S '96 - p41 [51-250]
    SLMQ - v24 - Sum '96 - p221 [51-250]
Harmon, Claude - *The Four Cornerstones of Winning Golf*
    LJ - v121 - O 1 '96 - p53 [1-50]
Harmon, Michael M - *Responsibility as Paradox*
    PAR - v56 - N '96 - p593+ [501+]
    PAR - v56 - N '96 - p596+ [501+]
    PAR - v56 - N '96 - p599+ [501+]
Harmon, Robert B - *John Steinbeck: An Annotated Guide to Biographical Sources*
  r AL - v69 - Mr '97 - p256+ [51-250]
  r ARBA - v28 - '97 - p446 [51-250]
  r Choice - v34 - Mr '97 - p1137 [51-250]
  r R&R Bk N - v12 - F '97 - p89 [51-250]
Harmon, Roy L - *Reinventing the Business*
    Choice - v34 - S '96 - p172 [51-250]
    HR Mag - v41 - Je '96 - p186 [51-250]
Harmony: Forum of the Symphony Orchestra Institute
  p Notes - v53 - D '96 - p535+ [51-250]
Harnack, Andrew - *Animal Rights*
  y Ch BWatch - v6 - My '96 - p5 [51-250]
  y SLJ - v42 - S '96 - p233 [51-250]
  y VOYA - v19 - O '96 - p226 [251-500]
Harness, Cheryl - *Abe Lincoln Goes to Washington 1837-1865 (Illus. by Cheryl Harness)*
  c BL - v93 - Ja '97 - p863+ [251-500]
  c KR - v65 - Ja 1 '97 - p58 [51-250]
  c PW - v244 - Ja 6 '97 - p73 [51-250]
  c SLJ - v43 - Mr '97 - p175 [51-250]
  They're Off! (Illus. by Cheryl Harness)
  c BL - v93 - N 15 '96 - p582 [51-250]
  c HB Guide - v8 - Spr '97 - p173 [1-50]
  c KR - v64 - N 15 '96 - p1669 [51-250]
  c SLJ - v42 - D '96 - p113+ [51-250]
  Young Abe Lincoln
  c BL - v93 - S 1 '96 - p139 [51-250]
  c HB Guide - v7 - Fall '96 - p372 [51-250]
Harnett, Penelope - *History KS1*
    TES - D 13 '96 - p43 [51-250]
Harp, Bill - *Reading and Writing. 2nd Ed.*
    R&R Bk N - v11 - N '96 - p55 [51-250]
Harp, Gillis J - *Positivist Republic*
    AHR - v101 - D '96 - p1630+ [501+]
    Ethics - v107 - O '96 - p192+ [51-250]

Harper, Andrew - *Bad Karma*
    KR - v65 - Mr 15 '97 - p402 [251-500]
    PW - v244 - Mr 24 '97 - p60 [51-250]
Harper, Charles A - *Active Electronic Component Handbook. 2nd Ed.*
    r SciTech - v21 - Mr '97 - p90 [51-250]
Harper, David A - *Entrepreneurship and the Market Process*
    JEL - v34 - D '96 - p2091 [51-250]
    R&R Bk N - v11 - N '96 - p25 [51-250]
Harper, Donna Akiba Sullivan - *Not So Simple*
    NYTBR - v101 - O 27 '96 - p48 [51-250]
Harper, Isabelle - *My Cats Nick and Nora (Illus. by Barry Moser)*
    c RT - v50 - O '96 - p134 [1-50]
    My Dog Rosie (Illus. by Barry Moser)
    c LA - v73 - S '96 - p353 [51-250]
    Our New Puppy (Illus. by Barry Moser)
    c BL - v93 - S 1 '96 - p142+ [51-250]
    c HB Guide - v8 - Spr '97 - p12 [51-250]
    c SLJ - v42 - O '96 - p96 [51-250]
Harper, Jo - *Outrageous, Bodacious Boliver Boggs! (Illus. by JoAnn Adinolfi)*
    c HB Guide - v7 - Fall '96 - p258+ [51-250]
Harper, John - *Inherited Skin Disorders*
    SciTech - v21 - Mr '97 - p66 [51-250]
Harper, Keith - *The Quality of Mercy*
    Choice - v34 - D '96 - p628 [51-250]
Harper, Kimball T - *Natural History of the Colorado Plateau and Great Basin*
    Am Ant - v61 - Ap '96 - p428+ [501+]
Harper, Michael S - *Every Shut Eye Ain't Asleep*
    y BL - v93 - F 15 '97 - p1014 [1-50]
    Honorable Amendments
    ABR - v17 - Ag '96 - p25 [501+]
Harper, Phillip Brian - *Are We Not Men?*
    Bl S - v26 - Fall '96 - p103 [51-250]
    Framing the Margins
    ASInt - v34 - O '96 - p114+ [501+]
Harper, Sue - *Picturing the Past*
    FQ - v49 - Sum '96 - p54+ [501+]
Harper, Tara K - *Grayheart*
    y Kliatt - v30 - N '96 - p14 [51-250]
Harper, Timothy - *The Good Beer Book*
    BL - v93 - Mr 15 '97 - p1216 [51-250]
Harper-Bill, Christopher - *Charters of the Medieval Hospitals of Bury St. Edmunds*
    EHR - v112 - Ap '97 - p438 [251-500]
The HarperCollins Bible Dictionary
    r BL - v93 - Mr 15 '97 - p1259+ [251-500]
    r Ch Today - v41 - Ja 6 '97 - p51+ [51-250]
    r LJ - v122 - F 15 '97 - p127 [51-250]
The HarperCollins Encyclopedia of Catholicism
    r CLW - v66 - Je '96 - p29+ [251-500]
Harpham, Trudy - *Urban Health in Developing Countries*
    GJ - v162 - N '96 - p341 [51-250]
    SciTech - v20 - N '96 - p37 [51-250]
Harpham, Wendy S - *After Cancer*
    LJ - v122 - Ja '97 - p57 [51-250]
    When a Parent Has Cancer
    BL - v93 - F 15 '97 - p974+ [51-250]
    LJ - v122 - F 15 '97 - p156 [51-250]
Harpinski, Richard - *Beyond HTML*
    CBR - v14 - N '96 - p34 [51-250]
Harpley, Avril - *Learning through Play*
    TES - F 14 '97 - p16* [251-500]
Harpman, Jacqueline - *I Who Have Never Known Men*
    BL - v93 - My 1 '97 - p1478 [51-250]
    KR - v65 - My 1 '97 - p679 [51-250]
    LJ - v122 - Ap 1 '97 - p125 [51-250]
    PW - v244 - Ap 21 '97 - p60 [51-250]
Harpprecht, Klaus - *Thomas Mann: Eine Biographie*
    WLT - v70 - Aut '96 - p955+ [501+]
Harpur, James - *Revelations: The Medieval World*
    y SLJ - v42 - D '96 - p33 [1-50]
Harpur, Patrick - *Daimonic Reality*
    Folkl - v107 - '96 - p121 [251-500]
Harpur, Tom - *The Thinking Person's Guide to God*
    CSM - v89 - Ja 8 '97 - p13 [501+]
Harr, Jonathan - *A Civil Action*
    BW - v26 - O 27 '96 - p12 [51-250]
    Ent W - S 27 '96 - p75 [51-250]
    y Kliatt - v31 - Ja '97 - p25 [51-250]
    NYTBR - v101 - S 22 '96 - p40 [51-250]
Harrah, Madge - *My Brother, My Enemy*
    c BL - v93 - My 1 '97 - p1493+ [51-250]
    c KR - v65 - My 1 '97 - p721+ [51-250]
    c PW - v244 - Ap 21 '97 - p73 [51-250]

Harrap, Simon - *Chickadees, Tits, Nuthatches and Treecreepers*
    Choice - v34 - S '96 - p155 [51-250]
    Wildbird - v10 - O '96 - p25 [51-250]
Harrell, Bryan - *Cycling Japan*
    r FEER - v160 - Mr 27 '97 - p51+ [501+]
Harrell, Loree - *Body Speaking Words*
    Quill & Q - v62 - Ag '96 - p36 [251-500]
Harrell, Stevan - *Chinese Historical Microdemography*
    Ch Rev Int - v4 - Spr '97 - p149+ [501+]
    JIH - v27 - Aut '96 - p376+ [501+]
    Cultural Encounters on China's Ethnic Frontiers
    Pac A - v69 - Fall '96 - p404+ [501+]
Harrelson, Walter - *Jews and Christians*
    Rel Ed - v91 - Fall '96 - p612 [1-50]
Harries, Jill - *Sidonius Apollinaris and the Fall of Rome A.D. 407-485*
    AJP - v117 - Win '96 - p663+ [501+]
Harries, Meirion - *The Last Days of Innocence*
    KR - v65 - F 1 '97 - p196 [251-500]
    LJ - v122 - Mr 15 '97 - p73 [51-250]
    PW - v244 - Mr 3 '97 - p58 [51-250]
Harries, Richard - *A Gallery of Reflections*
    CC - v113 - D 11 '96 - p1234 [51-250]
Harrill, Suzanne E - *Empowering You to Love Yourself*
    Rapport - v19 - 4 '96 - p40 [251-500]
Harrington, Ann M - *Japan's Hidden Christians*
    CH - v66 - Mr '97 - p147+ [501+]
Harrington, Anne - *Reenchanted Science*
    Choice - v34 - Ap '97 - p1360 [51-250]
    New Sci - v153 - Mr 1 '97 - p49 [51-250]
    TLS - N 15 '96 - p10+ [501+]
Harrington, Barry - *Unbelievably Good Deals That You Absolutely Can't Get Unless You're a Teacher*
    r EL - v54 - O '96 - p91 [51-250]
Harrington, Brian - *The Flight of the Red Knot*
    NYTBR - v101 - S 1 '96 - p17 [51-250]
    VQR - v72 - Aut '96 - p138*+ [51-250]
Harrington, C Lee - *Soap Fans*
    CS - v25 - N '96 - p812+ [501+]
    SF - v75 - S '96 - p394+ [251-500]
Harrington, Daniel J - *Paul on the Mystery of Israel*
    Rel Ed - v91 - Fall '96 - p603 [1-50]
Harrington, Denis J - *Sports Great Jim Kelly*
    c HB Guide - v7 - Fall '96 - p361 [51-250]
Harrington, Fred Harvey - *Hanging Judge*
    Roundup M - v4 - D '96 - p21 [251-500]
Harrington, Joel F - *Reordering Marriage and Society in Reformation Germany*
    AJS - v102 - S '96 - p638+ [501+]
    CEH - v29 - 2 '96 - p236+ [501+]
    CH - v65 - D '96 - p701+ [501+]
    CHR - v83 - Ja '97 - p99+ [251-500]
    J Soc H - v30 - Win '96 - p534+ [501+]
Harrington, Karen - *Faisons Le Point*
    MLJ - v81 - Spr '97 - p128+ [251-500]
Harrington, Walt - *At the Heart of It*
    BW - v27 - Ja 12 '97 - p12 [51-250]
Harrington, William - *Columbo: The Game Show Killer*
    BL - v92 - Ag '96 - p1886 [51-250]
    Columbo: The Glitter Murder
    BL - v93 - Mr 15 '97 - p1229 [51-250]
    KR - v65 - Ja 1 '97 - p23 [51-250]
    LJ - v122 - F 1 '97 - p111 [1-50]
    PW - v243 - D 16 '96 - p45 [51-250]
    Town on Trial
    Arm Det - v29 - Sum '96 - p338 [51-250]
Harris, A W - *Helicobacter Pylori*
    SciTech - v21 - Mr '97 - p58 [1-50]
Harris, Alex - *A New Life*
    BW - v27 - F 2 '97 - p13 [51-250]
    LJ - v122 - Ja '97 - p152 [51-250]
    PW - v243 - N 18 '96 - p67+ [51-250]
    S Liv - v32 - Mr '97 - p62 [51-250]
Harris, Alice - *The White T*
    Advocate - N 12 '96 - p77+ [501+]
Harris, Anita M - *Broken Patterns*
    BusLR - v21 - 3 '96 - p185+ [501+]
Harris, Anne - *The Nature of Smoke*
    BWatch - v17 - S '96 - p7 [51-250]
    Rapport - v19 - 5 '96 - p37 [251-500]
    y VOYA - v19 - D '96 - p279 [251-500]
Harris, Arthur T - *Despatch on War Operations 23rd February 1942 to 8th May 1945*
    For Aff - v75 - S '96 - p143 [51-250]
Harris, Charlaine - *Dead over Heels*
    KR - v64 - S 1 '96 - p1277 [51-250]
    PW - v243 - S '96 - p116 [51-250]
    Shakespeare's Landlord
    LJ - v121 - O 15 '96 - p112 [51-250]

Harris, Charles Wesley - *Congress and the Governance of the Nation's Capital*
    PSQ - v111 - Fall '96 - p564+ [501+]
Harris, D J - *Law of the European Convention on Human Rights*
    Law Q Rev - v112 - O '96 - p684+ [501+]
Harris, Dan R - *Diet and Nutrition Sourcebook*
    r BWatch - v18 - Mr '97 - p2 [51-250]
    r Choice - v34 - F '97 - p995+ [51-250]
    r R&R Bk N - v12 - F '97 - p96 [51-250]
Harris, Daniel - *The Rise and Fall of Gay Culture*
    Advocate - Ap 29 '97 - p71+ [501+]
    KR - v65 - Mr 15 '97 - p437 [251-500]
    LJ - v122 - Ap 15 '97 - p103 [51-250]
    PW - v244 - Ap 14 '97 - p67+ [251-500]
Harris, David - *The Last Stand*
    Trib Bks - My 11 '97 - p8 [1-50]
    Our War
    BL - v93 - S 15 '96 - p216 [51-250]
    BW - v26 - N 24 '96 - p8 [501+]
    FEER - v159 - O 24 '96 - p55 [251-500]
    LATBR - S 8 '96 - p1+ [501+]
    NYTBR - v101 - S 29 '96 - p21 [51-250]
Harris, Dean A - *Multiculturalism from the Margins*
    WorldV - v12 - O '96 - p7 [51-250]
Harris, Derek - *The Spanish Avantgarde*
    Hisp - v79 - S '96 - p446+ [501+]
Harris, Diane - *The Treasures of the Parthenon and Erechtheion*
    r Rel St Rev - v23 - Ja '97 - p61 [51-250]
Harris, Dorothy Joan - *Cameron and Me (Illus. by Marilyn Mets)*
    c Quill & Q - v63 - Mr '97 - p79 [251-500]
Harris, Eddy L - *Still Life in Harlem*
    KR - v64 - O 1 '96 - p1444 [251-500]
    LATBR - Ja 26 '97 - p6 [501+]
    NYTBR - v101 - D 22 '96 - p10+ [501+]
    PW - v243 - S 9 '96 - p69+ [51-250]
Harris, Elizabeth - *A Good Man's Love*
    BL - v93 - D 1 '96 - p641 [51-250]
    PW - v243 - N 18 '96 - p63 [51-250]
Harris, Errol E - *The Substance of Spinoza*
    RM - v50 - S '96 - p156+ [501+]
Harris, Frank - *The Bomb*
    NS - v126 - Ja 24 '97 - p48 [501+]
Harris, H S - *Hegel: Phenomenology and System*
    CPR - v16 - Ap '96 - p110+ [251-500]
Harris, Henry - *The Cells of the Body*
    Isis - v87 - D '96 - p712+ [501+]
    Identity
    IPQ - v37 - Mr '97 - p105+ [501+]
Harris, Ian - *The Mind of John Locke*
    EHR - v111 - S '96 - p986+ [251-500]
Harris, Irving B - *Children in Jeopardy*
    Choice - v34 - My '97 - p1583 [51-250]
    JEL - v35 - Mr '97 - p235 [51-250]
    PW - v243 - S 2 '96 - p108 [51-250]
Harris, J P - *Men, Ideas and Tanks*
    Albion - v28 - '96 - p726+ [501+]
Harris, Jacqueline L - *The Tuskegee Airmen*
    y BL - v93 - S 1 '96 - p113+ [51-250]
    c HB Guide - v7 - Fall '96 - p380 [51-250]
    y Kliatt - v30 - N '96 - p22 [51-250]
    y SLJ - v42 - S '96 - p233 [51-250]
Harris, James B - *Masted Structures in Architecture*
    Choice - v34 - Mr '97 - p1190+ [51-250]
    SciTech - v20 - N '96 - p60 [51-250]
Harris, James C - *Developmental Neuropsychiatry. Vols. 1-2*
    AJMR - v101 - Jl '96 - p95+ [501+]
Harris, Janet C - *Athletes and the American Hero Dilemma*
    Aethlon - v13 - Fall '95 - p153+ [501+]
Harris, Jay M - *How Do We Know This?*
    Rel St Rev - v22 - O '96 - p350 [51-250]
Harris, Jennifer, 1954- - *The Cultural Meaning of Deafness*
    R&R Bk N - v11 - N '96 - p44 [51-250]
Harris, Jessica - *The Welcome Table*
    PW - v243 - N 25 '96 - p70 [1-50]
Harris, Jim, 1953- - *Getting Employees to Fall in Love with Your Company*
    J Car P&E - v57 - Win '97 - p20+ [51-250]
Harris, Joel Chandler - *Brer Rabbit and the Wonderful Tar Baby (Glover). Audio Version*
    c Trib Bks - F 2 '97 - p7 [1-50]
    Dearest Chums and Partners
    Sew R - v104 - O '96 - pR84+ [501+]

Harris, John, 1931- - *Sir William Chambers: Architect to George III*
   BM - v139 - Ja '97 - p56+ [501+]
   Choice - v34 - Ap '97 - p1326 [51-250]
   TLS - N 8 '96 - p9 [501+]
Harris, Jonathan - *Federal Art and National Culture*
   Art J - v55 - Fall '96 - p95+ [501+]
   J Am Cult - v19 - Sum '96 - p159+ [51-250]
Harris, Jose - *Private Lives, Public Spirit*
   HT - v46 - S '96 - p57 [51-250]
Harris, Joseph Claude - *The Cost of Catholic Parishes and Schools*
   CLW - v67 - Mr '97 - p42+ [51-250]
   Comw - v123 - S 13 '96 - p26+ [501+]
Harris, Kristina - *Vintage Fashions for Women 1920s-1940s*
   Ant & CM - v101 - D '96 - p33 [1-50]
Harris, Lawrence - *Satellite Projects Handbook*
   SciTech - v20 - N '96 - p73 [51-250]
Harris, Lee - *The Passover Murder*
   Arm Det - v29 - Fall '96 - p488 [251-500]
Harris, Lis - *Rules of Engagement*
   NYTBR - v101 - N 10 '96 - p68 [51-250]
Harris, Marcia B - *Helping Your College Student Succeed*
   C&U - v72 - Win '97 - p40 [501+]
   The Parent's Crash Course in Career Planning
   J Car P&E - v57 - Win '97 - p19+ [51-250]
Harris, Mark, 1922- - *Bang the Drum Slowly*
   Aethlon - v13 - Spr '96 - p79+ [501+]
   Diamond: Baseball Writings of Mark Harris
   Aethlon - v13 - Fall '95 - p144+ [251-500]
   It Looked like For Ever
   Aethlon - v13 - Spr '96 - p79+ [501+]
   The Southpaw
   Aethlon - v13 - Spr '96 - p79+ [501+]
   A Ticket for a Seamstitch
   Aethlon - v13 - Spr '96 - p79+ [501+]
Harris, Mary - *My Kid's Allergic to Everything Dessert Cookbook*
   LJ - v122 - Ja '97 - p134 [51-250]
   PW - v243 - N 18 '96 - p73 [51-250]
Harris, Maureen - *Judaism*
   TES - D 6 '96 - pR7 [501+]
Harris, Michael - *The Judas Kiss*
   Arm Det - v30 - Win '97 - p118 [251-500]
Harris, Michael H - *History of Libraries in the Western World. 4th Ed.*
   LQ - v66 - O '96 - p494+ [501+]
Harris, Morgan H - *Hyde Yesterdays*
   EGH - v50 - N '96 - p178 [51-250]
Harris, Nathaniel - *Crown and Parliament*
   c Sch Lib - v44 - N '96 - p174 [51-250]
Harris, Neil - *The Denver Art Museum*
   Bloom Rev - v17 - Ja '97 - p22+ [51-250]
Harris, Neville - *The Law Relating to Schools. 1995 Ed.*
   TES - Ja 24 '97 - p11* [51-250]
Harris, Nicholas - *Oceans: A Fold-Out Book (Illus. by Peter David Scott)*
   c PW - v243 - N 18 '96 - p78 [51-250]
   Rain Forest (Illus. by Colin Woolf)
   c PW - v243 - N 18 '96 - p78 [51-250]
Harris, Nigel - *The Latin and German Etymachia*
   MLR - v91 - O '96 - p1029+ [501+]
Harris, Nigel, 1935- - *The New Untouchables*
   APSR - v90 - S '96 - p697+ [501+]
   TLS - Ag 2 '96 - p12 [501+]
Harris, Nigel G E, 1940- - *Professional Codes of Conduct in the United Kingdom. 2nd Ed.*
   r Choice - v34 - O '96 - p252 [51-250]
Harris, Paul - *The Fire of Silence and Stillness*
   RR - v55 - N '96 - p660+ [1-50]
   The Pantomine Book
   TES - O 11 '96 - p8* [51-250]
Harris, Peter - *Mouse Creeps (Illus. by Reg Cartwright)*
   c CCB-B - v50 - Mr '97 - p249 [51-250]
   c PW - v244 - My 5 '97 - p208 [51-250]
Harris, Philip R - *Managing Cultural Differences. 4th Ed.*
   Choice - v34 - O '96 - p326 [51-250]
Harris, R I D - *Using Cointegration Analysis in Econometric Modelling*
   Econ J - v106 - S '96 - p1465 [51-250]
Harris, Richard, 1942- - *The Sun and Other Stars (Illus. by Dennis Davidson)*
   c SB - v32 - O '96 - p209 [51-250]
Harris, Richard, 1947- - *Hidden Southwest. 3rd Ed.*
   r BWatch - v17 - S '96 - p5 [1-50]
   The Pacific Northwest Travel-Smart Trip Planner
   Bloom Rev - v17 - Ja '97 - p21 [51-250]
   Unique Oregon
   r BL - v93 - S 15 '96 - p210 [1-50]

Harris, Richard, 1952- - *Unplanned Suburbs*
   Choice - v34 - O '96 - p348 [51-250]
   GJ - v163 - Mr '97 - p96 [501+]
   JEL - v34 - D '96 - p2098+ [51-250]
Harris, Richard G - *The Asia Pacific Region in the Global Economy*
   Choice - v34 - My '97 - p1545 [51-250]
Harris, Robert, 1957- - *Enigma*
   Books - v9 - S '95 - p22 [1-50]
   PW - v243 - S 23 '96 - p74 [1-50]
   y SLJ - v42 - D '96 - p33 [1-50]
   TES - Jl 19 '96 - pR6 [51-250]
Harris, Robert L - *Information Graphics*
   r ARBA - v28 - '97 - p622 [51-250]
   r CBR - v15 - Spr '97 - p10 [51-250]
   r Choice - v34 - N '96 - p430 [51-250]
   r RQ - v36 - Win '96 - p297+ [251-500]
Harris, Robie H - *Happy Birth Day! (Illus. by Michael Emberley)*
   c BL - v93 - Ja '97 - p767 [1-50]
   c CBRS - v25 - S '96 - p3 [1-50]
   c HB Guide - v8 - Spr '97 - p30 [51-250]
   c JB - v60 - D '96 - p232 [51-250]
   c Magpies - v11 - S '96 - p28 [51-250]
   c NYTBR - v102 - Mr 30 '97 - p18 [501+]
   c Par Ch - v20 - O '96 - p28 [1-50]
   c Sch Lib - v44 - N '96 - p146 [51-250]
   c SLJ - v42 - D '96 - p29 [1-50]
   c SLJ - v42 - D '96 - p94 [51-250]
Harris, Robin - *Valois Guyenne*
   EHR - v112 - Ap '97 - p453+ [501+]
   Specu - v72 - Ja '97 - p163+ [501+]
Harris, Roma M - *Barriers to Information*
   LQ - v66 - O '96 - p475+ [501+]
Harris, Rosemary - *The Haunting of Joey M'basa (Illus. by Bethan Matthews)*
   c Sch Lib - v44 - Ag '96 - p104 [51-250]
Harris, Roy - *Signs of Writing*
   R&R Bk N - v11 - N '96 - p62 [51-250]
Harris, Ruth-Ann M - *The Nearest Place That Wasn't Ireland*
   JIH - v27 - Aut '96 - p309+ [501+]
   The Search for Missing Friends. Vol. 4
   r Am Geneal - v71 - Ap '96 - p124+ [51-250]
Harris, Ruth Elwin - *Beyond the Orchid House*
   y Magpies - v11 - My '96 - p53 [1-50]
Harris, Sally - *Out of Control*
   Choice - v34 - Ja '97 - p856 [51-250]
Harris, Sharon M - *American Women Writers to 1800*
   W&M Q - v53 - O '96 - p819+ [501+]
Harris, Sheldon H - *Factories of Death*
   Hast Cen R - v26 - S '96 - p37+ [501+]
Harris, Sidney - *There Goes the Neighborhood*
   VQR - v72 - Aut '96 - p139* [51-250]
Harris, Stephen E - *WordPerfect 7 for Windows 95 Bible*
   r Quill & Q - v62 - N '96 - p31 [51-250]
Harris, Stuart - *HTML Publishing for Netscape. Windows Ed.*
   R&R Bk N - v11 - N '96 - p76 [51-250]
Harris, Sue - *Science in Primary Schools*
   TES - Ja 3 '97 - pR14 [51-250]
Harris, Tim - *Popular Culture in England c. 1500-1850*
   Albion - v28 - Sum '96 - p303+ [501+]
Harris, Valentina - *Simply Italian*
   y Kliatt - v31 - My '97 - p30+ [51-250]
Harris, Wendell V - *Literary Meaning*
   TLS - D 6 '96 - p24 [51-250]
Harris, William - *The Middle East after the Cold War*
   MEJ - v51 - Spr '97 - p312 [51-250]
Harris, William W - *Faces of Lebanon*
   For Aff - v76 - My '97 - p143+ [51-250]
   LJ - v121 - O 1 '96 - p104+ [51-250]
   MEQ - v4 - Mr '97 - p86+ [51-250]
Harris, Wilson - *Jonestown*
   Obs - S 1 '96 - p18* [501+]
Harrison, Anthony H - *Gender and Discourse in Victorian Literature and Art*
   VS - v39 - Aut '95 - p79+ [501+]
Harrison, B D - *Polyhedral Virions and Bipartite RNA Genomes*
   SciTech - v20 - S '96 - p26 [51-250]
Harrison, Barbara Grizzuti - *An Accidental Autobiography*
   BW - v26 - Jl 7 '96 - p8 [251-500]
   Comw - v123 - S 13 '96 - p31+ [501+]
   LATBR - Jl 7 '96 - p6 [501+]
   LATBR - D 29 '96 - p10 [51-250]
   NYTBR - v101 - D 8 '96 - p84 [1-50]
   PW - v244 - My 5 '97 - p206 [1-50]
   Trib Bks - My 11 '97 - p8 [1-50]
   Wom R Bks - v14 - N '96 - p20+ [501+]

Harrison, Ben - *Undying Love*
   PW - v243 - S 23 '96 - p67 [51-250]
Harrison, Beverly Wildung - *Our Right to Choose*
   Cons - v17 - Aut '96 - p35+ [501+]
Harrison, Brian - *The Transformation of British Politics 1860-1995*
   CR - v269 - D '96 - p327+ [501+]
   TLS - Ja 3 '97 - p4+ [501+]
Harrison, Christina - *The Paleo-Indian of Southern St. Louis Co., Minnesota*
   Am Ant - v61 - O '96 - p821 [501+]
Harrison, Colin - *Manhattan Nocturne*
   BL - v92 - Ag '96 - p1854 [251-500]
   Ent W - O 25 '96 - p105+ [51-250]
   LATBR - v263 - S 29 '96 - p4+ [501+]
   NYTBR - v101 - O 13 '96 - p13 [501+]
   NYTBR - v101 - O 8 '96 - p80 [1-50]
   PW - v243 - Jl 22 '96 - p226 [51-250]
   Time - v148 - O 7 '96 - p96+ [501+]
   VV - v41 - O 1 '96 - p39+ [501+]
   Manhattan Nocturne (Rubenstein). Audio Version
   PW - v243 - N 4 '96 - p30+ [51-250]
Harrison, D M - *The Organization of Europe*
   Wil Q - v21 - Win '97 - p38 [51-250]
Harrison, David - *Experiments in Virtual Reality*
   SciTech - v20 - N '96 - p11 [51-250]
Harrison, David L - *The Animals' Song (Illus. by Chris L Demarest)*
   c BL - v93 - Ap 1 '97 - p1337 [51-250]
   c KR - v65 - Mr 1 '97 - p381 [51-250]
   c SLJ - v43 - Mr '97 - p160 [51-250]
   A Thousand Cousins (Illus. by Betsy Lewin)
   c HB Guide - v7 - Fall '96 - p367 [1-50]
Harrison, G Ainsworth - *The Human Biology of the English Village*
   Nature - v383 - O 3 '96 - p406 [501+]
Harrison, George H - *The Backyard Bird Watcher*
   LJ - v121 - D '96 - p66 [1-50]
   Garden Birds of America
   Wildbird - v10 - O '96 - p25 [51-250]
Harrison, Harry - *King and Emperor*
   KR - v64 - My 1 '96 - p649+ [251-500]
   The Stainless Steel Rat Goes to Hell
   KR - v64 - S 1 '96 - p1282 [51-250]
   LJ - v121 - O 15 '96 - p93 [51-250]
   PW - v243 - O 21 '96 - p74 [51-250]
Harrison, Henry Ford - *Jimbo on Board the Nettie Quill (Illus. by Jeffrey Hurst)*
   c HB Guide - v7 - Fall '96 - p259 [51-250]
Harrison, James - *The Young People's Atlas of the United States. Rev. 1996, New Ed.*
   cr BL - v93 - D 15 '96 - p749+ [251-500]
   cr PW - v243 - S 16 '96 - p85 [51-250]
   cr SLJ - v42 - N '96 - p137 [51-250]
Harrison, James P - *Mastering the Sky*
   LJ - v121 - N 1 '96 - p105 [51-250]
Harrison, Jamie - *The Edge of the Crazies*
   Arm Det - v29 - Sum '96 - p281 [51-250]
   Going Local
   Arm Det - v30 - Win '97 - p88+ [251-500]
   LATBR - Ag 18 '96 - p10 [501+]
Harrison, Jeffrey - *Signs of Arrival*
   LJ - v121 - S 15 '96 - p72 [51-250]
Harrison, Jennifer - *Cabramatta/Cudmirrah*
   Aust Bk R - F '97 - p44+ [501+]
   Mosaics and Mirrors
   Aust Bk R - Ag '96 - p59+ [501+]
Harrison, Joanna - *When Mom Turned into a Monster*
   c BL - v93 - N 15 '96 - p594 [51-250]
Harrison, Joseph - *The Spanish Economy*
   JEL - v34 - D '96 - p2119 [51-250]
Harrison, Joyce - *Instructional Strategies for Secondary School Physical Education. 4th Ed.*
   R&R Bk N - v11 - N '96 - p22 [51-250]
Harrison, Kathryn - *The Kiss*
   BL - v93 - Mr 1 '97 - p1094 [51-250]
   CSM - v89 - Ap 3 '97 - p14 [51-250]
   KR - v65 - F 15 '97 - p271+ [251-500]
   New R - v216 - Mr 31 '97 - p32+ [501+]
   NW - v129 - F 17 '97 - p62 [501+]
   NYTBR - v102 - Mr 30 '97 - p11 [501+]
   NYTLa - v146 - F 27 '97 - pC18 [501+]
   Obs - Ap 13 '97 - p17* [501+]
   PW - v244 - F 10 '97 - p71 [51-250]
   Time - v149 - Mr 10 '97 - p90 [251-500]
   Trib Bks - Ap 20 '97 - p3 [501+]
   VLS - Spr '97 - p16+ [501+]
   WSJ-Cent - v99 - Mr 4 '97 - pA16 [501+]
   Poison
   NYTBR - v101 - S 8 '96 - p36 [51-250]

Harrison, Kathryn, 1958- - *Risk, Science, and Politics*
  CS - v25 - S '96 - p651+ [501+]
  Pol Stud J - v24 - Sum '96 - p333 [51-250]
  SSQ - v77 - Je '96 - p466 [251-500]
Harrison, Lawrence E - *The Pan-American Dream*
  BL - v93 - N 1 '96 - p464 [51-250]
  BW - v27 - Ja 19 '97 - p5 [501+]
  Econ - v342 - Mr 15 '97 - p5*+ [501+]
  For Aff - v76 - My '97 - p137+ [251-500]
  KR - v64 - N 1 '96 - p1581 [51-250]
  LJ - v121 - D '96 - p110 [51-250]
  WSJ-Cent - v99 - My 22 '97 - pA13 [501+]
Harrison, Lowell H - *A New History of Kentucky*
  LJ - v122 - My 1 '97 - p120 [51-250]
Harrison, Lynn C - *Practicing Responsible Tourism*
  R&R Bk N - v11 - D '96 - p19 [1-50]
Harrison, Mark - *Public Health in British India*
  EHR - v111 - N '96 - p1330+ [501+]
Harrison, Martin - *Lisa Fonssagrives, a Portrait*
  NYTBR - v102 - F 9 '97 - p21 [251-500]
  VV - v52 - Ja 28 '97 - p48+ [501+]
Harrison, Maureen - *Freedom of Religion Decisions of the United States Supreme Court*
  r ARBA - v28 - '97 - p538+ [51-250]
  Freedom of Speech Decisions of the United States Supreme Court
  r ARBA - v28 - '97 - p244 [51-250]
  Freedom of the Press Decisions of the United States Supreme Court
  r ARBA - v28 - '97 - p350+ [51-250]
  Thinking about God
  y TES - D 6 '96 - pR6 [251-500]
Harrison, Michael - *New Oxford Treasury of Children's Poems*
  c Emerg Lib - v24 - Mr '97 - p45 [1-50]
  The Oxford Treasury of Classic Poems
  c Bks Keeps - Ja '97 - p24+ [251-500]
  y BL - v93 - D 15 '96 - p723 [51-250]
  c JB - v60 - D '96 - p267 [51-250]
  c Sch Lib - v45 - F '97 - p43 [51-250]
  A Year Full of Poems
  c Bks Keeps - Ja '97 - p21 [51-250]
  c Ch BWatch - v6 - N '96 - p5 [51-250]
Harrison, Michael J G - *Clinical Skills in Neurology*
  SciTech - v20 - N '96 - p41 [51-250]
Harrison, Michael R - *Atlas of Fetal Surgery*
  r SciTech - v20 - D '96 - p52 [51-250]
Harrison, Patricia - *Science in Action Books 1-4*
  c TES - S 27 '96 - pR8 [51-250]
Harrison, Paul - *Caring for the Future*
  CF - v75 - N '96 - p42+ [501+]
Harrison, Pegram - *Frankenthaler: A Catalogue Raisonne, Prints 1961-1994*
  r AB - v99 - Mr 3 '97 - p694 [51-250]
  r NYTBR - v102 - Ja 19 '97 - p19 [51-250]
  r PW - v243 - D 9 '96 - p58 [51-250]
Harrison, Peter - *Claude Monet*
  c CCB-B - v50 - S '96 - p13+ [51-250]
  c Ch BWatch - v6 - Jl '96 - p1 [1-50]
  c HB Guide - v8 - Spr '97 - p138 [51-250]
  c SLJ - v42 - Ag '96 - p156 [51-250]
  Vincent Van Gogh
  c CCB-B - v50 - S '96 - p13+ [51-250]
  c Ch BWatch - v6 - Jl '96 - p1 [51-250]
  c HB Guide - v8 - Spr '97 - p138 [51-250]
  c SLJ - v42 - Ag '96 - p156 [51-250]
Harrison, Robert T - *Gladstone's Imperialism in Egypt*
  AHR - v102 - F '97 - p109+ [501+]
  Albion - v28 - '96 - p745+ [51-250]
  Historian - v59 - Fall '96 - p190+ [251-500]
Harrison, S J - *Homage to Horace*
  Rel St Rev - v23 - Ja '97 - p65 [51-250]
Harrison, Sarah - *Life after Lunch*
  Woman's J - F '97 - p16 [1-50]
Harrison, Selig S - *UN Peacekeeping*
  NWCR - v50 - Win '97 - p140+ [501+]
  The United States, Japan, and the Future of Nuclear Weapons
  Arm F&S - v23 - Fall '96 - p118+ [501+]
  Parameters - v26 - Aut '96 - p146+ [501+]
Harrison, Taylor - *Enterprise Zones*
  LJ - v121 - O 1 '96 - p78 [51-250]
  Quill & Q - v62 - Ag '96 - p25 [251-500]
  TLS - Ja 3 '97 - p18+ [501+]
Harrison, Teresa M - *Computer Networking and Scholarly Communication in the Twenty-First-Century University*
  Choice - v34 - O '96 - p315 [51-250]
  R&R Bk N - v12 - F '97 - p97 [51-250]

Harrison, Thomas J - *1910: The Emancipation of Dissonance*
  ABR - v18 - D '96 - p24+ [501+]
  Choice - v34 - S '96 - p187 [51-250]
  Notes - v53 - Mr '97 - p767+ [501+]
  Essayism: Conrad, Musil and Pirandello
  CLS - v33 - 2 '96 - p225+ [501+]
Harrison, Tony - *Permanently Bard*
  WLT - v71 - Win '97 - p157 [501+]
Harrison, Trevor - *Of Passionate Intensity*
  Can Hist R - v77 - S '96 - p454+ [501+]
  CS - v26 - Ja '97 - p30+ [501+]
Harrison, Troon - *Aaron's Awful Allergies (Illus. by Eugenie Fernandes)*
  c Quill & Q - v62 - S '96 - p73 [251-500]
  Don't Dig So Deep, Nicholas! (Illus. by Gary Clement)
  c Quill & Q - v63 - F '97 - p59 [251-500]
Harriss, John - *The New Institutional Economics and Third World Development*
  Econ J - v107 - Ja '97 - p280 [251-500]
  JEL - v34 - D '96 - p2109+ [51-250]
  R&R Bk N - v11 - D '96 - p22 [51-250]
Harrisson, Barbara - *Later Ceramics in South-East Asia Sixteenth to Twentieth Centuries*
  Ceram Mo - v44 - O '96 - p30 [251-500]
  Choice - v34 - O '96 - p267 [51-250]
Harriss-White, Barbara - *A Political Economy of Agricultural Markets in South India*
  R&R Bk N - v12 - F '97 - p15 [51 250]
Harrisville, Roy A - *The Bible in Modern Culture*
  Bks & Cult - v2 - Mr '96 - p31 [251-500]
  Intpr - v51 - Ja '97 - p100+ [251-500]
  TT - v53 - O '96 - p414+ [501+]
Harris-Warrick, Rebecca - *Musical Theatre at the Court of Louis XIV*
  Dance RJ - v28 - Fall '96 - p75+ [501+]
  MLR - v91 - Jl '96 - p720+ [501+]
Harrod-Eagles, Cynthia - *Blood Lines*
  y BL - v93 - D 15 '96 - p712 [51-250]
  KR - v64 - O 1 '96 - p1427+ [251-500]
  LJ - v121 - N 1 '96 - p111 [1-50]
  NYTBR - v101 - D 8 '96 - p50 [51-250]
  PW - v243 - O 21 '96 - p73 [251-500]
  Grave Music
  Arm Det - v29 - Sum '96 - p281 [51-250]
  PW - v243 - O 14 '96 - p81 [1-50]
Harrold, Peter - *Practical Lessons for Africa from East Asia in Industrial and Trade Policies*
  JEL - v34 - D '96 - p2119+ [51-250]
Harrold, Stanley - *The Abolitionists and the South 1831-1861*
  AHR - v101 - O '96 - p1283 [501+]
  Historian - v58 - Sum '96 - p859 [251-500]
Harron, Mary - *I Shot Andy Warhol*
  Obs - Ja 26 '97 - p18* [51-250]
  Si & So - v6 - N '96 - p36 [1-50]
Harrop, Jeffrey - *Structural Funding and Employment in the European Union*
  Econ J - v107 - Ja '97 - p277 [251-500]
  JEL - v34 - D '96 - p2048 [51-250]
  R&R Bk N - v11 - D '96 - p25 [51-250]
Harrow, Kenneth W - *The Marabout and the Muse*
  Bl S - v26 - Fall '96 - p103 [51-250]
  Choice - v34 - F '97 - p961 [51-250]
Harrowitz, Nancy A - *Jews and Gender*
  Ger Q - v69 - Spr '96 - p219+ [501+]
  TLS - Ag 2 '96 - p9+ [501+]
  Tainted Greatness
  MLR - v92 - Ja '97 - p143+ [501+]
Harrs, Norma - *Love Minus One and Other Stories*
  Can Lit - Spr '97 - p214+ [501+]
Harsany, Stephen C - *Principles of Microwave Technology*
  SciTech - v20 - D '96 - p79 [51-250]
Harsch, Donna - *German Social Democracy and the Rise of Nazism*
  EHR - v111 - S '96 - p1022+ [501+]
  JMH - v68 - S '96 - p629+ [501+]
Harsch, Rick - *The Driftless Zone*
  KR - v65 - My 1 '97 - p663 [251-500]
  PW - v244 - My 5 '97 - p199 [51-250]
Hart, Alison - *Haunted Horseback Holiday*
  c SLJ - v42 - S '96 - p202 [51-250]
Hart, Avery - *Kids Garden!*
  c Ch BWatch - v6 - My '96 - p7 [51-250]
  c CSM - v89 - F 27 '97 - pB2 [51-250]
Hart, Carolyn - *Deadly Valentine (Reading). Audio Version*
  LJ - v121 - D '96 - p169+ [51-250]

Death in Lovers' Lane
  BL - v93 - Ja '97 - p825 [51-250]
  KR - v64 - D 1 '96 - p1705+ [51-250]
  LATBR - F 16 '97 - p10 [51-250]
  LJ - v122 - Ja '97 - p153 [1-50]
  PW - v243 - D 9 '96 - p62+ [51-250]
Hart, Catherine - *Charmed*
  PW - v243 - N 4 '96 - p71 [51-250]
Hart, Clive - *Heaven and the Flesh*
  Choice - v34 - S '96 - p112+ [51-250]
Hart, D G - *Defending the Faith*
  CH - v65 - D '96 - p753+ [501+]
  Fighting the Good Fight
  CH - v65 - D '96 - p771+ [501+]
Hart, E Richard - *Zuni and the Courts*
  WHQ - v28 - Spr '97 - p78+ [501+]
Hart, Ellen - *The Oldest Sin*
  PW - v243 - N 18 '96 - p70 [51-250]
  Robber's Wine
  BL - v93 - S 1 '96 - p67 [51-250]
  Bloom Rev - v16 - Jl '96 - p21 [1-50]
Hart, Gail K - *Tragedy in Paradise*
  Choice - v34 - O '96 - p284 [51-250]
Hart, Gary - *The Patriot: An Exhortation to Liberate America from the Barbarians*
  BW - v26 - Ag 18 '96 - p4 [251-500]
  KR - v64 - My 1 '96 - p664+ [251-500]
Hart, Henry - *Robert Lowell and the Sublime*
  AL - v68 - S '96 - p654+ [251-500]
Hart, James D - *The Oxford Companion to American Literature. 6th Ed.*
  r Ant R - v54 - Sum '96 - p379 [51-250]
  r ARBA - v28 - '97 - p441 [251-500]
  r Nine-C Lit - v51 - D '96 - p423 [51-250]
Hart, Janet - *New Voices in the Nation*
  AJS - v102 - Ja '97 - p1216+ [501+]
  Choice - v34 - O '96 - p339+ [51-250]
Hart, John, 1948- - *Storm over Mono*
  Choice - v34 - D '96 - p631 [51-250]
  TLS - My 24 '96 - p36 [1-50]
  WHQ - v28 - Spr '97 - p103 [1-50]
Hart, Jonathan - *Imagining Culture*
  R&R Bk N - v11 - N '96 - p65 [51-250]
  Reading the Renaissance
  Choice - v34 - S '96 - p118+ [51-250]
Hart, Josephine - *Oblivion*
  PW - v244 - Ap 21 '97 - p69 [1-50]
Hart, M B - *Biotic Recovery from Mass Extinction Events*
  Sci - v274 - N 8 '96 - p936 [251-500]
Hart, Philip S - *Up in the Air*
  c BL - v92 - Ag '96 - p1898 [51-250]
  c HB Guide - v8 - Spr '97 - p158 [51-250]
  c SLJ - v42 - Ag '96 - p156 [51-250]
Hart, Richard E - *Philosophy in Experience*
  LJ - v121 - D '96 - p97 [51-250]
Hart, Robert A - *Human Capital, Employment and Bargaining*
  JEL - v34 - S '96 - p1446 [51-250]
Hart, Robert A De J - *Forest Gardening*
  LJ - v121 - N 15 '96 - p80 [51-250]
Hart, Sergiu - *Game and Economic Theory*
  Econ J - v107 - Ja '97 - p215+ [501+]
Hart, Stephen - *The Language of Animals*
  y SB - v32 - O '96 - p205+ [251-500]
Hart, Tom - *Wei Jingsheng and the Prospects for Democracy in China*
  Ch Rev Int - v4 - Spr '97 - p153+ [501+]
Hart, Trevor - *Faith Thinking*
  BL - v93 - Ja '97 - p784 [51-250]
Hart, Ursula Kingsmill - *Behind the Courtyard Door*
  MEJ - v50 - Sum '96 - p452 [51-250]
Hart, Vaughan - *Art and Magic in the Court of the Stuarts*
  EHR - v112 - Ap '97 - p468+ [501+]
  HT - v46 - Jl '96 - p57 [501+]
Hart, Vivien - *Bound by Our Constitution*
  J Am St - v30 - Ap '96 - p186+ [251-500]
Hart, W D - *The Philosophy of Mathematics*
  SciTech - v20 - D '96 - p4 [51-250]
Harte, John - *The Green Fuse*
  LATBR - Mr 17 '96 - p11 [1-50]
Hartel, Lynda Jones - *Sexual Harassment*
  r RQ - v36 - Fall '96 - p136+ [501+]
Hartel, Paul - *The Kidnapping of the Painter Miro*
  PW - v244 - F 24 '97 - p70 [1-50]
Harter, Deborah A - *Bodies in Pieces*
  Choice - v34 - Ja '97 - p794+ [51-250]
Harter, H Leon - *CRC Handbook of Tables for the Use of Order Statistics in Estimation*
  Choice - v34 - D '96 - p647 [51-250]

Hartfield-Mendez, Vialla - *Woman and the Infinite*
Choice - v34 - N '96 - p464 [51-250]
Hartford, William F - *Where Is Our Responsibility?*
Choice - v34 - Ap '97 - p1387 [51-250]
Harthan, John - *Books of Hours and Their Owners*
AB - v99 - Mr 3 '97 - p685+ [501+]
Hartigan, Karelisa V - *Greek Tragedy on the American Stage*
r Theat J - v49 - Mr '97 - p92+ [501+]
Harting, Toni - *French River*
BIC - v25 - S '96 - p10+ [501+]
Hartje, Tod - *From behind the Red Line*
Mac - v109 - D 16 '96 - p73 [51-250]
Hartle, Ann - *Self-Knowledge in the Age of Theory*
Cres - v60 - Christmas '96 - p29+ [501+]
Hartley, John - *The Politics of Pictures*
JPC - v29 - Spr '96 - p235+ [501+]
Hartley, Marsden - *Somehow a Past*
NYTBR - v101 - D 22 '96 - p22 [501+]
PW - v243 - D 2 '96 - p48 [51-250]
Hartman, Bob - *A Night the Stars Danced for Joy (Illus. by Tim Jonke)*
c Bks Keeps - N '96 - p19 [1-50]
c PW - v243 - S 30 '96 - p92 [51-250]
c TES - D 6 '96 - p17* [501+]
Hartman, Charles O - *Virtual Muse*
BL - v93 - S 1 '96 - p56 [51-250]
Hartman, Cherry - *The Fearless Flyer*
J Account - v182 - D '96 - p99 [51-250]
The Well-Heeled Murders
Arm Det - v30 - Win '97 - p95 [251-500]
Hartman, Donald K - *Historical Figures in Fiction*
r RQ - v36 - Win '96 - p209+ [51-250]
Hartman, Edwin M - *Organizational Ethics and the Good Life*
Rel St Rev - v23 - Ap '97 - p160+ [51-250]
Hartman, Geoffrey H - *The Longest Shadow*
Nat - v263 - N 11 '96 - p30+ [501+]
Salm - Fall '96 - p226+ [501+]
TLS - Mr 7 '97 - p3+ [501+]
Hartman, Keith - *Congregations in Conflict*
HG&LRev - v3 - Fall '96 - p44+ [501+]
Rel St Rev - v23 - Ja '97 - p93+ [51-250]
Hartman, Linda - *Gallery of Teddy Bears*
Ant & CM - v101 - O '96 - p55 [51-250]
Hartman, Moshe - *Gender Equality and American Jews*
Choice - v34 - Mr '97 - p1244+ [51-250]
R&R Bk N - v11 - D '96 - p14 [51-250]
Hartmann, Frederick H - *America's Foreign Policy in a Changing World*
NWCR - v50 - Win '97 - p139+ [501+]
Hartmann, Wendy - *The Dinosaurs Are Back and It's All Your Fault, Edward! (Illus. by Niki Daly)*
c JB - v60 - D '96 - p232 [51-250]
c KR - v65 - Mr 15 '97 - p461 [51-250]
c PW - v244 - Ap 14 '97 - p74 [51-250]
c TES - Ja 10 '97 - p8* [501+]
Hartmann, William K - *Mars Underground*
PW - v244 - My 12 '97 - p62+ [51-250]
Hartnett, Sonya - *The Devil Latch*
y Magpies - v11 - My '96 - p50 [51-250]
Hartog, Diana - *The Photographer's Sweethearts*
ABR - v18 - O '96 - p20+ [501+]
Rapport - v19 - 4 '96 - p25 [251-500]
Hartshorn, Nick - *Catch: A Discovery of America*
BL - v93 - N 1 '96 - p476+ [51-250]
LJ - v121 - D '96 - p127 [51-250]
PW - v243 - S 23 '96 - p66+ [51-250]
Trib Bks - Mr 30 '97 - p3 [501+]
Hartwell, David G - *Age of Wonders*
Analog - v117 - Ja '97 - p141+ [51-250]
VOYA - v19 - F '97 - p356 [51-250]
The Science Fiction Century
y BL - v93 - My 15 '97 - p1567 [51-250]
Visions of Wonder
Analog - v117 - Ap '97 - p147+ [51-250]
BW - v26 - N 24 '96 - p6 [251-500]
LJ - v121 - N 15 '96 - p92 [51-250]
PW - v243 - O 14 '96 - p80 [51-250]
Hartwell, R M - *A History of the Mont Pelerin Society*
Econ J - v107 - Ja '97 - p261 [51-250]
TLS - Jl 19 '96 - p32 [251-500]
Hartwig, Andreas - *Algebraic 3-D Modeling*
SciTech - v20 - D '96 - p13 [51-250]
Hartzell, Gary N - *The Work Lives of First-Year Assistant Principals*
EL - v54 - S '96 - p88 [251-500]
Hartzmark, Gini - *Bitter Business*
PW - v243 - O 14 '96 - p81 [1-50]

Harvard, Gareth - *Action and Reflection in Teacher Education*
MLJ - v80 - Fall '96 - p400+ [501+]
Harvard Conference on the Internet and Society (1996: Cambridge, Mass.) - *The Harvard Conference on the Internet and Society*
LJ - v122 - My 1 '97 - p133 [51-250]
The Harvard International Journal of Press/Politics
p LJ - v121 - N 15 '96 - p94 [51-250]
p TLS - Mr 7 '97 - p28 [501+]
Harvard University. Art Museums - *Harvard's Art Museums*
Choice - v34 - D '96 - p602 [51-250]
LJ - v121 - S 15 '96 - p63+ [51-250]
Harvard University. Library - *A Catalogue of the Fifteenth-Century Printed Books in the Harvard University Library. Vol. 4*
r ARBA - v28 - '97 - p247 [51-250]
Harvey, A D - *Sex in Georgian England*
Eight-C St - v30 - Spr '97 - p324+ [501+]
RES - v47 - Ag '96 - p432+ [501+]
Harvey, A E - *Renewal through Suffering*
TLS - Ja 17 '97 - p31 [501+]
Harvey, Anne - *Criminal Records (Illus. by Peter Viccars)*
c Bks Keeps - v100 - S '96 - p13 [51-250]
c TES - N 8 '96 - p9* [51-250]
Swings and Shadows
c JB - v60 - D '96 - p267 [51-250]
Harvey, Anthony - *The Funeral Effigies of Westminster Abbey*
EHR - v112 - Ap '97 - p465+ [501+]
Harvey, Barry - *Politics of the Theological*
JR - v77 - Ap '97 - p320+ [501+]
Harvey, Brian M A - *The New Russian Space Programme*
Choice - v34 - N '96 - p480+ [51-250]
Harvey, Brian W - *The Violin Family and Its Makers in the British Isles*
r Notes - v53 - D '96 - p442+ [501+]
Harvey, Charles, M A - *Constraints on the Success of Structural Adjustment Programmes in Africa*
JEL - v34 - S '96 - p1482 [51-250]
Harvey, Charles - *Databases in Historical Research*
R&R Bk N - v11 - N '96 - p9 [51-250]
Harvey, Clay - *A Flash of Red*
LATBR - Jl 7 '96 - p10+ [51-250]
Rapport - v19 - 4 '96 - p23 [251-500]
A Whisper of Black
KR - v65 - F 15 '97 - p243 [251-500]
LJ - v122 - Mr 15 '97 - p90 [51-250]
PW - v244 - Mr 3 '97 - p66 [51-250]
Harvey, David - *Justice, Nature and the Geography of Difference*
Lon R Bks - v19 - Ap 24 '97 - p22+ [501+]
Harvey, Elizabeth - *Youth and the Welfare State in Weimar Germany*
JMH - v68 - S '96 - p629+ [501+]
Harvey, Graham - *The Killing of the Countryside*
NS - v126 - Mr 21 '97 - p52+ [501+]
Obs - Mr 2 '97 - p15* [501+]
Woman's J - Ap '97 - p18 [51-250]
Harvey, Haila - *The Envelope Mill*
Learning - v25 - Mr '97 - p70 [1-50]
Harvey, James Neal - *Dead Game*
BL - v93 - My 1 '97 - p1482 [51-250]
KR - v65 - Ap 1 '97 - p486 [251-500]
LJ - v122 - Ap 1 '97 - p125+ [51-250]
PW - v244 - Mr 10 '97 - p53 [51-250]
Harvey, Janet - *Traditional Textiles of Central Asia*
Choice - v34 - S '96 - p113 [51-250]
TCI - v30 - N '96 - p76+ [501+]
Harvey, John - *Easy Meat*
BL - v92 - Ag '96 - p1854 [251-500]
BL - v93 - Ja '97 - p762 [1-50]
NYTBR - v101 - S 29 '96 - p28 [51-250]
Woman's J - S '96 - p10 [51-250]
Living Proof
Books - v9 - S '95 - p18 [51-250]
Harvey, John Robert - *Men in Black*
Choice - v34 - S '96 - p109+ [51-250]
Harvey, Karen D - *How to Teach about American Indians*
Choice - v34 - S '96 - p180 [51-250]
r Emerg Lib - v24 - S '96 - p39 [51-250]
VOYA - v19 - F '97 - p357 [251-500]
Harvey, Miles - *Deion Sanders: Prime Time*
c HB Guide - v7 - Fall '96 - p359 [1-50]
Women's Voting Rights
c HB Guide - v8 - Spr '97 - p92 [51-250]
c SLJ - v43 - F '97 - p92 [51-250]
Harvey, P D A - *A Guide to British Medieval Seals*
R&R Bk N - v11 - N '96 - p9 [51-250]

Mappa Mundi
BC - v45 - Aut '96 - p389 [51-250]
Choice - v34 - D '96 - p662 [51-250]
R&R Bk N - v11 - D '96 - p19 [51-250]
Harvey, Paul - *New Uses for New Phylogenies*
New Sci - v151 - S 28 '96 - p49 [1-50]
Harvey, Robert C - *The Art of the Funnies*
Humor - v9 - 3 '96 - p410+ [501+]
J Am Cult - v19 - Sum '96 - p138 [501+]
Harvey, Roland - *Roland Harvey's Drawing Book*
c Magpies - v11 - Jl '96 - p40+ [51-250]
Harvey, Ross - *An Index of Civilisation*
r Lib & Cul - v32 - Win '97 - p151+ [501+]
Harvey, Sally Peltier - *Redefining the American Dream*
WAL - v31 - Sum '96 - p185+ [251-500]
Harvey, Van A - *Feuerbach and the Interpretation of Religion*
CC - v114 - Ap 9 '97 - p362+ [501+]
Choice - v34 - D '96 - p626 [51-250]
CPR - v16 - O '96 - p350+ [501+]
Rel St - v32 - D '96 - p521+ [501+]
Harvor, Elisabeth - *Let Me Be the One*
BL - v93 - Ap 1 '97 - p1281 [51-250]
KR - v65 - F 1 '97 - p160 [251-500]
Mac - v109 - N 18 '96 - p82 [501+]
Mac - v109 - D 9 '96 - p64 [1-50]
PW - v244 - F 17 '97 - p209 [51-250]
Quill & Q - v62 - S '96 - p65 [251-500]
Harwell, Ernie - *The Babe Signed My Shoe*
Aethlon - v13 - Spr '96 - p226+ [251-500]
Harwit, Martin - *An Exhibit Denied*
Apo - v144 - D '96 - p13 [251-500]
A & S Sm - v11 - F '97 - p87* [501+]
BW - v27 - Mr 2 '97 - p1+ [501+]
Choice - v34 - Ap '97 - p1360 [51-250]
J Mil H - v61 - Ap '97 - p419+ [501+]
LJ - v121 - D '96 - p116 [51-250]
Nature - v384 - D 12 '96 - p525+ [501+]
New Sci - v153 - F 8 '97 - p44 [51-250]
Harwood, Jonathan - *Styles of Scientific Thought*
Isis - v87 - D '96 - p748+ [501+]
Harwood, Richard - *Talking Tidewater*
BW - v26 - Jl 14 '96 - p12 [51-250]
Hasan, Mushirul - *Legacy of a Divided Nation*
LJ - v122 - Mr 15 '97 - p76 [51-250]
Haseler, Stephen - *The English Tribe*
Choice - v34 - N '96 - p517+ [51-250]
Spec - v277 - N 23 '96 - p45 [1-50]
Haseley, Dennis - *Crosby (Illus. by Jonathan Green)*
c CBRS - v25 - Win '97 - p63 [51-250]
c HB Guide - v8 - Spr '97 - p30 [51-250]
c Par - v72 - F '97 - p149 [51-250]
c PW - v243 - S 2 '96 - p131 [51-250]
c SLJ - v42 - S '96 - p180 [51-250]
Haseloff, Cynthia - *The Chains of Sarai Stone (Merlington). Audio Version*
y Kliatt - v30 - N '96 - p38 [51-250]
Man without Medicine
y BL - v93 - N 15 '96 - p570 [51-250]
Roundup M - v4 - D '96 - p27 [51-250]
Hasenyager, Bruce W - *Managing the Information Ecology*
R&R Bk N - v12 - F '97 - p37 [51-250]
Hashimoto, Koichi - *Visual Servoing*
Robotica - v14 - S '96 - p585+ [501+]
Hasian, Marouf Arif - *The Rhetoric of Eugenics in Anglo-American Thought*
Isis - v88 - Mr '97 - p163+ [501+]
Haskell, Harry - *The Attentive Listener*
Choice - v34 - S '96 - p136 [51-250]
FF - v20 - S '96 - p471+ [251-500]
ON - v61 - O '96 - p66 [51-250]
Haskell, Molly - *Holding My Own in No Man's Land*
BL - v93 - Ja '97 - p803 [51-250]
Ent W - F 7 '97 - p64 [51-250]
KR - v64 - N 1 '96 - p1581+ [251-500]
LATBR - Ja 19 '97 - p10 [501+]
NYTBR - v102 - F 9 '97 - p21 [51-250]
NYTLa - v146 - Ja 3 '97 - pC19 [501+]
Haskin, David - *The Complete Idiot's Guide to Multimedia*
Quill & Q - v62 - Ag '96 - p23 [51-250]
Haskin, Dayton - *Milton's Burden of Interpretation*
MP - v94 - F '97 - p390+ [501+]
Ren Q - v49 - Win '96 - p891+ [501+]
Haskins, Francine - *I Remember 121*
c Learning - v25 - Mr '97 - p54 [1-50]

Haskins, James - *Bayard Rustin: Behind the Scenes of the Civil Rights Movement*
c   BL - v93 - F 15 '97 - p1020 [251-500]
y   CBRS - v25 - Mr '97 - p94+ [51-250]
c   KR - v64 - D 1 '96 - p1737 [51-250]
c   NYTBR - v102 - F 16 '97 - p25 [1-50]
Count Your Way through Brazil (Illus. by Liz Brenner Dodson)
c   BL - v93 - S 15 '96 - p243 [51-250]
c   HB Guide - v8 - Spr '97 - p179 [51-250]
c   SLJ - v42 - Ag '96 - p138 [51-250]
Count Your Way through France (Illus. by Andrea Shine)
c   HB Guide - v8 - Spr '97 - p168 [51-250]
c   SLJ - v42 - Ag '96 - p138 [51-250]
Count Your Way through Greece (Illus. by Janice Lee Porter)
c   BL - v93 - S 15 '96 - p243 [51-250]
c   HB Guide - v8 - Spr '97 - p168 [51-250]
c   SLJ - v42 - Ag '96 - p138 [51-250]
Count Your Way through Ireland (Illus. by Beth Wright)
c   HB Guide - v8 - Spr '97 - p168 [51-250]
c   SLJ - v42 - Ag '96 - p138 [51-250]
From Afar to Zulu
cr   BL - v92 - Ag '96 - p1918 [51-250]
The Harlem Renaissance
y   BL - v93 - S 1 '96 - p116 [51-250]
y   HB Guide - v7 - Fall '96 - p386 [51-250]
y   SLJ - v42 - S '96 - p233 [51-250]
y   VOYA - v19 - D '96 - p288 [51-250]
Louis Farrakhan and the Nation of Islam
y   BL - v93 - O 1 '96 - p328+ [51-250]
y   CBRS - v25 - O '96 - p21 [51-250]
y   Ch BWatch - v7 - Ja '97 - p4 [51-250]
y   HB Guide - v8 - Spr '97 - p158 [51-250]
y   KR - v64 - S 15 '96 - p1401 [51-250]
c   SLJ - v43 - Ja '97 - p126+ [51-250]
Power to the People
y   BL - v93 - Mr 15 '97 - p1233 [51-250]
c   BW - v27 - Ap 6 '97 - p8 [251-500]
y   CBRS - v25 - F '97 - p82 [51-250]
y   KR - v64 - D 1 '96 - p1737 [51-250]
y   SLJ - v43 - Mr '97 - p201 [51-250]
Spike Lee: By Any Means Necessary
y   BL - v93 - My 1 '97 - p1488 [51-250]
y   CBRS - v25 - Ap '97 - p106 [51-250]
y   CCB-B - v50 - My '97 - p323 [51-250]
y   KR - v65 - Ap 1 '97 - p556 [51-250]
Thurgood Marshall: A Life for Justice
y   BL - v93 - D 15 '96 - p716 [1-50]
Haskins, Mark E - *The CFO Handbook. Rev. Ed.*
r   Choice - v34 - F '97 - p1008 [51-250]
R&R Bk N - v12 - F '97 - p48 [51-250]
Haskins, Susan - *Mary Magdalen: Myth and Metaphor*
Six Ct J - v27 - Win '96 - p1189+ [501+]
Haslam, Alexandra R - *Where Coyotes Howl and Wind Blows Free*
WAL - v31 - Win '97 - p396 [251-500]
Haslam, Andrew - *Arctic Peoples*
c   Magpies - v11 - S '96 - p41+ [251-500]
Make It Work! Sound
c   Am MT - v46 - D '96 - p56+ [251-500]
Maps
c   BL - v93 - N 15 '96 - p582+ [51-250]
North American Peoples
c   Magpies - v11 - S '96 - p41+ [251-500]
Rivers
c   BL - v93 - N 15 '96 - p582+ [51-250]
Space (Illus. by Jon Barnes)
c   Bks Keeps - v100 - S '96 - p21 [51-250]
Time (Illus. by Jon Barnes)
c   Bks Keeps - v100 - S '96 - p21 [51-250]
Hasler, Julie - *500 Flower and Animal Cross Stitch Designs*
LJ - v121 - D '96 - p91+ [51-250]
Stitch Charted Designs
CAY - v16 - Fall '95 - p5 [51-250]
Haslett, David W - *Capitalism with Morality*
CPR - v16 - D '96 - p408+ [501+]
RM - v50 - D '96 - p405+ [501+]
Haslinger, J - *Finite Element Approximation for Optimal Shape, Material and Topology Design. 2nd Ed.*
Choice - v34 - My '97 - p1529+ [251-500]
Hass, Aaron - *The Aftermath: Living with the Holocaust*
y   Kliatt - v31 - Mr '97 - p32 [51-250]
In the Shadow of the Holocaust
y   Kliatt - v31 - Mr '97 - p32 [51-250]

Hass, Robert - *Sun under Wood*
BL - v93 - S 15 '96 - p205 [51-250]
BW - v27 - Ja 26 '97 - p8+ [251-500]
LATBR - Ap 13 '97 - pG [51-250]
LJ - v121 - O 1 '96 - p82 [51-250]
NY - v72 - Ja 6 '97 - p73 [51-250]
PW - v243 - S 30 '96 - p82 [51-250]
Hassam, Andrew - *Sailing to Australia*
VS - v39 - Win '96 - p274+ [501+]
Hassan, Ihab - *Between the Eagle and the Sun*
WLT - v70 - Sum '96 - p769 [501+]
Rumors of Change
WLT - v70 - Sum '96 - p697+ [251-500]
Hassan, John - *The European Water Environment in a Period of Transformation*
R&R Bk N - v11 - N '96 - p31 [51-250]
Hassanpour, Amir - *Nationalism and Language in Kurdistan 1918-1985*
MEJ - v51 - Spr '97 - p300+ [501+]
Hasselstrom, Linda M - *Leaning into the Wind*
PW - v244 - Ap 28 '97 - p57 [51-250]
Hassett, John - *Charles of the Wild (Illus. by John Hassett)*
c   BL - v93 - Ap 1 '97 - p1337 [51-250]
c   CBRS - v25 - Mr '97 - p87 [51-250]
c   KR - v65 - F 15 '97 - p299 [51-250]
c   PW - v244 - F 10 '97 - p83 [51-250]
Hassig, Debra - *Medieval Bestiaries*
RM - v138 - Ag '96 - p548 [501+]
Hassig, Ross - *Aztec Warfare*
Historian - v58 - Sum '96 - p860 [251-500]
Hassig, Susan M - *Panama*
c   HB Guide - v7 - Fall '96 - p392 [51-250]
Somalia
c   Ch BWatch - v7 - Ja '97 - p3 [1-50]
Hassine, Juliette - *Marranisme Et Hebraisme Dans L'Oeuvre De Proust*
MLR - v91 - Jl '96 - p737+ [501+]
Hassine, Victor - *Life without Parole*
Fed Prob - v60 - D '96 - p63+ [251-500]
Hassler, Jon - *The Dean's List*
BL - v93 - My 15 '97 - p1561 [51-250]
KR - v65 - Ap 1 '97 - p486+ [251-500]
LJ - v122 - My 1 '97 - p140 [51-250]
PW - v244 - Ap 14 '97 - p54 [51-250]
Rookery Blues
CC - v113 - Ag 28 '96 - p822+ [251-500]
Hassoun, Mohamad H - *Fundamentals of Artificial Neural Networks*
Am Sci - v84 - S '96 - p504+ [501+]
Hastings, Adrian - *The Church in Africa 1450-1950*
AHR - v101 - D '96 - p1592+ [501+]
CH - v65 - D '96 - p794+ [501+]
Historian - v59 - Fall '96 - p136+ [501+]
Hastings, Anne Stirling - *Body and Soul*
Choice - v34 - F '97 - p1040 [51-250]
LJ - v121 - O 1 '96 - p107+ [51-250]
PW - v243 - S 9 '96 - p77 [51-250]
R&R Bk N - v12 - F '97 - p7 [51-250]
Hastings, Daniel - *Spacecraft-Environment Interactions*
Choice - v34 - Ap '97 - p1370 [51-250]
Hastings, Juliet - *Aria Appasionata*
Quill & Q - v62 - Jl '96 - p42 [501+]
Hasty, Olga Peters - *Tsvetaeva's Orphic Journeys in the Worlds of the Word*
R&R Bk N - v11 - N '96 - p64 [51-250]
Haswell, Peter - *The Megamogs and the Dangerous Doughnut (Illus. by Peter Haswell)*
c   KR - v64 - D 1 '96 - p1738 [51-250]
Haswell, Susan Olsen - *A Garden Apart*
Pub Hist - v18 - Sum '96 - p85+ [501+]
Hatab, Lawrence J - *A Nietzschean Defense of Democracy*
Choice - v34 - S '96 - p208 [51-250]
CPR - v16 - Je '96 - p167+ [501+]
Hatanaka, Michio - *Time-Series-Based Econometrics*
Econ J - v107 - Ja '97 - p263 [51-250]
JEL - v34 - D '96 - p2019 [51-250]
Hatar, Gyozo - *Eletut. 3. Vol. 3*
WLT - v70 - Sum '96 - p733+ [501+]
Hatch, James V - *Black Theatre, U.S.A.*
Bl S - v26 - Fall '96 - p103 [51-250]
Lost Plays of the Harlem Renaissance 1920-1940
Bloom Rev - v17 - Ja '97 - p20 [51-250]
LJ - v121 - O 15 '96 - p58 [51-250]
Hatch, Thom - *Custer and the Battle of the Little Bighorn*
r   LJ - v122 - F 15 '97 - p127+ [51-250]
Hatch, Walter - *Asia in Japan's Embrace*
Choice - v34 - Ap '97 - p1388 [51-250]
JEL - v35 - Mr '97 - p216 [251-500]

Hatcher, John - *Laurence Binyon: Poet, Scholar of East and West*
Choice - v34 - S '96 - p126 [51-250]
CR - v270 - Ja '97 - p54+ [501+]
Hatcher, Patricia Law - *Producing a Quality Family History*
NGSQ - v84 - S '96 - p233 [251-500]
Hatfield, Kate - *Drowning in Honey*
BL - v93 - N 15 '96 - p570 [51-250]
KR - v64 - O 1 '96 - p1421+ [251-500]
LJ - v121 - O 15 '96 - p90 [51-250]
PW - v243 - O 14 '96 - p63+ [51-250]
Hather, Jon G - *Tropical Archaeobotany*
Am Ant - v61 - Jl '96 - p614+ [501+]
Hathorn, Libby - *The Climb*
y   Aust Bk R - N '96 - p57+ [501+]
Grandma's Shoes (Illus. by Elivia Savadier)
c   LA - v73 - S '96 - p357 [51-250]
Juke-Box Jive
c   Sch Lib - v44 - Ag '96 - p105 [51-250]
Way Home (Illus. by Gregory Rogers)
c   Bks Keeps - N '96 - p10 [51-250]
c   RT - v50 - F '97 - p422 [51-250]
The Wonder Thing (Illus. by Peter Gouldthorpe)
c   HB Guide - v7 - Fall '96 - p259 [51-250]
c   JB - v60 - D '96 - p232+ [251-500]
c   Sch Lib - v44 - Ag '96 - p99 [51-250]
Hatrick, Gloria - *Masks*
c   CBRS - v24 - Ag '96 - p167 [51-250]
y   HB Guide - v7 - Fall '96 - p302 [51-250]
y   JAAL - v40 - S '96 - p73 [51-250]
Hattaway, Herman - *Shades of Blue and Gray*
KR - v65 - Mr 1 '97 - p352 [51-250]
PW - v244 - Ap 28 '97 - p63 [51-250]
Hattendorf, John B - *The Age of Discovery. Vol. 1*
Sea H - Aut '96 - p42 [51-250]
British Naval Documents 1204-1960
EHR - v111 - S '96 - p1038 [251-500]
Hatvary, George Egon - *The Murder of Edgar Allan Poe*
y   BL - v93 - Mr 15 '97 - p1229 [51-250]
BW - v27 - F 16 '97 - p5 [501+]
KR - v65 - Ja 1 '97 - p23+ [51-250]
PW - v244 - Ja 20 '97 - p396+ [51-250]
Hatzis, Dimitris - *The End of Our Small Town*
TLS - D 20 '96 - p23 [251-500]
Haublein, Gernot - *Memo: Wortschatz- Und Fertigkeitstraining Zum Zertifikat Deutsch Als Fremdsprache*
MLJ - v80 - Fall '96 - p419 [251-500]
Hauck, Dennis William - *Haunted Places. Rev. Ed.*
r   ARBA - v28 - '97 - p287+ [251-500]
Hauer, F Richard - *Methods in Stream Ecology*
SciTech - v20 - N '96 - p27 [51-250]
Hauerwas, Stanley - *In Good Company*
Bks & Cult - v2 - Mr '96 - p30 [251-500]
Ch Today - v41 - Ja 6 '97 - p50+ [501+]
Theol St - v57 - D '96 - p782 [251-500]
Where Resident Aliens Live
Ch Today - v41 - Ja 6 '97 - p50+ [501+]
Rel St Rev - v23 - Ja '97 - p50 [51-250]
Haugen, Robert A - *Modern Investment Theory. 4th Ed.*
R&R Bk N - v12 - F '97 - p49 [51-250]
Haugerud, Angelique - *The Culture of Politics in Modern Kenya*
Africa T - v43 - 4 '96 - p438+ [501+]
Am Ethnol - v23 - Ag '96 - p646+ [501+]
Haught, James A - *2000 Years of Disbelief*
r   BL - v93 - Ap 1 '97 - p1358 [251-500]
Haughton, Graham - *Sustainable Cities*
AAAGA - v86 - D '96 - p800+ [501+]
Haughton, Hugh - *John Clare in Context*
RES - v47 - Ag '96 - p430+ [501+]
Haunts
p   SF Chr - v18 - O '96 - p83 [1-50]
Hauptman, Laurence M - *Between Two Fires*
AHR - v101 - D '96 - p1626 [251-500]
JSH - v62 - N '96 - p813+ [251-500]
PHR - v66 - F '97 - p105+ [251-500]
Tribes and Tribulations
AHR - v102 - F '97 - p177+ [251-500]
Hauptmann, Emily - *Putting Choice before Democracy*
R&R Bk N - v11 - N '96 - p47 [51-250]
Hauptmann, Gerhart - *Tagebucher 1906 Bis 1913*
MLR - v91 - O '96 - p1045+ [501+]
Hausch, Donald B - *Efficiency of Racetrack Betting Markets*
Econ J - v106 - S '96 - p1466+ [251-500]
Hauschild, Jan-Christoph - *Georg Buchner*
MLN - v112 - Ap '97 - p470+ [501+]
Hausen, E - *Human History at the Crossroads*
R&R Bk N - v12 - F '97 - p8 [51-250]

Hauser, Barbara A - *Practical Manual of Wastewater Chemistry*
  SciTech - v20 - N '96 - p68 [51-250]
Hauser, Barbara R - *Women's Legal Guide*
  r Choice - v34 - N '96 - p440 [51-250]
Hauser, Jill Frankel - *Super Science Concoctions*
  c BL - v93 - Mr 1 '97 - p1158 [51-250]
Hauser, Marc D - *The Evolution of Communication*
  Choice - v34 - Ja '97 - p818 [51-250]
  Nature - v382 - Ag 15 '96 - p592+ [501+]
  R&R Bk N - v12 - F '97 - p94 [51-250]
  SciTech - v20 - S '96 - p21 [51-250]
Hauser, Pierre - *Illegal Aliens*
  y HB Guide - v8 - Spr '97 - p90 [51-250]
  c SLJ - v43 - F '97 - p116+ [51-250]
Hauser, Thomas - *Muhammad Ali: In Perspective*
  B Ent - v27 - F '97 - p215 [1-50]
Hauser, Walter - *Swami Sahajanand and the Peasants of Jharkhand*
  Pac A - v69 - Sum '96 - p272+ [501+]
Hausherr, Rosmarie - *Celebrating Families (Illus. by Rosmarie Hausherr)*
  c BL - v93 - Mr 1 '97 - p1165 [51-250]
  c SLJ - v43 - Mr '97 - p175 [51-250]
  What Food Is This?
  c Emerg Lib - v23 - My '96 - p45 [51-250]
Hausman, Daniel M - *Economic Analysis and Moral Philosophy*
  Choice - v34 - N '96 - p507 [51-250]
  JEL - v34 - D '96 - p2008 [51-250]
Hausman, Gerald - *Coyote Walks on Two Legs (Illus. by Floyd Cooper)*
  c Inst - v105 - My '96 - p69 [1-50]
  Eagle Boy (Illus. by Cara Moser)
  c Emerg Lib - v24 - Mr '97 - p64+ [51-250]
  c HB Guide - v7 - Fall '96 - p321 [51-250]
  c RT - v50 - Ap '97 - p594 [51-250]
  The Mythology of Dogs
  KR - v64 - N 15 '96 - p1651+ [251-500]
  Trib Bks - F 9 '97 - p1+ [501+]
  Night Flight
  c HB Guide - v7 - Fall '96 - p293 [51-250]
  y VOYA - v19 - O '96 - p209+ [251-500]
Hausmanis, Viktors - *Trimdas Lugas. Vols. 1-2*
  WLT - v70 - Sum '96 - p735+ [501+]
Hausmann, Klaus - *Protozoology. 2nd Ed.*
  Choice - v34 - O '96 - p303 [51-250]
Hausmann, Ricardo - *Securing Stability and Growth in Latin America*
  JEL - v34 - D '96 - p2115 [51-250]
  Volatile Capital Flows
  JEL - v34 - D '96 - p2048+ [51-250]
Hausner, Jerzy - *Strategic Choice and Path-Dependency in Post-Socialism*
  Econ J - v107 - Ja '97 - p286 [51-250]
Hauss, Charles - *Beyond Confrontation*
  Choice - v34 - Ja '97 - p870 [51-250]
  For Aff - v75 - N '96 - p146 [51-250]
Haut, Woody - *Pulp Culture*
  J Am St - v30 - Ag '96 - p328+ [501+]
Hautala, Rick - *Beyond the Shroud*
  Rapport - v19 - 5 '96 - p32 [251-500]
  The Mountain King
  LJ - v121 - S 15 '96 - p96 [51-250]
Hauter, Janet - *Guide to Career Success*
  BWatch - v18 - F '97 - p2+ [1-50]
Hauth, Katherine B - *Night Life of the Yucca (Illus. by Kay Sather)*
  c HB Guide - v8 - Spr '97 - p118 [51-250]
Hautman, Pete - *The Mortal Nuts*
  Arm Det - v29 - Sum '96 - p357 [501+]
  KR - v64 - My 1 '96 - p622 [251-500]
  NYTBR - v101 - D 8 '96 - p94 [1-50]
  Mr. Was
  y BL - v93 - S 15 '96 - p230 [51-250]
  y BL - v93 - Ap 1 '97 - p1292 [1-50]
  y CBRS - v25 - D '96 - p45 [51-250]
  y CCB-B - v50 - N '96 - p98 [51-250]
  y HB Guide - v8 - Spr '97 - p80 [51-250]
  y JAAL - v40 - S '96 - p72 [51-250]
  y KR - v64 - Ag 15 '96 - p1235 [51-250]
  y SLJ - v42 - O '96 - p147 [51-250]
  y VOYA - v19 - D '96 - p279+ [51-250]
Hautzig, David - *Pedal Power*
  c HB Guide - v7 - Fall '96 - p350 [51-250]
Hautzig, Esther - *The Endless Steppe (Bresnahan). Audio Version*
  y BL - v93 - My 15 '97 - p1595 [1-50]
  c HB - v72 - S '96 - p566+ [501+]
  y SLJ - v42 - Ag '96 - p62 [51-250]

Havas, Randall - *Nietzsche's Genealogy*
  Ethics - v107 - O '96 - p165+ [501+]
Havel, James T - *U.S. Presidential Candidates and the Elections. Vols. 1-2*
  r ARBA - v28 - '97 - p266 [251-500]
  r BL - v93 - Ja '97 - p901 [251-500]
  r Choice - v34 - Mr '97 - p1137+ [251-500]
  r LJ - v121 - O 1 '96 - p68 [51-250]
  r R&R Bk N - v11 - D '96 - p47 [51-250]
Havel, Vaclav - *The Art of the Impossible*
  BL - v93 - Ap 1 '97 - p1266+ [51-250]
  KR - v65 - Ap 1 '97 - p520+ [251-500]
  PW - v244 - Mr 31 '97 - p51 [51-250]
Havelock, Christine Mitchell - *The Aphrodite of Knidos and Her Successors*
  AJA - v100 - O '96 - p794+ [501+]
  Art Bull - v79 - Mr '97 - p148+ [501+]
Haveman, Robert - *Succeeding Generations*
  Soc Ser R - v71 - Mr '97 - p165+ [251-500]
  SSQ - v77 - S '96 - p715+ [501+]
Haven, Kendall F - *Great Moments in Science*
  SLMQ - v24 - Sum '96 - p221 [51-250]
  VOYA - v19 - O '96 - p242 [51-250]
Haver, William - *The Body of This Death*
  Choice - v34 - My '97 - p1533 [51-250]
Haverkamp, Anselm - *Leaves of Mourning*
  Choice - v34 - O '96 - p284 [51-250]
Haverstock, Nathan A - *Cuba in Pictures*
  y SLJ - v42 - O '96 - p45 [1-50]
  Fifty Years at the Front
  BW - v26 - Ag 4 '96 - p4 [501+]
  Choice - v34 - N '96 - p447 [51-250]
Haverty, Anne - *One Day as a Tiger*
  NS - v126 - Mr 14 '97 - p46+ [501+]
  Obs - Mr 23 '97 - p18* [251-500]
  TLS - Mr 7 '97 - p21 [501+]
Haviaras, Stratis - *Seamus Heaney: A Celebration*
  ILS - v15 - Fall '96 - p31 [51-250]
Havig, Bettina - *Amish Kinder Komforts*
  BL - v93 - S 15 '96 - p201+ [51-250]
Haviland, Virginia - *Told in Greece*
  c Ch BWatch - v6 - N '96 - p7 [1-50]
  Told in Italy
  c Ch BWatch - v6 - N '96 - p7 [1-50]
  Told in Norway
  c Ch BWatch - v6 - N '96 - p7 [1-50]
Havill, Juanita - *El Hallazgo De Jamaica (Illus. by Anne Sibley O'Brien)*
  c BL - v93 - My 1 '97 - p1507 [1-50]
Havill, Steven F - *Privileged to Kill*
  BL - v93 - F 15 '97 - p1006 [51-250]
  KR - v64 - D 15 '96 - p1768 [51-250]
  LJ - v122 - F 1 '97 - p111 [51-250]
  PW - v243 - D 16 '96 - p45+ [51-250]
Havinden, Michael - *Colonialism and Development*
  WorldV - v13 - Ja '97 - p5+ [51-250]
Havlik, Lubomir E - *Kronia O Velke Morave. Rev. Ed.*
  Slav R - v55 - Sum '96 - p452+ [501+]
Hawcock, David - *Beetle (Illus. by Lee Montgomery)*
  c HB Guide - v7 - Fall '96 - p341 [51-250]
  Fly (Illus. by Lee Montgomery)
  c HB Guide - v7 - Fall '96 - p341 [51-250]
  Wasp (Illus. by Lee Montgomery)
  c HB Guide - v7 - Fall '96 - p341 [51-250]
Hawdon, James - *Emerging Organization Forms*
  R&R Bk N - v12 - F '97 - p62 [51-250]
Hawes, C J - *Poor Relations*
  TLS - Ja 17 '97 - p29 [501+]
Hawes, Clement - *Mania and Literary Style*
  Choice - v34 - Ja '97 - p795 [51-250]
Hawes, J M - *A White Merc with Fins*
  LATBR - My 26 '96 - p10 [51-250]
  PW - v244 - F 3 '97 - p102 [1-50]
  Rapport - v19 - 5 '96 - p38 [251-500]
Hawke, Ethan - *The Hottest State*
  BW - v26 - O 6 '96 - p4 [501+]
  Ent W - O 18 '96 - p70+ [251-500]
  Ent W - O 27 '96 - p143 [51-250]
  NW - v128 - S 30 '96 - p80 [501+]
  NYTBR - v101 - N 3 '96 - p19 [51-250]
  PW - v243 - Jl 22 '96 - p225+ [51-250]
  Rapport - v19 - 5 '96 - p28 [251-500]
Hawke, John - *The New World Tattoo*
  Aust Bk R - F '97 - p47+ [501+]
Hawke, Simon - *The Ambivalent Magician*
  y Kliatt - v30 - N '96 - p14 [51-250]
Hawkes, David - *Ideology*
  Choice - v34 - Mr '97 - p1158 [251-500]
Hawkes, Dean - *The Environmental Tradition*
  Choice - v34 - Ja '97 - p783 [51-250]

Hawkes, G W - *Playing out of the Deep Woods*
  Aethlon - v13 - Spr '96 - p199 [251-500]
Hawkes, Gail - *A Sociology of Sex and Sexuality*
  R&R Bk N - v11 - N '96 - p40 [51-250]
Hawkes, John, 1925- - *The Frog*
  Ant R - v55 - Spr '97 - p243+ [251-500]
  Atl - v278 - Jl '96 - p109 [51-250]
  LATBR - S 8 '96 - p10+ [51-250]
  NYTBR - v101 - D 22 '96 - p11 [501+]
  VQR - v73 - Win '97 - p22*+ [51-250]
  Whistlejacket: A Novel
  Critiq - v37 - Sum '96 - p289+ [501+]
Hawkes, Judith - *My Soul to Keep*
  Arm Det - v29 - Sum '96 - p377 [51-250]
Hawkes, Terence - *Alternative Shakespeares. Vol. 2*
  NS - v125 - O 11 '96 - p46+ [501+]
Hawkin, David J - *The Johannine World*
  Choice - v34 - D '96 - p628 [51-250]
  R&R Bk N - v11 - D '96 - p5 [51-250]
Hawking, Stephen - *A Brief History of Time*
  y BL - v93 - Ja '97 - p832 [1-50]
  PSR - v25 - '96 - p273+ [501+]
  The Illustrated A Brief History of Time. Updated and Expanded Ed.
  Astron - v25 - Ja '97 - p103 [51-250]
  BW - v26 - D 8 '96 - p12 [51-250]
  New Sci - v152 - N 23 '96 - p44 [51-250]
  The Nature of Space and Time
  Astron - v24 - N '96 - p100 [51-250]
  S&T - v92 - N '96 - p60 [51-250]
Hawkins, Alan J - *Generative Fathering*
  R&R Bk N - v12 - F '97 - p52 [51-250]
Hawkins, Anne Hunsaker - *Time to Go*
  Rel St Rev - v22 - O '96 - p342 [51-250]
Hawkins, Colin - *Here's a Happy Elephant*
  c HB Guide - v7 - Fall '96 - p239 [51-250]
  Here's a Happy Kitten
  c HB Guide - v7 - Fall '96 - p239 [51-250]
  Here's a Happy Pig
  c HB Guide - v7 - Fall '96 - p239 [51-250]
  Here's a Happy Puppy
  c HB Guide - v7 - Fall '96 - p239 [51-250]
  Snap! Snap!
  c Bks Keeps - v100 - S '96 - p8 [51-250]
  c Books - v10 - Je '96 - p25 [1-50]
Hawkins, Darnell F - *Ethnicity, Race, and Crime*
  CS - v25 - S '96 - p668+ [501+]
Hawkins, Elizabeth - *The Lollipop Witch (Illus. by Nick Sharratt)*
  c Bks Keeps - Ja '97 - p20+ [51-250]
  Runner
  y TES - F 7 '97 - p9* [51-250]
Hawkins, Joyce - *Oxford School Dictionary*
  cr Bks Keeps - v100 - S '96 - p22+ [501+]
  Oxford Shorter School Dictionary
  cr Bks Keeps - v100 - S '96 - p22+ [501+]
  Oxford Study Dictionary
  cr Bks Keeps - v100 - S '96 - p22+ [501+]
Hawkins, Norma - *Chokecherry*
  BIC - v25 - D '96 - p41+ [51-250]
Hawkins-Dady, Mark - *Reader's Guide to Literature in English*
  r ARBA - v28 - '97 - p420 [51-250]
  r BL - v93 - S 15 '96 - p284 [501+]
  r Choice - v34 - D '96 - p594 [51-250]
  r Sch Lib - v44 - N '96 - p177 [51-250]
  r TLS - N 1 '96 - p12+ [501+]
Hawksley, Gerald - *Mr. MacMurdo's Guide to Ghostkeeping*
  c Bks Keeps - Mr '97 - p20 [51-250]
Hawksley, Humphrey - *Dragon Strike*
  Books - v11 - Ap '97 - p17 [501+]
  FEER - v160 - My 8 '97 - p39 [251-500]
Hawley, John C - *Reform and Counterreform*
  CH - v66 - Mr '97 - p176+ [501+]
Hawley, John Stratton - *Devi: Goddesses of India*
  Choice - v34 - O '96 - p296 [51-250]
  Sati, the Blessing and the Curse
  Wom R Bks - v13 - S '96 - p26+ [501+]
Hawley, Richard, 1963- - *Women in Antiquity*
  Rel St Rev - v23 - Ap '97 - p171 [51-250]
Hawley, Richard A - *Papers from the Headmaster*
  BWatch - v17 - N '96 - p5+ [51-250]
  Choice - v34 - Ap '97 - p1390+ [51-250]
  PW - v243 - S 23 '96 - p67 [51-250]
Haworth, John - *Psychological Research*
  SciTech - v21 - Mr '97 - p51 [51-250]
Haworth-Attard, Barbara - *Home Child*
  c Quill & Q - v63 - F '97 - p55 [251-500]
  The Truthsinger
  c Quill & Q - v62 - S '96 - p74 [251-500]

Hawthorn, Jeremy - *A Glossary of Contemporary Literary Theory. 2nd Ed.*
  r   RES - v47 - N '96 - p633+ [501+]
Hawthorne, Nathaniel - *The Blithedale Romance*
     HMR - Win '96 - p16 [501+]
The Scarlet Letter
     Cres - v60 - Christmas '96 - p5+ [501+]
     MLN - v111 - D '96 - p835+ [501+]
A Wonder Book for Girls and Boys (Illus. by Walter Crane)
  c   Ch BWatch - v7 - F '97 - p1 [51-250]
  c   PW - v243 - D 9 '96 - p69 [51-250]
Hawxhurst, Joan C - *Bubbe and Gram (Illus. by Jane K Bynum)*
  c   BL - v93 - Ja '97 - p866+ [251-500]
  c   PW - v244 - Ja 27 '97 - p98 [51-250]
Interfaith Wedding Ceremonies
     BL - v92 - Ag '96 - p1861 [51-250]
Hax, Herbert - *Economic Transformation in Eastern Europe and East Asia*
     JEL - v34 - D '96 - p2042 [51-250]
Hay, Carole - *Computers*
  c   Sch Lib - v44 - N '96 - p163 [51-250]
Hay, Colin - *Re-Stating Social and Political Change*
     R&R Bk N - v11 - N '96 - p46 [51-250]
Hay, Eldon - *The Chignecto Covenanters*
     R&R Bk N - v12 - F '97 - p12 [51-250]
Hay, Harry - *Radically Gay*
     HG&LRev - v3 - Fall '96 - p39+ [501+]
     Prog - v61 - Ja '97 - p34+ [251-500]
Hay, Ida - *Science in the Pleasure Ground*
     AHR - v101 - O '96 - p1278+ [501+]
Hay, James - *The Audience and Its Landscape*
     Choice - v34 - D '96 - p605 [51-250]
Hay, Jane - *Art Deco Ceramics*
     Ceram Mo - v44 - S '96 - p32 [51-250]
Hay, John - *The Great House of Birds*
  y   BL - v93 - O 1 '96 - p312 [51-250]
     BWatch - v17 - D '96 - p4 [1-50]
     SciTech - v20 - D '96 - p33 [1-50]
Hay, Louise L - *Empowering Women*
     LJ - v122 - F 1 '97 - p97 [51-250]
Hayashi, Brian Masaru - *For the Sake of Our Japanese Brethren*
     Bks & Cult - v2 - N '96 - p30+ [501+]
     RAH - v24 - D '96 - p663+ [501+]
     Rel St Rev - v23 - Ja '97 - p94 [51-250]
Haycox, Stephen W - *An Alaska Anthology*
     Choice - v34 - F '97 - p1023 [51-250]
Hayden, Dolores - *The Power of Place*
     EG - v73 - Ja '97 - p135+ [501+]
     Pub Hist - v18 - Sum '96 - p52+ [501+]
Hayden, Richard - *The Influencing Engine*
     TLS - O 18 '96 - p22 [251-500]
Hayden, Robert - *Collected Poems*
     HR - v49 - Aut '96 - p503+ [501+]
Hayden, Tom - *Irish Hunger*
     PW - v244 - My 12 '97 - p67 [51-250]
The Lost Gospel of the Earth
     BL - v93 - S 1 '96 - p38 [51-250]
     BW - v26 - N 17 '96 - p8 [501+]
     Econ - v342 - F 15 '97 - p7* [51-250]
     LJ - v121 - S 15 '96 - p73 [51-250]
     NYTBR - v101 - S 29 '96 - p23 [501+]
     PW - v243 - S 2 '96 - p127 [51-250]
Haydn, Joseph - *La Mesure De Son Siecle*
     TLS - S 13 '96 - p36 [501+]
Hayduk, Leslie A - *LISREL Issues, Debates, and Strategies*
     JEL - v34 - S '96 - p1409 [51-250]
Hayek, Friedrich A Von - *Contra Keynes and Cambridge*
     Econ J - v106 - S '96 - p1463 [51-250]
Individualism and Economic Order
     Bloom Rev - v16 - S '96 - p24 [51-250]
     JEL - v34 - D '96 - p2015 [51-250]
Hayes, Alan L - *Church and Society in Documents 100-600 A.D.*
     CH - v66 - Mr '97 - p186+ [51-250]
Hayes, Allan - *Southwestern Pottery*
     Bloom Rev - v16 - N '96 - p23 [51-250]
     LJ - v122 - Ja '97 - p93 [51-250]
     Nat Peop - v10 - '97 - p78+ [501+]
Hayes, Ann H - *Debugging and Performance Tuning for Parallel Computing Systems*
     SciTech - v20 - N '96 - p7 [51-250]
Hayes, Bascom Barry - *Bismarck and Mitteleuropa*
     JMH - v68 - S '96 - p729+ [501+]

Hayes, Daniel - *Flyers*
  y   BL - v93 - S 15 '96 - p230 [51-250]
  y   HB - v73 - Ja '97 - p56+ [51-250]
  y   HB Guide - v8 - Spr '97 - p80 [51-250]
  y   KR - v64 - S 1 '96 - p1322+ [51-250]
  y   PW - v243 - N 4 '96 - p77+ [51-250]
  y   SLJ - v42 - N '96 - p120 [51-250]
  y   VOYA - v19 - F '97 - p327 [251-500]
Hayes, Deborah - *Infants and Hearing*
     SciTech - v21 - Mr '97 - p62 [51-250]
Hayes, Diana L - *And Still We Rise*
     Theol St - v58 - Mr '97 - p196 [251-500]
Hayes, Joe - *Here Comes the Storyteller*
     CCB-B - v50 - Mr '97 - p263 [51-250]
A Spoon for Every Bite (Illus. by Rebecca Leer)
  c   CLW - v67 - Mr '97 - p57+ [51-250]
  c   HB Guide - v7 - Fall '96 - p259 [51-250]
Hayes, Karen - *Finding My Father*
  c   JB - v60 - D '96 - p268 [251-500]
  y   Sch Lib - v44 - N '96 - p170 [51-250]
Hayes, Kathleen - *Women on the Threshold*
     OS - v32 - Jl '96 - p43 [51-250]
Hayes, Katy - *Curtains*
     Obs - F 23 '97 - p17* [51-250]
Hayes, Kevin J - *A Colonial Woman's Bookshelf*
     Choice - v34 - F '97 - p1024 [51-250]
Henry James: The Contemporary Reviews
     AL - v68 - S '96 - p667 [1-50]
     Choice - v34 - F '97 - p966 [51-250]
The Library of William Byrd of Westover
     LJ - v122 - Ap 15 '97 - p96 [51-250]
Hayes, Malcolm - *Anton Von Webern*
     M Ed J - v83 - N '96 - p54 [1-50]
     TLS - Jl 7 '96 - p19 [501+]
Hayes, Mason H - *Statistical Digital Signal Processing and Modeling*
     SciTech - v20 - S '96 - p54 [1-50]
Hayes, Patricia - *Children of History*
     WorldV - v13 - Ja '97 - p15 [251-500]
Hayes, Peter - *Space Power Interests*
     SciTech - v20 - S '96 - p63 [51-250]
Hayes, Robert Mayo - *Strategic Management for Public Libraries*
     LJ - v121 - N 1 '96 - p113 [51-250]
  r   R&R Bk N - v12 - F '97 - p102 [51-250]
Hayes, Sarah - *This Is the Bear (Illus. by Helen Craig)*
  c   PW - v244 - F 10 '97 - p84 [1-50]
Hayes, Sheila - *The Tinker's Daughter*
  c   RT - v50 - N '96 - p256 [51-250]
Hayes-Renshaw, Fiona - *The Council of Ministers*
     For Aff - v76 - My '97 - p136+ [51-250]
Haygood, Wil - *The Haygoods of Columbus*
     KR - v65 - F 1 '97 - p197 [251-500]
     LJ - v122 - Ap 1 '97 - p100 [51-250]
     NYTBR - v102 - Ap 13 '97 - p22 [501+]
     PW - v244 - F 3 '97 - p85 [51-250]
Hayhoe, Ruth - *China's Universities 1895-1995*
     Choice - v34 - O '96 - p333 [51-250]
East-West Dialogue in Knowledge and Higher Education
     R&R Bk N - v11 - D '96 - p52 [51-250]
Ma Xiangbo and the Mind of Modern China 1840-1939
     Ch Rev Int - v4 - Spr '97 - p159+ [501+]
     R&R Bk N - v11 - N '96 - p9 [51-250]
Haykin, Michael A G - *The Spirit of God*
     CH - v66 - Mr '97 - p83+ [251-500]
Hayles, Karen - *The Star That Fell. Book and Audio Version*
  c   TES - O 25 '96 - p12*
The Star That Fell (Illus. by Karen Hayles). Book and Audio Version
  c   Sch Lib - v44 - N '96 - p146 [51-250]
Haylock, Julian - *Gustav Mahler: An Essential Guide to His Life and Work*
  y   BL - v93 - My 1 '97 - p1472 [51-250]
Sergei Rachmaninov: An Essential Guide to His Life and Work
  y   BL - v93 - My 1 '97 - p1472 [51-250]
Hayman, David - *Probes: Genetic Studies in Joyce*
     ILS - v15 - Fall '96 - p13 [501+]
Hayman, Richard - *Riddles in Stone*
     New Sci - v153 - Mr 22 '97 - p47 [51-250]
Hayman, Ronald - *Thomas Mann: A Biography*
     Ger Q - v69 - Fall '96 - p450+ [501+]
     Lon R Bks - v18 - S 5 '96 - p3+ [501+]
Haymes, Edward R - *Heroic Legends of the North*
     Choice - v34 - N '96 - p463 [51-250]
Haymon, S T - *Death and the Pregnant Virgin*
     Arm Det - v29 - Fall '96 - p437 [51-250]

Death of a Hero
     Arm Det - v30 - Win '97 - p106 [251-500]
     KR - v64 - N 1 '96 - p1566 [51-250]
     LJ - v121 - D '96 - p151 [51-250]
     PW - v243 - N 4 '96 - p66+ [51-250]
Haynes, Alan - *The Gunpowder Plot*
     EHR - v112 - F '97 - p195+ [251-500]
Invisible Power
     HT - v46 - Jl '96 - p53 [501+]
Haynes, B R - *Bonechillers: Teacher Creature*
  c   Bks Keeps - Jl '96 - p11 [51-250]
Haynes, Colin - *How to Succeed in Cyberspace*
     LR - v45 - 8 '96 - p45+ [501+]
Haynes, David - *Live at Five*
     Bloom Rev - v16 - S '96 - p7 [501+]
     Bl S - v26 - Fall '96 - p103 [1-50]
Somebody Else's Mama
  y   Kliatt - v30 - S '96 - p10 [51-250]
     NYTBR - v101 - Ap 7 '96 - p24 [1-50]
Haynes, John E - *Red Scare or Red Menace?*
     Nat R - v48 - N 11 '96 - p62 [51-250]
Haynes, Raymond - *Explorers of the Southern Sky*
     Choice - v34 - Ap '97 - p1361 [51-250]
     SB - v33 - Mr '97 - p38 [51-250]
     SciTech - v20 - D '96 - p20 [51-250]
Haynes, Roslynn D - *From Faust to Strangelove*
     Isis - v87 - S '96 - p526+ [501+]
Haynes, Stephen R - *Reluctant Witnesses*
     Intpr - v51 - Ja '97 - p104+ [251-500]
Haynie, W Preston - *Records of Indentured Servants and of Certificates for Land, Northumberland County, Virginia 1650-1795*
  r   EGH - v50 - N '96 - p190+ [51-250]
Hays, David - *My Old Man and the Sea*
  y   Kliatt - v30 - N '96 - p28 [51-250]
My Old Man and the Sea (Guidall). Audio Version
     BL - v92 - Ag '96 - p1917 [51-250]
  y   Kliatt - v31 - Ja '97 - p49+ [251-500]
My Old Man and the Sea (Hays). Audio Version
  y   Kliatt - v31 - My '97 - p48 [51-250]
     Quill & Q - v62 - My '96 - p25 [1-50]
Hays, Mary - *Memoirs of Emma Courtney. 1st Annotated Ed.*
     TLS - O 18 '96 - p27 [501+]
Hays, Michael - *Melodrama: The Cultural Emergence of a Genre*
     Choice - v34 - Ap '97 - p1350 [51-250]
     R&R Bk N - v12 - F '97 - p80 [51-250]
Hays, Otis, Jr. - *The Alaska-Siberia Connection*
     A & S Sm - v11 - F '97 - p90+ [51-250]
Hays, Richard B - *The Moral Vision of the New Testament*
     Am - v176 - Mr 8 '97 - p31 [51-250]
Hays, Sharon - *The Cultural Contradictions of Motherhood*
     Choice - v34 - Mr '97 - p1245 [51-250]
     KR - v64 - Ag 15 '96 - p1209+ [251-500]
     LJ - v121 - O 1 '96 - p108+ [51-250]
     Nat - v263 - O 14 '96 - p29+ [501+]
     NYRB - v43 - N 28 '96 - p22+ [501+]
     PW - v243 - S 16 '96 - p64+ [51-250]
Haysom, Cari - *Stamp Craft*
     BL - v93 - N 1 '96 - p468 [51-250]
     LJ - v122 - F 15 '97 - p134 [51-250]
Hayter, Alethea - *Charlotte Yonge*
     Spec - v277 - D 14 '96 - p63+ [501+]
Hayter, Sparkle - *Nice Girls Finish Last*
     PW - v244 - Mr 24 '97 - p81 [1-50]
Revenge of the Cootie Girls
     KR - v65 - F 1 '97 - p175 [51-250]
     PW - v244 - Ja 20 '97 - p396 [51-250]
Haythornthwaite, Philip - *Napoleon: The Final Verdict*
     HT - v46 - O '96 - p57 [1-50]
Hayward, Jack - *Governing the New Europe*
     Wil Q - v21 - Win '97 - p38 [51-250]
Hayward, Susan - *French National Cinema*
     FQ - v49 - Fall '95 - p46 [501+]
Key Concepts in Cinema Studies
  r   Choice - v34 - F '97 - p944 [51-250]
     Si & So - v6 - N '96 - p38 [51-250]
Hayward, Vicky - *Madrid 1996*
  r   BL - v93 - S 15 '96 - p210 [1-50]
Haywood, C Robert - *Tough Daisies*
     WHQ - v27 - Win '96 - p545+ [251-500]
Haywood, Gar Anthony - *Bad News Travels Fast*
  y   Kliatt - v31 - Ja '97 - p8 [51-250]
It's Not a Pretty Sight
     Arm Det - v29 - Fall '96 - p497 [251-500]
     BL - v93 - S 1 '96 - p67 [51-250]
     BW - v26 - Ag 18 '96 - p8 [251-500]
     Ent W - N 8 '96 - p63 [51-250]

Haywood, John - *The Romans*
  c Ch BWatch - v6 - S '96 - p6 [51-250]
  c Cur R - v36 - D '96 - p12 [51-250]
  c HB Guide - v8 - Spr '97 - p165 [51-250]
  c SLJ - v42 - S '96 - p214 [51-250]
Haywood, Trevor - *Info-Rich--Info-Poor*
  LR - v45 - 7 '96 - p44+ [501+]
Hazan, Ann - *The Reading Terminal Market Cookbook*
  BL - v93 - My 15 '97 - p1552 [51-250]
Hazard, Edith - *Singing for Your Supper*
  BL - v92 - Ag '96 - p1874 [51-250]
Hazelaar, Cor - *Zoo Dreams (Illus. by Cor Hazelaar)*
  c HB - v73 - Mr '97 - p192 [51-250]
  c KR - v65 - Ja 15 '97 - p142 [51-250]
  c PW - v244 - Ja 27 '97 - p105 [51-250]
  c SLJ - v43 - Mr '97 - p160 [51-250]
Hazell, Rebecca - *Heroines: Great Women through the Ages (Illus. by Rebecca Hazell)*
  c HB Guide - v8 - Spr '97 - p162 [51-250]
  c KR - v64 - O 1 '96 - p1467 [51-250]
  c SLJ - v42 - D '96 - p129+ [51-250]
Hazen, Barbara Shook - *Digby (Illus. by Barbara J Phillips-Duke)*
  c BL - v93 - N 15 '96 - p596+ [51-250]
  c KR - v64 - D 1 '96 - p1738 [51-250]
  c SLJ - v43 - F '97 - p81 [51-250]
Hazen, Robert M - *The Physical Sciences*
  New Sci - v151 - S 28 '96 - p54+ [501+]
  Why Aren't Black Holes Black?
  y BL - v93 - My 15 '97 - p1549 [51-250]
Hazen-Hammond, Susan - *Timelines of Native American History*
  r PW - v244 - Ap 21 '97 - p57 [51-250]
Hazenwinkel, M - *Handbook of Algebra. Vol. 1*
  SciTech - v20 - D '96 - p15 [51-250]
Hazlitt, Henry - *Economics in One Lesson (Riggenbach). Audio Version*
  LJ - v121 - N 1 '96 - p120 [51-250]
  LJ - v122 - F 15 '97 - p115 [1-50]
H D - *Kora and Ka*
  RCF - v16 - Fall '96 - p197 [501+]
He, Jingwen - *Nie Yu*
  BL - v93 - My 1 '97 - p1484 [1-50]
He, Li - *Chinese Ceramics*
  Ceram Mo - v45 - Mr '97 - p26+ [501+]
  FEER - v159 - D 19 '96 - p54+ [251-500]
He, Zhou - *Mass Media and Tiananmen Square*
  R&R Bk N - v12 - F '97 - p82 [51-250]
Head, David M - *The Ebbs and Flows of Fortune*
  Six Ct J - v27 - Win '96 - p1213+ [501+]
Head, Ivan - *The Canadian Way*
  BIC - v25 - S '96 - p14+ [501+]
  BIC - v25 - D '96 - p31 [501+]
Head, John W - *Introducing and Managing Academic Library Automation Projects*
  A Lib - v27 - Ag '96 - p70 [51-250]
  r RQ - v36 - Win '96 - p315 [251-500]
Head, Randolph C - *Early Modern Democracy in the Grisons*
  AHR - v101 - D '96 - p1572+ [501+]
  Six Ct J - v27 - Win '96 - p1113+ [501+]
  Six Ct J - v27 - Win '96 - p1114+ [501+]
Head, William - *The Eagle in the Desert*
  MEJ - v50 - Sum '96 - p455 [51-250]
  Every Inch a Soldier
  Pub Hist - v18 - Sum '96 - p66+ [501+]
Head, Wilson - *A Life on the Edge*
  CF - v75 - N '96 - p46+ [501+]
Headlam, Dave - *The Music of Alban Berg*
  Choice - v34 - F '97 - p974 [51-250]
Headlee, Sue - *The Cost of Being Female*
  Choice - v34 - My '97 - p1583+ [51-250]
Headon, David - *The League of a Nation*
  Aust Bk R - Je '96 - p26+ [501+]
Headrick, Daniel R - *The Tentacles of Progress*
  JC - v46 - Sum '96 - p183+ [501+]
Head's Legal Guide 1985-
  TES - Ja 24 '97 - p11* [51-250]
Heal, Felicity - *The Gentry in England and Wales 1500-1700*
  AHR - v101 - O '96 - p1202+ [501+]
  JIH - v27 - Aut '96 - p301+ [501+]
Heal, Gillian - *Grandpa Bear's Fantastic Scarf (Illus. by Gillian Heal)*
  c BL - v93 - Ap 1 '97 - p1337 [51-250]
  c KR - v65 - Mr 1 '97 - p390 [51-250]
  c PW - v244 - F 24 '97 - p91 [51-250]
Heald, Chris - *Journeys*
  TES - D 13 '96 - p43 [51-250]
Healey, John - *Votes and Budgets*
  APSR - v91 - Mr '97 - p215 [501+]

Healey, Thomas S - *The Two Deaths of George Wallace*
  BL - v93 - N 1 '96 - p478 [51-250]
Healki, Thomas - *Creative Ritual: Combining Yoruba, Santeria, and Western Magic Traditions*
  BWatch - v17 - S '96 - p12 [51-250]
Health and Safety/Risk Abstracts. Electronic Media Version
  Choice - v34 - D '96 - p644 [51-250]
Health and Safety (Time-Life)
  c HB Guide - v8 - Spr '97 - p129 [51-250]
  c SB - v33 - Ja '97 - p20 [51-250]
  c SLJ - v43 - Mr '97 - p174 [51-250]
Health Care Real Estate Institute Conference (1st: 1995: Los Angeles, Calif.) - *Real Estate Issues in the Health Care Industry*
  SciTech - v20 - N '96 - p38 [51-250]
Health Economics
  p JEL - v35 - Mr '97 - p308 [51-250]
The Health of Manitoba's Children
  J Gov Info - v23 - S '96 - p628 [51-250]
The Health Rationale for Family Planning
  J Gov Info - v23 - S '96 - p677 [1-50]
Health Resource Management Plan 1996-1999
  J Gov Info - v23 - S '96 - p595+ [51-250]
Healthy Cooking Deluxe. Electronic Media Version
  LJ - v121 - O 15 '96 - p96+ [501+]
Healthy Meals Fast
  BWatch - v17 - D '96 - p9 [1-50]
Healy, Chris - *From the Ruins of Colonialism*
  Aust Bk R - F '97 - p7+ [501+]
Healy, David - *The Psychopharmacologists*
  Sci - v275 - Mr 7 '97 - p1438+ [501+]
Healy, Dermot - *The Bend for Home*
  Obs - O 27 '96 - p17* [501+]
  Spec - v277 - O 26 '96 - p54+ [501+]
  TLS - S 27 '96 - p31 [501+]
Healy, James N - *Love Songs of the Irish*
  CAY - v17 - Win '96 - p11 [51-250]
Healy, Thomas - *A Hurting Business*
  NS & S - v9 - My 24 '96 - p36+ [501+]
Heaney, Seamus - *Crediting Poetry*
  Poet - v168 - S '96 - p337+ [501+]
  The Redress of Poetry
  HR - v49 - Aut '96 - p521+ [501+]
  NYTBR - v101 - D 1 '96 - p36 [1-50]
  Obs - O 6 '96 - p18* [51-250]
  Poet - v168 - S '96 - p337+ [501+]
  WLT - v70 - Sum '96 - p698 [501+]
  The School Bag
  NS - v126 - Ap 25 '97 - p48+ [501+]
  Obs - Mr 23 '97 - p16* [501+]
  TLS - Ap 11 '97 - p23 [501+]
  The Spirit Level
  BL - v93 - Ap 1 '97 - p1285 [1-50]
  LJ - v122 - Ja '97 - p49 [1-50]
  LJ - v122 - Ap 1 '97 - p94 [1-50]
  NS & S - v9 - Ap 26 '96 - p32 [251-500]
  NYTBR - v101 - Jl 21 '96 - p6 [501+]
  NYTBR - v101 - D 8 '96 - p82 [1-50]
  NYTBR - v102 - Ap 20 '97 - p32 [251-250]
  Poet - v168 - S '96 - p337+ [501+]
  y SLJ - v42 - N '96 - p141 [51-250]
  Spec - v276 - My 11 '96 - p42+ [251-500]
  TES - D 27 '96 - p16+ [51-250]
  TLS - N 29 '96 - p13 [51-250]
  TPR - v17 - Win '97 - p8+ [501+]
  VLS - Win '96 - p9 [51-250]
  WLT - v70 - Aut '96 - p963 [251-500]
  YR - v84 - O '96 - p166+ [501+]
  Stepping Stones (Pennington). Audio Version
  Kliatt - v30 - N '96 - p51 [51-250]
Heap, Nick - *Information Technology and Society*
  SocSciComR - v14 - Win '96 - p494+ [501+]
Heard, Georgia - *Writing toward Home*
  Inst - v106 - N '96 - p41 [1-50]
Hearder, Harry - *Cavour*
  EHR - v112 - F '97 - p237+ [251-500]
Hearle, Kevin - *Each Thing We Know Is Changed Because We Know It and Other Poems*
  WAL - v31 - Fall '96 - p273+ [251-500]
Hearn, Chester G - *The Capture of New Orleans 1862*
  J Mil H - v61 - Ja '97 - p165+ [251-500]
  George Washington's Schooners
  Sea H - Sum '96 - p29 [501+]
  Six Years of Hell
  Choice - v34 - My '97 - p1562+ [51-250]
  KR - v64 - S 15 '96 - p1373 [51-250]
  LJ - v121 - N 1 '96 - p88 [51-250]
  PW - v243 - O 14 '96 - p73+ [51-250]
Hearn, Donald - *Computer Graphics. 2nd Ed.*
  SciTech - v20 - D '96 - p59 [51-250]

Hearn, Jeff - *Sex at Work. Rev. Ed.*
  R&R Bk N - v11 - N '96 - p38 [51-250]
Hearn, Mark - *One Big Union*
  TLS - F 7 '97 - p30 [501+]
Hearne, Betsy - *Eliza's Dog (Illus. by Erica Thurston)*
  c HB - v72 - S '96 - p596 [51-250]
  c HB Guide - v7 - Fall '96 - p293 [51-250]
Hearne, Robert R - *Water Allocation and Water Markets*
  JEL - v34 - S '96 - p1497+ [51-250]
Hearnshaw, J B - *The Measurement of Starlight*
  Choice - v34 - F '97 - p985 [51-250]
Hearon, Reed - *Bocaditos: The Little Dishes of Mexico*
  BL - v93 - F 15 '97 - p988+ [51-250]
Hearst, Patty - *Murder at San Simeon*
  Arm Det - v30 - Win '97 - p39 [251-500]
Heartz, Daniel - *Haydn, Mozart and the Viennese School 1740-1780*
  Eight-C St - v30 - Win '96 - p199+ [501+]
  Notes - v53 - Mr '97 - p765+ [501+]
HEAT
  p Aust Bk R - Ag '96 - p55 [501+]
Heat Transfer, Houston 1996
  SciTech - v20 - D '96 - p73 [51-250]
Heater, Derek, 1931- - *Our World This Century*
  y TES - S 6 '96 - pR7 [501+]
Heater, Derek Benjamin - *World Citizenship and Government*
  Choice - v34 - Ja '97 - p872+ [51-250]
  R&R Bk N - v11 - D '96 - p46 [51-250]
Heath, Alan - *Common Threads*
  r BL - v93 - Mr 1 '97 - p1177 [51-250]
Heath, Dwight B - *International Handbook on Alcohol and Culture*
  Am Ethnol - v23 - Ag '96 - p656+ [501+]
Heath, Jim - *Clark County, Wisconsin Cemeteries. Vol. 1*
  r EGH - v50 - N '96 - p191+ [51-250]
Heath, Michael J - *Rabelais*
  Choice - v34 - My '97 - p1504 [51-250]
Heath, Roy - *Kwaku, or, The Man Who Could Not Keep His Mouth Shut*
  BL - v93 - Ap 1 '97 - p1281 [51-250]
  Kwaku, or, the Man Who Could Not Keep His Mouth Shut
  KR - v65 - F 15 '97 - p243+ [251-500]
  Kwaku, or, The Man Who Could Not Keep His Mouth Shut
  LJ - v122 - Ap 1 '97 - p126 [51-250]
  The Ministry of Hope
  BL - v93 - Mr 1 '97 - p1110 [51-250]
  KR - v64 - D 1 '96 - p1691 [251-500]
  LJ - v121 - N 15 '96 - p88 [51-250]
  PW - v243 - N 18 '96 - p63 [251-500]
  The Shadow Bride
  W&I - v11 - Jl '96 - p279+ [501+]
Heath, Steve - *Multimedia and Communications Technology*
  SciTech - v20 - N '96 - p7 [51-250]
Heath, William - *The Children Bob Moses Led*
  BWatch - v17 - N '96 - p10 [51-250]
Heathcote, T A - *The Military in British India*
  EHR - v111 - N '96 - p1320+ [501+]
Heaton, E W - *The School Tradition of the Old Testament*
  Intpr - v51 - Ap '97 - p200 [251-500]
  Theol St - v57 - Mr '96 - p180+ [251-500]
Heaton, Tim - *Education and Training*
  y TES - F 21 '97 - p20* [251-500]
Hebblethwaite, Peter - *The Next Pope*
  Theol St - v57 - Je '96 - p360+ [501+]
Hebden, Mark - *Pel and the Parked Car*
  Books - v9 - S '95 - p19 [51-250]
Hebeda, Ronald E - *Baked Goods Freshness*
  SciTech - v20 - S '96 - p63 [51-250]
Hebel, Johann Peter - *The Treasure Chest*
  MLR - v91 - O '96 - p1042+ [251-500]
Heber, David - *Dietary Fats, Lipids, Hormones, and Tumorigenesis*
  SciTech - v21 - Mr '97 - p50 [51-250]
Heberle, Marianna Olszweska - *German Cooking*
  BWatch - v17 - N '96 - p1 [51-250]
Hebert, Holly - *60 Super Simple Crafts (Illus. by Leo Abbett)*
  c SLJ - v43 - F '97 - p92 [51-250]
Hebert, Jean-Paul - *Production D'Armement*
  J Gov Info - v23 - S '96 - p658 [1-50]
Hebert, Mary - *Not Black and White*
  y Kliatt - v30 - N '96 - p18 [51-250]
Hebron Presbyterian Church
  EGH - v50 - N '96 - p165 [51-250]
Hechler, Ellen - *A Mathematical Word Search Puzzle Book*
  y Math T - v89 - D '96 - p784 [251-500]

Hecht, Anthony - *Collected Earlier Poems*
  LJ - v122 - Ap 1 '97 - p95 [1-50]
  Flight among the Tombs
    BL - v93 - N 15 '96 - p567 [51-250]
    BW - v27 - Ja 26 '97 - p8 [251-500]
    LJ - v121 - O 1 '96 - p82 [51-250]
    NYRB - v44 - Mr 27 '97 - p18+ [501+]
    YR - v85 - Ap '97 - p161+ [501+]
  The Hidden Law
    South CR - v28 - Spr '96 - p286+ [501+]
Hecht, Jonathan - *Opening to Reform?*
  For Aff - v76 - My '97 - p146+ [51-250]
Hecht, Julie - *Do the Windows Open?*
  BL - v93 - Ja '97 - p820 [51-250]
  Ent W - F 7 '97 - p65 [51-250]
  KR - v64 - D 1 '96 - p1691 [251-500]
  NYTBR - v102 - Ja 26 '97 - p8 [501+]
  NYTLa - v146 - Ja 24 '97 - pC31 [501+]
  PW - v243 - D 30 '96 - p56 [51-250]
  Time - v149 - F 10 '97 - p82 [251-500]
  VV - v42 - F 4 '97 - p51+ [251-500]
Hecht, N S - *An Introduction to the History and Sources of Jewish Law*
  MEJ - v51 - Spr '97 - p313 [51-250]
Hecht, Robert A - *An Unordinary Man*
  Am - v175 - N 30 '96 - p28+ [501+]
  Comw - v124 - Ap 11 '97 - p26 [251-500]
  R&R Bk N - v12 - F '97 - p11 [51-250]
Hechtman, Llly - *Do They Grow out of It?*
  Readings - v11 - D '96 - p30 [51-250]
Heck, Andre - *Introduction to Maple. 2nd Ed.*
  JEL - v35 - Mr '97 - p198 [51-250]
Heck, Peter J - *A Connecticut Yankee in Criminal Court*
  y BL - v93 - N 15 '96 - p574 [51-250]
  BWatch - v18 - F '97 - p7 [1-50]
  KR - v64 - O 1 '96 - p1428 [251-500]
  PW - v243 - S 23 '96 - p59 [51-250]
  Death on the Mississippi
  y Kliatt - v31 - Ja '97 - p8 [51-250]
Heck, Vera - *The Brandt History 1854-1994*
  r EGH - v50 - N '96 - p192 [51-250]
Heckel, Theo K - *Der Innere Mensch*
  Rel St Rev - v23 - Ap '97 - p185 [51-250]
Heckler, Jonellen - *Final Tour*
  Books - v9 - S '95 - p25 [51-250]
Heckler-Feltz, Cheryl - *Heart and Soul of the Nation*
  KR - v65 - Ja 1 '97 - p37+ [251-500]
  LJ - v122 - F 15 '97 - p138 [51-250]
  PW - v243 - D 2 '96 - p51 [51-250]
Heckman, Philip - *Waking Upside Down (Illus. by Dwight Been)*
  c HB Guide - v7 - Fall '96 - p259 [51-250]
  c KR - v64 - My 1 '96 - p689 [51-250]
Heckscher, Charles C - *The New Unionism*
  JEL - v35 - Mr '97 - p240 [51-250]
  White-Collar Blues
    CS - v26 - Mr '97 - p220+ [501+]
    ILRR - v50 - O '96 - p172+ [501+]
Hedaya, Robert J - *Understanding Biological Psychiatry*
  Readings - v12 - Mr '97 - p25 [51-250]
Hedderwick, Mairi - *The Big Katie Morag Storybook (Illus. by Mairi Hedderwick)*
  c JB - v60 - D '96 - p252+ [251-500]
  c PW - v243 - N 25 '96 - p77 [51-250]
  c Sch Lib - v44 - N '96 - p146 [51-250]
Heder, Steven R - *Propaganda, Politics and Violence in Cambodia*
  NYRB - v43 - N 14 '96 - p41+ [501+]
  Propaganda, Politics, and Violence in Cambodia
    Pac A - v69 - Fall '96 - p447+ [501+]
Hedetoft, Ulf - *Signs of Nations*
  R&R Bk N - v12 - F '97 - p14 [51-250]
Hedgecoe, John - *John Hedgecoe's Workbook of Photo Techniques*
  Pet PM - v25 - Jl '96 - p36 [51-250]
Hedgepeth, Sonia M - *Uberall Blicke Ich Nacheinem, Heimatlichen Boden Aus*
  Ger Q - v70 - Win '97 - p82+ [501+]
Hedges, Elaine - *Listening to Silences*
  Signs - v22 - Win '97 - p484+ [501+]
Hedges, G - *Issues in Librarianship 2*
  LAR - v98 - S '96 - p482 [51-250]
Hedin, Raymond - *Married to the Church*
  Rel St Rev - v23 - Ja '97 - p95 [51-250]
Hedin, Robert - *The Great Machines*
  CAY - v17 - Fall '96 - p5 [51-250]
  y Kliatt - v30 - S '96 - p23+ [51-250]
Hedin, Sven - *My Life as an Explorer*
  LJ - v122 - Ja '97 - p155 [1-50]

Hedlund, Carey - *Night Fell at Harry's Farm (Illus. by Carey Hedlund)*
  c KR - v65 - My 1 '97 - p722 [51-250]
Hedren, Paul L - *Traveler's Guide to the Great Sioux War*
  r Roundup M - v4 - O '96 - p26 [51-250]
  r WHQ - v28 - Spr '97 - p103 [1-50]
Hedrick, James L - *Step-Growth Polymers for High-Performance Materials*
  SciTech - v20 - S '96 - p61 [51-250]
Heel, K Donker Van - *The Illustrated Encyclopedia of World History*
  r HT - v46 - O '96 - p59 [1-50]
Heelas, Paul - *Detraditionalization*
  CS - v26 - Mr '97 - p246+ [501+]
  The New Age Movement
    Socio R - v45 - My '97 - p352+ [501+]
Heer, David M - *Immigration in America's Future*
  Choice - v34 - N '96 - p537+ [51-250]
Heersink, Mary - *E. Coli 0157*
  KR - v64 - My 1 '96 - p665 [251-500]
Heertje, Arnold - *The Makers of Modern Economics. Vol. 2*
  Econ J - v107 - Ja '97 - p260 [51-250]
Heery, Mike - *Practical Strategies for the Modern Academic Library*
  LAR - v99 - F '97 - p102 [51-250]
Heffer, Simon - *Moral Desperado*
  BL - v93 - D 15 '96 - p705 [51-250]
  Choice - v34 - F '97 - p965 [51-250]
  KR - v64 - N 1 '96 - p1582 [251-500]
  LJ - v122 - F 15 '97 - p142 [51-250]
  Nine-C Lit - v51 - Mr '97 - p558 [1-50]
Heffernan, Carol Falvo - *The Melancholy Muse*
  RMR - v50 - 2 '96 - p189+ [501+]
Heffernan, William - *The Dinosaur Club*
  LJ - v122 - Ap 15 '97 - p117 [51-250]
  PW - v244 - My 12 '97 - p58 [51-250]
  Winter's Gold
    PW - v243 - D 30 '96 - p63 [51-250]
Heffley, Mike - *The Music of Anthony Braxton*
  M Ed J - v83 - N '96 - p54 [1-50]
Heffron, Dorris - *A Shark in the House*
  Quill & Q - v62 - My '96 - p26+ [501+]
Heffron, Jack - *The Best Writing on Writing. Vol. 2*
  Col Comp - v47 - O '96 - p438 [51-250]
Heflick, David - *How to Make Money Performing in Schools*
  BL - v93 - Ja '97 - p803 [51-250]
  LJ - v122 - Ap 15 '97 - p83 [51-250]
Hefling, Charles - *Our Selves, Our Souls and Bodies*
  CC - v114 - Ja 1 '97 - p25 [51-250]
  TT - v53 - Ja '97 - p508+ [51-250]
Heflinger, Craig Anne - *Families and the Mental Health System for Children and Adolescents*
  Choice - v34 - O '96 - p313 [51-250]
Heftrich, Eckhard - *Getraumte Taten*
  MLR - v91 - Jl '96 - p798+ [501+]
Hegarty, Frances - *Let's Dance*
  Obs - S 8 '96 - p18* [51-250]
  Woman's J - S '96 - p10 [1-50]
Hegde, M N - *A Coursebook on Language Disorders in Children*
  SciTech - v20 - N '96 - p52 [51-250]
Hegel, G W F - *Lectures on Natural Right and Political Science*
  Ethics - v107 - Ja '97 - p393+ [51-250]
Heggen, Thomas - *Mister Roberts*
  J Am St - v30 - Ap '96 - p47+ [501+]
Heggeness, Fred - *Goldmine Country Western Record and CD Guide*
  r CAY - v17 - Win '96 - p5 [51-250]
Hegi, Ursula - *Floating in My Mother's Palm*
  SFR - v21 - N '96 - p48 [1-50]
  Salt Dancers
    BW - v26 - O 6 '96 - p12 [51-250]
    NYTBR - v101 - S 29 '96 - p32 [51-250]
    PW - v243 - Jl 22 '96 - p234 [1-50]
  Stones from the River
    Ent W - Mr 21 '97 - p65+ [501+]
  Tearing the Silence
    KR - v65 - My 1 '97 - p694 [251-500]
Hegland, Jean - *Into the Forest*
  KR - v64 - My 1 '96 - p622+ [251-500]
  Wom R Bks - v14 - Mr '97 - p16+ [501+]
Hegmon, Michelle - *The Social Dynamics of Pottery Style in the Early Puebloan Southwest*
  Am Craft - v56 - Ag '96 - p66 [1-50]
Heibel, Yule F - *Reconstructing the Subject*
  AHR - v101 - O '96 - p1238 [501+]
  BM - v139 - Ja '97 - p53 [51-250]

Heidbreder, Robert - *Eenie, Meenie, Manitoba (Illus. by Scot Ritchie)*
  c BIC - v25 - N '96 - p32 [251-500]
  Eenie Meenie Manitoba (Illus. by Scot Ritchie)
  c Emerg Lib - v24 - Mr '97 - p26 [1-50]
  Eenie, Meenie, Manitoba (Illus. by Scot Ritchie)
  c Quill & Q - v62 - N '96 - p45 [251-500]
Heide, Florence Parry - *The Day of Ahmed's Secrets*
  c Inst - v42 - Ag '96 - p44 [1-50]
  Oh, Grow Up! (Illus. by Nadine Bernard Westcott)
  c HB Guide - v7 - Fall '96 - p367+ [51-250]
Heide, Margaret - *Television Culture and Women's Lives*
  QJS - v83 - F '97 - p90+ [501+]
Heide, Sigrid - *In the Hands of My Enemies*
  PW - v243 - N 4 '96 - p61 [51-250]
Heidegger, Martin - *Aristotle's Metaphysics, Theta 1-3*
  Choice - v34 - D '96 - p626 [51-250]
  IPQ - v36 - D '96 - p492+ [501+]
  Being and Time
    Choice - v34 - Mr '97 - p1174+ [51-250]
    LJ - v121 - O 1 '96 - p132 [1-50]
    R&R Bk N - v12 - F '97 - p3 [51-250]
  Ecrits Politiques 1933-1966
    FR - v70 - O '96 - p103+ [501+]
  The Fundamental Concepts of Metaphysics
    IPQ - v37 - Mr '97 - p109+ [501+]
    RM - v50 - S '96 - p158+ [501+]
Heideking, Jurgen - *American Intelligence and the German Resistance to Hitler*
  NYRB - v44 - Ja 9 '97 - p49+ [501+]
Heidenry, John - *What Wild Ecstasy*
  BL - v93 - Mr 15 '97 - p1208 [51-250]
  BW - v27 - Ap 13 '97 - p11 [501+]
  KR - v65 - Mr 15 '97 - p437 [251-500]
  LJ - v122 - Mr 15 '97 - p78 [51-250]
  PW - v244 - F 10 '97 - p74 [51-250]
  WSJ-Cent - v99 - Ap 10 '97 - pA12 [501+]
Heidlberger, Frank - *Carl Maria Von Weber Und Hector Berlioz*
  Notes - v53 - S '96 - p73+ [501+]
Heidler, David S - *Old Hickory's War*
  Pres SQ - v26 - Sum '96 - p893+ [501+]
Heiferman, Marvin - *Love Is Blind*
  Ent W - F 14 '97 - p56 [51-250]
Heifetz, Milton D - *A Walk through the Heavens*
  y Kliatt - v30 - N '96 - p29 [51-250]
  S&T - v93 - Mr '97 - p66 [1-50]
Heighton, Steven - *The Admen Move on Lhasa*
  Quill & Q - v63 - Mr '97 - p74 [501+]
  Flight Paths of the Emperor
    Obs - F 16 '97 - p17* [501+]
    TLS - F 7 '97 - p21 [501+]
Heijmans, H G - *Wetenschap Tussen Universiteit En Industrie*
  T&C - v37 - Ap '96 - p383+ [501+]
Heikkonen, Esko - *Reaping the Bounty*
  BHR - v70 - Aut '96 - p412+ [501+]
Heil, John - *Mental Causation*
  Dialogue - v36 - Win '97 - p177+ [501+]
Heilbroner, Robert - *The Crisis of Vision in Modern Economic Thought*
  JEL - v34 - S '96 - p1406+ [51-250]
  Nat - v262 - Je 10 '96 - p25+ [501+]
  Teachings from the Worldly Philosophy
    BL - v93 - Ja '97 - p757 [1-50]
    Choice - v34 - S '96 - p176 [51-250]
    Nat - v262 - Je 10 '96 - p25+ [501+]
Heilbrun, Carolyn G - *The Education of a Woman*
  PW - v243 - S 2 '96 - p121 [1-50]
  The Last Gift of Time
    BL - v93 - Mr 15 '97 - p1221 [51-250]
    BW - v27 - Mr 30 '97 - p5+ [501+]
    KR - v65 - F 15 '97 - p272 [251-500]
    LJ - v122 - Mr 15 '97 - p70 [51-250]
    NYTBR - v102 - Ap 6 '97 - p31 [501+]
    PW - v244 - Mr 3 '97 - p55 [51-250]
Heilbut, Anthony - *Thomas Mann: Eros and Literature*
  BW - v26 - Jl 7 '96 - p8 [251-500]
  Lon R Bks - v18 - S 5 '96 - p3+ [501+]
  PW - v244 - Ja 13 '97 - p73 [1-50]
  RMR - v50 - 2 '96 - p191+ [501+]
Heiligman, Deborah - *From Caterpillar to Butterfly (Illus. by Bari Weissman)*
  c HB Guide - v7 - Fall '96 - p341 [51-250]
  c SLJ - v42 - Ag '96 - p138 [51-250]
  On the Move (Illus. by Lizzy Rockwell)
  c CLW - v67 - D '96 - p61 [51-250]
  c HB Guide - v7 - Fall '96 - p348 [1-50]
  c SLJ - v42 - Ag '96 - p138 [51-250]

Heilman, Robert Leo - *Overstory--Zero*
Bloom Rev - v17 - Ja '97 - p21 [51-250]
BW - v26 - O 20 '96 - p12 [51-250]
LATBR - O 13 '96 - p15 [51-250]
Heilman, Samuel C - *Portrait of American Jews*
CS - v25 - N '96 - p753+ [501+]
Heim, Dawn McLeod - *Step-by-Step Guide to Painting Realistic Watercolors*
y BL - v93 - Mr 15 '97 - p1219 [51-250]
Heim, Greg - *U.S. Half Cent Quickfinder. 3rd Ed.*
r Coin W - v38 - Ja 20 '97 - p16 [1-50]
Heim, Scott - *In Awe*
PW - v244 - My 12 '97 - p59 [51-250]
Mysterious Skin
Books - v10 - Je '96 - p24 [51-250]
TLS - Ag 30 '96 - p22+ [501+]
Mysterious Skin (Ciccolini). Audio Version
y Kliatt - v31 - Mr '97 - p49 [51-250]
Heimann, Mary - *Catholic Devotion in Victorian England*
Albion - v28 - '96 - p719+ [51-250]
HRNB - v25 - Fall '96 - p21+ [251-500]
Heimel, Cynthia - *If You Leave Me, Can I Come Too?*
Obs - F 23 '97 - p18* [51-250]
Hein, Hilde - *Aesthetics in Feminist Perspective*
Signs - v22 - Win '97 - p469+ [501+]
Hein, Jeremy - *From Vietnam, Laos, and Cambodia*
CS - v25 - S '96 - p653+ [501+]
Hein, Rolland - *George MacDonald: Victorian Mythmaker*
VS - v39 - Aut '95 - p91+ [501+]
Heinamaa, Anna - *The Soldiers' Story*
Slav R - v55 - Sum '96 - p496+ [501+]
Heineman, Kenneth J - *Campus Wars*
JSH - v63 - F '97 - p210+ [501+]
Heinemann, Edward A - *L'Art Metrique De La Chanson De Geste*
Specu - v71 - O '96 - p958+ [501+]
Heinemann, Ronald L - *Harry Byrd of Virginia*
BW - v26 - Ag 4 '96 - p5+ [501+]
Choice - v34 - O '96 - p348 [51-250]
HRNB - v25 - Fall '96 - p43+ [251-500]
Heinemann, Sue - *Timelines of American Women's History*
r CLW - v67 - D '96 - p51 [51-250]
Heinemann Modular Mathematics for London AS and A-Level: Mechanics 3
y TES - O 4 '96 - pR12 [501+]
Heinemann Modular Mathematics for London AS and A-Level: Pure Mathematics 3
y TES - O 4 '96 - pR12 [501+]
Heinen, Renata - *Model Guide*
Books - v10 - Je '96 - p21 [1-50]
Heiney, Paul - *Grumpers' Farm (Illus. by Penny Ives)*
c JB - v60 - D '96 - p253 [51-250]
Heinich, Nathalie - *The Glory of Van Gogh*
AJS - v102 - Ja '97 - p1194+ [501+]
Choice - v34 - O '96 - p267 [51-250]
Heinlein, Robert A - *Friday (McQuay). Audio Version*
LJ - v122 - My 1 '97 - p154 [51-250]
The Moon Is a Harsh Mistress
BWatch - v17 - S '96 - p7 [1-50]
Stranger in a Strange Land (Hurt). Audio Version
y Kliatt - v30 - N '96 - p46 [51-250]
LJ - v121 - N 15 '96 - p106+ [51-250]
Heinrich, Bernd - *The Thermal Warriors*
Choice - v34 - Mr '97 - p1186 [51-250]
LJ - v121 - S 15 '96 - p90 [51-250]
New Sci - v152 - N 16 '96 - p47 [51-250]
NH - v105 - O '96 - p12 [51-250]
Sci - v274 - D 13 '96 - p1848 [501+]
A Year in the Maine Woods
y Kliatt - v31 - Ja '97 - p28 [51-250]
Heinrichs, Ann - *Nepal*
c HB Guide - v7 - Fall '96 - p383 [51-250]
Tibet
c HB Guide - v8 - Spr '97 - p170 [51-250]
Heins, Ethel - *The Cat and the Cook and Other Fables of Krylov (Illus. by Anita Lobel)*
c ECEJ - v24 - Fall '96 - p38 [51-250]
Heinselman, Miron - *The Boundary Waters Wilderness Ecosystem*
Choice - v34 - Mr '97 - p1182 [51-250]
Heinz, Brian J - *Kayuktuk: An Arctic Quest (Illus. by Jon Van Zyle)*
c HB Guide - v8 - Spr '97 - p30 [51-250]
c SLJ - v42 - N '96 - p81 [51-250]
Kiyuktuk: Shadow without a Body (Illus. by Jon Van Zyle)
c KR - v64 - S 15 '96 - p1401 [51-250]

The Monsters' Test (Illus. by Sal Murdocca)
c CBRS - v25 - N '96 - p26 [51-250]
c HB Guide - v8 - Spr '97 - p30+ [51-250]
c PW - v243 - S 30 '96 - p86 [51-250]
c SLJ - v42 - O '96 - p96 [51-250]
The Wolves (Illus. by Bernie Fuchs)
c BL - v93 - Ja '97 - p767 [1-50]
c BL - v93 - S 15 '96 - p240 [51-250]
c HB Guide - v8 - Spr '97 - p31 [51-250]
c Inst - v106 - Mr '97 - p29 [1-50]
c KR - v64 - Ag 15 '96 - p1235 [51-250]
c SLJ - v42 - O '96 - p114 [51-250]
Heinz, Daniel - *Church, State, and Religious Dissent*
CH - v66 - Mr '97 - p210 [51-250]
Heinze, Kurt - *Cost Management of Capital Projects*
SciTech - v20 - D '96 - p6 [51-250]
Heinzelmann, Martin - *Gregor Von Tours 538-594*
EHR - v111 - N '96 - p1231+ [501+]
Specu - v71 - O '96 - p959+ [501+]
Heinzen, Thomas E - *Many Things to Tell You*
PW - v243 - O 14 '96 - p80 [51-250]
Heinzle, Joachim - *Geschichte Der Deutschen Literatur Bis Zum Beginn Der Neuzeit. Rev. Ed., Vol. 1, Pts. 1-2; Vol. 2, Pt. 2*
MLR - v92 - Ap '97 - p499+ [501+]
Heip, C H R - *Major Biological Processes in European Tidal Estuaries*
SciTech - v20 - D '96 - p29 [51-250]
Heiple, Daniel L - *Garcilaso De La Vega and the Italian Renaissance*
MLR - v92 - Ap '97 - p479+ [501+]
Heise, Hans-Jurgen - *Heiterkeit Ohne Grund*
WLT - v70 - Aut '96 - p953+ [251-500]
Heisel, Sharon E - *Eyes of a Stranger*
y HB Guide - v7 - Fall '96 - p302 [51-250]
Heisey, John W - *Genealogy: Helps, Hints, and Hope*
NGSQ - v84 - S '96 - p232+ [251-500]
Heising, Willetta L - *Detecting Women 2*
Arm Det - v29 - Fall '96 - p490 [251-500]
Heiss, Gayle - *Finding the Way Home*
BL - v93 - Ja '97 - p781+ [51-250]
BWatch - v18 - Mr '97 - p2 [51-250]
Heiss, Gernot - *Das Millennium*
TLS - D 20 '96 - p6 [501+]
Heit, Michael - *GIS Applications in Natural Resources 2*
SciTech - v20 - D '96 - p2 [51-250]
Heither, Theresia - *Translatio Religionis*
Rel St Rev - v22 - O '96 - p301+ [501+]
Heitzenrater, Richard P - *Wesley and the People Called Methodists*
Rel St Rev - v23 - Ap '97 - p192+ [51-250]
Hejaiej, Monia - *Behind Closed Doors*
CSM - v88 - O 31 '96 - pB1+ [501+]
Hek, Gill - *Making Sense of Research*
Choice - v34 - F '97 - p996 [51-250]
Hekman, Susan J - *Feminist Interpretations of Michel Foucault*
Choice - v34 - My '97 - p1539 [51-250]
Moral Voices, Moral Selves
Ethics - v107 - O '96 - p186+ [51-250]
Helal, Abdelsalam A - *Replication Techniques in Distributed Systems*
SciTech - v21 - Mr '97 - p12 [51-250]
Helal, Basil - *Surgery of Disorders of the Foot and Ankle*
SciTech - v20 - N '96 - p50 [51-250]
Helander, Brock - *The Rock Who's Who. 2nd Ed.*
r ARBA - v28 - '97 - p494 [51-250]
r LJ - v122 - Mr 15 '97 - p54 [51-250]
Helbig, Alethea - *Dictionary of American Children's Fiction 1990-1994*
r ARBA - v28 - '97 - p428+ [251-500]
r Ch BWatch - v7 - Ja '97 - p6 [51-250]
The Phoenix Award of the Children's Literature Association 1990-1994
r CCB-B - v50 - My '97 - p340+ [51-250]
r Sch Lib - v45 - F '97 - p54 [51-250]
This Land Is Our Land
r J Am Cult - v19 - Sum '96 - p139 [51-250]
Helbig, Gerhard - *Deutsche Partikeln--Richtig Gebraucht?*
MLJ - v80 - Fall '96 - p419+ [501+]
Held, David - *Democracy and the Global Order*
Socio R - v45 - F 1 '97 - p179+ [501+]
Models of Democracy. 2nd Ed.
Choice - v34 - My '97 - p1574 [51-250]
Held, Gilbert - *Data and Image Compression. 4th Ed.*
SciTech - v20 - N '96 - p11 [51-250]
Netware Login Scripts
CBR - v14 - S '96 - p30+ [51-250]
Heldenfels, R D - *Television's Greatest Year 1954*
J Pop F&TV - v24 - Win '97 - p183+ [501+]

Heldman, Marilyn E - *The Marian Icons of the Painter Fre Seyon*
Six Ct J - v27 - Fall '96 - p855+ [501+]
Helfert, Erich Anton - *Valley of the Shadow*
PW - v243 - D 9 '96 - p55 [51-250]
Helfgott, Gillian - *Love You to Bits and Pieces*
Lon R Bks - v19 - Ap 3 '97 - p30+ [51-250]
Obs - Ja 19 '97 - p15* [501+]
Trib Bks - F 2 '97 - p8 [1-50]
Trib Bks - Ap 6 '97 - p3 [501+]
Helg, Aline - *Our Rightful Share*
Historian - v58 - Sum '96 - p860+ [251-500]
Helgesen, Sally - *The Web of Inclusion*
Per Psy - v49 - Aut '96 - p759+ [501+]
Hell, Richard - *Go Now*
LJ - v121 - O 1 '96 - p47 [1-50]
Helland, Janice - *The Studios of Frances and Margaret Macdonald*
R&R Bk N - v11 - N '96 - p60 [51-250]
TLS - O 18 '96 - p21 [501+]
Helldorfer, M C - *Carnival (Illus. by Dan Yaccarino)*
c HB Guide - v7 - Fall '96 - p259 [51-250]
Harmonica Night (Illus. by Alexi Natchev)
c KR - v65 - My 1 '97 - p722 [51-250]
c PW - v244 - Ap 28 '97 - p75 [51-250]
Jack, Skinny Bones, and the Golden Pancakes (Illus. by Elise Primavera)
c CCB-B - v50 - D '96 - p137 [51-250]
c HB Guide - v8 - Spr '97 - p31 [51-250]
c PW - v243 - N 11 '96 - p73 [51-250]
c SLJ - v42 - O '96 - p96+ [51-250]
Helleiner, Eric - *States and the Reemergence of Global Finance*
JEL - v34 - D '96 - p2049 [51-250]
Helleiner, G K - *Manufacturing for Export in the Developing World*
JEL - v34 - S '96 - p1427 [51-250]
Heller, Charles E - *Portrait of an Abolitionist*
Bl S - v26 - Sum '96 - p65 [1-50]
Heller, Dana - *Family Plots*
J Pop F&TV - v24 - Win '97 - p184 [501+]
Heller, David - *Multimedia Business Presentations*
CBR - v15 - Spr '97 - p8 [1-50]
Heller, Francis H - *The United States and the Integration of Europe*
For Aff - v75 - S '96 - p146 [51-250]
JEL - v34 - D '96 - p2106 [51-250]
Heller, Henry - *Labour, Science and Technology in France 1500-1620*
Choice - v34 - N '96 - p518 [51-250]
Heller, Jan Christian - *Human Genome Research and the Challenge of Contingent Future Persons*
BWatch - v17 - S '96 - p11 [1-50]
Choice - v34 - D '96 - p636 [51-250]
Hast Cen R - v26 - S '96 - p40 [1-50]
SciTech - v20 - N '96 - p27 [51-250]
Heller, Jane - *Princess Charming*
BL - v93 - Mr 1 '97 - p1110 [51-250]
Ent W - Ap 18 '97 - p63 [51-250]
KR - v65 - F 1 '97 - p160+ [251-500]
Heller, Joseph - *The Stern Gang*
Choice - v34 - N '96 - p523 [51-250]
MEJ - v51 - Win '97 - p124+ [501+]
TLS - Jl 7 '96 - p8 [501+]
Heller, Karl - *Antonio Vivaldi: The Red Priest of Venice*
BL - v93 - Mr 15 '97 - p1218 [51-250]
LJ - v122 - Ap 1 '97 - p93+ [51-250]
Heller, Klaus - *Die Normannen in Osteuropa*
Russ Rev - v55 - O '96 - p712 [251-500]
Heller, Michael, 1937- - *Carl Rakosi: Man and Poet*
J Am St - v30 - Ag '96 - p271+ [501+]
Heller, Michal - *Lemaitre, Big Bang, and the Quantum Universe*
Choice - v34 - Ja '97 - p816 [51-250]
SciTech - v20 - N '96 - p17 [51-250]
Heller, Nicholas - *This Little Piggy (Illus. by Sonja Lamut)*
c BL - v93 - F 15 '97 - p1026 [51-250]
c KR - v65 - Ap 1 '97 - p556 [51-250]
c PW - v244 - Ap 7 '97 - p91 [51-250]
Heller, Peter - *Bad Intentions*
NYTBR - v101 - Ap 7 '96 - p24 [1-50]
In This Corner...!
Aethlon - v13 - Fall '95 - p161+ [251-500]
In Transit
R&R Bk N - v12 - F '97 - p91 [51-250]
Heller, Richard F - *The Carbohydrate Addict's Lifespan Program*
BL - v93 - N 1 '96 - p468+ [51-250]
LJ - v121 - D '96 - p131 [51-250]
PW - v243 - N 18 '96 - p72+ [51-250]

Heller, Ruth - *Behind the Mask (Illus. by Ruth Heller)*
c Inst - v106 - Ag '96 - p42 [51-250]
c LA - v73 - D '96 - p621 [51-250]
Color (Illus. by Ruth Heller)
c Inst - v106 - Ja '97 - p4* [1-50]
c RT - v50 - O '96 - p136 [1-50]
Fine Lines (Illus. by Michael Emery)
c BL - v93 - S 1 '96 - p121 [51-250]
c HB - v72 - S '96 - p613 [51-250]
c HB Guide - v7 - Fall '96 - p372 [51-250]
c Inst - v106 - Ag '96 - p42 [1-50]
c SLJ - v43 - Ja '97 - p102 [51-250]
Heller, Steve, 1949, Apr., 4- - *Who's Afraid of C++?*
SciTech - v21 - Mr '97 - p8 [1-50]
Heller, Steven - *Cover Story*
LATBR - O 6 '96 - p15 [51-250]
Heller, Vivian - *Joyce, Decadence, and Emancipation*
Choice - v34 - S '96 - p126 [51-250]
Hellier, Chris - *Monasteries of Greece*
NYTBR - v101 - D 8 '96 - p56 [51-250]
Hellman, Ben - *Poets of Hope and Despair*
WLT - v70 - Sum '96 - p721+ [501+]
Hellman, Hal - *The Story of Gold*
c HB Guide - v8 - Spr '97 - p112 [51-250]
c SB - v33 - Ja '97 - p20 [51-250]
Hellmann, Monika - *Judit--Eine Frau Im Spannungsfeld Von Autonomie Und Gottlicher Fuhrung*
Rel St Rev - v22 - O '96 - p350+ [51-250]
Hello, Poldy!
c HB Guide - v7 - Fall '96 - p240 [51-250]
Helly, Mathilde - *Montezuma and the Aztecs*
y SLJ - v43 - Mr '97 - p201 [51-250]
Helm, June - *Prophecy and Power among the Dogrib Indians*
JR - v76 - O '96 - p675+ [501+]
Helman, Cecil - *Culture, Health and Illness*
TLS - Ja 31 '97 - p29 [51-250]
Helmi, Rio - *Bali Style*
BWatch - v17 - S '96 - p3 [51-250]
Helmke, Uwe - *Optimization and Dynamical Systems*
SIAM Rev - v38 - S '96 - p531+ [501+]
Helmridge-Marsillian, Veronique - *Stewart MacFarlane: Riddles of Life*
Aust Bk R - Ag '96 - p31+ [501+]
Helms, Alan - *Young Man from the Provinces*
Bloom Rev - v16 - N '96 - p18 [501+]
Helms, Mary - *Creations of the Rainbow Serpent*
LA Ant - v7 - D '96 - p374+ [501+]
Helmstadter, Ernst - *Behavioral Norms, Technological Progress, and Economic Dynamics*
JEL - v35 - Mr '97 - p281 [51-250]
Helping Kids Get Organized
Ch BWatch - v6 - O '96 - p1 [51-250]
Helping Students Develop Their IEPs
EL - v54 - S '96 - p106 [51-250]
Helprin, Mark - *A City in Winter (Illus. by Chris Van Allsburg)*
y BW - v27 - Ja 5 '97 - p11 [501+]
c CBRS - v25 - D '96 - p46 [51-250]
y CCB-B - v50 - Ja '97 - p173 [51-250]
c Emerg Lib - v24 - Mr '97 - p44 [1-50]
c HB - v73 - Ja '97 - p57 [51-250]
c HB Guide - v8 - Spr '97 - p67 [51-250]
c LATBR - D 8 '96 - p18+ [1-50]
c NYTBR - v101 - N 24 '96 - p20 [501+]
c PW - v243 - S 9 '96 - p84 [51-250]
c SLJ - v42 - N '96 - p106 [51-250]
y VOYA - v19 - F '97 - p336 [251-500]
Helsel, Robert - *Visual Programming with HP VEE*
SciTech - v20 - S '96 - p6 [51-250]
Helvetia Sacra. Pt. 8, Vol. 1
CH - v65 - S '96 - p509+ [501+]
Helwig, David - *A Random Gospel*
CF - v75 - Ja '97 - p46+ [501+]
Hemelrijck, Danny Van - *Non Destructive Testing*
SciTech - v20 - N '96 - p62 [51-250]
Hemesath, James B - *Where Past Meets Present*
WAL - v31 - Sum '96 - p191 [251-500]
Hemingway, Ernest - *Ernest Hemingway Short Stories (Scourby). Audio Version*
CSM - v89 - Mr 27 '97 - pB2 [1-50]

The Only Thing That Counts
Choice - v34 - Ap '97 - p1336 [51-250]
Ent W - N 29 '96 - p85 [51-250]
HMR - Win '96 - p8+ [501+]
KR - v64 - S 15 '96 - p1366 [251-500]
LATBR - Ja 19 '97 - p9 [501+]
LJ - v121 - O 1 '96 - p76 [51-250]
NYTBR - v101 - D 15 '96 - p24 [51-250]
NYTLa - v146 - N 19 '96 - pC15 [501+]
PW - v243 - S 23 '96 - p63 [51-250]
TLS - N 8 '96 - p30 [501+]
Hemming, T D - *The Secular City*
MLR - v92 - Ja '97 - p191+ [251-500]
Hemmingson, Michael - *Crack Hotel*
ABR - v17 - Ag '96 - p7 [501+]
Nice Little Stories Jam-Packed with Depraved Sex and Violence
ABR - v17 - Ag '96 - p7 [501+]
Hemmons, Willa Mae - *Black Women in the New World Order*
Bl S - v26 - Fall '96 - p103 [51-250]
Choice - v34 - N '96 - p546 [51-250]
Hempel, Amy - *Tumble Home*
BL - v93 - My 1 '97 - p1478+ [51-250]
BW - v27 - Ap 13 '97 - p6 [251-500]
KR - v65 - Mr 15 '97 - p402+ [251-500]
PW - v244 - Mr 10 '97 - p47+ [51-250]
Hempel, Lamont C - *Environmental Governance*
Choice - v34 - O '96 - p356 [51-250]
Hemphill, Paul - *The Heart of the Game*
Econ - v340 - S 14 '96 - p4*+ [501+]
Wheels: A Season on NASCAR's Winston Cup Circuit
KR - v65 - My 1 '97 - p694 [251-500]
PW - v244 - My 12 '97 - p66+ [51-250]
Hempstead County, Arkansas Marriages January 1, 1900 through December 31, 1912
r EGH - v50 - N '96 - p163 [51-250]
Hempstead County, Arkansas United States Census of 1830, 1840, 1850 and Tax Lists of 1828, 1829, 1830, 1831, 1832, 1839, 1841, 1842, 1847, 1848, 1849
r EGH - v50 - N '96 - p162+ [51-250]
Hempton, David - *Evangelical Protestantism in Ulster Society 1740-1890*
Bks & Cult - v2 - Ja '96 - p11+ [501+]
Religion and Political Culture in Britain and Ireland from the Glorious Revolution to the Decline of Empire
CR - v269 - S '96 - p167 [51-250]
The Religion of the People
Bks & Cult - v2 - Ja '96 - p11+ [501+]
CR - v269 - S '96 - p166 [51-250]
Henbest, Nigel - *The New Astronomy. 2nd Ed.*
Astron - v25 - Ja '97 - p102+ [51-250]
SciTech - v20 - D '96 - p20 [51-250]
Hendee, W R - *Health Effects of Exposure to Low-Level Ionizing Radiation*
Phys Today - v49 - O '96 - p66+ [501+]
Hendel, Yehudit - *Aruhat Boker Temimah*
BL - v93 - Mr 1 '97 - p1115 [1-50]
Hendershott, Anne B - *Moving for Work*
CS - v26 - Ja '97 - p71+ [501+]
Henderson, Amy - *Red, Hot and Blue*
Choice - v34 - F '97 - p974 [51-250]
Econ - v341 - D 7 '96 - p16* [51-250]
PW - v243 - S 2 '96 - p100+ [51-250]
Henderson, Ann - *Language through Play*
TES - O 25 '96 - p12* [51-250]
Wood Play
TES - O 25 '96 - p12* [51-250]
Henderson, Bill - *Minutes of the Lead Pencil Club*
PW - v243 - N 25 '96 - p70 [51-250]
Henderson, Carrol L - *Landscaping for Wildlife*
LJ - v121 - D '96 - p66 [1-50]
Henderson, Carter - *Free Enterprise Moves East*
AB - v98 - O 7 '96 - p1152+ [51-250]
Choice - v34 - F '97 - p1008 [51-250]
Henderson, Errol Anthony - *Afrocentrism and World Politics*
APSR - v91 - Mr '97 - p232+ [501+]
Henderson, George - *Social Work Interventions*
Soc Ser R - v70 - S '96 - p500 [1-50]
Time - v57 - S '96 - p426 [251-500]
Henderson, Harry - *Modern Mathematicians*
y HB Guide - v7 - Fall '96 - p376 [51-250]
The Scientific Revolution
y HB Guide - v8 - Spr '97 - p110 [51-250]
Henderson, Hazel - *Building a Win-Win World*
Choice - v34 - Ja '97 - p844 [51-250]
Henderson, Helene - *Holidays and Festivals Index*
r CAY - v16 - Fall '95 - p5 [51-250]

Henderson, James G - *Transformative Curriculum Leadership*
ES - v27 - Sum '96 - p128+ [501+]
Henderson, John - *Piety and Charity in Late Medieval Florence*
AHR - v101 - D '96 - p1537+ [501+]
CHR - v82 - Jl '96 - p546+ [501+]
EHR - v111 - N '96 - p1260+ [251-500]
Ren Q - v50 - Spr '97 - p262+ [501+]
Poor Women and Children in the European Past
EHR - v112 - Ap '97 - p551+ [251-500]
Henderson, Johnny - *Boundary Value Problems for Functional Differential Equations*
SIAM Rev - v38 - D '96 - p713 [51-250]
Henderson, Kathy - *The Little Boat (Illus. by Patrick Benson)*
c RT - v50 - Mr '97 - p500 [51-250]
A Year in the City (Illus. by Paul Howard)
c BL - v93 - Ja '97 - p869 [251-500]
c CBRS - v25 - F '97 - p75 [1-50]
c HB Guide - v8 - Spr '97 - p31 [51-250]
c KR - v64 - O 15 '96 - p1533 [51-250]
c PW - v243 - N 18 '96 - p75 [51-250]
c Sch Lib - v45 - F '97 - p19 [51-250]
c SLJ - v43 - Ja '97 - p102 [51-250]
c TES - Ja 10 '97 - p8* [501+]
Henderson, Lauren - *Dead White Female*
Books - v10 - Je '96 - p13 [1-50]
Too Many Blondes
TLS - N 15 '96 - p25 [51-250]
Henderson, Lesley - *Reference Guide to World Literature. 2nd Ed., Vols. 1-2*
r ARBA - v28 - '97 - p421 [251-500]
Henderson, Mary C - *Theater in America. New, Updated Ed.*
Choice - v34 - S '96 - p139 [51-250]
Henderson, Richard A - *Plant Species Composition of Wisconsin Prairies*
J Gov Info - v23 - S '96 - p596 [51-250]
Henderson, Sally - *A Quiet Country*
Aust Bk R - D '96 - p93 [1-50]
Henderson, Willie - *Economics as Literature*
Econ J - v107 - Ja '97 - p245+ [501+]
Henderson-Sellers, Brian - *A Book of Object-Oriented Knowledge. 2nd Ed.*
SciTech - v20 - D '96 - p10 [51-250]
Hendin, David - *Guide to Biblical Coins. 3rd Ed.*
r Coin W - v37 - N 25 '96 - p68 [51-250]
Hendin, Herbert - *Seduced by Death*
AB - v99 - Mr 31 '97 - p1048+ [501+]
BL - v93 - N 15 '96 - p551 [51-250]
Choice - v34 - My '97 - p1533 [51-250]
KR - v64 - S 15 '96 - p1373+ [251-500]
LJ - v121 - N 1 '96 - p100 [51-250]
Nat - v263 - N 18 '96 - p25+ [501+]
NYTBR - v101 - N 24 '96 - p33 [501+]
PW - v243 - S 23 '96 - p65 [51-250]
Hendon, Donald W - *Cross-Cultural Business Negotiations*
R&R Bk N - v11 - D '96 - p28 [51-250]
Hendon, Sarah - *Success Skills Curriculum for Teen Single Parents*
J Gov Info - v23 - S '96 - p596+ [51-250]
Hendra, Sue - *Oliver's Wood (Illus. by Sue Hendra)*
c CBRS - v24 - Ag '96 - p159 [1-50]
c HB Guide - v8 - Spr '97 - p31 [51-250]
c Sch Lib - v44 - N '96 - p147+ [51-250]
c SLJ - v42 - S '96 - p180 [51-250]
Hendrick, J - *The Whole Child. 6th Ed.*
ECEJ - v24 - Win '96 - p113 [251-500]
Hendrick, Mary Jean - *If Anything Ever Goes Wrong at the Zoo (Illus. by Jane Dyer)*
c Par Ch - v20 - O '96 - p21 [51-250]
Hendricks, Bonnie L - *International Encyclopedia of Horse Breeds*
r ARBA - v28 - '97 - p588 [51-250]
Hendricks, William - *Coaching, Mentoring and Managing*
HR Mag - v41 - Je '96 - p184 [51-250]

Hendrickson, Paul - *The Living and the Dead*
BL - v92 - Ag '96 - p1851 [251-500]
BL - v93 - Ja '97 - p760 [1-50]
BW - v26 - S 15 '96 - p1+ [501+]
Comw - v123 - N 8 '96 - p28+ [501+]
LATBR - S 8 '96 - p1+ [501+]
Mar Crp G - v81 - Ja '97 - p72+ [501+]
NY - v72 - N 11 '96 - p119 [51-250]
NYTBR - v101 - S 29 '96 - p8+ [501+]
NYTBR - v101 - D 8 '96 - p88 [1-50]
NYTLa - v145 - S 6 '96 - pC27 [501+]
PW - v243 - Jl 22 '96 - p220 [51-250]
PW - v243 - N 4 '96 - p44 [51-250]
Time - v148 - S 23 '96 - p74 [501+]
The Living and the Dead (Hendrickson). Audio Version
LJ - v122 - Ja '97 - p170 [51-250]
Hendrickson, Robert - *Yankee Talk*
r ARBA - v28 - '97 - p384+ [251-500]
Hendrix, Lewellyn - *Illegitimacy and Social Structures*
R&R Bk N - v11 - D '96 - p41 [51-250]
Hendry, Chris - *Strategy through People*
Per Psy - v49 - Win '96 - p1001+ [501+]
Hendry, David F - *Econometrics: Alchemy or Science?*
Econ J - v106 - S '96 - p1398+ [501+]
The Foundations of Econometric Analysis
Econ J - v106 - N '96 - p1815+ [501+]
Hendry, Diana - *Dog Dottington (Illus. by Margaret Chamberlain)*
c Magpies - v11 - My '96 - p53 [1-50]
Flower Street Friends (Illus. by Julie Douglas)
c Bks Keeps - v100 - S '96 - p10 [51-250]
Happy Old Birthday, Owl (Illus. by Sue Heap)
c SLJ - v42 - O '96 - p98 [51-250]
The Thing on Two Legs
c Magpies - v11 - Jl '96 - p28 [1-50]
Hendy, Jenny - *Hanging Baskets*
BWatch - v17 - N '96 - p5 [51-250]
Heneghan, James - *Torn Away*
y Can Lit - Spr '97 - p250+ [501+]
y Kliatt - v30 - S '96 - p10 [51-250]
Wish Me Luck
c CCB-B - v50 - Ap '97 - p284 [51-250]
y KR - v65 - Mr 15 '97 - p461+ [51-250]
y PW - v244 - My 5 '97 - p211 [51-250]
Heneveld, Ward - *Schools Count*
JEL - v34 - S '96 - p1477+ [51-250]
Hengel, Martin - *Paul between Damascus and Antioch*
TLS - Mr 28 '97 - p3+ [501+]
Hengeveld, R - *Embargo: Apartheid's Oil Secrets Revealed*
WorldV - v13 - Ja '97 - p6 [251-500]
Henggeler, Paul R - *The Kennedy Persuasion*
AAPSS-A - v548 - N '96 - p229+ [251-500]
Henham, Ralph J - *Criminal Justice and Sentencing Policy*
Choice - v34 - Ja '97 - p883 [51-250]
Henig, Martin - *The Art of Roman Britain*
AJA - v100 - O '96 - p804+ [501+]
Henig, Robin Marantz - *The People's Health*
BL - v93 - D 1 '96 - p624 [51-250]
LJ - v121 - N 1 '96 - p100 [51-250]
Nature - v385 - F 13 '97 - p594 [501+]
Henighan, Tom - *The Presumption of Culture*
BIC - v25 - O '96 - p38+ [501+]
CF - v75 - S '96 - p38+ [501+]
Heninger, S K, Jr. - *The Subtext of Form in the English Renaissance*
MLR - v92 - Ap '97 - p443+ [501+]
Henisch, Heinz K - *The Painted Photograph 1839-1914*
Bloom Rev - v16 - N '96 - p23 [51-250]
Choice - v34 - My '97 - p1486 [51-250]
CSM - v88 - O 31 '96 - pB1+ [501+]
Henke, Klaus-Dietmar - *Die Amerikanische Besetzung Deutschlands*
r RP - v58 - Fall '96 - p840+ [501+]
Henke, Shirl - *Deep as the Rivers*
PW - v244 - Ja 13 '97 - p72 [51-250]
Henken, Elissa R - *National Redeemer*
Choice - v34 - Ja '97 - p856 [51-250]
Henkes, Kevin - *Chrysanthemum*
c PW - v243 - S 2 '96 - p133 [51-250]
Good-bye, Curtis (Illus. by Marisabina Russo)
c LA - v73 - S '96 - p355 [51-250]
Jessica (Illus. by Kevin Henkes)
c SLJ - v43 - Ja '97 - p36 [1-50]

Lilly's Purple Plastic Purse (Illus. by Kevin Henkes)
c BL - v92 - Ag '96 - p1904 [51-250]
c BL - v93 - Ja '97 - p767 [1-50]
c BL - v93 - Ap 1 '97 - p1296 [1-50]
c CCB-B - v50 - O '96 - p62 [51-250]
c CSM - v88 - S 26 '96 - pB1 [51-250]
c HB - v72 - S '96 - p577 [251-500]
c HB Guide - v8 - Spr '97 - p31 [51-250]
c LATBR - O 6 '96 - p15 [51-250]
c Learning - v25 - N '96 - p29 [51-250]
c NW - v128 - D 2 '96 - p86 [1-50]
c NY - v72 - N 18 '96 - p101 [1-50]
c NYTBR - v101 - N 10 '96 - p41 [501+]
c Par Ch - v21 - Mr '97 - p8 [1-50]
c PW - v243 - N 4 '96 - p48 [51-250]
c SLJ - v42 - Ag '96 - p122 [51-250]
c SLJ - v42 - D '96 - p30 [1-50]
Protecting Marie
y Kliatt - v31 - Mr '97 - p8 [51-250]
y PW - v243 - S 2 '96 - p133 [51-250]
c RT - v50 - N '96 - p255 [51-250]
Sheila Rae, the Brave. Electronic Media Version
c BW - v26 - D 15 '96 - p11 [51-250]
Two under Par (Illus. by Kevin Henkes)
c PW - v244 - F 17 '97 - p220 [1-50]
Words of Stone
c SLJ - v43 - Ja '97 - p36 [1-50]
c SLJ - v43 - Mr '97 - p113 [1-50]
y TES - Jl 5 '96 - pR8 [51-250]
Henkes, Victoria E - *Science of Whitewares*
SciTech - v21 - Mr '97 - p96 [51-250]
Henkin, Joshua - *Swimming across the Hudson*
y BL - v93 - Ap 1 '97 - p1281 [51-250]
BW - v27 - Ap 13 '97 - p6 [251-500]
KR - v65 - F 15 '97 - p244 [251-500]
LJ - v122 - Ap 1 '97 - p126 [51-250]
PW - v244 - Mr 10 '97 - p50+ [51-250]
Henley, Tricia - *Starting from Shops and Markets*
TES - F 14 '97 - p16* [51-250]
Henley, Virginia - *Dream Lover*
BL - v93 - Ja '97 - p820 [51-250]
KR - v64 - D 1 '96 - p1692 [251-500]
PW - v244 - Ja 6 '97 - p65 [51-250]
Henn, Raymond W - *Practical Guide to Grouting of Underground Structures*
SciTech - v20 - S '96 - p50 [51-250]
Henn, William - *One Faith*
CH - v65 - D '96 - p670+ [251-500]
CLW - v66 - Je '96 - p33+ [501+]
Intpr - v51 - Ja '97 - p103+ [251-500]
r Theol St - v57 - D '96 - p741+ [501+]
Henneman, John Bell - *Olivier De Clisson and Political Society in France under Charles V and Charles VI*
Choice - v34 - Ja '97 - p856 [51-250]
J Mil H - v61 - Ja '97 - p149+ [251-500]
R&R Bk N - v11 - N '96 - p12 [51-250]
Hennen, John C - *The Americanization of West Virginia*
Choice - v34 - O '96 - p348 [51-250]
Hennepin County Library - *Unreal! Hennepin County Library Subject Headings for Fictional Characters and Places. 2nd Ed.*
r RQ - v36 - Win '96 - p220 [51-250]
Hennessy, Anne - *The Galilee of Jesus*
Rel St Rev - v23 - Ja '97 - p68 [51-250]
Hennessy, B G - *Corduroy's Birthday (Illus. by Lisa McCue)*
c KR - v65 - Ja 1 '97 - p58+ [51-250]
c PW - v244 - Ja 13 '97 - p77 [51-250]
Olympics! (Illus. by Michael Chesworth)
c HB Guide - v7 - Fall '96 - p361 [51-250]
Hennessy, Peter - *The Hidden Wiring*
CR - v270 - F '97 - p110 [1-50]
Muddling Through
BW - v26 - D 8 '96 - p7 [51-250]
CR - v270 - Ja '97 - p45+ [501+]
NS - v125 - O 11 '96 - p45+ [501+]
Hennezel, Marie De - *Living with Death*
BL - v93 - F 15 '97 - p975 [51-250]
PW - v244 - Ja 20 '97 - p389 [51-250]
Hennig, Jean-Luc - *The Rear View*
KR - v65 - F 15 '97 - p272+ [251-500]
PW - v244 - F 10 '97 - p74+ [51-250]
VLS - Spr '97 - p14+ [501+]
Henning, Hans - *Faust-Variationen: Beitrage Zur Editionsgeschichte Vom 16. Bis Zum 20. Jahrhundert*
Ger Q - v69 - Spr '96 - p210 [51-250]
Henning, Randall - *Reviving the European Union*
Wil Q - v21 - Win '97 - p38 [51-250]
Henri, Adrian - *The Mersey Sound (Henri). Audio Version*
Obs - F 16 '97 - p18* [51-250]

One of Your Legs Is Both the Same (Illus. by Colin McNaughton)
c JB - v60 - Ag '96 - p150 [51-250]
Henrich, Dieter - *The Unity of Reason*
Phil R - v105 - Ja '96 - p122+ [501+]
Henricson, Mats - *Industrial Strength C++*
SciTech - v21 - Mr '97 - p7 [51-250]
Henriksen, Margot A - *Dr. Strangelove's America*
KR - v65 - My 1 '97 - p695 [251-500]
Henrique, Risha - *The Lighted Path*
LJ - v122 - F 1 '97 - p86+ [51-250]
Henriques, Diana B - *Fidelity's World*
NYTBR - v102 - Mr 2 '97 - p28 [51-250]
Trib Bks - F 23 '97 - p8 [1-50]
Henry, Alexandra - *If I Should Die*
Books - v9 - S '95 - p22 [51-250]
Books - v10 - Je '96 - p24 [51-250]
Henry, Alison - *Belfast English and Standard English*
Lang Soc - v25 - S '96 - p471+ [501+]
Henry, Christopher - *The Electoral College*
c BL - v93 - S 1 '96 - p122 [51-250]
c HB Guide - v8 - Spr '97 - p92 [51-250]
c SLJ - v42 - O '96 - p132+ [51-250]
Presidential Conventions
c BL - v93 - S 1 '96 - p122 [51-250]
c HB Guide - v8 - Spr '97 - p92 [51-250]
c SLJ - v42 - O '96 - p132+ [51-250]
Presidential Elections
c BL - v93 - S 1 '96 - p122 [51-250]
c HB Guide - v8 - Spr '97 - p92 [51-250]
c SLJ - v42 - O '96 - p132+ [51-250]
Henry, Clement M - *The Mediterranean Debt Crescent*
Choice - v34 - O '96 - p330 [51-250]
For Aff - v75 - S '96 - p156 [51-250]
MEJ - v51 - Win '97 - p139+ [251-500]
Henry, Donald O - *Prehistoric Cultural Ecology and Evolution*
Am Ant - v61 - O '96 - p819 [501+]
Henry, Eric - *To Be a Teacher*
EL - v54 - F '97 - p86 [251-500]
Henry, J David - *The Catlike Canine. 2nd Ed.*
y SB - v32 - N '96 - p236+ [51-250]
Red Fox
Choice - v34 - D '96 - p638 [51-250]
Henry, J Glynn - *Environmental Science and Engineering. 2nd Ed.*
BioSci - v47 - Ap '97 - p258+ [501+]
Henry, Jeanne - *If Not Now*
JAAL - v40 - N '96 - p235+ [501+]
Henry, John F - *John Bates Clark: The Making of a Neoclassical Economist*
JEH - v56 - S '96 - p756+ [501+]
Henry, Lenny - *Charlie and the Big Chill (Illus. by Chris Burke). Book and Audio Version*
c TES - Ag 30 '96 - p28 [51-250]
Charlie and the Big Chill (Illus. by Chris Burke)
c PW - v243 - D 2 '96 - p60 [51-250]
Charlie, Queen of the Desert (Illus. by Chris Burke)
c JB - v60 - O '96 - p184 [51-250]
c PW - v243 - D 2 '96 - p60 [51-250]
Henry, Madeleine M - *Prisoner of History*
AJP - v117 - Win '96 - p648+ [501+]
Rel St Rev - v23 - Ap '97 - p171+ [51-250]
Henry, Maeve - *Listen to the Dark*
c Bks Keeps - Mr '97 - p27 [51-250]
y TES - Ja 3 '97 - p22 [51-250]
Midwinter
c TES - Mr 7 '97 - p12* [51-250]
Henry, Margaret - *Young Children, Parents and Professionals*
TES - N 15 '96 - p7* [51-250]
Henry, Marguerite - *Brown Sunshine of Sawdust Valley (Illus. by Bonnie Shields)*
c BL - v93 - O 1 '96 - p348+ [51-250]
c CCB-B - v50 - O '96 - p62 [51-250]
c Ch BWatch - v7 - Ja '97 - p4 [51-250]
c HB Guide - v8 - Spr '97 - p67 [51-250]
c PW - v243 - S 9 '96 - p83 [51-250]
c SLJ - v42 - S '96 - p202 [51-250]
Misty of Chincoteague (McDonough). Audio Version
y Kliatt - v31 - My '97 - p42 [51-250]
Henry, Mary E - *Parent-School Collaboration*
Choice - v34 - O '96 - p333 [51-250]
ES - v27 - Sum '96 - p131+ [501+]
R&R Bk N - v12 - F '97 - p68 [1-50]
Henry, Patrick - *Approaches to Teaching Montaigne's Essays*
FR - v70 - F '97 - p465+ [501+]
Henry, Paul, 1959- - *Captive Audience*
TLS - Mr 7 '97 - p32 [51-250]

Henry, Paul David - *Strategic Networking*
    CBR - v14 - Jl '96 - p20+ [1-50]
Henry, Richard - *Pretending and Meaning*
    Choice - v34 - D '96 - p607 [51-250]
    R&R Bk N - v11 - N '96 - p67 [1-50]
Henry, Scott D - *Fatigue Data Book*
  r ARBA - v28 - '97 - p596+ [51-250]
  r SciTech - v20 - D '96 - p64 [51-250]
Henry, Sue - *Sleeping Lady*
  y BL - v93 - S 1 '96 - p67 [51-250]
    BW - v26 - S 15 '96 - p6 [51-250]
    PW - v243 - Jl 22 '96 - p229 [51-250]
    PW - v244 - Mr 31 '97 - p72 [1-50]
Henry, Tom, 1961- - *Dogless in Metchosin (Henry). Audio Version*
    Quill & Q - v62 - Jl '96 - p52 [251-500]
  Paul Bunyan on the West Coast (Illus. by Kim La Fave)
  c Can CL - v22 - Fall '96 - p107+ [501+]
Henry, Will - *One More River to Cross (Hammer). Audio Version*
  y Kliatt - v31 - My '97 - p42+ [51-250]
Henry Francis Du Pont Winterthur Museum - *Metalwork in Early America*
    Choice - v34 - F '97 - p956 [51-250]
Henshall, Kenneth G - *A Guide to Remembering Japanese Characters*
    MLJ - v80 - Fall '96 - p422+ [501+]
Hensher, Phillip - *Kitchen Venom*
    Obs - Mr 23 '97 - p18* [51-250]
Henson, Burt - *Furman v. Georgia*
  y HB Guide - v8 - Spr '97 - p93 [51-250]
  y SB - v33 - Mr '97 - p43 [51-250]
Henson, Carol - *English and Communication for Colleges. 2nd Ed.*
    R&R Bk N - v12 - F '97 - p78 [51-250]
Henson, Kevin D - *Just a Temp*
    AJS - v102 - N '96 - p898+ [501+]
    CS - v26 - Mr '97 - p223+ [501+]
    JEL - v34 - S '96 - p1446+ [51-250]
    SF - v75 - D '96 - p762+ [501+]
Henson, Margaret Swett - *Lorenzo De Zavala: The Pragmatic Idealist*
    Roundup M - v4 - O '96 - p26+ [251-500]
Henson, Michael A - *Nonlinear Process Control*
    SciTech - v21 - Mr '97 - p84 [51-250]
Henson, Stuart - *Who Can Tell? (Illus. by Wayne Anderson)*
  c Sch Lib - v45 - F '97 - p19 [51-250]
  c TES - Ja 10 '97 - p8* [501+]
Hensperger, Beth - *Beth's Basic Bread Book*
  y Kliatt - v31 - Ja '97 - p32 [51-250]
Hentschel, Klaus - *Physics and National Socialism*
    Isis - v88 - Mr '97 - p157+ [501+]
    SciTech - v20 - S '96 - p2 [51-250]
Hentzen, Whil - *The Pros Talk Microsoft Visual FoxPro 3*
    SciTech - v20 - N '96 - p12 [51-250]
Heo, Yumi - *The Green Frogs (Illus. by Yumi Heo)*
  c CBRS - v25 - S '96 - p3 [51-250]
  c CCB-B - v50 - O '96 - p62+ [51-250]
  c Ch BWatch - v6 - N '96 - p6 [1-50]
  c HB - v72 - N '96 - p748+ [51-250]
  c HB Guide - v8 - Spr '97 - p102 [51-250]
Hepburn, Elizabeth - *Of Life and Death*
    Aust Bk R - O '96 - p69 [1-50]
    Hast Cen R - v26 - Jl '96 - p41 [1-50]
Hepp, Aloysius F - *Covalent Ceramics III*
    SciTech - v20 - N '96 - p80 [51-250]
Heppenheimer, T A - *Countdown: A History of Space Flight*
    BL - v93 - My 15 '97 - p1546 [51-250]
    KR - v65 - Ap 1 '97 - p521 [251-500]
    PW - v244 - Ap 14 '97 - p65 [51-250]
  Turbulent Skies
    Choice - v34 - S '96 - p149 [51-250]
Hepplewhite, Peter - *Romans*
    TES - D 13 '96 - p43 [51-250]
  Social Change
  c Sch Lib - v44 - N '96 - p174 [51-250]
Herald, Diana Tixier - *Genreflecting: A Guide to Reading Interests in Genre Fiction. 4th Ed.*
  r CLW - v67 - D '96 - p48+ [251-500]
  r RQ - v36 - Win '96 - p208 [51-250]
Herb, Angela M - *Beyond the Mississippi*
  c CBRS - v25 - S '96 - p12 [51-250]
  y CCB-B - v50 - D '96 - p137 [51-250]
  y Ch BWatch - v6 - N '96 - p6 [51-250]
  y HB Guide - v8 - Spr '97 - p174 [51-250]
  c KR - v64 - S 1 '96 - p1323 [51-250]
  y SLJ - v42 - N '96 - p128 [51-250]
  y VOYA - v19 - F '97 - p348 [251-500]

Herbers, Jill - *Tile*
    BL - v93 - O 1 '96 - p315 [51-250]
    LJ - v121 - S 15 '96 - p66 [51-250]
    WSJ-MW - v78 - D 5 '96 - pA18 [51-250]
Herbert, James - *'48*
    KR - v65 - My 1 '97 - p663 [251-500]
    PW - v244 - My 12 '97 - p56 [51-250]
  Portent
    KR - v64 - My 1 '96 - p623 [251-500]
  y VOYA - v19 - D '96 - p280 [251-500]
Herbert, Jeffery G - *Index of Death Notices Appearing in the Cincinnati Commercial 1858-1899*
  r EGH - v50 - N '96 - p181 [51-250]
Herbert, Mary H - *Winged Magic*
  y Kliatt - v30 - N '96 - p14 [51-250]
Herbert, Robert L - *Monet on the Normandy Coast*
    BM - v138 - S '96 - p610+ [501+]
    PW - v243 - O 21 '96 - p78 [1-50]
Herbert, Tony - *The Decorative Tile in Architecture and Interiors*
    Am Craft - v56 - Ag '96 - p27 [1-50]
Herbert, Trevor - *Post-War Wales*
    Albion - v28 - Sum '96 - p371+ [501+]
Herbert, W N - *Cabaret McGonagall*
    TLS - D 27 '96 - p25 [501+]
Herbst, Jurgen - *The Once and Future School*
    Cur R - v36 - Ap '97 - p3* [51-250]
Herbst, L J - *Integrated Circuit Engineering*
    Choice - v34 - My '97 - p1530 [51-250]
Herbst, Phil - *The Color of Words*
  r LJ - v122 - My 1 '97 - p96 [51-250]
Herbst, Sharon Tyler - *Never Eat More than You Can Lift, and Other Food Quotes and Quips*
  r LJ - v122 - My 1 '97 - p98 [51-250]
Herbst, Susan - *Numbered Voices*
    RAH - v25 - Mr '97 - p146+ [501+]
Herd, Meg - *Learn and Play in the Garden*
  c PW - v244 - Mr 10 '97 - p68 [51-250]
Herda, D J - *Earl Warren, Chief Justice for Social Change*
  y CLW - v66 - Je '96 - p48 [251-500]
  Sandra Day O'Connor, Independent Thinker
  y CLW - v66 - Je '96 - p48 [251-500]
  Thurgood Marshall, Civil Rights Champion
  y CLW - v66 - Je '96 - p48 [251-500]
  United States v. Nixon
  y HB Guide - v7 - Fall '96 - p314 [51-250]
Herdegen, Lance J - *The Men Stood like Iron*
    KR - v65 - Ja 1 '97 - p38 [251-500]
    LJ - v122 - Ap 1 '97 - p106 [51-250]
Herder, Johann Gottfried - *Johann Gottfried Herder: Selected Early Works 1764-1767*
  r MLR - v92 - Ap '97 - p503+ [501+]
    MLR - v92 - Ap '97 - p503+ [501+]
  On World History
    R&R Bk N - v12 - F '97 - p13 [51-250]
Herek, Gregory M - *Out in Force*
    For Aff - v76 - My '97 - p130 [51-250]
Herenda, Drago C - *Poultry Diseases and Meat Hygiene*
  r SciTech - v20 - N '96 - p59 [51-250]
Hereniko, Vilsoni - *Woven Gods*
    Cont Pac - v9 - Spr '97 - p279+ [501+]
Herera, Sue - *Women of the Street*
    BL - v93 - D 1 '96 - p627 [51-250]
    BWatch - v18 - Mr '97 - p11 [51-250]
    PW - v243 - N 11 '96 - p62 [51-250]
Here's How (Illus. by Laura Cornell)
  c PW - v243 - S 9 '96 - p85 [51-250]
Hergenhahn, B R - *An Introduction to the History of Psychology. 3rd Ed.*
    R&R Bk N - v12 - F '97 - p5 [51-250]
Hergenhan, Laurie - *No Casual Traveller*
    Quad - v40 - Jl '96 - p92+ [501+]
Herget, James E - *Contemporary German Legal Philosophy*
    R&R Bk N - v12 - F '97 - p62 [51-250]
Hergott, Fabrice - *Francis Bacon*
    BM - v138 - D '96 - p842+ [501+]
Hering, Rainer - *Theologie Im Spannungsfeld Von Kirche Und Staat*
    CEH - v29 - 2 '96 - p252+ [501+]
Heriot, M Jean - *Blessed Assurance*
    JR - v76 - O '96 - p650 [251-500]
Heritage, J - *Introductory Microbiology*
    Choice - v34 - S '96 - p152 [51-250]
Heriteau, Jacqueline - *Glorious Gardens*
    Hort - v94 - Ap '97 - p80 [51-250]
    PW - v243 - O 7 '96 - p70 [51-250]
Herlihy, David - *Women, Family and Society in Medieval Europe*
    Historian - v59 - Win '97 - p464 [251-500]

Herlin, Denis - *Catalogue Du Fonds Musical De La Bibliotheque De Versailles*
  r Notes - v53 - S '96 - p57+ [501+]
Herling, Gustaw - *The Island: Three Tales*
    TranslRevS - v1 - My '95 - p26+ [51-250]
  Volcano and Miracle
    LATBR - O 20 '96 - p10+ [501+]
    NY - v72 - O 14 '96 - p100 [51-250]
    Obs - F 9 '97 - p18* [501+]
    Spec - v278 - F 15 '97 - p28 [51-250]
Herlinghaus, Hermann - *Posmodernidad En La Periferia*
    Hisp - v79 - S '96 - p456+ [501+]
Herman, Arthur - *The Idea of Decline in Western History*
    BL - v93 - F 1 '97 - p923 [51-250]
    BW - v27 - F 23 '97 - p1+ [501+]
    For Aff - v76 - Ja '97 - p153+ [501+]
    KR - v65 - Ja 1 '97 - p38+ [251-500]
    LATBR - F 9 '97 - p6+ [501+]
    LJ - v122 - F 15 '97 - p146 [51-250]
    NYTBR - v102 - Mr 30 '97 - p20 [501+]
    PW - v244 - Ja 27 '97 - p89 [51-250]
    WSJ-Cent - v99 - F 24 '97 - pA20 [501+]
Herman, Charlotte - *Millie Cooper and Friends (Illus. by Helen Coganchery)*
  c RT - v50 - Mr '97 - p498 [51-250]
Herman, David - *Universal Grammar and Narrative Form*
    ELT - v39 - 4 '96 - p526+ [51-250]
Herman, Didi - *The Antigay Agenda*
    KR - v65 - Mr 15 '97 - p438 [251-500]
    PW - v244 - My 12 '97 - p73 [51-250]
  Rights of Passage
    APSR - v90 - D '96 - p938+ [501+]
Herman, Edward S - *Triumph of the Market*
    Bl S - v26 - Sum '96 - p65 [51-250]
Herman, Ellen - *The Romance of American Psychology*
    AHR - v101 - O '96 - p1308+ [501+]
    Bks & Cult - v1 - N '95 - p21 [501+]
    J Am St - v30 - Ap '96 - p166+ [501+]
Herman, Emily - *The Missing Fossil Mystery (Illus. by Andrew Glass)*
  c HB Guide - v8 - Spr '97 - p58 [51-250]
  c SLJ - v42 - D '96 - p94 [51-250]
Herman, Gail - *Flower Girl (Illus. by Paige Billin-Frye)*
  c CCB-B - v50 - S '96 - p14 [51-250]
  c SLJ - v42 - Ag '96 - p122 [51-250]
  The Haunted Bike (Illus. by Blanche Sims)
  c SLJ - v42 - Ag '96 - p121 [51-250]
  The Littlest Duckling (Illus. by Ann Schweninger)
  c HB Guide - v7 - Fall '96 - p240 [1-50]
Herman, George - *Tears of the Madonna*
    Arm Det - v29 - Sum '96 - p371 [251-500]
Herman, Irving P - *Optical Diagnostics of Thin Film Processing*
    SciTech - v21 - Mr '97 - p22 [51-250]
Herman, Jan - *A Talent for Trouble*
    FIR - v48 - Ja '97 - p104+ [501+]
    LATBR - D 29 '96 - p9 [51-250]
    TPR - v17 - Fall '96 - p33+ [501+]
Herman, Jerry - *Showtune: A Memoir*
    BL - v93 - N 15 '96 - p563 [51-250]
    BW - v27 - Mr 2 '97 - p13 [51-250]
    KR - v64 - S 15 '96 - p1374 [251-500]
    LJ - v121 - N 1 '96 - p69 [51-250]
    NYTBR - v101 - N 17 '96 - p24 [51-250]
    PW - v243 - O 21 '96 - p66 [51-250]
Herman, John - *The Light of Common Day*
  y BL - v93 - Mr 15 '97 - p1204 [51-250]
    KR - v65 - Mr 15 '97 - p403 [51-250]
    PW - v244 - Ap 7 '97 - p71 [51-250]
Herman, Jonathan R - *I and Tao*
    Choice - v34 - N '96 - p475 [51-250]
Herman, Michael - *Intelligence Power in Peace and War*
    Choice - v34 - Ap '97 - p1414 [51-250]
Herman, R A - *Pal the Pony*
  c BL - v92 - Ag '96 - p1910 [51-250]
Herman, Richard - *Power Curve*
    BL - v93 - My 1 '97 - p1479 [51-250]
    KR - v65 - Mr 1 '97 - p325 [51-250]
    LJ - v122 - Ap 15 '97 - p117 [51-250]
    PW - v244 - Ap 7 '97 - p76 [51-250]
Herman, Vimala - *Dramatic Discourse*
    Choice - v34 - O '96 - p272 [51-250]
Hermann, Spring - *R.C. Gorman, Navajo Artist*
  c CLW - v66 - Je '96 - p49+ [251-500]
Hermans, Jos. M M - *Boeken In De Late Middeleeuwen*
    Lib - v18 - Je '96 - p160+ [501+]
Hermes, Joke - *Reading Women's Magazines*
    Arena - Ap '96 - p54+ [501+]
Hermes, Jules - *The Children of Bolivia*
  c HB Guide - v7 - Fall '96 - p392 [51-250]

Hermes, Matthew E - *Enough for One Lifetime*
  Choice - v34 - N '96 - p486 [51-250]
  R&R Bk N - v12 - F '97 - p93 [51-250]
  SciTech - v20 - S '96 - p16 [51-250]
Hermes, Patricia - *Fly Away Home*
  y VOYA - v19 - F '97 - p327+ [251-500]
  Mama, Let's Dance
  c SLJ - v43 - Mr '97 - p113 [1-50]
  On Winter's Wind
  c New Ad - v9 - Fall '96 - p327+ [501+]
  When Snow Lay Soft on the Mountain (Illus. by Leslie Baker)
  c CBRS - v25 - D '96 - p39 [51-250]
  c Ch BWatch - v6 - D '96 - p3 [1-50]
  c HB Guide - v8 - Spr '97 - p31 [51-250]
  c KR - v64 - S 15 '96 - p1401 [51-250]
  c PW - v243 - O 21 '96 - p82 [51-250]
  c SLJ - v43 - Ja '97 - p83 [51-250]
  c Smith - v27 - N '96 - p175 [1-50]
Hermes, Trismegistus - *De Triginta Sex Decanis*
  Specu - v72 - Ja '97 - p165+ [501+]
Hermogenes - *On Issues (Heath)*
  TLS - Ag 2 '96 - p27 [501+]
Hermon, John - *Holding the Line*
  NS - v126 - Mr 27 '97 - p58 [501+]
Hern, Candice - *A Garden Folly*
  LJ - v121 - N 15 '96 - p48 [51-250]
Hernandez, Anthony - *Landscapes for the Homeless*
  LATBR - Mr 24 '96 - p11 [251-500]
Hernandez, Eugenio - *A First Course on Wavelets*
  Choice - v34 - Mr '97 - p1197 [51-250]
  SciTech - v20 - D '96 - p19 [51-250]
Hernandez, Gilbert - *Luba Conquers the World*
  BL - v93 - N 15 '96 - p563 [51-250]
Hernandez, Irene Beltran - *The Secret of Two Brothers*
  y JOYS - v9 - Sum '96 - p416 [51-250]
Hernandez, Jaime - *Chester Square*
  BL - v93 - S 1 '96 - p53 [51-250]
Hernandez, Jo Farb - *A.G. Rizzoli: Architect of Magnificent Visions*
  PW - v244 - Mr 24 '97 - p66 [51-250]
Hernandez, Mauro - *A La Sombra De La Corona*
  AHR - v102 - F '97 - p133+ [501+]
  Choice - v34 - D '96 - p567 [1-50]
Hernandez, Michael J - *Relational Database Design for Mere Mortals*
  LJ - v122 - My 1 '97 - p132 [1-50]
Hernandez-Calderon, I - *Surfaces, Vacuum, and Their Applications*
  SciTech - v20 - D '96 - p23 [51-250]
Herndl, Carl G - *Green Culture*
  Choice - v34 - N '96 - p478 [51-250]
  Col Comp - v47 - D '96 - p617 [51-250]
  JEL - v34 - D '96 - p2133 [51-250]
  TLS - F 21 '97 - p12 [501+]
Herndon, Nancy - *Lethal Statues*
  Arm Det - v30 - Win '97 - p110 [251-500]
Hernon, Joseph Martin - *Profiles in Character*
  Choice - v34 - Mr '97 - p1239+ [51-250]
Hernon, Peter - *Federal Information Policies in the 1990s*
  LJ - v121 - D '96 - p156 [51-250]
  Service Quality in Academic Libraries
  LAR - v98 - Je '96 - p317 [51-250]
Hernon, Peter, 1947- - *The Kindling: A Novel*
  y BL - v93 - S 1 '96 - p62 [51-250]
Hero, Alfred Olivier - *Louisiana and Quebec*
  Choice - v34 - O '96 - p348 [51-250]
Herodotus - *The Histories (De Selincourt)*
  TranslRevS - v2 - D '96 - p5 [51-250]
Herold, Maggie Rugg - *A Very Important Day (Illus. by Catherine Stock)*
  c Inst - v106 - S '96 - p54+ [51-250]
  c RT - v50 - D '96 - p340+ [51-250]
Heron, Liz - *A Red River*
  TES - Jl 26 '96 - p18 [51-250]
Herotica 3
  Quill & Q - v62 - Jl '96 - p42 [501+]
Herr, Cheryl Temple - *Critical Regionalism and Cultural Studies*
  Choice - v34 - Ap '97 - p1322 [51-250]
Herr, Ethel - *The Dove and the Rose*
  BL - v93 - O 1 '96 - p304 [501+]
Herr, Michael - *Dispatches*
  Parameters - v26 - Win '96 - p148+ [501+]
Herrera, Juan Felipe - *Calling the Doves (Illus. by Elly Simmons)*
  c RT - v50 - N '96 - p244 [51-250]
  Love after the Riots
  Sm Pr R - v28 - Jl '96 - p1 [251-500]
  Mayan Drifter
  PW - v244 - Ja 6 '97 - p57 [251-250]

Herrera-Sobek, Maria - *Chicana Creativity and Criticism*
  AL - v69 - Mr '97 - p258 [1-50]
  The Mexican Corrido
  JTWS - v13 - Spr '96 - p362+ [501+]
Herrero, Concha - *Tapices Y Cartones De Goya*
  BM - v138 - S '96 - p630+ [501+]
Herrick, Steven - *Love, Ghosts and Nose Hair*
  y Kliatt - v30 - N '96 - p19 [51-250]
  y Magpies - v11 - Jl '96 - p33 [51-250]
Herriman, Michael - *Language Policies in English-Dominant Countries*
  R&R Bk N - v11 - D '96 - p59 [51-250]
Herring, Eric - *Danger and Opportunity*
  J Pol - v59 - F '97 - p321+ [501+]
  JPR - v33 - Ag '96 - p380 [251-500]
  PSQ - v111 - Win '96 - p741+ [501+]
Herring, Patricia Roche - *General Jose Cosme Urrea: His Life and Times 1797-1849*
  J Mil H - v60 - O '96 - p776+ [251-500]
  WHQ - v27 - Win '96 - p536+ [501+]
Herring, Phillip - *Djuna: The Life and Work of Djuna Barnes*
  NS & S - v9 - Ap 26 '96 - p35+ [251-500]
  WLT - v70 - Sum '96 - p702+ [501+]
Herring, Richard J - *Financial Regulation in the Global Economy*
  Econ J - v106 - S '96 - p1472 [51-250]
Herriot, James - *If Only They Could Talk (Timothy). Audio Version*
  y Kliatt - v31 - Mr '97 - p49 [51-250]
  It Shouldn't Happen to a Vet (Timothy). Audio Version
  y Kliatt - v31 - Ja '97 - p49 [51-250]
  James Herriot's Favorite Dog Stories
  y BL - v93 - S 15 '96 - p194 [51-250]
  Dog Fan - v28 - Ja '97 - p39 [51-250]
  James Herriot's Favorite Dog Stories (Timothy). Audio Version
  CSM - v88 - O 31 '96 - pB4 [51-250]
  y Kliatt - v31 - Mr '97 - p49 [51-250]
  y SLJ - v43 - Mr '97 - p143+ [51-250]
Herrmann, David G - *The Arming of Europe and the Making of the First World War*
  AAPSS-A - v550 - Mr '97 - p170+ [501+]
  HRNB - v25 - Fall '96 - p33 [251-500]
Herrnstein, Richard - *The Bell Curve*
  New Sci - v153 - F 1 '97 - p49 [501+]
Herron, Carolivia - *Nappy Hair (Illus. by Joe Cepeda)*
  c BL - v93 - F 1 '97 - p946 [51-250]
  c CCB-B - v50 - F '97 - p208 [51-250]
  c Emerg Lib - v24 - Mr '97 - p66 [1-50]
  c KR - v64 - N 15 '96 - p1670 [51-250]
  c NYTBR - v102 - F 16 '97 - p25 [1-50]
  c PW - v244 - Ja 6 '97 - p72 [51-250]
  c SLJ - v43 - Ja '97 - p83 [51-250]
Herron, J Dudley - *The Chemistry Classroom*
  SciTech - v20 - N '96 - p21 [51-250]
Herron, Nancy L - *The Social Sciences. 2nd Ed.*
  r ARBA - v28 - '97 - p42+ [251-500]
  r R&R Bk N - v11 - N '96 - p23 [51-250]
Herscher, Ermine - *Picasso Bon Vivant*
  BL - v93 - D 15 '96 - p703 [51-250]
  PW - v243 - S 2 '96 - p125 [51-250]
Hersen, Michel - *Psychological Treatment of Older Adults*
  SciTech - v20 - N '96 - p42 [51-250]
Hersey, George - *The Evolution of Allure*
  Econ - v340 - S 14 '96 - p13* + [501+]
Hersey, George L - *The Evolution of Allure*
  Choice - v34 - Mr '97 - p1152 [51-250]
  TLS - F 28 '97 - p32 [251-500]
Hersey, John - *Key West Tales*
  NYTBR - v101 - N 10 '96 - p68 [51-250]
Hersh, Burton - *The Shadow President*
  BL - v93 - My 15 '97 - p1559 [51-250]
  KR - v65 - Mr 15 '97 - p438 [251-500]
  PW - v244 - Ap 7 '97 - p86 [51-250]
Hersh, Jacques - *The Aftermath of Real Existing Socialism in Eastern Europe. Vol. 1*
  Choice - v34 - Mr '97 - p1385 [51-250]
Hershatter, Gail - *Remapping China*
  Hist & T - v36 - F '97 - p108+ [251-500]
Hershey, Fritz Lynn - *Optics and Focus for Camera Assistants*
  R&R Bk N - v12 - F '97 - p99 [1-50]
Hershfield, Joanne - *Mexican Cinema/Mexican Woman 1940-1950*
  Choice - v34 - My '97 - p1507 [51-250]
Hershman, Marcie - *Safe in America*
  y Kliatt - v30 - S '96 - p10+ [51-250]
Hershman-Leeson, Lynn - *Clicking In*
  Afterimage - v24 - Ja '97 - p22 [1-50]
  LJ - v121 - D '96 - p87 [51-250]

  Clicking In. Book and Electronic Media Version
  Choice - v34 - Mr '97 - p1195 [51-250]
Herskowitz, Suzan - *Legal Malpractice and Other Claims against Your Lawyer*
  LJ - v121 - O 15 '96 - p76 [51-250]
Hertzman, Clyde - *Environment and Health in Central and Eastern Europe*
  J Gov Info - v23 - S '96 - p685 [51-250]
Hertzog, Mark - *The Lavender Vote*
  Choice - v34 - F '97 - p1036 [51-250]
  R&R Bk N - v11 - D '96 - p40 [51-250]
Hervey, Sandor - *Thinking German Translation*
  TranslRevS - v2 - D '96 - p13 [1-50]
  Thinking Spanish Translation
  TranslRevS - v2 - D '96 - p13 [51-250]
Herwig, Holger H - *The First World War*
  Choice - v34 - My '97 - p1557 [51-250]
  HT - v46 - O '96 - p57 [1-50]
  LJ - v122 - Mr 15 '97 - p73+ [51-250]
Herz, J C - *Joystick Nation*
  KR - v65 - My 1 '97 - p695 [251-500]
Herz, Sarah K - *From Hinton to Hamlet*
  CCB-B - v50 - S '96 - p40 [51-250]
  JOYS - v10 - Win '97 - p219+ [251-500]
  SLJ - v42 - S '96 - p136 [51-250]
  SLMQ - v25 - Fall '96 - p64 [1-50]
  VOYA - v19 - D '96 - p296 [51-250]
Herzl, Theodor - *Der Judenstaat*
  TLS - Jl 7 '96 - p6+ [501+]
Herzlinger, Regina E - *Market-Driven Health Care*
  BL - v93 - Ja '97 - p794 [251-500]
  LJ - v122 - Ja '97 - p134 [51-250]
  WSJ-Cent - v99 - Ja 7 '97 - pA16 [501+]
Herzog, Brad - *HoopMania! The Jam-Packed Book of Basketball Trivia*
  y Emerg Lib - v24 - S '96 - p26 [1-50]
Herzog, Chaim - *Living History*
  BL - v93 - N 15 '96 - p568 [51-250]
  BW - v26 - N 17 '96 - p4+ [501+]
  For Aff - v76 - Mr '97 - p194 [51-250]
  KR - v64 - S 15 '96 - p1374+ [251-500]
  LJ - v121 - N 15 '96 - p68 [51-250]
  NYTBR - v101 - D 8 '96 - p62 [501+]
  Obs - Ap 6 '97 - p17* [501+]
  PW - v243 - S 30 '96 - p68 [51-250]
Herzog, Dagmar - *Intimacy and Exclusion*
  Choice - v34 - S '96 - p187 [51-250]
  HRNB - v25 - Fall '96 - p27+ [251-500]
Herzog, Juliet - *Implementing S/NVQs in the Information and Library Sector*
  r LAR - v99 - F '97 - p101 [51-250]
Herzog, Madeleine - *Ich Bin...Nicht Ich*
  Ger Q - v70 - Win '97 - p94+ [501+]
Herzog, Thomas - *Solar Energy in Architecture and Urban Planning*
  New Sci - v151 - S 28 '96 - p48 [51-250]
  TLS - N 29 '96 - p21 [501+]
Herzog, William R, II - *Parables as Subversive Speech*
  TT - v53 - O '96 - p423 [51-250]
Hesburgh, Theodore M - *The Challenge and Promise of a Catholic University*
  Rel St Rev - v23 - Ja '97 - p49 [51-250]
Heschel, Abraham J - *Prophetic Inspiration after the Prophets*
  Choice - v34 - Mr '97 - p1177 [51-250]
Heschel, Abraham Joshua - *Moral Grandeur and Spiritual Audacity*
  OS - v32 - Jl '96 - p43 [51-250]
Hesketh, Anthony - *Beg, Borrow or Starve?*
  TES - N 29 '96 - p10* [51-250]
Hesketh, Howard E - *Air Pollution Control*
  SciTech - v20 - N '96 - p68 [51-250]
Heskett, James L - *The Service Profit Chain*
  BL - v93 - Ap 1 '97 - p1273 [51-250]
  PW - v244 - F 24 '97 - p75+ [51-250]
Heskett, Sandra L - *Workplace Violence*
  HR Mag - v41 - S '96 - p140 [51-250]
Hess, David J - *Science and Technology in a Multicultural World*
  Isis - v87 - S '96 - p527+ [251-500]
Hess, Joan - *Closely Akin to Murder*
  Arm Det - v29 - Sum '96 - p366 [251-500]
  y SLJ - v42 - N '96 - p140 [51-250]
  The Maggody Militia
  BL - v93 - F 15 '97 - p1007 [51-250]
  KR - v65 - F 1 '97 - p175 [51-250]
  PW - v244 - Ja 13 '97 - p57 [51-250]
Hess, Karl - *Hot Carriers in Semiconductors*
  SciTech - v20 - D '96 - p25 [51-250]
Hess, Kathleen - *Environmental Sampling for Unknowns*
  SciTech - v20 - D '96 - p39 [51-250]

Hess, Paul - *Farmyard Animals (Illus. by Paul Hess)*
c   CCB-B - v50 - S '96 - p23 [51-250]
c   Sch Lib - v44 - Ag '96 - p99 [51-250]
Polar Animals (Illus. by Paul Hess)
c   HB Guide - v8 - Spr '97 - p150 [51-250]
c   SLJ - v42 - D '96 - p116 [51-250]
Rainforest Animals (Illus. by Paul Hess)
c   HB Guide - v8 - Spr '97 - p150 [51-250]
c   SLJ - v42 - D '96 - p116 [51-250]
Hess, Robert E - *International Approaches to Prevention*
in Mental Health and Human Services
AJPsych - v153 - Ag '96 - p1104 [501+]
Hess, Stephen - *Drawn and Quartered*
LATBR - O 27 '96 - p10 [251-500]
International News and Foreign Correspondents
AJS - v102 - Ja '97 - p1187+ [501+]
Choice - v34 - S '96 - p116+ [51-250]
CJR - v35 - N '96 - p53+ [501+]
JMCQ - v73 - Win '96 - p1003+ [501+]
News and Newsmaking
JMCQ - v73 - Aut '96 - p763+ [501+]
Hessayon, D G - *The New Bedding Plant Expert*
BL - v93 - O 1 '96 - p314 [51-250]
Hesse, Hermann - *The Fairy Tales of Hermann Hesse*
(Donovan). Audio Version
Mag Bl - Mr '97 - p62 [51-250]
y   SLJ - v43 - Mr '97 - p143 [51-250]
Narziss and Goldmund
Spec - v277 - N 16 '96 - p46 [1-50]
Hesse, Joachim Jens - *Constitutional Policy and Change*
in Europe
APSR - v91 - Mr '97 - p215+ [501+]
Hesse, Karen - *Lester's Dog*
c   CLW - v67 - Mr '97 - p14 [1-50]
The Music of Dolphins
y   BL - v93 - Ap 1 '97 - p1292 [1-50]
y   CBRS - v25 - O '96 - p21 [51-250]
c   CCB-B - v50 - D '96 - p137+ [51-250]
y   Emerg Lib - v24 - Mr '97 - p54 [51-250]
c   HB Guide - v8 - Spr '97 - p67 [51-250]
y   JAAL - v40 - F '97 - p407 [51-250]
c   KR - v64 - Ag 15 '96 - p1235 [51-250]
c   PW - v243 - S 2 '96 - p131 [51-250]
c   PW - v243 - N 4 '96 - p48 [1-50]
y   SLJ - v42 - N '96 - p120+ [51-250]
y   SLJ - v42 - D '96 - p30 [1-50]
y   VOYA - v19 - F '97 - p328 [251-500]
A Time of Angels
y   RT - v50 - N '96 - p248 [51-250]
Hesse-Biber, Sharlene - *Am I Thin Enough Yet?*
Choice - v34 - O '96 - p364 [51-250]
CS - v25 - S '96 - p693+ [501+]
Hesselbein, Frances - *The Leader of the Future*
Choice - v34 - O '96 - p326 [51-250]
HR Mag - v41 - Ag '96 - p121 [501+]
Per Psy - v49 - Win '96 - p991+ [501+]
The Organization of the Future
BL - v93 - F 15 '97 - p984 [51-250]
Choice - v34 - My '97 - p1544 [51-250]
ChrPhil - v9 - Ja 9 '97 - p36 [51-250]
HR Mag - v42 - Mr '97 - p133 [501+]
PW - v243 - D 16 '96 - p51 [51-250]
Hessler, Gene - *Comprehensive Catalog of U.S. Paper*
Money. 6th Ed.
r   Coin W - v38 - Mr 10 '97 - p42 [51-250]
Hest, Amy - *Baby Duck and the Bad Eyeglasses (Illus. by*
Jill Barton)
c   BL - v92 - Ag '96 - p1905 [51-250]
c   BL - v93 - Ja '97 - p767 [1-50]
c   CCB-B - v50 - O '96 - p63 [51-250]
c   Ch BWatch - v6 - S '96 - p1 [1-50]
c   HB - v72 - S '96 - p577+ [51-250]
c   HB Guide - v8 - Spr '97 - p12 [51-250]
c   Inst - v106 - Ja '97 - p51 [51-250]
c   SLJ - v42 - O '96 - p98 [51-250]
In the Rain with Baby Duck (Illus. by Jill Barton)
c   HB - v73 - Mr '97 - p186 [1-50]
Jamaica Louise James (Illus. by Sheila White Samton)
c   BL - v93 - S 1 '96 - p143 [51-250]
c   CBRS - v25 - S '96 - p3+ [51-250]
c   CCB-B - v50 - S '96 - p14 [51-250]
c   Emerg Lib - v24 - Mr '97 - p66 [1-50]
c   HB - v72 - S '96 - p578+ [251-500]
c   HB Guide - v8 - Spr '97 - p31 [51-250]
c   PW - v243 - Jl 22 '96 - p241+ [51-250]
c   SLJ - v42 - D '96 - p94 [51-250]
The Private Notebook of Katie Roberts, Age 11 (Illus. by
Sonja Lamut)
c   LA - v73 - O '96 - p432 [51-250]
c   RT - v50 - D '96 - p344 [51-250]

Hester, Colin - *Diamond Sutra*
KR - v65 - Ap 1 '97 - p487 [251-500]
PW - v244 - Mr 3 '97 - p66 [51-250]
Hester, Gwendolyn Lynette - *Freedmen and Colored*
Marriage Records 1865-1890, Sumter County, Alabama
r   BL - v93 - S 1 '96 - p166 [1-50]
r   EGH - v50 - N '96 - p161 [51-250]
Hester, Joseph P - *Encyclopedia of Values and Ethics*
r   ARBA - v28 - '97 - p530 [51-250]
r   BL - v93 - Ap 1 '97 - p1354 [501+]
r   LJ - v122 - Ap 15 '97 - p68 [51-250]
Hester, M L - *Another Jackie Robinson*
PW - v243 - S 9 '96 - p65+ [51-250]
Hester, M Thomas - *John Donne's Desire of More*
Choice - v34 - Mr '97 - p1163 [51-250]
Hester, R E - *Agricultural Chemicals and the Environment*
SciTech - v20 - N '96 - p67 [51-250]
Hetfield, Jamie - *The Yoruba of West Africa*
c   SLJ - v42 - N '96 - p98 [51-250]
Hetherington, Barry - *A Chronicle of Pre-Telescopic*
Astronomy
Choice - v34 - Ap '97 - p1362 [51-250]
r   S&T - v92 - D '96 - p66 [1-50]
Hetherington, E Mavis - *Stress, Coping, and Resiliency in*
Children and Families
SB - v32 - N '96 - p228+ [51-250]
Hetherington, Norriss S - *Encyclopedia of Cosmology*
r   Skeptic - v3 - '95 - p101 [51-250]
Hubble's Cosmology
Choice - v34 - F '97 - p985 [51-250]
SciTech - v20 - D '96 - p22 [51-250]
Hettche, Thomas - *Nox*
WLT - v70 - Sum '96 - p683 [501+]
Hettinga, Donald R - *British Children's Writers*
1914-1960
r   ARBA - v28 - '97 - p427 [51-250]
Hetzner, C N - *In the War for Peace*
KR - v65 - Ja 15 '97 - p81 [251-500]
PW - v244 - F 10 '97 - p64+ [51-250]
Heuberger, Georg - *The Rothschilds: Essays on the*
History of a European Family
JEH - v57 - Mr '97 - p214+ [501+]
Heuberger, Valeria - *Nationen, Nationalitaten,*
Minderheiten
Slav R - v55 - Fall '96 - p662+ [501+]
Heuer, Gerald A - *Silverman's Game*
JEL - v34 - D '96 - p2022 [51-250]
Heuer, Hans-Joachim - *Geheime Staatspolizei*
Arm F&S - v23 - Fall '96 - p125+ [501+]
Heugten, Sjraar Van - *Vincent Van Gogh: Drawings. Vol.*
1
BM - v138 - Ag '96 - p559+ [501+]
LJ - v122 - Ap 1 '97 - p90+ [51-250]
Heuman, Gad - *The Killing Time*
AHR - v101 - O '96 - p1319+ [501+]
Heusch, Luc De - *Objects: Signs of Africa*
BWatch - v17 - S '96 - p3 [51-250]
Heuser, Magdalene - *Ich Wunschte So Gar Gelehrt Zu*
Werden
MLR - v91 - O '96 - p1039+ [501+]
Heusinkveld, Paula - *Inside Mexico*
MLJ - v81 - Spr '97 - p143+ [251-500]
Heusler, Eugen E - *Switzerland*
r   BL - v93 - S 15 '96 - p210 [1-50]
Heuvelmans, Bernard - *On the Track of Unknown*
Animals. Rev. 3rd Ed.
Choice - v34 - S '96 - p155 [51-250]
Hevia, James L - *Cherishing Men from Afar*
Ch Rev Int - v3 - Fall '96 - p430+ [501+]
Heward, John - *The Country Houses of Northamptonshire*
TLS - Ja 10 '97 - p19 [501+]
Hewett, Lorri - *Soulfire*
y   HB Guide - v8 - Spr '97 - p80 [51-250]
y   JAAL - v40 - N '96 - p233 [51-250]
y   VOYA - v19 - O '96 - p210 [251-500]
Hewins, R H - *Chondrules and the Protoplanetary Disk*
Sci - v274 - N 8 '96 - p935+ [501+]
Hewitt, Andrew - *Political Inversions*
Choice - v34 - Ap '97 - p1342+ [51-250]
Hewitt, David - *Horizons One*
J Gov Info - v23 - S '96 - p614 [51-250]
Hewitt, George - *Georgian: A Learner's Grammar*
R&R Bk N - v11 - N '96 - p65 [51-250]
Hewitt, Martin - *The Emergence of Stability in the*
Industrial City
Choice - v34 - D '96 - p669 [51-250]
R&R Bk N - v11 - N '96 - p40 [51-250]
Hewitt, Nancy - *Talking Gender*
Choice - v34 - Mr '97 - p1200 [51-250]

Hewitt, Nicholas - *Literature and the Right in Postwar*
France
TLS - F 28 '97 - p24 [501+]
Hewitt, Paolo - *Getting High*
KR - v65 - F 15 '97 - p273 [251-500]
LJ - v122 - Ap 15 '97 - p83 [51-250]
PW - v244 - Mr 10 '97 - p60 [51-250]
Hewitt, Richard - *A Cottage in Portugal*
LATBR - Mr 17 '96 - p10+ [51-250]
Hewitt, Sally - *The Aztecs*
c   HB Guide - v7 - Fall '96 - p390 [51-250]
c   Sch Lib - v44 - Ag '96 - p112 [51-250]
Measuring
c   HB Guide - v7 - Fall '96 - p329 [51-250]
c   SB - v32 - O '96 - p208 [51-250]
Numbers
c   HB Guide - v7 - Fall '96 - p329 [51-250]
c   SB - v32 - O '96 - p208 [51-250]
The Plains People
c   HB Guide - v7 - Fall '96 - p390 [51-250]
c   Sch Lib - v44 - Ag '96 - p112 [51-250]
Puzzles
c   HB Guide - v7 - Fall '96 - p329 [51-250]
c   SB - v32 - O '96 - p208 [51-250]
Shapes
c   HB Guide - v7 - Fall '96 - p329 [51-250]
c   SB - v32 - O '96 - p208 [51-250]
Sorting and Sets
c   HB Guide - v7 - Fall '96 - p329 [51-250]
c   SB - v32 - O '96 - p208 [51-250]
Time
c   HB Guide - v7 - Fall '96 - p328 [51-250]
c   SB - v32 - O '96 - p208 [51-250]
Hewitt, W E - *Base Christian Communities and Social*
Change in Brazil
CH - v66 - Mr '97 - p175+ [501+]
Hewlett, Barry S - *Father-Child Relations*
RA - v25 - 3 '96 - p195+ [501+]
Hey, David - *The Oxford Companion to Local and Family*
History
r   ARBA - v28 - '97 - p164 [51-250]
r   BL - v93 - O 1 '96 - p372 [251-500]
r   R&R Bk N - v11 - D '96 - p6 [251-500]
r   TES - Jl 26 '96 - pR6 [1-50]
The Oxford Guide to Family History
TES - Jl 26 '96 - pR6 [51-250]
Hey, Jeanne A K - *Theories of Dependent Foreign Policy*
and the Case of Ecuador in the 1980s
APSR - v91 - Mr '97 - p233+ [501+]
Hey, Stan - *A Sudden and Unprovided Death*
Books - v10 - Je '96 - p23 [51-250]
Heyck, Denis Lynn - *Barrios and Borderlands*
Hisp - v79 - S '96 - p457+ [501+]
Heyd, David - *Toleration: An Elusive Virtue*
APSR - v91 - Mr '97 - p170+ [501+]
Rel St Rev - v23 - Ap '97 - p159 [51-250]
RM - v50 - D '96 - p406+ [501+]
TLS - Ag 30 '96 - p13 [501+]
Heydenreich, Ludwig H - *Architecture in Italy 1400-1500*
Six Ct J - v27 - Fall '96 - p960+ [501+]
Six Ct J - v27 - Fall '96 - p963+ [501+]
Heyen, William - *Crazy Horse in Stillness*
Chel - 61 '96 - p137+ [501+]
Sm Pr R - v28 - D '96 - p4 [51-250]
Heyer, Marilee - *Iron Hans*
c   PW - v243 - Jl 22 '96 - p243 [1-50]
Heyerdahl, Thor - *Green Was the Earth on the Seventh*
Day
Obs - Ja 5 '97 - p17* [501+]
Pyramids of Tucume
HAHR - v77 - My '97 - p297+ [501+]
Heyes, Cecilia M - *Social Learning in Animals*
SciTech - v20 - N '96 - p30 [51-250]
Hey'l, Bettina - *Geschichtsdenken Und Literarische*
Moderne
MLR - v91 - O '96 - p1050+ [501+]
Heylin, Clinton - *Bob Dylan: A Life in Stolen Moments*
BL - v92 - Ag '96 - p1871 [51-250]
Heyman, Jacques - *Arches, Vaults, and Buttresses*
SciTech - v21 - Mr '97 - p83 [51-250]
Elements of the Theory of Structures
SciTech - v20 - D '96 - p64 [51-250]
Heyman, Neil M - *Western Civilization*
r   ARBA - v28 - '97 - p510+ [51-250]
r   RQ - v35 - Sum '96 - p566+ [251-500]
Heymann, Daniel - *High Inflation*
Econ J - v106 - S '96 - p1439+ [501+]
Heyn, Dalma - *Marriage Shock*
KR - v65 - F 15 '97 - p273 [251-500]
PW - v244 - F 3 '97 - p85+ [51-250]

Heyns, Michiel - *Expulsion and the Nineteenth-Century Novel*
MLR - v92 - Ap '97 - p457+ [501+]
RES - v48 - F '97 - p127+ [501+]
Heyrman, Christine Leigh - *Southern Cross*
KR - v65 - Mr 1 '97 - p353 [51-250]
LJ - v122 - Ap 15 '97 - p86 [51-250]
Heyward, Vivian H - *Applied Body Composition Assessment*
Choice - v34 - O '96 - p303 [251-500]
Heywood, Colin - *The Development of the French Economy 1750-1914*
JEL - v35 - Mr '97 - p258 [51-250]
Heywood, Leslie - *Dedication to Hunger*
Choice - v34 - S '96 - p118 [51-250]
Heywood, V H - *Global Biodiversity Assessment*
Env - v38 - O '96 - p27 [51-250]
Heyworth, Peter - *Otto Klemperer: His Life and Times. Vol. 2*
NYRB - v43 - O 31 '96 - p22+ [501+]
Otto Klemperer: His Life and Times. Vols. 1-2
AS - v66 - Spr '97 - p307+ [501+]
TLS - S 13 '96 - p13+ [501+]
Hezel, Francis X - *Strangers in Their Own Land*
Cont Pac - v9 - Spr '97 - p272+ [501+]
Hiaasen, Carl - *Naked Came the Manatee*
BL - v93 - N 15 '96 - p549 [51-250]
BW - v27 - F 9 '97 - p13 [51-250]
Ent W - Mr 14 '97 - p75 [51-250]
KR - v64 - D 15 '96 - p1755 [251-500]
LJ - v122 - Ja '97 - p146 [51-250]
NYTBR - v102 - Mr 2 '97 - p18 [51-250]
PW - v244 - Ja 13 '97 - p53+ [51-250]
Trib Bks - F 2 '97 - p4 [51-250]
Stormy Weather
Arm Det - v29 - Sum '96 - p281 [51-250]
Strip Tease (Asner). Audio Version
BL - v93 - N 15 '96 - p604 [51-250]
Hiatt, Fred - *If I Were Queen of the World (Illus. by Mark Graham)*
c BL - v93 - My 1 '97 - p1501 [51-250]
c CBRS - v25 - Mr '97 - p87 [51-250]
c KR - v65 - Mr 15 '97 - p462 [51-250]
c PW - v244 - Mr 31 '97 - p74 [51-250]
Hibbeler, R C - *Mechanics of Materials. 3rd Ed.*
SciTech - v21 - Mr '97 - p76 [51-250]
Structural Analysis. 3rd Ed., Rev.
SciTech - v20 - D '96 - p64 [51-250]
Hibbert, Christopher - *Cavaliers and Roundheads (Crossley). Audio Version*
y Kliatt - v31 - Mr '97 - p47+ [51-250]
Nelson: A Personal History
NYTBR - v101 - S 22 '96 - p40 [1-50]
VQR - v72 - Aut '96 - p141* [1-50]
Wellington: A Personal History
Books - v11 - Ap '97 - p20 [51-250]
Obs - Mr 30 '97 - p16* [501+]
Hibbing, John R - *Congress as Public Enemy*
Choice - v34 - Mr '97 - p1240 [51-250]
Hibbs, Euthymia D - *Psychosocial Treatment for Child and Adolescent Disorders*
SciTech - v20 - N '96 - p54 [1-50]
Hibbs, Thomas S - *Dialectic and Narrative in Aquinas*
Theol St - v58 - Mr '97 - p163+ [501+]
Hick, John - *Disputed Questions in Theology and Philosophy of Religion*
JAAR - v64 - Win '96 - p884+ [501+]
More than One Way?
Rel St Rev - v23 - Ja '97 - p47 [51-250]
Hickel, Erika - *Frauen Und Naturwissenschaften*
Isis - v88 - Mr '97 - p171+ [501+]
Hickerson, Nancy Parrott - *The Jumanos: Hunters and Traders of the South Plains*
WHQ - v28 - Spr '97 - p101 [1-50]
Hickey, Anthony J - *Inhalation Aerosols*
SciTech - v20 - N '96 - p54 [51-250]
Hickey, Dave - *The Invisible Dragon*
Art J - v55 - Fall '96 - p97+ [501+]
Hickey, Dennis Van Vranken - *United States-Taiwan Security Ties*
JTWS - v13 - Spr '96 - p258+ [501+]
Hickey, Donald R - *Nebraska Moments*
Roundup M - v3 - Ag '96 - p25 [51-250]
Hickey, James E - *Government Structures in the U.S.A. and the Sovereign States of the Former U.S.S.R.*
R&R Bk N - v11 - D '96 - p47 [51-250]
Hickey, Joseph V - *Ghost Settlement on the Prairie*
PHR - v65 - Ag '96 - p485+ [251-500]
Hickey, Tina - *Language, Education and Society in a Changing World*
MLJ - v81 - Spr '97 - p133+ [501+]

Hickman, Cleveland P - *Integrated Principles of Zoology. 10th Ed.*
SciTech - v20 - N '96 - p29 [51-250]
Hickman, Janet - *Jericho*
y Kliatt - v30 - N '96 - p8+ [51-250]
Hickman, Martha Whitmore - *Such Good People*
LJ - v121 - N 1 '96 - p132 [51-250]
Hickman, Money L - *Japan's Golden Age*
Choice - v34 - F '97 - p956 [51-250]
FEER - v159 - D 19 '96 - p54 [501+]
VQR - v73 - Win '97 - p30*+ [51-250]
Hickman, Pamela M - *At the Seashore*
c Ch Bk News - v19 - Sum '96 - p31 [51-250]
c Quill & Q - v62 - Jl '96 - p58 [1-50]
Hungry Animals (Illus. by Heather Collins)
c Quill & Q - v63 - F '97 - p59 [51-250]
The Jumbo Book of Nature Science (Illus. by Judie Shore)
c Quill & Q - v62 - S '96 - p75 [251-500]
Kids Canadian Bug Book
c Emerg Lib - v24 - Mr '97 - p28 [1-50]
Kids Canadian Plant Book
c Emerg Lib - v24 - Mr '97 - p28 [1-50]
A New Butterfly (Illus. by Heather Collins)
c Quill & Q - v63 - F '97 - p59 [51-250]
A Seed Grows (Illus. by Heather Collins)
c Quill & Q - v63 - F '97 - p59 [51-250]
Hickman, Tom - *What Did You Do in the War, Auntie?*
BL - v93 - O 1 '96 - p309 [51-250]
LJ - v121 - N 15 '96 - p73 [51-250]
Hickman, Tracy - *The Immortals*
y VOYA - v19 - O '96 - p218 [251-500]
Hickox, Rebecca - *Zorro and Quwi (Illus. by Kim Howard)*
c BL - v93 - D 15 '96 - p730 [51-250]
c CCB-B - v50 - F '97 - p208+ [51-250]
c KR - v64 - D 1 '96 - p1738 [51-250]
c PW - v243 - D 9 '96 - p68 [51-250]
c SLJ - v43 - F '97 - p92+ [51-250]
Hicks, Barbara - *Environmental Politics in Poland*
R&R Bk N - v12 - F '97 - p61 [1-50]
Hicks, Doris Lynn - *Flannelboard Classic Tales*
BL - v93 - Mr 1 '97 - p1177 [51-250]
Hicks, George - *The Comfort Women*
CS - v25 - S '96 - p630+ [501+]
Hicks, John - *Dating Violence*
y BL - v93 - N 15 '96 - p578 [51-250]
y HB Guide - v8 - Spr '97 - p96 [51-250]
SLJ - v42 - N '96 - p128+ [51-250]
Hicks, Peter - *Pompeii and Herculaneum*
c TES - N 8 '96 - p13* [501+]
Troy and Knossos
c TES - N 8 '96 - p13* [501+]
Hicks, Philip - *Neoclassical History and English Culture*
Choice - v34 - F '97 - p1019 [51-250]
Hicks, Terry C - *Complications of Colon and Rectal Surgery*
SciTech - v20 - D '96 - p49 [51-250]
Hicks, Tyler G - *Standard Handbook of Consulting Engineering Practice. 2nd Ed.*
r SciTech - v20 - D '96 - p60 [1-50]
Hickson, Joyce - *Multicultural Counseling in a Divided and Traumatized Society*
Choice - v34 - N '96 - p543 [51-250]
Hickson, Linda - *Mental Retardation*
AJMR - v101 - Ja '97 - p430+ [501+]
Hicok, Bob - *The Legend of Light*
BL - v93 - Ap 1 '97 - p1285 [1-50]
Poet - v169 - Mr '97 - p345+ [501+]
Hicyilmaz, Gaye - *Watching the Watcher*
c JB - v60 - Ag '96 - p156+ [51-250]
y Sch Lib - v44 - Ag '96 - p117+ [51-250]
c TES - Ag 30 '96 - p28 [51-250]
Hidaka, Hiroyoshi - *Intracellular Signal Transduction*
SciTech - v20 - N '96 - p33 [51-250]
Hidalgo De Jesus, Amarilis - *La Novela Moderna En Venezuela*
WLT - v71 - Win '97 - p124 [51-250]
Hide, Louise - *The Big Break*
y JB - v60 - O '96 - p210+ [251-500]
y Magpies - v11 - N '96 - p37 [51-250]
y Sch Lib - v44 - Ag '96 - p118 [51-250]
Hiden, John - *Republican and Fascist Germany*
HRNB - v25 - Win '97 - p75 [251-500]
Hidore, John J - *Global Environmental Change*
Am Sci - v84 - S '96 - p498+ [251-500]
Hiebert, Fredrik Talmage - *Origins of the Bronze Age Civilization in Central Asia*
Am Ant - v61 - Jl '96 - p618+ [501+]

Hiebert, Murray - *Chasing the Tigers*
FEER - v160 - F 13 '97 - p36+ [501+]
KR - v64 - S 15 '96 - p1375 [251-500]
LJ - v121 - O 15 '96 - p72 [51-250]
PW - v243 - O 14 '96 - p74 [51-250]
Hiebert, Theodore - *The Yahwist's Landscape*
Choice - v34 - D '96 - p628 [51-250]
Hiery, Hermann Joseph - *Das Deutsche Reich In Der Sudsee 1900-1921*
AHR - v102 - F '97 - p123+ [501+]
The Neglected War
AHR - v102 - F '97 - p123+ [501+]
J Mil H - v61 - Ja '97 - p175+ [251-500]
Higashi, Sumiko - *Cecil B. DeMille and American Culture*
FQ - v49 - Sum '96 - p43+ [501+]
J Pop F&TV - v24 - Spr '96 - p45+ [501+]
PHR - v65 - Ag '96 - p496+ [501+]
Higbee, Joan F - *Western Europe since 1945*
r ARBA - v28 - '97 - p200+ [51-250]
Higginbotham, A Leon - *Shades of Freedom*
Choice - v34 - Mr '97 - p1240 [51-250]
New R - v215 - D 9 '96 - p27+ [501+]
NYTBR - v101 - N 24 '96 - p10 [501+]
NYTBR - v101 - D 8 '96 - p92 [1-50]
PW - v243 - O 7 '96 - p53 [51-250]
Higginbotham, Evelyn Brooks - *Righteous Discontent*
Signs - v22 - Win '97 - p479+ [501+]
Higginbotham, Jack - *Applications of New Technology*
SciTech - v20 - N '96 - p40 [51-250]
Higgins, Aidan - *Donkey's Years*
TES - Ag 2 '96 - p15 [51-250]
Flotsam and Jetsam
TLS - Mr 21 '97 - p23 [501+]
Higgins, E Tory - *Social Psychology*
Choice - v34 - F '97 - p1041 [51-250]
R&R Bk N - v11 - D '96 - p38 [51-250]
Higgins, George V - *Sandra Nichols Found Dead (Esmo). Audio Version*
LJ - v121 - D '96 - p170 [51-250]
Higgins, Gregory C - *Where Do You Stand?*
y CLW - v67 - Mr '97 - p38+ [51-250]
Higgins, Iain Macleod - *Writing East*
LJ - v122 - Ap 15 '97 - p96 [51-250]
Higgins, Ian - *Swift's Politics*
RES - v47 - Ag '96 - p419+ [501+]
Higgins, Jack - *Luciano's Luck (Macnee). Audio Version*
LJ - v122 - Ap 1 '97 - p145 [51-250]
The President's Daughter
BL - v93 - Mr 15 '97 - p1204 [51-250]
KR - v65 - Mr 15 '97 - p403+ [251-500]
LJ - v122 - My 1 '97 - p140 [51-250]
PW - v244 - Mr 24 '97 - p57+ [51-250]
Year of the Tiger
y BL - v93 - S 15 '96 - p220 [51-250]
y Kliatt - v31 - Mr '97 - p8 [51-250]
PW - v243 - S 23 '96 - p74 [1-50]
Higgins, James - *Myths of the Emergent*
Hisp - v79 - D '96 - p807+ [501+]
Higgins, Lynn A - *New Novel, New Wave, New Politics*
ABR - v18 - O '96 - p23+ [501+]
Choice - v34 - O '96 - p285 [51-250]
Higgins, Michael Denis - *A Geological Companion to Greece and the Aegean*
Choice - v34 - Mr '97 - p1189 [51-250]
Higgins, P J - *Handbook of Australian, New Zealand and Antarctic Birds. Vol. 3*
r Choice - v34 - Ja '97 - p821 [51-250]
Higgins, Patrick - *Heterosexual Dictatorship*
Obs - Ja 26 '97 - p16* [501+]
Higgins, Richard B - *The Search for Corporate Strategic Credibility*
R&R Bk N - v11 - N '96 - p29 [51-250]
Higgins, Richard S - *Deregulating Telecommunications*
Econ J - v106 - S '96 - p1476+ [51-250]
Higgins, Rita Ann - *Sunny Side Plucked*
Obs - Ja 5 '97 - p17* [51-250]
PW - v244 - F 24 '97 - p85 [51-250]
Higgs, Liz Curtis - *The Parable of the Lily (Illus. by Nancy Munger)*
c PW - v244 - Mr 24 '97 - p76 [51-250]
Higgs, Richard - *Bringing in the Sheaves*
LATBR - O 27 '96 - p11 [51-250]
LJ - v121 - D '96 - p104 [51-250]
PW - v243 - S 30 '97 - p79+ [51-250]
Higgs, Robert J - *Appalachia Inside Out. Vols. 1-2*
J Am Cult - v19 - Spr '96 - p100+ [51-250]
High, Linda Oatman - *The Summer of the Great Divide*
c HB Guide - v7 - Fall '96 - p293 [51-250]
High School Senior Magazine
yp SLJ - v42 - N '96 - p36 [1-50]

High School Senior's Guide to Merit and Other No-Need Funding. 1st Ed.
yr VOYA - v19 - D '96 - p301 [51-250]
High-Speed Europe
J Gov Info - v23 - S '96 - p669 [1-50]
Higham, Charles - *The Bronze Age of Southeast Asia*
Choice - v34 - Ap '97 - p1380 [51-250]
Higham, N J - *The English Conquest*
EHR - v112 - F '97 - p155 [251-500]
Specu - v72 - Ja '97 - p167+ [501+]
An English Empire
Albion - v28 - Win '96 - p658+ [501+]
Higham, Nicholas J - *Accuracy and Stability of Numerical Algorithms*
Choice - v34 - O '96 - p318 [51-250]
SIAM Rev - v39 - Mr '97 - p164+ [501+]
Highcrest, Alexandra - *At Home on the Stroll*
Quill & Q - v63 - Ja '97 - p13 [51-250]
The Higher Education Money Book for Women and Minorities. 1997 Ed.
r ARBA - v28 - '97 - p140 [251-500]
Highlights for Children - *Ashanti Festival*
c SLJ - v43 - Ja '97 - p77 [51-250]
Highlights for Children, Inc. - *The Timbertoes 123 Counting Book (Illus. by Judith Hunt)*
c BL - v93 - Mr 1 '97 - p1174 [51-250]
c PW - v244 - Mr 3 '97 - p77 [51-250]
The Timbertoes ABC Alphabet Book (Illus. by Judith Hunt)
c BL - v93 - Mr 1 '97 - p1174 [51-250]
c PW - v244 - Mr 3 '97 - p77 [51-250]
Highstein, Stephen M - *New Directions in Vestibular Research*
SciTech - v20 - N '96 - p32 [1-50]
Hightower, Lynn S - *Eyeshot*
Arm Det - v30 - Win '97 - p108+ [501+]
BL - v93 - O 1 '96 - p325 [51-250]
KR - v64 - Ag 15 '96 - p1190 [51-250]
PW - v243 - S 23 '96 - p58+ [51-250]
Flashpoint
Books - v10 - Je '96 - p24 [51-250]
PW - v243 - O 21 '96 - p79 [1-50]
Hightower, Paul - *Galileo: Astronomer and Physicist*
c KR - v65 - Ap 1 '97 - p557 [51-250]
Hightower, Susan - *Twelve Snails to One Lizard (Illus. by Matt Novak)*
c KR - v65 - Mr 15 '97 - p462 [51-250]
c PW - v244 - Mr 24 '97 - p82 [51-250]
Highwater, Jamake - *The Mythology of Transgression*
BL - v93 - D 1 '96 - p624+ [51-250]
KR - v64 - N 1 '96 - p1582+ [251-500]
NYTBR - v102 - Mr 9 '97 - p18 [51-250]
Rama (Guidall). Audio Version
c BL - v93 - My 15 '97 - p1595 [1-50]
c HB - v72 - S '96 - p566+ [501+]
Higle, Julia L - *Stochastic Decomposition*
SciTech - v20 - N '96 - p59 [1-50]
Higman, Barry W - *Slave Population and Economy in Jamaica 1807-1834*
JEL - v34 - D '96 - p2099 [51-250]
Higonnet, Margaret R - *Borderwork: Feminist Engagements with Comparative Literature*
Signs - v22 - Win '97 - p484+ [501+]
Reconfigured Spheres
Legacy - v13 - 2 '96 - p159+ [501+]
Higson, Andrew - *Waving the Flag*
FQ - v49 - Sum '96 - p62+ [501+]
Higson, Charles - *Getting Rid of Mr. Kitchen*
TLS - O 25 '96 - p24 [51-250]
Higson, Nigel - *Risk Management*
R&R Bk N - v12 - F '97 - p38 [1-50]
Higuera, Henry - *Eros and Empire*
RP - v59 - Spr '97 - p373+ [501+]
Hijiya-Kirschnereit, Irmela - *Rituals of Self-Revelation*
Choice - v34 - F '97 - p962 [51-250]
Hijuelos, Oscar - *Mr. Ives' Christmas*
Bks & Cult - v2 - My '96 - p6+ [501+]
Comw - v123 - D 6 '96 - p22 [51-250]
Comw - v123 - D 6 '96 - p26+ [251-500]
NYTBR - v101 - N 3 '96 - p28 [51-250]
Obs - O 27 '96 - p18* [51-250]
WLT - v71 - Win '97 - p151+ [251-500]
YR - v84 - O '96 - p151+ [501+]
Hikmet, Nazim - *Poems of Nazim Hikmet*
TranslRevS - v1 - My '95 - p33 [51-250]
Hilberg, Raul - *The Politics of Memory*
BL - v92 - Ag '96 - p1877 [51-250]
BW - v26 - S 1 '96 - p1+ [501+]
Choice - v34 - D '96 - p662 [51-250]
TLS - Mr 7 '97 - p3+ [501+]

Hilda's Tea Party
c Ch BWatch - v6 - My '96 - p3 [51-250]
Hildebrand, John - *Mapping the Farm*
LATBR - Ag 18 '96 - p15 [51-250]
Sew R - v104 - O '96 - p701+ [501+]
Hildebrand, Klaus - *Das Vergangene Reich*
Choice - v34 - D '96 - p568 [1-50]
Hildebrand, Reginald F - *The Times Were Strange and Stirring*
AHR - v102 - F '97 - p194+ [501+]
JR - v77 - Ja '97 - p147+ [501+]
JSH - v62 - N '96 - p823+ [251-500]
Hildebrandt, Stefan - *The Parsimonious Universe*
Choice - v34 - Ja '97 - p833+ [51-250]
Nature - v383 - O 31 '96 - p773 [51-250]
Hildegard, Saint - *Creation and Christ*
RR - v55 - N '96 - p661 [1-50]
The Letters of Hildegard of Bingen
CHR - v82 - Jl '96 - p542+ [501+]
Theol St - v57 - Mr '96 - p184+ [251-500]
Hildenbrand, Suzanne - *Reclaiming the American Library Past*
LAR - v98 - N '96 - p595 [51-250]
Hildick, E W - *The Case of the Wiggling Wig*
c HB Guide - v7 - Fall '96 - p293 [51-250]
Hile, Steve - *Rock Island Color Guide to Freight and Passenger Equipment*
Model R - v64 - F '97 - p53+ [51-250]
Hilfiker, David - *Not All of Us Are Saints*
Hast Cen R - v26 - Jl '96 - p39+ [501+]
Hilkert, Mary Catherine - *Naming Grace*
BL - v93 - D 15 '96 - p694 [51-250]
Hill, Anthony - *The Burnt Stick (Illus. by Mark Sofilas)*
c Magpies - v11 - Jl '96 - p45 [1-50]
Spindrift (Illus. by Mark Sofilas)
c Magpies - v11 - My '96 - p32 [501+]
Hill, Barbara Albers - *Time-Out for Children*
PW - v243 - D 16 '96 - p57 [51-250]
Hill, Brad - *World Wide Web Searching for Dummies*
New Sci - v153 - F 15 '97 - p45 [1-50]
Hill, Brian - *The Early Parties and Politics in Britain 1688-1832*
HRNB - v25 - Fall '96 - p20+ [251-500]
Hill, Bridget - *Servants: English Domestics in the Eighteenth Century*
HT - v46 - O '96 - p58 [1-50]
TLS - Ja 24 '97 - p30 [501+]
Hill, Charles C - *The Group of Seven*
Archiv - Spr '96 - p256+ [501+]
LJ - v121 - O 1 '96 - p74 [51-250]
Hill, Chris - *Rewind: Video Art and Alternative Media in the United States*
Afterimage - v24 - N '96 - p4 [1-50]
Hill, Christopher, 1912- - *Liberty against the Law*
BL - v93 - N 1 '96 - p478 [51-250]
CR - v269 - N '96 - p272+ [251-500]
Econ - v340 - S 21 '96 - p90 [251-500]
KR - v64 - O 1 '96 - p1444+ [251-500]
Lon R Bks - v243 - N 11 '96 - p23+ [501+]
Nat - v264 - Ap 21 '97 - p28+ [501+]
NYTBR - v102 - F 9 '97 - p21 [51-250]
Hill, Christopher, 1948- - *The Actors in Europe's Foreign Policy*
CR - v270 - Ja '97 - p56 [51-250]
Hill, Christopher R - *Olympic Politics. 2nd Ed.*
Choice - v34 - Mr '97 - p1199 [51-250]
R&R Bk N - v11 - D '96 - p21 [51-250]
Hill, Clara E - *Working with Dreams in Psychotherapy*
SciTech - v20 - N '96 - p44 [51-250]
Hill, Clara M - *John Thornbury in Tennessee and Alabama*
EGH - v50 - N '96 - p195 [51-250]
Hill, David - *Sacred Dust*
LJ - v121 - D '96 - p180 [51-250]
Rapport - v19 - 4 '96 - p26 [251-500]
Hill, David, 1943- - *Jakob Michael Reinhold Lenz: Studien Zum Gesamtwerk*
MLR - v91 - Jl '96 - p782+ [501+]
Hill, David, 1953- - *Turner in the North*
Choice - v34 - Ap '97 - p1324 [51-250]
Hill, Donna - *Intimate Betrayal*
PW - v244 - Mr 31 '97 - p72 [51-250]
Hill, Douglas - *Galaxy's Edge*
y Sch Lib - v44 - N '96 - p170 [51-250]
Hill, Eric - *Spot Bakes a Cake (Illus. by Eric Hill)*
c Bks Keeps - Ja '97 - p18+ [51-250]
Spot Visits His Grandparents
c Emerg Lib - v24 - Mr '97 - p45 [1-50]
c HB Guide - v8 - Spr '97 - p12 [1-50]
Where's Spot?
c HB - v73 - Mr '97 - p186 [1-50]

Hill, Ernest - *Satisfied with Nothin'*
y BL - v92 - Ag '96 - p1881 [51-250]
y BL - v92 - Ag '96 - p1891 [1-50]
Bl S - v26 - Fall '96 - p103+ [51-250]
Hill, Frances - *A Delusion of Satan*
NS - v126 - Ja 10 '97 - p46 [501+]
Hill, Geoffrey - *Canaan*
Agenda - v34 - Sum '96 - p29+ [501+]
NS - v125 - D 13 '96 - p46 [501+]
Obs - N 10 '96 - p17* [501+]
Spec - v277 - O 26 '96 - p57 [501+]
TLS - Ja 17 '97 - p23 [501+]
Hill, Grant - *Change the Game*
y BL - v93 - Ap 1 '97 - p1308 [1-50]
Hill, Hal - *The Indonesian Economy since 1966*
Choice - v34 - O '96 - p330 [51-250]
JEL - v34 - D '96 - p2120 [51-250]
Hill, J D - *Ritual and Rubbish in the Iron Age of Wessex*
Am Ant - v61 - Jl '96 - p631 [251-500]
Hill, John - *Big Picture, Small Screen*
Si & So - v6 - N '96 - p35 [51-250]
Hill, John Lawrence - *The Case for Vegetarianism*
Choice - v34 - D '96 - p631 [51-250]
Hill, John M - *Chaucerian Belief*
Comp L - v48 - Fall '96 - p377+ [501+]
The Cultural World in Beowulf
MP - v94 - N '96 - p207+ [501+]
Hill, John Spencer - *Ghirlandaio's Daughter*
BL - v93 - Mr 15 '97 - p1229 [51-250]
KR - v65 - Ja 15 '97 - p98 [51-250]
PW - v244 - Ja 27 '97 - p81 [51-250]
Hill, Joyce - *Old English Minor Heroic Poems*
Specu - v72 - Ja '97 - p169+ [251-500]
Hill, Kim - *Ache Life History*
Choice - v34 - S '96 - p168 [51-250]
Hill, Leonard - *Shells: Treasures of the Sea*
BL - v93 - Mr 1 '97 - p1099 [51-250]
Nature - v384 - D 12 '96 - p527 [51-250]
PW - v243 - O 14 '96 - p74 [51-250]
Hill, Lynda Marion - *Social Rituals and the Verbal Art of Zora Neale Hurston*
BWatch - v17 - N '96 - p9 [51-250]
Choice - v34 - Mr '97 - p1162 [51-250]
Hill, Marcia - *Classism and Feminist Therapy*
SciTech - v21 - Mr '97 - p54 [51-250]
Hill, Mark - *Ecclesiastical Law*
Law Q Rev - v112 - O '96 - p691+ [501+]
Hill, Michael R - *Archival Strategies and Techniques*
Archiv - Fall '94 - p191 [251-500]
Hill, Pamela Smith - *Ghost Horses*
y CCB-B - v50 - S '96 - p15 [51-250]
y HB Guide - v7 - Fall '96 - p302 [51-250]
y VOYA - v19 - O '96 - p210 [251-500]
Hill, Patricia Evridge - *Dallas: The Making of a Modern City*
Choice - v34 - Ap '97 - p1404 [51-250]
Hill, Paul R - *Unconventional Flying Objects*
Rapport - v19 - 4 '96 - p42 [51-250]
Hill, Peter - *The Messiaen Companion*
Notes - v53 - S '96 - p76+ [501+]
Hill, R Carter - *Bayesian Computational Methods and Applications*
JEL - v34 - D '96 - p2018 [51-250]
Hill, Raymond - *Hungary*
y KR - v64 - N 15 '96 - p1670 [51-250]
Hill, Reginald - *Asking for the Moon*
LJ - v121 - O 1 '96 - p131 [1-50]
PW - v243 - O 7 '96 - p64+ [51-250]
Matlock's System
BL - v93 - Ja '97 - p826 [51-250]
PW - v243 - D 30 '96 - p59 [51-250]
The Wood Beyond
Arm Det - v29 - Sum '96 - p373+ [251-500]
Books - v11 - Ap '97 - p22 [1-50]
LJ - v121 - O 15 '96 - p112 [51-250]
Spec - v277 - S 7 '96 - p37 [51-250]
Hill, Richard - *A Black Corps D'Elite*
MEQ - v3 - S '96 - p81 [251-500]
Hill, Robert - *Elementary Linear Algebra with DERIVE*
y New Sci - v151 - S 28 '96 - p44+ [501+]
Hill, Robert A - *The FBI's RACON*
RAH - v24 - S '96 - p495+ [501+]
Hill, Samuel S - *One Name but Several Faces*
Choice - v34 - S '96 - p144 [51-250]
Hill, Stephen - *The Early Byzantine Churches of Cilicia and Isauria*
r R&R Bk N - v11 - N '96 - p61 [51-250]
Hill, Susan, 1942- - *Listening to the Orchestra*
Obs - D 8 '96 - p15* [501+]
Spec - v277 - O 26 '96 - p46+ [501+]
TLS - N 15 '96 - p25 [251-500]

Reflections from a Garden
  Hort - v74 - N '96 - p57+ [501+]
Hill, T L - *Morris and the Kingdom of Knoll (Illus. by Jeff Colson)*
  c Ch BWatch - v6 - S '96 - p7 [1-50]
Hill, Tobias - *Midnight in the City of Clocks*
  Obs - S 29 '96 - p18* [51-250]
Hill, Tom - *Creation's Journey*
  GJ - v163 - Mr '97 - p105 [51-250]
  Pub Hist - v18 - Sum '96 - p44+ [501+]
Hill, William E - *The Mormon Trail*
  WHQ - v28 - Spr '97 - p103 [1-50]
Hillel, Margot - *Celebrate!*
  c Magpies - v11 - My '96 - p41 [251-500]
The Hillel Guide to Jewish Life on Campus. 1996 Ed.
  r ARBA - v28 - '97 - p142 [51-250]
Hillenbrand, Robert - *The Art of the Saljuqs in Iran and Anatolia*
  SDA - v4 - Spr '97 - p137+ [501+]
Islamic Architecture
  SDA - v4 - Fall '96 - p135+ [501+]
Hiller, Catherine - *Skin: Sensual Tales*
  KR - v65 - Mr 15 '97 - p404 [251-500]
  PW - v244 - Ap 14 '97 - p54+ [51-250]
Hiller, Ilo - *The White-Tailed Deer*
  y Choice - v34 - N '96 - p484 [51-250]
Hiller, J K - *The Newfoundland National Convention 1946-1948. Vols. 1-2*
  Can Hist R - v78 - Mr '97 - p116+ [501+]
Hillerman, Tony - *The Fallen Man*
  Atl - v279 - Ja '97 - p97 [51-250]
  y BL - v93 - N 1 '96 - p459 [51-250]
  CSM - v89 - D 19 '96 - p14 [51-250]
  CSM - v89 - Ja 6 '97 - p13 [501+]
  CSM - v89 - Ja 16 '97 - p14 [51-250]
  CSM - v89 - F 20 '97 - p10 [51-250]
  Ent W - N 15 '96 - p67 [51-250]
  KR - v64 - O 1 '96 - p1428 [251-500]
  LJ - v121 - O 15 '96 - p90 [51-250]
  NYTBR - v101 - D 8 '96 - p50 [51-250]
  PW - v243 - O 21 '96 - p73 [51-250]
The Fallen Man (Guidall). Audio Version
  CSM - v89 - Ja 30 '97 - pB4 [51-250]
  LJ - v122 - Mr 15 '97 - p102 [51-250]
The Fallen Man (Silverbird). Abridged Ed. Audio Version
  CSM - v89 - Ja 30 '97 - pB4 [51-250]
Finding Moon
  LATBR - S 1 '96 - p11 [51-250]
The Oxford Book of American Detective Stories
  Spec - v277 - S 7 '96 - p32+ [501+]
  TLS - N 29 '96 - p23 [501+]
  WSJ-MW - v78 - D 9 '96 - pA12 [1-50]
Hillert, Margaret - *The Sky Is Not So Far Away (Illus. by Thomas Werner)*
  c CBRS - v25 - Ja '97 - p50 [51-250]
  c CCB-B - v50 - N '96 - p98 [51-250]
  c CLW - v67 - Mr '97 - p51 [51-250]
  c HB Guide - v8 - Spr '97 - p152 [51-250]
  c SLJ - v42 - S '96 - p197 [51-250]
Hillesum, Etty - *An Interrupted Life. Letters from Westerbork*
  BL - v93 - F 1 '97 - p910 [1-50]
  NYTBR - v102 - Ja 26 '97 - p28 [51-250]
Hillgarth, J N - *Readers and Books in Majorca 1229-1550. Vols. 1-2*
  Lib & Cul - v32 - Win '97 - p133+ [501+]
Hilliard, Robert L - *Surviving the Americans*
  BL - v93 - D 1 '96 - p640 [51-250]
  Choice - v34 - My '97 - p1557+ [51-250]
  LJ - v122 - Ja '97 - p120 [51-250]
Hillier, Jim - *Cahiers Du Cinema. Vols. 1-2*
  TLS - Ja 17 '97 - p4+ [501+]
Hillier, Malcolm - *The Herb Garden*
  BL - v93 - S 15 '96 - p195 [51-250]
Hillman, Brenda - *Loose Sugar*
  PW - v244 - Mr 31 '97 - p71 [51-250]
Hillman, Eugene - *Toward an African Christianity*
  Rel St Rev - v23 - Ja '97 - p48 [51-250]
Hillman, James - *Beauty without Nature (Hillman). Audio Version*
  y Kliatt - v30 - N '96 - p46+ [51-250]
The Soul's Code
  BW - v26 - O 20 '96 - p4 [501+]
  CSM - v89 - D 12 '96 - p14 [51-250]
  LATBR - S 15 '96 - p4 [501+]
  NW - v129 - Ja 13 '97 - p64 [501+]
  NYTBR - v101 - S 15 '96 - p34 [501+]
Hillmer, Timothy - *The Hookmen*
  Aethlon - v13 - Spr '96 - p199+ [501+]
  WAL - v31 - Sum '96 - p176+ [251-500]

Hillocks, George, Jr. - *Teaching Writing as Reflective Practice*
  JAAL - v40 - S '96 - p74+ [501+]
Hills, D A - *Solution of Crack Problems*
  SciTech - v20 - S '96 - p49 [51-250]
Hills, John - *Private Welfare Insurance and Social Security*
  NS - v126 - Mr 7 '97 - p13 [51-250]
Hills, Ken - *Enciclopedia Visual: Historia Del Mundo*
  cr BL - v93 - Mr 1 '97 - p1196 [51-250]
Hills, Richard L - *Power from Wind*
  Nature - v384 - D 19 '96 - p618 [1-50]
Hills, Stephen M - *Employment Relations and the Social Sciences*
  ILRR - v50 - O '96 - p174+ [501+]
Hillston, Jane - *A Compositional Approach to Performance Modelling*
  SciTech - v20 - D '96 - p6 [51-250]
Hillyard, Paul - *The Book of the Spider*
  BL - v93 - D 1 '96 - p630 [1-50]
  KR - v64 - My 1 '96 - p665+ [251-500]
  NYTBR - v101 - O 20 '96 - p23 [51-250]
  VV - v41 - N 12 '96 - p84 [51-250]
Spiders and Scorpions (Illus. by Steve Johnson)
  c HB Guide - v7 - Fall '96 - p341 [51-250]
Hilmer, Frederick G - *Management Redeemed*
  Choice - v34 - F '97 - p1008 [51-250]
  HR Mag - v42 - F '97 - p122 [51-250]
Hilmes, Michele - *Radio Voices*
  KR - v65 - F 1 '97 - p197 [251-500]
  PW - v244 - Mr 3 '97 - p60+ [51-250]
Hilsman, Roger - *The Cuban Missile Crisis*
  Choice - v34 - S '96 - p194 [51-250]
  Parameters - v26 - Win '96 - p144+ [501+]
Hilton, James - *Goodbye, Mr. Chips (Jarvis). Audio Version*
  Obs - Ap 13 '97 - p18* [51-250]
Hilton, Margot - *Whiteley: An Unauthorised Life*
  Aust Bk R - S '96 - p44+ [501+]
Hilton, Michael - *The Christian Effect on Jewish Life*
  CH - v65 - S '96 - p538+ [501+]
The Gospels and Rabbinic Judaism
  Rel Ed - v91 - Fall '96 - p604 [1-50]
Hilton, R H - *English and French Towns in Feudal Society*
  JEH - v56 - S '96 - p710+ [501+]
Hilton, Sylvia L - *Fuentes Manuscritas Para La Historia De Iberoamerica*
  r HAHR - v76 - Ag '96 - p538+ [251-500]
Hilts, Philip J - *Smokescreen: The Truth behind the Tobacco Industry Cover-Up*
  ABA Jour - v82 - Ag '96 - p104 [501+]
  Bus W - D 16 '96 - p19 [51-250]
  New R - v215 - N 4 '96 - p27+ [501+]
  Reason - v28 - D '96 - p46+ [501+]
  Sci - v273 - Ag 9 '96 - p744+ [501+]
Hilty, Steven L - *A Guide to the Birds of Colombia*
  r AB - v97 - Je 17 '96 - p2398+ [51-250]
Himelblau, Jack J - *The Indian in Spanish America. Vol. 1*
  LA Ant - v7 - Mr '96 - p92 [251-500]
The Indian in Spanish America. Vol. 2
  HAHR - v76 - Ag '96 - p618+ [251-500]
Himelfarb, Richard - *Catastrophic Politics*
  APSR - v90 - D '96 - p911+ [501+]
  PSQ - v111 - Win '96 - p728+ [501+]
Himes, Chester - *The End of a Primitive*
  NYTBR - v102 - F 2 '97 - p22 [51-250]
  PW - v243 - D 2 '96 - p53 [51-250]
  VV - v42 - F 11 '97 - p53 [501+]
If He Hollers Let Him Go
  SAQ - v95 - Fall '96 - p979+ [501+]
Pinktoes
  AL - v69 - Mr '97 - p258 [1-50]
Himes, Michael J - *Finding God in All Things*
  Am - v176 - Mr 22 '97 - p30+ [51-250]
Himmelfarb, Gertrude - *The De-Moralization of Society*
  BIC - v26 - F '97 - p29+ [501+]
  RP - v58 - Sum '96 - p636+ [501+]
Himmelman, John - *Honest Tulio (Illus. by John Himmelman)*
  c KR - v65 - Ja 1 '97 - p59 [51-250]
  c PW - v244 - Ja 13 '97 - p74 [51-250]
J.J. versus the Baby-Sitter
  c HB Guide - v7 - Fall '96 - p259 [51-250]
Lights Out! (Illus. by John Himmelman). Book and Audio Version
  c SLJ - v42 - Ag '96 - p63+ [51-250]
Himmelstrand, Ulf - *African Perspectives on Development*
  For Aff - v75 - S '96 - p160+ [51-250]

Hinchcliffe, John - *Print Style*
  LJ - v121 - S 15 '96 - p67 [51-250]
Hinchcliffe, Tanis - *North Oxford*
  J Urban H - v23 - N '96 - p108+ [501+]
Hinckley, Barbara - *American Best Sellers*
  r RQ - v36 - Win '96 - p220+ [501+]
Hinckley, Ted C - *The Canoe Rocks*
  Choice - v34 - S '96 - p194 [51-250]
War, Wings, and a Western Youth 1925-1945
  WHQ - v28 - Spr '97 - p94 [251-500]
Hindcliffe, Alan - *Modelling Molecular Structures*
  Phys Today - v50 - Ja '97 - p69 [251-500]
Hindess, Barry - *Discourses of Power*
  AJS - v102 - N '96 - p869+ [501+]
  APSR - v90 - D '96 - p892 [501+]
Hindley, Joanne - *In the Company of Children*
  Inst - v106 - N '96 - p41 [1-50]
  Learning - v25 - Mr '97 - p9 [51-250]
Hindley, Judy - *The Big Red Bus (Illus. by William Benedict)*
  c Bks Keeps - N '96 - p6 [51-250]
Funny Walks. Book and Audio Version
  c SLJ - v42 - Ag '96 - p63 [51-250]
Hindman, Sandra - *Sealed in Parchment*
  EHR - v112 - F '97 - p167 [501+]
Hinds, James R - *South Atlantic Conflict*
  J Mil H - v61 - Ap '97 - p415+ [501+]
Hinds, Kathryn - *The Ancient Romans*
  c Ch BWatch - v7 - Ja '97 - p3 [1-50]
  c HB Guide - v8 - Spr '97 - p165 [51-250]
  y SLJ - v43 - Mr '97 - p201+ [51-250]
The Celts of Northern Europe
  c Ch BWatch - v7 - Ja '97 - p3 [1-50]
  c HB Guide - v8 - Spr '97 - p165 [51-250]
  y SLJ - v43 - Mr '97 - p202 [51-250]
India's Gupta Dynasty
  c HB Guide - v7 - Fall '96 - p378 [51-250]
Hine, Darlene Clark - *Facts on File Encyclopedia of Black Women in America. Vols. 1-11*
  r LJ - v122 - Ap 15 '97 - p66+ [51-250]
Hine Sight
  NWSA Jnl - v8 - Sum '96 - p126+ [501+]
Speak Truth to Power
  R&R Bk N - v11 - D '96 - p15 [51-250]
Hine, Thomas - *The Total Package*
  J Con A - v30 - Win '96 - p480+ [501+]
  Reason - v28 - D '96 - p42 [51-250]
Hines, Anna Grossnickle - *Miss Emma's Wild Garden (Illus. by Anna Grossnickle Hines)*
  c BL - v93 - Mr 1 '97 - p1172 [51-250]
  c CCB-B - v50 - My '97 - p324 [51-250]
  c KR - v65 - F 15 '97 - p310 [51-250]
When We Married Gary (Illus. by Anna Grossnickle Hines)
  c HB Guide - v7 - Fall '96 - p259 [51-250]
  c NYTBR - v101 - S 8 '96 - p28 [51-250]
Hines, I J - *ATM: The Key to High-Speed Broadband Networking*
  SciTech - v21 - Mr '97 - p88 [51-250]
Hines, Thomas S - *William Faulkner and the Tangible Past*
  BW - v27 - F 23 '97 - p13 [51-250]
  CHE - v43 - Mr 7 '97 - pA17 [51-250]
  NYTBR - v102 - F 9 '97 - p7 [501+]
Hiney, Tom - *Raymond Chandler: A Biography*
  KR - v65 - Ap 1 '97 - p521+ [251-500]
  LJ - v122 - Ap 1 '97 - p92 [51-250]
  PW - v244 - Mr 31 '97 - p52 [51-250]
Hing, Bill Ong - *To Be an American*
  y BL - v93 - F 15 '97 - p980 [251-500]
Hinkelman, Edward G - *Argentina Business*
  r ARBA - v28 - '97 - p115 [251-500]
Philippines Business
  r ARBA - v28 - '97 - p111+ [251-500]
Hinks, Peter P - *To Awaken My Afflicted Brethren*
  Choice - v34 - My '97 - p1563 [51-250]
Hinnant, Charles H - *The Poetry of Anne Finch*
  MLR - v91 - Jl '96 - p702+ [501+]
Hinnells, John R - *A New Dictionary of Religions. Rev. Ed.*
  r ARBA - v28 - '97 - p537 [51-250]
A New Handbook of Living Religions
  r LJ - v122 - Ap 1 '97 - p84 [51-250]
Who's Who of Religions
  r CR - v269 - S '96 - p166 [51-250]
Hinojosa, Maria - *Crews: Gang Members Talk to Maria Hinojosa*
  HAHR - v76 - N '96 - p760+ [501+]
Hinsdale, Mary Ann - *It Comes from the People*
  Am Ethnol - v24 - F '97 - p236+ [501+]

Hinsey, Ellen - *Cities of Memory*
  Choice - v34 - F '97 - p966 [51-250]
Hinshaw, Randall - *The World Economy in Transition*
  Econ J - v107 - Ja '97 - p267 [51-250]
  JEL - v34 - S '96 - p1434 [51-250]
Hinsley, Curtis M - *The Smithsonian and the American Indian*
  Pub Hist - v18 - Sum '96 - p43+ [501+]
Hinson, E Glenn - *The Church Triumphant*
  Rel St Rev - v23 - Ap '97 - p189 [51-250]
Hintikka, Jaakko - *From Dedekind to Godel*
  SciTech - v20 - D '96 - p4 [51-250]
  The Principles of Mathematics Revisited
  Choice - v34 - Mr '97 - p1197+ [51-250]
Hinton, Jeanne - *Walking in the Same Direction*
  Rel St Rev - v22 - O '96 - p340 [51-250]
Hinton, S E - *Big David, Little David (Illus. by Alan Daniel)*
  c PW - v244 - Mr 10 '97 - p69 [1-50]
  The Puppy Sister (Illus. by Jacqueline Rogers)
  c Magpies - v11 - My '96 - p43 [51-250]
Hintz, Martin - *Farewell, John Barleycorn*
  y BL - v92 - Ag '96 - p1893 [51-250]
  c CCB-B - v50 - O '96 - p63+ [51-250]
  c HB Guide - v8 - Spr '97 - p93 [51-250]
  c SLJ - v42 - O '96 - p134 [51-250]
Hintz, Suzanne S - *Rosario Ferre: A Search for Identity*
  WLT - v70 - Sum '96 - p670+ [501+]
Hinz, Evelyn J - *Adversaria: Literature and Law*
  Sev Cent N - v54 - Spr '96 - p15+ [501+]
Hinze, Christine Firer - *Comprehending Power in Christian Social Ethics*
  JR - v77 - Ap '97 - p326+ [501+]
Hinze, Jimmie W - *Construction Safety*
  SciTech - v20 - D '96 - p71 [51-250]
Hinze, Sarah - *Coming from the Light*
  LJ - v122 - Ja '97 - p106 [51-250]
  PW - v243 - D 9 '96 - p58 [51-250]
Hippel, Theodor Gottlieb Von - *On Marriage*
  TranslRevS - v1 - My '95 - p8 [51-250]
Hippely, Hilary Horder - *A Song for Lena (Illus. by Leslie Baker)*
  c BL - v93 - N 1 '96 - p507 [51-250]
  c HB Guide - v8 - Spr '97 - p32 [51-250]
  c SLJ - v42 - O '96 - p98 [51-250]
Hipple, F Steb - *Multinational Companies in United States International Trade*
  BusLR - v21 - 3 '96 - p244+ [251-500]
Hirano, Hiroyuki - *5S for Operators*
  SciTech - v20 - S '96 - p62 [51-250]
Hirata, Hosea - *The Poetry and Poetics of Nishiwaki Junzaburo*
  CLS - v33 - 2 '96 - p211+ [501+]
Hiro, Dilip - *Dictionary of the Middle East*
  r ARBA - v28 - '97 - p72 [251-500]
  r BL - v93 - S 1 '96 - p164 [51-250]
  r Choice - v34 - D '96 - p589+ [51-250]
  r MEJ - v50 - Aut '96 - p624 [51-250]
  r MEQ - v3 - D '96 - p82 [51-250]
  The Middle East
  yr BL - v92 - Ag '96 - p1920 [51-250]
  yr JAAL - v40 - N '96 - p238 [51-250]
  r MEJ - v50 - Aut '96 - p625 [51-250]
  yr R&R Bk N - v11 - N '96 - p14 [51-250]
  r WorldV - v12 - O '96 - p7 [51-250]
  Sharing the Promised Land
  TLS - F 14 '97 - p28 [501+]
Hirokawa, Randy Y - *Communication and Group Decision Making. 2nd Ed.*
  R&R Bk N - v11 - D '96 - p27 [51-250]
Hiroshi, Miyajima - *Yangban: Ri Chosen Shakai No Tokken Kaiso*
  Pac A - v69 - Fall '96 - p432+ [501+]
Hirsch, Arlene S - *Love Your Work and Success Will Follow*
  J Car P&E - v57 - Win '97 - p15 [51-250]
Hirsch, E D - *Cultural Literacy (Whitener). Audio Version*
  y Kliatt - v30 - N '96 - p47 [51-250]
  A First Dictionary of Cultural Literacy. 2nd Ed., Rev. and Updated
  cr ARBA - v28 - '97 - p137 [51-250]
  cr Cur R - v36 - N '96 - p12 [51-250]

The Schools We Need and Why We Don't Have Them
  Am - v175 - S 21 '96 - p33 [51-250]
  BL - v93 - S 15 '96 - p188 [251-500]
  Cng - v29 - Ja '97 - p63 [51-250]
  LJ - v121 - O 1 '96 - p96 [51-250]
  NASSP-B - v81 - My '97 - p121+ [501+]
  NYTBR - v101 - S 29 '96 - p14+ [501+]
  NYTBR - v101 - D 8 '96 - p92 [1-50]
  Pub Int - Win '97 - p124+ [501+]
  Rapport - v19 - 6 '96 - p34 [251-500]
  Trib Bks - Ja 12 '97 - p5 [51-250]
  W&I - v11 - D '96 - p255+ [501+]
Hirsch, Herbert - *Genocide and the Politics of Memory*
  AHR - v101 - D '96 - p1570 [251-500]
Hirsch, Karen D - *Mind Riot*
  y PW - v244 - Ap 7 '97 - p93 [51-250]
Hirsch, Moshe - *Whither Jerusalem?*
  TLS - Mr 7 '97 - p8+ [501+]
Hirsch, Robin - *Last Dance at the Hotel Kempinski*
  NYTBR - v101 - S 8 '96 - p36 [51-250]
Hirsch, Seev - *Outsiders' Response to European Integration*
  JEL - v34 - S '96 - p1427 [51-250]
Hirschfeld, Lawrence A - *Race in the Making*
  Choice - v34 - D '96 - p650+ [51-250]
  New Sci - v153 - F 1 '97 - p49 [501+]
Hirschfelder, Gunther - *Die Kolner Handelsbeziehungen Im Spatmittelalter*
  EHR - v111 - N '96 - p1259+ [251-500]
  JEH - v56 - S '96 - p708+ [501+]
Hirschheim, Rudy - *Information System Development and Data Modeling*
  LQ - v67 - Ap '97 - p196+ [501+]
Hirschhorn, Larry - *Reworking Authority*
  LJ - v122 - My 1 '97 - p118 [51-250]
Hirschi, Ron - *People of Salmon and Cedar (Illus. by Deborah Cooper)*
  c CBRS - v25 - Ja '97 - p57 [51-250]
  c HB Guide - v8 - Spr '97 - p177 [51-250]
  c SB - v33 - Ja '97 - p21 [51-250]
  c SLJ - v42 - S '96 - p216 [51-250]
Hirschield, Yizhar - *The Palestinian Dwelling in the Roman-Byzantine Period*
  Rel St Rev - v23 - Ja '97 - p88+ [51-250]
Hirschman, Albert O - *A Propensity to Self-Subversion*
  TLS - My 24 '96 - p35 [501+]
Hirschman, Dave - *Hijacked: The True Story of the Heroes of Flight 705*
  BL - v93 - My 1 '97 - p1465 [51-250]
Hirschmann, Nancy J - *Revisioning the Political*
  Choice - v34 - Mr '97 - p1237 [51-250]
  R&R Bk N - v12 - F '97 - p53 [51-250]
Hirsch-Pasek, Kathy - *The Origins of Grammar*
  Choice - v34 - Ja '97 - p788 [51-250]
Hirsh, John C - *The Boundaries of Faith*
  R&R Bk N - v12 - F '97 - p10 [51-250]
Hirsh, Sandra Krebs - *Work It Out*
  HR Mag - v41 - O '96 - p150+ [51-250]
Hirshberg, Caryle - *Remarkable Recovery*
  LJ - v122 - Ja '97 - p57 [1-50]
  Readings - v11 - D '96 - p10+ [501+]
Hirshberg, Daniel - *Emitt Smith*
  c HB Guide - v7 - Fall '96 - p359 [1-50]
Hirshberg, Jehoash - *Music in the Jewish Community of Palestine 1880-1948*
  MEJ - v50 - Sum '96 - p437+ [501+]
Hirshfield, Jane - *The October Palace*
  PS - v70 - Fall '96 - p186+ [501+]
Hirshhorn Museum and Sculpture Garden - *Hirshhorn Museum and Sculpture Garden: 150 Works of Art*
  BW - v26 - D 22 '96 - p13 [51-250]
  PW - v244 - Ja 13 '97 - p68 [51-250]
  WSJ-MW - v78 - D 5 '96 - pA18 [1-50]
Hirshman, Marc - *A Rivalry of Genius*
  Rel St Rev - v23 - Ja '97 - p89 [51-250]
Hirshon, Arnold - *Outsourcing Library Technical Services*
  IRLA - v32 - N '96 - p12 [51-250]
  LJ - v122 - Ja '97 - p156 [51-250]
  R&R Bk N - v12 - F '97 - p103 [51-250]
Hirshson, Stanley P - *The White Tecumseh*
  BL - v93 - My 15 '97 - p1559 [51-250]
  KR - v65 - Mr 15 '97 - p438+ [251-500]
  LJ - v122 - My 1 '97 - p114 [51-250]
  PW - v244 - Ap 14 '97 - p63+ [51-250]
Hirst, Paul - *Globalization in Question*
  AJS - v102 - My '97 - p1182+ [501+]
  Choice - v34 - S '96 - p176 [51-250]
  CS - v25 - S '96 - p585+ [501+]
Hirt, Paul W - *A Conspiracy of Optimism*
  AHR - v101 - D '96 - p1645+ [501+]

Hiscock, Andrew - *Authority and Desire*
  R&R Bk N - v12 - F '97 - p85 [51-250]
Hiscott, Gillian - *Emily Bronte's Wuthering Heights*
  c Sch Lib - v44 - Ag '96 - p116 [51-250]
Hise, Phaedra - *Growing Your Business Online*
  BL - v93 - N 1 '96 - p465 [51-250]
  BWatch - v18 - Mr '97 - p4 [51-250]
  LJ - v121 - N 1 '96 - p74 [51-250]
Hislop, P D - *Introduction to Spectral Theory*
  SIAM Rev - v39 - Mr '97 - p150+ [501+]
Hissey, Jane - *Hoot (Illus. by Jane Hissey)*
  c JB - v60 - D '96 - p233 [51-250]
  c KR - v65 - Mr 15 '97 - p462 [51-250]
  c PW - v244 - Mr 17 '97 - p85 [51-250]
  Ruff
  c Bks Keeps - Jl '96 - p6 [51-250]
  c Magpies - v11 - S '96 - p45 [1-50]
Histoire Militaire De La France. Vol. 4
  EHR - v111 - S '96 - p1034+ [501+]
Histoire Naturelle Des Indes
  BW - v26 - D 22 '96 - p13 [51-250]
  Mag Antiq - v151 - Mr '97 - p394 [51-250]
  PW - v243 - N 25 '96 - p66+ [51-250]
Historia General Del Peru. Vols. 1-10
  LA Ant - v7 - S '96 - p281+ [501+]
Historical Publications 1994. Electronic Media Version
  r J Gov Info - v23 - S '96 - p652 [51-250]
Historical Statistics 1960-1994
  r ARBA - v28 - '97 - p107 [51-250]
Historical Studies in Industrial Relations
  p BHR - v70 - Aut '96 - p406+ [501+]
A History of British Art
  TLS - Jl 7 '96 - p21 [501+]
The History of Decorative Arts. Vol. 1
  SDA - v4 - Fall '96 - p120+ [501+]
The History of Decorative Arts. Vols. 2-3
  SDA - v4 - Spr '97 - p126+ [501+]
The History of Printmaking
  c HB Guide - v7 - Fall '96 - p355 [51-250]
History of Sculpture
  Spec - v277 - D 14 '96 - p75+ [51-250]
A History of the University in Europe. Vol. 2
  TES - N 29 '96 - p10* [51-250]
A History of Women in the West. Vol. 4
  FR - v70 - D '96 - p370+ [501+]
Hitchcock, Alfred - *Hitchcock on Hitchcock*
  Am - v176 - Ja 4 '97 - p20+ [501+]
  CSM - v89 - D 6 '96 - p10 [51-250]
  Obs - Mr 16 '97 - p18* [51-250]
Hitchcock, Henry-Russell - *The International Style*
  Comw - v123 - S 13 '96 - p40+ [501+]
Hitchcock, Michael - *Islam and Identity in Eastern Indonesia*
  Choice - v34 - D '96 - p652 [51-250]
Hitchens, Christopher - *The Missionary Position*
  PW - v244 - Mr 3 '97 - p72 [1-50]
  Skeptic - v4 - 2 '96 - p105 [501+]
Hitchens, Susan Hayes - *Ross Lee Finney: A Bio-Bibliography*
  r ARBA - v28 - '97 - p475 [51-250]
  r R&R Bk N - v12 - F '97 - p69 [51-250]
Hitchins, Keith - *The Romanians 1774-1866*
  Choice - v34 - D '96 - p669+ [51-250]
  Rumania 1866-1947
  EHR - v111 - N '96 - p1344+ [501+]
  J Mil H - v61 - Ja '97 - p169+ [501+]
  Slav R - v55 - Fall '96 - p671+ [501+]
Hite, Kenneth - *Secret Societies*
  c Ch BWatch - v6 - D '96 - p7 [51-250]
Hite, Sid - *An Even Break*
  y Kliatt - v31 - My '97 - p6 [51-250]
  c PW - v244 - Ap 21 '97 - p74 [1-50]
  Those Darn Dithers
  c BL - v93 - D 15 '96 - p721 [51-250]
  y HB Guide - v8 - Spr '97 - p80 [51-250]
  y KR - v64 - O 1 '96 - p1467 [51-250]
  c NYTBR - v101 - N 24 '96 - p20 [1-50]
  y PW - v243 - N 25 '96 - p76 [51-250]
  c SLJ - v42 - D '96 - p121 [51-250]
Hitler, Adolph - *Hitler: Speeches and Proclamations 1932-1945. Vols. 1-2*
  J Mil H - v61 - Ja '97 - p184+ [251-500]
Hittner, Arthur D - *Honus Wagner: The Life of Baseball's Flying Dutchman*
  Choice - v34 - Ja '97 - p835+ [251-500]
HIV and AIDS Treatment Directory 1997
  r New Sci - v153 - F 22 '97 - p43 [51-250]
Hixson, Walter L - *Parting the Curtain*
  LJ - v122 - F 1 '97 - p94+ [51-250]
  Trib Bks - Ja 26 '97 - p4 [501+]

Hizlan, Dogan - *Kitaplar Kitabi*
WLT - v70 - Aut '96 - p1024 [51-250]
Hjelmeland, Andy - *Prisons: Inside the Big House*
y HB Guide - v8 - Spr '97 - p96 [51-250]
y SLJ - v42 - S '96 - p233 [51-250]
Hjelmstad, Keith D - *Fundamentals of Structural Mechanics*
SciTech - v20 - D '96 - p64 [51-250]
Hlavach, Laura - *Reporting the Kennedy Assassination*
LATBR - N 24 '96 - p3+ [501+]
HMO/PPO Directory 1996
r ARBA - v28 - '97 - p603 [51-250]
Ho, Bieu Chanh - *Cay Dang Mui Doi*
BL - v93 - My 15 '97 - p1568 [1-50]
Ho, Minfong - *Brother Rabbit (Illus. by Jennifer Hewitson)*
c BL - v93 - My 1 '97 - p1499+ [51-250]
c CCB-B - v50 - My '97 - p324 [51-250]
c HB - v73 - My '97 - p333+ [51-250]
c PW - v244 - Ap 14 '97 - p75 [51-250]
Hush! A Thai Lullaby (Illus. by Holly Meade)
c BL - v93 - Ap 1 '97 - p1296 [1-50]
c HB - v72 - N '96 - p725+ [51-250]
c HB Guide - v7 - Fall '96 - p368 [51-250]
c NYTBR - v102 - Mr 2 '97 - p25 [1-50]
The Two Brothers (Illus. by Jean Tseng)
c RT - v50 - N '96 - p254 [51-250]
Ho, Paul S - *Stress-Induced Phenomena in Metallization*
SciTech - v20 - N '96 - p75 [51-250]
Ho, Thomas S Y - *Fixed Income Solutions*
R&R Bk N - v11 - N '96 - p37 [51-250]
Ho, Truong An - *Thuo Sen Hong Phuong Tham*
BL - v93 - My 15 '97 - p1568 [1-50]
Hoag, Tami - *Guilty as Sin*
PW - v243 - N 4 '96 - p71 [1-50]
A Thin Dark Line
BL - v93 - Ja '97 - p778 [51-250]
CSM - v89 - Mr 20 '97 - p14 [51-250]
Ent W - Mr 28 '97 - p63 [51-250]
KR - v65 - Ja 15 '97 - p81+ [251-500]
LJ - v122 - F 15 '97 - p162 [51-250]
NYTBR - v102 - Mr 2 '97 - p20 [51-250]
PW - v244 - Ja 13 '97 - p52 [51-250]
Trib Bks - Ap 6 '97 - p5 [51-250]
Hoage, R J - *New Worlds, New Animals*
SciTech - v20 - N '96 - p29 [51-250]
Hoagland, Mahlon - *The Way Life Works*
Sci - v273 - Ag 9 '96 - p745 [251-500]
Hoagwood, Terence Allan - *Politics, Philosophy, and the Production of Romantic Texts*
Choice - v34 - Ja '97 - p795 [51-250]
Nine-C Lit - v51 - Mr '97 - p558+ [51-250]
TLS - D 6 '96 - p24 [51-250]
Hoak, Dale - *Tudor Political Culture*
EHR - v112 - Ap '97 - p458+ [501+]
HT - v46 - Ag '96 - p58+ [501+]
Six Ct J - v27 - Fall '96 - p820+ [501+]
The World of William and Mary
HRNB - v25 - Fall '96 - p20 [251-500]
HT - v47 - Mr '97 - p53 [501+]
Hoang, Khoi Phong - *Cay Tung Truoc Bao*
BL - v93 - S 1 '96 - p70 [51-250]
Nhung Con Chuot Thoi Tho Au
BL - v93 - S 1 '96 - p70 [51-250]
Viet Len Troi Xanh
BL - v93 - My 15 '97 - p1568 [1-50]
Hoard, G Richard - *Alone among the Living*
y Kliatt - v30 - S '96 - p26 [51-250]
Hoare, Philip - *Noel Coward: A Biography*
BL - v92 - Ag '96 - p1874 [51-250]
BW - v26 - Ag 18 '96 - p3 [501+]
LATBR - N 17 '96 - p8 [501+]
Nat R - v48 - S 16 '96 - p60+ [501+]
NY - v72 - S 9 '96 - p86+ [501+]
NYTBR - v101 - Ag 25 '96 - p7 [501+]
NYTBR - v101 - D 8 '96 - p89 [1-50]
Hoban, Lillian - *Arthur's Back to School Day (Illus. by Lillian Hoban)*
c BL - v93 - S 15 '96 - p253 [51-250]
c HB Guide - v8 - Spr '97 - p55 [51-250]
c SLJ - v42 - S '96 - p180 [51-250]
Big Little Lion (Illus. by Lillian Hoban)
c PW - v244 - Ja 6 '97 - p74 [51-250]
Big Little Otter (Illus. by Lillian Hoban)
c KR - v64 - D 1 '96 - p1738 [51-250]
c PW - v244 - Ja 6 '97 - p74 [51-250]
Hoban, Russell - *Bread and Jam for Frances*
c Ch BWatch - v6 - My '96 - p1 [1-50]
El Gran Negocio De Francisca (Illus. by Lillian Hoban)
c SLJ - v42 - N '96 - p132 [51-250]

Monster Film
c TES - Jl 5 '96 - pR8 [51-250]
The Trokeville Way
y Bks Keeps - v100 - S '96 - p33 [51-250]
c BL - v93 - N 15 '96 - p588 [51-250]
y CCB-B - v50 - F '97 - p209 [51-250]
y HB Guide - v8 - Spr '97 - p80 [51-250]
c JB - v60 - Ag '96 - p157 [51-250]
y KR - v64 - O 15 '96 - p1533 [51-250]
c PW - v243 - N 11 '96 - p77 [51-250]
y Sch Lib - v44 - Ag '96 - p118 [251-500]
y SLJ - v42 - D '96 - p136 [51-250]
Hoban, Tana - *Colors Everywhere (Illus. by Tana Hoban)*
c RT - v50 - D '96 - p346 [51-250]
Construction Zone (Illus. by Tana Hoban)
c BL - v93 - Ap 1 '97 - p1335 [51-250]
c CCB-B - v50 - Ap '97 - p284+ [51-250]
c KR - v65 - Ap 1 '97 - p557 [51-250]
c SLJ - v43 - Mr '97 - p175+ [51-250]
Is It Rough? Is It Smooth? Is It Shiny?
c Inst - v106 - S '96 - p92 [1-50]
Just Look (Illus. by Tana Hoban)
c HB Guide - v7 - Fall '96 - p259+ [51-250]
c Par Ch - v20 - O '96 - p3 [51-250]
What Is That? (Illus. by Tana Hoban)
c ECEJ - v24 - Win '96 - p109 [51-250]
Hobb, Robin - *Assassin's Apprentice*
MFSF - v91 - D '96 - p98 [51-250]
Assassin's Quest
BL - v93 - F 1 '97 - p929 [51-250]
KR - v65 - F 1 '97 - p177 [51-250]
PW - v244 - F 24 '97 - p68 [51-250]
Royal Assassin
MFSF - v91 - D '96 - p98 [51-250]
y VOYA - v19 - D '96 - p280 [51-250]
Hobbes, Thomas - *The Correspondence of Thomas Hobbes. Vols. 1-2*
RM - v49 - Je '96 - p926+ [501+]
Three Discourses
RP - v58 - Fall '96 - p813+ [501+]
TLS - N 29 '96 - p13 [51-250]
TLS - D 20 '96 - p27 [501+]
Hobbet, Anastasia - *Pleasure of Believing*
y BL - v93 - F 15 '97 - p1003 [51-250]
KR - v65 - Mr 1 '97 - p325+ [51-250]
PW - v244 - F 24 '97 - p63 [51-250]
Hobbie, Douglas - *Being Brett*
VLS - Win '96 - p9+ [51-250]
Hobbs, Anne Stevenson - *Beatrix Potter: The V and A Collection*
r RSR - v24 - 3 '96 - p23 [51-250]
Beatrix Potter's Art. Rev. Ed.
RSR - v24 - 3 '96 - p23 [51-250]
Hobbs, Catherine - *Nineteenth-Century Women Learn to Write*
Lib & Cul - v32 - Win '97 - p142+ [501+]
R&R Bk N - v11 - D '96 - p54 [51-250]
Hobbs, Dick - *Bad Business*
TLS - Ag 2 '96 - p28 [501+]
Hobbs, Joseph J - *Mount Sinai*
MEJ - v50 - Aut '96 - p627+ [51-250]
Hobbs, Susan - *The Art of Thomas Wilmer Dewing*
A Art - v61 - Ja '97 - p88 [501+]
Hobbs, Valerie - *Get It While It's Hot--or Not*
y CBRS - v25 - Mr '97 - p95 [51-250]
y CCB-B - v50 - N '96 - p99 [51-250]
y HB - v72 - N '96 - p744 [251-500]
y HB Guide - v8 - Spr '97 - p80 [51-250]
y JAAL - v40 - N '96 - p230 [51-250]
y KR - v64 - Ag 15 '96 - p1236 [51-250]
y PW - v243 - O 7 '96 - p76+ [51-250]
y SLJ - v42 - O '96 - p147 [51-250]
y VOYA - v19 - D '96 - p270 [51-250]
How Far Would You Have Gotten If I Hadn't Called You Back?
y Emerg Lib - v23 - My '96 - p58 [251-500]
y Emerg Lib - v24 - S '96 - p24 [1-50]
Hobbs, Vicki - *Virtual Classrooms*
H Sch M - v4 - Mr '97 - p56 [51-250]
Hobbs, Will - *Beardream (Illus. by Jill Kastner)*
c CBRS - v25 - Ap '97 - p99 [51-250]
c KR - v65 - Mr 15 '97 - p462 [51-250]
Bearstone
y Kliatt - v30 - S '96 - p3 [1-50]
Downriver
y Kliatt - v30 - S '96 - p3 [1-50]

Far North
y BL - v93 - Ap 1 '97 - p1292 [1-50]
y BL - v93 - Ap 1 '97 - p1310 [1-50]
c CBRS - v25 - N '96 - p34 [51-250]
y HB - v72 - N '96 - p745+ [251-500]
y HB Guide - v8 - Spr '97 - p80 [51-250]
c SLJ - v42 - S '96 - p227 [51-250]
y VOYA - v19 - F '97 - p328 [251-500]
Ghost Canoe
y BL - v93 - My 1 '97 - p1489 [51-250]
c CCB-B - v50 - Ap '97 - p285 [51-250]
y KR - v65 - Ap 1 '97 - p557 [51-250]
Hoberman, John - *Darwin's Athletes*
Econ - v343 - Ap 26 '97 - p83+ [501+]
KR - v65 - Ja 15 '97 - p119 [251-500]
LJ - v122 - F 15 '97 - p151 [51-250]
PW - v244 - Ja 20 '97 - p383 [51-250]
Trib Bks - Mr 16 '97 - p1+ [501+]
Wil Q - v21 - Win '97 - p95+ [501+]
WSJ-Cent - v99 - F 19 '97 - pA17 [501+]
Hoberman, Mary Ann - *The Seven Silly Eaters (Illus. by Marla Frazee)*
c BL - v93 - Mr 1 '97 - p1172 [51-250]
c CBRS - v25 - Mr '97 - p87 [51-250]
c CCB-B - v50 - My '97 - p324+ [51-250]
c HB - v73 - My '97 - p308 [51-250]
c KR - v65 - F 1 '97 - p223 [51-250]
c PW - v244 - F 3 '97 - p106 [51-250]
c SLJ - v43 - Mr '97 - p160 [51-250]
c Trib Bks - Mr 9 '97 - p7 [51-250]
Hobica, George - *Gay USA*
r Quill & Q - v62 - S '96 - p24 [51-250]
Hobsbaum, Philip - *Metre, Rhythm and Verse Form*
Choice - v34 - Mr '97 - p1158 [251-500]
Hobsbawm, Eric - *The Age of Extremes*
S&S - v60 - Win '96 - p497+ [501+]
Nations and Nationalism since 1780. 2nd Ed.
Crit R - v10 - Spr '96 - p285+ [501+]
Hobsbawn-Smith, Dees - *Skinny Feasts*
Quill & Q - v63 - Mr '97 - p21 [251-500]
Hobson, Archie - *The Cambridge Gazetteer of the United States and Canada*
r ARBA - v28 - '97 - p175 [51-250]
r RQ - v36 - Fall '96 - p123+ [251-500]
Hobson, Charles F - *The Great Chief Justice*
Choice - v34 - Ja '97 - p875 [51-250]
LJ - v121 - S 15 '96 - p82 [51-250]
New R - v216 - F 17 '97 - p38+ [501+]
WSJ-MW - v78 - D 10 '96 - pA20 [501+]
Hobson, Fred - *Mencken: A Life*
AL - v68 - D '96 - p861+ [501+]
Hobson, J Allan - *The Chemistry of Conscious States*
NYTBR - v101 - S 1 '96 - p24 [1-50]
Sleep
AJPsych - v153 - N '96 - p1497 [501+]
Hobson, Margaret - *AAL Picture Book Index. 3rd Ed.*
r LAR - v98 - D '96 - p652 [1-50]
Hoch, Jeffrey C - *NMR Data Processing*
SciTech - v20 - D '96 - p27 [51-250]
Hoch, Peter C - *Experimental and Molecular Approaches to Plant Biosystematics*
BioSci - v46 - O '96 - p715+ [501+]
Hochman, Elaine S - *Bauhaus: Crucible of Modernism*
KR - v65 - Ap 1 '97 - p522 [251-500]
PW - v244 - Ap 14 '97 - p63 [51-250]
Hochschild, Adam - *Finding the Trapdoor*
PW - v244 - Ap 21 '97 - p50 [51-250]
The Unquiet Ghost
Slav R - v55 - Sum '96 - p491+ [501+]
Hochschild, Arlie Russell - *The Time Bind*
BL - v93 - My 1 '97 - p1467 [51-250]
KR - v65 - Mr 15 '97 - p439 [251-500]
LJ - v122 - My 1 '97 - p118 [51-250]
PW - v244 - Mr 24 '97 - p69 [51-250]
Hochschild, Jennifer L - *Facing up to the American Dream*
AAPSS-A - v546 - Jl '96 - p170+ [501+]
J Pol - v59 - F '97 - p267+ [501+]
Pub Op Q - v60 - Sum '96 - p332+ [501+]
Hockaday, Mary - *Kafka, Love and Courage*
KR - v65 - Mr 1 '97 - p353 [51-250]
LJ - v122 - Ap 15 '97 - p81 [51-250]
PW - v244 - F 10 '97 - p76 [51-250]
VLS - Spr '97 - p5+ [51-250]
Hockenberry, John - *Declarations of Independence*
Obs - Ja 19 '97 - p18* [51-250]
Moving Violations
Ant R - v54 - Sum '96 - p371+ [251-500]
BW - v26 - S 22 '96 - p12 [51-250]
y Emerg Lib - v24 - S '96 - p23 [1-50]
y Kliatt - v30 - N '96 - p22 [51-250]

Hockey, Thomas - *The Comet Hale-Bopp Book*
  Astron - v25 - Mr '97 - p103 [51-250]
  Choice - v34 - Ap '97 - p1362 [51-250]
  S&T - v93 - F '97 - p56+ [501+]
Hockey Guide. 1996-97 Ed.
  r ARBA - v28 - '97 - p299 [51-250]
Hockey Superstars Album 1986-
  Emerg Lib - v24 - Mr '97 - p26 [1-50]
Hocking, John C - *Conan and the Emerald Lotus*
  Necro - Fall '96 - p7+ [501+]
Hocking, Mary - *The Meeting Place*
  Books - v10 - Je '96 - p22 [51-250]
Hocking, Ronald R - *Methods and Applications of Linear Models*
  Choice - v34 - F '97 - p999+ [51-250]
  SciTech - v20 - N '96 - p14 [51-250]
Hockney, David - *That's the Way I See It*
  NYTBR - v102 - Ja 19 '97 - p28 [1-50]
Hocquard, Emmanuel - *The Gardens of Sallust and Other Writings*
  TLS - D 13 '96 - p32 [251-500]
Hoddinott, Keith B - *Superfund Risk Assessment in Soil Contamination Studies. Vol. 2*
  SciTech - v20 - D '96 - p70 [51-250]
Hodel, Robert - *Betrachtungen Zum Skaz Bei N.S. Leskov and Dragoslav Mihailovic*
  Slav R - v55 - Sum '96 - p508+ [501+]
Hodge, Charlie - *Golly Gee It's Me!*
  Mac - v109 - D 16 '96 - p72 [1 50]
Hodge, Deborah - *Simple Machines (Illus. by Ray Boudreau)*
  c BIC - v25 - D '96 - p37 [251-500]
  c Emerg Lib - v24 - Mr '97 - p28 [1-50]
  c Quill & Q - v62 - D '96 - p39 [251-500]
  Whales: Killer Whales, Blue Whales and More (Illus. by Pat Stephens)
  c Quill & Q - v63 - Ja '97 - p38 [51-250]
  Wild Dogs (Illus. by Pat Stephens)
  c Quill & Q - v63 - Ja '97 - p38 [51-250]
Hodge, Dino - *The Fall Upward*
  Aust Bk R - D '96 - p93 [1-50]
Hodge, Jane Aiken - *Passion and Principle*
  CR - v269 - O '96 - p224 [51-250]
Hodge, John - *Trainspotting: A Screenplay*
  Ent W - Mr 28 '97 - p61 [51-250]
Hodge, Merle - *For the Life of Laetitia*
  c Bks Keeps - N '96 - p11 [51-250]
Hodges, Donald Clark - *America's New Economic Order*
  JEL - v35 - Mr '97 - p287 [51-250]
  Mexican Anarchism after the Revolution
  AHR - v102 - F '97 - p236+ [51-250]
  HAHR - v77 - F '97 - p136+ [501+]
Hodges, Graham Russell - *Slavery and Freedom in the Rural North*
  LJ - v122 - Mr 15 '97 - p74 [51-250]
  THe Black Loyalist Directory
  r W&M Q - v53 - O '96 - p831+ [501+]
Hodges, Margaret - *Comus (Illus. by Trina Schart Hyman)*
  c HB Guide - v7 - Fall '96 - p260 [51-250]
  c RT - v50 - Ap '97 - p594 [51-250]
  Gulliver in Lilliput (Illus. by Kimberly Bulcken Root)
  c PW - v244 - F 24 '97 - p93 [1-50]
  c RT - v50 - S '96 - p54 [51-250]
  Molly Limbo (Illus. by Elizabeth Miles)
  c BL - v93 - S 15 '96 - p243 [51-250]
  c CBRS - v25 - Ja '97 - p51 [51-250]
  c CCB-B - v50 - O '96 - p64 [51-250]
  c Ch BWatch - v6 - N '96 - p6 [51-250]
  c HB - v72 - N '96 - p749+ [251-500]
  c HB Guide - v8 - Spr '97 - p102 [51-250]
  c KR - v64 - S 1 '96 - p1323 [51-250]
  c SLJ - v42 - S '96 - p197 [51-250]
  Saint George and the Dragon
  c New Ad - v9 - Fall '96 - p267+ [501+]
  c New Ad - v9 - Fall '96 - p309+ [501+]
Hodgins, Michael C - *Reluctant Warrior*
  BL - v93 - Ja '97 - p812+ [51-250]
  KR - v64 - N 15 '96 - p1652 [251-500]
  LJ - v122 - F 15 '97 - p142 [51-250]
  PW - v243 - D 9 '96 - p56 [51-250]
Hodgkinson, Neville - *AIDS*
  New Sci - v152 - D 7 '96 - p50 [51-250]
Hodgkinson, Peter - *Capital Punishment*
  Law Q Rev - v113 - Ap '97 - p344+ [501+]
Hodgkinson, Tom - *The Idler's Companion*
  TLS - N 22 '96 - p7 [501+]
Hodgman, Helen - *Passing Remarks*
  Aust Bk R - S '96 - p29+ [501+]
Hodgson, Ann - *Dearing and Beyond*
  NS - v126 - Mr 7 '97 - p13 [51-250]

Hodgson, Barbara - *The Tattooed Map*
  LJ - v121 - S 15 '96 - p124 [51-250]
Hodgson, Godfrey - *The World Turned Right Side Up*
  BL - v93 - O 1 '96 - p309 [51-250]
  BW - v26 - N 3 '96 - p3 [501+]
  Choice - v34 - Ap '97 - p1404+ [51-250]
  Econ - v341 - N 2 '96 - p85 [501+]
  KR - v64 - S 15 '96 - p1375 [251-500]
  NYRB - v43 - O 17 '96 - p30+ [501+]
  NYTBR - v101 - O 27 '96 - p27 [501+]
  Rapport - v19 - 6 '96 - p31 [251-500]
  Reason - v28 - Mr '97 - p64+ [501+]
  W&I - v12 - F '97 - p247+ [501+]
  WSJ-MW - v78 - O 28 '96 - pA13 [501+]
Hodgson, Peter C - *Winds of the Spirit*
  TT - v53 - O '96 - p378+ [501+]
Hodgson, Peter John - *Benjamin Britten: A Guide to Research*
  r ARBA - v28 - '97 - p475+ [51-250]
  r Choice - v34 - F '97 - p944 [51-250]
  r R&R Bk N - v11 - D '96 - p56 [51-250]
Hodgson, William Hope - *The House on the Borderland*
  Necro - Fall '96 - p18+ [501+]
  Terrors of the Sea
  Necro - Fall '96 - p18+ [501+]
Hodson, Joel C - *Lawrence of Arabia and American Culture*
  ELT - v39 - 3 '96 - p361+ [501+]
  MEJ - v50 - Sum '96 - p454 [51 250]
Hoeg, Peter - *Borderliners (Guidall). Audio Version*
  y Kliatt - v30 - N '96 - p36+ [51-250]
  The History of Danish Dreams
  BW - v26 - O 6 '96 - p2 [51-250]
  NYTBR - v101 - O 13 '96 - p32 [1-50]
  PW - v243 - S 30 '96 - p79 [1-50]
  Smilla's Sense of Snow
  TranslRevS - v1 - My '95 - p17 [51-250]
  The Woman and the Ape
  BL - v93 - Ja '97 - p761 [1-50]
  BL - v93 - O 1 '96 - p291 [51-250]
  Ent W - Ja 17 '97 - p59 [51-250]
  KR - v64 - S 15 '96 - p1343 [251-500]
  LJ - v122 - Ja '97 - p49 [51-250]
  LJ - v121 - O 1 '96 - p126+ [51-250]
  NYTBR - v101 - D 22 '96 - p8+ [501+]
  NYTLa - v146 - D 4 '96 - pC17 [501+]
  Obs - D 22 '96 - p17* [501+]
  PW - v243 - O 21 '96 - p69 [251-500]
  Time - v148 - D 2 '96 - p87+ [501+]
  TLS - N 29 '96 - p24 [501+]
  Trib Bks - Ja 5 '97 - p2 [501+]
  VLS - Win '96 - p6 [501+]
  The Woman and the Ape (Guidall). Audio Version
  BWatch - v18 - Mr '97 - p6 [1-50]
  y Kliatt - v31 - Mr '97 - p47 [51-250]
  LJ - v122 - F 15 '97 - p114+ [1-50]
Hoehler-Fatton, Cynthia - *Women of Fire and Spirit*
  Choice - v34 - N '96 - p500 [51-250]
Hoek, C Van Den - *Algae: An Introduction to Phycology*
  r BioSci - v46 - O '96 - p720+ [501+]
Hoek, M Peter Van Der - *Conditions for Direct Foreign Investments in the Baltic States*
  JEL - v34 - D '96 - p2046 [51-250]
Hoekema, David A - *Christianity and Culture in the Crossfire*
  PW - v244 - Mr 24 '97 - p73+ [51-250]
Hoekman, Bernard M - *The Political Economy of the World Trading System*
  Econ J - v107 - Ja '97 - p268 [251-500]
  JEL - v34 - S '96 - p1427 [51-250]
Hoekstra, Rik - *Two Worlds Merging*
  HAHR - v77 - F '97 - p115 [251-500]
Hoerder, Dirk - *American Labor History*
  r RQ - v36 - Fall '96 - p55 [51-250]
  European Migrants
  HRNB - v25 - Win '97 - p77+ [251-500]
  RAH - v25 - Mr '97 - p68+ [501+]
  The Immigrant Labor Press in North America 1840s-1970s. Vols. 1-3
  r RQ - v36 - Fall '96 - p53 [251-500]
Hoesterey, Ingeborg - *Intertextuality: German Literature and Visual Art from the Renaissance to the Twentieth Century*
  Ger Q - v69 - Fall '96 - p437+ [501+]
Hoestlandt, Jo - *Star of Fear, Star of Hope (Illus. by Johanna Kang)*
  c RT - v50 - S '96 - p57 [51-250]
  c RT - v50 - N '96 - p245+ [51-250]
Hoeveler, Diane Long - *Approaches to Teaching Bronte's Jane Eyre*
  VS - v39 - Aut '95 - p55+ [501+]

Hoezee, Scott - *The Riddle of Grace*
  Ch Today - v40 - N 11 '96 - p54+ [51-250]
Hoff, B J - *Masquerade*
  LJ - v121 - N 1 '96 - p54 [51-250]
  The Tangled Web
  LJ - v122 - Ap 1 '97 - p78 [51-250]
Hoff, Charles - *The Fights*
  LATBR - D 8 '96 - p2 [51-250]
Hoff, Syd - *Bernard on His Own*
  c Par Ch - v20 - N '96 - p3 [51-250]
  Danny and the Dinosaur Go to Camp (Illus. by Syd Hoff)
  c BL - v92 - Ag '96 - p1910 [51-250]
  c HB Guide - v7 - Fall '96 - p284 [51-250]
  c KR - v64 - My 1 '96 - p689 [51-250]
  Happy Birthday, Danny and the Dinosaur! (Illus. by Syd Hoff)
  c RT - O '96 - p130 [1-50]
Hoffer, Abram - *Hoffer's Law of Natural Nutrition*
  Quill & Q - v62 - Ag '96 - p31 [51-250]
Hoffer, Peter Charles - *The Devil's Disciples*
  Choice - v34 - N '96 - p525 [51-250]
Hoffer, William - *Volcano: The Search for Vesuvius*
  y Kliatt - v31 - Mr '97 - p5 [51-250]
Hoffert, Sylvia D - *When Hens Crow*
  AHR - v102 - F '97 - p183+ [251-500]
Hoffman, Allan M - *Schools, Violence, and Society*
  Choice - v34 - Ja '97 - p850 [51-250]
  H Sch M - v4 - S '96 - p49 [51-250]
Hoffman, Allen - *Small Worlds*
  BL - v93 - O 1 '96 - p322 [51-250]
  Choice - v34 - Ap '97 - p1336 [51-250]
  NYTBR - v102 - Ja 19 '97 - p18 [51-250]
Hoffman, Amy - *Hospital Time*
  LJ - v122 - Ap 1 '97 - p115 [51-250]
  PW - v244 - Mr 10 '97 - p61+ [51-250]
Hoffman, Andrew - *Inventing Mark Twain*
  BL - v93 - Mr 15 '97 - p1220 [51-250]
  Econ - v342 - Mr 15 '97 - p13* [501+]
  KR - v65 - Ja 1 '97 - p39 [251-500]
  PW - v244 - Ja 20 '97 - p382+ [51-250]
Hoffman, Barry - *Hungry Eyes*
  PW - v244 - Ap 21 '97 - p62 [51-250]
Hoffman, Charles - *Bruce Lee, Brandon Lee, and the Dragon's Curse*
  y BL - v93 - Ap 1 '97 - p1308 [1-50]
Hoffman, Daniel - *Middens of the Tribe*
  HR - v49 - Sum '96 - p337+ [501+]
Hoffman, Dennis L - *Aggregate Money Demand Functions*
  JEL - v34 - D '96 - p2035+ [51-250]
  R&R Bk N - v11 - D '96 - p36 [51-250]
Hoffman, E J - *Power Cycles and Energy Efficiency*
  SciTech - v20 - N '96 - p70 [51-250]
Hoffman, Edward - *The Drive for Self*
  J ClinPsyc - v57 - Jl '96 - p313+ [501+]
Hoffman, Edward G - *Setup Reduction through Effective Workholding*
  SciTech - v20 - S '96 - p63 [51-250]
Hoffman, Eva - *Lost in Translation*
  SFR - v21 - Jl '96 - p48 [1-50]
Hoffman, F G - *Decisive Force*
  Choice - v34 - D '96 - p690 [51-250]
Hoffman, Katherine - *Concepts of Identity*
  NYTBR - v101 - D 22 '96 - p14 [51-250]
Hoffman, Lawrence A - *Covenant of Blood*
  Rel St Rev - v23 - Ap '97 - p196 [51-250]
  R&R Bk N - v11 - N '96 - p7 [51-250]
  Tikkun - v11 - N '96 - p72+ [501+]
Hoffman, Marvin - *Chasing Hellhounds*
  Trib Bks - Ja 12 '97 - p2 [1-50]
Hoffman, Mary - *La Asombrosa Graciela (Illus. by Caroline Binch)*
  c SLJ - v42 - Ag '96 - p178 [51-250]
  Boundless Grace (Illus. by Caroline Binch)
  c RT - v50 - N '96 - p242 [51-250]
  c SE - v60 - N '96 - p400 [51-250]
  Earth, Fire, Water, Air (Illus. by J Ray)
  c RT - v50 - Mr '97 - p477 [51-250]
Hoffman, Mary Ann - *Counseling Clients with HIV Disease*
  Readings - v11 - S '96 - p29 [51-250]
Hoffman, Patricia L - *AIDS and the Sleeping Church*
  CLW - v67 - D '96 - p42 [251-500]
Hoffman, Philip T - *Growth in a Traditional Society*
  AHR - v102 - F '97 - p117+ [501+]
  Choice - v34 - O '96 - p340 [51-250]
  JEL - v34 - D '96 - p1470+ [51-250]
Hoffman, Richard - *Half the House*
  LATBR - D 22 '96 - p6 [51-250]
  PW - v243 - S 23 '96 - p73 [1-50]

Hoffman, Ronald, 1941- - *The Transforming Hand of Revolution*
 Choice - v34 - S '96 - p199 [51-250]
 HRNB - v25 - Win '97 - p61 [251-500]
Hoffman, Valerie J - *Sufism, Mystics, and Saints in Modern Egypt*
 MEJ - v51 - Win '97 - p147+ [501+]
 Rel St Rev - v23 - Ap '97 - p201 [51-250]
 R&R Bk N - v12 - F '97 - p9 [51-250]
Hoffman, William, 1925- - *Follow Me Home*
 Sew R - v104 - Jl '96 - pR52 [51-250]
Hoffmann, Charlotte - *Language, Culture, and Communication in Contemporary Europe*
 R&R Bk N - v11 - D '96 - p58 [1-50]
Hoffmann, David - *The Complete Illustrated Holistic Herbal*
 r LJ - v121 - D '96 - p82 [51-250]
 Herbs to Relieve Headaches
 BWatch - v18 - Mr '97 - p1 [1-50]
 Herbs to Relieve Stress
 BWatch - v17 - N '96 - p4 [51-250]
Hoffmann, David L - *Peasant Metropolis*
 JMH - v68 - S '96 - p745+ [501+]
Hoffmann, Donald - *Frank Lloyd Wright's Dana House*
 BWatch - v17 - N '96 - p1+ [51-250]
 Choice - v34 - Mr '97 - p1152 [51-250]
Hoffmann, E T A - *The Nutcracker (Illus. by Nan Brooks)*
 c PW - v243 - S 30 '96 - p92+ [1-50]
 Nutcracker (Illus. by Roberto Innocenti)
 c BW - v26 - N 3 '96 - p10 [251-500]
 c KR - v64 - Ag 15 '96 - p1228 [51-250]
 c PW - v243 - S 30 '96 - p92 [51-250]
 The Nutcracker and the Mouse King (Reed). Audio Version
 c PW - v243 - N 11 '96 - p35 [51-250]
Hoffmann, Hartmut - *Bucher Und Urkunden Aus Helmarshausen Und Corvey*
 Specu - v72 - Ja '97 - p169+ [501+]
 Monchskonig Und Rex Idiota
 Specu - v72 - Ja '97 - p171+ [501+]
Hoffmann, Hilmar - *The Triumph of Propaganda*
 Choice - v34 - S '96 - p135 [51-250]
Hoffmann, Joachim - *Stalins Vernichtungskrieg 1941-1945*
 Slav R - v55 - Sum '96 - p493+ [501+]
Hoffmann, Joyce - *Theodore H. White and Journalism as Illusion*
 AHR - v102 - F '97 - p215 [251-500]
Hoffmann, Lis - *Libido*
 Aust Bk R - S '96 - p53+ [501+]
Hoffmann, Manfred - *Rhetoric and Theology*
 Ren Q - v49 - Win '96 - p902+ [501+]
Hoffmann, Paul - *Studien Zur Fruhgeschichte Der Jesus-Bewegung*
 Rel St Rev - v23 - Ap '97 - p178 [51-250]
Hoffmann, Peter - *Stauffenberg: A Family History 1905-1944*
 HRNB - v25 - Fall '96 - p30+ [251-500]
 NYRB - v43 - Je 6 '96 - p20+ [501+]
 NYRB - v44 - Ja 9 '97 - p49+ [501+]
 Parameters - v26 - Aut '96 - p161+ [501+]
Hoffmann, R Joseph - *The Secret Gospels*
 R&R Bk N - v11 - D '96 - p5 [51-250]
Hoffmann, Roald - *The Same and Not the Same*
 Am Sci - v84 - My '96 - p288+ [501+]
Hoffmann-Riem, Wolfgang - *Regulating Media*
 R&R Bk N - v11 - D '96 - p51 [51-250]
Hoffmeister, Gerhart - *A Reassessment of Weimar Classicism*
 Choice - v34 - N '96 - p463 [51-250]
Hofhansel, Claus - *Commercial Competition and National Security*
 R&R Bk N - v11 - D '96 - p33 [51-250]
Hofheinz, Thomas C - *Joyce and the Invention of Irish History*
 ELT - v39 - 3 '96 - p389+ [501+]
Hofmann, Gert - *The Film Explainer*
 NYTBR - v101 - S 1 '96 - p11 [501+]
 TranslRevS - v2 - D '96 - p25+ [51-250]
Hofmann, James R - *Andre-Marie Ampere: Enlightenment and Electrodynamics*
 Nature - v385 - F 20 '97 - p693+ [501+]
Hofmann, Karl H - *Semigroup Theory and Its Applications*
 SciTech - v21 - Mr '97 - p13 [51-250]
Hofmann, Paul - *The Seasons of Rome*
 BL - v93 - D 15 '96 - p706 [51-250]
 KR - v64 - O 15 '96 - p1511 [51-250]
 LJ - v121 - N 15 '96 - p78 [51-250]
 NYTBR - v102 - Mr 16 '97 - p20 [51-250]
 PW - v243 - N 4 '96 - p58 [51-250]

Hofmeister-Hunger, Andrea - *Pressepolitik Und Staatsreform*
 CEH - v29 - 1 '96 - p124+ [501+]
Hofmeyr, Dianne - *Blue Train to the Moon*
 y VOYA - v19 - O '96 - p199+ [501+]
 Boikie, You Better Believe It
 y VOYA - v19 - O '96 - p199+ [501+]
 A Red Kite in a Pale Sky
 y VOYA - v19 - O '96 - p199+ [501+]
Hofrenning, Daniel J B - *In Washington But Not of It*
 J Pol - v58 - N '96 - p1208+ [501+]
Hofsommer, Don L - *Grand Trunk Corporation*
 R&R Bk N - v11 - D '96 - p71 [51-250]
Hofstadter, Dan - *The Love Affair as a Work of Art*
 New R - v215 - S 16 '96 - p34+ [501+]
 NYTBR - v101 - D 8 '96 - p88 [1-50]
 PW - v244 - My 5 '97 - p206 [51-250]
Hofstadter, Douglas R - *Le Ton Beau De Marot*
 KR - v65 - F 15 '97 - p274 [251-500]
 LJ - v122 - Ap 1 '97 - p92 [51-250]
 PW - v244 - Mr 3 '97 - p55 [51-250]
Hogan, Ben - *Five Lessons*
 LJ - v121 - O 1 '96 - p53 [1-50]
Hogan, Ed - *From Three Worlds*
 KR - v64 - S 15 '96 - p1353 [51-250]
 LATBR - F 9 '97 - p11 [51-250]
 PW - v243 - S 16 '96 - p76+ [51-250]
Hogan, J Michael - *The Nuclear Freeze Campaign*
 QJS - v82 - N '96 - p431+ [501+]
Hogan, James P - *Bug Park*
 y BL - v93 - F 1 '97 - p929 [51-250]
 KR - v65 - F 15 '97 - p261 [51-250]
 LJ - v122 - Mr 15 '97 - p93 [1-50]
 PW - v244 - Mr 24 '97 - p63+ [51-250]
Hogan, Judy - *The Shade*
 BL - v93 - F 15 '97 - p1003 [51-250]
Hogan, Linda - *The Book of Medicines*
 PS - v70 - Fall '96 - p193+ [501+]
 Dwellings: A Spiritual History of the Living World
 WAL - v31 - Win '97 - p398+ [251-500]
 Solar Storms
 Bloom Rev - v16 - Jl '96 - p9+ [501+]
 NYTBR - v102 - F 23 '97 - p24 [51-250]
 Trib Bks - F 23 '97 - p8 [1-50]
 WLT - v70 - Aut '96 - p1007 [501+]
Hogan, Michael J - *America in the World*
 Choice - v34 - O '96 - p344 [51-250]
 For Aff - v75 - S '96 - p146 [51-250]
 Hiroshima in History and Memory
 PHR - v66 - F '97 - p130+ [501+]
 Sea H - Sum '96 - p31 [51-250]
Hogan, Ray - *Soldier in Buckskin*
 BWatch - v17 - N '96 - p10 [51-250]
Hogan, Robyn - *A Breath in May*
 y Magpies - v11 - My '96 - p48 [51-250]
Hoge, Dean R - *Money Matters*
 PW - v243 - O 14 '96 - p77 [51-250]
Hogervorst, Ron - *Design of Low-Voltage, Low-Power Operational Amplifier Cells*
 SciTech - v21 - Mr '97 - p90 [51-250]
Hogg, Frank N - *Looking Ahead*
 Sch Lib - v44 - Ag '96 - p129 [251-500]
Hogg, Ian V - *Battles: A Concise Dictionary*
 r Choice - v34 - S '96 - p100 [51-250]
 yr Kliatt - v30 - S '96 - p33 [51-250]
Hogg, James - *La Certosa Di Pavia. Vols. 1-2*
 CH - v66 - Mr '97 - p201+ [51-250]
 Die Kartauser Und Ihre Welt
 CH - v66 - Mr '97 - p189 [51-250]
Hogg, James, 1770-1835 - *A Queer Book*
 LR - v45 - 7 '96 - p62+ [501+]
 The Shepherd's Calendar
 LR - v45 - 7 '96 - p62+ [501+]
 The Three Perils of Woman
 LR - v45 - 7 '96 - p62+ [501+]
Hogg, Judy - *Splitting Up*
 Aust Bk R - Ag '96 - p67 [1-50]
Hoggart, K - *Rural Europe*
 GJ - v163 - Mr '97 - p97+ [251-500]
Hoggart, Richard - *The Way We Live Now*
 CR - v269 - N '96 - p277 [1-50]
 New Sci - v152 - N 9 '96 - p44 [1-50]
Hoggart, Simon - *Life Briefs*
 Spec - v277 - D 7 '96 - p54 [51-250]
Hoggarth, Peter - *Roar! (Illus. by Woody)*
 c Sch Lib - v44 - N '96 - p163 [51-250]
Hogue, John - *The Prophecies*
 Books - v11 - Ap '97 - p23 [51-250]
Hogue, W Lawrence - *Race, Modernity, Postmodernity*
 Choice - v34 - Mr '97 - p1162 [51-250]
 R&R Bk N - v12 - F '97 - p87 [51-250]

Hoh, Diane - *Virus*
 y Kliatt - v30 - S '96 - p11 [51-250]
Hohenberg, John - *The Pulitzer Diaries*
 KR - v65 - F 1 '97 - p197+ [251-500]
 PW - v244 - F 24 '97 - p76 [51-250]
Hohl, Anne Mullen - *Exoticism in Salammbo*
 FR - v70 - O '96 - p118 [251-500]
Hohmann, Hasso - *Die Architektur Der Sepulturas-Region Von Copan In Honduras. Vols. 1-2*
 LA Ant - v7 - D '96 - p375+ [501+]
Hoig, Stan - *Night of the Cruel Moon*
 y HB Guide - v7 - Fall '96 - p390+ [51-250]
Hoinacki, Lee - *El Camino: Walking to Santiago De Compostela*
 LJ - v121 - O 1 '96 - p112 [51-250]
 Utne R - Ja '97 - p96 [1-50]
Hoisington, William A, Jr. - *Lyautey and the French Conquest of Morocco*
 MEJ - v51 - Win '97 - p135+ [501+]
Hojman, David E - *Neo-Liberalism with a Human Face?*
 Econ J - v106 - N '96 - p1849+ [251-500]
Hokanson, Drake - *Reflecting a Prairie Town*
 CAY - v16 - Fall '95 - p6 [51-250]
Holahan, Carole K - *The Gifted Group in Later Maturity*
 AJS - v102 - Jl '96 - p316+ [501+]
Holappa, Pentti - *Jokapaivaista Aikaa*
 WLT - v70 - Sum '96 - p732+ [501+]
Holborn, Mark - *Issey Miyake*
 Bloom Rev - v16 - S '96 - p31 [51-250]
Holbrook, Kenneth A - *Unimolecular Reactions. 2nd Ed.*
 SciTech - v20 - S '96 - p17 [51-250]
Holbrook, Teri - *The Grass Widow*
 LJ - v121 - N 15 '96 - p88 [51-250]
 PW - v243 - N 4 '96 - p70+ [51-250]
Holbrook, Thomas M - *Do Campaigns Matter?*
 Choice - v34 - Ja '97 - p875 [51-250]
 R&R Bk N - v11 - N '96 - p49 [51-250]
Holcombe, Charles - *In the Shadow of the Han*
 AHR - v101 - D '96 - p1596 [251-500]
Holcombe, Randall G - *The Economic Foundations of Government*
 Econ J - v106 - S '96 - p1474 [51-250]
 Public Policy and the Quality of Life
 BusLR - v21 - 3 '96 - p245+ [51-250]
Holdaway, Simon - *The Racialisation of British Policing*
 Choice - v34 - O '96 - p367 [51-250]
Holden, Anthony - *Tchaikovsky*
 Books - v9 - S '95 - p23 [1-50]
 Tchaikovsky: A Biography
 Advocate - Ja 21 '97 - p94 [1-50]
 HG&LRev - v3 - Fall '96 - p31+ [501+]
Holden, Craig - *The River Sorrow (Ferrone). Audio Version*
 y Kliatt - v30 - N '96 - p44 [51-250]
Holden, Geoffrey - *Thermoplastic Elastomers. 2nd Ed.*
 SciTech - v21 - Mr '97 - p99 [51-250]
Holden, George W - *Parents and the Dynamics of Child Rearing*
 Choice - v34 - Ap '97 - p1420 [51-250]
Holden, Jonathan - *Guns and Boyhood in America*
 PW - v244 - Ap 28 '97 - p59 [251-500]
 The Sublime: Poems
 NYTBR - v101 - O 20 '96 - p22 [51-250]
Holden, Matthew - *Continuity and Disruption*
 Choice - v34 - Ja '97 - p867 [51-250]
 Pol Stud J - v24 - Aut '96 - p519 [51-250]
 R&R Bk N - v11 - D '96 - p47 [51-250]
Holden, Merle - *Economic Integration and Trade Liberalization in Southern Africa*
 JEL - v35 - Mr '97 - p213+ [51-250]
Holden, Mike - *The Common Fisheries Policy*
 SciTech - v20 - D '96 - p58 [51-250]
Holden, Paul - *Unshackling the Private Sector*
 J Gov Info - v23 - S '96 - p689 [51-250]
Holden, Philip - *Orienting Masculinity, Orienting Nation*
 Choice - v34 - Ja '97 - p795 [51-250]
 R&R Bk N - v11 - D '96 - p64 [51-250]
Holden, Robert H - *Mexico and the Survey of Public Lands*
 AHR - v101 - D '96 - p1657+ [501+]
 HAHR - v76 - N '96 - p797+ [251-500]
Holder, Charlotte - *Grayson County, Texas Miscellaneous Wills and Probates 1833-1923*
 r EGH - v50 - N '96 - p188 [51-250]
Holder, Heidi - *Carmine the Crow (Illus. by Heidi Holder)*
 c Par Ch - v20 - N '96 - p8 [51-250]
 c PW - v243 - S 23 '96 - p78 [51-250]

Holder, R W - *A Dictionary of Euphemisms*
  r AB - v99 - Ja 13 '97 - p80+ [501+]
  r ARBA - v28 - '97 - p381 [251-500]
  r Choice - v34 - N '96 - p430 [51-250]
  r Utne R - Jl '96 - p106 [51-250]
Holderlin, Friedrich - *Poems and Fragments*
    TranslRevS - v1 - My '95 - p5 [51-250]
  Samtliche Werke Und Briefe. Vols. 1-3
    Ger Q - v69 - Spr '96 - p199+ [501+]
Holdgate, Martin W - *From Care to Action*
    Choice - v34 - Ja '97 - p813+ [51-250]
    Env - v39 - Ja '97 - p25 [251-500]
Holdrege, Barbara A - *Veda and Torah*
    Rel St Rev - v23 - Ap '97 - p149 [51-250]
Holdrege, Craig - *Genetics and the Manipulation of Life*
    Hast Cen R - v26 - S '96 - p40+ [1-50]
Holdren, John - *Books to Build On*
  r BL - v93 - F 1 '97 - p962 [251-500]
Holdstock, Robert - *Ancient Echoes*
  y Kliatt - v30 - N '96 - p14 [51-250]
    MFSF - v91 - O '96 - p52+ [501+]
  y VOYA - v19 - D '96 - p280 [51-250]
  Unknown Regions
    BW - v27 - F 23 '97 - p11 [251-500]
  y Kliatt - v31 - Mr '97 - p18 [51-250]
Holeman, Linda - *Promise Song*
  y Quill & Q - v63 - F '97 - p55+ [251-500]
Holian, Timothy J - *The German-Americans and World War II*
    Choice - v34 - Mr '97 - p1227 [51-250]
Holing, Dwight - *Nature Travel*
  r E Mag - v7 - N '96 - p50 [51-250]
  The Smithsonian Guides to Natural America: The Far West
  r BL - v93 - S 15 '96 - p212 [1-50]
Holinshed, Raphael - *Chronicles of England, Scotland, and Ireland. Vol. 3*
    Six Ct J - v27 - Fall '96 - p705+ [501+]
Holladay, Carl R - *Fragments from Hellenistic Jewish Authors. Vol. 3*
  r Rel St Rev - v23 - Ja '97 - p89 [51-250]
Holladay, Hilary - *Ann Petry*
    AL - v69 - Mr '97 - p250 [51-250]
Holladay, William L - *Long Ago God Spoke*
    Intpr - v51 - Ja '97 - p88+ [251-500]
    Theol St - v58 - Mr '97 - p149+ [501+]
    TT - v53 - Ja '97 - p564 [51-250]
Hollahan, Eugene - *Gerard Manley Hopkins and Critical Discourse*
    VS - v39 - Spr '96 - p453+ [501+]
  Saul Bellow and the Struggle at the Center
    Choice - v34 - Mr '97 - p1166 [51-250]
    R&R Bk N - v12 - F '97 - p89 [51-250]
Hollan, Douglas W - *The Thread of Life*
    Choice - v34 - Ap '97 - p1380 [51-250]
Holland, Ben - *Wilhelmi: The Clay's the Thing*
    Am Craft - v56 - Ag '96 - p66 [1-50]
Holland, Cecelia, 1943- - *The Bear Flag*
    PW - v243 - Jl 22 '96 - p234 [1-50]
  Jerusalem
  y Kliatt - v31 - My '97 - p6 [51-250]
Holland, Clive - *Farthest North*
    GJ - v162 - N '96 - p340+ [51-250]
Holland, Francis Schmid - *Feminist Jurisprudence*
  r ARBA - v28 - '97 - p337+ [251-500]
Holland, Gini - *Airplanes*
  c HB Guide - v7 - Fall '96 - p349+ [51-250]
  Nuclear Energy
  c Ch BWatch - v6 - My '96 - p6 [51-250]
  c HB Guide - v7 - Fall '96 - p349+ [51-250]
  c SB - v32 - Ag '96 - p176 [51-250]
  c SLJ - v42 - S '96 - p216 [51-250]
  Photography
  c HB Guide - v7 - Fall '96 - p349+ [51-250]
  Telephones
  c HB Guide - v7 - Fall '96 - p349+ [51-250]
Holland, Heinrich D - *Living Dangerously*
    Am Sci - v85 - Ja '97 - p71+ [501+]
  y New Sci - v151 - S 28 '96 - p50+ [501+]
    SB - v32 - N '96 - p229 [51-250]
Holland, Isabelle - *The Promised Land*
  c HB Guide - v7 - Fall '96 - p293 [51-250]
  c RT - v50 - My '97 - p682 [51-250]
  c SLJ - v42 - Ag '96 - p144 [51-250]
Holland, James F - *Cancer Medicine. 4th Ed., Vols. 1-2*
    SciTech - v21 - Mr '97 - p50 [51-250]
Holland, John - *Hidden Order*
    Reason - v28 - D '96 - p59+ [501+]
Holland, Matthew F - *America and Egypt*
    Choice - v34 - Ja '97 - p870+ [51-250]
    R&R Bk N - v11 - D '96 - p13 [51-250]

Holland, Norman Norwood - *The Critical I*
    MLR - v92 - Ja '97 - p146+ [501+]
  Death in a Delphi Seminar
    TCR - v98 - Spr '97 - p537+ [501+]
Hollander, John - *American Poetry. Electronic Media Version*
    Choice - v34 - My '97 - p1493 [51-250]
  Committed to Memory
  y BL - v93 - N 15 '96 - p567 [51-250]
    LJ - v122 - Ja '97 - p103 [51-250]
    PW - v243 - N 25 '96 - p73 [51-250]
Hollanders, J M G - *Male Infertility from A to Z*
  r SciTech - v21 - Mr '97 - p58 [51-250]
Hollands, Marjorie - *More Choice Menus*
    Quill & Q - v62 - Ag '96 - p30 [51-250]
Hollandsworth, James G, Jr. - *The Louisiana Native Guards*
    JSH - v63 - F '97 - p183+ [501+]
Hollar, Barry Penn - *On Being the Church in the United States*
    Theol St - v57 - S '96 - p561+ [501+]
Hollas, J Michael - *Modern Spectroscopy. 3rd Ed.*
    SciTech - v20 - D '96 - p24 [51-250]
Holldobler, Bert - *The Ants*
    BW - v26 - D 8 '96 - p4 [51-250]
Hollenbeck, Cliff - *Great Travel Photography*
    LJ - v121 - N 1 '96 - p64 [51-250]
Hollenbeck, Kathleen M - *Lobster's Secret (Illus. by Jon Weiman). Book and Audio Version*
  c Inst - v106 - N '96 - p7 [51-250]
Holler, Clyde - *Black Elk's Religion*
    CHR - v83 - Ja '97 - p140+ [251-500]
Holleran, Andrew - *The Beauty of Men*
    LJ - v122 - Ja '97 - p49 [51-250]
    NYTBR - v101 - D 8 '96 - p76 [1-50]
    TLS - F 21 '97 - p21 [501+]
Hollerman, Leon - *The Effect of Japanese Investment on the World Economy*
    Choice - v34 - Mr '97 - p1207+ [51-250]
Hollett, David - *Passage to the New World*
    NEQ - v69 - D '96 - p665+ [501+]
Holley, Beth - *A Kaleidoscope of Choices*
    CLW - v66 - Je '96 - p41+ [501+]
Holley, Robert P - *Subject Indexing. Vol. 15*
    LRTS - v40 - Ap '96 - p185+ [51-250]
Holley, Tara Elgin - *My Mother's Keeper*
    KR - v65 - F 15 '97 - p274 [251-500]
    LJ - v122 - Ap 15 '97 - p101+ [51-250]
    PW - v244 - Ja 27 '97 - p84 [51-250]
    Trib Bks - Ap 27 '97 - p3+ [501+]
Holleyman, Sonia - *Little Vampire's Diary*
  c Books - v9 - S '95 - p26 [1-50]
Hollick, Helen - *Pendragon's Banner*
    PW - v243 - N 11 '96 - p58 [51-250]
Holliday, Laurel - *Children in the Holocaust and World War II*
  y Kliatt - v30 - N '96 - p22 [51-250]
    SS - v87 - S '96 - p232+ [501+]
  Children of the Troubles
    KR - v65 - Ja 15 '97 - p120 [251-500]
Hollifield, James F - *Immigrants, Markets, and States*
    WP - v49 - O '96 - p130+ [51-250]
Hollinger, David A - *Postethnic America*
    Bks & Cult - v2 - N '96 - p34 [501+]
    RAH - v24 - S '96 - p519+ [501+]
  Science, Jews, and Secular Culture
    BW - v26 - S 29 '96 - p6 [501+]
    RAH - v24 - D '96 - p706+ [501+]
    Rel St Rev - v23 - Ap '97 - p197+ [51-250]
    Sci - v275 - F 7 '97 - p787+ [501+]
Hollinger, Robert - *The Dark Side of Liberalism*
    Choice - v34 - F '97 - p1033 [51-250]
    R&R Bk N - v11 - D '96 - p46 [51-250]
  Pragmatism: From Progressivism to Postmodernism
    CPR - v16 - D '96 - p410+ [501+]
Hollinghurst, Alan - *The Swimming Pool Library*
    J Homosex - v31 - 3 '96 - p95+ [501+]
Hollingshead, Greg - *The Roaring Girl*
    BL - v93 - Mr 1 '97 - p1110 [51-250]
    KR - v65 - F 1 '97 - p161 [251-500]
    LJ - v122 - Mr 15 '97 - p92 [51-250]
    NYTBR - v102 - Ap 20 '97 - p20 [51-250]
    Obs - F 9 '97 - p18* [51-250]
    PW - v244 - Ja 27 '97 - p76 [51-250]
Hollingsworth, Mark - *The Ultimate Spin Doctor*
    NS - v126 - Mr 27 '97 - p49+ [501+]
    Obs - F 23 '97 - p18* [501+]
Hollingsworth, Mary - *Patronage in Renaissance Italy from 1400 to the Early Sixteenth Century*
    CH - v66 - Mr '97 - p108+ [501+]
    Six Ct J - v27 - Win '96 - p1154+ [501+]

  Patronage in Sixteenth-Century Italy
    Apo - v144 - S '96 - p79 [501+]
Hollingsworth, Sandra - *Teacher Research and Urban Literacy Education*
    TCR - v97 - Sum '96 - p660+ [501+]
Hollingsworth, William G - *Ending the Explosion*
    Choice - v34 - Ja '97 - p883+ [51-250]
Hollis, James - *The Middle Passage*
    Rel St Rev - v22 - O '96 - p344 [51-250]
  Swamplands of the Soul
    Choice - v34 - Ja '97 - p879 [51-250]
Hollis, Martin - *The Philosophy of Social Science*
    Ethics - v107 - O '96 - p157+ [501+]
  Reason in Action
    APSR - v91 - Mr '97 - p171+ [501+]
    IPQ - v37 - Je '97 - p235+ [501+]
Hollis, Susan Tower - *Feminist Theory and the Study of Folklore*
    Signs - v22 - Win '97 - p491+ [501+]
Holloway, Immy - *Qualitative Research for Nurses*
    SciTech - v20 - S '96 - p43 [51-250]
Holloway, Steven W - *The Pitcher Is Broken*
    Rel St Rev - v23 - Ap '97 - p162+ [51-250]
Holly, Carol - *Intensely Family*
    AL - v68 - D '96 - p859+ [501+]
    Biography - v19 - Fall '96 - p430 [1-50]
    ELT - v40 - 2 '97 - p206+ [501+]
Holly, Ellen - *One Life*
  y BL - v93 - N 15 '96 - p563 [51-250]
    BWatch - v18 - Mr '97 - p4 [51-250]
    TCI - v30 - O '96 - p57 [1-50]
    Wom R Bks - v14 - D '96 - p11+ [501+]
Hollywood, Amy - *The Soul as Virgin Wife*
    RR - v56 - Ja '97 - p106 [1-50]
Holm, Bill - *The Heart Can Be Filled Anywhere on Earth*
    Bloom Rev - v16 - S '96 - p27+ [51-250]
Holm, Don - *The Complete Sourdough Cookbook for Camp, Trail, and Kitchen*
    CAY - v17 - Fall '96 - p11 [51-250]
Holm, Pamela - *Objects of Desire*
    Obs - F 9 '97 - p18* [51-250]
Holm, Stef Ann - *Forget Me Not*
    PW - v244 - Mr 24 '97 - p80 [51-250]
  Portraits
    PW - v243 - Jl 22 '96 - p235 [51-250]
Holm, Tom - *Strong Hearts, Wounded Souls*
    Choice - v34 - O '96 - p348 [51-250]
    WHQ - v27 - Win '96 - p550+ [51-250]
Holman, Brian - *Instant JavaScript*
    CBR - v15 - Spr '97 - p4 [51-250]
    SciTech - v20 - D '96 - p9 [1-50]
Holman, David Marion - *A Certain Slant of Light*
    AL - v69 - Mr '97 - p231+ [251-500]
Holman, J Alan - *Pleistocene Amphibians and Reptiles in North America*
    Choice - v34 - D '96 - p640 [51-250]
Holman, J K - *Wagner's Ring*
    ON - v61 - Ap 5 '97 - p53 [51-250]
Holman, J P - *Heat Transfer. 8th Ed.*
    SciTech - v21 - Mr '97 - p23 [51-250]
Holman, Otto - *Integrating Southern Europe*
    JEL - v34 - D '96 - p2037 [51-250]
    R&R Bk N - v11 - N '96 - p27 [51-250]
Holman, Peter - *Henry Purcell*
    Notes - v53 - Mr '97 - p791+ [501+]
    Sev Cent N - v54 - Spr '96 - p24+ [501+]
Holman, Sheri - *A Stolen Tongue*
    BW - v27 - F 16 '97 - p11 [51-250]
    Ent W - Ja 24 '97 - p53 [51-250]
    KR - v64 - N 1 '96 - p1553+ [251-500]
    LJ - v121 - D '96 - p150 [51-250]
    PW - v243 - N 4 '96 - p62 [51-250]
    SFR - v22 - Ja '97 - p32+ [51-250]
Holmas, Stig - *Apache Pass (Illus. by John Hurford)*
  y SLJ - v43 - Ja '97 - p112 [51-250]
Holmer, Joan Ozark - *The Merchant of Venice*
    Shakes Q - v47 - Fall '96 - p349+ [501+]
Holmes, Barbara Ware - *Letters to Julia*
  y KR - v65 - Mr 1 '97 - p381 [51-250]
Holmes, Brian - *Russian Education*
    ES - v27 - Sum '96 - p150+ [501+]
Holmes, David S - *Minerals Bioprocessing II*
    SciTech - v20 - N '96 - p77 [51-250]
Holmes, Diana - *French Women's Writing 1848-1994*
    Choice - v34 - N '96 - p464 [51-250]
Holmes, Finlay - *Our Irish Presbyterian Heritage*
    Bks & Cult - v2 - Ja '96 - p11+ [501+]
Holmes, Frank, 1947- - *The Hank Wiescamp Story*
  y Cur R - v36 - F '97 - p12 [51-250]

Holmes, George, 1927- - *Renaissance*
LJ - v122 - Ap 15 '97 - p76 [51-250]
PW - v244 - Mr 24 '97 - p72 [51-250]
TLS - D 6 '96 - p26 [501+]
Holmes, George R - *Helping Teenagers into Adulthood*
Readings - v11 - S '96 - p22 [51-250]
Holmes, Janice - *Coming into the Light*
Bks & Cult - v2 - Ja '96 - p11+ [501+]
Holmes, John W - *The United States and Europe after the Cold War*
LJ - v122 - Mr 15 '97 - p76 [51-250]
Holmes, Joseph - *Canyons of the Colorado*
CSM - v89 - D 5 '96 - pB2+ [51-250]
Holmes, Judy - *Eye on Nature*
Pet PM - v25 - Jl '96 - p36 [51-250]
Holmes, Kenneth L - *Covered Wagon Women. Vol. 2*
Roundup M - v4 - O '96 - p27 [251-500]
Covered Wagon Women. Vol. 3
Roundup M - v4 - F '97 - p24+ [501+]
Holmes, Larry - *Sotsial'naia Istoriia Rossii 1917-1941*
Slav R - v55 - Fall '96 - p694+ [501+]
Holmes, M H - *Introduction to Perturbation Methods*
SIAM Rev - v38 - S '96 - p538 [251-500]
Holmes, Madelyn - *Lives of Women Public Schoolteachers*
NWSA Jnl - v8 - Sum '96 - p152+ [501+]
Holmes, Martin - *The Eurosceptical Reader*
Econ - v342 - F 15 '97 - p5*+ [501+]
NS - v125 - N 29 '96 - p42+ [501+]
Holmes, Oliver Wendell - *The Collected Works of Justice Holmes. Vols. 1-3*
New R - v215 - N 11 '96 - p47+ [501+]
Holmes and Frankfurter
KR - v64 - O 1 '96 - p1448+ [251-500]
LJ - v121 - D '96 - p120+ [51-250]
NYTBR - v101 - D 15 '96 - p16+ [501+]
Holmes, Philip - *Turbulence, Coherent Structures, Dynamical Systems and Symmetry*
New Sci - v153 - F 1 '97 - p42+ [501+]
Holmes, Ray - *Working Cowboy*
CAY - v16 - Fall '95 - p6 [51-250]
Holmes, Roger - *Taylor's Guide to Fruits and Berries*
r ARBA - v28 - '97 - p573 [51-250]
Holmes, Stephen F - *Passions and Constraints*
SSQ - v77 - D '96 - p943+ [501+]
Holmgren, Jennifer - *Marriage, Kinship, and Power in Northern China*
R&R Bk N - v11 - N '96 - p22 [51-250]
Holmlund, Chris - *Between the Sheets, in the Streets*
LJ - v122 - Ap 1 '97 - p93 [51-250]
Holm-Nielsen, Lauritz - *Institutional and Entrepreneurial Leadership in the Brazilian Science and Technology Sector*
JEL - v34 - D '96 - p2110 [51-250]
Holmstrom, John - *The Moving Picture Boy*
r Si & So - v6 - N '96 - p38 [51-250]
Holmwood, Ruth - *Buddhism*
TES - D 6 '96 - pR7 [501+]
Christianity. Pt. 2
TES - D 6 '96 - pR7 [501+]
Holroyd, Michael - *Augustus John: The New Biography*
CR - v270 - Ja '97 - p55+ [51-250]
NY - v73 - Ap 14 '97 - p78+ [501+]
NYRB - v44 - Mr 6 '97 - p24+ [501+]
Obs - Ag 18 '96 - p16* [501+]
TLS - Ag 30 '96 - p18+ [501+]
George Bernard Shaw. Vols. 1-3
Obs - D 1 '96 - p16* [51-250]
Lytton Strachey: The New Biography
Biography - v19 - Fall '96 - p430 [1-50]
Holschneider, M - *Wavelets: An Analysis Tool*
Phys Today - v49 - Ag '96 - p65+ [501+]
SIAM Rev - v39 - Mr '97 - p172+ [501+]
Holsinger, Erik - *How Multimedia Works*
Quill & Q - v62 - Ag '96 - p23 [51-250]
Holsti, K J - *The State, War, and the State of War*
Choice - v34 - My '97 - p1574 [51-250]
Holsti, Ole R - *Public Opinion and American Foreign Policy*
Choice - v34 - My '97 - p1572 [51-250]
Holt, A J - *Watch Me*
PW - v243 - N 18 '96 - p70 [1-50]
Holt, Daniel M - *A Surgeon's Civil War*
J Am Cult - v18 - Win '95 - p115+ [251-500]
Holt, David - *Mostly Ghostly Stories (Holt). Audio Version*
c Ch BWatch - v6 - Jl '96 - p7 [1-50]
y Kliatt - v30 - S '96 - p50 [51-250]
Holt, Hazel - *Mrs. Malory: Death of a Dean*
BL - v93 - D 15 '96 - p712 [51-250]
KR - v64 - O 15 '96 - p1496 [51-250]
LJ - v121 - O 1 '96 - p131 [1-50]
PW - v243 - S 16 '96 - p72+ [51-250]

Holt, Marilyn Irvin - *Linoleum, Better Babies, and the Modern Farm Woman 1890-1930*
AAPSS-A - v550 - Mr '97 - p190+ [501+]
Historian - v58 - Sum '96 - p844+ [501+]
JSH - v62 - N '96 - p829+ [251-500]
Holt, Richard - *The Medieval Town*
J Urban H - v22 - My '96 - p516+ [501+]
Holt, Stephen - *A Veritable Dynamo*
Aust Bk R - Jl '96 - p26+ [501+]
Holt, Tom - *Djinn Rummy*
Books - v9 - S '95 - p22 [1-50]
Odds and Gods
Books - v9 - S '95 - p27 [1-50]
Holton, Gerald James - *Einstein, History, and Other Passions*
Bloom Rev - v16 - N '96 - p28 [51-250]
Cng - v29 - Ja '97 - p63 [51-250]
NYTBR - v101 - S 22 '96 - p26 [501+]
Holton, Hugh - *Violent Crimes*
BL - v93 - F 1 '97 - p928 [51-250]
KR - v64 - D 15 '96 - p1756 [251-500]
PW - v243 - D 9 '96 - p63+ [51-250]
Holton, Sandra Stanley - *Suffrage Days*
TLS - Mr 21 '97 - p13 [251-500]
Holtze, Sally Holmes - *Seventh Book of Junior Authors and Illustrators*
cr ARBA - v28 - '97 - p428 [251-500]
Holtzman, Elizabeth - *Who Said It Would Be Easy?*
BL - v92 - Ag '96 - p1862+ [501+]
BW - v26 - Ag 18 '96 - p4 [251-500]
Holtzman, Jerome - *The Chicago Cubs Encyclopedia*
r LJ - v122 - F 1 '97 - p83 [51-250]
Holub, Miroslav - *Supposed to Fly*
TLS - Mr 28 '97 - p23 [501+]
TranslRevS - v2 - D '96 - p20 [51-250]
Holub, Robert C - *Friedrich Nietzsche*
Ger Q - v69 - Sum '96 - p334+ [501+]
Holum, John R - *Elements of General, Organic, and Biological Chemistry. 9th Ed.*
J Chem Ed - v73 - Je '96 - pA135 [251-500]
Holway, John B - *Red Tails, Black Wings*
LJ - v122 - F 15 '97 - p146 [51-250]
PW - v243 - D 9 '96 - p52 [51-250]
Holyoke, Nancy - *More Help! (Illus. by Scott Nash)*
c PW - v243 - S 9 '96 - p85 [51-250]
Holzem, Andreas - *Kirchenreform Und Sektenstiftung*
CHR - v83 - Ja '97 - p116+ [251-500]
Holzer, Hans - *The Secret of Healing*
Rapport - v19 - 5 '96 - p43 [251-500]
Holzer, Harry J - *What Employers Want*
Choice - v34 - D '96 - p654 [51-250]
JEL - v35 - Mr '97 - p238 [51-250]
Soc Ser R - v71 - Mr '97 - p164 [51-250]
Holzherr, George - *The Rule of Benedict*
CH - v65 - S '96 - p452+ [501+]
Holznagel, Franz-Josef - *Wege In Die Schriftlichkeit*
Specu - v72 - Ja '97 - p173+ [501+]
Holzner, Steven - *Advanced Visual Basic 4.0 Programming*
SciTech - v20 - S '96 - p6 [51-250]
Advanced Visual C++ 4
CBR - v14 - S '96 - p31 [1-50]
SciTech - v20 - N '96 - p8 [51-250]
Homan, Gerlof D - *American Mennonites and the Great War 1914-1918*
J Ch St - v38 - Sum '96 - p656+ [251-500]
Homans, Peter - *Jung in Context. 2nd Ed.*
Rel St Rev - v23 - Ja '97 - p44 [51-250]
Homberger, Eric - *Scenes from the Life of a City*
PW - v243 - S 23 '96 - p73 [1-50]
Hombs, Mary Ellen - *Welfare Reform*
r Choice - v34 - My '97 - p1475 [51-250]
Home, Stewart - *Slow Death*
Books - v10 - Je '96 - p24 [1-50]
KR - v64 - My 1 '96 - p640 [51-250]
NS & S - v9 - Ap 26 '96 - p31+ [251-500]
TLS - Ag 30 '96 - p22+ [501+]
Home Improvement 1-2-3
LJ - v122 - F 1 '97 - p52 [1-50]
Home Repair and Improvement. Vols. 1-24
LJ - v122 - F 1 '97 - p52 [1-50]
Homer - *Homer in English*
BW - v26 - D 8 '96 - p15 [51-250]
New R - v216 - F 24 '97 - p30+ [501+]
TranslRevS - v2 - D '96 - p27 [51-250]
The Iliad
TLS - N 29 '96 - p14 [51-250]
The Iliad (Jacobi). Audio Version
Obs - Mr 23 '97 - p16* [501+]
The Iliad (Pope)
BW - v26 - D 15 '96 - p12 [51-250]

The Odyssey
Reason - v28 - D '96 - p45 [51-250]
The Odyssey (Illus. by Victor G Ambrus)
c Bks Keeps - N '96 - p11 [51-250]
The Odyssey (Bodkin). Audio Version
y Kliatt - v31 - Ja '97 - p43+ [251-500]
The Odyssey (Fagles)
BL - v93 - N 1 '96 - p476 [1-50]
BW - v26 - D 8 '96 - p15 [51-250]
LATBR - D 8 '96 - p8 [51-250]
LJ - v121 - O 15 '96 - p58 [51-250]
New R - v216 - F 24 '97 - p30+ [501+]
NY - v72 - Ja 27 '97 - p74+ [501+]
NYRB - v43 - N 28 '96 - p52+ [501+]
NYTBR - v101 - D 22 '96 - p7 [501+]
Obs - D 22 '96 - p18* [501+]
Parabola - v22 - F '97 - p120 [1-50]
Spec - v278 - Mr 22 '97 - p37+ [501+]
Time - v148 - D 23 '96 - p86 [51-250]
The Odyssey (Jacobi). Audio Version
y Kliatt - v31 - Ja '97 - p43+ [251-500]
The Odyssey (McKellen). Audio Version
LJ - v122 - F 15 '97 - p115 [1-50]
LJ - v122 - F 15 '97 - p176 [51-250]
New R - v216 - F 24 '97 - p30+ [501+]
The Homeric Hymns (Shelmerdine)
Rel St Rev - v22 - O '96 - p345 [51-250]
Homerin, Th. Emil - *From Arab Poet to Muslim Saint*
Rel St Rev - v23 - Ap '97 - p199 [51-250]
Homes, A M - *The End of Alice*
Ent W - D 27 '96 - p143 [1-50]
Ent W - F 7 '97 - p65 [1-50]
LATBR - My 26 '96 - p6+ [501+]
Necro - Fall '96 - p11+ [501+]
NYTBR - v102 - F 9 '97 - p32 [51-250]
PW - v244 - Ja 13 '97 - p73 [1-50]
Homes, Ruth - *The Flying Trapeze (Illus. by Andrew McLean)*
c Magpies - v11 - Jl '96 - p30 [51-250]
Homeworking in the European Union
J Gov Info - v23 - S '96 - p669 [51-250]
Homeworks: A Book of Tennessee Writers
AL - v69 - Mr '97 - p258 [1-50]
Honan, Park - *Jane Austen: Her Life*
Trib Bks - Ja 5 '97 - p2 [51-250]
Honderich, Ted - *The Oxford Companion to Philosophy*
r ARBA - v28 - '97 - p531 [251-500]
r Ethics - v107 - O '96 - p198+ [51-250]
Hone, Joseph - *Firesong*
Spec - v278 - Ap 5 '97 - p33 [501+]
TLS - Mr 21 '97 - p22 [501+]
Hone, Lucy - *The Good Honeymoon Guide*
LJ - v122 - Ap 15 '97 - p104 [51-250]
Honea, Charla H - *A Reader's Companion to Crossing the Threshold of Hope*
PW - v243 - S 16 '96 - p66 [51-250]
Honey, Elizabeth - *Not a Nibble! (Illus. by Elizabeth Honey)*
c Aust Bk R - D '96 - p91+ [501+]
Honey, Maureen - *Breaking the Ties That Bind*
JPC - v29 - Spr '96 - p236+ [251-500]
Honeycombe, Robert - *Steels: Microstructure and Properties. 2nd Ed.*
Choice - v34 - S '96 - p159 [51-250]
Honeycutt, Natalie - *Twilight in Grace Falls*
c BL - v93 - Mr 15 '97 - p1239 [51-250]
y KR - v65 - F 15 '97 - p300 [51-250]
y PW - v244 - Ja 27 '97 - p107+ [51-250]
Honeygosky, Stephen R - *Milton's House of God*
Ren Q - v49 - Aut '96 - p658+ [501+]
Hong, Lily Toy - *The Empress and the Silkworm (Illus. by Lily Toy Hong)*
c CLW - v66 - Je '96 - p46 [51-250]
How the Ox Star Fell from Heaven (Illus. by Lily Toy Hong)
c CLW - v66 - Je '96 - p46 [51-250]
Hongo, Garret Kaoru - *Under Western Eyes*
Amerasia J - v22 - 3 '96 - p169+ [501+]
Hongo, Garrett Kaoru - *Volcano: A Memoir of Hawai'i*
y Kliatt - v30 - N '96 - p22+ [51-250]
Honig, Bonnie - *Feminist Interpretations of Hannah Arendt*
APSR - v90 - S '96 - p628+ [501+]
J Pol - v58 - Ag '96 - p894+ [501+]
Political Theory and the Displacement of Politics
Am Q - v48 - D '96 - p700+ [501+]
Honig, Donald - *The Ghost of Major Pryor*
KR - v65 - Ja 1 '97 - p11 [251-500]
LJ - v122 - F 1 '97 - p110 [51-250]
NYTBR - v102 - Mr 30 '97 - p16 [51-250]
PW - v244 - Ja 6 '97 - p67+ [51-250]

The Sword of General Englund
  Arm Det - v29 - Sum '96 - p370+ [51-250]
  VQR - v72 - Aut '96 - p132* [51-250]
Honig, Jan Willem - *Srebrenica: Record of a War Crime*
  y BL - v93 - F 1 '97 - p923+ [51-250]
     Cu H - v96 - Mr '97 - p141 [51-250]
     KR - v65 - Ja 1 '97 - p39+ [251-500]
     LJ - v122 - F 1 '97 - p96 [51-250]
     Obs - D 8 '96 - p16* [501+]
     PW - v244 - F 3 '97 - p87 [51-250]
Honneth, Axel - *The Fragmented World of the Social*
  Ethics - v107 - O '96 - p189 [51-250]
  The Struggle for Recognition
  APSR - v90 - D '96 - p892+ [501+]
  J Phil - v94 - Ja '97 - p46+ [501+]
Honore, Tony - *About Law*
  Choice - v34 - Mr '97 - p1230 [51-250]
Honour, Hugh - *A World History of Art. 4th Ed.*
  TES - Ag 30 '96 - p26 [1-50]
Honsberger, Ross - *From Erdos to Kiev*
  Choice - v34 - N '96 - p496 [51-250]
  Math T - v89 - N '96 - p695+ [51-250]
  y New Sci - v151 - S 28 '96 - p44+ [501+]
Hoobler, Dorothy - *The Cuban American Family Album*
  y AB - v98 - N 18 '96 - p1728 [51-250]
  y BL - v93 - Ja '97 - p836 [251-500]
  c HB Guide - v8 - Spr '97 - p90 [51-250]
  c KR - v64 - N 15 '96 - p1670 [51-250]
  The German American Family Album
  yr AB - v98 - N 18 '96 - p1728 [51-250]
  c Ch BWatch - v6 - My '96 - p1 [51-250]
  c HB Guide - v7 - Fall '96 - p312 [51-250]
  yr Par Ch - v21 - Mr '97 - p10 [1-50]
  y SLJ - v43 - Mr '97 - p202 [51-250]
  The Japanese American Family Album
  c HB Guide - v7 - Fall '96 - p312 [51-250]
  yr Par Ch - v21 - Mr '97 - p10 [1-50]
  The Jewish American Family Album
  yr Par Ch - v21 - Mr '97 - p10 [1-50]
Hood, Alison - *The Wolf Watcher (Illus. by Andy DaVolls)*
  c TES - F 21 '97 - p16* [51-250]
Hood, Ann - *The Properties of Water*
  Rapport - v19 - 5 '96 - p30 [251-500]
Hood, Christopher, 1947- - *Accident and Design*
  Nature - v385 - Ja 9 '97 - p129+ [501+]
  Explaining Economic Policy Reversals
  Econ J - v107 - Ja '97 - p275 [51-250]
Hood, Jean - *The Dragon of Brog (Illus. by Peter Kavanagh)*
  c Magpies - v11 - S '96 - p45 [1-50]
Hood, John Bell - *Advance and Retreat*
  LJ - v122 - Mr 15 '97 - p94 [1-50]
Hood, John M - *The Heroic Enterprise*
  Choice - v34 - N '96 - p503 [51-250]
  LJ - v122 - Mr 15 '97 - p36 [1-50]
  Nat R - v48 - S 16 '96 - p65+ [501+]
Hood, John Y B - *Aquinas and the Jews*
  CHR - v82 - Jl '96 - p550+ [501+]
  JR - v77 - Ja '97 - p133+ [501+]
  Theol St - v57 - S '96 - p567 [251-500]
Hood, Mary - *Familiar Heat*
  Am - v175 - N 16 '96 - p21 [501+]
  Ent W - N 8 '96 - p63 [1-50]
  NYTBR - v101 - N 17 '96 - p40 [1-50]
  PW - v243 - S 30 '96 - p79 [1-50]
  Sew R - v104 - Jl '96 - p468+ [501+]
  Trib Bks - Ja 12 '97 - p2 [1-50]
Hood, Ralph W - *The Psychology of Religion. 2nd Ed.*
  R&R Bk N - v11 - D '96 - p4 [51-250]
Hood, Robert E - *Begrimed and Black*
  JR - v76 - O '96 - p652+ [501+]
  Theol St - v57 - Mr '96 - p191+ [251-500]
Hood, Steven J - *The Kuomintang and the Democratization of Taiwan*
  Choice - v34 - Ap '97 - p1410 [51-250]
  R&R Bk N - v12 - F '97 - p61 [51-250]
Hood, William - *Fra Angelico at San Marco*
  Art Bull - v78 - S '96 - p559+ [501+]
Hooft, G 'T - *In Search of the Ultimate Building Blocks*
  Nature - v385 - Ja 16 '97 - p217+ [501+]
  New Sci - v153 - Ja 18 '97 - p40 [501+]
  Phys Today - v50 - Mr '97 - p80 [251-500]
Hooft, Stan Van - *Caring: An Essay in the Philosophy of Ethics*
  Ethics - v107 - O '96 - p195 [51-250]
Hoogenboom, Ari - *Rutherford B. Hayes: Warrior and President*
  SSQ - v77 - S '96 - p716+ [501+]
Hook, Sidney - *John Dewey: An Intellectual Portrait*
  Bks & Cult - v2 - Ja '96 - p31 [501+]
  Ethics - v107 - O '96 - p194 [51-250]

Hook, Steven W - *National Interest and Foreign Aid*
  J Pol - v59 - F '97 - p314+ [501+]
Hooker, Mark T - *The Military Uses of Literature*
  Choice - v34 - N '96 - p466 [51-250]
Hooker, Morna D - *The Gospel according to Saint Mark*
  BTB - v27 - Sum '97 - p72 [501+]
  Not Ashamed of the Gospel
  Rel St Rev - v23 - Ja '97 - p70 [51-250]
Hooker, Richard - *Of the Laws of Ecclesiastical Polity. Pts. 1-2*
  Ren Q - v49 - Aut '96 - p649+ [501+]
  RES - v47 - Ag '96 - p408+ [501+]
Hooks, Bell - *Art on My Mind*
  Art J - v55 - Fall '96 - p91+ [501+]
  JAAC - v54 - Fall '96 - p389+ [501+]
  Black Looks
  Signs - v22 - Aut '96 - p243+ [501+]
  Bone Black
  y BL - v93 - Ja '97 - p762 [1-50]
  y BL - v93 - S 15 '96 - p189 [51-250]
     Bloom Rev - v17 - Ja '97 - p19+ [501+]
     BW - v27 - F 16 '97 - p8 [51-250]
     KR - v64 - Ag 15 '96 - p1210 [251-500]
     LJ - v121 - S 15 '96 - p75 [51-250]
     NYTBR - v101 - D 15 '96 - p32+ [51-250]
  y SLJ - v43 - Mr '97 - p217 [51-250]
  Outlaw Culture
  QJS - v82 - N '96 - p402+ [501+]
  Reel to Real
  Afterimage - v24 - Ja '97 - p23 [51-250]
  LATBR - N 10 '96 - p14 [51-250]
  PW - v243 - S 30 '96 - p78 [51-250]
  Teaching to Transgress
  HER - v66 - Win '96 - p848+ [501+]
  QJS - v83 - F '97 - p129+ [501+]
Hooks, William H - *Freedom's Fruit (Illus. by James Ransome)*
  c CCB-B - v50 - S '96 - p16 [51-250]
  c HB Guide - v7 - Fall '96 - p260 [51-250]
  The Three Little Pigs and the Fox (Illus. by S D Schindler)
  c PW - v244 - F 10 '97 - p85 [1-50]
Hooper, Caroline - *Nursery Rhyme Songbook*
  c Books - v10 - Je '96 - p25 [51-250]
Hooper, Kay - *After Caroline*
  y BL - v93 - N 15 '96 - p570 [51-250]
     KR - v64 - O 15 '96 - p1485 [251-500]
     PW - v243 - O 14 '96 - p63 [51-250]
  y SLJ - v43 - F '97 - p134 [51-250]
Hooper, Mary - *Mad about the Boy*
  y Sch Lib - v44 - Ag '96 - p118 [51-250]
Hooper, Meredith - *The Pebble in My Pocket (Illus. by Chris Coady)*
  c Bks Keeps - Jl '96 - p23 [51-250]
  c CBRS - v24 - Ag '96 - p164 [51-250]
  c HB Guide - v7 - Fall '96 - p332 [51-250]
  c JB - v60 - Ag '96 - p149 [51-250]
  c RT - v50 - My '97 - p685 [51-250]
  c SB - v33 - Ja '97 - p16+ [251-500]
  c Sch Lib - v44 - Ag '96 - p112 [51-250]
Hooper, Nicholas - *The Cambridge Illustrated Atlas of Warfare: The Middle Ages*
  r ARBA - v28 - '97 - p251+ [51-250]
  r J Mil H - v61 - Ja '97 - p148+ [251-500]
  yr Sch Lib - v44 - Ag '96 - p127 [51-250]
  yr SLJ - v42 - Ag '96 - p182 [51-250]
  r SLMQ - v24 - Sum '96 - p221 [51-250]
Hooper, Paul D - *Physical Modalities*
  SciTech - v20 - N '96 - p57 [51-250]
Hooper, Trevor - *Adventures in Asian Tapas and Wild Sushi*
  Quill & Q - v63 - Mr '97 - p21 [51-250]
Hooper, Walter - *C.S. Lewis: A Companion and Guide*
  r Ch Today - v41 - F 3 '97 - p66+ [501+]
     TLS - F 21 '97 - p25 [501+]
Hoopes, Lyn Littlefield - *The Unbeatable Bread (Illus. by Brad Sneed)*
  c HB Guide - v7 - Fall '96 - p260 [51-250]
  c Par Ch - v20 - O '96 - p11 [1-50]
Hoopes, Townsend - *FDR and the Creation of the U.N.*
  BL - v93 - Mr 1 '97 - p1094 [51-250]
  For Aff - v76 - My '97 - p132 [51-250]
  KR - v65 - Ja 15 '97 - p120 [251-500]
  LJ - v122 - Mr 15 '97 - p74 [51-250]
  NYTBR - v102 - Ap 20 '97 - p17 [501+]
  PW - v244 - F 3 '97 - p88 [51-250]
Hoose, Bernard - *Received Wisdom?*
  Theol St - v57 - S '96 - p573+ [251-500]
Hooson, David - *Geography and National Identity*
  GJ - v162 - N '96 - p343 [51-250]

Hooten, Anthony J - *Sustainable Financing Mechanisms for Coral Reef Conservation*
  J Gov Info - v23 - S '96 - p689 [51-250]
Hoover, H M - *The Dawn Palace*
  y Kliatt - v30 - S '96 - p4 [1-50]
Hoover, Kenneth - *The Elements of Social Scientific Thinking. 6th Ed.*
  LQ - v66 - O '96 - p479+ [501+]
Hoover, Kevin D - *Macroeconometrics: Developments, Tensions, and Prospects*
  JEL - v34 - S '96 - p1418 [51-250]
  Monetarism and the Methodology of Economics
  JEL - v34 - S '96 - p1351+ [501+]
Hoover, R A - *Forever Flying*
  A & S Sm - v11 - O '96 - p90+ [51-250]
  BL - v92 - Ag '96 - p1867 [51-250]
Hoover's Directory of Human Resources Executives 1996
  r ARBA - v28 - '97 - p119 [251-500]
Hoover's Guide to the Top Chicago Companies. 1st Ed.
  r Choice - v34 - S '96 - p100 [51-250]
Hoover's Guide to the Top New York Companies. 1st Ed.
  r Choice - v34 - N '96 - p430 [51-250]
Hoover's Handbook of American Business 1996. Vols. 1-2
  r Choice - v34 - O '96 - p253 [51-250]
Hoover's Masterlist of Major Latin American Companies 1996-1997
  r BL - v93 - S 1 '96 - p166+ [251-500]
  r Choice - v34 - N '96 - p430+ [51-250]
Hoover's Masterlist of Major U.S. Companies 1996-1997
  r ARBA - v28 - '97 - p83 [51-250]
Hooyman, Nancy R - *Feminist Perspective on Family Care*
  Soc Ser R - v70 - D '96 - p669 [51-250]
Hopcke, Robert H - *There Are No Accidents*
  PW - v244 - My 5 '97 - p190 [51-250]
Hopcraft, Xan - *How It Was with Dooms (Illus. by Xan Hopcraft)*
  c BL - v93 - My 15 '97 - p1577 [51-250]
Hope
  p LJ - v122 - My 1 '97 - p43 [51-250]
  p Utne R - S '96 - p98+ [251-500]
Hope, Bob - *Bob Hope's Dear Prez, I Wanna Tell Ya!*
  SEP - v268 - N '96 - p42+ [501+]
Hope, Christopher - *Darkest England*
  BL - v93 - S 15 '96 - p220+ [51-250]
  BW - v26 - S 15 '96 - p5 [501+]
  NYTBR - v101 - S 29 '96 - p20 [51-250]
  VV - v41 - O 1 '96 - p39+ [251-500]
Hope, Jacqueline - *Big, Bold and Beautiful*
  Quill & Q - v62 - S '96 - p68 [501+]
Hope, Mary - *Towards Evening*
  LJ - v122 - My 1 '97 - p145 [1-50]
  PW - v244 - Mr 24 '97 - p74+ [51-250]
Hope, Murry - *The Sirius Connection*
  BWatch - v17 - N '96 - p4 [51-250]
Hope, Quentin M - *L'Art De Lire. 2nd Ed.*
  FR - v70 - O '96 - p155+ [251-500]
Hope, Tony - *Transforming the Bottom Line*
  Choice - v34 - Ja '97 - p841 [51-250]
Hopkin, Bart - *Musical Instrument Design*
  LJ - v122 - F 1 '97 - p80 [51-250]
Hopkins, Adam - *Essential French Riviera*
  r BL - v93 - S 15 '96 - p206 [1-50]
Hopkins, Andrea - *Harald the Ruthless (Illus. by Leo Duranona)*
  c HB Guide - v8 - Spr '97 - p68 [51-250]
  c KR - v64 - O 1 '96 - p1467 [51-250]
  c SLJ - v42 - N '96 - p106 [51-250]
Hopkins, Ann Branigar - *So Ordered*
  Wom R Bks - v14 - Ja '97 - p16+ [501+]
Hopkins, Antony - *The Seven Concertos of Beethoven*
  LJ - v122 - F 15 '97 - p137 [51-250]
Hopkins, Bruce - *The Smithsonian Guides to Natural America: Central Appalachia*
  r BL - v93 - S 15 '96 - p212 [1-50]
Hopkins, Budd - *Witnessed: The True Story of the Brooklyn Bridge UFO Abductions*
  BL - v93 - S 15 '96 - p181 [51-250]
  Books - v11 - Ap '97 - p8+ [51-250]
  PW - v244 - Ap 14 '97 - p72 [1-50]
Hopkins, Eric - *Childhood Transformed*
  EHR - v111 - N '96 - p1317+ [501+]
  JMH - v68 - D '96 - p987+ [501+]
  VS - v39 - Aut '95 - p112+ [501+]
  Working-Class Self-Help in Nineteenth-Century England
  Albion - v28 - '96 - p711+ [501+]
Hopkins, Jack W - *Policymaking for Conservation in Latin America*
  APSR - v90 - S '96 - p673+ [501+]

Hopkins, Jasper - *A Miscellany on Nicholas of Cusa*
    Ren Q - v49 - Win '96 - p901+ [501+]
Hopkins, Jerry - *The Jimi Hendrix Experience*
    Obs - F 16 '97 - p17* [501+]
Hopkins, John C - *Strategic Views from the Second Tier*
    Arm F&S - v23 - Fall '96 - p131+ [501+]
    Parameters - v26 - Aut '96 - p146+ [501+]
Hopkins, Julie M - *Towards a Feminist Christology*
    JR - v77 - Ja '97 - p157+ [501+]
Hopkins, Lee Bennett - *Been to Yesterdays (Illus. by Charlene Rendeiro)*
  y Emerg Lib - v24 - S '96 - p23 [1-50]
  c SLJ - v43 - Mr '97 - p113 [1-50]
  Blast Off! (Illus. by Melissa Sweet)
  c Inst - v106 - O '96 - p68 [1-50]
  Opening Days (Illus. by Scott Medlock)
  c HB Guide - v7 - Fall '96 - p365 [51-250]
  c RT - v50 - Ap '97 - p592 [51-250]
  School Supplies (Illus. by Renee Flower)
  c BL - v92 - Ag '96 - p1903 [51-250]
  c HB Guide - v8 - Spr '97 - p150 [51-250]
  c SLJ - v42 - N '96 - p98 [51-250]
  Song and Dance (Illus. by Cheryl Munro Taylor)
  c PW - v244 - Mr 31 '97 - p77 [51-250]
Hopkins, MaryCarol - *Braving a New World*
    Choice - v34 - Ap '97 - p1380+ [51-250]
Hopkins, Pauline E - *Contending Forces*
    AL - v69 - Mr '97 - p139+ [501+]
Hopkins, Terence K - *The Age of Transition*
    Choice - v34 - Mr '97 - p1208 [51-250]
Hopkinson, Deborah - *Birdie's Lighthouse (Illus. by Kimberly Bulcken Root)*
  c KR - v65 - My 1 '97 - p722 [51-250]
  c PW - v244 - Ap 14 '97 - p74+ [51-250]
Hopkinson, Neil - *Greek Poetry of the Imperial Period*
    CW - v89 - Jl '96 - p505+ [251-500]
Hopkirk, Frannie - *Brett: A Portrait of Brett Whiteley by His Sister*
    Aust Bk R - S '96 - p44+ [501+]
    Aust Bk R - S '96 - p46 [501+]
Hopkirk, Peter - *Quest for Kim*
    FEER - v159 - O 31 '96 - p46+ [501+]
    Spec - v277 - S 28 '96 - p47+ [501+]
    Spec - v277 - N 30 '96 - p58 [1-50]
    TLS - N 8 '96 - p29 [501+]
Hopkirk, Vivian - *Meditations of a Flawed Bridegroom*
    Aust Bk R - F '97 - p59 [51-250]
Hopmann, P Terrence - *The Negotiation Process and the Resolution of International Conflicts*
    APSR - v91 - Mr '97 - p234+ [501+]
    Choice - v34 - N '96 - p532 [51-250]
Hoppe, Flo - *Contemporary Wicker Basketry*
    LJ - v122 - F 15 '97 - p134 [51-250]
Hoppe, Goran - *Peasantry to Capitalism*
    EG - v72 - O '96 - p450+ [501+]
    JIH - v27 - Win '97 - p534+ [501+]
Hoppe, Leslie J - *The Synagogues and Churches of Ancient Palestine*
    CHR - v82 - Jl '96 - p493+ [251-500]
Hoppenstand, Gary - *The Gothic World of Anne Rice*
    R&R Bk N - v12 - F '97 - p90 [51-250]
Hopper, Helen M - *A New Woman of Japan*
    Pac A - v69 - Fall '96 - p419+ [501+]
Hopps, June Gary - *The Power to Care*
    JMSW - v4 - 4 '96 - p137+ [501+]
Hopps, Walter - *Edward Kienholz 1954-1962*
    BM - v138 - Jl '96 - p484+ [501+]
Hopwood, Anthony G - *Accounting as Social and Institutional Practice*
    AR - v71 - O '96 - p593+ [501+]
Hopwood, Clive - *Dinosaur Fun File (Illus. by Barry Green)*
  c PW - v244 - My 5 '97 - p211 [51-250]
Horace - *Horace in English*
    Agenda - v34 - Spr '96 - p182+ [501+]
    BW - v26 - D 8 '96 - p15 [501+]
  Horace Odes I: Carpe Diem
    Rel St Rev - v23 - Ja '97 - p65 [51-250]
Horak, Jan-Christopher - *Lovers of Cinema*
    AB - v98 - D 9 '96 - p1996 [51-250]
Horban', Mykola - *Slovo I Dilo Hosudareve*
    BL - v93 - N 15 '96 - p577 [1-50]
Horch, John W - *Practical Guide to Software Quality Management*
    SciTech - v20 - N '96 - p10 [51-250]
Hord, Fred Lee - *I Am Because We Are*
    Ethics - v107 - Ja '97 - p397+ [51-250]
    IPQ - v36 - S '96 - p379 [51-250]
Hordern, Michael - *Gone Fishing*
    Books - v9 - S '95 - p24 [1-50]

Horel, Catherine - *Juifs De Hongrie 1825-1849*
    AHR - v102 - F '97 - p137+ [251-500]
Horenstein, Henry - *Baseball in the Barrios*
  c Trib Bks - Mr 30 '97 - p5 [51-250]
Horgan, A D - *Johnson on Language*
    RES - v47 - N '96 - p593+ [501+]
Horgan, John - *The End of Science*
    Am Sci - v84 - S '96 - p495+ [501+]
    BAS - v52 - N '96 - p60+ [501+]
    BioSci - v47 - Mr '97 - p183+ [501+]
    Bks & Cult - v2 - N '96 - p5 [501+]
    Choice - v34 - N '96 - p479 [51-250]
    Nature - v382 - Ag 29 '96 - p769+ [501+]
    NYTBR - v101 - D 8 '96 - p87 [1-50]
    PW - v244 - My 12 '97 - p74 [1-50]
    Reason - v28 - O '96 - p61+ [501+]
    SB - v32 - O '96 - p199 [251-500]
    SciTech - v20 - S '96 - p2 [51-250]
    Time - v148 - S 9 '96 - p56 [501+]
    VQR - v73 - Win '97 - p26*+ [251-500]
Horgan, Terence - *Connectionism and the Philosophy of Psychology*
    Choice - v34 - My '97 - p1512+ [51-250]
    CPR - v16 - D '96 - p413+ [501+]
    SciTech - v20 - D '96 - p1 [1-50]
Horiuchi, Annick - *Les Mathematiques Japonaises A L'Epoque D'Edo*
    Isis - v87 - S '96 - p548+ [251-500]
Hormander, Lars - *Partial Differential Equations and Mathematical Physics*
    SIAM Rev - v39 - Mr '97 - p176 [51-250]
Horn, Barbara Lee - *Maxwell Anderson: A Research and Production Sourcebook*
    R&R Bk N - v11 - N '96 - p72 [51-250]
Horn, Gabriel - *Contemplations of a Primal Mind*
    BL - v93 - Ja '97 - p813 [51-250]
Horn, Jason Gary - *Mark Twain and William James*
    Choice - v34 - Ap '97 - p1336 [51-250]
Horn, John - *Mystical Healing*
    Am - v176 - F 15 '97 - p33 [51-250]
Horn, Murray J - *The Political Economy of Public Administration*
    J Pol - v59 - F '97 - p262+ [501+]
Horn, Nancy E - *Cultivating Customers*
    EG - v72 - Jl '96 - p353+ [501+]
Horn, Shifra - *Shalom, Japan*
    NYTBR - v101 - D 8 '96 - p31 [251-500]
    PW - v243 - O 7 '96 - p57 [51-250]
Hornblower, Malabar - *The Plimoth Plantation New England Cookery Book*
    BWatch - v17 - D '96 - p9 [51-250]
Hornblower, Simon - *The Oxford Classical Dictionary. 3rd Ed.*
  yr BL - v93 - My 1 '97 - p1533 [251-500]
  r BW - v26 - D 8 '96 - p15 [51-250]
  r Choice - v34 - My '97 - p1478 [501+]
  r Obs - F 2 '97 - p16* [501+]
  r TLS - F 14 '97 - p6 [501+]
Hornby, A S - *Oxford Advanced Learner's Dictionary of Current English. 5th Ed.*
  r MLJ - v80 - Fall '96 - p412+ [251-500]
Hornby, Nick - *High Fidelity*
    NS & S - v9 - Ap 26 '96 - p32 [1-50]
    Spec - v277 - N 16 '96 - p42 [1-50]
    Spec - v277 - N 23 '96 - p46 [1-50]
    TES - Jl 19 '96 - pR6 [51-250]
  High Fidelity (Carrington). Audio Version
    Obs - Ja 12 '97 - p18* [51-250]
Horne, Aaron - *Brass Music of Black Composers*
  r ARBA - v28 - '97 - p476 [51-250]
  r Choice - v34 - F '97 - p944 [51-250]
  r R&R Bk N - v11 - N '96 - p58 [51-250]
Horne, Alan - *The Dictionary of 20th Century British Book Illustrators*
  r Lib - v18 - Je '96 - p166+ [501+]
Horne, Alistair - *How Far from Austerlitz?*
    Spec - v277 - D 7 '96 - p48+ [501+]
    TLS - Ja 24 '97 - p29 [501+]
    WSJ-Cent - v99 - My 19 '97 - pA16 [501+]
Horne, Ann Mitchell - *Descendants of Jeremiah Mitchell of North Carolina (circa 1770-circa 1835) and Allied Families*
  r EGH - v50 - N '96 - p194 [51-250]
Horne, Gerald - *Black Liberation/Red Scare*
    S&S - v61 - Sum '97 - p284+ [501+]
  Fire This Time
    AAPSS-A - v549 - Ja '97 - p202+ [501+]
    PHR - v66 - F '97 - p99+ [501+]
Horne, Peter - *Outlooks: Lesbian and Gay Sexualities and Visual Cultures*
    Obs - N 3 '96 - p16* [51-250]

Horner, David - *Inside the War Cabinet*
    NWCR - v49 - Aut '96 - p155+ [501+]
Horner, John - *Dinosaur Lives*
    KR - v65 - My 1 '97 - p695+ [251-500]
    PW - v244 - My 12 '97 - p69 [251-500]
Horniman, Joanne - *Bad Behaviour*
  y Aust Bk R - Je '96 - p62 [501+]
  c Magpies - v11 - Jl '96 - p34 [51-250]
Horning, Kathleen T - *From Cover to Cover*
    BL - v93 - Mr 1 '97 - p1177 [51-250]
    CCB-B - v50 - My '97 - p341 [501+]
    PW - v244 - Mr 10 '97 - p69 [51-250]
    SLJ - v43 - Mr '97 - p115 [501+]
Hornstein, Harvey A - *Brutal Bosses and Their Prey*
    Econ - v339 - My 18 '96 - p11* [51-250]
    Per Psy - v49 - Aut '96 - p730+ [501+]
Horovitz, David Phillip - *Shalom, Friend*
    Choice - v34 - S '96 - p204 [51-250]
    MEP - v5 - 1 '97 - p207+ [501+]
Horowitz, Anthony - *Death Walks Tonight*
  y Kliatt - v30 - N '96 - p17 [51-250]
  The Falcon's Malteser
  c Magpies - v11 - My '96 - p53 [1-50]
  The Switch
  c JB - v60 - Ag '96 - p157 [51-250]
  c Magpies - v11 - S '96 - p33 [51-250]
  y Sch Lib - v44 - Ag '96 - p118 [51-250]
Horowitz, Asher - *The Barbarism of Reason*
    APSR - v90 - S '96 - p629+ [501+]
    BIC - v25 - D '96 - p39+ [501+]
Horowitz, Brian - *The Myth of A.S. Pushkin in Russia's Silver Age*
    R&R Bk N - v11 - D '96 - p60 [51-250]
Horowitz, David, 1939- - *Radical Son*
    BL - v93 - Ja '97 - p813 [501+]
    BW - v27 - F 9 '97 - p3 [501+]
    KR - v64 - N 15 '96 - p1652 [251-500]
    LATBR - F 9 '97 - p5 [501+]
    LJ - v121 - D '96 - p104+ [51-250]
  y Nat - v264 - F 17 '97 - p30+ [501+]
    NL - v79 - D 16 '96 - p5+ [501+]
    NYTBR - v102 - F 16 '97 - p34 [501+]
    PW - v243 - D 30 '96 - p49 [51-250]
    Reason - v28 - Mr '97 - p62+ [501+]
    WSJ-Cent - v99 - F 3 '97 - pA12 [501+]
Horowitz, David A - *Beyond Left and Right*
    NL - v80 - Ap 7 '97 - p16+ [501+]
Horowitz, Irving Louis - *Taking Lives. 4th Ed., Expanded and Rev.*
    Choice - v34 - F '97 - p1029 [51-250]
    JEL - v35 - Mr '97 - p305 [51-250]
Horowitz, Joy - *Tessie and Pearlie*
    KR - v64 - My 1 '96 - p666 [251-500]
    Trib Bks - My 4 '97 - p8 [1-50]
Horowitz, Leonard G - *Emerging Viruses*
    Choice - v34 - O '96 - p303 [51-250]
Horowitz, Maryanne Cline - *Race, Gender, and Rank*
    Six Ct J - v27 - Win '96 - p1220+ [501+]
Horowitz, Renee B - *RX for Murder*
    PW - v243 - D 9 '96 - p65 [51-250]
Horowitz, Ruth - *Teen Mothers*
    AAPSS-A - v549 - Ja '97 - p203+ [501+]
    Adoles - v31 - Win '96 - p993 [51-250]
    SF - v75 - D '96 - p759+ [501+]
Horrigan, Bonnie J - *Red Moon Passage*
    KR - v64 - My 1 '96 - p666 [251-500]
Horrocks, Anita - *Breath of a Ghost*
  c BIC - v25 - N '96 - p32 [251-500]
Horrocks, Roger - *Masculinity in Crisis*
    Socio R - v44 - N '96 - p746+ [501+]
Horrors: An Earthdawn Sourcebook
  cr Ch BWatch - v6 - O '96 - p2 [51-250]
Horrox, Rosemary - *Fifteenth-Century Attitudes*
    EHR - v112 - F '97 - p178+ [251-500]
    MLR - v92 - Ap '97 - p432+ [501+]
    Specu - v71 - Jl '96 - p718+ [501+]
Horse, Harry - *A Friend for Little Bear (Illus. by Harry Horse)*
  c CBRS - v25 - S '96 - p4 [51-250]
  c Ch BWatch - v6 - S '96 - p1 [1-50]
  c HB Guide - v8 - Spr '97 - p32 [51-250]
  c SLJ - v42 - S '96 - p180 [51-250]
  The Last Polar Bears (Illus. by Harry Horse)
  c Bks Keeps - Ja '97 - p21+ [51-250]
Horsfall, Paul - *The Touchstone*
    Econ - v341 - N 16 '96 - p18*+ [501+]
Horsley, Gloria Call - *The In-Law Survival Manual*
    LJ - v121 - D '96 - p124+ [51-250]

Horsley, Kate - *A Killing in New Town*
    Bloom Rev - v16 - S '96 - p16 [501+]
    LJ - v122 - Ap 1 '97 - p156 [51-250]
    PW - v243 - S 9 '96 - p79 [51-250]
Horsley, Richard A - *Archaeology, History and Society in Galilee*
    Am - v176 - Mr 8 '97 - p25 [51-250]
    Galilee: History, Politics, People
    Rel St Rev - v23 - Ja '97 - p87 [51-250]
    Theol St - v58 - Mr '97 - p155+ [501+]
Horsman, Reginald - *Frontier Doctor*
    Choice - v34 - N '96 - p492 [51-250]
Horst - *Horst: Sixty Years of Photography*
    BW - v26 - D 22 '96 - p12 [51-250]
Horst, Arend Jan Van Der - *Art of the Formal Garden*
    BL - v93 - F 15 '97 - p992 [51-250]
Horst, Gert J Ter - *Clinical Pharmacology of Cerebral Ischemia*
    SciTech - v21 - Mr '97 - p52 [51-250]
Horst, K Van Der - *Illuminated and Decorated Medieval Manuscripts in the University Library, Utrecht*
    Lib - v18 - Je '96 - p158+ [501+]
Horst, Reiner - *Global Optimization. 3rd Ed.*
    JEL - v35 - Mr '97 - p196 [51-250]
Horstman, Dorothy - *Sing Your Heart Out, Country Boy. Newly Rev. and Expanded Ed.*
    r AB - v98 - D 9 '96 - p2003 [51-250]
    LJ - v121 - N 1 '96 - p41 [1-50]
    South CR - v29 - Fall '96 - p284+ [501+]
Horstmann, Ignatius J - *Ensuring Competition*
    JEL - v34 - D '96 - p2055 [51-250]
Horton, Casey - *Apes*
    c HB Guide - v7 - Fall '96 - p345 [51-250]
    Bears
    c HB Guide - v7 - Fall '96 - p345 [51-250]
    Dolphins
    c HB Guide - v7 - Fall '96 - p345 [51-250]
    Eagles
    c HB Guide - v7 - Fall '96 - p343+ [51-250]
    Parrots
    c HB Guide - v7 - Fall '96 - p343+ [51-250]
    c SB - v32 - O '96 - p211+ [251-500]
    c SLJ - v42 - S '96 - p217 [51-250]
    Wolves
    c HB Guide - v7 - Fall '96 - p345 [51-250]
Horton, George Moses - *The Black Bard of North Carolina*
    LJ - v122 - Ap 1 '97 - p92 [51-250]
Horton, H Robert - *Principles of Biochemistry. 2nd Ed.*
    J Chem Ed - v74 - F '97 - p190 [501+]
Horton, James Oliver - *In Hope of Liberty*
    AB - v99 - F 17 '97 - p525+ [501+]
Horton, John - *The Politics of Diversity*
    CS - v26 - Ja '97 - p204+ [501+]
Horton, Madelyn - *Mother Jones*
    c HB Guide - v7 - Fall '96 - p370 [1-50]
Horton, Merrill - *Annotations to William Faulkner's The Town*
    r AL - v68 - S '96 - p668 [51-250]
Horton, Michael S - *In the Face of God*
    LJ - v121 - O 1 '96 - p86 [51-250]
Horton, Susan - *Women and Industrialization in Asia*
    JEL - v34 - D '96 - p2067 [51-250]
    R&R Bk N - v11 - N '96 - p27 [51-250]
Horton, Tom - *An Island out of Time*
    Bloom Rev - v16 - N '96 - p26 [51-250]
    NYTBR - v101 - S 15 '96 - p31 [51-250]
    y SLJ - v42 - D '96 - p153 [51-250]
Horvat, Branko - *The Political Economy of Socialism*
    IndRev - v1 - Spr '97 - p591+ [501+]
    The Theory of Value, Capital and Interest
    Econ J - v106 - S '96 - p1447+ [501+]
    IndRev - v1 - Spr '97 - p591+ [501+]
    JEL - v34 - S '96 - p1350+ [501+]
Horvath, Brooke - *Consolation at Ground Zero*
    RCF - v16 - Fall '96 - p204+ [251-500]
Horvath, Polly - *When the Circus Came to Town*
    c BL - v93 - N 15 '96 - p588 [51-250]
    c CBRS - v25 - N '96 - p34 [51-250]
    c CCB-B - v50 - N '96 - p138 [51-250]
    c HB - v73 - Ja '97 - p57+ [51-250]
    c HB Guide - v8 - Spr '97 - p68 [51-250]
    c KR - v64 - S 15 '96 - p1401 [51-250]
    c PW - v243 - S 16 '96 - p84 [51-250]
    c SLJ - v42 - D '96 - p122 [51-250]
Horve, Leslie A - *Shaft Seals for Dynamic Applications*
    SciTech - v20 - N '96 - p70 [51-250]
Horwitz, Henry - *Chancery Equity Records and Proceedings 1600-1800*
    Albion - v28 - Fall '96 - p488 [251-500]

Horwitz, Leonard - *Borderline Personality Disorder*
    AJPsych - v154 - F '97 - p281+ [501+]
    Readings - v11 - S '96 - p26 [51-250]
Horwitz, Margot F - *A Female Focus*
    y BL - v93 - Mr 15 '97 - p1233+ [51-250]
    y CCB-B - v50 - F '97 - p209 [51-250]
    y HB Guide - v8 - Spr '97 - p138 [51-250]
    c SLJ - v43 - F '97 - p117 [51-250]
Horwood, William - *Toad Triumphant (Illus. by Patrick Benson)*
    c CSM - v88 - N 21 '96 - pB4 [51-250]
    y KR - v64 - O 1 '96 - p1467+ [51-250]
    Wanderers of the Wolfways
    Books - v10 - Je '96 - p23 [51-250]
    The Willows in Winter
    c ChLAQ - v21 - Fall '96 - p126+ [501+]
Hosek, George - *Iowa Merchant Trade Token Town Rarity List. 4th Ed.*
    r Coin W - v37 - Je 10 '96 - p25 [51-250]
    Nebraska Merchant Trade Tokens, Town/Place Rarity Listing, and Other Exonumia. 6th Ed.
    r Coin W - v37 - Je 10 '96 - p25 [51-250]
Hosey, Henry P, II - *This Man Cries*
    Sm Pr R - v28 - S '96 - p9 [51-250]
Hoskin, Michael - *The Cambridge Illustrated History of Astronomy*
    r Astron - v25 - My '97 - p114 [51-250]
    yr BWatch - v18 - Mr '97 - p10 [51-250]
    LJ - v122 - My 1 '97 - p134 [51-250]
    y SB - v33 - My '97 - p106+ [251-500]
Hosking, David - *Common Birds of East Africa*
    r New Sci - v153 - Mr 8 '97 - p45 [1-50]
    Larger Animals of East Africa
    r New Sci - v153 - Mr 8 '97 - p45 [51-250]
Hosking, Geoffrey - *Russia: People and Empire 1552-1917*
    LJ - v122 - My 1 '97 - p120 [51-250]
    Obs - Mr 9 '97 - p17* [501+]
    PW - v244 - Ap 21 '97 - p54 [51-250]
    Spec - v278 - Mr 15 '97 - p35 [501+]
Hoskins, Irene - *Combining Work and Elder Care*
    ILR - v135 - 5 '96 - p598 [51-250]
    JEL - v34 - Mr '97 - p235 [51-250]
Hoskins, Jim - *Exploring the IBM PC Power Series*
    BWatch - v17 - S '96 - p4+ [51-250]
    IBM AS/400. 6th Ed.
    SciTech - v20 - D '96 - p12 [51-250]
Hoskyns, Barney - *The Lonely Planet Boy*
    KR - v65 - Mr 15 '97 - p404 [251-500]
Hoskyns, Catherine - *Integrating Gender*
    For Aff - v75 - S '96 - p148 [51-250]
    JEL - v34 - D '96 - p2067+ [51-250]
Hoskyns, Tam - *The Talking Cure*
    Obs - F 23 '97 - p17* [501+]
    TLS - Mr 28 '97 - p22 [251-500]
Hosley, William - *Colt: The Making of an American Legend*
    BL - v93 - Ja '97 - p797 [51-250]
    Choice - v34 - My '97 - p1519 [51-250]
    PW - v243 - N 18 '96 - p68+ [51-250]
Hospital, Carolina - *A Century of Cuban Writers in Florida*
    BW - v27 - Ja 19 '97 - p9 [501+]
Hospital, Janette Turner - *Oyster*
    Aust Bk R - O '96 - p40+ [501+]
    BIC - v25 - D '96 - p20+ [501+]
    Econ - v341 - N 16 '96 - p18*+ [501+]
    Lon R Bks - v19 - Mr 6 '97 - p26 [501+]
    Obs - S 8 '96 - p17* [501+]
    Obs - D 1 '96 - p17* [51-250]
    Quill & Q - v62 - S '96 - p63 [251-500]
    TES - O 4 '96 - p7* [51-250]
    TLS - S 13 '96 - p22 [501+]
Hospital Financing in Seven Countries
    J Gov Info - v23 - S '96 - p555+ [51-250]
Hossain, Akhtar - *Macroeconomic Issues and Policies*
    JEL - v35 - Mr '97 - p277 [51-250]
    R&R Bk N - v12 - F '97 - p36 [51-250]
Hossfeld, Mok - *Dona Juana*
    ABR - v18 - O '96 - p27 [501+]
Hostak, John Michael - *Characterization of Environmental Radiation and Radioactivity Near Albuquerque, New Mexico*
    J Gov Info - v23 - S '96 - p589 [51-250]
Hostelling USA 1996
    r ARBA - v28 - '97 - p178 [51-250]
Hostetler, Mark - *That Gunk on Your Car*
    New Sci - v152 - N 23 '96 - p44 [51-250]
Hostetter, Edwin C - *Old Testament Introduction*
    r ARBA - v28 - '97 - p540 [51-250]

Hostyn, Norbert - *Dictionary of Belgian and Dutch Flower Painters Born between 1750 and 1880*
    r BM - v138 - N '96 - p761 [251-500]
Hot Sand
    Aust Bk R - F '97 - p26+ [501+]
Hot Type
    Aust Bk R - Ag '96 - p54 [501+]
Hotaling, Andrew J - *Pediatric Otolaryngology for the General Otolaryngologist*
    SciTech - v20 - S '96 - p40 [51-250]
Hotchkiss, Valerie R - *Clothes Make the Man*
    Choice - v34 - D '96 - p670 [51-250]
Hotchner, A E - *Louisiana Purchase*
    KR - v64 - My 1 '96 - p623 [251-500]
Hotle, C Patrick - *Thorns and Thistles*
    HT - v46 - O '96 - p56 [1-50]
Hottong, Lisa - *Die Sprache Ist Ein Labyrinth Von Wegen*
    Ger Q - v69 - Spr '96 - p230+ [501+]
Houarner, Gerard Daniel - *Painfreak*
    Sm Pr R - v28 - D '96 - p1 [51-250]
Houbein, Lolo - *Lily Makes a Living*
    Aust Bk R - S '96 - p59+ [501+]
Houck, John W - *Is the Good Corporation Dead?*
    Choice - v34 - Ja '97 - p841 [51-250]
Houck, Lynne D - *Foundations of Animal Behavior*
    SciTech - v20 - N '96 - p30 [1-50]
Houfe, Simon - *The Dictionary of 19th Century British Book Illustrators and Caricaturists. Rev. Ed.*
    r BC - v46 - Spr '97 - p132+ [501+]
    r Choice - v34 - F '97 - p944 [51-250]
    r LJ - v122 - F 1 '97 - p72 [51-250]
    r TLS - F 7 '97 - p10 [501+]
    The Work of Charles Samuel Keene
    Nine-C Lit - v51 - S '96 - p272+ [51-250]
Houff, Richard D - *Exits*
    Sm Pr R - v28 - N '96 - p4 [251-500]
Hough, Harry E - *Purchasing for Manufacturing*
    R&R Bk N - v11 - N '96 - p29 [51-250]
Hough, Libby - *If Somebody Lived Next Door (Illus. by Laura McGee)*
    c PW - v244 - My 12 '97 - p75 [51-250]
Hough, Peter - *Supernatural Britain*
    r SF Chr - v18 - O '96 - p82 [1-50]
Hough, Richard - *Captain James Cook*
    Historian - v58 - Sum '96 - p905+ [501+]
    PW - v244 - F 17 '97 - p217 [1-50]
    Trib Bks - Ap 20 '97 - p8 [1-50]
    W&M Q - v54 - Ja '97 - p253+ [501+]
    Victoria and Albert
    KR - v64 - O 1 '96 - p1445 [251-500]
    LJ - v121 - O 15 '96 - p72 [51-250]
    PW - v243 - S 16 '96 - p60 [51-250]
    TLS - My 24 '96 - p9+ [501+]
Houghton, J T - *Climate Change 1995: The Science of Climate Change*
    JEL - v35 - Mr '97 - p299 [51-250]
Houghton, Philip - *People of the Great Ocean*
    New Sci - v152 - D 21 '96 - p75 [51-250]
Houk, Clifford C - *Chemistry: Concepts and Problems. 2nd Ed.*
    y SB - v32 - Ag '96 - p173+ [251-500]
Houk, James T - *Spirits, Blood and Drums*
    CAY - v17 - Win '96 - p5 [51-250]
Houk, Randy - *Hope (Illus. by Randy Houk). Book and Audio Version*
    c E Mag - v8 - Mr '97 - p48 [1-50]
    Wolves in Yellowstone (Illus. by Randy Houk). Book and Audio Version
    c E Mag - v8 - Mr '97 - p48 [1-50]
Houk, Walter - *The Botanical Gardens at the Huntington*
    Hort - v74 - O '96 - p71 [251-500]
    SciTech - v21 - Mr '97 - p37 [51-250]
Houlihan, Elaine Burke - *Tipperary: A Treasure Chest*
    ILS - v15 - Fall '96 - p31 [1-50]
Houlihan, Patrick F - *The Animal World of the Pharaohs*
    NH - v106 - F '97 - p13 [1-50]
House, Ellen Renshaw - *A Very Violent Rebel*
    BL - v93 - N 15 '96 - p568 [51-250]
    Choice - v34 - Ap '97 - p1405 [51-250]
A House Divided. Electronic Media Version
    y LJ - v121 - O 1 '96 - p134+ [501+]
Houselander, Caryll - *The Essential Rosary*
    RR - v55 - N '96 - p661 [1-50]
    Wood of the Cradle, Wood of the Cross
    RR - v55 - N '96 - p659 [1-50]
House-Midamba, Bessie - *African Market Women and Economic Power*
    JEH - v57 - Mr '97 - p231+ [501+]
Houser, Nathan - *Studies in the Logic of Charles Sanders Peirce*
    LJ - v122 - F 1 '97 - p84 [51-250]

Housewright, David - *Penance*
Arm Det - v29 - Fall '96 - p436 [251-500]
Arm Det - v30 - Win '97 - p18 [51-250]

Housman, A E - *Unkind to Unicorns*
TLS - N 29 '96 - p32 [251-500]

Houston, Gail Turley - *Consuming Fictions*
Nine-C Lit - v50 - Mr '96 - p554 [1-50]

Houston, Gloria - *Littlejim's Dreams (Illus. by Thomas B Allen)*
c KR - v65 - Ap 1 '97 - p557+ [51-250]
c PW - v244 - Mr 24 '97 - p84 [51-250]
My Great-Aunt Arizona (Illus. by Susan Condie Lamb)
c PW - v244 - Ap 21 '97 - p74 [1-50]

Houston, J - *Reported Miracles*
JR - v77 - Ja '97 - p155+ [501+]
Rel St Rev - v23 - Ap '97 - p151 [51-250]

Houston, James A - *Confessions of an Igloo Dweller*
SLJ - v42 - D '96 - p43 [51-250]

Houston, James D - *Continental Drift*
LJ - v122 - F 1 '97 - p112 [1-50]
In the Ring of Fire
KR - v65 - Mr 15 '97 - p439+ [251-500]
PW - v244 - Ap 14 '97 - p68 [51-250]

Houston, Pam - *Men before Ten A.M.*
BL - v93 - N 1 '96 - p471 [51-250]
Ent W - N 29 '96 - p84 [51-250]
LATBR - D 8 '96 - p26 [1-50]

Houston, Peter - *A Sketch of the Life and Character of Daniel Boone*
LJ - v122 - Mr 15 '97 - p70 [51-250]

Houston, R A - *Social Change in the Age of Enlightenment*
Albion - v28 - Sum '96 - p306+ [501+]
EHR - v112 - Ap '97 - p483+ [501+]
JIH - v27 - Win '97 - p511 [251-500]

Houston, Sam - *The Personal Correspondence of Sam Houston. Vol. 1*
Choice - v34 - N '96 - p525 [51-250]
Roundup M - v3 - Ag '96 - p26 [251-500]

Houthakker, Hendrik S - *The Economics of Financial Markets*
Choice - v34 - Mr '97 - p1208 [51-250]
JEL - v35 - Mr '97 - p222 [51-250]

Houtman, Cees - *Der Pentateuch: Die Geschichte Seiner Erforschung Neben Einer Auswertung*
JAAR - v64 - Win '96 - p875+ [501+]

Houtz, Phillip - *AIX for Breakfast*
SciTech - v20 - S '96 - p6 [51-250]

Houwen, L A J R - *Loyal Letters*
RES - v48 - F '97 - p77+ [501+]

Houze, Herbert G - *Colt Rifles and Muskets from 1847 to 1870*
Ant & CM - v101 - N '96 - p31 [1-50]

Hove, Chenjerai - *Ancestors*
Obs - Ja 12 '97 - p18* [1-50]
TLS - D 6 '96 - p23 [501+]

Hoving, Thomas - *False Impressions*
Apo - v144 - D '96 - p13+ [51-250]
Obs - Ja 5 '97 - p18* [501+]
Sew R - v104 - O '96 - pR92+ [501+]
VQR - v72 - Aut '96 - p140* [501+]

How to Do Just About Everything
BW - v26 - D 8 '96 - p3 [51-250]

How to Fly
c LATBR - v263 - S 29 '96 - p15 [51-250]

Howard, Arthur - *When I Was Five (Illus. by Arthur Howard)*
c HB - v72 - S '96 - p579 [51-250]
c HB Guide - v7 - Fall '96 - p260 [51-250]
c New Ad - v9 - Fall '96 - p327+ [501+]

Howard, Audrey - *Promises Lost*
Books - v11 - Ap '97 - p23 [51-250]
The Shadowed Hills
PW - v244 - Ap 28 '97 - p55 [1-50]

Howard, Blair - *Adventure Guide to the Great Smoky Mountains*
r BL - v93 - S 15 '96 - p210 [1-50]
r BWatch - v17 - S '96 - p5+ [51-250]
r BWatch - v17 - N '96 - p12 [51-250]

Howard, Coltia - *Romans in Britain*
c TES - Ap 4 '97 - p12* [501+]

Howard, Dale E - *India*
c HB Guide - v7 - Fall '96 - p359 [51-250]
c SLJ - v42 - N '96 - p112 [51-250]

Howard, David S - *The Choice of the Private Trader*
Mag Antiq - v151 - Ap '97 - p516 [251-500]

Howard, Deborah - *The Architectural History of Scotland*
BM - v138 - Jl '96 - p466+ [501+]

Howard, Dick - *Political Judgments*
Choice - v34 - N '96 - p534 [51-250]

Howard, Edmond - *Italia: The Art of Living Italian Style*
BL - v93 - D 15 '96 - p706 [51-250]

Howard, Elizabeth Fitzgerald - *America as Story*
r RQ - v36 - Win '96 - p221+ [51-250]
What's in Aunt Mary's Room? (Illus. by Cedric Lucas)
c HB Guide - v7 - Fall '96 - p260 [51-250]

Howard, Elizabeth Jane - *Casting Off (Balcon). Audio Version*
y Kliatt - v31 - Mr '97 - p40 [51-250]
Odd Girl Out
Trib Bks - Ja 12 '97 - p2 [1-50]

Howard, Ellen - *A Different Kind of Courage*
y BL - v93 - S 15 '96 - p230 [51-250]
c HB - v72 - N '96 - p736 [251-500]
c HB Guide - v8 - Spr '97 - p68 [51-250]
y LATBR - O 13 '96 - p15 [51-250]
c SLJ - v42 - N '96 - p106+ [51-250]
The Log Cabin Quilt (Illus. by Ronald Himler)
c BL - v93 - D 15 '96 - p731 [51-250]
c CBRS - v25 - S '96 - p4 [51-250]
c CCB-B - v50 - O '96 - p64 [51-250]
c HB Guide - v8 - Spr '97 - p32 [51-250]
c Inst - v106 - Ja '97 - p54 [1-50]
c KR - v64 - S 15 '96 - p1402 [51-250]
c Par Ch - v20 - O '96 - p28 [51-250]
c SLJ - v42 - O '96 - p122 [51-250]

Howard, Evan Drake - *Centered in God*
CC - v114 - Ja 15 '97 - p59+ [501+]

Howard, Jane R - *Cuando Tengo Sueno (Illus. by Lynne Cherry)*
c HB Guide - v8 - Spr '97 - p108 [51-250]
c SLJ - v42 - N '96 - p132 [51-250]
When I'm Sleepy (Illus. by Lynne Cherry)
c HB Guide - v8 - Spr '97 - p12 [51-250]

Howard, Jean - *Hollywood Memoirs*
Obs - Ap 13 '97 - p17* [51-250]
Jean Howard's Hollywood
LJ - v122 - Mr 15 '97 - p94 [51-250]

Howard, Jean E, 1948- - *The Stage and Social Struggle in Early Modern England*
Comp L - v48 - Fall '96 - p383+ [501+]
Sev Cent N - v54 - Spr '96 - p17+ [501+]
Shakes Q - v47 - Sum '96 - p204+ [501+]

Howard, Jeremy - *Art Nouveau*
Choice - v34 - My '97 - p1486 [51-250]

Howard, John - *Performing and Responding*
y Sch Lib - v44 - Ag '96 - p124 [51-250]

Howard, Joseph Jackson - *Visitation of England and Wales. Vols. 7-9*
EGH - v50 - N '96 - p155+ [51-250]

Howard, Judith A - *Gendered Situations, Gendered Selves*
Choice - v34 - F '97 - p1004 [51-250]

Howard, Kathleen L - *Inventing the Southwest*
LJ - v122 - Ja '97 - p93 [51-250]

Howard, Linda - *Shades of Twilight*
LJ - v122 - F 15 '97 - p184 [51-250]
Son of the Morning
PW - v244 - F 10 '97 - p81 [51-250]

Howard, Michael - *The Laws of War*
EHR - v112 - Ap '97 - p550+ [251-500]

Howard, Nancy Shroyer - *Jacob Lawrence: American Scenes, American Struggles*
c BL - v93 - N 1 '96 - p492 [51-250]
c HB Guide - v8 - Spr '97 - p138 [51-250]
c KR - v64 - O 1 '96 - p1468 [51-250]
c PW - v243 - N 4 '96 - p76+ [51-250]

Howard, Patricia - *Gluck: An Eighteenth-Century Portrait in Letters and Documents*
Eight-C St - v30 - Win '96 - p199+ [501+]

Howard, Peter - *Practise Your Language Skills Series*
c Quill & Q - v62 - O '96 - p50 [51-250]

Howard, Rebecca Moore - *The Bedford Guide to Teaching Writing in the Disciplines*
r Col Comp - v47 - O '96 - p438 [51-250]

Howard, Rhoda E - *Human Rights and the Search for Community*
CS - v25 - S '96 - p636+ [501+]

Howard, Richard - *Like Most Revelations*
LJ - v122 - Ap 1 '97 - p95 [1-50]

Howard, Robert E - *Beyond the Borders*
LJ - v121 - O 15 '96 - p93 [51-250]
Solomon Kane
Necro - Fall '96 - p7+ [501+]

Howard, Ron - *Distance Education for Language Teachers*
MLJ - v80 - Fall '96 - p401+ [251-500]

Howard, Victor B - *The Evangelical War against Slavery and Caste*
Choice - v34 - Ap '97 - p1405 [251-500]

Howard Hughes Medical Institute - *The Race against Lethal Microbes*
SB - v33 - Mr '97 - p40 [251-500]

Howard Worner International Symposium on Injection in Pyrometallurgy (1996: Melbourne, Australia) - *Injection in Pyrometallurgy*
SciTech - v20 - N '96 - p77 [51-250]

Howarth, Glennys - *Last Rites*
AJS - v102 - Ja '97 - p1210+ [501+]
CS - v26 - Mr '97 - p226+ [501+]

Howarth, Lesley - *Fort Biscuit (Illus. by Ann Kronheimer)*
c Sch Lib - v45 - F '97 - p24 [51-250]
Maphead
y Kliatt - v31 - Ja '97 - p14 [51-250]
c RT - v50 - F '97 - p423 [51-250]
The Pits
y Bks Keeps - v100 - S '96 - p33 [51-250]
y CBRS - v25 - O '96 - p22 [51-250]
y CCB-B - v50 - D '96 - p138+ [51-250]
c HB - v73 - Mr '97 - p200 [51-250]
y JB - v60 - Ag '96 - p164+ [51-250]
c Magpies - v11 - My '96 - p21 [251-500]
y Sch Lib - v44 - Ag '96 - p118 [51-250]
Weather Eye
y Ch BWatch - v7 - F '97 - p4 [51-250]

Howarth, Peter - *Fatherhood: An Anthology of New Writing*
NS - v126 - Ap 25 '97 - p46+ [501+]

Howarth, Sarah - *What Do We Know about the Middle Ages?*
c HB Guide - v7 - Fall '96 - p378 [51-250]

Howarth, William D - *Beaumarchais and the Theatre*
MLR - v92 - Ja '97 - p194+ [251-500]

Howe, Christopher - *The Origins of Japanese Trade Supremacy*
JEH - v57 - Mr '97 - p229+ [501+]
JEL - v34 - S '96 - p1474 [51-250]

Howe, Daniel Walker - *Making the American Self*
LJ - v122 - My 1 '97 - p120 [51-250]

Howe, David J - *Doctor Who Companions*
r SF Chr - v18 - O '96 - p82 [1-50]

Howe, Elisabeth A - *The Dramatic Monologue*
Choice - v34 - My '97 - p1496 [51-250]

Howe, James - *Pinky and Rex and the Bully (Illus. by Melissa Sweet)*
c HB Guide - v7 - Fall '96 - p286 [51-250]
Pinky and Rex and the New Neighbors (Illus. by Melissa Sweet)
c BL - v93 - My 1 '97 - p1503 [51-250]
The Watcher
y HB - v73 - My '97 - p321+ [251-500]
y KR - v65 - Mr 15 '97 - p463 [51-250]
y PW - v244 - Mr 31 '97 - p75+ [51-250]

Howe, John, 1957- - *The Knight with the Lion (Illus. by John Howe)*
c CCB-B - v50 - F '97 - p209+ [51-250]
c Ch BWatch - v6 - D '96 - p3 [1-50]
c HB Guide - v8 - Spr '97 - p102 [51-250]
c SLJ - v42 - S '96 - p217 [51-250]

Howe, John R - *Bear Man of Admiralty Island*
Choice - v34 - Ap '97 - p1360 [51-250]

Howe, K R - *Tides of History*
WorldV - v13 - Ja '97 - p12 [251-500]

Howe, Leroy T - *The Image of God*
Theol St - v57 - Je '96 - p389 [251-500]
TT - v53 - Ja '97 - p568 [51-250]

Howe, Roger T - *Microelectronics: An Integrated Approach*
SciTech - v20 - D '96 - p78 [51-250]

Howe, Rufus S - *Clinical Pathways for Ambulatory Care Case Management*
SciTech - v20 - D '96 - p41 [51-250]

Howe, Susan - *Frame Structures*
Sulfur - Fall '96 - p139+ [501+]

Howell, Colin D - *Northern Sandlots*
AHR - v101 - D '96 - p1654 [501+]

Howell, David L - *Capitalism from Within*
JIH - v27 - Win '97 - p571+ [501+]

Howell, Hannah - *Unconquered*
PW - v243 - S 9 '96 - p81 [51-250]
Wild Roses
PW - v244 - Ap 28 '97 - p73 [51-250]

Howell, Joel D - *Technology in the Hospital*
AHR - v102 - F '97 - p199 [251-500]
Isis - v87 - D '96 - p757+ [501+]
Nature - v385 - Ja 30 '97 - p408 [1-50]

Howell, Lis - *The Director's Cut*
PW - v243 - N 25 '96 - p59 [51-250]

Howell, P P - *The Nile: Sharing a Scarce Resource*
GJ - v162 - Jl '96 - p221 [251-500]

Howell, Patrick J - *A Spiritguide: Through Times of Darkness*
Am - v175 - O 12 '96 - p27 [501+]
RR - v55 - N '96 - p656+ [251-500]
Howells, Bernard - *Baudelaire: Individualism, Dandyism and the Philosophy of History*
TLS - Ja 24 '97 - p25 [501+]
Howells, Christina - *Sartre*
MLR - v91 - O '96 - p1001 [251-500]
Howells, Dion - *The Story of David*
y BL - v93 - My 15 '97 - p1546 [51-250]
PW - v244 - My 5 '97 - p190+ [51-250]
Howells, Robin - *Disabled Powers*
MLR - v92 - Ap '97 - p468+ [501+]
Hower, Edward - *Night Train Blues*
NYTBR - v101 - Ag 25 '96 - p19 [51-250]
Howes, Karen - *Making the Most of Bedrooms*
PW - v244 - Ap 7 '97 - p89 [51-250]
Howes, Ruth H - *Women and the Use of Military Force*
NWCR - v49 - Aut '96 - p144+ [501+]
Howker, Janni - *Badger on the Barge*
y Magpies - v11 - S '96 - p45 [1-50]
Isaac Campion
y Magpies - v11 - S '96 - p45 [1-50]
Howland, D R - *Borders of Chinese Civilization*
Choice - v34 - Ja '97 - p853 [51-250]
Howlett, Colin - *The Concise Oxford Russian Dictionary*
r ARBA - v28 - '97 - p398 [51-250]
Howlett, Jana - *The Violent Muse*
JAAC - v54 - Fall '96 - p409+ [501+]
Howlett, Virginia - *Visual Interface Design for Windows*
CBR - v15 - Spr '97 - p9 [51-250]
Howlings: Wild Women of the West
p Bloom Rev - v16 - Jl '96 - p17 [51-250]
Howorth, Lisa - *Yellow Dogs, Hushpuppies, and Bluetick Hounds*
VQR - v72 - Aut '96 - p138* [51-250]
Howren, Suzanne - *Stitches for Effect*
McCall Nee - v42 - S '96 - p13 [51-250]
Howson, Susan - *British Monetary Policy 1945-51*
Econ J - v106 - N '96 - p1848 [251-500]
Howze, Hamilton H - *A Cavalryman's Story*
For Aff - v76 - My '97 - p130 [51-250]
Hoxie, Frederick E - *Encyclopedia of North American Indians*
r BL - v93 - D 15 '96 - p747 [251-500]
r Choice - v34 - Ap '97 - p1307 [51-250]
r LJ - v121 - D '96 - p84 [51-250]
r LJ - v122 - Ap 15 '97 - p39 [51-250]
Parading through History
AHR - v102 - F '97 - p180+ [501+]
RAH - v24 - S '96 - p407+ [501+]
WHQ - v27 - Win '96 - p516+ [501+]
Hoy, Jim - *Cowboys and Kansas*
J Am Cult - v19 - Spr '96 - p101 [51-250]
Hoy, Suellen - *Chasing Dirt*
AHR - v102 - F '97 - p162+ [251-500]
J Am Cult - v19 - Spr '96 - p101 [251-500]
J Soc H - v30 - Fall '96 - p277+ [501+]
RAH - v24 - S '96 - p461+ [501+]
Hoyer, Eva Maria - *Sachsischer Serpentin*
SDA - v4 - Spr '97 - p120+ [501+]
Hoyer, Svennik - *Towards a Civic Society*
JC - v46 - Aut '96 - p171+ [501+]
Hoyle, Brian - *Cityports, Coastal Zones, and Regional Change*
Choice - v34 - Mr '97 - p1213+ [51-250]
R&R Bk N - v12 - F '97 - p55 [51-250]
Hoyle, David - *ISO 9000 Quality System Assessment Handbook*
SciTech - v21 - Mr '97 - p98 [1-50]
Hoyle, Leonard H - *Managing Conventions and Group Business*
R&R Bk N - v11 - N '96 - p79 [51-250]
Hoyo, Josep Del - *Handbook of the Birds of the World. Vol. 3*
r New Sci - v152 - N 2 '96 - p48 [51-250]
Hoyt, Erich - *The Earth Dwellers*
Choice - v34 - O '96 - p303+ [51-250]
SB - v32 - Ag '96 - p168 [51-250]
y SLJ - v42 - N '96 - p141 [51-250]
SLJ - v42 - D '96 - p42 [51-250]
Trib Bks - Mr 23 '97 - p6 [1-50]
Hoyt, Michael F - *Constructive Therapies. Vol. 2*
SciTech - v20 - N '96 - p43 [51-250]
Hoyt, Richard - *Red Card*
Aethlon - v13 - Fall '95 - p138+ [251-500]
Hoyt-Goldsmith, Diane - *Angela from the Arctic (Illus. by Lawrence Migdale)*
c Cur R - v36 - F '97 - p12 [51-250]

April: A Pueblo Storyteller (Illus. by Lawrence Migdale)
c SB - v33 - Ja '97 - p15 [51-250]
Celebrating Hanukkah (Illus. by Lawrence Migdale)
c BL - v93 - S 1 '96 - p135 [51-250]
c CCB-B - v50 - N '96 - p99 [51-250]
c CLW - v67 - D '96 - p53 [51-250]
c HB Guide - v8 - Spr '97 - p89 [51-250]
c PW - v243 - S 30 '96 - p87+ [51-250]
c SLJ - v42 - O '96 - p37 [51-250]
Clay Hernandez, a Mexican American (Illus. by Lawrence Migdale)
c Cur R - v36 - F '97 - p12 [51-250]
Migrant Worker (Illus. by Lawrence Migdale)
c HB Guide - v7 - Fall '96 - p312 [51-250]
c New Ad - v9 - Fall '96 - p327+ [501+]
Potlatch: A Tsimshian Celebration
c BL - v93 - My 1 '97 - p1491 [51-250]
Hrabal, Bohumil - *The Little Town Where Time Stood Still*
TranslRevS - v1 - My '95 - p17 [51-250]
Too Loud a Solitude
AJPsych - v153 - D '96 - p1640+ [501+]
Hristofis, Hristoforos - *Rosa T' Oniro*
WLT - v70 - Sum '96 - p742 [51-250]
Hritonenko, Natali - *Modeling and Optimization of the Lifetime of Technologies*
SciTech - v20 - D '96 - p2 [51-250]
Hron, Tom - *Whispers of the Mountain*
Roundup M - v4 - D '96 - p27 [51-250]
Hru, Dakari - *The Magic Moonberry Jump Ropes (Illus. by E B Lewis)*
c ECEJ - v24 - Spr '97 - p175 [51-250]
c HB Guide - v7 - Fall '96 - p260 [51-250]
c LA - v73 - D '96 - p622 [51-250]
Hrushevs'kyi, Mykhailo - *IAk Zhyv Ukrains'kyi Narod*
BL - v93 - N 15 '96 - p577 [1-50]
Hsia, R Po-chia - *In and Out of the Ghetto*
Six Ct J - v27 - Win '96 - p1057+ [501+]
Hsiang, W Y - *A Concise Introduction to Calculus*
Choice - v34 - O '96 - p318 [51-250]
Hsiao, T'ung - *Wen Xuan. Vol. 3*
Rel St Rev - v23 - Ap '97 - p204 [51-250]
TranslRevS - v2 - D '96 - p4 [51-250]
Hsieh, H P - *Inorganic Membranes for Separation and Reaction*
SciTech - v21 - Mr '97 - p95 [51-250]
Hsu, John Y - *Computer Networks*
SciTech - v20 - N '96 - p73 [51-250]
Hsu, Kenneth J - *The Geology of Switzerland*
Am Sci - v84 - S '96 - p498 [501+]
Hsu, Madeleine - *Olivier Messiaen, the Musical Mediator*
Choice - v34 - D '96 - p623 [51-250]
Hsun-Tzu - *Xunzi--A Translation and Study of the Complete Works. Vol. 3*
Rel St Rev - v22 - O '96 - p359 [51-250]
Hu, An-Kang - *Tiao Zhan Zhong Guo*
BL - v93 - N 1 '96 - p484 [51-250]
Hu, Shizhang - *Stanley K. Hornbeck and the Open Door Policy 1919-1937*
PHR - v65 - Ag '96 - p505+ [251-500]
Huang, Chun-Chieh - *Norms and the State in China*
Ch Rev Int - v3 - Fall '96 - p434+ [501+]
Time and Space in Chinese Culture
Ch Rev Int - v4 - Spr '97 - p5+ [501+]
Huang, H K - *PACS: Picture Archiving and Communication Systems in Biomedical Imaging*
SciTech - v20 - S '96 - p27 [51-250]
Huang, Kuang-Kuo - *Min Cui Wang Tai Lun*
BL - v93 - N 1 '96 - p484 [1-50]
Huang, Martin W - *Literati and Self-Re/presentation*
Ch Rev Int - v4 - Spr '97 - p162+ [501+]
Huang, Yasheng - *Inflation and Investment Controls in China*
JEL - v35 - Mr '97 - p290+ [51-250]
Hubanig, Alfred A - *Living in the Spirit's Fire*
RR - v56 - Mr '97 - p221 [1-50]
Hubbard, Barbara Burke - *The World according to Wavelets*
Am Sci - v85 - Ja '97 - p85+ [501+]
Choice - v34 - D '96 - p646 [51-250]
Math T - v90 - Ja '97 - p72 [251-500]
Nature - v385 - Ja 9 '97 - p130 [51-250]
Hubbard, Jim - *Lives Turned Upside Down*
c BL - v93 - N 15 '96 - p583 [51-250]
c CBRS - v25 - N '96 - p34 [51-250]
c CCB-B - v50 - Ja '97 - p173 [51-250]
c HB Guide - v8 - Spr '97 - p96 [51-250]
c SLJ - v42 - D '96 - p130 [51-250]
Hubbard, Ken - *The Best of Ken Hubbard*
CAY - v17 - Fall '96 - p11 [51-250]
Hubbard, Linda S - *Notable Americans. 4th Ed.*
r ASInt - v34 - O '96 - p13 [51-250]

Hubbard, Merton R - *Statistical Quality Control for the Food Industry. 2nd Ed.*
SciTech - v20 - N '96 - p80 [51-250]
Hubbard, Patricia - *My Crayons Talk (Illus. by G Brian Karas)*
c HB Guide - v7 - Fall '96 - p260 [1-50]
c LA - v73 - D '96 - p624 [51-250]
Hubbard, Ruth - *A Workshop of the Possible*
Choice - v34 - S '96 - p180 [51-250]
New Ad - v9 - Fall '96 - p309+ [501+]
Hubbert, William T - *Food Safety and Quality Assurance. 2nd Ed.*
SciTech - v20 - S '96 - p27 [51-250]
Hubchick, Dennis P - *Conflict and Chaos in Eastern Europe*
AAPSS-A - v548 - N '96 - p225+ [501+]
Culture and History in Eastern Europe
AAPSS-A - v548 - N '96 - p225+ [501+]
Hubel, Teresa - *Whose India?*
VQR - v73 - Win '97 - p14* [51-250]
Huber, Jeffrey T - *HIV/AIDS and HIV/AIDS-Related Terminology*
r ARBA - v28 - '97 - p241+ [251-500]
r BL - v93 - O 1 '96 - p370 [251-500]
r Choice - v34 - Ja '97 - p828 [51-250]
SLMQ - v25 - Fall '96 - p64 [51-250]
HIV/AIDS Community Information Services
Choice - v34 - N '96 - p492 [51-250]
SciTech - v20 - S '96 - p28 [51-250]
r SLMQ - v25 - Fall '96 - p64 [51-250]
Huber, John D - *Rationalizing Parliament*
JEL - v35 - Mr '97 - p202+ [51-250]
Huber, Wolfgang - *Violence: The Unrelenting Assault on Human Dignity*
Choice - v34 - D '96 - p628 [51-250]
Hubert, Jane - *Life after Head Injury*
SciTech - v20 - D '96 - p49 [51-250]
Hubert, Maria - *Jane Austen's Christmas*
CR - v269 - D '96 - p335 [51-250]
Hubin, Allen J - *Crime Fiction II. Vols. 1-2*
r RQ - v36 - Win '96 - p210+ [51-250]
Hubinger, Gangolf - *Kulturprotestantismus Und Politik*
JMH - v68 - S '96 - p733+ [501+]
Hubner, Hans - *Biblische Theologie Als Hermeneutik*
Rel St Rev - v23 - Ja '97 - p69 [51-250]
Hubner, John - *Somebody Else's Children*
BW - v27 - Ja 12 '97 - p4 [501+]
KR - v64 - O 15 '96 - p1512 [251-500]
LJ - v121 - N 15 '96 - p77 [51-250]
PW - v243 - O 14 '96 - p68 [51-250]
Trib Bks - Ap 13 '97 - p6 [501+]
Huck, Charlotte - *Toads and Diamonds (Illus. by Anita Lobel)*
c BL - v93 - N 1 '96 - p496 [51-250]
c CBRS - v25 - S '96 - p4 [51-250]
c CCB-B - v50 - Ja '97 - p173+ [51-250]
c HB - v72 - N '96 - p750+ [51-250]
c HB Guide - v8 - Spr '97 - p102 [51-250]
c SLJ - v42 - S '96 - p197 [51-250]
Huckabay, Calvin - *John Milton: An Annotated Bibliography 1968-1988*
r Choice - v34 - N '96 - p431 [51-250]
Huckell, Bruce B - *Of Marshes and Maize*
Am Ant - v61 - O '96 - p820+ [251-500]
Hucker, Hazel - *A Dangerous Happiness*
KR - v64 - My 1 '96 - p624 [251-500]
Huckfeldt, Robert - *Citizens, Politics, and Social Communication*
J Pol - v58 - N '96 - p1221+ [501+]
PSQ - v111 - Win '96 - p725+ [501+]
Pub Op Q - v60 - Win '96 - p650+ [501+]
Huckle, John - *Education for Sustainability*
TES - O 11 '96 - p9* [501+]
Hucklenbroich, Frankie - *A Crystal Diary*
PW - v244 - Mr 31 '97 - p65 [51-250]
Hucko, Bruce - *A Rainbow at Night*
c BL - v93 - Mr 15 '97 - p1236+ [51-250]
c Bloom Rev - v16 - S '96 - p29 [51-250]
c CBRS - v25 - F '97 - p82 [51-250]
c Nat Peop - v10 - Spr '97 - p83 [501+]
c PW - v244 - Ap 6 '97 - p74 [51-250]
c SLJ - v43 - Mr '97 - p176 [51-250]
Where There Is No Name for Art
c Bloom Rev - v16 - S '96 - p29 [51-250]
Huddleston, Kathryn - *Back on the Quality Track*
Per Psy - v49 - Aut '96 - p762+ [501+]
Huddleston, Mark W - *The Higher Civil Service in the United States*
APSR - v91 - Mr '97 - p188+ [501+]
Choice - v34 - N '96 - p538 [51-250]
Pol Stud J - v24 - Aut '96 - p520 [51-250]

Huddy, Delia - *The Nearly Ghost Baby (Illus. by David William)*
　　c　Sch Lib - v44 - Ag '96 - p107 [51-250]
Hudgins, Edward L - *The Last Monopoly*
　　Choice - v34 - Ja '97 - p844 [51-250]
Hudlicky, Milos - *Reductions in Organic Chemistry. 2nd Ed.*
　　SciTech - v21 - Mr '97 - p30 [51-250]
Hudson, Barbara A - *Race, Crime, and Justice*
　　R&R Bk N - v11 - D '96 - p44 [51-250]
　　Understanding Justice
　　R&R Bk N - v12 - F '97 - p63 [51-250]
Hudson, Benjamin T - *Kings of Celtic Scotland*
　　EHR - v112 - Ap '97 - p426+ [501+]
　　Prophecy of Berchan
　　ILS - v15 - Fall '96 - p31 [1-50]
　　R&R Bk N - v11 - D '96 - p59 [1-50]
Hudson, Charles - *The Forgotten Centuries*
　　Am Ant - v61 - Ap '96 - p438+ [501+]
　　Knights of Spain, Warriors of the Sun
　　LJ - v122 - My 1 '97 - p120 [51-250]
Hudson, Cheryl - *Kids' Book of Wisdom*
　　c　PW - v243 - N 11 '96 - p77 [51-250]
Hudson, Hud - *Kant's Compatibilism*
　　Phil R - v105 - Ja '96 - p125+ [501+]
Hudson, Jan - *Sweetgrass*
　　c　SLJ - v42 - N '96 - p41 [1-50]
Hudson, John - *The Formation of the English Common Law*
　　Choice - v34 - Ja '97 - p856 [51-250]
　　The History of English Law
　　TLS - Ja 3 '97 - p30 [501+]
　　Land, Law, and Lordship in Anglo-Norman England
　　Specu - v72 - Ja '97 - p174+ [501+]
Hudson, John C - *Making the Corn Belt*
　　T&C - v37 - Ap '96 - p362+ [501+]
Hudson, Larry E, Jr. - *Working toward Freedom*
　　J Am St - v30 - Ag '96 - p297+ [501+]
Hudson, Michael - *Privatization in the Ancient Near East and Classical World*
　　Sci - v275 - F 28 '97 - p1276 [1-50]
Hudson, Parker - *The President*
　　BW - v26 - D 8 '96 - p4 [51-250]
Hudson, Robert - *Companions for the Soul*
　　Ch Today - v40 - Ag 12 '96 - p46+ [501+]
Hudson, Wade - *How Sweet the Sound (Illus. by Floyd Cooper)*
　　c　CAY - v17 - Fall '96 - p5 [51-250]
　　In Praise of Our Fathers and Our Mothers
　　y　BL - v93 - Ap 1 '97 - p1321 [51-250]
　　c　BW - v27 - Ap 6 '97 - p8 [51-250]
　　c　HB - v73 - Mr '97 - p217+ [501+]
　　c　PW - v244 - Ja 20 '97 - p400 [51-250]
　　Pass It On (Illus. by Floyd Cooper)
　　c　BL - v93 - F 15 '97 - p1014 [1-50]
Huelin, Gordon - *Vanished Churches of the City of London*
　　LAR - v99 - F '97 - p103 [1-50]
Huet, Marie-Helene - *Monstrous Imagination*
　　Ren Q - v49 - Aut '96 - p664+ [501+]
Huet, Michel - *The Dances of Africa*
　　Atl - v278 - Jl '96 - p110 [51-250]
Huet, Sylvie - *Statistical Tools for Nonlinear Regression*
　　Choice - v34 - F '97 - p1000 [51-250]
Huey, George H H - *Wild Cactus*
　　Bloom Rev - v16 - Jl '96 - p12 [51-250]
Hufbauer, Gary Clyde - *Fundamental Tax Reform and Border Tax Adjustments*
　　JEL - v34 - S '96 - p1439 [51-250]
Huff, C Ronald - *Gangs in America. 2nd Ed.*
　　BWatch - v17 - D '96 - p5 [1-50]
　　R&R Bk N - v11 - D '96 - p44 [51-250]
Huff, Peter A - *Allen Tate and the Catholic Revival*
　　Am - v176 - Mr 22 '97 - p32+ [251-500]
Huff, Richard - *Behind the Wall*
　　Aethlon - v13 - Fall '95 - p164+ [251-500]
Huff, Tanya - *No Quarter*
　　y　VOYA - v19 - O '96 - p218 [251-500]
　　Scholar of Decay
　　MFSF - v91 - S '96 - p42+ [251-500]
Huff, Toby E - *The Rise of Early Modern Science*
　　Ch Rev Int - v3 - Fall '96 - p438+ [501+]
　　MEJ - v50 - Sum '96 - p448+ [501+]
　　SF - v75 - S '96 - p364+ [251-500]
Huff, W G - *The Economic Growth of Singapore*
　　AHR - v101 - D '96 - p1601+ [501+]
Huffman, Karen - *Psychology in Action. 4th Ed.*
　　R&R Bk N - v12 - F '97 - p5 [1-50]
Huffman, Ru Story - *Nursery Rhyme Time (Illus. by Nancy Story)*
　　c　CLW - v67 - D '96 - p57 [51-250]

Hufford, Charlie - *The Toy Soldier's Heart*
　　Rapport - v19 - 4 '96 - p31 [251-500]
Hufford, Mary - *Conserving Culture*
　　Pub Hist - v19 - Win '97 - p109+ [501+]
Hufton, Olwen - *Historical Change and Human Rights*
　　JIH - v27 - Spr '97 - p665+ [501+]
　　The Prospect before Her. Vol. 1
　　BL - v93 - N 1 '96 - p477 [51-250]
　　BW - v26 - N 17 '96 - p1+ [501+]
　　HT - v47 - Ja '97 - p52 [501+]
　　LJ - v121 - N 15 '96 - p73 [51-250]
　　New R - v216 - Ja 27 '97 - p38+ [501+]
　　NYRB - v44 - F 6 '97 - p4+ [501+]
　　NYTBR - v101 - D 15 '96 - p11 [501+]
　　PW - v243 - S 23 '96 - p63 [51-250]
　　PW - v243 - N 4 '96 - p44 [51-250]
　　W&I - v12 - Ap '97 - p286+ [501+]
Hugdahl, Kenneth - *Psychophysiology: The Mind-Body Perspective*
　　Choice - v34 - O '96 - p313 [51-250]
Hugenholz, D Bernt - *The Future of Copyright in a Digital Environment*
　　LAR - v99 - Mr '97 - p164 [251-500]
Huggan, Graham - *Critical Perspectives on J.M. Coetzee*
　　Bl S - v26 - Sum '96 - p65 [1-50]
　　Choice - v34 - S '96 - p120 [51-250]
　　Territorial Disputes
　　Can Lit - Win '96 - p177+ [501+]
Huggett, R J - *Geoecology: An Evolutionary Approach*
　　GJ - v162 - Jl '96 - p227 [251-500]
Huggins, David - *The Big Kiss*
　　Spec - v277 - S 7 '96 - p37 [51-250]
Huggins, Kevin - *Parenting Adolescents*
　　VOYA - v19 - F '97 - p317 [51-250]
Huggins, Nathan Irvin - *Revelations: American History, American Myths*
　　AHR - v101 - O '96 - p1270+ [501+]
Hugh Johnson's Pocket Encyclopedia of Wine 1997
　　r　LJ - v122 - Ap 1 '97 - p64 [1-50]
Hughes, Alex - *French Erotic Fiction*
　　RCF - v16 - Fall '96 - p201+ [251-500]
　　R&R Bk N - v12 - F '97 - p83 [51-250]
　　Violette Leduc: Mothers, Lovers, and Language
　　MLR - v91 - O '96 - p1002+ [251-500]
Hughes, Carol - *Toots and the Upside Down House*
　　c　Sch Lib - v44 - N '96 - p150+ [51-250]
Hughes, David - *Himself and Other Animals*
　　Books - v11 - Ap '97 - p20 [51-250]
Hughes, Dean - *Team Picture*
　　y　BL - v93 - N 15 '96 - p584 [51-250]
　　c　CCB-B - v50 - Ja '97 - p174 [51-250]
　　c　HB - v73 - Ja '97 - p58 [51-250]
　　c　HB Guide - v8 - Spr '97 - p68 [51-250]
　　c　SLJ - v42 - N '96 - p107 [51-250]
Hughes, Derek - *English Drama 1660-1700*
　　Choice - v34 - Ja '97 - p795 [51-250]
Hughes, Francesca - *The Architect: Reconstructing Her Practice*
　　Ms - v7 - N '96 - p81 [251-500]
Hughes, Gerard J - *The Nature of God*
　　Rel St - v32 - S '96 - p413+ [501+]
Hughes, Glyn - *Bronte*
　　BW - v26 - N 24 '96 - p5 [501+]
　　LJ - v121 - S 15 '96 - p96 [51-250]
　　NYTBR - v101 - N 10 '96 - p56 [51-250]
　　TLS - Jl 19 '96 - p21 [501+]
Hughes, J A, 1941- - *Understanding Classical Sociology*
　　Socio R - v45 - My '97 - p337+ [501+]
Hughes, John - *The Devil Himself*
　　BL - v93 - F 1 '97 - p921+ [51-250]
　　ILS - v15 - Fall '96 - p10 [501+]
Hughes, John Jay - *Pontiffs: Popes Who Shaped History*
　　CHR - v82 - Jl '96 - p476+ [251-500]
Hughes, Judith M - *From Freud's Consulting Room*
　　AHR - v101 - D '96 - p1520+ [501+]
　　JIH - v27 - Aut '96 - p323+ [501+]
　　JMH - v69 - Mr '97 - p125+ [501+]
Hughes, Kirsty - *Evaluation of Technical Assistance to Hungary*
　　JEL - v34 - D '96 - p2071 [51-250]
Hughes, Langston - *The Block (Illus. by Romare Bearden)*
　　y　Emerg Lib - v24 - S '96 - p23 [1-50]
　　The Dream Keeper and Other Poems (Illus. by J Brian Pinkney)
　　c　BW - v26 - D 8 '96 - p20 [51-250]
　　y　Kliatt - v31 - Mr '97 - p23 [1-50]
　　c　PW - v243 - D 9 '96 - p69 [1-50]

Short Stories
　　BW - v26 - S 8 '96 - p13 [51-250]
　　BWatch - v17 - D '96 - p8 [51-250]
　　Ent W - S 13 '96 - p127 [51-250]
　　NYTBR - v101 - S 1 '96 - p8+ [501+]
　　NYTBR - v101 - D 8 '96 - p82 [1-50]
Hughes, Larry - *Introduction to Data Communications*
　　SciTech - v21 - Mr '97 - p88 [51-250]
Hughes, Laura - *Bright Eyes and the Buffalo Hunt (Illus. by Laura Hughes)*
　　c　HB Guide - v7 - Fall '96 - p260 [51-250]
Hughes, Libby - *Colin Powell: A Man of Quality*
　　c　HB Guide - v7 - Fall '96 - p372+ [51-250]
　　y　SLJ - v42 - Ag '96 - p170+ [51-250]
Hughes, Mark - *The Unpublished Roll of Honor*
　　r　EGH - v50 - N '96 - p196 [51-250]
Hughes, Michael - *Ireland Divided*
　　Bks & Cult - v2 - Ja '96 - p11+ [501+]
Hughes, Monica - *A Handful of Seeds (Illus. by Luis Garay)*
　　c　Can CL - v22 - Fall '96 - p132+ [501+]
　　c　HB Guide - v7 - Fall '96 - p260 [51-250]
　　c　Smith - v27 - N '96 - p171+ [1-50]
　　The Seven Magpies
　　y　BIC - v26 - Mr '97 - p36 [501+]
　　y　Quill & Q - v63 - Ja '97 - p39 [251-500]
　　Where Have You Been, Billy Boy?
　　y　Can CL - v22 - Sum '96 - p92+ [251-500]
Hughes, Morgan E - *Mario Lemieux: Beating the Odds*
　　c　HB Guide - v8 - Spr '97 - p144 [51-250]
　　c　SLJ - v42 - S '96 - p217 [51-250]
Hughes, Nancy S - *The New Chili Cuisine*
　　BWatch - v18 - F '97 - p7 [51-250]
　　y　Kliatt - v31 - Mr '97 - p36 [51-250]
Hughes, Nathaniel Cheairs - *Bentonville: The Final Battle of Sherman and Johnston*
　　BL - v93 - S 15 '96 - p214 [51-250]
　　Choice - v34 - Mr '97 - p1227 [51-250]
Hughes, Richard T - *The American Quest for the Primitive Church*
　　CHR - v83 - Ja '97 - p131+ [501+]
　　The Primitive Church in the Modern World
　　CHR - v83 - Ja '97 - p131+ [501+]
　　J Ch St - v38 - Sum '96 - p665+ [251-500]
　　Reviving the Ancient Faith
　　Choice - v34 - O '96 - p297 [51-250]
Hughes, Robert - *American Visions*
　　BL - v93 - Mr 1 '97 - p1066 [251-500]
　　BW - v27 - Ap 13 '97 - p1+ [501+]
　　KR - v65 - Mr 1 '97 - p353+ [51-250]
　　LJ - v122 - My 1 '97 - p100 [51-250]
　　PW - v244 - F 24 '97 - p72 [51-250]
Hughes, Robin - *Australian Lives*
　　Aust Bk R - D '96 - p21+ [501+]
Hughes, Shirley - *Alfie's Feet*
　　c　HB - v73 - Mr '97 - p187 [1-50]
　　Chatting (Illus. by Shirley Hughes)
　　c　Bks Keeps - Mr '97 - p7 [51-250]
　　c　RT - v50 - F '97 - p420 [51-250]
　　Enchantment in the Garden (Illus. by Shirley Hughes)
　　c　BL - v93 - My 15 '97 - p1575 [51-250]
　　c　HB - v73 - Mr '97 - p192 [51-250]
　　c　JB - v60 - D '96 - p253+ [251-500]
　　c　KR - v65 - Ap 1 '97 - p558 [51-250]
　　c　PW - v244 - Mr 17 '97 - p83+ [51-250]
　　c　Spec - v277 - D 14 '96 - p76 [51-250]
　　c　TES - O 11 '96 - p9* [501+]
　　Rhymes for Annie Rose (Illus. by Shirley Hughes)
　　c　Magpies - v11 - My '96 - p37 [51-250]
　　c　RT - v50 - F '97 - p420 [51-250]
　　Tales of Trotter Street (Illus. by Shirley Hughes)
　　c　Bks Keeps - Mr '97 - p19 [51-250]
　　c　BL - v93 - F 1 '97 - p946 [51-250]
Hughes, Ted - *Difficulties of a Bridegroom*
　　Atl - v278 - N '96 - p122 [51-250]
　　BL - v93 - O 1 '96 - p321 [251-500]
　　KR - v64 - Ag 15 '96 - p1174 [251-500]
　　LATBR - N 10 '96 - p14 [51-250]
　　NYTBR - v101 - O 13 '96 - p21 [51-250]
　　Obs - N 10 '96 - p18* [51-250]
　　PW - v243 - S 2 '96 - p111 [51-250]
　　The Iron Woman (Illus. by Barry Moser)
　　c　RT - v50 - Mr '97 - p497 [51-250]
　　The Iron Woman (Hughes). Audio Version
　　c　Obs - Ja 12 '97 - p18* [51-250]
Hughes, Terry - *Quality Assurance. 2nd Ed.*
　　SciTech - v20 - S '96 - p48 [51-250]
Hughes, Tim - *Cycling Great Britain*
　　r　BL - v93 - S 15 '96 - p206 [1-50]

Hughes, Virginia Hayden - *Hughes, Hardee, McCumbee, Milligan Connection of the Carolinas*
r   EGH - v50 - N '96 - p194 [51-250]
Hugill, Peter J - *Upstate Arcadia*
AHR - v101 - D '96 - p1618+ [501+]
Hugo, Daniel - *Monnikewerk*
WLT - v70 - Aut '96 - p1018 [501+]
Hugo, Victor - *The Hunchback of Notre-Dame*
y   Ch BWatch - v6 - S '96 - p3 [1-50]
LJ - v121 - O 1 '96 - p132 [1-50]
Hugo, William R - *Studying the Life of Saint Francis of Assisi*
Comw - v123 - S 27 '96 - p28+ [251-500]
Hugon, Philippe - *L'Afrique Des Incertitudes*
JEL - v34 - D '96 - p2110 [51-250]
Hugo Primas, Aurelianensis - *Hugh Primas and the Archpoet*
RES - v48 - F '97 - p80+ [501+]
Huijing, Richard - *The Dedalus Book of Dutch Fantasy*
TranslRevS - v1 - My '95 - p2 [51-250]
Huitema, Christian - *IPv6: The New Internet Protocol*
New Sci - v151 - S 14 '96 - p46 [51-250]
Huizinga, Johan - *The Autumn of the Middle Ages*
NY - v72 - S 9 '96 - p91 [51-250]
R&R Bk N - v11 - N '96 - p12 [51-250]
Hukanovic, Rezak - *The Tenth Circle of Hell*
BW - v26 - N 17 '96 - p5 [51-250]
KR - v64 - Ag 15 '96 - p1210+ [251-500]
LATBR - N 10 '96 - p4 [501+]
NYTBR - v101 - D 1 '96 - p29 [501+]
PW - v243 - S 9 '96 - p76 [51-250]
Hulbert, Elizabeth - *The Memory Quilt*
c   Ch BWatch - v7 - F '97 - p1 [51-250]
Hulit, Lloyd M - *Straight Talk on Stuttering*
J Rehab RD - v34 - Ja '97 - p121 [51-250]
Hull, D - *An Introduction to Composite Materials. 2nd Ed.*
Choice - v34 - F '97 - p994 [51-250]
Hull, Isabel V - *Sexuality, State, and Civil Society in Germany 1700-1815*
Eight-C St - v30 - Spr '97 - p319+ [501+]
TLS - N 15 '96 - p11 [501+]
VQR - v73 - Win '97 - p8*+ [51-250]
Hull, John C - *Options, Futures, and Other Derivatives. 3rd Ed.*
R&R Bk N - v12 - F '97 - p50 [51-250]
Hull, Lynda - *The Only World*
Parnassus - v22 - 1 '97 - p282+ [501+]
Hull, Suzanne W - *Women according to Men*
Ren Q - v50 - Spr '97 - p346+ [501+]
VQR - v73 - Win '97 - p8* [51-250]
Hullar, Link - *West (Montana Shootout. Bones, Bullets, and Badmen)*
Roundup M - v3 - Ag '96 - p29+ [51-250]
Hulliung, Mark - *The Autocritique of Enlightenment*
EHR - v112 - F '97 - p214 [251-500]
Hulll, Robert - *Christmas Poetry (Illus. by Annabel Spenceley)*
c   Bks Keeps - N '96 - p24 [51-250]
Hulme, Joy N - *How to Write, Recite, and Delight in All Kinds of Poetry*
c   HB Guide - v8 - Spr '97 - p148 [51-250]
c   SLJ - v42 - D '96 - p130 [51-250]
Sea Sums (Illus. by Carol Schwartz)
c   BL - v93 - D 1 '96 - p662 [51-250]
c   CCB-B - v50 - D '96 - p139 [51-250]
c   HB Guide - v8 - Spr '97 - p110 [51-250]
c   Learning - v25 - Ja '97 - p56 [1-50]
c   SLJ - v42 - D '96 - p114 [51-250]
Hulme, T E - *The Collected Writings of T.E. Hulme*
RES - v47 - N '96 - p624+ [501+]
Hulpach, Vladimir - *Ahaiyute and Cloud Eater (Illus. by Marek Zawadzki)*
c   Ch BWatch - v6 - My '96 - p5 [1-50]
c   Emerg Lib - v24 - Mr '97 - p65 [51-250]
c   HB Guide - v7 - Fall '96 - p321 [51-250]
c   RT - v50 - My '97 - p686 [51-250]
Hulsebus, Marjorie - *Miniature Victorian Lamps*
r   Ant & CM - v101 - Jl '96 - p25 [1-50]
Hultgren, Arland J - *The Earliest Christian Heretics*
Choice - v34 - My '97 - p1515 [51-250]
Hults, Linda C - *The Print in the Western World*
Bloom Rev - v17 - Ja '97 - p23 [251-500]
r   Choice - v34 - N '96 - p444 [51-250]
R&R Bk N - v11 - N '96 - p61 [51-250]
y   SLJ - v42 - Ag '96 - p186 [51-250]
Human Anatomy
yr Sch Lib - v44 - Ag '96 - p124 [51-250]
Human Development Report 1996
JEL - v35 - Mr '97 - p274+ [51-250]
The Human Factor
J Gov Info - v23 - S '96 - p595 [51-250]

Human Gene Mapping 1995
SciTech - v20 - D '96 - p30 [51-250]
The Human Machine
c   CLW - v66 - Je '96 - p53 [51-250]
c   HB Guide - v7 - Fall '96 - p348 [51-250]
Human Rights and Gender
J Gov Info - v23 - S '96 - p665 [51-250]
Human Rights Watch/Africa - *Behind the Red Line*
For Aff - v76 - My '97 - p147+ [51-250]
Human Rights Watch (Organization) - *Civilian Pawns*
MEJ - v50 - Aut '96 - p626 [51-250]
Slaughter among Neighbors
Choice - v34 - S '96 - p206 [51-250]
Human Rights Watch World Report 1997
MEJ - v51 - Spr '97 - p308+ [51-250]
NYRB - v44 - Mr 27 '97 - p48 [501+]
Humana Festival '96
BL - v93 - F 1 '97 - p920+ [51-250]
Humanities Index 1974-
r   ASInt - v34 - O '96 - p19 [1-50]
Humber, James M - *Reproduction, Technology, and Rights*
CPR - v16 - Je '96 - p171+ [501+]
Hast Cen R - v26 - Mr '96 - p48 [1-50]
Humber, William - *All I Thought about was Baseball*
BIC - v25 - O '96 - p4+ [501+]
Humbert, Jean-Marcel - *Egyptomania: Egypt in Western Art 1730-1930*
AJA - v101 - Ja '97 - p158+ [501+]
Art Bull - v78 - D '96 - p739+ [501+]
Humble, Richard - *Ships*
c   Magpies - v11 - Jl '96 - p43 [51-250]
Hume, David - *Political Essays*
Ethics - v107 - O '96 - p180 [251-500]
Humes, Charles Warren - *Descendants of Nicholas Humes of Massachusetts. Vol. 1*
NGSQ - v84 - D '96 - p310+ [251-500]
Humes, Edward - *No Matter How Loud I Shout*
y   BL - v93 - Ja '97 - p762 [1-50]
CS - v26 - Ja '97 - p86+ [501+]
Econ - v339 - My 18 '96 - p3*+ [501+]
Fed Prob - v60 - D '96 - p65 [251-500]
LATBR - Mr 24 '96 - p1+ [501+]
Trib Bks - My 4 '97 - p8 [1-50]
Humes, Harry - *The Bottomland*
Sm Pr R - v28 - D '96 - p11 [251-500]
Humes, James C - *Confessions of a White House Ghost Writer*
BL - v93 - My 1 '97 - p1476 [51-250]
LJ - v122 - Ap 15 '97 - p100 [51-250]
Humez, Alexander - *Zero to Lazy Eight*
y   BL - v93 - Ap 1 '97 - p1342 [1-50]
Humez, Jean M - *Mother's First-Born Daughters*
CH - v65 - S '96 - p515+ [501+]
Humfrey, Peter - *Painting in Renaissance Venice*
Ren Q - v50 - Spr '97 - p318+ [501+]
Hummel, Dietrich O - *Analysis of Surfactants*
r   SciTech - v20 - N '96 - p19 [51-250]
Hummel, Joan M - *Starting and Running a Nonprofit Organization. 2nd Ed.*
JEL - v35 - Mr '97 - p245+ [51-250]
Hummel, Richard - *Hunting and Fishing for Sport*
Aethlon - v13 - Spr '96 - p216+ [251-500]
Hummer, T R - *Walt Whitman in Hell*
Am - v175 - O 26 '96 - p24+ [501+]
The Humongous Book of Dinosaurs
c   PW - v244 - My 5 '97 - p211 [51-250]
Humphrey, Carol Sue - *The Press of the Young Republic 1783-1833*
Choice - v34 - Ap '97 - p1329 [51-250]
R&R Bk N - v12 - F '97 - p82 [51-250]
Humphrey, Caroline - *The Archetypal Actions of Ritual*
JR - v76 - O '96 - p673+ [501+]
Rel St Rev - v23 - Ap '97 - p103+ [501+]
Shamans and Elders
Choice - v34 - Ap '97 - p1381 [501+]
Humphrey, John T - *Pennsylvania Births Lebanon County 1714-1800*
r   EGH - v50 - N '96 - p185 [51-250]
Understanding and Using Baptismal Records
EGH - v50 - N '96 - p154 [51-250]
Humphrey, Nicholas - *Leaps of Faith*
Skeptic - v4 - 2 '96 - p104 [501+]
Soul Searching
Nature - v385 - Ja 9 '97 - p130 [1-50]
New Sci - v152 - D 21 '96 - p68 [1-50]
Humphrey, Watts S - *Managing Technical People*
SciTech - v21 - Mr '97 - p9 [51-250]
Humphrey, William - *Home from the Hill*
Bloom Rev - v16 - S '96 - p28 [51-250]
VQR - v72 - Aut '96 - p143* [1-50]

Humphreys, Emyr - *Unconditional Surrender*
KR - v64 - O 15 '96 - p1485+ [251-500]
PW - v243 - O 14 '96 - p66 [51-250]
Humphreys, J F - *A Course in Group Theory*
y   New Sci - v151 - S 28 '96 - p44+ [501+]
Humphreys, Leonard A - *The Way of the Heavenly Sword*
AHR - v101 - D '96 - p1598+ [501+]
Historian - v59 - Fall '96 - p173+ [501+]
Humphreys, Margaret - *Yellow Fever and the South*
J Urban H - v22 - My '96 - p531+ [501+]
Humphreys, Robert - *Sin, Organized Charity and the Poor Law in Victorian England*
AHR - v102 - F '97 - p107 [251-500]
Albion - v28 - Fall '96 - p515+ [501+]
Humphries, Barry - *Women in the Background*
Quad - v40 - My '96 - p78+ [501+]
WLT - v70 - Aut '96 - p1037 [51-250]
Humphries, Jane - *The Economics of Equal Opportunities*
Econ J - v107 - Ja '97 - p207+ [501+]
J Gov Info - v23 - S '96 - p645 [51-250]
Gender and Economics
ILR - v135 - 2 '96 - p239+ [501+]
Humphries, Jefferson - *The Future of Southern Letters*
Choice - v34 - Mr '97 - p1161 [51-250]
Humphries, Mary - *Fabric Reference*
r   SciTech - v20 - D '96 - p86 [51-250]
Humphries, Patrick - *Richard Thompson: Strange Affair*
Books - v10 - Je '96 - p8+ [51-250]
Richard Thompson: The Biography
BL - v93 - F 1 '97 - p918 [51-250]
KR - v65 - F 1 '97 - p198 [251-500]
PW - v244 - Ja 13 '97 - p68 [1-50]
Humphries, Steve - *A Man's World*
Econ - v339 - My 18 '96 - p3*+ [501+]
Hundert, E J - *The Enlightenment's Fable*
JHI - v57 - O '96 - p725+ [501+]
Hundert, Edward M - *Lessons from an Optical Illusion*
AJPsych - v153 - D '96 - p1649+ [501+]
Hundhausen, Felicitas - *Heinrich Schneider, Bibliothekar Und Gelehrter*
Lib - v18 - S '96 - p572 [51-250]
Hunefeldt, Christine - *Paying the Price of Freedom*
AHR - v102 - F '97 - p241+ [501+]
HAHR - v77 - F '97 - p149+ [51-250]
Historian - v58 - Sum '96 - p861+ [501+]
Hung, Chang-Tai - *War and Popular Culture*
HJAS - v56 - 2 '96 - p540+ [51-250]
Hungary: Poverty and Social Transfers
JEL - v34 - D '96 - p2060 [51-250]
Hungary: Structural Reforms for Sustainable Growth
J Gov Info - v23 - S '96 - p686 [51-250]
Hunger, Bill - *Clearcut: A Novel of Bio-Consequences*
LJ - v121 - O 15 '96 - p93 [51-250]
Hunn, Bruce D - *Fundamentals of Building Energy Dynamics*
Choice - v34 - F '97 - p993+ [51-250]
Hunnicutt, Benjamin Kline - *Kellogg's Six-Hour Day*
BWatch - v18 - Mr '97 - p5 [51-250]
Choice - v34 - My '97 - p1543+ [51-250]
NYTBR - v101 - D 22 '96 - p9 [501+]
PW - v243 - O 7 '96 - p67 [51-250]
Hunnisett, Jean - *Period Costume for Stage and Screen*
LJ - v121 - D '96 - p90 [51-250]
TCI - v30 - N '96 - p75 [501+]
Hunsberger, George R - *Between Gospel and Culture*
CC - v113 - O 16 '96 - p983 [51-250]
Hunsinger, Deborah Van Deusen - *Theology and Pastoral Counseling*
JR - v77 - Ap '97 - p322+ [501+]
Rel St Rev - v22 - O '96 - p336 [51-250]
Hunt, Alan - *Governance of the Consuming Passions*
Choice - v34 - Mr '97 - p1214 [51-250]
Hunt, Albert - *Peter Brook*
Choice - v34 - S '96 - p139 [51-250]
Hunt, Angela Elwell - *Dreamers*
y   SLJ - v42 - Ag '96 - p184 [51-250]
Gentle Touch
LJ - v122 - Ap 1 '97 - p78 [51-250]
The Proposal
BL - v93 - N 15 '96 - p571 [501+]
Hunt, Brian - *The Japanese Advantage?*
R&R Bk N - v11 - N '96 - p28 [51-250]
Hunt, Caroline C - *British Children's Writers since 1960. 1st Ser.*
r   ARBA - v28 - '97 - p427+ [51-250]
Hunt, Christopher - *Sparring with Charlie*
Econ - v340 - S 14 '96 - p7*+ [51-250]
Hunt, Conover - *JFK for a New Generation*
BWatch - v17 - N '96 - p2 [51-250]
PW - v243 - O 7 '96 - p68 [51-250]
y   SLJ - v43 - Ja '97 - p142 [51-250]

Hunt, D Trinidad - *The Operator's Manual for Planet Earth*
    PW - v243 - S 2 '96 - p112 [51-250]
Hunt, David - *The Magician's Tale*
    BL - v93 - Mr 15 '97 - p1204 [51-250]
    BL - v93 - Ap 1 '97 - p1268 [51-250]
    KR - v65 - Ap 1 '97 - p487 [251-500]
    LJ - v122 - Ap 1 '97 - p126 [51-250]
    PW - v244 - My 5 '97 - p195+ [51-250]
Hunt, Donald - *Great Names in Black College Sports*
  y BL - v93 - Ja '97 - p806 [51-250]
Hunt, E Howard - *Dragon Teeth*
    KR - v65 - F 15 '97 - p244+ [251-500]
    PW - v244 - Ap 21 '97 - p60+ [51-250]
Hunt, Earl - *Will We Be Smart Enough?*
    Per Psy - v49 - Aut '96 - p766+ [501+]
Hunt, Edwin S - *The Medieval Super-Companies*
    EHR - v112 - F '97 - p171+ [501+]
Hunt, Harry T - *On the Nature of Consciousness*
    AJPsych - v153 - S '96 - p1223 [501+]
Hunt, John M - *Petroleum Geochemistry and Geology. 2nd Ed.*
  y New Sci - v151 - S 28 '96 - p46 [501+]
Hunt, Jonathan - *Leif's Saga*
  c Ch BWatch - v6 - My '96 - p4 [1-50]
  c HB Guide - v7 - Fall '96 - p261 [51-250]
Hunt, Karen - *Equivocal Feminists*
    Choice - v34 - Mr '97 - p1220 [51-250]
Hunt, Lynn - *The Invention of Pornography*
    NYTBR - v102 - Ja 19 '97 - p28 [51-250]
Hunt, Margaret R - *The Middling Sort*
    Choice - v34 - My '97 - p1558 [51-250]
Hunt, Michael H - *Crises in U.S. Foreign Policy*
    AAPSS-A - v550 - Mr '97 - p172 [251-500]
    CR - v269 - S '96 - p157+ [501+]
    The Genesis of Chinese Communist Foreign Policy
    APSR - v91 - Mr '97 - p235 [501+]
    JPR - v34 - F '97 - p112 [251-500]
    Lyndon Johnson's War
  y BL - v92 - Ag '96 - p1877 [51-250]
  y BL - v92 - Ag '96 - p1890 [1-50]
    For Aff - v76 - My '97 - p133 [51-250]
    HRNB - v25 - Win '97 - p54 [251-500]
    Toward a History of Chinese Communist Foreign Relations 1920s-1960s
    Ch Rev Int - v3 - Fall '96 - p441+ [501+]
Hunt, Nan - *Like a Pebble in Your Shoe (Illus. by Beth Norling)*
  c Magpies - v11 - Jl '96 - p30+ [51-250]
Hunt, Peter - *International Companion Encyclopedia of Children's Literature*
  r CCB-B - v50 - F '97 - p230+ [501+]
  r Ch BWatch - v7 - Ja '97 - p6 [251-500]
  r Choice - v34 - F '97 - p944+ [51-250]
  r R&R Bk N - v12 - F '97 - p80 [51-250]
  r Sch Lib - v44 - N '96 - p177 [501+]
Hunt, Richard - *Murder Benign*
    Arm Det - v30 - Win '97 - p110+ [251-500]
    KR - v64 - Ag 15 '96 - p1190 [51-250]
Hunt, Richard H - *Helicobacter Pylori*
    SciTech - v21 - Mr '97 - p58 [51-250]
Hunt, Roderick - *My Home (Illus. by Cliff Wright)*
  c TES - Mr 7 '97 - p6* [501+]
Hunt, Sally - *Competition and Choice in Electricity*
    JEL - v34 - D '96 - p2089+ [51-250]
Hunt, Sylvia - *The Romance of the Rose and Its Medieval Readers*
    MP - v94 - Ag '96 - p67+ [501+]
Hunt, Thomas C - *Religious Higher Education in the United States*
  r ARBA - v28 - '97 - p139+ [51-250]
  r Choice - v34 - O '96 - p256+ [51-250]
Hunt, Tony - *Anglo-Norman Medicine*
    EHR - v112 - Ap '97 - p432 [51-250]
    Villon's Last Will
    TLS - Ja 24 '97 - p24 [501+]
Hunter, Allan - *The Therapeutic Uses of Writing*
    SciTech - v21 - Mr '97 - p54 [51-250]
Hunter, Anne - *Possum's Harvest Moon (Illus. by Anne Hunter)*
  c BL - v93 - S 1 '96 - p127 [51-250]
  c CBRS - v24 - Ag '96 - p159 [51-250]
  c CCB-B - v50 - O '96 - p64+ [51-250]
  c Ch BWatch - v6 - N '96 - p6 [1-50]
  c HB - v72 - S '96 - p579+ [51-250]
  c HB Guide - v8 - Spr '97 - p32 [51-250]
  c SLJ - v42 - Ag '96 - p122+ [51-250]
  c SLJ - v42 - D '96 - p30 [1-50]
Hunter, David - *Music Publishing and Collecting*
    LR - v45 - 7 '96 - p69+ [501+]

Hunter, Douglas - *War Games*
    Mac - v109 - D 16 '96 - p73 [51-250]
    Quill & Q - v62 - N '96 - p38+ [251-500]
Hunter, Evan - *Privileged Conversation (Whitener). Audio Version*
    LJ - v122 - Ja '97 - p172 [51-250]
Hunter, Fred - *Government Gay*
    KR - v65 - Ap 1 '97 - p506 [251-500]
Hunter, Fred W - *Ransom for Our Sins*
    Arm Det - v29 - Fall '96 - p494 [51-250]
    BL - v93 - S 1 '96 - p67+ [51-250]
    BWatch - v18 - F '97 - p6 [1-50]
Hunter, Jana - *Pet Detectives*
  c Magpies - v11 - Jl '96 - p28 [51-250]
Hunter, Jessie - *One, Two, Buckle My Shoe*
    KR - v65 - Mr 15 '97 - p405 [251-500]
    LJ - v122 - Ap 15 '97 - p117+ [51-250]
    PW - v244 - Ap 14 '97 - p54 [51-250]
    Trib Bks - My 18 '97 - p6 [51-250]
Hunter, Kendall - *Black Taxi*
  y BIC - v26 - F '97 - p33 [251-500]
Hunter, Kenneth W - *International Rights and Responsibilities for the Future*
    R&R Bk N - v12 - F '97 - p63 [51-250]
Hunter, M S - *The Final Bell*
    Aethlon - v13 - Spr '96 - p200+ [251-500]
Hunter, Mic - *The American Barbershop*
    HMR - Spr '97 - p11 [51-250]
Hunter, Michael Cyril William - *Robert Boyle Reconsidered*
    CH - v66 - Mr '97 - p127+ [501+]
    Science and the Shape of Orthodoxy
    Albion - v28 - Fall '96 - p489+ [501+]
    HT - v46 - D '96 - p52+ [501+]
Hunter, Mollie - *The Walking Stones*
  c Ch BWatch - v6 - Jl '96 - p3 [51-250]
  y SF Chr - v18 - O '96 - p79 [51-250]
Hunter, Richard - *Theocritus and the Archaeology of Greek Poetry*
    TLS - Ja 3 '97 - p13 [501+]
Hunter, Ruth - *A Part of the Ribbon*
  c Ch BWatch - v6 - N '96 - p3 [51-250]
  c SLJ - v43 - Mr '97 - p187 [51-250]
Hunter, Sally M - *Four Seasons of Corn (Illus. by Joe Allen)*
  c BL - v93 - F 1 '97 - p937 [51-250]
  c KR - v64 - D 15 '96 - p1798 [51-250]
  c SLJ - v43 - Mr '97 - p176 [51-250]
Hunter, Sara Hoagland - *The Unbreakable Code (Illus. by Julia Miner)*
  c HB Guide - v7 - Fall '96 - p261 [51-250]
  c SLJ - v42 - Ag '96 - p123 [51-250]
  c Smith - v27 - N '96 - p169 [1-50]
Hunter, Shelagh - *Harriet Martineau: The Poetics of Moralism*
    R&R Bk N - v12 - F '97 - p85 [51-250]
Hunter, Shireen T - *Central Asia since Independence*
    Choice - v34 - D '96 - p683 [51-250]
    R&R Bk N - v11 - N '96 - p13 [51-250]
    The Transcaucasus in Transition
    MEJ - v51 - Win '97 - p121+ [501+]
Hunter, Stephen - *Black Light*
    Arm Det - v29 - Fall '96 - p499+ [251-500]
    NYTBR - v101 - D 8 '96 - p94 [1-50]
    PW - v244 - Ap 14 '97 - p72 [1-50]
    Black Light (Bridges). Audio Version
    LJ - v121 - S 15 '96 - p112 [51-250]
Hunter, Susan - *Enforcing the Law*
    R&R Bk N - v11 - D '96 - p44 [51-250]
Hunter, Tera W - *To 'Joy My Freedom*
    KR - v65 - Ap 1 '97 - p522 [251-500]
Hunter-Cevera, Jennie C - *Maintaining Cultures for Biotechnology and Industry*
    SciTech - v20 - N '96 - p79 [51-250]
Huntington, Anna Seaton - *Making Waves*
    LJ - v121 - N 15 '96 - p67 [51-250]
    Yacht - v181 - Ap '97 - p14 [1-50]
Huntington, June - *Managing the Practice*
    SciTech - v20 - D '96 - p37 [51-250]

Huntington, Samuel P - *The Clash of Civilizations and the Remaking of World Order*
    BL - v93 - O 1 '96 - p318 [51-250]
    Bus W - N 25 '96 - p16+ [51-250]
    BW - v26 - D 1 '96 - p4+ [501+]
    BW - v26 - D 8 '96 - p7 [51-250]
    FEER - v160 - F 6 '97 - p39+ [501+]
    KR - v64 - S 1 '96 - p1295+ [251-500]
    LJ - v121 - O 1 '96 - p106 [51-250]
    Lon R Bks - v19 - Ap 24 '97 - p3+ [501+]
    Nat R - v48 - O 28 '96 - p69+ [501+]
    NYRB - v44 - Ja 9 '97 - p18+ [501+]
    NYTBR - v101 - D 1 '96 - p13 [501+]
    NYTLa - v146 - N 6 '96 - pC17 [501+]
    Obs - F 23 '97 - p16* [501+]
    PW - v243 - S 9 '96 - p69 [51-250]
    TLS - Ap 11 '97 - p10+ [501+]
    WSJ-MW - v78 - N 7 '96 - pA20 [501+]
Huntley, E D - *V.C. Andrews: A Critical Companion*
    SLMQ - v25 - Fall '96 - p64 [51-250]
Huot, Helene - *La Linguistique Appliquee Aujourd'hui*
    FR - v70 - D '96 - p361+ [251-500]
Huovinen, Veikko - *Pietari Suuri Hatun Polki*
    WLT - v70 - Aut '96 - p1001 [51-250]
Hupchick, Dennis P - *A Concise Historical Atlas of Eastern Europe*
  r ARBA - v28 - '97 - p203+ [51-250]
  r Choice - v34 - Ap '97 - p1310 [51-250]
Hupp, James R - *The 5 Minute Clinical Consult for Dental Professionals*
  r SciTech - v20 - D '96 - p53 [1-50]
Huq, A M Abdul - *World Librarianship*
  r CLW - v66 - Je '96 - p45+ [251-500]
  r LAR - v98 - Ag '96 - p427 [251-500]
Hurd, Jerrie - *Kate Burke Shoots the Old West*
    PW - v243 - D 2 '96 - p55 [51-250]
    Roundup M - v4 - Ap '97 - p27 [251-500]
Hurd, Thacher - *Art Dog (Illus. by Thacher Hurd)*
  c HB Guide - v7 - Fall '96 - p261 [51-250]
  c LATBR - Mr 24 '96 - p11 [51-250]
Hurley, Andrew - *Environmental Inequalities*
    AHR - v102 - F '97 - p218+ [51-250]
    JIH - v27 - Aut '96 - p357+ [501+]
Hurley, Donna W - *An Historical and Historiographical Commentary on Suetonius' Life of C. Caligula*
    CW - v89 - Jl '96 - p504+ [251-500]
Hurley, Judith Benn - *Savoring the Day*
    BL - v93 - N 15 '96 - p559 [51-250]
    LJ - v121 - D '96 - p132 [51-250]
    PW - v243 - N 18 '96 - p71+ [51-250]
Hurley, W N - *Neikirk, Newkirk, Nikirk and Related Families. Vol. 1*
  r EGH - v50 - N '96 - p194+ [51-250]
Hurrelmann, Klaus - *International Handbook of Public Health*
    Choice - v34 - Ap '97 - p1372 [51-250]
    SciTech - v20 - D '96 - p39 [51-250]
    Social Problems and Social Contexts in Adolescence
    Adoles - v31 - Win '96 - p993 [51-250]
    Readings - v11 - D '96 - p29+ [51-250]
Hurst, Christon J - *Manual of Environmental Microbiology*
    SciTech - v21 - Mr '97 - p43 [51-250]
Hurst, Ronald - *The Golden Rock*
    TLS - S 27 '96 - p32 [251-500]
Hurst, Steven - *The Carter Administration and Vietnam*
    Choice - v34 - F '97 - p1032 [51-250]
Hurst, W Jeffrey - *Automation in the Laboratory*
    J Chem Ed - v73 - Je '96 - pA136+ [51-250]
Hursthouse, Rosalind - *Virtues and Reasons*
    IPQ - v37 - Je '97 - p242+ [501+]
    Lon R Bks - v18 - S 5 '96 - p22+ [501+]
    TLS - Jl 19 '96 - p26+ [501+]
Hurston, Zora Neale - *The Complete Stories*
    NYTBR - v101 - S 15 '96 - p44 [51-250]
    Dust Tracks on a Road
    NYTBR - v101 - S 15 '96 - p44 [51-250]
    Their Eyes Were Watching God
    WestFolk - v55 - Spr '96 - p137+ [501+]
    Zora Neale Hurston: Stories (Joshua-Porter). Audio Version
    Bloom Rev - v17 - Ja '97 - p22 [51-250]
    CSM - v89 - Mr 27 '97 - pB2 [1-50]
Hurt, Henry, III - *Chasing the Dream*
    PW - v244 - Ap 14 '97 - p68 [51-250]
Hurt, R Douglas - *American Farms*
    Choice - v34 - My '97 - p1563 [51-250]
Hurten, Heinz - *Katholiken, Kirche Und Staat Als Problem Der Historie*
    CHR - v82 - Jl '96 - p485+ [251-500]

Hurth, Robert - *Wedding Photographer's Handbook*
Pet PM - v25 - Jl '96 - p8 [51-250]
Hurtig, Mel - *At Twilight in the Country*
BIC - v26 - Mr '97 - p25+ [501+]
Mac - v109 - D 16 '96 - p74 [501+]
Quill & Q - v62 - O '96 - p35 [251-500]
Hurwin, Davida Wills - *A Time for Dancing*
y Emerg Lib - v24 - S '96 - p24 [1-50]
Hurwitz, Hilda Abramson - *Dear Hope...Love, Grandma*
c LA - v73 - S '96 - p354 [251-500]
Hurwitz, Jane - *High Performance through Effective Budgeting*
y Cur R - v36 - N '96 - p13 [51-250]
y SLJ - v42 - O '96 - p156 [51-250]
y VOYA - v19 - F '97 - p348 [251-500]
Hurwitz, Johanna - *Birthday Surprises*
c LA - v73 - O '96 - p429 [51-250]
The Down and Up Fall (Illus. by Gail Owens)
c CCB-B - v50 - S '96 - p16 [51-250]
c Ch BWatch - v6 - N '96 - p3 [51-250]
c HB Guide - v8 - Spr '97 - p68 [51-250]
c SLJ - v42 - S '96 - p202 [51-250]
Even Stephen
c HB Guide - v7 - Fall '96 - p293 [51-250]
y Par Ch - v20 - O '96 - p11 [1-50]
Spring Break (Illus. by Karen Dugan)
c CCB-B - v50 - Ap '97 - p285 [51-250]
c PW - v244 - Mr 3 '97 - p76 [51-250]
Hurwitz, Sue - *High Performance through Effective Scheduling*
y Cur R - v36 - N '96 - p13 [51-250]
y SLJ - v42 - D '96 - p146 [51-250]
y VOYA - v19 - F '97 - p348 [251-500]
Husain, Kamran - *JavaScript Developer's Resource*
SciTech - v21 - Mr '97 - p7 [51-250]
Husain, Shahrukh - *Handsome Heroines*
y BL - v93 - O 1 '96 - p322 [51-250]
LJ - v121 - O 1 '96 - p88 [51-250]
PW - v243 - S 16 '96 - p78 [51-250]
Husband, Janet - *Sequels: An Annotated Guide to Novels in Series. 2nd Ed.*
r RQ - v36 - Win '96 - p214 [51-250]
Husband, Timothy B - *The Luminous Image*
BM - v138 - N '96 - p755+ [501+]
Husbands, Christopher - *What Is History Teaching?*
R&R Bk N - v11 - D '96 - p7 [51-250]
Huse, Roy - *Who Else Writes Like...?. 2nd Ed.*
r LAR - v99 - Mr '97 - p160 [51-250]
r Sch Lib - v45 - F '97 - p54 [51-250]
Huss, Judson - *River of Mirrors*
BWatch - v18 - F '97 - p4 [51-250]
Hussainmiya, B A - *Sultan Omar Ali Saifuddin III and Britain*
Choice - v34 - Ja '97 - p853 [51-250]
Hussey, D E - *The Implementation Challenge*
Choice - v34 - F '97 - p1008 [51-250]
Hussey, Mark - *Virginia Woolf A to Z*
r ELT - v39 - 3 '96 - p384+ [501+]
r RMR - v50 - 2 '96 - p169+ [501+]
Hussey, Stanley - *The English Language*
Col Comp - v47 - O '96 - p438+ [51-250]
Huston, Nancy - *The Goldberg Variations*
Quill & Q - v62 - D '96 - p35 [501+]
Slow Emergencies
Quill & Q - v62 - D '96 - p35 [501+]
Huston-Somerville, Mary - *Networks and Resource Sharing in the 21st Century*
LR - v45 - 7 '96 - p70+ [501+]
Hustvedt, Siri - *The Enchantment of Lily Dahl*
Ent W - N 22 '96 - p130+ [51-250]
NY - v72 - D 2 '96 - p115 [51-250]
NYTBR - v101 - O 20 '96 - p30 [501+]
Obs - N 24 '96 - p17* [501+]
TLS - N 29 '96 - p22 [501+]
VV - v41 - O 8 '96 - p49+ [501+]
Woman's J - Ja '97 - p13 [51-250]
WSJ-MW - v77 - S 20 '96 - pA12 [251-500]
The Enchantment of Lily Dahl (Hustvedt). Audio Version
PW - v243 - N 4 '96 - p32 [51-250]
Huszar, Karen - *Meet Matt and Roxy (Illus. by Susan Huszar)*
c Quill & Q - v62 - S '96 - p73 [251-500]
Huszczo, Gregory E - *Tools for Team Excellence*
HR Mag - v41 - S '96 - p138 [51-250]
Hutcheon, Linda, 1947- - *Irony's Edge*
Essays CW - Spr '96 - p151+ [501+]
QJS - v82 - N '96 - p428+ [501+]
Opera: Desire, Disease, Death
Choice - v34 - S '96 - p137 [51-250]
ON - v61 - O '96 - p66 [501+]

Hutcheon, Pat Duffy - *Leaving the Cave*
New Sci - v153 - Mr 1 '97 - p49 [51-250]
R&R Bk N - v11 - N '96 - p23 [51-250]
Hutcherson, Hilda - *Having Your Baby*
LJ - v122 - Ap 15 '97 - p108 [51-250]
Hutcheson, Polly - *Directory of College Cooperative Education Programs*
r ARBA - v28 - '97 - p141 [251-500]
yr BL - v93 - Ja '97 - p769 [1-50]
r Choice - v34 - F '97 - p942 [51-250]
r R&R Bk N - v11 - D '96 - p54 [51-250]
Hutchings, Janet - *Once upon a Crime II*
Arm Det - v29 - Fall '96 - p469+ [51-250]
Hutchings, Merry - *Study Skills*
TES - D 13 '96 - p43 [51-250]
Hutchings, Raymond - *Historical Dictionary of Albania*
r ARBA - v28 - '97 - p60 [51-250]
Hutchings, W B - *Thomas Gray: Contemporary Essays*
MLR - v91 - Jl '96 - p703+ [501+]
Hutchins, Elizabeth - *Operation Teddy (Illus. by Liesbeth Pockett)*
c Magpies - v11 - S '96 - p29 [51-250]
Hutchins, Hazel - *Tess (Illus. by Ruth Ohi)*
c Ch Bk News - v19 - Spr '96 - p24 [251-500]
Within a Painted Past (Illus. by Ruth Ohi)
y Can CL - v22 - Sum '96 - p89+ [501+]
Yancy and Bear (Illus. by Ruth Ohi)
c BIC - v25 - O '96 - p32 [251-500]
c Quill & Q - v62 - O '96 - p46+ [251-500]
Hutchins, Pat - *Curse of the Egyptian Mummy. Audio Version*
c Ch BWatch - v6 - O '96 - p2 [1-50]
Llaman A La Puerta. Book and Audio Version
c SLJ - v43 - Ja '97 - p70 [51-250]
Shrinking Mouse (Illus. by Pat Hutchins)
c BL - v93 - F 15 '97 - p1026 [51-250]
c HB - v73 - My '97 - p309 [51-250]
c PW - v244 - F 24 '97 - p91 [51-250]
Titch and Daisy (Illus. by Pat Hutchins)
c HB Guide - v7 - Fall '96 - p261 [51-250]
c JB - v60 - D '96 - p233 [51-250]
Hutchins, Robert Maynard - *The Higher Learning in America*
ES - v27 - Fall '96 - p227+ [501+]
ES - v27 - Sum '96 - p111+ [501+]
Hutchinson, Allan C - *The Law School Book*
Quill & Q - v62 - D '96 - p29 [251-500]
Hutchinson, Earl Ofari - *The Assassination of the Black Male Image*
LJ - v121 - N 1 '96 - p86 [1-50]
Betrayed: A History of Presidential Failure to Protect Black Lives
Choice - v34 - S '96 - p194+ [51-250]
Blacks and Reds
AHR - v101 - D '96 - p1641+ [501+]
Soc - v34 - Mr '97 - p93+ [501+]
Hutchinson, George - *The Harlem Renaissance in Black and White*
TLS - Ja 10 '97 - p18 [501+]
Hutchinson, Gloria - *A Retreat with Gerard Manley Hopkins and Hildegard of Bingen*
CLW - v66 - Je '96 - p32 [51-250]
Hutchinson, John F - *Champions of Charity*
Choice - v34 - D '96 - p663 [51-250]
Hutchinson, Robert - *Their Kingdom Come*
Books - v11 - Ap '97 - p20 [51-250]
Hutchinson, Scott - *Inside ArcView*
SciTech - v20 - S '96 - p1 [51-250]
Hutchinson, William R - *Many Are Chosen*
Rel St Rev - v23 - Ja '97 - p83 [51-250]
Hutchinson History Library. Electronic Media Version
HT - v46 - D '96 - p48 [51-250]
The Hutchinson Illustrated Encyclopedia of British History
r HT - v46 - O '96 - p59 [1-50]
Hutchinson Multimedia Encyclopedia 1995. Electronic Media Version
cr Magpies - v11 - My '96 - p51+ [51-250]
Hutchison, Don - *The Great Pulp Heroes*
Arm Det - v29 - Fall '96 - p491 [251-500]
SF Chr - v18 - O '96 - p82 [1-50]
Northern Frights 3
SF Chr - v18 - O '96 - p80 [1-50]
Hutchison, Gillian - *Medieval Ships and Shipping*
EHR - v112 - Ap '97 - p445+ [501+]
Hutchison, Robert - *Meteorites*
RocksMiner - v72 - Ja '97 - p67+ [501+]
Hutchison, Sandra - *Chinese Brushstrokes*
Quill & Q - v62 - Ag '96 - p38 [251-500]

Hutchisson, James M - *The Rise of Sinclair Lewis 1920-1930*
Choice - v34 - D '96 - p613 [51-250]
Huth, Angela - *Casting a Spell and Other Poems (Illus. by Jane Ray)*
c Bks Keeps - v100 - S '96 - p12 [51-250]
Land Girls
y BL - v93 - Ap 1 '97 - p1292 [1-50]
NYTBR - v101 - D 8 '96 - p80 [1-50]
y SLJ - v42 - O '96 - p162 [51-250]
Huth, Holly Young - *Darkfright (Illus. by Jenny Stow)*
c BL - v93 - N 1 '96 - p507 [51-250]
c CBRS - v25 - Win '97 - p63 [51-250]
c CCB-B - v50 - Ap '97 - p174 [51-250]
c HB Guide - v8 - Spr '97 - p32 [51-250]
c SLJ - v43 - Ja '97 - p84 [51-250]
Huth, Paul K - *Standing Your Ground*
Choice - v34 - O '96 - p356+ [51-250]
Hutnyk, John - *The Rumour of Calcutta*
Choice - v34 - My '97 - p1541 [51-250]
Huttar, Charles A - *The Rhetoric of Vision*
Choice - v34 - Ap '97 - p1339 [51-250]
Hutter, Ulrich - *Martin Luther Und Die Reformation In Ostdeutschland Und Sudosteuropa*
CH - v66 - Mr '97 - p112+ [501+]
Hutterer, Robert - *Client-Centered and Experiental Psychotherapy*
SciTech - v20 - D '96 - p45 [51-250]
Huttner, Harry J M - *The Multilevel Design*
HER - v66 - Win '96 - p892 [51-250]
Huttner, Hilary - *Mystical Delights*
Rapport - v19 - 5 '96 - p40 [251-500]
Huttner, Markus - *Britische Presse Und Nationalsozialistischer Kirchenkampf*
CHR - v83 - Ja '97 - p128+ [501+]
Hutto, Joe - *Illumination in the Flatwoods*
Smith - v27 - Ja '97 - p103 [501+]
Hutton, Frankie - *Outsiders in 19th-Century Press History*
AL - v68 - S '96 - p665 [51-250]
Choice - v34 - S '96 - p117 [51-250]
Hutton, John G - *Neo-Impressionism and the Search for Solid Ground*
FR - v70 - O '96 - p131+ [501+]
JMH - v68 - S '96 - p704+ [501+]
Hutton, Ronald - *The Rise and Fall of Merry England*
EHR - v111 - N '96 - p1274+ [501+]
JIH - v27 - Win '97 - p507+ [501+]
The Stations of the Sun
Lon R Bks - v19 - Mr 6 '97 - p34 [501+]
TLS - O 11 '96 - p4 [501+]
Hutton, Warwick - *The Trojan Horse (Illus. by Warwick Hutton)*
c SLJ - v42 - N '96 - p39 [1-50]
Hutton, Will - *The State We're In*
TES - D 27 '96 - p17 [51-250]
Huxford, Sharon - *The Collector's Encyclopedia of Brush-McCoy Pottery*
r Ant & CM - v101 - Ja '97 - p45 [51-250]
Huxford's Collectible Advertising
r Ant & CM - v101 - Ja '97 - p44 [51-250]
Huxford's Old Book Value Guide. 8th Ed.
r ARBA - v28 - '97 - p357+ [51-250]
Huxley, Aldous - *Aldous Huxley's Hearst Essays*
Clio - v25 - Spr '96 - p293+ [501+]
Antic Hay
PW - v244 - Mr 17 '97 - p81 [1-50]
Between the Wars
Clio - v25 - Spr '96 - p293+ [501+]
Brave New World
MA - v38 - Fall '96 - p332+ [501+]
Point Counter Point
LJ - v122 - F 15 '97 - p166 [51-250]
PW - v243 - S 2 '96 - p122 [1-50]
Huxley, Mike - *Twentieth Century Performance Reader*
TCI - v30 - O '96 - p59 [51-250]
Huxtable, Ada Louise - *The Unreal America*
LATBR - Ap 6 '97 - p6 [501+]
LJ - v122 - Ap 1 '97 - p89 [51-250]
NYTBR - v102 - Ap 6 '97 - p13 [501+]
PW - v244 - F 24 '97 - p72+ [51-250]
Trib Bks - My 11 '97 - p6+ [501+]
WSJ-Cent - v99 - Ap 9 '97 - pA12 [501+]
Huxtable, Ryan J - *Taurine 2*
SciTech - v21 - Mr '97 - p43 [51-250]
Huyen, Chau Nu - *Vuot Bien*
BL - v93 - S 1 '96 - p70 [51-250]
Huygens, Daniel Johannes - *Opposite the Lion's Den*
Aust Bk R - Je '96 - p25 [251-500]
Huyghe, Patrick - *The Anomalist*
Skeptic - v4 - '96 - p106 [51-250]

Huyler, Stephen P - *Gifts of Earth*
    Ceram Mo - v44 - S '96 - p28 [251-500]
Huynh, Sanh Thong - *An Anthology of Vietnamese Poems*
    Choice - v34 - Ja '97 - p790 [251-500]
    TranslRevS - v2 - D '96 - p1 [51-250]
Huynh, Van Phu - *O Mot Noi De Tim Thay Thien Duong*
    BL - v93 - S 1 '96 - p70 [51-250]
Huyssen, Andreas - *Twilight Memories*
    Ger Q - v70 - Win '97 - p69+ [501+]
Hviding, Edvard - *Guardians of Marovo Lagoon*
    Choice - v34 - F '97 - p1006 [51-250]
Hvinden, Bjorn - *Divided against Itself*
    Soc Ser R - v71 - Mr '97 - p167 [51-250]
Hwang, Jennie S - *Modern Solder Technology for Competitive Electronics Manufacturing*
    r SciTech - v20 - S '96 - p57 [51-250]
Hwang, Ned H C - *Fundamentals of Hydraulic Engineering Systems. 3rd Ed.*
    SciTech - v20 - N '96 - p66 [51-250]
Hyatt, Brenda - *Auriculas: Their Care and Cultivation*
    BL - v93 - O 1 '96 - p314 [51-250]
Hyatt, Kathryn - *Marilyn: Story of a Woman*
    ABR - v18 - O '96 - p13 [501+]
Hyatt, Vera Lawrence - *Race, Discourse, and the Origin of the Americas*
    W&M Q - v53 - Jl '96 - p641+ [501+]
Hybels, Bill - *The God You're Looking For*
    PW - v244 - Ap 14 '97 - p70 [51-250]
Hyde, Catherine Ryan - *Funerals for Horses*
    PW - v244 - Ap 28 '97 - p52 [51-250]
Hyde, Christopher - *A Gathering of Saints*
    KR - v64 - My 1 '96 - p624 [251-500]
    Rapport - v19 - 5 '96 - p34 [251-500]
    A Gathering of Saints (Page). Audio Version
    y Kliatt - v30 - N '96 - p40 [51-250]
Hyde, Dayton - *Yamsi: A Year in the Life of a Wilderness Ranch*
    LJ - v122 - F 15 '97 - p166 [51-250]
Hyde, Dudley - *Betty and Me*
    Aust Bk R - Ag '96 - p67 [1-50]
Hyde, Margaret O - *AIDS: What Does It Mean to You?*
    y HB Guide - v7 - Fall '96 - p348 [51-250]
    Know about Mental Illness
    c BL - v93 - S 1 '96 - p116 [51-250]
    c HB Guide - v7 - Fall '96 - p348 [1-50]
    The Sexual Abuse of Children and Adolescents
    y BL - v93 - F 15 '97 - p1012+ [51-250]
    y KR - v64 - D 15 '96 - p1798 [51-250]
    y SLJ - v43 - Mr '97 - p202 [51-250]
Hyde, Samuel C - *Pistols and Politics*
    Choice - v34 - My '97 - p1563 [51-250]
Hyde, Thomas E - *Conservative Management of Sports Injuries*
    SciTech - v21 - Mr '97 - p69 [51-250]
Hyden, Goran - *Governance and Politics in Africa*
    WP - v49 - O '96 - p92+ [501+]
Hyde-Price, Adrian - *The International Politics of East Central Europe*
    Choice - v34 - O '96 - p357 [51-250]
    Parameters - v27 - Spr '97 - p169+ [501+]
Hydrick, Janie - *Parent's Guide to Literacy for the 21st Century*
    Learning - v25 - S '96 - p14 [51-250]
Hyegyonggung Hong Ssi - *The Memoirs of Lady Hyegyong*
    TranslRevS - v2 - D '96 - p9 [51-250]
    VV - v41 - O 8 '96 - p50+ [501+]
Hyland, Ann - *The Medieval Warhorse from Byzantium to the Crusades*
    EHR - v112 - Ap '97 - p430+ [501+]
Hyland, Drew A - *Finitude and Transcendence in the Platonic Dialogues*
    Rel St Rev - v23 - Ja '97 - p61 [51-250]
    RM - v49 - Je '96 - p928+ [501+]
Hyland, Gary - *White Crane Spreads Wings*
    Quill & Q - v62 - S '96 - p66 [251-500]
Hyland, Pat - *Presidential Libraries and Museums*
    r J Gov Info - v24 - Ja '97 - p71+ [501+]
    r Pres SQ - v26 - Sum '96 - p908 [51-250]
Hyland, Paul - *Backwards out of the Big World*
    Spec - v277 - S 7 '96 - p35+ [501+]
    TLS - O 11 '96 - p36 [501+]
Hyland, Peter - *An Introduction to Shakespeare*
    Choice - v34 - F '97 - p966 [51-250]
Hyland, Sara - *I Call to the Eye of the Mind*
    ILS - v16 - Spr '97 - p19 [501+]
Hyland, Sue - *Enquire Within*
    r Sch Lib - v45 - F '97 - p53 [51-250]
Hylson-Smith, Kenneth - *High Churchmanship in the Church of England*
    Theol St - v57 - Mr '96 - p150+ [501+]

Hylton, Sara - *Melissa*
    LJ - v121 - N 15 '96 - p88 [51-250]
    PW - v243 - O 21 '96 - p71 [51-250]
Hyman, Leonard S - *The Privatization of Public Utilities*
    En Jnl - v17 - 4 '96 - p163+ [501+]
Hyman, Paul E - *Pediatric GI Problems*
    SciTech - v21 - Mr '97 - p64 [51-250]
Hyman, Paula E - *Gender and Assimilation in Modern Jewish History*
    AHR - v102 - F '97 - p87 [501+]
Hymer, Dian - *Starting Out*
    BL - v93 - F 15 '97 - p983+ [51-250]
    LJ - v122 - Mr 15 '97 - p71 [51-250]
    PW - v244 - Ja 27 '97 - p100 [51-250]
Hymes, Dell - *Ethnography, Linguistics, Narrative Inequality*
    R&R Bk N - v11 - N '96 - p62 [51-250]
Hynd, Noel - *Rage of Spirits*
    BL - v93 - F 15 '97 - p1003 [51-250]
    KR - v65 - Ja 1 '97 - p11+ [251-500]
    LJ - v122 - F 1 '97 - p105 [51-250]
    PW - v244 - Ja 20 '97 - p396 [251-500]
Hyne, Anthony - *David Jones: A Fusilier at the Front*
    Quad - v40 - D '96 - p85+ [501+]
Hynes, H Patricia - *A Patch of Eden*
    CSM - v89 - F 27 '97 - pB3 [251-500]
    Ms - v7 - S '96 - p83 [1-50]
Hynes, James - *Publish and Perish*
    LJ - v122 - Ap 15 '97 - p122 [51-250]
    PW - v244 - My 5 '97 - p195 [51-250]
Hynes, Maureen - *Rough Skin*
    BIC - v25 - D '96 - p24+ [501+]
Hynes, Samuel - *The Soldiers' Tale*
    y BL - v93 - D 15 '96 - p695 [51-250]
    BW - v27 - Mr 30 '97 - p5 [501+]
    KR - v64 - N 1 '96 - p1583 [251-500]
    LJ - v121 - D '96 - p116 [51-250]
    NYTBR - v102 - Ap 13 '97 - p6+ [501+]
    PW - v243 - N 25 '96 - p64 [51-250]
    WSJ-Cent - v99 - Mr 27 '97 - pA20 [501+]
Hynes, William H - *Mythical Trickster Figures*
    JPC - v29 - Spr '96 - p237+ [51-250]
Hynson, Jerry M - *Maryland Freedom Papers. Vol. 1*
    NGSQ - v84 - D '96 - p317 [51-250]
Hyppolite, Jean - *Introduction to Hegel's Philosophy of History*
    Choice - v34 - Mr '97 - p1175 [51-250]
Hyppolite, Joanne - *Seth and Samona (Illus. by Colin Bootman)*
    c PW - v243 - D 30 '96 - p68 [51-250]
Hyslop, Lois Boe - *Charles Baudelaire Revisited*
    FR - v70 - F '97 - p469+ [501+]

I

I.A. Bunin I Russkaia Literatura XX Veka
  WLT - v70 - Sum '96 - p721 [251-500]
I Know an Old Lady Who Swallowed a Fly (Illus. by Glen Rounds)
  c Par Ch - v20 - N '96 - p3 [1-50]
I Say, I Play!
  c HB Guide - v7 - Fall '96 - p240 [51-250]
Iaccino, James F - *Psychological Reflections on Cinematic Terror*
  JPC - v30 - Fall '96 - p207+ [251-500]
Iacobucci, Dawn - *Networks in Marketing*
  Choice - v34 - Mr '97 - p1205 [51-250]
  R&R Bk N - v11 - D '96 - p34 [51-250]
Iacobucci, Edward - *Value for Money*
  JEL - v35 - Mr '97 - p253+ [51-250]
Iacocca, Lee - *I Gotta Tell You*
  QJS - v83 - F '97 - p130+ [501+]
Iacono, Frank P - *Rhode Island Public Library Trustees Handbook. Rev. and Updated Ed.*
  J Gov Info - v23 - S '96 - p594 [51-250]
IAHR International Symposium on Stochastic Hydraulics (7th: 1996: Mackay, Queensland, Australia) - *Stochastic Hydraulics 1996*
  SciTech - v20 - N '96 - p66 [51-250]
Iakovou, Takis - *So Dear to Wicked Men*
  KR - v64 - S 15 '96 - p1357 [51-250]
  LJ - v121 - N 1 '96 - p111 [51-250]
  PW - v243 - S 23 '96 - p59 [51-250]
Iannucci, Amilcare A - *Dante E La Bella Scola Della Poesia*
  MLR - v91 - Jl '96 - p749+ [501+]
  Specu - v71 - O '96 - p962+ [501+]
Iannucci, Armando - *Facts and Fancies*
  Books - v11 - Ap '97 - p9 [501+]
  Obs - Mr 2 '97 - p17* [251-500]
IArema, Volodymyr - *Dyvnyi Svit Ikon*
  BL - v93 - N 15 '96 - p577 [1-50]
Iatrides, John O - *Greece at the Crossroads*
  PSQ - v111 - Fall '96 - p555+ [501+]
Ibbotson, Eva - *Dial a Ghost (Illus. by Kerstin Meyer)*
  y JB - v60 - O '96 - p202+ [251-500]
  c Sch Lib - v44 - N '96 - p151 [51-250]
  The Haunting of Hiram (Scales). Audio Version
  c BL - v93 - N 1 '96 - p522 [51-250]
Ibnlfassi, Laila - *African Francophone Writing*
  R&R Bk N - v12 - F '97 - p83 [51-250]
Ibrahim, Saad Eddin - *Egypt, Islam and Democracy*
  Choice - v34 - Ap '97 - p1410 [51-250]
ICD-9-CM: International Classification of Diseases. 9th Revision, 5th Ed.
  SciTech - v21 - Mr '97 - p48 [51-250]
ICD-9-CM: International Classification of Diseases, 9th Revision, Clinical Modification, Fifth Edition, Color Coded, Volumes 1, 2, and 3, 1997. Hospital Ed.
  r SciTech - v21 - Mr '97 - p48 [51-250]
Ichida, Takashi - *Product Design Review*
  SciTech - v20 - S '96 - p63 [51-250]
Ichihashi, Yamato - *Morning Glory, Evening Shadow*
  LJ - v121 - D '96 - p118 [51-250]
  PW - v243 - O 21 '96 - p65 [51-250]
ICOLD Symposium on Reservoirs in River Basin Development (1995: Oslo, Norway) - *Reservoirs in River Basin Development. Vol. 2*
  SciTech - v20 - S '96 - p51 [51-250]
Icon Thoughtstyle Magazine
  p LJ - v122 - My 1 '97 - p43 [51-250]
I'd Like to Be a Chemist
  c Ch BWatch - v6 - S '96 - p8 [1-50]
I'd Like to Be a Meteorologist
  c Ch BWatch - v6 - S '96 - p8 [1-50]

I'd Like to Be a Physicist
  c Ch BWatch - v6 - S '96 - p8 [1-50]
I'd Like to Be a Zoologist
  c Ch BWatch - v6 - S '96 - p8 [1-50]
The Ideas That Changed the World. Electronic Media Version
  r LJ - v122 - My 1 '97 - p147 [51-250]
Idel, Moshe - *Hasidism: Between Ecstacy and Magic*
  JR - v77 - Ja '97 - p190+ [501+]
  Mystical Union in Judaism, Christianity and Islam
  MEJ - v51 - Win '97 - p155 [51-250]
Idemon, Richard - *The Magic Thread*
  BWatch - v17 - S '96 - p11 [1-50]
  Horoscope - v63 - F '97 - p14+ [501+]
Idilbi, Ulfat - *Sabriya*
  KR - v65 - My 1 '97 - p678 [51-250]
Idle, Eric - *The Quite Remarkable Adventures of the Owl and the Pussycat (Illus. by Edward Lear)*
  c KR - v64 - O 1 '96 - p1468 [251-500]
IEEE Computer Society Conference on Computer Vision and Pattern Recognition (1996: San Francisco, CA) - *Computer Vision and Pattern Recognition*
  SciTech - v20 - D '96 - p66 [1-50]
IEEE Infocom '96. Vols. 1-3
  SciTech - v20 - S '96 - p55 [51-250]
IEEE Information Visualization Symposium (2nd: 1996: San Francisco, CA) - *IEEE Symposium on Information Visualization '96*
  SciTech - v21 - Mr '97 - p80 [51-250]
IEEE International Conference on Engineering of Complex Computer Systems (2nd: 1996: Montreal, Quebec) - *Second IEEE International Conference on Engineering of Complex Computer Systems*
  SciTech - v21 - Mr '97 - p93 [51-250]
IEEE International Symposium on High Performance Distributed Computing (5th: 1996: Syracuse, NY) - *Proceedings of the 1996 International Symposium on High Performance Distributed Computing*
  SciTech - v20 - D '96 - p6 [51-250]
IEEE International Workshop on IDDQ Testing (1996: Washington, D.C.) - *Digest of Papers*
  SciTech - v21 - Mr '97 - p90 [51-250]
IEEE International Workshop on Rapid System Prototyping (7th: 1996: Thessaloniki, Greece) - *Rapid System Prototyping*
  SciTech - v20 - S '96 - p48 [51-250]
IEEE International Workshop on Systems Management (2nd: 1996: Toronto, Ont.) - *Proceedings of the IEEE Second International Workshop on Systems Management, June 19-21, 1996, Toronto, Ontario, Canada*
  SciTech - v20 - D '96 - p14 [51-250]
IEEE SP Workshop on Statistical Signal and Array Processing (8th: 1996: Corfu, Greece) - *8th IEEE Signal Processing Workshop on Statistical Signal and Array Processing*
  SciTech - v21 - Mr '97 - p80 [51-250]
IEEE Symposium on Security and Privacy (1996: Oakland, CA) - *Security and Privacy*
  SciTech - v20 - N '96 - p6 [51-250]
IEEE VLSI Test Symposium (14th: 1996: Princeton, N.J.) - *14th IEEE VLSI Test Symposium*
  SciTech - v20 - N '96 - p75 [51-250]
Iesan, Dorin - *Thermoelastic Deformations*
  SciTech - v21 - Mr '97 - p78 [51-250]
IFAC/IFORS/IMAC Symposium Large Scale Systems (7th: 1995: London, England) - *Large Scale Systems: Theory and Applications 1995. Vols. 1-2*
  SciTech - v20 - D '96 - p59 [51-250]

IFCIS International Conference Cooperative Information Systems (1st: 1996: Brussells, Belgium) - *Cooperative Information Systems*
  SciTech - v20 - S '96 - p8 [51-250]
IFLA Round Table on Research in Reading (1993: Haifa, Israel). Mid-Term Seminar - *Reading, a Comparative View*
  LQ - v67 - Ap '97 - p194+ [501+]
Iggers, Jeremy - *The Garden of Eating*
  Choice - v34 - F '97 - p996 [51-250]
  Utne R - N '96 - p93 [51-250]
Iggers, Wilma Abeles - *Women of Prague*
  Slav R - v55 - Fall '96 - p667+ [501+]
Iglehart, Alfreda P - *Social Services and the Ethnic Community*
  Soc Ser R - v70 - S '96 - p493+ [501+]
Igliori, Paolo - *American Magus Harry Smith*
  VV - v41 - O 15 '96 - p45 [501+]
Ignatiev, Noel - *How the Irish Became White*
  Bl S - v26 - Sum '96 - p65 [51-250]
  CS - v25 - N '96 - p749+ [501+]
  NEQ - v69 - D '96 - p667+ [501+]
Ignatius, of Loyola, Saint - *Personal Writings*
  BW - v27 - F 9 '97 - p12 [51-250]
Ignatius, David - *The Bank of Fear (Guidall). Audio Version*
  CSM - v89 - Mr 27 '97 - pB2 [1-50]
  y Kliatt - v30 - S '96 - p42+ [51-250]
  A Firing Offense
  BL - v93 - Mr 1 '97 - p1068 [251-500]
  KR - v65 - Mr 15 '97 - p405 [251-500]
  LJ - v122 - Ap 1 '97 - p126 [51-250]
  PW - v244 - Mr 17 '97 - p74+ [51-250]
  Time - v149 - My 19 '97 - p95 [501+]
Ignatow, David - *I Have a Name*
  BL - v93 - S 1 '96 - p57 [51-250]
Igus, Toyomi - *Two Mrs. Gibsons (Illus. by Daryl Wells)*
  c Ch BWatch - v6 - My '96 - p4 [1-50]
  c HB Guide - v7 - Fall '96 - p261 [51-250]
  c RT - v50 - Ap '97 - p590 [51-250]
  c SLJ - v42 - O '96 - p98+ [51-250]
Ihimaera, Witi - *Te Ao Marama. Vol. 5*
  Meanjin - v55 - '96 - p704+ [501+]
Iida, Deborah - *Middle Son*
  BL - v93 - Ap 1 '97 - p1285 [1-50]
  CC - v113 - N 20 '96 - p1169 [51-250]
  LJ - v121 - S 15 '96 - p124 [51-250]
  y SLJ - v43 - Ja '97 - p140 [51-250]
Ikeda, Stewart David - *What the Scarecrow Said*
  Choice - v34 - F '97 - p966+ [51-250]
  KR - v64 - My 1 '96 - p624+ [251-500]
  Rapport - v19 - 5 '96 - p22 [51-250]
Ikegami, Eiko - *The Taming of the Samurai*
  HJAS - v56 - 2 '96 - p535+ [501+]
  J Soc H - v30 - Fall '96 - p282+ [501+]
  TLS - O 25 '96 - p13 [251-500]
Ikels, Charlotte - *The Return of the God of Wealth*
  Choice - v34 - D '96 - p665 [51-250]
Ikenberry, G John - *American Foreign Policy*
  For Aff - v76 - Mr '97 - p184+ [251-500]
Ilan, Amitzur - *The Origin of the Arab-Israeli Arms Race*
  Choice - v34 - D '96 - p674 [51-250]
  MEJ - v51 - Spr '97 - p283+ [501+]
  MEQ - v4 - Mr '97 - p90+ [51-250]
Ilan, Tal - *Jewish Women in Greco-Roman Palestine*
  JR - v77 - Ja '97 - p123+ [501+]
  Rel St Rev - v23 - Ja '97 - p88 [51-250]
Ilarion, Metropolitan of Winnipeg and Canada - *Dokhristiians'ki Viruvannia Ukrains'koho Narodu*
  BL - v93 - N 15 '96 - p577 [1-50]

Ilatovskaya, Tatiana - *Master Drawings Rediscovered*
Choice - v34 - Ap '97 - p1324 [51-250]
LJ - v122 - Ap 1 '97 - p89+ [51-250]
Obs - Ja 19 '97 - p16* [51-250]

Iles, Francis - *Malice Aforethought (Montague). Audio Version*
y Kliatt - v30 - S '96 - p50 [51-250]

Iles, Greg - *Mortal Fear*
BL - v93 - D 15 '96 - p692 [51-250]
KR - v64 - D 1 '96 - p1692 [251-500]
LJ - v122 - Ja '97 - p146 [51-250]
NYTBR - v102 - F 16 '97 - p28 [51-250]
PW - v243 - D 9 '96 - p59 [51-250]

Ilie, Paul - *The Age of Minerva. Vols. 1-2*
Isis - v87 - S '96 - p551 [251-500]

Iliescu, Ion - *Toamna Diplomatica*
BL - v93 - D 15 '96 - p714 [1-50]

Ilko, John A - *Ojibwa Chiefs 1690-1890*
r ARBA - v28 - '97 - p159 [51-250]

Illes, Louise Moser - *Sizing Down*
ILRR - v50 - Ap '97 - p521+ [501+]
JEL - v34 - S '96 - p1460 [51-250]
M Lab R - v119 - Ag '96 - p64
Per Psy - v49 - Aut '96 - p754+ [501+]

Illingworth, Mark - *Real-Life Math Problem Solving*
Learning - v25 - Ja '97 - p57 [1-50]

Illustrated Factopedia
cr Books - v9 - S '95 - p26 [51-250]

Ilott, Terry - *Budgets and Markets*
R&R Bk N - v12 - F '97 - p81 [51-250]
Si & So - v6 - N '96 - p36 [51-250]

Ilton, Phil - *Capsules*
Aust Bk R - Ag '96 - p67 [1-50]

Im, James S - *Thermodynamics and Kinetics of Phase Transformations*
SciTech - v20 - N '96 - p18 [1-50]

I'm Going to the Dentist (Illus. by Maxie Chambliss)
c Cur R - v36 - Ap '97 - p13 [51-250]
c PW - v244 - Mr 24 '97 - p85 [51-250]

I'm Going to the Doctor (Illus. by Maxie Chambliss)
c Cur R - v36 - Ap '97 - p13 [51-250]
c PW - v244 - Mr 24 '97 - p85 [51-250]

IMACS-GAMM International Symposium on Numerical Methods and Error Bounds (1995: Oldenburg, Germany) - *Numerical Methods and Error Bounds*
SciTech - v21 - Mr '97 - p15 [51-250]

Images of America
CAY - v17 - Fall '96 - p11 [51-250]

Imagineers (Group) - *Walt Disney Imagineering*
y BL - v93 - D 15 '96 - p704 [51-250]
LJ - v121 - N 15 '96 - p63 [51-250]

Imai, Masaaki - *Gemba Kaizen*
LJ - v122 - Ap 15 '97 - p92 [51-250]
PW - v244 - Mr 24 '97 - p66 [51-250]

Imamura, Keiji - *Prehistoric Japan*
New Sci - v153 - F 1 '97 - p42 [1-50]

Imbeau, Louis M - *Comparing Government Activity*
Pol Stud J - v24 - Sum '96 - p333 [51-250]
R&R Bk N - v11 - N '96 - p48 [51-250]

Imber, Gerald - *The Youth Corridor*
BL - v93 - D 15 '96 - p700 [51-250]

Imboden, Gabriel - *Documents Diplomatiques Suisses 1848-1945*
EHR - v112 - Ap '97 - p532+ [501+]

Im Hof, Ulrich - *The Enlightenment*
EHR - v112 - F '97 - p208+ [501+]

Imhoff, Kathleen R T - *Making the Most of New Technology*
IRLA - v32 - Jl '96 - p11 [51-250]
IRLA - v32 - S '96 - p11+ [51-250]

Imielinski, Tomasz - *Mobile Computing*
SciTech - v20 - D '96 - p8 [51-250]

Imig, Douglas R - *Poverty and Power*
APSR - v90 - D '96 - p912+ [501+]
CS - v26 - Ja '97 - p39+ [501+]

Immigrant Women and Integration
J Gov Info - v23 - S '96 - p665 [51-250]

Immroth, Barbara Froling - *Achieving School Readiness*
Emerg Lib - v23 - My '96 - p38 [251-500]

Immunobiology Bookshelf on CD-ROM. Electronic Media Version
r SB - v33 - My '97 - p119 [251-500]

Impacts of Antibiotic Resistant Bacteria
J Gov Info - v23 - S '96 - p554 [51-250]

Imperato, Ayn - *Greyhound to Wherever*
Sm Pr R - v28 - S '96 - p6 [51-250]

Imperato, Pascal James - *Historical Dictionary of Mali. 3rd Ed.*
r ARBA - v28 - '97 - p53+ [251-500]

Impey, Oliver - *The Early Porcelain Kilns of Japan*
Ceram Mo - v45 - F '97 - p20+ [251-500]
Choice - v34 - Ja '97 - p783 [51-250]

Impey, Rose - *Fireballs from Hell*
c Sch Lib - v44 - Ag '96 - p107 [51-250]
y TES - Jl 5 '96 - pR8 [51-250]
The Girls' Gang
y TES - Jl 5 '96 - pR8 [51-250]

Importers Manual USA and the Dictionary of International Trade. 1996-97 Ed. Electronic Media Version
r ARBA - v28 - '97 - p125+ [251-500]

Improving the Implementation of the Individuals with Disabilities Education Act
J Gov Info - v23 - S '96 - p554 [51-250]

Improving the Prospects for Future International Peace Operations
J Gov Info - v23 - S '96 - p556 [51-250]

Improving the Software Process through Process Definition and Modeling
CBR - v14 - Jl '96 - p25 [51-250]

Improving Women's Health in India
JEL - v34 - D '96 - p2062+ [51-250]

In/Sight: African Photographers 1940 to the Present
LJ - v121 - D '96 - p88 [51-250]
LJ - v121 - N 1 '96 - p80 [1-50]

In the Family
p Utne R - My '96 - p108+ [251-500]

In Their Own Voices. Vols. 1-4. Audio Version
Trib Bks - F 2 '97 - p6 [51-250]

Inada, Lawson Fusao - *Drawing the Line*
BL - v93 - Mr 1 '97 - p1106 [51-250]

Inagaki, N - *Plasma Surface Modification and Plasma Polymerization*
SciTech - v20 - N '96 - p22 [51-250]

Inalcik, Halil - *An Economic and Social History of the Ottoman Empire 1300-1914*
Historian - v59 - Fall '96 - p138+ [501+]
HT - v47 - Ja '97 - p55+ [501+]
JEH - v56 - S '96 - p731+ [501+]
JIH - v27 - Aut '96 - p371+ [501+]
JMH - v69 - Mr '97 - p191+ [501+]

Inamori, Kazuo - *A Passion for Success*
Rapport - v19 - 4 '96 - p18+ [501+]

Inati, Shams - *Ibn Sina and Mysticism. Pt. 4*
Choice - v34 - Mr '97 - p1175 [51-250]
R&R Bk N - v11 - D '96 - p1 [51-250]

Inayat Khan - *The Inner Life*
BL - v93 - Mr 15 '97 - p1207 [51-250]
PW - v244 - Ja 27 '97 - p96 [51-250]

Inbar, Omri - *The Wingate Anaerobic Test*
SciTech - v20 - S '96 - p22 [51-250]

Inbari, Pinhas - *The Palestinians between Terrorism and Statehood*
MEJ - v50 - Aut '96 - p627 [51-250]

Ince, C - *Oxygen Transport to Tissue XVII*
SciTech - v20 - D '96 - p34 [51-250]

Inchbald, Elizabeth - *A Simple Story*
Eight-C St - v30 - Spr '97 - p255+ [501+]

Inches, Alison - *Go to Bed, Fred (Illus. by Lauren Attinello)*
c PW - v243 - N 18 '96 - p77 [51-250]

Income Distribution in OECD Countries
J Gov Info - v23 - S '96 - p674 [51-250]

Income of the Population 55 or Older 1994
JEL - v34 - D '96 - p2026 [51-250]

The Incredible Journey to the Centre of the Atom. The Incredible Journey to the Edge of the Universe
c Sch Lib - v45 - F '97 - p37 [51-250]

The Independent American Indian Review
p SLMQ - v25 - Fall '96 - p65 [51-250]

Independent Review: A Journal of Political Economy
p JEL - v34 - D '96 - p2143+ [51-250]

The Independent Study Catalog. 6th Ed.
r ARBA - v28 - '97 - p134 [51-250]

Index
p LJ - v122 - My 1 '97 - p43 [51-250]

Index of Certificates of Naturalization from the Board of Elections Lucas County, Ohio
r EGH - v50 - N '96 - p179 [51-250]

Index of Economic Freedom. 1997 Ed.
r HE - v53 - Ja 24 '97 - p10 [501+]

The Index of Middle English Prose. Handlists 9-10
r MLR - v91 - O '96 - p956+ [501+]

Index on Censorship
p Utne R - Jl '96 - p118+ [51-250]

Index to International Public Opinion 1994-1995
r R&R Bk N - v11 - N '96 - p39 [51-250]

Index to Labor Articles 1926-
r RQ - v36 - Fall '96 - p54 [51-250]

Index to Labor Periodicals 1926-
r RQ - v36 - Fall '96 - p54 [51-250]

Index to Marriage Notices in the Religious Herald 1828-1938
r EGH - v50 - N '96 - p189 [51-250]

Index to Marriage Notices in the Southern Churchman 1835-1941
r EGH - v50 - N '96 - p188+ [51-250]

Index to Obituary Notices in the Religious Herald 1828-1938
r EGH - v50 - N '96 - p189 [51-250]

India: Recent Economic Developments and Prospects
J Gov Info - v23 - S '96 - p686+ [51-250]

Indian Subcontinent
r BL - v93 - S 15 '96 - p212 [1-50]

Indiana, Gary - *Let It Bleed*
Nat - v263 - O 21 '96 - p31+ [501+]

Indiana. Division of Outdoor Recreation - *SCORP: Continuing the Tradition*
J Gov Info - v23 - S '96 - p583 [51-250]

Indiana's Dedicated Nature Preserves
r J Gov Info - v23 - S '96 - p583 [51-250]

Indigenous Knowledge and Development Monitor
p WorldV - v12 - Jl '96 - p11+ [51-250]

Indo-French Conference on Geometry (1989) -
Geometry: Proceedings
SciTech - v20 - N '96 - p16 [51-250]

Indochina Interchange
p WorldV - v13 - Ja '97 - p14 [51-250]

Industrial Commodity Statistics Yearbook 1994
r ARBA - v28 - '97 - p96 [51-250]

Info New York. Electronic Media Version
r J Gov Info - v23 - S '96 - p589+ [1-50]

Infopedia. Electronic Media Version
yr SLJ - v42 - O '96 - p58+ [51-250]

Information Disclosure of the State-Related Universities
J Gov Info - v23 - S '96 - p593 [51-250]

Information Please Almanac, Atlas, and Yearbook 1996
r ARBA - v28 - '97 - p5 [251-500]

Information Sources 1997
r BL - v93 - F 1 '97 - p965 [51-250]

Information Superhighway
J Gov Info - v23 - S '96 - p568+ [51-250]

Information Technologies for the Control of Money Laundering
J Gov Info - v23 - S '96 - p556 [51-250]

The Informed Librarian
A Lib - v27 - Ag '96 - p70 [1-50]

An Infrastructure Initiative for Latin America and the Caribbean
J Gov Info - v23 - S '96 - p687 [51-250]

Ingall, Marjorie - *The Field Guide to North American Males*
PW - v243 - D 2 '96 - p55 [51-250]

Ingebretsen, Edward J - *Maps of Heaven, Maps of Hell*
Am - v176 - Mr 1 '97 - p37+ [501+]
CC - v113 - N 6 '96 - p1088 [51-250]
Choice - v34 - D '96 - p613+ [51-250]
JPC - v30 - Fall '96 - p229+ [501+]
R&R Bk N - v11 - N '96 - p72 [51-250]
Robert Frost's Star in a Stone Boat
Theol St - v57 - Mr '96 - p194 [251-500]

Ingersoll, Barbara D - *Lonely, Sad and Angry*
Adoles - v31 - Fall '96 - p752 [51-250]

Ingersoll, Earl G - *Engendered Trope in Joyce's Dubliners*
Choice - v34 - S '96 - p122 [51-250]

Ingersoll, John G - *Natural Gas Vehicles*
Choice - v34 - S '96 - p159 [51-250]

Ingesman, Per - *Danmark I Senmiddellalderen*
EHR - v112 - Ap '97 - p451+ [501+]

Ingle, H Larry - *First among Friends*
JMH - v69 - Mr '97 - p132+ [501+]

Ingleby, Richard - *Christopher Wood*
Obs - D 29 '96 - p28 [51-250]

Inglehart, Ronald - *Modernization and Postmodernization*
For Aff - v76 - My '97 - p125 [51-250]
The North American Trajectory
Choice - v34 - F '97 - p1031 [51-250]
JEL - v35 - Mr '97 - p214 [51-250]

Ingleton, Roy - *The Gentlemen at War*
EHR - v112 - F '97 - p264+ [51-250]

Inglis, Amirah - *The Hammer and the Sickle and the Washing Up*
Meanjin - v55 - 3 '96 - p487+ [501+]

Inglis, Andrew F - *Video Engineering. 2nd Ed.*
SciTech - v20 - N '96 - p74 [51-250]

Inglis, Dorothy - *Bread and Roses*
CF - v75 - O '96 - p45+ [501+]

Inglis, Fred - *Raymond Williams*
Spec - v277 - N 16 '96 - p43 [1-50]

Ingman, Bruce - *When Martha's Away*
  c Bks Keeps - Ja '97 - p19 [51-250]
Ingoglia, Gina - *Disney's Treasury of Children's Classics*
  c Ch BWatch - v7 - Ja '97 - p3 [1-50]
Ingold, Jeanette - *The Window*
  y BL - v93 - N 1 '96 - p490 [51-250]
  y BL - v93 - Ap 1 '97 - p1292 [1-50]
  y CBRS - v25 - O '96 - p22 [51-250]
  y CCB-B - v50 - Ja '97 - p174+ [51-250]
  y HB Guide - v8 - Spr '97 - p80 [51-250]
  y KR - v64 - Ag 15 '96 - p1236 [51-250]
  y SLJ - v42 - D '96 - p136 [51-250]
  y VOYA - v19 - D '96 - p270 [51-250]
Ingoldsby, Bron B - *Families in Multicultural Perspective*
  Fam Relat - v45 - Jl '96 - p353+ [251-500]
  Soc Ser R - v70 - S '96 - p500+ [51-250]
Ingpen, Robert - *Events That Changed the World.
Electronic Media Version*
  Quill & Q - v62 - My '96 - p31 [501+]
Ingraffia, Brian D - *Postmodern Theory and Biblical
Theology*
  Choice - v34 - N '96 - p475+ [51-250]
  TT - v53 - Ja '97 - p560+ [501+]
Ingraham, Patricia Wallace - *The Foundation of Merit*
  AAPSS-A - v550 - Mr '97 - p183 [251-500]
  APSR - v90 - S '96 - p652+ [501+]
  Pol Stud J - v24 - Sum '96 - p333 [51-250]
Ingram, David - *Reason, History, and Politics*
  Ethics - v107 - Ja '97 - p366 [501+]
  IPQ - v37 - Je '97 - p248+ [501+]
Ingram, Edward - *Empire-Building and Empire-Builders*
  HT - v46 - Ag '96 - p56+ [501+]
Ingram, Jay - *The Burning House*
  TES - O 11 '96 - p8* [51-250]
Ingram, Scott - *More Scary Stories for Stormy Nights
(Illus. by Eric Angeloch)*
  c SLJ - v43 - Ja '97 - p112 [51-250]
Ingrams, Richard - *I Once Met*
  Spec - v277 - D 14 '96 - p73 [501+]
Ingrao, Charles W - *The Habsburg Monarchy 1618-1815*
  EHR - v111 - S '96 - p989 [251-500]
  State and Society in Early Modern Austria
  CEH - v29 - 1 '96 - p126+ [501+]
  EHR - v111 - S '96 - p989+ [251-500]
  Six Ct J - v27 - Fall '96 - p916+ [501+]
Inhorn, Marcia Claire - *Quest for Conception*
  Am Ethnol - v24 - F '97 - p251+ [501+]
  Signs - v22 - Aut '96 - p227+ [501+]
Inkeles, Alex - *National Character*
  For Aff - v76 - Mr '97 - p174 [51-250]
Inkpen, Mick - *Kipper's Book of Counting*
  c Bks Keeps - Jl '96 - p7 [51-250]
  Kipper's Book of Opposites
  c Bks Keeps - Jl '96 - p7 [51-250]
  Kipper's Book of Weather
  c Bks Keeps - Jl '96 - p7 [51-250]
  Kipper's Snowy Day (Illus. by Mick Inkpen)
  c Bks Keeps - N '96 - p21 [51-250]
  c HB Guide - v8 - Spr '97 - p32 [51-250]
  c SLJ - v42 - D '96 - p94 [51-250]
  Lullabyhullaballoo (Illus. by Mick Inkpen)
  c Books - v9 - S '95 - p26 [1-50]
  *Nothing (Holm) (Illus. by Mick Inkpen). Book and Audio
Version*
  c Sch Lib - v44 - N '96 - p146 [51-250]
  Nothing (Illus. by Mick Inkpen)
  c Bks Keeps - N '96 - p6 [51-250]
  c JB - v60 - O '96 - p184+ [51-250]
Inlander, Charles B - *The Consumer's Medical Desk
Reference*
  r BL - v93 - F 1 '97 - p957 [1-50]
  Stress: 63 Ways to Relieve Tension and Stay Healthy
  BL - v93 - D 15 '96 - p694 [51-250]
  PW - v243 - D 2 '96 - p58 [51-250]
Inman, Arthur, 1895- - *From a Darkened Room*
  NYTBR - v101 - N 24 '96 - p32 [51-250]
Inman, Arthur Crew, 1845- - *From a Darkened Room*
  PW - v243 - S 2 '96 - p121 [51-250]
Inman, Arthur Crew, 1895- - *From a Darkened Room*
  LJ - v121 - O 15 '96 - p58 [51-250]
Inman, Robert - *Dairy Queen Days*
  y BL - v93 - F 1 '97 - p925+ [51-250]
  KR - v65 - Ja 15 '97 - p82 [251-500]
  LJ - v121 - N 15 '96 - p88 [51-250]
  PW - v243 - N 25 '96 - p54 [51-250]
Inmon, W H - *Building the Data Warehouse. 2nd Ed.*
  CBR - v14 - S '96 - p28 [1-50]
  Managing the Data Warehouse
  SciTech - v21 - Mr '97 - p11 [1-50]
Inn Places. 9th Ed.
  r Quill & Q - v62 - S '96 - p24 [51-250]

Innerhofer, Ronald - *Deutsche Science Fiction 1870-1914*
  SFS - v24 - Mr '97 - p169+ [501+]
Innes, Doreen - *Ethics and Rhetoric*
  TLS - Ag 2 '96 - p27 [501+]
Innes, Miranda - *Fabric Painting*
  y Kliatt - v30 - S '96 - p38 [51-250]
  y VOYA - v19 - O '96 - p232 [51-250]
  Jewelry: A Practical Guide to Creative Crafts
  y Kliatt - v30 - S '96 - p38 [51-250]
  y VOYA - v19 - O '96 - p232 [51-250]
Innes, Stephen - *Creating the Commonwealth*
  Historian - v58 - Sum '96 - p863+ [501+]
  RAH - v25 - Mr '97 - p19+ [501+]
Inorganic Syntheses. Vol. 30
  Am Sci - v84 - N '96 - p615+ [501+]
Inoue, Yasushi - *Aru Onna No Shi*
  CLS - v33 - 1 '96 - p69+ [501+]
Inquisitor
  p LJ - v122 - Ja '97 - p158 [51-250]
Insall, John N - *Current Concepts in Primary and
Revision Total Knee Arthroplasty*
  SciTech - v20 - S '96 - p38 [51-250]
Inside Science Plus. Electronic Media Version
  r LAR - v99 - Mr '97 - p161 [51-250]
InsideOUT
  yp SLJ - v42 - N '96 - p36 [1-50]
Inskeep, Carolee R - *The Children's Aid Society of New
York*
  r EGH - v50 - N '96 - p176 [51-250]
Insley, John - *Scandinavian Personal Names in Norfolk*
  r Names - v45 - Mr '97 - p63+ [501+]
**INSPEC List of Journals and Other Serial Sources
1996/7**
  r ARBA - v28 - '97 - p596 [51-250]
Inspector
  p Sm Pr R - v28 - D '96 - p22 [51-250]
Inspiring Reform
  LJ - v122 - My 1 '97 - p100+ [51-250]
  Mag Antiq - v151 - Mr '97 - p382 [501+]
  PW - v244 - Ap 28 '97 - p68 [51-250]
Instabilities and Nonequilibrium Structures V
  SciTech - v21 - Mr '97 - p18 [51-250]
**Institute of Laboratory Animal Resources (U.S.).
Committee on Care and Use of Laboratory
Animals** - *Guide for the Care and Use of Laboratory
Animals*
  r BioSci - v46 - D '96 - p876 [51-250]
  r Choice - v34 - F '97 - p990 [51-250]
Institute of Medicine (U.S.) - *WIC Nutrition Risk Criteria*
  SciTech - v20 - S '96 - p36 [51-250]
**Institute of Medicine (U.S.). Committee on Evaluating
Clinical Applications of Telemedicine** - *Telemedicine:
A Guide to Assessing Telecommunications in Health
Care*
  SciTech - v21 - Mr '97 - p44 [51-250]
**Institute of Medicine (U.S.). Committee on Food
Chemicals Codex** - *Food Chemicals Codex. 4th Ed.*
  SciTech - v20 - S '96 - p60 [51-250]
**Institute of Physics (Great Britain). Applied Optics
Division. Divisional Conference (4th: 1996: Reading,
England)** - *Applied Optics and Optoelectronics 1996*
  SciTech - v21 - Mr '97 - p24 [51-250]
**Instituto Da Biblioteca Nacional E Do Livro
(Portugal)** - *Edicoes Aldinas Da Biblioteca Nacional,
Seculos XV-XVI*
  r Lib - v18 - S '96 - p274 [1-50]
Instructional Course Lectures. Vol. 44
  SciTech - v20 - S '96 - p39 [51-250]
Insurance Directory
  r R&R Bk N - v12 - F '97 - p50 [51-250]
**Integrity of Structures and Fluid Systems, Hazardous
Release Protection, Piping and Pipe Supports, and
Pumps and Valves**
  SciTech - v20 - N '96 - p83 [51-250]
Interactive
  p TES - O 18 '96 - p43U [51-250]
The Interactive Multimedia Sourcebook 1997
  r Choice - v34 - My '97 - p1476 [51-250]
Interactive Periodic Table. Electronic Media Version
  yr BL - v93 - D 1 '96 - p684+ [251-500]
Interactive Skeleton. Electronic Media Version
  r SciTech - v20 - N '96 - p30 [51-250]
InterActivity
  p LJ - v121 - O 15 '96 - p95 [51-250]
**Interconnect: For Grassroots Movement-Building and
Sharing of Resources within the US-Latin America
Solidarity Community**
  p WorldV - v13 - Ja '97 - p14 [51-250]

**Intermediate Sanctions for Female Offenders Policy
Group (Or.)** - *Intermediate Sanctions for Women
Offenders*
  J Gov Info - v23 - S '96 - p592 [51-250]
**International Air Transportation Conference (24th:
1996: Louisville, KY)** - *Rebuilding Inner City Airports*
  SciTech - v20 - D '96 - p81 [51-250]
**International Astronomical Union. Colloquium (153rd:
1995: Makuhari, Japan)** - *Magnetodynamic
Phenomena in the Solar Atmosphere*
  SciTech - v21 - Mr '97 - p19 [51-250]
**International Astronomical Union. Colloquium (158th:
1995: Keele, Staffordshire)** - *Cataclysmic Variables
and Related Objects*
  SciTech - v21 - Mr '97 - p19 [51-250]
**International Astronomical Union. Symposium (172nd:
1995: Paris, France)** - *Dynamics, Ephemerides, and
Astrometry of the Solar System*
  SciTech - v20 - D '96 - p21 [51-250]
**International Astronomical Union. Symposium (174th:
1995: Tokyo, Japan)** - *Dynamical Evolution of Star
Clusters*
  SciTech - v20 - D '96 - p21 [51-250]
**International Astronomical Union. Symposium (175th:
1995: Bologna, Italy)** - *Extragalactic Radio Sources*
  SciTech - v21 - Mr '97 - p20 [51-250]
**International Astronomical Union. Symposium (176th:
1995: Vienna, Austria)** - *Stellar Surface Structure*
  SciTech - v20 - N '96 - p16 [51-250]
International Bibliography of Theatre 1992-1993
  r ARBA - v28 - '97 - p523 [51-250]
**International Biochemistry of Exercise Conference (9th:
1994: Aberdeen, Scotland)** - *Biochemistry of Exercise
IX*
  SciTech - v20 - D '96 - p34 [51-250]
International Broadcasting Convention 1995
  SciTech - v20 - S '96 - p56 [1-50]
**International Centennial Chebotarev Conference (1994:
Kazan, Russia)** - *Algebra and Analysis*
  SciTech - v20 - N '96 - p12 [51-250]
**International Clean Water Conference (1995: La Jolla,
Calif.)** - *Clean Water*
  SciTech - v20 - D '96 - p69 [51-250]
**International COADS Winds Workshop (1994: Kiel,
Germany)** - *Proceedings of the International COADS
Winds Workshop, Kiel, Germany, 31 May-2 June 1994*
  J Gov Info - v23 - S '96 - p570 [51-250]
International Commission on the Balkans - *Unfinished
Peace*
  Cu H - v96 - Mr '97 - p141 [51-250]
  NYRB - v43 - D 19 '96 - p10+ [501+]
**International Conference Duracosys (1995: Brussels,
Belgium)** - *Progress in Durability Analysis of
Composite Systems*
  SciTech - v20 - N '96 - p63 [51-250]
**International Conference of Agricultural Economists
(22nd: 1994: Harare, Zimbabwe)** - *Agricultural
Competitiveness*
  JEL - v34 - S '96 - p1495 [51-250]
**International Conference of the Computer Graphics
Society (14th: 1996: Pohang, Korea)** - *Computer
Graphics International*
  SciTech - v20 - N '96 - p6 [51-250]
**International Conference on Arithmetic, Geometry and
Coding Theory (1993: Luminy, France)** - *Arithmetic,
Geometry, and Coding Theory*
  SciTech - v20 - N '96 - p13 [51-250]
**International Conference on Automatic Face and
Gesture Recognition (2nd: 1996: Killington, VT)** -
Automatic Face and Gesture Recognition
  SciTech - v21 - Mr '97 - p80 [51-250]
**International Conference on Burns and Fire Disasters
(2nd)** - *The Management of Burns and Fire Disasters*
  SciTech - v20 - D '96 - p49 [51-250]
**International Conference on Carcinogenesis and Risk
Assessment (8th: 1994: Austin, Tex.)** - *Genetics and
Cancer Susceptibility*
  BioSci - v46 - N '96 - p787+ [501+]
**International Conference on Coastal Research in Terms
of Large Scale Experiments (1995: Gdansk,
Poland)** - *Coastal Dynamics '95*
  SciTech - v20 - D '96 - p2 [51-250]
**International Conference on Cold Regions Engineering
(8th: 1996: University of Alaska Fairbanks)** - *Cold
Regions Engineering*
  SciTech - v20 - D '96 - p65 [51-250]
**International Conference on Computer Aided Design in
Composite Material Technology (5th: 1996: Udine,
Italy)** - *Computer Aided Design in Composite Material
Technology*
  SciTech - v20 - N '96 - p62 [51-250]

International Conference on Computer Communications and Networks (4th: 1995: Las Vegas, Nev.) - *Fourth International Conference on Computer Communications and Networks*
SciTech - v20 - S '96 - p54 [51-250]
SciTech - v21 - Mr '97 - p86 [51-250]

International Conference on Computer Design (1996: Austin, TX) - *Computer Design*
SciTech - v21 - Mr '97 - p91 [51-250]

International Conference on Computer Modelling of Seas and Coastal Regions (2nd: 1995: Cancun, Mexico) - *Computer Modelling of Seas and Coastal Regions*
Am Sci - v84 - S '96 - p497+ [251-500]

International Conference on Configurable Distributed Systems (3rd: 1996: Annapolis, Maryland) - *Configurable Distributed Systems*
SciTech - v20 - N '96 - p11 [1-50]

International Conference on Culinary Arts and Sciences (1st: 1996: London, England) - *Culinary Arts and Sciences*
SciTech - v20 - D '96 - p87 [51-250]

International Conference on Distributed Computing Systems (16th: 1996: Hong Kong) - *Distributed Computing Systems*
SciTech - v20 - D '96 - p6 [1-50]

International Conference on Dynamics and Control of Structures in Space (3rd: 1996: Cranfield Institute of Technology) - *Dynamics and Control of Structures in Space*
SciTech - v20 - D '96 - p81 [51-250]

International Conference on Earthquake Geotechnical Engineering (1st: 1995: Tokyo, Japan) - *Earthquake Geotechnical Engineering. Vols. 1-3*
SciTech - v20 - S '96 - p18 [51-250]

International Conference on Earthquake Resistant Engineering Structures (1st: 1996: Thessaloniki, Greece) - *Earthquake Resistant Engineering Structures*
SciTech - v21 - Mr '97 - p79 [51-250]

International Conference on Effect of Hydrogen on the Behavior of Materials (5th: 1994: Moran, Wyo.) - *Hydrogen Effects in Materials*
SciTech - v20 - D '96 - p28 [51-250]

International Conference on Energy and Environment (1995: Shanghai, China) - *Energy and Environment*
SciTech - v20 - N '96 - p3 [51-250]

International Conference on Environment Problems in Coastal Regions (1st: 1996) - *Coastal Environment*
SciTech - v20 - D '96 - p67 [51-250]

International Conference on Environmental Engineering Education and Training (1st: 1996: Southampton, UK) - *Environmental Engineering Education and Training*
SciTech - v20 - S '96 - p51 [51-250]

International Conference on Environmentally Sustainable Development (2nd: 1994: World Bank) - *The Human Face of the Urban Environment*
Env - v38 - N '96 - p25+ [501+]
J Gov Info - v23 - S '96 - p686 [51-250]

International Conference on Event-Related Potentials of the Brain (11th: 1995: Okinawa-Shi, Japan) - *Recent Advances in Event-Related Brain Potential Research*
SciTech - v20 - D '96 - p43 [51-250]

International Conference on Experimental Methods for Microgravity Materials Science (7th: 1995: Las Vegas, NV) - *Experimental Methods for Microgravity Materials Science*
SciTech - v20 - N '96 - p62 [51-250]

International Conference on Fundamentals of Adsorption (5th: 1995: Pacific Grove, CA) - *Fundamentals of Adsorption*
SciTech - v21 - Mr '97 - p31 [51-250]

International Conference on Greek Architectural Terracottas of the Classical and Hellenistic Periods (1991: American School of Classical Studies) - *Proceedings of the International Conference on Greek Architectural Terracottas of the Classical and Hellenistic Periods, December 12-15, 1991*
AJA - v100 - O '96 - p793+ [501+]

International Conference on Hydrology and Water Resources (1993: New Delhi, India) - *Hydrology and Water Resources. Vols. 1-4*
SciTech - v20 - N '96 - p2 [51-250]

International Conference on Image Management and Communication (4th: 1995: Oahu Island, Hawaii) - *Image Management and Communication*
SciTech - v20 - D '96 - p37 [51-250]

International Conference on Intelligent Systems in Process Engineering (1st: 1995: Snowmass, Colo.) - *International Conference on Intelligent Systems in Process Engineering*
SciTech - v20 - N '96 - p79 [51-250]

International Conference on Ion Beam Modification of Materials (9th: 1995: Canberra, A.C.T.) - *Ion Beam Modification of Materials*
SciTech - v21 - Mr '97 - p77 [51-250]

International Conference on Laser Interaction and Related Plasma Phenomena (12th: 1995: Osaka, Japan) - *Laser Interaction and Related Plasma Phenomena. Pts. 1-2*
SciTech - v20 - N '96 - p20 [51-250]

International Conference on Mobile and Rapidly Assembled Structures (2nd: 1996: Seville, Spain) - *Mobile and Rapidly Assembled Structures II*
SciTech - v21 - Mr '97 - p83 [51-250]

International Conference on Multimedia Computing and Systems (1996: Hiroshima, Japan) - *Multimedia Computing and System*
SciTech - v20 - D '96 - p7 [51-250]

International Conference on Multiphase Flow (2nd: 1995: Kyoto, Japan) - *Multiphase Flow 1995*
SciTech - v20 - D '96 - p61 [51-250]

International Conference on New Promising Electrochemical Systems for Rechargeable Batteries (1995: Kiev, Ukraine) - *New Promising Electrochemical Systems for Rechargeable Batteries*
SciTech - v20 - N '96 - p72 [51-250]

International Conference on North American Tunneling and the General Assembly of the International Tunneling Association (22nd: 1996) - *North American Tunneling '96. Vols. 1-2*
SciTech - v20 - N '96 - p65 [51-250]

International Conference on Offshore Mechanics and Arctic Engineering (15th: 1996: Florence, Italy) - *Offshore Mechanics and Arctic Engineering. Vol. 1, Pts. 1-2; Vols. 2-6*
SciTech - v20 - N '96 - p78+ [251-500]

International Conference on Parallel and Distributed Systems (1996: Tokyo, Japan) - *Proceedings 1996 International Conference on Parallel and Distributed Systems*
SciTech - v20 - D '96 - p8 [51-250]

International Conference on Parallel Computational Fluid Dynamics (1995: Pasadena, Calif.) - *Parallel Computational Fluid Dynamics*
SciTech - v20 - N '96 - p16 [51-250]

International Conference on Parallel Processing (1996: Cornell University, Ithaca, NY) - *Parallel Processing. Vols. 1-4*
SciTech - v21 - Mr '97 - p6 [1-50]

International Conference on Pressure Vessel Technology (8th: 1996: Montreal, Quebec) - *Proceedings of the 8th International Conference on Pressure Vessel Technology. Vols. 1-2*
SciTech - v20 - N '96 - p83 [51-250]

International Conference on Requirements Engineering (2nd: 1996: Colorado Springs, CO) - *Proceedings of the Second International Conference on Requirements Engineering*
SciTech - v20 - N '96 - p9 [51-250]

International Conference on Scientific and Statistical Database Systems (8th: 1996: Stockholm, Sweden) - *Scientific and Statistical Database Systems*
SciTech - v20 - N '96 - p5 [1-50]

International Conference on Software for Electrical Engineering Analysis and Design (3rd: 1996: Pisa, Italy) - *Software for Electrical Engineering Analysis and Design*
SciTech - v20 - N '96 - p71 [51-250]

International Conference on Software Reuse (4th: 1996: Orlando, FL) - *Software Reuse*
SciTech - v20 - N '96 - p7 [51-250]

International Conference on Surface Modication Technologies (9th: 1995: Cleveland, Ohio) - *Surface Modification Technologies IX*
SciTech - v20 - D '96 - p81 [51-250]

International Conference on Sustainability of Irrigated Agriculture (1994: Vimeiro, Portugal) - *Sustainability of Irrigated Agriculture*
SciTech - v20 - N '96 - p57 [51-250]

International Conference on the Economics of Design, Test, and Manufacturing (3rd: 1994: Austin, TX) - *Third International Conference on the Economics of Design, Test, and Manufacturing*
SciTech - v20 - S '96 - p56 [51-250]

International Conference on the Engineering of Sport (1st: 1996: Sheffield, UK) - *The Engineering of Sport*
SciTech - v20 - N '96 - p61 [51-250]

International Conference on Worldwide Advances in Structural Concrete and Masonry (14th: 1996: Chicago, Ill.) - *Worldwide Advances in Structural Concrete and Masonry*
SciTech - v20 - N '96 - p65 [51-250]

International Conference Software Engineering; Education and Practice (1996: Dunedin, New Zealand) - *Software Engineering*
SciTech - v20 - N '96 - p12 [51-250]

International Congress of EMG and Clinical Neurophysiology (10th: 1995: Kyoto, Japan) - *Recent Advances in Clinical Neurophysiology*
SciTech - v21 - Mr '97 - p49 [51-250]

International Congress on Catalysis (11th: 1996: Baltimore, MD) - *11th International Congress on Catalysis*
SciTech - v21 - Mr '97 - p31 [51-250]

International Congress on Industrial and Applied Mathematics (3rd: 1995: Hamburg, Germany) - *ICIAM '95*
SciTech - v20 - N '96 - p5 [51-250]

International Congress on Interventional Neuroradiology and Intravascular Neurosurgery (1995: Kyoto, Japan) - *Advances in Interventional Neuroradiology and Intravascular Neurosurgery*
r   SciTech - v20 - D '96 - p50 [51-250]

International Congress on Pathophysiology of Pregnancy (27th: 1995: Quezon City, Philippines) - *Increasingly Safe and Successful Pregnancies*
SciTech - v20 - D '96 - p52 [51-250]

International Congress on Surgical and Prosthetic Voice Restoration after Total Laryngectomy (6th: 1995: San Sebastian, Spain) - *Surgery and Prosthetic Voice Restoration after Total and Subtotal Laryngectomy*
SciTech - v20 - D '96 - p51 [51-250]

International Congress on the Dead Sea Scrolls (1991: Madrid, Spain) - *The Madrid Qumran Conference. Vols. 1-2*
Rel St Rev - v23 - Ap '97 - p194 [51-250]

International Dairy Federation - *Dictionary of Dairy Terminology. 2nd Rev. Ed.*
r   SciTech - v20 - N '96 - p58 [51-250]

International Dictionary of Theatre. Vol. 3
r   ARBA - v28 - '97 - p523 [51-250]

The International Directory of Business Information Sources and Services 1996
r   ARBA - v28 - '97 - p103 [251-500]
r   Bus Bk R - v13 - 4 '96 - p123 [51-250]
r   J Gov Info - v24 - Ja '97 - p66+ [501+]

International Directory of Company Histories. Vols. 12-14
r   ARBA - v28 - '97 - p103+ [251-500]

International Directory of Educational Audiovisuals. Electronic Media Version
r   BL - v93 - D 1 '96 - p682+ [251-500]

The International Directory of Government. 2nd Ed.
r   BL - v92 - Ag '96 - p1920 [251-250]

International Energy Agency - *Middle East Oil and Gas*
J Gov Info - v23 - S '96 - p674 [51-250]
Oil, Gas and Coal Supply Outlook
J Gov Info - v23 - S '96 - p675 [51-250]

The International Executive
p   JEL - v34 - S '96 - p1507 [51-250]

International Food Data Base Conference (1st: 1993: Sydney, Australia) - *Quality and Accessibility of Food-Related Data*
SciTech - v20 - D '96 - p86 [51-250]

The International Foundation Directory 1996
r   ARBA - v28 - '97 - p315 [251-500]
r   ChrPhil - v8 - Jl 11 '96 - p44 [51-250]
r   R&R Bk N - v11 - N '96 - p43 [51-250]

International GIS Sourcebook 1994
r   GJ - Jl '96 - p237 [51-250]

International Hotels Environment Initiatives (Firm) - *Environmental Management for Hotels. 2nd Ed.*
r   SciTech - v20 - D '96 - p87 [1-50]

International Index to Music Periodicals. Electronic Media Version
r   Choice - v34 - Mr '97 - p1148 [251-500]

International Ion Exchange Conference (7th: 1996: Churchill College, Cambridge, UK) - *Ion Exchange Developments and Applications*
SciTech - v20 - N '96 - p23 [51-250]

International Journal of Electronic Commerce
p   LJ - v122 - Ap 15 '97 - p127 [51-250]

International Journal of Forensic Document Examiners
p   Nature - v383 - S 5 '96 - p44 [51-250]

International Journal of Polymer Analysis and Characterization
p   Nature - v383 - S 5 '96 - p44 [51-250]

International Labour Conference, 83rd Session, 1996 -
Report III. Pts. 4A-4B
   ILR - v135 - '96 - p122 [501+]
Report V
   ILR - v135 - '96 - p119+ [501+]
Report VI
   ILR - v135 - '96 - p121+ [251-500]
International Labour Office - *Accident Prevention on
Board Ship at Sea and in Port. 2nd Rev. Ed.*
   ILR - v135 - 5 '96 - p597+ [251-500]
**International Lake Ladoga Symposium (1st: 1993: St.
Petersburg, Russia) -** *The First International Lake
Ladoga Symposium*
   SciTech - v20 - D '96 - p29 [51-250]
**International Lecture Series TBM Tunnelling Trends
(1995: Hagenberg, Austria) -** *Tunnel Boring Machines*
   SciTech - v20 - N '96 - p65 [51-250]
The International Legalization Handbook
   r AB - v98 - S 16 '96 - p840 [251-500]
**International Meeting on the Biology of Nitric Oxide
(4th: 1995: Amelia Island, FL) -** *The Biology of Nitric
Oxide. Pt. 5*
   SciTech - v20 - N '96 - p31 [51-250]
International Motion Picture Almanac 1996
   r ARBA - v28 - '97 - p355 [51-250]
International Movement ATD Fourth World - *This Is
How We Live*
   HER - v66 - Win '96 - p881+ [501+]
**International Parallel Processing Symposium (10th:
1996: Honolulu, HI) -** *International Parallel
Processing Symposium*
   SciTech - v20 - N '96 - p6 [51-250]
**International Photosynthesis Congress (10th: 1995:
Montpellier, France) -** *Photosynthesis*
   SciTech - v20 - N '96 - p28 [51-250]
**International Pipeline Conference (IPC'96) (1st: 1996:
Calgary, Alberta, Canada) -** *International Pipeline
Conference 1996. Vols. 1-2*
   SciTech - v20 - D '96 - p73 [51-250]
International Policy Review
   p JEL - v34 - D '96 - p2144 [51-250]
International Relations Research Directory. 1st Ed.
   r ARBA - v28 - '97 - p279 [51-250]
   r JPR - v33 - Ag '96 - p380 [251-500]
**International School of Mathematics G. Stampacchia
Workshop on Nonlinear Optimization and
Application (21st: 1995: Erice, Italy) -** *Nonlinear
Optimization and Applications*
   SciTech - v20 - N '96 - p15 [51-250]
**International Space Conference of Pacific Basin Societies
(6th: 1995: Marina Del Rey, CA) -** *Advances in the
Astronautical Sciences*
   SciTech - v20 - S '96 - p58 [51-250]
International Stamp Dealers' Directory 1996
   r Am Phil - v110 - S '96 - p829 [1-50]
   r Am Phil - v110 - D '96 - p1087+ [51-250]
**International Symposium and Workshop on
Desertification in Developed Countries: Why Can't
We Control It? (1994: Tuscon, Ariz.) -** *Desertification
in Developed Countries*
   R&R Bk N - v11 - D '96 - p19 [51-250]
**International Symposium in Economic Theory and
Econometrics -** *Dynamic Disequilibrium Modeling*
   JEL - v35 - Mr '97 - p204 [51-250]
**International Symposium of GLA (1st: 1995: San
Antonio, Tex.) -** *Gamma-Linolenic Acid*
   SciTech - v20 - D '96 - p36 [51-250]
**International Symposium on Acoustical Imaging (22nd:
1995: Florence, Italy) -** *Acoustical Imaging*
   SciTech - v20 - N '96 - p18 [51-250]
**International Symposium on Assessment of Software
Tools (4th: 1996: Toronto, Ont.) -** *Proceedings of the
Fourth International Symposium on Assessment of
Software Tools, May 22-24, 1996, Toronto, Canada*
   SciTech - v20 - S '96 - p4 [51-250]
**International Symposium on Biological Reactive
Intermediates (5th: 1995: Munich, Germany) -**
Biological Reactive Intermediates V
   SciTech - v20 - N '96 - p38 [51-250]
**International Symposium on Blood Transfusion (20th:
1995: Groningen, Netherlands) -** *Trigger Factors in
Transfusion Medicine*
   SciTech - v21 - Mr '97 - p67 [51-250]
**International Symposium on Computer and
Communication Systems for Image Guided Diagnosis
and Therapy (1996: Paris, France) -** *Computer
Assisted Radiology*
   SciTech - v20 - D '96 - p42 [51-250]

**International Symposium on Corrosion of Reinforcement
in Concrete Construction (4th: 1996: Cambridge,
UK) -** *Corrosion of Reinforcement in Concrete
Construction*
   SciTech - v20 - N '96 - p63 [51-250]
**International Symposium on Fault-Tolerant
Computing -** *Proceedings of the 1996 International
Symposium on Fault-Tolerant Computing*
   SciTech - v20 - N '96 - p12 [51-250]
**International Symposium on Headwater Control (3rd:
1995: New Delhi) -** *Sustainable Reconstruction of
Highland and Headwater Regions*
   SciTech - v20 - S '96 - p1 [51-250]
**International Symposium on Insect-Plant Relationships
(9th: 1995: Gwatt, Switzerland) -** *Proceedings of the
9th International Symposium on Insect-Plant
Relationships*
   SciTech - v20 - D '96 - p32 [51-250]
**International Symposium on Interactions between
Sediments and Water (6th: 1993: Santa Barbara,
Calif.) -** *Interactions between Sediments and Water*
   SciTech - v21 - Mr '97 - p32 [51-250]
**International Symposium on Landslides (7th: 1996:
Trondheim) -** *Landslides: Glissements De Terrain*
   SciTech - v20 - N '96 - p24 [51-250]
**International Symposium on Melanogenesis and
Malignant Melanoma (1995: Fukuoka-Shi, Japan) -**
Melanogenesis and Malignant Melanoma
   SciTech - v20 - D '96 - p42 [51-250]
International Symposium on Multiple-Valued Logic -
*Proceedings of the 26th International Symposium on
Multiple-Valued Logic*
   SciTech - v20 - N '96 - p12 [51-250]
**International Symposium on Natural Draught Cooling
Towers (4th: Kaiserslautern, Germany) -** *Natural
Draught Cooling Towers*
   SciTech - v20 - N '96 - p70 [51-250]
**International Symposium on Offshore Engineering (9th:
1995: COPPE) -** *International Offshore Engineering*
   SciTech - v20 - N '96 - p67 [51-250]
**International Symposium on River Sedimentation (6th:
1995: New Delhi, India) -** *Management of Sediment*
   SciTech - v20 - S '96 - p1 [51-250]
**International Symposium on Turner Syndrome (4th:
1995: Goteborg, Sweden) -** *Turner Syndrome in a Life
Span Perspective*
   SciTech - v20 - D '96 - p53 [51-250]
**International Symposium, Recycling of Metals and
Engineered Materials (3rd: 1995: Point Clear,
Ala.) -** *Third International Symposium, Recycling of
Metals and Engineered Materials*
   SciTech - v21 - Mr '97 - p81 [51-250]
International Television and Video Almanac 1996
   r ARBA - v28 - '97 - p355 [51-250]
International Trade Statistics Yearbook 1994. Vols. 1-2
   r R&R Bk N - v11 - D '96 - p32 [51-250]
The International Who's Who 1996-97
   r R&R Bk N - v11 - D '96 - p7 [51-250]
**International Who's Who in Music and Musician's
Directory. Vol. 1, 15th Ed.; Vol. 2, 1st Ed.**
   r LAR - v99 - Ja '97 - p47 [251-500]
**International Who's Who in Music and Musician's
Directory. Vol. 2, 1st Ed.**
   r ARBA - v28 - '97 - p485+ [251-500]
**International Workshop on Aerosol Inhalation, Lung
Transport, Deposition and the Relation to the
Environment (1995: Warsaw, Poland) -** *Aerosol
Inhalation, Recent Research Frontiers*
   SciTech - v20 - D '96 - p40 [51-250]
**International Workshop on Fetal Genetic Pathology
(3rd: 1993: Perugia, Italy) -** *Gene Regulation and
Fetal Development*
   SciTech - v20 - S '96 - p40 [51-250]
**International Workshop on High-Level Programming
Models and Supportive Environments (1st: 1996:
Honolulu, HI) -** *First International Workshop on High-
Level Programming Models and Supportive
Environments*
   SciTech - v20 - S '96 - p4 [51-250]
**International Workshop on Maximum Entropy and
Bayesian Methods (13th: 1993: Santa Barbara,
Calif.) -** *Maximum Entropy and Bayesian Methods*
   SciTech - v21 - Mr '97 - p24 [51-250]
**International Workshop on Multi-Media Database
Management Systems: Proceedings, August 14-16,
1996, Blue Mountain Lake, N.Y.**
   SciTech - v20 - D '96 - p7 [1-50]

**International Workshop on Neural Networks for
Identification, Control, Robotics, and Signal/Image
Processing (1996: Venice, Italy) -** *Proceedings:
International Workshop on Neural Networks for
Identification, Control, Robotics, and Signal/Image
Processing*
   SciTech - v20 - D '96 - p75 [51-250]
**International Workshop on Paediatric Osteology (1st:
1995: Cologne, Germany) -** *Paediatric Osteology*
   SciTech - v20 - D '96 - p52 [51-250]
**International Workshop on Services in Distributed and
Networked Environments (3rd: 1996: Macau) -** *Third
International Workshop on Services in Distributed and
Networked Environments*
   SciTech - v20 - S '96 - p9 [51-250]
**International Workshop on Temporal Representation
and Reasoning (3rd: 1996: Key West, FL) -** *Third
International Workshop on Temporal Representation and
Reasoning*
   SciTech - v20 - S '96 - p3 [51-250]
International Yearbook of Industrial Statistics 1996
   r ARBA - v28 - '97 - p96 [51-250]
   r JEL - v34 - D '96 - p2086+ [51-250]
International Youth Library - *Children's Literature
Research*
   ChLAQ - v20 - Fall '95 - p99 [1-50]
**Internationales Eriugena-Colloquium (8th: 1991:
Chicago, Ill., and Notre Dame, Ind.) -** *Eriugena: East
und West*
   CHR - v82 - Jl '96 - p519+ [501+]
   JR - v76 - O '96 - p629+ [501+]
Internet Life
   p TES - O 18 '96 - p43U [51-250]
Internet Reference Services Quarterly
   p LJ - v122 - Ja '97 - p156 [51-250]
**The Internet Resource Directory for K-12 Teachers and
Librarians. 96/97 Ed.**
   r Emerg Lib - v24 - Mr '97 - p42 [51-250]
The Internet Unleashed 1996
   r New Sci - v151 - S 14 '96 - p46 [51-250]
Interweave Knits
   p LJ - v121 - N 15 '96 - p94 [51-250]
Intner, Sheila S - *Standard Cataloging for School and
Public Libraries. 2nd Ed.*
   SLJ - v42 - S '96 - p114 [1-50]
   SLMQ - v25 - Fall '96 - p64 [51-250]
Intrarea In Casa
   BL - v93 - D 15 '96 - p714 [1-50]
An Introduction to Edgar Degas
   c TES - Ag 23 '96 - p24 [51-250]
An Introduction to Pieter Breugel
   c TES - Ag 23 '96 - p24 [51-250]
Introvigne, Massimo - *Indagine Sul Satanismo*
   Folkl - v107 - '96 - p118+ [501+]
Invertebrate Neuroscience
   p Nature - v383 - S 5 '96 - p34 [251-500]
Investigacion Economica
   p JEL - v35 - Mr '97 - p308 [51-250]
Investing in Today's Joy, Tomorrow's Wealth
   J Gov Info - v23 - S '96 - p656 [51-250]
Ion, A Hamish - *The Cross and the Rising Sun. Vols. 1-2*
   CH - v66 - Mr '97 - p163+ [501+]
Ion Channels. Vol. 4
   SciTech - v20 - S '96 - p20 [51-250]
Ionazzi, Daniel A - *The Stagecraft Handbook*
   TCI - v30 - O '96 - p56 [1-50]
Iordanskaia, L N - *A Russian-English Collocational
Dictionary of the Human Body*
   r ARBA - v28 - '97 - p399 [251-500]
Iowa Hydraulics Colloquium (1995: Iowa City, Iowa) -
Issues and Directions in Hydraulics
   SciTech - v20 - D '96 - p67 [51-250]
Ippisch, Hanneke - *Sky: A True Story of Resistance during
World War II*
   c HB - v72 - N '96 - p759+ [251-500]
   y HB Guide - v7 - Fall '96 - p373 [51-250]
Irani, K D - *Social Justice in the Ancient World*
   Ethics - v107 - Ja '97 - p400+ [51-250]
Irbinskas, Karen - *How Jackrabbit Got His Very Long
Ears*
   c CLW - v67 - Mr '97 - p14 [1-50]
Ireland, Ann - *The Instructor*
   BL - v93 - Ap 1 '97 - p1281 [51-250]
   BW - v27 - Ap 13 '97 - p6 [251-500]
   LJ - v122 - Ap 1 '97 - p126 [51-250]
   PW - v244 - F 24 '97 - p63 [51-250]
Ireland, Karin - *How to Have All the Answers when the
Questions Keep Changing*
   BL - v93 - N 1 '96 - p465 [51-250]

Wonderful Nature, Wonderful You (Illus. by Christopher Canyon)
  c Ch BWatch - v6 - N '96 - p1 [51-250]
  c HB Guide - v8 - Spr '97 - p118 [51-250]
Ireland, Kenneth - *A Treasury of Ghost Stories (Illus. by Tony Morris)*
  c CLW - v67 - Mr '97 - p52 [251-500]
Ireland, Owen S - *Religion, Ethnicity, and Politics*
     AHR - v102 - F '97 - p171+ [501+]
     Historian - v59 - Win '97 - p429+ [501+]
     W&M Q - v54 - Ap '97 - p447+ [501+]
Ireland, Patricia - *What Women Want*
     KR - v64 - My 1 '96 - p667 [251-500]
     LATBR - Ag 11 '96 - p6+ [501+]
     Utne R - Jl '96 - p107+ [501+]
Ireland, Patrick John - *Fashion Design Illustration: Men*
     LJ - v122 - Mr 15 '97 - p63 [51-250]
Ireland (Insight Compact Guides)
  r BL - v93 - S 15 '96 - p210 [1-50]
Ireland. Dept. of Justice - *Management of Offenders*
     J Gov Info - v23 - S '96 - p658 [51-250]
Irele, Dipo - *In the Tracks of African Predicament*
     Africa T - v44 - 1 '97 - p87+ [251-500]
  Introduction to Contemporary Social and Political Thinkers
     Africa T - v44 - 1 '97 - p86+ [251-500]
Ireson, Carol J - *Field, Forest and Family*
     R&R Bk N - v12 - F '97 - p20 [51-250]
Irfan-Ul-Haque - *Trade, Technology, and International Competitiveness*
     JEL - v34 - S '96 - p1477 [51-250]
Irigaray, Luce - *An Ethics of Sexual Difference*
     TranslRevS - v2 - D '96 - p18 [51-250]
  Thinking the Difference
     CPR - v16 - Je '96 - p174+ [501+]
     South HR - v30 - Fall '96 - p390+ [501+]
Irish Almanac and Yearbook of Facts 1997
  r Am - v176 - Mr 22 '97 - p2 [501+]
The Irish Review
  p TLS - N 15 '96 - p35 [501+]
The Irish Scientist. 1996 Ed.
  r New Sci - v152 - D 21 '96 - p66 [1-50]
Iritz, Maxine Haren - *Super Science Fair Sourcebook*
  yr SB - v32 - O '96 - p204 [251-500]
Irmer, Thomas - *Metafiction, Moving Pictures, Moving Histories*
     Can Lit - Win '96 - p161+ [501+]
Ironside, Elizabeth - *The Accomplice*
     Spec - v277 - D 14 '96 - p74 [51-250]
IRPTC Legal File 1994/1995. Vols. 1-2
     SciTech - v21 - Mr '97 - p82 [51-250]
Irreverent Guides: Chicago
  r BL - v93 - S 15 '96 - p210 [1-50]
Irtz, Hilma R - *Figural Nodders*
     Ant & CM - v101 - F '97 - p33 [51-250]
Irvin, Dale T - *The Agitated Mind of God*
     Am - v176 - F 15 '97 - p31+ [51-250]
Irvin, Monte - *Monte Irvin: Nice Guys Finish First*
     BW - v26 - Jl 7 '96 - p1+ [501+]
     NYTBR - v101 - Ap 7 '96 - p16 [51-250]
Irvine, Demar - *Massenet: A Chronicle of His Life and Times*
     South HR - v30 - Sum '96 - p282+ [501+]
Irvine, G Brent - *Neuropeptide Protocols*
     SciTech - v21 - Mr '97 - p42 [51-250]
Irvine, Jacqueline Jordan - *Growing Up African American in Catholic Schools*
     HER - v67 - Spr '97 - p144+ [501+]
     JNE - v65 - Win '96 - p100+ [501+]
     Urban Ed - v31 - Ja '97 - p609+ [501+]
Irvine, Janice M - *Sexual Cultures and the Construction of Adolescent Identities*
     Adoles - v32 - Spr '97 - p246 [51-250]
Irvine, Joan - *How to Make Holiday Pop-Ups (Illus. by Linda Hendry)*
  c BL - v93 - S 15 '96 - p235 [51-250]
  c CCB-B - v50 - S '96 - p16+ [51-250]
  c Ch BWatch - v6 - D '96 - p1 [1-50]
  c HB Guide - v8 - Spr '97 - p135 [51-250]
  c SLJ - v42 - S '96 - p217 [51-250]
Irvine, Martin - *The Making of Textual Culture*
     MLR - v92 - Ap '97 - p405+ [501+]
Irving, Clifford - *The Spring*
     BL - v92 - Ag '96 - p1886 [51-250]
Irving, David - *Goebbels: Mastermind of the Third Reich*
     NL - v79 - Ag 12 '96 - p3+ [501+]
     NYRB - v43 - S 19 '96 - p8+ [501+]
  Nuremberg: The Last Battle
     Spec - v278 - F 15 '97 - p30 [501+]
Irving, Helen - *A Woman's Constitution?*
     Aust Bk R - F '97 - p58 [51-250]

Irving, Howard H - *Family Mediation*
     JMF - v58 - Ag '96 - p805 [251-500]
Irving, John - *Trying to Save Piggy Sneed*
  y Kliatt - v31 - My '97 - p19 [51-250]
     LATBR - Mr 17 '96 - p10 [51-250]
     NYTBR - v102 - Mr 23 '97 - p28 [1-50]
Irving, Shae - *Nolo's Everyday Law Book*
     LJ - v122 - Ja '97 - p122 [51-250]
Irving, Washington - *The Legend of Sleepy Hollow (Illus. by Michael Garland)*
  c PW - v243 - S 16 '96 - p85 [1-50]
  Old Christmas
     LJ - v122 - Ap 15 '97 - p125 [1-50]
Irwin, Alan - *Citizen Science*
     Choice - v34 - S '96 - p148 [51-250]
  Misunderstanding Science?
     Sci - v274 - O 25 '96 - p523 [1-50]
Irwin, Douglas A - *Against the Tide*
     Choice - v34 - N '96 - p507+ [51-250]
     Econ - v341 - D 7 '96 - p9* [251-500]
     For Aff - v75 - S '96 - p138+ [51-250]
     JEL - v34 - D '96 - p2011 [51-250]
     NYTBR - v101 - S 15 '96 - p29 [501+]
     Reason - v28 - F '97 - p60+ [501+]
     TLS - S 13 '96 - p28 [501+]
  Trade in the Pre-Modern Era 1400-1700. Vols. 1-2
     JEL - v34 - D '96 - p1474 [51-250]
Irwin, Geoffrey - *The Prehistoric Exploration and Colonisation of the Pacific*
     Pac A - v69 - Sum '96 - p299+ [501+]
Irwin, Hadley - *The Original Freddie Ackerman*
  c SLJ - v42 - N '96 - p41 [1-50]
  The Original Freddie Ackerman (McDonough). Audio Version
  c BL - v93 - My 15 '97 - p1595 [1-50]
  Sarah with an H
  y BL - v93 - S 1 '96 - p119 [51-250]
  y CCB-B - v50 - N '96 - p99 [51-250]
  y HB Guide - v8 - Spr '97 - p81 [51-250]
  c KR - v64 - O 1 '96 - p1468 [51-250]
  y PW - v243 - O 7 '96 - p77 [51-250]
  c SLJ - v43 - F '97 - p103 [51-250]
  y VOYA - v19 - D '96 - p270 [51-250]
Irwin, John T - *Doubling and Incest/Repetition and Revenge. Expanded Ed.*
     AL - v68 - D '96 - p879 [1-50]
  The Mystery to a Solution
     CLS - v33 - 1 '96 - p129+ [501+]
Irwin, Judith Westphal - *Empowering Ourselves and Transforming Schools*
     Choice - v34 - My '97 - p1551 [51-250]
     R&R Bk N - v12 - F '97 - p68 [51-250]
Irwin, Lee - *The Dream Seekers*
     Rapport - v19 - 5 '96 - p40 [251-500]
  Visionary Worlds
     Choice - v34 - S '96 - p141 [51-250]
     R&R Bk N - v12 - F '97 - p2 [1-50]
Irwin, Mark - *Quick, Now, Always*
     ABR - v17 - Ag '96 - p19 [501+]
     Chel - 61 '96 - p137+ [501+]
Irwin, Michael R - *Visual dBASE Programming*
     SciTech - v20 - D '96 - p14 [51-250]
Irwin, Robert - *Exquisite Corpse*
     KR - v65 - Mr 1 '97 - p326 [51-250]
     LJ - v122 - Ap 1 '97 - p126 [51-250]
     NS & S - v9 - Ap 26 '96 - p32 [1-50]
     PW - v244 - Mr 3 '97 - p65 [51-250]
     VV - v42 - Ap 15 '97 - p54 [501+]
Irwin, Sarah - *Rights of Passage, Social Change and the Transition from Youth to Adulthood*
     TES - Jl 5 '96 - p8* [501+]
Irwin, Terence - *Plato's Ethics*
     Ethics - v107 - O '96 - p146+ [501+]
     Phil R - v105 - Ap '96 - p235+ [501+]
     RM - v50 - S '96 - p159+ [501+]
     TLS - Ja 3 '97 - p12 [501+]
Irwin, William - *The New Niagara*
     Choice - v34 - N '96 - p525 [51-250]
     NYRB - v44 - Ja 9 '97 - p46+ [501+]
     Pub Hist - v19 - Win '97 - p88+ [501+]
     VQR - v73 - Win '97 - p7* [501+]
Isaac, John - *Bosnia: Civil War in Europe (Illus. by John Isaac)*
  c HB Guide - v8 - Spr '97 - p167 [51-250]
  c SLJ - v42 - D '96 - p129 [51-250]
  The Middle East: Struggle for a Homeland (Illus. by John Isaac)
  c HB Guide - v8 - Spr '97 - p167 [51-250]
  Rwanda: Fierce Clashes in Central Africa (Illus. by John Isaac)
  c HB Guide - v8 - Spr '97 - p167 [51-250]

  Vietnam: The Boat People Search for a Home (Illus. by John Isaac)
  c HB Guide - v8 - Spr '97 - p167 [51-250]
Isaacman, Allen - *Cotton Is the Mother of Poverty*
     AHR - v102 - F '97 - p150+ [501+]
Isaacs, Ronald H - *Close Encounters*
     PW - v243 - O 14 '96 - p76 [51-250]
  Sacred Seasons
     LJ - v122 - Ap 15 '97 - p86+ [51-250]
Isaacs, Susan - *Lily White*
     BW - v26 - Jl 7 '96 - p7 [501+]
     CSM - v88 - S 19 '96 - p14 [51-250]
     Ent W - Ap 18 '97 - p63 [1-50]
     KR - v64 - My 1 '96 - p625 [251-500]
     NYTBR - v102 - Ap 13 '97 - p32 [51-250]
  y SLJ - v42 - D '96 - p152 [51-250]
  Lily White (Estabrook). Audio Version
     BWatch - v17 - D '96 - p10 [1-50]
  Lily White (Conlin). Audio Version
     LJ - v122 - F 15 '97 - p175 [51-250]
Isaacson, Keith B - *Office Hysteroscopy*
     SciTech - v20 - S '96 - p40 [51-250]
Isaacson, Philip M - *Round Buildings, Square Buildings, and Buildings that Wiggle like a Fish*
  c HB Guide - v7 - Fall '96 - p355+ [51-250]
  A Short Walk around the Pyramids and through the World of Art
  c HB Guide - v7 - Fall '96 - p356 [51-250]
Isachsen, Olaf - *Joining the Entrepreneurial Elite*
     LJ - v121 - N 1 '96 - p74+ [51-250]
Isadora, Rachel - *Lili Backstage (Illus. by Rachel Isadora)*
  c BL - v93 - Mr 15 '97 - p1247 [51-250]
  c KR - v65 - Mr 15 '97 - p463 [51-250]
  c PW - v244 - Mr 10 '97 - p69 [51-250]
  The Steadfast Tin Soldier (Illus. by Rachel Isadora)
  c HB Guide - v7 - Fall '96 - p261 [51-250]
  Young Mozart (Illus. by Rachel Isadora)
  c BL - v93 - My 1 '97 - p1500 [51-250]
  c KR - v65 - Ap 1 '97 - p558 [51-250]
  c PW - v244 - Mr 31 '97 - p73 [51-250]
Isager, Jacob - *Pliny on Art and Society*
     CW - v89 - Jl '96 - p511+ [251-500]
Isard, Peter - *Exchange Rate Economics*
  r Econ J - v106 - S '96 - p1441+ [501+]
Isasi-Diaz, Ada Maria - *Mujerista Theology*
     OS - v32 - N '96 - p33 [51-250]
     Rel St Rev - v23 - Ap '97 - p154 [51-250]
Isay, David - *Holding On*
     PW - v244 - Mr 31 '97 - p72 [1-50]
Isbell, John Claiborne - *The Birth of European Romanticism*
     MLR - v91 - O '96 - p996+ [251-500]
Isenberg, Barbara - *Making It Big*
     LJ - v122 - Mr 15 '97 - p65 [51-250]
     PW - v243 - O 14 '96 - p74+ [51-250]
     TCI - v30 - O '96 - p57+ [51-250]
     TCI - v31 - Mr '97 - p54 [501+]
Isenberg, Michael T - *John L. Sullivan and His America*
     Aethlon - v13 - Spr '96 - p220+ [501+]
Isensee, Scott - *Art of Rapid Prototyping*
     CBR - v14 - Jl '96 - p24+ [51-250]
Iserson, Kenneth V - *Death to Dust*
     Rel St Rev - v22 - O '96 - p342 [51-250]
Isham, C J - *Lectures on Quantum Theory*
     New Sci - v151 - S 28 '96 - p54+ [501+]
     Phys Today - v49 - Ag '96 - p66 [501+]
Isham, Valerie - *Models for Infectious Human Diseases*
     SciTech - v20 - D '96 - p39 [51-250]
Ishay, Micheline R - *Internationalism and Its Betrayal*
     CPR - v16 - D '96 - p414+ [501+]
Isherwood, Charles - *Wonder Bread and Ecstasy*
     PW - v243 - O 21 '96 - p77 [51-250]
Isherwood, Christopher - *Christopher and His Kind*
     LATBR - N 10 '96 - p15 [51-250]
  Diaries. Vol. 1
     Advocate - Mr 4 '97 - p57 [251-500]
     BL - v93 - D 1 '96 - p639 [51-250]
     KR - v64 - N 15 '96 - p1653 [251-500]
     LATBR - F 2 '97 - p6 [501+]
     LJ - v121 - D '96 - p93+ [51-250]
     Lon R Bks - v19 - Ja 2 '97 - p32+ [501+]
     Nat - v264 - F 10 '97 - p27+ [501+]
     NS - v125 - D 20 '96 - p122 [251-500]
     NYRB - v44 - F 20 '97 - p11+ [501+]
     NYTBR - v102 - Ja 5 '97 - p6 [501+]
     Obs - N 10 '96 - p15* [501+]
     PW - v243 - N 11 '96 - p63+ [51-250]
     Spec - v277 - N 16 '96 - p54 [501+]
     Spec - v277 - N 23 '96 - p44 [1-50]
     Time - v149 - Ja 13 '97 - p74 [501+]
     TLS - Ja 10 '97 - p5 [501+]

Goodbye to Berlin (Cumming). Audio Version
  CR - v270 - Ja '97 - p56 [1-50]
Isherwood, Sheila - *My Grandad*
  c Magpies - v11 - My '96 - p53 [1-50]
Isherwood, Shirley - *Something for James (Illus. by Neil Reed)*
  c HB Guide - v7 - Fall '96 - p261 [51-250]
Ishiguro, Kazuo - *The Unconsoled*
  HR - v49 - Sum '96 - p316+ [501+]
  NYTBR - v101 - O 20 '96 - p36 [51-250]
  PW - v243 - S 2 '96 - p122 [1-50]
Ishiguro, Masayasu - *Energy Demand in Five Major Asian Developing Countries*
  J Gov Info - v23 - S '96 - p685 [51-250]
Ishihara, Kenji - *Soil Behaviour in Earthquake Geotechnics*
  Choice - v34 - My '97 - p1530 [51-250]
Ishikawa, K - *Brain Processes and Memory*
  SciTech - v21 - Mr '97 - p41 [51-250]
Isichei, Elizabeth - *A History of Christianity in Africa*
  CHR - v82 - O '96 - p745+ [501+]
  JR - v77 - Ja '97 - p187+ [501+]
Isil, Olivia A - *When a Loose Cannon Flogs a Dead Horse, There's the Devil to Pay*
  Am - v175 - N 30 '96 - p2 [501+]
Islam, Syed Manzuru - *The Ethics of Travel*
  TLS - N 29 '96 - p32 [251-500]
Islamoglu-Inan, Huri - *State and Peasant in the Ottoman Empire*
  JEH - v57 - Mr '97 - p234+ [501+]
Isler, Alan - *The Bacon Fancier*
  KR - v65 - Ap 1 '97 - p488 [251-500]
  PW - v244 - My 5 '97 - p198 [51-250]
  Kraven Images
  Books - v11 - Ap '97 - p23 [51-250]
  PW - v244 - My 12 '97 - p74 [1-50]
  Op. Non Cit.
  Obs - F 23 '97 - p17* [501+]
  Spec - v278 - F 22 '97 - p29+ [501+]
  TLS - F 7 '97 - p22 [501+]
  The Prince of West End Avenue
  Books - v10 - Je '96 - p24 [1-50]
  TES - Jl 26 '96 - pR5 [51-250]
Isler, Charlotte - *The Watts Teen Health Dictionary*
  yr BL - v93 - Ja '97 - p770 [1-50]
  yr BL - v93 - S 1 '96 - p172 [251-500]
  yr Kliatt - v31 - Ja '97 - p22 [51-250]
  yr SB - v33 - Ja '97 - p13+ [251-500]
  yr SLJ - v42 - N '96 - p137+ [51-250]
  yr VOYA - v19 - O '96 - p232 [251-500]
Ismagilov, R S - *Representations of Infinite-Dimensional Groups*
  SciTech - v20 - S '96 - p10 [51-250]
Ison, Tara - *A Child Out of Alcatraz*
  KR - v65 - F 15 '97 - p245 [251-500]
  LJ - v122 - Ap 1 '97 - p126 [51-250]
  PW - v244 - Mr 24 '97 - p61 [51-250]
Israel, Fred L - *The Amish*
  c HB Guide - v7 - Fall '96 - p312 [1-50]
  c SLJ - v42 - O '96 - p134 [51-250]
Israel, Jonathan - *The Dutch Republic*
  AHR - v101 - D '96 - p1562+ [501+]
  EHR - v111 - S '96 - p943+ [501+]
  Six Ct J - v27 - Fall '96 - p892+ [501+]
Israel Conference on Computer Systems and Software Engineering (7th: 1996: Hertseliyah, Israel) - *Proceedings of the Seventh Israeli Conference on Computer Systems and Software Engineering, June 12-13, 1996, Herzliya, Israel*
  SciTech - v20 - S '96 - p8 [51-250]
Israel Studies
  p LJ - v122 - Ap 15 '97 - p127 [51-250]
Issawi, Charles Philip - *The Middle East Economy*
  MEJ - v50 - Sum '96 - p453 [51-250]
  Rel St Rev - v22 - O '96 - p356+ [51-250]
Isser, Steve - *The Economics and Politics of the United States Oil Industry 1920-1990*
  Choice - v34 - D '96 - p658 [51-250]
  JEL - v34 - S '96 - p1456 [51-250]
Issue Update on Information Security and Privacy in Network Environments
  J Gov Info - v23 - S '96 - p557 [51-250]
Issues in Accounting Education
  p JEL - v34 - S '96 - p1505 [51-250]
Istanbul (Essential Travel Guides)
  r BL - v93 - S 15 '96 - p206 [1-50]
L'Italia Tra Rivoluzione E Riforme 1831-1846
  EHR - v112 - Ap '97 - p501 [251-500]
Italiano, Francesca - *Crescendo! A Thematic Approach to Intermediate Italian Language and Culture*
  MLJ - v80 - Win '96 - p552+ [501+]

Italy. Commissione Per La Pubblicazione Dei Documenti Diplomatici - *I Documenti Diplomatici Italiani. 2nd Ser., Vols. 15-16*
  EHR - v112 - Ap '97 - p512+ [251-500]
  I Documenti Diplomatici Italiani. 2nd Ser., Vols. 17-18
  EHR - v112 - F '97 - p245 [501+]
  I Documenti Diplomatici Italiani. 10th Ser., Vol. 1
  EHR - v111 - S '96 - p1028+ [501+]
  I Documenti Diplomatici Italiani. 10th Ser., Vol. 2
  EHR - v111 - N '96 - p1350+ [251-500]
Italy (Eyewitness Travel Guides)
  r ARBA - v28 - '97 - p180+ [51-250]
  r BL - v93 - S 15 '96 - p206 [1-50]
  yr Kliatt - v30 - N '96 - p28 [51-250]
  yr SLJ - v42 - S '96 - p242 [51-250]
Ito, Takatoshi - *Financial Deregulation and Integration in East Asia*
  JEL - v34 - D '96 - p2053 [51-250]
  Growth Theories in Light of the East Asian Experience
  Econ J - v107 - Ja '97 - p280+ [51-250]
Ito, Tom - *The California Gold Rush*
  y HB Guide - v8 - Spr '97 - p173 [51-250]
  y SLJ - v43 - Mr '97 - p202 [51-250]
  John Muir
  c HB Guide - v7 - Fall '96 - p371 [51-250]
Itoh, Tatsuo - *Finite Element Software for Microwave Engineering*
  SciTech - v20 - D '96 - p79 [51-250]
ITP Nelson Canadian Dictionary of the English Language
  r BIC - v26 - Mr '97 - p2+ [501+]
It's about Our Health
  J Gov Info - v23 - S '96 - p615 [51-250]
IT's English
  TES - Ja 3 '97 - p47U [1-50]
Ittmann, Karl - *Work, Gender, and Family in Victorian England*
  AHR - v102 - F '97 - p106+ [501+]
  Albion - v28 - Sum '96 - p331+ [501+]
  Historian - v59 - Win '97 - p464+ [501+]
  JIH - v27 - Win '97 - p515+ [501+]
Iturbide, Graciela - *Images of the Spirit*
  BWatch - v18 - F '97 - p9 [1-50]
  LATBR - D 8 '96 - p26 [51-250]
  NYTBR - v102 - F 23 '97 - p17 [51-250]
  WSJ-MW - v78 - D 5 '96 - pA18 [51-250]
Itzin, Catherine - *Gender, Culture and Organizational Change*
  Socio R - v45 - F 1 '97 - p171+ [501+]
Itzkoff, Seymour W - *Children Learning to Read*
  LJ - v121 - O 1 '96 - p96 [51-250]
Itzkowitz, Gary - *Contingency Theory*
  Choice - v34 - Mr '97 - p1245 [51-250]
IUTAM Symposium on Asymptotic Methods for Turbulent Shear Flows at High Reynolds Numbers (1995: Bochum, Germany) - *Asymptotic Methods for Turbulent Shear Flows at High Reynolds Numbers*
  SciTech - v21 - Mr '97 - p15 [51-250]
IUTAM Symposium on Nonlinear Instability and Transition in Three-Dimensional Boundary Layers (1995: Manchester, England) - *IUTAM Symposium on Nonlinear Instability and Transition in Three-Dimensional Boundary Layers*
  SciTech - v20 - D '96 - p61 [51-250]
Ivashkin, Alexander - *Alfred Schnittke*
  PW - v243 - S 30 '96 - p79 [1-50]
Ivell, Richard - *Oxytocin: Cellular and Molecular Approaches in Medicine and Research*
  SciTech - v20 - S '96 - p23 [51-250]
Ivers, Gregg - *To Build a Wall*
  J Ch St - v38 - Aut '96 - p923+ [251-500]
  J Pol - v58 - N '96 - p1208+ [501+]
Iversen, Theodore - *Games Real Estate Agents Play*
  Rapport - v19 - 4 '96 - p36 [251-500]
Iverson, Diane - *Discover the Seasons*
  c CLW - v67 - D '96 - p60 [51-250]
Iverson, Peter - *When Indians Became Cowboys*
  WHQ - v27 - Win '96 - p516 [501+]
Ives, Colta - *Toulouse-Lautrec in the Metropolitan Museum of Art*
  Choice - v34 - D '96 - p602 [51-250]
Ives, Edward D - *The Tape-Recorded Interview. 2nd Ed.*
  Pub Hist - v18 - Fall '96 - p183+ [501+]
Ives, Penny - *Millie and the Mermaid*
  c Sch Lib - v44 - N '96 - p146 [51-250]
Ives, Richard - *Of Tigers and Men*
  NYTBR - v102 - Mr 9 '97 - p28 [1-50]
  PW - v244 - F 17 '97 - p217 [1-50]
  Trib Bks - Mr 2 '97 - p8 [1-50]
Ivry, Benjamin - *Francis Poulenc*
  PW - v243 - S 30 '96 - p79 [1-50]

Ivy, Marilyn - *Discourses of the Vanishing*
  Pac A - v69 - Fall '96 - p418+ [501+]
Iwago, Mitsuaki - *Mitsuaki Iwago's Penguins*
  Trib Bks - Ap 6 '97 - p6+ [51-250]
Iwami, Toru - *Japan in the International Financial System*
  Econ J - v106 - N '96 - p1836+ [251-500]
Iyam, David Uru - *The Broken Hoe*
  AAPSS-A - v549 - Ja '97 - p189+ [501+]
  Am Ethnol - v23 - N '96 - p909+ [501+]
Iyer, Pico - *Cuba and the Night*
  Obs - N 10 '96 - p18* [51-250]
  Tropical Classical
  BL - v93 - Ap 1 '97 - p1276+ [51-250]
  BW - v27 - Mr 30 '97 - p13 [51-250]
  KR - v65 - F 15 '97 - p274+ [251-500]
  LJ - v122 - Ap 15 '97 - p104 [51-250]
  NYTLa - v146 - My 2 '97 - pC37 [501+]
  PW - v244 - F 17 '97 - p201+ [51-250]
Iyob, Ruth - *The Eritrean Struggle for Independence*
  Africa T - v43 - 4 '96 - p434+ [501+]
  APSR - v90 - S '96 - p698+ [501+]
Iyun, B Folasade - *The Health of Nations*
  GJ - v162 - N '96 - p341+ [51-250]
Izen, Judith - *Collector's Guide to Vogue Dolls*
  r Ant & CM - v102 - Ap '97 - p68 [251-500]
Izzi, Eugene - *A Matter of Honor*
  Time - v149 - Ap 28 '97 - p76 [501+]

J

J., Angelica - *Fermentation*
    LJ - v122 - My 1 '97 - p136 [51-250]
J. Paul Getty Museum - *European Clocks in the J. Paul Getty Museum*
    WSJ-MW - v78 - D 5 '96 - pA18 [1-50]
Jabbari, Bijan - *Multiaccess, Mobility and Teletraffic for Personal Communications*
    SciTech - v20 - N '96 - p73 [51-250]
Jabbur, Jibrail S - *The Bedouins and the Desert*
    MEJ - v50 - Sum '96 - p439+ [501+]
Jabes, Edmond - *The Book of Margins*
    TranslRevS - v2 - D '96 - p11 [51-250]
Jablonski, David - *Evolutionary Paleobiology*
    Choice - v34 - Ap '97 - p1368 [51-250]
Jablonski, Edward - *Harold Arlen: Rhythm, Rainbows, and Blues*
    BW - v26 - Jl 7 '96 - p3 [501+]
    Choice - v34 - N '96 - p470 [51-250]
    KR - v64 - My 1 '96 - p667 [251-500]
    Rapport - v19 - 5 '96 - p43 [251-500]
Jablonski, Nina G - *Theropithecus: The Rise and Fall of a Primate Genus*
    RA - v25 - 3 '96 - p205+ [501+]
Jablonsky, David - *Paradigm Lost?*
    Arm F&S - v22 - Sum '96 - p651+ [501+]
    Time's Cycle and National Military Strategy
    J Gov Info - v23 - S '96 - p573 [51-250]
Jabri, Vivienne - *Discourses on Violence*
    Choice - v34 - N '96 - p546 [51-250]
    JPR - v34 - F '97 - p112+ [251-500]
Jaccard, James - *Statistics for the Behavioral Sciences. 3rd Ed.*
    R&R Bk N - v12 - F '97 - p5 [51-250]
Jaccard, Roland - *Le Cimetiere De La Morale*
    FR - v70 - Mr '97 - p591+ [501+]
Jaccomard, Helene - *Lecteur Et Lecture Dans L'Autobiographie Francaise Contemporaine*
    FR - v70 - F '97 - p462+ [501+]
Jack, Belinda Elizabeth - *Negritude and Literary Criticism*
    Bl S - v26 - Sum '96 - p65 [1-50]
    Choice - v34 - S '96 - p133 [51-250]
Jack, Donald - *Hitler Versus Me*
    BIC - v25 - N '96 - p12+ [501+]
Jack, George - *Beowulf: A Student Edition*
    RES - v47 - Ag '96 - p400+ [501+]
    Specu - v72 - Ja '97 - p176+ [501+]
Jackall, Robert - *Propaganda*
    Col Comp - v47 - D '96 - p617+ [51-250]
Jackaway, Gwenyth L - *Media at War*
    JMCQ - v73 - Win '96 - p1006+ [501+]
Jackley, John L - *Below the Beltway*
    BL - v92 - Ag '96 - p1862+ [501+]
    BW - v26 - Ag 18 '96 - p7 [501+]
    Pres SQ - v27 - Win '97 - p153+ [501+]
Jackowski, Karol - *Divine Madness*
    RR - v56 - Mr '97 - p222 [1-50]
Jacks, Philip - *The Antiquarian and the Myth of Antiquity*
    CW - v90 - S '96 - p65+ [251-500]
    Specu - v71 - O '96 - p964+ [501+]
Jackson, A R W - *Environmental Science*
    y New Sci - v151 - S 28 '96 - p50+ [501+]
Jackson, Alvin - *Colonel Edward Saunderson: Land and Loyalty in Victorian Ireland*
    AHR - v101 - O '96 - p1217 [501+]
    EHR - v112 - Ap '97 - p513+ [501+]
Jackson, Bernard S - *Making Sense in Law*
    Choice - v34 - N '96 - p534 [51-250]

Jackson, Brian Keith - *The View from Here*
    BL - v93 - F 15 '97 - p1003 [51-250]
    CSM - v89 - Mr 10 '97 - p12 [251-500]
    KR - v64 - D 15 '96 - p1756 [251-500]
    LJ - v122 - F 1 '97 - p106 [51-250]
    PW - v243 - D 30 '96 - p55 [251-500]
    y SLJ - v43 - Mr '97 - p215+ [51-250]
Jackson, Carlton - *Forgotten Tragedy*
    Choice - v34 - My '97 - p1552 [51-250]
    PW - v243 - D 16 '96 - p53 [251-500]
Jackson, Charles - *The Lost Weekend*
    BWatch - v17 - N '96 - p10 [51-250]
Jackson, Charles O - *The Other Americans*
    R&R Bk N - v11 - D '96 - p40 [51-250]
Jackson, Chris - *Edmund and Hillary (Illus. by Chris Jackson)*
    c Quill & Q - v63 - Ja '97 - p38 [251-500]
Jackson, Christopher - *Healing Your Mind, Healing Your Heart. Audio Version*
    BWatch - v18 - Mr '97 - p8 [1-50]
Jackson, Colin - *The Young Track and Field Athlete*
    c HB Guide - v7 - Fall '96 - p361 [51-250]
    c SLJ - v42 - Ag '96 - p156 [51-250]
Jackson, Dave - *Hero Tales*
    c HB Guide - v8 - Spr '97 - p87 [51-250]
    Quest for the Lost Prince (Illus. by Julian Jackson)
    c BL - v93 - O 1 '96 - p335 [51-250]
Jackson, David - *Taboos in German Literature*
    R&R Bk N - v11 - N '96 - p74 [51-250]
    TLS - S 20 '96 - p32 [51-250]
Jackson, Donald C - *Building the Ultimate Dam*
    Choice - v34 - S '96 - p149 [51-250]
    PHR - v66 - F '97 - p116+ [251-500]
    SciTech - v20 - S '96 - p51 [51-250]
    WHQ - v27 - Win '96 - p525+ [501+]
Jackson, Donna M - *The Bone Detectives (Illus. by Charlie Fellenbaum)*
    c BL - v93 - Ap 1 '97 - p1298 [1-50]
    y BL - v93 - Ap 1 '97 - p1308 [1-50]
    c HB Guide - v7 - Fall '96 - p317 [51-250]
    c SLJ - v42 - D '96 - p30 [1-50]
Jackson, Ellen - *The Book of Slime (Illus. by Jan Davey Ellis)*
    c BL - v93 - Mr 15 '97 - p1246 [51-250]
    c KR - v65 - Ja 15 '97 - p143 [51-250]
    Cinder Edna
    c Emerg Lib - v24 - S '96 - p45 [51-250]
    The Precious Gift (Illus. by Woodleigh Marx Hubbard)
    c Ch BWatch - v6 - My '96 - p4 [1-50]
    c Emerg Lib - v24 - Mr '97 - p65 [51-250]
    c HB Guide - v7 - Fall '96 - p321+ [51-250]
Jackson, Frank - *Dictionary of Canine Terms*
    yr ARBA - v28 - '97 - p588 [51-250]
Jackson, Guida M - *Encyclopedia of Literary Epics*
    yr ARBA - v28 - '97 - p409+ [251-500]
Jackson, Harvey H, III - *Rivers of History*
    Pub Hist - v18 - Fall '96 - p158+ [501+]
Jackson, Helen Hunt - *Ramona: The Heart and Conscience of Early California (Martin). Audio Version*
    BL - v93 - S 15 '96 - p264 [51-250]
Jackson, Howard - *An Introduction to the Nature and Functions of Language*
    TES - S 20 '96 - pR8 [251-500]
Jackson, Isaac - *Somebody's New Pajamas (Illus. by David Soman)*
    c BL - v93 - Ja '97 - p767+ [1-50]
    c HB Guide - v7 - Fall '96 - p261 [1-50]
Jackson, Jeremy B C - *Evolution and Environment in Tropical America*
    SciTech - v21 - Mr '97 - p33 [251-250]

Jackson, Jerry R - *Java by Example. 1st Ed.*
    CBR - v14 - Jl '96 - p21+ [51-250]
    Java by Example. 2nd Ed.
    SciTech - v21 - Mr '97 - p7 [51-250]
Jackson, Jesse - *Legal Lynching*
    y BL - v93 - S 15 '96 - p179 [51-250]
    BW - v26 - S 22 '96 - p8 [501+]
    NYTBR - v101 - D 15 '96 - p24 [51-250]
Jackson, John C - *Children of the Fur Trade*
    Beav - v76 - O '96 - p39+ [501+]
    WHQ - v27 - Win '96 - p521 [251-500]
Jackson, Jon A - *Dead Folks*
    NYTBR - v101 - Jl 21 '96 - p25 [251-500]
Jackson, Keith - *Historical Dictionary of New Zealand*
    r ARBA - v28 - '97 - p73+ [251-500]
    r Choice - v34 - Mr '97 - p1138 [51-250]
Jackson, Kennell - *America Is Me*
    Bl S - v26 - Sum '96 - p65 [51-250]
Jackson, Kenneth T - *The Encyclopedia of New York City*
    r Ant R - v54 - Sum '96 - p372+ [251-500]
    r Choice - v34 - S '96 - p96 [501+]
Jackson, Laura - *Mercury: The King of Queen*
    Books - v10 - Je '96 - p21 [1-50]
Jackson, Marie - *The Museum of Bad Art*
    PW - v243 - S 30 '96 - p80 [51-250]
Jackson, Mark - *New-Born Child Murder*
    Choice - v34 - Ap '97 - p1397 [51-250]
    Obs - O 20 '96 - p17* [501+]
    TLS - Mr 21 '97 - p10 [501+]
Jackson, Marvin - *Marketization, Restructuring and Competition in Transition Industries of Central and Eastern Europe*
    R&R Bk N - v12 - F '97 - p36 [51-250]
Jackson, Mary S - *Marriage Notices from Washington County, New York Newspapers 1799-1880*
    r EGH - v50 - N '96 - p176 [51-250]
Jackson, Michael, 1942- - *Michael Jackson's Beer Companion*
    LJ - v122 - Ap 1 '97 - p63 [1-50]
    Michael Jackson's World Beer Hunter. Electronic Media Version
    r LJ - v122 - Ap 1 '97 - p63 [1-50]
    The Simon and Schuster Pocket Guide to Beer
    r LJ - v122 - Ap 1 '97 - p64 [1-50]
Jackson, Michael S - *Human Genome Evolution*
    Choice - v34 - Ja '97 - p821+ [51-250]
Jackson, Mick - *The Underground Man*
    KR - v65 - My 1 '97 - p663+ [251-500]
    Obs - Ja 19 '97 - p15* [251-500]
    PW - v244 - My 5 '97 - p199 [251-500]
    Spec - v278 - Ja 25 '97 - p43 [251-500]
    TLS - Ja 31 '97 - p21 [501+]
Jackson, Nancy - *Photographers: History and Culture through the Camera*
    y BL - v93 - My 1 '97 - p1485 [51-250]
    c KR - v65 - Mr 15 '97 - p463 [51-250]
Jackson, Patricia Ludder - *Primary Care of the Child with a Chronic Condition. 2nd Ed.*
    SciTech - v20 - S '96 - p41 [51-250]
Jackson, Peter M - *Privatisation and Regulation*
    Econ J - v106 - N '96 - p1845 [51-250]
Jackson, Richard A - *Ordines Coronationis Franciae*
    CHR - v82 - Jl '96 - p517+ [501+]
Jackson, Robert H - *Indians, Franciscans, and Spanish Colonization*
    AHR - v101 - O '96 - p1272+ [501+]
    HAHR - v76 - N '96 - p771+ [501+]
Jackson, Rosie - *Frieda Lawrence*
    Books - v9 - S '95 - p24+ [1-50]

Jackson, Sandra - *Beyond Comfort Zones in Multiculturalism*
  Choice - v34 - S '96 - p179 [51-250]
Jackson, Sheneska - *Caught Up in the Rapture*
  Ant R - v55 - Spr '97 - p243 [251-500]
  Bloom Rev - v17 - Ja '97 - p19 [1-50]
  LJ - v121 - N 15 '96 - p116 [51-250]
  y SLJ - v42 - Ag '96 - p184 [51-250]
Li'l Mama's Rules
  BL - v93 - My 1 '97 - p1479 [51-250]
  KR - v65 - Ap 1 '97 - p488 [251-500]
  LJ - v122 - My 1 '97 - p140 [51-250]
  PW - v244 - Ap 21 '97 - p60 [51-250]
Jackson, Shirley - *Just an Ordinary Day*
  BL - v93 - O 1 '96 - p291 [51-250]
  BW - v27 - Ja 5 '97 - p4 [51-250]
  CSM - v89 - Mr 17 '97 - p13 [501+]
  Ent W - D 6 '96 - p59 [51-250]
  KR - v64 - N 1 '96 - p1554 [251-500]
  Nat - v263 - D 23 '96 - p25+ [501+]
  NW - v129 - Ja 13 '97 - p70 [251-500]
  NYTBR - v101 - D 29 '96 - p10 [501+]
  PW - v243 - O 14 '96 - p63 [51-250]
  VV - v42 - Ja 14 '97 - p53 [501+]
Jackson, Stephen - *Franz Schubert: An Essential Guide to His Life and Work*
  y BL - v93 - My 1 '97 - p1472 [51-250]
Jackson, Susan E - *Diversity in Work Teams*
  Per Psy - v50 - Spr '97 - p2091 [501+]
  R&R Bk N - v12 - F '97 - p45 [1-50]
Jackson, Terence - *From Polynomials to Sums of Squares*
  y New Sci - v151 - S 28 '96 - p44+ [501+]
Jackson, Tim - *Material Concerns*
  Choice - v34 - Ja '97 - p844 [51-250]
  New Sci - v152 - O 26 '96 - p47 [51-250]
Jackson, Valerie - *Racism and Child Protection*
  TES - F 28 '97 - p7* [51-250]
Jackson, Vera R - *The Abusive Elder*
  SciTech - v21 - Mr '97 - p53 [51-250]
Jackson, W H - *Chivalry in Twelfth-Century Germany*
  EHR - v112 - Ap '97 - p433+ [501+]
Jackson, Wes - *Becoming Native to This Place*
  NYTBR - v101 - D 15 '96 - p41 [501+]
  PW - v243 - S 23 '96 - p73 [1-50]
  Utne R - N '96 - p87+ [51-250]
Jacob, Francois - *La Souris, La Mouche Et L'Homme*
  Nature - v386 - Ap 17 '97 - p668+ [501+]
Jacob, Herbert - *Courts, Law, and Politics in Comparative Perspective*
  APSR - v91 - Mr '97 - p216+ [501+]
Jacob, Jane - *Cities and the Wealth of Nations*
  NCR - v85 - Spr '96 - p64 [51-250]
Jacob, Jeffrey - *New Pioneers*
  PW - v244 - Ap 7 '97 - p86 [51-250]
Jacob, Joseph M - *The Republican Crown*
  TLS - S 20 '96 - p9 [501+]
Jacob, Judith M - *The Traditional Literature of Cambodia*
  Choice - v34 - N '96 - p451 [51-250]
Jacob, Kathryn Allamong - *Capital Elites*
  J Am Cult - v18 - Win '95 - p111+ [251-500]
Jacob, Mary Jane - *Culture in Action*
  Afterimage - v23 - Sum '96 - p21 [501+]
  Art J - v55 - Fall '96 - p95+ [501+]
  CS - v25 - S '96 - p681+ [501+]
Jacob, Max - *The Story of King Kabul the First and Gawain the Kitchen-Boy*
  TranslRevS - v2 - D '96 - p23 [51-250]
Jacob, Merle - *To Be Continued*
  r ARBA - v28 - '97 - p432+ [251-500]
  r RQ - v36 - Win '96 - p208 [51-250]
Jacob, Suzanne - *Les Ecrits De L'Eau Suivi Les Sept Fenetres*
  WLT - v71 - Win '97 - p103+ [251-500]
Jacob, W M - *Crown and Mitre*
  EHR - v111 - S '96 - p1041 [251-500]
Jacobelli, Lucianna - *Le Pitture Erotiche Delle Terme Suburbane Di Pompei*
  TLS - O 18 '96 - p5+ [501+]
Jacobi, Friedrich Heinrich - *The Main Philosophical Writings and the Novel Allwill*
  Phil R - v105 - Ap '96 - p248+ [501+]
  RM - v50 - S '96 - p161+ [501+]
Jacobs, A J - *America Off-Line*
  BYTE - v22 - Ja '97 - p34 [51-250]
  Ent W - N 15 '96 - p66 [51-250]
Jacobs, Aletta - *Memories: My Life as an International Leader in Health, Suffrage, and Peace*
  Choice - v34 - D '96 - p670 [51-250]
  LJ - v121 - S 15 '96 - p76 [51-250]
  TranslRevS - v2 - D '96 - p8 [51-250]

Jacobs, Anna - *High Street*
  BL - v93 - D 15 '96 - p709 [51-250]
  PW - v244 - Ja 13 '97 - p56 [51-250]
Jacobs, Arthur - *The Penguin Dictionary of Music. 6th Ed.*
  r ARBA - v28 - '97 - p471 [51-250]
Jacobs, Claude - *Replacement of Renal Function by Dialysis. 4th Ed.*
  SciTech - v20 - N '96 - p48 [51-250]
Jacobs, Eric - *Kingsley Amis: A Biography*
  AS - v65 - Aut '96 - p624+ [501+]
  Sew R - v104 - Jl '96 - p452+ [501+]
Jacobs, Francine - *Follow That Trash! (Illus. by Mavis Smith)*
  c SLJ - v43 - Mr '97 - p177 [51-250]
Jacobs, J Bruce - *Bitter Peaches and Plums*
  Ch Rev Int - v4 - Spr '97 - p166+ [501+]
Jacobs, James A - *Engineering Materials Technology. 3rd Ed.*
  SciTech - v20 - D '96 - p62 [51-250]
Jacobs, Jane M - *Edge of Empire*
  Choice - v34 - D '96 - p663 [51-250]
Jacobs, Janet Liebman - *Victimized Daughters*
  Fam in Soc - v77 - O '96 - p515+ [501+]
Jacobs, Jennifer - *The Encyclopedia of Alternative Medicine*
  r ARBA - v28 - '97 - p611+ [51-250]
  r PW - v243 - N 4 '96 - p73 [51-250]
Jacobs, John - *A Rage for Justice*
  BW - v26 - D 8 '96 - p9 [51-250]
Jacobs, Jonathan A - *Practical Realism and Moral Psychology*
  Ethics - v107 - Ja '97 - p384+ [51-250]
  Theol St - v57 - Je '96 - p385+ [251-500]
Jacobs, Jonnie - *Evidence of Guilt*
  BL - v93 - Mr 15 '97 - p1229+ [51-250]
  KR - v65 - Ja 1 '97 - p24 [51-250]
  PW - v243 - D 30 '96 - p57 [51-250]
Jacobs, Kate - *A Sister's Wish (Illus. by Nancy Carpenter)*
  c Ch BWatch - v6 - My '96 - p5 [51-250]
  c HB Guide - v7 - Fall '96 - p261 [51-250]
Jacobs, Louis - *The Jewish Religion*
  Books - v9 - S '95 - p22 [51-250]
  The Schocken Book of Jewish Mystical Testimonies
  PW - v244 - Ja 13 '97 - p69 [51-250]
Jacobs, Michael - *In Search of Supervision*
  SciTech - v20 - S '96 - p33 [51-250]
Jacobs, Moises - *Atlas of Laparoscopic Colon Surgery*
  r SciTech - v20 - D '96 - p49 [51-250]
Jacobs, Nellie - *Grading the Teacher*
  Quill & Q - v62 - O '96 - p27 [501+]
Jacobs, Paul H - *Fungal Disease*
  SciTech - v20 - D '96 - p36 [51-250]
Jacobs, Paul Samuel - *James Printer: A Novel of Rebellion*
  y CCB-B - v50 - Mr '97 - p250 [51-250]
  c KR - v65 - Ja 15 '97 - p143 [51-250]
Jacobs, Pieter A - *Thermal Infrared Characterization of Ground Targets and Backgrounds*
  SciTech - v20 - D '96 - p66 [1-50]
Jacobs, Sheldon - *Sheldon Jacobs' Guide to Successful No-Load Investing*
  WSJ-MW - v77 - S 19 '96 - pA16 [51-250]
Jacobs, Steve - *The Enemy Within*
  WLT - v70 - Aut '96 - p1018+ [501+]
Jacobs, William Jay - *World Religions*
  cr BL - v93 - O 1 '96 - p339 [1-50]
  y Emerg Lib - v23 - My '96 - p43 [1-50]
  c HB Guide - v7 - Fall '96 - p309 [51-250]
Jacobsen, John Kurt - *Chasing Progress in the Irish Republic*
  Econ J - v106 - N '96 - p1803+ [501+]
Jacobsen, Josephine - *In the Crevice of Time*
  Comw - v123 - D 6 '96 - p21 [51-250]
  What Goes without Saying
  LJ - v121 - S 15 '96 - p99 [51-250]
  PW - v243 - N 18 '96 - p64 [51-250]
Jacobsen, Judith E - *Population Growth*
  y SB - v33 - Mr '97 - p42+ [51-250]
Jacobsen, Peter - *Buried Lies*
  Aethlon - v13 - Fall '95 - p160+ [251-500]
Jacobsen, Rolf - *Night Open*
  TranslRevS - v1 - My '95 - p26 [51-250]
Jacobsen, Roy - *The New Water*
  KR - v65 - My 1 '97 - p664 [251-500]
Jacobsohn, Gary Jeffrey - *Diversity and Citizenship*
  APSR - v91 - Mr '97 - p189+ [501+]
Jacobsohn, Rachel W - *The Reading Group Handbook*
  r RQ - v36 - Win '96 - p216 [51-250]
Jacobson, Arthur Lee - *North American Landscape Trees*
  r ARBA - v28 - '97 - p584 [51-250]

Jacobson, Bernard - *A Polish Renaissance*
  FF - v20 - N '96 - p517+ [251-500]
Jacobson, David - *Rights across Borders*
  APSR - v90 - D '96 - p894+ [501+]
  CS - v26 - Ja '97 - p65+ [501+]
Jacobson, Howard - *Seriously Funny*
  NS - v126 - Ja 31 '97 - p45+ [501+]
  Obs - Ja 26 '97 - p18* [501+]
  Spec - v278 - F 8 '97 - p36+ [501+]
  TLS - F 21 '97 - p18 [501+]
Jacobson, John W - *Manual of Diagnosis and Professional Practice in Mental Retardation*
  Choice - v34 - Mr '97 - p1243 [51-250]
  SciTech - v20 - S '96 - p42 [51-250]
Jacobson, Jon - *When the Soviet Union Entered World Politics*
  EHR - v112 - Ap '97 - p526+ [501+]
  Slav R - v55 - Fall '96 - p693+ [501+]
Jacobson, Kerri - *Mei Lin's Message (Illus. by Frances Luke)*
  c Magpies - v11 - Jl '96 - p25 [51-250]
Jacobson, Matthew Frye - *Special Sorrows*
  AHR - v101 - O '96 - p1296+ [501+]
Jacobson, Michael F - *Marketing Madness*
  ACI - v7 - Fall '95 - p25+ [501+]
Jacobson, Neil S - *Clinical Handbook of Couple Therapy*
  Readings - v11 - S '96 - p27+ [51-250]
Jacobson, Stephen L - *School Administration*
  Choice - v34 - My '97 - p1551 [51-250]
Jacobus, Donald Lines - *Genealogy as Pastime and Profession*
  BWatch - v17 - D '96 - p8+ [51-250]
Jacoby, Jean - *Abimbolu*
  c Bkbird - v34 - Spr '96 - p54 [1-50]
Jacoby, Russell - *The Bell Curve Debate*
  Soc - v34 - Mr '97 - p78+ [501+]
Jacoby, Sanford M - *The Workers of Nations*
  CS - v26 - Mr '97 - p188+ [501+]
  ILRR - v50 - O '96 - p159+ [501+]
Jacoff, Michael - *The Horses of San Marco and the Quadriga of the Lord*
  Ren Q - v49 - Aut '96 - p680+ [501+]
  Specu - v71 - O '96 - p965+ [501+]
Jacq, Christian - *Les Egyptiennes*
  BL - v93 - Ja '97 - p827 [1-50]
Jacquart, Danielle - *La Formation Du Vocabulaire Scientifique Et Intellectual Dans Le Monde Grabe*
  Specu - v71 - Jl '96 - p721 [501+]
Jacques, Brian - *The Great Redwall Feast (Illus. by Christopher Denise)*
  c HB Guide - v8 - Spr '97 - p58 [51-250]
  c JB - v60 - D '96 - p234 [251-500]
  c SLJ - v42 - D '96 - p95 [51-250]
  Mossflower (Keith). Audio Version
  y BL - v93 - N 15 '96 - p604 [51-250]
  y HB - v73 - Ja '97 - p85+ [501+]
  The Outcast of Redwall (Illus. by Allan Curless)
  y HB Guide - v7 - Fall '96 - p302 [51-250]
  c PW - v244 - F 24 '97 - p93 [1-50]
  y VOYA - v19 - O '96 - p218 [251-500]
  Pearls of Lutra (Illus. by Allan Curless)
  c BL - v93 - F 15 '97 - p1023 [51-250]
  c Books - v10 - Je '96 - p25 [51-250]
  c CCB-B - v50 - Ap '97 - p285+ [51-250]
  c JB - v60 - D '96 - p268 [51-250]
  c KR - v65 - Ja 1 '97 - p59 [51-250]
  c PW - v243 - D 30 '96 - p67 [51-250]
  c SLJ - v43 - Mr '97 - p187 [51-250]
  Redwall (Keith). Audio Version
  c HB - v72 - S '96 - p566+ [501+]
  Seven Strange and Ghostly Tales (Jacques). Audio Version
  y BL - v93 - D 15 '96 - p740 [51-250]
  c Emerg Lib - v24 - Mr '97 - p24 [51-250]
  y Kliatt - v30 - N '96 - p44 [51-250]
Jacques, Geoffrey - *Free within Ourselves*
  y BL - v93 - F 15 '97 - p1013 [51-250]
  y HB Guide - v8 - Spr '97 - p174 [51-250]
  y SLJ - v43 - Ja '97 - p127 [51-250]
Jacquet-Francillon, Vincent - *Film Composers Guide. 3rd Ed.*
  r ARBA - v28 - '97 - p474+ [51-250]
Jadjor, Kofi Buenor - *Another America*
  J Bl St - v27 - S '96 - p127+ [501+]
Jaeger, C Stephen - *The Envy of Angels*
  CH - v65 - S '96 - p459+ [501+]
  Specu - v71 - O '96 - p722+ [501+]
Jaegly, Peggy J - *Romantic Hearts*
  r RQ - v36 - Win '96 - p224 [51-250]
Jaekle, Charles - *Angels: Their Mission and Message*
  RR - v55 - S '96 - p553+ [51-250]

Jafek, Bruce W - *ENT Secrets*
SciTech - v20 - D '96 - p50 [51-250]

Jaffe, Azriela - *Honey, I Want to Start My Own Business*
BWatch - v18 - Mr '97 - p4 [51-250]

Jaffe, David B - *South American Consumer Protection Laws*
JEL - v35 - Mr '97 - p244 [51-250]

Jaffe, Harold - *Othello Blues*
ABR - v17 - Ag '96 - p8 [501+]
Straight Razor
Chel - 61 '96 - p154+ [501+]

Jaffe, Jerome H - *Encyclopedia of Drugs and Alcohol. Vols. 1-4*
yr ARBA - v28 - '97 - p320 [251-500]
r BL - v93 - F 1 '97 - p959 [1-50]

Jaffe, Jody - *Chestnut Mare, Beware*
BW - v27 - Ja 19 '97 - p11 [251-500]

Jaffe, Marjorie - *The Muscle Memory Method*
BL - v93 - My 1 '97 - p1470+ [51-250]

Jaffe, Michael - *The Devonshire Collection of Italian Drawings. Vols. 1-4*
BM - v138 - O '96 - p696+ [501+]

Jaffe, Michael Grant - *Dance Real Slow*
CSM - v88 - S 9 '96 - p14 [251-500]
LATBR - D 29 '96 - p8 [51-250]
LJ - v121 - O 1 '96 - p47 [1-50]

Jaffe, Murray - *The Perfect Recipe Baking Book*
BL - v93 - N 15 '96 - p559+ [51-250]
LJ - v121 - D '96 - p135+ [51-250]
PW - v243 - O 7 '96 - p71 [51-250]

Jaffe, Nina - *The Golden Flower (Illus. by Enrique O Sanchez)*
c CBRS - v24 - Ag '96 - p159 [51-250]
c Ch BWatch - v6 - N '96 - p7 [1-50]
c HB Guide - v7 - Fall '96 - p322 [51-250]
c SS - v88 - Ja '97 - p29+ [501+]
The Mysterious Visitor (Illus. by Elivia Savadier)
c BL - v93 - My 1 '97 - p1491+ [51-250]
c PW - v244 - F 24 '97 - p83+ [51-250]
Older Brother, Younger Brother (Illus. by Wenhai Ma)
c RT - v50 - N '96 - p254 [51-250]

Jaffe, Rona - *Five Women*
BL - v93 - My 15 '97 - p1541 [51-250]

Jaffe, Sherril - *Ground Rules*
KR - v65 - Mr 1 '97 - p354 [51-250]
PW - v244 - F 24 '97 - p70 [51-250]

Jaffe, Steven H - *Who Were the Founding Fathers?*
y BL - v93 - D 1 '96 - p653 [51-250]
y CBRS - v25 - D '96 - p46 [51-250]
y CCB-B - v50 - N '96 - p100 [51-250]
c HB Guide - v8 - Spr '97 - p174 [51-250]
c NYTBR - v102 - Mr 2 '97 - p25 [1-50]
y SLJ - v43 - Ja '97 - p127 [51-250]

Jaffee, Martin S - *Early Judaism*
Rel St Rev - v23 - Ap '97 - p193 [51-250]

Jaffrey, Madhur - *Market Days (Illus. by Marti Shohet)*
c Sch Lib - v44 - Ag '96 - p112 [51-250]

Jaffrey, Zia - *The Invisibles: A Tale of the Eunuchs of India*
BL - v93 - N 15 '96 - p553+ [51-250]
KR - v64 - S 1 '96 - p1296 [251-500]
NY - v72 - Ja 20 '97 - p97 [51-250]
NYTBR - v101 - N 24 '96 - p24 [501+]
NYTLa - v146 - N 20 '96 - pC22 [501+]
PW - v243 - S 23 '96 - p65 [51-250]

Jager, Rama D - *In the Company of Giants*
BL - v93 - My 1 '97 - p1468 [51-250]

Jaggi, Andreas - *Die Rahmenerzahlung Im 19. Jahrhundert*
MLR - v92 - Ap '97 - p513+ [51-250]

Jaggi, Carola - *Die Stadtkirche St. Laurentius In Winterthur*
Specu - v71 - Jl '96 - p723+ [501+]

Jagoe, Catherine - *Ambiguous Angels*
HAHR - v76 - N '96 - p765+ [251-500]

Jaham, Marie-Reine De - *L'Or Des Iles*
BL - v93 - F 1 '97 - p930 [1-50]

Jahan, Rounaq - *The Elusive Agenda*
AAPSS-A - v549 - Ja '97 - p204+ [251-500]
JEL - v34 - S '96 - p1478 [51-250]
WorldV - v12 - Jl '96 - p6 [51-250]

Jaher, Frederic Cople - *A Scapegoat in the New Wilderness*
Rel St Rev - v23 - Ap '97 - p198 [51-250]

Jahn, Michael - *Murder on Theatre Row*
BL - v93 - F 15 '97 - p1006 [51-250]
KR - v65 - Ja 15 '97 - p98 [51-250]
NYTBR - v102 - Mr 16 '97 - p28 [51-250]
PW - v244 - Ja 13 '97 - p58 [51-250]

Jahn-Clough, Lisa - *ABC Yummy (Illus. by Lisa Jahn-Clough)*
c BL - v93 - Ap 1 '97 - p1337+ [51-250]
c KR - v65 - Mr 1 '97 - p381+ [51-250]
c PW - v244 - Mr 3 '97 - p77 [51-250]
My Happy Birthday Book
c HB Guide - v7 - Fall '96 - p261 [1-50]

Jahnigen, Dennis - *Geriatric Medicine. 2nd Ed.*
SciTech - v21 - Mr '97 - p59 [51-250]

Jahnke, Roger - *The Healer Within*
PW - v244 - My 5 '97 - p205 [51-250]

Jain, B M - *Nuclear Politics in South Asia*
JTWS - v13 - Spr '96 - p262+ [501+]

Jain, K K - *Drug-Induced Neurological Disorders*
AJPsych - v154 - Ja '97 - p126+ [251-500]

Jain, Ravi - *Input/Output in Parallel and Distributed Computer Systems*
SciTech - v20 - D '96 - p8 [51-250]

Jaine, Tom - *Building a Wood-Fired Oven for Bread and Pizza*
TLS - N 22 '96 - p14 [501+]

Jaini, Padmanabh S - *Gender and Salvation*
Rel St Rev - v23 - Ap '97 - p113+ [501+]

Jaivin, Linda - *Eat Me*
KR - v65 - My 1 '97 - p664+ [251-500]
LJ - v122 - Ap 1 '97 - p126+ [51-250]
PW - v244 - My 5 '97 - p193 [51-250]
TLS - Ag 30 '96 - p22+ [501+]
Rock n Roll Babes from Outer Space
Aust Bk R - D '96 - p45+ [501+]

Jakeman, A J - *Modeling Change in Environmental Systems*
Env - v38 - O '96 - p27 [51-250]

Jakle, John A - *The Gas Station in America*
AAAGA - v87 - Mr '97 - p181+ [501+]
The Motel in America
BWatch - v18 - Mr '97 - p2+ [51-250]
Ent W - Ja 31 '97 - p54 [51-250]
HMR - Spr '97 - p10 [51-250]

Jakob, Donna - *My New Sandbox (Illus. by Julia Gorton)*
c HB Guide - v7 - Fall '96 - p261 [51-250]

Jakobsson, Kristin M - *Contingent Valuation and Endangered Species*
SciTech - v20 - D '96 - p29 [51-250]

Jakowatz, Charles V - *Spotlight-Mode Synthetic Aperture Radar*
SciTech - v20 - D '96 - p77 [51-250]

Jakubovich, Paul J - *Good for Children*
J Gov Info - v23 - S '96 - p603 [51-250]

Jakubowski, Maxim - *Life in the World of Women*
KR - v65 - Mr 15 '97 - p422 [51-250]
The Mammoth Book of Pulp Fiction
Bloom Rev - v17 - Ja '97 - p17 [51-250]
VV - v42 - Ja 7 '97 - p43 [1-50]
WSJ-MW - v78 - D 9 '96 - pA12 [1-50]

Jalal, Ayesha - *Democracy and Authoritarianism in South Asia*
JIH - v27 - Spr '97 - p745+ [251-500]

Jalland, Pat - *Death in the Victorian Family*
HT - v46 - O '96 - p58 [1-50]
Lon R Bks - v19 - Mr 6 '97 - p31+ [501+]
Spec - v277 - N 9 '96 - p48+ [501+]
TLS - N 29 '96 - p30 [501+]

Jam, Teddy - *The Charlotte Stories (Illus. by Harvey Chan)*
c CBRS - v25 - O '96 - p19 [51-250]
c Ch BWatch - v6 - S '96 - p7 [1-50]
c SLJ - v42 - D '96 - p95 [51-250]
Jacob's Best Sisters (Illus. by Joanne Fitzgerald)
c KR - v65 - F 1 '97 - p224 [51-250]
c Quill & Q - v62 - N '96 - p47 [251-500]

Jamaica (Essential Travel Guides)
r BL - v93 - S 15 '96 - p206 [1-50]

James, Alan - *Britain and the Congo Crisis 1960-63*
Choice - v34 - O '96 - p335 [51-250]

James, Bill, 1929- - *Gospel*
KR - v65 - Mr 1 '97 - p337 [51-250]
PW - v244 - Mr 10 '97 - p53 [51-250]

James, Bill, 1949- - *Bill James' Guide to Baseball Managers from 1870 to Today*
BL - v93 - My 15 '97 - p1555+ [51-250]

James, C L R - *C.L.R. James on the Negro Question*
Bloom Rev - v17 - Ja '97 - p20 [51-250]
Bl S - v26 - Fall '96 - p104+ [51-250]
Special Delivery
NYTBR - v101 - S 8 '96 - p12 [501+]

James, Caroline - *Nez Perce Women in Transition 1877-1990*
Choice - v34 - Ja '97 - p862 [51-250]
PHR - v66 - F '97 - p108+ [501+]
R&R Bk N - v12 - F '97 - p22 [51-250]

James, Clive - *The Silver Castle*
NS - v125 - O 25 '96 - p46 [51-250]
Obs - v54 - O 13 '96 - p17* [501+]
Spec - v277 - O 12 '96 - p44+ [501+]
TLS - S 20 '96 - p25 [501+]

James, Darius - *That's Blaxploitation!*
ABR - v18 - O '96 - p7 [251-500]

James, David E - *The Hidden Foundation*
Afterimage - v24 - Ja '97 - p23 [51-250]

James, E D - *Racine, Phedre*
MLR - v91 - Jl '96 - p725+ [501+]

James, E O - *Season Feasts and Festivals*
r JPC - v29 - Spr '96 - p258+ [51-250]

James, Elizabeth - *Social Smarts (Illus. by Martha Weston)*
c BL - v93 - S 1 '96 - p122 [51-250]
c HB Guide - v8 - Spr '97 - p134 [51-250]
c SLJ - v42 - S '96 - p217 [51-250]

James, Erica - *A Breath of Fresh Air*
PW - v243 - O 21 '96 - p70+ [51-250]

James, Frances W - *The Late Bronze Egyptian Garrison at Beth Shan. Vols. 1-2*
AJA - v100 - O '96 - p787+ [51-250]

James, Francis G - *Lords of the Ascendancy*
Albion - v28 - '96 - p738+ [501+]

James, Genie - *Making Managed Care Work*
R&R Bk N - v12 - F '97 - p95 [51-250]

James, Gerald - *In the Public Interest*
TLS - F 28 '97 - p25 [501+]

James, Henry - *The Awkward Age*
AL - v69 - Mr '97 - p105+ [501+]
The Europeans (Bron). Audio Version
BL - v93 - F 15 '97 - p1038 [51-250]
Portrait of a Lady
LJ - v122 - F 1 '97 - p112 [1-50]
Portrait of a Lady (Bloom). Audio Version
Obs - F 16 '97 - p18* [51-250]
Roderick Hudson
AL - v68 - D '96 - p739+ [501+]
The Tragic Muse
AL - v68 - D '96 - p739+ [501+]
LATBR - D 29 '96 - p8 [51-250]
Washington Square
LATBR - D 8 '96 - p8 [51-250]
LJ - v121 - O 1 '96 - p132 [1-50]

James, Ian N - *Introduction to Circulating Atmospheres*
Am Sci - v84 - N '96 - p602+ [501+]

James, Jennifer - *Thinking in the Future Tense*
HR Mag - v42 - F '97 - p121 [501+]

James, John A - *Capitalism in Context*
BHR - v70 - Sum '96 - p282+ [501+]
EHR - v112 - Ap '97 - p553 [501+]
JIH - v27 - Aut '96 - p280+ [251-500]

James, Joy - *Resisting State Violence*
Choice - v34 - Mr '97 - p1245 [51-250]
Wom R Bks - v14 - D '96 - p16+ [501+]
Spirit, Space and Survival
JNE - v65 - Win '96 - p102+ [501+]
Transcending the Talented Tenth
BW - v27 - F 2 '97 - p12 [51-250]
LJ - v121 - N 1 '96 - p92 [51-250]

James, Kelvin Christopher - *A Fling with a Demon Lover*
LATBR - Ag 11 '96 - p9 [501+]
NY - v72 - N 11 '96 - p119 [51-250]
NYTBR - v101 - S 15 '96 - p30 [51-250]

James, Liz - *Light and Colour in Byzantine Art*
Choice - v34 - D '96 - p602 [51-250]

James, Mary - *Shoebag Returns*
c BL - v93 - F 1 '97 - p941 [51-250]
c CCB-B - v50 - F '97 - p210 [51-250]
c HB Guide - v8 - Spr '97 - p68 [51-250]
c KR - v64 - O 15 '96 - p1533 [51-250]
c SLJ - v43 - F '97 - p103 [51-250]

James, Oliver - *Juvenile Violence in a Winner-Loser Culture*
Adoles - v32 - Spr '97 - p246 [51-250]

James, P D - *Original Sin*
Arm Det - v29 - Sum '96 - p281+ [51-250]

James, Paul T J - *Total Quality Management*
R&R Bk N - v11 - D '96 - p29 [51-250]

James, Peter - *Getting Wired! (Illus. by Derek Brazell)*
c JB - v60 - D '96 - p268+ [51-250]
c Sch Lib - v45 - F '97 - p24 [51-250]

James, Peter, 1946- - *The Politics of Bavaria--an Exception to the Rule*
R&R Bk N - v12 - F '97 - p16 [51-250]

James, Russell - *Count Me Out*
KR - v65 - Mr 1 '97 - p338 [51-250]
PW - v244 - Mr 24 '97 - p62 [51-250]

James, Samantha - *Every Wish Fulfilled*
  PW - v243 - D 2 '96 - p56 [1-50]
  PW - v243 - D 16 '96 - p55 [51-250]
James, Sian - *Storm at Arberth*
  KR - v65 - Mr 1 '97 - p334 [51-250]
James, Simon - *Leon and Bob (Illus. by Simon James)*
  c BL - v93 - F 1 '97 - p946 [51-250]
  c CCB-B - v50 - Mr '97 - p250 [51-250]
  c KR - v64 - D 15 '96 - p1799 [51-250]
  c Obs - Mr 30 '97 - p17* [51-250]
  c PW - v244 - Ja 27 '97 - p106 [51-250]
James, Stanlie M - *Theorizing Black Feminisms*
  Signs - v22 - Win '97 - p462+ [501+]
James, Susan Niner - *Puppet Theater (Illus. by Emma Carlow)*
  c PW - v243 - N 11 '96 - p77 [51-250]
James, T G H - *A Short History of Ancient Egypt*
  BL - v93 - S 15 '96 - p216 [51-250]
James, Tony - *Dream, Creativity, and Madness in Nineteenth-Century France*
  Choice - v34 - S '96 - p214+ [51-250]
James, Valentine Udoh - *Women and Sustainable Development in Africa*
  Wom R Bks - v14 - Ja '97 - p19+ [501+]
James, Will - *Lone Cowboy*
  BW - v27 - Mr 2 '97 - p12 [51-250]
  Sand
  BWatch - v17 - S '96 - p4 [1-50]
James, William - *The Correspondence of William James. Vol. 4*
  AL - v68 - S '96 - p662 [51-250]
  Nine-C Lit - v51 - S '96 - p273 [51-250]
  The Will to Believe and Other Essays
  JAAR - v64 - Fall '96 - p633+ [501+]
  William and Henry James
  LJ - v122 - F 1 '97 - p78+ [51-250]
  PW - v244 - Ja 13 '97 - p60+ [51-250]
James, William H - *Doin' Drugs*
  BWatch - v18 - Mr '97 - p3+ [51-250]
James, Willis Laurence - *Stars in De Elements*
  J Am St - v30 - Ag '96 - p325+ [251-500]
James Madison and the American Nation 1751-1836
  r W&M Q - v53 - Jl '96 - p675+ [501+]
James of Viterbo, Archbishop of Naples - *On Christian Government*
  CH - v65 - D '96 - p681+ [501+]
Jameson, Elizabeth - *Writing the Range*
  BL - v93 - Mr 15 '97 - p1209+ [51-250]
Jameson, Fredric - *The Seeds of Time*
  MP - v94 - F '97 - p422+ [501+]
  Salm - Sum '96 - p213+ [501+]
Jameson, John - *The Story of Big Bend National Park*
  BWatch - v17 - S '96 - p7 [51-250]
  Choice - v34 - Ja '97 - p862 [51-250]
Jameson, Mary - *Self-Study Course for Optometric Assisting. 2nd Ed.*
  SciTech - v21 - Mr '97 - p62 [51-250]
Jameson, Michael H - *A Greek Countryside*
  AHR - v101 - O '96 - p1188+ [501+]
Jamieson, Dale - *Language, Mind and Art*
  JAAC - v54 - Fall '96 - p386+ [501+]
Jamieson, Doug - *NPO Webmaster*
  ChrPhil - v8 - S 19 '96 - p51 [51-250]
Jamieson, Kathleen Hall - *Beyond the Double Bind*
  QJS - v82 - Ag '96 - p306+ [501+]
  Spiral of Cynicism
  BL - v93 - Ap 1 '97 - p1270 [51-250]
Jamieson, Marshall - *Beginnings: From the First Nations to the Great Migration*
  y Can CL - v22 - Fall '96 - p112+ [251-500]
Jamieson, Perry D - *Crossing the Deadly Ground*
  J Am St - v30 - Ap '96 - p136+ [251-500]
  Parameters - v26 - Aut '96 - p152+ [501+]
Jamison, Kay Redfield - *Touched with Fire*
  Nature - v385 - Ja 2 '97 - p30 [1-50]
  PW - v243 - S 2 '96 - p121+ [1-50]
  An Unquiet Mind
  Books - v10 - Je '96 - p21 [1-50]
  NS & S - v9 - My 17 '96 - p39 [251-500]
  NYTBR - v102 - F 2 '97 - p28 [51-250]
  PW - v243 - S 2 '96 - p121 [1-50]
  TLS - Ag 2 '96 - p13 [501+]
Jamison, Stephanie W - *Sacrificed Wife/Sacrificer's Wife*
  Rel St Rev - v23 - Ja '97 - p95 [51-250]
Jampolsky, Gerald G - *Listen to Me*
  BL - v93 - S 1 '96 - p41 [51-250]
Jamsa, Kris - *Rescued by Upgrading Your PC. 2nd Ed.*
  y BL - v93 - Mr 1 '97 - p1101 [501+]
  Success with Windows 95
  BL - v92 - Ag '96 - p1868 [501+]

  Web Programming
  LJ - v122 - Ja '97 - p138 [51-250]
Jamshidi, Mohammad - *Large-Scale Systems*
  SciTech - v20 - D '96 - p59 [51-250]
Janal, Daniel S - *101 Businesses You Can Start on the Internet*
  CBR - v14 - N '96 - p36 [51-250]
  R&R Bk N - v12 - F '97 - p39 [51-250]
  Online Marketing Handbook: How to Promote, Advertise, and Sell Your Products and Services on the Internet
  BWatch - v18 - F '97 - p3 [51-250]
  CBR - v15 - Spr '97 - p7 [51-250]
Janan, Micaela - *When the Lamp Is Shattered*
  CW - v89 - Jl '96 - p503 [251-500]
Janangelo, Joseph - *Resituating Writing*
  Col Comp - v47 - D '96 - p618 [51-250]
Janaway, Christopher - *Images of Excellence*
  Class Out - v74 - Fall '96 - p39+ [251-500]
Jancar-Webster, Barbara - *Environmental Action in Eastern Europe*
  Slav R - v55 - Sum '96 - p439+ [501+]
Jance, J A - *Dead to Rights*
  BL - v93 - S 15 '96 - p224 [51-250]
  KR - v64 - Ag 15 '96 - p1190+ [51-250]
  PW - v243 - S 2 '96 - p117 [51-250]
  Name Witheld
  PW - v244 - F 24 '97 - p88 [1-50]
  Shoot/Don't Shoot (Critt). Audio Version
  BWatch - v18 - Mr '97 - p7 [1-50]
Jancovich, Mark - *Rational Fears*
  Choice - v34 - F '97 - p973 [51-250]
  LJ - v121 - O 15 '96 - p60 [51-250]
  Si & So - v6 - N '96 - p35 [51-250]
Jandt, Fred E - *Using the Internet in Your Job Search*
  J Car P&E - v57 - Win '97 - p18 [251-500]
Janeczko, Paul - *Pocket Poems*
  y JAAL - v40 - D '96 - p319 [51-250]
Janelli, Roger L - *Making Capitalism*
  RA - v25 - 3 '96 - p185+ [501+]
Janes, Clara - *Rosas De Fuego*
  WLT - v71 - Win '97 - p122+ [501+]
Janes, J Robert - *Stonekiller*
  LJ - v122 - My 1 '97 - p144 [1-50]
  PW - v244 - F 24 '97 - p66 [51-250]
Jane's Air Traffic Control 1996-97
  r ARBA - v28 - '97 - p654 [51-250]
Jane's Aircraft Upgrades 1996-97
  r ARBA - v28 - '97 - p257+ [51-250]
  r SciTech - v21 - Mr '97 - p94 [51-250]
Jane's All the World's Aircraft 1996-97
  r ARBA - v28 - '97 - p654 [51-250]
Jane's Armour and Artillery 1995-96
  r ARBA - v28 - '97 - p259 [51-250]
Jane's Avionics 1996-97
  r ARBA - v28 - '97 - p654 [51-250]
Jane's Fighting Ships 1996-97
  r ARBA - v28 - '97 - p258 [501+]
  r Esq - v126 - D '96 - p40 [1-50]
  r R&R Bk N - v12 - F '97 - p100 [51-250]
Jane's High-Speed Marine Transportation 1996-97
  r R&R Bk N - v11 - D '96 - p73 [51-250]
Jane's International ABC Aerospace Directory 1996
  r ARBA - v28 - '97 - p104 [251-500]
Jane's International Defence Directory 1997
  r ARBA - v28 - '97 - p104+ [251-500]
Jane's NBC Protection Equipment 1996-97
  r ARBA - v28 - '97 - p257 [51-250]
Jane's Sentinel, the Unfair Advantage: Central America and the Caribbean. 1996 Ed.
  r ARBA - v28 - '97 - p67+ [501+]
Jane's Space Directory 1995-96. Electronic Media Version
  r Choice - v34 - Ja '97 - p780 [51-250]
Jane's Space Directory 1996-97
  r ARBA - v28 - '97 - p593+ [51-250]
Jang, Jyh-Shing Roger - *Neuro-Fuzzy and Soft Computing*
  SciTech - v20 - D '96 - p14 [51-250]
Jankovic, Sava - *Na Prelomu*
  WLT - v71 - Win '97 - p184+ [51-250]
Jankowiak, William - *Romantic Passion*
  Ant R - v55 - Spr '97 - p249 [51-250]
Janovitz, Marilyn - *Bowl Patrol! (Illus. by Marilyn Janovitz)*
  c HB Guide - v8 - Spr '97 - p12 [51-250]
  c SLJ - v42 - D '96 - p95+ [51-250]
  Can I Help? (Illus. by Marilyn Janovitz)
  c HB Guide - v7 - Fall '96 - p240 [51-250]
  c Smith - v27 - N '96 - p167 [1-50]

  Es Hora (Illus. by Marilyn Janovitz)
  c HB Guide - v7 - Fall '96 - p327 [1-50]
  c SLJ - v42 - N '96 - p132 [51-250]
Janovy, John, Jr. - *Back in Keith County*
  Sew R - v104 - O '96 - p665+ [501+]
  Keith County Journal
  Sew R - v104 - O '96 - p665+ [501+]
  On Becoming a Biologist
  Sew R - v104 - O '96 - p665+ [501+]
Janowitz, Tama - *By the Shores of Gitchee Gumee*
  BW - v26 - O 20 '96 - p6 [501+]
  Ent W - S 13 '96 - p125 [51-250]
  LATBR - v263 - S 29 '96 - p14 [51-250]
  NYTBR - v101 - O 20 '96 - p13 [51-250]
  VV - v41 - S 17 '96 - p47+ [251-500]
Jans, Nick - *A Place Beyond*
  BL - v93 - S 15 '96 - p216 [51-250]
Jansen, Hans-Heinrich - *Grossbritannien, Das Scheitern Der EVG Und Der NATO-Beitritt Der Bundesrepublik Deutschland*
  EHR - v112 - F '97 - p269+ [251-500]
Jansen, John - *Class Act (Illus. by Susan Slattery Burke)*
  c RT - v50 - O '96 - p136 [1-50]
Jansen, Sharon L - *Dangerous Talk and Strange Behavior*
  Choice - v34 - My '97 - p1558 [51-250]
  LJ - v122 - Ja '97 - p120 [51-250]
Jansen, Walfried - *Not a Prairie River*
  BIC - v25 - S '96 - p10+ [51-250]
Janson, H W - *History of Art. 5th Ed., Vols. 1 2*
  Art J - v55 - Sum '96 - p99+ [501+]
  History of Art for Young People. 5th Ed.
  y BL - v93 - F 1 '97 - p931 [51-250]
  cr KR - v65 - F 15 '97 - p310 [51-250]
  c PW - v243 - D 16 '96 - p61 [51-250]
Janson, Lee W - *Brew Chem 101*
  BL - v93 - S 15 '96 - p196 [51-250]
Janson-Smith, Deirdre - *Earth's Restless Surface*
  New Sci - v153 - Ja 25 '97 - p44 [51-250]
Janssen, Jacques - *Advances in Stochastic Modelling and Data Analysis*
  SciTech - v20 - N '96 - p2 [51-250]
Janssen, Karl-Heinz - *Der Sturz Der Generale*
  CEH - v29 - 2 '96 - p265+ [501+]
  EHR - v111 - N '96 - p1346 [251-500]
Janssens, Angelique - *Family and Social Change*
  EHR - v111 - S '96 - p1008 [251-500]
Jansson, Bruce S - *The Reluctant Welfare State. 3rd Ed.*
  R&R Bk N - v11 - D '96 - p39 [51-250]
Jansson, Maija - *England and the North*
  EHR - v112 - Ap '97 - p467+ [501+]
  Slav R - v55 - Sum '96 - p479+ [501+]
Jantra, Ingrid - *The Houseplant Encyclopedia*
  r LJ - v122 - Mr 15 '97 - p56 [51-250]
  r PW - v244 - Mr 24 '97 - p79 [51-250]
  r Quill & Q - v63 - Mr '97 - p22 [251-500]
Jantzen, Grace - *Power, Gender, and Christian Mysticism*
  Choice - v34 - S '96 - p144 [51-250]
  Comw - v123 - N 22 '96 - p29+ [501+]
  Theol St - v57 - D '96 - p751+ [501+]
Janvier, Philippe - *Early Vertebrates*
  Choice - v34 - My '97 - p1526 [51-250]
  Nature - v386 - Ap 10 '97 - p568 [51-250]
  New Sci - v151 - S 28 '96 - p55 [1-50]
  Sci - v276 - Ap 4 '97 - p46 [501+]
Janz, Oliver - *Burger Besonderer Art*
  CH - v65 - S '96 - p528+ [501+]
Janzen, David - *Fire, Salt, and Peace*
  OS - v33 - Mr '97 - p35 [51-250]
Japanese Studies in Canada
  r Choice - v34 - Mr '97 - p1135+ [501+]
Japanese Studies in the United States, the 1990s
  r Choice - v34 - Mr '97 - p1135+ [501+]
Jappe, Anselm - *Guy Debord*
  TLS - O 4 '96 - p8 [501+]
Japrisot, Sebastien - *A Very Long Engagement*
  Comw - v123 - D 6 '96 - p24 [251-500]
  SFR - v21 - Jl '96 - p48 [1-50]
  TranslRevS - v1 - My '95 - p19 [51-250]
Jaquette, Jane S - *The Women's Movement in Latin America. 2nd Ed.*
  HAHR - v77 - My '97 - p286+ [251-500]
Jaramillo, Stephan - *Going Postal*
  KR - v65 - Ap 1 '97 - p488+ [251-500]
  PW - v244 - Ap 14 '97 - p56 [51-250]
Jaramillo Levi, Enrique - *Contemporary Short Stories from Central America*
  TranslRev - 51 '96 - p49+ [501+]
  TranslRevS - v1 - My '95 - p1 [51-250]
  Duplications and Other Stories
  TranslRevS - v1 - My '95 - p30 [51-250]

The Shadow: Thirteen Stories in Opposition
TranslRevS - v2 - D '96 - p32 [51-250]
Jarausch, Konrad H - *The Rush to German Unity*
EHR - v112 - F '97 - p271+ [251-500]
Jardetzky, Oleg - *Dynamics and the Problem of Recognition in Biological Macromolecules*
SciTech - v21 - Mr '97 - p41 [51-250]
Jardin, Alexandre - *L'Ile Des Gauchers*
FR - v70 - D '96 - p350+ [251-500]
Jardine, Lisa - *Erasmus, Man of Letters*
Comp L - v48 - Fall '96 - p381+ [501+]
Reading Shakespeare Historically
Lon R Bks - v18 - O 31 '96 - p24+ [501+]
Worldly Goods
BL - v93 - N 1 '96 - p478 [51-250]
BW - v27 - Mr 2 '97 - p13 [51-250]
Econ - v341 - O 19 '96 - p6* [251-500]
KR - v64 - O 1 '96 - p1445+ [251-500]
NS - v125 - S 6 '96 - p44+ [501+]
NY - v72 - D 9 '96 - p119 [501+]
NYTBR - v102 - Ja 5 '97 - p30 [501+]
NYTLa - v146 - Ja 6 '97 - pC18 [501+]
Obs - S 8 '96 - p15* [501+]
PW - v243 - O 14 '96 - p69 [51-250]
TLS - O 11 '96 - p21 [501+]
Jardine, N - *Cultures of Natural History*
Am Sci - v85 - Mr '97 - p194+ [501+]
TLS - S 6 '96 - p28+ [501+]
Jardine, Quintin - *Skinner's Ordeal*
Books - v11 - Ap '97 - p23 [51-250]
Skinner's Round
Arm Det - v30 - Win '97 - p112 [251-500]
BL - v93 - D 1 '96 - p643 [51-250]
KR - v64 - O 15 '96 - p1496 [51-250]
Skinner's Trail
KR - v64 - My 1 '96 - p644 [51-250]
Jargowsky, Paul A - *Poverty and Place*
LJ - v122 - Ap 1 '97 - p112 [51-250]
PW - v244 - Ja 27 '97 - p85+ [51-250]
Jarlet, Anders - *The Oxford Group, Group Revivalism, and the Churches in Northern Europe 1930-1940*
CH - v65 - D '96 - p755+ [501+]
Jarman, Derek - *Chroma*
Obs - Ag 18 '96 - p18* [1-50]
Kicking the Pricks
Advocate - F 18 '97 - p59+ [501+]
KR - v64 - D 1 '96 - p1717 [251-500]
LJ - v122 - F 15 '97 - p142 [51-250]
PW - v244 - Ja 6 '97 - p58 [251-500]
Up in the Air
TLS - O 25 '96 - p21 [501+]
Jarman, Julia - *The Crow Haunting*
c JB - v60 - Ag '96 - p157+ [51-250]
Gertie and the Bloop
c Sch Lib - v44 - N '96 - p151 [51-250]
Jarman, Mark - *Questions for Ecclesiastes*
BL - v93 - Ja '97 - p809 [51-250]
LJ - v122 - Ja '97 - p103 [51-250]
PW - v243 - D 30 '96 - p62 [251-500]
Rebel Angels
LJ - v121 - O 1 '96 - p82+ [51-250]
PW - v243 - S 30 '96 - p82 [51-250]
WSJ-Cent - v99 - Ja 6 '97 - pA10 [501+]
Jarmon, Leslie Hope - *An Ecology of Embodied Interaction*
QJS - v83 - My '97 - p230+ [501+]
Jarnot, Lisa - *Some Other Kind of Mission*
TLS - N 29 '96 - p11 [51-250]
VV - v42 - Ap 29 '97 - p55 [501+]
Jarrard, Kyle - *Over There*
KR - v64 - N 15 '96 - p1622 [251-500]
LJ - v121 - D '96 - p145+ [51-250]
PW - v243 - D 2 '96 - p42 [51-250]
Jarrell, Randall - *Pictures from an Institution*
Nat R - v48 - D 23 '96 - p55 [51-250]
Jarrett, Clare - *Catherine and the Lion (Illus. by Clare Jarrett)*
c BL - v93 - D 15 '96 - p731+ [51-250]
c KR - v64 - D 1 '96 - p1739 [51-250]
c SLJ - v43 - F '97 - p81+ [51-250]
Jarrow, Gail - *The Naked Mole-Rat Mystery (Illus. by Raymond A Mendez)*
y BL - v93 - S 1 '96 - p116 [51-250]
c HB Guide - v8 - Spr '97 - p127 [51-250]
y SLJ - v42 - Ag '96 - p172 [51-250]
Naked Mole-Rats
y BL - v93 - Ap 1 '97 - p1308 [1-50]
c Ch BWatch - v6 - O '96 - p5+ [1-50]
c HB Guide - v8 - Spr '97 - p127 [51-250]
c SLJ - v42 - O '96 - p134 [51-250]

Jarva, Eero - *Archaiologia on Archaic Greek Body Armour*
AJA - v101 - Ja '97 - p194 [251-500]
Jarvik, Laurence - *PBS: Behind the Screen*
ChrPhil - v9 - Ja 9 '97 - p36 [51-250]
Nat R - v49 - F 10 '97 - p54+ [501+]
WSJ-MW - v78 - D 23 '96 - pA10 [501+]
Jarvis, Kila - *Owls: Whoo Are They? (Illus. by Leslie Leroux)*
c BL - v92 - Ag '96 - p1898 [51-250]
c CBRS - v24 - Ag '96 - p167 [1-50]
c Ch BWatch - v6 - S '96 - p6 [1-50]
c SLJ - v42 - D '96 - p130 [51-250]
Jarvis, Lovell S - *The Potential Effect of Two New Biotechnologies on the World Dairy Industry*
JEL - v34 - D '96 - p2129 [51-250]
SciTech - v20 - S '96 - p2 [51-250]
Jarvis, Robin - *The Raven's Knot*
y TES - Mr 21 '97 - p14* [501+]
The Whitby Witches (McKenzie). Audio Version
c Sch Lib - v45 - F '97 - p33 [51-250]
Jasanoff, Sheila - *Science at the Bar*
CS - v25 - S '96 - p664+ [501+]
Jaschinski, Britta - *Zoo*
Bloom Rev - v16 - N '96 - p23 [51-250]
LATBR - O 6 '96 - p14 [51-250]
Jasen, Patricia - *Wild Things*
AHR - v102 - F '97 - p225+ [501+]
Can Hist R - v77 - D '96 - p611+ [501+]
JIH - v27 - Spr '97 - p732+ [501+]
Jason, Philip K - *The Critical Response to Anais Nin*
r AL - v69 - Mr '97 - p256 [51-250]
Choice - v34 - Ja '97 - p793 [51-250]
R&R Bk N - v11 - D '96 - p6 [1-50]
Jason, Victoria - *Kabloona in the Yellow Kayak*
BIC - v25 - S '96 - p10+ [501+]
Jasper, David - *In Good Company*
JR - v76 - O '96 - p683+ [51-250]
Jasper, Herbert H - *Epilepsy and the Functional Anatomy of the Frontal Lobe*
r AJPsych - v153 - N '96 - p1498 [251-500]
Jaspers, Karl - *The Great Philosophers. Vol. 3*
TranslRevS - v1 - My '95 - p13 [51-250]
The Great Philosophers. Vols. 3-4
IPQ - v36 - S '96 - p351+ [501+]
Karl Jaspers: Basic Philosophical Writings
IPQ - v36 - S '96 - p351+ [501+]
Jaspersohn, William - *Timber!*
c HB Guide - v7 - Fall '96 - p352 [51-250]
Jassem, Zaidan Ali - *Impact of the Arab-Israeli Wars on Language and Social Change in the Arab World*
Rel St Rev - v23 - Ja '97 - p91 [51-250]
Jasso, Gayle - *Special Events from A to Z*
SLJ - v42 - N '96 - p42 [51-250]
Jastrow, Robert - *God and the Astronomers. 2nd Ed.*
PSR - v25 - '96 - p273+ [501+]
Skeptic - v3 - '95 - p100 [251-500]
Jaumain, Claire - *La Derniere Repetition*
FR - v70 - Mr '97 - p613+ [501+]
Jauss, David - *Black Maps*
Choice - v34 - D '96 - p614 [51-250]
KR - v64 - My 1 '96 - p639 [51-250]
Java Report
p LJ - v121 - O 15 '96 - p95 [51-250]
Javilier, Jean-Claude - *Droit Du Travail. 5th Ed.*
ILR - v135 - '96 - p117+ [51-250]
Jawad, H A - *The Middle East in the New World Order*
JTWS - v13 - Spr '96 - p373+ [501+]
Jaworski, Anna Marie - *Hypoplastic Left Heart Syndrome*
LJ - v122 - Ja '97 - p134 [51-250]
Jay, Antony - *The Oxford Dictionary of Political Quotations*
r Obs - N 3 '96 - p15* [501+]
r Spec - v277 - D 14 '96 - p70 [501+]
Jay, Eileen - *A Victorian Naturalist*
RSR - v24 - 3 '96 - p25 [51-250]
Jay, Elisabeth - *Mrs. Oliphant: A Fiction to Herself*
RES - v48 - F '97 - p130+ [501+]
VS - v39 - Win '96 - p246+ [501+]
Jay, Martin - *Downcast Eyes*
FR - v70 - F '97 - p486+ [501+]
Jay, Peter - *Sappho through English Poetry*
Obs - D 15 '96 - p18* [501+]
Jayarajah, Carl - *Social Dimensions of Adjustment*
JEL - v34 - D '96 - p2115 [501+]
Jayawardena, Kumari - *The White Woman's Other Burden*
Albion - v28 - Sum '96 - p377+ [501+]
J Soc H - v30 - Win '96 - p543+ [501+]
VS - v39 - Spr '96 - p418+ [501+]

Jayawardene, S A - *The Scientific Revolution*
r ARBA - v28 - '97 - p559 [51-250]
r Choice - v34 - My '97 - p1476 [51-250]
Jayne, T S - *Effects of Market Reform on Access to Food by Low-Income Households*
JEL - v34 - S '96 - p1478 [51-250]
Jay's Journal of Anomalies
p BC - v46 - Spr '97 - p127+ [251-500]
Jayyusi, Lena - *The Adventures of Sayf Ben Dhi Yazan*
TranslRevS - v2 - D '96 - p18 [51-250]
Jayyusi, Salma Khadra - *Anthology of Palestinian Literature*
MEJ - v51 - Spr '97 - p297+ [501+]
The Legend of Muslim Spain. Vols. 1-2
Ren Q - v50 - Spr '97 - p286+ [501+]
Modern Arabic Drama
MEJ - v50 - Aut '96 - p628 [51-250]
WLT - v70 - Aut '96 - p1021 [251-500]
Jazouli, Adil - *Une Saison En Banlieue*
FR - v70 - Mr '97 - p630+ [501+]
Jazz, Jimmy - *The Sub*
BL - v92 - Ag '96 - p1881 [51-250]
Sm Pr R - v29 - Ja '97 - p12 [501+]
Jazz: The Ultimate Guide
r TES - Ja 10 '97 - p7* [501+]
Jeal, Tim - *For God and Glory*
BL - v92 - Ag '96 - p1882 [51-250]
W&I - v12 - Mr '97 - p266+ [501+]
The Missionary's Wife
TLS - Ja 10 '97 - p20 [501+]
Jean, Francois - *Life, Death and Aid*
Arm F&S - v23 - Fall '96 - p136+ [501+]
Jean Fautrier: Musee National Fernand Leger, Biot, 20 Juin - 15 Septembre 1996 Et Mucsarnok, Budapest, 15 Octobre - 10 Novembre 1996
BM - v138 - S '96 - p625+ [501+]
Jeancolas, Jean-Pierre - *Histoire Du Cinema Francais*
FR - v70 - D '96 - p368+ [251-500]
Jean Renart - *The Romance of the Rose or of Guillaume De Dole*
MLR - v92 - Ja '97 - p185+ [251-500]
Jeansonne, Glen - *Women of the Far Right*
BW - v26 - Ag 4 '96 - p6 [501+]
Choice - v34 - O '96 - p348+ [51-250]
Dis - v44 - Spr '97 - p112+ [501+]
NYTBR - v102 - Ja 12 '97 - p20 [251-500]
TLS - S 20 '96 - p32 [251-500]
Jeauneau, Edouard - *L'Age D'Or Des Ecoles De Chartres*
Specu - v71 - O '96 - p967+ [501+]
Jedrzejewski, Jan - *Thomas Hardy and the Church*
Nine-C Lit - v51 - S '96 - p273 [51-250]
Rel St Rev - v23 - Ap '97 - p161 [51-250]
Jeffares, A Norman - *Images of Invention*
Choice - v34 - My '97 - p1496 [51-250]
TLS - S 27 '96 - p13 [501+]
W.B. Yeats, Man and Poet. 3rd Ed.
Choice - v34 - S '96 - p126 [51-250]
ELT - v40 - 2 '97 - p252 [51-250]
Jefferies, William McK. - *Safe Uses of Cortisol. 2nd Ed.*
SciTech - v20 - N '96 - p55 [51-250]
Jeffers, H Paul - *The Good Cigar*
BL - v93 - O 1 '96 - p309 [51-250]
PW - v243 - S 16 '96 - p65 [51-250]
Reader's Guide to Murder
Arm Det - v30 - Win '97 - p111 [251-500]
KR - v64 - O 1 '96 - p1432 [51-250]
Jefferson, Alan - *Elisabeth Schwarzkopf*
BL - v92 - Ag '96 - p1871 [51-250]
FF - v20 - Ja '97 - p375+ [501+]
Jefferson, Thomas - *The Papers of Thomas Jefferson. Vol. 26*
JSH - v63 - F '97 - p159+ [501+]
The Republic of Letters. Vols. 1-3
HT - v46 - Jl '96 - p56+ [501+]
RP - v58 - Fall '96 - p821+ [501+]
W&M Q - v53 - Jl '96 - p672+ [501+]
Jefferson-Brown, Michael - *The Rock Garden Month-by-Month*
BL - v93 - F 15 '97 - p987 [51-250]
Jeffery, Debby Ann - *Literate Beginnings*
Emerg Lib - v24 - S '96 - p39+ [251-500]
Jeffery, Keith - *An Irish Empire?*
R&R Bk N - v11 - N '96 - p11 [51-250]
TLS - S 27 '96 - p6 [501+]
Jeffery, Paul - *The City Churches of Sir Christopher Wren*
TLS - Ja 17 '97 - p36 [501+]
Jeffery, Roger - *Girls' Schooling, Women's Autonomy, and Fertility Change in South Asia*
R&R Bk N - v12 - F '97 - p34 [51-250]
Jeffery, Sally - *The Mansion House*
EHR - v112 - Ap '97 - p547+ [251-500]

Jefferys, Kevin - *The Labour Party since 1945*
EHR - v111 - S '96 - p1035 [51-250]
Jefford, Clayton N - *The Didache in Context*
Rel St Rev - v23 - Ja '97 - p77 [51-250]
Reading the Apostolic Fathers
CHR - v83 - Ja '97 - p166+ [51-250]
Jeffords, Susan - *Hard Bodies*
FQ - v49 - Fall '95 - p47+ [501+]
Jeffrey, David Lyle - *A Dictionary of Biblical Tradition in English Literature*
r CH - v65 - S '96 - p563+ [251-500]
People of the Book
BL - v93 - S 1 '96 - p38 [51-250]
Choice - v34 - Mr '97 - p1162+ [51-250]
Jeffrey, Laura S - *American Inventors of the Twentieth Century*
c HB Guide - v7 - Fall '96 - p376 [1-50]
Barbara Jordan: Congresswoman, Lawyer, Educator
y SLJ - v43 - Mr '97 - p202 [51-250]
Great American Businesswomen
c BL - v93 - S 1 '96 - p122 [51-250]
c HB Guide - v8 - Spr '97 - p161 [51-250]
y SLJ - v42 - S '96 - p233 [51-250]
Jeffrey, R Brooke - *Spiral CT of the Body*
SciTech - v21 - Mr '97 - p49 [51-250]
Jeffreys-Jones, Rhodri - *Changing Differences*
AAPSS-A - v546 - Jl '96 - p154+ [501+]
Historian - v58 - Sum '96 - p864+ [501+]
Jeffries, Ian - *A Guide to the Economies in Transition*
JEL - v34 - D '96 - p2124 [51-250]
Problems of Economic and Political Transformation in the Balkans
Choice - v34 - F '97 - p1013 [51-250]
Jeffries, John W - *Wartime America*
LJ - v121 - O 15 '96 - p72 [51-250]
Jeffries, Roderic - *An Arcadian Death*
Rapport - v19 - 4 '96 - p25 [251-500]
Jeffries, Thomas W - *Enzymes for Pulp and Paper Processing*
SciTech - v21 - Mr '97 - p99 [51-250]
Jegouzo, Yves - *Archeologie Et Droit De L'Urbanisme En Europe*
AJA - v101 - Ja '97 - p197 [251-500]
Jehenson, Myriam Yvonne - *Latin-American Women Writers*
Hisp - v79 - D '96 - p808+ [501+]
NWSA Jnl - v9 - Spr '97 - p126+ [501+]
Jejeebhoy, Shireen J - *Women's Education, Autonomy, and Reproductive Behaviour*
Choice - v34 - S '96 - p218 [51-250]
JEL - v34 - S '96 - p1444+ [501+]
Jelavich, Peter - *Berlin Cabaret*
CEH - v29 - 1 '96 - p138+ [501+]
Jelbert, Wendy - *Painting Nature's Details*
LJ - v122 - Mr 15 '97 - p62 [51-250]
Jeleff, Sophia - *The Gender Perspective*
J Gov Info - v23 - S '96 - p664 [51-250]
Jelen, Ted G - *Public Attitudes toward Church and State*
APSR - v90 - D '96 - p913+ [501+]
J Pol - v58 - N '96 - p1208+ [501+]
Pub Op Q - v60 - Fall '96 - p466+ [501+]
Jelin, Elizabeth - *Constructing Democracy*
For Aff - v75 - S '96 - p150 [51-250]
Jelinek, Elfriede - *Die Kinder Der Toten*
WLT - v70 - Aut '96 - p946+ [501+]
Jen, Gish - *Mona in the Promised Land*
FEER - v159 - O 31 '96 - p47 [251-500]
HR - v49 - Win '97 - p687+ [501+]
LATBR - My 26 '96 - p2 [501+]
LATBR - D 29 '96 - p11 [1-50]
Nat - v262 - Je 17 '96 - p35+ [501+]
NYTBR - v101 - D 8 '96 - p82 [1-50]
PW - v244 - Mr 17 '97 - p81 [1-50]
TLS - Mr 21 '97 - p24 [501+]
Wom R Bks - v13 - S '96 - p25 [501+]
Jenal, Georg - *Herrschaft, Kirche, Kultur*
EHR - v112 - F '97 - p155+ [251-500]
Jendresen, Erik - *The First Story Ever Told (Illus. by Yoshi)*
c BL - v93 - D 15 '96 - p733 [51-250]
c HB Guide - v8 - Spr '97 - p32 [51-250]
c KR - v64 - N 1 '96 - p1601 [51-250]
c SLJ - v42 - D '96 - p96 [51-250]
Jeng, Trio Jan - *Sing 'n Learn Chinese. Book and Audio Version*
c PW - v244 - Mr 17 '97 - p47 [51-250]
Jenicek, Milos - *Epidemiology: The Logic of Modern Medicine*
AJPsych - v153 - N '96 - p1499 [251-500]
Jenish, D'Arcy - *Money to Burn*
CF - v75 - S '96 - p41+ [501+]

Jenkin, Len - *The Secret Life of Billie's Uncle Myron*
c CBRS - v25 - O '96 - p22 [1-50]
c HB Guide - v8 - Spr '97 - p68 [51-250]
c KR - v64 - O 1 '96 - p1469 [51-250]
c PW - v243 - O 14 '96 - p84 [51-250]
c SLJ - v42 - N '96 - p107 [51-250]
Jenkin-Pearce, S - *Annie Angel (Illus. by S Jenkin-Pearce)*
c JB - v60 - D '96 - p234 [1-50]
Jenkins, Brian - *Henry Goulburn 1784-1856*
Choice - v34 - O '96 - p340 [51-250]
Jenkins, Carol Brennan - *Inside the Writing Portfolio*
HER - v66 - Fall '96 - p695+ [51-250]
Jenkins, Edward Sidney - *To Fathom More*
Choice - v34 - Ap '97 - p1358+ [51-250]
SciTech - v20 - S '96 - p2 [51-250]
Jenkins, Elaine Brown - *Jumping Double Dutch*
BW - v26 - Ag 18 '96 - p4 [51-250]
Jenkins, Ella - *This Is Rhythm*
c CAY - v17 - Fall '96 - p11 [51-250]
Jenkins, Emyl - *The Book of American Traditions*
LJ - v121 - D '96 - p126+ [51-250]
PW - v243 - S 23 '96 - p70 [51-250]
Emyl Jenkins' Southern Hospitality
JSH - v62 - N '96 - p864 [51-250]
Jenkins, Everett, Jr. - *Pan-African Chronology*
r ARBA - v28 - '97 - p196 [51-250]
Jenkins, Fred W - *Classical Studies*
r ARBA - v28 - '97 - p209 [51-250]
Jenkins, Henry - *Science Fiction Audiences*
Lon R Bks - v18 - My 23 '96 - p34+ [501+]
Jenkins, Ian - *Archaeologists and Aesthetes*
AJA - v100 - Jl '96 - p633+ [501+]
Jenkins, J Craig - *The Politics of Social Protest*
APSR - v90 - D '96 - p874+ [501+]
CS - v26 - Mr '97 - p181+ [501+]
Socio R - v45 - F 1 '97 - p147+ [501+]
Jenkins, Jerrold R - *Inside the Bestsellers*
PW - v243 - N 11 '96 - p67 [51-250]
Jenkins, Jerry B - *The Rookie*
y BL - v93 - Mr 1 '97 - p1111 [51-250]
Jenkins, Keith - *On What Is History?*
J Am St - v30 - Ag '96 - p344 [251-500]
Jenkins, Lyll Becerra De - *So Loud a Silence*
y BL - v93 - S 15 '96 - p230+ [51-250]
y CCB-B - v50 - Ja '97 - p175 [51-250]
y HB - v73 - Ja '97 - p58+ [51-250]
y HB Guide - v8 - Spr '97 - p81 [51-250]
y KR - v64 - Ag 15 '96 - p1236 [51-250]
y Par Ch - v20 - O '96 - p12 [1-50]
y PW - v243 - O 7 '96 - p76 [51-250]
y SLJ - v42 - D '96 - p136 [51-250]
y VOYA - v19 - F '97 - p328 [251-500]
Jenkins, Lynn B - *Adult Literacy in Indiana*
J Gov Info - v23 - S '96 - p582 [51-250]
Jenkins, Mark - *To Timbuktu*
KR - v65 - Ap 1 '97 - p523 [251-500]
PW - v244 - Ap 7 '97 - p78 [51-250]
Jenkins, Martin - *Deserts*
c Ch BWatch - v6 - S '96 - p5 [1-50]
c HB Guide - v8 - Spr '97 - p97 [51-250]
c SLJ - v42 - N '96 - p113 [51-250]
Fly Traps! (Illus. by David Parkins)
c Bks Keeps - Ja '97 - p21 [51-250]
c CCB-B - v50 - Ja '97 - p175+ [51-250]
c HB - v73 - Ja '97 - p76+ [51-250]
c HB Guide - v8 - Spr '97 - p121 [51-250]
c SLJ - v42 - D '96 - p114 [51-250]
Wings, Stings, and Wriggly Things (Illus. by Sandra Doyle)
c Bks Keeps - Mr '97 - p21 [501+]
c BL - v93 - D 1 '96 - p658 [51-250]
c HB Guide - v8 - Spr '97 - p122 [51-250]
c JB - v60 - D '96 - p254 [51-250]
c New Sci - v152 - N 16 '96 - p53 [51-250]
c Sch Lib - v45 - F '97 - p38 [51-250]
c SLJ - v43 - F '97 - p93 [51-250]
Jenkins, Mary - *House and Garden Samplers*
LJ - v122 - F 15 '97 - p134 [51-250]
Jenkins, Nancy Harmon - *Flavors of Puglia*
BL - v93 - My 15 '97 - p1552 [51-250]
PW - v244 - Ap 21 '97 - p66 [51-250]
Jenkins, Pamela - *Witnessing for Sociology*
R&R Bk N - v11 - N '96 - p53 [51-250]
Jenkins, Phil - *An Acre of Time*
CF - v75 - Mr '97 - p44+ [501+]
CG - v117 - Ja '97 - p74+ [501+]
Mac - v110 - F 24 '97 - p60 [501+]
Quill & Q - v63 - Ja '97 - p31 [251-500]
Jenkins, Philip - *A History of the United States*
y BL - v93 - My 1 '97 - p1476 [51-250]
LJ - v122 - Ap 1 '97 - p106 [51-250]

Pedophiles and Priests
AJS - v102 - S '96 - p635+ [501+]
Choice - v34 - S '96 - p218+ [51-250]
Jenkins, Priscilla Belz - *Falcons Nest on Skyscrapers (Illus. by Megan Lloyd)*
c BL - v92 - Ag '96 - p1902+ [51-250]
c CLW - v67 - Mr '97 - p54 [51-250]
c HB Guide - v7 - Fall '96 - p344 [51-250]
Jenkins, Ron - *Introduction to X-Ray Powder Diffractometry*
Choice - v34 - Ja '97 - p834 [51-250]
SciTech - v20 - D '96 - p24 [51-250]
Jenkins, Ronald Scott - *Subversive Laughter*
TDR - v40 - Fall '96 - p192+ [501+]
Jenkins, Roy - *Gladstone*
AS - v65 - Aut '96 - p610+ [501+]
CR - v269 - S '96 - p162+ [501+]
CR - v270 - F '97 - p110 [1-50]
HT - v47 - Ja '97 - p54 [501+]
Gladstone: A Biography
Atl - v279 - Ja '97 - p88+ [501+]
BL - v93 - F 15 '97 - p998+ [51-250]
BW - v27 - F 2 '97 - p3+ [501+]
KR - v64 - D 1 '96 - p1717 [251-500]
LJ - v122 - Ja '97 - p112 [51-250]
Nat R - v49 - Ap 7 '97 - p46+ [501+]
NW - v129 - Mr 10 '97 - p70 [501+]
NY - v72 - F 10 '97 - p78+ [501+]
NYRB - v44 - Mr 27 '97 - p10+ [501+]
NYTBR - v102 - F 23 '97 - p7+ [501+]
PW - v243 - D 9 '96 - p51 [51-250]
WSJ-Cent - v99 - F 21 '97 - pA12 [501+]
Jenkins, Ruth Y - *Reclaiming Myths of Power*
RES - v48 - F '97 - p128+ [501+]
VS - v39 - Win '96 - p244+ [501+]
Jenkins, Sally - *Men Will Be Boys*
PW - v243 - S 9 '96 - p77 [51-250]
Jenkins, Sandra - *Flip-Flap*
c RT - v50 - Mr '97 - p500 [51-250]
My Book about Me (Illus. by Grahame Corbett)
c PW - v244 - Ap 14 '97 - p77 [51-250]
Jenkins, Speight - *Enjoying Wagner's Ring (Jenkins). Audio Version*
LJ - v122 - F 1 '97 - p127 [51-250]
Jenkins, Starr - *Smokejumpers '49*
WAL - v31 - Sum '96 - p179+ [251-500]
Jenkins, Steve - *Big and Little (Illus. by Steve Jenkins)*
c BL - v93 - O 1 '96 - p358 [51-250]
c HB Guide - v8 - Spr '97 - p118 [51-250]
c KR - v64 - S 15 '96 - p1402 [51-250]
c SLJ - v42 - O '96 - p99 [51-250]
c SLJ - v43 - Mr '97 - p30 [51-250]
Jenkins, Steven W - *Cheese Primer*
LJ - v121 - N 15 '96 - p82 [51-250]
PW - v243 - O 21 '96 - p81 [51-250]
Jenkins, Susan C - *A Pocket Reference for Psychiatrists. 2nd Ed.*
r AJPsych - v153 - Ag '96 - p1106 [251-500]
Jenkins, T A - *The Liberal Ascendancy 1830-1886*
EHR - v112 - F '97 - p237 [251-500]
Jenkins, Virginia Scott - *The Lawn: A History of an American Obsession*
J Am Cult - v18 - Win '95 - p114+ [501+]
Jenkins, W Kenneth - *Advanced Concepts in Adaptive Signal Processing*
SciTech - v21 - Mr '97 - p86 [51-250]
Jenkins, Wendy - *Killer Boots*
c Aust Bk R - Jl '96 - p60+ [501+]
c Magpies - v11 - Jl '96 - p31 [51-250]
Jenks, Robert D - *Insurgency and Social Disorder in Guizhou*
Ch Rev Int - v3 - Fall '96 - p443+ [501+]
Jenkyns, Richard - *The Legacy of Rome*
Class Out - v74 - Win '97 - p75+ [501+]
Jenner, Bruce - *Finding the Champion Within*
BL - v93 - D 1 '96 - p622 [51-250]
LJ - v122 - Ja '97 - p126 [51-250]
PW - v243 - N 18 '96 - p57 [51-250]
Jenner, Caryn - *Dig and Dug with Daisy (Illus. by Alex Wilson)*
c HB Guide - v8 - Spr '97 - p32 [51-250]
c KR - v64 - O 1 '96 - p1469 [51-250]
Trouble with Trucks
c CLW - v67 - Mr '97 - p55 [51-250]
Jennings, Anne M - *The Nubians of West Aswan*
MEJ - v50 - Sum '96 - p430+ [501+]
Jennings, Dana Andrew - *Lonesome Standard Time*
LJ - v121 - N 15 '96 - p116 [51-250]

Me, Dad and Number 6 (Illus. by Goro Sasaki)
c CBRS - v25 - Ap '97 - p99 [51-250]
c CCB-B - v50 - My '97 - p325 [51-250]
c PW - v244 - Ap 7 '97 - p91 [51-250]
c Trib Bks - My 4 '97 - p6 [51-250]
Jennings, Elizabeth - *A Spell of Words*
c TES - F 14 '97 - p7* [501+]
Jennings, Francis - *Benjamin Franklin, Politician*
Choice - v34 - Ap '97 - p1405 [251-250]
LJ - v121 - S 15 '96 - p76 [51-250]
The Founders of America
J Am St - v30 - Ap '96 - p178+ [251-500]
Jennings, Gary - *Aztec Autumn*
BL - v93 - My 1 '97 - p1461 [51-250]
Jennings, Jesse D - *Accidental Archaeologist*
Am Ant - v61 - Ap '96 - p427+ [501+]
Jennings, Kate - *Snake*
Aust Bk R - Ag '96 - p45+ [501+]
BL - v93 - Ap 1 '97 - p1281 [51-250]
LJ - v122 - Ap 1 '97 - p127 [51-250]
PW - v244 - Mr 10 '97 - p50 [51-250]
Jennings, Ken - *Changing Health Care*
BL - v93 - Ja '97 - p794 [251-500]
Jennings, Linda - *The Best Christmas Present of All (Illus. by Catherine Walters)*
c BL - v93 - S 1 '96 - p136+ [51-250]
c HB Guide - v8 - Spr '97 - p32 [51-250]
c PW - v243 - S 30 '96 - p93 [1-50]
c SLJ - v42 - O '96 - p37 [51-250]
The Brave Little Bunny (Illus. by Catherine Walters)
c RT - v50 - O '96 - p132 [1-50]
Come Back, Buster (Illus. by Catherine Walters)
c Bks Keeps - N '96 - p21 [51-250]
c Sch Lib - v44 - N '96 - p148 [51-250]
Easy Peasy! (Illus. by Tanya Linch)
c BL - v93 - Ap 1 '97 - p1338 [51-250]
c CBRS - v25 - Ap '97 - p99 [51-250]
c KR - v65 - F 15 '97 - p300 [51-250]
c PW - v244 - Mr 3 '97 - p74+ [51-250]
A Treasury of Pony Stories (Illus. by Anthony Lewis)
c CLW - v67 - Mr '97 - p52 [251-500]
Jennings, Patrick - *Faith and the Electric Dogs (Illus. by Patrick Jennings)*
c BL - v93 - Ja '97 - p766 [1-50]
c BL - v93 - D 1 '96 - p653 [51-250]
c CCB-B - v50 - Ja '97 - p176 [51-250]
c HB Guide - v8 - Spr '97 - p68 [51-250]
c KR - v64 - S 15 '96 - p1402+ [51-250]
c SLJ - v42 - D '96 - p122+ [51-250]
Jennings, Paul - *The Cabbage Patch Fib (Illus. by Keith McEwan)*
c Bks Keeps - N '96 - p9 [51-250]
The Cabbage Patch War (Illus. by Craig Smith)
c Magpies - v11 - S '96 - p33+ [51-250]
Duck for Cover
c Magpies - v11 - S '96 - p45 [1-50]
Freeze a Crowd
c Aust Bk R - D '96 - p90+ [501+]
The Gizmo Again (Illus. by Keith McEwan)
c Bks Keeps - v100 - S '96 - p16 [51-250]
c Sch Lib - v44 - Ag '96 - p107 [51-250]
The Paw Thing (Illus. by Keith McEwan)
c Bks Keeps - N '96 - p9 [51-250]
Unbearable! More Bizarre Stories
y Emerg Lib - v24 - S '96 - p27 [1-50]
c New Ad - v9 - Fall '96 - p327+ [501+]
Uncovered! Weird, Weird Stories
c Bks Keeps - v100 - S '96 - p16 [51-250]
c HB Guide - v7 - Fall '96 - p293 [51-250]
c New Ad - v9 - Fall '96 - p327+ [501+]
c Sch Lib - v44 - Ag '96 - p107 [51-250]
Jennings, R E - *The Genealogy of Disjunction*
Dialogue - v36 - Win '97 - p208+ [501+]
Phil R - v105 - Ja '96 - p87+ [501+]
Jennings, Ruth - *Lofty Aims and Lowly Duties*
VS - v39 - Win '96 - p268+ [501+]
Jennings, Terry - *101 Optical Illusions (Illus. by Alex Pang)*
c Bks Keeps - Ja '97 - p26 [51-250]
c KR - v65 - Ap 1 '97 - p558 [51-250]
c New Sci - v153 - F 8 '97 - p46 [51-250]
The Oxford Children's A to Z of Science
cr New Sci - v152 - D 14 '96 - p45 [1-50]
Pushes and Pulls
c Sch Lib - v44 - N '96 - p163 [51-250]
Rocks
c Sch Lib - v44 - N '96 - p163 [51-250]
Jennings, Waylon - *Waylon: An Autobiography*
BL - v92 - Ag '96 - p1850+ [251-500]
BWatch - v18 - F '97 - p8 [51-250]
Ent W - S 27 '96 - p74 [51-250]

Waylon: An Autobiography (Jennings). Audio Version
y Kliatt - v31 - Mr '97 - p51 [51-250]
PW - v243 - S 2 '96 - p47+ [51-250]
Jenny, Carole - *Medical Evaluation of Physically and Sexually Abused Children*
SciTech - v20 - N '96 - p38 [51-250]
Jensen, Claus - *Contest for the Heavens*
NS - v125 - S 13 '96 - p47 [251-500]
Jensen, Frede - *Tuscan Poetry of the Duecento*
TranslRevS - v1 - My '95 - p4 [51-250]
Jensen, Jens Ledet - *Saddlepoint Approximations*
SIAM Rev - v38 - D '96 - p696+ [51-250]
Jensen, Jerry L - *Statistics for Petroleum Engineers and Geoscientists*
SciTech - v20 - D '96 - p17 [51-250]
Jensen, Julie - *Beginning Basketball (Illus. by Andy King)*
c Ch BWatch - v6 - S '96 - p5 [1-50]
c HB Guide - v8 - Spr '97 - p144 [51-250]
Beginning Hockey (Illus. by Andy King)
c HB Guide - v7 - Fall '96 - p361 [1-50]
Beginning Mountain Biking (Illus. by Andy King)
c HB Guide - v8 - Spr '97 - p144 [51-250]
c SLJ - v43 - F '97 - p117 [51-250]
Beginning Snowboarding (Illus. by Jimmy Clarke)
c HB Guide - v7 - Fall '96 - p361 [1-50]
Jensen, Klaus Bruhn - *The Social Semiotics of Mass Communication*
JC - v47 - Win '97 - p166+ [501+]
Jensen, Marvin - *Strike Swiftly!*
KR - v65 - F 1 '97 - p198+ [251-500]
Jensen, Mary Brandt - *Does Your Project Have a Copyright Problem?*
LJ - v122 - F 1 '97 - p114 [51-250]
Jensen, Paul M - *The Men Who Made the Monsters*
PW - v243 - N 25 '96 - p66 [51-250]
Jensen, Richard S - *Pilot Judgment and Crew Resource Management*
SciTech - v20 - D '96 - p81 [1-50]
Jensen, Robert - *Marketing Modernism in Fin-De-Siecle Europe*
Art Bull - v78 - D '96 - p745+ [501+]
FR - v70 - D '96 - p375+ [501+]
Jensen, Vickie - *Carving a Totem Pole (Illus. by Vickie Jensen)*
y AB - v98 - N 18 '96 - p1729 [51-250]
c HB Guide - v7 - Fall '96 - p391 [51-250]
Jensen-Dudley, Claudia - *The Fragrant Fire*
Sm Pr R - v28 - D '96 - p7 [251-500]
Jensen-Stevenson, Monika - *Spite House*
KR - v65 - F 1 '97 - p214 [1-50]
LJ - v122 - My 1 '97 - p120 [51-250]
NYTBR - v102 - Mr 30 '97 - p12 [501+]
NYTLa - v146 - Ap 2 '97 - pC16 [501+]
PW - v244 - F 24 '97 - p78 [51-250]
Jenson, Richard L - *Management Accounting in Support of Manufacturing Excellence*
Choice - v34 - Ja '97 - p841 [51-250]
Jenssen, Hans - *Jets (Illus. by Hans Jenssen)*
c Ch BWatch - v6 - S '96 - p5 [1-50]
c Par Ch - v20 - N '96 - p8 [51-250]
c SLJ - v43 - Mr '97 - p198 [51-250]
Jentleson, Bruce W - *Encyclopedia of U.S. Foreign Relations. Vols. 1-4*
r For Aff - v76 - My '97 - p133+ [51-250]
r LJ - v122 - Ap 1 '97 - p82 [51-250]
With Friends like These
J Am St - v30 - Ap '96 - p153 [251-500]
Pres SQ - v26 - Sum '96 - p907+ [501+]
Jereb, James F - *Arts and Crafts of Morocco*
Am Craft - v56 - O '96 - p52 [51-250]
Jernigan, E Jay - *William Lindsay White 1900-1973*
LJ - v122 - Ap 1 '97 - p106 [51-250]
Jerome, Saint - *A Translation of Jerome's Chronicon with Historical Commentary*
CHR - v83 - Ja '97 - p163 [51-250]
Jerome, Brenda Joyce - *Caldwell County, Kentucky Vital Statistics--Births 1852-1910*
r EGH - v50 - N '96 - p167 [51-250]
Jerome, Carl - *100 Simple Sauces for Today's Healthy Home Cooking*
PW - v244 - My 5 '97 - p203 [51-250]
Jerome, John - *Blue Rooms*
PW - v244 - My 5 '97 - p190 [51-250]
Stone Work
LATBR - Jl 7 '96 - p11 [51-250]
LATBR - Jl 14 '96 - p11 [51-250]
Truck: On Rebuilding a Worn-Out Pickup and Other Post-Technological Adventures
LATBR - Jl 14 '96 - p10+ [51-250]
LJ - v122 - Ap 1 '97 - p134 [1-50]

Jerri, Abdul J - *Linear Difference Equations with Discrete Transform Methods*
SciTech - v20 - S '96 - p11 [51-250]
Jersild, P C - *En Gammal Karlek*
WLT - v70 - Aut '96 - p980 [251-500]
The Jerusalem Report Five Year CD-ROM. Electronic Media Version
r MEQ - v4 - Mr '97 - p89 [51-250]
Jespersen, James - *Mummies, Dinosaurs, Moon Rocks (Illus. by Bruce Hiscock)*
y BL - v93 - O 1 '96 - p332 [51-250]
c CCB-B - v50 - D '96 - p139 [51-250]
c Ch BWatch - v6 - D '96 - p8 [1-50]
c HB Guide - v8 - Spr '97 - p165 [51-250]
y SLJ - v42 - S '96 - p233+ [51-250]
Jespersen, T Christopher - *American Images of China 1931-1949*
Ch Rev Int - v4 - Spr '97 - p170+ [501+]
Jessing, Benedikt - *Johann Wolfgang Goethe*
MLR - v91 - O '96 - p1036+ [501+]
Jessome, Phonse - *Somebody's Daughter*
Quill & Q - v62 - D '96 - p29 [251-500]
Jestaz, Bertrand - *Art of the Renaissance*
Six Ct J - v27 - Fall '96 - p960+ [501+]
Le Livre Journal De La Fabrique Da La Chapelle Salviati A Saint-Marc De Florence 1579-1594
BM - v138 - O '96 - p699 [51-250]
Jester, Thomas C - *Twentieth-Century Building Materials*
FHB - Ap '97 - p136 [251-500]
SB - v32 - Ag '96 - p168+ [251-500]
SciTech - v20 - S '96 - p48 [51-250]
Jeter, K W - *Blade Runner*
BW - v26 - N 24 '96 - p6 [251-500]
Blade Runner 2
MFSF - v92 - F '97 - p43 [51-250]
Replicant Night
LJ - v121 - S 15 '96 - p100 [51-250]
PW - v243 - S 23 '96 - p61 [51-250]
Jets Series
c Magpies - v11 - Jl '96 - p28 [1-50]
Jeunesse Gallimard - *Atlas of Countries (Illus. by Donald Grant)*
cr HB Guide - v7 - Fall '96 - p377 [51-250]
cr SLJ - v42 - S '96 - p195 [51-250]
Jewell, Helen M - *The North-South Divide*
EHR - v111 - N '96 - p1244+ [251-500]
J Urban H - v23 - N '96 - p94+ [501+]
Women in Medieval England
Choice - v34 - N '96 - p518 [51-250]
R&R Bk N - v11 - N '96 - p42 [51-250]
Jewell, Nancy - *Silly Times with Two Silly Trolls (Illus. by Lisa Thiesing)*
c HB Guide - v7 - Fall '96 - p284 [51-250]
Jewell, Nicholas P - *Lifetime Data*
SciTech - v20 - N '96 - p14 [51-250]
The Jewish Quarterly
p TLS - N 15 '96 - p35 [501+]
Jeyaretnam, Philip - *Abraham's Promise*
WLT - v70 - Sum '96 - p765 [501+]
Jezer, Marty - *Stuttering: A Life Bound Up in Words*
BL - v93 - My 15 '97 - p1551 [51-250]
KR - v65 - Ap 1 '97 - p523 [51-250]
PW - v244 - Ap 14 '97 - p62 [51-250]
Jha, Dayanatha - *Research Priorities in Indian Agriculture*
JEL - v34 - D '96 - p2129+ [51-250]
Jhabvala, Ruth Prawer - *Shards of Memory*
NYTBR - v101 - Ag 25 '96 - p28 [1-50]
Jhung, Paula - *Guests without Grief*
PW - v244 - Mr 24 '97 - p80 [51-250]
Jicai, Feng - *Let One Hundred Flowers Bloom*
y HB Guide - v7 - Fall '96 - p302 [51-250]
Ten Years of Madness
LJ - v122 - Ja '97 - p119 [51-250]
PW - v243 - N 4 '96 - p68 [51-250]
Jiggins, Janice - *Changing the Boundaries*
JTWS - v13 - Fall '96 - p360 [51-250]
Jiles, Paulette - *North Spirit*
Can Lit - Spr '97 - p241+ [501+]
LJ - v121 - N 1 '96 - p98 [51-250]
Wom R Bks - v14 - Mr '97 - p5+ [501+]
Jillson, Calvin - *Congressional Dynamics*
JIH - v27 - Aut '96 - p337+ [501+]
RAH - v25 - Mr '97 - p44+ [501+]
Jimenez, Emmanuel - *Public and Private Secondary Education in Developing Countries*
J Gov Info - v23 - S '96 - p688 [51-250]

Jimenez, Juan Ramon - *The Complete Perfectionist*
  BL - v93 - F 15 '97 - p994 [51-250]
  LJ - v122 - Ap 15 '97 - p81 [51-250]
  PW - v244 - Ja 13 '97 - p62 [51-250]
  Utne R - Mr '97 - p85 [1-50]
Jimenez, Luis A - *El Arte Autobiografico En Cuba En El Siglo XIX*
  Hisp - v79 - D '96 - p809+ [501+]
Jimenez Paton, Bartolome - *Elocuencia Espanola En Arte*
  Hisp - v79 - S '96 - p448+ [501+]
Jin, Ha - *Facing Shadows*
  Choice - v34 - O '96 - p278 [51-250]
  Sm Pr R - v28 - N '96 - p12 [251-500]
Ocean of Words
  Choice - v34 - N '96 - p451 [51-250]
  Ch Rev Int - v4 - Spr '97 - p175+ [501+]
Jin, Leroy - *Monetary Policy and the Design of Financial Institutions in China 1978-90*
  JEL - v34 - S '96 - p1391+ [501+]
Jinks, Catherine - *An Evening with the Messiah*
  Aust Bk R - N '96 - p52+ [501+]
Pagan's Scribe
  Aust Bk R - S '96 - p57 [501+]
  y Magpies - v11 - S '96 - p35 [501+]
Jirasinghe, Dilum - *The Competent Head*
  R&R Bk N - v11 - N '96 - p56 [51-250]
Jirgl, Reinhard - *Abschied Von Den Feinden*
  WLT - v70 - Aut '96 - p947+ [501+]
Joachimsthaler, Anton - *The Last Days of Hitler*
  HT - v46 - O '96 - p57 [1-50]
  LJ - v122 - My 1 '97 - p120 [51-250]
Joas, Hans - *Pragmatism and Social Theory*
  SF - v75 - S '96 - p337+ [251-500]
Job, Amy G - *Reference Work in School Library Media Centers*
  Emerg Lib - v24 - Mr '97 - p42 [1-50]
  Sch Lib - v45 - F '97 - p54 [51-250]
Job, Enrico - *Il Pittore Felice*
  WLT - v70 - Aut '96 - p932 [251-500]
Job, Rueben P - *A Guide to Spiritual Discernment*
  PW - v243 - N 11 '96 - p68+ [51-250]
Jobs and Skill Requirements for Entry-Level Workers
  J Gov Info - v23 - S '96 - p580 [51-250]
Jochens, Jenny - *Old Norse Images of Women*
  Choice - v34 - Ja '97 - p801 [51-250]
  R&R Bk N - v11 - D '96 - p67 [51-250]
  TLS - N 29 '96 - p25 [501+]
Women in Old Norse Society
  R&R Bk N - v11 - D '96 - p41 [51-250]
Jodorowsky, Alexandro - *The Madwoman of the Sacred Heart*
  PW - v243 - Jl 22 '96 - p234 [51-250]
Jody, Marilyn - *Computer Conversations*
  JOYS - v10 - Fall '96 - p100+ [251-500]
  VOYA - v19 - D '96 - p296 [251-500]
Joe, Rita - *Song of Rita Joe*
  BL - v92 - Ag '96 - p1874+ [51-250]
  Quill & Q - v62 - Jl '96 - p51 [251-500]
Joe, Yolanda - *He Say, She Say*
  y BL - v93 - S 1 '96 - p31 [51-250]
  BW - v27 - F 23 '97 - p6 [501+]
  KR - v64 - N 15 '96 - p1622+ [51-250]
  PW - v243 - N 18 '96 - p62 [51-250]
He Say, She Say. Audio Version
  LJ - v122 - Ap 1 '97 - p145 [51-250]
Joes, Anthony James - *Guerrilla Conflict before the Cold War*
  Choice - v34 - Ja '97 - p871 [51-250]
  R&R Bk N - v11 - D '96 - p7 [51-250]
Guerrilla Warfare
  r Choice - v34 - D '96 - p680+ [51-250]
  r R&R Bk N - v11 - D '96 - p72 [51-250]
Joffe, Carole E - *Doctors of Conscience*
  CS - v25 - S '96 - p691+ [501+]
  MHR - v10 - Fall '96 - p80+ [501+]
  NWSA Jnl - v8 - Fall '96 - p154+ [501+]
Joffe, Russell T - *Anticonvulsants in Mood Disorders*
  AJPsych - v153 - S '96 - p1227+ [501+]
Johannes, De Hauvilla - *Architrenius (Wetherbee)*
  RES - v48 - F '97 - p79+ [501+]
Johannes, Von Tepl - *Civis Zacensis, Epistola Cum Libello Ackerman Und Das Buchlein Ackerman. Vols. 1-2*
  MLR - v92 - Ap '97 - p501+ [501+]
Johannessen, Matthias - *Hvildarlaus Fero Inni Drauminn*
  WLT - v71 - Win '97 - p170 [251-500]
Johannesson, Magnus - *Theory and Methods of Economic Evaluation of Health Care*
  JEL - v35 - Mr '97 - p228 [51-250]
  SciTech - v20 - D '96 - p38 [51-250]

Johansen, Bruce E - *The Encyclopedia of Native American Biography*
  r BL - v93 - My 1 '97 - p1522+ [251-500]
  r BW - v27 - Mr 2 '97 - p13 [51-250]
  r LJ - v122 - Ap '97 - p88 [51-250]
Native American Political Systems and the Evolution of Democracy
  r Choice - v34 - N '96 - p432 [51-250]
Johansen, Flemming - *Roman Portraits. Vols. 1-3*
  AJA - v100 - O '96 - p795 [501+]
Johansen, Iris - *Long after Midnight*
  y BL - v93 - D 1 '96 - p620 [51-250]
  KR - v64 - D 15 '96 - p1757 [251-500]
  PW - v243 - D 30 '96 - p54 [51-250]
The Ugly Duckling
  PW - v243 - N 18 '96 - p70 [1-50]
Johansen, Julian - *Sufism and Islamic Reform in Egypt*
  Choice - v34 - N '96 - p476 [51-250]
Johansen, Ruthann Knechel - *The Narrative Secret of Flannery O'Connor*
  South HR - v31 - Win '97 - p77+ [501+]
Johansen, Soren - *Likelihood-Based Inference in Co-Integrated Vector Autoregressive Models*
  JEL - v34 - S '96 - p1409 [51-250]
Johanson, Donald C - *From Lucy to Language*
  BW - v26 - D 8 '96 - p12 [51-250]
  KR - v64 - O 1 '96 - p1460 [51-250]
  LJ - v121 - N 15 '96 - p85 [51-250]
  Nature   v385 - Ja 16 '97 - p215 [51-250]
  New Sci - v152 - N 16 '96 - p46 [501+]
  New Sci - v153 - F 1 '97 - p49 [51-250]
  NH - v106 - F '97 - p10 [1-50]
  NYTBR - v101 - D 1 '96 - p7 [501+]
  NYTBR - v101 - D 8 '96 - p87 [1-50]
  PW - v243 - S 30 '96 - p66 [51-250]
  PW - v243 - N 4 '96 - p44 [51-250]
  Sci - v275 - Ja 3 '97 - p37 [1-50]
Johansson, Per-Olov - *Evaluating Health Risks*
  JEL - v35 - Mr '97 - p152+ [501+]
John, of Worcester - *The Chronicle of John of Worcester. Vol. 2*
  Specu - v72 - Ja '97 - p177+ [501+]
  Albion - v28 - Win '96 - p662+ [501+]
John, of Salisbury, Bishop of Chartres - *Le Policratique De Jean De Salisbury 1372. Bks. 1-3*
  Specu - v72 - Ja '97 - p149+ [501+]
John, Angela V - *Elizabeth Robins: Staging a Life 1862-1952*
  AHR - v101 - D '96 - p1545+ [251-500]
  Albion - v28 - Fall '96 - p526+ [501+]
  ELT - v39 - 4 '96 - p487+ [501+]
John, Augustus - *Themes and Variations*
  NYRB - v44 - Mr 6 '97 - p24+ [501+]
  Obs - Ag 18 '96 - p16* [51-250]
John, Brian - *Reading the Ground*
  Choice - v34 - D '96 - p614 [51-250]
John, Eric - *Reassessing Anglo-Saxon England*
  HT - v46 - O '96 - p55 [1-50]
John, Geraint - *Handbook of Sports and Recreational Building Design. 2nd Ed., Vol. 3*
  R&R Bk N - v11 - N '96 - p22 [51-250]
John, J - *Campaign Dossier*
  WorldV - v12 - O '96 - p17 [51-250]
John, Katherine - *Murder of a Dead Man*
  BL - v93 - D 15 '96 - p712 [51-250]
  KR - v64 - N 1 '96 - p1566 [51-250]
  PW - v243 - D 2 '96 - p44 [51-250]
John, Martha Tyler - *Cultural Adaptation in the Workplace*
  JEL - v34 - S '96 - p1460+ [51-250]
John, Mary - *Children in Charge: The Child's Right to a Fair Hearing*
  TES - S 6 '96 - p8* [51-250]
Children in Charge: The Child's Right to Resources
  Readings - v12 - Mr '97 - p29 [51-250]
  TES - S 6 '96 - p8* [51-250]
John, Mary E - *Discrepant Dislocations*
  Critm - v39 - Win '97 - p229+ [501+]
John, Richard R - *Spreading the News*
  Am Phil - v110 - S '96 - p844 [501+]
  BHR - v70 - Sum '96 - p273+ [501+]
  JC - v47 - Win '97 - p155+ [501+]
  JEH - v56 - S '96 - p734+ [501+]
  NEQ - v70 - Mr '97 - p168+ [501+]
  Phil Lit R - v45 - 3 '96 - p257+ [501+]
  RAH - v24 - D '96 - p596+ [501+]
  W&M Q - v54 - Ap '97 - p448+ [501+]
John Ash's Wine Country Cuisine. Electronic Media Version
  LJ - v122 - F 15 '97 - p169 [51-250]

John of the Cross, Saint - *The Living Flame of Love: Versions A and B*
  Rel St Rev - v23 - Ja '97 - p81 [51-250]
  Six Ct J - v27 - Fall '96 - p875+ [501+]
John Paul II, Pope - *The Encyclicals of John Paul II on CD ROM. Electronic Media Version*
  r ARBA - v28 - '97 - p552+ [51-250]
Gift and Mystery
  BL - v93 - D 15 '96 - p690 [1-50]
  CSM - v89 - Ja 23 '97 - p12 [51-250]
Pope John Paul II on Jews and Judaism 1979-1986
  Rel Ed - v91 - Fall '96 - p609 [1-50]
Spiritual Pilgrimage
  Rel Ed - v91 - Fall '96 - p609 [1-50]
Johns, Catherine - *The Jewellery of Roman Britain*
  TLS - S 20 '96 - p32 [51-250]
Johns, Christina Jacqueline - *The Origins of Violence in Mexican Society*
  HAHR - v76 - N '96 - p781+ [501+]
Johns, Christopher M S - *Papal Art and Cultural Politics*
  CH - v65 - S '96 - p503+ [501+]
Johns, Jasper - *Johns (Abrams)*
  y BL - v93 - O 1 '96 - p314+ [51-250]
Johnsen, William T - *Deciphering the Balkan Enigma. 1st Rev. Ed.*
  J Gov Info - v23 - S '96 - p565+ [51-250]
Johnsgard, Paul A - *Ruddy Ducks and Other Stifftails*
  Choice - v34 - N '96 - p484 [51-250]
  R&R Bk N - v11 - N '96 - p77 [51 250]
Johnson, Alexandra - *The Hidden Writer*
  KR - v65 - Mr 1 '97 - p354+ [51-250]
  LJ - v122 - Ap 1 '97 - p92 [51-250]
  PW - v244 - Ap 21 '97 - p57 [51-250]
Johnson, Alice Jane Holland - *Information Brokers*
  LR - v45 - 7 '96 - p42+ [251-500]
Johnson, Allan G - *The Blackwell Dictionary of Sociology*
  r BL - v93 - D 1 '96 - p683+ [251-500]
  r SF - v75 - S '96 - p397 [51-250]
Johnson, Allen, Jr. - *Picker McClikker (Illus. by Stephen Hanson)*
  c Ch BWatch   v6 - O '96 - p4 [51-250]
Johnson, Angela - *The Aunt in Our House (Illus. by David Soman)*
  c HB Guide - v7 - Fall '96 - p261+ [51-250]
Humming Whispers
  y Kliatt - v31 - Ja '97 - p8 [51-250]
  y PW - v243 - O 21 '96 - p85 [1-50]
  y Sch Lib - v45 - F '97 - p46 [51-250]
Julius (Illus. by Dav Pilkey)
  c SLJ - v43 - Ja '97 - p36+ [1-50]
The Rolling Store (Illus. by Peter Catalanotto)
  c BL - v93 - F 15 '97 - p1026+ [51-250]
  c CCB-B - v50 - My '97 - p325+ [51-250]
  c KR - v65 - F 15 '97 - p300 [51-250]
  c PW - v244 - Mr 17 '97 - p82+ [51-250]
Shoes like Miss Alice's (Illus. by Ken Page)
  c RT - v50 - N '96 - p257 [51-250]
Toning the Sweep
  y Kliatt - v30 - S '96 - p3 [1-50]
  y Sch Lib - v44 - Ag '96 - p118 [51-250]
Johnson, Anne Akers - *Chinese Jump Rope*
  c PW - v244 - Ap 7 '97 - p94 [1-50]
Hair: A Book of Braiding and Styles
  y Emerg Lib - v24 - S '96 - p26 [1-50]
Johnson, Anne E - *A Student's Guide to African American Genealogy*
  yr ARBA - v28 - '97 - p167 [51-250]
  y NGSQ - v84 - S '96 - p224 [51-250]
A Student's Guide to British American Genealogy
  yr ARBA - v28 - '97 - p167 [51-250]
  y NGSQ - v84 - S '96 - p231+ [501+]
Johnson, Anne M - *The Essence of Parenting*
  CLW - v67 - Mr '97 - p39 [251-500]
Sailing on a Budget
  BL - v93 - D 1 '96 - p639 [51-250]
Johnson, B J - *Baby Farm Animals*
  c PW - v244 - F 10 '97 - p85 [51-250]
Baby Friends
  c PW - v244 - F 10 '97 - p85 [51-250]
Johnson, Barbara - *The Wake of Deconstruction*
  MLR - v92 - Ja '97 - p151+ [51-250]
Johnson, Barbara E - *Living Somewhere between Estrogen and Death*
  PW - v244 - Mr 10 '97 - p64 [51-250]
Johnson, Carmen - *Wave-Rings in the Water*
  BWatch - v17 - S '96 - p4 [51-250]
  Rapport - v19 - 6 '96 - p35 [251-500]
Wave Rings in the Water
  Rapport - v19 - 6 '96 - p35 [251-500]

Johnson, Cecil - *Guts: Legendary Black Rodeo Cowboy Bill Pickett*
y BL - v93 - D 15 '96 - p716 [1-50]

Johnson, Chalmers - *Japan, Who Governs?*
AAPSS-A - v547 - S '96 - p176+ [501+]
APH - v43 - Fall '96 - p64+ [501+]

Johnson, Charles S - *Shadow of the Plantation*
Bl S - v26 - Fall '96 - p104 [51-250]

Johnson, Cherry L F - *Half Moon Pocosin*
CSM - v89 - Ja 13 '97 - p13 [501+]
PW - v243 - N 11 '96 - p58 [51-250]
Trib Bks - Mr 2 '97 - p3 [501+]

Johnson, Christopher H - *The Life and Death of Industrial Languedoc 1700-1920*
J Soc H - v30 - Fall '96 - p286+ [501+]

Johnson, Claudia Durst - *Understanding Adventures of Huckleberry Finn*
y Ch BWatch - v6 - S '96 - p7 [1-50]
Nine-C Lit - v51 - D '96 - p423 [1-50]
y SLJ - v42 - D '96 - p146 [51-250]

Johnson, Claudia L - *Equivocal Beings*
Albion - v28 - Sum '96 - p313+ [501+]

Johnson, Curt - *Artillery Hell*
Pub Hist - v18 - Sum '96 - p61+ [501+]

Johnson, Curt, 1928- - *Thanksgiving in Vegas*
Sm Pr R - v28 - D '96 - p10 [251-500]

Johnson, Curtis D - *Redeeming America*
Rel St Rev - v23 - Ja '97 - p92 [51-250]

Johnson, D Gale - *Agricultural Policy and U.S.-Taiwan Trade*
Ch Rev Int - v3 - Fall '96 - p445+ [501+]

Johnson, Dale A - *Women and Religion in Britain and Ireland*
r ARBA - v28 - '97 - p533 [251-500]

Johnson, Dave, 1963- - *Aim High*
Aethlon - v13 - Spr '96 - p207+ [501+]

Johnson, David E - *Electric Circuit Analysis. 3rd Ed.*
SciTech - v20 - D '96 - p74 [51-250]

Johnson, David G - *Ritual and Scripture in Chinese Popular Religion*
Ch Rev Int - v3 - Fall '96 - p447+ [501+]

Johnson, David R - *Illegal Tender*
AHR - v102 - F '97 - p194 [251-500]
BusLR - v21 - 3 '96 - p246 [51-250]
HRNB - v25 - Win '97 - p57 [251-500]
JEH - v57 - Mr '97 - p257+ [501+]

Johnson, David S - *Cliques, Coloring, and Satisfiability*
SciTech - v21 - Mr '97 - p10 [51-250]

Johnson, David Thomas - *Poverty, Inequality and Social Welfare in Australia*
JEL - v35 - Mr '97 - p233 [51-250]

Johnson, Deidre - *Edward Stratemeyer and the Stratemeyer Syndicate*
JPC - v29 - Spr '96 - p238+ [251-500]

Johnson, Denis - *The Throne of the Third Heaven of the Nations Millennium General Assembly*
SFR - v22 - Ja '97 - p48 [51-250]

Johnson, Diane - *Le Divorce*
BL - v93 - D 1 '96 - p641 [51-250]
CSM - v89 - F 20 '97 - p10 [51-250]
KR - v64 - N 1 '96 - p1554+ [251-500]
LATBR - D 29 '96 - p2 [501+]
LJ - v121 - N 15 '96 - p88 [51-250]
NY - v73 - Mr 10 '97 - p93 [51-250]
NYRB - v44 - F 6 '97 - p16+ [501+]
NYTBR - v102 - F 2 '97 - p10 [501+]
NYTLa - v146 - Ja 23 '97 - pC21 [501+]
Obs - Ja 19 '97 - p17* [501+]
PW - v243 - O 21 '96 - p70 [51-250]
Spec - v278 - Ja 18 '97 - p34+ [501+]
TES - Ja 17 '97 - p9* [51-250]
TLS - Ja 24 '97 - p23 [501+]
Trib Bks - Ja 5 '97 - p6 [501+]
WSJ-Cent - v99 - Ja 10 '97 - pA9 [251-500]

Johnson, Dolores - *The Children's Book of Kwanzaa (Illus. by Dolores Johnson)*
c BL - v93 - S 1 '96 - p134 [51-250]
c Bloom Rev - v16 - N '96 - p31 [1-50]
c CBRS - v25 - O '96 - p22 [51-250]
c CCB-B - v50 - N '96 - p100 [51-250]
c Ch BWatch - v6 - D '96 - p1 [1-50]
c HB Guide - v8 - Spr '97 - p98 [51-250]
c PW - v243 - S 30 '96 - p88 [51-250]
c SLJ - v42 - O '96 - p37 [51-250]
Now Let Me Fly (Illus. by Dolores Johnson)
c PW - v244 - Ja 20 '97 - p403 [1-50]
She Dared to Fly
c Ch BWatch - v7 - F '97 - p7 [1-50]
c HB Guide - v8 - Spr '97 - p156 [51-250]

Johnson, Donald D - *The United States in the Pacific*
Pac A - v69 - Fall '96 - p458 [501+]
PHR - v65 - N '96 - p697+ [501+]

Johnson, Donald S - *Phantom Islands of the Atlantic*
BL - v93 - D 15 '96 - p697 [51-250]
KR - v64 - O 1 '96 - p1446 [251-500]
LJ - v121 - D '96 - p130 [51-250]
NYTBR - v102 - F 16 '97 - p19 [51-250]
PW - v243 - O 14 '96 - p69+ [51-250]

Johnson, Doug - *James and the Dinosaurs (Illus. by Bill Basso)*
c RT - v50 - O '96 - p133 [1-50]
Never Ride Your Elephant to School (Illus. by Abby Carter)
c RT - v50 - O '96 - p134 [1-50]

Johnson, Douglas H - *Nuer Prophets*
Am Ethnol - v23 - N '96 - p907+ [501+]

Johnson, Eileen - *Ancient Peoples and Landscapes*
Am Ant - v61 - O '96 - p802+ [501+]

Johnson, Ellwood - *The Pursuit of Power*
AL - v68 - S '96 - p663 [51-250]
J Am St - v30 - D '96 - p480+ [251-500]

Johnson, Elmer H - *Japanese Corrections*
Choice - v34 - O '96 - p367 [51-250]

Johnson, Eric A - *Urbanization and Crime*
AJS - v102 - S '96 - p622+ [501+]
JIH - v27 - Spr '97 - p698+ [501+]

Johnson, Ernest W - *Practical Electromyography. 3rd Ed.*
SciTech - v21 - Mr '97 - p49 [51-250]

Johnson, Eugene J - *Drawn from the Source*
NYTBR - v101 - D 8 '96 - p58+ [51-250]

Johnson, Everett A - *The Economic Era of Health Care*
R&R Bk N - v11 - D '96 - p69 [51-250]
SciTech - v21 - Mr '97 - p45 [51-250]

Johnson, Fenton - *Geography of the Heart*
NYTBR - v101 - S 22 '96 - p24+ [51-250]
SFR - v21 - N '96 - p48 [1-50]

Johnson, Frances - *Kitchen Antiques with Values*
r Ant & CM - v101 - D '96 - p30 [51-250]

Johnson, George - *Fire in the Mind*
NYTBR - v101 - N '96 - p32 [51-250]

Johnson, Graham - *The Songmakers' Almanac*
r Spec - v278 - F 8 '97 - p37 [501+]

Johnson, Greg - *I Am Dangerous*
BL - v92 - Ag '96 - p1882 [51-250]
LATBR - S 1 '96 - p11 [51-250]
NYTBR - v101 - O 27 '96 - p39 [51-250]

Johnson, H - *Super Vixens' Dymaxion Lounge*
KR - v65 - My 1 '97 - p696 [251-500]
PW - v244 - Ap 14 '97 - p62 [51-250]

Johnson, Haynes - *The System: The American Way of Politics at the Breaking Point*
BW - v26 - D 8 '96 - p9 [1-50]
NYRB - v43 - Je 6 '96 - p11+ [501+]

Johnson, Hillary - *Osler's Web*
Choice - v34 - N '96 - p493 [51-250]
PW - v244 - Ja 27 '97 - p103 [1-50]

Johnson, Hugh - *Principles of Gardening. Rev. Ed.*
Hort - v94 - Ap '97 - p78+ [501+]
PW - v244 - Ja 6 '97 - p70 [51-250]

Johnson, J David - *Information Seeking*
Choice - v34 - D '96 - p654+ [51-250]
R&R Bk N - v11 - N '96 - p28 [51-250]

Johnson, James A - *Showing America a New Way Home*
LJ - v121 - O 15 '96 - p68+ [51-250]

Johnson, James E - *Hydraulics for Engineering Technology*
SciTech - v20 - N '96 - p71 [51-250]

Johnson, James H - *The Human Geography of Ireland*
AAAGA - v87 - Mr '97 - p183+ [501+]
GJ - v162 - Jl '96 - p219 [251-500]

Johnson, James M - *Militiamen, Rangers, and Redcoats*
J Mil H - v61 - Ap '97 - p370+ [251-500]

Johnson, James Weldon - *The Autobiography of an Ex-Colored Man (Gilmore). Audio Version*
LJ - v121 - S 15 '96 - p112 [51-250]

Johnson, Jeff - *Careers for Music Lovers and Other Tuneful Types*
y Kliatt - v31 - Ja '97 - p21 [51-250]

Johnson, Jinny - *Prehistoric Life Explained*
c BL - v93 - D 1 '96 - p658 [51-250]
cr HB Guide - v8 - Spr '97 - p114 [51-250]
c PW - v243 - N 18 '96 - p78 [51-250]
Simon and Schuster Children's Guide to Birds
c HB Guide - v8 - Spr '97 - p344 [51-250]
Simon and Schuster Children's Guide to Insects and Spiders
c BL - v93 - My 1 '97 - p1492 [51-250]

Johnson, Julie - *Bullies and Gangs*
c Sch Lib - v45 - F '97 - p39 [51-250]

Johnson, K Paul - *The Masters Revealed*
Skeptic - v4 - '96 - p106 [1-50]

Johnson, Keith - *Language Teaching and Skill Learning*
Choice - v34 - N '96 - p511 [51-250]

Johnson, Kevin - *Catch the Wave!*
y VOYA - v19 - F '97 - p350 [251-500]
Does Anybody Know What Planet My Parents Are From?
y BL - v93 - O 1 '96 - p333 [51-250]
y VOYA - v19 - F '97 - p350 [251-500]
Why Is God Looking for Friends?
y VOYA - v19 - F '97 - p319 [51-250]

Johnson, Kristin - *Unfortunate Emigrants*
Roundup M - v4 - D '96 - p21+ [251-500]

Johnson, Lee - *Delacroix Pastels*
BM - v138 - S '96 - p608+ [501+]

Johnson, Leland - *Oak Ridge National Laboratory*
Pub Hist - v18 - Sum '96 - p72+ [251-500]

Johnson, Linda Cooke - *Cities of Jiangnan in Late Imperial China*
Ch Rev Int - v3 - Fall '96 - p450+ [501+]
Shanghai: From Market Town to Treaty Port 1074-1858
Ch Rev Int - v4 - Spr '97 - p177+ [501+]

Johnson, Loch K - *Secret Agencies*
Choice - v34 - F '97 - p1036 [51-250]
LJ - v121 - N 1 '96 - p92+ [51-250]
NYTBR - v101 - O 27 '96 - p40 [501+]
PW - v243 - O 7 '96 - p52 [51-250]

Johnson, Lois S - *Happy Birthdays Round the World*
r JPC - v29 - Spr '96 - p258+ [51-250]

Johnson, Lois Walfrid - *Midnight Rescue*
c BL - v93 - Ja '97 - p860 [251-500]
Secret of the Best Choice
y VOYA - v19 - F '97 - p318 [51-250]
Thanks for Being My Friend
y VOYA - v19 - F '97 - p318 [51-250]
You Are Wonderfully Made!
y VOYA - v19 - F '97 - p318 [51-250]
You're Worth More than You Think
y VOYA - v19 - F '97 - p318 [51-250]

Johnson, Lonnie R - *Central Europe*
BL - v93 - S 15 '96 - p214 [51-250]
Choice - v34 - My '97 - p1558 [51-250]
For Aff - v76 - My '97 - p140+ [51-250]

Johnson, Loretta - *Scholarships, Grants, Fellowships, and Endowments*
yr BL - v93 - F 1 '97 - p962+ [251-500]

Johnson, Luke Timothy - *The Real Jesus*
Rel St Rev - v23 - Ap '97 - p178 [51-250]
Theol St - v57 - Je '96 - p377 [251-500]
Scripture and Discernment
Intpr - v51 - Ap '97 - p208+ [251-500]

Johnson, Manuel H - *Monetary Policy, a Market Price Approach*
R&R Bk N - v12 - F '97 - p47 [51-250]

Johnson, Marael - *Outback Australia Handbook. 2nd Ed.*
r BL - v93 - S 15 '96 - p212 [1-50]
r BWatch - v17 - N '96 - p12 [51-250]

Johnson, Marilynn S - *Second Gold Rush*
Historian - v59 - Win '97 - p405 [1-50]

Johnson, Mark - *Moral Imagination*
Rel St Rev - v22 - O '96 - p340 [51-250]

Johnson, Maxwell E - *Living Water, Sealing Spirit*
CH - v65 - S '96 - p559+ [501+]

Johnson, Merv - *In Search of Steam Donkeys*
Model R - v64 - Ja '97 - p61 [251-500]

Johnson, Michael - *Slaying the Dragon*
Ent W - N 29 '96 - p85 [51-250]

Johnson, Michael L - *New Westers*
PHR - v66 - F '97 - p135+ [501+]
WHQ - v28 - Spr '97 - p69+ [251-500]

Johnson, Mike - *The Aspiring Manager's Survival Guide*
TES - F 14 '97 - p19U [251-500]

Johnson, Neil - *Ghost Night (Illus. by Neil Johnson)*
c KR - v64 - S 1 '96 - p1331 [51-250]
c PW - v243 - S 23 '96 - p78 [51-250]
c SLJ - v42 - S '96 - p202 [51-250]

Johnson, Nel - *Web Developer's Guide to Multimedia and Video*
LJ - v121 - O 1 '96 - p120 [1-50]

Johnson, Norman - *Private Markets in Health and Welfare*
J Con A - v31 - Sum '97 - p171+ [501+]

Johnson, Oliver - *The Mind of David Hume*
CPR - v16 - O '96 - p353+ [501+]

Johnson, Paul - *Children Making Books*
Sch Lib - v44 - Ag '96 - p129+ [51-250]

Johnson, Paul, 1928- - *A History of the Jews (May). Audio Version*
y Kliatt - v31 - Mr '97 - p48 [51-250]

The Quest for God
CSM - v88 - S 12 '96 - p13 [501+]
CSM - v88 - S 19 '96 - p14 [51-250]
HR - v49 - Win '97 - p669+ [501+]
Lon R Bks - v18 - O 3 '96 - p3+ [501+]
NY - v72 - My 20 '96 - p93+ [501+]
Spec - v277 - N 23 '96 - p43 [1-50]
W&I - v11 - O '96 - p270+ [501+]
To Hell with Picasso and Other Essays
Spec - v277 - N 9 '96 - p50 [501+]
TLS - D 27 '96 - p36 [501+]
Johnson, Paul, 1956- - *Twentieth-Century Britain*
EHR - v111 - N '96 - p1351+ [251-500]
Johnson, Paul Brett - *Farmers' Market (Illus. by Paul Brett Johnson)*
c BL - v93 - Mr 15 '97 - p1247 [51-250]
c CCB-B - v50 - Ap '97 - p286 [51-250]
c KR - v65 - F 15 '97 - p300+ [51-250]
Lost (Illus. by Paul Brett Johnson)
c HB Guide - v7 - Fall '96 - p262 [51-250]
c SLJ - v42 - D '96 - p30 [1-50]
Johnson, Paul E - *African-American Christianity*
JAAR - v64 - Fall '96 - p702+ [501+]
The Kingdom of Matthias
J Soc H - v30 - Spr '97 - p739+ [501+]
Johnson, Peggy - *The Searchable Internet Bibliography. Electronic Media Version*
r SLMQ - v24 - Sum '96 - p220 [51-250]
Johnson, Pete - *The Ghost Dog (Illus. by Peter Dennis)*
c Bks Keeps - Jl '96 - p12 [51-250]
c JB - v60 - O '96 - p193 [51-250]
The Vision
c Bks Keeps - Mr '97 - p26 [51-250]
y Sch Lib - v45 - F '97 - p46+ [51-250]
y TES - Ja 3 '97 - p22 [51-250]
Johnson, Phillip E - *Darwin on Trial. 2nd Ed.*
Bks & Cult - v2 - Ja '96 - p16+ [501+]
Reason in the Balance
Bks & Cult - v2 - Ja '96 - p16+ [501+]
Reason - v28 - O '96 - p53+ [501+]
Johnson, Pierre Marc - *The Environment and NAFTA*
Choice - v34 - O '96 - p357 [51-250]
Johnson, R W - *Launching Democracy in South Africa*
Choice - v34 - S '96 - p203 [51-250]
r J Pol - v59 - F '97 - p302+ [501+]
PSQ - v111 - Win '96 - p742+ [501+]
Johnson, Rebecca L - *Braving the Frozen Frontier*
c BL - v93 - F 15 '97 - p1018 [51-250]
y CCB-B - v50 - Mr '97 - p250+ [51-250]
c KR - v65 - Ja 1 '97 - p59 [51-250]
c SLJ - v43 - Mr '97 - p202 [51-250]
Johnson, Robert David - *The Peace Progressives and American Foreign Relations*
HAHR - v76 - N '96 - p838+ [501+]
Historian - v59 - Fall '96 - p147+ [501+]
RAH - v24 - S '96 - p466+ [501+]
Johnson, Robert Flynn - *Peter Milton: Complete Prints 1960-1996*
r BW - v27 - Ja 5 '97 - p13 [51-250]
r Choice - v34 - Ap '97 - p1324+ [51-250]
r SFR - v22 - Ja '97 - p44 [51-250]
Johnson, S - *Hungry Ghosts*
Aust Bk R - O '96 - p42+ [501+]
Women Love Sex
Aust Bk R - D '96 - p46+ [501+]
Johnson, Samuel - *A Dictionary of the English Language on CD-ROM. Electronic Media Version*
r Choice - v34 - Mr '97 - p1155+ [251-500]
r HT - v46 - D '96 - p55 [501+]
r HT - v46 - F 12 '97 - p48 [51-250]
The Latin and Greek Poems of Samuel Johnson
RES - v47 - N '96 - p592+ [501+]
Johnson, Sherry - *Pale Grace*
BIC - v25 - N '96 - p6+ [501+]
Johnson, Stanley - *The Politics of Population*
GJ - v162 - Jl '96 - p235 [251-500]
World Population
GJ - v162 - Jl '96 - p239 [51-250]
Johnson, Stanley R - *Conservation of Great Plains Ecosystems*
JEL - v34 - S '96 - p1498 [51-250]
Johnson, Stephen T - *Alphabet City (Illus. by Stephen T Johnson)*
c Inst - v42 - Ag '96 - p44+ [1-50]
c RT - v50 - D '96 - p347 [51-250]
Johnson, Susan - *Microfinance and Poverty Reduction*
New Sci - v153 - F 15 '97 - p42 [51-250]
Johnson, Susan, 1939- - *Wicked*
PW - v243 - N 25 '96 - p70 [51-250]
Johnson, Susan M - *Creating Connection*
SB - v33 - My '97 - p104+ [51-250]

The Practice of Emotionally Focused Marital Therapy
SciTech - v20 - D '96 - p45 [51-250]
Johnson, Susan Moore - *Leading to Change*
AJE - v105 - My '97 - p319+ [501+]
Choice - v34 - D '96 - p661 [51-250]
Johnson, Sylvia A - *Callie and the Prince*
c Magpies - v11 - Jl '96 - p31 [51-250]
Raptor Rescue (Illus. by Ron Winch)
c LA - v73 - O '96 - p438 [51-250]
Tomatoes, Potatoes, Corn, and Beans
c KR - v65 - F 15 '97 - p301 [51-250]
Johnson, Thomas C - *The Limnology, Climatology and Paleoclimatology of the East African Lakes*
SciTech - v21 - Mr '97 - p34 [51-250]
Johnson, Todd M - *China: Issues and Options in Greenhouse Gas Emissions Control*
JEL - v35 - Mr '97 - p299 [51-250]
Johnson, Tom - *Hammer Films*
r ARBA - v28 - '97 - p511 [51-250]
Johnson, Troy R - *The Occupation of Alcatraz Island*
PW - v243 - O 14 '96 - p78+ [51-250]
Johnson, Uwe - *Heute Neunzig Jahr*
WLT - v71 - Win '97 - p137 [501+]
Johnson, Venice - *Voices of the Dream*
c BL - v93 - F 15 '97 - p1014 [1-50]
Johnson, W J - *Harmless Souls*
Rel St Rev - v22 - O '96 - p359 [251-500]
Johnson, W S - *Life Prediction Methodology for Titanium Matrix Composites*
SciTech - v20 - S '96 - p50 [51-250]
Johnson, Whittington B - *Black Savannah 1788-1864*
Choice - v34 - D '96 - p676 [51-250]
Johnson, Will - *The Posture of Meditation*
BL - v93 - N 15 '96 - p551 [51-250]
Utne R - S '96 - p92 [1-50]
Johnson-Jahrbuch. Vol. 1
MLR - v92 - Ja '97 - p251+ [501+]
The Johnson Mortuary Death Records 1904-1937
r EGH - v50 - N '96 - p161 [51-250]
Johnsonbaugh, Richard - *C for Scientists and Engineers*
Choice - v34 - Mr '97 - p1195 [51-250]
SciTech - v21 - Mr '97 - p7 [51-250]
Discrete Mathematics. 4th Ed.
SciTech - v21 - Mr '97 - p4 [51-250]
Johnson-Feelings, Dianne - *The Best of the Brownies' Book*
CCB-B - v50 - D '96 - p156 [51-250]
Johnson-Hill, Jack A - *I-Sight: The World of Rastafari*
CS - v25 - S '96 - p642+ [501+]
JR - v76 - O '96 - p679+ [251-500]
Johnston, Alastair Iain - *Cultural Realism*
AAPSS-A - v547 - S '96 - p177+ [501+]
Pac A - v69 - Sum '96 - p261+ [501+]
RP - v59 - Win '97 - p191+ [501+]
Johnston, Andrea - *Girls Speak Out*
c CBRS - v25 - F '97 - p82+ [1-50]
c CCB-B - v50 - F '97 - p210 [51-250]
y Ms - v7 - Mr '97 - p80 [51-250]
c PW - v244 - Ja 6 '97 - p74 [51-250]
c SLJ - v43 - F '97 - p117 [51-250]
Johnston, Barry V - *Pitirim A. Sorokin: An Intellectual Biography*
Choice - v34 - S '96 - p219 [51-250]
Johnston, Basil - *The Manitous: The Supernatural World of the Ojibway*
y Kliatt - v30 - S '96 - p30 [51-250]
Johnston, David - *Stages of Translation*
TLS - N 8 '96 - p35 [501+]
Johnston, Douglas - *Religion, the Missing Dimension of Statecraft*
Bks & Cult - v2 - Ja '96 - p30 [51-250]
Johnston, Elin - *Dodoima: Tales of Oro*
Aust Bk R - Je '96 - p67 [1-50]
Johnston, H - *Social Movements and Culture*
Socio R - v45 - F 1 '97 - p147+ [501+]
Johnston, Ian - *Bad Seed*
Aust Bk R - O '96 - p31+ [501+]
Johnston, Ian A - *Animals and Temperature*
New Sci - v153 - F 1 '97 - p47 [51-250]
Johnston, Jill - *Jasper Johns: Privileged Information*
BL - v93 - S 15 '96 - p200 [51-250]
BW - v26 - N 3 '96 - p4 [501+]
Choice - v34 - Ap '97 - p1325 [51-250]
KR - v64 - Ag 15 '96 - p1211 [251-500]
LATBR - D 8 '96 - p28 [51-250]
NYTBR - v102 - F 9 '97 - p28 [501+]
PW - v243 - S 16 '96 - p62+ [51-250]

Johnston, Julie - *Adam and Eve and Pinch-Me*
y Bks Keeps - Ja '97 - p27 [51-250]
y Sch Lib - v45 - F '97 - p47 [51-250]
y SLJ - v43 - Ja '97 - p37 [1-50]
c TES - N 29 '96 - p10* [51-250]
Hero of Lesser Causes
c Bks Keeps - N '96 - p10 [51-250]
y Sch Lib - v45 - F '97 - p47 [51-250]
Johnston, Marianne - *Dealing with Anger*
c Ch BWatch - v7 - F '97 - p6 [1-50]
c SLJ - v42 - S '96 - p197+ [51-250]
Dealing with Bullying
c Ch BWatch - v7 - F '97 - p6 [1-50]
c SLJ - v43 - Ja '97 - p102 [51-250]
Dealing with Fighting
c Ch BWatch - v7 - F '97 - p6 [1-50]
Dealing with Insults
c Ch BWatch - v7 - F '97 - p6 [1-50]
Johnston, Mark - *At the Front Line*
Aust Bk R - N '96 - p26 [501+]
Choice - v34 - Ap '97 - p1394+ [51-250]
TLS - Ja 31 '97 - p29 [251-500]
Johnston, Mark D - *The Evangelical Rhetoric of Ramon Llull*
TLS - D 13 '96 - p32 [51-250]
Johnston, Mary - *Cease Firing*
LJ - v122 - Mr 15 '97 - p94 [1-50]
The Long Roll
BW - v27 - Mr 2 '97 - p12 [51-250]
LJ - v122 - Mr 15 '97 - p94 [1-50]
Johnston, Moira - *Spectral Evidence*
KR - v65 - My 1 '97 - p696+ [251-500]
Johnston, Norma - *Lotta's Progress*
y KR - v65 - My 1 '97 - p722+ [51-250]
Johnston, Patricia Irwin - *Launching a Baby's Adoption*
BWatch - v18 - F '97 - p6 [51-250]
LJ - v122 - F 15 '97 - p156+ [51-250]
Johnston, Paul, 1951- - *Success while Others Fail*
CS - v26 - Mr '97 - p169+ [501+]
Johnston, Ray - *Help! I'm a Sunday School Teacher*
Adoles - v32 - Spr '97 - p247 [51-250]
Johnston, Richard - *The Challenge of Direct Democracy*
Choice - v34 - My '97 - p1568 [51-250]
Johnston, Susanna - *Parties: A Literary Companion*
BL - v93 - D 15 '96 - p752 [51-250]
LJ - v121 - D '96 - p94 [51-250]
PW - v243 - D 30 '96 - p60 [51-250]
Johnston, Terry C - *Buffalo Palace*
LJ - v121 - S 15 '96 - p96 [51-250]
PW - v243 - S 16 '96 - p70 [51-250]
Roundup M - v4 - D '96 - p27 [51-250]
Wolf Mountain Moon
Roundup M - v4 - F '97 - p27 [51-250]
Johnston, Tony - *The Bull and the Fire Truck (Illus. by R W Alley)*
c BL - v93 - F 1 '97 - p949 [51-250]
Fishing Sunday (Illus. by Barry Root)
c HB Guide - v7 - Fall '96 - p262 [51-250]
c LATBR - My 26 '96 - p11 [51-250]
c New Ad - v9 - Fall '96 - p327+ [501+]
The Ghost of Nicholas Greebe (Illus. by S D Schindler)
c CCB-B - v50 - O '96 - p45+ [501+]
c HB - v72 - N '96 - p725+ [51-250]
c HB Guide - v8 - Spr '97 - p33 [51-250]
c LATBR - O 20 '96 - p8 [51-250]
c SLJ - v42 - S '96 - p180 [51-250]
c SLJ - v42 - D '96 - p30 [1-50]
How Many Miles to Jacksonville? (Illus. by Bart Forbes)
c CBRS - v25 - Ja '97 - p51 [51-250]
c HB Guide - v8 - Spr '97 - p33 [51-250]
c SLJ - v42 - D '96 - p96 [51-250]
The Magic Maguey (Illus. by Elisa Kleven)
c HB Guide - v8 - Spr '97 - p33 [51-250]
c PW - v243 - O 21 '96 - p82 [51-250]
c SLJ - v42 - O '96 - p37 [51-250]
c Smith - v27 - N '96 - p164 [1-50]
My Mexico (Illus. by F John Sierra)
c CLW - v67 - Mr '97 - p58 [51-250]
c HB Guide - v7 - Fall '96 - p368 [51-250]
Once in the Country (Illus. by Thomas B Allen)
c HB - v73 - Ja '97 - p74 [51-250]
c HB Guide - v8 - Spr '97 - p152 [51-250]
c SLJ - v42 - D '96 - p114 [51-250]
Slither McCreep and His Brother Joe (Illus. by Victoria Chess)
c PW - v243 - O 21 '96 - p85 [1-50]

The Wagon (Illus. by James E Ransome)
  c BL - v93 - Ja '97 - p869 [251-500]
  c CBRS - v25 - S '96 - p8 [51-250]
  c CCB-B - v50 - S '96 - p17 [51-250]
  c HB Guide - v8 - Spr '97 - p33 [51-250]
  c NYTBR - v102 - F 2 '97 - p18 [1-50]
  c NYTLa - v146 - D 9 '96 - pC18 [51-250]
  c PW - v243 - S 16 '96 - p83 [251-250]
  c SLJ - v43 - Mr '97 - p160 [51-250]
  c Smith - v27 - N '96 - p174 [1-50]
Johnston, William, 1925- - *Mystical Theology*
  CC - v113 - O 16 '96 - p964+ [501+]
  RR - v55 - S '96 - p551+ [251-500]
Johnston, William, 1955- - *The Modern Epidemic*
  Isis - v87 - D '96 - p751+ [501+]
  T&C - v37 - O '96 - p856+ [501+]
Johnston, William M, 1936- - *Recent Reference Books in Religion*
  r BL - v93 - D 15 '96 - p750 [251-500]
Johnston-Des Rochers, Janeen - *Export Financing and Insurance Vocabulary*
  r ARBA - v28 - '97 - p100 [251-500]
Johnstone, Alan - *Immunochemistry in Practice. 3rd Ed.*
  SciTech - v20 - S '96 - p26 [51-250]
Johnstone, Barbara - *The Linguistic Individual*
  Choice - v34 - N '96 - p450 [51-250]
Johnstone, Christopher Lyle - *Theory, Text, Context*
  Choice - v34 - Mr '97 - p1157 [251-500]
  R&R Bk N - v12 - F '97 - p77 [251-500]
Johnstone, Maxine Sheets - *The Roots of Power*
  Dance RJ - v28 - Fall '96 - p92+ [501+]
Johnstone, Robert A W - *Mass Spectrometry for Chemists and Biochemists. 2nd Ed.*
  New Sci - v153 - Mr 1 '97 - p39 [51-250]
Johnstone-Bryden, Ian M - *Managing Risk*
  R&R Bk N - v11 - N '96 - p30 [51-250]
Johri, V B - *The Early Universe*
  SciTech - v20 - N '96 - p17 [51-250]
Joint COST 227/231 Workshop on Mobile and Personal Communications (2nd: 1995: Florence, Italy) - *Mobile and Personal Communications*
  SciTech - v20 - N '96 - p73 [51-250]
Joint Electronic Library on CD-ROM 1993
  r RSR - v24 - 3 '96 - p45 [51-250]
Joint Review Committee Right-to-Work Study Final Report
  J Gov Info - v23 - S '96 - p623 [51-250]
Joint Summer Research Conference on Finsler Geometry (1995: Seattle, Wash.) - *Finsler Geometry*
  SciTech - v20 - N '96 - p15 [51-250]
Jolin, Dominique - *It's Not Fair! (Illus. by Dominique Jolin)*
  c HB Guide - v8 - Spr '97 - p33 [51-250]
  c SLJ - v42 - Ag '96 - p123 [51-250]
Jolink, Albert - *The Evolutionist Economics of Leon Walras*
  JEL - v34 - D '96 - p2015 [51-250]
  R&R Bk N - v11 - D '96 - p22 [51-250]
Jolles, P - *Lysozymes: Model Enzymes in Biochemistry and Biology*
  SciTech - v20 - D '96 - p35 [51-250]
Jolley, Nicholas - *The Cambridge Companion to Leibniz*
  Phil R - v105 - Ap '96 - p245+ [501+]
  Sev Cent N - v54 - Fall '96 - p63 [501+]
Jolly, Margaret - *Women of the Place*
  Cont Pac - v8 - Fall '96 - p458+ [501+]
Jolly, Rosemary Jane - *Colonization, Violence, and Narration in White South African Writing*
  Choice - v34 - O '96 - p273 [51-250]
Joly, Dominique - *How Does Your Garden Grow? (Illus. by Nathalie Locoste)*
  c HB Guide - v8 - Spr '97 - p121 [51-250]
Jomo, K S - *Japan and Malaysian Development*
  Econ J - v107 - Ja '97 - p281 [251-500]
Jonas, Ann - *Color Dance*
  c Inst - v106 - Ja '97 - p4* [1-50]
Watch William Walk (Illus. by Ann Jonas)
  c BL - v93 - Ap 1 '97 - p1338 [51-250]
  c PW - v244 - Mr 24 '97 - p82 [51-250]
Jonas, Hans - *Mortality and Morality*
  Choice - v34 - Mr '97 - p1176 [51-250]
  New R - v216 - Ja 20 '97 - p30+ [501+]
Jonas, Kirby - *Season of the Vigilante. Bks. 1-2*
  Roundup M - v4 - O '96 - p31 [251-500]
Jonas, Steven - *Just the Weigh You Are*
  PW - v244 - Mr 24 '97 - p80 [51-250]
Jonas, Susan - *Friends for Life*
  PW - v244 - Mr 24 '97 - p66 [51-250]
Jonas, Susanne, 1941- - *Latin America Faces the Twenty-First Century*
  JTWS - v13 - Fall '96 - p294+ [501+]

Jonassen, David H - *Handbook of Research for Educational Communications and Technology*
  r BL - v93 - Ap 1 '97 - p1356 [251-500]
  r Choice - v34 - My '97 - p1551 [51-250]
  r Cont Ed - v68 - Win '97 - p149+ [251-500]
  R&R Bk N - v12 - F '97 - p66 [51-250]
Joncas, Jan Michael - *The Catechism of the Catholic Church on Liturgy and Sacraments*
  CLW - v66 - Je '96 - p28+ [51-250]
Preaching the Rites of Christian Initiation. Vol. 4
  CLW - v66 - Je '96 - p31+ [251-500]
Jones, Mother - *The Speeches and Writings of Mother Jones*
  CAY - v17 - Fall '96 - p12 [51-250]
Jones, Alan Frewin - *Burning Issues*
  c Bks Keeps - Jl '96 - p13 [51-250]
Jones, Alan W - *The Soul's Journey*
  CC - v113 - N 20 '96 - p1147+ [501+]
Jones, Aled - *Powers of the Press*
  Choice - v34 - Mr '97 - p1154 [51-250]
Jones, Alun - *The New Germany*
  GJ - v162 - Jl '96 - p224+ [251-500]
Jones, Amelia - *Sexual Politics*
  Am Craft - v56 - Ag '96 - p62 [1-50]
  Bloom Rev - v17 - Ja '97 - p23 [501+]
  Choice - v34 - D '96 - p604 [51-250]
Jones, Andy - *1001 Guitar Tips and Tricks*
  Teach Mus - v4 - Ag '96 - p51 [1-50]
Jones, Archer - *Civil War Command and Strategy*
  J Mil H - v60 - O '96 - p777+ [501+]
Elements of Military Strategy
  J Mil H - v61 - Ap '97 - p421+ [501+]
  R&R Bk N - v12 - F '97 - p99 [51-250]
Jones, Barry Alan - *The Formation of the Book of the Twelve*
  Rel St Rev - v23 - Ap '97 - p163 [51-250]
Jones, Betty - *Language Exercises*
  c Quill & Q - v62 - O '96 - p50 [51-250]
Jones, Bill T - *Last Night on Earth*
  TDR - v41 - Spr '97 - p160 [51-250]
Jones, Bruce - *Maximum Velocity*
  BL - v93 - D 15 '96 - p712 [51-250]
  KR - v64 - O 1 '96 - p1422 [251-500]
  LJ - v121 - O 15 '96 - p90 [51-250]
  PW - v243 - O 14 '96 - p62+ [51-250]
Jones, Bryan D - *The New American Politics*
  Pol Stud J - v24 - Sum '96 - p316+ [501+]
Jones, Bryan L - *Mark Twain Made Me Do It and Other Plains Adventures*
  PW - v244 - F 24 '97 - p79 [251-500]
Jones, Calvin N - *The Literary Reputation of Else Lasker-Schuler*
  MLR - v91 - O '96 - p1048+ [251-500]
Negation and Utopia
  MLR - v91 - Jl '96 - p803+ [251-500]
Jones, Capers - *Applied Software Measurement. 2nd Ed.*
  SciTech - v21 - Mr '97 - p8 [51-250]
Patterns of Software Systems Failure and Success
  CBR - v14 - Jl '96 - p25 [51-250]
Jones, Carol - *Goddess of Cool*
  y Aust Bk R - Je '96 - p60+ [501+]
  y Magpies - v11 - Jl '96 - p34 [51-250]
The Hare and the Tortoise (Illus. by Carol Jones)
  c BL - v93 - S 1 '96 - p139 [51-250]
  c HB Guide - v8 - Spr '97 - p102 [51-250]
  c SLJ - v42 - S '96 - p198 [51-250]
Jones, Charles Edwin - *The Charismatic Movement. Vols. 1-2*
  r ARBA - v28 - '97 - p547 [51-250]
Jones, Charles O - *The Presidency in a Separated System*
  AAPSS-A - v546 - Jl '96 - p155+ [501+]
Jones, Charlotte Foltz - *Accidents May Happen (Illus. by John O'Brien)*
  y BL - v93 - Ap 1 '97 - p1308 [1-50]
  c BW - v26 - Jl 7 '96 - p15 [51-250]
  c CCB-B - v50 - S '96 - p17+ [51-250]
  c HB Guide - v8 - Fall '96 - p350 [51-250]
  c KR - v64 - My 1 '96 - p689 [51-250]
  c Smith - v27 - N '96 - p175 [1-50]
Jones, Christopher - *Crystallographic Methods and Protocols*
  SciTech - v20 - S '96 - p23 [51-250]
Jones, Christopher V - *Visualization and Optimization*
  SciTech - v21 - Mr '97 - p72 [51-250]
Jones, Chuck - *Chuck Reducks*
  BL - v93 - S 15 '96 - p200 [51-250]
  BW - v27 - Ja 12 '97 - p8 [51-250]
  KR - v64 - S 1 '96 - p1296+ [51-250]
  LJ - v121 - S 15 '96 - p70 [51-250]

Jones, Clive - *Soviet Jewish Aliyah 1989-1992*
  MEJ - v51 - Spr '97 - p305+ [501+]
  MEQ - v4 - Mr '97 - p93 [51-250]
Jones, Clyve - *The Scots and Parliament*
  TLS - S 20 '96 - p12 [501+]
Jones, Colin - *The Cambridge Illustrated History of France*
  Rel St Rev - v23 - Ja '97 - p84 [51-250]
Jones, Constance - *Sexual Harassment*
  r ARBA - v28 - '97 - p318 [51-250]
Jones, Constance, 1961- - *R.I.P.: The Complete Book of Death and Dying*
  BL - v93 - F 15 '97 - p979 [51-250]
  PW - v243 - D 30 '96 - p50 [51-250]
Jones, D B - *The Best Butler in the Business*
  Si & So - v6 - N '96 - p35 [51-250]
Jones, David - *Directions. Bks. 1-2*
  y Sch Lib - v45 - F '97 - p50+ [51-250]
  y TES - Mr 28 '97 - pR7 [251-500]
Jones, David E - *Women Warriors*
  y BL - v93 - F 15 '97 - p979+ [51-250]
  KR - v64 - D 15 '96 - p1783+ [251-500]
  LJ - v122 - F 15 '97 - p146 [51-250]
  PW - v243 - D 30 '96 - p48 [251-500]
Jones, David L - *Palms throughout the World*
  Am Sci - v85 - Ja '97 - p82 [501+]
  r ARBA - v28 - '97 - p584+ [501+]
Jones, David Seth - *Graziers, Land Reform, and Political Conflict in Ireland*
  Albion - v28 - Fall '96 - p549+ [501+]
Jones, David Wyn - *Beethoven: Pastoral Symphony*
  TLS - D 20 '96 - p20 [501+]
Music in Eighteenth-Century Austria
  CR - v268 - Je '96 - p334 [51-250]
Jones, Denise - *Life, Love, and Other Mysteries*
  y BL - v93 - S 1 '96 - p39 [51-250]
Jones, DeWitt - *Portrait of California*
  BWatch - v17 - S '96 - p5 [1-50]
Jones, Diana Wynne - *The Crown of Dalemark*
  y SLJ - v42 - Ag '96 - p164 [51-250]
Hexwood
  y Kliatt - v30 - S '96 - p18 [51-250]
The Time of the Ghost
  y BL - v92 - Ag '96 - p1894+ [51-250]
  y CCB-B - v50 - O '96 - p65 [51-250]
  c HB - v72 - N '96 - p736+ [51-250]
  c HB Guide - v8 - Spr '97 - p68 [51-250]
  y SLJ - v42 - N '96 - p123 [51-250]
Jones, Dilwyn - *Boats*
  AJA - v100 - Jl '96 - p635+ [251-500]
Jones, Dolores Blythe - *Special Collections in Children's Literature. 3rd Ed.*
  r JOYS - v9 - Sum '96 - p410+ [251-500]
  r Sch Lib - v44 - Ag '96 - p130 [51-250]
Jones, Donald D - *Former Major League Teams*
  r ARBA - v28 - '97 - p295 [251-500]
Jones, Doug - *Physical Attractiveness and the Theory of Sexual Selection*
  New Sci - v153 - F 22 '97 - p43 [51-250]
Jones, Dylan - *Meaty, Beaty, Big and Bouncy*
  TLS - D 6 '96 - p28 [501+]
Ultra Lounge
  NYTBR - v102 - Ap 13 '97 - p21 [51-250]
Unnatural Acts
  BL - v93 - N 15 '96 - p574 [51-250]
  KR - v64 - O 15 '96 - p1496+ [51-250]
  PW - v243 - O 14 '96 - p63 [51-250]
  Trib Bks - Ja 5 '97 - p4 [51-250]
Jones, E Michael - *John Cardinal Krol and the Cultural Revolution*
  CHR - v83 - Ja '97 - p149+ [501+]
Living Machines
  Comw - v123 - S 13 '96 - p40+ [501+]
Jones, Edgar - *True and Fair*
  BHR - v70 - Aut '96 - p428+ [501+]
Jones, Eric D - *Optoelectronic Materials*
  SciTech - v20 - N '96 - p65 [51-250]
Jones, F Stanley - *An Ancient Jewish Christian Source on the History of Christianity*
  Rel St Rev - v23 - Ja '97 - p78 [51-250]
Jones, Frank - *The Save Your Heart Wine Guide*
  BL - v93 - S 15 '96 - p194 [51-250]
Jones, Frederic J - *The Structure of Petrarch's Canzoniere*
  Specu - v72 - Ja '97 - p180+ [501+]
Jones, Gail - *Fetish Lives*
  Aust Bk R - F '97 - p22+ [501+]
Jones, Gareth E - *Human Cell Culture Protocols*
  SciTech - v20 - S '96 - p20 [51-250]

Jones, Geoffrey - *British Multinational Banking 1830-1990*
    Econ J - v107 - Ja '97 - p233+ [501+]
    The Evolution of International Business
    Econ J - v106 - S '96 - p1477 [251-500]
Jones, George - *My First Book of How Things Are Made*
    c LATBR - Mr 17 '96 - p11 [51-250]
Jones, Georgia - *Women on a Wire*
    BWatch - v17 - D '96 - p7 [51-250]
Jones, Gwyneth - *North Wind*
    Analog - v116 - Jl '96 - p273+ [251-500]
    Obs - F 2 '97 - p17* [501+]
    Phoenix Cafe
    New Sci - v153 - Mr 15 '97 - p45 [51-250]
    Obs - F 2 '97 - p17* [501+]
    Seven Tales and a Fable
    BW - v26 - S 1 '96 - p11 [51-250]
    White Queen
    Obs - F 2 '97 - p17* [501+]
Jones, H G - *Historical Consciousness in the Early Republic*
    JSH - v63 - F '97 - p156+ [251-500]
    North Carolina History
    r JSH - v62 - N '96 - p858 [51-250]
Jones, Helen - *Health and Society in Twentieth-Century Britain*
    EHR - v111 - S '96 - p1030+ [501+]
Jones, Hettie - *How I Became Hettie Jones*
    BW - v27 - F 2 '97 - p12 [51-250]
Jones, Howard - *Prologue to Manifest Destiny*
    BWatch - v18 - Mr '97 - p2 [51-250]
Jones, Ivor H - *The Matthean Parables*
    Rel St Rev - v23 - Ap '97 - p181 [51-250]
Jones, J D F - *The Buchan Papers*
    BW - v27 - F 16 '97 - p5 [501+]
    KR - v64 - D 15 '96 - p1768+ [51-250]
    LJ - v122 - F 1 '97 - p110 [51-250]
    Obs - O 27 '96 - p18* [51-250]
    PW - v243 - D 9 '96 - p63 [51-250]
    Spec - v277 - N 9 '96 - p54+ [501+]
    TLS - O 11 '96 - p28 [501+]
    Through Fortress and Rock
    Econ - v340 - S 14 '96 - p10* [501+]
Jones, J Gwynfor - *Early Modern Wales c. 1525-1640*
    EHR - v111 - N '96 - p1273+ [251-500]
Jones, J V - *Master and Fool*
    KR - v64 - S 1 '96 - p1282 [51-250]
    LJ - v121 - O 15 '96 - p93 [1-50]
Jones, James W - *In the Middle of This Road We Call Our Life*
    CLW - v66 - Je '96 - p31 [51-250]
    Religion and Psychology in Transition
    Choice - v34 - My '97 - p1579 [51-250]
Jones, Jane Anderson - *Florida in Poetry*
    Sm Pr R - v28 - O '96 - p1 [51-250]
Jones, Jeanne - *Healthy Cooking for People Who Don't Have Time to Cook*
    PW - v244 - F 17 '97 - p216 [51-250]
Jones, Jenny - *The House of Birds*
    y Sch Lib - v44 - Ag '96 - p118 [51-250]
Jones, John Henry - *The English Faust Book*
    MLR - v91 - O '96 - p1030+ [501+]
    RES - v48 - F '97 - p92+ [501+]
Jones, Jonah - *Clough Williams-Ellis*
    NS - v126 - Ja 31 '97 - p48 [251-500]
Jones, Judy - *Let Sleeping Bags Lie*
    c TES - Ja 3 '97 - pR15 [51-250]
    Polyethylene Terphthalate in Plastic Pop Bottles
    y TES - Ja 3 '97 - pR15 [1-50]
    Product Design
    y TES - Ja 3 '97 - pR15 [51-250]
Jones, K Maurice - *Spike Lee and the African American Filmmakers*
    y BL - v93 - Ja '97 - p836+ [251-500]
    y CCB-B - v50 - F '97 - p211 [51-250]
    y HB Guide - v8 - Spr '97 - p141 [51-250]
    c SLJ - v43 - F '97 - p117+ [51-250]
Jones, L Gregory - *Embodying Forgiveness*
    JR - v77 - Ap '97 - p319+ [501+]
    Rel St Rev - v22 - O '96 - p336 [51-250]
    Theol St - v57 - D '96 - p784 [251-500]
    TT - v53 - Ja '97 - p522+ [501+]
    Rethinking Metaphysics
    TT - v53 - Ja '97 - p552+ [501+]
Jones, Laura - *The Portrait of a Lady*
    Trib Bks - Ja 12 '97 - p2 [51-250]
Jones, LeAlan - *Our America*
    PW - v244 - Ap 21 '97 - p50 [51-250]
Jones, Leslie - *Happy Is the Bride the Sun Shines On*
    CAY - v17 - Fall '96 - p12 [51-250]

Jones, Lizard - *Two Ends of Sleep*
    BL - v93 - My 15 '97 - p1561+ [51-250]
Jones, Lou - *Final Exposure*
    LJ - v122 - F 15 '97 - p147+ [51-250]
    PW - v244 - F 17 '97 - p207 [51-250]
    R&R Bk N - v12 - F '97 - p57 [1-50]
Jones, Madison - *Nashville 1864*
    BL - v93 - My 15 '97 - p1563 [51-250]
    KR - v65 - Mr 15 '97 - p405+ [251-500]
    PW - v244 - Ap 14 '97 - p56 [251-500]
Jones, Margaret - *Patsy: The Life and Times of Patsy Cline*
    LJ - v121 - N 1 '96 - p42 [1-50]
Jones, Mark - *Designs on Posterity*
    Apo - v145 - Ja '97 - p61+ [501+]
Jones, Martin D W - *The Counter Reformation*
    CH - v66 - Mr '97 - p198 [51-250]
    Rel St Rev - v23 - Ap '97 - p192 [51-250]
    Six Ct J - v27 - Fall '96 - p814+ [501+]
Jones, Matthew - *Britain, the United States and the Mediterranean War 1942-44*
    HRNB - v25 - Win '97 - p65 [501+]
    J Mil H - v61 - Ap '97 - p408+ [501+]
Jones, Matthew F - *Blind Pursuit*
    KR - v65 - Mr 15 '97 - p406 [251-500]
    LJ - v122 - Ap 15 '97 - p118 [51-250]
    PW - v244 - My 12 '97 - p60 [51-250]
    A Single Shot
    Arm Det - v29 - Fall '96 - p503 [51-250]
    BW - v26 - Jl 7 '96 - p6 [501+]
    LATBR - My 12 '96 - p10 [51-250]
    PW - v244 - Ap 14 '97 - p72 [1-50]
    A Single Shot (Choate). Audio Version
    LJ - v121 - O 1 '96 - p144 [51-250]
    LJ - v122 - F 15 '97 - p115 [1-50]
Jones, Michael - *The Balloon Detectives (Illus. by Michael Bailey)*
    c TES - O 25 '96 - p12* [1-50]
Jones, Michael E - *The End of Roman Britain*
    Choice - v34 - D '96 - p670 [51-250]
Jones, Moyra - *Gentlecare: Changing the Experience of Alzheimer's Disease in a Positive Way*
    Quill & Q - v62 - D '96 - p23 [251-500]
Jones, Nancy L - *Atlas of Forensic Pathology*
    r SciTech - v20 - S '96 - p29 [51-250]
Jones, Nicholas - *Soundbites and Spin Doctors*
    CR - v270 - F '97 - p110 [51-250]
Jones, Noragh - *Power of Raven, Wisdom of Spirit*
    RR - v55 - S '96 - p553 [51-250]
Jones, Patricia Clunn - *Campos, Vigil, Barreras and Rubi Families of New Mexico*
    EGH - v50 - N '96 - p193 [51-250]
Jones, Paul H - *Christ's Eucharistic Presence*
    Theol St - v57 - Mr '96 - p169+ [501+]
Jones, Peter - *Introducing International Politics*
    y TES - F 21 '97 - p20* [501+]
Jones, Peter, 1945- - *Party, Parliament and Personality*
    R&R Bk N - v11 - N '96 - p50 [51-250]
    Rights
    APSR - v90 - S '96 - p631+ [501+]
Jones, Peter C - *Hero Dogs*
    PW - v244 - My 5 '97 - p192 [51-250]
Jones, Prudence - *A History of Pagan Europe*
    Folkl - v107 - '96 - p114+ [501+]
    JR - v76 - O '96 - p628+ [501+]
Jones, R - *Early Stages of Oxygen Precipitation in Silicon*
    SciTech - v21 - Mr '97 - p90 [51-250]
Jones, Rebecca C - *Great-Aunt Martha (Illus. by Shelley Jackson)*
    c RT - v50 - N '96 - p256+ [51-250]
    The President Has Been Shot!
    c CCB-B - v50 - S '96 - p18 [51-250]
    c HB Guide - v8 - Spr '97 - p174 [51-250]
    c LATBR - Jl 14 '96 - p11 [51-250]
    y SLJ - v42 - S '96 - p234 [51-250]
Jones, Rhonda - *Producing a School Newsletter Parents Will Read!*
    Learning - v25 - S '96 - p90 [51-250]
Jones, Richard C - *Ambivalent Journey*
    HAHR - v77 - F '97 - p164+ [251-500]
    JTWS - v13 - Fall '96 - p304+ [501+]
    WHQ - v27 - Win '96 - p548 [1-50]
Jones, Richard G - *Cybersex*
    LJ - v121 - S 15 '96 - p101 [51-250]
Jones, Robert F - *Blood Sport*
    PW - v244 - Mr 31 '97 - p72 [1-50]
    Dancers in the Sunset Sky
    BL - v92 - Ag '96 - p1874 [51-250]
    Choice - v34 - D '96 - p639 [51-250]

    Tie My Bones to Her Back
    y BL - v92 - Ag '96 - p1882 [51-250]
    y BL - v92 - Ag '96 - p1891 [1-50]
    BW - v26 - O 6 '96 - p8 [251-500]
    KR - v64 - My 1 '96 - p625+ [251-500]
    NYTBR - v101 - S 1 '96 - p16 [51-250]
Jones, Robert Tyre - *Bobby Jones on Golf*
    LJ - v121 - O 1 '96 - p53 [1-50]
Jones, Rod, 1953- - *Billy Sunday*
    NYTBR - v101 - S 15 '96 - p35 [501+]
    RCF - v16 - Fall '96 - p193+ [251-500]
    YR - v85 - Ja '97 - p144+ [501+]
Jones, Rodney, 1950- - *Things that Happen Once*
    PW - v243 - N 4 '96 - p47 [1-50]
Jones, Scott J - *John Wesley's Conception and Use of Scripture*
    TT - v53 - Ja '97 - p543+ [501+]
Jones, Seaborn - *Lost Keys*
    Sm Pr R - v29 - Ja '97 - p11 [501+]
    A Poetry Reading
    Sm Pr R - v29 - Ja '97 - p11 [501+]
Jones, Serene - *Calvin and the Rhetoric of Piety*
    Intpr - v51 - Ap '97 - p210+ [501+]
    Rel St Rev - v23 - Ap '97 - p152 [51-250]
    Six Ct J - v27 - Fall '96 - p955+ [501+]
    Theol St - v58 - Mr '97 - p166+ [501+]
Jones, Stephen - *Dark Terrors*
    Necro - Sum '96 - p23+ [501+]
    The Illustrated Werewolf Movie Guide
    r Necro - Win '97 - p27 [51-250]
    The Mammoth Book of Dracula
    y BL - v93 - My 1 '97 - p1480 [51-250]
    The Mammoth Book of Werewolves
    Necro - Sum '96 - p8+ [501+]
Jones, Stephen R G - *The Persistence of Unemployment*
    JEL - v35 - Mr '97 - p156+ [501+]
Jones, Sterling Scott - *The Lira Da Braccio*
    Notes - v53 - S '96 - p64+ [501+]
Jones, Steve - *In the Blood*
    Nature - v382 - Ag 1 '96 - p413+ [501+]
    NS & S - v9 - My 17 '96 - p36+ [501+]
Jones, Steven E - *Shelley's Satire*
    MLR - v91 - O '96 - p979+ [501+]
    MP - v94 - N '96 - p246+ [501+]
Jones, Steven G - *Cybersociety: Computer Mediated Communication and Community*
    SocSciComR - v14 - Fall '96 - p355+ [501+]
Jones, Syl - *Rescuing Little Roundhead*
    y Bloom Rev - v17 - Ja '97 - p19 [51-250]
Jones, Terry - *The Goblin Companion (Illus. by Brian Froud)*
    c LATBR - O 20 '96 - p8 [51-250]
Jones, Theodore - *Carnegie Libraries across America*
    PW - v244 - Ap 21 '97 - p57 [51-250]
Jones, Thom - *Cold Snap*
    NYTBR - v101 - Jl 21 '96 - p28 [51-250]
Jones, Tim, 1942- - *Dog Heroes*
    Dog Fan - v27 - N '96 - p24 [51-250]
Jones, Timothy K, 1955- - *The Art of Prayer*
    PW - v244 - F 24 '97 - p81 [51-250]
Jones, Tudor - *Remaking the Labour Party*
    Obs - S 29 '96 - p15* [501+]
Jones, W Gareth - *Tolstoi and Britain*
    TLS - O 4 '96 - p13 [501+]
Jones, W Kinzy - *Multichip Modules with Integrated Sensors*
    SciTech - v21 - Mr '97 - p92 [51-250]
Jones, William, Sir - *Sir William Jones: Selected Poetical and Prose Works*
    TLS - Mr 21 '97 - p25 [501+]
Jones-Wilson, Faustine C - *Encyclopedia of African-American Education*
    r ARBA - v28 - '97 - p132 [51-250]
    r BL - v93 - D 15 '96 - p746+ [251-500]
    r Choice - v34 - F '97 - p942 [51-250]
    r LJ - v121 - N 1 '96 - p86 [1-50]
    r R&R Bk N - v11 - D '96 - p54 [51-250]
Jong, Erica - *Inventing Memory*
    BL - v93 - My 1 '97 - p1461+ [51-250]
    KR - v65 - My 1 '97 - p665 [51-250]
    PW - v244 - My 5 '97 - p193 [51-250]
    Megan's Two Houses (Illus. by Freya Tanz)
    c PW - v243 - Jl 22 '96 - p240 [51-250]
Jongsma, Arthur E - *The Child and Adolescent Psychotherapy Treatment Planner*
    SciTech - v20 - D '96 - p53 [51-250]
Jonnes, Jill - *Hep-Cats, Narcs, and Pipe Dreams*
    BL - v93 - Ja '97 - p757 [1-50]
    BW - v26 - Ag 18 '96 - p6 [501+]

Jonson, Ben - *The Devil Is an Ass*
    LJ - v121 - O 15 '96 - p94 [1-50]
    RES - v47 - Ag '96 - p414+ [501+]
    The New Inn
    MLR - v91 - Jl '96 - p545+ [501+]
    Poetaster
    LJ - v121 - O 15 '96 - p94 [1-50]
    TLS - Ja 31 '97 - p23 [501+]
Jonson, Lena - *Peacekeeping and the Role of Russia in Eurasia*
    JPR - v33 - Ag '96 - p381 [251-500]
Jonsson, Einar Mar - *Le Miroir: Naissance D'un Genre Litteraire*
    Choice - v34 - D '96 - p566 [1-50]
    Specu - v72 - Ja '97 - p181+ [501+]
Jonsson, Lars - *Birds of Europe with North Africa and the Middle East*
    r AB - v97 - Je 17 '96 - p2400 [51-250]
Joos, Irene - *Computers in Small Bytes*
    SciTech - v20 - D '96 - p38 [51-250]
Joosse, Barbara M - *I Love You the Purplest (Illus. by Mary Whyte)*
    c CBRS - v25 - Ja '97 - p51 [51-250]
    c Ch BWatch - v6 - N '96 - p5 [51-250]
    c HB Guide - v8 - Spr '97 - p33 [51-250]
    c Par - v71 - D '96 - p251 [1-50]
    c PW - v243 - S 16 '96 - p82 [51-250]
    Nugget and Darling (Illus. by Sue Truesdell)
    c BL - v93 - Mr 1 '97 - p1172 [51-250]
    c KR - v65 - F 15 '97 - p301 [51-250]
    c PW - v244 - F 24 '97 - p91 [51-250]
Joppich, W - *Multigrid Methods for Process Simulation*
    SIAM Rev - v38 - S '96 - p543 [251-500]
Joppke, Christian - *East German Dissidents and the Revolution of 1989*
    AHR - v101 - O '96 - p1238+ [501+]
Jordan, Alan - *Displaced Homeless Adolescent Claimants for Social Security Payments*
    J Gov Info - v23 - S '96 - p652 [51-250]
Jordan, Barbara A - *Audiovisual Resources for Family Programming*
    r ARBA - v28 - '97 - p145 [51-250]
Jordan, Carsten - *Batching and Scheduling*
    JEL - v35 - Mr '97 - p254 [51-250]
Jordan, David M - *New World Regionalism*
    AAAGA - v86 - S '96 - p595+ [501+]
Jordan, David P - *Transforming Paris*
    T&C - v37 - Ap '96 - p370+ [501+]
Jordan, David R - *Surgical Anatomy of the Ocular Adnexa*
    SciTech - v20 - N '96 - p30 [1-50]
Jordan, Donald E - *Land and Popular Politics in Ireland*
    AHR - v101 - O '96 - p1215+ [501+]
    EHR - v111 - S '96 - p1007+ [251-500]
Jordan, Ervin L, Jr. - *Black Confederates and Afro-Yankees in Civil War Virginia*
    AHR - v101 - O '96 - p1625+ [501+]
Jordan, Helene J - *Como Crece Una Semilla (Illus. by Loretta Krupinski)*
    c SLJ - v42 - N '96 - p132 [51-250]
Jordan, Isolde - *Introduccion Al Analisis Linguistico Del Discurso*
    Hisp - v79 - S '96 - p465+ [501+]
Jordan, J R - *Serial Networked Field Instrumentation*
    SciTech - v20 - S '96 - p53 [51-250]
Jordan, Jeff - *Faith, Freedom, and Rationality*
    CPR - v16 - O '96 - p355+ [501+]
Jordan, John O - *Literature in the Marketplace*
    Nine-C Lit - v50 - Mr '96 - p554 [51-250]
Jordan, Mark D - *The Invention of Sodomy in Christian Theology*
    KR - v65 - Ap 1 '97 - p524 [251-500]
    LJ - v122 - Mr 15 '97 - p67 [51-250]
Jordan, Martin - *Amazon Alphabet (Illus. by Martin Jordan)*
    c AB - v98 - N 18 '96 - p1730 [51-250]
    c Emerg Lib - v24 - S '96 - p43 [1-50]
    c HB Guide - v7 - Fall '96 - p336 [1-50]
    c Inst - v106 - Mr '97 - p28 [51-250]
Jordan, Michele Anna - *Polenta: 100 Innovative Recipes, from Appetizers to Desserts*
    LJ - v121 - D '96 - p136 [51-250]
    PW - v243 - D 2 '96 - p57 [51-250]
Jordan, Neil - *Nightlines*
    WLT - v70 - Sum '96 - p692 [501+]
Jordan, Peter - *Staff Management In Library and Information Work. 3rd Ed.*
    LR - v45 - 5 '96 - p69+ [501+]
Jordan, Robert - *A Crown of Swords*
    y VOYA - v19 - F '97 - p336 [51-250]

The Eye of the World. Audio Version
    SF Chr - v18 - O '96 - p76 [51-250]
Jordan, Ruth - *Fromental Halevy: His Life and Music 1799-1862*
    FF - v20 - N '96 - p516 [251-500]
    ON - v61 - Ja 11 '97 - p50 [51-250]
Jordan, Sandra - *Down on Casey's Farm (Illus. by Sandra Jordan)*
    c HB Guide - v8 - Spr '97 - p12 [51-250]
    c KR - v64 - S 15 '96 - p1403 [51-250]
    c PW - v243 - S 9 '96 - p82 [51-250]
    c SLJ - v42 - O '96 - p99 [51-250]
Jordan, Sherryl - *Wolf-Woman*
    y Kliatt - v30 - S '96 - p11 [51-250]
Jordan, Tanis - *Angel Falls (Illus. by Martin Jordan)*
    c Inst - v106 - Mr '97 - p28 [1-50]
    c JOYS - v9 - Sum '96 - p416 [51-250]
Jordan, Teresa - *The Stories That Shape Us*
    LATBR - S 15 '96 - p11 [51-250]
Jordan, Tom - *Pre: The Story of America's Greatest Running Legend, Steve Prefontaine. 2nd Ed.*
    y BL - v93 - Mr 15 '97 - p1220 [51-250]
    PW - v244 - Mr 3 '97 - p58 [51-250]
Jordan, William - *Ancient Concepts of Philosophy*
    CPR - v16 - Je '96 - p176+ [501+]
Jordan, William A - *Crossfire Education*
    Choice - v34 - D '96 - p661 [51-250]
Jordan, William B - *Spanish Still Life from Velazquez to Goya*
    Six Ct J - v27 - Fall '96 - p883+ [501+]
Jordan, William C - *The Great Famine*
    Choice - v34 - D '96 - p670 [51-250]
    HRNB - v25 - Win '97 - p81+ [501+]
    HT - v46 - O '96 - p55 [51-250]
    JEL - v34 - D '96 - p2104+ [51-250]
    y SLJ - v43 - F '97 - p137 [51-250]
    The Middle Ages. Vols. 1-4
    yr ARBA - v28 - '97 - p213+ [51-250]
    yr BL - v93 - Ja '97 - p770 [51-250]
    yr BL - v93 - S 1 '96 - p168 [251-500]
    yr CLW - v67 - Mr '97 - p44+ [51-250]
    cr RQ - v36 - Win '96 - p302+ [251-500]
    yr R&R Bk N - v11 - N '96 - p9 [51-250]
    cr SLJ - v42 - N '96 - p138 [51-250]
Jorde, Lynn B - *Medical Genetics*
    SciTech - v20 - D '96 - p41 [51-250]
Jordon, Dale R - *Overcoming Dyslexia in Children, Adolescents, and Adults. 2nd Ed.*
    SciTech - v20 - S '96 - p31 [51-250]
Jorg, C J A - *Oriental Porcelain*
    Ceram Mo - v44 - O '96 - p28+ [251-500]
Jorgensen, Christine T - *Curl Up and Die*
    BL - v93 - D 15 '96 - p712 [51-250]
    KR - v64 - O 15 '96 - p1497 [51-250]
    LJ - v121 - D '96 - p151 [51-250]
    PW - v243 - O 21 '96 - p73 [51-250]
Jorgensen, Gail - *Gotcha! (Illus. by Kerry Argent)*
    c BL - v93 - F 1 '97 - p946 [51-250]
    c CCB-B - v50 - Ap '97 - p286+ [51-250]
    c PW - v244 - F 3 '97 - p105 [51-250]
    c SLJ - v43 - Mr '97 - p160 [51-250]
Jorgensen, Karen - *Pay for Results*
    HR Mag - v42 - Ja '97 - p148 [51-250]
Jorgenson, Dale A - *The Life and Legacy of Franz Xaver Hauser*
    AB - v98 - D 9 '96 - p1994 [51-250]
Jorgenson, Dale Weldeau - *Investment. Vols. 1-2*
    JEL - v34 - D '96 - p2033 [51-250]
    R&R Bk N - v12 - F '97 - p48 [51-250]
Jorion, Philippe - *Big Bets Gone Bad*
    JEL - v34 - D '96 - p2061 [51-250]
    Value at Risk
    R&R Bk N - v12 - F '97 - p50 [51-250]
Joris, Yvonne G J M - *Terra Sculptura, Terra Pictura--Ceramics from the Classic Modernists*
    Am Craft - v56 - Ag '96 - p66 [1-50]
Jose, F Sionil - *Sins*
    BW - v26 - S 8 '96 - p13 [51-250]
    WLT - v70 - Aut '96 - p1034+ [51-250]
Jose, Nicholas - *The Rose Crossing*
    BL - v93 - Ja '97 - p761 [1-50]
Joseph, Alison - *The Hour of Our Death*
    KR - v65 - F 15 '97 - p258 [51-250]
    PW - v244 - F 10 '97 - p71 [1-50]
Joseph, Gilbert M - *Everyday Forms of State Formation*
    HAHR - v77 - F '97 - p132+ [501+]
    I Saw a City Invincible
    HAHR - v77 - My '97 - p284+ [51-250]

Joseph, Lawrence - *Lawyerland*
    KR - v65 - Mr 1 '97 - p355 [51-250]
    LJ - v122 - Ap 1 '97 - p109 [51-250]
    NYTLa - v146 - My 29 '97 - pC20 [501+]
    PW - v244 - Mr 3 '97 - p54 [51-250]
Joseph, Rhawn - *Neuropsychiatry, Neuropsychology, and Clinical Neuroscience*
    SciTech - v20 - D '96 - p43 [51-250]
Joseph-Gaudet, Frances - *He Leadeth Me*
    AL - v68 - S '96 - p669 [51-250]
Josephine, Diana - *Fair Girls and Gray Horses*
    TLS - D 13 '96 - p32 [251-500]
Joseph's Coat of Colors
    c HB Guide - v7 - Fall '96 - p308 [1-50]
Josephson, Erland - *A Story about Mr. Silberstein*
    BIC - v25 - O '96 - p23 [501+]
Josephson, Judith Pinkerton - *Allan Pinkerton: The Original Private Eye*
    c HB Guide - v8 - Spr '97 - p158 [51-250]
    y SLJ - v42 - O '96 - p156+ [51-250]
    Mother Jones: Fierce Fighter for Workers' Rights
    y BL - v93 - F 1 '97 - p931+ [51-250]
Josephson, Paul R - *Totalitarian Science and Technology*
    Choice - v34 - Mr '97 - p1179 [51-250]
Josephson, Susan G - *From Idolatry to Advertising*
    Choice - v34 - Ja '97 - p783+ [51-250]
    R&R Bk N - v11 - D '96 - p57 [51-250]
Josephus, Flavius - *Les Antiquites Juives. Vol. 2*
    Rel St Rev - v23 - Ja '97 - p89 [51-250]
    Josephus: The Essential Works
    CH - v66 - Mr '97 - p185 [51-250]
Joshi, S T - *H.P. Lovecraft: A Life*
    Necro - Fall '96 - p3+ [501+]
    NYRB - v43 - O 31 '96 - p46+ [501+]
Joshi, Vijay - *India: Macroeconomics and Political Economy 1964-1991*
    JEL - v34 - S '96 - p1381+ [501+]
    India's Economic Reforms 1991-2001
    Econ - v341 - O 19 '96 - p8* [501+]
    Lon R Bks - v18 - Jl 18 '96 - p6+ [501+]
    TLS - Ja 24 '97 - p31 [501+]
Josipovici, Gabriel - *Touch*
    NS - v125 - O 18 '96 - p45+ [501+]
    TLS - Ap 11 '97 - p24 [501+]
Josselson, Ruthellen - *Revising Herself*
    Choice - v34 - Mr '97 - p1245 [51-250]
    PW - v243 - S 23 '96 - p69 [51-250]
    The Space between Us
    JMF - v58 - N '96 - p1042+ [251-500]
Jotischky, Andrew - *The Perfection of Solitude*
    AHR - v101 - D '96 - p1533+ [251-500]
    CHR - v82 - Jl '96 - p537+ [251-500]
    JR - v77 - Ja '97 - p132+ [501+]
Jouanard, Gil - *Plutot Que D'En Pleurer*
    WLT - v70 - Sum '96 - p663 [51-250]
Jouet, Jacques - *La Montagne R*
    WLT - v70 - Sum '96 - p651 [501+]
Jourdain, Robert - *Music, the Brain, and Ecstasy*
    BL - v93 - F 1 '97 - p918 [51-250]
    KR - v65 - Ja 15 '97 - p121 [251-500]
    LATBR - Mr 16 '97 - p4 [501+]
    LJ - v122 - Ja '97 - p101 [51-250]
    NYTLa - v146 - Ap 7 '97 - pC14 [501+]
    PW - v243 - D 30 '96 - p43 [51-250]
Jourde, Pierre - *L'Alcool Du Silence*
    FR - v70 - D '96 - p333+ [251-500]
Journal Chretien Dedie A La Reine
    p MLR - v92 - Ja '97 - p36+ [501+]
Journal of Accounting, Auditing and Finance
    p JEL - v35 - Mr '97 - p308 [251-500]
Journal of American Studies of Turkey
    p J Am Cult - v19 - Sum '96 - p162+ [501+]
Journal of Biomedical Science
    p Nature - v383 - S 5 '96 - p35 [251-500]
Journal of Customer Service in Marketing and Management: Innovations for Service, Quality and Value
    p BusLR - v21 - 3 '96 - p262 [251-500]
Journal of Economic Growth
    p JEL - v34 - S '96 - p1505 [51-250]
Journal of Energy Finance and Development
    p JEL - v35 - Mr '97 - p308+ [51-250]
Journal of HIV/AIDS Prevention and Education for Adolescents and Children
    p BioSci - v46 - D '96 - p876+ [51-250]
Journal of Human Resource Costing and Accounting
    p JEL - v35 - Mr '97 - p309 [51-250]
Journal of International and Comparative Economics
    p JEL - v34 - S '96 - p1505+ [51-250]
Journal of Internet Cataloging
    p LJ - v122 - Ap 15 '97 - p127 [51-250]

Journal of Management Accounting Research
p JEL - v35 - Mr '97 - p309 [51-250]
Journal of Market-Focused Management
p JEL - v35 - Mr '97 - p309 [51-250]
Journal of Material Culture
p AJA - v101 - Ja '97 - p191+ [251-500]
The Journal of Medieval and Early Modern Studies
p TLS - N 15 '96 - p34+ [501+]
Journal of Molecular Medicine
p Nature - v383 - S 5 '96 - p35 [251-500]
Journal of Poverty
p JEL - v34 - D '96 - p2144 [51-250]
Journal of Public and International Affairs
p JEL - v35 - Mr '97 - p309 [51-250]
Journal of Real Estate Portfolio Management
p JEL - v34 - S '96 - p1506 [51-250]
Journal of Synchrotron Radiation
p Nature - v383 - S 5 '96 - p42 [251-500]
Journal of the International Neuropsychological Society
p Nature - v383 - S 5 '96 - p33 [501+]
Journal of Undergraduate Sciences
p Nature - v383 - S 5 '96 - p44 [501+]
Jouve, Pierre Jean - *The Desert World*
KR - v64 - S 15 '96 - p1354 [51-250]
LJ - v121 - S 15 '96 - p96 [51-250]
LJ - v121 - O 1 '96 - p127 [51-250]
NYTBR - v102 - Ja 12 '97 - p21 [51-250]
PW - v243 - S 2 '96 - p114 [51-250]
Helene (Dans Les Annees Profondes)
ABR - v17 - Ag '96 - p13 [501+]
Paulina 1880
ABR - v17 - Ag '96 - p13 [501+]
Jowett, Garth S - *Children and the Movies*
Choice - v34 - O '96 - p289 [51-250]
Si & So - v6 - N '96 - p38 [1-50]
TLS - Ja 17 '97 - p7 [501+]
Jowitt, Susannah - *Out of My Head*
Books - v11 - Ap '97 - p23 [51-250]
Joy, Margaret - *The Torc and the Ring*
c JB - v60 - Ag '96 - p158 [251-500]
c Sch Lib - v44 - Ag '96 - p107 [51-250]
y TES - Jl 5 '96 - pR8 [501+]
Joyce, Brenda - *The Finer Things*
PW - v244 - F 17 '97 - p216 [51-250]
Joyce, Graham - *Requiem*
BL - v93 - O 1 '96 - p307 [51-250]
PW - v243 - S 23 '96 - p60+ [51-250]
Joyce, James - *Dubliners*
Critiq - v37 - Sum '96 - p261+ [501+]
y SLMQ - v25 - Fall '96 - p64 [51-250]
Finnegans Wake
Critiq - v37 - Sum '96 - p261+ [501+]
MLN - v111 - D '96 - p872+ [501+]
Listen and Read James Joyce's Dubliners (Keating). Book and Audio Version
c BL - v93 - Mr 15 '97 - p1253 [51-250]
The Lost Notebook
ILS - v15 - Fall '96 - p13 [501+]
Ulysses
Critiq - v37 - Sum '96 - p261+ [501+]
TLS - N 29 '96 - p14 [51-250]
Joyce, James A - *Manual on Elastic-Plastic Fracture*
SciTech - v20 - D '96 - p62 [51-250]
Joyce, Kristin - *Trees*
PW - v244 - F 3 '97 - p91 [51-250]
Vegetables
PW - v244 - F 3 '97 - p91 [51-250]
Joyce, Patrick - *Democratic Subjects*
EHR - v112 - F '97 - p236+ [251-500]
J Soc H - v30 - Fall '96 - p229+ [501+]
VS - v39 - Spr '96 - p405+ [501+]
Visions of the People
HT - v47 - Mr '97 - p55 [251-500]
Joyce, William - *The Ballad of Dinosaur Bob (Hemingway). Book and Audio Version*
c Ch BWatch - v6 - Jl '96 - p5 [1-50]
c PW - v243 - S 30 '96 - p43 [51-250]
Bently and Egg (Illus. by William Joyce)
c PW - v244 - F 3 '97 - p108 [1-50]
c SLJ - v43 - Ja '97 - p37 [1-50]

The Leaf Men and the Brave Good Bugs (Illus. by William Joyce)
c BL - v93 - O 1 '96 - p358+ [51-250]
c BW - v26 - D 8 '96 - p23 [51-250]
c CBRS - v25 - S '96 - p4 [51-250]
c Ch BWatch - v6 - N '96 - p6 [1-50]
c HB Guide - v8 - Spr '97 - p33 [51-250]
c LATBR - D 8 '96 - p18+ [1-50]
c NYTBR - v101 - N 10 '96 - p26 [501+]
c SLJ - v42 - O '96 - p100 [51-250]
c Smith - v27 - N '96 - p170 [1-50]
c Time - v148 - D 9 '96 - p78 [51-250]
Santa Calls Gift Box
c PW - v243 - S 30 '96 - p92 [1-50]
Joyce, William, 1945- - *Miller, Bukowski, and Their Enemies*
LJ - v121 - N 1 '96 - p67 [51-250]
Joyrich, Lynne - *Re-Viewing Reception*
Afterimage - v24 - Ja '97 - p23 [1-50]
LJ - v121 - D '96 - p96 [51-250]
Joysmith, Claire - *Las Formas De Nuestras Voces*
Bloom Rev - v17 - Ja '97 - p5+ [501+]
Juana Ines De La Cruz, Sister - *The Answer: Including a Selection of Poems*
HAHR - v76 - N '96 - p791+ [251-500]
TranslRevS - v1 - My '95 - p29+ [51-250]
Primero Sueano
Hisp - v79 - D '96 - p752+ [501+]
Juda, Lawrence - *International Law and Ocean Use Management*
Choice - v34 - My '97 - p1566+ [51-250]
Judah, Tim - *The Serbs: History, Myth, and the Destruction of Yugoslavia*
KR - v65 - F 1 '97 - p199 [251-500]
LJ - v122 - Mr 15 '97 - p76 [51-250]
PW - v244 - Mr 17 '97 - p67 [51-250]
Utne R - Mr '97 - p85+ [51-250]
Judd, Cameron - *The Shadow Warriors*
BL - v93 - Mr 15 '97 - p1225+ [51-250]
y Kliatt - v31 - My '97 - p6+ [51-250]
Judd, Denis - *Empire: The British Imperial Experience from 1765 to the Present*
CR - v270 - Ja '97 - p52+ [251-500]
Econ - v339 - My 18 '96 - p9*+ [501+]
Lon R Bks - v18 - Jl 18 '96 - p8+ [501+]
Quad - v40 - O '96 - p82+ [501+]
Judith, Anodea - *Eastern Body, Western Mind*
LJ - v122 - F 15 '97 - p138 [51-250]
Judovitz, Dalia - *Unpacking Duchamp*
TLS - O 25 '96 - p21 [501+]
Judson, Don - *Bird-Self Accumulated*
RCF - v16 - Fall '96 - p191+ [251-500]
Judson, Horace Freeland - *The Eighth Day of Creation. Expanded Ed.*
Choice - v34 - My '97 - p1523 [51-250]
Nature - v386 - Mr 27 '97 - p344+ [501+]
Sci - v274 - D 20 '96 - p2033 [1-50]
SciTech - v21 - Mr '97 - p36 [51-250]
Judson, Jeremy - *The Macintosh Bible. 6th Ed.*
r CBR - v15 - Spr '97 - p1 [1-50]
r New Sci - v152 - O 5 '96 - p48 [51-250]
Judson, Karen - *The Constitution of the United States*
y HB Guide - v7 - Fall '96 - p314 [51-250]
The Presidency of the United States
y HB Guide - v7 - Fall '96 - p314 [51-250]
Judt, Tony - *A Grand Illusion?*
BL - v93 - S 15 '96 - p214 [251-500]
For Aff - v76 - Ja '97 - p139+ [501+]
PW - v243 - Jl 22 '96 - p224 [51-250]
RP - v59 - Spr '97 - p386+ [501+]
Wil Q - v20 - Aut '96 - p99+ [251-500]
Wil Q - v21 - Win '97 - p38 [51-250]
Jue, Joyce - *Far East Cafe*
CSM - v89 - D 13 '96 - p11 [1-50]
Juel, Donald H - *A Master of Surprise*
Intpr - v51 - Ja '97 - p91+ [251-500]
Juhnke, James C - *Creative Crusader*
CH - v66 - Mr '97 - p211 [51-250]
Jukes, Mavis - *Expecting the Unexpected*
y BL - v93 - O 1 '96 - p342 [51-250]
c CBRS - v25 - D '96 - p46 [51-250]
c CCB-B - v50 - D '96 - p140 [51-250]
c HB Guide - v8 - Spr '97 - p68 [51-250]
c KR - v64 - Ag 15 '96 - p1236+ [51-250]
c SLJ - v42 - S '96 - p202+ [51-250]
y VOYA - v19 - D '96 - p270 [51-250]
Human Interactions with Mrs. Gladys Furley, R.N.
y JAAL - v40 - N '96 - p231 [51-250]

It's a Girl Thing (Illus. by Debbie Tilley)
y BL - v93 - Ap 1 '97 - p1308 [1-50]
c HB - v72 - S '96 - p614 [51-250]
y HB Guide - v7 - Fall '96 - p311 [1-50]
c NYTBR - v101 - Ag 25 '96 - p23 [251-500]
Julia, Isabelle - *Les Annees Romantiques*
BM - v138 - Ag '96 - p560+ [501+]
Julian, of Norwich - *The Life of the Soul*
RR - v55 - N '96 - p661 [1-50]
Juliano, Benjoe A - *Tracing Chains-of-Thought*
JEL - v35 - Mr '97 - p305 [51-250]
Julien, Nadia - *The Mammoth Dictionary of Symbols*
r ARBA - v28 - '97 - p288 [51-250]
Juliet, Charles - *Lambeaux*
FR - v70 - F '97 - p499+ [251-500]
Julig, Patrick J - *The Cummins Site Complex and Paleoindian Occupations in the Northwestern Lake Superior Region*
Am Ant - v62 - Ja '97 - p173 [251-500]
Julius, Anthony - *T.S. Eliot, Anti-Semitism, and Literary Form*
AS - v66 - Win '97 - p140+ [501+]
HM - v294 - Ja '97 - p62+ [501+]
Nat R - v48 - S 30 '96 - p62+ [501+]
NYRB - v43 - Je 6 '96 - p34+ [501+]
TLS - Jl 7 '96 - p13 [501+]
Julius, Edward H - *More Rapid Math Tricks and Tips*
c Learning - v25 - Ja '97 - p57 [1-50]
c Math T - v89 - O '96 - p609 [51-250]
Julius, Marshall - *Action! The Action Movie A-Z*
yr Kliatt - v31 - My '97 - p30 [51-250]
r LJ - v122 - F 15 '97 - p128 [51-250]
r PW - v244 - Ja 20 '97 - p390 [51-250]
Julivert, Maria Angels - *Los Escarabajos (Illus. by Estudio Marcel Socias)*
c BL - v93 - F 15 '97 - p1032 [1-50]
Los Murcielagos (Illus. by Estudio Marcel Socias)
c SLJ - v42 - N '96 - p132 [51-250]
Los Osos (Illus. by Estudio Marcel Socias)
c SLJ - v42 - N '96 - p132 [51-250]
Julliard, Jacques - *Dictionnaire Des Intellectuels Francais*
r TLS - F 7 '97 - p7 [501+]
Jullien, Francois - *The Propensity of Things*
Ch Rev Int - v3 - Fall '96 - p458+ [501+]
Julyan, Robert - *The Place Names of New Mexico*
r Names - v45 - Mr '97 - p73+ [501+]
Place Names of the White Mountains. Rev. Ed.
r Names - v44 - S '96 - p243+ [501+]
Juneja, Om P - *Post Colonial Novel*
WLT - v70 - Sum '96 - p769+ [501+]
Jung, C G - *The Psychology of Kundalini Yoga*
Choice - v34 - N '96 - p542 [51-250]
Parabola - v21 - Ag '96 - p120 [1-50]
Jung, Heidrun - *Barriers and Bridges*
MLJ - v81 - Spr '97 - p115+ [501+]
Jung, Patricia Beattie - *Abortion and Catholicism*
Cons - v17 - Aut '96 - p35+ [501+]
Junger, Sebastian - *The Perfect Storm*
KR - v65 - Mr 15 '97 - p440 [251-500]
PW - v244 - Ap 7 '97 - p83 [51-250]
Jungman, Ann - *Septimouse. Supermouse and Septimouse. Big Cheese (Lambert). Audio Version*
c BL - v93 - N 1 '96 - p522 [51-250]
Jungnickel, Dieter - *Designs and Finite Geometries*
SciTech - v21 - Mr '97 - p12 [51-250]
Jungreis, Ervin - *Spot Test Analysis. 2nd Ed.*
SciTech - v21 - Mr '97 - p29 [51-250]
Junion-Metz, Gail - *K-12 Resources on the Internet*
JOYS - v10 - Win '97 - p220+ [251-500]
Juniper, Tony - *Threatened Planet*
c Sch Lib - v44 - N '96 - p163 [51-250]
Junkin, Angus - *The Garden Tutor*
BWatch - v18 - F '97 - p11 [51-250]
Junod, Dominique-D - *The Imperiled Red Cross and the Palestine-Eretz-Yisrael Conflict 1945-1952*
Choice - v34 - D '96 - p674 [51-250]
Junor, Penny - *From Brixton to Downing Street*
TES - Jl 5 '96 - p7* [51-250]
Juravich, Tom - *Commonwealth of Toil*
R&R Bk N - v12 - F '97 - p41 [1-50]
Jurenka, Nancy Allen - *Cultivating a Child's Imagination through Gardening*
Cur R - v36 - F '97 - p3* [251-500]
Jurey, Philomena - *A Basement Seat to History*
JMCQ - v73 - Win '96 - p995 [251-500]
Pres SQ - v26 - Sum '96 - p909 [251-500]
Jurgensen, Carsten - *Demokratie Und Menschenrechte In Der Arabischen Welt*
MEJ - v51 - Win '97 - p153 [1-50]
Jurgensen, Manfred - *A Sporting Declaration*
Aust Bk R - D '96 - p74 [51-250]

Juristo, Juan Angel - *Alfredo Bryce Echenique: Para Que Duela Menos*
    LJ - v122 - Ja '97 - p79 [51-250]
Jurow, Susan - *Integrating Total Quality Management in a Library Setting*
    LR - v45 - 6 '96 - p67+ [251-500]
Jussawalla, Meheroo - *Telecommunications: A Bridge to the 21st Century*
    JEL - v34 - S '96 - p1458 [51-250]
Jussek, Nicole - *Seymour and Opal (Illus. by Ana Lopez Escriva)*
  c BL - v93 - D 1 '96 - p668 [51-250]
  c Emerg Lib - v24 - Mr '97 - p45 [1-50]
  c KR - v64 - O 1 '96 - p1469 [51-250]
  c PW - v243 - N 11 '96 - p73 [51-250]
  c SLJ - v42 - D '96 - p96 [51-250]
  c HB Guide - v8 - Spr '97 - p33 [51-250]
Just, Marion R - *Crosstalk: Citizens, Candidates, and the Media in a Presidential Campaign*
    Choice - v34 - N '96 - p537 [51-250]
    R&R Bk N - v11 - N '96 - p48 [51-250]
Just, Rick - *Keeping Private Idaho*
    BWatch - v17 - D '96 - p6 [51-250]
Just, Ward - *Echo House*
    KR - v65 - Mr 1 '97 - p326+ [51-250]
    PW - v244 - F 17 '97 - p209 [251-500]
    Time - v149 - My 19 '97 - p93 [501+]
    WSJ-Cent - v99 - Ap 30 '97 - pA12 [501+]
Juster, Norton - *The Phantom Tollbooth (Illus. by Jules Feiffer)*
  c HB Guide - v8 - Spr '97 - p69 [51-250]
A Woman's Place
    LATBR - Ag 18 '96 - p15 [51-250]
Juster, Susan - *Disorderly Women*
    J Ch St - v38 - Sum '96 - p657+ [251-500]
    Signs - v22 - Win '97 - p479+ [501+]
A Mighty Baptism
    AL - v69 - Mr '97 - p253 [51-250]
    CC - v113 - N 6 '96 - p1087+ [51-250]
Justice, Donald - *New and Selected Poems*
    Ant R - v54 - Sum '96 - p377+ [251-500]
    LJ - v122 - Ap 1 '97 - p95 [1-50]
    NYRB - v43 - S 19 '96 - p49+ [501+]
Justice, Steven - *Writing and Rebellion*
    Specu - v72 - Ja '97 - p183+ [501+]
Jutte, Robert - *Poverty and Deviance in Early Modern Europe*
    EHR - v111 - S '96 - p977+ [251-500]
Juusola, Detta - *Sunny Goes to School (Illus. by Lavona Keskey)*
  c Dog Fan - v27 - N '96 - p89 [51-250]
Juutilainen, Eino Ilmari - *Double Fighter Knight*
    A & S Sm - v11 - D '96 - p94 [51-250]
Juvenal - *Satires. Bk. 1*
    Choice - v34 - F '97 - p962 [51-250]
Juvonen, Jaana - *Social Motivation*
    Choice - v34 - My '97 - p1580 [51-250]

K

Kabdebo, Tamas - *Arapaly*
WLT - v70 - Aut '96 - p998+ [501+]
Pezsdules
WLT - v70 - Aut '96 - p998+ [501+]
Kabir, Ihtisham - *High Performance Computer Imaging*
SciTech - v20 - D '96 - p6 [1-50]
Kabuki: Five Classic Plays
TranslRevS - v1 - My '95 - p5 [51-250]
Kacapyr, Elia - *Economic Forecasting*
Choice - v34 - D '96 - p658 [51-250]
JEL - v34 - D '96 - p2032 [51-250]
R&R Bk N - v11 - D '96 - p23 [51-250]
Kacmarcik, Frank - *Seeing and Believing*
Am - v175 - N 2 '96 - p30 [51-250]
Comw - v123 - D 6 '96 - p21+ [51-250]
Kaczmarek, Ludger - *Destructiones Modorum Significandi*
Specu - v71 - Jl '96 - p726 [501+]
Kaczmarek, Zdzislaw - *Water Resources Management in the Face of Climatic/Hydrologic Uncertainties*
SciTech - v20 - N '96 - p67 [51-250]
Kadane, Joseph B - *A Probabilistic Analysis of the Sacco and Vanzetti Evidence*
R&R Bk N - v11 - N '96 - p52 [51-250]
Kadare, Ismail - *L'Aigle*
WLT - v70 - Aut '96 - p1008 [51-250]
Dialogue Avec Alain Bosquet
WLT - v70 - Aut '96 - p1005 [51-250]
Shkaba
WLT - v70 - Aut '96 - p1008 [51-250]
The Three-Arched Bridge
BL - v93 - F 15 '97 - p1003+ [51-250]
KR - v64 - D 15 '96 - p1757 [251-500]
LATBR - F 9 '97 - p2 [501+]
LJ - v122 - F 1 '97 - p106 [51-250]
NY - v73 - Ap 28 '97 - p227 [51-250]
NYTBR - v102 - Mr 2 '97 - p30 [501+]
PW - v243 - D 30 '96 - p54 [251-500]
Kadel, Andrew - *Matrology: A Bibliography of Writings by Christian Women from the First to the Fifteenth Centuries*
r CH - v66 - Mr '97 - p193+ [51-250]
Kaderabek, Todd - *A Field Guide to Hot Sauces*
BL - v93 - F 15 '97 - p989 [51-250]
Kadi, Joanna - *Thinking Class*
BWatch - v18 - F '97 - p9 [51-250]
OS - v33 - Mr '97 - p35 [51-250]
Kadir, Djelal - *The Other Writing*
MLR - v91 - O '96 - p1027+ [501+]
Kadish, Alon - *The Corn Laws. Vols. 1-2*
JEL - v34 - D '96 - p2011+ [51-250]
The Corn Laws. Vols. 1-6
R&R Bk N - v11 - D '96 - p33 [51-250]
The Corn Laws. Vols. 3-6
JEL - v34 - D '96 - p2012 [51-250]
Kadish, Doris Y - *Translating Slavery*
TranslRevS - v1 - My '95 - p10 [51-250]
Kadlec, Robert H - *Treatment Wetlands*
Choice - v34 - F '97 - p994 [51-250]
SciTech - v20 - S '96 - p51 [51-250]
Kadodwala, Dilip - *Hinduism*
TES - D 6 '96 - pR7 [501+]
My Hindu Life
TES - F 14 '97 - p16* [51-250]
Kael, Pauline - *For Keeps*
Ent W - S 20 '96 - p75 [51-250]
LATBR - O 13 '96 - p15 [51-250]
Raising Kane and Other Essays
TES - N 22 '96 - p8* [51-250]
TLS - Ja 17 '97 - p6 [501+]

Kaela, Laurent C W - *The Question of Namibia*
Choice - v34 - Ap '97 - p1411 [51-250]
Kaelbling, Leslie Pack - *Recent Advances in Reinforcement Learning*
R&R Bk N - v11 - D '96 - p67 [51-250]
Kaemmer, John E - *Music in Human Life*
RA - v25 - 4 '96 - p225+ [501+]
Kaes, Anton - *The Weimar Republic Sourcebook*
JMH - v68 - S '96 - p629+ [501+]
Kaestli, Jean-Daniel - *Le Mystere Apocryphe*
Rel St Rev - v23 - Ap '97 - p195 [51-250]
Kafadar, Cemal - *Between Two Worlds*
AHR - v101 - D '96 - p1588+ [251-500]
Historian - v59 - Fall '96 - p139+ [501+]
JIH - v27 - Win '97 - p564+ [501+]
Kafeh Ham Ba-Boker
BL - v93 - Mr 1 '97 - p1115 [1-50]
Kafengauz, Lev Borisovich - *Evolution of Industrial Output of Russia*
JEH - v57 - Mr '97 - p196+ [501+]
Kaffka, Alexander V - *Sea-Dumped Chemical Weapons*
SciTech - v20 - D '96 - p69 [51-250]
Kafka, Franz - *The Metamorphosis: The Translation, Backgrounds and Contexts, Criticism*
CR - v269 - O '96 - p222 [51-250]
Kafka, Paul - *Love Enter*
PW - v244 - My 5 '97 - p206 [1-50]
Kagal, Ayesha - *Present Imperfect*
Choice - v34 - O '96 - p288 [51-250]
TLS - Ja 3 '97 - p23 [501+]
Wom R Bks - v13 - S '96 - p19+ [501+]
Kagan, Donald - *On the Origins of War and the Preservation of Peace*
Parameters - v27 - Spr '97 - p179+ [501+]
PSQ - v111 - Win '96 - p722+ [501+]
Soc - v34 - N '96 - p99+ [501+]
Kagan, Elaine - *Blue Heaven*
Rapport - v19 - 4 '96 - p24 [251-500]
Kagan, Richard - *Turmoil to Turning Points*
Choice - v34 - Ja '97 - p884 [51-250]
Kagan, Robert - *A Twilight Struggle*
LATBR - O 6 '96 - p8 [501+]
Kaganoff, Penny - *Men on Divorce*
BL - v93 - F 15 '97 - p980 [51-250]
KR - v64 - D 15 '96 - p1784 [251-500]
PW - v243 - N 25 '96 - p61 [51-250]
Women on Divorce
PW - v243 - O 7 '96 - p68 [1-50]
Rapport - v19 - 5 '96 - p39 [251-500]
Kagawa-Singer, Marjorie - *Health Issues for Minority Adolescents*
Adoles - v31 - Fall '96 - p752+ [51-250]
Choice - v34 - N '96 - p492 [51-250]
Kagda, Sakina - *Norway*
c HB Guide - v7 - Fall '96 - p382 [1-50]
c SLJ - v42 - S '96 - p217 [51-250]
Kagel, John H - *Economic Choice Theory*
Econ J - v106 - N '96 - p1810+ [501+]
The Handbook of Experimental Economics
APSR - v90 - S '96 - p632+ [501+]
JEL - v34 - D '96 - p1950+ [501+]
Kagitcibasi, Cigdem - *Family and Human Development across Cultures*
SB - v32 - O '96 - p197 [251-500]
Kahan, Steven - *Take a Look at a Good Book*
Math T - v90 - Mr '97 - p249 [51-250]
Kahana-Carmon, Amalia - *Kan Nagur*
BL - v93 - Mr 1 '97 - p1115 [1-50]

Kahane, Claire - *Passions of the Voice*
ELT - v39 - 4 '96 - p527 [51-250]
ELT - v40 - 2 '97 - p252+ [51-250]
Nine-C Lit - v51 - S '96 - p273 [51-250]
Kahane, Howard - *Contract Ethics*
Choice - v34 - O '96 - p294 [51-250]
Kahane, Itzhak - *Toward Anti-Adhesion Therapy for Microbial Diseases*
SciTech - v20 - D '96 - p36 [51-250]
Kahane, Reuven - *Educational Advancement and Distributive Justice*
CS - v26 - Mr '97 - p207+ [501+]
Kahaner, Larry - *Competitive Intelligence*
LJ - v122 - Mr 15 '97 - p36 [1-50]
Kahaney, Phyllis - *Theoretical and Critical Perspectives on Teacher Change*
MLJ - v80 - Fall '96 - p402 [501+]
Kahin, Audrey R - *Subversion as Foreign Policy*
TLS - My 24 '96 - p30+ [501+]
Kahin, Brian - *Public Access to the Internet*
JEL - v34 - D '96 - p1986+ [501+]
J Gov Info - v23 - S '96 - p739+ [501+]
LQ - v67 - Ap '97 - p204+ [501+]
SocSciComR - v14 - Fall '96 - p361+ [501+]
Kahl, Jonathan D - *Weather Watch*
c HB Guide - v7 - Fall '96 - p332 [51-250]
Kahlenberg, Richard D - *The Remedy: Class, Race, and Affirmative Action*
BW - v26 - D 8 '96 - p9 [1-50]
Choice - v34 - D '96 - p690 [51-250]
KR - v64 - My 1 '96 - p668 [251-500]
NY - v72 - N 25 '96 - p106+ [501+]
Prog - v60 - N '96 - p41+ [501+]
Kahler, Miles - *Europe and America*
For Aff - v75 - S '96 - p148 [51-250]
Regional Futures and Transatlantic Economic Relations
JEL - v34 - S '96 - p1427+ [51-250]
Kahn, Arthur D - *The Many Faces of Gay*
LJ - v122 - Mr 15 '97 - p78 [51-250]
PW - v244 - F 3 '97 - p91 [51-250]
Kahn, David - *The Codebreakers: The Story of Secret Writing. Rev. Ed.*
BW - v27 - Mr 2 '97 - p13 [51-250]
For Aff - v76 - My '97 - p129 [51-250]
Kahn, Leora - *When They Came to Take My Father*
SS - v87 - N '96 - p283+ [501+]
Kahn, Michael A - *Sheer Gall*
KR - v64 - Ag 15 '96 - p1191 [51-250]
LJ - v121 - S 15 '96 - p101 [51-250]
Kahn, Michael D - *Between Therapist and Client. Rev. Ed.*
LJ - v122 - Ap 15 '97 - p125 [1-50]
Kahn, Olivier - *Magnetism: A Supramolecular Function*
SciTech - v20 - D '96 - p25 [51-250]
Kahn, Peter B - *Mathematical Methods for Scientists and Engineers*
SciTech - v20 - N '96 - p4 [51-250]
Kahn, Robbie Pfeufer - *Bearing Meaning*
Choice - v34 - S '96 - p167 [51-250]
CS - v26 - Mr '97 - p211+ [501+]
MHR - v10 - Fall '96 - p113+ [501+]
Kahn, Robert A - *Sickness and Healing*
AAPSS-A - v548 - N '96 - p232+ [501+]
Kahn, Robert S - *Other People's Blood*
Choice - v34 - Mr '97 - p1240 [51-250]
Kahn, Roger - *Joe and Marilyn (Estell). Audio Version*
y Kliatt - v30 - S '96 - p57 [51-250]

Memories of Summer
- BL - v93 - Mr 1 '97 - p1066+ [51-250]
- Bus W - Ap 7 '97 - p18 [501+]
- KR - v65 - F 15 '97 - p275 [251-500]
- LJ - v122 - F 1 '97 - p82 [1-50]
- NYTBR - v102 - Ap 6 '97 - p12 [501+]
- PW - v244 - Mr 24 '97 - p69+ [51-250]

Kahn, Victoria - *Machiavellian Rhetoric*
- QJS - v82 - Ag '96 - p298+ [501+]

Kahne, Joseph - *Reframing Educational Policy*
- Choice - v34 - S '96 - p180 [51-250]

Kahr, Brett - *D.W. Winnicott: A Biographical Portrait*
- Choice - v34 - F '97 - p1040 [51-250]
- Readings - v12 - Mr '97 - p23 [51-250]
- R&R Bk N - v11 - D '96 - p2 [51-250]

Kahrs, Kristin - *CyberHound's Guide to Publications on the Internet*
- r BL - v93 - F 1 '97 - p963+ [251-500]

Kaim, Wolfgang - *Bioinorganic Chemistry*
- J Chem Ed - v74 - Ap '97 - p382+ [501+]

Kain, Karen - *Karen Kain: Movement Never Lies*
- Bloom Rev - v16 - N '96 - p24 [251-500]

Kain, Kathleen - *All about How Things Are Made (Illus. by Robert Byrd)*
- c CLW - v66 - Je '96 - p45+ [51-250]
- c HB Guide - v7 - Fall '96 - p350+ [51-250]
All about Pets (Illus. by Yoshi Miyake)
- c CLW - v66 - Je '96 - p45+ [51-250]
- c HB Guide - v7 - Fall '96 - p346 [51-250]

Kain, Roger J P - *The Tithe Maps of England and Wales*
- r GJ - v162 - N '96 - p337 [501+]

Kainz, Howard P - *Democracy and the Kingdom of God*
- Rel St Rev - v22 - O '96 - p338 [51-250]
G.W.F. Hegel: The Philosophical System
- LJ - v122 - Ja '97 - p103 [51-250]

Kaiser, Harvey H - *Great Camps of the Adirondacks*
- LJ - v122 - F 1 '97 - p112 [51-250]

Kaiser, Janice - *Last Night in Rio*
- PW - v243 - N 4 '96 - p71 [51-250]

Kaiser, Wolfram - *Using Europe, Abusing the Europeans*
- Econ - v342 - F 15 '97 - p5*+ [501+]
- NS - v125 - N 29 '96 - p42+ [501+]

Kaiserlian, Dominique - *Antigen Presentation by Intestinal Epithelial Cells*
- SciTech - v20 - N '96 - p35 [51-250]

Kajanto, Iiro - *The Tragic Mission of Bishop Paul Juusten to Tsar Ivan the Terrible*
- Ren & Ref - v19 - Fall '96 - p101+ [501+]

Kakar, Sudhir - *The Colors of Violence*
- Rel St Rev - v23 - Ja '97 - p96 [51-250]

Kakazu, Hiroshi - *Sustainable Development of Small Island Economies*
- Pac A - v69 - Sum '96 - p300+ [501+]

Kalaidjian, Walter - *American Culture between the Wars*
- Poetics T - v18 - Spr '97 - p113+ [501+]

Kalan, Robert - *Moving Day (Illus. by Yossi Abolafia)*
- c HB Guide - v7 - Fall '96 - p240 [51-250]
Salta, Ranita, Salta! (Illus. by Byron Barton). Book and Audio Version
- c SLJ - v43 - Ja '97 - p70 [51-250]

Kalantar, Ashkharbek - *Armenia from the Stone Age to the Middle Ages*
- AJA - v100 - Jl '96 - p638+ [251-500]

Kalb, Rosalind C - *Multiple Sclerosis*
- BWatch - v17 - D '96 - p4 [51-250]
- LJ - v121 - N 1 '96 - p101+ [51-250]

Kaldor, Andras - *Opera Houses of Europe*
- LJ - v122 - Ap 15 '97 - p76+ [51-250]

Kaldor, Nicholas - *Causes of Growth and Stagnation in the World Economy*
- JEL - v35 - Mr '97 - p204+ [51-250]

Kaleidoscope
- p Sm Pr R - v28 - D '96 - p22 [51-250]

Kaler, James B - *The Ever-Changing Sky*
- Astron - v24 - N '96 - p102+ [51-250]
- Choice - v34 - O '96 - p301 [51-250]
- r New Sci - v153 - F 22 '97 - p45 [1-50]
- SLMQ - v24 - Sum '96 - p221 [51-250]
- S&T - v92 - O '96 - p54+ [501+]
Stars and Their Spectra
- S&T - v92 - S '96 - p53+ [51-250]

Kaler, James Otis - *Toby Tyler (Purinton). Audio Version*
- BL - v93 - My 15 '97 - p1596 [51-250]

Kaletsky, Richard - *OSHA Inspections*
- SciTech - v21 - Mr '97 - p71 [51-250]

Kalfatovic, Martin R - *The New Deal Fine Arts Projects 1933-1992*
- r RQ - v35 - Sum '96 - p486 [51-250]

Kalfatovic, Mary C - *Montgomery Clift: A Bio-Bibliography*
- r J Am Cult - v19 - Sum '96 - p138+ [51-250]

Kalichman, Seth C - *Understanding AIDS*
- Choice - v34 - S '96 - p162 [51-250]
- Readings - v11 - D '96 - p22 [51-250]

Kalinak, Kathryn - *Settling the Score*
- J Film & Vid - v48 - Spr '96 - p99+ [501+]

Kalinina, Natallia - *Mest' Zhenshchiny*
- BL - v93 - O 1 '96 - p327 [1-50]

Kalinke, Marianne E - *The Book of Reykjaholar*
- R&R Bk N - v12 - F '97 - p91 [1-50]

Kalish, Nancy - *Lost and Found Lovers*
- BL - v93 - F 15 '97 - p980 [51-250]
- BW - v27 - F 23 '97 - p6 [501+]
- KR - v64 - D 15 '96 - p1784+ [251-500]
- PW - v244 - Ja 6 '97 - p60 [251-500]

Kall, Peter - *Stochastic Programming*
- SIAM Rev - v38 - D '96 - p681+ [501+]

Kalland, Arne - *Fishing Villages in Tokugawa Japan*
- AHR - v102 - F '97 - p155+ [501+]

Kallberg, Jeffrey - *Chopin at the Boundaries*
- Choice - v34 - N '96 - p470 [51-250]
- TLS - D 6 '96 - p20 [501+]

Kalleberg, Arne L - *Organizations in America*
- Choice - v34 - O '96 - p326 [51-250]
- R&R Bk N - v11 - N '96 - p30 [51-250]

Kallet-Marx, Robert - *Hegemony to Empire*
- HRNB - v25 - Fall '96 - p41+ [251-500]

Kallifatides, Theodor - *Det Sista Ljuset*
- WLT - v70 - Sum '96 - p717+ [501+]

Kalman, Bobbie - *A...B...Sea (Illus. by Christopher Hartley)*
- c HB Guide - v7 - Fall '96 - p335 [51-250]
A Child's Day (Illus. by Antoinette DeBiasi)
- c Can CL - v22 - Fall '96 - p115+ [501+]
Customs and Traditions (Illus. by Barbara Bedell)
- c Can CL - v22 - Fall '96 - p115+ [501+]
Fort Life (Illus. by Tammy Everts)
- c Can CL - v22 - Fall '96 - p115+ [501+]
Games from Long Ago (Illus. by Barbara Bedell)
- c Can CL - v22 - Fall '96 - p115+ [501+]
The General Store
- c Ch BWatch - v7 - Ja '97 - p7 [51-250]
How a Book Is Published
- c HB Guide - v7 - Fall '96 - p307 [1-50]
- c RT - v50 - S '96 - p56 [51-250]
How a Plant Grows
- c Ch BWatch - v7 - F '97 - p5 [1-50]
How Animals Communicate
- c Ch BWatch - v7 - F '97 - p5 [1-50]
Life in the Coral Reef
- c Ch BWatch - v7 - F '97 - p5 [1-50]
Nicola's Floating Home
- c HB Guide - v7 - Fall '96 - p318 [1-50]
Old-Time Toys (Illus. by Barbara Bedell)
- c Can CL - v22 - Fall '96 - p115+ [501+]
A One Room School (Illus. by Antoinette DeBiasi)
- c Can CL - v22 - Fall '96 - p115+ [501+]
Penguins
- c HB Guide - v7 - Fall '96 - p344 [51-250]
Sea Otters
- c Ch BWatch - v7 - F '97 - p5 [1-50]
Settler Sayings (Illus. by Barbara Bedell)
- c Can CL - v22 - Fall '96 - p115+ [501+]
Spanish Missions (Illus. by Barbara Bedell)
- c Ch BWatch - v7 - Ja '97 - p7 [51-250]
Victorian Christmas
- c Ch BWatch - v6 - D '96 - p1 [51-250]
The Victorian Home (Illus. by Barbara Bedell)
- c Ch BWatch - v7 - Ja '97 - p7 [51-250]
Vietnam: The Culture
- c HB Guide - v7 - Fall '96 - p383+ [51-250]
- c SLJ - v42 - N '96 - p114 [51-250]
Vietnam: The Land
- c HB Guide - v7 - Fall '96 - p383+ [51-250]
- c SLJ - v42 - N '96 - p114 [51-250]
Vietnam: The People
- c HB Guide - v7 - Fall '96 - p383+ [51-250]
- c SLJ - v42 - N '96 - p114 [51-250]
Web Weavers and Other Spiders
- c Ch BWatch - v7 - F '97 - p5 [51-250]
- c Quill & Q - v63 - Mr '97 - p82 [251-500]
What Do You See under the Sea? (Illus. by Christopher Hartley)
- c HB Guide - v7 - Fall '96 - p335 [51-250]
Why Do Animals Do That?
- c Ch BWatch - v7 - F '97 - p5 [1-50]
- c Quill & Q - v63 - Mr '97 - p81 [251-500]

Kalman, Laura - *The Strange Career of Legal Liberalism*
- Choice - v34 - Ja '97 - p867 [51-250]
- NYTBR - v101 - S 15 '96 - p33 [501+]

Kalman, Maira - *Hey Willy, See the Pyramids (Illus. by Maira Kalman)*
- c HB Guide - v8 - Spr '97 - p33 [51-250]
Sayonara, Mrs. Kackleman (Illus. by Maira Kalman)
- c HB Guide - v8 - Spr '97 - p33 [51-250]

Kalnina, Laima - *Briniskigas Pukes*
- WLT - v71 - Win '97 - p195 [251-500]

Kalogridis, Jeanne - *Children of the Vampire. Abridged Ed. Audio Version*
- y Kliatt - v30 - S '96 - p46 [51-250]
Children of the Vampire. Unabridged Ed. Audio Version
- y Kliatt - v30 - S '96 - p46 [51-250]
Lord of the Vampires
- KR - v64 - S 1 '96 - p1257 [251-500]
- LJ - v121 - S 15 '96 - p96 [51-250]
- PW - v243 - O 14 '96 - p64 [251-500]

Kalson, Albert E - *Laughter in the Dark*
- RES - v47 - N '96 - p636 [251-500]

Kalthoff, Mark A - *Creation and Evolution in the Early American Scientific Affiliation*
- Isis - v88 - Mr '97 - p160+ [501+]

Kalton, Nigel - *Interaction between Functional Analysis, Harmonic Analysis, and Probability*
- SIAM Rev - v38 - D '96 - p713 [1-50]

Kalupahana, David J - *Ethics in Early Buddhism*
- JR - v77 - Ap '97 - p337+ [501+]
- Theol St - v58 - Mr '97 - p197+ [251-500]

Kaluza, Roman - *The Life of Stefan Banach*
- Sci - v274 - N 1 '96 - p734 [51-250]
Through a Reporter's Eyes
- Choice - v34 - F '97 - p1000 [51-250]
- Math T - v89 - D '96 - p782 [251-500]

Kamalipour, Yahya R - *Mass Media in the Middle East*
- JC - v46 - Aut '96 - p177+ [501+]
- Rel St Rev - v22 - O '96 - p357 [51-250]

Kamau, Kwadwo Agymah - *Flickering Shadows*
- BW - v26 - N 10 '96 - p7 [501+]
- BWatch - v17 - D '96 - p6 [1-50]
- HMR - Fall '96 - p21 [501+]
- LJ - v121 - S 15 '96 - p93 [51-250]
- LJ - v122 - Mr 15 '97 - p41 [1-50]
- NYTBR - v101 - D 15 '96 - p25 [51-250]

Kamboureli, Smaro - *Making a Difference*
- BIC - v25 - S '96 - p7+ [501+]

Kamen, Gloria - *Hidden Music (Illus. by Gloria Kamen)*
- c HB - v72 - S '96 - p615+ [51-250]
- c HB Guide - v7 - Fall '96 - p373 [51-250]

Kamenjarzh, Jacov A - *Limit Analysis of Solids and Structures*
- SciTech - v20 - N '96 - p64 [51-250]

Kamerman, Sheila - *Starting Right*
- Soc Ser R - v70 - D '96 - p653+ [501+]

Kamhi, Alan G - *Communication Development and Disorders in African American Children*
- R&R Bk N - v11 - D '96 - p70 [51-250]
- SciTech - v20 - N '96 - p52 [51-250]

Kamijima, Kenkichi - *Centre and Circumference*
- Nine-C Lit - v50 - Mr '96 - p554 [51-250]

Kamin, Ben - *Thinking Passover*
- BL - v93 - F 1 '97 - p909 [51-250]
- LJ - v122 - F 15 '97 - p138+ [51-250]
- PW - v244 - F 10 '97 - p79+ [51-250]

Kaminer, Reuven - *The Politics of Protest*
- Choice - v34 - N '96 - p530 [51-250]
- MEJ - v51 - Spr '97 - p295+ [501+]

Kaminer, Wendy - *True Love Waits*
- Wom R Bks - v13 - S '96 - p17+ [501+]

Kaminski, Bartlomiej - *Economic Transition in Russia and the New States of Eurasia*
- Choice - v34 - Ap '97 - p1386 [51-250]
- R&R Bk N - v12 - F '97 - p36 [51-250]
Foreign Trade in the Transition
- JEL - v34 - D '96 - p2126 [51-250]

Kaminski, John P - *A Necessary Evil?*
- JSH - v62 - N '96 - p796+ [501+]

Kaminsky, Amy Katz - *Water Lilies*
- Choice - v34 - S '96 - p134 [51-250]
- VQR - v73 - Win '97 - p12*+ [51-250]

Kaminsky, Joel S - *Corporate Responsibility in the Hebrew Bible*
- Intpr - v51 - Ja '97 - p86 [251-500]

Kaminsky, Stuart M - *Blood and Rubles (Murdock). Audio Version*
- BL - v93 - N 1 '96 - p522 [51-250]
- BWatch - v18 - Mr '97 - p8 [1-50]
Buried Caesars (Guidall). Audio Version
- LJ - v122 - My 1 '97 - p153 [51-250]
Dancing in the Dark (Guidall). Audio Version
- BWatch - v18 - Mr '97 - p7 [1-50]

Dancing in the Dark (Kohen). Audio Version
  BL - v93 - N 1 '96 - p522 [51-250]
  BWatch - v18 - Mr '97 - p8 [1-50]
  y Kliatt - v30 - S '96 - p46 [51-250]
  LJ - v121 - S 15 '96 - p112+ [51-250]
Dancing in the Dark (Parker). Audio Version
  BL - v93 - N 15 '96 - p604 [51-250]
  LJ - v121 - N 15 '96 - p104 [51-250]
A Fatal Glass of Beer
  KR - v65 - Ap 1 '97 - p507 [51-250]
  LJ - v122 - My 1 '97 - p144 [1-50]
  PW - v244 - My 5 '97 - p202 [51-250]
Lieberman's Law. Audio Version
  BWatch - v17 - D '96 - p10 [1-50]
Poor Butterfly (Parker). Audio Version
  LJ - v122 - Ja '97 - p172 [51-250]
The Rockford Files
  y BL - v93 - S 15 '96 - p224 [51-250]
  KR - v64 - Ag 15 '96 - p1191 [51-250]
Kamins'kyi, Anatol' - *Na Perekhidnomu Etapi*
  BL - v93 - N 15 '96 - p577 [1-50]
Kamler, Howard - *Identification and Character*
  CPR - v16 - Ap '96 - p111+ [501+]
Kamm, Henry - *Dragon Ascending*
  y SLJ - v42 - O '96 - p166 [51-250]
Kamman, Madeleine - *The New Making of a Cook*
  BL - v93 - My 15 '97 - p1552 [51-250]
Kammen, Michael - *The Lively Arts*
  AL - v69 - Mr '97 - p233+ [251-500]
  Choice - v34 - Ja '97 - p862+ [51-250]
  JC - v47 - Win '97 - p185+ [51-250]
  NYTBR - v101 - D 8 '96 - p88 [1-50]
Kammrath, Julaine - *Make a Christmas Memory*
  c SLJ - v42 - O '96 - p37 [51-250]
Kamp, Di - *The Excellent Trainer*
  R&R Bk N - v11 - D '96 - p34 [51-250]
Kan, Pao - *In Search of the Supernatural*
  Ch Rev Int - v4 - Spr '97 - p118+ [501+]
  Rel St Rev - v23 - Ap '97 - p204+ [51-250]
Kanaganayakam, Chelva - *Configurations of Exile*
  WLT - v70 - Sum '96 - p760 [501+]
Kanarek, Lisa - *101 Home Office Success Secrets*
  LJ - v122 - My 1 '97 - p52 [1-50]
Kanas, Nick - *Group Therapy for Schizophrenic Patients*
  SciTech - v20 - S '96 - p33 [51-250]
Kanatani, Kenichi - *Statistical Optimization for Geometric Computation*
  SciTech - v20 - N '96 - p69 [51-250]
Kandall, Stephen R - *Substance and Shadow*
  BL - v92 - Ag '96 - p1862 [51-250]
  BW - v27 - F 16 '97 - p13 [51-250]
  Choice - v34 - Mr '97 - p1245 [51-250]
Kandel, Michael - *Panda Ray*
  Analog - v116 - D '96 - p145+ [251-500]
  BW - v26 - S 1 '96 - p11 [251-500]
Kandiah, Michael David - *Ideas and Think Tanks in Contemporary Britain. Vol. 1*
  TLS - Ja 3 '97 - p4+ [501+]
Kandinsky, Wassily - *Wassily Kandinsky and Gabriele Munter*
  Art J - v55 - Fall '96 - p84+ [501+]
Kandiyoti, Deniz - *Gendering the Middle East*
  APSR - v91 - Mr '97 - p217+ [501+]
  MEJ - v50 - Sum '96 - p457 [51-250]
  Wom R Bks - v14 - D '96 - p24+ [501+]
Kane, Andrea - *Legacy of the Diamond*
  PW - v243 - D 30 '96 - p63 [51-250]
Kane, Cheikh Hamidou - *Les Gardiens Du Temple*
  WLT - v70 - Aut '96 - p1017+ [501+]
Kane, Elizabeth - *A Gentile Account of Life in Utah's Dixie 1872-73*
  WHQ - v28 - Spr '97 - p83 [251-500]
Kane, Gordon - *The Particle Garden*
  BWatch - v17 - S '96 - p11 [51-250]
  Nature - v383 - O 24 '96 - p682 [1-50]
Kane, Joe - *Savages*
  Ant R - v54 - Sum '96 - p372 [251-500]
  BW - v27 - F 23 '97 - p12 [51-250]
  LATBR - O 27 '96 - p11 [51-250]
  NYTBR - v101 - D 15 '96 - p40 [51-250]
  Smith - v28 - Ap '97 - p135+ [501+]
Kane, Kathleen - *A Pocketful of Paradise*
  PW - v243 - D 9 '96 - p65 [51-250]
Kane, Leslie - *David Mamet's Glengarry Glen Ross*
  Choice - v34 - F '97 - p964 [51-250]
  R&R Bk N - v12 - F '97 - p90 [51-250]
Kane, Paul - *Australian Poetry*
  Choice - v34 - Mr '97 - p1163 [51-250]
Kane, Rosalie - *Delegation of Nursing Activities*
  Hast Cen R - v26 - Mr '96 - p48+ [1-50]

Family Caregiving in an Aging Society
  Soc Ser R - v70 - S '96 - p502+ [51-250]
Kane, Russell D - *Wet H2S Cracking of Carbon Steels and Weldments*
  SciTech - v20 - D '96 - p63 [51-250]
Kane, Stephanie C - *The Phantom Gringo Boat*
  Am Ethnol - v23 - N '96 - p926+ [501+]
Kanellos, Nicholas - *Hispanic American Chronology*
  cr ARBA - v28 - '97 - p155 [51-250]
  cr SLJ - v42 - N '96 - p138 [51-250]
Kaner, Sam - *Facilitator's Guide to Participatory Decision Making*
  Workbook - v21 - Win '96 - p174+ [501+]
Kanfer, Stefan - *Serious Business*
  y BL - v93 - Ap 1 '97 - p1275 [51-250]
  Ent W - Ap 18 '97 - p62 [51-250]
  KR - v65 - F 15 '97 - p275+ [251-500]
  NYTBR - v102 - Ap 20 '97 - p11 [501+]
  PW - v244 - Mr 3 '97 - p56 [51-250]
Kang, Henry R - *Color Technology for Electronic Imaging Devices*
  SciTech - v21 - Mr '97 - p93 [51-250]
Kang, K Connie - *Home Was the Land of Morning Calm*
  Bks & Cult - v2 - Ja '96 - p30+ [51-250]
Kani, John - *More Market Plays*
  Theat J - v49 - Mr '97 - p85+ [501+]
Kanigel, Robert - *The One Best Way*
  BL - v93 - My 1 '97 - p1467 [51-250]
  KR - v65 - Mr 1 '97 - p355 [51-250]
  LJ - v122 - Ap 15 '97 - p92 [51-250]
  PW - v244 - Mr 17 '97 - p62 [251-500]
  Trib Bks - My 18 '97 - p1+ [501+]
Kankainen, Kathy - *Treading in the Past*
  Am Ant - v61 - Jl '96 - p629 [51-250]
Kannan, R - *Advanced Analysis on the Real Line*
  Choice - v34 - N '96 - p496 [51-250]
Kanon, Joseph - *Los Alamos*
  BL - v93 - Mr 15 '97 - p1204 [51-250]
  KR - v65 - Ap 1 '97 - p489 [251-500]
  LJ - v122 - Mr 15 '97 - p90 [51-250]
  NW - v129 - My 19 '97 - p85 [51-250]
  NYTLa - v146 - My 15 '97 - pC22 [501+]
  PW - v244 - F 10 '97 - p64 [251-500]
Kansas Quarterly/Arkansas Review
  p LMR - v15 - Fall '96 - p16+ [501+]
Kanski, Jack J - *Glaucoma: A Colour Manual of Diagnosis and Treatment. 2nd Ed.*
  SciTech - v20 - N '96 - p50 [51-250]
Kant, Immanuel - *The Metaphysics of Morals*
  TLS - Ja 3 '97 - p10+ [501+]
Religion and Rational Theology
  Choice - v34 - My '97 - p1513 [51-250]
Kantaris, Elia Geoffrey - *The Subversive Psyche*
  WLT - v70 - Aut '96 - p926+ [251-500]
Kanter, Laurence B - *Painting and Illumination in Early Renaissance Florence 1300-1450*
  Ren Q - v50 - Spr '97 - p315+ [501+]
Kantha, Sachi Sri - *An Einstein Dictionary*
  r ARBA - v28 - '97 - p638+ [251-500]
  r Choice - v34 - O '96 - p253 [51-250]
Kantoff, Philip - *Prostate Cancer*
  LJ - v121 - O 1 '96 - p116 [51-250]
  PW - v243 - O 21 '96 - p81 [51-250]
Kantor, Herman I - *The Matzo Mitzvah (Illus. by Jan Golden)*
  y Kliatt - v31 - Mr '97 - p24 [51-250]
Kantor, Paul - *The Dependent City Revisited*
  Pol Stud J - v24 - Sum '96 - p327+ [501+]
Kantor, Paul B - *Studying the Cost and Value of Library Services: Final Report*
  J Gov Info - v23 - S '96 - p572 [51-250]
Kantrowitz, Arnie - *Under the Rainbow*
  LATBR - S 1 '96 - p11 [51-250]
Kanungo, Rabindra N - *Ethical Dimensions of Leadership*
  Per Psy - v49 - Win '96 - p994+ [501+]
Kanwal, R P - *Asymptotic Analysis*
  SIAM Rev - v38 - D '96 - p706+ [501+]
Kao, Mary Liu - *Cataloging and Classification for Library Technicians*
  LAR - v98 - Mr '96 - p162 [51-250]
  LR - v45 - 7 '96 - p76+ [251-500]
Kao, Shang-Chuan - *China's Economic Reform*
  Choice - v34 - O '96 - p329 [51-250]
  JEL - v34 - D '96 - p2123+ [51-250]
Kapadia, Karin - *Siva and Her Sisters*
  CS - v26 - Mr '97 - p194+ [501+]
Kapchan, Deborah A - *Gender on the Market*
  Choice - v34 - O '96 - p323 [51-250]
Kaplan, Benjamin J - *Calvinists and Libertines*
  Six Ct J - v27 - Fall '96 - p891+ [501+]
  TLS - Ag 30 '96 - p33 [501+]

Kaplan, Burton - *Winning People Over*
  BL - v92 - Ag '96 - p1858 [51-250]
Kaplan, Caren - *Questions of Travel*
  Choice - v34 - Mr '97 - p1156 [51-250]
Kaplan, Carola M - *Seeing Double*
  Choice - v34 - Ap '97 - p1340 [51-250]
Kaplan, David E - *The Cult at the End of the World*
  Books - v10 - Je '96 - p21 [51-250]
  BW - v26 - Ag 4 '96 - p3 [51-250]
  Spec - v277 - N 23 '96 - p43 [1-50]
Kaplan, Edward K - *Holiness in Words*
  Choice - v34 - S '96 - p144 [51-250]
Kaplan, Edward S - *American Trade Policy 1923-1995*
  Choice - v34 - S '96 - p176 [51-250]
  JEH - v57 - Mr '97 - p252+ [251-500]
  JEL - v34 - S '96 - p1428 [51-250]
Prelude to Trade Wars
  BusLR - v21 - 3 '96 - p192+ [501+]
Kaplan, Elizabeth - *Taiga*
  c Ch BWatch - v6 - My '96 - p6 [51-250]
  c HB Guide - v7 - Fall '96 - p336 [51-250]
Temperate Forest
  c HB Guide - v7 - Fall '96 - p336 [51-250]
Tundra
  c HB Guide - v7 - Fall '96 - p336 [51-250]
Kaplan, Gerald S - *AS/400 Application Development Using COBOL/400*
  SciTech - v20 - N '96 - p11 [1-50]
Kaplan, Giscla - *The Meagre Harvest*
  Aust Bk R - O '96 - p22 [501+]
Kaplan, Harold I - *Comprehensive Textbook of Psychiatry. 6th Ed., Vols. 1-2*
  AJPsych - v153 - O '96 - p1357 [501+]
Concise Textbook of Clinical Psychiatry
  SciTech - v20 - S '96 - p32 [51-250]
Kaplan and Sadock's Synopsis of Psychiatry. 7th Ed.
  r AJPsych - v153 - O '96 - p1357 [501+]
Pocket Handbook of Primary Care Psychiatry
  SciTech - v21 - Mr '97 - p53 [51-250]
Kaplan, Herbert H - *Russian Overseas Commerce with Great Britain during the Reign of Catherine II*
  Choice - v34 - S '96 - p187 [51-250]
  R&R Bk N - v12 - F '97 - p44 [51-250]
Kaplan, Jack - *Smart Cards*
  CBR - v14 - Jl '96 - p20 [51-250]
Kaplan, James - *The Airport: Planes, People, Triumphs, and Disasters at John F. Kennedy International*
  NYTBR - v102 - F 16 '97 - p32 [1-50]
Kaplan, Janice - *The Whole Truth*
  PW - v243 - D 9 '96 - p65 [51-250]
Kaplan, Jeffrey - *Radical Religion in America*
  BL - v93 - Ja '97 - p784+ [51-250]
  LJ - v122 - F 1 '97 - p87 [51-250]
Kaplan, Jerry - *Startup: A Silicon Valley Adventure*
  NYTBR - v101 - O 20 '96 - p36 [51-250]
  PW - v243 - S 23 '96 - p73 [1-50]
Kaplan, Joel H - *Theatre and Fashion*
  RES - v47 - Ag '96 - p439+ [501+]
  VS - v39 - Win '96 - p260+ [501+]
Kaplan, John - *Mom and Me*
  c HB Guide - v7 - Fall '96 - p311 [1-50]
  c Par - v71 - D '96 - p252 [1-50]
Kaplan, Justin - *The Language of Names*
  BL - v93 - Ja '97 - p814 [51-250]
  KR - v64 - N 15 '96 - p1653 [251-500]
  LATBR - Mr 23 '97 - p10 [501+]
  LJ - v122 - Ap 15 '97 - p81 [51-250]
  NYTBR - v102 - F 16 '97 - p7 [501+]
  NYTLa - v146 - Ja 30 '97 - pC17 [501+]
  PW - v243 - D 9 '96 - p52+ [51-250]
Kaplan, Laura - *The Story of Jane*
  NWSA Jnl - v8 - Fall '96 - p154+ [501+]
  OOB - v26 - Jl '96 - p12+ [501+]
Kaplan, Laura G - *Emergency and Disaster Planning Manual*
  SB - v32 - N '96 - p229 [51-250]
Kaplan, Louis - *A Bibliography of American Autobiographies*
  r ASInt - v34 - O '96 - p14 [1-50]
Laszlo Moholy-Nagy: Biographical Writings
  AHR - v102 - F '97 - p88+ [501+]
Kaplan, Mark - *Decision Theory as Philosophy*
  CPR - v16 - Je '96 - p179+ [501+]
Kaplan, Martha - *Neither Cargo nor Cult*
  Cont Pac - v9 - Spr '97 - p270+ [501+]
Kaplan, Mike - *The New Hotel*
  R&R Bk N - v12 - F '97 - p73 [51-250]
Kaplan, Philip - *Wolfpack: U-Boats at War 1939-1945*
  y BL - v93 - My 15 '97 - p1559 [51-250]

Kaplan, Rachel - *Little-Known Museums in and around Paris*
r Choice - v34 - Ja '97 - p770 [51-250]
CR - v270 - F '97 - p110 [1-50]
LJ - v121 - N 1 '96 - p98 [51-250]

Kaplan, Robert D - *The Ends of the Earth*
Bks & Cult - v2 - S '96 - p16 [501+]
FEER - v159 - S 12 '96 - p52+ [501+]
LATBR - Mr 17 '96 - p1+ [501+]
MEJ - v51 - Spr '97 - p302+ [501+]
NYRB - v43 - S 19 '96 - p20+ [501+]
NYTBR - v101 - D 8 '96 - p87 [1-50]
PW - v244 - Ja 27 '97 - p103 [1-50]
VQR - v73 - Win '97 - p27* [51-250]
W&I - v11 - Ag '96 - p266+ [501+]

Kaplan, Robert E - *Forgotten Crisis*
HRNB - v25 - Win '97 - p76+ [251-500]

Kaplan, Robert M - *Psychological Testing. 4th Ed.*
R&R Bk N - v12 - F '97 - p6 [51-250]

Kaplan, Robert S - *The Balanced Scorecard*
AR - v72 - Ja '97 - p178+ [501+]
BL - v93 - S 1 '96 - p45 [51-250]
Bus Bk R - v14 - 1 '97 - p42+ [501+]
Choice - v34 - Ja '97 - p841 [51-250]
HR Mag - v41 - Ag '96 - p124+ [51-250]
JEL - v35 - Mr '97 - p254 [51-250]
LJ - v122 - Mr 15 '97 - p36 [1-50]

Kaplan, Sandra J - *Family Violence*
AJPsych - v154 - F '97 - p280+ [501+]
Choice - v34 - S '96 - p214 [51-250]

Kaplan, Steven - *Indigenous Responses to Western Christianity*
HAHR - v76 - Ag '96 - p619+ [501+]

Kaplan, Steven M - *English-Spanish, Spanish-English Electrical and Computer Engineering Dictionary*
r ARBA - v28 - '97 - p591 [51-250]
r Choice - v34 - O '96 - p252 [51-250]
r SciTech - v20 - S '96 - p53 [51-250]

Kaplan, Victoria - *The A-to-Z Book of Managing People*
BL - v93 - D 1 '96 - p627 [51-250]
BWatch - v18 - Mr '97 - p4 [51-250]
PW - v243 - N 25 '96 - p69 [51-250]

Kaplan, Wendy - *Charles Rennie Mackintosh*
Atl - v278 - S '96 - p113+ [51-250]
BL - v93 - S 1 '96 - p52 [51-250]
Choice - v34 - D '96 - p601 [51-250]
NYRB - v44 - F 20 '97 - p7+ [501+]
NYTBR - v101 - D 8 '96 - p58 [51-250]
Designing Modernity
Art J - v55 - Sum '96 - p86+ [501+]

Kaplan, William - *Bad Judgment*
Beav - v76 - D '96 - p46+ [251-500]
BIC - v25 - S '96 - p28+ [501+]
R&R Bk N - v11 - N '96 - p52 [51-250]

Kaplar, Richard T - *The Government Factor*
JMCQ - v73 - Win '96 - p1000+ [251-500]

Kaple, Deborah A - *Dream of a Red Factory*
EHR - v111 - N '96 - p1354+ [251-500]

Kapleau, Philip - *Awakening to Zen*
BL - v93 - Mr 1 '97 - p1071 [51-250]
LJ - v122 - F 15 '97 - p139 [51-250]
PW - v244 - Ja 27 '97 - p95 [51-250]

Kaplinski, Jaan - *Through the Forest*
Obs - S 29 '96 - p18* [51-250]
TLS - O 18 '96 - p25 [51-250]

Kaplowitz, Neil - *Liver and Biliary Diseases. 2nd Ed.*
SciTech - v20 - S '96 - p36 [51-250]

Kapr, Albert - *Johann Gutenberg: The Man and His Invention*
Choice - v34 - O '96 - p263 [51-250]

Kapral, Raymond - *Chemical Waves and Patterns*
Am Sci - v85 - Ja '97 - p77+ [501+]

Kapteyn, Paul - *The Stateless Market*
JEL - v34 - D '96 - p2039 [51-250]
TLS - S 20 '96 - p13 [501+]

Kaptur, Marcy - *Women of Congress*
r BL - v93 - F 15 '97 - p1043 [251-500]
Choice - v34 - Mr '97 - p1240 [51-250]

Kapur, Anil - *Airport Infrastructure*
JEL - v34 - S '96 - p1501+ [51-250]

Kapur, Basant K - *Communitarian Ethics and Economics*
Econ J - v107 - Ja '97 - p264 [251-500]

Kaput, Jim - *Research in Collegiate Mathematics Education*
SciTech - v20 - D '96 - p4 [51-250]

Karageorghis, Vassos - *The Coroplastic Art of Ancient Cyprus. Vol. 4*
AJA - v101 - Ja '97 - p174+ [501+]

Karalis, Edward - *Digital Design Principles and Computer Architecture*
SciTech - v20 - D '96 - p78 [51-250]

Karas, G Brian - *Home on the Bayou (Illus. by G Brian Karas)*
c BL - v93 - S 15 '96 - p247 [51-250]
c CBRS - v25 - Win '97 - p63 [51-250]
c CCB-B - v50 - Ja '97 - p176 [51-250]
c HB - v73 - Ja '97 - p52 [51-250]
c HB Guide - v8 - Spr '97 - p34 [51-250]
c NYTBR - v101 - N 10 '96 - p42 [51-250]
c SLJ - v42 - O '96 - p100 [51-250]
I Know an Old Lady (Illus. by G Brian Karas)
c RT - v50 - O '96 - p133 [1-50]

Karas, Nick - *Brook Trout*
BL - v93 - Ap 1 '97 - p1273 [51-250]
KR - v65 - F 1 '97 - p199+ [251-500]
PW - v244 - Mr 31 '97 - p56+ [51-250]

Karas, Phyllis - *Cry Baby*
y Kliatt - v31 - Mr '97 - p8+ [51-250]
y PW - v243 - N 18 '96 - p77 [51-250]

Karatzas, Ioannis - *Lectures on the Mathematics of Finance*
SciTech - v21 - Mr '97 - p2 [1-50]

Kara-Vasyleva, Tat'iana - *Ukrains'ka Vyshyvka*
BL - v93 - N 15 '96 - p577 [1-50]

Karay, Felicja - *Death Comes in Yellow*
Choice - v34 - F '97 - p1019 [51-250]

Karayiannis, Vasilios - *Maxime Le Confesseur: Essence Et Energies De Dieu*
Theol St - v57 - S '96 - p531+ [501+]

Karch, Steven B - *The Pathology of Drug Abuse. 2nd Ed.*
SciTech - v20 - D '96 - p55 [51-250]

Karcher, Carolyn L - *The First Woman in the Republic*
Legacy - v13 - 2 '96 - p152+ [501+]
NWSA Jnl - v8 - Sum '96 - p157+ [501+]
W&M Q - v53 - O '96 - p847+ [501+]

Kardash, Peter - *Ukraintsi V Sviti. 2nd Ed.*
BL - v93 - N 15 '96 - p577 [1-50]

Kardel, Troels - *Steno: Life, Science, Philosophy*
Isis - v87 - D '96 - p727+ [501+]

Kardell, Caroline Lewis - *Vital Records of Sandwich, Massachusetts to 1885. Vols. 1-3*
r Am Geneal - v71 - Jl '96 - p191+ [251-500]

Karger, Barry L - *High Resolution Separation and Analysis of Biological Macromolecules. Pt. B*
SciTech - v20 - N '96 - p27 [51-250]

Kari, Daven Michael - *Bibliography of Sources in Christianity and the Arts*
r ARBA - v28 - '97 - p547+ [51-250]

Karihaloo, B L - *Mechanics of Transformation Toughening and Related Topics*
SciTech - v20 - S '96 - p49 [51-250]

Karimi-Hakkak, Ahmad - *Recasting Persian Poetry*
Choice - v34 - O '96 - p273 [51-250]
WLT - v70 - Aut '96 - p1021+ [251-500]

Karin, Roberta - *Soundbites*
TES - D 6 '96 - pR5 [251-500]

Kariotis, Manthos - *Oudheteri Zoni*
WLT - v70 - Sum '96 - p739 [251-500]

Karjalainen, E J - *Data Analysis for Hyphenated Techniques*
SciTech - v20 - N '96 - p21 [51-250]

Kark, Ruth - *Yerushalayim Ve-Svivoteyah*
BL - v93 - Mr 1 '97 - p1115 [1-50]

Karl, Frederick R - *George Eliot: Voice of a Century*
NYTBR - v101 - N 17 '96 - p40 [51-250]
PW - v243 - S 9 '96 - p81 [1-50]

Karl, George - *This Game's the Best! So Why Don't They Quit Screwing with It?*
BL - v93 - My 1 '97 - p1474 [51-250]

Karl, Thomas R - *Long-Term Climate Monitoring by the Global Climate Observing System*
SciTech - v20 - N '96 - p20 [51-250]

Karlin, Daniel - *Browning's Hatreds*
VS - v39 - Aut '95 - p118+ [501+]

Karlin, Fred - *Listening to Movies*
FQ - v49 - Fall '95 - p64 [51-250]

Karlin, Nurit - *The Fat Cat Sat on the Mat (Illus. by Nurit Karlin)*
c BL - v93 - S 15 '96 - p253 [51-250]
c CCB-B - v50 - O '96 - p65+ [51-250]
c HB Guide - v8 - Spr '97 - p55 [51-250]
c NYTBR - v101 - Ag 25 '96 - p23 [1-50]
c SLJ - v42 - D '96 - p96+ [51-250]
I See, You Saw (Illus. by Nurit Karlin)
c KR - v65 - My 1 '97 - p723 [51-250]

Karlin, Wayne - *The Other Side of Heaven*
ABR - v17 - Ag '96 - p24 [501+]

Rumors and Stones
BL - v93 - O 1 '96 - p318 [51-250]
BW - v27 - Mr 2 '97 - p6 [501+]
KR - v64 - Ag 15 '96 - p1211+ [251-500]
LJ - v121 - O 15 '96 - p67 [51-250]
Nat - v263 - O 28 '96 - p28+ [501+]
NY - v72 - D 2 '96 - p115 [51-250]

Karlstadt, Andreas Rudolff-Bodenstein Von - *The Essential Carlstadt*
CH - v65 - D '96 - p695+ [501+]
Ren Q - v50 - Spr '97 - p300+ [501+]

Karlstrom, Paul J - *On the Edge of America*
Choice - v34 - My '97 - p1487 [51-250]
LATBR - D 8 '96 - p6 [51-250]

Karman, James - *Robinson Jeffers: Poet of California. Rev. Ed.*
RMR - v50 - 2 '96 - p214+ [501+]

Karmazyn, M - *Myocardial Ischemia*
SciTech - v21 - Mr '97 - p57 [51-250]

Karmi, Ghada - *Jerusalem Today*
TLS - Mr 7 '97 - p8+ [501+]

Karna, Shashi P - *Nonlinear Optical Materials*
SciTech - v20 - S '96 - p15 [51-250]

Karnes, Frances A - *Competitions: Maximizing Your Abilities*
r ARBA - v28 - '97 - p138+ [251-500]

Karney, Robyn - *Burt Lancaster: A Singular Man*
PW - v243 - D 9 '96 - p58 [51-250]

Karnick, Kristine Brunovska - *Classical Hollywood Comedy*
Can Lit - Spr '97 - p221+ [501+]

Karoleff, Brad - *Bust Half Dollar Bibliomania*
r Coin W - v37 - S 30 '96 - p68 [51-250]

Karolides, Nicholas J - *Reader Response in the Classroom*
New Ad - v9 - Fall '96 - p309+ [501+]

Karolyi, Bela - *Feel No Fear*
Aethlon - v13 - Fall '95 - p156+ [251-500]

Karolyi, Otto - *Modern American Music*
Choice - v34 - Mr '97 - p1172 [51-250]

Karon, Jan - *At Home in Mitford (McDonough). Audio Version*
y Kliatt - v31 - Mr '97 - p39 [51-250]
At Home in Mitford (Karon). Audio Version
y Kliatt - v31 - Mr '97 - p39 [51-250]
A Light in the Window (McDonough). Audio Version
y Kliatt - v31 - Mr '97 - p39 [51-250]
Out to Canaan
BL - v93 - Ap 1 '97 - p1268+ [51-250]
KR - v65 - Mr 15 '97 - p406+ [251-500]
LJ - v122 - My 1 '97 - p140 [51-250]
PW - v244 - Ap 14 '97 - p52+ [51-250]
These High, Green Hills
BW - v26 - N 10 '96 - p10 [251-500]
PW - v244 - Mr 24 '97 - p81 [1-50]

Karp, Cheryl L - *Treatment Strategies for Abused Children*
SciTech - v20 - S '96 - p41 [51-250]

Karp, David A - *Speaking of Sadness*
AJS - v102 - S '96 - p652+ [501+]
CS - v26 - Ja '97 - p109+ [501+]

Karp, Rashelle S - *Part-Time Public Relations with Full-Time Results*
CLW - v66 - Je '96 - p43 [51-250]
LAR - v98 - Mr '96 - p164 [1-50]
Plays for Children and Young Adults. 1st Suppl.
r ARBA - v28 - '97 - p430 [51-250]
r VOYA - v19 - D '96 - p300 [51-250]

Karp, Regina Cowen - *Central and Eastern Europe*
Parameters - v27 - Spr '97 - p169+ [501+]

Karpel, Bernard - *Arts in America. Vols. 1-4*
r ASInt - v34 - O '96 - p9 [51-250]

Karpf, Anne - *The War After*
TES - D 27 '96 - p16 [1-50]
TLS - Ag 30 '96 - p36 [501+]

Karpf, Ronald J - *The Ultimate Sin*
Choice - v34 - O '96 - p364 [51-250]

Karpiski, Jakub - *Poland since 1944*
Historian - v58 - Sum '96 - p906+ [251-500]

Karr, Kathleen - *Go West, Young Women!*
c HB Guide - v7 - Fall '96 - p293 [51-250]
y Kliatt - v31 - My '97 - p8+ [51-250]
In the Kaiser's Clutch
c Ch BWatch - v6 - N '96 - p3 [51-250]
Phoebe's Folly
c BL - v93 - D 1 '96 - p654+ [51-250]
c HB Guide - v8 - Spr '97 - p69 [51-250]
y Kliatt - v31 - My '97 - p8+ [51-250]
Spy in the Sky (Illus. by Thomas F Yezerski)
c KR - v65 - Mr 15 '97 - p463+ [51-250]

Karr, Mary - *The Liar's Club*
Obs - N 24 '96 - p18* [51-250]
South R - v33 - Win '97 - p150+ [501+]

Karras, Alan L - *Sojourners in the Sun*
AHR - v101 - D '96 - p1655 [501+]

Karras, Ruth Mazo - *Common Women*
Choice - v34 - N '96 - p518 [51-250]

Karras, Thomas - *A Concise English-Russian Phrase Book*
MLJ - v80 - Win '96 - p557+ [501+]

Karsh, Efraim - *Between War and Peace*
For Aff - v75 - N '96 - p164 [51-250]
MEJ - v50 - Sum '96 - p451 [51-250]
R&R Bk N - v11 - N '96 - p14 [51-250]

Karsh, Yousuf - *Karsh: A Sixty-Year Retrospective*
Ent W - S 13 '96 - p126 [51-250]
LATBR - D 8 '96 - p12 [51-250]

Karstedt, Mark J - *Chuffs: A Quitter's Guide to Smoking*
BWatch - v17 - D '96 - p4 [51-250]

Die Kartause Aggsbach 1995
CH - v66 - Mr '97 - p191 [251-500]

Kartiganer, Donald M - *Faulkner and the Artist*
AL - v69 - Mr '97 - p252 [51-250]

Kartographisches Institut Bertelsmann - *The Book of the World*
r   Choice - v34 - S '96 - p93 [251-500]
r   Ent W - Mr 21 '97 - p68 [51-250]
r   LATBR - D 8 '96 - p35 [51-250]
r   LJ - v122 - Ap 15 '97 - p37 [51-250]
r   RQ - v36 - Win '96 - p289+ [501+]

Kartsatos, Athanassios G - *Theory and Applications of Nonlinear Operators of Accretive and Monotone Type*
SIAM Rev - v39 - Mr '97 - p177 [51-250]

Karttunen, Hannu - *Fundamental Astronomy. 2nd Ed.*
S&T - v92 - S '96 - p54 [51-250]

Karvelis, Albert - *Proceedings of the 7th ASME International Transmission and Gearing Committee*
SciTech - v21 - Mr '97 - p85 [51-250]

Karvoskaia, Natacha - *Dounia (Illus. by Natacha Karvoskaia)*
c   RT - v50 - F '97 - p425 [51-250]

Karvoski, Ed, Jr. - *A Funny Time to Be Gay*
LJ - v122 - Ja '97 - p98+ [51-250]

Karwatka, Dennis - *Technology's Past*
Choice - v34 - O '96 - p301 [51-250]
yr   SLJ - v42 - Ag '96 - p182 [51-250]

Kasdorf, Julia - *Sleeping Preacher*
Shen - v46 - Win '96 - p118+ [501+]

Kaser-Leisibach, Ursula - *Kein Einig Volk*
Ger Q - v69 - Sum '96 - p359+ [501+]

Kasher, Steven - *The Civil Rights Movement*
B Ent - v27 - F '97 - p215 [1-50]
CC - v114 - F 5 '97 - p171+ [251-500]
LJ - v122 - Ja '97 - p93 [51-250]
VV - v41 - D 17 '96 - p51 [501+]

Kashner, Sam - *Hollywood Kryptonite*
BL - v93 - O 1 '96 - p315 [51-250]
KR - v64 - S 1 '96 - p1297 [251-500]
LJ - v121 - O 1 '96 - p80 [51-250]
PW - v243 - S 9 '96 - p73 [51-250]

Kasischke, Laura - *Housekeeping in a Dream*
MQR - v35 - Fall '96 - p734+ [501+]
Suspicious River
LATBR - Ag 4 '96 - p6 [501+]
Obs - D 22 '96 - p17* [51-250]
TLS - Ja 17 '97 - p20 [501+]

Kasl, Charlotte Sophia - *A Home for the Heart*
PW - v244 - Ap 21 '97 - p56+ [51-250]

Kaslow, Florence - *Projective Genogramming*
Adoles - v32 - Spr '97 - p247 [51-250]

Kaslyn, Robert J - *Communion with the Church and the Code of Canon Law*
Theol St - v57 - D '96 - p780+ [251-500]

Kasmir, Sharryn - *The Myth of Mondragon*
Choice - v34 - Ja '97 - p884 [51-250]
R&R Bk N - v11 - N '96 - p32 [51-250]

Kaspit, Ben - *Ha-Hitabdut: Miflagah Mevateret Al Shilton*
BL - v93 - Mr 1 '97 - p1115 [1-50]

Kass, Ilana - *The Deadly Embrace*
Choice - v34 - Ap '97 - p1414 [51-250]

Kassel, Marleen - *Tokugawa Confucian Education*
R&R Bk N - v12 - F '97 - p3 [51-250]

Kassirer, Sue - *Hidden Spirits (Illus. by Judy Larson)*
c   HB Guide - v7 - Fall '96 - p358 [51-250]
c   SLJ - v42 - Ag '96 - p138 [51-250]

Kastfelt, Niels - *Religion and Politics in Nigeria*
J Ch St - v38 - Sum '96 - p659+ [251-500]
JR - v77 - Ja '97 - p187+ [501+]

Kasties, Bert - *Walter Hasenclever: Eine Biographie Der Deutschen Moderne*
MLR - v92 - Ja '97 - p247+ [501+]

Kastner, Laura S - *The Seven-Year Stretch*
LJ - v122 - My 1 '97 - p134 [51-250]
PW - v244 - F 17 '97 - p215 [51-250]

Kasza, Gregory J - *The Conscription Society*
AJS - v102 - S '96 - p611+ [501+]

Kasza, Keiko - *Don't Laugh, Joe! (Illus. by Keiko Kasza)*
c   KR - v65 - Ap 1 '97 - p558+ [51-250]
c   PW - v244 - Mr 17 '97 - p83 [51-250]
Grandpa Toad's Secrets (Illus. by Keiko Kasza)
c   RT - v50 - O '96 - p157 [51-250]

Katahn, Martin - *How to Quit Smoking without Gaining Weight*
PW - v243 - O 21 '96 - p78 [1-50]

Katcher, Philip - *Great Gambles of the Civil War*
PW - v243 - S 16 '96 - p65 [51-250]

Katchor, Ben - *Julius Knipl, Real Estate Photographer*
NY - v72 - N 25 '96 - p117 [51-250]
NYTBR - v101 - D 22 '96 - p4 [501+]
NYTLa - v146 - O 1 '96 - pC15 [501+]

Kater, Michael H - *The Twisted Muse*
LJ - v122 - Ja '97 - p101 [51-250]
PW - v243 - N 11 '96 - p63 [51-250]

Kateregga, Badru D - *A Muslim and a Christian in Dialogue*
LJ - v122 - My 1 '97 - p110 [51-250]
PW - v244 - F 10 '97 - p79 [51-250]

Kates, Erica - *On the Couch*
BL - v93 - Ja '97 - p809 [51-250]
KR - v64 - D 15 '96 - p1758 [251-500]
PW - v243 - D 16 '96 - p44 [51-250]

Kates, Gary - *Monsieur D'Eon Is a Woman*
AHR - v101 - D '96 - p1554+ [501+]

Kathelyn, Dina - *Le Nez De Marmouset*
c   BL - v93 - N 1 '96 - p500 [1-50]

Kathuria, Sanjay - *Competing through Technology and Manufacturing*
JEL - v35 - Mr '97 - p249 [51-250]

Katihabwa, Sebastien - *Magume, Ou Les Ombres Du Sentier*
FR - v70 - O '96 - p144+ [251-500]

Kato, Pamela M - *Handbook of Diversity Issues in Health Psychology*
SciTech - v20 - D '96 - p37 [51-250]

Katoh, Amy Sylvester - *Blue and White Japan*
BL - v93 - S 1 '96 - p53 [51-250]

Katz, Avner - *The Little Pickpocket (Illus. by Avner Katz)*
c   Ch BWatch - v6 - My '96 - p4 [1-50]
c   HB Guide - v7 - Fall '96 - p262 [51-250]

Katz, Bernard S - *Biographical Dictionary of the United States Secretaries of the Treasury 1789-1995*
r   ARBA - v28 - '97 - p265+ [251-500]
r   Choice - v34 - My '97 - p1472 [51-250]

Katz, Bobbi - *Germs! Germs! Germs! (Illus. by Steve Bjorkman)*
c   BL - v93 - F 1 '97 - p950 [51-250]
Truck Talk (Illus. by Bobbi Katz)
c   BL - v93 - Ap 1 '97 - p1335 [51-250]
c   KR - v65 - F 15 '97 - p301 [51-250]
c   SLJ - v43 - Mr '97 - p177 [51-250]

Katz, Burton S - *Justice Overruled*
PW - v244 - My 5 '97 - p185 [51-250]

Katz, David S - *The Jews in the History of England 1485-1850*
EHR - v112 - Ap '97 - p474+ [501+]

Katz, Donald - *Just Do It*
Aethlon - v13 - Fall '95 - p155+ [251-500]

Katz, Elena D - *High Performance Liquid Chromatography*
SciTech - v20 - S '96 - p60 [51-250]

Katz, Ellis - *Federalism and Rights*
Choice - v34 - N '96 - p534 [51-250]

Katz, Fred E - *Dr. Shivers' Carnival of Terror*
c   Ch BWatch - v6 - Jl '96 - p1 [51-250]

Katz, J - *Virtuous Reality*
AJR - v19 - Ap '97 - p55 [251-500]
BL - v93 - Ja '97 - p792 [51-250]
BW - v27 - Ja 19 '97 - p6 [501+]
KR - v64 - N 15 '96 - p1654 [251-500]
LATBR - F 2 '97 - p3 [501+]
LJ - v121 - N 15 '96 - p69 [51-250]
NYTBR - v102 - F 23 '97 - p17 [51-250]
PW - v243 - D 2 '96 - p45 [51-250]

Katz, Jane B - *We Rode the Wind*
c   Ch BWatch - v6 - Jl '96 - p7 [51-250]
c   HB Guide - v7 - Fall '96 - p391 [51-250]

Katz, Jon - *The Father's Club*
KR - v64 - My 1 '96 - p644 [51-250]

Katz, Jonathan Ned - *The Invention of Heterosexuality*
JMF - v58 - N '96 - p1041 [251-500]

Katz, Judith - *The Escape Artist*
BL - v93 - My 1 '97 - p1479+ [51-250]
PW - v244 - Ap 21 '97 - p62+ [51-250]

Katz, Leo - *Ill-Gotten Gains*
JEL - v34 - D '96 - p2080+ [51-250]

Katz, Louise - *Myfanwy's Demon*
y   Magpies - v11 - S '96 - p37 [51-250]

Katz, Marshall P - *Palissy Ware*
BM - v139 - Ja '97 - p47+ [501+]
Ceram Mo - v44 - O '96 - p24 [51-250]

Katz, Michael - *Environmental Management Tools on the Internet*
Choice - v34 - Mr '97 - p1191 [51-250]
SciTech - v20 - D '96 - p2 [1-50]

Katz, Michael B - *Improving Poor People*
AAPSS-A - v546 - Jl '96 - p171+ [501+]
AHR - v101 - O '96 - p1294+ [501+]
CS - v25 - S '96 - p616+ [501+]
Historian - v59 - Fall '96 - p148+ [501+]
Pub Hist - v19 - Win '97 - p106+ [501+]
Soc Ser R - v70 - S '96 - p500 [51-250]
SSQ - v77 - S '96 - p714+ [501+]
In the Shadow of the Poorhouse
Trib Bks - Ja 19 '97 - p8 [1-50]

Katz, Michael Jay - *Buckeye Legends*
J Am Cult - v18 - Win '95 - p111 [51-250]

Katz, Nathan - *The Last Jews of Cochin*
JAAR - v64 - Sum '96 - p435+ [501+]

Katz, Richard S - *Italian Politics*
Choice - v34 - O '96 - p354 [51-250]

Katz, Sandor - *Anne Frank*
c   HB Guide - v7 - Fall '96 - p380 [51-250]
Whoopi Goldberg
c   Ch BWatch - v7 - Ja '97 - p4 [1-50]
c   HB Guide - v8 - Spr '97 - p158 [51-250]
c   SLJ - v43 - Ja '97 - p127+ [51-250]

Katz, Stephen - *Disciplining Old Age*
AB - v99 - Mr 31 '97 - p1050+ [501+]
R&R Bk N - v11 - N '96 - p41 [51-250]
Socio R - v45 - My '97 - p328+ [501+]

Katz, Steven T - *The Holocaust in Historical Context. Vol. 1*
Hist & T - v35 - 3 '96 - p375+ [501+]

Katz, Vincent - *Boulevard Transportation*
PW - v243 - D 30 '96 - p62 [1-50]

Katz, Welwyn Wilton - *False Face*
c   Quill & Q - v62 - My '96 - p13 [501+]
Out of the Dark (Illus. by Martin Springett)
y   Can CL - v22 - Sum '96 - p81+ [501+]
y   CBRS - v25 - Ja '97 - p57+ [51-250]
c   Ch BWatch - v7 - F '97 - p4 [51-250]
c   HB - v72 - N '96 - p737 [51-250]
c   HB Guide - v8 - Spr '97 - p69 [51-250]
y   SLJ - v42 - S '96 - p227 [51-250]
y   VOYA - v19 - D '96 - p270+ [51-250]
Time Ghost
y   Can CL - v22 - Sum '96 - p89+ [501+]

Katz, William A - *Dahl's History of the Book. 3rd Ed.*
LR - v45 - 7 '96 - p58+ [501+]

Katz, William Loren - *Black Legacy*
y   BL - v93 - F 15 '97 - p1012 [51-250]
y   CCB-B - v50 - Ap '97 - p287 [51-250]

Katzenbach, John - *State of Mind*
BL - v93 - My 15 '97 - p1541 [51-250]

Katzenstein, Peter J - *Cultural Norms and National Security*
Choice - v34 - Mr '97 - p1200 [51-250]
For Aff - v75 - S '96 - p157+ [51-250]
The Culture of National Security
For Aff - v76 - My '97 - p123+ [51-250]
R&R Bk N - v12 - F '97 - p100 [51-250]

Katznelson, Ira - *Liberalism's Crooked Circle*
Choice - v34 - N '96 - p535 [51-250]
For Aff - v75 - S '96 - p126+ [501+]
Marxism and the City
J Urban H - v23 - Ja '97 - p221+ [501+]

Katzner, Kenneth - *The Languages of the World. New Ed.*
r   ARBA - v28 - '97 - p375 [51-250]

Kaufer, David S - *Rhetoric and the Arts of Design*
Choice - v34 - O '96 - p271 [51-250]

Kauffman, Christopher J - *Ministry and Meaning*
AHR - v101 - O '96 - p1268+ [501+]
CH - v66 - Mr '97 - p171+ [501+]
CHR - v83 - Ja '97 - p135+ [501+]

Kauffman, Janet - *Characters on the Loose*
BL - v93 - My 1 '97 - p1479 [251-500]
KR - v65 - Mr 15 '97 - p407 [251-500]
PW - v244 - Mr 31 '97 - p61+ [51-250]

Kauffman, Louis H - *The Interface of Knots and Physics*
SIAM Rev - v38 - S '96 - p545 [1-50]

Kauffman, Ruth - *The Latter Day Saints*
  Historian - v58 - Sum '96 - p865+ [501+]
Kauffman, Stuart - *At Home in the Universe*
  BIC - v25 - O '96 - p35+ [501+]
  Nature - v385 - Ja 2 '97 - p36 [1-50]
  New Sci - v152 - D 21 '96 - p72 [1-50]
  NYTBR - v102 - Ja 12 '97 - p32 [51-250]
  VLS - S '96 - p14+ [501+]
Kaufman, Allan - *Technology Projects for the Classroom*
  y SB - v33 - Mr '97 - p46 [51-250]
Kaufman, Allen - *Managers vs. Owners*
  JEL - v34 - S '96 - p1377+ [501+]
Kaufman, Barry Neil - *Out-Smarting Your Karma and Other Preordained Conditions*
  PW - v243 - S 2 '96 - p121 [51-250]
Kaufman, Bob - *Cranial Guitar*
  ABR - v18 - D '96 - p11 [501+]
  Bl S - v26 - Fall '96 - p104 [1-50]
  BWatch - v17 - D '96 - p7 [51-250]
Kaufman, Burton I - *The Arab Middle East and the United States*
  Choice - v34 - F '97 - p1032 [51-250]
  For Aff - v75 - S '96 - p156 [51-250]
  MEJ - v50 - Aut '96 - p610+ [501+]
Kaufman, Gerald - *How to Be a Minister*
  NS - v126 - F 7 '97 - p44+ [501+]
  Obs - F 2 '97 - p15* [501+]
  TES - F 28 '97 - p8* [501+]
Kaufman, Gordon D - *God, Mystery, Diversity*
  Rel St Rev - v23 - Ja '97 - p47 [51-250]
Kaufman, Jonathan - *A Hole in the Heart of the World*
  y BL - v93 - D 1 '96 - p640 [51-250]
  BW - v27 - F 2 '97 - p4+ [501+]
  KR - v64 - O 15 '96 - p1512 [251-500]
  LJ - v121 - D '96 - p116 [51-250]
  NL - v80 - F 24 '97 - p17+ [501+]
  PW - v243 - O 21 '96 - p60 [51-250]
  WSJ-Cent - v99 - Mr 6 '97 - pA12 [501+]
Kaufman, Kenn - *Kingbird Highway*
  y BL - v93 - My 15 '97 - p1549 [51-250]
  KR - v65 - My 1 '97 - p697 [251-500]
  PW - v244 - My 12 '97 - p71 [51-250]
  Lives of North American Birds
  r LJ - v122 - Ja '97 - p88 [51-250]
  Utne R - Ja '97 - p96 [1-50]
Kaufman, Kenneth C - *Dred Scott's Advocate*
  LJ - v121 - O 15 '96 - p67 [51-250]
Kaufman, Louis - *Moe Berg: Athlete, Scholar, Spy*
  Aethlon - v13 - Fall '95 - p175+ [501+]
Kaufman, Perry - *Smarter Trading*
  BusLR - v21 - 3 '96 - p247 [51-250]
Kaufman, Peter Iver - *Church, Book, and Bishop*
  Choice - v34 - F '97 - p980 [51-250]
  CHR - v83 - Ja '97 - p167 [51-250]
  Prayer, Despair, and Drama
  CC - v113 - N 13 '96 - p1124 [51-250]
  Rel St Rev - v23 - Ap '97 - p191 [51-250]
  TLS - F 14 '97 - p24 [251-500]
Kaufman, Polly Welts - *National Parks and the Woman's Voice*
  BW - v26 - S 29 '96 - p13 [51-250]
  Choice - v34 - D '96 - p633+ [51-250]
  Pub Hist - v19 - Win '97 - p84+ [501+]
  TLS - Mr 21 '97 - p13 [251-500]
Kaufman, Robert Gordon - *Arms Control during the Pre-Nuclear Era*
  JIH - v27 - Aut '96 - p356+ [501+]
Kaufman, Shirley - *Roots in the Air*
  Wom R Bks - v14 - O '96 - p15+ [501+]
Kaufmann, Doris - *Aufklarung, Burgerliche Selbsterfahrung Und Die Erfindung Der Psychiatrie In Deutschland 1770-1850*
  Choice - v34 - D '96 - p569 [1-50]
Kaufmann, J E - *The Sleeping Giant*
  Choice - v34 - F '97 - p1025 [51-250]
  R&R Bk N - v11 - D '96 - p72 [51-250]
Kaufmann, Johannes - *Parasitic Infections of Domestic Animals*
  r SciTech - v20 - S '96 - p45 [51-250]
Kaufmann, Walter - *The Future of the Humanities*
  ES - v27 - Sum '96 - p145+ [501+]
Kaufmann, Wanda Ostrowska - *The Anthropology of Wisdom Literature*
  R&R Bk N - v12 - F '97 - p80 [51-250]
Kaufmann, William J, III - *Universe. 4th Ed.*
  S&T - v92 - S '96 - p53 [51-250]
Kaufmann, Yogi - *City at Sea*
  APH - v43 - Win '96 - p59+ [251-500]
Kauppi, Niilo - *The Making of an Avant Garde*
  Lon R Bks - v18 - D 12 '96 - p5+ [501+]

Kauranen, Anja - *Pelon Maantiede*
  WLT - v70 - Sum '96 - p733 [251-500]
Kausler, Donald H - *The Graying of America*
  r ARBA - v28 - '97 - p304 [51-250]
  r Choice - v34 - Ja '97 - p770 [51-250]
Kautz, Steven - *Liberalism and Community*
  Ethics - v107 - Ja '97 - p390+ [51-250]
  RP - v58 - Fall '96 - p809+ [501+]
  WSJ-MW - v77 - S 26 '96 - pA10 [51-250]
Kavaler-Adler, Susan - *The Compulsion to Create*
  Signs - v22 - Win '97 - p469+ [501+]
  The Creative Mystique
  BL - v93 - S 15 '96 - p181 [51-250]
  Choice - v34 - F '97 - p1040 [51-250]
Kavanagh, Gaynor - *A Bibliography for History, History Curatorship and Museums*
  r Choice - v34 - D '96 - p590 [51-250]
  r R&R Bk N - v11 - N '96 - p9 [51-250]
  Museums and the First World War
  J Mil H - v61 - Ja '97 - p181+ [251-500]
Kavanagh, Julie - *Secret Muses*
  Dance - v71 - F '97 - p122+ [501+]
  Econ - v342 - Mr 15 '97 - p15* [501+]
  KR - v65 - Ap 1 '97 - p524 [251-500]
  Obs - N 24 '96 - p15* [501+]
  PW - v244 - Ap 21 '97 - p55 [51-250]
  Spec - v277 - N 9 '96 - p53 [501+]
  Spec - v277 - N 16 '96 - p43 [1-50]
  Spec - v277 - N 23 '96 - p44 [51-250]
  TLS - N 22 '96 - p19 [501+]
  WSJ-Cent - v99 - My 15 '97 - pA21 [501+]
Kavanagh, Patrick - *Gaff Topsails*
  BIC - v25 - D '96 - p41 [251-500]
  Quill & Q - v63 - F '97 - p47 [251-500]
Kavanagh, Peter - *The Little Prince and the Great Treasure Hunt*
  c Bks Keeps - v100 - S '96 - p9 [51-250]
  c Sch Lib - v44 - Ag '96 - p99 [51-250]
Kavanagh, Thomas M - *Chance, Culture and the Literary Text*
  FR - v70 - Mr '97 - p592+ [501+]
  Esthetics of the Moment
  Choice - v34 - My '97 - p1486 [51-250]
Kavanagh, Thomas W - *Comanche Political History*
  Choice - v34 - D '96 - p676 [51-250]
Kavanaugh, John F - *The Word Encountered*
  Am - v175 - N 2 '96 - p32 [51-250]
Kavanaugh, Robert D - *Emotion: Interdisciplinary Perspectives*
  A J Psy - v110 - Spr '97 - p137+ [501+]
Kavasch, E Barrie - *A Student's Guide to Native American Genealogy*
  yr ARBA - v28 - '97 - p168 [51-250]
  y Ch BWatch - v6 - S '96 - p3 [51-250]
  R&R Bk N - v11 - D '96 - p12 [51-250]
Kawabata, Yasunari - *Palm-of-the-Hand Stories*
  LATBR - N 17 '96 - p14 [51-250]
  NYTBR - v102 - Ja 5 '97 - p28 [1-50]
  Thousand Cranes
  NYTBR - v102 - Ja 5 '97 - p28 [51-250]
  Trib Bks - F 2 '97 - p8 [1-50]
Kawar, Amal - *Daughters of Palestine*
  MEJ - v51 - Spr '97 - p290+ [501+]
  R&R Bk N - v12 - F '97 - p54 [51-250]
  Wom R Bks - v14 - Ja '97 - p14+ [501+]
Kaxiras, Efthimios - *Materials Theory, Simulations, and Parallel Algorithms*
  SciTech - v20 - N '96 - p62 [51-250]
Kay, Brian K - *Phage Display of Peptides and Proteins*
  SciTech - v21 - Mr '97 - p43 [51-250]
Kay, J A - *The Business of Economics*
  BL - v93 - My 15 '97 - p1548 [51-250]
  Econ - v341 - N 16 '96 - p12* [501+]
  Foundations of Corporate Success
  Econ J - v106 - N '96 - p1780+ [501+]
Kay, Jane Holtz - *Asphalt Nation*
  BL - v93 - Mr 15 '97 - p1208 [51-250]
  BW - v27 - Ap 6 '97 - p3 [501+]
  KR - v65 - F 1 '97 - p200 [251-500]
  PW - v244 - Ja 27 '97 - p85 [51-250]
Kay, Margarita Artschwager - *Healing with Plants in the American and Mexican West*
  Bloom Rev - v16 - N '96 - p14 [51-250]
  BWatch - v17 - N '96 - p3 [51-250]
  Choice - v34 - Ja '97 - p820 [51-250]
  R&R Bk N - v11 - D '96 - p70 [51-250]

Kay, Marvin L Michael - *Slavery in North Carolina 1748-1775*
  AHR - v102 - F '97 - p190 [501+]
  Historian - v59 - Fall '96 - p126 [51-250]
  JIH - v27 - Spr '97 - p710+ [501+]
  JSH - v62 - N '96 - p793+ [501+]
  W&M Q - v53 - Jl '96 - p664+ [501+]
Kay, Philip - *Out with It*
  y BL - v93 - My 1 '97 - p1502 [1-50]
  y VOYA - v19 - F '97 - p345 [251-500]
Kay, Richard - *Dante's Christian Astrology*
  MLR - v91 - Jl '96 - p749+ [501+]
  Specu - v72 - Ja '97 - p185+ [501+]
Kay, Sarah - *The Chansons De Geste in the Age of Romance*
  Choice - v34 - S '96 - p133 [51-250]
  MLR - v92 - Ja '97 - p185 [251-500]
  Framing Medieval Bodies
  EHR - v112 - F '97 - p176 [251-500]
Kay, W D - *Can Democracies Fly in Space?*
  APSR - v90 - S '96 - p653 [501+]
Kaye, Barbara - *The Company We Kept*
  BC - v44 - Win '95 - p480 [1-50]
  Second Impression
  BC - v44 - Win '95 - p480+ [251-500]
Kaye, Barry - *Die Rich*
  PW - v244 - Ap 21 '97 - p69 [1-50]
Kaye, Elaine - *Mansfield College Oxford*
  CR - v269 - O '96 - p219+ [501+]
Kaye, Geraldine - *Someone Else's Baby*
  y Kliatt - v31 - My '97 - p8 [51-250]
Kaye, Les - *Zen at Work*
  BL - v93 - F 1 '97 - p909 [51-250]
  LJ - v122 - F 15 '97 - p144 [51-250]
  PW - v243 - D 2 '96 - p52 [51-250]
Kaye, Marilyn - *Jill's Happy Un-Birthday*
  c PW - v243 - D 2 '96 - p61 [51-250]
Kaynak, Erdener - *International Business Teaching*
  JEL - v34 - D '96 - p2090 [51-250]
Kaysen, Carl - *The American Corporation Today*
  BL - v93 - D 1 '96 - p626 [51-250]
  Choice - v34 - Mr '97 - p1202+ [51-250]
Kazan, Fayad E - *Mass Media, Modernity, and Development*
  JC - v46 - Aut '96 - p177+ [501+]
Kazantzakis, Nikos - *Zorba the Greek (Guidall). Audio Version*
  y Kliatt - v30 - S '96 - p55 [51-250]
Kazdin, Alan E - *Methodological Issues and Strategies in Clinical Research*
  AJCH - v39 - Jl '96 - p73+ [501+]
Kazez, Daniel - *The Rhythm Book. 2nd Ed.*
  Am MT - v46 - O '96 - p51+ [501+]
Kazin, Alfred - *An American Procession*
  BW - v26 - N 24 '96 - p12 [51-250]
  A Lifetime Burning in Every Moment
  LATBR - My 26 '96 - p11 [51-250]
  NYTBR - v101 - D 8 '96 - p88 [1-50]
  Writing Was Everything
  J Am St - v30 - Ag '96 - p326+ [251-500]
Kazin, Michael - *The Populist Persuasion*
  AHR - v101 - O '96 - p1295+ [501+]
  CS - v25 - N '96 - p758+ [501+]
  Soc - v34 - Ja '97 - p92+ [501+]
Kazmierski, Carl R - *John the Baptist: Prophet and Evangelist*
  Rel St Rev - v23 - Ja '97 - p70 [51-250]
Kazovsky, Leonid G - *Optical Fiber Communication Systems*
  SciTech - v21 - Mr '97 - p87 [51-250]
Kealey, Gregory S - *Workers and Canadian History*
  Can Hist R - v78 - Mr '97 - p101+ [501+]
Kealey, Terence - *The Economic Laws of Scientific Research*
  Econ - v340 - S 14 '96 - p10*+ [501+]
  JEL - v34 - D '96 - p2117 [51-250]
  Reason - v28 - F '97 - p64+ [501+]
Keams, Geri - *Grandmother Spider Brings the Sun (Illus. by James Bernardin)*
  c RT - v50 - Mr '97 - p501+ [51-250]
Keane, Fergal - *Letter to Daniel*
  Obs - D 8 '96 - p18* [51-250]
  TES - Mr 14 '97 - p8* [51-250]
  TLS - Ja 17 '97 - p33 [51-250]
  Season of Blood
  y BL - v93 - S 1 '96 - p58+ [51-250]
  BW - v26 - Ag 25 '96 - p9 [501+]
  For Aff - v75 - N '96 - p169 [51-250]
  LATBR - Ag 4 '96 - p3 [501+]
  NYTBR - v101 - Jl 21 '96 - p7 [501+]
  NYTBR - v101 - D 8 '96 - p92 [1-50]

Keane, John - *Reflections on Violence*
NS & S - v9 - My 3 '96 - p37 [1-50]
Tom Paine: A Political Life
HT - v46 - S '96 - p53+ [501+]
NS - v125 - D 20 '96 - p116 [1-50]
Keane, Marc - *Japanese Garden Design*
BL - v93 - Ap 1 '97 - p1274 [51-250]
Keane, Maureen - *What to Eat if You Have Cancer*
LJ - v122 - Ja '97 - p57 [51-250]
LJ - v121 - O 1 '96 - p116 [51-250]
The What to Eat if You Have Cancer Cookbook
BL - v93 - My 15 '97 - p1552 [51-250]
Keane, Patrick J - *Coleridge's Submerged Politics*
RES - v47 - N '96 - p601+ [501+]
Kear, Lynn - *Reincarnation: A Selected Annotated Bibliography*
r Choice - v34 - Mr '97 - p1138 [51-250]
r R&R Bk N - v11 - D '96 - p4 [51-250]
Kearey, Philip - *Global Tectonics*
Nature - v384 - N 7 '96 - p38 [1-50]
The New Penguin Dictionary of Geology
r ARBA - v28 - '97 - p635 [51-250]
Kearfott, R Baker - *Rigorous Global Search*
SciTech - v21 - Mr '97 - p17 [51-250]
Kearney, Michael - *Mortally Wounded*
BL - v93 - S 15 '96 - p181 [51-250]
Kearney, Richard - *Postnationalist Ireland*
Obs - Ja 5 '97 - p18* [501+]
TLS - Ap 11 '97 - p6+ [501+]
Kearney, Robert - *Hole in the Water*
y BL - v93 - F 15 '97 - p1004 [51-250]
KR - v64 - D 15 '96 - p1758 [251-500]
PW - v244 - Ja 20 '97 - p395 [51-250]
Kearney, Robert J - *Within the Wall of Denial*
Readings - v11 - S '96 - p31 [51-250]
Kearns, Gerry - *Urbanising Britain*
J Urban H - v22 - My '96 - p524+ [501+]
Kearns, John T - *Reconceiving Experience*
Choice - v34 - Mr '97 - p1176 [51-250]
R&R Bk N - v11 - D '96 - p1 [51-250]
Kearny, Milo - *Border Cuates*
HAHR - v77 - F '97 - p163+ [251-500]
Kearsley, Susanna - *The Splendour Falls*
Quill & Q - v62 - Jl '96 - p43 [251-500]
Keates, Jonathan - *Purcell: A Biography*
Choice - v34 - Mr '97 - p1172 [51-250]
LJ - v121 - N 1 '96 - p69 [51-250]
PW - v243 - S 9 '96 - p73+ [51-250]
Stendhal
BW - v27 - Ap 13 '97 - p9 [501+]
LJ - v122 - Ap 1 '97 - p92 [51-250]
PW - v244 - F 10 '97 - p72 [51-250]
WSJ-Cent - v99 - Mr 25 '97 - pA16 [501+]
Keating, AnaLouise - *Women Reading, Women Writing*
Choice - v34 - N '96 - p456 [51-250]
Keating, H R F - *Asking Questions*
BL - v93 - F 15 '97 - p1007 [51-250]
KR - v65 - Ja 15 '97 - p98+ [51-250]
PW - v244 - Ja 20 '97 - p397 [51-250]
TLS - N 29 '96 - p23 [251-500]
Crime and Mystery
BW - v26 - D 29 '96 - p12 [51-250]
Keating, Michael - *Nations against the State*
Econ - v339 - My 18 '96 - p5* [501+]
R&R Bk N - v11 - N '96 - p47 [51-250]
Keating, Thomas - *Intimacy with God*
BL - v93 - O 1 '96 - p308 [1-50]
Keating, W Dennis - *Revitalizing Urban Neighborhoods*
Choice - v34 - Ap '97 - p1424 [51-250]
Keats, Ezra Jack - *Peter's Chair (Illus. by Ezra Jack Keats)*
c HB - v73 - Mr '97 - p187 [1-50]
La Silla De Pedro (Illus. by Ezra Jack Keats)
c HB Guide - v7 - Fall '96 - p327 [1-50]
c SLJ - v42 - Ag '96 - p178 [1-50]
The Snowy Day (Illus. by Ezra Jack Keats)
c HB Guide - v7 - Fall '96 - p240 [1-50]
Keats, J Bert - *Statistical Applications in Process Control*
SciTech - v20 - S '96 - p62 [51-250]
Keats, Victor - *Chess among the Jews*
Obs - D 1 '96 - p15* [501+]
Chess: Its Origins
Obs - D 1 '96 - p15* [501+]
Chess, Jews and History
Obs - D 1 '96 - p15* [501+]
Keay, John - *Collins Encyclopaedia of Scotland*
r NGSQ - v84 - S '96 - p225 [51-250]
Empire's End
BL - v93 - My 15 '97 - p1559 [51-250]
KR - v65 - Ap 1 '97 - p525 [251-500]
PW - v244 - Mr 24 '97 - p68 [51-250]

Last Post
Obs - Ap 6 '97 - p18* [501+]
Keay, Wally - *Expedition Guide. 3rd Ed.*
r TES - F 7 '97 - p3* [251-500]
Keays, Sara - *The Black Book*
Spec - v277 - O 12 '96 - p49 [501+]
Kebede, Ashenafi - *Roots of Black Music. 2nd Ed.*
CAY - v17 - Fall '96 - p12 [51-250]
Kechichian, Joseph A - *Oman and the World*
MEJ - v50 - Sum '96 - p435+ [501+]
Keck, David - *Forgetting Whose We Are*
Comw - v124 - Mr 14 '97 - p26+ [501+]
Keckley, Elizabeth - *Behind the Scenes (Jones). Audio Version*
LJ - v122 - F 15 '97 - p174 [51-250]
Kecmanovic, Dusan - *The Mass Psychology of Ethnonationalism*
SciTech - v20 - D '96 - p43 [51-250]
Keddie, Nikki R - *Debating Revolutions*
Hist & T - v35 - 3 '96 - p358+ [501+]
Iran and the Muslim World
AHR - v101 - D '96 - p1591 [501+]
CS - v25 - S '96 - p628+ [501+]
Kedourie, Elie - *Democracy and Arab Political Culture*
JTWS - v13 - Spr '96 - p372+ [501+]
Kee, Howard Clark - *The Cambridge Companion to the Bible*
r BL - v93 - Mr 15 '97 - p1207 [51-250]
LJ - v122 - Ap 1 '97 - p99 [51-250]
PW - v244 - Mr 24 '97 - p75 [51-250]
Removing Anti-Judaism from the Pulpit
CSM - v89 - D 26 '96 - p12 [501+]
Who Are the People of God?
AHR - v101 - O '96 - p1188 [501+]
Theol St - v57 - S '96 - p523+ [501+]
TT - v53 - O '96 - p411+ [501+]
Keech, William R - *Economic Politics*
JEL - v34 - S '96 - p1415 [51-250]
Keefe, James W - *Instruction and the Learning Environment*
NASSP-B - v81 - Ap '97 - p118 [251-500]
Keefe, Terry - *Autobiography and the Existential Self*
Biography - v19 - Fall '96 - p430 [1-50]
Keefer, Janice Kulyk - *The Green Library*
BIC - v26 - F '97 - p17 [501+]
Mac - v109 - S 9 '96 - p52 [501+]
Mac - v109 - D 9 '96 - p64 [1-50]
Quill & Q - v62 - My '96 - p24 [501+]
Keefer, Michael - *Lunar Perspectives*
BIC - v26 - F '97 - p31 [501+]
Quill & Q - v62 - My '96 - p31 [51-250]
Keegan, John - *The Battle for History*
J Mil H - v60 - O '96 - p798+ [251-500]
y Kliatt - v30 - S '96 - p33 [51-250]
Sea H - Aut '96 - p44 [251-500]
Fields of Battle
BW - v26 - Jl 7 '96 - p3+ [501+]
BYTE - v22 - Ja '97 - p147 [51-250]
Choice - v34 - N '96 - p525 [51-250]
Nat R - v48 - S 30 '96 - p64 [501+]
NYTBR - v101 - D 8 '96 - p87 [1-50]
RAH - v25 - Mr '97 - p31+ [501+]
Rapport - v19 - 6 '96 - p27 [251-500]
Who's Who in Military History from 1453 to the Present Day
r J Mil H - v61 - Ja '97 - p150+ [251-500]
Keegan, William F - *The People Who Discovered Columbus*
JTWS - v13 - Fall '96 - p321+ [501+]
Keehn, Amy - *Love and War between the Signs*
LJ - v122 - F 1 '97 - p96 [51-250]
Keehn, J D - *Master Builders of Modern Psychology*
Choice - v34 - S '96 - p215 [51-250]
Keele, Wendy - *Poems of Color*
Am Craft - v56 - Ag '96 - p62 [1-50]
Keeler, Patricia - *Unraveling Fibers*
c LA - v73 - O '96 - p438 [51-250]
Keeley, Lawrence H - *War before Civilization*
For Aff - v75 - N '96 - p150 [51-250]
Nat R - v48 - S 2 '96 - p92+ [501+]
NYTBR - v101 - N 17 '96 - p24+ [51-250]
Keen, Benjamin - *Latin American Civilization. 6th Ed., Rev. and Updated*
Parameters - v26 - Win '96 - p155 [1-50]
Keen, David - *The Benefits of Famine*
RP - v58 - Sum '96 - p664+ [501+]
Keen, Ian - *Knowledge and Secrecy in an Aboriginal Religion*
Am Ethnol - v24 - F '97 - p268+ [501+]

Keen, Mary - *Creating a Garden*
Hort - v94 - Ap '97 - p80 [51-250]
LJ - v122 - Ja '97 - p130 [51-250]
Keen, Maurice - *Nobles, Knights and Men-at-Arms in the Middle Ages*
HT - v47 - F '97 - p60+ [501+]
R&R Bk N - v11 - N '96 - p11 [1-50]
Keen, Peter G W - *Every Manager's Guide to Business Processes*
r ARBA - v28 - '97 - p123+ [251-500]
Keen SF
p SF Chr - v18 - O '96 - p83 [1-50]
Keenan, James F - *The Context of Casuistry*
Rel St Rev - v23 - Ap '97 - p156+ [51-250]
Keenan, Sheila - *More or Less a Mess! (Illus. by Patrick Girouard)*
c BL - v93 - My 1 '97 - p1503+ [51-250]
Scholastic Encyclopedia of Women in the United States
cr BL - v93 - N 15 '96 - p614 [501+]
cr PW - v243 - S 16 '96 - p85 [51-250]
cr SLJ - v43 - F '97 - p130 [51-250]
Keenan, Stella - *Concise Dictionary of Library and Information Science*
r ARBA - v28 - '97 - p237 [51-250]
r Choice - v34 - O '96 - p253 [51-250]
r LQ - v67 - Ap '97 - p180+ [501+]
Keene, Carolyn - *False Friends*
y VOYA - v19 - D '96 - p262 [51-250]
The Lost Locket
c TES - Mr 21 '97 - p9 [501+]
The Slumber Party Secret
c TES - Mr 21 '97 - p9* [501+]
Keene, Donald - *The Blue-Eyed Tarokaja*
Econ - v341 - N 16 '96 - p17*+ [251-500]
NY - v72 - O 7 '96 - p96 [501+]
TranslRevS - v2 - D '96 - p8 [51-250]
Modern Japanese Diaries
Biography - v19 - Fall '96 - p430 [1-50]
WLT - v71 - Win '97 - p228+ [251-500]
Seeds in the Heart
South HR - v30 - Sum '96 - p286+ [501+]
TranslRevS - v1 - My '95 - p11+ [51-250]
Keene, Kerry - *The Babe in Red Stockings*
LJ - v122 - F 1 '97 - p82 [1-50]
Keene, Michael - *Christianity: A Dictionary*
yr Sch Lib - v45 - F '97 - p51 [51-250]
Keens-Douglas, Richardo - *La Diablesse and the Baby (Illus. by Marie Lafrance)*
c Can CL - v22 - Fall '96 - p132+ [501+]
Freedom Child of the Sea (Illus. by Julia Gukova)
c Bks Keeps - Mr '97 - p20 [51-250]
Grandpa's Visit (Illus. by Frances Clancy)
c Ch Bk News - v20 - Win '97 - p29 [51-250]
c Quill & Q - v62 - N '96 - p46 [251-500]
Keep, John L H - *Last of the Empires*
r AHR - v102 - F '97 - p144 [501+]
Russ Rev - v56 - Ja '97 - p143+ [251-500]
Keery, James - *That Stranger, the Blues*
TLS - F 7 '97 - p24 [501+]
Keeshan, Bob - *Alligator in the Basement (Illus. by Kyle Corkum)*
c HB Guide - v7 - Fall '96 - p262 [1-50]
Good Morning, Captain
LJ - v122 - F 15 '97 - p137 [51-250]
PW - v243 - S 9 '96 - p80 [51-250]
Itty Bitty Kitty (Illus. by Jane Maday)
c PW - v244 - Ap 14 '97 - p73+ [51-250]
Keesing's Record of World Events CD-ROM Full Archive 1960-1994. Electronic Media Version
r MEQ - v4 - Mr '97 - p89+ [51-250]
Kefala, Antigone - *Alexia: A Tale for Advanced Children*
c Aust Bk R - Je '96 - p67 [1-50]
c WLT - v70 - Aut '96 - p1037 [51-250]
Kegan, Robert - *In Over Our Heads*
HER - v66 - Fall '96 - p689+ [501+]
Kegel, James A - *North with Lee and Jackson*
J Mil H - v61 - Ja '97 - p167+ [251-500]
Kegg, Maude - *Portage Lake*
CAY - v17 - Win '96 - p11 [51-250]
Kegl, Rosemary - *The Rhetoric of Concealment*
MLR - v92 - Ap '97 - p448+ [501+]
Kehayan, Nina - *Essentially Eggplant*
BWatch - v18 - F '97 - p7 [51-250]
Kehoe, Brendan - *Children and the Internet*
LJ - v122 - F 1 '97 - p102 [1-50]
Kehoe, Louise - *In This Dark House*
NS - v125 - S 20 '96 - p46 [501+]
PW - v244 - F 24 '97 - p88 [1-50]
Spec - v277 - N 2 '96 - p50 [501+]
Spec - v277 - N 30 '96 - p58 [1-50]
TLS - O 4 '96 - p30 [501+]

Kehoe, Patrick J - *Modeling North American Economic Integration*
  JEL - v34 - S '96 - p1428 [51-250]
Kehret, Peg - *Bone Breath and the Vandals (Montbertrand). Audio Version*
  y Kliatt - v31 - Mr '97 - p40 [51-250]
Danger at the Fair
  y Emerg Lib - v24 - S '96 - p27 [1-50]
  c RT - v50 - O '96 - p139 [1-50]
Desert Danger (Montbertrand). Audio Version
  y Kliatt - v31 - My '97 - p36 [51-250]
Earthquake Terror
  c HB Guide - v7 - Fall '96 - p293+ [51-250]
Small Steps
  c BL - v93 - N 1 '96 - p492+ [51-250]
  c BL - v93 - Ap 1 '97 - p1298 [1-50]
  y BL - v93 - Ap 1 '97 - p1308 [1-50]
  c CBRS - v25 - F '97 - p83 [51-250]
  c CCB-B - v50 - N '96 - p100+ [51-250]
  c HB - v73 - Ja '97 - p77 [51-250]
  c HB Guide - v8 - Spr '97 - p158+ [51-250]
  c KR - v64 - O 1 '96 - p1469 [51-250]
  c SLJ - v42 - N '96 - p114 [51-250]
Keighley, Michael - *Atlas of Colorectal Surgery*
  r SciTech - v20 - N '96 - p49 [51-250]
Keillor, Garrison - *Cat, You Better Come Home (Illus. by Steve Johnson)*
  c Magpies - v11 - My '96 - p43 [51-250]
  c RT - v50 - D '96 - p342 [51-250]
  c Sch Lib - v44 - Ag '96 - p99 [51-250]
The Old Man Who Loved Cheese (Illus. by Anne Wilsdorf)
  c HB Guide - v7 - Fall '96 - p262 [51-250]
  c JB - v60 - D '96 - p234+ [251-500]
  c NY - v72 - N 18 '96 - p102 [51-250]
  c Obs - Mr 30 '97 - p17* [51-250]
  c Sch Lib - v45 - F '97 - p19 [51-250]
The Sandy Bottom Orchestra
  c BL - v93 - Ja '97 - p860 [251-500]
  y BL - v93 - Ap 1 '97 - p1292 [1-50]
  c CBRS - v25 - Ja '97 - p58 [51-250]
  y CCB-B - v50 - F '97 - p211 [51-250]
  c HB Guide - v8 - Spr '97 - p69 [51-250]
  y KR - v64 - N 1 '96 - p1601+ [51-250]
  c NYTBR - v102 - Mr 2 '97 - p25 [1-50]
  c PW - v243 - D 2 '96 - p61+ [51-250]
  c SLJ - v43 - Ja '97 - p112 [51-250]
Keillor, Steven J - *This Rebellious House*
  Bks & Cult - v2 - N '96 - p4 [51-250]
  BL - v93 - O 1 '96 - p301 [51-250]
  Ch Today - v40 - N 11 '96 - p59 [501+]
  LJ - v121 - O 15 '96 - p64 [51-250]
Keim, Kevin P - *An Architectural Life*
  NY - v72 - S 30 '96 - p87 [51-250]
Kein, Sybil - *An American South*
  Choice - v34 - Ja '97 - p795 [51-250]
Keister, Douglas - *Fernando's Gift*
  c RT - v50 - F '97 - p426 [51-250]
Keith, Don - *Wizard of the Wind*
  BL - v93 - D 1 '96 - p641 [51-250]
  KR - v64 - N 15 '96 - p1623 [251-500]
  LJ - v121 - N 15 '96 - p88+ [51-250]
  PW - v243 - N 4 '96 - p63 [51-250]
Keith, Jeanette - *Country People in the New South*
  AHR - v101 - D '96 - p1639 [251-500]
  Historian - v59 - Win '97 - p431+ [501+]
  JSH - v62 - N '96 - p830+ [251-500]
Keith, Lois - *What Happened to You?*
  Wom R Bks - v14 - N '96 - p23 [501+]
Keizer, Bert - *Dancing with Mister D*
  BL - v93 - Mr 1 '97 - p1096 [51-250]
  KR - v65 - Ja 15 '97 - p121 [251-500]
  LJ - v122 - Mr 15 '97 - p80 [51-250]
  NS & S - v9 - My 17 '96 - p37 [51-250]
  PW - v244 - Ja 13 '97 - p59 [51-250]
  Spec - v276 - My 11 '96 - p38+ [501+]
  TLS - Ag 2 '96 - p13 [251-500]
Keizer, Gregg - *The Family PC Guide to Homework*
  c LJ - v122 - F 1 '97 - p102 [51-250]
Kekes, John - *Moral Wisdom and Good Lives*
  Theol St - v58 - Mr '97 - p179+ [501+]
Kekewich, Jim - *Spelling Connections*
  c Quill & Q - v62 - O '96 - p50 [51-250]
Keleras, Julius - *Sauja Medaus*
  WLT - v71 - Win '97 - p195 [501+]
Kellaway, Deborah - *The Virago Book of Women Gardeners*
  Hort - v74 - N '96 - p56+ [251-500]
  TES - Ag 23 '96 - p22 [51-250]
Kelle, Udo - *Computer-Aided Qualitative Data Analysis*
  MLJ - v81 - Spr '97 - p134+ [501+]

Kelleher, Michael D - *New Arenas for Violence*
  HR Mag - v42 - Mr '97 - p136 [51-250]
  R&R Bk N - v12 - F '97 - p46 [51-250]
Kelleher, Victor - *Earthsong*
  y JB - v60 - Ag '96 - p165 [251-500]
  y Sch Lib - v44 - Ag '96 - p120 [51-250]
Fire Dancer
  y Aust Bk R - N '96 - p61+ [51-250]
Johnny Wombat (Illus. by Craig Smith)
  c Aust Bk R - Je '96 - p63 [501+]
  c Magpies - v11 - Jl '96 - p25+ [51-250]
Parkland
  y Magpies - v11 - S '96 - p45 [1-50]
Storyman
  Aust Bk R - N '96 - p49 [501+]
Kellein, Sandra - *Gold Oder Rabenschwarz*
  Econ - v341 - O 19 '96 - p16*+ [501+]
Kellen, Vince - *Delphi 2*
  SciTech - v20 - N '96 - p9 [51-250]
Kellenbach, Katharina Von - *Anti-Judaism in Feminist Religious Writings*
  Rel Ed - v91 - Fall '96 - p612 [1-50]
  Theol St - v57 - Mr '96 - p190 [251-500]
Kellenberger, James - *Relationship Morality*
  Ethics - v107 - Ja '97 - p385+ [51-250]
Keller, Barbara G - *The Middle Ages Reconsidered*
  MLR - v92 - Ja '97 - p195+ [251-500]
Keller, Beverly - *The Amazon Papers*
  y BL - v93 - Ja '97 - p844 [251-500]
  y CCB-B - v50 - N '96 - p101 [51-250]
  y HB Guide - v8 - Spr '97 - p81 [51-250]
  y Kliatt - v31 - Ja '97 - p8 [51-250]
  y KR - v64 - Ag 15 '96 - p1237 [51-250]
  y SLJ - v42 - O '96 - p147+ [51-250]
  y VOYA - v19 - D '96 - p271 [51-250]
Keller, Edward A - *Environmental Geology. 7th Ed.*
  SciTech - v20 - N '96 - p24 [51-250]
Keller, Emily - *Margaret Bourke-White: A Photographer's Life*
  y CCB-B - v50 - S '96 - p18 [51-250]
  c Ch BWatch - v6 - Jl '96 - p3 [51-250]
  y HB Guide - v8 - Spr '97 - p138 [51-250]
  c SLJ - v42 - Ag '96 - p156 [51-250]
Keller, Evelyn Fox - *Refiguring Life*
  BioSci - v46 - S '96 - p627+ [501+]
  BWatch - v18 - Mr '97 - p10 [1-50]
  Isis - v88 - Mr '97 - p159+ [501+]
  New Sci - v152 - N 2 '96 - p47 [1-50]
Keller, Gary D - *A Biographical Handbook of Hispanics and United States Film*
  r BL - v93 - Mr 1 '97 - p1183+ [251-500]
Hispanics and United States Film
  Post Script - v16 - Fall '96 - p64+ [501+]
Keller, Holly - *Geraldine First (Illus. by Holly Keller)*
  c HB Guide - v7 - Fall '96 - p262 [51-250]
I Am Angela
  c BL - v93 - My 15 '97 - p1575+ [51-250]
Keller, John T S - *Chirac's Challenge*
  For Aff - v76 - Mr '97 - p187 [51-250]
Keller, Joseph B - *Surveys in Applied Mathematics*
  SIAM Rev - v38 - S '96 - p546 [1-50]
Keller, Kathryn - *Mothers and Work in Popular American Magazines*
  J Am Cult - v18 - Win '95 - p103+ [501+]
Keller, Lynn - *Feminist Measures*
  Can Lit - Win '96 - p173+ [501+]
Keller, Morton - *Regulating a New Society*
  JIH - v27 - Aut '96 - p350+ [501+]
Keller, Nora Okja - *Comfort Woman*
  BL - v93 - Mr 15 '97 - p1226 [51-250]
  KR - v65 - F 1 '97 - p161+ [251-500]
  LATBR - Mr 23 '97 - p9 [501+]
  LJ - v122 - Ja '97 - p146+ [51-250]
  NYTLa - v146 - Mr 25 '97 - pC16 [501+]
  PW - v244 - Ja 6 '97 - p61 [251-500]
  Time - v149 - My 5 '97 - p101+ [501+]
  Trib Bks - Ap 13 '97 - p1+ [501+]
Keller, Olivier - *Prehistoire De La Geometrie*
  Isis - v87 - D '96 - p713+ [501+]
Keller, Rosemary Skinner - *In Our Own Voices*
  CH - v65 - S '96 - p560+ [501+]
  Rel St Rev - v23 - Ja '97 - p91 [51-250]
Keller, Tsipi - *Ha-Navi Me-Rehov Eser*
  BL - v93 - Mr 1 '97 - p1115 [1-50]
Kellerman, Aharon - *Telecommunications and Geography*
  JC - v47 - Win '97 - p136+ [501+]

Kellerman, Faye - *Prayers for the Dead*
  BW - v26 - Ag 18 '96 - p8 [251-500]
  LATBR - S 22 '96 - p8 [51-250]
  NYTBR - v101 - S 8 '96 - p26 [51-250]
  PW - v243 - N 4 '96 - p40 [1-50]
  Rapport - v19 - 6 '96 - p22 [251-500]
Prayers for the Dead (Schirner). Audio Version
  y Kliatt - v31 - My '97 - p43 [51-250]
Kellerman, Frank R - *Introduction to Health Sciences Librarianship*
  LJ - v122 - Ja '97 - p156 [51-250]
Kellerman, Jonathan - *The Clinic*
  y BL - v93 - S 15 '96 - p180 [51-250]
  CSM - v89 - Ja 16 '97 - p14 [51-250]
  CSM - v89 - F 20 '97 - p10 [51-250]
  KR - v64 - O 15 '96 - p1486 [251-500]
  LATBR - F 16 '97 - p10 [251-500]
  LJ - v121 - O 15 '96 - p90 [51-250]
  NYTBR - v102 - F 23 '97 - p16 [51-250]
  TLS - D 20 '96 - p24 [51-250]
  Trib Bks - Ja 19 '97 - p6 [51-250]
The Clinic (Rubinstein). Audio Version
  LJ - v122 - Ap 15 '97 - p136 [51-250]
The Web
  PW - v243 - S 23 '96 - p74 [1-50]
Kellert, Stephen R - *The Biophilia Hypothesis*
  AAAGA - v86 - D '96 - p782+ [501+]
The Value of Life
  Env - v39 - Ja '97 - p27 [51-250]
  Nature - v382 - Ag 15 '96 - p594 [501+]
  PW - v244 - Mr 24 '97 - p81 [1-50]
Kelley, D - *Unrugged Individualism*
  Reason - v28 - Ap '97 - p61+ [501+]
Kelley, David - *The New French Poetry*
  TLS - D 20 '96 - p26 [501+]
  TranslRevS - v2 - D '96 - p4 [1-50]
  TranslRevS - v2 - D '96 - p4 [1-50]
Kelley, Edith Summers - *Weeds*
  NYTBR - v101 - D 29 '96 - p20 [51-250]
  PW - v243 - N 25 '96 - p70 [1-50]
Kelley, Klara Bonsack - *Navajo Sacred Places*
  J Ch St - v38 - Aut '96 - p920+ [251-500]
Kelley, Maria Felicia - *The Choice I Made*
  BWatch - v17 - N '96 - p6 [51-250]
Kelley, Patricia - *Companion to Grief*
  PW - v244 - Mr 24 '97 - p72+ [51-250]
Kelley, Robin D G - *Into the Fire*
  y Ch BWatch - v6 - My '96 - p5 [51-250]
  y HB Guide - v7 - Fall '96 - p386 [51-250]
Kelley, Stephen J - *Standards for Preservation and Rehabilitation*
  SciTech - v20 - S '96 - p52 [51-250]
Kelley, Wyn - *Melville's City*
  Choice - v34 - Ap '97 - p1337 [51-250]
Kelliher, Daniel - *Peasant Power in China*
  Ch Rev Int - v3 - Fall '96 - p463+ [501+]
Kelling, George L - *Fixing Broken Windows*
  Choice - v34 - My '97 - p1584 [51-250]
  KR - v64 - S 15 '96 - p1376 [251-500]
  LJ - v121 - D '96 - p121 [51-250]
  Nat R - v48 - N 11 '96 - p52+ [501+]
  Pub Int - Win '97 - p102+ [501+]
  PW - v243 - S 16 '96 - p60 [51-250]
  TLS - Ja 10 '97 - p9+ [501+]
Managing Squeegeeing
  J Gov Info - v23 - S '96 - p604 [51-250]
Kellner, Bruce - *Donald Windham: A Bio-Bibliography*
  r J Am Cult - v19 - Sum '96 - p150 [251-500]
Kellner, Douglas - *Media Culture*
  QJS - v82 - Ag '96 - p308+ [501+]
Kellner, Mark - *God on the Internet*
  CBR - v14 - N '96 - p35 [1-50]
Kellogg, Jefferson - *Sources for American Studies*
  r ASInt - v34 - O '96 - p7 [1-50]
Kellogg, Marne Davis - *Bad Manners*
  Arm Det - v29 - Sum '96 - p282 [51-250]
Kellogg, Steven - *La Bruja De Navidad (Illus. by Steven Kellogg)*
  c BL - v93 - My 1 '97 - p1507 [1-50]
I Was Born about 10,000 Years Ago (Illus. by Steven Kellogg)
  c CCB-B - v50 - O '96 - p66 [51-250]
  c Emerg Lib - v24 - Mr '97 - p44+ [1-50]
  c HB - v72 - N '96 - p753 [51-250]
  c HB Guide - v8 - Spr '97 - p140 [51-250]
  c LATBR - N 10 '96 - p15 [51-250]
  c NYTBR - v102 - Ja 19 '97 - p24 [1-50]
  c SLJ - v42 - S '96 - p180+ [51-250]

*Sally Ann Thunder Ann Whirlwind Crockett (Illus. by
Steven Kellogg)*
  c RT - v50 - O '96 - p137 [1-50]
  c RT - v50 - D '96 - p345 [51-250]
Yankee Doodle
  c HB Guide - v7 - Fall '96 - p357 [51-250]
  c Par Ch - v20 - O '96 - p21 [51-250]
Kellogg, Susan - *Law and the Transformation of Aztec
Culture 1500-1700*
    AHR - v102 - F '97 - p232+ [501+]
    JIH - v27 - Win '97 - p555+ [251-500]
Kellough, Gail - *Aborting Law*
    Choice - v34 - Ja '97 - p837+ [51-250]
    R&R Bk N - v11 - N '96 - p41 [51-250]
Kellow, Aynsley - *Transforming Power*
    Choice - v34 - F '97 - p1029 [51-250]
    JEL - v35 - Mr '97 - p251+ [51-250]
Kelly, Brigit Pegeen - *Song*
    South R - v32 - Aut '96 - p76+ [501+]
Kelly, Charles - *The Outlaw Trail*
    Roundup M - v4 - D '96 - p22 [251-500]
Kelly, Don C - *National Bank Notes. 3rd Ed.*
  r Coin W - v38 - Mr 10 '97 - p42 [251-500]
Kelly, Francis - *Window on a Catholic Parish*
    ILS - v16 - Spr '97 - p36 [1-50]
Kelly, Gary - *British Reform Writers 1789-1832*
  r ARBA - v28 - '97 - p447 [51-250]
Women, Writing, and Revolution 1790-1827
    Eight-C St - v29 - Sum '96 - p440+ [501+]
Kelly, Gavin - *Stakeholder Capitalism*
    TLS - Ap 11 '97 - p5+ [501+]
Kelly, Geoff - *Stuck with Baby (Illus. by Geoff Kelly)*
  c Cur R - v36 - F '97 - p13 [51-250]
Kelly, Gerard - *Recognition: Advancing Ecumenical
Thinking*
    Theol St - v58 - Mr '97 - p196+ [251-500]
Kelly, Henry Ansgar - *Ideas and Forms of Tragedy from
Aristotle to the Middle Ages*
    MLR - v91 - Jl '96 - p681+ [251-500]
Kelly, J N D - *Golden Mouth*
    Bks & Cult - v2 - Jl '96 - p31 [251-500]
    CH - v66 - Mr '97 - p85+ [501+]
    Theol St - v57 - Je '96 - p346+ [501+]
Kelly, Jason - *The Neatest Little Guide to Mutual Fund
Investing*
    BL - v93 - N 1 '96 - p465 [51-250]
Kelly, Jeffrey A - *Changing HIV Risk Behavior*
    Fam in Soc - v77 - O '96 - p520 [251-500]
    Soc Ser R - v70 - D '96 - p668 [1-50]
Kelly, Joanne - *The Beverly Cleary Handbook*
    Cur R - v36 - D '96 - p3* [51-250]
    Emerg Lib - v24 - Mr '97 - p39 [51-250]
Kelly, John - *Growing Plants from Seed*
    BL - v93 - D 1 '96 - p636 [51-250]
Kelly, Joyce - *An Archaeological Guide to Northern
Central America*
    Nature - v386 - Mr 13 '97 - p139 [1-50]
Kelly, Katherine E - *Modern Drama by Women
1880s-1930s*
    Choice - v34 - Ja '97 - p788 [51-250]
Kelly, Kathleen Coyne - *A.S. Byatt*
    BL - v93 - D 15 '96 - p705 [51-250]
Kelly, Kevin - *Out of Control*
    Reason - v28 - D '96 - p38 [51-250]
    Reason - v28 - D '96 - p44 [51-250]
    VLS - S '96 - p14+ [501+]
Kelly, Linda - *Richard Brinsley Sheridan: A Life*
    Obs - Ap 13 '97 - p17* [501+]
Kelly, Mary Pat - *Proudly We Served*
    Arm F&S - v22 - Sum '96 - p656+ [501+]
Kelly, Matthew - *A Call to Joy*
    LJ - v122 - My 1 '97 - p110 [51-250]
Kelly, Mike - *Color Lines*
    AAPSS-A - v546 - Jl '96 - p173+ [501+]
Kelly, Nigel - *The Modern World*
  y TES - Mr 28 '97 - p13* [501+]
Kelly, Orr - *From a Dark Sky*
  y BL - v92 - Ag '96 - p1862 [51-250]
  y BL - v92 - Ag '96 - p1890 [1-50]
Never Fight Fair!
  y Kliatt - v30 - S '96 - p33 [51-250]
Kelly, P T - *Television Violence*
  r Choice - v34 - Ap '97 - p1317 [51-250]
  r R&R Bk N - v12 - F '97 - p81 [1-50]
Kelly, Richard Michael - *The Art of George Du Maurier*
    Choice - v34 - O '96 - p267 [51-250]
    Nine-C Lit - v51 - Mr '97 - p559 [51-250]
    R&R Bk N - v12 - F '97 - p74 [51-250]
Kelly, Rob - *A Series for New York*
    LJ - v122 - F 1 '97 - p82 [1-50]

Kelly, Robert L - *The Foraging Spectrum*
    Am Ant - v61 - O '96 - p797+ [501+]
Kelly, Sean - *Who in Hell*
    VQR - v73 - Win '97 - p31*+ [51-250]
Kelly, Thomas - *Payback*
    BL - v93 - Ja '97 - p778 [51-250]
    KR - v65 - Ja 1 '97 - p12 [251-500]
    LJ - v122 - Ja '97 - p147 [51-250]
    NYTBR - v102 - Ap 13 '97 - p20 [51-250]
    NYTLa - v146 - Mr 13 '97 - pC17 [501+]
    Obs - Ja 26 '97 - p15* [501+]
    PW - v244 - Ja 6 '97 - p65 [251-500]
    Time - v149 - Mr 17 '97 - p69 [501+]
Kelly, Thomas R - *A Testament of Devotion*
    BL - v93 - O 1 '96 - p308 [1-50]
Kelly, Tom - *The Season*
    BL - v93 - N 1 '96 - p473 [51-250]
    KR - v64 - O 1 '96 - p1446 [251-500]
    PW - v243 - N 25 '96 - p65 [251-500]
Kelly, Valerie - *Cash Crop and Foodgrain Productivity in
Senegal*
    JEL - v34 - D '96 - p2130 [51-250]
Kelly, William Melvin - *A Drop of Patience*
    BW - v26 - Jl 14 '96 - p12 [51-250]
Kelm, George L - *Timnah: A Biblical City in the Sorek
Valley*
    Rel St Rev - v23 - Ja '97 - p55 [251-250]
Kelman, James - *Busted Scotch*
    BL - v93 - My 1 '97 - p1480 [51-250]
    Econ - v343 - Ap 26 '97 - p83+ [501+]
    KR - v65 - Ap 1 '97 - p489+ [251-500]
    LJ - v122 - My 1 '97 - p142 [51-250]
    PW - v244 - Ap 21 '97 - p59+ [251-500]
Kelman, Judith - *Fly Away Home*
    KR - v64 - O 15 '96 - p1486 [251-500]
    LJ - v121 - N 1 '96 - p107 [51-250]
    PW - v243 - O 7 '96 - p64 [51-250]
More than You Know
    Arm Det - v29 - Sum '96 - p376+ [51-250]
Kelsey, Michael - *Marriage and Death Notices from the
South Western Baptist Newspaper*
  r EGH - v50 - N '96 - p160 [51-250]
Kelsh, Nick - *Naked Babies*
    BL - v93 - N 1 '96 - p472 [51-250]
    CSM - v89 - D 5 '96 - pB1 [51-250]
    KR - v64 - O 1 '96 - p1460 [51-250]
    LATBR - D 8 '96 - p10 [51-250]
    NYTBR - v101 - D 29 '96 - p15 [51-250]
    PW - v243 - O 7 '96 - p50 [51-250]
Kelso, Scott - *Dynamic Patterns*
    Nature - v386 - Ap 3 '97 - p454 [1-50]
Keltic Fringe
  p Sm Pr R - v28 - Je '96 - p17 [51-250]
Kelton, Elmer - *Cloudy in the West*
    KR - v65 - F 1 '97 - p162 [251-500]
    PW - v244 - F 3 '97 - p93 [51-250]
    Roundup M - v4 - Ap '97 - p28 [251-500]
Kemal, Salim - *The Poetics of Alfarabi and Avicenna*
    Col Lit - v23 - Je '96 - p202+ [501+]
Kemble, Frances A - *Principles and Privilege*
    Legacy - v14 - 1 '97 - p70+ [501+]
Kemmis, Daniel - *The Good City and the Good Life*
    Ken R - v18 - Sum '96 - p206+ [501+]
Kemmy, Jim - *The Limerick Anthology*
    ILS - v16 - Spr '97 - p35 [51-250]
Kemp, Anthony E - *The Musical Temperament*
    Choice - v34 - Ap '97 - p1347 [51-250]
Kemp, Gene - *Dog's Journey (Illus. by Paul Howard)*
  c Bks Keeps - v100 - S '96 - p32 [51-250]
  c Bks Keeps - N '96 - p8 [51-250]
  c JB - v60 - D '96 - p269 [51-250]
Kemp, Geoffrey - *Powder Keg in the Middle East*
    MEP - v4 - 4 '96 - p151+ [501+]
    NWCR - v50 - Win '97 - p145+ [501+]
Kemp, Murray C - *The Gains from Trade and the Gains
from Aid*
    JEL - v34 - D '96 - p2042 [51-250]
    R&R Bk N - v11 - N '96 - p34 [51-250]
Kemp, Paul - *Underwater Warriors*
    J Mil H - v61 - Ap '97 - p400 [251-500]
Kemp, Peter - *H.G. Wells and the Culminating Ape*
    Spec - v277 - N 16 '96 - p46 [1-50]
Kemp, Simon - *Cognitive Psychology in the Middle Ages*
    Choice - v34 - Ap '97 - p1420 [51-250]
Kempker, Debra - *Totally Unauthorized Myst*
    Quill & Q - v62 - Ag '96 - p22 [501+]
Kemple, Thomas M - *Reading Marx Writing*
    AJS - v102 - Ja '97 - p1234+ [501+]
    APSR - v91 - Mr '97 - p171+ [501+]
Kempner, Ken - *The Social Role of Higher Education*
    R&R Bk N - v11 - D '96 - p54 [51-250]

Kemprecos, Paul - *The Mayflower Murder*
    KR - v64 - My 1 '96 - p644 [51-250]
Kempthorne, Charley - *For All Time*
  y BL - v93 - S 1 '96 - p59 [51-250]
    LJ - v121 - S 15 '96 - p77 [51-250]
Kempton, Linda - *Who'll Catch the Nightmares?*
  c Bks Keeps - Jl '96 - p13 [51-250]
  y JB - v60 - Ag '96 - p166 [251-500]
Kempton, Willett - *Environmental Values in American
Culture*
    Am Sci - v84 - N '96 - p608+ [501+]
Kemske, Floyd - *Human Resources*
    Kiplinger - v51 - F '97 - p112 [51-250]
Kendall, Brian - *Shutout: The Legend of Terry Sawchuk*
    Mac - v109 - D 16 '96 - p72 [51-250]
    Quill & Q - v62 - N '96 - p38 [251-500]
Kendall, Richard - *Degas: Beyond Impressionism*
    BL - v93 - N 1 '96 - p471+ [51-250]
    BM - v138 - S '96 - p615+ [501+]
    Choice - v34 - Ja '97 - p784 [51-250]
    LJ - v121 - N 15 '96 - p58+ [51-250]
    NYRB - v43 - O 3 '96 - p48+ [501+]
    NYRB - v43 - O 17 '96 - p14+ [501+]
    TES - Ag 30 '96 - p26 [1-50]
Kendall, Tim - *Paul Muldoon*
    Choice - v34 - Ja '97 - p796 [51-250]
    PW - v243 - S 9 '96 - p79 [51-250]
Kendrick, John W - *The New System of National
Accounts*
    JEL - v35 - Mr '97 - p206 [51-250]
Kendrick, Robert L - *Celestial Sirens*
    Choice - v34 - Ja '97 - p806 [51-250]
    TLS - F 28 '97 - p19 [501+]
Kendrick, Walter - *The Secret Museum*
    NYTBR - v102 - Ja 19 '97 - p28 [51-250]
    Obs - Mr 23 '97 - p18* [51-250]
Keneally, Thomas - *A River Town*
    WLT - v70 - Aut '96 - p1025+ [501+]
Kenen, Peter B - *Economic and Monetary Union in
Europe*
    JEL - v34 - S '96 - p1432+ [51-250]
The International Monetary System
    Econ J - v106 - S '96 - p1442+ [501+]
Understanding Interdependence
    JEL - v34 - S '96 - p1360+ [501+]
Kenet, Barney J - *Saving Your Skin*
    LJ - v122 - Ja '97 - p56 [1-50]
Kenna, Kathleen - *A People Apart (Illus. by Andrew
Stawicki)*
  c Can CL - v22 - Fall '96 - p111 [51-250]
Kenna, Stephanie - *Networking in the Humanities*
    LQ - v67 - Ja '97 - p90+ [501+]
Kennan, George F - *At a Century's Ending*
    Choice - v34 - S '96 - p195 [51-250]
    NYRB - v43 - Ag 8 '96 - p4+ [501+]
    NYTBR - v101 - Ap 7 '96 - p6 [501+]
    NYTBR - v101 - D 8 '96 - p84 [1-50]
    Pres SQ - v27 - Win '97 - p171+ [501+]
    PSQ - v111 - Win '96 - p701+ [501+]
    Spec - v276 - My 18 '96 - p35+ [501+]
    Trib Bks - My 25 '97 - p8 [1-50]
*George F. Kennan and the Origins of Containment
1944-1946*
    KR - v65 - Ja 1 '97 - p40 [251-500]
    LJ - v122 - F 15 '97 - p149 [51-250]
Kennard, Roy - *Teaching Mathematically Able Children*
    TES - O 4 '96 - pR13 [501+]
Kennealy, Jerry - *All That Glitters*
    BL - v93 - D 15 '96 - p712 [51-250]
    KR - v64 - N 1 '96 - p1569 [51-250]
    PW - v243 - N 18 '96 - p65 [51-250]
The Conductor (Kohen). Audio Version
  y Kliatt - v31 - Mr '97 - p40 [51-250]
The Conductor (Lane). Audio Version
  y Kliatt - v31 - Mr '97 - p40 [51-250]
Kennedy, A L - *Original Bliss*
    NS - v126 - Ja 10 '97 - p47 [501+]
    Obs - Ja 19 '97 - p15* [501+]
    Spec - v278 - Ja 18 '97 - p35+ [501+]
    TLS - Ja 24 '97 - p21 [501+]
So I Am Glad
    Econ - v343 - Ap 26 '97 - p83+ [501+]
    TLS - N 29 '96 - p16 [51-250]
Kennedy, Angus J - *Christine De Pizan: A
Bibliographical Guide. 1st Suppl.*
  r MLR - v92 - Ap '97 - p461+ [501+]
Kennedy, Brian - *A Passion to Oppose*
    TLS - My 24 '96 - p28 [501+]
Kennedy, Dane Keith - *The Magic Mountains*
    Choice - v34 - S '96 - p183 [51-250]
    R&R Bk N - v11 - N '96 - p15 [51-250]

Kennedy, Danielle - *Seven Figure Selling*
 BL - v93 - O 1 '96 - p311 [51-250]
Kennedy, Dennis - *Looking at Shakespeare*
 Shakes Q - v47 - Fall '96 - p345+ [501+]
Kennedy, Des - *The Garden Club and the Kumquat Campaign*
 BIC - v25 - O '96 - p41 [51-250]
 CF - v75 - O '96 - p37+ [501+]
Kennedy, Douglas - *The Big Picture*
 BL - v93 - F 15 '97 - p971 [51-250]
 Ent W - Mr 28 '97 - p62 [51-250]
 KR - v65 - Ja 15 '97 - p82 [251-500]
 NYTLa - v146 - Mr 27 '97 - pC15 [501+]
 PW - v243 - D 30 '96 - p53 [251-500]
 Trib Bks - Ap 13 '97 - p8 [51-250]
 Trib Bks - Ap 20 '97 - p5+ [501+]
Kennedy, Eugene - *This Man Bernardin*
 BL - v92 - Ag '96 - p1859 [51-250]
Kennedy, Felicitas - *The Wiley Dictionary of Civil Engineering and Construction: English-Spanish, Spanish-English*
 r ARBA - v28 - '97 - p595 [51-250]
 r Choice - v34 - O '96 - p253 [51-250]
Kennedy, Hugh - *Original Color*
 BL - v93 - O 1 '96 - p323 [51-250]
 Ent W - N 15 '96 - p67 [51-250]
 KR - v64 - Ag 15 '96 - p1174 [251-500]
 LJ - v121 - S 15 '96 - p96 [51-250]
 NYTBR - v101 - O 20 '96 - p22 [251-500]
Kennedy, Hugh N - *Crusader Castles*
 EHR - v111 - N '96 - p1239+ [501+]
 Specu - v72 - Ja '97 - p187+ [501+]
Kennedy, J Gerald - *Modern American Short Story Sequences*
 J Am St - v30 - Ap '96 - p165 [251-500]
Kennedy, Jenny - *Primary Science*
 TES - F 28 '97 - p16* [251-500]
Kennedy, Jimmy - *The Teddy Bears' Picnic (Illus. by Bruce Whatley). Book and Audio Version*
 c SLJ - v43 - Ja '97 - p84 [51-250]
Kennedy, Joyce Lain - *Cover Letters for Dummies*
 J Car P&E - v57 - Fall '96 - p20+ [251-500]
 J Car P&E - v57 - Win '97 - p20+ [251-500]
 Job Interviews for Dummies
 J Car P&E - v57 - Fall '96 - p20+ [251-500]
 J Car P&E - v57 - Win '97 - p20+ [251-500]
 Resumes for Dummies
 J Car P&E - v57 - Fall '96 - p20+ [251-500]
 J Car P&E - v57 - Win '97 - p20+ [251-500]
Kennedy, Liam, 1946- - *Colonialism, Religion and Nationalism in Ireland*
 TLS - S 27 '96 - p5+ [501+]
Kennedy, Liam, 1961- - *Susan Sontag: Mind as Passion*
 J Am St - v30 - D '96 - p475+ [251-500]
 WLT - v70 - Sum '96 - p698+ [501+]
Kennedy, Ludovic - *In Bed with an Elephant*
 Books - v9 - S '95 - p23 [1-50]
Kennedy, Michael, 1926- - *A Catalogue of the Works of Ralph Vaughan Williams. 2nd Ed.*
 Choice - v34 - Ap '97 - p1347+ [51-250]
 The Concise Oxford Dictionary of Music. 4th Ed.
 r ARBA - v28 - '97 - p470 [251-500]
Kennedy, Michael, 1939- - *The Global Positioning System and GIS*
 SciTech - v20 - N '96 - p77 [51-250]
Kennedy, Michael D - *Envisioning Eastern Europe*
 CS - v26 - Mr '97 - p175+ [501+]
Kennedy, Mimi - *Taken to the Stage*
 BL - v93 - S 1 '96 - p53 [51-250]
Kennedy, N Brent - *The Melungeons: The Resurrection of a Proud People*
 NGSQ - v84 - Je '96 - p134+ [501+]
Kennedy, Randall - *Race, Crime, and the Law*
 BL - v93 - My 1 '97 - p1465 [51-250]
 KR - v65 - Ap 1 '97 - p525 [251-500]
 LJ - v122 - My 1 '97 - p123 [51-250]
 PW - v244 - Mr 31 '97 - p49 [51-250]
 Wil Q - v21 - Spr '97 - p100+ [501+]
Kennedy, Richard - *Hans Christian Andersen's The Snow Queen (Illus. by Edward S Gazsi)*
 c CCB-B - v50 - Ja '97 - p162+ [51-250]
 c SLJ - v43 - F '97 - p74 [51-250]
Kennedy, Robert E - *Zen Spirit, Christian Spirit*
 CLW - v67 - D '96 - p38+ [251-500]
Kennedy, Roger G - *Hidden Cities*
 y Kliatt - v31 - Mr '97 - p32 [51-250]
Kennedy, Sheila Suess - *What's a Nice Republican Girl Like Me Doing in the ACLU?*
 PW - v244 - Ap 21 '97 - p52 [51-250]
Kennedy, Teresa - *Sensual Healing*
 BWatch - v17 - N '96 - p4 [51-250]

Kennedy, Thomas E - *Unreal City*
 RCF - v16 - Fall '96 - p190+ [501+]
 Sm Pr R - v29 - Ja '97 - p8 [51-250]
Kennedy, William, 1928- - *An Albany Trio*
 PW - v244 - Mr 17 '97 - p81 [1-50]
 The Flaming Corsage
 Am - v175 - S 14 '96 - p28+ [501+]
 BL - v93 - Ja '97 - p761 [1-50]
 Comw - v123 - S 13 '96 - p36+ [501+]
 ILS - v16 - Spr '97 - p15 [501+]
 LATBR - Jl 14 '96 - p6+ [501+]
 NY - v72 - My 27 '96 - p132 [51-250]
 NYTBR - v101 - D 8 '96 - p80 [1-50]
 PW - v244 - Mr 17 '97 - p81 [1-50]
 Rapport - v19 - 5 '96 - p33 [251-500]
 Trib Bks - Ap 27 '97 - p8 [1-50]
 The Flaming Corsage (Kennedy). Audio Version
 y Kliatt - v31 - Mr '97 - p42 [51-250]
Kennedy, William P - *Siren's Lullaby*
 KR - v65 - Mr 15 '97 - p407+ [251-500]
 LJ - v122 - Ap 15 '97 - p118 [51-250]
 PW - v244 - Ap 7 '97 - p74+ [51-250]
Kennedy, X J - *Uncle Switch (Illus. by John O'Brien)*
 c BL - v93 - My 1 '97 - p1500 [51-250]
 c CCB-B - v50 - Ap '97 - p287 [51-250]
 c KR - v65 - Mr 15 '97 - p464 [51-250]
 c PW - v244 - Mr 31 '97 - p77 [51-250]
Kennelly, Brendan - *Poetry My Arse*
 WLT - v70 - Sum '96 - p696+ [501+]
Kennemore, Tim - *Alice's World Record (Illus. by Alex De Wolf)*
 c Sch Lib - v44 - Ag '96 - p104 [51-250]
Kennerdell, John - *Tokyo Journal's Tokyo Restaurant Guide*
 r FEER - v160 - Mr 27 '97 - p51+ [501+]
Kennerly, David H - *PhotoOp*
 JMCQ - v73 - Win '96 - p1010+ [251-500]
Kennett, Lee - *Marching through Georgia*
 AHR - v101 - D '96 - p1626+ [501+]
 y Kliatt - v30 - S '96 - p33+ [501+]
Kennett, Shirley - *Gray Matter*
 y BL - v93 - S 1 '96 - p68 [51-250]
Kenney, Charles - *Hammurabi's Code*
 Arm Det - v29 - Sum '96 - p282 [51-250]
Kenney, Milli S - *What's News in Coos County?. Vol. 1*
 r EGH - v50 - N '96 - p173+ [51-250]
Kenny, Chris - *Women's Business*
 Aust Bk R - F '97 - p8+ [501+]
Kenny, Mary - *Goodbye to Catholic Ireland*
 NS - v126 - Ap 25 '97 - p55 [501+]
 Obs - Mr 16 '97 - p15* [501+]
Kent, Allegra - *Once a Dancer...*
 Dance - v71 - Ja '97 - p98 [51-250]
 KR - v64 - N 15 '96 - p1654 [251-500]
 NYTBR - v102 - Ja 19 '97 - p6 [501+]
 NYTLa - v146 - Ap 22 '97 - pC14 [501+]
 PW - v243 - D 2 '96 - p49 [51-250]
 WSJ-Cent - v99 - Ja 16 '97 - pA16 [501+]
Kent, Arthur - *Risk and Redemption*
 Mac - v109 - O 21 '96 - p82 [501+]
 Quill & Q - v62 - S '96 - p71 [251-500]
Kent, Assunta Bartolomucci - *Maria Irene Fornes and Her Critics*
 Choice - v34 - D '96 - p624+ [51-250]
 R&R Bk N - v11 - N '96 - p74 [51-250]
Kent, Bonnie - *Virtues of the Will*
 J Phil - v93 - D '96 - p628+ [501+]
 Rel St Rev - v23 - Ja '97 - p50 [51-250]
 Theol St - v57 - S '96 - p555+ [501+]
Kent, Deborah - *African-Americans in the Thirteen Colonies*
 c HB Guide - v7 - Fall '96 - p386 [1-50]
 c SLJ - v42 - N '96 - p114 [51-250]
 Beijing
 c HB Guide - v8 - Spr '97 - p170 [1-50]
 c SLJ - v43 - F '97 - p118 [51-250]
 China: Old Ways Meet New
 c HB Guide - v8 - Spr '97 - p169 [1-50]
 The Disability Rights Movement
 c HB Guide - v7 - Fall '96 - p314 [1-50]
 Dorothy Day: Friend to the Forgotten
 y HB Guide - v7 - Fall '96 - p373 [1-50]
 y Kliatt - v30 - S '96 - p28 [51-250]
 y SLJ - v42 - Ag '96 - p172 [51-250]
 Extraordinary People with Disabilities
 c BL - v93 - My 1 '97 - p1158 [51-250]
 c SLJ - v43 - Mr '97 - p202+ [51-250]
 The Lincoln Memorial
 c HB Guide - v8 - Spr '97 - p138 [1-50]
 c SLJ - v43 - F '97 - p92 [51-250]

 Mexico: Rich in Spirit and Tradition
 c HB Guide - v7 - Fall '96 - p386 [1-50]
 New York City
 c SLJ - v43 - Mr '97 - p177+ [51-250]
 Rio De Janeiro
 c HB Guide - v8 - Spr '97 - p179 [51-250]
 c SLJ - v42 - S '96 - p217+ [51-250]
 Tokyo
 c BL - v93 - N 1 '96 - p493 [51-250]
 c HB Guide - v8 - Spr '97 - p170 [1-50]
 c SLJ - v42 - O '96 - p134 [51-250]
Kent, J P C - *The Roman Imperial Coinage. Vol. 10*
 AJA - v100 - Jl '96 - p628+ [501+]
Kent, Jack - *There's No Such Thing as a Dragon (Illus. by Jack Kent)*
 c Bks Keeps - Ja '97 - p19 [51-250]
Kent, Jacqueline - *No Thanks or Regrets*
 Aust Bk R - S '96 - p67 [501+]
Kent, John - *The Internationalization of Colonialism*
 JMH - v69 - Mr '97 - p170+ [501+]
Kent, Marian - *The Great Powers and the End of the Ottoman Empire*
 MEJ - v50 - Aut '96 - p629 [51-250]
Kent, Michael - *The Oxford Dictionary of Sports Science and Medicine*
 r BL - v93 - F 1 '97 - p956 [1-50]
Kent, Michael R - *Bringing the Word to Life. Vol. 2*
 CLW - v67 - D '96 - p42 [251-500]
Kent, Peter - *A Slice through a City (Illus. by Peter Kent)*
 c CBRS - v25 - Ja '97 - p58 [1-50]
 c Ch BWatch - v7 - Ja '97 - p1 [51-250]
 c HB Guide - v8 - Spr '97 - p164 [51-250]
 c SLJ - v43 - Mr '97 - p203 [51-250]
Kent, Susan - *Cultural Diversity among Twentieth-Century Foragers*
 Choice - v34 - Ja '97 - p838 [51-250]
Kenton, Leslie - *Beat Stress*
 PW - v244 - F 17 '97 - p216 [1-50]
 Boost Energy
 PW - v244 - F 17 '97 - p216 [1-50]
 Get Fit
 PW - v244 - F 17 '97 - p216 [1-50]
 Look Great
 PW - v244 - F 17 '97 - p216 [1-50]
 Lose Fat
 PW - v244 - F 17 '97 - p216 [1-50]
 Sleep Deep
 PW - v244 - F 17 '97 - p216 [1-50]
Kenvin, Natalie - *Bruise Theory*
 A Lib - v27 - Ag '96 - p71 [1-50]
Kenward, Jean - *The Odd Job Man and the Thousand Mile Boots (Illus. by Val Biro)*
 c Bks Keeps - Jl '96 - p6+ [51-250]
Kenwood, Albert G - *Australian Economic Institutions since Federation*
 JEL - v34 - D '96 - p2095+ [51-250]
Kenworthy, Christopher - *Will You Hold Me?*
 KR - v65 - Mr 1 '97 - p334 [51-250]
Kenworthy, Eldon - *America/Americas*
 HAHR - v76 - Ag '96 - p614+ [501+]
 J Pol - v58 - N '96 - p1253+ [501+]
Kenworthy, Lane - *In Search of National Economic Success*
 CS - v25 - S '96 - p605+ [501+]
Kenyon, Jane - *Otherwise: New and Selected Poems*
 Bks & Cult - v3 - Ja '97 - p22+ [501+]
 BL - v93 - Ap 1 '97 - p1285 [1-50]
 HR - v49 - Win '97 - p659+ [501+]
 NY - v72 - S 9 '96 - p90+ [501+]
 NYTBR - v102 - Ja 5 '97 - p12 [501+]
 y SLJ - v42 - S '96 - p242 [51-250]
 VQR - v72 - Aut '96 - p136* [501+]
 VV - v42 - Ja 7 '97 - p41 [1-50]
Kenyon, Kay - *The Seeds of Time*
 PW - v244 - Ap 21 '97 - p68 [51-250]
Kenyon, Michael - *Durable Tumblers*
 SN - v111 - N '96 - p14 [251-500]
Kenyon, Tony - *The Crocodile in the Piano*
 c TES - Jl 5 '96 - pR6 [1-50]
Keogh, Daire - *The French Disease*
 AHR - v101 - D '96 - p1549 [251-500]
Keogh, Dermot - *Ireland and the Vatican*
 AHR - v101 - D '96 - p1550+ [251-500]
 CHR - v83 - Ja '97 - p126+ [251-500]
Keohane, Robert O - *Institutions for Environmental Aid*
 Choice - v34 - F '97 - p1012 [51-250]
 JEL - v35 - Mr '97 - p277+ [51-250]
 Internationalization and Domestic Politics
 JEL - v34 - D '96 - p2042+ [51-250]

Local Commons and Global Interdependence
 APSR - v91 - Mr '97 - p236 [501+]
 SSQ - v77 - D '96 - p942+ [501+]
Keon, Michael - *Glad Morning Again*
 Aust Bk R - F '97 - p16+ [501+]
Keonjian, Edward - *Survived to Tell*
 PW - v243 - N 18 '96 - p59+ [51-250]
Keown, Damien - *Buddhism and Bioethics*
 Ethics - v107 - Ja '97 - p399+ [51-250]
 Hast Cen R - v26 - Jl '96 - p41 [1-50]
 JR - v77 - Ap '97 - p341+ [501+]
 Rel St Rev - v23 - Ja '97 - p51 [51-250]
 The Nature of Buddhist Ethics
 Ethics - v107 - O '96 - p196+ [51-250]
Keown, John - *Euthanasia Examined*
 Hast Cen R - v26 - Mr '96 - p49 [1-50]
Kephalaia. English - *The Kephalaia of the Teacher*
 Rel St Rev - v23 - Ja '97 - p77 [51-250]
Kepler, Lynne - *Windowsill Science Centers*
 c SB - v33 - Mr '97 - p48 [51-250]
Kepner, Susan Fulop - *The Lioness in Bloom*
 TranslRevS - v2 - D '96 - p3 [51-250]
Keppel, Ben - *The Work of Democracy*
 AHR - v101 - O '96 - p1308 [501+]
Keppler, Michael - *Emerging Markets*
 Choice - v34 - Ap '97 - p1388 [251-500]
 R&R Bk N - v12 - F '97 - p49 [51-250]
Kerber, L L - *Stalin's Aviation Gulag*
 A & S Sm - v11 - F '97 - p91 [51-250]
Kerber, Linda K - *Toward an Intellectual History of Women*
 LJ - v122 - Ap 15 '97 - p96 [51-250]
 U.S. History as Women's History
 CS - v26 - Mr '97 - p158+ [501+]
 NWSA Jnl - v8 - Sum '96 - p126+ [501+]
Kerbo, Harold R - *Who Rules Japan?*
 CS - v26 - Mr '97 - p180+ [501+]
Kerckhoff, Alan C - *Generating Social Stratification*
 SF - v75 - Mr '97 - p1129+ [501+]
 Going Comprehensive in England and Wales
 TES - Ja 24 '97 - p9* [501+]
Keren, Michael - *Professionals against Populism*
 APSR - v90 - S '96 - p674+ [501+]
The Kerf
 p LMR - v15 - Win '96 - p11+ [501+]
Kerf, Michel - *Privatizing Africa's Infrastructure*
 JEL - v35 - Mr '97 - p246 [51-250]
Kerins, Tony - *The Brave Ones*
 c CBRS - v24 - Ag '96 - p159 [51-250]
 c HB Guide - v7 - Fall '96 - p240 [51-250]
 Little Clancy's New Drum (Illus. by Tony Kerins)
 c Ch BWatch - v6 - N '96 - p6 [1-50]
 c HB Guide - v8 - Spr '97 - p13 [51-250]
 c SLJ - v43 - Ja '97 - p84 [51-250]
Kerkhoff, Blair - *Phog Allen: The Father of Basketball Coaching*
 PW - v243 - N 18 '96 - p59 [51-250]
Kerl, Mary Ann - *Angel on Trial*
 BWatch - v17 - N '96 - p10 [51-250]
Kermode, Frank - *Not Entitled*
 Comw - v123 - D 6 '96 - p20 [51-250]
 Comw - v123 - D 6 '96 - p28 [251-500]
 CR - v269 - O '96 - p223+ [51-250]
 NS & S - v9 - My 17 '96 - p37+ [251-500]
 NYTBR - v101 - D 8 '96 - p90 [1-50]
 Obs - Mr 23 '97 - p18* [251-500]
 Sew R - v104 - O '96 - p692+ [501+]
 TLS - Jl 7 '96 - p29 [501+]
 WLT - v70 - Aut '96 - p970 [51-250]
 The Oxford Book of Letters
 Sew R - v104 - Jl '96 - p483+ [501+]
Kermode, Mo - *The Great Skeleton Race*
 c JB - v60 - D '96 - p269 [251-500]
 c Sch Lib - v45 - F '97 - p33 [51-250]
Kermode, P M C - *Manx Crosses*
 Folkl - v107 - '96 - p122+ [501+]
Kern, Elfriede - *Etude Fur Adele Und Einen Hund*
 WLT - v71 - Win '97 - p148 [251-500]
Kern, Gary - *The Last Snow Leopard*
 Chel - 61 '96 - p151+ [501+]
Kern, Robert W - *The Regions of Spain*
 yr ARBA - v28 - '97 - p205+ [251-500]
 yr RQ - v35 - Sum '96 - p564+ [251-500]
Kern, Stephen - *The Culture of Love*
 ASInt - v34 - O '96 - p96 [251-500]
 Eyes of Love
 Choice - v34 - Ja '97 - p784 [51-250]
 ELT - v40 - 2 '97 - p253 [51-250]

Kernan, Alvin - *Shakespeare, the King's Playwright*
 NYRB - v43 - Je 6 '96 - p52+ [501+]
 Ren Q - v50 - Spr '97 - p281+ [501+]
 RMR - v50 - 2 '96 - p194+ [501+]
 Six Ct J - v27 - Fall '96 - p975+ [501+]
 What's Happened to the Humanities?
 BL - v93 - Ap 1 '97 - p1270 [51-250]
 LJ - v122 - Ap 15 '97 - p94 [51-250]
 Wil Q - v21 - Spr '97 - p105+ [501+]
Kerner, Elizabeth - *Song in the Silence*
 y BL - v93 - F 15 '97 - p1008 [51-250]
 KR - v64 - D 15 '96 - p1772 [51-250]
 LJ - v122 - F 15 '97 - p165 [1-50]
 PW - v244 - Ja 27 '97 - p81+ [51-250]
Kerouac, Jack - *A Jack Kerouac ROMnibus. Electronic Media Version*
 BW - v26 - D 15 '96 - p11 [51-250]
 LJ - v121 - N 1 '96 - p114+ [501+]
 y SLJ - v42 - D '96 - p56 [51-250]
 TLS - Ja 24 '97 - p32 [251-500]
 Jack Kerouac: Selected Letters 1940-1956
 Atl - v278 - Ag '96 - p88+ [501+]
 The Portable Jack Kerouac
 Atl - Ag '96 - p88+ [501+]
 Visions of Cody (Parker). Audio Version
 BWatch - v18 - Mr '97 - p6 [1-50]
 PW - v243 - D 2 '96 - p30 [51-250]
The Kerouac Connection
 p Sm Pr R - v29 - F '97 - p41 [501+]
Kerr, Alex - *Lost Japan*
 LATBR - O 20 '96 - p15 [51-250]
 r Quill & Q - v62 - S '96 - p23 [251-500]
Kerr, Ann Zwicker - *Come with Me from Lebanon*
 MEP - v4 - 4 '96 - p154+ [501+]
Kerr, Daisy - *Ancient Egyptians (Illus. by John James)*
 c HB Guide - v8 - Spr '97 - p166 [51-250]
 Ancient Romans (Illus. by John James)
 c HB Guide - v8 - Spr '97 - p166 [51-250]
 Ships (Illus. by Gerald Wood)
 c HB Guide - v7 - Fall '96 - p351 [1-50]
Kerr, David - *African Popular Theatre*
 Theat J - v49 - Mr '97 - p83+ [501+]
 WLT - v70 - Sum '96 - p745+ [501+]
Kerr, Donal - *A Nation of Beggars?*
 AHR - v101 - O '96 - p1216+ [251-500]
 Albion - v28 - Sum '96 - p373+ [501+]
 CHR - v82 - O '96 - p729+ [251-500]
 EHR - v112 - F '97 - p233+ [501+]
 VS - v39 - Win '96 - p205+ [501+]
Kerr, Donald - *World Directory of Defence and Security*
 r ARBA - v28 - '97 - p255+ [251-500]
 r RQ - v36 - Fall '96 - p143+ [251-500]
Kerr, Frances - *Glimpses of Life in Victoria by a Resident*
 Aust Bk R - Ag '96 - p18+ [501+]
Kerr, Graham - *Graham Kerr's Swiftly Seasoned*
 BL - v93 - Ja '97 - p800 [51-250]
 PW - v243 - N 18 '96 - p71 [51-250]
Kerr, Joan Paterson - *A Bully Father*
 Pres SQ - v26 - Sum '96 - p904 [501+]
Kerr, John - *A Most Dangerous Method*
 AHR - v101 - O '96 - p1181+ [501+]
Kerr, Judith - *When Hitler Stole Pink Rabbit (Illus. by Judith Kerr)*
 c New Ad - v9 - Fall '96 - p297+ [501+]
Kerr, Katharine - *Palace*
 New Sci - v152 - O 5 '96 - p50 [51-250]
 The Shimmering Door
 y VOYA - v19 - F '97 - p340 [251-500]
Kerr, M E - *Deliver Us from Evie*
 y SLJ - v43 - Mr '97 - p113 [1-50]
 Gentlehands (Woodman). Audio Version
 c HB - v72 - S '96 - p566+ [501+]
 Hello, I Lied
 y KR - v65 - Mr 1 '97 - p382 [51-250]
 y PW - v244 - Mr 31 '97 - p75 [51-250]
Kerr, Peg - *Emerald House Rising*
 PW - v244 - Ap 21 '97 - p69 [51-250]
Kerr, Philip - *Esau*
 y BL - v93 - F 15 '97 - p971 [51-250]
 KR - v65 - F 1 '97 - p162+ [251-500]
 LJ - v122 - F 15 '97 - p162 [51-250]
 PW - v244 - Mr 3 '97 - p63 [51-250]
 Spec - v277 - O 19 '96 - p47+ [251-500]
 TLS - O 18 '96 - p24 [251-500]
 The Grid
 Arm Det - v30 - Win '97 - p116 [251-500]
 y Kliatt - v31 - Mr '97 - p18 [51-250]
 PW - v243 - D 2 '96 - p56 [51-250]
 Rapport - v19 - 4 '96 - p33 [51-250]
 The Grid (Spiner). Audio Version
 y Kliatt - v30 - S '96 - p48 [51-250]

 The Grid (Howard). Audio Version
 y Kliatt - v31 - Ja '97 - p41 [51-250]
 Gridiron
 Necro - Win '97 - p27+ [51-250]
Kerrigan, John - *Revenge Tragedy*
 Choice - v34 - D '96 - p607 [51-250]
 Lon R Bks - v18 - S 19 '96 - p10+ [501+]
 NYRB - v43 - N 28 '96 - p29+ [501+]
 TLS - Ag 2 '96 - p4 [501+]
Kerrigan, William - *Hamlet's Perfection*
 RES - v47 - N '96 - p585+ [501+]
Kerrod, Robin - *Machines (Illus. by George Fryer)*
 c HB Guide - v7 - Fall '96 - p351 [51-250]
 c SB - v32 - N '96 - p243 [51-250]
 c SLJ - v42 - Ag '96 - p156+ [51-250]
 Matter and Materials (Illus. by Terry Hadler)
 c HB Guide - v7 - Fall '96 - p331 [51-250]
 c SB - v32 - N '96 - p240 [251-500]
 c SLJ - v42 - Ag '96 - p156+ [51-250]
 The Night Sky (Illus. by Terry Hadler)
 c HB Guide - v7 - Fall '96 - p330 [1-50]
 c SB - v32 - N '96 - p239 [51-250]
 c SLJ - v42 - Ag '96 - p156+ [51-250]
 Technology
 c Sch Lib - v45 - F '97 - p38 [51-250]
Kerry, John - *The New War*
 PW - v244 - Ap 21 '97 - p53 [51-250]
Kersavage, Carol J - *Outdoor Writers Association of America Style Manual*
 r BL - v93 - My 1 '97 - p1514 [1-50]
Kersbergen, Kees Van - *Social Capitalism*
 AJS - v102 - Ja '97 - p1169+ [501+]
 Choice - v34 - S '96 - p208 [51-250]
 JEL - v34 - D '96 - p2064+ [51-250]
Kerschbaumer, Marie-Therese - *Woman's Face of Resistance*
 Choice - v34 - My '97 - p1502 [51-250]
Kerschner, Helen K - *365 Ways--*
 r ARBA - v28 - '97 - p304+ [51-250]
 r BL - v93 - F 1 '97 - p961 [51-250]
Kersenboom, Saskia - *Word, Sound, Image*
 R&R Bk N - v12 - F '97 - p30 [51-250]
Kershaw, Robert J - *It Never Snows in September*
 Mar Crp G - v81 - Mr '97 - p70+ [501+]
Kersten, Holger - *The Jesus Conspiracy*
 Quill & Q - v62 - D '96 - p18+ [51-250]
Kersten, Rikki - *Democracy in Postwar Japan*
 Choice - v34 - Ja '97 - p868 [51-250]
 R&R Bk N - v11 - N '96 - p50 [51-250]
Kerszenbaum, Isidor - *Inspection of Large Synchronous Machines*
 SciTech - v20 - N '96 - p71 [51-250]
Kertes, Joseph - *The Gift (Illus. by Peter Perko)*
 c BL - v93 - N 1 '96 - p498 [51-250]
 c KR - v64 - O 15 '96 - p1534 [51-250]
 c PW - v243 - S 30 '96 - p87 [51-250]
Kertess, Klaus - *Joan Mitchell*
 PW - v244 - Mr 17 '97 - p69 [51-250]
Kerth, Thomas - *Life's Golden Tree*
 R&R Bk N - v11 - N '96 - p74 [51-250]
Kertzer, David I - *Aging in the Past*
 JIH - v27 - Win '97 - p497+ [501+]
 J Soc H - v30 - Win '96 - p538+ [501+]
 The Kidnapping of Edgardo Mortara
 BL - v93 - My 15 '97 - p1559 [51-250]
 KR - v65 - Ap 1 '97 - p526 [251-500]
 LJ - v122 - My 1 '97 - p120+ [51-250]
 PW - v244 - Mr 31 '97 - p50 [51-250]
 Politics and Symbols
 Choice - v34 - Ja '97 - p868 [51-250]
 For Aff - v75 - N '96 - p157 [51-250]
 Sacrificed for Honor
 Am Ethnol - v23 - N '96 - p923+ [501+]
Kerven, David - *HTML 3 How-To*
 SciTech - v20 - D '96 - p11 [51-250]
Kerven, Rosalind - *The Mythical Quest*
 LAR - v98 - S '96 - p438 [1-50]
 Sch Lib - v44 - N '96 - p151 [51-250]
 TLS - Jl 19 '96 - p32 [1-50]
Kery, Lotte - *Die Errichtung Des Bistums Arras 1093/1094*
 EHR - v111 - N '96 - p1238+ [251-500]
Keshen, Jeffrey A - *Propaganda and Censorship during Canada's Great War*
 Choice - v34 - F '97 - p1025 [51-250]
Kesidis, George - *ATM Network Performance*
 SciTech - v20 - D '96 - p76 [51-250]
Kess, Joseph F - *Japanese Psycholinguistics*
 r MLJ - v80 - Fall '96 - p423 [251-500]

Kessel, John - *Corrupting Dr. Nice*
    Analog - v117 - Ap '97 - p147+ [501+]
 y BL - v93 - Ja '97 - p826 [51-250]
    BW - v26 - D 29 '96 - p6 [501+]
    KR - v64 - N 15 '96 - p1640 [51-250]
    LJ - v121 - D '96 - p152 [1-50]
    NYTBR - v102 - Ja 26 '97 - p22 [51-250]
    PW - v243 - D 30 '96 - p58 [51-250]
Kessler, Brad - *Brer Rabbit and Boss Lion (Glover) (Illus. by Bill Mayer). Book and Audio Version*
 c Ch BWatch - v6 - My '96 - p6 [51-250]
 c SLJ - v43 - Ja '97 - p102 [51-250]
Kessler, Carol Farley - *Charlotte Perkins Gilman: Her Progress toward Utopia with Selected Writings*
    AHR - v101 - O '96 - p1292+ [251-500]
Kessler, Cristina - *Muhamad's Desert Night (Illus. by Ian Schoenherr)*
 c Sch Lib - v44 - N '96 - p146 [51-250]
Kessler, David - *The Falashas: A Short History of the Ethiopian Jews. 3rd Ed.*
    R&R Bk N - v11 - D '96 - p11 [51-250]
Kessler, Dianne - *Encounters for Unity*
    RR - v55 - S '96 - p549+ [251-500]
Kessler, Donna J - *The Making of Sacagawea*
    Choice - v34 - Ja '97 - p863 [51-250]
Kessler, Eckhard - *Girolamo Cardano: Philosoph, Naturforscher, Arzt*
    Ren Q - v49 - Win '96 - p840+ [501+]
Kessler, Gary C - *ISDN: Concepts, Facilities, and Services. 3rd Ed.*
    SciTech - v20 - D '96 - p75 [51-250]
Kessler, Hilda - *Treating Couples*
    SciTech - v20 - N '96 - p44 [1-50]
Kessler, Jack - *Internet Digital Libraries*
    SciTech - v21 - Mr '97 - p106 [51-250]
Kessler, James H - *Distinguished African American Scientists of the 20th Century*
 cr ARBA - v28 - '97 - p560 [51-250]
 yr JAAL - v40 - S '96 - p78 [51-250]
Kessler, Lauren - *Full Court Press*
    BL - v93 - Mr 15 '97 - p1219 [51-250]
    KR - v65 - Ja 15 '97 - p121+ [251-500]
    PW - v243 - D 16 '96 - p47 [51-250]
Kessler, Lawrence D - *The Jiangyin Mission Station*
    Choice - v34 - O '96 - p336+ [51-250]
    PHR - v66 - F '97 - p138+ [251-500]
Kessler, Leonard - *Kick, Pass, and Run (Illus. by Leonard Kessler)*
 c BL - v93 - N 15 '96 - p597 [51-250]
 c HB Guide - v8 - Spr '97 - p55 [51-250]
Kessler, Ronald - *The FBI (Riggenbach). Audio Version*
 y Kliatt - v31 - Ja '97 - p48 [51-250]
Kessler, Sanford - *Tocqueville's Civil Religion*
    Rel St Rev - v23 - Ja '97 - p92 [51-250]
Kessler, Sheila - *Measuring and Managing Customer Satisfaction*
    Choice - v34 - F '97 - p1008 [51-250]
Kestenberg, Judith S - *The Last Witness*
    Choice - v34 - N '96 - p542+ [51-250]
Kester-Shelton, Pamela - *Feminist Writers*
 r ARBA - v28 - '97 - p408 [51-250]
 r BL - v93 - D 15 '96 - p748 [251-500]
Kesting, Jurgen - *Luciano Pavarotti: The Myth of the Tenor*
    BL - v93 - S 1 '96 - p53+ [51-250]
    Choice - v34 - F '97 - p974+ [51-250]
    KR - v64 - Ag 15 '96 - p1212 [251-500]
    ON - v61 - D 14 '96 - p73 [251-500]
Kestner, Joseph A - *Masculinities in Victorian Painting*
    Albion - v28 - Sum '96 - p338+ [501+]
    Art Bull - v78 - S '96 - p568+ [501+]
    Art J - v55 - Win '96 - p88+ [501+]
Ketchian, Sonia I - *The Poetic Craft of Bella Akhmadulina*
    MLR - v92 - Ja '97 - p267+ [251-500]
    MP - v94 - Ag '96 - p137+ [501+]
Ketchin, Susan - *25 and Under: Fiction*
    KR - v65 - Mr 1 '97 - p327 [51-250]
    LJ - v122 - Mr 15 '97 - p92+ [51-250]
    PW - v244 - Ap 28 '97 - p52 [51-250]
Ketchum, Jack - *The Girl Next Door*
    PW - v243 - Jl 22 '96 - p232 [51-250]
Ketchum, Liza - *Blue Coyote*
 y KR - v65 - Mr 1 '97 - p382 [51-250]
    The Gold Rush
 c BL - v92 - Ag '96 - p1897 [51-250]
 c CBRS - v25 - S '96 - p7 [51-250]
 c Ch BWatch - v7 - Ja '97 - p7 [1-50]
 c HB Guide - v8 - Spr '97 - p173 [51-250]
 c PW - v243 - S 2 '96 - p132+ [51-250]
 y SLJ - v42 - O '96 - p156 [51-250]

Ketchum, Robert Glenn - *Northwest Passage*
 y BL - v93 - N 15 '96 - p568+ [51-250]
    Bloom Rev - v17 - Ja '97 - p21 [51-250]
    LATBR - D 8 '96 - p3 [501+]
Ketelsen, Uwe-K - *Literatur Und Drittes Reich*
    Ger Q - v69 - Fall '96 - p453+ [501+]
Ketover, Karen Sherman - *Westbrook, Maine Cemeteries*
 r EGH - v50 - N '96 - p169 [51-250]
Kets De Vries, Manfred F R - *Life and Death in the Executive Fast Lane*
    Per Psy - v49 - Aut '96 - p743+ [501+]
Kettelhack, Guy - *Dancing around the Volcano*
    Advocate - F 18 '97 - p61 [51-250]
    KR - v64 - Ag 15 '96 - p1212 [251-500]
    LJ - v122 - F 15 '97 - p150 [51-250]
Kettelkamp, Larry - *ETs and UFOs*
 c BL - v93 - D 15 '96 - p723 [51-250]
 c HB Guide - v8 - Spr '97 - p86 [51-250]
 c SLJ - v43 - Ja '97 - p128 [51-250]
Ketteman, Helen - *Grandma's Cat (Illus. by Marsha Lynn Winborn)*
 c HB Guide - v7 - Fall '96 - p240 [51-250]
 c NYTBR - v101 - Ag 25 '96 - p23 [1-50]
Kettl, Donald F - *The State of Public Management*
    Choice - v34 - F '97 - p1029 [51-250]
    JEL - v35 - Mr '97 - p203 [51-250]
    R&R Bk N - v12 - F '97 - p59 [51-250]
Kettler, David - *Karl Mannheim and the Crisis of Liberalism*
    Isis - v87 - S '96 - p581+ [501+]
Keulman, Kenneth - *Critical Moments in Religious History*
    J Ch St - v38 - Aut '96 - p915+ [251-500]
Kevelson, Roberta - *Peirce, Science, Signs*
    SciTech - v20 - D '96 - p3 [1-50]
Keville, Kathi - *Herbs for Health and Healing*
    BL - v92 - Ag '96 - p1869 [51-250]
    SciTech - v20 - N '96 - p55 [51-250]
Kevles, Bettyann - *Naked to the Bone*
    BL - v93 - N 1 '96 - p470 [51-250]
    BW - v27 - F 9 '97 - p13 [51-250]
    LJ - v122 - Ja '97 - p140 [51-250]
    Nature - v386 - Ap 10 '97 - p567+ [501+]
    New Sci - v153 - Ja 18 '97 - p38+ [501+]
    NYTLa - v146 - My 5 '97 - pC16 [501+]
    PW - v243 - N 25 '96 - p63 [51-250]
Kew, Richard - *Toward 2015*
    PW - v244 - Ja 13 '97 - p70 [51-250]
Key, Mary Ritchie - *Male/Female Language. 2nd Ed.*
 r R&R Bk N - v12 - F '97 - p76 [51-250]
Key Indicators of Developing Asian and Pacific Countries. Vol. 26
 r JEL - v34 - S '96 - p1487 [1-50]
Key Maths (Year 8)
 y TES - O 4 '96 - pR14 [501+]
Key Organisations 96
 r Sch Lib - v44 - Ag '96 - p130 [51-250]
Key Technologies for the 21st Century
 y Kliatt - v30 - S '96 - p36 [51-250]
 y SB - v32 - Ag '96 - p175 [51-250]
    SF Chr - v18 - O '96 - p82 [1-50]
Keyes, J Gregory - *The Blackgod*
 y BL - v93 - Mr 1 '97 - p1068 [51-250]
    KR - v65 - F 15 '97 - p261 [51-250]
    LJ - v122 - Ap 15 '97 - p123 [51-250]
    PW - v244 - Mr 24 '97 - p63 [51-250]
    Waterborn
 y BL - v93 - Ja '97 - p763 [1-50]
Keyes, Jessica - *How to Be a Successful Internet Consultant. 1st Ed.*
    CBR - v15 - Spr '97 - p4 [1-50]
    Technology Trendlines
    CBR - v14 - N '96 - p34 [51-250]
    The Ultimate Multimedia Handbook. 2nd Ed.
 r LJ - v122 - My 1 '97 - p132 [1-50]
Keyes, W Noel - *Life, Death, and the Law. Vols. 1-2*
    Hast Cen R - v26 - Mr '96 - p49 [1-50]
Keyishian, Harry - *The Shapes of Revenge*
    Six Ct J - v27 - Win '96 - p1152+ [501+]
Keynes, Edward - *Liberty, Property, and Privacy*
    J Pol - v59 - F '97 - p274+ [501+]
Keys, Jane - *Australia*
 c Sch Lib - v44 - Ag '96 - p113 [51-250]
Keys, Roger - *The Reluctant Modernist*
    Choice - v34 - F '97 - p972 [251-500]
Keyser, Elizabeth Lennox - *Whispers in the Dark*
    AL - v68 - S '96 - p646+ [251-500]
Khademian, Anne M - *Checking on Banks*
    JEL - v35 - Mr '97 - p222 [51-250]

Khairi, Saad R - *Jinnah Reinterpreted*
    AAPSS-A - v547 - S '96 - p178+ [251-500]
    AHR - v101 - D '96 - p1607+ [251-500]
Khalfa, Jean - *What Is Intelligence?*
    New Sci - v152 - N 16 '96 - p46 [1-50]
Khalidi, Rashid - *Palestinian Identity*
    For Aff - v76 - My '97 - p141+ [51-250]
    KR - v65 - Mr 1 '97 - p356 [51-250]
    LJ - v122 - Mr 15 '97 - p76+ [51-250]
Khalidi, Tarif - *Arabic Historical Thought in the Classical Period*
    EHR - v112 - Ap '97 - p441 [251-500]
Khalil, Elias L - *Evolution, Order and Complexity*
    JEL - v35 - Mr '97 - p189 [51-250]
Khalsa, Dayal Kaur - *How Pizza Came to Queens (Illus. by Dayal Kaur Khalsa)*
 c Par Ch - v20 - N '96 - p8 [51-250]
Khalsa, Dharma Singh - *Brain Longevity*
    BL - v93 - Ap 1 '97 - p1267 [51-250]
    LJ - v122 - My 1 '97 - p133 [51-250]
Khambata, Dara - *The Practice of Multinational Banking. 2nd Ed.*
 r R&R Bk N - v11 - N '96 - p36 [1-50]
Khan, Adib - *Solitude of Illusions*
    Aust Bk R - N '96 - p17+ [501+]
Khan, Badrul - *Web-Based Instruction*
    LJ - v122 - My 1 '97 - p132 [51-250]
Khan, Javed Ahmad - *Islamic Economics and Finance*
 r ARBA - v28 - '97 - p110 [251-500]
 r R&R Bk N - v11 - D '96 - p22 [51-250]
Khan, L Ali - *The Extinction of Nation-States*
    R&R Bk N - v11 - D '96 - p46 [51-250]
Khan, M I Gabriel - *Heart Disease Diagnosis and Therapy*
 r SciTech - v20 - S '96 - p35 [51-250]
Khan, M Rashid - *Conversion and Utilization of Waste Materials*
    SciTech - v20 - S '96 - p61 [51-250]
Khandker, Shahidur R - *The Bangladesh Rural Advancement Committee's Credit Programs*
    JEL - v35 - Mr '97 - p278 [51-250]
    Education Achievements and School Efficiency in Rural Bangladesh
    JEL - v34 - D '96 - p2110 [51-250]
    Sustainability of a Government Targeted Credit Program
    JEL - v34 - S '96 - p1478 [51-250]
Khanna, Jane - *Southern China, Hong Kong, and Taiwan*
    Ch Rev Int - v4 - Spr '97 - p181+ [501+]
    JEL - v34 - S '96 - p1428 [51-250]
Kharbanda, O P - *What Made Gertie Gallop?*
    Choice - v34 - Ja '97 - p841+ [51-250]
Khare, Jitendra B - *From Contamination to Defects, Faults, and Yield Loss*
    SciTech - v20 - N '96 - p75 [51-250]
Kharitidi, Olga - *Entering the Circle*
    Utne R - N '96 - p89 [1-50]
Kharitonov, Mark - *Izbrannaia Proza. Vols. 1-2*
    BL - v93 - O 1 '96 - p327 [1-50]
    Lines of Fate
    Choice - v34 - S '96 - p135 [51-250]
    NYTBR - v101 - D 8 '96 - p80 [1-50]
    WLT - v70 - Aut '96 - p984+ [251-500]
Kharms, Daniil - *First, Second (Illus. by Marc Rosenthal)*
 c HB - v72 - S '96 - p581 [51-250]
 c HB Guide - v7 - Fall '96 - p262 [51-250]
 c Par Ch - v20 - O '96 - p28 [51-250]
 c Time - v148 - D 9 '96 - p79 [51-250]
Kharrat, Idwar - *Girls of Alexandria*
    TranslRevS - v1 - My '95 - p14 [51-250]
Khashoggi, Soheir - *Mirage*
    LJ - v121 - O 1 '96 - p47 [1-50]
Khavinson, S Ya. - *Best Approximation by Linear Superpositions (Approximate Nomography)*
    SciTech - v21 - Mr '97 - p13 [51-250]
Khazanov, Anatoly M - *After the USSR*
    Choice - v34 - O '96 - p357 [51-250]
Kheir, Michael - *The M68HC11 Microcontroller*
    SciTech - v21 - Mr '97 - p85 [51-250]
Khenpo Karthar Rinpoche - *The Instructions of Gampopa*
    BL - v93 - O 1 '96 - p301 [51-250]
Kherdian, David - *Beat Voices*
 y Kliatt - v31 - Mr '97 - p23+ [51-250]
    Road from Home
 y Kliatt - v30 - S '96 - p4 [1-50]
Khesin, Boris E - *Interpretation of Geophysical Fields in Complicated Environments*
    Choice - v34 - F '97 - p992 [51-250]
    SciTech - v20 - S '96 - p15 [51-250]
Khisamutdinov, Amir - *The Russian Far East*
    Historian - v59 - Fall '96 - p191+ [251-500]

Khlevniuk, Oleg V - *In Stalin's Shadow*
   AHR - v102 - F '97 - p141+ [501+]
   Russ Rev - v55 - O '96 - p721+ [501+]
Khoo, Iam-Choon - *Novel Optical Materials and Applications*
  r SciTech - v21 - Mr '97 - p24 [51-250]
Khoo, Michael C K - *Bioengineering Approaches to Pulmonary Physiology and Medicine*
   SciTech - v20 - D '96 - p47 [51-250]
Khoo, Rosemary - *Towards Global Multilingualism*
   Lang Soc - v25 - S '96 - p485+ [501+]
Khorana, Meena - *Africa in Literature for Children and Young Adults*
  r New Ad - v9 - Fall '96 - p348 [51-250]
  British Children's Writers 1800-1880
  r ARBA - v28 - '97 - p427 [51-250]
  r Choice - v34 - D '96 - p586 [51-250]
Khosoo, T N - *Mahatma Gandhi: An Apostle of Applied Human Ecology*
   BioSci - v46 - S '96 - p626+ [501+]
Khoury, Nabil F - *Gender and Development in the Arab World*
   CS - v26 - Mr '97 - p183+ [501+]
Khuri, Andre I - *Response Surfaces. 2nd Ed.*
   SciTech - v20 - D '96 - p17 [51-250]
Kiberd, Declan - *Inventing Ireland*
   ILS - v15 - Fall '96 - p19+ [501+]
   ILS - v15 - Fall '96 - p20 [501+]
   LJ - v122 - Ja '97 - p49+ [1-50]
   Obs - D 1 '96 - p16* [1-50]
   WLT - v71 - Win '97 - p160 [501+]
Kibler, W Ben - *ACSM's Handbook for the Team Physician*
  r SciTech - v20 - N '96 - p49 [51-250]
Kibler, William W - *The Lancelot-Grail Cycle*
   Specu - v72 - Ja '97 - p189+ [501+]
  Medieval France
  r CH - v65 - D '96 - p689+ [501+]
Kibria, Nazli - *Family Tightrope*
   Amerasia J - v22 - 2 '96 - p182+ [501+]
   Signs - v22 - Win '97 - p440+ [501+]
Kibzun, A I - *Stochastic Programming Problems with Probability and Quantile Functions*
   SciTech - v21 - Mr '97 - p72 [51-250]
Kich, Martin - *Western American Novelists. Vol. 1*
  r AL - v68 - S '96 - p667 [1-50]
  r WAL - v31 - Win '97 - p405+ [251-500]
Kidd, Bruce - *Contested Identities*
   Quill & Q - v62 - Jl '96 - p48 [251-500]
  The Struggle for Canadian Sport
   CF - v75 - D '96 - p44+ [501+]
   Choice - v34 - Ja '97 - p836 [51-250]
   R&R Bk N - v11 - N '96 - p23 [51-250]
Kidd, Chip - *Batman Collected*
   Ent W - N 1 '96 - p64 [51-250]
   Obs - N 24 '96 - p18* [501+]
   PW - v243 - O 14 '96 - p75 [51-250]
   VLS - Win '96 - p20 [51-250]
Kidd, David - *Peking Story*
   Obs - Ag 25 '96 - p16* [251-500]
   TLS - D 13 '96 - p32 [51-250]
Kidd, Mae Street - *Passing for Black*
  y BL - v93 - F 15 '97 - p998 [51-250]
Kidd, Richard - *Almost Famous Daisy! (Illus. by Richard Kidd)*
  c HB Guide - v7 - Fall '96 - p262 [51-250]
  c JB - v60 - Ag '96 - p142 [51-250]
  c SLJ - v42 - S '96 - p182 [51-250]
Kidder, Tracy - *The Soul of a New Machine*
   Inc. - v18 - D '96 - p55 [251-500]
Kids Discover
  cp Par Ch - v20 - O '96 - p15 [1-50]
Kids' Voices
   Teach Mus - v3 - Ap '96 - p21 [1-50]
Kidwell, Clara Sue - *Choctaws and Missionaries in Mississippi 1818-1918*
   AHR - v102 - F '97 - p181+ [251-500]
   PHR - v65 - Ag '96 - p480+ [251-500]
Kiefer, Frederick - *Writing on the Renaissance Stage*
   Choice - v34 - Mr '97 - p1164 [51-250]
Kiefer, Peter T - *The Fred Waring Discography*
  r ARBA - v28 - '97 - p479 [51-250]
Kiejna, A - *Metal Surface Electron Physics*
   SciTech - v20 - N '96 - p18 [51-250]
Kiel, L Douglas - *Chaos Theory in the Social Sciences*
   JEL - v34 - S '96 - p1420+ [51-250]
  Managing Chaos and Complexity in Government
   PAR - v56 - S '96 - p491+ [501+]
Kielhofner, Gary - *A Model of Human Occupation. 2nd Ed.*
   SciTech - v20 - N '96 - p56 [51-250]

Kieling, Jared T - *The Gift of Prayer*
   RR - v55 - N '96 - p660 [1-50]
Kiell, Norman - *Food and Drink in Literature*
  r ARBA - v28 - '97 - p406 [51-250]
  r Choice - v34 - N '96 - p432 [51-250]
Kielly, Shiela - *Advent and Lent Activities for Children*
   CLW - v67 - N '96 - p39 [51-250]
Kielmansegg, Peter, Graf - *Hannah Arendt and Leo Strauss*
   TLS - Ag 2 '96 - p11 [501+]
Kiely, Benedict - *The Cards of the Gambler*
   LJ - v121 - O 1 '96 - p132 [1-50]
Kiely, David M - *John Millington Synge: A Biography*
   Bloom Rev - v16 - N '96 - p20+ [501+]
Kiely, Ray - *Sociology and Development*
   SF - v75 - S '96 - p397 [501+]
Kienast, Burkhart - *Die Sumerischen Und Akkadischen Briefen*
   Rel St Rev - v23 - Ja '97 - p56 [51-250]
Kienberger, Silvia - *Poesie, Revolte Und Revolution*
   Ger Q - v69 - Spr '96 - p226+ [501+]
Kiene, Ronald P - *Biological and Environmental Chemistry of DMSP and Related Sulfonium Compounds*
   SciTech - v20 - N '96 - p28 [51-250]
Kienitz, Sabine - *Sexualitat, Macht Und Moral*
   AHR - v101 - D '96 - p1566+ [501+]
Kienzle, William X - *The Man Who Loved God*
   PW - v244 - Mr 17 '97 - p79 [51-250]
  Requiem for Moses
   Rapport - v19 - 5 '96 - p38 [251-500]
Kierkegaard, Soren - *Papers and Journals*
   CR - v268 - Je '96 - p335 [51-250]
   TranslRevS - v2 - D '96 - p18 [51-250]
  Works of Love
   RM - v50 - D '96 - p408+ [501+]
Kiernan, Ben - *The Pol Pot Regime*
   Choice - v34 - Ja '97 - p868 [51-250]
   Econ - v339 - My 18 '96 - p10* [501+]
   Lon R Bks - v18 - O 3 '96 - p11+ [501+]
   NS & S - v9 - My 3 '96 - p36+ [501+]
   NYRB - v43 - N 14 '96 - p41+ [501+]
   RP - v59 - Win '97 - p186+ [501+]
Kiernan, Pauline - *Shakespeare's Theory of Drama*
   Choice - v34 - F '97 - p967 [501+]
Kiernan, V G - *Imperialism and Its Contradictions*
   HT - v46 - Ag '96 - p56+ [501+]
  Shakespeare: Poet and Citizen
   Queens U - v103 - Win '96 - p807+ [501+]
Kies, Cosette - *Supernatural Fiction for Teens. 2nd Ed.*
  yr RQ - v36 - Win '96 - p224 [51-250]
Kiesling, Eugenia C - *Arming against Hitler*
   Choice - v34 - Ja '97 - p856+ [51-250]
   J Mil H - v61 - Ja '97 - p187 [251-500]
   R&R Bk N - v11 - N '96 - p10 [51-250]
Kiewe, Amos - *A Shining City on a Hill*
   JC - v46 - Sum '96 - p176+ [501+]
Kigunga, Raphael - *The Anthropology of Self-Person and Myth in Africa*
   R&R Bk N - v12 - F '97 - p4 [1-50]
Kihlstrom, April - *The Widowed Bride*
   LJ - v121 - N 15 '96 - p48 [1-50]
Kihn, Greg - *Horror Show*
   KR - v64 - Ag 15 '96 - p1174+ [251-500]
   Necro - Win '97 - p18+ [501+]
   PW - v243 - S 16 '96 - p72 [51-250]
Kijewski, Karen - *Honky Tonk Kat*
   Arm Det - v29 - Fall '96 - p496+ [251-500]
El-Kikhia, Mansour O - *Libya's Qaddafi*
   BL - v93 - Mr 1 '97 - p1108 [51-250]
   LJ - v122 - F 15 '97 - p148 [51-250]
Kiki - *Kiki's Memoirs*
   BL - v93 - N 15 '96 - p563 [51-250]
   LJ - v122 - F 1 '97 - p77 [51-250]
   NYTBR - v102 - Mr 16 '97 - p20 [51-250]
   PW - v243 - O 21 '96 - p66+ [51-250]
Kikoski, John F - *Reflexive Communication in the Culturally Diverse Workplace*
   Choice - v34 - D '96 - p655 [51-250]
   R&R Bk N - v11 - D '96 - p35 [51-250]
Kikuchi, June F - *Truth in Nursing Inquiry*
   Choice - v34 - O '96 - p314 [51-250]
Kil, David H - *Pattern Recognition and Prediction with Applications to Signal Characterization*
   SciTech - v20 - N '96 - p76 [51-250]
Kilbourne, Richard Holcombe, Jr. - *Debt, Investment, Slaves*
   AHR - v101 - D '96 - p1624+ [501+]
Kilcommons, Brian - *Mutts: America's Dogs*
   LJ - v121 - N 1 '96 - p99 [51-250]

Kilcup, Karen L - *Nineteenth-Century American Women Writers*
   Choice - v34 - My '97 - p1497+ [51-250]
Kilduff, Peter - *Richthofen: Beyond the Legend of the Red Baron*
   Historian - v58 - Sum '96 - p908+ [501+]
Kile, Robert W - *Strategic Board Recruitment*
   ChrPhil - v8 - O 3 '96 - p44 [51-250]
Killat, Ulrich - *Access to B-ISDN via PONs*
   SciTech - v20 - S '96 - p54 [51-250]
Killeen, Richard - *The Easter Rising*
  c TES - O 4 '96 - p17* [501+]
Killen, John - *The Famine Decade*
   ILS - v16 - Spr '97 - p35 [51-250]
Killick, Tony - *IMF Programmes in Developing Countries*
   Econ J - v107 - Ja '97 - p228+ [501+]
Killoran, Helen - *Edith Wharton: Art and Allusion*
   Choice - v34 - S '96 - p126 [51-250]
Kilmer, Nicholas - *A Place in Normandy*
   BL - v93 - D 15 '96 - p706+ [51-250]
   KR - v64 - O 15 '96 - p1513 [51-250]
   LJ - v121 - N 15 '96 - p78 [51-250]
   NYTBR - v101 - D 8 '96 - p31 [251-500]
   PW - v243 - N 11 '96 - p62 [51-250]
   Smith - v27 - F '97 - p129 [51-250]
Kilmer, Paulette D - *The Fear of Sinking*
   Choice - v34 - Ap '97 - p1405 [51-250]
Kilminster, Richard - *Culture, Modernity and Revolution*
   R&R Bk N - v11 - N '96 - p35 [51-250]
   Socio R - v45 - My '97 - p341+ [501+]
Kilner, John F - *Bioethics and the Future of Medicine*
   CC - v113 - N 6 '96 - p1087 [251-500]
   CC - v113 - N 20 '96 - p1157+ [501+]
  The Center for Bioethics and Human Dignity Presents Dignity and Dying
   Choice - v34 - Ap '97 - p1355 [51-250]
Kilov, Haim - *Object-Oriented Behavioral Specifications*
   SciTech - v21 - Mr '97 - p65 [51-250]
Kilpatrick, Andrew - *Of Permanent Value*
   Rapport - v19 - 6 '96 - p34 [251-500]
Kilroy, Phil - *Protestant Dissent and Controversy in Ireland 1660-1714*
   EHR - v111 - N '96 - p1288+ [251-500]
Kilworth, Garry - *Angel*
   SF Chr - v18 - O '96 - p78 [51-250]
  The Bronte Girls
  y JB - v60 - O '96 - p211 [251-500]
  Cybercats
  c Bks Keeps - Jl '96 - p12 [51-250]
  y Sch Lib - v44 - Ag '96 - p120 [51-250]
  The Raiders
  c JB - v60 - D '96 - p269 [51-250]
  y Sch Lib - v44 - N '96 - p171 [51-250]
  The Roof of Voyaging
  y TES - Jl 5 '96 - pR8 [501+]
Kim, Ai Ra - *Women Struggling for a New Life*
   CS - v26 - Mr '97 - p239 [501+]
   R&R Bk N - v12 - F '97 - p11 [51-250]
Kim, Bo-Kyung - *Sing 'n Learn Korean. Book and Audio Version*
  c PW - v244 - Mr 17 '97 - p47 [51-250]
Kim, C - *Microelectromechanical Systems*
   SciTech - v21 - Mr '97 - p86 [51-250]
Kim, Choong Soon - *The Culture of Korean Industry*
   RA - v25 - 3 '96 - p185+ [501+]
Kim, Dae Jung - *Mass-Participatory Economy. Rev. Ed.*
   R&R Bk N - v12 - F '97 - p37 [51-250]
Kim, Elaine H - *East to America*
   Amerasia J - v22 - 3 '96 - p175+ [501+]
   Bl S - v26 - Sum '96 - p65 [1-50]
   Comw - v123 - S 13 '96 - p34+ [501+]
  y SLJ - v42 - N '96 - p141 [51-250]
Kim, Helen - *The Long Season of Rain*
  y BL - v93 - N 1 '96 - p490 [51-250]
  c CBRS - v25 - Win '97 - p69 [51-250]
  y HB - v73 - Ja '97 - p59+ [51-250]
  y HB Guide - v8 - Spr '97 - p81 [51-250]
  y KR - v64 - O 15 '96 - p1534 [51-250]
  y NYTBR - v102 - Mr 16 '97 - p26 [51-250]
  c PW - v243 - N 4 '96 - p48 [1-50]
  y PW - v243 - N 4 '96 - p77 [51-250]
  y SLJ - v42 - D '96 - p30 [1-50]
  y SLJ - v42 - D '96 - p139 [51-250]
  y VOYA - v19 - F '97 - p328+ [251-500]
Kim, Hyung-Ki - *The Civil Service System and Economic Development*
   JEL - v35 - Mr '97 - p203 [51-250]
  The Japanese Civil Service and Economic Development
   APSR - v90 - D '96 - p939+ [501+]

Kim, In-Su - *Protestants and the Formation of Modern Korean Nationalism 1885-1920*
    Choice - v34 - My '97 - p1516 [51-250]
Kim, Jaegwon - *Philosophy of Mind*
    Choice - v34 - O '96 - p294 [51-250]
Kim, Kichung - *An Introduction to Classical Korean Literature*
    R&R Bk N - v12 - F '97 - p79 [51-250]
Kim, Patti - *A Cab Called Reliable*
    KR - v65 - My 1 '97 - p665 [251-500]
Kim, Sojin - *Chicano Graffiti and Murals*
    CAY - v17 - Fall '96 - p5 [51-250]
Kim, Sun-Jin - *Tuttle Dictionary of the Martial Arts of Korea, China and Japan*
  r ARBA - v28 - '97 - p300 [51-250]
Kim, Young C - *The Southeast Asian Economic Miracle*
    Econ J - v106 - S '96 - p1481 [251-500]
Kim, Young Jeh - *The New Pacific Community in the 1990s*
    For Aff - v76 - Mr '97 - p197 [51-250]
    R&R Bk N - v12 - F '97 - p21 [51-250]
Kimball, Christopher - *The Cook's Bible*
    BL - v93 - S 15 '96 - p196 [51-250]
    CSM - v89 - D 13 '96 - p10 [51-250]
    LJ - v121 - O 15 '96 - p85+ [51-250]
    PW - v243 - N 4 '96 - p47 [1-50]
Kimball, Gayle - *The Teen Trip*
  yr Kliatt - v31 - My '97 - p23+ [251-500]
Kimball, Herrick - *Making Plastic-Laminate Countertops*
    BL - v93 - O 1 '96 - p313 [51-250]
Kimball, Michael - *Undone*
    BL - v93 - S 15 '96 - p221 [51-250]
    LJ - v121 - S 15 '96 - p96+ [51-250]
    PW - v243 - S 16 '96 - p71 [51-250]
    Rapport - v19 - 6 '96 - p26 [51-250]
Kimball, Ralph - *The Data Warehouse Toolkit*
    CBR - v14 - N '96 - p40 [51-250]
    SciTech - v20 - S '96 - p8 [51-250]
Kimball, Stephen - *Death Duty*
    KR - v64 - S 15 '96 - p1343 [251-500]
    LJ - v121 - O 15 '96 - p90 [51-250]
    NYTBR - v102 - Mr 30 '97 - p16 [51-250]
    PW - v243 - O 14 '96 - p64 [51-250]
Kimball, Warren F - *Forged in War*
    BL - v93 - D 15 '96 - p707 [51-250]
    KR - v65 - Ja 1 '97 - p40+ [251-500]
    PW - v244 - Ja 13 '97 - p62+ [51-250]
Kimbel, William H - *Species, Species Concepts and Primate Evolution*
    RA - v25 - 3 '96 - p205+ [501+]
Kimble, Gregory A - *Psychology: The Hope of a Science*
    Choice - v34 - S '96 - p215 [51-250]
Kimbriel, Katharine Eliska - *Night Calls*
  y VOYA - v19 - O '96 - p218 [251-500]
Kimbro, Dennis P - *What Makes the Great Great*
    BL - v93 - Ja '97 - p783 [51-250]
    LJ - v121 - N 15 '96 - p70 [51-250]
    PW - v243 - N 18 '96 - p56 [51-250]
Kimbrough, David L - *Taking Up Serpents*
    AHR - v102 - F '97 - p195+ [501+]
    JSH - v62 - N '96 - p838+ [251-500]
Kimmel, Allan J - *Ethical Issues in Behavioral Research*
    Choice - v34 - S '96 - p215 [51-250]
    Hast Cen R - v26 - Jl '96 - p41 [1-50]
Kimmel, Eric A - *Bearhead: A Russian Folktale*
  c PW - v244 - Mr 10 '97 - p69 [1-50]
Billy Lazroe and the King of the Sea (Illus. by Michael Steirnagle)
  c BL - v93 - D 15 '96 - p730 [51-250]
  c CBRS - v25 - Win '97 - p63 [51-250]
  c CCB-B - v50 - D '96 - p140 [51-250]
  c HB Guide - v8 - Spr '97 - p103 [51-250]
  c PW - v243 - N 4 '96 - p75 [51-250]
  c SLJ - v42 - D '96 - p114 [51-250]
Count Silvernose (Illus. by Omar Rayyan)
  c HB Guide - v7 - Fall '96 - p322 [51-250]
  c NYTBR - v101 - O 13 '96 - p26 [1-50]
The Magic Dreidels (Illus. by Katya Krenina)
  c BL - v93 - S 1 '96 - p137 [51-250]
  c CBRS - v25 - O '96 - p15+ [51-250]
  c CCB-B - v50 - N '96 - p101+ [51-250]
  c Ch BWatch - v6 - O '96 - p4 [1-50]
  c CLW - v67 - D '96 - p53 [51-250]
  c HB Guide - v8 - Spr '97 - p34 [51-250]
  c NYTBR - v101 - D 8 '96 - p78 [1-50]
  c PW - v243 - S 30 '96 - p87 [51-250]
  c SLJ - v42 - O '96 - p37+ [51-250]

One Eye, Two Eyes, Three Eyes (Illus. by Dirk Zimmer)
  c BL - v93 - N 1 '96 - p503 [51-250]
  c HB - v73 - Ja '97 - p72+ [51-250]
  c HB Guide - v8 - Spr '97 - p103 [51-250]
  c PW - v243 - N 4 '96 - p75 [51-250]
  c SLJ - v43 - Ja '97 - p102 [51-250]
Onions and Garlic (Illus. by Katya Arnold)
  c HB Guide - v7 - Fall '96 - p322 [1-50]
Squash It! (Illus. by Robert Rayevsky)
  c PW - v244 - Ap 21 '97 - p72 [51-250]
The Tale of Ali Baba and the Forty Thieves (Illus. by Will Hillenbrand)
  c BL - v93 - D 1 '96 - p667 [51-250]
  c CCB-B - v50 - F '97 - p211+ [51-250]
  c HB - v73 - Ja '97 - p73 [51-250]
  c HB Guide - v8 - Spr '97 - p103 [51-250]
  c PW - v243 - S 16 '96 - p82 [51-250]
  c SLJ - v42 - D '96 - p114 [51-250]
Kimmel, Michael S - *Manhood in America*
    AJS - v102 - S '96 - p633+ [501+]
    CS - v26 - Ja '97 - p20+ [501+]
The Politics of Manhood
    Rapport - v19 - 4 '96 - p41 [251-500]
Kimmelman, Burt - *The Poetics of Authorship in the Later Middle Ages*
    R&R Bk N - v12 - F '97 - p80 [1-50]
Kimmelman, Leslie - *Hooray! It's Passover! (Illus. by John Himmelman)*
  c HB Guide - v7 - Fall '96 - p310 [1-50]
Kimmelman, Mira Ryczke - *Echoes from the Holocaust*
  y BL - v93 - D 1 '96 - p640 [51-250]
  y Kliatt - v31 - My '97 - p21 [251-500]
    PW - v243 - O 14 '96 - p79 [51-250]
Kimme-Smith, Carolyn - *Workbook for Quality Mammography. 2nd Ed.*
    SciTech - v21 - Mr '97 - p63 [51-250]
Kimpton, Diana - *The Bear Santa Claus Forgot (Illus. by Anna Kiernan)*
  c RT - v50 - O '96 - p132 [1-50]
Kinane, Vincent - *A History of the Dublin University Press 1734-1976*
    Lib - v18 - S '96 - p268+ [501+]
Kincaid, A Douglas - *Comparative National Development*
    CS - v25 - S '96 - p639+ [501+]
Kincaid, David - *Numerical Analysis. 2nd Ed.*
    SciTech - v20 - S '96 - p10 [51-250]
Kincaid, Harold - *Philosophical Foundations of the Social Sciences*
    Choice - v34 - N '96 - p499 [51-250]
    JEL - v34 - D '96 - p2016 [51-250]
Kincaid, Jamaica - *Annie John*
  y BL - v93 - Ja '97 - p832 [1-50]
The Autobiography of My Mother
    Ant R - v54 - Sum '96 - p368 [251-500]
    Ent W - Ja 17 '97 - p59 [51-250]
    HR - v49 - Aut '96 - p483+ [501+]
  y Kliatt - v31 - Mr '97 - p10 [51-250]
    LATBR - D 29 '96 - p11 [1-50]
    Lon R Bks - v19 - F 6 '97 - p25+ [501+]
    NS - v125 - O 11 '96 - p45 [501+]
    NYTBR - v101 - D 8 '96 - p76 [1-50]
    NYTBR - v102 - Ja 26 '97 - p28 [51-250]
    Obs - S 29 '96 - p18* [51-250]
    TLS - S 20 '96 - p22 [501+]
    Trib Bks - F 2 '97 - p8 [1-50]
    VLS - Win '96 - p10 [51-250]
    WLT - v71 - Win '97 - p202 [251-500]
Kincaid, James R - *Annoying the Victorians*
    VS - v39 - Spr '96 - p468+ [501+]
Child-Loving: The Erotic Child and Victorian Culture
    VS - v39 - Spr '96 - p468+ [501+]
Kincheloe, Joe L - *Measured Lies*
    Choice - v34 - N '96 - p543 [51-250]
Kindelan, Nancy - *Shadows of Realism*
    Choice - v34 - S '96 - p291+ [51-250]
Kinder, A Gordon - *Spanish Protestants and Reformers in the Sixteenth Century. 1st Suppl.*
    CH - v66 - Mr '97 - p198+ [51-250]
  r Six Ct J - v27 - Win '96 - p1147 [51-250]
Kinder, Donald R - *Divided by Color*
    Bl S - v26 - Fall '96 - p104 [51-250]
Kinder, Marsha - *Blood Cinema*
    Film Cr - v21 - Fall '96 - p75+ [501+]
Kinder, Peter - *Investing for Good*
    Kiplinger - v50 - O '96 - p32 [251-500]
Kinderman, William - *Beethoven*
    Notes - v53 - S '96 - p72+ [501+]

Kindersley, Barnabas - *Children Just like Me*
  c Emerg Lib - v24 - Mr '97 - p46 [51-250]
  c LA - v73 - O '96 - p430 [51-250]
  cr Par Ch - v21 - Mr '97 - p5 [1-50]
  c RT - v50 - Mr '97 - p476+ [51-250]
Kindl, Patrice - *The Woman in the Wall*
  y BL - v93 - Mr 15 '97 - p1236 [51-250]
  y CCB-B - v50 - Mr '97 - p251 [51-250]
  c KR - v65 - Mr 1 '97 - p382+ [51-250]
  c PW - v244 - F 17 '97 - p220 [51-250]
Kindleberger, Charles P - *Centralization Versus Pluralism*
    JEL - v34 - D '96 - p2103 [51-250]
World Economic Primacy 1500-1990
    For Aff - v75 - S '96 - p139 [51-250]
    JEH - v56 - S '96 - p702+ [501+]
    JEL - v34 - S '96 - p1464+ [51-250]
The World Economy and National Finance in Historical Perspective
    Econ J - v106 - N '96 - p1793+ [501+]
    JEH - v56 - S '96 - p702+ [501+]
    JEL - v34 - S '96 - p1464 [51-250]
Kindler, Seth - *Mind Games*
    Arm Det - v29 - Sum '96 - p373 [51-250]
Kinealy, Christine - *This Great Calamity*
    VS - v39 - Win '96 - p205+ [501+]
Kinesis
  p Sm Pr R - v29 - F '97 - p13+ [51-250]
King, Andy - *Fundamental Mountain Biking (Illus. by Andy King)*
  c HB Guide - v8 - Spr '97 - p145 [51-250]
  c SLJ - v43 - F '97 - p118 [51-250]
King, Anita - *Contemporary Quotations in Black*
  r LJ - v122 - My 1 '97 - p94+ [51-250]
King, Anthony D - *Re-Presenting the City*
    CS - v26 - Mr '97 - p193+ [501+]
King, Anthony Stephen - *Running Scared*
  y BL - v93 - N 15 '96 - p554 [51-250]
    Choice - v34 - My '97 - p1576 [51-250]
    Econ - v342 - F 15 '97 - p10*+ [501+]
    KR - v64 - N 1 '96 - p1583+ [251-500]
    LJ - v121 - D '96 - p122+ [51-250]
    PW - v243 - N 25 '96 - p63+ [51-250]
    WSJ-Cent - v99 - Ja 2 '97 - pA4 [501+]
King, B B - *Blues All around Me*
    BL - v93 - S 1 '96 - p3 [51-250]
King, Bernice A - *Hard Questions, Heart Answers*
    BL - v93 - D 15 '96 - p694 [51-250]
    PW - v243 - N 11 '96 - p69 [51-250]
King, Brian - *Lustmord: The Writings and Artifacts of Murderers*
    VLS - Spr '97 - p12 [501+]
King, Casey - *Oh, Freedom!*
  c BL - v93 - Ap 1 '97 - p1328 [51-250]
  c BW - v27 - Ap 6 '97 - p8 [251-500]
King, Celia - *Seven Great Explorations (Illus. by Celia King)*
  c Can CL - v22 - Fall '96 - p113+ [51-250]
  c HB Guide - v8 - Spr '97 - p162 [51-250]
King, Christopher R - *One Language, Two Scripts*
    AHR - v101 - D '96 - p1606+ [51-250]
King, Dave - *Farm Pops*
  c ECEJ - v24 - Win '96 - p109 [51-250]
This Is Me
  c ECEJ - v24 - Win '96 - p108+ [1-50]
King, David C - *Freedom of Assembly*
  c BL - v93 - My 15 '97 - p1574 [51-250]
The Right to Speak Out
  c BL - v93 - My 15 '97 - p1574 [51-250]
King, Dean - *Every Man Will Do His Duty*
    LJ - v122 - Ap 1 '97 - p105 [51-250]
    PW - v244 - F 24 '97 - p80+ [1-50]
Harbors and High Seas
  r LATBR - O 20 '96 - p3 [51-250]
King, Desmond - *Actively Seeking Work?*
    AAPSS-A - v546 - Jl '96 - p174+ [501+]
    APSR - v91 - Mr '97 - p218+ [501+]
Rethinking Local Democracy
    TLS - D 20 '96 - p28 [501+]
Separate and Unequal
    APSR - v90 - D '96 - p867+ [501+]
    Bl S - v26 - Sum '96 - p65+ [1-50]
King, Edmund - *The Anarchy of King Stephen's Reign*
    Albion - v28 - Sum '96 - p284+ [501+]
    EHR - v112 - F '97 - p163+ [501+]
    Specu - v71 - O '96 - p968+ [501+]
King, Edward - *Rubber Up!*
    Obs - N 3 '96 - p16* [251-500]
King, Eleace - *Culture of Recovery, Culture of Denial Alcoholism among Men and Women Religious*
    RR - v55 - S '96 - p547+ [501+]

King, Elizabeth - *Chile Fever (Illus. by Elizabeth King)*
  c JOYS - v9 - Sum '96 - p416 [51-250]
King, Florence - *The Florence King Reader*
  BW - v26 - S 8 '96 - p12 [51-250]
  LATBR - S 22 '96 - p15 [1-50]
King, Francis - *A Hand at the Shutter*
  Spec - v277 - N 30 '96 - p51+ [251-500]
  TLS - D 6 '96 - p22 [501+]
King, Gillian - *Reptiles and Herbivory*
  Choice - v34 - F '97 - p990 [51-250]
King, Greg - *The Mad King*
  LJ - v121 - O 15 '96 - p67 [51-250]
  PW - v243 - S 30 '96 - p71 [51-250]
King, Irving H - *The Coast Guard Expands 1865-1915*
  Choice - v34 - S '96 - p195 [51-250]
King, J E - *An Alternative Macroeconomic Theory*
  JEL - v35 - Mr '97 - p193 [51-250]
  Conversations with Post Keynesians
  Econ J - v106 - S '96 - p1462 [251-500]
  Post Keynesian Economics
  r ARBA - v28 - '97 - p76 [251-500]
  r Econ J - v106 - S '96 - p1462+ [51-250]
King, James - *Virginia Woolf*
  RMR - v50 - 2 '96 - p169+ [501+]
King, Jane - *Welcome to Chillsville Elementary*
  c PW - v243 - N 11 '96 - p76 [51-250]
King, John - *Central Asia*
  r BL - v93 - S 15 '96 - p210 [1-50]
  r FEER - v160 - Mr 27 '97 - p53 [501+]
King, Joseph - *Scale in Conscious Experience*
  AJPsych - v153 - N '96 - p1495+ [501+]
King, Julie - *Interviewing and Salary Negotiation*
  BWatch - v18 - F '97 - p3 [1-50]
  Resumes and Job Hunting
  BWatch - v18 - F '97 - p3 [1-50]
King, K N - *C Programming*
  Choice - v34 - S '96 - p164 [51-250]
King, Karen L - *Revelation of the Unknowable God*
  Rel St Rev - v23 - Ap '97 - p188 [51-250]
King, Katie - *Theory in Its Feminist Travels*
  NWSA Jnl - v8 - Fall '96 - p166+ [501+]
King, Kenneth - *Jua Kali Kenya*
  Choice - v34 - F '97 - p1012 [51-250]
  JEL - v35 - Mr '97 - p272 [51-250]
King, Kenneth D - *Designer Techniques*
  LJ - v122 - Ap 15 '97 - p79 [51-250]
King, Laurie R - *The Beekeeper's Apprentice*
  y Kliatt - v30 - S '96 - p2 [1-50]
  y Kliatt - v30 - S '96 - p11 [51-250]
  The Beekeeper's Apprentice (Follows). Audio Version
  BL - v93 - F 15 '97 - p1038 [51-250]
  y Kliatt - v31 - Ja '97 - p37 [51-250]
  A Grave Talent (Bresnahan). Audio Version
  y Kliatt - v31 - Ja '97 - p41 [51-250]
  LJ - v122 - Ja '97 - p172 [51-250]
  A Letter of Mary
  BL - v93 - Ja '97 - p825 [51-250]
  BW - v26 - D 15 '96 - p10 [251-500]
  KR - v64 - N 1 '96 - p1567 [51-250]
  NYTBR - v102 - Ja 5 '97 - p20 [51-250]
  PW - v243 - N 18 '96 - p64 [51-250]
  Trib Bks - Ja 5 '97 - p4 [51-250]
  WSJ-Cent - v99 - F 5 '97 - pA16 [51-250]
  A Letter of Mary (Follows). Audio Version
  y Kliatt - v31 - My '97 - p42 [51-250]
  A Monstrous Regiment of Women
  Arm Det - v29 - Fall '96 - p402 [51-250]
  y Kliatt - v31 - Ja '97 - p8 [51-250]
  PW - v243 - N 18 '96 - p70 [1-50]
  A Monstrous Regiment of Women (Follows). Audio Version
  BL - v93 - N 1 '96 - p522 [51-250]
  A Monstrous Regiment of Women (Sterlin). Audio Version
  y Kliatt - v31 - Mr '97 - p44 [51-250]
  With Child
  Arm Det - v29 - Sum '96 - p377 [51-250]
  PW - v244 - Mr 31 '97 - p72 [1-50]
King, Linda - *Roots of Identity*
  Lang Soc - v26 - Mr '97 - p150+ [501+]
King, Margaret L - *The Death of the Child Valerio Marcello*
  JIH - v27 - Aut '96 - p321+ [501+]
  Ren Q - v50 - Spr '97 - p266+ [501+]
King, Martin Luther, Jr. - *The Papers of Martin Luther King, Jr. Vol. 3*
  BL - v93 - F 15 '97 - p980 [51-250]
King, Nina - *Crimes of the Scene*
  r PW - v244 - F 10 '97 - p71 [51-250]

King, Penny - *Portraits*
  c Bks Keeps - v100 - S '96 - p20 [51-250]
  c Ch BWatch - v6 - O '96 - p5 [51-250]
  c PW - v243 - S 2 '96 - p133 [51-250]
  c Sch Lib - v44 - N '96 - p163 [51-250]
  c SLJ - v43 - Ja '97 - p103 [51-250]
  Stories
  c Bks Keeps - v100 - S '96 - p20 [51-250]
  c Ch BWatch - v6 - O '96 - p5 [51-250]
  c PW - v243 - S 2 '96 - p133 [51-250]
  c Sch Lib - v44 - N '96 - p163 [51-250]
  c SLJ - v43 - Ja '97 - p103 [51-250]
King, Penny, 1963- - *Animals*
  c Bks Keeps - v100 - S '96 - p20 [51-250]
  c Ch BWatch - v6 - O '96 - p5 [51-250]
  c PW - v243 - S 2 '96 - p133 [51-250]
  c Sch Lib - v44 - N '96 - p163 [51-250]
  c SLJ - v43 - Ja '97 - p103 [51-250]
  Landscapes
  c Ch BWatch - v6 - O '96 - p5 [51-250]
  c PW - v243 - S 2 '96 - p133 [51-250]
  c Sch Lib - v44 - N '96 - p163 [51-250]
  c SLJ - v43 - Ja '97 - p103 [51-250]
King, Peter - *Spiced to Death*
  KR - v65 - My 1 '97 - p681+ [251-500]
King, Preston - *Socialism and the Common Good*
  TLS - S 20 '96 - p10 [501+]
King, Reyahn - *Ignatius Sancho: An African Man of Letters*
  TLS - Mr 28 '97 - p17 [501+]
King, Richard - *Kindling Does for Firewood*
  Aust Bk R - O '96 - p46+ [501+]
King, Robert C - *A Dictionary of Genetics. 5th Ed.*
  r Nature - v386 - Ap 10 '97 - p567 [1-50]
King, Russell - *Mass Migration in Europe*
  GJ - v163 - Mr '97 - p98 [251-500]
King, Stephen - *The Bad Death of Eduard Delacroix*
  Ent W - Je 28 '96 - p98 [251-500]
  y Kliatt - v30 - S '96 - p18 [51-250]
  NYTBR - v101 - O 26 '96 - p16+ [501+]
  y VOYA - v19 - D '96 - p280+ [251-500]
  Christine
  Ext - v38 - Spr '97 - p66+ [501+]
  Coffey on the Mile
  Ent W - S 6 '96 - p67 [251-500]
  NYTBR - v101 - O 26 '96 - p16+ [501+]
  y VOYA - v19 - D '96 - p281 [251-500]
  Coffey's Hands
  y Kliatt - v30 - S '96 - p18 [51-250]
  NYTBR - v101 - O 26 '96 - p16+ [501+]
  y VOYA - v19 - D '96 - p280 [51-250]
  Desperation
  Bks & Cult - v3 - Mr '97 - p14+ [501+]
  y BL - v92 - Ag '96 - p1854 [251-500]
  BW - v26 - S 22 '96 - p5 [501+]
  CSM - v88 - N 14 '96 - p14 [51-250]
  CSM - v89 - D 19 '96 - p14 [51-250]
  CSM - v89 - Ja 16 '97 - p14 [51-250]
  Ent W - O 4 '96 - p54+ [501+]
  LATBR - S 22 '96 - p9 [501+]
  Necro - Win '97 - p9+ [501+]
  NY - v72 - S 30 '96 - p78+ [501+]
  NYTBR - v101 - O 20 '96 - p16+ [501+]
  PW - v243 - N 4 '96 - p42 [51-250]
  Desperation (King). Audio Version
  LJ - v122 - My 1 '97 - p154 [51-250]
  The Green Mile. Pts. 1-6
  Ent W - D 27 '96 - p142 [51-250]
  Misery
  JPC - v30 - Fall '96 - p137+ [501+]
  The Mountain on the Mile
  y VOYA - v19 - O '96 - p218+ [51-250]
  The Mouse on the Mile
  Analog - v116 - D '96 - p145+ [51-250]
  y Kliatt - v30 - S '96 - p18 [51-250]
  NYTBR - v101 - O 26 '96 - p16+ [501+]
  Night Journey
  y Kliatt - v30 - S '96 - p18 [51-250]
  NYTBR - v101 - O 26 '96 - p16+ [501+]
  y VOYA - v19 - D '96 - p281 [251-500]
  The Two Dead Girls
  Analog - v116 - D '96 - p145+ [51-250]
  y Kliatt - v30 - S '96 - p18 [51-250]
  LATBR - Mr 24 '96 - p10 [51-250]
  MFSF - v91 - S '96 - p35+ [501+]
  NYTBR - v101 - O 26 '96 - p16+ [501+]
  y VOYA - v19 - O '96 - p218+ [251-500]
King, Stephen Michael - *A Special Kind of Love*
  c ECEJ - v24 - Spr '97 - p175+ [51-250]
  c HB Guide - v7 - Fall '96 - p262 [51-250]

King, Susan - *The Raven's Moon*
  PW - v244 - Ja 27 '97 - p102 [51-250]
King, Susan Elizabeth - *Treading the Maze*
  PW - v244 - Mr 10 '97 - p54+ [51-250]
King, Tabitha - *Survivor*
  BL - v93 - Ja '97 - p820 [51-250]
  KR - v64 - D 1 '96 - p1692+ [251-500]
  LJ - v121 - N 15 '96 - p89 [51-250]
  PW - v243 - D 2 '96 - p39 [51-250]
King, Vandall T - *Mineralogy of Maine. Vol. 1*
  r J Gov Info - v23 - S '96 - p585 [51-250]
King, Wilma - *Stolen Childhood*
  JTWS - v13 - Spr '96 - p429+ [501+]
  NYTBR - v101 - O 27 '96 - p38+ [251-500]
Kingdon, Robert McCune - *Adultery and Divorce in Calvin's Geneva*
  AHR - v101 - O '96 - p1240 [501+]
  CHR - v82 - O '96 - p716+ [501+]
  Historian - v59 - Fall '96 - p192+ [501+]
  JIH - v27 - Aut '96 - p313+ [501+]
Kingery, W David - *Learning from Things*
  Choice - v34 - Ja '97 - p851 [51-250]
  R&R Bk N - v11 - N '96 - p22 [51-250]
Kingfisher, Catherine Pelissier - *Women in the American Welfare Trap*
  Choice - v34 - Mr '97 - p1245+ [51-250]
Kingfisher I Wonder Why Encyclopedia
  cr New Sci - v152 - O 19 '96 - p47 [51-250]
The Kingfisher Illustrated Children's Dictionary
  cr Ch BWatch - v6 - D '96 - p4+ [51-250]
Kinghorn, Harriet R - *Handy Dandy Reading Records K-3*
  SLMQ - v25 - Fall '96 - p64 [51-250]
Kingma, Bruce R - *The Economics of Access Versus Ownership*
  CLW - v67 - Mr '97 - p46+ [251-500]
  The Economics of Information
  LAR - v99 - F '97 - p102 [51-250]
  RQ - v36 - Fall '96 - p156+ [251-500]
  R&R Bk N - v11 - N '96 - p29 [51-250]
Kingma, Daphne Rose - *Finding True Love*
  Bloom Rev - v16 - N '96 - p15 [251-500]
  LJ - v121 - N 1 '96 - p94 [51-250]
Kingman, Rani - *A Taste of Madras*
  BL - v93 - D 15 '96 - p701+ [51-250]
Kingsbury, John M - *Trading in Santa Fe*
  Choice - v34 - D '96 - p676 [51-250]
  R&R Bk N - v11 - N '96 - p20 [51-250]
Kingsbury, Kate - *Chivalry Is Dead*
  Arm Det - v30 - Win '97 - p98+ [501+]
Kingsbury, Noel - *The New Perennial Garden*
  Fine Gard - S '96 - p69+ [251-500]
  Hort - v74 - D '96 - p56+ [251-500]
  TES - Ag 23 '96 - p22 [51-250]
  The Ultimate Planting Guide
  BL - v93 - Ap 1 '97 - p1274 [51-250]
Kingsbury, Paul - *The Country Reader*
  LJ - v121 - N 1 '96 - p41 [1-50]
  LJ - v121 - N 1 '96 - p68 [51-250]
  The Grand Ole Opry History of Country Music
  LJ - v121 - N 1 '96 - p42 [1-50]
Kingsbury, Stewart A - *Weather Wisdom*
  r SciTech - v21 - Mr '97 - p26 [51-250]
Kingsland, Robin - *Beanstalk*
  c Magpies - v11 - My '96 - p53 [1-50]
Kingsley, Amis - *The Biographer's Moustache*
  WLT - v70 - Sum '96 - p689+ [501+]
Kingsley, Charles - *The Water-Babies. Audio Version*
  c Ch BWatch - v7 - Ja '97 - p1 [1-50]
  The Water-Babies (Illus. by Jessie Willcox Smith)
  c PW - v244 - Mr 31 '97 - p77 [1-50]
Kingsley, J J - *Science, Technology and Commercialization of Powder Synthesis and Shape Forming Processes*
  SciTech - v20 - S '96 - p61 [51-250]
Kingsley, Katherine - *Once upon a Dream*
  PW - v244 - Mr 24 '97 - p81 [51-250]
Kingsley, Peter - *Ancient Philosophy, Mystery, and Magic*
  Parabola - v21 - N '96 - p110+ [501+]
King-Smith, Dick - *Animal Friends (Illus. by Anita Jeram)*
  c Sch Lib - v45 - F '97 - p39 [51-250]
  Animal Stories
  c Obs - Mr 30 '97 - p17* [51-250]
  Babe and Other Pig Tales (Illus. by Mary Rayner)
  c Spec - v277 - D 14 '96 - p77 [1-50]
  Babe, the Sheep Pig (Thorne). Audio Version
  c Ch BWatch - v6 - O '96 - p4 [51-250]
  c CSM - v89 - F 27 '97 - pB4 [51-250]
  c Emerg Lib - v24 - Mr '97 - p24 [51-250]
  y Kliatt - v31 - My '97 - p46 [51-250]

Clever Duck (Illus. by Mike Terry)
c JB - v60 - Ag '96 - p149 [51-250]
Dick King-Smith's Animal Friends (Illus. by Anita Jeram)
c BL - v93 - D 1 '96 - p650 [51-250]
c Ch BWatch - v6 - N '96 - p6 [1-50]
c HB - v73 - Mr '97 - p211+ [51-250]
c HB Guide - v8 - Spr '97 - p118 [51-250]
c KR - v64 - O 15 '96 - p1534 [51-250]
c SLJ - v42 - D '96 - p114 [51-250]
c Smith - v27 - N '96 - p168 [1-50]
Godhanger
y Bks Keeps - N '96 - p18 [501+]
c JB - v60 - D '96 - p270 [251-500]
y Sch Lib - v44 - N '96 - p171 [51-250]
Happy Mouseday
c TES - Jl 5 '96 - pR6 [1-50]
Harriet's Hare
c Magpies - v11 - Jl '96 - p45 [1-50]
Hogsel and Gruntel (Illus. by Liz Graham-Yooll)
c Bks Keeps - Mr '97 - p20 [51-250]
Jenius: The Amazing Guinea Pig (Illus. by Brian Floca)
c BL - v93 - O 1 '96 - p352 [51-250]
c HB - v73 - Ja '97 - p60 [51-250]
c HB Guide - v8 - Spr '97 - p58 [51-250]
c KR - v64 - Ag 15 '96 - p1237 [51-250]
c SLJ - v42 - N '96 - p87 [51-250]
King Max the Last (Illus. by Linda Birch)
c Bks Keeps - Ja '97 - p22 [51-250]
Lady Daisy (Lambert). Audio Version
c BL - v93 - S 15 '96 - p264 [51-250]
c Emerg Lib - v24 - Mr '97 - p25 [51-250]
c HB - v72 - S '96 - p566+ [501+]
c SLJ - v42 - S '96 - p165 [51-250]
Martin's Mice (Illus. by Jez Alborough)
c SLJ - v43 - Ja '97 - p37 [1-50]
Mr. Potter's Pet (Illus. by Mark Teague)
c HB Guide - v7 - Fall '96 - p294 [51-250]
c Par Ch - v20 - O '96 - p11 [1-50]
Omnibombulator (Illus. by Jim Kavanagh)
c Bks Keeps - N '96 - p8 [51-250]
The School Mouse (Illus. by Cynthia Fisher)
c Inst - v42 - Ag '96 - p44 [51-250]
c RT - v50 - O '96 - p137 [1-50]
Sophie's Lucky (Illus. by David Parkins)
c HB Guide - v7 - Fall '96 - p286+ [51-250]
c Magpies - v11 - Jl '96 - p45 [1-50]
The Spotty Pig (Illus. by Mary Wormell)
c BL - v93 - Mr 1 '97 - p1172 [51-250]
c KR - v65 - F 15 '97 - p301 [51-250]
c PW - v244 - Mr 10 '97 - p65 [51-250]
c Trib Bks - Ap 13 '97 - p7 [51-250]
The Stray (Illus. by Wayne Parmenter)
c BL - v93 - S 15 '96 - p238 [51-250]
c CCB-B - v50 - N '96 - p102 [51-250]
c HB Guide - v8 - Spr '97 - p69 [51-250]
c KR - v64 - Ag 15 '96 - p1237 [51-250]
c SLJ - v42 - N '96 - p87 [51-250]
The Terrible Trins (Illus. by Diz Wallis)
c Bks Keeps - Mr '97 - p23 [51-250]
Three Terrible Trins (Whitfield). Audio Version
c BL - v93 - D 15 '96 - p740 [51-250]
c BL - v93 - Ap 1 '97 - p1314 [1-50]
c SLJ - v42 - D '96 - p72+ [51-250]
What Sadie Saw
c Books - v11 - Ap '97 - p24 [51-250]
Yob (Illus. by Abigail Pizer)
c Bks Keeps - Mr '97 - p16 [51-250]
Kingsolver, Barbara - *Animal Dreams*
    J Am Cult - v18 - Win '95 - p77+ [501+]
The Bean Trees
    J Am Cult - v18 - Win '95 - p77+ [501+]
High Tide in Tucson
    Ent W - S 20 '96 - p75 [1-50]
    LATBR - O 20 '96 - p15 [51-250]
    NYTBR - v101 - O 13 '96 - p32 [51-250]
Homeland and Other Stories
    TLS - Ja 24 '97 - p22 [501+]
Homeland and Other Stories (Kingsolver). Audio Version
    Trib Bks - F 2 '97 - p6 [51-250]
Pigs in Heaven
    J Am Cult - v18 - Win '95 - p77+ [501+]
Kingson, Eric R - *Social Security in the 21st Century*
    Choice - v34 - Mr '97 - p1210+ [51-250]
    NYRB - v43 - D 19 '96 - p68+ [501+]
Kingston, Maxine Hong - *China Men*
    Col Lit - v23 - O '96 - p73+ [501+]

Kingwell, Mark - *Dreams of Millennium*
    KR - v65 - Ja 15 '97 - p122 [251-500]
    Mac - v109 - D 9 '96 - p64 [1-50]
    PW - v244 - Ja 20 '97 - p386 [51-250]
    VLS - Spr '97 - p7 [501+]
Kinkade, Sheila - *Children of the Philippines (Illus. by Elaine Little)*
c BL - v93 - D 1 '96 - p650+ [51-250]
c Ch BWatch - v6 - O '96 - p5+ [1-50]
c HB Guide - v8 - Spr '97 - p170 [51-250]
c SLJ - v42 - D '96 - p115 [51-250]
Kinkead-Weekes, Mark - *D.H. Lawrence: Triumph to Exile 1912-1922*
    BW - v26 - S 29 '96 - p13 [51-250]
    Choice - v34 - D '96 - p614 [51-250]
    Lon R Bks - v19 - Mr 6 '97 - p8+ [501+]
    NYTBR - v101 - D 15 '96 - p30+ [501+]
    Obs - S 1 '96 - p17* [501+]
Kinnane, Garry - *Colin Colahan: A Portrait*
    Aust Bk R - O '96 - p32+ [501+]
Kinnear, Karen L - *Gangs: A Reference Handbook*
r ARBA - v28 - '97 - p228+ [51-250]
r Choice - v34 - F '97 - p946 [51-250]
r R&R Bk N - v12 - F '97 - p57 [1-50]
yr SLJ - v43 - F '97 - p130 [51-250]
Kinnear, Mary - *In Subordination*
    Can Hist R - v77 - D '96 - p617+ [501+]
Kinneging, A A M - *Aristocracy, Antiquity, and History*
    Choice - v34 - Mr '97 - p1237 [51-250]
    R&R Bk N - v12 - F '97 - p55 [51-250]
Kinney, Anne Behnke - *Chinese Views of Childhood*
    Bkbird - v34 - Spr '96 - p57 [51-250]
    Rel St Rev - v23 - Ap '97 - p205 [51-250]
Kinney, Arthur F - *Go Down, Moses*
    AL - v69 - Mr '97 - p250+ [51-250]
    Bl S - v26 - Fall '96 - p104 [51-250]
    Choice - v34 - N '96 - p456+ [51-250]
Kinney, Harrison - *James Thurber: His Life and Times*
    JMCQ - v73 - Win '96 - p1005+ [251-500]
    LATBR - D 29 '96 - p10 [51-250]
Kinney, Jean - *Clinical Manual of Substance Abuse. 2nd Ed.*
r SciTech - v20 - S '96 - p34 [51-250]
Kinsale, Laura - *My Sweet Folly*
    PW - v244 - F 3 '97 - p99+ [51-250]
Kinsbruner, Jay - *Independence in Spanish America*
    HAHR - v77 - F '97 - p125+ [501+]
Kinsella, John - *Lightning Tree*
    Aust Bk R - O '96 - p54+ [501+]
The Silo: A Pastoral Symphony
    WLT - v70 - Sum '96 - p758 [501+]
The Undertow: New and Selected Poems
    TLS - F 7 '97 - p24 [501+]
Kinsella, Thomas - *Collected Poems 1956-1994*
    TLS - Ap 11 '97 - p28 [501+]
The Dual Tradition
    WLT - v70 - Aut '96 - p967 [251-500]
Kinsella, W P - *Diamonds Forever*
    PW - v244 - F 17 '97 - p207 [51-250]
    Quill & Q - v63 - F '97 - p45 [51-250]
If Wishes Were Horses
    Mac - v109 - D 16 '96 - p69 [251-500]
    Quill & Q - v62 - D '96 - p35 [251-500]
Kinsey, Joni L - *Plain Pictures*
    BW - v27 - Ja 19 '97 - p13 [51-250]
    LATBR - D 8 '96 - p5 [51-250]
    LJ - v121 - N 15 '96 - p59 [51-250]
    NH - v105 - N '96 - p16 [1-50]
Kinsey-Warnock, Natalie - *The Fiddler of the Northern Lights (Illus. by Leslie W Bowman)*
c BL - v93 - N 15 '96 - p594 [51-250]
c HB Guide - v8 - Spr '97 - p34 [51-250]
c PW - v243 - N 11 '96 - p74+ [51-250]
c SLJ - v42 - N '96 - p87 [51-250]
c Smith - v27 - N '96 - p164 [1-50]
The Summer of Stanley (Illus. by Donald Gates)
c KR - v65 - My 1 '97 - p723 [51-250]
c PW - v244 - Ap 21 '97 - p71 [51-250]
Sweet Memories Still (Illus. by Laurie Harden)
c BL - v93 - F 15 '97 - p1023 [51-250]
c KR - v64 - N 15 '96 - p1670+ [51-250]
c PW - v243 - D 30 '96 - p67+ [51-250]
c SLJ - v43 - Ja '97 - p84 [51-250]
Kinski, Klaus - *Kinski Uncut*
    BL - v93 - Ja '97 - p758 [1-50]
    Ent W - N 1 '96 - p64 [51-250]
    Obs - Ja 26 '97 - p18* [51-250]
    Si & So - v6 - N '96 - p35 [51-250]
    WSJ-MW - v77 - S 25 '96 - pA20 [501+]
Kinsley, David - *Ecology and Religion*
    JAAR - v64 - Win '96 - p907+ [501+]

Kinsley, Michael J - *Economic Renewal Guide*
    BL - v93 - Ja '97 - p793 [51-250]
Kinsolving, William - *Mister Christian*
y SLJ - v42 - N '96 - p140 [51-250]
Kintgen, Eugene R - *Reading in Tudor England*
    R&R Bk N - v11 - D '96 - p52 [1-50]
    TLS - Ja 31 '97 - p10+ [501+]
Kintz, Pascal - *Drug Testing in Hair*
    SciTech - v20 - D '96 - p41 [51-250]
Kinvig, Clifford - *Scapegoat: General Percival of Singapore*
    Spec - v278 - Mr 8 '97 - p31+ [501+]
Kinzey, Bert - *F6F Hellcat*
    A & S Sm - v11 - O '96 - p88 [1-50]
Kinzey, Warren G - *New World Primates*
    Sci - v276 - Ap 4 '97 - p47 [1-50]
Kinzo, Maria D'Alva G - *Growth and Development in Brazil*
    Econ J - v107 - Ja '97 - p279 [251-500]
Kiosterud, Erland - *Denne Gangen Horer Du Deg Selv. Vol. 2*
    WLT - v71 - Win '97 - p170 [251-500]
Kiourtsakis, Yannis - *San Mythistorima*
    WLT - v70 - Sum '96 - p739 [501+]
Kipfer, Barbara Ann - *The Order of Things*
r LJ - v122 - Ap 1 '97 - p84 [51-250]
y SLJ - v43 - F '97 - p137 [51-250]
Kipling, Rudyard - *The Irish Guards in the Great War*
    LJ - v121 - D '96 - p154 [51-250]
    Spec - v278 - F 15 '97 - p33 [501+]
The Jungle Book (Illus. by Christian Broutin)
y HB Guide - v7 - Fall '96 - p302 [51-250]
c Magpies - v11 - S '96 - p39+ [501+]
c TES - Ja 31 '97 - p7* [501+]
Just So Stories (Illus. by Barry Moser)
c BL - v93 - N 1 '96 - p498 [51-250]
c Ch BWatch - v6 - N '96 - p3 [51-250]
c HB Guide - v8 - Spr '97 - p69 [51-250]
The Letters of Rudyard Kipling. Vol. 3
    ELT - v40 - 2 '97 - p199+ [501+]
    Nine-C Lit - v51 - S '96 - p273+ [51-250]
Kipnis, Jeffrey - *Philip Johnson: Recent Work*
    TLS - N 8 '96 - p32 [251-500]
Kipnis, Laura - *Bound and Gagged*
    Choice - v34 - N '96 - p525+ [51-250]
    Nat - v263 - O 14 '96 - p31+ [501+]
    NYTBR - v101 - Ag 25 '96 - p18+ [51-250]
Kipp, Jonathan D - *Emergency Incident Risk Management*
    R&R Bk N - v12 - F '97 - p55 [51-250]
Kipp, Kathryn - *The Best of Flower Painting*
    LJ - v122 - Mr 15 '97 - p62 [51-250]
Kipple, Kenneth F - *The Cambridge World History of Human Disease*
r BL - v93 - F 1 '97 - p957 [1-50]
Kiraly, Bela K - *Lawful Revolution in Hungary 1989-94*
    Choice - v34 - N '96 - p531 [51-250]
Trianon and East Central Europe
    Slav R - v55 - Fall '96 - p661+ [501+]
Kiraly, Marie - *Madeline: After the Fall of Usher*
    PW - v243 - N 4 '96 - p71 [51-250]
Kiraly, Sherwood - *Big Babies*
    PW - v243 - O 7 '96 - p66 [51-250]
Kirby, David - *The Baltic World 1772-1993*
    AHR - v101 - O '96 - p1230+ [501+]
Kirby, Jack Temple - *Poquosin: A Study of Rural Landscape and Society*
    AHR - v102 - F '97 - p176+ [251-500]
    JSH - v63 - F '97 - p147+ [251-500]
    Pub Hist - v19 - Win '97 - p101+ [501+]
Kirby, James E - *The Methodists*
    Choice - v34 - Mr '97 - p1177+ [51-250]
    R&R Bk N - v12 - F '97 - p12 [51-250]
Kirby, John Lavan - *The Hungerford Cartulary*
r EHR - v112 - F '97 - p173+ [251-500]
Kirby, Lynne - *Parallel Tracks*
    Choice - v34 - My '97 - p1507 [51-250]
Kirby, Margaret - *My Body. My Blood*
    Aust Bk R - S '96 - p62+ [501+]
Kirby, Maurice W - *Business Enterprise in Modern Britain from the Eighteenth to the Twentieth Century*
    JEH - v56 - D '96 - p938+ [251-500]
Kirby, Susan - *Prairie Rose*
y Kliatt - v31 - Mr '97 - p10 [51-250]
Kirby-Smith, H T - *The Origins of Free Verse*
    Choice - v34 - Ap '97 - p1330 [51-250]
Kirch, Patrick Vinton - *The Wet and the Dry*
    AHR - v101 - D '96 - p1604+ [501+]
    Am Ant - v61 - O '96 - p817+ [51-250]
Kirchheimer, Sid - *Never Pay Retail*
    BL - v92 - Ag '96 - p1866 [51-250]

Kirchner, Audrey Burie - *In Days Gone By*
CAY - v17 - Fall '96 - p6 [51-250]
CAY - v17 - Win '96 - p5 [51-250]
SLMQ - v25 - Fall '96 - p64 [51-250]
Kirchner, Helmut O - *Computer Simulation in Materials Science*
SciTech - v20 - D '96 - p62 [51-250]
Kirk, Andrew M - *The Mirror of Confusion*
R&R Bk N - v12 - F '97 - p84 [51-250]
Kirk, Daniel - *Lucky's 24-Hour Garage (Illus. by Daniel Kirk)*
c BL - v93 - S 1 '96 - p143 [51-250]
c CBRS - v25 - O '96 - p16 [51-250]
c HB Guide - v8 - Spr '97 - p34 [51-250]
c NYTBR - v101 - D 22 '96 - p16 [501+]
c SLJ - v42 - S '96 - p182 [51-250]
Trash Trucks! (Illus. by Daniel Kirk)
c BL - v93 - My 15 '97 - p1579 [51-250]
c KR - v65 - My 1 '97 - p723 [51-250]
c PW - v244 - My 12 '97 - p75 [51-250]
Kirk, David - *Miss Spider's Tea Party (Illus. by David Kirk)*
c Magpies - v11 - My '96 - p39 [251-500]
c PW - v244 - Mr 24 '97 - p84+ [51-250]
c RT - v50 - Mr '97 - p503 [51-250]
c Sch Lib - v45 - F '97 - p19 [51-250]
Miss Spider's Wedding
c Magpies - v11 - My '96 - p39 [251-500]
c RT - v50 - Mr '97 - p503 [51-250]
Kirk, Donald - *Korean Dynasty*
Pac A - v69 - Fall '96 - p431+ [251-500]
Tell It To the Dead
LJ - v121 - S 15 '96 - p102 [1-50]
Kirk, Elizabeth J - *Assessing the Risks of Nuclear and Chemical Contamination in the Former Soviet Union*
SciTech - v20 - D '96 - p68 [51-250]
Kirk, J G - *Plasma Astrophysics*
Phys Today - v49 - Ag '96 - p72+ [501+]
Kirk, James - *The Books of Assumption of the Thirds of Benefices*
CHR - v83 - Ja '97 - p100+ [251-500]
Kirk, Neville - *Labour and Society in Britain and the USA. Vols. 1-2*
EHR - v111 - N '96 - p1222+ [501+]
Social Class and Marxism
R&R Bk N - v11 - N '96 - p43 [51-250]
Kirk, Robert - *Raw Feeling*
Phil R - v105 - Ja '96 - p94+ [501+]
Kirk, Russell - *The Sword of Imagination*
Bks & Cult - v1 - N '95 - p30+ [51-250]
CC - v113 - O 23 '96 - p1015+ [501+]
Kirk, Ruth - *The Enduring Forests*
Choice - v34 - Ja '97 - p819 [51-250]
Kirkendall, Tom - *Cross-Country Ski Tours: Washington's North Cascades. 2nd Ed.*
r BL - v93 - S 15 '96 - p212 [1-50]
Mountain Bike Adventures in Washington's North Cascades and Olympics. 2nd Ed.
r BL - v93 - S 15 '96 - p212 [1-50]
Mountain Bike Adventures in Washington's South Cascades and Puget Sound. 2nd Ed.
r BL - v93 - S 15 '96 - p212 [1-50]
Kirk-Greene, Anthony - *State and Society in Francophone Africa since Independence*
Africa T - v44 - 1 '97 - p84+ [501+]
Kirkham, Pat - *Charles and Ray Eames*
SDA - v4 - Fall '96 - p118+ [501+]
The Gendered Object
Choice - v34 - Ap '97 - p1419 [51-250]
Kirkland, Elithe Hamilton - *Leet's Christmas*
BWatch - v17 - D '96 - p1 [1-50]
Roundup M - v4 - D '96 - p28 [1-50]
Kirkland, Forrest - *The Rock Art of Texas Indians*
Roundup M - v4 - Ap '97 - p23 [51-250]
Kirkland, Martha - *The Honorable Thief*
LJ - v121 - N 15 '96 - p48 [51-250]
Kirkpatrick, Betty - *The Cassell Crossword Dictionary*
r LJ - v122 - Ja '97 - p88 [51-250]
Cliches
r PW - v244 - My 12 '97 - p72 [51-250]
Kirkpatrick, Colin - *Cost-Benefit Analysis and Project Appraisal in Developing Countries*
JEL - v35 - Mr '97 - p278 [51-250]
Kirkpatrick, Donald - *Evaluating Training Programs*
J Car P&E - v57 - Fall '96 - p16+ [51-250]
Kirkpatrick, James M - *Engineering Drawings and Models Using AutoCAD Solid Modeling and Designer*
SciTech - v20 - N '96 - p60 [51-250]
Kirkpatrick, Jane - *Love to Water My Soul*
y BL - v93 - S 1 '96 - p65 [501+]
Roundup M - v4 - D '96 - p27+ [251-250]

Kirkpatrick, Jay F - *Management of Wild Horses by Fertility Control*
J Gov Info - v23 - S '96 - p549 [1-50]
Kirkpatrick, Peter - *Wish You Were Here*
Aust Bk R - S '96 - p53+ [501+]
Kirkpatrick, Sidney D - *Lords of Sipan (McDonough). Audio Version*
y Kliatt - v30 - S '96 - p58 [51-250]
Kirkwood, Jon - *The Fantastic Cutaway Book of Giant Machines (Illus. by Alex Pang)*
c BL - v93 - F 15 '97 - p1018 [51-250]
c HB Guide - v8 - Spr '97 - p132 [51-250]
Kirmmse, Bruce H - *Encounters with Kierkegaard*
Choice - v34 - O '96 - p293 [51-250]
Comw - v124 - Ja 17 '97 - p20+ [501+]
Rel St Rev - v22 - O '96 - p335 [51-250]
VQR - v73 - Win '97 - p18* [51-250]
Kirp, David L - *Our Town*
Nat - v264 - Mr 31 '97 - p30+ [501+]
Tikkun - v12 - Ja '97 - p68+ [501+]
Kirsch, Clifford E - *The Financial Services Revolution*
Choice - v34 - Ja '97 - p844 [51-250]
R&R Bk N - v11 - D '96 - p35 [51-250]
Kirsch, George B - *Sports in North America. Vol. 4*
J Am Cult - v19 - Sum '96 - p134+ [501+]
Kirsch, Henry - *Drug Lessons and Education Programs in Developing Countries*
HAHR - v76 - N '96 - p837+ [251-500]
Kirsch, Jonathan - *The Harlot by the Side of the Road*
BL - v93 - My 15 '97 - p1545 [51-250]
KR - v65 - Mr 15 '97 - p440 [251-500]
PW - v244 - Ap 14 '97 - p69 [51-250]
Kirsch, Sarah - *Bodenlos*
WLT - v71 - Win '97 - p148 [51-250]
Kirschbaum, Stanislav J - *A History of Slovakia*
AHR - v101 - D '96 - p1578+ [501+]
Kirschke, Amy Helene - *Aaron Douglas: Art, Race, and the Harlem Renaissance*
AHR - v102 - F '97 - p203+ [501+]
Kirschner, Orin - *The Bretton-Woods-GATT System*
JEH - v56 - D '96 - p968+ [501+]
Kirschner, Suzanne R - *The Religious and Romantic Origins of Psychoanalysis*
Rel St Rev - v23 - Ap '97 - p150 [51-250]
Kirshner, Howard S - *Handbook of Neurological Speech and Language Disorders*
AJPsych - v154 - Ja '97 - p126 [251-500]
Kirshner, Jonathan - *Currency and Coercion*
APSR - v91 - Mr '97 - p236+ [501+]
JEH - v56 - D '96 - p966+ [501+]
Kirshner, Julius - *The Origins of the State in Italy 1300-1600*
R&R Bk N - v11 - D '96 - p9 [51-250]
Kirsop, Wallace - *Books for Colonial Readers*
BC - v45 - Win '96 - p573+ [501+]
Kirstein, Lincoln - *Mosaic: Memoirs*
Sew R - v104 - O '96 - pR87+ [501+]
Kirtland, Mark - *Why Do We Do That?*
c HB Guide - v8 - Spr '97 - p99 [51-250]
Kirtley, Clare - *Rhyme and Analogy*
c TES - Jl 5 '96 - pR7 [501+]
Kirvan, John - *Let Nothing Disturb You*
RR - v55 - N '96 - p661 [1-50]
Peace of Heart
RR - v55 - N '96 - p661 [1-50]
Simply Surrender
RR - v55 - N '96 - p661 [1-50]
True Serenity
RR - v55 - N '96 - p661 [1-50]
Where Only Love Can Go
RR - v55 - N '96 - p661 [1-50]
Kirwan, Anna - *Juliet: A Secret Takes Flight, England 1339 (Illus. by Lynne Marshall)*
c CCB-B - v50 - N '96 - p102+ [51-250]
c HB Guide - v8 - Spr '97 - p69 [51-250]
c PW - v243 - N 11 '96 - p76 [51-250]
c SLJ - v42 - S '96 - p204 [51-250]
Kis, Danilo - *Homo Poeticus*
TLS - O 4 '96 - p37 [501+]
Kisanga, Eliawony J - *Industrial and Trade Cooperation in Eastern and Southern Africa*
Econ J - v106 - S '96 - p1481 [51-250]
Kiser, Lisa J - *Truth and Textuality in Chaucer's Poetry*
Comp L - v48 - Fall '96 - p377+ [501+]
Kish-Goodling, Donna M - *Property Taxes and Local Economic Development*
JEL - v34 - S '96 - p1440 [51-250]
Kishi, Tetsuo - *Shakespeare and Cultural Traditions*
MLR - v91 - O '96 - p966+ [501+]

Kishlansky, Mark - *A Monarchy Transformed*
BL - v93 - Mr 15 '97 - p1222 [51-250]
HT - v46 - O '96 - p57 [51-250]
KR - v65 - F 1 '97 - p200+ [251-500]
Obs - D 1 '96 - p16* [1-50]
PW - v244 - Ja 27 '97 - p83 [51-250]
Spec - v278 - Ja 11 '97 - p31 [501+]
TLS - N 15 '96 - p9 [501+]
Kisiel, Theodore - *Reading Heidegger from the Start*
RM - v50 - S '96 - p162+ [501+]
Kismaric, Carole - *Growing Up with Dick and Jane*
BW - v26 - O 6 '96 - p11 [251-500]
Ent W - S 20 '96 - p74 [51-250]
Kisor, Henry - *What's That Pig Outdoors?*
y BL - v93 - D 15 '96 - p716 [1-50]
Kissane, Noel - *The Irish Famine*
r ILS - v16 - Spr '97 - p35 [1-50]
R&R Bk N - v11 - D '96 - p9 [51-250]
Kissane, Sharon F - *Career Success for People with Physical Disabilities*
y Kliatt - v31 - My '97 - p24 [51-250]
Kissel, Susan S - *Moving On*
Choice - v34 - Ja '97 - p796 [51-250]
R&R Bk N - v11 - D '96 - p65 [51-250]
Kissell, Thomas E - *Industrial Electronics*
SciTech - v20 - D '96 - p79 [51-250]
Kisseloff, Jeff - *The Box: An Oral History of Television 1920-1961*
JMCQ - v73 - Aut '96 - p754+ [501+]
Kissen, Morton - *Affect, Object, and Character Structure*
Rel St Rev - v23 - Ja '97 - p43+ [51-250]
Assessing Object Relations Phenomena
Rel St Rev - v23 - Ja '97 - p43 [51-250]
Kissen, Rita M - *The Last Closet*
Choice - v34 - F '97 - p1014 [51-250]
Kissick, William L - *Medicine's Dilemma*
AAPSS-A - v548 - N '96 - p232+ [501+]
Kistler, Don - *Sola Scriptura!*
Ch Today - v40 - O 7 '96 - p56 [51-250]
Kitaev, Igor - *Educational Finance in Central Asia and Mongolia*
JEL - v35 - Mr '97 - p230+ [51-250]
Kitamura, Satoshi - *Cat Is Sleepy (Illus. by Satoshi Kitamura)*
c HB Guide - v8 - Spr '97 - p13 [51-250]
c NYTBR - v102 - Ja 5 '97 - p22 [1-50]
c Par - v71 - D '96 - p251 [1-50]
c SLJ - v42 - Ag '96 - p124 [51-250]
Dog Is Thirsty (Illus. by Satoshi Kitamura)
c HB Guide - v8 - Spr '97 - p13 [51-250]
c Par - v71 - D '96 - p251 [1-50]
c SLJ - v42 - Ag '96 - p124 [51-250]
Duck Is Dirty (Illus. by Satoshi Kitamura)
HB Guide - v8 - Spr '97 - p13 [51-250]
c Par - v71 - D '96 - p251 [1-50]
c SLJ - v42 - Ag '96 - p124 [51-250]
Sheep in Wolves' Clothing (Illus. by Satoshi Kitamura)
c HB Guide - v7 - Fall '96 - p262 [51-250]
c SLJ - v42 - Ag '96 - p124 [51-250]
Squirrel Is Hungry (Illus. by Satoshi Kitamura)
c HB Guide - v8 - Spr '97 - p13 [51-250]
c Par - v71 - D '96 - p251 [1-50]
c SLJ - v42 - Ag '96 - p124 [51-250]
Kitch, Chris - *Pavement for My Pillow*
TLS - O 18 '96 - p31 [251-500]
Kitchen, Judith - *In Short*
BW - v26 - Ag 18 '96 - p12 [51-250]
LATBR - S 1 '96 - p6+ [501+]
Kitchen, Judith L - *Caring for Your Old House*
LJ - v122 - F 1 '97 - p52 [1-50]
Kitchen, Martin - *The Cambridge Illustrated History of Germany*
BL - v93 - O 1 '96 - p318 [51-250]
HT - v46 - O '96 - p57 [1-50]
R&R Bk N - v11 - D '96 - p9 [51-250]
y SLJ - v43 - Mr '97 - p217 [51-250]
Nazi Germany at War
EHR - v112 - Ap '97 - p535 [251-500]
Kitchen, Martin, 1947- - *Ephesians*
Rel St Rev - v23 - Ap '97 - p185 [51-250]
Kitchen (SnapShot)
c PW - v244 - Ja 6 '97 - p74 [1-50]
Kitchenham, Barbara - *Software Metrics*
SciTech - v20 - N '96 - p10 [51-250]
Kitchens, Susan A - *The KPT Bryce Book*
BYTE - v21 - O '96 - p168 [51-250]
Kitchens, William Michael - *Estimating and Project Management for Building Contractors*
SciTech - v20 - S '96 - p52 [51-250]

Kitcher, Philip - *The Lives to Come*
  BioSci - v46 - O '96 - p708+ [501+]
  Choice - v34 - S '96 - p153 [51-250]
  Hast Cen R - v26 - Jl '96 - p41 [1-50]
  Lon R Bks - v18 - N 14 '96 - p17+ [501+]
  Sci - v274 - N 15 '96 - p1147+ [501+]
Kite, L Patricia - *Blood-Feeding Bugs and Beasts*
  y BL - v93 - Ap 1 '97 - p1308 [1-50]
  c HB Guide - v7 - Fall '96 - p336 [51-250]
  c Learning - v25 - Mr '97 - p38 [1-50]
  c SB - v32 - N '96 - p241 [51-250]
  Insect-Eating Plants
  c RT - v50 - S '96 - p56 [51-250]
Kitromilides, Paschalis M - *Cyprus. Rev. Ed.*
  r JPR - v34 - F '97 - p113 [251-500]
Kitschelt, Herbert - *The Radical Right in Western Europe*
  AJS - v102 - Ja '97 - p1175+ [501+]
  Choice - v34 - N '96 - p530 [51-250]
  CS - v26 - Ja '97 - p29+ [501+]
  PSQ - v111 - Win '96 - p716+ [501+]
Kitson, Fulton G - *Gas Chromatography and Mass Spectrometry*
  SciTech - v20 - N '96 - p21 [51-250]
Kitson, Peter J - *Coleridge, Keats and Shelley*
  R&R Bk N - v12 - F '97 - p84 [51-250]
Kitsos, Christos P - *MODA4--Advances in Model-Oriented Data Analysis*
  JEL - v34 - D '96 - p2018 [51-250]
Kittinger, Jo S - *Dead Log Alive!*
  c HB Guide - v8 - Spr '97 - p118 [51-250]
Kittredge, Sonya - *Chickadee Rescue*
  c Ch BWatch - v6 - S '96 - p2 [1-50]
Kittredge, William - *Who Owns the West?*
  Bloom Rev - v16 - Jl '96 - p12 [251-500]
Kitts, Jennifer - *The Health Gap*
  Choice - v34 - F '97 - p997 [51-250]
  WorldV - v13 - Ja '97 - p8 [251-500]
Kitzinger, Sheila - *Becoming a Grandmother*
  PW - v243 - Jl 22 '96 - p221 [51-250]
  The Complete Book of Pregnancy and Childbirth. Rev. and Expanded Ed.
  y BL - v93 - S 15 '96 - p179 [51-250]
  LJ - v121 - N 1 '96 - p100+ [51-250]
  PW - v243 - S 16 '96 - p80 [51-250]
Kiyono, Hiroshi - *Mucosal Vaccines*
  SciTech - v21 - Mr '97 - p43 [51-250]
Kiyosaki, Wayne - *A Spy in Their Midst*
  WHQ - v28 - Spr '97 - p97 [251-500]
Kizer, Carolyn - *Harping On*
  BL - v93 - Ja '97 - p759 [1-50]
  BL - v93 - S 1 '96 - p57 [51-250]
  LJ - v122 - Ap 1 '97 - p95 [1-50]
  NL - v80 - F 24 '97 - p15 [251-500]
  VV - v41 - N 5 '96 - p51+ [501+]
Kizilyalli, Husnu - *Use of Inter-Regional Input-Output Models in Economic Analysis, Economic Development Planning and Project Appraisal*
  JEL - v35 - Mr '97 - p301+ [51-250]
Kizza, Joseph Migga - *Social and Ethical Effects of the Computer Revolution*
  LAR - v98 - D '96 - p651 [51-250]
  SL - v87 - Sum '96 - p238 [251-500]
Kjaergaard, Thorkild - *The Danish Revolution 1500-1800*
  EHR - v112 - Ap '97 - p475+ [501+]
Kjekshus, Helge - *Ecology Control and Economic Development in East African History*
  JEL - v34 - D '96 - p2096 [51-250]
Kjeldsberg, Carl R - *Practical Diagnosis of Hematologic Disorders. 2nd Ed.*
  SciTech - v20 - N '96 - p46 [51-250]
Kjellber, Paul - *Essays on Skepticism, Relativism, and Ethics in the Zhuangzi*
  Rel St Rev - v23 - Ja '97 - p97 [51-250]
Kjos, Berit - *Brave New Schools*
  VOYA - v19 - O '96 - p242+ [251-500]
Klaber, William F - *Shadow Play*
  KR - v65 - Ap 1 '97 - p526 [251-500]
  LJ - v122 - Ap 1 '97 - p109 [51-250]
Klafehn, Keith - *Computer Simulation in Operations Management*
  SciTech - v21 - Mr '97 - p98 [51-250]
Klagsbrun, Francine - *Jewish Days*
  LJ - v121 - S 15 '96 - p73 [51-250]
  PW - v243 - S 30 '96 - p76+ [51-250]
Klam, Marilyn Taylor - *My Mama Always Said*
  CAY - v17 - Win '96 - p5 [51-250]
Klammer, Martin - *Whitman, Slavery, and the Emergence of Leaves of Grass*
  AHR - v101 - O '96 - p1283+ [501+]
  AL - v68 - S '96 - p645+ [251-500]
  Nine-C Lit - v51 - S '96 - p274 [51-250]

Klapisch, Bob - *High and Tight*
  NYTBR - v101 - Ap 7 '96 - p13 [501+]
Klare, Michael - *Rogue States and Nuclear Outlaws*
  Parameters - v26 - Aut '96 - p146+ [501+]
Klarsfeld, Serge - *French Children of the Holocaust*
  BL - v93 - Ap 1 '97 - p1278 [251-500]
  Choice - v34 - My '97 - p1483 [51-250]
  LATBR - Ja 5 '97 - p4+ [501+]
  NYTBR - v102 - F 9 '97 - p21 [51-250]
  PW - v243 - N 25 '96 - p66 [51-250]
  Tikkun - v12 - Mr '97 - p73 [51-250]
Klass, David - *Danger Zone*
  y BL - v93 - Ap 1 '97 - p1292 [1-50]
  y Emerg Lib - v24 - S '96 - p53+ [51-250]
  y HB Guide - v7 - Fall '96 - p302 [51-250]
  y NY - v72 - N 18 '96 - p102 [1-50]
  y NYTBR - v101 - O 27 '96 - p44 [1-50]
Klass, Dennis - *Continuing Bonds*
  Readings - v11 - S '96 - p31 [51-250]
Klass, Morton - *Ordered Universes*
  Am Ethnol - v24 - F '97 - p217+ [501+]
  Rel St Rev - v23 - Ja '97 - p44+ [51-250]
  Theol St - v57 - Je '96 - p383 [251-500]
Klass, Sheila Solomon - *A Shooting Star*
  c BL - v93 - D 15 '96 - p726 [51-250]
  c HB - v73 - My '97 - p323 [51-250]
  c KR - v64 - N 15 '96 - p1671 [51-250]
  c PW - v243 - D 2 '96 - p61 [51-250]
Klassen, Duke - *The Dance Hall at Spring Hill and Other Stories*
  KR - v64 - Ag 15 '96 - p1175 [251-500]
Klassen, William - *Judas: Betrayer or Friend of Jesus?*
  CLW - v67 - D '96 - p39 [251-500]
  Lon R Bks - v19 - Ja 2 '97 - p23 [501+]
  TLS - O 18 '96 - p36 [501+]
Klatz, Ronald - *Grow Young with HGH*
  BL - v93 - Mr 15 '97 - p1202 [51-250]
Klaus, Carl H - *My Vegetable Love*
  BL - v93 - O 1 '96 - p314 [51-250]
Klaus, H Gustav - *Strong Words, Brave Deeds*
  RES - v47 - N '96 - p629+ [501+]
Klause, Annette Curtis - *The Silver Kiss*
  y Kliatt - v30 - S '96 - p2 [1-50]
  y SLJ - v42 - N '96 - p41 [1-50]
Klausmeier, Robert - *Cowboy (Illus. by Richard Erickson)*
  c HB Guide - v7 - Fall '96 - p386 [51-250]
Klavan, Andrew - *True Crime*
  Books - v9 - S '95 - p18+ [51-250]
  Books - v9 - S '95 - p22 [1-50]
  Books - v10 - Je '96 - p24+ [51-250]
Klavan, Ellen - *Vegetarian Factfinder (Illus. by Adrienne Hartman)*
  c PW - v243 - N 4 '96 - p78 [51-250]
Klawans, Harold L - *Why Michael Couldn't Hit and Other Tales of the Neurology of Sports*
  BWatch - v17 - D '96 - p3 [1-50]
  Choice - v34 - Ap '97 - p1378 [51-250]
  LJ - v121 - S 15 '96 - p74 [51-250]
  Nature - v383 - O 31 '96 - p776 [501+]
  New Sci - v152 - D 7 '96 - p49 [51-250]
  NYTLa - v146 - O 31 '96 - pC19 [501+]
  PW - v243 - S 9 '96 - p77 [51-250]
  Sci - v275 - Ja 31 '97 - p625 [1-50]
Klawans, Zander H - *Handbook of Ancient Greek and Roman Coins*
  r ARBA - v28 - '97 - p358 [51-250]
Klawitter, George - *The Enigmatic Narrator*
  Ren Q - v50 - Spr '97 - p339+ [501+]
Klee, Carol A - *Faces in a Crowd*
  MLJ - v80 - Fall '96 - p402+ [501+]
Klee, Sheila - *Working Together against School Violence*
  y SLJ - v43 - F '97 - p118 [51-250]
Kleeblatt, Norman L - *Too Jewish?*
  Choice - v34 - N '96 - p528 [51-250]
Kleeman, Terry F - *A God's Own Tale*
  Ch Rev Int - v4 - Spr '97 - p189+ [501+]
  JAAR - v64 - Sum '96 - p430+ [501+]
Kleffel, Kohnholdt, Gundermann
  SciTech - v20 - N '96 - p3 [1-50]
Klehr, Harvey - *The Amerasia Spy Case*
  HRNB - v25 - Fall '96 - p13 [251-500]
  PHR - v65 - N '96 - p692+ [501+]
  RAH - v24 - N '96 - p174+ [501+]
  The Secret World of American Communism
  AAPSS-A - v547 - S '96 - p183+ [251-500]
  PSQ - v111 - Win '96 - p730+ [501+]
  PW - v243 - S 23 '96 - p73 [1-50]
  RAH - v24 - N '96 - p500+ [501+]
  RP - v58 - Fall '96 - p838+ [501+]
  Soc - v34 - N '96 - p101+ [501+]

Kleiman, Devra G - *Wild Mammals in Captivity*
  Choice - v34 - D '96 - p639 [51-250]
  SciTech - v20 - N '96 - p58 [51-250]
Klein, Anne Carolyn - *Meeting the Great Bliss Queen*
  JAAR - v64 - Sum '96 - p427+ [501+]
Klein, Barry T - *Reference Encyclopedia of the American Indian. 7th Ed.*
  r R&R Bk N - v11 - D '96 - p12 [51-250]
Klein, Bob - *The Beer Lover's Rating Guide*
  r LJ - v122 - Ap 1 '97 - p64 [1-50]
Klein, Bonnie Sherr - *Slow Dance*
  Mac - v110 - Mr 31 '97 - p60 [501+]
  Quill & Q - v63 - Ja '97 - p31 [251-500]
Klein, Cornelis - *Mineralogy Tutorials. Electronic Media Version*
  Choice - v34 - N '96 - p487 [51-250]
Klein, David M - *Family Theories*
  JMF - v58 - N '96 - p1040+ [501+]
Klein, Donald F - *Current Psychotherapeutic Drugs*
  SB - v32 - Ag '96 - p169 [251-500]
Klein, Edward - *All Too Human*
  BW - v26 - S 22 '96 - p6 [501+]
  Ent W - S 13 '96 - p124+ [251-500]
  LATBR - S 8 '96 - p4+ [501+]
  NYTBR - v101 - S 1 '96 - p5 [501+]
Klein, Ellen R - *Feminism under Fire*
  RM - v50 - S '96 - p164+ [501+]
Klein, Etienne - *Conversations with the Sphinx*
  Nature - v384 - N 28 '96 - p325 [501+]
Klein, Frederick C - *Sunflower Seeds and Seoul Food*
  Trib Bks - My 18 '97 - p8 [1-50]
Klein, Gary A - *Decision Making in Action*
  A J Psy - v109 - Win '96 - p635+ [501+]
Klein, Hans - *The German Chancellors*
  Choice - v34 - O '96 - p354 [51-250]
Klein, Julie Thompson - *Crossing Boundaries*
  R&R Bk N - v12 - F '97 - p45 [51-250]
Klein, Laura F - *Women and Power in Native North America*
  Am Ethnol - v24 - F '97 - p233+ [501+]
  Historian - v59 - Win '97 - p432+ [251-500]
  WHQ - v28 - Spr '97 - p80+ [251-500]
Klein, Lawrence - *Shaftesbury and the Culture of Politeness*
  JHI - v57 - O '96 - p725+ [501+]
Klein, Malcolm W - *The American Street Gang*
  AJS - v102 - S '96 - p624+ [501+]
Klein, Marcus - *Easterns, Westerns, and Private Eyes*
  Nine-C Lit - v50 - Mr '96 - p538+ [501+]
Klein, Michael - *Track Conditions*
  BL - v93 - My 15 '97 - p1556 [51-250]
  PW - v244 - Mr 31 '97 - p49 [51-250]
  Trib Bks - Ap 27 '97 - p5 [501+]
Klein, Norman M - *Seven Minutes*
  JPC - v29 - Spr '96 - p239+ [501+]
Klein, Richard - *Eat Fat*
  BL - v93 - O 1 '96 - p309 [51-250]
  Ent W - Ja 10 '97 - p52 [51-250]
  KR - v64 - S 1 '96 - p1297 [51-250]
  NS - v126 - Ja 24 '97 - p46 [251-500]
  NYTBR - v101 - D 8 '96 - p33 [501+]
  NYTLa - v146 - N 15 '96 - pC31 [501+]
  Obs - F 16 '97 - p18* [251-500]
  PW - v243 - O 7 '96 - p57+ [51-250]
  Utne R - N '96 - p92 [251-500]
Klein, Robin - *Dresses of Red and Gold*
  Bks Keeps - N '96 - p11 [51-250]
  The Sky in Silver Lace
  y HB Guide - v7 - Fall '96 - p302 [51-250]
  y VOYA - v19 - D '96 - p271 [51-250]
Klein, Scott W - *The Fictions of James Joyce and Wyndham Lewis*
  Clio - v25 - Spr '96 - p338+ [501+]
  ELT - v39 - 3 '96 - p386+ [501+]
  RES - v47 - Ag '96 - p461+ [501+]
Klein, Susan - *A Book for Midwives*
  Workbook - v21 - Fall '96 - p128+ [501+]
Klein, Wilhelm - *Vienna. 2nd Ed.*
  r BL - v93 - S 15 '96 - p210 [1-50]
Klein, William - *New York 1954-55*
  Comw - v123 - D 6 '96 - p25+ [501+]
Klein, William W - *The Book of Ephesians*
  r ARBA - v28 - '97 - p540+ [51-250]
  r Choice - v34 - S '96 - p100 [51-250]
Kleinbaum, N H - *The Story of Doctor Doolittle (Illus. by Hugh Lofting)*
  c PW - v244 - Mr 3 '97 - p77 [1-50]
  The Voyages of Doctor Doolittle (Illus. by Hugh Lofting)
  c PW - v244 - Mr 3 '97 - p77 [1-50]

Kleindorfer, Paul R - *Energy, Environment and the Economy*
Econ J - v107 - Ja '97 - p288 [51-250]
JEL - v34 - D '96 - p2135 [51-250]
R&R Bk N - v11 - N '96 - p33 [51-250]
Kleine-Ahlbrandt, W Laird - *The Burden of Victory*
Choice - v34 - O '96 - p340 [51-250]
Kleiner, Art - *The Age of Heretics*
Bus Bk R - v13 - 4 '96 - p58+ [501+]
BW - v26 - S 22 '96 - p11+ [251-500]
WSJ-MW - v78 - N 5 '96 - pA20 [251-500]
Kleiner, Diana E E - *I, Claudia*
BWatch - v17 - D '96 - p8 [51-250]
Choice - v34 - Mr '97 - p1216 [51-250]
Kleiner, John - *Mismapping the Underworld*
MLR - v91 - O '96 - p1008+ [251-500]
Kleiner, Susan M - *The High Performance Vegetarian Cookbook*
BL - v93 - Mr 15 '97 - p1216 [51-250]
PW - v244 - F 17 '97 - p215 [51-250]
Kleinig, John - *The Ethics of Policing*
Hast Cen R - v26 - Jl '96 - p41 [1-50]
Kleinknecht, William - *The New Ethnic Mobs*
Nat R - v48 - N 25 '96 - p65+ [501+]
NYTLa - v145 - S 5 '96 - pC21 [51-250]
Kleinman, Daniel Lee - *Politics on the Endless Frontier*
AHR - v102 - F '97 - p213 [501+]
AJS - v102 - Jl '96 - p282+ [501+]
Isis - v87 - D '96 - p754+ [501+]
Kleinman, Sherryl - *Opposing Ambitions*
R&R Bk N - v11 - N '96 - p30 [51-250]
Kleinpenning, Jan M G - *Peopling the Purple Land*
HAHR - v77 - My '97 - p320+ [501+]
Kleinpeter, Maxime - *Energy Planning and Policy*
Choice - v34 - D '96 - p642 [51-250]
SciTech - v20 - S '96 - p53 [51-250]
Kleist, Heinrich Von - *Heinrich Von Kleist: Die Familie Ghonorez/Die Familie Schroffenstein*
MLR - v92 - Ap '97 - p506+ [501+]
Penthesilea
Ger Q - v69 - Spr '96 - p125+ [501+]
Klejment, Anne - *American Catholic Pacifism*
Choice - v34 - Ap '97 - p1354 [51-250]
Klemisch-Ahlert, Marlies - *Bargaining in Economic and Ethical Environments*
JEL - v35 - Mr '97 - p197 [51-250]
Klemp, P J - *Paradise Lost*
r AB - v99 - Ja 13 '97 - p82+ [501+]
r ARBA - v28 - '97 - p456 [51-250]
r Choice - v34 - Ja '97 - p770 [51-250]
Klemperer, Victor - *Ich Will Zeugnis Ablegen Bis Zum Letzten. Vols. 1-2*
TLS - Ja 24 '97 - p27+ [501+]
Leben Sammeln, Nicht Fragen Wozu Und Warum. Vols. 1-2
TLS - Ja 24 '97 - p27+ [501+]
Klemperer, W David - *Forest Resource Economics and Finance*
JEL - v34 - S '96 - p1498 [51-250]
Klenicki, Leon - *Jews and Christians*
Rel Ed - v91 - Fall '96 - p618 [1-50]
Toward a Theological Encounter
Rel Ed - v91 - Fall '96 - p612 [1-50]
Klenke, Karin - *Women and Leadership*
Readings - v11 - D '96 - p28 [51-250]
Klepper, Robert K - *Silent Films on Video*
r ARBA - v28 - '97 - p511 [51-250]
Klette, Reinhard - *Handbook of Image Processing Operators*
r SciTech - v20 - S '96 - p50 [51-250]
Kleven, Elisa - *Hooray! A Pinata! (Illus. by Elisa Kleven)*
c BL - v93 - Ja '97 - p768 [1-50]
c BL - v93 - S 15 '96 - p240 [51-250]
c CBRS - v25 - Win '97 - p63+ [51-250]
c HB Guide - v8 - Spr '97 - p34 [51-250]
c PW - v243 - S 16 '96 - p82 [51-250]
c SLJ - v42 - N '96 - p87 [51-250]
The Puddle Pail (Illus. by Elisa Kleven)
c PW - v244 - My 5 '97 - p208 [51-250]
Kley, Roland - *Hayek's Social and Political Thought*
APSR - v90 - D '96 - p895+ [501+]
Kleypas, Lisa - *Somewhere I'll Find You*
PW - v243 - S 2 '96 - p122 [51-250]
Kliebard, Herbert M - *The Struggle for the American Curriculum 1893-1958. 2nd Ed.*
ES - v27 - Fall '96 - p249+ [501+]
Kliemann, W H - *Nonlinear Dynamics and Stochastic Mechanics*
SciTech - v20 - S '96 - p14 [51-250]

Klier, John Doyle - *Imperial Russia's Jewish Question 1855-1881*
Slav R - v55 - Fall '96 - p684+ [501+]
Kliman, Bernice W - *Macbeth*
y Choice - v34 - O '96 - p292 [51-250]
Klimek, Antonin - *Vznik Ceskoslovenska 1918*
EHR - v112 - F '97 - p255+ [51-250]
Klimley, A Peter - *Great White Sharks*
SciTech - v21 - Mr '97 - p38 [51-250]
Klinck, David - *The French Counterrevolutionary Theorist, Louis De Bonald 1754-1840*
R&R Bk N - v12 - F '97 - p32 [51-250]
Kline, Christina Baker - *Child of Mine*
KR - v65 - Mr 1 '97 - p356 [51-250]
PW - v244 - F 24 '97 - p70 [51-250]
Kline, David - *All about Your Car*
BWatch - v18 - Mr '97 - p10 [51-250]
Kline, Nancy - *Elizabeth Blackwell: A Doctor's Triumph*
c BL - v93 - F 15 '97 - p1013 [51-250]
y Kliatt - v31 - My '97 - p22 [51-250]
Kline, S J - *Conceptual Foundations for Multidisciplinary Thinking*
New Sci - v151 - S 28 '96 - p51 [1-50]
Kline, Stephen - *Out of the Garden*
Econ - v339 - My 18 '96 - p4*+ [501+]
Kline, Suzy - *Horrible Harry and the Dungeon (Illus. by Frank Remkiewicz)*
c BL - v92 - Ag '96 - p1900 [501+]
c HB Guide - v8 - Spr '97 - p58 [51-250]
c SLJ - v42 - Ag '96 - p124+ [51-250]
Horrible Harry and the Green Slime (Heller). Audio Version
c HB - v73 - My '97 - p357+ [501+]
Horrible Harry in Room 2B (Heller). Audio Version
c HB - v73 - My '97 - p357+ [501+]
Marvin and the Mean Words (Illus. by Blanche Sims)
c BL - v93 - Ap 1 '97 - p1334 [51-250]
c PW - v244 - Mr 3 '97 - p76 [51-250]
Song Lee and the Leech Man (Illus. by Frank Remkiewicz)
c RT - v50 - N '96 - p252 [51-250]
Kling, Candace - *The Artful Ribbon*
LJ - v122 - F 15 '97 - p134 [51-250]
Klingaman, William K - *Encyclopedia of the McCarthy Era*
r ARBA - v28 - '97 - p267 [51-250]
r BL - v93 - Ja '97 - p770 [1-50]
yr BL - v93 - S 1 '96 - p165 [251-500]
r R&R Bk N - v12 - F '97 - p24 [51-250]
Klinge, Sven - *Cycling the Bush*
r Aust Bk R - Ag '96 - p67 [1-50]
Klingel, Gilbert - *Inagua: An Island Sojourn*
BW - v27 - F 16 '97 - p12 [51-250]
Klingemann, Hans-Dieter - *Parties, Policies, and Democracy*
Pol Stud J - v24 - Sum '96 - p311+ [501+]
Klingensmith, Samuel John - *The Utility of Splendor*
CEH - v29 - 2 '96 - p239+ [501+]
EHR - v111 - N '96 - p1293+ [251-500]
Klinger, Barbara - *Melodrama and Meaning*
FQ - v49 - Fall '95 - p55+ [501+]
Klinger, Monika - *Hermann Broch Und Die Demokratie*
Ger Q - v70 - Win '97 - p86+ [501+]
Klingler, Richard - *The New Information Industry*
R&R Bk N - v11 - N '96 - p33 [51-250]
Klingshirn, William E - *Caesarius of Arles*
AHR - v101 - D '96 - p1529+ [501+]
Klinkner, Philip A - *Midterm: The Elections of 1994 in Context*
APSR - v91 - Mr '97 - p190+ [501+]
Klinting, Lars - *Bruno the Carpenter (Illus. by Lars Klinting)*
c HB - v72 - N '96 - p726+ [51-250]
c HB Guide - v7 - Fall '96 - p262 [51-250]
Bruno the Tailor (Illus. by Lars Klinting)
c HB Guide - v8 - Spr '97 - p34 [51-250]
c PW - v243 - O 7 '96 - p73 [51-250]
c SLJ - v42 - D '96 - p97 [51-250]
Klintworth, Gary - *Asia-Pacific Security*
For Aff - v75 - N '96 - p168+ [51-250]
New Taiwan, New China
Ch Rev Int - v4 - Spr '97 - p192+ [51-250]
Klinzing, Jim - *Fundamental Basketball (Illus. by David Kyle)*
y Ch BWatch - v6 - S '96 - p5 [1-50]
c HB Guide - v8 - Spr '97 - p145 [51-250]
Klockenkamper, Reinhold - *Total-Reflection X-Ray Fluorescence Spectrometry*
SciTech - v21 - Mr '97 - p28 [51-250]
Kloczowski, Jerzy - *La Pologne Dans L'Eglise Medievale*
CHR - v82 - Jl '96 - p522+ [501+]

Kloefkorn, William - *Treehouse: New and Selected Poems*
PW - v243 - N 25 '96 - p72 [51-250]
Klonk, Charlotte - *Science and the Perception of Nature*
Choice - v34 - Ap '97 - p1325 [51-250]
Klonoff, Elizabeth A - *Preventing Misdiagnosis of Women*
SciTech - v21 - Mr '97 - p53 [51-250]
Klossowski De Rola, Stanislas - *Balthus*
BL - v93 - O 1 '96 - p315 [51-250]
BW - v26 - D 8 '96 - p10+ [251-500]
Spec - v277 - D 14 '96 - p76 [51-250]
Klotz, Audie - *Norms in International Relations*
For Aff - v76 - Mr '97 - p199 [51-250]
Klove, Lars - *I See a Sign (Illus. by Lars Klove)*
c HB Guide - v7 - Fall '96 - p326 [51-250]
c SLJ - v42 - S '96 - p198 [51-250]
Kluegel, James R - *Social Justice and Political Change*
APSR - v90 - S '96 - p676 [501+]
Pub Op Q - v60 - Win '96 - p655+ [501+]
Klug, Francesca - *The Three Pillars of Liberty*
NS - v125 - O 11 '96 - p45+ [501+]
Klug, Lyn - *Soul Weaving*
CLW - v67 - Mr '97 - p39 [51-250]
Kluge, P F - *Alma Mater*
AS - v65 - Aut '96 - p621+ [501+]
Biggest Elvis
Ent W - O 4 '96 - p57 [51-250]
LATBR - Ag 4 '96 - p2 [501+]
NYTBR - v101 - S 1 '96 - p16 [251-500]
Rapport - v19 - 5 '96 - p36 [501+]
Kluger, Richard - *Ashes to Ashes*
LJ - v122 - Ja '97 - p50 [1-50]
LJ - v122 - Mr 15 '97 - p37 [1-50]
New R - v215 - N 4 '96 - p27+ [501+]
NYTBR - v101 - D 8 '96 - p84 [1-50]
Reason - v28 - D '96 - p46+ [501+]
Sci - v273 - Ag 9 '96 - p744+ [501+]
VQR - v72 - Aut '96 - p134* [51-250]
Klump, G M - *Methods in Comparative Psychoacoustics*
SciTech - v20 - N '96 - p34 [51-250]
Klunder, Willard Carl - *Lewis Cass and the Politics of Moderation*
BWatch - v17 - S '96 - p8+ [51-250]
Choice - v34 - Ja '97 - p863 [51-250]
R&R Bk N - v12 - F '97 - p24 [51-250]
Klutz Press - *Coin Magic*
c PW - v244 - Ap 7 '97 - p94 [1-50]
Glove Compartment Games
c PW - v244 - Mr 17 '97 - p85 [51-250]
Klutzow, F W - *Neuropathology: The Practical Approach*
SciTech - v20 - D '96 - p43 [51-250]
Klyza, Christopher McGrory - *Who Controls Public Lands?*
APSR - v90 - D '96 - p914+ [501+]
Choice - v34 - S '96 - p149 [51-250]
JEL - v34 - S '96 - p1471 [51-250]
WHQ - v28 - Spr '97 - p88+ [251-500]
Knafla, Louis A - *Kent at Law 1602*
Albion - v28 - Fall '96 - p478+ [501+]
Law, Society, and the State
Can Hist R - v78 - Mr '97 - p181+ [501+]
Knapp, A Bernard - *Provenience Studies and Bronze Age Cyprus*
Am Ant - v61 - O '96 - p816+ [501+]
Knapp, Bettina L - *French Theater since 1968*
FR - v70 - D '96 - p342+ [501+]
Women in Myth
LJ - v122 - Ja '97 - p105 [51-250]
Knapp, Caroline - *Drinking: A Love Story*
NW - v127 - My 20 '96 - p72 [251-500]
PW - v244 - My 5 '97 - p206 [1-50]
Drinking: A Love Story (Knapp). Audio Version
PW - v244 - My 5 '97 - p40 [51-250]
Knapp, David W - *Behavioral Synthesis*
SciTech - v20 - D '96 - p78 [51-250]
Knapp, Gregory - *Andean Ecology*
AAAGA - v86 - D '96 - p784+ [501+]
Knapp, Jeffrey - *An Empire Nowhere*
Clio - v25 - Sum '96 - p421+ [501+]
Knapp, Julius Z - *Liquid- and Surface-Borne Particle Measurement Handbook*
SciTech - v20 - N '96 - p56 [51-250]
Knapp, Laurence F - *Directed by Clint Eastwood*
Choice - v34 - F '97 - p973 [51-250]
LJ - v121 - O 15 '96 - p60+ [51-250]
Knapp, Martin - *The Economic Evaluation of Mental Health Care*
SciTech - v20 - S '96 - p28 [51-250]
Knapp, Peter - *The Assault on Equality*
Choice - v34 - F '97 - p1028 [51-250]
R&R Bk N - v11 - D '96 - p46 [51-250]

Knapp, Ron - *American Legends of Rock*
  y BL - v93 - N 15 '96 - p578 [51-250]
  c HB Guide - v8 - Spr '97 - p161 [51-250]
  y SLJ - v42 - D '96 - p146 [51-250]
  y VOYA - v19 - F '97 - p350 [251-500]
  Bloodsuckers
  c HB Guide - v7 - Fall '96 - p336 [51-250]
  c SB - v32 - N '96 - p241 [51-250]
  c SB - v33 - Ja '97 - p25 [251-500]
  Charles Barkley: Star Forward
  c HB Guide - v7 - Fall '96 - p361+ [51-250]
  c SLJ - v42 - Ag '96 - p157 [51-250]
  Mummies
  c HB Guide - v7 - Fall '96 - p378 [51-250]
  c SB - v32 - Ag '96 - p177 [51-250]
  Sports Great Mario Lemieux
  c RT - v50 - O '96 - p142 [1-50]
  Steve Young: Star Quarterback
  c HB Guide - v7 - Fall '96 - p361+ [51-250]
Knapp, Steven - *Literary Interest*
  CLS - v33 - 2 '96 - p214+ [501+]
Knauff, Robert E - *Short Stories*
  Math T - v90 - Mr '97 - p249 [51-250]
Knaus, Denise - *Medicare Made Simple*
  SEP - v269 - Ja '97 - p14 [501+]
Knauss, John A - *Introduction to Physical Oceanography. 2nd Ed*
  R&R Bk N - v12 - F '97 - p29 [51-250]
Knaut, Andrew L - *The Pueblo Revolt of 1680*
  AHR - v101 - O '96 - p1272 [501+]
  Am Ethnol - v23 - N '96 - p924+ [501+]
  HAHR - v77 - F '97 - p106+ [51-250]
  PHR - v65 - N '96 - p661+ [251-500]
Knecht, R J - *Renaissance Warrior and Patron*
  EHR - v111 - N '96 - p1267 [251-500]
  HT - v47 - Mr '97 - p54 [501+]
  JMH - v69 - Mr '97 - p149+ [251-500]
  The Rise and Fall of Renaissance France 1483-1610
  TLS - O 11 '96 - p30+ [501+]
Knee, Philip - *Qui Perd Gagne*
  Dialogue - v35 - Sum '96 - p626+ [501+]
Knee, Stuart E - *Christian Science in the Age of Mary Baker Eddy*
  CH - v66 - Mr '97 - p156+ [501+]
Kneen, Maggie - *When You're Not Looking (Illus. by Maggie Kneen)*
  c CBRS - v24 - Ag '96 - p160 [1-50]
  c HB Guide - v8 - Spr '97 - p13 [51-250]
  c SLJ - v42 - D '96 - p97+ [51-250]
Knell, Heiner - *Die Nike Von Samothrake*
  AJA - v100 - O '96 - p794+ [501+]
Knelman, Martin - *Laughing on the Outside*
  Mac - v109 - D 23 '96 - p79 [251-500]
  Quill & Q - v62 - O '96 - p35 [501+]
Knevitt, Charles - *Shelter: Human Habitats from Around the World*
  Bloom Rev - v16 - Jl '96 - p26+ [501+]
Knief, Charles - *Diamond Head*
  Arm Det - v30 - Win '97 - p113 [251-500]
  BL - v93 - S 15 '96 - p224 [51-250]
  KR - v64 - S 1 '96 - p1277 [51-250]
Kniesche, Thomas W - *Korper/Kultur: Kalifornische Studien Zur Deutschen Moderne*
  MLN - v112 - Ap '97 - p486+ [501+]
Kniesner, Thomas J - *Simulating Workplace Safety Policy*
  JEL - v34 - S '96 - p1371+ [501+]
Kniffka, Hannes - *Recent Developments in Forensic Linguistics*
  R&R Bk N - v12 - F '97 - p76 [51-250]
Knight, Alfred H - *The Life of the Law*
  ABA Jour - v82 - O '96 - p101 [501+]
  NYTBR - v101 - Ag 25 '96 - p18 [51-250]
Knight, Amy - *Spies without Cloaks*
  Choice - v34 - N '96 - p530+ [51-250]
  For Aff - v75 - S '96 - p150+ [51-250]
  Spec - v277 - N 16 '96 - p44 [1-50]
  VQR - v72 - Aut '96 - p134* [51-250]
Knight, Arthur Winfield - *The Darkness Starts Up Where You Stand*
  BWatch - v17 - N '96 - p11 [51-250]
  The Secret Life of Jesse James
  Roundup M - v3 - Ag '96 - p30 [51-250]
  Sm Pr R - v28 - N '96 - p1 [501+]
Knight, Brenda - *Women of the Beat Generation*
  LATBR - N 17 '96 - p9 [501+]
  LJ - v121 - O 1 '96 - p102 [51-250]
  PW - v243 - S 16 '96 - p77 [51-250]
  Women of the Beat Generation (Weiss). Audio Version
  LJ - v122 - Mr 15 '97 - p103 [51-250]
Knight, Christopher - *Last Chance for Eden*
  Art J - v55 - Fall '96 - p97+ [501+]

Knight, Christopher, 1950- - *The Hiram Key*
  Mag Bl - Mr '97 - p60 [51-250]
Knight, Damon - *Humpty Dumpty*
  Analog - v117 - F '97 - p145+ [51-250]
  BL - v93 - S 15 '96 - p226 [51-250]
  BWatch - v18 - F '97 - p4 [51-250]
  LJ - v121 - S 15 '96 - p100 [51-250]
  MFSF - v91 - D '96 - p97+ [51-250]
  NYTBR - v101 - N 3 '96 - p24 [51-250]
  NYTBR - v101 - D 8 '96 - p94 [1-50]
  Rapport - v19 - 6 '96 - p23 [251-500]
  Rapport - v19 - 6 '96 - p23 [251-500]
Knight, David - *Humphry Davy: Science and Power*
  Nine-C Lit - v51 - D '96 - p423 [1-50]
Knight, Dawn - *Mischief, Mad Mary, and Me*
  c BL - v93 - My 15 '97 - p1576 [51-250]
  c HB - v73 - My '97 - p324 [51-250]
  c KR - v65 - My 1 '97 - p723+ [51-250]
  c PW - v244 - Ap 21 '97 - p73 [51-250]
Knight, Douglas A - *Ethics and Politics in the Hebrew Bible*
  Rel St Rev - v23 - Ap '97 - p169 [51-250]
Knight, Frances - *The Nineteenth-Century Church and English Society*
  Choice - v34 - O '96 - p297+ [51-250]
Knight, H Jackson - *Patent Strategy for Researchers and Research Managers*
  R&R Bk N - v11 - N '96 - p53 [51-250]
Knight, Henry H, III - *The Presence of God in the Christian Life*
  CH - v65 - S '96 - p507+ [501+]
Knight, Janice - *Orthodoxies in Massachusetts*
  CH - v65 - S '96 - p498+ [501+]
  JR - v76 - O '96 - p642+ [501+]
  Rel St Rev - v22 - O '96 - p357+ [501+]
  Sev Cent N - v54 - Spr '96 - p34+ [501+]
Knight, Joseph A - *Laboratory Medicine and the Aging Process*
  SciTech - v20 - D '96 - p41 [51-250]
Knight, Julia - *Diverse Practices*
  Si & So - v6 - N '96 - p34 [1-50]
Knight, Khadijah - *Islamic Festivals*
  c Sch Lib - v44 - Ag '96 - p112 [51-250]
Knight, Linda - *Winners: A Collection of Cooperatively Developed Teaching Units for Resource-Based Learning*
  r SLMQ - v25 - Fall '96 - p64 [1-50]
Knight, Margy Burns - *Las Paredes Hablan (Illus. by Anne Sibley O'Brien)*
  c SLJ - v42 - N '96 - p132+ [51-250]
  Talking Walls (Illus. by Anne Sibley O'Brien)
  c HB Guide - v8 - Spr '97 - p164 [51-250]
  c SLJ - v42 - O '96 - p134+ [51-250]
Knight, Nick - *Li Da and Marxist Philosophy in China*
  R&R Bk N - v11 - N '96 - p2 [51-250]
Knight, Stephen - *Dream City Cinema*
  Obs - Ja 5 '97 - p17* [51-250]
Knight, Stephen Thomas - *Robin Hood*
  MLR - v91 - O '96 - p962+ [501+]
  RES - v48 - F '97 - p87+ [501+]
The Knight of the Two Swords (Arthur)
  Choice - v34 - O '96 - p285 [51-250]
Knighton, Douglas W - *The Kingdom of Heaven Is Like...a Doctor and a Patient*
  LJ - v122 - Ja '97 - p106+ [51-250]
Knights, Mark - *Politics and Opinion in Crisis 1678-81*
  AHR - v101 - O '96 - p1204+ [501+]
  Historian - v59 - Fall '96 - p193+ [501+]
  Sev Cent N - v54 - Spr '96 - p19+ [501+]
Knippenberg, Joseph M - *Poets, Princes, and Private Citizens*
  Choice - v34 - Ap '97 - p1417 [51-250]
Knippling, Alpana Sharma - *New Immigrant Literatures in the United States*
  r AL - v69 - Mr '97 - p257 [51-250]
  yr BL - v93 - S 1 '96 - p168 [251-500]
  r Choice - v34 - D '96 - p592 [51-250]
  r R&R Bk N - v11 - N '96 - p71 [51-250]
Knipsheer, C P M - *Living Arrangements and Social Networks of Older Adults*
  JMF - v58 - Ag '96 - p803 [251-500]
Knitter, Paul F - *Jesus and the Other Names*
  Rel St Rev - v23 - Ja '97 - p47+ [51-250]
  One Earth, Many Religions
  ER - v49 - Ap '97 - p284+ [51-250]
Knitting Tips and Trade Secrets
  LJ - v122 - Ap 15 '97 - p78 [51-250]
Knobloch, Frieda - *The Culture of Wilderness*
  Choice - v34 - Ap '97 - p1405 [51-250]
Knoepfler, Denis - *Les Imagiers De L'Orestie*
  AJA - v101 - Ja '97 - p154+ [501+]

Knoepflmacher, U C - *Wuthering Heights*
  VS - v39 - Aut '95 - p55+ [501+]
Knoke, David - *Comparing Policy Networks*
  JEL - v34 - D '96 - p2075+ [51-250]
Knoke, William - *Bold New World*
  W&I - v11 - Jl '96 - p274+ [501+]
Knop, Karen - *Rethinking Federalism*
  R&R Bk N - v11 - N '96 - p47 [1-50]
Knopp, Lisa - *Field of Vision*
  Bloom Rev - v16 - Jl '96 - p20 [501+]
  Choice - v34 - D '96 - p692 [51-250]
  VQR - v73 - Win '97 - p31* [51-250]
Knoppers, Laura Lunger - *Historicizing Milton*
  MLR - v91 - O '96 - p970+ [501+]
  RES - v48 - F '97 - p105+ [501+]
Knott, Bill - *The Quicken Tree*
  ABR - v17 - Ag '96 - p26 [501+]
Knott, John R - *Discourses of Martyrdom in English Literature 1563-1694*
  MP - v94 - Ag '96 - p97+ [501+]
  RES - v47 - Ag '96 - p404+ [501+]
Knott, Stephen F - *Secret and Sanctioned*
  APSR - v91 - Mr '97 - p191+ [501+]
  Choice - v34 - S '96 - p210+ [51-250]
  Econ - v340 - S 14 '96 - p8* [251-500]
  For Aff - v75 - S '96 - p141+ [51-250]
Knouse, K C - *True Prosperity*
  BL - v93 - S 15 '96 - p191 [51-250]
  BWatch - v18 - F '97 - p10 [51-250]
Knouse, Stephen B - *Human Resource Management Perspectives on TQM*
  R&R Bk N - v12 - F '97 - p45 [51-250]
Knowdell, Richard L - *From Downsizing to Recovery*
  HR Mag - v42 - Ja '97 - p148 [51-250]
Knowles, David - *Medieval Religious Houses*
  Historian - v59 - Win '97 - p466 [251-500]
Knowles, Eric - *Discovering Antiques*
  r Ant & CM - v102 - Mr '97 - p33 [51-250]
  LJ - v121 - N 1 '96 - p64 [51-250]
Knowles, Ronald - *Gulliver's Travels*
  Choice - v34 - Mr '97 - p1164 [51-250]
Knowles, Sheena - *Edwina the Emu (Illus. by Rod Clement)*
  c Aust Bk R - v1 - Jl '96 - p61+ [501+]
  c Magpies - v11 - Jl '96 - p25 [501+]
Knowlson, James - *Damned to Fame*
  Am Theat - v14 - F '97 - p53+ [501+]
  BW - v26 - O 13 '96 - p1+ [501+]
  Comw - v124 - F 28 '97 - p25+ [501+]
  LATBR - D 15 '96 - p14 [501+]
  LJ - v122 - Ja '97 - p50 [1-50]
  LJ - v121 - S 15 '96 - p69 [51-250]
  Lon R Bks - v18 - N 14 '96 - p8+ [501+]
  New R - v215 - D 30 '96 - p29+ [501+]
  NS - v125 - S 27 '96 - p58+ [501+]
  NY - v72 - S 16 '96 - p92+ [501+]
  NYRB - v43 - N 14 '96 - p24+ [501+]
  NYTBR - v101 - N 24 '96 - p14 [501+]
  NYTBR - v101 - D 8 '96 - p85 [1-50]
  PW - v243 - S 30 '96 - p72 [51-250]
  Spec - v277 - S 21 '96 - p45+ [501+]
  Spec - v277 - N 16 '96 - p56 [1-50]
  TES - O 18 '96 - p7* [501+]
  TLS - S 27 '96 - p3+ [501+]
  TLS - N 29 '96 - p11+ [51-250]
  TLS - N 29 '96 - p13 [51-250]
  W&I - v12 - F '97 - p252+ [501+]
Knowlton, Jack - *Mapas Y Globos Terraqueos (Illus. by Harriett Barton)*
  c BL - v93 - My 1 '97 - p1506 [1-50]
Knowlton, Laurie Lazzaro - *Why Cowboys Need a Brand (Illus. by James Rice)*
  c HB Guide - v8 - Spr '97 - p34 [51-250]
  c Roundup M - v4 - Ap '97 - p29 [1-50]
Knox, Ann B - *Staying Is Nowhere*
  Sm Pr R - v28 - Jl '96 - p13 [251-500]
  Sm Pr R - v29 - F '97 - p12 [251-500]
Knox, Bernard - *Backing into the Future*
  Class Out - v74 - Win '97 - p84 [251-500]
  CW - v89 - Jl '96 - p500+ [501+]
  The Oldest Dead White European Males and Other Reflections on the Classics
  CW - v89 - Jl '96 - p500+ [501+]
Knox, Crawford - *Changing Christian Paradigms and Their Implications for Modern Thought*
  JAAR - v64 - Fall '96 - p683+ [501+]
Knox, George - *Antonio Pellegrini 1675-1741*
  BM - v138 - O '96 - p694+ [501+]
Knox, Melissa - *Oscar Wilde: A Long and Lovely Suicide*
  MLR - v91 - Jl '96 - p706+ [501+]
  Nine-C Lit - v51 - D '96 - p415+ [501+]

Knox, Michael - *The Private Diary of an O.J. Juror*
Esq - v126 - N '96 - p65 [1-50]
Knox, Paul L - *World Cities in a World-System*
APSR - v91 - Mr '97 - p237+ [501+]
GJ - v162 - Jl '96 - p231 [251-500]
JEL - v34 - D '96 - p2137+ [51-250]
Knox-Mawer, June - *The Shadow of Wings*
PW - v243 - S 23 '96 - p57 [51-250]
Knudsen, Olav F - *Strategic Analysis and the Management of Power*
R&R Bk N - v11 - N '96 - p51 [51-250]
Knudson, Ruthann - *The Public Trust and the First Americans*
Pub Hist - v18 - Fall '96 - p153+ [501+]
Knudtson, Peter - *Orca: Visions of the Killer Whale*
y BL - v93 - D 1 '96 - p632 [51-250]
Knuth, Donald E - *Selected Papers on Computer Science*
New Sci - v153 - Mr 1 '97 - p46+ [501+]
Ko, Dorothy - *Teachers of the Inner Chambers*
Historian - v58 - Sum '96 - p881+ [501+]
JIH - v27 - Spr '97 - p748+ [251-500]
Kobayashi, Shoshichi - *Foundations of Differential Geometry. Vol. 1*
SciTech - v20 - D '96 - p20 [51-250]
Kobliner, Beth - *Get a Financial Life (Kobliner). Audio Version*
LJ - v122 - Ap 15 '97 - p136 [51-250]
Koburger, Charles W - *Naval Warfare in the Baltic 1939-1945*
Mar Crp G - v80 - S '96 - p97 [501+]
Kobus, Ken - *The Pennsy in the Steel City*
Model R - v63 - O '96 - p54 [51-250]
Kobzev, Artyom I - *Ucheniye O Simvolakh I Chislakh V Kitaiskoi Klassicheskoi Filosofii*
Ch Rev Int - v3 - Fall '96 - p332+ [501+]
Koch, Carl - *Love: Daily Prayers for Virtue*
RR - v55 - N '96 - p661 [1-50]
Koch, Christopher - *Highways to a War*
Econ - v341 - N 16 '96 - p18*+ [501+]
Koch, Hans-Peter - *Gran Canaria*
r BL - v93 - S 15 '96 - p210 [1-50]
Koch, Kenneth - *The Gold Standard*
LJ - v121 - N 15 '96 - p62 [51-250]
On the Great Atlantic Rainway
MQR - v36 - Win '97 - p203+ [501+]
One Train
Econ - v342 - Mr 29 '97 - p92+ [51-250]
HR - v49 - Sum '96 - p341+ [501+]
MQR - v36 - Win '97 - p203+ [501+]
Koch, Maryjo - *Dragonfly Beetle, Butterfly Bee*
Aud - v99 - Mr '97 - p116 [1-50]
Koch, Rudolf - *Christian Symbols*
CC - v113 - D 4 '96 - p1208+ [51-250]
Koch, Stephen - *Double Lives*
JPR - v33 - N '96 - p499 [51-250]
Koch, Tom - *The Message Is the Medium*
Choice - v34 - Mr '97 - p1195 [51-250]
LJ - v121 - N 15 '96 - p82 [51-250]
R&R Bk N - v12 - F '97 - p92 [1-50]
Kochanowski, Jan - *Laments*
TranslRevS - v2 - D '96 - p30 [51-250]
Kocher, Eric - *International Jobs. 4th Ed.*
r Quill & Q - v63 - F '97 - p38 [501+]
Kochilas, Diane - *The Greek Vegetarian*
BL - v93 - N 15 '96 - p560 [51-250]
LJ - v122 - F 15 '97 - p158 [51-250]
PW - v243 - O 21 '96 - p79 [51-250]
Kochman, Stanley O - *Bordism, Stable Homotopy, and Adams Spectral Sequences*
SciTech - v20 - D '96 - p19 [51-250]
Kocka, Jurgen - *Bourgeois Society in Nineteenth-Century Europe*
EHR - v112 - Ap '97 - p503+ [251-500]
Kocsis, James H - *Diagnosis and Treatment of Chronic Depression*
AJPsych - v154 - Mr '97 - p433+ [501+]
J ClinPsyc - v57 - N '96 - p551 [501+]
Readings - v11 - S '96 - p23 [51-250]
Kodaira, Kunihiko - *Mathematics 1*
y SciTech - v20 - N '96 - p5 [1-50]
Mathematics 2
y SciTech - v21 - Mr '97 - p4 [51-250]
Kodama, Tatsuharu - *Shin's Tricycle (Illus. by Noriyuki Ando)*
c RT - v50 - S '96 - p57 [51-250]
c RT - v50 - O '96 - p138 [1-50]
Kodicek, Ann - *Diaghilev, Creator of the Ballets Russes*
Choice - v34 - S '96 - p139 [51-250]
Dance - v71 - Ja '97 - p98 [51-250]

Kodmani-Darwish, Bassma - *Le Liban Et Les Derives Du Processus De Paix*
MEJ - v51 - Win '97 - p151 [51-250]
Koea, Shonagh - *Sing to Me, Dreamer (Howley). Audio Version*
y Kliatt - v31 - Mr '97 - p46 [51-250]
Koeberland, Christian - *The Manson Impact Structure, Iowa*
SciTech - v21 - Mr '97 - p33 [51-250]
Koegel, Lynn Kern - *Positive Behavioral Support*
Readings - v11 - D '96 - p22 [51-250]
Koehler, Jerry W - *Transformational Leadership in Government*
R&R Bk N - v11 - D '96 - p47 [51-250]
Koehler, Ludwig - *The Hebrew and Aramaic Lexicon of the Old Testament. Vol. 2*
r ARBA - v28 - '97 - p544 [51-250]
Koehler, Phoebe - *The Day We Met You*
c PW - v244 - Ap 28 '97 - p77 [1-50]
Koehler-Pentacoff, Elizabeth - *Louise the One and Only (Illus. by R W Alley)*
c SLJ - v42 - Ag '96 - p125 [51-250]
Koehn, Daryl - *The Ground of Professional Ethics*
CPR - v16 - Je '96 - p181+ [501+]
Koehn, Nancy F - *The Power of Commerce*
EHR - v112 - F '97 - p213+ [251-500]
JMH - v68 - S '96 - p689+ [501+]
Koen, Karleen - *Now Face to Face*
Books - v10 - Je '96 - p22 [1-50]
Now Face to Face (Hart). Audio Version
y Kliatt - v31 - Ja '97 - p43 [51-250]
LJ - v121 - N 1 '96 - p121 [51-250]
Koenig, David - *Mouse under Glass*
y BL - v93 - Ja '97 - p803 [51-250]
Koenig, Harold G - *Is Religion Good for Your Health?*
PW - v244 - Ja 27 '97 - p96 [51-250]
Koenig-Bricker, Woodeene - *Prayers of the Saints*
BL - v92 - Ag '96 - p1859 [51-250]
Koerner, Michael - *PowerPC: An Inside View*
SciTech - v20 - S '96 - p7 [51-250]
Koertge, Ron - *Confess-O-Rama*
y BL - v93 - O 1 '96 - p342+ [51-250]
y CCB-B - v50 - N '96 - p103 [51-250]
y HB Guide - v8 - Spr '97 - p81 [51-250]
y JAAL - v40 - N '96 - p230 [51-250]
y KR - v64 - S 15 '96 - p1403 [51-250]
y SLJ - v42 - S '96 - p227 [51-250]
y SLJ - v42 - D '96 - p30 [1-50]
y VOYA - v19 - D '96 - p271+ [251-500]
Koestenbaum, Wayne - *Jackie under My Skin*
Books - v9 - S '95 - p23 [1-50]
Koester, Craig R - *Symbolism in the Fourth Gospel*
Intpr - v51 - Ap '97 - p201+ [251-500]
Koetzsch, Ronald E - *The Parents' Guide to Alternatives in Education*
LJ - v122 - My 1 '97 - p118 [251-500]
Koevoets, Pamela - *Schaduwboksen*
WLT - v70 - Aut '96 - p973 [251-500]
Koff-Chapin, Deborah - *Drawing Out Your Soul*
Mag Bl - Mr '97 - p58 [51-250]
Kofman, Sarah - *Rue Ordener, Rue Labat*
BL - v93 - S 15 '96 - p216 [51-250]
y Kliatt - v31 - Ja '97 - p19 [251-500]
PW - v243 - Jl 22 '96 - p232 [51-250]
TLS - Ja 31 '97 - p27 [501+]
Kofsky, Frank - *Harry S. Truman and the War Scare of 1948*
Pres SQ - v26 - Fall '96 - p1179 [501+]
Koga, Futoshi - *Lumiere! Les Freres Lumiere Et Le Japon 1895-1995*
FQ - v50 - Win '96 - p62+ [251-500]
Kogel, Renee - *Judaism in a Secular Age*
Rel St Rev - v23 - Ja '97 - p89+ [51-250]
Kohbach, Markus - *Die Eroberung Von Fulek Durch Die Osmanen 1554*
Slav R - v55 - Fall '96 - p669+ [501+]
Kohl, Benjamin G - *Major Problems in the History of the Italian Renaissance*
Ren Q - v50 - Spr '97 - p261+ [501+]
Kohl, Herbert - *Should We Burn Babar?*
ES - v27 - Fall '96 - p286+ [501+]
SFR - v21 - Jl '96 - p47 [251-500]
Kohl, Philip L - *Nationalism, Politics, and the Practice of Archaeology*
Am Ant - v62 - Ja '97 - p149 [501+]
Kohlas, Jurg - *A Mathematical Theory of Hints*
JEL - v34 - D '96 - p2018+ [51-250]
Kohlenberger, John R, III - *The Exhaustive Concordance to the Greek New Testament*
r ARBA - v28 - '97 - p544+ [51-250]

Kohler, Gabriele - *Questioning Development*
JEL - v34 - D '96 - p2110 [51-250]
Kohlhase, Thomas - *Internationales Cajkovskij-Symposium, Teubingen 1993*
Notes - v53 - D '96 - p472+ [501+]
Kohlhoff, Dean - *When the Wind Was a River*
PHR - v65 - N '96 - p689+ [501+]
Kohn, Alfie - *Beyond Discipline*
Learning - v25 - Mr '97 - p9 [51-250]
Kohn, Marek - *The Race Gallery*
Nature - v384 - D 5 '96 - p426 [1-50]
Soc - v34 - Mr '97 - p78+ [501+]
Koistinen, Paul A C - *Beating Plowshares into Swords*
Choice - v34 - Ap '97 - p1405+ [501+]
Koja, Kathe - *Kink*
LATBR - Ag 11 '96 - p10+ [51-250]
Necro - Sum '96 - p20+ [501+]
NYTBR - v102 - Ja 19 '97 - p18 [251-500]
RCF - v16 - Fall '96 - p189 [251-500]
Kojima, Hisaka - *Digital Image Creation*
BWatch - v17 - S '96 - p5 [51-250]
CBR - v14 - N '96 - p33 [51-250]
Quill & Q - v62 - N '96 - p33 [51-250]
Kojima, Kiyoshi - *Trade, Investment and Pacific Economic Integration*
JEL - v34 - D '96 - p2043 [51-250]
Kojin, Karatani - *Origins of Modern Japanese Literature*
TranslRevS - v1 - My '95 - p7 [51-250]
Kok, Peter N - *Governance and Conflict in the Sudan 1985-1995*
MEJ - v51 - Spr '97 - p293+ [501+]
Kokis, Sergio - *Negao Et Doralice*
WLT - v70 - Aut '96 - p908+ [251-500]
Kolakowski, Leszek - *God Owes Us Nothing*
JR - v76 - O '96 - p607+ [501+]
Rel St - v33 - Mr '97 - p127+ [501+]
W&I - v11 - Ag '96 - p280+ [501+]
Kolata, Alan L - *Tiwanaku and Its Hinterland*
R&R Bk N - v12 - F '97 - p28 [51-250]
Valley of the Spirits
NH - v105 - Ag '96 - p14 [51-250]
Kolatch, Alfred J - *Great Jewish Quotations*
r BL - v93 - F 1 '97 - p965 [251-500]
r Choice - v34 - Mr '97 - p1136+ [51-250]
The Second Jewish Book of Why (Bikel). Audio Version
y Kliatt - v31 - Ja '97 - p50 [51-250]
Kolb, Hugh - *Country Foxes*
New Sci - v153 - Mr 8 '97 - p45 [51-250]
Kolb, Rocky - *Blind Watchers of the Sky*
Astron - v24 - O '96 - p98 [501+]
Choice - v34 - O '96 - p301 [51-250]
Nature - v382 - Jl 18 '96 - p220 [51-250]
Phys Today - v50 - Ja '97 - p69+ [501+]
VQR - v72 - Aut '96 - p139* [51-250]
Kolbenschlag, Madonna - *Eastward toward Eve*
CLW - v67 - Mr '97 - p29+ [251-500]
Kolber-Stuart, Billy - *Out and About Gay Travel Guides*
r LJ - v122 - Ja '97 - p128 [51-250]
Kolbert, Colin - *The Idea of Property in History and Modern Times*
TLS - Mr 7 '97 - p13 [501+]
Kolin, Philip C - *Speaking on Stage*
Choice - v34 - Ja '97 - p807 [51-250]
Kolko, Gabriel - *Century of War*
S&S - v61 - Sum '97 - p286+ [501+]
Kollander, Patricia - *Frederick III: Germany's Liberal Emperor*
AHR - v102 - F '97 - p122+ [501+]
CEH - v29 - 2 '96 - p249+ [501+]
Kollar, Rene - *Abbot Aelred Carlyle, Caldey Island, and the Anglo-Catholic Revival in England*
Albion - v28 - Fall '96 - p520+ [501+]
Koller, Jackie French - *Dragon Quest (Illus. by Jackie French Koller)*
c BL - v93 - Mr 1 '97 - p1164 [51-250]
No Such Thing (Illus. by Betsy Lewin)
c BL - v93 - Ap 1 '97 - p1338 [51-250]
c CBRS - v25 - F '97 - p75 [1-50]
c CCB-B - v50 - Mr '97 - p237+ [251-500]
c KR - v65 - Ja 1 '97 - p60 [51-250]
c PW - v243 - D 30 '96 - p67 [51-250]
A Place to Call Home
y PW - v244 - Ap 21 '97 - p74 [51-250]
The Primrose Way
y Kliatt - v30 - S '96 - p3 [1-50]
Kolmanovskii, Vladimir B - *Control of Systems with Aftereffect*
SciTech - v21 - Mr '97 - p16 [51-250]

Kolmar, Gertrud - *A Jewish Mother from Berlin. Susanna*
  KR - v65 - My 1 '97 - p678 [51-250]
  LJ - v122 - Ap 1 '97 - p127 [51-250]
  PW - v244 - Mr 31 '97 - p65 [51-250]
Kolmogorov, A N - *Mathematics of the 19th Century*
  SciTech - v20 - S '96 - p11 [51-250]
Kolodziej, Edward A - *Coping with Conflict after the Cold War*
  Choice - v34 - O '96 - p356 [51-250]
  For Aff - v75 - S '96 - p136 [51-250]
Kolpas, Norman - *Pizza Presto*
  BWatch - v17 - N '96 - p1 [51-250]
  y Kliatt - v31 - Ja '97 - p32 [51-250]
Kolstoe, Paul - *Russians in the Former Soviet Republics*
  APSR - v90 - S '96 - p699 [501+]
  JPR - v33 - Ag '96 - p381 [251-500]
Koltsova, Vera A - *Post-Soviet Perspectives on Russian Psychology*
  Choice - v34 - O '96 - p365 [51-250]
Kolumban, Nicholas - *Surgery on My Soul*
  Sm Pr R - v28 - N '96 - p8 [51-250]
Komaiko, Leah - *Annie Bananie Moves to Barry Avenue (Illus. by Abby Carter)*
  c HB Guide - v8 - Spr '97 - p58 [51-250]
  c KR - v64 - N 1 '96 - p1602 [51-250]
  c SLJ - v43 - F '97 - p82 [51-250]
On Sally Perry's Farm (Illus. by Cat Bowman Smith)
  c HB Guide - v7 - Fall '96 - p263 [51-250]
  c KR - v64 - My 1 '96 - p690 [51-250]
  c LATBR - Jl 7 '96 - p11 [51-250]
Komanin, Zarko - *Gospod Nad Vojskama*
  WLT - v71 - Win '97 - p185 [501+]
Komarinski, Mark - *LINUX Companion*
  CBR - v14 - S '96 - p32 [1-50]
Komarnicki, Todd - *Famine*
  BL - v93 - D 15 '96 - p709 [51-250]
  Ent W - F 7 '97 - p64 [51-250]
  KR - v64 - N 15 '96 - p1623+ [251-500]
  LJ - v121 - D '96 - p146 [51-250]
  PW - v243 - N 18 '96 - p61 [51-250]
Komatsu, Yusaku - *Distortion Theorems in Relation to Linear Integral Operators*
  SciTech - v21 - Mr '97 - p17 [51-250]
Komenda-Soentgerath, Olly - *In the Shadow of Prague*
  KR - v64 - S 1 '96 - p1298 [251-500]
  TranslRevS - v2 - N '96 - p26 [51-250]
Komesaroff, Paul A - *Troubled Bodies*
  Bks & Cult - v3 - Ja '97 - p14+ [501+]
  MHR - v10 - Fall '96 - p56+ [501+]
Komlos, John - *The Biological Standard of Living in Europe and America 1700-1900*
  R&R Bk N - v12 - F '97 - p30 [51-250]
The Biological Standard of Living on Three Continents
  JIH - v27 - Aut '96 - p277+ [501+]
Stature, Living Conditions, and Economic Development
  JIH - v27 - Win '97 - p499+ [501+]
Kompatscher, Gottfried - *Volk Und Herrscher In Der Historischen Sage*
  Six Ct J - v27 - Win '96 - p1157+ [501+]
Kon, Igor S - *The Sexual Revolution in Russia*
  Slav R - v55 - Sum '96 - p502+ [501+]
Kondoleon, Christine - *Domestic and Divine*
  AJA - v101 - Ja '97 - p188+ [501+]
Kong, T Yung - *Topological Algorithms for Digital Image Processing*
  SciTech - v21 - Mr '97 - p80 [51-250]
Konhauser, Joseph D E - *Which Way Did the Bicycle Go? and Other Intriguing Mathematical Mysteries*
  New Sci - v153 - Mr 8 '97 - p42 [51-250]
  y SB - v33 - Mr '97 - p44+ [51-250]
  y SciTech - v21 - Mr '97 - p12 [51-250]
Konig, David Thomas - *Devising Liberty*
  Historian - v59 - Win '97 - p433+ [501+]
  RAH - v24 - S '96 - p395+ [501+]
  W&M Q - v53 - O '96 - p833+ [501+]
Konigsburg, E L - *From the Mixed-Up Files of Mrs. Basil E. Frankweiler*
  c JOYS - v10 - Fall '96 - p35+ [501+]
T-Backs, T-Shirts, Coat, and Suit
  c SLJ - v43 - Ja '97 - p37 [1-50]

The View from Saturday
  y BL - v93 - Ap 1 '97 - p1302 [1-50]
  c CBRS - v25 - O '96 - p22 [51-250]
  c CCB-B - v50 - N '96 - p103 [51-250]
  c HB - v73 - Ja '97 - p60+ [51-250]
  c HB Guide - v8 - Spr '97 - p70 [51-250]
  c LATBR - N 24 '96 - p10 [51-250]
  c NYTBR - v101 - N 10 '96 - p49 [251-500]
  c Par Ch - v21 - Mr '97 - p8+ [1-50]
  c PW - v243 - Jl 22 '96 - p242 [51-250]
  c SLJ - v42 - S '96 - p204 [51-250]
  c SLJ - v42 - D '96 - p30 [1-50]
Koninck, Rodolphe De - *Malay Peasants Coping with the World*
  Pac A - v69 - Sum '96 - p306 [251-500]
Koning, Niek - *The Failure of Agrarian Capitalism*
  JEH - v56 - D '96 - p965+ [501+]
Konneh, Augustine - *Religion, Commerce, and the Integration of the Mandingo in Liberia*
  Choice - v34 - Ja '97 - p852 [51-250]
Kono, Taeko - *Toddler-Hunting and Other Stories*
  Choice - v34 - F '97 - p962 [51-250]
Konrad, Christoph F - *Plutarch's Sertorius*
  CW - v90 - S '96 - p69+ [501+]
Konstantinos - *Vampires*
  BWatch - v17 - S '96 - p12 [51-250]
Konzak, Burt - *Noguchi the Samurai (Illus. by Johnny Wales)*
  c Can CL - v22 - Fall '96 - p132+ [501+]
Koo, Hagen - *State and Society in Contemporary Korea*
  Pac A - v69 - Fall '96 - p427+ [501+]
Kool, Clemens - *Essays on Money, Banking, and Regulation*
  JEL - v34 - D '96 - p2037 [51-250]
  R&R Bk N - v11 - D '96 - p36 [51-250]
Kooler, Donna - *Donna Kooler's Glorious Needlepoint*
  BL - v93 - O 1 '96 - p316 [51-250]
  LJ - v122 - Ap 15 '97 - p79 [51-250]
Koolhaas, Rem - *S, M, L, XL*
  NYRB - v43 - N 28 '96 - p42+ [501+]
Koon, George William - *Old Glory and the Stars and Bars*
  Nine-C Lit - v50 - Mr '96 - p554 [1-50]
Koontz, Dean - *Icebound*
  Books - v9 - S '95 - p25 [51-250]
Intensity
  Arm Det - v29 - Sum '96 - p376 [251-500]
  Ent W - D 13 '96 - p75 [1-50]
  PW - v244 - Mr 31 '97 - p72 [1-50]
Santa's Twin (Illus. by Phil Parks)
  c CBRS - v25 - Ja '97 - p55 [51-250]
  c NYTBR - v101 - D 8 '96 - p102 [1-50]
Santa's Twin (Sanders). Audio Version
  y BWatch - v17 - D '96 - p10 [1-50]
Sole Survivor
  y BL - v93 - Ja '97 - p778+ [51-250]
  CSM - v89 - F 20 '97 - p10 [51-250]
  CSM - v89 - Mr 20 '97 - p14 [51-250]
  Ent W - F 14 '97 - p54+ [251-500]
  KR - v65 - Ja 1 '97 - p12+ [251-500]
  LJ - v122 - F 15 '97 - p162 [51-250]
  NYTBR - v102 - Ap 20 '97 - p20 [51-250]
  PW - v244 - Ja 6 '97 - p63+ [251-500]
  Trib Bks - F 16 '97 - p6 [51-250]
Sole Survivor (Birney). Audio Version
  LJ - v122 - Ap 1 '97 - p146 [51-250]
Ticktock
  Books - v10 - Je '96 - p22 [1-50]
  Books - v11 - Ap '97 - p22 [51-250]
Koontz, Robin Michal - *Chicago and the Cat: The Family Reunion (Illus. by Robin Michal Koontz)*
  c HB Guide - v8 - Spr '97 - p55 [51-250]
  c SLJ - v42 - S '96 - p182 [51-250]
Kooper, Erik - *Medieval Dutch Literature in Its European Context*
  MLR - v92 - Ja '97 - p260+ [501+]
  Specu - v71 - Jl '96 - p727+ [501+]
Koopman, Douglas L - *Hostile Takeover*
  Choice - v34 - Ja '97 - p875 [51-250]
Koopmans, Jelle - *Rhetoric-Rhetoriqueurs-Rederijkers*
  Six Ct J - v27 - Fall '96 - p867+ [501+]
Koopmans, Ruud - *Democracy from Below*
  AJS - v102 - S '96 - p616+ [501+]
  CS - v25 - N '96 - p764+ [501+]
Koops, W R H - *Het Nieuwe Gebouw Van De Universiteitsbibliotheek Te Groningen*
  Lib & Cul - v32 - Win '97 - p137 [251-500]
Koortbojian, Michael - *Myth, Meaning and Memory on Roman Sarcophagi*
  Apo - v144 - Jl '96 - p65 [51-250]
  BM - v138 - Ag '96 - p546 [501+]

Kooser, Ted - *Weather Central*
  South HR - v30 - Fall '96 - p404+ [501+]
Kopcke, Gunter - *Greece between East and West*
  AJA - v100 - Jl '96 - p616+ [501+]
Kope, Spencer - *Everything Civil War*
  r BL - v93 - Mr 15 '97 - p1256+ [51-250]
Kopel, David B - *No More Wacos*
  BL - v93 - Mr 1 '97 - p1094 [51-250]
  PW - v244 - Ja 6 '97 - p55 [51-250]
Kopelman, Orion Moshe - *The Second Ten Commandments*
  Rapport - v19 - 4 '96 - p18+ [501+]
Kopelson, Kevin - *Beethoven's Kiss*
  Choice - v34 - O '96 - p291 [51-250]
Koperwas, Sam - *The Flash Effect*
  Aethlon - v13 - Fall '95 - p132+ [251-500]
Kopinak, Kathryn - *Desert Capitalism*
  Choice - v34 - D '96 - p658 [51-250]
  R&R Bk N - v11 - N '96 - p33 [51-250]
Kopkind, Andrew - *The Thirty Years' War*
  PW - v243 - S 23 '96 - p73 [1-50]
Koplan, Steven - *Exploring Wine*
  r LJ - v122 - Ap 1 '97 - p62 [1-50]
Kopnick, Lutz - *Nothungs Modernitat*
  Ger Q - v69 - Fall '96 - p433+ [501+]
Koponen, Juhani - *Development for Exploitation*
  AHR - v101 - D '96 - p1594+ [501+]
  Historian - v59 - Fall '96 - p140+ [501+]
Kopp, Jaine - *Frog Math*
  Inst - v106 - S '96 - p16 [51-250]
Koppel, Bruce M - *Induced Innovation Theory and International Agricultural Development*
  Econ J - v107 - Ja '97 - p288 [251-500]
Koppel, Ted - *Nightline: History in the Making and the Making of Television*
  BW - v26 - Ag 4 '96 - p4 [501+]
Koppelman, Susan - *Women in the Trees*
  Ms - v7 - Ja '97 - p77+ [501+]
  Wom R Bks - v14 - Mr '97 - p1+ [501+]
Kopper, Christopher - *Zwischen Marktwirtschaft Und Dirigismus*
  AHR - v101 - D '96 - p1568+ [501+]
Kopper, Lisa - *Daisy Is a Mommy (Illus. by Lisa Kopper)*
  c BL - v93 - D 1 '96 - p668+ [51-250]
  c KR - v64 - D 1 '96 - p1739 [51-250]
  c SLJ - v43 - F '97 - p82 [51-250]
Daisy Is a Mummy (Illus. by Lisa Kopper)
  c Sch Lib - v45 - F '97 - p19 [501+]
I'm a Baby, You're a Baby (Illus. by Lisa Kopper)
  c JB - v60 - O '96 - p185 [51-250]
Koppeschaar, Carl - *Moon Handbook*
  y SB - v32 - Ag '96 - p173 [51-250]
Koppett, Leonard - *Sports Illusion, Sports Reality*
  Aethlon - v13 - Spr '96 - p204+ [501+]
Kopple, Joel D - *Nutritional Management of Renal Disease*
  SciTech - v21 - Mr '97 - p58 [51-250]
Koppman, Lion - *A Treasury of American-Jewish Folklore*
  LJ - v121 - D '96 - p102 [51-250]
  PW - v243 - D 16 '96 - p53 [51-250]
Korbach, Ivan - *Sotnyky: Istorychnyi Romankhronika*
  BL - v93 - N 15 '96 - p577 [1-50]
Korchilov, Igor - *Translating History*
  BL - v93 - My 15 '97 - p1559+ [51-250]
  KR - v65 - Ap 1 '97 - p527 [251-500]
  PW - v244 - Ap 28 '97 - p56 [51-250]
Korda, Dyanne - *Spirit Food*
  Sm Pr R - v28 - Jl '96 - p11 [51-250]
Korda, Michael - *Man to Man*
  BL - v93 - Ja '97 - p758 [1-50]
  Choice - v34 - N '96 - p493 [51-250]
  New Sci - v153 - F 22 '97 - p46 [51-250]
  NYTBR - v101 - D 8 '96 - p88 [1-50]
  PW - v244 - Mr 31 '97 - p72 [1-50]
Kordesch, Karl - *Fuel Cells and Their Applications*
  SciTech - v20 - N '96 - p71 [51-250]
Korelitz, Jean Hanff - *A Jury of Her Peers*
  Rapport - v19 - 5 '96 - p33 [251-500]
  VQR - v72 - Aut '96 - p129*+ [51-250]
Koren, Herman - *Handbook of Environmental Health and Safety. 3rd Ed., Vols. 1-2*
  Choice - v34 - N '96 - p493+ [51-250]
Korf, Bruce R - *Human Genetics*
  SciTech - v21 - Mr '97 - p35 [51-250]
Korff, Kal K - *The Roswell UFO Crash*
  y BL - v93 - My 15 '97 - p1544 [51-250]
Koritz, Amy - *Gendering Bodies/Performing Art*
  Dance RJ - v28 - Fall '96 - p80+ [501+]
  TDR - v41 - Spr '97 - p152+ [501+]
Koriyama, Naoshi - *Like Underground Water*
  WLT - v70 - Sum '96 - p762+ [501+]

Korlek, Jenny - *A Treasury of Stories from Hans Christian Andersen (Illus. by Robin Lawrie)*
  c CLW - v67 - Mr '97 - p53 [51-250]
A Treasury of Stories from the Brothers Grimm (Illus. by Robin Lawrie)
  c CLW - v67 - Mr '97 - p53 [51-250]
Korman, Gordon - *The Chicken Doesn't Skate*
  c BIC - v25 - D '96 - p36+ [251-500]
  c BL - v93 - N 15 '96 - p588 [51-250]
  c CBRS - v25 - N '96 - p34+
  c HB Guide - v8 - Spr '97 - p70 [51-250]
  y JAAL - v40 - Mr '97 - p511+ [251-500]
  c Quill & Q - v62 - N '96 - p44 [51-250]
  c SLJ - v42 - N '96 - p107+ [51-250]
The D-Poems of Jeremy Bloom
  y JAAL - v40 - D '96 - p319 [51-250]
The Last-Place Sports Poems of Jeremy Bloom
  c Quill & Q - v62 - D '96 - p39 [251-500]
Something Fishy at MacDonald Hall
  c HB Guide - v7 - Fall '96 - p294 [51-250]
Korn, Jessica - *The Power of Separation*
     Choice - v34 - F '97 - p1036 [51-250]
Korn, Peter - *Lovejoy: A Year in the Life of an Abortion Clinic*
     BW - v27 - Ja 5 '97 - p8 [501+]
     Cons - v17 - Win '96 - p31 [1-50]
     KR - v64 - Ag 15 '96 - p1213 [251-500]
     LJ - v121 - O 1 '96 - p110 [51-250]
     NYTBR - v101 - O 20 '96 - p25 [501+]
     PW - v243 - S 9 '96 - p76 [51-250]
     Wom R Bks - v14 - Ja '97 - p21 [501+]
Kornberg, Grant - *The Largely Literary Legacy of the Late Leon Tolbert*
     BW - v26 - Jl 14 '96 - p12 [51-250]
Kornblatt, Judith Deutsch - *Russian Religious Thought*
     R&R Bk N - v12 - F '97 - p10 [51-250]
Kornbluth, C M - *His Share of Glory*
     BL - v93 - Ap 1 '97 - p1283 [51-250]
     KR - v65 - Mr 1 '97 - p315 [51-250]
     LJ - v122 - Mr 15 '97 - p93 [1-50]
     PW - v244 - Mr 31 '97 - p69 [1-50]
Kornbluth, Genevra Alisoun - *Engraved Gems of the Carolingian Empire*
     Apo - v145 - Ja '97 - p61 [501+]
     BM - v139 - Ja '97 - p51 [51-250]
Kornbluth, Jesse - *Airborne: The Truimph and Struggle of Michael Jordan*
  c RT - v50 - O '96 - p139 [1-50]
Kornbluth, Josh - *Red Diaper Baby*
     BL - v92 - Ag '96 - p1875 [51-250]
     LJ - v121 - N 1 '96 - p67+ [51-250]
Kornegay, E T - *Nutrient Management of Food Animals to Enhance and Protect the Environment*
     SciTech - v20 - D '96 - p57 [51-250]
Korner, Christian - *Carbon Dioxide, Populations, and Communities*
     SciTech - v20 - N '96 - p28 [51-250]
Korner, Tom - *The Pleasures of Counting*
     New Sci - v153 - F 15 '97 - p45 [51-250]
Kornfeld, Phyllis - *Cellblock Visions*
     PW - v244 - F 17 '97 - p207 [51-250]
Kornhaber, Arthur - *Contemporary Grandparenting*
     AAPSS-A - v550 - Mr '97 - p191+ [501+]
Kornstein, Daniel J - *Kill All the Lawyers?*
     TLS - N 29 '96 - p8 [501+]
Korntgen, Ludger - *Paenitentialia Franciae, Italiae Et Hispaniae Saeculi VIII-XI. Vol. 1*
     Specu - v71 - O '96 - p969+ [501+]
Korolko, Miroslaw - *Vincentius Lauro 1572-1578. Bk. 1*
     CHR - v82 - O '96 - p722+ [501+]
Korolkov, Dimitri V - *Electronic Structure and Properties of Non-Transition Element Compounds*
     SciTech - v21 - Mr '97 - p32 [51-250]
Korp, Maureen - *Sacred Art of the Earth*
     PW - v244 - Ap 14 '97 - p70+ [51-250]
Korpel, Adrian - *Acousto-Optics. 2nd Ed.*
     SciTech - v21 - Mr '97 - p22 [51-250]
Korprulu, Mehmed Fuad - *Islam in Anatolia after the Turkish Invasion*
     TranslRevS - v1 - My '95 - p13+ [51-250]
Korres, Manolis - *From Pentelicon to the Parthenon*
     AJA - v100 - Jl '96 - p601+ [501+]
     Arch - v49 - S '96 - p80+ [501+]
Korsgaard, Christine M - *The Sources of Normativity*
     Choice - v34 - My '97 - p1513 [51-250]
Kort, Michael - *Yitzhak Rabin: Israel's Soldier Statesman*
  y BL - v93 - Ja '97 - p838 [51-250]
  y CCB-B - v50 - Ja '97 - p176+ [51-250]
  y HB Guide - v8 - Spr '97 - p159 [51-250]
  y Kliatt - v31 - Ja '97 - p19 [51-250]
  y SLJ - v43 - F '97 - p118 [51-250]

Kortesis, Vasso - *The Duchess of York Uncensored*
     Spec - v277 - N 23 '96 - p54+ [501+]
Kortner, Ulrich H J - *The End of the World*
     Rel St Rev - v22 - O '96 - p335 [51-250]
     Theol St - v58 - Mr '97 - p175+ [501+]
Kortright, Brigitte E - *Fables of the Times Tables (Illus. by Dennis Nobel)*
  c Quill & Q - v63 - F '97 - p54+ [251-500]
Korzeniowski, Paul - *Windows NT Versus NetWare*
     SciTech - v20 - N '96 - p11 [51-250]
Koschmann, J Victor - *Revolution and Subjectivity in Postwar Japan*
     TLS - O 25 '96 - p7 [501+]
Kosenina, Alexander - *Anthropologie Und Schauspielkunst*
     MLR - v92 - Ja '97 - p241+ [501+]
Kosinski, Dahlia - *The Morning After*
  y VOYA - v19 - D '96 - p262 [51-250]
Koskas, Marco - *J'Ai Pas Ferme L'Oeil De L'Ete*
     BL - v93 - F 1 '97 - p930 [1-50]
Koslow, Philip - *Asante: The Gold Coast*
  y HB Guide - v7 - Fall '96 - p378 [51-250]
Benin: Lords of the River
  y HB Guide - v7 - Fall '96 - p378 [51-250]
Dahomey: The Warrior Kings
  c HB Guide - v8 - Spr '97 - p166 [51-250]
  c SLJ - v42 - D '96 - p130 [51-250]
Yorubaland: The Flowering of Genius
  y HB Guide - v7 - Fall '96 - p378 [51-250]
Koslow, Stephen H - *The Neuroscience of Mental Health II*
     J Gov Info - v23 - S '96 - p548 [51-250]
Koslowski, Barbara - *Theory and Evidence*
     Choice - v34 - Mr '97 - p1179 [51-250]
Koslowski, Peter - *Ethics of Capitalism and Critique of Sociobiology*
     JEL - v35 - Mr '97 - p287+ [51-250]
Koslowsky, Meni - *Commuting Stress*
     Per Psy - v49 - Win '96 - p1014+ [501+]
Kosman, Miriam - *Red, Blue and Yellow Yarn*
  c Ch BWatch - v6 - O '96 - p4 [51-250]
Kosnik, Clare - *Nelson Spelling*
  c Quill & Q - v62 - O '96 - p50 [51-250]
Kosof, Anna - *Living in Two Worlds*
  y BL - v93 - O 1 '96 - p332 [51-250]
  c Ch BWatch - v6 - N '96 - p2 [51-250]
  y SLJ - v42 - O '96 - p158 [51-250]
  y VOYA - v19 - F '97 - p346 [251-500]
Kosoff, Susan - *The I Could Eat Pasta Every Night Cookbook*
     BWatch - v17 - D '96 - p9 [1-50]
Kosok, Heinz - *Plays and Playwrights from Ireland in International Perspective*
     ILS - v15 - Fall '96 - p31 [1-50]
Kosslyn, Stephen M - *Image and Brain*
     AJPsych - v153 - S '96 - p1222+ [501+]
Kossowsky, Ram - *High Power Lasers*
     SciTech - v20 - D '96 - p66 [51-250]
Kostabi, Mark - *Conversations with Kostabi*
     BL - v93 - N 15 '96 - p563+ [51-250]
     NYTBR - v102 - Ja 26 '97 - p19 [251-500]
     PW - v243 - S 9 '96 - p78 [51-250]
Kostal, R W - *Law and English Railway Capitalism 1825-1875*
     EHR - v112 - F '97 - p234+ [501+]
Kostbare Illustrierte Bucher Des Sechzehnten Jahrhunderts In Der Stadtbibliothek Trier
     Six Ct J - v27 - Win '96 - p1182+ [501+]
Kostelanetz, Richard - *Writings on Glass*
     LJ - v122 - My 1 '97 - p107 [51-250]
     PW - v244 - F 3 '97 - p85 [51-250]
Kostenberger, Andreas J - *Women in the Church*
     Rel St Rev - v23 - Ja '97 - p75 [51-250]
Kostick, Conor - *Revolution in Ireland*
     HT - v46 - O '96 - p58 [1-50]
Kostiner, Joseph - *The Making of Saudi Arabia 1916-1936*
     EHR - v111 - Mr '97 - p1345+ [251-500]
Kostyrchenko, Gennadi - *Out of the Red Shadows*
     J Ch St - v38 - Aut '96 - p925+ [251-500]
     Russ Rev - v56 - Ja '97 - p141+ [501+]
Kosztolanyi, Dezso - *Skylark*
     TranslRevS - v2 - D '96 - p5+ [51-250]
Kotabe, Masaaki - *Anticompetitive Practices in Japan*
     R&R Bk N - v11 - D '96 - p30 [51-250]
Kotilainen, Markku - *Exchange Rate Unions*
     JEL - v34 - S '96 - p1433 [51-250]
Kotker, Norman - *Billy in Love*
     BL - v93 - O 1 '96 - p322 [51-250]
     BW - v27 - Ja 19 '97 - p8 [251-500]
     KR - v64 - Ag 15 '96 - p1175+ [251-500]
     PW - v243 - S 9 '96 - p78 [51-250]

Kotkin, Stephen - *Magnetic Mountain*
     AHR - v101 - D '96 - p1586+ [501+]
     JMH - v69 - Mr '97 - p197+ [501+]
     Russ Rev - v56 - Ja '97 - p140+ [501+]
Rediscovering Russia in Asia
     Pac A - v69 - Sum '96 - p251+ [501+]
Kotler, Philip - *Marketing Management. 9th Ed.*
     R&R Bk N - v12 - F '97 - p44 [51-250]
Principles of Marketing. European Ed.
     ILR - v135 - 5 '96 - p594+ [51-250]
Standing Room Only
     BL - v93 - D 1 '96 - p637 [51-250]
     BWatch - v18 - Mr '97 - p11 [51-250]
     TCI - v30 - O '96 - p56+ [51-250]
Kotlowitz, Robert - *Before Their Time*
     BL - v93 - Ja '97 - p814 [51-250]
     BW - v27 - F 16 '97 - p1+ [501+]
     KR - v64 - D 1 '96 - p1717+ [251-500]
     LJ - v122 - F 1 '97 - p90 [51-250]
     PW - v243 - D 30 '96 - p47 [51-250]
     Trib Bks - Ja 19 '97 - p7 [501+]
     WSJ-Cent - v99 - F 14 '97 - pA10 [501+]
Kotowicz, Zbigniew - *Fernando Pessoa: Voices of a Nomadic Soul*
     TLS - O 4 '96 - p38 [501+]
Kotsias, Telemahos - *To Telefteo Kanarini*
     WLT - v70 - Sum '96 - p740 [501+]
Kottek, Samuel S - *Medicine and Medical Ethics in Medievul and Eurly Modern Spain*
     Hast Cen R - v27 - Ja '97 - p47 [1-50]
Kotter, John P - *Leading Change*
     BL - v93 - S 1 '96 - p45 [51-250]
     LJ - v121 - S 15 '96 - p77 [51-250]
     LJ - v122 - Mr 15 '97 - p35 [1-50]
Matsushita Leadership
     BL - v93 - My 1 '97 - p1467 [51-250]
     KR - v65 - Mr 15 '97 - p441 [251-500]
     LJ - v122 - Ap 15 '97 - p92 [51-250]
     PW - v244 - Mr 17 '97 - p63 [51-250]
The New Rules
     Per Psy - v49 - Aut '96 - p746+ [501+]
Kottsieper, Ingo - *Wer Ist Wie Du, Herr, Unter De Gottern?*
     Rel St Rev - v23 - Ap '97 - p168+ [51-250]
Kotulak, Ronald - *Inside the Brain*
     NYTBR - v101 - S 8 '96 - p38 [501+]
     SciTech - v20 - N '96 - p32 [51-250]
Kotz, John C - *Chemistry and Chemical Reactivity. 3rd Ed.*
     J Chem Ed - v74 - Ap '97 - p378+ [501+]
Saunders Interactive General Chemistry CD-ROM. Electronic Media Version
     J Chem Ed - v74 - Ap '97 - p381+ [501+]
Kotzwinkle, William - *The Bear Went over the Mountain*
     BL - v92 - Ag '96 - p1855 [251-500]
The Bear Went Over the Mountain
     LATBR - N 10 '96 - p13 [501+]
     LATBR - D 29 '96 - p4 [51-250]
The Bear Went over the Mountain
     MFSF - v92 - Mr '97 - p32+ [501+]
The Bear Went Over the Mountain
     Nat - v263 - N 4 '96 - p31+ [501+]
The Bear Went over the Mountain
     NYTLa - v146 - O 17 '96 - pC19 [501+]
  y SLJ - v42 - D '96 - p152 [51-250]
The Bear Went over the Mountain (Prichard). Audio Version
     PW - v243 - N 4 '96 - p30 [51-250]
Tales from the Empty Notebook (Illus. by Joe Servello)
  c HB Guide - v8 - Spr '97 - p70 [51-250]
The World Is Big and I'm So Small (Illus. by Joe Servello)
  c PW - v243 - D 9 '96 - p69 [1-50]
Kou, Sindo - *Transport Phenomena and Materials Processing*
     Choice - v34 - Ap '97 - p1370 [51-250]
     SciTech - v21 - Mr '97 - p99 [51-250]
Koumoto, Kunihito - *Mass and Charge Transport in Ceramics*
     SciTech - v21 - Mr '97 - p96 [51-250]
Kouris, Michael - *Dictionary of Paper. 5th Ed.*
  r SciTech - v20 - D '96 - p86 [51-250]
Kourouma, Ahmadou - *Monnew*
     TranslRevS - v1 - My '95 - p19 [51-250]
Kourvetaris, George A - *The Impact of European Integration*
     JEL - v34 - S '96 - p1424 [51-250]
Koury, Joanne M - *Aquatic Therapy Programming*
     SciTech - v20 - S '96 - p43 [51-250]

Kovacs, Deborah - *Beneath Blue Waters (Illus. by Larry Madin)*
  c BL - v93 - D 1 '96 - p659 [51-250]
  y HB Guide - v8 - Spr '97 - p118 [51-250]
  c SLJ - v43 - Ja '97 - p128 [51-250]
Kovacs, Diane K - *Key Guide to Electronic Resources: Language and Literature*
  r R&R Bk N - v12 - F '97 - p75 [1-50]
Kovacs, Michael - *The Cybrarian's Guide to Developing Successful Internet Programs and Services*
  LJ - v122 - My 1 '97 - p146 [51-250]
Kovadloff, Santiago - *Lo Irremediable*
  BL - v93 - Mr 15 '97 - p1232 [1-50]
Koval, Ramona - *Samovar*
  Aust Bk R - Ag '96 - p48+ [51-250]
  Quad - v40 - O '96 - p85+ [501+]
Kovalainen, Anne - *At the Margins of the Economy*
  CS - v26 - Ja '97 - p23+ [501+]
Kovalenko, Igor Nikolaevich - *Models of Random Processes*
  Choice - v34 - D '96 - p647 [51-250]
  SciTech - v20 - N '96 - p13 [51-250]
Kovalevsky, Jean - *Modern Astrometry*
  Am Sci - v85 - Mr '97 - p184 [501+]
Kowaleski, Maryanne - *Local Markets and Regional Trade in Medieval Exeter*
  Albion - v28 - Sum '96 - p285+ [501+]
  BHR - v70 - Sum '96 - p286+ [501+]
  JIH - v27 - Spr '97 - p671+ [251-500]
Kowaleski-Wallace, Elizabeth - *Encyclopedia of Feminist Literary Theory*
  r Choice - v34 - Ap '97 - p1306+ [51-250]
Kowalewski, Michael - *Reading the West*
  AL - v68 - D '96 - p884 [51-250]
  Choice - v34 - My '97 - p1498+ [51-250]
Kowallis, Jon Eugene - *The Lyrical Lu Xun*
  Choice - v34 - D '96 - p608+ [51-250]
  Ch Rev Int - v4 - Spr '97 - p194+ [501+]
Kowalski, Kathiann M - *Hazardous Waste Sites*
  y HB Guide - v8 - Spr '97 - p97 [51-250]
Kowalski, Theodore J - *Keepers of the Flame*
  AJE - v105 - My '97 - p319+ [501+]
Kowarick, Lucio - *Social Struggles and the City*
  HAHR - v76 - Ag '96 - p596+ [501+]
Kowit, Steve - *In the Palm of Your Hand*
  Bloom Rev - v16 - S '96 - p11 [51-250]
Kozameh, Alicia - *Steps under Water*
  BL - v93 - N 15 '96 - p570 [51-250]
  Choice - v34 - Ap '97 - p1344 [51-250]
  KR - v64 - S 15 '96 - p1354 [51-250]
  LATBR - O 27 '96 - p10+ [51-250]
  LJ - v121 - O 15 '96 - p90 [51-250]
  NYTBR - v102 - Ja 12 '97 - p21 [251-500]
  PW - v243 - O 7 '96 - p67 [51-250]
  TLS - Ja 31 '97 - p19 [501+]
  TranslRevS - v2 - D '96 - p32 [1-50]
Kozhamthadam, Job - *The Discovery of Kepler's Laws*
  Theol St - v58 - Mr '97 - p190+ [251-500]
Kozinn, Allan - *The Beatles*
  M Ed J - v83 - N '96 - p54 [1-50]
  TLS - Jl 7 '96 - p19 [501+]
Kozloff, Eugene N - *Marine Invertebrates of the Pacific Northwest*
  R&R Bk N - v12 - F '97 - p94 [51-250]
Kozlov, V A - *Osobaia Papka I.V. Stalina*
  r Slav R - v55 - Fall '96 - p697 [51-250]
Kozlowski, Theodore T - *Physiology of Woody Plants. 2nd Ed.*
  Choice - v34 - Ap '97 - p1365 [51-250]
  SciTech - v21 - Mr '97 - p37 [51-250]
Kozodoy, Neal - *What to Do About...*
  Econ - v340 - S 14 '96 - p3*+ [501+]
Kozol, Jonathan - *Amazing Grace*
  y BL - v93 - Ap 1 '97 - p1286 [1-50]
  NYTBR - v101 - N 3 '96 - p28 [1-50]
Kozol, Wendy - *Life's America*
  AHR - v101 - O '96 - p1309+ [501+]
  Am Q - v48 - S '96 - p530+ [501+]
  Signs - v22 - Win '97 - p440+ [501+]
Kpundeh, Sahr John - *Politics and Corruption in Africa*
  JTWS - v13 - Fall '96 - p275+ [501+]
Kraak, Menno-Jan - *Cartography: Visualization of Spatial Data*
  Choice - v34 - F '97 - p992 [51-250]
Kraan, Dirk-Jan - *Budgetary Decisions*
  Choice - v34 - Mr '97 - p1230 [51-250]
  JEL - v35 - Mr '97 - p227 [51-250]
Kraan, Hanna - *Tales of the Wicked Witch (Illus. by Annemarie Van Haeringen)*
  c HB Guide - v7 - Fall '96 - p294 [51-250]

Kracauer, Siegfried - *The Mass Ornament*
  JAAC - v54 - Fall '96 - p397+ [501+]
Kradin, Richard L - *Immunopathology of Lung Disease*
  SciTech - v20 - S '96 - p36 [51-250]
Kraehmer, Steffen T - *Heroes: Embracing Your Role as Your Child's Hero*
  PW - v243 - S 23 '96 - p73 [1-50]
Kraemer, David - *Reading the Rabbis*
  Choice - v34 - Ja '97 - p811 [51-250]
Kraft, Betsey Harvey - *Mother Jones: One Woman's Fight for Labor*
  c RT - v50 - D '96 - p345 [51-250]
Kraft, Elizabeth - *Laurence Sterne Revisited*
  Choice - v34 - My '97 - p1496 [51-250]
Kraft, James P - *Stage to Studio*
  JEL - v35 - Mr '97 - p262+ [51-250]
Krafte-Jacobs, Lori - *Feminism and Modern Jewish Theological Method*
  R&R Bk N - v12 - F '97 - p9 [51-250]
Kragh, Helge - *Cosmology and Controversy*
  Choice - v34 - Ap '97 - p1362 [51-250]
  Nature - v384 - N 28 '96 - p323+ [501+]
  New Sci - v153 - F 15 '97 - p42+ [501+]
  NH - v106 - Mr '97 - p13 [1-50]
  SB - v33 - Mr '97 - p38+ [251-500]
  Sci - v275 - F 28 '97 - p1275+ [501+]
  TLS - Ap 11 '97 - p31 [501+]
Krahnen, Jan Pieter - *Development Finance as Institution Building*
  Econ J - v106 - S '96 - p1473+ [251-500]
Krahnke, K - *Reading Together. 2nd Ed.*
  MLJ - v81 - Spr '97 - p125+ [501+]
Krailing, Tessa - *The Green Hand (Illus. by Alex De Wolf)*
  c Sch Lib - v44 - Ag '96 - p107 [51-250]
Message from Venus
  y JB - v60 - O '96 - p211+ [51-250]
  y Obs - v54 - O 13 '96 - p18* [51-250]
  c Sch Lib - v44 - N '96 - p151 [51-250]
Trouble for Alberta (Illus. by Jacqueline East)
  c Sch Lib - v44 - Ag '96 - p104 [51-250]
Kraja, Mehmet - *Vdekje Pa Emer*
  WLT - v70 - Aut '96 - p1005+ [251-500]
Krajcinovic, Dusan - *Damage Mechanics*
  SciTech - v20 - N '96 - p62 [51-250]
Krakauer, Jon - *Eiger Dreams*
  HM - v293 - Ag '96 - p64+ [501+]
Into the Wild
  y BL - v93 - Ap 1 '97 - p1286 [1-50]
  BW - v27 - F 23 '97 - p12 [51-250]
  Ent W - D 27 '96 - p140 [51-250]
  NYTBR - v101 - D 8 '96 - p88 [1-50]
  NYTBR - v102 - Mr 2 '97 - p28 [51-250]
  SFR - v22 - Ja '97 - p48 [51-250]
  Trib Bks - Mr 23 '97 - p6 [1-50]
  VLS - Win '96 - p10 [51-250]
  WAL - v31 - Sum '96 - p163+ [501+]
Into Thin Air
  y BL - v93 - Ap 1 '97 - p1276 [51-250]
  KR - v65 - Mr 1 '97 - p357 [51-250]
  LJ - v122 - Ap 1 '97 - p117+ [51-250]
  NW - v129 - Ap 21 '97 - p76 [501+]
  NYTLa - v146 - My 6 '97 - pC16 [501+]
  PW - v244 - Mr 17 '97 - p63+ [251-500]
  Time - v149 - Ap 21 '97 - p123 [501+]
  WSJ-Cent - v99 - My 29 '97 - pA16 [501+]
Krakofsky, Shel - *Blind Messiah*
  BIC - v25 - O '96 - p21+ [501+]
Kralicek, V J - *The 25th Anniversary of Czechoslovak Independence*
  Am Phil - v110 - N '96 - p1038 [51-250]
Krall, Yung - *A Thousand Tears Falling*
  Rapport - v19 - 4 '96 - p35 [251-500]
Kramer, Arthur F - *Converging Operations in the Study of Visual Selective Attention*
  R&R Bk N - v12 - F '97 - p6 [51-250]
Kramer, Augustine - *The Samoa Islands. Vol. 2*
  Cont Pac - v9 - Spr '97 - p282+ [501+]
Kramer, B - *Quantum Transport in Semiconductor Submicron Structures*
  SciTech - v21 - Mr '97 - p24 [51-250]
Kramer, Barbara - *Amy Tan: Author of the Joy Luck Club*
  c HB Guide - v7 - Fall '96 - p371 [51-250]
  c SLJ - v42 - O '96 - p135 [51-250]
  y VOYA - v19 - O '96 - p234 [251-500]
Ken Griffey Junior: All-Around All-Star
  c HB Guide - v8 - Spr '97 - p144 [51-250]
Toni Morrison: Nobel Prize-Winning Author
  y HB Guide - v8 - Spr '97 - p159 [51-250]
  y KR - v64 - Ag 15 '96 - p1237+ [51-250]
  y SLJ - v42 - N '96 - p129 [51-250]

Kramer, Barbara, 1926- - *Nampeyo and Her Pottery*
  Ceram Mo - v45 - Ja '97 - p24 [251-500]
  Nat Peop - v10 - Fall '96 - p78+ [501+]
  R&R Bk N - v11 - D '96 - p13 [51-250]
Kramer, Bert - *N.E.W.S: A Model for the Evaluation of Non-Life Insurance Companies*
  JEL - v35 - Mr '97 - p222 [51-250]
Kramer, David Bruce - *The Imperial Dryden*
  MLR - v91 - Jl '96 - p701+ [501+]
  RES - v47 - Ag '96 - p416+ [501+]
Kramer, Donald E - *Guide to Northeast Pacific Flatfishes Families Bothidae, Cynoglossidae, and Pleuronectidae*
  r J Gov Info - v23 - S '96 - p577 [51-250]
Kramer, Gerhard W - *Berthold Schwarz: Chemie Und Waffentechnik Im 15. Jahrhundert*
  T&C - v37 - Ap '96 - p342+ [501+]
Kramer, Jane - *The Politics of Memory*
  BL - v93 - O 1 '96 - p319 [51-250]
  BW - v26 - N 17 '96 - p4 [501+]
  KR - v64 - Ag 15 '96 - p1213 [251-500]
  LJ - v121 - S 15 '96 - p82 [51-250]
  New R - v216 - F 10 '97 - p37+ [501+]
  NY - v72 - D 16 '96 - p108 [51-250]
  NYRB - v43 - O 31 '96 - p58+ [501+]
  NYTBR - v101 - O 20 '96 - p26 [501+]
  Time - v148 - O 28 '96 - p104+ [501+]
  Trib Bks - Ja 12 '97 - p6 [501+]
  WSJ-MW - v78 - O 18 '96 - pA12 [501+]
Kramer, Jon - *Bo Jackson*
  c HB Guide - v7 - Fall '96 - p361 [51-250]
Jim Abbott
  c HB Guide - v7 - Fall '96 - p361 [51-250]
Lee Trevino
  c HB Guide - v7 - Fall '96 - p361 [51-250]
Kramer, Jonathan - *Losing the Weight of the World*
  LJ - v122 - Mr 15 '97 - p77 [51-250]
Kramer, Lawrence - *Classical Music and Postmodern Knowledge*
  Notes - v53 - Mr '97 - p756+ [501+]
Kramer, Lloyd - *Lafayette in Two Worlds*
  HRNB - v25 - Win '97 - p91 [251-500]
Learning History in America
  Am Q - v48 - S '96 - p507+ [501+]
Kramer, Martin - *Arab Awakening and Islamic Revival*
  JEL - v34 - D '96 - p2142 [51-250]
  MEQ - v4 - Mr '97 - p85 [51-250]
Kramer, Matthew - *Critical Legal Theory and the Challenge of Feminism*
  Ethics - v107 - Ja '97 - p372+ [501+]
Kramer, Paul J - *Water Relations of Plants and Soils. 2nd Ed.*
  BioSci - v47 - Ap '97 - p256+ [501+]
Kramer, Stanley - *A Mad, Mad, Mad, Mad World*
  BL - v93 - My 1 '97 - p1458 [51-250]
Kramer, Stephen - *Eye of the Storm (Illus. by Warren Faidley)*
  c BL - v93 - Mr 15 '97 - p1241 [51-250]
  c CCB-B - v50 - Ap '97 - p288 [51-250]
  c HB - v73 - Mr '97 - p212 [51-250]
  c KR - v65 - F 1 '97 - p224 [51-250]
  c SLJ - v43 - Mr '97 - p203 [51-250]
Theodoric's Rainbow (Illus. by Daniel Mark Duffy)
  c RT - v50 - Mr '97 - p499 [51-250]
Kramer, Wendy - *Encomienda Politics in Early Colonial Guatemala 1524-1544*
  HAHR - v77 - F '97 - p120+ [251-500]
Kramnick, Isaac - *The Godless Constitution*
  CC - v113 - Ag 14 '96 - p793 [251-500]
  Ch Today - v40 - Ag 12 '96 - p42+ [501+]
  Cng - v28 - Jl '96 - p63 [51-250]
  J Ch St - v38 - Sum '96 - p644+ [501+]
  RAH - v24 - D '96 - p585+ [501+]
  TT - v53 - Ja '97 - p572 [51-250]
Krampner, Jon - *The Man in the Shadows*
  BL - v93 - F 1 '97 - p918+ [51-250]
  KR - v64 - D 1 '96 - p1718 [251-500]
  PW - v243 - D 16 '96 - p48 [51-250]
Kramsky, Jerry - *The Cranky Sun (Illus. by Lorenzo Mattotti)*
  c HB Guide - v7 - Fall '96 - p263 [51-250]
Kranes, David - *Low Tide in the Desert*
  KR - v64 - Ag 15 '96 - p1176 [251-500]
  NYTBR - v101 - O 27 '96 - p39 [51-250]
Kranidis, Rita S - *Subversive Discourse*
  ELT - v39 - 3 '96 - p363+ [501+]
Krannich, Ronald L - *The Directory of Federal Jobs and Employers*
  r ARBA - v28 - '97 - p120 [51-250]
Krantz, Judith - *Spring Collection*
  Ent W - F 21 '97 - p121 [51-250]

Krantz, Les - *The Peoplepedia: The Ultimate Reference on the American People*
  yr ARBA - v28 - '97 - p42 [251-500]
  r BL - v93 - Ap 1 '97 - p1357 [251-500]
  r Choice - v34 - D '96 - p590+ [51-250]
  yr SLJ - v43 - F '97 - p130 [51-250]
Kraske, Jochen - *Bankers with a Mission*
  Econ - v342 - Mr 15 '97 - p9* [251-500]
Krasnosel'skii, Alexander M - *Asymptotics of Nonlinearities and Operator Equations*
  SIAM Rev - v38 - S '96 - p533+ [501+]
Krasnow, Iris - *Surrendering to Motherhood*
  LJ - v122 - My 1 '97 - p128 [51-250]
  PW - v244 - Mr 31 '97 - p55 [51-250]
Kraszewski, Andrzej - *Microwave Aquametry*
  SciTech - v20 - N '96 - p63 [51-250]
Kratz, E Ulrich - *Southeast Asian Languages and Literatures*
  r Choice - v34 - N '96 - p436+ [51-250]
Kraujiete, Aina - *Divas Poemas*
  WLT - v70 - Sum '96 - p735 [251-500]
Kraus, Hans-Christof - *Ernst Ludwig Von Gerlach: Politisches Denken Und Handeln Eines Preussischen Altkonservativen. Vols. 1-2*
  AHR - v101 - O '96 - p1234+ [501+]
Kraus, Harry Lee - *Lethal Mercy*
  BL - v93 - Ja '97 - p819 [51-250]
  LJ - v121 - N 1 '96 - p54 [51-250]
Kraus, Ivan - *Rodinny Sjezd*
  WLT - v71 - Win '97 - p182 [251-500]
Kraus, Jim - *Pirates of the Heart*
  BL - v93 - Ja '97 - p819 [51-250]
Kraus, Michael, 1949- - *Russia and Eastern Europe after Communism*
  R&R Bk N - v11 - N '96 - p13 [51-250]
Kraus, Michael, 1965- - *Structured Biological Modelling*
  SciTech - v21 - Mr '97 - p36 [51-250]
Kraus, Richard G - *Research and Evaluation in Recreation, Parks and Leisure Studies. 2nd Ed.*
  R&R Bk N - v12 - F '97 - p31 [51-250]
Kraus, Robert - *Big Squeak, Little Squeak (Illus. by Kevin O'Malley)*
  c HB Guide - v8 - Spr '97 - p34 [51-250]
  c SLJ - v42 - O '96 - p100 [51-250]
  Fables Aesop Never Wrote
  c Emerg Lib - v24 - S '96 - p46 [51-250]
  Near Myths
  c HB Guide - v7 - Fall '96 - p263 [51-250]
Krause, Carol - *How Healthy Is Your Family Tree?*
  NGSQ - v84 - Je '96 - p151+ [251-500]
Krause, Chester L - *Standard Catalog of World Coins 1601-1700*
  r ARBA - v28 - '97 - p359 [51-250]
Krause, Donald G - *The Way of the Leader*
  PW - v243 - D 30 '96 - p53 [51-250]
Krause, Elliott A - *Death of the Guilds*
  Choice - v34 - Mr '97 - p1246 [51-250]
  JEL - v35 - Mr '97 - p263 [51-250]
Krause, Ernst-Georg - *Biochemical Mechanism in Heart Function*
  SciTech - v21 - Mr '97 - p39 [51-250]
Krause, Martin F - *Gustave Baumann: Nearer to Art*
  Am Craft - v56 - Ag '96 - p26 [1-50]
Krause, Shari Stamford - *Aircraft Safety*
  Choice - v34 - D '96 - p642 [51-250]
  SciTech - v20 - N '96 - p77 [51-250]
Krause, Staley - *Strange City*
  SF Chr - v18 - O '96 - p80 [1-50]
Krauss, Angela - *Die Uberfliegerin*
  WLT - v70 - Aut '96 - p948 [501+]
Krauss, Lawrence Maxwell - *Fear of Physics*
  New Sci - v153 - Ja 4 '97 - p38 [1-50]
  NS & S - v9 - My 17 '96 - p39 [1-50]
  The Physics of Star Trek
  Am Sci - v84 - N '96 - p597+ [501+]
  Ant R - v54 - Fall '96 - p488+ [251-500]
  NYTBR - v101 - D 8 '96 - p90+ [1-50]
  NYTBR - v102 - F 23 '97 - p24 [1-50]
  Skeptic - v3 - '95 - p102 [251-500]
  The Physics of Star Trek (Krauss). Audio Version
  y Kliatt - v30 - N '96 - p50 [51-250]
  The Physics of Star Trek (McKeever). Audio Version
  y Kliatt - v31 - Ja '97 - p50 [51-250]
Krauss, Ronnie - *Take a Look, It's in a Book (Illus. by Christopher Hornsby)*
  c BL - v93 - Mr 1 '97 - p1165+ [51-250]
  c CBRS - v25 - Mr '97 - p93 [51-250]
  c PW - v244 - Mr 10 '97 - p68 [51-250]
Krausz, A S - *Unified Constitutive Laws of Plastic Deformation*
  SciTech - v20 - N '96 - p62 [51-250]

Krausz, Michael - *Rightness and Reasons*
  RM - v50 - S '96 - p165+ [501+]
Kraut, Alan M - *Silent Travelers*
  Queens Q - v103 - Sum '96 - p403+ [501+]
Krauze, Enrique - *Mexico: Biography of Power*
  PW - v244 - My 5 '97 - p187 [251-500]
  Wil Q - v21 - Spr '97 - p107+ [501+]
Kravitt, Edward F - *The Lied: Mirror of Late Romanticism*
  Choice - v34 - D '96 - p624 [51-250]
  TLS - O 25 '96 - p18+ [501+]
Kraybill, Donald B - *Amish Enterprise*
  CS - v25 - S '96 - p670+ [501+]
Krebs, J R - *Behavioural Ecology. 4th Ed.*
  Nature - v386 - Ap 10 '97 - p567 [251-500]
Krebs, Peter - *Building Microsoft Exchange Applications*
  CBR - v15 - Spr '97 - p10 [1-50]
Krebs, Wolfgang - *Die Lateinische Evangelien-Motette Des 16. Jahrhunderts*
  Notes - v53 - Mr '97 - p788+ [501+]
Kreeft, Peter - *Angels (and Demons)*
  RR - v55 - S '96 - p554 [51-250]
  The Journey: A Spiritual Roadmap for Modern Christians
  PW - v244 - Ja 13 '97 - p70+ [51-250]
Kreifzman, Sue - *Low-Fat Vegetarian Cooking*
  BWatch - v18 - F '97 - p7 [1-50]
Kreimeier, Klaus - *The Ufa Story*
  BW - v26 - Ag 4 '96 - p13 [51-250]
  Choice - v34 - D '96 - p622 [51-250]
  KR - v64 - My 1 '96 - p668 [251-500]
  NYTBR - v101 - O 13 '96 - p20 [251-500]
Kreiner, Anna - *Creating Your Own Support System*
  y SLJ - v43 - Ja '97 - p128 [51-250]
  In Control
  y Cur R - v36 - Ap '97 - p12 [51-250]
  Let's Talk about Being Afraid
  c SLJ - v43 - Ja '97 - p103 [51-250]
  Let's Talk about Drug Abuse
  c BL - v93 - Mr 1 '97 - p1168 [51-250]
  c SLJ - v42 - D '96 - p130+ [51-250]
Kreinin, Mordechai E - *Contemporary Issues in Commercial Policy*
  Econ J - v107 - Ja '97 - p268 [51-250]
Kreinovich, V - *Problems of Reducing the Exhaustive Search*
  SciTech - v21 - Mr '97 - p14 [51-250]
Kreis, Thomas - *Holographic Interferometry*
  Choice - v34 - Ja '97 - p834 [51-250]
Kreiswirth, Martin - *Constructive Criticism*
  Dal R - v75 - Spr '95 - p123+ [501+]
Kreitzer, Larry J - *The Old Testament in Fiction and Film*
  Intpr - v51 - Ja '97 - p88 [251-500]
Krekorian, Michael - *Channel Zero*
  ABR - v17 - Ag '96 - p20 [501+]
Krell, Alan - *Manet and the Painters of Contemporary Life*
  BM - v138 - S '96 - p610 [501+]
Krell, David Farrell - *Nietzsche: A Novel*
  Choice - v34 - D '96 - p614 [51-250]
  R&R Bk N - v11 - D '96 - p66 [51-250]
Krell, Jonathan F - *Tournier Elementaire*
  FR - v70 - O '96 - p127+ [501+]
Krementsov, Nikolai - *Stalinist Science*
  Nature - v385 - F 27 '97 - p783+ [501+]
  New Sci - v154 - My 3 '97 - p47 [1-50]
Krementz, Jill - *The Writer's Desk*
  Ent W - F 7 '97 - p64 [51-250]
  NYTBR - v102 - F 16 '97 - p19 [251-500]
Kremer, Dieter - *Dictionnaire Historique Des Noms De Famille Romans: Actes Du 1er Colloque (Treves, 10-13 Decembre 1987)*
  r Names - v44 - Je '96 - p132+ [501+]
Kremer, Elmar J - *Interpreting Arnauld*
  R&R Bk N - v11 - D '96 - p2 [51-250]
Kremer, Rudiger - *The Color of the Snow*
  TranslRevS - v1 - My '95 - p22 [51-250]
Kren, Thomas, 1950- - *Renaissance Painting in Manuscripts*
  AB - v99 - Mr 3 '97 - p685+ [501+]
Krener, A J - *Nonlinear Control Systems Design 1995. Vol. 1-2*
  SciTech - v20 - D '96 - p72 [51-250]
Krenn, Michael L - *The Chains of Interdependence*
  Choice - v34 - Mr '97 - p1225 [51-250]
  R&R Bk N - v12 - F '97 - p27 [51-250]

Krensky, Stephen - *Breaking into Print (Illus. by Bonnie Christensen)*
  c CBRS - v25 - O '96 - p23 [51-250]
  c CCB-B - v50 - Ja '97 - p177 [51-250]
  c HB Guide - v8 - Spr '97 - p132 [51-250]
  c SLJ - v42 - O '96 - p114+ [51-250]
  Lionel and His Friends (Illus. by Susanna Natti)
  c BL - v93 - N 15 '96 - p594 [51-250]
  c CCB-B - v50 - F '97 - p212 [51-250]
  c HB Guide - v8 - Spr '97 - p55 [51-250]
  c SLJ - v42 - D '96 - p98 [51-250]
  My Teacher's Secret Life (Illus. by JoAnn Adinolfi)
  c BL - v93 - N 15 '96 - p594+ [51-250]
  c CBRS - v24 - Ag '96 - p160 [51-250]
  c CCB-B - v50 - D '96 - p140+ [51-250]
  c HB Guide - v8 - Spr '97 - p34+ [51-250]
  c NYTBR - v102 - Ja 5 '97 - p22 [501+]
  c SLJ - v42 - O '96 - p100+ [51-250]
  Striking It Rich (Illus. by Anna DiVito)
  c BL - v93 - S 15 '96 - p253 [51-250]
  c CCB-B - v50 - N '96 - p103+ [51-250]
  c HB Guide - v8 - Spr '97 - p174 [51-250]
  c SLJ - v43 - F '97 - p93 [51-250]
  Striking It Rich (Davidson). Audio Version
  c HB - v73 - My '97 - p357+ [501+]
Krentz, Jayne Ann - *Absolutely, Positively*
  PW - v243 - D 2 '96 - p56 [1-50]
  Rapport - v19 - 4 '96 - p31 [51-250]
  Deep Waters
  KR - v64 - D 1 '96 - p1693 [251-500]
  LJ - v122 - F 15 '97 - p162 [51-250]
  PW - v244 - Ja 13 '97 - p54 [51-250]
  Trib Bks - Mr 2 '97 - p4 [51-250]
Krepon, Michael L - *Crisis Prevention, Confidence Building, and Reconciliation in South Asia*
  R&R Bk N - v11 - N '96 - p15 [51-250]
Kreske, Diori L - *Environmental Impact Statements*
  SciTech - v20 - N '96 - p67 [51-250]
Kreskin - *How to Be a Fake Kreskin*
  Skeptic - v4 - 4 '96 - p98+ [501+]
Kresl, Peter Karl - *North American Cities and the Global Economy*
  NCR - v85 - Spr '96 - p65 [51-250]
Kress, Camille - *Tot Shabbat (Illus. by Camille Kress)*
  c BL - v93 - F 1 '97 - p946 [51-250]
  c PW - v244 - Ja 27 '97 - p98 [51-250]
Kress, Gunther - *Before Writing*
  New Sci - v153 - F 8 '97 - p42 [51-250]
  Reading Images
  Choice - v34 - D '96 - p598 [51-250]
Kress, Nancy - *Beggars Ride*
  Analog - v117 - Ap '97 - p147+ [501+]
  BL - v93 - N 15 '96 - p576 [51-250]
  KR - v64 - S 15 '96 - p1361 [51-250]
  LJ - v121 - O 15 '96 - p93 [51-250]
Kress, Stephen W - *The National Audubon Society: The Bird Garden*
  LJ - v121 - D '96 - p66 [1-50]
Kressel, Neil J - *Mass Hate*
  BW - v26 - S 29 '96 - p6+ [251-500]
  Choice - v34 - D '96 - p651 [51-250]
Kressin, Mark - *The Internet and the World Wide Web*
  SciTech - v21 - Mr '97 - p88 [51-250]
Kretzmann, Norman - *The Cambridge Companion to Aquinas*
  Specu - v71 - Jl '96 - p728+ [501+]
Kretzschmar, William A - *Handbook of the Linguistic Atlas of the Middle and South Atlantic States*
  J Am Cult - v18 - Win '95 - p111 [51-250]
  Introduction to Quantitative Analysis of Linguistic Survey Data
  R&R Bk N - v12 - F '97 - p77 [51-250]
Kreuter, Gretchen V - *Forgotten Promise*
  BWatch - v17 - N '96 - p5 [1-50]
  Wom R Bks - v14 - N '96 - p18+ [501+]
Kreuz, Roger J - *Empirical Approaches to Literature and Aesthetics*
  R&R Bk N - v11 - N '96 - p65 [51-250]
Krewson, Margrit B - *German-American Relations*
  r J Gov Info - v23 - S '96 - p551+ [51-250]
Kreyling, Christine - *Classical Nashville*
  Choice - v34 - Mr '97 - p1150 [51-250]
Kreyling, Michael - *New Essays on Wise Blood*
  J Am St - v30 - D '96 - p471+ [501+]
Krickus, Richard J - *Showdown: The Lithuanian Rebellion and the Breakup of the Soviet Empire*
  BL - v93 - D 15 '96 - p707 [51-250]
  LJ - v122 - F 1 '97 - p96 [51-250]
Kridel, Craig - *Teachers and Mentors*
  Choice - v34 - D '96 - p662 [51-250]
  ES - v27 - Sum '96 - p198+ [501+]

Kriebel, Robert C - *Blue Flame*
Rapport - v19 - 4 '96 - p13+ [501+]
Krieg, Paul A - *A Laboratory Guide to RNA*
SciTech - v20 - D '96 - p35 [51-250]
Kriegel, Blandine - *The State and the Rule of Law*
CPR - v16 - Ag '96 - p260+ [501+]
RP - v58 - Fall '96 - p850+ [501+]
Kriegel, Robert - *Sacred Cows Make the Best Burgers*
PW - v244 - Mr 17 '97 - p81 [1-50]
Krieger, Dolores - *Therapeutic Touch Inner Workbook*
BL - v93 - Ja '97 - p798 [51-250]
Krieger, Melanie Jacobs - *Means and Probabilities*
y HB Guide - v7 - Fall '96 - p328 [51-250]
y SB - v33 - Ja '97 - p12 [51-250]
y SLJ - v42 - S '96 - p234+ [51-250]
Krieger, Susan - *The Family Silver*
BL - v93 - N 1 '96 - p464 [51-250]
Choice - v34 - F '97 - p1042 [51-250]
Kriesi, Hanspeter - *New Social Movements in Western
Europe*
APSR - v90 - D '96 - p874+ [501+]
Choice - v34 - S '96 - p220 [51-250]
Krimsky, Sheldon - *Agricultural Biotechnology and the
Environment*
Choice - v34 - Ja '97 - p815 [51-250]
Krinard, Susan - *Twice a Hero*
PW - v244 - Ap 14 '97 - p71 [51-250]
Krinsky, Carol Herselle - *Contemporary Native American
Architecture*
Nat Peop - v10 - Spr '97 - p82+ [501+]
Kripal, Jeffrey J - *Kali's Child*
Rel St Rev - v23 - Ja '97 - p95+ [51-250]
Krips, Henry - *Science, Reason and Rhetoric*
Col Comp - v47 - D '96 - p618+ [51-250]
Krishan, Y - *The Buddha Image*
Choice - v34 - Ap '97 - p1323 [51-250]
Krisher, Trudy - *Spite Fences*
y Kliatt - v31 - Mr '97 - p10 [51-250]
y PW - v243 - S 2 '96 - p133 [51-250]
Krishna, Gopi - *Kundalini: Empowering Human Evolution*
LJ - v122 - F 15 '97 - p166 [51-250]
Krishnan, Rajam - *Lamps in the Whirlpool*
WLT - v71 - Win '97 - p222+ [501+]
Krishnaswami, Uma - *The Broken Tusk (Illus. by Maniam
Selven)*
c BL - v93 - O 1 '96 - p335+ [51-250]
y CCB-B - v50 - O '96 - p66 [51-250]
c HB Guide - v8 - Spr '97 - p103 [51-250]
y VOYA - v19 - D '96 - p288 [51-250]
Kristeva, Julia - *Black Sun*
South CR - v28 - Spr '96 - p160+ [501+]
Desire in Language
South CR - v28 - Spr '96 - p160+ [501+]
Essays in Semiotics
South CR - v28 - Spr '96 - p160+ [501+]
In the Beginning Was Love
South CR - v28 - Spr '96 - p160+ [501+]
The Kristeva Reader
South CR - v28 - Spr '96 - p160+ [501+]
Language the Unknown
South CR - v28 - Spr '96 - p160+ [501+]
On Chinese Women
South CR - v28 - Spr '96 - p160+ [501+]
Powers of Horror
South CR - v28 - Spr '96 - p160+ [501+]
Revolution in Poetic Language
South CR - v28 - Spr '96 - p160+ [501+]
Strangers to Ourselves
South CR - v28 - Spr '96 - p160+ [501+]
Tales of Love
South CR - v28 - Spr '96 - p160+ [501+]
Time and Sense
Choice - v34 - O '96 - p285+ [51-250]
TranslRevS - v2 - D '96 - p11 [51-250]
Kristof, Agota - *The Book of Lies*
Obs - Mr 9 '97 - p18* [51-250]
Hier
FR - v70 - Mr '97 - p614 [251-500]
WLT - v70 - Sum '96 - p651+ [501+]
The Third Lie
NYTBR - v101 - N 3 '96 - p19 [51-250]
Kristof, Nicholas D - *China Wakes*
Ch Rev Int - v4 - Spr '97 - p196+ [501+]
Kristol, Irving - *Neoconservatism: The Autobiography of
an Idea*
Bks & Cult - v2 - S '96 - p39 [251-500]
Econ - v340 - S 14 '96 - p3*+ [501+]

Kristy, Davida - *George Balanchine: American Ballet
Master*
y BL - v93 - S 1 '96 - p116 [51-250]
c HB Guide - v8 - Spr '97 - p156 [51-250]
c SLJ - v42 - Ag '96 - p157 [51-250]
Kritzman, Lawrence D - *Auschwitz and After*
FR - v70 - F '97 - p510+ [501+]
Historian - v59 - Fall '96 - p194+ [501+]
Realms of Memory. Vol. 1
R&R Bk N - v12 - F '97 - p15 [51-250]
TranslRevS - v2 - D '96 - p16 [51-250]
Krizek, Michal - *Mathematical and Numerical Modelling
in Electrical Engineering Theory and Applications*
SciTech - v21 - Mr '97 - p85 [51-250]
Krizmanic, Judy - *A Teen's Guide to Going Vegetarian*
y Emerg Lib - v23 - My '96 - p44 [1-50]
Kroeber, Clifton B - *El Hombre, La Tierra, Y El Agua*
HAHR - v76 - N '96 - p799 [251-500]
Kroeber, Karl - *American Indian Persistence and
Resurgence*
Am Ethnol - v24 - F '97 - p231+ [501+]
Ecological Literary Criticism
Critm - v38 - Sum '96 - p478+ [501+]
WAL - v31 - Sum '96 - p190+ [251-500]
Kroeger, Mary Kay - *Paperboy (Illus. by Ted Lewin)*
c HB - v72 - S '96 - p581 [51-250]
c HB Guide - v7 - Fall '96 - p263 [51-250]
c RT - v50 - My '97 - p682 [51-250]
c SLJ - v42 - Ag '96 - p125 [51-250]
Kroeker, P Travis - *Christian Ethics and Political
Economy in North America*
J Ch St - v38 - Sum '96 - p669+ [251-500]
JR - v76 - O '96 - p667+ [501+]
Theol St - v57 - Je '96 - p387 [251-500]
Kroes, Rob - *If You've Seen One, You've Seen the Mall*
CHE - v43 - S 13 '96 - pA25 [51-250]
Choice - v34 - Ja '97 - p851 [51-250]
VQR - v73 - Win '97 - p171+ [501+]
Krog, Antjie - *Gedigte 1989-1995*
WLT - v71 - Win '97 - p211 [501+]
Kroger, Jens - *Nishapur: Glass of the Early Islamic
Period*
AJA - v100 - O '96 - p812+ [251-500]
r BM - v139 - Ja '97 - p51 [51-250]
Krogt, Peter Van Der - *Bibliografie Van De Geschiedenis
Van De Kartografie Van De Nederlanden*
r GJ - v162 - N '96 - p342 [51-250]
Kroh, Aleksandra - *Lucien's Story*
LJ - v121 - S 15 '96 - p76 [51-250]
NYTBR - v102 - Mr 9 '97 - p24 [501+]
Trib Bks - F 2 '97 - p5 [501+]
Krohn, Jacqueline - *The Whole Way to Natural
Detoxification*
PW - v243 - N 18 '96 - p73 [51-250]
Quill & Q - v62 - Ag '96 - p32 [51-250]
Krohn, Lauren - *Consumer Protection and the Law*
r ARBA - v28 - '97 - p220 [51-250]
Kroker, Arthur - *Data Trash*
LQ - v66 - O '96 - p462+ [501+]
QJS - v83 - My '97 - p230+ [501+]
Krol, Gerrit - *De Mechanica Van Het Liegen*
WLT - v70 - Sum '96 - p709+ [501+]
Kroll, John A - *Closure in International Politics*
APSR - v90 - S '96 - p700+ [501+]
Kroll, Steven - *Pony Express! (Illus. by Dan Andreasen)*
c HB - v72 - S '96 - p616+ [51-250]
c HB Guide - v7 - Fall '96 - p386+ [51-250]
c RT - v50 - Ap '97 - p596 [51-250]
Kroll, Virginia - *Butterfly Boy (Illus. by Gerardo Suzan)*
c PW - v244 - Ap 28 '97 - p75 [51-250]
Can You Dance, Dalila? (Illus. by Nancy Carpenter)
c BL - v93 - N 15 '96 - p594 [51-250]
c HB Guide - v8 - Spr '97 - p35 [51-250]
c SLJ - v43 - F '97 - p82 [51-250]
*Fireflies, Peach Pies, and Lullabies (Illus. by Nancy
Cote)*
c HB Guide - v7 - Fall '96 - p263 [51-250]
Masai and I (Illus. by Nancy Carpenter)
c PW - v244 - Ja 27 '97 - p108 [1-50]
Krolop, Kurt - *Reflexionen Der Fackel*
MLR - v92 - Ja '97 - p244+ [501+]
Krommer, Anna - *Staub Von Stadten*
WLT - v70 - Aut '96 - p955 [251-500]
Kronbichler, Johann - *Michelangelo Unterperger
1695-1758*
BM - v138 - O '96 - p699+ [251-500]
Kronenwetter, Michael - *The Congress of the United
States*
y HB Guide - v8 - Spr '97 - p93 [51-250]
How to Write a News Article
yr Kliatt - v31 - My '97 - p17 [51-250]

Political Parties of the United States
y CLW - v66 - Je '96 - p53 [51-250]
y HB Guide - v7 - Fall '96 - p314 [51-250]
Protest!
y BL - v93 - Ja '97 - p838+ [251-500]
c Ch BWatch - v7 - Ja '97 - p2 [1-50]
y SLJ - v43 - Ja '97 - p128 [51-250]
The Supreme Court of the United States
y HB Guide - v8 - Spr '97 - p314 [51-250]
Kronish, Amy - *World Cinema: Israel*
Choice - v34 - N '96 - p468 [51-250]
Si & So - v6 - N '96 - p35 [51-250]
Kronmeyer, Robert - *Totally Fit Living*
BWatch - v17 - S '96 - p10 [51-250]
Kronowitz, Ellen L - *Your First Year of Teaching and
Beyond*
Learning - v25 - S '96 - p49 [51-250]
Kroodsma, Donald E - *Ecology and Evolution of Acoustic
Communication in Birds*
Choice - v34 - Ja '97 - p821 [51-250]
SciTech - v20 - N '96 - p29 [51-250]
Krooth, Richard - *The Middle East*
GJ - v163 - Mr '97 - p94 [251-500]
Kropf, David Glenn - *Authorship as Alchemy*
Russ Rev - v56 - Ja '97 - p128 [501+]
Kross, Joan - *The Conspiracy and Other Stories*
NYTBR - v101 - Jl 21 '96 - p19 [51-250]
Krotz, Larry - *Tourists: How Our Fastest Growing
Industry Is Changing the World*
BL - v93 - N 15 '96 - p556 [51-250]
KR - v64 - O 15 '96 - p1513 [251-500]
LJ - v121 - N 15 '96 - p78+ [51-250]
New Sci - v153 - Ja 4 '97 - p39 [251-500]
PW - v243 - O 14 '96 - p69 [51-250]
Krotzl, Christian - *Pilger, Mirakel Und Alltag*
AHR - v101 - O '96 - p1191 [501+]
CHR - v82 - O '96 - p689+ [251-500]
Krowinski, William J - *Measuring and Managing Patient
Satisfaction. 2nd Ed.*
SciTech - v21 - Mr '97 - p45 [51-250]
Krucker, Franz-Josef - *Beijing*
r BL - v93 - S 15 '96 - p210 [1-50]
Kruckmann, Peter O - *Tiepolo in Wurzburg. Vols. 1-2*
BM - v138 - Jl '96 - p476+ [501+]
Tiepolo: Masterpieces of the Wurzburg Years
NYRB - v44 - F 6 '97 - p35+ [501+]
Krueger, Anne O - *American Trade Policy*
JEL - v34 - S '96 - p1428+ [51-250]
The Political Economy of American Trade Policy
JEL - v34 - S '96 - p1361+ [501+]
JEL - v34 - S '96 - p1429 [51-250]
The Political Economy of Trade Protection
JEL - v34 - S '96 - p1361+ [501+]
JEL - v34 - S '96 - p1429 [51-250]
Krueger, Mark A - *Careless to Caring for Troubled Youth*
BWatch - v18 - F '97 - p6 [51-250]
Krueger, Robert - *The Dinosaurs*
c HB Guide - v7 - Fall '96 - p333 [51-250]
Krueger, Roberta L - *Women Readers and the Ideology of
Gender in Old French Verse Romance*
MP - v94 - F '97 - p360+ [501+]
Specu - v72 - Ja '97 - p191+ [501+]
Kruegle, Herman - *CCTV Surveillance*
SciTech - v20 - N '96 - p74 [51-250]
Kruger, Arnd - *The Story of Worker Sport*
Choice - v34 - Ja '97 - p836 [51-250]
R&R Bk N - v11 - N '96 - p23 [51-250]
Kruger, Barbara - *Remote Control*
J Am Cult - v18 - Win '95 - p110 [251-500]
Kruger, Irtraud Tarr - *Performance Power*
Teach Mus - v3 - Ap '96 - p69 [51-250]
Kruger, Lawrence - *Pain and Touch*
SciTech - v21 - Mr '97 - p1 [51-250]
Kruger, Mary - *Masterpiece of Murder*
KR - v64 - O 1 '96 - p1432 [51-250]
NYTBR - v102 - Ja 19 '97 - p22 [51-250]
PW - v243 - S 16 '96 - p72 [51-250]
Kruger, Michael - *Nachts, Unter Baumen*
WLT - v71 - Win '97 - p144 [501+]
Kruger, Steven F - *AIDS Narratives*
AL - v69 - Mr '97 - p250 [51-250]
Choice - v34 - D '96 - p598 [51-250]
HG&LRev - v3 - Fall '96 - p41+ [501+]
Kruger-Robbins, Jill - *Frames of Referents*
Choice - v34 - My '97 - p1504+ [51-250]
Krugman, Paul - *Development, Geography, and Economic
Theory*
Econ J - v106 - N '96 - p1832 [251-500]
JEL - v34 - D '96 - p2003+ [501+]

Pop Internationalism
  Dis - v44 - Win '97 - p124+ [501+]
  Econ J - v107 - Ja '97 - p268+ [51-250]
  JEL - v34 - S '96 - p1429 [51-250]
  Meanjin - v55 - 3 '96 - p556+ [501+]
  PW - v244 - Mr 3 '97 - p72 [1-50]
  TLS - S 13 '96 - p28 [501+]
Kruijt, Dirk - *Revolution by Decree*
  HAHR - v76 - N '96 - p811+ [501+]
Krull, Kathleen - *City within a City*
  y Kliatt - v30 - N '96 - p26 [51-250]
  Lives of the Artists (Illus. by Kathryn Hewitt)
  c HB Guide - v7 - Fall '96 - p356 [51-250]
  y RT - v50 - N '96 - p246 [51-250]
  Lives of the Artists (Brown). Audio Version
  c BL - v93 - D 15 '96 - p740 [51-250]
  c Bloom Rev - v16 - S '96 - p23 [51-250]
  y SLJ - v42 - O '96 - p77 [51-250]
  Lives of the Athletes (Illus. by Kathryn Hewitt)
  c BL - v93 - Mr 15 '97 - p1241 [51-250]
  c HB - v73 - My '97 - p340 [51-250]
  c PW - v244 - F 24 '97 - p93 [51-250]
  Lives of the Musicians (Brown). Audio Version
  c BL - v93 - D 15 '96 - p740 [51-250]
  c Bloom Rev - v16 - S '96 - p21 [51-250]
  Lives of the Writers (Brown). Audio Version
  c BL - v93 - D 15 '96 - p740 [51-250]
  c Bloom Rev - v16 - S '96 - p21 [51-250]
  y SLJ - v42 - O '96 - p78 [51-250]
  Wilma Unlimited (Illus. by David Diaz)
  c BL - v93 - Ja '97 - p768 [1-50]
  c BL - v93 - Ap 1 '97 - p1298 [1-50]
  c CLW - v67 - D '96 - p61 [51-250]
  c HB - v72 - S '96 - p617 [51-250]
  c HB Guide - v7 - Fall '96 - p362 [51-250]
  c Par Ch - v20 - O '96 - p28 [51-250]
  c RT - v50 - My '97 - p684 [51-250]
  c SLJ - v42 - D '96 - p30 [1-50]
  c SLJ - v42 - D '96 - p45 [51-250]
  Wish You Were Here (Illus. by Amy Schwartz)
  c CCB-B - v50 - My '97 - p326 [51-250]
Krummel, Donald William - *The Literature of Music Bibliography*
  r Lib - v19 - Mr '97 - p95+ [501+]
Krupat, Arnold - *Native American Autobiography Biography* - v19 - Sum '96 - p308+ [501+]
  The Turn to the Native
  LJ - v122 - F 1 '97 - p79 [51-250]
Krupinski, Loretta - *Bluewater Journal (Illus. by Loretta Krupinski)*
  c RT - v50 - D '96 - p344 [51-250]
  Heidi (Illus. by Loretta Krupinski)
  c BL - v93 - S 1 '96 - p145 [51-250]
  c HB Guide - v8 - Spr '97 - p49 [51-250]
  c SLJ - v43 - Ja '97 - p91 [51-250]
  Into the Woods (Illus. by Loretta Krupinski)
  c PW - v244 - Mr 31 '97 - p77 [51-250]
Krupp, E C - *Skywatchers, Shamans, and Kings*
  KR - v64 - O 1 '96 - p1447 [251-500]
  LJ - v121 - O 15 '96 - p88 [51-250]
  PW - v243 - O 14 '96 - p72+ [51-250]
  SciTech - v21 - Mr '97 - p19 [51-250]
Krupp, Robin Rector - *Let's Go Traveling in Mexico*
  c HB Guide - v7 - Fall '96 - p387 [51-250]
Kruschke, Earl R - *Gun Control*
  r ARBA - v28 - '97 - p229 [251-500]
Kruse, Douglas L - *Profit Sharing*
  NYRB - v44 - Ap 10 '97 - p38+ [501+]
Kruse, Robert L - *Data Structures and Program Design in C. 2nd Ed.*
  SciTech - v20 - D '96 - p9 [51-250]
Kruusval, Catarina - *Beach Day*
  c PW - v244 - Ap 7 '97 - p93+ [1-50]
  Birthday Flowers
  c PW - v244 - Ap 7 '97 - p93+ [1-50]
Krylov, N V - *Lectures on Elliptic and Parabolic Equations in Holder Spaces*
  SciTech - v20 - D '96 - p18 [51-250]
Kuang, Shanlong - *Geodetic Network Analysis and Optimal Design*
  SciTech - v20 - N '96 - p61 [51-250]
Kuark, John Y T - *Comparative Asian Economies*
  JEL - v34 - D '96 - p2120 [51-250]
Kube-McDowell, Michael P - *Before the Storm (Heald). Audio Version*
  y Kliatt - v30 - S '96 - p52 [51-250]
  Shield of Lies
  y Kliatt - v31 - Ja '97 - p14 [51-250]
  Shield of Lies (Heald). Audio Version
  y Kliatt - v31 - Ja '97 - p46 [51-250]

Tyrant's Test
  y Kliatt - v31 - My '97 - p14 [51-250]
Kuberski, Philip - *Chaosmos: Literature, Science, and Theory*
  South HR - v30 - Fall '96 - p382+ [501+]
Kubert, Joe - *Fax from Sarajevo*
  y BL - v93 - O 1 '96 - p315 [51-250]
  PW - v243 - S 23 '96 - p72 [51-250]
  VV - v42 - Ja 7 '97 - p43 [1-50]
Kubick, Dana - *Midnight Teddies*
  c PW - v244 - F 10 '97 - p85 [1-50]
Kubler-Ross, Elisabeth - *The Wheel of Life*
  BL - v93 - My 15 '97 - p1538 [51-250]
Kubo, Sakae - *A Beginner's New Testament Greek Grammar. New Ed., Rev.*
  Rel St Rev - v23 - Ja '97 - p66 [51-250]
Kubr, Milan - *Management Consulting. 3rd Ed.*
  JEL - v34 - D '96 - p2073 [51-250]
Kuch, K D - *The Babysitter's Handbook (Illus. by J J Smith Moore)*
  c PW - v244 - Ap 21 '97 - p74 [51-250]
Kucharski, Lisa - *Mirrors Blink*
  Sm Pr R - v29 - Ja '97 - p8 [501+]
Kuchler, Tilman - *Postmodern Gaming*
  Ger Q - v69 - Sum '96 - p336+ [501+]
Kucich, John - *The Power of Lies*
  MLR - v91 - O '96 - p981+ [501+]
  VS - v39 - Aut '95 - p67+ [501+]
Kuck, David J - *High Performance Computing*
  Choice - v34 - D '96 - p646 [51-250]
Kuckkan, Kevin G - *Career Basics*
  y JAAL - v40 - F '97 - p410+ [501+]
Kuczmarski, Thomas D - *Innovation: Leadership Strategies for the Competitive Edge*
  Bus Bk R - v3 - 3 '96 - p84+ [501+]
Kuczynski, Michael P - *Prophetic Song*
  MLR - v92 - Ap '97 - p431+ [501+]
  Specu - v72 - Ja '97 - p193+ [501+]
Kudlick, Catherine Jean - *Cholera in Post-Revolutionary Paris*
  Choice - v34 - N '96 - p494 [51-250]
  HRNB - v25 - Fall '96 - p28+ [251-500]
  J Soc H - v30 - Spr '97 - p788+ [501+]
  R&R Bk N - v11 - N '96 - p77 [51-250]
  SciTech - v20 - S '96 - p30 [51-250]
Kudlinski, Kathleen V - *Marie: An Invitation to Dance (Illus. by Lyn Durham)*
  c HB Guide - v8 - Spr '97 - p69 [51-250]
  c SLJ - v43 - Mr '97 - p187 [51-250]
  Shannon: A Chinatown Adventure, San Francisco 1880 (Illus. by Bill Farnsworth)
  c CCB-B - v50 - N '96 - p102+ [51-250]
  c HB Guide - v8 - Spr '97 - p69 [51-250]
  c PW - v243 - N 11 '96 - p76 [51-250]
  c SLJ - v42 - S '96 - p204 [51-250]
  Shannon, Lost and Found
  c BL - v93 - My 1 '97 - p1495 [51-250]
Kudryts'kyi, Anatolii - *Mytsi Ukrainy*
  r BL - v93 - N 15 '96 - p577 [1-50]
Kudszus, Winfried - *Poetic Process*
  Ger Q - v70 - Win '97 - p72+ [501+]
Kueh, Y Y - *Agricultural Instability in China 1931-1991*
  Ch Rev Int - v3 - Fall '96 - p465+ [501+]
  JEH - v57 - Mr '97 - p228+ [501+]
Kuehne, Dale S - *Massachusetts Congregationalist Political Thought 1760-1790*
  HRNB - v25 - Win '97 - p61+ [251-500]
Kuenzli, Rudolf E - *Dada and Surrealist Film*
  TCI - v30 - O '96 - p58 [51-250]
Kuester, Hildegard - *The Crafting of Chaos*
  Essays CW - Spr '97 - p65+ [501+]
Kuester, Martin - *Framing Truths*
  Essays CW - Spr '96 - p136+ [501+]
Kugler, Richard L - *Enlarging NATO*
  Choice - v34 - N '96 - p532+ [51-250]
  For Aff - v75 - S '96 - p151 [51-250]
Kugler, Robert A - *From Patriarch to Priest*
  R&R Bk N - v11 - N '96 - p7 [1-50]
Kuhl, Stefan - *The Nazi Connection*
  CEH - v29 - 2 '96 - p274+ [501+]
  Soc - v34 - Mr '97 - p78+ [501+]
Kuhles, Doris - *Herder-Bibliographie 1977-1992*
  r MLR - v92 - Ap '97 - p503+ [501+]
Kuhlthau, Carol Collier - *The Virtual School Library*
  LAR - v98 - O '96 - p538 [251-500]
  R&R Bk N - v11 - N '96 - p80 [51-250]
  Sch Lib - v45 - F '97 - p54 [51-250]
  SLMQ - v25 - Fall '96 - p64+ [51-250]
Kuhn, Anna K - *Playing for Stakes*
  Ger Q - v69 - Fall '96 - p444+ [501+]

Kuhn, James W - *Beyond Success*
  Rel St Rev - v23 - Ja '97 - p51 [51-250]
Kuhn, Karl F - *Basic Physics. 2nd Ed.*
  y SB - v32 - Ag '96 - p173 [51-250]
Kuhn, Steven L - *Mousterian Lithic Technology*
  Am Ant - v62 - Ja '97 - p166+ [501+]
Kuhn, William M - *Democratic Royalism*
  Choice - v34 - Mr '97 - p1220+ [51-250]
  Spec - v278 - Ja 18 '97 - p32+ [501+]
Kuhne, Cecil - *Inflatable Kayaking*
  BL - v93 - Mr 15 '97 - p1220 [51-250]
Kuhne, Thomas - *Dreiklassenwahlrecht Und Wahlkultur In Preussen 1867-1914*
  JMH - v68 - D '96 - p1019+ [501+]
Kuhre, W Lee - *ISO 14010 Environmental Auditing*
  Env - v39 - Ja '97 - p26+ [51-250]
Kuhrt, Amelie - *The Ancient Near East. Vols. 1-2*
  AJA - v101 - Ja '97 - p166+ [501+]
  Choice - v34 - D '96 - p665 [51-250]
  R&R Bk N - v11 - N '96 - p14 [51-250]
Kuiper, Koenrad - *Smooth Talkers*
  JC - v47 - Win '97 - p179+ [501+]
Kuipers, Barbara J - *American Indian Reference and Resource Books for Children and Young Adults. 2nd Ed.*
  r JOYS - v9 - Sum '96 - p411+ [251-500]
Kuipers, Dean - *Ray Gun*
  KR - v65 - Ap 1 '97 - p543+ [51-250]
  PW - v244 - Ap 14 '97 - p68 [51-250]
Kuklick, Bruce - *Puritans in Babylon*
  Bks & Cult - v3 - Ja '97 - p37 [251-500]
  RAH - v25 - Mr '97 - p73+ [501+]
  TLS - O 18 '96 - p9 [501+]
Kuklick, Henrika - *Science in the Field*
  SciTech - v21 - Mr '97 - p3 [51-250]
Kuklin, Susan - *Fireworks: The Science, the Art and the Magic (Illus. by Susan Kuklin)*
  c Ch BWatch - v6 - S '96 - p1 [1-50]
  c HB Guide - v8 - Spr '97 - p132 [51-250]
  Irrepressible Spirit
  y CCB-B - v50 - S '96 - p19 [51-250]
  y Ch BWatch - v6 - Jl '96 - p7 [51-250]
  y Emerg Lib - v23 - My '96 - p43 [1-50]
  y HB Guide - v7 - Fall '96 - p314+ [51-250]
  y JAAL - v40 - F '97 - p408 [51-250]
  y VOYA - v19 - F '97 - p350 [251-500]
  Kodomo: Children of Japan
  c RT - v50 - Mr '97 - p502 [51-250]
Kulas, John S - *Der Wanderer of St. Paul*
  R&R Bk N - v11 - D '96 - p62 [51-250]
Kulczycki, John J - *The Foreign Worker and the German Labor Movement*
  AHR - v101 - D '96 - p1567 [251-500]
  EHR - v112 - Ap '97 - p518 [51-250]
  JMH - v68 - D '96 - p1023+ [501+]
Kulke, Hermann - *The State in India 1000-1700*
  HRNB - v25 - Win '97 - p87+ [251-500]
Kulling, Monica - *Vanished! The Mysterious Disappearance of Amelia Earhart (Illus. by Ying-Hwa Hu)*
  c HB Guide - v8 - Spr '97 - p159 [51-250]
Kulp, Karel - *Frozen and Refrigerated Doughs and Batters*
  SciTech - v20 - N '96 - p80 [51-250]
Kulpa, Kathryn - *Short Takes*
  y Kliatt - v31 - Ja '97 - p17 [251-500]
  Taking Off and Other Coming of Age Stories by American Teen Writers
  y Kliatt - v31 - Ja '97 - p17 [251-500]
  Taking Off and Other Coming of Age Stories by American Teen Writers. Audio Version
  y Kliatt - v31 - Ja '97 - p46 [251-500]
Kul'tura Ukrains'koho Narodu
  BL - v93 - N 15 '96 - p577 [1-50]
Kumagai, Fumie - *Unmasking Japan Today*
  Choice - v34 - My '96 - p183 [51-250]
  Pac A - v69 - Fall '96 - p416+ [501+]
  SF - v75 - D '96 - p765 [51-250]
Kumar, Deepak - *Science and the Raj 1857-1905*
  TLS - O 11 '96 - p33 [501+]
Kumar, Devendra - *Towards a Tax Free Society*
  JEL - v35 - Mr '97 - p225 [51-250]
Kumar, Krishan - *From Post-Industrial to Post-Modern Society*
  AJS - v102 - S '96 - p597+ [501+]
  CS - v26 - Ja '97 - p121+ [501+]
Kumar, Nita - *Friends, Brothers, and Informants*
  RA - v25 - 4 '96 - p241+ [501+]
Kumar, Pradeep - *Unions and Workplace Change in Canada*
  ILRR - v50 - Ap '97 - p512+ [501+]

Kumin, Beat A - *The Shaping of a Community*
  Albion - v28 - Win '96 - p677+ [501+]
  Choice - v34 - S '96 - p187 [51-250]
  R&R Bk N - v12 - F '97 - p15 [51-250]
  Six Ct J - v27 - Win '96 - p1203+ [501+]
Kumin, Maxine - *Connecting the Dots*
  NY - v72 - S 9 '96 - p91 [51-250]
  Wom R Bks - v14 - O '96 - p15+ [501+]
Selected Poems 1960-1990
  BL - v93 - My 15 '97 - p1557+ [51-250]
  PW - v244 - Ap 28 '97 - p70 [251-500]
Kummer, Hans - *In Quest of the Sacred Baboon*
  TLS - My 24 '96 - p40 [501+]
Kummer, Patricia K - *Cote D'Ivoire (Ivory Coast)*
  c HB Guide - v7 - Fall '96 - p384 [51-250]
Kummerow, Jean M - *WORKTypes*
  BL - v93 - N 1 '96 - p465+ [51-250]
  LJ - v121 - D '96 - p126 [51-250]
  PW - v244 - Ja 20 '97 - p385 [51-250]
Kumta, Prashant N - *Role of Ceramics in Advanced Electrochemical Systems*
  SciTech - v21 - Mr '97 - p96 [51-250]
Kun, Janos - *Seigniorage and Burdens of Government Debt*
  JEL - v35 - Mr '97 - p294 [51-250]
Kundera, Milan - *The Joke*
  New ER - v18 - Win '97 - p93+ [501+]
Slowness
  BL - v93 - Ja '97 - p761 [1-50]
  Bloom Rev - v16 - Jl '96 - p7 [501+]
  Esq - v126 - Ag '96 - p34 [501+]
  LATBR - My 12 '96 - p2 [501+]
  LATBR - D 29 '96 - p11 [1-50]
  New R - v215 - S 9 '96 - p42+ [501+]
  NYTBR - v101 - D 8 '96 - p82 [1-50]
  Obs - Ja 5 '97 - p18* [51-250]
  RCF - v16 - Fall '96 - p182+ [501+]
  Spec - v277 - N 16 '96 - p43 [1-50]
  TES - Ja 17 '97 - p9* [51-250]
Testaments Betrayed
  Bloom Rev - v16 - Jl '96 - p7 [501+]
  NYTBR - v101 - N 10 '96 - p68 [51-250]
Kune, Gabriel A - *Causes and Control of Colorectal Cancer*
  SciTech - v21 - Mr '97 - p51 [51-250]
Kung, Hans - *Christianity: Essence, History and Future*
  CH - v65 - S '96 - p564+ [501+]
  LATBR - My 12 '96 - p6+ [501+]
  Theol St - v57 - Je '96 - p363+ [501+]
Dying with Dignity
  Choice - v34 - S '96 - p162 [51-250]
Great Christian Thinkers
  TT - v53 - O '96 - p423+ [51-250]
Kunin, Calvin M - *Urinary Tract Infections. 5th Ed.*
  SciTech - v21 - Mr '97 - p58 [51-250]
Kunin, Seth Daniel - *The Logic of Incest*
  Rel St Rev - v23 - Ja '97 - p57 [51-250]
Kunitz, Stanley - *Passing Through*
  Poet - v169 - F '97 - p291+ [501+]
Kunstler, James H - *Annie Oakley (Carradine) (Illus. by Fred Warter). Book and Audio Version*
  c Ch BWatch - v6 - My '96 - p6+ [51-250]
  c SLJ - v42 - Ag '96 - p125+ [51-250]
Kunstler, James Howard - *Home from Nowhere*
  BW - v26 - O 27 '96 - p7 [501+]
  HMR - Spr '97 - p6+ [501+]
  LJ - v121 - N 1 '96 - p96 [51-250]
  NYTBR - v101 - N 17 '96 - p26 [501+]
  PW - v243 - N 4 '96 - p44 [51-250]
  Utne R - N '96 - p89 [51-250]
  Utne R - Mr '97 - p84 [1-50]
  Wil Q - v20 - Aut '96 - p101 [251-500]
Kunstler, William Moses - *My Life as a Radical Lawyer (Kunstler). Audio Version*
  LJ - v122 - Mr 15 '97 - p101 [51-250]
  PW - v244 - Ja 6 '97 - p29 [51-250]
Kunt, Metin - *Suleyman the Magnificent and His Age*
  HRNB - v25 - Win '97 - p86 [251-500]
Kunz, Diane B - *Butter and Guns*
  BL - v93 - D 15 '96 - p697 [51-250]
  CHE - v43 - F 14 '97 - pA15 [51-250]
  Choice - v34 - My '97 - p1547 [51-250]
  CSM - v89 - Ja 30 '97 - pB2 [501+]
  For Aff - v76 - My '97 - p132 [51-250]
  LJ - v122 - Mr 15 '97 - p74 [51-250]
  PW - v243 - N 4 '96 - p54 [51-250]
Kunze, Horst - *Geschichte Der Buchillustration In Deutschland Das 16. Und 17. Jahrhundert. Vols. 1-2*
  BC - v44 - Win '95 - p584+ [501+]

Kuo, Cheng-Tian - *Global Competitiveness and Industrial Growth in Taiwan and the Philippines*
  Pac A - v69 - Fall '96 - p400+ [501+]
Kuo Li Ku Kung Po Wu Yuan - *Possessing the Past*
  Choice - v34 - Ja '97 - p785 [51-250]
  R&R Bk N - v11 - N '96 - p59 [51-250]
  y SLJ - v43 - Ja '97 - p142 [51-250]
  TLS - S 13 '96 - p18+ [501+]
Splendors of Imperial China
  Am Craft - v56 - Ag '96 - p66 [1-50]
  r Choice - v34 - N '96 - p444 [51-250]
  Time - v148 - N 18 '96 - p109 [1-50]
Kuon, Vuthy - *Humpty Dumpty (Illus. by Vuthy Kuon)*
  c Ch BWatch - v6 - O '96 - p1 [51-250]
Kupeli, Demir N - *Singular Semi-Riemannian Geometry*
  SciTech - v20 - S '96 - p12 [51-250]
Kuper, Adam - *The Chosen Primate*
  Nature - v384 - D 5 '96 - p426 [1-50]
  New Sci - v152 - N 2 '96 - p46 [1-50]
The Social Science Encyclopedia. 2nd Ed.
  r ARBA - v28 - '97 - p42 [251-500]
  r Choice - v34 - O '96 - p258 [51-250]
  r LAR - v98 - Je '96 - p318 [1-50]
Kupersmith, Joel - *The Pharmacologic Management of Heart Disease*
  SciTech - v20 - N '96 - p55 [51-250]
Kupferschmid, Gene S - *Testing Program for Con Mucho Gusto*
  Hisp - v79 - S '96 - p470+ [501+]
Y Tu, Que Dices. 3rd Ed.
  Hisp - v79 - S '96 - p466+ [501+]
Kupferschmid, Steve - *Simple Gifts of Christmas. Book and Audio Version*
  c CAY - v16 - Fall '95 - p11 [51-250]
Kupperman, Karen Ordahl - *America in European Consciousness 1493-1750*
  HAHR - v77 - F '97 - p78+ [501+]
  Sev Cent N - v54 - Spr '96 - p31+ [501+]
  W&M Q - v53 - O '96 - p797+ [501+]
Providence Island 1630-1641
  Historian - v58 - Sum '96 - p842 [51-250]
Kuppers, Gaby - *Campaneras: Voices from the Latin American Women's Movement*
  HAHR - v77 - F '97 - p85+ [251-500]
Kural, Orhan Cevdet - *Coal: Resources, Properties, Utilization, Pollution*
  SciTech - v20 - S '96 - p60 [51-250]
Kuralt, Charles - *Charles Kuralt's America*
  LATBR - N 17 '96 - p14 [51-250]
  NYTBR - v101 - D 22 '96 - p20 [1-50]
  PW - v243 - S 9 '96 - p81 [1-50]
Kuran, Timur - *Private Truths, Public Lies*
  AJS - v102 - N '96 - p874+ [501+]
  Econ J - v106 - S '96 - p1435+ [501+]
  JEH - v56 - S '96 - p757+ [501+]
  J Pol - v58 - Ag '96 - p889+ [501+]
  Pub Op Q - v60 - Sum '96 - p335+ [501+]
Kurani, Bharat - *Applied UNIX Programming. Vol. 2*
  SciTech - v20 - D '96 - p11 [51-250]
Kureishi, Hanif - *The Black Album*
  Books - v10 - Je '96 - p24 [1-50]
  LATBR - N 10 '96 - p15 [51-250]
  NYTBR - v101 - D 22 '96 - p20 [1-50]
  PW - v243 - S 2 '96 - p122 [1-50]
  Trib Bks - F 23 '97 - p9 [1-50]
The Faber Book of Pop
  TLS - D 6 '96 - p28 [501+]
Love in a Blue Time
  Obs - Ap 6 '97 - p16* [501+]
  TLS - Mr 28 '97 - p20 [501+]
My Beautiful Laundrette and Other Writings
  Si & So - v6 - N '96 - p36 [1-50]
Kurelek, William - *Lumberjack (Illus. by William Kurelek)*
  c Ch BWatch - v6 - S '96 - p3 [1-50]
A Northern Nativity (Illus. by William Kurelek)
  c Ch BWatch - v6 - S '96 - p3 [1-50]
A Prairie Boy's Summer (Illus. by William Kurelek)
  c Ch BWatch - v6 - S '96 - p3 [1-50]
A Prairie Boy's Winter (Illus. by William Kurelek)
  c Ch BWatch - v6 - S '96 - p3 [1-50]
They Sought a New World (Illus. by William Kurelek)
  c Ch BWatch - v6 - S '96 - p3 [1-50]
To My Father's Village (Illus. by William Kurelek)
  c Ch BWatch - v6 - S '96 - p3 [1-50]
Kurian, George Thomas - *Encyclopedia of Medical Media and Communications*
  r SciTech - v20 - N '96 - p35 [51-250]
Encyclopedia of the First World. Vols. 1-2
  r BL - v92 - Ag '96 - p1920 [51-250]

Encyclopedia of the Future. Vols. 1-2
  yr ARBA - v28 - '97 - p23+ [251-500]
  r RQ - v36 - Fall '96 - p127 [251-500]
The Encyclopedia of the Republican Party. The Encyclopedia of the Democratic Party. Vols. 1-4
  r BL - v93 - N 15 '96 - p605+ [501+]
  r Choice - v34 - Ap '97 - p1310 [51-250]
  r LJ - v121 - N 1 '96 - p58+ [51-250]
The Illustrated Book of World Rankings. 4th Ed.
  r BL - v93 - Mr 1 '97 - p1190+ [251-500]
Kuriansky, Judy - *The Complete Idiot's Guide to Dating*
  y CLW - v67 - Mr '97 - p59 [51-250]
Kurland, Michael - *Too Soon Dead*
  KR - v65 - Ja 15 '97 - p99 [51-250]
  PW - v244 - Ja 27 '97 - p80+ [51-250]
Kurland, Roselle - *Group Work Practice in a Troubled Society*
  Fam in Soc - v78 - Mr '97 - p222+ [501+]
Kurleto, Betsey - *Nutrition Secrets for Optimal Health*
  BWatch - v17 - D '96 - p3 [51-250]
Kuropas, Myron B - *Ukrainians in America*
  y HB Guide - v7 - Fall '96 - p312 [51-250]
Kurspahic, Kemal - *As Long as Sarajevo Exists*
  KR - v65 - F 15 '97 - p276 [251-500]
  PW - v244 - Mr 3 '97 - p57+ [501+]
Kursunoglu, Behram N - *Economics and Politics of Energy*
  SciTech - v20 - D '96 - p71 [51-250]
Neutrino Mass, Dark Matter, Gravitational Waves, Monopole Condensation, and Light Cone Quantization
  SciTech - v21 - Mr '97 - p20 [51-250]
Kurten, Bjorn - *Our Earliest Ancestors*
  RA - v25 - 4 '96 - p265+ [501+]
Kurth, Peter - *Tsar: The Lost World of Nicholas and Alexandra*
  HT - v46 - Jl '96 - p51 [1-50]
Zelda: An Illustrated Life
  y SLJ - v42 - O '96 - p166 [51-250]
Kurtis-Kleinman, Eileen - *When Aunt Lena Did the Rhumba (Illus. by Diane Greenseid)*
  c BL - v93 - My 15 '97 - p1579+ [51-250]
  c KR - v65 - My 1 '97 - p724 [51-250]
  c PW - v244 - Ap 21 '97 - p72 [51-250]
Kurtz, Carl - *Iowa's Wild Places*
  Choice - v34 - F '97 - p981 [51-250]
Kurtz, Howard - *Hot Air*
  Bus W - D 16 '96 - p19+ [51-250]
  JMCQ - v73 - Win '96 - p1002+ [501+]
Kurtz, Irma - *Dear London*
  NS - v126 - F 14 '97 - p46 [501+]
Kurtz, Jane - *Miro in the Kingdom of the Sun (Illus. by David Frampton)*
  c HB - v72 - N '96 - p751 [51-250]
  c HB Guide - v7 - Fall '96 - p322 [51-250]
Trouble (Illus. by Durga Bernhard)
  c BL - v93 - Mr 15 '97 - p1246 [51-250]
  c CCB-B - v50 - My '97 - p326+ [51-250]
  c KR - v65 - Mr 1 '97 - p383 [51-250]
Kurtz, Katherine - *Death of an Adept*
  y BL - v93 - D 1 '96 - p643 [51-250]
  KR - v64 - N 1 '96 - p1570 [51-250]
  PW - v243 - D 9 '96 - p62 [51-250]
Kurtz, Lester R - *Gods in the Global Village*
  SF - v75 - S '96 - p338+ [251-500]
Kurtz, Lisa A - *Handbook of Developmental Disabilities*
  SciTech - v20 - D '96 - p52 [51-250]
Kurz, Demie - *For Richer, for Poorer*
  SF - v75 - D '96 - p758+ [251-500]
Kurz, Heinz D - *Theory of Production*
  Econ J - v106 - N '96 - p1808+ [51-250]
  JEL - v34 - S '96 - p1344+ [501+]
Kurz, Kenneth Franklin - *The Reagan Years A to Z*
  r ARBA - v28 - '97 - p267 [51-250]
Kurzman, Dan - *Blood and Water*
  BL - v93 - Ja '97 - p814 [51-250]
  BW - v27 - F 9 '97 - p5 [501+]
  KR - v64 - N 1 '96 - p1584 [251-500]
  LJ - v122 - Ja '97 - p120 [51-250]
  NYTBR - v102 - Mr 9 '97 - p18 [51-250]
  NYTLa - v146 - F 12 '97 - pC17 [501+]
  PW - v243 - N 4 '96 - p54+ [51-250]
Kurzrock, Razelle - *Cytokines: Interleukins and Their Receptors*
  SciTech - v20 - D '96 - p36 [51-250]
Kurzweil, Edith - *A Partisan Century*
  BL - v93 - O 1 '96 - p293 [51-250]
  Dis - v44 - Spr '97 - p116+ [501+]
Kuschel, Karl-Josef - *Abraham: Sign of Hope for Jews, Christians and Muslims*
  JR - v77 - Ja '97 - p121+ [501+]

Kushner, Antony Robin Jeremy - *The Holocaust and the Liberal Imagination*
    EHR - v112 - Ap '97 - p538+ [501+]
Kushner, Eva - *La Problematique Du Sujet Chez Montaigne*
    Ren Q - v50 - Spr '97 - p251+ [501+]
Kushner, Eve - *Experiencing Abortion*
    PW - v244 - Ap 7 '97 - p86 [51-250]
Kushner, Harold S - *How Good Do We Have to Be?*
    CSM - v88 - N 7 '96 - p14 [51-250]
    CSM - v89 - N 25 '96 - p12 [51-250]
    CSM - v89 - Ja 23 '97 - p12 [51-250]
Kushner, Lawrence - *Invisible Lines of Connection*
    LJ - v121 - O 1 '96 - p86 [51-250]
Kushner, Michael G - *Employee Benefits Desk Encyclopedia*
    r ARBA - v28 - '97 - p118 [51-250]
    r HR Mag - v41 - D '96 - p125 [51-250]
    r R&R Bk N - v12 - F '97 - p40 [51-250]
Kushner, Tony - *Thinking about the Longstanding Problems of Virtue and Happiness*
    WLT - v70 - Sum '96 - p695 [251-500]
Kusiak, Andrew - *Designing Innovations in Industrial Logistics Modeling*
    SciTech - v21 - Mr '97 - p98 [51-250]
Kusler, Jon - *Our National Wetland Heritage. 2nd Ed.*
    BioSci - v47 - Ap '97 - p260 [51-250]
Kuster, Konrad - *Mozart: A Musical Biography*
    TLS - S 27 '96 - p20 [501+]
Kuster, Thomas - *Alte Armut Und Neues Burgertum*
    EHR - v112 - Ap '97 - p502+ [501+]
Kusugak, Michael - *My Arctic 1,2,3 (Illus. by Vladyana Krykorka)*
    c BIC - v25 - O '96 - p28 [51-250]
    c Ch Bk News - v19 - Sum '96 - p21 [501+]
    c Emerg Lib - v24 - Mr '97 - p27 [1-50]
    c Quill & Q - v62 - O '96 - p46 [251-500]
Kusukawa, Sachiko - *The Transformation of Natural Philosophy*
    CH - v65 - D '96 - p700+ [501+]
    Isis - v87 - S '96 - p541+ [251-500]
    Ren Q - v50 - Spr '97 - p336+ [501+]
    Six Ct J - v27 - Fall '96 - p815+ [501+]
    A Wittenberg University Library Catalogue of 1536
    LR - v45 - 7 '96 - p54+ [501+]
    Rel St Rev - v23 - Ja '97 - p82 [51-250]
    Six Ct J - v27 - Fall '96 - p815+ [501+]
Kutenplon, Deborah - *Young Adult Fiction by African American Writers 1968-1993*
    r Emerg Lib - v24 - S '96 - p41 [51-250]
Kuter, David J - *Thrombopoiesis and Thrombopoietins*
    SciTech - v21 - Mr '97 - p39 [51-250]
Kuti, Eva - *The Nonprofit Sector in Hungary*
    JEL - v35 - Mr '97 - p246 [51-250]
Kutler, Stanley I - *Encyclopedia of the United States in the Twentieth Century. Vols. 1-4*
    yr ARBA - v28 - '97 - p192 [51-250]
    r LJ - v122 - Ap 15 '97 - p39 [51-250]
    yr RQ - v35 - Sum '96 - p556+ [501+]
    Encyclopedia of the Vietnam War
    r ARBA - v28 - '97 - p199 [51-250]
    r BL - v93 - Ja '97 - p770 [1-50]
    r HRNB - v25 - Win '97 - p51+ [501+]
    r JTWS - v13 - Spr '96 - p250+ [501+]
    r LJ - v122 - Ja '97 - p86 [51-250]
    r WorldV - v12 - O '96 - p5+ [51-250]
Kutlu, Ayla - *Mekruh Kadinlar Mezarligi*
    WLT - v70 - Aut '96 - p1024 [51-250]
Kutner, Lawrence - *Making Sense of Your Teenager*
    BL - v93 - Mr 1 '97 - p1094+ [51-250]
    LJ - v122 - Ap 15 '97 - p109 [51-250]
    PW - v244 - Mr 24 '97 - p78 [51-250]
Kuttner, Ann L - *Dynasty and Empire in the Age of Augustus*
    AJA - v100 - O '96 - p800+ [501+]
    TLS - O 18 '96 - p6+ [501+]
Kuttner, Paul - *The Holocaust: Hoax or History?*
    AB - v99 - Mr 24 '97 - p963+ [501+]
Kuttner, Robert - *Everything for Sale*
    BW - v27 - F 2 '97 - p8 [501+]
    Comw - v124 - F 28 '97 - p21+ [501+]
    Econ - v342 - F 15 '97 - p3*+ [501+]
    KR - v64 - D 1 '96 - p1718+ [251-500]
    LATBR - Ja 26 '97 - p9 [501+]
    LJ - v122 - Ja '97 - p115 [51-250]
    NL - v79 - D 16 '96 - p34+ [501+]
    NW - v129 - F 10 '97 - p67 [501+]
    NYTBR - v102 - Ja 26 '97 - p11+ [501+]
    Prog - v61 - Mr '97 - p39+ [501+]
    PW - v243 - N 25 '96 - p65 [51-250]
    WSJ-Cent - v99 - Ja 22 '97 - pA12 [501+]

Ticking Time Bombs
    BL - v93 - S 1 '96 - p43 [51-250]
    Rapport - v19 - 6 '96 - p28 [251-500]
Kutulas, Judy - *The Long War*
    AAPSS-A - v549 - Ja '97 - p196+ [251-500]
    AL - v68 - D '96 - p865+ [501+]
    RAH - v25 - Mr '97 - p107+ [501+]
Kutzer, M Daphne - *Writers of Multicultural Fiction for Young Adults*
    r ARBA - v28 - '97 - p430+ [51-250]
    r JAAL - v40 - F '97 - p415 [1-50]
Kuusi, Osmo - *Innovation Systems and Competitiveness*
    JEL - v35 - Mr '97 - p281 [51-250]
Kuusisto, Stephen - *The Poet's Notebook*
    Bloom Rev - v16 - S '96 - p11 [51-250]
Kuypers, Janet - *Close Cover before Striking*
    Sm Pr R - v29 - F '97 - p10 [251-500]
Kuyt, Annelies - *The Descent to the Chariot*
    Rel St Rev - v22 - O '96 - p354 [51-250]
Kuzio, Taras - *Ukrainian Security Policy*
    Russ Rev - v56 - Ja '97 - p145+ [501+]
Kuznetsov, Andrei - *Foreign Investment in Contemporary Russia*
    Econ J - v106 - S '96 - p1472 [51-250]
Kuzniar, Alice A - *Outing Goethe and His Age*
    Choice - v34 - D '96 - p618+ [51-250]
Kuzych, Ingert - *Ukrainian Postage Stamps*
    r Am Phil - v111 - F '97 - p162+ [1-50]
    r Phil Lit R - v45 - '96 - p348+ [51-250]
Kvale, Steinar - *Interviews: An Introduction to Qualitative Research Interviewing*
    R&R Bk N - v11 - N '96 - p38 [51-250]
Kvanvig, Jonathan L - *The Problem of Hell*
    JAAR - v64 - Win '96 - p889+ [501+]
Kvasnicka, Robert M - *The Trans-Mississippi West 1804-1912. Pts. 1-3*
    WHQ - v28 - Spr '97 - p104 [1-50]
Kvasnosky, Laura McGee - *Mr. Chips! (Illus. by Laura McGee Kvasnosky)*
    c CBRS - v24 - Ag '96 - p160 [51-250]
    c CCB-B - v50 - N '96 - p104 [51-250]
    c HB Guide - v8 - Spr '97 - p35 [51-250]
    c SLJ - v42 - Ag '96 - p126 [51-250]
    See You Later, Alligator
    c LA - v73 - D '96 - p620 [51-250]
    What Shall I Dream? (Illus. by Judith Byron Schachner)
    c CCB-B - v50 - Ja '97 - p177+ [51-250]
    c HB Guide - v8 - Spr '97 - p35 [51-250]
    c SLJ - v42 - S '96 - p182 [51-250]
Kvet, Edward J - *Instructional Literature for Middle Level Band*
    Teach Mus - v3 - Ap '96 - p21 [51-250]
Kwak, Tae-Hwan - *The Major Powers of Northeast Asia*
    Choice - v34 - Mr '97 - p1235 [51-250]
    For Aff - v76 - Mr '97 - p197+ [51-250]
Kwasnicki, Witold - *Knowledge, Innovation and Economy*
    JEL - v34 - S '96 - p1418+ [51-250]
    R&R Bk N - v11 - N '96 - p24 [51-250]
Kwasny, Mark V - *Washington's Partisan War 1775-1783*
    Choice - v34 - My '97 - p1563 [51-250]
    LJ - v121 - D '96 - p117 [51-250]
Kwok, Pui-Lan - *Discovering the Bible in the Non-Biblical World*
    CLW - v67 - D '96 - p39 [251-500]
Kwolek-Folland, Angel - *Engendering Business*
    AHR - v101 - O '96 - p1290+ [501+]
    CS - v25 - N '96 - p799+ [501+]
    J Soc H - v30 - Fall '96 - p253+ [501+]
Kydland, Finn E - *Business Cycle Theory*
    Econ J - v106 - S '96 - p1470 [51-250]
    JEL - v35 - Mr '97 - p206+ [51-250]
Kyker, Keith - *Video Production for Elementary and Middle Schools*
    Emerg Lib - v23 - My '96 - p42 [1-50]
Kylatasku, Jussi - *Killeri Tulee*
    WLT - v71 - Win '97 - p188 [501+]
Kymlicka, Will - *Multicultural Citizenship*
    Dis - v44 - Win '97 - p135+ [501+]
    Ethics - v107 - O '96 - p153+ [501+]
    J Phil - v93 - S '96 - p480+ [501+]
    J Pol - v58 - N '96 - p1232+ [501+]
    RP - v59 - Win '97 - p127+ [501+]
    The Rights of Minority Cultures
    Ethics - v107 - Ja '97 - p356+ [501+]
Kyte, Jack - *Structure in Protein Chemistry*
    r Am Sci - v85 - Mr '97 - p187+ [501+]
Kythe, Prem K - *Fundamental Solutions for Differential Operators and Applications*
    Choice - v34 - Ja '97 - p834 [51-250]

Partial Differential Equations and Mathematica
    Choice - v34 - My '97 - p1536 [51-250]
    SciTech - v21 - Mr '97 - p16 [51-250]
Kytle, Elizabeth - *Home on the Canal*
    VQR - v72 - Aut '96 - p141* [1-50]
Kyvig, David E - *Explicit and Authentic Acts*
    Choice - v34 - Ap '97 - p1418 [51-250]
    LJ - v121 - O 15 '96 - p76 [51-250]
    New R - v216 - Mr 3 '97 - p38+ [501+]
    R&R Bk N - v12 - F '97 - p65 [51-250]

L

Laaksonen, Pirjo - *Consumer Involvement*
J Con A - v30 - Win '96 - p482+ [501+]
Laar, Bill - *The TES Guide to Surviving School Inspection*
TES - F 14 '97 - p19U [251-500]
LaBelle, Jacques - *Lexiques-Grammaires Compares en Francais*
FR - v70 - Mr '97 - p634+ [501+]
LaBelle, Patti - *Don't Block the Blessings*
BL - v93 - N 1 '96 - p459 [51-250]
BW - v27 - F 16 '97 - p8 [501+]
CSM - v88 - N 7 '96 - p14 [51-250]
Ent W - N 15 '96 - p64 [251-500]
LJ - v121 - N 1 '96 - p80 [1-50]
La Belle, Thomas J - *Ethnic Studies and Multiculturalism*
Choice - v34 - F '97 - p1015 [51-250]
Laberge, Marc - *Destins (Illus. by Frederic Eibner)*
c Can CL - v22 - Sum '96 - p107+ [251-500]
Laboda, Lawrence R - *From Selma to Appomattox*
JSH - v62 - N '96 - p816+ [251-500]
Labor in America
r RQ - v36 - Fall '96 - p55 [51-250]
Labor Institute - *Corporate Power and the American Dream*
Workbook - v21 - Win '96 - p168+ [251-500]
Labor-Personnel Index 1951-
r RQ - v36 - Fall '96 - p53+ [51-250]
Labor Research Association (U.S.) - *Labor Fact Book. Vols. 1-17*
r RQ - v36 - Fall '96 - p50+ [51-250]
La Bossiere, Camille R - *Context North America*
Essays CW - Spr '96 - p189+ [501+]
Labour Economics
p JEL - v35 - Mr '97 - p310 [51-250]
Labour File: A Monthly Journal of Labour and Economic Affairs
p WorldV - v12 - Jl '96 - p12 [51-250]
Labour Force Survey Report 1994
J Gov Info - v23 - S '96 - p655+ [1-50]
Labowitz, Shoni - *Miraculous Living*
BL - v93 - S 15 '96 - p182+ [51-250]
LJ - v121 - O 1 '96 - p86 [51-250]
PW - v243 - S 2 '96 - p126 [51-250]
LaBrake, Tammy - *How to Get Families More Involved in the Nursing Home*
SciTech - v21 - Mr '97 - p47 [1-50]
Labrie, Ross - *The Catholic Imagination in American Literature*
LJ - v122 - Mr 15 '97 - p64 [51-250]
LaCalamita, Tom - *The Ultimate Pressure Cooker Cookbook*
LJ - v122 - Mr 15 '97 - p82 [51-250]
Lacapa, Michael - *Antelope Woman*
c Learning - v25 - Mr '97 - p54 [1-50]
LaCapra, Dominick - *Representing the Holocaust*
JMH - v68 - S '96 - p673+ [501+]
MP - v94 - N '96 - p276+ [501+]
Lace, William W - *The Battle of Hastings*
y HB Guide - v7 - Fall '96 - p378+ [51-250]
The Little Princes in the Tower
y SLJ - v43 - Mr '97 - p203 [51-250]
The Wars of the Roses
y HB Guide - v7 - Fall '96 - p382 [51-250]
Lacey, A R - *A Dictionary of Philosophy. 3rd Ed.*
r ARBA - v28 - '97 - p530 [51-250]
Lacey, Sarah - *File Under: Jeopardy*
KR - v65 - Ja 15 '97 - p102 [51-250]
PW - v244 - F 3 '97 - p99 [51-250]
Lacey, Stephen - *Gardens of the National Trust*
BL - v93 - S 1 '96 - p54 [51-250]
TES - Ag 23 '96 - p22 [51-250]
TLS - Ag 2 '96 - p36 [501+]

Lacey, Theresa Jensen - *The Pawnee*
y HB Guide - v7 - Fall '96 - p391 [51-250]
Lach, Donald F - *Asia in the Making of Europe. Vol. 3, Bks. 1-4*
HT - v46 - Jl '96 - p49+ [501+]
LaChapelle, David - *LaChapelle Land*
Advocate - N 12 '96 - p77+ [501+]
BL - v93 - D 15 '96 - p703 [51-250]
Ent W - D 6 '96 - p58 [51-250]
LJ - v122 - Mr 15 '97 - p59 [51-250]
PW - v243 - S 16 '96 - p60 [51-250]
VLS - Win '96 - p31 [51-250]
Lachaud, Jean-Pierre - *Les Femmes Et Le Marche Du Travail Urbain En Afrique Subsaharienne*
ILR - v135 - 5 '96 - p595+ [501+]
The Labour Market in Africa
Econ J - v106 - N '96 - p1843 [251-500]
Lachele, Rainer - *Ein Volk, Ein Reich, Ein Glaube*
CEH - v29 - 2 '96 - p252+ [501+]
Lachman, Marvin - *A Reader's Guide to the American Novel of Detection*
r RQ - v36 - Win '96 - p216+ [51-250]
Lachner, Dorothea - *Look Out, Cinder! (Illus. by Eugen Sopko)*
c HB Guide - v7 - Fall '96 - p263 [51-250]
c KR - v64 - My 1 '96 - p690 [51-250]
c SLJ - v42 - O '96 - p101 [51-250]
Smoky's Special Easter Present (Illus. by Christa Unzner)
c HB Guide - v7 - Fall '96 - p263+ [51-250]
c SLJ - v42 - S '96 - p182 [51-250]
Lachnit, Carroll - *A Blessed Death*
Arm Det - v29 - Fall '96 - p477+ [51-250]
Lachs, John - *The Relevance of Philosophy to Life*
RM - v50 - S '96 - p167+ [501+]
Lachs, Lorraine - *Flowers for Mei-Ling*
KR - v65 - My 1 '97 - p666 [251-500]
LJ - v122 - My 1 '97 - p140+ [51-250]
PW - v244 - My 5 '97 - p194 [51-250]
Lack, Richard W - *Essentials of Safety and Health Management*
R&R Bk N - v11 - D '96 - p31 [51-250]
Lackey, Mercedes - *The Fire Rose*
y Kliatt - v31 - Ja '97 - p14 [51-250]
Firebird
y BL - v93 - Ja '97 - p826 [51-250]
KR - v64 - N 1 '96 - p1570 [51-250]
PW - v243 - N 18 '96 - p66 [51-250]
The Silver Gryphon
y SLJ - v42 - Ag '96 - p185 [51-250]
Storm Breaking
LJ - v121 - O 15 '96 - p93 [1-50]
PW - v243 - O 7 '96 - p66 [51-250]
y VOYA - v19 - F '97 - p336 [251-500]
Storm Rising
y Kliatt - v31 - Mr '97 - p18 [51-250]
Sword of Ice and Other Tales of Valdemar
y Kliatt - v31 - My '97 - p14 [51-250]
Lackmann, Ron - *Same Time...Same Station*
r ARBA - v28 - '97 - p352+ [251-500]
r RQ - v35 - Sum '96 - p565 [251-500]
Laclos, Choderlos De - *Les Liaisons Dangereuses*
MLN - v111 - S '96 - p671+ [501+]
Lacoe, Addie - *One, Two, and Three (Illus. by Anne Canevari Green)*
c RT - v50 - D '96 - p3346 [51-250]
Lacome, Susie - *Kids Country*
BL - v93 - D 1 '96 - p638 [51-250]
Lacquaniti, Francesco - *Neural Bases of Motor Behaviour*
SciTech - v20 - D '96 - p34 [51-250]

Lacranjan, Ion - *Cum Mor Taranii*
BL - v93 - D 15 '96 - p714 [1-50]
Lacy, Dan - *From Grunts to Gigabytes*
r Choice - v34 - N '96 - p447 [51-250]
Lacy, Norris J - *Text and Intertext in Medieval Arthurian Literature*
R&R Bk N - v11 - N '96 - p65 [51-250]
Lacy, Suzanne - *Mapping the Terrain*
Afterimage - v23 - Sum '96 - p21 [501+]
Lad, Frank - *Operational Subjective Statistical Methods*
SciTech - v20 - D '96 - p17 [51-250]
Ladd, Brian - *The Ghosts of Berlin*
LJ - v122 - Ap 1 '97 - p106 [51-250]
PW - v244 - Ap 28 '97 - p62 [251-500]
WSJ-Cent - v99 - Ap 28 '97 - pA17 [501+]
Ladd, Everett Carll - *Public Opinion in America and Japan*
For Aff - v75 - S '96 - p157 [51-250]
Ladd, Florence - *Sarah's Psalm*
BL - v92 - Ag '96 - p1882 [51-250]
Bl S - v26 - Fall '96 - p104 [1-50]
LATBR - Ag 25 '96 - p8 [501+]
NYTBR - v101 - S 29 '96 - p20 [51-250]
Ladd, Helen F - *Holding Schools Accountable*
JEL - v34 - D '96 - p2064 [51-250]
Ladd, Rosalind Ekman - *Children's Rights Re-Visioned*
Ethics - v107 - O '96 - p184+ [251-500]
Lade, Roger - *The Most Excellent Book of How to Be a Puppeteer (Illus. by Rob Shone)*
c HB Guide - v8 - Spr '97 - p142 [51-250]
c SLJ - v43 - F '97 - p89+ [51-250]
Laden, Nina - *My Family Tree*
c PW - v244 - Mr 24 '97 - p85 [51-250]
Ladenis, Nico - *Nico*
ILN - Christmas '96 - p90 [1-50]
Lader, Curt - *How to Prepare for the Advanced Placement Examination: AP U.S. Government and Politics*
y SLMQ - v25 - Fall '96 - p65 [1-50]
Ladero Quesada, Miguel-Angel - *Las Ferias De Castilla*
EHR - v111 - S '96 - p966+ [251-500]
Ladinsky, Daniel - *I Heard God Laughing*
Bloom Rev - v16 - N '96 - p14 [251-500]
Ladis, Andrew - *The Craft of Art*
Ren Q - v50 - Spr '97 - p317+ [501+]
Ladner, Gerhart B - *God, Cosmos, and Humankind*
Choice - v34 - S '96 - p144 [51-250]
Theol St - v57 - D '96 - p775+ [251-500]
TranslRevS - v2 - D '96 - p15 [51-250]
Ladous, Regis - *Des Nobel Au Vatican*
Isis - v88 - Mr '97 - p169+ [501+]
Ladybird Dictionary (Illus. by Peter Massey)
cr Sch Lib - v44 - N '96 - p163 [51-250]
Ladybugs: A Teacher's Guide
Inst - v105 - My '96 - p18 [51-250]
Lady Chablis - *Hiding My Candy*
BL - v92 - Ag '96 - p1872 [51-250]
BW - v26 - Ag 18 '96 - p13 [51-250]
LATBR - Ag 25 '96 - p10 [51-250]
PW - v243 - Jl 22 '96 - p224 [51-250]
Hiding My Candy. Audio Version
Advocate - O 1 '96 - p62+ [501+]
Laermer, Richard - *The Gay and Lesbian Handbook to New York City*
r Quill & Q - v62 - S '96 - p24 [51-250]
Laessoe, Thomas - *The Mushroom Book*
r ARBA - v28 - '97 - p582+ [251-500]
BL - v93 - S 1 '96 - p48 [51-250]
LaFarge, Albert - *U.S. Flea Market Directory. 2nd Ed.*
r BWatch - v17 - S '96 - p7 [1-50]

LaFarge, Tom - *Terror of Earth*
BW - v26 - S 1 '96 - p11 [51-250]
LaFargue, Michael - *Tao and Method*
Rel St Rev - v22 - O '96 - p359 [51-250]
Lafay, Arlette - *Georges Duhamel Et L'Idee De Civilisation*
FR - v70 - D '96 - p336+ [501+]
La Fayette, Madame De - *La Princesse De Cleves*
FR - v70 - O '96 - p24+ [501+]
Laferriere, Dany - *An Aroma of Coffee*
TranslRevS - v1 - My '95 - p19+ [51-250]
How to Make Love to a Negro
TranslRevS - v1 - My '95 - p20 [51-250]
Lafferty, Peter - *Heat and Cold (Illus. by Terry Hadler)*
c HB Guide - v7 - Fall '96 - p331 [51-250]
c SB - v32 - N '96 - p240 [251-500]
Light and Sound (Illus. by Terry Hadler)
c HB Guide - v7 - Fall '96 - p331 [51-250]
c SB - v32 - N '96 - p240 [251-500]
Laffineur, Robert - *Politeia: Society and State in the Aegean Bronze Age. Vols. 1-2*
AJA - v100 - Jl '96 - p612+ [501+]
Laffra, Chris - *Advanced Java*
CBR - v15 - Spr '97 - p3 [1-50]
SciTech - v21 - Mr '97 - p7 [51-250]
Lafont, Ghislain - *Imaginer L'Eglise Catholique*
Theol St - v57 - D '96 - p768+ [501+]
La Fontaine, Jean De - *La Fontaine's Bawdy*
TranslRevS - v1 - My '95 - p20 [51-250]
Lafore, Robert - *C++ Interactive Course*
SciTech - v20 - D '96 - p9 [51-250]
Laforest, Guy - *Trudeau and the End of a Canadian Dream*
Can Hist R - v78 - Mr '97 - p122+ [501+]
Dal R - v75 - Spr '95 - p107+ [501+]
Lafortune, Monique - *Oedipe A L'Universite*
Can Lit - Spr '97 - p209+ [501+]
LaFrance, Peter - *Cooking and Eating with Beer*
BL - v93 - My 15 '97 - p1552 [51-250]
LJ - v122 - Ap 1 '97 - p63 [1-50]
Lagasse, Emeril - *Louisiana Real and Rustic*
BL - v92 - Ag '96 - p1871 [51-250]
LJ - v121 - S 15 '96 - p89 [51-250]
Lagemann, Ellen Condliffe - *Brown v. Board of Education*
Choice - v34 - S '96 - p210 [51-250]
Lagnese, J E - *Modeling, Analysis and Control of Dynamic Elastic Multi-Link Structures*
SIAM Rev - v38 - S '96 - p537+ [251-500]
Lagon, Mark P - *The Reagan Doctrine*
Pres SQ - v26 - Sum '96 - p894+ [501+]
Lagorio, Gina - *Il Bastardo Ovvero Gli Amori, I Travagli E Le Lacrime Di Don Emanuel Di Savoia*
WLT - v70 - Aut '96 - p932+ [501+]
La Grange, Henry-Louis De - *Gustav Mahler. Vol. 2*
Notes - v53 - S '96 - p37+ [501+]
LaGuardia, Cheryl - *Teaching the New Library*
LJ - v122 - F 1 '97 - p114 [51-250]
R&R Bk N - v12 - F '97 - p102 [51-250]
Laham, Nicholas - *A Lost Cause*
Choice - v34 - My '97 - p1534 [51-250]
R&R Bk N - v12 - F '97 - p95 [51-250]
LaHaye, Tim - *Tribulation Force*
BL - v93 - O 1 '96 - p304 [501+]
CSM - v89 - N 25 '96 - p12 [51-250]
Lahman, James R - *Prayers of the Hours*
RR - v55 - N '96 - p661 [1-50]
Lahr, John - *Light Fantastic*
NY - v72 - D 16 '96 - p108 [51-250]
PW - v244 - F 24 '97 - p88 [1-50]
Spec - v277 - N 23 '96 - p44 [1-50]
Trib Bks - Mr 23 '97 - p6 [1-50]
Lai, Kuo-Yann - *Liquid Detergents*
SciTech - v21 - Mr '97 - p97 [51-250]
Laidlaw, James - *Riches and Renunciation*
Choice - v34 - S '96 - p165 [51-250]
Rel St Rev - v23 - Ja '97 - p96+ [51-250]
Rel St Rev - v23 - Ap '97 - p103+ [51-250]
Laidlaw, Marc - *The 37th Mandala*
MFSF - v91 - O '96 - p52+ [501+]
The Third Force
LJ - v121 - S 15 '96 - p101 [51-250]
PW - v243 - S 2 '96 - p121 [51-250]
Laimgruber, Monika - *Susannah and the Sandman (Illus. by Monika Laimgruber)*
c HB Guide - v8 - Spr '97 - p35 [51-250]
c SLJ - v43 - F '97 - p82 [51-250]
Laine, Pascal - *Fleur De Pave*
BL - v93 - Ja '97 - p827 [1-50]
WLT - v71 - Win '97 - p104 [501+]

Lainela, Seija - *The Baltic Economies in Transition*
Slav R - v55 - Fall '96 - p681+ [501+]
Laing, Jane - *Cecily Mary Barker and Her Art*
BC - v45 - Sum '96 - p274+ [251-500]
Laing, Lloyd - *Medieval Britain*
y BL - v93 - O 1 '96 - p319 [51-250]
Laing, R D - *Mad to Be Normal*
NYRB - v43 - N 14 '96 - p30+ [501+]
Laino, E J Miller - *Girl Hurt*
ABR - v18 - D '96 - p29+ [501+]
Laiou, Angeliki E - *Law and Society in Byzantium 9th-12th Centuries*
Rel St Rev - v23 - Ja '97 - p80 [51-250]
Specu - v71 - O '96 - p971+ [501+]
Laird, Brian Andrew - *To Bury the Dead*
KR - v65 - F 15 '97 - p258+ [51-250]
PW - v244 - Mr 3 '97 - p68 [51-250]
Laird, Crista - *But Can the Phoenix Sing?*
y Emerg Lib - v24 - S '96 - p24 [1-50]
Laird, Elizabeth - *Secret Friends (Illus. by Jason Cockcroft)*
c Bks Keeps - Mr '97 - p23 [51-250]
Laird, Ross - *Moanin' Low*
r ARBA - v28 - '97 - p486 [51-250]
r Choice - v34 - My '97 - p1476 [51-250]
Lake, Bernard - *Come to Y(our) Senses*
Aust Bk R - Ag '96 - p67 [1-50]
Lake, Mary Dixon - *The Royal Drum (Illus. by Carol O'Malia)*
c CBRS - v25 - S '96 - p8 [1-50]
c HB Guide - v8 - Spr '97 - p103 [51-250]
c SLJ - v42 - N '96 - p98 [51-250]
Lake, Tela Star Hawk - *Hawk Woman Dancing with the Moon*
BWatch - v17 - N '96 - p4 [51-250]
Laker, Rosalind - *The Fragile Hour*
PW - v244 - Ap 28 '97 - p55 [51-250]
Lake-Thom, Bobby - *Spirits of the Earth*
PW - v244 - Ap 21 '97 - p57 [51-250]
Lakoff, George - *Moral Politics*
Bks & Cult - v3 - Ja '97 - p34 [501+]
Choice - v34 - N '96 - p535 [51-250]
TLS - Ag 2 '96 - p12 [501+]
Lakoff, Sanford - *Democracy: History, Theory, Practice*
Choice - v34 - F '97 - p1033+ [51-250]
TLS - F 28 '97 - p27 [501+]
Lakos, John - *Large-Scale C++*
SciTech - v20 - N '96 - p8 [51-250]
Laks, Andre - *Justice and Generosity*
Rel St Rev - v22 - O '96 - p346 [51-250]
Lakshmikantham, V - *Dynamic Systems on Measure Chains*
SciTech - v21 - Mr '97 - p18 [51-250]
Lal, Deepak - *The Political Economy of Poverty, Equity, and Growth*
Choice - v34 - Ap '97 - p1388 [51-250]
JEL - v35 - Mr '97 - p285+ [51-250]
Lal, Vinay - *South Asian Cultural Studies*
r Choice - v34 - D '96 - p591 [51-250]
LaLande, Jeff - *An Environmental History of the Little Applegate River Watershed, Jackson County, Oregon*
Pub Hist - v18 - Sum '96 - p87+ [501+]
Lalande, Roxanne Decker - *Intruders in the Play World*
Choice - v34 - N '96 - p286 [51-250]
Lalic, Ivan V - *A Rusty Needle*
TLS - N 1 '96 - p23 [501+]
Lall, Sanjaya - *Technology and Enterprise Development*
Econ J - v106 - N '96 - p1850 [51-250]
Lalla, Barbara - *Defining Jamaican Fiction*
Choice - v34 - D '96 - p614 [51-250]
Lally, Kevin - *Wilder Times*
BW - v26 - Jl 7 '96 - p8 [251-500]
Choice - v34 - D '96 - p622 [51-250]
Econ - v340 - Ag 24 '96 - p70 [251-500]
Lalonde, Robert - *Le Petit Aigle A Tete Blanche*
FR - v70 - O '96 - p145+ [251-500]
Lalvani, Suren - *Photography, Vision, and the Production of Modern Bodies*
R&R Bk N - v12 - F '97 - p99 [51-250]
Lam, Willy Wo-Lap - *China after Deng Xiaoping*
Ch Rev Int - v3 - Fall '96 - p470+ [501+]
Lamar, Jake - *The Last Integrationist (Morton). Audio Version*
y Kliatt - v30 - N '96 - p42 [51-250]
Lamarca, Carlos Crovetto - *Stubble over the Soil*
Choice - v34 - Mr '97 - p1184 [51-250]
LaMarche, Gara - *Speech and Equality*
R&R Bk N - v11 - N '96 - p53 [1-50]
Lamarche-Vadel, Bernard - *Veterinaires*
FR - v70 - O '96 - p146+ [251-500]

Lamarque, Peter - *Fictional Points of View*
Choice - v34 - D '96 - p607 [51-250]
Truth, Fiction, and Literature
MLR - v91 - Jl '96 - p715+ [501+]
Phil R - v105 - Ja '96 - p84+ [501+]
LaMay, Craig L - *The Culture of Crime*
Fed Prob - v60 - Je '96 - p88+ [501+]
JMCQ - v73 - Win '96 - p996+ [251-500]
Lamb, Arnette - *True Heart*
LJ - v122 - F 15 '97 - p126 [51-250]
PW - v244 - Ja 13 '97 - p72 [51-250]
Lamb, Brian - *Booknotes: Writers and Their Stories from C-Span's Author Interviews*
BL - v93 - My 15 '97 - p1543 [51-250]
Lamb, Cynthia - *Brigid's Charge*
BL - v93 - F 15 '97 - p1004 [51-250]
Lamb, David - *Over the Hills*
LATBR - Jl 7 '96 - p10 [51-250]
Lamb, David, 1940- - *The Africans (Runger). Audio Version*
BL - v93 - My 15 '97 - p1596 [51-250]
y Kliatt - v31 - My '97 - p46 [51-250]
Lamb, David, 1942- - *Therapy Abatement, Autonomy and Futility*
R&R Bk N - v11 - D '96 - p69 [51-250]
Lamb, H H - *Climate, History and the Modern World. 2nd Ed.*
Choice - v34 - S '96 - p166 [51-250]
Lamb, John Lowry - *The End of Summer*
y Kliatt - v30 - S '96 - p12 [51-250]
Lamb, Nancy - *One April Morning (Illus. by Floyd Cooper)*
c CBRS - v24 - Ag '96 - p164 [51-250]
c HB Guide - v7 - Fall '96 - p387 [51-250]
c RT - v50 - Ap '97 - p593 [51-250]
Lamb, Richard - *War in Italy (Howard). Audio Version*
y Kliatt - v30 - N '96 - p52 [51-250]
Lamb, Robert - *Promising the Earth*
Nature - v383 - O 31 '96 - p781 [501+]
New Sci - v152 - N 23 '96 - p46 [51-250]
Lamb, Sharon - *The Trouble with Blame*
CC - v114 - Ja 15 '97 - p61+ [51-250]
Choice - v34 - S '96 - p215 [51-250]
Ethics - v107 - Ja '97 - p376+ [501+]
Fed Prob - v60 - S '96 - p85 [501+]
Lamb, Trevor - *Colour: Art and Science*
TLS - N 29 '96 - p16 [1-50]
Lamb, Ursula - *The Globe Encircled and the World Revealed*
HAHR - v77 - My '97 - p301+ [251-500]
Lamb, V B - *The Betrayal of Richard III*
CR - v269 - O '96 - p223 [51-250]
Lamb, Wally - *She's Come Undone*
Ent W - Mr 21 '97 - p65+ [501+]
Lambdin, Dewey - *A King's Commander*
KR - v64 - D 15 '96 - p1758+ [251-500]
PW - v243 - N 25 '96 - p55 [51-250]
Lambdin, Laura C - *Chaucer's Pilgrims*
yr ARBA - v28 - '97 - p452 [51-250]
Lambek, Michael - *Knowledge and Practice in Mayotte*
Am Ethnol - v24 - F '97 - p247+ [501+]
Lambersy, Werner - *Journal D'Un Athee Provisoire*
WLT - v71 - Win '97 - p108+ [501+]
Lambert, Bernard - *La Cavale: Memoire D'Albertine*
MLR - v91 - Jl '96 - p744+ [501+]
Lambert, David - *The Pacific Ocean*
c BL - v93 - Ja '97 - p850 [251-500]
c SB - v33 - Mr '97 - p49 [51-250]
Lambert, Gavin - *Inside Daisy Clover*
LJ - v121 - N 15 '96 - p93 [51-250]
Nazimova: A Biography
KR - v65 - F 15 '97 - p276+ [251-500]
PW - v244 - F 24 '97 - p72 [51-250]
Lambert, Joan Dahr - *Circles of Stone*
y BL - v93 - Mr 15 '97 - p1226 [51-250]
PW - v244 - F 24 '97 - p69+ [1-50]
Lambert, John - *Betrayed Trust*
Choice - v34 - S '96 - p182 [51-250]
Lambert, Matthew - *Joey's Birthday Wish (Illus. by Victoria Vebell Bruck)*
c RT - v50 - O '96 - p137 [1-50]
Lambert, Nicole - *12 Petits Europeens*
c BL - v93 - N 1 '96 - p500 [1-50]
Lambert, Page - *In Search of Kinship*
Bloom Rev - v16 - Jl '96 - p20 [501+]
Parabola - v21 - N '96 - p90+ [251-500]
Lambert, Phyllis - *Fortifications and the Synagogue*
AJA - v100 - O '96 - p808+ [501+]
Lambert, Tom - *The Power of Influence*
HR Mag - v41 - D '96 - p126 [51-250]

Lambeth, Benjamin S - *The Warrior Who Would Rule Russia*
LJ - v122 - Ja '97 - p124 [51-250]
Lambing, Peggy - *Entrepreneurship*
R&R Bk N - v11 - D '96 - p23 [51-250]
Lambourne, Lionel - *The Aesthetic Movement*
NYTLa - v146 - D 2 '96 - pC16 [51-250]
Lambrianou, Chris - *Escape*
Books - v9 - S '95 - p23 [1-50]
Lambright, W Henry - *Powering Apollo*
AHR - v102 - F '97 - p213+ [251-500]
Lambton, Lucinda - *A to Z of Britain*
TLS - Ja 10 '97 - p28 [251-500]
Lamers, Jos. M J - *Biochemistry of Signal Transduction in Myocardium*
SciTech - v20 - N '96 - p47 [51-250]
Lamm, C Drew - *Screech Owl at Midnight Hollow (Komisar) (Illus. by Joel Snyder). Book and Audio Version*
c SLJ - v42 - N '96 - p72 [51-250]
Lamm, Julia A - *The Living God*
Theol St - v58 - Mr '97 - p168+ [501+]
Lamm, Michael - *A Century of Automotive Style*
y BL - v93 - F 15 '97 - p986 [51-250]
Lamm, Richard - *The Immigration Time-Bomb*
BW - v26 - D 15 '96 - p1+ [51-250]
Lamm, Robert Carson - *The Humanities in Western Culture. 4th Ed.*
R&R Bk N - v11 - N '96 - p8 [51-250]
Lamm, Steven - *Thinner at Last*
PW - v243 - D 30 '96 - p64 [1-50]
Lammel, Gisold - *Deutsche Karikaturen*
MLR - v92 - Ap '97 - p536+ [501+]
Lammen, Michael - *Written in Water, Written in Stone*
PW - v243 - N 11 '96 - p69+ [51-250]
Lamonde, Yvan - *Louis-Antoine Dessaulles: Un Seigneur Liberal Et Anticlerical*
Can Hist R - v78 - Mr '97 - p149+ [501+]
LaMonte, Edward Shannon - *Politics and Welfare in Birmingham 1900-1975*
AHR - v101 - O '96 - p1293+ [501+]
Lamoreaux, Naomi R - *Coordination and Information*
JIH - v27 - Win '97 - p502+ [501+]
Insider Lending
JIH - v27 - Aut '96 - p345+ [51-250]
Lamorisse, Albert - *Le Ballon Rouge*
c BL - v93 - N 1 '96 - p500 [1-50]
Lamott, Anne - *Bird by Bird (Lamott). Audio Version*
BL - v93 - Ja '97 - p879 [51-250]
y Kliatt - v30 - N '96 - p47 [51-250]
Crooked Little Heart
y BL - v93 - Ap 1 '97 - p1281 [51-250]
BW - v27 - Ap 13 '97 - p6 [251-500]
KR - v65 - F 15 '97 - p245 [251-500]
LJ - v122 - Ap 1 '97 - p127+ [51-250]
PW - v244 - F 17 '97 - p208+ [251-500]
Trib Bks - Ap 20 '97 - p4 [501+]
Word by Word (Lamott). Audio Version
y Kliatt - v30 - N '96 - p47 [51-250]
L'Amour, Louis - *End of the Drive*
BL - v93 - My 1 '97 - p1480 [51-250]
KR - v65 - Ap 1 '97 - p490 [251-500]
PW - v244 - My 5 '97 - p198 [51-250]
Fork Your Own Broncs. Audio Version
LJ - v122 - My 1 '97 - p154 [51-250]
The Sixth Shotgun. Audio Version
LJ - v122 - My 1 '97 - p154 [51-250]
Lampert, Laurence - *Leo Strauss and Nietzsche*
APSR - v90 - S '96 - p633+ [501+]
CPR - v16 - Je '96 - p183+ [501+]
MLN - v111 - D '96 - p1022+ [501+]
RP - v59 - Win '97 - p158+ [501+]
Nietzsche and Modern Times
IPQ - v37 - Je '97 - p245+ [501+]
Lamperti, John W - *Probability: A Survey of the Mathematical Theory. 2nd Ed.*
SciTech - v20 - D '96 - p16 [51-250]
Lamphere, Louise - *Structuring Diversity*
BW - v26 - D 15 '96 - p1 [1-50]
Sunbelt Working Mothers
Am Ethnol - v24 - F '97 - p234+ [501+]
Signs - v22 - Win '97 - p440+ [501+]
Lampl, Patricia Ryan - *The Merry Christmas Postcard Story Book (Illus. by Emily Grossman)*
c PW - v243 - S 30 '96 - p93 [51-250]
Lampland, Martha - *The Object of Labor*
AJS - v102 - N '96 - p903+ [501+]
CS - v26 - Ja '97 - p95+ [501+]
R&R Bk N - v11 - D '96 - p29 [51-250]
Lampman, Archibald - *The Story of an Affinity*
Essays CW - Spr '96 - p158+ [501+]

Lamprell, Klay - *Scaly Things*
c BL - v93 - D 15 '96 - p728 [51-250]
c HB Guide - v8 - Spr '97 - p117 [1-50]
c SB - v33 - Ja '97 - p19 [51-250]
Lamsley, Terry - *Conference with the Dead*
Necro - Win '97 - p1+ [501+]
Lamy, Philip - *Millennium Rage*
y BL - v93 - N 15 '96 - p554 [51-250]
Choice - v34 - Ap '97 - p1423+ [51-250]
LJ - v121 - D '96 - p118 [51-250]
PW - v243 - N 4 '96 - p59 [51-250]
Lana, Robert E - *The Mass Flights of Italo Balbo*
Am Phil - v110 - O '96 - p909+ [51-250]
Lanagan, Margo - *Touching Earth Lightly*
y Aust Bk R - N '96 - p57+ [501+]
Lanahan, Eleanor Anne - *Scottie, the Daughter of--*
JPC - v30 - Sum '96 - p278+ [501+]
New ER - v18 - Win '97 - p174+ [501+]
Lancaster, Bill - *The Department Store*
Albion - v28 - Fall '96 - p535+ [501+]
J Soc H - v30 - Win '96 - p527+ [501+]
Lancaster, Jack - *Nitric Oxide*
SciTech - v20 - N '96 - p33 [51-250]
Lancaster, Kelvin - *Trade, Markets and Welfare*
JEL - v34 - D '96 - p2043 [51-250]
Lancaster, Lynn - *Folens Information Technology: Key Stage 1*
TES - Ja 3 '97 - p47U [51-250]
Folens Information Technology: Key Stage 2
TES - Ja 3 '97 - p47U [51-250]
Lancaster, Nicholas - *Geomorphology of Desert Dunes*
Choice - v34 - O '96 - p310 [51-250]
GJ - v162 - Jl '96 - p226 [251-500]
Lancaster, Peter - *Algebraic Riccati Equations*
SIAM Rev - v38 - D '96 - p694+ [501+]
Lectures on Operator Theory and Its Applications
SIAM Rev - v38 - D '96 - p713 [51-250]
Lancaster, Rosemary - *La Poesie Eclatee De Rene Char*
FR - v70 - O '96 - p128+ [251-500]
Lancaster, Roy - *What Plant Where?*
r RQ - v36 - Fall '96 - p143 [251-500]
Lancaster, Tony - *The Modern World*
y TES - Mr 28 '97 - p13* [501+]
Lance, Steven - *Written Out of Television*
r ARBA - v28 - '97 - p515 [51-250]
Ent W - Je 28 '96 - p97 [51-250]
Lanchester, John - *The Debt to Pleasure*
BIC - v25 - O '96 - p37+ [501+]
LJ - v121 - O 1 '96 - p47 [1-50]
NYRB - v43 - O 17 '96 - p48+ [501+]
NYTBR - v101 - D 8 '96 - p79 [1-50]
Obs - D 1 '96 - p17* [1-50]
Spec - v277 - N 16 '96 - p46 [1-50]
Trib Bks - Ap 6 '97 - p8 [1-50]
VLS - Win '96 - p10 [51-250]
The Debt to Pleasure (Ullett). Audio Version
y Kliatt - v30 - N '96 - p48 [51-250]
Lancon, Daniel - *Hibiscus Rouge*
WLT - v71 - Win '97 - p109 [501+]
Lancrey-Javal, Romain - *Le Langage Dramatique De La Reine Morte*
FR - v70 - Mr '97 - p602+ [251-500]
Land, Jon - *The Walls of Jericho*
KR - v65 - F 1 '97 - p163 [251-500]
LJ - v122 - Mr 15 '97 - p90 [51-250]
PW - v244 - F 17 '97 - p210 [51-250]
Land, Leslie - *The 3,000 Mile Garden*
Hort - v74 - N '96 - p69+ [501+]
Land, Philip S - *Catholic Social Teaching as I Have Lived, Loathed and Loved It*
Am - v175 - N 9 '96 - p25+ [501+]
Landa, Janet Tai - *Trust, Ethnicity, and Identity*
JEL - v35 - Mr '97 - p134+ [501+]
Landalf, Helen - *Movement Stories for Children Ages 3-6*
PW - v244 - Mr 10 '97 - p69 [51-250]
Landau, David - *The Renaissance Print 1470-1550*
PW - v243 - D 30 '96 - p64 [1-50]
Landau, Elaine - *The Abenaki*
c HB Guide - v7 - Fall '96 - p391 [51-250]
c SLJ - v43 - Ja '97 - p103 [51-250]
Alzheimer's Disease
y HB Guide - v8 - Spr '97 - p129 [51-250]
y SB - v33 - Mr '97 - p43+ [251-500]
c SLJ - v42 - Ag '96 - p157 [51-250]
The Curse of Tutankhamen
c Ch BWatch - v6 - D '96 - p6 [1-50]
c HB Guide - v8 - Spr '97 - p166 [51-250]
c SLJ - v42 - N '96 - p114+ [51-250]
Desert Mammals
c SLJ - v43 - Mr '97 - p178 [51-250]

ESP
c Ch BWatch - v6 - D '96 - p6 [1-50]
c HB Guide - v8 - Spr '97 - p86 [51-250]
c SLJ - v42 - N '96 - p114+ [51-250]
Fortune Telling
c Ch BWatch - v6 - D '96 - p6 [1-50]
c HB Guide - v8 - Spr '97 - p86 [51-250]
c SLJ - v42 - N '96 - p114+ [51-250]
Grassland Mammals
c SLJ - v43 - Mr '97 - p178 [51-250]
The Ottawa
c HB Guide - v7 - Fall '96 - p391 [51-250]
c SLJ - v43 - Ja '97 - p103 [51-250]
Stalking
y BL - v93 - F 15 '97 - p1013 [51-250]
y SLJ - v43 - F '97 - p118 [51-250]
Landau, Ellen G - *Lee Krasner: A Catalogue Raisonne*
r Art J - v55 - Fall '96 - p88+ [501+]
r Choice - v34 - S '96 - p113 [51-250]
Landau, Jacob M - *Pan-Turkism: From Irredentism to Cooperation. 2nd Rev. and Updated Ed.*
APSR - v90 - D '96 - p955+ [501+]
MEJ - v51 - Win '97 - p133+ [501+]
The Politics of Pan-Islam
JTWS - v13 - Spr '96 - p233+ [501+]
Landau, Paul Stuart - *The Realm of the Word*
AHR - v102 - F '97 - p149+ [501+]
Landau, Ralph - *The Mosaic of Economic Growth*
JEL - v34 - S '96 - p1486+ [51-250]
Landau, Sarah Bradford - *Rise of the New York Skyscraper 1865-1913*
ASInt - v34 - O '96 - p92+ [501+]
BW - v26 - S 1 '96 - p13 [51-250]
Choice - v34 - S '96 - p113 [51-250]
LATBR - D 8 '96 - p7 [251-500]
Nature - v382 - Ag 29 '96 - p771 [51-250]
SB - v32 - N '96 - p234 [51-250]
TLS - N 8 '96 - p4+ [501+]
Landau, Saul - *The Guerrilla Wars of Central America*
Parameters - v26 - Win '96 - p156 [1-50]
Landauer, Susan - *California Impressionists*
LATBR - D 8 '96 - p6 [51-250]
The San Francisco School of Abstract Expressionism
Choice - v34 - O '96 - p267+ [51-250]
LATBR - D 8 '96 - p6 [51-250]
WHQ - v27 - Win '96 - p551 [1-50]
Landauer, Thomas K - *The Trouble with Computers*
JEL - v34 - S '96 - p1383+ [501+]
SocSciComR - v14 - Sum '96 - p242+ [501+]
Lande, Aasulv - *Mission in a Pluralist World*
R&R Bk N - v12 - F '97 - p10 [51-250]
Landeck, Michael - *International Trade*
Econ J - v106 - S '96 - p1472+ [51-250]
Landers, Ann - *Wake Up and Smell the Coffee!*
Wom R Bks - v14 - Ja '97 - p11+ [501+]
Landers, John - *Death in the Metropolis*
J Urban H - v22 - S '96 - p727+ [501+]
Landesman, Peter - *The Raven*
y Kliatt - v31 - My '97 - p8 [51-250]
PW - v244 - Ja 27 '97 - p103 [1-50]
Trib Bks - F 2 '97 - p8 [1-50]
Landis, Jill Marie - *Just Once*
PW - v244 - Ap 28 '97 - p73 [51-250]
Landman, Christina - *The Piety of Afrikaans Women*
CH - v66 - Mr '97 - p162+ [501+]
Landman, Neil H - *Ammonoid Paleobiology*
Choice - v34 - Ja '97 - p824 [51-250]
SciTech - v20 - N '96 - p25 [51-250]
Landon, Brooks - *Science Fiction after 1900*
BL - v93 - Mr 15 '97 - p1221 [51-250]
Landon, H C Robbins - *The Mozart Compendium*
r CR - v269 - D '96 - p333+ [51-250]
Landow, George P - *Hyper/Text/Theory*
Dal R - v75 - Spr '95 - p121+ [501+]
Hypertext in Hypertext
QJS - v83 - My '97 - p230+ [501+]
Hypertext: The Convergence of Contemporary Critical Theory and Technology
QJS - v83 - My '97 - p230+ [501+]
Landrine, Hope - *African American Acculturation*
Bl S - v26 - Fall '96 - p104 [51-250]
Choice - v34 - N '96 - p546 [51-250]
Landrum, Gene N - *Profiles of Black Success*
y BL - v93 - F 15 '97 - p999 [51-250]
LJ - v122 - Mr 15 '97 - p78 [51-250]
PW - v244 - Ja 13 '97 - p62 [51-250]
Landrum, Graham - *The Historical Society Murder Mystery*
KR - v64 - My 1 '96 - p645 [251-500]
Landry, Dorothy Beaulieu - *Family Fallout*
Adoles - v31 - Fall '96 - p753 [51-250]

Landsberger, Stefan - *Chinese Propaganda Posters*
FEER - v159 - D 19 '96 - p57+ [501+]
R&R Bk N - v11 - N '96 - p50 [51-250]
Landskroner, Ronald A - *The Nonprofit Manager's Resource Directory*
r   Choice - v34 - Mr '97 - p1138 [51-250]
Landstrom, Olof - *Boo and Baa at Sea (Illus. by Olof Landstrom)*
c   PW - v244 - Ap 7 '97 - p93 [1-50]
Boo and Baa in a Party Mood (Illus. by Olof Landstrom)
c   BL - v93 - N 1 '96 - p507+ [51-250]
c   HB Guide - v8 - Spr '97 - p13 [51-250]
c   SLJ - v42 - N '96 - p87+ [51-250]
Boo and Baa in Windy Weather (Illus. by Olof Landstrom)
c   BL - v93 - N 1 '96 - p507+ [51-250]
c   HB Guide - v8 - Spr '97 - p13 [51-250]
c   JB - v60 - D '96 - p235 [51-250]
c   SLJ - v42 - N '96 - p87+ [51-250]
Boo and Baa on a Cleaning Spree
c   PW - v244 - Ap 7 '97 - p93 [1-50]
Landvik, Lorna - *Patty Jane's House of Curl*
Books - v11 - Ap '97 - p23 [51-250]
LJ - v121 - D '96 - p180 [51-250]
Patty Jane's House of Curl (Landvik). Audio Version
LJ - v122 - My 1 '97 - p154 [51-250]
Your Oasis on Flame Lake
PW - v244 - My 5 '97 - p193+ [51-250]
Landwehr, Ulrich - *Industrial Mobility and Public Policy*
JEL - v35 - Mr '97 - p304 [51-250]
Landy, Francis - *Hosea*
Rel St Rev - v23 - Ap '97 - p166 [51-250]
Landy, Marc K - *The New Politics of Public Policy*
Pol Stud J - v24 - Sum '96 - p316+ [501+]
Landy, Maria - *Inspecting Special Needs Provision in Schools*
TES - N 1 '96 - pR10 [51-250]
Landy, Robert J - *Essays in Drama Therapy*
Readings - v11 - S '96 - p26 [51-250]
Lane, Allison - *The Prodigal Daughter*
LJ - v121 - N 15 '96 - p48 [51-250]
Lane, Ann - *Britain, the Cold War and Yugoslav Unity 1941-1949*
Choice - v34 - F '97 - p1019+ [51-250]
R&R Bk N - v11 - D '96 - p8 [51-250]
Lane, Brian - *Cat and Mouse*
KR - v65 - F 15 '97 - p277 [251-500]
LJ - v122 - Mr 15 '97 - p75 [51-250]
PW - v244 - F 10 '97 - p78 [51-250]
The Investigation of Murder (Illus. by Rob Shone)
c   BL - v93 - Ja '97 - p850+ [251-500]
c   HB Guide - v8 - Spr '97 - p96 [51-250]
c   SLJ - v43 - Ja '97 - p103+ [51-250]
Lane, Christopher - *The Ruling Passion*
Albion - v28 - '96 - p749+ [501+]
Critm - v39 - Win '97 - p119+ [501+]
ELT - v39 - 4 '96 - p497+ [501+]
Lane, Dakota - *Johnny Voodoo*
y   BL - v93 - S 15 '96 - p232 [51-250]
y   BL - v93 - Ap 1 '97 - p1292 [1-50]
y   CBRS - v25 - F '97 - p83 [51-250]
y   CCB-B - v50 - Ja '97 - p178 [51-250]
c   Ch BWatch - v7 - F '97 - p4+ [1-50]
y   HB Guide - v8 - Spr '97 - p81 [51-250]
y   JAAL - v40 - N '96 - p231 [51-250]
y   KR - v64 - Ag 15 '96 - p1238 [51-250]
y   PW - v243 - N 18 '96 - p76+ [51-250]
y   SLJ - v42 - N '96 - p123 [51-250]
y   VOYA - v19 - O '96 - p210 [251-500]
Lane, David H - *The Phenomenon of Teilhard*
CC - v114 - Ja 15 '97 - p61 [51-250]
Theol St - v58 - Mr '97 - p193 [251-500]
Lane, David Stuart - *The Rise and Fall of State Socialism*
Choice - v34 - Ap '97 - p1411 [51-250]
Lane, Ed - *Florida's Geological History and Geological Resources*
J Gov Info - v23 - S '96 - p581 [51-250]
Lane, Harlan - *A Journey into the Deaf-World*
Choice - v34 - D '96 - p692+ [51-250]
R&R Bk N - v11 - N '96 - p44 [51-250]
Lane, Jan-Erik - *Constitutions and Political Theory*
Choice - v34 - Ap '97 - p1416 [51-250]
R&R Bk N - v12 - F '97 - p59 [51-250]
Lane, Kenneth Jay - *Kenneth Jay Lane: Faking It*
BL - v93 - N 15 '96 - p558 [51-250]
KR - v64 - S 15 '96 - p1391+ [51-250]
Lane, Maggie - *Jane Austen and Food*
RES - v48 - F '97 - p125+ [251-500]
Lane, Margaret - *The Tale of Beatrix Potter*
RSR - v24 - 3 '96 - p22 [51-250]

Lane, Nancy - *Understanding Eugene Ionesco*
MLR - v91 - Jl '96 - p743+ [251-500]
Lane, Peter - *Contemporary Porcelain*
Am Craft - v56 - Ag '96 - p27 [1-50]
Lane, Robert - *The Confetti Kid*
PW - v243 - D 30 '96 - p60 [1-50]
Lane, Roger - *Murder in America*
PW - v244 - Ap 14 '97 - p65+ [51-250]
Lane, Russell J M - *Handbook of Muscle Disease*
SciTech - v20 - N '96 - p48 [51-250]
Lane, Ruth - *Political Science in Theory and Practice*
Choice - v34 - Ap '97 - p1417 [51-250]
R&R Bk N - v12 - F '97 - p58 [51-250]
Lane, Wanda - *He's Got the Time, Have You Got the Money?*
Tric - v6 - Fall '96 - p142 [1-50]
Lang, Andrew - *The Rainbow Fairy Book (Illus. by Michael Hague)*
c   Par - v71 - S '96 - p209 [51-250]
Lang, Aubrey - *Loons*
Nature - v382 - Jl 25 '96 - p311 [1-50]
Lang, Berel - *Heidegger's Silence*
Choice - v34 - My '97 - p1513 [51-250]
LJ - v121 - S 15 '96 - p71 [51-250]
PW - v243 - S 9 '96 - p74+ [51-250]
Lang, Curt - *Database Publishing on the Web and Intranets*
LJ - v122 - Ja '97 - p138 [51-250]
Lang, Franz Peter - *International Economic Integration*
JEL - v34 - D '96 - p2039 [51-250]
Lang, James - *Feeding a Hungry Planet*
Choice - v34 - Mr '97 - p1184+ [51-250]
JEL - v35 - Mr '97 - p296 [51-250]
New Sci - v153 - Ja 4 '97 - p37 [1-50]
WorldV - v13 - Ja '97 - p6+ [251-500]
Lang, Kenneth R - *Sun, Earth and Sky*
New Sci - v153 - Mr 1 '97 - p42 [51-250]
S&T - v92 - N '96 - p59 [501+]
Lang, R G - *Two Tudor Subsidy Assessment Rolls for the City of London 1541 and 1582*
EHR - v111 - N '96 - p1267+ [251-500]
Lang, Susan S - *Teens and Tobacco*
y   Ch BWatch - v6 - Jl '96 - p7 [1-50]
You Don't Have to Suffer
LJ - v122 - Ja '97 - p57 [51-250]
Lang, Timothy - *The Victorians and the Stuart Heritage*
AHR - v102 - F '97 - p107+ [501+]
Lang, William L - *Stories from an Open Country*
Pub Hist - v19 - Win '97 - p99+ [501+]
WHQ - v27 - Win '96 - p526+ [251-500]
Langan, Celeste - *Romantic Vagrancy*
Nine-C Lit - v51 - Mr '97 - p533+ [501+]
TLS - My 24 '96 - p7 [501+]
Langan, Thomas - *Being and Truth*
R&R Bk N - v11 - N '96 - p3 [51-250]
Langdon, Susan - *From Pasture to Polis*
CW - v89 - Jl '96 - p506+ [251-500]
Lange, Armin - *Weisheit Und Pradestination*
JR - v77 - Ap '97 - p283+ [501+]
Rel St Rev - v22 - O '96 - p352 [51-250]
Lange, Charles H - *Bandelier: The Life and Adventures of Adolph Bandelier*
Choice - v34 - D '96 - p652 [51-250]
WHQ - v28 - Spr '97 - p102 [1-50]
Lange, David W - *The Complete Guide to Lincoln Cents*
r   Coin W - v37 - D 23 '96 - p18 [51-250]
r   Coin W - v38 - Ap 7 '97 - p62 [51-250]
Lange, Dorothea - *Ireland*
TLS - S 27 '96 - p22 [1-50]
Lange, Kurt - *Handbook of Metal Forming*
SciTech - v20 - N '96 - p82 [51-250]
Lange, Marjory E - *Telling Tears in the English Renaissance*
R&R Bk N - v12 - F '97 - p84 [51-250]
Lange, Tom - *Evidence Dismissed*
CSM - v89 - Mr 6 '97 - p14 [51-250]
NYTBR - v102 - Mr 9 '97 - p18 [51-250]
Langeler, Freddie - *Children of the Earth (Illus. by Freddie Langeler)*
c   Ch BWatch - v6 - S '96 - p3 [51-250]
c   SLJ - v43 - Ja '97 - p76 [51-250]
Children of the Stars (Illus. by Freddie Langeler)
c   Ch BWatch - v6 - S '96 - p3 [51-250]
c   SLJ - v43 - Ja '97 - p76 [51-250]
Fairies (Illus. by Freddie Langeler)
c   Ch BWatch - v6 - S '96 - p3 [51-250]
Lange-Muller, Katja - *Verfruhte Tierliebe*
WLT - v70 - Sum '96 - p683+ [501+]
Langen, Annette - *Felix Explores Planet Earth*
c   PW - v244 - Ap 14 '97 - p77 [51-250]

Langer, Ellen - *The Power of Mindful Learning*
KR - v65 - F 1 '97 - p201 [251-500]
Langer, Erick D - *The New Latin American Mission History*
HAHR - v76 - N '96 - p771+ [501+]
Langer, Howard J - *American Indian Quotations*
r   ARBA - v28 - '97 - p160 [251-500]
yr BL - v93 - N 15 '96 - p607+ [251-500]
r   Choice - v34 - Ja '97 - p765 [51-250]
r   LJ - v122 - Ag 15 '97 - p37 [51-250]
r   R&R Bk N - v11 - N '96 - p68 [51-250]
Langer, Maria - *America Online 3 for Macintosh*
LJ - v122 - My 1 '97 - p132 [1-50]
America Online 3 for Windows 95
CBR - v15 - Spr '97 - p2 [1-50]
LJ - v122 - My 1 '97 - p132 [1-50]
Pagemill 2 for Macintosh
CBR - v15 - Spr '97 - p1 [1-50]
Langerak, Tomas - *Andrei Platonov: Materialy Dlia Biografi 1899-1929 GG*
Slav R - v55 - Sum '96 - p515+ [501+]
Langewiesche, William - *Cutting for Sign*
BW - v26 - D 15 '96 - p4 [1-50]
Sahara Unveiled
y   BL - v92 - Ag '96 - p1876 [51-250]
y   BL - v92 - Ag '96 - p1890 [1-50]
NYTBR - v101 - D 8 '96 - p92 [1-50]
VQR - v73 - Win '97 - p32* [51-250]
Langford, Dave - *The Silence of the Langford*
Analog - v117 - Ap '97 - p147+ [51-250]
BW - v26 - S 1 '96 - p11 [51-250]
Langguth, A J - *A Noise of War (Blake). Audio Version*
BL - v92 - Ag '96 - p1917 [51-250]
Langhoff, June - *Telecom Made Easy. 2nd Ed.*
LJ - v122 - My 1 '97 - p53 [1-50]
Langland, Elizabeth - *Nobody's Angels*
Nine-C Lit - v51 - S '96 - p244+ [501+]
TSWL - v15 - Fall '96 - p365+ [501+]
VS - v39 - Win '96 - p251+ [501+]
Langland, William - *Piers Plowman. Vol. 1*
RES - v47 - N '96 - p558+ [501+]
Piers Plowman: A Facsimile of the Z-Text in Bodleian Library, Oxford, MS Bodley 851
MLR - v91 - O '96 - p959+ [501+]
Specu - v71 - Jl '96 - p702+ [501+]
Langley, Andrew - *100 Greatest Tyrants*
c   LAR - v98 - S '96 - p480 [1-50]
c   Sch Lib - v44 - N '96 - p174 [51-250]
The Illustrated Book of Questions and Answers
cr ARBA - v28 - '97 - p29+ [251-500]
Journey into Space (Illus. by Alex Pang)
c   SB - v33 - My '97 - p120 [501+]
Medieval Life (Illus. by Geoff Dann)
c   Ch BWatch - v6 - S '96 - p5 [51-250]
c   HB Guide - v7 - Fall '96 - p379 [51-250]
c   Magpies - v11 - Jl '96 - p39 [51-250]
c   Sch Lib - v44 - Ag '96 - p112 [51-250]
The Roman News
c   BL - v93 - O 1 '96 - p345+ [51-250]
c   CBRS - v25 - D '96 - p46+ [51-250]
c   HB Guide - v8 - Spr '97 - p166 [51-250]
c   JB - v60 - D '96 - p270 [51-250]
c   Magpies - v11 - S '96 - p41 [51-250]
c   SLJ - v43 - Ja '97 - p128+ [51-250]
c   Spec - v277 - D 14 '96 - p77 [51-250]
c   TES - N 8 '96 - p13* [51-250]
Langley, Harold D - *A History of Medicine in the Early U.S. Navy*
J Mil H - v61 - Ja '97 - p161+ [251-500]
Langley, Jonathan - *Little Red Riding Hood*
c   HB Guide - v7 - Fall '96 - p322 [51-250]
Three Little Pigs
c   HB Guide - v7 - Fall '96 - p322 [51-250]
Langley, Lester D - *The Americas in the Age of Revolution 1750-1850*
Choice - v34 - Ap '97 - p1393 [51-250]
CSM - v89 - Ja 30 '97 - pB1+ [501+]
LJ - v121 - N 15 '96 - p73 [51-250]
NYTBR - v102 - Mr 2 '97 - p27 [501+]
PW - v243 - O 14 '96 - p71+ [51-250]
The Banana Men
AAPSS-A - v547 - S '96 - p179+ [501+]
AHR - v101 - D '96 - p1636+ [251-500]
HAHR - v77 - My '97 - p331+ [251-500]
Langley, Myrtle - *Religion*
c   HB Guide - v8 - Spr '97 - p87 [51-250]
c   JB - v60 - D '96 - p270+ [51-250]
c   Sch Lib - v45 - F '97 - p39 [51-250]
c   SLJ - v42 - D '96 - p131 [51-250]

Langlois, Florence - *The Extraordinary Gift (Illus. by Florence Langlois)*
  c PW - v244 - F 24 '97 - p89 [51-250]

Langman, Larry - *A Guide to American Crime Films of the Forties and Fifties*
  r AB - v98 - D 9 '96 - p1997 [51-250]

Langmead, Donald - *Dutch Modernism*
  r ARBA - v28 - '97 - p368 [251-500]
  r Choice - v34 - Mr '97 - p1138 [51-250]
  r R&R Bk N - v12 - F '97 - p72 [51-250]

Langmuir, Erika - *National Gallery Companion Guide*
  TES - Ag 30 '96 - p26 [1-50]

Langmuir, Gavin I - *Toward a Definition of Antisemitism*
  Rel Ed - v91 - Fall '96 - p607 [1-50]

Langreuter, Jutta - *Little Bear Brushes His Teeth (Illus. by Vera Sobat)*
  c BL - v93 - F 1 '97 - p946+ [51-250]
  c KR - v65 - F 1 '97 - p230 [51-250]
  c PW - v244 - Ja 27 '97 - p105 [51-250]
Little Bear Goes to Kindergarten (Illus. by Vera Sobat)
  c BL - v93 - F 1 '97 - p946+ [51-250]
  c PW - v244 - Ja 27 '97 - p105 [51-250]

Langs, Robert - *The Evolution of the Emotion-Processing Mind*
  Readings - v12 - Mr '97 - p27+ [51-250]

Langsdorf, Lenore - *Phenomenology, Interpretation, and Community*
  R&R Bk N - v11 - N '96 - p2 [51-250]

Langsen, Richard C - *When Someone in the Family Drinks Too Much (Illus. by Nicole Rubel)*
  c CBRS - v24 - Ag '96 - p164 [51-250]
  c HB Guide - v7 - Fall '96 - p317 [51-250]
  c NY - v72 - N 18 '96 - p98 [1-50]

Langstaff, John - *Climbing Jacob's Ladder (Illus. by Ashley Bryan)*
  c BL - v93 - F 15 '97 - p1014 [1-50]

Langston, Nancy - *Forest Dreams, Forest Nightmares*
  PHR - v65 - N '96 - p679+ [251-500]

Langton, Jane - *Dead as a Dodo*
  Arm Det - v30 - Win '97 - p96 [251-500]
  KR - v64 - S 1 '96 - p1277+ [51-250]
  LJ - v121 - O 1 '96 - p131 [1-50]
  NYTBR - v101 - D 22 '96 - p21 [51-250]
The Shortest Day
  Arm Det - v29 - Fall '96 - p402 [51-250]
The Shortest Day (Reading). Audio Version
  y Kliatt - v30 - S '96 - p52 [51-250]

Langum, David J - *Crossing over the Line*
  AHR - v101 - D '96 - p1632+ [501+]
  RAH - v24 - S '96 - p471+ [501+]

Lang-Westcott, Martha - *The Orders of Light*
  Horoscope - v62 - N '96 - p32 [501+]

Lanham, Richard A - *The Electronic Word*
  QJS - v83 - My '97 - p230+ [501+]

Lanier, Virginia - *A Brace of Bloodhounds*
  KR - v65 - My 1 '97 - p682 [251-500]
  PW - v244 - My 5 '97 - p201 [51-250]
The House on Bloodhound Lane
  Arm Det - v29 - Fall '96 - p481 [251-500]

Lankford, John - *History of Astronomy*
  r Astron - v25 - My '97 - p114 [1-50]
  r Choice - v34 - Ap '97 - p1309+ [51-250]
  r LJ - v122 - Ja '97 - p86+ [51-250]
  r R&R Bk N - v12 - F '97 - p93 [51-250]

Lankford, Mary D - *Christmas around the World (Illus. by Karen Dugan)*
  c Emerg Lib - v23 - My '96 - p56 [51-250]
Jacks around the World (Illus. by Karen Dugan)
  c CBRS - v24 - Ag '96 - p164+ [51-250]
  c CCB-B - v50 - D '96 - p141 [51-250]
  c HB - v72 - S '96 - p617+ [51-250]
  c HB Guide - v8 - Spr '97 - p142 [51-250]
  c SLJ - v42 - S '96 - p198 [51-250]

Lankford, Mike - *Life in Double Time*
  BL - v93 - F 1 '97 - p919 [51-250]
  KR - v64 - D 1 '96 - p1719 [251-500]
  LJ - v122 - Ja '97 - p101 [51-250]
  PW - v243 - N 11 '96 - p61 [51-250]

Lankford, Nelson D - *The Last American Aristocrat*
  BL - v92 - Ag '96 - p1862+ [51-250]
  BW - v26 - Ag 4 '96 - p1+ [501+]
  Obs - v54 - O 13 '96 - p16* [501+]
  Spec - v277 - S 28 '96 - p49+ [501+]
  TLS - S 13 '96 - p30 [501+]

Lankford, Terrill - *Shooters*
  BL - v93 - Ja '97 - p825 [51-250]
  KR - v64 - N 15 '96 - p1624 [251-500]
  PW - v243 - N 25 '96 - p55 [51-250]

Lankhorst, G J - *Rehabilitation Activities Profile*
  J Rehab RD - v33 - O '96 - p440 [51-250]

Lanner, Ronald M - *Made for Each Other*
  Sci - v275 - Ja 31 '97 - p625 [1-50]

Lanning, Michael Lee - *The African-American Soldier from Crispus Attucks to Colin Powell*
  y BL - v93 - My 15 '97 - p1546 [51-250]
  PW - v244 - My 5 '97 - p188 [51-250]
The Military 100
  yr BL - v93 - D 1 '96 - p626 [51-250]
  r LJ - v121 - D '96 - p118 [51-250]
  r PW - v243 - N 11 '96 - p68 [51-250]

Lannoo, Michael J - *Okoboji Wetlands*
  Choice - v34 - N '96 - p482 [51-250]
  SB - v32 - N '96 - p230+ [51-250]

Lansdale, Joe R - *A Fist Full of Stories (and Articles)*
  BL - v93 - Mr 1 '97 - p1113+ [51-250]
The Lone Ranger and Tonto
  AL - v68 - S '96 - p609+ [501+]

Lansdowne, David - *Fund Raising Realities Every Board Member Must Face*
  ChrPhil - v8 - Jl 11 '96 - p44 [51-250]
The Relentlessly Practical Guide to Raising Serious Money
  ChrPhil - v9 - D 12 '96 - p48 [51-250]

Lansky, Bruce - *Sweet Dreams (Illus. by Vicki Wehrman)*
  c HB Guide - v8 - Spr '97 - p150 [51-250]
  c SLJ - v42 - O '96 - p115 [51-250]
You're Invited to Bruce Lansky's Poetry Party! (Illus. by Stephen Carpenter)
  c CCB-B - v50 - O '96 - p66+ [51-250]
  c Cur R - v36 - N '96 - p12 [51-250]
  c HB Guide - v8 - Spr '97 - p152 [51-250]

Lanspery, Susan - *Staying Put*
  R&R Bk N - v12 - F '97 - p73 [51-250]

Lantieri, Linda - *Waging Peace in Our Schools*
  Choice - v34 - Ap '97 - p1391 [51-250]
  EL - v54 - F '97 - p85+ [51-250]

Lanting, Frans - *Animal Athletes (Illus. by Frans Lanting)*
  c AB - v98 - N 18 '96 - p1730+ [51-250]
  c BL - v93 - D 1 '96 - p657+ [51-250]
  c HB Guide - v8 - Spr '97 - p116 [1-50]
  c SLJ - v43 - F '97 - p109+ [51-250]

Lantos, John D - *Do We Still Need Doctors?*
  KR - v65 - My 1 '97 - p697+ [251-500]

Lantz, Francess Lin - *Someone to Love*
  y CBRS - v25 - Mr '97 - p95 [51-250]
  y KR - v65 - F 1 '97 - p224 [51-250]
  y PW - v244 - Ja 6 '97 - p74 [51-250]

Lanyer, Aemilia - *The Poems of Aemilia Lanyer*
  Ren Q - v49 - Aut '96 - p666+ [501+]

Lanza, Joseph - *Elevator Music*
  JPC - v30 - Fall '96 - p208+ [251-500]

Lanza, Robert - *One World*
  BioSci - v47 - Mr '97 - p193+ [501+]

Lanzafame, Raymond J - *Prevention and Management of Complications in Minimally Invasive Surgery*
  SciTech - v20 - D '96 - p49 [51-250]

Lao-Hung - *Summer of Betrayal*
  PW - v244 - My 5 '97 - p196 [51-250]

Laorr, Alan - *MRI of Musculoskeletal Masses*
  SciTech - v20 - D '96 - p43 [51-250]

Lao-Tzu - *Lao-Tzu's Taoteching*
  LJ - v121 - O '96 - p84 [51-250]
  PW - v243 - Jl 22 '96 - p238 [51-250]
  Tric - v6 - Win '96 - p116 [1-50]

Lapan, Maureen T - *Learning and Intelligence*
  Choice - v34 - S '96 - p215 [51-250]

La Perouse, Jean-Francois De Galaup, Comte De - *The Journal of Jean-Francois De Galaup De La Perouse 1785-1788. Vol. 1*
  GJ - v162 - N '96 - p340 [51-250]

Lapham, Lewis H - *Hotel America*
  Dis - v43 - Fall '96 - p123+ [501+]
  PW - v243 - S 23 '96 - p73 [1-50]
The Wish for Kings
  Dis - v43 - Fall '96 - p123+ [501+]

Lapham, Robert - *Lapham's Raiders*
  Choice - v34 - O '96 - p349 [51-250]
  PHR - v66 - F '97 - p128+ [501+]

Lapica, Rey - *Derzhavna Zrada?*
  BL - v93 - N 15 '96 - p577 [1-50]

Lapid, Yosef - *The Return of Culture and Identity in IR Theory*
  APSR - v91 - Mr '97 - p238+ [501+]

Lapidge, Michael - *Archbishop Theodore: Commemorative Studies on His Life and Influence*
  Albion - v28 - Fall '96 - p459+ [501+]
  CH - v65 - D '96 - p671+ [501+]
  CHR - v82 - Jl '96 - p514+ [501+]

Lapidus, Morris - *Too Much Is Never Enough*
  NYTBR - v102 - Mr 2 '97 - p19 [51-250]
  PW - v243 - S 16 '96 - p65 [51-250]

Lapierre, Alexandra - *Fanny Stevenson: A Romance of Destiny*
  TranslRevS - v2 - D '96 - p8 [51-250]

LaPierre, Laurier L - *Sir Wilfrid Laurier and the Romance of Canada*
  Mac - v110 - Ja 13 '97 - p65 [501+]
  Quill & Q - v62 - N '96 - p34 [501+]

LaPierre, Wayne - *Guns, Crime, and Freedom*
  Soc - v33 - S '96 - p84+ [501+]

Lapine, Warren - *Absolute Magnitude*
  KR - v65 - Mr 15 '97 - p422 [51-250]
  LJ - v122 - Ap 15 '97 - p124 [51-250]
  PW - v244 - Ap 21 '97 - p65 [51-250]

La Place, Viana - *Unplugged Kitchen*
  LJ - v121 - O 15 '96 - p86 [51-250]
  PW - v243 - S 16 '96 - p78 [51-250]

La Plante, Lynda - *Cold Blood*
  Woman's J - Ag '96 - p11 [1-50]
Cold Shoulder
  Books - v9 - S '95 - p27 [51-250]
  LATBR - My 12 '96 - p11 [51-250]

Laplante, Phillip A - *Real-Time Imaging*
  SciTech - v20 - D '96 - p66 [51-250]

Lapomarda, Vincent A - *The Boston Mayor Who Became Truman's Secretary of Labor*
  NEQ - v69 - S '96 - p509+ [501+]

Laporte, Jean - *Theologie Liturgique De Philon D'Alexandrie Et D'Origene*
  Theol St - v57 - S '96 - p565+ [251-500]

Lappe, Marc - *The Body's Edge*
  Choice - v34 - Mr '97 - p1183 [51-250]
  Nature - v382 - Ag 15 '96 - p591 [501+]

Lappin, Elena - *Daylight in Nightclub Inferno*
  BL - v93 - F 1 '97 - p925 [51-250]
  KR - v65 - F 1 '97 - p171 [51-250]
  LJ - v122 - F 1 '97 - p109 [51-250]
  PW - v244 - Ja 13 '97 - p55+ [51-250]

La Prise, Larry - *The Hokey Pokey (Illus. by Sheila Hamanaka)*
  c BL - v93 - F 1 '97 - p940 [51-250]
  c KR - v65 - Ja 1 '97 - p60 [51-250]
  c PW - v244 - Ja 6 '97 - p72 [51-250]
  c SLJ - v43 - Mr '97 - p178 [51-250]

Lapsley, James T - *Bottled Poetry*
  BL - v93 - F 15 '97 - p989 [51-250]
  KR - v64 - O 1 '96 - p1447 [251-500]

La Puma, John - *Pocket Guide to Managed Care*
  Hast Cen R - v26 - Mr '96 - p49 [1-50]

Laqueur, Walter - *Fascism: Past, Present, Future*
  Choice - v34 - N '96 - p528+ [51-250]
  NYRB - v43 - N 28 '96 - p48+ [501+]
  NYTBR - v101 - D 22 '96 - p17 [501+]
  PSQ - v111 - Win '96 - p716+ [501+]

Lara, Brian - *Beating the Field*
  Books - v10 - Je '96 - p21 [1-50]

Lardet, Pierre - *L'Apologie De Jerome Contre Rufin*
  Rel St Rev - v22 - O '96 - p301+ [501+]

Lardner, George - *The Stalking of Kristin (Guidall). Audio Version*
  y Kliatt - v30 - S '96 - p59+ [51-250]

Lardner, Ring - *The Annotated Baseball Stories of Ring Lardner 1914-1919*
  JPC - v30 - Fall '96 - p206+ [501+]

Lareau, Alan - *The Wild Stage*
  Ger Q - v69 - Fall '96 - p432+ [501+]
  MLR - v92 - Ap '97 - p521+ [501+]

Larebo, Haile M - *The Building of an Empire*
  JEH - v57 - Mr '97 - p232+ [501+]
  JMH - v69 - Mr '97 - p170+ [501+]

Large, David Clay - *Germans to the Front*
  Choice - v34 - O '96 - p354 [51-250]

Lari, Sayyid - *Western Civilization through Muslim Eyes*
  JTWS - v13 - Fall '96 - p348+ [501+]

Larkcom, Joy - *Creative Vegetable Gardening*
  PW - v244 - My 5 '97 - p204 [51-250]

Larkham, Peter J - *Conservation and the City*
  CR - v269 - D '96 - p334 [51-250]

Larkin, Bruce D - *Nuclear Designs*
  APSR - v91 - Mr '97 - p239+ [501+]
  Choice - v34 - Ja '97 - p871 [51-250]
  Parameters - v26 - Win '96 - p147 [1-50]

Larkin, Colin - *The Guinness Encyclopedia of Popular Music. 2nd Ed., Vols. 1-6*
  r Choice - v34 - S '96 - p98+ [51-250]

Larkin, John - *Growing Payne*
  y Magpies - v11 - Jl '96 - p34+ [501+]

Larkin, Katrina J A - *Ruth and Esther*
  Rel St Rev - v23 - Ap '97 - p163+ [51-250]

Larkin, Maurice - *Religion, Politics, and Preferment in France since 1890*
  EHR - v112 - F '97 - p252+ [501+]

Larkin, Philip - *The Whitsun Weddings (Bennett). Audio Version*
  Spec - v277 - N 30 '96 - p56 [1-50]
Larkin, William J - *Acts*
  Rel St Rev - v23 - Ap '97 - p184 [51-250]
Larkins, William T - *Battleship and Cruiser Aircraft of the United States Navy 1910-1949*
  A & S Sm - v11 - D '96 - p92 [501+]
Larminie, Vivienne - *Wealth, Kinship and Culture*
  AHR - v102 - F '97 - p99+ [501+]
  Historian - v59 - Win '97 - p467+ [501+]
Larmore, Charles - *The Morals of Modernity*
  CPR - v16 - O '96 - p357+ [501+]
Larner, Gerald - *Maurice Ravel*
  LJ - v121 - D '96 - p96 [51-250]
  PW - v243 - S 30 '96 - p79 [1-50]
LaRoe, Edward T - *Our Living Resources*
  J Gov Info - v23 - S '96 - p550 [51-250]
La Rosa, Pablo - *Forbidden Fruit and Other Stories*
  Choice - v34 - O '96 - p278 [51-250]
LaRossa, Ralph - *The Modernization of Fatherhood*
  Choice - v34 - My '97 - p1584 [51-250]
  NS - v126 - Ap 25 '97 - p46+ [501+]
  PW - v243 - D 2 '96 - p54 [51-250]
Larousse, David Paul - *The Soup Bible*
  BL - v93 - Mr 15 '97 - p1216 [51-250]
  PW - v244 - Mr 3 '97 - p69 [51-250]
The Larousse Desk Reference
  r ARBA - v28 - '97 - p24+ [251-500]
Larousse Dictionary of Science and Technology
  r ARBA - v28 - '97 - p564+ [51-250]
Larousse English-Spanish, Spanish-English Dictionary. New Ed.
  r ARBA - v28 - '97 - p401+ [251-500]
Larousse Mini French-English, English-French Dictionary. New Ed.
  r ARBA - v28 - '97 - p390 [51-250]
Larousse Mini German-English, English-German Dictionary. New Ed.
  r ARBA - v28 - '97 - p391 [51-250]
Larousse Mini Italian-English, English-Italian Dictionary. New Ed.
  r ARBA - v28 - '97 - p394 [51-250]
Larousse Mini Spanish-English, English-Spanish Dictionary. New Ed.
  r ARBA - v28 - '97 - p402 [51-250]
Larrabee, F Stephen - *The Volatile Powder Kegs*
  Slav R - v55 - Sum '96 - p460+ [501+]
Larres, Klaus - *The Federal Republic of Germany since 1949*
  CR - v270 - F '97 - p111 [51-250]
  Politik Der Illusionen
  AHR - v101 - O '96 - p1213+ [501+]
Larrington, Caroline - *The Poetic Edda*
  SFS - v24 - Mr '97 - p181 [1-50]
Larroche, Caroline - *Corot from A to Z*
  c Ch BWatch - v6 - O '96 - p5 [51-250]
  c SLJ - v43 - Ja '97 - p130 [51-250]
Larsen, Clark Spencer - *Bioarchaeology of the Stillwater Marsh, Prehistoric Human Adaptation in the Western Great Basin*
  Am Sci - v85 - Ja '97 - p84+ [501+]
Larsen, Don - *The Perfect Yankee*
  NYTBR - v101 - O 13 '96 - p21 [51-250]
Larsen, Jeanne - *Manchu Palaces*
  KR - v64 - Ag 15 '96 - p1176 [251-500]
  LJ - v121 - S 15 '96 - p97 [51-250]
  PW - v243 - S 16 '96 - p70 [51-250]
  Tric - v6 - Spr '97 - p106+ [501+]
Larsen, Jeffrey A - *Arms Control*
  Parameters - v26 - Win '96 - p144+ [501+]
Larsen, Michael - *Uncertainty*
  BL - v92 - Ag '96 - p1886 [51-250]
  BW - v26 - O 6 '96 - p5 [501+]
  NYTBR - v101 - S 29 '96 - p20 [51-250]
Larsen, Mogens Trolle - *The Conquest of Assyria*
  LJ - v121 - N 15 '96 - p73 [51-250]
Larsen, Neil - *Reading North by South*
  Critm - v39 - Win '97 - p140+ [501+]
Larsen, Oivind - *The Shaping of a Profession*
  r BWatch - v18 - Mr '97 - p2 [51-250]
Larsen, Thor - *The Polar Bear Family Book*
  c Bks Keeps - N '96 - p15 [51-250]
Larson, Brooke - *Ethnicity, Markets, and Migration in the Andes*
  JEH - v56 - D '96 - p944+ [501+]
  JIH - v27 - Spr '97 - p738+ [251-500]
  J Soc H - v30 - Spr '97 - p793+ [501+]
Larson, C Kay - *'Til I Come Marching Home*
  Sea H - Win '96 - p45+ [251-500]

Larson, Charles R - *Under African Skies*
  LJ - v122 - Ap 15 '97 - p122+ [51-250]
Larson, David - *The Costly Consequences of Divorce*
  JMF - v58 - N '96 - p1044 [251-500]
Larson, Doran - *Marginalia*
  KR - v64 - N 1 '96 - p1555+ [251-500]
  NYTBR - v102 - F 16 '97 - p18 [251-500]
  PW - v243 - N 11 '96 - p57 [51-250]
Larson, Edward J - *Sex, Race, and Science*
  AHR - v101 - O '96 - p1293 [501+]
  Isis - v87 - D '96 - p759+ [501+]
  JIH - v27 - Aut '96 - p342+ [501+]
Larson, Gary - *Last Chapter and Worse*
  BL - v93 - N 15 '96 - p548 [1-50]
  BWatch - v17 - N '96 - p11 [51-250]
Larson, Gerald James - *India's Agony over Religion*
  JR - v77 - Ap '97 - p344+ [501+]
Larson, James L - *Interpreting Nature*
  AHR - v101 - O '96 - p1179+ [501+]
Larson, Kirby - *Cody and Quinn, Sitting in a Tree (Illus. by Nancy Poydar)*
  c CCB-B - v50 - S '96 - p19 [51-250]
  c HB Guide - v8 - Spr '97 - p59 [51-250]
Larson, Lois - *Software Directory for Fibre Artists. 3rd Ed.*
  r Choice - v34 - D '96 - p591 [51-250]
Larson, Reed - *Divergent Realities*
  CS - v25 - N '96 - p783+ [501+]
  Soc Ser R - v70 - S '96 - p489+ [501+]
  VOYA - v19 - D '96 - p256 [1-50]
Larson, Robert W - *Red Cloud: Warrior-Statesman of the Lakota Sioux*
  y BL - v93 - Mr 15 '97 - p1223 [51-250]
  KR - v65 - F 1 '97 - p201 [51-250]
  LJ - v122 - Ap 1 '97 - p106 [51-250]
Larson, Rodger - *What I Know Now*
  y BL - v93 - My 1 '97 - p1489 [51-250]
  y HB - v73 - Mr '97 - p200 [51-250]
  y KR - v65 - Mr 1 '97 - p383 [51-250]
  y PW - v244 - Mr 31 '97 - p76 [51-250]
Larsson, Bjorn - *The Celtic Ring*
  y BL - v93 - Mr 15 '97 - p1226 [51-250]
  PW - v244 - F 24 '97 - p70 [51-250]
Lartaguy, Jean - *Mourir Pour Jerusalem*
  BL - v93 - Ja '97 - p827 [1-50]
LaRue, C Steven - *Handel and His Singers*
  Albion - v28 - Fall '96 - p500+ [501+]
  Eight-C St - v30 - Win '96 - p199+ [501+]
  Notes - v53 - D '96 - p457+ [501+]
La Sale, Antoine De - *Saintre. Vols. 1-2*
  Specu - v72 - Ja '97 - p104+ [251-500]
LaSalle, Peter - *Hockey Sur Glace*
  CSM - v89 - Ja 14 '97 - p15 [51-250]
  KR - v64 - Ag 15 '96 - p1177 [251-500]
  LJ - v121 - S 15 '96 - p99 [51-250]
  NYTBR - v102 - F 2 '97 - p21 [251-500]
  PW - v243 - S 2 '96 - p113 [51-250]
  VLS - Win '96 - p27 [501+]
Lasater, Martin L - *The Changing of the Guard*
  AAPSS-A - v546 - Jl '96 - p161+ [501+]
  The New Pacific Community
  Choice - v34 - O '96 - p357 [51-250]
  U.S. Interests in the New Taiwan
  Ch Rev Int - v3 - Fall '96 - p473+ [501+]
Lasch, Christopher - *Women and the Common Life*
  KR - v64 - N 15 '96 - p1655 [251-500]
  LATBR - Ja 12 '97 - p10 [501+]
  LJ - v122 - Ja '97 - p127 [51-250]
  NS - v126 - Mr 21 '97 - p53+ [501+]
  NYTBR - v102 - Ja 19 '97 - p8 [501+]
  Obs - Mr 16 '97 - p17* [501+]
  Wil Q - v21 - Win '97 - p96+ [251-500]
LaScolea, Len J - *Quinolones in Pulmonary Tuberculosis Management*
  SciTech - v20 - D '96 - p43 [51-250]
Lasdun, James - *Woman Police Officer in Elevator*
  LJ - v122 - Ja '97 - p103+ [51-250]
Laselva, Samuel V - *The Moral Foundations of Canadian Federalism*
  Choice - v34 - Ja '97 - p868 [51-250]
Laser, Michael - *The Rain (Illus. by Jeffrey Greene)*
  c BL - v93 - Ap 1 '97 - p1338 [51-250]
  c CBRS - v25 - Mr '97 - p87+ [1-50]
  c PW - v244 - Ap 7 '97 - p91 [51-250]
Laserna, J J - *Modern Techniques in Raman Spectroscopy*
  SciTech - v20 - D '96 - p24 [51-250]
Laserna Gaitan, Antonio Ignacio - *Tierra, Gobierno Local, Y Actividad Misionera En La Comunidad Indigena Del Oriente Venezolano*
  HAHR - v76 - N '96 - p787+ [501+]

Lasers and Electro-Optics Society (Institute of Electrical and Electronics Engineers). Meeting (7th: 1994: Boston, Mass.) - *LEOS '94 Conference Proceedings. Vols. 1-2*
  SciTech - v20 - D '96 - p66 [51-250]
Lash, Nicholas - *The Beginning and the End of Religion*
  CR - v270 - F '97 - p112 [51-250]
Lasher, Margot - *And the Animals Will Teach You*
  y Kliatt - v31 - Mr '97 - p34 [51-250]
  PW - v243 - N 4 '96 - p70 [51-250]
Lashgari, Dierdre - *Violence, Silence and Anger*
  AL - v68 - D '96 - p882 [51-250]
Lashner, William - *Veritas*
  BL - v93 - D 15 '96 - p692 [51-250]
  KR - v64 - D 1 '96 - p1693+ [251-500]
  PW - v243 - D 9 '96 - p59 [51-250]
  Veritas (Howard). Audio Version
  PW - v244 - Mr 3 '97 - p30 [51-250]
Laskin, David - *Braving the Elements*
  BL - v93 - Ja '97 - p760 [1-50]
  y BL - v93 - D 1 '96 - p664 [1-50]
  A Common Life
  VQR - v72 - Aut '96 - p142* [1-50]
Lasky, Kathryn - *Beyond the Burning Time*
  y Kliatt - v30 - N '96 - p9 [51-250]
  Days of the Dead (Illus. by Christopher Knight)
  y SE - v60 - N '96 - p400 [51-250]
  The Gates of the Wind (Illus. by Janet Stevens)
  c New Ad - v9 - Fall '96 - p327+ [501+]
  A Journey to the New World
  c CBRS - v25 - S '96 - p11 [51-250]
  c CCB-B - v50 - O '96 - p55+ [51-250]
  c Ch BWatch - v6 - S '96 - p5 [1-50]
  c HB Guide - v8 - Spr '97 - p64 [51-250]
  c Par - v71 - D '96 - p254 [51-250]
  c PW - v243 - S 2 '96 - p131 [51-250]
  c SLJ - v42 - Ag '96 - p144 [51-250]
  c Trib Bks - My 4 '97 - p1+ [501+]
  y VOYA - v19 - O '96 - p210+ [251-500]
  The Librarian Who Measured the Earth (Illus. by Kevin Hawkes)
  c Math T - v90 - F '97 - p119 [51-250]
  Lunch Bunnies (Illus. by Marylin Hafner)
  c BL - v93 - S 15 '96 - p247 [51-250]
  c HB Guide - v8 - Spr '97 - p35 [51-250]
  c NYTBR - v102 - Ja 19 '97 - p24 [1-50]
  c PW - v243 - N 4 '96 - p48 [1-50]
  c SLJ - v42 - S '96 - p182 [51-250]
  The Most Beautiful Roof in the World (Illus. by Christopher G Knight)
  c BL - v93 - Ap 1 '97 - p1330 [51-250]
  c HB - v73 - My '97 - p341 [51-250]
  Pond Year (Illus. by Mike Bostock)
  c Bks Keeps - Jl '96 - p9 [51-250]
  c RT - v50 - O '96 - p154 [51-250]
  She's Wearing a Dead Bird on Her Head (Illus. by David Catrow)
  c LA - v73 - O '96 - p432 [51-250]
  c RT - v50 - O '96 - p137+ [1-50]
  c RT - v50 - O '96 - p154 [51-250]
  True North
  y BL - v93 - N 15 '96 - p579 [51-250]
  y BW - v26 - D 8 '96 - p21 [51-250]
  y CBRS - v25 - D '96 - p47 [51-250]
  y CCB-B - v50 - N '96 - p104 [51-250]
  y HB Guide - v8 - Spr '97 - p81 [51-250]
  y KR - v64 - O 1 '96 - p1470 [51-250]
  y SLJ - v42 - D '96 - p139 [51-250]
Laslett, Barbara - *Rethinking the Political*
  R&R Bk N - v11 - D '96 - p42 [1-50]
Laslett, John H M - *The United Mine Workers of America*
  Choice - v34 - F '97 - p1009 [51-250]
Laslett, Stephanie - *The Monster Party (Illus. by Nigel McMullen)*
  c PW - v243 - S 30 '96 - p86 [51-250]
  c SLJ - v42 - Ap '97 - p98 [51-250]
Lasley, Paul - *Beyond Amber Waves of Grain*
  CS - v26 - Ja '97 - p64+ [501+]
Lasner, Mark Samuels - *Mothers and Others*
  ELT - v39 - 4 '96 - p522+ [501+]
  A Selective Checklist of the Published Work of Aubrey Beardsley
  r AB - v98 - N 25 '96 - p1832 [51-250]
  r Nine-C Lit - v50 - Mr '96 - p535+ [501+]
Lasocki, David - *The Bassanos: Venetian Musicians and Instrument Makers in England 1531-1665*
  Notes - v53 - D '96 - p451+ [501+]
Lassell, Michael - *Two Hearts Desire*
  Advocate - F 18 '97 - p61 [51-250]
Lasserre, Philippe - *Strategies for Asia Pacific*
  Choice - v34 - S '96 - p172 [51-250]

Lassiter, Sybil M - *Multicultural Clients*
Soc Ser R - v70 - S '96 - p500 [51-250]
Lassner, Jacob - *Demonizing the Queen of Sheba*
JAAR - v64 - Win '96 - p874+ [501+]
Last Call: A Legacy of Madness
Sm Pr R - v29 - F '97 - p4+ [501+]
Laster, James - *Catalogue of Choral Music Arranged in Biblical Order. 2nd Ed.*
r ARBA - v28 - '97 - p481+ [251-500]
r Choice - v34 - Mr '97 - p1138 [51-250]
r R&R Bk N - v12 - F '97 - p69 [51-250]
Laszlo, Ervin - *Evolution: The General Theory*
SciTech - v21 - Mr '97 - p35 [1-50]
The Interconnected Universe
Choice - v34 - S '96 - p166 [51-250]
The Whispering Pond
Choice - v34 - Ap '97 - p1359 [51-250]
New Sci - v152 - N 23 '96 - p46 [1-50]
PW - v243 - O 7 '96 - p53+ [51-250]
Laszlo, Pierre - *Organic Reactions, Simplicity and Logic*
J Chem Ed - v74 - Ap '97 - p383 [51-250]
Latacz, Joachin - *Homer: His Art and His World*
Choice - v34 - N '96 - p452 [51-250]
Latash, Mark L - *Dexterity and Its Development*
Choice - v34 - O '96 - p321 [51-250]
Latawski, Paul - *Contemporary Nationalism in East Central Europe*
Slav R - v55 - Fall '96 - p662+ [501+]
Lateiner, Donald - *Sardonic Smile*
Choice - v34 - S '96 - p121 [51-250]
Historian - v59 - Fall '96 - p195+ [501+]
Latham, A J H - *Japanese Industrialisation and the Asian Economy*
EHR - v112 - F '97 - p209+ [251-500]
Latham, Aaron - *The Ballad of Gussie and Clyde*
PW - v244 - Ap 21 '97 - p51 [51-250]
Lathen, Emma - *Brewing Up a Storm*
BL - v93 - D 15 '96 - p712+ [51-250]
KR - v64 - O 15 '96 - p1497 [51-250]
LJ - v121 - D '96 - p151 [51-250]
NYTBR - v101 - D 8 '96 - p50 [51-250]
PW - v243 - O 21 '96 - p73+ [51-250]
Lathrop, Kathleen - *Amy Angel Goes Home*
c Ch BWatch - v6 - D '96 - p3 [51-250]
Latin America 1996
Parameters - v26 - Win '96 - p154 [1-50]
Latin America and the Caribbean
J Gov Info - v23 - S '96 - p682 [51-250]
Latina
p LJ - v122 - My 1 '97 - p43 [51-250]
Latins Anonymous
BL - v93 - Mr 1 '97 - p1104 [51-250]
Latour, Bruno - *Aramis or the Love of Technology*
Am Sci - v85 - Mr '97 - p196 [501+]
CS - v26 - Ja '97 - p90+ [501+]
Nature - v383 - S 19 '96 - p230 [501+]
NS - v125 - S 13 '96 - p47 [51-250]
NYTBR - v101 - Jl 21 '96 - p14 [501+]
VLS - S '96 - p10+ [501+]
LaTour, Susan - *Dead Reckoning*
Arm Det - v29 - Sum '96 - p361 [51-250]
LaTourrette, Joe - *Watching Wildlife*
LJ - v122 - Ap 15 '97 - p112 [51-250]
Latourrette, Victor - *Twelve Months of Monastery Soups*
LJ - v121 - S 15 '96 - p90 [51-250]
Lattany, Kristin Hunter - *Kinfolks*
Bloom Rev - v17 - Ja '97 - p19 [1-50]
KR - v64 - S 15 '96 - p1344 [251-500]
PW - v243 - S 30 '96 - p60 [51-250]
Lattimore, Deborah Nourse - *Arabian Nights (Illus. by Deborah Nourse Lattimore)*
c RT - v50 - S '96 - p59 [51-250]
Frida Maria
c PW - v244 - Ap 21 '97 - p74 [51-250]
The Winged Cat
c Magpies - v11 - Jl '96 - p27 [51-250]
Lattis, James M - *Between Copernicus and Galileo*
CH - v66 - Mr '97 - p120+ [501+]
Latzel, Monika - *Insight Compact Guides Dominican Republic*
r BL - v93 - S 15 '96 - p210 [1-50]
Lau, Evelyn - *Runaway*
y TES - O 25 '96 - p8* [251-500]
Lau, Joseph S M - *The Columbia Anthology of Modern Chinese Literature*
Ch Rev Int - v3 - Fall '96 - p476+ [501+]
Lau, Kwan - *Feng Shui for Today*
BWatch - v17 - N '96 - p4 [51-250]

Lauber, Patricia - *Flood: Wrestling with the Mississippi*
c HB Guide - v8 - Spr '97 - p174 [51-250]
c KR - v64 - O 1 '96 - p1470 [51-250]
c SLJ - v42 - N '96 - p115 [51-250]
c SLJ - v42 - D '96 - p30 [1-50]
How Dinosaurs Came to Be
c HB Guide - v7 - Fall '96 - p333 [51-250]
Hurricanes: Earth's Mightiest Storms
c BL - v93 - O 1 '96 - p346 [51-250]
y BL - v93 - Ap 1 '97 - p1308 [1-50]
c BW - v26 - S 1 '96 - p7 [251-500]
c CCB-B - v50 - O '96 - p67 [51-250]
c HB - v72 - S '96 - p618 [51-250]
c HB Guide - v8 - Spr '97 - p113 [51-250]
c LATBR - S 22 '96 - p15 [51-250]
c Par - v71 - D '96 - p254+ [51-250]
c SLJ - v42 - S '96 - p218 [51-250]
Who Eats What? (Illus. by Holly Keller)
c Emerg Lib - v23 - My '96 - p45 [51-250]
You're Aboard Spaceship Earth (Illus. by Holly Keller)
c BL - v92 - Ag '96 - p1903 [51-250]
c HB - v72 - S '96 - p618 [51-250]
c HB Guide - v7 - Fall '96 - p332 [51-250]
c SLJ - v42 - Ag '96 - p138+ [51-250]
Laubner, Ellie - *Fashions of the Roaring '20s*
Ant & CM - v102 - Mr '97 - p33 [51-250]
The Laude in the Middle Ages
TranslRevS - v1 - My '95 - p2 [51-250]
Lauderdale, James Maitland, Earl of - *Lauderdale's Notes on Adam Smith's Wealth of Nations*
JEL - v34 - D '96 - p2012 [51-250]
R&R Bk N - v11 - N '96 - p24 [51-250]
Lauderdale, John Vance - *After Wounded Knee*
Choice - v34 - N '96 - p526 [51-250]
WHQ - v28 - Spr '97 - p77+ [251-500]
Laue, Ingrid E - *Pictorialism in the Fictional Miniatures of Albert Paris Gutersloh*
R&R Bk N - v12 - F '97 - p91 [51-250]
Lauersen, Niels H - *The Complete Book of Breast Care*
BL - v93 - N 1 '96 - p470 [51-250]
LJ - v121 - O '96 - p84 [51-250]
PW - v243 - O 21 '96 - p80 [51-250]
Laufer, Gabriel - *Introduction to Optics and Lasers in Engineering*
r Choice - v34 - Mr '97 - p1191 [51-250]
SciTech - v20 - D '96 - p62 [51-250]
Laughing at the Tao
Rel St Rev - v23 - Ap '97 - p205 [51-250]
Laughland, John - *The Tainted Source*
Obs - Mr 9 '97 - p15* [501+]
TLS - Ap 11 '97 - p14 [501+]
Laughlin, Burgess - *The Aristotle Adventure*
CLW - v66 - Je '96 - p37 [251-500]
Laughlin, James - *The Secret Room*
BL - v93 - Ap 1 '97 - p1277 [51-250]
LJ - v122 - Ap 1 '97 - p97+ [51-250]
PW - v244 - F 24 '97 - p87 [51-250]
Laughlin, Karen - *Theatre and Feminist Aesthetics*
Theat J - v48 - O '96 - p398+ [501+]
Laughlin, Kay - *The Children's Song Index 1978-1993*
r ARBA - v28 - '97 - p473 [51-250]
r RQ - v35 - Sum '96 - p548+ [251-500]
Laughlin, Rosemary - *The Great Iron Link*
y Ch BWatch - v6 - D '96 - p2 [1-50]
c HB Guide - v8 - Spr '97 - p174 [51-250]
Laughton, Bruce - *Honore Daumier*
Atl - v279 - F '97 - p110 [51-250]
r Choice - v34 - Ap '97 - p1325 [51-250]
Laukel, Hans Gerold - *The Desert Fox Family Book (Illus. by Hans Gerold Laukel)*
c HB Guide - v7 - Fall '96 - p345 [51-250]
c NYTBR - v101 - S 8 '96 - p28 [1-50]
c RT - v50 - F '97 - p425 [51-250]
Laumann, Edward O - *The Social Organization of Sexuality*
AAPSS-A - v549 - Ja '97 - p205+ [501+]
Launius, Roger D - *Kingdom on the Mississippi Revisited*
Choice - v34 - O '96 - p349 [51-250]
WHQ - v28 - Spr '97 - p83+ [501+]
Laure - *Laure: The Collected Writings*
Lon R Bks - v18 - N 28 '96 - p26+ [501+]
Laurel County Historical Society - *A Pictorial History of World War II Veterans from Laurel County, Kentucky*
r EGH - v50 - N '96 - p168 [51-250]
Laurel Review
p Sm Pr R - v29 - F '97 - p13+ [51-250]
Lauren, Jill - *Succeeding with LD*
y Kliatt - v31 - My '97 - p22 [51-250]
Laurence, Anne - *Women in England 1500-1760*
EHR - v111 - S '96 - p982+ [251-500]
Theol St - v58 - Mr '97 - p189+ [251-500]

Laurence, Janet - *Death at the Table*
KR - v65 - Mr 1 '97 - p338 [51-250]
PW - v244 - F 17 '97 - p213 [51-250]
Laurence, K O - *A Question of Labour*
AHR - v101 - O '96 - p1320 [501+]
Laurence, Margaret - *A Very Large Soul*
Can Lit - Win '96 - p135+ [501+]
Dal R - v75 - Spr '95 - p99+ [501+]
Essays CW - Spr '96 - p145+ [501+]
Laurence, Mary Leefe - *Daughter of the Regiment*
Roundup M - v3 - Ag '96 - p25 [251-500]
WHQ - v27 - Win '96 - p543 [251-500]
Laurens, Du - *Imirce Ou La Fille De La Nature*
MLR - v91 - Jl '96 - p727 [51-250]
Laurens, Jacques - *Kleber En Egypte 1798-1800. Vols. 3-4*
MEJ - v50 - Aut '96 - p625 [51-250]
Laurentin, Marie - *Les Livres Africains Pour La Jeunesse*
r Bkbird - v34 - Spr '96 - p55 [51-250]
Lauret, Maria - *Liberating Literature*
Signs - v22 - Win '97 - p484+ [501+]
Lauria, Mickey - *Reconstructing Urban Regime Theory*
R&R Bk N - v12 - F '97 - p61 [51-250]
Laurie, Clayton D - *The Propaganda Warriors*
Choice - v34 - O '96 - p349 [51-250]
For Aff - v75 - S '96 - p147 [51-250]
J Mil H - v61 - Ja '97 - p185+ [251-500]
Parameters - v26 - Aut '96 - p155+ [501+]
Laurie, Hugh - *The Gun Seller*
KR - v65 - Ap 1 '97 - p490+ [251-500]
LJ - v122 - Ap 15 '97 - p118 [51-250]
PW - v244 - F 17 '97 - p208 [51-250]
Lauritzen, Steffen L - *Graphical Models*
Choice - v34 - My '97 - p1536 [51-250]
Lauture, Denize - *Running the Road to ABC (Illus. by Reynold Ruffins)*
c HB Guide - v7 - Fall '96 - p264 [51-250]
c LATBR - Jl 7 '96 - p11 [51-250]
Lauwerier, Hans - *Fractals: Endlessly Repeated Geometrical Figures*
Math T - v89 - My '96 - p436 [501+]
Lauwers-Rech, Magda - *Nazi Germany and the American Germanists*
Ger Q - v69 - Sum '96 - p341+ [501+]
Laux, Marcus - *Natural Woman, Natural Menopause*
LJ - v122 - My 1 '97 - p133+ [51-250]
PW - v244 - Ap 21 '97 - p67 [51-250]
Lav, Ercumend Behzad - *Butun Eserleri*
WLT - v71 - Win '97 - p219+ [501+]
Lavallee, Louis - *La Prairie En Nouvelle-France 1647-1760*
Can Hist R - v78 - Mr '97 - p147+ [501+]
Lavallee, Ronald - *Tchipayuk, or the Way of the Wolf*
TranslRevS - v1 - My '95 - p20 [1-50]
Lavatori, Gerard Ponziano - *Language and Money in Rabelais*
R&R Bk N - v11 - N '96 - p68 [1-50]
Lavelle, Sheila - *Harry's Aunt*
c TES - Jl 5 '96 - pR6 [1-50]
Snowy: The Christmas Dog (Illus. by Susan Scott)
c Bks Keeps - N '96 - p21 [1-50]
Lavenda, Bernard H - *Thermodynamics of Extremes*
Choice - v34 - S '96 - p166 [51-250]
Lavender, David - *Snowbound: The Tragic Story of the Donner Party*
c HB - v72 - S '96 - p618+ [51-250]
c HB Guide - v7 - Fall '96 - p387 [51-250]
Lavendhomme, Rene - *Basic Concepts of Synthetic Differential Geometry*
Choice - v34 - Ap '97 - p1376 [51-250]
SciTech - v20 - S '96 - p12 [51-250]
Laver, Michael - *Making and Breaking Governments*
JEL - v34 - D '96 - p2029 [51-250]
Lavergne, Gary M - *A Sniper in the Tower*
LJ - v122 - My 1 '97 - p123 [51-250]
PW - v244 - Ap 28 '97 - p65 [251-500]
Lavie, Peretz - *The Enchanted World of Sleep*
Choice - v34 - O '96 - p364+ [51-250]
Nature - v384 - N 7 '96 - p37 [501+]
Lavigne, Marie - *The Economics of Transition*
Econ J - v106 - S '96 - p1426+ [501+]
Lavigne, Yves - *Hells Angels: Into the Abyss*
BIC - v25 - N '96 - p30 [501+]
Lavin, Audrey A P - *Aspects of the Novelist*
ELT - v39 - 4 '96 - p494+ [501+]
Lavin, David E - *Changing the Odds*
AJS - v102 - Ja '97 - p1199+ [501+]
Choice - v34 - N '96 - p511 [51-250]
Lavin, Deborah - *From Empire to International Commonwealth*
Choice - v34 - S '96 - p187 [51-250]

Lavin, Michael R - *Understanding the Census*
  r ARBA - v28 - '97 - p324 [251-500]
  r BL - v93 - S 1 '96 - p172 [251-500]
  r Choice - v34 - N '96 - p432 [51-250]
  r JEL - v34 - D '96 - p2068 [51-250]
  r RQ - v36 - Fall '96 - p141+ [501+]
Lavine, Shaughan - *Understanding the Infinite*
     Phil R - v105 - Ap '96 - p256+ [501+]
Laving, A S - *Thermal Transport in Laser-Materials Interaction*
     SciTech - v21 - Mr '97 - p99 [51-250]
Lavington, Camille - *You've Only Got Three Seconds*
     BL - v93 - Ja '97 - p794 [51-250]
Lavis, Steve - *Cock-a-Doodle-Doo (Illus. by Steve Lavis)*
  c BL - v93 - N 15 '96 - p592 [51-250]
  c JB - v60 - O '96 - p185 [51-250]
  c KR - v64 - N 15 '96 - p1671 [51-250]
  c PW - v243 - D 16 '96 - p58 [51-250]
  c Sch Lib - v44 - Ag '96 - p99 [51-250]
  c SLJ - v43 - Ja '97 - p84 [51-250]
Lavrakas, Paul J - *Presidential Polls and the News Media*
     APSR - v90 - S '96 - p654 [501+]
Lavrentiev, Aleksandr Nikolaevich - *Alexander Rodchenko: Photography 1924-1954*
     BL - v93 - S 15 '96 - p200 [51-250]
     LJ - v121 - N 1 '96 - p64 [51-250]
     NYTBR - v101 - D 15 '96 - p36 [501+]
     PW - v243 - Jl 22 '96 - p219+ [51-250]
Lavrin, Asuncion - *Women, Feminism, and Social Change in Argentina, Chile, and Uruguay 1890-1940*
     AHR - v102 - F '97 - p245+ [501+]
     JIH - v27 - Spr '97 - p737+ [251-500]
Lavy, George - *Germany and Israel*
     R&R Bk N - v12 - F '97 - p16 [51-250]
Law, Alma - *Meyerhold, Eisenstein and Biomechanics*
     Theat J - v48 - D '96 - p519+ [501+]
Law, Janice - *Cross-Check*
     BL - v93 - My 1 '97 - p1482 [51-250]
     KR - v65 - Mr 15 '97 - p420 [51-250]
Law, Jonathan - *Brewer's Cinema*
  r TES - N 22 '96 - p8* [1-50]
Law, Jules David - *The Rhetoric of Empiricism*
     MLR - v91 - Jl '96 - p679+ [501+]
     MP - v94 - Ag '96 - p104+ [501+]
     Poetics T - v17 - Sum '96 - p270+ [501+]
Law Books and Serials in Print 1996. Vols. 1-3
  r ARBA - v28 - '97 - p217 [251-500]
Law in Humanitarian Crises. Vols. 1-2
     J Gov Info - v23 - S '96 - p669 [1-50]
Law of the Sea Institute. Conference (27th: 1993: Seoul, Korea) - *The Role of the Ocean in the 21st Century*
     NWCR - v49 - Aut '96 - p144 [251-500]
The Law of the Sea (United Nations)
     R&R Bk N - v11 - N '96 - p51 [51-250]
Law Society (Great Britain) - *Catalogue of the Law Society's Mendham Collection*
     CH - v65 - S '96 - p514+ [251-500]
Lawal, Ibironke O - *Metalworking in Africa South of the Sahara*
  r T&C - v38 - Ja '97 - p241+ [501+]
Lawall, Sarah - *Reading World Literature*
     Comp L - v49 - Win '97 - p76+ [501+]
Lawhead, Stephen R - *Byzantium*
     BL - v93 - S 1 '96 - p62 [51-250]
     Ch Today - v40 - D 9 '96 - p45+ [501+]
  y VOYA - v19 - F '97 - p336+ [51-250]
  Grail
     KR - v65 - My 1 '97 - p686 [51-250]
  Pendragon (Davidson). Audio Version
  y Kliatt - v31 - Ja '97 - p44 [51-250]
Lawler, Jennifer - *Songs of Life*
     LJ - v121 - N 1 '96 - p42 [1-50]
Lawler, Veronica - *I Was Dreaming to Come to America*
  c LA - v73 - O '96 - p430+ [51-250]
Lawless, Julia - *The Illustrated Encyclopedia of Essential Oils*
  r ARBA - v28 - '97 - p612 [51-250]
  r Quill & Q - v62 - Ag '96 - p32 [51-250]
Lawless, Richard I - *Algeria. Rev. Ed.*
  r ARBA - v28 - '97 - p51 [251-500]
  r Choice - v34 - O '96 - p253+ [51-250]
Lawliss, Chuck - *The Early American Sourcebook*
  r BL - v93 - S 15 '96 - p210 [1-50]
Lawlor, Laurie - *Come Away with Me*
  c SLJ - v42 - N '96 - p108 [51-250]
  Take to the Sky
  c SLJ - v42 - N '96 - p108 [51-250]

Where Will This Shoe Take You?
  c BL - v93 - N 15 '96 - p583 [51-250]
  c CCB-B - v50 - Ja '97 - p178 [51-250]
  c HB - v73 - Mr '97 - p212+ [51-250]
  c HB Guide - v8 - Spr '97 - p98 [51-250]
  c KR - v64 - N 1 '96 - p1602 [51-250]
  c NYTBR - v102 - Ja 19 '97 - p24 [1-50]
Lawniczak, Anna T - *Pattern Formation and Lattice Gas Automata*
     SIAM Rev - v38 - D '96 - p714 [1-50]
     SIAM Rev - v39 - Mr '97 - p176 [51-250]
Lawrence, Anthony - *The Viewfinder*
     Aust Bk R - O '96 - p55+ [501+]
Lawrence, Beverly Hall - *Reviving the Spirit*
     Bl S - v26 - Sum '96 - p66 [1-50]
Lawrence, Bruce B - *Defenders of God*
     MEJ - v50 - Aut '96 - p630 [51-250]
Lawrence, C H - *The Friars: The Impact of the Early Mendicant Movement on Western Society*
     EHR - v111 - S '96 - p955+ [251-500]
**Lawrence, Charles, 1943- ** - *We Won't Go Back*
  y BL - v93 - F 15 '97 - p981 [51-250]
     KR - v65 - F 1 '97 - p202 [251-500]
     PW - v244 - Ja 20 '97 - p388 [51-250]
Lawrence, Clifford M - *An Introduction to Dermatological Surgery*
     SciTech - v21 - Mr '97 - p60 [1-50]
Lawrence, D H - *Lady Chatterley's Lover*
     Crit Q - v38 - Aut '96 - p3+ [501+]
  The Selected Letters of D.H. Lawrence
     Obs - Ja 26 '97 - p16* [501+]
  Twilight in Italy and Other Essays
     RES - v47 - N '96 - p625+ [501+]
  The Woman Who Rode Away and Other Stories
     ELT - v39 - 4 '96 - p478+ [501+]
  Women in Love
     PQ - v74 - Fall '95 - p443+ [501+]
Lawrence, David G - *The Collapse of the Democratic Presidential Majority*
     Choice - v34 - O '96 - p361 [51-250]
Lawrence, Jacob - *Harriet and the Promised Land (Illus. by Jacob Lawrence)*
  c PW - v244 - Ja 13 '97 - p77 [1-50]
Lawrence, James - *Sweet Maple*
     CAY - v16 - Fall '95 - p6 [51-250]
Lawrence, Jo - *How to Sparkle at Alphabet Skills (Illus. by Kate Ford)*
  c TES - D 13 '96 - p43 [51-250]
  How to Sparkle at Nursery Rhymes (Illus. by Kate Ford)
  c TES - D 13 '96 - p43 [51-250]
  How to Sparkle at Phonics (Illus. by Kate Ford)
  c TES - D 13 '96 - p43 [51-250]
  How to Sparkle at Prediction Skills (Illus. by Kate Ford)
  c TES - D 13 '96 - p43 [51-250]
Lawrence, Karen R - *Penelope Voyages*
     MLR - v91 - O '96 - p978+ [501+]
Lawrence, Louise - *Children of the Dust*
  y TES - F 28 '97 - pR7 [501+]
  Dream-Weaver
  y BL - v93 - O 1 '96 - p349 [51-250]
  c Ch BWatch - v7 - F '97 - p4 [51-250]
  c Ch BWatch - v7 - F '97 - p4 [51-250]
  y HB Guide - v8 - Spr '97 - p81 [1-50]
  c KR - v64 - O 15 '96 - p1535 [51-250]
  y PW - v243 - O 7 '96 - p77 [51-250]
  c SLJ - v42 - O '96 - p148 [51-250]
  y VOYA - v19 - F '97 - p337 [251-500]
  Dreamweaver
  y TES - Mr 21 '97 - p14* [501+]
  Journey through Llandor
  c Magpies - v11 - S '96 - p34 [251-500]
  The Road to Irriyan
  c JB - v60 - D '96 - p278+ [51-250]
  c Magpies - v11 - S '96 - p34 [251-500]
  The Shadow of Mordican
  c JB - v60 - O '96 - p203 [51-250]
  c Magpies - v11 - S '96 - p34 [251-500]
  y Sch Lib - v45 - F '97 - p47 [51-250]
Lawrence, Margaret - *Hearts and Bones*
     BL - v93 - S 1 '96 - p67 [51-250]
Lawrence, Martha C - *The Cold Heart of Capricorn*
     BL - v93 - Ja '97 - p825 [51-250]
     KR - v64 - N 1 '96 - p1567 [51-250]
     LJ - v122 - Ja '97 - p153 [1-50]
     PW - v243 - N 18 '96 - p65 [51-250]
  Murder in Scorpio
     PW - v243 - O 21 '96 - p79 [1-50]
Lawrence, Peter - *Management in the USA*
     Per Psy - v50 - Spr '97 - p237+ [501+]
Lawrence, R D - *A Shriek in the Forest Night*
     BW - v27 - Ja 5 '97 - p13 [51-250]

Lawrence, Richard Russell - *The Period House*
  r LATBR - D 8 '96 - p4 [1-50]
     LJ - v121 - O 1 '96 - p74 [51-250]
Lawrence, Robert Z - *Regionalism, Multilateralism, and Deeper Integration*
     JEL - v34 - D '96 - p2082 [51-250]
     R&R Bk N - v11 - N '96 - p34 [51-250]
  A Vision for the World Economy
     For Aff - v75 - N '96 - p149+ [251-500]
     JEL - v34 - D '96 - p2052 [51-250]
Lawrence, Rod - *Painting Wildlife Textures Step by Step*
     LJ - v122 - Mr 15 '97 - p63 [51-250]
Lawrence, Starling - *Legacies: Stories*
     HR - v49 - Aut '96 - p483+ [501+]
     LATBR - My 12 '96 - p10 [51-250]
     Sew R - v104 - Jl '96 - pR50 [251-500]
     VQR - v72 - Aut '96 - p128*+ [51-250]
Lawrence, Sue - *Feasting on Herbs*
     BL - v93 - Ja '97 - p800 [51-250]
Lawrence, Susan C - *Charitable Knowledge*
     Choice - v34 - D '96 - p644 [51-250]
Lawrence, William - *The Pyramid and the Urn*
     EHR - v112 - F '97 - p203+ [501+]
Laws, Stephen - *Daemonic*
     Necro - Sum '96 - p25+ [251-500]
  Macabre
     Necro - Sum '96 - p25+ [251-500]
Lawson, Andrew - *The Gardener's Book of Color*
     Hort - v74 - D '96 - p55+ [251-500]
  The Gardener's Book of Colour
     TES - Ag 23 '96 - p22 [51-250]
Lawson, Colin - *The Cambridge Companion to the Clarinet*
  r Notes - v53 - Mr '97 - p779+ [501+]
  Mozart: Clarinet Concerto
     TLS - Ap 11 '97 - p19 [501+]
Lawson, Edward - *Encyclopedia of Human Rights. 2nd Ed.*
  r ARBA - v28 - '97 - p232 [51-250]
Lawson, Edwin D - *More Names and Naming*
  r ARBA - v28 - '97 - p170 [51-250]
  r Names - v44 - Je '96 - p143+ [501+]
Lawson, Fred H - *Why Syria Goes to War*
     Choice - v34 - Ap '97 - p1388 [51-250]
     For Aff - v76 - Mr '97 - p193+ [51-250]
Lawson, Julie - *Cougar Cove (Illus. by David Powell)*
  c Quill & Q - v62 - My '96 - p34 [51-250]
  c SLJ - v42 - S '96 - p204 [51-250]
  Danger Game
  y HB Guide - v7 - Fall '96 - p302 [51-250]
  y VOYA - v19 - O '96 - p211 [251-500]
  Too Many Suns (Illus. by Martin Springett)
  c BIC - v25 - N '96 - p34 [501+]
  Whatever You Do, Don't Go Near That Canoe! (Illus. by Werner Zimmermann)
  c BIC - v25 - O '96 - p28 [251-500]
  c Ch Bk News - v20 - Win '97 - p28+ [51-250]
  c Quill & Q - v62 - O '96 - p46 [251-500]
Lawson, Lewis A - *Walker Percy's Feminine Characters*
     AL - v69 - Mr '97 - p252 [51-250]
**Lawson, Mark, 1962- ** - *Idlewild or Everything Is Subject to Change*
     Obs - Ag 25 '96 - p18* [51-250]
  John Keane: Conflicts of Interest
     Choice - v34 - S '96 - p113 [51-250]
Lawson, Nigel - *The Nigel Lawson Diet Book*
     Spec - v277 - O 5 '96 - p55 [501+]
Lawson, Robert - *Mr. Revere and I (Porter). Audio Version*
  c BL - v93 - My 15 '97 - p1595 [1-50]
  Rabbit Hill (Caruso). Audio Version
  c SLJ - v42 - Ag '96 - p64 [51-250]
Lawson, Stephanie - *Tradition versus Democracy in the South Pacific*
     Choice - v34 - N '96 - p531 [51-250]
Lawson-Hall, Toni - *Hydrangeas: A Gardener's Guide*
     Hort - v74 - D '96 - p61 [51-250]
Lawton, Carol L - *Attic Document Reliefs*
     AJA - v100 - O '96 - p791+ [501+]
Lawton, David - *Blasphemy*
     CH - v66 - Mr '97 - p177+ [501+]
Lawton, John - *Black Out*
     Arm Det - v29 - Fall '96 - p402 [51-250]
Lawton, John H - *Extinction Rates*
     BioSci - v47 - Mr '97 - p192+ [501+]
Lawyers Committee for Human Rights (U.S.) - *Beset by Contradictions*
     For Aff - v76 - My '97 - p147+ [51-250]
     MEJ - v51 - Spr '97 - p309 [51-250]

In the National Interest: 1996 Quadrennial Report on Human Rights and U.S. Foreign Policy
  WorldV - v13 - Ja '97 - p8 [51-250]
Law-Yone, Wendy - *Irrawaddy Tango*
  Amerasia J - v22 - 2 '96 - p173+ [501+]
Lax, Eric - *Paul Newman: A Biography*
  BL - v93 - S 1 '96 - p52 [251-500]
  Ent W - O 4 '96 - p56 [51-250]
Lax, Peter D - *Linear Algebra*
  SciTech - v21 - Mr '97 - p13 [51-250]
Lax, Robert - *Love Had a Compass*
  Am - v175 - S 21 '96 - p31+ [51-250]
A Thing That Is
  BL - v93 - F 1 '97 - p922 [51-250]
  LJ - v122 - Ap 15 '97 - p85 [51-250]
  PW - v244 - Ja 27 '97 - p95 [51-250]
Laxer, James - *In Search of a New Left*
  Mac - v109 - O 28 '96 - p64 [501+]
  Quill & Q - v62 - Ag '96 - p38 [251-500]
Laxness, Halldor - *Independent People*
  BL - v93 - F 1 '97 - p910 [1-50]
  BW - v27 - Ja 12 '97 - p7 [501+]
  KR - v65 - Ja 1 '97 - p21 [51-250]
  NYTBR - v102 - F 2 '97 - p28 [1-50]
  NYTBR - v102 - Ap 20 '97 - p35 [501+]
  PW - v243 - N 25 '96 - p68 [251-500]
Mein Heiliger Stein
  WLT - v70 - Sum '96 - p712+ [501+]
Laxton, Edward - *The Famine Ships*
  LATBR - Mr 30 '97 - p8 [501+]
  LJ - v122 - Ap 15 '97 - p96 [51-250]
  NS - v126 - F 28 '97 - p46+ [501+]
  Obs - Ja 19 '97 - p18* [501+]
Lay, Shawn - *Hooded Knights on the Niagara*
  JSH - v63 - F '97 - p195+ [251-500]
Layard, P R G - *The Coming Russian Boom*
  BL - v93 - S 15 '96 - p192 [51-250]
  Bus W - N 4 '96 - p21+ [501+]
  Bus W - D 16 '96 - p19 [51-250]
  Choice - v34 - Mr '97 - p1209 [51-250]
  Econ - v341 - N 16 '96 - p9* [501+]
  For Aff - v75 - N '96 - p160+ [51-250]
  JEL - v35 - Mr '97 - p291 [51-250]
  LJ - v122 - Mr 15 '97 - p37 [1-50]
What Labour Can Do
  NS - v126 - F 21 '97 - p28+ [501+]
Laybourn, Keith - *The Evolution of British Social Policy and the Welfare State c. 1800-1993*
  VS - v39 - Spr '96 - p419+ [501+]
Laycock, Thomas - *To Ask the Suffrages of the Patrons*
  Isis - v88 - Mr '97 - p154+ [501+]
Layman, Kit - *The Falklands and the Dwarf*
  HT - v46 - Ag '96 - p57 [501+]
Layman, R D - *Naval Aviation in the First World War*
  R&R Bk N - v12 - F '97 - p101 [51-250]
Laynter, A I - *G.K. Derman--Pervyi Direktor Moskovskogo Instituta*
  Lib - v18 - D '96 - p365 [51-250]
Layton, Peter - *Glass Art*
  R&R Bk N - v12 - F '97 - p74 [51-250]
Layton, Susan - *Russian Literature and Empire*
  MLR - v92 - Ja '97 - p265+ [501+]
Lazard, Madeleine - *Pierre De Bourdeille, Seigneur De Brantome*
  Six Ct J - v27 - Fall '96 - p846+ [501+]
Lazare, Bernard - *Antisemitism: Its History and Causes*
  Historian - v59 - Fall '96 - p196+ [501+]
Lazare, Lucien - *Rescue as Resistance*
  Choice - v34 - D '96 - p670 [51-250]
  KR - v64 - My 1 '96 - p669 [251-500]
  TLS - O 4 '96 - p11 [501+]
Lazarescu, George - *Prezente Romanesti In Italia*
  BL - v93 - D 15 '96 - p714 [1-50]
Lazarre, Jane - *Beyond the Whiteness of Whiteness*
  BL - v93 - S 1 '96 - p41 [251-500]
  LATBR - O 6 '96 - p4 [501+]
  Wom R Bks - v14 - Ja '97 - p6+ [501+]
Lazarsfeld, Paul F - *On Social Research and Its Language*
  Soc - v33 - S '96 - p94+ [501+]
  Soc - v33 - S '96 - p94+ [501+]
Lazarus, Arthur - *Controversies in Managed Mental Health Care*
  AJPsych - v154 - Ja '97 - p125+ [501+]
Lazarus, Richard S - *Passion and Reason*
  y Kliatt - v30 - N '96 - p25 [251-500]
Lazear, Edward P - *Personnel Economics*
  BusLR - v21 - 3 '96 - p248 [51-250]
  JEL - v34 - S '96 - p1461 [251-500]
  JEL - v35 - Mr '97 - p170+ [501+]
  Per Psy - v50 - Spr '97 - p248+ [501+]

Lazenby, J F - *The First Punic War*
  Choice - v34 - O '96 - p336 [51-250]
  HRNB - v25 - Fall '96 - p40 [501+]
Lazerow, Jama - *Religion and the Working Class in Antebellum America*
  J Soc H - v30 - Fall '96 - p301+ [501+]
Lazic, Momir - *Ne Dam Se, Ljubavi*
  WLT - v70 - Sum '96 - p730 [251-500]
Lazin, Frederick A - *Israel in the Nineties*
  Choice - v34 - Mr '97 - p1233 [51-250]
Politics and Policy Implementation
  Pol Stud J - v24 - Aut '96 - p520 [51-250]
Lazo, Caroline - *Jimmy Carter: On the Road to Peace*
  c BL - v92 - Ag '96 - p1899 [51-250]
  c HB Guide - v7 - Fall '96 - p372+ [51-250]
  y SLJ - v42 - Ag '96 - p170+ [51-250]
Lazzaro, Joseph J - *Adapting PCs for Disabilities*
  BYTE - v21 - O '96 - p38 [51-250]
Le, Linda - *Slander*
  BW - v27 - Mr 2 '97 - p4 [501+]
  Choice - v34 - My '97 - p1505 [51-250]
  KR - v64 - S 15 '96 - p1354 [51-250]
  LJ - v121 - N 1 '96 - p107 [51-250]
  NYTBR - v101 - D 1 '96 - p23 [51-250]
  PW - v243 - S 30 '96 - p78 [51-250]
  TLS - F 14 '97 - p23 [501+]
Le, Luu - *A Time Far Past*
  KR - v65 - Ap 1 '97 - p504 [51-250]
  LJ - v122 - Mr 15 '97 - p90 [51-250]
  PW - v244 - Ap 28 '97 - p49+ [251-500]
Le, Minh Khue - *The Stars, the Earth, the River*
  KR - v65 - Mr 1 '97 - p335 [51-250]
  PW - v244 - Mr 24 '97 - p61 [51-250]
Le, My Huong - *Nua The Ky Pham Duy*
  BL - v93 - S 1 '96 - p70 [51-250]
Le, Thao Chuyen - *Cung Dan Dang Do*
  BL - v93 - My 15 '97 - p1568 [1-50]
Le, Van - *Bong Sac Giai Nhan Tren Duong Bac Va Nam Tien*
  BL - v93 - S 1 '96 - p70 [51-250]
Hat Ru Ba Mien
  BL - v93 - My 15 '97 - p1568 [1-50]
Lea, Christine - *The Oxford Paperback Spanish Dictionary*
  r MLJ - v80 - Fall '96 - p430 [501+]
Lea, D - *Concurrent Programming in Java*
  New Sci - v153 - Mr 1 '97 - p46+ [501+]
Lea, Peter W - *The Reference Sources Handbook. 4th Ed.*
  r ARBA - v28 - '97 - p9 [51-250]
  r Choice - v34 - Mr '97 - p1143 [51-250]
  r LAR - v99 - Mr '97 - p161 [251-500]
Lea, Sydney - *To the Bone*
  PW - v243 - S 30 '96 - p83 [51-250]
Lea, Thomas D - *The New Testament: Its Background and Message*
  Rel St Rev - v23 - Ap '97 - p176 [51-250]
Lea, Tom - *Tom Lea: An Oral History*
  R&R Bk N - v11 - N '96 - p73 [51-250]
Leab, Daniel J - *Labor History Archives in the United States*
  r RQ - v36 - Fall '96 - p52 [51-250]
Leach, Barbara J - *Toys*
  TES - D 13 '96 - p43 [51-250]
Leach, J H C - *Sparks of Reform*
  EHR - v111 - N '96 - p1318 [51-250]
Leach, Maria - *The Importance of Being a Wit*
  Trib Bks - Mr 30 '97 - p2 [1-50]
Leach, Mark Richard - *Michael Lucero: Sculpture 1976-1995*
  Am Craft - v56 - Ag '96 - p28 [1-50]
  Ceram Mo - v44 - O '96 - p28 [51-250]
Leach, Michael - *The Great Apes*
  y BL - v93 - D 1 '96 - p629+ [51-250]
  Nature - v385 - F 13 '97 - p593 [1-50]
  PW - v243 - S 23 '96 - p70 [51-250]
Leach, Neil - *Rethinking Architecture*
  TCI - v30 - O '96 - p59 [51-250]
Leach, Norman - *The Giant That Sneezed (Illus. by Toni Goffe)*
  c Ch BWatch - v6 - Jl '96 - p4 [51-250]
Leach, Robert - *Turncoats: Changing Party Allegiance by British Politicians*
  Albion - v28 - Sum '96 - p361+ [501+]
Leach, William - *Land of Desire*
  J Am Cult - v18 - Win '95 - p104 [251-500]
Leadbeater, Bonnie J Ross - *Urban Girls*
  Adoles - v31 - Win '96 - p994 [501+]
  R&R Bk N - v11 - N '96 - p44 [51-250]
  Soc Ser R - v71 - Mr '97 - p165 [1-50]

Leader, Darian - *Why Do Women Write More Letters than They Post?*
  TES - Mr 14 '97 - p8* [51-250]
Why Do Women Write More Letters than They Send?
  KR - v65 - Ja 1 '97 - p41 [251-500]
  LJ - v122 - Mr 15 '97 - p77 [51-250]
Leader, Mary - *Red Signature*
  LJ - v122 - Ap 15 '97 - p85 [51-250]
  PW - v244 - F 24 '97 - p86 [51-250]
Leader, Zachary - *Revision and Romantic Authorship*
  Nine-C Lit - v51 - Mr '97 - p559 [51-250]
  TLS - Ag 2 '96 - p5+ [501+]
Leadership Education 1996-1997. Vols. 1-2
  r BL - v93 - F 1 '97 - p965+ [251-500]
  r Choice - v34 - Ja '97 - p770 [51-250]
Leahy, James E - *Freedom Fighters of the United States Supreme Court*
  Choice - v34 - Ap '97 - p1418 [51-250]
Leahy, Linda Romanelli - *366 Healthful Ways to Cook Leafy Greens*
  BL - v93 - Mr 15 '97 - p1216 [51-250]
Leak, Andrew - *Barthes: Mythologies*
  MLR - v91 - Jl '96 - p742+ [501+]
Leak CD Magazine
  p Sm Pr R - v28 - S '96 - p16 [51-250]
Leakey, M D - *Olduvai Gorge. Vol. 5*
  Am Ant - v61 - Jl '96 - p627+ [501+]
Leakey, Richard - *The Origin of Humankind*
  y Kliatt - v31 - Ja '97 - p28 [251-500]
  NYTBR - v101 - S 15 '96 - p44 [1-50]
The Sixth Extinction
  Env - v38 - O '96 - p25 [51-250]
  Nature - v382 - Ag 15 '96 - p594 [501+]
  NYTBR - v101 - N 10 '96 - p68 [51-250]
  PW - v243 - O 7 '96 - p69 [1-50]
  y SB - v32 - Ag '96 - p172 [251-500]
  TLS - S 6 '96 - p29 [501+]
Leal, Rine - *Teatro: 5 Autores Cubanos*
  Hisp - v79 - D '96 - p812+ [501+]
Leaman, Oliver - *Evil and Suffering in Jewish Philosophy*
  Theol St - v58 - Mr '97 - p183+ [501+]
Friendship East and West
  TLS - Mr 21 '97 - p27 [251-500]
Leamer, Laurence - *Three Chords and the Truth*
  BL - v93 - My 1 '97 - p1458+ [51-250]
  PW - v244 - Ap 14 '97 - p61 [251-500]
Leaming, Barbara - *If This Was Happiness (Fields). Audio Version*
  LJ - v122 - My 1 '97 - p153 [51-250]
Orson Welles: A Biography (Conlin). Audio Version
  BL - v93 - N 1 '96 - p522 [51-250]
  y Kliatt - v31 - My '97 - p48 [51-250]
Leaming, Hugo Prosper - *Hidden Americans*
  W&M Q - v53 - Jl '96 - p666+ [501+]
Leaon-Borja, Istvan Szaszdi - *El Memorial Portugues De 1494*
  EHR - v112 - F '97 - p182+ [51-250]
Lear, Edward - *Book of Nonsense (Gielgud). Audio Version*
  c Sch Lib - v45 - F '97 - p43 [51-250]
Nonsense Songs (Illus. by Bee Willey)
  c BL - v93 - Ap 1 '97 - p1335 [51-250]
  c JB - v60 - D '96 - p255 [51-250]
  c PW - v244 - Ap 7 '97 - p91 [51-250]
The Owl and the Pussy Cat (Illus. by Ian Beck)
  c BL - v93 - O 1 '96 - p355 [51-250]
  c HB Guide - v8 - Spr '97 - p152 [1-50]
  c SLJ - v42 - D '96 - p98 [51-250]
Learn about Colors
  c HB Guide - v7 - Fall '96 - p240 [51-250]
Learn about Numbers
  c HB Guide - v7 - Fall '96 - p240 [51-250]
Learn about Opposites
  c HB Guide - v7 - Fall '96 - p240 [51-250]
Learn about Shapes
  c HB Guide - v7 - Fall '96 - p240 [51-250]
Learn about Size
  c HB Guide - v7 - Fall '96 - p240 [51-250]
Learn French with Teddy Berlitz. Book and Audio Version
  c PW - v244 - Mr 17 '97 - p47 [51-250]
Learn Spanish with Teddy Berlitz. Book and Audio Version
  c PW - v244 - Mr 17 '97 - p47 [1-50]
Learning, Walter - *Gifts to Last*
  Quill & Q - v62 - D '96 - p35 [251-500]
Learning to Work
  J Gov Info - v23 - S '96 - p558 [51-250]
Lears, T J Jackson - *Fables of Abundance*
  Historian - v58 - Sum '96 - p866+ [251-500]
  JC - v46 - Sum '96 - p195+ [501+]

Leary, Timothy - *Design for Dying*
  BL - v93 - My 15 '97 - p1538+ [51-250]
  Psychedelic Prayers and Other Meditations
  PW - v244 - Mr 24 '97 - p75 [51-250]
The Least Developed Countries 1995 Report
  R&R Bk N - v12 - F '97 - p35 [51-250]
The Least Developed Countries 1996 Report
  JEL - v34 - D '96 - p2112+ [51-250]
  R&R Bk N - v12 - F '97 - p35 [51-250]
Leatherbarrow, W J - *Dostoevskii and Britain*
  TLS - O 4 '96 - p13 [501+]
Leavell, Linda - *Marianne Moore and the Visual Arts*
  J Am St - v30 - Ag '96 - p333+ [501+]
Leavitt, David - *Arkansas: Three Novellas*
  Advocate - Ap 1 '97 - p59+ [501+]
  BL - v93 - Mr 1 '97 - p1110 [51-250]
  KR - v65 - F 1 '97 - p163 [251-500]
  LATBR - Ap 6 '97 - p8 [501+]
  LJ - v122 - F 1 '97 - p109 [51-250]
  NW - v129 - Mr 10 '97 - p71 [251-500]
  NYTBR - v102 - Mr 30 '97 - p15 [501+]
  NYTLa - v146 - Mr 11 '97 - pC17 [501+]
  PW - v244 - Ja 27 '97 - p75 [51-250]
  Time - v149 - Mr 17 '97 - p71 [501+]
  VLS - Spr '97 - p24 [501+]
  While England Sleeps
  NS - v125 - D 20 '96 - p117 [1-50]
Leavitt, Judith Walzer - *The Healthiest City*
  JEL - v35 - Mr '97 - p263 [51-250]
  Typhoid Mary: Captive to the Public's Health
  Choice - v34 - D '96 - p644+ [51-250]
  ILS - v15 - Fall '96 - p31 [51-250]
  KR - v64 - My 1 '96 - p669 [251-500]
  Nature - v383 - O 31 '96 - p781+ [501+]
  Sci - v274 - O 25 '96 - p523 [1-50]
  SciTech - v20 - S '96 - p28 [51-250]
  Wom R Bks - v14 - N '96 - p8+ [501+]
Leavy, Barbara Fass - *In Search of the Swan Maiden*
  Signs - v22 - Win '97 - p491+ [501+]
Leavy, Una - *Good-Bye, Papa (Illus. by Jennifer Eachus)*
  c HB Guide - v8 - Spr '97 - p35 [51-250]
  c Sch Lib - v44 - Ag '96 - p104+ [51-250]
  c SLJ - v42 - D '96 - p99 [51-250]
  c Trib Bks - F 9 '97 - p7 [51-250]
  The Orchard Book of Irish Fairy Tales and Legends (Illus. by Susan Field)
  c Bks Keeps - Mr '97 - p22 [51-250]
  c TES - Mr 14 '97 - p10* [501+]
LeBeau, Bryan F - *Religion in the Age of Exploration*
  Choice - v34 - O '96 - p298+ [51-250]
Lebedev, Viacheslav Ivanovich - *An Introduction to Functional Analysis in Computational Mathematics*
  SciTech - v21 - Mr '97 - p16 [51-250]
Lebel, Maurice - *D'Un Livre A L'Autre*
  Can Lit - Win '96 - p127+ [501+]
Le Bellac, Michel - *Thermal Field Theory*
  SciTech - v21 - Mr '97 - p21 [51-250]
Leben, Ulrich - *Bernard Molitor 1775-1833*
  SDA - v4 - Fall '96 - p138+ [501+]
Leber, Max - *The Handbook of Over-the-Counter Drugs and Pharmacy Products*
  r BL - v93 - F 1 '97 - p959 [1-50]
Lebergott, Stanley - *Consumer Expenditures*
  J Con A - v31 - Sum '97 - p175+ [501+]
  JEH - v56 - S '96 - p759+ [501+]
  JEL - v34 - S '96 - p1410+ [51-250]
Lebo, Harlan - *The Godfather Legacy*
  Am - v176 - Ap 5 '97 - p2 [501+]
  Ent W - Ap 4 '97 - p78 [51-250]
  PW - v244 - F 24 '97 - p78 [51-250]
Lebovic, James H - *Foregone Conclusions*
  Choice - v34 - D '96 - p690 [51-250]
  R&R Bk N - v11 - N '96 - p79 [51-250]
Lebow, Richard Ned - *The Art of Bargaining*
  For Aff - v75 - S '96 - p137 [51-250]
  JEL - v34 - D '96 - p2022 [51-250]
Lebrecht, Norman - *The Companion to 20th-Century Music*
  FF - v20 - Ja '97 - p375 [251-500]
  When the Music Stopped
  Spec - v277 - N 16 '96 - p43 [1-50]
  Who Killed Classical Music?
  PW - v244 - Mr 10 '97 - p62 [51-250]
Lebrun, Claude - *Little Brown Bear Does Not Want to Eat (Illus. by Daniele Bour)*
  c HB Guide - v7 - Fall '96 - p264 [1-50]
  c SLJ - v42 - S '96 - p182+ [51-250]
  Little Brown Bear Dresses Himself (Illus. by Daniele Bour)
  c HB Guide - v8 - Spr '97 - p35 [1-50]

Little Brown Bear Goes on a Trip (Illus. by Daniele Bour)
  c HB Guide - v8 - Spr '97 - p35 [1-50]
Little Brown Bear Helps His Mama (Illus. by Daniele Bour)
  c HB Guide - v8 - Spr '97 - p35 [1-50]
Little Brown Bear Is Growing Up (Illus. by Daniele Bour)
  c HB Guide - v7 - Fall '96 - p264 [1-50]
  c SLJ - v42 - S '96 - p182+ [1-50]
Little Brown Bear Takes a Bath (Illus. by Daniele Bour)
  c HB Guide - v8 - Spr '97 - p35 [1-50]
Little Brown Bear Wants to Be Read To (Illus. by Daniele Bour)
  c HB Guide - v7 - Fall '96 - p264 [1-50]
  c SLJ - v42 - S '96 - p182+ [51-250]
Lebrun, Richard A - *Joseph De Maistre: An Intellectual Militant*
  MA - v38 - Fall '96 - p392+ [501+]
  Maistre Studies
  MA - v38 - Fall '96 - p392+ [501+]
Leby, Deborah - *Billy and Girl*
  TLS - O 25 '96 - p24 [501+]
Lecanuet, Jean-Pierre - *Fetal Development*
  Am Sci - v84 - N '96 - p604+ [501+]
Le Carre, John - *Call for the Dead (Jayston). Audio Version*
  CSM - v89 - Mr 27 '97 - pB2 [1-50]
  Our Game (Davidson). Audio Version
  LJ - v122 - Ap 1 '97 - p145 [51-250]
  Our Game (Le Carre). Audio Version
  TLS - Ag 2 '96 - p24 [51-250]
  Smiley's People (Jayston). Audio Version
  LJ - v122 - O 15 '96 - p102 [51-250]
  The Tailor of Panama
  BL - v93 - Ja '97 - p762 [1-50]
  BL - v93 - S 1 '96 - p31 [51-250]
  CSM - v88 - N 4 '96 - p13 [251-500]
  CSM - v88 - N 14 '96 - p14 [51-250]
  CSM - v89 - D 19 '96 - p14 [51-250]
  Econ - v341 - D 7 '96 - p3*+ [501+]
  Ent W - N 15 '96 - p66+ [51-250]
  KR - v64 - Ag 15 '96 - p1177 [251-500]
  LATBR - O 20 '96 - p3+ [501+]
  LJ - v121 - O 15 '96 - p90+ [51-250]
  Nat R - v48 - D 23 '96 - p56 [51-250]
  NYRB - v43 - N 28 '96 - p16+ [501+]
  NYTBR - v101 - O 20 '96 - p11 [501+]
  NYTBR - v101 - D 8 '96 - p84 [1-50]
  NYTLa - v146 - O 18 '96 - pC37 [501+]
  Obs - O 6 '96 - p15* [501+]
  PW - v243 - S 2 '96 - p109 [51-250]
  PW - v243 - N 4 '96 - p37 [1-50]
  y SLJ - v43 - F '97 - p134+ [51-250]
  Spec - v277 - O 19 '96 - p53+ [501+]
  TES - O 4 '96 - p7* [51-250]
  Time - v148 - O 28 '96 - p102+ [501+]
  Time - v148 - D 23 '96 - p86 [51-250]
  TLS - O 18 '96 - p22 [501+]
  Tinker, Tailor, Soldier, Spy (Jayston). Audio Version
  LJ - v122 - Ap 1 '97 - p146 [51-250]
Lechago, Juan - *Bloodworth's Endocrine Pathology. 3rd Ed.*
  SciTech - v21 - Mr '97 - p56 [51-250]
Lechuga, Ruth D - *Mask Arts of Mexico*
  Am Craft - v56 - D '96 - p30 [51-250]
Lecker, Michael - *Muslims, Jews and Pagans*
  Rel St Rev - v23 - Ja '97 - p90 [51-250]
Lecker, Robert - *Canadian Writers and Their Works: Fiction Series. Vol. 12*
  r ARBA - v28 - '97 - p459 [51-250]
  r Choice - v34 - O '96 - p276 [251-500]
  Canadian Writers and Their Works: Poetry Series. Vol. 11
  r ARBA - v28 - '97 - p459 [51-250]
  r Choice - v34 - O '96 - p276 [251-500]
  Making It Real
  Can Lit - Spr '97 - p234+ [501+]
Leckie, Gloria J - *Directory of College and University Librarians in Canada. 2nd Ed.*
  r ARBA - v28 - '97 - p248 [51-250]
Leckie, Robert - *Okinawa: The Last Battle of World War II*
  y Kliatt - v30 - S '96 - p34 [51-250]
Leckie, Ross - *Hannibal*
  NYTBR - v101 - D 29 '96 - p14 [251-500]
  PW - v243 - S 2 '96 - p113 [51-250]
Leckie, Will - *Courage to Love*
  KR - v65 - My 1 '97 - p698 [251-500]
LeClair, Tom - *Passing Off*
  PW - v243 - N 4 '96 - p65 [51-250]

Le Clezio, J-M G - *Onitsha*
  KR - v65 - Mr 1 '97 - p335 [51-250]
  LJ - v122 - Ap 15 '97 - p118 [51-250]
  PW - v244 - Mr 17 '97 - p77 [51-250]
  La Quarantaine
  WLT - v70 - Aut '96 - p909 [501+]
Le Crom, Jean-Pierre - *Syndicats, Nous Voila!*
  AHR - v101 - D '96 - p1560+ [501+]
  EHR - v112 - Ap '97 - p536+ [501+]
  JMH - v68 - D '96 - p999+ [501+]
Ledbetter, Mark - *Victims and the Postmodern Narrative*
  Choice - v34 - Ja '97 - p796 [51-250]
Ledbetter, Suzann - *Deliverance Drive*
  Roundup M - v4 - O '96 - p31+ [251-500]
  Pure Justice
  PW - v244 - Mr 31 '97 - p72 [51-250]
  Redemption Trail
  Roundup M - v3 - Ag '96 - p30 [251-500]
Leddick, David - *My Worst Date*
  Advocate - S 17 '96 - p60 [1-50]
  BL - v93 - N 1 '96 - p481 [51-250]
  KR - v64 - S 1 '96 - p1257+ [251-500]
  PW - v243 - O 7 '96 - p61 [51-250]
Leddy, Mary Jo - *At the Border Called Hope*
  Quill & Q - v63 - Mr '97 - p72 [251-500]
Ledeen, Michael - *Freedom Betrayed*
  Nat R - v48 - O 28 '96 - p78 [51-250]
  WSJ-Cent - v99 - Mr 17 '97 - pA16 [501+]
Leder, Jane Mersky - *Grace and Glory*
  Choice - v34 - D '96 - p650 [501+]
  A Russian Jewish Family
  c BL - v93 - N 1 '96 - p493 [51-250]
  c Ch BWatch - v6 - O '96 - p5 [51-250]
  c HB Guide - v8 - Spr '97 - p90 [51-250]
  c SLJ - v42 - N '96 - p115+ [51-250]
Lederer, Helen - *Single Minding!*
  Books - v9 - S '95 - p23 [1-50]
  Books - v10 - Je '96 - p21 [1-50]
Lederer, Richard - *Nothing Risque, Nothing Gained*
  CAY - v16 - Fall '95 - p6 [51-250]
  Pun and Games
  y Kliatt - v30 - N '96 - p18 [51-250]
Lederer, Susan E - *Subjected to Science*
  Hast Cen R - v26 - S '96 - p38+ [501+]
  Isis - v88 - Mr '97 - p164+ [501+]
  RAH - v24 - D '96 - p652+ [501+]
Lederhendler, Eli - *Jewish Responses to Modernity*
  JAAR - v64 - Sum '96 - p437+ [501+]
Lederman, Ellen - *Vacations That Can Change Your Life*
  BL - v93 - S 15 '96 - p210 [1-50]
  r LJ - v121 - N 15 '96 - p79 [51-250]
Ledger, Sally - *Cultural Politics at the Fin De Siecle*
  ELT - v40 - 2 '97 - p188+ [501+]
  Nine-C Lit - v50 - Mr '96 - p554+ [1-50]
LeDoux, Joseph - *The Emotional Brain*
  y BL - v93 - N 15 '96 - p551+ [51-250]
  KR - v64 - S 15 '96 - p1376 [251-500]
  LJ - v121 - N 15 '96 - p85 [51-250]
  Nature - v385 - F 20 '97 - p694 [501+]
  New Sci - v153 - Ja 4 '97 - p36+ [501+]
  NYTBR - v101 - D 1 '96 - p30 [501+]
  PW - v243 - S 23 '96 - p62 [51-250]
  y SLJ - v43 - Mr '97 - p217 [51-250]
  W&I - v12 - Mr '97 - p281+ [501+]
  Wil Q - v21 - Win '97 - p92+ [501+]
LeDuc, Lawrence - *Comparing Democracies*
  R&R Bk N - v11 - D '96 - p46 [51-250]
Lee, A D - *Information and Frontiers*
  CW - v90 - S '96 - p71+ [251-500]
  Specu - v71 - O '96 - p973+ [501+]
Lee, A Robert - *Making America/Making American Literature*
  Nine-C Lit - v51 - Mr '97 - p559 [51-250]
  Other Britain, Other British
  WLT - v71 - Win '97 - p161+ [501+]
Lee, Adam - *The Dark Shore*
  KR - v65 - F 15 '97 - p261+ [51-250]
  LJ - v122 - Ap 15 '97 - p123 [51-250]
  PW - v244 - Mr 31 '97 - p68 [51-250]
Lee, Alex - *Force Recon Command*
  NWCR - v50 - Win '97 - p151+ [501+]
Lee, B H - *Fundamentals of Food Biotechnology*
  SciTech - v20 - S '96 - p60 [51-250]
Lee, Barbara - *The Financially Independent Woman*
  BL - v93 - D 1 '96 - p627 [51-250]
  Working in Health Care and Wellness
  y Ch BWatch - v6 - S '96 - p5 [1-50]
  y HB Guide - v8 - Spr '97 - p91 [51-250]

Working in Music
c BL - v93 - F 15 '97 - p1018+ [51-250]
y HB Guide - v8 - Spr '97 - p91 [51-250]
y SLJ - v43 - F '97 - p118 [51-250]
Working in Sports and Recreation
y Ch BWatch - v6 - S '96 - p5 [1-50]
y HB Guide - v8 - Spr '97 - p91 [51-250]
Working with Animals
c BL - v93 - F 15 '97 - p1018+ [51-250]
y Ch BWatch - v6 - S '96 - p5 [1-50]
y HB Guide - v8 - Spr '97 - p91 [51-250]
Lee, Bernard J - *Galilean Jewishness of Jesus*
Rel Ed - v91 - Fall '96 - p604 [1-50]
Lee, Blaine - *The Power Principle*
PW - v244 - Ap 21 '97 - p56 [51-250]
Lee, Byeong Gi - *Broadband Telecommunications Technology. 2nd Ed.*
SciTech - v21 - Mr '97 - p87 [51-250]
Lee, C C - *Chemical Guide to the Internet*
r ARBA - v28 - '97 - p628+ [51-250]
Lee, Carla A B - *Fluids and Electrolytes. 4th Ed.*
SciTech - v20 - S '96 - p35 [51-250]
Lee, Chae-Jin - *China and Korea*
Choice - v34 - Mr '97 - p1234+ [51-250]
Econ - v342 - F 15 '97 - p12*+ [501+]
For Aff - v76 - Mr '97 - p196+ [51-250]
Lee, Chang-Rae - *Native Speaker*
BW - v26 - D 15 '96 - p4 [1-50]
Obs - N 24 '96 - p18* [51-250]
Lee, Chin-Chuan - *China's Media, Media's China*
Ch Rev Int - v4 - Spr '97 - p198+ [501+]
Lee, Chin-Hui - *Automatic Speech and Speaker Recognition*
SciTech - v20 - S '96 - p58 [51-250]
Lee, D J - *Conflicts about Class*
Socio R - v45 - F 1 '97 - p181+ [501+]
Lee, Daniel E - *Generations and the Challenge of Justice*
Choice - v34 - Ja '97 - p876 [51-250]
Lee, David, 1944, Aug., 8- - *My Town*
WAL - v31 - Fall '96 - p266+ [251-500]
Lee, David, 1956- - *The Map-Building and Exploration Strategies of a Simple Sonar-Equipped Mobile Robot*
Robotica - v15 - Mr '97 - p235+ [501+]
Lee, David C J - *Ernest Renan: In the Shadow of Faith*
TLS - Mr 28 '97 - p10 [501+]
Lee, Deborah - *Having It All/Having Enough*
BWatch - v18 - Mr '97 - p5 [51-250]
Lee, Dennis, 1939- - *Dinosaur Dinner with a Slice of Alligator Pie (Illus. by Debbie Tilley)*
c BL - v93 - Ap 1 '97 - p1335 [51-250]
c PW - v244 - Mr 3 '97 - p76 [51-250]
Nightwatch: New and Selected Poems 1968-1996
Quill & Q - v62 - Jl '96 - p46 [501+]
Quill & Q - v62 - Jl '96 - p47 [251-500]
Lee, Dennis, 1943- - *Lord Lyndhurst: The Flexible Tory*
Albion - v28 - Sum '96 - p324+ [501+]
Lee, E Stanley - *Fuzzy and Evidence Reasoning*
JEL - v34 - D '96 - p2142 [51-250]
Lee, Eui W - *Light Weight Alloys for Aerospace Applications*
SciTech - v20 - D '96 - p81 [51-250]
Lee, Gentry - *Bright Messengers*
y Kliatt - v30 - S '96 - p18 [51-250]
Lee, Gerard A - *Leper Hospitals in Medieval Ireland*
r ILS - v16 - Spr '97 - p36 [1-50]
Lee, Gus - *Tiger's Tail*
Sew R - v104 - Jl '96 - p461+ [501+]
Lee, Hector Viveros - *I Had a Hippopotamus (Illus. by Hector Viveros Lee)*
c CBRS - v24 - Ag '96 - p160 [51-250]
c HB Guide - v7 - Fall '96 - p264 [1-50]
Lee, Helie - *Still Life with Rice*
Comw - v123 - S 13 '96 - p34+ [501+]
Lee, Henry - *Shaping National Responses to Climate Change*
Nature - v383 - S 12 '96 - p138 [501+]
Lee, Hermione - *Virginia Woolf*
BL - v93 - My 1 '97 - p1474 [51-250]
Econ - v341 - D 7 '96 - p12* [501+]
KR - v65 - Mr 15 '97 - p441 [251-500]
LJ - v122 - My 1 '97 - p104 [51-250]
Lon R Bks - v19 - Ja 23 '97 - p3+ [501+]
NS - v125 - S 6 '96 - p46+ [501+]
Obs - S 15 '96 - p16* [501+]
PW - v244 - Mr 24 '97 - p65 [251-500]
Spec - v277 - N 23 '96 - p44 [1-50]
TES - S 13 '96 - p7* [501+]
TES - D 27 '96 - p16+ [51-250]
TLS - S 20 '96 - p28+ [501+]
Lee, J A N - *Computer Pioneers*
T&C - v37 - O '96 - p860+ [501+]

Lee, James F - *Making Communicative Language Teaching Happen*
FR - v70 - F '97 - p488+ [501+]
Lee, Jane C Y - *Public Sector Reform in Hong Kong*
Ch Rev Int - v4 - Spr '97 - p201+ [501+]
Lee, John B - *Tongues of the Children*
Quill & Q - v62 - D '96 - p33 [251-500]
Lee, Julian C - *The Amphibians and Reptiles of the Yucatan Peninsula*
Choice - v34 - D '96 - p639 [51-250]
Lee, Jung Young - *The Trinity in Asian Perspective*
Rel St Rev - v23 - Ap '97 - p155 [51-250]
Lee, Kam Hing - *The Sultanate of Aceh*
Albion - v28 - Fall '96 - p552+ [501+]
Lee, Kathleen - *Illegal Immigration*
y HB Guide - v7 - Fall '96 - p312+ [51-250]
Lee, Kuan Yew - *The Battle for Merger*
FEER - Anniv '96 - p224 [251-500]
Lee, Lauren - *Japanese Americans*
yr Ch BWatch - v6 - O '96 - p5 [51-250]
c HB Guide - v7 - Fall '96 - p312 [51-250]
Lee, Lester W - *Human Tissue Monitoring and Specimen Banking*
J Gov Info - v23 - S '96 - p547 [51-250]
Lee, Li-Young - *The City in Which I Love You*
LJ - v122 - Ap 1 '97 - p95 [1-50]
Lee, M Owen - *First Intermissions*
M Ed J - v83 - S '96 - p58 [51-250]
Virgil as Orpheus
R&R Bk N - v12 - F '97 - p78 [51-250]
Lee, Marie G - *Necessary Roughness*
y BL - v93 - Ja '97 - p844 [251-500]
y CCB-B - v50 - Ja '97 - p178+ [51-250]
y HB - v73 - Ja '97 - p61+ [51-250]
y HB Guide - v8 - Spr '97 - p81 [51-250]
c KR - v64 - N 1 '96 - p1602 [51-250]
y NYTBR - v102 - Mr 16 '97 - p26 [1-50]
y PW - v243 - N 25 '96 - p76 [51-250]
y SLJ - v43 - Ja '97 - p112 [51-250]
Lee, Martha F - *Earth First!*
BioSci - v46 - S '96 - p628+ [501+]
The Nation of Islam
AJS - v102 - Ja '97 - p1224+ [501+]
Bl S - v26 - Fall '96 - p104 [51-250]
MEQ - v3 - S '96 - p85+ [251-500]
Lee, Milly - *Nim and the War Effort (Illus. by Yangsook Choi)*
c BL - v93 - F 1 '97 - p941 [51-250]
c CBRS - v25 - Mr '97 - p93 [51-250]
c CCB-B - v50 - Mr '97 - p252 [51-250]
c HB - v73 - Mr '97 - p193 [51-250]
c KR - v65 - Ja 1 '97 - p60 [51-250]
c Par Ch - v21 - Mr '97 - p4 [1-50]
c PW - v243 - D 30 '96 - p67 [51-250]
c SLJ - v43 - Mr '97 - p160 [51-250]
Lee, Patrick - *Abortion and Unborn Human Life*
Choice - v34 - F '97 - p978 [51-250]
Lee, Peter H - *Sourcebook of Korean Civilization. Vol. 2*
r R&R Bk N - v11 - D '96 - p11 [51-250]
Lee, Philip - *Home Pool*
CG - v117 - Mr '97 - p85 [51-250]
Lee, R Alton - *Encyclopedia USA. Vol. 22*
r ARBA - v28 - '97 - p192+ [51-250]
Encyclopedia USA. Vol. 23
r ARBA - v28 - '97 - p193 [51-250]
r R&R Bk N - v12 - F '97 - p35 [51-250]
Lee, Rachel - *A Fateful Choice*
LJ - v122 - F 15 '97 - p184 [51-250]
PW - v243 - S 23 '96 - p74 [51-250]
Lee, Robert E - *The ISDN Consultant*
CBR - v14 - N '96 - p38 [51-250]
SciTech - v20 - D '96 - p75 [51-250]
Lee, Robert L - *Everything about Theatre!*
y BL - v93 - D 1 '96 - p645 [51-250]
y Ch BWatch - v6 - Jl '96 - p2 [1-50]
y SLJ - v43 - F '97 - p137 [51-250]
TCI - v30 - O '96 - p58 [51-250]
Lee, Sander H - *Woody Allen's Angst*
Choice - v34 - Ap '97 - p1345 [51-250]
Lee, Sky - *Disappearing Moon Cafe*
Amerasia J - v22 - 3 '96 - p171+ [501+]
Lee, Spike - *Best Seat in the House*
y BL - v93 - Ap 1 '97 - p1267 [51-250]
KR - v65 - Ap 1 '97 - p527 [251-500]
PW - v244 - Ap 28 '97 - p60 [251-500]
Lee, Steven Hugh - *Outposts of Empire*
For Aff - v75 - N '96 - p154+ [51-250]
Lee, Sunggyu - *Alternative Fuels*
Choice - v34 - Mr '97 - p1191 [51-250]
Methane and Its Derivatives
r SciTech - v21 - Mr '97 - p96 [51-250]

Lee, Tan Chung - *Finland*
c HB Guide - v7 - Fall '96 - p382 [1-50]
Lee, Tanith - *The Gods Are Thirsty*
Atl - v278 - D '96 - p126 [51-250]
KR - v64 - S 15 '96 - p1344 [251-500]
LJ - v122 - My 1 '97 - p164 [51-250]
PW - v243 - S 9 '96 - p62+ [251-500]
Red as Blood
y VOYA - v19 - D '96 - p266 [51-250]
Lee, Vinny - *Bathrooms*
LJ - v121 - S 15 '96 - p66 [51-250]
Lee, W W - *Missing Eden*
Arm Det - v30 - Win '97 - p114 [251-500]
BL - v92 - Ag '96 - p1886 [51-250]
The Overland Trail
KR - v64 - My 1 '96 - p626 [251-500]
Lee, Yueh-Ting - *Stereotype Accuracy*
R&R Bk N - v12 - F '97 - p6 [51-250]
Leeb, Stephen - *The Agile Investor*
BL - v93 - Ja '97 - p794 [51-250]
LJ - v122 - F 15 '97 - p144 [51-250]
Leebron, Fred G - *Out West*
KR - v64 - S 1 '96 - p1258 [251-500]
PW - v243 - S 23 '96 - p56 [251-500]
SFR - v22 - Ja '97 - p22+ [501+]
Leech, Ben - *A Rare Breed*
Necro - Fall '96 - p27 [51-250]
Leedham-Green, Elisabeth - *A Concise History of the University of Cambridge*
New Sci - v152 - O 26 '96 - p46 [1-50]
TES - N 29 '96 - p10* [1-50]
TLS - Ja 3 '97 - p30 [501+]
Leedom, Tim C - *The Book Your Church Doesn't Want You to Read*
Skeptic - v4 - '96 - p107 [51-250]
Leeds, Anthony - *Cities, Classes, and the Social Order*
JTWS - v13 - Fall '96 - p340+ [501+]
Leeds, Marc - *The Vonnegut Encyclopedia*
r JPC - v30 - Fall '96 - p209+ [51-250]
Leeds-Hurwitz, Wendy - *Social Approaches to Communication*
JMCQ - v73 - Aut '96 - p767+ [501+]
QJS - v83 - My '97 - p262+ [501+]
Leedy, Loreen - *How Humans Make Friends*
c HB Guide - v7 - Fall '96 - p307 [51-250]
Leefmans, Alvarez - *Las Heuronas De Don Santiago*
y JAAL - v40 - S '96 - p77 [51-250]
Leeman, Richard W - *African-American Orators*
r Choice - v34 - Mr '97 - p1133 [51-250]
R&R Bk N - v11 - D '96 - p15 [51-250]
Leeming, David Adams - *Encyclopedia of Allegorical Literature*
yr ARBA - v28 - '97 - p410 [251-500]
r BL - v93 - F 1 '97 - p964 [251-500]
r Bloom Rev - v17 - Ja '97 - p15 [51-250]
r Choice - v34 - Ap '97 - p1310+ [51-250]
r LJ - v121 - N 15 '96 - p56 [51-250]
r R&R Bk N - v12 - F '97 - p79 [51-250]
yr SLJ - v43 - F '97 - p130 [51-250]
Leeming, Frank C - *Issues in Adolescent Sexuality*
Adoles - v31 - Win '96 - p994 [51-250]
Leenaars, Antoon A - *Treatment of Suicidal People*
J ClinPsyc - v57 - N '96 - p551+ [251-500]
Leerssen, Joep - *Remembrance and Imagination*
TLS - N 29 '96 - p13 [51-250]
Lees, Frank P - *Loss Prevention in the Process Industries. 2nd Ed., Vols. 1-3*
r SciTech - v21 - Mr '97 - p96 [51-250]
Lees, Gene - *Cats of Any Color*
MQ - v80 - Fall '96 - p392+ [501+]
Leader of the Band
Rapport - v19 - 4 '96 - p13+ [501+]
Lees, Sue - *Carnal Knowledge*
TLS - Jl 19 '96 - p29 [501+]
Lees-Milne, James - *Fourteen Friends*
Obs - S 15 '96 - p17* [501+]
Spec - v277 - S 21 '96 - p50+ [501+]
Spec - v277 - N 30 '96 - p58 [1-50]
TLS - S 13 '96 - p30 [501+]
Leeson, Robert - *The Dog Who Changed the World (Illus. by Alison Forsythe)*
c Bks Keeps - v100 - S '96 - p12 [51-250]
Red, White and Blue
y Sch Lib - v44 - Ag '96 - p120 [51-250]
Leeson, Ted - *The Gift of Trout*
KR - v64 - S 1 '96 - p1298 [251-500]
Leeuwenburgh, Todd - *Profiles of Worldwide Government Leaders*
r J Gov Info - v23 - Jl '96 - p535+ [501+]

Leeuwenhoek, Antoni Van - *The Collected Letters of Antoni Van Leeuwenhoek. Vol. 13*
     Isis - v87 - D '96 - p729+ [501+]
Le Fanu, Joseph Sheridan - *Carmilla*
     Critm - v38 - Fall '96 - p607+ [501+]
Lefcourt, Peter - *Abbreviating Ernie*
     BL - v93 - F 15 '97 - p1004 [51-250]
     BW - v27 - Mr 2 '97 - p5 [51+]
     KR - v64 - N 15 '96 - p1624 [251-500]
     LJ - v122 - F 1 '97 - p106 [51-250]
     NYTBR - v102 - Mr 2 '97 - p15 [501+]
     PW - v243 - D 2 '96 - p39 [51-250]
Lefebure, L D - *The Buddha and the Christ*
     JAAR - v64 - Fall '96 - p664+ [501+]
Le Fevre, Ralph - *History of New Paltz, New York and Its Old Families from 1678 to 1820. 2nd Ed.*
     EGH - v50 - N '96 - p174 [51-250]
Leff, Carol Skalnik - *The Czech and Slovak Republics*
     Choice - v34 - Ap '97 - p1411 [51-250]
Leff, Enrique - *Green Production*
     CS - v25 - S '96 - p652+ [501+]
Leff, Lawrence S - *EZ-101 Study Keys*
     Math T - v89 - S '96 - p514 [51-250]
     New Math Workbook for SAT I
     Math T - v89 - D '96 - p781 [251-500]
     y SLMQ - v25 - Fall '96 - p65 [1-50]
Lefferts, Vena - *Floral Style*
     BL - v93 - Ja '97 - p805+ [51-250]
     LJ - v122 - Ap 1 '97 - p89 [51-250]
     PW - v243 - O 7 '96 - p58 [51-250]
Lefkoe, Morty - *Re-Create Your Life*
     PW - v244 - Ap 28 '97 - p66 [251-500]
Lefkovitz, Lori Hope - *Textual Bodies*
     Choice - v34 - My '97 - p1492 [51-250]
Lefkowitz, Bernard - *Our Guys*
     KR - v65 - My 1 '97 - p698 [251-500]
     PW - v244 - My 12 '97 - p63 [51-250]
Lefkowitz, Frances - *David Letterman*
     y SLJ - v42 - D '96 - p146+ [51-250]
Lefkowitz, Mary R - *Black Athena Revisited*
     AJA - v100 - O '96 - p781+ [501+]
     Lon R Bks - v18 - D 12 '96 - p17+ [501+]
     Nat - v263 - O 28 '96 - p42+ [501+]
     Rel St Rev - v23 - Ja '97 - p63 [251-500]
     TLS - F 14 '97 - p3+ [501+]
     Not Out of Africa
     Ant R - v55 - Spr '97 - p239 [251-500]
     BYTE - v22 - Ap '97 - p151 [51-250]
     J Bl St - v27 - S '96 - p130+ [251-500]
     Lon R Bks - v18 - D 12 '96 - p17+ [501+]
     Nat - v263 - O 28 '96 - p42+ [501+]
     Skeptic - v4 - 2 '96 - p110 [251-500]
     TLS - F 14 '97 - p3+ [501+]
Lefley, Harriet P - *Family Caregiving in Mental Illness*
     Choice - v34 - S '96 - p162 [51-250]
     Readings - v12 - Mr '97 - p29 [51-250]
LeFranc, Elsie - *Consequences of Structural Adjustment*
     JEL - v34 - D '96 - p2116 [51-250]
The Left Index 1982-
     r RQ - v36 - Fall '96 - p54 [1-50]
The Left Index 1995
     r ARBA - v28 - '97 - p32+ [251-500]
Legacy, Sean - *Point Zero Bliss*
     PW - v244 - F 24 '97 - p79 [51-250]
Legacy of Light
     Mag Antiq - v151 - Ja '97 - p32 [251-500]
The Legal Researcher's Desk Reference 1996-97
     r ARBA - v28 - '97 - p224 [51-250]
     r RQ - v36 - Fall '96 - p146+ [501+]
Legato, Marianne - *What Women Need to Know*
     LJ - v122 - Ja '97 - p134 [51-250]
     PW - v243 - N 4 '96 - p71+ [51-250]
The Legend of Danny Boy. Book and Audio Version
     CAY - v17 - Fall '96 - p6 [51-250]
Legends of the Americas. Book and Electronic Media Version
     c BL - v93 - Ja '97 - p876 [51-250]
Legg, Keith R - *Modern Greece*
     R&R Bk N - v12 - F '97 - p16 [51-250]
Legge, Thomas - *Richardus Tertius*
     TranslRevS - v1 - My '95 - p26 [51-250]
     Solymitana Clades
     TranslRevS - v1 - My '95 - p26 [1-50]
Leggewie, Claus - *Republikschutz: Masstabe Fur Die Verteidigung Der Demokratie*
     Choice - v34 - D '96 - p569 [1-50]
Legler, Gretchen - *All the Powerful Invisible Things*
     Bloom Rev - v16 - Jl '96 - p21 [1-50]
Le Goff, Claude - *Le Nouveau French for Business. 3rd Ed.*
     FR - v70 - D '96 - p366+ [501+]

Legoux, Luc - *La Crise De L'Asile Politique En France*
     Choice - v34 - D '96 - p569 [1-50]
Legro, Jeffrey W - *Cooperation under Fire*
     AHR - v101 - O '96 - p1212 [501+]
     Soc - v33 - S '96 - p92+ [501+]
     Soc - v33 - S '96 - p92+ [501+]
Le Guin, Ursula K - *A Fisherman of the Inland Sea*
     New Sci - v153 - Ja 4 '97 - p40 [51-250]
     Four Ways to Forgiveness
     Books - v10 - Je '96 - p23 [51-250]
     The Left Hand of Darkness
     NWSA Jnl - v9 - Spr '97 - p22+ [501+]
     The Shobies' Story (Bruce). Audio Version
     BL - v93 - D 15 '96 - p740 [51-250]
     Unlocking the Air and Other Stories
     y Kliatt - v31 - My '97 - p14 [51-250]
     NYTBR - v101 - D 8 '96 - p84 [1-50]
     NYTBR - v102 - Ja 12 '97 - p32 [51-250]
     Trib Bks - F 2 '97 - p8 [51-250]
     Worlds of Exile and Illusion
     NYTBR - v102 - Ja 12 '97 - p32 [51-250]
Legum, Colin - *Mwalimu: The Influence of Nyerere*
     For Aff - v76 - Mr '97 - p200 [51-250]
Lehane, Brendan - *The Quest for Three Abbots*
     RR - v55 - S '96 - p553 [51-250]
Lehane, Dennis - *Darkness, Take My Hand*
     LATBR - Ag 11 '96 - p8 [251-500]
     A Drink before the War
     y Kliatt - v30 - S '96 - p12 [51 250]
     VV - v42 - Ja 7 '97 - p41 [51-250]
Lehman, Charles - *Psalm Refrains*
     CLW - v67 - Mr '97 - p35 [51-250]
Lehman, David, 1948- - *Ecstatic Occasions, Expedient Forms*
     PW - v243 - N 25 '96 - p72 [51-250]
     Valentine Place
     Ant R - v54 - Fall '96 - p498 [251-500]
     HR - v49 - Aut '96 - p503+ [501+]
Lehman, Doris - *The Riviera: Off Season and On*
     BL - v93 - S 15 '96 - p210 [1-50]
Lehman, Hugh - *Rationality and Ethics in Agriculture*
     CPR - v16 - Je '96 - p185+ [501+]
Lehman, Richard L - *Handbook on Continuous Fiber-Reinforced Ceramic Matrix Composites*
     SciTech - v21 - Mr '97 - p79 [51-250]
Lehman, Tim - *Public Values, Private Lands*
     AHR - v101 - D '96 - p1645 [251-500]
Lehman, Yvonne - *Tornado Alley*
     y VOYA - v19 - D '96 - p261 [51-250]
Lehmann, Arthur - *Magic, Witchcraft, and Religion. 3rd Ed.*
     Skeptic - v4 - '96 - p107 [51-250]
Lehmann, David - *Struggle for the Spirit*
     Choice - v34 - Mr '97 - p1225+ [51-250]
     TLS - Mr 28 '97 - p8 [501+]
Lehmann, Hartmut - *Paths of Continuity*
     EHR - v111 - S '96 - p1029+ [251-500]
Lehmann, Jennifer M - *Durkheim and Women*
     SF - v75 - S '96 - p350+ [251-500]
Lehmann, Paul L - *The Decalogue and a Human Future*
     Theol St - v57 - Je '96 - p373+ [501+]
Lehmann, Robert H - *Cooking for Life*
     LJ - v122 - Ja '97 - p134 [51-250]
     PW - v244 - Ja 6 '97 - p69 [51-250]
Lehmann-Haupt, Christopher - *A Crooked Man*
     Arm Det - v29 - Fall '96 - p402+ [51-250]
Lehmberg, Stanford E - *Cathedrals under Siege*
     Choice - v34 - N '96 - p518 [51-250]
Lehndorff, Peter - *60 Second Chronic Pain Relief*
     BWatch - v17 - D '96 - p3 [1-50]
Lehner, Philip N - *Handbook of Ethological Methods. 2nd Ed.*
     Choice - v34 - Ap '97 - p1366 [51-250]
Lehner, Urban C - *Let's Talk Turkey (About Japanese Turkeys) and Other Tales from The Asian Wall Street Journal*
     FEER - v159 - O 31 '96 - p47 [251-500]
Lehning, James R - *Peasant and French*
     JIH - v27 - Spr '97 - p687+ [501+]
     J Soc H - v30 - Win '96 - p559+ [501+]
Lehr, Susan - *Battling Dragons*
     Emerg Lib - v24 - S '96 - p38 [51-250]
Lehrer, Jamie - *The Magic Costumes (Illus. by Tracey Morgan)*
     c BL - v93 - D 15 '96 - p732 [1-50]
     c KR - v64 - S 1 '96 - p1331 [51-250]
Lehrer, Jim - *Crown Oklahoma*
     LJ - v122 - Ap 1 '97 - p134 [51-250]
     The Last Debate
     BW - v26 - D 8 '96 - p6 [51-250]

     The Sooner Spy
     LJ - v122 - Ap 1 '97 - p134 [1-50]
     White Widow
     BL - v93 - O 1 '96 - p291 [51-250]
     BW - v27 - Ja 5 '97 - p5 [501+]
     KR - v64 - O 15 '96 - p1487 [51-250]
     LJ - v121 - O 15 '96 - p91 [51-250]
     NYTBR - v102 - F 2 '97 - p21 [51-250]
     PW - v243 - O 14 '96 - p61 [51-250]
Lehrer, Kate - *Out of Eden*
     BW - v26 - S 15 '96 - p4 [501+]
     NYTBR - v102 - Ja 5 '97 - p18+ [51-250]
Lehrman, Karen - *The Lipstick Proviso*
     PW - v244 - Ap 7 '97 - p85 [51-250]
     Wil Q - v21 - Spr '97 - p105 [51-250]
Lehto, Kerry A - *Introducing Microsoft FrontPage*
     CBR - v14 - S '96 - p29 [1-50]
     TES - O 18 '96 - p41U [51-250]
Leiber, Fritz - *The Dealings of Daniel Kesserich*
     BL - v93 - F 1 '97 - p929 [51-250]
     BW - v27 - F 23 '97 - p11 [251-500]
     KR - v65 - Ja 1 '97 - p28 [51-250]
     LJ - v122 - F 15 '97 - p165 [51-250]
     PW - v244 - F 24 '97 - p68+ [51-250]
Leibfried, Stephan - *European Social Policy*
     CS - v25 - N '96 - p743+ [501+]
Leibman, Nina C - *Living Room Lectures*
     J Pop F&TV - v24 - Spr '96 - p46 [501+]
Leibniz, Gottfried Wilhelm, Freiherr Von - *La Caracteristique Geometrique*
     Isis - v87 - D '96 - p725+ [501+]
     L'Estime Des Apparences
     Isis - v87 - D '96 - p725+ [501+]
     La Reforme De La Dynamique
     Isis - v87 - D '96 - p725+ [501+]
Leibovich, Anna Feldman - *The Russian Concept of Work*
     Slav R - v55 - Fall '96 - p686+ [501+]
Leibovitz, Annie - *Olympic Portraits*
     CSM - v89 - D 5 '96 - pB4 [51-250]
Leibowitz, Yeshayahu - *Judaism, Human Values and the Jewish State*
     Rel St Rev - v22 - O '96 - p309+ [501+]
Leiby, Bruce R - *Howard Keel: A Bio-Bibliography*
     r ARBA - v28 - '97 - p492 [51-250]
Leichtman, Martin - *The Rorschach: A Developmental Perspective*
     Choice - v34 - S '96 - p215 [51-250]
Leider, Emily Wortis - *Becoming Mae West*
     BL - v93 - My 1 '97 - p1473 [51-250]
     KR - v65 - Ap 1 '97 - p527+ [251-500]
     LJ - v122 - Ap 1 '97 - p96 [51-250]
     PW - v244 - My 5 '97 - p189 [51-250]
Leiderman, Leonardo - *Inflation Targets*
     Econ J - v107 - Ja '97 - p211+ [501+]
Leiding, O - *Historische Stedenatlas Van Belgie. Vols. 1-3*
     r J Urban H - v22 - S '96 - p739+ [501+]
Leier, Mark - *Red Flags and Red Tape*
     Choice - v34 - O '96 - p349 [51-250]
Leifer, Eric Matheson - *Making the Majors*
     CS - v25 - N '96 - p804+ [501+]
     JEL - v35 - Mr '97 - p169+ [501+]
Leifer, Michael - *Dictionary of the Modern Politics of Southeast Asia*
     r Econ - v341 - O 19 '96 - p8* [51-250]
Leigh, Andrew - *Leading Your Team*
     Bus Bk R - v14 - 1 '97 - p112+ [501+]
Leigh, David - *Sleaze: The Corruption of Parliament*
     Lon R Bks - v19 - F 20 '97 - p22+ [501+]
     NS - v126 - F 14 '97 - p45 [501+]
     Obs - Ja 26 '97 - p15* [501+]
     TLS - F 21 '97 - p28 [501+]
Leigh, I M - *Skin Cancer*
     SciTech - v20 - D '96 - p50 [51-250]
Leigh, Nancey Green - *Stemming Middle-Class Decline*
     AAPSS-A - v546 - Jl '96 - p179+ [501+]
Leigh, Robert - *The Turner Journals*
     Arm Det - v29 - Fall '96 - p503+ [251-500]
Leigh, Wallace B - *Devices for Optoelectronics*
     SciTech - v20 - N '96 - p66 [51-250]
Leighton, Angela - *Victorian Women Poets*
     ELT - v39 - 4 '96 - p531 [51-250]
     Nine-C Lit - v50 - Mr '96 - p555 [1-50]
     Nine-C Lit - v51 - D '96 - p424 [51-250]
Leighton, Audrey O - *A Window of Time (Illus. by Rhonda Kyrias)*
     c LA - v73 - S '96 - p356+ [51-250]
Leighton, C D A - *Catholicism in a Protestant Kingdom*
     EHR - v111 - S '96 - p993+ [251-500]
Leighton, Mary S - *Model Strategies in Bilingual Education*
     J Gov Info - v23 - S '96 - p544 [51-250]

Leighton, Richard M - *Global Logistics and Strategy*
J Gov Info - v23 - S '96 - p543 [51-250]
Leiman, Melvin M - *The Political Economy of Racism*
S&S - v61 - Sum '97 - p275+ [501+]
Leimbach, Marti - *Love and Houses*
BL - v93 - Mr 15 '97 - p1226 [51-250]
KR - v65 - Ja 1 '97 - p13 [251-500]
LJ - v122 - F 15 '97 - p162 [51-250]
NYTBR - v102 - Ap 13 '97 - p20 [51-250]
PW - v244 - Ja 27 '97 - p77 [51-250]
Trib Bks - Ap 6 '97 - p5+ [51-250]
Leiner, Katherine - *First Children (Illus. by Katie Keller)*
c HB Guide - v7 - Fall '96 - p387 [51-250]
c LATBR - Jl 14 '96 - p11 [51-250]
Leiner, Marvin - *Sexual Politics in Cuba*
S&S - v60 - Win '96 - p514+ [501+]
Leinwand, Gerald - *Heroism in America*
y BL - v93 - F 1 '97 - p934 [51-250]
y HB Guide - v8 - Spr '97 - p174+ [51-250]
y SLJ - v43 - F '97 - p118+ [51-250]
Patriotism in America
y BL - v93 - My 15 '97 - p1571 [51-250]
Leipzig, Arthur - *Growing Up in New York*
R&R Bk N - v11 - N '96 - p19 [1-50]
Leiris, Michel - *Scraps*
LJ - v122 - Ap 1 '97 - p92+ [51-250]
Leitch, Patricia - *Cross-Country Gallop*
c SLJ - v43 - Ja '97 - p112+ [51-250]
Pony Club Rider
c SLJ - v42 - D '96 - p123 [51-250]
Leitch, Vincent B - *Postmodernism: Local Effects, Global Flows*
R&R Bk N - v11 - N '96 - p2 [51-250]
Leites, Edmund - *The Puritan Conscience and Modern Sexuality*
Sev Cent N - v54 - Fall '96 - p55+ [501+]
Leith, Prue - *Leith's Cookery Bible*
Obs - Ja 19 '97 - p18* [251-500]
Leithauser, Brad - *The Friends of Freeland*
BL - v93 - D 15 '96 - p709 [51-250]
KR - v64 - D 1 '96 - p1694 [251-500]
Nat - v264 - F 10 '97 - p34+ [501+]
NYRB - v44 - Ap 10 '97 - p54+ [501+]
NYTBR - v102 - F 23 '97 - p10+ [501+]
NYTLa - v146 - Ja 31 '97 - pC31 [501+]
PW - v243 - N 25 '96 - p56 [251-500]
Time - v149 - F 3 '97 - p70 [251-500]
WSJ-Cent - v99 - Ja 29 '97 - pA9 [501+]
Leithwood, Kenneth - *Effective School District Leadership*
AJE - v105 - My '97 - p319+ [501+]
Leitner, Michael J - *Leisure in Later Life. 2nd Ed.*
R&R Bk N - v11 - D '96 - p21 [51-250]
Leitzel, Jim - *Russian Economic Reform*
Econ J - v106 - S '96 - p1428+ [501+]
Lejeune, Claire - *Le Livre De La Soeur*
FR - v70 - D '96 - p351+ [251-500]
Leland, Christopher T - *Letting Loose*
BL - v93 - S 1 '96 - p62 [51-250]
Lele, Jayant - *Asia: Who Pays for Growth?*
R&R Bk N - v12 - F '97 - p36 [51-250]
Unravelling the Asian Miracle
R&R Bk N - v12 - F '97 - p36 [51-250]
Leledakis, Kanakis - *Society and Psyche*
AJS - v102 - Ja '97 - p1231+ [501+]
Leloudis, James L - *Schooling the New South*
Choice - v34 - N '96 - p511 [51-250]
HRNB - v25 - Win '97 - p56+ [251-500]
VQR - v72 - Aut '96 - p117* [51-250]
Lem, Stanislaw - *Highcastle: A Remembrance*
PW - v243 - O 7 '96 - p68+ [1-50]
WLT - v70 - Sum '96 - p726+ [501+]
Lemarchand, Rene - *Burundi: Ethnic Conflict and Genocide*
NYRB - v43 - Je 6 '96 - p58+ [501+]
Burundi: Ethnocide as Discourse and Practice
Am Ethnol - v23 - Ag '96 - p649 [501+]
Lemay, Laura - *3D Graphics and VRML 2*
New Sci - v153 - Ja 18 '97 - p41 [51-250]
Graphics and Web Page Design
New Sci - v153 - Ja 18 '97 - p41 [51-250]
Laura Lemay's Web Workshop
CBR - v15 - Spr '97 - p6 [1-50]
Teach Yourself Java in 21 Days
BL - v93 - S 15 '96 - p193 [501+]
Quill & Q - v62 - My '96 - p20+ [501+]
Lembede, Anton Muziwakhe - *Freedom in Our Lifetime*
Choice - v34 - My '97 - p1552 [51-250]
Lember, Barbara Hirsch - *The Shell Book (Illus. by Barbara Hirsch Lember)*
c KR - v65 - F 1 '97 - p224 [51-250]

Lembke, Janet - *Shake Them 'Simmons Down*
NH - v105 - Ag '96 - p14 [51-250]
Lemelle, Anthony J, Jr. - *Black Male Deviance*
SF - v75 - S '96 - p372+ [251-500]
Lemelle, Sidney - *Imagining Home*
Arena - Ag '96 - p50+ [501+]
Lemert, Charles - *Sociology after the Crisis*
AJS - v102 - Jl '96 - p260+ [501+]
SF - v75 - S '96 - p345+ [251-500]
LeMieux, A C - *Do Angels Sing the Blues?*
y Kliatt - v30 - N '96 - p9 [51-250]
Lemieux, Margo - *The Fiddle Ribbon (Illus. by Francis Livingston)*
c HB Guide - v7 - Fall '96 - p264 [51-250]
c SLJ - v42 - S '96 - p183 [51-250]
Paul and the Wolf (Illus. by Bill Nelson)
c HB Guide - v7 - Fall '96 - p264 [51-250]
c RT - v50 - Ap '97 - p594 [51-250]
Lemke, Jay L - *Textual Politics*
Lang Soc - v25 - S '96 - p456+ [501+]
Lemke, Nancy - *Missions of the Southern Coast*
c HB Guide - v8 - Spr '97 - p172 [51-250]
c SLJ - v42 - Ag '96 - p157+ [51-250]
Lemke-Santangelo, Gretchen - *Abiding Courage*
PHR - v65 - N '96 - p688+ [251-500]
Lemma, Alessandra - *Introduction to Psychopathology*
SciTech - v21 - Mr '97 - p53 [51-250]
Lemmon, David - *A Vision Achieved*
LAR - v98 - Ag '96 - p425 [1-50]
Lemon, Anthony - *The Geography of Change in South Africa*
AAAGA - v86 - S '96 - p599+ [501+]
GJ - v162 - Jl '96 - p221+ [251-500]
Lemon, Charles - *Early Visitors to Haworth*
TLS - Ag 2 '96 - p32 [51-250]
Lemon, M C - *The Discipline of History and the History of Thought*
AHR - v102 - F '97 - p91+ [501+]
Lemons, John - *Scientific Uncertainty and Environmental Problem Solving*
Nature - v385 - F 6 '97 - p499+ [501+]
R&R Bk N - v12 - F '97 - p29 [51-250]
Lemos, Noah M - *Intrinsic Value*
IPQ - v36 - S '96 - p370+ [501+]
Phil R - v105 - Ap '96 - p267+ [501+]
Lemos, Ramon M - *The Nature of Value*
RM - v50 - D '96 - p410+ [501+]
Lems-Dworkin, Carol - *Videos of African and African-Related Performance*
r ARBA - v28 - '97 - p521+ [51-250]
r CAY - v17 - Win '96 - p6 [51-250]
r R&R Bk N - v12 - F '97 - p70 [51-250]
Le Navenec, Carole-Lynne - *One Day at a Time*
Choice - v34 - O '96 - p313+ [51-250]
Readings - v11 - D '96 - p23 [51-250]
Le Nay, Louise - *The Hero*
Aust Bk R - O '96 - p46+ [501+]
PW - v244 - Ap 14 '97 - p58 [51-250]
Lendvai, Paul - *Auf Schwarzen Listen*
Econ - v342 - Mr 29 '97 - p94 [501+]
Zwischen Hoffnung Und Ernuchterung
Slav R - v55 - Sum '96 - p437+ [501+]
Leneouanic, Lionel - *Peekaboo Babies*
c PW - v244 - Mr 3 '97 - p77 [51-250]
Leng, Tse-Kang - *The Taiwan-China Connection*
For Aff - v76 - My '97 - p145+ [51-250]
Lenger, Friedrich - *Werner Sombart 1863-1941*
BusLR - v21 - 3 '96 - p223+ [501+]
L'Engle, Madeleine - *Love Letters*
Ch Today - v40 - N 11 '96 - p54 [51-250]
PW - v243 - S 23 '96 - p62 [51-250]
Mothers and Daughters
PW - v244 - F 24 '97 - p76 [51-250]
A Swiftly Tilting Planet (L'Engle). Audio Version
c BL - v93 - Mr 15 '97 - p1253 [51-250]
c Emerg Lib - v24 - Mr '97 - p24 [51-250]
y Kliatt - v31 - My '97 - p45 [51-250]
Wintersong: Christmas Readings
CC - v113 - D 11 '96 - p1232+ [1-50]
A Wrinkle in Time
c JOYS - v10 - Fall '96 - p35+ [501+]
c JOYS - v10 - Fall '96 - p46+ [501+]
Lenin, Vladimir Ilich - *The Unknown Lenin*
LATBR - N 17 '96 - p1+ [501+]
New R - v215 - O 14 '96 - p49+ [501+]
NYRB - v44 - Mr 6 '97 - p6+ [501+]
NYTBR - v101 - O 27 '96 - p32 [501+]
NYTLa - v146 - O 30 '96 - pC19 [501+]
TLS - Ja 31 '97 - p6+ [501+]
Wil Q - v20 - Aut '96 - p93+ [251-500]
WSJ-MW - v78 - O 23 '96 - pA16 [501+]

Lenk, John D - *McGraw-Hill Circuit Encyclopedia and Troubleshooting Guide. Vol. 3*
r Choice - v34 - D '96 - p642+ [51-250]
r SciTech - v20 - N '96 - p75 [51-250]
Simplified Design of IC Amplifiers
SciTech - v20 - S '96 - p57 [51-250]
Lennan, Richard - *The Ecclesiology of Karl Rahner*
JR - v77 - Ja '97 - p156+ [501+]
Rel St Rev - v23 - Ja '97 - p46 [51-250]
Theol St - v57 - S '96 - p540+ [501+]
Redefining the Church
CLW - v67 - D '96 - p38 [51-250]
Lenneberg, Hans - *The Dissemination of Music*
Notes - v53 - D '96 - p444+ [501+]
Lennon, Colm - *Sixteenth-Century Ireland*
EHR - v112 - Ap '97 - p460+ [501+]
Lennon, John - *In His Own Write. A Spaniard in the Works*
Obs - F 2 '97 - p18* [51-250]
Leno, Jay - *Leading with My Chin*
y BL - v93 - Ja '97 - p762 [1-50]
Ent W - O 11 '96 - p84+ [501+]
Ent W - D 27 '96 - p143 [51-250]
NYTBR - v101 - N 17 '96 - p24 [51-250]
Leading with My Chin (Leno). Audio Version
PW - v243 - O 7 '96 - p32 [51-250]
Lenox Avenue: A Journal of Interartistic Inquiry
p Notes - v53 - D '96 - p536+ [501+]
Lensink, Robert - *Structural Adjustment in Sub-Saharan Africa*
Econ J - v107 - Ja '97 - p281 [51-250]
Lent, John A - *Animation, Caricature, Gag and Political Cartoons in the United States and Canada*
r Humor - v10 - 1 '97 - p123+ [501+]
r RQ - v35 - Sum '96 - p486+ [51-250]
Asian Popular Culture
J Am Cult - v19 - Sum '96 - p141 [51-250]
Comic Art in Africa, Asia, Australia, and Latin America
r AB - v99 - Mr 3 '97 - p696+ [501+]
Comic Art of Europe
r Humor - v10 - 1 '97 - p123+ [501+]
r RQ - v35 - Sum '96 - p486+ [51-250]
Comic Books and Comic Strips in the United States
r Humor - v10 - 1 '97 - p123+ [501+]
Lenten, Roelie - *Cooking under the Volcanoes*
HAHR - v77 - My '97 - p345+ [251-500]
Lentricchia, Frank - *Johnny Critelli. The Knifemen*
Ent W - F 14 '97 - p56 [51-250]
KR - v64 - O 15 '96 - p1487 [251-500]
LJ - v121 - N 15 '96 - p91 [51-250]
LJ - v122 - Mr 15 '97 - p42 [1-50]
NYTBR - v101 - D 29 '96 - p7+ [501+]
PW - v243 - N 4 '96 - p64 [51-250]
Modernist Quartet
RES - v47 - N '96 - p635+ [501+]
Lentz, Harris M - *Western and Frontier Film and Television Credits 1903-1995. Vols. 1-2*
r ARBA - v28 - '97 - p515 [51-250]
r BL - v93 - N 1 '96 - p542 [51-250]
r Choice - v34 - Ja '97 - p770 [51-250]
r R&R Bk N - v11 - D '96 - p61 [51-250]
Lentzen, Manfred - *Italienische Lyrik Des 20. Jahrhunderts*
MLR - v91 - O '96 - p1015+ [501+]
Lenz, Frederick - *Snowboarding to Nirvana*
KR - v65 - F 15 '97 - p246 [251-500]
Snowboarding to Nirvana (Hawkins). Audio Version
PW - v244 - Ap 7 '97 - p34 [501+]
Surfing the Himalayas
y Kliatt - v31 - My '97 - p22 [51-250]
Rapport - v19 - 4 '96 - p33 [51-250]
Lenzenweger, Mark F - *Frontiers of Developmental Psychopathology*
AJPsych - v154 - F '97 - p280 [501+]
Leo, Vince - *Here and Now*
Afterimage - v24 - S '96 - p16 [251-500]
Leob, Kurt - *White Man's Burden*
JTWS - v13 - Fall '96 - p272+ [501+]
Leon, Burke - *The Insider's Guide to Buying a New or Used Car*
BL - v93 - D 15 '96 - p700 [51-250]
Leon, Donna - *Acqua Alta*
BL - v93 - O 1 '96 - p325 [51-250]
Books - v10 - Je '96 - p23 [51-250]
KR - v64 - Ag 15 '96 - p1194 [51-250]
NYTBR - v101 - O 27 '96 - p42 [51-250]
PW - v243 - S 2 '96 - p117 [51-250]
Leon, Philip W - *Walt Whitman and Sir William Osler*
AJPsych - v153 - D '96 - p1644+ [501+]

Leon, Pierre - *Pigou, Fiflard Et Compagnie (Illus. by Pierre Leon)*
  c Can CL - v22 - Sum '96 - p98+ [251-500]

Leonard, Buck - *Buck Leonard, the Black Lou Gehrig*
  Aethlon - v13 - Spr '96 - p224+ [251-500]

Leonard, Dick - *Elections in Britain Today*
  Econ - v342 - Mr 22 '97 - p106 [501+]

Leonard, Edmund A - *Packaging. 4th Ed.*
  SciTech - v20 - N '96 - p82 [51-250]

Leonard, Elmore - *The Big Bounce (Adams). Audio Version*
  y Kliatt - v30 - S '96 - p44 [51-250]
Cat Chaser (Muller). Audio Version
  y Kliatt - v30 - S '96 - p44 [51-250]
Cat Chaser (Adams). Audio Version
  y Kliatt - v30 - S '96 - p44 [51-250]
Freaky Deaky (Muller). Audio Version
  LJ - v121 - O 1 '96 - p142+ [51-250]
Get Shorty (Mantegna). Audio Version
  y Kliatt - v30 - S '96 - p48 [51-250]
Mr. Majestyk (Muller). Audio Version
  y Kliatt - v30 - S '96 - p50 [51-250]
Out of Sight
  CSM - v88 - S 19 '96 - p14 [51-250]
  LATBR - Ag 25 '96 - p3 [501+]
  LATBR - D 29 '96 - p5 [51-250]
  Mac - v109 - S 16 '96 - p66 [251-500]
  Nat - v263 - O 21 '96 - p33+ [501+]
  NYTBR - v101 - S 8 '96 - p8 [501+]
  y SLJ - v43 - Mr '97 - p216 [51-250]
Out of Sight (Mantegna). Audio Version
  Arm Det - v30 - Win '97 - p81 [51-250]
  y Kliatt - v30 - N '96 - p44 [51-250]
Riding the Rap
  Books - v9 - S '95 - p18 [51-250]
Stick (Muller). Audio Version
  LJ - v121 - O 1 '96 - p144+ [51-250]
Swag (Muller). Audio Version
  LJ - v121 - O 1 '96 - p144+ [51-250]

Leonard, Frank - *A Thousand Blunders*
  JEL - v34 - D '96 - p2107 [51-250]
  WHQ - v27 - Win '96 - p531+ [501+]

Leonard, John - *Smoke and Mirrors*
  y BL - v93 - F 1 '97 - p912 [51-250]
  Ent W - Mr 28 '97 - p62 [51-250]
  KR - v65 - Ja 1 '97 - p42 [251-500]
  NYTBR - v102 - Mr 2 '97 - p7 [501+]
  PW - v244 - Ja 6 '97 - p54+ [251-500]

Leonard, Karen Isaksen - *Making Ethnic Choices*
  HAHR - v77 - F '97 - p94 [251-500]

Leonard, Linda Schierse - *Creation's Heartbeat*
  Parabola - v22 - F '97 - p118+ [501+]
Meeting the Madwoman
  JPC - v29 - Spr '96 - p240+ [51-250]

Leonard, Paul - *Dancing the Code*
  SF Chr - v18 - O '96 - p77 [51-250]

Leonard, Richard G - *Nothing Diplomatic*
  PW - v243 - D 30 '96 - p50 [51-250]

Leonard, Thomas C - *News for All*
  Choice - v34 - S '96 - p117 [51-250]
  CJR - v35 - Jl '96 - p60+ [501+]

Leonard Maltin's Movie and Video Guide. 1997 Ed.
  yr Kliatt - v30 - N '96 - p30 [51-250]

Leonardi, Paolo - *On Quine*
  RM - v50 - S '96 - p168+ [501+]

Leonardi, Robert - *Convergence, Cohesion and Integration in the European Union*
  J Pol - v58 - N '96 - p1251+ [501+]

Leonardi, Susan J - *The Diva's Mouth*
  Choice - v34 - Ap '97 - p1348 [51-250]
  Nat - v264 - F 3 '97 - p33+ [501+]
  PW - v243 - N 18 '96 - p69 [51-250]

Leonardo Da Vinci. Electronic Media Version
  LJ - v122 - Ap 1 '97 - p136+ [51-250]
  r LJ - v122 - Ap 15 '97 - p40 [1-50]
  PW - v244 - F 24 '97 - p36 [51-250]

Leon Carpio, Ramiro De - *Riding the Tiger*
  HAHR - v77 - My '97 - p335+ [501+]

Leone, Daniel A - *The Spread of AIDS*
  y Kliatt - v31 - Mr '97 - p29 [51-250]

Leone, Diana - *Crazy with Cotton*
  BL - v93 - Mr 1 '97 - p1103 [51-250]
  LJ - v122 - Ap 15 '97 - p80 [51-250]

Leong, Frederick T L - *The Psychology Research Handbook*
  SciTech - v20 - N '96 - p1 [51-250]

Leong, Stanley P L - *Immunotherapy of Malignant Melanoma*
  SciTech - v20 - N '96 - p41 [51-250]

Leon-Portilla, Miguel - *The Aztec Image of Self and Society*
  Am Ethnol - v23 - N '96 - p927+ [501+]

Leopardi, Giacomo - *Scritti E Frammenti Autobiografici*
  MLR - v92 - Ja '97 - p219+ [501+]

Lepetit, Bernard - *The Pre-Industrial Urban System*
  EHR - v111 - N '96 - p1304 [251-500]
  JIH - v27 - Aut '96 - p316+ [501+]

Lepine, David - *A Brotherhood of Canons Serving God*
  Albion - v28 - Fall '96 - p469+ [501+]

Lepine, Luc - *Les Officiers De Milice Du Bascanada 1812-1815*
  r EGH - v50 - N '96 - p154 [51-250]

Le Pla, Frances - *Islam*
  TES - D 6 '96 - pR7 [501+]

Lepon, Shoshana - *Hillel Builds a House (Illus. by Marilynn Barr)*
  c Ch BWatch - v6 - Jl '96 - p5 [51-250]

Leppard, Lois Gladys - *Mandie and the Courtroom Battle*
  c SLJ - v43 - Mr '97 - p187+ [51-250]

Lepper, Marion J C De - *The Added Value of Geographical Information Systems in Public and Environmental Health*
  AAAGA - v86 - D '96 - p801+ [501+]

Leps, Marie-Christine - *Apprehending the Criminal*
  CLS - v33 - 2 '96 - p227+ [501+]

Lepthien, Emilie U - *Sea Turtles*
  c HB Guide - v8 - Spr '97 - p123 [1-50]
  c SB - v33 - My '97 - p113 [251-500]

Le Queux, William - *Spies of the Kaiser*
  TLS - D 27 '96 - p21 [501+]

Lerer, Seth - *Literary History and the Challenge of Philology*
  Choice - v34 - O '96 - p272 [51-250]
  YR - v85 - Ja '97 - p136+ [501+]

Lerman, Rory S - *Charlie's Checklist (Illus. by Alison Bartlett)*
  c CBRS - v25 - Ap '97 - p99 [51-250]
  c KR - v65 - Mr 15 '97 - p464 [51-250]
  c PW - v244 - Mr 24 '97 - p83 [51-250]
  c TES - Mr 21 '97 - p9* [501+]

Lerner, Carol - *Backyard Birds of Summer (Illus. by Carol Lerner)*
  c Emerg Lib - v23 - My '96 - p43 [1-50]
  c HB Guide - v7 - Fall '96 - p344 [51-250]
  cr SB - v32 - N '96 - p241+ [251-500]

Lerner, Eric J - *The Big Bang Never Happened*
  Skeptic - v3 - '95 - p101 [51-250]

Lerner, Gerda - *Why History Matters*
  BL - v93 - Ap 1 '97 - p1279 [51-250]
  KR - v65 - F 1 '97 - p202 [251-500]
  LJ - v122 - Mr 15 '97 - p74 [51-250]
  PW - v244 - F 3 '97 - p83+ [51-250]

Lerner, Harriet - *What's So Terrible about Swallowing an Apple Seed? (Illus. by Catharine O'Neill)*
  c CBRS - v25 - D '96 - p39+ [51-250]
  c HB Guide - v8 - Spr '97 - p36 [51-250]
  c SLJ - v42 - N '96 - p183+ [51-250]

Lerner, Lawrence S - *Physics for Scientists and Engineers*
  SciTech - v20 - D '96 - p22 [1-50]

Lerner, Max - *Wounded Titans*
  KR - v64 - S 1 '96 - p1298+ [251-500]
  LJ - v121 - O 15 '96 - p77 [51-250]
  PW - v243 - S 23 '96 - p65+ [51-250]

Lerner, Michael, 1943- - *Jews and Blacks*
  LATBR - Mr 24 '96 - p11 [51-250]
The Politics of Meaning
  Bloom Rev - v16 - S '96 - p23 [501+]
  CC - v113 - O 30 '96 - p1038+ [501+]
  TLS - Mr 21 '97 - p29 [501+]
  VQR - v73 - Win '97 - p25* [501+]

Lerner, Michael, 1943, Oct., 10- - *Choices in Healing*
  LJ - v122 - Ja '97 - p57 [1-50]
  Readings - v11 - D '96 - p10+ [501+]

Lerner, Michel-Pierre - *Tommaso Campanella En France*
  Isis - v87 - S '96 - p545+ [251-500]

Lerner, Richard M - *Final Solutions*
  Soc - v34 - Mr '97 - p78+ [501+]

Lerner, Robert - *American Elites*
  Choice - v34 - Ap '97 - p1424 [51-250]
  JEL - v35 - Mr '97 - p305+ [51-250]
  Nat R - v48 - D 9 '96 - p64+ [501+]
Molding the Good Citizen
  Pub Int - Sum '96 - p108+ [501+]
  SS - v87 - Jl '96 - p188+ [501+]
  TCR - v97 - Sum '96 - p664+ [501+]

Lerner, William J - *The Irwin Directory of Emerging Markets Brokers*
  r R&R Bk N - v12 - F '97 - p48 [1-50]

Lerner Publications Company. Geography Dept. - *Cambodia--in Pictures*
  c HB Guide - v8 - Spr '97 - p169 [51-250]
Laos--in Pictures
  c HB Guide - v8 - Spr '97 - p169 [51-250]
Libya--in Pictures
  c HB Guide - v8 - Spr '97 - p171 [51-250]
Switzerland--in Pictures
  c HB Guide - v7 - Fall '96 - p383 [51-250]
  c SLJ - v42 - Ag '96 - p160+ [51-250]

Lernout, Geert - *The Poet as Thinker*
  MLR - v91 - O '96 - p1041+ [251-500]

Leroe, Ellen - *Racetrack Robbery (Illus. by Bill Basso)*
  c HB Guide - v7 - Fall '96 - p287 [1-50]

LeRoith, Derek - *Diabetes Mellitus*
  SciTech - v20 - N '96 - p46 [51-250]

Leroux, Gaston - *Le Fantome De L'Opera*
  FR - v70 - F '97 - p416+ [501+]
Phantom of the Opera
  RM - v95 - Sum '96 - p821+ [501+]

Leroux, Odette - *Inuit Women Artists*
  BL - v92 - Ag '96 - p1871 [51-250]
  LATBR - Ag 18 '96 - p15 [51-250]

Leroux-Van Der Boon, Marzanne - *Soos Honde Van Die Hemel*
  WLT - v70 - Sum '96 - p751 [501+]

Le Roy Ladurie, Emmanuel - *The Ancien Regime*
  Choice - v34 - Ap '97 - p1397 [51-250]
  TLS - D 13 '96 - p9 [501+]
The Beggar and the Professor
  BL - v93 - F 1 '97 - p924 [51-250]
  KR - v65 - Ja 1 '97 - p41 [251-500]
  LJ - v121 - D '96 - p117 [51-250]
  Nat - v264 - Ap 21 '97 - p28+ [501+]
  NYTBR - v102 - Ap 13 '97 - p28 [501+]
  Obs - Ap 13 '97 - p15* [501+]
  PW - v244 - Ja 20 '97 - p383 [251-500]
The Royal French State 1460-1610
  EHR - v111 - S '96 - p972+ [501+]
Le Siecle Des Platter. Vol. 1
  Choice - v34 - D '96 - p567 [1-50]

Lerski, George J - *Historical Dictionary of Poland 966-1945*
  r Choice - v34 - S '96 - p100+ [51-250]

Le Ru, Veronique - *Jean Le Rond D'Alembert Philosophe*
  Dialogue - v35 - Fall '96 - p821+ [501+]

Lery, Jean De - *Histoire D'Un Voyage En Terre De Bresil*
  Poetics T - v18 - Spr '97 - p127+ [501+]

Le Saux, Francoise H M - *The Text and Tradition of Layamon's Brut*
  MLR - v92 - Ap '97 - p423+ [501+]
  RES - v48 - F '97 - p84+ [501+]

Lesch, David W - *The Middle East and the United States*
  Choice - v34 - S '96 - p206 [51-250]
  For Aff - v75 - S '96 - p157 [51-250]
  MEJ - v50 - Sum '96 - p455 [51-250]

Leschert, Dale F - *Hermeneutical Foundations of Hebrews*
  Rel St Rev - v23 - Ja '97 - p75 [51-250]

Lescroart, John T - *A Certain Justice (David). Audio Version*
  y Kliatt - v31 - My '97 - p35 [51-250]
Guilt
  KR - v65 - Ap 1 '97 - p491 [251-500]
  LJ - v122 - My 1 '97 - p141 [51-250]
  PW - v244 - Ap 14 '97 - p51+ [51-250]

Leseur, Elisabeth - *My Spirit Rejoices*
  RR - v56 - Ja '97 - p107 [501+]

Leshem, Nurit - *Ba-Midrakhot*
  BL - v93 - Mr 1 '97 - p1115 [1-50]

Lesieur, M - *Computational Fluid Dynamics*
  SciTech - v20 - D '96 - p20 [1-50]

Lesinski, Jeanne M - *Exotic Invaders*
  c Ch BWatch - v6 - Jl '96 - p6 [51-250]
  c HB Guide - v7 - Fall '96 - p336 [51-250]
  c SB - v33 - Ja '97 - p19 [51-250]

Lesley, Craig - *The Sky Fisherman*
  LATBR - N 17 '96 - p14 [51-250]
The Sky Fisherman (Sala). Audio Version
  CSM - v89 - F 27 '97 - pB4 [51-250]

Leslie, Amanda - *Let's Look inside the Red Car*
  c Bks Keeps - Mr '97 - p18 [51-250]
  c Books - v11 - Ap '97 - p24 [51-250]
  c PW - v244 - Ja 20 '97 - p403 [51-250]
Let's Look inside the Yellow Truck
  c Bks Keeps - Mr '97 - p18 [51-250]
  c Books - v11 - Ap '97 - p24 [51-250]
  c PW - v244 - Ja 20 '97 - p403 [51-250]

Leslie, David W - *Wise Moves in Hard Times*
  Choice - v34 - D '96 - p661 [51-250]

Leslie, Edward E - *The Devil Knows How to Ride*
    BL - v93 - S 15 '96 - p216 [51-250]
    NY - v72 - Ja 13 '97 - p79 [51-250]
    PW - v243 - S 9 '96 - p74 [51-250]
Leslie, John, 1940- - *The End of the World*
    Quill & Q - v62 - My '96 - p31 [501+]
    TLS - F 21 '97 - p10 [501+]
Universes
    NS & S - v9 - My 17 '96 - p39 [1-50]
Leslie, John, 1944- - *Love for Sale*
    BL - v93 - D 15 '96 - p713 [51-250]
    LJ - v121 - D '96 - p151 [51-250]
    PW - v243 - N 18 '96 - p65 [51-250]
Night and Day
    Arm Det - v29 - Fall '96 - p403 [51-250]
Leslie, Kent Anderson - *Woman of Color, Daughter of Privilege*
    Bloom Rev - v17 - Ja '97 - p18 [251-500]
Lesniewicz, Paul - *Bonsai in Your Home*
    r BL - v93 - Mr 1 '97 - p1102 [51-250]
Lesnik-Oberstein, Karin - *Children's Literature*
    RES - v47 - Ag '96 - p458+ [501+]
Lesourd, Jean-Baptiste - *Models for Energy Policy*
    JEL - v34 - D '96 - p2135+ [51-250]
Lessard, Suzannah - *The Architect of Desire*
    BL - v93 - N 1 '96 - p464 [51-250]
    BW - v26 - O 27 '96 - p3 [501+]
    Ent W - D 6 '96 - p58 [51-250]
    Ent W - D 27 '96 - p143 [51-250]
    KR - v64 - S 1 '96 - p1299 [251-500]
    LATBR - N 24 '96 - p4 [501+]
    LJ - v121 - O 15 '96 - p55 [51-250]
    Lon R Bks - v19 - Mr 6 '97 - p7 [501+]
    NY - v72 - D 16 '96 - p108 [51-250]
    NYTBR - v101 - N 3 '96 - p7 [501+]
    NYTBR - v101 - D 8 '96 - p84 [1-50]
    NYTLa - v146 - O 28 '96 - pC19 [51-250]
    Obs - Mr 9 '97 - p16* [501+]
    Prog - v61 - Ja '97 - p31+ [501+]
    PW - v243 - S 9 '96 - p70 [251-500]
    PW - v243 - N 4 '96 - p44 [51-250]
    SLJ - v42 - D '96 - p41 [251-500]
    TLS - Mr 28 '97 - p12 [501+]
Lessem, Don - *Dinosaur Worlds*
    c BL - v93 - N 15 '96 - p583+ [51-250]
    c CBRS - v25 - Ja '97 - p58 [51-250]
    c Ch BWatch - v6 - D '96 - p8 [51-250]
    c CLW - v67 - Mr '97 - p54+ [51-250]
    c HB Guide - v8 - Spr '97 - p115 [51-250]
    c PW - v243 - N 4 '96 - p78 [51-250]
    c SLJ - v42 - D '96 - p131 [51-250]
Ornithomimids, the Fastest Dinosaur (Illus. by Donna Bragenitz)
    c HB Guide - v7 - Fall '96 - p333+ [51-250]
Raptors! The Nastiest Dinosaurs (Illus. by David Peters)
    c BL - v93 - S 1 '96 - p121 [51-250]
    c HB Guide - v8 - Spr '97 - p115 [51-250]
    c PW - v243 - S 2 '96 - p133 [51-250]
    c SLJ - v42 - O '96 - p135+ [51-250]
Seismosaurus: The Longest Dinosaur (Illus. by Donna Bragenetz)
    c HB Guide - v8 - Spr '97 - p115 [51-250]
    c SB - v32 - O '96 - p209 [51-250]
    c SLJ - v42 - S '96 - p218 [51-250]
Troodon: The Smartest Dinosaur
    c HB Guide - v7 - Fall '96 - p334 [51-250]
Utahraptor: The Deadliest Dinosaur (Illus. by Donna Bragenitz)
    c HB Guide - v8 - Spr '97 - p115 [51-250]
    c SB - v32 - O '96 - p209+ [51-250]
    c SLJ - v42 - S '96 - p218 [51-250]
Lesser, Carolyn - *Dig Hole, Soft Mole (Illus. by Laura Regan)*
    c BL - v93 - O 1 '96 - p359 [51-250]
    c HB Guide - v8 - Spr '97 - p36 [51-250]
    c PW - v243 - O 7 '96 - p75 [51-250]
    c SLJ - v42 - D '96 - p99 [51-250]
Great Crystal Bear (Illus. by William Noonan)
    c HB Guide - v7 - Fall '96 - p264 [51-250]
Storm on the Desert (Illus. by Ted Rand)
    c BL - v93 - My 1 '97 - p1500 [51-250]
Lesser, Jeffrey - *Welcoming the Undesirables*
    AHR - v102 - F '97 - p243 [251-500]
    HAHR - v76 - N '96 - p818+ [501+]
Lessing, Doris May - *Going Home*
    NYTBR - v101 - Ap 7 '96 - p24 [1-50]
In Pursuit of the English
    NYTBR - v101 - Ap 7 '96 - p24 [51-250]

Love, Again
    Am - v175 - D 7 '96 - p25+ [501+]
    Ant R - v54 - Fall '96 - p493 [251-500]
    NYTBR - v102 - Mr 30 '97 - p24 [51-250]
    Trib Bks - Mr 30 '97 - p2 [1-50]
    WLT - v70 - Aut '96 - p959 [501+]
    Wom R Bks - v14 - O '96 - p11+ [501+]
Play with a Tiger and Other Plays
    Obs - Ja 12 '97 - p18* [51-250]
Under My Skin
    Soc - v34 - Ja '97 - p94+ [501+]
Lessoff, Alan - *The Nation and Its City*
    T&C - v37 - Ap '96 - p370+ [501+]
Lest We Forget. Electronic Media Version
    r LJ - v122 - Ap 15 '97 - p40 [1-50]
Lester, Alan - *From Colonization to Democracy*
    Choice - v34 - My '97 - p1552+ [51-250]
Lester, Alison - *When Frank Was Four*
    c HB Guide - v7 - Fall '96 - p264 [51-250]
    c Par - v71 - D '96 - p252 [1-50]
Yikes! In Seven Wild Adventures, Who Would You Be? (Illus. by Alison Lester)
    c JB - v60 - O '96 - p185+ [51-250]
Lester, Andrew D - *Hope in Pastoral Care and Counseling*
    Rel St Rev - v22 - O '96 - p336 [51-250]
    TT - v53 - O '96 - p428 [51-250]
Lester, G A - *The Language of Old and Middle English Poetry*
    R&R Bk N - v11 - N '96 - p69 [51-250]
Lester, Helen - *Author: A True Story (Illus. by Helen Lester)*
    c BL - v93 - Mr 15 '97 - p1246 [51-250]
    c CBRS - v25 - Ap '97 - p103 [51-250]
    c CCB-B - v50 - Ap '97 - p288 [51-250]
    c HB - v73 - My '97 - p341 [51-250]
    c KR - v65 - Ap '97 - p559 [51-250]
    c PW - v244 - F 3 '97 - p105 [51-250]
    c Trib Bks - My 4 '97 - p7 [51-250]
Princess Penelope's Parrot (Illus. by Lynn Munsinger)
    c BL - v93 - S 1 '96 - p143 [51-250]
    c CCB-B - v50 - Ja '97 - p179 [51-250]
    c HB - v72 - N '96 - p727 [51-250]
    c HB Guide - v8 - Spr '97 - p36 [51-250]
    c KR - v64 - O 15 '96 - p1540 [51-250]
    c PW - v243 - O 7 '96 - p74 [51-250]
    c SLJ - v42 - O '96 - p101 [51-250]
Three Cheers for Tacky (Illus. by Lynn Munsinger)
    c PW - v243 - O 7 '96 - p78 [1-50]
Lester, Jim - *Fallout*
    y HB Guide - v7 - Fall '96 - p302 [51-250]
Lester, Joan Steinau - *Taking Charge*
    Ms - v7 - N '96 - p82 [1-50]
    PW - v243 - S 16 '96 - p76 [51-250]
Lester, Joseph - *E. Ray Lankester and the Making of Modern British Biology*
    Isis - v87 - S '96 - p561 [501+]
Lester, Julius - *John Henry*
    c CLW - v67 - Mr '97 - p14 [1-50]
Othello
    y Emerg Lib - v24 - S '96 - p24 [1-50]
    y Emerg Lib - v24 - S '96 - p27 [1-50]
Sam and the Tigers (Illus. by Jerry Pinkney)
    c BL - v93 - Ja '97 - p768 [1-50]
    c BL - v93 - Ap 1 '97 - p1296 [1-50]
    c CBRS - v25 - N '96 - p26 [51-250]
    c ECEJ - v24 - Spr '97 - p176 [51-250]
    c HB - v72 - S '96 - p536+ [501+]
    c HB Guide - v8 - Spr '97 - p36 [51-250]
    c LATBR - D 8 '96 - p19 [51-250]
    c Learning - v25 - N '96 - p29 [51-250]
    c NY - v72 - N 18 '96 - p98+ [1-50]
    c NYTBR - v101 - N 10 '96 - p34 [501+]
    c SLJ - v42 - Ag '96 - p126 [51-250]
    c SLJ - v42 - D '96 - p30 [1-50]
    c Time - v148 - S 9 '96 - p72 [251-500]
    c VV - v41 - S 17 '96 - p49 [501+]
Lester, Patrick D - *The Biographical Directory of Native American Painters*
    yr ARBA - v28 - '97 - p370+ [251-500]
Lester, Paul Martin - *Images That Injure*
    Choice - v34 - O '96 - p270+ [251-500]
Lester, Ray - *Information Sources in Finance and Banking*
    r ARBA - v28 - '97 - p94+ [251-500]
Lester, Robin - *Stagg's University*
    RAH - v24 - D '96 - p629+ [501+]
Lester, V Markham - *Victorian Insolvency*
    AHR - v101 - D '96 - p1542+ [501+]
    BHR - v70 - Aut '96 - p426+ [501+]
Lestienne, Remy - *The Children of Time*
    CPR - v16 - Ag '96 - p263+ [501+]

Lestringant, Frank - *L'Experience Huguenote Au Nouveau Monde*
    Ren Q - v50 - Spr '97 - p251+ [501+]
Lesurf, J C G - *Information and Measurement*
    LQ - v66 - O '96 - p482+ [501+]
Lesynski, Loris - *Boy Soup (Illus. by Loris Lesynski)*
    c BIC - v25 - O '96 - p31+ [251-500]
    c Ch Bk News - v19 - Sum '96 - p21 [501+]
    c Quill & Q - v62 - N '96 - p47 [251-500]
Lethem, Jonathan - *As She Climbed across the Table*
    KR - v65 - Ja 15 '97 - p83 [251-500]
    LJ - v122 - Mr 15 '97 - p90 [51-250]
    PW - v244 - F 3 '97 - p93+ [51-250]
    VLS - Spr '97 - p18+ [501+]
The Wall of the Sky, the Wall of the Eye
    BL - v93 - S 1 '96 - p69 [51-250]
    BW - v26 - S 29 '96 - p11 [251-500]
    LATBR - v263 - S 29 '96 - p10 [501+]
Letourneau, P A - *Milwaukee Road 1850-1960 Photo Archive*
    Model R - v63 - D '96 - p74 [51-250]
LeTourneau, Tom - *Lighting Techniques for Video Production*
    SciTech - v20 - S '96 - p62 [51-250]
Let's Go Shopping (Snapshot)
    c Ch BWatch - v6 - D '96 - p8 [1-50]
    c PW - v243 - N 4 '96 - p78 [51-250]
Let's Play
    p TES - Ja 10 '97 - p14* [1-50]
Lette, Kathy - *Mad Cows*
    Aust Bk R - D '96 - p66+ [501+]
    PW - v243 - D 30 '96 - p56+ [251-500]
    Spec - v277 - D 7 '96 - p44 [501+]
    Woman's J - D '96 - p16 [51-250]
Letterman, David - *David Letterman's Book of Top Ten Lists and Zesty Lo-Cal Chicken Recipes*
    y BL - v93 - Ap 1 '97 - p1308 [1-50]
Lettres Des Souverains Portugais A Charles Quint Et A L'Imperatrice 1528-1532
    Six Ct J - v27 - Win '96 - p1116+ [51-250]
Letts, Barry - *The Ghosts of N-Space*
    SF Chr - v18 - O '96 - p77 [51-250]
Letts, Billie - *Where the Heart Is*
    y Kliatt - v30 - S '96 - p12 [51-250]
Leu, Corneliu - *Drumul Spre Damasc*
    BL - v93 - D 15 '96 - p714 [1-50]
Leuchtenburg, William Edward - *The FDR Years*
    JSH - v63 - F '97 - p199+ [501+]
    Rapport - v19 - 4 '96 - p35 [251-500]
The Supreme Court Reborn
    AHR - v101 - O '96 - p1303+ [501+]
    Am - v175 - Ag 17 '96 - p28+ [501+]
    Bks & Cult - v2 - N '96 - p27+ [501+]
    SE - v60 - S '96 - p302 [51-250]
Leuci, Robert - *The Snitch*
    KR - v65 - Ja 1 '97 - p13 [251-500]
    LJ - v122 - Ja '97 - p147 [51-250]
    PW - v244 - Ja 27 '97 - p76 [51-250]
Leuck, Laura - *My Baby Brother Has Ten Tiny Toes (Illus. by Clara Vulliamy)*
    c SLJ - v43 - Mr '97 - p160+ [51-250]
Sun Is Falling, Night Is Calling (Illus. by Ora Eitan)
    c Sch Lib - v44 - N '96 - p147 [51-250]
    c TES - S 27 '96 - p12* [501+]
Leuenberger, Hans Georg W - *A Multilingual Glossary of Biotechnological Terms*
    r SciTech - v20 - S '96 - p60 [51-250]
Leung, Albert - *Encyclopedia of Common Natural Ingredients Used in Food, Drugs, and Cosmetics. 2nd Ed.*
    r Am Sci - v85 - Ja '97 - p83 [251-500]
Leung, Joe C B - *Authority and Benevolence*
    Ch Rev Int - v3 - Fall '96 - p477+ [501+]
    Soc Ser R - v71 - Mr '97 - p167 [51-250]
Leupp, Gary P - *Male Colors*
    CS - v26 - Ja '97 - p73+ [501+]
Leuzzi, Linda - *A Matter of Style*
    y HB Guide - v8 - Spr '97 - p92 [51-250]
    c SLJ - v43 - F '97 - p117 [51-250]
Levant, Ronald F - *A New Psychology of Men*
    JMF - v59 - F '97 - p234+ [501+]
Levarie, Norma - *The Art and History of Books*
    Bloom Rev - v16 - N '96 - p22 [1-50]
    LR - v45 - 7 '96 - p71+ [251-500]
LeVay, Simon - *Albrick's Gold*
    PW - v244 - F 3 '97 - p97 [51-250]

Queer Science
Advocate - Ja 21 '97 - p94 [1-50]
BW - v26 - S 1 '96 - p9 [501+]
Choice - v34 - O '96 - p321 [51-250]
HG&LRev - v3 - Fall '96 - p42+ [501+]
NH - v105 - Ag '96 - p10+ [501+]
TLS - N 1 '96 - p14 [501+]

Levchev, Vladimir - *Leaves from the Dry Tree*
TranslRevS - v2 - D '96 - p19 [51-250]

Leveille, Paul - *Painting Expressive Portraits in Oil*
y BL - v93 - Mr 15 '97 - p1219 [51-250]

Levendosky, Charles - *Circle of Light*
WAL - v31 - Fall '96 - p281+ [251-500]

Levenduski, Cristine - *Peculiar Power*
Choice - v34 - Ja '97 - p811 [51-250]
HRNB - v25 - Win '97 - p228+ [501+]

Levenkron, Steven - *The Best Little Girl in the World*
y Kliatt - v30 - S '96 - p3 [1-50]
The Luckiest Girl in the World
y BL - v93 - Mr 1 '97 - p1110 [51-250]
KR - v65 - Ja 15 '97 - p83 [251-500]
PW - v244 - F 3 '97 - p97 [51-250]

Levenson, Hanna - *Time-Limited Dynamic Psychotherapy*
AJPsych - v153 - S '96 - p1228+ [501+]

Levenson, Jon D - *The Death and Resurrection of the Beloved Son*
CC - v113 - O 16 '96 - p982+ [501+]
The Hebrew Bible, the Old Testament, and Historical Criticism
Bks & Cult - v1 - N '95 - p3+ [501+]
TT - v53 - O '96 - p377+ [501+]

Levenspiel, Octave - *Understanding Engineering Thermo*
SciTech - v20 - S '96 - p53 [51-250]

Leventhal, F M - *Twentieth-Century Britain*
r Albion - v28 - Fall '96 - p541+ [501+]

Leveque, Francois - *Environmental Policy in Europe*
JEL - v34 - D '96 - p2133 [51-250]

Leveque, Pierre - *Cleisthenes the Athenian*
Choice - v34 - S '96 - p208 [51-250]

LeVeque, William J - *Fundamentals of Number Theory*
Math T - v89 - D '96 - p781 [251-500]

Lever, Evelyne - *Philippe Egalite*
TLS - F 28 '97 - p30 [501+]

Lever, Maurice - *Papiers De Famille*
FR - v70 - D '96 - p327+ [501+]

Lever, Richard - *Post-Colonial Literatures in English: Australia 1970-1992*
r ARBA - v28 - '97 - p458 [51-250]
r Choice - v34 - Ja '97 - p770+ [51-250]
r R&R Bk N - v11 - D '96 - p74 [51-250]

Leverich, Kathleen - *Daisy (Illus. by Lynne Woodcock Cravath)*
c HB - v73 - My '97 - p324+ [51-250]
Heather (Illus. by Lynne Woodcock Cravath)
c HB - v73 - My '97 - p324+ [51-250]
Rose (Illus. by Lynne Woodcock Cravath)
c HB - v73 - My '97 - p324+ [51-250]
Violet (Illus. by Lynne Woodcock Cravath)
c HB - v73 - My '97 - p324+ [51-250]
c PW - v244 - Ap 21 '97 - p72 [51-250]

Leverich, Lyle - *Tom: The Unknown Tennessee Williams*
Ent W - Ap 18 '97 - p63 [1-50]
NYTBR - v101 - D 8 '96 - p93 [1-50]
PW - v244 - Mr 24 '97 - p81 [1-50]
Trib Bks - My 11 '97 - p8 [1-50]
WLT - v70 - Sum '96 - p703 [501+]

Leverington, David - *A History of Astronomy from 1890 to the Present*
Isis - v87 - D '96 - p744+ [501+]
Phys Today - v49 - S '96 - p83 [501+]

Leverington, Karen - *The Vital Guide to Fighting Aircraft of World War II*
yr ARBA - v28 - '97 - p261 [51-250]
r BL - v93 - O 1 '96 - p367 [1-50]

LeVert, Marianne - *AIDS: A Handbook for the Future*
y BL - v93 - D 15 '96 - p715+ [51-250]
y HB Guide - v8 - Spr '97 - p129 [51-250]
y SB - v33 - Mr '97 - p46 [51-250]
y SLJ - v42 - N '96 - p129 [51-250]

Levert, Mireille - *Little Red Riding Hood (Illus. by Mireille Levert)*
c SLJ - v42 - S '96 - p198 [51-250]

Levertov, Denise - *Evening Train*
LJ - v122 - Ap 1 '97 - p95 [1-50]
Sands of the Well
Am - v175 - O 26 '96 - p25+ [501+]
Comw - v123 - D 20 '96 - p23 [501+]
HR - v49 - Win '97 - p659+ [501+]
Tesserae: Memories and Suppositions
PW - v243 - S 2 '96 - p121 [1-50]

Lever-Tracy, Constance - *The Chinese Diaspora and Mainland China*
Choice - v34 - Ap '97 - p1388+ [51-250]
R&R Bk N - v12 - F '97 - p49 [51-250]

Leveson, Nancy G - *Safeware: System Safety and Computers*
Am Sci - v84 - N '96 - p612+ [501+]

Levete, Sarah - *Looking after Yourself*
c Sch Lib - v45 - F '97 - p39 [51-250]

Levey, Michael - *Florence: A Portrait*
BL - v92 - Ag '96 - p1877 [51-250]
BW - v26 - S 29 '96 - p13 [51-250]
BWatch - v17 - D '96 - p8 [51-250]
CR - v270 - Ja '97 - p55 [501+]
LATBR - N 10 '96 - p14+ [51-250]
LJ - v121 - S 15 '96 - p64 [51-250]
NS & S - v9 - Ap 26 '96 - p39 [1-50]
NYRB - v43 - O 31 '96 - p54+ [501+]
NYTBR - v101 - S 15 '96 - p16 [501+]
NYTBR - v101 - D 8 '96 - p87 [1-50]

Levi, Antonia - *Samurai from Outer Space*
BL - v93 - N 1 '96 - p472 [51-250]
Choice - v34 - My '97 - p1488+ [51-250]
LJ - v121 - S 15 '96 - p64 [51-250]

Levi, Decio - *Symmetries and Integrability of Difference Equations*
SciTech - v20 - D '96 - p19 [51-250]

Levi, Erik - *BBC Music Magazine Top 1000 CDs Guide*
r ARBA - v28 - '97 - p482 [51-250]
Music in the Third Reich
CEH - v29 - 1 '96 - p93+ [501+]

Levi, Peter - *A Bottle in the Shade*
New Sci - v151 - S 14 '96 - p47 [51-250]
Spec - v276 - My 18 '96 - p42 [251-500]
Spec - v277 - N 30 '96 - p58 [1-50]
TLS - Ag 30 '96 - p31 [501+]
Eden Renewed
CR - v270 - Ja '97 - p53 [251-500]
Econ - v340 - S 21 '96 - p90 [251-500]
PW - v244 - Ap 14 '97 - p63 [51-250]
Spec - v277 - N 23 '96 - p43 [1-50]
WSJ-Cent - v99 - My 6 '97 - pA20 [501+]

Levi, Steven C - *Cowboys of the Sky*
c HB - v72 - S '96 - p619+ [51-250]
y HB Guide - v7 - Fall '96 - p351 [51-250]

Levin, Aryeh - *Envoy to Moscow*
R&R Bk N - v11 - D '96 - p11 [1-50]

Levin, B IA. - *Lectures on Entire Functions*
SciTech - v20 - N '96 - p14 [51-250]

Levin, Betty - *Fire in the Wind*
c RT - v50 - Mr '97 - p498 [51-250]
Gift Horse (Illus. by Jos. A Smith)
c BL - v93 - O 1 '96 - p352 [51-250]
c CCB-B - v50 - N '96 - p105 [51-250]
c Ch BWatch - v6 - D '96 - p5 [1-50]
c HB Guide - v8 - Spr '97 - p70 [51-250]
c KR - v64 - Ag 15 '96 - p1238 [51-250]
c SLJ - v42 - N '96 - p108 [51-250]

Levin, Carole - *The Heart and Stomach of a King*
EHR - v112 - F '97 - p190+ [51-250]
JMH - v68 - S '96 - p675+ [501+]
Shakes Q - v47 - Fall '96 - p339+ [501+]
Political Rhetoric, Power, and Renaissance Women
Albion - v28 - Sum '96 - p298+ [501+]
Ren Q - v50 - Spr '97 - p340+ [501+]
Sev Cent N - v54 - Fall '96 - p52+ [501+]

Levin, Christoph - *Der Jahwist*
Rel St Rev - v23 - Ja '97 - p22+ [501+]

Levin, Doron P - *Behind the Wheel at Chrysler*
NYTBR - v101 - D 29 '96 - p20 [1-50]

Levin, Frank S - *Coulomb Interactions in Nuclear and Atomic Few-Body Collisions*
SciTech - v20 - D '96 - p23 [51-250]

Levin, Gail - *Edward Hopper: A Catalogue Raisonne. Vols. 1-3. Electronic Media Version*
r Apo - v144 - N '96 - p55+ [501+]
Edward Hopper: An Intimate Biography
AS - v65 - Aut '96 - p628+ [501+]
RAH - v24 - S '96 - p454+ [501+]
Sew R - v104 - Jl '96 - p492+ [501+]

Levin, Harriet - *The Christmas Show*
PW - v244 - Ap 28 '97 - p72 [251-500]

Levin, Jenifer - *Love and Death and Other Disasters*
Advocate - D 24 '96 - p68+ [251-500]
BL - v93 - N 15 '96 - p570 [51-250]
LJ - v121 - D '96 - p149 [51-250]

Levin, Jonathan L - *The Guide to National Banking Law*
r R&R Bk N - v11 - D '96 - p51 [51-250]

Levin, Karen - *20-Minute One-Dish Gourmet*
BWatch - v18 - F '97 - p7 [1-50]

Levin, Lee - *King Tut's Private Eye*
KR - v64 - My 1 '96 - p645 [51-250]

Levin, Michael - *What Every Jew Needs to Know about God*
BL - v93 - D 1 '96 - p622 [51-250]
LJ - v122 - Ja '97 - p107 [51-250]

Levin, Miriam Ramsfelder - *In the Beginning (Illus. by Katherine Janus Kahn)*
c SLJ - v43 - Ja '97 - p84 [51-250]

Levin, Morris A - *Engineered Organisms in Environmental Settings*
Choice - v34 - My '97 - p1522 [51-250]
SciTech - v20 - D '96 - p30 [51-250]

Levin, Phillis - *The Afterimage*
HR - v49 - Aut '96 - p503+ [501+]

Levin, Roger - *Patterns in Evolution*
Nature - v386 - Ap 3 '97 - p456 [251-500]

Levin, Ross - *The Wealth Management Index*
r R&R Bk N - v12 - F '97 - p47 [51-250]

Levin, Theodore - *The Hundred Thousand Fools of God*
LJ - v121 - D '96 - p96 [51-250]
PW - v243 - D 30 '96 - p51 [51-250]

Levine, Alan J - *The Missile and Space Race*
PHR - v66 - F '97 - p132 [251-500]
The Pacific War
NWCR - v49 - Aut '96 - p152+ [501+]
Race Relations within Western Expansion
Choice - v34 - N '96 - p526 [51-250]
The United States and the Struggle for Southeast Asia 1945-1975
Pac A - v69 - Sum '96 - p282+ [251-500]

Levine, Arthur - *Beating the Odds*
TCR - v98 - Spr '97 - p561+ [501+]

Levine, Arthur A - *Bono and Nonno (Illus. by Judi Lanfredi)*
c LA - v73 - S '96 - p352+ [51-250]

Levine, Barbara - *Works about John Dewey 1886-1995*
r CPR - v16 - Je '96 - p188+ [501+]
r HER - v66 - Win '96 - p888+ [251-500]

Levine, David I - *Reinventing the Workplace*
NYRB - v44 - Ap 10 '97 - p38+ [501+]

Levine, Deborah J - *Teaching Christian Children about Judaism*
Rel Ed - v91 - Fall '96 - p618 [51-250]

Levine, Donald N - *Visions of the Sociological Tradition*
AJS - v102 - Jl '96 - p256+ [501+]
SF - v75 - S '96 - p336+ [251-500]

Levine, Ellen - *Freedom's Children*
y BL - v93 - F 15 '97 - p1014 [1-50]

Levine, Evan - *Not the Piano, Mrs. Medley!. Book and Audio Version*
c SLJ - v43 - Mr '97 - p143 [51-250]

Levine, Felice J - *Social Causes of Violence*
JEL - v34 - D '96 - p2081 [51-250]

Levine, Gail Carson - *Ella Enchanted*
c CCB-B - v50 - My '97 - p327 [51-250]
c HB - v73 - My '97 - p325 [51-250]
y KR - v65 - F 1 '97 - p225 [51-250]
c PW - v244 - Mr 31 '97 - p75 [51-250]

Levine, George - *Aesthetics and Ideology*
Clio - v25 - Sum '96 - p439+ [501+]
VS - v39 - Spr '96 - p441+ [501+]
Realism and Representation
Can Lit - Spr '97 - p212+ [501+]

Levine, Hedi - *Natural Recipes for the Good Life*
BL - v93 - My 15 '97 - p1552 [51-250]

Levine, Herbert J - *Sing unto God a New Song*
Theol St - v57 - Je '96 - p338+ [501+]

Levine, Hillel - *In Search of Sugihara*
BL - v93 - N 1 '96 - p479 [51-250]
Choice - v34 - Mr '97 - p1214 [51-250]
KR - v64 - S 15 '96 - p1377 [251-500]
LJ - v121 - N 1 '96 - p88 [51-250]
NYTLa - v146 - D 23 '96 - pC16 [501+]
PW - v243 - S 16 '96 - p57 [51-250]
Trib Bks - F 2 '97 - p5 [501+]

Levine, John - *The UNIX Dictionary of Commands, Terms, and Acronyms*
r ARBA - v28 - '97 - p623+ [51-250]
r BL - v93 - O 1 '96 - p373 [251-500]
r CBR - v14 - N '96 - p40 [1-50]
r SB - v32 - N '96 - p235 [501+]

Levine, Joyce - *Contacting Your Guardian Angel*
Horoscope - v63 - Mr '97 - p10 [51-250]

Levine, Laura - *Men in Women's Clothing*
MLR - v92 - Ap '97 - p448+ [501+]

Levine, Lawrence W - *The Opening of the American Mind*
BL - v93 - S 15 '96 - p181 [51-250]
BW - v26 - S 29 '96 - p3+ [501+]
Choice - v34 - Mr '97 - p1227+ [51-250]
Dis - v44 - Win '97 - p115+ [501+]
Nat - v263 - O 7 '96 - p25+ [501+]
NL - v79 - D 16 '96 - p7+ [501+]
NYTBR - v101 - O 27 '96 - p14+ [501+]
PW - v243 - Jl 22 '96 - p221 [51-250]
Wil Q - v20 - Aut '96 - p94+ [251-500]
Levine, Madeline - *Viewing Violence*
BL - v93 - O 1 '96 - p309 [51-250]
Choice - v34 - F '97 - p1042 [51-250]
LJ - v121 - O 1 '96 - p110 [51-250]
Levine, Marilyn A - *The Found Generation*
Ch Rev Int - v3 - Fall '96 - p479+ [501+]
Levine, Mark R - *Manual of Oculoplastic Surgery. 2nd Ed.*
SciTech - v20 - N '96 - p50 [51-250]
Levine, Michael G - *Writing through Repression*
MLN - v111 - D '96 - p1055+ [501+]
Levine, Michael L - *African Americans and Civil Rights from 1619 to the Present*
y JAAL - v40 - Mr '97 - p512 [51-250]
R&R Bk N - v11 - D '96 - p14 [51-250]
Levine, Neil - *The Architecture of Frank Lloyd Wright*
Apo - v144 - N '96 - p57+ [501+]
New R - v216 - Mr 17 '97 - p36+ [501+]
TLS - N 8 '96 - p3+ [501+]
Levine, Paul - *False Dawn*
Arm Det - v30 - Win '97 - p82+ [501+]
Flesh and Bones
BL - v93 - N 15 '96 - p574+ [51-250]
KR - v64 - O 15 '96 - p1497+ [51-250]
PW - v244 - Ja 13 '97 - p59 [51-250]
Fool Me Twice
Arm Det - v30 - Win '97 - p82+ [501+]
Mortal Sin
Arm Det - v30 - Win '97 - p82+ [501+]
Night Vision
Arm Det - v30 - Win '97 - p82+ [501+]
Slashback
Arm Det - v30 - Win '97 - p82+ [501+]
To Speak for the Dead
Arm Det - v30 - Win '97 - p82+ [501+]
Levine, Peter - *Nietzsche and the Modern Crisis of the Humanities*
Clio - v25 - Spr '96 - p329+ [501+]
Levine, Philip - *The Simple Truth*
LJ - v122 - Ap 1 '97 - p95 [1-50]
NYTBR - v102 - F 2 '97 - p28 [1-50]
Unselected Poems
LJ - v122 - Ap 15 '97 - p85 [51-250]
LeVine, Robert A - *Child Care and Culture*
Choice - v34 - Ap '97 - p1378+ [51-250]
Levine, Robert M - *Brazilian Legacies*
LJ - v122 - Ap 15 '97 - p100 [51-250]
The Life and Death of Carolina Maria De Jesus
HAHR - v76 - Ag '96 - p598+ [501+]
LeVine, Sarah - *Dolor Y Alegria*
JTWS - v13 - Spr '96 - p362+ [501+]
Levine, Shar - *The Microscope Book (Illus. by David Sovka)*
c Ch BWatch - v6 - Jl '96 - p1 [1-50]
c HB Guide - v7 - Fall '96 - p328 [51-250]
c SB - v32 - O '96 - p207 [251-500]
Science around the World (Illus. by Laurel Aiello)
c SB - v32 - O '96 - p207+ [251-500]
Leving, Jeffrey M - *Fathers' Rights*
PW - v244 - Mr 17 '97 - p66 [51-250]
Levinson, Bradley A - *The Cultural Production of the Educated Person*
Choice - v34 - O '96 - p332 [51-250]
Levinson, Daniel J - *The Seasons of a Woman's Life*
J Car P&E - v57 - Fall '96 - p22 [501+]
NYRB - v43 - N 28 '96 - p22+ [501+]
NYTBR - v102 - Mr 30 '97 - p24 [51-250]
Trib Bks - Ap 6 '97 - p8 [1-50]
Levinson, David - *Encyclopedia of Cultural Anthropology. Vols. 1-4*
r ARBA - v28 - '97 - p147+ [51-250]
r BL - v93 - Ja '97 - p770 [1-50]
r Choice - v34 - S '96 - p96 [251-500]
r CLW - v67 - Mr '97 - p44 [51-250]
r LJ - v122 - Ap 15 '97 - p38 [51-250]
r R&R Bk N - v11 - D '96 - p20 [51-250]
Encyclopedia of Marriage and the Family. Vols. 1-2
r Fam Relat - v45 - O '96 - p478+ [251-500]

Encyclopedia of World Sport. Vols. 1-3
yr BL - v93 - My 1 '97 - p1526+ [501+]
r LJ - v122 - Ap 15 '97 - p39 [51-250]
r LJ - v122 - Ap 15 '97 - p66 [51-250]
The Global Village Companion
yr ARBA - v28 - '97 - p213 [251-500]
yr BL - v93 - My 1 '97 - p1530 [251-500]
r LJ - v122 - Ap 15 '97 - p66 [51-250]
Religion: A Cross Cultural Encyclopedia
r ARBA - v28 - '97 - p536 [51-250]
Levinson, Jay Conrad - *Guerrilla Marketing Online Weapons*
BL - v92 - Ag '96 - p1865 [51-250]
Guerrilla Marketing Weapons. Audio Version
LJ - v122 - Ja '97 - p172 [51-250]
The Way of the Guerrilla
BL - v93 - D 15 '96 - p699 [51-250]
LJ - v122 - Ja '97 - p116 [51-250]
PW - v243 - D 30 '96 - p52 [51-250]
Levinson, Jerrold - *The Pleasures of Aesthetics*
Choice - v34 - O '96 - p294 [51-250]
CPR - v16 - D '96 - p416+ [501+]
Levinson, Luisa Mercedes - *The Two Siblings and Other Stories*
LJ - v122 - F 1 '97 - p109 [51-250]
PW - v243 - O 21 '96 - p76 [51-250]
Levinson, Ralph - *Science Today*
New Sci - v153 - F 15 '97 - p41 [51-250]
TES - F 21 '97 - p7* [501+]
Levinson, Riki - *Watch the Stars Come Out*
c Learning - v25 - Mr '97 - p54 [1-50]
Levinthal, David - *Mein Kampf*
LJ - v122 - Ap 1 '97 - p90 [51-250]
Levinton, Jeffrey S - *Marine Biology*
SciTech - v20 - N '96 - p25 [51-250]
Levi-Strauss, Claude - *The Jealous Potter*
NYTBR - v102 - F 2 '97 - p28 [1-50]
Look, Listen, Read
BL - v93 - My 1 '97 - p1473 [51-250]
KR - v65 - Ap 1 '97 - p528 [251-500]
PW - v244 - Ap 14 '97 - p66 [51-250]
Saudades Do Brasil
For Aff - v76 - Mr '97 - p189 [51-250]
The Story of Lynx
Am Ethnol - v23 - N '96 - p901+ [501+]
NYTBR - v102 - F 2 '97 - p28 [1-50]
TranslRevS - v2 - D '96 - p23 [51-250]
Levitan, Nadav - *Maakhal Taavah*
BL - v93 - Mr 1 '97 - p1115 [1-50]
Levitin, Sonia - *Annie's Promise*
c Ch BWatch - v6 - O '96 - p8 [51-250]
Evil Encounter
y CCB-B - v50 - O '96 - p67+ [51-250]
y HB Guide - v7 - Fall '96 - p303 [51-250]
y VOYA - v19 - F '97 - p329 [251-500]
Nine for California (Illus. by Cat Bowman Smith)
c CCB-B - v50 - D '96 - p141 [51-250]
c HB Guide - v8 - Spr '97 - p36 [51-250]
c LATBR - O 6 '96 - p15 [51-250]
c PW - v243 - S 9 '96 - p83 [51-250]
c SLJ - v42 - S '96 - p184 [51-250]
c SLJ - v42 - D '96 - p30+ [1-50]
A Piece of Home (Illus. by Juan Wijngaard)
c BL - v93 - N 15 '96 - p594+ [51-250]
c CBRS - v25 - F '97 - p76 [51-250]
c CCB-B - v50 - Ja '97 - p179 [51-250]
c HB Guide - v8 - Spr '97 - p36 [51-250]
c PW - v243 - N 18 '96 - p74 [51-250]
c SLJ - v42 - D '96 - p99 [51-250]
Yesterday's Child
y KR - v65 - My 1 '97 - p724 [51-250]
Levitt, Cheryl - *Survey of Routine Maternity Care and Practices in Canadian Hospitals*
J Gov Info - v23 - S '96 - p620 [51-250]
Levitt, Helen - *In the Street*
CAY - v17 - Win '96 - p11 [51-250]
LeVitus, Bob - *Cheap and Easy Internet Access*
CBR - v14 - N '96 - p34 [1-50]
Levy, Avigdor - *The Jews of the Ottoman Empire*
Rel St Rev - v22 - O '96 - p354+ [51-250]
Levy, Barrie - *What Parents Need to Know about Dating Violence*
VOYA - v19 - D '96 - p256 [1-50]
Levy, Bernard-Henri - *Adventures on the Freedom Road*
Lon R Bks - v18 - O 31 '96 - p32+ [501+]
Quad - v40 - Je '96 - p81+ [501+]
Levy, Brian - *Regulations, Institutions, and Commitment*
JEL - v35 - Mr '97 - p252 [51-250]

Levy, Constance - *When Whales Exhale and Other Poems (Illus. by Judy LaBrasca)*
c BL - v93 - D 15 '96 - p723 [51-250]
c HB Guide - v8 - Spr '97 - p153 [51-250]
c SLJ - v42 - D '96 - p131 [51-250]
Levy, Daniel C - *Building the Third Sector*
WorldV - v12 - O '96 - p5 [251-500]
Levy, David H - *Skywatching*
r E Mag - v7 - N '96 - p50 [51-250]
Stars and Planets
c HB Guide - v7 - Fall '96 - p330 [51-250]
c New Sci - v153 - F 8 '97 - p46 [51-250]
y Sch Lib - v44 - Ag '96 - p123 [51-250]
c S&T - v92 - O '96 - p57 [51-250]
c TES - N 8 '96 - p13* [51-250]
Levy, Donald - *Freud among the Philosophers*
Choice - v34 - Ap '97 - p1420 [51-250]
Levy, Elinor - *The Ten Best Tools to Boost Your Immune System*
BL - v93 - Ja '97 - p798 [51-250]
LJ - v122 - F 1 '97 - p99+ [51-250]
Levy, Elizabeth - *Cleo and the Coyote (Illus. by Diana Bryer)*
c HB Guide - v7 - Fall '96 - p264+ [51-250]
The Creepy Computer Mystery (Illus. by Denise Brunkus)
c BL - v93 - S 15 '96 - p253 [51-250]
The Karate Class Mystery (Illus. by Denise Brunkus)
c BL - v93 - F 1 '97 - p950 [51-250]
Wolfman Sam
c BL - v93 - N 15 '96 - p588 [51-250]
Levy, Faye - *The Low-Fat Jewish Cookbook*
BL - v93 - Ja '97 - p800 [51-250]
LJ - v122 - Mr 15 '97 - p84 [51-250]
PW - v244 - Ja 6 '97 - p69 [51-250]
Levy, Harlan - *And the Blood Cried Out*
New Sci - v152 - O 26 '96 - p46 [51-250]
WSJ-MW - v77 - S 4 '96 - pA10 [501+]
Levy, Janice - *El Espiritu De Tio Fernando (Illus. by Morella Fuenmayor)*
c SLJ - v42 - Ag '96 - p178 [51-250]
The Spirit of Tio Fernando (Illus. by Morella Fuenmayor)
c CLW - v66 - Je '96 - p51 [51-250]
c HB Guide - v7 - Fall '96 - p327 [51-250]
Levy, John M - *Contemporary Urban Planning. 4th Ed.*
R&R Bk N - v12 - F '97 - p55 [51-250]
Essential Microeconomics for Public Policy Analysis
SSQ - v78 - Mr '97 - p246+ [251-500]
Levy, Julien - *Surrealism*
Art J - v56 - Spr '97 - p95+ [501+]
Levy, Justine - *Le Rendez-vous*
FR - v70 - D '96 - p352+ [251-500]
Levy, Leonard W - *Blasphemy: Verbal Offense against the Sacred, from Moses to Salman Rushdie*
CH - v66 - Mr '97 - p177+ [501+]
QJS - v82 - Ag '96 - p304+ [501+]
A License to Steal
AHR - v102 - F '97 - p174 [501+]
Nat R - v48 - S 2 '96 - p98 [51-250]
Levy, M J - *The Mistresses of King George IV*
TLS - S 27 '96 - p32 [251-500]
Levy, Marilyn - *Run for Your Life*
y BL - v93 - Ap 1 '97 - p1294 [1-50]
c HB Guide - v8 - Spr '97 - p70 [51-250]
Levy, Marion J - *Modernization and the Structure of Societies. Vols. 1-2*
R&R Bk N - v12 - F '97 - p51 [51-250]
Levy, Matthys - *Why the Earth Quakes*
y Kliatt - v31 - Mr '97 - p15 [51-250]
Levy, Patricia Marjorie - *Puerto Rico*
c JOYS - v9 - Sum '96 - p416+ [51-250]
Sudan
c Ch BWatch - v7 - Ja '97 - p3 [1-50]
Tibet
c HB Guide - v7 - Fall '96 - p383 [1-50]
y SLJ - v42 - S '96 - p235 [51-250]
Levy, Paul - *The Turtle Who Lost His Shell (Illus. by Rick Grayson)*
c RT - v50 - O '96 - p135 [1-50]
Levy, Paul, 1941- - *Penguin Book of Food and Drink*
Obs - D 15 '96 - p18* [501+]
TLS - D 6 '96 - p29 [501+]
Levy, Peter B - *Encyclopedia of the Reagan-Bush Years*
r ARBA - v28 - '97 - p268 [251-500]
r BL - v93 - Ja '97 - p770 [1-50]
r Choice - v34 - O '96 - p254 [51-250]
yr SLJ - v43 - F '97 - p130 [51-250]
r SLMQ - v25 - Fall '96 - p65 [51-250]
The New Left and Labor in the 1960s
AHR - v101 - O '96 - p1301+ [501+]

Levy, Raymond - *Developments in Dementia and Functional Disorders in the Elderly*
  r AJPsych - v153 - O '96 - p1361+ [501+]
Levy, Shawn - *King of Comedy*
  Rapport - v19 - 4 '96 - p39 [251-500]
Levy, Sidney M - *Build, Operate, Transfer*
  R&R Bk N - v12 - F '97 - p35 [51-250]
Levy, Stephen - *Artificial Life*
  NS - v125 - D 20 '96 - p117 [1-50]
Levy, Steven - *Starting from Scratch*
  Inst - v106 - Ag '96 - p13 [51-250]
Levy, Susan L - *Your Body Can Talk*
  BL - v93 - S 1 '96 - p50 [51-250]
Levy-Leboyer, Maurice - *Histoire Generale De L'Electricite En France. Vol. 2*
  AHR - v101 - D '96 - p1561+ [501+]
Levy-Livermore, Amnon - *Economic Analyses of Financial Crises*
  Econ J - v107 - Ja '97 - p273+ [51-250]
Lew, Alan A - *Tourism in China*
  Ch Rev Int - v3 - Fall '96 - p481+ [251-500]
Lewalski, Barbara Kiefer - *Writing Women in Jacobean England*
  Sev Cent N - v54 - Fall '96 - p53+ [501+]
Lewandowski, J J - *Layered Materials for Structural Applications*
  SciTech - v21 - Mr '97 - p77 [51-250]
Lewellen, Ted C - *Dependency and Development*
  JTWS - v13 - Fall '96 - p335+ [501+]
Lewels, Joe - *The God Hypothesis*
  BL - v93 - My 15 '97 - p1544 [51-250]
Lewes, Darby - *Dream Revisionaries*
  AL - v69 - Mr '97 - p226+ [251-500]
Lewes, George Henry - *The Letters of George Henry Lewes. Vols. 1-2*
  ELT - v39 - 3 '96 - p406 [51-250]
  RMR - v50 - 2 '96 - p179+ [501+]
The Physical Basis of Mind
  Nature - v385 - Ja 16 '97 - p217 [501+]
Lewin, Betsy - *Chubbo's Pool (Illus. by Betsy Lewin)*
  c BL - v92 - Ag '96 - p1907 [51-250]
  c CCB-B - v50 - O '96 - p68 [51-250]
  c HB Guide - v8 - Spr '97 - p36 [51-250]
  c SLJ - v42 - S '96 - p184 [51-250]
Lewin, Ellen - *Inventing Lesbian Cultures in America*
  LJ - v122 - F 1 '97 - p97 [51-250]
  PW - v243 - N 18 '96 - p69 [51-250]
Out in the Field
  Choice - v34 - D '96 - p652+ [51-250]
Lewin, Jack - *Hydraulic Gates and Valves*
  SciTech - v20 - N '96 - p66 [51-250]
Lewin, Michael Z - *Hard Line*
  Arm Det - v29 - Fall '96 - p478 [501+]
Late Payments
  Arm Det - v29 - Fall '96 - p478 [501+]
Night Cover
  Arm Det - v29 - Fall '96 - p478 [501+]
Lewin, Roger A - *Compassion: The Core Value That Animates Psychotherapy*
  Choice - v34 - O '96 - p365 [51-250]
  Readings - v11 - D '96 - p28 [51-250]
Lewin, Ted - *Amazon Boy*
  c CLW - v67 - Mr '97 - p14 [1-50]
I Was a Teenage Professional Wrestler
  y BL - v93 - D 15 '96 - p716 [1-50]
Market! (Illus. by Ted Lewin)
  c CCB-B - v50 - S '96 - p19+ [51-250]
  c Ch BWatch - v6 - My '96 - p3+ [1-50]
  c Emerg Lib - v24 - S '96 - p43 [1-50]
  c HB Guide - v7 - Fall '96 - p318 [51-250]
  c NYTBR - v101 - O 27 '96 - p44 [1-50]
  c RT - v50 - My '97 - p686 [51-250]
  c SLJ - v42 - D '96 - p31 [1-50]
  c Smith - v27 - N '96 - p165+ [1-50]
Lewington, Anna - *Atlas of the Rain Forests*
  cr BL - v93 - My 15 '97 - p1610+ [251-500]
  yr SB - v33 - My '97 - p107 [51-250]
Mexico
  c HB Guide - v8 - Spr '97 - p175 [51-250]
  c SLJ - v43 - F '97 - p93 [51-250]
The Wayland Atlas of Rain Forests
  cr TES - F 28 '97 - p21* [251-500]
Lewis, Alan - *Ethics and Economic Affairs*
  Econ J - v106 - N '96 - p1832+ [251-500]
Lewis, Alcinda - *Butterfly Gardens*
  LJ - v121 - D '96 - p66 [1-50]
Lewis, Alfred - *EU and US Banking in the 1990s*
  JEL - v35 - Mr '97 - p222+ [51-250]
Lewis, Alison - *Subverting Patriarchy*
  Ger Q - v69 - Sum '96 - p361+ [501+]

Lewis, Amanda - *Lettering: Make Your Own Cards, Signs, Gifts and More (Illus. by Esperanca Melo)*
  c Ch Bk News - v19 - Spr '96 - p24 [251-500]
Lewis, Ann - *Children's Understanding of Disability*
  AJMR - v101 - Ja '97 - p433+ [501+]
Lewis, Bernard - *Cultures in Conflict*
  JTWS - v13 - Spr '96 - p233+ [501+]
Islam and the West
  JTWS - v13 - Spr '96 - p233+ [501+]
The Middle East: A Brief History of the Last 2,000 Years
  For Aff - v75 - S '96 - p153+ [251-500]
  MEQ - v3 - S '96 - p84+ [251-500]
  Nat R - v48 - O 28 '96 - p70+ [501+]
  NYTBR - v101 - D 8 '96 - p89 [1-50]
  WorldV - v13 - Ja '97 - p8+ [251-500]
Lewis, C S - *Mere Christianity*
  CSM - v89 - N 25 '96 - p12 [51-250]
  CSM - v89 - Ja 23 '97 - p12 [51-250]
Readings for Meditation and Reflection
  Bks & Cult - v3 - Mr '97 - p39 [251-500]
Lewis, Cam - *Around the World in Seventy-Nine Days*
  y Kliatt - v30 - N '96 - p28 [51-250]
Lewis, Catherine - *Dry Fire*
  Arm Det - v29 - Fall '96 - p438 [51-250]
Lewis, Catherine C - *Educating Hearts and Minds*
  EL - v54 - S '96 - p86+ [251-500]
Lewis, Charles A - *Green Nature/Human Nature*
  Choice - v34 - N '96 - p483 [51-250]
Lewis, Colin - *Bonsai Survival Manual*
  r ARBA - v28 - '97 - p572 [51-250]
  BL - v93 - S 1 '96 - p52 [51-250]
Lewis, Dan A - *Race and Educational Reform in the American Metropolis*
  JNE - v65 - Win '96 - p97+ [501+]
Lewis, David Rich - *Neither Wolf nor Dog*
  J Am St - v30 - Ap '96 - p175+ [251-500]
Lewis, Dennis - *The Tao of Natural Breathing*
  LJ - v121 - O 15 '96 - p64 [51-250]
  PW - v243 - S 2 '96 - p125 [51-250]
Lewis, Derek - *Hidden Agendas*
  TLS - Mr 21 '97 - p14 [501+]
Lewis, Donald M - *The Blackwell Dictionary of Evangelical Biography 1730-1860. Vols. 1-2*
  r ARBA - v28 - '97 - p548+ [51-250]
  r Bks & Cult - v2 - Jl '96 - p30 [251-500]
Lewis, Erica-Lee - *Help Yourself*
  yr Kliatt - v31 - Mr '97 - p27 [51-250]
Lewis, Eugene M - *Births, Deaths and Marriages on California's Mendocino Coast. Vol. 1*
  r EGH - v50 - N '96 - p164 [51-250]
Lewis, Flora - *Europe: Road to Unity*
  Wil Q - v21 - Win '97 - p37 [51-250]
Lewis, Gladys Sherman - *Message, Messenger, and Response*
  Rel St Rev - v23 - Ja '97 - p52+ [51-250]
Lewis, Herschell - *Selling on the Net*
  BWatch - v18 - F '97 - p2 [51-250]
Lewis, J D - *Journeys in Art*
  c HB Guide - v8 - Spr '97 - p137 [51-250]
  c JB - v60 - O '96 - p203 [51-250]
  c SLJ - v43 - Ja '97 - p130 [51-250]
Lewis, J Patrick - *The Boat of Many Rooms (Illus. by Reg Cartwright)*
  c BL - v93 - F 1 '97 - p948 [51-250]
  c CCB-B - v50 - F '97 - p212 [51-250]
  c KR - v64 - D 15 '96 - p1799 [51-250]
  c PW - v244 - Ja 13 '97 - p71 [51-250]
  c SLJ - v43 - Mr '97 - p161 [51-250]
The La-Di-Da Hare (Illus. by Diana Cain Bluthenthal)
  c KR - v65 - Mr 1 '97 - p383 [51-250]
  c PW - v244 - Mr 24 '97 - p83 [51-250]
Riddle-icious (Illus. by Debbie Tilley)
  c Ch BWatch - v6 - My '96 - p4 [1-50]
  c HB Guide - v7 - Fall '96 - p368 [51-250]
  c PW - v244 - Mr 3 '97 - p77 [1-50]
Lewis, James R - *Angels A to Z*
  r ARBA - v28 - '97 - p535+ [51-250]
  r RQ - v35 - Sum '96 - p545+ [251-500]
Lewis, Jane - *Implementing the New Community Care*
  SciTech - v20 - S '96 - p27 [51-250]
The Voluntary Sector, the State and Social Work in Britain
  Albion - v28 - Sum '96 - p344+ [501+]
  JEH - v57 - Mr '97 - p220+ [501+]
Lewis, Jayne Elizabeth - *The English Fable*
  Choice - v34 - Ap '97 - p1337 [51-250]
Lewis, Jessica H - *Comparative Hemostasis in Vertebrates*
  Choice - v34 - Ja '97 - p822 [51-250]
  SciTech - v20 - N '96 - p31 [51-250]

Lewis, Johanna Miller - *Artisans in the North Carolina Backcountry*
  AHR - v101 - D '96 - p1611+ [501+]
  JSH - v62 - N '96 - p792+ [251-500]
Lewis, John P - *Governance and Reform*
  PSQ - v111 - Win '96 - p736+ [501+]
Lewis, John S - *Mining the Sky*
  Astron - v25 - Ap '97 - p104+ [501+]
  Choice - v34 - My '97 - p1521 [501+]
  LJ - v121 - N 15 '96 - p85+ [51-250]
  NH - v105 - O '96 - p12 [1-50]
  Reason - v28 - Ap '97 - p59+ [501+]
  y SB - v33 - Mr '97 - p45 [51-250]
Rain of Iron and Ice
  Nat - v263 - O 28 '96 - p38+ [501+]
  Phys Today - v50 - F '97 - p65+ [501+]
Lewis, Jon - *True Swamp: The Memoirs of Lenny the Frog*
  p Quill & Q - v62 - Ag '96 - p26 [51-250]
Lewis, Jon, 1955- - *Whom God Wishes to Destroy...*
  FQ - v50 - Win '96 - p60+ [501+]
Lewis, Judith A - *Women's Health*
  NWSA Jnl - v9 - Spr '97 - p89+ [501+]
Lewis, Kim - *The Last Train*
  c Bks Keeps - N '96 - p8 [51-250]
One Summer Day (Illus. by Kim Lewis)
  c CBRS - v24 - Ag '96 - p160+ [51-250]
  c HB Guide - v8 - Spr '97 - p13 [51-250]
  c JB - v60 - D '96 - p235 [51-250]
  c Smith - v27 - N '96 - p170 [1-50]
Lewis, Lionel S - *Marginal Worth*
  Choice - v34 - F '97 - p1015 [51-250]
  JEL - v34 - D '96 - p2073+ [51-250]
Lewis, Marcia - *The Private Lives of the Three Tenors*
  NYTBR - v101 - D 29 '96 - p15 [51-250]
  PW - v243 - S 2 '96 - p124 [51-250]
Lewis, Mark - *The Growth of Nations*
  JEL - v35 - Mr '97 - p288 [51-250]
Lewis, Marvin A - *Afro-Argentine Discourse*
  Bl S - v26 - Sum '96 - p66 [1-50]
  Choice - v34 - O '96 - p286 [51-250]
Lewis, Melvin - *Child and Adolescent Psychiatry. 2nd Ed.*
  SciTech - v20 - D '96 - p53 [51-250]
Lewis, Michael - *Trail Fever*
  BL - v93 - My 15 '97 - p1539+ [51-250]
  KR - v65 - My 1 '97 - p699 [251-500]
  PW - v244 - My 12 '97 - p65 [51-250]
  WSJ-Cent - v99 - My 28 '97 - pA16 [501+]
Lewis, Naomi - *Classic Fairy Tales to Read Aloud (Illus. by Jo Worth)*
  c HB Guide - v8 - Spr '97 - p103 [51-250]
  c Sch Lib - v45 - F '97 - p33 [51-250]
  c TES - F 28 '97 - p8* [501+]
Lewis, Naphtali - *On Government and Law in Roman Egypt*
  Rel St Rev - v22 - O '96 - p346 [51-250]
Lewis, Norman - *Back to Mandalay*
  Time - v148 - N 18 '96 - p109 [1-50]
Norman Lewis Omnibus
  Lon R Bks - v18 - Jl 18 '96 - p17+ [501+]
The World, the World
  Lon R Bks - v18 - Jl 18 '96 - p17+ [501+]
  NS & S - v9 - Ap 26 '96 - p41 [251-500]
  Spec - v276 - My 11 '96 - p40 [501+]
Lewis, Paul G - *Shaping Suburbia*
  Choice - v34 - Ap '97 - p1406 [51-250]
  R&R Bk N - v12 - F '97 - p55 [51-250]
  TLS - Ja 24 '97 - p8 [501+]
Lewis, Paul G, 1945- - *Central Europe since 1945*
  EHR - v112 - F '97 - p275 [501+]
Lewis, Paul Owen - *Storm Boy*
  c Bks Keeps - v100 - S '96 - p12 [51-250]
  c Sch Lib - v44 - Ag '96 - p99 [51-250]
Lewis, Philip E - *Seeing through the Mother Goose Tales*
  Choice - v34 - Ap '97 - p1344 [51-250]
Lewis, Philip H - *Tomorrow by Design*
  Choice - v34 - Ja '97 - p814 [51-250]
Lewis, R Barry - *Kentucky Archaeology*
  Choice - v34 - F '97 - p1006 [51-250]
Lewis, R W - *The Finite Element Method in Heat Transfer Analysis*
  SciTech - v20 - D '96 - p73 [51-250]
Lewis, R W B - *The City of Florence*
  LATBR - My 12 '96 - p11 [51-250]
  NYTBR - v101 - Jl 21 '96 - p28 [1-50]
Lewis, Rand C - *The Neo-Nazis and German Unification*
  Choice - v34 - Ap '97 - p1411 [501+]
  R&R Bk N - v11 - D '96 - p9 [51-250]
Lewis, Richard D - *When Cultures Collide*
  Choice - v34 - D '96 - p655 [51-250]
  Econ - v341 - O 19 '96 - p12* [251-500]

Lewis, Richard J - *Sax's Dangerous Properties of Industrial Materials. 9th Ed., Vols. 1-3*
  r Choice - v34 - Mr '97 - p1188 [51-250]
    SciTech - v21 - Mr '97 - p71 [51-250]
Lewis, Richard W - *Absolut Book*
  Advocate - N 12 '96 - p77+ [501+]
  BL - v93 - O 1 '96 - p311+ [51-250]
  Bloom Rev - v16 - N '96 - p25 [51-250]
Lewis, Ricki - *Human Genetics. 2nd Ed.*
  SciTech - v20 - N '96 - p26 [51-250]
Lewis, Rob - *Grandpa Comes to Stay*
  c Bks Keeps - Jl '96 - p9 [51-250]
  Mr. Dunfilling and the Denture Adventure
  c Bks Keeps - v100 - S '96 - p9 [51-250]
  c Sch Lib - v44 - Ag '96 - p107 [51-250]
Lewis, Roger - *The Life and Death of Peter Sellers*
  BL - v93 - N 1 '96 - p459 [1-50]
  Ent W - D 6 '96 - p56+ [501+]
  LATBR - N 3 '96 - p5+ [501+]
  NYTBR - v101 - D 15 '96 - p26+ [501+]
  PW - v243 - O 7 '96 - p55 [51-250]
  The Real Life of Laurence Olivier
  NS - v125 - S 13 '96 - p45 [501+]
  Si & So - v6 - N '96 - p34 [51-250]
  Spec - v277 - S 14 '96 - p37+ [501+]
  Spec - v277 - N 23 '96 - p44 [1-50]
Lewis, Samuel - *A Topographical Dictionary of England*
  r EGH - v50 - N '96 - p155 [51-250]
Lewis, Sara - *But I Love You Anyway*
  LJ - v121 - N 1 '96 - p132 [51-250]
Lewis, Sherry - *No Place for Death*
  Arm Det - v30 - Win '97 - p96+ [51-250]
Lewis, Shon - *Brain Imaging in Psychiatry*
  SciTech - v21 - Mr '97 - p53 [51-250]
Lewis, Sian - *Cities in the Sea (Illus. by Jackie Morris)*
  c Sch Lib - v45 - F '97 - p33 [51-250]
  c TES - Ja 17 '97 - p13* [51-250]
Lewis, Sinclair - *Main Street (Caruso). Audio Version*
  BL - v93 - My 15 '97 - p1596 [51-250]
Lewis, Sydney - *A Totally Alien Life-Form*
  y BL - v93 - Ja '97 - p763 [1-50]
  y BL - v93 - S 15 '96 - p189 [51-250]
  Nat - v263 - O 21 '96 - p27+ [501+]
Lewis, Terry - *Conflict of Interest*
  KR - v65 - Mr 1 '97 - p327+ [51-250]
  PW - v244 - F 17 '97 - p210+ [51-250]
Lewis, Thomas M N - *The Prehistory of the Chickamauga Basin in Tennessee. Vols. 1-2*
  Am Ant - v61 - Jl '96 - p612+ [501+]
  JSH - v62 - N '96 - p787+ [501+]
Lewis, Trudy - *Private Correspondence*
  Trib Bks - My 4 '97 - p8 [1-50]
Lewis, W David - *Sloss Furnaces and the Rise of the Birmingham District*
  T&C - v37 - Ap '96 - p365+ [501+]
Lewis, William F - *Soul Rebels*
  CS - v25 - S '96 - p642+ [501+]
Lewis, William H - *Weapons of Mass Destruction*
  Parameters - v26 - Aut '96 - p146+ [501+]
Lewitt, S N - *Cybersong*
  y Kliatt - v30 - N '96 - p14 [51-250]
Lewitt, Shariann - *Interface Masque*
  BL - v93 - Ap 1 '97 - p1283 [51-250]
  KR - v65 - F 15 '97 - p262 [51-250]
  LJ - v122 - Mr 15 '97 - p93 [51-250]
  PW - v244 - F 24 '97 - p69 [51-250]
  Memento Mori
  BWatch - v18 - F '97 - p4 [1-50]
Lewon, Paul - *CyberHound's Guide to Internet Discussion Groups*
  r BL - v93 - F 1 '97 - p963+ [251-500]
Lewontin, Richard - *Human Diversity*
  Nature - v381 - My 16 '96 - p204 [1-50]
Lewty, Peter J - *Across the Columbia Plain*
  PHR - v65 - N '96 - p676+ [251-500]
Lewy, Guenter - *Why America Needs Religion*
  Choice - v34 - Mr '97 - p1178 [51-250]
  LJ - v121 - O 1 '96 - p84 [51-250]
Leyens, Erich - *Years of Estrangement*
  Choice - v34 - My '97 - p1558 [51-250]
  LJ - v121 - N 15 '96 - p68 [51-250]
  PW - v243 - N 18 '96 - p69 [51-250]
Leyerle, Betty - *The Private Regulation of American Health Care*
  J Con A - v30 - Win '96 - p485+ [501+]
Leys, Ad - *Ecclesiological Impacts of the Principle of Subsidiarity*
  Theol St - v57 - Je '96 - p370+ [501+]
Leys, Colin - *Namibia's Liberation Struggle*
  Africa T - v43 - 4 '96 - p417+ [501+]
  JTWS - v13 - Spr '96 - p313+ [501+]

  The Rise and Fall of Development Theory
  JEL - v34 - S '96 - p1478+ [51-250]
Leyser, Brady J - *Rock Stars/Pop Stars*
  r PMS - v19 - Win '95 - p105+ [501+]
Leyser, Henrietta - *Medieval Women*
  Albion - v28 - Fall '96 - p455+ [501+]
  JIH - v27 - Spr '97 - p672+ [251-500]
  R&R Bk N - v11 - N '96 - p42 [51-250]
  Six Ct J - v27 - Fall '96 - p925+ [501+]
Leyser, Karl - *Communications and Power in Medieval Europe*
  Historian - v58 - Sum '96 - p909+ [251-500]
  Communications and Power in Medieval Europe: The Carolingian and Ottoman Centuries
  EHR - v112 - Ap '97 - p412+ [501+]
  Communications and Power in Medieval Europe: The Gregorian Revolution and Beyond
  EHR - v112 - Ap '97 - p412+ [501+]
Leznoff, C C - *Phthalocyanines: Properties and Applications. Vol. 4*
  SciTech - v21 - Mr '97 - p30 [51-250]
L'Heureux, John - *The Handmaid of Desire*
  Atl - v278 - O '96 - p122 [51-250]
  BL - v92 - Ag '96 - p1882 [51-250]
  BW - v26 - O 13 '96 - p4 [501+]
  NYTBR - v101 - O 20 '96 - p14 [501+]
  WSJ-MW - v77 - S 9 '96 - pA16 [501+]
Li, Ang - *The Butcher's Wife and Other Stories*
  WLT - v70 - Aut '96 - p1028 [501+]
Li, Huishi - *Zariskian Filtrations*
  SciTech - v21 - Mr '97 - p13 [51-250]
Li, Jun - *Chinese Civilization in the Making 1766-221 BC*
  Choice - v34 - My '97 - p1554 [51-250]
Li, Kui-Wai - *Financial Repression and Economic Reform in China*
  Ch Rev Int - v3 - Fall '96 - p482+ [501+]
Li, Lincoln - *The China Factor in Modern Japanese Thought*
  R&R Bk N - v11 - N '96 - p15 [51-250]
  Student Nationalism in China 1924-1949
  TLS - O 25 '96 - p8+ [501+]
Li, Po-Yuan - *Modern Times*
  Choice - v34 - S '96 - p121 [51-250]
Li, Rex - *A Theory of Conceptual Intelligence*
  Choice - v34 - O '96 - p365 [51-250]
Li, Tse-Hou - *Gao Bie Ge Ming*
  BL - v93 - N 1 '96 - p484 [1-50]
  The Path of Beauty
  JAAC - v55 - Win '97 - p77+ [501+]
Li, Xiaoming - *Disequilibria, Economic Reforms and Economic Policies*
  Econ J - v106 - S '96 - p1481+ [51-250]
  R&R Bk N - v12 - F '97 - p36 [51-250]
Li, Yu - *The Carnal Prayer Mat*
  TranslRevS - v2 - D '96 - p6 [51-250]
Li, Yuehua - *Hong Yan Nan Zi*
  BL - v93 - My 1 '97 - p1484 [1-50]
Li, Zhisui - *The Private Life of Chairman Mao*
  Books - v10 - Je '96 - p21 [51-250]
Liao, Thomas T - *Advanced Educational Technology*
  R&R Bk N - v11 - N '96 - p54 [51-250]
Libanius - *Imaginary Speeches*
  TLS - Mr 7 '97 - p33 [251-500]
Libby, Gary R - *Celebrating Florida*
  BWatch - v18 - F '97 - p5 [51-250]
Libby, Lewis - *The Apprentice*
  BW - v26 - O 27 '96 - p4+ [501+]
  NYTBR - v101 - N 3 '96 - p19 [51-250]
Libby, Megan McNeill - *Postcards from France*
  PW - v244 - Ja 20 '97 - p387 [51-250]
Libecap, Gary D - *Reinventing Government and the Problem of Bureaucracy*
  JEL - v34 - D '96 - p2029+ [51-250]
Libera, Alain De - *La Philosophie Medievale*
  CPR - v16 - Ap '96 - p89+ [501+]
  Dialogue - v35 - Sum '96 - p611+ [501+]
Liberati, Annamaria - *Ancient Rome*
  y BL - v93 - D 15 '96 - p706 [51-250]
  NYTBR - v102 - Mr 30 '97 - p17 [251-500]
  PW - v243 - S 16 '96 - p61 [51-250]
  Time - v148 - N 18 '96 - p109 [1-50]
Liberatore, Paul - *The Road to Hell*
  BL - v92 - Ag '96 - p1861 [51-250]
  BL - v93 - Ja '97 - p757 [1-50]
  BW - v26 - Ag 25 '96 - p13 [51-250]
  SFR - v21 - Jl '96 - p4 [251-500]
Liberles, Robert - *Salo Wittmayer Baron: Architect of Jewish History*
  AHR - v102 - F '97 - p87+ [501+]
Liberman, Peter - *Does Conquest Pay?*
  JEL - v35 - Mr '97 - p145+ [51-250]

Liberman, Syd - *Streets and Alleys*
  CAY - v17 - Win '96 - p12 [51-250]
Librarianship and Information Work Worldwide 1994
  LQ - v67 - Ja '97 - p85+ [501+]
Librarianship and Information Work Worldwide 1995
  LAR - v98 - O '96 - p533 [251-500]
Libraries Unlimited Professional Collection CD 1995. Electronic Media Version
  r ARBA - v28 - '97 - p236 [251-500]
Library and Information Plan for Leicestershire Working Party on Local Government Reorganisation
  LAR - v98 - D '96 - p650 [51-250]
Library and Information Services Council (Northern Ireland) - *Libraries in Post Primary Schools*
  LAR - v98 - Jl '96 - p371 [51-250]
  Sch Lib - v44 - Ag '96 - p130 [51-250]
  Libraries in Primary Schools
  LAR - v98 - Jl '96 - p371 [251-500]
  Sch Lib - v44 - Ag '96 - p130 [51-250]
Library Literature 95
  r ARBA - v28 - '97 - p238+ [51-250]
Library of Congress - *Medieval and Renaissance Manuscript Books in the Library of Congress. Vol. 1*
  r Lib - v18 - Je '96 - p159+ [251-500]
  The National Union Catalog: Pre-1956 Imprints. Vols. 1-754
  r ASInt - v34 - O '96 - p6 [51-250]
  Special Collections in the Library of Congress
  r ASInt - v34 - O '96 - p11 [51-250]
Library of Congress. Federal Research Division - *Country Studies*
  r BL - v92 - Ag '96 - p1919 [51-250]
Library of Congress. General Reference and Bibliography Division - *A Guide to the Study of the United States of America*
  r ASInt - v34 - O '96 - p6 [1-50]
  A Guide to the Study of the United States of America. 1st Suppl.
  r ASInt - v34 - O '96 - p6 [1-50]
Library of Congress. Office for Subject Cataloging Policy - *Library of Congress Subject Headings. 19th Ed., Vols. 1-4*
  r ARBA - v28 - '97 - p240+ [251-500]
The Library of the Future. 4th Ed. Electronic Media Version
  r TES - Mr 14 '97 - p22U [51-250]
Libutti, Patricia O'Brien - *Teaching Information Retrieval Skills to Education Students and Practitioners*
  RQ - v36 - Fall '96 - p152+ [51-250]
Lichbach, Mark Irving - *The Cooperator's Dilemma*
  JEL - v35 - Mr '97 - p197 [51-250]
  JPR - v34 - F '97 - p113+ [51-250]
  The Rebel's Dilemma
  J Pol - v58 - Ag '96 - p863+ [501+]
Lichfield, Nathaniel - *Community Impact Evaluation*
  Choice - v34 - F '97 - p1016 [51-250]
Licht, Walter - *Industrializing America*
  Pub Hist - v19 - Win '97 - p113+ [501+]
  T&C - v37 - O '96 - p838+ [501+]
Lichtenstein, Alex - *Twice the Work of Free Labor*
  JEH - v57 - Mr '97 - p237+ [501+]
Lichtenstein, Diane - *Writing Their Nations*
  Signs - v22 - Aut '96 - p234+ [501+]
Lichtenstein, Nelson - *The Most Dangerous Man in Detroit*
  Am - v175 - N 16 '96 - p23+ [501+]
  CS - v26 - Mr '97 - p165+ [501+]
  Dis - v43 - Fall '96 - p128+ [501+]
  ILRR - v50 - Ja '97 - p363+ [501+]
  NYTBR - v101 - D 8 '96 - p89 [1-50]
  RAH - v24 - S '96 - p488+ [501+]
Lichter, Gerhard - *Fossil Collector's Handbook*
  r RocksMiner - v71 - S '96 - p361+ [251-500]
Lichter, S Robert - *Good Intentions Make Bad News*
  PSQ - v111 - Fall '96 - p535+ [501+]
Lickson, Charles - *Finance and Taxes for the Home-Based Business*
  LJ - v122 - My 1 '97 - p52 [1-50]
Licoppe, Christian - *La Formation De La Pratique Scientifique*
  Isis - v87 - D '96 - p731+ [501+]
Liddell, Caroline - *Frozen Desserts*
  BWatch - v17 - D '96 - p9 [1-50]
Liddell, Henry George - *A Greek-English Lexicon. Rev. and Augm. Throughout*
  r ARBA - v28 - '97 - p392 [51-250]
  r Rel St Rev - v23 - Ap '97 - p173 [51-250]
  r TLS - N 1 '96 - p9+ [501+]
Lie, J T - *Biopsy Diagnosis in Rheumatic Diseases*
  SciTech - v21 - Mr '97 - p58 [51-250]

Lieb, Elliott H - *Analysis*
    SciTech - v21 - Mr '97 - p15 [1-50]
Lieb, Michael - *Milton and the Culture of Violence*
    MP - v94 - N '96 - p237+ [501+]
Lieber, James B - *Friendly Takeover*
    NYRB - v44 - Ap 10 '97 - p38+ [501+]
Lieber, Robert J - *Eagle Adrift*
    For Aff - v76 - Mr '97 - p184+ [251-500]
Lieber, Werner - *Amethyst--Geschichte, Eigenschaften, Fundorte*
    RocksMiner - v71 - S '96 - p360 [51-250]
Lieberknecht, Sieglinde - *Die Canones Des Pseudo-Mesue*
    Isis - v87 - D '96 - p720+ [501+]
Lieberman, Carole - *Bad Boys*
    LJ - v122 - Ap 1 '97 - p111 [51-250]
Lieberman, Herbert - *The Girl with the Botticelli Eyes*
    y BL - v92 - Ag '96 - p1886 [51-250]
    BL - v92 - Ag '96 - p1891 [1-50]
Lieberman, Herbert A, 1920- - *Pharmaceutical Dosage Forms: Disperse Systems. 2nd Ed., Vols. 1-2*
    SciTech - v20 - N '96 - p56 [51-250]
Lieberman, Ira W - *Mass Privatization in Central and Eastern Europe and the Former Soviet Union*
    J Gov Info - v23 - S '96 - p687+ [51-250]
    Russia: Creating Private Enterprises and Efficient Markets
    J Gov Info - v23 - S '96 - p689 [51-250]
Lieberman, Laurence - *Beyond the Muse of Memory*
    Parnassus - v22 - 1 '97 - p326+ [501+]
    VQR - v72 - Aut '96 - p120* [51-250]
    The Creole Mephistopheles
    Parnassus - v22 - 1 '97 - p326+ [501+]
    Dark Songs
    HR - v49 - Win '97 - p659+ [501+]
    Parnassus - v22 - 1 '97 - p326+ [501+]
    New and Selected Poems 1962-92
    Parnassus - v22 - 1 '97 - p326+ [501+]
    The St. Kitts Monkey Feuds
    Parnassus - v22 - 1 '97 - p326+ [501+]
Lieberman, Philip A - *Radio's Morning Show Personalities*
    r ARBA - v28 - '97 - p351+ [51-250]
Lieberman, Richard K - *Steinway and Sons*
    Am MT - v46 - D '96 - p64+ [51-250]
    Notes - v53 - S '96 - p81+ [501+]
    NYTBR - v101 - D 8 '96 - p93 [1-50]
Lieberman, Ronald - *Principles of Drug Development in Transplantation and Autoimmunity*
    SciTech - v20 - S '96 - p26 [51-250]
Lieberman, Saul - *Greek in Jewish Palestine. Hellenism in Jewish Palestine*
    Rel St Rev - v23 - Ja '97 - p87 [51-250]
Lieberman, Sima - *Growth and Crisis in the Spanish Economy 1940-93*
    Econ J - v106 - S '96 - p1479 [51-250]
    JEL - v34 - S '96 - p1488 [51-250]
Liebert, Georges - *Nietzsche Et La Musique*
    TLS - N 29 '96 - p15 [51-250]
Lieberthal, Kenneth - *Governing China*
    Ch Rev Int - v3 - Fall '96 - p487+ [501+]
Lieblich, Amia - *Conversations with Dvora*
    LJ - v122 - My 1 '97 - p104 [51-250]
    El Leah
    BL - v93 - Mr 1 '97 - p1115 [1-50]
Lieblich, Julia - *Sisters: Lives of Devotion and Defiance*
    RR - v56 - Mr '97 - p221 [1-50]
Liebling, A J - *Neutral Corner*
    LATBR - D 8 '96 - p2 [1-50]
Liebman, Herbert - *The Dramatic Art of David Storey*
    Choice - v34 - F '97 - p967 [51-250]
    R&R Bk N - v11 - D '96 - p64 [51-250]
Liebman, Marcia C - *Multimodal Therapy in Oncology Nursing*
    SciTech - v20 - S '96 - p30 [51-250]
Liebman, Roy - *Silent Film Performers*
    r ARBA - v28 - '97 - p504+ [51-250]
Liebmann, George W - *The Little Platoons*
    CS - v26 - Mr '97 - p174+ [501+]
Liebovich, Louis W - *Bylines in Despair*
    JC - v46 - Sum '96 - p176+ [501+]
Liebregts, Peter - *Beauty and the Beast*
    Nine-C Lit - v51 - Mr '97 - p560 [1-50]
Liechtensteiner Briefmarkenkatalog 1995
    r Am Phil - v110 - Ag '96 - p754 [251-500]
Lied, Kate - *Potato: A Tale from the Great Depression (Illus. by Lisa Campbell Ernst)*
    c BL - v93 - Ap 1 '97 - p1338 [51-250]
    c HB - v73 - My '97 - p309 [51-250]
    c KR - v65 - F 15 '97 - p302 [51-250]
    c PW - v244 - Mr 10 '97 - p66 [51-250]

Liefeld, Walter L - *Interpreting the Book of Acts*
    Rel St Rev - v23 - Ap '97 - p184 [51-250]
Liehu, Rakel - *Readymade*
    WLT - v71 - Win '97 - p188+ [251-500]
Liem, C B - *The Splitting Extrapolation Method*
    SIAM Rev - v39 - Mr '97 - p161+ [501+]
Liep, John - *Komplekse Liv*
    Am Ethnol - v24 - F '97 - p244+ [501+]
Liepa, Anita - *Vejgaze*
    WLT - v70 - Aut '96 - p1001 [501+]
Lieu, Samuel N C - *From Constantine to Julian*
    Rel St Rev - v23 - Ja '97 - p63+ [51-250]
Lifshin, Lyn - *Madonna and Marilyn Ad Nausea*
    Sm Pr R - v29 - F '97 - p5 [251-500]
    Madonna Poems
    Sm Pr R - v29 - F '97 - p5 [251-500]
Lift-and-Peek into Noah's Ark
    c HB Guide - v7 - Fall '96 - p241 [51-250]
Lifton, Betty Jean - *Tell Me a Real Adoption Story (Illus. by Claire A Nivola)*
    c Inst - v106 - Ja '97 - p52 [1-50]
Lifton, Robert Jay - *Hiroshima in America*
    y Kliatt - v30 - N '96 - p27 [51-250]
Liggett, Stephen B - *The Genetics of Asthma*
    SciTech - v20 - D '96 - p46 [51-250]
Light, Andrew - *Environmental Pragmatism*
    Choice - v34 - D '96 - p631 [51-250]
Light, Ivan - *Race, Ethnicity, and Entrepreneurship in Urban America*
    AJS - v102 - N '96 - p920+ [501+]
    CS - v25 - S '96 - p673+ [501+]
    JEL - v34 - D '96 - p2091 [501+]
Light, Laura - *Catalogue of Medieval and Renaissance Manuscripts in the Houghton Library, Harvard University. Vol. 1*
    r ARBA - v28 - '97 - p246+ [51-250]
Light, Paul C - *The Tides of Reform*
    LJ - v122 - My 1 '97 - p124 [51-250]
Lightbody, Mark - *Canada: A Travel Survival Guide*
    r Quill & Q - v63 - F '97 - p40 [51-250]
Lighting Listings
    r TCI - v30 - O '96 - p59 [1-50]
Lightman, Alan - *Dance for Two*
    Obs - Ag 25 '96 - p17* [501+]
Lightman, Gavin - *The Law of Receivers of Companies. 2nd Ed.*
    Law Q Rev - v112 - O '96 - p680+ [501+]
Lightston, Jack N - *Ritual and Ethnic Identity*
    Rel St Rev - v23 - Ja '97 - p90 [51-250]
Ligotti, Thomas - *The Nightmare Factory*
    BL - v92 - Ag '96 - p1882 [51-250]
    Necro - Win '97 - p7+ [501+]
    Obs - S 1 '96 - p18* [51-250]
Lila Says
    Obs - Mr 30 '97 - p17* [51-250]
Liles, J N - *The Art and Craft of Natural Dyeing*
    CAY - v16 - Fall '95 - p12 [51-250]
Liles, Maurine - *The Littlest Vaquero*
    c HB Guide - v8 - Spr '97 - p70 [51-250]
Lilie, Ralph-Johannes - *Byzantium and the Crusader States 1096-1204*
    Historian - v59 - Fall '96 - p197+ [251-500]
    Byzanz: Kaiser Und Reich
    EHR - v112 - F '97 - p159+ [501+]
Lilienheim, Henry - *The Aftermath: A Survivor's Odyssey through War-Torn Europe*
    Essays CW - Spr '96 - p194+ [501+]
Lill, Wendy - *The Glace Bay Miners' Museum*
    Quill & Q - v62 - D '96 - p32 [501+]
Lilla, Mark - *New French Thought*
    Ethics - v107 - Ja '97 - p403+ [51-250]
    Historian - v58 - Sum '96 - p910 [251-500]
Lillegard, Dee - *The Day the Daisies Danced (Illus. by Rex Barron)*
    c HB Guide - v7 - Fall '96 - p265 [1-50]
    c NYTBR - v101 - S 8 '96 - p28 [51-250]
    Tortoise Brings the Mail (Illus. by Jillian Lund)
    c BL - v93 - My 15 '97 - p1580 [51-250]
    c PW - v244 - Mr 31 '97 - p73 [51-250]
Lilley, Stephen R - *The Conquest of Mexico*
    y HB Guide - v8 - Spr '97 - p173 [51-250]
    y SLJ - v43 - Mr '97 - p202 [51-250]
    Hernando Cortes
    c HB Guide - v7 - Fall '96 - p371 [51-250]
Lillie, Patricia - *Floppy Teddy Bear (Illus. by Karen Lee Baker)*
    c RT - v50 - N '96 - p254 [51-250]
    When This Box Is Full (Illus. by Donald Crews)
    c PW - v244 - Ja 20 '97 - p403 [51-250]

Lilliefors, Jim - *Bananaville*
    BW - v26 - N 17 '96 - p6 [51-250]
    LJ - v121 - O 1 '96 - p131 [51-250]
    PW - v243 - S 9 '96 - p68 [51-250]
Lillios, Katina T - *The Origins of Complex Societies in Late Prehistoric Iberia*
    AJA - v100 - Jl '96 - p609+ [501+]
    Am Ant - v61 - Jl '96 - p617+ [501+]
Lilliput Review
    p Sm Pr R - v28 - S '96 - p21 [51-250]
Lilly, Reginald - *The Ancients and the Moderns*
    Choice - v34 - Ap '97 - p1415 [51-250]
Lim, David - *Explaining Economic Growth*
    Econ J - v107 - Ja '97 - p282 [51-250]
    JEL - v34 - S '96 - p1487 [51-250]
Lim, Lin Lean - *More and Better Jobs for Women*
    JEL - v35 - Mr '97 - p235 [51-250]
    WorldV - v13 - Ja '97 - p9 [51-250]
Lim, Richard - *Public Disputation, Power, and Social Order in Late Antiquity*
    AHR - v101 - D '96 - p1528+ [501+]
    CH - v65 - D '96 - p669+ [501+]
    Theol St - v57 - S '96 - p529+ [501+]
Lim, Shirley - *Among the White Moon Faces*
    Amerasia J - v22 - 2 '96 - p153+ [501+]
    BW - v26 - D 15 '96 - p1+ [501+]
    Choice - v34 - Ja '97 - p796 [51-250]
    Ms - v7 - S '96 - p82+ [251-500]
    Monsoon History
    WLT - v70 - Aut '96 - p1033+ [501+]
    Writing S.E/Asia in English
    WLT - v70 - Aut '96 - p1030 [251-500]
Lima, Luiz Costa - *The Limits of Voice*
    Choice - v34 - N '96 - p450 [51-250]
Lima, Robert - *Dark Prisms*
    Hisp - v79 - D '96 - p791+ [501+]
Limb, Peter - *Bibliography of African Literatures*
    r AB - v99 - F 17 '97 - p522+ [501+]
    r ARBA - v28 - '97 - p458 [51-250]
    r Choice - v34 - F '97 - p946 [51-250]
    r R&R Bk N - v12 - F '97 - p80 [51-250]
Limb, Sue - *Passion Fruit*
    Obs - S 15 '96 - p18* [51-250]
Limbaugh, Ronald H - *John Muir's Stickeen and the Lessons of Nature*
    Choice - v34 - N '96 - p480 [51-250]
    WHQ - v28 - Spr '97 - p85+ [251-500]
Lim-Hing, Sharon - *The Very Inside*
    Amerasia J - v22 - 2 '96 - p161+ [501+]
Limoges, Raymonde - *American Limoges*
    r Ant & CM - v101 - Ag '96 - p18 [1-50]
Limon, Graciela - *Song of the Hummingbird*
    Choice - v34 - O '96 - p278+ [51-250]
Limon, Jose E - *Dancing with the Devil*
    JPC - v30 - Fall '96 - p210+ [51-250]
Limon, Martin - *Slicky Boys*
    KR - v65 - My 1 '97 - p666 [251-500]
    LJ - v122 - Ap 1 '97 - p128 [51-250]
    PW - v244 - Mr 24 '97 - p59 [51-250]
Limouris, Gennadios - *Orthodox Visions of Ecumenism*
    Rel St Rev - v22 - O '96 - p339 [51-250]
Lim-Wilson, Fatima - *Crossing the Snow Bridge*
    Ant R - v54 - Sum '96 - p376+ [51-250]
Lin, Bih-Jaw - *Contemporary China in the Post-Cold War Era*
    JEL - v34 - S '96 - p1493+ [51-250]
Lin, C T - *Neural Fuzzy Systems*
    SciTech - v20 - S '96 - p53 [51-250]
Lin, E C C - *Regulation of Gene Expression in Escherichia Coli*
    SciTech - v20 - N '96 - p26 [51-250]
Lin, Jing - *The Opening of the Chinese Mind*
    Ch Rev Int - v3 - Fall '96 - p490+ [501+]
Lin, Pai - *Qing Tai*
    BL - v93 - My 1 '97 - p1484 [1-50]
Lin, Ray Y - *Design Fundamentals of High Temperature Composites, Intermetallics, and Metal-Ceramics Systems*
    SciTech - v20 - D '96 - p62 [51-250]
Lin, Tan - *Lotion Bullwhip Giraffe*
    PW - v243 - Jl 22 '96 - p237 [51-250]
Lin, Wuu-Long - *Management of Developing Economies in Transition*
    JEL - v34 - S '96 - p1482+ [51-250]
Lin, Xiannuan - *China's Energy Strategy*
    Pac A - v69 - Sum '96 - p257 [251-500]
Lin, Yutang - *The Importance of Living*
    Wil Q - v20 - Aut '96 - p103 [251-500]
Linaham, Liz - *Pit Ghosts, Padfeet and Poltergeists*
    Folkl - v107 - '96 - p125+ [251-500]
Linaweaver, Brad - *Free Space*
    KR - v65 - My 1 '97 - p686 [51-250]

Linck, Ernestine Sewell - *How the Cimarron River Got Its Name and Other Stories about Coffee*
J Am Cult - v19 - Sum '96 - p161 [51-250]
Lincoln, Abraham - *The Gettysburg Address (Illus. by Michael McCurdy)*
c RT - v50 - N '96 - p245 [51-250]
Lincoln's Letters (Vail). Audio Version
CSM - v89 - Mr 27 '97 - pB2 [1-50]
Lincoln's Prose (Vail). Audio Version
CSM - v89 - Mr 27 '97 - pB2 [1-50]
Of the People, by the People, for the People, and Other Quotations from Abraham Lincoln
r ARBA - v28 - '97 - p35 [51-250]
Lincoln, Andrew - *Spiritual History*
Choice - v34 - S '96 - p126+ [51-250]
Lincoln, Bruce - *Authority: Construction and Corrosion*
QJS - v82 - Ag '96 - p311+ [501+]
Rel St Rev - v23 - Ja '97 - p50+ [51-250]
Lincoln, C Eric - *Coming through the Fire*
CC - v113 - N 13 '96 - p1119 [251-500]
Choice - v34 - O '96 - p349 [51-250]
JSH - v62 - N '96 - p861 [1-50]
VQR - v72 - Aut '96 - p134*+ [51-250]
Lincoln, Kenneth - *Men Down West*
PW - v244 - Ja 6 '97 - p56 [51-250]
Lincoln, William A - *The Complete Manual of Wood Veneering*
BWatch - v18 - Mr '97 - p10 [51-250]
Lind, Beth Beutler - *Multicultural Children's Literature*
r ARBA - v28 - '97 - p426 [51-250]
r BL - v93 - N 15 '96 - p612 [51-250]
r SLJ - v43 - Ja '97 - p38 [51-250]
r VOYA - v19 - F '97 - p358 [251-500]
Lind, Carla - *Lost Wright*
WSJ-MW - v78 - D 5 '96 - pA18 [51-250]
Lind, David - *The Physics of Skiing*
Sci - v275 - Ja 3 '97 - p37 [1-50]
SciTech - v21 - Mr '97 - p20 [51-250]
Lind, Michael - *The Alamo: An Epic*
BL - v93 - Mr 1 '97 - p1106 [51-250]
LATBR - Mr 9 '97 - p6 [501+]
LJ - v122 - My 1 '97 - p107 [51-250]
NYTBR - v102 - Mr 9 '97 - p14 [501+]
PW - v244 - Mr 31 '97 - p71 [51-250]
Trib Bks - Ap 27 '97 - p5 [251-500]
The Next American Nation
Am - v176 - F 15 '97 - p34 [501+]
NYTBR - v101 - Jl 21 '96 - p28 [51-250]
Powertown
BL - v93 - S 1 '96 - p62 [51-250]
LJ - v122 - Mr 15 '97 - p42+ [1-50]
Nat R - v48 - S 2 '96 - p91+ [501+]
NYTBR - v101 - O 20 '96 - p27 [501+]
Reason - v28 - Ja '97 - p64+ [501+]
Time - v148 - O 7 '96 - p96+ [501+]
VV - v41 - O 22 '96 - p58+ [501+]
Up from Conservatism
y BL - v92 - Ag '96 - p1862+ [501+]
y BL - v92 - Ag '96 - p1890 [1-50]
BW - v26 - Ag 18 '96 - p5+ [501+]
Choice - v34 - D '96 - p690+ [51-250]
Nat R - v48 - S 2 '96 - p89+ [501+]
NL - v79 - Ag 12 '96 - p6+ [501+]
NYRB - v43 - O 17 '96 - p30+ [501+]
NYTBR - v101 - D 8 '96 - p94 [1-50]
Prog - v60 - O '96 - p42+ [501+]
VV - v41 - O 22 '96 - p58+ [501+]
Lindahl, Anders - *The Aim of Laboratory Analyses of Ceramics in Archaeology*
Am Ant - v62 - Ja '97 - p150+ [501+]
Lindamood, Jean - *Road Trips, Head Trips and Other Car-Crazed Writings*
LJ - v122 - F 1 '97 - p103 [51-250]
Lindbeck, George - *The Nature of Doctrine*
Rel St - v33 - Mr '97 - p233+ [501+]
Lindberg, Carter - *The European Reformations*
Rel St Rev - v22 - O '96 - p349 [51-250]
Lindberg, David C - *Theories of Vision from Al-Kindi to Kepler*
Nature - v383 - O 24 '96 - p682 [1-50]
Lindberg, Jana Hauschild - *Scandinavian Cross Stitch Designs*
BL - v93 - S 1 '96 - p55 [51-250]
Lindberg, Kathryne V - *America's Modernisms*
AL - v69 - Mr '97 - p255 [51-250]
Nine-C Lit - v51 - S '96 - p274 [51-250]
Lindberg, Richard - *Ethnic Chicago*
Trib Bks - Mr 30 '97 - p2 [1-50]
Lindbergh, Peter - *10 Women by Peter Lindbergh*
Pet PM - v25 - D '96 - p20 [51-250]

Lindbergh, Reeve - *Nobody Owns the Sky (Illus. by Pamela Paparone)*
c BL - v93 - Ja '97 - p869 [251-500]
c BW - v26 - D 8 '96 - p23 [51-250]
c CBRS - v25 - F '97 - p76 [51-250]
c Ch BWatch - v7 - Ja '97 - p5 [51-250]
c HB Guide - v8 - Spr '97 - p36 [51-250]
c KR - v64 - N 1 '96 - p1603 [51-250]
c PW - v243 - N 18 '96 - p75 [51-250]
c Sch Lib - v45 - F '97 - p19 [51-250]
c SLJ - v42 - N '96 - p98+ [51-250]
North Country Spring (Illus. by Liz Sivertson)
c BL - v93 - My 15 '97 - p1580 [51-250]
c KR - v65 - F 15 '97 - p302 [51-250]
c PW - v244 - Mr 24 '97 - p82 [51-250]
View from the Air (Illus. by Richard Brown)
c CLW - v67 - Mr '97 - p14 [1-50]
y Kliatt - v30 - S '96 - p24 [51-250]
What Is the Sun? (Illus. by Stephen Lambert)
c LA - v73 - S '96 - p354 [51-250]
Lindbom, Tage - *The Myth of Democracy*
Univ Bkmn - v36 - Win '96 - p11 [51-250]
Linde, Charlotte - *Life Stories*
Lang Soc - v25 - D '96 - p620+ [501+]
Linde, Nancy - *The Orange Cat Bistro*
LJ - v122 - Mr 15 '97 - p112 [51-250]
Lindeburg, Michael R - *EIT Review Manual*
r RQ - v35 - Sum '96 - p554+ [251-500]
Lindee, M Susan - *Suffering Made Real*
CS - v25 - S '96 - p677+ [501+]
Lindekugel, D M - *Shooters: TV News Photographers and Their Work*
J Am Cult - v19 - Sum '96 - p142 [51-250]
SF - v75 - S '96 - p379+ [251-500]
Lindemann, Mary - *Health and Healing in Eighteenth-Century Germany*
Choice - v34 - My '97 - p1534 [51-250]
Lindemeyer, Paul - *Celebrating the Saxophone*
BW - v26 - S 8 '96 - p13 [51-250]
Linden, Anne Marie - *Emerald Blue (Illus. by Katherine Doyle)*
c Bks Keeps - N '96 - p8 [51-250]
c TES - O 18 '96 - p12* [1-50]
Linden, G - *Analytical Techniques for Foods and Agricultural Products*
SciTech - v20 - S '96 - p63 [51-250]
Linden, Marcel Van Der - *Racism and the Labour Market*
ILRR - v50 - O '96 - p171+ [501+]
Linden, Stanton J - *Darke Hierogliphicks*
Choice - v34 - Mr '97 - p1164 [51-250]
Linden, Tom - *Dr. Tom Linden's Guide to Online Medicine*
r BL - v93 - F 1 '97 - p956 [1-50]
Lindenberger, Jan - *Collecting Plastic Jewelry*
r Ant & CM - v101 - D '96 - p31 [1-50]
Lindenberger, Thomas - *Strassenpolitik: Zur Sozialgeschichte Der Offentlichen Ordnung In Berlin 1900 Bis 1914*
AHR - v102 - F '97 - p124+ [501+]
Lindenmayer, Clem - *Walking in Switzerland*
r BL - v93 - S 15 '96 - p210 [1-50]
Lindenmeyr, Adele - *Poverty Is Not a Vice*
Choice - v34 - D '96 - p670+ [51-250]
ChrPhil - v8 - Je 27 '96 - p34 [51-250]
Lindensmith, Mark - *Short-Term Losses*
NYTBR - v102 - Ja 19 '97 - p18 [51-250]
PW - v243 - N 18 '96 - p68 [51-250]
Lindenstrauss, Joram - *Classical Banach Spaces. Vols. 1-2*
JEL - v34 - S '96 - p1503 [51-250]
Linder, Ann P - *Princes of the Trenches*
Choice - v34 - My '97 - p1502+ [51-250]
Linder, Leslie - *A History of the Writings of Beatrix Potter. Rev. Ed.*
RSR - v24 - 3 '96 - p23 [51-250]
Linder, Rolf - *The Reportage of Urban Culture*
TLS - Ja 24 '97 - p12 [501+]
Linderman, Michael - *Developing Visual Programming Applications Using Smalltalk*
SciTech - v20 - N '96 - p8 [51-250]
Lindfors, Bernth - *Twentieth-Century Caribbean and Black African Writers: Third Series*
r ARBA - v28 - '97 - p462+ [51-250]
Lindgren, Astrid - *Pippi in the South Seas*
c Bkbird - v34 - Spr '96 - p5 [1-50]

Pippi Longstocking's After-Christmas Party (Illus. by Michael Chesworth)
c BL - v93 - S 1 '96 - p137 [51-250]
c HB Guide - v8 - Spr '97 - p36 [1-50]
c KR - v64 - S 15 '96 - p1403+ [51-250]
c PW - v243 - S 30 '96 - p93 [51-250]
c SLJ - v42 - O '96 - p38 [51-250]
Lindgren, Barbro - *Rosa Moves to Town (Illus. by Eva Eriksson)*
c KR - v65 - Mr 1 '97 - p384 [51-250]
Lindgren, H Elaine - *Land in Her Own Name*
Roundup M - v4 - F '97 - p25 [51-250]
Lindgren, James M - *Preserving Historic New England*
NEQ - v69 - S '96 - p506+ [501+]
W&M Q - v54 - Ap '97 - p463+ [501+]
Lindholm, T Sam - *Bone Morphogenetic Proteins*
SciTech - v20 - N '96 - p33 [51-250]
Lindholm, Tim - *The Java Virtual Machine Specification*
R&R Bk N - v12 - F '97 - p92 [51-250]
Lindley, Arthur - *Hyperion and the Hobbyhorse*
Choice - v34 - Ap '97 - p1337 [51-250]
Lindley, David, 1948- - *Court Masques*
TLS - N 29 '96 - p18+ [501+]
Lindley, David, 1956- - *Where Does the Weirdness Go?*
BW - v26 - S 1 '96 - p4 [251-500]
Choice - v34 - S '96 - p166 [51-250]
Nature - v383 - S 26 '96 - p310 [501+]
New Sci - v152 - O 19 '96 - p48 [501+]
New Sci - v152 - N 2 '96 - p47 [51-250]
New Sci - v153 - F 8 '97 - p44 [1-50]
Wil Q - v20 - Aut '96 - p96 [251-500]
Lindley, Susan Hill - *You Have Stept out of Your Place*
Bks & Cult - v2 - N '96 - p33 [501+]
Choice - v34 - Ja '97 - p811+ [51-250]
LJ - v121 - S 15 '96 - p73 [51-250]
Lindmier, Tom - *I See by Your Outfit*
WHQ - v27 - Win '96 - p552 [1-50]
Lindon, Mathieu - *Champion Du Monde*
FR - v70 - Mr '97 - p615 [501+]
Lindop, Edmund - *Dwight D. Eisenhower, John F. Kennedy, Lyndon B. Johnson*
c Ch BWatch - v6 - My '96 - p5 [51-250]
Political Parties
y SLJ - v42 - D '96 - p144 [51-250]
Richard M. Nixon, Jimmy Carter, Ronald Reagan
c Ch BWatch - v6 - My '96 - p5 [51-250]
Lindop, Laurie - *Athletes*
y BL - v93 - Ja '97 - p840 [251-500]
c Ch BWatch - v6 - N '96 - p2 [51-250]
y SLJ - v43 - F '97 - p120 [51-250]
Political Leaders
y BL - v93 - Ja '97 - p840 [251-500]
c Ch BWatch - v6 - N '96 - p2 [51-250]
y SLJ - v43 - Ja '97 - p130 [51-250]
y VOYA - v19 - F '97 - p350+ [251-500]
Lindquist, E E - *Eriophyoid Mites*
SciTech - v20 - D '96 - p56 [51-250]
Lindquist, Mary M - *Reaching Standards*
Math T - v90 - Mr '97 - p248+ [51-250]
Lindqvist, Sven - *Exterminate All the Brutes*
Bl S - v26 - Sum '96 - p66 [1-50]
For Aff - v75 - N '96 - p169 [51-250]
NS - v126 - Ap 25 '97 - p47+ [501+]
TranslRevS - v2 - D '96 - p16 [51-250]
The Skull Measurer's Mistake and Other Portraits of Men and Women Who Spoke Out against Racism
LJ - v122 - Ap 15 '97 - p96 [51-250]
PW - v244 - Mr 24 '97 - p64 [51-250]
Lindsay, Anne - *Smart Cooking. 10th Anniversary Ed.*
Quill & Q - v62 - Ag '96 - p30 [51-250]
Lindsay, Arturo - *Santeria Aesthetics in Contemporary Latin American Art*
BW - v26 - D 8 '96 - p10 [251-500]
VV - v41 - O 1 '96 - p40+ [501+]
Lindsay, Dennis R - *Josephus and Faith*
Rel St Rev - v22 - O '96 - p352+ [51-250]
Lindsay, Jeanne Warren - *Pregnant? Adoption Is an Option*
y BL - v93 - D 1 '96 - p645+ [51-250]
y HB Guide - v8 - Spr '97 - p89 [51-250]
y Kliatt - v31 - Ja '97 - p22 [51-250]
LJ - v122 - F 15 '97 - p157 [51-250]
y SLJ - v43 - F '97 - p120 [51-250]
Teenage Couples: Expectations and Reality
y HB Guide - v7 - Fall '96 - p311 [51-250]
Kliatt - v30 - S '96 - p30 [51-250]
Lindsay, Peter - *Creative Individualism*
JEL - v35 - Mr '97 - p200+ [51-250]
R&R Bk N - v11 - D '96 - p45 [51-250]

Lindsay, William M - *Total Quality and Organization Development*
  Choice - v34 - D '96 - p655 [51-250]
  R&R Bk N - v11 - D '96 - p28 [51-250]
Lindsey, David L - *An Absence of Light*
  Books - v9 - S '95 - p27 [1-50]
  Requiem for a Glass Heart
  BW - v26 - Ag 4 '96 - p8 [51-250]
Lindsey, Donal F - *Indians at Hampton Institute 1877-1923*
  AHR - v101 - O '96 - p1285 [251-500]
  PHR - v65 - Ag '96 - p488+ [251-500]
Lindsey, Duncan - *The Welfare of Children*
  Soc Ser R - v70 - D '96 - p655+ [501+]
  Soc Ser R - v71 - Mr '97 - p135+ [501+]
Lindsey, J K - *Parametric Statistical Inference*
  SciTech - v21 - Mr '97 - p15 [51-250]
Lindsey, Johanna - *Love Me Forever*
  PW - v243 - N 18 '96 - p70 [1-50]
  Say You Love Me
  BL - v93 - O 1 '96 - p291 [51-250]
  PW - v243 - O 14 '96 - p65 [51-250]
Lindskold, Jane - *Smoke and Mirrors*
  MFSF - v91 - O '96 - p65 [51-250]
Lindskoog, Kathryn - *C.S. Lewis, Mere Christian. 4th Ed.*
  PW - v244 - Ap 28 '97 - p70 [51-250]
  Finding the Landlord
  Bks & Cult - v2 - My '96 - p34 [251-500]
Lindskoog, Nils - *Long-Term Greedy*
  BL - v93 - S 1 '96 - p45 [51-250]
  LJ - v121 - O 15 '96 - p69 [51-250]
Lindvall, Terry - *Surprised by Laughter*
  Choice - v34 - My '97 - p1496+ [51-250]
  Ch Today - v41 - F 3 '97 - p66+ [501+]
Line, Maurice B - *National Libraries 3*
  LR - v45 - 7 '96 - p78+ [51-250]
Linedecker, Clifford - *O.J. A to Z*
  r Esq - v126 - N '96 - p65 [1-50]
Linehan, Thomas P - *East London for Mosley*
  TLS - F 28 '97 - p32 [251-500]
Linenthal, Edward T - *History Wars*
  BAS - v53 - Ja '97 - p63+ [501+]
  BW - v26 - Ag 18 '96 - p13 [51-250]
  BWatch - v17 - S '96 - p6 [51-250]
  CC - v113 - N 20 '96 - p1134+ [501+]
  y Kliatt - v30 - N '96 - p27 [51-250]
  LATBR - Ag 4 '96 - p1+ [501+]
  LATBR - D 29 '96 - p3 [51-250]
  Skeptic - v4 - 4 '96 - p101 [501+]
  Preserving Memory
  AHR - v101 - D '96 - p1652 [501+]
  Trib Bks - Ap 6 '97 - p8 [1-50]
Ling, Bettina - *Maya Lin*
  c BL - v93 - My 1 '97 - p1492 [51-250]
Ling, Frank W - *Primary Care in Gynecology*
  SciTech - v20 - S '96 - p30 [51-250]
Ling, Mary - *Asombrosos Lobos, Perros Y Zorros*
  c BL - v93 - F 15 '97 - p1032 [1-50]
  The Snake Book (Illus. by Frank Greenaway)
  c CCB-B - v50 - My '97 - p327 [51-250]
  c PW - v244 - Mr 3 '97 - p76+ [51-250]
Lingard, Joan - *Sulky Suzy. Jittery Jack (Illus. by Jacqui Thomas)*
  c Bks Keeps - Mr '97 - p20 [51-250]
Lingemann, Linda - *Beluga Passage (Illus. by Jon Wieman)*
  c SB - v33 - My '97 - p113 [51-250]
Lingle, Virginia - *World Wide Web and Other Internet Information Services in the Health Sciences*
  LJ - v121 - N 1 '96 - p113 [51-250]
Linguistics and Science Fiction
  p SF Chr - v18 - O '96 - p83 [1-50]
Link, Albert N - *Evaluating Public Sector Research and Development*
  JEL - v34 - D '96 - p2117 [51-250]
  Pol Stud J - v24 - Aut '96 - p520 [51-250]
  SciTech - v20 - S '96 - p46 [51-250]
Link, Luther - *The Devil: A Mask without a Face*
  BM - v138 - Ag '96 - p546+ [501+]
Link, P S - *Middle East Imbroglio*
  R&R Bk N - v12 - F '97 - p18 [51-250]
Link, William A - *William Friday: Power, Purpose, and American Higher Education*
  ES - v27 - Sum '96 - p139+ [501+]
Links, Paul S - *Clinical Assessment and Management of Severe Personality Disorders*
  AJPsych - v154 - F '97 - p283 [501+]
Linley, David - *Extraordinary Furniture*
  BL - v93 - N 15 '96 - p565 [51-250]
Linn, Ruth - *Conscience at War*
  MEJ - v50 - Sum '96 - p451+ [51-250]

Linnaeus, Carl - *The Lapland Journey*
  TranslRevS - v2 - D '96 - p33 [51-250]
Linnea, Ann - *Deep Water Passage*
  PW - v244 - F 17 '97 - p217 [1-50]
Linney, Mark - *Anyone Can Draw*
  Sch Lib - v45 - F '97 - p54 [51-250]
Linscott, Gillian - *Dead Man's Sweetheart*
  Arm Det - v30 - Win '97 - p99+ [251-500]
  y BL - v93 - D 15 '96 - p713 [51-250]
  KR - v64 - O 15 '96 - p1498 [51-250]
Linsky, Arnold S - *Stress, Culture and Aggression*
  CS - v25 - S '96 - p667+ [501+]
  Stress, Culture, and Aggression
  SF - v75 - D '96 - p747+ [501+]
Linton, David - *The Twentieth-Century Newspaper Press in Britain*
  r Albion - v28 - Sum '96 - p360+ [501+]
Linton, J P - *Love Story Classics (Linton). Audio Version*
  LJ - v121 - N 1 '96 - p121 [51-250]
Linton, Martin - *The Election: A Voter's Guide*
  r Econ - v342 - Mr 22 '97 - p106 [501+]
Lintott, Andrew - *Imperium Romanum*
  CW - v89 - Jl '96 - p514+ [251-500]
Linz, Juan J - *Problems of Democratic Transition and Consolidation*
  For Aff - v76 - Mr '97 - p173+ [51-250]
Linzey, Andrew - *Animal Theology*
  Rel St Rev - v22 - O '96 - p343+ [51-250]
Lionni, Leo - *Between Worlds*
  BL - v93 - Mr 1 '97 - p1103 [51-250]
  KR - v65 - F 15 '96 - p277 [251-500]
  LJ - v122 - My 1 '97 - p101 [51-250]
  PW - v244 - F 17 '97 - p202 [251-500]
  A Color of His Own
  c Inst - v106 - Ja '97 - p4* [1-50]
  Frederick
  c New Ad - v9 - Fall '96 - p309+ [501+]
Lions, P L - *Mathematical Topics in Fluid Mechanics. Vol. 1*
  SciTech - v21 - Mr '97 - p18 [51-250]
Lip, Evelyn - *Choosing Auspicious Chinese Names. Rev. Ed.*
  Names - v45 - Mr '97 - p60+ [501+]
Lipanov, Aleksei M - *Theory of Combustion of Powder and Explosives*
  SciTech - v21 - Mr '97 - p96 [51-250]
Lipari, Giuseppe - *Incunaboli E Cinquecentine Della Provincia Dei Cappuccini Di Messina*
  r Lib - v18 - D '96 - p362 [51-250]
Lipinski, Robert A - *Professional Beverage Management*
  r R&R Bk N - v12 - F '97 - p99 [51-250]
Lipkowitz, Myron A - *Allergies A-Z*
  r BL - v93 - F 1 '97 - p958 [1-50]
Lipman, Elinor - *Isabel's Bed*
  NYTBR - v102 - Mr 23 '97 - p28 [51-250]
  Isabel's Bed (Lipman). Audio Version
  y Kliatt - v31 - Ja '97 - p42 [51-250]
Lipman, Matthew - *Natasha: Vygotskian Dialogues*
  HER - v66 - Win '96 - p889 [251-500]
Lipman-Blumen, Jean - *The Connective Edge*
  Choice - v34 - N '96 - p503 [51-250]
Lipovetsky, Gilles - *The Empire of Fashion*
  JMH - v68 - D '96 - p974+ [501+]
Lipovsky, Igor P - *The Socialist Movement in Turkey 1960-1980*
  MEJ - v50 - Aut '96 - p627 [51-250]
Lipp, Solomon - *Crucible of Ideas*
  R&R Bk N - v12 - F '97 - p83 [51-250]
Lippard, Chris - *By Angels Driven*
  Choice - v34 - Ja '97 - p803 [51-250]
  Obs - Ag 18 '96 - p18* [1-50]
  R&R Bk N - v11 - D '96 - p62 [51-250]
  Si & So - v6 - N '96 - p37 [51-250]
Lippard, Lucy - *The Pink Glass Swan*
  JAAC - v55 - Win '97 - p61+ [501+]
Lipper, Ari - *Baby Stuff*
  LJ - v122 - Ap 15 '97 - p92 [51-250]
Lippincott, Catherine - *Well Rounded*
  LJ - v122 - Ja '97 - p126 [51-250]
Lippincott, Robin - *The Real, True Angel*
  NYTBR - v102 - Ja 26 '97 - p18 [51-250]
Lippman, Laura - *Baltimore Blues*
  PW - v243 - D 30 '96 - p64 [51-250]
Lippman, Stanley B - *C++ Gems*
  SciTech - v20 - D '96 - p9 [51-250]
Lipps, Susanne - *Madeira*
  r BL - v93 - S 15 '96 - p210 [1-50]
Lippy, Charles H - *Being Religious, American Style*
  Rel St Rev - v23 - Ja '97 - p93 [51-250]
  Christianity Comes to the Americas 1492-1776
  Rel St Rev - v23 - Ja '97 - p91 [51-250]

  Encyclopedia of the American Religious Experience. Vols. 1-3
  r ASInt - v34 - O '96 - p9 [51-250]
  Modern American Popular Religion
  r ARBA - v28 - '97 - p533+ [51-250]
  r Choice - v34 - S '96 - p102 [51-250]
Lipschutz, Ronnie D - *Global Civil Society and Global Environmental Governance*
  Choice - v34 - Ap '97 - p1364 [51-250]
  R&R Bk N - v12 - F '97 - p29 [51-250]
Lipscomb, Carolyn E - *Information Access and Delivery in Health Sciences Libraries*
  R&R Bk N - v12 - F '97 - p101 [51-250]
  SciTech - v20 - D '96 - p88 [51-250]
Lipscomb, Stephen - *Symmetric Inverse Semigroups*
  SciTech - v21 - Mr '97 - p13 [51-250]
Lipset, Seymour Martin - *American Exceptionalism*
  AJS - v102 - N '96 - p872+ [501+]
  APSR - v91 - Mr '97 - p192+ [501+]
  Comw - v123 - S 13 '96 - p38+ [501+]
  CS - v25 - N '96 - p760+ [501+]
  Jews and the New American Scene
  J Am St - v30 - Ap '96 - p155+ [251-500]
Lipsig, Ethan - *Downsizing: Law and Practice*
  R&R Bk N - v12 - F '97 - p65 [51-250]
Lipsitz, Gail Josephson - *Practical Parenting*
  LJ - v122 - Ap 15 '97 - p109 [51-250]
Lipski, Elizabeth - *Digestive Wellness*
  Quill & Q - v62 - Ag '96 - p31+ [51-250]
Lipski, John M - *Latin American Spanish*
  Hisp - v79 - S '96 - p467+ [501+]
Lipsky, David - *The Art Fair*
  LJ - v121 - O 1 '96 - p47 [51-250]
  Rapport - v19 - 4 '96 - p29 [51-250]
Lipson, Juliene G - *Self-Care Nursing in a Multicultural Context*
  SciTech - v20 - S '96 - p44 [51-250]
Lipsyte, Robert - *One Fat Summer*
  y JAAL - v40 - D '96 - p318 [51-250]
Lisandrelli, Elaine Slivinski - *Maya Angelou: More than a Poet*
  y BL - v93 - S 1 '96 - p116+ [51-250]
  c HB Guide - v7 - Fall '96 - p273 [51-250]
  y VOYA - v19 - O '96 - p234 [251-500]
Lisboa, Maria Manuel - *Machado De Assis and Feminism*
  Choice - v34 - D '96 - p619 [51-250]
Lischer, Richard - *The Preacher King*
  AHR - v101 - D '96 - p1642+ [501+]
Lish, Gordon - *Dear Mr. Capote*
  LJ - v122 - Ja '97 - p155 [1-50]
  NYTBR - v102 - Ja 26 '97 - p28 [51-250]
  TLS - Ja 31 '97 - p20 [501+]
  Epigraph
  BL - v93 - N 15 '96 - p570+ [51-250]
  KR - v64 - S 15 '96 - p1258+ [251-500]
  LATBR - Ap 13 '97 - pG [51-250]
  NYTBR - v101 - D 22 '96 - p15 [51-250]
  PW - v243 - S 9 '96 - p63 [251-500]
  SFR - v21 - N '96 - p34 [501+]
  What I Know So Far
  LJ - v122 - Ja '97 - p155 [1-50]
  NYTBR - v102 - Ja 26 '97 - p28 [51-250]
  TLS - Ja 31 '97 - p20 [501+]
Lishak, Antony - *Baby Bear Comes Home (Illus. by Ian Newsham)*
  c Bks Keeps - Jl '96 - p8 [51-250]
Lishman, Bill - *Father Goose*
  SciTech - v20 - S '96 - p21 [51-250]
Liskin, Jack - *Moving Medicine*
  BL - v93 - D 15 '96 - p701 [51-250]
  LJ - v122 - Ja '97 - p134 [51-250]
Lisle, Janet Taylor - *Afternoon of the Elves*
  c SLJ - v43 - Ja '97 - p37 [1-50]
  Afternoon of the Elves (Moore). Audio Version
  c HB - v72 - S '96 - p566+ [501+]
  Angela's Aliens
  c BL - v93 - N 1 '96 - p498+ [51-250]
  c HB Guide - v8 - Spr '97 - p70 [51-250]
  c KR - v64 - O 1 '96 - p1470 [51-250]
  c NYTBR - v102 - Ap 13 '97 - p27 [1-50]
  c PW - v243 - S 16 '96 - p84 [51-250]
  c SLJ - v42 - N '96 - p108 [51-250]
  Looking for Juliette
  c PW - v243 - O 21 '96 - p85 [1-50]
  A Message from the Match Girl
  c PW - v244 - Ap 7 '97 - p94 [1-50]
Lisle, Julia - *A Perfect Match*
  Woman's J - Ja '97 - p13 [1-50]
Lisle, Laurie - *Portrait of an Artist (Conlin). Audio Version*
  y Kliatt - v30 - S '96 - p58+ [51-250]

Lisowski, Marylin - *Wetlands*
  y BL - v93 - My 1 '97 - p1488 [51-250]
Lispector, Clarice - *Selected Cronicas*
    KR - v64 - O 1 '96 - p1447+ [251-500]
    LJ - v122 - Ja '97 - p99 [51-250]
    NYTBR - v101 - D 15 '96 - p20 [501+]
    PW - v243 - S 30 '96 - p78 [51-250]
    PW - v243 - N 4 '96 - p44 [51-250]
Lissauer, Robert - *Lissauer's Encyclopedia of Popular Music in America 1888 to the Present. Vols. 1-3*
  r ARBA - v28 - '97 - p486 [51-250]
  r BWatch - v17 - S '96 - p8 [51-250]
Lisska, Anthony J - *Aquinas's Theory of Natural Law*
    IPQ - v37 - Mr '97 - p95+ [501+]
Lisson, Deborah - *A Place of Safety*
  y Aust Bk R - D '96 - p88+ [501+]
Lister, Frederick K - *The European Union, the United Nations, and the Revival of Confederal Governance*
    R&R Bk N - v11 - N '96 - p47 [51-250]
Lister, Ruth - *Charles Murray and the Underclass*
    TLS - Ja 24 '97 - p3+ [501+]
Lister, Ted - *Classic Chemistry Demonstrations*
    J Chem Ed - v74 - Mr '97 - p344 [251-500]
    Upgrade Chemistry A-Level
  y TES - Ja 3 '97 - pR12 [251-500]
Listfield, Emily - *The Last Good Night*
    LJ - v122 - Ap 15 '97 - p118 [51-250]
Liszka, James Jakob - *A General Introduction to the Semeiotic of Charles Sanders Peirce*
    Choice - v34 - F '97 - p959 [51-250]
Litalien, Raymonde - *Les Explorateurs De L'Amerique Du Nord*
    Can Hist R - v77 - S '96 - p441+ [501+]
Litchfield, Michael W - *Renovation: A Complete Guide. 2nd Ed.*
    LJ - v122 - F 1 '97 - p52 [1-50]
Literacy, Economy, and Society
    JAAL - v40 - F '97 - p415 [51-250]
    J Gov Info - v23 - S '96 - p615+ [51-250]
Literacy Techniques for Building Successful Readers and Writers
  r Quill & Q - v63 - Mr '97 - p82 [251-500]
Literal Latte
  p LMR - v15 - Win '96 - p15+ [501+]
Literature Criticism from 1400 to 1800. Vols. 28-29
  r ARBA - v28 - '97 - p415+ [251-500]
Literature Criticism from 1400 to 1800. Vols. 30-31
  r ARBA - v28 - '97 - p416+ [501+]
Litfin, A Duane - *St. Paul's Theology of Proclamation*
    QJS - v82 - Ag '96 - p320+ [501+]
Litherland, Janet - *Broadway Costumes on a Budget*
  y BL - v93 - D 1 '96 - p645 [51-250]
  y Ch BWatch - Jl '96 - p2 [1-50]
    TCI - v30 - O '96 - p58 [51-250]
Litoff, Judy Barrett - *European Immigrant Women in the United States*
  r NWSA Jnl - v9 - Spr '97 - p110+ [501+]
Litsios, Socrates - *The Tomorrow of Malaria*
    Nature - v383 - S 12 '96 - p135 [501+]
Litt, Paul - *The Muses, the Masses, and the Massey Commission*
    Archiv - Fall '94 - p201+ [501+]
Litt, Toby - *Adventures in Capitalism*
    NS - v125 - Ag 30 '96 - p48 [251-500]
Littek, Wolfgang - *The New Division of Labour*
    CS - v26 - Mr '97 - p188+ [501+]
Littell, Marcia Sachs - *Liturgies on the Holocaust*
    Rel Ed - v91 - Fall '96 - p618 [1-50]
Littell, Mary Ann - *LSD*
  y BL - v93 - D 1 '96 - p655 [51-250]
  y HB Guide - v8 - Spr '97 - p98 [51-250]
Littell, Robert - *Walking Back the Cat*
    BL - v93 - My 15 '97 - p1567 [51-250]
    KR - v65 - My 1 '97 - p666+ [501+]
    LJ - v122 - My 1 '97 - p141 [51-250]
    PW - v244 - My 12 '97 - p57 [251-500]
Little, Benilde - *Good Hair*
    Bloom Rev - v17 - Ja '97 - p19 [1-50]
    Ent W - O 18 '96 - p75 [51-250]
    KR - v64 - S 1 '96 - p1259 [251-500]
    LATBR - O 27 '96 - p4 [501+]
    LATBR - D 29 '96 - p6 [51-250]
    LJ - v121 - N 1 '96 - p82 [1-50]
Little, Bentley - *The Ignored*
    PW - v244 - Ap 14 '97 - p71 [51-250]
Little, Blake - *Dichotomy*
    Advocate - N 12 '96 - p77+ [501+]
Little, Charles E - *The Dying of the Trees*
    PW - v244 - Mr 24 '97 - p81 [1-50]

Little, Colin - *The Biology of Rocky Shores*
    Choice - v34 - F '97 - p988 [51-250]
    SB - v33 - Ja '97 - p8 [251-500]
Little, Daniel - *On the Reliability of Economic Models*
    JEL - v35 - Mr '97 - p122+ [501+]
Little, Douglas - *Plutarch's Lives of Galba and Otho*
    CW - v90 - S '96 - p69+ [501+]
Little, Geraldine - *Woman in a Special House*
    PW - v244 - F 3 '97 - p96 [51-250]
Little, Jean - *Gruntle Piggle Takes Off (Illus. by Johnny Wales)*
  c CCB-B - v50 - My '97 - p328 [51-250]
  c Ch Bk News - v20 - Win '97 - p29 [51-250]
  c Emerg Lib - v24 - Mr '97 - p27 [1-50]
  c KR - v65 - F 15 '97 - p302 [51-250]
  c PW - v244 - Ja 20 '97 - p401 [51-250]
  c Quill & Q - v62 - S '96 - p72 [251-500]
Little, John - *The Warrior Within*
    LJ - v121 - O 15 '96 - p78 [51-250]
Little, Kate - *Jingle Bell Baby*
    LJ - v121 - N 15 '96 - p48 [51-250]
Little, Lester K - *Benedictine Maledictions*
    EHR - v111 - S '96 - p950 [251-500]
Little, Miles - *Humane Medicine*
    CPR - v16 - Ag '96 - p265+ [501+]
Little, Mimi Otey - *Yoshiko and the Foreigner (Illus. by Mimi Otey Little)*
  c BL - v93 - N 15 '96 - p595 [51-250]
  c CBRS - v25 - D '96 - p40 [51-250]
  c HB - v72 - N '96 - p727 [51-250]
  c HB Guide - v8 - Spr '97 - p36 [51-250]
  c Inst - v106 - Ja '97 - p53 [1-50]
  c NYTBR - v102 - Ap 13 '97 - p27 [1-50]
  c PW - v243 - N 11 '96 - p75 [51-250]
  c SLJ - v43 - Ja '97 - p84+ [51-250]
Little, Peter D - *Living under Contract*
    JIH - v27 - Aut '96 - p368+ [501+]
Little, Walter - *Political Corruption in Europe and Latin America*
    Choice - v34 - O '96 - p355 [501+]
Little Brother and Little Sister (Illus. by Bernadette Watts)
  c HB Guide - v7 - Fall '96 - p321 [51-250]
Little Oxford Dictionary of English Grammar
  r TES - Jl 5 '96 - p7* [1-50]
Little Red Readers Series
  c Inst - v105 - My '96 - p18 [51-250]
Little Theater (Illus. by Stef De Reuver)
  c HB Guide - v7 - Fall '96 - p238 [51-250]
Littlefield, Bill - *Champions: Stories of Ten Remarkable Athletes (Illus. by Bernie Fuchs)*
  c BL - v93 - D 15 '96 - p716 [1-50]
  y Kliatt - v30 - S '96 - p5 [1-50]
Littlefield, Daniel F, Jr. - *Seminole Burning*
    PW - v243 - O 21 '96 - p64 [51-250]
Littlefield, Holly - *Fire at the Triangle Factory (Illus. by Mary O'Keefe Young)*
  c BL - v92 - Ag '96 - p1900 [51-250]
  c HB Guide - v8 - Spr '97 - p59 [51-250]
  c SLJ - v42 - O '96 - p122 [51-250]
Littlejohn, David - *The Fate of the English Country House*
    BL - v93 - Ja '97 - p803+ [51-250]
    PW - v244 - Ja 20 '97 - p387 [51-250]
    WSJ-Cent - v99 - Ap 7 '97 - pA12 [501+]
Littlejohn, Richard - *You Couldn't Make It Up*
    NS - v125 - D 20 '96 - p117 [1-50]
Littlesugar, Amy - *Marie in Fourth Position (Illus. by Ian Schoenherr)*
  c Ch BWatch - v6 - D '96 - p2 [1-50]
  c Dance - v70 - D '96 - p53 [1-50]
  c HB Guide - v8 - Spr '97 - p37 [51-250]
  c KR - v64 - S 1 '96 - p1324 [51-250]
  c NW - v128 - D 2 '96 - p88 [1-50]
  c SLJ - v42 - O '96 - p101+ [51-250]
Littleton, C Scott - *Eastern Wisdom*
  y SLJ - v42 - O '96 - p166 [51-250]
    From Scythia to Camelot
    WestFolk - v55 - Spr '96 - p166+ [501+]
Littleton, Mark - *Pairin' Up*
  y VOYA - v19 - F '97 - p319 [51-250]
    When They Invited Me to FellowShip...
  y VOYA - v19 - F '97 - p319+ [51-250]
Littlewood, Ian - *The Idea of Japan*
    LJ - v121 - S 15 '96 - p80 [51-250]
    NYRB - v43 - Je 6 '96 - p31+ [501+]

Littman, Jonathan - *The Watchman: The Twisted Life and Crimes of Serial Hacker Kevin Poulsen*
    BL - v93 - F 15 '97 - p980 [51-250]
    KR - v65 - Ja 15 '97 - p122+ [251-500]
    LJ - v122 - F 15 '97 - p148 [51-250]
    NYTBR - v102 - Mr 30 '97 - p17 [51-250]
    PW - v244 - Ja 27 '97 - p88 [51-250]
Littrell, Helen E - *Stedman's OB-GYN Words. 2nd Ed.*
  r SciTech - v20 - N '96 - p51 [51-250]
Litva, John - *Digital Beamforming in Wireless Communications*
    SciTech - v20 - D '96 - p75 [51-250]
Litvack, Leon - *J.M. Neale and the Quest for Sobornost*
    JR - v76 - O '96 - p682+ [51-250]
Litvak, Marilyn M - *Edward James Lennox Builder of Toronto*
    Beav - v76 - D '96 - p47 [51-250]
Litvak, Simon - *Retroviral Reverse Transcriptases*
    SciTech - v20 - S '96 - p24 [51-250]
Litvan, Gyorgy - *The Hungarian Revolution of 1956*
    CR - v269 - N '96 - p278 [51-250]
    NYRB - v43 - N 14 '96 - p18+ [501+]
Litwin, George - *Mobilizing the Organization*
    Per Psy - v50 - Spr '97 - p203+ [501+]
Litwin, Howard - *The Social Networks of Older People*
    R&R Bk N - v12 - F '97 - p53 [51-250]
    Uprooted in Old Age
    MEJ - v50 - Sum '96 - p434+ [501+]
Litzinger, Rosanne - *The Old Woman and Her Pig*
  c PW - v244 - My 5 '97 - p211 [1-50]
Liu, Aimee - *Cloud Mountain*
    KR - v65 - My 1 '97 - p667 [251-500]
    PW - v244 - My 12 '97 - p57 [51-250]
Liu, Alan P L - *Mass Politics in the People's Republic*
    Choice - v34 - D '96 - p683 [51-250]
Liu, Chamond - *Smalltalk, Objects, and Design*
    SciTech - v20 - D '96 - p10 [51-250]
Liu, Cricket - *Managing Internet Information Services*
    LRTS - v40 - Ap '96 - p190+ [501+]
Liu, Cui-Rong - *Ji Jian Suo Zhi. Vols. 1-2*
    Ch Rev Int - v4 - Spr '97 - p203+ [501+]
Liu, Feng - *Xie Ji Tai Yang Qi*
    BL - v93 - My 1 '97 - p1484 [1-50]
Liu, Hong - *Mastering Miracles*
    BL - v93 - N 1 '96 - p470 [51-250]
    LJ - v122 - Ja '97 - p136 [51-250]
Liu, Hsin-Ju - *Silk and Religion*
    Choice - v34 - Ja '97 - p854 [51-250]
Liu, I-Ch'ang - *The Cockroach and Other Stories*
    WLT - v70 - Aut '96 - p1028+ [501+]
Liu, Kang - *Politics, Ideology, and Literary Discourse in Modern China*
    Ch Rev Int - v3 - Fall '96 - p455+ [501+]
Liu, Lewis-Guodo - *The Internet and Library and Information Services*
  r R&R Bk N - v12 - F '97 - p101 [51-250]
Liu, Ning-Jung - *Zhong Guo Ren She Chao*
    BL - v93 - My 1 '97 - p1484 [1-50]
Liu, Qingshan - *Chinese Fitness*
    BL - v93 - My 1 '97 - p1471 [51-250]
Liu, Shaoming - *Xiang Gang Yin Yuan*
    BL - v93 - N 1 '96 - p484 [1-50]
Liu, So-la - *Chaos and All That*
    Ch Rev Int - v3 - Fall '96 - p491+ [501+]
    South HR - v31 - Win '97 - p89+ [501+]
    TranslRevS - v1 - My '95 - p15 [51-250]
Liu, Timothy - *Burnt Offerings*
    VQR - v73 - Win '97 - p28* [51-250]
Liu, Xiaoyuan - *A Partnership for Disorder*
    Choice - v34 - Ap '97 - p1395 [51-250]
Liu, Yanpei - *Embeddability in Graphs*
    SciTech - v21 - Mr '97 - p12 [51-250]
Liu, Yen-Chih - *The Essential Book of Traditional Chinese Medicine. Vols. 1-2*
    Ch Rev Int - v3 - Fall '96 - p494+ [501+]
Livdahl, Barbara Smith - *Stories from Response-Centered Classrooms*
    JAAL - v40 - N '96 - p237+ [501+]
Livelton, Trevor - *Archival Theory, Records, and the Public*
    R&R Bk N - v12 - F '97 - p12 [51-250]
Lively, Penelope - *Astercote (Tomelty). Audio Version*
  c BL - v93 - My 15 '97 - p1595 [1-50]
    Good Night, Sleep Tight (Illus. by Adriano Gon)
  c Bks Keeps - Jl '96 - p9 [51-250]

Heat Wave
    BL - v92 - Ag '96 - p1854+ [251-500]
    LATBR - v263 - S 29 '96 - p3 [501+]
    LATBR - D 29 '96 - p6 [51-250]
    NY - v72 - O 7 '96 - p96 [51-250]
    NYTBR - v101 - N 10 '96 - p12 [501+]
    NYTBR - v101 - D 8 '96 - p80 [1-50]
    Spec - v276 - My 25 '96 - p29 [251-500]
    TLS - My 24 '96 - p27 [501+]
    VQR - v73 - Win '97 - p24* [51-250]
    WSJ-MW - v77 - S 20 '96 - pA12 [251-500]
Livermore, Mary - *My Story of the War*
    Arm F&S - v23 - Win '96 - p305+ [501+]
Liversidge, Michael - *Imagining Rome*
    Nine-C Lit - v51 - Mr '97 - p560 [51-250]
Lives and Works in the Arts from the Renaissance to the 20th Century. Vols. 1-9
    r BL - v93 - D 15 '96 - p749 [251-500]
    yr LJ - v122 - Ap 1 '97 - p84 [51-250]
Livesey, Margot - *Criminals*
    y BL - v93 - Ja '97 - p763 [1-50]
    NYTBR - v102 - Ap 20 '97 - p32 [51-250]
    Obs - Ag 25 '96 - p16* [501+]
    PW - v244 - Ja 27 '97 - p103 [1-50]
    Rapport - v19 - 4 '96 - p29 [51-250]
    Sew R - v104 - Jl '96 - p461+ [501+]
    Trib Bks - F 2 '97 - p8 [1-50]
    VQR - v72 - Aut '96 - p129* [51-250]
    W&I - v11 - Jl '96 - p284† [501†]
Livesey, Rupert - *Barron's Diccionario Juvenil Illustrado (Illus. by Gerald Chmielewski)*
    cr SLJ - v42 - Ag '96 - p178 [51-250]
Livesley, W John - *The DSM-IV Personality Disorders*
    SciTech - v20 - N '96 - p45 [51-250]
Livezeanu, Irina - *Cultural Politics in Greater Romania*
    AHR - v101 - O '96 - p1244 [501+]
    CS - v25 - N '96 - p740+ [501+]
Living Arrangements of Women and Their Children in Developing Countries
    r J Gov Info - v23 - S '96 - p678 [51-250]
Living Biographies of Great Scientists (May). Audio Version
    Kliatt - v30 - N '96 - p50 [51-250]
The Living Environment. Vols. 1-6
    c Cur R - v35 - S '96 - p3* [51-250]
Living with Low Vision. 4th Ed.
    r ARBA - v28 - '97 - p305+ [51-250]
    r SciTech - v20 - S '96 - p39 [51-250]
The Living World (Illus. by Sue Barclay)
    c CLW - v66 - Je '96 - p53 [51-250]
    c HB Guide - v7 - Fall '96 - p336+ [51-250]
Livingston, Carol - *Gecko Tails*
    LJ - v122 - Ap 15 '97 - p104 [51-250]
    NYRB - v43 - N 14 '96 - p41+ [501+]
    PW - v244 - Mr 24 '97 - p65 [51-250]
Livingston, James, 1949- - *Pragmatism and the Political Economy of Cultural Revolution 1850-1940*
    JEH - v57 - Mr '97 - p190+ [501+]
Livingston, James D - *Driving Force*
    y BL - v93 - D 1 '96 - p664 [1-50]
    Choice - v34 - N '96 - p497 [51-250]
    Phys Today - v50 - Ja '97 - p72 [501+]
    y SB - v32 - Ag '96 - p173 [51-250]
    SciTech - v20 - N '96 - p19 [51-250]
Livingston, Lili Cockerille - *American Indian Ballerinas*
    Dance - v71 - Ja '97 - p98 [51-250]
    KR - v64 - D 15 '96 - p1785 [251-500]
    LJ - v122 - Ap 1 '97 - p96 [51-250]
    NYTLa - v146 - Ap 22 '97 - pC14 [501+]
    Trib Bks - My 11 '97 - p3 [251-500]
    VV - v42 - Ap 15 '97 - p52 [251-500]
Livingston, Myra Cohn - *B Is for Baby (Illus. by Steel Stillman)*
    c HB Guide - v8 - Spr '97 - p153 [51-250]
    c SLJ - v42 - S '96 - p198 [51-250]
Cricket Never Does
    c BL - v93 - Mr 1 '97 - p1158 [51-250]
Festivals (Illus. by Leonard Everett Fisher)
    c Emerg Lib - v24 - S '96 - p43 [1-50]
    c HB Guide - v7 - Fall '96 - p368 [51-250]
    c LA - v73 - D '96 - p624+ [51-250]
    c RT - v50 - My '97 - p685 [51-250]
Livingstone, D W - *Recast Dreams*
    Choice - v34 - F '97 - p1044+ [51-250]
Livingstone, Marco - *David Hockney*
    NS & S - v9 - Ap 26 '96 - p31 [1-50]
Livo, Norma J - *Troubadour's Storybag*
    c PW - v243 - O 21 '96 - p85 [51-250]
Livsey, Karen E - *Western New York Land Transactions 1825-1835*
    Am Geneal - v71 - O '96 - p256+ [251-500]

Llamas, Andreu - *Birds Conquer the Sky (Illus. by Miriam Ferron)*
    c HB Guide - v7 - Fall '96 - p334 [51-250]
The Era of the Dinosaurs (Illus. by Luis Rizo)
    c HB Guide - v7 - Fall '96 - p334 [51-250]
The First Amphibians (Illus. by Luis Rizo)
    c HB Guide - v7 - Fall '96 - p334 [51-250]
The Great Plains (Illus. by Luis Rizo)
    c HB Guide - v7 - Fall '96 - p337 [51-250]
    y SB - v32 - O '96 - p204 [51-250]
Hearing (Illus. by Francisco Arredondo)
    c HB Guide - v7 - Fall '96 - p337 [51-250]
    c SB - v32 - N '96 - p242 [51-250]
Life Starts in the Sea (Illus. by Luis Rizo)
    c HB Guide - v7 - Fall '96 - p334 [51-250]
Mammals Dominate the Earth (Illus. by Carles Castellvi)
    c HB Guide - v7 - Fall '96 - p334 [51-250]
The Mysterious Jungles (Illus. by Luis Rizo)
    c HB Guide - v7 - Fall '96 - p337 [51-250]
    y SB - v32 - O '96 - p204 [51-250]
Plants of the Desert (Illus. by Luis Rizo)
    c HB Guide - v7 - Fall '96 - p337 [51-250]
    y SB - v32 - O '96 - p204 [51-250]
Plants of the Forest (Illus. by Miquel Ferron)
    c HB Guide - v7 - Fall '96 - p337 [51-250]
    y SB - v32 - O '96 - p205 [51-250]
Plants under the Sea (Illus. by Luis Rizo)
    c HB Guide - v7 - Fall '96 - p337 [51-250]
    y SB - v32 - O '96 - p205 [51-250]
Sight (Illus. by Francisco Arredondo)
    c HB Guide - v7 - Fall '96 - p337 [51-250]
    c SB - v32 - N '96 - p242 [51-250]
Smell (Illus. by Francisco Arredondo)
    c HB Guide - v7 - Fall '96 - p337 [51-250]
    c SB - v32 - N '96 - p242 [51-250]
Taste (Illus. by Francisco Arredondo)
    c HB Guide - v7 - Fall '96 - p337 [51-250]
Touch (Illus. by Francisco Arredondo)
    c HB Guide - v7 - Fall '96 - p337 [51-250]
    c SB - v32 - N '96 - p242 [51-250]
The Vegetation of Rivers, Lakes, and Swamps (Illus. by Luis Rizo)
    c HB Guide - v7 - Fall '96 - p337 [51-250]
    y SB - v32 - O '96 - p205 [51-250]
Llamas Ruiz, Andres - *Blood Circulation (Illus. by Luis Rizo)*
    c PW - v244 - Mr 31 '97 - p77 [1-50]
Evolution (Illus. by Ferron-Retana)
    c PW - v244 - Mr 31 '97 - p77 [1-50]
Metamorphosis (Illus. by Francisco Arredondo)
    c PW - v244 - Mr 31 '97 - p77 [1-50]
Rain (Illus. by Luis Rizo)
    c PW - v244 - Mr 31 '97 - p77 [1-50]
Reptiles and Amphibians (Illus. by Ali Garousi)
    c HB Guide - v8 - Spr '97 - p124 [51-250]
Rivers (Illus. by Francisco Arredondo)
    c PW - v244 - Mr 31 '97 - p77 [1-50]
Seasons (Illus. by Luis Rizo)
    c KR - v65 - Mr 15 '97 - p464 [51-250]
    c PW - v244 - Mr 31 '97 - p77 [1-50]
Stars (Illus. by Ali Garousi)
    c PW - v244 - Mr 31 '97 - p77 [1-50]
Trees (Illus. by Francisco Arredondo)
    c PW - v244 - Mr 31 '97 - p77 [1-50]
Llerena, Mario - *La Honda De David*
    BL - v93 - Ap 1 '97 - p1284 [1-50]
Llewellyn, Caroline - *False Light*
    KR - v64 - O 15 '96 - p1487+ [251-500]
Llewellyn, Claire - *Disguises and Surprises*
    c Bks Keeps - Mr '97 - p21 [51-250]
    c BL - v93 - D 1 '96 - p658 [51-250]
    c HB Guide - v8 - Spr '97 - p118 [51-250]
    c JB - v60 - D '96 - p254 [51-250]
    c Sch Lib - v45 - F '97 - p38 [51-250]
    c SLJ - v43 - F '97 - p93 [51-250]
Trucks (Illus. by Nicholas Hewetson)
    c HB Guide - v7 - Fall '96 - p351 [1-50]
Llewellyn, Kate - *Gorillas, Tea and Coffee*
    Aust Bk R - D '96 - p74 [51-250]
Llewellyn, Michael - *Twelfth Night*
    PW - v244 - Ja 13 '97 - p56 [51-250]
Llewellyn, Robert - *Thin He Was and Filthy-Haired*
    Woman's J - Ja '97 - p13 [51-250]
Llewellyn's 1997 Moon Sign Book
    r Horoscope - v63 - Ja '97 - p125 [1-50]
Llewellyn's 1997 Sun Sign Book
    r Horoscope - v63 - Ja '97 - p125 [1-50]
Llewelyn, John - *Emmanuel Levinas: The Genealogy of Ethics*
    Rel St Rev - v23 - Ap '97 - p151 [51-250]
Lloyd, Carole - *The Charles Barber Treatment*
    c TES - N 22 '96 - p5* [1-50]

The Midnight Detectives
    c JB - v60 - Ag '96 - p149 [51-250]
Lloyd, Christopher, 1921- - *Other People's Gardens*
    Hort - v74 - O '96 - p77 [51-250]
Lloyd, Christopher, 1945- - *Epidemics and Sickness in French Literature and Culture*
    MLR - v92 - Ja '97 - p199+ [501+]
Masterpieces in Little
    Mag Antiq - v151 - Mr '97 - p394 [251-500]
Mirbeau's Fictions
    TLS - S 20 '96 - p32 [51-250]
Lloyd, Errol - *Many Rivers to Cross*
    c Bks Keeps - Ja '97 - p25 [51-250]
    c TES - Ap 4 '97 - p8* [51-250]
Lloyd, Genevieve - *Part of Nature*
    Phil R - v105 - Ja '96 - p116+ [501+]
Lloyd, Janet E - *Joy and Wonder in All God's Works*
    SLJ - v42 - D '96 - p46 [51-250]
Lloyd, Michael - *Turner*
    PW - v243 - O 21 '96 - p77 [51-250]
Lloyd, Richmond M - *Fundamentals of Force Planning. Vol. 2*
    RSR - v24 - 3 '96 - p42 [51-250]
Lloyd, Roseann - *War Baby Express*
    HMR - Fall '96 - p30+ [501+]
    Wom R Bks - v14 - Mr '97 - p12+ [501+]
Lloyd, Rosemary - *Closer and Closer Apart*
    MLR - v92 - Ja '97 - p213+ [251-500]
Lloyd, Tim - *Poverty, Inequality and Rural Development*
    Econ J - v107 - Ja '97 - p276 [251-500]
Llywelyn, Morgan - *Irish Magic II*
    y BL - v93 - Mr 1 '97 - p1110 [51-250]
    KR - v65 - Ja 15 '97 - p83+ [251-500]
    PW - v244 - F 10 '97 - p69 [51-250]
Pride of Lions
    y Kliatt - v31 - My '97 - p8 [51-250]
Strongbow: The Story of Richard and Aoife
    y Ch BWatch - v6 - Jl '96 - p3 [51-250]
    y HB Guide - v7 - Fall '96 - p303 [51-250]
Lo, Andrew W - *The Industrial Organization and Regulation of the Securities Industry*
    Econ J - v107 - Ja '97 - p274 [251-500]
    JEL - v34 - S '96 - p1373+ [501+]
    JEL - v34 - S '96 - p1437 [251-500]
Lo, Chin-Shun - *Knowledge Painfully Acquired*
    CPR - v16 - D '96 - p419+ [501+]
Lo, Kuan-Chung - *Three Kingdoms*
    TranslRevS - v1 - My '95 - p15+ [51-250]
Loader, J A - *A Tale of Two Cities*
    Rel St Rev - v23 - Ja '97 - p88 [51-250]
Loades, D M - *John Dudley, Duke of Northumberland 1504-1553*
    HT - v47 - F '97 - p59+ [501+]
    TLS - N 1 '96 - p28 [501+]
Politics, Censorship and the English Reformation
    CH - v65 - S '96 - p489+ [501+]
The Politics of Marriage
    EHR - v112 - F '97 - p187+ [251-500]
Lobban, Marjorie - *Out of the Closet and into the Classroom. 2nd Ed.*
    r Magpies - v11 - Jl '96 - p15 [51-250]
Lobe, Mira - *Christoph Wants a Party (Illus. by Winfried Opgenoorth)*
    c RT - v50 - F '97 - p424 [51-250]
Lobel, Anita - *The Dwarf Giant*
    c HB Guide - v8 - Spr '97 - p37 [51-250]
Lobel, Arnold - *Frog and Toad (Lobel). Audio Version*
    c Trib Bks - F 2 '97 - p7 [1-50]
Frog and Toad Together
    c HMR - Win '96 - p45 [1-50]
Lobel, M D - *The British Atlas of Historic Towns. Vols. 1-3*
    r J Urban H - v22 - S '96 - p739+ [501+]
Lobinski, Ryszard - *Spectrochemical Trace Analysis for Metals and Metalloids*
    SciTech - v21 - Mr '97 - p28 [51-250]
Lobo, Raul F - *Microporous and Macroporous Materials*
    SciTech - v21 - Mr '97 - p95 [51-250]
LoBrutto, Vincent - *Sound-on-Film*
    FQ - v49 - Fall '95 - p64 [51-250]
Stanley Kubrick: A Biography
    BL - v93 - N 15 '96 - p564 [51-250]
    KR - v64 - O 15 '96 - p1513+ [251-500]
    LJ - v121 - D '96 - p96 [51-250]
    NYTLa - v146 - Ap 1 '97 - pC15 [501+]
    PW - v243 - O 21 '96 - p62 [51-250]
Local Computer Networks
    SciTech - v21 - Mr '97 - p88 [51-250]
Local Government in Europe. Electronic Media Version
    r Choice - v34 - My '97 - p1568 [51-250]
    r LAR - v99 - Ja '97 - p49 [251-500]

Localized Damage IV
SciTech - v20 - D '96 - p64 [51-250]
Lochead, Richard - *Beyond the Printed Word*
Archiv - Fall '94 - p189+ [501+]
Lochman, Katharine A - *The Earthly Paradise*
Archiv - Fall '94 - p214+ [501+]
Lochte, Dick - *The Neon Smile*
Arm Det - v29 - Fall '96 - p403 [51-250]
Lock, Dennis - *Project Management. 6th Ed.*
SciTech - v20 - N '96 - p59 [51-250]
Lock, Gary - *Archaeology and Geographical Information Systems*
AJA - v101 - Ja '97 - p163+ [501+]
Am Ant - v61 - O '96 - p801+ [501+]
Lock, Peter - *The Franks in the Aegean 1204-1500*
r Historian - v58 - Sum '96 - p911 [251-500]
Lock, Robert D - *Taking Charge of Your Career Direction*
J Car P&E - v57 - Fall '96 - p15 [251-500]
Locke, John - *Le Second Traite Du Gouvernement*
Dialogue - v35 - Fall '96 - p823+ [501+]
Locke, Meryl - *Jean-Luc Godard's Hail Mary*
FQ - v49 - Fall '95 - p64 [51-250]
Locke, Richard M - *Employment Relations in a Changing World Economy*
ILRR - v50 - Ap '97 - p534+ [501+]
Remaking the Italian Economy
ILRR - v50 - O '96 - p168+ [501+]
Locke, Robert R - *The Collapse of the American Management Mystique*
Choice - v34 - Mr '97 - p1204 [51-250]
Locke, Thomas - *The Delta Factor*
Books - v10 - Je '96 - p24 [1-50]
Locker, Thomas - *Sky Tree (Illus. by Thomas Locker)*
c RT - v50 - Mr '97 - p501 [51-250]
Water Dance (Illus. by Thomas Locker)
c BL - v93 - Mr 1 '97 - p1164 [51-250]
c CBRS - v25 - Mr '97 - p93+ [51-250]
c CCB-B - v50 - My '97 - p328 [51-250]
c KR - v65 - Mr 1 '97 - p384 [51-250]
c PW - v244 - Mr 17 '97 - p83 [51-250]
Lockhart, Douglas - *The Paradise Complex*
PW - v244 - Ja 20 '97 - p395 [251-500]
Lockhart, James - *We People Here*
HAHR - v76 - Ag '96 - p555+ [251-500]
Lockhart, Olive - *Mortgage Lifter and Other Stories*
Aust Bk R - Je '96 - p66 [251-500]
Lockhart, Paul Douglas - *Denmark in the Thirty Years' War 1618-1648*
Choice - v34 - D '96 - p671 [51-250]
Lockie, Andrew - *The Complete Guide to Homeopathy*
r ARBA - v28 - '97 - p612+ [51-250]
Locklin, Gerald - *The Cabo Conference*
Sm Pr R - v29 - Ja '97 - p1+ [501+]
The Macao/Hong Kong Trip
Sm Pr R - v29 - Ja '97 - p1+ [501+]
The Pittsburgh Poems
Sm Pr R - v29 - Ja '97 - p1+ [501+]
Lockman, Zachary - *Comrades and Enemies*
For Aff - v75 - N '96 - p166+ [51-250]
JEL - v34 - D '96 - p2099 [51-250]
Lockwood, Karen - *Lady's Choice*
PW - v243 - S 23 '96 - p74 [51-250]
Lockwood, Michael - *Opportunities for English in the Primary School*
Sch Lib - v44 - Ag '96 - p130 [51-250]
Locus: The Newspaper of the Science Fiction Field
p RQ - v36 - Win '96 - p227 [51-250]
Lodahl, Michael E - *Shekhinah/Spirit: Divine Presence in Jewish and Christian Religion*
Rel Ed - v91 - Fall '96 - p612 [1-50]
Loday, Jean-Louis - *Operads: Proceedings of Renaissance Conferences*
SciTech - v21 - Mr '97 - p12 [51-250]
Loder, James E - *The Knight's Move*
Zygon - v31 - D '96 - p731+ [501+]
Lodgaard, Sverre - *Arms and Technology Transfers*
J Gov Info - v23 - S '96 - p682+ [51-250]
Lodge, Bernard - *The Half-Mile Hat (Illus. by Bernard Lodge)*
c CLW - v66 - Je '96 - p47 [51-250]
Tanglebird (Illus. by Bernard Lodge)
c BL - v93 - Mr 1 '97 - p1172 [51-250]
c CBRS - v25 - Mr '97 - p88 [51-250]
c KR - v65 - Mr 1 '97 - p384 [51-250]
c PW - v244 - F 24 '97 - p90 [51-250]

Lodge, David - *The Practice of Writing*
BL - v93 - Ja '97 - p807 [51-250]
BW - v27 - Ja 12 '97 - p13 [501+]
KR - v64 - N 1 '96 - p1584 [251-500]
LJ - v121 - D '96 - p94 [51-250]
NYTBR - v102 - Ja 5 '97 - p19 [51-250]
NYTLa - v146 - D 31 '96 - pC20 [501+]
Spec - v277 - N 16 '96 - p52 [51-250]
TLS - Ja 3 '97 - p25 [501+]
W&I - v12 - Ap '97 - p282+ [501+]
Therapy
Books - v10 - Je '96 - p24 [51-250]
MA - v38 - Fall '96 - p403+ [501+]
Therapy (Clarke). Audio Version
y Kliatt - v30 - N '96 - p46 [51-250]
Lodge, Jeff - *Where This Lake Is*
KR - v65 - My 1 '97 - p667+ [251-500]
Lodge, Jo - *If You're Happy and You Know It*
c TES - N 29 '96 - p13* [51-250]
Patch and His Favorite Things
c PW - v243 - S 23 '96 - p78 [51-250]
Patch Bakes a Cake
c PW - v244 - Mr 24 '97 - p85 [51-250]
Patch Goes to the Park
c PW - v244 - Mr 24 '97 - p85 [51-250]
Patch Grows Flowers
c PW - v244 - Mr 24 '97 - p85 [51-250]
Patch in the Garden
c PW - v243 - S 23 '96 - p78 [51-250]
Patch Takes a Vacation
c PW - v244 - Mr 24 '97 - p85 [51-250]
This Is the Way We Pull a Face
c TES - N 29 '96 - p13* [51-250]
Lodge, Milton - *Political Judgment*
APSR - v90 - S '96 - p654+ [501+]
Lodge, R Anthony - *French: From Dialect to Standard*
MLJ - v81 - Spr '97 - p129+ [501+]
Lodoli, Marco - *Cani E Lupi*
WLT - v70 - Sum '96 - p673+ [501+]
Lodwick, Kathleen L - *Crusaders against Opium*
Ch Rev Int - v4 - Spr '97 - p211+ [501+]
Loeb, Gerald - *The Battle for Investment Survival*
Barron's - v76 - S 2 '96 - p43 [51-250]
Loeb, Lori Anne - *Consuming Angels*
J Con A - v30 - Win '96 - p489+ [501+]
JIH - v27 - Aut '96 - p305+ [251-500]
VS - v39 - Aut '95 - p108+ [501+]
Loeb, Paul - *Smarter than You Think*
BL - v93 - Mr 1 '97 - p1100 [51-250]
LJ - v122 - F 15 '97 - p155 [51-250]
Loehr, Mallory - *The Princess Book (Illus. by Jan Palmer)*
c HB Guide - v8 - Spr '97 - p135 [51-250]
Loesche-Scheller, Brigitta - *Reparations to Poverty*
Choice - v34 - F '97 - p1036+ [51-250]
Loeschnig, Louis V - *Simple Earth Science Experiments with Everyday Materials (Illus. by Frances Zweifel)*
c SB - v33 - Ja '97 - p17 [251-500]
c Smith - v27 - N '96 - p174 [1-50]
Loest, Erich - *Nikolaikirche*
WLT - v70 - Aut '96 - p948+ [501+]
Loewe, Michael - *Divination, Mythology and Monarchy in Han China*
JAAR - v64 - Fall '96 - p670+ [501+]
JIH - v27 - Aut '96 - p375+ [501+]
Early Chinese Texts
r Ch Rev Int - v3 - Fall '96 - p337+ [501+]
Loewen, Harry - *Through Fire and Water*
BL - v92 - Ag '96 - p1859 [51-250]
Loewen, James W - *Lies My Teacher Told Me*
Pub Int - Sum '96 - p108+ [501+]
PW - v243 - Jl 22 '96 - p235 [1-50]
SE - v60 - S '96 - p316+ [501+]
SE - v60 - S '96 - p317 [501+]
Skeptic - v4 - 2 '96 - p108 [51-250]
Loewen, Nancy - *Bicycle Safety (Illus. by Penny Dann)*
c HB Guide - v8 - Spr '97 - p134 [51-250]
c SLJ - v43 - Ja '97 - p104 [51-250]
Emergencies (Illus. by Penny Dann)
c HB Guide - v8 - Spr '97 - p134 [51-250]
c SLJ - v43 - Mr '97 - p178 [51-250]
Fire Safety (Illus. by Penny Dann)
c HB Guide - v8 - Spr '97 - p134 [51-250]
Home Safety (Illus. by Penny Dann)
c HB Guide - v8 - Spr '97 - p134 [51-250]
Outdoor Safety (Illus. by Penny Dann)
c HB Guide - v8 - Spr '97 - p134 [51-250]
School Safety (Illus. by Penny Dann)
c HB Guide - v8 - Spr '97 - p134 [51-250]
c SLJ - v43 - Mr '97 - p178 [51-250]

Traffic Safety (Illus. by Penny Dann)
c HB Guide - v8 - Spr '97 - p134 [51-250]
c SLJ - v43 - Ja '97 - p104 [51-250]
Water Safety (Illus. by Penny Dann)
c HB Guide - v8 - Spr '97 - p134 [51-250]
Loewenberg, Peter - *Fantasy and Reality in History*
AHR - v102 - F '97 - p93+ [501+]
Loewenstein, Jane - *Parents and Primary Mathematics*
TES - F 21 '97 - p13* [51-250]
Loewenthal, Kate Miriam - *An Introduction to Psychological Tests and Scales*
Choice - v34 - F '97 - p1040 [51-250]
Readings - v11 - D '96 - p25 [51-250]
Loewer, H Peter - *Pond Water Zoo (Illus. by Jean Jenkins)*
c BL - v93 - S 15 '96 - p235 [51-250]
c CCB-B - v50 - D '96 - p141+ [51-250]
c HB Guide - v8 - Spr '97 - p118 [51-250]
c SLJ - v43 - F '97 - p120 [51-250]
Thoreau's Garden
BL - v92 - Ag '96 - p1870 [51-250]
BW - v26 - S 29 '96 - p13 [51-250]
Loewy, Erich H - *Moral Strangers, Moral Acquaintance, and Moral Friends*
Choice - v34 - Ap '97 - p1352 [51-250]
Textbook of Healthcare Ethics
SciTech - v20 - S '96 - p26 [51-250]
Loewy, Ernst - *Gesellschaft Fur Exilforschung. Vols. 1-3*
MLR - v92 - Ja '97 - p249+ [251-500]
Lofficier, Randy - *Into the Twilight Zone*
r SF Chr - v18 - O '96 - p82 [51-250]
Lofstrom, William L - *Paita, Outpost of Empire*
Sea H - Win '96 - p46+ [51-250]
Loftas, Tony - *Dimensions of Need*
r J Gov Info - v23 - S '96 - p670 [51-250]
Lofton, J Mack, Jr. - *Healing Hands*
JSH - v62 - N '96 - p837+ [251-500]
Loftus, Elizabeth - *The Myth of Repressed Memory*
JPC - v30 - Fall '96 - p211+ [501+]
Loftus, John - *The Secret War against the Jews*
PW - v244 - Mr 17 '97 - p81 [1-50]
Logan, Bey - *Hong Kong Action Cinema*
y BL - v92 - Ag '96 - p1872 [501+]
y BL - v92 - Ag '96 - p1890 [1-50]
Logan, Chuck - *The Price of Blood*
BL - v93 - Mr 15 '97 - p1226 [51-250]
KR - v65 - Ja 15 '97 - p84 [251-500]
PW - v244 - F 17 '97 - p212 [51-250]
Trib Bks - Mr 16 '97 - p6 [51-250]
Logan, F Donald - *Runaway Religious in Medieval England c. 1240-1540*
Choice - v34 - F '97 - p1020 [51-250]
CR - v270 - F '97 - p111 [51-250]
TLS - Jl 19 '96 - p32 [251-500]
Logan, J David - *Applied Mathematics. 2nd Ed.*
SciTech - v21 - Mr '97 - p4 [51-250]
Logan, James C - *Theology and Evangelism in the Wesleyan Heritage*
JAAR - v64 - Win '96 - p898+ [501+]
Logan, John R - *Family Ties*
Choice - v34 - F '97 - p1044 [51-250]
Logan, Leandra - *Santa and Son*
LJ - v121 - N 15 '96 - p50 [51-250]
Logan, Pamela - *Among Warriors*
KR - v64 - S 1 '96 - p1299+ [251-500]
LJ - v121 - O 1 '96 - p112 [51-250]
NYTBR - v101 - D 8 '96 - p31 [251-500]
PW - v243 - S 23 '96 - p68 [51-250]
Utne R - Mr '97 - p84 [1-50]
Loggen, Karl Wilhelm - *Erzahlungen*
Can Lit - Spr '97 - p247+ [501+]
Logrippo, Ro - *In My World*
LJ - v122 - F 1 '97 - p53 [1-50]
Logsdon, John M - *Exploring the Unknown. Vol. 1*
APH - v43 - Win '96 - p63+ [251-500]
Logue, Christopher - *Selected Poems*
TLS - D 13 '96 - p24 [501+]
Logue, John - *Murder on the Links*
Arm Det - v29 - Sum '96 - p363 [51-250]
Logue, Larry M - *To Appomattox and Beyond*
JSH - v63 - F '97 - p178+ [501+]
Logue, Mary - *Halfway Home*
Bloom Rev - v16 - N '96 - p22 [51-250]
Logue, Victoria - *Kids Outdoors*
c BL - v93 - S 15 '96 - p228 [51-250]
Lohans, Alison - *Nathaniel's Violin (Illus. by Marlene Watson)*
c Quill & Q - v62 - My '96 - p34 [251-500]
Lohfink, Norbert - *Der Gott Israels Und Die Volker*
Rel St Rev - v23 - Ap '97 - p170 [51-250]

Lohlker, Rudiger - *Abhandlungen Fur Die Kunde Des Morgenlandes*
  MEJ - v51 - Win '97 - p154 [1-50]
Lohmann, Jeanne - *Granite under Water*
  BWatch - v17 - N '96 - p9 [51-250]
Lohr, Hermut - *Umkehr Und Sunde Im Hebraerbrief*
  Rel St Rev - v23 - Ap '97 - p186 [51-250]
Lohr, Winrich Alfried - *Basilides Und Seine Schule*
  Rel St Rev - v23 - Ap '97 - p188 [51-250]
Lohse, Bernhard - *Luthers Theologie In Ihrer Historischen Entwicklung Und In Ihrem Systematischen Zusammenhang*
  Rel St Rev - v22 - O '96 - p348+ [51-250]
Lohser, Beate - *Unorthodox Freud*
  Choice - v34 - F '97 - p1040 [51-250]
  SciTech - v20 - D '96 - p46 [51-250]
Lois, George - *Covering the 60's*
  BW - v26 - S 15 '96 - p12 [51-250]
  NYTBR - v101 - N 24 '96 - p19 [251-500]
  PW - v243 - S 30 '96 - p80 [51-250]
Loiselle, Andre - *Auteur/Provocateur: The Films of Denys Arcand*
  FR - v70 - F '97 - p483+ [501+]
Loitsianskii, L G - *Mechanics of Liquids and Gases. 6th Ed.*
  SciTech - v20 - N '96 - p16 [51-250]
Lokkeberg, Vibeke - *Jordens Skygge*
  WLT - v70 - Aut '96 - p977 [501+]
Lomas, Herbert - *Selected Poems*
  HR - v49 - Aut '96 - p513+ [501+]
Lomas, Kathryn - *Rome and the Western Greeks 350 B.C.-A.D. 200*
  CW - v90 - S '96 - p67 [251-500]
Lomas Garza, Carmen - *In My Family (Illus. by Carmen Lomas Garza)*
  c AB - v98 - N 18 '96 - p1729+ [51-250]
  c BL - v93 - N 1 '96 - p503+ [51-250]
  c BL - v93 - My 1 '97 - p1507 [1-50]
  c HB - v72 - N '96 - p760+ [51-250]
  c HB Guide - v8 - Spr '97 - p108 [51-250]
  c SLJ - v42 - N '96 - p134 [51-250]
Lomawaima, K Tsianina - *They Called It Prairie Light*
  JWomHist - v8 - Fall '96 - p205+ [501+]
Lomax, Eric - *The Railway Man*
  Books - v9 - S '95 - p23 [51-250]
  Ch Today - v41 - Mr 3 '97 - p47+ [501+]
  FEER - Anniv '96 - p228 [501+]
  y Kliatt - v30 - N '96 - p23 [51-250]
  Spec - v277 - N 23 '96 - p46 [1-50]
  The Railway Man (Paterson). Audio Version
  y Kliatt - v31 - My '97 - p48 [51-250]
Lombardi, Marilyn May - *The Body and the Song*
  NEQ - v70 - Mr '97 - p145+ [501+]
Lombardini, Siro - *Growth and Economic Development*
  Econ J - v107 - Ja '97 - p282 [51-250]
  JEL - v34 - S '96 - p1487 [51-250]
  R&R Bk N - v11 - N '96 - p31 [51-250]
Lombardo, Daniel - *A Hedge Away*
  LJ - v122 - My 1 '97 - p104 [51-250]
  PW - v244 - Ap 28 '97 - p67 [51-250]
LoMonaco, Palmyra - *Night Letters (Illus. by Normand Chartier)*
  c HB Guide - v7 - Fall '96 - p265 [51-250]
  c New Ad - v9 - Fall '96 - p327+ [501+]
  c RT - v50 - Ap '97 - p596 [51-250]
Lomperis, Timothy J - *From People's War to People's Rule*
  Bks & Cult - v3 - Ja '97 - p38 [251-500]
  Choice - v34 - Mr '97 - p1214 [51-250]
  LJ - v121 - S 15 '96 - p80 [51-250]
London, David - *Sun Dancer*
  KR - v64 - My 1 '96 - p626 [251-500]
  NYTBR - v101 - N 24 '96 - p18 [51-250]
London, Jack - *The Call of the Wild*
  y EJ - v85 - S '96 - p98+ [501+]
  The Call of the Wild (Illus. by Philippe Munch)
  y HB Guide - v7 - Fall '96 - p302 [51-250]
  c Magpies - v11 - S '96 - p39+ [501+]
  c TES - Ja 31 '97 - p7* [501+]
  The Call of the Wild (Hagon). Audio Version
  c TES - D 27 '96 - p27 [51-250]
  The Call of the Wild (Hootkins). Audio Version
  c Obs - Ja 12 '97 - p18* [51-250]
  c TES - D 27 '96 - p27 [51-250]
  White Fang (Hagon). Audio Version
  c TES - D 27 '96 - p27 [51-250]
  White Fang (Hootkins). Audio Version
  y Kliatt - v30 - N '96 - p46 [51-250]
  c TES - D 27 '96 - p27 [51-250]

London, Jonathan - *Ali, Child of the Desert (Illus. by Ted Lewin)*
  c BL - v93 - Mr 1 '97 - p1172+ [51-250]
  Fireflies, Fireflies, Light My Way (Illus. by Linda Messier)
  c HB Guide - v7 - Fall '96 - p265 [51-250]
  c Time - v148 - D 9 '96 - p78 [51-250]
  Froggy Goes to School (Illus. by Frank Remkiewicz)
  c HB Guide - v8 - Spr '97 - p37 [51-250]
  c SLJ - v42 - Ag '96 - p126 [51-250]
  Froggy Learns to Swim (Illus. by Frank Remkiewicz)
  c RT - v50 - O '96 - p130 [51-250]
  Honey Paw and Lightfoot (Illus. by Jon Van Zyle)
  c RT - v50 - O '96 - p155 [51-250]
  I See the Moon and the Moon Sees Me (Illus. by Peter Fiore)
  c HB Guide - v7 - Fall '96 - p368 [51-250]
  c LA - v73 - D '96 - p620 [51-250]
  Jackrabbit (Illus. by Deborah Kogan Ray)
  c CCB-B - v50 - S '96 - p20 [51-250]
  c HB Guide - v7 - Fall '96 - p265 [51-250]
  Let the Lynx Come In (Illus. by Patrick Benson)
  c BL - v93 - S 15 '96 - p247+ [51-250]
  c CBRS - v25 - F '97 - p76 [51-250]
  c Ch BWatch - v6 - N '96 - p6 [1-50]
  c HB Guide - v8 - Spr '97 - p37 [51-250]
  c SLJ - v42 - O '96 - p102 [51-250]
  c Smith - v27 - N '96 - p172 [1-50]
  c TES - Ja 10 '97 - p8* [501+]
  Liplap's Wish (Illus. by Sylvia Long)
  c LA - v73 - S '96 - p358 [251-500]
  Old Salt, Young Salt (Illus. by Todd L W Doney)
  c HB Guide - v8 - Spr '97 - p37 [51-250]
  c SLJ - v42 - O '96 - p102 [51-250]
  The Owl Who Became the Moon (Illus. by Ted Rand)
  c PW - v243 - D 2 '96 - p62 [1-50]
  Puddles (Illus. by G Brian Karas)
  c BL - v93 - My 15 '97 - p1580 [51-250]
  Red Wolf Country (Illus. by Daniel San Souci)
  c HB Guide - v7 - Fall '96 - p265 [51-250]
  c Inst - v106 - Mr '97 - p29 [1-50]
  c New Ad - v9 - Fall '96 - p327+ [501+]
  c RT - v50 - My '97 - p685 [51-250]
  c SLJ - v42 - D '96 - p31 [1-50]
  The Sugaring-Off Party (Illus. by Gilles Pelletier)
  c Can CL - v22 - Fall '96 - p129+ [51-250]
  The Village Basket Weaver (Illus. by George Crespo)
  c BL - v92 - Ag '96 - p1907 [51-250]
  c HB Guide - v7 - Fall '96 - p265 [51-250]
  c NY - v72 - N 18 '96 - p99 [1-50]
  What Newt Could Do for Turtle (Illus. by Louise Voce)
  c Bks Keeps - v - Mr '97 - p19 [51-250]
  c BL - v93 - D 15 '96 - p733 [51-250]
  c CBRS - v25 - F '97 - p76 [1-50]
  c CCB-B - v50 - F '97 - p213 [51-250]
  c HB Guide - v8 - Spr '97 - p37 [51-250]
  c KR - v64 - N 15 '96 - p1671 [51-250]
  c PW - v243 - N 11 '96 - p73 [51-250]
  c SLJ - v42 - D '96 - p99+ [51-250]
  c TES - Mr 21 '97 - p9* [501+]
London, Manuel - *Self and Interpersonal Insight*
  Readings - v11 - S '96 - p23 [51-250]
The London Philatelist
  p Am Phil - v110 - S '96 - p828 [51-250]
Lone, Stewart - *Japan's First Modern War*
  AHR - v101 - D '96 - p1598 [251-500]
Lonergan, Bernard F J - *The Collected Works of Lonergan. Vol. 6*
  CPR - v16 - Je '96 - p189+ [501+]
Long, Cathryn J - *The Middle East in Search of Peace. Updated Ed.*
  c HB Guide - v8 - Spr '97 - p167 [51-250]
  c SLJ - v43 - Ja '97 - p130+ [51-250]
Long, Charles - *How to Survive without a Salary*
  BWatch - v17 - N '96 - p7 [51-250]
Long, David - *Towards a New Liberal Internationalism*
  Choice - v34 - O '96 - p359 [51-250]
Long, David, 1948- - *The Falling Boy*
  PW - v244 - Ap 28 '97 - p47 [251-500]
Long, Eugene Thomas - *God, Reason, and Religions*
  R&R Bk N - v12 - F '97 - p1 [51-250]
Long, Gary J - *Mossbauer Spectroscopy Applied to Magnetism and Materials Science. Vol. 2*
  SciTech - v20 - N '96 - p22 [51-250]
Long, Jan Freeman - *The Bee and the Dream (Illus. by Kaoru Ono)*
  c HB Guide - v7 - Fall '96 - p322 [51-250]
  c KR - v64 - My 1 '96 - p690 [51-250]
  c NY - v72 - N 18 '96 - p101 [51-250]
  c NYTBR - v102 - Ap 13 '97 - p27 [1-50]
  c RT - v50 - My '97 - p683+ [51-250]

Long, John, 1954, Apr.- - *Rock Jocks, Wall Rats, and Hang Dogs*
  Aethlon - v13 - Fall '95 - p166+ [251-500]
Long, John A, 1957- - *The Rise of Fishes*
  Nature - v383 - O 17 '96 - p586 [1-50]
  New Sci - v152 - N 9 '96 - p43 [1-50]
Long, John Hamilton - *Atlas of Historical County Boundaries: Connecticut, Maine, Massachusetts, Rhode Island*
  r Am Geneal - v71 - Jl '96 - p192 [51-250]
Long, Kim - *Squirrels: A Wildlife Handbook*
  AB - v97 - Je 17 '96 - p2402+ [51-250]
  r ARBA - v28 - '97 - p589 [51-250]
Long, Lynette - *Domino Addition*
  c Cur R - v35 - S '96 - p12 [51-250]
  c HB Guide - v7 - Fall '96 - p329 [51-250]
  c Learning - v25 - Ja '97 - p56 [1-50]
  c SLJ - v42 - D '96 - p115 [51-250]
Long, Nicholas J - *Conflict in the Classroom. 5th Ed.*
  R&R Bk N - v11 - N '96 - p57 [51-250]
Long, Rob - *Conversations with My Agent*
  BL - v93 - N 15 '96 - p564 [51-250]
  Ent W - v - Ja 24 '97 - p52 [51-250]
  KR - v64 - O 15 '96 - p1514 [251-500]
  LATBR - O 27 '96 - p10 [51-250]
  LJ - v122 - Ja '97 - p101+ [51-250]
  PW - v243 - O 21 '96 - p60 [51-250]
Long, Roger D - *The Man on the Spot*
  Albion - v28 - Fall '96 - p554 [251-500]
  HRNB - v25 - Fall '96 - p22+ [501+]
Long, Sarah S - *Principles and Practice of Pediatric Infectious Diseases*
  SciTech - v20 - D '96 - p52 [51-250]
Long, Sheila M - *Never Drink Coffee from Your Saucer*
  Ent W - D 20 '96 - p71 [51-250]
Long, Sylvia - *Hush Little Baby (Illus. by Sylvia Long)*
  c CBRS - v25 - Ap '97 - p99+ [51-250]
  c KR - v65 - Mr 15 '97 - p464+ [51-250]
  c PW - v244 - Ja 20 '97 - p400 [51-250]
Long, Thomas G - *Whispering the Lyrics*
  TT - v53 - Ja '97 - p573 [51-250]
Long, Yingtai - *Zai Hai De Bao Zhui Ru Qing Wang*
  BL - v93 - N 1 '96 - p484 [1-50]
Longacre, Edward G - *Pickett, Leader of the Charge*
  J Mil H - v61 - Ap '97 - p377+ [251-500]
  JSH - v63 - F '97 - p175+ [251-500]
Longacre, Robert E - *The Grammar of Discourse. 2nd Ed.*
  R&R Bk N - v11 - N '96 - p63 [51-250]
Longair, Malcolm S - *Our Evolving Universe*
  Nature - v382 - Jl 18 '96 - p220 [51-250]
Longaker, Christine - *Facing Death and Finding Hope*
  PW - v244 - F 24 '97 - p81 [1-50]
Longest, Beaufort B - *Seeking Strategic Advantage through Health Policy Analysis*
  SciTech - v21 - Mr '97 - p45 [51-250]
Longfellow, Henry Wadsworth - *La Cabalgata De Paul Revere (Illus. by Ted Rand)*
  c HB Guide - v8 - Spr '97 - p108 [1-50]
  Hiawatha (Illus. by Susan Jeffers)
  c HB Guide - v8 - Spr '97 - p108 [51-250]
Longhi, Jim - *Woody, Cisco, and Me*
  BL - v93 - Mr 1 '97 - p1103 [51-250]
  LJ - v122 - Ap 1 '97 - p100 [51-250]
  PW - v244 - F 24 '97 - p73 [51-250]
  Trib Bks - Ap 27 '97 - p9 [501+]
Longhi, Roberto - *Three Studies*
  r Choice - v34 - N '96 - p445 [51-250]
Longhurst, Brian - *Popular Music and Society*
  PMS - v19 - Win '95 - p115+ [501+]
Longitude Symposium (1993: Harvard University) - *The Quest for Longitude*
  BL - v93 - Ap '97 - p795 [51-250]
  Choice - v34 - Ap '97 - p1360 [51-250]
  KR - v64 - O 1 '96 - p1459 [51-250]
  LJ - v121 - N 1 '96 - p105 [51-250]
  Nature - v385 - Ja 23 '97 - p309+ [501+]
  TLS - O 11 '96 - p34 [501+]
Longley, Lawrence D - *The Electoral College Primer*
  y BL - v93 - S 15 '96 - p187 [251-500]
  Choice - v34 - Ja '97 - p876 [51-250]
  LJ - v121 - O 15 '96 - p77 [51-250]
Longman, Cleaver - *Because I Said So*
  Tric - v6 - Fall '96 - p142 [1-50]
Longman, Tremper, III - *Old Testament Commentary Survey. 2nd Ed.*
  r ARBA - v28 - '97 - p541 [51-250]
Longsdon, John M - *Exploring the Unknown. Vol. 1*
  J Gov Info - v23 - S '96 - p552 [51-250]
Longstreth, Richard - *City Center to Regional Mall*
  PW - v244 - My 5 '97 - p189+ [51-250]

Longsworth, Polly - *The World of Emily Dickinson*
BW - v27 - Mr 30 '97 - p12 [51-250]
Longuenesse, Beatrice - *Kant Et Le Pouvoir De Juger*
Dialogue - v35 - Fall '96 - p832+ [501+]
Longyear, Barry B - *The Last Enemy*
Analog - v117 - Ja '97 - p141+ [251-500]
Lonier, Terri - *The Frugal Entrepreneur*
LJ - v122 - My 1 '97 - p52 [1-50]
Working Solo
LJ - v122 - My 1 '97 - p52 [1-50]
Lonigan, Paul R - *The Druids*
R&R Bk N - v11 - N '96 - p6 [51-250]
Lonsdale, Allison Beeby - *Teaching Translation from Spanish to English*
TranslRevS - v2 - D '96 - p13 [51-250]
Lontai, Endre - *Unification of Law in the Field of International Industrial Property*
SciTech - v21 - Mr '97 - p72 [51-250]
Looby, Christopher - *Voicing America*
AL - v69 - Mr '97 - p208+ [251-500]
Choice - v34 - S '96 - p127 [51-250]
A Look into Tokyo
r FEER - v160 - Mr 27 '97 - p51+ [501+]
Looking for Papito (Sacre). Audio Version
c BL - v93 - F 15 '97 - p1037 [51-250]
Loomie, Albert J - *Spain and the Early Stuarts 1585-1655*
R&R Bk N - v11 - N '96 - p11 [51-250]
Loomis, Christine - *Rush Hour (Illus. by Mari Takabayashi)*
c CBRS - v25 - S '96 - p5 [51-250]
c HB Guide - v8 - Spr '97 - p37 [51-250]
c SLJ - v42 - S '96 - p184 [51-250]
Loomis, Jennifer A - *A Duck in a Tree (Illus. by Jennifer A Loomis)*
c BL - v93 - F 1 '97 - p943 [51-250]
c HB Guide - v8 - Spr '97 - p125 [51-250]
c PW - v243 - N 25 '96 - p74 [51-250]
Loomis, Susan Herrmann - *French Farmhouse Cookbook*
BWatch - v18 - F '97 - p8 [51-250]
PW - v243 - N 18 '96 - p73 [51-250]
Loomis, Ted A - *Loomis's Essentials of Toxicology. 4th Ed.*
SciTech - v20 - N '96 - p38 [51-250]
Looney, Janice Soutee - *Cedar County Missouri 1870 Federal Census*
r EGH - v50 - N '96 - p173 [51-250]
McDonald County, Missouri 1870 Federal Census
r EGH - v50 - N '96 - p173 [1-50]
Looney, Robert E - *The Economics of Third World Defense Expenditures*
JEL - v34 - D '96 - p1975+ [501+]
Loori, John Daido - *Heart of Being*
BL - v93 - S 15 '96 - p182 [51-250]
LJ - v121 - O 1 '96 - p84 [51-250]
PW - v243 - S 2 '96 - p126 [51-250]
Looser, Devoney - *Jane Austen and Discourses of Feminism*
Critm - v38 - Fall '96 - p644+ [501+]
Nine-C Lit - v50 - Mr '96 - p555 [1-50]
Lopata, Helena Znaniecka - *Current Widowhood*
AJS - v102 - N '96 - p881+ [501+]
CS - v25 - N '96 - p787+ [501+]
JMF - v58 - N '96 - p1043+ [251-500]
Lopate, Phillip - *Portrait of My Body*
BL - v92 - Ag '96 - p1875 [51-250]
BW - v26 - S 22 '96 - p13 [51-250]
HMR - Win '96 - p14 [501+]
LATBR - S 8 '96 - p10 [251-500]
NYTBR - v101 - S 22 '96 - p24 [51-250]
Lopez, Antoinette Sedillo - *Historical Themes and Identity*
HAHR - v76 - Ag '96 - p547+ [501+]
Latina Issues
HAHR - v76 - Ag '96 - p547+ [501+]
Latino Employment, Labor Organizations, and Immigration
HAHR - v77 - F '97 - p91+ [251-500]
Lopez, Donald S - *Buddhism in Practice*
JAAR - v65 - Spr '97 - p230+ [501+]
JR - v77 - Ap '97 - p340+ [501+]
Curators of the Buddha
JR - v77 - Ja '97 - p180+ [501+]
Religions of China in Practice
JAAR - v65 - Spr '97 - p230+ [501+]
Religions of India in Practice
JAAR - v65 - Spr '97 - p230+ [501+]
Religions of Tibet in Practice
PW - v244 - Mr 10 '97 - p62 [51-250]
Lopez, Ericka - *Flaming Iguanas*
PW - v244 - My 5 '97 - p200 [51-250]

Lopez, Loretta - *The Birthday Swap (Illus. by Loretta Lopez)*
c BL - v93 - My 1 '97 - p1501 [51-250]
Lopez, Michael - *Emerson and Power*
NEQ - v70 - Mr '97 - p163+ [501+]
Nine-C Lit - v51 - Mr '97 - p560 [51-250]
Lopez, Steve - *The Sunday Macaroni Club*
BL - v93 - Mr 1 '97 - p1110+ [51-250]
KR - v65 - Ap 1 '97 - p491 [251-500]
LJ - v122 - F 15 '97 - p162 [51-250]
PW - v244 - Mr 24 '97 - p57 [51-250]
Third and Indiana
y Emerg Lib - v24 - S '96 - p24 [1-50]
Lopez De Mariscal, Blanca - *The Harvest Birds (Illus. by Enrique Flores)*
c RT - v50 - F '97 - p426 [51-250]
Lopez Pinero, Jose Maria - *Bibliographia Medica Hispanica 1475-1950. Vols. 2, 4, 8, 9*
r Isis - v87 - D '96 - p709+ [501+]
Clasicos Medicos Valencianos Del Siglo XVII
Isis - v87 - S '96 - p547+ [501+]
Historia De La Ciencia Al Pais Valencia
Isis - v87 - D '96 - p708+ [501+]
El Megaterio De Bru Y El Presidente Jefferson
Isis - v87 - D '96 - p733 [501+]
Lopez-Stafford, Gloria - *A Place in El Paso*
Choice - v34 - O '96 - p349+ [51-250]
Lopo, Lisbet De Castro - *A Family Affair*
Aust Bk R - F '97 - p58 [51-250]
Lopshire, Robert - *New Tricks I Can Do! (Illus. by Robert Lopshire)*
c HB Guide - v7 - Fall '96 - p284 [1-50]
c SLJ - v42 - S '96 - p184 [51-250]
Loptson, Peter - *Theories of Human Nature*
Dialogue - v35 - Sum '96 - p620+ [501+]
Loraux, Nicole - *The Children of Athena*
South HR - v30 - Sum '96 - p279+ [501+]
The Experiences of Tiresias
Rel St Rev - v22 - O '96 - p345 [51-250]
Lorber, Judith - *Paradoxes of Gender*
APSR - v90 - S '96 - p634+ [501+]
Lorbiecki, Marybeth - *Aldo Leopold: A Fierce Green Fire*
Choice - v34 - My '97 - p1520 [51-250]
LJ - v121 - N 1 '96 - p105 [51-250]
SB - v33 - Ja '97 - p11 [251-500]
Just One Flick of a Finger (Illus. by David Diaz)
y BL - v93 - Ap 1 '97 - p1308 [1-50]
c CBRS - v25 - Ja '97 - p51 [51-250]
c CCB-B - v50 - S '96 - p20+ [51-250]
c HB Guide - v8 - Spr '97 - p38 [51-250]
c HMR - Fall '96 - p39+ [501+]
c SLJ - v42 - S '96 - p204 [51-250]
My Palace of Leaves in Sarajevo (Illus. by Herbert Tauss)
c CCB-B - v50 - Mr '97 - p252 [51-250]
c Cur R - v36 - F '97 - p12 [51-250]
c KR - v64 - D 15 '96 - p1799 [51-250]
c PW - v244 - Ap 14 '97 - p76 [51-250]
Lorcin, Patricia M E - *Imperial Identities*
AHR - v101 - D '96 - p1594 [501+]
JIH - v27 - Win '97 - p557+ [51-250]
Lord, Bette Bao - *The Middle Heart*
NYTBR - v101 - D 8 '96 - p80+ [1-50]
Rapport - v19 - 4 '96 - p25 [51-250]
Lord, Christine - *Eighth Grade*
y Cur R - v36 - N '96 - p13 [51-250]
y PW - v243 - D 9 '96 - p69 [51-250]
Sophomores: Tales of Reality, Conflict, and the Road by Tenth Grade Writers
y Cur R - v36 - N '96 - p13 [51-250]
y PW - v243 - D 9 '96 - p69 [1-50]
Lord, Christopher - *Absent at the Creation*
R&R Bk N - v12 - F '97 - p36 [51-250]
British Entry to the European Community under the Heath Government 1970-74
EHR - v112 - Ap '97 - p547 [51-250]
Lord, James - *Giacometti: A Biography*
Obs - Ja 19 '97 - p18* [51-250]
Some Remarkable Men
KR - v64 - Ag 15 '96 - p1213+ [251-500]
LATBR - O 27 '96 - p6+ [501+]
Nat - v263 - O 28 '96 - p48+ [501+]
NYTBR - v101 - S 15 '96 - p7+ [501+]
NYTBR - v101 - D 8 '96 - p93 [1-50]
NYTLa - v145 - S 9 '96 - pC15 [501+]
WSJ-MW - v77 - S 30 '96 - pA16 [501+]
Lord, Mary E - *Search for Security. 3rd Ed.*
r ARBA - v28 - '97 - p317 [251-500]

Lord, Nancy - *Fishcamp: Life on an Alaskan Shore*
KR - v65 - Mr 1 '97 - p357 [51-250]
LJ - v122 - Ap 15 '97 - p112 [51-250]
PW - v244 - F 24 '97 - p71 [51-250]
Lord, Tony - *Gardening at Sissinghurst*
Hort - v74 - O '96 - p73+ [251-500]
Lord, Vicki - *Painting Acrylics*
LJ - v121 - N 15 '96 - p60 [51-250]
Lord, Walter - *A Night to Remember*
Reason - v28 - D '96 - p41 [51-250]
Loredo, Betsy - *Faraway Families (Illus. by Monisha Raja)*
c RT - v50 - N '96 - p257 [51-250]
Lorelli, John A - *To Foreign Shores*
Historian - v58 - Sum '96 - p867+ [501+]
Lorence, James J - *Organizing the Unemployed*
Choice - v34 - D '96 - p676+ [51-250]
R&R Bk N - v11 - N '96 - p32 [51-250]
Lorentz, H A - *The Centenary of a Paper on Slow Viscous Flow by the Physicist H.A. Lorentz*
SciTech - v20 - D '96 - p23 [51-250]
Lorenz, Albert - *Metropolis: Ten Cities, Ten Centuries*
c Bks Keeps - Mr '97 - p26 [51-250]
c BW - v26 - D 8 '96 - p23 [51-250]
c HB Guide - v8 - Spr '97 - p164 [51-250]
c KR - v64 - N 1 '96 - p1603 [51-250]
c NY - v72 - N 18 '96 - p101 [1-50]
c PW - v243 - N 18 '96 - p75 [51-250]
y Sch Lib - v45 - F '97 - p51 [51-250]
c Smith - v27 - N '96 - p170+ [1-50]
c VLS - Win '96 - p21 [51-250]
Lorenz, Juliane - *Chaos as Usual*
BW - v27 - Ap 13 '97 - p13 [51-250]
Lorenz, Konrad - *The Natural Science of the Human Species*
Isis - v87 - D '96 - p761+ [501+]
Lorenzen, David N - *Praises to a Formless God*
Rel St Rev - v23 - Ja '97 - p95 [51-250]
R&R Bk N - v12 - F '97 - p79 [51-250]
Lorenzen, Thorwald - *Resurrection and Discipleship*
Theol St - v57 - S '96 - p549+ [501+]
Lorenzo, Olga - *The Rooms in My Mother's House*
Aust Bk R - D '96 - p64+ [501+]
Quad - v40 - D '96 - p81+ [501+]
Lorgue, G - *Clinical Veterinary Toxoicology*
SciTech - v20 - D '96 - p57 [1-50]
Loria, Stefano - *Pablo Picasso (Illus. by Simone Boni)*
y HB Guide - v7 - Fall '96 - p356 [51-250]
Lorian, Victor - *Antibiotics in Laboratory Medicine. 4th Ed.*
r SciTech - v20 - D '96 - p36 [51-250]
Lorrain, Francois-Guillaume - *L'Eleve Trouble*
FR - v70 - Mr '97 - p616+ [501+]
Lorrain, Jean - *Monsieur De Phocas*
TranslRevS - v1 - My '95 - p20 [51-250]
Loshitzky, Yosefa - *The Radical Faces of Godard and Bertolucci*
FQ - v50 - Win '96 - p56+ [501+]
Losinger, Anton - *Gerechte Vermogensverteilung*
RM - v49 - Je '96 - p929+ [501+]
Losonsky, Terry - *McDonald's Happy Meal Toys around the World*
Ant & CM - v101 - Ja '97 - p44 [51-250]
Losse, Deborah N - *Sampling the Book*
FR - v70 - O '96 - p109+ [501+]
JC - v46 - Sum '96 - p206+ [51-250]
Poetics T - v18 - Spr '97 - p128+ [501+]
Ren Q - v50 - Spr '97 - p294+ [501+]
Lossky, Andrew - *Louis XIV and the French Monarchy*
EHR - v112 - Ap '97 - p479 [251-500]
Lost and Found Stories Jesus Told
c Ch BWatch - v7 - F '97 - p5 [1-50]
Loth, Calder - *Virginia Landmarks of Black History*
r R&R Bk N - v11 - D '96 - p15 [51-250]
Lott, Bernice - *The Social Psychology of Interpersonal Discrimination*
Per Psy - v49 - Win '96 - p1004+ [501+]
Lott, Bret - *Fathers, Sons, and Brothers*
BL - v93 - My 1 '97 - p1474+ [51-250]
KR - v65 - Mr 15 '97 - p442 [251-500]
PW - v244 - Ap 14 '97 - p61 [51-250]
How to Get Home
BL - v92 - Ag '96 - p1882 [51-250]
LATBR - Ag 25 '96 - p10+ [251-500]
Lott, Eric - *Love and Theft*
South CR - v28 - Spr '96 - p282+ [501+]
Lott, Tim - *The Scent of Dried Roses*
Lon R Bks - v18 - O 17 '96 - p30 [501+]
Obs - v54 - O 13 '96 - p16* [501+]
TLS - O 11 '96 - p35 [501+]

Lotterman, Andrew - *Specific Techniques for the Psychotherapy of Schizophrenic Patients*
Readings - v12 - Mr '97 - p26 [51-250]
SciTech - v20 - N '96 - p45 [51-250]

Lottman, Herbert R - *Albert Camus: A Biography*
PW - v244 - Ap 21 '97 - p69 [1-50]
Jules Verne: An Exploratory Biography
BL - v93 - D 15 '96 - p705 [51-250]
BW - v26 - D 15 '96 - p9+ [501+]
KR - v64 - N 1 '96 - p1585 [251-500]
LATBR - Ja 5 '97 - p3 [501+]
LJ - v121 - D '96 - p94 [51-250]
NYTBR - v102 - Ja 26 '97 - p4 [501+]
PW - v243 - N 4 '96 - p53+ [51-250]

Lottridge, Celia Barker - *Something Might Be Hiding (Illus. by Paul Zwolak)*
c BL - v92 - Ag '96 - p1908 [51-250]
c Ch BWatch - v6 - Jl '96 - p4 [1-50]

Lotz, Wolfgang - *Architecture in Italy 1500-1600*
Six Ct J - v27 - Fall '96 - p960+ [501+]
Six Ct J - v27 - Fall '96 - p963+ [501+]

Loudon, Jane - *The Mummy! A Tale of the Twenty-Second Century*
AB - v98 - N 4 '96 - p1516 [51-250]

Loughery, John - *John Sloan: Painter and Rebel*
Sew R - v104 - Jl '96 - p492+ [501+]

Loughlin, Gerard - *Telling God's Story*
CC - v113 - N 6 '96 - p1088+ [51-250]
TLS - S 6 '96 - p31 [501+]

Loughlin, James - *Ulster Unionism and British National Identity since 1885*
AHR - v101 - D '96 - p1549+ [501+]

Loughlin, Laurie - *Holiday Hounds*
Dog Fan - v27 - N '96 - p34 [51-250]
NYTBR - v101 - D 8 '96 - p102 [1-50]

Louis, Adrian C - *Skins*
Bloom Rev - v16 - Jl '96 - p14 [501+]
Vortex of Indian Fevers
Bloom Rev - v16 - Jl '96 - p14+ [501+]
WAL - v31 - Fall '96 - p285+ [251-500]
Wild Indians and Other Creatures
Bloom Rev - v16 - Jl '96 - p15 [251-500]
NYTBR - v101 - O 27 '96 - p36 [251-500]
WAL - v31 - Win '97 - p409+ [251-500]

Louis, Karen Seashore - *Professionalism and Community*
TCR - v97 - Sum '96 - p653+ [501+]

Louisiana Toxics Release Inventory 1994
J Gov Info - v23 - S '96 - p584+ [51-250]

Louis-Jacques, Lyonette - *Introduction to International Organizations*
r Choice - v34 - D '96 - p590 [51-250]

Loukides, Paul - *Beyond the Stars. Vol. 5*
Choice - v34 - Ja '97 - p803 [51-250]
R&R Bk N - v11 - D '96 - p61 [1-50]

Lourdes, Ayala - *Los Ninos Alfabeticos (Illus. by Kathryn Shoemaker)*
c SLJ - v42 - N '96 - p134 [51-250]

Loureiro, Joao - *Monetary Policy in the European Monetary System*
JEL - v34 - D '96 - p2049 [51-250]

Lourie, Peter - *In the Path of Lewis and Clark*
y BL - v93 - F 15 '97 - p1013 [51-250]

Louvish, Simon - *The Days of Miracles and Wonders*
Quill & Q - v63 - Ja '97 - p33+ [251-500]

Le Louvre: The Palace and Its Paintings. Electronic Media Version
r LJ - v122 - Ap 15 '97 - p40 [1-50]

Louw, P Eric - *South African Media Policy*
JC - v46 - Aut '96 - p162+ [501+]

Love, Bruce - *The Paris Codex*
HAHR - v76 - N '96 - p767+ [251-500]

Love, D Anne - *Bess's Log Cabin Quilt*
y Ch BWatch - v7 - F '97 - p5 [1-50]
c RT - v50 - N '96 - p256 [51-250]
My Lone Star Summer
c HB Guide - v7 - Fall '96 - p294 [51-250]
y VOYA - v19 - O '96 - p211+ [51-250]

Love, Davis, III - *Every Shot I Take*
PW - v244 - Mr 31 '97 - p56 [51-250]

Love, Harold - *Scribal Publication in Seventeenth-Century England*
Ren Q - v49 - Aut '96 - p663+ [501+]

Love, Jeff - *Swamp Cats*
SFR - v22 - Ja '97 - p21 [501+]

Love, John - *Penguins*
c PW - v244 - My 5 '97 - p192 [51-250]

Love, Joseph L - *Crafting the Third World*
Choice - v34 - O '96 - p330 [51-250]

Love, Nicholas J - *Sunscreens: Development, Evaluation, and Regulatory Aspects. 2nd Ed.*
SciTech - v21 - Mr '97 - p68 [51-250]

Love, Spencie - *One Blood*
BW - v26 - Jl 14 '96 - p14 [501+]
NYTBR - v101 - Ap 7 '96 - p26 [501+]
RAH - v24 - D '96 - p657+ [501+]

Love, Susan - *Dr. Susan Love's Breast Book. 2nd Ed.*
r BL - v93 - F 1 '97 - p959 [1-50]
Dr. Susan Love's Hormone Book
BL - v93 - F 15 '97 - p986 [251-500]
CSM - v89 - Ap 3 '97 - p14 [51-250]
PW - v244 - F 3 '97 - p102 [51-250]

Love Lyrics of Ancient Egypt
TranslRevS - v1 - My '95 - p2 [51-250]

Lovecraft, H P - *The Transition of H.P. Lovecraft*
PW - v243 - S 2 '96 - p120+ [51-250]

Loveday, John - *Goodbye Buffalo Sky*
y Magpies - v11 - Jl '96 - p31 [51-250]
c TES - N 29 '96 - p10* [51-250]

Lovejoy, Ann - *Cascadia: Inspired Gardening in the Pacific Northwest*
BL - v93 - Mr 1 '97 - p1102 [51-250]
LJ - v122 - Ap 15 '97 - p106 [51-250]
PW - v244 - F 3 '97 - p104 [51-250]
Fragrance in Bloom
Fine Gard - Ja '97 - p66 [251-500]

Lovelace, Ann - *Beliefs, Values and Traditions*
y TES - D 6 '96 - pR6 [251-500]

Lovelace, Earl - *Salt*
BL - v93 - F 15 '97 - p1002 [51-250]
BW - v27 - Mr 30 '97 - p11 [501+]
KR - v65 - Ja 1 '97 - p14 [251-500]
LJ - v122 - F 1 '97 - p106 [51-250]
NS - v125 - S 27 '96 - p60 [51-250]
NYTBR - v102 - Ap 20 '97 - p19 [501+]
Obs - Ag 25 '96 - p16* [501+]
PW - v244 - Ja 27 '97 - p78+ [51-250]
TLS - S 20 '96 - p24 [501+]
Trib Bks - Mr 23 '97 - p4+ [501+]

Lovelace, Merline - *Line of Duty*
PW - v243 - O 21 '96 - p78 [51-250]

Lovell, Caroline Couper - *The Light of Other Days*
JSH - v62 - N '96 - p824+ [251-500]

Lovell, W George - *A Beauty That Hurts*
HAHR - v77 - My '97 - p334+ [251-500]
Demography and Empire
LA Ant - v7 - Je '96 - p174 [51-250]

Loveloch, Damien - *Soccer*
c Magpies - v11 - Jl '96 - p39 [1-50]

Loverde, Joyce - *The Complete Eldercare Planner*
PW - v244 - Ap 21 '97 - p68 [51-250]

Loveridge, Catherine E - *Nursing Management in the New Paradigm*
SciTech - v21 - Mr '97 - p69 [51-250]

Lovesey, Peter - *Bloodhounds*
Arm Det - v30 - Win '97 - p105+ [251-500]
BL - v93 - N 15 '96 - p575 [51-250]
KR - v64 - O 1 '96 - p1429 [251-500]
LATBR - D 15 '96 - p12 [51-250]
NYTBR - v101 - D 22 '96 - p21 [51-250]
PW - v243 - N 25 '96 - p60 [51-250]

Lovett, Sarah, 1953- - *Bats*
c Ch BWatch - v6 - My '96 - p1 [1-50]
Endangered Species
c Ch BWatch - v6 - My '96 - p1 [1-50]
Extremely Weird Birds
c Ch BWatch - v7 - F '97 - p5 [1-50]
Fishes (Illus. by Mary Sundstrom)
c Ch BWatch - v6 - My '96 - p1 [1-50]
Frogs (Illus. by Mary Sundstrom)
c Ch BWatch - v6 - My '96 - p1 [1-50]
Reptiles
c Ch BWatch - v6 - My '96 - p1 [1-50]
Spiders
c Ch BWatch - v6 - My '96 - p1 [1-50]

Lovett, Sarah Poland - *Acquired Motives*
BL - v93 - S 15 '96 - p224 [51-250]
BWatch - v17 - '96 - p6+ [1-50]
LATBR - S 22 '96 - p8 [51-250]
Rapport - v19 - 6 '96 - p20 [51-250]
Acquired Motives (Crouse). Audio Version
y Kliatt - v31 - My '97 - p35 [51-250]
LJ - v121 - O 1 '96 - p142 [51-250]
Dangerous Attachments
Books - v9 - S '95 - p25 [1-50]

Lovett, William A - *United States Shipping Policies and the World Market*
Sea H - Aut '96 - p45+ [51-250]

Lovin, Robin W - *Reinhold Niebuhr and Christian Realism*
Ethics - v107 - O '96 - p196 [51-250]
JR - v77 - Ap '97 - p325+ [501+]

Lovisi, Gary - *Hellbent on Homicide*
Arm Det - v29 - Sum '96 - p310 [51-250]

Lovitt, Chip - *The Flamingos Are Tickled Pink (Illus. by Marshall Toomey)*
c RT - v50 - O '96 - p132 [1-50]

Lovric, Miroslav - *Riemannian Geometry*
SIAM Rev - v38 - D '96 - p714 [1-50]

Lovullo, Sam - *Life in the Kornfield*
BL - v93 - D 1 '96 - p637 [51-250]
PW - v243 - S 30 '96 - p80 [1-50]

Low, Alice - *Mommy's Briefcase (Illus. by Aliki)*
c RT - v50 - O '96 - p134 [1-50]
Stories to Tell a Five-Year-Old
SLJ - v43 - F '97 - p43 [51-250]

Low, Anthony - *The Reinvention of Love*
MLR - v92 - Ja '97 - p179+ [501+]

Low, D A - *The Egalitarian Moment*
For Aff - v76 - My '97 - p148+ [51-250]

Low, John - *Basic Biomechanics Explained*
SciTech - v20 - D '96 - p34 [51-250]

Low, Kathleen - *Legislative Reference Services and Sources*
J Gov Info - v23 - Jl '96 - p524+ [501+]
The Roles of Reference Librarians
CLW - v67 - Mr '97 - p46 [51-250]

Low, Lisa - *Milton, the Metaphysicals, and Romanticism*
RES - v48 - F '97 - p109+ [501+]

Low, Robert - *Peoples of the Arctic*
c SLJ - v42 - Ag '96 - p139 [51-250]
Peoples of the Desert
c SLJ - v43 - Ja '97 - p104 [51-250]
Peoples of the Mountains
c SLJ - v43 - Ja '97 - p104 [51-250]
Peoples of the Rain Forest
c SLJ - v42 - N '96 - p99 [51-250]
Peoples of the Savanna
c SLJ - v43 - Ja '97 - p104 [51-250]

Lowance, Mason I, Jr. - *The Stowe Debate*
Col Lit - v23 - O '96 - p196+ [501+]

Low-Beer, F H - *Questions of Judgement*
CPR - v16 - Ap '96 - p114+ [251-500]

Lowden, Pamela - *Moral Opposition to Authoritarian Rule in Chile 1973-90*
HAHR - v77 - My '97 - p358+ [501+]
R&R Bk N - v11 - N '96 - p48 [51-250]

Lowe, Bia - *Wild Ride*
LATBR - Mr 24 '96 - p11 [51-250]

Lowe, David - *Australia*
c HB Guide - v8 - Spr '97 - p179 [1-50]

Lowe, Donald M - *The Body in Late Capitalist America*
J Am St - v30 - Ag '96 - p331+ [251-500]

Lowe, Duncan - *Cushion Plants for the Rock Garden*
r ARBA - v28 - '97 - p572 [51-250]

Lowe, E J - *Subjects of Experience*
TLS - Ja 10 '97 - p27 [501+]

Lowe, Jacques - *Jacqueline Kennedy Onassis: The Making of a First Lady*
NYTBR - v101 - S 1 '96 - p5 [501+]

Lowe, John - *Jump at the Sun*
TSWL - v15 - Fall '96 - p358+ [501+]

Lowe, Malcolm - *Orthodox Christians and Jews on Continuity and Renewal*
Rel Ed - v91 - Fall '96 - p612+ [1-50]

Lowe, Warren - *Leroy's Zoo (Illus. by Leroy Ramon Archuleta)*
c PW - v244 - Ap 28 '97 - p76 [51-250]

Lowell, Elizabeth - *Winter Fire*
BL - v93 - O 1 '96 - p291+ [51-250]
KR - v64 - S 15 '96 - p1344+ [251-500]
PW - v243 - O 14 '96 - p65 [51-250]

Lowell, James - *Investing from Scratch*
BL - v93 - Ja '97 - p794 [51-250]
Ent W - Ja 24 '97 - p53 [1-50]
PW - v243 - D 2 '96 - p54 [51-250]

Lowell, Melissa - *A Leap Ahead*
y Ch BWatch - v6 - S '96 - p3 [1-50]
A New Move
c Ch BWatch - v6 - My '96 - p7 [1-50]

Lowell, Robert - *Life Studies*
New ER - v18 - Win '97 - p72+ [501+]

Lowell, Susan - *I Am Lavina Cumming (Caruso). Audio Version*
c BL - v93 - Ap 1 '97 - p1313 [1-50]
c CSM - v89 - Mr 27 '97 - pB6 [1-50]
Little Red Cowboy Hat (Illus. by Randy Cecil)
c CBRS - v25 - Mr '97 - p88 [51-250]
c KR - v65 - F 15 '97 - p302+ [51-250]
c PW - v244 - Mr 3 '97 - p75 [51-250]

Lowen, R - *Fuzzy Set Theory*
SciTech - v20 - D '96 - p16 [51-250]

Lowenfeld, Andreas F - *International Litigation and the Quest for Reasonableness*
  Law Q Rev - v113 - Ja '97 - p170+ [501+]

Lowenhardt, John - *The Reincarnation of Russia*
  AAPSS-A - v546 - Jl '96 - p164+ [501+]
  APSR - v90 - D '96 - p940+ [251-500]
  Russ Rev - v55 - O '96 - p723+ [251-500]

Lowenstein, C Jared - *A Descriptive Catalogue of the Jorge Luis Borges Collection at the University of Virginia Library*
  r TranslRevS - v1 - My '95 - p4+ [51-250]

Lowenstein, Felicia - *The Abortion Battle*
  y Cons - v17 - Win '96 - p31 [1-50]
  y HB Guide - v7 - Fall '96 - p316+ [51-250]
  y SLJ - v42 - S '96 - p235 [51-250]

Lowenstein, Jerome - *The Midnight Meal and Other Essays about Doctors, Patients, and Medicine*
  BL - v93 - F 1 '97 - p916 [51-250]

Lowenstein, Roger - *Buffett: The Making of an American Capitalist*
  Econ - v340 - S 14 '96 - p9* [251-500]
  NYTBR - v101 - D 1 '96 - p36 [1-50]

Lowenstein, Steven M - *The Berlin Jewish Community*
  CEH - v29 - 1 '96 - p129+ [501+]
  EHR - v112 - F '97 - p225+ [501+]

Lowenthal, Abraham F - *Latin America in a New World*
  Parameters - v26 - Win '96 - p154 [1-50]

Lowenthal, Anne W - *The Object as Subject*
  Choice - v34 - D '96 - p603 [51-250]

Lowenthal, Cynthia J - *Lady Mary Wortley Montagu and the Eighteenth-Century Familiar Letter*
  RES - v47 - Ag '96 - p421+ [501+]

Lowenthal, David - *The Heritage Crusade and the Spoils of History*
  NS - v126 - F 7 '97 - p45+ [501+]
  Possessed by the Past
  Choice - v34 - Ja '97 - p851 [51-250]

Lowery, Linda - *Georgia O'Keeffe (Illus. by Rochelle Draper)*
  c BL - v93 - S 1 '96 - p139 [51-250]
  c HB Guide - v8 - Spr '97 - p138 [51-250]
  c SLJ - v42 - Ag '96 - p139 [51-250]
  Twist with a Burger, Jitter with a Bug (Illus. by Pat Dypold)
  c LA - v73 - D '96 - p623 [51-250]
  c Magpies - v11 - My '96 - p37 [51-250]
  Wilma Mankiller (Illus. by Janice Lee Porter)
  c BL - v93 - S 1 '96 - p139 [51-250]
  c CCB-B - v50 - S '96 - p21 [51-250]
  c HB Guide - v8 - Spr '97 - p159 [51-250]
  c SLJ - v42 - S '96 - p198 [51-250]

Lowi, Miriam R - *Water and Power*
  GJ - v162 - Jl '96 - p241 [51-250]

Lowi, Theodore J - *The End of the Republican Era*
  CS - v26 - Ja '97 - p30+ [501+]
  RP - v58 - Sum '96 - p597+ [501+]
  RP - v58 - Sum '96 - p601+ [501+]

Lowis, Peter - *South Africa: Free at Last*
  c HB Guide - v7 - Fall '96 - p380 [51-250]

Lowitz, Leza - *A Long Rainy Season*
  TranslRevS - v1 - My '95 - p2 [51-250]
  Old Way to Fold New Paper
  SFR - v22 - Ja '97 - p23+ [501+]

Lowman, Margaret D - *Forest Canopies*
  Choice - v34 - O '96 - p306 [51-250]

Lown, Bernard - *The Lost Art of Healing*
  BL - v93 - S 1 '96 - p50+ [51-250]
  Nat - v263 - N 18 '96 - p28+ [501+]
  PW - v243 - S 16 '96 - p62 [51-250]

Lowry, Bullitt - *Armistice 1918*
  Choice - v34 - My '97 - p1558 [51-250]
  LJ - v121 - N 1 '96 - p88+ [51-250]
  PW - v243 - N 18 '96 - p58 [51-250]

Lowry, Lois - *Anastasia, Absolutely*
  c PW - v244 - Ap 14 '97 - p77 [1-50]
  El Dador
  y BL - v93 - F 15 '97 - p1032 [1-50]
  The Giver
  c JOYS - v10 - Fall '96 - p35+ [501+]
  c JOYS - v10 - Fall '96 - p46+ [501+]
  c JOYS - v10 - Fall '96 - p92+ [501+]
  y Kliatt - v30 - S '96 - p4 [1-50]
  y SLJ - v42 - O '96 - p45 [1-50]
  Number the Stars
  c JOYS - v10 - Fall '96 - p46+ [501+]
  c JOYS - v10 - Fall '96 - p92+ [501+]
  c SLJ - v42 - N '96 - p41 [1-50]

See You Around, Sam! (Illus. by Diane De Groat)
  c BL - v93 - Ja '97 - p766 [1-50]
  c BL - v93 - O 1 '96 - p349 [51-250]
  c CCB-B - v50 - N '96 - p105 [51-250]
  c HB - v72 - S '96 - p597 [51-250]
  c HB Guide - v8 - Spr '97 - p70 [51-250]
  c Inst - v106 - Ja '97 - p51 [51-250]
See You around, Sam! (Illus. by Diane De Groat)
  c KR - v64 - O 1 '96 - p1470 [51-250]
See You Around, Sam! (Illus. by Diane De Groat)
  c Par Ch - v21 - Mr '97 - p12 [1-50]
  c SLJ - v42 - O '96 - p102 [51-250]
  c SLJ - v42 - D '96 - p31 [51-250]

Lowry, Malcolm - *Malcolm Lowry's La Mordida. Scholarly Ed.*
  TLS - D 20 '96 - p11 [501+]

Lowry, Richard S - *Littery Man*
  Choice - v34 - D '96 - p614+ [51-250]

Lowry, Thomas P - *The Story the Soldiers Wouldn't Tell*
  J Am Cult - v19 - Sum '96 - p140+ [501+]
  WHQ - v27 - Win '96 - p549 [1-50]

Lowther, George - *The Adventures of Superman*
  LJ - v121 - O 1 '96 - p132 [51-250]

Lowy, Ilana - *Between Bench and Bedside*
  LJ - v122 - Ja '97 - p136 [51-250]
  Nature - v386 - Mr 13 '97 - p139+ [501+]

Lowy, Michael - *The War of Gods*
  Choice - v34 - Mr '97 - p1178 [51-250]
  TLS - Ja 10 '97 - p28 [251-500]

Loxterkamp, David - *A Measure of My Days*
  y BL - v93 - Ap 1 '97 - p1273+ [51-250]
  KR - v65 - F 15 '97 - p278 [251-500]
  LJ - v122 - Ap 1 '97 - p115+ [51-250]
  PW - v244 - Mr 24 '97 - p72 [51-250]
  Wil Q - v21 - Spr '97 - p104+ [251-500]

Loy, Mina - *The Lost Lunar Baedeker*
  ABR - v18 - O '96 - p16+ [501+]
  Atl - v278 - Ag '96 - p94 [51-250]
  Nat - v264 - F 10 '97 - p29+ [501+]
  NYRB - v43 - S 19 '96 - p57+ [501+]
  TLS - Ag 30 '96 - p3+ [501+]
  Wom R Bks - v14 - O '96 - p1+ [501+]

Lozansky, Edward - *Winning Solutions*
  Choice - v34 - Ap '97 - p1376 [51-250]

Lozowick, Louis - *Survivor from a Dead Age*
  KR - v65 - Ja 15 '97 - p123 [251-500]
  PW - v244 - F 17 '97 - p205 [51-250]

Lu, Guojun - *Communication and Computing for Distributed Multimedia Systems*
  SciTech - v21 - Mr '97 - p5 [51-250]

Lu, Yung-Tsai - *Industrial Intelligent Control*
  SciTech - v20 - S '96 - p46 [51-250]

Luard, Elisabeth - *Family Life*
  Spec - v277 - N 16 '96 - p46 [1-50]
  TLS - Jl 7 '96 - p28 [501+]

Lubarsky, Sandra B - *Jewish Theology and Process Thought*
  Choice - v34 - S '96 - p144 [51-250]
  CPR - v16 - O '96 - p360+ [501+]
  Rel St Rev - v23 - Ap '97 - p193 [51-250]
  Tolerance and Transformation
  Rel Ed - v91 - Fall '96 - p613 [1-50]

Lubbock, Jules - *The Tyranny of Taste*
  SDA - v4 - Fall '96 - p124+ [501+]
  Sev Cent N - v54 - Fall '96 - p68+ [501+]
  South CR - v29 - Fall '96 - p272+ [501+]

Lubensky, Sophia - *Random House Russian-English Dictionary of Idioms*
  r Slav R - v55 - Sum '96 - p522+ [501+]

Luber, Philip - *Deliver Us from Evil*
  PW - v244 - My 12 '97 - p74 [51-250]

Lubin, Bernard - *Research on Group Treatment Methods*
  r ARBA - v28 - '97 - p283 [51-250]
  r Choice - v34 - Ap '97 - p1314 [51-250]
  r R&R Bk N - v12 - F '97 - p6 [51-250]

Lubin, David M - *Picturing a Nation*
  Am Q - v49 - Mr '97 - p162+ [501+]

Lubinski, David - *Assessing Individual Differences in Human Behavior*
  Per Psy - v50 - Spr '97 - p225+ [51-250]

Lubitz, Rita - *Marital Power in Dickens' Fiction*
  R&R Bk N - v12 - F '97 - p85 [51-250]

Luborsky, Lester - *The Symptom-Context Method*
  SciTech - v20 - N '96 - p43 [51-250]

Lubove, Roy - *Twentieth Century Pittsburgh. Vol. 2*
  JEL - v34 - S '96 - p1502 [51-250]

Lucado, Max - *Alabaster's Song (Illus. by Michael Garland)*
  c PW - v244 - Ja 13 '97 - p72 [51-250]

Lucas, Ceil - *Multicultural Aspects of Sociolinguistics in Deaf Communities*
  R&R Bk N - v11 - D '96 - p58 [51-250]

Lucas, Christopher J - *American Higher Education*
  HRNB - v25 - Fall '96 - p4 [251-500]
  J Hi E - v67 - S '96 - p597+ [501+]
  LQ - v67 - Ap '97 - p179+ [501+]
  Rel St Rev - v23 - Ja '97 - p35+ [501+]
  VQR - v72 - Aut '96 - p132* [51-250]
  Crisis in the Academy
  BL - v93 - S 1 '96 - p41 [51-250]
  Choice - v34 - Mr '97 - p1212 [51-250]
  Cng - v29 - Ja '97 - p63 [51-250]
  Econ - v341 - O 19 '96 - p5*+ [501+]
  NL - v79 - D 16 '96 - p7+ [501+]
  Rapport - v19 - 6 '96 - p28 [251-500]
  Teacher Education in America
  LJ - v122 - Mr 15 '97 - p72 [51-250]

Lucas, Eileen - *Civil Rights*
  y CLW - v67 - Mr '97 - p59+ [251-500]
  y HB Guide - v8 - Spr '97 - p93 [51-250]
  y SB - v32 - N '96 - p235 [251-500]
  c SLJ - v42 - D '96 - p131+ [51-250]

Lucas, James - *Hitler's Enforcers*
  PW - v243 - O 21 '96 - p68 [1-50]

Lucas, Mike - *Antarctica*
  New Sci - v151 - S 21 '96 - p55 [51-250]

Lucas, Phillip Charles - *The Odyssey of a New Religion*
  AHR - v101 - O '96 - p1311+ [501+]

Lucas, Robert J - *Mastering Prolog*
  SciTech - v20 - D '96 - p10 [51-250]

Lucas, Robin - *Balancing Act*
  Aust Bk R - Je '96 - p66 [251-500]

Lucas, Scott - *Britain and Suez*
  R&R Bk N - v11 - N '96 - p16 [51-250]

Luccarelli, Mark - *Lewis Mumford and the Ecological Region*
  Isis - v88 - Mr '97 - p169 [501+]
  JEL - v34 - S '96 - p1502 [51-250]

Luce, Louise Fiber - *Litteratures En Contexte*
  FR - v70 - O '96 - p156+ [501+]

Luce, Solomon - *Zen Fixtures*
  Tric - v6 - Fall '96 - p142 [1-50]

Lucey, Kenneth G - *On Knowing and the Known*
  LJ - v121 - N 15 '96 - p64+ [51-250]

Luchetti, Cathy - *I Do!*
  BW - v26 - Jl 14 '96 - p12 [51-250]
  WHQ - v28 - Spr '97 - p104 [1-50]

Luchetti, Emily - *Four-Star Desserts*
  BL - v93 - S 15 '96 - p196 [51-250]
  CSM - v89 - D 13 '96 - p11 [51-250]
  LJ - v121 - S 15 '96 - p88 [51-250]

Luchs, Alison - *Tullio Lombardo and Ideal Portrait Sculpture in Renaissance Venice 1490-1530*
  BM - v138 - D '96 - p831+ [501+]
  Choice - v34 - O '96 - p268 [51-250]
  Six Ct J - v27 - Win '96 - p1096+ [501+]

Lucht, Irmgard - *The Red Poppy (Illus. by Irmgard Lucht)*
  c RT - v50 - N '96 - p243 [51-250]

Luciak, Ilja A - *The Sandinista Legacy*
  APSR - v90 - D '96 - p941+ [501+]
  HAHR - v76 - N '96 - p804+ [501+]
  J Pol - v58 - N '96 - p1246+ [501+]

Lucier, Armand Francis - *Jolly Old England*
  EGH - v50 - N '96 - p155 [51-250]

Lucier, Charles V - *Traditional Beluga Drives of the Inupiat of Kotzebue Sound*
  Am Ant - v62 - Ja '97 - p170+ [251-500]
  Am Ethnol - v24 - F '97 - p230+ [501+]

Lucie-Smith, Edward - *Art Deco Painting*
  LJ - v121 - N 15 '96 - p93 [1-50]
  The Art of Albert Paley
  Am Craft - v57 - Ap '97 - p24+ [51-250]
  PW - v243 - N 18 '96 - p60 [51-250]
  Visual Arts in the Twentieth Century
  PW - v244 - F 17 '97 - p207 [51-250]

Luckett, Dave - *The Best Batsman in the World*
  c Magpies - v11 - My '96 - p43+ [51-250]
  The Wizard and Me
  y Aust Bk R - D '96 - p86+ [501+]

Luckyj, George S N - *Modern Ukrainian Short Stories*
  WLT - v71 - Win '97 - p185+ [501+]

Lucretius Carus, Titus - *Lucy Hutchinson's Translation of Lucretius: De Rerum Natura*
  TLS - Ja 10 '97 - p28 [251-500]
  On the Nature of the Universe
  TranslRevS - v1 - My '95 - p5+ [51-250]

Lucy, Niall - *Debating Derrida*
Arena - Ag '96 - p51+ [501+]
Aust Bk R - Ag '96 - p21+ [501+]
Quad - v40 - Jl '96 - p98+ [501+]
Luczkovich, Joseph J - *Ecomorphology of Fishes*
SciTech - v20 - D '96 - p32 [51-250]
Ludden, David - *Agricultural Production and Indian History*
JEH - v56 - D '96 - p948+ [501+]
Ludden, LaVerne L - *Luddens' Adult Guide to Colleges and Universities*
r BL - v93 - Mr 15 '97 - p1258 [51-250]
Luddy, Maria - *Women and Philanthropy in Nineteenth-Century Ireland*
JIH - v27 - Spr '97 - p684+ [501+]
Ludema, Kenneth C - *Friction, Wear, Lubrication*
Choice - v34 - Ja '97 - p826 [51-250]
Ludemann, Gerd - *Heretics: The Other Side of Early Christianity*
BL - v93 - O 1 '96 - p301+ [51-250]
TLS - Ja 17 '97 - p31 [501+]
Ludlam, Steve - *Contemporary British Conservatism*
Pol Stud J - v24 - Sum '96 - p311+ [501+]
Ludlow, Peter - *High Noon on the Electronic Frontier*
Afterimage - v24 - Ja '97 - p23 [1-50]
Choice - v34 - D '96 - p646 [51-250]
NS - v125 - S 13 '96 - p47 [51-250]
Ludlum, Robert - *The Apocalypse Watch*
Books - v10 - Je '96 - p23 [51-250]
The Cry of the Halidon
PW - v243 - O 14 '96 - p81 [1-50]
Ludtke, Alf - *Eigen-Sinn: Fabrikalltag, Arbeitererfahrungen Und Politik Vom Kaiserreich Bis In Den Faschismus*
JMH - v68 - S '96 - p629+ [501+]
The History of Everyday Life
CS - v25 - S '96 - p698+ [501+]
Ludwig, Arnold M - *How Do We Know Who We Are?*
KR - v65 - Mr 15 '97 - p442 [251-500]
Luebbermann, Mimi - *Cactus and Succulents*
PW - v244 - Mr 24 '97 - p79 [51-250]
Luebke, Frederick C - *Nebraska: An Illustrated History*
J Gov Info - v23 - S '96 - p587 [51-250]
Luedemann, Gerd - *The Resurrection of Jesus*
Theol St - v57 - Je '96 - p341+ [501+]
Lueders, Bill - *An Enemy of the State*
AJR - v18 - D '96 - p45 [501+]
Nat - v264 - Ap 21 '97 - p30+ [501+]
Luere, Jeane - *Playwright versus Director*
Theat J - v49 - Mr '97 - p95+ [501+]
Luff, Rosemary - *Whither Environmental Archaeology?*
Am Ant - v61 - Jl '96 - p624+ [501+]
Luftig, Victor - *Seeing Together*
VS - v39 - Win '96 - p279+ [501+]
Luftman, Jerry N - *Competing in the Information Age*
BL - v92 - Ag '96 - p1865 [51-250]
Choice - v34 - Ja '97 - p840+ [51-250]
Luger, Harriett Mandelay - *Bye, Bye, Bali Kai*
c CBRS - v24 - Ag '96 - p168 [51-250]
c HB Guide - v7 - Fall '96 - p294 [51-250]
The Last Stronghold
c Ch BWatch - v6 - O '96 - p8 [51-250]
Lugg, Catherine A - *For God and Country*
Choice - v34 - My '97 - p1577 [51-250]
Lugo, Luis E - *Religion, Public Life, and the American Polity*
JR - v77 - Ja '97 - p150+ [501+]
Rel St Rev - v23 - Ap '97 - p157+ [501+]
Luhmann, Niklas - *Social Systems*
CS - v26 - Ja '97 - p117+ [501+]
Luhrmann, T M - *The Good Parsi*
Choice - v34 - Ja '97 - p838+ [51-250]
Luk, Y F - *Hong Kong's Economic and Financial Future*
Ch Rev Int - v4 - Spr '97 - p181+ [501+]
Lukacher, Ned - *Daemonic Figures*
MP - v94 - F '97 - p386+ [501+]
Six Ct J - v27 - Fall '96 - p837+ [501+]
Lukacs, Georg - *German Realists in the Nineteenth Century*
MLR - v91 - Jl '96 - p789+ [501+]
Lukacs, Yehuda - *Israel, Jordan, and the Peace Process*
BL - v93 - My 15 '97 - p1546 [51-250]
Lukas, Paul - *Inconspicuous Consumption*
LJ - v121 - N 1 '96 - p76 [51-250]
Nat - v264 - Mr 3 '97 - p31+ [501+]
PW - v243 - S 30 '96 - p62 [51-250]
VV - v42 - F 18 '97 - p56+ [501+]
Luke, Carmen - *Feminisms and Pedagogies of Everyday Life*
Choice - v34 - F '97 - p1014 [51-250]

Luke, Eric - *Ghost: Nocturnes*
p Quill & Q - v62 - Ag '96 - p26 [51-250]
Lukens, Nancy - *Daughters of Eve*
TranslRevS - v1 - My '95 - p2 [51-250]
Luker, Kristin - *Abortion and the Politics of Motherhood*
Cons - v17 - Aut '96 - p35+ [501+]
Dubious Conceptions
BL - v93 - Ap 1 '97 - p1285 [1-50]
Comw - v123 - S 27 '96 - p25+ [501+]
Hast Cen R - v26 - Jl '96 - p42 [1-50]
Nat - v263 - O 21 '96 - p27+ [501+]
New R - v215 - O 21 '96 - p30+ [501+]
NYTBR - v101 - S 1 '96 - p12+ [501+]
NYTBR - v101 - D 8 '96 - p87 [1-50]
Prog - v61 - Ja '97 - p32+ [251-500]
VOYA - v19 - O '96 - p243 [251-500]
Wom R Bks - v14 - N '96 - p11+ [501+]
Luker, Ralph E - *Historical Dictionary of the Civil Rights Movement*
r BL - v93 - F 15 '97 - p1042 [51-250]
Lukes, Bonnie L - *The American Revolution*
y Ch BWatch - v6 - Jl '96 - p2 [51-250]
y HB Guide - v7 - Fall '96 - p384+ [1-50]
Lukes, Igor - *Czechoslovakia between Stalin and Hitler*
Choice - v34 - D '96 - p671 [51-250]
HRNB - v25 - Win '97 - p74+ [501+]
Lukic, Reneo - *Europe from the Balkans to the Urals*
For Aff - v76 - Mr '97 - p191 [51-250]
Lukins, Sheila - *USA Cookbook*
PW - v244 - Ap 21 '97 - p65+ [51-250]
Lukitz, Liora - *Iraq: The Search for National Identity*
MEJ - v50 - Sum '96 - p433+ [501+]
MEP - v4 - 4 '96 - p147+ [501+]
Luksic, Irena - *Noci U Bijelom Satenu*
WLT - v70 - Sum '96 - p725 [501+]
Lum, Bernice - *If I Had a Dog*
c Books - v9 - S '95 - p26 [1-50]
If My Dog Went on Vacation
c Books - v9 - S '95 - p26 [1-50]
Lum, Doman - *Social Work Practice and People of Color. 3rd Ed.*
Soc Ser R - v70 - S '96 - p501 [51-250]
Lumet, Sidney - *Making Movies*
FQ - v50 - Win '96 - p63 [251-500]
Obs - F 9 '97 - p18* [51-250]
Lumley, Brian - *Fruiting Bodies and Other Fungi*
y Kliatt - v30 - S '96 - p18 [51-250]
Necroscope: Resurgence
KR - v64 - Ag 15 '96 - p1178 [251-500]
LJ - v121 - O 15 '96 - p93 [1-50]
PW - v243 - S 30 '96 - p63 [51-250]
Titus Crow. Vol. 1
BWatch - v18 - Mr '97 - p9 [51-250]
KR - v64 - N 1 '96 - p1556 [251-500]
PW - v243 - N 11 '96 - p57 [51-250]
Titus Crow. Vol. 2
KR - v65 - My 1 '97 - p668 [251-500]
Lummis, C Douglas - *Radical Democracy*
Choice - v34 - D '96 - p688 [51-250]
For Aff - v75 - S '96 - p135 [51-250]
Nat - v263 - S 9 '96 - p50+ [501+]
Lumpkin, Grace - *To Make My Bread*
AL - v68 - S '96 - p669 [1-50]
Nat - v263 - S 23 '96 - p30+ [501+]
Lumsden, Charles J - *Origins of the Human Mind (Riggenbach). Audio Version*
BL - v93 - F 15 '97 - p1038 [51-250]
Lumsden, Ian - *Machos, Maricones, and Gays*
Choice - v34 - D '96 - p695 [51-250]
Luna, Juan J - *Goya: 250 Aniversario*
BM - v138 - S '96 - p630+ [501+]
Lunan, Gordon - *The Making of a Spy*
Can Hist R - v78 - Mr '97 - p141+ [501+]
Lunardi, Alessandra - *Analytic Semigroups and Optimal Regularity in Parabolic Problems*
SciTech - v20 - D '96 - p18 [51-250]
Lunbeck, Elizabeth - *The Psychiatric Persuasion*
JIH - v27 - Aut '96 - p349 [251-500]
MQR - v36 - Spr '97 - p355+ [501+]
NYTBR - v101 - Jl 21 '96 - p28 [51-250]
Lund, Jens - *Flatheads and Spooneys*
CAY - v17 - Fall '96 - p6 [51-250]
Lund, Marcia - *Olympic Winners*
SLMQ - v25 - Fall '96 - p65 [1-50]
Lund, Michael S - *Preventing Violent Conflicts*
Choice - v34 - D '96 - p686 [51-250]
For Aff - v75 - S '96 - p134 [51-250]
Lund, Roy - *A Whole-School Behaviour Policy*
TES - Ja 24 '97 - p10* [501+]

Lund, William - *Integrating UNIX and PC Network Operating Systems*
SciTech - v20 - S '96 - p6 [51-250]
Lundahl, Mats - *Themes in Development Economics*
JEL - v34 - S '96 - p1479 [51-250]
Lundberg, Erik - *The Development of Swedish and Keynesian Macroeconomic Theory and Its Impact on Economic Policy*
JEL - v35 - Mr '97 - p191+ [51-250]
Studies in Economic Instability and Change
JEL - v35 - Mr '97 - p207 [51-250]
Lundberg, Ulla-Lena - *Allt Man Kan Onska Sig*
WLT - v71 - Win '97 - p173 [501+]
Lundbom, Jack R - *The Early Career of the Prophet Jeremiah*
Rel St Rev - v23 - Ja '97 - p59+ [51-250]
Lundeberg, Philip K - *The Gunboat Philadelphia and the Defense of Lake Champlain in 1776*
Sea H - Sum '96 - p29 [501+]
Lundell, Margo - *The Furry Bedtime Book (Illus. by David McPhail)*
c Par - v71 - D '96 - p251 [1-50]
c PW - v243 - N 4 '96 - p74 [51-250]
Lunden, Joan - *Joan Lunden's Healthy Living*
BL - v93 - Ap 1 '97 - p1274 [51-250]
LJ - v122 - Ap 15 '97 - p102 [51-250]
Lundgren, Mary Beth - *We Sing the City (Illus. by Donna Perrone)*
c PW - v244 - Mr 31 '97 - p74 [51-250]
Lundie, Catherine A - *Restless Spirits*
Choice - v34 - My '97 - p1499 [51-250]
KR - v64 - N 1 '96 - p1556+ [251-500]
Lundin, Anne - *Teaching Children's Literature*
r Emerg Lib - v23 - My '96 - p41 [51-250]
Lundin, G Edward - *Contemporary Religious Ideas*
r BL - v93 - O 1 '96 - p368 [51-250]
r Choice - v34 - F '97 - p940 [51-250]
r R&R Bk N - v11 - D '96 - p4 [51-250]
Lunelli, Clemente - *I Manoscritti Polifonici Della Biblioteca Musicale L. Feininger*
r Notes - v53 - D '96 - p446+ [501+]
Lunghi, Elvio - *The Basilica of St. Francis in Assisi*
LJ - v122 - My 1 '97 - p101 [51-250]
Lungo, Mario - *El Salvador in the Eighties*
Choice - v34 - Ja '97 - p869 [51-250]
Lunn, Janet - *The Root Cellar (Illus. by Scott Cameron)*
c Can CL - v22 - Fall '96 - p125 [51-250]
The Unseen: Scary Stories
c Quill & Q - v62 - My '96 - p13 [501+]
Lunsford, Andrea A - *Reclaiming Rhetoric*
QJS - v82 - Ag '96 - p300+ [501+]
Luntta, Karl - *Caribbean: The Lesser Antilles*
r BL - v93 - S 15 '96 - p212 [1-50]
Luo, Zhi-Quan - *Mathematical Programs with Equilibrium Constraints*
SciTech - v21 - Mr '97 - p17 [51-250]
Luoma, Heikki - *Kuparitaivas*
WLT - v71 - Win '97 - p189 [501+]
Luong, Hy V - *Revolution in the Village*
Am Ethnol - v23 - N '96 - p914+ [501+]
Luongo, Albert M - *The Soccer Handbook for Players, Coaches and Parents*
LJ - v121 - N 15 '96 - p67 [51-250]
Lupack, Barbara T - *Insanity as Redemption in Contemporary Fiction*
J Am St - v30 - Ag '96 - p286 [251-500]
Vision/Re-Vision: Adapting Contemporary American Fiction by Women to Film
LJ - v121 - D '96 - p97 [51-250]
Luper, Steven - *Invulnerability: On Securing Happiness*
Choice - v34 - N '96 - p473 [51-250]
Lupher, Mark - *Power Restructuring in China and Russia*
AJS - v102 - Ja '97 - p1166+ [501+]
Choice - v34 - O '96 - p354 [51-250]
Lupica, Mike - *Mad as Hell*
CSM - v89 - D 23 '96 - p15 [251-500]
KR - v64 - Ag 15 '96 - p1214 [251-500]
LJ - v121 - O 1 '96 - p87 [51-250]
Lupii, Oles' - *Padinnia Davn'oi Stolytsi*
BL - v93 - N 15 '96 - p577 [1-50]
Lupoff, Richard A - *Before...12:01...and After*
BWatch - v17 - S '96 - p7 [51-250]
The Silver Chariot Killer
Arm Det - v30 - Win '97 - p94 [251-500]
BL - v93 - O 1 '96 - p325 [51-250]
KR - v64 - S 15 '96 - p1357 [51-250]
Luppens, Michel - *What Do the Fairies Do with All Those Teeth?*
c Ch BWatch - v6 - My '96 - p3 [1-50]
Lupton, Deborah - *Food, the Body and the Self*
Socio R - v44 - N '96 - p780+ [501+]

Lupton, Ellen - *Design, Writing, Research*
 Choice - v34 - S '96 - p114 [51-250]
 Letters from the Avant-Garde
 Am Craft - v56 - Ag '96 - p28 [1-50]
 Choice - v34 - O '96 - p268 [51-250]
 Mixing Messages
 LJ - v122 - Mr 15 '97 - p60 [51-250]
 SFR - v21 - N '96 - p45 [51-250]
 TCI - v30 - O '96 - p58 [1-50]
Lupu, Coman - *Hommages Offerts A Maria Manoliu-Manea*
 MLR - v92 - Ap '97 - p401+ [501+]
Lupu, N - *Prin Lume*
 BL - v93 - D 15 '96 - p714 [1-50]
Luquet, Wade - *Short-Term Couples Therapy*
 SciTech - v20 - S '96 - p33 [1-50]
Luraghi, Raimondo - *A History of the Confederate Navy*
 Choice - v34 - Ja '97 - p863 [51-250]
Lurcat, Francois - *L'Autorite De La Science*
 Isis - v88 - Mr '97 - p125+ [501+]
Luria-Sukenick, Lynn - *Danger Wall May Fall*
 KR - v65 - Mr 1 '97 - p328 [51-250]
 LJ - v122 - Ap 15 '97 - p122 [51-250]
 PW - v244 - Ap 14 '97 - p57 [51-250]
Lurie, Alison - *The Heavenly Zoo (Illus. by Monica Beisner)*
 c Par Ch - v20 - O '96 - p21 [51-250]
Lurie, Jon - *Allison's Story (Illus. by Rebecca Dallinger)*
 c BL - v93 - N 1 '96 - p504 [51-250]
 c HB Guide - v8 - Spr '97 - p93 [51-250]
 c SLJ - v42 - D '96 - p115 [51-250]
 Fundamental Snowboarding (Illus. by Jimmy Clarke)
 y BL - v93 - Ap 1 '97 - p1308 [1-50]
 c HB Guide - v7 - Fall '96 - p360 [1-50]
Lurie, Morris - *Welcome to Tangier*
 Aust Bk R - F '97 - p29+ [501+]
Lurie, Patty - *Guide to Impressionist Paris*
 r LJ - v122 - F 15 '97 - p154 [51-250]
 r PW - v244 - Ja 27 '97 - p93 [51-250]
Lurigio, Arthur J - *Criminal Justice Statistics*
 R&R Bk N - v11 - D '96 - p22 [51-250]
Lury, Celia - *Consumer Culture*
 Choice - v34 - O '96 - p321+ [51-250]
Lusane, Clarence - *African-Americans at the Crossroads*
 SSQ - v77 - S '96 - p712+ [501+]
 No Easy Victories
 y BL - v93 - F 15 '97 - p1013+ [51-250]
 y HB Guide - v8 - Spr '97 - p92 [51-250]
Lusby, Philip - *Scottish Wild Plants*
 Nature - v385 - F 6 '97 - p500 [51-250]
Lustbader, Eric - *Dark Homecoming*
 BL - v93 - My 15 '97 - p1541+ [51-250]
Lustick, Ian - *Unsettled States, Disputed Lands*
 MEJ - v51 - Win '97 - p145+ [501+]
Lustig, Arnost - *The Unloved: From the Diary of Perla S.*
 LJ - v121 - O 1 '96 - p127
 PW - v243 - S 2 '96 - p122 [1-50]
Lustig, Irma S - *Boswell: Citizen of the World, Man of Letters*
 Albion - v28 - Win '96 - p698+ [501+]
Lustig, Nora - *Coping with Austerity*
 JEL - v34 - D '96 - p1977+ [501+]
Lustig, T J - *Henry James and the Ghostly*
 MLR - v91 - Jl '96 - p708+ [501+]
 Nine-C Lit - v51 - S '96 - p266+ [501+]
 RES - v48 - F '97 - p139+ [501+]
Lusztig, Michael - *Risking Free Trade*
 Choice - v34 - My '97 - p1547 [51-250]
Lutes, Jason - *Jar of Fools. Pts. 1-2*
 p Quill & Q - v62 - Ag '96 - p26 [51-250]
Luteyn, James L - *Flora Neotropica*
 R&R Bk N - v12 - F '97 - p94 [51-250]
Luth, Hans - *Surfaces and Interfaces of Solid Materials*
 Phys Today - v49 - S '96 - p88 [501+]
Luther, Sara F - *Diverse Perspectives on Marxist Philosophy*
 Slav R - v55 - Fall '96 - p709 [501+]
Lutjens, Sheryl - *The State, Bureaucracy, and the Cuban Schools*
 R&R Bk N - v11 - D '96 - p54 [51-250]
Lutkenhoff, Marlene - *SPINAbilities: A Young Person's Guide to Spina Bifida*
 y BL - v93 - F 15 '97 - p1016 [51-250]
Luton, Larry S - *The Politics of Garbage*
 Choice - v34 - My '97 - p1577 [51-250]
Luttig, Peter - *Der Palestrina-Stil Als Satzideal In Der Musiktheorie Zwischen 1750 Und 1900*
 Notes - v53 - S '96 - p71+ [501+]
Luttwak, Edward N - *The Endangered American Dream*
 YR - v84 - O '96 - p137+ [501+]

Lutz, Gary - *Stories in the Worst Way*
 Ant R - v55 - Spr '97 - p242 [251-500]
 KR - v64 - S 15 '96 - p1345 [251-500]
 LJ - v121 - N 1 '96 - p110 [51-250]
 NYTBR - v102 - Ja 5 '97 - p18 [51-250]
 PW - v243 - S 30 '96 - p60 [251-500]
Lutz, John - *The Ex*
 BL - v92 - Ag '96 - p1887+ [51-250]
 The Ex (Griffin). Audio Version
 y Kliatt - v31 - Ja '97 - p40 [51-250]
Lutz, Richard L - *Komodo, the Living Dragon. Rev. Ed.*
 BWatch - v18 - F '97 - p6 [51-250]
Lutz, Wolfgang - *The Future Population of the World*
 GJ - v163 - Mr '97 - p106 [51-250]
Lutzeler, Paul Michael - *Poetik Der Autoren*
 Ger Q - v69 - Spr '96 - p222+ [501+]
Lutzen, Karl F - *Brew Ware*
 BL - v92 - Ag '96 - p1867 [51-250]
Luu, Kim Loan - *Nhu Ao Nhu Thuc*
 BL - v93 - S 1 '96 - p70 [51-250]
Luukkanen, Arto - *The Party of Unbelief*
 Russ Rev - v56 - Ja '97 - p139 [501+]
Lux, Thomas - *The Blind Swimmer*
 LJ - v121 - D '96 - p98 [51-250]
Luxon, Thomas H - *Literal Figures*
 CH - v65 - D '96 - p712+ [501+]
 Shakes Q - v47 - Fall '96 - p340+ [501+]
Luxton, Steve - *Iridium*
 Can Lit - Win '96 - p189+ [501+]
Luykx, Felix F - *Radioecology and the Restoration of Radioactive-Contaminated Sites*
 SciTech - v20 - D '96 - p31 [51-250]
Luz, Ulrich - *Die Jesusgeschichte Des Matthaus*
 Rel St Rev - v23 - Ja '97 - p71+ [51-250]
 Matthew in History, Interpretation, Influence, and Effects
 Rel St Rev - v23 - Ap '97 - p180 [51-250]
 The Theology of the Gospel of Matthew
 JR - v77 - Ap '97 - p288+ [501+]
Luzzati, Michele - *L'Inquisizione E Gli Ebrei In Italia*
 JMH - v69 - Mr '97 - p168+ [501+]
Ly, Minh Hao - *Nguyen Trung Truc*
 BL - v93 - S 1 '96 - p70 [51-250]
Lyall, Francis - *James Blish: A Dusk of Idols and Other Stories*
 PW - v243 - N 18 '96 - p66+ [51-250]
Lyall, Gavin - *Flight from Honour*
 TLS - D 27 '96 - p21 [501+]
Lyandres, Semion - *The Bolsheviks' German Gold Revisitd*
 Slav R - v55 - Sum '96 - p486+ [501+]
Lycan, William G - *Consciousness and Experience*
 New Sci - v153 - Mr 1 '97 - p48 [51-250]
 TLS - F 7 '97 - p25+ [501+]
Lycett, Andrew - *Ian Fleming*
 Quad - v40 - O '96 - p83+ [501+]
Lydon, Susan Gordon - *The Knitting Sutra*
 BL - v93 - Mr 15 '97 - p1219 [51-250]
Lye, Keith - *Cold Climates*
 c TES - Mr 21 '97 - p18* [251-500]
 Dry Climates
 c TES - Mr 21 '97 - p18* [251-500]
 Equatorial Climates
 c TES - Mr 21 '97 - p18* [251-500]
 Passport to Russia
 c HB Guide - v7 - Fall '96 - p382 [51-250]
 The Portable World Factbook
 yr Kliatt - v30 - N '96 - p27 [51-250]
 Temperate Climates
 c TES - Mr 21 '97 - p18* [251-500]
Lykes, Dorothy Raitt - *Cobalt Blue*
 Sm Pr R - v28 - Je '96 - p4 [251-500]
Lyle, Emily - *Scottish Ballads*
 Folkl - v107 - '96 - p126 [501+]
Lyle, James R - *The Managed Care Handbook. 2nd Ed.*
 SciTech - v20 - D '96 - p38 [51-250]
Lyle, Katie Letcher - *The Foraging Gourmet*
 BL - v93 - Mr 15 '97 - p1216 [51-250]
 PW - v244 - Mr 3 '97 - p70 [51-250]
Lyly, John - *Endymion*
 Choice - v34 - Mr '97 - p1164 [51-250]
Lyman, Henry - *After Frost*
 PW - v243 - S 30 '96 - p84 [51-250]
Lyman, J Rebecca - *Christology and Cosmology*
 Rel St Rev - v22 - O '96 - p301+ [501+]
Lyman, Robert D - *Treating Children and Adolescents in Residential and Inpatient Settings*
 SciTech - v20 - D '96 - p53 [51-250]
Lynas, Bryan - *Snowdonia Rocky Rambles*
 r New Sci - v153 - Mr 22 '97 - p47 [51-250]

Lynch, Aaron - *Thought Contagion*
 BW - v26 - D 29 '96 - p8 [51-250]
 KR - v64 - S 1 '96 - p1300 [251-500]
 New Sci - v153 - Mr 8 '97 - p42+ [501+]
 New Sci - v153 - Mr 8 '97 - p42+ [501+]
 PW - v243 - S 2 '96 - p106 [51-250]
 Reason - v28 - Ap '97 - p57+ [501+]
Lynch, Allan - *Sweat Equity*
 Quill & Q - v63 - Ja '97 - p28 [251-500]
Lynch, Anne - *Great Buildings*
 c HB Guide - v8 - Spr '97 - p138+ [51-250]
 c SLJ - v43 - Mr '97 - p203+ [51-250]
Lynch, Chris - *Babes in the Woods*
 c BL - v93 - F 15 '97 - p1023 [51-250]
 c HB - v73 - My '97 - p325+ [251-500]
 c SLJ - v43 - Mr '97 - p188 [51-250]
 Blood Relations
 y HB - v72 - S '96 - p602+ [251-500]
 y HB Guide - v7 - Fall '96 - p303 [51-250]
 y JAAL - v40 - S '96 - p70+ [251-500]
 Dog Eat Dog
 y HB - v72 - S '96 - p602+ [251-500]
 y HB Guide - v7 - Fall '96 - p303 [51-250]
 y JAAL - v40 - S '96 - p70+ [251-500]
 Johnny Chesthair
 c BL - v93 - F 15 '97 - p1023 [51-250]
 c HB - v73 - My '97 - p325+ [251-500]
 c KR - v64 - N 15 '96 - p1671+ [51-250]
 c PW - v243 - D 9 '96 - p68+ [51-250]
 c SLJ - v43 - Mr '97 - p188 [51-250]
 Mick
 y HB - v72 - S '96 - p602+ [251-500]
 y HB Guide - v7 - Fall '96 - p303 [51-250]
 y JAAL - v40 - S '96 - p70+ [251-500]
 Political Timber
 y CCB-B - v50 - N '96 - p105+ [51-250]
 y HB - v73 - Mr '97 - p201 [51-250]
 y KR - v64 - S 1 '96 - p1324 [51-250]
 c PW - v243 - O 21 '96 - p84 [51-250]
 y SLJ - v43 - Ja '97 - p115 [51-250]
 y VOYA - v19 - F '97 - p329+ [251-500]
 Scratch and the Sniffs
 c HB - v73 - My '97 - p325+ [251-500]
 Shadow Boxer
 y Kliatt - v30 - S '96 - p5 [1-50]
 Slot Machine
 y Emerg Lib - v24 - S '96 - p24+ [1-50]
 y Emerg Lib - v24 - S '96 - p27 [1-50]
 y Kliatt - v31 - Ja '97 - p8+ [51-250]
Lynch, Claudia - *I Do Veils--So Can You*
 LJ - v121 - D '96 - p90+ [51-250]
Lynch, David K - *Color and Light in Nature*
 Am Sci - v84 - N '96 - p599+ [501+]
Lynch, Frederick R - *The Diversity Machine*
 BL - v93 - Ja '97 - p794 [51-250]
 PW - v243 - D 2 '96 - p50 [51-250]
 WSJ-Cent - v99 - Ja 9 '97 - pA8 [501+]
Lynch, John - *Latin American Revolutions 1808-1826*
 HAHR - v77 - F '97 - p125+ [501+]
Lynch, Lee - *Off the Rag*
 BL - v93 - S 1 '96 - p56+ [51-250]
 Utne R - Ja '97 - p96+ [1-50]
Lynch, Michael, 1948- - *Scientific Practice and Ordinary Action*
 Isis - v87 - D '96 - p766+ [501+]
 The Spectacle of History
 Choice - v34 - Ja '97 - p863+ [51-250]
Lynch, Richard Chigley - *Broadway, Movie, TV, and Studio Cast Musicals on Record*
 r ARBA - v28 - '97 - p471+ [51-250]
 r BL - v93 - Ap 1 '97 - p1352 [251-500]
 r Choice - v34 - F '97 - p946+ [51-250]
 r R&R Bk N - v12 - F '97 - p70 [51-250]
Lynch, Roslyn - *Gender Segregation in the Barbadian Labour Market 1946 and 1980*
 JEL - v34 - D '96 - p2071 [51-250]
Lynch, Thomas - *The Undertaking: Life Studies from the Dismal Trade*
 KR - v65 - My 1 '97 - p699 [251-500]
 Obs - Ap 6 '97 - p17* [501+]
 PW - v244 - My 5 '97 - p184 [51-250]
Lynch, Vincent J - *Caring for the HIV/AIDS Caregiver*
 SciTech - v21 - Mr '97 - p56 [51-250]
Lynch, Wayne - *A Is for Arctic (Illus. by Wayne Lynch)*
 y Kliatt - v31 - Mr '97 - p34 [51-250]
 y SB - v33 - Mr '97 - p46 [51-250]
Lynd, Staughton - *Living inside Our Hope*
 LJ - v122 - Ap 15 '97 - p103 [51-250]
 PW - v244 - Ap 21 '97 - p52+ [51-250]
Lynde, Stan - *The Bodacious Kid*
 Roundup M - v4 - D '96 - p28 [251-500]

Lynds, Gayle - *Masquerade*
    Arm Det - v29 - Fall '96 - p403 [51-250]
    Arm Det - v29 - Fall '96 - p437
Lyne, Alice - *A My Name Is... (Illus. by Lynne Cravath)*
    c PW - v244 - F 17 '97 - p218 [51-250]
Lyne, R O A M - *Horace: Behind the Public Poetry*
    AJP - v117 - Win '96 - p657+ [501+]
Lyne, Sandford - *Ten-Second Rainshowers (Illus. by Virginia Halstead)*
    c HB Guide - v7 - Fall '96 - p365 [51-250]
    c SLJ - v42 - D '96 - p132 [51-250]
    y VOYA - v19 - D '96 - p292 [51-250]
Lynn, Kenneth S - *Charlie Chaplin and His Times*
    BL - v93 - F 1 '97 - p919 [51-250]
    Ent W - Ap 18 '97 - p62 [51-250]
    KR - v65 - Ja 1 '97 - p42 [251-500]
    LATBR - Mr 16 '97 - p3+ [501+]
    Nat R - v49 - Ap 7 '97 - p48+ [501+]
    NYTBR - v102 - Mr 30 '97 - p6 [501+]
    NYTLa - v146 - Ap 9 '97 - pC19 [501+]
    PW - v244 - Ja 20 '97 - p384 [51-250]
    Wil Q - v21 - Spr '97 - p107 [251-500]
    WSJ-Cent - v99 - Mr 7 '97 - pA12 [501+]
Lynn, Lawrence E, Jr. - *Public Management as Art, Science, and Practice*
    Pol Stud J - v24 - Sum '96 - p333 [51-250]
Lynn, Loretta - *Coal Miner's Daughter*
    CAY - v17 - Win '96 - p6 [51-250]
    LJ - v121 - N 1 '96 - p42 [1 50]
Lynn, Matthew - *Birds of Prey*
    KR - v65 - F 15 '97 - p278 [251-500]
    LJ - v122 - Ap 15 '97 - p92 [51-250]
    PW - v244 - F 17 '97 - p203 [51-250]
Lynn, Stephen G - *Medical Emergency*
    r BL - v93 - F 1 '97 - p957 [1-50]
Lynn-Jones, Sean M - *Global Dangers*
    For Aff - v75 - S '96 - p142+ [51-250]
Lynton, Linda - *The Sari: Styles, Patterns, History, Techniques*
    Am Craft - v56 - Ag '96 - p62 [1-50]
    Surface DJ - v21 - Fall '96 - p34 [501+]
Lyon, Edwin A - *A New Deal for Southeastern Archaeology*
    r Am Ant - v62 - Ja '97 - p154+ [501+]
    Am Sci - v85 - Mr '97 - p190+ [501+]
Lyon, Eugene - *Pedro Menendez De Aviles*
    r HAHR - v76 - Ag '96 - p568 [251-500]
Lyon, George Ella - *Ada's Pal (Illus. by Marguerite Casparian)*
    c BL - v93 - S 15 '96 - p248 [51-250]
    c CBRS - v25 - Ja '97 - p51+ [51-250]
    c HB Guide - v8 - Spr '97 - p38 [51-250]
    c SLJ - v42 - S '96 - p184 [51-250]
    A Day at Damp Camp (Illus. by Peter Catalanotto)
    c HB Guide - v7 - Fall '96 - p265 [51-250]
    A Wordful Child (Illus. by Ann W Olson)
    c BL - v93 - S 1 '96 - p121 [51-250]
    c HB - v72 - S '96 - p613 [51-250]
    c HB Guide - v7 - Fall '96 - p372 [51-250]
    c SLJ - v43 - Ja '97 - p102 [51-250]
Lyon, James K - *Brecht Unbound*
    Ger Q - v70 - Win '97 - p87+ [501+]
Lyon, Jeff - *Altered Fates*
    New Sci - v153 - Mr 8 '97 - p44 [1-50]
    NYTBR - v101 - N 24 '96 - p32 [1-50]
    PW - v243 - S 23 '96 - p73 [1-50]
Lyon, William S - *Encyclopedia of Native American Healing*
    r ARBA - v27 - '96 - p158 [51-250]
    r LJ - v122 - Mr 15 '97 - p56 [51-250]
Lyons, Gene, 1943- - *Fools for Scandal*
    Atl - v278 - O '96 - p113+ [501+]
    y BL - v92 - Ag '96 - p1862+ [501+]
    y BL - v92 - Ag '96 - p1890 [1-50]
    CJR - v35 - S '96 - p58+ [501+]
Lyons, Gene Martin - *Beyond Westphalia?*
    APSR - v90 - D '96 - p956+ [501+]
Lyons, Genevieve - *Lucy Leighton's Journey*
    BL - v93 - Ap 1 '97 - p1280 [51-250]
Lyons, John D - *Critical Tales*
    Ren Q - v50 - Spr '97 - p345+ [501+]
    The Tragedy of Origins
    Choice - v34 - D '96 - p619 [51-250]
Lyons, Louis - *All You Wanted to Know about Mathematics...but Were Afraid to Ask*
    y New Sci - v151 - S 28 '96 - p44+ [501+]
Lyons, Lyman - *You Do Teach Atoms, Don't You?*
    J Chem Ed - v73 - Ap '96 - pA92+ [51-250]
Lyons, M C - *The Arabian Epic. Vols. 1-3*
    Choice - v34 - O '96 - p273+ [51-250]
    WLT - v70 - Sum '96 - p756 [51-250]

Lyons, Mary E - *Painting Dreams*
    c CCB-B - v50 - S '96 - p21 [51-250]
    c HB Guide - v7 - Fall '96 - p356 [51-250]
Lyons, Michael E G - *Electroactive Polymer Electrochemistry. Pt. 2*
    SciTech - v20 - S '96 - p16 [51-250]
Lyons, Paul - *New Left, New Right, and the Legacy of the Sixties*
    Choice - v34 - Mr '97 - p1200 [51-250]
Lyons, Renee F - *Relationships in Chronic Illness and Disability*
    JMF - v59 - F '97 - p236+ [251-500]
Lyons, Richard G - *Understanding Digital Signal Processing*
    SciTech - v21 - Mr '97 - p87 [51-250]
Lyons, Sherry H - *Accomack County, Virginia Early Marriage Records. Vols. 1-2*
    r EGH - v50 - N '96 - p189+ [51-250]
Lyons, Stephen J - *Landscape of the Heart*
    Bloom Rev - v16 - N '96 - p18 [51-250]
Lyons, Steve - *Time of Your Life*
    SF Chr - v18 - O '96 - p77+ [51-250]
Lyons, Thomas P - *The Economic Transformation of South China*
    Ch Rev Int - v3 - Fall '96 - p495+ [501+]
Lyotard, Jean-Francois - *Libidinal Economy*
    TranslRevS - v1 - My '95 - p8 [51-250]
Lyssiotis, Tess - *A White Sports Coat and Other Plays*
    Aust Bk R - D '96 - p78+ [501+]
Lytle, Andrew - *The Velvet Horn*
    W&I - v11 - Jl '96 - p251 [251-500]
    W&I - v11 - Jl '96 - p259+ [501+]

M

M. Boothe and Associates - *Promoting Issues and Ideas. Rev. Ed.*
JEL - v34 - S '96 - p1462 [51-250]

Ma, Bo - *Blood Red Sunset*
Ch Rev Int - v3 - Fall '96 - p501+ [501+]
Cu H - v95 - S '96 - p290 [251-500]
y Kliatt - v30 - S '96 - p26 [51-250]
NYTBR - v101 - Jl 21 '96 - p28 [51-250]

Ma, Zhi-Ming - *Dirichlet Forms and Stochastic Processes*
SIAM Rev - v38 - S '96 - p545 [1-50]

Maach, Mary Niles - *Aspirations and Mentoring in an Academic Environment*
CLW - v66 - Je '96 - p37+ [51-250]

Maag, Karin - *Seminary or University?*
R&R Bk N - v12 - F '97 - p66 [51-250]

Maalouf, Amin - *Les Echelles Du Levant*
BL - v93 - F 1 '97 - p930 [1-50]
The Gardens of Light
Econ - v342 - Mr 15 '97 - p15*+ [501+]
TLS - D 13 '96 - p22 [501+]
Samarkand: A Novel
Choice - v34 - S '96 - p133 [51-250]
MEJ - v50 - Sum '96 - p454 [51-250]
WLT - v70 - Sum '96 - p755+ [501+]

Maar, Paul - *El Dia En Que Desaparecio Tia Marga (Illus. by Raul)*
BL - v93 - F 15 '97 - p1032 [1-50]

Maas, Paula - *The MEND Clinic Guide to Natural Medicine for Menopause and Beyond*
LJ - v122 - My 1 '97 - p133+ [51-250]

Maas, Peter - *Underboss: Sammy the Bull Gravano's Story of Life in the Mafia*
BL - v93 - My 1 '97 - p1459 [51-250]
Time - My 12 '97 - p90 [51-250]

Maas, Stephen A - *Nonlinear Microwave Circuits*
SciTech - v20 - D '96 - p79 [51-250]

Maasdorp, Gavin - *Can South and Southern Africa Become Globally Competitive Economies?*
Choice - v34 - My '97 - p1546 [51-250]

Maass, Donald - *The Career Novelist*
Roundup M - v4 - D '96 - p29 [51-250]

Maass, Peter - *Love Thy Neighbor*
Ant R - v54 - Sum '96 - p380 [51-250]
NYRB - v43 - S 19 '96 - p34+ [501+]
NYTBR - v102 - Mr 9 '97 - p28 [51-250]
PW - v244 - F 24 '97 - p88 [1-50]
Trib Bks - My 4 '97 - p8 [1-50]
VV - v41 - D 31 '96 - p49 [501+]

Mabee, Carleton - *Sojourner Truth: Slave, Prophet, Legend*
NWSA Jnl - v8 - Fall '96 - p172+ [501+]

Mabes, Joni - *Everything Elvis*
PW - v244 - Ja 6 '97 - p61 [1-50]

Mabey, Richard - *Flora Britannica*
Nature - v384 - D 12 '96 - p528 [51-250]
New Sci - v152 - N 16 '96 - p56 [501+]
Obs - D 8 '96 - p17* [501+]
Spec - v277 - N 30 '96 - p58 [1-50]
TLS - D 6 '96 - p36 [501+]
The Oxford Book of Nature Writing
Nature - v386 - Ap 3 '97 - p454 [1-50]

Mabire, Jean - *Operation Minotaure*
BL - v93 - Ja '97 - p827 [1-50]

Mabro, Judy - *Veiled Half-Truths*
MEJ - v50 - Sum '96 - p457 [51-250]

The Mac
p TES - O 18 '96 - p43U [51-250]

Macafee, C I - *A Concise Ulster Dictionary*
r ILS - v16 - Spr '97 - p35 [51-250]
yr Sch Lib - v44 - N '96 - p176 [51-250]
r TLS - N 1 '96 - p10+ [501+]

Macalister, Robert Alexander Stewart - *Corpus Inscriptionum Insularum Celticarum. Vol. 1*
ILS - v16 - Spr '97 - p26 [1-50]

Macan, Edward L - *Rocking the Classics*
Books - v11 - Ap '97 - p21 [51-250]
LJ - v121 - O 15 '96 - p61 [51-250]

MacAndrew, Amanda - *Party Pieces*
PW - v243 - O 21 '96 - p72+ [51-250]

Mac An Ghaill, Mairtin - *Understanding Masculinities*
R&R Bk N - v11 - N '96 - p42 [1-50]

Mac Anna, Ferdia - *The Penguin Book of Irish Comic Writing*
TES - S 6 '96 - p8* [51-250]

Macaro, Ernesto - *Target Language, Collaborative Learning and Autonomy*
TES - Mr 14 '97 - p20* [501+]

MacArthur, Brian - *The Penguin Book of Historic Speeches*
y Kliatt - v31 - My '97 - p19+ [51-250]

Macaulay, Ambrose - *William Crolly: Archbishop of Armagh 1835-49*
EHR - v112 - F '97 - p231+ [251-500]

Macaulay, Catharine - *Letters on Education*
RES - v48 - F '97 - p121+ [501+]

Macaulay, David - *Black and White*
c New Ad - v9 - Fall '96 - p267+ [501+]
The Way Things Work. Electronic Media Version
yr Kliatt - v31 - Mr '97 - p38 [51-250]
The Way Things Work 2. Electronic Media Version
cr New Sci - v152 - D 14 '96 - p47 [51-250]

Macaulay, Rose - *Life among the English*
PW - v244 - Mr 24 '97 - p72 [1-50]
TLS - D 27 '96 - p32 [251-500]

Macauley, David - *Minding Nature*
Choice - v34 - N '96 - p479 [51-250]
JEL - v34 - D '96 - p2013 [51-250]
SB - v32 - Ag '96 - p164 [51-250]

MacBride, Roger Lea - *Little Town in the Ozarks (Illus. by David Gilleece)*
c HB Guide - v8 - Spr '97 - p71 [51-250]

MacCaffrey, Wallace T - *Elizabeth I*
HT - v46 - Jl '96 - p53 [51-250]
JMH - v68 - S '96 - p675+ [501+]
Elizabeth I: War and Politics 1588-1603
HT - v46 - Jl '96 - p53 [51-250]
Queen Elizabeth and the Making of Policy 1572-1603
HT - v46 - Jl '96 - p53 [51-250]
The Shaping of the Elizabethan Regime
HT - v46 - Jl '96 - p53 [51-250]

Maccarone, Grace - *The Gym Day Winner (Illus. by Betsy Lewin)*
c BL - v92 - Ag '96 - p1910 [51-250]
c SLJ - v43 - Ja '97 - p86 [51-250]
Monster Math (Illus. by Marge Hartelius)
c RT - O '96 - p130+ [1-50]
My Tooth Is about to Fall Out (Illus. by Betsy Lewin)
c Learning - v25 - Ag '96 - p96 [51-250]
c RT - O '96 - p131 [1-50]
Recess Mess (Illus. by Betsy Lewin)
c BL - v93 - F 1 '97 - p950 [51-250]
Sharing Time Troubles (Illus. by Betsy Lewin)
c BL - v93 - My 1 '97 - p1504 [51-250]

MacCarthy, Fiona - *William Morris: A Life for Our Times*
ELT - v39 - 4 '96 - p468+ [501+]

MacCaskill, Bridget - *The Blood Is Wild*
TLS - Ja 17 '97 - p33 [51-250]

Macchi, Jean-Daniel - *Les Samaritains: Histoire D'Une Legende Israel Et La Province De Samarie*
Rel St Rev - v22 - O '96 - p350 [51-250]

Macchia, Frank D - *Spirituality and Social Liberation*
CH - v65 - S '96 - p529+ [501+]

Macchiavelli, M - *Decoupage*
BWatch - v18 - F '97 - p2 [1-50]

Maccioli, Gerald A - *Intra-Aortic Balloon Pump Therapy*
SciTech - v20 - N '96 - p47 [51-250]

Maccoby, Hyam - *A Pariah People*
Obs - v54 - O 13 '96 - p15* [501+]

MacColl, Mary-Rose - *No Safe Place*
Aust Bk R - O '96 - p48+ [501+]
BL - v93 - My 15 '97 - p1563 [51-250]

Mac Cormac, Earl R - *Fractals of Brain, Fractals of Mind*
SciTech - v20 - D '96 - p34 [51-250]

Mac Cuarta, Brian - *Ulster 1641*
CH - v66 - Mr '97 - p126+ [501+]

MacCulloch, Diarmaid - *The Reign of Henry VIII*
Albion - v28 - Win '96 - p685+ [501+]
Historian - v59 - Win '97 - p469+ [501+]
HT - v47 - F '97 - p59+ [501+]
Thomas Cranmer: A Life
CC - v113 - D 11 '96 - p1231+ [501+]
Choice - v34 - Ja '97 - p857 [51-250]
Comw - v124 - Ap 11 '97 - p28+ [251-500]
Lon R Bks - v18 - O 31 '96 - p21+ [501+]
NYTBR - v101 - D 15 '96 - p24+ [51-250]
Spec - v276 - My 18 '96 - p38 [251-500]
TLS - My 24 '96 - p3+ [501+]
TLS - N 29 '96 - p11 [1-50]
WSJ-MW - v77 - S 12 '96 - pA12 [501+]

MacDonagh, Thomas - *Literature in Ireland*
ILS - v15 - Fall '96 - p31 [51-250]

MacDonald, A A - *The Renaissance in Scotland*
EHR - v112 - F '97 - p183+ [501+]
Lib - v18 - S '96 - p257+ [501+]

MacDonald, Amy - *Cousin Ruth's Tooth (Illus. by Marjorie Priceman)*
c HB Guide - v7 - Fall '96 - p266 [51-250]
No More Nice (Illus. by Cat Bowman Smith)
c BL - v93 - S 1 '96 - p130 [51-250]
c CCB-B - v50 - O '96 - p68+ [51-250]
c HB Guide - v8 - Spr '97 - p71 [51-250]
c KR - v64 - O 1 '96 - p1471 [51-250]
c SLJ - v42 - S '96 - p204 [51-250]
The Spider Who Created the World (Illus. by G Brian Karas)
c HB - v72 - S '96 - p582 [51-250]
c HB Guide - v7 - Fall '96 - p266 [51-250]

MacDonald, Ann-Marie - *Fall on Your Knees*
BIC - v25 - S '96 - p36+ [501+]
BL - v93 - Ap 1 '97 - p1281 [51-250]
CF - v75 - S '96 - p47 [501+]
KR - v65 - Ja 15 '97 - p84+ [251-500]
Mac - v109 - D 9 '96 - p64 [1-50]
Obs - O 27 '96 - p16* [51-250]
PW - v244 - F 24 '97 - p61 [51-250]
Quill & Q - v63 - F '97 - p50 [51-250]
TLS - O 11 '96 - p25 [501+]
Trib Bks - Ap 6 '97 - p9 [501+]

Macdonald, Anne L - *Feminine Ingenuity*
T&C - v38 - Ja '97 - p214+ [501+]

Macdonald, Cameron Lynne - *Working in the Service Society*
Choice - v34 - Mr '97 - p1247+ [51-250]

Macdonald, Caroline - *Spider Mansion*
y Magpies - v11 - My '96 - p53 [1-50]

Macdonald, Copthorne - *Toward Wisdom*
BWatch - v17 - N '96 - p4 [51-250]

MacDonald, Eleanor Kay - *A Window into History*
r Inst - v106 - Ja '97 - p54 [1-50]
r Sch Lib - v45 - F '97 - p54 [51-250]

Macdonald, Fiona - *American Frontier (Illus. by Mark Bergin)*
c Sch Lib - v45 - F '97 - p39 [51-250]
Ancient Romans (Illus. by Mark Bergin)
c Sch Lib - v45 - F '97 - p39 [51-250]
Exploring the World (Illus. by Gerald Wood)
c Ch BWatch - v7 - Ja '97 - p7 [1-50]
c HB Guide - v8 - Spr '97 - p162 [51-250]
c SLJ - v43 - Ja '97 - p97 [51-250]
First Facts about the American Frontier (Illus. by Mark Bergin)
c SLJ - v43 - Mr '97 - p204 [51-250]
First Facts about the Ancient Romans (Illus. by Mark Bergin)
c KR - v64 - N 15 '96 - p1672 [51-250]
c SLJ - v43 - Ja '97 - p104 [51-250]
A Greek Temple (Illus. by Fiona Macdonald)
y SLJ - v42 - N '96 - p39 [1-50]
A Samurai Castle (Illus. by David Antram)
c CLW - v66 - Je '96 - p47 [51-250]
A Viking Town (Illus. by Mark Bergin)
c CLW - v66 - Je '96 - p47 [51-250]
MacDonald, George - *The Gifts of the Child Christ and Other Stories and Fairy Tales. Rev. Ed.*
CC - v113 - D 11 '96 - p1233 [51-250]
Nine-C Lit - v51 - Mr '97 - p560 [1-50]
MacDonald, George F - *Haida Art*
BL - v93 - Mr 15 '97 - p1218 [51-250]
BWatch v18 F '97 p5 [51 250]
Choice - v34 - My '97 - p1486 [51-250]
LJ - v122 - My 1 '97 - p101 [51-250]
Mac - v109 - D 9 '96 - p66 [1-50]
Macdonald, Gina - *James Clavell: A Critical Companion*
y SLJ - v42 - O '96 - p158 [51-250]
SLMQ - v25 - Fall '96 - p65 [1-50]
Macdonald, J H - *The Free World*
Aust Bk R - O '96 - p45+ [501+]
MacDonald, John D - *Bright Orange for the Shroud (McGavin). Audio Version*
LJ - v122 - Mr 15 '97 - p102 [51-250]
A Deadly Shade of Gold (McGavin). Audio Version
LJ - v122 - Mr 15 '97 - p102 [51-250]
Macdonald, Kevin - *Emeric Pressburger: The Life and Death of a Screenwriter*
TES - N 22 '96 - p8* [51-250]
Imagining Reality
NS - v126 - Ja 10 '97 - p44+ [501+]
Obs - Ja 19 '97 - p16* [501+]
Macdonald, Malcolm - *The Trevarton Inheritance*
y BL - v93 - N 1 '96 - p481+ [51-250]
KR - v64 - S 1 '96 - p1260 [251-500]
LJ - v121 - N 15 '96 - p89 [51-250]
PW - v243 - S 23 '96 - p57 [51-250]
Macdonald, Mandy - *In the Mountains of Morazan*
Cu H - v96 - F '97 - p90 [251-500]
MacDonald, Margaret F - *James McNeill Whistler: Drawings, Pastels, and Watercolours*
r Art J - v55 - Win '96 - p99+ [501+]
MacDonald, Margaret Read - *Bookplay: 101 Creative Themes to Share with Young Children*
Emerg Lib - v23 - My '96 - p38 [51-250]
Old Woman Who Lived in a Vinegar Bottle (Illus. by Nancy Dunaway)
c Emerg Lib - v24 - S '96 - p46 [51-250]
Tuck-Me-In Tales (Illus. by Yvonne Davis)
c BL - v93 - O 1 '96 - p355 [51-250]
c Bloom Rev - v17 - Ja '97 - p21 [51-250]
c HB Guide - v8 - Spr '97 - p103 [51-250]
c SLJ - v42 - N '96 - p99 [51-250]
MacDonald, Michael - *Mystical Bedlam*
PQ - v74 - Fall '95 - p373+ [501+]
MacDonald, Robert H - *The Language of Empire*
EHR - v111 - N '96 - p1333+ [251-500]
VS - v39 - Aut '95 - p101+ [501+]
MacDonald, Robert I - *Great Lakes Archaeology and Paleoecology*
Am Ant - v62 - Ja '97 - p157+ [501+]
Macdonald, Ross - *The Barbarous Coast*
Arm Det - v29 - Sum '96 - p294 [1-50]
Black Money
Arm Det - v29 - Sum '96 - p295 [1-50]
Blue City
Arm Det - v29 - Sum '96 - p294 [1-50]
The Blue Hammer
Arm Det - v29 - Sum '96 - p295 [1-50]
The Blue Hammer (Parker). Audio Version
y Kliatt - v31 - My '97 - p35 [51-250]
The Chill
Arm Det - v29 - Sum '96 - p295 [1-50]
The Dark Tunnel
Arm Det - v29 - Sum '96 - p294 [1-50]

The Doomsters
Arm Det - v29 - Sum '96 - p294 [1-50]
The Drowning Pool
Arm Det - v29 - Sum '96 - p294 [1-50]
The Far Side of the Dollar
Arm Det - v29 - Sum '96 - p295 [1-50]
Bks & Cult - v3 - Mr '97 - p38 [51-250]
The Ferguson Affair
Arm Det - v29 - Sum '96 - p295 [1-50]
Find a Victim
Arm Det - v29 - Sum '96 - p294 [1-50]
The Galton Case
Arm Det - v29 - Sum '96 - p294+ [1-50]
Bks & Cult - v3 - Mr '97 - p38 [51-250]
The Goodbye Look
Arm Det - v29 - Sum '96 - p295 [1-50]
The Instant Enemy
Arm Det - v29 - Sum '96 - p295 [1-50]
The Ivory Grin
Arm Det - v29 - Sum '96 - p294 [1-50]
Meet Me at the Morgue
Arm Det - v29 - Sum '96 - p294 [1-50]
The Moving Target
Arm Det - v29 - Sum '96 - p294 [1-50]
Sleeping Beauty
Arm Det - v29 - Sum '96 - p295 [1-50]
The Three Roads
Arm Det - v29 - Sum '96 - p294 [1-50]
Trouble Follows Me
Arm Det - v29 - Sum '96 - p294 [1-50]
The Underground Man
Arm Det - v29 - Sum '96 - p295 [1-50]
Bks & Cult - v3 - Mr '97 - p38 [51-250]
The Way Some People Die
Arm Det - v29 - Sum '96 - p294 [1-50]
The Wycherly Woman
Arm Det - v29 - Sum '96 - p295 [1-50]
The Zebra Striped Hearse
Arm Det - v29 - Sum '96 - p295 [1-50]
MacDonald, Ruth K - *Beatrix Potter*
RSR - v24 - 3 '96 - p24 [51-250]
MacDonald, Scott B - *Fast Forward*
Parameters - v26 - Win '96 - p154 [1-50]
MacDonald, Sebastian K - *Moral Theology and Suffering*
Theol St - v57 - S '96 - p574 [251-500]
Macdonald, Sharon - *Theorizing Museums*
Socio R - v44 - N '96 - p775+ [501+]
MacDonald, Sharon, 1942- - *Squish, Sort, Paint and Build (Illus. by Rebecca Jones)*
Ch BWatch - v6 - S '96 - p8 [1-50]
MacDonald, Susan Peck - *Professional Academic Writing in the Humanities and Social Sciences*
Col Comp - v47 - O '96 - p439 [51-250]
MacDonald, Suse - *Peck, Slither and Slide (Illus. by Suse MacDonald)*
c BL - v93 - Ap 1 '97 - p1335+ [51-250]
c PW - v244 - Mr 31 '97 - p76 [51-250]
MacDonald, Thomas A - *The Time of the Wolf*
c Can CL - v22 - Fall '96 - p119+ [501+]
MacDonald, William L - *Hadrian's Village and Its Legacy*
Rel St Rev - v23 - Ja '97 - p66 [51-250]
Macdonell, A G - *Napoleon and His Marshals*
Spec - v278 - F 8 '97 - p39 [501+]
MacDonnell, Francis - *Insidious Foes*
Parameters - v26 - Aut '96 - p155+ [501+]
MacDougal, Bonnie - *Breach of Trust*
BL - v93 - O 1 '96 - p322 [51-250]
KR - v64 - Ag 15 '96 - p1178 [251-500]
Macdougall, J D - *A Short History of Planet Earth*
Choice - v34 - Mr '97 - p1189 [51-250]
Nature - v382 - Ag 1 '96 - p414 [51-250]
y SB - v33 - Mr '97 - p45 [51-250]
Macdougall, Lee - *High Life*
Quill & Q - v63 - Mr '97 - p76 [251-500]
Mace, Chris - *The Art and Science of Assessment in Psychotherapy*
SciTech - v20 - S '96 - p33 [1-50]
Mace, Jane - *Literacy Language and Community Publishing*
JAAL - v40 - D '96 - p323+ [501+]
Mace, Nancy A - *Henry Fielding's Novels and the Classical Tradition*
Choice - v34 - N '96 - p457 [51-250]
Macedo, Jorge Braga De - *Currency Convertibility*
JEL - v34 - D '96 - p2096+ [51-250]
R&R Bk N - v11 - D '96 - p36 [51-250]
Macedo, Stephen - *Reassessing the Sixties*
BW - v26 - N 24 '96 - p8 [501+]
Econ - v341 - O 19 '96 - p3*+ [501+]
PW - v243 - S 16 '96 - p59 [51-250]

MacEoin, Denis - *Rituals in Babism and Baha'ism*
Rel St Rev - v22 - O '96 - p356 [51-250]
MacEoin, Gary - *The People's Church*
Am - v175 - D 14 '96 - p26 [501+]
Macesich, George - *Integration and Stabilization*
JEL - v35 - Mr '97 - p218 [51-250]
R&R Bk N - v11 - N '96 - p34 [51-250]
Transformation and Emerging Markets
Choice - v34 - My '97 - p1547 [51-250]
Macfie, A L - *Ataturk*
EHR - v112 - Ap '97 - p525 [251-500]
MacGill-Callahan, Sheila - *And Still the Turtle Watched (Illus. by Barry Moser)*
c Inst - v105 - My '96 - p39 [1-50]
c PW - v243 - N 18 '96 - p78 [51-250]
MacGilvray, Marian W - *Electronic Capabilities of Federal Depository Libraries, Summer 1994*
J Gov Info - v23 - S '96 - p546 [51-250]
MacGinley, Rosa - *A Dynamic of Hope*
RR - v56 - Mr '97 - p221 [1-50]
MacGregor, Arthur - *Sir Hans Sloane: Collector, Scientist, Antiquary, Founding Father of the British Museum*
AJA - v100 - O '96 - p769+ [501+]
EHR - v112 - Ap '97 - p482 [251-500]
MacGregor, Greg - *Overland: The California Emigrant Trail of 1841-1870*
BWatch - v17 - S '96 - p6 [51-250]
NYTBR v101 D 8 '96 p74 [51 250]
MacGregor, James G - *Reinforced Concrete. 3rd Ed.*
SciTech - v20 - D '96 - p65 [51-250]
MacGregor, Rob - *Hawk Moon*
y HB Guide - v8 - Spr '97 - p81 [51-250]
y SLJ - v42 - N '96 - p123 [51-250]
y VOYA - v19 - F '97 - p330 [251-500]
MacGregor, Robert S - *WWW.Security: How to Build a Secure World Wide Web Connection*
SciTech - v21 - Mr '97 - p89 [51-250]
MacGregor, Roy - *Murder at Hockey Camp*
c Quill & Q - v63 - Mr '97 - p81 [51-250]
The Screech Owl's Northern Adventure
c Quill & Q - v62 - S '96 - p74 [51-250]
The Seven A.M. Practice
Mac - v109 - D 16 '96 - p71+ [51-250]
Quill & Q - v62 - N '96 - p39 [251-500]
MacGregor-Villarreal, Mary - *Brazilian Folk Narrative Scholarship*
r Hisp - v79 - D '96 - p814+ [501+]
r WestFolk - v55 - Sum '96 - p247+ [251-500]
Machado, Ana Maria - *Nina Bonita (Illus. by Rosana Faria)*
c HB Guide - v7 - Fall '96 - p266 [51-250]
c SLJ - v42 - D '96 - p100 [51-250]
Machan, Tibor R - *Liberty for the Twenty-First Century*
APSR - v90 - D '96 - p888+ [501+]
CPR - v16 - Je '96 - p192+ [501+]
RM - v50 - D '96 - p411+ [501+]
Machan, Tim William - *Textual Criticism and Middle English Texts*
MLR - v91 - O '96 - p954+ [501+]
Specu - v71 - O '96 - p975+ [501+]
Machann, Clinton - *The Genre of Autobiography in Victorian Literature*
Nine-C Lit - v50 - Mr '96 - p533+ [501+]
VS - v39 - Spr '96 - p409+ [501+]
Machholz, Don - *An Observer's Guide to Comet Hale-Bopp*
S&T - v93 - F '97 - p56+ [501+]
Machi, Junji - *Ultrasound for Surgeons*
SciTech - v21 - Mr '97 - p59 [51-250]
Machiavelli, Niccolo - *The Discourses (Crick)*
Ren Q - v49 - Aut '96 - p573+ [501+]
Discourses on Livy (Mansfield)
Choice - v34 - D '96 - p689 [51-250]
RP - v59 - Spr '97 - p404+ [501+]
TLS - S 20 '96 - p8 [501+]
Machiavelli and His Friends
LJ - v121 - N 1 '96 - p90 [51-250]
Machiavelli's The Prince
Ren Q - v49 - Aut '96 - p573+ [501+]
The Machineel Journal
p LMR - v15 - Fall '96 - p42+ [51-250]
Machlis, Gary E - *An Atlas of Social Indicators for the Upper Columbia River Basin*
r J Gov Info - v23 - S '96 - p582 [51-250]
Machlis, Joseph - *Allegro*
BL - v93 - My 15 '97 - p1563 [51-250]
KR - v65 - Mr 15 '97 - p408 [251-500]
PW - v244 - Ap 7 '97 - p75+ [51-250]
Macho, James - *Everyone's Guide to Outpatient Surgery*
r BL - v93 - F 1 '97 - p957 [1-50]

Machon, Kirsty - *Immortality*
　　Aust Bk R - D '96 - p65+ [501+]
Machotka, Pavel - *Cezanne: Landscape into Art*
　　A Art - v60 - Jl '96 - p80 [251-500]
　　Art J - v55 - Win '96 - p95+ [501+]
　　BM - v138 - S '96 - p612+ [501+]
　　Choice - v34 - S '96 - p114 [51-250]
Machover, Jacobo - *La Habana*
　　BL - v93 - Ap 1 '97 - p1284 [1-50]
　　El Heraldo De Las Malas Noticias
　　BL - v93 - Mr 15 '97 - p1232 [1-50]
Machover, Wilma - *Sound Choices*
　　Am MT - v46 - D '96 - p54 [501+]
Maciel, David R - *Chicanas/Chicanos at the Crossroads*
　　Choice - v34 - O '96 - p366 [51-250]
MacInnes, Gordon - *Wrong for All the Right Reasons*
　　Bl S - v26 - Sum '96 - p66 [51-250]
　　Rapport - v19 - 6 '96 - p30 [251-500]
MacInnes, Helen - *The Hidden Target (Pacey). Audio Version*
　　BWatch - v17 - D '96 - p10 [1-50]
MacInnis, Joseph - *Saving the Oceans*
　　BL - v93 - Ja '97 - p792 [51-250]
　　SB - v33 - Ja '97 - p6+ [251-500]
MacIntyre, R P - *Takes: Stories for Young Adults*
　　y BIC - v26 - F '97 - p32+ [501+]
　　y Quill & Q - v62 - My '96 - p334+ [501+]
MacIvor, Daniel - *Here Lies Henry*
　　Quill & Q - v63 - Ja '97 - p18 [1-50]
Mack, Burton L - *The Lost Gospel*
　　Bks & Cult - v1 - N '95 - p3+ [51-250]
　　Who Wrote the New Testament?
　　Rel St Rev - v23 - Ap '97 - p176 [51-250]
　　Skeptic - v4 - 2 '96 - p110 [51-250]
Mack, Dana - *The Assault on Parenthood*
　　BL - v93 - My 1 '97 - p1465 [51-250]
　　KR - v65 - Ap 1 '97 - p528+ [251-500]
　　PW - v244 - Ap 14 '97 - p62+ [51-250]
　　WSJ-Cent - v99 - My 8 '97 - pA20 [501+]
Mack, Daniel - *The Rustic Furniture Companion*
　　Am Craft - v56 - Ag '96 - p62 [1-50]
Mack, Dorothy - *The Counterfeit Widow*
　　LJ - v121 - N 15 '96 - p50 [51-250]
Mack, William C - *Worldwide Guide to Equivalent Nonferrous Metals and Alloys. 3rd Ed.*
　　r ARBA - v28 - '97 - p597 [51-250]
Mackail, J W - *The Life of William Morris*
　　CR - v269 - O '96 - p222 [51-250]
Mackay, Angus - *Atlas of Medieval Europe*
　　r HT - v46 - O '96 - p59 [1-50]
Mackay, Claire - *Touching All the Bases*
　　c Ch BWatch - v6 - Jl '96 - p2 [1-50]
MacKay, Donald - *Train Country*
　　Can Lit - Win '96 - p150+ [501+]
Mackay, Harvey - *Dig Your Well before You're Thirsty*
　　PW - v244 - Mr 31 '97 - p53 [51-250]
Mackay, James - *Michael Collins: A Life*
　　BL - v93 - Ja '97 - p811 [251-500]
　　Choice - v34 - Mr '97 - p1221 [51-250]
　　HT - v46 - O '96 - p58 [1-50]
　　KR - v64 - N 15 '96 - p1656 [251-500]
　　LJ - v122 - Ja '97 - p112 [51-250]
　　Mar Crp G - v81 - Mr '97 - p73+ [501+]
　　PW - v243 - D 9 '96 - p56 [51-250]
　　TLS - S 27 '96 - p7 [501+]
　　Vagabond of Verse
　　Can Lit - Win '96 - p181+ [501+]
MacKay, Ron - *20th Fighter Group*
　　A & S Sm - v11 - O '96 - p88 [1-50]
Mackay, Sheila - *Behind the Facade*
　　LJ - v122 - F 1 '97 - p77 [51-250]
Mackay, Shena - *The Orchard on Fire*
　　BL - v93 - S 15 '96 - p220 [51-250]
　　LJ - v121 - O 1 '96 - p127+ [51-250]
　　NYTBR - v101 - N 3 '96 - p11 [501+]
　　NYTBR - v101 - D 8 '96 - p82 [1-50]
　　PW - v243 - N 4 '96 - p37 [1-50]
　　TES - Ag 23 '96 - p27 [251-500]
Mackel, Kathy - *A Season of Comebacks*
　　c CCB-B - v50 - Ap '97 - p289 [51-250]
　　c KR - v65 - Mr 15 '97 - p465 [51-250]
Macken, Deirdre - *Smoke*
　　Aust Bk R - D '96 - p63 [501+]
MacKendrick, Paul - *The Speeches of Cicero*
　　r AJP - v117 - Win '96 - p654+ [501+]
Mackenzie, Ann L - *Francisco De Rojas Zorrilla Y Agustin Moreto*
　　Hisp - v79 - S '96 - p449+ [501+]
MacKenzie, David S - *Perennial Ground Covers*
　　PW - v244 - My 5 '97 - p205 [51-250]

MacKenzie, Donald - *Knowing Machines*
　　CS - v26 - Mr '97 - p243+ [501+]
　　JEL - v34 - S '96 - p1485 [51-250]
　　R&R Bk N - v12 - F '97 - p97 [51-250]
　　Socio R - v44 - N '96 - p767+ [501+]
　　SocSciComR - v14 - Fall '96 - p353+ [501+]
Mackenzie, G Calvin - *Bucking the Deficit*
　　JEL - v34 - S '96 - p1423 [51-250]
　　The Irony of Reform
　　Choice - v34 - O '96 - p361 [51-250]
Mackenzie, Harry - *Command Performance, USA!*
　　r ARBA - v28 - '97 - p355 [251-500]
Mackenzie, Hector - *Documents on Canadian External Relations. Vols. 14-15*
　　Can Hist R - v78 - Mr '97 - p118+ [501+]
Mackenzie, S P - *The Home Guard*
　　AHR - v102 - F '97 - p114+ [251-500]
　　Albion - v28 - Fall '96 - p538+ [501+]
　　J Mil H - v60 - O '96 - p791+ [251-500]
Mackerras, Colin - *China's Minority Cultures*
　　R&R Bk N - v11 - N '96 - p15 [51-250]
　　Eastern Asia
　　EHR - v111 - S '96 - p1042+ [251-500]
Mackesy, Piers - *British Victory in Egypt 1801*
　　EHR - v112 - Ap '97 - p497+ [501+]
　　J Mil H - v61 - Ja '97 - p162+ [251-500]
Mackey, James P - *Power and Christian Ethics*
　　Theol St - v57 - Mr '96 - p176+ [501+]
Mackey, Sandra - *The Iranians: Persia, Islam and the Soul of a Nation*
　　BW - v26 - Ag 4 '96 - p7 [501+]
　　For Aff - v75 - S '96 - p155+ [51-250]
　　LATBR - Jl 7 '96 - p3 [501+]
　　MEQ - v4 - Mr '97 - p88+ [251-500]
　　Nat - v263 - N 11 '96 - p32+ [501+]
　　NYTBR - v101 - Ag 25 '96 - p16+ [501+]
Mackey, Wade C - *The American Father*
　　Choice - v34 - My '97 - p1584 [51-250]
　　R&R Bk N - v12 - F '97 - p52 [51-250]
MacKillop, Ian - *F.R. Leavis: A Life in Criticism*
　　KR - v65 - Mr 15 '97 - p443 [251-500]
　　LJ - v122 - Ap 15 '97 - p81+ [51-250]
　　PW - v244 - My 5 '97 - p190 [51-250]
　　TES - Ag 23 '96 - p25 [501+]
MacKillop, Peigi - *Information for Scotland II*
　　LAR - v98 - S '96 - p482 [51-250]
　　LR - v45 - 8 '96 - p48 [251-500]
MacKinnon, Catharine A - *Only Words*
　　NYTBR - v102 - Ja 19 '97 - p28 [1-50]
　　QJS - v82 - N '96 - p433+ [501+]
　　Trib Bks - Ja 12 '97 - p2 [1-50]
MacKinnon, Debbie - *Billy's Boots (Illus. by Anthea Sieveking)*
　　c HB Guide - v7 - Fall '96 - p241 [51-250]
　　Cathy's Cake (Illus. by Anthea Sieveking)
　　c HB Guide - v7 - Fall '96 - p241 [51-250]
　　Daniel's Duck (Illus. by Anthea Sieveking)
　　c SLJ - v43 - Mr '97 - p162 [51-250]
　　In the Bathroom (Illus. by Geoff Dann)
　　c Books - v10 - Je '96 - p25 [51-250]
　　c Magpies - v11 - S '96 - p26 [51-250]
　　In the Bedroom (Illus. by Geoff Dann)
　　c Books - v10 - Je '96 - p25 [51-250]
　　c Magpies - v11 - S '96 - p26 [51-250]
　　In the Garden (Illus. by Geoff Dann)
　　c Books - v10 - Je '96 - p25 [51-250]
　　c JB - v60 - Ag '96 - p150 [51-250]
　　c Magpies - v11 - S '96 - p26 [51-250]
　　In the Kitchen (Illus. by Geoff Dann)
　　c Books - v10 - Je '96 - p25 [51-250]
　　c Magpies - v11 - S '96 - p26 [51-250]
　　Ken's Kitten (Illus. by Anthea Sieveking)
　　c HB Guide - v7 - Fall '96 - p241 [51-250]
　　Meg's Monkey (Illus. by Anthea Sieveking)
　　c HB Guide - v7 - Fall '96 - p241 [51-250]
　　Pippa's Puppy (Illus. by Anthea Sieveking)
　　c SLJ - v43 - Mr '97 - p162 [51-250]
　　Sarah's Shovel (Illus. by Anthea Sieveking)
　　c SLJ - v43 - Mr '97 - p162 [51-250]
　　Tom's Train (Illus. by Anthea Sieveking)
　　c SLJ - v43 - Mr '97 - p162 [51-250]
　　What Am I? (Illus. by Anthea Sieveking)
　　c HB Guide - v7 - Fall '96 - p241 [51-250]
MacKinnon, Douglas - *First Victim*
　　KR - v65 - My 1 '97 - p668+ [251-500]
MacKinnon, John - *Wild China*
　　FEER - v159 - D 19 '96 - p58+ [501+]
Mackintosh, Prudence - *Just as We Were*
　　LJ - v121 - O 1 '96 - p110 [51-250]
Macklem, Patrick - *Aboriginal Self-Government*
　　J Gov Info - v23 - S '96 - p610 [51-250]

Mackler, Tasha - *Murder...by Category*
　　r RQ - v36 - Win '96 - p223 [51-250]
Mackoff, Barbara - *Growing a Girl*
　　PW - v243 - S 16 '96 - p79+ [51-250]
Mack Smith, Denis - *Mazzini*
　　PW - v243 - D 9 '96 - p66 [1-50]
MacLachlan, Alastair - *The Rise and Fall of Revolutionary England*
　　Choice - v34 - N '96 - p518+ [51-250]
　　HRNB - v25 - Win '97 - p68+ [501+]
　　Lon R Bks - v18 - O 31 '96 - p23+ [501+]
MacLachlan, Liz - *Making Project Management Work for You*
　　LAR - v99 - Mr '97 - p164 [51-250]
MacLachlan, Patricia - *All the Places to Love (Illus. by Mike Wimmer)*
　　c LA - v73 - S '96 - p352 [51-250]
　　Skylark
　　c PW - v244 - F 3 '97 - p108 [1-50]
　　What You Know First (Illus. by Barry Moser)
　　c RT - v50 - O '96 - p153 [51-250]
Maclaine, Shirley - *My Lucky Stars*
　　PW - v243 - O 14 '96 - p81 [1-50]
MacLaverty, Bernard - *Walking the Dog and Other Stories*
　　NYTBR - v101 - S 8 '96 - p36 [1-50]
Maclay, William - *The Diary of William Maclay and Other Notes on Senate Debates*
　　W&M Q - v53 - O '96 - p836+ [501+]
Maclean, Charles - *The Silence*
　　Books - v10 - Je '96 - p23 [1-50]
　　Books - v11 - Ap '97 - p22 [51-250]
　　PW - v244 - Ja 13 '97 - p72 [51-250]
Maclean, D J H - *Optical Line Systems*
　　SciTech - v21 - Mr '97 - p87 [51-250]
Maclean, Kenneth - *Scotland's Changing Landscapes*
　　c Sch Lib - v44 - Ag '96 - p124 [51-250]
Maclean, Norman - *A River Runs through It and Other Stories*
　　Aethlon - v13 - Fall '95 - p79+ [501+]
　　Aethlon - v13 - Fall '95 - p87+ [501+]
　　Young Men and Fire
　　y Kliatt - v31 - Mr '97 - p5 [51-250]
MacLean, Rory - *The Oatmeal Ark*
　　Obs - Mr 2 '97 - p17* [501+]
　　Quill & Q - v63 - F '97 - p37 [501+]
Maclear, J F - *Church and State in the Modern Era*
　　Bks & Cult - v2 - Mr '96 - p31 [51-250]
MacLennan, Hugh - *Dear Marian, Dear Hugh*
　　Can Lit - Spr '97 - p237+ [501+]
　　Essays CW - Spr '96 - p145+ [501+]
MacLennan, Nigel - *Counselling for Managers*
　　R&R Bk N - v11 - N '96 - p35 [51-250]
MacLennan, Robert S - *Early Christian Texts on Jews and Judaism*
　　Rel Ed - v91 - Fall '96 - p604 [51-250]
MacLeod, Alison - *The Changeling*
　　BIC - v26 - Mr '97 - p40 [251-500]
　　BL - v93 - N 15 '96 - p572 [51-250]
　　KR - v64 - O 15 '96 - p1488 [251-500]
　　PW - v243 - N 4 '96 - p65 [51-250]
MacLeod, Anne Scott - *American Childhood*
　　ChLAQ - v21 - Fall '96 - p142+ [501+]
Macleod, Calum - *Uzbekistan*
　　r FEER - v160 - Mr 27 '97 - p53 [501+]
Macleod, Dianne Sachko - *Art and the Victorian Middle Class*
　　Lon R Bks - v19 - Ap 3 '97 - p14+ [501+]
　　TLS - Ja 31 '97 - p29 [251-500]
MacLeod, Elizabeth - *Stamp Collecting for Canadian Kids (Illus. by Esperanza Melo)*
　　c Emerg Lib - v24 - Mr '97 - p28 [1-50]
　　c Phil Lit R - v45 - '96 - p342+ [251-500]
　　c Quill & Q - v62 - S '96 - p75 [251-500]
MacLeod, Glen - *Wallace Stevens and Modern Art*
　　Poetics T - v17 - Sum '96 - p266+ [501+]
MacLeod, Jay - *Ain't No Makin' It*
　　Am Ethnol - v23 - Ag '96 - p644+ [501+]
Macleod, Joan - *The Hope Slide. Little Sister*
　　Can Lit - Win '96 - p183+ [501+]
Macleod, Mark - *Ready or Not*
　　y Magpies - v11 - My '96 - p46 [501+]
Macleod, Mary - *Why Me?*
　　c TES - S 6 '96 - p8* [51-250]
MacLeod, Norman - *Cretaceous-Tertiary Mass Extinctions*
　　Nature - v385 - Ja 2 '97 - p36 [501+]
　　New Sci - v152 - O 5 '96 - p48 [1-50]
MacLiammoir, Micheal - *The Importance of Being Oscar*
　　ELT - v39 - 4 '96 - p527 [51-250]
　　ILS - v15 - Fall '96 - p22+ [501+]

MacLochlainn, Alf - *The Corpus in the Library*
ILS - v15 - Fall '96 - p14 [501+]
Mac Low, Jackson - *Barnesbook*
PW - v243 - S 30 '96 - p84 [1-50]
MacManus, Susan A - *Young v. Old*
APSR - v90 - D '96 - p915+ [501+]
Pol Stud J - v24 - Aut '96 - p520 [51-250]
MacMillan, Dianne - *Missions of the Los Angeles Area*
c HB Guide - v8 - Spr '97 - p172 [51-250]
c LATBR - Ag 18 '96 - p15 [51-250]
c SLJ - v42 - Ag '96 - p157+ [51-250]
MacMillan, Dianne M - *Ramadan and Id-Al-Fitr*
TES - F 14 '97 - p16* [51-250]
MacMillan, Margaret - *Women of the Raj*
CR - v269 - N '96 - p277 [51-250]
LJ - v122 - Mr 15 '97 - p94 [1-50]
Macmillan Encyclopedia of Physics. Vols. 1-4
r ARBA - v28 - '97 - p639 [51-250]
r LJ - v122 - Mr 15 '97 - p56+ [51-250]
The Macmillan World Atlas
r Choice - v34 - S '96 - p93 [251-500]
r LATBR - D 8 '96 - p35 [51-250]
MacMullen, Ramsay - *Changes in the Roman Empire*
CH - v65 - D '96 - p664+ [251-500]
Macnair, Ian - *Teach Yourself New Testament Greek*
Rel St Rev - v23 - Ja '97 - p67 [51-250]
MacNally, Ralph C - *Ecological Versatility and Community Ecology*
Choice - v34 - O '96 - p304 [51-250]
MacNeil, Robert - *The Voyage*
PW - v243 - S 2 '96 - p122 [1-50]
MacNeill, Alastair - *Alistair MacLean's Red Alert (Hodson). Audio Version*
y Kliatt - v30 - N '96 - p36 [51-250]
Macnow, Glen - *Shaquille O'Neal: Star Center*
c HB Guide - v8 - Spr '97 - p145 [51-250]
Macomber, Debbie - *This Matter of Marriage*
PW - v244 - Mr 10 '97 - p64 [51-250]
Macomber, Roger - *Organic Chemistry. Vol. 1*
SB - v33 - Ja '97 - p7+ [51-250]
Organic Chemistry. Vol. 2
SB - v33 - Ja '97 - p8 [51-250]
Organic Chemistry. Vols. 1-2
SciTech - v21 - Mr '97 - p29 [51-250]
Macpherson, James - *The Poems of Ossian and Related Works*
Lon R Bks - v18 - O 3 '96 - p18 [501+]
MacPherson, Rett - *Family Skeletons*
BL - v93 - Mr 15 '97 - p1230 [51-250]
KR - v65 - Ja 1 '97 - p24 [51-250]
PW - v244 - Ja 13 '97 - p59 [51-250]
Macpherson, W J - *The Economic Development of Japan 1868-1941*
JEL - v34 - D '96 - p2096 [51-250]
Macquarrie, John - *A Guide to the Sacraments*
LJ - v122 - My 1 '97 - p110 [51-250]
Mediators between Human and Divine
Choice - v34 - N '96 - p476 [51-250]
Comw - v124 - Ja 17 '97 - p27+ [251-500]
Macqueen, J G - *The Hittites*
LJ - v121 - N 15 '96 - p93 [1-50]
MacQueen, Sheila - *The New Flower Arranging from Your Garden*
Bloom Rev - v16 - Jl '96 - p26 [51-250]
MacQuitty, Miranda - *Amazing Bugs*
c BL - v93 - D 1 '96 - p658 [51-250]
c CBRS - v25 - D '96 - p44 [51-250]
c CLW - v67 - Mr '97 - p55 [51-250]
c HB Guide - v8 - Spr '97 - p122 [51-250]
c New Sci - v152 - N 16 '96 - p53 [51-250]
c PW - v243 - N 4 '96 - p78 [51-250]
c SLJ - v42 - N '96 - p116 [51-250]
Macrae, C Neil - *Stereotypes and Stereotyping*
R&R Bk N - v12 - F '97 - p6 [51-250]
Macrakis, Kristie - *Surviving the Swastika*
JMH - v69 - Mr '97 - p184+ [501+]
MacSkimming, Roy - *Cold War*
Mac - v109 - D 16 '96 - p73 [1-50]
Quill & Q - v62 - N '96 - p38 [501+]
MacTaggart, Terrence J - *Restructuring Higher Education*
J Hi E - v68 - Mr '97 - p238+ [501+]
Macunovich, Janet - *Caring for Perennials*
BL - v93 - Mr 1 '97 - p1102 [51-250]
PW - v244 - F 3 '97 - p103+ [51-250]
Macura, Miroslav - *International Migration*
J Gov Info - v23 - S '96 - p678 [51-250]
Macy, Marianne - *Working Sex*
BL - v93 - N 1 '96 - p464 [51-250]
PW - v243 - S 9 '96 - p70 [51-250]

Macy, Sue - *Winning Ways*
y BL - v93 - Ja '97 - p764 [1-50]
y BL - v93 - Ap 1 '97 - p1286 [1-50]
y BL - v93 - Ap 1 '97 - p1302 [1-50]
c CLW - v67 - D '96 - p61 [51-250]
c HB - v72 - S '96 - p621 [251-500]
y HB Guide - v7 - Fall '96 - p362 [51-250]
c LATBR - Ag 18 '96 - p15 [51-250]
y SLJ - v42 - Ag '96 - p174 [51-250]
y SLJ - v42 - D '96 - p31 [1-50]
y VOYA - v19 - O '96 - p234 [251-500]
Maczak, Antoni - *Money, Price, and Power in Poland, Sixteenth and Seventeenth Centuries*
Six Ct J - v27 - Win '96 - p1086+ [501+]
Travel in Early Modern Europe
AHR - v101 - O '96 - p1198+ [501+]
J Soc H - v30 - Fall '96 - p271+ [251-500]
Madajczyk, Czeslaw - *Vom Generalplan Ost Zum Generalsiedlungsplan*
CEH - v29 - 2 '96 - p270+ [501+]
Madan, T N - *Muslim Communities of South Asia. Rev. and Enlarged Ed.*
Pac A - v69 - Fall '96 - p439+ [251-500]
Madden, David - *Sharpshooter: A Novel of the Civil War*
NYTBR - v101 - D 22 '96 - p15 [51-250]
PW - v243 - O 14 '96 - p65 [51-250]
Madden, Deirdre - *One by One in the Darkness*
TLS - My 24 '96 - p26 [501+]
Madden, John - *All Madden*
NYTBR - v101 - O 20 '96 - p23 [51-250]
Madden-Lunsford, Kerry - *Offsides*
LJ - v121 - S 15 '96 - p97 [51-250]
Maddex, Robert L - *Constitutions of the World*
r J Gov Info - v24 - Ja '97 - p75+ [251-500]
The Illustrated Dictionary of Constitutional Concepts
yr ARBA - v28 - '97 - p268 [251-500]
Maddison, Angus - *Explaining the Economic Performance of Nations*
Econ J - v106 - S '96 - p1479 [251-500]
R&R Bk N - v11 - D '96 - p29 [51-250]
Monitoring the World Economy 1820-1992
JEL - v34 - S '96 - p1378+ [501+]
Maddock, Richard C - *Marketing to the Mind*
Choice - v34 - Mr '97 - p1204 [51-250]
R&R Bk N - v12 - F '97 - p46 [51-250]
Maddocks, John - *Streetwise*
Aust Bk R - O '96 - p61 [501+]
Maddox, Brenda - *D.H. Lawrence (Peters). Audio Version*
y Kliatt - v30 - N '96 - p48 [51-250]
D.H. Lawrence: The Story of a Marriage
NYTBR - v101 - Ag 25 '96 - p28 [1-50]
Maddox, Donald - *Literary Aspects of Courtly Culture*
MLR - v91 - O '96 - p953+ [501+]
Maddox, Graham - *Religion and the Rise of Democracy*
Choice - v34 - F '97 - p1034 [51-250]
Maddox, Gregory - *Custodians of the Land*
JEL - v34 - D '96 - p2111 [51-250]
Maddox, Muriel - *Love and Betrayal*
PW - v244 - F 10 '97 - p69 [51-250]
Maddox, Robert James - *Weapons for Victory*
AHR - v102 - F '97 - p212+ [501+]
PHR - v65 - Ag '96 - p501+ [251-500]
Pres SQ - v26 - Fall '96 - p1175+ [501+]
RAH - v24 - S '96 - p529+ [501+]
Maddox, Sam - *The Quest for Cure*
J Rehab RD - v33 - Jl '96 - p337 [51-250]
Maddox, Tony - *Fergus' Big Splash (Illus. by Tony Maddox)*
c JB - v60 - O '96 - p186 [51-250]
Maddux, Vernon R - *John Hittson: Cattle King on the Texas and Colorado Frontier*
PHR - v65 - Ag '96 - p487+ [251-500]
Madeline European Adventure. Electronic Media Version
c HB - v73 - Mr '97 - p219+ [501+]
c Par - v72 - F '97 - p155 [51-250]
c PW - v244 - Ja 27 '97 - p36 [51-250]
Madelung, Wilferd - *The Succession to Muhammad*
TLS - F 7 '97 - p28 [501+]
Mader, Sylvia S - *Biology. 5th Ed.*
SciTech - v20 - N '96 - p26 [51-250]
Inquiry into Life. 8th Ed.
SciTech - v21 - Mr '97 - p35 [51-250]
Madhubuti, Haki R - *GroundWork: New and Selected Poems of Don L. Lee/Haki R. Madhubuti from 1966-1996*
Trib Bks - Ap 20 '97 - p1+ [501+]
Madigan, Michael T - *Brock Biology of Microorganisms. 8th Ed.*
SciTech - v20 - D '96 - p36 [1-50]

Madison, James - *The Papers of James Madison: Presidential Series. Vol. 3*
R&R Bk N - v11 - D '96 - p15 [51-250]
Madison, James G - *CNC Machining Handbook*
r SciTech - v20 - D '96 - p74 [51-250]
Madison Township, Williams County, Ohio Cemetery Records (Inclusive to August 1995)
r EGH - v50 - N '96 - p180 [51-250]
Madland, Helga Stipa - *Image and Text*
Ger Q - v70 - Win '97 - p78+ [501+]
Madrick, Jeffrey - *The End of Affluence*
Soc - v34 - Ja '97 - p88+ [501+]
TLS - Ag 30 '96 - p10+ [501+]
YR - v84 - O '96 - p137+ [501+]
Madsen, Axel - *The Sewing Circle*
Spec - v277 - N 2 '96 - p46+ [501+]
Madsen, Bjarne - *Modelling the Economy and the Environment*
JEL - v34 - D '96 - p2133+ [51-250]
Madsen, David B - *Across the West*
Am Ant - v61 - Ap '96 - p426+ [501+]
Madsen, Deborah L - *Allegory in America*
J Am St - v30 - D '96 - p495+ [251-500]
R&R Bk N - v11 - N '96 - p71 [51-250]
The Postmodernist Allegories of Thomas Pynchon
Poetics T - v18 - Spr '97 - p95+ [501+]
Madsen, Jean - *Private and Public School Partnerships*
R&R Bk N - v11 - D '96 - p53 [51-250]
Madsen, Mark S - *The Dynamic Cosmos*
Choice - v34 - O '96 - p301+ [51-250]
New Sci - v153 - Mr 1 '97 - p43 [51-250]
Madsen, Richard - *China and the American Dream*
CS - v25 - S '96 - p633+ [501+]
Madu, Christian N - *Strategic Planning in Technology Transfer to Less Developed Countries*
JC - v46 - Sum '96 - p183+ [501+]
Madura, Jeff - *Global Portfolio Management for Institutional Investors*
R&R Bk N - v12 - F '97 - p48 [1-50]
Maeda, Hiroshi - *Bismuth-Based High-Temperature Superconductors*
SciTech - v20 - D '96 - p25 [51-250]
Maeda, Seiji - *Sorbets and Granitas*
PW - v244 - Ap 21 '97 - p68 [51-250]
Maehr, Martin L - *Transforming School Cultures*
Choice - v34 - F '97 - p1015 [51-250]
Maekawa, Takeshi - *Drunken Master*
y Sch Lib - v44 - N '96 - p171 [501+]
Ironfist Chinmi: Titles 1 to 12
c TES - N 1 '96 - p8* [501+]
Journey to Mount Shen
c Books - v9 - S '95 - p26 [1-50]
Kung-Fu Boy
c Books - v9 - S '95 - p26 [1-50]
Pole Stars
y Sch Lib - v44 - N '96 - p171 [501+]
Maestre, Pedro - *Matando Dinosaurios Con Tirachinas*
WLT - v70 - Aut '96 - p923 [501+]
Maestro, Betsy - *Coming to America (Illus. by Susannah Ryan)*
c HB Guide - v7 - Fall '96 - p313 [51-250]
c Inst - v106 - S '96 - p54 [51-250]
c RT - v50 - My '97 - p681+ [51-250]
The Story of Religion (Illus. by Giulio Maestro)
c BL - v93 - O 1 '96 - p336 [51-250]
c CCB-B - v50 - S '96 - p23+ [51-250]
c Ch BWatch - v7 - Ja '97 - p4 [51-250]
c HB Guide - v8 - Spr '97 - p87 [51-250]
c SLJ - v42 - S '96 - p218 [51-250]
The Voice of the People
c HB Guide - v7 - Fall '96 - p315 [51-250]
Maestro, Marco - *What Do You Hear When Cows Sing? And Other Silly Riddles (Illus. by Giulio Maestro)*
c HB Guide - v7 - Fall '96 - p358 [1-50]
Maffei, Domenico - *Angelo Gambiglioni, Giuresconsulto Aretino Del Quattrocento*
MLR - v92 - Ap '97 - p478 [251-500]
Maffesoli, Michel - *The Contemplation of the World*
TranslRevS - v2 - O '96 - p12 [51-250]
The Time of the Tribes
AJS - v102 - Ja '97 - p1229+ [501+]
Maffi, Mario - *Gateway to the Promised Land*
AHR - v102 - F '97 - p201+ [251-500]
Historian - v58 - Sum '96 - p868+ [251-500]
Maffioli, Cesare S - *Out of Galileo*
T&C - v37 - Ap '96 - p348+ [501+]
Maga, Timothy P - *The World of Jimmy Carter*
AHR - v101 - O '96 - p1313+ [501+]
Magai, Carol - *Handbook of Emotion, Adult Development, and Aging*
Choice - v34 - My '97 - p1579 [51-250]

Magdanz, James - *Go Home, River (Illus. by Dianne Widom)*
  c BL - v93 - N 1 '96 - p508 [51-250]
  c HB Guide - v8 - Spr '97 - p39 [51-250]
  c SLJ - v43 - Ja '97 - p86 [51-250]
Magdassi, Shlomo - *Surface Activities of Proteins*
  SciTech - v20 - D '96 - p82 [51-250]
Magee, Bryan - *On Blindness*
  Lon R Bks - v19 - Ja 2 '97 - p9+ [501+]
Magee, Elaine - *Lighten Up!*
  PW - v244 - My 5 '97 - p204 [51-250]
Magee, Wes - *The Puffin Book of Christmas Poems (Illus. by Jill Bennett)*
  c Bks Keeps - N '96 - p24 [51-250]
Mageo, Jeannette Marie - *Spirits in Culture, History, and Mind*
  R&R Bk N - v11 - D '96 - p4 [51-250]
Maggin, Donald L - *Stan Getz: A Life in Jazz*
  AB - v98 - D 9 '96 - p1994+ [51-250]
  Choice - v34 - Ja '97 - p806 [51-250]
  Rapport - v19 - 4 '96 - p12 [501+]
Maggio, Rosalie - *The New Beacon Book of Quotations by Women*
  r ARBA - v28 - '97 - p36 [51-250]
  r LJ - v122 - F 1 '97 - p72+ [51-250]
  r PW - v243 - S 30 '96 - p74 [51-250]
Maggs, Peter B - *The Mandelstam and Der Nister Files*
  NYRB - v43 - O 3 '96 - p4+ [501+]
The Magic School Bus Explores in the Age of Dinosaurs. Electronic Media Version
  c PW - v244 - Ja 27 '97 - p37 [51-250]
The Magic Shoes. Book and Audio Version
  c SLJ - v42 - D '96 - p72 [51-250]
Magid, Lawrence J - *The Little PC Book. 2nd Ed.*
  y BL - v93 - Mr 1 '97 - p1101 [501+]
Magida, Arthur J - *How to Be a Perfect Stranger*
  r BL - v93 - Ja '97 - p770 [1-50]
  How to Be a Perfect Stranger. Vol. 2
    PW - v244 - Mr 10 '97 - p63 [51-250]
  Prophet of Rage
    BW - v26 - Ag 4 '96 - p1+ [501+]
    Choice - v34 - O '96 - p350 [51-250]
    MEQ - v4 - Mr '97 - p91+ [251-500]
    NYRB - v43 - S 19 '96 - p61+ [501+]
Magida, Phyllis - *Skinny Vegetarian Entrees*
  BWatch - v17 - N '96 - p1 [51-250]
Magill, Frank Northen - *Cyclopedia of Literary Characters II. Vols. 1-4*
  r RQ - v36 - Win '96 - p221 [51-250]
  Magill's Survey of World Literature. Vols. 1-2
  yr ARBA - v28 - '97 - p417 [51-250]
  Masterplots II: Short Story Series. Vols. 7-10
  r ARBA - v28 - '97 - p436 [251-500]
  Masterplots: 1,801 Plot Stories and Critical Evaluations of the World's Finest Literature. Rev. 2nd Ed., Vols. 1-12
  yr ARBA - v28 - '97 - p417+ [51-250]
  r BL - v93 - Mr 1 '97 - p1192+ [251-500]
  r R&R Bk N - v12 - F '97 - p79 [51-250]
  USA in Space. Vols. 1-3
  r ARBA - v28 - '97 - p594 [51-250]
  r Choice - v34 - My '97 - p1481 [51-250]
  r LJ - v122 - Ap 15 '97 - p74 [51-250]
    SciTech - v21 - Mr '97 - p94 [51-250]
Magill, Gerard - *Personality and Belief*
  CH - v65 - S '96 - p520+ [501+]
Magill, Michael - *Theory of Incomplete Markets. Vol. 1*
  JEL - v34 - D '96 - p2027 [51-250]
  R&R Bk N - v11 - N '96 - p24 [1-50]
Magill's Cinema Annual 1995
  r ARBA - v28 - '97 - p515+ [251-500]
  r RQ - v36 - Fall '96 - p147 [501+]
Magill's Guide to Science Fiction and Fantasy Literature. Vols. 1-4
  r ARBA - v28 - '97 - p433+ [251-500]
  r BL - v93 - Mr 1 '97 - p1192 [251-500]
  r Choice - v34 - Ap '97 - p1312 [51-250]
Maginn, Simon - *Methods of Confinement*
  Obs - D 22 '96 - p18* [51-250]
  Sheep
    PW - v243 - S 16 '96 - p71+ [51-250]
Magistrale, Tony - *A Dark Night's Dreaming*
  Choice - v34 - S '96 - p124 [51-250]
  Ext - v37 - Win '96 - p366+ [501+]
  J Am Cult - v19 - Sum '96 - p142+ [251-500]
Maglin, Nan Bauer - *Bad Girls/Good Girls*
  Cons - v17 - Win '96 - p31 [1-50]
  NYRB - v43 - N 28 '96 - p22+ [501+]
Magnasco, Alessandro - *Alessandro Magnasco 1667-1749*
  BM - v138 - O '96 - p710+ [501+]

Magnenat-Thalmann, Nadia - *Interactive Computer Animation*
  New Sci - v153 - Ja 18 '97 - p41 [1-50]
Magnet: Real Music Alternatives
  p LJ - v122 - F 15 '97 - p167 [51-250]
Magnier, Bernard - *Poesie D'Afrique Au Sud Du Sahara 1945-1995*
  WLT - v70 - Sum '96 - p747 [51-250]
Magnin, Andre - *Contemporary Art of Africa*
  BW - v26 - D 8 '96 - p10 [251-500]
  BWatch - v17 - S '96 - p3 [51-250]
  TLS - D 6 '96 - p21 [501+]
Magnus, Bernd - *Whither Marxism?*
  S&S - v61 - Sum '97 - p267+ [501+]
Magnus, Olaus - *Olaus Magnus. Vol. 1*
  Spec - v277 - N 16 '96 - p43 [1-50]
Magnuson, Mike - *The Right Man for the Job*
  KR - v64 - D 15 '96 - p1760 [251-500]
  PW - v244 - Ja 13 '97 - p52 [251-500]
Magnusson, David - *The Lifespan Development of Individuals*
  Choice - v34 - N '96 - p543 [51-250]
Magnusson, Warren - *The Search for Political Space*
  Choice - v34 - Mr '97 - p1230+ [51-250]
  R&R Bk N - v12 - F '97 - p61 [51-250]
Magny, Olivier De - *Les Trois Premiers Livres Des Odes De 1559*
  Ren Q - v50 - Spr '97 - p251+ [501+]
  Six Ct J - v27 - Fall '96 - p949+ [501+]
Magocsi, Paul Robert - *A History of Ukraine*
  For Aff - v76 - Mr '97 - p192 [51-250]
  Our People. 3rd Ed.
    Slav R - v55 - Fall '96 - p680+ [501+]
Magorian, Michelle - *Good Night Mr. Tom*
  c New Ad - v9 - Fall '96 - p297+ [501+]
Magowska, Anita - *Polska Prasa Studencka W II Rzeczypospolitej*
  AHR - v102 - F '97 - p138+ [51-250]
Magrs, Paul - *Does It Show?*
  Obs - F 2 '97 - p18* [51-250]
  TLS - Ja 17 '97 - p21 [51-250]
Maguin, Jean-Marie - *French Essays on Shakespeare and His Contemporaries*
  Shakes Q - v47 - Fall '96 - p348+ [501+]
Maguire, Carmel - *Information Services for Innovative Organizations*
  LRTS - v41 - Ja '97 - p58+ [501+]
Maguire, Gregory - *The Good Liar*
  y Aust Bk R - N '96 - p60 [501+]
  Oasis
  y BL - v93 - S 15 '96 - p232 [51-250]
  y CCB-B - v50 - Ja '97 - p179+ [51-250]
  y HB Guide - v8 - Spr '97 - p82 [51-250]
  y KR - v64 - Ag 15 '96 - p1239 [51-250]
  c SLJ - v42 - N '96 - p108 [51-250]
  y VOYA - v19 - F '97 - p330 [251-500]
Maguire, Henry - *Byzantine Magic*
  CH - v65 - D '96 - p684+ [501+]
  HRNB - v25 - Fall '96 - p36+ [1-50]
  Rel St Rev - v23 - Ja '97 - p79 [51-250]
Maguire, Robert A - *Exploring Gogol*
  Russ Rev - v55 - O '96 - p699+ [501+]
Magyar, Karl P - *Challenge and Response*
  APH - v44 - Spr '97 - p54 [251-500]
  RSR - v24 - 3 '96 - p46 [51-250]
  Prolonged Wars
    NWCR - v50 - Win '97 - p142 [251-500]
Mahaffie, Charles D, Jr. - *A Land of Discord Always*
  AHR - v102 - F '97 - p225 [251-500]
Mahaim, Ivan - *Beethoven: Naissance Et Renaissance Des Derniers Quatuors. Vols. 1-2*
  MQ - v80 - Fall '96 - p525+ [501+]
Mahan, Harold E - *Benson J. Lossing and Historical Writing in the United States 1830-1890*
  Choice - v34 - S '96 - p195 [51-250]
Mahan, Sue - *Crack Cocaine, Crime, and Women*
  R&R Bk N - v11 - D '96 - p43 [1-50]
Mahapatra, Anuradha - *Another Spring Darkness*
  TranslRevS - v2 - D '96 - p19 [51-250]
Mahapatra, Jayanta - *The Best of Jayanta Mahapatra*
  WLT - v71 - Win '97 - p223+ [501+]
Maharaj, Rabrindranath - *The Interloper*
  BIC - v26 - F '97 - p18+ [501+]
Maharam, Lewis G - *Backs in Motion*
  BL - v92 - Ag '96 - p1869 [51-250]
Maharatna, Arup - *The Demography of Famines*
  Choice - v34 - Ap '97 - p1424 [51-250]
  JEL - v35 - Mr '97 - p236 [51-250]

Maharidge, Dale - *The Coming White Minority*
  y BL - v93 - S 15 '96 - p190 [51-250]
  BW - v26 - D 15 '96 - p4 [1-50]
  BW - v26 - D 15 '96 - p5 [501+]
  Econ - v342 - F 15 '97 - p9*+ [501+]
  KR - v64 - Ag 15 '96 - p1214+ [251-500]
  LATBR - O 27 '96 - p5+ [501+]
  LJ - v121 - S 15 '96 - p84 [51-250]
Mahathir Bin Mohamad - *The Malay Dilemma*
  FEER - Anniv '96 - p224 [251-500]
Maher, Bill - *Political Incorrections (Maher). Audio Version*
  LJ - v122 - Mr 15 '97 - p103 [51-250]
Maher, Jane - *Mina P. Shaughnessy: Her Life and Work*
  PW - v244 - Mr 24 '97 - p73 [51-250]
  Seeing Language in Sign
    Choice - v34 - O '96 - p272 [51-250]
Maher, John C, 1951- - *Chomsky for Beginners*
  New Sci - v153 - Ja 4 '97 - p36 [1-50]
  TES - D 27 '96 - p16 [1-50]
Maher, John Christopher - *Diversity in Japanese Culture and Language*
  Pac A - v69 - Sum '96 - p266+ [501+]
Maher, Richard - *The Roald Dahl Quiz Book (Illus. by Quentin Blake)*
  c PW - v243 - D 16 '96 - p61 [51-250]
Maheu, Louis - *Social Movements and Social Classes*
  CS - v25 - N '96 - p767+ [501+]
  SF - v75 - S '96 - p356+ [501+]
  Socio R - v45 - F 1 '97 - p147+ [501+]
Mahfouz, Naguib - *Arabian Days and Nights*
  NS & S - v9 - My 17 '96 - p40 [1-50]
  Children of the Alley
    BW - v26 - D 22 '96 - p12 [51-250]
    NYTBR - v101 - D 1 '96 - p36 [51-250]
    PW - v243 - S 30 '96 - p79 [1-50]
    SFR - v21 - N '96 - p48 [1-50]
    Trib Bks - Ja 5 '97 - p2 [51-250]
  Echoes of an Autobiography
    BL - v93 - N 15 '96 - p547 [51-250]
    Econ - v342 - Mr 15 '97 - p15*+ [501+]
    KR - v64 - N 1 '96 - p1585 [251-500]
    PW - v243 - N 11 '96 - p66 [51-250]
    Spec - v278 - F 22 '97 - p28 [501+]
  Miramar
    Econ - v342 - Mr 15 '97 - p15*+ [501+]
Mahias, Marie-Claude - *Delivrance Et Convivialite*
  Rel St Rev - v23 - Ap '97 - p103+ [501+]
Mahieu, Vincent - *The Hunt for the Heart*
  WLT - v71 - Win '97 - p167+ [501+]
Mahir, Behcet - *A Turkish Folktale*
  CAY - v17 - Win '96 - p9 [51-250]
Mahjoub, Jamal - *In the Hour of Signs*
  KR - v64 - N 15 '96 - p1631 [51-250]
  TLS - F 28 '97 - p23 [501+]
Mahler, Sarah J - *American Dreaming*
  AAPSS-A - v549 - Ja '97 - p207+ [501+]
  AJS - v102 - S '96 - p631+ [501+]
  CS - v26 - Ja '97 - p68+ [501+]
Mahmood, Cynthia Keppley - *Fighting for Faith and Nation*
  LJ - v122 - Ja '97 - p124 [51-250]
Mahnke, Frank H - *Color, Environment, and Human Response*
  R&R Bk N - v12 - F '97 - p73 [51-250]
Mahnken, Jan - *The Backyard Bird-Lover's Guide*
  y BL - v92 - Ag '96 - p1867 [51-250]
  y BL - v92 - Ag '96 - p1890 [1-50]
Mahon, Derek - *Journalism: Selected Prose 1970-1995*
  ILS - v16 - Spr '97 - p20 [501+]
  PW - v244 - Ja 27 '97 - p92+ [51-250]
  TLS - N 29 '96 - p26 [501+]
Mahon, James E - *Mobile Capital and Latin American Development*
  Choice - v34 - F '97 - p1012 [51-250]
  JEL - v35 - Mr '97 - p218 [51-250]
Mahon, John F - *Industry as a Player in the Political and Social Arena*
  Choice - v34 - Mr '97 - p1204 [51-250]
  R&R Bk N - v11 - N '96 - p32 [51-250]
Mahoney, Dan - *Edge of the City*
  PW - v243 - S 23 '96 - p74 [1-50]
  Hyde
    BL - v93 - F 1 '97 - p928 [51-250]
    KR - v64 - N 15 '96 - p1626 [251-500]
    NYTBR - v102 - Ja 19 '97 - p22 [51-250]
    PW - v243 - N 18 '96 - p62 [51-250]
Mahoney, Daniel J - *De Gaulle: Statesmanship, Grandeur, and Modern Democracy*
  Choice - v34 - N '96 - p519 [51-250]
  For Aff - v75 - S '96 - p146+ [51-250]

Mahoney, Dennis F - *The Critical Fortunes of a Romantic Novel*
    Ger Q - v69 - Sum '96 - p349+ [501+]
    MLR - v91 - Jl '96 - p787+ [251-500]
Mahoney, John L - *William Wordsworth: A Poetic Life*
    PW - v244 - Ja 27 '97 - p90 [251-500]
Mahoney, Judy - *Teach Me Chinese (Illus. by Amy Xiaomin Wang). Book and Audio Version*
    c PW - v244 - Mr 17 '97 - p47 [51-250]
Mahoney, Michael Sean - *The Mathematical Career of Pierre De Fermat 1601-1665. 2nd Ed.*
    Ren Q - v50 - Spr '97 - p334+ [501+]
Mahoney, Rhona - *Kidding Ourselves*
    Fam Relat - v45 - Jl '96 - p351+ [251-500]
Mahony, Patrick J - *Freud's Dora*
    Choice - v34 - Ja '97 - p880 [51-250]
    LJ - v121 - O 1 '96 - p107 [51-250]
    SciTech - v21 - Mr '97 - p55 [51-250]
Mahony, Robert - *Jonathan Swift: The Irish Identity*
    ILS - v16 - Spr '97 - p33+ [501+]
Mahood, Linda - *The Magdalenes: Prostitution in the Nineteenth Century*
    J Urban H - v23 - Ja '97 - p231+ [501+]
    Policing Gender, Class and Family
    Choice - v34 - Ap '97 - p1424 [51-250]
Mahrer, Alvin R - *The Complete Guide to Experiential Psychotherapy*
    Readings - v11 - D '96 - p22+ [51-250]
Mahy, Brian W J - *Immunobiology and Pathogenesis of Persistent Virus Infections*
    Choice - v34 - Mr '97 - p1182+ [51-250]
    SciTech - v21 - Mr '97 - p50 [51-250]
Mahy, Margaret - *Boom, Baby, Boom, Boom! (Illus. by Patricia MacCarthy)*
    c BL - v93 - Mr 1 '97 - p1173 [51-250]
    c KR - v65 - F 15 '97 - p303 [51-250]
    c PW - v244 - F 17 '97 - p218 [51-250]
    The Boy with Two Shadows (Illus. by Jenny Williams)
    c Bks Keeps - N '96 - p7 [51-250]
    The Catalogue of the Universe
    y Kliatt - v30 - S '96 - p4 [1-50]
    The Five Sisters (Illus. by Patricia MacCarthy)
    c Bks Keeps - Mr '97 - p21 [51-250]
    c BL - v93 - F 1 '97 - p941 [51-250]
    c CCB-B - v50 - My '97 - p329 [51-250]
    c HB - v73 - Mr '97 - p201+ [251-500]
    c KR - v64 - D 15 '96 - p1800 [51-250]
    c PW - v243 - D 9 '96 - p68 [51-250]
    c SLJ - v43 - Mr '97 - p162 [51-250]
    c Spec - v277 - D 14 '96 - p77 [51-250]
    c TES - Ja 24 '97 - p8* [251-500]
    A Fortune Branches Out (Mitchley). Audio Version
    c Ch BWatch - v6 - O '96 - p2+ [1-50]
    The Great White Man-Eating Shark (Illus. by Jonathan Allen)
    c HB - v73 - Mr '97 - p189 [1-50]
    The Greatest Show off Earth
    c PW - v243 - D 9 '96 - p69 [1-50]
    Tingleberries, Tuckertubs, and Telephones (Illus. by Robert Staermose)
    c HB Guide - v7 - Fall '96 - p294 [51-250]
    Underrunners
    y SLJ - v42 - N '96 - p41 [1-50]
Maier, Carol - *Ramon Maria Del Valle-Inclan: Questions of Gender*
    MP - v94 - N '96 - p258+ [501+]
Maier, Charles S - *Dissolution: The Crisis of Communism and the End of East Germany*
    For Aff - v76 - My '97 - p139+ [51-250]
    LJ - v122 - Ap 1 '97 - p110 [51-250]
Maier, Christoph T - *Preaching the Crusades*
    CH - v65 - S '96 - p463+ [501+]
    EHR - v112 - F '97 - p169+ [501+]
Maier, Ernest L - *The Business Library and How to Use It*
    r ARBA - v27 - '96 - p239 [51-250]
    r Choice - v34 - D '96 - p586+ [51-250]
    r RQ - v36 - Fall '96 - p156 [251-500]
Maier, Gunther - *Spatial Search*
    JEL - v34 - D '96 - p2031 [51-250]
Maier, John R - *Desert Songs*
    Choice - v34 - D '96 - p608 [51-250]
    R&R Bk N - v11 - N '96 - p15 [51-250]
Maier, Karl - *Angola: Promises and Lies*
    BL - v93 - S 1 '96 - p58+ [51-250]
    PW - v243 - Jl 22 '96 - p232+ [251-250]
    TLS - Ja 3 '97 - p15 [501+]
Maier, Pauline - *American Scripture*
    KR - v65 - My 1 '97 - p700 [251-500]
Maifair, Linda Lee - *Batter Up, Bailey Benson!*
    c BL - v93 - Mr 15 '97 - p1242 [51-250]

The Case of the Bashed-Up Bicycle
    c BL - v93 - N 15 '96 - p588 [51-250]
The Case of the Nearsighted Neighbor
    c BL - v93 - N 15 '96 - p588 [51-250]
Go Figure, Gabriella Grant!
    c BL - v93 - Mr 15 '97 - p1242 [51-250]
    c PW - v244 - Mr 24 '97 - p76 [51-250]
Maihafer, Harry J - *Oblivion: The Mystery of West Point Cadet Richard Cox*
    LJ - v121 - N 15 '96 - p74 [51-250]
Mailer, Adele - *The Last Party*
    BL - v93 - My 15 '97 - p1556+ [51-250]
    PW - v244 - Mr 31 '97 - p49 [51-250]
Mailer, Nicholas - *The UK School Internet Primer*
    TES - Ja 3 '97 - p47U [51-250]
Mailer, Norman - *The Gospel according to the Son*
    Ent W - My 16 '97 - p108+ [51-250]
    KR - v65 - Mr 15 '97 - p409 [251-500]
    NYTLa - v146 - Ap 14 '97 - pC15 [501+]
    PW - v244 - Mr 31 '97 - p59 [251-500]
    Time - v149 - Ap 28 '97 - p75 [501+]
    Trib Bks - My 18 '97 - p3 [501+]
    WSJ-Cent - v99 - Ap 18 '97 - pA16 [501+]
    Oswald's Tale
    Books - v9 - S '95 - p23+ [51-250]
    Portrait of Picasso as a Young Man
    Lon R Bks - v19 - Mr 6 '97 - p3+ [501+]
    NS - v125 - N 15 '96 - p15+ [501+]
    Obs - D 1 '96 - p15* [501+]
    TLS - N 8 '96 - p11+ [501+]
Maillard, Keith - *Hazard Zones*
    LJ - v122 - My 1 '97 - p164 [51-250]
    Two Strand River
    KR - v64 - Ag 15 '96 - p1178+ [251-500]
    PW - v243 - S 23 '96 - p71 [51-250]
Maillol (Flammarion/Musees Des Beaux-Arts)
    BM - v138 - S '96 - p627+ [501+]
Mailloux, Steven - *Rhetoric, Sophistry, Pragmatism*
    AL - v68 - D '96 - p882 [51-250]
Maimon, Arye - *Germania Judaica. Vol. 3, Pt. 2*
    Six Ct J - v27 - Win '96 - p1057+ [501+]
Main, Jan - *The Lactose-Free Family Cookbook*
    Quill & Q - v62 - Ag '96 - p30 [51-250]
Main Developments in Trade
    J Gov Info - v23 - S '96 - p674 [51-250]
Maine Association for Supervision and Curriculum Development - *Using Assessment to Drive School Change*
    EL - v54 - D '96 - p88 [51-250]
Maines, Mahin D - *Nitric Oxide Synthase*
    Sci - v275 - F 14 '97 - p939 [251-500]
    SciTech - v20 - D '96 - p35 [51-250]
Maingon, Charles - *La Medecine Dans L'Oeuvre De J.K. Huysmans*
    MLR - v92 - Ja '97 - p199+ [501+]
Mainguet, Monique - *L'Homme Et La Secheresse*
    Env - v38 - N '96 - p29 [51-250]
Maino, Donatello Biagi - *Gaetano Gandolfi*
    BM - v138 - O '96 - p694+ [501+]
Mainwaring, Scott - *Building Democratic Institutions*
    HAHR - v76 - Ag '96 - p612+ [501+]
    J Pol - v58 - Ag '96 - p924+ [501+]
Mainzer, Klaus - *Symmetries of Nature*
    J Chem Ed - v74 - Ap '97 - p381 [251-500]
    Nature - v382 - Ag 29 '96 - p771 [501+]
    SciTech - v20 - N '96 - p4 [51-250]
Maio, Samuel - *Creating Another Self*
    Bloom Rev - v16 - S '96 - p11 [51-250]
Mair, George - *The Barry Diller Story*
    BL - v93 - My 1 '97 - p1467+ [51-250]
    KR - v65 - Mr 15 '97 - p444 [251-500]
    LJ - v122 - My 1 '97 - p114 [51-250]
    PW - v244 - Ap 7 '97 - p81+ [51-250]
    Rosie O'Donnell: Her True Story
    y BL - v93 - Ap 1 '97 - p1267 [51-250]
Maira, Arun - *The Accelerating Organization*
    LJ - v122 - Mr 15 '97 - p35+ [1-50]
Mairowitz, David Zane - *Kafka*
    Utne R - S '96 - p92 [1-50]
Mairs, Nancy - *Waist-High in the World*
    y BL - v93 - Ja '97 - p790 [51-250]
    BW - v27 - F 2 '97 - p4 [501+]
    KR - v64 - N 1 '96 - p1585+ [251-500]
    LJ - v121 - D '96 - p132 [51-250]
    Nat - v264 - Ap 14 '97 - p32+ [501+]
    NYTBR - v102 - Mr 2 '97 - p19 [51-250]
    Prog - v61 - Mr '97 - p41+ [501+]
    PW - v243 - N 4 '96 - p56 [51-250]
    Wom R Bks - v14 - Mr '97 - p8+ [501+]

Maisel, Ephraim - *The Foreign Office and Foreign Policy 1919-1926*
    HT - v47 - Ja '97 - p59 [501+]
Maisey, John G - *Discovering Fossil Fishes*
    BL - v93 - S 1 '96 - p47 [251-500]
    Choice - v34 - D '96 - p639 [51-250]
    LJ - v121 - S 15 '96 - p90 [51-250]
    R&R Bk N - v11 - N '96 - p76 [51-250]
    r SB - v32 - N '96 - p234 [51-250]
    y SLJ - v42 - D '96 - p153 [1-50]
Maisner, Heather - *The Magic Crystal (Illus. by Peter Joyce)*
    c HB Guide - v8 - Spr '97 - p118 [51-250]
    c SLJ - v42 - D '96 - p115 [51-250]
    The Magic Globe (Illus. by Alan Baron)
    y Emerg Lib - v24 - S '96 - p26 [1-50]
    The Magic Hourglass (Illus. by Peter Joyce)
    y Emerg Lib - v24 - S '96 - p26 [1-50]
    Planet Monster (Illus. by Alan Rowe)
    c HB Guide - v8 - Spr '97 - p142 [51-250]
    c SLJ - v42 - D '96 - p115+ [51-250]
    Save Brave Ted (Illus. by Charlotte Hard)
    c HB Guide - v8 - Spr '97 - p39 [51-250]
    c SLJ - v43 - Ja '97 - p86 [51-250]
Maister, David H - *True Professionalism*
    BL - v93 - My 15 '97 - p1548+ [51-250]
Maistre, Joseph Marie, Comte De - *Against Rousseau*
    Choice - v34 - F '97 - p1034 [51-250]
    R&R Bk N - v11 - D '96 - p46 [51-250]
    Considerations on France
    MA - v38 - Fall '96 - p392+ [501+]
    St. Petersburg Dialogues
    MA - v38 - Fall '96 - p392+ [501+]
Maitino, John R - *Teaching American Ethnic Literatures*
    AL - v68 - D '96 - p883+ [51-250]
Maitland, Barbara - *The Bear Who Didn't Like Honey (Illus. by Odilon Moraes)*
    c BL - v93 - F 15 '97 - p1027 [51-250]
    c CBRS - v25 - Mr '97 - p88 [51-250]
    c CCB-B - v50 - My '97 - p329+ [51-250]
    c KR - v65 - F 1 '97 - p225 [51-250]
    c PW - v244 - F 24 '97 - p89 [51-250]
Maitland, Barry - *All My Enemies*
    Aust Bk R - D '96 - p79+ [501+]
    TLS - O 25 '96 - p23 [51-250]
Maitland, Sara - *Angel Maker*
    Ms - v7 - S '96 - p82 [251-500]
    A Big-Enough God
    CC - v113 - N 20 '96 - p1144+ [501+]
    NYTBR - v101 - D 22 '96 - p20 [1-50]
Maitra, Amit K - *Building a Corporate Internet Strategy*
    BWatch - v17 - N '96 - p11 [51-250]
    r R&R Bk N - v12 - F '97 - p37 [51-250]
Maitra, Ashok P - *Discrete Gambling and Stochastic Games*
    JEL - v34 - D '96 - p2022+ [51-250]
Maitra, Priyatosh - *The Globalization of Capitalism in Third World Countries*
    Choice - v34 - Ja '97 - p845 [51-250]
    JEL - v35 - Mr '97 - p272 [51-250]
    R&R Bk N - v11 - D '96 - p23 [51-250]
Maizels, Jennie - *The Amazing Pop-Up Grammar Book (Illus. by Kate Petty)*
    y BL - v93 - Ap 1 '97 - p1308 [1-50]
    c HB Guide - v8 - Spr '97 - p39 [51-250]
    c KR - v64 - S 1 '96 - p1331 [51-250]
    The Great Grammar Book
    c Bks Keeps - Ja '97 - p23 [51-250]
Maizels, John - *Raw Creation*
    Am Craft - v56 - D '96 - p33 [51-250]
    Atl - v278 - N '96 - p121+ [51-250]
    Bloom Rev - v16 - N '96 - p24 [51-250]
    BWatch - v17 - S '96 - p3 [51-250]
    Choice - v34 - D '96 - p602+ [51-250]
    LJ - v121 - O 1 '96 - p74 [51-250]
    TLS - Ag 2 '96 - p13 [1-50]
Maizlish, Lisa - *The Ring (Illus. by Lisa Maizlish)*
    c CLW - v67 - D '96 - p57 [51-250]
    c HB Guide - v7 - Fall '96 - p266 [51-250]
    c Par - v71 - D '96 - p252 [1-50]
Majno, Guido - *Cells, Tissues, and Disease*
    SciTech - v21 - Mr '97 - p47 [51-250]
Majok, Aggrey Ayuen - *Development among Africa's Migratory Pastoralists*
    Choice - v34 - Ja '97 - p839 [51-250]
    R&R Bk N - v11 - D '96 - p20 [51-250]
Major, Clarence - *Calling the Wind*
    y BL - v93 - F 15 '97 - p1014 [1-50]
    Dirty Bird Blues
    LJ - v121 - N 15 '96 - p116 [51-250]

The Garden Thrives
  Bl S - v26 - Sum '96 - p66 [51-250]
  VQR - v72 - Aut '96 - p137* [51-250]
Major, Devorah - *An Open Weave*
  Bloom Rev - v16 - Jl '96 - p21 [1-50]
  y Kliatt - v31 - My '97 - p8 [51-250]
Street Smarts
  Bl S - v26 - Sum '96 - p66 [1-50]
Major, J Russell - *From Renaissance Monarchy to*
  Absolute Monarchy
  JMH - v68 - S '96 - p693+ [501+]
  Ren Q - v50 - Spr '97 - p290+ [501+]
Major, Norma - *Chequers: The Prime Minister's Country*
  House and Its History
  BL - v93 - Mr 1 '97 - p1103 [51-250]
  PW - v244 - Mr 3 '97 - p61 [51-250]
  Woman's J - D '96 - p16 [1-50]
Major, Robert - *The American Dream in Nineteenth-*
  Century Quebec
  Choice - v34 - F '97 - p970+ [51-250]
  R&R Bk N - v11 - D '96 - p63 [51-250]
Jean Rivard Ou L'Art De Reussir
  Can Lit - Win '96 - p47+ [501+]
Major Authors on CD-ROM. Electronic Media Version
  yr HT - v46 - F 12 '97 - p48 [51-250]
Major Business Organisations of Eastern Europe and
  the Commonwealth of Independent States 1995/96
  r ARBA - v28 - '97 - p115 [251-500]
  r J Gov Info - v24 - Ja '97 - p55+ [501+]
Major Characters in American Fiction
  yr Kliatt - v30 - S '96 - p22+ [51-250]
  r RQ - v36 - Win '96 - p214+ [51-250]
Major Companies of Africa South of the Sahara 1996
  r ARBA - v28 - '97 - p105 [251-500]
Major Companies of Central and Eastern Europe and
  the Commonwealth of Independent States 1996/97
  r ARBA - v28 - '97 - p105 [251-500]
Major Companies of Latin America 1996
  r ARBA - v28 - '97 - p116 [251-500]
Major Companies of the Arab World 1996/97
  r ARBA - v28 - '97 - p110 [251-500]
  r MEJ - v51 - Win '97 - p149 [251-500]
  r R&R Bk N - v12 - F '97 - p18 [51-250]
Major U.S. Companies. 3rd Ed.
  r BWatch - v18 - F '97 - p3 [1-50]
Majorca (Kingdom). Sovereign (1324-1349: Jaime III) -
  Leyes Palatinas
  Specu - v71 - Jl '96 - p725+ [501+]
Majure, Janet - *Elections*
  y HB Guide - v8 - Spr '97 - p93 [51-250]
  y VOYA - v19 - O '96 - p234 [51-250]
Mak, Grace C L - *Women, Education, and Development*
  in Asia
  R&R Bk N - v12 - F '97 - p69 [51-250]
Makanin, Vladimir - *Baize-Covered Table with Decanter*
  WLT - v70 - Sum '96 - p723 [501+]
Escape Hatch. The Long Road Ahead
  Choice - v34 - D '96 - p621 [51-250]
  NYTBR - v101 - S 8 '96 - p25 [51-250]
  WLT - v70 - Aut '96 - p985 [501+]
Zwei Einsamkeiten
  WLT - v70 - Aut '96 - p985+ [501+]
Makarushka, Irena S M - *Religious Imagination and*
  Language in Emerson and Nietzsche
  JR - v76 - O '96 - p660+ [251-500]
Make It Safe
  TES - O 4 '96 - p16* [1-50]
  TES - N 29 '96 - p12* [51-250]
Makel, William - *Cleaning Recreation Sites*
  J Gov Info - v23 - S '96 - p565 [51-250]
Makela, Hannu - *Mestari: Eino Leinon Elama Ja*
  Kuolema
  WLT - v70 - Aut '96 - p994+ [251-500]
Makela, Klaus - *Alcoholics Anonymous as a Mutual-Help*
  Movement
  Choice - v34 - N '96 - p544 [51-250]
  R&R Bk N - v11 - N '96 - p44 [51-250]
Makepeace, Maggie - *Travelling Hopefully*
  Books - v10 - Je '96 - p24 [1-50]
Makepeace-Warne, Antony - *Brassey's Companion to the*
  British Army
  r HT - v46 - S '96 - p54+ [501+]
Maker, C June - *Curriculum Development and Teaching*
  Strategies for Gifted Learners. 2nd Ed.
  Choice - v34 - Ap '97 - p1391 [51-250]
Maker, Eve - *Developing SGML DTDs*
  BYTE - v21 - S '96 - p34 [251-500]
Makhijani, Arjun - *Nuclear Wastelands*
  r Am Sci - v84 - S '96 - p506+ [501+]
  r Env - v38 - N '96 - p29 [51-250]

Makin, Jirjis Ibn Al-Amid - *Chronique Des Ayyoubides*
  602-658/1205-6-1259-60
  EHR - v112 - Ap '97 - p441+ [251-500]
  Specu - v71 - Jl '96 - p731 [251-500]
Makin, Peter - *Bunting: The Shaping of His Verse*
  TLS - N 29 '96 - p13 [51-250]
Makin, Peter J - *Organizations and the Psychological*
  Contract
  R&R Bk N - v11 - D '96 - p34 [51-250]
Makine, Andrei - *Le Testament Francais*
  FR - v70 - O '96 - p147+ [501+]
Making the Grade
  Inst - v106 - O '96 - p14 [51-250]
Makino, Yasuko - *Japan and the Japanese*
  r R&R Bk N - v11 - N '96 - p16 [51-250]
Makinson, Larry - *Open Secrets. 4th Ed.*
  r R&R Bk N - v12 - F '97 - p60 [51-250]
Makowicki, Jim - *Making Heirloom Toys*
  BL - v93 - O 1 '96 - p313 [51-250]
Makowski, Colleen Lahan - *Charles Burchfield: An*
  Annotated Bibliography
  r Choice - v34 - My '97 - p1476 [51-250]
Makowski, Krzysztof - *Vicus*
  LA Ant - v7 - S '96 - p280+ [251-500]
Makus, Ingrid - *Women, Politics, and Reproduction*
  Choice - v34 - Mr '97 - p1176 [51-250]
  R&R Bk N - v12 - F '97 - p54 [51-250]
Makward, Christiane P - *Plays by French and*
  Francophone Women
  Theat J - v48 - O '96 - p397+ [501+]
Malaguzzi, Francesco - *De Libris Compactis*
  BC - v45 - Sum '96 - p275+ [251-500]
  Lib - v18 - D '96 - p363 [51-250]
Legatura De Pregio In Valle D'Aosta
  BC - v45 - Sum '96 - p275+ [251-500]
Regiam Sibi Bibliothecam Instruxit
  BC - v45 - Sum '96 - p275+ [251-500]
Malam, John - *Claude Monet*
  c Bks Keeps - Mr '97 - p24 [51-250]
Highest, Longest, Deepest (Illus. by Gary Hincks)
  c HB Guide - v8 - Spr '97 - p114 [51-250]
  c KR - v64 - N 1 '96 - p1603+ [51-250]
Isambard Kingdom Brunel
  c Bks Keeps - Mr '97 - p24 [51-250]
Vincent Van Gogh
  c Bks Keeps - Mr '97 - p24 [51-250]
Malamud, Bernard - *Talking Horse*
  WLT - v71 - Win '97 - p164 [251-500]
Malamud Goti, Jaime E - *Game without End*
  BL - v93 - O 1 '96 - p293+ [51-250]
Malan, Lucas - *Hongergrond*
  WLT - v70 - Aut '96 - p1020 [51-250]
Malanga, Gerard - *Mythologies of the Heart*
  LATBR - My 26 '96 - p4 [501+]
Malat, Randy - *Passport Mexico*
  r LJ - v121 - S 15 '96 - p85 [51-250]
Malatesta, Maria - *Society and the Professions in Italy*
  1860-1914
  AHR - v102 - F '97 - p135+ [501+]
  AJS - v102 - Ja '97 - p1212+ [501+]
  JIH - v27 - Spr '97 - p695+ [501+]
Malavis, Nicholas George - *Bless the Pure and Humble*
  JEL - v35 - Mr '97 - p266 [51-250]
Malawi Demographic and Health Survey 1992
  J Gov Info - v23 - S '96 - p659 [1-50]
Malcata, F Xavier - *Engineering of/with Lipases*
  SciTech - v20 - S '96 - p24 [51-250]
Malchow, H L - *Gothic Images of Race in Nineteenth-*
  Century Britain
  Choice - v34 - Mr '97 - p1164 [51-250]
  ELT - v40 - 2 '97 - p253 [51-250]
Malcolm, Andrew H - *Mississippi Currents*
  LJ - v121 - S 15 '96 - p85 [51-250]
  NYTBR - v102 - Ja 12 '97 - p20 [251-500]
  PW - v243 - S 16 '96 - p59 [51-250]
  Trib Bks - Ja 26 '97 - p6 [251-500]
Malcolm, Jahnna N - *Rebel Angels*
  y Kliatt - v31 - Mr '97 - p18 [51-250]
Winging It
  y Kliatt - v31 - Mr '97 - p18 [51-250]
Malcolm, Janet - *The Purloined Clinic*
  NS & S - v9 - Ap 26 '96 - p31 [251-500]
  Spec - v277 - N 16 '96 - p43 [1-50]
Malcolm, Joyce Lee - *To Keep and Bear Arms*
  EHR - v111 - N '96 - p1290+ [251-500]
  J Mil H - v61 - Ja '97 - p158 [251-500]
Malcolm, Noel - *Bosnia: A Short History*
  CR - v269 - Ag '96 - p112 [51-250]
Malcolm, Norman - *Wittgenstein: A Religious Point of*
  View?
  IPQ - v36 - S '96 - p362+ [501+]

Wittgensteinian Themes
  RM - v49 - Je '96 - p931+ [501+]
Malden, R H - *Nine Ghosts*
  Necro - Sum '96 - p13+ [501+]
Maldifassi, Jose O - *Defense Industries in Latin American*
  Countries
  JTWS - v13 - Spr '96 - p357+ [501+]
Maldonado, Rafael - *Neurobiological Mechanisms of*
  Opiate Withdrawal
  SciTech - v20 - N '96 - p45 [51-250]
Malenfant, Paul Chanel - *La Partie Et Le Tout*
  Can Lit - Win '96 - p163+ [501+]
Males, Anne Marie - *Great Careers for People Fascinated*
  by Government and the Law
  y SLJ - v42 - N '96 - p129 [51-250]
  y SLMQ - v24 - Sum '96 - p221 [51-250]
Males, Mike A - *The Scapegoat Generation*
  Nat - v263 - O 21 '96 - p27+ [501+]
  Prog - v61 - Ja '97 - p32+ [251-500]
  Readings - v11 - D '96 - p25 [51-250]
Malettke, Klaus - *Frankreich, Deutschland Und Europa*
  Im 17. Und 18. Jahrhundert
  EHR - v112 - F '97 - p205+ [501+]
Malevich, Kazimir - *Malevich (Faerna)*
  y BL - v93 - O 1 '96 - p314+ [51-250]
  LJ - v121 - N 1 '96 - p64 [51-250]
Maley, Willy - *A Spenser Chronology*
  r MLR - v91 - Jl '96 - p700+ [501+]
Malfer, Stefan - *Die Protokolle Des Osterreichischen*
  Ministerrates 1848-1867
  Slav R - v55 - Sum '96 - p450+ [501+]
Malhuish, M - *Oh, What a Feeling*
  y Emerg Lib - v24 - Mr '97 - p28 [1-50]
Malice Domestic 5
  y Kliatt - v30 - N '96 - p17 [51-250]
Maliepaard, Marc - *Mitosenes and Related Antitumor*
  Drugs
  SciTech - v20 - N '96 - p40 [51-250]
Malik, Jamal - *Colonialization of Islam*
  Choice - v34 - My '97 - p1554 [51-250]
Malik, Kenan - *The Meaning of Race*
  BW - v26 - O 13 '96 - p12 [51-250]
  New Sci - v153 - F 1 '97 - p49 [51-250]
  NS - v125 - D 13 '96 - p45+ [501+]
  R&R Bk N - v11 - D '96 - p42 [51-250]
  Socio R - v45 - My '97 - p357+ [501+]
Malin, David - *Hartung's Astronomical Objects for*
  Southern Telescopes. 2nd Ed.
  Am Sci - v85 - Mr '97 - p182 [51-250]
Malina, Bruce J - *On the Genre and Message of*
  Revelation
  Theol St - v57 - D '96 - p775 [251-500]
  TT - v53 - O '96 - p433 [51-250]
Malinowski, Sharon - *Native North American Biography.*
  Vols. 1-2
  yr ARBA - v28 - '97 - p157 [51-250]
  cr SLJ - v42 - Ag '96 - p182 [51-250]
Malinvaud, Edmond - *Diagnosing Unemployment*
  JEL - v35 - Mr '97 - p135+ [501+]
Malitz, Jerome - *Plants for the Future*
  BWatch - v18 - F '97 - p11 [1-50]
Malkki, Liisa H - *Purity and Exile*
  AJS - v102 - S '96 - p607+ [501+]
  Am Ethnol - v24 - F '97 - p252+ [501+]
  CS - v25 - N '96 - p733+ [501+]
  Historian - v59 - Win '97 - p412+ [501+]
  NYRB - v43 - Je 6 '96 - p58+ [501+]
Mall, David - *When Life and Choice Collide*
  CLW - v66 - Je '96 - p35 [51-250]
El Mallakh, Dorothea H - *Energy Watchers VII*
  JEL - v34 - D '96 - p2135 [51-250]
El-Mallakh, Rif S - *Lithium: Actions and Mechanisms*
  AJPsych - v154 - F '97 - p285+ [501+]
Mallama, Anthony - *Eclipses, Atmospheres, and Global*
  Change
  S&T - v92 - D '96 - p66 [51-250]
Mallan, Chicki - *Guide to Catalina*
  r BWatch - v17 - S '96 - p5 [51-250]
Mallarme, Stephane - *Collected Poems*
  APR - v25 - N '96 - p33+ [501+]
Mallat, Chibli - *The Middle East into the 21st Century*
  Choice - v34 - F '97 - p1032 [51-250]
Mallat, Kathy - *The Picture That Mom Drew (Illus. by*
  Bruce McMillan)
  c BL - v93 - Ja '97 - p856 [51-250]
  c KR - v64 - D 15 '96 - p1800 [51-250]
Malle, Louis - *Malle on Malle*
  TES - Ag 2 '96 - pR6 [51-250]
Mallett, David - *Inch by Inch (Illus. by Ora Eitan)*
  c PW - v244 - My 5 '97 - p211 [1-50]

Mallett, Jane - *The Royal Marsden NHS Trust Manual of Clinical Nursing Procedures. 4th Ed.*
  SciTech - v21 - Mr '97 - p69 [51-250]
Malley, Robert - *The Call from Algeria*
  For Aff - v76 - Mr '97 - p192+ [51-250]
  MEJ - v51 - Spr '97 - p309 [51-250]
Mallgrave, Harry Francis - *Gottfried Semper: Architect of the Nineteenth Century*
  BWatch - v17 - N '96 - p2 [51-250]
  Choice - v34 - D '96 - p603 [51-250]
  NYRB - v43 - N 14 '96 - p51+ [501+]
  NYTBR - v101 - D 8 '96 - p57 [51-250]
  R&R Bk N - v11 - N '96 - p61 [51-250]
Mallick, Ross - *Development Policy of a Communist Government*
  JTWS - v13 - Fall '96 - p238+ [501+]
Indian Communism
  Pac A - v69 - Sum '96 - p268+ [501+]
Mallie, Eamonn - *The Fight for Peace*
  Spec - v276 - My 25 '96 - p34 [501+]
  TES - Jl 5 '96 - p7* [51-250]
Mallin, Eric S - *Inscribing the Time*
  Albion - v28 - Win '96 - p692+ [501+]
  Six Ct J - v27 - Win '96 - p1209+ [501+]
Mallin, Samuel B - *Art Line Thought*
  R&R Bk N - v12 - F '97 - p2 [51-250]
Mallon, Florencia E - *Peasant and Nation*
  HAHR - v76 - Ag '96 - p617+ [501+]
  Historian - v59 - Win '97 - p434+ [251-500]
Mallon, Thomas - *Dewey Defeats Truman*
  BL - v93 - N 15 '96 - p572 [51-250]
  Ent W - F 21 '97 - p120 [51-250]
  KR - v64 - O 15 '96 - p1488+ [251-500]
  LATBR - Ja 5 '97 - p2 [501+]
  LJ - v121 - N 15 '96 - p89 [51-250]
  Nat R - v49 - F 24 '97 - p58 [51-250]
  NL - v79 - D 16 '96 - p26+ [501+]
  NY - v73 - Mr 24 '97 - p83 [51-250]
  NYTBR - v102 - F 2 '97 - p13 [501+]
  NYTLa - v146 - Ja 16 '97 - pC22 [501+]
  Trib Bks - Ja 26 '97 - p1+ [501+]
  WSJ-Cent - v99 - Ja 15 '97 - pA12 [501+]
Mallorca, Jacqueline - *Cooking Basics*
  BWatch - v17 - S '96 - p2 [51-250]
  CSM - v89 - D 13 '96 - p11 [1-50]
Malloy, Catharine - *Seamus Heaney: The Shaping Spirit*
  Choice - v34 - N '96 - p460 [51-250]
Malloy, Jerry - *Sol White's History of Colored Baseball*
  J Am Cult - v19 - Spr '96 - p101+ [501+]
Malm, William P - *Music Cultures of the Pacific, the Near East, and Asia. 3rd Ed.*
  M Ed J - v83 - S '96 - p58 [51-250]
Malmquist, Carl P - *Homicide: A Psychiatric Perspective*
  Choice - v34 - S '96 - p215+ [51-250]
Malnes, Raino - *Valuing the Environment*
  Choice - v34 - S '96 - p148 [51-250]
Malone, Bill C - *Country Music, USA*
  LJ - v121 - N 1 '96 - p42 [51-250]
Malone, Caroline - *The Memory Bird*
  TES - N 1 '96 - p8* [501+]
Malone, Jacqui - *Steppin' on the Blues*
  CAY - v17 - Fall '96 - p7 [51-250]
  Choice - v34 - Ap '97 - p1350 [251-500]
Malone, Mary - *Will Rogers: Cowboy Philosopher*
  c HB Guide - v7 - Fall '96 - p371 [51-250]
Malone, Michael - *Time's Witness*
  SFR - v21 - Jl '96 - p48 [51-250]
Malone, Michael, 1956- - *A Guatemalan Family*
  c Ch BWatch - v6 - O '96 - p5 [51-250]
  c HB Guide - v8 - Spr '97 - p90 [51-250]
  c SLJ - v43 - Ja '97 - p125 [51-250]
Malone, Michael P - *James J. Hill: Empire Builder of the Northwest*
  WHQ - v27 - Win '96 - p530+ [251-500]
Malone, Michael S, 1954- - *The Microprocessor: A Biography*
  LQ - v67 - Ja '97 - p97+ [501+]
Maloney, Mike - *Flash! Splash! Crash! All at Sea with Cap'n Bob*
  Obs - v54 - O 13 '96 - p16* [1-50]
Malotki, Ekkehart - *The Bedbugs' Night Dance and Other Hopi Sexual Tales*
  TranslRevS - v2 - D '96 - p27 [51-250]
The Magic Hummingbird (Illus. by Michael Lacapa)
  c SLJ - v42 - N '96 - p99 [51-250]
Malott, Gene - *The Mature Traveler's Book of Deals*
  r LJ - v122 - F 1 '97 - p98 [51-250]

Malouf, David - *The Conversations at Curlow Creek*
  Atl - v279 - F '97 - p109 [51-250]
  Aust Bk R - S '96 - p8+ [501+]
  BL - v93 - D 1 '96 - p641 [51-250]
  Econ - v341 - N 16 '96 - p18*+ [501+]
  KR - v64 - N 1 '96 - p1557 [251-500]
  LATBR - Ja 12 '97 - p2 [501+]
  LJ - v121 - N 15 '96 - p89 [51-250]
  Lon R Bks - v18 - D 12 '96 - p27 [501+]
  NY - v73 - Ap 7 '97 - p95 [51-250]
  NYRB - v44 - Ap 10 '97 - p19+ [501+]
  NYTBR - v102 - Ja 19 '97 - p10 [501+]
  NYTLa - v146 - Ja 22 '97 - pC17 [501+]
  PW - v243 - N 4 '96 - p62+ [51-250]
  Spec - v277 - S 7 '96 - p32 [501+]
  TES - O 4 '96 - p7* [51-250]
  TLS - S 13 '96 - p22 [501+]
  W&I - v12 - Ap '97 - p253+ [251-500]
  W&I - v12 - Ap '97 - p263+ [501+]
Harland's Half Acre
  NYTBR - v102 - Mr 30 '97 - p24 [51-250]
  PW - v243 - D 30 '96 - p64 [1-50]
An Imaginary Life
  LATBR - Ag 11 '96 - p11 [51-250]
Remembering Babylon
  SFR - v21 - N '96 - p36+ [501+]
Malouf, Melissa - *It Had to Be You*
  KR - v65 - F 15 '97 - p246 [51-250]
  PW - v244 - Mr 3 '97 - p66 [51-250]
Maloy, Stanley R - *Genetic Analysis of Pathogenic Bacteria*
  SciTech - v20 - S '96 - p19 [51-250]
Maloy, Timothy K - *The Internet Research Guide*
  r Choice - v34 - Ja '97 - p832 [51-250]
  yr Kliatt - v30 - N '96 - p29+ [51-250]
  r LJ - v122 - Ja '97 - p89 [51-250]
Malpass, Michael Andrew - *Daily Life in the Inca Empire*
  R&R Bk N - v11 - D '96 - p18 [51-250]
Malphrus, Benjamin K - *The History of Radio Astronomy and the National Radio Astronomy Observatory*
  Choice - v34 - D '96 - p634 [51-250]
  S&T - v93 - F '97 - p60 [51-250]
Malroux, Claire - *Edge*
  WLT - v71 - Win '97 - p114 [251-500]
Malsberger, Brian M - *Covenants Not to Compete. 2nd Ed.*
  r ARBA - v28 - '97 - p222+ [51-250]
Maltenfort, George G - *Corrugated Shipping Containers. Rev. Ed.*
  SciTech - v20 - D '96 - p85 [51-250]
Malti-Douglas, Fedwa - *Men, Women, and God(s)*
  TLS - Ja 10 '97 - p24+ [501+]
Maltz, Alan S - *Miami: City of Dreams*
  BL - v93 - F 1 '97 - p922 [51-250]
  PW - v244 - Ja 20 '97 - p390 [1-50]
Maltz, Wendy - *In the Garden of Desire*
  KR - v65 - Ap 1 '97 - p529+ [251-500]
  PW - v244 - Ap 7 '97 - p79+ [51-250]
Maltzman, Jeffrey - *Jobs in Paradise*
  r Quill & Q - v63 - F '97 - p38 [501+]
Maluka, Zulfikar Khalid - *The Myth of Constitutionalism in Pakistan*
  Choice - v34 - S '96 - p203 [51-250]
Malz, Russell E, Jr. - *Catalysis of Organic Reactions*
  SciTech - v20 - D '96 - p27 [51-250]
Mamadi, Kaba - *Anthologie De Chansons Mandingues (Cote D'Ivoire, Guinee, Mali)*
  BL - v93 - F 1 '97 - p930 [1-50]
Maman, Marie - *Women in Agriculture*
  r ARBA - v28 - '97 - p567 [51-250]
Mamdani, Mahmood - *Citizen and Subject*
  Choice - v34 - D '96 - p683 [51-250]
  For Aff - v76 - Mr '97 - p199+ [51-250]
  JTWS - v13 - Spr '96 - p282+ [501+]
  Nat - v263 - D 16 '96 - p28+ [501+]
Mamet, David - *The Duck and the Goat (Illus. by Maya Kennedy)*
  c Bloom Rev - v16 - N '96 - p29 [1-50]
  c Ch BWatch - v6 - D '96 - p7 [51-250]
  c NY - v72 - N 18 '96 - p102 [1-50]
Make-Believe Town
  Si & So - v6 - N '96 - p38 [51-250]
  TLS - D 6 '96 - p19 [501+]
Mammana, Dennis - *Other Suns, Other Worlds?*
  Astron - v24 - N '96 - p109 [51-250]
Mammano, Julie - *Rhinos Who Surf*
  c HB Guide - v7 - Fall '96 - p267 [51-250]
Management (University of Split)
  p JEL - v35 - Mr '97 - p310 [51-250]

Management of Alcohol- and Drug-Related Issues in the Workplace
  ILR - v135 - 5 '96 - p599+ [501+]
The Management of Forests on Reserve
  J Gov Info - v23 - S '96 - p616 [51-250]
Management of Water Treatment Plant Residuals
  SciTech - v20 - D '96 - p70 [51-250]
Managing Capital Flows in East Asia
  JEL - v34 - D '96 - p2047 [51-250]
Managing Saskatchewan Rangeland. Rev. Ed.
  J Gov Info - v23 - S '96 - p640 [51-250]
Manas, Jose Angel - *Historias Del Kronen*
  Hisp - v79 - D '96 - p825+ [501+]
Mancall, Peter C - *Deadly Medicine*
  AHR - v101 - D '96 - p1616+ [501+]
  Can Hist R - v78 - Mr '97 - p169+ [501+]
  J Am St - v30 - D '96 - p463 [501+]
  JIH - v27 - Win '97 - p538+ [251-500]
  JSH - v63 - F '97 - p142+ [501+]
  J Soc H - v30 - Win '96 - p562+ [501+]
  Six Ct J - v27 - Fall '96 - p835+ [501+]
  W&M Q - v53 - O '96 - p805+ [501+]
Envisioning America
  Sev Cent N - v54 - Spr '96 - p33+ [501+]
Land of Rivers
  LJ - v121 - O 1 '96 - p112 [51-250]
Manchester, William - *A World Lit Only by Fire*
  CR - v269 - O '96 - p222 [51-250]
Mancinelli, Fabrizio - *The Sistine Chapel*
  LJ - v122 - Ja '97 - p93+ [251-500]
Mancini, Matthew J - *One Dies, Get Another*
  Choice - v34 - N '96 - p526 [51-250]
  HRNB - v25 - Win '97 - p57 [251-500]
  R&R Bk N - v11 - N '96 - p46 [51-250]
Mancoff, Debra N - *Victorian Urban Settings*
  Nine-C Lit - v51 - Mr '97 - p560+ [51-250]
  R&R Bk N - v11 - D '96 - p8 [51-250]
Mancosu, Paolo - *Philosophy of Mathematics and Mathematical Practice in the Seventeenth Century*
  Choice - v34 - O '96 - p318 [51-250]
  Isis - v88 - Mr '97 - p140+ [501+]
Mancuso, Chuck - *Popular Music and the Underground*
  JPC - v30 - Sum '96 - p280+ [51-250]
Mancuso, Maureen - *The Ethical World of British MPs*
  J Pol - v58 - Ag '96 - p914+ [501+]
Mandado, Enrique - *Programmable Logic Devices and Logic Controllers*
  SciTech - v21 - Mr '97 - p91 [51-250]
Mandate Review Committee, CBC, NFB, Telefilm (Canada) - *Making Our Voices Heard*
  J Gov Info - v23 - S '96 - p616 [51-250]
Mandava, Bhargavi C - *Where the Oceans Meet*
  KR - v64 - O 1 '96 - p1422+ [251-500]
  LJ - v121 - N 1 '96 - p107 [51-250]
  LJ - v122 - Mr 15 '97 - p43 [1-50]
  PW - v243 - O 14 '96 - p66 [51-250]
Mandel, Brett H - *Minor Players, Major Dreams*
  y BL - v93 - F 15 '97 - p993 [51-250]
  KR - v64 - D 1 '96 - p1720 [251-500]
  LJ - v122 - F 1 '97 - p82 [51-250]
  PW - v243 - D 9 '96 - p53 [51-250]
Mandel, Ernest - *Long Waves of Capitalist Development. 2nd Rev. Ed.*
  S&S - v61 - Sum '97 - p264+ [501+]
Mandel, Michael J - *The High-Risk Society*
  KR - v64 - S 15 '96 - p1377 [251-500]
  NYTBR - v101 - N 10 '96 - p70 [501+]
  PW - v243 - O 7 '96 - p53 [51-250]
Mandela, Nelson - *Long Walk to Freedom*
  y BL - v93 - D 15 '96 - p716 [1-50]
Mandela: An Illustrated Autobiography
  y BL - v93 - Ja '97 - p763 [1-50]
  y BL - v93 - N 15 '96 - p547 [51-250]
  LJ - v121 - D '96 - p108 [51-250]
Mandelaro, Jim - *Silver Seasons*
  Choice - v34 - F '97 - p1002 [51-250]
Mandelbaum, Michael - *The Dawn of Peace in Europe*
  Choice - v34 - Mr '97 - p1235 [51-250]
  For Aff - v75 - N '96 - p156 [51-250]
  NYTBR - v101 - D 29 '96 - p17 [501+]
  TLS - Mr 28 '97 - p28 [501+]
  WSJ-MW - v78 - N 29 '96 - pA5 [501+]
Postcommunism: Four Perspectives
  JEL - v34 - D '96 - p2124 [51-250]
Mandeles, Mark D - *Managing Command and Control in the Persian Gulf War*
  For Aff - v76 - My '97 - p130+ [51-250]
  R&R Bk N - v12 - F '97 - p100 [51-250]
Mandelker, Amy - *Framing Anna Karenina*
  Signs - v22 - Win '97 - p501+ [501+]

Mandell, Daniel R - *Behind the Frontier*
NEQ - v70 - Mr '97 - p143+ [501+]
W&M Q - v54 - Ap '97 - p424+ [501+]
Mandell, Gerald L - *External Manifestations of Systemic Infections*
SciTech - v21 - Mr '97 - p50 [51-250]
Intra-Abdominal Infections, Hepatitis, and Gastroenteritis
SciTech - v20 - D '96 - p48 [51-250]
Pleuropulmonary and Bronchial Infections
SciTech - v20 - N '96 - p47 [51-250]
Mandelson, Peter - *The Blair Revolution*
Spec - v277 - N 23 '96 - p45 [1-50]
Mandelstam, Osip - *The Complete Critical Prose*
PW - v244 - My 12 '97 - p74 [1-50]
Selected Poems
TES - D 27 '96 - p16 [51-250]
The Voronezh Notebooks
BL - v93 - S 15 '96 - p205 [51-250]
PW - v243 - Jl 22 '96 - p236+ [51-250]
TLS - S 6 '96 - p6 [501+]
TranslRevS - v2 - D '96 - p31 [51-250]
Mander, Jerry - *The Case against the Global Economy*
BL - v93 - O 1 '96 - p310 [51-250]
Choice - v34 - Mr '97 - p1206 [51-250]
Prog - v61 - Ja '97 - p38 [501+]
Utne R - Ja '97 - p96 [1-50]
Manderino, John - *Sam and His Brother Len*
Aethlon - v13 - Fall '95 - p133+ [251-500]
Mandeville, A Glen - *Doll Fashion Anthology and Price Guide. 5th Ed.*
r Ant & CM - v101 - N '96 - p31 [51-250]
Mandic, Ranko - *Katalog Metalnog Novca Jugoslavije 1700-1994*
r Coin W - v37 - D 2 '96 - p100 [51-250]
Mandino, Og - *The Greatest Mystery in the World*
PW - v244 - Mr 3 '97 - p67 [51-250]
Mandle, Jay R - *Caribbean Hoops*
CS - v25 - S '96 - p687+ [501+]
Persistent Underdevelopment
Choice - v34 - N '96 - p508 [51-250]
Mandler, Peter - *Aristocratic Government in the Age of Reform*
AHR - v101 - O '96 - p1207+ [501+]
The Fall and Rise of the Stately Home
Obs - Ap 13 '97 - p16* [501+]
Manea, Norman - *The Black Envelope*
NYTBR - v101 - O 27 '96 - p48 [51-250]
TranslRevS - v2 - D '96 - p30 [51-250]
WLT - v70 - Aut '96 - p943+ [501+]
Manent, Pierre - *An Intellectual History of Liberalism*
RM - v49 - Je '96 - p933+ [501+]
TranslRevS - v1 - My '95 - p8+ [51-250]
Tocqueville and the Nature of Democracy
APSR - v91 - Mr '97 - p173+ [501+]
Choice - v34 - O '96 - p359 [51-250]
Pub Int - Sum '96 - p101+ [501+]
RP - v59 - Spr '97 - p392+ [501+]
Manera, Tony - *A Dream Betrayed*
CF - v75 - Ja '97 - p36+ [501+]
Quill & Q - v62 - N '96 - p35 [501+]
Manery, Phyllis J - *Ancestor Charts Preserving Yesterday for Tomorrow. Vols. 1-2*
r EGH - v50 - N '96 - p184 [51-250]
Maness, Larry - *A Once Perfect Place*
KR - v64 - O 1 '96 - p1429 [51-250]
Manfredi, Antonio - *I Codici Latini Di Niccolo V*
Specu - v72 - Ja '97 - p195+ [501+]
Manfull, Helen - *In Other Words*
LJ - v122 - Ja '97 - p100+ [51-250]
PW - v243 - N 4 '96 - p58 [51-250]
Mangan, James Clarence - *Poems. Vol. 1*
ILS - v16 - Spr '97 - p35 [1-50]
Mangan, Kathy - *Above the Tree Line*
South R - v32 - Aut '96 - p761+ [501+]
Mangan, Mark - *Java Programming Basics*
Quill & Q - v62 - My '96 - p20+ [501+]
Mangan, Michael - *A Preface to Shakespeare's Comedies 1594-1603*
Choice - v34 - O '96 - p279 [51-250]
Mangan, Richard - *Investigating Wildland Fire Entrapments*
J Gov Info - v23 - S '96 - p569 [51-250]
Mangelsen, Thomas D - *Polar Dance*
PW - v244 - My 5 '97 - p192 [51-250]
Manger, Jason - *Essential Java*
CBR - v14 - N '96 - p35 [1-50]
JavaScript Essentials
CBR - v15 - Spr '97 - p5 [1-50]
LJ - v121 - D '96 - p138 [51-250]

Manger, William Muir - *Clinical and Experimental Pheochromocytoma. 2nd Ed.*
SciTech - v20 - N '96 - p40 [51-250]
Mangini, Shirley - *Memories of Resistance*
NWSA Jnl - v8 - Sum '96 - p143+ [501+]
Mango, Cyril - *Constantinople and Its Hinterland*
Specu - v72 - Ja '97 - p196+ [501+]
Manguel, Alberto - *A History of Reading*
BIC - v25 - D '96 - p42 [501+]
BL - v93 - Ja '97 - p759 [1-50]
BL - v93 - S 1 '96 - p34 [51-250]
BL - v93 - Ap 1 '97 - p1285 [1-50]
BW - v26 - S 29 '96 - p3 [501+]
BWatch - v17 - D '96 - p7 [1-50]
Mac - v109 - N 4 '96 - p67 [501+]
Mac - v109 - D 9 '96 - p64 [1-50]
NY - v73 - Mr 17 '97 - p118+ [501+]
NYTBR - v101 - N 17 '96 - p37 [501+]
NYTLa - v146 - D 3 '96 - pC17 [501+]
Quad - v40 - N '96 - p78+ [501+]
Quill & Q - v62 - S '96 - p67 [501+]
Quill & Q - v63 - F '97 - p50 [51-250]
SLJ - v42 - D '96 - p40 [51-250]
Spec - v277 - N 30 '96 - p58 [1-50]
TES - Jl 5 '96 - p8* [501+]
Time - v148 - S 9 '96 - p68 [51-250]
TLS - Ag 2 '96 - p8 [501+]
YR - v85 - Ap '97 - p145+ [501+]
Lost Words
Obs - N 3 '96 - p18* [51-250]
Manheimer, Ronald J - *Older Adult Education*
Cng - v28 - S '96 - p62 [51-250]
Maniam, K S - *Sensuous Horizons*
WLT - v71 - Win '97 - p231+ [501+]
Maniatty, Taramesha - *Glory Trail*
c HB Guide - v7 - Fall '96 - p294 [51-250]
Maniero, Lina - *American Women Writers. Vols. 1-5*
r ASInt - v34 - O '96 - p14 [1-50]
Manifold
p LMR - v15 - Win '96 - p45+ [51-250]
Manitoba Lottery Policy Review Working Group Report
J Gov Info - v23 - S '96 - p628 [51-250]
Mankell, Henning - *Faceless Killers*
BL - v93 - F 15 '97 - p1008 [251-500]
KR - v65 - Ja 1 '97 - p24+ [51-250]
LJ - v121 - D '96 - p150 [51-250]
PW - v243 - D 16 '96 - p45 [51-250]
Trib Bks - Mr 2 '97 - p5 [51-250]
WSJ-Cent - v99 - Mr 28 '97 - pA14 [51-250]
Mankin, Don - *Teams and Technology*
Choice - v34 - O '96 - p326 [51-250]
HR Mag - v41 - Je '96 - p186 [51-250]
Per Psy - v50 - Spr '97 - p213+ [51-250]
Manley, Bill - *The Penguin Historical Atlas of Ancient Egypt*
yr Kliatt - v31 - Mr '97 - p33 [51-250]
Manley, Joan H - *Qu'est-Ce Qu'on Dit?*
FR - v70 - O '96 - p157+ [251-500]
Manley, K A - *Careering Along with Books*
LAR - v99 - Mr '97 - p162 [251-500]
Manley, Lawrence - *Literature and Culture in Early Modern London*
Albion - v28 - Sum '96 - p294+ [501+]
Six Ct J - v27 - Fall '96 - p805+ [501+]
Manley, Rachel - *Drumblair: Memories of a Jamaican Childhood*
Mac - v109 - O 21 '96 - p84 [251-500]
Quill & Q - v62 - S '96 - p70 [251-500]
Manley, Will - *The Truth about Catalogers*
LR - v45 - 4 '96 - p62+ [251-500]
The Truth about Reference Librarians
LAR - v98 - O '96 - p533 [1-50]
Manlove, Colin - *Christian Fantasy from 1200 to the Present*
Rel St Rev - v23 - Ja '97 - p52 [51-250]
Mann, A - *The Dilemma of Einstein, Podolsky, and Rosen, 60 Years Later*
SciTech - v21 - Mr '97 - p21 [51-250]
Mann, Alfred K - *Shadow of a Star*
y BL - v93 - F 15 '97 - p985 [51-250]
New Sci - v153 - F 22 '97 - p44 [251-500]
NH - v106 - Mr '97 - p13 [1-50]
Mann, Bill - *Politics on the Net*
SocSciComR - v14 - Win '96 - p489+ [501+]
Mann, Carol - *Paris: Artistic Life in the Twenties and Thirties*
NS - v125 - N 29 '96 - p46 [1-50]
Obs - D 8 '96 - p15* [1-50]
Mann, Charles C - *Noah's Choice*
NYRB - v44 - F 20 '97 - p30+ [501+]

Mann, Charles F - *Madeleine Delbrel: A Life beyond Boundaries*
Rel St Rev - v22 - O '96 - p349+ [51-250]
Mann, Coramae Richey - *When Women Kill*
R&R Bk N - v12 - F '97 - p57 [51-250]
Mann, David D - *Women Playwrights in England, Ireland, and Scotland 1660-1823*
r AB - v99 - Mr 17 '97 - p870+ [501+]
r Choice - v34 - Mr '97 - p1140 [51-250]
Mann, Elizabeth - *The Brooklyn Bridge (Illus. by Alan Witschonke)*
c BL - v93 - F 1 '97 - p937 [51-250]
c Ch BWatch - v7 - Ja '97 - p7 [1-50]
c CLW - v67 - Mr '97 - p56 [51-250]
c HB - v73 - My '97 - p342 [51-250]
c PW - v243 - N 11 '96 - p75 [51-250]
The Great Pyramid (Illus. by Laura Lo Turco)
c Ch BWatch - v7 - Ja '97 - p7 [1-50]
c BL - v93 - F 1 '97 - p937 [51-250]
Mann, Golo - *The History of Germany since 1789*
CR - v269 - N '96 - p277 [1-50]
Mann, John - *Bacteria and Antibacterial Agents*
BioSci - v47 - Mr '97 - p185+ [501+]
Mann, Jonathan M - *AIDS in the World II*
r BL - v93 - D 1 '96 - p682 [1-50]
LJ - v121 - O 1 '96 - p114 [51-250]
Mann, Judy - *The Difference: Discovering the Hidden Ways We Silence Girls*
BW - v26 - S 22 '96 - p12 [51-250]
y Kliatt - v31 - Ja '97 - p25 [251-500]
PW - v243 - S 23 '96 - p73 [1-50]
The Difference: Growing Up Female in America
VOYA - v19 - D '96 - p256 [1-50]
Mann, K H - *Dynamics of Marine Ecosystems. 2nd Ed.*
SciTech - v20 - D '96 - p30 [51-250]
Mann, Kenny - *Ghana, Mali, Songhay*
c HB Guide - v7 - Fall '96 - p379 [1-50]
c SLJ - v42 - S '96 - p218+ [51-250]
Kongo Ndongo
c HB Guide - v8 - Spr '97 - p171 [51-250]
y SLJ - v43 - F '97 - p120+ [51-250]
y VOYA - v19 - F '97 - p351+ [251-500]
Monomotapa, Zulu, Basuto
c HB Guide - v8 - Spr '97 - p171 [51-250]
y SLJ - v43 - F '97 - p120+ [51-250]
y VOYA - v19 - F '97 - p351+ [251-500]
Oyo, Benin, Ashanti
c HB Guide - v7 - Fall '96 - p379 [1-50]
Mann, Paul - *The Burning Ghats*
BL - v93 - D 15 '96 - p713 [51-250]
KR - v64 - S 15 '96 - p1345+ [251-500]
LJ - v121 - N 1 '96 - p110 [51-250]
NYTBR - v101 - D 22 '96 - p21 [51-250]
PW - v243 - S 30 '96 - p64+ [51-250]
Mann, Robert - *The Walls of Jericho*
NYTBR - v101 - Ag 25 '96 - p13 [501+]
Mann, Thomas - *The Magic Mountain*
Ant R - v54 - Sum '96 - p370 [251-500]
TLS - O 25 '96 - p27 [501+]
Tagebucher 1953-55
WLT - v71 - Win '97 - p145+ [501+]
Der Zauberberg
Ger Q - v69 - Sum '96 - p305+ [501+]
Mann, Thomas E - *Intensive Care*
APSR - v91 - Mr '97 - p193+ [501+]
PSQ - v111 - Fall '96 - p542+ [501+]
Mann, Thomas W - *Deuteronomy*
Am - v176 - Mr 8 '97 - p23 [51-250]
Rel St Rev - v23 - Ap '97 - p165 [51-250]
Mann, Vivian B - *From Court Jews to the Rothschilds*
Mag Antiq - v150 - S '96 - p240+ [501+]
NYRB - v44 - Ja 9 '97 - p37+ [501+]
Mann, William J - *The Men from the Boys*
KR - v65 - My 1 '97 - p669 [251-500]
LJ - v122 - My 1 '97 - p141 [51-250]
PW - v244 - My 12 '97 - p60 [51-250]
Mann, William J, 1947- - *Gynecologic Surgery*
SciTech - v20 - D '96 - p51 [51-250]
Manna, Anthony L - *Many Faces, Many Voices*
Emerg Lib - v23 - My '96 - p40 [51-250]
Mr. Semolina-Semolinus (Illus. by Giselle Potter)
c HB - v73 - My '97 - p334 [251-500]
c KR - v65 - Mr 1 '97 - p385 [51-250]
c PW - v244 - F 3 '97 - p106 [51-250]
Manne, Robert - *The Culture of Forgetting*
Aust Bk R - Jl '96 - p8+ [51-250]
Meanjin - v55 - 3 '96 - p523+ [501+]
Quad - v40 - Jl '96 - p94+ [501+]
Mannikka, Eleanor - *Angkor Wat*
PW - v243 - N 11 '96 - p67 [51-250]

Manning, Catherine - *Fortunes a Faire*
Choice - v34 - Ap '97 - p1395 [51-250]
Manning, Martha - *Chasing Grace*
BL - v92 - Ag '96 - p1860 [51-250]
NYTBR - v101 - O 27 '96 - p30 [501+]
Manning, Mick - *Art School (Illus. by Mick Manning)*
c PW - v243 - S 2 '96 - p133 [51-250]
c SLJ - v42 - D '96 - p116 [51-250]
My Body, Your Body
c Bks Keeps - Ja '97 - p21 [51-250]
c Sch Lib - v45 - F '97 - p19 [51-250]
Nature Watch (Illus. by Brita Granstrom)
c PW - v244 - Mr 31 '97 - p77 [51-250]
A Ruined House
c CLW - v67 - Mr '97 - p14 [1-50]
What's Under the Bed?
c Bks Keeps - v100 - S '96 - p20 [51-250]
c TES - Mr 7 '97 - p7* [501+]
The World Is Full of Babies! (Illus. by Mick Manning)
c Bks Keeps - v100 - S '96 - p20 [51-250]
c CBRS - v25 - F '97 - p77 [51-250]
c HB Guide - v8 - Spr '97 - p90 [51-250]
c KR - v64 - S 15 '96 - p1404 [51-250]
c NYTBR - v102 - Mr 30 '97 - p18 [501+]
c PW - v243 - N 4 '96 - p74 [51-250]
c SLJ - v42 - O '96 - p115 [51-250]
Manning, Richard - *Grassland: The History, Biology, Politics, and Promise of the American Prairie*
Bloom Rev - v16 - S '96 - p26 [501+]
Manning, Robert John Sheffler - *Interpreting Otherwise than Heidegger*
JR - v77 - Ja '97 - p176+ [501+]
Manning, Sturt W - *The Absolute Chronology of the Aegean Early Bronze Age*
AJA - v100 - O '96 - p784+ [501+]
Mannoni, Laurent - *Light and Movement*
TLS - F 7 '97 - p18 [501+]
Mano, M Morris - *Logic and Computer Design Fundamentals*
SciTech - v21 - Mr '97 - p93 [51-250]
Manogaran, Chelvadurai - *The Sri Lankan Tamils*
GJ - v162 - Jl '96 - p237 [51-250]
Manolis, Argie - *Crafts Marketplace*
r LJ - v122 - F 15 '97 - p133 [51-250]
Manos, Constantine - *American Color*
NS & S - v9 - My 17 '96 - p41 [1-50]
Manrai, Lalita A - *Global Perspectives in Cross-Cultural and Cross-National Consumer Research*
JEL - v35 - Mr '97 - p255 [51-250]
R&R Bk N - v11 - D '96 - p34 [51-250]
Manrique, Jaime - *Twilight at the Equator*
KR - v65 - F 1 '97 - p164 [251-500]
PW - v244 - F 17 '97 - p211+ [51-250]
A Man's Guide to Coping with Disability
r BL - v93 - D 1 '96 - p685+ [51-250]
LJ - v121 - N 1 '96 - p101 [51-250]
Mansel, Philip - *Constantinople: City of the World's Desire 1453-1924*
BL - v93 - O 1 '96 - p319 [51-250]
BW - v27 - F 2 '97 - p7+ [501+]
HT - v47 - Ja '97 - p55+ [501+]
KR - v64 - S 15 '96 - p1378 [251-500]
LJ - v121 - S 15 '96 - p80 [51-250]
NYTBR - v101 - D 29 '96 - p9 [501+]
Manser, A G R - *Practical Handbook of Processing and Recycling of Municipal Waste*
SciTech - v20 - D '96 - p70 [51-250]
Mansfield, Bob - *Towards a Competent Workforce*
TES - F 28 '97 - p32 [251-500]
Mansfield, Harvey C - *Machiavelli's Virtue*
Choice - v34 - S '96 - p208 [51-250]
Lon R Bks - v18 - Ag 22 '96 - p12+ [501+]
RP - v59 - Spr '97 - p404+ [501+]
TLS - S 20 '96 - p8 [501+]
Mansfield, Helen - *Mathematics for Tomorrow's Young Children*
SciTech - v20 - D '96 - p15 [51-250]
Mansfield, Katherine - *Short Stories by Katherine Mansfield*
y TES - S 20 '96 - pR6 [251-500]
Mansfield, Mary C - *The Humiliation of Sinners*
AHR - v101 - D '96 - p1534+ [501+]
FR - v70 - F '97 - p507+ [501+]
JR - v76 - O '96 - p632+ [501+]
Mansfield, Richard - *Windows 95 Power Toolkit*
SciTech - v20 - D '96 - p12 [51-250]
Mansfield, Ron - *Excel for Windows 95 for Busy People*
CBR - v14 - Jl '96 - p25 [1-50]
PowerPoint for Windows 95 for Busy People
BL - v92 - Ag '96 - p1868 [501+]
CBR - v14 - Jl '96 - p24 [1-50]

Windows 95 for Busy People. 2nd Ed.
LJ - v122 - Ap 1 '97 - p118 [51-250]
Mansingh, Surjit - *Historical Dictionary of India*
r ARBA - v28 - '97 - p57+ [251-500]
r Choice - v34 - Ap '97 - p1312 [51-250]
r R&R Bk N - v12 - F '97 - p19 [51-250]
Manski, Charles F - *Identification Problems in the Social Sciences*
CS - v25 - N '96 - p820+ [501+]
Manson, Ainslie - *Just like New (Illus. by Karen Reczuch)*
c BL - v93 - N 15 '96 - p594 [51-250]
c CCB-B - v50 - Ja '97 - p180 [51-250]
c Ch BWatch - v6 - S '96 - p7 [1-50]
c SLJ - v42 - D '96 - p100+ [51-250]
Manson, Cynthia - *The Haunted Hour*
SF Chr - v18 - O '96 - p80 [1-50]
Murder by the Book
y Kliatt - v31 - Mr '97 - p21 [51-250]
Murder Intercontinental
KR - v64 - O 15 '96 - p1499 [51-250]
LJ - v121 - N 1 '96 - p111 [1-50]
PW - v243 - O 14 '96 - p67 [51-250]
Win, Lose or Die
KR - v64 - My 1 '96 - p648 [51-250]
PW - v243 - D 2 '96 - p56 [51-250]
Mansour, Camille - *Beyond Alliance*
JTWS - v13 - Fall '96 - p331+ [501+]
Mantel, Hilary - *Eight Months on Ghazzah Street*
TES - Ag 23 '96 - p21 [51-250]
An Experiment in Love
Books - v10 - Je '96 - p24 [51-250]
NY - v72 - S 30 '96 - p87 [51-250]
NYRB - v43 - Ag 8 '96 - p35+ [501+]
NYTBR - v101 - D 8 '96 - p79 [1-50]
An Experiment in Love (Walter). Audio Version
y Kliatt - v30 - N '96 - p40 [51-250]
An Experiment in Love (Whitelaw). Audio Version
Obs - Ja 12 '97 - p18* [51-250]
Mantell, Michael R - *Don't Sweat the Small Stuff (Hall). Audio Version*
LJ - v121 - N 15 '96 - p107 [51-250]
Mantena, P R - *Advanced Materials for Vibro-Acoustic Applications*
SciTech - v21 - Mr '97 - p83 [51-250]
Manthorne, Jackie - *Final Take*
Quill & Q - v62 - O '96 - p32 [51-250]
Manthorne, Katherine E - *The Landscapes of Louis Remy Mignot*
Choice - v34 - My '97 - p1487 [51-250]
Manthorpe, Victoria - *Children of the Empire*
CR - v269 - D '96 - p334 [51-250]
TLS - Ag 30 '96 - p36 [501+]
Mantilla R, Luis Carlos - *Historia De La Arquidiocesis De Bogota*
CHR - v82 - O '96 - p743+ [501+]
Mantius, Peter - *Shell Game*
Nat - v262 - Je 10 '96 - p28+ [501+]
Mantle, Jonathan - *Car Wars*
LJ - v121 - O 1 '96 - p95 [51-250]
PW - v243 - S 23 '96 - p67 [51-250]
Mantle, Merlyn - *A Hero All His Life*
y BL - v93 - S 1 '96 - p3 [51-250]
KR - v64 - S 1 '96 - p1300+ [251-500]
Manuale Enciclopedico Della Bibliofilia
r BC - v46 - Spr '97 - p135 [51-250]
Manuel, David - *Bosnia: Hope in the Ashes*
BWatch - v18 - F '97 - p12 [51-250]
Manuel, Frank E - *A Requiem for Karl Marx*
CEH - v29 - 1 '96 - p147+ [501+]
Manuel, Lynn - *The Night the Moon Blew Kisses (Illus. by Robin Spowart)*
c CBRS - v24 - Ag '96 - p161 [51-250]
c HB Guide - v8 - Spr '97 - p39 [51-250]
c Quill & Q - v62 - O '96 - p46 [51-250]
c SLJ - v42 - N '96 - p88 [51-250]
Manuel, Paul Christopher - *The Challenges of Democratic Consolidation in Portugal*
R&R Bk N - v11 - D '96 - p48 [51-250]
Manuel, Peter - *Caribbean Currents*
Notes - v53 - S '96 - p89+ [501+]
Manufacturing Science and Engineering 1996
SciTech - v21 - Mr '97 - p99 [51-250]
Manufacturing Worldwide. 1st Ed.
r ARBA - v28 - '97 - p97 [251-500]
r RQ - v36 - Fall '96 - p133+ [501+]
Many, Paul - *These Are the Rules*
y BL - v93 - My 1 '97 - p1489 [51-250]
y CCB-B - v50 - Ap '97 - p289 [51-250]
y KR - v65 - Ap 1 '97 - p559+ [51-250]
y PW - v244 - Ap 28 '97 - p76 [51-250]

Many Mountains Moving
p Sm Pr R - v28 - O '96 - p16 [51-250]
Manzhelii, Vadim G - *Physics of Cryocrystals*
SciTech - v21 - Mr '97 - p20 [51-250]
Manzo, Kathryn A - *Creating Boundaries*
Choice - v34 - D '96 - p681+ [51-250]
Mao, Tse-Tung - *Mao's Road to Power. Vol. 3*
Ch Rev Int - v4 - Spr '97 - p238+ [501+]
Quotations from Chairman Mao Tse-Tung
FEER - Anniv '96 - p222+ [501+]
Mao, Tun - *Rainbow*
TranslRevS - v1 - My '95 - p16 [51-250]
Maples, William R - *Dead Men Do Tell Tales*
Rapport - v19 - 4 '96 - p41 [251-500]
Maples in the Mist (Illus. by Jean Tseng)
c BL - v93 - O 1 '96 - p355 [51-250]
c BL - v93 - Ap 1 '97 - p1305 [1-50]
c CCB-B - v50 - S '96 - p15 [51-250]
c HB Guide - v8 - Spr '97 - p150 [51-250]
c Par - v72 - F '97 - p149 [51-250]
c SLJ - v42 - S '96 - p216 [51-250]
Mapplethorpe, Robert - *Pistils*
LJ - v121 - D '96 - p88 [51-250]
VLS - Win '96 - p30 [51-250]
Mara, Mary Jane - *Head for the Web*
CBR - v15 - Spr '97 - p4 [1-50]
Mara, William P - *The Fragile Frog (Illus. by John R Quinn)*
c BL - v93 - N 1 '96 - p493 [51-250]
c HB Guide - v8 - Spr '97 - p123 [51-250]
c SLJ - v42 - N '96 - p116 [51-250]
Marable, Manning - *Beyond Black and White*
J Pol - v59 - F '97 - p267+ [501+]
Black Liberation in Conservative America
BL - v93 - F 15 '97 - p999+ [51-250]
BW - v27 - F 16 '97 - p12 [51-250]
PW - v244 - Ja 13 '97 - p67 [51-250]
Maracotta, Lindsay - *The Dead Hollywood Moms Society*
Ent W - S 27 '96 - p75 [51-250]
LATBR - S 22 '96 - p8 [51-250]
Maragos, Petros - *Mathematical Morphology and Its Applications to Image and Signal Processing*
SciTech - v20 - D '96 - p66 [51-250]
Maragoudakis, Michael E - *Molecular, Cellular, and Clinical Aspects of Angiogenesis*
SciTech - v20 - N '96 - p31 [51-250]
Maraire, J Nozipo - *Zenzele: A Letter for My Daughter*
Ms - v7 - S '96 - p83 [1-50]
NYTBR - v101 - D 8 '96 - p84 [1-50]
PW - v244 - Ap 14 '97 - p72 [1-50]
W&I - v11 - N '96 - p269+ [501+]
WLT - v71 - Win '97 - p212 [501+]
Maran, Meredith - *Notes from an Incomplete Revolution*
KR - v65 - Mr 15 '97 - p444 [251-500]
LJ - v122 - Ap 1 '97 - p112 [51-250]
PW - v244 - F 24 '97 - p71 [51-250]
Maran, Ruth - *Teach Yourself Computers and the Internet Visually*
LJ - v121 - N 1 '96 - p104 [51-250]
Maraniss, David - *Tell Newt to Shut Up*
NYRB - v43 - Je 6 '96 - p11+ [501+]
Marans, Steven - *The Police-Mental Health Partnership*
Readings - v11 - D '96 - p22 [51-250]
Soc Ser R - v71 - Mr '97 - p166 [1-50]
Maranto, Gina - *Quest for Perfection*
BW - v26 - O 20 '96 - p8 [251-500]
Nature - v384 - N 14 '96 - p127+ [501+]
Mararike, C G - *Grassroots Leadership*
Choice - v34 - S '96 - p219 [51-250]
Marberry, Sara O - *The Power of Color*
FHB - D '96 - p144 [251-500]
Marble, Allan Everett - *Surgeons, Smallpox, and the Poor*
Can Hist R - v77 - S '96 - p442+ [501+]
Marbrouk, S T - *The Organic Chemistry Survival Manual*
J Chem Ed - v74 - Mr '97 - p343+ [251-500]
Marc, David - *Bonfire of the Humanities*
J Am Cult - v19 - Sum '96 - p160 [51-250]
Marcantel, Pamela - *An Army of Angels*
y BL - v93 - F 15 '97 - p1004 [51-250]
KR - v65 - Ja 15 '97 - p85 [251-500]
LJ - v121 - D '96 - p146 [51-250]
PW - v243 - D 2 '96 - p38+ [51-250]
Marceau, Gabrielle Z - *Anti-Dumping and Anti-Trust Issues in Free-Trade Areas*
JEL - v34 - D '96 - p1968+ [501+]
Marcellini, Paolo - *Partial Differential Equations and Applications*
SIAM Rev - v38 - D '96 - p714 [51-250]
Marcellino, Dennis - *Why Are We Here?*
BWatch - v18 - Mr '97 - p10 [51-250]

March, G Patrick - *Eastern Destiny*
    Choice - v34 - My '97 - p1558+ [51-250]
    R&R Bk N - v12 - F '97 - p17 [51-250]
March, Ivan - *The Penguin Guide to Compact Discs*
    r FF - v20 - Mr '97 - p424+ [501+]
March, Karen - *The Stranger Who Bore Me*
    CS - v25 - N '96 - p789+ [501+]
March, N H - *Electron Correlation in Molecules and Condensed Phases*
    Sci - v275 - Mr 21 '97 - p1749 [501+]
    SciTech - v21 - Mr '97 - p28 [51-250]
Marchac, Daniel - *Male Aesthetic Surgery*
    SciTech - v20 - N '96 - p49 [51-250]
Marchak, M Patricia - *Logging the Globe*
    CS - v25 - S '96 - p598+ [251-500]
    Racism, Sexism, and the University
    Quill & Q - v62 - O '96 - p38 [251-500]
Marchand, Marianne -
    Feminism/Postmodernism/Development
    CS - v26 - Ja '97 - p48+ [501+]
Marchand, Patrick - *Graphics and GUIs with MATLAB*
    Choice - v34 - N '96 - p495 [51-250]
Marchand, Pierre - *The Story of Printmaking*
    c Sch Lib - v44 - Ag '96 - p114 [51-250]
    c TES - Ag 23 '96 - p24 [51-250]
Marchand, Suzanne L - *Down from Olympus*
    Choice - v34 - Ja '97 - p857 [51-250]
    TLS - D 13 '96 - p26+ [501+]
Marchant, Kerena - *Diwali*
    c Sch Lib - v45 - F '97 - p39 [51-250]
    Id-Ul-Fitr
    c TES - F 14 '97 - p16* [51-250]
Marchena Fernandez, Juan - *Ejercito Y Milicias En El Mundo Colonial Americano*
    HAHR - v76 - N '96 - p770+ [501+]
    La Vida De Guarnicion En Las Ciudades Americanas De La Ilustracion
    HAHR - v76 - N '96 - p770+ [501+]
Marchessault, Janine - *Mirror Machine*
    Afterimage - v24 - N '96 - p4 [1-50]
Marchionini, Gary - *Information Seeking in Electronic Environments*
    LQ - v66 - O '96 - p483+ [501+]
Marciniak, Barbara - *Bringers of the Dawn (Marciniak). Audio Version*
    BL - v93 - F 15 '97 - p1038 [51-250]
Marcinko, Richard - *Leadership Secrets of the Rogue Warrior (Marcinko). Audio Version*
    BL - v93 - N 15 '96 - p604 [51-250]
    Rogue Warrior--Designation Gold
    KR - v65 - Ja 15 '97 - p85+ [251-500]
    PW - v244 - F 10 '97 - p68 [51-250]
    Rogue Warrior--Task Force Blue
    PW - v244 - Ja 27 '97 - p103 [1-50]
    The Rogue Warrior's Strategy for Success
    PW - v244 - My 5 '97 - p191+ [51-250]
Marco, Guy A - *Checklist of Writings on American Music 1640-1992*
    r LJ - v121 - N 1 '96 - p62 [51-250]
    Literature of American Music III
    r ARBA - v28 - '97 - p467+ [251-500]
    r LJ - v121 - N 1 '96 - p62 [51-250]
Marcombe, David - *Sounding Boards*
    Pub Hist - v18 - Fall '96 - p183+ [501+]
Marcone, Stephen - *Managing Your Band*
    Teach Mus - v4 - F '97 - p51+ [51-250]
Marconi, Clemente - *Selinunte: Le Metope Dell'Heraion*
    AJA - v100 - Jl '96 - p624+ [501+]
Marconi, Joe - *Image Marketing*
    Choice - v34 - Ap '97 - p1384 [51-250]
Marcos, Subcomandante - *Shadows of Tender Fury*
    AAAGA - v86 - S '96 - p614+ [501+]
    HAHR - v76 - N '96 - p801 [251-500]
    Workbook - v21 - Fall '96 - p137 [501+]
Marcos Marin, Francisco - *Informatica Y Humanidades*
    Compt & H - v30 - 1 '96 - p85+ [501+]
Marcum, Betty E - *The New Cairn Terrier*
    Dog Fan - v27 - N '96 - p24 [1-50]
Marcus, Alan I - *Cancer from Beef*
    T&C - v37 - Ap '96 - p396+ [501+]
    Plague of Strangers
    J Urban H - v22 - My '96 - p531+ [501+]
Marcus, Alan Rudolph - *Relocating Eden*
    AHR - v102 - F '97 - p230 [251-500]
Marcus, Ben - *The Age of Wire and String*
    ABR - v18 - O '96 - p8+ [501+]
Marcus, Clare Cooper - *House as a Mirror of Self*
    FHB - Ag '96 - p136 [251-500]
Marcus, David - *The Irish Eros*
    TLS - S 27 '96 - p21 [51-250]

Marcus, George E - *With Malice toward Some*
    APSR - v90 - D '96 - p916+ [501+]
    Choice - v34 - N '96 - p529 [51-250]
    Pub Op Q - v60 - Win '96 - p653+ [501+]
Marcus, Greil - *Invisible Republic*
    BL - v93 - My 1 '97 - p1473 [51-250]
    KR - v65 - Mr 1 '97 - p358+ [51-250]
    LJ - v122 - My 1 '97 - p105 [51-250]
    PW - v244 - Mr 17 '97 - p62 [51-250]
Marcus, Ivan G - *Rituals of Childhood*
    Choice - v34 - S '96 - p145 [51-250]
    HRNB - v25 - Win '97 - p82 [251-500]
Marcus, Jacob Rader - *The American Jew 1585-1990*
    Choice - v34 - D '96 - p677 [51-250]
Marcus, Joel - *Jesus and the Holocaust*
    PW - v244 - Mr 24 '97 - p74 [51-250]
Marcus, Joyce - *Caciques and Their People*
    HAHR - v76 - N '96 - p766+ [501+]
    Zapotec Civilization
    Sci - v273 - Ag 30 '96 - p1178+ [501+]
Marcus, Leonard J - *Renegotiating Health Care*
    AJN - v96 - D '96 - p16N [51-250]
Marcus, Leonard S - *The Making of Goodnight Moon*
    c PW - v244 - F 3 '97 - p108 [51-250]
Marcus, P - *Corrosion Mechanisms in Theory and Practice*
    Choice - v34 - O '96 - p311 [51-250]
Marcus, Robert - *Osteoporosis*
    r SciTech - v20 - S '96 - p37 [51-250]
Marcus, Ruth Barcan - *Modalities: Philosophical Essays*
    Dialogue - v36 - Win '97 - p157+ [501+]
Marcuse, Peter M - *Disease: In Search of Remedy*
    Choice - v34 - N '96 - p494 [51-250]
    y SB - v32 - O '96 - p206 [51-250]
Marcuzzo, Maria Cristina - *The Economics of Joan Robinson*
    R&R Bk N - v12 - F '97 - p33 [1-50]
Marcy, Jean - *Cemetery Murders*
    KR - v65 - Ap 1 '97 - p508 [51-250]
    LJ - v122 - My 1 '97 - p143 [51-250]
Maree, Kathy - *500 Anos Del Ensayo En Hispanoamerica*
    Hisp - v79 - S '96 - p458+ [501+]
Marek, Jayne E - *Women Editing Modernism*
    AL - v69 - Mr '97 - p232+ [251-500]
    ELT - v40 - 2 '97 - p214+ [501+]
    JMCQ - v73 - Aut '96 - p773+ [501+]
Marek, Milos - *Chaotic Behavior of Deterministic Dissipative Systems*
    SIAM Rev - v38 - D '96 - p695+ [501+]
Maren, Michael - *The Road to Hell*
    BL - v93 - D 1 '96 - p626 [51-250]
    For Aff - v76 - Ja '97 - p132+ [501+]
    KR - v64 - N 1 '96 - p1586 [251-500]
    LJ - v121 - D '96 - p123 [51-250]
    NYTBR - v102 - Mr 23 '97 - p23 [501+]
Margalit, Avishai - *The Decent Society*
    Choice - v34 - Mr '97 - p1237 [51-250]
    JEL - v35 - Mr '97 - p201 [51-250]
    TLS - Mr 7 '97 - p10+ [501+]
Margenau, Henry - *Cosmos, Bios, Theos*
    PSR - v25 - '96 - p273+ [501+]
Margherita, Gayle - *The Romance of Origins*
    MLR - v92 - Ja '97 - p167+ [501+]
Margolies, Edward - *The Several Lives of Chester Himes*
    PW - v244 - My 5 '97 - p189 [51-250]
Margolin, Jean-Claude - *Erasme, Precepteur De L'Europe*
    Choice - v34 - D '96 - p567 [1-50]
    Ren Q - v49 - Win '96 - p904+ [501+]
    Six Ct J - v27 - Fall '96 - p865+ [501+]
Margolin, Phillip - *The Burning Man*
    y BL - v92 - Ag '96 - p1855 [251-500]
    Books - v11 - Ap '97 - p23 [51-250]
    BWatch - v17 - D '96 - p6 [51-250]
    CSM - v88 - S 19 '96 - p14 [51-250]
    PW - v243 - Jl 22 '96 - p227 [51-250]
    The Burning Man (Scott). Audio Version
    y Kliatt - v31 - Mr '97 - p40 [51-250]
Margolin, Victor - *The Struggle for Utopia*
    PW - v244 - Ap 21 '97 - p50+ [51-250]
Margolis, David - *The Stepman*
    KR - v64 - S 15 '96 - p1346 [251-500]
    LJ - v121 - N 1 '96 - p107 [51-250]
    PW - v243 - S 9 '96 - p63 [51-250]
Margolis, Howard - *Dealing with Risk*
    Choice - v34 - Mr '97 - p1179 [51-250]
    Nature - v385 - Ja 9 '97 - p129+ [501+]
    New Sci - v152 - O 26 '96 - p45 [51-250]
Margolis, Jonathan - *Bernard Manning*
    NS - v126 - Ja 17 '97 - p47 [501+]

Margolis, Joseph - *Life without Principles*
    Choice - v34 - O '96 - p294 [51-250]
Margolis, Philip E - *Random House Personal Computer Dictionary. 2nd Ed.*
    r Choice - v34 - S '96 - p102 [51-250]
Margolis, Seth - *Perfect Angel*
    BL - v93 - Mr 15 '97 - p1230 [51-250]
    KR - v65 - Ja 1 '97 - p14+ [251-500]
    LJ - v122 - F 15 '97 - p163 [51-250]
    PW - v244 - Ja 13 '97 - p51 [51-250]
    Trib Bks - Mr 16 '97 - p6 [51-250]
Margolis, Simon - *Johns Hopkins Symptoms and Remedies*
    r BL - v93 - F 1 '97 - p958 [1-50]
Margolis, Susanna - *Adventuring in the Pacific. 2nd Ed.*
    r BL - v93 - S 15 '96 - p212 [1-50]
Margoshes, Dave - *Long Distance Calls*
    BIC - v26 - Mr '97 - p4+ [501+]
Margulies, Donald - *Sight Unseen and Other Plays*
    Choice - v34 - S '96 - p127+ [51-250]
Margulies, Edward - *Bad Movies We Love*
    r TES - Ag 2 '96 - pR6 [1-50]
Margulies, Herbert F - *Reconciliation and Revival*
    R&R Bk N - v11 - N '96 - p19 [51-250]
Mariani, Paul - *The Great Wheel*
    Am - v175 - O 26 '96 - p24+ [501+]
    Lost Puritan
    CR - v269 - N '96 - p277 [1-50]
    Obs - F 9 '97 - p18* [51-250]
    WLT - v70 - Sum '96 - p703+ [501+]
Marias, Javier - *All Souls*
    BL - v93 - N 1 '96 - p482 [51-250]
    KR - v64 - N 1 '96 - p1558 [251-500]
    Trib Bks - Ja 12 '97 - p2 [1-50]
    A Heart So White
    BW - v26 - Jl 7 '96 - p6 [501+]
    Tomorrow in the Battle Think on Me
    Lon R Bks - v19 - Ap 24 '97 - p13+ [501+]
    Obs - N 10 '96 - p18* [51-250]
    TLS - N 15 '96 - p24 [501+]
Mariategui, Jose Carlos - *The Heroic and Creative Meaning of Socialism*
    HAHR - v77 - My '97 - p288+ [251-500]
Marie, Claude-Valentin - *The EC Member States and Immigration 1993*
    J Gov Info - v23 - S '96 - p667 [51-250]
Marie, Linda - *The Menace of the Sublime to the Individual Self*
    CPR - v16 - Je '96 - p159+ [501+]
Marien, Michael - *Environmental Issues and Sustainable Futures*
    r BioSci - v46 - O '96 - p721 [51-250]
    r BL - v93 - S 15 '96 - p284 [251-500]
    r Choice - v34 - D '96 - p592 [51-250]
    r New Sci - v152 - O 26 '96 - p47 [51-250]
Marietta, Don E - *Philosophy of Sexuality*
    Choice - v34 - Ap '97 - p1352 [51-250]
    R&R Bk N - v12 - F '97 - p52 [51-250]
Marie-Victoire, Louis - *Le Droit De Cuissage*
    FR - v70 - F '97 - p509+ [501+]
Marik, Paul Ellis - *The ICU Therapeutics Handbook*
    SciTech - v20 - S '96 - p30 [51-250]
Marika, Wandjuk - *Wandjuk Marika: Life Story*
    Aust Bk R - S '96 - p66 [251-500]
Maril, Robert Lee - *The Bay Shrimpers of Texas*
    CS - v25 - S '96 - p644+ [501+]
    JSH - v63 - F '97 - p212 [251-500]
Marin, Gustavo Adolfo - *La Locura De Fidel Castro*
    BL - v93 - Ap 1 '97 - p1284 [1-50]
Marin, Lise - *Ploumette Et Ploum Partagent Leurs Jouets*
    c BL - v93 - N 1 '96 - p500 [1-50]
Marinatos, Nanno - *Greek Sanctuaries*
    CW - v89 - Jl '96 - p518+ [51-250]
Marino, Bruno - *Heart Disease in Persons with Down Syndrome*
    SciTech - v20 - N '96 - p47 [51-250]
Marino, Jan - *The Day That Elvis Came to Town*
    y SLJ - v43 - Ja '97 - p37 [1-50]
    y SLJ - v43 - Mr '97 - p113 [1-50]
Marino, Vinny - *Journey from Hell*
    BL - v92 - Ag '96 - p1863 [51-250]
Marion Zimmer Bradley's Fantasy Magazine
    p SF Chr - v18 - O '96 - p83 [1-50]
Marissen, Michael - *The Social and Religious Designs of J.S. Bach's Brandenburg Concertos*
    CH - v65 - D '96 - p717+ [501+]
Maristed, Kai - *Fall*
    LATBR - S 1 '96 - p3 [501+]
Maritain, Jacques - *The Degrees of Knowledge*
    LQ - v66 - O '96 - p471+ [501+]

Marius, Richard - *The Columbia Book of Civil War Poetry*
JSH - v62 - N '96 - p860+ [51-250]
Marjoribanks, Augustus - *Lucky!*
Books - v9 - S '95 - p24 [1-50]
Mark, Barbara - *Angelspeake*
CSM - v89 - N 25 '96 - p12 [51-250]
Mark, James E - *Physical Properties of Polymers Handbook*
Choice - v34 - D '96 - p643 [51-250]
r SciTech - v20 - N '96 - p64 [51-250]
Physical Properties of Polymers Handbook. Electronic Media Version
r SciTech - v20 - N '96 - p63 [1-50]
Mark, Jan - *The Tale of Tobias (Illus. by Rachel Merriman)*
c CBRS - v25 - Win '97 - p68 [1-50]
c CCB-B - v50 - D '96 - p142 [51-250]
c HB - v73 - Ja '97 - p77+ [51-250]
c HB Guide - v8 - Spr '97 - p87 [51-250]
c KR - v64 - O 1 '96 - p1471 [51-250]
c SLJ - v42 - O '96 - p115 [51-250]
Mark, Michael L - *Contemporary Music Education. 3rd Ed.*
Choice - v34 - Mr '97 - p1212 [51-250]
Markel, Geraldine - *Performance Breakthroughs for Adolescents with Learning Disabilities or ADD*
VOYA - v19 - F '97 - p358+ [251-500]
Markel, Howard - *The Practical Pediatrician*
r ARBA - v28 - '97 - p615 [51-250]
r BL - v93 - S 1 '96 - p170 [251-500]
r LJ - v121 - N 1 '96 - p62 [51-250]
Quarantine! East European Jewish Immigrants and the New York City Epidemics of 1892
KR - v65 - My 1 '97 - p701 [251-500]
Markel, Michael H - *Technical Communication. 4th Ed.*
SciTech - v20 - D '96 - p58 [51-250]
Marken, Amy Van - *Johnny Rolf: Her Ceramics/Her Gouaches*
Am Craft - v57 - F '97 - p31+ [501+]
Ceram Mo - v45 - Ja '97 - p26+ [251-500]
Marker, Sherry - *The Plains Indian Wars*
y HB Guide - v8 - Spr '97 - p178 [51-250]
The Market Guide for Young Writers. 5th Ed.
cr ARBA - v28 - '97 - p347 [51-250]
Market Information 1995/96
r ARBA - v28 - '97 - p126 [51-250]
Markey, Peter - *Nodding Farm*
c PW - v244 - Mr 10 '97 - p68 [51-250]
Nodding Safari
c PW - v244 - Mr 10 '97 - p68 [51-250]
Markham, Beryl - *West with the Night (Harris). Audio Version*
CSM - v89 - Mr 27 '97 - pB1 [1-50]
Markham, Lois - *Avi*
c SLJ - v42 - Ag '96 - p158 [51-250]
Jacques-Yves Cousteau: Exploring the Wonders of the Deep
c HB Guide - v8 - Spr '97 - p159 [51-250]
Markham, Ursula - *The Ultimate Stress Handbook for Women*
r Books - v11 - Ap '97 - p21 [1-50]
Markides, Constantinos C - *Diversification, Refocusing, and Economic Performance*
JEL - v34 - S '96 - p1437+ [51-250]
R&R Bk N - v12 - F '97 - p40 [51-250]
Markle, Sandra - *Creepy, Crawly Baby Bugs*
c BL - v93 - N 15 '96 - p592 [51-250]
c HB Guide - v8 - Spr '97 - p122 [51-250]
Creepy, Spooky Science (Illus. by Cecile Schoberle)
c HB Guide - v8 - Spr '97 - p110 [51-250]
c Learning - v25 - Mr '97 - p38 [1-50]
c SLJ - v42 - O '96 - p136 [51-250]
Icky, Squishy Science (Illus. by Cecile Schoberle)
c HB Guide - v7 - Fall '96 - p328+ [51-250]
c Learning - v25 - Mr '97 - p38 [1-50]
c SLJ - v42 - Ag '96 - p158 [51-250]
Outside and inside Sharks
c Ch BWatch - v6 - My '96 - p4 [51-250]
c HB Guide - v7 - Fall '96 - p343 [51-250]
Pioneering Frozen Worlds
c Ch BWatch - v6 - My '96 - p4 [51-250]
c HB Guide - v7 - Fall '96 - p392 [51-250]
Marklew, Victoria - *Cash, Crisis, and Corporate Governance*
APSR - v90 - S '96 - p677+ [501+]
Markman, Maurie - *Expert Consultations in Gynecological Cancers*
SciTech - v21 - Mr '97 - p50 [51-250]

Markoe, Merrill - *Merrill Markoe's Guide to Love*
BL - v93 - F 1 '97 - p912 [51-250]
KR - v64 - D 1 '96 - p1720+ [251-500]
PW - v243 - D 9 '96 - p54 [51-250]
Trib Bks - F 9 '97 - p6 [501+]
Markolin, Caroline - *Modern Austrian Literature*
Ger Q - v69 - Fall '96 - p458+ [501+]
Markova, Dawna - *The Open Mind*
LJ - v121 - N 1 '96 - p94 [51-250]
Markowe, Laura A - *Redefining the Self*
Choice - v34 - F '97 - p1044 [51-250]
Markowitz, Gerald - *Children, Race, and Power*
BL - v93 - S 1 '96 - p42 [51-250]
NYTBR - v101 - N 17 '96 - p36 [501+]
PW - v243 - S 23 '96 - p67+ [51-250]
Marks, Alan - *Ring-a-Ring O'Roses and a Ding, Dong, Bell (Illus. by Alan Marks)*
c Bks Keeps - N '96 - p9 [51-250]
c HB Guide - v8 - Spr '97 - p107 [51-250]
Marks, Anthony - *Learn to Play Blues*
y Sch Lib - v44 - Ag '96 - p124 [51-250]
The Usborne French Songbook for Beginners
c Sch Lib - v44 - Ag '96 - p113 [51-250]
Marks, Elaine - *Marrano as Metaphor*
Choice - v34 - O '96 - p286 [51-250]
Marks, Gil - *The World of Jewish Cooking*
BL - v93 - S 15 '96 - p196 [51-250]
LJ - v121 - S 15 '96 - p89 [51-250]
Marks, Graham - *Fault Line*
y Bks Keeps - v100 - S '96 - p17 [51-250]
y Sch Lib - v44 - Ag '96 - p120 [51-250]
Wallace and Gromit in A Close Shave
c PW - v243 - N 11 '96 - p77 [51-250]
Wallace and Gromit in The Wrong Trousers
c PW - v243 - N 11 '96 - p77 [51-250]
Marks, Howard - *Mr. Nice*
Lon R Bks - v19 - Ja 23 '97 - p26+ [501+]
Obs - S 8 '96 - p15* [501+]
TLS - O 4 '96 - p30 [501+]
Marks, Joel - *Emotions in Asian Thought*
Ch Rev Int - v4 - Spr '97 - p216+ [501+]
Marks, Lara V - *Metropolitan Maternity*
JEL - v35 - Mr '97 - p263+ [51-250]
Model Mothers
EHR - v111 - N '96 - p1336+ [501+]
VS - v39 - Win '96 - p287+ [501+]
Marks, Lynne - *Revivals and Roller Rinks*
Choice - v34 - Mr '97 - p1228 [51-250]
R&R Bk N - v11 - D '96 - p18 [51-250]
Marks, Marlene Adler - *Nice Jewish Girls*
y Kliatt - v30 - S '96 - p25 [51-250]
Marks, Paula Mitchell - *Hands to the Spindle*
Choice - v34 - O '96 - p350 [51-250]
Roundup M - v3 - Ag '96 - p25+ [251-500]
Marks, Sheldon - *Cancer De La Prostata*
LJ - v122 - Ja '97 - p79 [51-250]
Marks, Thomas A - *Maoist Insurgency since Vietnam*
Choice - v34 - S '96 - p205+ [51-250]
Parameters - v26 - Aut '96 - p160+ [501+]
Marks' Electronic Handbook for Mechanical Engineers. Electronic Media Version
r Choice - v34 - N '96 - p489 [51-250]
r SciTech - v20 - N '96 - p69 [51-250]
Marks' Standard Handbook for Mechanical Engineers. 10th Ed.
r Choice - v34 - F '97 - p994 [51-250]
r SciTech - v20 - D '96 - p71 [51-250]
Markson, David - *Reader's Block*
BW - v26 - N 3 '96 - p9+ [501+]
KR - v64 - S 15 '96 - p1346+ [251-500]
LJ - v121 - O 15 '96 - p91 [51-250]
NYTBR - v102 - Ja 12 '97 - p21 [251-500]
PW - v243 - N 4 '96 - p37 [51-250]
Marku, Rudolf - *Vdekja Lexon Gazeten*
WLT - v70 - Aut '96 - p1006 [251-500]
Markun, Patricia Maloney - *The Little Painter of Sabana Grande*
c CLW - v67 - Mr '97 - p14 [1-50]
Markus, R A - *Sacred and Secular*
CHR - v83 - Ja '97 - p168 [51-250]
Markusen, Eric - *The Holocaust and Strategic Bombing*
AHR - v102 - F '97 - p89+ [501+]
APH - v43 - Win '96 - p60 [251-500]
Arm F&S - v23 - Win '96 - p299+ [501+]
CS - v25 - S '96 - p623+ [501+]
Markwick, Margaret - *Trollope and Women*
NS - v126 - F 14 '97 - p46+ [501+]
Obs - F 9 '97 - p16* [501+]
Spec - v278 - Mr 8 '97 - p36+ [501+]
Marland, Hilary - *The Art of Midwifery*
EHR - v112 - F '97 - p201+ [501+]

Marland, Michael - *Scenes from Plays*
y TES - F 28 '97 - pR7 [501+]
Marlatt, Daphne - *Ana Historic*
Essays CW - Spr '96 - p93+ [501+]
Marlatt, David - *A Hog Slaughtering Woman*
BL - v93 - N 1 '96 - p476 [51-250]
Marley, Anne - *Fair's Fair*
Sch Lib - v44 - Ag '96 - p130 [51-250]
Marley, Louise - *Sing the Warmth*
y Kliatt - v31 - Mr '97 - p18+ [51-250]
Marling, Karal Ann - *As Seen on TV*
J Am Cult - v19 - Spr '96 - p102+ [251-500]
Graceland: Going Home with Elvis
LATBR - v263 - S 29 '96 - p4 [501+]
LJ - v121 - O 1 '96 - p80 [51-250]
Nat - v263 - D 9 '96 - p29+ [501+]
NYTBR - v101 - Ag 25 '96 - p9 [501+]
Marlow, Eugene - *The Breakdown of Hierarchy*
PW - v244 - Ja 27 '97 - p87 [51-250]
Marlow, James E - *Charles Dickens: The Uses of Time*
RES - v47 - N '96 - p614+ [501+]
Marlowe, Christopher - *Edward II*
RES - v48 - F '97 - p94+ [501+]
Marlowe, Sam - *Learning about Dedication from the Life of Frederick Douglass*
c SLJ - v43 - Ja '97 - p104+ [51-250]
Marlowe, Stephen, 1928- - *The Death and Life of Miguel De Cervantes*
CSM - v89 - F 6 '97 - p13 [501+]
KR - v64 - S 15 '96 - p1347 [251-500]
LJ - v121 - N 1 '96 - p107+ [51-250]
NYTBR - v101 - N 10 '96 - p56 [51-250]
PW - v243 - S 9 '96 - p63+ [51-250]
The Lighthouse at the End of the World
BW - v26 - N 17 '96 - p12 [51-250]
y Kliatt - v31 - Mr '97 - p10 [51-250]
Marmo, Constantino - *Semiotica E Linguaggio Nella Scolastica*
Specu - v71 - O '96 - p978+ [501+]
Marmon, Shaun Elizabeth - *Eunuchs and Sacred Boundaries in Islamic Society*
MEJ - v50 - Sum '96 - p456 [51-250]
Rel St Rev - v23 - Ap '97 - p200 [51-250]
Marmontel, Jean-Francois - *Belisaire*
MLR - v92 - Ap '97 - p469+ [251-500]
Marnef, Guido - *Antwerp in the Age of Reformation*
HRNB - v25 - Fall '96 - p26+ [251-500]
TLS - Ag 30 '96 - p33 [501+]
Marney-Petix, V C - *Bridges, Routers, Gateways*
SciTech - v20 - N '96 - p73 [51-250]
Marokvia, Mireille - *Immortelles: Memoir of a Will-o'-the-Wisp*
y BL - v93 - S 15 '96 - p204 [51-250]
KR - v64 - Ag 15 '96 - p1215 [251-500]
LJ - v121 - O 15 '96 - p68 [51-250]
NY - v72 - Ja 13 '97 - p79 [51-250]
PW - v243 - S 9 '96 - p75 [51-250]
Maromonte, Kevin R - *Building the Invisible Quality Corporation*
R&R Bk N - v11 - N '96 - p30 [51-250]
Maron, Margaret - *Killer Market*
BL - v93 - My 15 '97 - p1542 [51-250]
Shooting at Loons (Critt). Audio Version
BWatch - v18 - Mr '97 - p7 [1-50]
Up Jumps the Devil
y BL - v92 - Ag '96 - p1887 [51-250]
y BL - v92 - Ag '96 - p1891 [1-50]
y BL - v93 - Ja '97 - p763 [1-50]
NYTBR - v101 - S 29 '96 - p28 [51-250]
Maron, Monika - *Animal Triste*
Econ - v341 - O 19 '96 - p16*+ [501+]
WLT - v71 - Win '97 - p137 [501+]
Marona, Christopher - *Colorado Cowboys*
LATBR - D 8 '96 - p5 [1-50]
Maroncelli, Dorothy - *Britain on Your Own*
LJ - v121 - F 15 '97 - p154 [51-250]
Marot, Clement - *Cinquante Pseaumes De David Mis En Francoys Selon La Verite Hebraique*
CML - v16 - Spr '96 - p265+ [501+]
Marotti, Arthur F - *Critical Essays on John Donne*
Ren Q - v49 - Win '96 - p880+ [501+]
Manuscript, Print, and the English Renaissance Lyric
Lib - v18 - S '96 - p261+ [501+]
MLR - v92 - Ap '97 - p445+ [501+]
MP - v94 - F '97 - p380+ [501+]
Marotti, Maria Ornella - *Italian Women Writers from the Renaissance to the Present*
Choice - v34 - F '97 - p970 [51-250]
Marowitz, Charles - *Alarums and Excursions*
TCI - v30 - O '96 - p55 [51-250]

Marples, David R - *Belarus: From Soviet Rule to Nuclear Catastrophe*
 Choice - v34 - D '96 - p671 [51-250]
Marquand, David - *The Ideas That Shaped Post-War Britain*
 TLS - Ja 3 '97 - p6+ [501+]
Marquardt, Michael J - *Building the Learning Organization*
 Choice - v34 - N '96 - p503 [51-250]
Marquez-Sterling, Manuel - *La Cupula*
 BL - v93 - Ap 1 '97 - p1284 [1-50]
Marquina Barrio, Antonio - *La Diplomacia Vaticana Y La Espana De Franco 1936-1945*
 CHR - v82 - O '96 - p661+ [501+]
Marquis, Alice Goldfarb - *Art Lessons*
 AHR - v101 - D '96 - p1651+ [501+]
 Bks & Cult - v2 - Mr '96 - p22 [501+]
 RP - v58 - Fall '96 - p857+ [501+]
Marquis, Don - *Archyology: The Long Lost Tales of Archy and Mehitable (Illus. by Ed Frascino)*
 y SLJ - v43 - F '97 - p137 [51-250]
Marquis, Susan - *Unconventional Warfare*
 PW - v244 - My 5 '97 - p191 [51-250]
Marqusee, Mike - *War Minus the Shooting*
 NS - v125 - N 29 '96 - p43+ [501+]
 TLS - D 6 '96 - p31 [501+]
Marr, David - *Vietnam 1945*
 Am - v175 - D 14 '96 - p27+ [501+]
 Lon R Bks - v19 - F 20 '97 - p28+ [501+]
Marra, Ben - *Powwow: Images Along the Red Road*
 y BL - v93 - O 1 '96 - p310 [51-250]
 Nat Peop - v10 - '97 - p78+ [501+]
Marranca, Bonnie - *Ecologies of Theater*
 Am Theat - v13 - D '96 - p20 [1-50]
 Am Theat - v14 - Ja '97 - p70+ [501+]
Marren, Peter - *Postcards from the Country*
 New Sci - v152 - O 26 '96 - p47 [1-50]
Marrin, Albert - *Empires Lost and Won*
 y CCB-B - v50 - My '97 - p330 [51-250]
 Plains Warrior
 c CLW - v67 - D '96 - p64 [51-250]
 c HB - v72 - S '96 - p621+ [251-500]
 y HB Guide - v7 - Fall '96 - p391 [51-250]
 Virginia's General
 y Emerg Lib - v24 - S '96 - p23 [1-50]
Marriott, Janice - *Hope's Rainbow*
 c Magpies - v11 - Jl '96 - p35 [51-250]
Marris, Robin - *How to Save the Underclass*
 Choice - v34 - My '97 - p1548 [51-250]
 Obs - D 15 '96 - p17* [51-250]
 TLS - Ja 24 '97 - p3+ [501+]
Marrison, Andrew - *British Business and Protection 1903-1932*
 Choice - v34 - My '97 - p1559 [51-250]
Marron, Kevin - *The Slammer: The Crisis in Canada's Prisons*
 Mac - v109 - D 9 '96 - p64 [1-50]
Marrow, James H - *As Horas De Margarida De Cleves*
 BM - v138 - N '96 - p754+ [501+]
 The Hours of Simon De Varie
 Ren Q - v49 - Aut '96 - p681+ [501+]
Marrow, Stanley B - *The Gospel of John*
 BTB - v26 - Win '96 - p174 [501+]
 Rel St Rev - v22 - O '96 - p347 [501+]
Marrs, Jim - *Alien Agenda*
 PW - v244 - My 5 '97 - p188 [51-250]
Marrs, Richard - *Dr. Richard Marrs' Fertility Book*
 LJ - v121 - D '96 - p132 [51-250]
 PW - v243 - D 2 '96 - p57+ [51-250]
Marrs, Timothy C - *Chemical Warfare Agents*
 SciTech - v20 - S '96 - p28 [51-250]
Mars, Phil - *Learning Algorithms*
 Choice - v34 - Mr '97 - p1192 [51-250]
Marsa, Linda - *Prescription for Profits*
 PW - v244 - Mr 17 '97 - p64 [51-250]
Marschall, Laurence - *The Supernova Story*
 S&T - v92 - S '96 - p53 [51-250]
Marsden, George M - *The Outrageous Idea of Christian Scholarship*
 Am - v176 - Mr 22 '97 - p29+ [251-250]
 Comw - v124 - Mr 28 '97 - p22+ [501+]
 KR - v64 - D 15 '96 - p1785 [251-500]
 PW - v244 - Ja 13 '97 - p69 [51-250]
 The Secularization of the Academy
 Rel St Rev - v23 - Ja '97 - p35+ [501+]
 The Soul of the American University
 Cres - v59 - Sum '96 - p31+ [501+]
 Rel St Rev - v23 - Ja '97 - p35+ [501+]
Marsden, Jerrold E - *Integration Algorithms and Classical Mechanics*
 SciTech - v20 - N '96 - p16 [51-250]

Introduction to Mechanics and Symmetry
 SIAM Rev - v39 - Mr '97 - p152 [501+]
Marsden, John - *Checkers*
 y Aust Bk R - Je '96 - p60+ [501+]
 y Magpies - v11 - My '96 - p48 [51-250]
 Creep St.
 y Aust Bk R - Jl '96 - p59+ [501+]
 Darkness Be My Friend
 y Aust Bk R - D '96 - p85+ [501+]
 Letters from the Inside
 y Kliatt - v30 - S '96 - p3 [1-50]
 y SLJ - v42 - O '96 - p45 [1-50]
 y SLJ - v43 - Ja '97 - p37 [1-50]
 So Much to Tell You
 y SLJ - v42 - O '96 - p45 [1-50]
 The Third Day, the Frost
 y Magpies - v11 - My '96 - p53 [1-50]
 This I Believe
 y Aust Bk R - S '96 - p17+ [501+]
 Tomorrow, When the War Began
 y Ch BWatch - v7 - F '97 - p6 [1-50]
 y Emerg Lib - v24 - S '96 - p25 [1-50]
 y Kliatt - v31 - Mr '97 - p10 [1-50]
 y PW - v243 - D 2 '96 - p62 [1-50]
Marsden, Philip - *The Bronski House*
 KR - v65 - My 1 '97 - p701 [251-500]
 Obs - D 22 '96 - p18* [51-250]
 PW - v244 - Ap 28 '97 - p59+ [51-250]
Marsden, Vera - *A Victorian Seaside Resort*
 TES - Ap 4 '97 - p12* [251-500]
Marsella, Anthony J - *Ethnocultural Aspects of Posttraumatic Stress Disorder*
 Choice - v34 - F '97 - p1039 [51-250]
 R&R Bk N - v12 - F '97 - p96 [51-250]
Marsella, Gail B C - *Reasonings in Chemistry*
 SB - v32 - N '96 - p230 [251-500]
Marsh, Carole - *Asteroids, Comets, and Meteors*
 c BL - v93 - D 15 '96 - p722 [51-250]
 c Ch BWatch - v6 - D '96 - p6 [1-50]
 c SLJ - v43 - Ja '97 - p118 [51-250]
 Unidentified Flying Objects and Extraterrestrial Life
 c BL - v93 - D 1 '96 - p660 [51-250]
 c Ch BWatch - v6 - D '96 - p6 [1-50]
 c SLJ - v42 - D '96 - p132 [51-250]
Marsh, Christopher W - *The Family of Love in English Society 1550-1630*
 JMH - v68 - S '96 - p678+ [501+]
Marsh, David - *Germany and Europe*
 WP - v49 - Ja '97 - p282+ [501+]
Marsh, James L - *Critique, Action, and Liberation*
 IPQ - v36 - S '96 - p359+ [501+]
Marsh, Jan - *Christina Rossetti: A Literary Biography*
 CR - v269 - D '96 - p333 [1-50]
 Christina Rossetti: A Writer's Life
 Bks & Cult - v2 - Jl '96 - p17 [501+]
 South HR - v31 - Win '97 - p74+ [501+]
 The Pre-Raphaelites
 Books - v10 - Je '96 - p21 [51-250]
Marsh, Jean - *Fiennders Keepers*
 BL - v93 - My 1 '97 - p1480 [51-250]
 PW - v244 - Ap 7 '97 - p76 [51-250]
Marsh, Linda - *Highlights from 19th-Century Novels*
 y TES - S 20 '96 - pR6 [251-500]
 Landmarks
 y TES - F 28 '97 - pR7 [501+]
 Travel Writing
 y TES - S 20 '96 - pR6 [251-500]
Marsh, Margaret - *The Empty Cradle*
 Choice - v34 - S '96 - p162 [51-250]
 J Soc H - v30 - Spr '97 - p785+ [501+]
 SciTech - v20 - S '96 - p37 [51-250]
Marsh, Ngaio - *Death at the Dolphin (Saxon). Audio Version*
 y Kliatt - v31 - My '97 - p36 [51-250]
 A Man Lay Dead
 Arm Det - v29 - Fall '96 - p438 [1-50]
Marsh, Peter T - *Joseph Chamberlain: Entrepreneur in Politics*
 JMH - v68 - D '96 - p989+ [501+]
Marsh, Robert M - *The Great Transformation*
 Choice - v34 - F '97 - p1018 [51-250]
 R&R Bk N - v11 - D '96 - p39 [51-250]
Marsh, Rosalind - *History and Literature in Contemporary Russia*
 Russ Rev - v55 - O '96 - p726+ [501+]
Marsh, Valerie - *Beyond Worlds (Illus. by Patrick K Luzadder)*
 c CLW - v66 - Je '96 - p38 [51-250]
Marshak, Boris - *Treasures from the Ob'Basin*
 BM - v139 - Ja '97 - p44+ [501+]

Marshall, Alan - *Intelligence and Espionage in the Reign of Charles II 1660-1685*
 EHR - v112 - F '97 - p202+ [251-500]
Marshall, Alexandra - *Something Borrowed*
 BL - v93 - Ap 1 '97 - p1281+ [51-250]
 KR - v65 - Mr 15 '97 - p409 [251-500]
 PW - v244 - Mr 24 '97 - p56+ [251-500]
Marshall, Alfred - *The Correspondence of Alfred Marshall, Economist. Vol. 1*
 JEL - v34 - D '96 - p2015+ [51-250]
 The Correspondence of Alfred Marshall, Economist. Vols. 2-3
 JEL - v34 - D '96 - p2016 [51-250]
 Official Papers of Alfred Marshall: A Supplement
 JEL - v35 - Mr '97 - p192+ [51-250]
Marshall, Anne - *The World's Healthiest Food*
 NYTLa - v146 - D 2 '96 - pC16 [1-50]
Marshall, Brenda K - *Mavis*
 NYTBR - v101 - S 15 '96 - p30 [51-250]
 Rapport - v19 - 5 '96 - p31 [251-500]
Marshall, Bruce - *Father Malachy's Miracle*
 Nat R - v48 - D 23 '96 - p55 [51-250]
Marshall, Byron K - *Learning to Be Modern*
 AHR - v102 - F '97 - p157+ [251-500]
 r Historian - v58 - Sum '96 - p883+ [501+]
Marshall, Catherine - *Designing Qualitative Research. 2nd Ed.*
 MLJ - v80 - Fall '96 - p403+ [501+]
Marshall, Donald G - *Contemporary Critical Theory*
 r MLR - v91 - O '96 - p946+ [501+]
 r Poetics T - v18 - Spr '97 - p121+ [501+]
Marshall, Edward - *Fox All Week*
 c New Ad - v9 - Fall '96 - p309+ [501+]
 Zorro En La Escuela (Illus. by James Marshall)
 c BL - v93 - My 1 '97 - p1507 [1-50]
Marshall, Elizabeth L - *The Human Genome Project*
 y BL - v93 - D 1 '96 - p654 [51-250]
 y HB Guide - v8 - Spr '97 - p119 [51-250]
 A Student's Guide to the Internet
 y BL - v93 - D 15 '96 - p719 [1-50]
 y HB Guide - v8 - Spr '97 - p85 [51-250]
 y SB - v33 - Mr '97 - p42 [51-250]
Marshall, George Catlett - *The Papers of George Catlett Marshall. Vol. 4*
 J Mil H - v61 - Ja '97 - p195+ [501+]
 R&R Bk N - v11 - D '96 - p15 [51-250]
Marshall, Howard Wright - *Paradise Valley, Nevada*
 Pub Hist - v19 - Win '97 - p98+ [501+]
Marshall, I Howard - *New Bible Dictionary. 3rd Ed.*
 r BL - v93 - Mr 15 '97 - p1259+ [251-500]
Marshall, Ian - *Who's Afraid of Schrodinger's Cat?*
 y BL - v93 - Mr 15 '97 - p1211 [51-250]
Marshall, Ingeborg - *A History and Ethnography of the Beothuk*
 Choice - v34 - Ja '97 - p864 [51-250]
 R&R Bk N - v12 - F '97 - p22 [501+]
Marshall, James - *George and Martha*
 c HMR - Win '96 - p45 [1-50]
 Goldilocks and the Three Bears (Illus. by James Marshall)
 c PW - v243 - O 7 '96 - p77 [51-250]
 Ricitos Dorados Y Los Tres Osos (Illus. by James Marshall)
 c BL - v93 - My 1 '97 - p1507 [1-50]
 c SLJ - v42 - Ag '96 - p179 [51-250]
Marshall, Janet - *Look Once, Look Twice (Illus. by Janet Marshall)*
 c RT - O '96 - p130 [1-50]
 c RT - v50 - D '96 - p345 [51-250]
Marshall, Joe - *On Behalf of the Wolf and the First Peoples*
 Bloom Rev - v16 - Jl '96 - p3+ [501+]
Marshall, John, 1755-1835 - *The Papers of John Marshall. Vol. 8*
 JSH - v63 - F '97 - p160+ [501+]
Marshall, John, 1961- - *John Locke: Resistance, Religion, and Responsibility*
 JMH - v69 - Mr '97 - p135+ [501+]
 Theol St - v57 - Je '96 - p356+ [501+]
Marshall, John Douglas - *Home Field*
 KR - v65 - F 15 '97 - p280 [251-500]
 PW - v244 - F 17 '97 - p201 [51-250]
Marshall, Jonathan - *To Have and Have Not*
 Historian - v58 - Sum '96 - p926+ [501+]
 JIH - v27 - Win '97 - p569+ [501+]
Marshall, Joseph, Jr. - *Street Soldier (Marshall). Audio Version*
 y Kliatt - v30 - N '96 - p51 [51-250]
Marshall, Judith - *Literacy, Power and Democracy in Mozambique*
 Am Ethnol - v23 - N '96 - p908+ [501+]

Marshall, Margaret J - *Contesting Cultural Rhetorics*
   AHR - v102 - F '97 - p165+ [251-500]
   Col Comp - v47 - D '96 - p619 [51-250]
Marshall, Muriel - *Where Rivers Meet*
   Roundup M - v4 - D '96 - p28 [1-50]
   WHQ - v27 - Win '96 - p547 [51-250]
Marshall, P J - *The Cambridge Illustrated History of the British Empire*
   Lon R Bks - v18 - Jl 18 '96 - p8+ [501+]
   Quad - v40 - O '96 - p82+ [501+]
  y Sch Lib - v44 - Ag '96 - p127 [251-250]
  r SLMQ - v24 - Sum '96 - p221+ [51-250]
Marshall, Paul A - *A Kind of Life Imposed on Man*
   Choice - v34 - Ap '97 - p1352 [51-250]
   R&R Bk N - v12 - F '97 - p10 [51-250]
  Their Blood Cries Out
   PW - v244 - Mr 24 '97 - p76 [51-250]
Marshall, Peter - *The Catholic Priesthood and the English Reformation*
   EHR - v111 - N '96 - p1266 [251-500]
   Rel St Rev - v23 - Ap '97 - p191 [51-250]
Marshall, Richard H, Jr. - *Hryhorij Savyc Skovoroda*
   Slav R - v55 - Sum '96 - p476+ [501+]
Marshall, Suzanne - *Violence in the Black Patch of Kentucky and Tennessee*
   AHR - v101 - O '96 - p1281+ [501+]
Marshall, Sybil - *Strip the Willow*
   Books - v11 - Ap '97 - p22 [51-250]
Marshall, Tim - *Murdering to Dissect*
   Nine-C Lit - v51 - S '96 - p274 [51-250]
   SFS - v24 - Mr '97 - p119+ [501+]
Marshall, W J - *O Come Emmanuel*
   CLW - v66 - Je '96 - p31 [51-250]
Marshall, William - *Nightmare Syndrome*
   BL - v93 - My 15 '97 - p1567 [51-250]
Marshall, William J - *Clinical Biochemistry*
   SciTech - v20 - S '96 - p29 [51-250]
Marsiglio, William - *Fatherhood: Contemporary Theory, Research, and Social Policy*
   Fam Relat - v45 - Jl '96 - p354 [251-500]
Marsili, Ray - *Techniques for Analyzing Food Aroma*
  r SciTech - v21 - Mr '97 - p99 [51-250]
Marsilius, of Padua - *Defensor Minor. De Translatione Imperii*
   RM - v50 - D '96 - p413+ [501+]
Mars-Jones, Adam - *Blind Bitter Happiness*
   Obs - Ja 19 '97 - p17* [501+]
   TES - F 21 '97 - p7* [51-250]
   TLS - Mr 7 '97 - p36 [501+]
Marsland, David - *Welfare or Welfare State?*
   JEL - v34 - D '96 - p2065 [51-250]
Marsonet, Michele - *The Primacy of Practical Reason*
   Choice - v34 - S '96 - p141 [51-250]
Marston, Edward - *The Laughing Hangman*
   Arm Det - v30 - Win '97 - p101 [251-500]
   BL - v93 - S 1 '96 - p68 [51-250]
  The Lions of the North
   BL - v93 - S 15 '96 - p224+ [51-250]
  The Roaring Boy
  y Kliatt - v31 - Mr '97 - p10+ [51-250]
Marston, Elsa - *The Ancient Egyptians*
  c HB Guide - v7 - Fall '96 - p378 [51-250]
  The Fox Maiden (Illus. by Tatsuro Kiuchi)
  c Ch BWatch - v7 - F '97 - p2 [1-50]
  c HB Guide - v8 - Spr '97 - p39 [51-250]
  c KR - v64 - N 1 '96 - p1604 [51-250]
  c PW - v243 - N 18 '96 - p75 [51-250]
  c SLJ - v42 - D '96 - p101 [51-250]
Marston, Gwen - *Liberated Quiltmaking*
   LJ - v122 - Ap 15 '97 - p79+ [51-250]
Marston, Hope Irvin - *Fire Trucks (Illus. by Hope Irvin Marston)*
  c HB Guide - v8 - Spr '97 - p132 [51-250]
  c SLJ - v42 - S '96 - p198+ [51-250]
Marston, R M - *Newnes Digital Logic IC Pocket Book*
   SciTech - v21 - Mr '97 - p89 [1-50]
Marston, Richard C - *International Financial Integration*
   JEL - v34 - D '96 - p2049+ [51-250]
Martel, John - *Conflicts of Interest*
   Books - v9 - S '95 - p24 [51-250]
Martel, Yann - *Self*
   CF - v75 - N '96 - p43+ [501+]
   TES - D 13 '96 - p33 [51-250]
   TLS - N 22 '96 - p24 [501+]
Martell, Hazel Mary - *The Celts*
  c HB Guide - v7 - Fall '96 - p379 [51-250]
  Food and Feasts with the Vikings
  c HB Guide - v7 - Fall '96 - p378 [51-250]
Martens, Lorna - *Shadow Lines*
   Choice - v34 - D '96 - p618 [51-250]

Marthaler, Berard L - *The Catechism Yesterday and Today*
   Theol St - v57 - S '96 - p570 [251-500]
Marti, Jose - *En Un Domingo De Mucha Luz*
   BL - v93 - Ap 1 '97 - p1284 [1-50]
Marti, Kurt - *Stochastic Programming*
   JEL - v34 - D '96 - p2142+ [51-250]
Martial - *Epigrams. Vols. 1, 3*
   TranslRevS - v1 - My '95 - p26 [51-250]
  Epigrams V
   Choice - v34 - D '96 - p609+ [51-250]
  Martial in English
   BW - v26 - D 8 '96 - p15 [51-250]
Martin, A Lynn - *Plague? Jesuit Accounts of Epidemic Disease in the 16th Century*
   CH - v66 - Mr '97 - p117+ [501+]
   Choice - v34 - S '96 - p162 [51-250]
Martin, Alexander C - *American Wildlife and Plants*
   LJ - v121 - D '96 - p67 [51-250]
Martin, Allana - *Death of a Healing Woman*
   BL - v93 - O 1 '96 - p325 [51-250]
   KR - v64 - S 1 '96 - p1278 [51-250]
Martin, Andrew John - *Savoldos Sogenanntes Bildnis Des Gaston De Foix*
   BM - v138 - Jl '96 - p470 [51-250]
Martin, Andy - *Waiting for Bardot*
   NS - v125 - N 1 '96 - p46 [251-500]
Martin, Ann M - *Leo the Magnificat (Illus. by Emily Arnold McCully)*
  c BL - v93 - S 1 '96 - p143+ [51-250]
  c CBRS - v25 - N '96 - p27 [51-250]
  c CCB-B - v50 - D '96 - p142+ [51-250]
  c HB Guide - v8 - Spr '97 - p39 [51-250]
  c PW - v243 - S 2 '96 - p131 [51-250]
  c SLJ - v42 - N '96 - p88 [51-250]
Martin, Augustine - *Bearing Witness*
   ILS - v16 - Spr '97 - p35 [51-250]
Martin, Bill, 1916- - *Brown Bear, Brown Bear, What Do You See? (Illus. by Eric Carle)*
  c HB Guide - v8 - Spr '97 - p13 [51-250]
  c Inst - v106 - Ja '97 - p4* [1-50]
  Fire! Fire! Said Mrs. McGuire (Illus. by Richard Egielski)
  c Emerg Lib - v24 - S '96 - p43 [1-50]
  c HB Guide - v7 - Fall '96 - p325 [51-250]
  c NYTBR - v101 - O 13 '96 - p26 [251-500]
Martin, Bill, 1956- - *Music of Yes*
   BL - v93 - N 15 '96 - p564+ [51-250]
   BWatch - v18 - F '97 - p8 [51-250]
   LJ - v121 - N 15 '96 - p64 [51-250]
  Politics in the Impasse
   R&R Bk N - v12 - F '97 - p58 [1-50]
Martin, Brian G - *The Shanghai Green Gang*
   Choice - v34 - O '96 - p337 [51-250]
   HRNB - v25 - Win '97 - p87 [251-500]
   RP - v59 - Win '97 - p189+ [501+]
   R&R Bk N - v11 - N '96 - p16 [51-250]
Martin, C J F - *An Introduction to Medieval Philosophy*
   Rel St - v33 - Mr '97 - p132 [51-250]
Martin, Carol - *Martha Black: Gold Rush Pioneer*
  y Beav - v76 - D '96 - p47 [51-250]
  c BIC - v26 - F '97 - p34 [251-500]
  y Can CL - v22 - Fall '96 - p105+ [251-500]
  c Quill & Q - v62 - D '96 - p39+ [501+]
  North: Landscape of the Imagination
   Archiv - Fall '94 - p207+ [501+]
Martin, Charles, 1942- - *What the Darkness Proposes*
   PW - v243 - S 30 '96 - p84 [51-250]
Martin, Cheryl English - *Governance and Society in Colonial Mexico*
   Choice - v34 - S '96 - p190 [51-250]
   HRNB - v25 - Fall '96 - p16 [251-500]
   W&M Q - v54 - Ap '97 - p422+ [501+]
Martin, Christopher - *Classic Poems*
  y TES - S 20 '96 - pR6 [501+]
Martin, Chuck, 1949- - *The Digital Estate*
   BL - v93 - D 1 '96 - p627 [51-250]
   LJ - v121 - N 15 '96 - p70 [51-250]
   LJ - v122 - Mr 15 '97 - p36+ [1-50]
   PW - v243 - N 4 '96 - p60 [51-250]
Martin, Claire - *The Race of the Golden Apples (Illus. by Leo Dillon)*
  c SLJ - v42 - N '96 - p39 [1-50]
Martin, Constance R - *Dictionary of Endocrinology and Related Biomedical Sciences*
  r ARBA - v28 - '97 - p614+ [51-250]
Martin, Dale B - *The Corinthian Body*
   JR - v77 - Ap '97 - p290+ [501+]
   Rel St Rev - v23 - Ja '97 - p73 [51-250]
   Theol St - v57 - D '96 - p740+ [501+]
   TT - v53 - Ja '97 - p540+ [501+]

Martin, Dave - *Communicating Skills. 2nd Ed.*
  c Quill & Q - v62 - O '96 - p50 [51-250]
Martin, David, 1944- - *Little Chicken Chicken (Illus. by Sue Heap)*
  c HB Guide - v7 - Fall '96 - p267 [51-250]
  c JB - v60 - O '96 - p186 [51-250]
  c Magpies - v11 - S '96 - p27 [51-250]
Martin, David, 1965- - *Geographic Information Systems*
   GJ - v163 - Mr '97 - p104 [51-250]
Martin, David Lozell, 1946- - *Cul-De-Sac*
   BL - v93 - Mr 15 '97 - p1230 [51-250]
   KR - v65 - Ja 15 '97 - p86 [251-500]
   LJ - v122 - Ja '97 - p148 [51-250]
   PW - v243 - D 30 '96 - p53 [51-250]
   Trib Bks - Ap 13 '97 - p5+ [51-250]
  Tap, Tap
   Ent W - Ag 23 '96 - p119 [1-50]
Martin, Denis-Constant - *Les Democraties Antillaises En Crise*
   BL - v93 - F 1 '97 - p930 [1-50]
Martin, Edward C, Jr. - *Home Landscapes*
   Hort - v74 - My '96 - p77+ [251-500]
Martin, Fenton S - *How to Research Congress*
  r ARBA - v28 - '97 - p265 [251-500]
  r BL - v93 - O 1 '96 - p370+ [251-500]
  r Choice - v34 - D '96 - p592 [51-250]
  How to Research the Presidency
  r ARBA - v28 - '97 - p265 [251-500]
  r BL - v93 - O 1 '96 - p370+ [251-500]
  r Choice - v34 - D '96 - p592 [51-250]
Martin, Francis - *The Feminist Question*
   Bks & Cult - v1 - N '95 - p24+ [501+]
Martin, Fred - *Environmental Change*
  c Sch Lib - v44 - N '96 - p163 [251-500]
  c TES - Mr 21 '97 - p18* [251-500]
  Rivers
  c Sch Lib - v44 - N '96 - p163 [251-500]
  c TES - Mr 21 '97 - p18* [251-500]
  Settlements
  c TES - Mr 21 '97 - p18* [251-500]
  Weather
  c TES - Mr 21 '97 - p18* [251-500]
Martin, Frederick N - *Introduction to Audiology. 6th Ed.*
   SciTech - v20 - D '96 - p51 [1-50]
Martin, Ged - *Britain and the Origins of Canadian Confederation 1837-67*
   EHR - v112 - Ap '97 - p505+ [501+]
Martin, George R R - *A Game of Thrones*
  y BL - v92 - Ag '96 - p1889 [51-250]
  y BL - v92 - Ag '96 - p1891 [1-50]
   PW - v243 - N 4 '96 - p42 [1-50]
   SF Chr - v18 - O '96 - p76 [251-500]
Martin, Henri-Jean - *The History and Power of Writing*
   Sev Cent N - v54 - Spr '96 - p14+ [501+]
  Print, Power and People in 17th-Century France
   Lib & Cul - v32 - Win '97 - p137+ [501+]
Martin, Henry - *Charlie Parker and Thematic Improvisation*
   AB - v98 - D 9 '96 - p1996 [501+]
Martin, Irene - *A Newspaper Index and Guide for Genealogy in Wahkiakum County and Naselle Area of Pacific County*
  r EGH - v50 - N '96 - p191 [51-250]
Martin, Jacqueline Briggs - *Grandmother Bryant's Pocket (Illus. by Petra Mathers)*
  c BL - v93 - Ap 1 '97 - p1305 [1-50]
  c HB Guide - v7 - Fall '96 - p287 [51-250]
  c SLJ - v42 - D '96 - p31 [1-50]
  The Green Truck Garden Giveaway (Illus. by Alec Gillman)
  c BL - v93 - My 1 '97 - p1501+ [51-250]
  c PW - v244 - Ap 7 '97 - p92 [51-250]
  Washing the Willow Tree Loon (Illus. by Nancy Carpenter)
  c New Ad - v9 - Fall '96 - p327+ [501+]
Martin, James - *Cybercorp: The New Business Revolution*
   Choice - v34 - Ap '97 - p1384 [51-250]
Martin, James A - *The Gulf War and Mental Health*
   R&R Bk N - v12 - F '97 - p18 [51-250]
Martin, James D - *Proverbs*
   Rel St Rev - v23 - Ap '97 - p163 [51-250]
Martin, Jane Read - *Now I Will Never Leave the Dinner Table (Illus. by Roz Chast)*
  c HB - v72 - S '96 - p582+ [51-250]
  c HB Guide - v7 - Fall '96 - p267 [51-250]
Martin, Jane Roland - *Changing the Educational Landscape*
   Ed Theory - v46 - Fall '96 - p525+ [501+]
Martin, Jeremy - *Togo: The Postal History of the Anglo-French Occupation 1914-1922*
   Am Phil - v110 - N '96 - p1037 [51-250]

Martin, Jodean McGuffin - *The Mangum Star Weekly 1898-1900*
 r EGH - v50 - N '96 - p184 [51-250]
Martin, Joel - *Love beyond Life*
 PW - v244 - F 24 '97 - p79 [51-250]
Martin, Joel W - *Screening the Sacred*
 J Am St - v30 - Ag '96 - p327+ [251-500]
 Rel St Rev - v23 - Ap '97 - p161 [51-250]
Martin, John - *Venice's Hidden Enemies*
 Ren Q - v49 - Win '96 - p853+ [501+]
Martin, Judith - *Miss Manners Basic Training: Communication*
 BL - v93 - N 15 '96 - p547 [51-250]
 Ent W - Ja 10 '97 - p52 [51-250]
 KR - v64 - O 15 '96 - p1514+ [251-500]
 LJ - v122 - F 1 '97 - p88 [51-250]
 PW - v243 - N 18 '96 - p55 [51-250]
 Time - v149 - Ja 13 '97 - p76 [501+]
 Miss Manners on (Painfully Proper) Weddings
 LATBR - Mr 17 '96 - p4 [501+]
 Miss Manners Rescues Civilization
 Nat R - v48 - Je 3 '96 - p55+ [501+]
 Reason - v28 - Ap '97 - p61+ [501+]
 Wom R Bks - v14 - Ja '97 - p11+ [501+]
Martin, Kat - *Innocence Undone*
 PW - v243 - N 25 '96 - p70 [51-250]
Martin, Laura C - *The Folklore of Birds*
 BWatch - v17 - S '96 - p4 [1-50]
 Wildlife Folklore
 y Kliatt - v30 - S '96 - p36 [51-250]
Martin, Lee - *The Least You Need to Know*
 NAR - v282 - Mr '97 - p43+ [501+]
Martin, Les - *Die, Bug, Die!*
 c SLJ - v43 - Mr '97 - p188 [51-250]
 Humbug
 y BL - v93 - Ap 1 '97 - p1310 [1-50]
Martin, Linette - *Practical Praying*
 BL - v93 - F 15 '97 - p976 [501+]
Martin, Lynne M - *Library Instruction Revisited*
 LAR - v99 - Ja '97 - p47 [251-500]
 LR - v45 - 8 '96 - p56+ [501+]
Martin, Malachi - *Windswept House*
 KR - v64 - My 1 '96 - p627 [251-500]
 Rapport - v19 - 5 '96 - p33 [251-500]
Martin, Marvin - *The Beatles: The Music Was Never the Same*
 y BL - v93 - F 1 '97 - p934 [51-250]
 y SLJ - v43 - Mr '97 - p204 [51-250]
Martin, Mary Jane - *From Anne to Zach (Illus. by Michael Grejniec)*
 c CBRS - v25 - Win '97 - p64 [1-50]
 c CLW - v67 - D '96 - p57 [51-250]
 c HB Guide - v8 - Spr '97 - p13 [51-250]
 c KR - v64 - S 1 '96 - p1324 [51-250]
 c SLJ - v42 - D '96 - p116 [51-250]
Martin, Michael, 1932, Feb., 2- - *The Big Domino in the Sky and Other Atheistic Tales*
 PW - v243 - D 30 '96 - p60 [51-250]
Martin, Michael T - *Cinemas of the Black Diaspora*
 Bl S - v26 - Sum '96 - p66 [51-250]
 Choice - v34 - Ja '97 - p803+ [51-250]
 Film Cr - v21 - Win '96 - p62+ [501+]
Martin, Michelle - *Stolen Hearts*
 LJ - v122 - F 15 '97 - p126 [51-250]
Martin, Mike W - *Love's Virtues*
 R&R Bk N - v12 - F '97 - p4 [51-250]
Martin, Nancy - *Vanilla Blood*
 BWatch - v17 - N '96 - p8 [1-50]
Martin, Nicholas - *Nietzsche and Schiller*
 Choice - v34 - D '96 - p626+ [51-250]
Martin, Norman M - *Closure Spaces and Logic*
 SciTech - v20 - D '96 - p19 [51-250]
Martin, Patricia - *Travels with Rainie Marie*
 c BL - v93 - My 15 '97 - p1576 [51-250]
 c KR - v65 - Mr 15 '97 - p465 [51-250]
 c PW - v244 - Ap 14 '97 - p76 [51-250]
Martin, Paul - *The Sickening Mind*
 New Sci - v153 - F 15 '97 - p44 [1-50]
 Obs - F 2 '97 - p15* [501+]
Martin, Peter J - *Sounds and Society*
 Notes - v53 - D '96 - p488+ [501+]
Martin, Phyllis M - *Leisure and Society in Colonial Brazzaville*
 Choice - v34 - O '96 - p335 [51-250]
Martin, Rafe - *The Boy Who Loved Mammoths (Illus. by Richard Wehrman)*
 c Par Ch - v20 - O '96 - p21 [1-50]
 The Monkey Bridge (Illus. by Fahimeh Amiri)
 c BL - v93 - My 15 '97 - p1577+ [51-250]
 c KR - v65 - My 1 '97 - p724 [51-250]
 c PW - v244 - Ap 21 '97 - p70 [51-250]

 Mysterious Tales of Japan (Illus. by Tatsuro Kiuchi)
 c BL - v93 - Ap 1 '97 - p1298 [1-50]
 c HB - v72 - S '96 - p605 [51-250]
 c HB Guide - v7 - Fall '96 - p322 [51-250]
 c NYTBR - v101 - S 8 '96 - p28 [1-50]
Martin, Ralph - *Teaching Science for All Children. 2nd Ed.*
 SciTech - v20 - D '96 - p4 [51-250]
Martin, Randy - *Socialist Ensembles*
 CS - v25 - N '96 - p815+ [501+]
Martin, Renee J - *Practicing What We Teach*
 EL - v54 - S '96 - p87 [251-500]
Martin, Rick - *Vintage Illustration*
 Ant & CM - v102 - Mr '97 - p32 [51-250]
 BWatch - v18 - F '97 - p5 [51-250]
Martin, Robin - *Gel Electrophoresis*
 Choice - v34 - Mr '97 - p1188 [51-250]
Martin, Ruth R - *Oral History in Social Work*
 Soc Ser R - v70 - S '96 - p497+ [501+]
Martin, Scott C - *Killing Time*
 J Soc H - v30 - Spr '97 - p738+ [501+]
Martin, Stephanie - *The Teaching Voice*
 SciTech - v20 - N '96 - p51 [51-250]
Martin, Stephen - *The Economics of Offsets*
 JEL - v35 - Mr '97 - p226 [51-250]
Martin, Stephen, 1951- - *A History of Antarctica*
 Aust Bk R - F '97 - p20+ [501+]
Martin, Stephen Hawley - *Soul Survivor*
 LJ - v121 - N 15 '96 - p89 [51-250]
 PW - v243 - O 21 '96 - p70 [51-250]
Martin, Steve, 1945- - *Picasso at the Lapin Agile and Other Plays*
 BL - v93 - S 15 '96 - p204 [51-250]
 LJ - v121 - O 1 '96 - p76+ [51-250]
Martin, Susan - *Decade of Protest*
 LATBR - My 26 '96 - p11 [1-50]
Martin, Susan Ehrlich - *Doing Justice, Doing Gender*
 Choice - v34 - S '96 - p211 [51-250]
Martin, Suzanne - *Awesome Almanac--Texas*
 cr ARBA - v28 - '97 - p49 [51-250]
Martin, T P - *Large Clusters of Atoms and Molecules*
 SciTech - v20 - S '96 - p14 [51-250]
Martin, Terence - *Parables of Possibility*
 J Am St - v30 - Ag '96 - p292+ [501+]
Martin, Teresa A - *The Project Cool Guide to HTML*
 CBR - v15 - Spr '97 - p7 [1-50]
 LJ - v122 - F 1 '97 - p102 [51-250]
Martin, Terry - *Why Are Zebras Black and White?*
 c BL - v93 - D 1 '96 - p663 [51-250]
 c CBRS - v25 - N '96 - p32+ [1-50]
 c HB Guide - v8 - Spr '97 - p119 [51-250]
 c Sch Lib - v44 - N '96 - p166 [51-250]
 c SLJ - v43 - Ja '97 - p105 [51-250]
 Why Do Sunflowers Face the Sun?
 c CBRS - v25 - N '96 - p32+ [1-50]
 c HB Guide - v8 - Spr '97 - p119 [51-250]
 c Sch Lib - v44 - N '96 - p166 [51-250]
 c SLJ - v43 - Ja '97 - p105 [51-250]
 Why Do We Laugh?
 c BL - v93 - D 1 '96 - p663 [51-250]
 c CBRS - v25 - N '96 - p32+ [1-50]
 c HB Guide - v8 - Spr '97 - p130 [51-250]
 c Sch Lib - v44 - N '96 - p166 [51-250]
 c SLJ - v43 - Ja '97 - p105 [51-250]
 Why Does Lightening Strike?
 c CBRS - v25 - N '96 - p32+ [1-50]
 Why Does Lightning Strike?
 c HB Guide - v8 - Spr '97 - p114 [51-250]
 c Sch Lib - v44 - N '96 - p166 [51-250]
 c SLJ - v43 - Ja '97 - p105 [51-250]
Martin, Thomas R - *Ancient Greece*
 y BL - v93 - S 15 '96 - p216+ [51-250]
Martin, Tovah - *Window Boxes*
 PW - v244 - Ja 27 '97 - p100 [51-250]
Martin, Troy W - *By Philosophy and Empty Deceit*
 Rel St Rev - v23 - Ja '97 - p74 [51-250]
Martin, Trude - *Obee and Mungedeech*
 c CBRS - v24 - Ag '96 - p168 [51-250]
 c HB Guide - v7 - Fall '96 - p294 [51-250]
Martin, Vincent - *A House Divided*
 y CLW - v66 - Je '96 - p30 [51-250]
Martin, Will - *The Uruguay Round and the Developing Economies*
 J Gov Info - v23 - S '96 - p689+ [51-250]
Martin, William, 1950- - *Annapolis*
 NYTBR - v101 - Jl 21 '96 - p19 [51-250]
Martin, William A, 1946- - *A Martin Genealogy Tied to the History of Germanna, Virginia*
 Am Geneal - v71 - Ap '96 - p123+ [251-500]

Martin, William C, 1937- - *With God on Our Side*
 y BL - v92 - Ag '96 - p1851 [251-500]
 BW - v26 - O 27 '96 - p3+ [501+]
 CC - v113 - N 20 '96 - p1151+ [501+]
 Choice - v34 - Mr '97 - p1228 [51-250]
 CSM - v89 - D 26 '96 - p12 [501+]
 Econ - v341 - N 2 '96 - p86 [501+]
 LJ - v122 - Ja '97 - p105+ [51-250]
Martin, William F - *Maintaining Energy in a Global Context*
 MEJ - v51 - Spr '97 - p310 [51-250]
Martin, William J, 1938- - *The Global Information Society*
 Choice - v34 - N '96 - p495 [51-250]
 LAR - v98 - D '96 - p649 [251-500]
Martinac, Paula - *K.D. Lang*
 y HB Guide - v8 - Spr '97 - p160 [51-250]
 y SLJ - v42 - N '96 - p129+ [51-250]
Martindale, Charles - *Horace Made New*
 MP - v94 - Ag '96 - p79+ [501+]
Martin del Campo, David - *El Ano Del Fuego*
 LJ - v122 - Ja '97 - p79 [51-250]
Martineau, Harriet - *Illustrations of Political Economy. Vols. 1-9*
 VS - v39 - Aut '95 - p33+ [501+]
Martines, Lauro - *An Italian Renaissance Sextet*
 Ren Q - v49 - Win '96 - p859+ [501+]
Martinet, Claire - *L'Abbaye Premontre Du Lac De Joux Des Origines Au XIVe Siecle*
 CHR - v82 - Jl '96 - p554+ [251-500]
Martinet, Jeanne - *The Art of Mingling (Martinet). Audio Version*
 BL - v93 - Ja '97 - p879 [51-250]
Martinez, Demetria - *Lengua Madre*
 LJ - v122 - Ja '97 - p79 [51-250]
 MotherTongue
 WAL - v31 - Sum '96 - p169+ [251-500]
Martinez, Elena M - *Lesbian Voices from Latin America*
 NWSA Jnl - v9 - Spr '97 - p126+ [501+]
Martinez, Hildeberto - *Codiciaban La Tierra*
 HAHR - v77 - F '97 - p110+ [501+]
Martinez, Javier - *Chile: The Great Transformation*
 Choice - v34 - Mr '97 - p1209 [51-250]
 JEL - v35 - Mr '97 - p286 [51-250]
Martinez, Joseph G R - *Math without Fear*
 SciTech - v20 - Mr '97 - p3 [51-250]
Martinez, Max - *White Leg*
 Bloom Rev - v16 - S '96 - p20+ [251-500]
Martinez, Rafael - *El Arquitecto Del Cosmos*
 y JAAL - v40 - S '96 - p77 [51-250]
Martinez, Samuel - *Peripheral Migrants*
 Choice - v34 - S '96 - p219+ [51-250]
Martinez, Tomas Eloy - *Santa Evita*
 Ant R - v55 - Spr '97 - p241+ [251-500]
 BL - v92 - Ag '96 - p1855 [251-500]
 BW - v26 - D 8 '96 - p6 [1-50]
 KR - v64 - Ag 15 '96 - p1179 [51-250]
 LATBR - D 22 '96 - p3 [501+]
 LATBR - D 29 '96 - p9 [501+]
 Lon R Bks - v19 - F 20 '97 - p13+ [501+]
 Nat - v263 - O 28 '96 - p50+ [501+]
 New R - v216 - F 10 '97 - p31+ [501+]
 NYRB - v44 - F 20 '97 - p27+ [501+]
 NYTBR - v101 - S 29 '96 - p27 [501+]
 NYTBR - v101 - D 8 '96 - p82 [1-50]
 NYTLa - v146 - S 20 '96 - pC31 [501+]
 Obs - Ja 12 '97 - p16* [501+]
 Spec - v278 - Ja 11 '97 - p34 [501+]
 TLS - Ja 3 '97 - p22 [501+]
 W&I - v12 - F '97 - p268+ [501+]
 WSJ-MW - v78 - N 14 '96 - pA18 [51-250]
 Santa Evita (Grifasi). Audio Version
 y Kliatt - v31 - My '97 - p44 [51-250]
Martinez, Victor - *Parrot in the Oven*
 y BW - v27 - Ja 12 '97 - p9 [251-500]
 y CBRS - v25 - D '96 - p47 [51-250]
 y CCB-B - v50 - D '96 - p143 [51-250]
 y CSM - v88 - N 12 '96 - p14 [51-250]
 y HB - v73 - Ja '97 - p62+ [51-250]
 y HB Guide - v8 - Spr '97 - p82 [51-250]
 y KR - v64 - S 1 '96 - p1324+ [51-250]
 y NYTBR - v102 - Mr 30 '97 - p18 [1-50]
 y PW - v243 - N 4 '96 - p48+ [1-50]
 y SLJ - v42 - N '96 - p123 [51-250]
Martinez Baracs, Andrea - *Suma Y Epiloga De Toda La Desripcion De Tlaxcala*
 HAHR - v76 - N '96 - p777+ [251-500]
Martinez Neira, Manuel - *Revolucion Y Fiscalidad Municipal*
 Choice - v34 - D '96 - p568 [1-50]
 Choice - v34 - D '96 - p568 [1-50]

Martinez-Taboas, Alfonso - *Multiple Personality*
AJCH - v39 - O '96 - p150+ [501+]
Martini, Steve - *The Judge*
Ent W - N 29 '96 - p85 [1-50]
The Judge (Guidall). Audio Version
y Kliatt - v30 - N '96 - p42 [51-250]
The Judge (Tucci). Audio Version
y Kliatt - v30 - N '96 - p42 [51-250]
The List
BL - v93 - Ja '97 - p779 [51-250]
CSM - v89 - Mr 20 '97 - p14 [51-250]
Ent W - Mr 21 '97 - p68+ [51-250]
KR - v64 - D 15 '96 - p1760+ [251-500]
LJ - v122 - F 15 '97 - p163 [51-250]
PW - v244 - Ja 20 '97 - p394+ [51-250]
Trib Bks - F 16 '97 - p6 [51-250]
Martinich, A P - *A Hobbes Dictionary*
r ARBA - v28 - '97 - p530+ [51-250]
Thomas Hobbes
Choice - v34 - Mr '97 - p1176 [51-250]
Martinich, Joseph Stanislaus - *Production and Operations Management*
SciTech - v21 - Mr '97 - p98 [51-250]
Martiniello, Marco - *Migration, Citizenship and Ethno-National Identities in the European Union*
CS - v26 - Ja '97 - p65+ [501+]
Martin Martinez, Magdalena M - *National Sovereignty and International Organizations*
R&R Bk N - v11 - D '96 - p19 [51-250]
Martino, Teresa Tsimmu - *The Wolf, the Woman, the Wilderness*
LJ - v122 - Ap 15 '97 - p103 [51-250]
Martin-Perdue, Nancy J - *Talk about Trouble*
Choice - v34 - Ap '97 - p1408 [51-250]
Martin-Santos, Martin - *Tiempo De Silencio*
Hisp - v79 - S '96 - p429+ [501+]
Martinson, Linda - *The Poetry of Pain*
Sm Pr R - v28 - S '96 - p4 [51-250]
Martinson, Steven D - *Harmonious Tensions*
Choice - v34 - Mr '97 - p1168 [51-250]
Martis, Kenneth C - *The Historical Atlas of the Congresses of the Confederate States of America 1861-1865*
r JSH - v62 - N '96 - p857 [51-250]
Marton, Kati - *A Death in Jerusalem*
Queens Q - v103 - Win '96 - p729+ [501+]
Martorella, Peter H - *Interactive Technologies and the Social Studies*
R&R Bk N - v12 - F '97 - p32 [51-250]
Marty, Martin E - *Accounting for Fundamentalisms*
JAAR - v65 - Spr '97 - p161+ [501+]
Fundamentalisms and Society
JAAR - v65 - Spr '97 - p161+ [501+]
Fundamentalisms and the State
JAAR - v65 - Spr '97 - p161+ [501+]
JEL - v34 - D '96 - p2008+ [51-250]
Fundamentalisms Comprehended
APSR - v90 - S '96 - p678+ [501+]
CS - v26 - Ja '97 - p106+ [501+]
JAAR - v65 - Spr '97 - p161+ [501+]
J Ch St - v38 - Sum '96 - p641+ [251-500]
Rel St - v32 - S '96 - p421+ [501+]
Fundamentalisms Observed
JAAR - v65 - Spr '97 - p161+ [501+]
Modern American Religion. Vol. 3
BL - v92 - Ag '96 - p1860 [51-250]
CC - v114 - Ja 29 '97 - p105+ [501+]
Ch Today - v40 - Ag 12 '96 - p47 [51-250]
Comw - v124 - Ja 17 '97 - p26 [501+]
HRNB - v25 - Win '97 - p54 [251-500]
NYTBR - v101 - O 27 '96 - p37 [501+]
The One and the Many
KR - v65 - F 15 '97 - p280 [251-500]
LJ - v122 - My 1 '97 - p109 [51-250]
Varieties of Protestantism
CH - v66 - Mr '97 - p183+ [501+]
Marty, Michael - *Manual of GM-CSF*
SciTech - v20 - S '96 - p43 [51-250]
Martyn, John R C - *Pedro Nunes 1502-1578*
SciTech - v21 - Mr '97 - p3 [51-250]
Martz, John D - *The Politics of Clientelism*
Choice - v34 - Mr '97 - p1233 [51-250]
United States Policy in Latin America
Parameters - v26 - Win '96 - p155 [1-50]
SSQ - v77 - D '96 - p939+ [501+]
Martz, Sandra Haldeman - *Grow Old along with Me, the Best Is Yet to Be (Asner). Audio Version*
BL - v93 - N 15 '96 - p603+ [51-250]
Threads of Experience
BWatch - v17 - D '96 - p7 [51-250]
PW - v243 - S 30 '96 - p84 [1-50]

Marucci, Franco - *The Fine Delight That Fathers Thought*
RM - v50 - S '96 - p170+ [501+]
VS - v39 - Win '96 - p264+ [501+]
Marullo, Clara - *The Last Forbidden Kingdom, Mustang*
GJ - v162 - Jl '96 - p238+ [51-250]
Marun, Gioconda - *El Modernismo Argentino Incognito En La Ondina Del Plata Y Revista Literaria 1875-1880*
Hisp - v79 - D '96 - p815+ [501+]
Maruska, Edward - *Salamanders*
c Ch BWatch - v6 - N '96 - p7+ [1-50]
c HB Guide - v8 - Spr '97 - p123 [51-250]
Maruya, Saiichi - *A Mature Woman*
Books - v9 - S '95 - p22 [1-50]
Marvel, William - *The Alabama and the Kearsarge*
Choice - v34 - F '97 - p1025 [51-250]
J Mil H - v61 - Ap '97 - p380+ [251-500]
Marven, Craig - *A Simple Approach to Digital Signal Processing*
Choice - v34 - Ja '97 - p826 [51-250]
SciTech - v20 - S '96 - p54 [51-250]
Marven, Nigel - *Incredible Journeys*
Obs - Ja 19 '97 - p17* [501+]
Marvin, Elizabeth West - *Concert Music, Rock, and Jazz since 1945*
Notes - v53 - Mr '97 - p773+ [501+]
Marvin, Garry - *Bullfight*
Aethlon - v13 - Spr '96 - p218+ [501+]
Marvis, Barbara J - *Famous People of Hispanic Heritage. Vol. 4*
c SLJ - v43 - Ja '97 - p131 [51-250]
Famous People of Hispanic Heritage. Vols. 4-6
c BL - v93 - D 15 '96 - p719+ [51-250]
c Ch BWatch - v6 - N '96 - p2 [51-250]
c HB Guide - v8 - Spr '97 - p162 [51-250]
y VOYA - v19 - F '97 - p352 [51-250]
Marwell, Gerald - *The Critical Mass in Collective Action*
SF - v75 - S '96 - p343+ [251-500]
Marwick, Arthur - *British Society since 1945*
CR - v269 - Ag '96 - p112 [51-250]
Marwick, Thomas H - *Cardiac Stress Testing and Imaging*
SciTech - v20 - D '96 - p47 [51-250]
Marwood, Lorraine - *Skinprint*
Aust Bk R - S '96 - p53+ [501+]
Marx, C W - *The Devil's Rights and the Redemption in the Literature of Medieval England*
Albion - v28 - Win '96 - p670+ [501+]
Marx, Karl - *Capital. Vol. 3*
S&S - v60 - Win '96 - p452+ [501+]
Karl Marx, Frederick Engels. Vol. 35
JEL - v35 - Mr '97 - p191 [51-250]
Marx, Leo - *Progress: Fact or Illusion?*
TLS - F 28 '97 - p26 [501+]
Marx, Trish - *I Heal (Illus. by Cindy Karp)*
c BL - v93 - D 1 '96 - p651 [51-250]
c CCB-B - v50 - D '96 - p143+ [51-250]
c HB Guide - v8 - Spr '97 - p130 [51-250]
c SLJ - v42 - O '96 - p136 [51-250]
Mary Francis, Mother - *Summon Spirit's Cry*
RR - v55 - N '96 - p660 [1-50]
Maryland. Joint Executive-Legislative Task Force to Study Commercial Gaming Activities in Maryland - *Final Report of the Joint Executive-Legislative Task Force to Study Commercial Gaming Activities in Maryland*
J Gov Info - v23 - S '96 - p585 [1-50]
Marysmith, Joan - *Holy Aspic*
Woman's J - Ja '97 - p13 [51-250]
Marz, Ron - *DC Versus Marvel/Marvel Versus DC*
y VOYA - v19 - F '97 - p324 [251-500]
Marzal, Manuel M - *The Indian Face of God in Latin America*
CC - v114 - Ja 1 '97 - p22 [251-500]
Marzan, Julio - *Luna, Luna*
Kliatt - v31 - My '97 - p26 [51-250]
The Spanish American Roots of William Carlos Williams
HAHR - v76 - Ag '97 - p549+ [251-500]
Marzollo, Jean - *Home Sweet Home (Illus. by Ashley Wolff)*
c BL - v93 - Ap 1 '97 - p1338 [51-250]
c CCB-B - v50 - My '97 - p330 [51-250]
c KR - v65 - F 15 '97 - p303 [51-250]
c PW - v244 - F 24 '97 - p90+ [51-250]
I Am Water (Illus. by Judith Moffatt)
c BL - v93 - S 15 '96 - p241 [51-250]
I Spy Spooky Night (Illus. by Walter Wick)
c Ch BWatch - v7 - F '97 - p2 [1-50]
Pretend You're a Cat (Illus. by Jerry Pinkney)
c PW - v244 - Mr 3 '97 - p77 [1-50]
Mas Alla De La Isla
BL - v93 - Ap 1 '97 - p1284 [1-50]

Masaryk, T G - *Masaryk A Benes Ve Svych Dopisech Z Doby Parizskych Mirovych Jednani V Roce 1919. Vols. 1-2*
EHR - v112 - F '97 - p256+ [501+]
Maschio, Thomas - *To Remember the Faces of the Dead*
Cont Pac - v9 - Spr '97 - p268+ [501+]
Maschner, Herbert D G - *New Methods, Old Problems*
Choice - v34 - F '97 - p1016+ [51-250]
Masci, Joseph R - *Outpatient Management of HIV Infection. 2nd Ed.*
SciTech - v20 - S '96 - p34 [51-250]
Mascull, Bill - *Collins COBUILD Key Words in the Media*
MLJ - v80 - Fall '96 - p413+ [251-500]
Maser, Chris - *Sustainable Community Development*
Choice - v34 - F '97 - p1044 [51-250]
R&R Bk N - v12 - F '97 - p35 [51-250]
Masera, M - *Dried Flowers*
BL - v93 - O 1 '96 - p316 [51-250]
LJ - v121 - O 15 '96 - p56+ [51-250]
Mash, Eric J - *Child Psychopathology*
SB - v32 - N '96 - p232+ [51-250]
SciTech - v20 - S '96 - p41 [51-250]
Mashuta, Mary - *Stripes in Quilts*
BL - v93 - S 15 '96 - p201+ [51-250]
Masing-Delic, Irene - *Abolishing Death*
Slav R - v55 - Sum '96 - p506+ [501+]
Masini, Donna - *About Yvonne*
KR - v65 - My 1 '97 - p670 [251-500]
That Kind of Danger
Ken R - v18 - Sum '96 - p191+ [501+]
Maskell, Brian H - *Making the Numbers Count*
Choice - v34 - D '96 - p655 [51-250]
Maslac, Evelyn Hughes - *Finding a Job for Daddy (Illus. by Kay Life)*
c Ch BWatch - v6 - N '96 - p1 [51-250]
c HB Guide - v7 - Fall '96 - p267 [51-250]
Masliah, Leo - *La Buena Noticia Y Otros Cuentos*
BL - v93 - Mr 15 '97 - p1232 [1-50]
Maslow, Jonathan - *Footsteps in the Jungle*
Aud - v99 - Mr '97 - p118+ [501+]
BWatch - v18 - F '97 - p6 [51-250]
Choice - v34 - My '97 - p1523 [51-250]
KR - v64 - Ag 15 '96 - p1215+ [251-500]
TLS - Mr 21 '97 - p32 [501+]
Maslowski, Peter - *Armed with Cameras*
Arm F&S - v22 - Sum '96 - p659+ [501+]
Maso, Carole - *Aureole*
KR - v64 - Ag 15 '96 - p1179 [251-500]
LATBR - N 24 '96 - p1+ [501+]
LJ - v121 - N 1 '96 - p108 [51-250]
PW - v243 - S 30 '96 - p63 [51-250]
Ghost Dance
SFR - v21 - S '96 - p48 [51-250]
Masoliver, Juan Antonio - *The Origins of Desire*
TranslRevS - v1 - My '95 - p3 [51-250]
Mason, Adrienne - *Living Things (Illus. by Ray Boudreau)*
c Quill & Q - v63 - Ja '97 - p38 [51-250]
Mason, Antony - *Biblical Times (Illus. by Michael Welply)*
c HB Guide - v8 - Spr '97 - p166 [51-250]
c PW - v244 - Ja 13 '97 - p72 [51-250]
c SLJ - v43 - Ja '97 - p105 [51-250]
Medieval Times (Illus. by Richard Berridge)
c HB Guide - v8 - Spr '97 - p166 [51-250]
c KR - v64 - N 1 '96 - p1604 [51-250]
c PW - v244 - Ja 13 '97 - p72 [1-50]
c SLJ - v43 - Ja '97 - p105 [51-250]
The Time Trekkers Visit the Stone Age
c HB Guide - v7 - Fall '96 - p334 [51-250]
Mason, Bobbie Ann - *In Country*
y BL - v93 - Ja '97 - p832 [1-50]
Mason, David - *The Country I Remember*
HR - v49 - Sum '96 - p331+ [501+]
Mason, Felicia - *Rhapsody*
PW - v244 - My 5 '97 - p206 [51-250]
Mason, H E - *Moral Dilemmas and Moral Theory*
Choice - v34 - Ja '97 - p809 [51-250]
Hast Cen R - v27 - Ja '97 - p47 [51-250]
Mason, Harriet - *The Power of Storytelling*
Emerg Lib - v24 - S '96 - p40+ [51-250]
Learning - v25 - Mr '97 - p14 [51-250]
Mason, Helen - *Great Careers for People Interested in Food*
y SLJ - v42 - S '96 - p230 [51-250]
Mason, Keith - *Restitution Law in Australia*
Law Q Rev - v112 - O '96 - p689+ [501+]
Mason, Lesley - *Crafty Little Fingers (Illus. by Bettina Paterson)*
c Sch Lib - v45 - F '97 - p19 [51-250]
Mason, Lisa - *The Golden Nineties*
y VOYA - v19 - F '97 - p337+ [251-500]

Mason, Marilyn - *Seven Mountains*
　　PW - v243 - D 9 '96 - p56 [51-250]
Mason, Michael - *The Making of Victorian Sexual
　　Attitudes*
　　AHR - v101 - O '96 - p1210+ [501+]
　　EHR - v112 - F '97 - p240+ [501+]
　　JIH - v27 - Spr '97 - p681+ [251-500]
　　JR - v76 - O '96 - p648+ [501+]
　　RES - v47 - Ag '96 - p432+ [501+]
　　VS - v39 - Spr '96 - p466+ [501+]
　　The Making of Victorian Sexuality
　　EHR - v111 - N '96 - p1325+ [501+]
　　HT - v46 - S '96 - p57 [51-250]
　　RES - v47 - Ag '96 - p432+ [501+]
　　VS - v39 - Spr '96 - p466+ [501+]
Mason, Paul - *Atlas of Threatened Cultures*
　　cr BL - v93 - My 15 '97 - p1610+ [251-500]
　　cr SB - v33 - My '97 - p115 [251-500]
Mason, Richard - *The World of Suzie Wong*
　　FEER - Anniv '96 - p226+ [251-500]
Mason, T David - *Japan, NAFTA and Europe*
　　Econ J - v107 - Ja '97 - p269 [51-250]
Mason, Timothy W - *Nazism, Fascism and the Working
　　Class*
　　HT - v47 - Ja '97 - p51 [501+]
Mason, Tony - *Passion of the People?*
　　HAHR - v76 - Ag '96 - p542+ [501+]
Mason, Wendy H - *CyberHound's Guide to Companies on
　　the Internet*
　　r BL - v93 - F 1 '97 - p963+ [251-500]
Mason-Robinson, Sally - *Developing and Managing Video
　　Collections*
　　BL - v93 - N 1 '96 - p514 [51-250]
　　Emerg Lib - v24 - Mr '97 - p40 [51-250]
　　LJ - v121 - N 1 '96 - p113 [51-250]
Mason's Coin and Stamp Collector's Magazine. Vols. 1-2
　　Coin W - v38 - Ja 27 '97 - p42 [51-250]
Masood, Shahla - *Cytopathology of the Breast*
　　SciTech - v20 - N '96 - p40 [51-250]
Massa, Renato - *The Breathing Earth*
　　c Ch BWatch - v7 - F '97 - p5 [1-50]
　　y HB Guide - v8 - Spr '97 - p119 [51-250]
　　The Tropical Forest
　　c Ch BWatch - v7 - F '97 - p5 [1-50]
Massachusetts Community Profiles. Vols. 1-5
　　r J Gov Info - v23 - S '96 - p586 [1-50]
Massel, Norma - *Into Israel*
　　c TES - Mr 28 '97 - pR6 [51-250]
Massengale, John D - *The History of Exercise and Sport
　　Science*
　　Choice - v34 - My '97 - p1539 [51-250]
　　R&R Bk N - v12 - F '97 - p31 [51-250]
Massey, Calvin R - *Silent Rights*
　　HLR - v110 - D '96 - p560+ [51-250]
Massey, Doreen B - *A Place in the World?*
　　GJ - v163 - Mr '97 - p102+ [501+]
　　Space, Place and Gender
　　Signs - v22 - Win '97 - p456+ [501+]
Massey, Ed - *Milton (Illus. by Kristy Chu)*
　　c HB Guide - v7 - Fall '96 - p267 [51-250]
　　c SLJ - v42 - Ag '96 - p126 [51-250]
Massey, Irving - *Identity and Community*
　　Col Lit - v23 - Je '96 - p199+ [501+]
Massialas, Byron G - *Crucial Issues in Teaching Social
　　Studies K-12*
　　SS - v88 - Ja '97 - p44 [501+]
Massie, Gabriele - *Employ Your PC. Vol. 1*
　　BWatch - v18 - F '97 - p3 [51-250]
　　LJ - v122 - My 1 '97 - p53 [1-50]
Massie, Robert K - *The Romanovs: The Final Chapter*
　　y Kliatt - v31 - Mr '97 - p32 [51-250]
　　LATBR - D 22 '96 - p6 [51-250]
　　NYTBR - v102 - Ja 12 '97 - p32 [51-250]
　　PW - v243 - S 23 '96 - p73 [1-50]
Massie-Ferch, Kathleen M - *Warrior Enchantresses*
　　y Kliatt - v30 - S '96 - p20 [51-250]
　　SF Chr - v18 - O '96 - p80 [1-50]
Massing, Jean Michel - *Erasmian Wit and Proverbial
　　Wisdom*
　　BM - v138 - N '96 - p756+ [501+]
Massingberd, Hugh - *The Daily Telegraph Second Book
　　of Obituaries*
　　Spec - v277 - N 16 '96 - p43 [1-50]
　　Heroes and Adventures
　　Spec - v277 - N 23 '96 - p44 [1-50]
Massis, Bruce Edward - *Serving Print Disabled Library
　　Patrons*
　　A Lib - v27 - Ag '96 - p70 [51-250]
Masson, Alain - *Le Recit Au Cinema*
　　FR - v70 - Mr '97 - p608+ [51-250]

Masson, J Moussaieff - *Dogs Never Lie about Love*
　　Woman's J - Ap '97 - p18 [51-250]
　　When Elephants Weep
　　y Kliatt - v31 - Ja '97 - p28+ [51-250]
　　Queens Q - v103 - Fall '96 - p607+ [501+]
Masson, Sophie - *Birds of a Feather*
　　y Aust Bk R - N '96 - p60 [501+]
　　Carabas
　　y Aust Bk R - D '96 - p89+ [501+]
　　The Secret
　　c Aust Bk R - Jl '96 - p59+ [501+]
　　c Magpies - v11 - Jl '96 - p31+ [51-250]
　　The Sun Is Rising
　　c Magpies - v11 - My '96 - p48 [51-250]
Massoud, Mary - *Literary Inter-Relations*
　　TLS - S 27 '96 - p13 [501+]
Massy, William F - *Resource Allocation in Higher
　　Education*
　　JEL - v34 - D '96 - p2064 [51-250]
Mast, Greg - *State Troops and Volunteers. Vol. 1*
　　J Gov Info - v23 - S '96 - p590 [51-250]
Mastel, Greg - *American Trade Laws after the Uruguay
　　Round*
　　For Aff - v76 - Mr '97 - p178 [51-250]
　　R&R Bk N - v12 - F '97 - p64 [51-250]
Masten, Scott E - *Case Studies in Contracting and
　　Organization*
　　JEL - v35 - Mr '97 - p244 [51-250]
Masters, Anthony - *Bypass*
　　c Bks Keeps - Mr '97 - p25+ [51-250]
　　Deadly Games
　　y Sch Lib - v45 - F '97 - p47 [51-250]
　　Haunted School
　　y Sch Lib - v45 - F '97 - p47 [51-250]
　　Poltergeist
　　y Sch Lib - v45 - F '97 - p47 [251-500]
　　True Stories
　　c TES - O 18 '96 - p12* [51-250]
Masters, Brian - *She Must Have Known*
　　TES - D 27 '96 - p16 [1-50]
Masters, Colin - *The Peroxisome: A Vital Organelle*
　　Sci - v274 - O 4 '96 - p62 [251-500]
Masters, D C - *Henry John Cody: An Outstanding Life*
　　Can Hist R - v77 - D '96 - p623+ [501+]
Masters, Roger D - *Machiavelli, Leonardo, and the
　　Science of Power*
　　RP - v59 - Spr '97 - p408+ [501+]
Masters, William A - *Government and Agriculture in
　　Zimbabwe*
　　JTWS - v13 - Fall '96 - p278+ [501+]
Masterson, Josephine - *County Cork, Ireland*
　　r EGH - v50 - N '96 - p156+ [51-250]
Masterson, Paul - *Herbert Richardson*
　　c Can CL - v22 - Fall '96 - p106+ [251-500]
Masterton, Graham - *The House That Jack Built*
　　LJ - v122 - Ja '97 - p148 [51-250]
　　Necro - Fall '96 - p26 [51-250]
　　PW - v243 - S 30 '96 - p61 [51-250]
　　y VOYA - v19 - F '97 - p338 [251-500]
　　Rook
　　KR - v65 - F 15 '97 - p246+ [51-250]
　　PW - v244 - Mr 10 '97 - p51 [51-250]
Mastny, Vojtech - *The Cold War and Soviet Insecurity*
　　Choice - v34 - F '97 - p1020 [51-250]
　　Turkey between East and West
　　Choice - v34 - S '96 - p207 [51-250]
　　MEJ - v50 - Sum '96 - p452 [51-250]
Mastretta, Angeles - *Lovesick*
　　BL - v93 - Mr 1 '97 - p1068 [51-250]
　　KR - v65 - F 15 '97 - p247 [251-500]
　　LJ - v122 - Ap 1 '97 - p128 [51-250]
　　PW - v244 - Mr 10 '97 - p49 [51-250]
　　Tear This Heart Out
　　PW - v244 - Ap 14 '97 - p72 [1-50]
Masud, Muhammad Khalid - *Islamic Legal Interpretation*
　　MEJ - v51 - Spr '97 - p313 [51-250]
Masui, Kazuko - *French Cheeses*
　　BL - v93 - N 15 '96 - p560 [51-250]
　　BWatch - v18 - Mr '97 - p5 [1-50]
　　r LJ - v121 - O 15 '96 - p52 [51-250]
Matane, Paulias - *Pawa Na Pipel!*
　　WorldV - v13 - Ja '97 - p17 [251-500]
Matanle, Ivor - *Collecting and Using Classic SLRs*
　　LJ - v121 - D '96 - p88 [51-250]
　　r Pet PM - v25 - D '96 - p20 [51-250]

Matas, Carol - *After the War*
　　y BIC - v25 - N '96 - p32+ [501+]
　　y BL - v93 - Ja '97 - p764 [1-50]
　　y BL - v93 - Ap 1 '97 - p1294 [1-50]
　　y BL - v93 - Ap 1 '97 - p1310 [1-50]
　　y Ch Bk News - v20 - Win '97 - p30 [51-250]
　　y Emerg Lib - v24 - Mr '97 - p27 [1-50]
　　y HB Guide - v8 - Spr '97 - p82 [51-250]
　　y JAAL - v40 - D '96 - p324+ [501+]
　　y Quill & Q - v62 - O '96 - p49 [251-500]
　　Daniel's Story
　　c New Ad - v9 - Fall '96 - p297+ [501+]
　　The Freak
　　y Quill & Q - v63 - Mr '97 - p79 [251-500]
　　The Garden
　　y BL - v93 - Ap 1 '97 - p1322 [51-250]
　　c CCB-B - v50 - My '97 - p330+ [51-250]
　　More Minds
　　c CCB-B - v50 - F '97 - p214 [51-250]
　　c HB Guide - v8 - Spr '97 - p71 [51-250]
　　y SLJ - v42 - O '96 - p148 [51-250]
　　The Primrose Path
　　y BIC - v25 - O '96 - p30 [501+]
　　y Ch Bk News - v19 - Sum '96 - p29+ [51-250]
Mateer, John - *Anachronism*
　　Aust Bk R - F '97 - p46+ [501+]
Mateljan, George - *Baking without Fat*
　　y Kliatt - v30 - S '96 - p38 [51-250]
　　Cooking without Fat
　　y Kliatt - v30 - S '96 - p38 [51-250]
Matelski, Marilyn J - *Vatican Radio*
　　CHR - v82 - Jl '96 - p480+ [251-500]
Matera, Frank J - *New Testament Ethics*
　　Am - v176 - Mr 8 '97 - p30 [51-250]
　　Rel St Rev - v23 - Ap '97 - p186 [51-250]
Matera, Lia - *Last Chants*
　　KR - v64 - My 1 '96 - p645 [51-250]
　　Star Witness
　　KR - v65 - My 1 '97 - p682 [251-500]
　　PW - v244 - Ap 14 '97 - p59 [51-250]
Materer, Timothy - *Modernist Alchemy*
　　Choice - v34 - S '96 - p128 [51-250]
Material for Thought
　　p Parabola - v21 - Ag '96 - p112+ [501+]
Materials Reliability in Microelectronics VI
　　SciTech - v21 - Mr '97 - p92 [51-250]
Materials Research Centres. 6th Ed.
　　r RQ - v36 - Fall '96 - p134 [251-500]
Matero, Robert - *The Birth of a Humpback Whale (Illus.
　　by Pamela Johnson)*
　　c Ch BWatch - v6 - My '96 - p4 [51-250]
　　c HB Guide - v7 - Fall '96 - p345 [51-250]
Mathabane, Mark - *African Women*
　　Africa T - v43 - 3 '96 - p329+ [501+]
Mathematical Methods of Operations Research
　　p JEL - v34 - S '96 - p1506 [51-250]
Mather, Anne - *Dangerous Temptation*
　　PW - v243 - D 16 '96 - p54+ [51-250]
Mather, Cotton - *The Christian Philosopher*
　　Bks & Cult - v2 - My '96 - p34 [251-500]
　　The Threefold Paradise of Cotton Mather
　　Sev Cent N - v54 - Spr '96 - p34 [251-500]
Mather, Cynthia L - *How Long Does It Hurt?*
　　y Fam Relat - v45 - Jl '96 - p353 [251-500]
Mather, John C - *The Very First Light*
　　y BL - v93 - N 15 '96 - p557+ [51-250]
　　KR - v64 - O 1 '96 - p1448 [51-250]
　　LJ - v121 - D '96 - p139 [51-250]
　　Nature - v385 - F 20 '97 - p691+ [501+]
　　New Sci - v152 - N 30 '96 - p43 [501+]
　　SciTech - v21 - Mr '97 - p20 [51-250]
Mather, Paul M - *Terra-2: Understanding the Terrestrial
　　Environment*
　　GJ - v162 - Jl '96 - p219+ [501+]
Mather, Stephen J - *Current Directions in
　　Radiopharmaceutical Research and Development*
　　SciTech - v21 - Mr '97 - p67 [51-250]
Mather, Victoria - *Absolutely Typical*
　　Spec - v277 - D 7 '96 - p54+ [51-250]
Matherne, Beverly - *La Grande Pointe*
　　TranslRevS - v2 - D '96 - p19 [51-250]
Mathers, Petra - *Kisses from Rosa (Illus. by Petra
　　Mathers)*
　　c NYTBR - v101 - Ap 7 '96 - p21 [1-50]
　　c RT - v50 - O '96 - p152 [51-250]
Mathes, Charles - *The Girl Who Remembered Snow*
　　Arm Det - v29 - Sum '96 - p362 [251-500]
　　LJ - v122 - Ja '97 - p51 [1-50]
Matheson, Ian - *Passing Higher History*
　　y Sch Lib - v44 - N '96 - p176 [51-250]

Matheson, Lister M - *Popular and Practical Science of Medieval England*
RES - v47 - Ag '96 - p402+ [501+]

Matheson, Susan B - *Polygnotos and Vase Painting in Classical Athens*
AB - v99 - Mr 3 '97 - p692 [51-250]
Choice - v34 - S '96 - p114 [51-250]

Mathew, Brian - *Growing Bulbs*
r BL - v93 - Ap 1 '97 - p1274 [51-250]
PW - v244 - Mr 24 '97 - p79 [51-250]

Mathewes-Green, Frederica - *Facing East*
Bks & Cult - v3 - Mr '97 - p4 [51-250]
Ch Today - v41 - F 3 '97 - p60+ [501+]
KR - v64 - N 15 '96 - p1656 [251-500]
LJ - v122 - Ja '97 - p106 [51-250]
PW - v243 - D 2 '96 - p52 [51-250]

Mathews, Adrian - *The Hat of Victor Noir*
TLS - N 15 '96 - p24 [251-500]

Mathews, David - *Politics for People*
RP - v59 - Win '97 - p127+ [501+]

Mathews, Francine - *Death in a Mood Indigo*
PW - v244 - Ap 21 '97 - p63 [51-250]

Mathews, Gordon - *What Makes Life Worth Living?*
SF - v75 - D '96 - p765 [51-250]

Mathews, Nancy Mowll - *Cassatt: A Retrospective*
LJ - v122 - Ap 15 '97 - p76 [51-250]
PW - v243 - O 7 '96 - p55+ [51-250]

Mathews, Nieves - *Francis Bacon: The History of a Character Assassination*
Choice - v34 - D '96 - p671 [51-250]
TLS - O 11 '96 - p3+ [501+]

Mathews, Robin - *The Death of Socialism and Other Poems*
Can Lit - Spr '97 - p232+ [501+]
Treason of the Intellectuals
Can Lit - Spr '97 - p232+ [501+]

Mathews, Thomas F - *Art and Architecture in Byzantium and Armenia*
R&R Bk N - v12 - F '97 - p72 [51-250]

Mathias, Barbara - *40 Ways to Raise a Nonracist Child*
LATBR - Jl 7 '96 - p10 [51-250]

Mathias, Peter - *Enterprise and Labour*
JEL - v34 - D '96 - p2099 [51-250]
TLS - Ja 24 '97 - p30 [501+]

Mathiasen, Patrick - *An Ocean of Time*
KR - v65 - Mr 1 '97 - p359 [51-250]

Mathiesen, Michael - *Marketing on the Internet. 2nd Ed.*
BWatch - v17 - N '96 - p11 [51-250]

Mathieu, Jacques - *Les Dynamismes De La Recherche Au Quebec*
Can Hist R - v77 - S '96 - p458+ [501+]

Mathieu, Nicolas - *Industrial Restructuring*
JEL - v35 - Mr '97 - p278 [51-250]

Mathieu, Pierre - *D'Est En Quest*
c Can CL - v22 - Sum '96 - p99 [251-500]

Mathieu, Richard G - *Manufacturing and the Internet*
SciTech - v20 - D '96 - p84 [51-250]

Maths in Action. Rev. Ed., Bks. 1-4B
y TES - O 4 '96 - pR15 [501+]

Maths in Action Plus. Bks. 1-4
y TES - O 4 '96 - pR15 [501+]

Matias Alonso, Marcos - *Rituales Agricolas Y Otras Costumbres Guerrences Siglos XVI-XX*
HAHR - v77 - My '97 - p291+ [501+]

Matibag, Eugenio - *Afro-Cuban Religious Experience*
Choice - v34 - D '96 - p620 [51-250]
WLT - v71 - Win '97 - p125 [501+]

Matijevich, Elke - *The Zeitroman of the Late Weimar Republic*
Ger Q - v70 - Win '97 - p88+ [501+]

Matlins, Antoinette L - *The Pearl Book*
LJ - v122 - Mr 15 '97 - p59 [51-250]

Matlock, Jack F, Jr. - *Autopsy on an Empire*
Ant R - v54 - Sum '96 - p358 [251-500]
NYTBR - v101 - D 8 '96 - p85 [1-50]
TLS - D 27 '96 - p7 [501+]

Matos, Maria Antonia Pinto De - *Chinese Export Porcelain from the Museum of Anastacio Goncalves, Lisbon*
Spec - v277 - D 14 '96 - p76 [1-50]

Matos Mendieta, Ramiro - *Pumpu: Centro Administrativo Inka De La Puna De Junin*
LA Ant - v7 - S '96 - p279+ [501+]

Matott, Justin - *My Garden Visits*
PW - v244 - Ja 27 '97 - p95 [51-250]

Matousek, Mark - *Sex, Death, Enlightenment*
LATBR - My 26 '96 - p4+ [501+]
TLS - Ja 3 '97 - p32 [51-250]
Trib Bks - Mr 23 '97 - p6 [1-50]
Tric - v6 - Fall '96 - p144+ [501+]

Matovina, Timothy M - *Tejano Religion and Ethnicity*
JSH - v62 - N '96 - p803+ [251-500]

Matson, P A - *Biogenic Trace Gases*
Am Sci - v85 - Ja '97 - p79+ [501+]

Matsuda, Mari J - *Where Is Your Body? and Other Essays on Race, Gender, and the Law*
BWatch - v18 - Mr '97 - p11 [51-250]
KR - v64 - N 1 '96 - p1586+ [251-500]
LJ - v121 - D '96 - p121 [51-250]
Ms - v7 - Ja '97 - p79 [251-500]
PW - v243 - O 7 '96 - p48+ [51-250]

Matsui, Makinosuke - *Sin-Itiro Tomonaga: Life of a Japanese Physicist*
Isis - v87 - D '96 - p750+ [501+]

Matsumoto, David - *Unmasking Japan*
Choice - v34 - Mr '97 - p1200 [51-250]

Matsumoto, Valerie J - *Farming the Home Place*
AAPSS-A - v549 - Ja '97 - p197+ [251-500]
Amerasia J - v22 - 3 '96 - p180+ [501+]
Am Q - v49 - Mr '97 - p203+ [501+]

Matsuura, Rieko - *Oyayubi P No Shugyo Jidal*
Econ - v342 - F 15 '97 - p17*+ [501+]

Matt, Daniel Chanan - *The Essential Kabbalah*
Rel St Rev - v23 - Ap '97 - p196+ [51-250]
The Essential Kabbalah (Asner). Audio Version
BL - v93 - N 15 '96 - p603+ [51-250]
y Kliatt - v31 - My '97 - p47 [51-250]
God and the Big Bang
BL - v93 - S 1 '96 - p38 [51-250]
CLW - v67 - D '96 - p36 [51-250]
LJ - v121 - S 15 '96 - p73+ [51-250]

Matt, Paul - *Paul Matt Scale Airplane Drawings. Vols. 1-2*
FSM - v15 - Ja '97 - p79 [1-50]

Matter, E Ann - *Creative Women in Medieval and Early Modern Italy*
CHR - v82 - O '96 - p694+ [501+]
JR - v76 - O '96 - p637+ [251-500]

Mattern, David B - *Benjamin Lincoln and the American Revolution*
NEQ - v70 - Mr '97 - p156+ [501+]
VQR - v72 - Aut '96 - p764+ [501+]
W&M Q - v53 - O '96 - p829+ [501+]

Mattes, Hanspeter - *Qaddafi Und Die Islamistische Opposition In Libyen*
MEJ - v51 - Win '97 - p151 [51-250]

Matteson, Richard - *An Application Christmas*
CAY - v16 - Fall '95 - p12 [51-250]

Matteson, Stefanie - *Murder among the Angels*
Arm Det - v29 - Sum '96 - p368 [251-500]
Murder under the Palms
BL - v93 - Mr 15 '97 - p1230 [51-250]
KR - v65 - Ja 15 '97 - p99 [51-250]
PW - v244 - Ja 6 '97 - p68 [51-250]

Mattfeld, Dirk C - *Evolutionary Search and the Job Shop*
JEL - v34 - D '96 - p2091+ [51-250]

Matthaei, Gay - *The Journal of Julia Singing Bear (Illus. by Adam Cvijanovic)*
c PW - v243 - O 7 '96 - p75+ [51-250]
c Smith - v27 - N '96 - p170 [1-50]

Matthai, Sandra Higgins - *Faith Matters*
OS - v33 - Mr '97 - p35 [51-250]

Matthee, Dalene - *Fiela's Child*
y TES - F 28 '97 - pR7 [501+]

Mattheij, R M M - *Ordinary Differential Equations in Theory and Practice*
Choice - v34 - F '97 - p1000 [51-250]

Matthen, Mohan - *Biology and Society*
CPR - v16 - Ap '96 - p115+ [501+]

Matthew, H C G - *Gladstone 1875-1898*
AHR - v101 - D '96 - p1543+ [501+]
Albion - v28 - Sum '96 - p343+ [501+]
Historian - v58 - Sum '96 - p912+ [501+]
HT - v47 - Ja '97 - p54 [501+]

Matthews, Alex - *Satan's Silence*
PW - v244 - Ja 6 '97 - p68 [51-250]

Matthews, Andrew - *Alfred the Great (Illus. by Peter Kent)*
c Bks Keeps - Ja '97 - p24 [251-500]
c Sch Lib - v45 - F '97 - p39 [51-250]
The Beasts of Boggart Hollow (Illus. by Chris Fisher)
c Magpies - v11 - Jl '96 - p45 [1-50]
c Sch Lib - v44 - Ag '96 - p108+ [51-250]
Dick Whittington (Illus. by Lesley Bisseker)
c Bks Keeps - Ja '97 - p24 [251-500]
c Sch Lib - v45 - F '97 - p37 [51-250]
Marduk the Mighty and Other Stories of Creation (Illus. by Sheila Moxley)
c CBRS - v25 - Ap '97 - p103 [51-250]

Matthews, Anne, 1957- - *Bright College Years*
KR - v65 - F 1 '97 - p203+ [251-500]
NYTBR - v102 - Ap 20 '97 - p6 [501+]
PW - v244 - Mr 3 '97 - p56 [51-250]

Matthews, Anne McLean - *The Cave*
KR - v64 - D 1 '96 - p1695 [251-500]
LJ - v121 - D '96 - p146 [51-250]
PW - v243 - D 30 '96 - p56 [251-500]

Matthews, Birch - *Cobra! Bell Aircraft Corporation 1934-1946*
APH - v43 - Win '96 - p60 [251-500]

Matthews, Christopher - *Kennedy and Nixon*
Ant R - v54 - Fall '96 - p492+ [251-500]
Choice - v34 - N '96 - p538 [51-250]
NL - v79 - Ag 12 '96 - p10+ [501+]
SFR - v21 - S '96 - p21 [501+]

Matthews, Downs - *Harp Seal Pups (Illus. by Dan Guravich)*
c BL - v93 - Ja '97 - p852 [251-500]
c KR - v64 - D 1 '96 - p1739 [51-250]
c SLJ - v43 - F '97 - p93+ [51-250]

Matthews, Elizabeth W - *The Law Library Reference Shelf. 3rd Ed., Rev.*
r ARBA - v28 - '97 - p218 [51-250]
r Choice - v34 - S '96 - p102 [51-250]

Matthews, Gordon - *An Australian Son*
Aust Bk R - S '96 - p22 [501+]

Matthews, Graham - *Disaster Management in British Libraries*
LAR - v99 - Ja '97 - p49 [51-250]

Matthews, J Rosser - *Quantification and the Quest for Medical Certainty*
AJS - v102 - Jl '96 - p278+ [501+]
Isis - v87 - D '96 - p710+ [501+]

Matthews, Janice R - *Successful Scientific Writing*
LR - v45 - 7 '96 - p67+ [501+]

Matthews, John - *The Druid Source Book*
LJ - v121 - O 15 '96 - p64 [51-250]
PW - v243 - S 2 '96 - p108 [51-250]
The Unknown Arthur (Illus. by Mark Robertson)
c Bloom Rev - v16 - Jl '96 - p27 [1-50]

Matthews, Kent - *Macroeconomics and the Market*
Econ J - v107 - Ja '97 - p265 [51-250]

Matthews, Mary - *Magid Fasts for Ramadan (Illus. by E B Lewis)*
c BL - v93 - O 1 '96 - p339 [1-50]
c HB Guide - v7 - Fall '96 - p287 [51-250]

Matthews, Mervyn - *The Passport Society*
Slav R - v55 - Fall '96 - p687+ [501+]

Matthews, Richard H - *Virtue, Corruption, and Self-Interest*
EHR - v112 - F '97 - p210+ [501+]

Matthews, William - *Time and Money*
Ant R - v54 - Fall '96 - p497 [251-500]

Matthiessen, Peter - *The Snow Leopard*
LATBR - Ag 25 '96 - p11 [51-250]

Matthys, Eric F - *Melt-Spinning, Strip Casting and Slab Casting*
SciTech - v20 - N '96 - p82 [51-250]

Mattick, Paul, Jr. - *Eighteenth-Century Aesthetics and the Reconstruction of Art*
BM - v138 - O '96 - p700 [1-50]

Mattingley, Christobel - *Asmir in Vienna*
c Magpies - v11 - My '96 - p45 [501+]
Escape from Sarajevo
c Magpies - v11 - My '96 - p45 [501+]
The Magic Saddle (Illus. by Patricia Mullins)
c BL - v93 - S 1 '96 - p137 [51-250]
c CBRS - v25 - F '97 - p77 [51-250]
c Ch BWatch - v6 - D '96 - p1 [1-50]
c HB Guide - v8 - Spr '97 - p39 [51-250]
c Magpies - v11 - Jl '96 - p26 [51-250]
c PW - v243 - S 30 '96 - p90 [51-250]
c SLJ - v42 - O '96 - p38 [51-250]
No Gun for Asmir
c Magpies - v11 - My '96 - p45 [501+]

Mattingly, David J - *Tripolitania*
AJA - v100 - O '96 - p803+ [501+]

Mattingly, Rozella - *Management of Health Information*
SciTech - v20 - S '96 - p27 [51-250]

Mattison, Chris - *Rattler! A Natural History of Rattlesnakes*
y BL - v93 - D 1 '96 - p632+ [51-250]
New Sci - v151 - S 21 '96 - p55 [51-250]

Matto De Turner, Clorinda - *Birds without a Nest*
KR - v64 - N 15 '96 - p1631 [51-250]

Mattox, Cheryl Warren - *Shake It to the One That You Love the Best (Illus. by Warren-Mattox)*
c BL - v93 - F 15 '97 - p1014 [1-50]

Mattson, James - *The Pioneers of NMR and Magnetic Resonance in Medicine*
  Phys Today - v50 - Ja '97 - p66+ [501+]
Mattson, Mark T - *Macmillan Color Atlas of the States*
  yr ARBA - v28 - '97 - p46+ [251-500]
  r BL - v93 - N 1 '96 - p536+ [251-500]
  r Choice - v34 - Mr '97 - p1140 [51-250]
  yr LJ - v121 - O 15 '96 - p52 [51-250]
  yr R&R Bk N - v12 - F '97 - p29 [51-250]
Maturi, Richard J - *The 105 Best Investments for the 21st Century*
  r ARBA - v28 - '97 - p107+ [51-250]
Matus, Jill L - *Unstable Bodies*
  Nine-C Lit - v51 - D '96 - p403+ [501+]
  VS - v39 - Win '96 - p289+ [501+]
Matustik, Martin J - *Kierkegaard in Post-Modernity*
  IPQ - v36 - S '96 - p374+ [501+]
Matute, Ana Maria - *Celebration in the Northwest*
  KR - v65 - F 1 '97 - p172 [51-250]
  The Trap
  PW - v243 - S 16 '96 - p77 [51-250]
Matveeva, N M - *Ordered Phases in Metallic Systems*
  SciTech - v21 - Mr '97 - p94 [51-250]
Matyas, Laszlo - *The Econometrics of Panel Data. 2nd Ed.*
  JEL - v34 - D '96 - p2019 [51-250]
  R&R Bk N - v12 - F '97 - p33 [51-250]
Matyjaszewski, Krzysztof - *Cationic Polymerization*
  r SciTech - v20 - S '96 - p16 [51-250]
Matza, Diane - *Sephardic American Voices*
  BL - v93 - F 1 '97 - p921 [51-250]
  LJ - v122 - Ja '97 - p100 [51-250]
Mau, Vladimir - *The Political History of Economic Reform in Russia 1985-1994*
  JEL - v34 - S '96 - p1491 [51-250]
Mauceri, Philip - *State under Siege*
  Choice - v34 - My '97 - p1568+ [51-250]
  R&R Bk N - v11 - D '96 - p48 [51-250]
Mauck, Jeffrey - *The Education of a Soldier*
  WHQ - v28 - Spr '97 - p102 [1-50]
Maude, R B - *Seedborne Diseases and Their Control*
  Choice - v34 - Mr '97 - p1183 [51-250]
Maudlin, Tim - *Quantum Non-Locality and Relativity*
  Phil R - v105 - Ap '96 - p259+ [501+]
Mauger, Thierry - *Impressions of Arabia*
  BL - v93 - Mr 1 '97 - p1103 [51-250]
  LJ - v121 - D '96 - p88 [51-250]
Maulik, Sunil - *Molecular Biotechnology*
  New Sci - v153 - Mr 1 '97 - p42 [1-50]
  SciTech - v20 - D '96 - p82 [51-250]
Maulpoix, Jean-Michel - *Un Dimanche Apres-Midi Dans La Tete*
  FR - v70 - Mr '97 - p617+ [501+]
  WLT - v70 - Aut '96 - p918 [51-250]
  La Poesie Malgre Tout
  FR - v70 - F '97 - p500+ [501+]
  WLT - v70 - Aut '96 - p915 [251-500]
Maupassant, Guy De - *Afloat*
  TranslRevS - v2 - D '96 - p9 [51-250]
  Short Stories by Guy De Maupassant
  y TES - S 20 '96 - pR6 [251-500]
Maupin, Melissa - *The Ultimate Kids' Club Book*
  c SLJ - v43 - F '97 - p43 [51-250]
  y VOYA - v19 - F '97 - p352 [51-250]
Maurer, Boris - *R and D, Innovation and Industrial Structure*
  JEL - v34 - D '96 - p2117 [51-250]
Maurer, Donna - *Eating Agendas*
  CS - v26 - Ja '97 - p94+ [501+]
Maurer, John G - *Encyclopedia of Business. Vols. 1-2*
  r ARBA - v28 - '97 - p78+ [251-500]
  r Bus Bk R - v13 - 3 '96 - p121 [51-250]
  r Choice - v34 - S '96 - p96 [251-500]
Maurer-Alvarez, Pansy - *Dolores: The Alpine Years*
  y Kliatt - v30 - N '96 - p19 [51-250]
Maurice, Catherine - *Behavioral Intervention for Young Children with Autism*
  SciTech - v20 - S '96 - p41 [51-250]
Mauries, Patrick - *Christian Lacroix: The Diary of a Collection*
  BL - v93 - F 1 '97 - p911 [51-250]
Maus, Didier - *Election Presidentielle Des 23 Avril Et 7 Mai 1995*
  J Gov Info - v23 - S '96 - p657+ [1-50]
Maus, Katharine Eisaman - *Inwardness and Theater in the English Renaissance*
  Albion - v28 - Win '96 - p682+ [501+]
  Clio - v25 - Sum '96 - p421+ [501+]
  MP - v94 - F '97 - p366+ [501+]
Mauss, Armand L - *The Angel and the Beehive*
  AJS - v102 - Jl '96 - p312 [251-500]

Mavissakalian, Matig R - *Long-Term Treatments of Anxiety Disorders*
  SciTech - v20 - S '96 - p34 [51-250]
Mavor, Carol - *Pleasures Taken*
  VS - v39 - Spr '96 - p391+ [501+]
Mawe, S M - *Grown Men*
  KR - v65 - Mr 15 '97 - p409+ [251-500]
  PW - v244 - Mr 31 '97 - p61 [51-250]
Mawson, Douglas - *The Home of the Blizzard*
  Aust Bk R - F '97 - p20+ [501+]
Max, Aggie - *The Last Resort*
  BL - v93 - My 15 '97 - p1546 [51-250]
  PW - v244 - Mr 24 '97 - p69 [51-250]
Max Beckmann in Exile
  NYRB - v43 - N 28 '96 - p13 [501+]
Maxfield, Clive - *Bebop to the Boolean Boogie*
  BYTE - v21 - N '96 - p38 [51-250]
Maxfield, James F - *The Fatal Woman*
  Choice - v34 - O '96 - p289+ [51-250]
Maxford, Howard - *The A-Z of Horror Films*
  r LJ - v122 - F 15 '97 - p128 [51-250]
  r PW - v244 - Ja 20 '97 - p390 [51-250]
Maxim, John R - *The Shadow Box*
  PW - v243 - Jl 22 '96 - p227 [51-250]
Maximin, Daniel - *L'Ile Et Une Nuit*
  WLT - v70 - Sum '96 - p748 [501+]
Maximov's Companion to Who Governs the Russian Federation. Vol. 2, No. 1
  r ARBA - v28 - '97 - p275 [251-500]
Maxwell, Cathy - *You and No Other*
  PW - v243 - Jl 22 '96 - p235 [51-250]
Maxwell, Christine - *McKinley Internet Yellow Pages*
  r RQ - v36 - Win '96 - p301+ [501+]
Maxwell, Glyn - *Rest for the Wicked*
  WLT - v70 - Aut '96 - p963+ [501+]
Maxwell, James Clerk - *Maxwell on Heat and Statistical Mechanics*
  Isis - v87 - S '96 - p511+ [501+]
  The Scientific Letters and Papers of James Clerk Maxwell. Vol. 2
  Isis - v87 - S '96 - p511+ [501+]
Maxwell, Jessica - *I Don't Know Why I Swallowed the Fly*
  KR - v65 - Mr 15 '97 - p444+ [251-500]
  LJ - v122 - Ap 15 '97 - p87 [51-250]
Maxwell, Joseph Alex - *Qualitative Research Design*
  SciTech - v20 - S '96 - p3 [51-250]
Maxwell, Kenneth, 1941- - *The Making of Portuguese Democracy*
  For Aff - v76 - Mr '97 - p188 [51-250]
  Pombal: Paradox of the Enlightenment
  AHR - v101 - D '96 - p1577+ [501+]
  HT - v47 - Mr '97 - p52+ [501+]
Maxwell, Kenneth E, 1908- - *A Sexual Odyssey*
  New Sci - v152 - N 30 '96 - p45 [51-250]
Maxwell, Robin - *The Secret Diary of Anne Boleyn*
  KR - v65 - F 15 '97 - p247+ [251-500]
  LJ - v122 - Mr 15 '97 - p90 [51-250]
  PW - v244 - F 24 '97 - p62 [51-250]
Maxwell, William, 1908- - *All the Days and Nights*
  Lon R Bks - v19 - Mr 6 '97 - p24+ [501+]
  Obs - F 2 '97 - p16* [501+]
  Spec - v278 - Ja 25 '97 - p38+ [501+]
  The Folded Leaf
  NYTBR - v102 - F 23 '97 - p24 [1-50]
  Mrs. Donald's Dog Bun and His Home Away from Home (Illus. by James Stevenson)
  c HB Guide - v7 - Fall '96 - p267 [51-250]
  c RT - v50 - Mr '97 - p496 [51-250]
  So Long, See You Tomorrow
  Lon R Bks - v19 - Mr 6 '97 - p24+ [501+]
  Obs - F 2 '97 - p16* [501+]
  Spec - v278 - Ja 25 '97 - p38+ [501+]
  Time Will Darken It
  NYTBR - v102 - F 23 '97 - p24 [51-250]
May, Bella J - *Amputations and Prosthetics*
  SciTech - v20 - N '96 - p50 [51-250]
May, Dean L - *Three Frontiers*
  RAH - v24 - S '96 - p432+ [501+]
May, Derwent - *Feather Reports*
  TLS - D 6 '96 - p27 [501+]
May, Elaine Tyler - *Barren in the Promised Land*
  AHR - v102 - F '97 - p221 [501+]
  CS - v25 - N '96 - p788+ [501+]
  J Soc H - v30 - Fall '96 - p260+ [501+]
May, Georges - *La Perruque De Dom Juan*
  MLR - v91 - Jl '96 - p726+ [251-500]
May, Glenn Anthony - *Inventing a Hero*
  Choice - v34 - My '97 - p1554+ [51-250]
May, Graham H - *The Future Is Ours*
  Choice - v34 - F '97 - p1004 [51-250]
  Fut - v30 - N '96 - p57 [501+]

May, J Peter - *Equivariant Homotopy and Cohomology Theory*
  SciTech - v21 - Mr '97 - p17 [51-250]
May, Jill P - *Children's Literature and Critical Theory*
  Bkbird - v34 - Spr '96 - p57 [1-50]
May, Jim - *The Farm on Nippersink Creek*
  y Kliatt - v31 - Mr '97 - p26 [51-250]
May, Julian - *Sky Trillium*
  y BL - v93 - Ja '97 - p826 [51-250]
  PW - v243 - D 30 '96 - p58+ [51-250]
May, Katja - *African Americans in the Creek and Cherokee Nations 1830s to 1920s*
  Bl S - v26 - Fall '96 - p104 [51-250]
May, Larry - *Hannah Arendt: Twenty Years Later*
  Choice - v34 - Ja '97 - p808 [51-250]
  R&R Bk N - v11 - N '96 - p47 [51-250]
  Mind and Morals
  Ethics - v107 - Ja '97 - p349+ [501+]
  Sharing Responsibility
  Hast Cen R - v27 - Ja '97 - p38+ [501+]
May, Peter, 1951, Feb., 2- - *The Last Banner*
  BL - v93 - D 1 '96 - p639 [51-250]
  LJ - v121 - D '96 - p101 [51-250]
  PW - v243 - N 11 '96 - p66 [51-250]
May, Peter Herman - *Pricing the Planet*
  Choice - v34 - F '97 - p1013 [51-250]
  R&R Bk N - v11 - D '96 - p24 [51-250]
May, Rachel - *The Translator in the Text*
  Slav R - v55 - Sum '96 - p518 [501+]
May, Robert E - *The Union, the Confederacy, and the Atlantic Rim*
  Historian - v59 - Fall '96 - p149+ [251-500]
May, Steve - *Closer, Closer*
  y Bks Keeps - v100 - S '96 - p13 [51-250]
  Egghead
  c Bks Keeps - N '96 - p10 [51-250]
  c JB - v60 - D '96 - p271+ [51-250]
  y Sch Lib - v44 - N '96 - p171 [51-250]
May, William D - *Edges of Reality*
  Choice - v34 - O '96 - p316 [51-250]
  SB - v33 - My '97 - p100 [51-250]
May, William F - *Testing the Medical Covenant*
  BL - v93 - S 1 '96 - p34 [51-250]
  Choice - v34 - My '97 - p1534 [51-250]
Mayall, Berry - *Children, Health and the Social Order*
  Socio R - v45 - My '97 - p330+ [501+]
Mayall, James - *The New Interventionism 1991-1994*
  Choice - v34 - D '96 - p687 [51-250]
  For Aff - v75 - S '96 - p137 [51-250]
Mayberry, Sara O - *Healthcare Design*
  r SciTech - v21 - Mr '97 - p47 [51-250]
Maychell, Karen - *Providing for Young People*
  LAR - v98 - Ag '96 - p424 [1-50]
Mayer, Ann Elizabeth - *Artists in Dylan Thomas's Prose Works*
  Choice - v34 - S '96 - p128 [51-250]
  Islam and Human Rights. 2nd Ed.
  Rel St Rev - v23 - Ja '97 - p3+ [501+]
Mayer, Bernadette - *Proper Name and Other Stories*
  KR - v64 - My 1 '96 - p639 [51-250]
  RCF - v16 - Fall '96 - p198+ [251-500]
Mayer, Bob - *Z: A Dave Riley Novel*
  KR - v64 - D 15 '96 - p1761 [251-500]
  LJ - v122 - F 1 '97 - p106 [51-250]
  PW - v244 - Ja 13 '97 - p57 [51-250]
Mayer, Colin - *Capital Markets and Financial Intermediation*
  Econ J - v107 - Ja '97 - p274 [51-250]
Mayer, David N - *The Constitutional Thought of Thomas Jefferson*
  IndRev - v1 - Spr '96 - p135+ [501+]
Mayer, Eugen Friedrich - *Armas Y Herramientas De Metal Prehispanicas En Bolivia*
  LA Ant - v7 - S '96 - p285+ [251-500]
Mayer, Frank A - *Adenauer and Kennedy*
  HRNB - v25 - Win '97 - p53 [251-500]
Mayer, Hans - *Erinnerung An Brecht*
  WLT - v71 - Win '97 - p146+ [501+]
Mayer, Holly A - *Belonging to the Army*
  Choice - v34 - Ap '97 - p1406 [51-250]
Mayer, Marianna - *Turandot (Illus. by Winslow Pels)*
  c RT - v50 - Mr '97 - p496+ [51-250]

Mayer, Martin - *The Bankers: The Next Generation*
  BL - v93 - D 1 '96 - p628 [51-250]
  Bus W - Ja 27 '97 - p13 [501+]
  BW - v27 - Ja 5 '97 - p6 [251-500]
  Choice - v34 - My '97 - p1548 [51-250]
  KR - v64 - N 1 '96 - p1587 [251-500]
  LATBR - Ja 19 '97 - p5 [501+]
  LJ - v121 - D '96 - p110+ [51-250]
  NYTBR - v102 - Ja 12 '97 - p10+ [501+]
  WSJ-MW - v78 - D 30 '96 - pA10 [501+]
Mayer, Mercer - *Bun Bun's Birthday (Illus. by Mercer Mayer)*
  c HB Guide - v7 - Fall '96 - p267 [51-250]
  Just Me and My Dad. Electronic Media Version
  c SLJ - v43 - Ja '97 - p50+ [51-250]
  Just Me and My Little Brother
  c Par - v71 - N '96 - p114 [1-50]
  Just Me and My Mom. Electronic Media Version
  c Par - v72 - F '97 - p155 [51-250]
  Little Sister's Bracelet (Illus. by Mercer Mayer)
  c HB Guide - v7 - Fall '96 - p267 [51-250]
  Old Howl Hall (Illus. by Mercer Mayer)
  c LATBR - O 20 '96 - p8 [1-50]
Mayer, Thomas F - *The Rhetorics of Life-Writing in Early Modern Europe*
  Six Ct J - v27 - Fall '96 - p943+ [501+]
Mayer, William G - *The Divided Democrats*
  Choice - v34 - F '97 - p1037 [51-250]
  In Pursuit of the White House
  APSR - v90 - S '96 - p655+ [501+]
Mayers, David - *The Ambassadors and America's Soviet Policy*
  AAPSS-A - v547 - S '96 - p174+ [501+]
  AHR - v102 - F '97 - p222+ [251-500]
  Historian - v58 - Sum '96 - p928 [501+]
  HRNB - v25 - Fall '96 - p13 [251-500]
Mayers, Eileen - *Foster Parent Retention and Recruitment*
  Soc Ser R - v70 - D '96 - p670 [501+]
Mayers, Florence Cassen - *Basketball ABC*
  c HB Guide - v8 - Spr '97 - p145 [51-250]
  c KR - v64 - O 15 '96 - p1535 [51-250]
Mayers, Gregory - *Listen to the Desert*
  BL - v93 - O 1 '96 - p305 [51-250]
Mayerson, Charlotte - *The Death Cycle Machine*
  Bloom Rev - v16 - N '96 - p20 [251-500]
Mayes, David G - *Sources of Productivity Growth*
  JEL - v35 - Mr '97 - p283 [51-250]
Mayes, Frances - *Under the Tuscan Sun*
  BL - v93 - S 15 '96 - p217 [51-250]
  NYTBR - v101 - N 17 '96 - p10 [501+]
  NYTBR - v101 - D 8 '96 - p93 [1-50]
Mayes, Susan - *Smart Art*
  c PW - v243 - D 30 '96 - p68 [51-250]
  Starting Painting (Illus. by T Burton)
  c JB - v60 - D '96 - p256 [1-50]
Mayeski, Marie Anne - *Dhuoda, Ninth Century Mother and Theologian*
  Theol St - v58 - Mr '97 - p188+ [251-500]
Mayeur, Jean Marie - *Histoire Du Christianisme, Des Origines A Nos Jours. Vol. 4*
  CH - v66 - Mr '97 - p92+ [501+]
Mayeux, Peter E - *Broadcast News. 2nd Ed.*
  R&R Bk N - v11 - N '96 - p66 [51-250]
Mayfield, Katherine - *Smart Actors, Foolish Choices*
  Am Theat - v13 - D '96 - p21 [1-50]
The Mayflower Descendant. Vols. 17-18
  r EGH - v50 - N '96 - p196 [51-250]
Mayflower Families though Five Generations. Vol. 9
  Am Geneal - v71 - Ap '96 - p125+ [501+]
Mayhew, James - *Miranda the Castaway (Illus. by James Mayhew)*
  c JB - v60 - O '96 - p186 [51-250]
  c Magpies - v11 - S '96 - p29 [51-250]
  c Sch Lib - v44 - Ag '96 - p100 [51-250]
Mayle, Peter - *Anything Considered*
  PW - v244 - Mr 17 '97 - p81 [1-50]
  Rapport - v19 - 5 '96 - p31 [251-500]
  Anything Considered (Curry). Audio Version
  LJ - v121 - O 1 '96 - p142 [51-250]
  Chasing Cezanne
  BL - v93 - My 1 '97 - p1462 [51-250]
  KR - v65 - My 1 '97 - p670 [251-500]
  PW - v244 - My 12 '97 - p59 [51-250]
  A Dog's Life
  y Kliatt - v30 - S '96 - p12 [51-250]
  LATBR - Jl 14 '96 - p11 [51-250]
Mayle, Simon - *The Burial Brothers*
  BL - v92 - Ag '96 - p1877 [51-250]
  NYTBR - v101 - D 8 '96 - p29+ [51-250]

Maynard, Caitlin - *Rain Forests and Reefs (Illus. by Stan Rullman)*
  c BL - v93 - F 15 '97 - p1019 [51-250]
  c SLJ - v43 - Mr '97 - p204+ [51-250]
Maynard, Donald E - *A Handbook of SOPs for Good Clinical Practice*
  SciTech - v21 - Mr '97 - p35 [51-250]
Maynard, Isabelle - *China Dreams*
  y Kliatt - v31 - Mr '97 - p26+ [51-250]
  KR - v64 - S 15 '96 - p1378 [251-500]
  LJ - v121 - D '96 - p108 [51-250]
  PW - v243 - S 30 '96 - p77 [51-250]
  SFR - v22 - Ja '97 - p5 [501+]
Maynard, John - *Victorian Literature and Culture*
  RES - v47 - N '96 - p611+ [501+]
Maynard, Mary - *New Frontiers in Women's Studies*
  R&R Bk N - v11 - D '96 - p41 [51-250]
Maynard, Thane - *Komodo Dragons*
  c Ch BWatch - v6 - N '96 - p7 [1-50]
  c HB Guide - v8 - Spr '97 - p123 [51-250]
  c SLJ - v43 - Mr '97 - p178+ [51-250]
  Ostriches
  c Ch BWatch - v6 - N '96 - p7 [1-50]
  c HB Guide - v8 - Spr '97 - p125 [51-250]
Maynard-Moody, Steven - *The Dilemma of the Fetus*
  APSR - v90 - D '96 - p917+ [501+]
Maynard-Reid, Pedrito Uriah - *Complete Evangelism*
  BL - v93 - Ja '97 - p785 [51-250]
Mayne, Andrew - *The Language Book*
  y Sch Lib - v45 - F '97 - p51 [51-250]
Mayne, Judith - *Cinema and Spectatorship*
  Signs - v22 - Aut '96 - p248+ [51-250]
  Directed by Dorothy Arzner
  FQ - v49 - Sum '96 - p44+ [501+]
Mayne, Seymour - *Jerusalem: An Anthology of Jewish Canadian Poetry*
  Queens Q - v103 - Win '96 - p785+ [501+]
Mayne, William - *The Fairy Tales of London Town. Vol. 2*
  c Sch Lib - v45 - F '97 - p33 [51-250]
  c TES - F 28 '97 - p8* [501+]
  The Fairy Tales of London Town. Vols. 1-2
  c JB - v60 - D '96 - p272 [51-250]
  The Fox Gate and Other Stories (Illus. by William Geldart)
  c JB - v60 - D '96 - p256+ [51-250]
  c Spec - v277 - D 14 '96 - p77 [51-250]
  Lady Muck (Illus. by Jonathan Heale)
  c BL - v93 - Mr 1 '97 - p1167 [51-250]
  c Books - v11 - Ap '97 - p24 [51-250]
  c CBRS - v25 - Mr '97 - p88 [51-250]
  c CCB-B - v50 - Ap '97 - p290 [251-500]
  c KR - v65 - Mr 1 '97 - p386 [51-250]
  c PW - v244 - Ja 27 '97 - p106 [51-250]
  Pandora (Illus. by Dietland Blech)
  c BL - v93 - S 15 '96 - p248 [51-250]
  c HB - v72 - S '96 - p583+ [51-250]
  c HB Guide - v7 - Fall '96 - p267+ [51-250]
  c Par Ch - v20 - O '96 - p3 [51-250]
  A Parcel of Trees (Illus. by Margery Gill)
  y JB - v60 - O '96 - p176+ [501+]
Maynes, Charles William - *U.S. Foreign Policy and the United Nations System*
  Pres SQ - v27 - Win '97 - p160+ [501+]
Maynes, Mary Jo - *Taking the Hard Road*
  AHR - v101 - D '96 - p1560 [501+]
  JIH - v27 - Spr '97 - p690+ [501+]
Maynes, William - *Supernatural Stories (Illus. by Martin Salisbury)*
  c CLW - v67 - D '96 - p56 [51-250]
The Maynooth University Record
  p ILS - v16 - Spr '97 - p34 [51-250]
Mayo, C M - *Sky over El Nido*
  Comw - v123 - O 11 '96 - p25+ [501+]
  VQR - v72 - Aut '96 - p129* [51-250]
Mayo, Deborah G - *Error and the Growth of Experimental Knowledge*
  Nature - v383 - O 24 '96 - p682 [501+]
  SciTech - v20 - N '96 - p13 [51-250]
Mayo, J K - *The Masterless Men*
  Econ - v341 - D 7 '96 - p3*+ [501+]
Mayo, Margaret - *How to Count Crocodiles (Illus. by Emily Bolam)*
  c Bks Keeps - v100 - S '96 - p8 [51-250]
  c Magpies - v11 - Jl '96 - p45 [51-250]
  Mythical Birds and Beasts from Many Lands (Illus. by Jane Ray)
  c BL - v93 - My 1 '97 - p1496 [51-250]
  c KR - v65 - My 1 '97 - p725 [51-250]
  c PW - v244 - Ap 14 '97 - p73 [51-250]

  Orchard Book of Mythical Birds and Beasts (Illus. by Jane Ray)
  c Bks Keeps - Ja '97 - p8+ [501+]
  The Orchard Book of Mythical Birds and Beasts (Illus. by Jane Ray)
  c Bks Keeps - Ja '97 - p8+ [501+]
  Orchard Book of Mythical Birds and Beasts (Illus. by Jane Ray)
  c Sch Lib - v45 - F '97 - p33 [51-250]
  c TES - D 6 '96 - p16 [501+]
  When the World Was Young (Illus. by Louise Brierley)
  c BL - v93 - S 1 '96 - p122+ [51-250]
  c CCB-B - v50 - F '97 - p214 [51-250]
  c HB Guide - v8 - Spr '97 - p103 [51-250]
  c KR - v64 - O 1 '96 - p1471 [51-250]
  c PW - v243 - O 21 '96 - p85 [51-250]
  c SLJ - v42 - O '96 - p116 [51-250]
Mayo, Terry - *The Illustrated Rules of Inline Hockey (Illus. by Ned Butterfield)*
  c SLJ - v42 - Ag '96 - p158 [51-250]
Mayo, Virginia - *Remembering*
  c Sch Lib - v45 - F '97 - p20 [51-250]
Mayo, Wendell - *Centaur of the North*
  BL - v93 - S 15 '96 - p221 [51-250]
  Choice - v34 - F '97 - p967+ [51-250]
  KR - v64 - S 1 '96 - p1266 [51-250]
  NYTBR - v101 - D 15 '96 - p25 [51-250]
Mayo Clinic Complete Book of Pregnancy and Baby's First Year
  r BL - v93 - F 1 '97 - p960 [1-50]
The Mayo Clinic Family Health Book. 1996 Ed. Book and Electronic Media Version
  r BL - v93 - F 1 '97 - p957 [1-50]
Mayo Clinic Family Health Book. 1996 Ed. Electronic Media Version
  yr Emerg Lib - v23 - My '96 - p60 [51-250]
Mayo Clinic Women's Healthsource
  p LJ - v122 - Mr 15 '97 - p95 [51-250]
Mayor, Anne - *Strong Hearts, Inspired Minds*
  LATBR - D 8 '96 - p11 [51-250]
Mayor, Archer - *The Ragman's Memory*
  BL - v93 - N 15 '96 - p574 [51-250]
  BW - v27 - Ja 19 '97 - p11 [251-500]
  KR - v64 - O 1 '96 - p1429 [251-500]
  LATBR - F 16 '97 - p10 [51-250]
  NYTBR - v101 - D 22 '96 - p21 [51-250]
  PW - v243 - O 14 '96 - p66+ [51-250]
Mayou, Richard - *Treatment of Functional Somatic Symptoms*
  AJPsych - v154 - F '97 - p277+ [501+]
Mayr, Ernst - *This Is Biology*
  KR - v65 - Ja 15 '97 - p124 [251-500]
  PW - v244 - F 17 '97 - p205 [51-250]
Mayr, Helmut - *A Guide to Fossils*
  yr Kliatt - v31 - Mr '97 - p33 [51-250]
Mays, James Luther - *Old Testament Interpretation*
  Rel St Rev - v23 - Ja '97 - p56 [51-250]
Mays, June - *Women's Guide to Financial Self-Defense*
  BL - v93 - Mr 1 '97 - p1098 [51-250]
  PW - v244 - Mr 3 '97 - p58 [51-250]
Mays, Larry W - *Water Resources Handbook*
  r SB - v33 - Ja '97 - p7 [51-250]
  r SciTech - v20 - N '96 - p67 [51-250]
Mays, Terry M - *Historical Dictionary of Multinational Peacekeeping*
  r ARBA - v28 - '97 - p277+ [251-500]
  r Choice - v34 - Ap '97 - p1312 [51-250]
Mazda, Fraidoon - *Analytical Techniques in Telecommunications*
  r SciTech - v20 - N '96 - p72 [51-250]
  Mobile Communications
  r SciTech - v20 - N '96 - p72 [51-250]
  Packet Based Communications
  r SciTech - v20 - N '96 - p72 [51-250]
  Principles of Radio Communication
  r SciTech - v20 - N '96 - p72 [51-250]
  Switching Systems and Applications
  r SciTech - v20 - N '96 - p72 [51-250]
  Telecommunication Networks
  r SciTech - v20 - N '96 - p72 [51-250]
  Telecommunication Systems and Applications
  r SciTech - v20 - N '96 - p72 [51-250]
  Telecommunication Transmission Principles
  r SciTech - v20 - N '96 - p72 [51-250]
Maze, Stephanie - *I Want to Be...a Veterinarian*
  c CCB-B - v50 - My '97 - p321 [51-250]
  c HB - v73 - My '97 - p342+ [251-500]
  c PW - v244 - Ap 7 '97 - p94 [51-250]
  c Trib Bks - My 4 '97 - p6 [51-250]

I Want to Be...an Astronaut
  c CCB-B - v50 - My '97 - p321 [51-250]
  c HB - v73 - My '97 - p342+ [251-500]
  c PW - v244 - Ap 7 '97 - p94 [51-250]
Mazel, Michelle - *Retsah Be-Layl Ha-Skadim*
     BL - v93 - Mr 1 '97 - p1115 [1-50]
Mazel-Tov Cocktail
  p Utne R - Jl '96 - p112 [251-500]
Mazer, Anne - *Disney's 101 Dalmations*
  c Ch BWatch - v7 - Ja '97 - p3 [1-50]
     Going Where I'm Coming From
  y Kliatt - v30 - S '96 - p4 [1-50]
     A Sliver of Glass and Other Uncommon Tales
  c BL - v93 - S 15 '96 - p242 [51-250]
  y CCB-B - v50 - N '96 - p107 [51-250]
  c HB Guide - v8 - Spr '97 - p71 [51-250]
  c KR - v64 - S 15 '96 - p1404 [51-250]
  c SLJ - v43 - F '97 - p104 [51-250]
Mazer, Harry - *The Dog in the Freezer*
  y BL - v93 - Mr 15 '97 - p1236 [51-250]
  c KR - v65 - Mr 15 '97 - p466 [51-250]
  c PW - v244 - F 10 '97 - p84 [51-250]
Mazer, Norma Fox - *Missing Pieces*
  y Kliatt - v30 - N '96 - p9 [51-250]
  y PW - v243 - S 16 '96 - p85 [51-250]
Mazlish, Bruce - *The Fourth Discontinuity*
     Reason - v28 - D '96 - p37 [51-250]
Mazo, Judith F - *Providing Health Care Benefits in Retirement*
     ILRR - v50 - Ja '97 - p351+ [501+]
Mazor, Emanuel - *Chemical and Isotopic Groundwater Hydrology. 2nd Ed.*
     SciTech - v21 - Mr '97 - p81 [51-250]
Mazor, Yair - *Missadot Sheba'emek Ad Rekhov Hamasger*
     WLT - v71 - Win '97 - p217+ [501+]
     The Triple Cord
     Rel St Rev - v22 - O '96 - p355 [51-250]
Mazuka, Reiko - *Japanese Sentence Processing*
     A J Psy - v109 - Fall '96 - p475+ [501+]
     MLJ - v80 - Fall '96 - p424 [501+]
Mazumder, Pinaki - *Testing and Testable Design of High-Density Random-Access Memories*
     SciTech - v21 - Mr '97 - p93 [51-250]
Mazur, Grace Dane - *Silk: Stories*
     BL - v93 - S 15 '96 - p221 [51-250]
     BW - v26 - N 3 '96 - p12 [51-250]
     KR - v64 - S 1 '96 - p1266 [51-250]
     LJ - v121 - O 1 '96 - p130 [51-250]
     NYTBR - v101 - N 17 '96 - p27 [501+]
     PW - v243 - Jl 22 '96 - p233 [51-250]
Mazza, Cris - *Dog People*
     KR - v65 - Mr 1 '97 - p328 [51-250]
     LJ - v122 - Ap 1 '97 - p128 [51-250]
     PW - v244 - Ap 7 '97 - p72 [51-250]
Mazza, Enrico - *The Origins of the Eucharistic Prayer*
     Theol St - v57 - S '96 - p526+ [501+]
Mazza, Samuele - *Spectacles*
     Ent W - N 15 '96 - p66 [51-250]
Mazzarella, Merete - *Tanten Och Krokodilen*
     WLT - v70 - Aut '96 - p980 [501+]
Mazzeno, Laurence W - *Victorian Poetry*
  r ARBA - v28 - '97 - p457 [51-250]
  r Nine-C Lit - v50 - Mr '96 - p555 [51-250]
Mazzeo, Cristina Ana - *El Comercio Libre En El Peru*
     HAHR - v77 - My '97 - p319+ [251-500]
Mazzola, Anthony T - *The Best Families*
     PW - v243 - S 23 '96 - p70 [51-250]
     High Society
     BW - v26 - D 8 '96 - p12+ [51-250]
     Pet PM - v25 - Ap '97 - p96 [51-250]
     PW - v243 - S 23 '96 - p70 [51-250]
     WSJ-MW - v78 - D 5 '96 - pA18 [51-250]
Mazzola, Frank - *Counting Is for the Birds (Illus. by Frank Mazzola)*
  c CBRS - v25 - Ap '97 - p100 [51-250]
  c KR - v65 - F 1 '97 - p225 [51-250]
  c PW - v244 - F 3 '97 - p105+ [51-250]
Mazzoni, Cristina - *Saint Hysteria*
     Choice - v34 - Ap '97 - p1420 [51-250]
McAdams, Dona Ann - *Caught in the Act*
     Afterimage - v24 - Ja '97 - p22 [1-50]
     BL - v93 - D 15 '96 - p703 [51-250]
     VV - v41 - D 24 '96 - p59 [251-500]
McAdams, Jerry L - *The Reward Plan Advantage*
     HR Mag - v41 - S '96 - p138 [51-250]
McAdoo, H R - *The Mystery of the Eucharist in the Anglican Tradition*
     ER - v49 - Ja '97 - p114+ [501+]
McAdoo, Harriette Pipes - *Black Families. 3rd Ed.*
     BWatch - v17 - D '96 - p5 [1-50]
     R&R Bk N - v11 - D '96 - p15 [51-250]

McAleavy, Tony - *Modern World History*
  y TES - S 6 '96 - pR7 [501+]
McAleer, Dave - *The All Music Book of Hit Albums*
  r ARBA - v28 - '97 - p486+ [51-250]
     The All Music Book of Hit Singles
  r ARBA - v28 - '97 - p486+ [51-250]
McAleer, Kevin - *Dueling: The Cult of Honor in Fin-De-Siecle Germany*
     Aethlon - v13 - Fall '95 - p146 [251-500]
     EHR - v112 - Ap '97 - p518+ [501+]
McAllister, Andrew - *The Objectivists*
     TLS - Ja 3 '97 - p27 [501+]
McAllister, James W - *Beauty and Revolution in Science*
     Choice - v34 - F '97 - p983 [51-250]
McAllister, Lisa S - *Collectors Guide to Yellow Ware*
  r Ant & CM - v101 - D '96 - p32 [51-250]
McAllister, P K - *Orion's Dagger*
  y Kliatt - v30 - S '96 - p20 [51-250]
McAllister, Robert - *Cancer: What Cutting-Edge Science Can Tell You and Your Doctor about the Causes and the Impact on Diagnosis and Treatment*
  r BL - v93 - F 1 '97 - p958 [51-250]
McAllister, Ted V - *Revolt against Modernity*
     AAPSS-A - v548 - N '96 - p230+ [251-500]
     RAH - v25 - Mr '97 - p95+ [501+]
McAlpine, Alistair - *Once a Jolly Bagman*
     Econ - v342 - Mr 22 '97 - p106 [501+]
     Lon R Bks - v19 - Ap 3 '97 - p7 [501+]
     Obs - Mr 16 '97 - p16* [501+]
     Spec - Mr 15 '97 - p41 [501+]
McAlpine, Trevor - *The Partition Principle*
     Quill & Q - v63 - Ja '97 - p30 [51-250]
McAndrew, Bill - *Liberation: The Canadians in Europe*
     J Gov Info - v23 - S '96 - p615 [51-250]
McAndrew, John P - *Urban Usurpation*
     Pac A - v69 - Sum '96 - p289+ [501+]
McArdle, William D - *Exercise Physiology. 4th Ed.*
     SciTech - v20 - D '96 - p34 [51-250]
McArthur, Glenn - *William Thomas, Architect 1799-1860*
     Choice - v34 - My '97 - p1487 [51-250]
McArthur, Stuart - *Veterinary Management of Tortoises and Turtles*
  r SciTech - v20 - S '96 - p45 [51-250]
McArthur, Tom - *The Oxford Companion to the English Language*
  yr Sch Lib - v44 - N '96 - p176 [51-250]
McArthur, William - *Healthy Incentives*
     Quill & Q - v62 - D '96 - p26+ [501+]
McAteer, Michael R - *The Man in the Scarlet Robe*
     Quill & Q - v62 - D '96 - p18 [51-250]
McAuley, Paul J - *Fairyland*
     BW - v26 - N 24 '96 - p6 [251-500]
     The Invisible Country
     New Sci - v153 - Ja 4 '97 - p40 [51-250]
McAuliffe, Chris - *Art and Surburbia*
     Aust Bk R - F '97 - p30+ [501+]
McAuslan, Ian - *Women in Antiquity*
     Rel St Rev - v23 - Ja '97 - p64 [51-250]
McBain, Ed - *Gladly the Cross-Eyed Bear*
     NYTBR - v101 - S 8 '96 - p26 [51-250]
     Gladly the Cross-Eyed Bear (Heald). Audio Version
     BWatch - v17 - D '96 - p11 [1-50]
     Nocturne
     PW - v244 - Mr 24 '97 - p62 [51-250]
     Romance
     Arm Det - v30 - Win '97 - p18 [51-250]
     Books - v9 - S '95 - p18 [51-250]
McBratney, Sam - *The Caterpillow Fight (Illus. by Jill Barton)*
  c CBRS - v24 - Ag '96 - p161 [51-250]
  c HB Guide - v7 - Fall '96 - p241 [1-50]
  c RT - v50 - Ap '97 - p590 [51-250]
  c Sch Lib - v44 - Ag '96 - p99+ [51-250]
     The Dark at the Top of the Stairs (Illus. by Ivan Bates)
  c BL - v93 - Ja '97 - p768 [1-50]
  c HB Guide - v7 - Fall '96 - p265 [51-250]
  c Sch Lib - v44 - Ag '96 - p100 [51-250]
     Guess How Much I Love You (Illus. by Anita Jeram)
  c Ch BWatch - v6 - O '96 - p6 [1-50]
  c HB Guide - v8 - Spr '97 - p13 [51-250]
     In Crack Willow Wood (Illus. by Ivan Bates)
  c Bks Keeps - Jl '96 - p9 [51-250]
     Little Red Riding Hood (Illus. by Emma Chichester Clark)
  c Sch Lib - v45 - F '97 - p20 [51-250]
     Long, Tall, Short and Hairy Poems (Illus. by Stephen Lewis)
  c Sch Lib - v44 - N '96 - p167 [1-50]
McBrearty, James C - *American Labor History and Comparative Labor Movements*
  r RQ - v36 - Fall '96 - p55+ [51-250]

McBride, Alfred - *A Retreat with Pope John XXIII*
     CLW - v67 - Mr '97 - p40+ [501+]
     The Story of the Church
     CLW - v67 - Mr '97 - p40 [251-500]
McBride, Douglas F - *Learning Veterinary Terminology*
     SciTech - v20 - S '96 - p45 [51-250]
McBride, Francis R - *Iceland. Rev. Ed.*
  r ARBA - v28 - '97 - p62 [51-250]
  r R&R Bk N - v12 - F '97 - p17 [51-250]
McBride, James - *The Color of Water*
     BL - v93 - Ap 1 '97 - p1285 [1-50]
     Bl S - v26 - Sum '96 - p66 [1-50]
     Ch Today - v41 - F 3 '97 - p61+ [51-250]
  y Kliatt - v31 - Mr '97 - p27 [51-250]
     NYTBR - v102 - Mr 2 '97 - p28 [51-250]
     Trib Bks - F 16 '97 - p8 [1-50]
     The Color of Water (Braugher). Audio Version
     LJ - v122 - F 15 '97 - p115 [1-50]
McBride, Joseph - *Frank Capra: The Catastrophe of Success*
     TES - N 22 '96 - p8* [51-250]
     Steven Spielberg
     Obs - Ap 13 '97 - p18* [501+]
     Steven Spielberg: A Biography
     KR - v65 - F 15 '97 - p278+ [251-500]
     LJ - v122 - Ap 15 '97 - p83+ [51-250]
     PW - v244 - Ap 28 '97 - p65 [251-500]
McBride, Peter - *Internet Clear and Simple*
     CBR - v14 - Jl '96 - p21 [1-50]
     The Internet for Windows 95 Made Simple
     New Sci - v151 - S 28 '96 - p57 [51-250]
     Windows 95 Clear and Simple
     CBR - v14 - Jl '96 - p24 [1-50]
McBrien, Philip J - *The Word of the Lord. Vol. 2*
     CLW - v67 - D '96 - p42 [51-250]
McBrien, Richard P - *Responses to 101 Questions on the Church*
     CLW - v67 - D '96 - p38 [251-500]
McBurney, Melissa - *Key Guide to Electronic Resources: Engineering*
  r Choice - v34 - S '96 - p100 [51-250]
McCabe, Gerard B - *Academic Libraries*
     LQ - v66 - O '96 - p473+ [501+]
McCabe, Patrick - *Carn*
     BL - v93 - F 1 '97 - p926 [51-250]
     BW - v27 - Ja 26 '97 - p4 [501+]
     KR - v64 - D 1 '96 - p1694+ [251-500]
     LJ - v122 - F 1 '97 - p106 [51-250]
     NYTBR - v102 - F 9 '97 - p20 [51-250]
     PW - v243 - D 9 '96 - p60+ [51-250]
     Trib Bks - Mr 9 '97 - p8 [1-50]
McCabe, Richard A - *Incest, Drama and Nature's Law 1550-1700*
     MLR - v92 - Ja '97 - p176+ [501+]
     MP - v94 - Ag '96 - p92+ [501+]
McCaffery, Edward J - *Taxing Women*
     BL - v93 - My 1 '97 - p1465+ [51-250]
     KR - v65 - F 15 '97 - p279 [251-500]
     LJ - v122 - F 15 '97 - p148 [51-250]
     PW - v244 - Mr 10 '97 - p57 [51-250]
McCaffery, Larry - *Some Other Frequency*
     PW - v243 - S 16 '96 - p77 [51-250]
     R&R Bk N - v12 - F '97 - p88 [51-250]
McCaffery, Steve - *The Cheat of Words*
     BIC - v26 - Mr '97 - p18 [501+]
     Quill & Q - v62 - Jl '96 - p47 [251-500]
     Sulfur - Fall '96 - p139+ [501+]
McCaffray, Susan P - *The Politics of Industrialization in Tsarist Russia*
     Choice - v34 - O '96 - p340 [51-250]
     JEL - v34 - D '96 - p2099+ [51-250]
McCaffrey, Anne - *Acorna: The Unicorn Girl*
     KR - v65 - My 1 '97 - p684 [51-250]
     Black Horses for the King
  y Emerg Lib - v24 - S '96 - p43 [1-50]
  y Emerg Lib - v24 - S '96 - p53 [51-250]
  y HB Guide - v7 - Fall '96 - p303 [51-250]
  c JB - v60 - Ag '96 - p158 [51-250]
  y Magpies - v11 - S '96 - p38 [51-250]
  y Sch Lib - v44 - Ag '96 - p120 [51-250]
  y TES - Jl 5 '96 - pR8 [501+]
  y VOYA - v19 - D '96 - p272 [251-500]
     Dragonseye
  y BL - v93 - D 15 '96 - p692+ [51-250]
     CSM - v89 - F 20 '97 - p10 [51-250]
     KR - v64 - D 15 '96 - p1773 [51-250]
     LJ - v122 - F 15 '97 - p165 [51-250]
     PW - v244 - Ja 20 '97 - p398 [51-250]
     Freedom's Choice
  y BL - v93 - Ap 1 '97 - p1269 [51-250]
     KR - v65 - Ap 1 '97 - p509 [51-250]

Freedom's Landing
BWatch - v17 - S '96 - p8 [51-250]
No One Noticed the Cat
y PW - v243 - S 30 '96 - p66 [51-250]
Space Opera
LJ - v121 - N 15 '96 - p92 [51-250]
McCaffrey, Robert J - *The Practice of Forensic Neuropsychology*
SciTech - v21 - Mr '97 - p47 [51-250]
McCahill, Bob - *Dialogue of Life*
Rel St Rev - v23 - Ja '97 - p48 [51-250]
McCaig, C D - *Nerve Growth and Guidance*
Sci - v275 - Ja 24 '97 - p497 [251-500]
SciTech - v20 - N '96 - p32 [51-250]
McCain, Charles H - *Plugged In and Turned On*
H Sch M - v4 - D '96 - p54 [51-250]
McCain, Thomas A - *The 1,000 Hour War*
JPC - v30 - Fall '96 - p200+ [501+]
McCall, Bruce - *Thin Ice*
LJ - v122 - My 1 '97 - p114 [51-250]
PW - v244 - Ap 21 '97 - p52 [51-250]
McCall, Christina - *Trudeau and Our Times. Vol. 2*
Can Hist R - v78 - Mr '97 - p122+ [501+]
McCall, Dinah - *Dreamcatcher*
LJ - v122 - Ja '97 - p51 [1-50]
Tallchief
LJ - v122 - F 15 '97 - p125+ [51-250]
PW - v244 - F 24 '97 - p87+ [51-250]
McCall, G J II - *Urban Geoscience*
New Sci - v153 - Mr 1 '97 - p48 [251-500]
McCall, Storrs - *A Model of the Universe*
Dialogue - v36 - Win '97 - p171+ [501+]
McCall, Thomas - *Beyond Ice, Beyond Death*
Arm Det - v29 - Fall '96 - p403+ [51-250]
McCalley, Russell W - *Marketing Channel Management*
R&R Bk N - v11 - D '96 - p34 [51-250]
McCall Smith, Alexander - *The Watermelon Boys*
c TES - Jl 5 '96 - pR6 [1-50]
The Watermelon Boys (Illus. by Lis Toft)
c Sch Lib - v44 - Ag '96 - p104 [51-250]
McCallum, Bennett T - *International Monetary Economics*
JEL - v34 - D '96 - p2050 [51-250]
McCallum, Donald F - *Zenkoji and Its Icon*
HJAS - v56 - 2 '96 - p559+ [501+]
JR - v76 - O '96 - p674+ [251-500]
McCalpin, James P - *Paleoseismology*
SciTech - v20 - N '96 - p24 [51-250]
McCampbell, Debbie Lynn - *Natural Bridges*
KR - v64 - D 1 '96 - p1695 [251-500]
PW - v244 - Ja 13 '97 - p55 [51-250]
McCann, Colum - *Fishing the Sloe-Black River*
BL - v93 - O 1 '96 - p321 [251-500]
BW - v26 - D 15 '96 - p6 [501+]
KR - v64 - S 1 '96 - p1259+ [251-500]
LATBR - Ap 13 '97 - pF [51-250]
NYTBR - v101 - D 1 '96 - p12 [501+]
PW - v243 - S 23 '96 - p55 [51-250]
Songdogs
NYTBR - v101 - D 22 '96 - p20 [1-50]
McCann, Dermot - *Small States, Open Markets and the Organization of Business Interests*
JEL - v34 - S '96 - p1415 [51-250]
McCann, Graham - *Cary Grant: A Class Apart*
BL - v93 - Jl '97 - p804 [51-250]
Ent W - Mr 14 '97 - p74 [51-250]
KR - v64 - D 1 '96 - p1719 [251-500]
LJ - v122 - F 15 '97 - p137 [51-250]
Lon R Bks - v19 - Mr 6 '97 - p27+ [501+]
NYTBR - v102 - Ap 13 '97 - p21 [51-250]
PW - v244 - Ja 6 '97 - p58 [51-250]
Si & So - v6 - N '96 - p36 [51-250]
TLS - N 22 '96 - p10 [501+]
McCann, James C - *People of the Plow*
Historian - v59 - Win '97 - p413+ [501+]
McCann, Joseph T - *Forensic Assessment with the Millon Inventories*
SciTech - v20 - N '96 - p38 [51-250]
McCants, William - *Much Ado about Prom Night*
y Emerg Lib - v24 - S '96 - p25 [1-50]
y Emerg Lib - v24 - S '96 - p27 [1-50]
McCarter, William - *My Life in the Irish Brigade*
ILS - v16 - Spr '97 - p36 [1-50]
McCarthy, Bill - *On the Streets*
J Gov Info - v23 - S '96 - p627 [51-250]
McCarthy, Brendon - *Fertility and Faith*
New Sci - v154 - My 3 '97 - p46 [1-50]
McCarthy, Carmel - *Saint Ephrem's Commentary on Tatian's Diatessaron*
CH - v65 - S '96 - p443+ [501+]

McCarthy, Claire - *Learning How the Heart Beats*
y Kliatt - v31 - My '97 - p22 [51-250]
Trib Bks - F 2 '97 - p8 [1-50]
McCarthy, Cormac - *The Gardener's Son*
BL - v93 - S 15 '96 - p200 [251-500]
McCarthy, E Doyle - *Knowledge as Culture*
R&R Bk N - v12 - F '97 - p4 [51-250]
TLS - Ap 11 '97 - p28 [251-500]
McCarthy, Ed - *Wine for Dummies*
LJ - v122 - Ap 1 '97 - p62 [1-50]
McCarthy, Gary - *Rivers West*
Roundup M - v4 - D '96 - p28 [51-250]
McCarthy, George - *The Wild Mushroom*
Nature - v385 - Ja 2 '97 - p34 [1-50]
New Sci - v152 - D 21 '96 - p74 [1-50]
McCarthy, Helen - *The Anime Movie Guide*
r Si & So - v6 - N '96 - p36 [1-50]
McCarthy, J - *Are Sweet Dreams Made of This?*
WorldV - v13 - Ja '97 - p15 [251-500]
McCarthy, J Thomas - *McCarthy's Desk Encyclopedia of Intellectual Property. 2nd Ed.*
r ARBA - v28 - '97 - p233 [51-250]
McCarthy, John - *Hurricane*
y Kliatt - v31 - Mr '97 - p5 [51-250]
McCarthy, John A - *The Future of Germanistik in the USA*
MLJ - v80 - Win '96 - p548+ [501+]
McCarthy, Justin - *Death and Exile*
Choice - v34 - O '96 - p343 [51-250]
MEJ - v51 - Win '97 - p141+ [501+]
TLS - Mr 21 '97 - p31 [501+]
McCarthy, Margaret William - *Amy Fay: America's Notable Woman of Music*
Notes - v53 - D '96 - p469+ [501+]
McCarthy, Michael - *Language as Discourse*
MLR - v91 - Jl '96 - p677 [251-500]
McCarthy, Patrick - *The Crisis of the Italian State*
APSR - v90 - S '96 - p670+ [501+]
TLS - Jl 19 '96 - p6 [501+]
Disintegration or Transformation
PSQ - v111 - Fall '96 - p552+ [501+]
McCarthy, Tara - *Been There, Haven't Done That*
PW - v244 - My 12 '97 - p68 [51-250]
McCarthy, Thomas - *The Lost Province*
TLS - Mr 7 '97 - p24 [51-250]
McCarthy, Todd - *Howard Hawks: The Grey Fox of Hollywood*
BL - v93 - My 15 '97 - p1554 [51-250]
PW - v244 - My 5 '97 - p187 [51-250]
WSJ-Cent - v99 - Je 4 '97 - pA16 [501+]
McCarthy, Wil - *The Fall of Sirius*
BL - v93 - S 15 '96 - p226 [51-250]
Murder in the Solid State
Analog - v116 - D '96 - p145+ [251-500]
KR - v64 - My 1 '96 - p650 [51-250]
MFSF - v92 - F '97 - p44 [51-250]
McCarthy, William Bernard - *Jack in Two Worlds*
Folkl - v107 - '96 - p117 [501+]
McCartney, Donal - *W.E.H. Lecky: Historian and Politician 1838-1903*
EHR - v111 - N '96 - p1323+ [501+]
McCartney, Linda - *Roadworks*
BL - v92 - Ag '96 - p1872 [51-250]
McCaskie, T C - *State and Society in Pre-Colonial Asante*
JIH - v27 - Aut '96 - p367+ [501+]
McCaskill, Mizzy - *Irish Tin Whistle Book*
CAY - v17 - Win '96 - p6 [51-250]
McCaughrean, Geraldine - *The Canterbury Tales (Illus. by Victor G Ambrus)*
c HB Guide - v7 - Fall '96 - p364 [1-50]
Cowboy Jess (Illus. by Lizzie Sanders)
c Bks Keeps - v100 - S '96 - p32 [51-250]
c JB - v60 - O '96 - p193 [51-250]
c Sch Lib - v44 - Ag '96 - p107 [51-250]
The Golden Hoard (Illus. by Bee Willey)
c Ch BWatch - v6 - My '96 - p4 [51-250]
c HB Guide - v7 - Fall '96 - p322 [51-250]
c SLJ - v42 - D '96 - p31 [51-250]
Moby-Dick (Illus. by Victor G Ambrus)
y Cur R - v36 - F '97 - p13 [51-250]
Moby Dick (Illus. by Victor G Ambrus)
c KR - v65 - Ja 15 '97 - p143 [51-250]
c Spec - v277 - D 14 '96 - p77 [51-250]
Myths and Legends of the World. Vol. 2 (Illus. by Bee Willey)
c TES - D 6 '96 - p16* [501+]
The Orchard Book of Stories from the Ballet
c TES - D 6 '96 - p16* [1-50]

Plundering Paradise
c Bks Keeps - Jl '96 - p12+ [51-250]
y JB - v60 - O '96 - p203+ [51-250]
y Magpies - v11 - S '96 - p36 [51-250]
y Sch Lib - v44 - Ag '96 - p120 [51-250]
c TES - Ag 30 '96 - p28 [51-250]
The Silver Treasure (Illus. by Bee Willey)
c JB - v60 - D '96 - p256 [51-250]
c KR - v65 - Mr 15 '97 - p465 [51-250]
c Sch Lib - v45 - F '97 - p33 [51-250]
McCauley, Deborah Vansau - *Appalachian Mountain Religion*
AHR - v101 - D '96 - p1613+ [251-500]
CH - v65 - D '96 - p773+ [501+]
McCauley, Martin - *The Origins of the Cold War 1941-1949*
NWCR - v50 - Win '97 - p160+ [501+]
Stalin and Stalinism
NWCR - v50 - Win '97 - p160+ [501+]
McCauley, Shane - *Shadow behind the Heart*
Aust Bk R - N '96 - p55 [501+]
McCauley, Stephen - *The Man of the House*
Advocate - Ja 21 '97 - p94 [1-50]
Obs - F 9 '97 - p18* [51-250]
PW - v243 - S 30 '96 - p79 [1-50]
TLS - F 21 '97 - p21 [251-500]
McCawley, Patrick - *Guide to Civil War Records*
r JSH - v62 - N '96 - p859 [51-250]
McCawly, William - *The First Angelinos*
Choice - v34 - O '96 - p323 [51-250]
WHQ - v28 - Spr '97 - p101 [1-50]
McChesney, Robert W - *Telecommunications, Mass Media, and Democracy*
BHR - v70 - Aut '96 - p416+ [501+]
McChristian, Douglas C - *The U.S. Army in the West 1870-1880*
Pub Hist - v18 - Sum '96 - p62+ [501+]
McClain, Ellen Jaffe - *No Big Deal*
y PW - v244 - Ja 13 '97 - p77 [1-50]
McClain, James L - *Edo and Paris*
CS - v25 - N '96 - p773+ [501+]
EHR - v112 - Ap '97 - p466+ [251-500]
JIH - v27 - Aut '96 - p382+ [501+]
McClain, Liz - *Ridgeback Joe and the Boy*
c Bkbird - v34 - Spr '96 - p54 [51-250]
McClanahan, Ed - *A Congress of Wonders*
SFR - v21 - Jl '96 - p7 [501+]
McClaran, Robbie - *Angry White Men*
Afterimage - v24 - Ja '97 - p22 [51-250]
McClary, Andrew - *Toys with Nine Lives*
y BL - v93 - F 15 '97 - p1015 [51-250]
c KR - v64 - N 1 '96 - p1603 [51-250]
McClatchy, J D - *The Vintage Book of Contemporary World Poetry*
y Kliatt - v31 - Ja '97 - p17+ [251-500]
VQR - v73 - Win '97 - p28* [51-250]
McClaurin, Irma - *Women of Belize*
Choice - v34 - Mr '97 - p1201+ [51-250]
McCleary, Dick - *The Logic of Imaginative Education*
CPR - v16 - Ap '96 - p120+ [501+]
McClelland, Marilyn R - *Conservation-Tillage Systems for Cotton*
J Gov Info - v23 - S '96 - p578 [51-250]
McClendon, James William - *Systematic Theology. Vol. 2*
JR - v77 - Ap '97 - p316+ [501+]
McClendon, Sarah - *Mr. President, Mr. President!*
LJ - v121 - D '96 - p108 [51-250]
NYTBR - v102 - Ja 26 '97 - p19 [51-250]
Rapport - v19 - 6 '96 - p33 [251-500]
Mr. President, Mr. President
Rapport - v19 - 6 '96 - p33 [251-500]
McClintock, Anne - *Imperial Leather*
Can Hist R - v78 - Mr '97 - p175+ [501+]
McClintock, Barbara - *The Fantastic Drawings of Danielle (Illus. by Barbara McClintock)*
c CBRS - v25 - Win '97 - p64 [51-250]
c CCB-B - v50 - F '97 - p213 [51-250]
c Ch BWatch - v6 - N '96 - p6 [1-50]
c HB Guide - v8 - Spr '97 - p38 [51-250]
c NYTBR - v101 - O 27 '96 - p44 [1-50]
c SLJ - v42 - S '96 - p184 [51-250]
c Smith - v27 - N '96 - p175 [1-50]
c Time - v148 - D 9 '96 - p79 [51-250]
McCloskey, Donald N - *Knowledge and Persuasion in Economics*
BHR - v70 - Sum '96 - p262+ [501+]
Econ J - v107 - Ja '97 - p241+ [501+]
McCloskey, Robert - *Abran Paso A Los Patitos (Illus. by Robert McCloskey)*
c SLJ - v42 - N '96 - p134 [51-250]

Burt Dow, Deep-Water Man
c HB - v73 - Mr '97 - p188 [1-50]
McCloskey, Walter - *Risking Elizabeth*
y BL - v93 - Ja '97 - p820 [51-250]
Ent W - Mr 28 '97 - p63 [51-250]
KR - v64 - N 15 '96 - p1635+ [51-250]
LJ - v121 - D '96 - p150 [51-250]
PW - v243 - N 25 '96 - p56 [51-250]
McCloud, Aminah Beverly - *African American Islam*
JR - v76 - O '96 - p676+ [501+]
McCloud, Barry - *Definitive Country*
r LJ - v121 - N 1 '96 - p41 [51-250]
McCloud, Kevin - *Kevin McCloud's Complete Book of Paint and Decorative Techniques*
PW - v244 - Ap 7 '97 - p89 [51-250]
McClure, Amy A - *Books That Invite Talk, Wonder, and Play*
r BL - v93 - Mr 1 '97 - p1176+ [51-250]
Cur R - v36 - D '96 - p3* [51-250]
Emerg Lib - v24 - Mr '97 - p39 [51-250]
Inst - v106 - Ja '97 - p36 [1-50]
McClure, J Derrick - *Scots and Its Literature*
WLT - v71 - Win '97 - p199+ [501+]
McClure, Kirstie M - *Judging Rights*
Choice - v34 - Ap '97 - p1417 [51-250]
McClure, Lynne Falkin - *Risky Business*
BL - v92 - Ag '96 - p1865+ [51-250]
JEL - v35 - Mr '97 - p240 [51-250]
Readings - v12 - Mr '97 - p26 [51-250]
R&R Bk N - v12 - F '97 - p46 [51-250]
McColley, Diane Kelsey - *A Gust for Paradise*
MP - v94 - Ag '96 - p85+ [501+]
Ren Q - v49 - Aut '96 - p658+ [501+]
McColley, Kevin - *Switch*
y KR - v65 - Mr 1 '97 - p384+ [51-250]
McCollum, Audrey - *Smart Moves*
LJ - v121 - O 15 '96 - p78 [51-250]
PW - v243 - S 9 '96 - p80 [51-250]
McComas, Alan J - *Skeletal Muscle*
Choice - v34 - O '96 - p304 [51-250]
SciTech - v20 - S '96 - p22 [51-250]
McComb, Gordon - *JavaScript Sourcebook*
CBR - v14 - N '96 - p36 [51-250]
SciTech - v20 - D '96 - p10 [51-250]
McConkey, Kevin M - *Hypnosis, Memory, and Behavior in Criminal Investigation*
Readings - v11 - S '96 - p24 [51-250]
McConnell, Bob - *SABR Presents the Home Run Encyclopedia*
r NYTBR - v101 - Ap 7 '96 - p16 [251-500]
McConnell, Malcolm - *Inside Hanoi's Secret Archives*
S&S - v61 - Sum '97 - p292+ [501+]
McConnell, Robert - *Far Out in the New Age*
JP - v60 - S '96 - p262+ [501+]
McConnell, William F - *Remember Reno*
LJ - v121 - O 1 '96 - p90 [51-250]
PW - v243 - S 16 '96 - p65 [51-250]
McConville, James - *Shipping Business and Maritime Economics*
r R&R Bk N - v11 - D '96 - p32 [51-250]
McCooey, David - *Artful Histories*
Aust Bk R - Jl '96 - p17+ [501+]
Choice - v34 - Ap '97 - p1337 [51-250]
McCook, Kathleen De La Pena - *Developing Readers' Advisory Services*
RQ - v36 - Win '96 - p214 [51-250]
McCool, Daniel C - *Waters of Zion*
PHR - v65 - N '96 - p686+ [501+]
McCool, Gerald A - *The Neo-Thomists*
IPQ - v36 - D '96 - p475+ [501+]
RM - v50 - D '96 - p415+ [501+]
McCoole, Sinead - *Hazel: A Life of Lady Lavery 1880-1935*
KR - v65 - My 1 '97 - p700 [251-500]
Spec - v277 - O 26 '96 - p47+ [501+]
McCord, Gary - *Just a Range Ball in a Box of Titleists*
BL - v93 - F 15 '97 - p970 [51-250]
KR - v65 - Mr 15 '97 - p443 [251-500]
PW - v244 - Mr 10 '97 - p58+ [51-250]
McCord, Louisa S - *Louisa S. McCord: Poems, Drama, Biography, Letters*
Nine-C Lit - v51 - D '96 - p424 [51-250]
McCord, Margaret - *The Calling of Katie Makanya*
BL - v93 - F 15 '97 - p1000 [51-250]
KR - v65 - Ja 15 '97 - p123 [251-500]
LJ - v122 - Mr 15 '97 - p70 [51-250]
NYTBR - v102 - Ap 6 '97 - p20 [51-250]
PW - v244 - Ja 20 '97 - p383 [51-250]
McCord, Nancy - *Please Don't Eat My Garden!*
LJ - v121 - D '96 - p67 [1-50]

McCord, Richard - *The Chain Gang*
AB - v98 - N 4 '96 - p1514+ [501+]
AJR - v18 - S '96 - p53 [501+]
BL - v93 - Ja '97 - p757 [1-50]
NYTBR - v101 - S 22 '96 - p19 [501+]
SFR - v22 - Ja '97 - p6+ [501+]
Utne R - Jl '96 - p109 [501+]
McCord, Robert - *Traveler's and TV Viewer's Golf Tournament Guide*
BL - v93 - S 15 '96 - p210+ [1-50]
McCord, Wilson - *Biology for Beginners*
New Sci - v152 - D 21 '96 - p67 [1-50]
McCordick, David - *Scottish Literature. Vols. 1-2*
Choice - v34 - My '97 - p1500 [51-250]
McCorkle, Constance M - *Ethnoveterinary Research and Development*
Sci - v275 - F 28 '97 - p1276 [1-50]
McCorkle, Jill - *Carolina Moon*
Am - v175 - S 21 '96 - p36 [51-250]
BL - v92 - Ag '96 - p1855 [251-500]
BL - v93 - Ja '97 - p761 [1-50]
Ent W - S 27 '96 - p74+ [51-250]
LJ - v121 - N 1 '96 - p107 [51-250]
NYTBR - v101 - D 15 '96 - p12 [501+]
S Liv - v31 - O '96 - p108 [51-250]
y SLJ - v43 - Ja '97 - p140 [51-250]
McCormack, Bruce L - *Karl Barth's Critically Realistic Dialectical Theology*
Intpr - v51 - Ap '97 - p191+ [501+]
JR - v77 - Ap '97 - p308+ [501+]
Theol St - v57 - D '96 - p755+ [501+]
TT - v53 - Ja '97 - p524+ [501+]
McCormack, Derek - *Dark Rides*
BIC - v25 - O '96 - p41 [51-250]
McCormack, Gavan - *The Emptiness of Japanese Affluence*
For Aff - v75 - N '96 - p148 [51-250]
McCormack, Mark H - *On Managing*
LJ - v121 - N 1 '96 - p102+ [51-250]
PW - v243 - S 9 '96 - p78 [51-250]
McCormack, Thomas W - *The Canadian Demand for Household Furniture and Trends. 5th Ed.*
R&R Bk N - v12 - F '97 - p42 [51-250]
McCormick, Anita Louise - *Native Americans and the Reservation in American History*
y BL - v93 - Ja '97 - p833+ [251-500]
c HB Guide - v8 - Spr '97 - p177 [51-250]
c SLJ - v43 - F '97 - p120 [51-250]
McCormick, Barrett L - *China after Socialism*
Pac A - v69 - Fall '96 - p403 [251-500]
McCormick, Brian - *Japanese Companies--British Factories*
JEL - v35 - Mr '97 - p245 [51-250]
McCormick, Donald - *Spy Fiction*
r RQ - v36 - Win '96 - p225 [51-250]
McCormick, Harold J - *Two Years behind the Mast*
BWatch - v18 - F '97 - p5+ [51-250]
McCormick, Ian - *Secret Sexualities*
Obs - F 16 '97 - p16* [501+]
McCormick, John - *The Global Environmental Movement. 2nd Ed.*
GJ - v163 - Mr '97 - p103 [251-500]
McCormick, Joseph B - *Level 4*
Am Sci - v85 - Ja '97 - p80+ [501+]
y BL - v93 - D 1 '96 - p664 [1-50]
BW - v26 - S 1 '96 - p4 [251-500]
Sci - v273 - Ag 30 '96 - p1180 [51-250]
McCormick, Kathleen - *The Culture of Reading and the Teaching of English*
Col Comp - v47 - O '96 - p424+ [501+]
McCormick, Patty - *Patty McCormick's Pieces of an American Quilt*
BL - v93 - S 15 '96 - p201+ [51-250]
McCormick, Scott, Jr. - *Behold the Man*
Intpr - v51 - Ja '97 - p90+ [251-500]
Rel St Rev - v23 - Ap '97 - p177 [51-250]
McCosker, Karen - *A Poem a Day*
y BL - v93 - N 15 '96 - p567 [51-250]
LJ - v121 - D '96 - p99 [51-250]

McCourt, Frank - *Angela's Ashes*
y BL - v92 - Ag '96 - p1851 [251-500]
BL - v93 - Ap 1 '97 - p1285 [1-50]
Bloom Rev - v16 - N '96 - p17+ [501+]
BW - v26 - S 29 '96 - p1+ [501+]
BW - v26 - D 8 '96 - p6 [51-250]
Comw - v123 - N 8 '96 - p26+ [501+]
CSM - v89 - D 4 '96 - p13 [501+]
CSM - v89 - D 12 '96 - p14 [51-250]
CSM - v89 - Ja 9 '97 - p14 [51-250]
CSM - v89 - F 6 '97 - p14 [51-250]
CSM - v89 - Mr 6 '97 - p14 [51-250]
CSM - v89 - Ap 3 '97 - p14 [51-250]
Ent W - S 20 '96 - p74 [51-250]
Ent W - D 27 '96 - p140 [51-250]
ILS - v15 - Fall '96 - p31 [51-250]
LATBR - v263 - S 29 '96 - p6 [501+]
LJ - v122 - Ja '97 - p50 [1-50]
Mac - v110 - Mr 3 '97 - p69+ [501+]
NS - v125 - N 1 '96 - p45 [501+]
NYTBR - v101 - S 15 '96 - p13 [501+]
NYTBR - v101 - D 8 '96 - p11 [51-250]
NYTLa - v145 - S 17 '96 - pC15 [501+]
PW - v243 - N 4 '96 - p44+ [1-50]
Time - v148 - S 23 '96 - p74 [251-500]
Time - v148 - D 23 '96 - p86 [51-250]
TLS - Ja 3 '97 - p32 [51-250]
Woman's J - N '96 - p12 [1-50]
Angela's Ashes (McCourt). Audio Version
CSM - v89 - F 27 '97 - pB4 [51-250]
CSM - v89 - Mr 27 '97 - pB1 [1-50]
LJ - v122 - F 1 '97 - p125 [51-250]
LJ - v122 - F 15 '97 - p115 [1-50]
PW - v244 - F 3 '97 - p43 [51-250]
McCoy, Clyde B - *Intervening with Drug-Involved Youth*
R&R Bk N - v11 - D '96 - p44 [51-250]
McCoy, Horace - *Kiss Tomorrow Goodbye*
KR - v65 - Mr 1 '97 - p333+ [51-250]
LJ - v122 - Mr 15 '97 - p94 [1-50]
McCoy, J J - *The Hunt for the Whooping Cranes*
BWatch - v17 - D '96 - p4 [51-250]
PW - v243 - O 7 '96 - p69 [1-50]
McCoy, Jennifer - *Venezuelan Democracy under Stress*
HAHR - v76 - Ag '96 - p586+ [251-500]
JTWS - v13 - Fall '96 - p311+ [501+]
McCoy, Kathy - *Life Happens*
y Kliatt - v30 - S '96 - p29 [51-250]
McCoy, Michael - *The Wild West*
r CAY - v17 - Fall '96 - p6 [51-250]
McCoy, Thomas J - *Creating an Open Book Organization*
Bus Bk R - v13 - 4 '96 - p72+ [501+]
McCracken, David - *The Scandal of the Gospels*
Theol St - v57 - Je '96 - p378 [251-500]
McCracken, Elizabeth - *The Giant's House*
BW - v26 - N 10 '96 - p6 [501+]
Ent W - D 27 '96 - p142 [51-250]
KR - v64 - My 1 '96 - p627 [251-500]
LATBR - S 15 '96 - p6 [501+]
LATBR - D 29 '96 - p6 [51-250]
LJ - v121 - O 1 '96 - p47 [51-250]
NYTBR - v101 - D 8 '96 - p80 [1-50]
Obs - D 8 '96 - p17* [51-250]
PW - v243 - N 4 '96 - p37+ [1-50]
Rapport - v19 - 5 '96 - p31 [251-500]
y SLJ - v42 - N '96 - p140 [51-250]
TLS - N 29 '96 - p22 [501+]
McCracken, J L - *New Light at the Cape of Good Hope*
EHR - v111 - N '96 - p1319+ [51-250]
McCracken, Robert D - *Las Vegas: The Great American Playground*
WHQ - v27 - Win '96 - p550 [1-50]
McCreadie, Mary - *Canoeing Canada's Northwest Territories*
r BIC - v25 - S '96 - p10+ [501+]
McCredden, Lyn - *The Space of Poetry. Vol. 3*
Aust Bk R - S '96 - p47+ [501+]
McCreery, David - *Rural Guatemala 1760-1940*
Historian - v58 - Sum '96 - p869+ [501+]
McCreery, Elaine - *Christianity*
c TES - O 4 '96 - p16* [251-500]
McCrum, Robert - *Suspicion*
Books - v10 - Je '96 - p10 [51-250]
KR - v65 - Ja 1 '97 - p14 [51-250]
LATBR - Ap 13 '97 - pH [501+]
LJ - v122 - F 15 '97 - p163 [51-250]
NYTBR - v102 - Ap 6 '97 - p21 [51-250]
PW - v244 - Ja 13 '97 - p52 [51-250]
Woman's J - S '96 - p10 [51-250]
McCrumb, Sharyn - *The Rosewood Casket (Darling). Audio Version*
y Kliatt - v31 - My '97 - p44 [51-250]

The Rosewood Casket (Herbert). Audio Version
y Kliatt - v31 - My '97 - p43+ [51-250]
McCue, Margi Laird - *Domestic Violence*
r ARBA - v28 - '97 - p307 [51-250]
McCuen, Gary - *The Conservative Agenda*
y Ch BWatch - v6 - S '96 - p6 [51-250]
The Militia Movement and Hate Groups in America
y Ch BWatch - v6 - S '96 - p6 [51-250]
Welfare Reform
y Ch BWatch - v6 - S '96 - p6 [51-250]
McCuen, Gary E - *Homosexuality and Gay Rights*
y Ch BWatch - v6 - Jl '96 - p8 [51-250]
McCuen, Richard H - *The Elements of Academic Research*
SciTech - v20 - D '96 - p59 [51-250]
McCulla, L Cleaves, II - *How to Buy Stocks Factory Direct and Save*
r BWatch - v17 - N '96 - p12 [51-250]
McCuller, Carson - *Reflections in a Golden Eye*
LATBR - D 29 '96 - p5 [51-250]
McCulloch, Jock - *Colonial Psychiatry and the African Mind*
AJPsych - v154 - Mr '97 - p430+ [501+]
JIH - v27 - Win '97 - p560+ [501+]
McCulloch, John A - *Macnab's Backache. 3rd Ed.*
SciTech - v20 - N '96 - p50 [51-250]
McCullough, Bill - *Listen to the Howl of the Wolf*
c SLJ - v43 - F '97 - p103+ [51-250]
McCullough, Colleen - *Caesar's Women*
PW - v244 - Ja 27 '97 - p103 [1-50]
McCullough, David - *The Great Bridge*
Reason - v28 - D '96 - p42 [51-250]
Truman (McCullough). Audio Version
CSM - v89 - Mr 27 '97 - pB1 [1-50]
McCullough, Donald W - *The Trivialization of God*
TT - v53 - Ja '97 - p566 [51-250]
McCullough, Frances - *Classic American Food without Fuss*
BL - v93 - Ja '97 - p800+ [51-250]
LJ - v122 - F 15 '97 - p158 [51-250]
PW - v243 - D 2 '96 - p56 [51-250]
McCullough, L E - *Plays of America from American Folklore for Children Grades K-6*
c SLJ - v42 - Ag '96 - p158 [51-250]
Plays of America from American Folklore for Young Actors
y BL - v92 - Ag '96 - p1893 [51-250]
y SLJ - v42 - Ag '96 - p172+ [51-250]
The Plays of the Songs of Christmas
c PW - v243 - S 30 '96 - p92 [1-50]
c SLJ - v42 - O '96 - p38 [51-250]
McCullough, Laurence B - *Ethics in Obstetrics and Gynecology*
Hast Cen R - v26 - Mr '96 - p45+ [501+]
McCullough, Malcolm - *Abstracting Craft*
Wil Q - v21 - Win '97 - p104 [251-500]
McCully, Emily Arnold - *The Ballot Box Battle (Illus. by Emily Arnold McCully)*
c BL - v93 - S 1 '96 - p140 [51-250]
c CCB-B - v50 - S '96 - p22 [51-250]
c HB Guide - v8 - Spr '97 - p159 [51-250]
c HMR - Fall '96 - p40 [501+]
c Inst - v106 - S '96 - p53+ [1-50]
c SLJ - v42 - S '96 - p198 [51-250]
c Smith - v27 - N '96 - p168 [1-50]
The Bobbin Girl (Illus. by Emily Arnold McCully)
c HB - v72 - S '96 - p581+ [51-250]
c HB Guide - v7 - Fall '96 - p266 [51-250]
c LATBR - Ag 4 '96 - p11 [251-500]
c Par Ch - v20 - O '96 - p28 [51-250]
c RT - v50 - My '97 - p682 [51-250]
Mirette on the High Wire
c CLW - v67 - Mr '97 - p14 [1-50]
c New Ad - v9 - Fall '96 - p267+ [501+]
The Pirate Queen (Illus. by Emily Arnold McCully)
c RT - v50 - S '96 - p57+ [51-250]
c SLJ - v42 - D '96 - p45 [51-250]
Starring Mirette and Bellini (Illus. by Emily Arnold McCully)
c KR - v65 - Ap 1 '97 - p559 [51-250]
c Par Ch - v21 - Mr '97 - p4 [51-250]
c PW - v244 - F 17 '97 - p219 [51-250]
McCumber, David - *Playing Off the Rail*
BL - v93 - Ja '97 - p759 [1-50]
PW - v244 - Mr 3 '97 - p72 [1-50]
McCune, Don - *Trail to the Klondike*
PW - v244 - Mr 31 '97 - p58 [51-250]
McCunn, Ruthanne Lum - *Wooden Fish Songs*
y Kliatt - v30 - S '96 - p12 [51-250]

McCurry, Stephanie - *Masters of Small Worlds*
AHR - v101 - D '96 - p1624 [251-500]
Historian - v59 - Win '97 - p435+ [251-500]
J Am St - v30 - Ag '96 - p313 [251-500]
JSH - v63 - F '97 - p164+ [501+]
McCusker, Paul - *Catacombs*
LJ - v122 - Ap 1 '97 - p78 [51-250]
McCutcheon, John - *Happy Adoption Day! (Illus. by Julie Paschkis)*
c BL - v93 - D 1 '96 - p667 [51-250]
c CBRS - v25 - S '96 - p5 [51-250]
c HB Guide - v8 - Spr '97 - p140 [51-250]
c SLJ - v42 - N '96 - p88 [51-250]
McCutcheon, Sandy - *In Wolf's Clothing*
Aust Bk R - F '97 - p55+ [501+]
McDade, Lucinda A - *La Selva: Ecology and Natural History of a Neotropical Rain Forest*
GJ - v163 - Mr '97 - p108 [51-250]
McDaniel, Antonio - *Swing Low, Sweet Chariot*
AHR - v101 - D '96 - p1593+ [501+]
JIH - v27 - Win '97 - p558+ [501+]
McDaniel, Jay B - *With Roots and Wings*
Am - v175 - N 23 '96 - p26+ [501+]
McDaniel, Lurlene - *Angels Watching over Me*
y Ch BWatch - v7 - F '97 - p6 [1-50]
y Kliatt - v31 - Mr '97 - p12 [51-250]
y SLJ - v43 - Mr '97 - p188 [51-250]
I Want to Live
c Ch BWatch - v6 - N '96 - p7 [1-50]
I'll Be Seeing You
y Ch BWatch - v6 - S '96 - p2 [1-50]
y Kliatt - v30 - S '96 - p12 [51-250]
y SLJ - v42 - D '96 - p139 [51-250]
No Time to Cry
c Ch BWatch - v6 - My '96 - p7 [1-50]
Saving Jessica
y Ch BWatch - v6 - S '96 - p2 [1-50]
y Kliatt - v30 - S '96 - p12 [51-250]
A Season for Goodbye
y Emerg Lib - v24 - S '96 - p27 [1-50]
Six Months to Live
c Ch BWatch - v6 - My '96 - p7 [1-50]
y Ch BWatch - v7 - F '97 - p6 [1-50]
So Much to Live For
y Ch BWatch - v7 - F '97 - p6 [1-50]
McDaniel, Melissa - *Ernest Hemingway*
c Ch BWatch - v7 - F '97 - p7 [1-50]
y SLJ - v43 - Mr '97 - p204 [51-250]
McDaniel, Tim - *The Agony of the Russian Idea*
Choice - v34 - F '97 - p1031 [51-250]
For Aff - v76 - Mr '97 - p191+ [51-250]
HRNB - v25 - Win '97 - p82 [251-500]
Spec - v277 - O 26 '96 - p53 [501+]
McDaniel, Wilma Elizabeth - *The Last Dust Storm*
WAL - v31 - Fall '96 - p282+ [251-500]
McDannell, Colleen - *Material Christianity*
AJS - v102 - S '96 - p644+ [501+]
CH - v65 - D '96 - p793+ [501+]
CS - v26 - Mr '97 - p235+ [501+]
Rel St Rev - v23 - Ja '97 - p92+ [51-250]
TLS - Ja 17 '97 - p32 [501+]
McDargh, Eileen - *Work for a Living and Still Be Free to Live*
J Car P&E - v57 - Win '97 - p22 [51-250]
McDarrah, Fred W - *Beat Generation*
Choice - v34 - My '97 - p1484 [51-250]
LATBR - D 8 '96 - p26 [51-250]
McDermid, Richard T - *Beverley Minster Fasti*
EHR - v111 - N '96 - p1253+ [251-500]
McDermid, Val - *Blue Genes*
BL - v93 - F 1 '97 - p928 [51-250]
KR - v64 - N 15 '96 - p1636 [51-250]
PW - v243 - N 11 '96 - p59 [51-250]
Booked for Murder
TLS - D 20 '96 - p24 [251-500]
Deadline for Murder
BL - v93 - Mr 1 '97 - p1114 [51-250]
KR - v65 - F 15 '97 - p260 [51-250]
PW - v244 - Ja 27 '97 - p80 [51-250]
The Mermaids Singing
BL - v93 - D 15 '96 - p713 [51-250]
BW - v27 - Ja 19 '97 - p11 [251-500]
KR - v64 - O 15 '96 - p1498 [51-250]
LJ - v121 - D '96 - p151 [1-50]
NYTBR - v101 - D 22 '96 - p21 [51-250]
McDermott, E Patrick - *Alternative Dispute Resolution in the Workplace*
R&R Bk N - v12 - F '97 - p65 [51-250]
McDermott, Gerald R - *One Holy and Happy Society*
Rel St Rev - v22 - O '96 - p358 [51-250]

McDermott, Ian - *Practical NLP for Managers*
R&R Bk N - v12 - F '97 - p46 [51-250]
McDermott, Kevin - *The Comintern: A History of International Communism from Lenin to Stalin*
Choice - v34 - Mr '97 - p1221 [51-250]
McDermott, Nancie - *The Curry Book*
PW - v244 - Ap 21 '97 - p66 [51-250]
Real Vegetarian Thai
PW - v244 - Mr 24 '97 - p80 [51-250]
McDermott, Patrice - *Politics and Scholarship*
Signs - v22 - Win '97 - p453+ [501+]
McDevitt, Jack - *Ancient Shores*
Analog - v116 - Jl '96 - p273+ [501+]
New Sci - v152 - O 5 '96 - p50 [51-250]
y VOYA - v19 - O '96 - p219 [251-500]
Eternity Road
y BL - v93 - My 15 '97 - p1567 [51-250]
KR - v65 - Mr 15 '97 - p423 [51-250]
PW - v244 - Ap 21 '97 - p65 [51-250]
Standard Candles
Analog - v116 - D '96 - p145+ [501+]
McDonagh, Eileen L - *Breaking the Abortion Deadlock*
Choice - v34 - Ap '97 - p1418 [51-250]
McDonagh, Josephine - *De Quincey's Disciplines*
RES - v47 - N '96 - p605+ [501+]
McDonagh, Maitland - *The 50 Most Erotic Films of All Time*
Si & So - v6 - N '96 - p33 [51-250]
McDonagh, Sean - *Passion for the Earth*
Cres - v59 - S '96 - p38+ [501+]
McDonald, Douglas C - *Managing Prison Health Care and Costs*
J Gov Info - v23 - S '96 - p550 [51-250]
McDonald, Forrest - *The American Presidency*
MA - v38 - Fall '96 - p401+ [501+]
McDonald, Gail - *Learning to Be Modern*
MP - v94 - Ag '96 - p124+ [501+]
Mcdonald, Gregory - *Skylar in Yankeeland*
BL - v93 - F 15 '97 - p1007 [51-250]
KR - v64 - N 1 '96 - p1567 [51-250]
PW - v243 - N 4 '96 - p66 [51-250]
McDonald, Ian - *Revolution in the Head*
Books - v9 - S '95 - p25 [1-50]
Sacrifice of Fools
New Sci - v153 - Mr 15 '97 - p45 [51-250]
McDonald, John K - *House of Eternity*
HT - v46 - O '96 - p55 [1-50]
Nature - v385 - Ja 23 '97 - p312 [1-50]
McDonald, Joseph P - *Redesigning School*
NASSP-B - v81 - Ap '97 - p119+ [501+]
McDonald, Joyce - *Comfort Creek*
c BL - v93 - N 15 '96 - p588 [51-250]
c CBRS - v25 - F '97 - p83 [51-250]
c CCB-B - v50 - F '97 - p213+ [51-250]
c Ch BWatch - v7 - F '97 - p4 [1-50]
c HB - v73 - Ja '97 - p62 [51-250]
c HB Guide - v8 - Spr '97 - p71 [51-250]
y JAAL - v40 - F '97 - p407 [51-250]
c PW - v243 - N 25 '96 - p75+ [51-250]
c SLJ - v42 - N '96 - p108 [51-250]
y VOYA - v19 - O '96 - p212 [251-500]
McDonald, Julie Jensen - *Danish Proverbs*
CAY - v17 - Fall '96 - p12 [51-250]
McDonald, Keiko I - *Japanese Classical Theater in Films*
FQ - v49 - Sum '96 - p47+ [501+]
McDonald, Kendall - *Divers*
c Ch BWatch - v6 - Jl '96 - p6 [51-250]
McDonald, Lee M - *The Formation of the Christian Biblical Canon. Rev. and Expanded Ed.*
Rel St Rev - v23 - Ja '97 - p77 [51-250]
McDonald, Mary Ann - *Boas (Illus. by Dwight Kuhn)*
c Ch BWatch - v6 - N '96 - p7+ [1-50]
c HB Guide - v8 - Spr '97 - p123 [51-250]
Cobras (Illus. by Dwight Kuhn)
c Ch BWatch - v6 - N '96 - p7+ [1-50]
c HB Guide - v8 - Spr '97 - p123 [51-250]
Grizzlies
c Ch BWatch - v6 - N '96 - p7+ [1-50]
c HB Guide - v8 - Spr '97 - p127 [51-250]
Sunflowers
c HB Guide - v8 - Spr '97 - p121 [51-250]
Woodpeckers
c Ch BWatch - v6 - N '96 - p7+ [1-50]
c HB Guide - v8 - Spr '97 - p125 [51-250]
McDonald, Megan - *Insects Are My Life (Illus. by Paul Brett Johnson)*
c RT - v50 - Mr '97 - p501 [51-250]

My House Has Stars (Illus. by Peter Catalanotto)
 c BL - v93 - N 1 '96 - p508 [51-250]
 c CCB-B - v50 - N '96 - p106 [51-250]
 c HB Guide - v8 - Spr '97 - p38 [51-250]
 c KR - v64 - Ag 15 '96 - p1238 [51-250]
 c SLJ - v42 - O '96 - p102+ [51-250]
McDonald, Patrick - *Can Your Marriage Be a Friendship?*
 CLW - v67 - Mr '97 - p41 [51-250]
McDonald, Peter, 1952- - *The Literature of Forestry and Agroforestry*
 Choice - v34 - N '96 - p483 [51-250]
 SciTech - v20 - N '96 - p58 [51-250]
McDonald, Peter, 1962- - *Adam's Dream*
 Lon R Bks - v18 - Ag 22 '96 - p25+ [501+]
 TLS - Ag 2 '96 - p25 [251-500]
McDonald, Richard E - *Food Lipids and Health*
 SciTech - v20 - N '96 - p34 [51-250]
McDonald, Robert A J - *Making Vancouver*
 Choice - v34 - O '96 - p350 [51-250]
 WHQ - v27 - Win '96 - p550 [51-250]
McDonald, Roger - *The Slap*
 Aust Bk R - Ag '96 - p46+ [501+]
McDonald, Russ - *Shakespeare Reread*
 Ren Q - v50 - Spr '97 - p280+ [501+]
McDonnell, Flora - *Flora McDonnell's ABC*
 c Obs - Mr 30 '97 - p17* [51-250]
 c PW - v244 - Mr 3 '97 - p77 [51-250]
McDonnell, Hector - *The Wild Geese of the Antrim MacDonnells*
 ILS - v16 - Spr '97 - p36 [51-250]
 TLS - F 7 '97 - p29 [501+]
McDonnell, Janet - *Success (Illus. by Mechelle Ann)*
 c HB Guide - v8 - Spr '97 - p86 [51-250]
 Thankfulness (Illus. by Mechelle Ann)
 c HB Guide - v8 - Spr '97 - p86 [51-250]
McDonogh, Gary W - *Black and Catholic in Savannah, Georgia*
 Am Ethnol - v24 - F '97 - p235 [251-500]
 The Florida Negro
 RA - v25 - 4 '96 - p275+ [501+]
McDonough, Ann - *New Monologues for Mature Actors*
 TCI - v30 - O '96 - p56 [51-250]
McDonough, Carla J - *Staging Masculinity*
 Choice - v34 - Ap '97 - p1338 [51-250]
McDougall, Len - *The Complete Tracker*
 LJ - v122 - Ap 15 '97 - p112 [51-250]
McDougall, Walter A - *Promised Land, Crusader State*
 For Aff - v76 - My '97 - p131 [51-250]
 KR - v65 - F 15 '97 - p279+ [251-500]
 LJ - v122 - Ap 1 '97 - p110 [51-250]
 PW - v244 - Mr 10 '97 - p56 [51-250]
McDowall, David - *A Modern History of the Kurds*
 HRNB - v25 - Win '97 - p84+ [251-500]
 MEJ - v50 - Aut '96 - p600+ [501+]
 MEQ - v3 - S '96 - p85 [251-500]
McDowell, Christopher - *A Tamil Asylum Diaspora*
 R&R Bk N - v11 - D '96 - p10 [51-250]
McDowell, Colin - *Forties Fashion and the New Look*
 NS - v126 - F 28 '97 - p47+ [501+]
 Woman's J - F '97 - p16 [51-250]
McDowell, Deborah E - *The Changing Same*
 RMR - v50 - 2 '96 - p197+ [501+]
 TSWL - v15 - Fall '96 - p349+ [501+]
 Leaving Pipe Shop
 BW - v27 - F 16 '97 - p8 [251-500]
 KR - v64 - N 15 '96 - p1655 [251-500]
 LJ - v122 - F 1 '97 - p90 [51-250]
 PW - v243 - D 2 '96 - p46 [51-250]
 Trib Bks - F 9 '97 - p3+ [501+]
McDowell, Joan R S - *Diabetes: Caring for Patients in the Community*
 SciTech - v20 - D '96 - p47 [51-250]
McDowell, John Holmes - *So Wise Were Our Elders*
 WestFolk - v55 - Sum '96 - p245+ [501+]
McDowell, Josh - *The Best of Josh McDowell*
 y VOYA - v19 - F '97 - p317 [51-250]
 Don't Check Your Brains at the Door
 y VOYA - v19 - F '97 - p320 [51-250]
 Right from Wrong
 y VOYA - v19 - F '97 - p317 [51-250]
 The Teenage Q and A Book
 y VOYA - v19 - F '97 - p318+ [51-250]
McDowell, Robert - *The Diviners*
 HR - v49 - Sum '96 - p331+ [501+]
 y Sch Lib - v44 - Ag '96 - p116 [51-250]
McDowell, Ruth B - *Art and Inspirations*
 y BL - v93 - Ja '97 - p805 [51-250]
 LJ - v121 - D '96 - p92 [51-250]
McEachin, James - *Farewell to the Mockingbirds*
 PW - v244 - Ap 14 '97 - p60 [51-250]

Tell Me a Tale
 y SLJ - v42 - S '96 - p239+ [51-250]
McEldowney, Eugene - *A Stone of the Heart*
 Arm Det - v29 - Fall '96 - p404 [51-250]
McElhone, Alice - *Mail It!*
 BWatch - v17 - S '96 - p2 [51-250]
McElligott, Matthew - *The Truth about Cousin Ernie's Head (Illus. by Matthew McElligott)*
 c CBRS - v25 - F '97 - p76+ [51-250]
 c HB Guide - v8 - Spr '97 - p38 [51-250]
 c KR - v64 - S 15 '96 - p1404 [51-250]
 c NW - v128 - D 2 '96 - p86+ [51-250]
 c PW - v243 - N 11 '96 - p74 [51-250]
 c SLJ - v42 - N '96 - p88 [51-250]
 c BL - v93 - D 1 '96 - p669 [51-250]
McElmeel, Sharron L - *Educator's Companion to Children's Literature. Vol. 2*
 BL - v93 - S 15 '96 - p254 [51-250]
McElroy, Colleen J - *A Long Way from St. Louie*
 KR - v65 - Mr 1 '97 - p357+ [51-250]
 LJ - v122 - Ap 15 '97 - p104+ [51-250]
 PW - v244 - Mr 10 '97 - p57 [51-250]
McElroy, Lorie Jenkins - *Women's Voices. Vols. 1-2*
 yr SLJ - v43 - F '97 - p132 [51-250]
McElroy, Michael B - *The Macroeconomy: Private Choices, Public Actions, and Aggregate Outcomes*
 JEL - v34 - S '96 - p1418 [51-250]
McElroy, Susan Chernak - *Animals as Teachers and Healers*
 LJ - v122 - Ap 15 '97 - p139 [51-250]
 PW - v244 - Ja 6 '97 - p61 [51-250]
McElroy, Wendy - *XXX: A Woman's Right to Pornography*
 ABR - v18 - O '96 - p25 [501+]
 BW - v27 - Mr 30 '97 - p12 [51-250]
McEnery, Tony - *Corpus Linguistics*
 New Sci - v153 - Mr 1 '97 - p46 [1-50]
McEnroy, Carmel - *Guests in Their Own House*
 Comw - v123 - S 27 '96 - p29 [251-500]
McEvedy, Colin - *The Penguin Atlas of African History. New Ed., Rev. Ed. 1995*
 r ARBA - v28 - '97 - p196+ [251-500]
McEwan, Barbara - *White House Landscapes*
 Hort - v94 - Mr '97 - p80 [51-250]
McEwan, Chris - *The Nine Tasks of Mistry*
 c HB Guide - v7 - Fall '96 - p358 [51-250]
McEwan, Vera - *Education Law*
 TES - Ja 24 '97 - p11* [1-50]
McEwen, Christian - *Jo's Girls*
 PW - v244 - Ap 28 '97 - p58+ [251-500]
McEwen, Currier - *The Siberian Iris*
 Choice - v34 - S '96 - p154 [51-250]
 R&R Bk N - v11 - N '96 - p78 [51-250]
McEwen, Gwendolyn - *Gwendolyn MacEwen (Exile Editions). Vols. 1-2*
 Can Lit - Spr '97 - p244+ [501+]
McEwen, R F - *Heartwood and Other Poems*
 PS - v70 - Win '96 - p184+ [501+]
McFadden, David W - *An Innocent in Ireland*
 ILS - v15 - Fall '96 - p30 [501+]
McFadden, Mary Ann - *Eye of the Blackbird*
 PW - v244 - Ap 28 '97 - p71 [251-500]
McFadyen, Deidre - *Haiti: Dangerous Crossroads*
 Bks & Cult - v3 - Ja '97 - p8+ [501+]
McFall, Gardner - *The Pilot's Daughter*
 ABR - v18 - D '96 - p29+ [501+]
McFalls, Laurence H - *Communism's Collapse, Democracy's Demise?*
 Slav R - v55 - Sum '96 - p464+ [501+]
McFarland, Dennis - *A Face at the Window*
 BL - v93 - F 15 '97 - p1004 [51-250]
 KR - v64 - D 15 '96 - p1759 [251-500]
 LJ - v122 - Ja '97 - p147+ [51-250]
 NYTBR - v102 - Mr 16 '97 - p10+ [501+]
 NYTLa - v146 - Mr 14 '97 - pC34 [501+]
 PW - v243 - N 25 '96 - p54+ [251-500]
 Trib Bks - Ap 6 '97 - p5 [51-250]
 WSJ-Cent - v99 - Mr 20 '97 - pA14 [51-250]
McFarland, E W - *Ireland and Scotland in the Age of Revolution*
 Albion - v28 - Fall '96 - p544+ [501+]
McFarland, Stephen L - *America's Pursuit of Precision Bombing 1910-1945*
 T&C - v37 - Ap '96 - p387+ [501+]
McFarland, Thomas C - *X Windows on the World*
 SciTech - v20 - S '96 - p7 [51-250]
McFarlane, Anthony - *The British in the Americas 1480-1815*
 J Am St - v30 - Ag '96 - p290+ [251-500]

McFarlane, Brian - *Hockey for Kids (Illus. by Bill Slavin)*
 c HB Guide - v8 - Spr '97 - p145 [51-250]
 c PW - v243 - O 14 '96 - p85 [51-250]
McFarlane, Brian, 1934- - *Novel to Film*
 Choice - v34 - F '97 - p973 [51-250]
 Si & So - v6 - N '96 - p34 [1-50]
McFarlane, Marilyn - *Sacred Myths*
 c BL - v93 - O 1 '96 - p336 [51-250]
 c Ch BWatch - v6 - S '96 - p3 [51-250]
 y SLJ - v43 - Ja '97 - p131 [51-250]
McFarlane, Peter - *The Enemy You Killed*
 y Magpies - v11 - My '96 - p50 [251-500]
McFarlane, Sheryl - *Eagle Dreams (Illus. by Ron Lightburn)*
 c RT - v50 - D '96 - p343+ [51-250]
 Going to the Fair (Illus. by Sheena Lott)
 c BL - v93 - N 1 '96 - p508 [51-250]
McFate, Katherine - *Poverty, Inequality, and the Future of Social Policy*
 ILRR - v50 - Ap '97 - p535+ [501+]
McFedries, Paul - *The Complete Idiot's Guide to Creating an HTML Web Page*
 Quill & Q - v62 - N '96 - p32 [51-250]
 The Complete Idiot's Guide to Windows 95
 TES - O 18 '96 - p43U [251-500]
McFee, Michael - *Colander*
 VQR - v72 - Aut '96 - p137* [51-250]
 The Language They Speak Is Things to Eat
 South HR - v31 - Win '97 - p96+ [501+]
McGabee-Kovac, Marcy - *A Student's Guide to the IEP*
 EL - v54 - S '96 - p106 [51-250]
McGahan, Andrew - *1988*
 BL - v93 - Ja '97 - p821 [51-250]
 KR - v64 - N 15 '96 - p1625 [251-500]
 LJ - v122 - Ja '97 - p148 [51-250]
 NYTBR - v102 - F 23 '97 - p11 [501+]
 PW - v243 - D 2 '96 - p41 [51-250]
McGahan, Jerry - *A Condor Brings the Sun*
 BL - v93 - S 1 '96 - p62+ [51-250]
 Choice - v34 - Ap '97 - p1338 [51-250]
 Parabola - v22 - F '97 - p120 [1-50]
 y SLJ - v43 - F '97 - p135 [51-250]
McGahey, Robert - *The Orphic Moment*
 Comp L - v49 - Win '97 - p86+ [501+]
McGann, Jerome - *The Poetics of Sensibility*
 Choice - v34 - D '96 - p615 [51-250]
 TLS - D 27 '96 - p11+ [501+]
 VQR - v73 - Win '97 - p12* [51-250]
McGarrity, Michael - *Mexican Hat*
 BL - v93 - My 15 '97 - p1567 [51-250]
 LJ - v122 - My 1 '97 - p141 [51-250]
 PW - v244 - Mr 24 '97 - p61 [51-250]
 Trib Bks - My 4 '97 - p4 [51-250]
 Tularosa
 Bloom Rev - v16 - Jl '96 - p16 [51-250]
 BWatch - v17 - S '96 - p1 [51-250]
 PW - v243 - N 4 '96 - p40 [1-50]
 PW - v244 - Mr 24 '97 - p81 [1-50]
 y SLJ - v43 - Ja '97 - p140 [51-250]
 VQR - v73 - Win '97 - p20* [51-250]
McGarry, Daniel D - *World Historical Fiction Guide. 2nd Ed.*
 r RQ - v36 - Win '96 - p222 [51-250]
McGaugh, James L - *Plasticity in the Central Nervous System*
 SB - v32 - Ag '96 - p170 [51-250]
McGaughey, Neil - *The Best Money Murder Can Buy*
 Arm Det - v30 - Win '97 - p86 [501+]
McGaw, Judith A - *Early American Technology*
 JIH - v27 - Aut '96 - p340+ [501+]
 T&C - v37 - Ap '96 - p356+ [501+]
McGee, Glenn - *The Perfect Baby*
 Choice - v34 - My '97 - p1534 [51-250]
McGee, Jim - *Main Justice*
 BW - v26 - D 22 '96 - p11 [501+]
 NYTBR - v101 - S 15 '96 - p38 [501+]
McGee, Robert W - *A Trade Policy for Free Societies*
 BusLR - v21 - 3 '96 - p192+ [501+]
McGee, T G - *The Mega-Urban Regions of Southeast Asia*
 Pac A - v69 - Sum '96 - p278+ [501+]
McGee, Timothy J - *Singing Early Music*
 Choice - v34 - Ja '97 - p806 [51-250]
 M Ed J - v83 - N '96 - p54+ [51-250]
McGeer, Eric - *Sowing the Dragon's Teeth*
 J Mil H - v61 - Ap '97 - p361+ [501+]
McGeorge, Constance W - *Boomer Goes to School (Illus. by Mary Whyte)*
 c HB Guide - v7 - Fall '96 - p266 [51-250]
McGhee, George R - *The Late Devonian Mass Extinction*
 Choice - v34 - S '96 - p153 [51-250]
 SB - v32 - Ag '96 - p168 [51-250]

McGhee, Robert - *Ancient People of the Arctic*
  CG - v117 - Mr '97 - p80 [251-500]
  Quill & Q - v62 - Ag '96 - p39 [251-500]
McGill, Dan M - *Fundamentals of Private Pensions. 7th Ed.*
  R&R Bk N - v12 - F '97 - p41 [51-250]
McGilligan, Patrick - *Backstory 3*
  BL - v93 - Mr 15 '97 - p1220 [51-250]
  Fritz Lang: The Nature of the Beast
  LJ - v122 - Ap 1 '97 - p96 [51-250]
  PW - v244 - Ap 14 '97 - p61 [51-250]
McGillis, Roderick - *The Nimble Reader*
  CCB-B - v50 - My '97 - p341 [51-250]
McGinity, James W - *Aqueous Polymeric Coatings for Pharmaceutical Dosage Forms. 2nd Ed.*
  SciTech - v21 - Mr '97 - p68 [51-250]
McGinn, Bernard - *Antichrist: Two Thousand Years of the Human Fascination with Evil*
  Am - v175 - S 21 '96 - p37+ [501+]
  Bks & Cult - v2 - My '96 - p9+ [501+]
  JR - v76 - O '96 - p623+ [501+]
  Rel St Rev - v23 - Ja '97 - p82 [51-250]
  Theol St - v57 - Mr '96 - p140+ [501+]
  Apocalypticism in the Western Tradition
  CHR - v82 - Jl '96 - p528+ [501+]
  The Growth of Mysticism
  Am - v175 - S 21 '96 - p37+ [501+]
  Meister Eckhart and the Beguine Mystics
  CH - v65 - S '96 - p167+ [501+]
  CHR - v82 - Jl '96 - p552+ [251-500]
McGinn, Colin - *The Problem of Consciousness*
  Zygon - v31 - D '96 - p735+ [501+]
  Problems in Philosophy
  Phil R - v105 - Ap '96 - p253+ [501+]
McGinn, Noel F - *Crossing Lines*
  R&R Bk N - v12 - F '97 - p69 [51-250]
McGinness, Frederick J - *Right Thinking and Sacred Oratory in Counter-Reformation Rome*
  CH - v65 - D '96 - p702+ [501+]
  CHR - v82 - O '96 - p714+ [501+]
  J Ch St - v38 - Sum '96 - p647+ [501+]
  Theol St - v57 - Je '96 - p352+ [501+]
McGinnis, Bruce - *Reflections in Dark Glass*
  Roundup M - v3 - Ag '96 - p30+ [251-500]
McGlothlin, Bruce - *Choosing a Career in Transportation*
  y SLJ - v43 - Mr '97 - p196+ [51-250]
  High Performance through Understanding Systems
  y SLJ - v43 - Mr '97 - p204 [51-250]
McGoldrick, James Edward - *Baptist Successionism*
  CH - v66 - Mr '97 - p205+ [51-250]
McGoldrick, Monica - *Ethnicity and Family Therapy. 2nd Ed.*
  SciTech - v20 - D '96 - p44 [51-250]
McGonagle, John J - *A New Archetype for Competitive Intelligence*
  Choice - v34 - Ja '97 - p842 [51-250]
  R&R Bk N - v11 - N '96 - p29 [51-250]
McGoogan, Ken - *Kerouac's Ghost*
  Quill & Q - v62 - S '96 - p64 [501+]
McGorrin, Robert J - *Flavor-Food Interactions*
  SciTech - v21 - Mr '97 - p96 [51-250]
McGough, Roger - *The Kingfisher Book of Poems about Love*
  c TES - F 14 '97 - p7* [501+]
  The Kite and Caitlin (Illus. by John Prater)
  c JB - v60 - D '96 - p235+ [51-250]
  c Sch Lib - v44 - N '96 - p151 [51-250]
  c TES - S 6 '96 - p7* [501+]
  The Magic Fountain by HRH Princess Gloriana (Illus. by Philip Hopman)
  c Bks Keeps - v100 - S '96 - p12 [51-250]
McGovern, George - *Terry: My Daughter's Life-and-Death Struggle with Alcoholism*
  CC - v113 - N 6 '96 - p1083+ [501+]
  Nat R - v48 - S 2 '96 - p94 [501+]
  NW - v127 - My 20 '96 - p72 [51-250]
  y SLJ - v42 - S '96 - p242 [51-250]
McGowan, Richard - *Business, Politics, and Cigarettes*
  JEL - v34 - D '96 - p2086 [51-250]
McGowan, Susan - *With Undefending Heart*
  Aust Bk R - Ag '96 - p67 [1-50]
McGown, Jill - *Verdict Unsafe*
  PW - v244 - Ap 14 '97 - p60 [51-250]
McGrail, Anna - *Blood Sisters*
  Books - v9 - S '95 - p22 [1-50]
McGrath, Ann - *Contested Ground*
  Choice - v34 - S '96 - p183 [51-250]
McGrath, Barbara Barbieri - *The M & M's Brand Chocolate Candies Counting Board Book*
  c PW - v244 - Ja 27 '97 - p108 [1-50]

McGrath, Bob - *Uh Oh! Gotta Go! (Illus. by Shelley Dieterichs)*
  c SLJ - v43 - Ja '97 - p86 [51-250]
McGrath, Campbell - *Spring Comes to Chicago*
  HMR - Spr '97 - p39+ [501+]
McGrath, John - *Six-Pack: Plays for Scotland*
  TLS - Ag 30 '96 - p19 [501+]
McGrath, Melanie - *Motel Nirvana*
  Books - v9 - S '95 - p23 [1-50]
McGrath, Patrick - *Asylum*
  BL - v93 - D 1 '96 - p620 [51-250]
  Ent W - Mr 7 '97 - p60+ [51-250]
  KR - v64 - D 15 '96 - p1759+ [251-500]
  LATBR - Mr 23 '97 - p10 [501+]
  LJ - v122 - F 1 '97 - p106 [51-250]
  Lon R Bks - v18 - O 31 '96 - p7 [501+]
  NS - v125 - S 13 '96 - p48 [251-500]
  NY - v72 - Ja 27 '97 - p78+ [501+]
  NYTBR - v102 - F 23 '97 - p6 [501+]
  NYTLa - v146 - F 14 '97 - pC38 [501+]
  Obs - Ag 25 '96 - p16* [501+]
  Obs - D 1 '96 - p17* [51-250]
  PW - v243 - D 16 '96 - p41 [51-250]
  Trib Bks - Mr 30 '97 - p2 [501+]
  VV - v42 - F 25 '97 - p51 [251-500]
McGraw, Eloise - *The Moorchild*
  y BL - v93 - Ap 1 '97 - p1302+ [1-50]
  c HB - v72 - S '96 - p598+ [51-250]
  c HB Guide - v7 - Fall '96 - p294 [51-250]
  c SLJ - v42 - D '96 - p31 [1-50]
McGraw, Erin - *Lies of the Saints*
  LATBR - Jl 14 '96 - p10 [51-250]
  NYTBR - v101 - S 1 '96 - p8 [501+]
  NYTBR - v101 - D 8 '96 - p80 [1-50]
McGraw, Gary - *Java Security*
  CBR - v15 - Spr '97 - p5 [1-50]
  New Sci - v153 - Mr 1 '97 - p46+ [501+]
  SciTech - v21 - Mr '97 - p7 [1-50]
McGraw, Mary Jo - *Making Greeting Cards with Rubber Stamps*
  BL - v93 - Ja '97 - p806 [51-250]
  LJ - v122 - F 15 '97 - p134 [51-250]
McGraw-Hill Yearbook of Science and Technology 1996
  r ARBA - v28 - '97 - p566 [51-250]
McGraw-Hill's National Electrical Code Handbook. 22nd Ed.
  SciTech - v20 - N '96 - p71 [51-250]
McGreal, Wilfrid - *John of the Cross*
  TES - F 21 '97 - p7* [1-50]
McGreevy, John T - *Parish Boundaries*
  AHR - v101 - D '96 - p1640+ [501+]
  BW - v26 - S 29 '96 - p6 [501+]
  Choice - v34 - N '96 - p526 [51-250]
  CLW - v67 - Mr '97 - p41+ [251-500]
  NYTBR - v101 - Ag 25 '96 - p24+ [501+]
McGreevy, Patrick V - *Imagining Niagara*
  AAAGA - v86 - S '96 - p590+ [501+]
McGregor, Douglas - *The Human Side of Enterprise*
  Inc. - v18 - D '96 - p55 [251-500]
McGregor, Richard - *Japan Swings*
  Aust Bk R - Je '96 - p22+ [501+]
McGregor, Rob - *Peter Norton's Guide to Windows 95/NT 4 Programming with MFC*
  BYTE - v22 - Mr '97 - p148 [51-250]
McGrew, Timothy J - *The Foundations of Knowledge*
  Choice - v34 - O '96 - p294 [51-250]
  CPR - v16 - D '96 - p421+ [501+]
McGrew, William C - *Great Ape Societies*
  Nature - v384 - N 7 '96 - p35 [1-50]
McGuckian, Medbh - *Captain Lavender*
  Lon R Bks - v18 - Jl 18 '96 - p24+ [501+]
  PS - v70 - Fall '96 - p175+ [501+]
McGuigan, Jim - *Culture and the Public Sphere*
  Socio R - v45 - My '97 - p345+ [501+]
McGuigan, Mary Ann - *Where You Belong*
  y CCB-B - v50 - My '97 - p328+ [51-250]
  c KR - v65 - Mr 1 '97 - p385 [51-250]
McGuire, Bob - *The Line*
  PW - v243 - N 11 '96 - p72 [51-250]
McGuire, Christine - *Until Death Do Us Part*
  PW - v243 - D 2 '96 - p55 [51-250]
Mcguire, Laurie E - *Shakespearean Suspect Texts*
  Choice - v34 - N '96 - p457 [51-250]
McGuire, Patrick - *From the Left Bank to the Mainstream*
  CS - v25 - S '96 - p704+ [501+]
McGuire, Philip C - *Shakespeare: The Jacobean Plays*
  Shakes Q - v47 - Sum '96 - p221+ [501+]
McGuire, Richard - *What Goes around Comes Around (Illus. by Richard McGuire)*
  c RT - v50 - O '96 - p131 [1-50]
  c Tric - v6 - Win '96 - p117 [1-50]

  What's Wrong with This Book? (Illus. by Richard McGuire)
  c BL - v93 - F 1 '97 - p948 [51-250]
  c CCB-B - v50 - Ap '97 - p288+ [51-250]
  c HB - v73 - Mr '97 - p194 [51-250]
  c KR - v64 - D 15 '96 - p1799 [51-250]
  c PW - v243 - D 2 '96 - p59 [51-250]
  c SLJ - v43 - Mr '97 - p161+ [51-250]
McGuire, W J - *Volcano Instability on the Earth and Other Planets*
  Sci - v275 - Ja 24 '97 - p496+ [501+]
McHam, Sarah Blake - *The Chapel of St. Anthony at the Santo and the Development of Venetian Renaissance Sculpture*
  Specu - v72 - Ja '97 - p198+ [501+]
McHarg, Ian L - *A Quest for Life*
  BW - v26 - Jl 7 '96 - p13 [51-250]
  Choice - v34 - O '96 - p300 [51-250]
McHoul, A W - *Semiotic Investigations*
  Choice - v34 - D '96 - p598 [1-50]
  Writing Pynchon
  Poetics T - v18 - Spr '97 - p95+ [501+]
McIlvanney, William - *The Kiln*
  Obs - O 20 '96 - p18* [501+]
  Spec - v277 - S 21 '96 - p49+ [501+]
  TLS - O 4 '96 - p27 [501+]
McIlwain, Harris H - *The Fibromyalgia Handbook*
  BL - v93 - N 1 '96 - p470 [51-250]
  LJ - v121 - N 1 '96 - p101 [51-250]
  PW - v243 - O 21 '96 - p81 [51-250]
  Stop Osteoarthritis Now!
  BL - v93 - S 15 '96 - p194+ [51-250]
McIlwaine, John - *Africa: A Guide to Reference Material*
  r GJ - v163 - Mr '97 - p106 [1-50]
  Writings on African Archives
  r ARBA - v28 - '97 - p50+ [251-500]
  r Choice - v34 - N '96 - p432 [51-250]
McInerney, Jay - *Dressed to Kill*
  BW - v26 - O 27 '96 - p13 [51-250]
  Obs - O 20 '96 - p15* [1-50]
  The Last of the Savages
  Atl - v278 - Jl '96 - p106+ [501+]
  HR - v49 - Win '97 - p687+ [501+]
  Nat - v262 - Je 10 '96 - p30+ [501+]
  Rapport - v19 - 5 '96 - p29 [501+]
  y SLJ - v42 - S '96 - p240 [51-250]
  Woman's J - Ag '96 - p11 [51-250]
McInerny, Ralph - *The Tears of Things*
  Arm Det - v30 - Win '97 - p97+ [251-500]
  y BL - v93 - N 15 '96 - p575 [51-250]
  Ent W - O 25 '96 - p109 [51-250]
  KR - v64 - S 15 '96 - p1357+ [51-250]
  LJ - v121 - N 1 '96 - p111 [1-50]
  PW - v243 - S 16 '96 - p73 [51-250]
McIntire, Sandra - *Job Analysis Kit*
  Per Psy - v49 - Aut '96 - p769+ [501+]
McIntosh, William S - *Location Portraiture*
  Pet PM - v25 - Ag '96 - p10 [51-250]
McIntosh, Wm. Alex - *Sociologies of Food and Nutrition*
  Choice - v34 - Mr '97 - p1246 [51-250]
  R&R Bk N - v11 - D '96 - p20 [51-250]
McIntyre, Anne - *Flower Power*
  y SLJ - v43 - F '97 - p137 [51-250]
McIntyre, Don - *Two Below Zero*
  Aust Bk R - F '97 - p20+ [501+]
McIntyre, Ian - *Dirt and Deity*
  Choice - v34 - O '96 - p279 [51-250]
McIntyre, Lee C - *Laws and Explanation in the Social Sciences*
  Choice - v34 - S '96 - p168 [51-250]
McIntyre, Lisa J - *Law in the Sociological Enterprise*
  SSQ - v77 - Je '96 - p454+ [501+]
McIntyre, Mike - *The Kindness of Strangers*
  y Kliatt - v31 - Ja '97 - p19 [51-250]
  PW - v243 - O 7 '96 - p68 [51-250]
McIntyre, Rick - *A Society of Wolves*
  SciTech - v20 - N '96 - p30 [51-250]
McIntyre, W David - *Background to the ANZUS Pact*
  r AHR - v101 - D '96 - p1603 [501+]
  EHR - v112 - Ap '97 - p541+ [251-500]
McIntyre, W John - *Children of Peace*
  JR - v77 - Ja '97 - p148+ [501+]
McIver, Bruce - *Teaching with Shakespeare*
  Shakes Q - v47 - Sum '96 - p223+ [501+]
McKague, Ormond - *Racism in Canada*
  Can Lit - Win '96 - p129+ [501+]
McKane, William - *A Late Harvest*
  Rel St Rev - v23 - Ap '97 - p168 [51-250]
McKay, David - *Rush to Union*
  Choice - v34 - Ap '97 - p1414 [51-250]

McKay, Don - *Apparatus*
   Quill & Q - v63 - Mr '97 - p76 [251-500]
McKay, Duncan - *Effective Financial Planning for Library and Information Services*
   LR - v45 - 6 '96 - p61 [51-250]
McKay, Elizabeth Norman - *Franz Schubert: A Biography*
   BL - v93 - O 1 '96 - p315 [51-250]
   Choice - v34 - Ap '97 - p1348 [51-250]
   LJ - v121 - O 1 '96 - p80 [51-250]
McKay, Helen - *About Storytelling*
   Magpies - v11 - Jl '96 - p14+ [251-500]
McKay, Hilary - *The Amber Cat. Audio Version*
   c Ch BWatch - v6 - O '96 - p2 [1-50]
   The Echo in the Chimney (Illus. by Tony Kenyon)
   c Sch Lib - v44 - N '96 - p151 [51-250]
   The Exiles in Love
   c JB - v60 - D '96 - p271 [251-500]
   y TES - F 14 '97 - p7* [251-500]
   The Magic in the Mirror (Illus. by Tony Kenyon)
   c Sch Lib - v44 - N '96 - p151 [51-250]
   Practically Perfect (Illus. by H Offen)
   c JB - v60 - D '96 - p256 [51-250]
   Why Didn't You Tell Me? (Illus. by John Eastwood)
   c Sch Lib - v44 - N '96 - p151 [51-250]
McKay, Ian - *The Quest of the Folk*
   Can Lit - Spr '97 - p210+ [501+]
   CAY - v16 - Fall '95 - p6 [51-250]
McKay, Judith - *The Chemotherapy Survival Guide*
   LJ - v122 - Ja '97 - p57 [51-250]
McKay, Sharon - *Have a Heart! (Illus. by Marilyn Mets)*
   c PW - v243 - D 30 '96 - p68 [51-250]
McKean, Lise - *Divine Enterprise*
   Choice - v34 - N '96 - p500 [51-250]
   Rel St Rev - v23 - Ja '97 - p96 [51-250]
McKee, David - *Charlotte's Piggy Bank (Illus. by David McKee)*
   c JB - v60 - Ag '96 - p142 [51-250]
   c Sch Lib - v44 - Ag '96 - p107 [51-250]
   Elmer and Wilbur (Illus. by David McKee)
   c BL - v93 - N 1 '96 - p508 [51-250]
   c HB Guide - v8 - Spr '97 - p38 [51-250]
   c SLJ - v42 - N '96 - p88 [51-250]
   The Sad Story of Veronica Who Played the Violin
   c Bks Keeps - N '96 - p8 [51-250]
   c TES - O 18 '96 - p12* [51-250]
McKee, David L - *External Linkages and Growth in Small Economies*
   JTWS - v13 - Spr '96 - p410+ [501+]
   Urban Environments in Emerging Economies
   BusLR - v21 - 3 '96 - p193+ [501+]
McKee, Elsie Anne - *Reforming Popular Piety in Sixteenth-Century Strasbourg*
   CH - v66 - Mr '97 - p195 [51-250]
McKeehan, Julie - *Programming for the Newton Using Windows*
   SciTech - v21 - Mr '97 - p9 [51-250]
   Safe Surfing
   CBR - v14 - N '96 - p37 [1-50]
McKeganey, Neil - *Sex Work on the Streets*
   R&R Bk N - v11 - D '96 - p40 [51-250]
McKellar, Margaret Maud - *Life on a Mexican Ranch*
   HAHR - v77 - My '97 - p325+ [251-500]
McKelvey, Douglas Kaine - *The Angel Knew Papa and the Dog*
   c BL - v93 - S 15 '96 - p242 [51-250]
   c CBRS - v25 - N '96 - p31 [51-250]
   c CCB-B - v50 - S '96 - p22 [51-250]
   c HB Guide - v8 - Spr '97 - p71 [51-250]
McKelvey, Maureen D - *Evolutionary Innovations*
   Choice - v34 - Mr '97 - p1209 [51-250]
   JEL - v35 - Mr '97 - p249+ [51-250]
McKemmish, Jan - *Common Knowledge*
   Aust Bk R - S '96 - p27 [501+]
McKemmish, Sue - *The Records Continuum*
   Archiv - Spr '96 - p251+ [501+]
McKendry, Ruth - *Classic Quilts*
   Quill & Q - v63 - Mr '97 - p23 [251-500]
McKenna, Erin - *A Student's Guide to Irish American Genealogy*
   cr ARBA - v28 - '97 - p168 [51-250]
   c Ch BWatch - v7 - F '97 - p8 [1-50]
   cr LJ - v122 - My 1 '97 - p98 [51-250]
McKenna, Mark - *The Captive Republic*
   Aust Bk R - F '97 - p10+ [501+]
McKenna, Megan - *Angels Unawares*
   RR - v55 - S '96 - p553 [51-250]
McKenna, Virginia - *Back to the Blue (Illus. by Ian Andrew)*
   c TES - F 21 '97 - p16* [51-250]

Journey to Freedom (Illus. by Nick Mountain)
   c TES - F 21 '97 - p16* [51-250]
McKenty, Elizabeth J - *The Literature of the Nonprofit Sector. Vol. 7*
   r ARBA - v28 - '97 - p309 [51-250]
McKenzie, James F - *Planning, Implementing, and Evaluating Health Promotion Programs. 2nd Ed.*
   SciTech - v20 - D '96 - p39 [51-250]
McKenzie, John D - *Uncertain Glory*
   KR - v64 - D 1 '96 - p1720 [251-500]
   LJ - v122 - Ja '97 - p120 [51-250]
   PW - v244 - Ja 6 '97 - p57 [51-250]
   WSJ-Cent - v99 - F 26 '97 - pA16 [501+]
McKenzie, Richard B - *The Paradox of Progress*
   BL - v93 - Ap 1 '97 - p1272 [51-250]
   KR - v65 - F 1 '97 - p202+ [251-500]
McKenzie, Robert Tracy - *One South or Many?*
   JEH - v56 - S '96 - p741+ [501+]
McKenzie, Shirlyn B - *Textbook of Hematology. 2nd Ed.*
   SciTech - v20 - S '96 - p29 [51-250]
McKenzie, Vashti - *Not without a Struggle*
   OS - v32 - S '96 - p59 [51-250]
McKercher, B J C - *The Operational Art*
   R&R Bk N - v12 - F '97 - p99 [51-250]
McKerrow, Ronald B - *An Introduction to Bibliography for Literary Students*
   Lib & Cul - v32 - Win '97 - p155+ [501+]
McKetta, John J - *Encyclopedia of Chemical Processing and Design. Vol. 56*
   r ARBA - v28 - '97 - p627 [51-250]
McKevett, G A - *Killer Calories*
   KR - v65 - Ap 1 '97 - p507 [251-500]
   LJ - v122 - Ap 1 '97 - p133 [1-50]
   PW - v244 - F 24 '97 - p66 [51-250]
McKey, JoAnn Riley - *Baptismal Records of the Dutch Reformed Churches in the City of Groningen, Netherlands. Vols. 1-2*
   r EGH - v50 - N '96 - p157 [51-250]
McKibben, Bill - *The Comforting Whirlwind*
   Ch Today - v40 - D 9 '96 - p45+ [51-250]
   Hope, Human and Wild
   Ken R - v18 - Sum '96 - p206+ [501+]
   PW - v244 - Mr 3 '97 - p72 [1-50]
McKibbon, Hugh William - *The Token Gift (Illus. by Scott Cameron)*
   c BL - v93 - F 1 '97 - p941 [51-250]
   c Quill & Q - v62 - O '96 - p44+ [251-500]
   c SLJ - v43 - Ja '97 - p104 [51-250]
McKiernan, Dennis L - *The Dragonstone*
   KR - v64 - S 1 '96 - p1281 [251-500]
   PW - v243 - O 21 '96 - p74 [51-250]
McKillip, Patricia A - *The Book of Atrix Wolfe*
   y Kliatt - v31 - Ja '97 - p14 [51-250]
   Winter Rose
   y BL - v93 - Ja '97 - p763 [1-50]
   BWatch - v17 - N '96 - p8 [1-50]
   MFSF - v91 - O '96 - p65 [51-250]
   y VOYA - v19 - F '97 - p338 [251-500]
McKillop, A B - *Matters of Mind*
   Dal R - v75 - Spr '95 - p110+ [501+]
McKim, Donald K - *Westminster Dictionary of Theological Terms*
   r BL - v93 - O 1 '96 - p373 [51-250]
McKim, Mark G - *Emil Brunner: A Bibliography*
   r ARBA - v28 - '97 - p534 [51-250]
McKinley, Edward H - *Marching to Glory. 2nd Ed., Rev. and Expanded*
   Bks & Cult - v2 - S '96 - p38 [51-250]
   CC - v113 - Ag 28 '96 - p825+ [251-500]
McKinley, Mary B - *Les Terrains Vagues Des Essais*
   Ren Q - v50 - Spr '97 - p251+ [501+]
McKinley, Michael - *Legends: Legends of the Hockey Hall of Fame*
   Beav - v76 - O '96 - p46 [51-250]
   Legends of Hockey
   y LJ - v122 - F 1 '97 - p87 [51-250]
   Mac - v109 - D 16 '96 - p73 [1-50]
McKinley, Robin - *Beauty*
   y Kliatt - v30 - S '96 - p4 [1-50]
   y VOYA - v19 - D '96 - p266 [1-50]
   Deerskin
   y VOYA - v19 - D '96 - p266 [1-50]
   The Door in the Hedge
   y HB Guide - v7 - Fall '96 - p303 [51-250]
   The Hero and the Crown
   c JOYS - v10 - Fall '96 - p46+ [501+]
McKinley, Terry - *The Distribution of Wealth in Rural China*
   Econ J - v106 - N '96 - p1840 [251-500]

McKinney, Anne - *Resumes and Cover Letters That Have Worked for Military Professionals*
   BL - v93 - N 1 '96 - p474+ [51-250]
McKinney, Hannah J - *The Development of Local Public Services 1650-1860*
   BusLR - v21 - 3 '96 - p250+ [51-250]
   JIH - v27 - Win '97 - p537+ [51-250]
McKinney, Jordan - *Pumpkin Painting*
   c LATBR - O 20 '96 - p8 [1-50]
   c PW - v243 - S 30 '96 - p86 [51-250]
McKinney, Meagan - *Gentle from the Night*
   KR - v64 - N 15 '96 - p1625 [251-500]
   PW - v244 - Ja 6 '97 - p67 [251-500]
McKinney-Whetstone, Diane - *Tumbling*
   LATBR - Ag 25 '96 - p10 [51-250]
   LJ - v121 - O 1 '96 - p47 [1-50]
   LJ - v121 - O 1 '96 - p156 [51-250]
   Trib Bks - Ap 27 '97 - p8 [1-50]
McKinnis, Lynn N - *Fundamentals of Orthopedic Radiology*
   SciTech - v21 - Mr '97 - p61 [51-250]
McKinnon, Leonie - *Exploring Shape and Space*
   TES - D 13 '96 - p43 [51-250]
McKinnon, Ronald I - *The Rules of the Game*
   JEL - v35 - Mr '97 - p219 [51-250]
McKinty, Adrian - *Orange Rhymes with Everything*
   KR - v64 - N 1 '96 - p1557 [251-500]
   LJ - v121 - N 15 '96 - p89 [51-250]
   NYTBR - v102 - Mr 2 '97 - p18 [51-250]
   PW - v243 - N 4 '96 - p63 [51-250]
McKissack, Pat - *Black Diamond*
   y Kliatt - v30 - S '96 - p5 [1-50]
   Dark-Thirty: Southern Tales of the Supernatural
   c JOYS - v10 - Fall '96 - p46+ [501+]
   Ma Dear's Aprons (Illus. by Floyd Cooper)
   c BL - v93 - F 15 '97 - p1027 [51-250]
   c HB - v73 - My '97 - p310 [51-250]
   c KR - v65 - Mr 1 '97 - p385 [51-250]
   c PW - v244 - Ja 20 '97 - p401 [51-250]
   A Million Fish...More or Less
   c CLW - v67 - Mr '97 - p14 [1-50]
   Mirandy and Brother Wind (Illus. by Jerry Pinkney)
   c PW - v244 - Ja 27 '97 - p108 [1-50]
   A Picture of Freedom
   c PW - v244 - F 24 '97 - p93 [1-50]
   c Trib Bks - My 4 '97 - p1+ [501+]
   Rebels against Slavery
   y BL - v93 - Ap 1 '97 - p1286+ [1-50]
   y Ch BWatch - v6 - My '96 - p5 [51-250]
   y HB Guide - v7 - Fall '96 - p387 [51-250]
   Red-Tail Angels
   y RT - v50 - N '96 - p247 [51-250]
   Sojourner Truth: Ain't I a Woman?
   y Kliatt - v30 - S '96 - p4 [1-50]
McKitterick, David - *The Making of the Wren Library, Trinity College, Cambridge*
   Apo - v144 - O '96 - p60+ [501+]
McKitterick, Rosamond - *The New Cambridge Medieval History. Vol. 2*
   CH - v65 - D '96 - p674+ [501+]
   TLS - Jl 7 '96 - p31+ [501+]
McKiven, Henry M, Jr. - *Iron and Steel*
   AHR - v101 - D '96 - p1637+ [501+]
McKnight, Reginald - *Wisdom of the African World*
   Bl S - v26 - Sum '96 - p66 [1-50]
McLachlan, Geoffrey J - *The EM Algorithm and Extensions*
   SciTech - v21 - Mr '97 - p14 [51-250]
McLachlan, Keith - *The Boundaries of Modern Iran*
   Historian - v58 - Sum '96 - p850+ [501+]
McLane, Bobbie Jones - *1850 Census of North Central Arkansas*
   r EGH - v50 - N '96 - p161+ [51-250]
McLaren, Clemence - *Inside the Walls of Troy*
   y CBRS - v25 - D '96 - p47 [51-250]
   y CCB-B - v50 - N '96 - p106+ [51-250]
   y HB Guide - v8 - Spr '97 - p82 [51-250]
   y KR - v64 - Ag 15 '96 - p1238+ [51-250]
   y SLJ - v42 - O '96 - p148 [51-250]
   y VOYA - v19 - F '97 - p338+ [251-500]
McLaren, John - *Writing in Hope and Fear*
   Aust Bk R - Jl '96 - p34+ [501+]
   Choice - v34 - Ap '97 - p1338 [51-250]
   Meanjin - v55 - '96 - p688+ [501+]
McLaren, Peter - *Rethinking Media Literacy*
   Afterimage - v23 - Sum '96 - p25+ [501+]
McLaren, Peter L - *Politics of Liberation*
   AE - v47 - Win '97 - p238+ [501+]
McLaren, Tim - *MCSE Study Guide*
   SciTech - v21 - Mr '97 - p6 [51-250]

McLarey, Myra - *Water from the Well*
    NYTBR - v101 - S 22 '96 - p40 [51-250]
McLaughlin, Eve - *Interviewing Elderly Relatives*
    TES - Jl 26 '96 - pR6 [1-50]
    No Time for Family History?
    TES - Jl 26 '96 - pR6 [1-50]
McLaughlin, Glen - *The Mapping of California as an Island*
    GJ - v162 - Jl '96 - p222+ [251-500]
McLaughlin, Kevin - *Writing in Parts*
    MLN - v111 - D '96 - p1057+ [251-500]
    Nine-C Lit - v51 - S '96 - p274 [51-250]
McLaughlin, Martin L - *Literary Imitation in the Italian Renaissance*
    Choice - v34 - D '96 - p620 [51-250]
McLaughlin, Megan - *Consorting with Saints*
    EHR - v112 - F '97 - p157+ [501+]
    Specu - v71 - Jl '96 - p731+ [501+]
McLaughlin, Roberta - *Folk Songs of Africa*
    c CAY - v17 - Fall '96 - p12 [51-250]
    Latin American Folk Song
    c CAY - v17 - Fall '96 - p12 [51-250]
McLaughlin, Terence - *The Contemporary Catholic School*
    Am - v176 - Ja 18 '97 - p26+ [501+]
    R&R Bk N - v11 - N '96 - p57 [51-250]
    TES - N 15 '96 - p7* [51-250]
McLaughlin, Thomas - *Street Smarts and Critical Theory*
    CHE - v43 - F 14 '97 - pA18 [51-250]
    Choice - v34 - My '97 - p1490+ [51-250]
McLaurin, David - *Mortal Sins*
    Spec - v277 - N 16 '96 - p43 [1-50]
McLean, Andrew - *Cats' Whiskers*
    c Sch Lib - v44 - Ag '96 - p100 [51-250]
McLean, David - *War, Diplomacy and Informal Empire*
    AHR - v102 - F '97 - p108+ [251-500]
    EHR - v112 - Ap '97 - p506+ [501+]
McLean, Deckle - *Privacy and Its Invasion*
    CPR - v16 - Ap '96 - p118+ [501+]
McLean, Dirk - *Steel Drums and Ice Skates (Illus. by Ho Che Anderson)*
    c Quill & Q - v62 - D '96 - p36+ [251-500]
McLean, Duncan - *Bunker Man*
    BL - v93 - My 15 '97 - p1563 [51-250]
    KR - v65 - Ap 1 '97 - p492 [51-250]
    PW - v244 - Ap 21 '97 - p59 [51-250]
McLean, Ian - *The Art of Gordon Bennett*
    Aust Bk R - F '97 - p33+ [501+]
McLean, Jim - *The Eight-Step Swing*
    LJ - v121 - O 1 '96 - p53 [1-50]
McLean, Ruari - *Typographers on Type*
    LR - v45 - S 17 '96 - p57+ [251-500]
Mclean, Stuart - *When We Were Young*
    Quill & Q - v62 - D '96 - p35 [251-500]
McLeay, Alison - *After Shanghai*
    y BL - v92 - Ag '96 - p1882 [51-250]
    y BL - v92 - Ag '96 - p1891 [1-50]
    The Summer House
    KR - v65 - My 1 '97 - p669 [51-250]
McLeish, Ewan - *Oceans and Seas*
    c HB Guide - v8 - Spr '97 - p118 [51-250]
McLeish, Kenneth - *Myth: Myths and Legends of the World Explored*
    yr ARBA - v28 - '97 - p498 [51-250]
    The Prentice Hall Good Reading Guide
    r RQ - v36 - Win '96 - p221 [51-250]
McLellan, David - *Ideology. 2nd Ed.*
    JEL - v34 - S '96 - p1503 [51-250]
McLennan, Gregor - *Pluralism*
    JEL - v34 - S '96 - p1503 [51-250]
McLennan, Karen Jacobsen - *Nature's Ban*
    AL - v68 - S '96 - p670 [1-50]
    Ms - v7 - Ja '97 - p77+ [501+]
McLennan, Rob - *Poems from the Blue Horizon*
    BIC - v25 - O '96 - p41+ [251-500]
    We Live at the End of the 20th Century
    BIC - v25 - O '96 - p41+ [251-500]
McLeod, Donald W - *Lesbian and Gay Liberation in Canada*
    r ARBA - v28 - '97 - p308+ [51-250]
McLeod, Hugh - *European Religion in the Age of Great Cities 1830-1930*
    EHR - v112 - Ap '97 - p504+ [501+]
    Piety and Poverty
    Choice - v34 - D '96 - p663+ [51-250]
    JEL - v35 - Mr '97 - p264 [51-250]
    Religion and Society in England 1850-1914
    CH - v66 - Mr '97 - p157+ [501+]
    Choice - v34 - S '96 - p145 [51-250]
    HRNB - v25 - Win '97 - p67 [251-500]

McLeod, Ken - *The Stone Canal*
    New Sci - v152 - N 23 '96 - p48 [51-250]
McLeRoy, Sherrie - *More Passages*
    EGH - v50 - N '96 - p190 [51-250]
    Red River Women
    Roundup M - v4 - D '96 - p22 [51-250]
McLerran, Alice - *The Ghost Dance (Illus. by Paul Morin)*
    c HB Guide - v7 - Fall '96 - p368 [51-250]
    The Year of the Ranch (Illus. by Kimberly Bulcken Root)
    c CBRS - v24 - Ag '96 - p165 [51-250]
    c HB Guide - v7 - Fall '96 - p266 [51-250]
McLeskey, Charles H - *Geriatric Anesthesiology*
    SciTech - v21 - Mr '97 - p60 [51-250]
McLindon, Michael P - *Privatization and Capital Market Development*
    Choice - v34 - F '97 - p1012 [51-250]
    R&R Bk N - v12 - F '97 - p48 [51-250]
McLoughlin, Andrea - *Simple Science Experiments (Illus. by Lynn Adams)*
    c SLJ - v42 - Ag '96 - p139 [51-250]
McLuhan, Marshall - *On McLhan*
    LJ - v122 - Ja '97 - p140 [51-250]
McLuhan, T C - *Cathedrals of the Spirit*
    Books - v10 - Je '96 - p21 [1-50]
    Smith - v27 - S '96 - p114+ [501+]
McLuskie, Kathleen E - *Dekker and Heywood*
    MLR - v92 - Ja '97 - p177+ [501+]
McLynn, Frank - *Carl Gustav Jung*
    Econ - v340 - S 14 '96 - p6* [501+]
    TLS - S 27 '96 - p29 [501+]
McLynn, Neil B - *Ambrose of Milan: Church and Court in a Christian Capital*
    CHR - v82 - Jl '96 - p499+ [501+]
McMahan, Chris - *Buddy Concrackle's Amazing Adventure*
    y BIC - v25 - N '96 - p33+ [501+]
    c Quill & Q - v62 - Ag '96 - p43 [51-250]
McMahon, Christopher - *Authority and Democracy*
    Phil R - v105 - Ap '96 - p272+ [501+]
    RM - v49 - Je '96 - p934+ [501+]
McMahon, Eileen M - *What Parish Are You From?*
    AHR - v101 - D '96 - p1640+ [501+]
    CHR - v83 - Ja '97 - p145+ [251-500]
    CLW - v67 - Mr '97 - p41 [251-500]
McMahon, Franci - *Staying the Distance*
    Aethlon - v13 - Fall '95 - p136+ [251-500]
McMahon, Gary - *Lessons in Economic Policy for Eastern Europe from Latin America*
    JEL - v34 - S '96 - p1483 [51-250]
McMahon, Katherine - *Footsteps*
    TES - Ja 17 '97 - p9* [51-250]
    TLS - Ja 10 '97 - p21 [251-500]
McMahon, Martha - *Engendering Motherhood*
    JMF - v58 - Ag '96 - p806+ [501+]
McMahon, Patricia - *Listen for the Bus (Illus. by John Godt)*
    c LA - v73 - O '96 - p440 [51-250]
    Summer Tunes (Illus. by Peter Simon)
    c HB Guide - v8 - Spr '97 - p159 [51-250]
    c SLJ - v42 - O '96 - p136 [51-250]
McMains, Joel - *Dog Training Projects for Young People*
    c Dog Fan - v27 - N '96 - p88 [501+]
McManamon, John M - *Pierpaolo Vergerio the Elder*
    Choice - v34 - My '97 - p1484 [51-250]
McMane, Fred - *Scottie Pippen*
    c HB Guide - v7 - Fall '96 - p360 [51-250]
McMann, Evelyn De R - *Biographical Index to Artists in Canada*
    r Quill & Q - v62 - Jl '96 - p50 [51-250]
McManners, Hugh - *Biking: An Outdoor Adventure Handbook*
    c CLW - v67 - D '96 - p64 [51-250]
    c Sch Lib - v45 - F '97 - p39 [51-250]
    The Outdoor Adventure Handbook
    c BL - v93 - D 1 '96 - p651 [51-250]
    c HB Guide - v7 - Fall '96 - p362 [51-250]
    y Kliatt - v30 - N '96 - p31 [51-250]
    c Par Ch - v20 - O '96 - p25 [51-250]
    c SB - v32 - O '96 - p212 [51-250]
    c Sch Lib - v44 - Ag '96 - p112+ [51-250]
    Top Guns
    A & S Sm - v11 - F '97 - p87 [1-50]
McManus, James - *Going to the Sun*
    A Lib - v27 - Ag '96 - p71 [1-50]
    BW - v27 - Mr 2 '97 - p4 [501+]
    PW - v244 - Ja 27 '97 - p103 [1-50]
McManus, Patrick - *Mountain Goats Never Say Cheese. Audio Version*
    BWatch - v17 - D '96 - p11 [1-50]

McManus, Patrick F - *Never Cry Arp! and Other Great Adventures*
    y BL - v92 - Ag '96 - p1896 [51-250]
    c CCB-B - v50 - S '96 - p22+ [51-250]
    c HB Guide - v7 - Fall '96 - p294 [51-250]
    c KR - v64 - My 1 '96 - p690+ [51-250]
McManus, Ron - *Structured Exercises for Promoting Family and Group Strengths*
    J ClinPsyc - v57 - D '96 - p598+ [501+]
McMaster, H R - *Dereliction of Duty*
    KR - v65 - Ap 1 '97 - p529 [251-500]
    PW - v244 - Ap 21 '97 - p56 [51-250]
McMaster, Juliet - *Jane Austen's Business*
    R&R Bk N - v11 - Je '96 - p64 [51-250]
McMaster, Shawn - *60 Super Simple Magic Tricks (Illus. by Leo Abbett)*
    c SLJ - v43 - F '97 - p92 [51-250]
McMenamin, Donna - *Popular Arts of Mexico 1850-1950*
    LJ - v122 - F 15 '97 - p131 [51-250]
McMichael, Philip - *Food and Agrarian Orders in the World-Economy*
    BusLR - v21 - 3 '96 - p251+ [251-500]
    CS - v25 - S '96 - p600+ [501+]
McMillan, Bruce - *Counting Wildflowers*
    cr BL - v93 - Ap 1 '97 - p1341 [1-50]
    Eating Fractions
    c BL - v93 - Ap 1 '97 - p1341 [1-50]
    Grandfather's Trolley (Illus. by Bruce McMillan)
    c ECEJ - v23 - Sum '96 - p222 [51-250]
    c RT - v50 - D '96 - p346 [51-250]
    Jelly Beans for Sale (Illus. by Bruce McMillan)
    c BL - v93 - S 1 '96 - p139+ [51-250]
    c BL - v93 - Ap 1 '97 - p1296 [1-50]
    c CCB-B - v50 - O '96 - p69 [51-250]
    c HB Guide - v8 - Spr '97 - p110 [51-250]
    c Learning - v25 - Ja '97 - p56 [1-50]
    c SLJ - v42 - O '96 - p115 [51-250]
    Summer Ice
    c LA - v73 - O '96 - p439 [251-500]
McMillan, John - *Reforming Asian Socialism*
    JEL - v35 - Mr '97 - p291 [51-250]
McMillan, Katharine Kaye - *House Comfortable*
    BL - v93 - S 1 '96 - p49 [51-250]
    LJ - v121 - S 15 '96 - p66 [51-250]
McMillan, Lisa - *Positive Cooking*
    LJ - v122 - Mr 15 '97 - p80+ [51-250]
    PW - v244 - Ja 27 '97 - p99 [51-250]
McMillan, Rosalyn - *Knowing*
    Bloom Rev - v17 - Ja '97 - p19 [1-50]
    PW - v244 - Mr 17 '97 - p81 [1-50]
McMillan, Terry - *How Stella Got Her Groove Back*
    Bloom Rev - v17 - Ja '97 - p20 [501+]
    CSM - v88 - S 19 '96 - p14 [51-250]
    Lon R Bks - v19 - F 6 '97 - p25+ [501+]
McMillen, Margot Ford - *Paris, Tightwad, and Peculiar*
    r Names - v44 - S '96 - p245+ [501+]
McMinn, W G - *Nationalism and Federalism in Australia*
    AHR - v101 - O '96 - p1264 [501+]
McMorris, Mark - *The Black Reeds*
    VV - v42 - Ap 29 '97 - p55 [501+]
McMullan, Gordon - *The Politics of Unease in the Plays of John Fletcher*
    Ren Q - v49 - Aut '96 - p652+ [501+]
McMullan, Jim - *Cheatin' Hearts, Broken Dreams, and Stomped-On Love*
    r BL - v93 - N 15 '96 - p616 [51-250]
McMullan, Kate - *If You Were My Bunny (Illus. by David McPhail)*
    c HB Guide - v7 - Fall '96 - p266 [51-250]
    c Par - v71 - D '96 - p251 [1-50]
    Noel the First (Illus. by Jim McMullan)
    c BL - v93 - Ja '97 - p870 [251-500]
    c Dance - v70 - D '96 - p53 [1-50]
    c HB Guide - v8 - Spr '97 - p38 [51-250]
    c KR - v64 - O 15 '96 - p1535 [51-250]
    c PW - v243 - O 7 '96 - p73+ [51-250]
    c SLJ - v42 - D '96 - p100 [51-250]
McMullen, Joanne Halleran - *Writing against God*
    Choice - v34 - N '96 - p457 [51-250]
McMurry, Sally Ann - *Transforming Rural Life*
    AHR - v101 - D '96 - p1620+ [501+]
    HRNB - v25 - Fall '96 - p6 [251-500]
    J Am St - v30 - Ap '96 - p176+ [501+]
McMurtry, Larry - *The Late Child*
    PW - v243 - N 4 '96 - p71 [1-50]

Zeke and Ned
    BL - v93 - N 15 '96 - p549 [51-250]
    BW - v27 - Ja 5 '97 - p5 [501+]
    Ent W - Ja 24 '97 - p52 [51-250]
    KR - v64 - N 15 '96 - p1625+ [251-500]
    LATBR - Ja 19 '97 - p6 [501+]
    LJ - v122 - Ja '97 - p148 [51-250]
    NYTBR - v102 - Ja 19 '97 - p18 [51-250]
    PW - v243 - D 2 '96 - p40+ [51-250]
    Time - v149 - F 10 '97 - p82 [251-500]
McNab, Andy - *Immediate Action*
    Mar Crp G - v80 - O '96 - p76+ [501+]
McNab, Claire - *Inner Circle*
    Advocate - S 17 '96 - p60 [1-50]
    Aust Bk R - D '96 - p79+ [501+]
McNair, Elisabeth Jane - *Robert Burns: Maker of Rhymes*
(Illus. by Scoular Anderson)
  c Bks Keeps - Mr '97 - p24 [51-250]
McNair, James - *James McNair's Beans and Grains*
  y Kliatt - v31 - Mr '97 - p36 [51-250]
McNair, Wesley - *The Town of No. My Brother Running*
    LJ - v122 - Ap 1 '97 - p134 [1-50]
McNall, Rebecca - *Angel of God, What's Your Name?*
(Illus. by Joan Hutson)
  c CLW - v67 - Mr '97 - p35+ [51-250]
McNally, Raymond T - *Dracula: Truth and Terror.*
Electronic Media Version
    Trib Bks - F 2 '97 - p7 [51-250]
McNally, Terrence - *Terrence McNally: Collected Plays.*
Vol. 2
    BL - v93 - S 15 '96 - p203 [251-500]
    LJ - v122 - Ja '97 - p98 [51-250]
McNally, Vincent J - *Reform, Revolution and Reaction*
    CHR - v83 - Ja '97 - p111+ [251-500]
    Historian - v59 - Win '97 - p470+ [501+]
McNamara, Brooks - *Day of Jubilee*
    LJ - v122 - Ap 1 '97 - p106+ [51-250]
    PW - v244 - Mr 24 '97 - p73 [51-250]
Step Right Up. Rev. Ed.
    JPC - v30 - Sum '96 - p277+ [251-500]
McNamara, Dennis L - *Textiles and Industrial Transition*
in Japan
    Pac A - v69 - Fall '96 - p414+ [501+]
    T&C - v38 - Ja '97 - p267+ [501+]
Trade and Transformation in Korea 1876-1945
    Choice - v34 - Ja '97 - p846 [51-250]
    R&R Bk N - v11 - N '96 - p34 [51-250]
McNamara, Jo Ann Kay - *Sisters in Arms*
    Am - v176 - Mr 29 '97 - p26+ [501+]
    BL - v93 - S 1 '96 - p39 [51-250]
    BW - v26 - N 24 '96 - p4+ [501+]
    Choice - v34 - Ja '97 - p812 [51-250]
    Comw - v123 - N 22 '96 - p28+ [501+]
    New R - v215 - O 14 '96 - p39+ [501+]
    NYRB - v43 - D 19 '96 - p31+ [501+]
    NYTBR - v101 - O 13 '96 - p16+ [501+]
    RR - v56 - Mr '97 - p212+ [501+]
    TLS - Mr 28 '97 - p6 [501+]
McNamara, Kenneth J - *Evolutionary Change and*
Heterochrony
    Choice - v34 - N '96 - p481+ [51-250]
McNamara, Kevin R - *Urban Verbs*
    Choice - v34 - Ja '97 - p781 [51-250]
McNamara, Robert P - *Sex, Scams, and Street Life*
    Am Ethnol - v24 - F '97 - p213+ [501+]
    SF - v75 - S '96 - p395+ [251-500]
The Times Square Hustler
    SF - v75 - S '96 - p395+ [251-500]
McNamara, Sheila - *Traditional Chinese Medicine*
    Books - v11 - Ap '97 - p21 [1-50]
McNamee, Eoin - *The Last of Deeds. Love in History*
    BL - v93 - N 15 '96 - p572 [51-250]
    KR - v64 - S 1 '96 - p1260 [251-500]
    LATBR - N 24 '96 - p1+ [501+]
    LATBR - D 29 '96 - p5+ [51-250]
    NYTBR - v101 - N 17 '96 - p21 [501+]
    PW - v243 - S 30 '96 - p61 [51-250]
Resurrection Man
    NYTBR - v101 - D 22 '96 - p20 [1-50]
McNamee, Gregory - *A Desert Bestiary*
    CAY - v17 - Win '96 - p7 [51-250]
    PW - v243 - N 25 '96 - p69+ [51-250]
McNamee, John - *Clay Vessels*
    RR - v55 - N '96 - p660 [1-50]
McNamee, Thomas - *The Return of the Wolf to*
Yellowstone
  y BL - v93 - My 1 '97 - p1466 [51-250]
    KR - v65 - Mr 1 '97 - p358 [51-250]
    PW - v244 - Ap 28 '97 - p66 [51-250]
McNaron, Toni A H - *Poisoned Ivy*
    LJ - v122 - Mr 15 '97 - p72 [51-250]

McNaspy, Clement J - *Play On!*
    Am - v175 - S 21 '96 - p31 [51-250]
McNaught, Brian - *Now That I'm Out, What Do I Do?*
    LJ - v122 - My 1 '97 - p128 [51-250]
    PW - v244 - Mr 31 '97 - p55 [51-250]
McNaughton, Colin - *Boo! (Illus. by Colin McNaughton)*
  c CBRS - v25 - S '96 - p5 [1-50]
  c HB Guide - v8 - Spr '97 - p38 [51-250]
  c SLJ - v42 - S '96 - p184+ [51-250]
Captain Abdul's Pirate School
  c Magpies - v11 - Jl '96 - p45 [1-50]
Here Come the Aliens! (Illus. by Colin McNaughton)
  c Inst - v105 - My '96 - p71 [51-250]
  c RT - O '96 - p130 [1-50]
Oops! (Illus. by Colin McNaughton)
  c JB - v60 - D '96 - p236 [51-250]
  c Sch Lib - v44 - N '96 - p147 [51-250]
Suddenly!
  c Magpies - v11 - Jl '96 - p45 [1-50]
Watch Out for the Giant-Killers!
  c Bks Keeps - Jl '96 - p12 [51-250]
McNaughton, Janet - *To Dance at the Palais Royale*
  y Quill & Q - v62 - Ag '96 - p42 [251-500]
McNeal, Tom - *The Dog Who Lost His Bob (Illus. by John*
Sandford)
  c BL - v93 - S 1 '96 - p144 [51-250]
  c CBRS - v25 - Win '97 - p64 [51-250]
  c CCB-B - v50 - O '96 - p69 [51-250]
  c HB Guide - v8 - Spr '97 - p39 [51-250]
  c SLJ - v42 - N '96 - p88 [51-250]
McNee, Mona - *Step by Step. Rev. and Expanded Ed.*
    TES - Ja 10 '97 - p14* [501+]
McNeely, Connie L - *Constructing the Nation-State*
    AAPSS-A - v550 - Mr '97 - p172+ [251-500]
    AJS - v102 - S '96 - p601+ [501+]
    CS - v25 - N '96 - p742+ [501+]
McNeely, Jeffrey A - *Expanding Partnerships in*
Conservation
    Env - v39 - Ja '97 - p25+ [251-500]
McNeil, Alex - *Total Television. 4th Ed.*
  r ARBA - v28 - '97 - p516 [51-250]
McNeil, Beth - *Patron Behavior in Libraries*
    LAR - v98 - N '96 - p594 [51-250]
    RQ - v36 - Fall '96 - p157 [251-500]
McNeil, Florence - *Breathing Each Other's Air*
    Can Lit - Spr '97 - p236+ [501+]
McNeil, Ian - *An Encyclopedia of the History of*
Technology
  r New Sci - v153 - F 8 '97 - p43 [51-250]
McNeil, Jean - *Hunting down Home*
    BIC - v25 - O '96 - p40 [251-500]
    Wom R Bks - v14 - N '96 - p16 [501+]
McNeil, Keith - *Colonial and Revolution Songbook*
  c SLJ - v42 - D '96 - p132 [51-250]
McNeil, Legs - *Please Kill Me*
    TLS - D 6 '96 - p28 [501+]
    Utne R - Jl '96 - p109 [51-250]
McNeil, W K - *Appalachian Images in Folk and Popular*
Culture. 2nd Ed.
    J Am Cult - v19 - Spr '96 - p101 [51-250]
McNeil, William - *Europe's Steppe Frontier*
    Wil Q - v21 - Win '97 - p37 [51-250]
McNeil, William F - *The King of Swat*
    LJ - v122 - F 1 '97 - p82+ [1-50]
McNeil, William Hardy - *The Pursuit of Power*
    Reason - v28 - D '96 - p40 [51-250]
McNeill, J R - *The Mountains of the Mediterranean World*
    AAAGA - v86 - D '96 - p780+ [501+]
McNeill, John J - *Freedom, Glorious Freedom*
    Rel St Rev - v22 - O '96 - p336 [51-250]
McNeill, Robert - *UPI Stylebook. 3rd Ed.*
  r BL - v93 - My 1 '97 - p1514 [1-50]
McNeill, Sarah - *Ancient Egyptian People*
  c SLJ - v43 - Mr '97 - p204 [51-250]
Ancient Egyptian Places
  c SLJ - v43 - Mr '97 - p204 [51-250]
Roman Fort
  c Bks Keeps - Ja '97 - p23+ [51-250]
  c Sch Lib - v45 - F '97 - p39 [51-250]
McNeill, William H - *Keeping Together in Time*
    Comw - v123 - O 11 '96 - p19+ [501+]
    JIH - v27 - Spr '97 - p664+ [251-500]
McNeilly, Mark - *Sun Tzu and the Art of Business*
    Choice - v34 - Ap '97 - p1384 [51-250]
McNerney, Kathleen - *Double Minorities of Spain*
  r MLR - v91 - O '96 - p1024+ [501+]
McNey, Martha - *Leslie's Story (Illus. by Martha McNey)*
  c Cur R - v36 - N '96 - p12 [51-250]
  c HB Guide - v8 - Spr '97 - p95 [1-50]
  c SLJ - v42 - S '96 - p195 [51-250]

McNichol, Tom - *Barking at Prozac*
    Dog Fan - v28 - Ja '97 - p37 [1-50]
McNickle, Chris - *To Be Mayor of New York*
    J Urban H - v22 - Jl '96 - p656+ [501+]
McNitt, Robert W - *Sailing at the U.S. Naval Academy*
    BL - v93 - S 15 '96 - p203 [51-250]
McNulty, Faith - *Endangered Animals (Illus. by Carol*
Schwartz)
  c Learning - v25 - Ag '96 - p96 [51-250]
McNulty, Sara - *Report to the Governor's Hemp and*
Related Fiber Crops Task Force (Kentucky)
    J Gov Info - v23 - S '96 - p584 [51-250]
McNulty, Tim - *Olympic National Park*
  r BL - v93 - S 15 '96 - p212 [1-50]
  y Kliatt - v30 - S '96 - p35 [51-250]
McNutt, Charles H - *Prehistory of the Central Mississippi*
Valley
    R&R Bk N - v11 - N '96 - p16 [51-250]
McNutt, John - *Running Wild*
    BL - v93 - Mr 15 '97 - p1212 [51-250]
    LJ - v122 - Mr 15 '97 - p84+ [51-250]
    PW - v244 - F 24 '97 - p80 [51-250]
  y SB - v33 - My '97 - p108 [51-250]
McPartlan, Paul - *Sacrament of Salvation*
    ER - v48 - Jl '96 - p422+ [501+]
McPhail, Catherine - *Run, Zan, Run*
  c Sch Lib - v44 - Ag '96 - p96+ [501+]
McPhail, David - *Edward and the Pirates (Illus. by David*
McPhail)
  c KR - v65 - Ap 1 '97 - p559 [51-250]
  c PW - v244 - F 10 '97 - p82+ [51-250]
  c Trib Bks - My 4 '97 - p6 [51-250]
In Flight with David McPhail
  c HB - v72 - S '96 - p609 [51-250]
  c HB Guide - v7 - Fall '96 - p371 [51-250]
Pigs Ahoy! (Illus. by David McPhail)
  c Magpies - v11 - S '96 - p27 [51-250]
  c RT - O '96 - p131 [1-50]
  c RT - v50 - Mr '97 - p503 [51-250]
Pigs Aplenty, Pigs Galore!
  c PW - v243 - N 18 '96 - p78 [51-250]
Those Can-Do Pigs (Illus. by David McPhail)
  c Ch BWatch - v6 - O '96 - p5 [1-50]
  c Emerg Lib - v24 - Mr '97 - p45 [1-50]
  c HB Guide - v8 - Spr '97 - p39 [1-50]
  c SLJ - v42 - S '96 - p185 [51-250]
McPhail, Mark Lawrence - *Zen in the Art of Rhetoric*
    R&R Bk N - v12 - F '97 - p76 [51-250]
McPhee, John - *Irons in the Fire*
    BL - v93 - Ja '97 - p777 [51-250]
    BW - v27 - Ap 13 '97 - p13 [51-250]
    KR - v65 - F 1 '97 - p203 [251-500]
    LJ - v122 - F 15 '97 - p136 [51-250]
    NYTBR - v102 - Ap 13 '97 - p21 [51-250]
    PW - v244 - Ja 27 '97 - p84 [51-250]
Reader (Runger). Audio Version
    BWatch - v18 - Mr '97 - p8 [1-50]
McPhee, Martha A - *Bright Angel Time*
    KR - v65 - Mr 15 '97 - p408 [251-500]
    LJ - v122 - Ap 1 '97 - p128 [51-250]
    PW - v244 - Ap 7 '97 - p74 [51-250]
McPhee, Peter - *A Way with Horses*
  c Quill & Q - v62 - Jl '96 - p56 [51-250]
McPherson, Christopher - *Everything but the Truth*
    BIC - v25 - N '96 - p24 [501+]
McPherson, James M - *Drawn with the Sword*
    CC - v114 - Ja 1 '97 - p25 [51-250]
    HRNB - v25 - Fall '96 - p7+ [251-500]
    VQR - v72 - Aut '96 - p116* [51-250]
For Cause and Comrades
  y BL - v93 - F 1 '97 - p924 [51-250]
    KR - v65 - Ja 1 '97 - p42+ [251-500]
    LATBR - Mr 30 '97 - p8 [501+]
    LJ - v122 - Mr 15 '97 - p74 [51-250]
    NYTBR - v102 - Mr 23 '97 - p22 [501+]
    NYTLa - v146 - Mr 6 '97 - pC22 [501+]
    PW - v244 - Ja 27 '97 - p89 [251-500]
    Wil Q - v21 - Spr '97 - p109 [501+]
    WSJ-Cent - v99 - Mr 21 '97 - pA17 [501+]
We Cannot Escape History
    J Gov Info - v23 - S '96 - p582 [1-50]
McPherson, Karen S - *Incriminations: Guilty Women/*
Telling Stories
    FR - v70 - O '96 - p104+ [501+]
    MP - v94 - F '97 - p412+ [501+]
McPherson, Kenneth - *The Indian Ocean*
    AHR - v102 - F '97 - p159+ [501+]
McPherson, Natalie - *Machines and Economic Growth*
    BusLR - v21 - 3 '96 - p252+ [251-500]
McPherson, Sandra - *Edge Effect*
    Poet - v169 - Mr '97 - p341+ [501+]

The Spaces between Birds
Poet - v169 - Mr '97 - p343+ [501+]
McPherson, Stephanie Sammartino - *TV's Forgotten Hero*
c BL - v93 - F 1 '97 - p937 [51-250]
c Cur R - v36 - D '96 - p13 [51-250]
c HB Guide - v8 - Spr '97 - p159 [51-250]
c SLJ - v43 - F '97 - p120 [51-250]
McPhillimy, Bill - *Controlling Your Class*
TES - Ja 24 '97 - p10* [501+]
McQuade, Jacqueline - *Christmas with Teddy Bear (Illus. by Jacqueline McQuade)*
c BL - v93 - S 1 '96 - p137 [51-250]
c CBRS - v25 - D '96 - p40 [51-250]
c HB Guide - v8 - Spr '97 - p39 [51-250]
c KR - v64 - O 1 '96 - p1476 [51-250]
c PW - v243 - S 30 '96 - p89 [51-250]
c SLJ - v42 - O '96 - p38 [51-250]
Cosy Christmas with Teddy Bear
c Bks Keeps - N '96 - p21 [51-250]
Cosy Moments with Teddy Bear
c Books - v11 - Ap '97 - p24 [51-250]
McQuade, Joe - *Baptized in Dirty Water*
Sm Pr R - v29 - F '97 - p12 [51-250]
McQuarrie, Edward F - *The Market Research Toolbox*
Choice - v34 - S '96 - p172 [51-250]
McQueen, Rod - *Who Killed Confederation Life?*
Quill & Q - v62 - N '96 - p37 [251-500]
McRae, Hamish - *The World in 2020*
JEL - v35 - Mr '97 - p211 [51-250]
McRae, W C - *Montana Handbook. 3rd Ed.*
r BL - v93 - S 15 '96 - p212 [1-50]
Montana Handbook. 3rd Rev. Ed.
r BWatch - v17 - S '96 - p5 [51-250]
McRandle, James H - *The Antique Drums of War*
JIH - v27 - Aut '96 - p281+ [251-500]
McRedmond, Louis - *Modern Irish Lives*
r Choice - v34 - My '97 - p1478 [51-250]
McReynolds, Mary - *Wells of Glory*
y VOYA - v19 - D '96 - p272 [51-250]
McRobbie, Angela - *Postmodernism and Popular Culture*
J Am Cult - v19 - Sum '96 - p144+ [251-500]
JPC - v30 - Fall '96 - p212+ [251-500]
McRobbie, David - *See How They Run*
y Aust Bk R - Ag '96 - p63+ [501+]
y Magpies - v11 - S '96 - p38 [51-250]
McRobbie, Narelle - *Who's That Jumbun in the Log? (Illus. by Grace Fielding)*
c Aust Bk R - S '96 - p61+ [501+]
McSean, Tony - *Health Information--New Possibilities*
LR - v45 - 8 '96 - p55+ [251-500]
McShane, Clay - *Down the Asphalt Path*
HRNB - v25 - Fall '96 - p10 [501-500]
McShane, Marilyn D - *Encyclopedia of American Prisons*
r ARBA - v28 - '97 - p227 [51-250]
r Choice - v34 - S '96 - p95 [51-250]
r LJ - v122 - Ap 15 '97 - p37 [51-250]
r RQ - v36 - Fall '96 - p125+ [251-500]
McSmith, Andy - *Faces of Labour*
NS - v125 - S 27 '96 - p63 [501+]
Obs - S 29 '96 - p15* [501+]
TLS - O 18 '96 - p12 [501+]
McSween, Harry Y - *Fanfare for Earth*
y BL - v93 - Mr 15 '97 - p1212 [51-250]
KR - v65 - Ja 1 '97 - p43 [251-500]
PW - v244 - Ja 20 '97 - p384 [251-500]
McWhirter, Darien A - *The End of Affirmative Action*
Choice - v34 - Ja '97 - p876 [51-250]
McWilliam, Candia - *Debateable Land*
Econ - v343 - Ap 26 '97 - p83+ [501+]
McWilliam, Neil - *A Bibliography of Salon Criticism in Paris from the Ancien Regime to the Restoration 1699-1827*
r FR - v70 - D '96 - p371+ [501+]
A Bibliography of Salon Criticism in Paris from the July Monarchy to the Second Republic 1831-1851
r FR - v70 - D '96 - p371+ [501+]
McWilliam, P J - *Practical Strategies for Family-Centered Early Intervention*
SciTech - v21 - Mr '97 - p62 [51-250]
Mda, Zakes - *When People Play People*
Theat J - v49 - Mr '97 - p83+ [501+]
Meacham, Cory J - *How the Tiger Lost Its Stripes*
y BL - v93 - My 1 '97 - p1466 [51-250]
LJ - v122 - My 1 '97 - p135 [51-250]
Meacham, Margaret - *Oyster Moon (Illus. by Marcy Dunn Ramsey)*
c SLJ - v42 - N '96 - p109 [51-250]

Meachum, Virginia - *Steven Spielberg: Hollywood Filmmaker*
c HB Guide - v7 - Fall '96 - p371 [51-250]
c SLJ - v42 - O '96 - p136 [51-250]
Mead, Alice - *Adem's Cross*
y BL - v93 - N 15 '96 - p579+ [51-250]
y BL - v93 - Ap 1 '97 - p1294 [1-50]
c CBRS - v25 - Ja '97 - p58+ [51-250]
y CCB-B - v50 - Ja '97 - p180 [51-250]
y HB Guide - v8 - Spr '97 - p82 [51-250]
y JAAL - v40 - F '97 - p406 [51-250]
c KR - v64 - O 15 '96 - p1535+ [51-250]
c PW - v243 - O 21 '96 - p84 [51-250]
c SLJ - v42 - N '96 - p109 [51-250]
y VOYA - v19 - D '96 - p272 [251-500]
Junebug
c PW - v244 - F 3 '97 - p108 [1-50]
c RT - v50 - Mr '97 - p502+ [51-250]
Mead, Jane - *The Lord and the General Din of the World*
Ant R - v55 - Spr '97 - p246 [251-500]
Sm Pr R - v29 - F '97 - p1+ [501+]
Mead, Juliette - *Intimate Strangers*
KR - v64 - S 1 '96 - p1261 [251-500]
Mead, Richard - *I Wonder Why the Telephone Rings and Other Questions about Communication*
c HB Guide - v8 - Spr '97 - p132 [51-250]
c JB - v60 - O '96 - p196+ [51-250]
c Sch Lib - v44 - N '96 - p163 [51-250]
Meade, Glenn - *Brandenburg*
BL - v93 - My 1 '97 - p1482 [51-250]
KR - v65 - Ap 1 '97 - p492 [251-500]
PW - v244 - Ap 28 '97 - p47 [251-500]
Snow Wolf
BW - v26 - Ag 4 '96 - p8 [51-250]
LJ - v121 - O 1 '96 - p47 [1-50]
PW - v244 - Mr 31 '97 - p72 [1-50]
Snow Wolf (Michael). Audio Version
y Kliatt - v30 - N '96 - p45 [51-250]
LJ - v121 - N 15 '96 - p106 [51-250]
Meade, J E, 1907- - *Full Employment Regained?*
JEL - v34 - S '96 - p1423 [51-250]
Meade, Marion - *Cut to the Chase*
Spec - v277 - N 16 '96 - p43 [1-50]
Meadowcroft, James - *Conceptualizing the State*
TLS - Mr 28 '97 - p26 [501+]
The Liberal Political Tradition
APSR - v91 - Mr '97 - p174+ [501+]
R&R Bk N - v11 - N '96 - p48 [51-250]
TLS - S 20 '96 - p3+ [501+]
Meadowcroft, T J - *Aramaic Daniel and Greek Daniel*
Rel St Rev - v23 - Ja '97 - p86 [51-250]
Meadows, Anne - *Digging Up Butch and Sundance. Rev. Ed.*
Roundup M - v4 - F '97 - p25 [51-250]
Meadows, Eddie S - *Jazz Research and Performance Materials. 2nd Ed.*
r Notes - v53 - D '96 - p480+ [501+]
Meadows, Kenneth - *Rune Power*
Horoscope - v62 - N '96 - p30+ [501+]
Meadows, Matthew - *Edgar Degas*
c Sch Lib - v44 - N '96 - p161 [51-250]
Pablo Picasso
c BL - v93 - F 1 '97 - p937 [51-250]
c HB Guide - v8 - Spr '97 - p139 [51-250]
c KR - v64 - O 15 '96 - p1808 [51-250]
c PW - v243 - D 30 '96 - p68 [51-250]
c SLJ - v43 - Mr '97 - p179 [51-250]
Meale, Carol M - *Readings in Medieval English Romance*
MLR - v92 - Ap '97 - p426+ [501+]
Mean Streets
p Arm Det - v29 - Sum '96 - p322 [1-50]
Meaney, Gerardine - *(Un)like Subjects*
MLR - v91 - Jl '96 - p686+ [501+]
Means, Russell - *Where White Men Fear to Tread*
y BL - v93 - D 15 '96 - p717 [1-50]
Measday, Stephen - *A Pig Called Francis Bacon*
Aust Bk R - S '96 - p60+ [501+]
Measell, James - *Imperial Glass Encyclopedia. Vol. 1*
r Ant & CM - v101 - Ag '96 - p18 [1-50]
Measham, Anthony R - *India's Family Welfare Program*
JEL - v34 - D '96 - p2068 [51-250]
Supplement to India's Family Welfare Program
JEL - v34 - D '96 - p2068+ [51-250]
Mebane, Robert C - *Adventures with Atoms and Molecules*
c CLW - v66 - Je '96 - p45+ [51-250]
Mechanic, David - *Inescapable Decisions*
AAPSS-A - v547 - S '96 - p185+ [251-500]

Meckelnborg, Christina - *Bartholomaei Coloniensis Ecloga Bucolici Carminis. Silva Carminum*
Ren Q - v49 - Win '96 - p840+ [501+]
Medawar, Mardi Oakley - *Death at Rainy Mountain*
Arm Det - v29 - Fall '96 - p489 [251-500]
Medawar, Peter - *The Case of the Spotted Mice and Other Classic Essays on Science*
Books - v10 - Je '96 - p22 [1-50]
Meddaugh, Susan - *Hog-Eye*
c Inst - v105 - My '96 - p70 [1-50]
Martha Blah Blah (Illus. by Susan Meddaugh)
c BL - v93 - S 15 '96 - p248 [51-250]
c CCB-B - v50 - D '96 - p144 [51-250]
c HB - v72 - N '96 - p727+ [51-250]
c HB Guide - v8 - Spr '97 - p39 [51-250]
c KR - v64 - S 1 '96 - p1325 [51-250]
c Par Ch - v20 - O '96 - p3 [51-250]
c PW - v243 - N 4 '96 - p48 [1-50]
c SLJ - v42 - N '96 - p88+ [51-250]
c SLJ - v42 - D '96 - p31 [51-250]
c Trib Bks - Ja 12 '97 - p5 [51-250]
Martha Calling (Illus. by Susan Meddaugh)
c PW - v243 - O 21 '96 - p85 [1-50]
Medearis, Angela Shelf - *The Freedom Riddle (Illus. by John Ward)*
c RT - v50 - O '96 - p154 [51-250]
Haunts: Five Hair-Raising Tales (Illus. by Trina Schart Hyman)
c BL - v93 - F 1 '97 - p941 [51-250]
c CCB-B - v50 - F '97 - p214+ [51-250]
c HB Guide - v8 - Spr '97 - p59 [51-250]
c KR - v64 - N 1 '96 - p1604 [51-250]
c PW - v243 - D 2 '96 - p62 [51-250]
Here Comes the Snow (Illus. by Maxie Chambliss)
c BL - v92 - Ag '96 - p1910 [51-250]
c SLJ - v42 - S '96 - p185 [51-250]
Rum-a-Tum-Tum (Illus. by James E Ransome)
c BL - v93 - My 1 '97 - p1502 [51-250]
c PW - v244 - Ap 14 '97 - p74 [51-250]
Skin Deep and Other Teenage Reflections (Illus. by Michael Bryant)
y RT - v50 - O '96 - p142 [1-50]
y RT - v50 - Mr '97 - p479 [51-250]
The Spray-Paint Mystery
c BL - v93 - F 15 '97 - p1023 [51-250]
Tailypo: A Newfangled Tall Tale (Illus. by Sterling Brown)
c BL - v93 - N 1 '96 - p504 [51-250]
c Ch BWatch - v6 - D '96 - p3 [51-250]
c HB Guide - v8 - Spr '97 - p104 [51-250]
c SLJ - v43 - Ja '97 - p105+ [51-250]
Too Much Talk (Illus. by Stefano Vitale)
c Bks Keeps - Mr '97 - p20 [51-250]
c RT - v50 - O '96 - p157 [51-250]
The Zebra-Riding Cowboy (Illus. by Maria Cristina Brusca)
c PW - v244 - Mr 17 '97 - p85 [1-50]
Medeiros, Teresa - *Touch of Enchantment*
PW - v244 - Ap 21 '97 - p68 [51-250]
Medhurst, Martin J - *Beyond the Rhetorical Presidency*
Choice - v34 - Ja '97 - p873 [51-250]
R&R Bk N - v11 - D '96 - p16 [51-250]
Landmark Essays on American Public Address
QJS - v82 - Ag '96 - p302+ [501+]
Media Courses UK 1996
r LAR - v98 - D '96 - p652 [51-250]
Media Review Digest 1996
r ARBA - v28 - '97 - p7 [251-500]
Medic, Kris - *Pruning*
Hort - v94 - F '97 - p66 [251-500]
Medicott, Mary - *The Big-Wide-Mouthed Toad-Frog and Other Stories (Illus. by Sue Williams)*
c Bks Keeps - Jl '96 - p7 [51-250]
The King with Dirty Feet and Other Stories (Illus. by Sue Williams)
c Bks Keeps - Jl '96 - p7 [51-250]
The River That Went to the Sky (Illus. by Ademola Akintola)
c CLW - v66 - Je '96 - p50+ [51-250]
Medieval Knighthood V
Albion - v28 - Win '96 - p666+ [501+]
The Medieval Year Diary 1997
LAR - v98 - D '96 - p649 [1-50]
Medina, John J - *The Clock of Ages*
Am Sci - v85 - Mr '97 - p186 [501+]
Mediterranean Politics
p TLS - N 15 '96 - p26+ [501+]
Mediterranean Strategies
J Gov Info - v23 - S '96 - p665 [51-250]
Medlin, William K - *Fire Mountain*
WHQ - v27 - Win '96 - p547 [51-250]

Mednick, Christina Singleton - *San Cristobal: Voices and Visions of the Galisteo Basin*
    Bloom Rev - v16 - S '96 - p27 [501+]
Mednick, Fred - *Rebel without a Car*
    H Sch M - v4 - D '96 - p54 [51-250]
Mednicki, Bernard - *Never Be Afraid*
    BL - v93 - Ap 1 '97 - p1279 [51-250]
Medoff, James - *The Indebted Society*
    BL - v93 - S 15 '96 - p190 [51-250]
    Bus W - O 28 '96 - p22 [501+]
    BW - v26 - S 22 '96 - p11 [251-500]
    KR - v64 - Ag 15 '96 - p1216 [251-500]
    LJ - v121 - O 1 '96 - p95 [51-250]
    NYTLa - v146 - S 26 '96 - pC21 [501+]
Medoff, Jillian - *Hunger Point*
    BL - v93 - Ja '97 - p821 [51-250]
    KR - v64 - D 1 '96 - p1696 [251-500]
    LJ - v122 - Ja '97 - p148 [51-250]
    PW - v243 - D 9 '96 - p60 [51-250]
Medwed, Mameve - *Mail*
    BL - v93 - Ap 1 '97 - p1282 [51-250]
    KR - v65 - Mr 15 '97 - p410 [251-500]
    PW - v244 - Mr 3 '97 - p62 [51-250]
Mee, Susie - *Downhome: An Anthology of Southern Women Writers*
    AL - v68 - S '96 - p670 [51-250]
Meehan, Bridget Mary - *God Delights in You*
    CLW - v67 - D '96 - p47 [251-500]
Meehan, Christopher H - *Deadly Waters*
    Arm Det - v29 - Sum '96 - p309 [51-250]
Meehan, Patricia - *The Unnecessary War*
    NYRB - v44 - Ja 9 '97 - p49+ [501+]
Meehan, Paula - *Mysteries of the Home*
    Obs - Ja 5 '97 - p17* [51-250]
Meek, Gary K - *Country Studies in International Accounting: Americas and the Far East*
    JEL - v35 - Mr '97 - p256 [51-250]
    R&R Bk N - v11 - D '96 - p35 [51-250]
Meek, M R D - *Postscript to Murder*
    PW - v244 - My 5 '97 - p202 [51-250]
Meek, Margaret - *Information and Book Learning*
    Bks Keeps - Ja '97 - p18 [51-250]
    Sch Lib - v45 - F '97 - p54+ [51-250]
    TES - Ja 24 '97 - p17* [501+]
Meeker, Clare Hodgson - *Who Wakes Rooster? (Illus. by Megan Halsey)*
    c BL - v93 - N 1 '96 - p508 [51-250]
    c CBRS - v25 - Ja '97 - p52 [1-50]
    c HB Guide - v8 - Spr '97 - p14 [51-250]
    Who Wakes Rooster (Illus. by Megan Halsey)
    c NY - v72 - N 18 '96 - p101 [1-50]
    Who Wakes Rooster? (Illus. by Megan Halsey)
    c SLJ - v42 - S '96 - p185+ [51-250]
Meeker-Lowry, Susan - *Invested in the Common Good*
    Kiplinger - v50 - O '96 - p35 [251-500]
Meeks, Dimitri - *Daily Life of the Egyptian Gods*
    LJ - v121 - O 1 '96 - p84 [51-250]
Meeks, Wayne A - *The Origins of Christian Morality*
    CW - v90 - S '96 - p65 [251-500]
Meer, Ameena - *Bombay Talkie*
    Amerasia J - v22 - 2 '96 - p169+ [501+]
Meer Lecha-Marzo, Fernando De - *El Partido Nacionalista Vasco Ante La Guerra De Espana 1936-1937*
    CHR - v82 - O '96 - p661+ [501+]
Meester, Ronald - *Continuum Percolation*
    SciTech - v20 - D '96 - p23 [51-250]
Meeting the Challenges of Local Government: Final Report
    J Gov Info - v23 - S '96 - p628+ [51-250]
Megantz, Robert C - *How to License Technology*
    SciTech - v20 - N '96 - p3 [51-250]
Megarry, Tim - *Society in Prehistory*
    Choice - v34 - S '96 - p168 [51-250]
Meggers, Betty Jane - *Amazonia: Man and Culture in a Counterfeit Paradise. Rev. Ed.*
    New Sci - v153 - F 15 '97 - p44 [51-250]
Megill, Donald D - *Introduction to Jazz History. 4th Ed.*
    Teach Mus - v4 - F '97 - p49 [51-250]
Mehan, Hugh - *Constructing School Success*
    AJE - v105 - My '97 - p346+ [501+]
    AJS - v102 - Ja '97 - p1198+ [501+]
Mehl-Madrona, Lewis - *Coyote Medicine*
    BL - v93 - F 1 '97 - p916+ [51-250]
    KR - v64 - D 1 '96 - p1721 [251-500]
    LJ - v122 - F 15 '97 - p156 [51-250]
    PW - v244 - Ja 6 '97 - p57+ [51-250]
Mehrer, Mark W - *Cahokia's Countryside*
    Am Ant - v61 - O '96 - p803+ [501+]

Mehta, Gita - *Snakes and Ladders*
    BL - v93 - My 1 '97 - p1477 [51-250]
    KR - v65 - Mr 15 '97 - p445 [251-500]
    LJ - v122 - My 1 '97 - p124 [51-250]
    PW - v244 - Ap 7 '97 - p82 [51-250]
Mehta, Ved - *Rajiv Gandhi and Rama's Kingdom*
    PW - v243 - N 25 '96 - p70 [1-50]
    TLS - D 13 '96 - p32 [251-500]
MEI Structured Mathematics: Mechanics 5-6
    y TES - O 4 '96 - pR12 [501+]
MEI Structured Mathematics: Pure Mathematics 3-4
    y TES - O 4 '96 - pR12 [501+]
Meidinger, Claude - *Science Economique*
    JEL - v34 - D '96 - p2016+ [51-250]
Meier, Christian - *Caesar*
    Books - v9 - S '95 - p23 [51-250]
Meier, Deborah - *The Power of Their Ideas*
    EL - v54 - S '96 - p15 [501+]
    JNE - v65 - Win '96 - p93+ [501+]
    NASSP-B - v81 - Mr '97 - p121+ [501+]
Meier, Heinrich - *Carl Schmitt and Leo Strauss*
    TLS - Ag 2 '96 - p11 [501+]
Meier, John P - *A Marginal Jew. Vols. 1-2*
    Bks & Cult - v1 - N '95 - p3+ [501+]
Meier, Leslie - *Trick or Treat Murder*
    KR - v64 - Ag 15 '96 - p1195 [51-250]
Meier, Levi - *Ancient Secrets*
    BL - v93 - O 1 '96 - p305 [51-250]
Meier, Matt S - *Notable Latino Americans*
    r LJ - v122 - Ap 15 '97 - p70 [51-250]
Meier, Paul - *The Third Millennium*
    HM - v293 - S '96 - p64+ [501+]
Meihy, Jose Carlos Sebe Bom - *Cinderela Negra A Saga De Carolina Maria De Jesus*
    HAHR - v76 - Ag '96 - p598+ [501+]
Meijer, Laurent - *Progress in Cell Cycle Research. Vol. 2*
    SciTech - v21 - Mr '97 - p36 [51-250]
Meikle, Denis - *A History of Horrors*
    Choice - v34 - D '96 - p622 [51-250]
    Si & So - v6 - N '96 - p34 [51-250]
Meikle, Jeffrey L - *American Plastic*
    Am Sci - v84 - S '96 - p505+ [501+]
    New R - v215 - D 2 '96 - p50+ [501+]
    RAH - v25 - Mr '97 - p140+ [501+]
    SDA - v4 - Spr '97 - p110+ [501+]
Meilach, Dona - *Making Your Own Biscotti and Dunking Delights*
    BWatch - v18 - F '97 - p8 [1-50]
Meilaender, Gilbert - *Bioethics: A Primer for Christians*
    BL - v93 - S 1 '96 - p34+ [51-250]
    LJ - v121 - D '96 - p99 [51-250]
    Body, Soul, and Bioethics
    CC - v114 - F 5 '97 - p164+ [501+]
    Theol St - v57 - D '96 - p786 [251-500]
    Letters to Ellen
    Ch Today - v40 - Ag 12 '96 - p47 [51-250]
    Cres - v59 - S '96 - p40 [51-250]
Meincke, Mark - *The Complete Guide to Stationary Gas Engines*
    r SciTech - v20 - N '96 - p70 [51-250]
Meindl, Dieter - *American Fiction and the Metaphysics of the Grotesque*
    Choice - v34 - My '97 - p1497 [51-250]
Meindl, James R - *Cognition within and between Organizations*
    R&R Bk N - v11 - N '96 - p29 [51-250]
Meinecke, Michael - *Patterns of Stylistic Changes in Islamic Architecture*
    MEJ - v51 - Win '97 - p153 [51-250]
    R&R Bk N - v11 - D '96 - p57 [51-250]
Meinig, D W - *The Shaping of America. Vol. 2*
    W&M Q - v54 - Ap '97 - p460+ [51-250]
Meinke, Peter - *Scars*
    VQR - v73 - Win '97 - p27* [51-250]
Meirovitch, Leonard - *Principles and Techniques of Vibrations*
    SciTech - v21 - Mr '97 - p22 [51-250]
Meisel, Jacqueline Drobis - *South Africa: A Tapestry of Peoples and Traditions*
    c Ch BWatch - v6 - D '96 - p6 [1-50]
    c HB Guide - v8 - Spr '97 - p171 [51-250]
Meisler, Stanley - *United Nations*
    Pres SQ - v27 - Win '97 - p160+ [501+]
Meisner, Maurice - *The Deng Xiaoping Era*
    BL - v93 - S 15 '96 - p217 [51-250]
    Bus W - Ja 13 '96 - p18 [501+]
    Cu H - v95 - S '96 - p292 [51-250]
    For Aff - v75 - N '96 - p167 [51-250]
    New R - v216 - Mr 10 '97 - p45+ [501+]
    Wil Q - v21 - Win '97 - p99 [251-500]

Meissner, Bill - *Hitting into the Wind*
    Trib Bks - Mr 30 '97 - p3 [501+]
Meissner, Jochen - *Eine Elite Im Umbruch*
    HAHR - v76 - N '96 - p779+ [501+]
Meissner, W W - *Ignatius of Loyola: The Psychology of a Saint*
    CHR - v82 - Jl '96 - p469+ [501+]
    Thy Kingdom Come
    JR - v77 - Ap '97 - p333+ [501+]
    Rel St Rev - v23 - Ja '97 - p44 [51-250]
    Theol St - v57 - S '96 - p577 [251-500]
Mejia, Maria - *Somos Iglesia*
    Cons - v17 - Win '96 - p31 [1-50]
Mekler, Eva - *Sunrise Shows Late*
    BL - v93 - Mr 15 '97 - p1226+ [51-250]
    CSM - v89 - Mr 10 '97 - p12 [251-500]
    KR - v65 - F 1 '97 - p164 [251-500]
    LJ - v122 - F 15 '97 - p163 [51-250]
    PW - v244 - F 3 '97 - p93 [51-250]
Melamed, Leo - *Leo Melamed: Escape to the Futures*
    Barron's - v76 - S 2 '96 - p43 [51-250]
    Econ - v340 - S 14 '96 - p9* [51-250]
    NYTBR - v101 - S 22 '96 - p22 [501+]
Melancon, Michael - *The Socialist Revolutionaries and the Russian Anti-War Movement 1914-17*
    EHR - v111 - S '96 - p1018+ [501+]
Melaragno, Michele - *Severe Storm Engineering for Structural Design*
    Choice - v34 - N '96 - p489 [51-250]
Melcher, Mary - *Mommy, Who Does God Love? (Illus. by Mary Melcher)*
    c PW - v244 - Mr 24 '97 - p76 [51-250]
Mel'cuk, Igor A - *Introduction A La Lexicologie Explicative Et Combinatoire*
    FR - v70 - F '97 - p481+ [501+]
Meldolesi, Luca - *Discovering the Possible*
    JEL - v34 - D '96 - p1947+ [501+]
Mele, Alfred R - *Autonomous Agents*
    Ethics - v107 - Ja '97 - p346+ [501+]
    RM - v50 - D '96 - p416+ [501+]
Melendy, H Brett - *Walter Francis Dillingham 1875-1963*
    Choice - v34 - S '96 - p195 [51-250]
Melford, Michael - *Big Sky Country*
    CSM - v88 - N 21 '96 - pB1 [51-250]
Melhuish, Clare - *Odile Decq Benoit Cornette*
    TLS - N 8 '96 - p32 [51-250]
Melhuus, Marit - *Machos, Mistresses, Madonnas*
    LJ - v121 - N 1 '96 - p96 [51-250]
Meliteniote, Theodore - *Tribiblos Astronomique. Bk. 2, Vols. 1-2*
    Isis - v88 - Mr '97 - p133+ [501+]
Mell, Donald C - *Pope, Swift, and Women Writers*
    Choice - v34 - Mr '97 - p1165 [51-250]
Mellars, Paul - *Modelling the Early Human Mind*
    New Sci - v153 - F 1 '97 - p44 [51-250]
    The Neanderthal Legacy
    Am Ant - v62 - Ja '97 - p165+ [501+]
    Choice - v34 - O '96 - p323 [51-250]
Mellen, Frank - *If Only I Could Whistle Loudly!*
    c Ch BWatch - v7 - F '97 - p2 [1-50]
Mellen, Joan - *Hellman and Hammett*
    Choice - v34 - N '96 - p457 [51-250]
    LATBR - D 29 '96 - p9+ [51-250]
    Nat R - v48 - S 30 '96 - p65+ [501+]
    NYTBR - v101 - D 8 '96 - p88 [1-50]
Mellencamp, Patricia - *A Fine Romance*
    Bloom Rev - v16 - Mr '96 - p24 [51-250]
    Choice - v34 - D '96 - p622+ [51-250]
Mellentin, Kath - *Dear Tooth Fairy (Illus. by Fran Thatcher)*
    c PW - v244 - Mr 31 '97 - p76 [51-250]
Mellers, Wilfrid - *Francis Poulenc*
    FR - v70 - O '96 - p133+ [501+]
Melleuish, Gregory - *Cultural Liberalism in Australia*
    Choice - v34 - O '96 - p337 [51-250]
Mellin, Laurel - *The Solution: The 6 Causes and 6 Cures of Weight Problems*
    BL - v93 - D 15 '96 - p691 [51-250]
Melling, John Kennedy - *Murder Done to Death*
    TLS - O 11 '96 - p28 [501+]
Melling, Joseph - *Management, Labour, and Industrial Politics in Modern Europe*
    JEL - v34 - D '96 - p2100 [51-250]
    R&R Bk N - v11 - N '96 - p27 [51-250]
Melling, O R - *My Blue Country*
    y JAAL - v40 - D '96 - p326 [251-500]
Mellinger, Philip J - *Race and Labor in Western Copper*
    AHR - v101 - D '96 - p1635+ [501+]
    PHR - v65 - Ag '96 - p493+ [501+]
Mello, Michael - *Against the Death Penalty*
    Choice - v34 - O '96 - p361+ [51-250]

Mellor, Corinne - *Bruce the Balding Moose (Illus. by Jonathan Allen)*
   c KR - v64 - S 1 '96 - p1332 [51-250]
   c PW - v243 - N 25 '96 - p77 [51-250]

Mellor, George L - *Introduction to Physical Oceanography*
     Choice - v34 - My '97 - p1528 [51-250]
     SciTech - v21 - Mr '97 - p2 [51-250]

Melman, Billie - *Women's Orients*
     JMH - v68 - S '96 - p617+ [501+]
     MEJ - v50 - Sum '96 - p449+ [501+]

Melmed, Laura Krauss - *The Marvelous Market on Mermaid (Illus. by Maryann Kovalski)*
   c HB Guide - v7 - Fall '96 - p268 [51-250]
Rainbabies
   c CLW - v67 - Mr '97 - p14 [1-50]

Melnick, Mimi - *Manhole Covers*
     BW - v26 - Ag 4 '96 - p12 [51-250]

Melnik, Jan - *How to Start a Home-Based Secretarial Services Business. 2nd Ed.*
     BWatch - v18 - Mr '97 - p5 [1-50]

Mel'nychuk, IAroslav - *Kozats'ki Stravy*
     BL - v93 - N 15 '96 - p577 [1-50]

Melnyczuk, Askold - *Take Three 2*
     PW - v244 - F 24 '97 - p85 [51-250]

Melnyk, Steven A - *Operations Management*
     SciTech - v20 - S '96 - p62 [51-250]

Melot, Michel - *The Impressionist Print*
     LJ - v122 - Mr 15 '97 - p60 [51-250]

Melrose, A R - *The Pooh Bedside Reader (Illus. by Ernest H Shepard)*
   c HB Guide - v8 - Spr '97 - p148 [51-250]
The Pooh Dictionary (Illus. by Ernest H Shepard)
   cr HB Guide - v7 - Fall '96 - p295 [51-250]

Melrose, Richard B - *Geometric Scattering Theory*
     SIAM Rev - v38 - D '96 - p702+ [501+]

Melton, H Keith - *The Ultimate Spy Book*
   y BL - v93 - Ap 1 '97 - p1308 [1-50]
   r Choice - v34 - S '96 - p102 [51-250]
     NYTLa - v146 - D 2 '96 - pC16 [1-50]
   y VOYA - v19 - O '96 - p234+ [51-250]
     WSJ-MW - v78 - D 9 '96 - pA12 [1-50]

Melton, J Gordon - *The Encyclopedia of American Religions. 4th Ed.*
   r ASInt - v34 - O '96 - p8+ [51-250]
Encyclopedia of Occultism and Parapsychology. 4th Ed., Vols. 1-2
   r ARBA - v28 - '97 - p287 [51-250]
Prime-Time Religion
   r BL - v93 - D 1 '96 - p686 [251-500]
   r Ch Today - v41 - Mr 3 '97 - p48 [51-250]

Meltzer, Brad - *The Tenth Justice*
   y BL - v93 - F 1 '97 - p907 [51-250]
     KR - v65 - Mr 1 '97 - p329 [51-250]
     LJ - v122 - F 15 '97 - p163 [51-250]
     PW - v244 - F 10 '97 - p63 [51-250]

Meltzer, David - *Reading Jazz*
     MQ - v80 - Fall '96 - p392+ [501+]

Meltzer, Milton - *Brother, Can You Spare a Dime?*
   y SE - v60 - S '96 - p303 [1-50]
Nonfiction for the Classroom
   y New Ad - v9 - Fall '96 - p347 [251-500]
Theodore Roosevelt and His America
   y BL - v93 - D 15 '96 - p717 [1-50]
Tom Paine: Voice of Revolution
     BL - v93 - D 15 '96 - p720 [51-250]
   c HB Guide - v8 - Spr '97 - p160 [51-250]
   y SLJ - v42 - D '96 - p148 [51-250]
   y VOYA - v19 - F '97 - p352 [251-500]
Weapons and Warfare (Illus. by Sergio Martinez)
   c BL - v93 - D 1 '96 - p660 [51-250]
   y BL - v93 - Ap 1 '97 - p1308 [1-50]
   c CCB-B - v50 - F '97 - p215 [51-250]
   c HB - v73 - Mr '97 - p213 [51-250]
   c KR - v64 - N 1 '96 - p1604+ [51-250]
   y SLJ - v43 - Ja '97 - p131 [51-250]

Meltzer, Richard - *The Night (Alone)*
     ABR - v18 - O '96 - p26 [501+]

Melucci, Alberto - *Challenging Codes*
     Choice - v34 - Mr '97 - p1246 [51-250]
     Socio R - v45 - My '97 - p347+ [501+]
The Playing Self
     Choice - v34 - Ap '97 - p1420 [51-250]

Melville, Anne - *Role Play*
     BL - v93 - Mr 15 '97 - p1230 [51-250]

Melville, Herman - *The Piazza Tales*
     LJ - v121 - N 1 '96 - p112 [1-50]
Pierre, or, The Ambiguities
     Lon R Bks - v18 - O 3 '96 - p19+ [501+]

Melville, Jennie - *The Morbid Kitchen*
     Arm Det - v30 - Win '97 - p110 [251-500]
     KR - v64 - O 15 '96 - p1499 [501+]
     PW - v243 - N 4 '96 - p67 [51-250]

Melville, Stephen - *Vision and Textuality*
     Afterimage - v24 - Ja '97 - p23 [51-250]
     Critm - v39 - Win '97 - p148+ [501+]
     LAR - v98 - Mr '96 - p164 [51-250]

Melvin, Neil - *Russians beyond Russia*
     Choice - v34 - S '96 - p203 [51-250]

Melzer, Arthur M - *History and the Idea of Progress*
     Ethics - v107 - O '96 - p192 [51-250]

Melzer, Richard - *Ernie Pyle in the American Southwest*
     Bloom Rev - v16 - Jl '96 - p12 [51-250]
     WHQ - v28 - Spr '97 - p96+ [251-500]

Memo #70
   p Sm Pr R - v28 - Jl '96 - p27 [51-250]

Men, Aleksandr - *Christianity for the Twenty-First Century*
     Ch Today - v40 - Ag 12 '96 - p47 [1-50]
     CLW - v67 - D '96 - p37+ [251-500]
     TLS - N 29 '96 - p32 [251-500]

Men on Men 6
     BL - v93 - S 15 '96 - p221 [51-250]
     KR - v64 - Ag 15 '96 - p1168 [251-500]

Menache, Sophia - *Communication in the Jewish Diaspora*
     R&R Bk N - v12 - F '97 - p19 [51-250]

Menand, Louis - *The Future of Academic Freedom*
     CHE - v43 - F 7 '97 - pA17 [51-250]
     Econ - v341 - O 19 '96 - p5*+ [501+]
     PW - v243 - D 2 '96 - p50 [51-250]
     TLS - Ja 24 '97 - p9 [501+]

Menander, of Athens - *The Bad Tempered Man (Dyskolos)*
     Class Out - v74 - Win '97 - p76+ [501+]

Menant, Sylvain - *L'Esthetique De Voltaire*
     MLR - v91 - Jl '96 - p728 [251-500]

MENC Committee on Performance Standards - *Performance Standards for Music*
     Teach Mus - v3 - Ap '96 - p20 [51-250]

MENC Task Force for National Standards in the Arts - *The School Music Program*
     Teach Mus - v3 - Ap '96 - p20 [51-250]

Mencher, George T - *Audiology and Auditory Dysfunction*
   r SciTech - v20 - D '96 - p50 [51-250]

Menchini, Pat - *The Beatrix Potter Knitting Book*
     RSR - v24 - 3 '96 - p25 [51-250]
The Beatrix Potter Needlepoint Book
     RSR - v24 - 3 '96 - p25 [51-250]

Mencken, H L - *Do You Remember?*
     LJ - v121 - O 15 '96 - p58 [51-250]
Happy Days 1880-1892
     AL - v69 - Mr '97 - p257 [51-250]
Heathen Days 1890-1936
     AL - v69 - Mr '97 - p257 [51-250]
In Defense of Marion
     Choice - v34 - D '96 - p615 [51-250]
     NYTBR - v101 - Ag 25 '96 - p18 [51-250]
A Mencken Chrestomathy
     BW - v26 - D 8 '96 - p3 [51-250]
Newspaper Days 1899-1906
     AL - v69 - Mr '97 - p257 [51-250]
On Politics
     AL - v69 - Mr '97 - p257 [51-250]
Prejudices: A Selection
     AL - v69 - Mr '97 - p257 [51-250]
Thirty-Five Years of Newspaper Work
     AL - v69 - Mr '97 - p248 [51-250]

Mendel, Lisa Lucks - *Audiologic Evaluation and Management and Speech Perception Assessment*
     SciTech - v21 - Mr '97 - p62 [51-250]

Mendel, Matthew Parynik - *The Male Survivor*
     HER - v66 - Fall '96 - p688+ [501+]

Mendele Mokher Sefarim - *Tales of Mendele the Book Peddler*
     NYTBR - v101 - D 1 '96 - p28 [501+]

Mendel-Reyes, Meta - *Reclaiming Democracy*
     APSR - v91 - Mr '97 - p175+ [501+]

Mendelsohn, Jane - *I Was Amelia Earhart*
     A & S Sm - v11 - Ag '96 - p82 [51-250]
     Ent W - My 16 '97 - p109 [51-250]
     LJ - v121 - O 1 '96 - p48 [1-50]
     New R - v214 - Je 17 '96 - p38+ [501+]
     NW - v127 - My 20 '96 - p74 [51-250]
     NY - v72 - My 20 '96 - p96+ [501+]
     NYTBR - v102 - Mr 23 '97 - p28 [1-50]
     PW - v244 - Ja 13 '97 - p73 [1-50]
     Sew R - v104 - Jl '96 - pR56+ [501+]
   y SLJ - v42 - O '96 - p162+ [51-250]
     Trib Bks - Ap 20 '97 - p8 [1-50]
     VV - v42 - Ja 7 '97 - p44 [1-50]

Mendelson, Anne - *Stand Facing the Stove*
     BL - v93 - N 15 '96 - p560 [51-250]
     BW - v26 - N 10 '96 - p3 [501+]
     Econ - v341 - D 7 '96 - p14* [251-500]
     Ent W - Ja 17 '97 - p58 [51-250]
     KR - v64 - S 1 '96 - p1301 [251-500]
     LJ - v121 - O 1 '96 - p90 [51-250]
     NW - v128 - N 11 '96 - p94 [501+]
     NY - v72 - Ja 6 '97 - p66+ [501+]
     NYTBR - v102 - Mr 23 '97 - p6 [501+]
     PW - v243 - S 16 '96 - p60+ [51-250]

Mendelson, Edward - *W.H. Auden: Prose 1926-1938*
     Spec - v278 - Mr 8 '97 - p29+ [501+]

Mendelssohn, Fanny - *Sixteen Songs*
     Am MT - v46 - D '96 - p62 [51-250]

Mendes, Anthony - *Inspiring Commitment*
     HR Mag - v41 - Je '96 - p181 [501+]

Mendez Ferrin, X L - *Them and Other Stories*
     TES - D 13 '96 - p33 [51-250]

Mendicutti, Eduardo - *Fuego De Marzo*
     WLT - v70 - Aut '96 - p923+ [501+]

Mendle, Michael - *Henry Parker and the English Civil War*
     Albion - v28 - Fall '96 - p482+ [501+]

Mendlowitz, Benjamin - *The Guide to Wooden Boats (Illus. by Benjamin Mendlowitz)*
   y BW - v26 - D 8 '96 - p11+ [51-250]
   c Sea H - Aut '96 - p47 [51-250]

Mendoza, Eduardo - *The Year of the Flood*
     NY - v72 - S 30 '96 - p87 [51-250]
     NYTBR - v101 - S 1 '96 - p16 [51-250]

Mendoza, Elmer - *Buenos Muchachos*
     WLT - v71 - Win '97 - p119 [501+]

Mendoza, Jonathan - *Official Duke Nukem 3D Strategies and Secrets*
     Quill & Q - v62 - Ag '96 - p22 [501+]

Mendoza, Plinio Apuleyo - *Manual Del Perfecto Idiota Latinoamericano*
     LJ - v122 - Ja '97 - p79 [51-250]

Mendoza, Vincent L - *Son of Two Bloods*
     Rapport - v19 - 6 '96 - p30 [251-500]

Meneley, Anne - *Tournaments of Value*
     Choice - v34 - Ap '97 - p1381 [51-250]
     R&R Bk N - v12 - F '97 - p54 [51-250]

Menendez, Albert J - *Evangelicals at the Ballot Box*
     Choice - v34 - F '97 - p1037 [51-250]
The Subject Is Murder. Vols. 1-2
   r RQ - v36 - Win '96 - p217 [51-250]

Menendez Pidal De Navascues, Faustino - *Sellos Medievales De Navarra*
     Specu - v71 - Jl '96 - p733+ [501+]

Menezes, Alfred J - *Handbook of Applied Cryptography*
     Choice - v34 - Ap '97 - p1373 [51-250]
     SciTech - v21 - Mr '97 - p11 [51-250]

Mengel, Ewald - *On First Looking into Arden's Goethe*
     MLR - v92 - Ap '97 - p538+ [501+]

Mengel, Mark B - *Fundamentals of Clinical Practice*
     SciTech - v21 - Mr '97 - p44 [51-250]

Menino, Holly - *Forward Motion*
     KR - v64 - Ag 15 '96 - p1216 [251-500]
     PW - v243 - S 9 '96 - p75 [51-250]

Menna, Larry K - *Sports in North America. Vol. 3*
     J Am Cult - v18 - Win '95 - p101 [51-250]
Sports in North America. Vol. 5
   r ARBA - v28 - '97 - p292+ [251-500]

Mennel, Wolfgang - *Henry and Horace Clean Up (Illus. by Gisela Durr)*
   c BL - v93 - N 15 '96 - p595 [51-250]
   c HB Guide - v8 - Spr '97 - p40 [51-250]
   c PW - v243 - N 18 '96 - p75 [51-250]
   c SLJ - v42 - D '96 - p101 [51-250]
   c Smith - v27 - N '96 - p167 [1-50]

Mennen, Ingrid - *Somewhere in Africa (Illus. by Nicolaas Maritz)*
   c PW - v244 - My 12 '97 - p77 [1-50]

Menning, Carol Bresnahan - *Charity and State in Late Renaissance Italy*
     JMH - v68 - S '96 - p709+ [501+]

Menninghaus, Winfried - *Lob Des Unsinns*
Ger Q - v69 - Fall '96 - p428+ [501+]
Menocal, Maria Rosa - *Shards of Love*
MLN - v111 - D '96 - p990+ [501+]
Specu - v71 - O '96 - p980+ [501+]
Writing in Dante's Cult of Truth from Borges to Boccaccio
CLS - v33 - 3 '96 - p307+ [501+]
Menon, Dilip M - *Caste, Nationalism and Communism in South India, Malabar 1900-1948*
JIH - v27 - Aut '96 - p373+ [501+]
Menon, Jayant - *Exchange Rates and Prices*
JEL - v34 - D '96 - p2043 [51-250]
Men's Travel in Your Pocket. 13th Ed.
r Quill & Q - v62 - S '96 - p24 [51-250]
Mensch, James Richard - *Knowing and Being*
Choice - v34 - F '97 - p978 [51-250]
Menta, Ed - *The Magic World behind the Curtain*
Theat J - v48 - O '96 - p390+ [501+]
Mentor Program
ABA Jour - v83 - Ja '97 - p97 [51-250]
Mentre, Mireille - *Illuminated Manuscripts of Medieval Spain*
Choice - v34 - My '97 - p1487 [51-250]
Spec - v277 - D 14 '96 - p76 [51-250]
Mentzer, Raymond A - *Sin and the Calvinists*
CH - v65 - S '96 - p490+ [501+]
CHR - v82 - O '96 - p717+ [501+]
Ren Q - v50 - Spr '97 - p302+ [501+]
Six Ct J - v27 - Fall '96 - p921+ [501+]
Menuhin, Yehudi - *Unfinished Journey*
PW - v244 - Ap 7 '97 - p85 [51-250]
The Violin
Esq - v126 - D '96 - p40 [1-50]
Menzel, Adolph - *Adolph Menzel 1815-1905: Between Romanticism and Impressionism*
Choice - v34 - Ja '97 - p782 [51-250]
PW - v243 - N 18 '96 - p60 [51-250]
Menzel, Donald C - *The American County*
Choice - v34 - F '97 - p1035 [51-250]
JEL - v35 - Mr '97 - p304 [51-250]
Menzel, Manfred - *Klatsch, Gerucht Und Wirklichkeit Bei Nathaniel Hawthorne*
Nine-C Lit - v51 - Mr '97 - p561 [51-250]
Menzel, Peter - *Material World*
CC - v114 - Ja 1 '97 - p22+ [251-500]
y Kliatt - v30 - S '96 - p3 [1-50]
Material World. Electronic Media Version
WorldV - v13 - Ja '97 - p24 [51-250]
Menzel, Sewall H - *Fire in the Andes*
Choice - v34 - My '97 - p1560 [51-250]
Menzies, Heather - *Whose Brave New World?*
BIC - v26 - Mr '97 - p22+ [501+]
Quill & Q - v62 - My '96 - p18 [251-500]
Menzies, John - *Past Glacial Environments*
SciTech - v20 - S '96 - p18 [51-250]
Meranze, Michael - *Laboratories of Virtue*
Choice - v34 - O '96 - p350 [51-250]
HRNB - v25 - Fall '96 - p6 [251-500]
Meras, Icchokas - *Apverstas Pasaulis*
WLT - v70 - Sum '96 - p738 [501+]
Merbreier, W Carter - *Television: What's Behind What You See (Illus. by Michael Chesworth)*
c HB Guide - v7 - Fall '96 - p351 [1-50]
Mercer, Cavalie - *Journal of the Waterloo Campaign*
Parameters - v26 - Aut '96 - p164+ [501+]
Mercer, Helen - *Constructing a Competitive Order*
Econ J - v106 - S '96 - p1430+ [501+]
Mercer, Jonathan - *Reputation and International Politics*
APSR - v91 - Mr '97 - p240+ [501+]
Mercer, Judy - *Fast Forward*
PW - v244 - My 12 '97 - p74 [1-50]
Mercer, Mary E - *The Art of Becoming Human*
BL - v93 - F 1 '97 - p908 [51-250]
Mercer Commentary on the Bible
Intpr - v50 - O '96 - p412+ [501+]
Merchant, Carolyn - *Earthcare: Women and the Environment*
PHR - v66 - F '97 - p134+ [251-500]
Merchant Culture in Fourteenth-Century Venice
Ren Q - v49 - Aut '96 - p627+ [501+]
Mercier, Raymond - *An Almanac for Trebizond for the Year 1336*
Isis - v87 - S '96 - p540+ [251-500]
Mercier, S C - *Muslims*
TES - D 6 '96 - pR6 [251-500]
Mercier, Vivian - *Modern Irish Literature*
RES - v47 - Ag '96 - p457+ [501+]
Meredith, Howard - *Dancing on Common Ground*
AHR - v102 - F '97 - p180 [251-500]

Meredith, Owen - *Parish Activities Handbook*
r CLW - v67 - Mr '97 - p42 [51-250]
Meredith, Susan - *Starting Gardening (Illus. by T Gower)*
c JB - v60 - D '96 - p254 [51-250]
c Sch Lib - v44 - N '96 - p163 [51-250]
Merelman, Richard M - *Representing Black Culture*
Bl S - v26 - Fall '96 - p105 [1-50]
Merer, Jane - *The Upside-Down Mice and Other Animal Stories*
c Bks Keeps - v100 - S '96 - p12+ [51-250]
Mergler, Wayne - *The Last New Land*
BL - v93 - Ja '97 - p809 [51-250]
Bloom Rev - v17 - Ja '97 - p21 [51-250]
LJ - v121 - N 15 '96 - p79 [51-250]
Meriam, J L - *Engineering Mechanics. 4th Ed., Vol. 1*
SciTech - v20 - D '96 - p61 [51-250]
Merians, Linda E - *The Secret Malady*
AB - v99 - Mr 31 '97 - p1049+ [501+]
LJ - v121 - D '96 - p134 [51-250]
Merini, Alda - *A Rage for Love*
TranslRevS - v2 - D '96 - p28 [51-250]
Merkel, Jeanean D - *Creating a Home*
RR - v56 - Mr '97 - p215+ [501+]
Merkelbach, Reinhold - *Isis Regina, Zeus Sarapis*
Choice - v34 - D '96 - p566 [1-50]
Merkin, Daphne - *Dreaming of Hitler*
BL - v93 - My 15 '97 - p1557 [51-250]
KR - v65 - My 1 '97 - p702 [251-500]
PW - v244 - Ap 14 '97 - p62 [51-250]
Merkle, John C - *Abraham Joshua Heschel: Exploring His Life and Thought*
Rel Ed - v91 - Fall '96 - p613 [1-50]
Merla, Patrick - *Boys like Us*
BW - v26 - S 29 '96 - p13 [51-250]
LJ - v121 - N 15 '96 - p77 [51-250]
Merle, Gabriel - *Emile Combes*
EHR - v112 - Ap '97 - p517+ [501+]
Merlin, Helene - *Public Et Litterature En France Au XVIIe Siecle*
MLN - v111 - S '96 - p806+ [501+]
Merlis, Mark - *American Studies*
SFR - v21 - S '96 - p48 [51-250]
Merlo, Pat - *Screw: Observations and Revelations of a Prison Officer*
Aust Bk R - Je '96 - p67 [1-50]
Merluzzi, Vincent J - *The Search for Anti-Inflammatory Drugs*
SciTech - v20 - N '96 - p35 [51-250]
Meron, Theodor - *Henry's Wars and Shakespeare's Laws*
EHR - v111 - S '96 - p964+ [501+]
Merrell, Floyd - *Signs Grow*
R&R Bk N - v12 - F '97 - p2 [51-250]
Merriam, Eve - *The Inner City Mother Goose (Illus. by David Diaz)*
y BL - v93 - Ap 1 '97 - p1308 [1-50]
y HB Guide - v8 - Spr '97 - p153 [51-250]
y HMR - Fall '96 - p39+ [501+]
Merriam, Louise A - *United States History*
r ARBA - v28 - '97 - p187+ [251-500]
r Choice - v34 - O '96 - p254 [51-250]
The Merriam-Webster Dictionary. Home and Office Ed.
cr ARBA - v28 - '97 - p378 [51-250]
Merriam-Webster's Collegiate Dictionary. Deluxe Electronic Ed. Electronic Media Version
r Choice - v34 - Ja '97 - p780+ [501+]
Merriam-Webster's Crossword Puzzle Dictionary. 2nd Ed.
r ARBA - v28 - '97 - p385 [51-250]
Merriam-Webster's Dictionary of Law
r ARBA - v28 - '97 - p220 [51-250]
Merriam-Webster's Pocket Biographical Dictionary
r ARBA - v28 - '97 - p13+ [51-250]
Merriam-Webster's Pocket Geographical Dictionary
r ARBA - v28 - '97 - p175 [51-250]
Merrians, Deborah - *Earthquakes and Volcanoes (Illus. by Greg Harris)*
c SB - v32 - O '96 - p209 [51-250]
Merrick, Anne - *A Mouse in Winter*
c TES - N 22 '96 - p12* [51-250]
Someone Came Knocking
c Sch Lib - v44 - Ag '96 - p96+ [501+]
Merricks, Linda - *The World Made New*
Sci - v274 - D 6 '96 - p1628 [501+]
Merrill, James - *A Scattering of Salts*
NYTBR - v102 - Ja 19 '97 - p28 [1-50]
Selected Poems
Lon R Bks - v18 - Ag 22 '96 - p10+ [501+]
TLS - Ja 17 '97 - p22 [501+]
Merrill, Nan C - *Psalms for Praying*
BL - v93 - O 1 '96 - p300 [501+]
LJ - v121 - O 1 '96 - p86 [51-250]

Merrill, Richard - *Calls from the Granite State*
PW - v244 - Ap 28 '97 - p50 [251-500]
Merrill, Ronald T - *The Magnetic Field of the Earth*
Choice - v34 - F '97 - p1001+ [51-250]
SciTech - v20 - D '96 - p25 [51-250]
Merrill, Yvonne Y - *Hands-On Rocky Mountains*
c BL - v93 - Ja '97 - p852 [251-500]
Merriman, John - *A History of Modern Europe*
TES - N 1 '96 - p7* [51-250]
TLS - D 20 '96 - p3+ [501+]
Merrin, Jeredith - *Shift*
BL - v93 - S 15 '96 - p205 [51-250]
Choice - v34 - Ja '97 - p796 [51-250]
PW - v243 - Jl 22 '96 - p237 [51-250]
Merritt, Frederick S - *Standard Handbook for Civil Engineers. 4th Ed.*
Choice - v34 - S '96 - p160 [51-250]
Merritt, J F - *The Political World of Thomas Wentworth, Earl of Strafford 1621-1641*
EHR - v112 - F '97 - p143+ [501+]
ILS - v16 - Spr '97 - p29 [501+]
Merritt, Richard L - *Democracy Imposed*
APSR - v91 - Mr '97 - p241+ [501+]
RP - v58 - Fall '96 - p845+ [501+]
Merritt, Susan E - *Her Story*
y Can CL - v22 - Fall '96 - p104+ [501+]
Her Story II
y Can CL - v22 - Fall '96 - p104+ [501+]
The Stone Orchard
Beav - v77 - F '97 - p47 [51-250]
c Quill & Q - v63 - Ja '97 - p39 [251-500]
Merritt Publishing - *How to Insure Your Income*
BWatch - v18 - F '97 - p10 [51-250]
Merry, Emma - *First Names*
r J Gov Info - v23 - S '96 - p645 [51-250]
Merry, Robert W - *Taking on the World*
NYTBR - v101 - D 8 '96 - p93 [1-50]
PW - v244 - Mr 24 '97 - p81 [1-50]
Trib Bks - Ap 27 '97 - p8 [1-50]
Merryfield, Merry M - *Teaching about International Conflict and Peace*
TCR - v97 - Sum '96 - p666+ [501+]
Merskey, Harold - *The Analysis of Hysteria. 2nd Ed.*
AJPsych - v154 - F '97 - p284 [501+]
Mertens, Dieter - *Der Alte Heratempel In Paestum Und Die Archaische Baukunst In Unteritalien*
AJA - v100 - Jl '96 - p624 [501+]
Mertens, Pierre - *Une Paix Royale*
WLT - v70 - Sum '96 - p652 [501+]
Mertins, Lisa - *Ginkgo and Moon (Illus. by Lisa Mertins)*
c HB Guide - v7 - Fall '96 - p268 [51-250]
Merton, Andrew H - *Enemies of Choice*
Cons - v17 - Aut '96 - p35+ [501+]
Merton, Robert King - *On Social Structure and Science*
New Sci - v153 - Mr 1 '97 - p49 [1-50]
Sci - v274 - N 1 '96 - p734 [51-250]
Merton, Thomas - *At Home in the World*
CHR - v83 - Ja '97 - p171+ [51-250]
Basic Principles of Monastic Spirituality
RR - v56 - Mr '97 - p220 [1-50]
Conjectures of a Guilty Bystander
BL - v93 - O 1 '96 - p308 [1-50]
Contemplative Prayer
BL - v93 - O 1 '96 - p308 [1-50]
Dancing in the Water of Life
PW - v244 - Ap 14 '97 - p69 [51-250]
Entering the Silence
TLS - Jl 19 '96 - p30 [501+]
Life and Holiness
BL - v93 - O 1 '96 - p308 [1-50]
A Search for Solitude
Am - v175 - N 9 '96 - p24+ [501+]
Striving towards Being
BL - v93 - F 1 '97 - p909 [51-250]
BW - v27 - Mr 30 '97 - p13 [51-250]
KR - v64 - D 1 '96 - p1721+ [251-500]
LJ - v121 - D '96 - p100 [51-250]
PW - v243 - D 2 '96 - p51 [51-250]
A Thomas Merton Reader. Rev. Ed.
BL - v93 - O 1 '96 - p308 [1-50]
Turning toward the World
Am - v176 - F 15 '97 - p30 [51-250]
BL - v93 - N 1 '96 - p462 [51-250]
KR - v64 - S 15 '96 - p1379 [251-500]
LJ - v121 - O 1 '96 - p85 [51-250]
PW - v243 - S 30 '96 - p75 [51-250]
Mertus, Julie - *The Suitcase: Refugee Voices from Bosnia and Croatia*
y BL - v93 - Ja '97 - p814 [51-250]
KR - v64 - O 15 '96 - p1515 [251-500]
LJ - v121 - D '96 - p124 [51-250]

Mertvago, Peter - *The Comparative Russian-English Dictionary of Russian Proverbs and Sayings*
  r MLJ - v80 - Fall '96 - p428+ [501+]
Dictionary of 1000 Spanish Proverbs with English Equivalents
  r ARBA - v28 - '97 - p497+ [251-500]
Mertz, D W - *Moderate Realism and its Logic*
  R&R Bk N - v11 - N '96 - p2 [51-250]
Mervin, David - *George Bush and the Guardianship Presidency*
  Choice - v34 - S '96 - p211 [51-250]
Merwin, W S - *The First Four Books of Poems*
  LJ - v122 - Ap 1 '97 - p95 [1-50]
Flower and Hand
  PW - v244 - F 24 '97 - p86 [51-250]
Lament for the Makers
  BL - v93 - N 1 '96 - p476 [51-250]
  LJ - v121 - N 1 '96 - p71 [51-250]
  NL - v80 - Ja 13 '97 - p15 [501+]
  NYRB - v44 - Mr 27 '97 - p18+ [501+]
  PW - v243 - S 30 '96 - p81 [51-250]
The Second Four Books of Poems
  LJ - v122 - Ap 1 '97 - p95 [1-50]
The Vixen: Poems
  NYRB - v44 - Mr 27 '97 - p18+ [501+]
  Parabola - v21 - Ag '96 - p106+ [501+]
  WLT - v70 - Aut '96 - p964+ [501+]
Meryman, Richard - *Andrew Wyeth: A Secret Life*
  A Art - v61 - Ap '97 - p70+ [501+]
  Choice - v34 - Mr '97 - p1152 [51-250]
  LATBR - D 1 '96 - p1+ [501+]
  LJ - v121 - D '96 - p88 [51-250]
  NYTBR - v101 - N 24 '96 - p8 [501+]
  NYTBR - v101 - D 8 '96 - p84 [1-50]
  NYTLa - v146 - Ja 17 '97 - pC31 [501+]
  PW - v243 - O 7 '96 - p50+ [51-250]
Merz, Kenneth M, Jr. - *Biological Membranes*
  SciTech - v20 - D '96 - p31 [51-250]
Mesa-Lago, Carmelo - *Breve Historia Economica De La Cuba Socialista*
  HAHR - v76 - Ag '96 - p584+ [501+]
Mesechabe
  p Sm Pr R - v28 - D '96 - p14 [51-250]
Meserve, Walter J - *On Stage, America!*
  LJ - v121 - D '96 - p94 [51-250]
Meskimmon, Marsha - *The Art of Reflection*
  Ms - v7 - N '96 - p73 [51-250]
  R&R Bk N - v12 - F '97 - p71 [1-50]
Messadie, Gerald - *La Fortune D'Alexandrie*
  BL - v93 - Ja '97 - p827 [1-50]
A History of the Devil
  R&R Bk N - v12 - F '97 - p8 [51-250]
Messaoudi, Khalida - *Une Algerienne Debout*
  FR - v70 - Mr '97 - p626+ [501+]
Messaris, Paul - *Visual Persuasion*
  BWatch - v18 - F '97 - p3 [51-250]
Messenger, Phyllis Mauch - *The Ethics of Collecting Cultural Property*
  AJA - v100 - O '96 - p769+ [501+]
Messent, Jan - *Jan Messent's World of Embroidery*
  BL - v93 - F 15 '97 - p992+ [51-250]
  LJ - v122 - Ap 15 '97 - p79 [51-250]
Messer, Jane - *Bedlam: An Anthology of Sleepless Nights*
  Aust Bk R - N '96 - p25 [501+]
Messer, Thomas - *Lucio Fontana Retrospektive*
  BM - v138 - O '96 - p704+ [501+]
Messerli, Bruno - *Himalayan Environment*
  AAAGA - v86 - S '96 - p584+ [501+]
Messerli, Douglas - *From the Other Side of the Century*
  South HR - v31 - Win '97 - p92+ [501+]
Messerly, John G - *Piaget's Conception of Evolution*
  Choice - v34 - My '97 - p1580 [51-250]
Messie, Pierre - *Homelies Sur Les Juges*
  Rel St Rev - v22 - O '96 - p301+ [501+]
Messina, Mark - *The Dietitian's Guide to Vegetarian Diets*
  SciTech - v20 - N '96 - p55 [51-250]
Messmer, Otto - *Nine Lives to Live*
  BL - v93 - S 1 '96 - p54 [51-250]
  Ent W - O 18 '96 - p74 [51-250]
Messner, Michael A - *Sex, Violence and Power in Sports*
  Aethlon - v13 - Fall '95 - p152 [251-500]
Messner, Reinhold - *Reinhold Messner, Free Spirit*
  HM - v293 - Ag '96 - p64+ [501+]
Messner, Roberta L - *Increasing Patient Satisfaction*
  Choice - v34 - N '96 - p494 [51-250]
Messner, Tammy Faye - *Tammy: Telling It My Way*
  BL - v93 - S 15 '96 - p179 [51-250]
  KR - v64 - S 15 '96 - p1379 [251-500]
  LJ - v121 - N 15 '96 - p66 [51-250]
  PW - v243 - O 14 '96 - p77+ [51-250]

Mestrovic, Stjepan G - *The Coming Fin De Siecle*
  SF - v75 - S '96 - p347+ [501+]
Genocide after Emotion
  Choice - v34 - O '96 - p338 [51-250]
Meszaros, Istvan - *Beyond Capital*
  Choice - v34 - S '96 - p176 [51-250]
  Nat - v262 - Je 10 '96 - p27+ [501+]
  R&R Bk N - v12 - F '97 - p33 [51-250]
Metakides, George - *Principles of Logic and Logic Programming*
  SciTech - v21 - Mr '97 - p7 [51-250]
Metaxas, A C - *Foundations of Electroheat*
  SciTech - v21 - Mr '97 - p86 [51-250]
Metaxas, Eric - *David and Goliath (Illus. by Douglas Fraser). Book and Audio Version*
  c Ch BWatch - v6 - My '96 - p6 [51-250]
  c SLJ - v43 - Ja '97 - p106 [51-250]
Pinocchio: The Classic Italian Tale (Illus. by Brian Ajhar). Book and Audio Version
  c Ch BWatch - v6 - My '96 - p6+ [51-250]
  c SLJ - v42 - Ag '96 - p126 [51-250]
Squanto and the First Thanksgiving (Greene) (Illus. by Michael Donato). Book and Audio Version
  c PW - v243 - N 11 '96 - p35 [51-250]
Metcalf, Barbara Daly - *Making Muslim Space in North America and Europe*
  Choice - v34 - My '97 - p1541 [51-250]
  MEJ - v51 - Spr '97 - p314 [51-250]
Metcalf, Fred - *The Penguin Dictionary of Jokes*
  yr Kliatt - v30 - S '96 - p25 [51-250]
Metcalf, Linda - *Parenting toward Solutions*
  LJ - v122 - Ja '97 - p126 [51-250]
  PW - v243 - D 16 '96 - p56+ [51-250]
Metcalf, Paul - *Paul Metcalf: Collected Works 1956-1976*
  BL - v93 - N 15 '96 - p566 [51-250]
  LJ - v121 - N 15 '96 - p65 [51-250]
  PW - v243 - S 9 '96 - p67 [51-250]
Metcalf, Thomas R - *Ideologies of the Raj*
  AHR - v101 - D '96 - p1605+ [501+]
Metcalfe, Mike - *Business Research through Argument*
  R&R Bk N - v11 - D '96 - p27 [51-250]
Meter, Leo - *Letters to Barbara*
  c TES - Mr 28 '97 - p7* [51-250]
Methods in Enzymology. Vol. 273
  SciTech - v21 - Mr '97 - p42 [51-250]
Methold, Ken - *A-Z of Authorship*
  r Aust Bk R - D '96 - p97 [1-50]
Metin, Kivilcim - *The Analysis of Inflation*
  JEL - v34 - D '96 - p2035 [51-250]
Metras, Gary - *Seagull Beach*
  Sm Pr R - v28 - Je '96 - p8 [251-500]
Metraux, Guy P R - *Sculptors and Physicians in Fifth-Century Greece*
  Art Bull - v79 - Mr '97 - p148+ [501+]
  Isis - v87 - S '96 - p535+ [251-500]
Metre: A Magazine of International Poetry
  p ILS - v16 - Spr '97 - p34 [51-250]
Metress, Christopher - *The Critical Response to Dashiell Hammett*
  Arm Det - v30 - Win '97 - p74 [251-500]
Metrika
  p JEL - v34 - S '96 - p1506 [51-250]
Metropolitan Governance Handbook
  NCR - v85 - Spr '96 - p63 [51-250]
Metropolitan Museum of Art (New York, NY) - *European Paintings in the Metropolitan Museum of Art by Artists Born before 1865*
  r ARBA - v28 - '97 - p369 [51-250]
Metropolitan Organization
  NCR - v85 - Spr '96 - p63 [51-250]
Mettee, Stephen Blake - *The Portable Writer's Conference*
  BL - v93 - F 15 '97 - p994+ [51-250]
  PW - v244 - Ja 27 '97 - p93 [51-250]
Mettenheim, Kurt Von - *The Brazilian Voter*
  APSR - v90 - S '96 - p688+ [501+]
Metter, Ellen - *The Writer's Ultimate Research Guide*
  r ARBA - v28 - '97 - p347 [51-250]
Mettinger, Tryggve N D - *No Graven Image?*
  Rel St Rev - v23 - Ja '97 - p55 [51-250]
Mettler, Rene - *Penguins*
  c Ch BWatch - v7 - Ja '97 - p2 [1-50]
Metz, Allan - *A NAFTA Bibliography*
  r Choice - v34 - My '97 - p1476+ [51-250]
  r R&R Bk N - v12 - F '97 - p64 [51-250]
Metz, G Harold - *Shakespeare's Earliest Tragedy*
  Choice - v34 - Ap '97 - p1338 [51-250]
Metz, Helen Chapin - *Turkey: A Country Study*
  MEJ - v50 - Aut '96 - p627 [51-250]

Metz, Leon Claire - *John Wesley Hardin: Dark Angel of Texas*
  Roundup M - v4 - F '97 - p25+ [251-500]
The Shooters
  LJ - v121 - O 15 '96 - p94 [1-50]
Metz, Ray E - *Using the World Wide Web and Creating Home Pages*
  IRLA - v32 - Jl '96 - p11+ [51-250]
  LJ - v121 - S 15 '96 - p104 [51-250]
  SLJ - v43 - Ja '97 - p38 [51-250]
Metzenthen, David - *Animal Instinct*
  y Aust Bk R - D '96 - p86+ [501+]
Johnny Hart's Heroes
  Aust Bk R - Jl '96 - p60+ [501+]
  y Magpies - v11 - My '96 - p50 [51-250]
Metzger, Erika A - *Reading Andreas Gryphius*
  MLR - v91 - O '96 - p1032+ [501+]
Metzger, Marcel - *Les Sacramentaires*
  Specu - v72 - Ja '97 - p200+ [251-500]
Metzger, Phil - *The North Light Artist's Guide to Materials and Techniques*
  A Art - v61 - Ap '97 - p80 [51-250]
  LJ - v121 - N 15 '96 - p60 [51-250]
Metzger, Stephen - *Colorado Handbook. 3rd Ed.*
  r BL - v93 - S 15 '96 - p212 [1-50]
  r BWatch - v17 - S '96 - p5 [51-250]
Metzger, Th. - *Blood and Volts*
  ABR - v17 - Ag '96 - p6 [501+]
Metzger, Thomas A - *Greater China and U.S. Foreign Policy*
  For Aff - v76 - My '97 - p144+ [51-250]
Metzidakis, Stamos - *Difference Unbound*
  L'Esprit - v36 - Win '96 - p102+ [501+]
Understanding French Poetry
  MLR - v91 - Jl '96 - p748+ [501+]
Metzner, Rainer - *Die Rezeption Des Matthausevangeliums Im 1. Petrusbrief*
  Rel St Rev - v23 - Ja '97 - p75+ [251-500]
Meunier, Bernard - *DNA and RNA Cleavers and Chemotherapy of Cancer and Viral Diseases*
  SciTech - v20 - S '96 - p24 [51-250]
Mews, Peter - *Maritime*
  Aust Bk R - D '96 - p52+ [501+]
The Mexican War of Independence
  y SLJ - v43 - F '97 - p121 [51-250]
Meyer, Ben F - *Reality and Illusion in New Testament Scholarship*
  Theol St - v57 - Mr '96 - p143+ [501+]
Meyer, Carolyn - *Gideon's People*
  y BL - v93 - Ap 1 '97 - p1294 [1-50]
  y HB Guide - v7 - Fall '96 - p303 [51-250]
  y JAAL - v40 - S '96 - p71 [51-250]
In a Different Light (Illus. by John McDonald)
  y HB - v72 - S '96 - p622+ [51-250]
  y HB Guide - v7 - Fall '96 - p391 [51-250]
Meyer, Elisa - *Feeding Your Allergic Child*
  BL - v93 - Mr 15 '97 - p1214 [51-250]
  LJ - v122 - Ja '97 - p134 [51-250]
  PW - v244 - F 3 '97 - p104 [51-250]
Meyer, Esther Da Costa - *The Work of Antonio Sant'Ella*
  TLS - Jl 19 '96 - p8 [501+]
Meyer, G J - *Executive Blues*
  BW - v26 - S 29 '96 - p12 [51-250]
  Ent W - O 4 '96 - p57 [51-250]
  LATBR - O 6 '96 - p15 [51-250]
  PW - v243 - S 23 '96 - p73 [1-50]
Meyer, Gerald J - *Molecular Level Artificial Photosynthetic Materials*
  SciTech - v21 - Mr '97 - p29 [51-250]
Meyer, Helga - *The Contemporary Craft of Paper Mache*
  BL - v93 - F 15 '97 - p993 [51-250]
Meyer, John R - *A Guide to the Frogs and Toads of Belize*
  Choice - v34 - D '96 - p639 [51-250]
Meyer, Laure - *Masters of English Landscape*
  CSM - v88 - N 21 '96 - pB3 [1-50]
Meyer, Leisa D - *Creating GI Jane*
  Choice - v34 - My '97 - p1563 [51-250]
  LJ - v121 - O 15 '96 - p72 [51-250]
  Ms - v7 - S '96 - p82 [251-500]
  R&R Bk N - v12 - F '97 - p100 [51-250]
  Wom R Bks - v14 - Mr '97 - p20+ [501+]
Meyer, Linda - *Teenspeak*
  y VOYA - v19 - D '96 - p256 [1-50]
Meyer, Marvin - *Ancient Magic and Ritual Power*
  Rel St Rev - v23 - Ja '97 - p64 [51-250]
Meyer, Mary Keysor - *A Directory of Cayuga County Residents Who Supported Publication of the History of Cayuga County, New York*
  r EGH - v50 - N '96 - p175 [1-50]

Genealogical Abstracts from Palmyra, Wayne County, New York Newspapers 1810-1854
  r EGH - v50 - N '96 - p176+ [51-250]
Meyer, Michel - *Questions De Rhetorique*
  Poetics T - v18 - Spr '97 - p131+ [251-500]
Meyer, Nicholas - *The Canary Trainer*
  Sew R - v104 - Jl '96 - p461+ [501+]
Meyer, Richard J - *Stories from the Heart*
  A J Psy - v110 - Spr '97 - p153+ [501+]
Meyer, Susan, 1960- - *Imperialism at Home*
  Choice - v34 - My '97 - p1497 [51-250]
  Nine-C Lit - v51 - Mr '97 - p561 [51-250]
Meyer, Susan E - *A Treasury of the Great Children's Book Illustrators*
  PW - v244 - Ap 14 '97 - p72 [1-50]
Meyer, William B - *Changes in Land Use and Land Cover*
  AAAGA - v87 - Mr '97 - p182+ [501+]
  Human Impact on the Earth
  Choice - v34 - O '96 - p304 [51-250]
  r Nature - v384 - N 7 '96 - p38 [1-50]
  SB - v32 - O '96 - p197+ [501+]
Meyerhoff, Arthur A - *Phanerozoic Faunal and Floral Realms of the Earth*
  SciTech - v21 - Mr '97 - p33 [51-250]
Meyerowitz, Joanne - *Not June Cleaver*
  J Am St - v30 - Ap '96 - p166+ [501+]
Meyerowitz, Rick - *Elvis the Bulldozer (Illus. by Rick Meyerowitz)*
  c HB Guide - v8 - Spr '97 - p40 [51-250]
  c SLJ - v42 - D '96 - p102 [51-250]
Meyers, Annette - *The Groaning Board*
  KR - v65 - My 1 '97 - p682+ [251-500]
  LJ - v122 - My 1 '97 - p144 [1-50]
  PW - v244 - Ap 14 '97 - p60 [51-250]
Meyers, Carolyn - *Drummers of Jericho*
  y Emerg Lib - v24 - S '96 - p25 [1-50]
Meyers, Jeffrey - *Bogart: A Life in Hollywood*
  BL - v93 - F 1 '97 - p906 [51-250]
  KR - v65 - F 15 '97 - p281 [251-500]
  LATBR - Ap 6 '97 - p3 [501+]
  LJ - v122 - Ap 1 '97 - p96 [51-250]
  NYTBR - v102 - Ap 20 '97 - p7 [501+]
  NYTLa - v146 - Ap 17 '97 - pC20 [501+]
  PW - v244 - F 17 '97 - p202 [51-250]
  Edmund Wilson: A Biography
  WLT - v70 - Aut '96 - p969+ [501+]
  Robert Frost: A Biography
  Choice - v34 - N '96 - p558 [51-250]
  CR - v269 - N '96 - p275+ [501+]
  y SLJ - v42 - S '96 - p242 [51-250]
  TLS - Ag 30 '96 - p4+ [501+]
  VQR - v72 - Aut '96 - p122*+ [51-250]
Meyers, Margaret - *Swimming in the Congo*
  LJ - v121 - S 15 '96 - p124 [51-250]
Meyers, Marian - *News Coverage of Violence against Women*
  R&R Bk N - v12 - F '97 - p82 [51-250]
Meyers, Odette - *Doors to Madame Marie*
  KR - v65 - Mr 1 '97 - p359 [51-250]
  LJ - v122 - My 1 '97 - p114+ [51-250]
  PW - v244 - Ap 14 '97 - p63 [51-250]
Meyers, Randall - *Film Music*
  FQ - v49 - Sum '96 - p51+ [501+]
Meyers, Robert A - *Encyclopedia of Molecular Biology and Molecular Medicine. Vol. 3*
  r SciTech - v20 - N '96 - p27 [51-250]
  Encyclopedia of Molecular Biology and Molecular Medicine. Vols. 1-3
  r ARBA - v28 - '97 - p577+ [51-250]
  r Choice - v34 - Ja '97 - p768 [51-250]
Meyers, Scott - *More Effective C++*
  SciTech - v20 - O '96 - p10 [51-250]
Meyers, Terry L - *The Sexual Tensions of William Sharp*
  ELT - v40 - 2 '97 - p253+ [51-250]
Mezey, Susan Gluck - *Children in Court*
  AAPSS-A - v550 - Mr '97 - p183+ [251-500]
  APSR - v91 - Mr '97 - p194+ [501+]
MFC Smartlabs
  SciTech - v21 - Mr '97 - p5 [1-50]
Mfume, Kweisi - *No Free Ride*
  Bl S - v26 - Fall '96 - p105 [1-50]
  Bus W - S 9 '96 - p18 [51-250]
  BW - v26 - O 6 '96 - p1+ [501+]
  ChrPhil - v9 - O 17 '96 - p35 [51-250]
  LJ - v121 - N 1 '96 - p80 [1-50]
  No Free Ride (Mfume). Audio Version
  LJ - v122 - F 1 '97 - p125 [51-250]
  PW - v243 - O 7 '96 - p32+ [51-250]

Mi, Yaoming - *Three-Dimensional Analysis of Crack Growth*
  SciTech - v21 - Mr '97 - p79 [51-250]
Miall, Andrew D - *The Geology of Fluvial Deposits*
  Choice - v34 - D '96 - p640+ [51-250]
  y New Sci - v151 - S 28 '96 - p46 [501+]
Miall, Hugh - *Minority Rights in Europe*
  CS - v25 - S '96 - p593+ [501+]
Miano, Mark - *Flesh and Stone*
  KR - v64 - N 15 '96 - p1636 [51-250]
  LJ - v121 - D '96 - p150 [51-250]
  PW - v243 - D 2 '96 - p44 [51-250]
Micale, Mark S - *Approaching Hysteria*
  Bks & Cult - v3 - Ja '97 - p17+ [501+]
  JMH - v68 - D '96 - p970+ [501+]
Miceli, Thomas J - *Compensation for Regulatory Takings*
  JEL - v35 - Mr '97 - p299 [51-250]
Michael, James J - *From A to Z39.50*
  LRTS - v40 - O '96 - p381+ [501+]
Michael, Jan - *Hill of Darkness*
  c TES - Jl 5 '96 - pR8 [51-250]
Michael, Judith - *Acts of Love*
  BL - v93 - D 1 '96 - p620+ [51-250]
  KR - v65 - Ja 15 '97 - p86 [251-500]
  LJ - v122 - Ja '97 - p148 [51-250]
  PW - v244 - Ja 6 '97 - p62+ [251-500]
Michael, Livi - *All the Dark Air*
  Obs - Ja 26 '97 - p18* [51-250]
  TLS - D 27 '96 - p22 [501+]
Michael, Magali Cornier - *Feminism and the Postmodern Impulse*
  Choice - v34 - F '97 - p968 [51-250]
Michael, Michele - *The New Apartment Book*
  PW - v243 - O 21 '96 - p81 [51-250]
Michael, Mike - *Constructing Identities*
  New Sci - v153 - Mr 1 '97 - p49 [51-250]
Michael, Robert T - *Sex in America*
  J Am Cult - v19 - Sum '96 - p143+ [501+]
Michaels, Anne - *Fugitive Pieces*
  BL - v93 - F 15 '97 - p1003 [51-250]
  Bloom Rev - v17 - Ja '97 - p8 [501+]
  BW - v27 - Mr 23 '97 - p5 [501+]
  CSM - v89 - Mr 10 '97 - p12 [251-500]
  KR - v65 - Ja 1 '97 - p15 [251-500]
  Mac - v109 - D 9 '96 - p64 [1-50]
  Nat - v264 - Ap 7 '97 - p35+ [501+]
  NYTBR - v102 - Ap 20 '97 - p10 [501+]
  NYTLa - v146 - Mr 7 '97 - pC35 [501+]
  Obs - Ja 12 '97 - p15* [501+]
  PW - v243 - D 30 '96 - p55 [501+]
  Quill & Q - v62 - My '96 - p27 [251-500]
  Quill & Q - v63 - F '97 - p50 [51-250]
  Spec - v278 - Mr 22 '97 - p44 [501+]
  Time - v149 - Mr 3 '97 - p74 [501+]
  TLS - F 7 '97 - p23 [501+]
  Trib Bks - Mr 30 '97 - p7 [501+]
  VV - v42 - Ap 22 '97 - p55+ [501+]
  WSJ-Cent - v99 - Mr 3 '97 - pA16 [51-250]
Michaels, Barbara - *The Dancing Floor*
  y BL - v93 - Ja '97 - p779 [51-250]
  KR - v64 - D 15 '96 - p1761 [251-500]
  PW - v244 - Ja 13 '97 - p53 [51-250]
Michaels, Eileen - *When Are You Entitled to New Underwear and Other Major Financial Decisions*
  BL - v93 - D 15 '96 - p699 [51-250]
  LJ - v122 - Ap 1 '97 - p104 [51-250]
  PW - v243 - N 11 '96 - p65 [51-250]
Michaels, Fern - *Vegas Heat*
  KR - v65 - Ja 15 '97 - p87 [251-500]
  LJ - v122 - Mr 15 '97 - p90+ [51-250]
  PW - v244 - F 10 '97 - p67 [51-250]
  Vegas Rich (Merlington). Audio Version
  PW - v243 - D 2 '96 - p30 [51-250]
Michaels, Jennifer E - *Franz Werfel and the Critics*
  MLR - v92 - Ap '97 - p524+ [501+]
Michaels, Kasey - *The Untamed*
  PW - v243 - O 7 '96 - p69 [51-250]
Michaels, Laura - *A Most Deadly Retirement*
  Arm Det - v29 - Fall '96 - p404 [51-250]
Michaels, Susan - *Sightings: Beyond Imagination Lies the Truth*
  Arm Det - v29 - Fall '96 - p506 [251-500]
Michaels, Walter Benn - *Our America*
  J Am St - v30 - D '96 - p483+ [501+]
  NY - v72 - F 3 '97 - p81+ [501+]
  RMR - v50 - 2 '96 - p199+ [501+]
Michaelson, Carol - *Ancient China*
  c Sch Lib - v44 - Ag '96 - p109+ [51-250]
Michaud, Francine - *Un Signe Des Temps*
  Specu - v71 - O '96 - p983+ [251-500]

Michaux, Henri - *Darkness Moves*
  TranslRevS - v1 - My '95 - p20 [51-250]
Michel, Prince of Greece - *Living with Ghosts*
  KR - v64 - S 1 '96 - p1301 [251-500]
  LJ - v121 - O 15 '96 - p77 [51-250]
Michel, Frere - *The Revelation of Ares*
  Mag Bl - Mr '97 - p70 [51-250]
Michelangelo: Selected Scholarship in English. Vols. 1-5
  Six Ct J - v27 - Fall '96 - p852+ [501+]
Michelangelo Buonarroti - *The Poems (Ryan)*
  Choice - v34 - Ap '97 - p1344 [51-250]
  The Poems (Ryan)
  TLS - Ja 3 '97 - p26 [501+]
  The Sonnets of Michelangelo (Jennings)
  TLS - Ja 3 '97 - p26 [501+]
Micheli, Enrico - *Il Ritorno Di Andrea*
  WLT - v70 - Aut '96 - p933+ [501+]
Michelin Canada
  r Quill & Q - v63 - F '97 - p41 [51-250]
Michelin Tyre Public Limited Company - *In Your Pocket--Greek Islands*
  r Books - v10 - Je '96 - p9 [51-250]
  In Your Pocket--New York
  r Books - v10 - Je '96 - p9 [51-250]
  In Your Pocket--Paris
  r Books - v10 - Je '96 - p9 [51-250]
  In Your Pocket--Prague
  r Books - v10 - Je '96 - p9 [51-250]
  In Your Pocket--Southern Spain
  r Books - v10 - Je '96 - p9 [51-250]
  In Your Pocket--the French Riviera
  r Books - v10 - Je '96 - p9 [51-250]
  In Your Pocket--Tuscany
  r Books - v10 - Je '96 - p9 [51-250]
Michelin's In Your Pocket Guide Books
  r CR - v269 - N '96 - p279 [51-250]
Michell, John - *Who Wrote Shakespeare?*
  PW - v243 - Jl 22 '96 - p223 [51-250]
Michelman, Irving S - *The Moral Limitations of Capitalism*
  Econ J - v107 - Ja '97 - p260 [51-250]
Michelotti, Leo - *Intermediate Classical Dynamics with Applications to Beam Physics*
  SIAM Rev - v38 - D '96 - p685+ [501+]
Michelsen, P - *Vand Til Torstig Jord*
  GJ - v162 - Jl '96 - p236 [51-250]
Michelson, Bruce - *Mark Twain on the Loose*
  Nine-C Lit - v51 - S '96 - p263+ [501+]
Michelson, Larry K - *Handbook of Dissociation*
  SciTech - v20 - S '96 - p34 [51-250]
Michelson, Peter - *Speaking the Unspeakable*
  JPC - v29 - Spr '96 - p241+ [51-250]
  Utne R - Jl '96 - p106 [51-250]
Michelson, Richard - *Animals That Ought to Be (Illus. by Leonard Baskin)*
  c CCB-B - v50 - O '96 - p69+ [51-250]
  c HB - v72 - N '96 - p754 [51-250]
  c HB Guide - v8 - Spr '97 - p153 [51-250]
  c KR - v64 - Ag 15 '96 - p1239 [51-250]
  c NYTBR - v102 - F 2 '97 - p18 [501+]
  c PW - v243 - S 23 '96 - p76+ [51-250]
  c SLJ - v42 - S '96 - p199 [51-250]
Michener, James A - *This Noble Land*
  BL - v93 - S 1 '96 - p3+ [51-250]
  BW - v26 - N 24 '96 - p13 [51-250]
  KR - v64 - Ag 15 '96 - p1217 [251-500]
  LJ - v121 - O 15 '96 - p79+ [51-250]
  NYTBR - v101 - N 17 '96 - p24 [51-250]
  PW - v243 - S 2 '96 - p102 [51-250]
  This Noble Land. Audio Version
  BWatch - v17 - D '96 - p11 [1-50]
Michette, Alan - *X-Rays: The First Hundred Years*
  New Sci - v152 - O 12 '96 - p42 [1-50]
Michi, Josef - *Spectroscopy with Polarized Light*
  J Chem Ed - v73 - Je '96 - pA137 [51-250]
Michie, Lindsay W - *Portrait of an Appeaser*
  R&R Bk N - v12 - F '97 - p15 [51-250]
Michiels, Ivo - *Daar Komen Scherven Van*
  WLT - v70 - Sum '96 - p710 [501+]
Michigan Quarterly Review
  p Utne R - Jl '96 - p118+ [51-250]
Michod, Richard E - *Eros and Evolution*
  Skeptic - v4 - 4 '96 - p105 [251-500]
  VLS - Win '96 - p25+ [501+]
Michon, Pierre - *La Grande Beune*
  TLS - O 4 '96 - p28 [501+]
  Le Roi Du Bois
  TLS - O 4 '96 - p28 [501+]

Micklethwait, John - *The Witch Doctors*
    BW - v27 - Ja 5 '97 - p6 [251-500]
    Choice - v34 - Mr '97 - p1204 [51-250]
    Econ - v341 - N 16 '96 - p12*+ [501+]
    Har Bus R - v75 - Mr '97 - p142+ [501+]
    LJ - v121 - D '96 - p112 [51-250]
    LJ - v122 - Mr 15 '97 - p35 [1-50]
    Nat R - v49 - Ap 7 '97 - p50+ [501+]
    NYTBR - v102 - Ja 12 '97 - p34 [501+]
    PW - v243 - O 21 '96 - p67 [51-250]
    WSJ-MW - v78 - N 1 '96 - pA11 [501+]
Micklethwait, Lucy - *A Child's Book of Play in Art*
  c BL - v93 - O 1 '96 - p350 [51-250]
  c KR - v64 - S 15 '96 - p1404+ [51-250]
  c Sch Lib - v45 - F '97 - p39 [51-250]
  c SLJ - v42 - N '96 - p99 [51-250]
  c TES - Mr 21 '97 - p10* [501+]
I Spy a Freight Train
  c CSM - v88 - N 21 '96 - pB1+ [51-250]
  c HB Guide - v8 - Spr '97 - p139 [51-250]
  c SLJ - v42 - Ag '96 - p139 [51-250]
Transport in Art
  c Bks Keeps - N '96 - p14 [51-250]
Micozzi, Marc S - *Fundamentals of Complementary and Alternative Medicine*
    SciTech - v20 - N '96 - p36 [51-250]
Microbial Drug Resistance
  p Nature - v383 - S 5 '96 - p36 [51-250]
Micrologus: Natura, Scienze E Società Medievali. Vol. 2
    EHR - v112 - Ap '97 - p442+ [501+]
Microscopic Anatomy of Invertebrates. Vol. 6, Pts. A-B
    SciTech - v21 - Mr '97 - p37 [51-250]
Microsoft BackOffice. Pt. 1
    SciTech - v21 - Mr '97 - p11 [51-250]
Microsoft Bookshelf 1996-97. Electronic Media Version
  r CLW - v67 - Mr '97 - p61+ [251-500]
  yr Kliatt - v30 - S '96 - p40 [51-250]
  r LJ - v121 - O 15 '96 - p96+ [501+]
  r SLMQ - v25 - Fall '96 - p65 [51-250]
Microsoft Bookshelf Internet Directory. 1996-1997 Ed.
  r CBR - v14 - Jl '96 - p22 [1-50]
  r Choice - v34 - Ja '97 - p772 [251-500]
  r R&R Bk N - v11 - O '96 - p68 [51-250]
Microsoft Corporation - *Microsoft Project/Visual Basic Reference*
  r SciTech - v20 - D '96 - p11 [51-250]
Microsoft Encarta 96 World Atlas. Electronic Media Version
  cr SLJ - v42 - N '96 - p58 [51-250]
Microsoft Encarta 97 World Atlas. Electronic Media Version
  r Choice - v34 - Ap '97 - p1320 [51-250]
  yr Kliatt - v31 - Ja '97 - p34 [51-250]
Microsoft Press Programmer's Bookshelf for Windows 95. Electronic Media Version
  r CBR - v14 - N '96 - p40 [1-50]
Microsoft Wine Guide. Electronic Media Version
  r LJ - v122 - Ap 1 '97 - p63 [1-50]
Microwave Processing of Materials V
    SciTech - v21 - Mr '97 - p78 [51-250]
Microwaves: Theory and Application in Materials Processing III
    SciTech - v20 - S '96 - p61 [51-250]
Micu, Dumitru - *Scurta Istorie A Literaturii Romane*
    BL - v93 - D 15 '96 - p714 [1-50]
Micucci, Charles - *The Life and Times of the Honeybee*
  c LA - v73 - O '96 - p438 [51-250]
The Life and Times of the Peanut (Illus. by Charles Micucci)
  c BL - v93 - My 1 '97 - p1496 [51-250]
  c CCB-B - v50 - My '97 - p331 [51-250]
  c KR - v65 - F 15 '97 - p303 [51-250]
Middione, Carlo - *Traditional Pasta*
    BWatch - v17 - S '96 - p2 [51-250]
The Middle East and North Africa 1996
  r MEJ - v50 - Sum '96 - p451 [51-250]
The Middle East and North Africa 1997
  r ARBA - v28 - '97 - p72 [51-250]
Middle East Contemporary Survey. Vol. 17
  r MEJ - v50 - Aut '96 - p625 [51-250]
  r MEQ - v3 - D '96 - p85 [51-250]
Middlebrook, Christina - *Seeing the Crab*
    Nat - v263 - D 9 '96 - p33+ [501+]
Middlebrook, Kevin J - *The Paradox of Revolution*
    AHR - v101 - D '96 - p1658+ [501+]
    CS - v25 - N '96 - p776+ [501+]
    HAHR - v76 - Ag '96 - p577+ [501+]
    PSQ - v111 - Fall '96 - p553+ [501+]
Middlebrook, Martin - *Arnhem 1944*
    Mar Crp G - v80 - O '96 - p75 [501+]

Middlekauff, Robert - *Benjamin Franklin and His Enemies*
    Choice - v34 - S '96 - p195+ [51-250]
    Lon R Bks - v18 - N 14 '96 - p16 [501+]
    NEQ - v69 - D '96 - p655+ [501+]
    NYRB - v43 - Je 6 '96 - p47+ [501+]
    NYTBR - v101 - S 22 '96 - p37 [501+]
    W&M Q - v53 - O '96 - p827+ [501+]
Middleton, Andrew - *Rugs and Carpets*
    BL - v93 - N 15 '96 - p565 [51-250]
Middleton, Darren J N - *God's Struggler*
    Choice - v34 - D '96 - p600 [51-250]
Middleton, David - *An Introduction to Statistical Communication Theory*
  r SciTech - v20 - D '96 - p74 [51-250]
Middleton, Harry - *The Earth Is Enough*
    LATBR - Mr 24 '96 - p11 [51-250]
Middleton, Richard G - *Medical and Surgical Management of Prostate Cancer*
    SciTech - v20 - S '96 - p31 [51-250]
Middleton, Roger - *Government Versus the Market*
    Choice - v34 - S '96 - p176+ [51-250]
    JEL - v34 - D '96 - p2096 [51-250]
    R&R Bk N - v11 - D '96 - p30 [51-250]
Middleton, Stanley - *Live and Learn*
    PW - v244 - Ap 28 '97 - p55 [51-250]
Middleton, Thomas - *The Changeling*
    PQ - v74 - Fall '95 - p373+ [501+]
A Mad World, My Masters and Other Plays
    Sev Cent N - v54 - Fall '96 - p58 [501+]
Midelfort, H C Erik - *Mad Princes of Renaissance Germany*
    EHR - v111 - N '96 - p1263+ [501+]
Midge, Tiffany - *Outlaws, Renegades, and Saints*
    WLT - v71 - Win '97 - p200 [251-500]
Midgley, Graham - *University Life in Eighteenth-Century Oxford*
    Obs - O 6 '96 - p16* [501+]
    TES - N 29 '96 - p10* [51-250]
Midgley, James - *Challenges to Social Security*
    Choice - v34 - O '96 - p329 [51-250]
Midgley, Mary - *The Ethical Primate*
    J Ch St - v38 - Sum '96 - p663+ [501+]
    NS & S - v9 - Ap 26 '96 - p35 [1-50]
Utopias, Dolphins and Computers
    New Sci - v153 - Ja 25 '97 - p44 [251-500]
A Midsummer Night's Dream. Electronic Media Version
  y Sch Lib - v45 - F '97 - p28 [251-500]
Midwest Art History Society - *Drawings in Midwestern Collections. Vol. 1*
    R&R Bk N - v11 - N '96 - p61 [51-250]
Midwinter, Eric - *State Educator*
    TES - Ag 30 '96 - p32 [51-250]
Mieczkowski, Z - *Environmental Issues of Tourism and Recreation*
    GJ - v162 - N '96 - p338 [251-500]
Miernowski, Jan - *Dialectique Et Connaissance Dans La Sepmaine De Du Bartas*
    FR - v70 - F '97 - p464+ [501+]
Mierop, Caroline - *Skyscrapers Higher and Higher*
    Choice - v34 - S '96 - p114 [51-250]
Mies, Maria - *Ecofeminism*
    Signs - v22 - Win '97 - p496+ [501+]
Migdal, Joel S - *State Power and Social Forces*
    HAHR - v76 - Ag '96 - p613+ [501+]
Mighetto, Lisa - *Saving the Salmon*
    PHR - v66 - F '97 - p123+ [501+]
    WHQ - v27 - Win '96 - p547 [51-250]
Migliore, Leonard - *Laser Materials Processing*
    SciTech - v20 - S '96 - p63 [51-250]
Mignola, Mike - *Hellboy*
    VV - v42 - Ja 7 '97 - p43 [1-50]
Mignolo, Walter D - *The Darker Side of the Renaissance*
    NYRB - v44 - Ap 10 '97 - p57+ [501+]
    Six Ct J - v27 - Fall '96 - p946+ [501+]
Migrants against HIV/AIDS
  p WorldV - v12 - O '96 - p12 [51-250]
Miguel-Alfonso, Ricardo - *Reconstructing Foucault*
    FR - v70 - F '97 - p476+ [501+]
Mihesuah, Devon A - *Cultivating the Rosebuds*
    JWomHist - v8 - Fall '96 - p205+ [501+]
Mihevc, John - *The Market Tells Them So*
    Choice - v34 - Ap '97 - p1389 [51-250]
    R&R Bk N - v12 - F '97 - p37 [51-250]
Mikaelsen, Ben - *Countdown*
  y BL - v93 - Ja '97 - p856 [51-250]
  c CBRS - v25 - Ja '97 - p59 [51-250]
  c CCB-B - v50 - N '96 - p107 [51-250]
  c HB Guide - v8 - Spr '97 - p71 [51-250]
  c SLJ - v43 - Mr '97 - p188 [51-250]

Rescue Josh McGuire (Sala). Audio Version
  y BL - v93 - N 15 '96 - p604 [51-250]
Stranded
  y Kliatt - v31 - Ja '97 - p9 [51-250]
Mikanagi, Yumiko - *Japan's Trade Policy*
    JEL - v34 - D '96 - p2043+ [51-250]
Mikat, Paul - *Die Inzestgesetzgebung Der Merowingisch-Frankischen Konzilien 511-626/27*
    CHR - v82 - Jl '96 - p511+ [501+]
Mikics, David - *The Limits of Moralizing*
    Ren Q - v49 - Win '96 - p875+ [51-250]
Miklowitz, Gloria - *Past Forgiving*
  y Emerg Lib - v24 - S '96 - p27 [1-50]
Mikocki, Tomasz - *Sub Specie Deae*
    AJA - v100 - O '96 - p797+ [501+]
Mikos, Michal Jacek - *W Pogoni Za Sienkiewiczem*
    Slav R - v55 - Sum '96 - p469 [501-500]
Mikula, Rick - *Garden Butterflies of America*
    BL - v93 - My 15 '97 - p1549+ [51-250]
Mikulski, Barbara - *Capitol Offense*
    NYTBR - v101 - Ag 25 '96 - p19 [51-250]
    PW - v243 - Jl 22 '96 - p229 [51-250]
Milande, Veronique - *Michelangelo and His Times*
  y HB Guide - v8 - Spr '97 - p139 [51-250]
  y SLJ - v42 - D '96 - p148 [51-250]
Milanese, Mario - *Bounding Approaches to System Identification*
    SciTech - v20 - N '96 - p69 [51-250]
Milani, Abbas - *Tales of Two Cities*
    BW - v26 - D 15 '96 - p1+ [501+]
    MEJ - v51 - Win '97 - p138+ [501+]
Milanich, Jerald T - *Florida Indians and the Invasion from Europe*
    AHR - v102 - F '97 - p179 [251-500]
    HAHR - v76 - Ag '96 - p566+ [251-500]
    JSH - v63 - F '97 - p139+ [501+]
Hernando De Soto and the Indians of Florida
    RA - v25 - 4 '96 - p275+ [501+]
Tacachale: Essays on the Indians of Florida and Southeastern Georgia during the Historic Period
    HAHR - v76 - N '96 - p783+ [251-500]
The Timucua
    Choice - v34 - F '97 - p1025 [51-250]
Milburn, Gerard - *Quantum Technology*
    Aust Bk R - D '96 - p93 [1-50]
Milburn, Michael A - *The Politics of Denial*
    BL - v93 - S 15 '96 - p186 [251-500]
    Choice - v34 - Ja '97 - p876 [51-250]
    TLS - D 6 '96 - p9 [501+]
Milch, David - *True Blue*
    Ent W - Ja 10 '97 - p53 [51-250]
Mildren, K W - *Information Sources in Engineering. 3rd Ed.*
  r ARBA - v28 - '97 - p591 [51-250]
  r Choice - v34 - N '96 - p432 [51-250]
The Milepost: Alaska. Spring '96-Spring '97
    Pet PM - v25 - Jl '96 - p8+ [51-250]
Miles, Betty - *Hey! I'm Reading! (Illus. by Sylvie Wickstrom)*
  c Inst - v42 - Ag '96 - p44 [1-50]
Miles, D C - *Polymer Technology. 3rd Ed.*
    SciTech - v20 - D '96 - p83 [51-250]
Miles, Gary B - *Livy: Reconstructing Ancient Rome*
    Rel St Rev - v23 - Ja '97 - p63 [51-250]
Miles, Geoffrey - *Shakespeare and the Constant Romans*
    Rel St Rev - v23 - Ap '97 - p172 [51-250]
Miles, Jack - *God: A Biography*
    Biography - v19 - Fall '96 - p430 [1-50]
    CSM - v89 - N 25 '96 - p12 [51-250]
    NS - v125 - D 20 '96 - p117 [51-250]
    TES - O 11 '96 - p8* [51-250]
    VV - v42 - Ja 7 '97 - p44 [51-250]
Miles, James A R - *The Legacy of Tiananmen*
    BW - v26 - O 6 '96 - p6 [501+]
    Choice - v34 - N '96 - p515 [51-250]
    Econ - v341 - O 19 '96 - p8* [51-250]
    FEER - v160 - My 8 '97 - p39 [251-500]
    NYRB - v44 - Ja 9 '97 - p33+ [501+]
Miles, John C - *Guardians of the Parks*
    Env - v39 - Ja '97 - p27 [251-500]
    Pub Hist - v18 - Fall '96 - p166+ [501+]
Miles, Jonathan - *David Jones: The Maker Unmade*
    Quad - v40 - N '96 - p85+ [501+]
Miles, Keith - *Murder in Perspective*
  y BL - v93 - F 15 '97 - p1007 [51-250]
    KR - v65 - Ja 1 '97 - p25 [51-250]
    LJ - v122 - F 1 '97 - p111 [1-50]
    PW - v244 - Ja 13 '97 - p58 [51-250]
Miles, Lisa - *Atlas of World History*
  yr Sch Lib - v44 - Ag '96 - p124 [51-250]

Miles, Margaret R - *Seeing and Believing*
    Choice - v34 - S '96 - p135+ [51-250]
    Comw - v123 - O 25 '96 - p22+ [501+]
Miles, Robert - *Migration and European Integration*
    CS - v25 - S '96 - p593+ [501+]
Miles, Robert H - *Corporate Comeback*
    BL - v93 - N 1 '96 - p466 [51-250]
    LJ - v121 - N 1 '96 - p76 [51-250]
    LJ - v122 - Mr 15 '97 - p37 [1-50]
Miles, Sarah - *Bolt from the Blue*
    Spec - v277 - N 23 '96 - p44 [1-50]
Milestones in Rock Engineering
    SciTech - v21 - Mr '97 - p79 [51-250]
Miletich, Leo N - *Dan Stuart's Fistic Carnival*
    Aethlon - v13 - Spr '96 - p220+ [501+]
    JPC - v30 - Fall '96 - p213+ [51-250]
Miley, Karla Krogsrud - *Generalist Social Work Practice*
    Soc Ser R - v70 - D '96 - p669 [51-250]
Milgrim, David - *Dog Brain (Illus. by David Milgrim)*
  c BL - v93 - S 1 '96 - p144 [51-250]
  c HB Guide - v8 - Spr '97 - p40 [51-250]
  c SLJ - v42 - S '96 - p186 [51-250]
Milhaud, Darius - *My Happy Life*
    TLS - S 13 '96 - p10+ [501+]
Milhaud, Madeleine - *Conversations with Madeleine Milhaud*
    TLS - S 13 '96 - p10+ [501+]
Milich, Melissa - *Miz Fannie Mae's Fine New Easter Hat (Illus. by Yong Chen)*
  c BL - v93 - My 15 '97 - p1580 [51-250]
  c CBRS - v25 - Mr '97 - p88+ [51-250]
  c PW - v244 - Ap 7 '97 - p90 [51-250]
Milkman, Ruth - *Farewell to the Factory*
    BL - v93 - My 1 '97 - p1468 [51-250]
Mill, John Stuart - *The Correspondence of John Stuart Mill and Auguste Comte*
    VS - v39 - Aut '95 - p72+ [501+]
Millam, Rosalind - *Anti-Discriminatory Practice*
    TES - N 22 '96 - p9* [251-500]
Millan, Jim - *Serpent Kills*
    Can Lit - Spr '97 - p229+ [501+]
Millar, Cam - *In-Line Skating Basics (Illus. by Bruce Curtis)*
  c HB Guide - v7 - Fall '96 - p362 [1-50]
    Roller Hockey (Illus. by Bruce Curtis)
  c HB Guide - v7 - Fall '96 - p362 [1-50]
Millar, David - *The Cambridge Dictionary of Scientists*
  yr BL - v93 - N 15 '96 - p608+ [251-500]
  r BWatch - v17 - S '96 - p11 [51-250]
  r Choice - v34 - Ja '97 - p772 [51-250]
  r LJ - v121 - S 15 '96 - p54+ [51-250]
  r Sci - v274 - O 25 '96 - p523 [1-50]
Millar, Delia - *The Victorian Watercolours and Drawings in the Collection of Her Majesty the Queen. Vols. 1-2*
    Apo - v144 - Ag '96 - p72 [501+]
    TLS - F 28 '97 - p20 [501+]
Millar, Fergus - *The Roman Near East 31 B.C.-A.D. 337*
    CW - v89 - Jl '96 - p510 [51-250]
Millar, Heather - *China's Tang Dynasty*
  c HB Guide - v7 - Fall '96 - p378 [51-250]
    The Kingdom of Benin in West Africa
  c Ch BWatch - v7 - Ja '97 - p3 [1-50]
  c HB Guide - v8 - Spr '97 - p165 [51-250]
  y SLJ - v43 - Mr '97 - p200 [51-250]
Millard, A J - *America on Record*
    AHR - v102 - F '97 - p198+ [251-500]
    T&C - v38 - Ja '97 - p256+ [501+]
    Edison Laboratory. Vols. 1-2
    J Gov Info - v23 - S '96 - p550 [51-250]
Millard, Anne - *Explorers and Traders*
  c HB Guide - v8 - Spr '97 - p163 [51-250]
    Lost Civilisations
  y Sch Lib - v45 - F '97 - p52 [51-250]
    Mysteries of Lost Civilizations
  c HB Guide - v8 - Spr '97 - p166 [51-250]
    Mysteries through the Ages
  cr PW - v243 - S 16 '96 - p85 [51-250]
    Pyramids
  c HB Guide - v7 - Fall '96 - p379 [51-250]
  c Sch Lib - v44 - Ag '96 - p113 [51-250]
Millard, Bob - *Country Music*
  r LJ - v121 - N 1 '96 - p41 [1-50]
    Country Music What's What
  r LJ - v121 - N 1 '96 - p41 [1-50]
Millard, Kerry - *Gordon's Biscuit*
  c Magpies - v11 - S '96 - p27 [51-250]

Millen, C M - *A Symphony for the Sheep (Illus. by Mary Azarian)*
  c BL - v92 - Ag '96 - p1908 [51-250]
  c CBRS - v25 - Win '97 - p64 [1-50]
  c CCB-B - v50 - D '96 - p144 [51-250]
  c HB Guide - v8 - Spr '97 - p40 [51-250]
  c Par Ch - v20 - O '96 - p3 [51-250]
  c SLJ - v43 - Ja '97 - p86 [51-250]
Millen, Rochelle L - *New Perspectives on the Holocaust*
    Choice - v34 - F '97 - p1017 [51-250]
Miller, Alice - *The Drama of the Gifted Child*
    Trib Bks - Ja 19 '97 - p8 [1-50]
Miller, Andrew, 1961- - *Ingenious Pain*
    BL - v93 - Mr 1 '97 - p1112 [51-250]
    KR - v65 - Ja 15 '97 - p87 [251-500]
    LJ - v122 - Ja '97 - p148+ [51-250]
    NYTBR - v102 - Ap 13 '97 - p10+ [501+]
    Obs - F 23 '97 - p17* [501+]
    PW - v244 - Ja 20 '97 - p391 [51-250]
    TLS - F 28 '97 - p21 [251-500]
Miller, Andrew H - *Novels behind Glass*
    Nine-C Lit - v51 - D '96 - p424 [1-50]
Miller, Andrew H, 1964- - *Novels behind Glass*
    MLN - v111 - D '96 - p1058 [251-500]
Miller, Andy - *Pupil Behaviour and Teacher Culture*
    TES - Ja 24 '97 - p10* [501+]
Miller, Arthur - *The Crucible: Screenplay*
    Ent W - Mr 28 '97 - p60 [51-250]
    Obs - Mr 23 '97 - p18* [51-250]
    Focus
    NYTBR - v102 - Mr 16 '97 - p32 [51-250]
    Homely Girl, a Life and Other Stories
    NYTBR - v102 - Mr 16 '97 - p32 [51-250]
    PW - v243 - N 25 '96 - p70 [1-50]
Miller, Arthur I - *Insights of Genius*
    Choice - v34 - My '97 - p1518 [51-250]
    New Sci - v153 - Ja 4 '97 - p37 [1-50]
Miller, Arthur P, Jr. - *Trails across America*
  y Kliatt - v30 - S '96 - p35 [51-250]
Miller, Barbara Stoler - *Masterworks of Asian Literature in Comparative Perspective*
    Ch Rev Int - v3 - Fall '96 - p502+ [501+]
Miller, Bonnie J - *Why Not?*
    Am Craft - v56 - Ag '96 - p66 [1-50]
Miller, Brandon Marie - *Buffalo Gals*
  y RT - v50 - N '96 - p246 [51-250]
Miller, Brian - *Prairie Night*
    New Sci - v152 - O 26 '96 - p44 [51-250]
    SB - v33 - Ja '97 - p8+ [251-500]
Miller, Calvin - *An Owner's Manual for the Unfinished Soul*
    PW - v244 - F 24 '97 - p82 [51-250]
Miller, Calvin Craig - *Spirit like a Storm*
  y Ch BWatch - v6 - Jl '96 - p3 [51-250]
  y HB Guide - v7 - Fall '96 - p373 [1-50]
Miller, Charles - *Praying the Eucharist*
    CLW - v67 - Mr '97 - p34 [51-250]
Miller, Christina G - *Air Alert*
  y HB Guide - v7 - Fall '96 - p317 [51-250]
  y VOYA - v19 - D '96 - p288 [251-500]
Miller, Cristanne - *Marianne Moore: Questions of Authority*
    Critm - v39 - Win '97 - p144+ [501+]
    J Am St - v30 - Ag '96 - p333+ [501+]
    NEQ - v70 - Mr '97 - p148+ [501+]
    TLS - Ag 30 '96 - p28 [501+]
Miller, Cynthia D - *Creating a Peaceable Kingdom*
    LJ - v122 - Ja '97 - p130 [51-250]
Miller, Dan B - *Erskine Caldwell: The Journey from Tobacco Road*
    AHR - v101 - O '96 - p1307+ [501+]
Miller, Daniel - *Domination and Resistance*
    R&R Bk N - v11 - N '96 - p8 [51-250]
    Unwrapping Christmas
    RA - v25 - 3 '96 - p175+ [501+]
    Worlds Apart
    Am Ethnol - v23 - N '96 - p937+ [501+]
Miller, David - *You Can Do Thousands of Things with String (Illus. by David Miller)*
  c Cur R - v36 - N '96 - p12 [51-250]
  c JB - v60 - D '96 - p272 [51-250]
Miller, David Lee - *The Production of English Renaissance Culture*
    MLR - v91 - Jl '96 - p699+ [501+]
    MP - v94 - F '97 - p372+ [501+]
    Ren Q - v49 - Win '96 - p867+ [501+]
    Shakes Q - v47 - Sum '96 - p209+ [501+]
Miller, David Leslie - *On Nationality*
    APSR - v90 - D '96 - p894+ [501+]
    RP - v58 - Fall '96 - p852+ [501+]

    Pluralism, Justice, and Equality
    APSR - v90 - S '96 - p635+ [501+]
    J Pol - v58 - Ag '96 - p897+ [501+]
Miller, David M O - *The Wreck of the Isabella*
    CR - v268 - Je '96 - p328+ [51-250]
    CR - v269 - S '96 - p165 [251-500]
    HT - v46 - Ag '96 - p57 [501+]
Miller, David Philip - *Visions of Empire*
    Choice - v34 - Ja '97 - p820 [51-250]
    TLS - Ag 30 '96 - p26 [501+]
Miller, David W - *Peep O'Day Boys and Defenders*
    Bks & Cult - v2 - Ja '96 - p11+ [501+]
Miller, Davis - *The Tao of Muhammad Ali*
    BL - v93 - S 15 '96 - p179 [51-250]
    KR - v64 - S 15 '96 - p1379+ [251-500]
    PW - v243 - O 14 '96 - p72 [51-250]
    TLS - F 14 '97 - p36 [501+]
    The Tao of Muhammad Ali (Miller). Audio Version
    PW - v244 - F 3 '97 - p43 [51-250]
Miller, Dawn - *The Journal of Callie Wade*
    LJ - v122 - Ja '97 - p184 [51-250]
    Roundup M - v3 - Ag '96 - p31 [251-500]
Miller, Debbie S - *Disappearing Lake (Illus. by Jon Van Zyle)*
  c BL - v93 - Mr 15 '97 - p1246 [51-250]
  c CCB-B - v50 - F '97 - p215 [51-250]
  c KR - v64 - D 15 '96 - p1800 [51-250]
    Flight of the Golden Plover (Illus. by Daniel Van Zyle)
  c Ch BWatch - v6 - S '96 - p6 [51-250]
  c HB Guide - v8 - Spr '97 - p125 [51-250]
Miller, Donald L - *City of the Century*
    HRNB - v25 - Fall '96 - p9+ [251-500]
    Nat R - v48 - S 16 '96 - p70 [51-250]
    RAH - v24 - D '96 - p635+ [501+]
Miller, Donna - *Developing an Integrated Library Program*
    Emerg Lib - v24 - Mr '97 - p39+ [51-250]
    SLJ - v43 - F '97 - p43 [51-250]
Miller, Dorothy Reynolds - *The Clearing: A Mystery*
  c BL - v93 - N 1 '96 - p501 [51-250]
  c CBRS - v25 - Win '97 - p69 [1-50]
  c CCB-B - v50 - N '96 - p108 [51-250]
  c HB Guide - v8 - Spr '97 - p71 [51-250]
  c KR - v64 - O 1 '96 - p1471 [51-250]
  c PW - v243 - N 4 '96 - p77 [51-250]
  c SLJ - v42 - O '96 - p122 [51-250]
Miller, E Willard - *United States Immigration*
  r ARBA - v28 - '97 - p280 [251-500]
  r Choice - v34 - Ap '97 - p1312 [51-250]
  r R&R Bk N - v12 - F '97 - p61 [1-50]
Miller, Edward, 1915- - *Medieval England*
    Albion - v28 - Sum '96 - p282+ [501+]
    EHR - v111 - S '96 - p939+ [501+]
    TLS - Jl 7 '96 - p32 [501+]
Miller, Edward A, Jr., 1927- - *Gullah Statesman*
    J Am St - v30 - Ap '96 - p149+ [251-500]
    Lincoln's Abolitionist General
    LJ - v122 - F 1 '97 - p90 [51-250]
Miller, Eileen - *The Edinburgh International Festival 1947-1996*
    LAR - v98 - N '96 - p593 [1-50]
Miller, Eugene D - *A Holy Alliance?*
    Choice - v34 - Ap '97 - p1400 [51-250]
    R&R Bk N - v12 - F '97 - p41 [51-250]
Miller, Frank - *Martha Washington Goes to War (Illus. by Dave Gibbons)*
  c Par Ch - v20 - N '96 - p11 [1-50]
Miller, Fred D, Jr. - *Nature, Justice, and Rights in Aristotle's Politics*
    APSR - v91 - Mr '97 - p176+ [501+]
    J Pol - v58 - N '96 - p1239+ [501+]
    RP - v58 - Sum '96 - p644+ [501+]
Miller, G Tyler - *Environmental Science. 6th Ed.*
    R&R Bk N - v11 - N '96 - p21 [1-50]
Miller, Gary M - *Modern Electronic Communication. 5th Ed.*
  r SciTech - v20 - N '96 - p72 [51-250]
Miller, Geoffrey - *Superior Force*
    J Mil H - v61 - Ja '97 - p176+ [501+]
Miller, George A - *The Science of Words*
  y Kliatt - v30 - S '96 - p23 [51-250]
Miller, Gordon L - *The Way of the English Mystics*
    CLW - v67 - Mr '97 - p32+ [251-500]
Miller, Gordon L, 1954- - *Wisdom of the Earth. Vol. 1*
    PW - v244 - Mr 10 '97 - p63 [51-250]
Miller, H Lyman - *Science and Dissent in Post-Mao China*
    FEER - v160 - Ja 30 '97 - p37 [501+]
    Nature - v385 - F 27 '97 - p783+ [501+]
    NYRB - v43 - O 17 '96 - p43+ [501+]
    Sci - v274 - O 25 '96 - p521 [501+]

Miller, Henry I - *Biotechnology Regulation*
NS - v126 - Ja 31 '97 - p11 [1-50]
Miller, Irwin - *American Health Care Blues*
Choice - v34 - D '96 - p645 [51-250]
JEL - v35 - Mr '97 - p228+ [51-250]
Miller, J Hillis - *Topographies*
VS - v39 - Spr '96 - p414+ [501+]
Miller, J R - *Shingwauk's Vision*
Choice - v34 - Mr '97 - p1212 [51-250]
Quill & Q - v62 - My '96 - p30 [251-500]
R&R Bk N - v11 - N '96 - p16 [51-250]
Miller, James D - *Improving Fundraising with Technology*
ChrPhil - v8 - S 19 '96 - p51 [51-250]
Miller, Jane - *Memory at These Speeds*
LJ - v122 - Ja '97 - p104 [51-250]
School for Women
TLS - Mr 21 '97 - p13 [51-250]
Miller, Jay - *American Indian Festivals*
c BL - v93 - Mr 1 '97 - p1158 [51-250]
American Indian Foods
c BL - v93 - Mr 1 '97 - p1158 [51-250]
Miller, Jeffrey H - *Discovering Molecular Genetics*
Sci - v274 - O 25 '96 - p523 [1-50]
SciTech - v20 - S '96 - p19 [51-250]
Miller, Jerome G - *Search and Destroy*
BW - v26 - S 22 '96 - p8 [501+]
Choice - v34 - D '96 - p695+ [51-250]
Fed Prob - v60 - S '96 - p88+ [501+]
PW - v243 - N 4 '96 - p46 [51-250]
TLS - Ja 10 '97 - p9+ [501+]
Miller, John, 1959- - *Cape Cod Stories*
Bloom Rev - v16 - Jl '96 - p20 [51-250]
Gluttony: Ample Tales of Epicurean Excess
Ent W - N 1 '96 - p64 [51-250]
Miller, John A - *Cutdown*
BL - v93 - Mr 15 '97 - p1230 [51-250]
KR - v65 - F 15 '97 - p248 [251-500]
PW - v244 - F 17 '97 - p213 [51-250]
Jackson Street and Other Soldier Stories
PW - v244 - F 17 '97 - p217 [1-50]
Miller, John Lester - *Photonics Rules of Thumb*
r SciTech - v20 - N '96 - p66 [51-250]
Miller, John Ramsey - *The Last Family (McRaney). Audio Version*
y Kliatt - v30 - N '96 - p42 [51-250]
Miller, Jon - *The Social Control of Religious Zeal*
CH - v65 - S '96 - p524+ [501+]
Miller, Joseph C - *Slavery and Slaving in World History*
r JSH - v62 - N '96 - p856 [51-250]
Miller, Joshua - *Democratic Temperament*
PW - v244 - Ap 14 '97 - p66 [51-250]
The Mao Game
PW - v244 - Ap 21 '97 - p62 [51-250]
Miller, Judith - *God Has Ninety-Nine Names*
BL - v93 - Ap 1 '97 - p1285+ [1-50]
Comw - v124 - Ja 31 '97 - p27+ [501+]
LATBR - Jl 7 '96 - p3 [501+]
NWCR - v50 - Win '97 - p146+ [501+]
NY - v72 - My 27 '96 - p132 [51-250]
NYTBR - v101 - D 8 '96 - p87 [1-50]
Trib Bks - My 11 '97 - p8 [1-50]
Miller, Justin - *Cooking with Justin*
c PW - v244 - Ap 21 '97 - p74 [51-250]
Miller, Kathy - *God's Vitamin C for the Christmas Spirit*
BWatch - v17 - D '96 - p3 [51-250]
Miller, Keith Graber - *Wise as Serpents, Innocent as Doves*
CC - v114 - My 7 '97 - p456+ [501+]
Choice - v34 - Ap '97 - p1356 [51-250]
Miller, Kent C - *Ministry for the Homebound*
CLW - v67 - Mr '97 - p42 [51-250]
Miller, Kenton R - *Balancing the Scales*
BioSci - v46 - O '96 - p721+ [51-250]
Miller, Larry L - *Ohio Place Names*
Names - v45 - Mr '97 - p34 [251-500]
Miller, Lee - *From the Heart*
y Kliatt - v30 - S '96 - p25 [51-250]
TES - D 6 '96 - p6* [501+]
VQR - v73 - Win '97 - p27* [501+]
Miller, Lillian B - *The Peale Family*
Atl - v279 - F '97 - p108+ [251-500]
Choice - v34 - My '97 - p1488 [51-250]
LJ - v122 - Mr 15 '97 - p62 [51-250]
Miller, Linda Lael - *Knights*
PW - v243 - N 18 '96 - p70 [1-50]
My Outlaw
PW - v244 - Mr 17 '97 - p80 [51-250]
Miller, Lyle H - *Stress and Marriage*
PW - v243 - S 23 '96 - p72+ [51-250]

Miller, M L - *The Enormous Snore (Illus. by Kevin Hawkes)*
c HB Guide - v7 - Fall '96 - p268 [51-250]
Miller, Marc H - *Louis Armstrong: A Cultural Legacy*
JPC - v30 - Fall '96 - p214 [51-250]
Miller, Margaret - *At the Shore (Illus. by Margaret Miller)*
c SLJ - v42 - Ag '96 - p126+ [51-250]
Family Time (Illus. by Margaret Miller)
c SLJ - v42 - Ag '96 - p126+ [51-250]
Happy Days (Illus. by Margaret Miller)
c SLJ - v42 - Ag '96 - p126+ [51-250]
My Best Friends (Illus. by Margaret Miller)
c SLJ - v42 - Ag '96 - p126+ [51-250]
My Five Senses
c Inst - v106 - S '96 - p92 [1-50]
Now I'm Big (Illus. by Margaret Miller)
c HB - v72 - S '96 - p584+ [51-250]
c HB Guide - v7 - Fall '96 - p241 [51-250]
c New Ad - v9 - Fall '96 - p327+ [501+]
Miller, Marian A L - *The Third World in Global Environmental Politics*
APSR - v90 - S '96 - p701+ [501+]
Env - v38 - N '96 - p31 [51-250]
Miller, Marilyn - *Behind the Scenes at the Airport (Illus. by Ingo Fast)*
c HB Guide - v7 - Fall '96 - p313 [51-250]
c SLJ - v42 - D '96 - p116 [51-250]
Behind the Scenes at the Hospital (Illus. by Ingo Fast)
c HB Guide - v7 - Fall '96 - p313 [51-250]
c SLJ - v42 - D '96 - p116 [51-250]
Behind the Scenes at the Shopping Mall (Illus. by Ingo Fast)
c HB Guide - v7 - Fall '96 - p313 [51-250]
c SLJ - v42 - D '96 - p116 [51-250]
Behind the Scenes at the TV News Studio (Illus. by Ingo Fast)
c HB Guide - v7 - Fall '96 - p313 [51-250]
c SLJ - v42 - D '96 - p116 [51-250]
Miller, Mark - *Troubleshooting TCP/IP. 2nd Ed.*
SciTech - v21 - Mr '97 - p89 [51-250]
Miller, Mark A - *Christopher Lee and Peter Cushing and Horror Cinema*
r FQ - v49 - Sum '96 - p64+ [51-250]
Miller, Mark C - *Making Moral Choices*
y CLW - v67 - D '96 - p46 [251-500]
Miller, Mark Charles - *Flavored Breads*
BL - v93 - Ja '97 - p801 [51-250]
Miller, Marlane - *Brainstyles: Change Your Life without Changing Who You Are*
LJ - v122 - Ja '97 - p126 [51-250]
PW - v243 - D 2 '96 - p50 [51-250]
Miller, Marlene - *An Intricate Weave*
y BL - v93 - Ap 1 '97 - p1276 [51-250]
BWatch - v18 - F '97 - p9 [51-250]
PW - v244 - Mr 10 '97 - p58 [51-250]
Miller, Mary Jane - *Rewind and Search*
CF - v75 - Ja '97 - p36+ [501+]
Choice - v34 - D '96 - p605+ [51-250]
Quill & Q - v62 - My '96 - p29+ [251-500]
Miller, Maryann - *Drugs and Violent Crime*
c SLJ - v43 - Mr '97 - p205 [51-250]
Miller, Monica Migliorino - *Sexuality and Authority in the Catholic Church*
Theol St - v57 - Je '96 - p368+ [251-500]
Miller, Nancy K - *Bequest and Betrayal*
KR - v64 - S 15 '96 - p1380 [251-500]
PW - v243 - O 21 '96 - p65 [51-250]
Wom R Bks - v14 - D '96 - p7+ [501+]
Miller, Naomi J - *Changing the Subject*
Choice - v34 - N '96 - p458 [51-250]
R&R Bk N - v11 - N '96 - p69 [51-250]
TSWL - v15 - Fall '96 - p361+ [501+]
Miller, Oscar, Jr. - *Employee Turnover in the Public Sector*
JEL - v34 - D '96 - p2078 [51-250]
Miller, P J - *Miniature Vertebrates*
SB - v33 - My '97 - p103 [251-500]
Miller, Patricia Cox - *Dreams in Late Antiquity*
CH - v65 - S '96 - p445+ [501+]
CHR - v82 - O '96 - p675+ [51-250]
JAAR - v64 - Sum '96 - p444+ [501+]
Miller, Patricia Martens - *Sex Is Not a Four-Letter Word!*
Adoles - v31 - Fall '96 - p753 [51-250]
Miller, Patrick D - *They Cried to the Lord*
Intpr - v51 - Ja '97 - p77+ [501+]
JR - v76 - O '96 - p615+ [501+]
Miller, Paul Allen - *Lyric Texts and Lyric Consciousness*
Class Out - v74 - Fall '96 - p40+ [251-500]
CW - v90 - S '96 - p72+ [501+]

Miller, Peter, 1934- - *People of the Great Plains*
BL - v93 - O 1 '96 - p319 [51-250]
LJ - v121 - D '96 - p127 [51-250]
Miller, Peter N - *Defining the Common Good*
EHR - v111 - N '96 - p1294+ [251-500]
JMH - v68 - S '96 - p681+ [501+]
RM - v49 - Je '96 - p936+ [501+]
Miller, Philip - *Media Law for Producers. 2nd Ed.*
R&R Bk N - v12 - F '97 - p65 [51-250]
Miller, Phyllis D - *Encyclopedia of Designs for Quilting*
r LJ - v122 - Ap 15 '97 - p80 [51-250]
Miller, Randall M - *American Reform and Reformers*
r ARBA - v28 - '97 - p188+ [51-250]
Miller, Rhea - *Cloudhand, Clenched Fist*
OS - v32 - N '96 - p33 [51-250]
Miller, Richard Lawrence - *Nazi Justiz*
Historian - v59 - Win '97 - p472+ [251-500]
Miller, Richard W - *Flow Measurement Engineering Handbook. 3rd Ed.*
SciTech - v20 - S '96 - p48 [51-250]
Miller, Robert H - *A Pony for Jeremiah (Illus. by Nneka Bennett)*
c BL - v93 - F 15 '97 - p1023 [51-250]
c SLJ - v43 - Mr '97 - p162 [51-250]
The Story of Stagecoach Mary Fields (Illus. by Cheryl Hanna)
c SLJ - v42 - D '96 - p45 [51-250]
Miller, Robert Ryal - *Captain Richardson: Mariner, Ranchero, and Founder of San Francisco*
PHR - v65 - N '96 - p667+ [251-500]
Miller, Ron - *Mystery! A Celebration*
BL - v93 - Ja '97 - p804 [51-250]
Miller, Rowland S - *Embarrassment: Poise and Peril in Everyday Life*
Choice - v34 - F '97 - p1041 [51-250]
Miller, Sally M - *American Labor in the Era of World War II*
ILRR - v50 - Ja '97 - p365+ [501+]
Miller, Sara Swan - *Three Stories You Can Read to Your Cat (Illus. by True Kelley)*
c BL - v93 - Mr 1 '97 - p1164+ [51-250]
c PW - v244 - F 3 '97 - p107 [51-250]
Three Stories You Can Read to Your Dog (Illus. by True Kelley)
c Inst - v105 - My '96 - p68 [1-50]
Miller, Sasha - *Ladylord*
MFSF - v91 - O '96 - p66 [51-250]
Miller, Scott D - *Escape from Babel*
Adoles - v32 - Spr '97 - p247 [51-250]
Handbook of Solution-Focused Brief Therapy
SciTech - v20 - N '96 - p44 [51-250]
Miller, Simon - *Landlords and Haciendas in Modernizing Mexico*
HAHR - v77 - F '97 - p131+ [501+]
Miller, Stephen A - *Zoology. 3rd Ed.*
SciTech - v20 - N '96 - p29 [51-250]
Miller, Stephen W - *Cardiac Radiology*
SciTech - v20 - S '96 - p35 [51-250]
Miller, Steven E - *Civilizing Cyberspace*
New Sci - v151 - S 14 '96 - p46 [51-250]
Miller, Stuart - *Understanding Europeans. 2nd Rev. Ed.*
r BL - v93 - S 15 '96 - p210 [1-50]
Miller, Sue - *The Distinguished Guest*
CC - v114 - Mr 12 '97 - p271+ [501+]
The Distinguished Guest (Cassidy). Audio Version
y Kliatt - v30 - S '96 - p46 [51-250]
For Love (Reading). Audio Version
LJ - v121 - O 15 '96 - p101+ [51-250]
Miller, Sukie - *After Death*
KR - v65 - F 1 '97 - p204 [251-500]
LJ - v122 - My 1 '97 - p110 [51-250]
PW - v244 - F 24 '97 - p77 [51-250]
Miller, Tan C - *Equilibrium Facility Location on Networks*
JEL - v34 - D '96 - p2139 [51-250]
Miller, Thomas W - *Theory and Assessment of Stressful Life Events*
Readings - v11 - D '96 - p23 [51-250]
Miller, Timothy - *America's Alternative Religions*
Rel St Rev - v23 - Ap '97 - p203 [51-250]
Miller, Toby - *The Well-Tempered Self*
Afterimage - v24 - Ja '97 - p23 [51-250]
Miller, Walter M, Jr. - *A Canticle for Leibowitz*
Ext - v37 - Fall '96 - p257+ [501+]
Miller, Warren E - *The New American Voter*
Choice - v34 - Mr '97 - p1240 [51-250]
LJ - v121 - O 15 '96 - p77+ [51-250]
Miller, Will - *Why We Watch*
PW - v243 - S 30 '96 - p80 [51-250]
Miller, William - *The Conjure Woman (Illus. by Terea D Shaffer)*
c HB Guide - v7 - Fall '96 - p268 [51-250]

A House by the River (Illus. by Cornelius Van Wright)
c BL - v93 - My 15 '97 - p1580 [51-250]
c PW - v244 - Ap 28 '97 - p74+ [51-250]
Zora Hurston and the Chinaberry Tree (Illus. by Cornelius Van Wright)
c SLJ - v42 - D '96 - p44 [51-250]
Miller, William Ian - *The Anatomy of Disgust*
BL - v93 - Mr 15 '97 - p1206 [51-250]
KR - v65 - Ja 15 '97 - p124 [251-500]
LJ - v122 - My 1 '97 - p128 [51-250]
NYTBR - v102 - Mr 16 '97 - p34 [501+]
Obs - Ap 13 '97 - p16* [501+]
PW - v244 - Ja 27 '97 - p88+ [51-250]
VLS - Spr '97 - p12 [501+]
Miller, William J - *The Peninsula Campaign of 1862*
JSH - v62 - N '96 - p820+ [251-500]
Miller, William Lee - *Arguing about Slavery*
BL - v93 - Ja '97 - p760 [51-250]
BW - v26 - S 1 '96 - p13 [51-250]
CC - v113 - S 11 '96 - p868+ [501+]
NYRB - v43 - N 14 '96 - p46+ [501+]
NYTBR - v101 - D 8 '96 - p84 [1-50]
Smith - v27 - D '96 - p137+ [501+]
Miller, Zell - *Corps Values*
PW - v244 - My 5 '97 - p190 [51-250]
They Heard Georgia Singing
BWatch - v17 - S '96 - p8 [51-250]
Milleret, Margo - *Homenagem A Alexandrino Severino*
Hisp - v79 - D '96 - p792+ [501+]
Miller Frank, Felicia - *The Mechanical Song*
FR - v70 - Mr '97 - p600+ [501+]
MLN - v111 - D '96 - p1016+ [501+]
Miller-Lachmann, Lyn - *Global Voices, Global Visions*
r ARBA - v28 - '97 - p7+ [251-500]
CLW - v66 - Je '96 - p40 [51-250]
y JAAL - v40 - N '96 - p234 [501+]
Miller-McLemore, Bonnie J - *Also a Mother*
JAAR - v64 - Win '96 - p892+ [501+]
Millet, Lydia - *Omnivores*
BIC - v25 - O '96 - p40 [51-250]
Ent W - Je 28 '96 - p101 [51-250]
Quill & Q - v62 - My '96 - p27 [501+]
Millet, Marietta S - *Light Revealing Architecture*
R&R Bk N - v12 - F '97 - p73 [51-250]
Millett, Larry - *Sherlock Holmes and the Red Demon*
Arm Det - v30 - Win '97 - p115 [251-500]
Millett, Richard L - *Beyond Praetorianism*
For Aff - v76 - Mr '97 - p189 [51-250]
Millhauser, Steven - *Martin Dressler: The Tale of an American Dreamer*
HR - v49 - Win '97 - p687+ [501+]
LATBR - My 26 '96 - p10 [51-250]
LJ - v122 - Ja '97 - p50 [1-50]
NY - v72 - Ag 12 '96 - p73 [51-250]
NYTBR - v101 - D 8 '96 - p80 [1-50]
PW - v243 - N 4 '96 - p38 [1-50]
RCF - v16 - Fall '96 - p185+ [501+]
W&I - v11 - O '96 - p251 [251-500]
W&I - v11 - O '96 - p261+ [501+]
YR - v85 - Ja '97 - p144+ [501+]
Millhiser, Marlys - *It's Murder Going Home*
KR - v64 - O 1 '96 - p1430 [51-250]
PW - v243 - O 7 '96 - p64 [51-250]
Millican, Edward - *One United People*
J Am Cult - v18 - Win '95 - p114 [251-500]
Millican, Peter - *Machines and Thought. Vols. 1-2*
New Sci - v153 - F 1 '97 - p42 [51-250]
Milligan, Barry - *Pleasures and Pains*
Nine-C Lit - v50 - Mr '96 - p555 [1-50]
Milligan, Bryce - *Daughters of the Fifth Sun*
Bloom Rev - v16 - N '96 - p22 [1-50]
JSH - v62 - N '96 - p9 [51-250]
VQR - v73 - Win '97 - p12* [51-250]
WLT - v71 - Win '97 - p161 [251-500]
Working the Stone
Sm Pr R - v28 - Jl '96 - p4 [501+]
Milliken, Diane - *Capitol Cuisine*
PW - v243 - S 16 '96 - p80 [51-250]
Milliken, Mary Sue - *Cooking with Too Hot Tamales*
LJ - v122 - F 15 '97 - p157 [51-250]
PW - v243 - D 2 '96 - p56 [51-250]
Milliman, John D - *Sea-Level Rise and Coastal Subsidence*
SciTech - v20 - D '96 - p2 [51-250]
Millin, Sarah Gertrude - *Rhodes*
Econ - v341 - O 5 '96 - p80+ [501+]
Millington, Thomas - *Colombia's Military and Brazil's Monarchy*
Choice - v34 - F '97 - p1022 [51-250]
R&R Bk N - v11 - D '96 - p18 [51-250]

Millman, Dan - *The Laws of Spirit*
BWatch - v17 - N '96 - p2 [1-50]
Millonas, Mark - *Fluctuations and Order*
Phys Today - v50 - F '97 - p69+ [501+]
Mills, Barbara K - *Ceramic Production in the American Southwest*
Am Ant - v61 - Jl '96 - p625+ [501+]
Mills, Claudia - *Gus and Grandpa (Illus. by Catherine Stock)*
c BL - v93 - F 1 '97 - p950 [51-250]
c KR - v65 - F 1 '97 - p225 [51-250]
c PW - v244 - F 3 '97 - p107 [51-250]
Losers, Inc.
c BL - v93 - Mr 1 '97 - p1165 [51-250]
c CCB-B - v50 - Ap '97 - p290 [51-250]
c KR - v65 - Ja 15 '97 - p144 [51-250]
c PW - v244 - Ja 20 '97 - p402 [51-250]
Mills, Daniel Quinn - *Broken Promises*
Choice - v34 - N '96 - p504 [51-250]
Mills, Deanie Francis - *Ordeal*
y BL - v93 - Mr 15 '97 - p1227 [51-250]
KR - v65 - Ap 1 '97 - p492+ [251-500]
PW - v244 - Mr 24 '97 - p58+ [51-250]
Mills, Kenneth - *An Evil Lost to View?*
HAHR - v76 - N '96 - p789+ [501+]
Mills, Kenneth George - *Change Your Standpoint, Change Your World*
Mag Bl - Mr '97 - p60 [51-250]
Mills, Kevin - *Justifying Language*
Rel St Rev - v23 - Ap '97 - p184+ [51-250]
Mills, Patricia Jagentowicz - *Feminist Interpretations of G.W.F. Hegel*
MLN - v111 - D '96 - p1026+ [501+]
Mills, W E - *The Deanna Durbin Fairy Tale*
Si & So - v6 - N '96 - p35 [1-50]
Mills, Watson E - *The Acts of the Apostles*
r Choice - v34 - N '96 - p434 [51-250]
Bibliographies for Biblical Research. Vol. 3
r Rel St Rev - v23 - Ap '97 - p184 [51-250]
Romans
r Choice - v34 - N '96 - p434 [51-250]
Millspaugh, Ben P - *Let's Build Airplanes and Rockets! (Illus. by Saundra Carmical)*
c Ch BWatch - v6 - S '96 - p4 [51-250]
c SB - v32 - N '96 - p243 [51-250]
Millward, Robert - *The Political Economy of Nationalisation in Britain 1920-1950*
EHR - v112 - Ap '97 - p539+ [251-500]
Historian - v59 - Fall '96 - p198+ [501+]
Milne, A A - *The Complete Tales of Winnie-the-Pooh (Illus. by Ernest H Shepard)*
c HB Guide - v8 - Spr '97 - p40 [51-250]
c PW - v243 - S 16 '96 - p85 [51-250]
Eeyore Has a Birthday (Illus. by Ernest H Shepard)
c HB Guide - v7 - Fall '96 - p241 [1-50]
Pooh and Some Bees (Illus. by Ernest H Shepard)
c HB Guide - v7 - Fall '96 - p241 [1-50]
Pooh Goes Visiting (Illus. by Ernest H Shepard)
c HB Guide - v7 - Fall '96 - p241 [1-50]
Pooh's Parade. retold (Illus. by Ernest H Shepard)
c PW - v244 - Ja 6 '97 - p74 [1-50]
Tigger Has Breakfast (Illus. by Ernest H Shepard)
c HB Guide - v7 - Fall '96 - p241 [1-50]
Milne, Antony - *Beyond the Warming*
Choice - v34 - Ja '97 - p834+ [51-250]
Milne, Frank - *Finance Theory and Asset Pricing*
JEL - v34 - D '96 - p1972+ [501+]
Milne, Lesley - *Bulgakov: The Novelist-Playwright*
Choice - v34 - Ja '97 - p802 [51-250]
Milne, Lyndsay - *Fun Factory (Illus. by Lyndsay Milne)*
c HB Guide - v7 - Fall '96 - p354 [51-250]
Milner, Anthony - *The Invention of Politics in Colonial Malaya*
AHR - v101 - D '96 - p1600 [501+]
Milner, Chris - *Policy Adjustment in Africa*
Econ J - v106 - S '96 - p1482 [51-250]
Milner, Clyde A - *The Oxford History of the American West*
yr Kliatt - v31 - Mr '97 - p32 [51-250]
Milner, Henry - *Social Democracy and Rational Choice*
RP - v58 - Fall '96 - p793+ [501+]
Milner, Murray, Jr. - *Status and Sacredness*
Am Ethnol - v24 - F '97 - p255 [501+]
Milne-Thomson, L M - *Theoretical Hydrodynamics. Dover Ed.*
SciTech - v20 - S '96 - p12 [1-50]
Milord, Susan - *Tales Alive! (Illus. by Michael A Donato)*
c CAY - v16 - Fall '95 - p7 [51-250]
Tales of the Shimmering Sky (Illus. by JoAnn E Kitchel)
c PW - v243 - Jl 22 '96 - p243 [51-250]
c SLJ - v43 - F '97 - p94 [51-250]

Milosavljevic, M - *Atomic Collision Processes and Laser Beam Interactions with Solids*
SciTech - v21 - Mr '97 - p25 [51-250]
Low Temperature and General Plasmas
SciTech - v21 - Mr '97 - p81 [51-250]
Milosz, Czeslaw - *A Book of Luminous Things*
BL - v93 - S 1 '96 - p57 [51-250]
Facing the River
HR - v49 - Win '97 - p659+ [501+]
LJ - v122 - Ap 1 '97 - p94 [1-50]
Poet - v169 - F '97 - p293+ [501+]
South R - v33 - Win '97 - p136+ [501+]
VQR - v72 - Aut '96 - p136* [51-250]
A Year of the Hunter
WLT - v70 - Sum '96 - p727 [501+]
Milroy, Lesley - *One Speaker, Two Languages*
RMR - v50 - 2 '96 - p200+ [501+]
Milstein, Linda - *Miami-Nanny Stories (Illus. by Oki S Han)*
c LA - v73 - S '96 - p353 [51-250]
Milstein, Uri - *History of the War of Independence. Vol. 1*
Choice - v34 - Ap '97 - p1402 [51-250]
MEQ - v4 - Mr '97 - p88 [51-250]
Milteer, Lee - *Feel and Grow Rich*
Rapport - v19 - 4 '96 - p18+ [501+]
Milton, Anthony - *Catholic and Reformed*
AHR - v102 - F '97 - p100+ [501+]
Albion - v28 - Fall '96 - p477+ [251-500]
CHR - v83 - Ja '97 - p104+ [501+]
HT - v46 - Jl '96 - p50+ [501+]
Milton, Giles - *The Riddle and the Knight*
Spec - v277 - D 7 '96 - p50 [501+]
Milton, John - *Dynamics of Small Neural Populations*
SciTech - v20 - S '96 - p22 [51-250]
Milton, John, 1608-1674 - *Paradise Lost*
Comp L - v48 - Sum '96 - p189+ [501+]
Critm - v39 - Win '97 - p55+ [501+]
Ren Q - v49 - Aut '96 - p573+ [501+]
Poems
Bloom Rev - v17 - Ja '97 - p17 [1-50]
Milton, Joyce - *Gorillas: Gentle Giants of the Forest (Illus. by Bryn Barnard)*
c BL - v93 - My 1 '97 - p1504 [51-250]
Mummies (Illus. by Susan Swan)
c BL - v93 - N 15 '96 - p597 [51-250]
c HB Guide - v8 - Spr '97 - p166 [1-50]
Milton, Steve - *Skate: 100 Years of Figure Skating*
Mac - v109 - D 9 '96 - p66 [1-50]
Super Skaters
c Emerg Lib - v24 - Mr '97 - p26 [1-50]
Milton Studies. Vol. 29
Sev Cent N - v54 - Spr '96 - p4+ [501+]
Milton-Edwards, Beverley - *Islamic Politics in Palestine*
Choice - v34 - D '96 - p686+ [51-250]
Milward, Alan S - *Britain's Place in the World*
JEL - v35 - Mr '97 - p268 [51-250]
R&R Bk N - v12 - F '97 - p43 [51-250]
Milward, Peter - *A Challenge to C.S. Lewis*
Bks & Cult - v2 - My '96 - p34 [251-500]
Theol St - v57 - Je '96 - p380+ [251-500]
Mimouni, Rachid - *Chroniques De Tanger Janvier 1994-Janvier 1995*
WLT - v70 - Sum '96 - p743 [501+]
Une Paix A Vivre
BL - v93 - F 1 '97 - p930 [1-50]
Le Printemps N'En Sera Que Plus Beau
WLT - v70 - Sum '96 - p743+ [501+]
Mimouni, Simon Claude - *Dormition Et Assomption De Marie*
Theol St - v58 - Mr '97 - p187+ [251-500]
Min, Anchee - *Katherine*
Books - v9 - S '95 - p22 [1-50]
LATBR - My 12 '96 - p11 [51-250]
Obs - O 20 '96 - p18* [51-250]
VQR - v72 - Aut '96 - p143* [1-50]
Min, Pyong Gap - *Caught in the Middle*
Choice - v34 - Mr '97 - p1246 [51-250]
JEL - v35 - Mr '97 - p236 [51-250]
LATBR - Ja 12 '97 - p6 [501+]
VV - v41 - D 10 '96 - p60+ [501+]
Minahan, James - *Nations without States*
r ARBA - v28 - '97 - p264 [51-250]
r RQ - v36 - Fall '96 - p134 [251-500]
Minahan, John A - *Abigail's Drum (Illus. by Robert Quackenbush)*
c HB Guide - v7 - Fall '96 - p295 [51-250]
Minami, Ryoshin - *Acquiring, Adapting and Developing Technologies*
Econ J - v107 - Ja '97 - p282+ [251-500]
Minas, Anne - *Gender Basics*
Dialogue - v35 - Spr '96 - p412+ [501+]

Minatra, Mary Ann - *Before Night Falls*
    BL - v93 - O 1 '96 - p304 [501+]
Mindell, Earl - *What You Should Know about Homeopathic Remedies*
    BWatch - v17 - N '96 - p3 [51-250]
Minden, Karen - *Bamboo Stone*
    Pac A - v69 - Sum '96 - p257+ [501+]
Mindscape Student Reference Library. Electronic Media Version
    yr BL - v93 - My 15 '97 - p1608+ [501+]
Minear, Larry - *The News Media, Civil War, and Humanitarian Action*
    For Aff - v75 - N '96 - p145+ [51-250]
Minear, Paul Sevier - *The Golgotha Earthquake*
    Rel St Rev - v23 - Ap '97 - p187 [51-250]
Minear, Roger A - *Water Disinfection and Natural Organic Matter*
    SciTech - v21 - Mr '97 - p82 [51-250]
Miner, Brad - *The Concise Conservative Encyclopedia*
    r BL - v93 - D 15 '96 - p746 [251-500]
    r PW - v243 - S 2 '96 - p121 [51-250]
    r Utne R - Jl '96 - p109 [51-250]
    r WSJ-MW - v78 - O 28 '96 - pA13 [501+]
Miner, Craig - *Wolf Creek Station*
    T&C - v37 - Ap '96 - p394+ [251-500]
Miner, Earl - *Naming Properties*
    Choice - v34 - My '97 - p1491 [51-250]
Miner, John B - *The 4 Routes to Entrepreneurial Success*
    yr BWatch - v17 - N '96 - p11 [51-250]
    Choice - v34 - Mr '97 - p1204 [51-250]
    How Honesty Testing Works
    HR Mag - v42 - F '97 - p122 [51-250]
    R&R Bk N - v12 - F '97 - p45 [51-250]
Miner, Margaret - *American Heritage Dictionary of American Quotations*
    r AH - v47 - D '96 - p9 [501+]
    r BL - v93 - F 15 '97 - p1040 [51-250]
    r LJ - v122 - Ja '97 - p82 [51-250]
Miner, Valerie - *Winter's Edge*
    BW - v26 - D 22 '96 - p12 [51-250]
Mineral Resources Development and Investment Opportunities
    J Gov Info - v23 - S '96 - p659 [51-250]
Mingay, G E - *Land and Society in England 1750-1980*
    EHR - v112 - Ap '97 - p511 [251-500]
Minger, Elda - *Christmas with Eve*
    LJ - v121 - N 15 '96 - p50 [51-250]
Minghella, Anthony - *The English Patient*
    Ent W - Mr 28 '97 - p60 [51-250]
    Obs - Mr 9 '97 - p15* [501+]
Ming-Kang Liu, Max - *Principles and Applications of Optical Communications*
    SciTech - v20 - N '96 - p73 [51-250]
Mingroot, Erik Van - *Sapientie Immarcessibilis*
    CHR - v83 - Ja '97 - p91+ [501+]
Minhinnick, Robert - *Badlands*
    KR - v64 - D 15 '96 - p1786 [251-500]
Miniatury: Catalogue of Miniatures
    BM - v139 - Ja '97 - p52 [51-250]
Minick, Scott - *Arts and Crafts of China*
    TLS - O 25 '96 - p13 [51-250]
Mink, Gwendolyn - *The Wages of Motherhood*
    JEH - v57 - Mr '97 - p241+ [501+]
    JIH - v27 - Spr '97 - p726+ [251-500]
    NWSA Jnl - v8 - Sum '96 - p107+ [501+]
    RAH - v24 - D '96 - p647+ [501+]
    Wom R Bks - v14 - D '96 - p14+ [501+]
Minkoff, Debra C - *Organizing for Equality*
    CS - v25 - N '96 - p761+ [501+]
    SF - v75 - S '96 - p383+ [251-500]
Minks, Louise - *Traditional Africa*
    y HB Guide - v7 - Fall '96 - p384 [51-250]
Minnaert, M G J - *Light and Color in the Outdoors*
    S&T - v92 - S '96 - p55 [51-250]
Minnesota and the Global Community
    J Gov Info - v23 - S '96 - p586 [51-250]
Minns, Denis - *Irenaeus*
    CH - v65 - S '96 - p441+ [501+]
    JR - v76 - O '96 - p624+ [501+]
    Specu - v71 - O '96 - p984 [251-500]
Minogue, Coll - *Impressed and Incised Ceramics*
    Ceram Mo - v44 - O '96 - p24+ [251-500]
Minogue, Kenneth - *Conservative Realism*
    TLS - Ja 3 '97 - p3 [501+]
    TLS - Ja 3 '97 - p3+ [501+]
Minois, Georges - *Censure Et Culture Sous L'Ancien Regime*
    Choice - v34 - D '96 - p567 [1-50]
Minoli, Daniel - *Distance Learning Technology and Applications*
    R&R Bk N - v11 - N '96 - p58 [51-250]

Planning and Managing ATM Networks
    SciTech - v21 - Mr '97 - p88 [51-250]
Minor, Mark - *Literary-Critical Approaches to the Bible*
    r ARBA - v28 - '97 - p541 [51-250]
    r R&R Bk N - v11 - D '96 - p74 [51-250]
Minor, Vernon Hyde - *Art History's History*
    BM - v138 - O '96 - p700 [51-250]
Minore, Renato - *Il Dominio Del Cuore*
    BL - v93 - D 1 '96 - p644 [1-50]
Minority Rights Group - *Polar Peoples*
    GJ - v162 - N '96 - p342 [51-250]
Minow, Newton N - *Abandoned in the Wasteland*
    Choice - v34 - O '96 - p271 [51-250]
Minsker, Karl S - *Fast Polymerization Processes*
    Choice - v34 - N '96 - p486 [51-250]
Minter, David - *A Cultural History of the American Novel*
    Col Lit - v23 - Je '96 - p195+ [501+]
    MLR - v92 - Ja '97 - p180+ [501+]
Minters, Frances - *Cinder-Elly (Illus. by G Brian Karas)*
    c Emerg Lib - v24 - S '96 - p45 [51-250]
    c PW - v244 - Ap 21 '97 - p74 [1-50]
    Sleepless Beauty (Illus. by G Brian Karas)
    c BL - v93 - N 1 '96 - p508+ [51-250]
    c CCB-B - v50 - N '96 - p108 [51-250]
    c HB - v72 - N '96 - p751+ [51-250]
    c HB Guide - v8 - Spr '97 - p104 [51-250]
    c KR - v64 - S 1 '96 - p1325 [51-250]
    c LATBR - N 10 '96 - p15 [51-250]
    c NYTBR - v101 - N 10 '96 - p40 [501+]
    c SLJ - v42 - S '96 - p199 [51-250]
Mintz, F J - *Safety Engineering and Risk Analysis*
    SciTech - v21 - Mr '97 - p71 [51-250]
Mintz, Jack M - *Putting Consumers First*
    JEL - v35 - Mr '97 - p223 [51-250]
Mintz, Joel A - *Enforcement at the EPA*
    Choice - v34 - S '96 - p168 [51-250]
Mintz, Sidney W - *Tasting Food, Tasting Freedom*
    BL - v92 - Ag '96 - p1863 [51-250]
    NYTBR - v101 - S 15 '96 - p31 [51-250]
Mintz, Steven - *Moralists and Modernizers*
    AHR - v102 - F '97 - p184 [251-500]
    CH - v65 - D '96 - p732+ [501+]
    JSH - v63 - F '97 - p169+ [501+]
    Soc Ser R - v70 - S '96 - p499 [1-50]
Miola, Robert S - *Shakespeare and Classical Comedy*
    MLR - v91 - O '96 - p964+ [501+]
    Ren Q - v50 - Spr '97 - p270+ [501+]
Miranda, Anne - *The Elephant at the Waldorf. Book and Audio Version*
    c SLJ - v42 - Ag '96 - p62 [51-250]
    Pignic (Illus. by Rosekrans Hoffman)
    c Ch BWatch - v6 - My '96 - p3 [1-50]
    c HB Guide - v7 - Fall '96 - p268 [51-250]
Miranda, Julia - *Entrelazos*
    BL - v93 - Ap 1 '97 - p1284 [1-50]
Mirel, Jeffrey - *The Rise and Fall of an Urban School System*
    J Urban H - v23 - N '96 - p113+ [501+]
Mirho, Charles A - *Communications Programming for Windows 95*
    SciTech - v20 - D '96 - p76 [51-250]
Mirikitani, Janice - *We, the Dangerous*
    Amerasia J - v22 - 3 '96 - p155+ [501+]
Miron, Jeffrey A - *The Economics of Seasonal Cycles*
    Choice - v34 - Mr '97 - p1209 [51-250]
    JEL - v35 - Mr '97 - p207 [51-250]
Mirosevich, Toni - *The Rooms We Make Our Own*
    BL - v93 - N 15 '96 - p566 [51-250]
Mirowitz, Scott A - *Pitfalls, Variants, and Artifacts in Body MR Imaging*
    SciTech - v20 - D '96 - p42 [51-250]
Mirrer, Louise - *Women, Jews, and Muslims in the Texts of Reconquest Castile*
    Choice - v34 - Ja '97 - p802 [51-250]
Mirsky, Georgiy I - *On Ruins of Empire*
    For Aff - v76 - My '97 - p140 [51-250]
Mirzoeff, Nicholas - *Bodyscape: Art, Modernity and the Ideal Figure*
    CC - v113 - D 18 '96 - p1261 [51-250]
Misa, Thomas J - *A Nation of Steel*
    AHR - v102 - F '97 - p196+ [251-500]
    BHR - v70 - Aut '96 - p410+ [501+]
    Isis - v87 - S '96 - p567+ [501+]
Mishchenko, Mykola - *Narodynyi Kalendarl*
    BL - v93 - N 15 '96 - p577 [1-50]
Mishima, Yukio - *The Temple of the Golden Pavilion*
    FEER - Anniv '96 - p226 [501+]
Mishima, Yutaka - *Cancer Neutron Capture Therapy*
    SciTech - v21 - Mr '97 - p50 [51-250]

Mishkin, Tracy - *Literary Influence and African-American Writers*
    AL - v69 - Mr '97 - p254 [51-250]
Mishne, Judith Marks - *The Learning Curve*
    Choice - v34 - Ja '97 - p849 [51-250]
    Readings - v12 - Mr '97 - p23 [51-250]
Mishra, Shiraz I - *AIDS Crossing Borders*
    Choice - v34 - D '96 - p694 [51-250]
    SciTech - v20 - N '96 - p37 [51-250]
Mishra, Vijay - *The Gothic Sublime*
    Clio - v25 - Spr '96 - p333+ [501+]
    South HR - v30 - Fall '96 - p393+ [501+]
Missar, Charles D - *Management of Federally Sponsored Libraries*
    CLW - v66 - Je '96 - p42+ [51-250]
    J Gov Info - v23 - S '96 - p736+ [501+]
Missimer, Thomas M - *A Lender's Guide to Environmental Liability Management*
    SciTech - v21 - Mr '97 - p2 [51-250]
The Missing Cat (Illus. by Chris Demarest). Book and Audio Version
    c LATBR - D 22 '96 - p6 [51-250]
    c PW - v244 - Mr 17 '97 - p47 [51-250]
Missouri. Dept. of Public Safety - *The State of Juvenile Justice*
    J Gov Info - v23 - S '96 - p587 [51-250]
Mistral, Gabriela - *Poemas De Las Madres*
    Bloom Rev - v16 - N '96 - p7+ [501+]
    WLT - v71 - Win '97 - p126 [51-250]
Mistry, Percy S - *Resolving Africa's Multilateral Debt Problem*
    JEL - v35 - Mr '97 - p219 [51-250]
Mistry, Rohinton - *A Fine Balance*
    BL - v93 - Ap 1 '97 - p1285 [1-50]
    Choice - v34 - O '96 - p279 [51-250]
    Comw - v123 - D 6 '96 - p20 [51-250]
    FEER - v160 - F 20 '97 - p48+ [501+]
    NYTBR - v101 - D 8 '96 - p80 [1-50]
    NYTBR - v102 - Ap 6 '97 - p32 [51-250]
    Obs - F 2 '97 - p18* [51-250]
    PW - v244 - Ja 13 '97 - p73 [1-50]
    WLT - v71 - Win '97 - p224+ [501+]
    Swimming Lessons and Other Stories from Firozsha Baag
    NYTBR - v102 - Ap 6 '97 - p32 [1-50]
    PW - v244 - Ja 13 '97 - p73 [1-50]
Misztal, Barbara A - *Trust in Modern Societies*
    Choice - v34 - O '96 - p367+ [51-250]
    TLS - Ag 30 '96 - p15 [501+]
Mitcham, Allison - *Poetic Voices of the Maritimes*
    Quill & Q - v63 - F '97 - p46 [251-500]
Mitcham, Judson - *The Sweet Everlasting*
    LJ - v122 - Mr 15 '97 - p112 [51-250]
Mitcham, Samuel W, Jr. - *Why Hitler?*
    LJ - v121 - D '96 - p118 [51-250]
Mitchard, Jacquelyn - *The Deep End of the Ocean*
    CSM - v88 - S 9 '96 - p14 [251-500]
    CSM - v88 - S 19 '96 - p14 [51-250]
    CSM - v88 - N 14 '96 - p14 [51-250]
    CSM - v89 - D 19 '96 - p14 [51-250]
    CSM - v89 - Ja 16 '97 - p14 [51-250]
    CSM - v89 - F 20 '97 - p10 [51-250]
    CSM - v89 - Mr 20 '97 - p14 [51-250]
    Ent W - Mr 21 '97 - p65+ [501+]
    LATBR - Jl 14 '96 - p4+ [501+]
    PW - v243 - N 4 '96 - p38 [51-250]
    Rapport - v19 - 5 '96 - p35 [251-500]
    The Deep End of the Ocean (Cassidy). Audio Version
    y Kliatt - v31 - My '97 - p36 [51-250]
    The Deep End of the Ocean (Ivey). Audio Version
    y Kliatt - v31 - Ja '97 - p38+ [51-250]
Mitchelhill, Barbara - *Eric and the Striped Horror (Illus. by Bridget MacKeith)*
    c Sch Lib - v44 - Ag '96 - p108 [51-250]
    c TES - Jl 5 '96 - pR6 [1-50]
Mitchell, Adrian - *Blue Coffee*
    PW - v243 - S 30 '96 - p83+ [51-250]
    Gynormous! (Illus. by Sally Gardner)
    c Sch Lib - v45 - F '97 - p24 [51-250]
    Maudie and the Green Children (Illus. by Signue Hamann)
    c TES - Jl 5 '96 - pR2 [501+]
    The Orchard Book of Poems
    c TES - N 8 '96 - p9* [51-250]
    c Bks Keeps - Ja '97 - p26 [51-250]

Steadfast Tin Soldier (Illus. by Jonathan Heale)
c   BL - v93 - N 1 '96 - p509 [51-250]
c   CCB-B - v50 - Ja '97 - p163 [51-250]
c   Ch BWatch - v6 - D '96 - p2 [1-50]
c   HB Guide - v8 - Spr '97 - p17 [51-250]
c   Sch Lib - v45 - F '97 - p17 [51-250]
c   SLJ - v43 - Ja '97 - p75 [51-250]
Mitchell, Barbara - *Red Bird (Illus. by Todd L W Doney)*
c   CCB-B - v50 - S '96 - p24 [51-250]
c   Ch BWatch - v6 - Jl '96 - p4 [1-50]
c   HB Guide - v7 - Fall '96 - p268 [51-250]
c   KR - v64 - My 1 '96 - p691 [51-250]
Waterman's Child (Illus. by Daniel San Souci)
c   CCB-B - v50 - Ap '97 - p291 [51-250]
c   PW - v244 - Mr 31 '97 - p75 [51-250]
Mitchell, Bruce, 1920- - *An Invitation to Old English and Anglo-Saxon England*
RES - v48 - F '97 - p75+ [501+]
Specu - v71 - Jl '96 - p734+ [501+]
Mitchell, Bruce M - *Multicultural Education*
r   ARBA - v28 - '97 - p131 [51-250]
Choice - v34 - F '97 - p1015 [51-250]
r   JAAL - v40 - Mr '97 - p512 [1-50]
r   R&R Bk N - v11 - D '96 - p54 [51-250]
r   WorldV - v12 - O '96 - p7 [51-250]
Mitchell, C Thomas - *New Thinking in Design*
r   Choice - v34 - N '96 - p445 [51-250]
R&R Bk N - v12 - F '97 - p74 [51-250]
Mitchell, Cecily Harper - *Cecily Small and the Rainy Day Adventure*
c   HB Guide - v7 - Fall '96 - p268 [51-250]
Mitchell, Chris - *Mathematics of Dependable Systems*
SIAM Rev - v38 - D '96 - p713+ [51-250]
Mitchell, Craig - *Teach to Reach*
Learning - v25 - Mr '97 - p7 [1-50]
Mitchell, David A - *Oxford Handbook of Clinical Dentistry. 2nd Ed.*
r   ARBA - v28 - '97 - p614 [51-250]
Mitchell, Edgar - *The Way of the Explorer (Mitchell). Audio Version*
BL - v93 - Ja '97 - p879 [51-250]
Mitchell, Eleanor - *Document Delivery Services*
SciTech - v20 - S '96 - p63 [1-50]
Mitchell, Ellinor R - *Fighting Drug Abuse with Acupuncture*
Choice - v34 - S '96 - p163 [51-250]
Mitchell, George J - *Not for America Alone*
KR - v65 - Mr 15 '97 - p445+ [251-500]
LJ - v122 - Ap 15 '97 - p100 [51-250]
PW - v244 - F 17 '97 - p199+ [51-250]
Mitchell, Harvey - *Individual Choice and the Structures of History*
Choice - v34 - N '96 - p519 [51-250]
CR - v269 - N '96 - p275 [501+]
Mitchell, J F - *Foundations for Programming Languages*
New Sci - v153 - Mr 1 '97 - p46+ [501+]
Mitchell, Jerome - *More Scott Operas*
Nine-C Lit - v51 - D '96 - p424 [51-250]
Mitchell, John C - *Foundations for Programming Languages*
Choice - v34 - F '97 - p999 [51-250]
Mitchell, John Hanson - *Walking towards Walden*
ABR - v18 - D '96 - p6 [501+]
Mitchell, John J - *Adolescent Vulnerability*
Adoles - v32 - Spr '97 - p247+ [51-250]
Mitchell, Joseph - *Up in the Old Hotel*
SFR - v21 - N '96 - p48 [1-50]
Mitchell, Joshua - *The Fragility of Freedom*
Ethics - v107 - Ja '97 - p401 [51-250]
J Pol - v58 - N '96 - p1236+ [501+]
Mitchell, Judith - *The Stone and the Scorpion*
VS - v39 - Aut '95 - p86+ [501+]
Mitchell, Kirk - *Deep Valley Malice*
Arm Det - v29 - Sum '96 - p372+ [51-250]
Mitchell, Lee Clark - *Westerns: Making the Man in Fiction and Film*
LJ - v121 - S 15 '96 - p70 [51-250]
Lon R Bks - v19 - F 6 '97 - p27+ [501+]
Obs - D 1 '96 - p18* [1-50]
SFR - v21 - N '96 - p33 [501+]
Mitchell, Margaree King - *Granddaddy's Gift (Illus. by Larry Johnson)*
c   BL - v93 - F 15 '97 - p1027+ [51-250]
c   KR - v65 - Ja 1 '97 - p60 [51-250]
c   PW - v244 - Ja 6 '97 - p73 [51-250]
c   Trib Bks - F 9 '97 - p7 [51-250]
Uncle Jed's Barbershop
c   CLW - v67 - Mr '97 - p14 [1-50]
Mitchell, Margaret - *Lost Laysen (Fellows). Audio Version*
y   Kliatt - v31 - Mr '97 - p44 [51-250]

Mitchell, Mark - *The Penguin Book of International Gay Writing*
TES - O 11 '96 - p8* [51-250]
Mitchell, Marybelle - *From Talking Chiefs to a Native Corporate Elite*
Choice - v34 - F '97 - p1025+ [51-250]
R&R Bk N - v11 - D '96 - p13 [51-250]
Mitchell, Melanie - *An Introduction to Genetic Algorithms*
Choice - v34 - S '96 - p164 [51-250]
Mitchell, P - *The Duchovny Files*
Quill & Q - v62 - D '96 - p30 [501+]
Mitchell, P M - *Johann Christoph Gottsched 1700-1766*
MLR - v92 - Ja '97 - p239+ [501+]
Mitchell, Paul - *Frameworks: Form, Function and Ornament in European Portrait Frames*
TLS - Mr 7 '97 - p32 [1-50]
Mitchell, Pratima - *The Ramayana*
c   Sch Lib - v44 - Ag '96 - p113 [51-250]
Mitchell, Reid - *A Man Under Authority*
KR - v65 - My 1 '97 - p671 [251-500]
Mitchell, Rhonda - *The Talking Cloth (Illus. by Rhonda Mitchell)*
c   BL - v93 - F 15 '97 - p1028 [51-250]
c   CBRS - v25 - Mr '97 - p89 [51-250]
c   PW - v244 - F 17 '97 - p218+ [51-250]
Mitchell, Richard H - *Political Bribery in Japan*
Choice - v34 - Ap '97 - p1411 [51-250]
Mitchell, Rita Phillips - *One for Me, One for You*
c   Bks Keeps - Jl '96 - p9 [51-250]
Mitchell, Robert H - *Ride the Lightning*
KR - v65 - F 15 '97 - p248+ [251-500]
PW - v244 - Mr 10 '97 - p52 [51-250]
Mitchell, Roger - *The Word for Everything*
Ant R - v55 - Spr '97 - p246+ [251-500]
Mitchell, Ruth - *Learning in Overdrive*
Math T - v89 - S '96 - p515+ [51-250]
Mitchell, Sally - *Daily Life in Victorian England*
R&R Bk N - v12 - F '97 - p15 [51-250]
Mitchell, Sally, 1937- - *The New Girl*
ELT - v40 - 2 '97 - p217+ [501+]
NWSA Jnl - v8 - Fall '96 - p144+ [501+]
Mitchell, Samuel - *Tidal Waves of Reform*
R&R Bk N - v12 - F '97 - p68 [51-250]
Mitchell, Susan, Ph.D. - *I'd Kill for a Cookie*
BL - v93 - F 1 '97 - p917 [51-250]
PW - v244 - Ja 27 '97 - p99+ [51-250]
Mitchell, Susan, 1945- - *The Scent of Power*
Arena - Ag '96 - p46+ [501+]
Aust Bk R - Je '96 - p11+ [501+]
Mitchell, Susan, 1958- - *The Official Guide to American Attitudes*
r   ARBA - v28 - '97 - p325+ [251-500]
r   Choice - v34 - O '96 - p254 [51-250]
The Official Guide to the Generations
r   ACI - v9 - Spr '97 - p37 [51-250]
Mitchell, Timothy - *Colonising Egypt*
JMH - v68 - S '96 - p617+ [501+]
Mitchell, Timothy J - *Flamenco Deep Song*
Am Ethnol - v23 - N '96 - p922+ [501+]
Notes - v53 - S '96 - p86+ [501+]
Mitchell, William J - *City of Bits*
AAAGA - v86 - S '96 - p605+ [501+]
JC - v47 - Win '97 - p136+ [501+]
SocSciComR - v14 - Sum '96 - p238+ [501+]
Mitford, Nancy - *The Letters of Nancy Mitford and Evelyn Waugh*
BL - v93 - Mr 15 '97 - p1221 [51-250]
BW - v27 - Ap 13 '97 - p1+ [501+]
KR - v65 - Ja 15 '97 - p125 [251-500]
Lon R Bks - v19 - F 6 '97 - p19+ [501+]
Obs - O 27 '96 - p17* [501+]
PW - v244 - Ja 13 '97 - p60 [51-250]
Spec - v277 - O 12 '96 - p40+ [501+]
Spec - v277 - N 16 '96 - p46 [1-50]
Spec - v277 - N 30 '96 - p58 [1-50]
TLS - O 25 '96 - p32 [501+]
WSJ-Cent - v99 - Ap 29 '97 - pA20 [501+]
Mitgang, Herbert - *Dangerous Dossiers*
NYTBR - v101 - N 3 '96 - p28 [1-50]
The Man Who Rode the Tiger
NYTBR - v101 - N 3 '96 - p28 [1-50]
Mitgutsch, Waltraud Anna - *Abschied Von Jerusalem*
WLT - v70 - Aut '96 - p949+ [501+]
Mithen, Steven - *The Prehistory of the Mind*
Choice - v34 - Ap '97 - p1379 [51-250]
LJ - v121 - D '96 - p139 [51-250]
Lon R Bks - v18 - N '96 - p22+ [501+]
Nature - v383 - O 31 '96 - p775+ [501+]
New Sci - v152 - O 26 '96 - p44+ [501+]
NS - v125 - O 18 '96 - p42+ [501+]
Obs - D 15 '96 - p15* [501+]

Mitra, Subrata K - *Subnational Movements in South Asia*
R&R Bk N - v12 - F '97 - p19 [51-250]
Mitrofanow, Ilja - *Der Zeuge*
WLT - v70 - Aut '96 - p987 [501+]
Mitropulu, Costula - *Sei Ruoli Per Solisti*
WLT - v70 - Aut '96 - p1004 [51-250]
Mitsui, T - *Numerical Analysis of Ordinary Differential Equations and Its Applications*
SIAM Rev - v38 - D '96 - p714 [1-50]
Mittal, Gauris S - *Computerized Control Systems in the Food Industry*
SciTech - v20 - D '96 - p83 [51-250]
Mittelhammer, Ron C - *Mathematical Statistics for Economics and Business*
r   JEL - v34 - S '96 - p1409 [51-250]
Mittelman, James H - *Globalization: Critical Reflections*
CS - v25 - S '96 - p585+ [501+]
Out from Underdevelopment Revisited
Choice - v34 - My '97 - p1548 [51-250]
Mitter, Partha - *Art and Nationalism in Colonial India 1850-1922*
Art J - v55 - Fall '96 - p93+ [501+]
Mitterand, Francois - *De L'Allemagne, De La France*
Econ - v339 - My 18 '96 - p5*+ [251-500]
Memoires Interrompus
Econ - v339 - My 18 '96 - p5*+ [251-500]
Mitterand, Henri - *L'Illusion Realiste*
MLN - v111 - S '96 - p803+ [501+]
Mitterer, Felix - *Siberia and Other Plays*
TranslRevS - v1 - My '95 - p22 [51-250]
Mittermayer, Manfred - *Thomas Bernhard*
Ger Q - v70 - Win '97 - p93+ [501+]
Mitterrand, Danielle - *En Toute Liberte*
BL - v93 - Ja '97 - p827 [51-250]
Mitterrand, Francois - *Memoir in Two Voices*
AB - v98 - Ag 19 '96 - p566+ [501+]
LATBR - Jl 7 '96 - p2 [501+]
Mittleman, Alan L - *The Politics of Torah*
R&R Bk N - v12 - F '97 - p9 [51-250]
Mitton, Jacqueline - *Gems of Hubble*
Astron - v25 - Mr '97 - p103 [1-50]
y   SB - v33 - Mr '97 - p45 [51-250]
S&T - v92 - D '96 - p63+ [501+]
Mitton, Michael - *The Soul of Celtic Spirituality in the Lives of Its Saints*
CLW - v66 - Je '96 - p34+ [251-500]
RR - v55 - S '96 - p552+ [51-250]
Mitton, Simon - *The Young Oxford Book of Astronomy*
y   HB Guide - v7 - Fall '96 - p330 [51-250]
yr Par Ch - v21 - Mr '97 - p5 [1-50]
Miwa, Yoshiro - *Firms and Industrial Organization in Japan*
JEL - v34 - D '96 - p2082 [51-250]
Mix: The Magazine of Artist-Run Culture
p   Utne R - Mr '97 - p89 [51-250]
Mixner, David B - *Stranger among Friends*
BL - v92 - Ag '96 - p1862+ [501+]
HG&LRev - v3 - Fall '96 - p35+ [501+]
Nat - v263 - S 9 '96 - p44+ [501+]
Mixon, Wayne - *The People's Writer*
AL - v69 - Mr '97 - p236+ [251-500]
Mixter, Keith E - *General Bibliography for Music Research. 3rd Ed.*
r   ARBA - v28 - '97 - p468 [251-500]
Miyabe, Miyuki - *All She Was Worth*
Arm Det - v30 - Win '97 - p85+ [251-500]
BW - v27 - F 23 '97 - p8 [501+]
KR - v64 - N 15 '96 - p1636+ [51-250]
LJ - v121 - N 1 '96 - p110 [51-250]
NYTBR - v102 - F 16 '97 - p28 [51-250]
PW - v243 - N 11 '96 - p59 [51-250]
Trib Bks - Mr 2 '97 - p5 [51-250]
Miyamoto, Masao - *Straitjacket Society*
J Con A - v30 - Win '96 - p493+ [501+]
Miyazawa, Kenji - *Milky Way Railroad*
LATBR - v263 - S 29 '96 - p15 [51-250]
Once and Forever
TranslRevS - v1 - My '95 - p25 [51-250]
Mizell, Louis R, Jr. - *Masters of Deception*
PW - v243 - O 21 '96 - p61 [51-250]
Miziolek, Andrzej W - *Halon Replacements*
SciTech - v20 - S '96 - p60 [51-250]
Mizoguchi, Toshiyuki - *Reforms of Statistical System under Socio-Economic Changes*
r   JEL - v34 - S '96 - p1353+ [501+]
Mizrachi, Eli - *Two Americans within the Gates*
Nat R - v48 - O 28 '96 - p78 [51-250]
Mizuno, Kogen - *Essentials of Buddhism*
PW - v244 - Ap 14 '97 - p71 [51-250]
Mizuno, Kosuke - *Rural Industrialization in Indonesia*
JEL - v35 - Mr '97 - p272+ [51-250]

MLA International Bibliography of Books and Articles on the Modern Languages and Literatures 1922-
r ASInt - v34 - O '96 - p18 [51-250]
Mlyn, Eric - *The State, Society, and Limited Nuclear War*
J Pol - v58 - N '96 - p1262+ [501+]
Mo, Shen - *Nian Hua*
BL - v93 - N 1 '96 - p484 [1-50]
Mo, Yan - *Feng Ru Fei Tun*
BL - v93 - N 1 '96 - p484 [1-50]
Mo, Yen - *The Garlic Ballads*
NYTBR - v101 - Jl 21 '96 - p28 [1-50]
Red Sorghum
TranslRevS - v1 - My '95 - p16 [51-250]
Moaddel, Mansoor - *Class, Politics, and Ideology in the Iranian Revolution*
JTWS - v13 - Spr '96 - p379+ [501+]
Moat, A G - *Microbial Physiology. 3rd Ed.*
BioSci - v46 - O '96 - p704 [501+]
Moats, Louisa Cook - *Spelling: Development, Disability, and Instruction*
HER - v66 - Fall '96 - p692+ [501+]
Moatti, Christiane - *Notre Siecle Au Miroir Des Limbes*
FR - v70 - D '96 - p338+ [501+]
Mobius, J Mark - *Mobius on Emerging Markets*
BL - v93 - S 1 '96 - p45 [51-250]
BWatch - v17 - N '96 - p7 [51-250]
Choice - v34 - Ap '97 - p1388 [251-500]
PW - v243 - O 14 '96 - p71 [51-250]
Mobley, Joe A - *Ship Ashore!*
Pub Hist - v18 - Fall '96 - p172+ [501+]
Mobley, Marilyn Sanders - *Folk Roots and Mythic Wings in Sarah Orne Jewett and Toni Morrison*
Signs - v22 - Aut '96 - p243+ [501+]
Mochizuki, Ken - *Heroes (Illus. by Dom Lee)*
c RT - v50 - N '96 - p245 [51-250]
Passage to Freedom (Illus. by Dom Lee)
c BL - v93 - My 15 '97 - p1574 [51-250]
c PW - v244 - Ap 21 '97 - p71 [51-250]
Mock, Irene - *Inappropriate Behaviour*
Quill & Q - v63 - Mr '97 - p70+ [251-500]
Mockaitis, Thomas R - *British Counterinsurgency in the Post-Imperial Era*
Albion - v28 - Sum '96 - p365+ [501+]
Mockler, Anthony - *Graham Greene: Three Lives*
AS - v66 - Win '97 - p128+ [501+]
Modarressi, Mitra - *The Beastly Visits (Illus. by Mitra Modarressi)*
c BL - v93 - O 1 '96 - p359 [51-250]
c CBRS - v25 - Mr '97 - p89 [51-250]
c HB Guide - v8 - Spr '97 - p40 [51-250]
c KR - v64 - Ag 15 '96 - p1239 [51-250]
c PW - v243 - Jl 22 '96 - p241 [51-250]
c SLJ - v42 - S '96 - p186 [51-250]
The Parent Thief (Illus. by Mitra Modarressi)
c NYTBR - v101 - Ap 7 '96 - p21 [1-50]
Modell, Martin E - *Professional's Guide to Systems Analysis. 2nd Ed.*
CBR - v14 - N '96 - p40 [51-250]
A Professional's Guide to Systems Analysis. 2nd Ed.
SciTech - v20 - N '96 - p12 [51-250]
Modelski, George - *Leading Sectors and World Powers*
JEL - v34 - S '96 - p1421 [51-250]
R&R Bk N - v12 - F '97 - p34 [51-250]
Modern Aspects of Electrochemistry. No. 28
SciTech - v20 - S '96 - p17 [51-250]
Modern Aspects of Electrochemistry. No. 30
SciTech - v21 - Mr '97 - p32 [51-250]
Modern Spectroscopy of Solids, Liquids, and Gases
SciTech - v20 - N '96 - p24 [51-250]
Modesitt, L E - *Adiamante*
Analog - v117 - F '97 - p145+ [251-500]
LJ - v121 - S 15 '96 - p101 [51-250]
NYTBR - v101 - D 29 '96 - p16 [51-250]
PW - v243 - S 23 '96 - p61 [51-250]
y VOYA - v19 - F '97 - p339 [51-250]
The Ecolitan Enigma
KR - v65 - My 1 '97 - p685 [51-250]
PW - v244 - My 12 '97 - p62 [51-250]
The Soprano Sorceress
y BL - v93 - F 1 '97 - p929 [51-250]
KR - v64 - D 15 '96 - p1773 [51-250]
PW - v244 - Ja 20 '97 - p398 [51-250]
Modesitt, L E, Jr. - *The Parafaith War*
Analog - v116 - Jl '96 - p273+ [251-500]
Modeste, Naomi N - *Dictionary of Public Health Promotion and Education*
r ARBA - v28 - '97 - p601 [51-250]
Modiano, Patrick - *Du Plus Loin De L'Oubli*
BL - v93 - Ja '97 - p827 [1-50]
WLT - v70 - Aut '96 - p909+ [251-500]

Modica, Andrea - *Treadwell: Photographs*
VV - v52 - Ja 28 '97 - p48+ [501+]
Modin, Yuri - *My Five Cambridge Friends*
JPR - v33 - N '96 - p499+ [51-250]
Modinos, A - *Quantum Theory of Matter*
Choice - v34 - D '96 - p648+ [51-250]
SciTech - v20 - S '96 - p14 [51-250]
Modleski, Tania - *Studies in Entertainment*
CAY - v17 - Fall '96 - p13 [51-250]
Modrzejewski, Joseph Meleze - *The Jews of Egypt*
Historian - v59 - Win '97 - p415+ [251-500]
Moe, Barbara A - *A Question of Timing*
y Cur R - v36 - Ap '97 - p12 [51-250]
Moench, Doug - *Batman vs. Predator II*
p Quill & Q - v62 - Ag '96 - p26 [51-250]
Moens, Alexander - *Disconcerted Europe*
Parameters - v27 - Spr '97 - p169+ [501+]
Moessinger, Pierre - *Irrationalite Individuelle Et Ordre Social*
TLS - N 29 '96 - p14 [51-250]
Moeyes, Paul - *Siegfried Sassoon: Scorched Glory*
LJ - v122 - Ap 1 '97 - p93 [51-250]
Moffat, Riley Moore - *Population History of Western U.S. Cities and Towns 1850-1990*
r ARBA - v28 - '97 - p328 [51-250]
r Choice - v34 - F '97 - p947 [51-250]
R&R Bk N - v12 - F '97 - p34 [51-250]
Moffat, Frank - *Farmer Beans and the Dog with No Name*
c Magpies - v11 - Jl '96 - p26 [51-250]
Moffatt, Judith - *Who Stole the Cookies? (Illus. by Judith Moffatt)*
c BL - v92 - Ag '96 - p1910 [51-250]
c SLJ - v42 - S '96 - p186 [51-250]
Moffi, Larry - *This Side of Cooperstown*
BW - v26 - Jl 7 '96 - p1+ [501+]
Econ - v340 - S 14 '96 - p4*+ [501+]
Moffit, Gisela - *Bonds and Bondage*
Ger Q - v69 - Sum '96 - p360+ [501+]
Moffitt, John F - *O Brave New People*
Choice - v34 - N '96 - p526 [51-250]
Moffitt, Leonard C - *Connected Community*
R&R Bk N - v12 - F '97 - p51 [51-250]
Mogelonsky, Marcia - *Everybody Eats*
ACI - v8 - Fall '96 - p36+ [251-500]
Mogensen, Gunnar Viby - *The Shadow Economy in Denmark 1994*
JEL - v34 - S '96 - p1439 [51-250]
Mogensen, Ole Erik - *Positron Annihilation in Chemistry*
Am Sci - v84 - N '96 - p600+ [501+]
Mogensen, Vernon L - *Office Politics*
Choice - v34 - Mr '97 - p1193 [51-250]
Moggach, Deborah - *Close Relations*
Books - v11 - Ap '97 - p4 [501+]
Moghadam, Valentine M - *Democratic Reform and the Position of Women in Transitional Economies*
APSR - v90 - S '96 - p679+ [501+]
Gender and National Identity
JTWS - v13 - Spr '96 - p420+ [501+]
Patriarchy and Economic Development
Choice - v34 - Mr '97 - p1209 [51-250]
Mogil, H Michael - *Anytime Weather Everywhere*
cr SB - v32 - N '96 - p238 [51-250]
Mohan, Brij - *Democracies of Unfreedom*
Choice - v34 - F '97 - p1031 [51-250]
R&R Bk N - v12 - F '97 - p51 [1-50]
Mohan, Claire Jordan - *The Young Life of Mother Teresa of Calcutta (Illus. by Jane Robbins)*
c CLW - v67 - Mr '97 - p54 [51-250]
c SLJ - v43 - Ja '97 - p106 [51-250]
Mohanram, Radhika - *English Postcoloniality*
Choice - v34 - S '96 - p125 [51-250]
Mohler, Johann Adam - *Unity in the Church or the Principle of Catholicism*
Rel St Rev - v23 - Ap '97 - p153 [51-250]
Theol St - v58 - Mr '97 - p192 [51-250]
Mohler, R Albert, Jr. - *Theological Education in the Theological Tradition*
PW - v244 - Ja 13 '97 - p70 [51-250]
Mohr, James - *SCO Companion*
SciTech - v20 - D '96 - p7 [1-50]
Mohr, James C - *Abortion in America*
Cons - v17 - Aut '96 - p35+ [501+]
Mohr, Joseph - *Silent Night (Illus. by Susan Jeffers)*
c TES - D 6 '96 - p16* [1-50]
Mohr, Nicholasa - *Old Letivia and the Mountain of Sorrows (Illus. by Rudy Gutierrez)*
c HB Guide - v8 - Spr '97 - p40 [51-250]
c RT - v50 - My '97 - p683 [51-250]
c SLJ - v42 - Ag '96 - p127 [51-250]

El Regalo Magico (Illus. by Rudy Gutierrez)
c BL - v93 - My 1 '97 - p1506 [1-50]
The Song of El Coq and Other Tales of Puerto Rico
c SS - v88 - Ja '97 - p29+ [51-250]
La Vieja Letivia Y El Monte De Los Pesares (Illus. by Rudy Gutierrez)
c BL - v93 - My 1 '97 - p1506 [1-50]
c SLJ - v42 - N '96 - p134 [51-250]
Moi, Toril - *Simone De Beauvoir: The Making of an Intellectual Woman*
FR - v70 - O '96 - p125+ [501+]
NWSA Jnl - v8 - Fall '96 - p177+ [501+]
Moise, Edwin E - *Tonkin Gulf and the Escalation of the Vietnam War*
Choice - v34 - My '97 - p1563+ [51-250]
KR - v64 - O 1 '96 - p1449 [251-500]
Moiz, Azra - *Taiwan*
c HB Guide - v7 - Fall '96 - p383 [1-50]
c SLJ - v42 - S '96 - p217 [51-250]
Moje, Steven W - *Paper Clip Science*
c HB Guide - v8 - Spr '97 - p110 [51-250]
Mokeddem, Malika - *Des Reves Et Des Assassins*
WLT - v70 - Aut '96 - p1010+ [501+]
Mokhtari, Fariborz L - *Peacemaking, Peacekeeping and Coalition Warfare*
RSR - v24 - 3 '96 - p44 [51-250]
Mokotoff, Gary - *How to Document Victims and Locate Survivors of the Holocaust*
NGSQ - v85 - Mr '97 - p61+ [501+]
Mokros, Hartmut B - *Interaction and Identity*
Readings - v11 - S '96 - p24 [51-250]
Mol, Pieter Laurens - *Grand Promptness*
LJ - v121 - N 15 '96 - p59 [51-250]
Mola, Luca - *La Comunita Dei Lucchesi A Venezia*
EHR - v112 - Ap '97 - p449+ [501+]
Specu - v71 - Jl '96 - p736+ [501+]
Molarsky, Osmond - *A Sky Full of Kites (Illus. by Helen Hipshman)*
c HB Guide - v7 - Fall '96 - p268 [51-250]
Moldea, Dan E - *The Killing of Robert F. Kennedy*
PW - v244 - F 3 '97 - p100 [1-50]
Trib Bks - Mr 2 '97 - p8 [1-50]
Moldi-Ravenna, Cristiana - *Secret Gardens in Venice*
LJ - v122 - Ja '97 - p130 [51-250]
PW - v243 - N 25 '96 - p66 [51-250]
Mole, John - *Hot Air (Illus. by Peter Bailey)*
c Sch Lib - v44 - N '96 - p167 [51-250]
c TES - Jl 26 '96 - pR8 [51-250]
Mole, Sandra - *Colours of the Rainbow*
Sch Lib - v44 - Ag '96 - p130 [51-250]
Molecular Breeding: New Strategies in Plant Improvement
p Nature - v383 - S 5 '96 - p39 [251-500]
Molecular Physics and Hypersonic Flows (1995: Maratea, Italy) - *Molecular Physics and Hypersonic Flows*
SciTech - v20 - N '96 - p17 [51-250]
Molen, Ron - *My New Life*
NYTBR - v102 - Ja 5 '97 - p18 [51-250]
Molenaar, Cor - *Interactive Marketing*
R&R Bk N - v12 - F '97 - p44 [51-250]
Molesworth, Mrs. - *The Cuckoo Clock*
c ChLAQ - v21 - Win '96 - p170+ [501+]
Molho, Anthony - *Marriage Alliance in Late Medieval Florence*
EHR - v112 - F '97 - p179+ [501+]
Historian - v59 - Win '97 - p406+ [501+]
JIH - v27 - Aut '96 - p320+ [501+]
Ren Q - v49 - Aut '96 - p621+ [501+]
Specu - v72 - Ja '97 - p201+ [501+]
Moliere - *Dom Juan*
MLN - v111 - D '96 - p918+ [501+]
L'Ecole Des Femmes
FR - v70 - F '97 - p407+ [501+]
Molina, Tirso De - *El Burlador De Sevilla Y Convidado De Piedra*
MLR - v91 - O '96 - p1017+ [501+]
Molina-Foix, Vicente - *La Misa De Baroja*
WLT - v71 - Win '97 - p119+ [251-500]
Molinet, Jean - *Le Mystere De Judith Et Holofernes*
Ren Q - v50 - Spr '97 - p251+ [501+]
Moll, Louise B - *Baffling Cryptograms*
c SLJ - v42 - Ag '96 - p158 [51-250]
Moll, Lucy - *The Vegetarian Child*
PW - v244 - F 3 '97 - p104 [51-250]
Mollel, Tololwa M - *Big Boy (Illus. by E B Lewis)*
c PW - v244 - Ja 27 '97 - p108 [1-50]
Kele's Secret (Illus. by Catherine Stock)
c PW - v244 - My 12 '97 - p76 [51-250]
c Quill & Q - v63 - F '97 - p57 [251-500]

Mollenkopf, John - *A Phoenix in the Ashes*
J Urban H - v22 - Jl '96 - p656+ [501+]
Moller, Bjorn - *Defence Doctrines and Conversion*
R&R Bk N - v12 - F '97 - p35 [51-250]
Moller, David Wendell - *Confronting Death*
Hast Cen R - v26 - S '96 - p41 [51-250]
Mollier, Jean-Yves - *La Plus Longue Des Republiques 1870-1940*
EHR - v112 - F '97 - p252+ [501+]
Mollin, Richard A - *Quadratics*
Choice - v34 - Ap '97 - p1376 [51-250]
Molloy, Scott - *Trolley Wars*
HRNB - v25 - Win '97 - p56 [501+]
T&C - v38 - Ja '97 - p255+ [501+]
Molloy, Sylvia - *Signs of Borges*
TranslRevS - v1 - My '95 - p30+ [51-250]
Molloy, William - *What Are We Going to Do Now?*
Quill & Q - v63 - F '97 - p46 [501+]
Molnar, Geza Von - *Goethes Kantstudien*
MLR - v91 - Jl '96 - p785+ [501+]
Moloney, James - *A Bridge to Wiseman's Cove*
y Aust Bk R - D '96 - p88+ [501+]
Moloney, Kevin - *Lobbyists for Hire*
R&R Bk N - v11 - N '96 - p49 [51-250]
Moloney, Norah - *The Young Oxford Book of Archaeology*
c Magpies - v11 - Jl '96 - p40 [251-500]
c Sch Lib - v44 - Ag '96 - p124+ [51-250]
Molson, Karen - *Complain, Complain, Complain*
r Quill & Q - v63 - Mr '97 - p73 [251-500]
Molstad, Stephen - *Independence Day*
y Books - v10 - Je '96 - p25 [51-250]
Moltesen, Mette - *Excavations at La Giostra*
AJA - v101 - Ja '97 - p196 [251-500]
Moltmann, Jurgen - *The Coming of God*
CC - v114 - Ja 1 '97 - p21+ [251-500]
Rel St Rev - v23 - Ap '97 - p154 [51-250]
Moltmann-Wendel, Elisabeth - *I Am My Body*
ER - v48 - Jl '96 - p420+ [501+]
Theol St - v57 - Mr '96 - p191 [51-250]
TT - v53 - Ja '97 - p563 [51-250]
Momaday, N Scott - *House Made of Dawn*
Bloom Rev - v16 - N '96 - p15 [51-250]
The Man Made of Words
KR - v65 - Mr 1 '97 - p360 [51-250]
LJ - v122 - My 1 '97 - p104 [51-250]
PW - v244 - Mr 24 '97 - p67 [251-500]
The Names: A Memoir
Bloom Rev - v16 - N '96 - p15 [51-250]
Trib Bks - Ja 19 '97 - p3+ [501+]
The Way to Rainy Mountain
Bloom Rev - v16 - N '96 - p15 [51-250]
Trib Bks - Ja 19 '97 - p3+ [501+]
Mommaers, Paul - *Mysticism, Buddhist and Christian*
JR - v77 - Ja '97 - p179+ [501+]
Mommen, Andre - *The Belgian Economy in the Twentieth Century*
BusLR - v21 - 3 '96 - p248+ [501+]
Econ J - v106 - N '96 - p1848+ [251-500]
Mommsen, Hans - *The Rise and Fall of Weimar Democracy*
Choice - v34 - N '96 - p519 [51-250]
HRNB - v25 - Fall '96 - p30 [251-500]
Die Verspielte Freiheit
JMH - v68 - S '96 - p629+ [501+]
Mommsen, Theodor - *A History of Rome under the Emperors*
BWatch - v18 - F '97 - p2 [51-250]
CR - v269 - N '96 - p278+ [51-250]
New R - v215 - D 16 '96 - p42+ [501+]
Spec - v277 - O 5 '96 - p45+ [501+]
Spec - v277 - N 16 '96 - p44 [1-50]
Mommsen, Wolfgang J - *Das Ringen Um Den Nationalen Staat*
JMH - v68 - S '96 - p730+ [501+]
Momsen, Janet Henshall - *St. Lucia*
r ARBA - v28 - '97 - p74 [51-250]
r Choice - v34 - Mr '97 - p1140 [51-250]
r R&R Bk N - v12 - F '97 - p27 [51-250]
Monaghan, Daniel T - *The Ionotropic Glutamate Receptors*
SciTech - v21 - Mr '97 - p40 [51-250]
Monaghan, John - *The Covenants with Earth and Rain*
Am Ethnol - v24 - F '97 - p229+ [501+]
Monahan, Arthur P - *From Personal Duties towards Personal Rights*
Specu - v71 - Jl '96 - p737+ [501+]
Monahan, Brent - *The Bell Witch*
KR - v65 - Ja 1 '97 - p15+ [251-500]
PW - v244 - F 3 '97 - p94 [51-250]

Monahan, Michael A - *California Environmental Law Handbook. 9th Ed.*
r R&R Bk N - v11 - N '96 - p53 [51-250]
Monahan, Patricia - *The Watercolor Painter's Handbook*
LJ - v122 - Mr 15 '97 - p63 [51-250]
Monassebian, Jeff - *Survival Guide to Computer Contracts*
CBR - v14 - N '96 - p33 [51-250]
Monastysky, Michael - *Modern Mathematics in the Light of the Fields Medals*
Sci - v276 - Ap 4 '97 - p47 [1-50]
Monchak, Ronald W - *The Last White Christmas*
BWatch - v17 - D '96 - p3 [51-250]
Monckton, Stephen G - *Huron Paleoethnobotany*
Am Ant - v62 - Ja '97 - p173+ [251-500]
Moncrieff, Elspeth - *Farm Animal Portraits*
Mag Antiq - v151 - Ja '97 - p50 [251-500]
Moncur, Andrew - *A Good Looking Man*
TLS - N 1 '96 - p26 [501+]
Woman's J - N '96 - p12 [1-50]
Moncure, Jane Belk - *Caring (Illus. by Mechelle Ann)*
c HB Guide - v8 - Spr '97 - p86 [51-250]
Courage (Illus. by Mechelle Ann)
c HB Guide - v8 - Spr '97 - p86 [51-250]
Joy (Illus. by Mechelle Ann)
c HB Guide - v8 - Spr '97 - p86 [51-250]
Kindness (Illus. by Mechelle Ann)
c HB Guide - v8 - Spr '97 - p86 [51-250]
Monda, Virgiliu - *Aurul*
BL - v93 - D 15 '96 - p714 [1-50]
Mondak, Jeffrey J - *Nothing to Read*
APSR - v90 - D '96 - p918+ [501+]
J Pol - v58 - Ag '96 - p882+ [501+]
PSQ - v111 - Win '96 - p726+ [501+]
Pub Op Q - v60 - Sum '96 - p338+ [501+]
Mondimore, Francis Mark - *A Natural History of Homosexuality*
BW - v27 - F 2 '97 - p13 [51-250]
Choice - v34 - My '97 - p1584 [51-250]
LJ - v122 - Ja '97 - p127+ [51-250]
PW - v243 - S 30 '96 - p67+ [51-250]
TLS - N 1 '96 - p14 [501+]
Mondini De Leuciis - *Exposito Super Capitulum De Generatione Embrionis Canonis Avicennae Cum Quibusdam Quaestionibus*
Specu - v71 - O '96 - p984+ [501+]
Monet, Jean - *The Cassock and the Crown*
Beav - v76 - D '96 - p46+ [51-250]
Monette, Paul - *Afterlife*
Obs - N 3 '96 - p16* [51-250]
TLS - O 11 '96 - p27 [51-250]
Sanctuary: A Tale of Life in the Woods
Advocate - Mr 18 '97 - p77 [51-250]
BL - v93 - N 15 '96 - p572 [51-250]
KR - v64 - N 15 '96 - p1626+ [251-500]
LATBR - F 16 '97 - p9 [501+]
LJ - v121 - D '96 - p146 [51-250]
NYTBR - v102 - Mr 9 '97 - p19 [51-250]
PW - v243 - N 11 '96 - p55 [51-250]
Money: A History (CCNB)
Coin W - v38 - F 10 '97 - p75 [1-50]
Money and Morals Worldwide: First Annual Report
BWatch - v17 - S '96 - p9 [51-250]
Choice - v34 - D '96 - p659 [51-250]
R&R Bk N - v11 - D '96 - p36 [51-250]
Money Coach Guide to Top Funds 1997
r Quill & Q - v63 - Ja '97 - p24+ [51-250]
Money for Graduate Students in the Humanities 1996-1998
r Choice - v34 - Mr '97 - p1140+ [251-500]
Money for Graduate Students in the Sciences 1996-1998
r Choice - v34 - Mr '97 - p1140+ [251-500]
Money for Graduate Students in the Social Sciences 1996-1998
r Choice - v34 - Mr '97 - p1140+ [251-500]
Monfasani, John - *Byzantine Scholars in Renaissance Italy*
CHR - v83 - Ja '97 - p95+ [501+]
Monfredo, Miriam Grace - *Through a Gold Eagle*
Arm Det - v29 - Fall '96 - p489+ [51-250]
BWatch - v17 - S '96 - p1 [51-250]
Monga, Celestin - *The Anthropology of Anger*
Choice - v34 - Ap '97 - p1411 [51-250]
Mongredien, Jean - *French Music from the Enlightenment to Romanticism 1789-1830*
AB - v98 - D 9 '96 - p1994 [51-250]
Choice - v34 - Mr '97 - p1172 [51-250]
Monicat, Benedicte - *Itineraires De L'Ecriture Au Feminin*
FR - v70 - Mr '97 - p599+ [501+]

Monk, Gerald - *Narrative Therapy in Practice*
SciTech - v21 - Mr '97 - p54 [51-250]
Monk, Karyn - *Once a Warrior*
PW - v244 - Mr 17 '97 - p80 [51-250]
The Rebel and the Redcoat
Quill & Q - v62 - Jl '96 - p43 [251-500]
Monk, Linda R - *Ordinary Americans*
SE - v61 - Mr '97 - p173+ [501+]
Monk, Ray - *Bertrand Russell: The Spirit of Solitude*
BL - v93 - S 1 '96 - p35 [51-250]
CHE - v43 - N 15 '96 - pA24 [51-250]
CPR - v16 - Ag '96 - p267+ [501+]
LATBR - N 3 '96 - p4+ [501+]
New R - v215 - D 2 '96 - p46+ [501+]
NL - v79 - D 16 '96 - p3+ [501+]
NY - v72 - D 9 '96 - p104+ [501+]
NYRB - v43 - N 28 '96 - p39+ [501+]
NYTBR - v101 - D 29 '96 - p5 [501+]
NYTLa - v146 - D 6 '96 - pC35 [501+]
Quad - v40 - Je '96 - p78+ [501+]
R&R Bk N - v12 - F '97 - p33 [51-250]
WSJ-MW - v77 - S 27 '96 - pA12 [501+]
Monks, Robert A G - *Watching the Watchers*
Choice - v34 - D '96 - p655 [51-250]
Monmonier, Mark - *Cartographies of Danger*
BL - v93 - Ap 1 '97 - p1272 [51-250]
LJ - v122 - Ap 1 '97 - p119 [51-250]
New Sci - v154 - My 3 '97 - p46+ [501+]
Monod, David - *Store Wars*
JEL - v34 - D '96 - p2107 [51-250]
Quill & Q - v62 - Jl '96 - p50 [501+]
R&R Bk N - v11 - N '96 - p35 [51-250]
Monroe, Dan L - *Gifts of the Spirit*
Am Craft - v57 - Ap '97 - p28 [1-50]
LJ - v122 - Ap 15 '97 - p76 [51-250]
Mag Antiq - v150 - D '96 - p760 [501+]
PW - v244 - Ja 27 '97 - p93+ [51-250]
Monroe, Judy - *Phobias: Everything You Wanted to Know, but Were Afraid to Ask*
y HB Guide - v7 - Fall '96 - p348 [51-250]
Monroe, Kristen Renwick - *The Heart of Altruism*
AAPSS-A - v550 - Mr '97 - p192+ [251-500]
Choice - v34 - N '96 - p543 [51-250]
ChrPhil - v8 - Je 27 '96 - p34 [51-250]
New R - v215 - O 28 '96 - p36+ [501+]
NL - v79 - O 7 '96 - p18+ [501+]
Rel St Rev - v23 - Ap '97 - p159 [51-250]
Monroe, Marilyn - *Marilyn: Her Life in Her Own Words*
Obs - D 22 '96 - p16* [501+]
Monroe, Valerie - *In the Weather of the Heart*
KR - v64 - My 1 '96 - p669+ [251-500]
Monseau, Virginia R - *Responding to Young Adult Literature*
EJ - v85 - N '96 - p125+ [501+]
JAAL - v40 - Mr '97 - p508+ [501+]
SLJ - v42 - Ag '96 - p36 [51-250]
Monser, George J - *Antenna Design*
SciTech - v20 - S '96 - p57 [51-250]
Monshipouri, Mahmood - *Democratization Liberalization and Human Rights in the Third World*
JPR - v33 - Ag '96 - p381+ [251-500]
Monsma, Stephen V - *When Sacred and Secular Mix*
Choice - v34 - Mr '97 - p1240+ [51-250]
Monson, A M - *Wanted: Best Friend (Illus. by Lynn Munsinger)*
c BL - v93 - D 15 '96 - p733+ [51-250]
c KR - v64 - N 15 '96 - p1672 [51-250]
c PW - v243 - D 16 '96 - p59 [51-250]
c SLJ - v43 - Ja '97 - p86+ [51-250]
Monson, Craig A - *Disembodied Voices*
Notes - v53 - D '96 - p426+ [501+]
Sev Cent N - v54 - Fall '96 - p76+ [501+]
Six Ct J - v27 - Fall '96 - p940+ [501+]
Monster Faces
c CCB-B - v50 - Ja '97 - p169 [51-250]
Monsters (Hologram World)
c Ch BWatch - v6 - N '96 - p6 [1-50]
Montada, Leo - *Current Societal Concerns about Justice*
R&R Bk N - v12 - F '97 - p58 [51-250]
Montagnes, Anne - *Jade Slash Laverna*
PW - v243 - S 30 '96 - p63 [51-250]
Montagu, Jennifer - *The Expression of the Passions*
Eight-C St - v29 - Sum '96 - p438+ [501+]
FR - v70 - Mr '97 - p625+ [501+]
JAAC - v54 - Fall '96 - p384+ [501+]
Gold, Silver, and Bronze
Choice - v34 - O '96 - p268 [51-250]
SDA - v4 - Spr '97 - p112+ [501+]
Montagu, Mary Wortley, Lady - *Romance Writings*
Lon R Bks - v18 - O 31 '96 - p14+ [501+]

Montague, John - *Collected Poems*
  Shen - v46 - Fall '96 - p113+ [501+]
  TLS - Ag 2 '96 - p25 [501+]
  WLT - v71 - Win '97 - p155 [501+]
Montale, Eugenio - *Cuttlefish Bones*
  TranslRevS - v1 - My '95 - p24 [51-250]
  Prose E Racconti
  MLR - v92 - Ap '97 - p484+ [501+]
Montana, Monte, Jr. - *Cowboy Cuisine*
  BWatch - v17 - S '96 - p2 [51-250]
Montandon, Alain - *Bibliographie Des Traites De Savoir-Vivre En Europe Du Moyen Age A Nos Jours. Vols. 1-2*
  r MLR - v91 - O '96 - p1005+ [501+]
  Dictionnaire Raisonne De La Politesse Et Du Savoir-Vivre
  r MLR - v91 - O '96 - p1005+ [501+]
  r Ren Q - v50 - Spr '97 - p292+ [501+]
  Pour Une Histoire Des Traites De Savoir-Vivre En Europe
  MLR - v91 - O '96 - p1005+ [501+]
Montanez, Jose - *The Medical Device Quality Assurance Manual*
  SciTech - v21 - Mr '97 - p44 [51-250]
Montauk, Richard - *How to Get into the Top MBA Programs*
  LJ - v121 - N 15 '96 - p70 [51-250]
Monteath, Peter - *The Spanish Civil War in Literature, Film, and Art*
  r TranslRevS - v1 - My '95 - p5 [1-50]
Montefiore, Janet - *Men and Women Writers of the 1930s*
  BW - v26 - D 8 '96 - p6+ [51-250]
  TLS - F 28 '97 - p24 [501+]
Montefiore, Judith Cohen, Lady - *The Jewish Manual*
  AB - v99 - Mr 24 '97 - p962 [251-500]
Monteiro, George - *The Presence of Camoes*
  AL - v69 - Mr '97 - p249 [51-250]
  Choice - v34 - D '96 - p620 [51-250]
Monteith, Ann - *The Business of Wedding Photography*
  Pet PM - v25 - Ap '97 - p96 [51-250]
Montejo, Victor - *Sculpted Stones*
  WLT - v70 - Sum '96 - p667+ [251-500]
  Testimonio: Muerte De Una Comunidad Indigena En Guatemala
  BL - v93 - S 15 '96 - p227 [1-50]
Monteleone, John - *The Louisville Slugger Ultimate Book of Hitting*
  LJ - v122 - F 1 '97 - p83 [51-250]
Monteleone, Thomas F - *Night of Broken Souls*
  KR - v65 - Ja 1 '97 - p16 [251-500]
  LJ - v122 - Ja '97 - p149 [51-250]
  PW - v244 - F 10 '97 - p66+ [51-250]
Monter, William - *Frontiers of Heresy*
  CH - v66 - Mr '97 - p123+ [501+]
Montero, Mayra - *In the Palm of Darkness*
  LJ - v122 - Ap 1 '97 - p128 [51-250]
  PW - v244 - Mr 31 '97 - p61 [51-250]
  Tu, La Oscuridad
  BL - v93 - Ap 1 '97 - p1284 [1-50]
Monterroso, Augusto - *Complete Works and Other Stories*
  TranslRev - 51 '96 - p52+ [501+]
  WLT - v70 - Aut '96 - p928 [501+]
  Cuentos, Fabulas Y Lo Demas Es Silencio
  LJ - v122 - Ja '97 - p79 [51-250]
  WLT - v71 - Win '97 - p120 [251-500]
Montes, Graciela - *Federico Va A La Escuela (Illus. by Claudia Legnazzi)*
  BL - v93 - F 15 '97 - p1033 [51-250]
  Federico Y El Mar (Illus. by Claudia Legnazzi)
  c SLJ - v42 - Ag '96 - p179 [51-250]
Montes, Manuel F - *Macroeconomic Management in Southeast Asia's Transitional Economies*
  Pac A - v69 - Sum '96 - p281+ [501+]
Monteverdi, Claudio - *The Letters of Claudio Monteverdi*
  Sev Cent N - v54 - Fall '96 - p73+ [501+]
Montfort, Catherine R - *Literate Women and the French Revolution of 1789*
  FR - v70 - Mr '97 - p598+ [501+]
Montgomery, Carla W - *Earth: Then and Now. 3rd Ed.*
  SciTech - v21 - Mr '97 - p32 [51-250]
  Fundamentals of Geology. 3rd Ed.
  SciTech - v21 - Mr '97 - p32 [51-250]
Montgomery, Diane - *Educating the Able*
  Choice - v34 - N '96 - p511 [51-250]
Montgomery, Douglas C - *Introduction to Statistical Quality Control. 3rd Ed.*
  SciTech - v20 - D '96 - p84 [51-250]
Montgomery, John - *Hacker's Guide to Visual Basic*
  R&R Bk N - v12 - F '97 - p92 [51-250]
Montgomery, L M - *Anne of Green Gables. Audio Version*
  c TES - Ag 30 '96 - p28 [51-250]

Christmas with Anne and Other Holiday Stories
  c BIC - v25 - D '96 - p33+ [501+]
  c BL - v93 - S 1 '96 - p134 [51-250]
  y Ch BWatch - v6 - D '96 - p1 [1-50]
  c HB Guide - v8 - Spr '97 - p71 [51-250]
  c KR - v64 - S 15 '96 - p1411 [51-250]
  c PW - v243 - S 30 '96 - p93 [1-50]
  c SLJ - v42 - O '96 - p38 [51-250]
Montgomery, Lee - *Absolute Disaster*
  PW - v243 - D 16 '96 - p45 [51-250]
Montgomery, Maxine Lavon - *The Apocalypse in African-American Fiction*
  AL - v69 - Mr '97 - p223+ [251-500]
  Choice - v34 - Ja '97 - p797 [51-250]
Montgomery, Paula Kay - *Approaches to Literature through Literary Form*
  JAAL - v40 - D '96 - p321+ [501+]
Montgomery, Robert E - *The Visionary D.H. Lawrence*
  RES - v47 - N '96 - p625+ [501+]
Montgomery, Scott L - *The Scientific Voice*
  Isis - v87 - D '96 - p707+ [501+]
  Sci - v273 - S 20 '96 - p1672 [501+]
Montgomery, Tommie Sue - *Revolution in El Salvador*
  HAHR - v76 - Ag '96 - p579+ [501+]
Montgomery, Vickie L, 1956- - *The Smart Woman's Guide to Starting a Business*
  BWatch - v18 - F '97 - p3 [1-50]
  LJ - v122 - My 1 '97 - p53 [1-50]
Montgomery, William W - *Surgery of the Upper Respiratory System. 3rd Ed.*
  SciTech - v20 - N '96 - p50 [51-250]
Monti, James - *The Week of Salvation*
  CHR - v82 - O '96 - p669+ [501+]
Monti, Joseph - *Arguing about Sex*
  Theol St - v57 - Je '96 - p375+ [501+]
  TT - v53 - Ja '97 - p547+ [501+]
Monti-Belkaoui, Janice - *Fairness in Accounting*
  Choice - v34 - S '96 - p172 [51-250]
Monticelli, Carlo - *European Integration, Monetary Co-ordination and the Demand for Money*
  JEL - v35 - Mr '97 - p219 [51-250]
Montier, Jean-Pierre - *Henri Cartier-Bresson and the Artless Art*
  BL - v93 - Ja '97 - p804 [51-250]
  Econ - v341 - D 7 '96 - p15* [1-50]
  LJ - v122 - F 15 '97 - p131+ [51-250]
  Obs - N 10 '96 - p17* [51-250]
Montoya, Rodrigo - *Al Borde Del Naufragio*
  HAHR - v76 - N '96 - p810 [251-500]
Montpetit, Charles - *The First Time. Vol. 2*
  y BL - v93 - Ap 1 '97 - p1306 [1-50]
  The First Time. Vols. 1-2
  y SLJ - v42 - Ag '96 - p174 [51-250]
Montreal Protocol on Substances That Deplete the Ozone Layer: 1994 Report of the Methyl Bromide Technical Options Committee
  SciTech - v21 - Mr '97 - p29 [51-250]
Montreal Protocol on Substances That Deplete the Ozone Layer: 1994 Report of the Solvents, Coatings, and Adhesives Technical Options Committee
  SciTech - v21 - Mr '97 - p29 [51-250]
Montrose, Louis - *The Purpose of Playing*
  Choice - v34 - N '96 - p472 [51-250]
  Lon R Bks - v18 - O 31 '96 - p24+ [501+]
Montrose, Mark I - *Printed Circuit Board Design Techniques for EMC Compliance*
  SciTech - v20 - D '96 - p77 [1-50]
Montserrat, Dominic - *Sex and Society in Graeco-Roman Egypt*
  TLS - O 18 '96 - p5+ [501+]
Montupet, Janine - *La Jeune Amante*
  BL - v93 - Ja '97 - p827 [1-50]
Monture, Joel - *Cloudwalker: Contemporary Native American Stories (Illus. by Carson Waterman)*
  c HB Guide - v7 - Fall '96 - p295 [51-250]
Moodie, Andrew - *Riot*
  Quill & Q - v63 - Mr '97 - p76 [251-500]
Moodie, Fiona - *Nabulela (Illus. by Fiona Moodie)*
  c PW - v244 - Ja 13 '97 - p74 [51-250]
  c Sch Lib - v45 - F '97 - p20 [51-250]
  c SLJ - v43 - Mr '97 - p179 [51-250]
Moodie, T Dunbar - *Going for Gold*
  CS - v25 - S '96 - p624+ [501+]
Moody, A David - *The Cambridge Companion to T.S. Eliot*
  ASInt - v34 - O '96 - p102+ [501+]
  Thomas Stearns Eliot: Poet. 2nd Ed.
  ASInt - v34 - O '96 - p102+ [501+]
  ELT - v39 - 4 '96 - p527 [51-250]
  TLS - Jl 7 '96 - p13 [501+]

Moody, Bill - *The Sound of the Trumpet*
  BL - v93 - F 15 '97 - p1007 [51-250]
  KR - v64 - D 15 '96 - p1769 [51-250]
  LJ - v122 - Ja '97 - p152+ [51-250]
  NYTBR - v102 - F 16 '97 - p28 [51-250]
  PW - v243 - D 16 '96 - p45 [51-250]
  Trib Bks - F 2 '97 - p4 [51-250]
Moody, Fred - *I Sing the Body Electronic*
  yr Kliatt - v30 - N '96 - p30 [51-250]
  LATBR - Ag 25 '96 - p11 [51-250]
  y SLJ - v43 - F '97 - p137+ [51-250]
Moody, Greg - *Two Wheels*
  Bloom Rev - v16 - S '96 - p21 [251-500]
Moody, Linda A - *Women Encounter God*
  BL - v93 - N 1 '96 - p462 [51-250]
Moody, Rick - *Garden State*
  Trib Bks - My 4 '97 - p8 [1-50]
  Purple America
  BL - v93 - Mr 15 '97 - p1227 [51-250]
  Esq - v127 - Ap '97 - p50 [501+]
  KR - v65 - F 1 '97 - p164+ [251-500]
  LATBR - Ap 20 '97 - p12 [501+]
  LJ - v122 - F 15 '97 - p163 [51-250]
  PW - v244 - F 17 '97 - p208 [51-250]
  Time - v149 - Ap 14 '97 - p89+ [501+]
  Trib Bks - My 11 '97 - p5 [501+]
  The Ring of Brightest Angels around Heaven
  BW - v27 - Ja 12 '97 - p12 [51-250]
  NYTBR - v101 - D 29 '96 - p20 [1-50]
Moody, Skye Kathleen - *Rain Dance*
  y BL - v93 - S 1 '96 - p68 [51-250]
Moody, Susan - *Doubled in Spades*
  KR - v65 - Mr 15 '97 - p420+ [51-250]
  PW - v244 - F 10 '97 - p70 [51-250]
  Misselthwaite
  Books - v10 - Je '96 - p13 [51-250]
Moody-Adams, Michelle - *Morality, Culture and Philosophy*
  Hast Cen R - v27 - Ja '97 - p38+ [501+]
Moolten, David - *Plums and Ashes*
  South R - v32 - Aut '96 - p761+ [501+]
Moon, Bruce R - *Dilemmas of International Trade*
  AAPSS-A - v550 - Mr '97 - p173+ [501+]
Moon, Elizabeth - *Once a Hero*
  y BL - v93 - F 1 '97 - p929 [51-250]
  KR - v65 - Ja 1 '97 - p28 [51-250]
  LJ - v122 - Mr 15 '97 - p93 [51-250]
  PW - v244 - F 24 '97 - p69 [51-250]
  Remnant Population
  y SLJ - v43 - Ja '97 - p140+ [51-250]
  y VOYA - v19 - O '96 - p219+ [251-500]
Moon, Marilyn - *Entitlements and the Elderly*
  Choice - v34 - O '96 - p368 [51-250]
  ILRR - v50 - Ja '97 - p352+ [501+]
Moon, Michael - *Subjects and Citizens*
  Nine-C Lit - v50 - Mr '96 - p555 [1-50]
Moon, Nicola - *Something Special (Illus. by Alex Ayliffe)*
  c PW - v244 - F 10 '97 - p82 [51-250]
Moon, Pat - *Ready, Steady, Go, Cheetah*
  c TES - Jl 5 '96 - pR6 [1-50]
Moon, Warren G - *Polykleitos, the Doryphoros, and Tradition*
  AJA - v101 - Ja '97 - p177+ [501+]
  Art Bull - v79 - Mr '97 - p148+ [501+]
Moon Travel Handbooks
  r E Mag - v7 - N '96 - p49 [51-250]
Moonan, Lawrence - *Divine Power*
  Specu - v71 - O '96 - p985+ [501+]
Mooney, Bel - *The Voices of Silence*
  c BL - v93 - Ap 1 '97 - p1322 [51-250]
  y CCB-B - v50 - Ap '97 - p291 [51-250]
  c HB - v73 - Mr '97 - p203 [51-250]
  c KR - v65 - Ja 1 '97 - p61 [51-250]
  c PW - v244 - Ja 27 '97 - p107 [51-250]
  c SLJ - v43 - Mr '97 - p190 [51-250]
Mooney, Christopher F - *Theology and Scientific Knowledge*
  Am - v175 - O 5 '96 - p28+ [501+]
Mooney, Patrick H - *Farmers' and Farm Workers' Movements*
  CS - v26 - Ja '97 - p38+ [501+]
  Farmers' and Farm Workers Movements
  SF - v75 - D '96 - p753+ [501+]
Mooney, William - *The Storyteller's Guide*
  CCB-B - v50 - N '96 - p120 [51-250]
  Emerg Lib - v24 - Mr '97 - p42 [1-50]
  SLJ - v42 - O '96 - p46 [51-250]
Moonrabbit Review: Asian Pacific American Voices
  p Sm Pr R - v28 - S '96 - p13+ [51-250]

Moorcock, Michael - *Fabulous Harbors*
  y BL - v93 - Mr 1 '97 - p1114 [51-250]
     KR - v64 - D 15 '96 - p1773 [51-250]
     LJ - v122 - F 15 '97 - p165 [51-250]
     PW - v244 - Ja 20 '97 - p398+ [51-250]
  The Roads between the Worlds
     LJ - v122 - Ap 15 '97 - p148 [51-250]
  Von Bek
     AB - v98 - D 2 '96 - p1924 [51-250]
Moorcraft, Paul L - *African Nemesis*
     JTWS - v13 - Spr '96 - p303+ [501+]
Moorcroft, Christine - *Christianity*
     TES - D 13 '96 - p43 [51-250]
  Hinduism
  c TES - O 4 '96 - p16* [251-500]
  Islam
  c TES - O 4 '96 - p16* [251-500]
  Tudor Times
     TES - D 13 '96 - p43 [51-250]
Moore, Alison - *Synonym for Love*
     NYTBR - v101 - S 22 '96 - p40 [1-50]
Moore, Andrew - *The Mighty Bears!*
     Aust Bk R - S '96 - p20 [501+]
Moore, Brian - *The Statement*
     Am - v176 - F 22 '97 - p27 [251-500]
     Atl - v278 - Jl '96 - p110 [51-250]
     BW - v26 - D 8 '96 - p6 [1-50]
     Comw - v123 - O 25 '96 - p24+ [501+]
     ILS - v16 - Spr '97 - p11+ [501+]
     NL - v79 - Ag 12 '96 - p30+ [501+]
     NYRB - v43 - O 3 '96 - p36+ [501+]
     NYTBR - v101 - D 8 '96 - p82 [1-50]
     PW - v243 - N 4 '96 - p38 [51-250]
     W&I - v11 - N '96 - p262+ [501+]
     WLT - v71 - Win '97 - p152 [501+]
  The Statement (Sachs). Audio Version
  y Kliatt - v31 - My '97 - p44+ [51-250]
Moore, C J - *Ishtar and Tammuz (Illus. by Christina Balit)*
  c Bks Keeps - v100 - S '96 - p32 [51-250]
  c BL - v93 - S 1 '96 - p123 [51-250]
  c CCB-B - v50 - D '96 - p144+ [51-250]
  c CLW - v67 - D '96 - p62 [51-250]
  c HB Guide - v8 - Spr '97 - p104 [51-250]
  c JB - v60 - O '96 - p186+ [51-250]
  c PW - v243 - Jl 22 '96 - p242 [51-250]
  c Sch Lib - v44 - N '96 - p151 [51-250]
  c SLJ - v42 - D '96 - p132 [51-250]
Moore, Charles B - *Cemetery Records of the Township of Fort Ann, Washington County, NY*
  r EGH - v50 - N '96 - p175+ [51-250]
Moore, Charlotte - *Martha's Ark*
     Spec - v277 - N 16 '96 - p50+ [251-500]
Moore, Christopher - *Bloodsucking Fiends*
     PW - v243 - S 9 '96 - p80+ [1-50]
Moore, Clayton - *I Was That Masked Man*
     BL - v93 - S 15 '96 - p200+ [51-250]
     NYTBR - v101 - N 10 '96 - p57 [51-250]
Moore, Clement Clarke - *The Night before Christmas (Illus. by Nan Brooks)*
  c PW - v243 - S 30 '96 - p92+ [1-50]
  The Night before Christmas (Illus. by Howard Finster)
  c HB Guide - v8 - Spr '97 - p153 [51-250]
  c PW - v243 - S 30 '96 - p89 [51-250]
  The Night before Christmas (Illus. by Anita Lobel)
  c PW - v243 - S 30 '96 - p92 [51-250]
  The Night before Christmas (Streep) (Illus. by William Cone). Book and Audio Version
  c PW - v243 - N 11 '96 - p35 [51-250]
Moore, David - *To Build a Bridge*
     Aust Bk R - O '96 - p69 [1-50]
Moore, Dennis D - *More Letters from the American Farmer*
     CH - v65 - S '96 - p510+ [501+]
Moore, Dinty W - *The Emperor's Virtual Clothes*
     J Am Cult - v19 - Sum '96 - p145+ [501+]
     VQR - v72 - Aut '96 - p132* [51-250]
Moore, Donald J - *Martin Buber: Prophet of Religious Secularism*
     Comw - v124 - Ja 17 '97 - p26+ [251-500]
Moore, Edward - *The Foundling: A Comedy. The Gamester: A Tragedy*
     Choice - v34 - My '97 - p1497 [51-250]
Moore, Edward P - *Polypropylene Handbook*
     SciTech - v20 - N '96 - p81 [51-250]
Moore, Eileen - *Dark at the Foot of the Stairs (Illus. by Moira Kemp)*
  c Bks Keeps - v100 - S '96 - p12 [51-250]
Moore, Elaine - *Good Morning, City (Illus. by William Low)*
  c HB Guide - v7 - Fall '96 - p268 [1-50]

Roly-Poly Puppies (Illus. by Jacqueline Rogers)
  c BL - v93 - S 15 '96 - p248 [51-250]
  c HB Guide - v8 - Spr '97 - p14 [51-250]
  c SLJ - v42 - D '96 - p102 [51-250]
Moore, Elizabeth - *Mimi and Jean-Paul's Cajun Mardi Gras (Illus. by Marilyn Carter Rougelot)*
  c HB Guide - v7 - Fall '96 - p268 [1-50]
Moore, Eva - *Buddy: The First Seeing Eye Dog (Illus. by Don Bolognese)*
  c BL - v93 - N 15 '96 - p597 [51-250]
Moore, F C T - *Bergson: Thinking Backwards*
     CPR - v16 - D '96 - p424+ [501+]
Moore, Floyd C - *I Gave Thomas Edison My Sandwich (Illus. by Donna Kae Nelson)*
  c Inst - v106 - O '96 - p67 [1-50]
Moore, Gary - *Ten Golden Rules for Financial Success*
     BL - v92 - Ag '96 - p1866 [51-250]
Moore, Henry, 1898- - *Henry Moore: Sculture, Disegni, Incisioni, Arazzi*
     BM - v138 - D '96 - p836 [1-50]
Moore, Honor - *The White Blackbird*
     NYRB - v43 - O 3 '96 - p45+ [501+]
     NYTBR - v101 - D 8 '96 - p94 [1-50]
Moore, Ishbel L - *The Summer of the Hand*
  y Can CL - v22 - Sum '96 - p89+ [51-250]
Moore, Jack B - *Skinheads: Shaved for Battle*
     CAY - v17 - Win '96 - p12 [51-250]
Moore, James F - *The Death of Competition*
     Bus Bk R - v14 - 1 '97 - p4+ [501+]
     Bus W - D 16 '96 - p19+ [51-250]
Moore, James R - *The Darwin Legend*
     CH - v65 - S '96 - p524 [251-500]
Moore, Jean M - *The John Metcalf Papers*
  r ARBA - v28 - '97 - p459 [51-250]
Moore, Jerry D - *Architecture and Power in the Ancient Andes*
     Choice - v34 - Mr '97 - p1202 [51-250]
Moore, Jim - *Swan: The Second Voyage*
     Aethlon - v13 - Fall '95 - p168+ [251-500]
Moore, Joan - *In the Barrios*
     HAHR - v76 - N '96 - p759+ [251-500]
Moore, John - *Slay and Rescue*
  y VOYA - v19 - D '96 - p266 [1-50]
  The Wrong Stuff
  y BL - v93 - Mr 15 '97 - p1213 [51-250]
Moore, John H - *Legacies of the Collapse of Marxism*
     Slav R - v55 - Sum '96 - p439 [251-500]
Moore, John Hammond - *The Confederate Housewife*
     PW - v244 - My 12 '97 - p72 [51-250]
Moore, John L - *The Limits of Mercy*
     BL - v93 - N 15 '96 - p571 [501+]
     Roundup M - v4 - F '97 - p28 [51-250]
Moore, Judith - *Never Eat Your Heart Out*
     BL - v93 - F 15 '97 - p989 [51-250]
     BW - v27 - Ap 13 '97 - p10+ [501+]
     NYTBR - v102 - Mr 9 '97 - p8 [501+]
     PW - v243 - D 16 '96 - p52+ [51-250]
Moore, Julia - *While You Sleep (Illus. by Lyn Gilbert)*
  c CBRS - v24 - Ag '96 - p161 [51-250]
  c HB Guide - v7 - Fall '96 - p241 [1-50]
  c SLJ - v42 - Ag '96 - p127 [51-250]
Moore, Kathleen Dean - *Riverwalking*
     Bloom Rev - v16 - S '96 - p17 [501+]
Moore, Kathleen M - *Al-Mughtaribun: American Law and the Transformation of Muslim Life in the United States*
     Rel St Rev - v23 - Ap '97 - p203 [51-250]
Moore, Kristin A - *Adolescent Sex, Contraception, and Childbearing*
     J Gov Info - v23 - S '96 - p563+ [51-250]
Moore, Lorrie - *The Faber Book of Contemporary Stories about Childhood*
     Obs - Ja 12 '97 - p17* [501+]
     TES - Ja 17 '97 - p8* [501+]
     TLS - Ja 17 '97 - p20 [501+]
Moore, Mack Arthur - *Descendants of John Moore (Revolutionary War Soldier) and Mary Keller Moore*
     NGSQ - v84 - D '96 - p310 [251-500]
Moore, Marat - *Women in the Mines*
     Wom R Bks - v14 - O '96 - p17+ [501+]
Moore, Marilyn - *A Guide to Licensing Artwork*
     LJ - v121 - O 15 '96 - p55 [51-250]
Moore, Mark H - *Creating Public Value*
     AAPSS-A - v550 - Mr '97 - p174+ [251-500]
     J Pol - v59 - F '97 - p257+ [501+]
Moore, Martha - *Under the Mermaid Angel*
  y Emerg Lib - v24 - S '96 - p25 [1-50]
  y PW - v244 - Ap 28 '97 - p77 [1-50]
Moore, Mary Tyler - *After All*
     Ent W - O 18 '96 - p75 [51-250]
     PW - v243 - O 14 '96 - p81 [1-50]

Moore, Melinda K - *AIDS Education*
     Choice - v34 - Ja '97 - p827 [51-250]
     SciTech - v20 - N '96 - p37 [51-250]
Moore, Melodie - *Vim and Vinegar*
     PW - v244 - Mr 24 '97 - p80 [51-250]
Moore, Michael - *Downsize This!*
  y BL - v92 - Ag '96 - p1851 [251-500]
  y BL - v93 - Ja '97 - p763 [1-50]
     Bus W - S 9 '96 - p15 [501+]
     CSM - v88 - N 7 '96 - p14 [51-250]
     Ent W - O 11 '96 - p86 [51-250]
     Mac - v109 - N 25 '96 - p126 [251-500]
     NYTBR - v101 - D 29 '96 - p11 [501+]
     VV - v41 - N 5 '96 - p51+ [251-500]
  Downsize This! (Moore). Audio Version
     LJ - v121 - O 15 '96 - p103 [51-250]
     Trib Bks - F 2 '97 - p6 [51-250]
Moore, Miriam - *The Kwanzaa Contest (Illus. by Laurie Spencer)*
  c BL - v93 - S 15 '96 - p242 [51-250]
  c HB Guide - v8 - Spr '97 - p59 [51-250]
  c SLJ - v42 - O '96 - p38+ [51-250]
Moore, Moses Nathaniel - *Orishatukeh Faduma: Liberal Theology and Evangelical Pan-Africanism 1857-1946*
     R&R Bk N - v11 - D '96 - p5 [51-250]
Moore, Olive - *Fugue*
     LJ - v122 - F 1 '97 - p112 [1-50]
  Spleen
     LJ - v122 - F 1 '97 - p112 [1-50]
     PW - v243 - S 9 '96 - p81 [1-50]
Moore, Oscar - *PWA: Looking AIDS in the Face*
     Lon R Bks - v19 - F 6 '97 - p3+ [501+]
     NS - v125 - N 22 '96 - p47+ [501+]
     Obs - N 3 '96 - p16* [501+]
  PWA: Looking AIDS in the Face (Moore). Audio Version
     Books - v11 - Ap '97 - p19 [1-50]
     Obs - Ja 12 '97 - p18* [501+]
Moore, Patrick - *Brilliant Stars*
     New Sci - v152 - N 30 '96 - p44 [51-250]
  Comets and Shooting Stars (Illus. by Paul Doherty)
  c New Sci - v153 - F 8 '97 - p46 [1-50]
  Mission to the Planets
     S&T - v92 - O '96 - p57 [1-50]
  The Planet Neptune
     S&T - v93 - F '97 - p60 [51-250]
  The Planets (Illus. by Paul Doherty)
  c New Sci - v153 - F 8 '97 - p46 [1-50]
  Small Astronomical Observatories
     Astron - v25 - Mr '97 - p103 [1-50]
     Choice - v34 - Ap '97 - p1362 [51-250]
  The Stars (Illus. by Paul Doherty)
  c New Sci - v153 - F 8 '97 - p46 [1-50]
  The Sun and Moon (Illus. by Paul Doherty)
  c New Sci - v153 - F 8 '97 - p46 [1-50]
Moore, Robert C - *Logic and Representation*
     CPR - v16 - Ap '96 - p122+ [501+]
Moore, Sara - *Peace without Victory for the Allies 1918-1932*
     EHR - v111 - N '96 - p1343+ [501+]
Moore, Sharon - *News from Marion*
  r EGH - v50 - N '96 - p179+ [51-250]
Moore, Simon W - *Multithreaded Processor Design*
     SciTech - v20 - N '96 - p7 [51-250]
Moore, Stephen - *Spilling the Magic*
  c Bks Keeps - Jl '96 - p12 [51-250]
Moore, Stephen D - *God's Gym*
     CC - v114 - Ja 1 '97 - p23+ [51-250]
     HG&LRev - v3 - Fall '96 - p43 [1-50]
     LJ - v121 - O 1 '96 - p85 [51-250]
Moore, Steven - *Ronald Firbank: An Annotated Bibliography of Secondary Materials 1905-1995*
  r ELT - v40 - 2 '97 - p254 [51-250]
Moore, Susan - *Youth, AIDS, and Sexually Transmitted Diseases*
     SciTech - v21 - Mr '97 - p64 [51-250]
Moore, Susanna - *In the Cut*
     Ant R - v54 - Sum '96 - p379+ [51-250]
     Necro - Fall '96 - p11+ [501+]
     NYTBR - v101 - D 15 '96 - p40 [51-250]
     Obs - D 1 '96 - p16* [1-50]
Moore, Thomas, 1940- - *Care of the Soul*
     CSM - v89 - N 25 '96 - p12 [51-250]
     CSM - v89 - Ja 23 '97 - p12 [51-250]
  The Education of the Heart
     BL - v93 - N 15 '96 - p547 [51-250]
  The Re-Enchantment of Everyday Life
     CC - v113 - N 6 '96 - p1072+ [501+]
     Obs - F 2 '97 - p18* [501+]
     W&I - v11 - S '96 - p290+ [501+]
  The Re-Enchantment of Everyday Life. Audio Version
     Quill & Q - v62 - My '96 - p31 [1-50]

Moore, Thomas R - *A Thick and Darksome Veil*
NEQ - v69 - D '96 - p684+ [501+]
Moore, Thomas S - *The Disposable Work Force*
Choice - v34 - S '96 - p172 [51-250]
Moore, Wayne D - *Constitutional Rights and Powers of the People*
Choice - v34 - F '97 - p1037 [51-250]
Moore-Gilbert, Bart - *Writing India 1757-1990*
Choice - v34 - O '96 - p618 [51-250]
Moorehead, Caroline - *Lost and Found*
KR - v64 - My 1 '96 - p670 [251-500]
NYRB - v43 - D 19 '96 - p15+ [501+]
Moorey, Teresa - *Herbs for Magic and Ritual*
BL - v93 - Ja '97 - p798 [51-250]
Moorhead, John - *Justinian*
EHR - v111 - N '96 - p1230+ [251-500]
Moorhead, Rex K - *Moorhead-Bear Ancestry*
r EGH - v50 - N '96 - p194 [51-250]
Moorhen, John - *English Choral Practice 1400-1650*
FF - v20 - Mr '97 - p422+ [501+]
Moorhouse, Frank - *Grand Days*
Sew R - v104 - Jl '96 - pR64+ [501+]
Moorhouse, Geoffrey - *A People's Game*
Books - v9 - S '95 - p23 [51-250]
Moorman, Margaret - *Waiting to Forget*
BL - v93 - S 1 '96 - p41 [251-500]
BW - v27 - Mr 23 '97 - p13 [51-250]
NYTBR - v101 - D 8 '96 - p67 [501+]
Moors, Annelies - *Women, Property and Islam*
Choice - v34 - O '96 - p343 [51-250]
Moosa, Matti - *The Early Novels of Naguib Mahfouz*
JTWS - v13 - Fall '96 - p361+ [501+]
Moosewood Collective - *Moosewood Restaurant Low-Fat Favorites*
BL - v93 - S 15 '96 - p196+ [51-250]
BWatch - v18 - F '97 - p7+ [1-50]
y Kliatt - v31 - Ja '97 - p30+ [251-500]
PW - v243 - S 16 '96 - p78 [51-250]
Mootoo, Shani - *Cereus Blooms at Night*
BIC - v26 - F '97 - p37 [251-500]
Quill & Q - v62 - D '96 - p34 [251-500]
Moo-Young, Murray - *Environmental Biotechnology*
SciTech - v20 - N '96 - p67 [51-250]
Mor, Caiseal - *The Song of Earth*
Aust Bk R - O '96 - p69 [1-50]
Mora, Jo - *Budgee Budgee Cottontail (Illus. by Jo Mora)*
c Ch BWatch - v6 - O '96 - p4 [51-250]
Mora, Pat - *Confetti: Poems for Children (Illus. by Enrique O Sanchez)*
c BL - v93 - N 15 '96 - p592 [51-250]
c CBRS - v25 - Win '97 - p68 [51-250]
c HB Guide - v8 - Spr '97 - p153 [51-250]
c KR - v64 - O 1 '96 - p1476 [51-250]
c SLJ - v42 - N '96 - p100 [51-250]
House of Houses
BL - v93 - My 1 '97 - p1475 [51-250]
KR - v65 - Mr 15 '97 - p446 [251-500]
LJ - v122 - Ap 15 '97 - p88+ [51-250]
PW - v244 - Mr 24 '97 - p68 [51-250]
The Race of Toad and Deer (Illus. by M I Brooks)
c SS - v88 - Ja '97 - p29+ [501+]
Uno, Dos, Tres (Illus. by Barbara Lavallee)
c HB Guide - v7 - Fall '96 - p268+ [51-250]
Morabito, Fabio - *Toolbox*
TranslRevS - v2 - D '96 - p33 [51-250]
Morabito, Yvonne - *Dollar Signs*
BL - v93 - Mr 1 '97 - p1098 [51-250]
Morachiello, Paolo - *Fra Angelico: The San Marco Frescoes*
Choice - v34 - Ap '97 - p1325 [51-250]
Spec - v277 - D 14 '96 - p76 [51-250]
Morad, Martin - *Molecular Physiology and Pharmacology of Cardiac Ion Channels and Transporters*
SciTech - v21 - Mr '97 - p39 [51-250]
Moraes, Marcia - *Bilingual Education*
R&R Bk N - v11 - N '96 - p57 [1-50]
Moragne, Wendy - *Attention Deficit Disorder*
y HB Guide - v8 - Spr '97 - p129 [51-250]
y SLJ - v43 - F '97 - p114 [51-250]
Dyslexia
y BL - v93 - My 1 '97 - p1488 [51-250]
c SLJ - v43 - Mr '97 - p205 [51-250]
Morales, Edmund - *The Guinea Pig*
HAHR - v76 - N '96 - p768+ [501+]
Morales, Juan Antonio - *Economic Policy and the Transition to Democracy*
JEL - v34 - D '96 - p2122 [51-250]
R&R Bk N - v11 - N '96 - p27 [51-250]
Morales, Maino R - *Senor Bajo Los Arboles O Brevisima Relacion De La Destruccion De Los Indios*
BL - v93 - S 15 '96 - p227 [1-50]

Moran, Amanda M - *CyberHound's Guide to Associations and Nonprofit Organizations on the Internet*
r BL - v93 - F 1 '97 - p963+ [251-500]
r LJ - v122 - F 1 '97 - p70 [51-250]
Moran, Emilio F - *Through Amazonian Eyes*
Am Ethnol - v23 - N '96 - p928+ [501+]
Moran, Gabriel - *A Grammar of Responsibility*
Choice - v34 - O '96 - p294+ [51-250]
Moran, Kerry - *Nepal Handbook*
r BWatch - v17 - S '96 - p5 [51-250]
r Quill & Q - v62 - S '96 - p22+ [51-250]
Nepal Handbook. 2nd Ed.
r BL - v93 - S 15 '96 - p212 [1-50]
Moran, Leslie - *The Homosexual(ity) of Law*
R&R Bk N - v12 - F '97 - p64 [51-250]
Moran, Michael - *Prepare to Be Healed. Audio Version*
BWatch - v18 - Mr '97 - p8 [1-50]
Moran, Sean Farrell - *Patrick Pearse and the Politics of Redemption*
EHR - v112 - F '97 - p254 [501+]
Moran, Thomas - *The Man in the Box*
Atl - v279 - F '97 - p110 [51-250]
y BL - v93 - Ja '97 - p821+ [51-250]
KR - v64 - D 1 '96 - p1696 [251-500]
LJ - v122 - Ja '97 - p149 [51-250]
NYTBR - v102 - Mr 2 '97 - p9 [501+]
PW - v243 - D 16 '96 - p43 [51-250]
Moran, Thomas, 1837-1926 - *Thomas Moran: The Field Sketches 1856-1923*
Choice - v34 - My '97 - p1487 [51-250]
Moran, Victoria - *Shelter for the Spirit*
LJ - v122 - F 15 '97 - p150 [51-250]
Morandi, Patrick - *Field and Galois Theory*
Choice - v34 - My '97 - p1536+ [51-250]
Moran-Lopez, J L - *Theory and Applications of the Cluster Variation and Path Probability Methods*
SciTech - v20 - D '96 - p22 [51-250]
Morash, Chris - *Fearful Realities*
ILS - v15 - Fall '96 - p16 [501+]
Moravia, Sergio - *The Enigma of the Mind*
RM - v50 - S '96 - p171+ [501+]
Morawska, Ewa - *Insecure Prosperity*
AJS - v102 - N '96 - p918+ [501+]
Choice - v34 - S '96 - p196 [51-250]
CS - v26 - Mr '97 - p154+ [501+]
HRNB - v25 - Fall '96 - p10+ [251-500]
Morazzoni, Marta - *L'Estuario*
BL - v93 - D 1 '96 - p644 [1-50]
WLT - v71 - Win '97 - p130 [251-500]
Morck, Irene - *Tiger's New Cowboy Boots (Illus. by Georgia Graham)*
c Quill & Q - v63 - Ja '97 - p39 [251-500]
Mordden, Ethan - *Make Believe*
BL - v93 - My 15 '97 - p1554+ [51-250]
PW - v244 - Mr 31 '97 - p52 [51-250]
Some Men Are Lookers
KR - v65 - My 1 '97 - p671 [251-500]
PW - v244 - My 12 '97 - p60+ [51-250]
More, Julian - *Pagnol's Provence*
PW - v243 - D 30 '96 - p51 [51-250]
More, Thomas - *Utopia*
PQ - v75 - Sum '96 - p267+ [501+]
Moreau, C X - *Distant Valor*
BL - v93 - S 15 '96 - p221 [51-250]
KR - v64 - Ag 15 '96 - p1180 [251-500]
PW - v243 - S 23 '96 - p58 [51-250]
Moreau, Daniel - *Take Charge of Your Career*
BL - v93 - N 1 '96 - p466 [51-250]
Morehead, Debby - *A Special Place for Charlee (Illus. by Karen Cannon)*
c BL - v93 - N 15 '96 - p588 [51-250]
c Dog Fan - v28 - F '97 - p8 [51-250]
Morehead, Joe - *Introduction to United States Government Information Sources. 5th Ed.*
r ARBA - v28 - '97 - p28 [251-500]
LQ - v67 - Ap '97 - p199+ [501+]
Morehouse, Barbara J - *A Place Called Grand Canyon*
Choice - v34 - O '96 - p350 [51-250]
WHQ - v27 - Win '96 - p547 [51-250]
Morehouse, David - *Psychic Warrior*
KR - v64 - O 1 '96 - p1449+ [251-500]
PW - v243 - O 7 '96 - p55 [51-250]
Morehouse, David A - *Nonlethal Weapons*
SciTech - v21 - Mr '97 - p99 [51-250]
Moreland, Kim Ileen - *The Medievalist Impulse in American Literature*
R&R Bk N - v11 - N '96 - p71 [51-250]
VQR - v73 - Win '97 - p10* [51-250]
Morell, Virginia - *Ancestral Passions*
y BL - v93 - D 15 '96 - p717 [1-50]
Nature - v384 - D 5 '96 - p426 [1-50]

Morella, Joseph - *Genius and Lust*
Si & So - v6 - N '96 - p35 [51-250]
Morelli, Jim - *Poison! How to Handle the Hazardous Substances in Your Home*
y BL - v93 - My 15 '97 - p1551 [51-250]
Moreno, Antonio Montero - *Historia De La Persecucion Religiosa En Espana 1936-1939*
CHR - v82 - O '96 - p661+ [501+]
Moreno, Dario - *The Struggle for Peace in Central America*
HAHR - v77 - My '97 - p333+ [501+]
Moreno, Paolo - *Lisippo: L'Arte E La Fortuna*
Choice - v34 - D '96 - p570 [1-50]
Moreno, Pedro C - *Handbook on Religious Liberty around the World*
r MEQ - v3 - D '96 - p83+ [501+]
Moreno Villarreal, Jaime - *Jose Luis Cuevas: El Monstruo Y El Monumento*
LJ - v122 - Ja '97 - p80 [51-250]
Morerod, Charles - *Cajetan Et Luther En 1518. Vols. 1-2*
CHR - v82 - O '96 - p697+ [501+]
Moreton, Romaine - *The Callused Stick of Wanting*
Aust Bk R - D '96 - p73 [501+]
Moretti, Franco - *The Modern Epic*
Econ - v341 - D 7 '96 - p14*+ [501+]
Lon R Bks - v18 - My 23 '96 - p14 [501+]
Morey, Janet - *Famous Hispanic Americans*
c HB Guide - v7 - Fall '96 - p376 [51-250]
Morgain, Stephane-Marie - *Pierre De Berulle Et Les Carmelites De France*
CHR - v83 - Ja '97 - p103+ [251-500]
Morgan, Bill - *The Response to Allen Ginsberg 1926-1994*
r AL - v68 - D '96 - p885 [51-250]
r ARBA - v28 - '97 - p444 [251-500]
r Choice - v34 - S '96 - p102 [51-250]
Morgan, David, 1957- - *Icons of American Protestantism*
CC - v113 - Ag 14 '96 - p789+ [501+]
CH - v66 - Mr '97 - p167+ [501+]
Choice - v34 - S '96 - p113 [51-250]
Rel St Rev - v23 - Ja '97 - p93 [51-250]
TLS - Ja 17 '97 - p32 [501+]
Morgan, David H J, 1957- - *Family Connections*
Socio R - v45 - My '97 - p332+ [501+]
Morgan, David T - *The Devious Dr. Franklin, Colonial Agent*
Choice - v34 - Ja '97 - p864 [51-250]
NYRB - v43 - Je 6 '96 - p47+ [501+]
The New Crusades, the New Holy Land
VQR - v72 - Aut '96 - p133* [51-250]
Morgan, Ed - *Analytical Chemistry by Open Learning*
J Chem Ed - v73 - Ag '96 - pA179 [1-50]
Morgan, Elizabeth Shelfer - *Uncertain Seasons*
y Kliatt - v31 - Ja '97 - p19 [51-250]
Morgan, Frank - *Calculus Lite*
Choice - v34 - D '96 - p646 [51-250]
y New Sci - v151 - S 28 '96 - p44+ [501+]
Geometric Measure Theory
y New Sci - v151 - S 28 '96 - p44+ [501+]
Morgan, Gareth - *Images of Organization. 2nd Ed.*
Choice - v34 - My '97 - p1544 [51-250]
Morgan, Harry - *Historical Perspectives on the Education of Black Children*
ES - v27 - Fall '96 - p267+ [501+]
Morgan, Ivan W - *Beyond the Liberal Consensus*
J Am St - v30 - Ap '96 - p146+ [251-500]
Morgan, James - *If These Walls Had Ears*
BL - v92 - Ag '96 - p1878 [51-250]
CSM - v88 - O 2 '96 - p15 [501+]
Morgan, Janet - *North Carolina Tracings*
r EGH - v50 - N '96 - p177 [51-250]
Morgan, Jill - *Blood Brothers*
c BL - v93 - D 1 '96 - p665 [51-250]
c SLJ - v43 - Ja '97 - p115 [51-250]
Morgan, Jinx - *The Sugar Mill Caribbean Cookbook*
PW - v243 - S 16 '96 - p79 [51-250]
Morgan, Judith - *Dr. Seuss and Mr. Geisel*
LATBR - N 10 '96 - p15 [51-250]
NYTBR - v102 - Ja 5 '97 - p28 [51-250]
Morgan, Kenneth - *Bristol and the Atlantic Trade in the Eighteenth Century*
JMH - v68 - S '96 - p689+ [501+]
W&M Q - v53 - O '96 - p813+ [501+]
Morgan, Kenneth O - *Modern Wales*
Albion - v28 - Fall '96 - p546+ [501+]
Morgan, Kevin - *Harry Pollitt*
S&S - v61 - Spr '97 - p147+ [501+]
Morgan, Marcyliena - *Language and the Social Construction of Identity in Creole Situations*
Lang Soc - v25 - S '96 - p487+ [501+]

Morgan, Marjorie - *Manners, Morals, and Class in England 1774-1858*
    EHR - v111 - N '96 - p1307 [251-500]
Morgan, Nina - *The Caribbean and the Gulf of Mexico*
  c BL - v93 - Ja '97 - p850 [251-500]
  c SB - v33 - Mr '97 - p49 [251-500]
  The North Sea and the Baltic Sea
  c SB - v33 - Mr '97 - p49 [251-500]
Morgan, R P C - *Soil Erosion and Conservation. 2nd Ed.*
    GJ - v162 - Jl '96 - p233+ [251-500]
Morgan, Robert - *The Truest Pleasure*
    Rapport - v19 - 4 '96 - p29 [251-500]
Morgan, Robert C - *Art into Ideas*
    TLS - N 8 '96 - p33 [51-250]
Morgan, Robert J - *Tiny Talks (Illus. by Ann S Hogue)*
  c SLJ - v43 - F '97 - p94 [51-250]
Morgan, Ronald B - *Staffing the New Workplace*
    Choice - v34 - S '96 - p172+ [51-250]
    Per Psy - v50 - Spr '97 - p231+ [501+]
Morgan, Sally - *Animals and Their World*
  c BL - v93 - D 1 '96 - p662+ [51-250]
  c SB - v33 - Ja '97 - p15+ [251-500]
  Butterflies, Bugs, and Worms
  c SB - v33 - Ja '97 - p15+ [251-500]
  Flowers, Trees, and Fruits
  c BL - v93 - D 1 '96 - p662+ [51-250]
  c SB - v33 - Ja '97 - p15+ [251-500]
  The Human Body
  c SB - v33 - Ja '97 - p15+ [251-500]
  Inside the Body
  c New Sci - v152 - N 16 '96 - p54 [51-250]
  Weather
  c Emerg Lib - v24 - Mr '97 - p45 [1-50]
  c HB Guide - v8 - Spr '97 - p114 [51-250]
Morgan, Stephen - *On the Road around New England*
  r BL - v93 - S 15 '96 - p212 [1-50]
Morgan, Steve - *Performance Assessment in Academic Libraries*
    LR - v45 - 5 '96 - p68+ [501+]
Morgan, Susan - *Place Matters*
    TSWL - v15 - Fall '96 - p369+ [501+]
Morgan, Terri - *Capturing Childhood Memories*
    BL - v93 - D 15 '96 - p703+ [51-250]
    LJ - v122 - F 1 '97 - p77 [51-250]
  Junior Seau: High-Voltage Linebacker
  c HB Guide - v8 - Spr '97 - p144 [51-250]
Morgen, Sharon Drew - *Selling with Integrity*
    PW - v244 - Ap 28 '97 - p57 [51-250]
Morgenstern, Mira - *Rousseau and the Politics of Ambiguity*
    Choice - v34 - My '97 - p1513 [51-250]
Mori, Kyoko - *One Bird*
  y Emerg Lib - v24 - S '96 - p25 [1-50]
  y Kliatt - v31 - Ja '97 - p9 [51-250]
Mori, Masaki - *Epic Grandeur*
    Choice - v34 - My '97 - p1491 [51-250]
Moriarty, Laura - *Symmetry*
    ABR - v18 - O '96 - p30 [501+]
Moriarty, Michael - *The Voyeur*
    BL - v93 - My 1 '97 - p1482+ [51-250]
    KR - v65 - My 1 '97 - p683 [51-250]
    LJ - v122 - My 1 '97 - p144 [51-250]
    PW - v244 - Mr 31 '97 - p65+ [51-250]
Morice, David - *Alphabet Avenue*
    PW - v244 - My 12 '97 - p72 [51-250]
Moriceau, Jean-Marc - *Les Fermiers De L'Ile-De-France*
    AHR - v101 - O '96 - p1217+ [501+]
    EHR - v111 - N '96 - p1275+ [251-500]
Moricz, Zsigmond - *Be Faithful Unto Death*
    TranslRevS - v2 - D '96 - p27 [51-250]
    WLT - v71 - Win '97 - p193+ [501+]
Morillo, Stephen - *Warfare under the Anglo-Norman Kings 1066-1135*
    EHR - v112 - Ap '97 - p431+ [501+]
    Specu - v72 - Ja '97 - p203+ [501+]
Morimoto, Anri - *Jonathan Edwards and the Catholic Vision of Salvation*
    CH - v65 - D '96 - p721+ [501+]
    Theol St - v57 - S '96 - p568+ [251-500]
    W&M Q - v53 - O '96 - p817+ [501+]
Morin, Carole - *Dead Glamorous*
    KR - v64 - D 1 '96 - p1722 [251-500]
    PW - v243 - N 25 '96 - p61 [51-250]
    TLS - F 14 '97 - p32 [501+]
Morin, Isobel V - *Impeaching the President*
  y HB Guide - v7 - Fall '96 - p315 [51-250]
  y VOYA - v19 - O '96 - p236 [251-500]
Morina, Mimmo - *Democraticon: For a Democratic Democracy*
    WLT - v71 - Win '97 - p130 [251-500]

Moring, Marcel - *The Great Longing*
    TLS - D 20 '96 - p23 [51-250]
Morison, John - *Tall Stories?*
    R&R Bk N - v11 - N '96 - p65 [51-250]
Morison, Samuel Eliot - *The European Discovery of America*
    Sea H - Aut '96 - p42 [51-250]
    Sea H - Win '96 - p42 [1-50]
Morison, Stanley - *First Principles of Typography*
    BC - v45 - Aut '96 - p390 [51-250]
Moritz, Karl Philipp - *Anton Reiser*
    TranslRevS - v2 - D '96 - p26 [51-250]
Morkot, Robert - *The Penguin Historical Atlas of Ancient Greece*
  r ARBA - v28 - '97 - p205 [51-250]
  yr Kliatt - v31 - Mr '97 - p33 [51-250]
Morland, Kjell Arne - *The Rhetoric of Curse in Galatians*
    Rel St Rev - v23 - Ja '97 - p74 [51-250]
Morley, Christine - *Cat (Illus. by Brita Granstrom)*
  c Sch Lib - v45 - F '97 - p39+ [51-250]
  Dog (Illus. by Brita Granstrom)
  c Sch Lib - v45 - F '97 - p39+ [51-250]
Morley, Jacqueline - *The Ancient Egyptian Facts of Life*
  c Sch Lib - v45 - F '97 - p39 [51-250]
  Exploring North America (Illus. by David Antram)
  c Ch BWatch - v7 - Ja '97 - p7 [1-50]
  c HB Guide - v8 - Spr '97 - p162 [51-250]
  c SLJ - v42 - D '96 - p132 [51-250]
  First Facts about the Ancient Egyptians (Illus. by Mark Bergin)
  c SLJ - v43 - Ja '97 - p104 [51-250]
  First Facts about the Vikings
  c SLJ - v43 - Mr '97 - p204 [51-250]
  How Would You Survive in the American West? (Illus. by David Antram)
  c HB Guide - v7 - Fall '96 - p387 [51-250]
  Viking
  c Sch Lib - v45 - F '97 - p39 [51-250]
Morley, John David - *The Anatomy Lesson*
    Obs - N 24 '96 - p18* [51-250]
Morley, Sheridan - *Gene Kelly: A Celebration*
    Obs - D 1 '96 - p16* [51-250]
    PW - v244 - Mr 3 '97 - p61 [51-250]
Morneau, Robert - *Ashes to Easter*
    RR - v56 - Ja '97 - p104+ [51-250]
Morocco: The Journal of the Society for Moroccan Studies
  p TLS - N 15 '96 - p26+ [501+]
Moroff, Diane Lynn - *Fornes: Theater in the Present Tense*
    Choice - v34 - Ap '97 - p1351 [51-250]
Morot-Sir, Edouard - *The Imagination of Reference II*
    CPR - v16 - Ag '96 - p270+ [501+]
Morowitz, Harold J - *Entropy and the Magic Flute*
    Nature - v385 - Ja 9 '97 - p130 [1-50]
Morpeth, F F - *Preservation of Surfactant Formulations*
    SciTech - v20 - S '96 - p61 [51-250]
Morpurgo, Michael - *Arthur, High King of Britain (Illus. by Michael Foreman)*
  c Bks Keeps - Ja '97 - p23 [51-250]
  c RT - v50 - F '97 - p424 [51-250]
  Beyond the Rainbow Warrior
  c TES - Ja 17 '97 - p13* [51-250]
  The Butterfly Lion
  c PW - v244 - My 12 '97 - p76+ [51-250]
  The Butterfly Lion (Illus. by Christian Birmingham)
  c JB - v60 - O '96 - p204 [251-500]
  c Sch Lib - v44 - Ag '96 - p108 [51-250]
  The Dancing Bear (Illus. by Christian Birmingham)
  c HB Guide - v7 - Fall '96 - p295 [51-250]
  The Ghost of Grania O'Malley
  c Ch BWatch - v6 - N '96 - p3 [1-50]
  c HB Guide - v8 - Spr '97 - p71 [51-250]
  c JB - v60 - Ag '96 - p159 [51-250]
  c Sch Lib - v45 - F '97 - p33 [51-250]
  Ghostly Haunts
  y BL - v93 - Mr 15 '97 - p1236 [51-250]
  The Marble Crusher (Illus. by Frances Thatcher)
  c Bks Keeps - Mr '97 - p16 [51-250]
  Mums the Word
  c Magpies - v11 - Jl '96 - p28 [1-50]
  Robin of Sherwood (Illus. by Michael Foreman)
  c BL - v93 - O 1 '96 - p350 [51-250]
  y BL - v93 - Ap 1 '97 - p1308 [1-50]
  c CCB-B - v50 - Ja '97 - p181 [51-250]
  c HB Guide - v8 - Spr '97 - p104 [51-250]
  c SLJ - v43 - F '97 - p104 [51-250]
  c Spec - v277 - D 14 '96 - p77 [51-250]
  y VOYA - v19 - F '97 - p330 [251-500]
  Sam's Duck (Illus. by Keith Bowen)
  c TES - Ja 17 '97 - p13* [51-250]

  Waiting for Anya
  c PW - v244 - Ja 20 '97 - p403 [51-250]
  c SLJ - v42 - N '96 - p41 [1-50]
  The War of Jenkins' Ear
  y BL - v93 - O 1 '96 - p339 [1-50]
  y EJ - v85 - N '96 - p133+ [251-500]
  y Emerg Lib - v24 - S '96 - p25 [1-50]
  y Emerg Lib - v24 - S '96 - p53 [51-250]
  y SLJ - v42 - N '96 - p41 [1-50]
  The Wreck of the Zanzibar (Illus. by Christian Birmingham)
  c RT - v50 - F '97 - p422 [51-250]
Morreim, E Haavi - *Balancing Act*
    Theol St - v57 - Je '96 - p388+ [251-500]
Morrell, David - *Extreme Denial*
    PW - v244 - Mr 3 '97 - p72 [1-50]
Morrell, Gordon W - *Britain Confronts the Stalin Revolution*
    AHR - v102 - F '97 - p113 [251-500]
    Russ Rev - v55 - O '96 - p717+ [501+]
Morressy, John - *The Juggler*
  y Emerg Lib - v24 - S '96 - p54 [51-250]
  y HB Guide - v7 - Fall '96 - p303 [51-250]
Morrice, David - *Philosophy, Science and Ideology in Political Thought*
    Choice - v34 - My '97 - p1574 [51-250]
Morrill, Calvin - *The Executive Way*
    CS - v26 - Mr '97 - p220+ [501+]
Morrill, John - *The Oxford Illustrated History of Tudor and Stuart Britain*
    BL - v93 - N 1 '96 - p478 [51-250]
    LJ - v122 - My 1 '97 - p119 [51-250]
Morris, Alan - *By Honor Bound*
    BL - v93 - O 1 '96 - p304 [501+]
  Patrick Modiano
    R&R Bk N - v12 - F '97 - p83 [1-50]
Morris, Alistair - *Antiques from the Garden*
    BL - v93 - F 15 '97 - p987 [51-250]
    LJ - v122 - Ap 1 '97 - p90 [51-250]
Morris, Ann - *El Chico Karateka (Illus. by David Katzenstein)*
  c BL - v93 - My 1 '97 - p1507 [1-50]
  Karate Boy (Illus. by David Katzenstein)
  c BL - v92 - Ag '96 - p1903 [51-250]
  c CCB-B - v50 - S '96 - p24+ [51-250]
  c HB Guide - v8 - Spr '97 - p145 [51-250]
  c SLJ - v42 - Ag '96 - p139+ [51-250]
  Tengo Seis Anos (Illus. by Nancy Sheehan)
  c SLJ - v42 - N '96 - p134 [51-250]
Morris, Beryl - *First Steps in Management*
    LAR - v98 - O '96 - p533 [51-250]
Morris, Bill - *All Souls' Day*
    KR - v65 - Ap 1 '97 - p493 [251-500]
    PW - v244 - Ap 21 '97 - p58+ [51-250]
Morris, Brian - *Anthropology of the Self*
    Am Ethnol - v24 - F '97 - p215+ [501+]
Morris, Charles R - *The AARP: America's Most Powerful Lobby and the Clash of Generations*
    KR - v64 - My 1 '96 - p670+ [251-500]
    Nat - v263 - Ag 26 '96 - p29+ [501+]
    NYTBR - v101 - O 20 '96 - p12 [501+]
Morris, Christopher - *Becoming Southern*
    AHR - v101 - D '96 - p1623+ [501+]
    JIH - v27 - Win '97 - p540+ [251-500]
    JSH - v62 - N '96 - p802+ [251-500]
  Southern Writers and Their Worlds
    Choice - v34 - O '96 - p282 [51-250]
Morris, Cindy E - *Aerial Plant Surface Microbiology*
    SciTech - v21 - Mr '97 - p44 [51-250]
Morris, Claud - *The Last Inch*
    Spec - v278 - Ap 5 '97 - p35 [501+]
Morris, D L - *Hepatic Metastases*
    SciTech - v20 - S '96 - p31 [51-250]
Morris, Daniel - *The Writings of William Carlos Williams*
    J Am St - v30 - Ag '96 - p294+ [501+]
Morris, David Joseph - *Market Power and Business Strategy*
    Choice - v34 - D '96 - p656 [51-250]
    R&R Bk N - v11 - D '96 - p27 [51-250]
Morris, Desmond - *Babywatching*
    Books - v9 - S '95 - p23 [1-50]
  Cat World
  r BL - v93 - F 1 '97 - p962 [251-500]
  r LJ - v121 - D '96 - p86 [51-250]

Morris, Dick - *Behind the Oval Office*
BL - v93 - F 15 '97 - p971 [1-50]
CSM - v89 - F 6 '97 - p14 [51-250]
Ent W - Ja 31 '97 - p52+ [501+]
LATBR - Ja 19 '97 - p4+ [501+]
LJ - v122 - Ap 1 '97 - p110 [51-250]
Lon R Bks - v19 - F 20 '97 - p25+ [501+]
Nat - v264 - Mr 3 '97 - p27+ [501+]
New R - v216 - F 24 '97 - p26+ [501+]
NYRB - v44 - F 20 '97 - p4+ [501+]
NYTBR - v102 - F 2 '97 - p15+ [501+]
NYTLa - v146 - Ja 14 '97 - pC20 [501+]
Spec - v278 - F 22 '97 - p34 [501+]
WSJ-Cent - v99 - Ja 24 '97 - pA12 [501+]
Morris, Evan - *The Book Lover's Guide to the Internet*
r BW - v27 - Ap 6 '97 - p15 [501+]
Morris, Gay - *Moving Words*
Choice - v34 - F '97 - p977 [51-250]
Morris, Gilbert - *Over the Misty Mountains*
BL - v93 - Mr 1 '97 - p1111 [51-250]
LJ - v122 - F 1 '97 - p66 [51-250]
Vanishing Clues
c BL - v93 - O 1 '96 - p336 [51-250]
Morris, Glenn E - *Epitope Mapping Protocols*
SciTech - v20 - N '96 - p35 [51-250]
Morris, Gregory L - *Talking up a Storm*
WAL - v31 - Win '97 - p394+ [251-500]
Morris, Guy - *Airborne Pulsed Doppler Radar. 2nd Ed.*
SciTech - v21 - Mr '97 - p89 [51-250]
Morris, Holly - *A Different Angle*
Aethlon - v13 - Spr '96 - p216 [501+]
Morris, Irwin - *From the Glittering World*
PW - v244 - Ja 6 '97 - p67 [51-250]
Morris, James - *On Mozart*
Eight-C St - v30 - Win '96 - p199+ [501+]
Morris, James G - *Aluminum Alloys for Packaging II*
SciTech - v20 - N '96 - p82 [51-250]
Morris, James McGrath - *Grant Seekers Guide. 4th Ed.*
r ARBA - v28 - '97 - p314 [251-500]
Morris, Jeffrey - *The FDR Way*
c HB Guide - v7 - Fall '96 - p387+ [51-250]
The Lincoln Way
c HB Guide - v7 - Fall '96 - p387+ [51-250]
The Reagan Way
c HB Guide - v7 - Fall '96 - p387+ [51-250]
Morris, Jenny - *Growing*
TES - D 13 '96 - p43 [51-250]
Morris, Judy K - *Nightwalkers*
c BL - v93 - D 1 '96 - p665 [51-250]
c CBRS - v25 - O '96 - p23 [51-250]
c CCB-B - v50 - D '96 - p145 [51-250]
c HB Guide - v8 - Spr '97 - p72 [51-250]
c SLJ - v42 - D '96 - p123+ [51-250]
Morris, Katherine - *Odyssey of Exile*
R&R Bk N - v11 - D '96 - p18 [51-250]
Morris, Kathleen V - *Pulmonary Rehabilitation Administration and Patient Education Manual*
SciTech - v20 - D '96 - p47 [51-250]
Morris, Kenneth E - *Jimmy Carter, American Moralist*
Am - v176 - Mr 22 '97 - p31+ [251-500]
Bks & Cult - v3 - Mr '97 - p16+ [501+]
BL - v93 - N 1 '96 - p479 [51-250]
CC - v114 - Mr 19 '97 - p307+ [501+]
Choice - v34 - Ap '97 - p1406 [51-250]
KR - v64 - S 15 '96 - p1380+ [251-500]
LJ - v121 - S 15 '96 - p76 [51-250]
PW - v243 - S 30 '96 - p69 [51-250]
Morris, Libby V - *Multiculturalism in Academe*
r Choice - v34 - O '96 - p254 [51-250]
Morris, Lydia - *Social Divisions*
SF - v75 - D '96 - p765 [1-50]
Soc Ser R - v70 - D '96 - p671 [51-250]
Morris, Lynn - *Secret Place of Thunder*
LJ - v121 - N 1 '96 - p54 [51-250]
Toward the Sunrising
y SLJ - v42 - Ag '96 - p185 [51-250]
y VOYA - v19 - O '96 - p212 [251-500]
Morris, Mary - *House Arrest*
NY - v72 - Ag 12 '96 - p73 [51-250]
The Lifeguard: Stories
KR - v65 - My 1 '97 - p671+ [251-500]
Morris, Michael A - *Caribbean Maritime Security*
HAHR - v76 - N '96 - p844+ [501+]
Morris, Miranda - *Pink Triangle*
Aust Bk R - Jl '96 - p67 [51-250]
Morris, Nancy - *Puerto Rico: Culture, Politics, and Identity*
HAHR - v77 - My '97 - p336+ [501+]
Hisp - v79 - D '96 - p816+ [501+]
Morris, Neil - *Caves*
c HB Guide - v7 - Fall '96 - p332+ [51-250]

Deserts (Wonders of Our World)
c HB Guide - v7 - Fall '96 - p337 [51-250]
Deserts (World's Top Ten) (Illus. by Vanessa Card)
c HB Guide - v8 - Spr '97 - p163 [51-250]
Islands (Illus. by Vanessa Card)
c HB Guide - v8 - Spr '97 - p163 [51-250]
Mountain Ranges (Illus. by Vanessa Card)
c HB Guide - v8 - Spr '97 - p163 [51-250]
Mountains
c HB Guide - v7 - Fall '96 - p332+ [51-250]
Oceans
c HB Guide - v7 - Fall '96 - p332+ [51-250]
Rivers (Illus. by Vanessa Card)
c HB Guide - v8 - Spr '97 - p163 [51-250]
Volcanoes
c HB Guide - v7 - Fall '96 - p332+ [51-250]
Morris, Norval - *The Oxford History of the Prison*
Comw - v123 - O 25 '96 - p21+ [501+]
J Soc H - v30 - Spr '97 - p746+ [501+]
Morris, R J - *The Victorian City*
J Urban H - v22 - My '96 - p516+ [501+]
Morris, R Winston - *The Tuba Source Book*
r Am MT - v46 - F '97 - p67+ [501+]
M Ed J - v83 - S '96 - p58 [51-250]
r Notes - v53 - Mr '97 - p813+ [501+]
Morris, Richard - *Achilles in the Quantum Universe*
KR - v65 - Mr 15 '97 - p446 [251-500]
LJ - v122 - Ap 15 '97 - p112+ [51-250]
PW - v244 - Ap 28 '97 - p66 [251-500]
Morris, Robert - *The Papers of Robert Morris 1781-1784. Vol. 8*
JEL - v34 - S '96 - p1469 [51-250]
The Papers of Robert Morris 1781-1784. Vols. 7-8
J Mil H - v61 - Ja '97 - p160+ [501+]
Morris, Roger - *Partners in Power*
Atl - v278 - O '96 - p109+ [501+]
y BL - v92 - Ag '96 - p1862+ [501+]
y BL - v92 - Ag '96 - p1890 [1-50]
Nat - v263 - S 9 '96 - p40+ [501+]
NYRB - v43 - Ag 8 '96 - p25+ [501+]
Pres SQ - v27 - Win '97 - p153+ [501+]
TLS - Ag 30 '96 - p9 [501+]
W&I - v11 - N '96 - p254+ [501+]
Morris, Roy - *Ambrose Bierce: Alone in Bad Company*
Rapport - v19 - 5 '96 - p42 [251-500]
VQR - v72 - Aut '96 - p128* [51-250]
Morris, Stephen D - *Political Reformism in Mexico*
APSR - v90 - D '96 - p942+ [501+]
Morris, Susan - *A Traveler's Guide to Pioneer Jewish Cemeteries of the California Gold Rush*
LJ - v121 - D '96 - p130 [51-250]
Morris, Sylvia Jukes - *Rage for Fame*
BL - v93 - My 15 '97 - p1539 [51-250]
NYTLa - v146 - My 30 '97 - pC30 [501+]
WSJ-Cent - v99 - My 30 '97 - pA16 [501+]
Morris, Thomas D - *Southern Slavery and the Law 1619-1860*
AHR - v102 - F '97 - p188+ [501+]
BW - v26 - D 8 '96 - p8 [51-250]
HRNB - v25 - Fall '96 - p7 [251-500]
RAH - v24 - D '96 - p590+ [501+]
W&M Q - v54 - Ja '97 - p269+ [501+]
Morris, Timothy, 1959- - *Becoming Canonical in American Poetry*
Col Lit - v23 - O '96 - p171+ [501+]
Making the Team
LJ - v122 - F 1 '97 - p83 [1-50]
Morris, Ting - *Communication (Illus. by Ed Dovey)*
c HB Guide - v7 - Fall '96 - p354 [51-250]
Morris, Tudor - *German Notgeld*
Coin W - v38 - Ap 7 '97 - p62 [51-250]
Morris, William, 1834-1896 - *The Collected Letters of William Morris. Vols. 3-4*
Am Craft - v56 - Ag '96 - p27 [1-50]
ELT - v39 - 4 '96 - p463+ [501+]
Nine-C Lit - v51 - S '96 - p275 [1-50]
NY - v72 - S 23 '96 - p90+ [501+]
VQR - v72 - Aut '96 - p128* [251-500]
News from Nowhere or, An Epoch of Rest
Nine-C Lit - v51 - S '96 - p275 [1-50]
Morris, William Sparkes - *The Young Jonathan Edwards*
CH - v65 - D '96 - p720+ [501+]

Morris, Winifred - *Liar*
y BL - v93 - D 1 '96 - p646 [51-250]
y CBRS - v25 - F '97 - p84 [1-50]
y CCB-B - v50 - Ja '97 - p181 [51-250]
c Ch BWatch - v7 - F '97 - p4 [51-250]
y HB Guide - v8 - Spr '97 - p82 [51-250]
y KR - v65 - S 15 '96 - p1405 [51-250]
y PW - v243 - N 18 '96 - p77 [51-250]
y SLJ - v43 - Ja '97 - p115 [51-250]
y VOYA - v19 - D '96 - p272 [51-250]
Morris, Wright - *Plains Song*
WAL - v31 - Win '97 - p291+ [501+]
Morrisey, Will - *A Political Approach to Pacifism. Bks. 1-2*
r Choice - v34 - O '96 - p353 [51-250]
Morris-Hale, Walter - *Conflict and Harmony in Multi-Ethnic Societies*
Choice - v34 - Ap '97 - p1411+ [51-250]
Morrison, Arthur - *Tales of Mean Streets*
Trib Bks - Mr 23 '97 - p6 [1-50]
Morrison, Blake - *As If*
Books - v11 - Ap '97 - p20 [51-250]
Econ - v342 - F 15 '97 - p6* [251-500]
Lon R Bks - v19 - Mr 6 '97 - p13+ [501+]
NS - v126 - F 14 '97 - p44+ [501+]
Obs - F 9 '97 - p15* [501+]
Spec - v278 - F 1 '97 - p29+ [501+]
TLS - F 14 '97 - p27 [501+]
Morrison, Connie - *A Practical Approach to Microsoft Word for Windows 95*
R&R Bk N - v12 - F '97 - p101 [51-250]
Morrison, Craig - *Go Cat Go!*
BL - v93 - S 1 '96 - p54 [51-250]
Choice - v34 - Ap '97 - p1348 [51-250]
Morrison, Dane - *A Praying People*
W&M Q - v53 - Jl '96 - p647+ [501+]
Morrison, David - *Threads of Arctic Prehistory*
Am Ant - v61 - Jl '96 - p626+ [501+]
Morrison, Gail - *Medical Nutrition and Disease*
SciTech - v20 - D '96 - p54 [51-250]
Morrison, Grant - *The Invisibles. Vol. 1*
p VLS - Spr '97 - p29+ [501+]
Morrison, Ian R - *Rabelais: Tiers Livre, Quart Livre, Ve Livre*
MLR - v91 - Jl '96 - p719+ [501+]
Morrison, J Ian - *The Second Curve*
Bus Bk R - v14 - 1 '97 - p30+ [501+]
Morrison, James H - *Alfred Fitzpatrick*
c Can CL - v22 - Fall '96 - p107+ [501+]
Morrison, K - *Marx, Durkheim, Weber*
Socio R - v45 - My '97 - p337+ [501+]
Morrison, Lillian - *Slam Dunk (Illus. by Bill James)*
c RT - v50 - O '96 - p142 [1-50]
Morrison, Marion - *Belize*
c HB Guide - v7 - Fall '96 - p392 [51-250]
Brazil
c Sch Lib - v45 - F '97 - p36+ [51-250]
Mexico
c Sch Lib - v44 - Ag '96 - p113 [51-250]
Morrison, Robert - *Tales of Terror from Blackwood's Magazine*
ELT - v39 - 4 '96 - p527 [1-50]
Morrison, Roy D - *Science, Theology and the Transcendental Horizon*
Theol St - v57 - Mr '96 - p171+ [501+]
Morrison, Steven A - *The Evolution of the Airline Industry*
Econ J - v106 - S '96 - p1477+ [251-500]
Morrison, Taylor - *Antonio's Apprenticeship*
c HB Guide - v7 - Fall '96 - p356 [51-250]
The Neptune Fountain (Illus. by Taylor Morrison)
c KR - v65 - Mr 1 '97 - p386 [51-250]
Morrison, Terri - *Dun and Bradstreet's Guide to Doing Business around the World*
BL - v93 - F 15 '97 - p984 [51-250]
r LJ - v122 - Mr 15 '97 - p57 [51-250]
Morrison, Toni - *Beloved*
y BL - v93 - Ja '97 - p832 [1-50]
Col Lit - v23 - O '96 - p117+ [501+]
Critiq - v37 - Sum '96 - p243+ [501+]
Birth of a Nation'hood
Ent W - Ap 4 '97 - p78+ [51-250]
LJ - v122 - Mr 15 '97 - p78 [51-250]
Playing in the Dark
Signs - v22 - Aut '96 - p243+ [501+]
Song of Solomon
Ent W - Mr 21 '97 - p65+ [501+]
Names - v44 - S '96 - p189+ [501+]
Sula
Col Lit - v23 - O '96 - p88+ [501+]

Tar Baby
  ASInt - v34 - O '96 - p76+ [501+]
Morrisroe, Patricia - *Mapplethorpe: A Biography*
  Art J - v55 - Fall '96 - p99 [501+]
Morriss, Roger - *Nelson: The Life and Letters of a Hero*
  BL - v93 - D 15 '96 - p697 [51-250]
  PW - v243 - D 2 '96 - p51 [51-250]
Morrissey, Bill - *Edson*
  LJ - v121 - N 15 '96 - p116 [51-250]
  Rapport - v19 - 4 '96 - p28 [251-500]
Morrissey, Gabrielle - *Sex in the Time of Generation X*
  Aust Bk R - D '96 - p43+ [501+]
Morrissey, Mary Manin - *Building Your Field of Dreams*
  BL - v92 - Ag '96 - p1860 [51-250]
Morrissey, Stephen - *The Compass*
  Can Lit - Win '96 - p189+ [501+]
The Yoni Rocks
  BIC - v25 - S '96 - p35+ [251-500]
Morris-Suzuki, Tessa - *The Technological Transformation of Japan*
  Historian - v58 - Sum '96 - p885+ [251-500]
  Isis - v88 - Mr '97 - p129+ [501+]
Morrissy, Mary - *A Lazy Eye*
  NYTBR - v101 - D 8 '96 - p80 [1-50]
  W&I - v11 - D '96 - p272+ [501+]
Morrissy, Raymond T - *Atlas of Pediatric Orthopaedic Surgery. 2nd Ed.*
  r SciTech - v20 - N '96 - p50 [51-250]
Morrone, Wenda Wardell - *No Time for an Everyday Woman*
  PW - v244 - My 5 '97 - p202 [51-250]
Morrow, Bradford - *Giovanni's Gift*
  BW - v27 - F 2 '97 - p1+ [501+]
  KR - v64 - N 15 '96 - p1627 [251-500]
  NYTBR - v102 - Mr 9 '97 - p7+ [501+]
  PW - v243 - N 18 '96 - p60 [51-250]
  Trib Bks - Mr 9 '97 - p3 [501+]
  WSJ-Cent - v99 - Mr 3 '97 - pA16 [51-250]
Giovanni's Gift (Muller). Audio Version
  CSM - v89 - Mr 27 '97 - p8B [51-250]
  PW - v244 - Ap 7 '97 - p33 [51-250]
Morrow, C Paul - *Gynecologic Cancer Surgery*
  SciTech - v20 - D '96 - p51 [51-250]
Morrow, James - *Bible Stories for Adults*
  BL - v93 - Ja '97 - p762 [1-50]
Blameless in Abaddon
  Analog - v117 - Ja '97 - p141+ [251-500]
  BW - v26 - S 1 '96 - p11 [251-500]
  NYTBR - v101 - S 15 '96 - p40 [251-500]
  NYTBR - v101 - D 8 '96 - p94 [1-50]
Only Begotten Daughter
  NYTBR - v101 - Ap 7 '96 - p24 [1-50]
Morrow, Laurie - *Shooting Sports for Women*
  BL - v93 - N 1 '96 - p473 [51-250]
  LJ - v121 - O 1 '96 - p87 [51-250]
Morrow, Mark - *Images of the Southern Writer*
  S Liv - v31 - Jl '96 - p80 [51-250]
Morrow, Susan Brind - *The Names of Things*
  KR - v65 - My 1 '97 - p702 [251-500]
Morrow, William G - *Northern Justice*
  Beav - v76 - Ag '96 - p45 [501+]
Morse, Christopher - *Not Every Spirit*
  Intpr - v50 - O '96 - p418+ [501+]
  JAAR - v64 - Sum '96 - p455+ [501+]
Morse, Janice M - *Preventing Patient Falls*
  SciTech - v21 - Mr '97 - p47 [51-250]
Morse, Jennifer - *Apprentice to Power*
  LJ - v121 - S 15 '96 - p83 [51-250]
  Mag Bl - Mr '97 - p61 [51-250]
Morse, Melvin - *Transformed by the Light*
  JP - v60 - Je '96 - p171+ [501+]
  Rel St Rev - v23 - Ap '97 - p141+ [501+]
Morse, Richard - *Grassroot Horizons*
  JEL - v34 - S '96 - p1479 [51-250]
Morse, Ruth - *The Medieval Medea*
  TLS - F 14 '97 - p4+ [501+]
Morse, Stephen - *People and Environment*
  Choice - v34 - O '96 - p300 [51-250]
  GJ - v163 - Mr '97 - p108+ [51-250]
  JEL - v34 - D '96 - p2111 [51-250]
Morsi, Pamela - *The Love Charm*
  LJ - v122 - Ja '97 - p51 [1-50]
  LJ - v121 - N 15 '96 - p52 [51-250]
No Ordinary Princess
  PW - v244 - Ap 14 '97 - p71 [51-250]
Morson, Gary Saul - *Mikhail Bakhtin: Creation of a Prosaics*
  Bks & Cult - v2 - Ja '96 - p26 [1-50]
Narrative and Freedom
  Soc - v33 - Jl '96 - p88+ [501+]

Morson, Ian - *Falconer and the Face of God*
  BL - v93 - Mr 15 '97 - p1230 [51-250]
  KR - v65 - Ja '97 - p102 [51-250]
Morss, John R - *Growing Critical*
  Choice - v34 - O '96 - p365 [51-250]
Mort, Frank - *Cultures of Consumption*
  Choice - v34 - N '96 - p546 [51-250]
  NS & S - v9 - Ap 26 '96 - p32 [1-50]
Mortensen, Jorgen - *Improving Economic and Social Cohesion in the European Community*
  Econ J - v106 - N '96 - p1837 [251-500]
Mortimer, Jeylan T - *Adolescents, Work, and Family*
  R&R Bk N - v11 - D '96 - p40 [51-250]
Mortimer, John - *Rumpole and the Angel of Death*
  Arm Det - v29 - Fall '96 - p468 [51-250]
  PW - v244 - F 3 '97 - p102 [1-50]
  Trib Bks - My 4 '97 - p8 [1-50]
Rumpole and the Angel of Death (May). Audio Version
  LJ - v121 - N 1 '96 - p122 [51-250]
Mortimer, Richard - *Angevin England 1154-1258*
  EHR - v112 - Ap '97 - p436+ [501+]
Mortimore, Jim - *Cracker: The Mad Woman in the Attic*
  BL - v93 - D 1 '96 - p643 [51-250]
  KR - v64 - O 1 '96 - p1432 [51-250]
  PW - v243 - S 23 '96 - p59 [501+]
Mortman, Doris - *The Lucky Ones*
  BL - v93 - My 1 '97 - p1462 [51-250]
  KR - v65 - My 1 '97 - p672 [251-500]
Morton, Adam - *Benacerraf and His Critics*
  SciTech - v20 - D '96 - p6 [51-250]
Morton, Brian - *The Blackwell Guide to Recorded Contemporary Music*
  r Choice - v34 - N '96 - p434 [51-250]
Morton, Carlos - *The Fickle Finger of Lady Death and Other Plays*
  Choice - v34 - N '96 - p464 [51-250]
Morton, Charles - *Aristotelian and Cartesian Logic at Harvard*
  NEQ - v69 - S '96 - p520+ [501+]
Morton, Desmond - *Shaping a Nation*
  y Quill & Q - v62 - Jl '96 - p58 [51-250]
The United Nations: Its History and the Canadians Who Shaped It
  c Ch Bk News - v19 - Sum '96 - p32 [51-250]
Morton, F L - *Pro-Choice vs. Pro-Life*
  CHR - v82 - O '96 - p741+ [501+]
Morton, Helen - *Becoming Tongan*
  Choice - v34 - Ap '97 - p1381 [51-250]
Morton, Jerry - *Romania*
  BWatch - v17 - N '96 - p9 [51-250]
Morton, Margaret - *The Tunnel: The Underground Homeless of New York City*
  Afterimage - v24 - N '96 - p12 [51-250]
  CS - v26 - Ja '97 - p58+ [501+]
  LATBR - D 8 '96 - p9 [501+]
Morton, Mark - *Cupboard Love*
  r Quill & Q - v63 - F '97 - p45 [251-500]
Morton, Mary - *Five Steps to Selecting the Best Alternative Medicine*
  BWatch - v18 - Mr '97 - p1 [51-250]
  Mag Bl - Mr '97 - p70 [51-250]
Morton, Patricia - *Discovering the Women in Slavery*
  Legacy - v14 - 1 '97 - p73+ [51-250]
Morton, Ron L - *Music of the Earth*
  Choice - v34 - O '96 - p310 [51-250]
  Nature - v382 - Ag 1 '96 - p414 [501+]
  SB - v32 - Ag '96 - p167 [51-250]
Morton, Suzanne - *Ideal Surroundings*
  AHR - v101 - O '96 - p1317+ [501+]
  Can Hist R - v77 - D '96 - p613+ [501+]
Morton, Timothy - *Shelley and the Revolution in Taste*
  Critm - v39 - Win '97 - p153+ [501+]
  MLR - v91 - O '96 - p979+ [501+]
  Nine-C Lit - v51 - S '96 - p275 [251-500]
Morville, Peter - *The Internet Searcher's Handbook*
  LAR - v98 - O '96 - p534 [51-250]
  SL - v87 - Sum '96 - p237+ [501+]
Morykan, Dana Gehman - *Warman's Country Antiques and Collectibles. 3rd Ed.*
  r BWatch - v17 - S '96 - p7 [1-50]
Mosby's Complete Drug Reference 1997
  r SciTech - v21 - Mr '97 - p68 [51-250]
Mosby's Medical, Nursing, and Allied Health Dictionary. 4th Ed.
  r BL - v93 - F 1 '97 - p956 [1-50]
Moschis, George P - *Gerontographics: Life-Stage Segmentation for Marketing Strategy Development*
  Choice - v34 - Mr '97 - p1204+ [51-250]
  R&R Bk N - v11 - D '96 - p34 [51-250]
Moscoe, Mike - *First Dawn*
  y Kliatt - v31 - Mr '97 - p20 [51-250]

Moscow and St. Petersburg (Essential Travel Guides)
  r BL - v93 - S 15 '96 - p206 [1-50]
Moseley, Eva Steiner - *Women, Information, and the Future*
  LQ - v66 - O '96 - p492+ [501+]
  NWSA Jnl - v8 - Sum '96 - p145+ [501+]
Moseley, Fred - *Heterodox Economic Theories*
  Econ J - v106 - S '96 - p1445+ [501+]
Moseley, Mary June - *Communication Therapy*
  Choice - v34 - Ap '97 - p1372 [51-250]
  J Rehab RD - v34 - Ap '97 - p241 [251-500]
  SciTech - v20 - D '96 - p51 [51-250]
Moser, Barry Kurt - *Linear Models*
  SciTech - v21 - Mr '97 - p15 [1-50]
Moser, Caroline O N - *Confronting Crisis*
  JEL - v35 - Mr '97 - p233 [51-250]
Moser, Charles - *Bound to Be Free*
  LJ - v121 - N 1 '96 - p94+ [51-250]
Moser, Diane K - *Disease Fighters since 1950*
  c KR - v65 - Ja 1 '97 - p61 [51-250]
Moser, Edward P - *The Politically Correct Guide to American History*
  VQR - v73 - Win '97 - p31* [51-250]
The Politically Correct Guide to the Bible
  PW - v244 - My 12 '97 - p73 [51-250]
Moser, Joann - *Singular Impressions*
  Mag Antiq - v151 - Ap '97 - p510+ [501+]
Moser, Johann M - *O Holy Night*
  RR - v55 - N '96 - p659 [1-50]
Moser, Madeline - *Ever Heard of an Aardwolf? (Illus. by Barry Moser)*
  c BL - v93 - S 15 '96 - p243 [51-250]
  c CBRS - v25 - N '96 - p31 [51-250]
  c Ch BWatch - v6 - N '96 - p7 [1-50]
  c HB Guide - v8 - Spr '97 - p119 [51-250]
  c KR - v64 - Ag 15 '96 - p1239 [51-250]
  c NYTBR - v102 - F 2 '97 - p18 [501+]
  c SLJ - v42 - O '96 - p115+ [51-250]
Moser, Mary Anne - *Immersed in Technology*
  Afterimage - v24 - Ja '97 - p23 [1-50]
Moser, Richard - *The New Winter Soldiers*
  RAH - v25 - Mr '97 - p151+ [501+]
Moser, William R - *Advanced Catalyst and Nanostructured Materials*
  SciTech - v21 - Mr '97 - p95 [51-250]
Moses, A D A - *Matthew's Transfiguration Story and Jewish-Christian Controversy*
  Rel St Rev - v23 - Ap '97 - p180 [51-250]
Moses, Amy - *Doctors Help People*
  c HB Guide - v8 - Spr '97 - p91 [51-250]
  c SLJ - v43 - Mr '97 - p174 [51-250]
Zookeepers Care for Animals
  c HB Guide - v8 - Spr '97 - p91 [51-250]
Moses, Brian - *Performance Poems*
  Sch Lib - v44 - N '96 - p167+ [51-250]
  TES - D 6 '96 - p12* [501+]
Moses, Emmanuel - *Opus 100*
  WLT - v70 - Aut '96 - p914 [251-500]
Moses, Greg - *Revolution of Conscience*
  BWatch - v18 - Mr '97 - p4 [51-250]
Moses, Harry - *Pickups: Classic American Trucks*
  y BL - v93 - Ja '97 - p797 [51-250]
  WSJ-MW - v78 - D 5 '96 - pA18 [51-250]
Moses, L G - *Wild West Shows and the Images of American Indians 1883-1933*
  Choice - v34 - Mr '97 - p1228 [51-250]
  NYTBR - v101 - O 27 '96 - p38 [251-500]
  WHQ - v28 - Spr '97 - p69 [251-500]
Moses, Michael Valdez - *The Novel and the Globalization of Culture*
  ELT - v39 - 4 '96 - p528 [51-250]
  MP - v94 - F '97 - p418+ [501+]
Moses, Russell Leigh - *Freeing the Hostages*
  Choice - v34 - D '96 - p687 [51-250]
  R&R Bk N - v11 - D '96 - p13 [51-250]
Moses, Wilson Jeremiah - *Classical Black Nationalism rvey*
  Bl S - v26 - Sum '96 - p66+ [501+]
Mosher, Bill - *Visionaries*
  Rapport - v19 - 4 '96 - p41 [51-250]
Mosher, Howard Frank - *North Country*
  KR - v65 - Mr 1 '97 - p360 [51-250]
  LJ - v122 - Ap 15 '97 - p105 [51-250]
  PW - v244 - F 17 '97 - p199 [51-250]
Mosher, Kiki - *Learning about Bravery from the Life of Harriet Tubman*
  c SLJ - v43 - Ja '97 - p104+ [51-250]
Learning about Fairness from the Life of Susan B. Anthony
  c SLJ - v42 - D '96 - p132+ [51-250]

Learning about Honesty from the Life of Abraham Lincoln
  c SLJ - v42 - D '96 - p132+ [51-250]
Learning about Leadership from the Life of George Washington
  c SLJ - v42 - D '96 - p132+ [51-250]
Mosher, Merrill Hill - *John Freeman of Norfolk County, Virginia*
  NGSQ - v84 - D '96 - p309 [251-500]
Mosher, Richard - *The Taxi Navigator*
  c BL - v93 - S 15 '96 - p242 [51-250]
  c CBRS - v25 - Mr '97 - p95 [51-250]
  c HB Guide - v8 - Spr '97 - p72 [51-250]
  c KR - v64 - S 1 '96 - p1325 [51-250]
  c SLJ - v43 - Ja '97 - p115 [51-250]
Mosk, Carl - *Competition and Cooperation in Japanese Labour Markets*
  JEL - v34 - D '96 - p1978+ [501+]
Moskin, J Robert - *Mr. Truman's War*
  BW - v26 - Jl 14 '96 - p9 [501+]
  Choice - v34 - O '96 - p677 [51-250]
  Mar Crp G - v80 - S '96 - p96 [501+]
  NL - v79 - Ag 12 '96 - p12+ [501+]
  NYTBR - v101 - S 15 '96 - p30+ [51-250]
  Rapport - v19 - 5 '96 - p42 [501+]
Moskos, Charles C - *All That We Can Be*
  BL - v93 - S 1 '96 - p41 [51-250]
  Bl S - v26 - Fall '96 - p105 [51-250]
  BWatch - v17 - D '96 - p5 [51-250]
  Choice - v34 - Ja '97 - p864 [51-250]
  LJ - v121 - S 15 '96 - p84+ [51-250]
  Wil Q - v20 - Aut '96 - p98+ [251-500]
  WSJ-Cent - v99 - F 12 '97 - pA12 [501+]
Moskovitz, Richard A - *Lost in the Mirror*
  BL - v93 - S 1 '96 - p51 [51-250]
Moskowitz-Mateu, Lysa - *Poison Pen*
  PW - v243 - D 9 '96 - p58 [51-250]
Mosley, Don - *With Our Own Eyes*
  BL - v93 - S 15 '96 - p183 [51-250]
  OS - v32 - S '96 - p59 [51-250]
Mosley, Jenny - *Quality Circle Time in the Primary Classroom*
  TES - O 4 '96 - p16* [501+]
Mosley, Pat - *Sensor Materials*
  SciTech - v20 - N '96 - p60 [51-250]
Mosley, Paul - *Aid and Power. 2nd Ed., Vol. 1*
  JEL - v34 - S '96 - p1479 [51-250]
Mosley, Walter - *Devil in a Blue Dress (Windfield). Audio Version*
  Obs - Ja 12 '97 - p18* [51-250]
Gone Fishin'
  BL - v93 - D 1 '96 - p621 [51-250]
  BW - v27 - F 2 '97 - p1+ [501+]
  Ent W - Ja 24 '97 - p53 [51-250]
  KR - v64 - N 1 '96 - p1568 [51-250]
  LATBR - F 2 '97 - p10 [501+]
  LJ - v121 - D '96 - p146 [51-250]
  NYTBR - v102 - Ja 26 '97 - p18 [51-250]
  Obs - Mr 30 '97 - p15* [501+]
  PW - v243 - N 18 '96 - p65 [51-250]
  Trib Bks - Ja 5 '97 - p4 [51-250]
A Little Yellow Dog
  Arm Det - v29 - Fall '96 - p482+ [251-500]
  LATBR - Jl 14 '96 - p2 [501+]
  LJ - v122 - Ja '97 - p51 [1-50]
  NYTBR - v101 - D 8 '96 - p94 [1-50]
  y SLJ - v42 - O '96 - p164 [51-250]
A Little Yellow Dog (Winfield). Audio Version
  Arm Det - v29 - Fall '96 - p473 [51-250]
  LJ - v121 - O 1 '96 - p144 [51-250]
  Trib Bks - F 2 '97 - p6 [51-250]
Mariposa Blanca
  LJ - v122 - Ja '97 - p79 [51-250]
RL's Dream
  Obs - D 8 '96 - p18* [51-250]
RL's Dream (Kramer). Audio Version
  y Kliatt - v30 - N '96 - p44 [51-250]
Mosquera, Gerardo - *Beyond the Fantastic*
  r Choice - v34 - N '96 - p443 [51-250]
Moss, Ann - *Printed Commonplace-Books and the Structuring of Renaissance Thought*
  TLS - Ja 31 '97 - p10+ [501+]
Moss, Carolyn - *The Charles Dickens-Thomas Powell Vendetta*
  Nine-C Lit - v51 - Mr '97 - p561 [51-250]

Moss, Cynthia - *Little Big Ears (Illus. by Martyn Colbeck)*
  c BL - v93 - Ja '97 - p864 [251-500]
  c CCB-B - v50 - F '97 - p216 [51-250]
  c HB Guide - v8 - Spr '97 - p127 [51-250]
  c KR - v64 - D 1 '96 - p1739+ [51-250]
  c PW - v243 - D 9 '96 - p68 [1-50]
  c SLJ - v43 - Mr '97 - p179 [51-250]
Moss, Cynthia E - *Neuroethological Studies of Cognitive and Perceptual Processes*
  Choice - v34 - S '96 - p153 [51-250]
Moss, Elaine - *The Signal Companion*
  Sch Lib - v44 - N '96 - p176 [51-250]
Moss, Ian G - *Quantum Theory, Black Holes, and Inflation*
  SciTech - v20 - S '96 - p13 [51-250]
Moss, Joyce - *Profiles in World History. Vols. 1-8*
  cr ARBA - v28 - '97 - p214 [51-250]
  cr SLJ - v42 - Ag '96 - p182 [51-250]
Moss, Kary L - *Man-Made Medicine*
  Hast Cen R - v27 - Ja '97 - p47 [1-50]
  Wom R Bks - v14 - D '96 - p23+ [501+]
Moss, Kevin - *Out of the Blue*
  Advocate - Ap 1 '97 - p62 [51-250]
  Choice - v34 - My '97 - p1506 [51-250]
  LJ - v121 - D '96 - p149+ [51-250]
Moss, Marc - *Prospects: The Congressionally Mandated Study of Educational Growth and Opportunity*
  J Gov Info - v23 - S '96 - p544 [51-250]
Moss, Marissa - *Amelia Writes Again (Illus. by Marissa Moss)*
  c BL - v93 - N 1 '96 - p501 [51-250]
  c HB Guide - v8 - Spr '97 - p40 [51-250]
  c Inst - v106 - N '96 - p26 [51-250]
  c SLJ - v42 - O '96 - p122+ [51-250]
Amelia's Notebook
  c Inst - v106 - N '96 - p26 [51-250]
The Ugly Menorah (Illus. by Marissa Moss)
  c CCB-B - v50 - N '96 - p108+ [51-250]
  c HB Guide - v8 - Spr '97 - p41 [51-250]
  c NY - v72 - N 18 '96 - p99+ [1-50]
  c PW - v243 - S 30 '96 - p87 [51-250]
  c SLJ - v42 - O '96 - p39 [51-250]
Moss, Nathaniel - *W.E.B. DuBois: Civil Rights Leader*
  c HB Guide - v7 - Fall '96 - p373 [51-250]
Moss, P Buckley - *Reuben and the Blizzard (Illus. by P Buckley Moss)*
  c HB Guide - v7 - Fall '96 - p257 [51-250]
Moss, Richard J - *The Life of Jedidiah Morse*
  AHR - v101 - O '96 - p1275 [501+]
Moss, Robert - *The Interpreter: A Story of Two Worlds*
  y BL - v93 - Mr 15 '97 - p1227 [51-250]
  KR - v65 - Ja 15 '97 - p87+ [251-500]
  LJ - v122 - F 1 '97 - p106+ [51-250]
  PW - v244 - F 3 '97 - p97 [51-250]
Mosse, George L - *The Image of Man*
  Econ - v339 - My 18 '96 - p3*+ [501+]
  New R - v214 - Je 10 '96 - p38+ [501+]
  Obs - S 15 '96 - p17* [501+]
  R&R Bk N - v11 - D '96 - p41 [51-250]
  TLS - Ja 24 '97 - p10 [501+]
Mosse, Kate - *Eskimo Kissing*
  Books - v11 - Ap '97 - p23 [1-50]
  Woman's J - D '96 - p16 [1-50]
Mosse, W E - *An Economic History of Russia 1856-1914*
  JEL - v35 - Mr '97 - p259 [51-250]
Mossman, Carol A - *Politics and Narratives of Birth*
  MLR - v91 - O '96 - p991+ [251-500]
Mossman, Judith - *Wild Justice*
  Rel St Rev - v23 - Ja '97 - p62+ [51-250]
Most, Bernard - *Catbirds and Dogfish*
  c RT - v50 - D '96 - p346 [51-250]
Cock-a-Doodle-Moo! (Illus. by Bernard Most)
  c BL - v93 - S 1 '96 - p144 [51-250]
  c HB Guide - v8 - Spr '97 - p14 [51-250]
  c Par - v71 - D '96 - p251 [1-50]
  c SLJ - v42 - D '96 - p102 [51-250]
If the Dinosaurs Came Back (Illus. by Bernard Most)
  c HB Guide - v7 - Fall '96 - p269 [51-250]
Moo-Ha!
  c PW - v244 - Mr 31 '97 - p76 [51-250]
Oink-Ha!
  c PW - v244 - Mr 31 '97 - p76 [51-250]
Whatever Happened to the Dinosaurs? (Illus. by Bernard Most)
  c HB Guide - v7 - Fall '96 - p269 [51-250]
Where to Look for a Dinosaur
  c PW - v244 - Ap 14 '97 - p77 [1-50]
Mostly Murder: Your Guide to Reading Mysteries
  p RQ - v36 - Win '96 - p227 [1-50]
Mostow, Joshua S - *Pictures of the Heart*
  Choice - v34 - Ap '97 - p1332 [51-250]

Mostyn, David - *Captain Daylight's Birthday Bash*
  c Magpies - v11 - Jl '96 - p28 [51-250]
Mota, Antonio - *O Lobisomem (Illus. by Bayard Christ)*
  c Bkbird - v34 - Spr '96 - p52 [1-50]
Mote, Dave - *Contemporary Popular Writers*
  r BL - v93 - Mr 1 '97 - p1183 [501+]
Mother Goose: A Canadian Sampler
  c Ch BWatch - v6 - My '96 - p4 [51-250]
Mother Jones
  p Utne R - Jl '96 - p118+ [51-250]
Motion, Andrew - *Philip Larkin: A Writer's Life*
  South CR - v28 - Spr '96 - p284+ [501+]
Salt Water
  Econ - v342 - Mr 29 '97 - p93 [51-250]
  Obs - Mr 2 '97 - p18* [51-250]
Motsapi, Seitlhamo - *Earthstepper/The Ocean Is Very Shallow*
  Bl S - v26 - Sum '96 - p33+ [501+]
Mott, Evelyn Clarke - *Cool Cat*
  c HB Guide - v7 - Fall '96 - p241 [1-50]
Dancing Rainbows
  c HB Guide - v7 - Fall '96 - p391 [51-250]
Hot Dog
  c HB Guide - v7 - Fall '96 - p241 [51-250]
Mott, Frank Luther - *A History of American Magazines. Vols. 1-5*
  ASInt - v34 - O '96 - p15 [51-250]
Mott, Kathleen O'Sullivan - *Leadership Skills for the Nurse Manager*
  SciTech - v20 - S '96 - p43 [51-250]
Mott, Stephen Paul - *A Christian Perspective on Political Thought*
  Rel St Rev - v23 - Ja '97 - p50 [51-250]
Mott, Wesley T - *Biographical Dictionary of Transcendentalism*
  r AL - v69 - Mr '97 - p256 [1-50]
  r ARBA - v28 - '97 - p439 [51-250]
  r Choice - v34 - Ja '97 - p766 [51-250]
  r Nine-C Lit - v51 - Mr '97 - p561+ [51-250]
  r R&R Bk N - v11 - D '96 - p1 [51-250]
Encyclopedia of Transcendentalism
  r ARBA - v28 - '97 - p440 [51-250]
  r Choice - v34 - F '97 - p943 [51-250]
  r R&R Bk N - v12 - F '97 - p88 [51-250]
Motta, Giuseppe - *Le Cinquecentine Della Biblioteca San Benedetto Di Seregno*
  r Lib - v19 - Mr '97 - p100 [51-250]
Motte, Warren - *Playtexts: Ludics in Contemporary Literature*
  L'Esprit - v36 - Win '96 - p100+ [251-500]
Motter, Alton M - *Ecumenism 101*
  CC - v114 - My 7 '97 - p457 [51-250]
Motz, Lloyd - *The Story of Astronomy*
  Am Sci - v85 - Mr '97 - p182+ [501+]
Motz, Marilyn Ferris - *Making the American Home*
  CAY - v17 - Win '96 - p12 [51-250]
Mouat, Jeremy - *Roaring Days*
  Can Hist R - v78 - Mr '97 - p105+ [501+]
  JEL - v34 - D '96 - p2105 [51-250]
  PHR - v65 - N '96 - p677+ [251-500]
Mouffe, Chantal - *The Return of the Political*
  Ger Q - v69 - Spr '96 - p196+ [501+]
Moughtin, Cliff - *Urban Design*
  R&R Bk N - v11 - D '96 - p58 [51-250]
Mould, Richard F - *Mould's Medical Anecdotes*
  New Sci - v152 - D 7 '96 - p49 [51-250]
Mould's Medical Anecdotes Omnibus Edition
  SciTech - v21 - Mr '97 - p44 [51-250]
Moulin, Herve - *Cooperative Microeconomics*
  JEL - v34 - D '96 - p1955+ [501+]
Moulton, Candy - *Wagon Wheels*
  Roundup M - v4 - Ap '97 - p22+ [251-500]
Moulton, Gary E - *The Journals of the Lewis and Clark Expedition. Vol. 9*
  Roundup M - v3 - Ag '96 - p26 [51-250]
The Journals of the Lewis and Clark Expedition. Vol. 10
  Roundup M - v4 - D '96 - p22 [51-250]
The Journals of the Lewis and Clark Expedition. Vols. 5-9
  W&M Q - v54 - Ja '97 - p274+ [501+]
Mountjoy, P A - *Mycenaean Athens*
  AJA - v101 - Ja '97 - p193 [251-500]
Mountstephens, Tessa - *The Good Life Guide to Sydney*
  r FEER - v160 - Mr 27 '97 - p52+ [501+]
Moura, Ann - *Green Witchcraft*
  BWatch - v17 - S '96 - p12 [1-50]
Mouroulis, Pantazis - *Geometrical Optics and Optical Design*
  Choice - v34 - Ap '97 - p1377 [51-250]

Moussis, Nicholas - *Handbook of European Union. 2nd Rev. Ed.*
  r Choice - v34 - S '96 - p102+ [51-250]
Mouth: The Voice of Disability Rights
  p Utne R - Jl '96 - p118+ [51-250]
Mouzelis, Nicos - *Sociological Theory*
  AJS - v102 - S '96 - p595+ [501+]
  CS - v26 - Mr '97 - p252+ [501+]
  Socio R - v45 - My '97 - p341+ [501+]
Mowat, Farley - *Aftermath: Travels in a Post-War World*
  BL - v93 - S 1 '96 - p59 [51-250]
Mowery, David C - *The International Computer Software Industry*
  Choice - v34 - S '96 - p164 [51-250]
  JEL - v34 - S '96 - p1457 [51-250]
Mowitt, John - *Text: The Genealogy of an Antidisciplinary Object*
  MLR - v91 - O '96 - p946+ [501+]
Mowl, Timothy - *Horace Walpole: The Great Outsider*
  Apo - v144 - O '96 - p60 [501+]
  CR - v270 - F '97 - p111+ [51-250]
  Spec - v277 - S 14 '96 - p41+ [501+]
  Spec - v277 - N 23 '96 - p43 [1-50]
  TLS - O 4 '96 - p33 [501+]
Mowry, Jess - *Babylon Boyz*
  y BL - v93 - F 15 '97 - p1020 [251-500]
  y PW - v244 - F 3 '97 - p107 [51-250]
  Ghost Train
  y BL - v93 - Ap 1 '97 - p1310 [1-50]
  y CBRS - v25 - O '96 - p23 [51-250]
  c CCB-B - v50 - D '96 - p145 [51-250]
  c HB Guide - v8 - Spr '97 - p72 [51-250]
  c PW - v243 - S 16 '96 - p84 [51-250]
  c SFR - v22 - Ja '97 - p47 [251-500]
  y SLJ - v42 - D '96 - p139 [51-250]
  y VOYA - v19 - F '97 - p330 [251-500]
Moxey, Keith - *The Practice of Theory*
  AHR - v101 - O '96 - p1175+ [501+]
Moxley, Jennifer - *Imagination Verses*
  PW - v243 - N 25 '96 - p71 [51-250]
Moxley, Joseph M - *The Politics and Processes of Scholarship*
  Cng - v28 - Jl '96 - p61+ [501+]
Moyano, Maria Jose - *Argentina's Lost Patrol*
  AHR - v102 - F '97 - p246 [251-500]
  Historian - v59 - Win '97 - p436+ [251-500]
Moya Pons, Frank - *The Dominican Republic*
  HAHR - v77 - F '97 - p142+ [251-500]
Moyers, Bill D - *Genesis: A Living Conversation*
  y BL - v93 - S 1 '96 - p4 [51-250]
  Bloom Rev - v16 - N '96 - p9+ [501+]
  BW - v26 - D 8 '96 - p5 [501+]
  CSM - v88 - N 6 '96 - p12 [51-250]
  CSM - v89 - N 25 '96 - p12 [51-250]
  CSM - v89 - Ja 23 '97 - p12 [51-250]
  Nat R - v48 - D 9 '96 - p61+ [501+]
  PW - v243 - O 14 '96 - p76 [51-250]
  Genesis: A Living Conversation (Patinkin). Audio Version
  y Kliatt - v31 - Ja '97 - p48+ [51-250]
  Talking about Genesis
  CSM - v89 - N 25 '96 - p12 [51-250]
Moyes, Howard A - *Restoring Balance to the American Federal System*
  PAR - v57 - Ja '97 - p91 [501+]
Moyes, Norman B - *Battle Eye*
  Pet PM - v25 - S '96 - p8 [51-250]
Moyes, Patricia - *Who Killed Father Christmas? and Other Unseasonable Demises*
  Arm Det - v30 - Win '97 - p119 [251-500]
Moynahan, Julian - *Anglo-Irish: The Literary Imagination in a Hyphenated Culture*
  Dal R - v75 - Spr '95 - p130+ [501+]
  ELT - v40 - 2 '97 - p235+ [501+]
Moynihan, Daniel Patrick - *Miles to Go*
  Am - v175 - S 21 '96 - p34+ [51-250]
  BL - v93 - S 15 '96 - p190 [51-250]
  Bus W - N 18 '96 - p19+ [501+]
  BW - v26 - D 8 '96 - p6 [51-250]
  Choice - v34 - F '97 - p1004 [51-250]
  Comw - v123 - N 8 '96 - p17+ [501+]
  KR - v64 - Ag 15 '96 - p1217 [251-500]
  LJ - v121 - O 1 '96 - p110 [51-250]
  Nat - v263 - O 21 '96 - p25+ [501+]
  NS - v125 - N 22 '96 - p48 [501+]
  NYTBR - v101 - N 10 '96 - p14+ [501+]
  PW - v243 - S 16 '96 - p62 [51-250]
Moynihan, Michael - *The Coming American Renaissance*
  BL - v93 - S 1 '96 - p45 [51-250]
  BW - v26 - N 24 '96 - p13 [51-250]

Moynihan, Ruth Barnes - *Second to None. Vols. 1-2*
  J Am St - v30 - Ap '96 - p135+ [251-500]
Moyo, Sam - *The Land Question in Zimbabwe*
  JTWS - v13 - Spr '96 - p320+ [501+]
Moyse, Sarah - *Chinese New Year*
  TES - F 14 '97 - p16* [51-250]
Mozzi, Giulio - *La Felicita Terrena*
  BL - v93 - D 1 '96 - p644 [1-50]
MPI Developer's Conference (2nd: 1996: Notre Dame, Indiana) - *MPI Developer's Conference*
  SciTech - v20 - N '96 - p8 [51-250]
Mr. Potato Head's Mix'n Match Book (Illus. by Rick Farley)
  c HB Guide - v7 - Fall '96 - p238 [51-250]
MRI Bankers' Guide to Foreign Currency, Spring 1997
  r Coin W - v38 - My 12 '97 - p34 [51-250]
MRI Bankers' Guide to Foreign Currency, Winter 1996
  r Coin W - v38 - Mr 10 '97 - p42 [51-250]
Mrkvicka, Edward F, Jr. - *Your Bank Is Ripping You Off*
  LJ - v122 - Ap 15 '97 - p92+ [51-250]
  PW - v243 - D 30 '96 - p45 [51-250]
Mrozowski, Stephen A - *Living on the Boott*
  Choice - v34 - Ap '97 - p1406 [51-250]
Mrs. Hen's Secret! (Illus. by Cathy Beylon)
  c HB Guide - v7 - Fall '96 - p237 [51-250]
MSA Profile 1996
  r ARBA - v28 - '97 - p328+ [251-500]
MSI-2000: Multivariate Statistical Analysis in Honor of Professor Minoru Siotani. Vol. 34
  SciTech - v20 - N '96 - p14 [51-250]
Mubarak, Jamil Abdalla - *From Bad Policy to Chaos in Somalia*
  Choice - v34 - Ja '97 - p846 [51-250]
  R&R Bk N - v11 - N '96 - p28 [51-250]
Mucciaroni, Gary - *Reversals of Fortune*
  PSQ - v111 - Win '96 - p727+ [501+]
Muchinsky, Paul M - *Psychology Applied to Work. 5th Ed.*
  R&R Bk N - v12 - F '97 - p45 [51-250]
Muchmore, Jo Ann - *Johnny Rides Again*
  c RT - v50 - N '96 - p255 [51-250]
Muckleroy, D V - *Elmore County, Alabama Marriage Records 1881-1893*
  r EGH - v50 - N '96 - p160 [51-250]
Mudd-Ruth, Maria - *The Ultimate Ocean Book*
  cr Par Ch - v21 - Mr '97 - p5 [1-50]
Mudrooroo - *Us Mob*
  TLS - S 13 '96 - p32 [251-500]
Mueller, Cookie - *Ask Dr. Mueller*
  BL - v93 - Mr 1 '97 - p1104 [51-250]
  KR - v65 - Ja 15 '97 - p88 [251-500]
  PW - v244 - Ja 20 '97 - p387 [251-500]
Mueller, John, 1958- - *The CA-Visual Objects Interface Handbook*
  SciTech - v20 - S '96 - p5 [51-250]
  Novell CNA/CNE Study Guide. 2nd Ed.
  CBR - v15 - Spr '97 - p1+ [501+]
Mueller, Margrit - *Structure and Strategy of Small and Medium Size Enterprises since the Industrial Revolution*
  JEH - v57 - Mr '97 - p263+ [501+]
Mueller, Milton - *China in the Information Age*
  For Aff - v76 - My '97 - p146 [51-250]
Mueller, Robert Kirk - *Anchoring Points for Corporate Directors*
  R&R Bk N - v11 - D '96 - p29 [51-250]
Muellner, Leonard - *The Anger of Achilles*
  Choice - v34 - D '96 - p610 [51-250]
Muesterberger, Werner - *Collecting: An Unruly Passion*
  Rapport - v19 - 4 '96 - p39 [51-250]
Mufti, Malik - *Sovereign Creations*
  For Aff - v75 - N '96 - p166 [51-250]
Mugerauer, Robert - *Interpreting Environments*
  AAAGA - v87 - Mr '97 - p188+ [501+]
Mugglestone, Lynda - *Talking Proper*
  J Soc H - v30 - Fall '96 - p284+ [501+]
  RES - v47 - N '96 - p550+ [501+]
Muhammad, Askia - *Behind Enemy Lines*
  BW - v26 - N 10 '96 - p12 [51-250]
Muhlbauer, W Kent - *Pipeline Risk Management Manual. 2nd Ed.*
  SciTech - v20 - N '96 - p71 [51-250]
Muhlenberg, Ekkehard - *Predigt In Der Alten Kirche*
  CH - v65 - D '96 - p667 [251-500]
Muhlenberg, Henry Melchior - *The Correspondence of Henry Melchior Muhlenberg. Vol. 1*
  CH - v66 - Mr '97 - p131+ [501+]
Muhlhausler, Peter - *Linguistic Ecology*
  R&R Bk N - v11 - N '96 - p65 [51-250]
Muhr, Ursula - *Easter Egg Farm*
  c Ch BWatch - v6 - My '96 - p2 [1-50]

Muhringer, Doris - *Reisen Wir*
  WLT - v70 - Aut '96 - p954 [501+]
Muhyi Al-Din, Khaled - *Memories of a Revolution*
  Choice - v34 - S '96 - p191 [51-250]
Muhyi Al-Din, Khalid - *Memories of a Revolution*
  HRNB - v25 - Win '97 - p84 [251-500]
  MEJ - v51 - Win '97 - p136+ [501+]
Muir, D - *Optical Illusions*
  c JB - v60 - D '96 - p257 [51-250]
Muir, Elizabeth Gillan - *Changing Roles of Women within the Christian Church in Canada*
  Can Hist R - v77 - D '96 - p619+ [501+]
  CH - v65 - D '96 - p779+ [501+]
Muir, Jane - *Of Men and Numbers*
  Math T - v89 - D '96 - p781 [251-500]
Muir, John - *John Muir: His Life and Letters and Other Writings*
  Choice - v34 - Mr '97 - p1180 [51-250]
  My First Summer in the Sierra
  BW - v27 - F 9 '97 - p12 [51-250]
  Nature Writings
  Trib Bks - Ap 20 '97 - p6 [251-500]
  Stickeen
  WAL - v31 - Sum '96 - p139+ [501+]
  Travels in Alaska (Waterman). Audio Version
  y Kliatt - v31 - Ja '97 - p51 [251-500]
Muir, Lynette R - *The Biblical Drama of Medieval Europe*
  MLR - v92 - Ap '97 - p409+ [501+]
  Six Ct J - v27 - Win '96 - p1109+ [501+]
  Theol St - v57 - Je '96 - p380 [251-500]
Muir, Malcolm, Jr. - *Black Shoes and Blue Water*
  J Mil H - v61 - Ap '97 - p413+ [251-500]
Muir, Percy - *Minding My Own Business*
  BC - v44 - Win '95 - p480 [51-250]
Muir, Rory - *Britain and the Defeat of Napoleon 1807-1815*
  Choice - v34 - O '96 - p340+ [51-250]
  HRNB - v25 - Fall '96 - p21 [501+]
  HT - v47 - Ja '97 - p60+ [501+]
  J Mil H - v60 - O '96 - p774+ [501+]
Muir, Star A - *Earthtalk: Communication Empowerment for Environmental Action*
  Choice - v34 - S '96 - p116 [51-250]
Muirden, James - *Enciclopedia Visual: El Universo*
  cr BL - v93 - Mr 1 '97 - p1196 [51-250]
Muirden, Sallie - *Revelations of a Spanish Infanta*
  Aust Bk R - O '96 - p44+ [501+]
Mukherjee, Bharati - *Leave It to Me*
  PW - v244 - Ap 21 '97 - p59 [51-250]
Mukta, Parita - *Upholding the Common Life*
  Rel St Rev - v23 - Ja '97 - p96 [51-250]
Mulamoottil, George - *Wetlands: Environmental Gradients, Boundaries, and Buffers*
  Choice - v34 - Mr '97 - p1184 [51-250]
  SciTech - v20 - N '96 - p2 [51-250]
Mulberg, Jon - *Social Limits to Economic Theory*
  JEL - v34 - D '96 - p1948+ [501+]
Mulcahy, Greg - *Constellation*
  BL - v92 - Ag '96 - p1883 [51-250]
Mulcahy, John J - *Diagnosis and Management of Male Sexual Dysfunction*
  SciTech - v21 - Mr '97 - p58 [51-250]
Mulcahy, Robert - *Diseases: Finding the Cure*
  c CBRS - v25 - S '96 - p10 [51-250]
  y HB Guide - v8 - Spr '97 - p130 [51-250]
  y SLJ - v42 - O '96 - p158 [51-250]
Mulcahy, Rosemarie - *The Decoration of the Royal Basilica of El Escorial*
  Specu - v71 - Jl '96 - p739+ [501+]
Mulcaster, Richard - *Positions Concerning the Training Up of Children*
  Ren Q - v49 - Aut '96 - p638+ [501+]
Mulder, Marcel - *Basic Principles of Membrane Technology. 2nd Ed.*
  SciTech - v21 - Mr '97 - p95 [51-250]
Mulder, Monique Borgerhoff - *I've Been Gone Far Too Long*
  y BL - v93 - D 1 '96 - p629 [51-250]
  LJ - v121 - D '96 - p102 [51-250]
  New Sci - v152 - D 21 '96 - p74 [51-250]
  PW - v243 - N 25 '96 - p67 [51-250]
Muldoon, Brian - *The Heart of Conflict*
  LJ - v121 - S 15 '96 - p77+ [51-250]
  PW - v243 - Jl 22 '96 - p221+ [51-250]
Muldoon, James - *The Americas in the Spanish World Order*
  EHR - v111 - N '96 - p1281+ [501+]
  JMH - v68 - S '96 - p720+ [501+]
  Ren Q - v49 - Aut '96 - p629+ [501+]

Muldoon, Paul - *The Noctuary of Narcissus Batt (Illus. by Marketa Prachaticka)*
  c Obs - Mr 30 '97 - p17* [1-50]
Muldoon, Paul, 1951- - *Kerry Slides*
  BL - v93 - Ja '97 - p809+ [51-250]
  PW - v243 - D 30 '96 - p62 [51-250]
  TLS - S 27 '96 - p23 [1-50]
  New Selected Poems 1968-1994
  Obs - D 1 '96 - p16* [1-50]
Mulford, Charles W - *Financial Warnings*
  Choice - v34 - N '96 - p504 [51-250]
Mulgan, Geoff - *Connexity: How to Live in a Connected World*
  NS - v126 - Mr 27 '97 - p48+ [501+]
  Life after Politics
  NS - v126 - Ja 31 '97 - p11 [1-50]
  NS - v126 - Mr 27 '97 - p48+ [501+]
  TES - Ja 31 '97 - p8* [501+]
Mulhern, Kathy - *Finding God in the Craziness of Life*
  y CLW - v67 - D '96 - p44 [51-250]
Mulholland, S Grant - *Antibiotic Therapy in Urology*
  SciTech - v20 - S '96 - p37 [51-250]
Mulisch, Harry - *Bij Gelegenheid*
  WLT - v70 - Aut '96 - p973+ [501+]
  The Discovery of Heaven
  BW - v26 - O 27 '96 - p5 [501+]
  KR - v64 - O 15 '96 - p1489 [251-500]
  LATBR - N 10 '96 - p2 [501+]
  LJ - v121 - O 15 '96 - p91 [51-250]
  NY - v72 - N 25 '96 - p115+ [501+]
  NYRB - v44 - Mr 6 '97 - p40+ [501+]
  NYTBR - v102 - Ja 5 '97 - p8 [501+]
  PW - v243 - S 23 '96 - p55 [51-250]
  PW - v243 - N 4 '96 - p38 [51-250]
  TranslRevS - v2 - D '96 - p20 [51-250]
  WSJ-MW - v78 - O 30 '96 - pA16 [501+]
  Last Call
  BW - v26 - D 8 '96 - p4 [501+]
Mulkey, Stephen S - *Tropical Forest Plant Ecophysiology*
  SciTech - v20 - D '96 - p32 [51-250]
Mullan, Don - *Eyewitness Bloody Sunday*
  NS - v126 - F 7 '97 - p46 [501+]
Mullan, John - *Lives of the Great Romantics. Vols. 1-3*
  R&R Bk N - v11 - D '96 - p63 [51-250]
Mullane, R Mike - *Lift Off!*
  y JAAL - v40 - D '96 - p308+ [501+]
Mullaney, Steven - *The Place of the Stage*
  Six Ct J - v27 - Win '96 - p1214+ [501+]
Mullard, Maurice - *Policy-Making in Britain*
  JEL - v34 - D '96 - p2037 [51-250]
Mullen, Bill - *Radical Revisions*
  AL - v69 - Mr '97 - p253 [51-250]
  Choice - v34 - Ja '97 - p797 [51-250]
Muller, Andreas - *Hydroinformatics '96. Vols. 1-2*
  SciTech - v21 - Mr '97 - p86 [51-250]
Muller, Christian - *Helmut Kohl*
  Econ - v341 - N 16 '96 - p8* [51-250]
Muller, Eddie - *Grindhouse: The Forbidden World of Adults Only Cinema*
  BL - v93 - N 1 '96 - p472 [51-250]
  VLS - Win '96 - p22 [51-250]
Muller, Henning - *Exil--Asyl: Tatort Deutschland*
  MLR - v91 - Jl '96 - p800+ [501+]
Muller, Herta - *The Land of Green Plums*
  BL - v93 - N 15 '96 - p570 [51-250]
  KR - v64 - S 15 '96 - p1347 [251-500]
  LJ - v121 - N 1 '96 - p108 [51-250]
  NYTBR - v101 - D 1 '96 - p38 [501+]
  PW - v243 - O 7 '96 - p60+ [51-250]
Muller, Jerry Z - *Conservatism: An Anthology of Social and Political Thought from David Hume to the Present*
  LJ - v122 - Ap 15 '97 - p100 [51-250]
  PW - v244 - Ap 28 '97 - p67+ [51-250]
  Wil Q - v21 - Spr '97 - p103+ [251-500]
Muller, Kal - *Borneo: Journey into the Tropical Rainforest. 2nd Ed.*
  r BL - v93 - S 15 '96 - p212 [1-50]
Muller, Klaus-Jurgen - *The Military in Politics and Society in France and Germany in the Twentieth Century*
  Historian - v59 - Fall '96 - p200+ [501+]
Muller, Marcia - *Both Ends of the Night*
  BL - v93 - My 1 '97 - p1462 [51-250]
  PW - v244 - My 5 '97 - p200+ [51-250]
  The Broken Promise Land
  KR - v64 - My 1 '96 - p646 [51-250]
  The Broken Promise Land (Reed-Bahle). Audio Version
  y Kliatt - v31 - Ja '97 - p37 [51-250]

Muller, Nathan J - *Network Planning, Procurement, and Management*
  CBR - v14 - N '96 - p38 [51-250]
  SciTech - v20 - S '96 - p56 [51-250]
Muller, Rene J - *Anatomy of a Splitting Borderline*
  AJPsych - v153 - N '96 - p1500+ [501+]
Muller, Richard A - *God, Creation, and Providence in the Thought of Jacob Arminius*
  CH - v66 - Mr '97 - p118+ [501+]
Muller, Steven - *Universities in the Twenty-First Century*
  Choice - v34 - N '96 - p334 [51-250]
Muller, Wolfgang P - *Huguccio: The Life, Works, and Thought of a Twelfth-Century Jurist*
  CH - v66 - Mr '97 - p96+ [501+]
  CHR - v82 - Jl '96 - p543+ [501+]
Muller-Brockmann, Josef - *Josef Muller-Brockmann, Designer*
  Choice - v34 - O '96 - p268 [51-250]
Muller De Morogues, Ines - *Le Probleme Feminin Et Les Portraits De Femmes Dans L'Oeuvre De Nikolaj Leskov*
  Russ Rev - v55 - O '96 - p700+ [501+]
Muller-Fahrenholz, Geiko - *God's Spirit*
  Theol St - v57 - D '96 - p779+ [251-500]
Muller-Hill, Benno - *The lac Operon*
  Sci - v275 - F 14 '97 - p938 [501+]
Mullett, Michael - *James II and English Politics 1678-1688*
  HT - v46 - D '96 - p56 [251-500]
Mulligan, Mary - *Wine for Dummies*
  Books - v10 - Je '96 - p22 [1-50]
Mullin, Glenn - *The Mystical Arts of Tibet*
  Tric - v6 - Win '96 - p117 [1-50]
Mullin, Michael - *Design by Motley*
  Choice - v34 - S '96 - p139+ [51-250]
Mullin, Robert Bruce - *Miracles and the Modern Religious Imagination*
  Choice - v34 - Ap '97 - p1356 [51-250]
  LJ - v121 - N 15 '96 - p66 [51-250]
  Reimagining Denominationalism
  Bks & Cult - v2 - Ja '96 - p30 [51-250]
  JR - v76 - O '96 - p651+ [501+]
Mullineux, Andrew - *Financial Innovation, Banking and Monetary Aggregates*
  JEL - v34 - D '96 - p2036 [51-250]
Mullings, Christine - *New Technologies for the Humanities*
  R&R Bk N - v12 - F '97 - p1 [51-250]
Mullins, Linda - *Tribute to Teddy Bear Artists. 2nd Ser.*
  Ant & CM - v101 - O '96 - p55 [51-250]
Mulroy, Elizabeth A - *The New Uprooted*
  Fam Relat - v45 - O '96 - p477 [501+]
Mulryan, John - *Through a Glass Darkly*
  Choice - v34 - Mr '97 - p1165 [51-250]
  R&R Bk N - v12 - F '97 - p85 [51-250]
Multhauf, Robert P - *Neptune's Gift*
  JEL - v35 - Mr '97 - p266 [51-250]
  New Sci - v153 - Ja 4 '97 - p39 [1-50]
Multidimensional Systems Signal Processing Algorithms and Applications Techniques. Vol. 77
  SciTech - v20 - S '96 - p54 [51-250]
Multilateral Treaties Deposited with the Secretary-General 1995
  R&R Bk N - v11 - D '96 - p50 [51-250]
The Multimedia and CD-ROM Directory 1996 on CD-ROM. Electronic Media Version
  r LJ - v121 - N 15 '96 - p95+ [501+]
  r RQ - v36 - Win '96 - p285+ [501+]
  r WorldV - v12 - O '96 - p24 [51-250]
The Multimedia Bird Book. Electronic Media Version
  cr Ch BWatch - v6 - Jl '96 - p8 [51-250]
The Multimedia Encyclopedia of Science Fiction. Electronic Media Version
  r LJ - v122 - Ja '97 - p162 [51-250]
The Multimedia I Ching. Electronic Media Version
  LJ - v122 - F 15 '97 - p169 [51-250]
Multimedia: The Complete Guide
  r ARBA - v28 - '97 - p619 [51-250]
  Choice - v34 - S '96 - p164 [51-250]
  y VOYA - v19 - O '96 - p236 [251-500]
The Multimedia Yearbook 1996
  r Choice - v34 - O '96 - p256 [51-250]
  r SLMQ - v25 - Fall '96 - p61 [51-250]
Mulvaney, Kieran - *Witness: 25 Years on the Environmental Front Line*
  Obs - Ja 12 '97 - p18* [51-250]
Mumford, Laura Stempel - *Love and Ideology in the Afternoon*
  J Pop F&TV - v24 - Win '97 - p185+ [501+]
Mumford, Lewis - *Lewis Mumford and Patrick Geddes*
  T&C - v37 - O '96 - p828+ [501+]

The Lewis Mumford Reader
  Soc - v33 - Jl '96 - p77+ [501+]
Mumtaz, Khawar - *Pakistan: Tradition and Change*
  WorldV - v13 - Ja '97 - p16+ [251-500]
Munch, Edvard - *Munch (Faerna)*
  y BL - v93 - O 1 '96 - p314+ [51-250]
  LJ - v121 - N 1 '96 - p64 [51-250]
Munda, Giuseppe - *Multicriteria Evaluation in a Fuzzy Environment*
  JEL - v34 - D '96 - p2134 [51-250]
Mund-Dopchie, Monique - *La Fortune Du Periple D'Hannon*
  Ren Q - v50 - Spr '97 - p251+ [501+]
Mundo, Anscario M - *Biblioteca De Catalunya*
  r Specu - v71 - O '96 - p987+ [501+]
El Mundo De Los Ninos. Vols. 1-16
  cr CLW - v67 - D '96 - p63 [51-250]
Mundy, Barbara E - *The Mapping of New Spain*
  Choice - v34 - Ap '97 - p1400 [51-250]
  Nature - v385 - Ja 2 '97 - p35 [1-50]
Mundy, John Hine - *Men and Women at Toulouse in the Age of the Cathars*
  JWomHist - v8 - Fall '96 - p228+ [501+]
Mundy, Martha - *Domestic Government*
  MEJ - v50 - Aut '96 - p607+ [501+]
  Rel St Rev - v23 - Ja '97 - p91 [51-250]
Mungello, D E - *The Forgotten Christians of Hangzhou*
  CHR - v82 - O '96 - p747+ [501+]
Mungo, Ray - *Famous Long Ago*
  HMR - Win '96 - p16+ [501+]
Munhall, Edgar - *Whistler and Montesquiou*
  Art J - v55 - Win '96 - p99+ [501+]
Munich, Adrienne - *Queen Victoria's Secrets*
  Choice - v34 - D '96 - p671 [51-250]
  Nine-C Lit - v51 - D '96 - p425 [51-250]
  TLS - My 24 '96 - p9+ [501+]
Munif, Abd Al-Rahman - *Cities of Salt*
  Econ - v342 - Mr 15 '97 - p15*+ [501+]
  Story of a City
  Econ - v342 - Mr 15 '97 - p15*+ [501+]
  Obs - F 16 '97 - p18* [51-250]
Munk, Walter H - *Ocean Acoustic Tomography*
  SIAM Rev - v38 - D '96 - p683+ [501+]
Munn, Felicity - *Eastern Canada*
  r BL - v93 - S 15 '96 - p210 [1-50]
Munn, Vella - *Daughter of the Forest (Klein). Audio Version*
  y Kliatt - v30 - S '96 - p46 [51-250]
  Seminole Song
  PW - v244 - Mr 17 '97 - p78 [51-250]
Munoz, Victoria I - *Where Something Catches*
  CS - v25 - S '96 - p657+ [501+]
Munro, Alice - *Selected Stories*
  BIC - v25 - D '96 - p8+ [501+]
  BL - v92 - Ag '96 - p1856 [251-500]
  BW - v26 - N 10 '96 - p1+ [501+]
  KR - v64 - S 1 '96 - p1269 [51-250]
  LATBR - O 13 '96 - p3+ [501+]
  LATBR - D 29 '96 - p5 [51-250]
  LJ - v122 - Ja '97 - p50 [51-250]
  LJ - v121 - O 1 '96 - p130 [51-250]
  Mac - v109 - D 9 '96 - p64 [1-50]
  Ms - v7 - N '96 - p81+ [501+]
  NW - v128 - O 21 '96 - p88 [501+]
  NY - v72 - D 16 '96 - p109 [51-250]
  NYRB - v44 - F 20 '97 - p19+ [501+]
  NYTBR - v101 - O 27 '96 - p11+ [501+]
  NYTBR - v101 - D 8 '96 - p11 [51-250]
  Obs - N 24 '96 - p17* [501+]
  Obs - D 1 '96 - p16* [1-50]
  PW - v243 - N 4 '96 - p38 [1-50]
  Quill & Q - v62 - O '96 - p33 [501+]
  Spec - v277 - N 9 '96 - p47 [501+]
  TLS - N 8 '96 - p26 [501+]
  TLS - N 29 '96 - p13 [51-250]
  VLS - Win '96 - p10 [51-250]
  VV - v41 - O 29 '96 - p63+ [501+]
  WSJ-MW - v78 - O 25 '96 - pA12 [501+]
Munro, David - *The Oxford Dictionary of the World*
  r Choice - v34 - N '96 - p434+ [51-250]
Munro, Jane Southwell - *Grief Notes and Animal Dreams*
  BIC - v26 - Mr '97 - p19+ [501+]

Munro, Roxie - *The Inside-Outside Book of Libraries (Illus. by Roxie Munro)*
c BW - v26 - O 13 '96 - p13 [51-250]
c CBRS - v25 - N '96 - p30 [51-250]
c CCB-B - v50 - O '96 - p53 [51-250]
c HB - v72 - S '96 - p611 [51-250]
c HB Guide - v8 - Spr '97 - p85 [51-250]
c LATBR - S 22 '96 - p15 [51-250]
c NYTBR - v101 - N 24 '96 - p20 [1-50]
c SLJ - v42 - Ag '96 - p134 [51-250]
c SLJ - v42 - D '96 - p28 [1-50]
c Smith - v27 - N '96 - p169 [1-50]
Munro-Hay, Stuart - *Ethiopia*
r Lib - v18 - D '96 - p355+ [501+]
Munro-Kua, Anne - *Authoritarian Populism in Malaysia*
Choice - v34 - My '97 - p1569 [51-250]
Munsch, Robert - *From Far Away*
c Emerg Lib - v24 - Mr '97 - p46 [51-250]
Stephanie's Ponytail (Illus. by Michael Martchenko)
c BIC - v25 - O '96 - p32 [51-250]
c Emerg Lib - v24 - Mr '97 - p26 [1-50]
c Quill & Q - v62 - O '96 - p45+ [251-500]
c SLJ - v42 - N '96 - p89 [51-250]
Munson, Paul L - *Principles of Pharmacology. Rev. Ed.*
SciTech - v21 - Mr '97 - p67 [51-250]
Munson, Sammye - *Los Vaqueros: Our First Cowboys*
c KR - v64 - D 15 '96 - p1801 [51-250]
Munsterberg, Peggy - *Beastly Banquet (Illus. by Tracy Gallup)*
c BL - v93 - Ja '97 - p864 [251-500]
c Ch BWatch - v7 - F '97 - p3 [1-50]
c KR - v64 - D 15 '96 - p1801 [51-250]
c PW - v243 - D 2 '96 - p61 [51-250]
c SLJ - v43 - Ja '97 - p106 [51-250]
Munting, Roger - *An Economic and Social History of Gambling in Britain and the USA*
R&R Bk N - v11 - N '96 - p45 [51-250]
TLS - Ag 2 '96 - p28 [501+]
Muntzer, Thomas - *Revelation and Revolution*
CH - v66 - Mr '97 - p109+ [501+]
Mura, David - *Where the Body Meets Memory*
A Lib - v27 - Ag '96 - p71 [1-50]
Murakami, Haruki - *Nejimaki Tori Kuronikuru*
Econ - v342 - F 15 '97 - p17*+ [501+]
Murakami, Ryu - *Coin Locker Babies*
WLT - v70 - Sum '96 - p763 [501+]
Rabu Ando Poppu
Econ - v342 - F 15 '97 - p17*+ [501+]
Murakami, Yasusuke - *An Anticlassical Political-Economic Analysis*
Choice - v34 - Ap '97 - p1389 [51-250]
Murasugi, Kunio - *Knot Theory and Its Applications*
Choice - v34 - F '97 - p1000 [51-250]
SciTech - v20 - S '96 - p12 [51-250]
Murata, Hiroshi - *Handbook of Optical Fibers and Cables. 2nd Ed.*
SciTech - v20 - N '96 - p66 [51-250]
Muravchik, Joshua - *The Imperative of American Leadership*
BW - v26 - S 29 '96 - p6 [251-500]
Choice - v34 - S '96 - p211+ [51-250]
Murav'eva, Irina - *Kudriavyi Leitenant*
WLT - v71 - Win '97 - p176+ [501+]
Murawski, Darlyne - *The World of Reptiles*
c SB - v33 - My '97 - p114 [51-250]
Murchison, Kenneth M - *Federal Criminal Law Doctrines*
AHR - v101 - D '96 - p1633+ [501+]
Murcia, Claude - *Un Chien Andalou, L'Age D'Or*
FR - v70 - O '96 - p163+ [251-500]
Murck, Barbara W - *Dangerous Earth*
Choice - v34 - My '97 - p1528 [51-250]
SciTech - v21 - Mr '97 - p2 [51-250]
Murdoch, Brian - *The Germanic Hero*
Choice - v34 - N '96 - p463 [51-250]
Murdoch, G - *Amputation: Surgical Practice and Patient Management*
SciTech - v20 - S '96 - p38 [51-250]
Murdoch, Iris - *Jackson's Dilemma*
Bks & Cult - v2 - Mr '96 - p31 [251-500]
NYTBR - v101 - D 8 '96 - p80 [1-50]
NYTBR - v102 - Mr 2 '97 - p28 [51-250]
PW - v244 - F 17 '97 - p217 [1-50]
Trib Bks - My 18 '97 - p8 [1-50]
WLT - v70 - Sum '96 - p692+ [501+]
Murdoch, J - *Iesna Lighting Ready Reference*
r TCI - v30 - O '96 - p57 [1-50]
Murdoch, Norman H - *Origins of the Salvation Army*
AHR - v101 - O '96 - p1208 [501+]
Bks & Cult - v2 - Ja '96 - p30 [51-250]
CH - v65 - D '96 - p745+ [501+]

Murdoch, Tom - *Streamkeeper's Field Guide. 5th Ed.*
r Workbook - v21 - Win '96 - p182+ [251-500]
Murdy, Edward O - *Fishes of Chesapeake Bay*
r LJ - v122 - Ja '97 - p89 [51-250]
Murfett, Malcolm H - *The First Sea Lords*
Albion - v28 - '96 - p733+ [501+]
Arm F&S - v23 - Win '96 - p315+ [501+]
Murhall, J J - *Stinkerbell (Illus. by Tony Blundell)*
c Bks Keeps - Jl '96 - p7 [51-250]
Murnane, Richard J - *Teaching the New Basic Skills*
JEL - v35 - Mr '97 - p231 [51-250]
Murov, Steven - *Experiments in Basic Chemistry. 4th Ed.*
SciTech - v21 - Mr '97 - p28 [51-250]
Murph, Roxane C - *The Wars of the Roses in Fiction*
r Albion - v28 - Win '96 - p679+ [501+]
Murphy, Ann Pleshette - *Parents Magazine's It Worked for Me!*
LJ - v121 - D '96 - p126 [51-250]
PW - v244 - Ja 27 '97 - p99 [51-250]
Murphy, Anne - *Thomas More*
TES - F 21 '97 - p7* [1-50]
Murphy, Arthur Edward - *Reason, Reality, and Speculative Philosophy*
Choice - v34 - F '97 - p979 [51-250]
R&R Bk N - v12 - F '97 - p2 [51-250]
Murphy, Brian P - *John Chartres: Mystery Man of the Treaty*
ILS - v15 - Fall '96 - p16+ [501+]
Murphy, Brian R - *Fisheries Techniques. 2nd Ed.*
SciTech - v20 - D '96 - p35 [51-250]
Murphy, Bruce - *Benet's Reader's Encyclopedia. 4th Ed.*
yr BL - v93 - N 15 '96 - p608 [51-250]
r Bloom Rev - v17 - Ja '97 - p21 [51-250]
Murphy, Carol J - *The Allegorical Impulse in the Works of Julien Gracq*
L'Esprit - v36 - Win '96 - p99+ [251-500]
Murphy, Christina - *Landmark Essays on Writing Centers*
Col Comp - v47 - O '96 - p439+ [51-250]
Writing Centers
r ARBA - v28 - '97 - p131 [51-250]
r Choice - v34 - F '97 - p947 [51-250]
r R&R Bk N - v11 - D '96 - p60 [51-250]
Murphy, Cornelius F, Jr. - *Beyond Feminism*
Theol St - v57 - S '96 - p552+ [501+]
Murphy, Daniel - *Comenius: A Critical Reassessment of His Life and Work*
Slav R - v55 - Sum '96 - p453+ [501+]
Murphy, Daniel P - *An Illustrated Guide to Attracting Birds*
LJ - v121 - D '96 - p66 [1-50]
Murphy, Donal A - *The Two Tipperarys*
ILS - v15 - Fall '96 - p31 [51-250]
Murphy, Francesca Aran - *Christ, the Form of Beauty*
Rel St Rev - v23 - Ja '97 - p53 [51-250]
Murphy, Frederick J - *The Religious World of Jesus*
Rel Ed - v91 - Fall '96 - p605 [1-50]
Murphy, Gerald P - *Informed Decisions*
BL - v93 - Mr 1 '97 - p1066 [51-250]
LJ - v122 - Ap 1 '97 - p116 [51-250]
PW - v244 - F 17 '97 - p215 [51-250]
Murphy, Ignatius - *Before the Famine Struck*
ILS - v16 - Spr '97 - p36 [51-250]
A People Starved
ILS - v16 - Spr '97 - p36 [51-250]
Murphy, J David - *Plunder and Preservation*
FEER - v159 - N 28 '96 - p63 [251-500]
Murphy, Jane - *Stay Tuned*
BL - v92 - Ag '96 - p1867 [51-250]
BL - v93 - N 1 '96 - p514 [51-250]
Murphy, Jill - *Geoffrey Strangeways (Sacks). Audio Version*
c BL - v93 - My 15 '97 - p1595 [1-50]
The Last Noo-Noo
c ECEJ - v23 - Sum '96 - p223+ [51-250]
A Piece of Cake
c PW - v244 - F 17 '97 - p220 [1-50]
Worlds Apart
c TES - Ap 4 '97 - p8* [51-250]
Murphy, Jim - *The Great Fire*
y Emerg Lib - v24 - S '96 - p23+ [1-50]
y Emerg Lib - v24 - S '96 - p26 [1-50]
c LA - v73 - O '96 - p436+ [251-500]
Into the Deep Forest with Henry David Thoreau (Illus. by Kate Kiesler)
c RT - v50 - S '96 - p57 [51-250]
A Young Patriot
c HB - v72 - S '96 - p623 [51-250]
c HB Guide - v7 - Fall '96 - p388 [51-250]
y SLJ - v42 - D '96 - p31 [1-50]

Murphy, Josette L - *Gender Issues in World Bank Lending*
J Gov Info - v23 - S '96 - p686 [51-250]
Murphy, Julien S - *The Constructed Body*
Ethics - v107 - Ja '97 - p399 [51-250]
SciTech - v20 - N '96 - p46 [51-250]
Murphy, L A - *Heavensbee (Illus. by Ronnie Rooney)*
c SLJ - v43 - Mr '97 - p162 [51-250]
Murphy, Lizz - *Wee Girls*
Aust Bk R - F '97 - p58+ [51-250]
PW - v244 - Ja 20 '97 - p393 [51-250]
Murphy, Martha Watson - *A New England Fish Tale*
PW - v244 - Ap 7 '97 - p88 [51-250]
Murphy, Mary - *I Like It When... (Illus. by Mary Murphy)*
c BL - v93 - Ap 1 '97 - p1338 [51-250]
c CBRS - v25 - Mr '97 - p89 [51-250]
c KR - v65 - Mr 15 '97 - p466 [51-250]
c PW - v244 - Ja 27 '97 - p105 [51-250]
Murphy, Michael J - *A Field Guide to Common Animal Poisons*
r ARBA - v28 - '97 - p574 [51-250]
r SciTech - v20 - N '96 - p58 [51-250]
Murphy, Michael P - *What Is Life?*
Am Sci - v84 - My '96 - p299+ [501+]
Murphy, Nancey - *On the Moral Nature of the Universe*
Choice - v34 - Ap '97 - p1352 [51-250]
Murphy, P J - *Critique of Beckett Criticism*
MLR - v91 - Jl '96 - p688+ [501+]
Murphy, Pat - *Pigasus (Illus. by Graham Percy)*
c HB Guide - v7 - Fall '96 - p269 [51-250]
The Science Explorer (Illus. by Jason Gorski)
c SB - v33 - Mr '97 - p48 [51-250]
Murphy, Pat, 1955- - *The Color of Nature (Illus. by William Neill)*
Aud - v98 - N '96 - p136 [51-250]
y Kliatt - v31 - Ja '97 - p29 [251-500]
Nadya: The Wolf Chronicles
BL - v93 - N 15 '96 - p572 [51-250]
KR - v64 - S 15 '96 - p1361 [51-250]
LJ - v121 - O 15 '96 - p93 [51-250]
PW - v243 - O 21 '96 - p74 [51-250]
Rapport - v19 - 6 '96 - p21 [251-500]
Murphy, Pat, 1958- - *Complete Conditioning for Baseball*
LJ - v122 - F 1 '97 - p83 [51-250]
Murphy, Paud - *National Assessments*
JEL - v35 - Mr '97 - p231 [51-250]
Murphy, Paul Thomas - *Toward a Working-Class Canon*
Critm - v38 - Sum '96 - p475+ [501+]
Murphy, Philip - *Party Politics and Decolonization*
AHR - v101 - D '96 - p1595+ [501+]
Albion - v28 - Fall '96 - p556+ [501+]
EHR - v112 - Ap '97 - p545+ [501+]
Historian - v59 - Win '97 - p416+ [501+]
TLS - D 27 '96 - p29 [501+]
Murphy, R Taggart - *The Weight of the Yen*
Bus W - D 16 '96 - p19 [51-250]
Rapport - v19 - 4 '96 - p38 [251-500]
Trib Bks - Ap 6 '97 - p8 [1-50]
Murphy, Roland E - *Responses to 101 Questions on the Biblical Torah*
Am - v176 - Mr 8 '97 - p22 [51-250]
Murphy, S T - *Closing the Shop*
AJMR - v101 - N '96 - p328+ [501+]
Murphy, Shirley Rousseau - *Cat on the Edge*
Analog - v117 - F '97 - p145+ [51-250]
Arm Det - v30 - Win '97 - p95+ [251-500]
Cat under Fire
y BL - v93 - Mr 15 '97 - p1230+ [51-250]
Murphy, Stuart J - *The Best Bug Parade (Illus. by Holly Keller)*
c HB Guide - v7 - Fall '96 - p269 [51-250]
The Best Vacation Ever (Illus. by Nadine Bernard Westcott)
c BL - v93 - F 1 '97 - p943 [51-250]
c KR - v64 - D 15 '96 - p1801 [51-250]
c SLJ - v43 - Mr '97 - p179+ [51-250]
Divide and Ride (Illus. by George Ulrich)
c BL - v93 - F 1 '97 - p943 [51-250]
c SLJ - v43 - Mr '97 - p179+ [51-250]
Every Buddy Counts (Illus. by Fiona Dunbar)
c BL - v93 - F 1 '97 - p943 [51-250]
c SLJ - v43 - Mr '97 - p179+ [51-250]
Get Up and Go! (Illus. by Diane Greenseid)
c HB Guide - v8 - Spr '97 - p110 [51-250]
Get Up and Go (Illus. by Diane Greenseid)
c Learning - v25 - Ja '97 - p56 [1-50]
Get Up and Go! (Illus. by Diane Greenseid)
c SLJ - v42 - D '96 - p116 [51-250]
Give Me Half! (Illus. by G Brian Karas)
c BL - v93 - Ap 1 '97 - p1341 [1-50]
c HB Guide - v7 - Fall '96 - p329 [51-250]

A Pair of Socks (Illus. by Lois Ehlert)
  c BL - v93 - O 1 '96 - p355 [51-250]
  c HB Guide - v8 - Spr '97 - p110 [51-250]
  c Learning - v25 - Ja '97 - p56 [1-50]
  c SLJ - v42 - D '96 - p116 [51-250]
Ready, Set, Hop! (Illus. by Jon Buller)
  c HB Guide - v7 - Fall '96 - p330 [51-250]
Too Many Kangaroo Things to Do! (Illus. by Kevin O'Malley)
  c HB Guide - v8 - Spr '97 - p111 [51-250]
  c Learning - v25 - Ja '97 - p56 [1-50]
  c SLJ - v42 - D '96 - p116 [51-250]
Murphy, T M - *The Secrets of Cain's Castle*
  y SLJ - v43 - F '97 - p104 [51-250]
The Secrets of Cranberry Beach
  c SLJ - v43 - Ja '97 - p115 [51-250]
Murphy, Timothy - *Getting Off Clean*
     Advocate - Ap 1 '97 - p62 [51-250]
     KR - v65 - Ja 15 '97 - p88+ [251-500]
     PW - v244 - F 10 '97 - p68 [51-250]
Murphy, Virginia Reed - *Across the Plains in the Donner Party*
  c HB Guide - v7 - Fall '96 - p388 [51-250]
  y SLJ - v42 - Ag '96 - p174 [51-250]
Murphy, William J - *Irish Airmail 1919-1990*
     Phil Lit R - v45 - 3 '96 - p250 [51-250]
Murphy, Yannick - *The Sea of Trees*
     KR - v65 - Mr 1 '97 - p329 [51-250]
     LJ - v122 - Ap 15 '97 - p118 [51-250]
     PW - v244 - Mr 10 '97 - p48 [51-250]
Murphy-Milano, Susan - *Defending Our Lives*
     BL - v93 - S 1 '96 - p42 [51-250]
     PW - v243 - S 16 '96 - p76 [51-250]
Murphy-O'Connor, Jerome - *Paul: A Critical Life*
     Am - v176 - Mr 8 '97 - p28 [51-250]
     BL - v92 - Ag '96 - p1860 [51-250]
     BL - v93 - Ja '97 - p756 [1-50]
     Choice - v34 - Ja '97 - p812 [51-250]
     CR - v269 - N '96 - p274 [501+]
     TLS - Mr 28 '97 - p4 [501+]
Murray, Albert - *The Seven League Boots*
     BW - v27 - Mr 23 '97 - p12 [51-250]
     LATBR - Mr 17 '96 - p6 [501+]
     NYTBR - v102 - Ap 20 '97 - p32 [51-250]
     PW - v244 - Ja 27 '97 - p103 [1-50]
     W&I - v11 - D '96 - p235 [251-500]
     W&I - v11 - D '96 - p247+ [501+]
Murray, Bill - *The World's Game*
     Choice - v34 - Ja '97 - p836 [51-250]
Murray, Charles A - *What It Means to Be a Libertarian*
  y BL - v93 - D 1 '96 - p618 [51-250]
     BW - v27 - Ja 5 '97 - p1+ [501+]
     Econ - v342 - F 15 '97 - p4*+ [501+]
     HE - v53 - F 7 '97 - p17+ [251-500]
     KR - v64 - N 15 '96 - p1657 [251-500]
     LATBR - Ja 19 '97 - p6+ [501+]
     LJ - v122 - Ja '97 - p124 [51-250]
     Nat R - v49 - F 24 '97 - p48+ [501+]
     NL - v80 - F 10 '97 - p13+ [501+]
     NYRB - v44 - F 20 '97 - p16+ [501+]
     NYTBR - v102 - Ja 19 '97 - p21 [501+]
     NYTLa - v146 - F 10 '97 - pC16 [501+]
     PW - v243 - N 18 '96 - p25 [51-250]
     Reason - v28 - Mr '97 - p56+ [501+]
     Trib Bks - Mr 9 '97 - p5 [501+]
     VV - v42 - F 4 '97 - p52+ [501+]
     WSJ-Cent - v99 - Ja 13 '97 - pA14 [501+]
What It Means to Be a Libertarian (Murray). Audio Version
     LJ - v122 - Ap 15 '97 - p139 [51-250]
Murray, Charles J - *The Supermen: The Story of Seymour Cray and the Technical Wizards behind the Supercomputer*
     Bus W - F 17 '97 - p15 [501+]
     Bus W - F 17 '97 - p15 [501+]
     KR - v64 - D 1 '96 - p1722+ [251-500]
     LJ - v122 - F 15 '97 - p155 [51-250]
     PW - v243 - D 16 '96 - p50 [51-250]
Murray, Don, 1947- - *A Democracy of Despots*
     For Aff - v75 - S '96 - p152 [51-250]
Murray, Donald Morison - *Crafting a Life in Essay, Story, Poem*
     Inst - v106 - N '96 - p41 [1-50]
Murray, Donna Huston - *Final Arrangements*
     Arm Det - v29 - Sum '96 - p367 [251-500]
School of Hard Knocks
     PW - v244 - Ja 20 '97 - p399 [51-250]
Murray, Douglass L - *Cultivating Crisis*
     CS - v25 - S '96 - p600+ [501+]

Murray, Earl - *Spirit of the Moon*
  y BL - v93 - O 1 '96 - p322 [51-250]
     PW - v243 - S '97 - p66+ [51-250]
     Roundup M - v4 - O '96 - p32 [251-500]
Murray, Frank - *Ginkgo Biloba*
     BWatch - v17 - N '96 - p3+ [51-250]
Murray, G Douglas - *2000 Postmarks of Prince Edward Island 1814-1995*
  r Am Phil - v110 - N '96 - p1039 [51-250]
Murray, Geoffrey - *Singapore: The Global City-State*
     JEL - v34 - S '96 - p1488 [51-250]
Murray, Heather - *Working in English*
     R&R Bk N - v11 - N '96 - p69 [51-250]
Murray, Iain H - *Revival and Revivalism*
     CH - v66 - Mr '97 - p204+ [251-500]
     W&M Q - v53 - Jl '96 - p662+ [501+]
Murray, Irena Zantovska - *Moshe Safdie: Buildings and Projects 1967-1992*
     R&R Bk N - v11 - N '96 - p60 [51-250]
Murray, Jerome T - *The Year 2000 Computing Crisis*
     CBR - v14 - S '96 - p28 [51-250]
     Choice - v34 - O '96 - p316 [51-250]
     SciTech - v20 - N '96 - p11 [1-50]
Murray, Jesse - *Teddy Bear Figurines*
     Ant & CM - v101 - O '96 - p14 [51-250]
Murray, John - *Reiver Blues*
     Obs - D 1 '96 - p16* [1-50]
     TLS - D 6 '96 - p22 [501+]
Murray, John A - *Cactus Country*
  yr Kliatt - v31 - My '97 - p30 [51-250]
The Sierra Club Nature Writing Handbook
     Workbook - v21 - Fall '96 - p130+ [501+]
Murray, John G - *A Gentleman Publisher's Commonplace Book*
     Obs - F 16 '97 - p16* [251-500]
     Spec - v277 - S 28 '96 - p50+ [501+]
     Spec - v277 - N 23 '96 - p46 [1-50]
     Spec - v277 - N 30 '96 - p58 [1-50]
     TLS - O 11 '96 - p40 [501+]
Murray, Judith Sargent - *Selected Writings of Judith Sargent Murray*
     AL - v68 - S '96 - p661 [51-250]
     W&M Q - v53 - O '96 - p819+ [501+]
Murray, Les - *Subhuman Redneck Poems*
     Aust Bk R - N '96 - p9+ [501+]
     Obs - S 29 '96 - p18* [51-250]
     PW - v244 - Mr 31 '97 - p69 [51-250]
     TLS - Ja 10 '97 - p8 [501+]
Murray, Mary M - *Artwork of the Mind*
     Col Comp - v47 - O '96 - p440 [51-250]
Murray, Michael T - *Encyclopedia of Nutritional Supplements*
  r ARBA - v28 - '97 - p613 [51-250]
Murray, Nicholas - *A Life of Matthew Arnold*
     BW - v27 - F 23 '97 - p4 [501+]
     NYTBR - v102 - Mr 16 '97 - p14+ [501+]
     Spec - v277 - N 23 '96 - p43 [1-50]
Murray, Paul - *A Fantastic Journey*
     CLS - v33 - 1 '96 - p82+ [501+]
Murray, Peter, 1920- - *The Oxford Companion to Christian Art and Architecture*
  r AB - v99 - Mr 3 '97 - p692 [51-250]
  r BL - v93 - F 15 '97 - p1043 [51-250]
  r LJ - v122 - Ja '97 - p89 [51-250]
Murray, Peter, 1952, Sep., 9- - *Deserts*
  c Ch BWatch - v6 - D '96 - p6 [1-50]
  c HB Guide - v8 - Spr '97 - p119 [51-250]
Floods
  c HB Guide - v8 - Spr '97 - p114 [51-250]
Lightning
  c HB Guide - v8 - Spr '97 - p114 [51-250]
Mountains
  c Ch BWatch - v6 - D '96 - p6 [1-50]
  c HB Guide - v8 - Spr '97 - p119 [51-250]
Prairies
  c Ch BWatch - v6 - D '96 - p6 [1-50]
  c HB Guide - v8 - Spr '97 - p119 [51-250]
Rainforests
  c Ch BWatch - v6 - D '96 - p6 [1-50]
  c HB Guide - v8 - Spr '97 - p119 [51-250]
Redwoods
  c HB Guide - v8 - Spr '97 - p121 [51-250]
  c SLJ - v43 - Mr '97 - p180 [51-250]
Scorpions
  c Ch BWatch - v6 - N '96 - p7 [1-50]
  c HB Guide - v8 - Spr '97 - p122 [51-250]
Murray, Rupert Wolfe - *IFOR on IFOR*
     Obs - D 8 '96 - p16* [501+]
Murray, Shoon Kathleen - *Anchors against Change*
     Choice - v34 - My '97 - p1572 [51-250]

Murray, Stephen, 1945- - *Notre-Dame, Cathedral of Amiens*
     Apo - v144 - D '96 - p69+ [501+]
Murray, Stephen O - *American Gay*
     Choice - v34 - N '96 - p546 [51-250]
     R&R Bk N - v11 - N '96 - p40 [51-250]
Latin American Male Homosexualities
     Am Ethnol - v24 - F '97 - p193+ [501+]
     CS - v26 - Ja '97 - p74+ [501+]
Theory Groups and the Study of Language in North America
     Lang Soc - v25 - S '96 - p445+ [501+]
Murray, Stuart - *Norman Rockwell's Four Freedoms*
  c SE - v60 - S '96 - p304 [1-50]
Murray, Thomas H, 1926- - *The Human Genome Project and the Future of Health Care*
     Choice - v34 - My '97 - p1533 [51-250]
     LJ - v121 - D '96 - p131 [51-250]
Murray, Thomas H, 1946- - *The Worth of a Child*
     LJ - v121 - O 15 '96 - p63 [51-250]
     New Sci - v153 - Ja 25 '97 - p42 [51-250]
Murray, Thomson C - *Official License Plate Book*
  r ARBA - v28 - '97 - p657 [51-250]
Murray, Timothy - *Like a Film*
     Can Lit - Win '96 - p160+ [501+]
Murray, William - *A Fine Italian Hand*
     Arm Det - v29 - Fall '96 - p486+ [251-500]
Murray, William H - *The Visual J++ Handbook*
     BYTE - v22 - Mr '97 - p34 [51-250]
Windows 95 and NT Programming with the Microsoft Foundation Class Library
     CBR - v14 - Jl '96 - p23 [1-50]
     SciTech - v20 - N '96 - p10 [51-250]
Murray, Williamson - *Air War in the Persian Gulf*
     J Mil H - v60 - O '96 - p806+ [501+]
The Making of Strategy
     EHR - v112 - Ap '97 - p482+ [501+]
Military Innovation in the Interwar Period
     For Aff - v76 - My '97 - p128 [51-250]
     J Mil H - v61 - Ja '97 - p183+ [501+]
Murray, Yxta Maya - *Locas*
     KR - v65 - Mr 1 '97 - p329+ [51-250]
     LJ - v122 - Ap 1 '97 - p128 [51-250]
     PW - v244 - Mr 3 '97 - p62 [51-250]
     Trib Bks - My 11 '97 - p6 [501+]
Murrin, Michael - *History and Warfare in Renaissance Epic*
     Comp L - v49 - Win '97 - p89+ [501+]
Mursky, Gregory - *Introduction to Planetary Volcanism*
     SciTech - v20 - S '96 - p13 [51-250]
     S&T - v93 - Ap '97 - p62+ [501+]
Musallam, Musallam Ali - *The Iraqi Invasion of Kuwait*
     Choice - v34 - S '96 - p206 [51-250]
Muschard, Jutta - *Relevant Translations*
     R&R Bk N - v12 - F '97 - p76 [51-250]
Muschell, David - *What in the Word?*
  cr ARBA - v28 - '97 - p379 [51-250]
Muschla, Judith A - *The Math Teacher's Book of Lists*
  r Math T - v89 - D '96 - p781 [51-250]
Muscio, Giuliana - *Hollywood's New Deal*
     BL - v93 - F 15 '97 - p992 [51-250]
Muse
  cp BL - v93 - D 1 '96 - p658 [51-250]
Muse, Robert L - *The Book of Revelation*
  r ARBA - v28 - '97 - p541+ [51-250]
  r Choice - v34 - S '96 - p103 [51-250]
Musella, Marco - *The Money Supply in the Economic Process*
     JEL - v34 - S '96 - p1421+ [51-250]
Museum of Fine Arts, Boston - *Alfred Stieglitz: Photographer*
     CSM - v89 - D 5 '96 - pB2 [51-250]
     WSJ-MW - v78 - D 5 '96 - pA18 [51-250]
Museum Premieres and Exhibitions, Special Events 1996
  r BL - v93 - Ja '97 - p896 [51-250]
  r BL - v93 - S 15 '96 - p212 [1-50]
  r Choice - v34 - Ja '97 - p772 [51-250]
  r LJ - v121 - O 15 '96 - p50+ [51-250]
Musgrave, James - *Relationship Dynamics*
     BL - v92 - Ag '96 - p1866 [51-250]
Musgrave, James Ray - *The Digital Scribe*
     CBR - v14 - S '96 - p27 [1-50]
     CBR - v14 - N '96 - p39 [1-50]
Musgrave, Michael - *The Musical Life of the Crystal Palace*
     Albion - v28 - Fall '96 - p500+ [501+]
     Notes - v53 - S '96 - p44+ [501+]
     VS - v39 - Spr '96 - p462+ [501+]
Mushketyk, IUrii - *Hetmans'kyi Skarb*
     BL - v93 - N 15 '96 - p577 [1-50]

Music, David W - *Hymnology: A Collection of Source Readings*
 R&R Bk N - v12 - F '97 - p70 [51-250]
Music Educators National Conference (U.S.) -
 Opportunity-to-Learn Standards for Music Instruction, Grades PreK-12
 Teach Mus - v3 - Ap '96 - p20 [51-250]
Musiker, Reuben - *South African Bibliography. 3rd Ed.*
 r ARBA - v28 - '97 - p249 [51-250]
 Southern Africa Bibliography
 r ARBA - v28 - '97 - p54+ [51-250]
Musil, Caryn McTighe - *Diversity in Higher Education*
 HER - v66 - Win '96 - p890 [51-250]
Musil, Robert - *The Man without Qualities. Vols. 1-2*
 NYTBR - v102 - Ja 26 '97 - p28 [51-250]
 Obs - D 1 '96 - p16* [51-250]
Muske, Carol - *Dear Digby*
 MQR - v35 - Fall '96 - p720+ [501+]
 Red Trousseau
 MQR - v35 - Fall '96 - p720+ [501+]
 Saving St. Germ
 MQR - v35 - Fall '96 - p720+ [501+]
Musolff, Andreas - *Conceiving of Europe*
 R&R Bk N - v11 - D '96 - p8 [51-250]
Mussini, Massimo - *Correggio Tradotto*
 BM - v138 - O '96 - p692+ [501+]
Musso, Pierre - *The Printed Press and Television in the Regions of Europe*
 J Gov Info - v23 - S '96 - p665 [51-250]
Mustafa, Fawzia - *V.S. Naipaul*
 Choice - v34 - O '96 - p279 [51-250]
Muster, Nori J - *Betrayal of the Spirit*
 PW - v243 - O 14 '96 - p77 [51-250]
Musu, Ignazio - *National Accounts and the Environment*
 R&R Bk N - v12 - F '97 - p46 [51-250]
Muszynski, Alicja - *Cheap Wage Labour*
 R&R Bk N - v11 - D '96 - p31 [51-250]
Mutz, Diana C - *Political Persuasion and Attitude Change*
 Choice - v34 - Ja '97 - p787 [51-250]
Muysken, J - *Measurement and Analysis of Job Vacancies*
 Econ J - v106 - N '96 - p1843+ [51-250]
Muzzio, J C - *Chaos in Gravitational N-Body Systems*
 SciTech - v21 - Mr '97 - p19 [51-250]
The MVR Book Motor Sources Guide 1996
 r AJR - v18 - O '96 - p62 [501+]
My Kind of Town
 r J Gov Info - v23 - S '96 - p600 [51-250]
My Nose, My Toes! (Illus. by Sandra Lousada)
 c HB Guide - v7 - Fall '96 - p240 [51-250]
Myer, Valerie Grosvenor - *Jane Austen: Obstinate Heart*
 KR - v65 - Mr 1 '97 - p360+ [51-250]
 LJ - v122 - My 1 '97 - p102 [51-250]
 NYTLa - v146 - Ap 16 '97 - pC17 [501+]
 PW - v244 - Mr 10 '97 - p57 [51-250]
Myerly, Scott Hughes - *British Military Spectacle*
 Choice - v34 - Mr '97 - p1222 [51-250]
 J Mil H - v61 - Ap '97 - p375+ [501+]
 KR - v64 - S 1 '96 - p1302 [251-500]
 LJ - v121 - O 15 '96 - p72+ [51-250]
 Lon R Bks - v18 - D 12 '96 - p20 [501+]
 TLS - Ja 10 '97 - p12 [501+]
Myers, Amy - *Murder Makes an Entree*
 Arm Det - v30 - Win '97 - p101+ [251-500]
 PW - v243 - Jl 22 '96 - p230 [51-250]
Myers, Anna - *Fire in the Hills*
 y HB Guide - v7 - Fall '96 - p303+ [51-250]
 y Par Ch - v20 - O '96 - p12 [1-50]
 Graveyard Girl
 c RT - v50 - Mr '97 - p499 [51-250]
 Spotting the Leopard
 c CCB-B - v50 - F '97 - p216 [51-250]
 c HB - v73 - Ja '97 - p63 [51-250]
 c HB Guide - v8 - Spr '97 - p72 [51-250]
 c KR - v64 - S 15 '96 - p1405 [51-250]
 c SLJ - v42 - N '96 - p109+ [51-250]
Myers, Anne - *Experimental Psychology. 4th Ed.*
 R&R Bk N - v12 - F '97 - p6 [51-250]
Myers, Arthur - *Communicating with Animals*
 PW - v244 - Ap 28 '97 - p67 [51-250]
 Drugs and Emotions
 c SLJ - v43 - Mr '97 - p205 [51-250]
Myers, Bill - *Blood of Heaven*
 BL - v93 - O 1 '96 - p304 [501+]
 The Spell
 y VOYA - v19 - O '96 - p202 [501+]
Myers, David - *Re-Inventing the Jewish Past*
 Tikkun - v11 - My '96 - p67+ [501+]
Myers, Edward - *Climb or Die*
 y Kliatt - v31 - Ja '97 - p10 [51-250]
 Hostage
 c HB Guide - v7 - Fall '96 - p295 [51-250]

Myers, Gloria E - *A Municipal Mother*
 PHR - v65 - N '96 - p684+ [251-500]
 WHQ - v27 - Win '96 - p532+ [501+]
Myers, Jonathan - *Essentials of Cardiopulmonary Exercise Testing*
 SciTech - v20 - S '96 - p35 [51-250]
Myers, Jorge - *Orden Y Virtud*
 HAHR - v76 - Ag '96 - p602+ [501+]
Myers, K Sara - *Ovid's Causes*
 CW - v90 - S '96 - p61 [251-500]
Myers, Kenneth D - *False Security*
 J Con A - v30 - Win '96 - p497+ [501+]
Myers, Marie L - *Shortcuts to Beginning Reading*
 Cur R - v36 - F '97 - p3* [51-250]
Myers, Michael W - *Let the Cow Wander*
 Rel St Rev - v23 - Ja '97 - p95 [51-250]
Myers, Norma - *Reconstructing the Black Past*
 Choice - v34 - Mr '97 - p1222 [51-250]
 Lon R Bks - v19 - F 20 '97 - p23+ [501+]
Myers, Ralph - *Quantification of Brain Function Using PET*
 SciTech - v20 - D '96 - p35 [51-250]
Myers, Robert M - *Reluctant Expatriate*
 ELT - v39 - 4 '96 - p528 [51-250]
Myers, Robin - *Antiquaries, Book Collectors and the Circles of Learning*
 TLS - Mr 21 '97 - p33 [251-500]
 A Genius for Letters
 LR - v45 - 7 '96 - p74+ [501+]
 A Millennium of the Book
 LQ - v67 - Ap '97 - p208+ [501+]
Myers, Tamar - *Gilt by Association*
 PW - v243 - N 11 '96 - p72 [51-250]
 Parsley, Sage, Rosemary, and Crime
 Arm Det - v29 - Fall '96 - p404 [51-250]
Myers, W David - *Poor, Sinning Folk*
 Choice - v34 - D '96 - p629 [51-250]
 Theol St - v58 - Mr '97 - p190 [251-500]
Myers, Walter Dean - *Glorious Angels*
 c RT - v50 - O '96 - p156 [51-250]
 The Glory Field
 y Kliatt - v30 - S '96 - p4 [1-50]
 Harlem (Illus. by Christopher Myers)
 y BL - v93 - F 15 '97 - p1021 [51-250]
 c CBRS - v25 - F '97 - p80 [1-50]
 y CCB-B - v50 - Mr '97 - p252+ [51-250]
 c KR - v64 - D 15 '96 - p1801 [51-250]
 c Par Ch - v21 - Mr '97 - p8 [1-50]
 c PW - v244 - Ja 13 '97 - p76 [51-250]
 y SLJ - v43 - F '97 - p121 [51-250]
 How Mr. Monkey Saw the Whole World (Illus. by Synthia Saint James)
 c HB Guide - v7 - Fall '96 - p269 [51-250]
 Malcolm X: By Any Means Necessary
 y BL - v93 - D 15 '96 - p717 [1-50]
 y Kliatt - v30 - S '96 - p4 [1-50]
 One More River to Cross
 y BL - v93 - Ap 1 '97 - p1288 [1-50]
 y SLJ - v42 - Ag '96 - p186 [51-250]
 Scorpions
 y SLJ - v42 - O '96 - p45 [1-50]
 Shadow of the Red Moon (Illus. by Christopher Myers)
 c RT - v50 - Mr '97 - p502 [51-250]
 Slam!
 y BL - v93 - N 15 '96 - p579 [51-250]
 y BL - v93 - Ap 1 '97 - p1294 [1-50]
 y BL - v93 - Ap 1 '97 - p1310 [1-50]
 y BW - v27 - Ja 12 '97 - p9 [251-500]
 y CBRS - v25 - Win '97 - p69+ [51-250]
 y CCB-B - v50 - F '97 - p216+ [51-250]
 y HB - v73 - Ja '97 - p63+ [51-250]
 y HB Guide - v8 - Spr '97 - p82 [51-250]
 y JAAL - v40 - F '97 - p408 [51-250]
 y KR - v64 - O 15 '96 - p1536 [51-250]
 y PW - v243 - N 25 '96 - p76 [51-250]
 y SLJ - v42 - N '96 - p123+ [51-250]
 y VOYA - v19 - F '97 - p330+ [251-500]
 Smiffy Blue: Ace Crime Detective (Illus. by David J A Sims)
 c Emerg Lib - v24 - S '96 - p51 [51-250]
 c HB Guide - v7 - Fall '96 - p295 [51-250]
 c SLJ - v42 - N '96 - p89 [51-250]
 The Story of the Three Kingdoms (Illus. by Ashley Bryan)
 c PW - v244 - Ja 27 '97 - p108 [1-50]

 Toussaint L'Ouverture: The Fight for Haiti's Freedom (Illus. by Jacob Lawrence)
 c BL - v93 - S 1 '96 - p123 [51-250]
 c BL - v93 - Ap 1 '97 - p1298 [1-50]
 c CBRS - v25 - O '96 - p19 [1-50]
 c CCB-B - v50 - Ja '97 - p181+ [51-250]
 c HB Guide - v8 - Spr '97 - p178 [51-250]
 c KR - v64 - O 1 '96 - p1472 [51-250]
 c NYTBR - v101 - N 24 '96 - p20 [1-50]
 c PW - v243 - N 4 '96 - p76 [51-250]
 c SLJ - v42 - N '96 - p116 [51-250]
 c Trib Bks - F 9 '97 - p7 [51-250]
Myerson, Allan S - *Crystal Growth of Organic Materials*
 SciTech - v21 - Mr '97 - p95 [51-250]
Myerson, George - *Rhetoric, Reason and Society*
 QJS - v82 - N '96 - p427+ [501+]
Myerson, Joel - *The Cambridge Companion to Henry David Thoreau*
 J Am St - v30 - D '96 - p469+ [501+]
Myerson, Julie - *The Touch*
 NYTBR - v101 - Jl 21 '96 - p19 [51-250]
Myers-Schaffer, Christina - *How to Prepare for the SAT II: Literature*
 yr SLMQ - v25 - Fall '96 - p65 [1-50]
Myles, Gareth D - *Public Economics*
 JEL - v34 - S '96 - p1438 [51-250]
Myles, Robert - *Chaucerian Realism*
 MLR - v92 - Ja '97 - p169+ [251-500]
Mylynarczyk, R - *In Our Own Words. 2nd Ed.*
 MLJ - v81 - Spr '97 - p125+ [501+]
Mynors, Lavinia - *A Wise Woman*
 TLS - Ja 17 '97 - p18 [51-250]
Mynors, R A B - *Catalogue of the Manuscripts of Hereford Cathedral Library*
 r Specu - v72 - Ja '97 - p205+ [501+]
Myrick, Roger - *AIDS, Communication, and Empowerment*
 Choice - v34 - O '96 - p314 [51-250]
Myss, Caroline - *Anatomy of the Spirit*
 PW - v243 - S 9 '96 - p72+ [51-250]
 Energy Anatomy (Myss). Audio Version
 BL - v93 - S 15 '96 - p264 [51-250]
Mysterious Erotic Tales
 Woman's J - F '97 - p16 [51-250]
Mysterious Women
 p Arm Det - v29 - Sum '96 - p322 [1-50]

N

Naas, Bernard G - *American Labor Union Periodicals*
  r RQ - v36 - Fall '96 - p52 [51-250]
Naasner, Walter - *Neue Machtzentren In Der Deutschen Kriegswirtschaft 1942-1945*
  EHR - v111 - N '96 - p1348+ [251-500]
Naastepad, C W M - *The State and the Economic Process*
  JEL - v34 - D '96 - p2122 [51-250]
  R&R Bk N - v11 - D '96 - p23 [51-250]
Nabokov, Vladimir Vladimirovich - *Collected Stories*
  Spec - v277 - N 16 '96 - p42 [1-50]
Lolita (Irons). Audio Version
  LJ - v122 - Ap 15 '97 - p138 [51-250]
  PW - v244 - Mr 3 '97 - p30 [51-250]
  Quill & Q - v62 - D '96 - p31 [1-50]
  Trib Bks - F 2 '97 - p6+ [51-250]
Novels 1955-1962
  Bloom Rev - v17 - Ja '97 - p17 [51-250]
  LATBR - D 8 '96 - p8 [51-250]
  LJ - v121 - O 15 '96 - p94 [51-250]
  PW - v243 - S 23 '96 - p62 [51-250]
  WSJ-MW - v78 - D 27 '96 - pA5 [501+]
Novels 1969-1974
  Bloom Rev - v17 - Ja '97 - p17 [51-250]
  LJ - v121 - O 15 '96 - p94 [51-250]
  PW - v243 - S 23 '96 - p62 [51-250]
  WSJ-MW - v78 - D 27 '96 - pA5 [501+]
Novels and Memoirs 1941-1951
  Bloom Rev - v17 - Ja '97 - p17 [51-250]
  LATBR - D 8 '96 - p8 [51-250]
  LJ - v121 - O 15 '96 - p94 [51-250]
  PW - v243 - S 23 '96 - p62 [51-250]
  WSJ-MW - v78 - D 27 '96 - pA5 [501+]
The Stories of Vladimir Nabokov
  Bks & Cult - v1 - N '95 - p26+ [501+]
  LATBR - D 29 '96 - p4 [51-250]
  NYTBR - v102 - Ja 19 '97 - p28 [51-250]
  PW - v243 - N 25 '96 - p70 [1-50]
  South R - v32 - Aut '96 - p820+ [501+]
  TLS - Ag 2 '96 - p21+ [501+]
Nace, Vaughn M - *Nonionic Surfactants*
  r SciTech - v20 - S '96 - p61 [51-250]
Nachel, Marty - *Beer for Dummies*
  LJ - v122 - Ap 1 '97 - p63 [1-50]
Nachman, Patricia - *You and Your Only Child*
  LJ - v122 - Mr 15 '97 - p82 [51-250]
Nackenoff, Carol - *The Fictional Republic*
  AHR - v101 - O '96 - p1289+ [501+]
  J Pol - v59 - F '97 - p275+ [501+]
Nacos, Brigitte L - *Terrorism and the Media*
  JMCQ - v73 - Aut '96 - p770+ [501+]
  y Kliatt - v30 - S '96 - p32 [51-250]
Nadakavukaren, Anne - *Our Global Environment. 4th Ed.*
  SciTech - v20 - D '96 - p39 [51-250]
Nadal, Rafael - *Antonio Torres Y La Politica Espanola Del Foreign Office 1940-1944*
  Econ - v342 - Mr 29 '97 - p94 [501+]
De La BBC A The Observer
  Econ - v342 - Mr 29 '97 - p94 [501+]
Nadas, Peter - *A Book of Memories*
  LJ - v122 - Ap 15 '97 - p118+ [51-250]
  PW - v244 - Ap 21 '97 - p59 [51-250]
Esszek
  WLT - v70 - Aut '96 - p999 [501+]
Nadeau, Kathleen G - *Adventures in Fast Forward*
  SB - v32 - Ag '96 - p170 [51-250]
A Comprehensive Guide to Attention Deficit Disorder in Adults
  Fam in Soc - v78 - Ja '97 - p105+ [501+]
Nadeau, Robert L - *S/He Brain*
  PW - v243 - S 30 '96 - p74 [51-250]

Nadel, Alan - *Containment Culture*
  AL - v68 - D '96 - p875+ [501+]
  J Am St - v30 - D '96 - p494+ [251-500]
Nadel, Ira Bruce - *Joyce and the Jews*
  ELT - v40 - 2 '97 - p254 [51-250]
Various Positions
  BL - v93 - S 15 '96 - p204 [51-250]
  BW - v26 - N 24 '96 - p13 [51-250]
  Can Lit - Spr '97 - p216+ [501+]
  Ent W - O 25 '96 - p108 [51-250]
  Esq - v126 - D '96 - p40 [1-50]
  LJ - v121 - N 1 '96 - p69 [51-250]
  Mac - v109 - D 2 '96 - p91 [251-500]
  NYTBR - v101 - N 24 '96 - p19 [251-500]
  Prog - v61 - Ja '97 - p36+ [51-250]
  Quill & Q - v62 - S '96 - p70 [251-500]
  Spec - v278 - Mr 22 '97 - p39 [501+]
Nadel, Jack - *There's No Business like Your Business*
  BL - v93 - S 1 '96 - p45 [51-250]
Nadelstern, Paula - *Kaleidoscopes and Quilts*
  BL - v93 - Mr 1 '97 - p1103+ [51-250]
  LJ - v122 - Ap 15 '97 - p80 [51-250]
Nader, Laura - *Naked Science*
  Sci - v274 - D 20 '96 - p2033 [1-50]
Nader, Ralph - *No Contest*
  BL - v93 - Ag '96 - p4 [51-250]
  Bus W - N 11 '96 - p18 [501+]
  BW - v26 - O 13 '96 - p8 [501+]
  Choice - v34 - Mr '97 - p1241 [51-250]
  LJ - v121 - O 1 '96 - p104 [51-250]
  Prog - v61 - Ap '97 - p42+ [501+]
Nadir, Shams - *The Astrolabe of the Sea*
  TranslRevS - v2 - D '96 - p23 [51-250]
Naef, Adam - *The Barbury Hall Murders*
  LJ - v121 - D '96 - p150 [51-250]
Naef, Weston - *In Focus*
  Art J - v55 - Sum '96 - p105+ [501+]
The J. Paul Getty Museum
  BM - v138 - Ag '96 - p552 [251-500]
Naes, Tormod - *Multivariate Analysis of Data in Sensory Science*
  SciTech - v20 - N '96 - p32 [51-250]
Naeve, Jean - *Therapeutic Uses of Trace Elements*
  SciTech - v21 - Mr '97 - p56 [51-250]
Naficy, Hamid - *Otherness and Media*
  FQ - v49 - Fall '95 - p58+ [501+]
Nafziger, E Wayne - *Learning from the Japanese*
  JTWS - v13 - Fall '96 - p241+ [501+]
Nagai, Althea K - *Giving for Social Change*
  SF - v75 - S '96 - p353+ [251-500]
Nagarjuna - *The Fundamental Wisdom of the Middle Way*
  IPQ - v36 - D '96 - p503 [251-500]
Nagarkar, Kiran - *Seven Sixes Are Forty-Three*
  WLT - v70 - Sum '96 - p767 [251-500]
Nagata, Linda - *Deception Well*
  NYTBR - v102 - F 23 '97 - p20 [51-250]
  PW - v243 - D 30 '96 - p62+ [51-250]
Nagel, James - *Ernest Hemingway: The Oak Park Legacy*
  AL - v69 - Mr '97 - p252 [51-250]
Nagel, Joane - *American Indian Ethnic Renewal*
  Choice - v34 - N '96 - p547 [51-250]
Nagel, Karen Berman - *The Lunch Line (Illus. by Jerry Zimmerman)*
  c BL - v93 - F 1 '97 - p950 [51-250]
  c BL - v93 - Ap 1 '97 - p1341 [1-50]
Nagel, Thomas - *Egalite Et Partialite*
  Dialogue - v35 - Spr '96 - p416+ [501+]
Other Minds
  J Phil - v93 - Ag '96 - p425+ [501+]
Nagele, Sabine - *Laubhutte Davids Und Wolkensohn*
  Rel St Rev - v23 - Ap '97 - p167 [51-250]

Nageswara Rao, B D - *NMR as a Structural Tool for Macromolecules*
  SciTech - v20 - N '96 - p33 [51-250]
Nagibin, IUrii - *Dafnis I Khloia Epokhi Kullta Lichnosti, Voliuntarizma I Zastoia*
  BL - v93 - O 1 '96 - p327 [1-50]
Nagle, Garrett - *A Geography of the European Union*
  TES - Mr 28 '97 - pR5 [251-500]
Investigating Geography
  TES - O 18 '96 - pR3 [251-500]
Nagle, J F - *Collins, the Courts and the Colony*
  Aust Bk R - Ag '96 - p17+ [501+]
Nagorsen, David W - *Opossums, Shrews and Moles of British Columbia*
  SciTech - v20 - S '96 - p21 [1-50]
Nagy, Gregory - *Homeric Questions*
  Choice - v34 - F '97 - p962 [51-250]
Poetry as Performance
  Choice - v34 - F '97 - p962 [51-250]
  TLS - Ag 2 '96 - p27 [501+]
Nahavandi, Afsaneh - *The Art and Science of Leadership*
  R&R Bk N - v11 - D '96 - p3 [51-250]
Naher, Gaby - *The Underwharf*
  TLS - Ag 30 '96 - p22+ [501+]
Nahohai, Milford - *Dialogues with Zuni Potters*
  Bloom Rev - v16 - S '96 - p31 [251-500]
  Ceram Mo - v44 - D '96 - p28 [51-250]
Nahumck, Nadia Chilkovsky - *Isadora Duncan: The Dances*
  Choice - v34 - S '96 - p139 [501+]
  Dance - v70 - N '96 - p80+ [501+]
  Dance RJ - v28 - Fall '96 - p99+ [501+]
Naiditch, P G - *Problems in the Life and Writings of A.E. Housman*
  TLS - S 13 '96 - p32 [251-500]
Naidoo, Beverley - *Journey to Jo'burg*
  c TES - Jl 5 '96 - pR8 [51-250]
  y VOYA - v19 - O '96 - p199+ [501+]
No Turning Back
  c BL - v93 - D 15 '96 - p724 [51-250]
  c CBRS - v25 - Mr '97 - p95+ [51-250]
  y CCB-B - v50 - F '97 - p217 [51-250]
  c HB - v73 - Mr '97 - p203 [51-250]
  y KR - v64 - D 1 '96 - p1740 [51-250]
  c PW - v243 - D 16 '96 - p60 [51-250]
  c Sch Lib - v44 - Ag '96 - p96+ [501+]
  c SLJ - v43 - F '97 - p104 [51-250]
Naidu, Prabhakar S - *Modern Spectrum Analysis of Time Series*
  Choice - v34 - Mr '97 - p1198 [51-250]
Naik, Anita - *Families: Can't Live with Them, Can't Live without Them! (Illus. by Carol Morley)*
  c Sch Lib - v44 - N '96 - p174 [51-250]
Naiman, Robert J - *The Freshwater Imperative*
  Choice - v34 - O '96 - p302 [51-250]
Naimark, Norman - *The Russians in Germany*
  CEH - v29 - 1 '96 - p142+ [501+]
Naimer, Lucille - *The Zen of Cooking*
  BL - v92 - Ag '96 - p1871 [51-250]
  BWatch - v17 - D '96 - p9 [51-250]
Naipaul, V S - *A Bend in the River*
  Col Lit - v23 - O '96 - p58+ [501+]
Nair, K M - *Hybrid Microelectronic Materials*
  SciTech - v21 - Mr '97 - p90 [51-250]
Nairn, Alan E M - *The Ocean Basins and Margins. Vol. 8*
  SciTech - v20 - D '96 - p28 [51-250]
Nairne, James S - *Psychology: The Adaptive Mind*
  SciTech - v20 - D '96 - p1 [51-250]

Naisbitt, John - *Megatrends Asia*
 Bus Bk R - v13 - 3 '96 - p4+ [501+]
 Pac A - v69 - Fall '96 - p397+ [501+]
 W&I - v11 - Jl '96 - p274+ [501+]
Najam, Adil - *Nongovernmental Organizations as Policy Entrepreneurs*
 ChrPhil - v9 - N 14 '96 - p39 [1-50]
Najemy, John M - *Between Friends*
 Ren Q - v49 - Aut '96 - p625+ [501+]
Najstarsze Druki Cerkiewnoslowianskie I Ich Stosunek Do Tradycji Rekopismiennej
 Lib - v18 - D '96 - p365 [51-250]
Nakagawa, Soen - *Endless Vow*
 Choice - v34 - N '96 - p476 [51-250]
Nakai, S - *Food Proteins*
 r SciTech - v20 - S '96 - p60 [51-250]
Nakamura, Shuji - *The Blue Laser Diode*
 New Sci - v154 - My 3 '97 - p45 [501+]
Nakano, Makiko - *Makiko's Diary*
 TLS - Mr 7 '97 - p32 [51-250]
Nakano, Minoru - *The Policy-Making Process in Contemporary Japan*
 Choice - v34 - My '97 - p1569 [51-250]
Nakao, Shigeo - *The Political Economy of Japan Money*
 JEL - v35 - Mr '97 - p142+ [501+]
Nakashima, S - *Silicon Carbide and Related Materials 1995*
 SciTech - v20 - N '96 - p75 [51-250]
Nakazawa, Teruko - *Molecular Biology of Pseudomonads*
 SciTech - v20 - N '96 - p34 [51-250]
Nakhaeizadeh, G - *Machine Learning and Statistics*
 SciTech - v21 - Mr '97 - p14 [51-250]
Nalty, Bernard C - *With Courage*
 J Gov Info - v23 - S '96 - p543 [51-250]
Nalven, Gail - *Plant Operation and Optimization*
 SciTech - v20 - N '96 - p79 [51-250]
Namboodiri, N Krishnan - *A Primer of Population Dynamics*
 R&R Bk N - v11 - D '96 - p23 [51-250]
Nambu, Y - *Broken Symmetry*
 Phys Today - v49 - O '96 - p72+ [501+]
Namibia. National Planning Commission - *Women and Men in Namibia*
 J Gov Info - v23 - S '96 - p660 [1-50]
Namioka, Lensey - *Den of the White Fox*
 c HB - v73 - Mr '97 - p203+ [51-250]
 y KR - v65 - My 1 '97 - p725 [51-250]
 The Loyal Cat (Illus. by Aki Sogabe)
 c RT - v50 - Mr '97 - p502 [51-250]
 Yang the Third and Her Impossible Family (Illus. by Kees De Kiefte)
 c PW - v243 - Jl 22 '96 - p243 [1-50]
 c RT - v50 - D '96 - p343 [51-250]
 Yang the Youngest and His Terrible Ear
 c HMR - Win '96 - p45 [1-50]
Nan, Yujian - *Huang Tian Hou Tu*
 BL - v93 - N 1 '96 - p484 [1-50]
Nanao, Jun - *Contemplating Your Bellybutton (Illus. by Tomoko Hasegawa)*
 c LATBR - Mr 17 '96 - p11 [51-250]
Nancarrow, Loren - *Dead Snails Leave No Trails*
 BL - v92 - Ag '96 - p1870 [51-250]
Nance, John J - *Medusa's Child*
 y BL - v93 - D 15 '96 - p693 [51-250]
 KR - v64 - D 15 '96 - p1762 [251-500]
 LJ - v122 - Ja '97 - p149 [51-250]
 PW - v244 - Ja 6 '97 - p64 [51-250]
 Trib Bks - Ja 19 '97 - p6 [51-250]
 Pandora's Clock
 y BL - v93 - Ap 1 '97 - p1310 [1-50]
 Ent W - N 1 '96 - p65 [1-50]
 PW - v243 - O 21 '96 - p79 [1-50]
Nancy, Jean-Luc - *The Muses*
 Choice - v34 - Mr '97 - p1176 [51-250]
Nanda, B R - *Jawaharlal Nehru*
 Econ - v341 - N 16 '96 - p8* [51-250]
Nanda, Bikram Narayan - *Contours of Continuity and Change*
 CS - v26 - Mr '97 - p194+ [501+]
Nandy, Ashis - *The Savage Freud and Other Essays on Possible and Retrievable Selves*
 Am Ethnol - v23 - N '96 - p936+ [501+]
 Rel St Rev - v23 - Ja '97 - p44 [51-250]
Nanji, Azim - *The Muslim Almanac*
 ARBA - v28 - '97 - p553 [51-250]
 r RQ - v35 - Sum '96 - p561 [251-500]
Nankivell, Owen - *Economics, Society and Values*
 JEL - v34 - S '96 - p1404 [51-250]
Nann, Lizzie - *Brush! Brush! Bunny*
 c PW - v244 - Ap 21 '97 - p73 [1-50]

Bubble Monkey
 c PW - v244 - Ap 21 '97 - p73 [1-50]
Comb! Comb! Puppy
 c PW - v244 - Ap 21 '97 - p73 [1-50]
Nanos, Mark D - *The Mystery of Romans*
 CC - v113 - S 25 '96 - p905+ [501+]
Nanton, Isabel - *Adventuring in British Columbia. 2nd Ed.*
 r BL - v93 - S 15 '96 - p212 [1-50]
Naparstek, Belleruth - *A Meditation to Help You Recover from Alcohol and Other Drugs. Audio Version*
 BWatch - v18 - Mr '97 - p8 [51-250]
 A Meditation to Help You Recover from Smoking. Audio Version
 BWatch - v18 - Mr '97 - p8 [51-250]
 A Meditation to Help You Recover from Weight Loss. Audio Version
 BWatch - v18 - Mr '97 - p8 [51-250]
 Your Sixth Sense
 PW - v244 - Mr 24 '97 - p70 [51-250]
Naphy, William G - *Calvin and the Consolidation of the Genevan Reformation*
 JMH - v68 - D '96 - p1017+ [501+]
 Six Ct J - v27 - Win '96 - p1161+ [501+]
Napier, A David - *Foreign Bodies*
 RA - v25 - 3 '96 - p175+ [501+]
Napier, Kristine - *Cigarettes: What the Warning Label Doesn't Tell You*
 Choice - v34 - Mr '97 - p1193 [51-250]
 New Sci - v153 - F 22 '97 - p46 [51-250]
Napier, Nancy J - *Sacred Practices for Conscious Living*
 PW - v244 - Ap 28 '97 - p69 [51-250]
Napier, Nancy K, 1952- - *Western Women Working in Japan*
 Pac A - v69 - Fall '96 - p420+ [501+]
Napoleon: Europe and the Empire. Electronic Media Version
 HT - v46 - D '96 - p48 [51-250]
Napoli, Donna Jo - *The Bravest Thing*
 c RT - v50 - Mr '97 - p501 [51-250]
 On Guard
 c BL - v93 - D 15 '96 - p726+ [51-250]
 c CCB-B - v50 - F '97 - p217 [51-250]
 c KR - v64 - D 1 '96 - p1740 [51-250]
 The Prince of the Pond
 c Inst - v105 - My '96 - p69 [51-250]
 The Song of the Magdalene
 y BL - v93 - O 1 '96 - p333 [51-250]
 y BL - v93 - Ap 1 '97 - p1294 [1-50]
 y CBRS - v25 - Ja '97 - p59 [51-250]
 y CCB-B - v50 - Ja '97 - p182 [51-250]
 y Emerg Lib - v24 - Mr '97 - p55 [51-250]
 y HB Guide - v8 - Spr '97 - p82 [51-250]
 y JAAL - v40 - F '97 - p408+ [51-250]
 y KR - v64 - S 1 '96 - p1326 [51-250]
 y PW - v243 - N 4 '96 - p77 [51-250]
 y SLJ - v42 - N '96 - p124 [51-250]
 y VOYA - v19 - F '97 - p331 [251-500]
 Trouble on the Tracks
 c BL - v93 - F 1 '97 - p941 [51-250]
 c CBRS - v25 - Ap '97 - p106 [51-250]
 c CCB-B - v50 - Mr '97 - p253 [51-250]
 c KR - v65 - Ja 15 '97 - p144 [51-250]
 c SLJ - v43 - Mr '97 - p190 [51-250]
 Zel
 y BL - v93 - S 1 '96 - p118 [51-250]
 y Ch BWatch - v6 - N '96 - p3 [51-250]
 y HB - v72 - S '96 - p603 [51-250]
 y HB Guide - v8 - Spr '97 - p82 [51-250]
 y KR - v64 - My 1 '96 - p691 [51-250]
 c PW - v243 - N 4 '96 - p49 [1-50]
 y SLJ - v42 - S '96 - p227+ [51-250]
 y SLJ - v42 - D '96 - p31 [1-50]
Naqvi, Syed Nawab Haider - *PIDE's Research Programme for 1993-96*
 JEL - v34 - D '96 - p2116 [51-250]
Narayan, Deepa - *Toward Participatory Research*
 JEL - v34 - D '96 - p2023+ [51-250]
Narayan, Kirin - *Mondays on the Dark Night of the Moon*
 LJ - v122 - My 1 '97 - p114 [51-250]
Narayan, R K - *A Writer's Nightmare*
 Spec - v277 - N 16 '96 - p43 [1-50]
Narayan-Parker, Deepa - *The Contribution of People's Participation*
 J Gov Info - v23 - S '96 - p684 [51-250]
Nardi, Bonnie A - *Context and Consciousness*
 R&R Bk N - v12 - F '97 - p92 [51-250]
Nardi, Thomas - *Karate and Judo (Illus. by Art Seiden)*
 c HB Guide - v7 - Fall '96 - p360 [51-250]

Nardin, Terry - *The Ethics of War and Peace*
 Choice - v34 - O '96 - p296 [51-250]
 CPR - v16 - O '96 - p362+ [501+]
 Rel St Rev - v23 - Ja '97 - p52 [51-250]
Nardo, Don - *The Age of Augustus*
 y HB Guide - v8 - Spr '97 - p165 [51-250]
 c SLJ - v43 - F '97 - p112 [51-250]
 The Age of Pericles
 y Ch BWatch - v6 - Jl '96 - p2 [51-250]
 y HB Guide - v7 - Fall '96 - p379 [51-250]
 The Battle of Zama
 y HB Guide - v7 - Fall '96 - p379 [51-250]
 Caesar's Conquest of Gaul
 y HB Guide - v7 - Fall '96 - p379 [51-250]
 Julius Caesar
 c HB Guide - v8 - Spr '97 - p157 [1-50]
 y SLJ - v43 - Mr '97 - p205 [51-250]
 Life in Ancient Greece
 y HB Guide - v7 - Fall '96 - p379 [51-250]
 Life on a Medieval Pilgrimage
 y HB Guide - v7 - Fall '96 - p379 [51-250]
 Mozart
 y BL - v93 - F 15 '97 - p1015 [51-250]
 y SLJ - v43 - Mr '97 - p205 [51-250]
 The Punic Wars
 y HB Guide - v7 - Fall '96 - p379 [51-250]
 Readings on Sophocles
 y SLJ - v43 - F '97 - p122 [51-250]
 Readings on The Canterbury Tales
 y BL - v93 - D 15 '96 - p720 [51-250]
 y SLJ - v43 - F '97 - p122 [51-250]
 The Scopes Trial
 y BL - v93 - My 1 '97 - p1489 [51-250]
 Teen Sexuality
 y HB Guide - v8 - Spr '97 - p90 [1-50]
 y SLJ - v43 - F '97 - p122 [51-250]
Nardon, J David - *Bridge and Structure Estimating*
 SciTech - v20 - N '96 - p69 [51-250]
Nargi, Lela - *All U Can Eat*
 y Kliatt - v31 - Ja '97 - p32 [51-250]
Naroola, Gurmeet - *How to Achieve ISO 9000 Registration Economically and Efficiently*
 SciTech - v20 - S '96 - p62 [51-250]
 QS-9000 Implementation and Registration
 SciTech - v20 - D '96 - p80 [51-250]
Narula, Rajneesh - *Multinational Investment and Economic Structure*
 JEL - v34 - D '96 - p2046 [51-250]
 R&R Bk N - v11 - N '96 - p34 [51-250]
Nas, Tevfik F - *Cost-Benefit Analysis*
 JEL - v34 - D '96 - p2056+ [51-250]
Nasaw, David - *Going Out*
 Am Q - v48 - S '96 - p523+ [501+]
Nasaw, Jonathan - *The World on Blood*
 PW - v244 - Ap 14 '97 - p72 [1-50]
Nash, Carol Rust - *Sexual Harassment*
 y HB Guide - v7 - Fall '96 - p316 [51-250]
 y SLJ - v42 - O '96 - p158+ [51-250]
Nash, Dennison - *Anthropology of Tourism*
 Choice - v34 - D '96 - p652 [51-250]
Nash, George - *Do-It-Yourself Housebuilding*
 LJ - v122 - F 1 '97 - p52 [1-50]
 Renovating Old Houses
 LJ - v122 - F 1 '97 - p52 [1-50]
Nash, George H - *The Life of Herbert Hoover. Vol. 3*
 Choice - v34 - Ja '97 - p864 [51-250]
 WSJ-MW - v77 - O 1 '96 - pA20 [501+]
Nash, Gerald D - *A.P. Giannini and the Bank of America*
 BHR - v70 - Sum '96 - p277+ [501+]
 Historian - v59 - Fall '96 - p150+ [501+]
Nash, Jerry C - *A Sceve Celebration*
 MP - v94 - N '96 - p222+ [501+]
Nash, Jonell - *Low-Fat Soul*
 LJ - v121 - O 15 '96 - p86 [51-250]
 LJ - v121 - N 1 '96 - p82 [1-50]
 PW - v243 - O 7 '96 - p72 [51-250]
Nash, Knowlton - *Cue the Elephant*
 Quill & Q - v62 - N '96 - p35 [501+]
Nash, Mary - *Defying Male Civilization*
 Choice - v34 - Sum '96 - p341 [51-250]
Nash, N Richard - *Selected Plays*
 Am Theat - v13 - D '96 - p20 [1-50]
Nash, Ogden - *Custard the Dragon and the Wicked Knight (Illus. by Lynn Munsinger)*
 c HB Guide - v7 - Fall '96 - p368 [51-250]
Nash, Paul W - *The Corvinus Press*
 r BC - v44 - Win '95 - p582+ [501+]
Nash, Ronald H - *Why the Left Is Not Right*
 Bks & Cult - v2 - N '96 - p20+ [501+]
Nash, Steven A - *Facing Eden*
 BM - v138 - D '96 - p836 [1-50]

Nash, Sunny - *Bigmama Didn't Shop at Woolworth's*
  LJ - v121 - O 15 '96 - p68 [51-250]
  PW - v243 - S 16 '96 - p63 [51-250]
  y SLJ - v42 - D '96 - p153 [51-250]
Nash, Susan Smith - *Channel-Surfing the Apocalypse*
  RCF - v16 - Fall '96 - p200+ [501+]
Nashif, Taysir N - *Nuclear Weapons in Israel*
  MEJ - v51 - Spr '97 - p283+ [501+]
Nasr, Kameel - *Cycling the Mediterranean*
  r BL - v93 - S 15 '96 - p206 [1-50]
Nasr, Seyyed Hossein - *History of Islamic Philosophy.*
  Vols. 1-2
  Choice - v34 - O '96 - p293+ [51-250]
  R&R Bk N - v11 - N '96 - p1 [51-250]
Nasr, Seyyed Vali Reza - *Mawdudi and the Making of
  Islamic Revivalism*
  AJS - v102 - N '96 - p907+ [501+]
Nassal, Joe - *Faith Walkers*
  CLW - v67 - D '96 - p44 [51-250]
  RR - v56 - Ja '97 - p105 [1-50]
Nassib, Selim - *Oum*
  FR - v70 - Mr '97 - p618+ [501+]
Nassif, Bradley - *New Perspectives in Historical Theology*
  Rel St Rev - v22 - O '96 - p347+ [51-250]
Nastorescu-Balcesti, Horia - *Ordinul Masonic Roman*
  BL - v93 - D 15 '96 - p714 [1-50]
Nata, Sebastiano - *Il Dipendente*
  BL - v93 - D 1 '96 - p644 [1-50]
Nataf, Daniel - *Democratization and Social Settlements*
  AJS - v102 - Jl '96 - p297+ [501+]
  J Pol - v59 - F '97 - p298+ [501+]
Natarajan, Nalini - *Handbook of Twentieth-Century
  Literatures of India*
  Choice - v34 - Mr '97 - p1156+ [51-250]
  R&R Bk N - v12 - F '97 - p79 [51-250]
Nath, Nathalie - *Lou. Vol. 3*
  c BL - v93 - N 1 '96 - p500 [1-50]
Nathan, Amy - *Conflict Resolution*
  y SLJ - v43 - Ja '97 - p128 [51-250]
  Surviving Homework (Illus. by Anne Canevari Green)
  c HB Guide - v8 - Spr '97 - p93 [51-250]
Nathan, Andrew J - *The Great Wall and the Empty
  Fortress*
  WSJ-Cent - v99 - My 16 '97 - pA16 [501+]
Nathan, David M - *Diabetes*
  LJ - v122 - My 1 '97 - p134 [51-250]
Nathan, Debbie - *Satan's Silence*
  Skeptic - v4 - 2 '96 - p101+ [501+]
Nathan, Joe - *Charter Schools*
  CSM - v89 - Mr 3 '97 - p12 [501+]
Nathan, Leonard - *Diary of a Left-Handed Birdwatcher*
  BL - v93 - O 1 '96 - p312 [51-250]
  KR - v64 - Ag 15 '96 - p1218 [251-500]
  LJ - v121 - O 1 '96 - p122 [51-250]
  PW - v243 - S 16 '96 - p64 [51-250]
Nathan, Paul - *Count Your Enemies*
  BL - v93 - Mr 15 '97 - p1231 [51-250]
  KR - v65 - Ja 1 '97 - p26 [51-250]
  PW - v244 - Ja 6 '97 - p68 [51-250]
Nathanielsz, Peter W - *Life before Birth*
  y SB - v32 - Ag '96 - p175 [51-250]
Nathanson, Donald L - *Knowing Feeling*
  Readings - v12 - Mr '97 - p22+ [51-250]
  Shame and Pride
  Bks & Cult - v2 - Mr '96 - p3+ [501+]
Nathanson, Laura Walther - *The Portable Pediatrician's
  Guide to Kids*
  BL - v93 - S 1 '96 - p51 [51-250]
Nathanson, Stephen - *The Ideal of Rationality*
  CPR - v16 - Ap '96 - p125+ [501+]
  Ethics - v107 - O '96 - p176 [251-500]
**National 5-Digit Zip Code and Post Office Directory
  1996. Vols. 1-2**
  r ARBA - v28 - '97 - p28 [51-250]
National Accounts Studies of the ESCWA Region
  R&R Bk N - v12 - F '97 - p18 [51-250]
**National Ag Safety Disc (NASD). Electronic Media
  Version**
  r J Gov Info - v23 - S '96 - p569 [51-250]
National Archives of Canada - *Facing History*
  Archiv - Fall '94 - p209+ [501+]
The National Archives Preparing for a New Records Age
  J Gov Info - v23 - S '96 - p541+ [51-250]
**National Audubon Society Interactive CD-ROM Guide
  to North American Birds. Electronic Media Version**
  r ARBA - v27 - '96 - p587+ [51-250]
  r BWatch - v17 - S '96 - p4 [51-250]
  r Choice - v34 - Mr '97 - p1186 [51-250]
  r LJ - v122 - Ap 1 '97 - p138 [51-250]
  c SB - v32 - Ag '96 - p186+ [251-500]

National Center for History in the Schools - *National
  Standards for United States History*
  Pub Hist - v18 - Fall '96 - p145+ [501+]
**National Conference on Business Ethics (10th: 1994:
  Bentley College)** - *The Ethics of Accounting and
  Finance*
  R&R Bk N - v11 - D '96 - p33 [51-250]
**National Conference on Intermodalism (1994: New
  Orleans, Louisiana)** - *National Conference of
  Intermodalism*
  R&R Bk N - v12 - F '97 - p43 [51-250]
**National Defense University. Institute for National
  Strategic Studies** - *Strategic Assessment 1995*
  RSR - v24 - 3 '96 - p46 [51-250]
**National Development Planning and the Regions of
  Namibia**
  J Gov Info - v23 - S '96 - p659+ [51-250]
**The National Directory of Addresses and Telephone
  Numbers 1996**
  r BusLR - v21 - 3 '96 - p253 [51-250]
**National Directory of Grantmaking Public Charities. 1st
  Ed.**
  r ARBA - v28 - '97 - p315+ [251-500]
**National Directory of Woman-Owned Business Firms.
  8th Ed.**
  r Choice - v34 - My '97 - p1478 [51-250]
**National Education Longitudinal Study of 1988: High
  School Seniors' Instructional Experiences in Science
  and Mathematics**
  SLMQ - v25 - Fall '96 - p61+ [51-250]
National Fax Directory 1996
  r ARBA - v28 - '97 - p27+ [251-500]
National Gallery (Great Britain) - *Giotto to Durer*
  TES - Ag 30 '96 - p26 [51-250]
  The National Gallery Complete Illustrated Catalogue
  r ARBA - v28 - '97 - p365+ [251-500]
National Geographic World
  cp Par Ch - v20 - O '96 - p15 [1-50]
National Greenhouse Advisory Committee - *Warming to
  the Issue*
  J Gov Info - v23 - S '96 - p653 [1-50]
**National Guide to Funding for Children, Youth, and
  Families. 3rd Ed.**
  r ARBA - v28 - '97 - p316 [251-500]
National Health Directory 1996
  r ARBA - v28 - '97 - p603 [51-250]
**The National Literacy Trust's Guide to Books on
  Literacy Published during 1995**
  r JAAL - v40 - D '96 - p328 [1-50]
**National LOEX Library Instruction Conference (21st:
  1993: Racine, Wis.)** - *The Impact of Technology on
  Library Instruction*
  LQ - v67 - Ja '97 - p83+ [501+]
**National Meeting of the American Chemical Society
  (206th: 1993: Chicago, IL)** - *Hydrophilic Polymers*
  SciTech - v20 - N '96 - p23 [51-250]
**National Meeting of the American Chemical Society
  (208th: 1994: Washington, DC)** - *Hydrogels and
  Biodegradable Polymers for Bioapplications*
  SciTech - v20 - N '96 - p36 [51-250]
  Irradiation of Polymers
  SciTech - v20 - N '96 - p22 [51-250]
**National Meeting of the American Chemical Society
  (209th: 1995: Anaheim, CA)** - *Nitration: Recent
  Laboratory and Industrial Developments*
  SciTech - v20 - N '96 - p21 [51-250]
**National Meeting of the American Chemical Society
  (210th: 1995: Chicago, IL)** - *Nanotechnology:
  Molecularly Designed Materials*
  SciTech - v20 - N '96 - p63 [51-250]
**National Museum and Archive of Lesbian and Gay
  History (U.S.)** - *The Gay Almanac*
  r ARBA - v28 - '97 - p307+ [51-250]
  r Choice - v34 - D '96 - p589 [51-250]
  The Lesbian Almanac
  r ARBA - v27 - '96 - p308 [51-250]
  r Choice - v34 - D '96 - p592 [51-250]
**The National Museum of American Art. Electronic
  Media Version**
  cr LJ - v122 - F 1 '97 - p116+ [51-250]
National Party Conventions 1831-1992
  r CLW - v66 - Je '96 - p39 [251-500]
**National Report for the Fourth World Conference on
  Women**
  J Gov Info - v23 - S '96 - p656 [51-250]
National Research Council (U.S.) - *Improving the
  Environment*
  J Gov Info - v23 - S '96 - p568 [51-250]

**National Research Council (U.S.). Climate Research
  Committee** - *Natural Climate Variability on Decade-to-
  Century Time Scales*
  SciTech - v21 - Mr '97 - p26 [51-250]
**National Research Council (U.S.) Committee on Coatings
  for High-Temperature Structural Materials** -
  Coatings for High-Temperature Structural Materials
  SciTech - v20 - N '96 - p62 [51-250]
**National Research Council (U.S.). Committee on
  Comparative Toxicity of Naturally Occurring
  Carcinogens** - *Carcinogens and Anticarcinogens in the
  Human Diet*
  Choice - v34 - Ap '97 - p1372 [51-250]
  SB - v33 - My '97 - p105 [51-250]
**National Research Council (U.S.). Committee on Criteria
  for Federal Support of Research and Development** -
  Allocating Federal Funds for Science and Technology
  J Gov Info - v23 - S '96 - p564 [51-250]
**National Research Council (U.S.). Committee on
  Fracture Characterization and Fluid Flow** - *Rock
  Fractures and Fluid Flow*
  SciTech - v20 - D '96 - p65 [51-250]
**National Research Council (U.S.). Committee on Inland
  Aquatic Ecosystems** - *Freshwater Ecosystems*
  SciTech - v21 - Mr '97 - p34 [51-250]
**National Research Council (U.S.). Committee on
  National Needs in Maritime Technology** -
  Shipbuilding Technology and Education
  SciTech - v20 - S '96 - p63 [51-250]
**National Research Council (U.S.). Committee on Pest
  and Pathogen Control** - *Ecologically Based Pest
  Management*
  Choice - v34 - Ja '97 - p818 [51-250]
  SciTech - v20 - S '96 - p44 [51-250]
**National Research Council (U.S.). Committee on
  Protection and Management of Pacific Northwest
  Anadromous Salmonids** - *Upstream: Salmon and
  Society in the Pacific Northwest*
  Choice - v34 - F '97 - p991 [51-250]
  SciTech - v20 - N '96 - p29 [51-250]
**National Research Council (U.S.). Committee on Prudent
  Practices for Handling, Storage, and Disposal of
  Chemicals in Laboratories** - *Prudent Practices in the
  Laboratory*
  Choice - v34 - O '96 - p308 [51-250]
**National Research Council (U.S.). Committee on
  Scientific Issues in the Endangered Species Act** -
  Science and the Endangered Species Act
  J Gov Info - v23 - S '96 - p572 [51-250]
**National Research Council (U.S.). Committee on
  Separations Technology and Transmutation
  Systems** - *Nuclear Wastes*
  SciTech - v20 - S '96 - p51 [51-250]
**National Research Council (U.S.). Committee on the
  Strategic Assessment of the U.S. Department of
  Energy's Coal Program** - *Coal: Energy for the Future*
  Env - v38 - O '96 - p25+ [251-500]
**National Research Council (U.S.). Committee on
  Toxicological and Performance Aspects of
  Oxygenated Motor Vehicle Fuels** - *Toxicological and
  Performance Aspects of Oxygenated Motor Vehicle Fuels*
  SciTech - v20 - N '96 - p68 [51-250]
**National Research Council (U.S.). NII 2000 Steering
  Committee** - *The Unpredictable Certainty*
  Choice - v34 - Ja '97 - p833 [51-250]
  JEL - v35 - Mr '97 - p250+ [51-250]
**National Research Council (U.S.). Office of International
  Affairs** - *Bridge Builders*
  R&R Bk N - v11 - D '96 - p12 [51-250]
**National Research Council (U.S.). Panel on Aerosol
  Radiative Forcing and Climate Change** - *A Plan for a
  Research Program on Aerosol Radiative Forcing and
  Climate Change*
  SciTech - v20 - S '96 - p51 [51-250]
**National Research Council (U.S.). Steering Committee,
  Workshop Series on High Performance Computing
  and Communications** - *Computing and
  Communications in the Extreme*
  SciTech - v20 - N '96 - p7 [51-250]
National Safety Council - *First Aid and CPR. 3rd Ed.*
  SciTech - v20 - D '96 - p42 [51-250]
National Science Education Standards
  Math T - v89 - S '96 - p516 [51-250]
National Science Resources Center (U.S.) - *Resources for
  Teaching Elementary School Science*
  r EL - v54 - O '96 - p92 [51-250]
  r SB - v30 - O '96 - p199 [251-500]
  r SLMQ - v25 - Fall '96 - p66 [51-250]
  Science for All Children
  BioSci - v46 - N '96 - p790 [51-250]

The National Space Transportation Policy
J Gov Info - v23 - S '96 - p557 [51-250]
National Storytelling Directory 1996
r ARBA - v28 - '97 - p248 [51-250]
National Systems for Financing Innovation
J Gov Info - v23 - S '96 - p674 [51-250]
National Task Force on African-American Men and Boys - *Repairing the Breach*
Choice - v34 - D '96 - p696 [51-250]
National Television Violence Study. Vol. 1
R&R Bk N - v12 - F '97 - p81 [51-250]
National Trade and Professional Associations of the United States. 31st Ed.
r LJ - v122 - Ja '97 - p90 [51-250]
The National Trust Guide to Historic Bed and Breakfasts, Inns, and Small Hotels. 4th Ed.
r ARBA - v28 - '97 - p178+ [51-250]
National Union Catalog of Manuscript Collections 1959/61-
r ASInt - v34 - O '96 - p10 [51-250]
The Native Americans (Turner Publishing). Electronic Media Version
NYTBR - v101 - S 15 '96 - p26 [501+]
Natividad, Irene - *The Asian American Almanac*
yr Par Ch - v21 - Mr '97 - p5 [1-50]
NATO Advanced Research Workshop (ARW) Pulsed Metal Vapour Lasers, Physics and Emerging Applications (1995: University of St. Andrews) - *Pulsed Metal Vapour Lasers*
SciTech - v20 - D '96 - p67 [51-250]
NATO Advanced Research Workshop on Heterostructure Epitaxy and Devices (1995: Smolenice Castle) - *Heterostructure Epitaxy and Devices*
SciTech - v20 - D '96 - p77 [51-250]
NATO Advanced Research Workshop on Photoactive Organic Materials: Science and Applications (1995: Avignon, France) - *Photoactive Organic Materials*
SciTech - v20 - D '96 - p24 [51-250]
NATO Advanced Research Workshop on Science and Innovation as Strategic Tools for Industrial and Economic Growth (1994: Moscow, Russia) - *Science and Innovation as Strategic Tools for Industrial and Economic Growth*
SciTech - v20 - N '96 - p60 [51-250]
NATO Advanced Research Workshop on Scientific Advances in Alternative Demilitarization Technologies (1995: Warsaw, Poland) - *Scientific Advances in Alternative Demilitarization Technologies*
SciTech - v20 - D '96 - p88 [51-250]
NATO Advanced Research Workshop on the Chemical Physics of Fullerenes 10 (and 5) Years Later (1995: Varenna, Italy) - *The Chemical Physics of Fullerenes 10 (and 5) Years Later*
SciTech - v21 - Mr '97 - p29 [51-250]
NATO Advanced Research Workshop on Ventilation and Indoor Air Quality in Hospitals (1996: Milan, Italy) - *Ventilation and Indoor Air Quality in Hospitals*
SciTech - v20 - N '96 - p37 [51-250]
NATO Advanced Study Institute on Advances in Morphometrics (1993: Tuscany, Italy) - *Advances in Morphometrics*
SciTech - v20 - N '96 - p26 [51-250]
NATO Advanced Study Institute on Crystallography of Supramolecular Compounds (1995: Erice, Italy) - *Crystallography of Supramolecular Compounds*
SciTech - v20 - N '96 - p22 [51-250]
NATO Advanced Study Institute on Laser Processing: Surface Treatment and Film Deposition (1994: Sezimbra, Portugal) - *Laser Processing*
SciTech - v20 - D '96 - p67 [51-250]
NATO Advanced Study Institute on Light as Energy Source and Information Carrier in Plant Photophysiology (1994: Volterra, Italy) - *Light as an Energy Source and Information Carrier in Plant Physiology*
SciTech - v20 - N '96 - p28 [51-250]
NATO Advanced Study Institute on Mechanical Behaviour of Materials at High Temperature (1995: Sesimbra, Portugal) - *Mechanical Behaviour of Materials at High Temperature*
SciTech - v20 - D '96 - p63 [51-250]
NATO Advanced Study Institute on Physics and Chemistry of Low-Dimensional Inorganic Conductors (1995: Les Houches, Frances) - *Physics and Chemistry of Low-Dimensional Inorganic Conductors*
SciTech - v20 - N '96 - p18 [51-250]
NATO Advanced Study Institute on Stability of Materials (1994: Corfu, Greece) - *Stability of Materials*
SciTech - v20 - N '96 - p18 [51-250]

Natoli, Joseph - *Hauntings: Popular Film and American Culture 1990-1992*
J Pop F&TV - v24 - Win '97 - p184+ [501+]
Natter, Wolfgang - *Objectivity and Its Other*
Hist & T - v35 - 3 '96 - p391+ [501+]
Nattrass, Leonora - *William Cobbett: The Politics of Style*
Nine-C Lit - v51 - S '96 - p275 [51-250]
Natural Hazard Phenomena and Mitigation 1996
SciTech - v20 - N '96 - p83 [51-250]
Natural History Museum (London). General Library - *A Catalogue of Manuscripts and Drawings in the General Library of the Natural History Museum, London*
R&R Bk N - v11 - D '96 - p68 [51-250]
Nature Medicine
p Nature - v383 - S 5 '96 - p35 [251-500]
Nau, Jim - *Ball Perennial Manual*
r ARBA - v28 - '97 - p580 [51-250]
Naud, Andre - *Un Aggiornamento Et Son Eclipse*
Theol St - v58 - Mr '97 - p194+ [251-500]
Naude, Charl-Pierre - *Die Nomadiese Oomblik*
WLT - v70 - Aut '96 - p1019 [51-250]
Nauen, Elinor - *Ladies, Start Your Engines*
BL - v93 - Ja '97 - p809 [51-250]
LJ - v122 - F 1 '97 - p79 [51-250]
Ms - v7 - Ja '97 - p82 [1-50]
PW - v243 - D 2 '96 - p49+ [51-250]
Naufftus, William F - *British Short-Fiction Writers 1880-1914*
r ARBA - v28 - '97 - p447+ [51-250]
Naughton, Barry - *Growing Out of the Plan*
APSR - v91 - Mr '97 - p209+ [501+]
Ch Rev Int - v4 - Spr '97 - p219+ [501+]
Naughton, Jim - *Catholics in Crisis*
Am - v176 - F 1 '97 - p27+ [501+]
BW - v26 - O 20 '96 - p5 [501+]
Comw - v124 - Mr 14 '97 - p17+ [501+]
KR - v64 - S 1 '96 - p1302 [251-500]
LJ - v121 - D '96 - p100 [51-250]
PW - v243 - S 2 '96 - p126 [51-250]
Naughton, Patrick - *Java Handbook*
CBR - v14 - N '96 - p36 [51-250]
Naugle, Matthew G - *Local Area Networking. 2nd Ed.*
CBR - v14 - N '96 - p38 [51-250]
SciTech - v20 - S '96 - p56 [51-250]
Naum, Gellu - *Zenobia*
WLT - v70 - Sum '96 - p679+ [501+]
Naumann, Claudia - *Der Kreuzzug Kaiser Heinrichs VI*
Specu - v71 - Jl '96 - p740+ [501+]
Naumuk, O M - *Russkaia Lubochnaia Kniga XVII-XIX Vekov*
r Lib - v18 - D '96 - p365 [1-50]
Nauright, John - *Making Men*
Choice - v34 - O '96 - p321 [51-250]
Lon R Bks - v18 - N 14 '96 - p26+ [501+]
Socio R - v44 - N '96 - p782+ [501+]
Nava, Michael - *The Death of Friends*
Advocate - S 17 '96 - p60 [1-50]
BL - v92 - Ag '96 - p1887 [51-250]
BW - v26 - Ag 18 '96 - p8 [501+]
Ent W - S 6 '96 - p71 [51-250]
NYTBR - v101 - O 27 '96 - p42 [51-250]
The Naval Institute Guide to World Military Aviation 1996. Electronic Media Version
r Choice - v34 - F '97 - p952 [51-250]
Navaratna-Bandara, Abeysinghe M - *The Management of Ethnic Secessionist Conflict*
Choice - v34 - S '96 - p206 [51-250]
Navari, Cornelia - *British Politics and the Spirit of the Age*
TLS - S 13 '96 - p29 [501+]
Navarra, Tova - *Encyclopedia of Vitamins, Minerals and Supplements*
r ARBA - v28 - '97 - p575+ [51-250]
r BL - v93 - F 1 '97 - p959 [1-50]
r Choice - v34 - S '96 - p103+ [251-500]
yr SLJ - v42 - N '96 - p141+ [51-250]
Navarrete, Ignacio - *Orphans of Petrarch*
Comp L - v48 - Fall '96 - p385+ [501+]
Navarro, Angel M - *La Pintura Holandesa Y Flamenca (Siglos XVI Al XVIII) En El Museo Nacional De Bellas Artes De Buenos Aires*
BM - v138 - N '96 - p760 [251-500]
Navarro, Armando - *Mexican American Youth Organization*
APSR - v90 - S '96 - p656+ [501+]
WHQ - v27 - Win '96 - p538+ [251-500]
Navarro, Jose Antonio - *Defending Mexican Valor in Texas*
WHQ - v27 - Win '96 - p548 [1-50]

Navarro, Jose Maria - *Configuracion Textual De La Recopilacion Historial De Venezuela De Pedro De Aguado*
HAHR - v77 - My '97 - p316+ [501+]
Mastering Spanish Vocabulary
r ARBA - v28 - '97 - p402+ [51-250]
Navarro, Juan Carlos - *Community Organizations in Latin America*
HAHR - v76 - N '96 - p836+ [251-500]
Navarro, Julio A - *Integrated Active Antennas and Spatial Power Combining*
SciTech - v20 - D '96 - p78 [51-250]
Navarro, Yvonne - *Deadrush*
Necro - Win '97 - p23+ [501+]
Navarro, Yvonne, 1957- - *First Name Reverse Dictionary*
r Names - v45 - Mr '97 - p76 [251-500]
Navascues, Javier De - *El Esperpento Controlado*
Hisp - v79 - S '96 - p459+ [501+]
Naves, Elaine Kalman - *Journey to Vaja*
Quill & Q - v62 - O '96 - p34 [501+]
Navia, Luis E - *Classical Cynicism*
R&R Bk N - v12 - F '97 - p1 [1-50]
Navran, Frank - *Truth and Trust*
Per Psy - v49 - Aut '96 - p756+ [501+]
Nawawi - *Al-Maqasid: Imam Nawawi's Manual of Islam*
Rel St Rev - v22 - O '96 - p356 [51-250]
Naydler, Jeremy - *Temple of the Cosmos*
Parabola - v21 - N '96 - p120 [1-50]
Nayler, G H F - *Dictionary of Mechanical Engineering. 4th Ed.*
r ARBA - v28 - '97 - p597 [51-250]
Naylor, Gloria - *Children of the Night*
Ant R - v54 - Sum '96 - p365+ [251-500]
BW - v27 - F 9 '97 - p12 [51-250]
PW - v244 - Ja 27 '97 - p103 [1-50]
Trib Bks - Mr 9 '97 - p8 [1-50]
Naylor, James - *The New Democracy*
Can Hist R - v77 - S '96 - p452+ [501+]
Naylor, Phyllis Reynolds - *Alice In-Between*
c Ch BWatch - v6 - Jl '96 - p5 [1-50]
Alice in Lace
c HB Guide - v7 - Fall '96 - p295 [51-250]
The Bomb in the Bessledorf Bus Depot
c HB Guide - v7 - Fall '96 - p295 [51-250]
Ducks Disappearing (Illus. by Tony Maddox)
c BL - v93 - F 1 '97 - p948 [51-250]
c CCB-B - v50 - F '97 - p217+ [51-250]
c KR - v64 - D 15 '96 - p1802 [51-250]
c Par Ch - v21 - Mr '97 - p4 [1-50]
c PW - v243 - D 16 '96 - p59 [51-250]
c SLJ - v43 - Mr '97 - p162 [51-250]
The Healing of Texas Jake
c BL - v93 - My 1 '97 - p1495 [51-250]
Ice
c New Ad - v9 - Fall '96 - p327+ [501+]
c RT - v50 - D '96 - p345 [51-250]
Outrageously Alice
y BL - v93 - My 15 '97 - p1573 [51-250]
c PW - v244 - Ap 21 '97 - p73+ [1-50]
Shiloh
c JOYS - v10 - Fall '96 - p46+ [501+]
Shiloh Season
c BL - v93 - Ja '97 - p766 [1-50]
c BL - v93 - N 15 '96 - p584 [51-250]
c BW - v26 - O 6 '96 - p11 [501+]
c CBRS - v25 - S '96 - p12 [51-250]
y CCB-B - v50 - D '96 - p145+ [51-250]
c Ch BWatch - v7 - Ja '97 - p4 [51-250]
c HB - v72 - N '96 - p737+ [51-250]
c HB Guide - v8 - Spr '97 - p72 [51-250]
c NYTBR - v102 - Ja 5 '97 - p22 [1-50]
c PW - v243 - N 4 '96 - p49 [51-250]
c SLJ - v42 - N '96 - p110 [51-250]
Nazar, David - *There Is a Tomorrow*
Mag Bl - Mr '97 - p58+ [51-250]
Sm Pr R - v28 - S '96 - p7 [251-500]
Nazmi, Nader - *Economic Policy and Stabilization in Latin America*
Choice - v34 - S '96 - p177 [51-250]
NBER Macroeconomics Annual 1995
JEL - v34 - S '96 - p1417 [51-250]
NCAA Basketball 1997
r ARBA - v28 - '97 - p297 [51-250]
NCAA Final Four 1997
r ARBA - v28 - '97 - p298 [251-500]
NCEA/Ganley's Catholic Schools in America 1995
r ARBA - v28 - '97 - p542 [51-250]
Ndiaye, Marie - *La Sorciere*
Econ - v340 - S 14 '96 - p14*+ [501+]

Ndulu, Benno - *Agenda for Africa's Economic Renewal*
 JEL - v34 - D '96 - p2116+ [51-250]
 TLS - Ja 3 '97 - p14+ [501+]
Neagoe, Stelian - *Istoria Guvernelor Romaniei*
 BL - v93 - D 15 '96 - p714 [1-50]
Neagu, Fanus - *Partida De Pocher*
 BL - v93 - D 15 '96 - p714 [1-50]
Neal, Kenneth - *A Wise Extravagance*
 R&R Bk N - v11 - D '96 - p57 [51-250]
Neal, Tommy - *Lawmaking and the Legislative Process*
 r BL - v93 - S 1 '96 - p166 [51-250]
Neary, J Peter - *International Trade. Vols. 1-2*
 Econ J - v106 - S '96 - p1473 [51-250]
Neat, Timothy - *The Summer Walkers*
 TLS - N 22 '96 - p13 [501+]
Nebauer, Alan - *Against All Odds*
 KR - v65 - Ja 15 '97 - p125 [251-500]
 PW - v244 - Ja 20 '97 - p388 [51-250]
Nebraska Alternative Transportation Fuels Handbook
 J Gov Info - v23 - S '96 - p588 [51-250]
Nebula Awards 30
 BWatch - v17 - S '96 - p7 [1-50]
 SF Chr - v18 - O '96 - p80 [1-50]
Nebula Awards 31
 y BL - v93 - Mr 15 '97 - p1231 [51-250]
 KR - v65 - Mr 1 '97 - p342 [51-250]
 LJ - v122 - Ap 15 '97 - p124 [51-250]
 PW - v244 - Mr 31 '97 - p67 [51-250]
Necipoglu, Gulru - *The Topkapi Scroll*
 Choice - v34 - Ja '97 - p784 [51-250]
Neck, Raymond W - *A Field Guide to Butterflies of Texas*
 Choice - v34 - S '96 - p153 [51-250]
Necrofile
 p SF Chr - v18 - O '96 - p83 [1-50]
NecronomicoN. Bk. 1
 Afterimage - v24 - N '96 - p16 [51-250]
Nederman, Cary J - *Community and Consent*
 Ethics - v107 - O '96 - p181+ [51-250]
 Specu - v71 - Jl '96 - p741+ [501+]
Nederveen Pieterse, Jan - *Christianity and Hegemony*
 JTWS - v13 - Spr '96 - p423+ [501+]
Nedo, Michael - *Ludwig Wittgenstein: Wiener Ausgabe*
 Dialogue - v35 - Fall '96 - p777+ [501+]
Needham, Joseph - *Science and Civilisation in China. Vol. 5, Pt. 6*
 HJAS - v56 - 2 '96 - p508+ [501+]
 Isis - v87 - S '96 - p536+ [501+]
 TLS - O 25 '96 - p13 [251-500]
 Science and Civilisation in China. Vol. 6, Pt. 3
 Nature - v383 - S 12 '96 - p136 [1-50]
 The Shorter Science and Civilisation in China. Vol. 5
 Ch Rev Int - v4 - Spr '97 - p226+ [501+]
Needham, Kate - *First Pony (Illus. by M Rain)*
 c Bks Keeps - N '96 - p14+ [51-250]
 c JB - v60 - D '96 - p257 [51-250]
 c Sch Lib - v44 - N '96 - p163 [51-250]
 The Time Trekkers Visit the Middle Ages
 c HB Guide - v7 - Fall '96 - p379 [51-250]
Needle, Jan - *The Bully*
 c Sch Lib - v44 - Ag '96 - p96+ [501+]
Needleman, Jacob - *Gurdjieff: Essays and Reflections on the Man and His Teaching*
 Choice - v34 - D '96 - p628 [51-250]
 Parabola - v22 - F '97 - p90+ [501+]
 TLS - F 14 '97 - p31 [501+]
 A Little Book on Love
 Parabola - v21 - Ag '96 - p94 [501+]
Needler, Martin C - *Mexican Politics. 3rd Ed.*
 HAHR - v77 - F '97 - p136+ [501+]
Neel, David - *The Great Canoes*
 BIC - v25 - S '96 - p10+ [501+]
Neel, Janet - *A Timely Death*
 BL - v93 - Ja '97 - p825 [51-250]
 Books - v10 - Je '96 - p10 [1-50]
 BW - v27 - F 16 '97 - p11 [51-250]
 KR - v64 - N 15 '96 - p1637 [51-250]
 PW - v243 - N 11 '96 - p60 [51-250]
 Spec - v277 - D 14 '96 - p75 [51-250]
Neely, Richard - *Tragedies of Our Own Making*
 ILRR - v50 - O '96 - p162+ [501+]
Neely, Teresa - *In Our Own Voices*
 LAR - v98 - S '96 - p651 [51-250]
Ne'eman, Yuval - *The Particle Hunters. 2nd Ed.*
 New Sci - v151 - S 14 '96 - p44 [51-250]
Neenan, Colin - *In Your Dreams*
 y Emerg Lib - v24 - S '96 - p27 [1-50]

Live a Little
 y BL - v93 - S 1 '96 - p119 [51-250]
 y CBRS - v25 - O '96 - p23 [51-250]
 y CCB-B - v50 - O '96 - p70+ [51-250]
 y HB Guide - v8 - Spr '97 - p82 [51-250]
 y Kliatt - v31 - Ja '97 - p10 [51-250]
 y SLJ - v43 - Mr '97 - p190 [51-250]
 y VOYA - v19 - D '96 - p272+ [251-500]
Neff, Donald - *Fallen Pillars*
 JTWS - v13 - Fall '96 - p331+ [501+]
 MEJ - v50 - Sum '96 - p440+ [501+]
Neff, Miriam - *Helping Teens in Crisis*
 VOYA - v19 - F '97 - p317+ [51-250]
Neff, Robert - *Japan's Hidden Hot Springs*
 r FEER - v160 - Mr 27 '97 - p51+ [501+]
Negash, Tekeste - *Dimensions of Development with Emphasis on Africa*
 JEL - v34 - S '96 - p1479+ [51-250]
Negativeland - *Fair Use*
 ABR - v18 - D '96 - p20 [501+]
Neggers, Carla - *Just before Sunrise*
 PW - v244 - F 10 '97 - p81 [51-250]
Negus, George - *The Trev Series (Illus. by Craig Smith)*
 c Aust Bk R - D '96 - p91+ [501+]
Negus, Joan - *The Book of Uranus*
 Horoscope - v62 - D '96 - p16+ [501+]
Neibauer, Alan - *Microsoft Word for Windows 95 Made Easy*
 CBR - v14 - Jl '96 - p26 [1-50]
Neidermeier, Otto - *Nobody Home*
 Tric - v6 - Fall '96 - p142 [1-50]
Neighbors, Harold W - *Mental Health in Black America*
 SciTech - v20 - S '96 - p32 [1-50]
Neihart, Ben - *Hey, Joe*
 VQR - v72 - Aut '96 - p130*+ [51-250]
 VV - v42 - Ja 7 '97 - p41 [51-250]
Neiiendam, Klaus - *The Art of Acting in Antiquity*
 AJA - v101 - Ja '97 - p154+ [501+]
Neil, Alexander - *Alexander Neil and the Last Shenandoah Valley Campaign*
 PW - v243 - O 21 '96 - p68 [1-50]
Neil, Andrew - *Full Disclosure*
 Econ - v341 - O 26 '96 - p108 [501+]
 ILN - Christmas '96 - p90 [51-250]
 Lon R Bks - v18 - D 12 '96 - p24 [501+]
 NS - v125 - N 1 '96 - p47+ [501+]
 Obs - N 3 '96 - p15* [501+]
 Spec - v277 - O 26 '96 - p56+ [501+]
 TLS - D 20 '96 - p32 [501+]
Neillands, Robin - *The Conquest of the Reich*
 Historian - v59 - Win '97 - p473+ [251-500]
 The Dervish Wars
 TLS - Ag 2 '96 - p31 [501+]
 A Fighting Retreat
 NS - v125 - D 20 '96 - p119 [501+]
Neilson, D - *Computational Approaches to Novel Condensed Matter Systems*
 Am Sci - v85 - Ja '97 - p76+ [501+]
Neilson, Keith - *Britain and the Last Tsar*
 Albion - v28 - '96 - p722+ [501+]
 Choice - v34 - S '96 - p188 [51-250]
 HRNB - v25 - Fall '96 - p23 [251-500]
Neiman, LeRoy - *LeRoy Neiman on Safari*
 KR - v65 - F 15 '97 - p292 [51-250]
 PW - v244 - Mr 17 '97 - p73 [51-250]
Neimanis, George J - *The Collapse of the Soviet Empire*
 LJ - v122 - My 1 '97 - p124+ [51-250]
Neimark, Anne E - *Myth Maker (Illus. by Brad Weinman)*
 c HB Guide - v8 - Spr '97 - p160 [51-250]
 c KR - v64 - Ag 15 '96 - p1240 [51-250]
 c SLJ - v42 - O '96 - p136+ [51-250]
Neinstein, Lawrence S - *Adolescent Health Care. 3rd Ed.*
 SciTech - v20 - S '96 - p42 [51-250]
Neirynck, Frans - *Q-Synopsis: The Double Tradition Passages in Greek. Rev. Ed.*
 Rel St Rev - v23 - Ja '97 - p71 [51-250]
Neitzel, Shirley - *We're Making Breakfast for Mother (Illus. by Nancy Winslow Parker)*
 c BL - v93 - Mr 1 '97 - p1173 [51-250]
 c CCB-B - v50 - My '97 - p331 [51-250]
Nelken, David - *Law as Communication*
 R&R Bk N - v11 - D '96 - p50 [51-250]
Nelken, Israel - *Option-Embedded Bonds*
 R&R Bk N - v11 - D '96 - p36 [51-250]
Nelkin, Dorothy - *The DNA Mystique*
 New Sci - v152 - D 21 '96 - p71 [51-250]
Nell, Edward J - *Making Sense of a Changing Economy*
 JEL - v34 - D '96 - p2122+ [51-250]
Nellen, Henk J M - *Hugo Grotius, Theologian*
 CH - v65 - S '96 - p496+ [501+]

Nelligan, Emile - *Selected Poems*
 BIC - v25 - S '96 - p17+ [501+]
 TranslRevS - v2 - D '96 - p6 [51-250]
Nelmes, Jill - *An Introduction to Film Studies*
 Si & So - v6 - N '96 - p32+ [501+]
Nelson, Alan H - *Early Cambridge Theatres*
 MLR - v91 - Jl '96 - p696+ [501+]
 RES - v47 - N '96 - p566+ [501+]
 Shakes Q - v47 - Sum '96 - p217+ [501+]
Nelson, Albert J - *Democrats under Siege in the Sunbelt Megastates*
 R&R Bk N - v12 - F '97 - p60 [51-250]
Nelson, Antonya - *Family Terrorists and Other Stories*
 Obs - F 2 '97 - p18* [51-250]
 Talking in Bed
 NYTBR - v101 - D 8 '96 - p84 [1-50]
Nelson, Barbara J - *Women and Politics Worldwide*
 Signs - v22 - Win '97 - p466+ [501+]
Nelson, Blake - *Exile*
 KR - v65 - My 1 '97 - p672+ [251-500]
 PW - v244 - My 12 '97 - p58+ [51-250]
Nelson, Bob - *Managing for Dummies*
 HR Mag - v42 - Ja '97 - p149 [51-250]
 LJ - v122 - Mr 15 '97 - p35 [1-50]
Nelson, Byron C - *The Creationist Writing of Byron C. Nelson*
 Isis - v88 - Mr '97 - p160+ [501+]
Nelson, Claudia - *The Girl's Own*
 NWSA Jnl - v8 - Fall '96 - p144+ [501+]
 VS - v39 - Aut '95 - p114+ [501+]
Nelson, Cynthia - *Doria Shafik, Egyptian Feminist*
 Choice - v34 - Ap '97 - p1402 [51-250]
 LJ - v121 - N 15 '96 - p68 [51-250]
Nelson, Daniel, 1941- - *Farm and Factory*
 JEH - v56 - S '96 - p745+ [501+]
 Managers and Workers. 2nd Ed.
 Choice - v34 - S '96 - p173 [51-250]
 JEL - v34 - S '96 - p1467 [51-250]
Nelson, Emmanuel S - *Contemporary Gay American Novelists*
 r RQ - v36 - Win '96 - p222 [51-250]
Nelson, Hilde Lindemann - *The Patient in the Family*
 Ethics - v107 - O '96 - p185+ [251-500]
 Hast Cen R - v27 - Ja '97 - p45+ [501+]
 MHR - v10 - Fall '96 - p93+ [501+]
Nelson, J Robert - *On the New Frontiers of Genetics and Religion*
 Rel St Rev - v23 - Ja '97 - p51 [51-250]
Nelson, James B - *Moral Nexus*
 BL - v93 - O 1 '96 - p308 [1-50]
Nelson, James L - *By Force of Arms*
 VQR - v72 - Aut '96 - p129* [51-250]
 The Maddest Idea
 BL - v93 - F 1 '97 - p926 [51-250]
Nelson, James Lindemann - *Alzheimer's: Answers to Hard Questions for Families*
 BL - v93 - N 15 '96 - p554 [51-250]
 Hast Cen R - v27 - Ja '97 - p47 [1-50]
 LJ - v121 - N 15 '96 - p82 [51-250]
Nelson, John K - *A Year in the Life of a Shinto Shrine*
 Choice - v34 - O '96 - p298 [51-250]
 NYRB - v43 - Je 6 '96 - p31+ [501+]
Nelson, Julie A - *Feminism, Objectivity and Economics*
 Choice - v34 - S '96 - p177 [51-250]
 JEL - v34 - S '96 - p2069 [51-250]
Nelson, Kay Yarborough - *Optimizing Windows 95*
 BYTE - v21 - Ag '96 - p142 [51-250]
 Windows 95 Is Driving Me Crazy
 BL - v92 - Ag '96 - p1868 [501+]
 BYTE - v21 - Ag '96 - p133 [251-500]
 CBR - v14 - Jl '96 - p24 [51-250]
Nelson, Keith L - *The Making of Detente*
 AHR - v101 - O '96 - p1650 [501+]
 RAH - v24 - S '96 - p513+ [501+]
 RP - v58 - Sum '96 - p663+ [501+]
Nelson, Lynn, 1957- - *Desktop Guide to Creating CL Commands*
 SciTech - v20 - N '96 - p11 [51-250]
Nelson, Lynn D, 1943- - *Property to the People*
 Econ J - v106 - N '96 - p1846 [51-250]
Nelson, Margaret Cecile - *Equity Issues for Women in Archeology*
 Am Ant - v61 - Ap '96 - p421+ [501+]
 LA Ant - v7 - Je '96 - p175 [251-500]
Nelson, Marion J - *Material Culture and People's Art among Norwegians in America*
 CAY - v16 - Fall '95 - p9 [51-250]
 Norwegian Folk Art
 Am Craft - v56 - Ag '96 - p28 [1-50]
 SDA - v4 - Fall '96 - p126+ [501+]

Nelson, Michael - *Guide to the Presidency. 2nd Ed., Vols. 1-2*
  r BL - v93 - F 1 '97 - p963 [251-500]
  r Choice - v34 - Mr '97 - p1137 [51-250]
  r LAR - v99 - F '97 - p103 [1-50]
Nelson, Miriam E - *Strong Women Stay Young*
    CSM - v89 - F 6 '97 - p14 [51-250]
    LJ - v122 - Ja '97 - p136 [51-250]
    PW - v243 - D 2 '96 - p58 [51-250]
Nelson, Nan Ferring - *My Day with Anka (Illus. by Bill Farnsworth)*
  c BL - v93 - S 15 '96 - p249 [51-250]
  c CBRS - v25 - D '96 - p40 [1-50]
  c HB Guide - v8 - Spr '97 - p41 [51-250]
  c KR - v64 - Ag 15 '96 - p1240 [51-250]
  c SLJ - v42 - S '96 - p186+ [51-250]
Nelson, Nancy Owen - *Private Voices, Public Lives*
    AL - v68 - D '96 - p883 [51-250]
    WAL - v31 - Sum '96 - p167+ [501+]
Nelson, Nigel - *Looking into My Body (Illus. by Simone Able)*
  c Ch BWatch - v7 - F '97 - p6 [51-250]
  c Cur R - v36 - Ja '97 - p13 [51-250]
  c HB Guide - v8 - Spr '97 - p130 [51-250]
Nelson, Paul David - *Sir Charles Grey, First Earl Grey*
    Choice - v34 - Ja '97 - p864+ [51-250]
    W&M Q - v54 - Ap '97 - p438+ [501+]
Nelson, Paul J - *The World Bank and Non-Governmental Organizations*
    TLS - S 6 '96 - p27 [501+]
Nelson, Paula M - *The Prairie Winnows Out Its Own*
    WHQ - v28 - Spr '97 - p90+ [251-500]
Nelson, Ray - *Connie and Bonnie's Birthday Blastoff*
  c HB Guide - v7 - Fall '96 - p330 [51-250]
  A Dinosaur Ate My Homework
  c Ch BWatch - v6 - N '96 - p1 [51-250]
  c Ch BWatch - v7 - F '97 - p3 [1-50]
  c Ch BWatch - v7 - F '97 - p3 [1-50]
  c HB Guide - v8 - Spr '97 - p41 [51-250]
  c KR - v64 - N 1 '96 - p1605 [51-250]
  c SLJ - v43 - Mr '97 - p162 [51-250]
  Greetings from America
  c HB Guide - v7 - Fall '96 - p269 [1-50]
  Seven Seas of Billy's Bathtub
  c HB Guide - v7 - Fall '96 - p337 [1-50]
  Wooden Teeth and Jelly Beans
  c HB Guide - v7 - Fall '96 - p388 [51-250]
Nelson, Richard - *The General from America*
    Am Theat - v13 - D '96 - p20 [1-50]
Nelson, Richard, 1950- - *Making Plays*
    Theat J - v49 - Mr '97 - p95+ [501+]
Nelson, Richard Alan - *A Chronology and Glossary of Propaganda in the United States*
  r ARBA - v28 - '97 - p268+ [251-500]
  r Choice - v34 - Mr '97 - p1141 [51-250]
  r R&R Bk N - v12 - F '97 - p51 [51-250]
Nelson, Richard E - *The Power to Prevent Suicide*
    Adoles - v31 - Fall '96 - p753 [51-250]
Nelson, Richard R - *National Innovation Systems*
    Econ J - v106 - N '96 - p1850 [251-500]
  The Sources of Economic Growth
    BW - v27 - F 16 '97 - p6 [251-500]
Nelson, Robert H - *Public Lands and Private Rights*
    APSR - v91 - Mr '97 - p195+ [501+]
    JEL - v34 - D '96 - p2000+ [501+]
Nelson, Robert S - *Critical Terms for Art History*
    Choice - v34 - Ja '97 - p783 [51-250]
Nelson, Sarah Milledge - *The Archaeology of Northeast China*
    Am Ant - v61 - Jl '96 - p619+ [501+]
Nelson, Sharlene - *Bull Whackers to Whistle Punks*
  c BL - v92 - Ag '96 - p1899 [51-250]
  c HB Guide - v7 - Fall '96 - p385 [51-250]
Nelson, Stanley - *Immigrant. Bk. 3*
    Sm Pr R - v28 - O '96 - p12 [51-250]
Nelson, Stephen L - *Office 97 for Busy People. 2nd Ed.*
    LJ - v122 - Ap 1 '97 - p118 [51-250]
  Windows NT 4 for Busy People
    LJ - v122 - Ja '97 - p138 [1-50]
  The World Wide Web for Busy People
    CBR - v15 - Spr '97 - p7 [1-50]
    LJ - v121 - O 1 '96 - p120 [1-50]
Nelson, Suzanne - *Fast, Fun, and Fabulous Quilts*
    McCall Nee - v42 - D '96 - p13 [51-250]
Nelson, T G A - *Children, Parents, and the Rise of the Novel*
    Bkbird - v34 - Spr '96 - p57 [51-250]
Nelson, Theresa - *Earthshine*
  y SLJ - v43 - Ja '97 - p37 [1-50]
Nelson, Vaunda Micheaux - *Possibles*
  c RT - v50 - Mr '97 - p498 [51-250]

Nelson, W Dale - *The President Is at Camp David*
    Pres SQ - v27 - Win '97 - p176 [51-250]
Nelson, Willie - *Willie Nelson Lyrics 1957-1994*
    CAY - v16 - Fall '95 - p1 [51-250]
    CAY - v17 - Fall '96 - p2 [51-250]
Nelson-Atkins Museum of Art - *The Collection of the Nelson-Atkins Museum of Art*
  r Choice - v34 - F '97 - p956+ [51-250]
    LJ - v121 - D '96 - p90 [51-250]
    PW - v243 - N 18 '96 - p60 [51-250]
    R&R Bk N - v12 - F '97 - p74 [51-250]
  Durer to Matisse
    Choice - v34 - F '97 - p957 [51-250]
Nelson-Anderson, Danette L - *Genetic Connections*
    NGSQ - v84 - Je '96 - p150+ [501+]
Nembach, Eckhard - *Particle Strengthening of Metals and Alloys*
    SciTech - v21 - Mr '97 - p79 [51-250]
Nembhard, Jessica Gordon - *Capital Control, Financial Regulation, and Industrial Policy in South Korea and Brazil*
    JEL - v34 - S '96 - p1483 [51-250]
Nemec, David - *The Great Encyclopedia of 19th-Century Major League Baseball*
  r LJ - v122 - F 1 '97 - p83 [1-50]
  r PW - v243 - D 30 '96 - p52 [51-250]
Nemiroff, Diana - *Land Spirit Power*
    Afterimage - v24 - N '96 - p16 [1-50]
Nenner, Howard - *The Right to Be King*
    Albion - v28 - Win '96 - p696+ [501+]
    Sev Cent N - v54 - Fall '96 - p65+ [501+]
    Six Ct J - v27 - Win '96 - p1217+ [501+]
Nenno, Mary K - *Ending the Stalemate*
    Choice - v34 - N '96 - p538 [51-250]
Nenzel, Reinhard - *Kleinkarierte Avantgarde*
    MLR - v91 - Jl '96 - p795+ [501+]
Nepomnyashchy, Catherine Theimer - *Abram Tertz and the Poetics of Crime*
    Slav R - v55 - Sum '96 - p516+ [501+]
Nerburn, Kent - *A Haunting Reverence*
    BWatch - v17 - N '96 - p2 [51-250]
Nerhot, Patrick - *Law, Writing, Meaning*
    JC - v47 - Win '97 - p128+ [501+]
Nerlove, Miriam - *Flowers on the Wall (Illus. by Miriam Nerlove)*
  c HB Guide - v7 - Fall '96 - p287 [51-250]
  c NYTBR - v102 - Ap 13 '97 - p27 [1-50]
Nerone, John C - *Last Rights*
    JC - v47 - Win '97 - p150+ [501+]
Nersesian, Roy L - *Computer Simulation in Logistics*
    R&R Bk N - v11 - D '96 - p27 [51-250]
Nersessian, Edward - *Textbook of Psychoanalysis*
    AJPsych - v153 - Ag '96 - p1100+ [501+]
    Choice - v34 - S '96 - p216 [51-250]
Neruda, Jan - *Prague Tales*
    TranslRevS - v2 - D '96 - p6 [51-250]
Neruda, Pablo - *Ceremonial Songs*
    BL - v93 - N 15 '96 - p567 [51-250]
    LJ - v121 - D '96 - p98 [51-250]
  Heaven Stones
    TranslRevS - v1 - My '95 - p31 [51-250]
  Seaquake
    TranslRevS - v1 - My '95 - p31 [51-250]
Nerval, Gerard De - *Aurelia Followed by Sylvie*
    TranslRevS - v1 - My '95 - p20+ [51-250]
Nerve Cowboy
  p Sm Pr R - v29 - F '97 - p23 [51-250]
Nesaule, Agate - *A Woman in Amber*
  y Kliatt - v31 - My '97 - p22+ [51-250]
    NYTBR - v102 - Ja 26 '97 - p28 [1-50]
    PW - v243 - D 30 '96 - p64 [1-50]
    Trib Bks - F 23 '97 - p9 [1-50]
Nesbit, E - *The Deliverers of Their Country (Illus. by Lisbeth Zwerger)*
  c HB Guide - v8 - Spr '97 - p59 [51-250]
  c PW - v243 - N 25 '96 - p77 [1-50]
  Five Children and It
  c Bks Keeps - Mr '97 - p28 [51-250]
Nesbitt, John - *Twin Rivers*
    Roundup M - v4 - F '97 - p28 [51-250]
Nesbitt, Kate - *Theorizing a New Agenda for Architecture*
    Choice - v34 - O '96 - p269+ [51-250]
Ness, Caroline - *The Ocean of Story (Illus. by Jacqueline Mair)*
  c HB Guide - v7 - Fall '96 - p322 [51-250]
Ness, Stanley - *Nondestructive Testing Handbook. 2nd Ed.*
    SciTech - v21 - Mr '97 - p78 [51-250]
Nesset, Kirk - *The Stories of Raymond Carver*
    WAL - v31 - Sum '96 - p186+ [251-500]

Nester, William R - *Power across the Pacific*
    Choice - v34 - F '97 - p1032 [51-250]
    R&R Bk N - v11 - D '96 - p14 [51-250]
Nestle, Joan - *Women on Women 3*
    HG&LRev - v3 - Fall '96 - p44 [501+]
Nestroy, Johann - *Samtliche Werke*
    MLR - v92 - Ap '97 - p508+ [501+]
Net.Genesis (Firm) - *Build a World Wide Web Commerce Center*
    CBR - v14 - S '96 - p28 [1-50]
    Quill & Q - v62 - My '96 - p22+ [501+]
Netanyahu, Benzion - *The Origins of the Inquisition in Fifteenth Century Spain*
    Lon R Bks - v18 - O 31 '96 - p19+ [501+]
Netanyahu, Binyamin - *Fighting Terrorism*
    TLS - Mr 7 '97 - p7 [501+]
Neth, Mary - *Preserving the Family Farm*
    AHR - v101 - O '96 - p1298 [501+]
    J Am St - v30 - Ap '96 - p176+ [501+]
Nethery, Mary - *Hannah and Jack (Illus. by Mary Morgan)*
  c HB Guide - v7 - Fall '96 - p269 [51-250]
NetPages: The Internationally Renowned Resource Guide to the Internet. 3rd Ed.
  r Choice - v34 - Ja '97 - p772 [251-500]
Netstudy: Your Guide to Getting Better Grades Using the Internet and Online Services
  y BL - v93 - S 15 '96 - p252 [51-250]
Nettell, Stephanie - *Collins Christmas Treasury (Illus. by Ian Penney)*
  c Bks Keeps - N '96 - p20 [51-250]
  c Spec - v277 - D 14 '96 - p77 [51-250]
Nettl, Bruno - *Heartland Excursions*
    Am Ethnol - v23 - Ag '96 - p658+ [501+]
    M Ed J - v83 - Jl '96 - p50 [51-250]
    Notes - v53 - S '96 - p32+ [501+]
Netton, Ian Richard - *Text and Trauma*
    MEJ - v51 - Win '97 - p140+ [501+]
Netzer, Amnon - *Padyavand. Vol. 1*
    MEJ - v51 - Win '97 - p155 [51-250]
Netzer, Nancy - *Cultural Interplay in the Eighth Century*
    CHR - v82 - O '96 - p687+ [501+]
Netzley, Patricia D - *Queen Victoria*
  c HB Guide - v7 - Fall '96 - p371 [51-250]
Netzorg, Morton J - *The Philippines in World War II and to Independence (December 8, 1941-July 4, 1946). 2nd Ed., Vols. 1-2*
  r ARBA - v28 - '97 - p198+ [51-250]
  r Choice - v34 - S '96 - p104 [51-250]
Neubach, Keren - *Ha-Meruts: Behirot 96*
    BL - v93 - Mr 1 '97 - p1115 [1-50]
Neubauer, Joan R - *Dear Diary*
    EGH - v50 - N '96 - p154 [51-250]
Neuberger, Joan - *Hooliganism: Crime, Culture and Power in St. Petersburg 1900-1914*
    EHR - v111 - S '96 - p1014+ [501+]
Neuberger, Julia - *On Being Jewish*
    Obs - v54 - O 13 '96 - p15* [501+]
Neuberger, Verena E - *Margery Kempe: A Study in Early English Feminism*
    Six Ct J - v27 - Fall '96 - p870 [251-500]
Neuer, Werner - *Adolf Schlatter: A Biography of Germany's Premier Biblical Theologian*
    Rel St Rev - v23 - Ap '97 - p176 [251-500]
Neufeld, David - *Chilkoot Trail*
    CG - v116 - N '96 - p83+ [501+]
Neufeld, James - *Power to Rise*
    BIC - v26 - Mr '97 - p5+ [501+]
    Choice - v34 - Mr '97 - p1173 [51-250]
    R&R Bk N - v12 - F '97 - p32 [51-250]
Neufeld, John - *Gaps in Stone Walls*
  y BW - v26 - D 8 '96 - p21 [51-250]
  y HB Guide - v7 - Fall '96 - p304 [51-250]
  A Small Civil War
  y HB Guide - v8 - Spr '97 - p83 [51-250]
  c PW - v243 - S 2 '96 - p133 [51-250]
  y SLJ - v42 - N '96 - p124 [51-250]
  y VOYA - v19 - F '97 - p331 [251-500]
Neufeld, Mark A - *The Restructuring of International Relations Theory*
    Choice - v34 - D '96 - p687 [51-250]
Neufeld, Maurice F - *American Working Class History*
  r RQ - v36 - Fall '96 - p56 [51-250]
Neufeld, Michael J - *The Rocket and the Reich*
    J Mil H - v60 - O '96 - p796+ [251-500]
Neugarten, Bernice L - *The Meanings of Age*
    LJ - v121 - N 1 '96 - p95 [51-250]
Neugeboren, Bernard - *Environmental Practice in the Human Services*
    Choice - v34 - O '96 - p368 [51-250]

Neugeboren, Jay - *Imagining Robert*
  BL - v93 - D 1 '96 - p628+ [51-250]
  BW - v27 - Mr 2 '97 - p6 [51-250]
  KR - v64 - D 15 '96 - p1786 [251-500]
  LJ - v121 - N 1 '96 - p95 [51-250]
  NYTBR - v102 - F 9 '97 - p10 [501+]
  PW - v243 - D 30 '96 - p48+ [51-250]
  Trib Bks - Ap 27 '97 - p3+ [501+]
Neuhauser, Rudolf - *F.M. Dostojevskij: Die Grossen Romane Und Erzahlungen*
  Slav R - v55 - Sum '96 - p510+ [501+]
Neuhold, Martin - *Achim Von Arnims Kunsttheorie Und Sein Roman Die Kronenwachter Im Kontext Ihrer Epoche*
  MLR - v91 - Jl '96 - p788+ [251-500]
Neuls-Bates, Carol - *Women in Music. Rev. Ed.*
  TLS - D 27 '96 - p20 [501+]
Neumaier, Diane - *Reframings: New American Feminist Photographies*
  Choice - v34 - S '96 - p114 [51-250]
  LJ - v121 - S 15 '96 - p65 [51-250]
Neuman, Johanna - *Lights, Camera, War*
  CJR - v35 - N '96 - p53+ [501+]
Neuman, Robert - *Robert De Cotte and the Perfection of Architecture in Eighteenth-Century France*
  FR - v70 - F '97 - p508+ [501+]
Neumann, A W - *Applied Surface Thermodynamics*
  SciTech - v20 - N '96 - p17 [51-250]
Neumann, Bernd - *Uwe Johnson*
  MLR - v91 - O '96 - p1052+ [501+]
Neumann, Diane - *Choosing a Divorce Mediator*
  BL - v93 - D 15 '96 - p697 [51-250]
  LJ - v121 - D '96 - p121+ [51-250]
Neumann, Dietrich - *Film Architecture*
  Si & So - v6 - N '96 - p34 [51-250]
  TLS - N 8 '96 - p32 [251-500]
Neumann, Joseph - *Historia De Las Sublevaciones Indias En La Tarahumara*
  HAHR - v77 - F '97 - p116+ [501+]
Neupert, Richard - *The End: Narration and Closure in the Cinema*
  FQ - v50 - Win '96 - p57+ [501+]
Neuroimmunomodulation
  p Nature - v383 - S 5 '96 - p36 [251-500]
The Neuroscientist: A Review Journal Bridging Neurobiology, Neurology and Psychiatry
  p Nature - v383 - S 5 '96 - p33 [501+]
Neuse, Steven M - *David E. Lilienthal: The Journey of an American Liberal*
  LJ - v121 - O 1 '96 - p90 [51-250]
  Nature - v386 - Ap 3 '97 - p453+ [501+]
Neusner, Jacob - *The Book of Jewish Wisdom*
  MEJ - v51 - Spr '97 - p312+ [51-250]
The Classics of Judaism
  JAAR - v65 - Spr '97 - p203+ [501+]
Dictionary of Judaism in the Biblical Period 450 B.C.E. to 600 C.E. Vols. 1-2
  r ARBA - v28 - '97 - p554+ [51-250]
  r Choice - v34 - S '96 - p94+ [251-500]
  yr SLJ - v42 - Ag '96 - p183 [51-250]
Forging a Common Future
  PW - v244 - Mr 24 '97 - p74 [51-250]
Judaisms and Their Messiahs at the Turn of the Christian Era
  Rel Ed - v91 - Fall '96 - p605 [1-50]
The Price of Excellence
  CLW - v67 - D '96 - p51+ [251-500]
Rabbinic Literature and the New Testament
  Rel St Rev - v22 - O '96 - p353 [51-250]
Revelation: The Torah and the Bible
  Rel St Rev - v23 - Ap '97 - p170 [51-250]
World Religions in America
  CH - v66 - Mr '97 - p215 [51-250]
Neustadt, Kathy - *Clambake: A History and Celebration of an American Tradition*
  CAY - v17 - Fall '96 - p13 [51-250]
Neutens, James J - *Research Techniques for the Health Sciences. 2nd Ed.*
  SciTech - v21 - Mr '97 - p46 [51-250]
Neuzil, Mark - *Mass Media and Environmental Conflict*
  Choice - v34 - My '97 - p1489 [51-250]
  R&R Bk N - v12 - F '97 - p75 [51-250]
Nevada County, Arkansas United States Census of 1880
  r EGH - v50 - N '96 - p163 [51-250]
Nevada Youth Risk Behavior Survey 1995
  J Gov Info - v23 - S '96 - p588 [51-250]
Nevaer, Louis E V - *New Business Opportunities in Latin America*
  Choice - v34 - S '96 - p173 [51-250]
Strategies for Business in Mexico
  HAHR - v77 - F '97 - p166+ [251-500]

Nevai, Lucia - *Normal: Stories*
  BL - v93 - Ap 1 '97 - p1282 [51-250]
  KR - v65 - F 15 '97 - p249 [251-500]
  PW - v244 - F 10 '97 - p64 [51-250]
  VLS - Spr '97 - p7+ [501+]
Nevanlinna, Saara - *St. Katherine of Alexandria*
  Specu - v71 - Jl '96 - p743+ [501+]
Neve, Kim A - *The Dopamine Receptors*
  SciTech - v21 - Mr '97 - p42 [51-250]
Neves, Joao Luis Cesar Das - *The Portuguese Economy*
  JEL - v34 - D '96 - p2032 [51-250]
Neville, Emily Cheney - *It's like This Cat*
  c JOYS - v10 - Fall '96 - p35+ [501+]
Neville, Jill - *The Day We Cut the Lavender*
  Obs - Ja 26 '97 - p18* [51-250]
  Spec - v277 - O 26 '96 - p54 [501+]
  TLS - N 22 '96 - p23 [501+]
Neville, Richard - *Out of My Mind*
  TLS - Ag 2 '96 - p14 [501+]
Neville, Robert C - *The Truth of Broken Symbols*
  R&R Bk N - v12 - F '97 - p8 [51-250]
Nevin, David - *1812 (Hill). Audio Version*
  y Kliatt - v31 - Mr '97 - p40+ [51-250]
Nevin, Michael - *World of Soccer*
  c Bks Keeps - Jl '96 - p23 [51-250]
  c Sch Lib - v44 - Ag '96 - p113 [51-250]
Nevin, Thomas - *Ernst Junger and Germany*
  Choice - v34 - Ap '97 - p1343 [51-250]
  LJ - v122 - Ja '97 - p121 [51-250]
  NS - v126 - F 7 '97 - p46+ [501+]
  Obs - F 16 '97 - p16* [501+]
  TLS - F 28 '97 - p3+ [501+]
Nevins, Francis M, Jr. - *Bar-20: The Life of Clarence E. Mulford, Creator of Hopalong Cassidy*
  JPC - v30 - Fall '96 - p214+ [251-500]
Into the Same River Twice
  Arm Det - v29 - Fall '96 - p481+ [251-500]
  KR - v64 - My 1 '96 - p646 [51-250]
Nevins, Linda - *Renaissance Moon*
  KR - v65 - F 15 '97 - p249 [251-500]
  LJ - v122 - Mr 15 '97 - p91 [51-250]
  PW - v244 - Mr 10 '97 - p51 [51-250]
Nevitte, Neil - *The Decline of Deference*
  Choice - v34 - Ap '97 - p1412 [51-250]
New, Elisa - *The Regenerate Lyric*
  MP - v94 - Ag '96 - p118+ [501+]
New, W H - *Science Lessons*
  Quill & Q - v62 - Ag '96 - p36 [251-500]
The New Age Information Guide to the Federal Government 1995
  r J Gov Info - v24 - Ja '97 - p59+ [501+]
New Approaches to Poverty Analysis and Policy. Vols. 1-3
  Econ J - v107 - Ja '97 - p225+ [501+]
The New Book of Knowledge 1996. Vols. 1-21
  cr BL - v93 - S 15 '96 - p274+ [501+]
The New Cambridge History of India. Vol. 3, Pt. 4
  Historian - v58 - Sum '96 - p884+ [501+]
A New Context, A New Vision
  J Gov Info - v23 - S '96 - p623+ [51-250]
The New Criterion
  p LMR - v15 - Win '96 - p38+ [501+]
New Delta Review
  p LMR - v15 - Fall '96 - p19+ [501+]
New Developments in Transmission and Driveline Design
  SciTech - v20 - D '96 - p80 [51-250]
The New Encyclopaedia Britannica. Vols. 1-32
  r BL - v93 - F 1 '97 - p960+ [501+]
The New Georgia Guide
  r BL - v93 - S 15 '96 - p212 [1-50]
The New Interpreter's Bible. Vol. 1
  Rel St Rev - v23 - Ja '97 - p57 [51-250]
The New Interpreter's Bible. Vol. 4
  Am - v176 - Mr 8 '97 - p24 [51-250]
The New Interpreter's Bible. Vols. 9-10
  Rel St Rev - v23 - Ap '97 - p179 [51-250]
New Jersey's Women Legislators 1921-1995
  r J Gov Info - v23 - S '96 - p589 [51-250]
New Left Review
  p Dis - v44 - Spr '97 - p103+ [501+]
New Lincoln Cent Book
  Coin W - v37 - S 30 '96 - p68 [51-250]
New Moon
  cp Par Ch - v20 - O '96 - p26 [1-50]
New Scientist
  p Utne R - Jl '96 - p118+ [51-250]
New Serial Titles 1953-
  r ASInt - v34 - O '96 - p15 [51-250]
The New Shape of World Affairs
  For Aff - v76 - Mr '97 - p184+ [251-500]

New Standard Encyclopedia 1996. Vols. 1-20
  yr BL - v93 - S 15 '96 - p276+ [501+]
New Statesman
  p Dis - v44 - Spr '97 - p103+ [501+]
New Stories from the South: The Year's Best 1996
  BL - v93 - S 15 '96 - p221 [51-250]
  S Liv - v32 - F '97 - p80 [51-250]
New Teacher Orientation
  H Sch M - v4 - S '96 - p49 [51-250]
New Way
  c TES - Jl 5 '96 - pR7 [501+]
New Writing 6
  TLS - Ap 11 '97 - p27 [501+]
New Writing Scotland 14
  Obs - N 24 '96 - p17* [501+]
New York Giving Guide 1996-1997
  r ChrPhil - v9 - D 12 '96 - p48 [51-250]
The New York State Directory 1996/1997
  r Choice - v34 - F '97 - p947+ [51-250]
The New York Times Film Reviews 1993-1994
  r ARBA - v28 - '97 - p516+ [51-250]
The New Yorker
  p LMR - v15 - Fall '96 - p24+ [501+]
New Zealand. Maori Language Commission - *Te Matatiki: Contemporary Maori Words. New, Rev. Ed.*
  r ARBA - v28 - '97 - p397 [251-500]
Newall, Alexander S - *British External Airmails Until 1934. 2nd Ed.*
  r Am Phil - v110 - N '96 - p1036+ [51-250]
Newall, Paul - *Japan and the City of London*
  TLS - O 25 '96 - p6 [501+]
Newark, Tim - *Warlords: Ancient-Celtic-Medieval*
  PW - v243 - S 16 '96 - p65+ [1-50]
Newberg, Paula R - *Judging the State*
  AHR - v101 - D '96 - p1608 [501+]
Newbery, Elizabeth - *Tudor Warship*
  c Bks Keeps - Ja '97 - p23+ [51-250]
  c Sch Lib - v45 - F '97 - p39 [51-250]
Newbery, Linda - *A Fear of Heights*
  y Sch Lib - v44 - Ag '96 - p120 [51-250]
The Newbery and Caldecott Awards. 1996 Ed.
  A Lib - v27 - Ag '96 - p70 [1-50]
  Sch Lib - v44 - N '96 - p176 [51-250]
  SLMQ - v24 - Sum '96 - p220 [51-250]
Newbigin, Lesslie - *Proper Confidence*
  Bks & Cult - v2 - Ja '96 - p27 [501+]
A Word in Season
  Bks & Cult - v2 - Ja '96 - p27 [501+]
Newbolt, Peter - *G.A. Henty 1832-1902*
  r Nine-C Lit - v51 - Mr '97 - p562 [51-250]
  r R&R Bk N - v12 - F '97 - p85 [51-250]
Newbould, Brian - *Schubert: The Music and the Man*
  BL - v93 - Ap 1 '97 - p1275 [51-250]
  LJ - v122 - Mr 15 '97 - p65 [51-250]
  NYTLa - v146 - Ap 17 '97 - pC33 [501+]
  PW - v244 - Ap 14 '97 - p65 [51-250]
  WSJ-Cent - v99 - My 13 '97 - pA21 [501+]
Newcastle, Margaret Cavendish - *Grounds of Natural Philosophy*
  R&R Bk N - v11 - D '96 - p68 [51-250]
Margaret Cavendish: Sociable Letters
  Choice - v34 - My '97 - p1497 [51-250]
Newcomb, Benjamin H - *Political Partisanship in the American Middle Colonies 1700-1776*
  AHR - v102 - F '97 - p169+ [501+]
  JIH - v27 - Spr '97 - p709+ [251-500]
  W&M Q - v53 - Jl '96 - p654+ [501+]
Newcomb, Jack - *The Ticket: Recollections of 50 Years of Sports Classics*
  PW - v244 - Mr 17 '97 - p62 [51-250]
Newcome, Zita - *Toddlerobics*
  c ECEJ - v24 - Win '96 - p109+ [51-250]
  c HB Guide - v7 - Fall '96 - p242 [51-250]
  c Magpies - v11 - S '96 - p26+ [51-250]
  c New Ad - v9 - Fall '96 - p327+ [501+]
Newdick, Christopher - *Who Should We Treat?*
  JEL - v34 - S '96 - p1441 [51-250]
Newdick, Jane - *The Tuscan Table*
  Books - v11 - Ap '97 - p20 [51-250]
Ultimate Christmas
  CLW - v67 - D '96 - p52+ [51-250]
  LJ - v121 - O 15 '96 - p56 [51-250]
  PW - v243 - S 2 '96 - p125 [51-250]
Newell, Clayton R - *Lee vs. McClellan*
  Parameters - v27 - Spr '97 - p177+ [501+]
Newell, Susan - *The Healthy Organization*
  Per Psy - v49 - Aut '96 - p726+ [51-250]
Newey, Vincent - *Mortal Pages, Literary Lives*
  Choice - v34 - Mr '97 - p1165 [51-250]
  Nine-C Lit - v51 - Mr '97 - p562 [51-250]
  TLS - N 8 '96 - p29 [501+]

Newfield, Christopher - *The Emerson Effect*
  R&R Bk N - v11 - N '96 - p72 [51-250]
Newfield, Nancy L - *Hummingbird Gardens*
  LJ - v121 - D '96 - p66 [1-50]
Newlands, Anne - *The Group of Seven and Tom Thomson*
  c Ch Bk News - v19 - Sum '96 - p32+ [251-500]
Newlands, Carole E - *Playing with Time*
  Rel St Rev - v23 - Ja '97 - p65 [51-250]
Newlin, Gary - *Simple Kaleidoscopes!*
  c Ch BWatch - v7 - F '97 - p8 [1-50]
Newlin, George - *Every Thing in Dickens*
  r ARBA - v28 - '97 - p453+ [251-500]
  r Choice - v34 - F '97 - p948 [51-250]
  r R&R Bk N - v11 - N '96 - p70 [51-250]
  Everyone in Dickens. Vols. 1-3
  r ARBA - v28 - '97 - p454 [251-500]
Newlin, Nicholas Paul - *Adelhelm Abbey*
  Rapport - v19 - 5 '96 - p31 [251-500]
Newlyn, Lucy - *Paradise Lost and the Romantic Reader*
  Ren Q - v49 - Aut '96 - p658+ [501+]
Newman, Barbara - *From Virile Woman to WomanChrist*
  CH - v65 - S '96 - p465+ [501+]
  CHR - v82 - Jl '96 - p525+ [501+]
  JR - v76 - O '96 - p635+ [501+]
  Specu - v71 - O '96 - p988+ [501+]
Newman, Christopher - *Knock-Off (Murdock). Audio Version*
  y Kliatt - v30 - S '96 - p49 [51-250]
Newman, Donald J - *James Boswell's Psychological Interpretations*
  Albion - v28 - Fall '96 - p496+ [501+]
Newman, Graham - *Essential Skills in Maths. Bks. 1-3*
  y TES - Mr 21 '97 - pR10 [51-250]
Newman, Harvey B - *History of Original Ideas and Basic Discoveries in Particle Physics*
  Sci - v275 - F 7 '97 - p788 [251-500]
  SciTech - v20 - N '96 - p19 [51-250]
Newman, James L - *The Peopling of Africa*
  AHR - v101 - D '96 - p1592 [251-500]
Newman, Jay - *Religion vs. Television*
  CC - v113 - N 20 '96 - p1134+ [501+]
  Choice - v34 - Ja '97 - p812 [51-250]
  R&R Bk N - v11 - D '96 - p5 [51-250]
Newman, John, 1942- - *Vietnam War Literature. 2nd Ed.*
  r RQ - v36 - Win '96 - p225 [1-50]
Newman, John Henry - *The Idea of a University*
  Am - v175 - S 21 '96 - p32 [251-500]
  BW - v26 - Ag 18 '96 - p12 [1-50]
  TES - Ja 24 '97 - p8* [51-250]
  TLS - Ja 24 '97 - p9 [501+]
  WSJ-MW - v77 - S 16 '96 - pA14 [501+]
Newman, Karen, 1949- - *Fetal Positions*
  SciTech - v20 - N '96 - p52 [51-250]
Newman, Katherine D - *Never without a Song*
  Notes - v53 - S '96 - p47+ [501+]
Newman, Kim - *The BFI Companion to Horror*
  r TLS - Ap 11 '97 - p20 [501+]
  The Bloody Red Baron
  y Kliatt - v31 - My '97 - p14 [51-250]
  PW - v243 - D 2 '96 - p56 [1-50]
Newman, Leslea - *Fat Chance*
  y Kliatt - v30 - N '96 - p9+ [51-250]
  Remember That (Illus. by Karen Ritz)
  c HB Guide - v7 - Fall '96 - p269+ [1-50]
Newman, Marjorie - *Yo Ho Ho!*
  c TES - Jl 5 '96 - pR6 [1-50]
Newman, Martha G - *The Boundaries of Charity*
  CH - v66 - Mr '97 - p95+ [501+]
  Choice - v34 - O '96 - p298 [51-250]
  HRNB - v25 - Fall '96 - p25 [501+]
  RR - v56 - Mr '97 - p220 [1-50]
Newman, Michael - *Defining the Enemy*
  AE - v47 - Win '97 - p117+ [501+]
Newman, Michael, 1946- - *Democracy, Sovereignty and the European Union*
  Choice - v34 - F '97 - p1032 [51-250]
  R&R Bk N - v11 - N '96 - p49 [51-250]
  TLS - S 20 '96 - p13 [501+]
Newman, P R - *The Old Service*
  EHR - v111 - S '96 - p984+ [251-500]
  Sev Cent N - v54 - Spr '96 - p21+ [501+]
Newman, Richard - *Words like Freedom*
  Choice - v34 - D '96 - p677 [51-250]
Newman, Robert - *Centuries' Ends, Narrative Means*
  Choice - v34 - F '97 - p960 [51-250]
Newman, Robert D, 1951- - *Pedagogy, Praxis, Ulysses*
  ELT - v40 - 2 '97 - p243+ [501+]
  Transgressions of Reading
  MLR - v91 - O '96 - p950+ [501+]

Newman, Robert P - *Truman and the Hiroshima Cult*
  PHR - v65 - Ag '96 - p502+ [251-500]
  Pres SQ - v26 - Fall '96 - p1177+ [501+]
  QJS - v83 - My '97 - p257+ [501+]
  RP - v58 - Sum '96 - p659+ [501+]
Newman, Rochelle - *Space, Structure and Form*
  Math T - v89 - O '96 - p610 [51-250]
Newman, Roger K - *Hugo Black: A Biography*
  AHR - v101 - O '96 - p1305 [501+]
Newman, Saul - *Ethnoregional Conflict in Democracies*
  AAPSS-A - v550 - Mr '97 - p175+ [501+]
Newman, Sharan - *Strong as Death*
  y BL - v93 - S 1 '96 - p68 [51-250]
Newman, Shirlee P - *The Creek*
  c HB Guide - v8 - Spr '97 - p178 [51-250]
Newman, Velda - *Velda Newman: A Painter's Approach to Quilt Design*
  LJ - v121 - D '96 - p92 [51-250]
Newman, William R - *Gehennical Fire*
  Ren Q - v50 - Spr '97 - p331+ [501+]
Newmeyer, Frederick J - *Generative Linguistics*
  R&R Bk N - v11 - N '96 - p62 [51-250]
Newport, Kenneth G C - *The Sources and Sitz Im Leben of Matthew 23*
  Rel St Rev - v23 - Ap '97 - p180 [51-250]
Newsinger, John - *Fenianism in Mid-Victorian Britain*
  Historian - v59 - Fall '96 - p201+ [251-500]
Newsletter Inago
  p Sm Pr R - v28 - Je '96 - p17 [51-250]
Newsom, Iris - *Performing Arts: Music*
  AB - v98 - D 9 '96 - p2002 [51-250]
Newsom, Vera - *Emily Bronte Re-Collects and Other Poems*
  Aust Bk R - Jl '96 - p56 [501+]
Newson, Lesley - *Growing Older*
  c Sch Lib - v44 - N '96 - p164 [51-250]
  Language
  c JB - v60 - O '96 - p204 [51-250]
  c Sch Lib - v44 - N '96 - p164 [51-250]
  Sleep
  c Sch Lib - v44 - N '96 - p164 [51-250]
  Time
  c Sch Lib - v44 - N '96 - p164 [51-250]
Newson, Linda A - *Life and Death in Early Colonial Ecuador*
  AHR - v101 - D '96 - p1660+ [501+]
  HAHR - v76 - Ag '96 - p565+ [501+]
  Historian - v59 - Win '97 - p437+ [251-500]
Newspapers in Microform: U.S. Newspapers 1948-1983. Vols. 1-2
  r ASInt - v34 - O '96 - p16 [51-250]
Newsplan: Report of the Newsplan Project in the London and South Eastern Library Region (Laser), January 1992-December 1995
  LAR - v98 - N '96 - p594 [51-250]
Newth, Mette - *The Abduction*
  y SLJ - v42 - N '96 - p41 [1-50]
Newton, Adam Zachary - *Narrative Ethics*
  Critm - v38 - Sum '96 - p485+ [501+]
Newton, Candelas - *Understanding Federico Garcia Lorca*
  MLR - v91 - O '96 - p1020 [251-500]
Newton, David, 1933- - *Tainted Justice 1914*
  Beav - v76 - D '96 - p46 [51-250]
Newton, David E - *Environmental Justice*
  r ARBA - v28 - '97 - p650+ [51-250]
  r Choice - v34 - Mr '97 - p1141 [51-250]
  yr LJ - v122 - F 1 '97 - p74 [51-250]
  r R&R Bk N - v12 - F '97 - p59 [1-50]
  Makers of Modern Science. Vol. 9
  J Chem Ed - v74 - Ap '97 - p380 [51-250]
  Violence and the Media
  yr ARBA - v28 - '97 - p345+ [251-500]
  r Choice - v34 - F '97 - p948 [51-250]
  r R&R Bk N - v11 - D '96 - p59 [51-250]
  yr SLJ - v42 - D '96 - p148 [51-250]
Newton, Helmut - *The Best of Helmut Newton*
  BWatch - v18 - Mr '97 - p10 [1-50]
  Ent W - D 20 '96 - p70 [51-250]
Newton, Isaac, Sir - *Newton's Principia*
  Isis - v87 - D '96 - p701+ [501+]
  Phys Today - v49 - D '96 - p58 [501+]
Newton, Jill - *Crocodile*
  c PW - v244 - Mr 10 '97 - p68 [51-250]
  Elephant
  c PW - v244 - Mr 10 '97 - p68 [51-250]
  Giraffe
  c PW - v244 - Mr 10 '97 - p68 [51-250]
  Penguin
  c PW - v244 - Mr 10 '97 - p68 [51-250]

Newton, John Sefton - *The Man Who Painted Women*
  Aust Bk R - Jl '96 - p50+ [501+]
  Wogfood: An Oral History with Recipes (Illus. by Grenville Turner)
  Aust Bk R - N '96 - p21 [501+]
Newton, Judith - *Starting Over*
  VS - v39 - Aut '95 - p84+ [501+]
Newton, Merlin Owen - *Armed with the Constitution*
  AHR - v101 - D '96 - p1642 [501+]
Newton, Miller - *Adolescence: Guiding Youth through the Perilous Ordeal*
  Soc Ser R - v70 - S '96 - p501+ [51-250]
Newton, Natika - *Foundations of Understanding*
  Choice - v34 - My '97 - p1580 [51-250]
Newton, Sam - *The Origins of Beowulf*
  Folkl - v107 - '96 - p118 [251-500]
Newton, Scott - *Profits of Peace*
  Choice - v34 - D '96 - p671+ [51-250]
Newton, Verne - *FDR and the Holocaust*
  SE - v60 - S '96 - p302 [51-250]
Next Generation
  p LJ - v121 - O 15 '96 - p95 [51-250]
Ng, Jack - *Julian Schwinger: The Physicist, the Teacher and the Man*
  y Phys Today - v49 - O '96 - p68 [501+]
Ng, Linda Fung-Yee - *Three Chinese Economies*
  JEL - v34 - D '96 - p2128 [51-250]
Ngaosyvathn, Pheuiphanh - *Strategic Involvement and International Partnership*
  Pac A - v69 - Sum '96 - p297 [51-250]
Ngara, Emmanuel - *New Writing from Southern Africa*
  WLT - v71 - Win '97 - p204+ [501+]
Ngien, Dennis - *The Suffering of God According to Martin Luther's Theologia Crucis*
  Rel St Rev - v23 - Ja '97 - p81 [51-250]
Ngo, Nguyen Dung - *Am Ban*
  BL - v93 - S 1 '96 - p70 [51-250]
Ngoc, Thuy - *Qua Bong Tuoi Tho*
  BL - v93 - My 15 '97 - p1568 [1-50]
Nguyen, Ba Trac - *Ngon Co Bong Toan Tap*
  BL - v93 - S 1 '96 - p70 [51-250]
Nguyen, Chi Thien - *Hoa Dia Nguc*
  BL - v93 - My 15 '97 - p1568 [1-50]
Nguyen, Dinh Hoa - *NTC's Vietnamese-English Dictionary. New Updated Ed.*
  r ARBA - v28 - '97 - p403+ [51-250]
Nguyen, Dinh Toan - *Dong Co*
  BL - v93 - S 1 '96 - p70 [51-250]
Nguyen, Duc An - *Sau Con Mua*
  BL - v93 - My 15 '97 - p1568 [1-50]
Nguyen, Hung T - *A First Course in Fuzzy Logic*
  Choice - v34 - Mr '97 - p1195+ [51-250]
  SciTech - v20 - D '96 - p12 [51-250]
Nguyen, Ngoc Nga - *Kiep Phu Sinh*
  BL - v93 - My 15 '97 - p1568 [1-50]
Nguyen, Ngoc Ngan - *Nang Qua Pho Cu*
  BL - v93 - My 15 '97 - p1568 [1-50]
  Nhin Lai Mot Thap Nien
  BL - v93 - S 1 '96 - p70 [51-250]
Nguyen, Sa - *Lich Su Ngan Nguoi Viet*
  BL - v93 - S 1 '96 - p70 [51-250]
Nguyen, Thanh T - *Poems from Captured Documents*
  TranslRevS - v1 - My '95 - p3 [51-250]
Nguyen, Thi Ngoc Dung - *Phuong Van No Ben Troi Ha Noi*
  BL - v93 - S 1 '96 - p70 [51-250]
  Sai Gon Nang Nho Mua Thuong
  BL - v93 - My 15 '97 - p1568 [1-50]
Nguyen, Tuong Bach - *Tren Song Hong Cuon Cuon*
  BL - v93 - My 15 '97 - p1568 [1-50]
Nguyen, Van Huy - *Nguoi Hoa Tai Vietnam*
  BL - v93 - S 1 '96 - p70 [51-250]
Nguyen, Van Ly - *Ba Chi Em Nha Ho Tong*
  BL - v93 - My 15 '97 - p1568 [1-50]
Nguyen, Vu - *Mot Ngay Co 26 Gio*
  BL - v93 - My 15 '97 - p1568 [1-50]
Nhat Hanh, Thich - *The Blooming of a Lotus*
  TranslRevS - v1 - My '95 - p33+ [51-250]
  The Heart of the Buddha's Teaching
  PW - v243 - N 11 '96 - p69 [51-250]
  Living Buddha, Living Christ
  CC - v113 - O 16 '96 - p964+ [501+]
  OS - v32 - Jl '96 - p43 [51-250]
  The Stone Boy and Other Stories
  WLT - v71 - Win '97 - p234 [501+]
Niall, Mani - *Sweet and Natural Baking*
  y Kliatt - v31 - Ja '97 - p32 [51-250]
Niblo, Stephen R - *War, Diplomacy, and Development*
  HAHR - v76 - Ag '96 - p616 [251-500]

Niccoli, Ottavia - *Il Seme Della Violenza*
Ren Q - v49 - Aut '96 - p598+ [501+]
Six Ct J - v27 - Win '96 - p1159+ [501+]
Nice, David - *Edward Elgar: An Essential Guide to His Life and Work*
y BL - v93 - My 1 '97 - p1472 [51-250]
Nice, David C, 1952- - *Policy Innovation in State Government*
Pol Stud J - v24 - Sum '96 - p321+ [501+]
Niche Markets as a Rural Development Strategy
J Gov Info - v23 - S '96 - p674+ [51-250]
Nichiren - *Letters of Nichiren*
Tric - v6 - Win '96 - p112+ [501+]
Nichol, James P - *Diplomacy in the Former Soviet Republics*
APSR - v90 - S '96 - p692+ [501+]
Russ Rev - v55 - O '96 - p722 [251-500]
Nicholas, Jane - *Stumpwork Embroidery*
BL - v93 - F 15 '97 - p992+ [51-250]
LJ - v122 - Ap 15 '97 - p79 [51-250]
Nicholas, Jeremy - *The Classic FM Guide to Classical Music*
r BL - v93 - N 1 '96 - p534 [251-500]
r Choice - v34 - N '96 - p434 [51-250]
Nicholas, Kilmer - *Harmony in Flesh and Black*
Arm Det - v29 - Fall '96 - p402 [51-250]
Nicholas, Sian - *The Echo of War*
Choice - v34 - N '96 - p519 [51-250]
Nicholas, Ted - *Advanced Materials*
SciTech - v21 - Mr '97 - p76 [51-250]
Nicholas II, Emperor of Russia - *A Lifelong Passion*
BW - v27 - Ap 6 '97 - p6 [501+]
KR - v65 - Ja 1 '97 - p43+ [251-500]
LJ - v122 - Ap 1 '97 - p100+ [51-250]
Obs - N 10 '96 - p16* [501+]
PW - v244 - Ja 13 '97 - p67 [51-250]
Spec - v277 - O 12 '96 - p47+ [501+]
TLS - D 6 '96 - p10+ [501+]
Nicholls, C S - *The Dictionary of National Biography 1986-1990*
r ARBA - v28 - '97 - p19+ [251-500]
r CSM - v88 - N 21 '96 - pB2 [51-250]
r Lon R Bks - v18 - Ag 22 '96 - p21 [501+]
r R&R Bk N - v12 - F '97 - p14 [51-250]
r TLS - N 29 '96 - p14 [1-50]
Nicholls, David - *God and Government in an Age of Reason*
R&R Bk N - v12 - F '97 - p9 [51-250]
The Lost Prime Minister
JMH - v69 - Mr '97 - p146+ [501+]
The Pluralist State
CH - v65 - S '96 - p530+ [501+]
Nicholls, Judith - *Otherworlds: Poems of the Mysterious (Illus. by Shirley Felts)*
c Bks Keeps - v100 - S '96 - p12 [51-250]
c TES - N 8 '96 - p9* [51-250]
Who Am I? (Illus. by Robin Davies)
c Sch Lib - v45 - F '97 - p20 [51-250]
Nicholls, Peter - *Modernisms: A Literary Guide*
r ELT - v40 - 1 '97 - p105+ [501+]
J Am St - v30 - D '96 - p482+ [501+]
Nicholls, Stan - *The Book of Shadows*
y Sch Lib - v44 - N '96 - p171 [51-250]
Nicholls, William - *Christian Antisemitism*
Rel Ed - v91 - Fall '96 - p607 [51-250]
Nichols, Ann Eljenholm - *Seeable Signs*
EHR - v112 - F '97 - p179 [251-500]
Specu - v71 - O '96 - p991+ [501+]
Nichols, Bill - *Blurred Boundaries*
FQ - v49 - Sum '96 - p41+ [501+]
Nichols, Bradford - *Pthreads Programming*
SciTech - v20 - D '96 - p11 [51-250]
Nichols, Bridget - *Liturgical Hermeneutics*
R&R Bk N - v12 - F '97 - p11 [51-250]
Nichols, Francis W - *Christianity and the Stranger*
Rel St Rev - v22 - O '96 - p338 [51-250]
Nichols, Grace - *Can I Buy a Slice of Sky?*
c TES - N 8 '96 - p9* [51-250]
Give Yourself a Hug (Illus. by Kim Harley)
c Bks Keeps - Jl '96 - p12 [51-250]
Nichols, Jack - *The Gay Agenda*
LJ - v122 - F 1 '97 - p97+ [51-250]
PW - v243 - S 16 '96 - p63 [51-250]
Nichols, John A - *Medieval Religious Women. Vol. 3, Bks. 1-2*
JR - v77 - Ja '97 - p135 [251-500]
RR - v56 - Mr '97 - p220 [1-50]
Nichols, Judith E - *Global Demographics*
ChrPhil - v8 - Jl 11 '96 - p44 [51-250]

Nichols, Michael - *Keepers of the Kingdom*
y BL - v93 - F 15 '97 - p985 [501+]
LJ - v122 - Ja '97 - p139 [51-250]
Nichols, Michael P - *Family Therapy. 3rd Ed.*
Fam Relat - v45 - Jl '96 - p352 [251-500]
No Place to Hide
Adoles - v31 - Fall '96 - p754 [51-250]
Nichols, Nichelle - *Beyond Uhura*
Lon R Bks - v18 - My 23 '96 - p34+ [501+]
Saturn's Child
Bl S - v26 - Sum '96 - p67 [51-250]
Nichols, Nina Da Vinci - *Pirandello and Film*
Theat J - v48 - D '96 - p526+ [501+]
Nichols, Peter - *Sea Change*
KR - v65 - Ap 1 '97 - p530 [251-500]
LJ - v122 - My 1 '97 - p129 [51-250]
PW - v244 - My 5 '97 - p185 [51-250]
Nichols, Preston - *Encounter in the Pleiades*
BWatch - v17 - S '96 - p12 [51-250]
Nichols, Stephen G - *The Whole Book*
Choice - v34 - My '97 - p1492 [51-250]
Nicholson, Colin - *Writing and the Rise of Finance*
Albion - v28 - Fall '96 - p490+ [501+]
EHR - v112 - F '97 - p207+ [251-500]
RES - v47 - N '96 - p589+ [501+]
Nicholson, D H S - *The Oxford Book of English Mystical Verse*
BW - v27 - Ap 13 '97 - p12 [51-250]
Nicholson, Dorinda Makanaonalani - *Pearl Harbor Child*
c Ch BWatch - v6 - N '96 - p8 [51-250]
Nicholson, Emma - *Secret Society Inside--and Outside--the Conservative Party*
CR - v270 - F '97 - p110 [1-50]
Nicholson, Geoff - *Footsucker*
BW - v26 - D 29 '96 - p9 [501+]
NY - v72 - Ja 6 '97 - p73 [501+]
Nicholson, H B - *Mixteca-Puebla: Discoveries and Research in Mesoamerican Art and Archaeology*
LA Ant - v7 - Mr '96 - p87+ [501+]
Nicholson, John - *The Cruelest Place on Earth*
c Cur R - v36 - F '97 - p12 [51-250]
Nicholson, Linda J - *Feminism/Postmodernism*
JPC - v29 - Spr '96 - p245+ [51-250]
Nicholson, Mavis - *What Did You Do in the War, Mummy?*
CR - v269 - D '96 - p333 [1-50]
Nicholson, Michael - *Causes and Consequences in International Relations*
Choice - v34 - O '96 - p357+ [501+]
Nicholson, Nigel - *The Blackwell Encyclopedic Dictionary of Organizational Behavior*
r Per Psy - v49 - Aut '96 - p724+ [501+]
Nicholson, Stuart - *Billie Holiday*
Rapport - v19 - 4 '96 - p14+ [501+]
Ella Fitzgerald 1917-1996
TLS - N 22 '96 - p31 [251-500]
Nichter, Mark - *Anthropological Approaches to the Study of Ethnomedicine*
RA - v25 - 3 '96 - p167+ [501+]
Nickel, Barbara Kathleen - *The Secret Wish of Nannerl Mozart*
c Can CL - v22 - Fall '96 - p127+ [501+]
Nickelodeon
cp Par Ch - v20 - O '96 - p15 [1-50]
Nickerson, Camilla - *Fashion: Photography of the Nineties*
LJ - v122 - F 15 '97 - p131 [51-250]
VLS - Win '96 - p31 [251-500]
VV - v52 - Ja 28 '97 - p48+ [501+]
Nickerson, Sheila - *Disappearances: A Map*
PW - v244 - Mr 17 '97 - p81 [1-50]
Nicklaus, Jack - *Golf My Way*
LJ - v121 - O 1 '96 - p53 [1-50]
Jack Nicklaus: My Story
BL - v93 - Mr 15 '97 - p1202 [51-250]
LJ - v122 - Ap 15 '97 - p87 [51-250]
PW - v244 - Mr 10 '97 - p58 [51-250]
Nickson, Chris - *Keanu Reeves*
y Kliatt - v30 - Jl '96 - p23 [51-250]
Nickson, R Andrew - *Local Government in Latin America*
HAHR - v76 - N '96 - p835+ [251-500]
Nicol, Donald M - *The Byzantine Lady*
Specu - v71 - Jl '96 - p745+ [501+]
The Reluctant Emperor
Choice - v34 - N '96 - p519 [51-250]
TLS - F 7 '97 - p28 [501+]
Nicol, Mike - *Horseman*
LATBR - Mr 17 '96 - p6 [501+]
NYTBR - v101 - N 24 '96 - p32 [51-250]
PW - v243 - S 2 '96 - p122 [1-50]

Nicolaides, Roy - *Maple: A Comprehensive Introduction*
Choice - v34 - Mr '97 - p1196 [51-250]
Nicolaou, K C - *Classics in Total Synthesis*
New Sci - v153 - Mr 1 '97 - p38 [51-250]
Nicolaus, De Autricuria - *Nicholas of Autrecourt: His Correspondence with Master Giles and Bernard of Arezzo*
Specu - v71 - O '96 - p990+ [501+]
Nicolay, John G - *An Oral History of Abraham Lincoln*
Choice - v34 - N '96 - p526+ [51-250]
Nicolet-Monnier, Michel - *Quantitative Risk Assessment of Hazardous Materials Transport Systems*
SciTech - v20 - D '96 - p58 [51-250]
Nicolis, G - *Introduction to Nonlinear Science*
Am Sci - v84 - N '96 - p610+ [501+]
J Chem Ed - v73 - Ap '96 - pA93 [51-250]
y New Sci - v151 - S 28 '96 - p44+ [501+]
Nicoll, David - *Fearsome Hunters of the Wild*
c HB Guide - v8 - Spr '97 - p119 [51-250]
c Sch Lib - v45 - F '97 - p40 [51-250]
Nicolle, David - *Christendom and Its Neighbours*
HT - v46 - O '96 - p55 [1-50]
Medieval Warfare Source Book. Vol. 1
PW - v243 - S 16 '96 - p66 [1-50]
Nicollier, Alain - *Dictionnaire Des Ecrivains Suisses D'Expression Francaise. Vols. 1-2*
r MLR - v92 - Ja '97 - p210+ [501+]
Nicollier-De Weck, Beatrice - *Hubert Languet 1518-1581*
Six Ct J - v27 - Win '96 - p1130+ [501+]
Nicols, Jim - *Golf Resorts*
r BL - v93 - S 15 '96 - p210 [1-50]
Nicolson, Harold George, Sir - *Diaries and Letters 1930-1964*
CR - v269 - N '96 - p277 [51-250]
Nicolson, Nigel - *Mary Curzon*
Spec - v278 - Mr 1 '97 - p32+ [501+]
Ni Dhomhnaill, Nuala - *Pharaoh's Daughter*
TranslRevS - v1 - My '95 - p24 [1-50]
Niditch, Susan - *Ancient Israelite Religion*
KR - v65 - Mr 1 '97 - p361 [51-250]
Nie, Hualing - *Lu Yuan Qing Shi*
BL - v93 - My 1 '97 - p1484 [1-50]
Niebuhr, Gary Warren - *Reader's Guide to the Private Eye Novel*
r RQ - v36 - Win '96 - p217 [51-250]
Niebuhr, H Richard - *Theology, History, and Culture*
CC - v114 - Ap 2 '97 - p346+ [501+]
Choice - v34 - S '96 - p145 [51-250]
Rel St Rev - v22 - O '96 - p335 [51-250]
Niebuhr, Reinhold - *Love and Justice*
Rel St Rev - v23 - Ap '97 - p157 [51-250]
Niederhoffer, Victor - *The Education of a Speculator*
Barron's - v77 - Ja 27 '97 - p49 [501+]
BL - v93 - F 15 '97 - p984 [51-250]
Bus W - Mr 31 '97 - p22 [51-250]
KR - v64 - D 15 '96 - p1787 [251-500]
LJ - v122 - Ap 15 '97 - p93 [51-250]
NYTBR - v102 - Mr 23 '97 - p20 [501+]
PW - v243 - D 16 '96 - p49 [51-250]
WSJ-Cent - v99 - My 12 '97 - pA12 [51-250]
Niehoff, Arthur - *Takeover: How Euroman Changed the World*
BL - v92 - Ag '96 - p1878 [51-250]
Niehoff, Maren - *The Figure of Joseph in Post-Biblical Jewish Literature*
Rel St Rev - v23 - Ja '97 - p87+ [51-250]
Nielsen, Jorgen S - *Muslims in Western Europe. 2nd Ed.*
MEJ - v50 - Sum '96 - p455+ [51-250]
Nielsen, Kai - *Exploitation*
Choice - v34 - My '97 - p1547 [51-250]
Nielsen, Lee Brattland - *Blast Off!*
c Cur R - v36 - Ap '97 - p3* [51-250]
Nielsen, Marianne O - *Native Americans, Crime, and Justice*
R&R Bk N - v12 - F '97 - p22 [51-250]
Nielsen, Niels C - *Fundamentalism, Mythos, and World Religions*
JAAR - v65 - Spr '97 - p193+ [501+]
Nielsen, Ruth - *Employers' Prerogatives*
JEL - v34 - D '96 - p2080 [51-250]
Nielsen, Waldemar A - *Inside American Philanthropy*
ChrPhil - v8 - S 19 '96 - p51 [51-250]
CSM - v89 - D 9 '96 - p15 [501+]
Niemeyer, Lucian - *Shenandoah: Daughter of the Stars*
JSH - v62 - N '96 - p860 [51-250]
Niemiec, Maciej - *Male Wiersze 1976-1994*
WLT - v70 - Sum '96 - p727+ [501+]
Nienaber, Christoph A - *Imaging and Intervention in Cardiology*
SciTech - v20 - N '96 - p47 [51-250]

Niesink, Raymond J M - *Toxicology: Principles and Applications*
    SciTech - v20 - S '96 - p29 [51-250]
Nieto, Adelaida - *Olvidando Olvidos*
    WLT - v70 - Sum '96 - p666 [501+]
Nieto-Vesperinas, M - *Optics at the Nanometer Scale*
    SciTech - v20 - D '96 - p29 [51-250]
Nietzke, Ann - *Natalie on the Street*
    NAR - v281 - S '96 - p48 [501+]
Nietzsche, Friedrich - *On the Genealogy of Morality and Other Writings*
    Ethics - v107 - O '96 - p180+ [51-250]
    Philosophical Writings
    TranslRevS - v2 - D '96 - p26 [51-250]
Nieuwkerk, Karin Van - *A Trade Like Any Other*
    Dance RJ - v28 - Fall '96 - p77+ [501+]
Nigeria Democracy Action Update
    p WorldV - v12 - Jl '96 - p12 [51-250]
Nightingale, Andrea Wilson - *Genres in Dialogue*
    Choice - v34 - S '96 - p142 [51-250]
Nightingale, Demetra Smith - *The Work Alternative*
    ILRR - v50 - O '96 - p163+ [501+]
Nightingale, Florence - *Florence Nightingale in Egypt and Greece*
    Choice - v34 - My '97 - p1533 [51-250]
    SciTech - v21 - Mr '97 - p68 [51-250]
Nightingale, Pamela - *A Medieval Mercantile Community*
    TLS - Jl 7 '96 - p32 [501+]
Nightingale, Sandy - *Cider Apples (Illus. by Sandy Nightingale)*
    c BL - v93 - S 1 '96 - p144 [51-250]
    c HB Guide - v8 - Spr '97 - p41 [51-250]
    c Sch Lib - v45 - F '97 - p20 [51-250]
    c SLJ - v42 - N '96 - p89+ [51-250]
    c Smith - v27 - N '96 - p168+ [1-50]
Nightingale, Steven - *The Lost Coast*
    Rapport - v19 - 4 '96 - p23 [251-500]
Niimi, Hideyuki - *Microcirculatory Approach to Asian Traditional Medicine*
    SciTech - v20 - D '96 - p37 [51-250]
Nijkamp, Peter - *Telematics and Transport Behaviour*
    JEL - v35 - Mr '97 - p252 [51-250]
Nijssen, Rombout - *Bibliographie Courante Archivistique*
    r Archiv - Spr '96 - p255 [251-500]
Nikaido, Hukukane - *Prices, Cycles, and Growth*
    JEL - v34 - S '96 - p1421 [51-250]
    R&R Bk N - v12 - F '97 - p34 [51-250]
Nikitin, Yakov - *Asymptotic Efficiency of Nonparametric Tests*
    SIAM Rev - v39 - Mr '97 - p162+ [251-500]
Nikkel, David H - *Panentheism in Hartshorne and Tillich*
    Choice - v34 - S '96 - p142 [51-250]
Nikolajeva, Maria - *Children's Literature Comes of Age*
    Emerg Lib - v24 - S '96 - p38+ [501+]
Nikola-Lisa, W - *America: My Land, Your Land, Our Land*
    c PW - v244 - My 5 '97 - p209 [51-250]
    Bein' with You This Way (Illus. by Michael Bryant)
    c ECEJ - v24 - Spr '97 - p176+ [51-250]
    One Hole in the Road (Illus. by Dan Yaccarino)
    c BL - v93 - O 1 '96 - p359 [51-250]
    c CBRS - v25 - O '96 - p16 [1-50]
    c HB Guide - v8 - Spr '97 - p41 [51-250]
    c NYTBR - v102 - Mr 16 '97 - p26 [501+]
    c SLJ - v42 - O '96 - p103 [51-250]
    Tangletalk (Illus. by Jessica Clerk)
    c BL - v93 - My 1 '97 - p1500 [51-250]
    c PW - v244 - Mr 17 '97 - p82 [51-250]
Nile, Norman H - *Education and Democratic Citizenship in America*
    Choice - v34 - Mr '97 - p1241 [51-250]
Niles, Blair - *Black Haiti*
    Bks & Cult - v3 - Ja '97 - p8+ [501+]
Niles, Douglas - *Breach the Watershed*
    y Kliatt - v30 - N '96 - p14 [51-250]
    Darkenheight
    y Kliatt - v31 - Mr '97 - p20 [51-250]
Nilsen, Anna - *Drive Your Car (Illus. by Tony Wells)*
    c Ch BWatch - v6 - Jl '96 - p4 [1-50]
    c HB Guide - v7 - Fall '96 - p242 [51-250]
    Drive Your Tractor (Illus. by Tony Wells)
    c Ch BWatch - v6 - Jl '96 - p4 [1-50]
    c HB Guide - v7 - Fall '96 - p242 [51-250]
Nilsen, Don Lee Fred - *Humor in Irish Literature*
    r Choice - v34 - My '97 - p1478 [51-250]
    r Nine-C Lit - v51 - Mr '97 - p562 [51-250]
    r R&R Bk N - v12 - F '97 - p87 [51-250]
Nilson, Don Lee Fred - *Humor in Irish Literature*
    r ILS - v16 - Spr '97 - p35 [51-250]
    Humor Scholarship
    r JPC - v29 - Spr '96 - p247+ [51-250]

Nilson, Jon - *Nothing beyond the Necessary*
    CLW - v66 - Je '96 - p33+ [501+]
    Theol St - v57 - S '96 - p572+ [251-500]
Nilsson, Annika - *Ultraviolet Reflections*
    New Sci - v153 - Mr 1 '97 - p38 [1-50]
Nilsson, Eleanor - *Outside Permission*
    y Aust Bk R - N '96 - p62+ [501+]
Nilsson, Lennart - *How Was I Born? (Illus. by Lennart Nilsson)*
    c PW - v243 - D 30 '96 - p68 [1-50]
Nimier, Marie - *The Giraffe*
    TranslRevS - v2 - D '96 - p23 [51-250]
    Hypnotism Made Easy
    TranslRevS - v2 - D '96 - p23 [51-250]
Nimmo, Dan - *Political Commentators in the United States in the 20th Century*
    r LJ - v122 - Mr 15 '97 - p57 [51-250]
Nimmo, Jenny - *Alien on the 99th Floor (Illus. by M Chatterton)*
    c JB - v60 - Ag '96 - p150 [51-250]
    The Bronze Trumpeter
    c Bks Keeps - Ja '97 - p25 [51-250]
    Delilah and the Dishwasher Dogs (Illus. by Ben Cort)
    c JB - v60 - Ag '96 - p150+ [51-250]
    Delilah and the Dogspell (Illus. by Emma Chichester Clark)
    c Bks Keeps - Jl '96 - p11+ [51-250]
    Griffin's Castle
    c CCB-B - v50 - Ap '97 - p291+ [51-250]
    c KR - v65 - Ap 1 '97 - p560 [51-250]
    c RT - v50 - F '97 - p423 [51-250]
    c TES - Jl 5 '96 - pR8 [51-250]
    The Witch's Tears (Illus. by Paul Howard)
    c JB - v60 - O '96 - p194 [251-500]
    c Magpies - v11 - Jl '96 - p32 [51-250]
    c Sch Lib - v44 - Ag '96 - p108 [51-250]
Nimoy, Leonard - *I Am Spock*
    BWatch - v17 - N '96 - p8 [1-50]
    Ent W - N 8 '96 - p63 [51-250]
    Lon R Bks - v18 - My 23 '96 - p34+ [501+]
    PW - v243 - S 23 '96 - p74 [1-50]
Nimrod: The City
    p Sm Pr R - v29 - Ja '97 - p17 [51-250]
Nin, Anais - *Nearer the Moon*
    BL - v93 - N 15 '96 - p566 [51-250]
    KR - v64 - O 1 '96 - p1450 [51-250]
    LJ - v121 - N 15 '96 - p62+ [51-250]
    PW - v243 - S 23 '96 - p64 [51-250]
Nineteenth Avenue
    yp Par Ch - v20 - O '96 - p15 [1-50]
Nineteenth Century French Drawings and Some Sculpture
    BM - v138 - S '96 - p619+ [501+]
Nineteenth-Century Literature Criticism. Vols. 47-52
    r ARBA - v28 - '97 - p419+ [251-500]
Nineteenth-Century Literature Criticism Annual Cumulative Title Index for 1996
    r ARBA - v28 - '97 - p419+ [251-500]
Nineteenth Century Short Title Catalogue Series III. Electronic Media Version
    r HT - v46 - D '96 - p49 [51-250]
    r LJ - v122 - F 15 '97 - p169 [51-250]
Ning, Tien-Pi - *He Zhi Nu*
    BL - v93 - My 1 '97 - p1484 [1-50]
Ninkovich, Frank - *Modernity and Power*
    JIH - v27 - Aut '96 - p295+ [501+]
Nino, Carlos Santiago - *The Constitution of Deliberative Democracy*
    Choice - v34 - My '97 - p1574 [51-250]
    Radical Evil on Trial
    Choice - v34 - Mr '97 - p1231 [51-250]
    LJ - v121 - N 15 '96 - p74+ [51-250]
Niosi, Jorge - *Flexible Innovation*
    BIC - v25 - N '96 - p28+ [501+]
    SciTech - v21 - N '96 - p72 [1-50]
Nippel, Wilfried - *Public Order in Ancient Rome*
    TLS - S 20 '96 - p30 [501+]
Nipperdey, Thomas - *Germany from Napoleon to Bismarck 1800-1866*
    Choice - v34 - S '96 - p188 [51-250]
    HRNB - v25 - Fall '96 - p29+ [251-500]
    VQR - v73 - Win '97 - p4 [51-250]
Nippert-Eng, Christena E - *Home and Work*
    JEL - v34 - D '96 - p2143 [51-250]
    R&R Bk N - v11 - N '96 - p38 [51-250]
    Wom R Bks - v14 - N '96 - p5+ [501+]
Nirenberg, David - *Communities of Violence*
    Choice - v34 - N '96 - p519+ [251-500]
    HRNB - v25 - Fall '96 - p25+ [251-500]
    Theol St - v58 - Mr '97 - p165+ [501+]

Nirgiotis, Nicholas - *No More Dodos*
    c BL - v93 - F 15 '97 - p1021 [251-500]
    y CCB-B - v50 - F '97 - p218 [51-250]
    c KR - v64 - D 15 '96 - p1802 [51-250]
    c SB - v33 - Mr '97 - p53 [51-250]
    c SLJ - v43 - F '97 - p122 [51-250]
    Volcanoes: Mountains That Blow Their Tops (Illus. by Michael Radencich)
    c Ch BWatch - v6 - My '96 - p8 [51-250]
    c SLJ - v42 - Ag '96 - p140 [51-250]
Nisargadattam, Maharaj - *The Experience of Nothingness*
    Parabola - v22 - F '97 - p92 [251-500]
Nisbett, Richard E - *Culture of Honor*
    AJS - v102 - Ja '97 - p1225+ [501+]
    Nature - v384 - N 7 '96 - p36 [1-50]
    Reason - v28 - F '97 - p62+ [51-250]
Nischan, Bodo - *Prince, People, and Confession*
    EHR - v111 - N '96 - p1272+ [501+]
    JMH - v68 - S '96 - p724+ [501+]
Nisenson, Eric - *Round about Midnight. Updated Ed.*
    Rapport - v19 - 4 '96 - p15 [501+]
Nishimoto, Richard S - *Inside an American Concentration Camp*
    Bks & Cult - v2 - N '96 - p30+ [501+]
    CS - v26 - Mr '97 - p163+ [501+]
    PHR - v65 - N '96 - p691+ [251-500]
Nishioka, Kenji - *Polyamines in Cancer*
    SciTech - v20 - D '96 - p42 [51-250]
Nissen, Bruce - *Fighting for Jobs*
    ILRR - v50 - Ap '97 - p523+ [501+]
Nissenbaum, Stephen - *The Battle for Christmas*
    BL - v93 - O 1 '96 - p309+ [51-250]
    BW - v26 - D 1 '96 - p3 [501+]
    KR - v64 - S 1 '96 - p1303 [251-500]
    LJ - v121 - O 1 '96 - p100 [51-250]
    NW - v128 - D 16 '96 - p71 [501+]
    NYTBR - v101 - D 8 '96 - p43 [501+]
    PW - v243 - O 7 '96 - p53 [51-250]
Nistor, Ioan Liviu - *Istoria Romanilor Din Transilvania*
    BL - v93 - D 15 '96 - p714 [1-50]
Nitti, John - *501 Portuguese Verbs*
    r MLJ - v80 - Win '96 - p555 [251-500]
Nityananda, Swami - *The Sky of the Heart*
    Parabola - v21 - N '96 - p120 [1-50]
Nitzan, Bilha - *Qumran Prayer and Religious Poetry*
    Rel St Rev - v22 - O '96 - p352 [51-250]
Niven, Catherine A - *Conception, Pregnancy, and Birth*
    SciTech - v20 - N '96 - p51 [1-50]
Niven, Larry - *Beowulf's Children*
    y Kliatt - v31 - My '97 - p14+ [51-250]
    Destiny's Road
    PW - v244 - My 12 '97 - p63 [51-250]
    The Integral Trees (Bottino). Audio Version
    LJ - v121 - S 15 '96 - p114 [51-250]
    Ringworld (Parker). Audio Version
    y Kliatt - v31 - Mr '97 - p45 [51-250]
    The Ringworld Throne
    BW - v26 - O 27 '96 - p11 [501+]
    MFSF - v92 - F '97 - p45 [51-250]
    NYTBR - v101 - S 15 '96 - p40 [51-250]
Nivison, David S - *The Ways of Confucianism*
    Choice - v34 - My '97 - p1513+ [51-250]
Nivola, Claire A - *Elisabeth (Illus. by Claire A Nivola)*
    c BL - v93 - F 1 '97 - p946 [51-250]
    c CBRS - v25 - Ap '97 - p103 [51-250]
    c CCB-B - v50 - Mr '97 - p253+ [51-250]
    c HB - v73 - My '97 - p310+ [251-500]
    c HMR - Spr '97 - p29 [501+]
    c KR - v65 - F 1 '97 - p226 [51-250]
    c PW - v244 - Ja 6 '97 - p73 [51-250]
Nivola, Pietro S - *The Extra Mile*
    Pol Stud J - v24 - Sum '96 - p333 [51-250]
Nix, Don - *Road Stories and Recipes*
    BL - v93 - Ja '97 - p804 [51-250]
    KR - v64 - N 15 '96 - p1657 [51-250]
    LJ - v122 - Ja '97 - p102 [51-250]
Nix, Garth - *Sabriel*
    Aust Bk R - S '96 - p63+ [501+]
    y BL - v93 - O 1 '96 - p350 [51-250]
    y BL - v93 - Ap 1 '97 - p1294 [1-50]
    y BL - v93 - Ap 1 '97 - p1305 [1-50]
    y CBRS - v25 - N '96 - p35 [51-250]
    y CCB-B - v50 - D '96 - p146 [51-250]
    y Emerg Lib - v24 - Mr '97 - p55 [51-250]
    y HB - v73 - Ja '97 - p64+ [51-250]
    y HB Guide - v8 - Spr '97 - p83 [51-250]
    y PW - v243 - O 21 '96 - p84 [51-250]
    y SLJ - v42 - S '96 - p228 [51-250]
Nixon, Joan Lowery - *Circle of Love*
    c BL - v93 - Ap 1 '97 - p1334 [51-250]

Don't Scream
y HB Guide - v8 - Spr '97 - p83 [51-250]
y SLJ - v42 - N '96 - p124 [51-250]
y VOYA - v19 - F '97 - p331+ [251-500]
Search for the Shadowman
c BL - v93 - O 1 '96 - p352 [51-250]
c CCB-B - v50 - Ja '97 - p182 [51-250]
c HB - v73 - Ja '97 - p65 [51-250]
c HB Guide - v8 - Spr '97 - p72 [51-250]
y JAAL - v40 - N '96 - p232 [51-250]
c KR - v64 - S 15 '96 - p1405+ [51-250]
c SLJ - v42 - N '96 - p110 [51-250]
y VOYA - v19 - D '96 - p273 [51-250]
The Statue Walks at Night (Illus. by Kathleen Collins Howell)
c RT - v50 - O '96 - p136 [1-50]
Whispers from the Dead
y JAAL - v40 - D '96 - p317 [51-250]
Nizan, Paul - *Aden Arabie*
   FR - v70 - D '96 - p206+ [501+]
Njeri, Itabari - *The Last Plantation*
   BL - v93 - F 15 '97 - p980+ [51-250]
   BW - v27 - Ap 6 '97 - p4+ [501+]
   KR - v65 - Ja 1 '97 - p44 [251-500]
   LJ - v121 - N 1 '96 - p80 [1-50]
   NYTBR - v102 - Ap 20 '97 - p23 [501+]
   PW - v243 - D 16 '96 - p48 [51-250]
Nnadozie, Emmanuel U - *Oil and Socioeconomic Crisis in Nigeria*
   For Aff - v75 - N '96 - p170 [51-250]
No Rattling of Sabers
   Choice - v34 - S '96 - p120 [51-250]
   MEJ - v50 - Aut '96 - p628 [51-250]
Noah and the Ark (McGillis). Book and Audio Version
c BL - v93 - Ap 1 '97 - p1314 [1-50]
Noah's Ark of Animals (Little Moorings)
c HB Guide - v7 - Fall '96 - p308 [1-50]
Noback, Charles Robert - *The Human Nervous System. 5th Ed.*
   SciTech - v20 - N '96 - p32 [51-250]
Nobel Symposium (87th: 1993: Tromso, Norway) - *The Fall of Great Powers*
   JIH - v27 - Aut '96 - p294+ [501+]
Nobes, Christopher - *International Accounting*
   JEL - v35 - Mr '97 - p256 [1-50]
   R&R Bk N - v11 - D '96 - p35 [51-250]
International Harmonization of Accounting
   JEL - v35 - Mr '97 - p256 [1-50]
   R&R Bk N - v11 - D '96 - p35 [51-250]
Noble, Bruce J - *Perceived Exertion*
   Choice - v34 - N '96 - p498 [51-250]
r SciTech - v20 - S '96 - p22 [51-250]
Noble, Kate - *The Dragon of Navy Pier (Illus. by Rachel Bass)*
c CBRS - v24 - Ag '96 - p161 [51-250]
c Ch BWatch - v6 - O '96 - p4 [51-250]
c Ch BWatch - v6 - N '96 - p6 [51-250]
Noble, Keith Allan - *The International Education Quotations Encyclopaedia*
r ARBA - v28 - '97 - p133 [251-500]
Noble, Peter - *Hebert: Les Fous De Bassan*
   MLR - v91 - O '96 - p1004+ [251-500]
Noble, Scott - *Noble's International Guide to the Law Reports. 1995 Ed.*
r ARBA - v28 - '97 - p218 [251-500]
Noble, Thomas F X - *Soldiers of Christ*
   CHR - v82 - Jl '96 - p505+ [251-500]
Noble, William - *Human Evolution, Language and Mind*
   Choice - v34 - Ap '97 - p1381 [51-250]
   New Sci - v153 - F 1 '97 - p45 [251-500]
Nobleman, Tyler - *Felix Activity Book (Illus. by George Ulrich)*
c PW - v243 - N 4 '96 - p78 [51-250]
Nobles, Gregory H - *American Frontiers*
   BL - v93 - F 15 '97 - p1000 [51-250]
   LJ - v122 - F 15 '97 - p146 [51-250]
   NYTBR - v102 - Mr 16 '97 - p22 [501+]
   PW - v243 - D 2 '96 - p45 [51-250]
   Wil Q - v21 - Win '97 - p88 [51-250]
Noblit, George W - *The Social Construction of Virtue*
   Choice - v34 - Mr '97 - p1212 [51-250]
   R&R Bk N - v11 - D '96 - p54 [51-250]
Nocera, Joseph - *A Piece of the Action*
   Reason - v28 - D '96 - p43 [51-250]
Nochlin, Linda - *The Body in Pieces*
   JAAC - v54 - Fall '96 - p410+ [501+]
Nockles, Peter B - *The Oxford Movement in Context*
   EHR - v112 - F '97 - p229+ [251-500]
   Historian - v58 - Sum '96 - p913+ [501+]
   VS - v39 - Aut '95 - p93+ [501+]

Nocon, Andrew - *Outcomes of Community Care for Users and Carers*
   SciTech - v21 - Mr '97 - p46 [51-250]
Noda, Kaz - *Pre-Harvest Sprouting in Cereals 1995*
   SciTech - v20 - D '96 - p56 [51-250]
Nodaway County Genealogical Society - *Monroe Township Cemeteries, Nodaway County, Missouri 1960*
r EGH - v50 - N '96 - p173 [51-250]
Price Funeral Home Records 1960
r EGH - v50 - N '96 - p173 [51-250]
Nodelman, Perry - *The Pleasures of Children's Literature*
   SLJ - v42 - S '96 - p112 [1-50]
Noe, Kenneth W - *Southwestern Virginia's Railroad*
   T&C - v37 - Ap '96 - p360+ [501+]
Noel, Bernard - *Le Roman D'Adam Et Eve*
   Econ - v340 - S 14 '96 - p14*+ [501+]
   WLT - v71 - Win '97 - p105 [51-250]
Noel, Christopher - *In the Unlikely Event of a Water Landing*
   LATBR - Ag 18 '96 - p8 [501+]
Noel, Daniel C - *The Soul of Shamanism*
   BL - v93 - F 1 '97 - p909 [51-250]
   LJ - v122 - Ap 1 '97 - p98 [51-250]
Noel, Jan - *Canada Dry*
   AHR - v102 - F '97 - p226+ [251-500]
   Beav - v76 - Ag '96 - p46+ [251-500]
   Can Hist R - v77 - S '96 - p424+ [501+]
   CH - v66 - Mr '97 - p204 [51-250]
   CIIR - v83 - Ja '97 - p151+ [501+]
   Historian - v59 - Fall '96 - p151+ [251-500]
Noel, Rhya - *Pongee Goes to Paris*
c SLJ - v43 - F '97 - p82+ [51-250]
Noer, David M - *Breaking Free*
   HR Mag - v41 - D '96 - p126 [51-250]
Noffke, Suzanne - *Catherine of Siena: Vision through a Distant Eye*
   RR - v56 - Ja '97 - p106 [1-50]
Noguchi, Rick - *The Ocean inside Kenji Takezo*
   PW - v243 - N 4 '96 - p47 [1-50]
Noguera, Claudine - *Physics and Chemistry at Oxide Surfaces*
   SciTech - v21 - Mr '97 - p31 [51-250]
Noguere, Suzanne - *Whirling Round the Sun*
   LJ - v121 - N 1 '96 - p71 [51-250]
   PW - v243 - N 25 '96 - p73 [1-50]
Noiriel, Gerard - *The French Melting Pot*
   For Aff - v75 - N '96 - p156+ [51-250]
   TLS - Ja 24 '97 - p7 [501+]
   TranslRevS - v2 - D '96 - p16 [51-250]
Nokes, David - *John Gay: A Profession of Friendship*
   RES - v48 - F '97 - p118+ [501+]
Nokes, Kathleen M - *HIV/AIDS and the Older Adult*
   SciTech - v20 - S '96 - p34 [51-250]
Nolan, Alan T - *Lee Reconsidered*
y Kliatt - v31 - Ja '97 - p26 [251-500]
Nolan, Brian - *Resources, Deprivation and Poverty*
   JEL - v35 - Mr '97 - p233 [51-250]
Nolan, Cathal J - *Ethics and Statecraft*
   Ethics - v107 - Ja '97 - p391+ [51-250]
Nolan, Charles E - *St. Mary's of Natchez. Vols. 1-2*
   CH - v66 - Mr '97 - p211+ [51-250]
   CHR - v82 - O '96 - p738+ [501+]
Nolan, Emer - *James Joyce and Nationalism*
   TLS - D 20 '96 - p12 [501+]
Nolan, Han - *Send Me Down a Miracle*
y BL - v93 - O 1 '96 - p339 [1-50]
y Ch BWatch - v6 - D '96 - p5 [51-250]
y HB Guide - v7 - Fall '96 - p304 [1-50]
y JAAL - v40 - S '96 - p72 [51-250]
y Par Ch - v20 - O '96 - p12 [1-50]
Nolan, Helen - *How Much, How Many, How Far, How Heavy, How Long, How Tall Is 1000? (Illus. by Tracy Walker)*
c Ch Bk News - v19 - Sum '96 - p29 [51-250]
Nolan, James L - *Australia Business*
r ARBA - v28 - '97 - p112 [251-500]
Nolan, Mary - *Visions of Modernity*
   EHR - v112 - Ap '97 - p258+ [501+]
   JMH - v68 - S '96 - p629+ [501+]
   JMH - v69 - Mr '97 - p181+ [501+]
Nolan, Patricia - *Broken Windows*
   Quill & Q - v62 - Ag '96 - p35 [251-500]
Nolan, Peter - *China's Rise, Russia's Fall*
   Ch Rev Int - v4 - Spr '97 - p221+ [501+]
   JEL - v35 - Mr '97 - p1996+ [51-250]
Nolden, Thomas - *An Einen Jungen Dichter*
   Ger Q - v70 - Win '97 - p71+ [501+]
Nolens, Leonard - *De Vrek Van Missenburg*
   WLT - v70 - Sum '96 - p711 [501+]

Noll, Mark A - *Adding Cross to Crown*
   Bks & Cult - v2 - N '96 - p4 [51-250]
   BL - v93 - O 1 '96 - p305+ [51-250]
   PW - v243 - O 14 '96 - p76 [51-250]
Noll, Richard - *The Jung Cult*
   CEH - v29 - 2 '96 - p261+ [501+]
   New Sci - v152 - N 9 '96 - p44 [51-250]
   NYRB - v43 - O 3 '96 - p38+ [501+]
Noll, Steven - *Feeble-Minded in Our Midst*
   J Soc H - v30 - Spr '97 - p754+ [501+]
   RAH - v24 - D '96 - p618+ [501+]
Nolla, Olga - *El Castillo De La Memoria*
   LJ - v122 - Ja '97 - p79 [51-250]
Nollet, Leo M L - *Handbook of Food Analysis. Vols. 1-2*
   SciTech - v20 - D '96 - p87 [51-250]
Nolo News
p Sm Pr R - v29 - Ja '97 - p22 [251-500]
Nolte, Paul - *Gemeindeburgetum Und Liberalismus In Baden 1800-1850*
   EHR - v111 - N '96 - p1310 [251-500]
Noltze, Holger - *Gahmurets Orientfahrt*
   MLR - v91 - Jl '96 - p777+ [51-250]
Nomani, Farhad - *Islamic Economic Systems*
   JTWS - v13 - Spr '96 - p375+ [251-500]
Nomura, Noriko S - *I Am Shinto*
c SLJ - v42 - N '96 - p100 [51-250]
Nonneman, Gerd - *Muslim Communities in the New Europe*
   Choice - v34 - Ja '97 - p858 [51-250]
Political and Economic Liberalization
   Choice - v34 - N '96 - p508 [51-250]
   JEL - v34 - D '96 - p2126+ [51-250]
Nonprofit Almanac 1996-1997
r ChrPhil - v9 - O 17 '96 - p35 [51-250]
Noon, Jeff - *Automated Alice (Illus. by Harry Trumbore)*
y BL - v93 - O 1 '96 - p322+ [51-250]
   BW - v26 - D 29 '96 - p6 [251-500]
   LATBR - D 15 '96 - p15 [51-250]
Pollen
   Obs - N 10 '96 - p18* [51-250]
Noonan, Diana - *Hercules (Illus. by Margaret Power)*
c Magpies - v11 - My '96 - p39 [51-250]
Noonan, James-Charles, Jr. - *The Church Visible*
r CLW - v67 - D '96 - p50 [51-250]
Noonan, John T - *The Morality of Abortion*
   Cons - v17 - Aut '96 - p35+ [501+]
Nooteboom, Cees - *The Following Story*
   WLT - v70 - Aut '96 - p974 [251-500]
Roads to Santiago
   BL - v93 - Mr 15 '97 - p1221 [51-250]
   BW - v27 - Mr 30 '97 - p3+ [501+]
   Econ - v342 - Mr 15 '97 - p6* [501+]
   KR - v65 - F 1 '97 - p214 [1-50]
   LJ - v122 - Ap 15 '97 - p105 [51-250]
   NYTBR - v102 - Ap 6 '97 - p26 [501+]
   Obs - F 2 '97 - p16* [501+]
   PW - v244 - F 3 '97 - p89 [51-250]
Nooy, G C De - *The Role of European Naval Forces after the Cold War*
   R&R Bk N - v11 - N '96 - p12 [51-250]
Norbeck, Joseph M - *Hydrogen Fuel for Surface Transporation*
   Choice - v34 - Ap '97 - p1370 [51-250]
Norberg, Arthur L - *Transforming Computer Technology*
   Sci - v274 - D 6 '96 - p1627+ [501+]
   SciTech - v20 - N '96 - p6 [51-250]
Norby, Lisa - *Treasure Island (Illus. by Fernando Fernandez)*
c New Ad - v9 - Fall '96 - p309+ [501+]
Nord, Deborah Epstein - *Walking the Victorian Streets*
   Critm - v39 - Win '97 - p121+ [501+]
   ELT - v40 - 4 '96 - p528 [51-250]
   Nine-C Lit - v51 - Mr '97 - p544+ [501+]
Nord, Philip - *The Republican Moment*
   Historian - v59 - Win '97 - p474+ [251-500]
   TLS - Ag 30 '96 - p27 [501+]
Nord, Warren A - *Religion and American Education*
   Bks & Cult - v2 - S '96 - p28+ [501+]
   CC - v113 - N 20 '96 - p1134+ [501+]
   EL - v54 - O '96 - p88 [51-250]
   Rel St Rev - v23 - Ja '97 - p93 [51-250]
Nordan, Lewis - *Lightning Song*
   BL - v93 - Mr 1 '97 - p1068 [51-250]
   KR - v65 - Ap 1 '97 - p493+ [251-500]
   LJ - v122 - Ap 1 '97 - p128+ [51-250]
   PW - v244 - Mr 10 '97 - p47 [51-250]
Sugar Among the Freaks
   Bloom Rev - v16 - Jl '96 - p25 [51-250]
Nordell, John R, Jr. - *The Undetected Enemy*
   PHR - v66 - F '97 - p143+ [251-500]

Norden, Deborah L - *Military Rebellion in Argentina*
APSR - v90 - D '96 - p943+ [501+]
Choice - v34 - O '96 - p354+ [51-250]
Norden, Martin - *The Cinema of Isolation*
Lon R Bks - v18 - S 19 '96 - p14+ [501+]
Nordhaus, William D - *Managing the Global Commons*
Econ J - v106 - N '96 - p1852+ [251-500]
Nordhoff, Charles - *Mutiny on the Bounty (Reed). Audio Version*
y Sch Lib - v45 - F '97 - p47 [51-250]
Spec - v277 - N 30 '96 - p55 [51-250]
Nordlinger, Eric - *Isolationism Reconfigured*
IndRev - v1 - Spr '96 - p147+ [501+]
Nordquist, Joan - *Affirmative Action*
r ARBA - v28 - '97 - p218+ [51-250]
Asian Americans
r ARBA - v28 - '97 - p151+ [51-250]
Environmental Racism and the Environmental Justice Movement
r ARBA - v28 - '97 - p230 [51-250]
Feminism and Postmodern Theory
r ARBA - v28 - '97 - p332 [251-500]
Latinas in the United States
r ARBA - v28 - '97 - p332 [251-500]
Martin Heideggar II: A Bibliography
r ARBA - v28 - '97 - p527 [51-250]
Women of Color
r ARBA - v28 - '97 - p333 [51-250]
Nordstokke, Kjell - *Council and Context in Leonardo Boff's Ecclesiology*
Choice - v34 - F '97 - p980 [51-250]
Nordstrom, Rolf E A - *Tissue Expansion*
SciTech - v20 - D '96 - p49 [51-250]
Noren, Lars - *De Doda Pjaserna I-IV 1989-1994*
WLT - v70 - Aut '96 - p981 [501+]
Norfleet, Barbara P - *Looking at Death*
Afterimage - v23 - Sum '96 - p8+ [501+]
Norfolk, Lawrence - *The Pope's Rhinoceros*
BL - v93 - S 15 '96 - p221+ [51-250]
BW - v26 - S 15 '96 - p4 [501+]
NS & S - v9 - Ap 26 '96 - p39+ [251-500]
NYTBR - v101 - N 10 '96 - p60 [501+]
Spec - v277 - N 16 '96 - p46 [1-50]
Norgaard, Ole - *The Baltic States after Independence*
Choice - v34 - S '96 - p202 [51-250]
JEL - v34 - D '96 - p2124+ [51-250]
R&R Bk N - v11 - N '96 - p13 [51-250]
Noriega, Chon A - *The Ethnic Eye*
Afterimage - v24 - N '96 - p16 [51-250]
Choice - v34 - N '96 - p468 [51-250]
TDR - v41 - Spr '97 - p159+ [51-250]
VQR - v72 - Aut '96 - p122* [51-250]
Noriega, Manuel - *America's Prisoner*
BW - v27 - Ap 6 '97 - p1+ [501+]
Norland, Howard B - *Drama in Early Tudor Britain 1485-1558*
Albion - v28 - Sum '96 - p293+ [501+]
Ren Q - v50 - Spr '97 - p276+ [501+]
Norling, Donna Scott - *Patty's Journey*
LJ - v121 - O 15 '96 - p78 [51-250]
y SLJ - v43 - Mr '97 - p217+ [51-250]
Norman, Diana - *Siena, Florence and Padua. Vols. 1-2*
Ren Q - v50 - Spr '97 - p313+ [501+]
Norman, Greg - *Advanced Golf*
LJ - v121 - O 1 '96 - p53 [1-50]
Norman, Hilary - *The Pact*
PW - v244 - My 5 '97 - p194 [51-250]
Norman, Howard - *Northern Tales*
CAY - v17 - Win '96 - p12 [51-250]
Norman, Lisanne - *Fire Margins*
LJ - v121 - N 15 '96 - p91 [51-250]
Norman, Philip, 1943- - *Everyone's Gone to the Moon*
Obs - S 1 '96 - p18* [51-250]
Rave On
y BL - v93 - S 15 '96 - p201 [51-250]
Ent W - O 18 '96 - p74 [51-250]
LATBR - v263 - S 29 '96 - p3+ [501+]
LJ - v121 - S 15 '96 - p70 [51-250]
NYTBR - v101 - S 29 '96 - p21 [251-500]
Norman, Richard - *Ethics, Killing and War*
Ethics - v107 - O '96 - p159+ [501+]
Rel St Rev - v23 - Ap '97 - p160 [51-250]
Norman, Sandy - *Copyright in Further and Higher Education Libraries*
LAR - v99 - Ja '97 - p47 [251-500]
Copyright in Health Libraries
LAR - v99 - Ja '97 - p47 [251-500]
Copyright in Industrial and Commercial Libraries
LAR - v99 - Ja '97 - p47 [251-500]
Copyright in Public Libraries
LAR - v99 - Ja '97 - p47 [251-500]

Copyright in School Libraries
LAR - v99 - Ja '97 - p47 [251-500]
Copyright in Voluntary Sector Libraries
LAR - v99 - Ja '97 - p47 [251-500]
Normile, Dwight - *Gymnastics (Illus. by Dwight Normile)*
c HB Guide - v7 - Fall '96 - p360 [51-250]
Norrhem, Svante - *Uppkomlingarna: Kanslitjanstemannen I 1600-Talets*
EHR - v111 - N '96 - p1282+ [251-500]
Norris, Allen Wilkinson Hart - *Hyde County North Carolina Record of Deeds A 1736-1762*
r EGH - v50 - N '96 - p178 [51-250]
Norris, Charles Gilman - *Charles and Kathleen Norris*
WAL - v31 - Sum '96 - p189+ [251-500]
Norris, Christopher - *Reclaiming Truth*
Choice - v34 - My '97 - p1514 [51-250]
Norris, Frank - *The Apprenticeship Writings of Frank Norris 1896-1898*
AL - v68 - D '96 - p878 [1-50]
Nine-C Lit - v51 - D '96 - p425 [51-250]
Norris, Harry T - *Islam in the Balkans*
JAAR - v64 - Sum '96 - p423+ [501+]
Norris, John R - *The Historic Railroad*
r ARBA - v28 - '97 - p656 [51-250]
r RQ - v36 - Win '96 - p296 [251-500]
Norris, Kathleen - *The Cloister Walk*
Bks & Cult - v2 - Jl '96 - p21 [501+]
BL - v93 - Ja '97 - p756 [1-50]
BW - v26 - D 8 '96 - p6 [51-250]
BW - v27 - Mr 23 '97 - p12 [51-250]
CC - v113 - O 9 '96 - p940+ [501+]
Comw - v123 - My 17 '96 - p26+ [501+]
CSM - v89 - N 25 '96 - p12 [51-250]
LJ - v122 - Ja '97 - p50 [1-50]
NYTBR - v101 - D 8 '96 - p85 [1-50]
NYTBR - v102 - Ap 13 '97 - p32 [51-250]
PW - v243 - N 4 '96 - p46 [51-250]
Trib Bks - Ap 27 '97 - p8 [1-50]
VV - v42 - Ja 7 '97 - p44 [1-50]
Wom R Bks - v14 - N '96 - p26+ [501+]
The Cloister Walk (Winger). Audio Version
y Kliatt - v30 - S '96 - p56 [51-250]
Dakota: A Spiritual Biography
Rel St Rev - v22 - O '96 - p344 [51-250]
Little Girls in Church
Shen - v46 - Win '96 - p118+ [501+]
Norris, Ken - *Full Sun*
Essays CW - Spr '96 - p198+ [501+]
A New World
Essays CW - Spr '96 - p198+ [501+]
Norris, Leslie - *Collected Poems*
BL - v93 - S 15 '96 - p205 [51-250]
Collected Stories
KR - v64 - S 1 '96 - p1268 [51-250]
Norris, Mark - *Understanding Networking Technology*
r SciTech - v20 - D '96 - p75 [1-50]
Norris, Pippa - *Electoral Change Since 1945*
Econ - v342 - Mr 22 '97 - p106 [51-250]
Women, Media, and Politics
Choice - v34 - F '97 - p1039 [51-250]
Norris, Steven - *Changing Trains*
Lon R Bks - v18 - O 17 '96 - p10+ [501+]
Spec - v277 - O 26 '96 - p49+ [501+]
TLS - O 25 '96 - p31 [501+]
Norriss, Andrew - *Matt's Million (Illus. by Richard Jones)*
c Bks Keeps - v100 - S '96 - p13+ [51-250]
c JB - v60 - D '96 - p272 [51-250]
c Obs - v54 - O 13 '96 - p18* [51-250]
North, Anthony - *The Paranormal: A Guide to the Unexplained*
y BL - v93 - N 15 '96 - p552 [51-250]
PW - v243 - O 21 '96 - p68 [1-50]
North, Darian - *Thief of Souls*
BL - v93 - Mr 1 '97 - p1114 [51-250]
KR - v65 - Ja 15 '97 - p89 [251-500]
LJ - v122 - F 15 '97 - p163 [51-250]
PW - v244 - Ja 20 '97 - p392 [51-250]
Trib Bks - Ap 20 '97 - p7 [51-250]
North, Freya - *Sally*
Books - v11 - Ap '97 - p23 [51-250]
Woman's J - D '96 - p16 [1-50]
North, Gerald - *The Impact of Global Warming on Texas*
AAAGA - v87 - Mr '97 - p193+ [501+]
North, John D - *The Norton History of Astronomy and Cosmology*
Am Sci - v84 - My '96 - p307+ [501+]

North, John David - *Stonehenge: Neolithic Man and the Cosmos*
Lon R Bks - v18 - D 12 '96 - p19 [501+]
Nature - v383 - O 3 '96 - p403+ [501+]
New Sci - v152 - D 21 '96 - p75 [251-500]
Obs - Ag 18 '96 - p17* [501+]
TLS - O 18 '96 - p10 [501+]
North, Larry - *Living Lean*
BL - v93 - Ja '97 - p798 [51-250]
North, Percy - *Bernhard Gutmann: An American Impressionist*
LATBR - D 8 '96 - p14 [1-50]
North, Suzanne - *Seeing Is Deceiving*
Quill & Q - v62 - O '96 - p32 [51-250]
North American Brewers Resource Directory 1996-1997
r ARBA - v28 - '97 - p569+ [51-250]
North American Coins and Prices 1997
r Coin W - v37 - D 2 '96 - p100 [51-250]
North American Rock Mechanics Symposium (2nd: 1996: Montreal, Quebec) - *Rock Mechanics Tools and Techniques. Vols. 1-2*
SciTech - v21 - Mr '97 - p80 [51-250]
North American Water and Environment Congress (1996: Anaheim, Calif.) - *North American Water and Environment Congress and Destructive Water. Electronic Media Version*
SciTech - v21 - Mr '97 - p81 [51-250]
North Carolina. Adjutant-General's Dept. - *Muster Rolls of the Soldiers of the War of 1812*
r EGH - v50 - N '96 - p177 [51-250]
North Carolina. State Center for Health and Environmental Statistics - *North Carolina Environmental Indicators*
J Gov Info - v23 - S '96 - p590 [51-250]
North Coast Review
p Sm Pr R - v28 - S '96 - p19 [251-500]
North Dakota Quarterly
p LMR - v15 - Win '96 - p20+ [501+]
Northcutt, Wayne - *The Regions of France*
yr ARBA - v28 - '97 - p61 [251-500]
r BL - v93 - Ap 1 '97 - p1358 [251-500]
Northington, David K - *The Botanical World. 2nd Ed.*
SciTech - v20 - N '96 - p28 [51-250]
Northrup, David - *Indentured Labor in the Age of Imperialism 1834-1922*
Historian - v59 - Win '97 - p489+ [501+]
HRNB - v25 - Win '97 - p67 [251-500]
JEH - v56 - D '96 - p935+ [501+]
JIH - v27 - Spr '97 - p682+ [501+]
Northway, Jennifer - *Lucy's Rabbit*
c Bks Keeps - v100 - S '96 - p8 [51-250]
Norton, Andre - *Derelict for Trade*
y BL - v93 - F 1 '97 - p929 [51-250]
KR - v64 - D 1 '96 - p1707+ [51-250]
LJ - v121 - D '96 - p152 [51-250]
PW - v244 - Ja 27 '97 - p82 [51-250]
The Monster's Legacy (Illus. by Jody A Lee)
y Emerg Lib - v24 - S '96 - p43 [1-50]
y HB Guide - v7 - Fall '96 - p304 [51-250]
The Warding of Witch World
y BL - v93 - S 1 '96 - p69 [51-250]
KR - v64 - S 1 '96 - p1281 [51-250]
LJ - v121 - S 15 '96 - p101 [1-50]
PW - v243 - S 16 '96 - p75 [51-250]
y VOYA - v19 - F '97 - p339 [251-500]
Norton, Arthur P - *Norton's Star Atlas and Reference Handbook. 17th Ed.*
r S&T - v92 - S '96 - p52 [51-250]
Norton, Augustus Richard - *Civil Society in the Middle East. Vol. 2*
MEJ - v51 - Spr '97 - p311 [51-250]
Civil Society in the Middle East. Vols. 1-2
Choice - v34 - D '96 - p682 [51-250]
MEQ - v4 - Mr '97 - p86 [251-500]
Norton, Bruce H - *Sergeant Major, U.S. Marines*
Mar Crp G - v81 - Ja '97 - p73+ [501+]
Norton, Bryan A - *Ethics on the Ark*
Am Sci - v84 - S '96 - p500 [501+]
Norton, David Fate - *The David Hume Library*
TLS - D 27 '96 - p33 [251-500]
Norton, David L - *Imagination, Understanding, and the Virtue of Liberality*
Choice - v34 - S '96 - p142 [51-250]
Norton, Joseph J - *NAFTA and Beyond*
R&R Bk N - v12 - F '97 - p64 [51-250]
Norton, Judith A - *New England Planters in the Maritime Provinces of Canada 1759-1800*
Archiv - Fall '94 - p180+ [501+]
Norton, Kevin - *Anthropometrica: A Textbook of Body Measurement for Sports and Health Courses*
R&R Bk N - v11 - D '96 - p21 [51-250]

Norton, Lisa Dale - *Hawk Flies Above*
 BL - v93 - O 1 '96 - p319+ [51-250]
 Bloom Rev - v16 - N '96 - p19 [501+]
 KR - v64 - Ag 15 '96 - p1218 [251-500]
 LATBR - N 10 '96 - p14 [51-250]
 LJ - v121 - S 15 '96 - p76 [51-250]
Norton, Mary Beth - *Founding Mothers and Fathers*
 BW - v26 - Ag 4 '96 - p6 [501+]
 Choice - v34 - O '96 - p350+ [51-250]
 J Soc H - v30 - Spr '97 - p783+ [501+]
 NEQ - v70 - Mr '97 - p129+ [501+]
 NYRB - v43 - O 31 '96 - p66+ [501+]
 VQR - v72 - Aut '96 - p115* [51-250]
 Wom R Bks - v13 - S '96 - p23+ [501+]
Norton, O Richard - *Rocks from Space*
 RocksMiner - v71 - S '96 - p359+ [501+]
Norton, R D - *New Urban Strategies in Advanced Regional Economies*
 JEL - v35 - Mr '97 - p304 [51-250]
Norton, Robert Edward - *The Beautiful Soul*
 Eight-C St - v30 - Win '96 - p197+ [501+]
 JAAC - v55 - Win '97 - p62+ [501+]
The Norton Anthology of African American Literature
 B Ent - v27 - F '97 - p215 [1-50]
 y BL - v93 - Ja '97 - p809 [51-250]
 y BL - v93 - F 15 '97 - p1014 [1-50]
 Bloom Rev - v17 - Ja '97 - p18 [501+]
 Choice - v34 - Ap '97 - p1338 [51-250]
 Ch Today - v41 - F 3 '97 - p62 [1-50]
 LATBR - D 15 '96 - p1+ [501+]
 LJ - v121 - N 1 '96 - p84 [1-50]
 LJ - v122 - F 1 '97 - p79 [51-250]
 Nat R - v49 - Mr 10 '97 - p50+ [501+]
 NS - v126 - Ap 25 '97 - p52+ [501+]
 Obs - Ap 6 '97 - p17* [501+]
 PW - v243 - N 11 '96 - p60 [51-250]
Norton Anthology of Poetry. 4th Ed.
 VV - v42 - Ja 7 '97 - p44 [51-250]
Norton-Taylor, Richard - *Knee Deep in Dishonour*
 CR - v269 - N '96 - p269 [501+]
 TLS - F 28 '97 - p25+ [501+]
Norval, Aletta J - *Deconstructing Apartheid Discourse*
 Bl S - v26 - Fall '96 - p105 [51-250]
 CS - v26 - Ja '97 - p44+ [501+]
Norwich, John Julius - *Byzantium: The Decline and Fall*
 NYTBR - v101 - D 8 '96 - p85 [1-50]
 A Short History of Byzantium
 BW - v27 - Mr 23 '97 - p13 [51-250]
 Econ - v342 - Mr 22 '97 - p104+ [501+]
 LJ - v122 - Ap 1 '97 - p108 [51-250]
 PW - v244 - F 24 '97 - p77 [51-250]
Norwich, William - *Learning to Drive*
 LATBR - Jl 14 '96 - p10 [51-250]
 Spec - v277 - N 30 '96 - p46 [501+]
 TLS - N 15 '96 - p25 [51-250]
Norwood, Janet L - *Organizing to Count*
 CS - v26 - Ja '97 - p72+ [501+]
Nose, Throat, and Ear (Coding Illustrated)
 r SciTech - v20 - N '96 - p50 [51-250]
Nosek, Kathleen - *Dyslexia in Adults*
 PW - v244 - Mr 24 '97 - p80 [51-250]
Noskova, Albina F - *NKVD I Pol'Skoe Podpol'e 1944-1945. Vol. 1*
 Slav R - v55 - Sum '96 - p470+ [501+]
Noss, Richard - *Windows on Mathematical Meanings*
 SciTech - v20 - D '96 - p6 [51-250]
Nossiter, Joshua C - *Using Corel WordPerfect 7*
 Quill & Q - v62 - N '96 - p31 [51-250]
Nostradamus - *Les Premieres Centuries Ou Propheties*
 Ren Q - v50 - Spr '97 - p251+ [501+]
Nosworthy, Brent - *With Musket, Cannon, and Sword*
 J Mil H - v60 - O '96 - p773+ [251-500]
Notable American Women 1607-1950. Vols. 1-3
 r ASInt - v34 - O '96 - p13 [1-50]
Noteboom, Cess - *In the Dutch Mountains*
 PW - v244 - F 24 '97 - p88 [1-50]
Notelovitz, Morris - *Menopause and Midlife Health*
 r BL - v93 - F 1 '97 - p960 [1-50]
Nothomb, Amelie - *Les Catalinaires*
 FR - v70 - Mr '97 - p619+ [251-500]
Notley, Alice - *The Descent of Alette*
 Ant R - v55 - Spr '97 - p247+ [251-500]
Notre Dame Review
 p LMR - v15 - Fall '96 - p43+ [51-250]
Nott, Lewis Windermere - *Somewhere in France*
 Aust Bk R - Je '96 - p24+ [501+]
Nottingham, Ted - *Chess for Children*
 c Ch BWatch - v6 - My '96 - p1 [1-50]
Nottle, Trevor - *Gardens of the Sun*
 BL - v93 - S 15 '96 - p195 [51-250]
 PW - v243 - O 7 '96 - p70 [51-250]

Nouwen, Henri J M - *Can You Drink the Cup?*
 CC - v114 - Mr 19 '97 - p302+ [501+]
 The Inner Voice of Love
 BL - v93 - D 1 '96 - p622 [51-250]
 CC - v114 - Mr 19 '97 - p302+ [501+]
 LJ - v122 - Ja '97 - p107 [51-250]
 PW - v243 - S 16 '96 - p66 [51-250]
 The Return of the Prodigal Son
 RR - v55 - N '96 - p659 [1-50]
Nova, Craig - *The Universal Donor*
 KR - v65 - Ap 1 '97 - p494 [251-500]
 PW - v244 - Mr 31 '97 - p59 [51-250]
Novacek, Michael - *Dinosaurs of the Flaming Cliffs*
 y BL - v93 - S 1 '96 - p47 [251-500]
 BW - v26 - S 29 '96 - p8 [501+]
 Nature - v384 - D 5 '96 - p426 [501+]
 New Sci - v152 - D 21 '96 - p74 [251-500]
 NH - v105 - S '96 - p11 [1-50]
 NYTBR - v101 - N 10 '96 - p13 [501+]
 NYTBR - v101 - D 8 '96 - p87 [51-250]
Novak, David - *Jewish-Christian Dialogue*
 Rel Ed - v91 - Fall '96 - p613 [1-50]
 Leo Strauss and Judaism
 Choice - v34 - O '96 - p298 [51-250]
Novak, Elaine Adams - *Staging Musical Theatre*
 y SLJ - v43 - F '97 - p138 [51-250]
 TCI - v30 - O '96 - p56 [51-250]
Novak, Helga M - *Aufenthalt In Einem Irren Haus*
 WLT - v70 - Sum '96 - p688 [501+]
Novak, James J - *Bangladesh: Reflections on the Water*
 GJ - v162 - N '96 - p343 [51-250]
Novak, Jeannie - *Creating Internet Entertainment*
 LJ - v122 - F 1 '97 - p102 [51-250]
 SciTech - v21 - Mr '97 - p88 [51-250]
Novak, Jiri Tibor - *Birdman*
 c Magpies - v11 - Jl '96 - p45 [1-50]
 You Can Make Mobiles
 c Magpies - v11 - S '96 - p43 [51-250]
Novak, Matt - *Mouse TV*
 c Inst - v106 - N '96 - p35 [51-250]
 Newt
 c HB Guide - v7 - Fall '96 - p284 [51-250]
Novak, Michael - *Business as a Calling*
 Am - v176 - Ap 5 '97 - p30+ [501+]
 CC - v113 - D 4 '96 - p1200+ [501+]
 Comw - v124 - F 28 '97 - p28+ [501+]
 Nat R - v48 - S 16 '96 - p65+ [501+]
 The Guns of Lattimer
 JEL - v35 - Mr '97 - p264 [51-250]
Novak, Michael, 1968- - *The Glow-in-the-Dark Book of Human Skeletons (Illus. by Kate Sweeney)*
 c PW - v244 - Ap 14 '97 - p77 [1-50]
Novak, Miroslav M - *Fractal Reviews in the Natural and Applied Sciences*
 SIAM Rev - v39 - Mr '97 - p174+ [1-50]
Novak, William J - *The People's Welfare*
 Choice - v34 - Ap '97 - p1418+ [51-250]
 LJ - v121 - O 15 '96 - p76 [51-250]
Novaresio, Paolo - *The Explorers: From the Ancient World to the Present*
 CSM - v88 - N 21 '96 - pB1 [51-250]
 Mac - v109 - D 9 '96 - p66 [1-50]
 PW - v243 - O 14 '96 - p73 [51-250]
Novarina, Valere - *The Theater of the Ears*
 TranslRevS - v2 - D '96 - p24 [51-250]
Novel and Short Story Writer's Market 1996
 r ARBA - v28 - '97 - p348 [51-250]
 r SF Chr - v18 - O '96 - p81 [51-250]
Novello, John - *The Contemporary Keyboardist*
 Am MT - v46 - D '96 - p60 [251-500]
Novick, Jack - *Fearful Symmetry*
 Readings - v11 - D '96 - p25 [51-250]
Novick, Michael - *White Lies, White Power*
 Nat - v263 - O 28 '96 - p20+ [501+]
Novick, Sheldon M - *Henry James: The Young Master*
 BL - v93 - S 1 '96 - p56 [51-250]
 BW - v26 - D 1 '96 - p9 [501+]
 LJ - v121 - O 1 '96 - p77 [51-250]
 New R - v216 - Ap 14 '97 - p44+ [501+]
 NYTBR - v101 - N 3 '96 - p18 [51-250]
 NYTLa - v146 - N 1 '96 - pC35 [501+]
 TLS - D 6 '96 - p3+ [501+]
 WSJ-MW - v78 - O 17 '96 - pA20 [501+]
Novikov, Denis - *Okno V Ianvare*
 WLT - v71 - Win '97 - p179 [501+]
Novo, Salvador - *The War of the Fatties and Other Stories from Aztec History*
 TranslRevS - v1 - My '95 - p31 [251-500]
Nowak, Kurt - *Geschichte Des Christentums In Deutschland*
 CH - v65 - D '96 - p761+ [501+]

Nowell-Smith, Geoffrey - *The Companion to Italian Cinema*
 r Si & So - v6 - N '96 - p36 [51-250]
 The Oxford History of World Cinema
 AB - v98 - D 9 '96 - p1996 [51-250]
 Choice - v34 - Ap '97 - p1346 [51-250]
 r Econ - v341 - D 14 '96 - p88 [501+]
 LJ - v122 - F 15 '97 - p137 [51-250]
 Obs - N 3 '96 - p17* [501+]
 Obs - D 1 '96 - p16* [1-50]
 PW - v244 - Ja 20 '97 - p390 [51-250]
 r R&R Bk N - v12 - F '97 - p81 [1-50]
 r Si & So - v6 - N '96 - p38 [51-250]
Nowlan, Robert A - *Born This Day*
 r ARBA - v28 - '97 - p21 [51-250]
 yr BL - v93 - N 15 '96 - p608 [51-250]
 R&R Bk N - v11 - D '96 - p63 [51-250]
Nowotny, Helga - *After the Breakthrough*
 Nature - v385 - F 6 '97 - p498+ [501+]
Nowra, Louis - *Cosi: The Screenplay*
 Aust Bk R - Jl '96 - p42+ [501+]
Noyaya Iskra-1
 y TES - Mr 7 '97 - pR10 [51-250]
Noyce, Richard - *Contemporary Painting in Poland*
 r Choice - v34 - N '96 - p445 [51-250]
Nozick, Betsy - *Texas Tuxedos to Tacos*
 BL - v93 - My 15 '97 - p1552+ [51-250]
The NPR Interviews 1996
 Ent W - Ja 24 '97 - p52 [51-250]
 Trib Bks - Ja 19 '97 - p8 [1-50]
Ntuen, Celestine A - *Human Interaction with Complex Systems*
 SciTech - v21 - Mr '97 - p11 [51-250]
Nubola, Cecilia - *Conoscere Per Governare*
 EHR - v111 - S '96 - p977 [51-250]
Nuclear Safeguards and the International Atomic Energy Agency
 J Gov Info - v23 - S '96 - p557 [51-250]
Nuclear Test Ban: Glossary in English, French, and Arabic
 r ARBA - v28 - '97 - p260+ [51-250]
Nuclear Wastes in the Arctic
 J Gov Info - v23 - S '96 - p554 [51-250]
Nuffield National Curriculum Mathematics (Levels 7 and 8): Number and Algebra 4
 y TES - O 4 '96 - pR14 [501+]
Nuffield National Curriculum Mathematics (Levels 7 and 8): Shape, Space and Measures 4
 y TES - O 4 '96 - pR14 [501+]
Nugent, Beth - *Live Girls*
 Bloom Rev - v16 - S '96 - p19+ [51-250]
 LATBR - S 1 '96 - p10+ [51-250]
Nugent, Frances - *Drawing from Life*
 Woman's J - S '96 - p10 [1-50]
Nugent, Paul - *Big Men, Small Boys and Politics in Ghana*
 Choice - v34 - S '96 - p204 [51-250]
Nugent, Walter - *Crossings: The Great Transatlantic Migrations 1870-1914*
 J Soc H - v30 - Fall '96 - p268+ [501+]
Nuland, Sherwin B - *The Wisdom of the Body*
 BL - v93 - Mr 15 '97 - p1202+ [51-250]
 KR - v65 - Mr 1 '97 - p361+ [51-250]
 LJ - v122 - Ap 15 '97 - p108 [51-250]
 NYTLa - v146 - Ap 28 '97 - pC14 [501+]
 PW - v244 - Mr 24 '97 - p64 [51-250]
 Time - My 12 '97 - p91 [251-500]
 WSJ-Cent - v99 - My 7 '97 - pA16 [501+]
Null, Gary - *The Woman's Encyclopedia of Natural Healing*
 r LJ - v122 - Ja '97 - p90 [51-250]
 r PW - v244 - Ja 27 '97 - p100 [51-250]
Nulman, Philip - *Start Up Marketing*
 LJ - v122 - My 1 '97 - p52 [1-50]
Number Grids and Tiles
 TES - F 14 '97 - p16* [51-250]
Numbers, Ronald L - *Antievolution before World War I*
 Isis - v88 - Mr '97 - p160+ [501+]
 Creation-Evolution Debates
 Isis - v88 - Mr '97 - p160+ [501+]
 Early Creationist Journals
 Isis - v88 - Mr '97 - p160+ [501+]
 The Scientific Enterprise in America
 SciTech - v20 - S '96 - p2 [51-250]
Numeroff, Laura Joffe - *The Chicken Sisters (Illus. by Sharleen Collicott)*
 c BL - v93 - My 1 '97 - p1497 [51-250]
 c KR - v65 - My 1 '97 - p725 [51-250]
 c PW - v244 - Ap 7 '97 - p90 [51-250]

Two for Stew (Illus. by Sal Murdocca)
  c BL - v93 - S 15 '96 - p249 [51-250]
  c CBRS - v25 - S '96 - p5 [1-50]
  c HB Guide - v8 - Spr '97 - p41 [51-250]
  c SLJ - v42 - D '96 - p102+ [51-250]
Why a Disguise? (Illus. by David McPhail)
  c HB Guide - v7 - Fall '96 - p270 [1-50]
Nummi, Lassi - *Hengitys Yossa*
  WLT - v70 - Aut '96 - p1001 [51-250]
Numrich, Paul David - *Old Wisdom in the New World*
  AJS - v102 - N '96 - p915+ [501+]
  JAAR - v65 - Spr '97 - p235+ [501+]
Nunes, Terezinha - *Children Doing Mathematics*
  SciTech - v20 - N '96 - p12 [51-250]
  SciTech - v20 - D '96 - p14 [51-250]
Nunez, Benjamin - *Dictionary of Portuguese-African Civilization. Vol. 2*
  r ARBA - v28 - '97 - p196 [51-250]
  r Choice - v34 - O '96 - p256 [51-250]
  r LAR - v98 - Je '96 - p321 [1-50]
Dictionary of Portuguese-African Civilization. Vols. 1-2
  r LJ - v122 - Ap 15 '97 - p39 [51-250]
Nunez, Sigrid - *A Feather on the Breath of God*
  Shen - v46 - Sum '96 - p95+ [501+]
Naked Sleeper
  BL - v93 - S 1 '96 - p63 [51-250]
  LATBR - S 22 '96 - p6 [501+]
  Ms - v7 - N '96 - p82 [1-50]
  NYTBR - v101 - D 1 '96 - p23 [51-250]
  Time - v148 - O 7 '96 - p98 [51-250]
  WSJ-MW - v77 - S 20 '96 - pA12 [251-500]
Nunez Cabeza De Vaca, Alvar - *The Account: Alvar Nunez Cabeza De Vaca's Relacion*
  TranslRevS - v1 - My '95 - p10 [51-250]
Nunn, Chris - *Awareness: What It Is, What It Does*
  CPR - v16 - D '96 - p426+ [501+]
Nunn, Kem - *The Dogs of Winter*
  BL - v93 - D 1 '96 - p621 [51-250]
  BW - v27 - F 2 '97 - p1+ [501+]
  LJ - v121 - N 15 '96 - p89+ [51-250]
  NYTBR - v102 - Mr 23 '97 - p18 [51-250]
  PW - v243 - D 16 '96 - p41+ [51-250]
  Trib Bks - F 16 '97 - p5 [501+]
  VV - v42 - F 18 '97 - p55+ [501+]
Nunn, Pamela Gerrish - *Problem Pictures*
  R&R Bk N - v12 - F '97 - p74 [1-50]
Nunnally, Tiina - *Runemaker*
  y BL - v93 - S 15 '96 - p225 [51-250]
  PW - v243 - Je '96 - p120 [51-250]
  PW - v243 - S 16 '96 - p77 [51-250]
Nurcombe, Valerie J - *Information Sources in Architecture and Construction. 2nd Ed.*
  r ARBA - v28 - '97 - p592 [51-250]
Nursing Home Statistical Yearbook 1995
  r ARBA - v28 - '97 - p604+ [51-250]
Nursing96 Drug Handbook
  r ARBA - v28 - '97 - p618 [51-250]
Nuseibeh, Said - *The Dome of the Rock*
  y BL - v93 - D 15 '96 - p707 [51-250]
  LJ - v121 - D '96 - p88+ [51-250]
  Time - v148 - N 18 '96 - p109 [1-50]
Nussbaum, Felicity A - *Torrid Zones*
  TSWL - v15 - Fall '96 - p363+ [501+]
Nussbaum, Martha Craven - *For Love of Country*
  BL - v92 - Ag '96 - p1863+ [51-250]
  For Aff - v76 - Mr '97 - p173 [51-250]
  LATBR - Ag 18 '96 - p14 [51-250]
  Lon R Bks - v19 - Mr 6 '97 - p22+ [501+]
  TLS - D 27 '96 - p8+ [501+]
Poetic Justice
  APSR - v90 - S '96 - p636+ [501+]
  Choice - v34 - S '96 - p118 [51-250]
  Lon R Bks - v18 - O 17 '96 - p13+ [501+]
  NYTBR - v101 - Ap 7 '96 - p19 [501+]
  Trib Bks - My 25 '97 - p8 [1-50]
The Therapy of Desire
  NYTBR - v101 - S 8 '96 - p36 [1-50]
Women, Culture, and Development
  JEL - v34 - S '96 - p1445 [51-250]
Nussdorfer, Laurie - *Civic Politics in the Rome of Urban VIII*
  J Urban H - v23 - Ja '97 - p240+ [501+]
Nussey, Kent - *The War in Heaven*
  Quill & Q - v63 - Ja '97 - p35 [251-500]
Nutini, Hugo G - *The Wages of Conquest*
  Am Ethnol - v23 - Ag '96 - p642+ [501+]
  Six Ct J - v27 - Win '96 - p1216 [501+]
Nuttall, A D - *Why Does Tragedy Give Pleasure?*
  Choice - v34 - F '97 - p960 [51-250]
  Lon R Bks - v18 - S 19 '96 - p10+ [501+]

Nwosu, Kingsley C - *Multimedia Database Systems*
  SciTech - v20 - S '96 - p5 [51-250]
Nyala, Hannah - *Point Last Seen*
  BL - v93 - My 15 '97 - p1546+ [51-250]
  KR - v65 - My 1 '97 - p702+ [251-500]
Nye, David E, 1946- - *American Photographs in Europe*
  J Am St - v30 - Ag '96 - p310+ [501+]
American Technological Sublime
  Analog - v116 - D '96 - p145+ [501+]
  JEL - v35 - Mr '97 - p267 [51-250]
Nye, Mary Jo - *Before Big Science*
  Choice - v34 - My '97 - p1520 [51-250]
  Sci - v276 - Ap 11 '97 - p216+ [501+]
  TLS - Ap 11 '97 - p31 [501+]
Nye, Naomi Shihab - *I Feel a Little Jumpy around You*
  y BL - v93 - Ap 1 '97 - p1286 [1-50]
  y HB - v72 - N '96 - p755 [51-250]
  y HB Guide - v7 - Fall '96 - p365 [51-250]
  y JAAL - v40 - N '96 - p231+ [51-250]
Never in a Hurry
  y BL - v92 - Ag '96 - p1875 [51-250]
  y BL - v92 - Ag '96 - p1890 [1-50]
  y SLJ - v42 - N '96 - p142 [51-250]
  WAL - v31 - Fall '96 - p265+ [501+]
  Wom R Bks - v14 - D '96 - p1+ [501+]
That Tree Is Older than You Are
  y Emerg Lib - v24 - S '96 - p24 [1-50]
  c RT - v50 - F '97 - p425 [51-250]
  c RT - v50 - Mr '97 - p477 [51-250]
Words under the Words
  WAL - v31 - Fall '96 - p265+ [501+]
Nyeki, Jozsef - *Floral Biology of Temperate Zone Fruit Trees and Small Fruits*
  Choice - v34 - D '96 - p637 [51-250]
  SciTech - v20 - S '96 - p44 [51-250]
Nyeko, Balam - *Uganda. Rev. Ed.*
  r ARBA - v28 - '97 - p56 [51-250]
  r R&R Bk N - v12 - F '97 - p21 [1-50]
Nyer, Evan K - *In Situ Treatment Technology*
  Choice - v34 - Mr '97 - p1191 [51-250]
  SciTech - v20 - D '96 - p68 [51-250]
Nyerges, Timothy L - *Cognitive Aspects of Human-Computer Interaction for Geographic Information Systems*
  SciTech - v20 - D '96 - p1 [51-250]
Nyhart, Lynn K - *Biology Takes Form*
  TLS - F 21 '97 - p8+ [501+]
Nyhoff, Larry - *Fortran 90 for Engineers and Scientists*
  SciTech - v20 - D '96 - p9 [1-50]
Introduction to Fortran 90 for Engineers and Scientists
  SciTech - v20 - D '96 - p9 [51-250]
Nyiri, Janos - *Battlefields and Playgrounds*
  TranslRevS - v2 - D '96 - p27 [51-250]
Nyman, Mattias - *Photoshop in 4 Colors*
  CBR - v15 - Spr '97 - p9 [1-50]
Nyquist, Richard A - *Handbook of Infrared and Raman Spectra of Inorganic Compounds and Organic Salts. Vols. 1-4*
  Choice - v34 - Mr '97 - p1188 [51-250]
Nyzhankivs'kyi, Bohdan - *Vyrishal'ni Zustichi*
  WLT - v71 - Win '97 - p186 [501+]

O

Oakerson, Ronald J - *The Organization of Local Public Economies*
    NCR - v85 - Spr '96 - p63 [51-250]
Oakes, Baile - *Sculpting with the Environment*
    Art J - v55 - Sum '96 - p95+ [501+]
Oakes, Edward T - *German Essays on Religion*
    Rel St Rev - v22 - O '96 - p335 [51-250]
    TranslRevS - v2 - D '96 - p2 [1-50]
Oakes, Guy - *The Imaginary War*
    AIIR - v101 - O '96 - p1311 [501+]
    Historian - v59 - Fall '96 - p152+ [501+]
Oakes, Jill - *Our Boots*
    Am Craft - v56 - O '96 - p52 [51-250]
Oakeshott, Ewart - *A Knight and His Castle. Rev. and Updated Ed.*
    y Ch BWatch - v7 - F '97 - p1 [51-250]
Oakeshott, Michael - *The Politics of Faith and the Politics of Scepticism*
    Choice - v34 - D '96 - p689 [51-250]
Oakham, Ronald A - *One at the Table*
    CLW - v67 - Mr '97 - p35 [251-500]
Oakley, Allen - *Classical Economic Man*
    Econ J - v107 - Ja '97 - p261+ [51-250]
Oakley, Ann - *Man and Wife*
    NS - v125 - N 8 '96 - p47 [501+]
    Who's Afraid of Feminism?
    Obs - Mr 30 '97 - p17* [501+]
Oakley, R J - *Tirso De Molina: El Condenado Por Desconfiado*
    MLR - v91 - O '96 - p1017+ [501+]
Oaks, Scott - *Java Threads*
    LJ - v122 - Ap 1 '97 - p118 [51-250]
Oates, Joyce Carol - *American Gothic Tales*
    y BL - v93 - N 1 '96 - p480 [51-250]
    BW - v27 - Mr 30 '97 - p12 [51-250]
    y Kliatt - v31 - My '97 - p17 [51-250]
    KR - v64 - O 15 '96 - p1493 [51-250]
    LJ - v121 - N 15 '96 - p90+ [51-250]
    PW - v243 - N 11 '96 - p58 [51-250]
    Trib Bks - Ja 19 '97 - p8 [1-50]
    Bloodstained Bridal Gown (McDonough). Audio Version
    BWatch - v18 - Mr '97 - p7 [1-50]
    Demon and Other Tales
    MFSF - v91 - Ag '96 - p31 [251-500]
    First Love
    LATBR - S 8 '96 - p11 [51-250]
    NYTBR - v101 - S 15 '96 - p11 [501+]
    Tenderness
    PW - v243 - S 30 '96 - p84 [51-250]
    Unholy Loves
    Critiq - v37 - Sum '96 - p270+ [501+]
    The Virgin in the Rose Bower (McDonough). Audio Version
    BWatch - v17 - D '96 - p10 [1-50]
    y Kliatt - v31 - Mr '97 - p47 [51-250]
    Quill & Q - v62 - N '96 - p41 [1-50]
    We Were the Mulvaneys
    BL - v92 - Ag '96 - p1855 [251-500]
    BW - v26 - S 22 '96 - p4 [501+]
    BW - v26 - D 8 '96 - p6 [1-50]
    LATBR - S 15 '96 - p3+ [501+]
    LATBR - D 29 '96 - p6+ [51-250]
    Nat - v263 - O 28 '96 - p62+ [501+]
    NYTBR - v101 - S 15 '96 - p11 [501+]
    NYTBR - v101 - N 8 '96 - p84 [1-50]
    PW - v243 - N 4 '96 - p38 [51-250]
    Will You Always Love Me? and Other Stories
    NYTBR - v101 - D 8 '96 - p84 [1-50]
    W&I - v11 - Ag '96 - p274+ [501+]
    WLT - v70 - Aut '96 - p959+ [251-500]

Will You Always Love Me? and Other Stories (Guidall). Audio Version
    CSM - v88 - O 31 '96 - pB4 [51-250]
    y Kliatt - v31 - Ja '97 - p47+ [51-250]
    Zombie
    Necro - Fall '96 - p11+ [501+]
    NYTBR - v101 - O 13 '96 - p32 [51-250]
    WLT - v70 - Sum '96 - p693 [501+]
Oates, Mary J - *The Catholic Philanthropic Tradition in America*
    AHR - v101 - D '96 - p1614 [501+]
Oates, Stephen B - *The Approaching Fury*
    KR - v65 - Ja 1 '97 - p44+ [251-500]
    LJ - v122 - F 15 '97 - p146 [51-250]
    NYTBR - v102 - Ap 6 '97 - p34 [501+]
    PW - v244 - Ja 6 '97 - p57 [51-250]
Oates, Wallace E - *The Economics of Environmental Regulation*
    JEL - v34 - S '96 - p1498 [51-250]
    R&R Bk N - v11 - D '96 - p24 [51-250]
Oates, Wayne E - *Luck: A Secular Faith*
    Intpr - v51 - Ja '97 - p106 [51-250]
    TT - v53 - O '96 - p428 [51-250]
Obaldia, Claire De - *The Essayistic Spirit*
    Choice - v34 - D '96 - p606 [51-250]
O'Ballance, Edgar - *The Kurdish Struggle 1920-94*
    Choice - v34 - S '96 - p191 [51-250]
    R&R Bk N - v11 - N '96 - p14 [51-250]
    No Victor, No Vanquished
    BWatch - v18 - F '97 - p5 [51-250]
O'Barr, Jean F - *Feminism in Action*
    Signs - v22 - Win '97 - p453+ [501+]
Obbink, Dirk - *Philodemus and Poetry*
    Rel St Rev - v23 - Ap '97 - p172 [51-250]
Obejas, Achy - *Memory Mambo*
    Advocate - S 17 '96 - p60 [1-50]
    BL - v93 - S 1 '96 - p63 [51-250]
    BW - v26 - D 15 '96 - p7 [501+]
    Ms - v7 - S '96 - p83 [251-500]
Ober, Hal - *How Music Came to the World (Illus. by C Ober)*
    c SS - v88 - Ja '97 - p29+ [501+]
Oberhaus, Dorothy Huff - *Emily Dickinson's Fascicles*
    NEQ - v69 - D '96 - p672+ [501+]
    Nine-C Lit - v50 - Mr '96 - p556 [51-250]
Oberle, Gerard - *Auguste Poulet-Malassis*
    r BC - v45 - Win '96 - p578+ [501+]
Oberman, Cerise - *Russian-American Seminar on Critical Thinking and the Library*
    LR - v45 - 7 '96 - p72+ [501+]
Oberman, Sheldon - *The Always Prayer Shawl (Illus. by Ted Lewin)*
    c PW - v244 - F 24 '97 - p84 [1-50]
Oberoi, Harjot - *The Construction of Religious Boundaries*
    JR - v77 - Ja '97 - p182+ [501+]
Oberrecht, Ken - *How to Start a Home-Based Photography Business*
    BWatch - v18 - F '97 - p3 [1-50]
Obeyesekere, Gananath - *The Apotheosis of Captain Cook*
    W&M Q - v54 - Ja '97 - p253+ [501+]
Obi, Alexis - *Time for Bed*
    c Bks Keeps - N '96 - p7 [51-250]
Obituaries in the Performing Arts 1994
    r ARBA - v28 - '97 - p501+ [51-250]
    r BL - v93 - N 1 '96 - p539 [51-250]
Obituaries in the Performing Arts 1994-
    r Choice - v34 - Mr '97 - p1140 [51-250]

Obituaries in the Performing Arts 1995
    r ARBA - v28 - '97 - p501+ [51-250]
    r BL - v93 - N 1 '96 - p539 [51-250]
Obler, Martin - *Fatal Analysis*
    BL - v93 - F 1 '97 - p912 [51-250]
    LJ - v121 - D '96 - p122 [51-250]
    PW - v243 - N 18 '96 - p52+ [51-250]
O'Boyle, Edward J - *Social Economics*
    JEL - v34 - D '96 - p2009 [51-250]
O'Brian, Patrick - *The Commodore*
    Books - v9 - S '95 - p24 [1-50]
    The Golden Ocean
    NYTBR - v101 - O 20 '96 - p36 [51-250]
    The Unknown Shore
    NYTBR - v101 - O 20 '96 - p36 [1-50]
    The Yellow Admiral
    BL - v93 - S 15 '96 - p222 [51-250]
    Comw - v123 - N 8 '96 - p9+ [501+]
    CSM - v88 - O 24 '96 - p11 [51-250]
    CSM - v88 - N 14 '96 - p14 [51-250]
    KR - v64 - S 1 '96 - p1261 [251-500]
    LATBR - O 20 '96 - p3 [501+]
    NL - v79 - D 16 '96 - p22+ [501+]
    NY - v72 - Ja 13 '97 - p79 [51-250]
    NYTBR - v101 - N 3 '96 - p9 [501+]
    NYTBR - v101 - D 8 '96 - p84 [1-50]
    Obs - Ja 5 '97 - p15* [501+]
    PW - v243 - S 16 '96 - p70 [51-250]
    SFR - v22 - Ja '97 - p48 [51-250]
    Spec - v278 - Ja 4 '97 - p30+ [501+]
    TLS - Ja 10 '97 - p20 [501+]
    WSJ-Cent - v99 - Ja 27 '97 - pA20 [501+]
    The Yellow Admiral (Tull). Audio Version
    BWatch - v18 - Mr '97 - p7 [1-50]
O'Brien, Catherine - *Italian Women Poets of the Twentieth Century*
    Choice - v34 - My '97 - p1505 [51-250]
O'Brien, Conor Cruise - *Conor: A Biography of Conor Cruise O'Brien*
    Bks & Cult - v2 - Ja '96 - p11+ [501+]
    Can Hist R - v77 - D '96 - p646+ [501+]
    Can Hist R - v77 - D '96 - p646+ [501+]
    Conor: An Anthology
    Bks & Cult - v2 - Ja '96 - p11+ [501+]
    The Long Affair
    Am - v175 - S 21 '96 - p35+ [51-250]
    y BL - v93 - N 1 '96 - p479 [51-250]
    BW - v26 - N 24 '96 - p3+ [501+]
    KR - v64 - S 1 '96 - p1303 [251-500]
    LATBR - N 10 '96 - p1+ [501+]
    LJ - v121 - O 15 '96 - p73 [51-250]
    Nat R - v48 - N 25 '96 - p67+ [501+]
    New R - v216 - Mr 10 '97 - p32+ [501+]
    NL - v79 - D 16 '96 - p9+ [501+]
    NS - v125 - D 6 '96 - p55+ [501+]
    NYRB - v44 - F 20 '97 - p23+ [501+]
    NYTBR - v101 - N 17 '96 - p23 [501+]
    Obs - D 8 '96 - p15* [501+]
    PW - v243 - N 4 '96 - p52+ [51-250]
    TLS - N 15 '96 - p3+ [501+]
O'Brien, Dan, 1947- - *Brendan Prairie*
    Ant R - v54 - Fall '96 - p488 [251-500]
    LATBR - v263 - S 29 '96 - p14 [51-250]
    VQR - v73 - Win '97 - p22* [51-250]
    Equinox: Life, Love, and Falconry in the Great Outdoors
    BL - v93 - F 15 '97 - p994 [51-250]
    KR - v65 - Ja 1 '97 - p45 [251-500]
    PW - v244 - Ja 6 '97 - p54 [51-250]
O'Brien, Daniel - *Clint Eastwood, Film-Maker*
    Choice - v34 - F '97 - p973 [51-250]

O'Brien, David J - *Public Catholicism. 2nd Ed.*
Cons - v17 - Win '96 - p31 [1-50]
O'Brien, David M - *To Dream of Dreams*
APSR - v91 - Mr '97 - p219+ [501+]
Choice - v34 - Ja '97 - p869 [51-250]
O'Brien, Denis - *Plotinus on the Origin of Matter*
Dialogue - v35 - Spr '96 - p293+ [501+]
Theodicee Plotinienne, Theodicee Gnostique
Dialogue - v35 - Spr '96 - p293+ [501+]
O'Brien, Edna - *Down by the River*
BL - v93 - Mr 1 '97 - p1069 [51-250]
KR - v65 - F 15 '97 - p250 [251-500]
LJ - v122 - Ap 1 '97 - p130 [51-250]
NS - v125 - Ag 30 '96 - p46 [251-500]
Obs - S 15 '96 - p16* [501+]
PW - v244 - Mr 3 '97 - p62 [51-250]
TLS - S 27 '96 - p22 [501+]
Trib Bks - My 18 '97 - p3+ [501+]
O'Brien, Flann - *The Third Policeman*
TES - Ag 30 '96 - p25 [1-50]
O'Brien, Geoffrey - *The Reader's Catalog. 2nd Ed., Vols. 1-2*
r LJ - v122 - Mr 15 '97 - p58 [51-250]
r PW - v244 - Ja 20 '97 - p390 [51-250]
O'Brien, Jacqueline - *Ancient Ireland*
BL - v93 - N 1 '96 - p479 [51-250]
BWatch - v17 - D '96 - p8 [1-50]
LJ - v122 - F 15 '97 - p154 [51-250]
O'Brien, John - *Mother Hubbard's Christmas (Illus. by John O'Brien)*
c CBRS - v25 - O '96 - p16 [51-250]
c HB Guide - v8 - Spr '97 - p41 [1-50]
c PW - v243 - S 30 '96 - p89 [51-250]
c SLJ - v42 - O '96 - p39 [51-250]
O'Brien, John, 1954- - *Anacreon Redivivus*
MLR - v92 - Ap '97 - p465 [251-500]
MLR - v92 - Ap '97 - p465 [251-500]
O'Brien, John, 1960- - *The Assault on Tony's*
NYTBR - v101 - S 1 '96 - p16 [51-250]
O'Brien, John E - *Refreshed by the Word. Vol. 2*
CLW - v67 - Mr '97 - p34 [51-250]
O'Brien, Judith - *Maiden Voyage*
PW - v243 - D 9 '96 - p65 [51-250]
O'Brien, Kate - *Talk of Angels*
LJ - v122 - Ap 1 '97 - p130 [51-250]
PW - v244 - Mr 10 '97 - p50 [51-250]
O'Brien, Keith - *Cut Your Losses!*
Quill & Q - v62 - D '96 - p30 [51-250]
O'Brien, Kevin - *Only Son*
PW - v243 - N 4 '96 - p63 [51-250]
O'Brien, Michael, 1943- - *Philip Hart: The Conscience of the Senate*
Choice - v34 - Mr '97 - p1228 [51-250]
O'Brien, Michael, 1948- - *Father Elijah: An Apocalypse*
Bks & Cult - v3 - Mr '97 - p18+ [501+]
O'Brien, Michael D - *Strangers and Sojourners*
LJ - v122 - F 1 '97 - p66 [51-250]
PW - v244 - F 24 '97 - p70 [51-250]
O'Brien, Michael J, 1950- - *Evolutionary Archaeology*
Choice - v34 - My '97 - p1540 [51-250]
Sci - v275 - F 28 '97 - p1276 [1-50]
O'Brien, Patrick S - *Making College Count*
J Car P&E - v57 - Win '97 - p16 [251-500]
O'Brien, Robert C - *Z for Zachariah*
y Kliatt - v30 - S '96 - p4 [1-50]
O'Brien, Thomas F - *The Revolutionary Mission*
Choice - v34 - O '96 - p330+ [51-250]
O'Brien, Thomas G - *Handbook of Human Factors Testing and Evaluation*
Per Psy - v49 - Win '96 - p1034+ [501+]
O'Brien, Tim - *Family Adventure Guide: Tennessee*
Bloom Rev - v16 - Jl '96 - p24 [51-250]
O'Brien, Virginia - *The Fast Forward MBA in Business*
Bus Bk R - v13 - 4 '96 - p124 [51-250]
O'Brien, William Arctander - *Novalis: Signs of Revolution*
MLN - v111 - D '96 - p1047+ [501+]
MP - v94 - N '96 - p240+ [501+]
Observatory Techniques
p S&T - v93 - Mr '97 - p96 [51-250]
Observer's Handbook. 1st Ed.-
r S&T - v92 - S '96 - p55 [51-250]
Obst, Lynda - *Hello, He Lied and Other Truths from the Hollywood Trenches*
Ent W - S 13 '96 - p125 [51-250]
LATBR - S 8 '96 - p4 [501+]
LJ - v121 - O 1 '96 - p80 [51-250]
NYTBR - v101 - O 13 '96 - p34 [501+]
Obstfeld, Maurice - *Foundations of International Macroeconomics*
JEL - v35 - Mr '97 - p221 [51-250]

Obstfeld, Raymond - *Earth Angel*
Rapport - v19 - 4 '96 - p33 [251-500]
Obtaining Resources for Technology
H Sch M - v4 - D '96 - p60 [51-250]
O'Burns, Carl - *Imperial Carnival Glass*
Ant & CM - v101 - D '96 - p30 [1-50]
O'Callaghan, Joseph F - *The Learned King*
EHR - v111 - S '96 - p957+ [251-500]
O'Callaghan, Margaret - *British High Politics and a Nationalist Ireland*
AHR - v101 - D '96 - p1544+ [251-500]
Albion - v28 - '96 - p740+ [501+]
Ireland: Criminality, Land and the Law under Forster and Balfour
EHR - v112 - F '97 - p243+ [501+]
O'Callahan, Jay - *Herman and Marguerite (Illus. by Laura O'Callahan)*
c HB Guide - v7 - Fall '96 - p270 [1-50]
Tulips (Illus. by Debrah Santini)
c HB Guide - v8 - Spr '97 - p41 [51-250]
Ocana, Maria Teresa - *Picasso and Els 4 Gats*
LATBR - D 8 '96 - p28 [1-50]
LJ - v122 - F 1 '97 - p76+ [251-500]
Occelli, Mario L - *Hydrotreating Technology for Pollution Control*
SciTech - v20 - D '96 - p83 [51-250]
Synthesis of Porous Materials
SciTech - v20 - D '96 - p82 [51-250]
The Occupational Outlook Handbook. 1996-97 Ed.
r Fut - v31 - Ja '97 - p60+ [501+]
Oceanographic and Marine Resources. Vol. 1. Electronic Media Version
r Choice - v34 - My '97 - p1523 [251-500]
O Ceirin, Kit - *Women of Ireland*
r ILS - v16 - Spr '97 - p18 [501+]
LJ - v122 - Mr 15 '97 - p57+ [51-250]
Ochagi Trevogi V Vostochnoi Europe
Slav R - v55 - Sum '96 - p459+ [501+]
Ochsenbein, Peter - *Codices Sangallenses*
Specu - v71 - O '96 - p994+ [501+]
Ochshorn, Judith - *Women's Spirituality, Women's Lives*
NWSA Jnl - v9 - Spr '97 - p123+ [501+]
O'Clery, Conor - *Daring Diplomacy*
BL - v93 - Mr 15 '97 - p1223 [51-250]
PW - v244 - F 17 '97 - p204 [251-500]
O'Coileain, Seamas - *Voices of Ferrier*
TLS - O 18 '96 - p31 [251-500]
O'Collins, Gerald - *Christology: A Biblical, Historical, and Systematic Study of Jesus*
Rel St Rev - v23 - Ja '97 - p46+ [51-250]
Theol St - v57 - S '96 - p547+ [501+]
Experiencing Jesus
RR - v56 - Ja '97 - p105 [51-250]
O'Connell, Carol - *Killing Critics*
BL - v93 - Ja '97 - p762 [1-50]
Killing Critics (Merlington). Audio Version
y Kliatt - v30 - S '96 - p49 [51-250]
LJ - v121 - O 1 '96 - p144 [51-250]
The Man Who Cast Two Shadows
Arm Det - v30 - Win '97 - p18+ [51-250]
The Man Who Cast Two Shadows (Burton). Audio Version
Arm Det - v29 - Sum '96 - p355 [51-250]
O'Connell, David - *Francois Mauriac Revisited*
FR - v70 - O '96 - p121+ [501+]
O'Connell, Marvin R - *Critics on Trial*
CH - v65 - S '96 - p533+ [501+]
CHR - v82 - O '96 - p732+ [501+]
JAAR - v64 - Win '96 - p900+ [501+]
JMH - v69 - Mr '97 - p118+ [501+]
O'Connell, Patrick - *The Inn at Little Washington Cookbook*
BL - v93 - S 15 '96 - p197 [51-250]
O'Connell, Robert J - *Images of Conversion in St. Augustine's Confessions*
Theol St - v58 - Mr '97 - p160+ [501+]
O'Connell, Robert L - *Ride of the Second Horseman*
APH - v43 - Fall '96 - p65+ [501+]
O'Connell, Sanjida - *Theory of Mind*
Books - v10 - Je '96 - p10 [51-250]
O'Conner, Jim - *Call Me Gretzky*
c Emerg Lib - v24 - Mr '97 - p27 [1-50]
O'Conner, Joseph - *The Irish Male at Home and Abroad*
Obs - O 27 '96 - p18* [501+]
O'Conner, Patricia T - *Woe Is I*
NYTBR - v101 - S 15 '96 - p31 [51-250]
PW - v243 - Jl 22 '96 - p224 [51-250]
SLJ - v42 - D '96 - p41 [51-250]

O'Connor, Barbara - *Beethoven in Paradise*
c CCB-B - v50 - My '97 - p332 [51-250]
c KR - v65 - Mr 15 '97 - p466 [51-250]
c PW - v244 - Mr 3 '97 - p76 [51-250]
The Soldiers' Voice
c BL - v93 - S 1 '96 - p123+ [51-250]
y CCB-B - v50 - O '96 - p71 [51-250]
c HB Guide - v8 - Spr '97 - p160 [51-250]
c SLJ - v42 - Ag '96 - p158 [51-250]
O'Connor, Bonnie Blair - *Healing Traditions*
WestFolk - v55 - Sum '96 - p248+ [501+]
O'Connor, Brian C - *Explorations in Indexing and Abstracting*
LAR - v99 - Ja '97 - p47 [51-250]
R&R Bk N - v11 - N '96 - p80 [51-250]
O'Connor, Colin - *Roman Bridges*
AJA - v100 - Jl '96 - p627+ [501+]
O'Connor, David B - *Ancient Nubia*
AJA - v100 - O '96 - p783+ [501+]
O'Connor, Edwin - *Benjy: A Ferocious Fairy Tale (Illus. by Catharine O'Neill)*
c PW - v243 - Jl 22 '96 - p243 [51-250]
O'Connor, Flannery - *The Violent Bear It Away*
HM - v293 - S '96 - p64+ [501+]
O'Connor, Frank - *The Happiness of Getting It Down Right*
Bks & Cult - v3 - Mr '97 - p28+ [501+]
ILS - v15 - Fall '96 - p6 [501+]
Sew R - v104 - Jl '96 - pR48 [51-250]
O'Connor, Garry - *The Secret Woman*
TLS - Mr 21 '97 - p19 [501+]
O'Connor, Jane - *The Bad-Luck Penny (Illus. by Horatio Elena)*
c SLJ - v42 - Ag '96 - p121 [51-250]
O'Connor, Jill - *Phyllo: Easy Recipes for Sweet and Savory Treats*
BL - v93 - D 15 '96 - p702 [51-250]
PW - v244 - Ja 27 '97 - p102 [51-250]
O'Connor, Jim - *Sticking It Out*
c SLJ - v42 - Ag '96 - p144 [51-250]
O'Connor, John - *Unseen Warhol*
VV - v41 - O 15 '96 - p47 [501+]
O'Connor, Joseph - *Sweet Liberty*
ILS - v16 - Spr '97 - p36 [1-50]
NYTBR - v101 - D 8 '96 - p29 [51-250]
PW - v243 - Jl 22 '96 - p222 [51-250]
O'Connor, Karen, 1938- - *A Kurdish Family (Illus. by Rick Moncauskas)*
c BL - v93 - N 1 '96 - p493 [51-250]
c CCB-B - v50 - D '96 - p146 [51-250]
c Ch BWatch - v6 - O '96 - p5 [51-250]
c HB Guide - v8 - Spr '97 - p90 [51-250]
c SLJ - v42 - N '96 - p115+ [51-250]
O'Connor, Karen, 1952- - *No Neutral Ground?*
Choice - v34 - F '97 - p1037 [51-250]
Wom R Bks - v14 - F '97 - p7+ [501+]
O'Connor, Kathleen - *Robert Musil and the Tradition of the German Novelle*
Ger Q - v69 - Fall '96 - p451+ [501+]
O'Connor, Mallory McCane - *Lost Cities of the Ancient Southeast*
JSH - v62 - N '96 - p861+ [51-250]
O'Connor, Michael K - *The Mayo Clinic Manual of Nuclear Medicine*
SciTech - v20 - D '96 - p38 [51-250]
O'Connor, Paul - *Deactivation and Testing of Hydrocarbon-Processing Catalysts*
SciTech - v21 - Mr '97 - p96 [51-250]
O'Connor, Raymond G - *Origins of the American Navy*
EHR - v111 - S '96 - p998 [51-250]
O'Connor, Richard - *Bodyguards: The World of VIP Protection*
PW - v244 - Mr 17 '97 - p73 [51-250]
O'Connor, Richard F X - *How to Market You and Your Book*
r BWatch - v18 - F '97 - p4 [51-250]
O'Connor, Thomas - *An Irish Theologian in Enlightenment France*
Rel St Rev - v23 - Ja '97 - p83+ [51-250]
O'Connor, Thomas H - *The Boston Irish*
NYTBR - v102 - Mr 16 '97 - p32 [51-250]
Building a New Boston
J Urban H - v22 - Jl '96 - p665+ [501+]
O Croinin, Daibhi - *Early Medieval Ireland 400-1200*
HRNB - v25 - Fall '96 - p17+ [251-500]
TLS - Ja 3 '97 - p28 [501+]
TLS - Ja 3 '97 - p29 [501+]
O'Dair, Barbara - *The Rolling Stone Book of Women in Rock*
LJ - v122 - Ja '97 - p102 [51-250]
PW - v244 - Ja 6 '97 - p55 [51-250]

O'Day, Rosemary - *The Family and Family Relationships 1500-1900*
    Historian - v59 - Fall '96 - p210+ [251-500]
    JIH - v27 - Aut '96 - p302+ [501+]
The Longman Companion to the Tudor Age
    r Six Ct J - v27 - Fall '96 - p873+ [501+]
Oddie, Bill - *Follow That Bird!*
    BL - v93 - S 1 '96 - p48 [51-250]
Oddie, Geoffrey A - *Hindu and Christian in South-East India*
    JTWS - v13 - Spr '96 - p265+ [501+]
Oddy, Pat - *Future Libraries, Future Catalogues*
    LAR - v98 - D '96 - p649 [51-250]
Odean, Kathleen - *Great Books for Girls*
    r BL - v93 - Mr 1 '97 - p1176 [51-250]
    r Ent W - Mr 7 '97 - p60 [51-250]
    yr Kliatt - v31 - My '97 - p17+ [51-250]
    r LJ - v122 - Ja '97 - p99 [51-250]
    r Ms - v7 - Mr '97 - p83 [1-50]
    r PW - v243 - D 16 '96 - p61 [51-250]
Odell, George H - *Stone Tools*
    Choice - v34 - S '96 - p169 [51-250]
Stone Tools and Mobility in the Illinois Valley
    Choice - v34 - My '97 - p1542 [51-250]
O'Dell, Scott - *The Black Pearl*
    c Ch BWatch - v6 - My '96 - p7 [1-50]
Island of the Blue Dolphins
    c JOYS - v10 - Fall '96 - p46+ [501+]
Sarah Bishop (Haas). Audio Version
    y Kliatt - v31 - Ja '97 - p45 [51-250]
Odem, Mary E - *Delinquent Daughters*
    Historian - v59 - Win '97 - p439 [251-500]
    JIH - v27 - Spr '97 - p721+ [501+]
Oden, Amy - *In Her Words*
    CH - v66 - Mr '97 - p165+ [501+]
    Rel St Rev - v22 - O '96 - p347 [51-250]
Odenwald, Neil G - *Plants for American Landscapes*
    BL - v93 - O 1 '96 - p314 [51-250]
    Choice - v34 - My '97 - p1524+ [51-250]
    LJ - v121 - O 15 '96 - p82 [51-250]
    r PW - v243 - N 4 '96 - p73 [51-250]
Odenwald, Sylvia B - *Global Impact*
    HR Mag - v42 - Ja '97 - p147 [501+]
Oderman, Stuart - *Roscoe Fatty Arbuckle: A Biography of the Silent Film Comedian 1887-1933*
    FQ - v49 - Fall '95 - p64+ [51-250]
Odgers, Sally - *Bunyips Don't! (Illus. by Kim Gamble)*
    c Aust Bk R - S '96 - p61+ [501+]
    c Magpies - v11 - S '96 - p27 [51-250]
Odifreddi, Piergiorgio - *Kreiseliana: About and around Georg Kreisel*
    SciTech - v21 - Mr '97 - p4 [51-250]
Odo, of Tournai - *On Original Sin*
    CH - v66 - Mr '97 - p187+ [51-250]
Odom, William E - *Commonwealth or Empire?*
    MEJ - v51 - Win '97 - p121+ [501+]
Odone, Cristina - *The Shrine*
    Spec - v277 - N 23 '96 - p44 [1-50]
O'Donnell, Brennan - *The Passion of Meter*
    Nine-C Lit - v51 - S '96 - p233+ [501+]
O'Donnell, Edith - *Integrating Computers into the Classroom*
    Cur R - v36 - F '97 - p3* [51-250]
O'Donnell, Lillian - *The Goddess Affair*
    BL - v93 - Ja '97 - p825 [51-250]
    BW - v26 - D 15 '96 - p10 [51-250]
    KR - v64 - N 15 '96 - p1637 [51-250]
    LJ - v122 - Ja '97 - p153 [51-250]
    PW - v243 - N 11 '96 - p60 [51-250]
O'Donnell, Mark - *Getting over Homer*
    HG&LRev - v3 - Fall '96 - p43 [51-250]
    LJ - v122 - F 1 '97 - p136 [51-250]
O'Donnell, Patrick, 1948- - *New Essays on The Crying of Lot 49*
    Poetics T - v18 - Spr '97 - p95+ [501+]
O'Donoghue, Brian - *My Lead Dog Was a Lesbian*
    y Kliatt - v30 - S '96 - p39 [51-250]
    Rapport - v19 - 5 '96 - p44 [251-500]
O'Donoghue, Michael - *Rocks and Minerals*
    yr BWatch - v17 - N '96 - p7 [51-250]
O'Donohoe, Nick - *The Healing of Crossroads*
    y BL - v93 - D 1 '96 - p643 [51-250]
    BWatch - v18 - Mr '97 - p9+ [1-50]
    y Kliatt - v31 - My '97 - p15 [51-250]
O'Donovan, Donal - *God's Architect*
    Aust Bk R - N '96 - p43 [501+]
O'Donovan, Gerald - *Father Ralph*
    Rel St Rev - v23 - Ja '97 - p52 [51-250]

Odozor, Paulinus Ikechukwu - *Richard A. McCormick and the Renewal of Moral Theology*
    Rel St Rev - v23 - Ap '97 - p157 [51-250]
    Theol St - v57 - S '96 - p557+ [501+]
O'Driscoll, Gerald P - *The Economics of Time and Ignorance*
    JEL - v35 - Mr '97 - p205 [51-250]
Odum, Howard T - *Environmental Accounting*
    Choice - v34 - S '96 - p177 [51-250]
Ody, Penelope - *Home Herbal*
    r ARBA - v28 - '97 - p583 [51-250]
Odysseus '96
    r Quill & Q - v62 - S '96 - p24 [51-250]
Odyssey: The Glaxo Wellcome Journal of Innovation in Healthcare
    p Nature - v383 - S 5 '96 - p38 [251-500]
Oe, Emily - *Kaleidoscope of Play Therapy Stories*
    Readings - v11 - D '96 - p30 [51-250]
Oe, Kenzaburo - *An Echo of Heaven*
    BL - v93 - Ja '97 - p761 [1-50]
    LATBR - My 12 '96 - p4 [501+]
    Nat - v263 - S 30 '96 - p34+ [501+]
    WLT - v71 - Win '97 - p229 [501+]
A Healing Family
    BL - v92 - Ag '96 - p1852 [251-500]
    KR - v64 - S 1 '96 - p1304 [251-500]
    LATBR - O 20 '96 - p14 [51-250]
    LJ - v121 - O 1 '96 - p90 [51-250]
    Obs - D 15 '96 - p15* [501+]
    PW - v243 - O 7 '96 - p56 [51-250]
    TLS - D 27 '96 - p32 [51-250]
    YR - v85 - Ap '97 - p150+ [501+]
Hiroshima Notes
    y Kliatt - v30 - N '96 - p27+ [51-250]
Nip the Buds, Shoot the Kids
    LATBR - Ag 4 '96 - p11 [51-250]
    Obs - O 20 '96 - p18* [51-250]
Oinaru Hi Ni
    WLT - v70 - Aut '96 - p1033 [501+]
A Quiet Life
    Ent W - D 20 '96 - p71 [51-250]
    KR - v64 - S 1 '96 - p1262 [251-500]
    NYTBR - v101 - N 17 '96 - p19 [501+]
    PW - v243 - O 14 '96 - p64+ [51-250]
    YR - v85 - Ap '97 - p150+ [501+]
Seventeen and J
    LATBR - Ag 11 '96 - p2 [501+]
Two Novels
    BL - v92 - Ag '96 - p1852 [251-500]
    WLT - v71 - Win '97 - p229+ [501+]
    YR - v85 - Ap '97 - p150+ [501+]
OECD Statistical Compendium 1996/1. Electronic Media Version
    r ARBA - v28 - '97 - p108 [251-500]
Oelschlager, Max - *Postmodern Environmental Ethics*
    Ethics - v107 - O '96 - p184 [51-250]
Oermann, Robert K - *America's Music*
    LJ - v121 - N 1 '96 - p42 [1-50]
Oestmann, Cord - *Lordship and Community*
    EHR - v111 - S '96 - p970+ [251-500]
O'Faolain, Nuala - *Are You Somebody?*
    TLS - N 29 '96 - p15 [51-250]
O'Farrell, Brigid - *Rocking the Boat*
    Choice - v34 - D '96 - p677 [51-250]
    Wom R Bks - v14 - O '96 - p17+ [501+]
Offe, Claus - *Modernity and the State*
    Choice - v34 - My '97 - p1574+ [51-250]
    For Aff - v76 - Mr '97 - p175 [51-250]
    JEL - v35 - Mr '97 - p288 [51-250]
    TLS - Ja 24 '97 - p4+ [501+]
Offen, Hilda - *As Quiet as a Mouse*
    c Bks Keeps - N '96 - p6 [51-250]
The Bad Day ABC (Illus. by Hilda Offen)
    c Bks Keeps - Mr '97 - p18 [51-250]
    c JB - v60 - D '96 - p236 [51-250]
Good Girl, Gracie Growler!
    c Magpies - v11 - My '96 - p37+ [51-250]
Rita the Rescuer
    c TES - Jl 5 '96 - pR6 [1-50]
Scared of a Bear
    c Sch Lib - v44 - Ag '96 - p100 [51-250]
Watch Out for Witches! (Illus. by Hilda Offen)
    c Bks Keeps - Ja '97 - p22 [51-250]
Offer, Avner - *In Pursuit of the Quality of Life*
    TLS - F 28 '97 - p27 [501+]

Officer, Charles - *The Great Dinosaur Extinction Controversy*
    A & S Sm - v11 - O '96 - p88 [1-50]
    BWatch - v17 - S '96 - p11 [51-250]
    Choice - v34 - O '96 - p641 [51-250]
    Nature - v385 - Ja 2 '97 - p36 [51-250]
    Sci - v273 - S 27 '96 - p1808 [51-250]
    Skeptic - v4 - 3 '96 - p105+ [251-500]
Officer, Lawrence H - *Between the Dollar-Sterling Gold Points*
    Choice - v34 - Ja '97 - p846 [51-250]
    JEL - v35 - Mr '97 - p261 [51-250]
Official 1996 National Football League Record and Fact Book
    r ARBA - v28 - '97 - p298 [51-250]
The Official Country Music Directory 1994
    r LJ - v121 - N 1 '96 - p41 [1-50]
Official Heartbreak High Book
    y Books - v9 - S '95 - p26 [1-50]
Official Methods of Analysis of the AOAC International. 16th Ed., Vols. 1-2
    SciTech - v20 - S '96 - p44 [51-250]
Official Railway Equipment Register
    r Model R - v64 - Mr '97 - p51+ [51-250]
Official Records of the Human Rights Committee 1989/90. Vol. 2
    R&R Bk N - v11 - N '96 - p48 [51-250]
The Official UEFA Euro '96
    Books - v10 - Je '96 - p21 [51-250]
Offit, Sidney - *Memoir of the Bookie's Son*
    y Kliatt - v30 - S '96 - p26 [51-250]
    LATBR - Jl 14 '96 - p11 [51-250]
Offutt, Chris - *The Good Brother*
    PW - v244 - My 5 '97 - p194+ [51-250]
Offutt, William M, Jr. - *Of Good Laws and Good Men*
    AHR - v102 - F '97 - p168+ [501+]
    CH - v65 - D '96 - p715+ [501+]
    JR - v77 - Ap '97 - p323+ [501+]
    JSH - v62 - N '96 - p791+ [251-500]
    W&M Q - v53 - O '96 - p811+ [501+]
O'Flaherty, Brendan - *Making Room*
    JEL - v35 - Mr '97 - p302+ [51-250]
O'Flaherty, Liam - *The Black Soul*
    LJ - v121 - N 15 '96 - p93 [1-50]
The Wilderness
    LJ - v121 - N 15 '96 - p93 [51-250]
O'Flynn, Mark - *The Too Bright Sun*
    Aust Bk R - S '96 - p53+ [501+]
Ofosu-Appiah, L H - *The Encyclopedia Africana Dictionary of African Biography. Vol. 3*
    r ARBA - v28 - '97 - p50 [251-500]
Ofshe, Richard - *Making Monsters*
    Bks & Cult - v3 - Ja '97 - p17+ [501+]
Ogai, Mori - *The Wild Goose*
    TranslRevS - v2 - D '96 - p29 [51-250]
    WLT - v70 - Aut '96 - p1032+ [251-500]
Youth and Other Stories
    TranslRevS - v1 - My '95 - p25 [51-250]
Ogasapian, John - *English Cathedral Music in New York*
    VS - v39 - Spr '96 - p461+ [501+]
Ogata, Katsuhiko - *Modern Control Engineering. 3rd Ed.*
    SciTech - v20 - D '96 - p72 [51-250]
Ogawa, Joseph M - *Compendium of Stone Fruit Diseases*
    SciTech - v20 - D '96 - p56 [51-250]
Ogawa, Kikuko - *Isamu Noguchi/Rosanjin Kitaoji*
    LJ - v122 - Ap 1 '97 - p90 [51-250]
Ogden, Daniel - *Greek Bastardy in the Classical and Hellenistic Periods*
    HRNB - v25 - Win '97 - p88+ [501+]
    Rel St Rev - v22 - O '96 - p346 [51-250]
Ogden, Paul W - *The Silent Garden*
    BWatch - v18 - F '97 - p6 [51-250]
Ogden, R Todd - *Essential Wavelets for Statistical Applications and Data Analysis*
    Choice - v34 - My '97 - p1537 [51-250]
    r SciTech - v21 - Mr '97 - p17 [51-250]
L'Oggetto Libro '96
    AB - v98 - Ag 19 '96 - p580 [51-250]
    BC - v45 - Win '96 - p543 [51-250]
Ogilvie, Marilyn Bailey - *Women and Science*
    r ARBA - v28 - '97 - p333 [51-250]
    r Choice - v34 - Ja '97 - p772+ [51-250]
    r R&R Bk N - v11 - D '96 - p67 [51-250]
Ogilvie, Sheilagh C - *European Proto-Industrialization*
    Choice - v34 - Mr '97 - p1208 [51-250]
    JEL - v35 - Mr '97 - p259 [51-250]
Ogle, Maureen - *All the Modern Conveniences*
    Choice - v34 - Ja '97 - p815+ [51-250]
    SciTech - v21 - Mr '97 - p84 [51-250]
Ogletree, Charles J - *Beyond the Rodney King Story*
    CS - v25 - N '96 - p798+ [501+]

Ognjenovic, Vida - *Kuca Mrtvih Mirisa*
  WLT - v70 - Aut '96 - p991+ [501+]
Ogonowska, Ewa - *Oprawy Zabytkowe I Artystyczne XIII-XIX Wieku W Zbiorach Biblioteki Gdanskiej Polskiej Akademii Nauk*
  Lib - v18 - D '96 - p365 [1-50]
Ogot, Bethwell A - *Decolonization and Independence in Kenya 1940-93*
  Choice - v34 - N '96 - p513 [51-250]
  JEL - v34 - D '96 - p2103+ [51-250]
O Grada, Cormac - *The Great Irish Famine*
  JEL - v34 - D '96 - p2105 [51-250]
  Ireland: A New Economic History 1780-1939
  JEL - v34 - S '96 - p1465 [51-250]
  JIH - v27 - Win '97 - p517+ [501+]
  VS - v39 - Win '96 - p205+ [501+]
O'Grady, Scott - *Return with Honor*
  Mar Crp G - v81 - Ja '97 - p71+ [501+]
Ogunyemi, Chikwenye Okonjo - *Africa Wo/man Palava*
  Choice - v34 - S '96 - p120 [51-250]
Ohadi, M M - *Advances in Energy Efficiency, Heat/Mass Transfer Enhancement*
  SciTech - v21 - Mr '97 - p95 [51-250]
Ohadike, Don C - *Anioma: A Social History of the Western Igbo People*
  Historian - v58 - Sum '96 - p851+ [501+]
  JTWS - v13 - Spr '96 - p329+ [501+]
O'Hagan, Andrew - *The Missing*
  Bus W - N 4 '96 - p24 [51-250]
  KR - v64 - Ag 15 '96 - p1218+ [251-500]
  LJ - v121 - O 15 '96 - p76 [51-250]
  NYTBR - v101 - N 10 '96 - p58 [501+]
  Obs - O 6 '96 - p18* [51-250]
  PW - v243 - O 7 '96 - p57 [51-250]
  VLS - Win '96 - p10 [51-250]
  VV - v41 - N 5 '96 - p51 [501+]
O'Hagan, J W - *The Economy of Ireland*
  JEL - v35 - Mr '97 - p178+ [501+]
Ohanian, Susan - *Ask Ms. Class*
  EL - v54 - S '96 - p86 [501+]
Ohanian, Thomas A - *Digital Filmmaking*
  SciTech - v20 - S '96 - p62 [51-250]
O'Hanlon, Christine - *Professional Development through Action Research in Educational Settings*
  R&R Bk N - v11 - D '96 - p52 [51-250]
O'Hanlon, Redmond - *Congo Journey*
  Lon R Bks - v19 - Ap 24 '97 - p19+ [501+]
  Nature - v384 - D 12 '96 - p528 [1-50]
  NS - v125 - O 25 '96 - p45+ [501+]
  Obs - O 20 '96 - p16* [501+]
  Obs - D 1 '96 - p17* [1-50]
  Spec - v277 - N 2 '96 - p54 [501+]
  TLS - N '96 - p6 [501+]
  No Mercy
  y BL - v93 - F 15 '97 - p998 [51-250]
  KR - v65 - Ja 15 '97 - p126 [251-500]
  PW - v244 - F 3 '97 - p91 [51-250]
Ohanneson, Joan - *Scarlet Music*
  BL - v93 - Mr 1 '97 - p1111 [51-250]
  LJ - v122 - F 1 '97 - p66+ [51-250]
O'Hara, James J - *True Names*
  Choice - v34 - Ja '97 - p790+ [51-250]
O'Hara, Michael W - *Psychological Aspects of Women's Reproductive Health*
  AJPsych - v153 - S '96 - p1225 [251-500]
O'Hara, Valerie - *Wellness at Work*
  BWatch - v18 - Mr '97 - p4 [51-250]
O'Hare, Padraic - *The Enduring Covenant*
  PW - v244 - Ja 13 '97 - p70 [51-250]
O'Hear, Anthony - *Karl Popper: Philosophy and Problems*
  CPR - v16 - O '96 - p365+ [501+]
Ohio Genealogical Society. Wood County Chapter - *Lake Township Cemetery, Wood County, Ohio*
  r EGH - v50 - N '96 - p181 [51-250]
Ohlmeyer, Jane H - *Civil War and Restoration in the Three Stuart Kingdoms*
  Sev Cent N - v54 - Spr '96 - p22+ [501+]
  Ireland from Independence to Occupation 1641-1660
  Albion - v28 - Fall '96 - p548+ [501+]
  HT - v46 - S '96 - p55+ [501+]
Ohly, Friedrich - *Ausgewahlte und Neue Schriften Zur Literaturgeschichte Und Zur Bedeutungsforschung*
  TLS - Ja 24 '97 - p26 [501+]
Ohmann, Richard - *English in America*
  Col Comp - v47 - O '96 - p440 [51-250]
  TCR - v98 - Spr '97 - p537+ [501+]
  Selling Culture
  Nat - v262 - Je 3 '96 - p38+ [501+]
  Prog - v61 - Ja '97 - p36 [51-250]
  TLS - O 11 '96 - p10 [501+]

Ohno, Izumi - *Beyond the East Asian Miracle*
  JEL - v35 - Mr '97 - p248 [51-250]
Ojakangas, Beatrice - *Beatrice Ojakangas' Light and Easy Baking*
  BL - v93 - S 15 '96 - p197 [51-250]
  LJ - v121 - N 15 '96 - p84 [51-250]
  PW - v243 - O 7 '96 - p71 [51-250]
Ojo-Ade, Femi - *Of Dreams Deferred, Dead or Alive*
  AL - v69 - Mr '97 - p253+ [51-250]
  Bl S - v26 - Fall '96 - p105 [1-50]
  R&R Bk N - v11 - N '96 - p71 [51-250]
Okada, Kazuo - *Shock, from Molecular and Cellular Level to Whole Body*
  SciTech - v21 - Mr '97 - p48 [51-250]
O'Kane, Leslie - *Just the Fax, Ma'am*
  Ent W - O 11 '96 - p86+ [51-250]
O'Kane, Rosemary H T - *Terror, Force, and States*
  Choice - v34 - O '96 - p353 [51-250]
  R&R Bk N - v11 - N '96 - p47 [51-250]
Oke, Janette - *The Bluebird and the Sparrow (Haas).*
  Audio Version
  y Kliatt - v31 - My '97 - p35 [51-250]
  Drums of Change
  y VOYA - v19 - O '96 - p212 [251-500]
  Nana's Gift
  Rapport - v19 - 6 '96 - p21 [251-500]
  Return to Harmony
  y BL - v93 - S 1 '96 - p65 [501+]
O'Keefe, Claudia - *Famous Writers Celebrate Motherhood with a Treasury of Short Stories, Essays and Poems*
  Trib Bks - My 4 '97 - p8 [1-50]
O'Keefe, Frank - *If It Rains Again Tomorrow, Can We Go Home?*
  c Quill & Q - v62 - O '96 - p49+ [251-500]
O'Keefe, Garrett J - *Taking a Bite out of Crime*
  R&R Bk N - v11 - D '96 - p45 [51-250]
O'Keefe, Mark - *Becoming Good, Becoming Holy*
  Am - v175 - N 2 '96 - p28+ [251-500]
  RR - v56 - Mr '97 - p218+ [501+]
  Theol St - v57 - D '96 - p784+ [251-500]
O'Keefe, Richard R - *Mythic Archetypes in Ralph Waldo Emerson*
  Nine-C Lit - v51 - D '96 - p425 [51-250]
O'Keefe, Timothy J - *Columbus, Confrontation, Christianity*
  CHR - v82 - O '96 - p671+ [501+]
O'Keeffe, Linda - *Shoes: A Celebration of Pumps, Sandals, Slippers and More*
  Bloom Rev - v17 - Ja '97 - p23 [51-250]
  VLS - Win '96 - p20 [51-250]
Okely, John - *Own or Other Culture*
  Socio R - v45 - F 1 '97 - p162+ [501+]
Okihiro, Gary Y - *Margins and Mainstreams*
  RAH - v24 - D '96 - p663+ [501+]
  Whispered Silences
  Bks & Cult - v2 - N '96 - p32 [51-250]
  BW - v27 - Ja 5 '97 - p12 [51-250]
  Choice - v34 - D '96 - p677 [51-250]
  y Kliatt - v30 - N '96 - p28 [51-250]
  LATBR - Ag 11 '96 - p10 [51-250]
  y SLJ - v42 - N '96 - p142 [51-250]
  WHQ - v28 - Spr '97 - p101 [1-50]
Oklahoma. Governor's Commission on Government Performance - *A Government as Good as Our People*
  J Gov Info - v23 - S '96 - p592 [51-250]
Okpewho, Isidore - *African Oral Literature*
  RA - v25 - 3 '96 - p215+ [501+]
Okrand, Mark - *Star Trek: The Klingon Way*
  SF Chr - v18 - O '96 - p82 [1-50]
Okrend, Elise - *Blintzes for Blitzen (Illus. by Alice Io Oglesby)*
  c PW - v243 - S 30 '96 - p87 [51-250]
Oktavec, Eileen - *Answered Prayers*
  HAHR - v77 - My '97 - p290+ [251-500]
Oktenberg, Adrian - *The Bosnia Elegies*
  BL - v93 - F 15 '97 - p996 [51-250]
  Choice - v34 - Ap '97 - p1338 [51-250]
Okun, Barbara F - *Understanding Diverse Families*
  SciTech - v21 - Mr '97 - p54 [51-250]
Okwu, Julian C R - *Face Forward*
  PW - v244 - Mr 3 '97 - p54 [51-250]
Olafson, Frederick A - *What Is a Human Being?*
  CPR - v16 - Ag '96 - p271+ [501+]
  Ethics - v107 - Ja '97 - p403 [51-250]
  TLS - Jl 19 '96 - p27 [501+]
Olafsson, Einar - *Manadufur*
  WLT - v70 - Aut '96 - p982 [51-250]
Olalleye, Isaac - *The Distant Talking Drum (Illus. by F Lessac Honesdale)*
  c RT - v50 - Mr '97 - p477 [51-250]

Olaniyan, R Omotayo - *Foreign Aid, Self-Reliance, and Economic Development in West Africa*
  R&R Bk N - v12 - F '97 - p37 [51-250]
Olasky, Marvin - *Renewing American Compassion*
  BL - v93 - Ja '97 - p757 [1-50]
  Nat R - v48 - Je 3 '96 - p53+ [501+]
  Telling the Truth
  Bks & Cult - v2 - Jl '96 - p3+ [501+]
Olausen, Judy - *Mother*
  Bloom Rev - v16 - N '96 - p25+ [51-250]
  LATBR - My 26 '96 - p10 [251-500]
  Wom R Bks - v14 - N '96 - p12+ [501+]
Olav, Stokke - *Foreign Aid towards the Year 2000*
  R&R Bk N - v11 - N '96 - p25 [51-250]
Olbermann, Keith - *The Big Show*
  PW - v244 - Ap 14 '97 - p67 [51-250]
Old, Wendie C - *Duke Ellington: Giant of Jazz*
  y HB Guide - v8 - Spr '97 - p159 [51-250]
  y SLJ - v42 - N '96 - p130 [51-250]
Old House Journal
  p LJ - v122 - F 1 '97 - p53 [1-50]
Old South (Insight Guides)
  r BL - v93 - S 15 '96 - p210 [1-50]
Olde, Peter - *The Grevillea Book. Vols. 1-3*
  Hort - v74 - D '96 - p60 [251-500]
Olden, Anthony - *Libraries in Africa*
  LAR - v98 - O '96 - p537 [51-250]
  LQ - v67 - Ap '97 - p200+ [501+]
Olden, Kevin W - *Handbook of Functional Gastrointestinal Disorders*
  SciTech - v20 - S '96 - p36 [51-250]
Oldenburg, Manfred - *Die Trierer Kartause St. Alban Von Der Grundung 1330/31 Bis Zur Mitte Des 15. Jahrhunderts*
  CH - v66 - Mr '97 - p192+ [51-250]
Older, Effin - *Double Birthday Trouble*
  y Ch BWatch - v7 - F '97 - p5 [1-50]
Oldfield, Duane Murray - *The Right and the Righteous*
  CC - v113 - N 20 '96 - p1134+ [501+]
  Choice - v34 - Mr '97 - p1241 [51-250]
Oldfield, Homer R - *King of the Seven Dwarfs*
  Choice - v34 - D '96 - p646 [51-250]
  SciTech - v20 - S '96 - p4 [1-50]
Oldfield, J R - *Popular Politics and British Anti-Slavery*
  Albion - v28 - '96 - p705+ [501+]
Oldfield, Sara - *Rain Forests (Illus. by Still Pictures Firm)*
  c Ch BWatch - v6 - S '96 - p5 [1-50]
  c HB Guide - v8 - Spr '97 - p97 [51-250]
  c SLJ - v43 - Ja '97 - p106+ [51-250]
Oldham, Doug - *There Is Hope*
  BL - v93 - S 1 '96 - p39 [51-250]
Oldham, Gabriella - *Keaton's Silent Shorts*
  AB - v98 - D 9 '96 - p1997 [51-250]
  Choice - v34 - S '96 - p136 [51-250]
  Rapport - v19 - 4 '96 - p34 [251-500]
Oldham, John M - *Impulsivity and Compulsivity*
  AJPsych - v154 - Ja '97 - p127 [251-500]
  New Personality Self-Portrait
  J ClinPsyc - v57 - D '96 - p598 [501+]
Oldham, June - *Escape*
  c Bks Keeps - Mr '97 - p27 [51-250]
  y Sch Lib - v45 - F '97 - p47 [51-250]
  y TES - Ja 3 '97 - p22 [51-250]
  Found
  y BL - v93 - S 15 '96 - p232+ [51-250]
  y CBRS - v25 - Win '97 - p70 [51-250]
  y CCB-B - v50 - Ja '97 - p183 [51-250]
  c HB - v72 - N '96 - p738+ [51-250]
  c HB Guide - v8 - Spr '97 - p72 [51-250]
  c KR - v64 - S 15 '96 - p1406 [51-250]
  y SLJ - v43 - Ja '97 - p115+ [51-250]
  y VOYA - v19 - F '97 - p339 [51-250]
Oldroyd, D R - *Darwinian Impacts*
  BWatch - v18 - Mr '97 - p10 [51-250]
  Thinking about the Earth
  Choice - v34 - Ap '97 - p1368 [51-250]
  Nature - v383 - S 26 '96 - p309+ [501+]
  New Sci - v152 - N 9 '96 - p42 [51-250]
Oldroyd, Margaret - *Staff Development in Academic Libraries*
  LAR - v98 - Ag '96 - p424 [501+]
Olds, Bruce - *Raising Holy Hell*
  y Kliatt - v31 - My '97 - p8 [51-250]
  NS - v125 - O 25 '96 - p48 [501+]
  PW - v243 - D 30 '96 - p64 [1-50]
  TLS - O 11 '96 - p25 [251-500]
Olds, Fred A - *An Abstract of North Carolina Wills from about 1760 to about 1800*
  r EGH - v50 - N '96 - p177+ [51-250]
Olds, Patrick C - *The Barbie Doll Years 1959-1995*
  r Ant & CM - v101 - Jl '96 - p25 [1-50]

Olds, Sharon - *The Wellspring*
  Obs - D 1 '96 - p16* [1-50]
The Wellspring: Poems
  BL - v93 - Ja '97 - p759 [1-50]
  NYTBR - v101 - S 15 '96 - p15 [501+]
  VQR - v72 - Aut '96 - p137* [51-250]
O'Leary, A P - *Jane's Electro-Optic Systems*
  r Choice - v34 - S '96 - p100 [51-250]
O'Leary, Ann - *Women and AIDS*
  R&R Bk N - v12 - F '97 - p95 [51-250]
Women at Risk
  Readings - v11 - D '96 - p28 [51-250]
O'Leary, Elizabeth L - *At Beck and Call*
  R&R Bk N - v11 - N '96 - p61 [1-50]
O'Leary, J Patrick, 1941- - *The Physiologic Basis of Surgery. 2nd Ed.*
  SciTech - v20 - N '96 - p39 [51-250]
O'Leary, Joseph S - *La Verite Chretienne A L'Age Du Pluralisme Religieux*
  JR - v76 - O '96 - p661+ [501+]
O'Leary, Pamela - *Transportation Expressions*
  r J Gov Info - v23 - S '96 - p573 [1-50]
O'Leary, Patrick, 1952- - *Door Number Three*
  y Kliatt - v31 - My '97 - p15 [51-250]
O'Leary, Wayne M - *Maine Sea Fisheries*
  r Choice - v34 - My '97 - p1520 [51-250]
Oleksiw, Susan - *A Reader's Guide to the Classic British Mystery*
  r RQ - v36 - Win '96 - p217 [51-250]
Oleksy, Walter - *Business and Industry*
  y HB Guide - v7 - Fall '96 - p351 [51-250]
Entertainment
  y HB Guide - v7 - Fall '96 - p351 [51-250]
  y VOYA - v19 - O '96 - p236 [251-500]
Olevianus, Caspar - *A Firm Foundation*
  Six Ct J - v27 - Win '96 - p1089+ [501+]
Olgin, Howard - *Remote Intrusion*
  PW - v243 - S 30 '96 - p80+ [51-250]
Olin, John C - *Erasmus, Utopia and the Jesuits*
  Ren Q - v50 - Spr '97 - p305+ [501+]
Oliner, Samuel P - *Who Shall Live*
  y BL - v93 - N 1 '96 - p479+ [51-250]
  KR - v64 - N 1 '96 - p1587+ [251-500]
  LJ - v122 - F 1 '97 - p95 [51-250]
  Trib Bks - F 2 '97 - p5 [501+]
Oliphant, B J - *A Ceremonial Death*
  Arm Det - v29 - Sum '96 - p365+ [51-250]
Oliphant, Betty - *Miss O*
  Quill & Q - v62 - Jl '96 - p52 [251-500]
Oliphant, Dave - *Texan Jazz*
  AB - v98 - D 9 '96 - p1996 [51-250]
  Choice - v34 - N '96 - p470 [51-250]
Olitzky, Kerry M - *The American Synagogue*
  r ARBA - v28 - '97 - p554 [51-250]
  r Choice - v34 - D '96 - p593 [51-250]
  r LJ - v121 - O 1 '96 - p68+ [51-250]
  R&R Bk N - v11 - N '96 - p6 [51-250]
Striving toward Virtue
  BL - v93 - S 1 '96 - p39 [51-250]
Oliver, Dick - *Netscape 2 Unleashed*
  BL - v93 - S 15 '96 - p193 [501+]
Oliver, Geoff - *Reclaim It*
  c TES - Ja 3 '97 - pR15 [51-250]
Oliver, Jack - *Shocks and Rocks*
  Nature - v383 - O 24 '96 - p684 [251-500]
Oliver, Joseph - *Quality of Life and Mental Health Services*
  SciTech - v20 - S '96 - p28 [51-250]
Oliver, Kelly - *Ethics, Politics, and Difference in Julia Kristeva's Writing*
  Signs - v22 - Aut '96 - p254+ [501+]
Reading Kristeva
  Signs - v22 - Aut '96 - p254+ [501+]
Oliver, Marilyn Tower - *Drugs: Should They Be Legalized?*
  y HB Guide - v8 - Spr '97 - p98 [51-250]
  y SLJ - v43 - Mr '97 - p205+ [51-250]
Oliver, Mary - *Blue Pastures*
  Ant R - v54 - Sum '96 - p369 [251-500]
White Pine
  PS - v70 - Fall '96 - p186+ [501+]
Oliver, Melvin L - *Black Wealth/White Wealth*
  AAPSS-A - v548 - N '96 - p233+ [501+]
  JNE - v64 - Fall '95 - p477+ [501+]
  PSQ - v111 - Fall '96 - p523+ [501+]
  Soc Ser R - v70 - S '96 - p494+ [501+]
Oliver, Michael - *Benjamin Britten*
  LJ - v121 - N 1 '96 - p69 [51-250]
  PW - v243 - S 30 '96 - p79 [1-50]

Igor Stravinsky
  M Ed J - v83 - N '96 - p54 [1-50]
  TLS - Jl 7 '96 - p19 [501+]
Oliver, Roland - *A Short History of Africa (Howard). Audio Version*
  y Kliatt - v31 - Mr '97 - p50 [51-250]
  LJ - v121 - N 15 '96 - p107 [51-250]
Oliver, Simon - *Special Educational Needs and the Law*
  TES - N 1 '96 - pR8 [251-500]
  TES - Ja 24 '97 - p11* [51-250]
Oliver, Valerie Burnham - *Fashion and Costume in American Popular Culture*
  r ARBA - v28 - '97 - p499 [51-250]
  r BL - v93 - D 15 '96 - p748 [501+]
  Choice - v34 - Mr '97 - p1141+ [251-500]
  r R&R Bk N - v12 - F '97 - p103 [51-250]
Oliver Labra, Carilda - *Dust Disappears*
  TranslRevS - v2 - D '96 - p33 [51-250]
Ollard, Richard - *Cromwell's Earl*
  HT - v46 - S '96 - p55+ [501+]
Ollier, Brigitte - *Doisneau Paris*
  Afterimage - v24 - Ja '97 - p23 [1-50]
  BL - v93 - Ja '97 - p803 [51-250]
  PW - v243 - N 25 '96 - p69 [51-250]
Ollin, Ros - *Planning, Delivering and Assessing GNVQs*
  TES - F 28 '97 - p32 [251-500]
Ollivier, Emile - *Les Urnes Scellees*
  FR - v70 - Mr '97 - p620+ [501+]
  WLT - v70 - Sum '96 - p749+ [501+]
Olmstead, Robert - *Stay Here with Me*
  NYTBR - v101 - S 1 '96 - p19 [501+]
  TLS - Ag 30 '96 - p28 [501+]
Olmsted, Katherine S - *Challenging the Secret Government*
  HRNB - v25 - Fall '96 - p15 [251-500]
Olness, Karen - *Hypnosis and Hypnotherapy with Children. 3rd Ed.*
  SB - v32 - O '96 - p201+ [251-500]
  r SciTech - v20 - S '96 - p41 [51-250]
Olney, Ross Robert - *Lyn St. James: Driven to Be First*
  c BL - v93 - F 15 '97 - p1019 [51-250]
  c Ch BWatch - v7 - F '97 - p7 [1-50]
  c SLJ - v43 - Mr '97 - p206 [51-250]
Olof Palme International Center - *Estonia and Russia, Estonians and Russians*
  JPR - v34 - F '97 - p114 [51-250]
O'Looney, John - *Redesigning the Work of Human Services*
  Choice - v34 - O '96 - p368 [51-250]
O'Loughlin, Michael - *Another Nation*
  TLS - S 27 '96 - p12 [501+]
Olsen, Byron D - *Great Northern Railway 1945-1970 Photo Archive*
  Model R - v63 - D '96 - p74 [51-250]
Olsen, Dale A - *Music of the Warao of Venezuela*
  Choice - v34 - N '96 - p470+ [51-250]
Olsen, Gary - *Getting Started in Multimedia Design*
  BL - v93 - Mr 1 '97 - p1071 [51-250]
Olsen, Gregg - *Starvation Heights*
  PW - v244 - F 24 '97 - p87 [51-250]
Olsen, Jack - *Salt of the Earth*
  PW - v244 - F 17 '97 - p217 [1-50]
Salt of the Earth (Bottino). Audio Version
  PW - v243 - S 2 '96 - p48 [51-250]
Olsen, K H - *Continental Rifts*
  SciTech - v21 - Mr '97 - p33 [51-250]
Olsen, Monty - *Choctaw Emigration Records 1831-1856. Vols. 1-2*
  r EGH - v50 - N '96 - p183+ [51-250]
Olsen, Peer - *The Sophie's World Workbook*
  TES - F 14 '97 - p23* [501+]
Olsen, Penny - *Australian Birds of Prey*
  r SciTech - v21 - Mr '97 - p38 [51-250]
Olsen, Sandra L - *Horses through Time*
  y BL - v93 - N 15 '96 - p557 [51-250]
  LJ - v121 - O 15 '96 - p88 [51-250]
  Nature - v386 - Mr 27 '97 - p341+ [501+]
  y SB - v33 - My '97 - p108 [51-250]
Olsen, T V - *Deadly Pursuit (Addison). Audio Version*
  LJ - v121 - O 15 '96 - p101 [51-250]
Olsen, W Scott - *The Sacred Place*
  Bloom Rev - v16 - N '96 - p13 [51-250]
Olshan, Joseph - *Night Swimmer*
  Books - v9 - S '95 - p24 [1-50]
Olson, Alan M - *Heidegger and Jaspers*
  JAAR - v64 - Sum '96 - p452+ [501+]
Olson, David M - *The New Parliaments of Central and Eastern Europe*
  CR - v269 - N '96 - p279 [51-250]
  R&R Bk N - v11 - N '96 - p49 [51-250]

Olson, David R - *The Handbook of Education and Human Development*
  r Choice - v34 - Ja '97 - p849 [51-250]
The World on Paper
  MLR - v92 - Ap '97 - p411+ [501+]
  Nature - v384 - N 7 '96 - p37 [51-250]
Olson, Dennis T - *Numbers*
  Rel St Rev - v23 - Ap '97 - p164+ [51-250]
Olson, Ellen - *Controversies in Ethics in Long-Term Care*
  AJN - v96 - N '96 - p16D [51-250]
Olson, Gary - *Women Writing Culture*
  Col Comp - v47 - O '96 - p440+ [51-250]
Olson, Gregory Allen - *Mansfield and Vietnam*
  PHR - v66 - F '97 - p144+ [251-500]
  QJS - v83 - F '97 - p119+ [501+]
Olson, James Stuart - *Cuban Americans*
  HAHR - v77 - F '97 - p167+ [501+]
  JSH - v62 - N '96 - p849+ [251-500]
The Peoples of Africa
  r ARBA - v28 - '97 - p149 [51-250]
  r BL - v93 - S 1 '96 - p169 [51-250]
  r Choice - v34 - D '96 - p593 [51-250]
  r R&R Bk N - v11 - N '96 - p22 [51-250]
The Vietnam War
  r JTWS - v13 - Spr '96 - p252+ [501+]
Olson, Jenni - *The Ultimate Guide to Lesbian and Gay Film and Video*
  r ARBA - v28 - '97 - p514 [51-250]
  r BL - v93 - S 1 '96 - p171+ [251-500]
Olson, Richard P - *Midlife Journeys*
  PW - v243 - S 2 '96 - p127 [51-250]
Olson, Robert - *The Kurdish Nationalist Movement in the 1990s*
  BL - v93 - N 1 '96 - p478+ [51-250]
  Choice - v34 - My '97 - p1568 [51-250]
  MEJ - v51 - Spr '97 - p312 [51-250]
Olson, Walter - *The Excuse Factory*
  WSJ-Cent - v99 - My 20 '97 - pA16 [501+]
Olsson, Lars O - *Undergraduate Teaching of the History of Technology*
  T&C - v38 - Ja '97 - p271+ [501+]
Olsson, Mats - *De Ensamma Pojkarna*
  WLT - v70 - Aut '96 - p982 [51-250]
Olsson, Vibeke - *Molnfri Bombnatt*
  WLT - v70 - Sum '96 - p718 [501+]
Olster, David M - *Roman Defeat, Christian Response, and the Literary Construction of the Jew*
  EHR - v111 - N '96 - p1232+ [251-500]
Olster, Fredi - *A Midsummer Night's Dream*
  y BL - v93 - Ja '97 - p840 [251-500]
  y Kliatt - v30 - N '96 - p20 [51-250]
  y SLJ - v42 - D '96 - p148 [51-250]
  y VOYA - v19 - F '97 - p360+ [251-500]
Romeo and Juliet
  y BL - v93 - Ja '97 - p840 [251-500]
  y Kliatt - v30 - N '96 - p20 [51-250]
  y SLJ - v42 - D '96 - p148 [51-250]
  y VOYA - v19 - F '97 - p360+ [251-500]
The Taming of the Shrew
  y VOYA - v19 - F '97 - p360+ [251-500]
Olukoshi, Adebayo - *The Politics of Structural Adjustment in Nigeria*
  WP - v49 - O '96 - p92+ [501+]
O'Malley, Kevin - *Carl Caught a Flying Fish*
  c HB Guide - v7 - Fall '96 - p270 [1-50]
O'Malley, Tony - *Tony O'Malley (Lynch)*
  R&R Bk N - v11 - N '96 - p60 [51-250]
Oman, Lela Kiana - *The Epic of Qayaq*
  BL - v93 - N 15 '96 - p555 [51-250]
O'Mara, Carmel - *Good Morning, Good Night*
  c PW - v244 - F 10 '97 - p85 [1-50]
O'Mara, Michael - *Using Your PC. 2nd Ed.*
  y BL - v93 - Mr 1 '97 - p1101 [51-250]
O'Marie, Carol Anne - *Death of an Angel*
  BL - v93 - D 15 '96 - p713 [51-250]
  KR - v64 - N 15 '96 - p1638 [51-250]
  PW - v243 - N 4 '96 - p66 [51-250]
O'Meara, Dan - *Forty Lost Years*
  Choice - v34 - Ap '97 - p1412 [51-250]
O'Meara, John - *Delaware-English/English-Delaware Dictionary*
  r ARBA - v28 - '97 - p389 [51-250]
  r Choice - v34 - D '96 - p593 [51-250]
O'Meilia, Matt - *Garth Brooks: The Road out of Santa Fe*
  BL - v93 - F 1 '97 - p919 [51-250]
  LJ - v122 - F 1 '97 - p80+ [51-250]
  PW - v244 - Mr 17 '97 - p67 [51-250]
Omelianuk, J Scott - *Work Clothes*
  BL - v93 - S 1 '96 - p49 [51-250]
Omori, Hideki - *Infinite-Dimensional Lie Groups*
  SciTech - v21 - Mr '97 - p18 [51-250]

The OMRI Annual Survey of Eastern Europe and the Former Soviet Union 1995
   R&R Bk N - v12 - F '97 - p17 [51-250]
O Muirithe, Diarmaid - *A Dictionary of Anglo-Irish*
   r ILS - v16 - Spr '97 - p35 [1-50]
   The Words We Use
      ILS - v15 - Fall '96 - p31 [1-50]
O Muraile, Nollaig - *The Celebrated Antiquary*
   ILS - v16 - Spr '97 - p27 [501+]
O'Murchu, Diarmuid - *Quantum Theology*
   PW - v243 - D 2 '96 - p51 [51-250]
On Spec
   p SF Chr - v18 - O '96 - p83 [1-50]
O'Nan, Stewart - *The Names of the Dead*
   Bks & Cult - v2 - S '96 - p9 [501+]
   NYTBR - v101 - Ap 7 '96 - p18 [501+]
   PW - v244 - Mr 17 '97 - p81 [1-50]
   Trib Bks - Ap 27 '97 - p8 [1-50]
   Snow Angels
      Sew R - v104 - Jl '96 - pR59+ [501+]
   The Speed Queen
      BL - v93 - Ap 1 '97 - p1282 [51-250]
      KR - v65 - Ja 15 '97 - p89+ [251-500]
      LJ - v122 - F 1 '97 - p107 [51-250]
      PW - v244 - Ja 20 '97 - p391 [251-500]
      Trib Bks - Ap 6 '97 - p5 [501+]
Oncken, O - *Basement Tectonics 11*
   SciTech - v20 - D '96 - p28 [51-250]
Ondaatje, Christopher - *Sindh Revisited*
   Mac - v109 - My 20 '96 - p71 [501+]
   Quill & Q - v62 - My '96 - p29 [51-250]
Ondaatje, Michael - *The Collected Works of Billy the Kid*
   LATBR - Jl 14 '96 - p10 [51-250]
   In the Skin of a Lion
      BIC - v25 - S '96 - p35 [251-500]
   Running in the Family (Ondaatje). Audio Version
      Quill & Q - v62 - D '96 - p31 [251-500]
One Currency for Europe
   J Gov Info - v23 - S '96 - p668+ [51-250]
One-Dish Meals (Better Homes and Gardens)
   BWatch - v17 - D '96 - p9 [1-50]
One Hundred Years of Cinema
   c Books - v9 - S '95 - p26 [1-50]
O'Neal, Reagan - *The Fallon Pride*
   PW - v243 - S 9 '96 - p65 [51-250]
Onega, Susana - *Narratology: An Introduction*
   Choice - v34 - Mr '97 - p1156 [51-250]
O'Neil, Brian - *Actors Take Action*
   Am Theat - v13 - D '96 - p21 [1-50]
O'Neil, Buck - *I Was Right on Time*
   BW - v26 - Jl 7 '96 - p1+ [501+]
   y SLJ - v42 - N '96 - p142 [51-250]
O'Neil, Frank - *The Mammoth Book of Oddities*
   r BL - v93 - Mr 15 '97 - p1264 [251-500]
O'Neil, Robert M - *Free Speech in the College Community*
   KR - v65 - Ja 1 '97 - p45+ [251-500]
   PW - v244 - F 3 '97 - p90 [51-250]
O'Neill, Amanda - *I Wonder Why Snakes Shed Their Skin and Other Questions about Reptiles*
   c HB Guide - v7 - Fall '96 - p342 [51-250]
O'Neill, J C - *Who Did Jesus Think He Was?*
   Rel St Rev - v23 - Ja '97 - p71 [51-250]
O'Neill, Jean - *Athletic Activities for Juniors*
   c TES - N 22 '96 - p16* [251-500]
O'Neill, John - *Hegel's Dialectic of Desire and Recognition*
   CPR - v16 - Je '96 - p195+ [501+]
O'Neill, Joseph - *The Breezes*
   Books - v9 - S '95 - p24 [1-50]
   Obs - Ag 25 '96 - p18* [51-250]
O'Neill, Judith - *Hearing Voices*
   y Sch Lib - v45 - F '97 - p47 [51-250]
   y TES - Ja 3 '97 - p22 [51-250]
O'Neill, Laurie A - *The Boston Tea Party*
   c BL - v93 - Ja '97 - p852 [251-500]
   c HB Guide - v8 - Spr '97 - p172 [51-250]
   c SLJ - v43 - Mr '97 - p206 [51-250]
O'Neill, Mary - *Adventures in Color*
   c Inst - v106 - Ja '97 - p4* [1-50]
O'Neill, Molly - *The Pleasure of Your Company*
   BL - v93 - Mr 15 '97 - p1216 [51-250]
   LJ - v122 - Mr 15 '97 - p84 [51-250]
   PW - v244 - Mr 3 '97 - p68 [51-250]
O'Neill, Patricia - *Robert Browning and Twentieth-Century Criticism*
   Nine-C Lit - v50 - Mr '96 - p556 [1-50]
O'Neill, Patrick - *Acts of Narrative*
   R&R Bk N - v11 - F '97 - p91 [51-250]
   Fictions of Discourse
      MLR - v91 - Jl '96 - p746+ [501+]

O'Neill, Peter - *Environmental Chemistry. 2nd Ed.*
   J Chem Ed - v73 - N '96 - pA276 [251-500]
O'Neill, Rose Cecil - *The Story of Rose O'Neill*
   KR - v65 - Mr 1 '97 - p362 [51-250]
   PW - v244 - Ap 7 '97 - p82 [251-500]
O'Neill, Teresa - *The Homeless: Distinguishing between Fact and Opinion*
   y SLJ - v42 - O '96 - p45 [1-50]
O'Neill, William G - *Paper Laws, Steel Bayonets*
   JTWS - v13 - Spr '96 - p369+ [501+]
O'Neill, William R - *The Ethics of Our Climate*
   Ethics - v107 - Ja '97 - p404 [51-250]
   Theol St - v58 - Mr '97 - p181+ [501+]
O'Nell, Theresa DeLeane - *Disciplined Hearts*
   R&R Bk N - v11 - N '96 - p17 [51-250]
Onetti, Juan Carlos - *Esbjerg, En La Costa Y Otros Cuentos*
   MLR - v92 - Ap '97 - p496+ [501+]
   Let the Wind Speak
      KR - v64 - D 1 '96 - p1703+ [51-250]
      LJ - v122 - Ap 15 '97 - p125 [1-50]
Oney, Steven Thomas - *Cape Cod Radio Mystery Theater. Audio Version*
   BWatch - v17 - D '96 - p11 [1-50]
Ong, Paul - *The New Asian Immigration in Los Angeles and Global Restructuring*
   Pac A - v69 - Sum '96 - p303 [251-500]
Oni, Olusola O A - *How to Cope with University Life*
   TES - S 27 '96 - p8* [51-250]
Onimus, Jean - *Pour Lire Le Clezio*
   FR - v70 - Mr '97 - p606+ [501+]
Online-Offline
   p LJ - v121 - D '96 - p158 [51-250]
Onnepalu, Tonu - *Hind*
   WLT - v70 - Sum '96 - p731 [501+]
Ono, Yoshiyasu - *Money, Interest, and Stagnation*
   JEL - v34 - S '96 - p1354+ [501+]
Onstad, Dianne - *The Whole Foods Companion*
   BL - v93 - N 15 '96 - p560 [51-250]
   LJ - v121 - N 15 '96 - p56 [51-250]
   r PW - v243 - N 4 '96 - p73 [51-250]
Onyefulu, Ifeoma - *Emeka's Gift*
   c Emerg Lib - v24 - Mr '97 - p46 [51-250]
   Ogbo: Sharing Life in an African Village (Illus. by Ifeoma Onyefulu)
   c BL - v93 - Ap 1 '97 - p1298 [1-50]
   c HB - v72 - S '96 - p623+ [51-250]
   c HB Guide - v7 - Fall '96 - p311 [51-250]
   c New Ad - v9 - Fall '96 - p327+ [501+]
   One Big Family
   c Sch Lib - v44 - Ag '96 - p100 [51-250]
Ooms, Herman - *Tokugawa Village Practice*
   R&R Bk N - v11 - N '96 - p40 [51-250]
Oorschot, Wim Van - *Realizing Rights*
   Soc Ser R - v70 - D '96 - p671 [51-250]
Oostendorp, Herre Van - *Cognitive Aspects of Electronic Text Processing*
   SciTech - v21 - Mr '97 - p10 [51-250]
Oostindie, Gert - *Fifty Years Later*
   JEL - v34 - S '96 - p1467+ [51-250]
Oostrum, Duco Van - *Male Authors, Female Subjects*
   AL - v69 - Mr '97 - p224+ [251-500]
Oparenko, Christina - *Ukrainian Folk Tales*
   c Bks Keeps - Jl '96 - p11 [51-250]
   c JB - v60 - Ag '96 - p159 [51-250]
   c Magpies - v11 - Jl '96 - p42 [51-250]
Opatrny, Josef - *Cuba: Algunos Problemas De Su Historia*
   HAHR - v77 - F '97 - p118+ [251-500]
Opdyke, Neil D - *Magnetic Stratigraphy*
   Sci - v275 - Mr 28 '97 - p1894 [501+]
Open Doors 1994/95
   r ARBA - v28 - '97 - p144 [51-250]
Open House (Illus. by Steve Noon)
   c BL - v93 - D 15 '96 - p732 [1-50]
   c Ch BWatch - v6 - S '96 - p6 [1-50]
   c HB Guide - v8 - Spr '97 - p99 [51-250]
   c Sch Lib - v44 - N '96 - p164 [51-250]
   c Smith - v27 - N '96 - p169 [1-50]
   c TES - N 22 '96 - p12* [51-250]
Opening Universiteitsbibliotheek Groningen
   Lib & Cul - v32 - Win '97 - p137 [251-500]

Opie, Iona Archibald - *My Very First Mother Goose (Illus. by Rosemary Wells)*
   c Bks Keeps - Mr '97 - p7 [51-250]
   c BL - v93 - Ja '97 - p768 [51-250]
   c BL - v93 - S 1 '96 - p127 [51-250]
   c BL - v93 - Ap 1 '97 - p296 [1-50]
   c BW - v26 - D 8 '96 - p2 [51-250]
   c CBRS - v25 - N '96 - p27 [1-50]
   c CCB-B - v50 - D '96 - p147 [51-250]
   c Ch BWatch - v6 - O '96 - p6 [1-50]
   c CSM - v88 - N 21 '96 - pB1 [51-250]
   c HB - v72 - N '96 - p752 [251-500]
   c HB Guide - v8 - Spr '97 - p107 [51-250]
   c JB - v60 - D '96 - p236+ [51-250]
   c KR - v64 - S 15 '96 - p1411 [51-250]
   c NW - v128 - D 2 '96 - p86 [1-50]
   c NY - v72 - N 18 '96 - p101 [51-250]
   c NYTBR - v101 - N 10 '96 - p38 [501+]
   c Par Ch - v20 - O '96 - p3 [51-250]
   c PW - v243 - N 4 '96 - p48 [51-250]
   c Sch Lib - v45 - F '97 - p20 [51-250]
   c SLJ - v42 - O '96 - p116 [51-250]
   c SLJ - v42 - D '96 - p31 [1-50]
Opp, Karl-Dieter - *Origins of a Spontaneous Revolution*
   AJS - v102 - Ja '97 - p1171+ [501+]
   CS - v26 - Mr '97 - p176+ [501+]
   HRNB - v25 - Fall '96 - p33 [251-500]
   J Pol - v59 - F '97 - p306+ [501+]
Oppelland, Torsten - *Reichstag Uns Aussenpolitik Im Ersten Weltkrieg*
   AHR - v101 - O '96 - p1235+ [501+]
Oppenheim, Alan V - *Signals and Systems. 2nd Ed.*
   SciTech - v20 - D '96 - p18 [51-250]
Oppenheim, Joanne - *Have You Seen Bugs? (Illus. by Ron Broda)*
   c BIC - v25 - O '96 - p32 [51-250]
   c Emerg Lib - v24 - Mr '97 - p27 [1-50]
   c Quill & Q - v62 - O '96 - p47+ [251-500]
Oppenheim, Lois - *Beckett On and On...*
   Am Theat - v14 - F '97 - p56 [51-250]
Oppenheim, Shulamith Levey - *And the Earth Trembled (Illus. by Neil Waldman)*
   c BL - v93 - O 1 '96 - p337+ [51-250]
   c CCB-B - v50 - F '97 - p218+ [51-250]
   c HB Guide - v8 - Spr '97 - p87 [51-250]
   c SLJ - v42 - S '96 - p219 [51-250]
   The Hundredth Name (Illus. by Michael Hays)
   c BL - v93 - O 1 '96 - p339 [1-50]
Oppenheimer, Andres - *Bordering on Chaos*
   For Aff - v75 - S '96 - p148+ [51-250]
   LATBR - D 29 '96 - p3 [251-500]
   NYRB - v43 - O 3 '96 - p31+ [501+]
   Soc - v34 - Mr '97 - p95+ [501+]
Oppenheimer, Jess - *Laughs, Luck...and Lucy*
   BL - v93 - O 1 '96 - p315 [501+]
   PW - v243 - S 23 '96 - p68+ [251-500]
Oppenheimer, Paul - *Evil and the Demonic*
   Choice - v34 - Ja '97 - p781+ [51-250]
O'Pray, Michael - *Derek Jarman: Dreams of England*
   Choice - v34 - My '97 - p1507 [51-250]
Oprea, John - *Differential Geometry and Its Applications*
   SciTech - v21 - Mr '97 - p18 [51-250]
O'Prey, Kevin P - *A Farewell to Arms?*
   JEL - v34 - D '96 - p2059+ [51-250]
Options for Consolidation of Health Benefits Purchasing for State Employees
   J Gov Info - v23 - S '96 - p579 [51-250]
OR Spektrum
   p JEL - v34 - S '96 - p1506 [51-250]
O'Rahilly, Ronan - *Human Embryology and Teratology. 2nd Ed.*
   r SciTech - v20 - S '96 - p21 [51-250]
Oram, Alison - *Women Teachers and Feminist Politics 1900-1939*
   R&R Bk N - v11 - N '96 - p56 [51-250]
Oram, Hiawyn - *Badger's Bring Something Party (Illus. by Susan Varley)*
   c RT - v50 - N '96 - p252 [51-250]
Oram, Peter A - *Technologies for Rainfed Agriculture in Mediterranean Climates*
   JEL - v34 - S '96 - p1480 [51-250]
Orange, Donna M - *Emotional Understanding*
   Rel St Rev - v23 - Ja '97 - p43 [51-250]
Orange County Grand Jury Final Report 1994-95
   J Gov Info - v23 - S '96 - p604 [51-250]
Orans, Martin - *Not Even Wrong*
   SFR - v21 - Jl '96 - p8 [501+]
Oravec, Jo Ann - *Virtual Individuals, Virtual Groups*
   Choice - v34 - Ap '97 - p1373+ [51-250]
Orbach, Larry - *Soaring Underground*
   Rapport - v19 - 4 '96 - p36 [251-500]

Orchard, Andy - *The Poetic Art of Aldhelm*
MLR - v92 - Ja '97 - p164 [251-500]
MP - v94 - N '96 - p204+ [501+]
Orchard, Karin - *Blast: Vortizismus*
TLS - D 6 '96 - p21 [501+]
Orde, Anne - *The Eclipse of Great Britain*
Choice - v34 - Mr '97 - p1222 [51-250]
Ordelheide, Dieter - *Transnational Accounting. Vols. 1-2*
r RQ - v36 - Fall '96 - p139+ [501+]
OrderNow CD-ROM. Electronic Media Version
r BL - v93 - Mr 15 '97 - p1260 [251-500]
Ordine, Nuccio - *Giordano Bruno and the Philosophy of
the Ass*
R&R Bk N - v11 - N '96 - p2 [51-250]
**The Ordnance Survey Interactive Atlas of Great Britain.
Electronic Media Version**
r TES - Mr 14 '97 - p31U [251-500]
Ordonez, Elizabeth J - *Voices of Their Own*
MLR - v92 - Ap '97 - p495+ [501+]
O'Regan, Noel - *Institutional Patronage in Post-Tridentine
Rome*
Notes - v53 - Mr '97 - p787+ [501+]
Six Ct J - v27 - Win '96 - p1191+ [501+]
Oregon 1920 Deschutes County Census
r EGH - v50 - N '96 - p184 [51-250]
**The Oregon Health Plan Economic Impact Analysis for
the Employer Mandate**
J Gov Info - v23 - S '96 - p592 [51-250]
Oregon's Watershed Health Program. Vols. 1-2
J Gov Info - v23 - S '96 - p592+ [51-250]
O'Reilly, Emma-Louise - *Perfect Country Rooms*
LJ - v122 - Ja '97 - p95 [51-250]
O'Reilly, James - *San Francisco*
r BL - v93 - S 15 '96 - p212 [1-50]
Travelers' Tales India
WorldV - v12 - O '96 - p10 [51-250]
O'Reilly, James T, 1947- - *Environmental and Workplace
Safety*
Choice - v34 - S '96 - p159 [51-250]
O'Reilly, Kenneth - *Nixon's Piano*
Historian - v59 - Win '97 - p440 [251-500]
JSH - v63 - F '97 - p218+ [501+]
O'Reilly, Terence - *From Ignatius Loyola to John of the
Cross*
CHR - v82 - O '96 - p712+ [501+]
MLR - v92 - Ja '97 - p227+ [501+]
Rel St Rev - v23 - Ja '97 - p81 [51-250]
O'Reilly, Victor - *The Devil's Footprint*
KR - v64 - D 15 '96 - p1762 [251-500]
LJ - v122 - Ja '97 - p149 [51-250]
PW - v243 - D 16 '96 - p44 [51-250]
Orel, Harold - *The Brontes: Interviews and Recollections*
TLS - F 14 '97 - p24 [251-500]
Gilbert and Sullivan
JPC - v30 - Fall '96 - p215 [51-250]
South HR - v30 - Fall '96 - p401+ [501+]
Orel, Vitezslav - *Gregor Mendel: The First Geneticist*
Choice - v34 - My '97 - p1520 [51-250]
Sci - v275 - Mr 7 '97 - p1438 [501+]
SciTech - v21 - Mr '97 - p33 [1-50]
Orel, Vladimir E - *Hamito-Semitic Etymological
Dictionary*
r TLS - N 1 '96 - p10 [501+]
Orellana, Ignacio - *Descripcion Geografica Y Estadistica
Del Distrito De Cuernavaca 1826*
HAHR - v77 - My '97 - p323 [251-500]
Orengo, Nico - *L'Autunno Della Signora Waal*
WLT - v70 - Aut '96 - p934 [251-500]
Orenstein, Debra - *Lifecycles. Vol. 2*
PW - v244 - Mr 10 '97 - p62 [51-250]
Orenstein, Gloria Feman - *Multicultural Celebrations*
OS - v32 - Jl '96 - p43 [51-250]
Oresko, Robert - *Royal and Republican Sovereignty in
Early Modern Europe*
TLS - Ap 11 '97 - p30 [501+]
Oresme, Nicolaus - *Expositio Et Quaestiones In Aristotelis
De Anima*
Specu - v72 - Ja '97 - p206+ [501+]
Orfalea, Gregory - *Messengers of the Lost Battalion*
KR - v65 - F 1 '97 - p204 [51-250]
LJ - v122 - Ap 15 '97 - p96 [51-250]
PW - v244 - F 17 '97 - p205 [251-500]
Orfield, Gary - *Dismantling Desegregation*
Adoles - v31 - Win '96 - p993 [51-250]
BL - v92 - Ag '96 - p1864 [51-250]
Choice - v34 - Mr '97 - p1212+ [51-250]
Orfield, Myron - *Metropolitics: A Regional Agenda for
Community and Stability*
NCR - v85 - Spr '96 - p65+ [51-250]

**Organ Pipe Cactus National Monument Ecological
Monitoring Program Monitoring Protocol Manual**
J Gov Info - v23 - S '96 - p569+ [51-250]
Organic Reactions. Vol. 49
SciTech - v21 - Mr '97 - p31 [51-250]
**Organisation for Economic Co-Operation and
Development** - *Future Global Capital Shortages*
Econ J - v107 - Ja '97 - p269 [51-250]
JEL - v34 - S '96 - p1420 [51-250]
JEL - v35 - Mr '97 - p137+ [501+]
The Global Human Genome Programme
J Gov Info - v23 - S '96 - p673 [51-250]
Organised Sound
p TLS - Mr 7 '97 - p28+ [501+]
Orgel, Doris - *Don't Call Me Slob-O (Illus. by Bob
Dorsey)*
c BL - v93 - Ja '97 - p860 [251-500]
c HB Guide - v7 - Fall '96 - p295+ [51-250]
Friends to the Rescue (Illus. by Bob Dorsey)
c HB Guide - v8 - Spr '97 - p72 [51-250]
c SLJ - v43 - Mr '97 - p162 [51-250]
The Princess and the God
c Ch BWatch - v6 - O '96 - p3 [51-250]
y HB Guide - v7 - Fall '96 - p304 [51-250]
Orgel, Stephen - *Impersonations: The Performance of
Gender in Shakespeare's England*
Choice - v34 - Ap '97 - p1323 [51-250]
Lon R Bks - v18 - O 31 '96 - p24+ [501+]
Obs - v54 - O 13 '96 - p18* [51-250]
Orgill, Andrew - *The 1990-91 Gulf War*
r ARBA - v28 - '97 - p207+ [51-250]
r R&R Bk N - v11 - D '96 - p10 [51-250]
**Oriental Medicine: An Illustrated Guide to the Asian
Arts of Healing**
FEER - v159 - D 19 '96 - p57 [501+]
Origins of Mankind. Electronic Media Version
HT - v46 - D '96 - p48 [51-250]
Orioles, Filippo - *Il Riscatto D'Adamo Nella Morte Di
Gesu Cristo*
MLN - v112 - Ja '97 - p124+ [251-500]
O'Riordan, Tim - *Politics of Climate Change*
SciTech - v20 - N '96 - p20 [51-250]
Orleck, Annelise - *Common Sense and a Little Fire*
AHR - v101 - O '96 - p1297+ [501+]
NWSA Jnl - v8 - Fall '96 - p159+ [501+]
RAH - v24 - S '96 - p482+ [501+]
Orledge, Robert - *Satie Remembered*
Notes - v53 - D '96 - p476+ [501+]
Orlev, Uri - *The Lady with the Hat*
c Bkbird - v34 - Spr '96 - p52 [1-50]
c RT - v50 - F '97 - p424 [51-250]
The Man from the Other Side
y Kliatt - v30 - S '96 - p3 [1-50]
c New Ad - v9 - Fall '96 - p297+ [501+]
Orlich, Francisco J - *Plan Nacional De Desarrollo
1994/1998*
J Gov Info - v23 - S '96 - p657 [1-50]
Orlin, Lena Cowen - *Private Matters and Public Culture
in Post-Reformation England*
J Soc H - v30 - Fall '96 - p296+ [501+]
MLR - v92 - Ap '97 - p441+ [501+]
RES - v48 - F '97 - p88+ [501+]
Orman, Suze - *The 9 Steps to Financial Freedom*
LJ - v122 - My 1 '97 - p118 [51-250]
Orme, Nicholas - *The English Hospital 1070-1570*
Albion - v28 - Fall '96 - p471+ [501+]
R&R Bk N - v12 - F '97 - p96 [51-250]
Orme, Will A, Jr. - *Understanding NAFTA*
Workbook - v21 - Win '96 - p169+ [251-500]
Ormerod, Jan - *Ms. MacDonald Has a Class (Illus. by
Jan Ormerod)*
c BL - v93 - S 15 '96 - p249 [51-250]
c CBRS - v25 - Ja '97 - p52 [1-50]
c CCB-B - v50 - O '96 - p71 [51-250]
c HB Guide - v8 - Spr '97 - p41 [51-250]
c JB - v60 - Ag '96 - p142+ [51-250]
c NYTBR - v102 - Ja 5 '97 - p22 [501+]
c SLJ - v42 - Ag '96 - p127 [51-250]
Mum and Dad and Me (Illus. by Jan Ormerod)
c JB - v60 - O '96 - p187 [51-250]
c Magpies - v11 - S '96 - p26 [51-250]
To Baby with Love
c TES - Mr 28 '97 - p11* [1-50]
Ormerod, Roger - *The Vital Minute*
PW - v244 - Ap 28 '97 - p55 [1-50]
Ormond, Richard - *Frederic, Lord Leighton: Eminent
Victorian Artist*
Choice - v34 - S '96 - p112 [51-250]
Ormrod, W M - *Political Life in Medieval England
1300-1450*
Albion - v28 - Fall '96 - p465+ [501+]

Ormsby, Eric - *For a Modest God*
LJ - v122 - Ap 1 '97 - p98 [51-250]
PW - v244 - Mr 31 '97 - p70 [51-250]
Ormsby, Frank - *The Ghost Train*
BL - v93 - F 1 '97 - p921+ [51-250]
Orna, Mary Virginia - *Archaeological Chemistry*
Choice - v34 - N '96 - p485 [51-250]
SciTech - v20 - N '96 - p1 [51-250]
Orna-Ornstein, John - *The Story of Money*
c Coin W - v38 - F 10 '97 - p75 [1-50]
Ornish, Dean - *Everyday Cooking with Dr. Dean Ornish*
Quill & Q - v62 - Ag '96 - p30 [51-250]
O'Rourke, F M - *The Poison Tree*
Arm Det - v29 - Sum '96 - p308 [251-500]
y SLJ - v42 - D '96 - p152 [51-250]
O'Rourke, P J - *Age and Guile Beat Youth, Innocence,
and a Bad Haircut*
Bloom Rev - v16 - S '96 - p23 [51-250]
Orphee, Elvira - *Las Viejas Fantasiosas*
TSWL - v15 - Fall '96 - p241+ [501+]
Orr, Clarissa Campbell - *Women in the Victorian Art
World*
Art J - v55 - Win '96 - p88+ [501+]
Orr, F William - *Bone Metastasis*
SciTech - v20 - S '96 - p31 [51-250]
Orr, Gregory - *Poets Teaching Poets*
VQR - v73 - Win '97 - p27*+ [51-250]
Orr, Julian E - *Talking about Machines*
JEL - v35 - Mr '97 - p238 [51-250]
Orr, Larry L - *Does Training for the Disadvantaged
Work?*
ILRR - v50 - Ap '97 - p529+ [501+]
JEL - v34 - D '96 - p2071 [251-500]
Orr, Richard - *Nature Cross-Sections (Illus. by Richard
Orr)*
c RT - v50 - D '96 - p347 [51-250]
Orr, Robert M, Jr. - *The Emergence of Japan's Foreign
Aid Power*
JTWS - v13 - Spr '96 - p272+ [501+]
Orr, Wendy - *Ark in the Park (Illus. by Kerry Millard)*
c Bkbird - v34 - Spr '96 - p51 [51-250]
A Light in Space (Illus. by Ruth Ohi)
c Can CL - v22 - Sum '96 - p88+ [251-500]
Peeling the Onion
y BL - v93 - Ap 1 '97 - p1322 [51-250]
y KR - v65 - F 1 '97 - p226 [51-250]
y Magpies - v11 - S '96 - p38 [51-250]
y PW - v244 - Mr 10 '97 - p67 [51-250]
The Orrery
p S&T - v93 - Mr '97 - p96+ [251-500]
Orru, Marco - *The Economic Organization of East Asian
Capitalism*
Choice - v34 - Ap '97 - p1389 [51-250]
R&R Bk N - v12 - F '97 - p38 [51-250]
Orsborn, Carol - *The Art of Resilience*
PW - v244 - My 12 '97 - p72 [51-250]
Solved by Sunset
Rapport - v19 - 4 '96 - p37 [251-500]
Orser, Charles E - *A Historical Archaeology of the
Modern World*
Am Ant - v62 - Ja '97 - p163+ [501+]
Choice - v34 - S '96 - p182 [51-250]
Orser, Stanton - *Dancing with the Wind (Illus. by James
Bernardin)*
c CBRS - v25 - Mr '97 - p89 [51-250]
Orsi, Robert A - *Thank You, St. Jude*
Am - v176 - F 22 '97 - p26+ [501+]
BW - v26 - S 1 '96 - p13 [51-250]
CHE - v43 - S 20 '96 - pA26 [51-250]
Choice - v34 - D '96 - p629 [51-250]
Comw - v123 - N 8 '96 - p14+ [501+]
Orso, Steven N - *Velazquez, Los Borrachos, and Painting
at the Court of Philip IV*
Ren Q - v49 - Aut '96 - p676+ [501+]
Ortalli, Gherardo - *Gioco E Giustizia Nell'Italia Di
Comune*
EHR - v111 - S '96 - p960+ [251-500]
Ortega, Francisco - *Descripcion Geografica Y Estadistica
Del Distrito De Tulancingo 1825*
HAHR - v77 - My '97 - p322 [51-250]
Ortega, Julio - *Ayacucho, Goodbye. Moscow's Gold*
TranslRevS - v1 - My '95 - p31 [51-250]
Conquista Y Contraconquista
Hisp - v79 - D '96 - p818+ [501+]
Ortenburger, Leigh N - *A Climber's Guide to the Teton
Range. 3rd Ed.*
r BL - v93 - S 15 '96 - p212 [1-50]
Ortese, Anna Maria - *The Iguana*
LATBR - Ag 25 '96 - p7 [501+]

A Music behind the Wall. Vol. 1
LATBR - Ag 25 '96 - p7 [501+]
TranslRevS - v1 - My '95 - p24 [51-250]
Orth-Gomer, Kristina - *Behavioral Medicine Approaches to Cardiovascular Disease Prevention*
r SB - v32 - Ag '96 - p170 [251-500]
Orthopaedic Knowledge Update 5
SciTech - v20 - S '96 - p38 [51-250]
Ortiz, Altagracia - *Puerto Rican Women and Work*
Choice - v34 - Mr '97 - p1210 [51-250]
Ortiz Cofer, Judith - *An Island like You*
y Emerg Lib - v24 - S '96 - p24 [1-50]
y Emerg Lib - v24 - S '96 - p26 [1-50]
y Kliatt - v30 - S '96 - p3 [1-50]
y LA - v73 - O '96 - p431 [51-250]
y PW - v243 - D 2 '96 - p62 [1-50]
c RT - v50 - Mr '97 - p477 [51-250]
Ortkemper, Hubert - *Engel Wider Willen*
Notes - v53 - S '96 - p52+ [501+]
Ortman, Mark - *The Teacher's Book of Wit*
Learning - v25 - Mr '97 - p7 [1-50]
Ortner, Jon - *Where Every Breath Is a Prayer*
BL - v93 - N 15 '96 - p562+ [51-250]
LJ - v122 - F 15 '97 - p132 [51-250]
Ortner, Sherry B - *Making Gender*
LJ - v121 - D '96 - p102 [51-250]
Ms - v7 - N '96 - p82 [1-50]
NYTBR - v101 - N 24 '96 - p25 [501+]
PW - v243 - S 30 '96 - p68 [51-250]
Ortolani, Benito - *The Japanese Theatre*
Pac A - v69 - Fall '96 - p425+ [501+]
Orton, Anthony - *Insights into Teaching Mathematics*
Choice - v34 - O '96 - p333 [51-250]
Orttung, Robert W - *From Leningrad to St. Petersburg*
J Pol - v58 - Ag '96 - p926+ [501+]
Orucu, Esin - *Studies in Legal Systems*
R&R Bk N - v11 - D '96 - p50 [51-250]
Orum, Anthony M - *City Building in America*
CS - v26 - Ja '97 - p62+ [501+]
Pol Stud J - v24 - Sum '96 - p327+ [501+]
Orum, Margo - *Fairytales in Reality*
Aust Bk R - Je '96 - p30+ [501+]
Orwant, Jon - *Perl 5 Interactive Course*
BYTE - v22 - F '97 - p34 [51-250]
LJ - v121 - N 1 '96 - p104 [51-250]
SciTech - v21 - Mr '97 - p8 [51-250]
Orwell, George - *Animal Farm*
Books - v9 - S '95 - p22 [1-50]
Comw - v123 - My 17 '96 - p14+ [501+]
Animal Farm (West). Audio Version
y Kliatt - v30 - N '96 - p36 [51-250]
Burmese Days
FEER - Anniv '96 - p228+ [251-500]
Nineteen Eighty-Four (West). Audio Version
y Kliatt - v31 - My '97 - p42 [51-250]
Orwin, Clifford - *The Legacy of Rousseau*
LJ - v121 - D '96 - p97 [51-250]
Orzeck, Martin - *Dickinson and Audience*
Choice - v34 - F '97 - p964 [51-250]
Os, H W Van - *The Art of Devotion in the Late Middle Ages in Europe 1300-1500*
CHR - v82 - Jl '96 - p553+ [501+]
Osa, Osayimwense - *The All White World of Children's Books and African American Children's Literature*
TES - Jl 5 '96 - pR3 [501+]
Osberg, Lars - *Unnecessary Debts*
BIC - v25 - S '96 - p33+ [501+]
Osborn, Karen - *Between Earth and Sky*
LJ - v122 - Ja '97 - p184 [51-250]
Osborn, Kathy - *Wedding Pictures*
Ent W - Ap 18 '97 - p62+ [51-250]
KR - v65 - My 1 '97 - p677 [51-250]
PW - v244 - My 5 '97 - p196 [51-250]
Osborn, Torie - *Coming Home to America*
Advocate - O 15 '96 - p84+ [501+]
BW - v27 - Ja 12 '97 - p13 [51-250]
Osborne, Catherine - *Eros Unveiled*
Class Out - v74 - Fall '96 - p39+ [251-500]
JR - v77 - Ja '97 - p163+ [501+]
Osborne, Charles C - *Jubal: The Life and Times of General Jubal A. Early, C.S.A., Defender of the Lost Cause*
JSH - v63 - F '97 - p173+ [501+]
Osborne, David - *Banishing Bureaucracy*
KR - v64 - D 15 '96 - p1787 [251-500]
LJ - v122 - Ja '97 - p124 [51-250]
PW - v243 - D 9 '96 - p54 [51-250]
Osborne, Jon - *Mosaics and Wallpaintings in Roman Churches*
Apo - v144 - D '96 - p13 [51-250]

Osborne, Karen Lee - *Reclaiming the Heartland*
Advocate - O 29 '96 - p72+ [501+]
LJ - v121 - O 1 '96 - p108 [51-250]
Osborne, Laurie E - *The Trick of Singularity*
AB - v98 - D 9 '96 - p2004+ [251-500]
Choice - v34 - Ja '97 - p797 [51-250]
Osborne, Mary Pope - *Favorite Norse Myths (Illus. by Troy Howell)*
c HB Guide - v7 - Fall '96 - p322+ [51-250]
One World, Many Religions
c BL - v93 - O 1 '96 - p336 [51-250]
c CCB-B - v50 - Ja '97 - p183 [51-250]
y Ch BWatch - v6 - N '96 - p8 [51-250]
c HB Guide - v8 - Spr '97 - p88 [51-250]
c NW - v128 - D 2 '96 - p88 [51-250]
c SLJ - v42 - N '96 - p116+ [51-250]
Osborne, Peter - *The Politics of Time*
Hist & T - v35 - 3 '96 - p412+ [251-500]
Osborne, Roger - *Historical Atlas of the Earth*
yr BL - v93 - D 1 '96 - p664 [1-50]
Osborough, W N - *Law and the Emergence of Modern Dublin*
Choice - v34 - Mr '97 - p1222 [51-250]
Osen, James L - *Royalist Political Thought during the French Revolution*
AHR - v101 - O '96 - p1221 [251-500]
O'Shea, John M - *Villagers of the Maros*
Choice - v34 - My '97 - p1541+ [51-250]
R&R Bk N - v12 - F '97 - p30 [51-250]
O'Shea, Stephen - *Back to the Front*
BL - v93 - My 15 '97 - p1560 [51-250]
Mac - v110 - F 10 '97 - p59+ [501+]
PW - v244 - My 12 '97 - p70 [51-250]
O'Shea, Thomas J - *Population Biology of the Florida Manatee*
J Gov Info - v23 - S '96 - p570 [51-250]
Osherow, Jacqueline - *With a Moon in Transit*
HMR - Spr '97 - p38+ [501+]
LJ - v121 - D '96 - p98+ [51-250]
NY - v73 - Ap 14 '97 - p85 [51-250]
PW - v243 - S 30 '96 - p83 [51-250]
Oshinsky, David M - *Worse than Slavery*
Choice - v34 - S '96 - p196 [51-250]
NL - v79 - Jl 15 '96 - p19+ [501+]
NYTBR - v101 - D 8 '96 - p94 [1-50]
Trib Bks - Ap 20 '97 - p8 [1-50]
Osho - *Meditation: The First and Last Freedom*
LJ - v122 - Ja '97 - p107 [51-250]
Osiander, Andreas - *The States System of Europe 1640-1990*
EHR - v111 - N '96 - p1310+ [251-500]
Osio, Antonio Maria - *The History of Alta California*
Choice - v34 - N '96 - p527 [51-250]
TLS - S 6 '96 - p33 [251-500]
WHQ - v28 - Spr '97 - p101 [1-50]
Oskamp, Stuart - *Understanding and Preventing HIV Risk Behavior*
R&R Bk N - v11 - D '96 - p69 [51-250]
Osler, Margaret J - *Divine Will and the Mechanical Philosophy*
Phil R - v105 - Ja '96 - p119+ [501+]
Osman, Ibrahim H - *Meta-Heuristics: Theory and Applications*
SciTech - v20 - D '96 - p18 [51-250]
Osman, Karen - *The Italian Renaissance*
y HB Guide - v7 - Fall '96 - p382 [51-250]
Osman, Mohamed - *Successful C for Commercial UNIX Developers*
SciTech - v21 - Mr '97 - p8 [51-250]
Osmanczyk, Edmund Jan - *The Encyclopedia of the United Nations and International Agreements. 2nd Ed.*
r BL - v92 - Ag '96 - p1919 [51-250]
Osmer, Richard Robert - *Confirmation: Presbyterian Practices in Ecumenical Perspective*
Rel St Rev - v23 - Ap '97 - p156 [51-250]
Osmond, Jonathan - *Rural Protest in the Weimar Republic*
JMH - v68 - S '96 - p629+ [501+]
Osmont, Marie-Louise - *The Normandy Diary of Marie-Louise Osmont 1940-1944*
TranslRevS - v1 - My '95 - p10+ [51-250]
Osofisan, Femi - *The Oriki of a Grasshopper and Other Plays*
WLT - v71 - Win '97 - p207+ [501+]
Osofsky, Audrey - *Free to Dream*
y BL - v93 - Ap 1 '97 - p1308 [1-50]
c BW - v26 - D 8 '96 - p20 [51-250]
y HB Guide - v7 - Fall '96 - p373+ [51-250]
Ospina, Sonia - *Illusions of Opportunity*
Choice - v34 - Ja '97 - p842 [51-250]
JEL - v34 - D '96 - p2076 [51-250]

Ospina, William - *Too Late for Man*
ABR - v17 - Ag '96 - p16+ [501+]
Ossa, Alvaro De La - *Panama: La Integracion Con Los Otros Paises Del Istmo Centroamericano*
BL - v93 - S 15 '96 - p227 [1-50]
Ossenkopp, Klaus-Peter - *Measuring Movement and Locomotion*
SciTech - v20 - N '96 - p32 [51-250]
Ossman, Susan - *Picturing Casablanca*
Am Ethnol - v24 - F '97 - p252 [251-500]
Osteen, Mark - *The Economy of Ulysses*
ELT - v39 - 4 '96 - p510+ [501+]
Osten-Sacken, Peter Von Der - *Christian-Jewish Dialogue*
Rel Ed - v91 - Fall '96 - p613 [1-50]
Osterberg, Richard - *Silver Hollowware for Dining Elegance*
Ant & CM - v101 - D '96 - p30+ [1-50]
Osterbrock, Donald E - *Yerkes Observatory 1892-1950*
LJ - v122 - Ja '97 - p139 [51-250]
Sci - v275 - Mr 28 '97 - p1894 [1-50]
Ostergard, Derek E - *The Brilliance of Swedish Glass 1918-1939*
Am Craft - v57 - Ap '97 - p26 [51-250]
Ostergard, Donald R - *Urogynecology and Urodynamics. 4th Ed.*
r SciTech - v20 - D '96 - p52 [51-250]
Osterheld, Albert L - *Atomic Processes in Plasmas*
SciTech - v21 - Mr '97 - p25 [51-250]
Osterholm, J Roger - *Bing Crosby: A Bio-Bibliography*
r AB - v98 - D 9 '96 - p2003 [501+]
Osterman, Paul - *Broken Ladders*
Choice - v34 - Ap '97 - p1382+ [51-250]
HR Mag - v42 - Mr '97 - p136 [51-250]
Ostheeren, Ingrid - *The Blue Monster (Illus. by Christa Unzner)*
c HB Guide - v8 - Spr '97 - p42 [51-250]
c SLJ - v42 - D '96 - p103 [51-250]
c Smith - v27 - N '96 - p173 [1-50]
I'm the Real Santa Claus! (Illus. by Christa Unzner)
c Bks Keeps - N '96 - p20+ [1-50]
c Bloom Rev - v16 - N '96 - p31 [1-50]
Ostick, Stephen - *Superman's Song*
BIC - v25 - S '96 - p29+ [501+]
Ostler, James - *Zuni: A Village of Silversmiths*
Nat Peop - v10 - '97 - p78+ [501+]
Ostler, Larry J - *The Closing of American Library Schools*
LQ - v67 - Ja '97 - p76+ [501+]
LRTS - v40 - O '96 - p385+ [501+]
Ostler, Neal K - *Health Effects of Hazardous Materials*
SciTech - v20 - S '96 - p29 [51-250]
Ostor, Akos - *Vessels of Time*
JIH - v27 - Spr '97 - p663+ [501+]
Ostow, Mortimer - *Ultimate Intimacy*
AJPsych - v153 - N '96 - p1499+ [501+]
Rel St Rev - v23 - Ja '97 - p44 [51-250]
Ostrander, Gary K - *Techniques in Aquatic Toxicology*
SciTech - v20 - D '96 - p29 [51-250]
Ostrander, Sheila - *Super-Learning 2000*
TES - O 4 '96 - p7* [51-250]
Ostrander, Susan A - *Money for Change*
AJS - v102 - N '96 - p935+ [501+]
CS - v26 - Ja '97 - p91+ [501+]
Ostriker, Alicia - *The Crack in Everything*
HMR - Fall '96 - p28 [501+]
HR - v49 - Win '97 - p659+ [501+]
y Kliatt - v31 - My '97 - p18 [51-250]
PW - v243 - N 4 '96 - p47 [1-50]
VQR - v73 - Win '97 - p29* [51-250]
WLT - v71 - Win '97 - p156 [501+]
Wom R Bks - v14 - Mr '97 - p12+ [501+]
Ostrow, Jill - *A Room with a Different View*
New Ad - v9 - Fall '96 - p309+ [501+]
Ostrow, Steven F - *Art and Spirituality in Counter-Reformation Rome*
Choice - v34 - Mr '97 - p1152+ [51-250]
Ostrow, Vivian - *My Brother Is from Outer Space (Illus. by Eric Brace)*
c CLW - v66 - Je '96 - p50 [51-250]
c HB Guide - v7 - Fall '96 - p270 [51-250]
Ostrower, Francie - *Why the Wealthy Give*
CS - v26 - Mr '97 - p160+ [501+]
Ostrower, Gary B - *The League of Nations from 1919 to 1929*
Pres SQ - v27 - Win '97 - p160+ [501+]
Ostwald, Peter - *Glenn Gould: The Ecstasy and Tragedy of Genius*
BL - v93 - My 15 '97 - p1554 [51-250]
PW - v244 - Ap 7 '97 - p82 [51-250]

O'Sullivan, Arthur - *Property Taxes and Tax Revolts*
Econ J - v106 - S '96 - p1474 [251-500]
O'Sullivan, Donal - *Carolan: The Life, Times and Music of an Irish Harper. Vols. 1-2*
CAY - v17 - Fall '96 - p7 [51-250]
O'Sullivan, J N - *Xenophon of Ephesus: His Compositional Technique and the Birth of the Novel*
AJP - v117 - Win '96 - p660+ [501+]
O'Sullivan, Jerry - *Teaching English/Japan*
r Quill & Q - v63 - F '97 - p38 [501+]
O'Sullivan, Marie - *Financial Resources for International Study. 2nd Ed.*
r ARBA - v28 - '97 - p143 [51-250]
Funding for United States Study. 2nd Ed.
r ARBA - v28 - '97 - p141 [51-250]
O'Sullivan, Sue - *Positively Women. Rev. and Updated Ed.*
New Sci - v152 - D 7 '96 - p50 [51-250]
Oswald, Alice - *The Thing in the Gap-Stone Stile*
TLS - N 29 '96 - p16 [51-250]
Otfinoski, Steve - *Behind the Wheel*
c Ch BWatch - v6 - D '96 - p6 [1-50]
c HB Guide - v8 - Spr '97 - p132 [51-250]
c SLJ - v43 - F '97 - p94+ [51-250]
Into the Wind
c Ch BWatch - v6 - D '96 - p6 [1-50]
c HB Guide - v8 - Spr '97 - p132 [51-250]
c SLJ - v43 - F '97 - p94+ [51-250]
The Kid's Guide to Money
c HB Guide - v7 - Fall '96 - p353 [51-250]
Pedaling Along
c Ch BWatch - v6 - D '96 - p6 [1-50]
c HB Guide - v8 - Spr '97 - p132 [51-250]
Riding the Rails
c Ch BWatch - v6 - D '96 - p6 [1-50]
c HB Guide - v8 - Spr '97 - p132 [51-250]
Speaking Up, Speaking Out (Illus. by Carol Nicklaus)
c BL - v93 - Ja '97 - p852+ [251-500]
c HB Guide - v8 - Spr '97 - p134 [51-250]
c SLJ - v43 - Ja '97 - p131+ [51-250]
Taking Off
c Ch BWatch - v6 - D '96 - p6 [1-50]
c HB Guide - v8 - Spr '97 - p132 [51-250]
c SLJ - v43 - F '97 - p94+ [51-250]
To the Rescue
c Ch BWatch - v6 - D '96 - p6 [1-50]
c HB Guide - v8 - Spr '97 - p132 [51-250]
Other Dimensions 3
SF Chr - v18 - O '96 - p83 [1-50]
Other Voices
p LMR - v15 - Win '96 - p23+ [501+]
Otnes, Cele - *Gift Giving*
R&R Bk N - v11 - N '96 - p22 [51-250]
Oto, Ali M - *Practice and Progress in Cardiac Pacing and Electrophysiology*
SciTech - v20 - D '96 - p47 [1-50]
Otomo, Katsuhiro - *The Legend of Mother Sarah*
y VOYA - v19 - F '97 - p324 [251-500]
O'Toole, Jack - *Forming the Future*
BL - v93 - S 1 '96 - p45+ [51-250]
O'Toole, James M - *Militant and Triumphant*
CH - v65 - D '96 - p758+ [501+]
O'Toole, Peter - *Loitering with Intent. Vol. 1*
NYTBR - v102 - Mr 30 '97 - p24 [51-250]
PW - v244 - Ja 13 '97 - p73 [1-50]
Trib Bks - F 16 '97 - p8 [1-50]
Loitering with Intent. Vol. 2
BL - v93 - D 1 '96 - p619 [51-250]
BW - v27 - F 2 '97 - p3 [501+]
KR - v64 - D 1 '96 - p1723 [251-500]
LATBR - F 16 '97 - p14 [501+]
NYTBR - v102 - F 23 '97 - p26 [501+]
PW - v243 - D 9 '96 - p53 [251-500]
Si & So - v6 - N '96 - p35+ [1-50]
Ott, Katherine - *Fevered Lives*
BL - v93 - Ja '97 - p798 [51-250]
KR - v64 - N 1 '96 - p1588 [251-500]
LJ - v121 - D '96 - p132+ [51-250]
PW - v243 - D 9 '96 - p55 [51-250]
Sci - v275 - F 28 '97 - p1276 [1-50]
Ottati, Douglas F - *Jesus Christ and Christian Vision*
Rel St Rev - v22 - O '96 - p338 [51-250]
Reforming Protestantism
Intpr - v51 - Ap '97 - p193+ [501+]
Rel St Rev - v23 - Ap '97 - p156 [51-250]
Ottaway, David - *Chained Together*
JTWS - v13 - Spr '97 - p333+ [501+]
Ottenheimer, Martin - *Forbidden Relatives*
Choice - v34 - My '97 - p1542 [51-250]

Otter, Patrick - *Lincolnshire Airfields in the Second World War*
A & S Sm - v11 - F '97 - p87 [1-50]
Otterbein, Keith E - *Feuding and Warfare*
JPR - v33 - Ag '96 - p382 [251-500]
Ottesen, Carole - *The Native Plant Primer*
Fine Gard - N '96 - p70 [251-500]
Otteson, Paul - *World Awaits*
r BL - v93 - S 15 '96 - p210 [1-50]
Ottley, Matt - *What Faust Saw (Illus. by Matt Ottley)*
c HB Guide - v7 - Fall '96 - p270 [51-250]
c RT - v50 - My '97 - p683 [51-250]
Ottley, Ted - *Code of Deception*
y Kliatt - v30 - S '96 - p13 [51-250]
Code of the Roadies
y Kliatt - v30 - S '96 - p13 [51-250]
Otto, Carolyn - *What Color Is Camouflage? (Illus. by Megan Lloyd)*
c BL - v93 - N 1 '96 - p504 [51-250]
c HB Guide - v8 - Spr '97 - p119 [51-250]
c KR - v64 - Ag 15 '96 - p1240 [51-250]
c SLJ - v42 - D '96 - p111 [51-250]
Otto, Karl F - *Bibliographia Kleschiana*
r R&R Bk N - v11 - N '96 - p75 [51-250]
Otto, Whitney - *The Passion Dream Book*
BL - v93 - Mr 15 '97 - p1204 [51-250]
KR - v65 - Mr 1 '97 - p330 [51-250]
LJ - v122 - Ap 1 '97 - p130 [51-250]
PW - v244 - Mr 17 '97 - p74 [51-250]
The Passion Dream Book (Brown). Audio Version
PW - v244 - My 5 '97 - p40 [51-250]
Ottosen, Garry K - *Reducing Unemployment*
JEL - v34 - S '96 - p1420 [51-250]
M Lab R - v119 - S '96 - p47+ [501+]
O Tuama, Sean - *Repossessions: Selected Essays on the Irish Literary Heritage*
ILS - v15 - Fall '96 - p7 [501+]
TLS - S 27 '96 - p14 [501+]
O Tuathail, Gearoid - *Critical Geopolitics*
Choice - v34 - Mr '97 - p1238 [51-250]
Ouaknin, Marc-Alain - *The Burnt Book*
CPR - v16 - Ap '96 - p127+ [501+]
JC - v46 - Sum '96 - p207+ [251-500]
Symbols of Judaism
y BL - v93 - D 15 '96 - p704 [51-250]
PW - v243 - S 16 '96 - p67 [51-250]
Ouditt, Sharon - *Fighting Forces, Writing Women*
RES - v47 - Ag '96 - p448+ [501+]
Oudot, Susan - *Real Women*
Books - v10 - Je '96 - p24 [51-250]
Ouellette, Pierre - *The Third Pandemic*
BL - v93 - S 1 '96 - p63 [51-250]
PW - v244 - Mr 31 '97 - p72 [1-50]
Ouellette, Robert J - *Introduction to General, Organic, and Biological Chemistry. 4th Ed.*
SciTech - v20 - N '96 - p21 [51-250]
Organic Chemistry
SciTech - v20 - S '96 - p16 [51-250]
Oughton, Jerrie - *Music from a Place Called Half Moon*
c PW - v244 - Ap 7 '97 - p94 [1-50]
The War in Georgia
y BL - v93 - Ap 1 '97 - p1330 [251-500]
y KR - v65 - F 15 '97 - p304 [51-250]
c PW - v244 - F 17 '97 - p84 [51-250]
Ould-Mey, Mohameden - *Global Restructuring and Peripheral States*
Africa T - v44 - 1 '97 - p83+ [251-500]
Our Changing Planet
c Ch BWatch - v7 - Ja '97 - p2 [1-50]
c PW - v243 - N 18 '96 - p78 [51-250]
c SLJ - v42 - O '96 - p134 [51-250]
Our Experience
y Sch Lib - v45 - F '97 - p47 [51-250]
Our Gift of Love
BL - v93 - F 1 '97 - p912+ [51-250]
LJ - v121 - D '96 - p134 [51-250]
Our Glorious Century
Beav - v76 - O '96 - p46 [51-250]
Our Secret Century. Electronic Media Version
LJ - v121 - N 1 '96 - p114+ [501+]
Our Sunday Visitor's 1997 Catholic Almanac
r ARBA - v28 - '97 - p546 [51-250]
Our World in Danger
c CLW - v66 - Je '96 - p53 [51-250]
c HB Guide - v7 - Fall '96 - p317 [51-250]
Oursler, Fulton - *The Greatest Story Ever Told (Herrmann). Audio Version*
LJ - v122 - Ap 15 '97 - p139 [51-250]

Ousby, Ian - *The Cambridge Paperback Guide to Literature in English*
r ARBA - v28 - '97 - p412 [251-500]
r BL - v92 - Ag '96 - p1922 [1-50]
r Choice - v34 - O '96 - p256 [51-250]
yr CLW - v67 - D '96 - p51 [251-500]
yr Sch Lib - v44 - Ag '96 - p128 [51-250]
yr SLMQ - v25 - Fall '96 - p65 [51-250]
Ousseimi, Maria - *Caught in the Crossfire*
y BL - v93 - Ap 1 '97 - p1308 [1-50]
y Emerg Lib - v24 - S '96 - p24 [1-50]
Ousterhout, Robert - *The Sacred Image East and West*
CH - v65 - S '96 - p474+ [501+]
Out, H J - *Recombinant FSH (Puregon)*
SciTech - v21 - Mr '97 - p67 [51-250]
Out El Kouloub - *Zanouba*
KR - v64 - D 1 '96 - p1702 [501+]
LJ - v122 - Ja '97 - p145 [51-250]
Outhwaite, R B - *Clandestine Marriage in England 1580-1850*
JEH - v56 - S '96 - p712+ [501+]
Outside Magazine Adventure Guide to Northern California
r BL - v93 - S 15 '96 - p210 [1-50]
Outwater, Alice - *Water: A Natural History*
y BL - v93 - S 15 '96 - p192 [51-250]
BL - v93 - D 1 '96 - p630 [1-50]
y BL - v93 - D 1 '96 - p664 [1-50]
Choice - v34 - F '97 - p981 [51-250]
E Mag - v8 - Ja '97 - p49 [51-250]
KR - v64 - Ag 15 '96 - p1219 [251-500]
NH - v105 - O '96 - p12 [51-250]
NY - v72 - D 2 '96 - p115 [51-250]
SciTech - v21 - Mr '97 - p1 [51-250]
Oved, Iaacov - *The Witness of the Brothers*
Choice - v34 - D '96 - p629 [51-250]
R&R Bk N - v11 - D '96 - p6 [1-50]
TLS - Mr 21 '97 - p30 [501+]
Ovenden, Keith - *A Fighting Withdrawal*
TLS - D 27 '96 - p24 [501+]
Over the Moon
c Books - v10 - Je '96 - p25 [51-250]
Overby, Charlotte - *Missouri's Conservation Atlas*
r J Gov Info - v23 - S '96 - p586+ [51-250]
Overbye, Dennis - *Lonely Hearts of the Cosmos*
S&T - v92 - S '96 - p54 [51-250]
Overholser, Wayne - *Nugget City*
Roundup M - v4 - F '97 - p28+ [251-500]
Overholt, Thomas - *Cultural Anthropology and the Old Testament*
Choice - v34 - F '97 - p980 [51-250]
Overland, Orm - *The Western Home*
Choice - v34 - My '97 - p1564 [51-250]
Overman, J Andrew - *Church and Community in Crisis*
Am - v176 - Mr 8 '97 - p27 [51-250]
Rel St Rev - v23 - Ap '97 - p181+ [51-250]
Overton, Bill - *The Novel of Female Adultery*
NS - v126 - Ja 31 '97 - p48 [501+]
Overton, Julie - *Revolutionary War Veterans of Greene County, Ohio*
r EGH - v50 - N '96 - p179 [51-250]
Overton, Mark - *Agricultural Revolution in England*
Choice - v34 - Mr '97 - p1222 [51-250]
JEL - v35 - Mr '97 - p266+ [51-250]
Overy, R J - *The Nazi Economic Recovery 1932-1938. 2nd Ed.*
JEL - v35 - Mr '97 - p259 [51-250]
Overy, Richard - *Atlas of the Twentieth Century*
r TLS - N 1 '96 - p7 [501+]
War and the Economy in the Third Reich
HT - v46 - Jl '96 - p52+ [501+]
Why the Allies Won
APH - v44 - Spr '97 - p58 [251-500]
Choice - v34 - S '96 - p182 [51-250]
HRNB - v25 - Fall '96 - p44 [251-500]
J Mil H - v60 - O '96 - p797+ [251-500]
Nat R - v48 - S 16 '96 - p70 [51-250]
Pres SQ - v26 - Fall '96 - p1172+ [501+]
PW - v244 - Ap 14 '97 - p72 [1-50]
Rapport - v19 - 5 '96 - p44 [251-500]
Ovid - *Heroides--Select Epistles (Knox)*
Choice - v34 - O '96 - p274 [51-250]
The Metamorphoses of Ovid
TranslRevS - v1 - My '95 - p26 [51-250]
Ovington, Mary White - *Black and White Sat Down Together*
y Kliatt - v30 - N '96 - p23 [51-250]
Ovsyanikov, Nikita - *Polar Bears*
NH - v106 - F '97 - p13 [1-50]
PW - v243 - O 21 '96 - p66 [51-250]

Owen, Annie - *From Snowflakes to Sandcastles*
  c HB Guide - v7 - Fall '96 - p326 [51-250]
  c Obs - Mr 30 '97 - p17* [51-250]
Owen, David, 1938- - *Balkan Odyssey*
  PW - v244 - Mr 17 '97 - p81 [1-50]
  Slav R - v55 - Fall '96 - p677+ [501+]
Owen, David, 1955- - *Lure of the Links*
  PW - v244 - My 12 '97 - p69 [51-250]
Owen, David, 1964- - *Nietzsche, Politics and Modernity*
  AJS - v102 - Ja '97 - p1233+ [501+]
Owen, David G - *Philosophical Foundations of Tort Law*
  Law Q Rev - v112 - O '96 - p686+ [501+]
Owen, Gareth - *Rosie No-Name and the Forest of Forgetting*
  c BL - v93 - N 1 '96 - p501 [51-250]
  c CBRS - v25 - D '96 - p47+ [51-250]
  c CCB-B - v50 - Ja '97 - p183+ [51-250]
  c HB - v73 - Ja '97 - p65+ [51-250]
  c HB Guide - v8 - Spr '97 - p72 [51-250]
  c KR - v64 - O 15 '96 - p1536 [51-250]
  c SLJ - v42 - O '96 - p124 [51-250]
  Say Cheese! (Illus. by Tim Archbold)
  c Sch Lib - v45 - F '97 - p33 [51-250]
Owen, Gordon R - *The Two Alberts*
  Roundup M - v4 - O '96 - p27+ [251-500]
  WHQ - v28 - Spr '97 - p89 [51-250]
Owen, Guillermo - *Game Theory. 3rd Ed.*
  JEL - v34 - D '96 - p2023 [51-250]
Owen, Howard - *The Measured Man*
  BL - v93 - F 15 '97 - p1005 [51-250]
  KR - v64 - D 1 '96 - p1697 [251-500]
  LJ - v122 - F 1 '97 - p107 [51-250]
  PW - v243 - D 9 '96 - p59+ [51-250]
Owen, Joseph R - *Colder than Hell*
  BL - v93 - S 1 '96 - p59 [51-250]
Owen, Margaret - *A World of Widows*
  Choice - v34 - My '97 - p1584+ [51-250]
Owen, Robert - *Gen X TV*
  LJ - v122 - Mr 15 '97 - p65 [51-250]
  PW - v244 - Mr 17 '97 - p72 [51-250]
Owen, Sri - *Healthy Thai Cooking*
  PW - v244 - My 5 '97 - p205 [51-250]
Owen, Stephen - *An Anthology of Chinese Literature*
  Choice - v34 - N '96 - p451 [51-250]
  Ch Rev Int - v4 - Spr '97 - p23+ [501+]
  New R - v215 - S 9 '96 - p38+ [501+]
  The End of the Chinese Middle Ages
  Choice - v34 - D '96 - p609 [51-250]
Owen, Thomas C - *Russian Corporate Capitalism from Peter the Great to Perestroika*
  JEL - v34 - S '96 - p1472 [51-250]
  JIH - v27 - Spr '97 - p703+ [501+]
Owen, Tim - *Success at the Enquiry Desk*
  LAR - v98 - O '96 - p533 [251-500]
Owens, Allan - *Dramaworks*
  TES - F 28 '97 - pR7 [251-500]
Owens, Ann-Maureen - *Forts of Canada (Illus. by Don Kilby)*
  c Ch Bk News - v19 - Sum '96 - p31+ [51-250]
  c Emerg Lib - v24 - Mr '97 - p28 [1-50]
  c Quill & Q - v62 - Jl '96 - p58+ [251-500]
  c Quill & Q - v63 - F '97 - p51 [51-250]
Owens, Frank J - *The New Superconductors*
  SciTech - v21 - Mr '97 - p91 [51-250]
Owens, Ian - *Information and Business Performance*
  R&R Bk N - v11 - D '96 - p33 [51-250]
Owens, Janis - *My Brother Michael*
  KR - v65 - Ja 1 '97 - p16+ [251-500]
  LJ - v121 - D '96 - p146 [51-250]
  PW - v244 - Ja 20 '97 - p394 [51-250]
Owens, Joseph - *Cognition: An Epistemological Inquiry*
  Dialogue - v35 - Sum '96 - p616+ [501+]
Owens, Louis - *Nightland*
  BL - v92 - Ag '96 - p1887 [51-250]
  Bloom Rev - v16 - N '96 - p26 [51-250]
  BW - v26 - O 6 '96 - p8 [51-250]
Owens, Thomas S - *Collecting Baseball Memorabilia*
  c HB Guide - v7 - Fall '96 - p354 [51-250]
  y VOYA - v19 - O '96 - p236 [51-250]
  Inside Collectible Card Games
  c HB Guide - v8 - Spr '97 - p142+ [51-250]
Owings, Alison - *Frauen: German Women Recall the Third Reich*
  HT - v46 - Ag '96 - p60 [251-500]
Ownby, David - *Brotherhoods and Secret Societies in Early and Mid-Qing China*
  Choice - v34 - N '96 - p515 [51-250]
Ownby, Ted - *Black and White*
  CAY - v17 - Fall '96 - p13 [51-250]
Owram, Doug - *Born at the Right Time*
  Choice - v34 - Mr '97 - p1228 [51-250]

Oxenberg, Christina - *Royal Blue*
  PW - v244 - My 12 '97 - p61 [251-500]
  Trib Bks - My 25 '97 - p11 [51-250]
Oxenbury, Helen - *It's My Birthday*
  c Magpies - v11 - My '96 - p53 [1-50]
Oxenhandler, Neal - *Looking for Heroes in Postwar France*
  CC - v113 - Ag 14 '96 - p792+ [251-500]
The Oxfam Handbook of Development and Relief
  r Choice - v34 - S '96 - p104 [51-250]
Oxford 3-in-1 Bilingual Dictionary on CD-Rom. Electronic Media Version
  cr TES - Ja 3 '97 - p14U [501+]
Oxford Atlas of the World. 4th Ed.
  r ARBA - v28 - '97 - p173 [51-250]
  r LATBR - D 8 '96 - p35 [51-250]
Oxford Children's Encyclopedia. 2nd Ed., Vols. 1-9
  cr Bks Keeps - Mr '97 - p24+ [51-250]
  cr Sch Lib - v45 - F '97 - p40 [51-250]
  cr TES - N 8 '96 - p12* [501+]
Oxford Children's Encyclopedia. Rev. Ed. Electronic Media Version
  cr New Sci - v152 - D 14 '96 - p44 [1-50]
  cr Sch Lib - v45 - F '97 - p29 [501+]
The Oxford Dictionary and Thesaurus
  r LJ - v122 - Ja '97 - p90 [51-250]
The Oxford Dictionary of Current English. 2nd Ed.
  r ARBA - v28 - '97 - p378 [51-250]
The Oxford-Duden Pictorial Spanish and English Dictionary. 2nd Ed.
  yr BL - v93 - Mr 1 '97 - p1196 [51-250]
The Oxford Encyclopedia of Archaeology in the Near East. Vols. 1-5
  r BL - v93 - Mr 15 '97 - p1260 [51-250]
  r Choice - v34 - My '97 - p1478+ [251-500]
The Oxford Encyclopedia of the Reformation. Vols. 1-4
  r ARBA - v28 - '97 - p550 [251-500]
  r Comw - v124 - Ja 17 '97 - p28+ [501+]
  r HRNB - v25 - Fall '96 - p3+ [501+]
  r LJ - v122 - Ap 15 '97 - p39 [51-250]
  r Rel St Rev - v23 - Ap '97 - p121+ [501+]
  r RQ - v36 - Win '96 - p303+ [251-500]
  r TLS - N 1 '96 - p6 [501+]
Oxford Encyclopedic World Atlas. 3rd Ed.
  yr ARBA - v28 - '97 - p173+ [51-250]
Oxford English Dictionary. 2nd Ed. Electronic Media Version
  r ARBA - v28 - '97 - p388 [251-500]
  r TES - Mr 14 '97 - p22U [51-250]
The Oxford English-Hebrew Dictionary
  r ARBA - v28 - '97 - p393 [51-250]
  r Choice - v34 - Ja '97 - p773 [51-250]
  r R&R Bk N - v11 - N '96 - p64 [51-250]
  r TES - Ag 23 '96 - p27 [501+]
The Oxford History of Australia. Vol. 5
  Aust Bk R - Ag '96 - p67 [1-50]
The Oxford Large Print Dictionary. 2nd Ed.
  r ARBA - v28 - '97 - p377 [51-250]
Oxford Mathematics: Intermediate Link for Year 9
  y TES - O 4 '96 - pR14 [501+]
Oxford Primary Geography: Pupils' Book 3
  c TES - O 18 '96 - pR2 [51-250]
The Oxford Treasury of Children's Stories
  c Magpies - v11 - S '96 - p45 [1-50]
Oxford Visual Dictionary
  yr Sch Lib - v44 - Ag '96 - p125 [51-250]
Oxhorn, Philip D - *Organizing Civil Society*
  PSQ - v111 - Win '96 - p738+ [501+]
Oxlade, Chris - *Bridges*
  c HB Guide - v8 - Spr '97 - p132 [51-250]
  Flags: Facts, Things to Make, Activities (Illus. by Raymond Turvey)
  c HB Guide - v7 - Fall '96 - p354 [51-250]
  Plane (Illus. by George Fryer)
  c Sch Lib - v45 - F '97 - p20 [51-250]
  Skyscrapers and Towers
  c HB Guide - v8 - Spr '97 - p132 [51-250]
  c Sch Lib - v44 - Ag '96 - p113 [51-250]
Oxley, Deborah - *Convict Maids*
  Aust Bk R - Je '96 - p14+ [501+]
Oyen, Else - *Poverty--A Global Review*
  Choice - v34 - O '96 - p368+ [51-250]
Oyewole, Abiodun - *The Last Poets on a Mission*
  LJ - v122 - Ja '97 - p99 [51-250]
  PW - v243 - S 30 '96 - p84 [51-250]
O'Young, Brian - *PM&R Secrets*
  J Rehab RD - v34 - Ap '97 - p242+ [501+]
Oz, Amos - *Black Box*
  Nat - v263 - N 11 '96 - p25+ [501+]

  Don't Call It Night
  BL - v93 - S 15 '96 - p220 [51-250]
  BW - v26 - O 13 '96 - p5 [501+]
  LATBR - N 3 '96 - p5 [501+]
  Nat - v263 - N 11 '96 - p25+ [501+]
  NYTBR - v101 - S 29 '96 - p11 [501+]
  NYTBR - v101 - D 8 '96 - p79 [1-50]
  Obs - S 15 '96 - p18* [51-250]
  Fima
  Nat - v263 - N 11 '96 - p25+ [501+]
  TranslRevS - v1 - My '95 - p23 [51-250]
  In the Land of Israel
  Nat - v263 - N 11 '96 - p25+ [501+]
  Panter Ba-Martef
  BL - v93 - Mr 1 '97 - p1115 [1-50]
  The Slopes of Lebanon
  Nat - v263 - N 11 '96 - p25+ [501+]
Oz Clarke's Wine Advisor 1997
  r LJ - v122 - Ap 1 '97 - p64 [1-50]
Ozcan, Gul Berna - *Small Firms and Local Economic Development*
  R&R Bk N - v11 - D '96 - p29 [51-250]
Ozdamar, Emine Sevgi - *Das Leben Ist Eine Karawanserei*
  Ger Q - v69 - Fall '96 - p414+ [501+]
  Mother Tongue
  TranslRevS - v1 - My '95 - p22 [51-250]
Ozick, Cynthia - *Fame and Folly*
  WLT - v71 - Win '97 - p158 [501+]
  Portrait of the Artist as a Bad Character
  TES - S 6 '96 - p8* [51-250]
  The Puttermesser Papers
  BL - v93 - My 15 '97 - p1561 [51-250]
  PW - v244 - Ap 21 '97 - p58 [251-500]
Ozinga, James R - *The Recurring Dream of Equality*
  Choice - v34 - O '96 - p334+ [51-250]
Ozkul, Tarik - *Data Acquisition and Process Control Using Personal Computers*
  r SciTech - v20 - S '96 - p62 [51-250]
Ozment, Steven - *The Burgermeister's Daughter*
  NYTBR - v102 - Ap 6 '97 - p32 [51-250]
  Six Ct J - v27 - Win '96 - p1195+ [501+]
Ozouf, Mona - *Les Mots Des Femmes*
  AHR - v101 - O '96 - p1228+ [501+]
  Choice - v34 - D '96 - p565 [1-50]
  FR - v70 - D '96 - p318+ [501+]
Oz-Salzberger, Fania - *Translating the Enlightenment*
  AHR - v102 - F '97 - p120+ [251-500]
Oztopcu, Kurtulus - *Dictionary of the Turkic Languages*
  r ARBA - v28 - '97 - p403 [251-500]
  r R&R Bk N - v12 - F '97 - p79 [51-250]

P

P-Form: A Journal of Interdisciplinary and Performance
Art
  p Utne R - N '96 - p97 [251-500]
Paasilinna, Arto - *The Year of the Hare*
  TranslRevS - v2 - D '96 - p21 [51-250]
Paasilinna, Reino - *Glasnost and Soviet Television*
  Slav R - v55 - Fall '96 - p701+ [501+]
Pabel, Hilmar M - *Erasmus' Vision of the Church*
  Rel St Rev - v23 - Ap '97 - p190 [51-250]
  Six Ct J - v27 - Win '96 - p1204+ [501+]
Pabst, Bernhard - *Atomtheorien Des Lateinischen
Mittelalters*
  Specu - v71 - Jl '96 - p747+ [501+]
  *Prosimetrum: Tradition Und Wandel Einer Literaturform
Zwischen Spatantike Und Spatmittelalter. Vols. 1-2*
  Specu - v71 - Jl '96 - p749+ [501+]
Pace, DeWanna - *Our Town*
  PW - v243 - O 7 '96 - p69 [51-250]
Pace, Maria - *The Little Italy Cookbook*
  BWatch - v18 - F '97 - p8 [51-250]
Pace, Nicola - *Ricerche Sulla Tradizione Di Rufino Del De
Principiis Di Origene*
  Rel St Rev - v22 - O '96 - p301+ [501+]
Pachai, Bridglal - *William Hall*
  c Can CL - v22 - Fall '96 - p107+ [501+]
Pacheco, Ferdie - *Ybor City Chronicles*
  y BL - v93 - D 15 '96 - p717 [1-50]
Pacheco, Jose Emilio - *City of Memory and Other Poems*
  LJ - v122 - My 1 '97 - p107+ [51-250]
Pacherie, Elisabeth - *Naturaliser L'Intentionnalite*
  Dialogue - v35 - Spr '96 - p406+ [501+]
Pacht, Otto - *Book Illumination in the Middle Ages*
  AB - v99 - Mr 3 '97 - p685+ [501+]
Paci, Pierella - *Wage Differentials between Men and
Women*
  JEL - v34 - S '96 - p1447 [51-250]
Pacific Coast Journal
  p Sm Pr R - v28 - Je '96 - p18 [51-250]
Pacific Island Economies
  JEL - v34 - D '96 - p2121 [51-250]
Pacione, Michael - *Glasgow: The Socio-Spatial
Development of the City*
  GJ - v162 - N '96 - p334+ [251-500]
Pack, Robert - *Minding the Sun*
  R&R Bk N - v11 - N '96 - p74 [51-250]
Packard, Mary - *Bubble Trouble (Illus. by Elena
Kuckarik)*
  c Learning - v25 - Ag '96 - p96 [51-250]
  The Pet That I Want (Illus. by John Magino)
  c Learning - v25 - Ag '96 - p96 [51-250]
  We Are Monsters (Illus. by John Magine)
  c BL - v93 - F 1 '97 - p950 [51-250]
Packel, Ed - *Animating Calculus*
  Choice - v34 - Ap '97 - p1376 [51-250]
Packer, Craig - *Into Africa*
  y Kliatt - v31 - Mr '97 - p34 [51-250]
Packer, Lester - *Free Radicals in Brain Physiology and
Disorders*
  SciTech - v21 - Mr '97 - p52 [51-250]
Packer, Nancy Huddleston - *Jealous-Hearted Me*
  PW - v244 - Ja 13 '97 - p56 [51-250]
  Trib Bks - Mr 2 '97 - p8 [1-50]
Packull, Werner O - *Hutterite Beginnings*
  CC - v114 - Mr 19 '97 - p310+ [501+]
  TLS - D 20 '96 - p31 [501+]
Pacovska, Kveta - *The Little Flower King (Illus. by Kveta
Pacovska)*
  c HB Guide - v7 - Fall '96 - p270 [51-250]
  El Pequeno Rey De Las Flores
  c HB Guide - v7 - Fall '96 - p327 [51-250]

Pacquet, Jacques - *Les Matricules Universitaires*
  CHR - v82 - Jl '96 - p459+ [51-250]
Padberg, John W - *For Matters of Greater Moment*
  CHR - v82 - Jl '96 - p484+ [251-500]
  Together as a Companionship
  CHR - v83 - Ja '97 - p168+ [51-250]
Padberg, Manfred - *Location, Scheduling, Design and
Integer Programming*
  SciTech - v21 - Mr '97 - p71 [51-250]
Paddock, Lisa - *Facts about the Supreme Court of the
United States*
  r Choice - v34 - D '96 - p593 [51-250]
  r R&R Bk N - v11 - N '96 - p53 [51-250]
  yr VOYA - v19 - D '96 - p300+ [251-500]
Paddock, Lisa Olson - *A Student's Guide to Scandinavian
American Genealogy*
  yr ARBA - v28 - '97 - p167+ [251-500]
  y SLJ - v42 - O '96 - p152 [51-250]
Padel, Ruth - *Fusewire*
  TLS - N 29 '96 - p15 [51-250]
  Whom Gods Destroy
  AJP - v117 - Fall '96 - p485+ [501+]
Paden, Ann - *I Bought It at Polk Bros*
  LJ - v122 - Ja '97 - p116 [51-250]
Paden, William D - *The Future of the Middle Ages*
  Specu - v71 - Jl '96 - p686+ [501+]
Padfield, Peter - *War beneath the Sea*
  J Mil H - v60 - O '96 - p794+ [251-500]
Padgett, Abigail - *The Dollmaker's Daughters*
  BW - v27 - F 16 '97 - p11 [51-250]
  KR - v64 - D 15 '96 - p1769 [51-250]
  LJ - v122 - Ja '97 - p153 [51-250]
  PW - v243 - D 2 '96 - p44 [51-250]
  Moonbird Boy
  PW - v244 - Ja 27 '97 - p103 [1-50]
Padgett, Deborah K - *Handbook on Ethnicity, Aging, and
Mental Health*
  r Soc Ser R - v70 - D '96 - p667 [51-250]
Padgett, Ron - *New and Selected Poems*
  VLS - v93 - My 23 '96 - p21 [501+]
Padilla, Raymond V - *The Leaning Ivory Tower*
  CS - v25 - S '96 - p654+ [501+]
  HAHR - v77 - F '97 - p89+ [501+]
Padovani, Serena - *L'Eta Di Savonarola*
  BM - v138 - S '96 - p628+ [501+]
Padovano, Anthony T - *A Retreat with Thomas Merton*
  CLW - v66 - Je '96 - p32+ [251-500]
Padowicz, Julian - *Stalking the Corporate Dollar
(Padowicz). Audio Version*
  LJ - v122 - Mr 15 '97 - p101 [51-250]
Padwa, Lynette - *Everything You Pretend to Know and
Are Afraid Someone Will Ask*
  r ARBA - v28 - '97 - p30 [251-500]
Padwee, Howard - *The Cat Who Couldn't See in the Dark*
  y BL - v93 - My 15 '97 - p1550 [51-250]
Padwick, Constance E - *Muslim Devotions*
  MEJ - v50 - Aut '96 - p631 [51-250]
Pae, Mu-Gi - *Women's Wages and Employment in Korea*
  ILR - v135 - '96 - p115+ [501+]
Paehlke, Robert - *Conservation and Environmentalism*
  r ARBA - v28 - '97 - p647 [51-250]
Paek, Min - *Aekyung's Dream (Illus. by Min Paek)*
  c Learning - v25 - Mr '97 - p54 [1-50]
Paesler, Michael A - *Near-Field Optics*
  Choice - v34 - D '96 - p649 [51-250]
  r SciTech - v20 - S '96 - p18 [51-250]
Pafford, J H P - *John Clavell 1601-43*
  EHR - v111 - N '96 - p1277+ [51-250]
Pagan, Nicholas O - *Rethinking Literary Biography*
  South HR - v30 - Fall '96 - p399+ [501+]

Pagano, Michael A - *Cityscapes and Capital*
  APSR - v90 - D '96 - p919 [501+]
  J Pol - v58 - Ag '96 - p885+ [501+]
Pagano, Ugo - *Democracy and Efficiency in the Economic
Enterprise*
  JEL - v34 - D '96 - p2076 [51-250]
  R&R Bk N - v11 - D '96 - p30 [51-250]
Pagden, Anthony - *Lords of All the World*
  Can Hist R - v78 - Mr '97 - p173+ [501+]
  EHR - v111 - S '96 - p945+ [501+]
  HAHR - v77 - F '97 - p80+ [251-500]
  Lon R Bks - v18 - Jl 18 '96 - p8+ [501+]
  Six Ct J - v27 - Fall '96 - p965+ [501+]
  Six Ct J - v27 - Fall '96 - p966+ [51-250]
  TLS - My 24 '96 - p15 [501+]
Page, Benjamin I - *Who Deliberates?*
  AJS - v102 - Ja '97 - p1189+ [501+]
  Choice - v34 - N '96 - p538 [51-250]
Page, Carl - *Philosophical Historicism and the Betrayal of
First Philosophy*
  Hist & T - v35 - 3 '96 - p401+ [501+]
  JAAR - v65 - Spr '97 - p215+ [501+]
Page, Caroline - *U.S. Official Propaganda during the
Vietnam War 1965-1973*
  Choice - v34 - S '96 - p212 [51-250]
Page, Charles R, II - *Jesus and the Land*
  Rel St Rev - v23 - Ja '97 - p67 [51-250]
Page, Clarence - *Showing My Color*
  BL - v93 - Ap 1 '97 - p1286 [1-50]
  CC - v114 - F 26 '97 - p228+ [501+]
  y Kliatt - v31 - Mr '97 - p24 [51-250]
  NYTBR - v102 - Mr 2 '97 - p28 [1-50]
  PW - v244 - Ja 13 '97 - p73 [1-50]
Page, David W - *Body Trauma*
  BL - v92 - Ag '96 - p1874 [51-250]
Page, Jake - *The Lethal Partner*
  PW - v244 - Ja 27 '97 - p103 [1-50]
Page, Jason - *I'm a Genius Vet (Illus. by David Hart)*
  c Sch Lib - v44 - N '96 - p164 [51-250]
Page, Katherine Hall - *Christie and Company*
  c BL - v93 - D 1 '96 - p665+ [51-250]
  c CBRS - v25 - D '96 - p48 [51-250]
  c HB Guide - v8 - Spr '97 - p72 [51-250]
  c SLJ - v43 - Mr '97 - p190 [51-250]
  Christie and Company down East
  c BL - v93 - My 1 '97 - p1498 [51-250]
Page, Lynda - *Just by Chance*
  Books - v11 - Ap '97 - p22 [51-250]
Page, Myra - *Moscow Yankee*
  AL - v68 - S '96 - p669 [1-50]
  Nat - v263 - S 23 '96 - p30+ [501+]
Page, P K - *Brazilian Journal*
  Biography - v19 - Fall '96 - p355+ [501+]
  The Glass Air
  Essays CW - Spr '96 - p115+ [501+]
  P.K. Page: Poems Selected and New
  Essays CW - Spr '96 - p115+ [501+]
Page, Patricia - *Hope's Cadillac*
  KR - v64 - My 1 '96 - p627+ [251-500]
  NYTBR - v101 - S 22 '96 - p25 [51-250]
  Rapport - v19 - 5 '96 - p35 [251-500]
Page, Robin - *Working with Your Foreign Language
Assistant*
  TES - Mr 14 '97 - p20* [51-250]
Page, Sheila - *How Developing Countries Trade*
  Econ J - v106 - N '96 - p1795+ [501+]
Page, Susan - *How One of You Can Bring the Two of You
Together*
  LJ - v122 - F 15 '97 - p150 [51-250]
  PW - v244 - Ja 27 '97 - p100 [51-250]

The Shortest Distance between You and a Published Book
  PW - v244 - My 12 '97 - p67 [51-250]
Page, Sydney H T - *Powers of Evil*
  Intpr - v51 - Ap '97 - p206 [251-500]
  Rel St Rev - v23 - Ap '97 - p187 [51-250]
Page, Tim - *Page after Page*
  Parameters - v26 - Win '96 - p148+ [501+]
Pageler, Elaine - *The Condor Hoax*
  c Ch BWatch - v6 - Jl '96 - p5 [51-250]
Monarchs at Risk
  c Ch BWatch - v6 - Jl '96 - p5 [51-250]
Robbers of the Giant Cactus
  c Ch BWatch - v6 - Jl '96 - p5 [51-250]
Threat to the Sea Otters
  c Ch BWatch - v6 - Jl '96 - p5 [51-250]
Troubles in the Rain Forest
  c Ch BWatch - v6 - Jl '96 - p5 [51-250]
Pagels, Elaine - *The Origin of Satan*
  Ant R - v54 - Fall '96 - p494 [251-500]
  CR - v269 - Ag '96 - p104+ [501+]
  Skeptic - v4 - '96 - p101+ [501+]
  Theol St - v57 - Je '96 - p379 [251-500]
  TT - v53 - O '96 - p398+ [501+]
Pagonis, William G - *Moving Mountains*
  Mar Crp G - v80 - N '96 - p81+ [501+]
Pahl, Ray - *After Success*
  TLS - D 6 '96 - p7+ [501+]
Pahlen, Kurt - *The World of the Oratorio*
  TranslRevS - v1 - My '95 - p12 [51-250]
Pai, Hua - *The Remote Country of Women*
  TranslRevS - v1 - My '95 - p14 [51-250]
Paidar, Parvin - *Women and the Political Process in Twentieth-Century Iran*
  AHR - v102 - F '97 - p148+ [501+]
  AJS - v102 - Jl '96 - p295+ [501+]
  APSR - v90 - D '96 - p929+ [501+]
  CS - v25 - S '96 - p629+ [501+]
  MEJ - v50 - Sum '96 - p432+ [501+]
Paige, Frances - *The Confetti Bed*
  BL - v93 - D 1 '96 - p641 [51-250]
Paik, Keun-Wook - *Gas and Oil in Northeast Asia*
  En Jnl - v18 - 1 '97 - p132+ [501+]
  JEL - v34 - D '96 - p2136 [51-250]
Pailin, David A - *Probing the Foundations*
  JR - v77 - Ja '97 - p167+ [501+]
Pain, Robin - *Practical Electronic Fault Finding and Troubleshooting*
  SciTech - v20 - S '96 - p57 [51-250]
Pain, Stephen - *Find a Space!*
  r TES - Mr 14 '97 - p16* [1-50]
Painchaud, Louis - *Les Textes De Nag Hammadi Et Le Probleme De Leur Classification*
  Rel St Rev - v23 - Ja '97 - p76 [51-250]
Paine, Lauran - *Lockwood: A Western Story*
  Roundup M - v3 - Ag '96 - p31 [251-500]
Tears of the Heart (Weideman). Audio Version
  y Kliatt - v31 - Mr '97 - p46 [51-250]
Paine, Sarah C M - *Imperial Rivals*
  R&R Bk N - v11 - N '96 - p13 [51-250]
Paine, Thomas - *The Rights of Man. Common Sense*
  HT - v46 - S '96 - p53+ [501+]
Painted Bride Quarterly
  p Sm Pr R - v29 - F '97 - p13+ [51-250]
Painter, Charlotte - *Conjuring Tibet*
  BL - v93 - N 15 '96 - p572 [51-250]
  LJ - v121 - N 15 '96 - p90 [51-250]
  PW - v243 - O 14 '96 - p79 [51-250]
Painter, James - *Bolivia and Coca*
  HAHR - v76 - Ag '96 - p592+ [251-500]
Painter, Michael - *The Social Causes of Environmental Destruction in Latin America*
  HAHR - v77 - F '97 - p160+ [501+]
Painter, Nell Irvin - *Sojourner Truth: A Life, a Symbol*
  Bks & Cult - v3 - Mr '97 - p20 [501+]
  BL - v93 - Ja '97 - p760 [1-50]
  y BL - v93 - S 1 '96 - p43 [51-250]
  BL - v93 - Ap 1 '97 - p1286 [1-50]
  BW - v26 - S 15 '96 - p9+ [501+]
  BWatch - v17 - N '96 - p2 [51-250]
  Choice - v34 - Mr '97 - p1228+ [251-500]
  Ch Today - v41 - F 3 '97 - p61 [51-250]
  LATBR - O 6 '96 - p4+ [501+]
  LJ - v121 - N 1 '96 - p84 [1-50]
  Ms - v7 - S '96 - p83 [1-50]
  Ms - v7 - Ja '97 - p78 [251-500]
  Nat - v264 - Ja 13 '97 - p25+ [501+]
  New R - v215 - N 4 '96 - p37+ [501+]
  NYTBR - v101 - S 22 '96 - p29 [501+]
Painting Outside Painting
  ABR - v18 - D '96 - p12+ [501+]

Pais, Abraham - *Einstein Lived Here*
  Isis - v88 - Mr '97 - p156+ [501+]
A Tale of Two Continents
  KR - v65 - Mr 15 '97 - p447 [251-500]
  LJ - v122 - Mr 15 '97 - p86 [51-250]
  NYTLa - v146 - My 28 '97 - pC14 [501+]
  PW - v244 - Ap 7 '97 - p85+ [51-250]
PAIS Select. Electronic Media Version
  r BL - v93 - F 15 '97 - p1039 [251-500]
  yr Kliatt - v31 - Mr '97 - p38 [51-250]
  yr LJ - v122 - Ap 1 '97 - p138 [51-250]
Paisner, Emme - *True Beauty*
  PW - v243 - N 4 '96 - p55 [51-250]
Pak, Kyong-Ni - *Land*
  LATBR - S 15 '96 - p6 [501+]
Pak, Wan-So - *The Naked Tree*
  Choice - v34 - O '96 - p274 [51-250]
  WLT - v70 - Sum '96 - p764 [251-500]
Pakenham, Thomas, 1933- - *The Boer War*
  TLS - Ap 11 '97 - p28 [251-500]
Meetings with Remarkable Trees
  New Sci - v152 - D 21 '96 - p67 [1-50]
  Spec - v277 - N 30 '96 - p54 [501+]
Pakistan 1995
  GJ - v163 - Mr '97 - p108 [51-250]
  Pac A - v69 - Sum '96 - p274+ [501+]
Pakistan (Handbooks of the World)
  r BL - v93 - S 15 '96 - p210 [1-50]
Pakula, Hannah - *An Uncommon Woman*
  NYRB - v43 - Je 6 '96 - p20+ [501+]
  NYTBR - v101 - D 8 '96 - p93 [1-50]
  Spec - v277 - N 16 '96 - p42 [1-50]
Pakulski, Jan - *The Death of Class*
  Socio R - v44 - N '96 - p757+ [501+]
Palacios, Argentina - *The Hummingbird King (Illus. by F Davalos)*
  c SS - v88 - Ja '97 - p29+ [501+]
Palacios, Marco - *Entre La Legitimidad Y La Violencia*
  HAHR - v76 - N '96 - p808 [251-500]
Palac-McMiken, Evanor D - *Rescheduling, Credit-Worthiness and Market Prices*
  JEL - v34 - S '96 - p1433 [51-250]
Palaeologus, Jacobus - *Disputatio Scholastica*
  CH - v65 - D '96 - p696+ [251-500]
Palahniuk, Chuck - *Fight Club*
  BW - v26 - D 1 '96 - p6 [51-250]
  Ent W - S 6 '96 - p71 [51-250]
  LATBR - Ag 18 '96 - p1+ [501+]
  LJ - v122 - Mr 15 '97 - p43 [1-50]
  NY - v72 - D 23 '96 - p146 [51-250]
Palais, James B - *Confucian Statecraft and Korean Institutions*
  Choice - v34 - Mr '97 - p1216 [51-250]
  R&R Bk N - v11 - D '96 - p4 [51-250]
Palamar, Larysa - *Mova Dilovykh Paperiv*
  BL - v93 - N 15 '96 - p577 [1-50]
Palan, Ronen - *State Strategies in the Global Political Economy*
  Choice - v34 - F '97 - p1012+ [51-250]
Palatini, Margie - *Moosetache (Illus. by Henry Cole)*
  c KR - v65 - Mr 1 '97 - p386 [51-250]
  c PW - v244 - Mr 3 '97 - p74 [51-250]
Piggie Pie! (Illus. by Howard Fine)
  c Inst - v105 - My '96 - p70 [51-250]
  c LA - v73 - O '96 - p431 [51-250]
Palau I Fabre, Josep - *Pablo Picasso: Academic and Anti-Academic 1895-1900*
  BM - v138 - Ag '96 - p565+ [501+]
Palazchenko, Pavel - *My Years with Gorbachev and Shevardnadze*
  BL - v93 - My 15 '97 - p1559+ [51-250]
  PW - v244 - Mr 3 '97 - p59 [51-250]
Palazzo-Craig, Janet - *Bobo's Magic Wishes. Book and Audio Version*
  c SLJ - v42 - Ag '96 - p62 [51-250]
Emerald Tree. Book and Audio Version
  c SLJ - v42 - Ag '96 - p62 [51-250]
The Golden Flower. Book and Audio Version
  c SLJ - v42 - Ag '96 - p62 [51-250]
How Lama Saved the Day. Book and Audio Version
  c SLJ - v42 - Ag '96 - p62 [51-250]
How Night Came to Be. Book and Audio Version
  c SLJ - v42 - Ag '96 - p62 [51-250]
The Magic Peach. Book and Audio Version
  c SLJ - v42 - Ag '96 - p62 [51-250]
Tam's Slipper. Book and Audio Version
  c SLJ - v42 - Ag '96 - p62 [51-250]
When Sun Ruled the Land (Illus. by Dave Albers)
  c SLJ - v42 - Ag '96 - p140 [51-250]

When Sun Ruled the Land (Illus. by Dave Alpers). Book and Audio Version
  c SLJ - v42 - Ag '96 - p62 [51-250]
Why Opossum Is Gray (Illus. by Charles Reasoner). Book and Audio Version
  c SLJ - v42 - Ag '96 - p62 [51-250]
Why Opossum Is Gray (Illus. by Charles Reasoner)
  c SLJ - v42 - Ag '96 - p62 [51-250]
Why Owl Comes Out at Night (Illus. by Charles Reasoner). Book and Audio Version
  c SLJ - v42 - Ag '96 - p62 [51-250]
Why Owl Comes Out at Night (Illus. by Charles Reasoner)
  c SLJ - v42 - Ag '96 - p140 [51-250]
Why Spider Spins Tales. Book and Audio Version
  c SLJ - v42 - Ag '96 - p62 [51-250]
Palder, Edward - *The Catalog of Catalogs V*
  r LJ - v122 - F 15 '97 - p128 [51-250]
Paldiel, Mordecai - *Sheltering the Jews*
  CC - v114 - Mr 12 '97 - p275 [251-500]
  CH - v66 - Mr '97 - p209 [51-250]
Paley, Morton D - *Coleridge's Later Poetry*
  Nine-C Lit - v51 - Mr '97 - p563 [51-250]
Paley, Nicholas - *Finding Art's Place*
  Afterimage - v24 - S '96 - p13 [501+]
Paley, Vivian Gussin - *The Girl with the Brown Crayon*
  BL - v93 - F 15 '97 - p981 [51-250]
  KR - v65 - Ja 1 '97 - p46 [251-500]
  PW - v244 - F 17 '97 - p202+ [51-250]
Kwanzaa and Me
  BW - v26 - D 1 '96 - p12 [51-250]
Paley, William - *Natural Theology*
  Nature - v386 - Mr 6 '97 - p35 [501+]
Paling, Chris - *Morning All Day*
  TLS - Ap 11 '97 - p26 [501+]
Palisca, Claude V - *Musica Enchiriadis and Scolica Enchiriadis*
  Notes - v53 - S '96 - p60+ [501+]
Palko, Zsuzsanna - *Hungarian Folktales*
  Choice - v34 - Ap '97 - p1345 [51-250]
  TranslRevS - v2 - D '96 - p3 [51-250]
Palkovic, Mark - *Harp Music Bibliography*
  r M Ed J - v83 - Jl '96 - p50 [51-250]
  r Notes - v53 - S '96 - p58+ [501+]
Pall, Ellen - *Among the Ginzburgs*
  BW - v26 - Jl 14 '96 - p6 [251-500]
Palladino, Grace - *Teenagers: An American History*
  Ent W - Ap 4 '97 - p79 [1-50]
Palladino, Lucy Jo - *The Edison Trait*
  PW - v244 - Mr 24 '97 - p78 [51-250]
Pallasmaa, Juhani - *The Melnikov House, Moscow 1927-1929*
  TLS - D 27 '96 - p32 [251-500]
Palley, Thomas I - *Post Keynesian Economics*
  JEL - v35 - Mr '97 - p205 [51-250]
Palliser, Charles - *Betrayals*
  Ent W - Ag 23 '96 - p119 [1-50]
Pallone, Nathaniel J - *Tinder-Box Criminal Aggression*
  Nat R - v48 - N 11 '96 - p52+ [501+]
  R&R Bk N - v11 - N '96 - p45 [51-250]
Pallotta, Jerry - *The Airplane Alphabet Book (Illus. by Rob Bolster)*
  c BL - v93 - F 1 '97 - p943 [51-250]
  c Cur R - v36 - Ap '97 - p13 [51-250]
  c KR - v65 - Ja 15 '97 - p144 [51-250]
  c PW - v244 - Mr 3 '97 - p77 [51-250]
The Freshwater Alphabet Book (Illus. by David Biedrzycki)
  c HB Guide - v7 - Fall '96 - p337+ [1-50]
Pally, Marcia - *Sex and Sensibility*
  CSM - v89 - D 6 '96 - p10 [51-250]
Palma, Milagros - *Desencanto Al Amanecer*
  WLT - v70 - Aut '96 - p924 [501+]
El Pacto
  LJ - v122 - Ja '97 - p80 [51-250]
Palmen, Connie - *De Vriendschap*
  WLT - v70 - Sum '96 - p711+ [501+]
Palmer, Alan Warwick - *Dictionary of the British Empire and Commonwealth*
  r ARBA - v28 - '97 - p61+ [251-500]
  r Choice - v34 - O '96 - p256 [51-250]
Twilight of the Habsburgs
  BW - v27 - Mr 2 '97 - p12 [51-250]
Who's Who in World Politics from 1860 to the Present Day
  r CR - v270 - F '97 - p110 [51-250]
Palmer, Arnold - *Play Great Golf*
  LJ - v121 - O 1 '96 - p53 [1-50]
Palmer, Catherine - *The Treasure of Timbuktu*
  LJ - v122 - F 1 '97 - p68 [51-250]

Palmer, Charlie - *Great American Food*
    BL - v93 - S 15 '96 - p197 [51-250]
    LJ - v121 - S 15 '96 - p89 [51-250]
Palmer, Christopher M - *Principles of Contaminant Hydrogeology. 2nd Ed.*
    SciTech - v20 - D '96 - p69 [51-250]
Palmer, Edward - *Pumpkin Carving*
    c CAY - v16 - Fall '95 - p7 [51-250]
    c LATBR - O 20 '96 - p8 [51-250]
Palmer, Frank - *Nightwatch*
    BL - v92 - Ag '96 - p1887 [51-250]
Palmer, Janice B - *Varner, Verner, Werner Families of America*
    NGSQ - v84 - S '96 - p230+ [251-500]
Palmer, Jerry - *Taking Humour Seriously*
    Humor - v9 - 3 '96 - p401+ [501+]
Palmer, Jim - *Together We Were Eleven Foot Nine*
    NYTBR - v101 - Ap 7 '96 - p16 [251-500]
Palmer, Joy A - *Just Environments*
    CPR - v16 - D '96 - p428+ [501+]
Palmer, Marilyn - *Industry in the Landscape 1700-1900*
    GJ - v162 - Jl '96 - p236+ [51-250]
Palmer, Mary H - *Urinary Continence*
    SciTech - v21 - Mr '97 - p58 [51-250]
Palmer, Michael, 1942- - *Critical Judgment (Gallagher). Audio Version*
    y Kliatt - v31 - Mr '97 - p40 [51-250]
    Extreme Measures (Pankow). Audio Version
    BWatch - v17 - D '96 - p11 [1-50]
    BWatch - v18 - Mr '97 - p7 [1-50]
    Extreme Measures (Guidall). Audio Version
    y Kliatt - v31 - My '97 - p38 [51-250]
    Extreme Measures (Pankow). Audio Version
    y Kliatt - v31 - My '97 - p38 [51-250]
    LJ - v122 - Mr 15 '97 - p102 [51-250]
Palmer, Michael, 1943- - *At Passages*
    Nat - v263 - D 23 '96 - p26+ [501+]
Palmer, Michael, 1952- - *Political Philosophy and the Human Soul*
    APSR - v90 - S '96 - p637+ [501+]
    J Pol - v59 - F '97 - p279+ [501+]
Palmer, Pete - *The Web Server Handbook*
    BYTE - v22 - Mr '97 - p34 [51-250]
    SciTech - v20 - D '96 - p76 [51-250]
Palmer, Ransford W - *Pilgrims from the Sun*
    JEL - v35 - Mr '97 - p158+ [51-250]
Palmer, Robert - *Deep Blues*
    CSM - v88 - N 21 '96 - p11 [1-50]
Palmer, Robert C, 1947- - *English Law in the Age of the Black Death 1348-1381*
    Albion - v28 - Sum '96 - p290+ [501+]
Palmer, Sally E - *Maintaining Family Ties*
    Adoles - v31 - Fall '96 - p754 [51-250]
    Soc Ser R - v70 - D '96 - p669 [51-250]
Palmer, Stuart B - *Advanced University Physics*
    New Sci - v151 - S 28 '96 - p54+ [501+]
    Phys Today - v49 - D '96 - p59+ [501+]
Palmer, Tim - *America by Rivers*
    Hast Cen R - v26 - S '96 - p41 [1-50]
Palmer, William, 1945- - *Four Last Things*
    Obs - O 20 '96 - p18* [51-250]
    The Pardon of Saint Anne
    Spec - v278 - F 1 '97 - p36 [501+]
    TLS - Ja 10 '97 - p21 [501+]
Palmer, William, 1951- - *The Problem of Ireland in Tudor Foreign Policy 1485-1603*
    AHR - v101 - O '96 - p1215 [501+]
    EHR - v112 - Ap '97 - p459+ [501+]
Palmer, William J - *The Films of the Eighties*
    J Pop F&TV - v24 - Spr '96 - p48 [501+]
Palmer, William J, 1934- - *Construction Insurance, Bonding, and Risk Management*
    R&R Bk N - v12 - F '97 - p50 [51-250]
Palmer, William J, 1943- - *The Hoydens and Mr. Dickens*
    BL - v93 - F 15 '97 - p1007 [51-250]
    KR - v64 - D 15 '96 - p1769+ [51-250]
    PW - v243 - D 30 '96 - p58 [51-250]
Palmer-Fernandez, Gabriel - *Moral Issues*
    Rel St Rev - v23 - Ja '97 - p50 [51-250]
Palmie, Stephan - *Slave Cultures and the Cultures of Slavery*
    HAHR - v77 - F '97 - p157+ [251-500]
    W&M Q - v54 - Ja '97 - p259+ [501+]
Palmieri, Giovanni - *Schmitz, Svevo, Zeno*
    MLR - v91 - Jl '96 - p760+ [501+]
Palmieri, Patricia Ann - *In Adamless Eden*
    AHR - v101 - D '96 - p1630 [501+]
    HER - v66 - Win '96 - p858+ [501+]
    NEQ - v69 - S '96 - p518+ [501+]
    NWSA Jnl - v8 - Sum '96 - p152+ [501+]

Pals, Daniel L - *Seven Theories of Religion*
    Choice - v34 - S '96 - p146 [51-250]
    Rel St Rev - v23 - Ja '97 - p42 [51-250]
    Skeptic - v4 - 4 '96 - p102 [251-500]
Paludan, Philip Shaw - *A People's Conquest*
    HT - v46 - O '96 - p58 [1-50]
Paludi, Michele Antoinette - *Exploring/Teaching the Psychology of Women. 2nd Ed.*
    R&R Bk N - v12 - F '97 - p53 [51-250]
    Sexual Harassment on College Campuses
    Choice - v34 - D '96 - p661 [51-250]
Palumbo-Liu, David - *The Ethnic Canon*
    AL - v68 - D '96 - p883 [51-250]
    Amerasia J - v22 - 3 '96 - p157+ [501+]
    Col Lit - v23 - O '96 - p171+ [501+]
Pam, David Owen - *A History of Enfield. Vols. 2-3*
    EHR - v112 - F '97 - p246+ [251-500]
Pamuk, Orhan - *The Black Book*
    NS & S - v9 - My 17 '96 - p40 [1-50]
    TLS - N 29 '96 - p16 [251-500]
    The New Life
    BL - v93 - Mr 1 '97 - p1112 [51-250]
    KR - v65 - F 1 '97 - p165 [251-500]
    LJ - v122 - F 1 '97 - p107 [51-250]
    Nat - v264 - Ap 7 '97 - p38+ [501+]
    NYTBR - v102 - Ap 6 '97 - p8 [501+]
    PW - v244 - F 3 '97 - p93 [51-250]
    Trib Bks - Ap 13 '97 - p4 [251-500]
    WSJ Cent - v99 - Ap 4 '97 - pA7 [501+]
Pan, Zhongdang - *To See Ourselves*
    Ch Rev Int - v3 - Fall '96 - p505+ [501+]
Pan-American Aerobiology Association - *Aerobiology: Proceedings of the Pan-American Aerobiology Association*
    SciTech - v20 - D '96 - p36 [51-250]
Panas, John - *Aircraft Mishap Photography*
    SciTech - v20 - D '96 - p80 [51-250]
Panati, Charles - *Sacred Origins of Profound Things*
    y Kliatt - v31 - Mr '97 - p28 [51-250]
    LJ - v121 - D '96 - p100 [51-250]
    NYTBR - v102 - Ja 12 '97 - p20 [251-500]
Panayi, Panikos - *Germans in Britain since 1500*
    HT - v47 - F '97 - p58+ [501+]
Panayotakis, Costas - *Theatrum Arbitri*
    Rel St Rev - v23 - Ja '97 - p63 [51-250]
Pancheri, Jan - *The Twelve Poodle Princesses*
    c Bks Keeps - Jl '96 - p9 [51-250]
Pancrazi, Jean-Noel - *Madame Arnoul*
    FR - v70 - D '96 - p353+ [501+]
Pandell, Karen - *Animal Action ABC (Illus. by Art Wolfe)*
    c BL - v93 - N 15 '96 - p592 [51-250]
    c HB Guide - v8 - Spr '97 - p14 [51-250]
    c Inst - v106 - Mr '97 - p28 [1-50]
    c KR - v64 - S 15 '96 - p1406 [51-250]
    c PW - v243 - O 14 '96 - p85 [51-250]
    Learning from the Dalai Lama (Illus. by John B Taylor)
    c BL - v93 - O 1 '96 - p339 [1-50]
    y HB Guide - v7 - Fall '96 - p309 [51-250]
    c LA - v73 - O '96 - p442+ [51-250]
Pander Brothers - *Triple-X International*
    PW - v244 - Mr 31 '97 - p68 [1-50]
Pandiri, Ananda M - *A Comprehensive, Annotated Bibliography on Mahatma Gandhi. Vol. 1*
    r ARBA - v28 - '97 - p197+ [51-250]
Pang, Stella W - *Diagnostic Techniques for Semiconductor Materials Processing II*
    SciTech - v20 - S '96 - p53 [51-250]
Panik, Michael J - *Linear Programming*
    SciTech - v20 - N '96 - p59 [51-250]
Panitch, Leo - *Are There Alternatives?*
    TLS - S 13 '96 - p29 [501+]
    Why Not Capitalism
    CS - v25 - N '96 - p771+ [501+]
Pankey, Eric - *The Late Romances*
    NL - v79 - D 16 '96 - p31+ [501+]
    PW - v243 - D 30 '96 - p65 [51-250]
Pankhurst, Donna - *A Resolvable Conflict?*
    JPR - v33 - N '96 - p500 [51-250]
Pankowski, Marian - *Rudolf*
    KR - v64 - S 15 '96 - p1354 [51-250]
    LJ - v121 - O 1 '96 - p128 [51-250]
Pannell, David J - *Introduction to Practical Linear Programming*
    Choice - v34 - F '97 - p999 [51-250]
    JEL - v35 - Mr '97 - p196+ [51-250]
    SciTech - v20 - D '96 - p59 [51-250]
Pannenberg, Wolfhart - *Systematic Theology. Vol. 2*
    JAAR - v64 - Fall '96 - p685+ [501+]
Pannier, Dominique - *Corporate Governance of Public Enterprises in Transitional Economies*
    JEL - v34 - D '96 - p2083 [51-250]

Panofsky, Erwin - *Three Essays on Style*
    BM - v138 - O '96 - p700 [251-500]
    JAAC - v55 - Win '97 - p66+ [501+]
    Six Ct J - v27 - Fall '96 - p882+ [501+]
Panoramiques
    p Arena - Ap '96 - p56 [501+]
Panourgia, Neni - *Fragments of Death, Fables of Identity*
    Choice - v34 - S '96 - p168 [51-250]
    TLS - N 1 '96 - p29 [501+]
Pantel, Gerda - *The Canadian Bed and Breakfast Guide. 12th Ed.*
    r ARBA - v28 - '97 - p180 [51-250]
Panter, Nicole - *Unnatural Disasters*
    SFR - v21 - N '96 - p22 [501+]
    Sm Pr R - v29 - Ja '97 - p12 [501+]
Pantin, Isabelle - *La Poesie Du Ciel En France Dans La Seconde Moitie Du Seizieme Siecle*
    Ren Q - v50 - Spr '97 - p251+ [501+]
Panton, Ronald L - *Incompressible Flow. 2nd Ed.*
    Phys Today - v49 - N '96 - p89+ [501+]
Pantry, Sheila - *Dealing with Aggression and Violence in Your Workplace*
    LAR - v98 - S '96 - p481 [51-250]
Panych, Morris - *Vigil*
    Quill & Q - v62 - D '96 - p32 [501+]
Panzer, Richard A - *Condom Nation*
    Choice - v34 - My '97 - p1535 [51-250]
Paoletti, John T - *Art in Renaissance Italy*
    Choice - v34 - My '97 - p1487+ [51-250]
    LJ - v122 - F 15 '97 - p132 [51-250]
    Mag Antiq - v151 - Ap '97 - p518 [51-250]
Paolucci, Anne - *Queensboro Bridge and Other Poems*
    Sm Pr R - v28 - Je '96 - p10 [51-250]
Paolucci, Antonio - *The Origins of Renaissance Art*
    PW - v243 - N 18 '96 - p60 [51-250]
Papacosma, S Victor - *NATO in the Post-Cold War Era*
    Parameters - v27 - Spr '97 - p169+ [501+]
Papademetriou, George C - *Maimonides and Palamas on God*
    Rel St Rev - v23 - Ja '97 - p80 [51-250]
Papadimitriou, Dimitri B - *Aspects of Distribution of Wealth and Income*
    Econ J - v106 - N '96 - p1840 [251-500]
    Stability in the Financial System
    Choice - v34 - N '96 - p509 [51-250]
    JEL - v35 - Mr '97 - p223 [51-250]
Papaellinas, George - *More Beautiful Lies*
    Aust Bk R - D '96 - p54+ [501+]
Papandreou, Nick - *Father Dancing*
    BW - v27 - Ja 5 '97 - p3 [501+]
    TLS - D 27 '96 - p31 [501+]
Papanikolas, Helen - *The Apple Falls from the Apple Tree*
    LATBR - D 15 '96 - p15 [51-250]
Papanikolas, Zeese - *Trickster in the Land of Dreams*
    PHR - v66 - F '97 - p103+ [251-500]
    WAL - v31 - Win '97 - p419+ [251-500]
Papathanasiou, Vana - *Ase Tin Porta Anihti*
    WLT - v70 - Sum '96 - p740 [251-500]
Papayanis, Nicholas - *Horse-Drawn Cabs and Omnibuses in Paris*
    Choice - v34 - Ap '97 - p1397+ [51-250]
Papazian, Charlie - *The Home Brewer's Companion*
    LJ - v122 - Ap 1 '97 - p63 [1-50]
Pape, David Sholom - *A Chanuka Story for Night Number 3 (Illus. by Harris Mandel)*
    c Ch BWatch - v6 - D '96 - p8 [51-250]
Pape, Donna Lugg - *The Book of Foolish Machinery (Illus. by Fred Winkowski)*
    c New Ad - v9 - Fall '96 - p309+ [501+]
Pape, Walter - *Reflecting Senses*
    MLR - v92 - Ap '97 - p417+ [501+]
Paper, Jordan - *The Spirits Are Drunk*
    Ch Rev Int - v3 - Fall '96 - p507+ [501+]
Paper Boat
    p Sm Pr R - v28 - N '96 - p13 [51-250]
Paperback Books for Children
    r Inst - v105 - My '96 - p17 [51-250]
Paperbound: A Showcase of Contemporary Papermakers and Bookbinders
    Am Craft - v56 - D '96 - p29+ [1-50]
Papers in Regional Science
    p JEL - v34 - S '96 - p1506 [51-250]
Papert, Seymour - *The Connected Family*
    LJ - v121 - N 1 '96 - p99+ [51-250]
    PW - v243 - S 2 '96 - p108 [51-250]
Papineau, David - *Philosophical Naturalism*
    RM - v49 - Je '96 - p938+ [501+]
    The Philosophy of Science
    New Sci - v151 - S 28 '96 - p51 [1-50]
Pappano, Marilyn - *Suspicion*
    PW - v244 - Ja 20 '97 - p399 [51-250]

Pappas, Chris H - *C/C++ Programmer's Guide*
SciTech - v21 - Mr '97 - p7 [51-250]
Java with Borland C++
SciTech - v21 - Mr '97 - p7 [51-250]
Pappas, Marjorie L - *Searching Electronic Resources*
H Sch M - v4 - D '96 - p54 [51-250]
Pappas, Nickolas - *Plato and the Republic*
CPR - v16 - Ap '96 - p129+ [501+]
Pappas, Theoni - *The Music of Reason*
Math T - v89 - My '96 - p437 [51-250]
Papper, E M - *Romance, Poetry, and Surgical Sleep*
Nine-C Lit - v50 - Mr '96 - p556 [51-250]
Pappetti, F - *An Introduction to Parallel Computational Fluid Dynamics*
SciTech - v21 - Mr '97 - p18 [51-250]
Papworth, John - *Small Is Powerful*
CPR - v16 - Ag '96 - p277+ [251-500]
Utne R - N '96 - p89 [1-50]
Paquette, Robert L - *The Lesser Antilles in the Age of European Expansion*
Choice - v34 - Ap '97 - p1400 [51-250]
Para-Doxa: Studies in World Literary Genres
p LJ - v122 - Ja '97 - p158 [51-250]
Paradis, Adrian A - *The Labor Almanac*
r RQ - v36 - Fall '96 - p51 [51-250]
Opportunities in Airline Careers
y Kliatt - v31 - Ja '97 - p21 [51-250]
Paradis, Gerard W - *Demystifying ISO 9000*
SciTech - v20 - S '96 - p62 [51-250]
Paradise, Lois J - *Enteric Infections and Immunity*
SciTech - v20 - S '96 - p37 [51-250]
Paral, Vladimir - *Catapult*
TranslRevS - v1 - My '95 - p17 [51-250]
The Four Sonyas
TranslRevS - v1 - My '95 - p17 [51-250]
Paranagua, Paulo Antonio - *Mexican Cinema*
Choice - v34 - N '96 - p468 [51-250]
Paraskevas, Betty - *Cecil Bunions and the Midnight Train (Illus. by Michael Paraskevas)*
c CBRS - v25 - Win '97 - p65 [51-250]
c CCB-B - v50 - D '96 - p147 [51-250]
c HB Guide - v8 - Spr '97 - p42 [51-250]
c SLJ - v42 - D '96 - p103 [51-250]
The Ferocious Beast (Illus. by Michael Paraskevas)
c HB Guide - v7 - Fall '96 - p270 [51-250]
Paraskevopoulos, P N - *Digital Control Systems*
SciTech - v20 - S '96 - p53 [51-250]
Paravicini, Werner - *Die Preussenreisen Des Europaischen Adels. Vol. 2*
Specu - v71 - O '96 - p996 [51-250]
Paravisini-Gebert, Lizabeth - *Phyllis Shand Allfrey: A Caribbean Life*
AL - v68 - D '96 - p878+ [51-250]
Choice - v34 - D '96 - p616 [51-250]
TLS - O 25 '96 - p30 [501+]
Pardalos, P M - *Global Minimization of Nonconvex Energy Functions*
SIAM Rev - v38 - D '96 - p713 [51-250]
Pardo Tomas, Jose - *Ciencia Y Censura*
Lib - v18 - S '96 - p274 [51-250]
Pare, Ambroise - *On Monsters and Marvels*
r TranslRevS - v2 - D '96 - p6 [1-50]
Pare, Michael A - *Sports Stars. 2nd Ser., Vols. 1-2*
cr ARBA - v28 - '97 - p292 [251-500]
cr SLJ - v43 - F '97 - p132 [51-250]
Paredes, Ricardo - *Human Resources and the Adjustment Process*
Econ J - v107 - Ja '97 - p277+ [251-500]
Parelli, Robert J - *Medicolegal Issues for Radiographers. 3rd Ed.*
SciTech - v21 - Mr '97 - p51 [51-250]
Principles of Fluoroscopic Image Intensification and Television Systems
SciTech - v21 - Mr '97 - p89 [51-250]
Parens, Joshua - *Metaphysics as Rhetoric*
APSR - v90 - S '96 - p638+ [501+]
RP - v59 - Spr '97 - p371+ [501+]
Parent, Andre - *Human Neuroanatomy. 9th Ed.*
SciTech - v20 - N '96 - p30 [51-250]
Parent, Marc - *Turning Stones*
y BL - v93 - S 15 '96 - p190 [51-250]
LATBR - O 27 '96 - p5 [501+]
NYTBR - v101 - N 10 '96 - p15 [501+]
Parent, Michael - *Of Kings and Fools*
c Ch BWatch - v6 - D '96 - p2 [51-250]
y Kliatt - v31 - Mr '97 - p24 [51-250]
Parents and Computers
p TES - O 18 '96 - p43U [51-250]
Paretsky, Sara - *Windy City Blues*
PW - v243 - N 18 '96 - p70 [1-50]

Windy City Blues (Cassidy). Audio Version
y Kliatt - v30 - S '96 - p54 [51-250]
Women on the Case
Arm Det - v29 - Sum '96 - p347 [51-250]
KR - v64 - My 1 '96 - p648 [51-250]
Parfitt, Tudor - *The Road to Redemption*
R&R Bk N - v12 - F '97 - p19 [51-250]
Parham, David M - *Pediatric Neoplasia*
SciTech - v20 - S '96 - p31 [51-250]
Pariani, Laura - *Il Pettine*
WLT - v70 - Sum '96 - p674 [251-500]
La Spada E La Luna
WLT - v71 - Win '97 - p129 [251-500]
Parijs, Philippe Van - *Real Freedom for All*
APSR - v90 - D '96 - p900+ [501+]
Ethics - v107 - Ja '97 - p321+ [501+]
JEL - v35 - Mr '97 - p181+ [501+]
Parikh, Anoop - *The Home Decorator's Bible*
LJ - v122 - F 1 '97 - p52 [1-50]
Parini, Jay - *Benjamin's Crossing*
BL - v93 - My 15 '97 - p1563 [51-250]
KR - v65 - Mr 15 '97 - p410+ [251-500]
LJ - v122 - Ap 15 '97 - p120 [51-250]
PW - v244 - Mr 31 '97 - p60+ [51-250]
Gore Vidal: Writer against the Grain
J Am St - v30 - Ap '96 - p160+ [251-500]
John Steinbeck: A Biography
y Kliatt - v30 - S '96 - p26 [251-500]
Paris, Barry - *Audrey Hepburn*
BL - v93 - S 15 '96 - p179 [51-250]
KR - v64 - S 1 '96 - p1304 [251-500]
LJ - v121 - D '96 - p96 [51-250]
NYTBR - v101 - D 15 '96 - p24 [51-250]
Obs - F 9 '97 - p16* [51-250]
PW - v243 - S 9 '96 - p70+ [51-250]
Garbo: A Biography
NS & S - v9 - Ap 26 '96 - p36 [1-50]
Paris, Bernard J - *Karen Horney: A Psychoanalyst's Search for Self-Understanding*
NYTBR - v101 - O 27 '96 - p48 [1-50]
PW - v243 - D 9 '96 - p66 [1-50]
Paris, Bob - *Flawless: The Ten-Week, Total-Image Method for Transforming Your Physique*
Quill & Q - v62 - D '96 - p24+ [501+]
Paris, Erna - *The End of Days*
AB - v98 - O 14 '96 - p1235+ [501+]
y SLJ - v42 - N '96 - p142 [51-250]
Paris, Matthew - *The Life of St. Edmund*
CR - v268 - Je '96 - p334 [51-250]
Paris, Michael - *From the Wright Brothers to Top Gun*
Albion - v28 - '96 - p734+ [501+]
J Am St - v30 - Ag '96 - p302+ [251-500]
Paris, Peter J - *The Spirituality of African Peoples*
Theol St - v57 - Je '96 - p390 [251-500]
Paris (Travelers' Tales)
r BL - v93 - S 15 '96 - p212 [1-50]
Pariser, Harry S - *Adventure Guide to Costa Rica. 3rd Ed.*
r BL - v93 - S 15 '96 - p210 [1-50]
Parish, Herman - *Bravo, Amelia Bedelia! (Illus. by Lynn Sweat)*
c BL - v93 - My 1 '97 - p1504 [51-250]
c PW - v244 - Ja 13 '97 - p77 [51-250]
Parish, James Robert - *Rosie: Rosie O'Donnell's Biography*
y BL - v93 - Ap 1 '97 - p1267 [51-250]
KR - v65 - F 15 '97 - p281 [51-250]
PW - v244 - Mr 17 '97 - p68 [51-250]
Parish, Peggy - *Amelia Bedelia (Illus. by Fritz Siebel)*
c BL - v93 - My 1 '97 - p1507 [1-50]
Be Ready at Eight (Illus. by Cynthia Fisher)
c HB Guide - v7 - Fall '96 - p284 [51-250]
Granny and the Desperadoes (Illus. by Steven Kellogg)
c HB Guide - v7 - Fall '96 - p284 [51-250]
Play Ball, Amelia Bedelia (Illus. by Wallace Tripp)
c HB Guide - v7 - Fall '96 - p284 [51-250]
Teach Us, Amelia Bedelia (Illus. by Lynn Sweat)
c RT - v50 - O '96 - p138 [1-50]
Parish, Steven M - *Hierarchy and Its Discontents*
Choice - v34 - D '96 - p665+ [51-250]
R&R Bk N - v11 - N '96 - p15 [51-250]
Parisher, Roy A - *Pipe Drafting and Design*
SciTech - v20 - D '96 - p74 [51-250]
Park, Andrew Sung - *The Wounded Heart of God*
JAAR - v64 - Fall '96 - p667+ [501+]
Park, Barbara - *Junie B. Jones Loves Handsome Warren (Illus. by Denise Brunkus)*
c BL - v93 - F 1 '97 - p950 [51-250]
Park, David - *Stone Kingdoms*
TLS - My 24 '96 - p26 [501+]

Park, Geoff - *Nga Uruora*
Meanjin - v55 - 3 '96 - p395+ [501+]
Park, James William - *Latin American Underdevelopment*
AAPSS-A - v548 - N '96 - p224+ [251-500]
AHR - v102 - F '97 - p205+ [501+]
PHR - v65 - N '96 - p699+ [251-500]
Park, Kun Il - *Personal and Wireless Communications*
SciTech - v20 - D '96 - p75 [51-250]
Park, Kwan-Hwa - *Enzymes for Carbohydrate Engineering*
SciTech - v20 - D '96 - p82 [51-250]
Park, Nick - *A Close Shave*
c Ch BWatch - v7 - F '97 - p5 [1-50]
The Wrong Trousers
c Ch BWatch - v7 - F '97 - p5 [1-50]
Park, Paul - *The Gospel of Corax*
Atl - v278 - Jl '96 - p109+ [51-250]
BW - v26 - O 13 '96 - p4 [501+]
Utne R - N '96 - p88 [1-50]
VQR - v73 - Win '97 - p22* [51-250]
Park, Tom - *Runamok: A Novel about the Realities of Small Business*
Kiplinger - v51 - F '97 - p110 [51-250]
Parkany, M - *The Use of Recovery Factors in Trace Analysis*
SciTech - v20 - D '96 - p27 [51-250]
Parke, Frederic I - *Computer Facial Animation*
SciTech - v20 - D '96 - p84 [51-250]
Parke, Ross D - *Fatherhood*
Adoles - v31 - Fall '96 - p754 [51-250]
Parker, Alan, 1944- - *The Making of Evita*
y BL - v93 - F 1 '97 - p919 [51-250]
Ent W - D 13 '96 - p74 [51-250]
Lon R Bks - v19 - F 20 '97 - p13+ [501+]
NYRB - v44 - F 20 '97 - p27+ [501+]
Parker, Alan Michael - *Days like Prose*
PW - v244 - Ap 28 '97 - p71 [51-250]
Parker, Ann - *Hajj Paintings*
MEJ - v50 - Aut '96 - p609+ [501+]
Parker, Barbara - *Criminal Justice*
KR - v64 - N 15 '96 - p1627 [251-500]
LJ - v122 - Ja '97 - p149 [51-250]
NYTBR - v102 - Ap 13 '97 - p20 [51-250]
PW - v244 - Ja 6 '97 - p66 [51-250]
Parker, Barry - *Chaos in the Cosmos*
Choice - v34 - N '96 - p481 [51-250]
Parker, Christopher - *Gender Roles and Sexuality in Victorian Literature*
Nine-C Lit - v50 - Mr '96 - p556 [51-250]
Parker, D M - *Habitat Creation*
J Gov Info - v23 - S '96 - p646 [51-250]
Parker, David, 1943- - *Ethics, Theory and the Novel*
Quad - v40 - S '96 - p76+ [501+]
Parker, David, 1956- - *Macrocycle Synthesis*
SciTech - v20 - D '96 - p28 [51-250]
Parker, David, Ph.D. - *Class and State in Ancien Regime France*
TLS - O 11 '96 - p31+ [501+]
Parker, Deborah - *Commentary and Ideology*
CLS - v33 - 2 '96 - p205+ [501+]
Parker, Dorothy - *The Best of Dorothy Parker*
TLS - Jl 19 '96 - p32 [251-500]
Not Much Fun
Atl - v278 - S '96 - p114 [51-250]
BL - v92 - Ag '96 - p1876 [51-250]
SFR - v21 - Jl '96 - p36 [251-500]
Wom R Bks - v13 - S '96 - p12+ [501+]
YR - v85 - Ja '97 - p156+ [501+]
Parker, Edward - *Peru*
c HB Guide - v8 - Spr '97 - p179 [51-250]
c SLJ - v43 - F '97 - p93 [51-250]
Parker, Elisabeth - *Jumpstart Tutorial for Microsoft Internet Explorer 3.0*
CBR - v15 - Spr '97 - p5 [1-50]
Parker, Elizabeth C - *The Cloisters Cross*
EHR - v111 - N '96 - p1240+ [251-500]
Parker, Gabrielle - *Languages for the International Scientist*
MLR - v92 - Ap '97 - p402+ [501+]
Parker, Gary E - *Dark Road to Daylight*
LJ - v122 - Ap 1 '97 - p78+ [51-250]
Parker, Geoffrey - *The Military Revolution. 2nd Ed.*
J Mil H - v61 - Ap '97 - p347+ [501+]
J Mil H - v61 - Ap '97 - p349+ [501+]
J Mil H - v61 - Ap '97 - p351+ [501+]
Parker, George L - *The Clockmaker. 1st-3rd Ser.*
Can Lit - Spr '97 - p228+ [501+]
Parker, Glenn R - *Congress and the Rent-Seeking Society*
Choice - v34 - N '96 - p538 [51-250]
PSQ - v111 - Fall '96 - p563+ [501+]

Parker, Hershel - *Herman Melville: A Biography. Vol. 1*
  Am - v176 - Mr 29 '97 - p27+ [501+]
  Atl - v279 - Ja '97 - p96+ [251-500]
  BW - v26 - D 1 '96 - p8 [501+]
  KR - v64 - O 1 '96 - p1450 [251-500]
  LATBR - D 15 '96 - p8 [501+]
  LJ - v122 - Ja '97 - p50 [51-250]
  LJ - v121 - S 15 '96 - p69 [51-250]
  New R - v216 - Mr 17 '97 - p29+ [501+]
  NYTBR - v101 - D 22 '96 - p12+ [501+]
  PW - v243 - O 14 '96 - p70 [51-250]
  Spec - v278 - Ja 4 '97 - p32 [501+]
  TLS - Ja 10 '97 - p3+ [501+]
  WSJ-MW - v78 - N 22 '96 - pA14 [501+]
Parker, J Carlyle - *Going to Salt Lake City to Do Family History Research. 3rd Ed.*
  r RQ - v36 - Fall '96 - p128+ [501+]
Parker, J I - *Truth and Power*
  Ch Today - v40 - D 9 '96 - p49 [51-250]
Parker, James E, 1942- - *Codename Mule*
  Arm F&S - v22 - Sum '96 - p643+ [501+]
  Mar Crp G - v80 - S '96 - p95 [501+]
Parker, James E, Jr. - *Last Man Out*
  LJ - v122 - Mr 15 '97 - p74 [51-250]
  PW - v244 - F 17 '97 - p205 [51-250]
Parker, Jane - *Pyramids and Temples*
  c HB Guide - v8 - Spr '97 - p132 [51-250]
  c Sch Lib - v44 - Ag '96 - p113 [51-250]
Parker, John - *The Walking Dead*
  Books - v9 - S '95 - p19 [51-250]
Parker, John, 1938- - *The Killing Factory*
  Nature - v385 - Ja 16 '97 - p216+ [501+]
Parker, John P - *His Promised Land*
  Bloom Rev - v17 - Ja '97 - p18 [501+]
  Bl S - v26 - Fall '96 - p106 [1-50]
  y Ch BWatch - v7 - F '97 - p7 [51-250]
  KR - v64 - S 15 '96 - p1381 [251-500]
  LJ - v121 - O 1 '96 - p92 [51-250]
  Obs - Mr 23 '97 - p17* [501+]
  PW - v243 - S 9 '96 - p71 [51-250]
Parker, Julie F - *High Performance through Leadership*
  y Cur R - v36 - N '96 - p13 [51-250]
  y SLJ - v42 - D '96 - p146 [51-250]
Parker, Mary Ann - *Eighteenth-Century Music in Theory and Practice*
  Notes - v53 - D '96 - p462+ [501+]
Parker, Michael - *The Growth of Understanding*
  R&R Bk N - v11 - N '96 - p39 [51-250]
Parker, Michael W, 1959- - *Protein Toxin Structure*
  SciTech - v20 - D '96 - p36 [51-250]
Parker, Nancy Winslow - *Locks, Crocs, and Skeeters*
  c HB Guide - v7 - Fall '96 - p392 [51-250]
  Money, Money, Money (Illus. by Nancy Winslow Parker)
  c RT - v50 - S '96 - p55 [51-250]
Parker, P J - *Cell Signalling*
  SciTech - v21 - Mr '97 - p36 [51-250]
Parker, Patricia - *Shakespeare from the Margins*
  Choice - v34 - N '96 - p458 [51-250]
  Lon R Bks - v18 - O 31 '96 - p24+ [501+]
Parker, Peter - *A Reader's Guide to the Twentieth-Century Novel*
  r Ant R - v54 - Sum '96 - p379 [51-250]
  A Reader's Guide to Twentieth-Century Writers
  r ARBA - v28 - '97 - p420+ [51-250]
  r BL - v93 - S 1 '96 - p170+ [251-500]
  r Parnassus - v22 - 1 '97 - p338+ [501+]
  yr SLJ - v42 - Ag '96 - p183 [51-250]
  r WSJ-MW - v78 - D 17 '96 - pA16 [51-250]
Parker, R H - *Milestones in the British Accounting Literature*
  R&R Bk N - v11 - N '96 - p36 [51-250]
  Readings in True and Fair
  R&R Bk N - v11 - N '96 - p36 [51-250]
Parker, Richard B - *The Six-Day War*
  For Aff - v76 - Mr '97 - p194+ [51-250]
Parker, Robert, 1950- - *Athenian Religion*
  Choice - v34 - D '96 - p629 [51-250]
  TLS - N 29 '96 - p14 [51-250]
  TLS - D 13 '96 - p26 [501+]
Parker, Robert B - *Chance*
  Obs - S 29 '96 - p17* [251-500]
  Chance (Reynolds). Audio Version
  y Kliatt - v31 - Ja '97 - p38 [51-250]
  Small Vices
  BL - v93 - Ja '97 - p779 [51-250]
  KR - v65 - Ja 15 '97 - p90 [251-500]
  NYTBR - v102 - Ap 13 '97 - p24 [251-500]
  PW - v244 - Ja 27 '97 - p80 [51-250]
  Trib Bks - Ap 13 '97 - p5 [51-250]
  Thin Air (Dukes). Audio Version
  Arm Det - v29 - Sum '96 - p355 [51-250]

Parker, Robert E - *Flesh Peddlers and Warm Bodies*
  ILRR - v50 - Ja '97 - p353+ [251-500]
  SF - v75 - Mr '97 - p1135+ [251-500]
Parker, Robert M, Jr. - *Parker's Wine Buyer's Guide. 4th Ed.*
  r LJ - v122 - Ap 1 '97 - p62 [1-50]
Parker, Robert Nash - *Alcohol and Homicide*
  CS - v26 - Ja '97 - p88+ [501+]
Parker, Star - *Pimps, Whores and Welfare Brats*
  BL - v93 - F 15 '97 - p981 [51-250]
  KR - v65 - Ja 1 '97 - p52 [1-50]
  PW - v244 - Ja 13 '97 - p66 [51-250]
Parker, Steve - *53<1/2> Things That Changed the World (Illus. by David West)*
  c RT - v50 - O '96 - p141 [1-50]
  The Brain and Nervous System
  c TES - F 28 '97 - p16* [51-250]
  Computers
  c New Sci - v152 - D 14 '96 - p46 [1-50]
  c Sch Lib - v44 - N '96 - p174 [51-250]
  Deserts and Drylands
  c New Sci - v153 - Ja 25 '97 - p45 [51-250]
  c Sch Lib - v44 - N '96 - p164+ [51-250]
  Giraffes (Illus. by John Lobban)
  c Bks Keeps - Jl '96 - p22 [51-250]
  c HB Guide - v7 - Fall '96 - p345+ [1-50]
  High in the Sky and Making Tracks
  c PW - v244 - Ap 28 '97 - p77 [1-50]
  The Human Body
  c KR - v64 - N 15 '96 - p1672+ [51-250]
  y PW - v243 - N 25 '96 - p78 [51-250]
  c Sch Lib - v45 - F '97 - p40 [51-250]
  c TES - F 28 '97 - p16* [51-250]
  In the Footsteps of Frankenstein (Illus. by Susanna Addario)
  c RT - v50 - O '96 - p141 [1-50]
  Lungs
  c BL - v93 - N 1 '96 - p494 [51-250]
  c HB Guide - v8 - Spr '97 - p130 [51-250]
  c Sch Lib - v45 - F '97 - p40 [51-250]
  c TES - F 28 '97 - p16* [51-250]
  The Lungs and Respiratory System
  c TES - F 28 '97 - p16* [51-250]
  Natural World
  c JB - v60 - Ag '96 - p159 [51-250]
  yr Sch Lib - v44 - Ag '96 - p125 [51-250]
  Professor Protein's Fitness, Health, Hygiene and Relaxation Tonic (Illus. by Rob Shone)
  c Bks Keeps - N '96 - p15 [51-250]
  c HB Guide - v8 - Spr '97 - p130 [51-250]
  c SLJ - v43 - Ja '97 - p107 [51-250]
  Satellites
  c Sch Lib - v44 - N '96 - p174 [51-250]
  Sharks (Illus. by Tony Kenyon)
  c Bks Keeps - Jl '96 - p22 [51-250]
  c HB Guide - v7 - Fall '96 - p343 [51-250]
  Shocking Science (Illus. by John Kelly)
  c Bks Keeps - N '96 - p15 [51-250]
  c HB Guide - v7 - Fall '96 - p329 [51-250]
  y Sch Lib - v45 - F '97 - p52 [51-250]
  c SLJ - v42 - Ag '96 - p158 [51-250]
  Skeleton
  c BL - v93 - N 1 '96 - p494 [51-250]
  c HB Guide - v8 - Spr '97 - p130 [51-250]
  c Sch Lib - v45 - F '97 - p40 [51-250]
  c TES - F 28 '97 - p16* [51-250]
Parker, Sybil P - *McGraw-Hill Encyclopedia of Astronomy. 2nd Ed.*
  r S&T - v92 - S '96 - p55 [51-250]
  World Geographical Encyclopedia. Vols. 1-5
  r BL - v92 - Ag '96 - p1920 [51-250]
  r LQ - v67 - Ja '97 - p95+ [501+]
Parker, T H L - *Calvin: An Introduction to His Thought*
  Intpr - v51 - Ap '97 - p209+ [251-500]
  Rel St Rev - v22 - O '96 - p334 [51-250]
Parker, T Jefferson - *The Triggerman's Dance*
  Arm Det - v29 - Fall '96 - p503 [251-500]
  KR - v64 - My 1 '96 - p628 [251-500]
  NYTBR - v101 - Jl 21 '96 - p25 [51-250]
Parker, Tony - *Life after Life*
  NS - v125 - O 18 '96 - p43 [51-250]
  Lighthouse
  NS - v125 - O 18 '96 - p43 [51-250]
  May the Lord in His Mercy Be Kind to Belfast
  NS - v125 - O 18 '96 - p43 [51-250]
  The People of Providence
  NS - v125 - O 18 '96 - p43 [51-250]
  Obs - Ja 26 '97 - p18* [51-250]
  Spec - v277 - N 23 '96 - p46 [51-250]
  TLS - Ja 24 '97 - p32 [251-500]

  Studs Terkel: A Life in Words
  BL - v93 - S 15 '96 - p179 [51-250]
  KR - v64 - S 15 '96 - p1382 [251-500]
  LATBR - D 1 '96 - p6+ [501+]
  LJ - v121 - N 1 '96 - p73 [51-250]
  NS - v126 - Mr 14 '97 - p46 [501+]
  NYTBR - v101 - D 29 '96 - p15 [51-250]
  PW - v243 - S 2 '96 - p101 [51-250]
  The Violence of Our Lives
  NS - v125 - O 18 '96 - p43 [51-250]
Parker, Vic - *Bearobics: A Hip-Hop Counting Story (Illus. by Emily Bolam)*
  c BL - v93 - F 15 '97 - p1028 [51-250]
  c KR - v64 - D 15 '96 - p1802 [51-250]
  c PW - v243 - D 16 '96 - p58+ [51-250]
  c Sch Lib - v45 - F '97 - p20 [51-250]
  c SLJ - v43 - F '97 - p83 [51-250]
  c Spec - v277 - D 14 '96 - p77 [1-50]
Parker, Victoria - *Women's Rights (Illus. by Andrew McIntyre)*
  y Sch Lib - v44 - N '96 - p174 [51-250]
Parker, Walter C - *Educating the Democratic Mind*
  SE - v61 - F '97 - p114+ [501+]
Parker G, Cristian - *Popular Religion and Modernization in Latin America*
  CC - v114 - Ja 1 '97 - p22 [251-500]
  CLW - v67 - Mr '97 - p33 [51-250]
Parkes, Adam - *Modernism and the Theater of Censorship*
  Choice - v34 - O '96 - p279+ [51-250]
  ELT - v40 - 1 '97 - p107+ [501+]
Parkes, Graham - *Composing the Soul*
  RM - v49 - Je '96 - p939+ [501+]
Parkes, James - *The Conflict of the Church and Synagogue*
  Rel Ed - v91 - Fall '96 - p613 [1-50]
Parkin, Alan J - *Explorations in Cognitive Neuropsychology*
  SciTech - v20 - N '96 - p45 [51-250]
Parkin, Robert - *The Dark Side of Humanity*
  Choice - v34 - F '97 - p1006 [51-250]
Parkin, Stuart - *Trade Secret*
  Aust Bk R - v - Ag '96 - p66 [501+]
Parkinson, Brian - *Changing Moods*
  Choice - v34 - Ap '97 - p1419 [51-250]
  Ideas and Realities of Emotion
  Choice - v34 - S '96 - p216 [51-250]
Parkinson, David - *History of Film*
  LR - v45 - 8 '96 - p58+ [251-500]
Parkinson, Susan - *Taste of the Pacific*
  BWatch - v17 - D '96 - p9+ [51-250]
Parkison, Jami - *Amazing Mallika (Illus. by Itoko Maeno)*
  c KR - v64 - N 15 '96 - p1673 [51-250]
  c PW - v243 - N 25 '96 - p75 [51-250]
  Inger's Promise (Illus. by Andra Chase)
  c HB Guide - v7 - Fall '96 - p270 [51-250]
Parkman, Francis - *The Oregon Trail (Muller). Audio Version*
  LJ - v122 - Ap 1 '97 - p146 [51-250]
The Parkman Dexter Howe Library. Pt. 10
  NEQ - v69 - S '96 - p504+ [501+]
Parks, Carol - *Home Decorating with Fabric*
  BWatch - v17 - S '96 - p11 [1-50]
  Simple Upholstery and Slipcovers
  BL - v93 - D 1 '96 - p638 [51-250]
Parks, Deborah - *Climb Away!*
  c HB Guide - v7 - Fall '96 - p362 [51-250]
Parks, Rosa - *Dear Mrs. Parks*
  c BL - v93 - D 1 '96 - p654 [51-250]
  c Ch BWatch - v7 - Ja '97 - p1 [51-250]
  c HB Guide - v8 - Spr '97 - p93 [51-250]
  c KR - v64 - S 1 '96 - p1326 [51-250]
  c SLJ - v42 - D '96 - p133 [51-250]
  I Am Rosa Parks (Illus. by Wil Clay)
  c BL - v93 - My 1 '97 - p1504 [51-250]
  c HB - v73 - My '97 - p343+ [51-250]
  c KR - v64 - D 1 '96 - p1742 [51-250]
  c PW - v244 - Ja 20 '97 - p402 [51-250]
Parks, Sarah T - *A+ Certification Success Guide*
  SciTech - v20 - D '96 - p79 [51-250]
Parks, Tim - *Europa*
  Obs - Ap 6 '97 - p16* [501+]
  TLS - Ap 11 '97 - p26 [501+]
  An Italian Education
  Books - v10 - Je '96 - p21 [1-50]
  BW - v26 - S 8 '96 - p12 [51-250]
  LATBR - Mr 24 '96 - p6 [501+]
  NYTBR - v101 - O 20 '96 - p36 [1-50]
  TLS - Jl 19 '96 - p7 [501+]
  Italian Neighbours
  NS - v125 - D 20 '96 - p116 [1-50]

Parks, Van Dyke - *Jump! The Adventures of Brer Rabbit (Illus. by Barry Moser)*
  c PW - v244 - Ap 28 '97 - p77 [1-50]

Parlapiano, Ellen H - *Mompreneurs: A Mother's Practical Step-by-Step Guide to Work-at-Home Success*
  BL - v93 - S 15 '96 - p192 [51-250]

The Parliament and Government Pocket Book 1996
  r CR - v269 - D '96 - p331+ [251-500]

Parloff, Roger - *Triple Jeopardy*
  KR - v64 - My 1 '96 - p671 [251-500]

Parmelee, Dean X - *Child and Adolescent Psychiatry*
  SciTech - v20 - S '96 - p41 [51-250]

Parmentelot, Elizabeth - *Dans Mon Jardin*
  c BL - v93 - N 1 '96 - p500 [1-50]

Parmer, Lynette - *Collecting Occupied Japan with Values*
  Ant & CM - v101 - D '96 - p31 [51-250]

Parnell, James F - *Atlas of Colonial Waterbirds of North Carolina Estuaries 1993*
  r J Gov Info - v23 - S '96 - p564 [51-250]

Parnell, Laurel - *Transforming Trauma*
  LJ - v122 - Ap 15 '97 - p102 [51-250]
  PW - v244 - Ap 14 '97 - p64 [51-250]

Parr, Anthony - *Three Renaissance Travel Plays*
  Ren Q - v50 - Spr '97 - p277+ [501+]

Parr, Delia - *The Ivory Duchess*
  PW - v244 - Ap 21 '97 - p69 [51-250]

Parr, E A - *Control Engineering*
  Choice - v34 - F '97 - p994+ [51-250]
  SciTech - v20 - N '96 - p70 [51-250]

Parr, Jan - *The Young Vegetarian's Companion (Illus. by Sarah Durham)*
  c HB Guide - v8 - Spr '97 - p133 [51-250]
  y Kliatt - v31 - Ja '97 - p22 [51-250]
  y SLJ - v42 - D '96 - p148+ [51-250]

Parr, Joy - *A Diversity of Women*
  Can Hist R - v77 - D '96 - p614+ [501+]

Parr, Rob - *Rob Parr's Post-Pregnancy Workout*
  LJ - v122 - Ja '97 - p136 [51-250]

Parra, Marco Antonio De La - *The Secret Holy War of Santiago De Chile*
  TranslRevS - v1 - My '95 - p31 [51-250]

Parra, Nicanor - *Poesia Y Antipoesia*
  MLR - v91 - Jl '96 - p771+ [501+]

Parra, Teresa De La - *Iphigenia: The Diary of a Young Lady Who Wrote Because She Was Bored*
  TranslRevS - v1 - My '95 - p32 [51-250]
  Mama Blanca's Memoirs
  TranslRevS - v1 - My '95 - p31 [51-250]

Parramon, Jose M - *Oils*
  BWatch - v18 - Mr '97 - p3 [51-250]

Parrinder, Patrick - *Shadows of the Future*
  ELT - v39 - 3 '96 - p351+ [501+]
  SFS - v23 - N '96 - p529+ [501+]

Parris, Matthew - *Read My Lips*
  Spec - v277 - D 7 '96 - p54 [1-50]
  TLS - Ja 17 '97 - p33 [51-250]
  Scorn
  Obs - F 23 '97 - p18* [51-250]

Parris, Nicholas - *Macromolecular Interactions in Food Technology*
  SciTech - v21 - Mr '97 - p43 [51-250]

Parris, P B - *His Arms Are Full of Broken Things*
  Spec - v278 - F 15 '97 - p31+ [501+]
  TLS - F 28 '97 - p21 [501+]

Parris, Samuel - *The Sermon Notebook of Samuel Parris 1689-1694*
  Rel St Rev - v23 - Ja '97 - p91 [51-250]

Parris, Winston C V - *Cancer Pain Management*
  SciTech - v21 - Mr '97 - p50 [51-250]

Parrish, Michael - *The Lesser Terror*
  Choice - v34 - N '96 - p520 [51-250]

Parrish, Richard - *Wind and Lies*
  PW - v244 - Ja 27 '97 - p102 [51-250]

Parrish, Robert - *Words about Wizards*
  JPC - v30 - Fall '96 - p215+ [251-500]

Parrish, Thomas - *The Cold War Encyclopedia*
  r ARBA - v28 - '97 - p214 [51-250]
  yr SLJ - v42 - Ag '96 - p183 [51-250]

Parrott, Louiselle - *Evaluating Women's Health Messages*
  Choice - v34 - S '96 - p162 [51-250]

Parry, Caroline - *Eleanora's Diary*
  c Can CL - v22 - '96 - p122+ [501+]
  c Can CL - v22 - Fall '96 - p123+ [251-500]

Parry, Donald W - *A Comprehensive Annotated Book of Mormon Bibliography*
  r Choice - v34 - Mr '97 - p1142 [51-250]

Parry, Glyn - *Mosh*
  y Aust Bk R - Je '96 - p59+ [501+]
  c Magpies - v11 - Jl '96 - p35+ [251-500]

Parry, Graham - *The Trophies of Time*
  Sev Cent N - v54 - Fall '96 - p71+ [501+]
  TLS - S 13 '96 - p26 [501+]

Parry, Linda - *William Morris*
  BM - v138 - Jl '96 - p471+ [501+]
  BW - v26 - D 15 '96 - p13 [51-250]
  LATBR - D 8 '96 - p4 [51-250]

Parry, Martin - *The Economic Implications of Climate Change in Britain*
  GJ - v162 - N '96 - p343 [51-250]

Parry, Melanie - *Larousse Dictionary of Women*
  r BL - v93 - N 1 '96 - p536 [51-250]
  r Choice - v34 - F '97 - p946 [51-250]
  r LJ - v122 - Ja '97 - p82+ [51-250]

Parry, Richard, 1942- - *The Winter Wolf*
  BL - v93 - O 1 '96 - p323 [51-250]
  KR - v64 - Ag 15 '96 - p1180 [251-500]
  PW - v243 - S 9 '96 - p66 [51-250]
  Roundup M - v4 - F '97 - p29 [251-500]

Parry, Richard D - *Plato's Craft of Justice*
  R&R Bk N - v12 - F '97 - p1 [51-250]

Parsanis, Ila - *Cultural and Language Diversity and the Deaf Experience*
  Sci - v274 - N 15 '96 - p1149 [1-50]

Parsigian, Elise K - *Proposal Savvy*
  Si & So - v6 - N '96 - p38 [1-50]

Parslow, Christopher Charles - *Rediscovering Antiquity*
  BM - v138 - D '96 - p835 [501+]
  Choice - v34 - O '96 - p336 [51-250]
  TLS - O 18 '96 - p8 [501+]

Parson-Nesbitt, Julie - *Finders: Poems*
  ABR - v18 - D '96 - p18 [501+]
  Choice - v34 - O '96 - p280 [51-250]

Parsons, Alexandra - *An Amazing Machine (Illus. by John Shackell)*
  c HB Guide - v7 - Fall '96 - p348 [51-250]
  Being Me (Illus. by Teri Gower)
  c HB Guide - v8 - Spr '97 - p86 [1-50]
  c Sch Lib - v44 - Ag '96 - p113 [51-250]
  Fit for Life (Illus. by John Shackell)
  c HB Guide - v7 - Fall '96 - p348 [51-250]
  c SLJ - v42 - O '96 - p137 [51-250]
  Me and My World (Illus. by Teri Gower)
  c HB Guide - v8 - Spr '97 - p86 [51-250]
  c Sch Lib - v44 - Ag '96 - p113 [51-250]
  You're Special, Too
  c TES - Mr 21 '97 - p9* [501+]

Parsons, David - *Skills, Qualifications and Utilisation*
  JEL - v34 - D '96 - p2071 [51-250]

Parsons, Elsie Worthington Clews - *Tewa Tales*
  CAY - v17 - Fall '96 - p13 [51-250]

Parsons, John Carmi - *Eleanor of Castile: Queen and Society in Thirteenth-Century England*
  AHR - v101 - O '96 - p1198 [501+]
  Historian - v59 - Fall '96 - p202+ [251-500]
  Six Ct J - v27 - Fall '96 - p922+ [501+]
  Specu - v71 - Jl '96 - p752+ [501+]

Parsons, Martin - *Essential History Dates*
  yr Sch Lib - v44 - N '96 - p174+ [51-250]

Parsons, Patricia - *Hippocrates Now!*
  Theol St - v57 - Je '96 - p388 [251-500]

Parsons, Susan Frank - *Feminism and Christian Ethics*
  Intpr - v51 - Ap '97 - p220 [251-500]

Parsons, Tom - *Pierre Auguste Renoir*
  c BL - v93 - F 1 '97 - p937 [51-250]
  c HB Guide - v8 - Spr '97 - p139 [51-250]
  c PW - v243 - D 30 '96 - p68 [51-250]
  c SLJ - v43 - Mr '97 - p179 [51-250]

Parsons, Vic - *Ken Thomson: Canada's Enigmatic Billionaire*
  Quill & Q - v63 - Ja '97 - p29 [51-250]

Partington, Geoffrey - *Hasluck versus Coombs*
  Meanjin - v55 - '96 - p614+ [501+]

Partridge, Elizabeth - *Clara and the Hoodoo Man*
  c BL - v93 - S 1 '96 - p131 [51-250]
  c CBRS - v24 - Ag '96 - p165 [51-250]
  c CCB-B - v50 - S '96 - p25 [51-250]
  c HB - v72 - N '96 - p739 [51-250]
  c HB Guide - v8 - Spr '97 - p73 [51-250]
  c KR - v64 - My 1 '96 - p691 [51-250]

Partridge, Loren - *The Art of Renaissance Rome 1400-1600*
  Choice - v34 - Mr '97 - p1153 [51-250]
  LJ - v121 - N 1 '96 - p63 [51-250]
  NYTBR - v101 - D 8 '96 - p19 [51-250]
  Michelangelo: The Sistine Chapel Ceiling, Rome
  LJ - v122 - Ja '97 - p93 [51-250]
  PW - v243 - O 7 '96 - p50 [51-250]

Partridge, Norman - *Bad Intentions*
  SF Chr - v18 - O '96 - p80 [51-250]

  It Came from the Drive-In
  Necro - Fall '96 - p26+ [251-500]
  SF Chr - v18 - O '96 - p76 [51-250]

Partridge, R B - *3 K: The Cosmic Microwave Background Radiation*
  Sci - v274 - D 13 '96 - p1847+ [501+]

Parums, Dinah V - *Essential Clinical Pathology*
  SciTech - v20 - N '96 - p38 [51-250]

Parvin, Joy - *Pencils, Poems and Princesses*
  c TES - Ja 3 '97 - pR15 [51-250]

Parvin, Manoucher - *Avicenna and I*
  MEJ - v51 - Spr '97 - p310 [51-250]

Parvin, Roy - *The Loneliest Road in America*
  BL - v93 - D 15 '96 - p709 [51-250]
  Ent W - Mr 7 '97 - p61 [51-250]
  KR - v64 - N 1 '96 - p1558 [251-500]
  LJ - v122 - F 1 '97 - p110 [51-250]
  NYTBR - v102 - Mr 2 '97 - p12 [501+]
  PW - v243 - N 11 '96 - p70+ [51-250]

Pasachoff, Naomi - *Alexander Graham Bell: Making Connections*
  y HB Guide - v7 - Fall '96 - p374 [51-250]
  y SLJ - v43 - F '97 - p122 [51-250]
  Marie Curie and the Science of Radioactivity
  y BL - v93 - S 1 '96 - p118 [51-250]
  y HB Guide - v7 - Fall '96 - p374 [51-250]
  y KR - v64 - My 1 '96 - p692 [51-250]
  y SLJ - v42 - Ag '96 - p174+ [51-250]

Pascal, Francine - *Stephen Gets Even*
  y Books - v9 - S '95 - p26 [1-50]

Paschen, Elise - *Infidelities*
  Choice - v34 - Ap '97 - p1339 [51-250]
  PW - v243 - S 30 '96 - p81+ [51-250]
  Poetry in Motion
  y BL - v93 - Ap 1 '97 - p1288 [1-50]

Pascoe, Elaine - *Butterflies and Moths (Illus. by Dwight Kuhn)*
  c HB Guide - v8 - Spr '97 - p122 [51-250]
  c SB - v33 - Mr '97 - p51+ [51-250]
  Earthworms (Illus. by Dwight Kuhn)
  c BL - v93 - D 1 '96 - p660 [51-250]
  c HB Guide - v8 - Spr '97 - p122 [51-250]
  c SB - v33 - Mr '97 - p52 [51-250]
  Mexico and the United States
  y BL - v93 - D 1 '96 - p646 [51-250]
  c Ch BWatch - v6 - N '96 - p2 [1-50]
  y SLJ - v43 - Ja '97 - p132 [51-250]
  Racial Prejudice
  y BL - v93 - My 15 '97 - p1571+ [51-250]
  Seeds and Seedlings (Illus. by Dwight Kuhn)
  c BL - v93 - D 1 '96 - p660 [51-250]
  c HB Guide - v8 - Spr '97 - p110 [51-250]
  c SLJ - v43 - Mr '97 - p206 [51-250]
  Tadpoles (Illus. by Dwight Kuhn)
  c HB Guide - v8 - Spr '97 - p123 [51-250]
  c KR - v64 - N 1 '96 - p1605 [51-250]
  c SB - v33 - Mr '97 - p52 [251-500]
  c SLJ - v42 - O '96 - p137 [51-250]

Pascuzzi, Antonella - *Feste E Spettacoli Di Corte Nella Caserta Del Settecento*
  Choice - v34 - D '96 - p567 [1-50]

Paskin, Barbara - *Dudley Moore*
  Obs - Mr 16 '97 - p18* [501+]

Paso, Fernando Del - *Palinuro of Mexico*
  Bloom Rev - v16 - Jl '96 - p9+ [501+]
  BW - v26 - S 1 '96 - p6 [501+]
  PW - v243 - N 4 '96 - p37 [1-50]

Pasolini, Pier Paolo - *Petrolio*
  KR - v65 - F 1 '97 - p172 [51-250]
  LATBR - Mr 23 '97 - p9 [501+]
  NY - v73 - Ap 28 '97 - p227 [51-250]
  NYTBR - v102 - Mr 23 '97 - p8 [501+]
  PW - v244 - Ja 13 '97 - p53 [51-250]
  Storie Della Citta Di Dio
  BL - v93 - D 1 '96 - p644 [1-50]
  A Violent Life
  Obs - O 27 '96 - p18* [51-250]

Pasquerella, Lynn - *Ethical Dilemmas in Public Administration*
  R&R Bk N - v11 - N '96 - p48 [1-50]

Pasquino, Gianfranco - *La Politica Italiana*
  r Choice - v34 - D '96 - p569 [1-50]

Pass, Christopher - *Business and Macroeconomics*
  Econ J - v106 - S '96 - p1470 [51-250]

Passavant, Tom - *Birnbaum's Walt Disney World for Kids by Kids 1997*
  cr LJ - v121 - D '96 - p128 [51-250]

Passenger and Immigration Lists Index. 1996 Suppl.
  r ARBA - v28 - '97 - p169 [51-250]

Passerini, Luisa - *Autobiography of a Generation*
  VV - v42 - Ja 21 '97 - p53 [501+]

Passet, Joanne Ellen - *Cultural Crusaders*
    J Am Cult - v19 - Spr '96 - p103 [51-250]
    Lib & Cul - v32 - Win '97 - p145+ [501+]
Past and Present
    p TLS - N 15 '96 - p33+ [501+]
Past Imperfect
    Bks & Cult - v2 - Mr '96 - p16+ [501+]
    CR - v269 - O '96 - p224 [51-250]
    TES - N 22 '96 - p8* [51-250]
    TLS - Ja 3 '97 - p19 [501+]
    W&I - v11 - Jl '96 - p288+ [501+]
Pastan, Linda - *An Early Afterlife*
    HR - v49 - Aut '96 - p503+ [501+]
Pasternack, Carol Braun - *The Textuality of Old English Poetry*
    Choice - v34 - S '96 - p128 [51-250]
Pasternak, Anna - *Princess in Love*
    Obs - O 27 '96 - p18* [51-250]
Pasternak, Boris - *Doctor Zhivago*
    NS & S - v9 - My 3 '96 - p37 [1-50]
Pastor Bodmer, Beatriz - *The Armature of Conquest*
    HAHR - v77 - F '97 - p103+ [501+]
Pastourmatzi, Domna - *Bibliography of Science Fiction, Fantasy, and Horror 1960-1993*
    r Ext - v37 - Sum '96 - p187+ [501+]
Pastrana, Patricia Aceves - *Quimica, Botanica Y Farmacia En La Nueva Espana A Finales Del Siglo XVII*
    Isis - v87 - S '96 - p555+ [501+]
Pastuchiv, Olga - *Minas and the Fish (Illus. by Olga Pastuchiv)*
    c CBRS - v25 - Mr '97 - p90 [51-250]
    c CCB-B - v50 - My '97 - p332 [51-250]
, Pasuk Phongpaichit - *Thailand, Economy and Politics*
    Choice - v34 - My '97 - p1548 [51-250]
    JEL - v34 - S '96 - p1488 [51-250]
Pasztory, Esther - *Teotihuacan: An Experiment in Living*
    PW - v244 - Mr 17 '97 - p69+ [251-500]
Patai, Daphne - *Professing Feminism*
    Signs - v22 - Win '97 - p453+ [501+]
Patai, Raphael - *Jadid Al-Islam*
    LJ - v122 - My 1 '97 - p121 [51-250]
    The Jews of Hungary
    AB - v99 - Mr 24 '97 - p965+ [501+]
    R&R Bk N - v11 - N '96 - p14 [51-250]
Pataki, Caroly S - *Study Guide and Self-Examination Review for Kaplan and Sadock's Synopsis of Psychiatry. 5th Ed.*
    r AJPsych - v153 - O '96 - p1357 [501+]
Patanjali - *Yoga: Discipline of Freedom*
    BL - v93 - N 15 '96 - p552+ [51-250]
    LJ - v122 - F 1 '97 - p87 [51-250]
    Parabola - v22 - F '97 - p120 [1-50]
Pate, Alexs D - *Finding Makeba*
    y BL - v93 - D 1 '96 - p641+ [51-250]
    KR - v64 - N 1 '96 - p1559 [251-500]
    LJ - v121 - N 1 '96 - p84 [1-50]
    LJ - v121 - N 15 '96 - p90 [51-250]
    PW - v243 - N 4 '96 - p62 [51-250]
Patel, Ilyas - *Indian Telegraphs 1851-1914*
    Am Phil - v110 - N '96 - p1037+ [51-250]
Patel, Jagdish K - *Handbook of the Normal Distribution. 2nd Ed., Rev. and Expanded*
    Am Sci - v84 - N '96 - p504 [501+]
Patel, Pratik - *Java Database Programming with JDBC*
    LJ - v122 - Ja '97 - p138 [51-250]
Pateman, Robert - *Belgium*
    c HB Guide - v7 - Fall '96 - p382 [1-50]
    c SLJ - v42 - S '96 - p217 [51-250]
    Bolivia
    c HB Guide - v7 - Fall '96 - p392 [51-250]
Patent, Arnold M - *You Can Have It All*
    PW - v243 - D 30 '96 - p64 [1-50]
Patent, Dorothy Hinshaw - *Biodiversity (Illus. by William Munoz)*
    y BL - v93 - D 1 '96 - p654+ [51-250]
    c CCB-B - v50 - Mr '97 - p254 [51-250]
    c HB - v73 - Ja '97 - p78 [51-250]
    c HB Guide - v8 - Spr '97 - p97 [51-250]
    c KR - v64 - O 1 '96 - p1472 [51-250]
    c SLJ - v42 - D '96 - p133 [51-250]
    Children Save the Rain Forest (Illus. by Dan L Perlman)
    c CCB-B - v50 - O '96 - p79+ [51-250]
    c HB - v72 - N '96 - p761 [51-250]
    c HB Guide - v8 - Spr '97 - p120 [51-250]
    c SB - v33 - Mr '97 - p49 [51-250]
    c SLJ - v42 - S '96 - p219 [51-250]
    c Smith - v27 - N '96 - p172 [1-50]

Flashy Fantastic Rain Forest Frogs (Illus. by Kendahl Jan Jubb)
    c BL - v93 - F 1 '97 - p943 [51-250]
    c CCB-B - v50 - Mr '97 - p254 [51-250]
    c KR - v65 - Ja 15 '97 - p144 [51-250]
    c PW - v244 - F 24 '97 - p93 [1-50]
    c SLJ - v43 - Mr '97 - p180 [51-250]
Prairies (Illus. by William Munoz)
    c BL - v93 - N 1 '96 - p494 [51-250]
    c CCB-B - v50 - F '97 - p219 [51-250]
    c HB Guide - v8 - Spr '97 - p120 [1-50]
    c KR - v64 - O 15 '96 - p1536 [51-250]
    c SLJ - v43 - F '97 - p122 [51-250]
Quetzal: Sacred Bird of the Cloud Forest (Illus. by Neil Waldman)
    c BL - v92 - Ag '96 - p1899 [51-250]
    c HB - v73 - Ja '97 - p78+ [51-250]
    c HB Guide - v8 - Spr '97 - p125 [51-250]
    c SLJ - v42 - O '96 - p138 [51-250]
Why Mammals Have Fur (Illus. by William Munoz)
    c RT - v50 - S '96 - p55 [51-250]
    c SB - v32 - N '96 - p248 [51-250]
Pater, Walter - *Gaston De Latour: The Revised Text*
    ELT - v39 - 3 '96 - p345+ [501+]
    Nine-C Lit - v50 - Mr '96 - p556 [1-50]
Paternosto, Cesar - *The Stone and the Thread*
    r Choice - v34 - N '96 - p445 [51-250]
    R&R Bk N - v11 - D '96 - p18 [51-250]
Paterson, Andrew II - *Genome Mapping in Plants*
    SciTech - v20 - D '96 - p32 [51-250]
Paterson, Bettina - *I Go to Preschool*
    c PW - v243 - S 9 '96 - p84 [51-250]
Paterson, Isabel - *The God of the Machine*
    Reason - v28 - S '96 - p65 [501+]
Paterson, Janet M - *Postmodernism and the Quebec Novel*
    Dal R - v75 - Spr '95 - p111+ [501+]
    TranslRevS - v2 - D '96 - p12 [51-250]
Paterson, Jennifer - *Two Fat Ladies*
    Spec - v277 - N 23 '96 - p46 [1-50]
    Spec - v277 - D 7 '96 - p47+ [501+]
Paterson, John - *Edwardians: London Life and Letters 1901-1914*
    Choice - v34 - O '96 - p280 [51-250]
Paterson, Katherine - *The Angel and the Donkey (Illus. by Alexander Koshkin)*
    c BL - v93 - O 1 '96 - p339 [1-50]
    c Emerg Lib - v24 - S '96 - p43 [1-50]
    c HB Guide - v8 - Spr '97 - p42 [1-50]
    c RT - v50 - Ap '97 - p591 [51-250]
Bridge to Terabithia
    c HMR - Win '96 - p45 [1-50]
Bridge to Terabithia (Stechschulte). Audio Version
    c BL - v93 - Ap 1 '97 - p1313 [1-50]
    c CSM - v89 - Mr 27 '97 - pB6 [1-50]
Flip-Flop Girl
    c Bks Keeps - N '96 - p11 [51-250]
    y JB - v60 - O '96 - p205 [251-500]
    c Magpies - v11 - Jl '96 - p45 [1-50]
The Great Gilly Hopkins (Bresnahan). Audio Version
    c BL - v93 - My 15 '97 - p1595 [1-50]
Jip: His Story
    c BL - v93 - Ja '97 - p764 [1-50]
    c BL - v93 - S 1 '96 - p127 [51-250]
    y BL - v93 - Ap 1 '97 - p1294 [1-50]
    c BL - v93 - Ap 1 '97 - p1298 [1-50]
    c BW - v26 - D 8 '96 - p21 [51-250]
    c CCB-B - v50 - D '96 - p147 [51-250]
    c Ch BWatch - v7 - Ja '97 - p4 [51-250]
    c HB - v72 - N '96 - p739+ [251-500]
    c HB Guide - v8 - Spr '97 - p73 [51-250]
    c KR - v64 - O 15 '96 - p1537 [51-250]
    c Learning - v25 - N '96 - p30 [51-250]
    c NYTBR - v101 - N 10 '96 - p50 [501+]
    c Par Ch - v20 - O '96 - p11 [1-50]
    c PW - v243 - N 4 '96 - p49 [51-250]
    y Sch Lib - v45 - F '97 - p47+ [51-250]
    c SLJ - v42 - O '96 - p124 [51-250]
    c SLJ - v42 - D '96 - p31 [1-50]
The King's Equal (Illus. by Vladimir Vagin)
    c Magpies - v11 - Jl '96 - p27 [51-250]
A Midnight Clear
    c RT - v50 - N '96 - p259 [51-250]
Rebels of the Heavenly Kingdom (Guidall). Audio Version
    c HB - v72 - S '96 - p566+ [501+]
    y SLJ - v42 - O '96 - p78 [51-250]
Paterson, Linda M - *The World of the Troubadours*
    Comp L - v48 - Fall '96 - p373+ [501+]
Paterson, R W K - *Philosophy and the Belief in a Life after Death*
    Rel St - v32 - S '96 - p415+ [501+]

Paterson, Thomas G - *Major Problems in American Foreign Relations. 4th Ed., Vols. 1-2*
    For Aff - v76 - Mr '97 - p184+ [251-500]
Paterson, Wilma - *The Songs of Scotland*
    Obs - F 16 '97 - p18* [501+]
Patey, Stan - *The Coast of New England*
    LJ - v121 - N 1 '96 - p98 [51-250]
Pathria, R K - *Statistical Mechanics. 2nd Ed.*
    SciTech - v20 - S '96 - p4 [51-250]
Patneaude, David - *Dark Starry Morning*
    c Ch BWatch - v6 - N '96 - p3 [1-50]
    The Last Man's Reward
    c CLW - v67 - D '96 - p58 [51-250]
    c HB Guide - v7 - Fall '96 - p296 [51-250]
Paton, Bernadette - *Preaching Friars and the Civic Ethos*
    CH - v66 - Mr '97 - p105+ [501+]
Paton, Priscilla - *Howard and the Sitter Surprise (Illus. by Paul Meisel)*
    c CBRS - v25 - F '97 - p77 [51-250]
    c HB Guide - v8 - Spr '97 - p42 [51-250]
    c PW - v243 - N 4 '96 - p75 [51-250]
    c SLJ - v42 - O '96 - p103 [51-250]
Paton, T R - *Soils: A New Global View*
    GJ - v162 - Jl '96 - p225+ [251-500]
Paton Walsh, Jill - *Connie Came to Play (Illus. by Stephen Lambert)*
    c HB Guide - v7 - Fall '96 - p245 [51-250]
    c New Ad - v9 - Fall '96 - p327+ [501+]
Knowledge of Angels
    Comw - v123 - D 6 '96 - p22+ [251-500]
Knowledge of Angels (Scott). Audio Version
    BL - v93 - Mr 15 '97 - p1253 [51-250]
A Parcel of Patterns (Forsyth). Audio Version
    BL - v93 - D 15 '96 - p740 [51-250]
    y BL - v93 - My 15 '97 - p1595 [1-50]
    y Emerg Lib - v24 - Mr '97 - p24 [51-250]
    y HB - v73 - Ja '97 - p85+ [501+]
    y Kliatt - v31 - Ja '97 - p44 [51-250]
    y PW - v244 - Ja 13 '97 - p36 [51-250]
    y SLJ - v42 - O '96 - p78 [51-250]
A Piece of Justice (Forsyth). Audio Version
    y Kliatt - v30 - S '96 - p51 [51-250]
The Serpentine Cave
    TLS - Ja 31 '97 - p21 [251-500]
Patricia Smith's Doll Values. 12th Ed.
    r ARBA - v28 - '97 - p359 [51-250]
Patrick, Anne E - *Liberating Conscience*
    Am - v176 - Ja 18 '97 - p24+ [51-250]
    Choice - v34 - Ja '97 - p812 [51-250]
    Comw - v124 - Ap 11 '97 - p22+ [501+]
    Cons - v17 - Win '96 - p31 [1-50]
Patrick, Dale R - *Rotating Electrical Machines and Power Systems. 2nd Ed.*
    r SciTech - v21 - Mr '97 - p86 [51-250]
Patrick, Ellen - *Bunny's Tale (Illus. by Ernie Eldredge)*
    c Ch BWatch - v6 - My '96 - p3 [1-50]
    Magic Easter Egg (Illus. by Ernie Eldredge)
    c Ch BWatch - v6 - My '96 - p3 [1-50]
    Three Baby Chicks (Illus. by Ernie Eldredge)
    c Ch BWatch - v6 - My '96 - p3 [1-50]
    Very Little Duck (Illus. by Ernie Eldredge)
    c Ch BWatch - v6 - My '96 - p3 [1-50]
Patten, Barbara J - *The Basic Five Food Groups*
    c SLJ - v43 - Ja '97 - p107 [51-250]
    Digestion: Food at Work
    c SLJ - v43 - Ja '97 - p107 [51-250]
    Nutrients: Superstars of Good Health
    c SLJ - v43 - Ja '97 - p107 [51-250]
Patten, Lewis B - *Trail to Vicksburg*
    PW - v244 - Ap 14 '97 - p60 [51-250]
Patten, Rena - *How to Prepare Stuffings and Fillings*
    BWatch - v17 - D '96 - p9 [51-250]
Patten, Robert L - *George Cruikshank's Life, Times, and Art. Vol. 2*
    Choice - v34 - O '96 - p268 [51-250]
    Nine-C Lit - v51 - D '96 - p425+ [1-50]
Pattern Recognition. Vols. 1-4
    SciTech - v21 - Mr '97 - p92 [51-250]
Patterson, Alex - *A Field Guide to Rock Art Symbols of the Greater Southwest*
    r CAY - v17 - Win '96 - p13 [51-250]
Patterson, Annabel - *Reading Holinshed's Chronicles*
    r EHR - v112 - Ap '97 - p462+ [501+]
    MP - v94 - N '96 - p230+ [501+]
Patterson, Beverly Bush - *The Sound of the Dove*
    JSH - v63 - F '97 - p202+ [251-500]
    Notes - v53 - S '96 - p80+ [501+]
Patterson, Chris - *Client Access Token-Ring Connectivity*
    SciTech - v20 - S '96 - p55 [1-50]
Patterson, D J - *Free-Living Freshwater Protozoa*
    Choice - v34 - My '97 - p1523 [51-250]

Patterson, David - *Exile: The Sense of Alienation in Modern Russian Letters*
  Russ Rev - v55 - O '96 - p705+ [501+]
Patterson, Dennis - *Law and Truth*
  Choice - v34 - N '96 - p536 [51-250]
  CLR - v97 - Ja '97 - p133+ [501+]
  CPR - v16 - D '96 - p431+ [501+]
Patterson, Freeman - *ShadowLight: A Photographer's Life*
  Aud - v98 - N '96 - p137 [51-250]
  Mac - v109 - D 9 '96 - p66 [1-50]
  Mac - v110 - Ja 20 '97 - p62+ [501+]
  Quill & Q - v62 - O '96 - p36 [251-500]
Patterson, Gareth - *With My Soul amongst Lions*
  KR - v64 - S 15 '96 - p1382 [251-500]
  LJ - v121 - S 15 '96 - p91 [51-250]
  PW - v243 - S 23 '96 - p64+ [51-250]
Patterson, Geoffrey - *The Naughty Boy and the Strawberry Horse (Illus. by G Patterson)*
  c JB - v60 - D '96 - p237 [251-500]
Patterson, J H - *The Man-Eaters of Tsavo*
  LJ - v121 - N 15 '96 - p93 [1-50]
Patterson, James - *Hide and Seek*
  Books - v10 - Je '96 - p10 [51-250]
  Miracle on the 17th Green
  BL - v93 - S 1 '96 - p30 [51-250]
  KR - v64 - S 1 '96 - p1269+ [51-250]
  LJ - v121 - O 1 '96 - p128 [51-250]
  NYTBR - v101 - D 8 '96 - p102 [51-250]
  PW - v243 - S 16 '96 - p68 [51-250]
  Miracle on the 17th Green (Linden). Audio Version
  BWatch - v17 - D '96 - p11 [1-50]
  LJ - v122 - F 1 '97 - p126 [51-250]
Patterson, James, 1947- - *Jack and Jill*
  BL - v92 - Ag '96 - p1855 [251-500]
  Books - v11 - Ap '97 - p21 [51-250]
  CSM - v88 - S 19 '96 - p14 [51-250]
  CSM - v88 - N 14 '96 - p14 [51-250]
  Ent W - S 6 '96 - p68 [51-250]
Patterson, James T - *Grand Expectations*
  Atl - v278 - S '96 - p107+ [501+]
  Choice - v34 - O '96 - p351 [51-250]
  CR - v270 - F '97 - p103+ [501+]
  NYTBR - v101 - D 8 '96 - p87 [1-50]
  R&R Bk N - v11 - D '96 - p13 [51-250]
  VQR - v73 - Win '97 - p9* [501+]
Patterson, Lillie A - *A. Philip Randolph: Messenger for the Masses*
  y HB Guide - v7 - Fall '96 - p374 [51-250]
Patterson, Michael - *German Theatre*
  r Choice - v34 - Ja '97 - p773 [51-250]
Patterson, Richard, 1946- - *Aristotle's Modal Logic*
  CPR - v16 - Ag '96 - p278+ [501+]
Patterson, Richard North - *The Final Judgement*
  Books - v10 - Je '96 - p10 [51-250]
  Spec - v277 - S 7 '96 - p37 [51-250]
  The Final Judgment
  Ent W - Ja 24 '97 - p53 [51-250]
  y Kliatt - v31 - Mr '97 - p12 [51-250]
  PW - v243 - N 4 '96 - p71 [1-50]
  Silent Witness
  BL - v93 - N 15 '96 - p549 [51-250]
  BW - v27 - Ja 19 '97 - p11 [251-500]
  CSM - v89 - F 20 '97 - p10 [51-250]
  CSM - v89 - Mr 20 '97 - p14 [51-250]
  Ent W - Ja 17 '97 - p56+ [501+]
  KR - v64 - N 15 '96 - p1628 [251-500]
  LATBR - Ja 26 '97 - p10 [501+]
  PW - v243 - D 2 '96 - p40 [51-250]
  Trib Bks - Ja 19 '97 - p6 [51-250]
Patterson, Stephen - *Royal Insignia*
  R&R Bk N - v12 - F '97 - p14 [51-250]
Patterson, Thomas E - *Out of Order*
  JC - v46 - Sum '96 - p193+ [501+]
Patterson, Walt - *Rebuilding Romania*
  GJ - v162 - Jl '96 - p240 [51-250]
Patterson, William L - *Lao-English Dictionary*
  r ARBA - v28 - '97 - p395+ [251-500]
Patterson, William Patrick - *Struggle of the Magicians*
  Rapport - v19 - 4 '96 - p37 [251-500]
Pattiaratchi, Charitha - *Mixing in Estuaries and Coastal Seas*
  SciTech - v20 - S '96 - p1 [51-250]
Patton, Adell - *Physicians, Colonial Racism, and Diaspora in West Africa*
  Choice - v34 - N '96 - p494 [51-250]
Patton, Cindy - *Last Served?*
  CS - v26 - Ja '97 - p113+ [501+]
Patton, James R - *Transition and Students with Learning Disabilities*
  R&R Bk N - v11 - N '96 - p57 [1-50]

Patton, Jim - *Il Basket D'Italia*
  Aethlon - v13 - Fall '95 - p157+ [251-500]
Patton, Mark - *Islands in Time*
  Choice - v34 - Mr '97 - p1202 [51-250]
  R&R Bk N - v12 - F '97 - p30 [51-250]
Patton, Robert H - *Life between Wars*
  KR - v65 - Mr 15 '97 - p417+ [51-250]
  LJ - v122 - Ap 1 '97 - p130 [51-250]
  PW - v244 - Mr 31 '97 - p59 [51-250]
  Up, Down, and Sideways
  KR - v65 - Mr 15 '97 - p418 [51-250]
  LJ - v122 - Ap 1 '97 - p130 [51-250]
  PW - v244 - Mr 31 '97 - p59+ [51-250]
Patton-Hulce, Vicki R - *Environment and the Law*
  r ARBA - v28 - '97 - p230+ [251-500]
Pattullo, Polly - *Last Resorts*
  HAHR - v77 - F '97 - p170+ [251-500]
  WorldV - v13 - Ja '97 - p8 [251-500]
Patyra, M J - *Fuzzy Logic*
  Choice - v34 - Ja '97 - p832 [51-250]
  SciTech - v20 - S '96 - p53 [51-250]
Patzer, Gordon L - *Experiment-Research Methodology in Marketing*
  Choice - v34 - O '96 - p326 [51-250]
  Using Secondary Data in Marketing Research
  BusLR - v21 - 3 '96 - p253+ [51-250]
Patzold, Kurt - *Adolf Hitler: Eine Politische Biographie*
  Choice - v34 - D '96 - p568 [1-50]
Pauketat, Timothy R - *The Ascent of Chiefs*
  Am Ant - v61 - Ap '96 - p436+ [501+]
  Am Sci - v84 - S '96 - p503+ [251-500]
Paul, Ann Whitford - *The Seasons Sewn (Illus. by Michael McCurdy)*
  c HB Guide - v7 - Fall '96 - p356 [51-250]
  c NYTBR - v101 - N 10 '96 - p48 [501+]
  c RT - v50 - My '97 - p680+ [51-250]
  c Smith - v27 - N '96 - p171 [1-50]
Paul, Anthony - *The Tiger Who Lost His Stripes (Illus. by Michael Foreman)*
  c HB Guide - v7 - Fall '96 - p270 [51-250]
Paul, Bette - *Variations on a Dream*
  c Bks Keeps - Jl '96 - p13 [51-250]
  y JB - v60 - Ag '96 - p166 [51-250]
Paul, Bill - *Getting In*
  y Kliatt - v31 - My '97 - p24 [51-250]
Paul, Carolyn Keiler - *T'shuva*
  LJ - v121 - O 1 '96 - p48 [1-50]
Paul, Diane B - *Controlling Human Heredity 1865 to Present*
  Hast Cen R - v26 - Mr '96 - p49 [1-50]
Paul, Donna - *The Home Office Book*
  BL - v93 - S 15 '96 - p202 [51-250]
  LJ - v121 - S 15 '96 - p65+ [51-250]
  PW - v243 - O 7 '96 - p72 [51-250]
Paul, Eldor A - *Soil Microbiology and Biochemistry. 2nd Ed.*
  SciTech - v20 - D '96 - p36 [51-250]
Paul, Ellen Frankel - *The Just Society*
  CPR - v16 - Ag '96 - p280+ [501+]
Paul, Frances Lackey - *Kahtahah (Illus. by Rie Munoz)*
  c Smith - v27 - N '96 - p174+ [1-50]
Paul, Gerhard - *Aufstand Der Bilder*
  JMH - v68 - S '96 - p629+ [501+]
Paul, Gregory S - *Beyond Humanity*
  Choice - v34 - My '97 - p1535 [51-250]
Paul, Heather - *Discovering Scottish Plants (Illus. by Fhiona Galloway)*
  c Sch Lib - v45 - F '97 - p40 [51-250]
Paul, Jim - *Medieval in L.A.*
  Bloom Rev - v16 - Jl '96 - p15+ [251-500]
  NY - v72 - S 9 '96 - p91 [51-250]
Paul, Kathleen - *Whitewashing Britain*
  LJ - v122 - Ap 15 '97 - p100+ [51-250]
Paul, Richard - *The Magic Telescope (Illus. by Larry Salk)*
  c Ch BWatch - v7 - Ja '97 - p2 [51-250]
Paul, Robert A - *Moses and Civilization*
  Choice - v34 - O '96 - p365 [51-250]
  R&R Bk N - v11 - N '96 - p4 [51-250]
Paul, Swaraj - *Surface Coatings. 2nd Ed.*
  SciTech - v20 - S '96 - p59 [51-250]
Paul, William - *Sleeping Partner*
  BL - v93 - Mr 15 '97 - p1231 [51-250]
  KR - v65 - Ja 15 '97 - p99+ [51-250]
Paul Cezanne: Portrait of My World. Electronic Media Version
  NYTBR - v101 - S 15 '96 - p23 [501+]
Paulding County, Ohio Census Index 1830, 1840, 1850, 1860
  r EGH - v50 - N '96 - p180 [51-250]

Paulin, Roger - *Rilke's Duino Elegies*
  Choice - v34 - Ap '97 - p1343 [51-250]
  Lon R Bks - v18 - Ag 22 '96 - p8+ [501+]
Paulin, Tom - *Writing to the Moment*
  ILS - v16 - Spr '97 - p9 [501+]
  Spec - v277 - N 23 '96 - p52+ [501+]
  TLS - N 29 '96 - p26 [501+]
Pauling, Linus - *Linus Pauling in His Own Words*
  New Sci - v151 - S 21 '96 - p52 [51-250]
Paull, Irene - *Irene: Selected Writings of Irene Paull*
  LJ - v122 - Ja '97 - p121 [51-250]
Paulsen, Gary - *Brian's Winter*
  y BL - v93 - Ap 1 '97 - p1310 [1-50]
  y CLW - v66 - Je '96 - p53+ [251-500]
  y HB Guide - v7 - Fall '96 - p304 [51-250]
  y Par - v71 - D '96 - p254 [1-50]
  y VOYA - v19 - F '97 - p332 [251-500]
  Call Me Francis Tucket
  c Ch BWatch - v7 - F '97 - p5 [1-50]
  y Kliatt - v31 - Mr '97 - p12 [51-250]
  c PW - v243 - N 25 '96 - p78 [1-50]
  c RT - v50 - O '96 - p139 [1-50]
  Call Me Francis Tucket (Jones). Audio Version
  c SLJ - v42 - S '96 - p165 [51-250]
  Canyons
  c Magpies - v11 - Jl '96 - p45 [1-50]
  The Car
  c Bks Keeps - Mr '97 - p27 [51-250]
  Eastern Sun, Winter Moon
  Lon R Bks - v18 - My 23 '96 - p28+ [501+]
  Obs - Mr 30 '97 - p17* [51-250]
  Escape from Fire Mountain (Woodman). Audio Version
  c HB - v73 - My '97 - p357+ [501+]
  Father Water, Mother Woods
  y Kliatt - v30 - S '96 - p39 [51-250]
  Harris and Me
  c HMR - Win '96 - p45 [1-50]
  Hatchet: Winter
  y Sch Lib - v44 - Ag '96 - p120 [51-250]
  The Legend of Red Horse Cavern (Woodman). Audio Version
  c HB - v73 - My '97 - p357+ [501+]
  Mr. Tucket
  c Bks Keeps - Jl '96 - p13 [51-250]
  y Sch Lib - v44 - Ag '96 - p120 [51-250]
  Murphy's Ambush (Dietz). Audio Version
  y Kliatt - v30 - N '96 - p42 [51-250]
  Murphy's Trail
  y BL - v93 - S 1 '96 - p63 [51-250]
  LJ - v122 - Ap 1 '97 - p156 [51-250]
  Roundup M - v4 - F '97 - p29 [51-250]
  Nightjohn
  y SLJ - v42 - O '96 - p45 [1-50]
  Puppies, Dogs, and Blue Northers (Illus. by Ruth Wright Paulsen)
  y BL - v93 - Ap 1 '97 - p1288 [1-50]
  y BL - v93 - Ap 1 '97 - p1308 [1-50]
  c Ch BWatch - v7 - Ja '97 - p2 [51-250]
  y HB Guide - v8 - Spr '97 - p145 [51-250]
  c NYTBR - v101 - N 10 '96 - p46+ [501+]
  c PW - v243 - S 2 '96 - p132 [51-250]
  c PW - v243 - N 4 '96 - p49 [51-250]
  y SLJ - v42 - N '96 - p130 [51-250]
  y VOYA - v19 - F '97 - p352+ [251-500]
  The Rifle
  y Kliatt - v31 - My '97 - p8 [51-250]
  y PW - v244 - F 24 '97 - p93 [1-50]
  The Rifle (Dietz). Audio Version
  c BL - v93 - Ap 1 '97 - p1314 [51-250]
  c CSM - v89 - Mr 27 '97 - pB6 [1-50]
  Skydive! (Woodman). Audio Version
  c HB - v73 - My '97 - p357+ [501+]
  y Kliatt - v31 - My '97 - p44 [51-250]
  The Tent
  y Ch BWatch - v7 - F '97 - p6 [1-50]
  y Kliatt - v31 - Mr '97 - p12 [51-250]
  y PW - v243 - N 25 '96 - p78 [1-50]
  The Tortilla Factory (Illus. by Ruth Wright Paulsen)
  c Emerg Lib - v23 - My '96 - p45 [1-50]
  c RT - v50 - F '97 - p426 [51-250]
  The Treasure of El Patron
  c SLJ - v42 - Ag '96 - p144 [51-250]
  Tucket's Ride
  c BL - v93 - D 15 '96 - p727 [51-250]
  c KR - v64 - N 15 '96 - p1673 [51-250]
  c PW - v244 - Ja 6 '97 - p74 [1-50]
  c SLJ - v43 - Mr '97 - p190 [51-250]
  The Voyage of the Frog
  y SLJ - v42 - N '96 - p41 [51-250]
  Woodsong
  y Kliatt - v30 - S '96 - p5 [1-50]

Worksong (Illus. by Ruth Wright Paulsen)
   c BL - v93 - My 1 '97 - p1502 [51-250]
   c CBRS - v25 - Ap '97 - p100 [51-250]
   c KR - v65 - F 15 '97 - p304 [51-250]
   c PW - v244 - Mr 31 '97 - p74 [51-250]
   c Trib Bks - My 4 '97 - p6+ [51-250]
Paulsen, George E - *A Living Wage for the Forgotten Man*
      Choice - v34 - Ap '97 - p1384+ [51-250]
      LJ - v121 - N 15 '96 - p73+ [51-250]
Paulsen, Wolfgang - *Franz Werfel: Sein Weg In Den Roman*
      MLR - v92 - Ap '97 - p524+ [501+]
Paulson, Don - *An Evening at the Garden of Allah*
      TLS - O 4 '96 - p22 [501+]
Paulson, Lawrence C - *ML for the Working Programmer. 2nd Ed.*
      SciTech - v20 - D '96 - p10 [51-250]
Paulson, Ronald - *The Beautiful, Novel, and Strange*
      Eight-C St - v30 - Spr '97 - p329+ [501+]
      MLN - v111 - D '96 - p1014+ [501+]
      VQR - v72 - Aut '96 - p119* [51-250]
Paulston, Rolland G - *Social Cartography*
   r R&R Bk N - v12 - F '97 - p50 [51-250]
Pauly, Edward - *Homegrown Lessons*
      TCR - v98 - Win '96 - p357+ [501+]
Pauly, Louis W - *Who Elected the Bankers?*
      BL - v93 - Mr 15 '97 - p1210 [51-250]
      For Aff - v76 - My '97 - p125+ [51-250]
      LJ - v122 - Ap 15 '97 - p93 [51-250]
Pauphilet, Albert - *Dictionnaire Des Lettres Francaises*
   r TLS - N 1 '96 - p13 [501+]
Pausacker, Jenny - *Hide and Seek*
   y Magpies - v11 - My '96 - p46 [501+]
Pausewang, Gudrun - *The Final Journey*
   y BL - v93 - O 1 '96 - p344 [51-250]
   y BL - v93 - Ap 1 '97 - p1294 [1-50]
   y CCB-B - v50 - D '96 - p148 [51-250]
   y HB - v73 - Ja '97 - p66 [51-250]
   y HB Guide - v8 - Spr '97 - p83 [51-250]
   c JB - v60 - Ag '96 - p160 [51-250]
   c KR - v64 - O 15 '96 - p1537 [51-250]
   y Sch Lib - v44 - N '96 - p171 [51-250]
Pautrot, Jean-Louis - *La Musique Oubliee*
      FR - v70 - D '96 - p316+ [501+]
Pauwels, Jean-Pierre - *The Geopolitics of Energy Supply in the European Union in the 21st Century*
      En Jnl - v17 - 4 '96 - p165+ [501+]
Pauwels, Louis - *Les Orphelins*
      TLS - N 29 '96 - p15 [51-250]
Pavel, D Michael - *Characteristics of American Indian and Alaska Native Education*
      J Gov Info - v23 - S '96 - p545 [51-250]
Pavic, Milorad - *Sesir Od Riblje Koze*
      WLT - v70 - Aut '96 - p992 [501+]
Pavis, Patrice - *The Intercultural Performance Reader*
      Aftereimage - v24 - N '96 - p16 [51-250]
      Choice - v34 - Mr '97 - p1172+ [51-250]
Pavlenkov, Victor - *Russia: Yesterday, Today, Tomorrow*
   y BL - v93 - F 15 '97 - p1016 [51-250]
Pavlik, John V - *New Media Technology*
      JMCQ - v73 - Aut '96 - p762+ [501+]
Pavlischek, Keith J - *John Courtney Murray and the Dilemma of Religious Toleration*
      Theol St - v57 - S '96 - p569+ [251-500]
Pavlyshyn, Stefaniia - *Ihor Sovevyts'kyi*
      BL - v93 - N 15 '96 - p577 [1-50]
Pavord, Anna - *The New Kitchen Garden*
      Hort - v94 - Ja '97 - p80 [501+]
Pawel, Ernst - *The Labyrinth of Exile*
      Nat - v263 - N 11 '96 - p25+ [501+]
Pawlikowski, John T - *When Catholics Speak about Jews*
      Rel Ed - v91 - Fall '96 - p618 [1-50]
Pawlowski, Lucjan - *Chemistry for the Protection of the Environment 2*
      SciTech - v20 - D '96 - p68 [51-250]
Pawluch, Dorothy - *The New Pediatrics*
      Choice - v34 - F '97 - p997 [51-250]
Pawson, John - *Minimum*
      LATBR - D 8 '96 - p4 [51-250]
      LJ - v121 - N 15 '96 - p59 [51-250]
      Obs - S 1 '96 - p15* [1-50]
      Obs - D 1 '96 - p17* [1-50]
      VLS - Win '96 - p20 [51-250]
Paxson, James J - *The Poetics of Personification*
      MLR - v91 - Jl '96 - p713+ [501+]
Paxton, Robert O - *De Gaulle and the United States*
      EHR - v112 - Ap '97 - p546+ [501+]
Paxton, Tom - *A Car Full of Songs*
      CAY - v16 - Fall '95 - p12 [51-250]

Engelbert Joins the Circus (Illus. by Roberta Wilson)
   c BL - v93 - Mr 15 '97 - p1247 [51-250]
   c PW - v244 - Ja 13 '97 - p76 [51-250]
   c SLJ - v43 - Mr '97 - p162+ [51-250]
Going to the Zoo (Illus. by Karen Lee Schmidt)
   c HB Guide - v7 - Fall '96 - p357 [51-250]
The Marvelous Toy (Illus. by Elizabeth Sayles)
   c HB Guide - v8 - Spr '97 - p140 [51-250]
   c Par - v72 - F '97 - p149 [51-250]
   c SLJ - v42 - Ag '96 - p127+ [51-250]
The Story of the Tooth Fairy (Illus. by Robert Sauber)
   c BL - v92 - Ag '96 - p1908 [51-250]
   c Ch BWatch - v6 - My '96 - p3 [1-50]
Story of the Tooth Fairy (Illus. by Robert Sauber)
   c Emerg Lib - v24 - S '96 - p44 [1-50]
The Story of the Tooth Fairy (Illus. by Robert Sauber)
   c HB Guide - v7 - Fall '96 - p271 [1-50]
   c SLJ - v42 - S '96 - p187 [51-250]
Payant, Rene - *Video*
      Aftereimage - v24 - N '96 - p4 [1-50]
Paykel, Eugene S - *Prevention in Psychiatry*
      AJPsych - v154 - Mr '97 - p429+ [251-500]
Payn, Graham - *My Life with Noel Coward*
      LATBR - N 17 '96 - p8 [501+]
      NY - v72 - S 9 '96 - p86+ [501+]
Payne, Charles M - *I've Got the Light of Freedom*
      AHR - v101 - D '96 - p1643+ [501+]
      VQR - v72 - Aut '96 - p748+ [501+]
Payne, Daniel G - *Voices in the Wilderness*
      Choice - v34 - O '96 - p631 [51-250]
      LATBR - O 13 '96 - p14 [51-250]
      TLS - F 21 '97 - p12 [501+]
Payne, Joan - *Employment Training and Employment Action*
      JEL - v34 - D '96 - p2072 [51-250]
Payne, John C - *The Great Cruising Cookbook*
      BWatch - v18 - F '97 - p8 [51-250]
Payne, Michael - *A Dictionary of Cultural and Critical Theory*
   r ARBA - v28 - '97 - p344 [251-500]
Payne, Richard J - *The Clash with Distant Cultures*
      APSR - v90 - S '96 - p702+ [501+]
      Pres SQ - v26 - Fall '96 - p1184+ [501+]
Payne, Roger - *Among Whales*
   y Kliatt - v31 - Ja '97 - p29 [51-250]
      LATBR - O 6 '96 - p15 [51-250]
      PW - v243 - S 23 '96 - p73 [1-50]
      TLS - S 6 '96 - p36 [501+]
Payne, Stanley G - *A History of Fascism 1914-1945*
      Choice - v34 - O '96 - p359 [51-250]
      HRNB - v25 - Fall '96 - p31+ [51-250]
      NYRB - v43 - N 28 '96 - p48+ [501+]
      NYTBR - v101 - Ag 25 '96 - p28 [1-50]
      PW - v243 - Jl 22 '96 - p235 [1-50]
      TLS - N 15 '96 - p12 [501+]
      VQR - v72 - Aut '96 - p117* [51-250]
Spain's First Democracy
      JMH - v68 - S '96 - p722+ [501+]
Payne, Wardell J - *Directory of African American Religious Bodies. 2nd Ed.*
   r ARBA - v28 - '97 - p538 [51-250]
Payne-Palacio, June - *The Profession of Dietetics*
      SciTech - v20 - N '96 - p55 [51-250]
Paynter, Robert T - *Introductory Electronic Devices and Circuits. 4th Ed.*
      SciTech - v20 - D '96 - p78 [51-250]
Introductory Electronic Devices and Circuits: Conventional Flow Version. 4th Ed.
      SciTech - v20 - D '96 - p78 [51-250]
Payson, Stephen - *Quality Measurement in Economics*
      J Con A - v31 - Sum '97 - p178+ [501+]
Paz, D G - *Nineteenth-Century English Religious Traditions*
      CH - v65 - D '96 - p741+ [501+]
      CHR - v83 - Ja '97 - p114+ [251-500]
      ELT - v39 - 4 '96 - p528+ [51-250]
      Rel St Rev - v23 - Ja '97 - p83 [51-250]
Popular Anti-Catholicism in Mid-Victorian England
      CHR - v82 - O '96 - p730+ [501+]
Paz, Octavio - *The Double Flame*
      TLS - Ag 2 '96 - p7 [501+]
In Light of India
      BL - v93 - Mr 15 '97 - p1223 [51-250]
      KR - v64 - D 15 '96 - p1788 [251-500]
      LATBR - Mr 30 '97 - p4 [501+]
      LJ - v122 - F 15 '97 - p146 [51-250]
      NYTBR - v101 - Mr 30 '97 - p25 [501+]
      PW - v244 - Ja 13 '97 - p59 [51-250]
A Tale of Two Gardens
      BL - v93 - Mr 15 '97 - p1223 [51-250]
      NYTBR - v102 - Mr 30 '97 - p25 [501+]

Paz De Araujo, Carlos - *Ferroelectric Thin Films*
      SciTech - v21 - Mr '97 - p77 [51-250]
Pazzanita, Anthony G - *Historical Dictionary of Mauritania. 2nd Ed.*
   r ARBA - v28 - '97 - p54 [51-250]
Western Sahara
   r ARBA - v28 - '97 - p56 [51-250]
   r MEJ - v51 - Spr '97 - p309 [51-250]
   r R&R Bk N - v12 - F '97 - p21 [51-250]
Pazzi, Roberto - *Incerti Di Viaggio*
      BL - v93 - D 1 '96 - p644 [1-50]
PBS Teacher Connex
   p SLJ - v42 - D '96 - p48 [1-50]
PC Magazine 1997 Computer Buyer's Guide
   r LJ - v121 - D '96 - p138 [51-250]
PCs for Dummies. 4th Ed.
   y BL - v93 - Mr 1 '97 - p1101 [501+]
The Peacemaker's Journey (Swamp). Audio Version
      BL - v93 - F 15 '97 - p1038 [51-250]
Peach, Linden - *Toni Morrison*
      AL - v68 - S '96 - p663 [51-250]
Peach, Robert W - *The ISO 9000 Handbook. 3rd Ed.*
      SciTech - v21 - Mr '97 - p98 [51-250]
Peacock, Anthony - *Rethinking the Constitution*
      BIC - v26 - Mr '97 - p30+ [501+]
Peacock, Doug - *Grizzly Years*
   y Kliatt - v30 - S '96 - p36 [51-250]
Peacock, John - *Men's Fashion*
      BL - v93 - D 15 '96 - p697 [51-250]
   r Choice - v34 - Mr '97 - p1173 [51-250]
   r TCI - v30 - O '96 - p59 [1-50]
The Stage Designs of Inigo Jones
      Sev Cent N - v54 - Fall '96 - p58+ [51-250]
Peacock, Lindsay T - *Pilots*
   c Ch BWatch - v6 - Jl '96 - p6 [51-250]
Peacock, Martin - *Information Technology in the Hospitality Industry*
      R&R Bk N - v11 - D '96 - p72 [51-250]
Peacock, Molly - *Original Love*
      MQR - v35 - Fall '96 - p734+ [501+]
Peacock, Nancy - *Life without Water*
      BW - v27 - Ja 19 '97 - p8 [251-500]
      KR - v64 - Ag 15 '96 - p1180+ [251-500]
      LJ - v121 - O 1 '96 - p128 [51-250]
      NYTBR - v101 - N 24 '96 - p23 [501+]
      NYTBR - v101 - D 8 '96 - p80 [1-50]
      PW - v243 - S 9 '96 - p65 [51-250]
Peake, Mervyn Laurence - *Boy in Darkness (Illus. by P J Lynch)*
   y Bks Keeps - Ja '97 - p6+ [501+]
   y JB - v60 - D '96 - p279 [51-250]
   y TES - N 8 '96 - p11* [251-500]
Peale, Charles Willson - *The Selected Papers of Charles Willson Peale and His Family. Vol. 4*
      LJ - v122 - Mr 15 '97 - p62 [51-250]
Pean, Pierre - *Une Jeunesse Francaise*
      JMH - v69 - Mr '97 - p162+ [501+]
Pean, Stanley - *L'Emprise De La Nuit*
      BL - v93 - F 1 '97 - p930 [1-50]
La Memoire Ensanglantee
      BL - v93 - F 1 '97 - p930 [1-50]
Pearce, David - *Blueprint 4*
      JEL - v35 - Mr '97 - p299+ [51-250]
Pearce, Frank - *Corporate Crime*
      CS - v25 - N '96 - p794 [501+]
Pearce, Joseph - *Wisdom and Innocence*
      Lon R Bks - v18 - D 12 '96 - p22+ [501+]
      TLS - D 20 '96 - p9 [501+]
Pearce, Lynne - *Reading Dialogics*
      MLR - v92 - Ap '97 - p410+ [501+]
Pearce, Michael - *Mamur Zapt and the Camel of Destruction (Prebble). Audio Version*
      BWatch - v17 - D '96 - p10 [1-50]
Pearce, Philippa - *Beauty and the Beast (Illus. by James Mayhew)*
   c Sch Lib - v45 - F '97 - p20 [51-250]
The Little White Hen (Illus. by Gillian McClure)
   c JB - v60 - Ag '96 - p143 [51-250]
   c Sch Lib - v44 - Ag '96 - p100 [51-250]
Pearce, Susan M - *Interpreting Objects and Collections*
      AJA - v100 - O '96 - p769+ [501+]
On Collecting
      AJA - v100 - O '96 - p769+ [501+]
Pearl, Diane - *Spending, Saving and Managing Money*
      BWatch - v18 - F '97 - p2 [1-50]

Pearl, Sydelle - *Elijah's Tears (Illus. by Rossitza Skortcheva Penney)*
c BL - v93 - S 15 '96 - p242 [51-250]
c CCB-B - v50 - N '96 - p109 [51-250]
c HB Guide - v8 - Spr '97 - p73 [51-250]
c KR - v64 - Ag 15 '96 - p1240 [51-250]
c NYTBR - v101 - S 8 '96 - p28 [1-50]
c SLJ - v43 - Ja '97 - p88 [51-250]
Pearl: An Edition with Verse Translation
Choice - v34 - S '96 - p128 [51-250]
Pearlman, Dale Ann - *Stephen J. Gould and Immanuel Velikovsky*
Skeptic - v4 - 4 '96 - p107 [501+]
Pearlman, Daniel - *Black Flames*
BL - v93 - Ja '97 - p818 [51-250]
PW - v243 - D 9 '96 - p61 [51-250]
Pearlman, Edith - *Vaquita and Other Stories*
BL - v93 - N 15 '96 - p572+ [51-250]
Choice - v34 - Ap '97 - p1339 [51-250]
KR - v64 - S 15 '96 - p1348 [251-500]
LJ - v121 - O 15 '96 - p92 [51-250]
PW - v243 - S 30 '96 - p60 [51-250]
Pearlman, Laurie A - *Trauma and the Therapist*
AJCH - v38 - Ap '96 - p298+ [501+]
Pearlman, Mickey - *A Place Called Home*
BL - v93 - S 15 '96 - p204 [51-250]
Ent W - O 4 '96 - p56 [51-250]
SFR - v21 - N '96 - p41 [251-500]
What to Read
r RQ - v36 - Win '96 - p209 [51-250]
Pearlman, Rodney - *Formulation, Characterization, and Stability of Protein Drugs*
SciTech - v21 - Mr '97 - p68 [51-250]
Pearman, Roger R - *I'm Not Crazy, I'm Just Not You*
LJ - v122 - Mr 15 '97 - p77 [51-250]
Pears, Iain - *The Last Judgement*
Arm Det - v29 - Fall '96 - p487 [251-500]
VQR - v72 - Aut '96 - p130* [51-250]
Pears, Tim - *In a Land of Plenty*
Spec - v278 - Ap 5 '97 - p34 [501+]
Pearsall, Deborah M - *Current Research in Phytolith Analysis*
Am Ant - v61 - Ap '96 - p430+ [501+]
Pearsall, Judy - *The Oxford English Reference Dictionary. 2nd Ed.*
r TLS - N 1 '96 - p36 [501+]
Pearsall, Marilyn - *The Other within Us*
PW - v244 - Ja 27 '97 - p85 [51-250]
Pearsall, Paul - *The Pleasure Prescription*
LJ - v121 - D '96 - p126 [51-250]
Mag Bl - Mr '97 - p61 [51-250]
Pearson, Alan - *Nursing Models for Practice. 2nd Ed.*
SciTech - v20 - D '96 - p56 [51-250]
Pearson, Anne - *Ancient Greece*
c SLJ - v42 - N '96 - p39 [51-250]
Pearson, Anne Mackenzie - *Because It Gives Me Peace of Mind*
Choice - v34 - N '96 - p476 [51-250]
R&R Bk N - v11 - N '96 - p6 [51-250]
Pearson, Carol Lynn - *Morning Glory Mother*
KR - v65 - Mr 1 '97 - p330+ [51-250]
PW - v244 - Ap 14 '97 - p53+ [51-250]
A Stranger for Christmas
PW - v243 - S 2 '96 - p109 [51-250]
Pearson, Charles E - *The Last Voyage of El Nuevo Constante*
r HAHR - v76 - Ag '96 - p569 [251-500]
Pearson, Clifford A - *Modern American Houses*
WSJ-MW - v78 - D 5 '96 - pA18 [51-250]
Pearson, David, 1940- - *The Natural House Catalog*
FHB - O '96 - p144 [501+]
Pearson, David, 1955- - *Provenance Research in Book History*
r Lib - v19 - Mr '97 - p73+ [501+]
Pearson, Debora - *Cookie Count and Bake (Illus. by Jane Kurisu)*
c Quill & Q - v62 - D '96 - p39 [251-500]
Ready, Set, Grow! with the Earth Buddies (Illus. by Jane Kurisu)
c Ch Bk News - v19 - Spr '96 - p21+ [501+]
Pearson, Gaye - *The Secret Box*
c PW - v244 - Ap 28 '97 - p76 [51-250]
Pearson, K F - *The Apparition's Daybook*
Aust Bk R - N '96 - p55 [501+]
Pearson, Kit - *Awake and Dreaming*
y BIC - v26 - F '97 - p32 [251-500]
c CCB-B - v50 - My '97 - p332+ [51-250]
c Ch Bk News - v19 - Sum '96 - p30+ [51-250]
c PW - v244 - Ap 7 '97 - p92 [51-250]
y Quill & Q - v62 - Ag '96 - p41 [251-500]
c Quill & Q - v63 - F '97 - p51 [51-250]

Pearson, Lynn F - *Northern City*
LAR - v99 - F '97 - p101 [1-50]
Pearson, M N, 1941- - *Pilgrimage to Mecca*
Choice - v34 - S '96 - p191 [51-250]
Rel St Rev - v23 - Ap '97 - p199 [51-250]
The Portuguese in India
Quad - v40 - My '96 - p85+ [501+]
Pearson, Maggie - *Lord of the Winds (Illus. by Helen Ong)*
c Sch Lib - v44 - Ag '96 - p100 [51-250]
Owl Light
c JB - v60 - D '96 - p273 [51-250]
y Sch Lib - v44 - Ag '96 - p120+ [51-250]
y TES - Jl 5 '96 - pR8 [51-250]
A Treasury of Old Testament Stories (Illus. by Kate Aldous)
c CLW - v66 - Je '96 - p52 [51-250]
Pearson, Mary Rose - *Frogs in Pharaoh's Bed and Other Fun Devotions for Kids*
y CLW - v66 - Je '96 - p47 [51-250]
Pearson, Michael - *John McPhee*
BL - v93 - Mr 15 '97 - p1221 [51-250]
Pearson, Nathan W, Jr. - *Goin' to Kansas City*
Teach Mus - v3 - Ap '96 - p71 [51-250]
Pearson, Ridley - *Beyond Recognition*
BL - v93 - D 15 '96 - p693 [51-250]
KR - v64 - D 1 '96 - p1697 [251-500]
LJ - v122 - Ja '97 - p149+ [51-250]
PW - v243 - D 16 '96 - p42 [51-250]
Chain of Evidence
PW - v244 - Ja 27 '97 - p102+ [1-50]
Chain of Evidence. Audio Version
LJ - v121 - D '96 - p169 [51-250]
Pearson, Roger - *The Fables of Reason*
MLR - v92 - Ap '97 - p468+ [501+]
Pearson, Ryne Douglas - *Simple Simon. Audio Version*
LJ - v122 - Ap 15 '97 - p138 [51-250]
Simple Simon (Morton). Audio Version
y Kliatt - v31 - Mr '97 - p46 [51-250]
Pearson, Scott - *Agricultural Policy in Kenya*
JEL - v34 - D '96 - p2130 [51-250]
Pearson, Tracey Campbell - *The Purple Hat (Illus. by Tracey Campbell Pearson)*
c BL - v93 - F 1 '97 - p948+ [51-250]
c CCB-B - v50 - Mr '97 - p254+ [51-250]
c KR - v65 - Mr 15 '97 - p466 [51-250]
Peart, Jane - *The Pattern*
y BL - v93 - S 1 '96 - p65 [501+]
The Pledge
y BL - v93 - S 1 '96 - p65 [501+]
The Promise
y BL - v93 - S 1 '96 - p65 [501+]
Shadow of Fear
y BL - v93 - S 1 '96 - p65 [501+]
LJ - v121 - N 1 '96 - p54 [51-250]
Pease, Joseph A - *A Liberal Chronicle*
Albion - v28 - Fall '96 - p529 [251-500]
Pease, William D - *The Monkey's Fist*
BW - v26 - Jl 14 '96 - p3 [501+]
KR - v64 - My 1 '96 - p628+ [251-500]
LATBR - Jl 14 '96 - p10 [51-250]
Pease, William H - *James Louis Petigru: Southern Conservative, Southern Dissenter*
AHR - v102 - F '97 - p187 [501+]
JSH - v63 - F '97 - p170+ [501+]
Peat, F David - *Infinite Potential*
Choice - v34 - Ap '97 - p1359 [51-250]
LJ - v121 - N 1 '96 - p105 [51-250]
Nature - v385 - F 13 '97 - p592 [501+]
New Sci - v152 - N 16 '96 - p48+ [501+]
Phys Today - v50 - Mr '97 - p77+ [501+]
PW - v243 - O 14 '96 - p70 [51-250]
Sci - v275 - Mr 28 '97 - p1893+ [501+]
SciTech - v21 - Mr '97 - p20 [51-250]
WSJ-Cent - v99 - Ja 23 '97 - pA16 [501+]
Peattie, Noel - *Western Skyline*
Sm Pr R - v28 - N '96 - p9 [501+]
Peavler, Terry J - *Structures of Power*
Choice - v34 - S '96 - p134 [51-250]
R&R Bk N - v12 - F '97 - p83 [1-50]
WLT - v70 - Aut '96 - p928 [251-500]
Peavy, Linda - *Pioneer Women*
Bloom Rev - v16 - Jl '96 - p12 [51-250]
Pecci-Blunt, Donatella - *Io, Monna Lisa*
WLT - v70 - Aut '96 - p935 [501+]
Pechenik, Jan A - *Biology of the Invertebrates. 3rd Ed.*
SciTech - v20 - N '96 - p29 [51-250]
Pechter, Edward - *Textual and Theatrical Shakespeare*
AB - v98 - O 14 '96 - p1234+ [501+]
What Was Shakespeare
Ren Q - v50 - Spr '97 - p278+ [501+]

Peck, Amelia - *Period Rooms in the Metropolitan Museum of Art*
LJ - v122 - F 1 '97 - p77 [51-250]
WSJ-MW - v78 - D 5 '96 - pA18 [51-250]
Peck, Carole - *The Buffet Book*
PW - v244 - Mr 24 '97 - p77 [51-250]
Peck, Dale - *The Law of Enclosures*
Advocate - Ja 21 '97 - p94 [1-50]
BW - v27 - Ja 26 '97 - p12 [51-250]
Lon R Bks - v18 - My 23 '96 - p29 [501+]
Trib Bks - Mr 9 '97 - p8 [51-250]
Peck, Demaree C - *The Imaginative Claims of the Artist in Willa Cather's Fiction*
Choice - v34 - F '97 - p968 [51-250]
Peck, Donna - *Romantic Days and Nights in San Francisco*
LJ - v121 - N 15 '96 - p79 [51-250]
Peck, Jamie - *Work-Place: The Social Regulation of Labor Markets*
Choice - v34 - N '96 - p504 [51-250]
JEL - v34 - D '96 - p2139 [51-250]
SB - v32 - O '96 - p198 [51-250]
Peck, John - *M and Other Poems*
Choice - v34 - My '97 - p1498 [51-250]
Peck, Linda Levy - *Court Patronage and Corruption in Early Stuart England*
HT - v46 - D '96 - p56 [251-500]
The Mental World of the Jacobean Court
Ren Q - v49 - Aut '96 - p647+ [501+]
Peck, M Scott - *Denial of the Soul*
BL - v93 - Ja '97 - p777 [51-250]
KR - v65 - Ja 15 '97 - p126 [251-500]
LJ - v122 - Mr 15 '97 - p81 [51-250]
PW - v244 - Ja 20 '97 - p383 [51-250]
In Heaven as on Earth
Am - v176 - Ap 19 '97 - p26+ [501+]
The Road Less Traveled
Am - v176 - Ap 19 '97 - p26+ [501+]
The Road Less Traveled and Beyond
KR - v64 - O 15 '96 - p1515+ [251-500]
LJ - v121 - D '96 - p100 [51-250]
PW - v243 - N 4 '96 - p53 [51-250]
The Road Less Traveled and Beyond (Peck). Audio Version
Quill & Q - v62 - D '96 - p31 [1-50]
Trib Bks - F 2 '97 - p6 [51-250]
Peck, Malcolm C - *Historical Dictionary of the Gulf Arab States*
r LJ - v122 - F 1 '97 - p74 [51-250]
Peck, Patricia D - *Jones Family Genealogy*
r EGH - v50 - N '96 - p194 [51-250]
Kraus Family Genealogy
r EGH - v50 - N '96 - p194 [51-250]
Shepherd Family Genealogy
r EGH - v50 - N '96 - p195 [51-250]
Peck, Richard - *The Great Interactive Dream Machine*
c BL - v93 - S 1 '96 - p131 [51-250]
c CCB-B - v50 - N '96 - p109 [51-250]
y Emerg Lib - v24 - Mr '97 - p55+ [51-250]
c HB Guide - v8 - Spr '97 - p73 [51-250]
c KR - v64 - S 15 '96 - p1411 [51-250]
c PW - v243 - S 2 '96 - p131+ [51-250]
c SLJ - v42 - S '96 - p206 [51-250]
The Last Safe Place on Earth
y Emerg Lib - v24 - S '96 - p25 [1-50]
y Emerg Lib - v24 - S '96 - p27 [1-50]
y Kliatt - v30 - S '96 - p13 [51-250]
c NY - v72 - N 18 '96 - p100 [1-50]
c PW - v243 - Jl 22 '96 - p243 [1-50]
Sounds and Silences
y JAAL - v40 - D '96 - p319+ [51-250]
Peck, Robert Newton - *Soup 1776 (Illus. by Charles Robinson)*
c RT - v50 - Mr '97 - p498 [51-250]
Peck, Susan B - *Building Your Own Website*
LJ - v121 - O 1 '96 - p120 [51-250]
Peddicord, Richard - *Gay and Lesbian Rights*
Theol St - v58 - Mr '97 - p200 [251-500]
Pedelty, Mark - *War Stories*
CS - v26 - Ja '97 - p97+ [501+]
Socio R - v45 - F 1 '97 - p87+ [501+]
Pedersen, Charlott Hoffmann - *The Natufian Chipped Lithic Assemblage*
Am Ant - v61 - Jl '96 - p633 [251-500]
Pedersen, Susan - *After the Victorians*
EHR - v111 - S '96 - p1015+ [501+]
Family, Dependence, and the Origins of the Welfare State, Britain and France 1914-1945
JWomHist - v8 - Fall '96 - p219+ [501+]

Pedersen, Ted - *Buried Alive and Other True Stories Scarier than Fiction*
  y Kliatt - v30 - N '96 - p20 [51-250]
Pederson, Jay P - *St. James Guide to Science Fiction Writers. 4th Ed.*
  r ARBA - v28 - '97 - p435 [51-250]
  r Ext - v38 - Spr '97 - p85+ [501+]
Pedigo, Alan - *International Encyclopedia of Violin-Keyboard Sonatas and Composer Biographies. 2nd Ed.*
  r ARBA - v28 - '97 - p477 [51-250]
Pedlosky, Joseph - *Ocean Circulation Theory*
  Sci - v275 - F 21 '97 - p1076 [501+]
Pedoe, Dan - *Circles: A Mathematical View*
  Math T - v89 - My '96 - p434+ [251-500]
Pedraza, Silvia - *Origins and Destinies*
  CS - v26 - Mr '97 - p201+ [501+]
Pedraza Gracia, Manuel Jose - *Documentos Para El Estudio De La Historia Del Libro En Zaragoza Entre 1501 Y 1521*
  r Lib - v18 - S '96 - p274 [51-250]
Pedrazas, Allan - *The Harry Chronicles*
  Arm Det - v30 - Win '97 - p19 [51-250]
  Arm Det - v30 - Win '97 - p39+ [251-500]
Pedrero, Paloma - *Parting Gestures*
  TranslRevS - v1 - My '95 - p32 [51-250]
Pedrycz, Witold - *Fuzzy Modelling*
  SciTech - v20 - D '96 - p13 [51-250]
Peebles, Curtis - *Watch the Skies!*
  JPC - v30 - Fall '96 - p216+ [501+]
Peebles, Gavin - *The Singapore Economy*
  Choice - v34 - N '96 - p508 [51-250]
  JEL - v34 - D '96 - p2120 [51-250]
  R&R Bk N - v11 - D '96 - p26 [51-250]
Peek, Joe - *Is Bank Lending Important for the Transmission of Monetary Policy?*
  JEL - v34 - S '96 - p1422 [51-250]
Peek, Mary - *Mary Wore Her Red Dress and Henry Wore His Green Sneakers*
  c Inst - v106 - Ja '97 - p4* [1-50]
Peek, Robin P - *Scholarly Publishing*
  Cng - v28 - Jl '96 - p61+ [501+]
  JC - v46 - Sum '96 - p208 [51-250]
Peel, Colin D - *Blood of Your Sisters*
  KR - v65 - Ja 15 '97 - p90+ [251-500]
Peel, John - *The Death of Princes*
  y Kliatt - v31 - My '97 - p15 [51-250]
  Objective: Bajor
  y Kliatt - v30 - S '96 - p20 [51-250]
Peel, Lynnette J - *The Henty Journals*
  Aust Bk R - Ag '96 - p18+ [501+]
Peel, Mark - *The Land of Lost Content*
  TLS - S 27 '96 - p32 [251-500]
Peeling, W B - *Questions and Uncertainties in Prostate Cancer*
  SciTech - v21 - Mr '97 - p51 [51-250]
Peers, Douglas M - *Between Mars and Mammon*
  Albion - v28 - '96 - p743+ [501+]
Peers, Laura - *The Ojibwa of Western Canada 1780-1970*
  Can Hist R - v78 - Mr '97 - p167+ [501+]
Peery, Janet - *The River beyond the World*
  BL - v93 - O 1 '96 - p323 [501+]
  KR - v64 - Ag 15 '96 - p1181 [251-500]
  LJ - v122 - Mr 15 '97 - p43 [1-50]
  NYTBR - v101 - N 10 '96 - p23 [501+]
Peeters, Marga - *Time-to-Build: Interrelated Investment and Labour Demand Modelling with Applications to Six OECD Countries*
  JEL - v34 - D '96 - p2033+ [51-250]
Peeva, K - *Elsevier's Dictionary of Computer Science and Mathematics in English, German, French, and Russian*
  r ARBA - v28 - '97 - p621 [51-250]
Peffer-Engels, John - *The Benin Kingdom of West Africa*
  c SLJ - v43 - Ja '97 - p107 [51-250]
Peghini, Mauro - *Arnaldo Segarizzi: Un Intellettuale Trentino A Venezia Avio 1872-Asolo 1924*
  Lib - v18 - D '96 - p364 [51-250]
Pegler, Martin - *Lifestyle Stores*
  TCI - v30 - O '96 - p58 [1-50]
Peguero, Leone - *Lionel and Amelia (Illus. by Adrian Peguero)*
  c BL - v93 - Ja '97 - p870 [251-500]
Peirce, Andrea - *The American Pharmaceutical Association Parent's Guide to Childhood Medications*
  r BL - v93 - Mr 15 '97 - p1254 [51-250]
Peirce, Neal R - *Citistates: How Urban America Can Prosper in a Competitive World*
  NCR - v85 - Spr '96 - p65 [51-250]
  PAR - v57 - Ja '97 - p83+ [501+]

Peirce, William Spangar - *Economics of the Energy Industries. 2nd Ed.*
  Choice - v34 - Ja '97 - p846 [51-250]
  En Jnl - v18 - 1 '97 - p128+ [251-500]
  JEL - v34 - D '96 - p2136 [51-250]
Pei-Tao - *Forms of Distance*
  TranslRevS - v1 - My '95 - p14+ [51-250]
  Landscape over Zero
  TranslRevS - v2 - D '96 - p19+ [51-250]
Pei-Tao, 1949- - *Landscape over Zero*
  PW - v243 - S 30 '96 - p83 [51-250]
  SFR - v21 - S '96 - p33 [501+]
  TranslRevS - v2 - D '96 - p19+ [51-250]
Pejovich, Svetozar - *Economic Analysis of Institutions and Systems*
  IndRev - v1 - Spr '97 - p601+ [501+]
Peju, Pierre - *La Vie Courante*
  WLT - v70 - Aut '96 - p910 [251-500]
Pekar, Harvey - *American Splendor Presents Bob and Harv's Comics*
  BL - v93 - D 15 '96 - p704 [51-250]
Pekarik, Gene - *Psychotherapy Abbreviation*
  SciTech - v20 - S '96 - p33 [51-250]
Peleg, Ilan - *Human Rights in the West Bank and Gaza*
  APSR - v91 - Mr '97 - p220+ [501+]
  MEJ - v50 - Sum '96 - p453 [51-250]
Pelevin, Viktor - *The Life of Insects*
  Obs - F 16 '97 - p15* [501+]
  Omon Ra
  Choice - v34 - D '96 - p621 [51-250]
  VV - v41 - Ag 27 '96 - p57+ [251-500]
  The Yellow Arrow
  LATBR - S 15 '96 - p11 [51-250]
  PW - v244 - Ap 21 '97 - p69 [1-50]
  TranslRevS - v2 - D '96 - p31 [51-250]
Pelham, David - *Crawlies Creep*
  c HB Guide - v7 - Fall '96 - p242 [51-250]
  Sam's Pizza
  c PW - v243 - N 18 '96 - p77 [51-250]
  The Sensational Samburger (Illus. by Chris Moore)
  c RT - v50 - O '96 - p135 [1-50]
Pelikan, Jaroslav - *Christianity and Classical Culture*
  CH - v65 - S '96 - p446+ [501+]
  CHR - v82 - O '96 - p679+ [501+]
  CW - v89 - Jl '96 - p515+ [251-500]
  Faust the Theologian
  CH - v65 - D '96 - p727+ [501+]
  Eight-C St - v30 - Win '96 - p197+ [501+]
  TT - v53 - Ja '97 - p521+ [501+]
  Mary through the Centuries
  Am - v176 - Ap 5 '97 - p26+ [501+]
  BL - v93 - O 1 '96 - p306 [51-250]
  BW - v26 - D 8 '96 - p9 [501+]
  BWatch - v18 - F '97 - p2 [51-250]
  CC - v114 - Mr 5 '97 - p242+ [501+]
  Choice - v34 - Ap '97 - p1356 [51-250]
  Comw - v123 - N 8 '96 - p19+ [501+]
  HT - v46 - O '96 - p55 [1-50]
  LJ - v121 - O 15 '96 - p64 [51-250]
  NYTBR - v101 - O 27 '96 - p34+ [501+]
  NYTBR - v101 - D 8 '96 - p88+ [1-50]
  PW - v243 - N 4 '96 - p46 [1-50]
  Time - v148 - D 23 '96 - p66+ [501+]
  TLS - D 20 '96 - p31 [501+]
  Wil Q - v20 - Aut '96 - p101+ [251-500]
  The Reformation of the Bible, the Bible of the Reformation
  Am - v176 - Mr 8 '97 - p22 [51-250]
  BC - v45 - Win '96 - p563 [51-250]
  Bks & Cult - v3 - Mr '97 - p21+ [501+]
  CC - v114 - Ja 15 '97 - p58+ [251-500]
  Rel St Rev - v22 - O '96 - p348 [51-250]
Pelizzetti, Ezio - *Fine Particles Science and Technology*
  SciTech - v20 - N '96 - p63 [51-250]
Pell, Derek - *The Marquis De Sade's Elements of Style*
  ABR - v17 - Ag '96 - p5 [501+]
  X-Texts
  ABR - v17 - Ag '96 - p5 [501+]
Pella, Judith - *Blind Faith*
  LJ - v121 - N 1 '96 - p54 [51-250]
  Distant Dreams
  LJ - v122 - Ap 1 '97 - p80 [51-250]
  White Nights, Red Mornings
  LJ - v122 - F 1 '97 - p68 [51-250]
Pellant, Chris - *An Illustrated Guide to Fossils*
  yr Sch Lib - v44 - Ag '96 - p125 [51-250]
Pellegrini, Anthony D - *Observing Children in Their Natural Worlds*
  SB - v32 - O '96 - p196 [51-250]

Pellegrino, Charles - *Return to Sodom and Gomorrah (Davidson). Audio Version*
  y Kliatt - v31 - Mr '97 - p50 [51-250]
Pellegrino, Edmund D - *The Christian Virtues in Medical Practice*
  Rel St Rev - v23 - Ap '97 - p160 [51-250]
Pelletier, Cathie - *Beaming Sonny Home*
  LATBR - Ag 4 '96 - p10 [51-250]
  Quill & Q - v62 - Ag '96 - p35 [251-500]
Pelletier, David - *The Graphic Alphabet (Illus. by David Pelletier)*
  c BL - v93 - N 1 '96 - p494 [51-250]
  c BL - v93 - Ap 1 '97 - p1305 [1-50]
  c CCB-B - v50 - D '96 - p148 [51-250]
  c HB - v72 - N '96 - p730 [251-500]
  c HB Guide - v8 - Spr '97 - p42 [51-250]
  c NYTBR - v101 - N 10 '96 - p44 [251-500]
  c PW - v243 - S 16 '96 - p81 [51-250]
  c SLJ - v42 - N '96 - p100 [51-250]
Pelletier, Jacques - *Litterature Et Societe*
  Can Lit - Win '96 - p197+ [501+]
Pelletiere, Stephen C - *Terrorism: National Security Policy and the Home Front*
  J Gov Info - v23 - S '96 - p573 [51-250]
Pellowski, Michael - *The Art of Making Comic Books (Illus. by Howard Bender)*
  y Emerg Lib - v24 - S '96 - p26 [1-50]
  Baseball's Funniest People (Illus. by Sanford Hoffman)
  c LJ - v122 - F 1 '97 - p83 [1 50]
  Joke and Riddle Bonanza (Illus. by Sanford Hoffman)
  c Ch BWatch - v6 - My '96 - p1 [1-50]
Pells, Richard - *Not like Us*
  BL - v93 - Mr 15 '97 - p1208+ [51-250]
  KR - v65 - Mr 1 '97 - p362+ [51-250]
  LJ - v122 - Mr 15 '97 - p77 [51-250]
  PW - v244 - F 17 '97 - p199 [51-250]
Pellston Workshop on Whole Effluent Toxicity (1995: University of Michigan Biological Station, Douglas Lake) - *Whole Effluent Toxicity Testing*
  SciTech - v20 - D '96 - p31 [51-250]
Pelly, David F - *Thelon: A River Sanctuary*
  BIC - v26 - F '97 - p36 [251-500]
Pelteret, David A E - *Slavery in Early Mediaeval England*
  Albion - v28 - Win '96 - p664+ [501+]
  Specu - v72 - Ja '97 - p208+ [501+]
Peltier-Draine, Elsaida - *What's Up Girlfriend?*
  BWatch - v17 - N '96 - p10 [51-250]
Peltola, Pekka - *The Lost May Day*
  Africa T - v43 - 4 '96 - p417+ [501+]
Pelton, Robert Young - *Fielding's Borneo*
  r FEER - v160 - Mr 27 '97 - p49+ [501+]
  The World's Most Dangerous Places
  FEER - v160 - F 27 '97 - p36 [251-500]
Peltonen, Markku - *The Cambridge Companion to Bacon*
  TLS - O 11 '96 - p3+ [501+]
  Classical Humanism and Republicanism in English Political Thought 1570-1640
  HRNB - v25 - Win '97 - p70 [251-500]
  Six Ct J - v27 - Fall '96 - p812+ [501+]
Peltz, Carl F - *Minute Meditations*
  RR - v55 - N '96 - p661 [1-50]
  Psalms for All Occasions with Accompanying Prayers
  RR - v55 - N '96 - p661 [1-50]
Peltz, Gary - *Leukocyte Recruitment in Inflammatory Disease*
  SciTech - v20 - S '96 - p29 [51-250]
Peltzer, Karl - *Psychology and Health in African Cultures*
  Readings - v12 - Mr '97 - p25 [51-250]
Peltzer, Lilli - *Die Demontage Deutscher Naturwissenschaftlicher Intelligenz Nach Dem 2. Weltkrieg*
  Isis - v87 - D '96 - p749+ [51-250]
Pelyvas, Peter - *Subjectivity in English*
  R&R Bk N - v12 - F '97 - p78 [51-250]
Pema Donyo Nyinche, Tai Situpa XII - *Awakening the Sleeping Buddha*
  BL - v93 - O 1 '96 - p301 [51-250]
Pemberton, William E - *Exit with Honor*
  KR - v65 - My 1 '97 - p703 [251-500]
Pena, Milagros - *Theologies and Liberation in Peru*
  CS - v25 - S '96 - p627+ [501+]
  HAHR - v77 - F '97 - p152+ [501+]
Pena, Octavio G - *The Pena Files*
  BL - v92 - Ag '96 - p1864 [51-250]
Pena, Terri De La - *Margins*
  Bloom Rev - v16 - Jl '96 - p21 [1-50]
Penberthy, Jenny - *Lorine Niedecker: Woman and Poet*
  AL - v69 - Mr '97 - p253 [51-250]
Pencak, William - *Worldmaking*
  R&R Bk N - v12 - F '97 - p76 [51-250]

Pendergrast, Mark - *Victims of Memory*
    Am Sci - v84 - S '96 - p493+ [501+]
    Obs - F 9 '97 - p17* [501+]
    TES - Mr 21 '97 - p7* [501+]
Pendleton, Robert - *Graham Greene's Conradian Masterplot*
    Choice - v34 - N '96 - p458 [51-250]
Pendleton, Wade C - *Katutura: A Place Where We Stay*
    Choice - v34 - N '96 - p514 [51-250]
Pendleton-Jullian, Ann M - *The Road That Is Not a Road and the Open City, Ritoque, Chile*
    Choice - v34 - My '97 - p1488 [51-250]
Pendray, Shay - *Shay Pendray's Needlecraft Projects*
    LJ - v121 - O 15 '96 - p56 [51-250]
Penelhum, Terence - *Reason and Religious Faith*
    CPR - v16 - Je '96 - p197+ [501+]
    Rel St - v33 - Mr '97 - p105+ [501+]
Penelope, Julia - *Out of the Class Closet*
    NWSA Jnl - v8 - Fall '96 - p159+ [501+]
Penfield, Marc - *Solar Returns in Your Face*
    Horoscope - v63 - Mr '97 - p8+ [501+]
Penguin English Verse. Vol. 3. Audio Version
    LJ - v121 - D '96 - p171 [51-250]
Penguin Modern Poets 8
    Obs - S 29 '96 - p18* [51-250]
Penick, Harvey - *And if You Play Golf, You're My Friend*
    LJ - v121 - O 1 '96 - p54 [1-50]
    For All Who Love the Game
    LJ - v121 - O 1 '96 - p54 [1-50]
    Harvey Penick's Little Red Book
    LJ - v121 - O 1 '96 - p54 [1-50]
Penman, Danny - *The Price of Meat*
    New Sci - v153 - Ja 25 '97 - p42 [51-250]
Penman, Sharon Kay - *The Queen's Man*
    y BL - v93 - N 1 '96 - p483 [51-250]
    KR - v64 - O 1 '96 - p1430 [251-500]
    LJ - v121 - O 1 '96 - p130 [51-250]
    y SLJ - v43 - Mr '97 - p216 [51-250]
Penn, Malka - *The Hanukkah Ghosts*
    c RT - v50 - D '96 - p342 [51-250]
Penn, Roger - *Skill and Occupational Change*
    SF - v75 - S '96 - p378+ [251-500]
Penn, W S, 1949- - *All My Sins Are Relatives*
    LATBR - Ag 4 '96 - p11 [51-250]
    The Telling of the World
    LJ - v122 - F 15 '97 - p140 [51-250]
    Parabola - v22 - F '97 - p121 [1-50]
Penna, Romano - *Paul the Apostle. Vols. 1-2*
    Rel St Rev - v23 - Ja '97 - p73 [51-250]
Penna, Sandro - *Remember Me, God of Love*
    TranslRevS - v1 - My '95 - p24 [51-250]
Pennac, Daniel - *Better than Life*
    EJ - v85 - N '96 - p125 [251-500]
    TranslRevS - v1 - My '95 - p9 [51-250]
    Monsieur Malaussene
    FR - v70 - D '96 - p355 [251-500]
Pennebaker, James W - *Emotion, Disclosure, and Health*
    R&R Bk N - v12 - F '97 - p96 [51-250]
Pennebaker, Ruth - *Don't Think Twice*
    y BL - v93 - Ap 1 '97 - p1294 [1-50]
    y HB Guide - v7 - Fall '96 - p304 [51-250]
Penner, Lucille Recht - *Monster Bugs (Illus. by Pamela Johnson)*
    c Learning - v25 - Mr '97 - p38 [1-50]
    c SLJ - v42 - S '96 - p199 [51-250]
    The Pilgrims at Plymouth (Illus. by S D Schindler)
    c HB Guide - v8 - Spr '97 - p175 [51-250]
    Twisters! (Illus. by Kazushige Nitta)
    c BL - v93 - N 15 '96 - p597 [51-250]
Penney, David W - *Art of the American Indian Frontier*
    r CAY - v16 - Fall '95 - p13 [51-250]
Penney, Ian - *Ian Penney's Book of Fairy Tales*
    c ECEJ - v24 - Fall '96 - p40+ [51-250]
Penney, Jacqueline - *Painting Greeting Cards in Watercolor*
    BL - v93 - Mr 1 '97 - p1104 [51-250]
    LJ - v122 - Mr 15 '97 - p62+ [51-250]
Penney, Sue - *Buddhism*
    c HB Guide - v8 - Spr '97 - p88 [51-250]
    Christianity
    c HB Guide - v8 - Spr '97 - p88 [51-250]
    Judaism
    c HB Guide - v8 - Spr '97 - p88 [51-250]
Penning-Roswell, Edmund - *Floods across Europe*
    GJ - v162 - Jl '96 - p236 [51-250]
Penny, Malcolm - *How Bats See in the Dark*
    c HB Guide - v8 - Spr '97 - p128 [51-250]
    c SB - v33 - My '97 - p114 [51-250]
    c SLJ - v43 - F '97 - p95 [51-250]

How Plants Grow
    c Ch BWatch - v7 - Ja '97 - p3 [51-250]
    c HB Guide - v8 - Spr '97 - p121 [1-50]
    c SB - v33 - My '97 - p112 [51-250]
    c SLJ - v43 - F '97 - p86 [51-250]
Penrose, Roger - *The Large, the Small and the Human Mind*
    KR - v65 - F 15 '97 - p281+ [251-500]
    Nature - v386 - Ap 3 '97 - p456 [251-500]
    PW - v244 - Mr 10 '97 - p59 [51-250]
    Shadows of the Mind
    Bks & Cult - v2 - Ja '96 - p20+ [501+]
Pensinger, William L - *The Moon of Hoa Binh. Vols. 1-2*
    WLT - v70 - Sum '96 - p765+ [501+]
Pensky, Max - *Melancholy Dialectics*
    Ger Q - v69 - Sum '96 - p335+ [501+]
Penslar, Robin Levin - *Research Ethics*
    BioSci - v46 - O '96 - p705+ [501+]
    New Sci - v151 - S 28 '96 - p52 [1-50]
Pentland, John - *Exchanges Within*
    PW - v244 - Ap 14 '97 - p64 [51-250]
Penwill, John - *Two Essays on Virgil*
    Class Out - v74 - Fall '96 - p44 [251-500]
Penzler, Otto - *Murder for Love*
    Arm Det - v29 - Sum '96 - p347 [51-250]
    Murder for Love. Audio Version
    Arm Det - v29 - Fall '96 - p473 [51-250]
People and Other Animals
    Sch Lib - v45 - F '97 - p55 [51-250]
People in the News 1996
    R&R Bk N - v11 - N '96 - p9 [51-250]
    y SLJ - v42 - O '96 - p166 [51-250]
Peperzak, Adriaan Theodoor - *To the Other*
    JAAR - v64 - Win '96 - p905+ [501+]
Pepitone, James S - *Future Training*
    J Car P&E - v57 - Fall '96 - p22 [251-500]
Peppe, Rodney - *The Magic Toy Box (Illus. by Rodney Peppe)*
    c BL - v93 - S 15 '96 - p249 [51-250]
    c CBRS - v25 - N '96 - p27 [51-250]
    c Ch BWatch - v6 - O '96 - p6 [1-50]
    c HB Guide - v8 - Spr '97 - p14 [51-250]
    c JB - v60 - D '96 - p237 [51-250]
    c SLJ - v42 - N '96 - p90 [51-250]
Pepper, D W - *Natural Convection in a Horizontal Circular Cylinder*
    SciTech - v21 - Mr '97 - p22 [51-250]
Pepper, David - *Modern Environmentalism*
    Choice - v34 - D '96 - p631+ [51-250]
Pepper, Dennis - *The Oxford Book of Scary Tales*
    c LATBR - O 20 '96 - p8 [51-250]
    The Oxford Funny Story Book
    c JB - v60 - Ag '96 - p151 [251-500]
    c Sch Lib - v45 - F '97 - p34 [51-250]
Pepper, Ian L - *Pollution Science*
    SciTech - v20 - N '96 - p67 [51-250]
Pepper, Jane - *Jane Pepper's Garden*
    BL - v93 - Mr 15 '97 - p1215 [51-250]
    PW - v244 - Mr 24 '97 - p79 [51-250]
Pepper, Suzanne - *Radicalism and Education Reform in 20th-Century China*
    Choice - v34 - Ap '97 - p1391 [51-250]
Pepperell, Robert - *O D*
    TLS - Mr 21 '97 - p26 [501+]
    The Post-Human Condition
    TLS - Mr 21 '97 - p26 [501+]
Peppers, Don - *Enterprise One to One*
    LJ - v122 - Ap 15 '97 - p93 [51-250]
Peppers, Russel A - *Palynological Correlation of Major Pennsylvanian (Middle and Upper Carboniferous) Chronostratigraphic Boundaries in the Illinois and Other Coal Basins*
    SciTech - v21 - Mr '97 - p33 [51-250]
Peppiatt, Michael - *Francis Bacon: Anatomy of an Enigma*
    KR - v65 - Ap 1 '97 - p530 [251-500]
    Obs - D 29 '96 - p27 [501+]
    PW - v244 - Mr 31 '97 - p48+ [51-250]
    Spec - v277 - N 9 '96 - p54 [501+]
Pepys, Samuel - *The Diary of Samuel Pepys. Vols. 1-11*
    CSM - v88 - N 21 '96 - pB2 [51-250]
Pera, Pia - *Diario Di Lo*
    BL - v93 - D 1 '96 - p644 [1-50]
Perafita, Alexandre - *Uma Andorinha No Alpendre (Illus. by Manuel Mouta Faria)*
    c Bkbird - v34 - Spr '96 - p52 [1-50]
Peralta, Victoria - *El Ritmo Ludico Y Los En Bogota*
    HAHR - v76 - Ag '96 - p587+ [251-500]
Perceval-Maxwell, M - *The Outbreak of the Irish Rebellion of 1641*
    EHR - v111 - N '96 - p1283+ [501+]

Perchuk, Andrew - *The Masculine Masquerade*
    Art J - v55 - Win '96 - p88+ [501+]
Percival, Joyce - *Architecture for Dolls' Houses*
    LJ - v122 - F 15 '97 - p134 [51-250]
Percy, Graham - *24 Strange Little Animals (Illus. by Graham Percy)*
    c CBRS - v25 - O '96 - p16 [51-250]
    c HB Guide - v8 - Spr '97 - p42 [51-250]
    c SLJ - v43 - Ja '97 - p88+ [51-250]
Percy, John R - *Astronomy Education*
    S&T - v92 - O '96 - p57 [1-50]
Percy, Walker - *The Thanatos Syndrome*
    South R - v268 - Jl '96 - p603+ [501+]
Percy, William Armstrong - *Pederasty and Pedagogy in Archaic Greece*
    Choice - v34 - F '97 - p1017 [51-250]
Percy-Smith, Janie - *Needs Assessments in Public Policy*
    R&R Bk N - v11 - N '96 - p43 [51-250]
Perdomo, Willie - *Where a Nickel Costs a Dime*
    Choice - v34 - S '96 - p128 [51-250]
Perdue, Leo G - *Wisdom and Creation*
    JR - v76 - O '96 - p612+ [501+]
Perdue, Lewis - *The High-Technology Editorial Guide and Stylebook*
    r BL - v93 - My 1 '97 - p1511 [1-50]
Perdue, Theda - *The Cherokee Removal*
    WHQ - v27 - Win '96 - p521+ [501+]
Perea, Juan F - *Immigrants Out!*
    BW - v26 - D 15 '96 - p5 [501+]
    CHE - v43 - Ja 24 '97 - pA18 [51-250]
    LJ - v122 - F 15 '97 - p152 [51-250]
Perec, Georges - *Un Homme Qui Dort*
    MLN - v111 - S '96 - p775+ [501+]
Peregrine, Peter N - *Archaeology of the Mississippian Culture*
    Am Ant - v62 - Ja '97 - p171+ [251-500]
    r ARBA - v28 - '97 - p183 [51-250]
Perel, Shlomo - *Europa, Europa*
    y BL - v93 - My 15 '97 - p1560 [51-250]
    PW - v244 - Ap 21 '97 - p52 [51-250]
Perelman, Michael - *The End of Economics*
    JEL - v35 - Mr '97 - p259+ [251-500]
Perennials (Eyewitness Handbooks)
    r ARBA - v28 - '97 - p580 [51-250]
    SB - v32 - Ag '96 - p171 [51-250]
Perera, Victor - *The Cross and the Pear Tree*
    MEJ - v51 - Spr '97 - p314 [51-250]
    Unfinished Conquest
    Parameters - v26 - Win '96 - p156 [1-50]
Peres, Asher - *Quantum Theory*
    New Sci - v151 - S 28 '96 - p54+ [501+]
Peres, Shimon - *Battling for Peace*
    Am - v175 - N 30 '96 - p27+ [501+]
Peretti, Burton W - *Jazz in American Culture*
    LJ - v122 - Ap 15 '97 - p84 [51-250]
    PW - v244 - Ap 7 '97 - p82 [51-250]
Peretti, Frank E - *The Oath*
    CSM - v89 - N 25 '96 - p12 [51-250]
    CSM - v89 - Ja 23 '97 - p12 [51-250]
    HM - v293 - S '96 - p64+ [501+]
    This Present Darkness (Sondericker). Audio Version
    LJ - v122 - Ja '97 - p172 [51-250]
Peretz, Don - *The Arab-Israeli Dispute*
    r ARBA - v28 - '97 - p208 [51-250]
    One Land, Two Nations
    LJ - v121 - D '96 - p118 [51-250]
Peretz, Isaac Leib - *Selected Works of I.L. Peretz*
    R&R Bk N - v11 - N '96 - p65 [51-250]
Peretz, Paul - *The Politics of American Economic Policy Making. 2nd Ed.*
    JEL - v35 - Mr '97 - p224 [51-250]
    R&R Bk N - v11 - D '96 - p37 [51-250]
Perez, Emma - *Gulf Dreams*
    Choice - v34 - Ap '97 - p1339 [51-250]
Perez, Gladys E Garcia - *Insurrection and Revolution*
    HT - v46 - O '96 - p59 [1-50]
Perez, Janet - *Climate and Literature*
    RMR - v50 - 2 '96 - p203+ [501+]
Perez, Louis A, Jr. - *Essays on Cuban History*
    HAHR - v76 - Ag '96 - p582+ [501+]
Perez De Mendiola, Marina - *Bridging the Atlantic*
    HAHR - v77 - My '97 - p283+ [251-500]
Perez Firmat, Gustavo - *Life on the Hyphen*
    HAHR - v77 - F '97 - p167+ [501+]
    Next Year in Cuba
    y Kliatt - v31 - Ja '97 - p18+ [51-250]
    LATBR - O 20 '96 - p15 [51-250]
Perez Gonzalez, Domingo Julian - *Entre Tu Nombre Y El Mar*
    WLT - v70 - Sum '96 - p668 [251-500]

Perez-Lopez, Jorge F - *Cuba at a Crossroads*
    Parameters - v26 - Win '96 - p158 [1-50]
Cuba's Second Economy
    HAHR - v76 - N '96 - p828+ [501+]
    JEL - v34 - S '96 - p1393+ [501+]
Perez-Reverte, Arturo - *The Club Dumas*
    BL - v93 - O 1 '96 - p292 [51-250]
    KR - v64 - D 15 '96 - p1762+ [251-500]
    Lon R Bks - v19 - Ap 24 '97 - p13+ [501+]
    NY - v73 - Ap 28 '97 - p227 [51-250]
    NYTBR - v102 - Mr 23 '97 - p10 [501+]
    PW - v243 - N 18 '96 - p61 [51-250]
    TLS - S 6 '96 - p23 [251-500]
    Trib Bks - F 16 '97 - p6 [51-250]
The Flanders Panel
    Books - v9 - S '95 - p25 [1-50]
    NYTBR - v101 - S 22 '96 - p40 [1-50]
    Quill & Q - v62 - O '96 - p30 [51-250]
Perez-Stable, Marifeli - *The Cuban Revolution*
    HAHR - v76 - Ag '96 - p583+ [501+]
Perez-Torres, Rafael - *Movements in Chicano Poetry*
    J Am St - v30 - Ag '96 - p308+ [501+]
Perham, Molly - *Food (Illus. by Sallie Alane Reason)*
  c HB Guide - v8 - Spr '97 - p133 [51-250]
Landscapes (Illus. by Sallie Alane Reason)
  c HB Guide - v8 - Spr '97 - p114 [51-250]
  c SB - v33 - My '97 - p110 [51-250]
  c SLJ - v43 - Ja '97 - p108 [51-250]
People (Illus. by Sallie Alane Reason)
  c HB Guide - v8 - Spr '97 - p163 [51-250]
  c SLJ - v43 - Ja '97 - p108 [51-250]
Water (Illus. by Sallie Alane Reason)
  c HB Guide - v8 - Spr '97 - p114 [51-250]
Perillo, Lucia - *The Body Mutinies*
    VQR - v73 - Win '97 - p29* [51-250]
Periodicals in Print 1996
  r ARBA - v28 - '97 - p33+ [251-500]
Perissinotto, Renato M - *Classes Dominantes E Hegomonia Na Republica Velha*
    HAHR - v77 - My '97 - p347+ [251-500]
Perkin, Harold - *The Third Revolution*
    Econ - v339 - My 18 '96 - p11* [501+]
    TLS - Mr 21 '97 - p14 [501+]
Perkins, C R - *Mapping the UK*
  r R&R Bk N - v12 - F '97 - p29 [51-250]
Perkins, Carl - *Go, Cat, Go!*
    PW - v244 - My 12 '97 - p74 [1-50]
Perkins, Catherine - *The Most Excellent Book of How to Be a Clown (Illus. by Rob Shone)*
  c HB Guide - v7 - Fall '96 - p358 [51-250]
Perkins, Charles - *Swinging on a Rainbow (Illus. by Thomas Hamilton)*
  c Bks Keeps - v100 - S '96 - p9 [51-250]
Perkins, David - *Books of Passage*
    PW - v243 - D 30 '96 - p52+ [51-250]
Perkins, Derek - *Dylan Thomas and His World*
    BWatch - v17 - D '96 - p8 [51-250]
Perkins, Dorothy - *The Mastodon Mystery*
  c Ch Bk News - v20 - Win '97 - p30 [51-250]
Perkins, John - *Malice in Wonderland*
    Rapport - v19 - 6 '96 - p31 [251-500]
Perkins, Kathy A - *Contemporary Plays By Women of Color*
    BWatch - v17 - S '96 - p4 [51-250]
Contemporary Plays by Women of Color
    Choice - v34 - S '96 - p124 [51-250]
    TDR - v41 - Spr '97 - p159 [1-50]
Perkins, Mary Anne - *Coleridge's Philosophy*
    Nine-C Lit - v50 - Mr '96 - p529+ [501+]
Perkins, Pheme - *First and Second Peter, James, and Jude*
    Intpr - v51 - Ap '97 - p202 [251-500]
    TT - v53 - Ja '97 - p566+ [51-250]
Peter: Apostle for the Whole Church
    Intpr - v50 - O '96 - p410+ [501+]
Perkins, Robert F - *Talking to Angels*
    LATBR - My 12 '96 - p10+ [51-250]
Perkins, Robert L - *Either/Or. Pts. 1-2*
    IPQ - v37 - Je '97 - p241+ [501+]
Perkins, Warren S - *Textile Coloration and Finishing*
    Choice - v34 - My '97 - p1530 [51-250]
Perkowitz, Sidney - *Empire of Light*
  y BL - v93 - S 1 '96 - p48 [51-250]
  y BL - v93 - D 1 '96 - p664 [1-50]
    Choice - v34 - Ap '97 - p1377 [51-250]
    Phys Today - v50 - Mr '97 - p84* [501+]
    SciTech - v20 - N '96 - p19 [51-250]
Perl, Joseph - *Joseph Perl's Revealer of Secrets*
    KR - v65 - Ja 1 '97 - p20 [51-250]
    LJ - v122 - F 15 '97 - p164 [51-250]
    PW - v243 - N 18 '96 - p70 [51-250]

Perl, Lila - *Four Perfect Pebbles*
  c BL - v93 - Ap 1 '97 - p1298 [1-50]
  y BL - v93 - Ap 1 '97 - p1308 [1-50]
  c HB Guide - v7 - Fall '96 - p380 [51-250]
  c RT - v50 - Ap '97 - p588 [51-250]
It Happened in America (Illus. by Ib Ohlsson)
  c AB - v98 - N 18 '96 - p1727+ [51-250]
  c PW - v243 - Jl 22 '96 - p243 [1-50]
Perlman, Janet - *The Emperor Penguin's New Clothes (Illus. by Janet Perlman)*
  c Emerg Lib - v24 - S '96 - p45+ [51-250]
  c PW - v244 - F 10 '97 - p85 [1-50]
Perlman, Richard - *Sex Discrimination in the Labor Market*
    ILRR - v50 - O '96 - p170+ [501+]
Perlmutter, Philip - *The Dynamics of American Ethnic, Religious, and Racial Group Life*
    R&R Bk N - v11 - D '96 - p14 [51-250]
Perloff, Marjorie - *Radical Artifice*
    Can Lit - Spr '97 - p239+ [501+]
Wittgenstein's Ladder
    Choice - v34 - Ap '97 - p1331 [51-250]
    Wil Q - v20 - Aut '96 - p97* [251-500]
Perlstein, Steve - *Rebel Baseball*
    Aethlon - v13 - Fall '95 - p180+ [251-500]
Permaloff, Anne - *Political Power in Alabama*
    Choice - v34 - S '96 - p196 [51-250]
Pernetta, John - *Philip's Atlas of the Oceans*
  r GJ - v162 - Jl '96 - p240 [31-250]
Pernick, Martin S - *The Black Stork*
    Hast Cen R - v26 - Jl '96 - p42 [1-50]
    Nature - v382 - Jl 18 '96 - p217+ [501+]
    SF - v75 - Mr '97 - p1136+ [501+]
Pernot, Michel - *La Fronde*
    EHR - v111 - N '96 - p1286 [251-500]
Perols, Sylvaine - *The Human Body*
  c Ch BWatch - v7 - Ja '97 - p2 [1-50]
  c SLJ - v43 - F '97 - p88+ [51-250]
Peron, Eva - *In My Own Words*
    LATBR - D 22 '96 - p3 [501+]
    LJ - v121 - O 15 '96 - p66+ [51-250]
    Lon R Bks - v19 - F 20 '97 - p13+ [501+]
    Nat - v263 - O 28 '96 - p50+ [501+]
    NYRB - v44 - F 20 '97 - p27+ [501+]
    NYTBR - v101 - N 24 '96 - p27 [501+]
    PW - v243 - N 4 '96 - p70 [51-250]
    WSJ-MW - v78 - N 14 '96 - pA18 [51-250]
Perone, James E - *Musical Anthologies for Analytical Study*
  r ARBA - v28 - '97 - p468 [51-250]
Orchestration Theory
  r ARBA - v28 - '97 - p483 [51-250]
  r Choice - v34 - N '96 - p435 [51-250]
Perrault, Charles - *Peau D'Ane*
  c BL - v93 - N 1 '96 - p500 [1-50]
Perreault, Jeanne - *Writing Selves*
    Biography - v19 - Fall '96 - p435+ [501+]
    Choice - v34 - S '96 - p128 [51-250]
Perret, Geoffrey - *Old Soldiers Never Die*
    Choice - v34 - D '96 - p678 [51-250]
    Lon R Bks - v19 - F 6 '97 - p29+ [501+]
    NL - v79 - Ag 12 '96 - p16+ [501+]
    NYTBR - v101 - D 8 '96 - p90 [1-50]
    RAH - v25 - Mr '97 - p132+ [501+]
Perret, Patti - *The Faces of Fantasy*
    Bloom Rev - v17 - Ja '97 - p12 [51-250]
    BW - v26 - N 10 '96 - p13 [51-250]
Perrick, Penny - *Evermore*
    Books - v11 - Ap '97 - p21 [51-250]
Perrin, Wendy - *Wendy Perrin's Secrets Every Smart Traveler Should Know*
    PW - v243 - N 18 '96 - p69+ [51-250]
Perrine, Daniel M - *The Chemistry of Mind-Altering Drugs*
    SciTech - v21 - Mr '97 - p67 [51-250]
Perrings, Charles - *Biodiversity Conservation*
    BioSci - v46 - O '96 - p717+ [501+]
Biodiversity Loss
    BioSci - v46 - O '96 - p717+ [501+]
    JEL - v34 - S '96 - p1480+ [51-250]
Sustainable Development and Poverty Alleviation in Sub-Saharan Africa
    Choice - v34 - S '96 - p177 [51-250]
    ILR - v135 - '96 - p118+ [501+]
    JEL - v34 - S '96 - p1480+ [51-250]
Perrone, Lorenzo - *Il Cuore Indurito Del Faraone*
    Rel St Rev - v22 - O '96 - p301+ [501+]
Perrot, Philippe - *Fashioning the Bourgeoisie*
    JPC - v30 - Fall '96 - p218+ [501+]

Perrotta, Tom - *The Wishbones*
    BL - v93 - My 15 '97 - p1563+ [51-250]
    KR - v65 - Mr 15 '97 - p411 [251-500]
    LJ - v122 - Ap 15 '97 - p120 [51-250]
    PW - v244 - Mr 31 '97 - p61 [51-250]
Perry, Anne - *Ashworth Hall*
  y BL - v93 - Ja '97 - p779 [51-250]
    KR - v65 - Ja 1 '97 - p25 [51-250]
    LJ - v122 - F 1 '97 - p111 [51-250]
    NYTBR - v102 - Mr 16 '97 - p28 [51-250]
    PW - v244 - Ja 13 '97 - p58 [51-250]
    WSJ-Cent - v99 - Mr 28 '97 - pA14 [51-250]
Cain His Brother
    PW - v243 - O 14 '96 - p81 [1-50]
Defend and Betray (Porter). Audio Version
  y Kliatt - v30 - S '96 - p46 [51-250]
Pentecost Alley
    NYTBR - v101 - Ap 7 '96 - p23 [51-250]
A Sudden, Fearful Death (Porter). Audio Version
    BWatch - v17 - D '96 - p10 [1-50]
Weighed in the Balance
    Arm Det - v30 - Win '97 - p103+ [251-500]
    BL - v93 - S 1 '96 - p31 [51-250]
    KR - v64 - Ag 15 '96 - p1191+ [251-500]
    LATBR - N 10 '96 - p42 [51-250]
    NYTBR - v101 - O 27 '96 - p42 [51-250]
    PW - v243 - S 2 '96 - p116+ [51-250]
Weighed in the Balance (Jones). Audio Version
    BWatch - v18 - Mr '97 - p6 [1-50]
Perry, Charles - *Portrait of a Young Man Drowning*
    BW - v26 - S 1 '96 - p12 [51-250]
Perry, David B - *Bike Cult*
    Workbook - v21 - Fall '96 - p144+ [251-500]
Perry, Elizabeth A - *A Brief History of the Town of Glocester, Rhode Island*
  r EGH - v50 - N '96 - p185+ [51-250]
Perry, Elizabeth J - *Shanghai on Strike*
    APSR - v90 - D '96 - p874+ [501+]
Perry, Gill - *Women Artists and the Parisian Avant-Garde*
    Choice - v34 - O '96 - p269 [51-250]
Perry, Guillermo - *Public Finances, Stabilization, and Structural Reform in Latin America*
    HAHR - v76 - N '96 - p832+ [501+]
Perry, J Mitchell - *In the Zone*
    BL - v93 - Mr 15 '97 - p1211 [51-250]
Perry, James A - *Water Quality*
    R&R Bk N - v12 - F '97 - p35 [51-250]
Perry, James M - *Arrogant Armies*
  y SLJ - v42 - N '96 - p142 [51-250]
    TLS - S 6 '96 - p33 [251-500]
Perry, John Curtis - *Facing West*
    AHR - v101 - O '96 - p1288 [501+]
Perry, John Michael - *Exploring the Identity and Vision of Jesus*
    CLW - v67 - D '96 - p41 [251-500]
Perry, Marvin - *Arnold Toynbee and the Western Tradition*
    Hist & T - v36 - F '97 - p109 [51-250]
Perry, Michael C - *The Chemotherapy Source Book. 2nd Ed.*
  r SciTech - v20 - D '96 - p42 [51-250]
Perry, Michael J - *The Constitution in the Courts*
    J Ch St - v38 - Sum '96 - p653+ [251-500]
Perry, Phyllis J - *Ballooning*
  c BL - v93 - F 1 '97 - p937+ [51-250]
  c SLJ - v43 - F '97 - p95 [51-250]
Rainy, Windy, Snowy, Sunny Days
  c SB - v33 - My '97 - p109 [51-250]
    SLMQ - v24 - Sum '96 - p222 [51-250]
Sea Stars and Dragons
  c HB Guide - v7 - Fall '96 - p338 [51-250]
  c SLJ - v43 - Ag '96 - p159 [51-250]
The World's Regions and Weather
    SLMQ - v24 - Sum '96 - p222 [51-250]
    VOYA - v19 - D '96 - p296+ [51-250]
Perry, Richard D - *More Maya Missions*
    CHR - v83 - Ja '97 - p169+ [251-500]
Perry, Richard J - *From Time Immemorial*
    Choice - v34 - My '97 - p1564 [51-250]
Perry, Ritchie - *The Runton Werewolf and the Big Match*
  c JB - v60 - O '96 - p205 [51-250]
Perry, S D - *The Labyrinth*
    SF Chr - v18 - O '96 - p78 [51-250]
Perry, Sarah - *If...*
  c LA - v73 - D '96 - p620 [51-250]
Perry, Steve - *First Contact*
    LJ - v122 - Mr 15 '97 - p93 [1-50]
Leonard Nimoy's Primortals
    KR - v65 - Mr 1 '97 - p341 [51-250]
    PW - v244 - Mr 24 '97 - p64 [51-250]

Shadows of the Empire
  PW - v244 - Mr 17 '97 - p81 [1-50]
Target Earth
  y BL - v93 - Ap 1 '97 - p1283 [51-250]
Perry, Theresa - *Teaching Malcolm X*
  Bl S - v26 - Fall '96 - p105 [1-50]
  Choice - v34 - S '96 - p180 [51-250]
Perry, Thomas - *Dance for the Dead*
  Rapport - v19 - 4 '96 - p27 [251-500]
Dance for the Dead (Crouse). Audio Version
  BL - v93 - N 1 '96 - p522 [51-250]
  y Kliatt - v31 - My '97 - p36 [51-250]
Shadow Woman
  BL - v93 - My 1 '97 - p1462 [51-250]
  KR - v65 - My 1 '97 - p673 [251-500]
  LJ - v122 - My 1 '97 - p143+ [51-250]
  PW - v244 - Ap 21 '97 - p63 [51-250]
Perryman, Mark - *The Blair Agenda*
  TLS - O 18 '96 - p13 [501+]
Persaud, Rajen - *Making It through College*
  B Ent - v27 - O '96 - p62 [51-250]
Perschbacher, Gerald - *Wheels in Motion*
  BWatch - v18 - F '97 - p1 [1-50]
Perseus 2.0. Comprehensive Ed. Electronic Media Version
  BW - v26 - D 15 '96 - p11 [251-500]
Perseus 2.0. Concise Ed. Electronic Media Version
  BW - v26 - D 15 '96 - p11 [251-500]
Persico, Deborah A - *Mapp v. Ohio*
  y KR - v65 - Ja 1 '97 - p61 [51-250]
Persidsky, Andre - *Director 5 for Macintosh*
  CBR - v14 - N '96 - p33 [1-50]
Director 5 for Windows
  CBR - v14 - N '96 - p39 [1-50]
  LJ - v122 - Ja '97 - p138 [1-50]
Persing, David H - *PCR Protocols for Emerging Infectious Diseases*
  SciTech - v20 - S '96 - p24 [51-250]
Persky, Stan - *Boyopolis: Essays from Gay Eastern Europe*
  LJ - v121 - O 15 '96 - p80 [51-250]
Perspection, Inc. - *Microsoft Powerpoint for Windows 95 Step by Step*
  CBR - v14 - Jl '96 - p24 [1-50]
Perspectives on Arabic Linguistics VII
  MLJ - v81 - Spr '97 - p120+ [501+]
Persson, Lars Olof - *Microregional Fragmentation*
  JEL - v34 - D '96 - p2138+ [51-250]
Perthes, Volker - *The Political Economy of Syria under Asad*
  MEJ - v51 - Win '97 - p132+ [501+]
Pertzig, F - *Messes of Dresses (Illus. by Tova Leff)*
  c Ch BWatch - v7 - Ja '97 - p3 [51-250]
Peru (Insight Guides)
  r BL - v93 - S 15 '96 - p210 [1-50]
Perucca, Fabien - *The Rubbish on Our Plates*
  Econ - v342 - F 15 '97 - p7* [51-250]
  New Sci - v152 - O 19 '96 - p48 [51-250]
  PW - v243 - D 30 '96 - p49 [51-250]
Perusek, Glenn - *Trade Union Politics*
  ILRR - v50 - Ja '97 - p344+ [501+]
Perutz, Leo - *Turlupin*
  Obs - D 15 '96 - p18* [51-250]
  TLS - N 15 '96 - p25 [51-250]
Perutz, Vivien - *Edouard Manet*
  BM - v138 - S '96 - p610 [501+]
Pervin, Lawrence A - *Personality: Theory and Research. 7th Ed.*
  R&R Bk N - v11 - D '96 - p3 [51-250]
Pescador, Juan Jose - *De Bautizados A Fieles Difuntos*
  HAHR - v77 - F '97 - p113+ [501+]
Pescatello, Ann M - *Charles Seeger: A Life in American Music*
  J Am Cult - v19 - Sum '96 - p158+ [51-250]
Pesce, Dolores - *Hearing the Motet*
  Choice - v34 - Ap '97 - p1347 [51-250]
Pesci, David - *Amistad*
  y BL - v93 - My 15 '97 - p1563 [51-250]
  PW - v244 - Ap 28 '97 - p52 [51-250]
Pescio, Claudio - *Rembrandt and Seventeenth-Century Holland (Illus. by Sergio)*
  y HB Guide - v7 - Fall '96 - p356 [51-250]
  c SLJ - v42 - D '96 - p31 [1-50]
Van Gogh (Illus. by Francesca D'Ottavi)
  y SLJ - v42 - D '96 - p144 [51-250]
Pesek, Joseph J - *Chemically Modified Surfaces*
  SciTech - v20 - S '96 - p49 [51-250]
Peset Reig, Jose Luis - *Las Heridas De La Ciencia*
  Isis - v88 - Mr '97 - p151 [251-500]

Peskin, Michael E - *An Introduction to Quantum Field Theory*
  Phys Today - v49 - Ag '96 - p69+ [501+]
Peskine, Brigitte - *Les Eaux Douces D'Europe*
  WLT - v71 - Win '97 - p105+ [501+]
Peskine, Christian - *An Algebraic Introduction to Complex Projective Geometry. Vol. 1*
  Choice - v34 - D '96 - p647+ [51-250]
Pesman, Ros - *Duty Free*
  Meanjin - v55 - 3 '96 - p467+ [501+]
The Oxford Book of Australian Travel Writing
  Aust Bk R - D '96 - p12+ [501+]
El Peso De La Lengua Espanola En El Mundo
  Hisp - v79 - D '96 - p823+ [501+]
Pessarakli, Mohammad - *Handbook of Photosynthesis*
  r SciTech - v20 - D '96 - p31 [51-250]
Pessin, Andrew - *The Twin Earth Chronicles*
  R&R Bk N - v11 - N '96 - p63 [51-250]
Pestov, Stanislav - *Bomba: Tainy I Strasti Atomnoi Preispodnei*
  BL - v93 - O 1 '96 - p327 [1-50]
Petach, Heidi - *Goldilocks and the Three Hares*
  c Emerg Lib - v24 - S '96 - p46 [51-250]
Petchesky, Rosalind Pollack - *Abortion and Woman's Choice*
  Cons - v17 - Aut '96 - p35+ [501+]
Peter, Rodolphe - *Bibliotheca Calviniana. Vol. 2*
  r Lib - v18 - S '96 - p260 [251-500]
Peter Rabbit's Math Garden. Electronic Media Version
  c HB - v73 - Mr '97 - p219+ [501+]
Peters, Albrecht - *Kommentar Zu Luthers Katechismen. Vol. 5*
  Six Ct J - v27 - Fall '96 - p951+ [251-500]
Peters, Andrew - *The Weather's Getting Verse (Illus. by Alan Larkins)*
  c TES - S 27 '96 - p7* [51-250]
Peters, Arthur King - *Seven Trails West*
  yr SLJ - v42 - D '96 - p153 [51-250]
Peters, B Guy - *Agenda for Excellence 2*
  Pol Stud J - v24 - Aut '96 - p521 [51-250]
The Future of Governing
  Choice - v34 - Ap '97 - p1419 [51-250]
Peters, Bernard C - *Lake Superior Place Names*
  Names - v45 - Mr '97 - p74+ [501+]
Peters, C J - *Virus Hunter*
  y BL - v93 - My 1 '97 - p1471 [51-250]
  KR - v65 - Ap 1 '97 - p531 [251-500]
  PW - v244 - Ap 28 '97 - p64 [51-250]
Peters, Charles M - *The Ecology and Management of Non-Timber Forest Resources*
  JEL - v34 - D '96 - p2134 [51-250]
Peters, E K - *No Stone Unturned*
  New Sci - v153 - Mr 22 '97 - p47 [51-250]
Peters, Elizabeth - *The Camelot Caper*
  LJ - v122 - F 15 '97 - p166 [51-250]
The Hippopotamus Pool (Rosenblat). Audio Version
  y Kliatt - v31 - My '97 - p40 [51-250]
The Murders of Richard III
  Quill & Q - v62 - O '96 - p30 [51-250]
Seeing a Large Cat
  y BL - v93 - My 1 '97 - p1462 [51-250]
  PW - v244 - My 5 '97 - p201+ [51-250]
Peters, Ellis - *Saint Peter's Fair. Audio Version*
  Books - v9 - S '95 - p27 [1-50]
Peters, Emrys L - *The Bedouin of Cyrenaica*
  Am Ethnol - v23 - Ag '96 - p651+ [501+]
Peters, F E - *The Hajj*
  JAAR - v64 - Sum '96 - p421+ [501+]
Mecca: A Literary History of the Muslim Holy Land
  Historian - v59 - Fall '96 - p141+ [501+]
Muhammad and the Origins of Islam
  JAAR - v64 - Sum '96 - p419+ [501+]
Peters, George H - *Agricultural Economics*
  Econ - v106 - S '96 - p1484 [51-250]
Peters, Glen - *Beyond the Next Wave*
  Choice - v34 - Ap '97 - p1385 [51-250]
Peters, Julie Anne - *How Do You Spell Geek?*
  c BL - v93 - S 15 '96 - p242 [51-250]
  c CCB-B - v50 - O '96 - p72 [51-250]
  c HB Guide - v8 - Spr '97 - p73 [51-250]
  c KR - v64 - S 1 '96 - p1326 [51-250]
  c SLJ - v42 - O '96 - p124 [51-250]
Peters, Lisa Westberg - *The Hayloft (Illus. by K D Plum)*
  c RT - v50 - N '96 - p255 [51-250]
October Smiled Back (Illus. by Ed Young)
  c BL - v93 - N 1 '96 - p509 [51-250]
  c CBRS - v25 - S '96 - p5 [51-250]
  c HB Guide - v8 - Spr '97 - p42 [51-250]
  c KR - v64 - S 1 '96 - p1332 [51-250]
  c PW - v243 - S 16 '96 - p81 [51-250]
  c SLJ - v42 - O '96 - p104 [51-250]

Peters, Lynn - *Premature Infatuation*
  Books - v11 - Ap '97 - p21+ [51-250]
Peters, Margot - *May Sarton: A Biography*
  Advocate - Mr 18 '97 - p78 [251-500]
  BL - v93 - Mr 1 '97 - p1105 [51-250]
  BW - v27 - F 23 '97 - p4+ [501+]
  KR - v65 - Ja 1 '97 - p46 [251-500]
  LJ - v122 - F 15 '97 - p136 [51-250]
  NYTBR - v102 - Ap 6 '97 - p9 [501+]
  PW - v244 - Ja 13 '97 - p59+ [51-250]
Peters, Michael, 1948- - *Individualism and Community*
  R&R Bk N - v11 - N '96 - p56 [51-250]
Poststructuralism, Politics and Education
  Choice - v34 - S '96 - p212 [51-250]
Peters, Mitchell - *Fundamental Method for Mallets. Bk. 1*
  Teach Mus - v4 - F '97 - p49+ [51-250]
Peters, Pauline E - *Dividing the Commons*
  AAPSS-A - v546 - Jl '96 - p162 [501+]
Peters, Ralph - *Twilight of Heroes*
  PW - v243 - D 9 '96 - p65 [51-250]
Peters, Ray DeV - *Preventing Childhood Disorders, Substance Abuse, and Delinquency*
  R&R Bk N - v11 - N '96 - p78 [51-250]
Peters, Robert - *Twin Peaks Cherry Pie*
  WAL - v31 - Win '97 - p413+ [51-250]
Peters, Robert, 1924- - *Feather: A Child's Death and Life*
  KR - v65 - Mr 15 '97 - p447 [251-500]
For You, Lili Marlene
  VQR - v73 - Win '97 - p33* [1-50]
Peters, Ronald M, Jr. - *The Speaker: Leadership in the U.S. House of Representatives*
  SSQ - v77 - S '96 - p709+ [501+]
Peters, Rudolph - *Jihad in Classical and Modern Islam*
  Rel St Rev - v23 - Ap '97 - p200 [51-250]
Peters, Sally - *Bernard Shaw: The Ascent of the Superman*
  ABR - v18 - O '96 - p14+ [501+]
  BW - v26 - Jl 7 '96 - p8 [251-500]
  Choice - v34 - S '96 - p129 [51-250]
  Econ - v339 - My 18 '96 - p13*+ [251-500]
  ELT - v40 - 1 '97 - p72+ [501+]
Peters, Ted, 1941- - *Playing God?*
  LJ - v122 - Ja '97 - p103 [51-250]
  New Sci - v153 - Mr 15 '97 - p42+ [501+]
Peters, Theodore, 1922- - *All about Albumin*
  SciTech - v20 - N '96 - p31 [51-250]
Peters, Tom F - *Building the Nineteenth Century*
  Choice - v34 - F '97 - p984 [51-250]
  New Sci - v152 - N 23 '96 - p44+ [501+]
In Search of Excellence
  Inc. - v18 - D '96 - p63 [251-500]
Peters, Virginia Bergman - *Women of the Earth Lodges*
  AHR - v101 - O '96 - p1274 [501+]
Peters, Werner - *Society on the Run*
  R&R Bk N - v11 - N '96 - p39 [51-250]
Peterse, Hans - *Jacobus Hoogstraeten Gegen Johannes Reuchlin*
  Six Ct J - v27 - Win '96 - p1239+ [501+]
Peterseil, Tehila - *The Safe Place*
  c HB Guide - v8 - Spr '97 - p73 [51-250]
  c SLJ - v42 - D '96 - p124 [51-250]
Petersen, Andrew - *Dictionary of Islamic Architecture*
  r ARBA - v28 - '97 - p369 [251-500]
  r Choice - v34 - D '96 - p593 [51-250]
  r R&R Bk N - v11 - N '96 - p60 [51-250]
Petersen, Christian - *Bread and the British Economy c.1770-1870*
  Albion - v28 - Sum '96 - p323+ [501+]
  JEH - v57 - Mr '97 - p217+ [501+]
Petersen, Dan - *Human Error Reduction and Safety Management. 3rd Ed.*
  SciTech - v20 - S '96 - p46 [51-250]
Petersen, David - *Bryce Canyon National Park*
  c HB Guide - v8 - Spr '97 - p175 [51-250]
  c SB - v33 - My '97 - p115 [51-250]
Death Valley National Park
  c HB Guide - v8 - Spr '97 - p175 [51-250]
  c SB - v33 - My '97 - p115 [51-250]
Denali National Park and Preserve
  c HB Guide - v8 - Spr '97 - p175 [51-250]
Ghost Grizzlies
  WAL - v31 - Sum '96 - p161+ [501+]
A Hunter's Heart
  BL - v93 - S 15 '96 - p203 [51-250]
  Bloom Rev - v17 - Ja '97 - p9 [501+]
  LATBR - Ag 25 '96 - p1+ [501+]
Petrified Forest National Park
  c SB - v33 - My '97 - p115 [51-250]
Petersen, David C - *Sports, Convention and Entertainment Facilities*
  R&R Bk N - v12 - F '97 - p73 [51-250]

Petersen, David L - *Zechariah 9-14 and Malachi*
    Intpr - v51 - Ja '97 - p85+ [251-500]
Petersen, Elise - *Tracy's Mess (Illus. by Iza Trapani)*
    c HB Guide - v7 - Fall '96 - p271 [51-250]
Petersen, James B - *A Most Indispensable Art*
    Choice - v34 - F '97 - p1006 [51-250]
    R&R Bk N - v11 - D '96 - p12 [51-250]
Petersen, Keith - *River of Life, Channel of Death*
    PHR - v65 - N '96 - p675+ [251-500]
    Pub Hist - v19 - Win '97 - p104+ [501+]
Petersen, Keith C - *Controversy, Conflict, and Compromise*
    Pub Hist - v19 - Win '97 - p104+ [501+]
Peterson, Anna Lisa - *Martyrdom and the Politics of Religion*
    Choice - v34 - Mr '97 - p1178 [51-250]
    R&R Bk N - v12 - F '97 - p11 [51-250]
Peterson, Bernard L - *The African American Theatre Directory 1816-1960*
    r BL - v93 - F 15 '97 - p1039 [251-500]
    r LJ - v122 - F 15 '97 - p128+ [51-250]
Peterson, Beth - *No Turning Back*
    c HB Guide - v7 - Fall '96 - p296 [51-250]
Peterson, Brenda - *Sister Stories*
    y Kliatt - v31 - Mr '97 - p28 [251-500]
Peterson, Carla L - *Doers of the Word*
    Nine-C Lit - v50 - Mr '96 - p557 [51-250]
    NWSA Jnl - v8 - Fall '96 - p172+ [501+]
    QJS - v83 - My '97 - p234+ [501+]
    TSWL - v15 - Fall '96 - p352+ [501+]
Peterson, Christian A - *Alfred Stieglitz's Camera Notes*
    BW - v27 - Ja 19 '97 - p12 [51-250]
    Obs - N 3 '96 - p18* [51-250]
Peterson, Cris - *Harvest Year (Illus. by Alvis Upitis)*
    c BL - v93 - S 15 '96 - p244 [51-250]
    c CLW - v67 - Mr '97 - p55 [51-250]
    c HB Guide - v8 - Spr '97 - p133 [51-250]
    c SLJ - v42 - N '96 - p117 [51-250]
Horsepower: The Wonder of Draft Horses (Illus. by Alvis Upitis)
    c CCB-B - v50 - Ap '97 - p292 [51-250]
    c KR - v65 - F 1 '97 - p226 [51-250]
Peterson, David R - *An International Accounting Practice Set*
    JEL - v34 - S '96 - p1463 [51-250]
Peterson, Esther - *Restless: The Memoirs of Labor and Consumer Activist Esther Peterson*
    J Con A - v30 - Win '96 - p499+ [501+]
Peterson, Eugene H - *Leap over a Wall*
    Am - v176 - F 15 '97 - p33 [51-250]
    BL - v93 - F 15 '97 - p975+ [51-250]
    PW - v243 - D 16 '96 - p53 [51-250]
The Message
    BIC - v25 - D '96 - p43 [51-250]
Take and Read
    Bks & Cult - v2 - My '96 - p5 [51-250]
    r CC - v113 - O 16 '96 - p983 [51-250]
Peterson, Florence - *American Labor Unions, What They Are and How They Work. 2nd Rev. Ed.*
    r RQ - v36 - Fall '96 - p51 [51-250]
Handbook of Labor Unions
    r RQ - v36 - Fall '96 - p51 [51-250]
Peterson, J E - *Historical Dictionary of Saudi Arabia*
    r JTWS - v13 - Spr '96 - p393+ [501+]
Peterson, James - *Fish and Shellfish*
    PW - v243 - N 4 '96 - p47 [1-50]
Peterson, James, 1957- - *Dreams of Chaos, Visions of Order*
    FQ - v49 - Fall '95 - p43+ [501+]
Peterson, Jane T - *Women Playwrights of Diversity*
    r LJ - v122 - Ap 1 '97 - p84 [51-250]
Peterson, John - *The Littles Take a Trip*
    c New Ad - v9 - Fall '96 - p309+ [501+]
Peterson, Julienne - *Caterina, the Clever Farm Girl (Illus. by Enzo Giannini)*
    c HB Guide - v7 - Fall '96 - p323 [51-250]
    c RT - v50 - Ap '97 - p593+ [51-250]
Peterson, K Jean - *Health Care for Lesbians and Gay Men*
    SciTech - v21 - Mr '97 - p46 [51-250]
Peterson, Larry L - *Computer Networks*
    SciTech - v20 - S '96 - p55 [51-250]
Peterson, Lorraine - *Lord, I Haven't Talked to You since the Last Crisis, But...*
    y VOYA - v19 - F '97 - p320 [51-250]
Trying to Get the Toothpaste Back into the Tube
    y VOYA - v19 - F '97 - p320 [51-250]
Peterson, Mark - *Complete Entrepreneur*
    CBR - v15 - Spr '97 - p2 [1-50]

Peterson, Melissa - *Hasta La Vista, Blarney! (Illus. by S M Taggart)*
    c BL - v93 - F 1 '97 - p941+ [51-250]
    c SLJ - v43 - F '97 - p83+ [51-250]
Peterson, Michael Todd - *AutoCAD Performance Tuning Toolkit*
    SciTech - v20 - S '96 - p46 [51-250]
Peterson, Paul E - *Classifying by Race*
    APSR - v91 - Mr '97 - p196+ [501+]
The Price of Federalism
    AAPSS-A - v546 - Jl '96 - p172+ [501+]
    AJS - v102 - Jl '96 - p290+ [501+]
    J Pol - v58 - N '96 - p1226+ [501+]
Peterson, Peter G - *Will America Grow Up before It Grows Old?*
    Barron's - v76 - D 23 '96 - p51 [501+]
    BL - v93 - S 15 '96 - p190+ [51-250]
    BW - v26 - N 17 '96 - p11 [251-500]
    KR - v64 - Ag 15 '96 - p1219+ [251-500]
    NYRB - v43 - D 19 '96 - p68+ [501+]
    NYTBR - v101 - O 20 '96 - p12 [501+]
    NYTBR - v101 - D 8 '96 - p94 [1-50]
    NYTLa - v146 - N 7 '96 - pC26 [501+]
    Reason - v28 - Mr '97 - p60+ [501+]
    W&I - v15 - Mr '97 - p277+ [501+]
    WSJ-MW - v78 - O 16 '96 - pA18 [501+]
Peterson, Rai - *The Writing Teacher's Companion*
    Col Comp - v47 - O '96 - p441 [51-250]
Peterson, Richard T - *Democratic Philosophy and the Politics of Knowledge*
    Choice - v34 - Ap '97 - p1352+ [51-250]
Peterson, Robert W - *Pigskin: The Early Years of Pro Football*
    Ant R - v55 - Spr '97 - p240+ [251-500]
    BL - v93 - N 15 '96 - p565 [51-250]
    Choice - v34 - Ap '97 - p1378 [51-250]
    KR - v64 - O 15 '96 - p1516 [251-500]
    PW - v243 - N 11 '96 - p66+ [51-250]
Peterson, Roger Tory - *Birds of Britain and Europe*
    Wildbird - v10 - N '96 - p49 [51-250]
A Field Guide to the Birds. Commemorative Ed.
    r Sci - v274 - D 13 '96 - p1848 [1-50]
    r Wildbird - v11 - F '97 - p39 [51-250]
Mexican Birds
    Wildbird - v10 - N '96 - p49 [51-250]
Roger Tory Peterson's ABC of Birds (Illus. by Roger Tory Peterson)
    c HB Guide - v7 - Fall '96 - p344 [51-250]
Peterson, Rolf O - *The Wolves of Isle Royale*
    SciTech - v20 - S '96 - p21 [51-250]
Peterson, Shelley - *Dancer*
    y Quill & Q - v62 - D '96 - p40 [251-500]
Peterson, Susan, 1961- - *Crisis Bargaining and the State*
    Choice - v34 - N '96 - p533 [51-250]
Peterson, Susan Harnly - *The Craft and Art of Clay*
    R&R Bk N - v12 - F '97 - p22 [51-250]
Peterson, T Sarah - *Acquired Taste*
    FR - v70 - Mr '97 - p623+ [501+]
Peterson, Tracie - *Entangled*
    LJ - v122 - F 1 '97 - p68 [51-250]
Peterson, V Spike - *Global Gender Issues*
    Signs - v22 - Win '97 - p466+ [501+]
Peterson, Walt - *Exploring Baja by RV*
    BWatch - v17 - N '96 - p12 [51-250]
Peterson-Fleming, Judy - *Kitten Training and Critters, Too! (Illus. by Darryl Bush)*
    c HB Guide - v7 - Fall '96 - p346 [51-250]
Puppy Training and Critters, Too! (Illus. by Darryl Bush)
    c HB Guide - v7 - Fall '96 - p346 [51-250]
Peterson's Distance Learning 1997
    r ARBA - v28 - '97 - p134 [251-500]
    r BL - v93 - Mr 1 '97 - p1195+ [251-500]
    yr Kliatt - v31 - Ja '97 - p20 [51-250]
Peterson's Internships 1996
    r ARBA - v28 - '97 - p119+ [251-500]
Peterson's Paying Less for College 1996
    yr RQ - v35 - Sum '96 - p567+ [251-500]
Peterson's Study Abroad 1996
    yr RQ - v36 - Win '96 - p305+ [501+]
Peterson's Summer Opportunities for Kids and Teenagers 1996
    r ARBA - v28 - '97 - p83 [251-500]
Peterson's Top Colleges for Science. 1st Ed.
    r ARBA - v28 - '97 - p141+ [251-500]
    yr Choice - v34 - S '96 - p104 [51-250]
Petersson, Irmtraud - *And What Books Do You Read?*
    Aust Bk R - N '96 - p42+ [501+]

Petesch, Natalie L M - *The Immigrant Train and Other Stories*
    y Kliatt - v31 - Ja '97 - p17 [251-500]
    LATBR - v263 - S 29 '96 - p14 [51-250]
    NYTBR - v101 - D 22 '96 - p15 [251-500]
Petit, Chris - *The Psalm Killer*
    BL - v93 - Mr 1 '97 - p1069 [251-500]
    KR - v65 - Mr 1 '97 - p331 [251-500]
    LJ - v122 - Ap 1 '97 - p130 [51-250]
    PW - v244 - Mr 17 '97 - p78 [51-250]
    Spec - v277 - N 30 '96 - p52+ [501+]
    TLS - D 6 '96 - p22 [501+]
    Trib Bks - Ap 20 '97 - p7 [51-250]
Petit, Marc - *Le Troisieme Faust*
    FR - v70 - O '96 - p148+ [251-500]
Petitfils, Jean-Christian - *Louis XIV*
    Choice - v34 - D '96 - p567 [1-50]
Petit-Jean, Michele - *Baby Earth*
    c HB Guide - v7 - Fall '96 - p271 [1-50]
Petkov, Steven - *The Frank Sinatra Reader*
    Ant R - v54 - Sum '96 - p373 [251-500]
    J Am St - v30 - D '96 - p491+ [251-500]
Petkovic, Danielle - *Know Life*
    Aust Bk R - Jl '96 - p67 [51-250]
Petkovsek, Marko - *A=B*
    Choice - v34 - N '96 - p495 [51-250]
Petra, Basilio - *Il Matrimonio Puo Morire?*
    Theol St - v58 - Mr '97 - p201 [251-500]
Petraglia, Joseph - *Reconceiving Writing, Rethinking Writing Instruction*
    Col Comp - v47 - O '96 - p441 [51-250]
Petrarca, Francesco - *The Canzoniere or Rerum Vulgarium Fragmenta*
    TranslRevS - v2 - D '96 - p28 [51-250]
Letters of Old Age. Vols. 1-2
    Ren Q - v49 - Win '96 - p900+ [501+]
Petrarch: The Canzoniere
    Choice - v34 - N '96 - p464 [51-250]
Petrarch's Songbook
    Choice - v34 - S '96 - p133 [51-250]
Petras, James - *Empire or Republic*
    CS - v25 - S '96 - p608+ [501+]
Petrie, A Roy - *Alexander Graham Bell*
    c Can CL - v22 - Fall '96 - p106+ [251-500]
Petrie, Duncan - *The British Cinematographer*
    Choice - v34 - Mr '97 - p1170 [51-250]
Petrie, Glen - *Lucy and the Pirates (Illus. by Matilda Harrison)*
    c TES - Jl 5 '96 - pR2 [501+]
Petrie, Pat - *Communicating with Children and Adults*
    TES - Mr 28 '97 - p7* [51-250]
Petrinovich, Lewis - *Living and Dying Well*
    Choice - v34 - N '96 - p494 [51-250]
Petro, Nicolai N - *The Rebirth of Russian Democracy*
    APSR - v90 - S '96 - p680+ [501+]
Petro, Patrice - *Fugitive Images*
    Afterimage - v24 - S '96 - p14 [501+]
Petrobelli, Pierluigi - *Music in the Theater*
    Notes - v53 - D '96 - p433+ [501+]
Petroff, Elizabeth Alvilda - *Body and Soul*
    JWomHist - v8 - Fall '96 - p228+ [501+]
Petrone, Gerard S - *Tobacco Advertising*
    Ant & CM - v101 - N '96 - p32 [51-250]
    BW - v26 - S 8 '96 - p13 [51-250]
Petronius Arbiter - *Satyrica (Branham)*
    Class Out - v74 - Win '97 - p81+ [501+]
    New R - v215 - O 28 '96 - p42+ [501+]
    TranslRevS - v2 - D '96 - p29 [51-250]
The Satyricon (Walsh)
    Choice - v34 - D '96 - p610 [51-250]
    New R - v215 - O 28 '96 - p42+ [501+]
    VQR - v73 - Win '97 - p23* [51-250]
Petropoulos, J C B - *Heat and Lust*
    CW - v90 - S '96 - p61+ [251-500]
Petropoulos, Jonathan - *Art as Politics in the Third Reich*
    CS - v26 - Ja '97 - p101+ [501+]
    HRNB - v25 - Fall '96 - p32+ [251-500]
Petroski, Catherine - *A Bride's Passage*
    KR - v64 - D 1 '96 - p1723 [251-500]
    LJ - v122 - F 15 '97 - p142 [51-250]
    PW - v243 - D 9 '96 - p52 [51-250]
Petroski, Henry - *Engineers of Dreams*
    BW - v26 - D 1 '96 - p12 [51-250]
    NYTBR - v102 - F 9 '97 - p32 [1-50]
    PW - v243 - O 7 '96 - p69 [1-50]
    RAH - v24 - S '96 - p437+ [501+]
    Trib Bks - F 23 '97 - p8 [1-50]
The Evolution of Useful Things
    Reason - v28 - D '96 - p41+ [51-250]

Invention by Design
  BW - v26 - D 29 '96 - p8 [51-250]
  KR - v64 - S 15 '96 - p1382+ [251-500]
  Nature - v386 - Mr 27 '97 - p347 [501+]
  New Sci - v153 - Ja 4 '97 - p38 [251-500]
  NH - v105 - N '96 - p16 [1-50]
  PW - v243 - S 30 '96 - p69 [51-250]
  R&R Bk N - v12 - F '97 - p97 [51-250]
  Sci - v274 - D 13 '96 - p1848 [1-50]
Petrov, Valentin V - *Limit Theorems of Probability Theory*
  r SIAM Rev - v38 - S '96 - p527 [251-500]
Petrow, Stefan - *Policing Morals*
  EHR - v111 - S '96 - p1009+ [251-500]
  VS - v39 - Aut '95 - p99+ [501+]
Petrucha, Stefan - *The X-Files Collection. Vol. 1*
  yp VOYA - v19 - O '96 - p203+ [251-500]
Petrusewicz, Marta - *Latifundium: Moral Economy and Material Life in a European Periphery*
  Choice - v34 - Ap '97 - p1398 [51-250]
Petrushevskaya, Ludmilla - *Immortal Love*
  Nat - v262 - Je 10 '96 - p32 [251-500]
Petry, Carl F - *Protectors or Praetorians?*
  AHR - v101 - O '96 - p1256 [501+]
  Twilight of Majesty
  Specu - v71 - Jl '96 - p754+ [501+]
Pets (Time-Life)
  c HB Guide - v8 - Spr '97 - p128 [51-250]
Petsonk, Judy - *Taking Judaism Personally*
  BL - v93 - S 1 '96 - p39 [51-250]
Pettas, William - *A Sixteenth-Century Spanish Bookstore*
  Six Ct J - v27 - Fall '96 - p791+ [501+]
Pettegree, Andrew - *Calvinism in Europe 1540-1620*
  HT - v46 - Jl '96 - p50+ [501+]
  JMH - v68 - S '96 - p660+ [501+]
  Ren Q - v50 - Spr '97 - p302+ [501+]
  Six Ct J - v27 - Win '96 - p1107+ [501+]
Petti, Maria Rosario - *Luci Del Nord*
  BL - v93 - D 1 '96 - p644 [1-50]
Pettifer, Adrian - *English Castles*
  r ARBA - v28 - '97 - p180 [51-250]
Pettigrew, Jane - *The Tea Companion*
  r BL - v93 - My 15 '97 - p1554 [51-250]
Pettipas, Katherine - *Severing the Ties That Bind*
  Can Hist R - v78 - Mr '97 - p171+ [501+]
Pettis, Joyce - *Toward Wholeness in Paule Marshall's Fiction*
  AL - v68 - D '96 - p872+ [501+]
Pettit, Jayne - *Maya Angelou: Journey of the Heart*
  c HB Guide - v7 - Fall '96 - p374 [51-250]
  c RT - v50 - Ap '97 - p588 [51-250]
  A Time to Fight Back
  c HB Guide - v7 - Fall '96 - p380+ [51-250]
Pettit, Thomas - *Custom, Culture and Community in the Later Middle Ages*
  MLR - v92 - Ja '97 - p172+ [501+]
Pettiway, Leon E - *Honey, Honey, Miss Thang*
  PW - v243 - O 14 '96 - p78 [51-250]
Pettman, Jan Jindy - *Worlding Women*
  Aust Bk R - S '96 - p16+ [501+]
Petts, Geoffrey - *River Biota*
  SciTech - v20 - N '96 - p29 [51-250]
  River Flows and Channel Forms
  SciTech - v20 - D '96 - p2 [51-250]
  River Restoration
  SciTech - v20 - D '96 - p68 [51-250]
Petty, Kate - *The Great Grammar Book (Illus. by Jennie Maizels)*
  c Bks Keeps - Ja '97 - p23 [51-250]
  c JB - v60 - D '96 - p257+ [51-250]
  c Spec - v277 - D 14 '96 - p77 [51-250]
  c TES - N 22 '96 - p12* [51-250]
  Rosie Plants a Radish (Illus. by Axel Scheffler)
  c Books - v11 - Ap '97 - p24 [51-250]
  c Obs - Mr 30 '97 - p17* [51-250]
  Sam Plants a Sunflower (Illus. by Axel Scheffler)
  c Books - v11 - Ap '97 - p24 [51-250]
Petty, Michael W - *A Faith That Loves the Earth*
  Choice - v34 - Ap '97 - p1356+ [51-250]
Petzinger, Thomas, Jr. - *Hard Landing*
  NYTBR - v101 - D 8 '96 - p87+ [1-50]
  NYTBR - v102 - F 16 '97 - p32 [1-50]
Petzold, Charles - *Programming Windows 95. 4th Ed.*
  CBR - v14 - Jl '96 - p23 [1-50]
  SciTech - v20 - N '96 - p10 [51-250]
Peucker, Brigitte - *Incorporating Images*
  FQ - v50 - Win '96 - p52+ [501+]
Peurifoy, Reneau - *Overcoming Anxiety*
  PW - v244 - Ja 6 '97 - p71 [51-250]

Peurifoy, Robert L - *Formwork for Concrete Structures. 3rd Ed.*
  SciTech - v20 - S '96 - p50 [51-250]
Pevere, Geoff - *Mondo Canuck*
  y Emerg Lib - v24 - Mr '97 - p28 [1-50]
  Mac - v109 - D 9 '96 - p64 [1-50]
  Quill & Q - v62 - N '96 - p40 [251-500]
Pevsner, Stella - *Would My Fortune Cookie Lie?*
  c HB Guide - v7 - Fall '96 - p296 [51-250]
Pew, John A - *Instant Java*
  CBR - v14 - Jl '96 - p21 [51-250]
  SciTech - v20 - S '96 - p5 [51-250]
  Instant Java. 2nd Ed.
  SciTech - v21 - Mr '97 - p7 [51-250]
Pewsey, Elizabeth - *The Talking Head*
  y Sch Lib - v44 - N '96 - p171 [51-250]
Peynaud, Emile - *The Taste of Wine. 2nd Ed.*
  LJ - v122 - Ap 1 '97 - p62 [1-50]
Peyser, Joseph L - *Jacques Legardeur De Saint-Pierre: Officer, Gentleman, Entrepreneur*
  Choice - v34 - F '97 - p1024+ [51-250]
Peyton, K M - *The Swallow Summer (Illus. by K M Peyton)*
  c Sch Lib - v44 - Ag '96 - p108 [51-250]
  The Swallow Tale
  c Magpies - v11 - S '96 - p45 [1-50]
Pezdek, Kathy - *The Recovered Memory/False Memory Debate*
  SciTech - v20 - D '96 - p44 [1-50]
Pezeshkzad, Iraj - *My Uncle Napoleon*
  Atl - v278 - Ag '96 - p93 [251-500]
  BW - v26 - S 29 '96 - p4 [501+]
  Choice - v34 - Ja '97 - p789 [51-250]
  CSM - v89 - F 12 '97 - p12 [501+]
  TLS - N 1 '96 - p25 [501+]
  TranslRevS - v2 - D '96 - p29 [51-250]
  WLT - v71 - Win '97 - p217 [251-500]
Pfaelzer, Jean - *Parlor Radical*
  LJ - v121 - D '96 - p118+ [51-250]
Pfaffenberger, Bryan - *Netscape Navigator 3.0, Macintosh*
  CBR - v14 - N '96 - p36 [1-50]
  Netscape Navigator 3.0, Windows
  CBR - v14 - N '96 - p36 [51-250]
  Official Microsoft Internet Explorer Book
  CBR - v15 - Spr '97 - p7 [1-50]
  Publish It on the Web
  CBR - v14 - N '96 - p36 [51-250]
  Web Search Strategies
  BL - v93 - S 15 '96 - p193 [501+]
  World Wide Web Bible. 2nd Ed.
  CBR - v14 - S '96 - p30 [1-50]
  CBR - v14 - N '96 - p37 [51-250]
  Quill & Q - v62 - N '96 - p32 [51-250]
Pfanzagl, Johann - *Parametric Statistical Theory*
  SIAM Rev - v38 - S '96 - p527+ [501+]
Pfeffer, Cynthia R - *Severe Stress and Mental Disturbance in Children*
  Readings - v11 - S '96 - p27 [51-250]
Pfeffer, Paula F - *A. Philip Randolph, Pioneer of the Civil Rights Movement*
  Am Vis - v12 - F '97 - p26 [51-250]
Pfeffer, Susan Beth - *Justice for Emily*
  c BL - v93 - Ja '97 - p862 [251-500]
  c KR - v64 - D 15 '96 - p1802+ [51-250]
  c PW - v244 - Ja 6 '97 - p74 [1-50]
  c SLJ - v43 - F '97 - p104 [51-250]
  The Pizza Puzzle
  c BL - v93 - O 1 '96 - p352 [51-250]
  c HB Guide - v8 - Spr '97 - p73 [51-250]
  c SLJ - v42 - S '96 - p206 [51-250]
  The Trouble with Wishes (Illus. by Jennifer Plecas)
  c Emerg Lib - v24 - S '96 - p51+ [51-250]
  c HB Guide - v7 - Fall '96 - p287 [51-250]
  c Par Ch - v20 - O '96 - p11 [1-50]
  Twice Taken
  y Kliatt - v30 - S '96 - p13 [51-250]
Pfeffer, Wendy - *Mute Swans (Illus. by Wendy Pfeffer)*
  c HB Guide - v8 - Spr '97 - p125 [51-250]
  c KR - v64 - N 1 '96 - p1605 [51-250]
  c SLJ - v43 - F '97 - p95 [51-250]
  Polar Bears
  c BL - v92 - Ag '96 - p1903 [51-250]
  c CCB-B - v50 - O '96 - p72 [51-250]
  c HB Guide - v8 - Spr '97 - p128 [51-250]
  c SLJ - v42 - S '96 - p199+ [51-250]
  What's It like to Be a Fish? (Illus. by Holly Keller)
  c HB Guide - v7 - Fall '96 - p343 [51-250]
Pfeifer, Gerd P - *Technologies for Detection of DNA Damage and Mutations*
  SciTech - v20 - N '96 - p27 [51-250]

Pfeiffer, Friedrich - *Multibody Dynamics with Unilateral Contacts*
  SciTech - v20 - N '96 - p69 [51-250]
Pfeiffer, Steven I - *Outcome Assessment in Residential Treatment*
  SciTech - v20 - N '96 - p52 [51-250]
Pfiffner, George - *Earth-Friendly Outdoor Fun*
  c SB - v32 - O '96 - p207 [51-250]
Pfiffner, James P - *The Strategic Presidency. 2nd Ed., Rev.*
  Choice - v34 - Ja '97 - p876 [51-250]
Pfister, Joel - *Inventing the Psychological*
  LJ - v122 - F 15 '97 - p150 [51-250]
  Staging Depth
  MLR - v91 - O '96 - p985+ [501+]
Pfister, Marcus - *Hopper's Treetop Adventure (Illus. by Marcus Pfister)*
  c BL - v93 - Ap 1 '97 - p1338 [51-250]
  c KR - v65 - F 1 '97 - p226 [51-250]
  c SLJ - v43 - Mr '97 - p163 [51-250]
  I See the Moon (Illus. by Marcus Pfister)
  c JB - v60 - Ag '96 - p143 [51-250]
  Penguin Pete (Illus. by Marcus Pfister)
  c PW - v244 - Ja 27 '97 - p108 [1-50]
  Penguin Pete's New Friends (Illus. by Marcus Pfister)
  c PW - v244 - Ja 27 '97 - p108 [1-50]
  El Pez Arco Iris (Illus. by Marcus Pfister)
  c HB Guide - v8 - Spr '97 - p108 [51-250]
  El Pez Arco Iris Al Rescate! (Illus. by Marcus Pfister)
  c HB Guide - v8 - Spr '97 - p108 [51-250]
  El Pinguino Pedro (Illus. by Marcus Pfister)
  c HB Guide - v8 - Spr '97 - p108 [1-50]
  El Pinguino Pedro Y Sus Nuevos Amigos (Illus. by Marcus Pfister)
  c BL - v93 - My 1 '97 - p1507 [1-50]
  The Rainbow Fish
  c HB Guide - v7 - Fall '96 - p242 [1-50]
  Rainbow Fish to the Rescue! (Illus. by Marcus Pfister)
  c RT - v50 - O '96 - p135 [1-50]
  Saltarin (Illus. by Marcus Pfister)
  c SLJ - v42 - N '96 - p134 [51-250]
  Wake Up, Santa Claus! (Illus. by Marcus Pfister)
  c HB Guide - v8 - Spr '97 - p42 [51-250]
  c KR - v64 - Ag 15 '96 - p1246 [51-250]
  c PW - v243 - S 30 '96 - p91 [51-250]
  c SLJ - v42 - O '96 - p39 [51-250]
Pfleeger, Charles P - *Security in Computing. 2nd Ed.*
  SciTech - v20 - D '96 - p14 [51-250]
Pflueger, Lynda - *Stonewall Jackson*
  y KR - v64 - D 1 '96 - p1740 [51-250]
Pflug, Georg Ch. - *Optimization of Stochastic Models*
  SciTech - v21 - Mr '97 - p71 [51-250]
Pham, Cong Thien - *Triet Ly Ve Su Vuot Bien*
  BL - v93 - S 1 '96 - p70 [51-250]
Pham, Kim Vinh - *Viet Nam Theo Duong Nao Vao The Ky 21?*
  BL - v93 - S 1 '96 - p70 [51-250]
Pham, Quoc Bao - *Dau Vet Van Hoa Viet Nam Tren Bac My. Vols. 1-2*
  BL - v93 - S 1 '96 - p70 [51-250]
Pham, The Ngu - *Viet Nam Van Hoc Su Viet Van*
  BL - v93 - S 1 '96 - p70 [51-250]
Pham, Thi Hoai - *Marie Sen*
  BL - v93 - My 15 '97 - p1568 [1-50]
Pham, Xuan Dai - *Ha Noi Trong Mat Toi*
  BL - v93 - S 1 '96 - p70 [51-250]
Phan, Lac Tiep - *Que Nha Bon Muoi Nam Tro Lai*
  BL - v93 - S 1 '96 - p70 [51-250]
Phan, Nhat Nam - *Nhung Truyen Can Duoc Ke Lai*
  BL - v93 - S 1 '96 - p70 [51-250]
Pharmaceutical News
  p Nature - v383 - S 5 '96 - p38+ [251-500]
PharmFacts for Nurses
  r ARBA - v28 - '97 - p618 [51-250]
Phase Equilibria Diagrams. Vol. 12
  SciTech - v21 - Mr '97 - p91 [51-250]
Phelan, Carolyn - *Science Books for Young People*
  r SLJ - v42 - D '96 - p48 [1-50]
Phelan, Craig - *Divided Loyalties*
  ILRR - v50 - O '96 - p181+ [501+]
Phelan, James - *Narrative as Rhetoric*
  VQR - v73 - Win '97 - p12* [51-250]
Phelan, Nancy - *Pieces of Heaven*
  Aust Bk R - S '96 - p23 [501+]
  BWatch - v17 - N '96 - p9 [51-250]
Phelan, Patricia - *High Interest-Easy Reading. 7th Ed.*
  r CCB-B - v50 - D '96 - p156 [51-250]
  r New Ad - v9 - Fall '96 - p348 [51-250]
Phelan, Peter - *Argument and Evidence*
  JEL - v34 - D '96 - p2017 [51-250]

Phelan, Shane - *Getting Specific*
  J Pol - v58 - Ag '96 - p890+ [501+]
Phelan, Tom - *In the Season of the Daisies*
  KR - v64 - S 15 '96 - p1348 [251-500]
  LJ - v121 - O 1 '96 - p128 [51-250]
  PW - v243 - S 30 '96 - p61 [51-250]
Phelps, Susan - *A Lady without a Latitude*
  PW - v243 - D 30 '96 - p51 [51-250]
Phelts, Marsha Dean - *An American Beach for African Americans*
  PW - v244 - Ap 21 '97 - p51 [51-250]
Phenix, Katharine Joan - *Subject Guide to Women of the World*
  r ARBA - v28 - '97 - p339 [251-500]
Philabaum, Dabney Miller - *Ocean Buddies (Illus. by Dabney Miller Philabaum)*
  c SLJ - v43 - Mr '97 - p180 [51-250]
Philadelphia Mental Health and Mental Retardation Program
  J Gov Info - v23 - S '96 - p605 [51-250]
The Philatelic Exporter
  p Am Phil - v110 - S '96 - p829 [51-250]
Philbin, Regis - *I'm Only One Man*
  Ent W - S 6 '96 - p71 [1-50]
Philbin, Tobias R, III - *The Lure of Neptune*
  Slav R - v55 - Fall '96 - p695+ [501+]
Philbrick, Rodman - *The Fire Pony*
  y Emerg Lib - v24 - S '96 - p54 [51-250]
  o HB Guide - v7 - Fall '96 - p296 [51 250]
  y JAAL - v40 - N '96 - p231 [51-250]
  c SLJ - v42 - S '96 - p206 [51-250]
  y VOYA - v19 - O '96 - p212 [251-500]
Philip, Marlene Nourbese - *Frontiers: Essays and Writings on Racism and Culture*
  Can Lit - Win '96 - p129+ [501+]
Philip, Neil - *The Adventures of Odysseus (Illus. by Peter Malone)*
  c KR - v65 - F 1 '97 - p227 [51-250]
  c PW - v244 - Mr 17 '97 - p85 [1-50]
  c Sch Lib - v45 - F '97 - p34 [51-250]
  c TES - N 15 '96 - p7* [51-250]
  American Fairy Tales (Illus. by Michael McCurdy)
  y BL - v93 - D 15 '96 - p721 [51-250]
  y CCB-B - v50 - S '96 - p3+ [501+]
  c Ch BWatch - v7 - F '97 - p3 [1-50]
  c HB - v73 - Ja '97 - p66+ [51-250]
  c HB Guide - v8 - Spr '97 - p74 [51-250]
  c KR - v64 - N 1 '96 - p1606 [51-250]
  c PW - v243 - N 25 '96 - p76 [51-250]
  c SLJ - v42 - N '96 - p117 [51-250]
  Christmas Fairy Tales (Illus. by Isabelle Brent)
  c BL - v93 - S 1 '96 - p134 [51-250]
  c HB Guide - v8 - Spr '97 - p148 [51-250]
  c JB - v60 - D '96 - p258 [51-250]
  c PW - v243 - S 30 '96 - p88 [51-250]
  c SLJ - v42 - O '96 - p39 [51-250]
  Earth Always Endures (Illus. by Edward S Curtis)
  c BL - v93 - O 1 '96 - p346 [51-250]
  c BL - v93 - Ap 1 '97 - p1305+ [1-50]
  c HB Guide - v8 - Spr '97 - p150+ [51-250]
  c KR - v64 - O 15 '96 - p1537 [51-250]
  y SLJ - v42 - N '96 - p130 [51-250]
  The Golden Bird (Illus. by Isabelle Brent)
  c CLW - v67 - Mr '97 - p51 [51-250]
  c HB Guide - v7 - Fall '96 - p321 [51-250]
  c JB - v60 - Ag '96 - p142 [51-250]
  The Illustrated Book of Myths, Tales and Legends of the World (Illus. by Nilesh Mistry)
  c ILN - Christmas '96 - p88 [1-50]
  c Magpies - v11 - Jl '96 - p41+ [251-500]
  The New Oxford Book of Children's Verse
  c AB - v98 - N 18 '96 - p1732+ [251-500]
  c Bks Keeps - Ja '97 - p17+ [501+]
  c Choice - v34 - Mr '97 - p1156 [51-250]
  c JB - v60 - D '96 - p273 [51-250]
  c Sch Lib - v45 - F '97 - p43 [251-500]
  c Spec - v277 - D 14 '96 - p77 [51-250]
  c TES - N 8 '96 - p9*+ [501+]
  Odin's Family (Illus. by Maryclare Foa)
  c CCB-B - v50 - O '96 - p73 [51-250]
  c HB Guide - v8 - Spr '97 - p104 [51-250]
  c PW - v243 - S 9 '96 - p85 [51-250]
  c SLJ - v42 - N '96 - p117+ [51-250]
  The Penguin Book of Scottish Folktales
  y Kliatt - v31 - Ja '97 - p18 [51-250]
  Poems for Christmas (Illus. by John Lawrence)
  c Bks Keeps - N '96 - p24 [51-250]
  Robin Hood (Illus. by Nick Harris)
  c PW - v244 - My 12 '97 - p77 [51-250]
Philip Larkin and His Bibliographer
  BC - v45 - Aut '96 - p386 [51-250]

Philippart, Guy - *Hagiographies: Histoire Internationale De La Litterature Hagiographique Latine Et Vernaculaire En Occident Des Origines A 1550. Vol. 1*
  EHR - v112 - Ap '97 - p457+ [501+]
  Specu - v71 - O '96 - p996+ [501+]
Philippe, Daniel - *France from the Air*
  PW - v244 - Mr 3 '97 - p61 [51-250]
Phillips, Adam - *Monogamy*
  BW - v27 - F 9 '97 - p6 [501+]
  NS - v125 - S 20 '96 - p47+ [501+]
  Obs - S 1 '96 - p18* [501+]
  Obs - D 1 '96 - p16* [1-50]
  Obs - D 1 '96 - p17* [1-50]
  PW - v243 - N 4 '96 - p58 [51-250]
  TLS - S 27 '96 - p28 [501+]
  On Flirtation
  NYTBR - v101 - S 8 '96 - p36 [1-50]
  Terrors and Experts
  Lon R Bks - v19 - F 20 '97 - p9+ [501+]
  TES - Mr 14 '97 - p8* [501+]
Phillips, Anne - *The Politics of Presence*
  AAPSS-A - v550 - Mr '97 - p176+ [501+]
Phillips, C B - *A Regional History of England*
  EHR - v111 - My '96 - p997+ [251-500]
Phillips, Caryl - *The Nature of Blood*
  BL - v93 - Mr 15 '97 - p1204+ [51-250]
  Books - v11 - Ap '97 - p22 [51-250]
  LJ - v122 - Ap 15 '97 - p120 [51-250]
  Obs - Ja 26 '97 - p17* [501+]
  PW - v244 - Mr 24 '97 - p57 [251-500]
  Spec - v278 - F 15 '97 - p31 [501+]
  TES - F 14 '97 - p8* [501+]
  TLS - Ja 31 '97 - p21 [501+]
  WSJ-Cent - v99 - My 21 '97 - pA12 [501+]
Phillips, Charles - *Encyclopedia of the American West. Vols. 1-4*
  r ARBA - v28 - '97 - p191+ [251-500]
  yr BL - v93 - D 1 '96 - p680+ [501+]
  r Choice - v34 - F '97 - p943 [51-250]
  r LJ - v121 - N 1 '96 - p58 [51-250]
  r R&R Bk N - v11 - D '96 - p17 [51-250]
Phillips, D Z - *Can Religion Be Explained Away?*
  R&R Bk N - v12 - F '97 - p8 [51-250]
  Introducing Philosophy
  Rel St - v32 - D '96 - p530 [251-500]
Phillips, David - *Greek Americans*
  yr Ch BWatch - v6 - O '96 - p5 [51-250]
  c HB Guide - v7 - Fall '96 - p312 [51-250]
Phillips, Edward, 1931- - *The Mice Will Play*
  BIC - v26 - F '97 - p16 [501+]
  Quill & Q - v62 - S '96 - p65 [251-500]
Phillips, Ellen - *The VIII Olympiad*
  Choice - v34 - F '97 - p1002+ [501+]
Phillips, Faye - *Congressional Papers Management*
  LJ - v122 - Ja '97 - p156 [51-250]
Phillips, Gary W - *Technical Issues in Large-Scale Performance Assessment*
  SLMQ - v25 - Fall '96 - p62 [51-250]
Phillips, George Harwood - *Indians and Indian Agents*
  Choice - v34 - My '97 - p1564 [51-250]
Phillips, Graham - *The Shakespeare Conspiracy*
  HT - v46 - Jl '96 - p53 [501+]
Phillips, Henry - *Racine: Language and Theatre*
  MLR - v91 - Jl '96 - p725+ [501+]
Phillips, Jack J - *Accountability in Human Resource Management*
  HR Mag - v41 - O '96 - p147 [501+]
  Per Psy - v50 - Spr '97 - p245+ [501+]
Phillips, Jan - *Math Solutions*
  Math T - v89 - My '96 - p516 [51-250]
Phillips, Jan, 1949- - *Born Gay*
  Wom R Bks - v14 - Mr '97 - p6+ [501+]
Phillips, Jane - *The Magic Daughter*
  y Kliatt - v31 - Ja '97 - p22 [51-250]
  PW - v243 - S 2 '96 - p122 [1-50]
Phillips, Jim - *Essays in the History of Canadian Law. Vol. 5*
  Can Hist R - v78 - Mr '97 - p183+ [501+]
Phillips, Jo - *Poems Deep and Dangerous*
  c Sch Lib - v44 - Ag '96 - p116 [51-250]
  y TES - S 20 '96 - pR6 [501+]
Phillips, John, 1914-1996 - *Free Spirit in a Troubled World*
  LJ - v122 - Ap 1 '97 - p90 [51-250]
  NS - v126 - Mr 21 '97 - p54+ [501+]
Phillips, John A, 1949- - *Computing Parliamentary History*
  EHR - v112 - F '97 - p227+ [501+]
Phillips, John L, Jr. - *How to Think about Statistics. 5th Ed.*
  Math T - v89 - My '96 - p436 [251-500]

Phillips, Jonathan - *Defenders of the Holy Land*
  Choice - v34 - Ap '97 - p1398 [251-500]
Phillips, Julia - *Driving under the Affluence*
  Books - v10 - Je '96 - p21 [1-50]
  Ent W - Ja 17 '97 - p59 [51-250]
Phillips, Kate - *White Rabbit*
  Ent W - Ja 10 '97 - p53 [1-50]
  NYTBR - v102 - Mr 16 '97 - p32 [1-50]
  PW - v243 - D 9 '96 - p66 [1-50]
  Trib Bks - Ja 12 '97 - p2 [1-50]
Phillips, Katharine A - *The Broken Mirror*
  SciTech - v21 - Mr '97 - p56 [51-250]
Phillips, Kathryn - *Tracking the Vanishing Frogs*
  Am Sci - v85 - Ja '97 - p81+ [501+]
Phillips, Kathy J - *Virginia Woolf against Empire*
  RMR - v50 - 2 '96 - p169+ [501+]
  TLS - Ag 30 '96 - p6 [501+]
Phillips, Lisa - *Beat Culture and the New America 1950-1965*
  Advocate - O 15 '96 - p77+ [501+]
Phillips, Louis - *263 Brain Busters*
  c BL - v93 - Ap 1 '97 - p1341 [1-50]
  Hot Corner
  Sm Pr R - v28 - N '96 - p9 [501+]
  Keep 'em Laughing (Illus. by Michael Chesworth)
  c HB Guide - v7 - Fall '96 - p358 [51-250]
Phillips, Mark - *Science Fiction Television Series*
  r Choice - v34 - D '96 - p593 [51-250]
  r R&R Bk N - v11 - N '96 - p66 [51 250]
  r VOYA - v19 - F '97 - p365 [251-500]
Phillips, Max - *Snakebite Sonnet*
  NYTBR - v101 - S 15 '96 - p30 [51-250]
  Obs - D 22 '96 - p17* [51-250]
Phillips, Melanie - *All Must Have Prizes*
  CR - v270 - F '97 - p101+ [501+]
  Lon R Bks - v18 - O 3 '96 - p9+ [501+]
  NS - v125 - S 13 '96 - p44+ [501+]
  Obs - S 29 '96 - p16* [501+]
  Spec - v277 - O 12 '96 - p46+ [501+]
  TES - S 13 '96 - p7* [501+]
  TES - D 27 '96 - p17 [1-50]
  TLS - O 25 '96 - p29 [501+]
Phillips, Michael, 1946- - *The Braxtons of Miracle Springs*
  y BL - v93 - S 1 '96 - p65 [501+]
  Mercy and Eagleflight
  BL - v93 - O 1 '96 - p304 [501+]
Phillips, Michael K - *The Wolves of Yellowstone*
  BL - v93 - N 15 '96 - p557 [251-500]
  Choice - v34 - Ap '97 - p1366 [51-250]
  LJ - v122 - Ja '97 - p139 [51-250]
  Trib Bks - Mr 9 '97 - p6+ [501+]
Phillips, Michael R - *A Dangerous Love*
  LJ - v122 - Ap 1 '97 - p80 [51-250]
Phillips, Mike - *An Image to Die For*
  BL - v93 - F 15 '97 - p1007+ [51-250]
  KR - v65 - Ja 15 '97 - p100 [51-250]
  PW - v244 - Ja 20 '97 - p397 [51-250]
Phillips, Mildred - *The Sign in Mendel's Window (Illus. by Margot Zemach)*
  c PW - v243 - N 25 '96 - p78 [1-50]
Phillips, Newk - *The Papers*
  Sm Pr R - v28 - S '96 - p8 [51-250]
Phillips, Patrick - *Ruin*
  PW - v243 - Jl 22 '96 - p238 [1-50]
Phillips, Paul T - *A Kingdom on Earth*
  Choice - v34 - S '96 - p146 [51-250]
  HRNB - v25 - Win '97 - p55+ [501+]
  RAH - v25 - Mr '97 - p82+ [501+]
Phillips, Roger - *Perfect Plants*
  Books - v10 - Je '96 - p21 [1-50]
  A Photographic Garden History
  NYTBR - v101 - D 8 '96 - p42 [51-250]
Phillips, Sandra S - *Crossing the Frontier*
  Choice - v34 - Ap '97 - p1403 [51-250]
  LATBR - D 8 '96 - p5 [51-250]
Phillips, Shelley - *Beyond the Myths*
  KR - v64 - My 1 '96 - p671 [251-500]
Phillips, Stephen H - *Classical Indian Metaphysics*
  IPQ - v37 - Mr '97 - p124 [51-250]
Phillips, Steven - *The Soil Conservation Service Responds to the 1993 Midwest Floods*
  Pub Hist - v18 - Sum '96 - p87+ [501+]
Phillips, Sue - *The Garden Pack*
  PW - v243 - N 4 '96 - p73 [51-250]
  Patio Gardening
  BWatch - v17 - N '96 - p5 [51-250]
Phillips, Susan Elizabeth - *Hot Shot (Fields). Audio Version*
  y Kliatt - v31 - Mr '97 - p42+ [51-250]
  It Had to Be You (Fields). Audio Version
  y Kliatt - v30 - S '96 - p48 [51-250]

Nobody's Baby but Mine
  LJ - v122 - F 15 '97 - p126 [51-250]
Phillips, T J - *Woman in the Dark*
  KR - v64 - D 15 '96 - p1770 [51-250]
  PW - v244 - F 17 '97 - p214 [51-250]
Phillips, Timothy R - *The Nature of Confession*
  Bks & Cult - v2 - Jl '96 - p26+ [501+]
Philo, Chris - *Off the Map*
  GJ - v162 - Jl '96 - p240 [51-250]
Philpot, Lorna - *Anthony Ant's Treasure Hunt (Illus. by Graham Philpot)*
  c JB - v60 - D '96 - p238 [51-250]
Hide and Seek with Anthony Ant
  c HB Guide - v7 - Fall '96 - p242 [51-250]
Out and about with Anthony Ant
  c HB Guide - v7 - Fall '96 - p242 [51-250]
Who's at Home with Anthony Ant?
  c HB Guide - v7 - Fall '96 - p242 [51-250]
Philpott, Don - *St. Lucia*
  r BL - v93 - S 15 '96 - p206 [1-50]
U.S. Virgin Islands
  r BL - v93 - S 15 '96 - p206 [1-50]
Philpott, William James - *Anglo-French Relations and Strategy on the Western Front 1914-18*
  Choice - v34 - N '96 - p520 [51-250]
  J Mil H - v61 - Ap '97 - p389+ [501+]
  R&R Bk N - v11 - N '96 - p10 [51-250]
Phipps, William E - *Muhammad and Jesus*
  Choice - v34 - O '96 - p298 [51-250]
  Rel St Rev - v23 - Ja '97 - p48 [51-250]
Phlips, Louis - *Competition Policy*
  JEL - v34 - D '96 - p2084 [51-250]
Phoenix Irish Short Stories 1996
  TLS - O 25 '96 - p23 [501+]
Phosa, Matthews - *Deur Die Oog Van 'N Naald*
  WLT - v71 - Win '97 - p212 [251-500]
Photo Work: Art and Technique
  p LJ - v121 - N 15 '96 - p94 [51-250]
Photography (Make It Work!)
  c TES - Jl 19 '96 - pR8 [51-250]
Phya Khankhaak, the Toad King
  TranslRevS - v2 - D '96 - p34 [51-250]
Phythian, Mark - *Arming Iraq*
  Choice - v34 - Ap '97 - p1414+ [51-250]
  KR - v64 - O 15 '96 - p1516+ [251-500]
  LJ - v121 - S 15 '96 - p82 [51-250]
Phythian-Adams, Charles - *Societies, Cultures and Kinship 1580-1850*
  J Urban H - v23 - N '96 - p94+ [501+]
Piar, Carlos R - *Jesus and Liberation*
  TT - v53 - Ja '97 - p556+ [501+]
Piasentini, Stefano - *Alla Luce Della Luna*
  EHR - v111 - S '96 - p962+ [251-500]
Piattelli-Palmarini, Massimo - *Inevitable Illusions*
  Nature - v385 - Ja 9 '97 - p130 [1-50]
  New Sci - v152 - N 16 '96 - p46 [51-250]
Piau, J-M - *Rheology for Polymer Melt Processing*
  SciTech - v21 - Mr '97 - p97 [51-250]
Piazza, Donna - *When Love Is Not Enough*
  SciTech - v20 - N '96 - p54 [51-250]
Piazza, Tom - *Setting the Tempo*
  BL - v93 - S 15 '96 - p201 [51-250]
  LJ - v121 - O 1 '96 - p79 [51-250]
  PW - v243 - S 9 '96 - p80 [51-250]
  r Trib Bks - Ja 12 '97 - p8 [501+]
Picano, Felice - *A House on the Ocean, a House on the Bay*
  KR - v65 - F 15 '97 - p282 [251-500]
  PW - v244 - Mr 17 '97 - p70+ [251-500]
Like People in History
  Obs - N 3 '96 - p16* [251-500]
Picard, Elizabeth - *Lebanon: A Shattered Country*
  MEJ - v51 - Win '97 - p127+ [501+]
  TranslRevS - v2 - D '96 - p16 [51-250]
Picard, Robert G - *The Newspaper Publishing Industry*
  Choice - v34 - My '97 - p1489 [51-250]
Picasso's Paintings, Watercolors, Drawings and Sculpture. Vols. 3-4
  r Choice - v34 - O '96 - p269 [51-250]
Picavet, Emmanuel - *Approches Du Concret*
  Choice - v34 - D '96 - p565 [1-50]
Piccioni, Leone - *Profili: Saba, Cardarelli, Ungaretti, Montale*
  WLT - v70 - Sum '96 - p675 [501+]
Picciotto, Linda Pierce - *Student-Led Parent Conferences*
  Cur R - v36 - Ja '97 - p3* [51-250]
Piccirilli, Tom - *Shards*
  PW - v244 - Mr 17 '97 - p81 [1-50]

Piccoli, Sean - *Jimi Hendrix*
  c Ch BWatch - v6 - S '96 - p6 [51-250]
  c HB Guide - v8 - Spr '97 - p156 [51-250]
  y SLJ - v42 - N '96 - p127+ [51-250]
Piccolo, Alessandro - *Humic Substances in Terrestrial Ecosystems*
  SciTech - v20 - D '96 - p56 [51-250]
Pichois, Claude - *Auguste Poulet-Malassis: L'Editeur De Baudelaire*
  TLS - O 4 '96 - p9 [501+]
Pick, Albert - *Standard Catalog of World Paper Money. 7th Ed., Vol. 3*
  r Coin W - v37 - Je 10 '96 - p25 [51-250]
Standard Catalog of World Paper Money. 8th Ed., Vol. 2
  Coin W - v38 - Mr 31 '97 - p26 [51-250]
Pick, Hella - *Simon Wiesenthal: A Life in Search of Justice*
  y BL - v93 - S 15 '96 - p217 [51-250]
  BW - v26 - D 29 '96 - p4 [501+]
  NYTBR - v101 - O 27 '96 - p38 [51-250]
  PW - v243 - S 2 '96 - p104 [51-250]
  TLS - Ag 2 '96 - p9 [501+]
The Pick and Shop Marketplace (Illus. by Fran Thatcher)
  c KR - v64 - S 1 '96 - p1332 [51-250]
Pickard, James D - *North American Shortwave Frequency Guide. Vol. 3*
  r ARBA - v28 - '97 - p354 [251-500]
Pickard, Kate E R - *The Kidnapped and the Ransomed*
  Bl S - v26 - Sum '96 - p67 [51-250]
  TLS - Ag 2 '96 - p32 [51-250]
Pickard, Nancy - *Marriage Is Murder (Bernard). Audio Version*
  BWatch - v18 - Mr '97 - p8+ [1-50]
  y Kliatt - v31 - My '97 - p42 [51-250]
Pickard, Susan - *Living on the Front Line*
  R&R Bk N - v11 - N '96 - p41 [51-250]
Pickelhaupt, Bill - *Shanghaied in San Francisco*
  BWatch - v18 - F '97 - p2 [51-250]
Picken, Joseph C - *Mission Critical*
  Choice - v34 - Mr '97 - p1205 [51-250]
Pickering, Andrew - *The Mangle of Practice*
  AJS - v102 - S '96 - p599+ [501+]
  CS - v25 - N '96 - p809+ [501+]
  Isis - v87 - D '96 - p762+ [501+]
Pickering, Marianne - *Chile: Where the Land Ends*
  c Ch BWatch - v6 - D '96 - p6 [1-50]
  c HB Guide - v8 - Spr '97 - p179 [51-250]
Pickering, Mel - *Picture Reference Atlas*
  cr BL - v93 - D 15 '96 - p749+ [251-500]
  cr Sch Lib - v45 - F '97 - p40 [51-250]
Pickering, Robert - *The People (Illus. by Ted Finger)*
  c HB Guide - v7 - Fall '96 - p333 [51-250]
  c SB - v32 - Ag '96 - p182 [51-250]
Pickering, Sam - *The Blue Caterpillar and Other Essays*
  KR - v65 - Ja 1 '97 - p47 [251-500]
  LJ - v122 - Mr 15 '97 - p64 [51-250]
  PW - v244 - F 10 '97 - p79 [51-250]
Pickersgill, J W - *Seeing Canada Whole*
  Can Hist R - v78 - Mr '97 - p120+ [501+]
Pickett, James Carroll - *Sundays at Seven*
  LATBR - Mr 17 '96 - p11 [51-250]
Pickett, Terry H - *Inventing Nations*
  Choice - v34 - Ja '97 - p873 [51-250]
  R&R Bk N - v11 - N '96 - p47 [51-250]
Pickett, William B - *Dwight D. Eisenhower and American Power*
  J Mil H - v61 - Ja '97 - p196+ [251-500]
Pickle, Linda Schelbitzki - *Contented among Strangers*
  Choice - v34 - N '96 - p527 [51-250]
Pickles, John - *Ground Truth*
  AAAGA - v86 - S '96 - p608+ [501+]
  GJ - v162 - Jl '96 - p241 [51-250]
Pickover, Clifford A - *Black Holes*
  Astron - v24 - N '96 - p100 [251-500]
  S&T - v92 - N '96 - p57 [1-50]
Fractal Horizons
  Choice - v34 - Mr '97 - p1197 [51-250]
  SciTech - v20 - D '96 - p19 [51-250]
The Loom of God
  PW - v244 - Ap 28 '97 - p67 [1-50]
The Pattern Book
  Choice - v34 - O '96 - p318 [51-250]
Pickstone, Charles - *For Fear of the Angels*
  TLS - D 20 '96 - p30 [501+]
Pickvance, Ronald - *Manet*
  BM - v138 - O '96 - p709+ [501+]
Pico, Fernando - *El Dia Menos Pensado*
  HAHR - v76 - Ag '96 - p581 [251-500]

Picon-Parra, Roberto - *Fundadores, Primeros Moradores, Y Familias Coloniales De Merida 1558-1810. Vol. 3*
  HAHR - v77 - My '97 - p316+ [501+]
Picq, Pascal - *Lucy and Her Times*
  y SLJ - v43 - Mr '97 - p201 [51-250]
Picton, John - *The Art of African Textiles*
  Am Craft - v56 - Ag '96 - p26 [1-50]
Picture Word Book
  cr Bks Keeps - v100 - S '96 - p22+ [501+]
Pi De Cabanyes, Oriol - *Pel Bell Nord Glacat*
  WLT - v70 - Sum '96 - p677 [251-500]
Pidgeon, Charles - *Advanced Tutorials for the Biomedical Sciences*
  SciTech - v20 - S '96 - p27 [51-250]
Piehler, G Kurt - *Remembering War the American Way*
  AHR - v101 - D '96 - p1609+ [251-500]
Pienkowski, Jan - *Botticelli's Bed and Breakfast*
  KR - v64 - D 1 '96 - p1728 [51-250]
  PW - v244 - Ja 27 '97 - p93 [51-250]
  y TES - N 8 '96 - p14* [501+]
Pierangelo, Roger - *Parents' Complete Special Education Guide*
  r VOYA - v19 - F '97 - p365 [251-500]
Pierce, Charles - *The Chicken Parts Cookbook*
  LJ - v122 - Mr 15 '97 - p84 [51-250]
Pierce, Constance - *Hope Mills*
  y BL - v93 - Ap 1 '97 - p1282 [51-250]
  KR - v65 - F 15 '97 - p250 [251-500]
  LJ - v122 - Ap 1 '97 - p130 [51-250]
  PW - v244 - F 24 '97 - p64 [51-250]
Pierce, David - *Yeats's Worlds*
  LATBR - Ag 4 '96 - p10 [251-500]
Pierce, Donna - *Spanish New Mexico. Vols. 1-2*
  Am Craft - v57 - F '97 - p50 [51-250]
  LJ - v121 - N 15 '96 - p59+ [51-250]
Pierce, Gregory R - *Handbook of Social Support and the Family*
  Choice - v34 - Ja '97 - p883 [51-250]
  R&R Bk N - v11 - N '96 - p41 [51-250]
Pierce, Jennifer L - *Gender Trials*
  AJS - v102 - N '96 - p886+ [501+]
  CS - v26 - Mr '97 - p136+ [501+]
  SF - v75 - D '96 - p763+ [501+]
  Wom R Bks - v14 - O '96 - p14+ [501+]
Pierce, L D - *Human Prey*
  y Kliatt - v30 - N '96 - p10 [51-250]
Pierce, Meredith Ann - *The Son of Summer Stars*
  y HB Guide - v7 - Fall '96 - p304 [51-250]
Pierce, Olive - *Up River*
  y Kliatt - v31 - Ja '97 - p27 [51-250]
Pierce, Phyllis S - *The Dow Jones Averages 1885-1995*
  r ARBA - v28 - '97 - p91 [251-500]
  R&R Bk N - v11 - N '96 - p37 [51-250]
Pierce, Roy - *Choosing the Chief*
  J Pol - v59 - F '97 - p296+ [501+]
Pierce, Sydney J - *Weeding and Maintenance of Reference Collections*
  LR - v45 - 8 '96 - p42+ [501+]
Pierce, Tamora - *Alanna: The First Adventure*
  c PW - v244 - Mr 10 '97 - p69 [1-50]
Emperor Mage
  y Emerg Lib - v24 - S '96 - p25 [1-50]
In the Hand of the Goddess
  c PW - v244 - Mr 10 '97 - p69 [1-50]
Lioness Rampant
  c PW - v244 - Mr 10 '97 - p69 [1-50]
The Realms of the Gods
  c HB Guide - v8 - Spr '97 - p83 [51-250]
  y Sch Lib - v44 - Ag '96 - p121 [51-250]
  y SLJ - v42 - N '96 - p124 [51-250]
Wild Magic
  y Kliatt - v30 - S '96 - p4 [1-50]
The Woman Who Rides Like a Man
  c PW - v244 - Mr 10 '97 - p69 [1-50]
Piercy, Fred P - *Family Therapy Sourcebook. 2nd Ed.*
  SciTech - v21 - Mr '97 - p54 [51-250]
Piercy, Marge - *City of Darkness, City of Light*
  BL - v93 - O 1 '96 - p292 [51-250]
  KR - v64 - S 15 '96 - p1349 [251-500]
  Ms - v7 - Ja '97 - p81+ [251-500]
  NYTBR - v101 - N 24 '96 - p18 [51-250]
  PW - v243 - S 23 '96 - p54+ [51-250]
  Wom R Bks - v14 - F '97 - p5+ [501+]
What Are Big Girls Made Of?
  BL - v93 - F 1 '97 - p922 [51-250]
  LJ - v122 - F 1 '97 - p84+ [51-250]
  PW - v244 - Ja 27 '97 - p94+ [51-250]
Woman on the Edge of Time
  NWSA Jnl - v9 - Spr '97 - p22+ [501+]
Pieri, Christian - *Land Quality Indicators*
  JEL - v34 - S '96 - p1499 [51-250]

Pieroth, Doris H - *Their Day in the Sun*
  Choice - v34 - My '97 - p1539 [51-250]
  KR - v64 - Ag 15 '96 - p1220 [51-250]
Piers, Helen - *Is There Room on the Bus? (Illus. by Hannah Giffard)*
  c HB Guide - v7 - Fall '96 - p271 [51-250]
  c NW - v128 - D 2 '96 - p84+ [1-50]
  c Sch Lib - v44 - Ag '96 - p100 [51-250]
Piersen, William Dillon - *From Africa to America*
  Choice - v34 - F '97 - p1026 [51-250]
  SE - v61 - Mr '97 - p173+ [51-250]
  VQR - v73 - Win '97 - p9*+ [51-250]
Pierson, Christopher - *Socialism after Communism*
  APSR - v91 - Mr '97 - p221+ [501+]
  Ethics - v107 - Ja '97 - p393 [51-250]
  J Pol - v58 - N '96 - p1243+ [501+]
Pierson, John - *Spike, Mike, Slackers and Dykes*
  BW - v27 - Ja 26 '97 - p12 [51-250]
  Ent W - Ja 31 '97 - p55 [1-50]
  NYTBR - v101 - D 8 '96 - p93 [1-50]
  Obs - Ja 19 '97 - p15* [501+]
  PW - v244 - Ja 27 '97 - p103 [1-50]
Pierson, Melissa Holbrook - *The Perfect Vehicle*
  KR - v65 - F 15 '97 - p282+ [251-500]
  PW - v244 - Mr 10 '97 - p56+ [51-250]
  VV - v42 - Ap 22 '97 - p56 [501+]
Pierson, Paul - *Dismantling the Welfare State?*
  J Pol - v58 - Ag '96 - p917+ [501+]
Picsarskas, Dronius - *Lithuanian Dictionary. English-Lithuanian, Lithuanian-English*
  r ARBA - v28 - '97 - p396 [251-500]
Piesman, Marissa - *Survival Instincts*
  BL - v93 - F 15 '97 - p1008 [51-250]
  KR - v64 - D 1 '96 - p1706 [51-250]
  NYTBR - v102 - Mr 2 '97 - p20 [51-250]
  PW - v244 - Ja 20 '97 - p397+ [51-250]
Pietrangeli, Carlo - *Paintings in the Vatican*
  LJ - v122 - Mr 15 '97 - p62 [51-250]
  Sancta Sanctorum
  BM - v138 - D '96 - p836 [251-500]
Pietroni, Patrick - *The Family Guide to Alternative Health Care*
  Quill & Q - v62 - Ag '96 - p31 [51-250]
Pietropaolo, Laura - *Feminisms in the Cinema*
  Afterimage - v24 - Ja '97 - p23 [1-50]
Pietrusza, David - *The Battle of Waterloo*
  c HB Guide - v7 - Fall '96 - p382 [51-250]
  The Chinese Cultural Revolution
  y BL - v93 - Ja '97 - p836 [251-500]
  y HB Guide - v8 - Spr '97 - p170 [51-250]
  c SLJ - v43 - F '97 - p122+ [51-250]
  John F. Kennedy
  y HB Guide - v8 - Spr '97 - p96 [51-250]
  y SLJ - v43 - Ja '97 - p132 [51-250]
Pietsch, Theodore W - *Fishes, Crayfishes, and Crabs. Vols. 1-2*
  Isis - v87 - S '96 - p554 [251-500]
Pietsch, Ulrich - *Johann Gregorius Horoldt 1696-1775 Und Die Meissener Porzellan-Malerei*
  BM - v138 - O '96 - p705+ [501+]
Piette, John D - *Preventing Illness among People with Coronary Heart Disease*
  SciTech - v21 - Mr '97 - p57 [51-250]
Piglia, Ricardo - *Assumed Name*
  WLT - v70 - Aut '96 - p929 [251-500]
Pigott, Stuart - *Touring in Wine Country*
  r LJ - v122 - Ap 1 '97 - p113 [51-250]
Pike, Christopher - *Phantom*
  y Sch Lib - v45 - F '97 - p49 [51-250]
Pike, David Wingeate - *In the Service of Stalin*
  EHR - v111 - S '96 - p1027 [501+]
  JMH - v68 - D '96 - p1015+ [501+]
Pike, E Holly - *Family and Society in the Works of Elizabeth Gaskell*
  Nine-C Lit - v51 - D '96 - p426 [1-50]
Pike, Fredrick B - *FDR's Good Neighbor Policy*
  HAHR - v76 - N '96 - p840+ [251-500]
  Pres SQ - v26 - Fall '96 - p1171+ [501+]
  SSQ - v77 - D '96 - p938+ [251-500]
Pike, Royston - *Round the Year with the World's Religions*
  r JPC - v29 - Spr '96 - p258+ [51-250]
Pilarczyk, Daniel E - *Lenten Lunches*
  CLW - v67 - D '96 - p54 [51-250]
  RR - v56 - Ja '97 - p105 [51-250]
Pilarczyk, Krystian W - *Offshore Breakwaters and Shore Evolution Control*
  SciTech - v20 - D '96 - p67 [51-250]
Pilbrow, G - *Fetch! (Illus. by G Pilbrow)*
  c JB - v60 - D '96 - p238 [51-250]
Pilcher, Jane - *Thatcher's Children?*
  TES - N 22 '96 - p10* [501+]

Pilcher, Rosamunde - *Coming Home*
  Books - v9 - S '95 - p22 [1-50]
  Books - v10 - S '96 - p17 [51-250]
  Coming Home (Peters). Audio Version
  y Kliatt - v31 - Ja '97 - p38 [51-250]
  The Day of the Storm (Hunter). Audio Version
  y Kliatt - v31 - Ja '97 - p38 [51-250]
  The Day of the Storm (Redgrave). Audio Version
  y Kliatt - v31 - Ja '97 - p38 [51-250]
  The End of Summer (James). Audio Version
  Obs - Ja 12 '97 - p18* [51-250]
Pilcher, V Ennis - *Early Science and the First Century of Physics at Union College 1795-1895*
  Isis - v87 - S '96 - p566+ [51-250]
Pilditch, Jan - *The Critical Response to Katherine Mansfield*
  ELT - v39 - 4 '96 - p529 [51-250]
Pile, Steve - *The Body and the City*
  R&R Bk N - v12 - F '97 - p5 [51-250]
Pileggi, Nicholas - *Casino*
  Si & So - v6 - N '96 - p36 [51-250]
Pilger, Mary Anne - *Science Experiments Index for Young People. 2nd Ed.*
  cr ARBA - v28 - '97 - p566 [51-250]
  cr BL - v93 - N 1 '96 - p540 [51-250]
  r R&R Bk N - v11 - D '96 - p67 [51-250]
  r VOYA - v19 - F '97 - p365 [251-500]
Pilgrim, Aubrey - *Build Your Own Multimedia PC. 2nd Ed.*
  CBR - v14 - Jl '96 - p20 [1-50]
  Build Your Own Pentium Processor PC. 2nd Ed.
  CBR - v14 - Jl '96 - p20 [1-50]
Pilhofer, Peter - *Philippi. Vol. 1*
  Rel St Rev - v23 - Ja '97 - p74 [51-250]
Pilipp, Frank - *New Critical Perspectives on Martin Walser*
  MLR - v92 - Ap '97 - p535+ [501+]
Pilkey, Dav - *Big Dog and Little Dog (Illus. by Dav Pilkey)*
  c PW - v244 - F 10 '97 - p85 [51-250]
  Big Dog and Little Dog Going for a Walk (Illus. by Dav Pilkey)
  c PW - v244 - F 10 '97 - p85 [51-250]
  Dog Breath
  c Bks Keeps - N '96 - p9 [51-250]
  God Bless the Gargoyles (Illus. by Dav Pilkey)
  c BL - v93 - O 1 '96 - p336 [51-250]
  c CBRS - v25 - O '96 - p16+ [51-250]
  c HB Guide - v8 - Spr '97 - p42 [51-250]
  c KR - v64 - S 15 '96 - p1406 [51-250]
  c NY - v72 - N 18 '96 - p101 [51-250]
  c PW - v243 - O 14 '96 - p82 [51-250]
  c SLJ - v42 - N '96 - p90 [51-250]
  The Hallo-Wiener (Illus. by Dav Pilkey)
  c Inst - v105 - My '96 - p68 [1-50]
  c RT - v50 - O '96 - p158 [51-250]
  The Paperboy (Illus. by Dav Pilkey)
  c BL - v93 - Ja '97 - p768 [1-50]
  c BL - v93 - Ap 1 '97 - p1296 [1-50]
  c HB Guide - v7 - Fall '96 - p277 [51-250]
Pilkey, Orrin H - *The Corps and the Shore*
  Under Nat - v23 - 3 '96 - p30+ [501+]
Pilkington, Doris - *Follow the Rabbit Proof Fence*
  Aust Bk R - D '96 - p93 [1-50]
Pilling, Ann - *Mother's Daily Scream (Krapf). Audio Version*
  BL - v93 - N 1 '96 - p522 [51-250]
Pilling, Michael J - *Reaction Kinetics*
  Choice - v34 - F '97 - p992 [51-250]
Pillsbury, Richard - *Atlas of American Agriculture*
  r ARBA - v28 - '97 - p567 [51-250]
  r BL - v93 - Ja '97 - p769 [1-50]
  r Choice - v34 - Ja '97 - p820 [51-250]
  r R&R Bk N - v11 - N '96 - p20 [51-250]
Pillsbury Best Chicken Cookbook
  PW - v244 - My 5 '97 - p205 [51-250]
Pillsbury Best of the Bake-Off Cookbook
  BL - v93 - N 15 '96 - p560 [51-250]
Pimlott, Ben - *Hugh Dalton*
  NS - v125 - D 20 '96 - p117 [1-50]
  The Queen: A Biography of Elizabeth II
  Econ - v341 - N 16 '96 - p5*+ [501+]
  NS - v125 - O 11 '96 - p43+ [501+]
  NS - v125 - D 20 '96 - p117 [501+]
  Obs - O 6 '96 - p15* [501+]
  Spec - v277 - O 19 '96 - p44+ [501+]
  TLS - O 4 '96 - p31 [501+]
  TLS - N 29 '96 - p19 [501+]
Pimm, David - *Symbols and Meanings in School Mathematics*
  Math T - v89 - D '96 - p782 [251-500]

Pina, Leslie - *Designed and Signed*
  Ant & CM - v101 - Jl '96 - p25 [51-250]
  Fostoria: Designer George Sakier
  Ant & CM - v101 - D '96 - p31 [51-250]
  Tiffin Glass 1914-1940
  Ant & CM - v101 - F '97 - p33 [51-250]
Pincas, Stephane - *Versailles: The History of the Gardens and Their Sculpture*
  BL - v93 - F 1 '97 - p919 [51-250]
  Choice - v34 - Ap '97 - p1326 [51-250]
  LJ - v122 - F 15 '97 - p132 [51-250]
Pinch, William R - *Peasants and Monks in British India*
  Choice - v34 - D '96 - p653 [51-250]
Pinckaers, Servais - *The Sources of Christian Ethics*
  Theol St - v57 - Je '96 - p371+ [501+]
Pincus, Jonathan - *Class, Power, and Agrarian Change*
  R&R Bk N - v12 - F '97 - p39 [51-250]
Pincus, Leslie - *Authenticating Culture in Imperial Japan*
  CR - v270 - F '97 - p106+ [251-500]
Pincus, Steven - *Protestantism and Patriotism*
  Lon R Bks - v19 - F 6 '97 - p13+ [501+]
Pincus, Steven C A - *Protestantism and Patriotism*
  Choice - v34 - Ja '97 - p858 [51-250]
  HRNB - v25 - Win '97 - p69 [251-500]
Pinczes, Elinor J - *Arctic Fives Arrive (Illus. by Holly Berry)*
  c BL - v93 - S 15 '96 - p249+ [51-250]
  c HB Guide - v8 - Spr '97 - p42 [51-250]
  c PW - v243 - O 14 '96 - p83 [51-250]
  c SLJ - v42 - N '96 - p90 [51-250]
Pindell, Terry - *A Good Place to Live*
  PW - v243 - D 30 '96 - p64 [1-50]
  Yesterday's Train
  BL - v93 - Ja '97 - p814 [51-250]
  KR - v64 - N 1 '96 - p1588+ [251-500]
  LJ - v121 - D '96 - p130 [51-250]
  NYTBR - v102 - F 2 '97 - p20 [51-250]
  PW - v243 - N 11 '96 - p62+ [51-250]
Pine, Cynthia M - *Community Oral Health*
  SciTech - v21 - Mr '97 - p66 [51-250]
Pine, Richard - *Lawrence Durrell: The Mindscape*
  TLS - F 7 '97 - p32 [251-500]
  The Thief of Reason
  ELT - v40 - 2 '97 - p232+ [501+]
  ILS - v15 - Fall '96 - p22+ [501+]
Pineiro, R J - *Exposure*
  Arm Det - v30 - Win '97 - p116 [251-500]
  y BL - v93 - S 15 '96 - p222 [51-250]
  LJ - v121 - S 15 '96 - p97 [51-250]
  Retribution (Whitener). Audio Version
  LJ - v121 - O 1 '96 - p144 [51-250]
Pinello, Daniel R - *The Impact of Judicial-Selection Method on State-Supreme-Court Policy*
  AAPSS-A - v549 - Ja '97 - p198+ [251-500]
  APSR - v90 - D '96 - p920 [501+]
Pineo, Ronn F - *Social and Economic Reform in Ecuador*
  Choice - v34 - Ja '97 - p860 [51-250]
Pinfield, Lawrence T - *The Operation of Internal Labor Markets*
  ILRR - v50 - Ja '97 - p357+ [501+]
  Per Psy - v49 - Win '96 - p1025+ [501+]
Pingwa, Jia - *Le Porteur De Jeunes Mariees*
  WLT - v70 - Sum '96 - p759+ [501+]
Pink, Thomas - *The Psychology of Freedom*
  Choice - v34 - Mr '97 - p1243 [51-250]
Pinkard, Terry - *Hegel's Phenomenology*
  Ethics - v107 - O '96 - p163+ [501+]
Pinker, Steven - *Language, Learnability and Language Development*
  Nature - v384 - N 7 '96 - p37 [1-50]
Pinkney, Andrea Davis - *Bill Pickett: Rodeo-Ridin' Cowboy (Illus. by Brian Pinkney)*
  c BL - v93 - N 1 '96 - p504+ [51-250]
  Bill Pickett, Rodeo-Ridin' Cowboy (Illus. by Brian Pinkney)
  c BL - v93 - Ap 1 '97 - p1298 [1-50]
  Bill Pickett: Rodeo-Ridin' Cowboy (Illus. by Brian Pinkney)
  c CCB-B - v50 - N '96 - p110 [51-250]
  c HB - v72 - N '96 - p761+ [251-500]
  Bill Pickett, Rodeo-Ridin' Cowboy (Illus. by Brian Pinkney)
  c HB Guide - v8 - Spr '97 - p160 [51-250]
  Bill Pickett: Rodeo-Ridin' Cowboy (Illus. by Brian Pinkney)
  c NYTBR - v101 - N 10 '96 - p42 [501+]
  c SLJ - v42 - O '96 - p116 [51-250]
  Hold Fast to Dreams
  y Kliatt - v31 - Ja '97 - p10 [51-250]
  c RT - v50 - D '96 - p342 [51-250]

I Smell Honey (Illus. by Brian Pinkney)
  c PW - v244 - Mr 10 '97 - p65 [51-250]
Pretty Brown Face (Illus. by Brian Pinkney)
  c PW - v244 - Mr 10 '97 - p65 [51-250]
Pinkney, Brian - *The Adventures of Sparrowboy (Illus. by Brian Pinkney)*
  c BL - v93 - Ap 1 '97 - p1338+ [51-250]
  c KR - v65 - Mr 15 '97 - p467 [51-250]
  c PW - v244 - Mr 10 '97 - p66 [51-250]
Pinkston, Elizabeth - *High-Tech Highways*
     J Gov Info - v23 - S '96 - p559 [1-50]
Pinkwater, Daniel - *Wallpaper from Space (Illus. by Jill Pinkwater)*
  c BL - v93 - S 1 '96 - p131 [51-250]
  c CCB-B - v50 - O '96 - p73 [51-250]
  c HB Guide - v8 - Spr '97 - p59 [51-250]
  c Inst - v106 - O '96 - p68 [1-50]
  c NYTBR - v102 - Ja 5 '97 - p22 [1-50]
  c SLJ - v42 - O '96 - p104 [51-250]
Pinn, Anthony B - *Why, Lord?*
     Choice - v34 - S '96 - p146 [51-250]
Pinney, Estelle Runcie - *A Net Full of Honey*
  y Aust Bk R - O '96 - p61 [501+]
  y Magpies - v11 - Jl '96 - p36 [51-250]
Pinnock, Clark H - *Flame of Love*
     Ch Today - v40 - N 11 '96 - p52+ [501+]
Pinochet Ugarte, Augusto - *Camino Recorrido. Vols. 1-2; Vol. 3, Pts. 1-2*
     HAHR - v76 - Ag '96 - p604+ [501+]
Pinsky, Maxine A - *Marx Toys*
     Ant & CM - v101 - D '96 - p30 [1-50]
Pinsky, Robert - *The Figured Wheel*
     LJ - v122 - Ap 1 '97 - p95 [1-50]
     NYTBR - v101 - D 8 '96 - p79+ [1-50]
     NYTBR - v102 - Ap 20 '97 - p32 [51-250]
     Obs - D 1 '96 - p16* [1-50]
     TLS - Ja 24 '97 - p14 [501+]
Pinsof, William M - *Integrative Problem-Centered Therapy*
     AJPsych - v154 - Mr '97 - p431+ [501+]
Pinson, Linda - *The Home Based-Entrepreneur. 2nd Ed.*
     LJ - v122 - My 1 '97 - p52 [1-50]
Pinson, Mark - *The Muslims of Bosnia-Herzegovina. 2nd Ed.*
     MEJ - v51 - Spr '97 - p314 [51-250]
     New R - v215 - N 25 '96 - p31+ [501+]
Pinter, Harold - *99 Poems in Translation*
     Trib Bks - Mr 30 '97 - p2 [1-50]
Collected Poems and Prose
     WLT - v70 - Aut '96 - p965 [251-500]
Pinto, Constancio - *East Timor's Unfinished Struggle*
  y BL - v93 - F 1 '97 - p924 [51-250]
     LJ - v122 - F 1 '97 - p96 [51-250]
     Prog - v61 - F '97 - p41+ [501+]
Pinzer, Maimie - *The Maimie Papers*
     NYTBR - v102 - Ap 6 '97 - p32 [51-250]
Pipe, Jim - *Alien*
  c HB Guide - v8 - Spr '97 - p86 [51-250]
In the Footsteps of Dracula (Illus. by Francesca D'Ottavi)
  c RT - v50 - O '96 - p141 [1-50]
In the Footsteps of the Werewolf
  c HB Guide - v7 - Fall '96 - p323 [51-250]
Medieval Castle
  c Sch Lib - v45 - F '97 - p37+ [51-250]
Mystery History of a Medieval Castle
  c HB Guide - v8 - Spr '97 - p166 [51-250]
Piper, Adrian - *Out of Order, Out of Sight. Vols. 1-2*
     Nat - v264 - F 3 '97 - p25+ [501+]
Piper, Alan - *A History of Brixton*
     TLS - N 1 '96 - p31 [51-250]
Pipes, Daniel - *The Hidden Hand*
     For Aff - v75 - N '96 - p163 [51-250]
     MEJ - v51 - Spr '97 - p311 [51-250]
     WSJ-MW - v78 - D 26 '96 - p4 [501+]
Pipes, Richard - *Communism: The Vanished Specter*
     Historian - v59 - Fall '96 - p128+ [501+]
A Concise History of the Russian Revolution
  y Kliatt - v31 - My '97 - p29 [51-250]
     NYTBR - v102 - Ja 26 '97 - p28 [51-250]
     PW - v243 - N 11 '96 - p72 [1-50]
Russia under the Old Regime
     NYTBR - v102 - Ja 26 '97 - p28 [1-50]
Pipher, Mary Bray - *Reviving Ophelia*
     VOYA - v19 - D '96 - p256 [1-50]
Reviving Ophelia (Pipher). Audio Version
     LJ - v122 - F 15 '97 - p115 [1-50]
The Shelter of Each Other
     EL - v54 - D '96 - p85+ [251-500]
The Shelter of Each Other (Pipher). Audio Version
  y Kliatt - v30 - S '96 - p59 [51-250]

Pipkin, Turk - *Fast Greens*
     LATBR - My 26 '96 - p10+ [51-250]
     NYTBR - v101 - Jl 21 '96 - p19 [51-250]
Pirages, Dennis C - *Building Sustainable Societies*
     R&R Bk N - v11 - D '96 - p24 [51-250]
Pirandello, Luigi - *Pirandello's Love Letters to Marta Abba*
     MLR - v91 - Jl '96 - p758+ [501+]
Pirate Writings
  p SF Chr - v18 - O '96 - p83 [1-50]
Pirates: Terror on the High Seas from the Caribbean to the South China Sea
  y BL - v93 - D 15 '96 - p706 [51-250]
     BW - v26 - D 8 '96 - p11 [51-250]
     LJ - v122 - F 1 '97 - p95 [51-250]
Pirello, Christina - *Cooking the Whole Foods Way*
     LJ - v122 - Ap 15 '97 - p110 [51-250]
     PW - v244 - F 3 '97 - p102+ [51-250]
Piret, Pierre - *Les Illuminations: Un Autre Lecteur?*
     FR - v70 - D '96 - p331 [251-500]
Piron, Claude - *Le Defi Des Langues*
     Lang Soc - v26 - Mr '97 - p143+ [501+]
Pirotta, Saviour - *Fossils and Bones*
  c Sch Lib - v45 - F '97 - p40 [51-250]
Pirozhkova, A N - *At His Side*
     BL - v93 - N 1 '96 - p474 [51-250]
     BW - v27 - F 9 '97 - p4 [501+]
     Choice - v34 - Ap '97 - p1345 [51-250]
     KR - v64 - O 1 '96 - p1451 [251-500]
     LJ - v121 - O 15 '96 - p58+ [51-250]
     Nat - v263 - D 30 '96 - p28+ [501+]
     New R - v216 - F 3 '97 - p34+ [501+]
     NYRB - v44 - Ap 10 '97 - p26+ [501+]
     NYTBR - v101 - D 22 '96 - p6 [501+]
     NYTLa - v146 - N 25 '96 - pC16 [501+]
     PW - v243 - N 18 '96 - p59 [51-250]
Pirro, Vincenzo - *Gli Arabi E Noi*
     MEJ - v51 - Win '97 - p153 [51-250]
Pirsig, Robert M - *Zen and the Art of Motorcycle Maintenance (Pressman). Audio Version*
  y Kliatt - v31 - Ja '97 - p48 [51-250]
Pisani, Donald J - *Water, Land, and Law in the West*
     Choice - v34 - Ap '97 - p1406 [51-250]
Pisters, Peter W T - *Protein and Amino Acid Metabolism in Cancer Cachexia*
     SciTech - v20 - N '96 - p46 [51-250]
Pistolis, Donna Reidy - *Hit List: Frequently Challenged Books for Children*
     BL - v93 - S 15 '96 - p254 [51-250]
  r Emerg Lib - v24 - Mr '97 - p40 [51-250]
  r JOYS - v10 - Win '97 - p221+ [251-500]
  yr Kliatt - v30 - N '96 - p17+ [51-250]
Pistone, Joseph D - *Donnie Brasco (Pistone). Audio Version*
     LJ - v122 - Ap 1 '97 - p144 [51-250]
     PW - v244 - Mr 3 '97 - p31 [51-250]
Pitcher, Caroline - *The Snow Whale (Illus. by Jackie Morris)*
  c CBRS - v25 - F '97 - p77 [51-250]
  c CCB-B - v50 - D '96 - p148+ [51-250]
  c HB Guide - v8 - Spr '97 - p43 [51-250]
  c JB - v60 - D '96 - p238 [1-50]
  c Sch Lib - v45 - F '97 - p20 [51-250]
  c SLJ - v42 - D '96 - p103 [51-250]
  c TES - D 6 '96 - p17* [501+]
Pitcher, Patricia C - *The Drama of Leadership*
     LJ - v122 - Mr 15 '97 - p71 [51-250]
Pitchford, John - *The Current Account and Foreign Debt*
     Econ J - v107 - Ja '97 - p269+ [51-250]
Pitchfork, Colin E - *Renniks Australian Coin and Banknote Values. 17th Ed.*
     Coin W - v37 - D 23 '96 - p18 [51-250]
Pite, Ralph - *The Circle of Our Vision*
     RES - v47 - N '96 - p598+ [501+]
Pitkanen, Matti A - *The Grandchildren of the Vikings*
  c HB Guide - v8 - Spr '97 - p169 [51-250]
  c SLJ - v43 - F '97 - p96 [51-250]
Pitkin, Gary M - *The National Electronic Library*
     IRLA - v32 - Jl '96 - p10+ [51-250]
  r RQ - v36 - Win '96 - p315+ [251-500]
     R&R Bk N - v11 - N '96 - p80 [51-250]
Pitre, Felix - *Juan Bobo and the Pig*
  c SS - v88 - Ja '97 - p29+ [501+]
Pitre, Glen - *The Crawfish Book*
     JPC - v29 - Spr '96 - p248 [51-250]
Pitschen, Salome - *Peter Mettler: Making the Invisible Visible*
     Quill & Q - v62 - Jl '96 - p50 [251-500]

Pitt, Mark M - *Household and Intrahousehold Impact of the Grameen Bank and Similar Targeted Credit Programs in Bangladesh*
     JEL - v34 - D '96 - p2111 [51-250]
Pittau, Francesco - *Perry Poops! (Illus. by Bernadette Gervais)*
  c PW - v244 - Ap 21 '97 - p73 [1-50]
Terry Toots! (Illus. by Bernadette Gervais)
  c PW - v244 - Ap 21 '97 - p73 [1-50]
Pittman, Al - *Dancing in Limbo*
     Can Lit - Win '96 - p144+ [501+]
Pittman, C U, Jr. - *Metal-Containing Polymeric Materials*
     Am Sci - v85 - Ja '97 - p87 [501+]
Pittman, Don A - *Ministry and Theology in Global Perspective*
     Rel St Rev - v23 - Ap '97 - p155+ [51-250]
Pittman, Helena Clare - *One Quiet Morning (Illus. by Helena Clare Pittman)*
  c BL - v93 - S 1 '96 - p144 [51-250]
  c HB Guide - v8 - Spr '97 - p43 [51-250]
  c HMR - Win '96 - p40+ [501+]
  c SLJ - v42 - S '96 - p187 [51-250]
Pittock, Murray G H - *Poetry and Jacobite Politics in Eighteenth-Century Britain and Ireland*
     Albion - v28 - Sum '96 - p312+ [501+]
     EHR - v112 - Ap '97 - p484+ [501+]
Spectrum of Decadence
     MLR - v91 - Jl '96 - p684+ [501+]
Pitts, Walter F, Jr. - *Old Ship of Zion*
     Am Ethnol - v23 - Ag '96 - p645+ [501+]
Pitzer, Paul C - *Grand Coulee*
     PHR - v66 - F '97 - p125+ [51-250]
Pius II, Pope - *Historia De Duobus Amantibus*
     Lib - v18 - S '96 - p216+ [501+]
Pivato, Joseph - *Echo: Essays on Other Literatures*
     Can Lit - Win '96 - p185+ [501+]
Piver, M Steven - *Gilda's Disease*
     BL - v93 - S 15 '96 - p195 [51-250]
     BWatch - v17 - N '96 - p3 [51-250]
     Choice - v34 - F '97 - p997 [51-250]
     LJ - v122 - Ja '97 - p56 [51-250]
     Trib Bks - Ja 19 '97 - p9 [501+]
Pixton, Paul B - *The German Episcopacy and the Implementation of the Decrees of the Fourth Lateran Council 1216-1245*
     AHR - v101 - O '96 - p1191+ [251-500]
     CHR - v82 - Jl '96 - p545+ [501+]
     Specu - v72 - Ja '97 - p209+ [501+]
Pizer, Donald - *American Expatriate Writing and the Paris Moment*
     AL - v68 - D '96 - p879 [51-250]
     Choice - v34 - S '96 - p129 [51-250]
The Cambridge Companion to American Realism and Naturalism
     J Am St - v30 - Ag '96 - p322 [251-500]
Pizer, John - *Toward a Theory of Radical Origin*
     Ger Q - v70 - Win '97 - p67+ [501+]
Pizzigati, Sam - *The New Labor Press*
     JC - v46 - Sum '96 - p197+ [501+]
Place, Robin - *Bodies from the Past*
  y TES - N 8 '96 - p13* [51-250]
Place, Ron - *Educators Internet Yellow Pages*
  r Choice - v34 - S '96 - p106 [51-250]
Plach, Tom - *The Creative Use of Music in Group Therapy. 2nd Ed.*
     SciTech - v20 - S '96 - p33 [1-50]
Placher, William C - *The Domestication of Transcendence*
     Comw - v123 - D 20 '96 - p18+ [501+]
     Intpr - v51 - Ap '97 - p216 [501+]
     Theol St - v58 - Mr '97 - p171+ [501+]
Plachta, Bodo - *Damnatur--Toleratur--Admittitur*
     MLR - v91 - O '96 - p1035+ [251-500]
Plachy, Sylvia - *Red Light*
     NYTBR - v101 - Ag 25 '96 - p18 [251-500]
     Utne R - S '96 - p92+ [1-50]
Plaidy, Jean - *The Lady in the Tower (Jeater). Audio Version*
  y Kliatt - v31 - My '97 - p41+ [51-250]
Victoria Victorious (Franklin). Audio Version
     BL - v93 - Mr 15 '97 - p1253 [51-250]
Plain, Belva - *The Carousel (Brown). Audio Version*
  y Kliatt - v30 - S '96 - p44 [51-250]
Promises
     Books - v10 - Je '96 - p23 [51-250]
     KR - v64 - My 1 '96 - p629 [251-500]
     PW - v244 - Mr 31 '97 - p72 [1-50]
Random Winds (Fairman). Audio Version
  y Kliatt - v30 - S '96 - p51 [51-250]
Whispers (King). Audio Version
  y Kliatt - v30 - S '96 - p54 [51-250]

Plain, Gill - *Women's Fiction of the Second World War*
   Choice - v34 - Mr '97 - p1165 [51-250]
Plain, Nancy - *The Man Who Painted Indians*
   c   Ch BWatch - v7 - F '97 - p7 [1-50]
   c   HB Guide - v8 - Spr '97 - p156 [51-250]
   c   SLJ - v43 - F '97 - p96 [51-250]
Plaisance, Michel - *Fetes Urbaines En Italie A L'Epoque De La Renaissance, Verone, Florence, Sienne, Naples*
   Ren Q - v49 - Aut '96 - p619+ [501+]
Plaisted, Caroline - *Christmas Crackered*
   c   Bks Keeps - N '96 - p21 [1-50]
   I'm in the Wedding Too (Illus. by Joanna Walsh)
   c   KR - v65 - Ja 1 '97 - p61+ [51-250]
   c   PW - v244 - Ja 13 '97 - p77 [51-250]
Planchart, Alejandro Enrique - *Beneventanum Troporum Corpus. Vols. 1-2*
   Specu - v71 - Jl '96 - p756+ [501+]
Planer, Nigel - *Therapy and How to Avoid It!*
   Obs - v54 - O 13 '96 - p17* [501+]
Planet Dexter - *Planet Dexter's Calculator Mania! (Illus. by Jack Keely)*
   c   LATBR - O 27 '96 - p11 [51-250]
Planet Dexter (Firm) - *The Hairy Book (Illus. by Jack Keely)*
   c   Cur R - v36 - Ja '97 - p12 [51-250]
   c   LATBR - D 22 '96 - p6 [51-250]
   c   Learning - v25 - Mr '97 - p38 [51-250]
   c   PW - v243 - N 25 '96 - p78 [51-250]
Planet Earth. Electronic Media Version
   yr Sch Lib - v45 - F '97 - p27 [251-500]
A Planet with One Mind (Pinder). Audio Version
   c   BL - v92 - Ag '96 - p1917 [51-250]
The Planets. Electronic Media Version
   r   S&T - v93 - F '97 - p59 [501+]
The Planned Parenthood Women's Health Encyclopedia
   r   BL - v93 - N 1 '96 - p532+ [501+]
   r   LJ - v121 - S 15 '96 - p58 [51-250]
   r   PW - v243 - O 7 '96 - p72 [51-250]
Plant, Deborah - *Every Tub Must Sit on It's Own Bottom*
   TSWL - v15 - Fall '96 - p358+ [501+]
Plant, Stephen - *Simone Weil*
   TES - F 21 '97 - p7* [1-50]
Plant Systems/Components Aging Management 1996
   SciTech - v20 - N '96 - p83 [51-250]
Plante, Ellen M - *The American Kitchen 1700 to the Present*
   Historian - v59 - Fall '96 - p154 [251-500]
Plas, Jeanne M - *Person-Centered Leadership*
   Choice - v34 - O '96 - p326+ [51-250]
Plaschka, Richard G - *Was Heisst Osterreich?*
   TLS - D 20 '96 - p6 [501+]
Plasketes, George - *Images of Elvis Presley in American Culture 1977-1997*
   BL - v93 - Ap 1 '97 - p1275 [51-250]
   PW - v244 - Mr 17 '97 - p73 [51-250]
Plaskovitis, Spyros - *I Alli Kardhia*
   WLT - v70 - Sum '96 - p740+ [251-500]
Plass, Paul - *The Game of Death in Ancient Rome*
   Rel St Rev - v22 - O '96 - p346 [51-250]
Plaster, John L - *SOG: The Secret Wars of America's Commandos in Vietnam*
   y   BL - v93 - Ja '97 - p814 [51-250]
   KR - v64 - N 1 '96 - p1589 [251-500]
   NYTLa - v146 - Ja 21 '97 - pC15 [1-50]
   PW - v243 - N 18 '96 - p56 [51-250]
Plate, Peter - *Snitch Factory*
   PW - v243 - N 11 '96 - p71 [51-250]
Plath, Sylvia - *The Bell Jar*
   LJ - v121 - O 15 '96 - p94 [51-250]
   The Bell Jar (McDormand). Audio Version
   CSM - v89 - Mr 27 '97 - pB8 [51-250]
   Quill & Q - v62 - S '96 - p71 [1-50]
   The Bell Jar (Shaw). Audio Version
   Obs - Mr 23 '97 - p16* [501+]
   Spec - v277 - N 30 '96 - p56 [51-250]
   The It-Doesn't-Matter Suit (Illus. by Rotraut Susanne Berner)
   c   NY - v72 - N 18 '96 - p101+ [51-250]
   c   Sch Lib - v44 - Ag '96 - p108 [51-250]
Plato - *The Dialogues of Plato (Allen). Vol. 3*
   TranslRevS - v2 - D '96 - p18 [51-250]
   The Laws (Penguin)
   LATBR - D 29 '96 - p10 [51-250]
   Parmenide (Brisson)
   Dialogue - v35 - Spr '96 - p393+ [501+]
   Parmenides (Gill)
   CPR - v16 - D '96 - p398+ [501+]
   TLS - N 29 '96 - p11 [1-50]

Platonov, Andrei Platonovich - *The Foundation Pit*
   KR - v64 - N 15 '96 - p1633 [51-250]
   LJ - v122 - Ap 15 '97 - p125 [1-50]
   Lon R Bks - v19 - Ap 24 '97 - p15+ [501+]
   NYTBR - v102 - F 9 '97 - p20 [51-250]
   Obs - D 1 '96 - p16* [51-250]
   PW - v243 - O 21 '96 - p71 [51-250]
   Spec - v277 - D 14 '96 - p65+ [501+]
   TLS - N 29 '96 - p12 [51-250]
   TLS - D 6 '96 - p12+ [501+]
Platt, Charles - *Anarchy Online*
   PW - v244 - F 10 '97 - p78 [51-250]
   Protektor
   SF Chr - v18 - O '96 - p78 [51-250]
Platt, Colin - *The Great Rebuildings of Tudor and Stuart England*
   EHR - v112 - Ap '97 - p464+ [501+]
   King Death
   Choice - v34 - N '96 - p494+ [51-250]
   HRNB - v25 - Win '97 - p71 [251-500]
   SciTech - v20 - S '96 - p30 [51-250]
Platt, Donald - *Fresh Peaches, Fireworks, and Guns*
   Ken R - v18 - Sum '96 - p191+ [501+]
Platt, Ellen Spector - *How to Profit from Flower and Herb Crafts*
   LJ - v121 - O 15 '96 - p56 [51-250]
Platt, Jennifer - *A History of Sociological Research Methods in America 1920-1960*
   Choice - v34 - D '96 - p696 [51-250]
   Hist & T - v36 - F '97 - p109+ [251-500]
Platt, Jennifer M, 1945- - *Teaching Adolescents with Mild Disabilities*
   R&R Bk N - v12 - F '97 - p69 [1-50]
Platt, Lyman D - *Hispanic Surnames and Family History*
   r   ARBA - v28 - '97 - p165+ [51-250]
   r   BL - v93 - S 1 '96 - p166 [1-50]
Platt, Pamela - *Rock n' Roll Rainforest*
   c   Magpies - v11 - S '96 - p34 [51-250]
Platt, Randall Beth - *Honor Bright*
   y   BL - v93 - Ap 1 '97 - p1322 [51-250]
   y   CCB-B - v50 - Mr '97 - p255 [51-250]
   y   KR - v65 - Ja 1 '97 - p62 [51-250]
   y   SLJ - v43 - Mr '97 - p190+ [51-250]
   The Royalscope Fe-As-Ko
   PW - v244 - Ap 28 '97 - p50+ [51-250]
Platt, Richard - *Desde El Principio*
   c   BL - v93 - My 1 '97 - p1506 [1-50]
   Incredible Explosions (Illus. by Stephen Biesty)
   c   Magpies - v11 - S '96 - p42 [51-250]
   Pirate
   y   Emerg Lib - v24 - S '96 - p26 [1-50]
   Spy (Illus. by Geoff Dann)
   c   Bks Keeps - N '96 - p15 [51-250]
   c   BL - v93 - D 1 '96 - p654 [51-250]
   c   HB Guide - v8 - Spr '97 - p94 [51-250]
   c   Sch Lib - v45 - F '97 - p40 [51-250]
Platten, David - *Philippe Djian: 37° 2 Le Matin*
   MLR - v92 - Ja '97 - p206+ [251-500]
Plattner, Stuart - *High Art Down Home*
   JEL - v35 - Mr '97 - p304 [51-250]
   LJ - v121 - O 1 '96 - p74 [51-250]
Plaut, Eric A - *The Grand Opera*
   TCI - v30 - O '96 - p56 [1-50]
Plaut, Joshua Eli - *Greek Jewry in the Twentieth Century 1913-1983*
   Choice - v34 - D '96 - p672 [51-250]
Plautus, Titus Maccius - *Menaechmi*
   CW - v89 - Jl '96 - p495+ [501+]
Play Cleaning (Dorling Kindersley)
   c   PW - v243 - N 25 '96 - p77 [51-250]
Play Garage (Dorling Kindersley)
   c   PW - v243 - N 25 '96 - p77 [51-250]
Play Garden (Dorling Kindersley)
   c   PW - v243 - N 25 '96 - p77 [51-250]
Play Kitchen (Dorling Kindersley)
   c   PW - v243 - N 25 '96 - p77 [51-250]
Player, Gary - *Golf Begins at Fifty*
   LJ - v121 - O 1 '96 - p54 [1-50]
Playford, Phillip - *Carpet of Silver*
   Aust Bk R - F '97 - p9+ [501+]
Pleasant, Barbara - *Easy Garden Projects for All Seasons*
   BL - v93 - Mr 15 '97 - p1215 [51-250]
Plender, John - *A Stake in the Future*
   NS - v126 - F 21 '97 - p47+ [501+]
Plesu, Andrei - *Limba Pasarilor*
   RM - v49 - Je '96 - p941+ [251-500]
Plichta, Peter - *God's Secret Formula*
   Books - v11 - Ap '97 - p23 [51-250]
Ploeg, Durk Van Der - *Reis Nei De Kalkman*
   WLT - v70 - Aut '96 - p974+ [501+]

Plotinus - *Ennead III. 6*
   Rel St Rev - v23 - Ja '97 - p63 [51-250]
Plotke, David - *Building a Democratic Political Order*
   Choice - v34 - My '97 - p1577+ [51-250]
   RAH - v25 - Mr '97 - p101+ [501+]
Plotkin, Fred - *Italy for the Gourmet Traveler*
   r   BL - v93 - S 15 '96 - p212 [1-50]
Plotkin, Mariano Ben - *Manana Es San Peron*
   HAHR - v77 - My '97 - p353+ [501+]
Plotnik, Arthur - *The Elements of Expression*
   Choice - v34 - O '96 - p272+ [51-250]
Plotnikoff, Vi - *Head Cook at Weddings and Funerals and Other Stories of Doukhobor Life*
   Can Lit - Win '96 - p150+ [501+]
Plotz: The Zine for the Vaclempt
   p   Utne R - Jl '96 - p112 [251-500]
Plourde, Lynn - *Pigs in the Mud in the Middle of the Rud (Illus. by John Schoenherr)*
   c   CBRS - v25 - Mr '97 - p90 [1-50]
   c   CCB-B - v50 - F '97 - p219 [51-250]
   c   KR - v65 - Ja 15 '97 - p145 [51-250]
   c   PW - v243 - D 30 '96 - p66 [51-250]
   c   SLJ - v43 - Mr '97 - p163+ [51-250]
Plowden, Martha Ward - *Olympic Black Women (Illus. by Ronald Jones)*
   c   HB Guide - v7 - Fall '96 - p362 [1-50]
Pluckrose, Henry - *Beginnings and Endings*
   c   HB Guide - v7 - Fall '96 - p326 [1-50]
   Walls (Illus. by Steve Shott)
   c   HB Guide - v7 - Fall '96 - p326 [1-50]
Pluhar, Evelyn B - *Beyond Prejudice*
   Ethics - v107 - Ja '97 - p395+ [51-250]
   Rel St Rev - v22 - O '96 - p343 [51-250]
Plumb, Donald C - *Veterinary Drug Handbook. 2nd Ed.*
   r   ARBA - v28 - '97 - p574 [51-250]
Plumlee, Harry James - *Shadow of the Wolf*
   KR - v65 - Ja 1 '97 - p17 [251-500]
   LJ - v122 - Ja '97 - p150 [51-250]
   PW - v244 - Ja 27 '97 - p78 [51-250]
Plumly, Stanley - *The Marriage in the Trees*
   LJ - v122 - Ja '97 - p104 [51-250]
Plummer, Brenda Gayle - *Rising Wind*
   Choice - v34 - D '96 - p678 [51-250]
   TLS - Ja 3 '97 - p32 [51-250]
Plummer, Louise - *The Unlikely Romance of Kate Bjorkman*
   y   Kliatt - v30 - S '96 - p3 [1-50]
Plumwood, Val - *Feminism and the Mastery of Nature*
   EG - v72 - O '96 - p476+ [501+]
Plunka, Gene A - *Antonin Artaud and the Modern Theater*
   FR - v70 - O '96 - p122+ [251-500]
Plunket, Robert - *Love Junkie*
   TLS - Ag 30 '96 - p22+ [501+]
Plunkett, Jack W - *Plunkett's Financial Services Industry Almanac*
   r   LJ - v122 - Ap 15 '97 - p72 [51-250]
   Plunkett's Health Care Industry Almanac
   r   ARBA - v28 - '97 - p605 [51-250]
   Plunkett's InfoTech Industry Almanac
   r   ARBA - v28 - '97 - p243 [51-250]
   r   LJ - v122 - Ja '97 - p90+ [51-250]
   r   RQ - v36 - Win '96 - p304 [251-500]
Plunkett, John - *Mind Grenades*
   Quill & Q - v63 - F '97 - p30 [251-500]
   VV - v41 - O 29 '96 - p63 [251-500]
Plut-Pregelj, Leopoldina - *Historical Dictionary of Slovenia*
   r   Choice - v34 - Mr '97 - p1142 [51-250]
   r   R&R Bk N - v11 - D '96 - p10 [51-250]
Pluvier, Jan M - *Historical Atlas of South-East Asia*
   r   ARBA - v28 - '97 - p197 [51-250]
   r   Choice - v34 - Ja '97 - p774 [51-250]
Pochna, Marie-France - *Christian Dior: The Man Who Made the World Look New*
   BL - v93 - S 15 '96 - p201 [51-250]
   BWatch - v17 - N '96 - p2 [51-250]
   Econ - v342 - Mr 15 '97 - p3*+ [501+]
   LJ - v122 - Ja '97 - p94 [51-250]
   NYTBR - v102 - Ja 12 '97 - p14+ [501+]
Pochocki, Ethel - *The Mushroom Man*
   c   CLW - v67 - Mr '97 - p14 [1-50]
   One-of-a-Kind Friends
   c   CLW - v66 - Je '96 - p50 [51-250]
   A Penny for a Hundred (Illus. by Mary Beth Owens)
   c   HB Guide - v8 - Spr '97 - p59 [51-250]
   c   Smith - v27 - N '96 - p117 [1-50]
   Soup Pot (Illus. by Mary Beth Owens)
   c   CLW - v67 - Mr '97 - p43 [251-500]
   The Wind Harp and Other Angel Tales
   c   CLW - v66 - Je '96 - p52 [51-250]

The Pocket Factfile of 20th Century Events
r ARBA - v28 - '97 - p211+ [51-250]
The Pocket Factfile of 20th Century People
r ARBA - v28 - '97 - p14 [51-250]
Pocock, J G A - *The Machiavellian Moment*
RP - v58 - Fall '96 - p677+ [501+]
Pocock, Tom - *A Thirst for Glory*
Spec - v277 - N 16 '96 - p49+ [501+]
Podcameni, Silvio - *Distributed Relational Database*
SciTech - v20 - D '96 - p13 [51-250]
Podeh, Elie - *The Quest for Hegemony in the Arab World*
MEJ - v51 - Win '97 - p144+ [501+]
Poderis, Tony - *It's a Great Day to Fund-Raise!*
ChrPhil - v8 - S 5 '96 - p46 [51-250]
Podesta, Connie - *How to Be the Person Successful
Companies Fight to Keep*
BL - v93 - My 1 '97 - p1468 [51-250]
Podesta, Patti - *Resolutions: A Critique of Video Art*
Afterimage - v24 - N '96 - p4 [1-50]
Podgorecki, Adam - *Totalitarian and Post-Totalitarian
Law*
R&R Bk N - v12 - F '97 - p62 [51-250]
Podmore, Dave - *Pod Almighty*
Books - v10 - Je '96 - p23 [51-250]
Poe, Edgar Allan - *Classic Chilling Tales (Donovan). Vol.
2. Audio Version*
y Kliatt - v31 - Ja '97 - p37+ [51-250]
Le Corbeau
MLR - v91 - Jl '96 - p732 [251-500]
*The Fall of the House of Usher. The Phantom Island.
Audio Version*
BL - v92 - Ag '96 - p1917 [51-250]
*Listen and Read Edgar Allan Poe's The Tell-Tale Heart
and Other Stories (Hammond). Book and Audio Version*
c BL - v93 - Mr 15 '97 - p1253 [51-250]
c Ch BWatch - v6 - Jl '96 - p7 [1-50]
Poe, Robert - *Return to the House of Usher*
PW - v243 - S 16 '96 - p71 [51-250]
Poem Finder 95. Electronic Media Version
r ARBA - v28 - '97 - p465+ [51-250]
Poeschke, Joachim - *Michelangelo and His World*
NYTBR - v101 - Jl 21 '96 - p18 [51-250]
Sculpt R - v45 - Fall '96 - p35 [501+]
Poetry Flash
p Sm Pr R - v28 - S '96 - p19 [251-500]
Poetry Now
p Sm Pr R - v28 - N '96 - p22 [51-250]
Poetry Review
p Sm Pr R - v29 - F '97 - p16 [51-250]
Poey, Delia - *Little Havana Blues*
BL - v93 - Ja '97 - p808 [1-50]
Choice - v34 - Mr '97 - p1164 [51-250]
LJ - v121 - O 1 '96 - p78 [51-250]
Pogrebin, Letty Cottin - *Getting Over Getting Old*
Wom R Bks - v13 - S '96 - p1+ [501+]
Pohanish, Richard P - *Hazardous Materials Handbook*
r ARBA - v28 - '97 - p651 [51-250]
r Choice - v34 - Ap '97 - p1370+ [51-250]
Pohl, Frederik - *The Other End of Time*
Analog - v117 - Mr '97 - p148+ [251-500]
y BL - v93 - S 15 '96 - p226 [51-250]
BW - v26 - N 24 '96 - p6 [51-250]
LJ - v121 - S 15 '96 - p101 [51-250]
NYTBR - v101 - N 3 '96 - p24 [51-250]
PW - v243 - S 30 '96 - p66 [51-250]
Rapport - v19 - 6 '96 - p19 [251-500]
Pohl, John M D - *The Politics of Symbolism in the Mixtec
Codices*
LA Ant - v7 - Mr '96 - p91+ [501+]
Pohs, Henry A - *The Miner's Flame Light Book*
RocksMiner - v71 - S '96 - p359 [251-500]
R&R Bk N - v12 - F '97 - p98 [51-250]
Poinsett, Alex - *Walking with Presidents*
PW - v244 - Ap 7 '97 - p87 [51-250]
Pointer, Michael - *Charles Dickens on the Screen*
r ARBA - v28 - '97 - p511+ [51-250]
r Nine-C Lit - v51 - Mr '97 - p563 [1-50]
Pointon, Marcia - *Art Apart*
AJA - v100 - O '96 - p769+ [501+]
Poirier, Charles C - *Supply Chain Optimization*
Bus Bk R - v13 - 4 '96 - p98+ [501+]
Poirier, Guy - *L'Homosexualite Dans L'Imaginaire De La
Renaissance*
Ren Q - v50 - Spr '97 - p252+ [501+]
Poirier, Jean-Pierre - *Antoine Laurent De Lavoisier
1743-1794*
Isis - v87 - D '96 - p688+ [501+]
Lavoisier: Chemist, Biologist, Economist
LJ - v121 - N 1 '96 - p105 [51-250]
Poirier, Suzanne - *Chicago's War on Syphilis 1937-40*
MHR - v10 - Fall '96 - p97+ [501+]

Poirot, Luis - *Pablo Neruda: Absence and Presence*
BW - v26 - S 29 '96 - p12 [51-250]
Poirot-Delpech, Bertrand - *Diagonales*
WLT - v71 - Win '97 - p110 [501+]
Poirteir, Cathal - *The Great Irish Famine*
VS - v39 - Win '96 - p205+ [501+]
Poissenot, Benigne - *Nouvelles Histoires Tragiques*
Ren Q - v50 - Spr '97 - p252+ [501+]
Poitry, Guy - *Michel Leiris: Dualisme Et Totalite*
FR - v70 - Mr '97 - p601+ [501+]
Poivre D'Arvor, Patrick - *Un Hero De Passage*
BL - v93 - Ja '97 - p827 [1-50]
Poker, D B - *Ion-Solid Interactions for Materials
Modification and Processing*
SciTech - v20 - S '96 - p49 [51-250]
Pokhrel, Durga - *Shadow over Shangri-La*
y BL - v92 - Ag '96 - p1878 [51-250]
y BL - v92 - Ag '96 - p1890 [1-50]
Pola, Giancarlo - *Developments in Local Government
Finance*
JEL - v34 - D '96 - p2061+ [51-250]
Polacco, Patricia - *Aunt Chip and the Great Triple Creek
Dam Affair (Illus. by Patricia Polacco)*
c HB Guide - v7 - Fall '96 - p271 [1-50]
c New Ad - v9 - Fall '96 - p327+ [501+]
Babushka's Mother Goose
c ECEJ - v24 - Fall '96 - p39 [51-250]
The Bee Tree
c CLW - v67 - Mr '97 - p14 [1-50]
I Can Hear the Sun (Illus. by Patricia Polacco)
c BL - v93 - N 1 '96 - p509 [51-250]
c CLW - v67 - Mr '97 - p52 [51-250]
c HB Guide - v8 - Spr '97 - p43 [51-250]
c PW - v243 - S 2 '96 - p120 [51-250]
c SLJ - v42 - N '96 - p90+ [51-250]
In Enzo's Splendid Gardens (Illus. by Patricia Polacco)
c PW - v244 - F 24 '97 - p90 [51-250]
c Trib Bks - My 4 '97 - p6 [51-250]
The Keeping Quilt
c Learning - v25 - Mr '97 - p54 [1-50]
My Ol' Man
c LA - v73 - S '96 - p353+ [51-250]
Pink and Say
c HMR - Win '96 - p45 [1-50]
Tikvah Means Hope
c PW - v243 - S 2 '96 - p133 [51-250]
*The Trees of the Dancing Goats (Illus. by Patricia
Polacco)*
c BL - v93 - N 1 '96 - p509+ [51-250]
c HB Guide - v8 - Spr '97 - p43 [51-250]
c KR - v64 - N 1 '96 - p1606 [51-250]
c NYTBR - v101 - D 22 '96 - p16 [1-50]
c PW - v243 - S 30 '96 - p87 [51-250]
c SLJ - v43 - F '97 - p84 [51-250]
Polachek, Dora E - *Heroic Virtue, Comic Infidelity*
FR - v70 - O '96 - p108+ [501+]
Ren Q - v49 - Aut '96 - p631+ [501+]
Polain, Marcella - *Dumbstruck*
Aust Bk R - D '96 - p69+ [501+]
Poland, F - *Women and Senior Management*
LAR - v98 - S '96 - p481 [251-500]
Poland, Jeffrey - *Physicalism: The Philosophical
Foundations*
Phil R - v105 - Ja '96 - p92+ [501+]
Poland (Rough Guide). 3rd Ed.
r BL - v93 - S 15 '96 - p212 [1-50]
Polding, John Bede - *The Letters of John Bede Polding.
Vols. 1-2*
Aust Bk R - F '97 - p18+ [51-250]
Polhemus, Ted - *Style Surfing*
TCI - v30 - O '96 - p59 [51 250]
Polidora, Jim - *Mind-Body Wellness*
r SciTech - v20 - N '96 - p37 [51-250]
Poling, Clark V - *Surrealist Vision and Technique*
Art J - v56 - Spr '97 - p95+ [501+]
Polit, Denise F - *Nursing Research*
AJN - v96 - N '96 - p16G [51-250]
Political Handbook of the World 1995-1996
r BL - v92 - Ag '96 - p1919 [51-250]
Politique Pour Le Developpement Rural
J Gov Info - v23 - S '96 - p659 [1-50]
Polito, Robert - *Savage Art*
BW - v27 - Ja 5 '97 - p12 [51-250]
NYTBR - v102 - Ja 19 '97 - p28 [51-250]
TLS - Ag 30 '96 - p29 [501+]
Polizzotti, Mark - *Revolution of the Mind*
Art J - v56 - Spr '97 - p95+ [501+]
WLT - v71 - Win '97 - p111 [501+]

Polizzotto, Lorenzo - *The Elect Nation*
AHR - v101 - O '96 - p1240+ [251-500]
Historian - v58 - Sum '96 - p914+ [251-500]
JMH - v68 - D '96 - p1004+ [501+]
Polk, Dora Beale - *The Island of California*
J Am Cult - v19 - Sum '96 - p159 [251-500]
WAL - v31 - Sum '96 - p182+ [251-500]
Polk, Noel - *Children of the Dark House*
AL - v69 - Mr '97 - p235+ [251-500]
Choice - v34 - N '96 - p458+ [51-250]
Polking, Kirk - *Writing Family Histories and Memoirs*
NGSQ - v84 - S '96 - p233+ [251-500]
Polkinghorn, R S - *Pino Grande. 2nd Ed.*
Model R - v64 - Ap '97 - p53 [51-250]
Polkinghorne, John - *Beyond Science*
BL - v93 - S 1 '96 - p48 [51-250]
Choice - v34 - Mr '97 - p1179 [51-250]
Nature - v383 - O 31 '96 - p772 [501+]
The Faith of a Physicist
Skeptic - v3 - '95 - p101 [51-250]
Zygon - v32 - Mr '97 - p115+ [501+]
Serious Talk
Theol St - v57 - Je '96 - p383+ [251-500]
Polkinhorn, Harry - *Mount Soledad*
ABR - v17 - Ag '96 - p23 [501+]
Pollack, Jill S - *Women on the Hill*
y BL - v93 - Mr 15 '97 - p1233+ [51-250]
y HB Guide - v8 - Spr '97 - p94 [51-250]
y SLJ - v43 - Ja '97 - p132 [51-250]
y VOYA - v19 - F '97 - p350+ [51-250]
Pollack, Mark H - *Challenges in Clinical Practice*
SciTech - v20 - S '96 - p33 [51-250]
Pollack, Rachel - *Godmother Night*
BL - v93 - S 1 '96 - p64 [51-250]
BW - v26 - S 29 '96 - p11 [251-500]
Pollack, Sandra - *Contemporary Lesbian Writers of the
United States*
r RQ - v36 - Win '96 - p223 [51-250]
Pollack, Sheldon D - *The Failure of U.S. Tax Policy*
Choice - v34 - Mr '97 - p1209 [51-250]
JEL - v35 - Mr '97 - p224 [51-250]
WSJ-MW - v78 - D 24 '96 - pA7 [501+]
Pollak, Felix - *Print Quarterly: Index to Vols. 1-10*
r BM - v138 - Jl '96 - p470 [51-250]
Pollak, Jane - *Decorating Eggs*
LJ - v121 - O 15 '96 - p57 [51-250]
Pollak, Martha D - *Turin 1564-1680*
J Urban H - v23 - Ja '97 - p240+ [501+]
Pollak, Richard - *The Creation of Dr. B*
BL - v93 - Ja '97 - p798 [51-250]
KR - v64 - N 1 '96 - p1589+ [251-500]
LATBR - Ja 19 '97 - p3 [501+]
LJ - v122 - Ja '97 - p127 [51-250]
NY - v73 - Mr 24 '97 - p76+ [501+]
NYTBR - v102 - Ja 26 '97 - p14+ [501+]
NYTLa - v146 - Ja 13 '97 - pC18 [501+]
PW - v243 - N 18 '96 - p53 [51-250]
Readings - v12 - Mr '97 - p16+ [501+]
Time - v149 - Ja 27 '97 - p74 [501+]
Trib Bks - F 23 '97 - p1+ [501+]
Pollan, Michael - *A Place of My Own*
BL - v93 - F 15 '97 - p986 [51-250]
KR - v65 - Ja 15 '97 - p126+ [251-500]
LJ - v122 - F 15 '97 - p160 [51-250]
NYTBR - v102 - Mr 16 '97 - p8 [501+]
PW - v244 - Ja 13 '97 - p61 [51-250]
Trib Bks - My 25 '97 - p6+ [501+]
Second Nature
Spec - v277 - D 7 '96 - p55 [51-250]
Pollan, Stephen M - *Stephen Pollan's Foolproof Guide to
Renovating Your Kitchen*
BL - v93 - F 1 '97 - p916 [51-250]
Pollard, A J - *The North of England in the Age of Richard
III*
Albion - v28 - Win '96 - p679+ [501+]
HRNB - v25 - Win '96 - p70 [251-500]
The Wars of the Roses
Albion - v28 - Win '96 - p679+ [501+]
Pollard, A Mark - *Archaeological Chemistry*
Am Ant - v62 - Ja '97 - p152+ [501+]
Pollard, Irina - *A Guide to Reproduction*
Rel St Rev - v22 - O '96 - p342 [51-250]
Pollard, Jean - *Fly Eagle Fly (Illus. by Martine Gourbault)*
c Sch Lib - v45 - F '97 - p20 [51-250]
Pollard, Leslie J - *Complaint to the Lord*
Choice - v34 - N '96 - p547 [251-500]
Pollard, Michael - *Emmeline Pankhurst*
c Bks Keeps - Mr '97 - p24 [51-250]
Roads and Tunnels
c HB Guide - v8 - Spr '97 - p132 [51-250]

Pollard, Miriam - *The Other Face of Love*
Am - v175 - N 2 '96 - p32 [51-250]
BL - v92 - Ag '96 - p1860 [51-250]
LATBR - D 15 '96 - p15 [51-250]
Pollen, Daniel A - *Hannah's Heirs*
NGSQ - v84 - Je '96 - p152 [51-250]
Pollicott, Mark - *Ergodic Theory of Zd Actions*
SciTech - v20 - D '96 - p19 [51-250]
Pollin, Irene - *Medical Crisis Counseling*
Fam in Soc - v78 - Ja '97 - p107+ [501+]
Pollitt, Michael G - *Ownership and Performance in Electric Utilities*
JEL - v34 - S '96 - p1458 [51-250]
Pollock, John Charles - *Wilberforce (Davidson). Audio Version*
y Kliatt - v31 - Mr '97 - p51 [51-250]
Pollock, John L - *Cognitive Carpentry*
RM - v50 - D '96 - p418+ [501+]
Pollock, Lansing - *The Free Society*
WSJ-MW - v77 - S 26 '96 - pA10 [251-500]
Pollock, Linda - *With Faith and Physic*
Albion - v28 - Sum '96 - p301+ [501+]
Pollock, Penny - *The Turkey Girl (Illus. by Ed Young)*
c AB - v98 - N 18 '96 - p1726+ [251-500]
c CLW - v67 - Mr '97 - p58 [51-250]
c Emerg Lib - v24 - S '96 - p44 [1-50]
c Emerg Lib - v24 - Mr '97 - p65 [51-250]
c HB Guide - v7 - Fall '96 - p323 [51-250]
Pollock, Sudie - *Will the Dollars Stretch?*
y Ch BWatch - v6 - Jl '96 - p2 [51-250]
y Kliatt - v31 - Ja '97 - p20 [51-250]
y VOYA - v19 - F '97 - p353 [251-500]
Pollock, Zailig - *A.M. Klein: The Story of the Poet*
Can Lit - Win '96 - p175+ [501+]
Polloway, Edward A - *Strategies for Teaching Learners with Special Needs. 6th Ed.*
R&R Bk N - v12 - F '97 - p69 [51-250]
Polly, Jean - *The Internet Kids Yellow Pages. Special Ed.*
cr CBR - v14 - Jl '96 - p21 [1-50]
Polly, Jean Armour - *The Internet Kids Yellow Pages. Special Ed.*
c LJ - v122 - Ja '97 - p138 [51-250]
Polmar, Norman - *Spy Book*
r BW - v27 - Ja 26 '97 - p13 [51-250]
r Choice - v34 - My '97 - p1479 [51-250]
r LJ - v122 - Ap 15 '97 - p72 [51-250]
r Time - v148 - D 9 '96 - p86+ [501+]
World War II
r Choice - v34 - F '97 - p948 [51-250]
Polner, Murray - *Disarmed and Dangerous*
Am - v176 - Mr 22 '97 - p29 [51-250]
BL - v93 - D 1 '96 - p624 [51-250]
BW - v27 - Ja 12 '97 - p5 [501+]
Choice - v34 - My '97 - p1516 [51-250]
KR - v64 - N 1 '96 - p1590 [251-500]
LATBR - F 9 '97 - p5 [501+]
LJ - v122 - Ja '97 - p112 [51-250]
NYTBR - v102 - F 9 '97 - p16 [501+]
OS - v33 - Mr '97 - p35 [51-250]
PW - v243 - D 30 '96 - p52 [51-250]
Polowetzky, Michael - *Prominent Sisters*
Choice - v34 - Mr '97 - p1165 [51-250]
R&R Bk N - v12 - F '97 - p84 [51-250]
Pols, Edward - *Radical Realism*
IPQ - v36 - D '96 - p500+ [501+]
Polsgrove, Carol - *It Wasn't Pretty Folks, but Didn't We Have Fun?*
JPC - v30 - Fall '96 - p219+ [501+]
It Wasn't Pretty, Folks, but Didn't We Have Fun?
Rapport - v19 - 4 '96 - p35 [251-500]
Polyak, Ilya - *Computational Statistics in Climatology*
SciTech - v21 - Mr '97 - p26 [51-250]
Pombo, Richard - *This Land Is Our Land*
BL - v93 - S 1 '96 - p46 [51-250]
Pomeranc, Marion Hess - *The Hand-Me-Down Horse (Illus. by Joanna Yardley)*
c CBRS - v25 - Ja '97 - p55 [51-250]
c HB Guide - v8 - Spr '97 - p43 [51-250]
c PW - v243 - O 7 '96 - p75 [51-250]
c SLJ - v43 - Ja '97 - p89 [51-250]
c Smith - v27 - N '96 - p168 [1-50]
Pomerance, Michla - *The United States and the World Court as a Supreme Court of the Nations*
R&R Bk N - v11 - D '96 - p49 [51-250]
Pomerantz, Charlotte - *Mangaboom (Illus. by Anita Lobel)*
c BL - v93 - Ap 1 '97 - p1339 [51-250]
c CCB-B - v50 - My '97 - p333 [51-250]
c PW - v244 - Mr 31 '97 - p74+ [51-250]

Pomerantz, Gary M - *Where Peachtree Meets Sweet Auburn*
Ent W - Je 28 '96 - p100 [51-250]
NYTBR - v101 - Jl 21 '96 - p4 [501+]
NYTBR - v101 - D 8 '96 - p94 [1-50]
PW - v244 - Ap 14 '97 - p72 [1-50]
Pomerleau, Dean A - *Neural Network Perception for Mobile Robot Guidance*
Robotica - v14 - S '96 - p586+ [501+]
Pomeroy, Diana - *One Potato (Illus. by Diana Pomeroy)*
c HB Guide - v7 - Fall '96 - p271 [51-250]
c NYTBR - v101 - O 27 '96 - p44 [1-50]
Wildflower ABC (Illus. by Diana Pomeroy)
c BL - v93 - F 15 '97 - p1025 [51-250]
c KR - v65 - F 1 '97 - p227 [51-250]
c PW - v244 - Mr 3 '97 - p77 [51-250]
Pomeroy, Sarah B - *Xenophon, Oeconomicus*
AJP - v117 - Fall '96 - p492+ [501+]
RM - v49 - Je '96 - p942+ [251-500]
Pomfret, Richard W T - *Asian Economies in Transition*
Choice - v34 - N '96 - p508 [51-250]
Econ J - v106 - N '96 - p1852 [251-500]
JEL - v34 - S '96 - p1491 [51-250]
R&R Bk N - v11 - N '96 - p27 [51-250]
Australia's Trade Policies
JEH - v56 - D '96 - p953+ [501+]
Pomian, Raphaelle - *Gifts and Sorrows*
Aust Bk R - F '97 - p59 [51-250]
Pommaret-Imaeda, Francoise - *Bhutan*
r BL - v93 - S 15 '96 - p210 [1-50]
Pomp and Circumstantial Evidence
p Arm Det - v29 - Sum '96 - p322 [1-50]
Pomykala, Kenneth E - *The Davidic Dynasty Tradition in Early Judaism*
Rel St Rev - v22 - O '96 - p353+ [51-250]
Ponce, F A - *Gallium Nitride and Related Materials*
SciTech - v21 - Mr '97 - p90 [51-250]
Ponchillia, Paul E - *Foundations of Rehabilitation Teaching with Persons Who Are Blind or Visually Impaired*
J Rehab RD - v34 - Ap '97 - p242 [251-500]
Poncins, Gontran De - *Kabloona*
NYTBR - v101 - D 15 '96 - p40 [1-50]
Ponder, Rhinold Lamar - *The Wisdom of the Word: Faith*
Am - v176 - F 15 '97 - p32 [51-250]
B Ent - v27 - F '97 - p215 [1-50]
The Wisdom of the Word: Love
LJ - v121 - N 1 '96 - p86 [1-50]
Poniatowska, Elena - *Nothing, Nobody*
HAHR - v77 - F '97 - p141+ [251-500]
Paseo De La Reforma
LJ - v122 - Ja '97 - p80 [51-250]
Tinisima
BL - v93 - Ja '97 - p761 [1-50]
BL - v93 - S 15 '96 - p221 [51-250]
BW - v26 - D 22 '96 - p4 [501+]
KR - v64 - S 1 '96 - p1262 [251-500]
LATBR - N 17 '96 - p6+ [501+]
LJ - v121 - S 15 '96 - p97 [51-250]
Nat - v263 - O 28 '96 - p52+ [501+]
NYTBR - v101 - N 17 '96 - p25 [51-250]
Obs - O 27 '96 - p18* [501+]
PW - v243 - S 16 '96 - p69 [251-500]
TES - D 13 '96 - p33 [251-500]
TLS - O 25 '96 - p22 [501+]
Poniatowski, Marty - *Learning the HP-UX Operating System*
SciTech - v20 - D '96 - p11 [1-50]
Ponnuswamy, S - *Transportation Tunnels*
SciTech - v20 - N '96 - p66 [51-250]
Ponomarev, V N - *Krymskaia Voina I Russko-Amerikanskie Otnosheniia*
AHR - v101 - D '96 - p1583 [251-500]
Pons, Bruno - *Grands Decors Francais 1650-1800*
Lon R Bks - v18 - D 12 '96 - p8+ [501+]
Ponterotto, Joseph G - *Handbook of Multicultural Counseling*
Adoles - v31 - Fall '96 - p754+ [51-250]
Ponting, Clive - *Armageddon: The Reality behind the Distortions, Myths, Lies and Illusions of World War II*
NWCR - v50 - Win '97 - p168+ [501+]
Ponzek, Debra - *French Food, American Accent*
NYTBR - v101 - D 8 '96 - p71 [51-250]
Pool, Daniel - *Dickens' Fur Coat and Charlotte's Unanswered Letters*
KR - v65 - Mr 15 '97 - p448 [251-500]
LJ - v122 - Ap 15 '97 - p82 [51-250]
PW - v244 - Mr 31 '97 - p54 [51-250]
Pool, Harbison - *Beyond Tracking*
EL - v54 - O '96 - p90 [51-250]

Poole, Adrian - *The Oxford Book of Classical Verse in Translation*
Class Out - v74 - Win '97 - p83+ [251-500]
TLS - N 29 '96 - p15+ [51-250]
Poole, C P, Jr. - *Superconductivity*
Phys Today - v49 - S '96 - p90 [501+]
Poole, Jacob - *The Dialect of Forth and Bargy, Co. Wexford, Ireland*
r ILS - v15 - Fall '96 - p31 [1-50]
Poole, Josephine - *The Water Babies (Illus. by Jan Ormerod)*
c Sch Lib - v45 - F '97 - p33 [51-250]
Poole, Joyce - *Coming of Age with Elephants*
BL - v93 - D 1 '96 - p630 [1-50]
y BL - v93 - D 1 '96 - p664 [1-50]
Choice - v34 - S '96 - p155 [51-250]
y SB - v32 - Ag '96 - p175 [51-250]
Smith - v27 - Jl '96 - p123 [501+]
Poole, Julia E - *Italian Maiolica and Incised Slipware at the Fitzwilliam Museum*
Apo - v144 - N '96 - p58 [501+]
Poole, Roger - *The Unknown Virginia Woolf. 4th Ed.*
ELT - v40 - 2 '97 - p254+ [51-250]
Poole, Sara - *Etcherelli: Elise Ou La Vraie Vie*
MLR - v91 - O '96 - p1003+ [251-500]
Poole, Stafford - *Our Lady of Guadalupe*
AHR - v101 - D '96 - p1656+ [501+]
CHR - v83 - Ja '97 - p153+ [251-500]
HAHR - v76 - N '96 - p776+ [251-500]
Theol St - v57 - Je '96 - p382 [251-500]
Pooley, Colin F - *Migrants, Emigrants and Immigrants*
J Urban H - v22 - My '96 - p524+ [501+]
Pooley, Sarah - *Jump the World*
c PW - v244 - Ap 7 '97 - p94 [51-250]
Poor, Alfred - *Cross Country*
A & S Sm - v11 - O '96 - p88 [1-50]
Poorthuis, Marcel - *The Centrality of Jerusalem*
Rel St Rev - v23 - Ja '97 - p89 [51-250]
Poortvliet, Rien - *Bed-Time Alphabet Stories*
c Ch BWatch - v7 - Ja '97 - p1 [51-250]
The Sandman
c Ch BWatch - v7 - Ja '97 - p1 [51-250]
c PW - v243 - N 4 '96 - p74 [51-250]
Poovey, Mary - *Making a Social Body*
Choice - v34 - S '96 - p188 [51-250]
Critm - v39 - Win '97 - p119+ [501+]
Nine-C Lit - v51 - Mr '97 - p538+ [501+]
Popchock, Barry - *Soldier Boy*
JSH - v63 - F '97 - p186+ [251-500]
Popcorn, Faith - *Clicking: 16 Trends to Future Fit Your Life, Your Work, and Your Business*
LJ - v122 - Mr 15 '97 - p37 [1-50]
Clicking: 16 Trends to Future Fit Your Life, Your Work, and Your Business. Audio Version
BWatch - v17 - D '96 - p10 [1-50]
Pope, James - *Spin the Bottle*
y Books - v11 - Ap '97 - p24 [51-250]
Pope, Joyce - *Earthquakes*
c Sch Lib - v45 - F '97 - p37 [51-250]
Pope, Kenneth S - *Recovered Memories of Abuse*
Choice - v34 - My '97 - p1580 [51-250]
Pope, Liston - *Living like the Saints*
PW - v243 - D 2 '96 - p40 [51-250]
Pope, Loren - *Colleges That Change Lives*
yr SLJ - v42 - N '96 - p142 [51-250]
Pope, Nick - *Open Skies, Closed Minds*
Books - v10 - Je '96 - p23 [51-250]
Pope, Paul - *The One-Trick Rip-Off*
PW - v244 - Ap 28 '97 - p52+ [51-250]
Pope, Randolph D - *Understanding Juan Goytisolo*
WLT - v70 - Aut '96 - p927 [501+]
Pope, Stephen - *The Dictionary of the First World War*
r ARBA - v28 - '97 - p214+ [51-250]
r J Mil H - v60 - O '96 - p781 [251-500]
Pope-Hennessy, John Wyndham, Sir - *An Introduction to Italian Sculpture. 4th Ed., Vols. 1-3*
LJ - v122 - F 1 '97 - p77+ [51-250]
NYTBR - v101 - N 10 '96 - p57 [251-500]
TLS - N 8 '96 - p33 [251-500]
Popenoe, David - *Life without Father*
Choice - v34 - O '96 - p368 [51-250]
Econ - v339 - My 18 '96 - p3*+ [501+]
Promises to Keep
CC - v113 - N 20 '96 - p1178+ [51-250]
Choice - v34 - N '96 - p547 [51-250]
Soc Ser R - v71 - Mr '97 - p164 [1-50]
Popescu, Dumitru - *Am Fost Si Ciopfilitor De Himere*
BL - v93 - D 15 '96 - p714 [1-50]
Popescu, Petru - *Almost Adam*
PW - v244 - Ja 27 '97 - p103 [1-50]
Rapport - v19 - 4 '96 - p34 [51-250]

Popkin, Richard H - *Scepticism in the History of Philosophy*
R&R Bk N - v12 - F '97 - p2 [51-250]

Poplawski, Paul - *D.H. Lawrence: A Reference Companion*
r ARBA - v28 - '97 - p455 [51-250]
r Choice - v34 - D '96 - p593+ [51-250]
r R&R Bk N - v11 - N '96 - p70 [51-250]

Pople, Kenneth - *Stanley Spencer: A Biography*
PW - v244 - My 12 '97 - p68 [51-250]

Pople, Stephen - *Foundation Science to 14*
yr TES - Mr 21 '97 - p27* [51-250]

Poploff, Michelle - *Splash-a-Roo and Snowflakes (Illus. by Diane Palmisciano)*
c HB Guide - v7 - Fall '96 - p285 [51-250]

Popov, Eugeny - *Merry-Making in Old Russia*
Obs - S 29 '96 - p18* [51-250]

Popov, Nikolai - *Why? (Illus. by Nikolai Popov)*
c Bloom Rev - v16 - S '96 - p29 [51-250]
c HB Guide - v7 - Fall '96 - p271 [51-250]

Popov, V I - *Sovetnik Korolevy--Superagent Kremlia*
BL - v93 - O 1 '96 - p327 [1-50]

Poppema, Suzanne T - *Why I Am an Abortion Doctor*
Choice - v34 - O '96 - p314 [51-250]
Hast Cen R - v26 - Jl '96 - p42 [1-50]
SB - v32 - N '96 - p233 [51-250]
Wom R Bks - v14 - F '97 - p7+ [501+]

Popper, Karl Raimund, Sir - *The Lesson of This Century*
New Sci - v152 - N 30 '96 - p46 [1-50]
The Myth of the Framework
Ethics - v107 - Ja '97 - p405 [51-250]
Skeptic - v4 - 4 '96 - p104 [251-500]

Popular Mechanics
p LJ - v122 - F 1 '97 - p53 [1-50]

Population Summit (1993: New Delhi, India) - *Population: The Complex Reality*
GJ - v163 - Mr '97 - p105 [51-250]

Por, Francis Dov - *The Pantanal of Mato Grosso (Brazil)*
SciTech - v20 - D '96 - p33 [51-250]

Porat, Boaz - *A Course in Digital Signal Processing*
SciTech - v21 - Mr '97 - p86 [51-250]

Porcelli, Bruno - *Struttura E Lingua*
MLR - v92 - Ja '97 - p217+ [501+]

Porcelli, Joe - *The Photograph*
y SLJ - v42 - N '96 - p140 [51-250]

Porch, Douglas - *The French Secret Services*
TLS - Ag 2 '96 - p29 [501+]

Porcher, Richard D - *Wildflowers of the Carolina Lowcountry and Lower Pee Dee*
r AB - v97 - Je 17 '96 - p2397 [51-250]

Porete, Marguerite - *Marguerite Porete: The Mirror of Simple Souls*
CHR - v82 - Jl '96 - p552+ [251-500]

Porges, Amelia - *Analytical Index. Updated 6th Ed., Vols. 1-2*
r J Gov Info - v23 - S '96 - p741+ [501+]

Porges, Vivette - *Who Do You Say That I Am?*
CC - v114 - Ja 22 '97 - p86 [1-50]

Porket, J L - *Unemployment in Capitalist, Communist and Post-Communist Economies*
Econ J - v106 - S '96 - p1475 [51-250]
Slav R - v55 - Sum '96 - p442+ [501+]

Porshney, B F - *Muscovy and Sweden in the Thirty Years' War 1630-1635*
Choice - v34 - Mr '97 - p1222 [51-250]

Port, M H - *Imperial London*
EHR - v112 - Ap '97 - p509+ [501+]
Historian - v58 - Sum '96 - p915+ [501+]
VS - v39 - Spr '96 - p443+ [501+]

Porte, Barbara Ann - *Black Elephant with a Brown Ear (in Alabama) (Illus. by Bill Traylor)*
c HB Guide - v7 - Fall '96 - p296 [51-250]
Something Terrible Happened
y Kliatt - v31 - Ja '97 - p10 [51-250]

Portelli, Alessandro - *The Text and the Voice*
Col Lit - v23 - Je '96 - p181+ [501+]

Porteous, David J - *The Geography of Finance*
Econ J - v107 - Ja '97 - p290 [51-250]
R&R Bk N - v12 - F '97 - p47 [1-50]

Porter, Alison - *How Things Work*
c New Sci - v152 - D 14 '96 - p47 [51-250]

Porter, Anne - *An Altogether Different Language*
Comw - v123 - D 6 '96 - p21 [51-250]

Porter, Cecelia Hopkins - *The Rhine as Musical Metaphor*
Choice - v34 - My '97 - p1508+ [51-250]
R&R Bk N - v12 - F '97 - p71 [51-250]

Porter, Cheryl - *Gross Grub*
y Emerg Lib - v24 - S '96 - p26 [1-50]

Porter, Deborah Lynn - *From Deluge to Discourse*
R&R Bk N - v11 - N '96 - p6 [51-250]

Porter, Dennis - *Haunted Journeys*
JMH - v68 - S '96 - p617+ [501+]

Porter, Douglas R - *Housing for Seniors*
R&R Bk N - v11 - N '96 - p61 [51-250]

Porter, Eleanor H - *Pollyanna (Gordon). Audio Version*
c BL - v93 - My 15 '97 - p1595 [1-50]

Porter, Eliot - *Vanishing Songbirds*
CSM - v89 - D 5 '96 - pB3 [51-250]
LJ - v122 - Ja '97 - p139 [51-250]
Nature - v384 - D 12 '96 - p526 [51-250]

Porter, Francis Knowles - *From Belfast to Peking*
ILS - v16 - Spr '97 - p36 [1-50]

Porter, J R - *The Illustrated Guide to the Bible*
CLW - v66 - Je '96 - p30 [251-500]
LJ - v122 - F 15 '97 - p139 [51-250]
Rel St Rev - v23 - Ja '97 - p54 [51-250]

Porter, Jean - *Moral Action and Christian Ethics*
JR - v77 - Ja '97 - p172+ [501+]
Rel St Rev - v23 - Ap '97 - p157 [51-250]
RM - v50 - S '96 - p173+ [501+]
Theol St - v57 - Mr '96 - p190+ [251-500]

Porter, Jonathan - *Macau: The Imaginary City*
Choice - v34 - D '96 - p666 [51-250]

Porter, Katherine Anne - *Katherine Anne Porter's Poetry*
AL - v68 - D '96 - p880 [1-50]
VQR - v73 - Win '97 - p30* [51-250]

Porter, Kenneth W - *The Black Seminoles*
Choice - v34 - F '97 - p1026 [51-250]
LJ - v121 - O 1 '96 - p100 [51-250]

Porter, L J - *Assessing Business Excellence*
Choice - v34 - Ja '97 - p842 [51-250]
R&R Bk N - v11 - D '96 - p28 [51-250]

Porter, Laurence M - *Approaches to Teaching Flaubert's Madame Bovary*
Choice - v34 - S '96 - p132 [51-250]

Porter, Lynnette - *Research Strategies in Technical Communication*
CBR - v14 - S '96 - p27 [1-50]

Porter, Michael - *Competitive Strategy*
Inc. - v18 - D '96 - p56 [251-500]

Porter, Muriel - *Sex, Marriage and the Church*
Aust Bk R - Je '96 - p29+ [501+]

Porter, Norman - *Rethinking Unionism*
LJ - v122 - Ap 1 '97 - p108 [51-250]

Porter, Peter - *The Oxford Book of Modern Australian Verse*
Aust Bk R - N '96 - p16+ [501+]

Porter, R F - *Field Guide to the Birds of the Middle East*
r New Sci - v153 - Mr 8 '97 - p45 [51-250]

Porter, Robin - *Reporting the News from China*
Arm F&S - v22 - Sum '96 - p649+ [501+]

Porter, Roy - *The Cambridge Illustrated History of Medicine*
Bloom Rev - v16 - N '96 - p14 [51-250]
Nature - v384 - D 12 '96 - p528 [1-50]
New Sci - v154 - My 3 '97 - p49 [251-500]
Drugs and Narcotics in History
Historian - v59 - Win '97 - p491+ [251-500]
JEH - v56 - S '96 - p761+ [501+]
The Facts of Life
AHR - v101 - O '96 - p1210 [501+]
London: A Social History
AHR - v101 - O '96 - p1214+ [501+]
AJPsych - v153 - D '96 - p1651 [501+]
EHR - v112 - F '97 - p272+ [501+]
JMH - v69 - Mr '97 - p129+ [501+]
Obs - D 22 '96 - p18* [501+]
Rewriting the Self
HT - v46 - O '96 - p55 [1-50]
Obs - Mr 2 '97 - p18* [51-250]
Sexual Knowledge, Sexual Science
AHR - v101 - O '96 - p1178+ [501+]
EHR - v112 - F '97 - p151+ [501+]
JIH - v27 - Aut '96 - p282+ [501+]

Porter, Stanley E - *Approaches to New Testament Study*
Rel St Rev - v23 - Ap '97 - p177 [51-250]
New Testament Introduction
r ARBA - v28 - '97 - p542 [51-250]
Studies in the Greek New Testament
Rel St Rev - v23 - Ap '97 - p174 [51-250]
Verbal Aspect in the Greek of the New Testament
Rel St Rev - v23 - Ja '97 - p67 [51-250]

Porter, Sue - *Sweet Dreams (Illus. by Sue Porter)*
c HB Guide - v8 - Spr '97 - p14+ [51-250]
c KR - v64 - N 1 '96 - p1606 [51-250]
c PW - v243 - N 18 '96 - p77 [51-250]

Porter, Susan L - *Women of the Commonwealth*
Choice - v34 - S '96 - p200 [51-250]

Porter, Theodore M - *Trust in Numbers*
Bks & Cult - v3 - Ja '97 - p32+ [501+]
Isis - v87 - S '96 - p519+ [501+]
JEL - v35 - Mr '97 - p123+ [251-500]
T&C - v38 - Ja '97 - p259+ [501+]

Porter, Yves - *Painters, Paintings and Books*
MEJ - v50 - Aut '96 - p628+ [51-250]

Porterfield, Kay Marie - *Straight Talk about Post-Traumatic Stress Disorder*
y HB Guide - v7 - Fall '96 - p348 [51-250]

Porterfield, Nolan - *Jimmie Rodgers: The Life and Times of America's Blue Yodeler*
LJ - v121 - N 1 '96 - p42 [1-50]
Last Cavalier
BL - v93 - S 1 '96 - p54 [51-250]
Choice - v34 - F '97 - p975 [51-250]

Porterfield, Sally F - *Jung's Advice to the Players*
Shakes Q - v47 - Fall '96 - p353+ [501+]

Porter-Gaylord, Laurel - *I Love My Daddy Because... (Illus. by Ashley Wolff)*
c HB Guide - v7 - Fall '96 - p242 [51-250]
I Love My Mommy Because... (Illus. by Ashley Wolff)
c HB Guide - v7 - Fall '96 - p242 [51-250]

Portes, Alejandro - *Immigrant America. 2nd Ed.*
BW - v26 - D 15 '96 - p4 [501+]
The New Second Generation
BW - v26 - D 15 '96 - p4 [501+]
Choice - v34 - D '96 - p696 [51-250]
HER - v67 - Spr '97 - p160+ [251-500]
R&R Bk N - v11 - N '96 - p18 [51-250]

Portes, Richard - *Economic Transformation in Central Europe*
Econ J - v106 - S '96 - p1424+ [251-500]

Portner, Hans O - *Physiology of Cephalopod Molluscs*
Choice - v34 - S '96 - p155+ [51-250]

Portocarrero, Gonzalo - *Los Nuevos Limenos*
HAHR - v77 - My '97 - p346+ [251-500]
Racismo Y Mestizaje
HAHR - v76 - N '96 - p810 [251-500]

Porton, Gary G - *The Stranger within Your Gates*
BTB - v26 - Win '96 - p172 [501+]

Portugali, Juval - *The Construction of Cognitive Maps*
R&R Bk N - v11 - D '96 - p19 [51-250]

Posada-Carbo, Eduardo - *The Colombian Caribbean*
Choice - v34 - Ja '97 - p860 [51-250]

Posamentier, Alfred S - *Challenging Problems in Algebra*
Math T - v90 - Mr '97 - p248 [251-500]
Challenging Problems in Geometry
Math T - v90 - Ja '97 - p70 [251-500]

Posey, Carl - *Big Book of Weirdos*
y Emerg Lib - v24 - S '96 - p26 [1-50]

Posner, Gerald - *Citizen Perot*
BL - v93 - S 1 '96 - p29 [1-50]
BW - v26 - Ag 18 '96 - p5 [501+]
CSM - v88 - O 7 '96 - p15 [501+]
LATBR - Ag 11 '96 - p6 [501+]
NYTBR - v101 - Ag 25 '96 - p10+ [501+]
VQR - v73 - Win '97 - p18* [51-250]

Posner, Mitch - *Kai, a Big Decision*
c BL - v93 - My 1 '97 - p1495 [51-250]

Posner, Rebecca - *The Romance Languages*
Choice - v34 - My '97 - p1491 [51-250]

Posner, Richard A - *Aging and Old Age*
JEL - v35 - Mr '97 - p159+ [501+]
The Federal Courts
Choice - v34 - My '97 - p1578 [51-250]
LJ - v122 - Ja '97 - p122 [51-250]
A Guide to America's Sex Laws
r ARBA - v28 - '97 - p224 [51-250]
BW - v26 - N 3 '96 - p13 [51-250]
Overcoming Law
Law Q Rev - v112 - O '96 - p682+ [501+]
NYTBR - v101 - D 15 '96 - p40 [51-250]

Post, Emily - *Emily Post's Etiquette. 16th Ed.*
y BL - v93 - Ap 1 '97 - p1267 [51-250]

Post, Ken - *Regaining Marxism*
Choice - v34 - O '96 - p368 [51-250]

Post, Robert C - *High Performance*
Aethlon - v13 - Fall '95 - p163+ [251-500]

Post, Stephen Garrard - *The Moral Challenge of Alzheimer Disease*
MHR - v10 - Fall '96 - p108+ [501+]

Postel, Guillaume - *De Sommopere 1566. Le Miracle De Laon*
Ren Q - v50 - Spr '97 - p252+ [501+]

Postel, Sandra - *Dividing the Waters*
y SB - v33 - Mr '97 - p43 [51-250]

Postera Crescam Laude
Lib - v19 - Mr '97 - p101 [51-250]

Postgraduate Engineering and Technology Studies in Europe, the CIS and North America: 1996/97 Academic Year
  r Choice - v34 - D '96 - p594 [51-250]
Post-Lauria, Sheila - *Correspondent Colorings*
  Choice - v34 - D '96 - p616 [51-250]
  NEQ - v69 - D '96 - p645+ [501+]
Postle, Martin - *Sir Joshua Reynolds: The Subject Pictures*
  Albion - v28 - Win '96 - p697+ [501+]
Postman, Neil - *The End of Education*
  EL - v54 - D '96 - p84+ [501+]
  HER - v66 - Win '96 - p873+ [501+]
  Nat - v263 - O 28 '96 - p32+ [501+]
  PW - v243 - S 30 '96 - p79 [1-50]
Poston, Robert M - *Automated Specification-Based Software Testing*
  SciTech - v20 - S '96 - p6 [51-250]
Die Posttaxen Der Schweiz Ab 1875. Vol. 2
  Am Phil - v110 - O '96 - p909 [51-250]
Posusta, Steven - *Don't Panic*
  c Ch BWatch - v6 - Jl '96 - p1 [51-250]
Potash, Robert A - *The Army and Politics in Argentina 1962-1973. Vol. 3*
  Choice - v34 - O '96 - p343 [51-250]
  HRNB - v25 - Fall '96 - p17 [251-500]
  J Mil H - v61 - Ja '97 - p200+ [501+]
Poteau-Tralie, Mary L - *Voices of Authority*
  MLR - v92 - Ja '97 - p201+ [251-500]
Potkay, Adam - *Black Atlantic Writers of the 18th Century*
  JSH - v62 - N '96 - p861 [51-250]
  The Fate of Eloquence in the Age of Hume
  MP - v94 - F '97 - p396+ [501+]
  QJS - v83 - My '97 - p249+ [501+]
  RES - v48 - F '97 - p113+ [501+]
Potocki, Jan - *The Manuscript Found in Saragossa*
  AS - v66 - Win '97 - p152+ [501+]
  TranslRevS - v2 - D '96 - p24 [51-250]
Potok, Chaim - *The Gates of November*
  BL - v93 - N 1 '96 - p480 [51-250]
  KR - v64 - S 15 '96 - p1383 [251-500]
  LJ - v121 - N 1 '96 - p90 [51-250]
  NYTBR - v101 - D 1 '96 - p33 [501+]
  WSJ-MW - v78 - D 12 '96 - pA10 [501+]
Potparic, O - *A Dictionary of Sports Injuries and Disorders*
  r ARBA - v28 - '97 - p617 [51-250]
  r SciTech - v20 - D '96 - p48 [51-250]
Potpourri
  p Sm Pr R - v29 - F '97 - p22 [501+]
Potter, B G - *Synthesis and Application of Lanthanide-Doped Materials*
  SciTech - v21 - Mr '97 - p80 [51-250]
Potter, Beatrix - *The Adventures of Peter Rabbit and Benjamin Bunny. Electronic Media Version*
  c SLJ - v42 - S '96 - p144 [51-250]
  Beatrix Potter's Americans
  RSR - v24 - 3 '96 - p24 [51-250]
  Beatrix Potter's Letters
  RSR - v24 - 3 '96 - p24 [51-250]
  Bunnies
  c HB Guide - v7 - Fall '96 - p242 [51-250]
  Dear Peter Rabbit
  c HB Guide - v7 - Fall '96 - p271 [51-250]
  The Journal of Beatrix Potter from 1881 to 1897. Rev. Ed.
  RSR - v24 - 3 '96 - p24 [51-250]
  Letters to Children from Beatrix Potter
  RSR - v24 - 3 '96 - p25 [51-250]
  Mice
  c HB Guide - v7 - Fall '96 - p242 [51-250]
  The Peter Rabbit and Friends Treasury
  c PW - v244 - Mr 10 '97 - p68 [51-250]
  Scenes from Peter Rabbit
  c HB Guide - v7 - Fall '96 - p242 [51-250]
  Scenes from Tom Kitten
  c HB Guide - v7 - Fall '96 - p242 [51-250]
  The Tale of Jemima Puddle-Duck (Illus. by Beatrix Potter)
  c HB Guide - v7 - Fall '96 - p271 [1-50]
  The Tale of Peter Rabbit. Electronic Media Version
  c Ch BWatch - v6 - Jl '96 - p8 [51-250]
Potter, Ben - *An Introduction to Formal Specification and Z. 2nd Ed.*
  SciTech - v20 - D '96 - p11 [51-250]
Potter, D S - *Prophets and Emperors*
  QJS - v83 - My '97 - p260+ [501+]
Potter, David, 1931- - *NGOs and Environmental Policies*
  R&R Bk N - v11 - D '96 - p26 [1-50]
Potter, Harry - *Hanging in Judgment*
  Albion - v28 - Sum '96 - p327+ [501+]
  Rel St Rev - v23 - Ja '97 - p83 [51-250]

Potter, Janet Greenstein - *Great American Railroad Stations*
  Model R - v63 - N '96 - p60 [51-250]
Potter, Jeremy - *The Mystery of the Campden Wonder*
  Books - v9 - S '95 - p19 [51-250]
Potter, Jerry Allen - *Fatal Justice*
  PW - v244 - Ja 27 '97 - p103 [1-50]
Potter, Michelle A - *The Complete Saving Source Catalog*
  r BL - v92 - Ag '96 - p1866 [51-250]
Potter, Parker B, Jr. - *Public Archaeology in Annapolis*
  JIH - v27 - Aut '96 - p335+ [501+]
  Pub Hist - v18 - Sum '96 - p56+ [501+]
Potter, Robert B - *Low-Income Housing and the State in the Eastern Caribbean*
  GJ - v163 - Mr '97 - p107 [51-250]
  JEL - v34 - D '96 - p2139+ [501+]
Potter, Tessa - *Digger: The Story of a Mole in the Fall (Illus. by Kenneth Lilly)*
  c JB - v60 - D '96 - p238+ [51-250]
  Digger, the Story of a Mole in the Fall (Illus. by Kenneth Lilly)
  c Sch Lib - v44 - Ag '96 - p100+ [51-250]
  c TES - F 21 '97 - p16* [51-250]
  Fang, the Story of a Fox (Illus. by Kenneth Lilly)
  c JB - v60 - D '96 - p258 [51-250]
  c Sch Lib - v45 - F '97 - p20 [51-250]
  c TES - F 21 '97 - p16* [51-250]
  Greyfur, the Story of a Rabbit (Illus. by Kenneth Lilly)
  c JB - v60 - D '96 - p258 [51-250]
  c Sch Lib - v45 - F '97 - p20 [51-250]
  c TES - F 21 '97 - p16* [51-250]
  Louis Braille (Illus. by Helena Owen)
  c Bks Keeps - Ja '97 - p24 [251-500]
  c Sch Lib - v45 - F '97 - p37 [51-250]
  Sarn, the Story of an Otter (Illus. by Kenneth Lilly)
  c JB - v60 - D '96 - p238+ [51-250]
  c Sch Lib - v44 - Ag '96 - p100 [51-250]
  c TES - F 21 '97 - p16* [51-250]
Potter, Vincent G - *Peirce's Philosophical Perspectives*
  Choice - v34 - D '96 - p627 [51-250]
  IPQ - v37 - Je '97 - p225+ [501+]
Potterfield, Peter - *In the Zone*
  BL - v93 - S 1 '96 - p55 [51-250]
  Choice - v34 - Mr '97 - p1199 [51-250]
Potter-MacKinnon, Janice - *While the Women Only Wept*
  J Am Cult - v18 - Win '95 - p115 [51-250]
Potthoff, Wilfried - *Vuk Karadzic Im Europaischen Kontext*
  Slav R - v55 - Sum '96 - p456+ [501+]
Pottle, Russ - *Patriot Royal*
  PW - v243 - S 23 '96 - p62 [51-250]
Potts, Alex - *Flesh and the Ideal*
  AJA - v100 - Jl '96 - p631+ [501+]
Potts, D M - *Queen Victoria's Gene*
  CR - v269 - S '96 - p164 [251-500]
Potts, D T - *Mesopotamian Civilization*
  Choice - v34 - My '97 - p1553+ [51-250]
Potts, Timothy C - *Mesopotamia and the East*
  AJA - v101 - Ja '97 - p192+ [251-500]
  Structures and Categories for the Representation of Meaning
  Phil R - v105 - Ap '96 - p264+ [501+]
Poulakos, John - *Sophistical Rhetoric in Classical Greece*
  CW - v90 - S '96 - p64 [251-500]
Poularikas, Alexander D - *The Transforms and Applications Handbook*
  Choice - v34 - O '96 - p319 [51-250]
Poulin, Jacques - *Mr. Blue*
  TranslRevS - v1 - My '95 - p21 [51-250]
Poullada, Leon B - *The Kingdom of Afghanistan and the United States 1828-1973*
  MEJ - v50 - Aut '96 - p595+ [501+]
Poulle, Emmanuel - *Astronomie Planetaire Au Moyen Age Latin*
  SciTech - v20 - S '96 - p13 [51-250]
Poulsen, David A - *Billy and the Bearman*
  y Ch Bk News - v19 - Sum '96 - p30 [51-250]
  y Quill & Q - v62 - My '96 - p35 [251-500]
  The Vampire's Visit
  c Quill & Q - v62 - S '96 - p74 [251-500]
Poulson, Joan - *Girls Are like Diamonds (Illus. by H Dell)*
  y JB - v60 - Ag '96 - p160 [51-250]
  y Magpies - v11 - Jl '96 - p37 [51-250]
Poulsson, Emilie - *Baby's Breakfast (Illus. by Randy Cecil)*
  c HB Guide - v7 - Fall '96 - p242 [51-250]
Poulton, Hugh - *Who Are the Macedonians?*
  AHR - v102 - F '97 - p139+ [51-250]
  Historian - v58 - Sum '96 - p916+ [501+]
  TLS - Ja 31 '97 - p24 [501+]

Poulton, Terry - *No Fat Chicks*
  Quill & Q - v62 - S '96 - p68 [51-250]
Pouncy, Carolyn Johnston - *The Domostroi: Rules for Russian Households in the Time of Ivan the Terrible*
  Slav R - v55 - Sum '96 - p478+ [501+]
Pound, Ezra - *Dear Uncle George*
  Choice - v34 - Mr '97 - p1166 [51-250]
  Ezra Pound and Senator Bronson Cutting
  J Am St - v30 - D '96 - p485+ [501+]
  R&R Bk N - v11 - N '96 - p73 [501+]
  Pound/Cummings: The Correspondence of Ezra Pound and E.E. Cummings
  Choice - v34 - Mr '97 - p1166 [51-250]
  Selected Letters of Ezra Pound and William Carlos Williams
  AL - v68 - D '96 - p878 [1-50]
Pound, Richard W - *Five Rings over Seoul*
  Aethlon - v13 - Spr '96 - p206+ [501+]
Pounds, Norman John Greville - *The Culture of the English People*
  EHR - v111 - N '96 - p1229 [51-250]
  JIH - v27 - Aut '96 - p298+ [501+]
Poverman, C E - *On the Edge*
  KR - v65 - Ap 1 '97 - p494+ [251-500]
  LJ - v122 - Ap 1 '97 - p130+ [51-250]
  PW - v244 - Mr 24 '97 - p58 [51-250]
Povolo, Claudio - *Il Romanziere E L'Archivista*
  Ren Q - v49 - Aut '96 - p598+ [501+]
Puwaga, Wiesiek - *The Dedalus Book of Polish Fantasy*
  TLS - O 4 '96 - p38 [501+]
Powell, Agnes D - *The Duncans, by George!*
  r EGH - v50 - N '96 - p193 [501+]
Powell, Alan - *War by Stealth*
  Aust Bk R - S '96 - p15+ [501+]
  Choice - v34 - D '96 - p666 [51-250]
Powell, Anne - *The Fierce Light*
  CR - v269 - S '96 - p168 [51-250]
  TLS - O 11 '96 - p5 [501+]
Powell, Anthony - *Journals 1987-1989*
  Spec - v277 - N 16 '96 - p44 [1-50]
  TLS - N 29 '96 - p11 [1-50]
Powell, Anton - *The Greek News*
  c BL - v93 - D 1 '96 - p345+ [51-250]
  c CBRS - v25 - D '96 - p46+ [51-250]
  c HB Guide - v8 - Spr '97 - p166 [51-250]
  c KR - v64 - Ag 15 '96 - p1240+ [51-250]
  c Magpies - v11 - S '96 - p41 [51-250]
  c SLJ - v42 - N '96 - p39 [51-250]
  c SLJ - v43 - Ja '97 - p128+ [51-250]
  c Spec - v277 - D 14 '96 - p77 [51-250]
  c TES - N 8 '96 - p13* [251-500]
Powell, Arthur G - *Lessons from Privilege*
  LJ - v122 - F 1 '97 - p93 [51-250]
Powell, Barbara - *Windows into the Infinite*
  BL - v93 - S 15 '96 - p184 [51-250]
Powell, Charles C - *Ball Pest and Disease Manual. 2nd Ed.*
  SciTech - v21 - Mr '97 - p70 [51-250]
Powell, Colin - *My American Journey*
  JTWS - v13 - Spr '96 - p431+ [501+]
Powell, Dawn - *Angels on Toast*
  LJ - v121 - S 15 '96 - p102 [51-250]
  The Diaries of Dawn Powell 1931-1965
  NYTBR - v101 - D 8 '96 - p85+ [1-50]
  TLS - O 25 '96 - p32 [501+]
  WLT - v70 - Sum '96 - p705 [501+]
  The Locusts Have No King
  Nat R - v48 - D 23 '96 - p55 [501+]
  A Time to Be Born
  LJ - v121 - S 15 '96 - p102 [51-250]
  The Wicked Pavilion
  LJ - v121 - S 15 '96 - p102 [51-250]
Powell, Evan - *The Unfinished Gospel*
  JR - v76 - O '96 - p619+ [501+]
Powell, Geoffrey - *The Devil's Birthday*
  Mar Crp G - v81 - Mr '97 - p70+ [501+]
Powell, H Jefferson - *The Moral Tradition of American Constitutionalism*
  Bks & Cult - v2 - N '96 - p27+ [501+]
  JAAR - v64 - Win '96 - p883+ [501+]
Powell, Jillian - *Autumn on the Farm*
  c Sch Lib - v44 - N '96 - p165 [51-250]
  Bread
  c Bks Keeps - N '96 - p14 [51-250]
  Eggs
  c Sch Lib - v44 - Ag '96 - p113 [51-250]
  Fish
  c Bks Keeps - N '96 - p14 [51-250]
  A History of France through Art
  c HB Guide - v7 - Fall '96 - p382+ [51-250]

Pasta
c Bks Keeps - N '96 - p14 [51-250]
Potatoes
c Bks Keeps - N '96 - p14 [51-250]
Rice
c Sch Lib - v44 - Ag '96 - p113 [51-250]
Spring on the Farm
c Bks Keeps - Ja '97 - p23 [51-250]
c Sch Lib - v45 - F '97 - p40 [51-250]
Summer on the Farm
c Sch Lib - v44 - N '96 - p165 [51-250]
The Supernatural
c HB Guide - v7 - Fall '96 - p307 [1-50]
c SB - v32 - Ag '96 - p176 [51-250]
Winter on the Farm
c Bks Keeps - Ja '97 - p23 [51-250]
c Sch Lib - v45 - F '97 - p40 [51-250]
Powell, John - *Art, Truth, and High Politics*
r ARBA - v28 - '97 - p274 [51-250]
r Choice - v34 - Mr '97 - p1142 [251-500]
r R&R Bk N - v12 - F '97 - p15 [1-50]
Powell, Josh - *AIDS and HIV-Related Diseases*
Choice - v34 - F '97 - p997+ [51-250]
Powell, Lee Riley - *J. William Fulbright and His Time*
Choice - v34 - F '97 - p1026 [51-250]
Powell, Lynn - *Old and New Testaments*
ABR - v17 - Ag '96 - p12 [501+]
Shen - v46 - Win '96 - p118+ [501+]
Powell, Mark Allan - *God with Us*
Intpr - v51 - Ja '97 - p91 [251-500]
Rel St Rev - v23 - Ap '97 - p182 [51-250]
Powell, Neil - *Roy Fuller: Writer and Society*
WLT - v71 - Win '97 - p166 [251-500]
Powell, Padgett - *Edisto Revisited*
CSM - v88 - S 16 '96 - p13 [501+]
Powell, Patricia - *A Small Gathering of Bones*
JTWS - v13 - Fall '96 - p317+ [501+]
Powell, Polly - *Just Dessert (Illus. by Polly Powell)*
c HB Guide - v7 - Fall '96 - p271 [1-50]
c SLJ - v42 - Ag '96 - p128 [51-250]
Powell, Randy - *Dean Duffy*
y Emerg Lib - v24 - S '96 - p25 [1-50]
y Emerg Lib - v24 - S '96 - p27 [1-50]
Dean Duffy (Woodman). Audio Version
y Kliatt - v31 - My '97 - p36 [51-250]
The Whistling Toilets
y BL - v93 - S 15 '96 - p233 [51-250]
y CBRS - v25 - N '96 - p35 [51-250]
y CCB-B - v50 - N '96 - p110 [51-250]
y HB Guide - v8 - Spr '97 - p83 [1-50]
y JAAL - v40 - F '97 - p409 [51-250]
y SLJ - v42 - O '96 - p148 [51-250]
y VOYA - v19 - D '96 - p273 [51-250]
Powell, Richard J - *Black Art and Culture in the 20th Century*
y BL - v93 - F 15 '97 - p990 [51-250]
Bl S - v26 - Fall '96 - p105 [51-250]
LJ - v121 - S 15 '96 - p64 [51-250]
Powell, Robert - *Contributions to West Indian Herpetology*
SciTech - v20 - N '96 - p29 [51-250]
Powell, Sandra West - *When Wallflowers Die (Breck). Audio Version*
y Kliatt - v31 - My '97 - p46 [51-250]
Powell, Thomas J - *Understanding the Self-Help Organization*
Soc Ser R - v70 - S '96 - p503 [51-250]
Powell, William S - *Dictionary of North Carolina Biography. Vols. 2-6*
r JSH - v62 - N '96 - p858+ [51-250]
Powelson, Mark - *The Lost Gospel Q*
BL - v93 - D 1 '96 - p622 [51-250]
Power, Edward J - *Religion and the Public Schools in 19th Century America*
Choice - v34 - O '96 - p333 [51-250]
Power, Jack - *Crisis*
Aust Bk R - N '96 - p67 [51-250]
Power, Jo-Ann - *The Nightingale's Song*
PW - v244 - My 5 '97 - p206 [51-250]
Power, Kim - *Veiled Desire*
CC - v114 - Ja 15 '97 - p52+ [501+]
Power, Thomas Michael - *Environmental Protection and Economic Well-Being. 2nd Ed.*
Choice - v34 - D '96 - p660 [51-250]
JEL - v34 - D '96 - p141 [51-250]
Lost Landscapes and Failed Economies
Choice - v34 - Mr '97 - p1209+ [51-250]
JEL - v35 - Mr '97 - p302 [51-250]
Power, Vicki - *Vanity*
y Emerg Lib - v24 - S '96 - p26 [1-50]

PowerPC Microprocessor Common Hardware Reference Platform
SciTech - v20 - N '96 - p11 [51-250]
Powers, Alice Leccese - *Italy in Mind*
PW - v244 - Mr 17 '97 - p73 [51-250]
Powers, Celeste N - *Fine Needle Aspiration Biopsy of the Head and Neck*
SciTech - v20 - N '96 - p46 [51-250]
Powers, Charles T - *In the Memory of the Forest*
KR - v65 - F 1 '97 - p178 [1-50]
LATBR - Mr 23 '97 - p7 [501+]
NYTBR - v102 - Ap 13 '97 - p7 [501+]
PW - v243 - D 9 '96 - p58+ [51-250]
Powers, Margaret Fishback - *Margaret Fishback Powers Boxed Set*
BWatch - v17 - D '96 - p2 [51-250]
Powers, Mark - *The Shipping Forecast*
New Sci - v153 - F 8 '97 - p45 [51-250]
Powers, Richard, 1957- - *Galatea 2.2*
NYTBR - v101 - S 1 '96 - p24 [1-50]
The Gold Bug Variations
Critiq - v38 - Fall '96 - p12+ [501+]
Critiq - v38 - Fall '96 - p38+ [501+]
Operation Wandering Soul
Critiq - v38 - Fall '96 - p68+ [501+]
Powers, Richard Gid - *Not Without Honor*
NYTBR - v101 - D 8 '96 - p90 [1-50]
RAH - v24 - D '96 - p681+ [501+]
RP - v59 - Win '97 - p175+ [501+]
Powers, Stephen - *Hollywood's America*
Choice - v34 - D '96 - p623 [51-250]
Nat R - v48 - N 25 '96 - p70+ [501+]
TLS - Ja 17 '97 - p6 [501+]
Powers, Steven - *Afoot and Alone*
WHQ - v28 - Spr '97 - p102 [1-50]
Powers, Tim - *Expiration Date*
BYTE - v21 - Ag '96 - p142 [51-250]
y Kliatt - v31 - Mr '97 - p20 [51-250]
PW - v243 - N 4 '96 - p42 [1-50]
Powers, Treval C - *Leakage: The Bleeding of the American Economy*
NL - v79 - N 4 '96 - p12+ [501+]
R&R Bk N - v11 - D '96 - p23 [51-250]
Powling, Anne - *New Oxford English 2*
y TES - S 20 '96 - pR7 [501+]
Powling, Chris - *A Guide to Poetry 0-13*
Sch Lib - v44 - N '96 - p177 [251-500]
Harry the Superhero
c Magpies - v11 - Jl '96 - p28 [1-50]
Powning, Beth - *Home: Chronicle of a North Country Life*
Bloom Rev - v16 - N '96 - p20 [51-250]
Poydar, Nancy - *Cool Ali (Illus. by Nancy Poydar)*
c BL - v92 - Ag '96 - p1908 [51-250]
c CCB-B - v50 - O '96 - p73+ [51-250]
c HB - v72 - S '96 - p578+ [251-500]
c HB Guide - v8 - Spr '97 - p43 [51-250]
c SLJ - v42 - S '96 - p187+ [51-250]
Poyer, David - *Down to a Sunless Sea*
KR - v64 - S 1 '96 - p1263 [251-500]
LJ - v121 - O 15 '96 - p91 [51-250]
PW - v243 - O 7 '96 - p63 [51-250]
Poynter, Margaret - *Killer Asteroids*
c HB Guide - v7 - Fall '96 - p331 [51-250]
c SB - v32 - O '96 - p209 [51-250]
Poznansky, Alexander - *Tchaikovsky's Last Days*
Choice - v34 - Ap '97 - p1348 [51-250]
KR - v64 - Ag 15 '96 - p1220 [251-500]
LJ - v121 - O 1 '96 - p80 [51-250]
NYTBR - v102 - F 2 '97 - p20+ [51-250]
Spec - v277 - D 7 '96 - p52+ [501+]
Pozo, Susan - *Exploring the Underground Economy*
JEL - v34 - S '96 - p1419 [51-250]
Prabhakara, F S - *Industrial and Commercial Power Systems Handbook*
Choice - v34 - S '96 - p159+ [51-250]
Practical Guide to Interviewing Teachers
H Sch M - v4 - Mr '97 - p56 [51-250]
Practical Guide to Planned Giving 1996
r RQ - v36 - Fall '96 - p136 [501+]
The Practical Guide to Practically Everything 1997
r LATBR - D 22 '96 - p6 [51-250]
yr LJ - v121 - O 15 '96 - p52+ [51-250]
Practice Parameters for the Psychiatric Assessment of Children and Adolescents
Soc Ser R - v70 - S '96 - p502 [51-250]
Pradhan, Sanjay - *Evaluating Public Spending*
JEL - v34 - D '96 - p2060 [51-250]
Pradl, Gordon M - *Literature for Democracy*
Col Comp - v47 - D '96 - p619 [51-250]

Prager, Jan C - *Environmental Contaminant Reference Databook. Vols. 1-2*
r ARBA - v28 - '97 - p630 [51-250]
Prager, Karen J - *The Psychology of Intimacy*
JMF - v58 - Ag '96 - p805+ [251-500]
Readings - v11 - S '96 - p28+ [51-250]
Prager, M - *Structural Integrity, NDE, Risk and Material Performance for Petroleum, Process and Power*
SciTech - v20 - D '96 - p85 [51-250]
Prague and the Best of the Czech Republic
r BL - v93 - S 15 '96 - p210 [1-50]
Prahl, Roman - *Freie Richtungen*
BM - v139 - Ja '97 - p53 [501+]
Prahlad, Sw. Anand - *African-American Proverbs in Context*
Choice - v34 - Ja '97 - p797 [51-250]
Prakash, G K Surya - *Stable Carbocation Chemistry*
SciTech - v21 - Mr '97 - p30 [51-250]
Prakash, Gyan - *After Colonialism*
Am Ethnol - v24 - F '97 - p212+ [501+]
Cont Pac - v9 - Spr '97 - p295+ [501+]
HAHR - v76 - Ag '96 - p620+ [501+]
JTWS - v13 - Spr '96 - p401+ [501+]
Prang, Margaret - *A Heart at Leisure from Itself*
Can Hist R - v78 - Mr '97 - p157+ [501+]
Pranger, M B - *Bernard of Clairvaux and the Shape of Monastic Thought*
CH - v65 - S '96 - p457+ [501+]
Specu - v72 - Ja '97 - p211+ [501+]
Prantera, Amanda - *Zoe Trope*
TLS - N 22 '96 - p23 [501+]
Pranty, Bill - *A Birder's Guide to Florida. 4th Ed.*
r Wildbird - v11 - F '97 - p38 [51-250]
Prasad, Biren - *Concurrent Engineering Fundamentals. Vol. 2*
SciTech - v20 - D '96 - p85 [51-250]
Prasad, Ramjee - *CDMA for Wireless Personal Communications*
SciTech - v20 - S '96 - p55 [51-250]
Prasolov, V V - *Knots, Links, Braids and 3-Manifolds*
SciTech - v21 - Mr '97 - p17 [51-250]
Prassel, Frank Richard - *The Great American Outlaw*
SFR - v21 - N '96 - p28+ [501+]
Prat, Marie-Helene - *Les Mots Du Corps*
Ren Q - v50 - Spr '97 - p252+ [501+]
Pratchett, Terry - *Feet of Clay*
y BL - v93 - O 1 '96 - p326 [51-250]
BW - v26 - S 29 '96 - p11 [251-500]
LJ - v121 - O 15 '96 - p93 [51-250]
PW - v243 - S 30 '96 - p65 [51-250]
y VOYA - v19 - F '97 - p339+ [51-250]
Interesting Times
KR - v65 - Mr 1 '97 - p342 [51-250]
LJ - v122 - Ap 15 '97 - p124 [51-250]
PW - v244 - Mr 31 '97 - p67 [51-250]
Johnny and the Bomb
c Magpies - v11 - S '96 - p34 [51-250]
Johnny and the Bomb (Robinson). Audio Version
y Sch Lib - v44 - Ag '96 - p121 [51-250]
Men at Arms
LJ - v121 - O 15 '96 - p112 [51-250]
MFSF - v91 - S '96 - p39+ [501+]
y VOYA - v19 - O '96 - p220 [251-500]
Pratelidis, Konstantin - *Tafelrunde Und Gral*
MLR - v91 - Jl '96 - p779+ [501+]
Prater, Donald - *Thomas Mann: A Life*
Ant R - v54 - Sum '96 - p369+ [251-500]
Lon R Bks - v18 - S 5 '96 - p3+ [501+]
MLR - v92 - Ap '97 - p515+ [501+]
Prater, John - *No! Said Joe*
c Magpies - v11 - Jl '96 - p45 [1-50]
Once upon a Picnic (Illus. by John Prater)
c BL - v92 - Ag '96 - p1908 [51-250]
c HB Guide - v7 - Fall '96 - p256 [51-250]
c JB - v60 - O '96 - p183 [51-250]
c Sch Lib - v44 - Ag '96 - p101 [51-250]
c SLJ - v42 - Ag '96 - p122 [51-250]
Pratesi, Alessandro - *Frustula Paleographica*
Lib - v18 - Je '96 - p155+ [251-500]
Pratt, E J - *Pursuits Amateur and Academic*
Can Lit - Spr '97 - p237+ [501+]
Pratt, Kristin Joy - *A Fly in the Sky (Illus. by Kristin Joy Pratt)*
c CLW - v67 - D '96 - p57+ [51-250]
c SLJ - v42 - Ag '96 - p140 [51-250]
Pratt, Mary Louise - *Imperial Eyes*
JMH - v68 - S '96 - p617+ [501+]
Pratt, Minnie Bruce - *S/He*
VV - v42 - Ja 7 '97 - p42 [51-250]

Pratt, Paula Bryant - *Jane Goodall*
  c HB Guide - v8 - Spr '97 - p157 [1-50]
  y SLJ - v43 - F '97 - p123 [51-250]
Pratt, William - *Singing the Chaos*
  Ant R - v54 - Fall '96 - p495+ [251-500]
  Choice - v34 - O '96 - p280 [51-250]
  WLT - v70 - Aut '96 - p1039+ [501+]
Prawer, Joshua - *The History of Jerusalem*
  MEJ - v51 - Spr '97 - p313 [51-250]
Prazmowska, Anita J - *Britain and Poland 1939-1943*
  J Mil H - v61 - Ja '97 - p188+ [501+]
Prazniak, Roxann - *Dialogues across Civilizations*
  Ch Rev Int - v4 - Spr '97 - p224+ [501+]
Precoat Filtration. 2nd Ed.
  SciTech - v20 - N '96 - p68 [1-50]
Precursori Di Cristoforo Colombo
  EHR - v112 - F '97 - p172+ [501+]
  Specu - v71 - O '96 - p954+ [501+]
Pred, Allan - *Recognizing European Modernities*
  AAAGA - v87 - Mr '97 - p191+ [501+]
Pree, Wolfgang - *Framework Patterns*
  SciTech - v21 - Mr '97 - p5 [51-250]
Preece, Rod - *Animal Welfare and Human Values*
  Dal R - v75 - Spr '95 - p118+ [501+]
Preeg, Ernest H - *The Haitian Dilemma*
  Parameters - v26 - Win '96 - p156 [1-50]
  Traders in a Brave New World
  Econ J - v107 - Ja '97 - p270 [251-500]
Prehistorya Yazilari
  AJA - v100 - Jl '96 - p608+ [501+]
Preinreich, Gabriel A D - *A Landmark in Accounting Theory*
  AR - v72 - Ja '97 - p179+ [251-500]
  R&R Bk N - v11 - N '96 - p35 [51-250]
Preiskel, Harold W - *Overdentures Made Easy*
  SciTech - v21 - Mr '97 - p66 [51-250]
Preiss, Byron - *The Best Children's Books in the World*
  c BL - v93 - S 15 '96 - p252 [1-50]
  c HB - v73 - My '97 - p348 [51-250]
  c KR - v64 - N 15 '96 - p1677 [51-250]
  c PW - v243 - N 25 '96 - p76 [51-250]
  c SLJ - v42 - D '96 - p124 [51-250]
Prelec, Kresto - *Production and Neutralization of Negative Ions and Beams*
  SciTech - v21 - Mr '97 - p25 [51-250]
Prelinger, Catherine M - *Episcopal Women*
  CH - v66 - Mr '97 - p181+ [501+]
Prelinger, Elizabeth - *The Symbolist Prints of Edvard Munch*
  Obs - Mr 9 '97 - p16* [51-250]
Preller, James - *Hiccups for Elephant (Illus. by Hans Wilhelm)*
  c Learning - v25 - Ag '96 - p96 [51-250]
Prelutsky, Jack - *Monday's Troll (Illus. by Peter Sis)*
  c Ch BWatch - v6 - My '96 - p3 [1-50]
  c HB Guide - v7 - Fall '96 - p368 [51-250]
  c SLJ - v42 - D '96 - p31 [1-50]
  Monday's Troll (Prelutsky). Audio Version
  c BL - v93 - Mr 15 '97 - p1253 [51-250]
  c BL - v93 - Ap 1 '97 - p1314 [1-50]
  c Emerg Lib - v24 - Mr '97 - p23 [51-250]
  A Pizza the Size of the Sun (Illus. by James Stevenson)
  c BL - v93 - Ja '97 - p766 [1-50]
  c BL - v93 - S 15 '96 - p241 [51-250]
  c BW - v26 - O 13 '96 - p13 [51-250]
  c CCB-B - v50 - S '96 - p25 [51-250]
  c HB - v72 - S '96 - p605+ [51-250]
  c HB Guide - v8 - Spr '97 - p153 [51-250]
  c PW - v243 - N 4 '96 - p49 [1-50]
  c SLJ - v42 - S '96 - p219 [51-250]
  c SLJ - v42 - D '96 - p31 [1-50]
Premiers Mots Pour Bebes De 12-18 Mois
  c BL - v93 - N 1 '96 - p500 [1-50]
The Prentice Hall Directory of Online Business Information 1997
  r ARBA - v28 - '97 - p83+ [501+]
  r BL - v93 - Ja '97 - p900 [251-500]
  r LJ - v121 - N 1 '96 - p60 [51-250]
Prentzas, G S - *Mario Andretti*
  c HB Guide - v7 - Fall '96 - p359 [51-250]
  y SLJ - v42 - Ag '96 - p168 [51-250]
Prenzlau, Sheryl - *The Jewish Children's Bible: Genesis (Illus. by Daniel Goldberg)*
  c HB Guide - v8 - Spr '97 - p88 [51-250]
Preparing for the 21st Century
  J Gov Info - v23 - S '96 - p559 [51-250]
Prescott, Ellen - *Mondays Are Yellow, Sundays Are Gray*
  Obs - D 1 '96 - p17* [51-250]
Preserving Ontario's Harvest by Foodland Ontario
  J Gov Info - v23 - S '96 - p634 [1-50]

Presidential Elections 1789-1992
  r CLW - v66 - Je '96 - p39 [251-500]
  r J Gov Info - v23 - Jl '96 - p532+ [501+]
President's Council on Sustainable Development - *Sustainable America*
  BioSci - v47 - Mr '97 - p196 [51-250]
  J Gov Info - v23 - S '96 - p552+ [51-250]
Presilla, Maricel E - *Life around the Lake*
  c AB - v98 - N 18 '96 - p1730 [51-250]
  c HB Guide - v7 - Fall '96 - p391+ [51-250]
  c Smith - v27 - N '96 - p174 [1-50]
  Mola: Cuna Life Stories and Art
  c BL - v93 - O 1 '96 - p346 [51-250]
  c CCB-B - v50 - Ja '97 - p184 [51-250]
  c HB Guide - v8 - Spr '97 - p178 [51-250]
  c KR - v64 - Ag 15 '96 - p1241 [51-250]
  c PW - v243 - N 4 '96 - p76 [51-250]
  c SLJ - v42 - O '96 - p138 [51-250]
Presnall, Judith Janda - *Artificial Organs*
  y HB Guide - v7 - Fall '96 - p348 [51-250]
  Circuses: Under the Big Top
  c SLJ - v43 - Mr '97 - p195 [51-250]
Press, Margaret - *Counterpoint: A Murder in Massachusetts Bay*
  Arm Det - v29 - Fall '96 - p505 [251-500]
Press, Petra - *A Multicultural Portrait of Immigration*
  y HB Guide - v7 - Fall '96 - p313 [51-250]
  y SLJ - v42 - Ag '96 - p176 [51-250]
  Puerto Ricans
  yr Ch BWatch - v6 - O '96 - p5 [51-250]
  c HB Guide - v7 - Fall '96 - p312 [51-250]
Press, William H - *Numerical Recipes in Fortran 90*
  SB - v33 - My '97 - p100 [251-500]
Pressman, Alan H - *The GSH Phenomenon*
  BL - v93 - F 1 '97 - p917 [51-250]
Pressman, Roger - *Manager's Guide to Software Engineering*
  CBR - v14 - S '96 - p32 [1-50]
Pressman, Steven - *Interactions in Political Economy*
  JEL - v35 - Mr '97 - p205+ [51-250]
Presson, Leslie - *What in the World Is a Homophone?*
  cr SLMQ - v25 - Fall '96 - p65+ [1-50]
Pressure Vessels and Piping Codes and Standards. Vols. 1-2
  SciTech - v20 - N '96 - p83 [51-250]
Preston, Caroline - *Jackie by Josie*
  Ent W - F 7 '97 - p64+ [51-250]
  KR - v64 - D 1 '96 - p1697+ [251-500]
  LJ - v121 - D '96 - p146+ [51-250]
  NYTBR - v102 - F 23 '97 - p10 [501+]
  PW - v243 - N 25 '96 - p56 [51-250]
  Trib Bks - F 16 '97 - p6+ [501+]
Preston, Douglas - *Mount Dragon*
  Necro - Win '97 - p28 [51-250]
  Mount Dragon (Colacci). Audio Version
  y Kliatt - v30 - S '96 - p50 [51-250]
  LJ - v121 - S 15 '96 - p114 [51-250]
  Relic
  y Emerg Lib - v24 - S '96 - p25 [1-50]
  Reliquary
  y BL - v93 - Mr 15 '97 - p1205 [51-250]
  KR - v65 - Mr 15 '97 - p411+ [251-500]
  LJ - v122 - My 1 '97 - p143 [51-250]
  PW - v244 - Mr 3 '97 - p64 [51-250]
  Trib Bks - Ap 20 '97 - p7 [51-250]
  Talking to the Ground
  Smith - v27 - S '96 - p114+ [501+]
Preston, Ivan L - *The Great American Blow-Up. Rev. Ed.*
  Choice - v34 - Ap '97 - p1385 [51-250]
  JEL - v35 - Mr '97 - p255 [51-250]
  R&R Bk N - v12 - F '97 - p46 [51-250]
Preston, John - *Flesh and the Word*
  Quill & Q - v62 - Jl '96 - p42 [501+]
Preston, John, 1953- - *Ghosting*
  Obs - Ag 18 '96 - p19 [51-250]
  Spec - v277 - N 16 '96 - p46 [1-50]
  TLS - S 13 '96 - p24 [251-500]
Preston, Paul - *The Coming of the Spanish Civil War. 2nd Ed.*
  JMH - v68 - S '96 - p722+ [501+]
Preston, Richard - *First Light. 1st Rev. Ed.*
  Astron - v25 - My '97 - p112 [1-50]
  Choice - v34 - My '97 - p1521 [51-250]
  Nature - v384 - D 12 '96 - p528 [1-50]
  S&T - v92 - S '96 - p54 [1-50]
  S&T - v93 - Ap '97 - p65 [1-50]
  Hot Zone
  y Emerg Lib - v24 - S '96 - p24 [1-50]
Preston, Ronald H - *Confusions in Christian Ethics*
  Theol St - v58 - Mr '97 - p200+ [251-500]

Preston, Scott - *Canyonvue*
  WAL - v31 - Win '97 - p413+ [251-500]
  Letters from Elko
  WAL - v31 - Fall '96 - p280+ [251-500]
Preston, Tom - *The Double Eagle Guide to Western State Parks. Vol. 1, 2nd Ed.; Vols. 2-6*
  r LJ - v122 - F 15 '97 - p153 [51-250]
Preston, William, Jr. - *Aliens and Dissenters. 2nd Ed.*
  S&S - v60 - Win '96 - p517+ [501+]
Preston-Dunlop, Valerie - *Dance Words*
  r ARBA - v28 - '97 - p503 [251-500]
  r Choice - v34 - O '96 - p256 [51-250]
Preston-Mafham, Rod - *The Natural History of Insects*
  y BL - v93 - My 1 '97 - p1469 [51-250]
Prestwich, Michael - *Armies and Warfare in the Middle Ages*
  Choice - v34 - O '96 - p341 [51-250]
  HRNB - v25 - Win '97 - p71+ [501+]
  HT - v47 - F '97 - p60+ [501+]
  VQR - v72 - Aut '96 - p116* [51-250]
Preuss, Horst Dietrich - *Old Testament Theology. Vols. 1-2*
  Rel St Rev - v23 - Ap '97 - p169 [51-250]
  Theol St - v58 - Mr '97 - p150+ [501+]
Prevedello, Barbara - *Centro Cooks*
  Quill & Q - v62 - O '96 - p39 [51-250]
Prevention Magazine Health Books - *The Doctors Book of Home Remedies for Women*
  r BL - v93 - Ja '97 - p797 [51-250]
  The Female Body
  r BL - v93 - S 15 '96 - p194 [51-250]
  Prevention's Healing with Vitamins
  r BL - v93 - S 1 '96 - p167+ [251-500]
  Prevention's the Healthy Cook
  BL - v93 - F 15 '97 - p989 [51-250]
  LJ - v122 - Mr 15 '97 - p82 [51-250]
  PW - v244 - F 3 '97 - p102 [51-250]
Prevention, Response, and Oversight Five Years after the Exxon Valdez Oil Spill
  J Gov Info - v23 - S '96 - p577+ [1-50]
Prevost, Philippe - *La France Et La Canada*
  AHR - v102 - F '97 - p120 [501+]
Prevost-Marchilhacy, Pauline - *Les Rothschild: Batisseurs Et Mecenes*
  BM - v138 - Ag '96 - p551 [251-500]
Price, Alan - *The End of the Age of Innocence*
  AL - v69 - Mr '97 - p229+ [51-250]
  BW - v26 - Jl 7 '96 - p13 [51-250]
  Choice - v34 - O '96 - p280 [51-250]
  Legacy - v14 - 1 '97 - p74 [51-250]
  NYTBR - v101 - D 29 '96 - p15 [251-500]
Price, Catherine - *The Oglala People 1841-1879*
  Choice - v34 - S '96 - p196 [51-250]
  Roundup M - v4 - O '96 - p28 [51-250]
  WHQ - v27 - Win '96 - p520 [251-500]
Price, Charles F - *Hiwassee: A Novel of the Civil War*
  LATBR - Ag 25 '96 - p11 [51-250]
Price, Curtis - *Italian Opera in Late Eighteenth-Century London. Vol. 1*
  Albion - v28 - Sum '96 - p315+ [501+]
  Theat J - v49 - Mr '97 - p90+ [501+]
  Purcell Studies
  Notes - v53 - Mr '97 - p791+ [501+]
Price, Eugenia - *The Waiting Time*
  BL - v93 - Mr 15 '97 - p1205 [51-250]
  KR - v65 - Ap 1 '97 - p495 [251-500]
  LJ - v122 - Ap 15 '97 - p120 [51-250]
  PW - v244 - Mr 24 '97 - p58 [51-250]
Price, Frank - *Loving Work*
  R&R Bk N - v12 - F '97 - p44 [51-250]
Price, George McCready - *Selected Works of George McCready Price*
  Isis - v88 - Mr '97 - p160+ [501+]
Price, Huw - *Time's Arrow and Archimedes' Point*
  Choice - v34 - N '96 - p497 [51-250]
  Nature - v383 - S 19 '96 - p228+ [501+]
  Parabola - v21 - Ag '96 - p120 [1-50]
  Phys Today - v50 - Ja '97 - p68+ [501+]
Price, J L - *Holland and the Dutch Republic in the Seventeenth Century*
  EHR - v111 - S '96 - p994+ [251-500]
  Ren Q - v50 - Spr '97 - p298+ [501+]
Price, Jacob M - *The Atlantic Frontier of the Thirteen Colonies and States*
  R&R Bk N - v11 - N '96 - p34 [51-250]
  Tobacco in Atlantic Trade
  JEH - v57 - Mr '97 - p213 [251-500]
  R&R Bk N - v12 - F '97 - p41 [51-250]
Price, Jerome A - *Power and Compassion*
  SciTech - v21 - Mr '97 - p65 [51-250]

Price, Jody - *A Map with Utopia*
    Choice - v34 - My '97 - p1498 [51-250]
Price, Jonathan - *Video-Visions*
    Afterimage - v24 - N '96 - p4 [1-50]
Price, Kenneth M - *Periodical Literature in Nineteenth-Century America*
    AL - v68 - S '96 - p664 [51-250]
    Nine-C Lit - v51 - S '96 - p275+ [51-250]
    Walt Whitman: The Contemporary Reviews
    r AL - v69 - Mr '97 - p256 [51-250]
    Choice - v34 - F '97 - p966 [51-250]
    Nine-C Lit - v51 - Mr '97 - p563 [51-250]
Price, Martin F - *Mountain Environments and Geographic Information Systems*
    GJ - v162 - Jl '96 - p234 [51-250]
Price, Monroe E - *Television: The Public Sphere and National Identity*
    Choice - v34 - S '96 - p117 [51-250]
Price, Munro - *Preserving the Monarchy*
    EHR - v112 - Ap '97 - p494+ [501+]
    HT - v47 - Mr '97 - p52+ [501+]
Price, Nicholas Stanley - *Historical and Philosophical Issues in the Conservation of Cultural Heritage*
    Apo - v145 - F '97 - p60 [501+]
    Choice - v34 - F '97 - p956 [51-250]
    LJ - v122 - Ap 1 '97 - p89 [51-250]
Price, Nick - *The Swing: Mastering the Principles of the Game*
    LJ - v122 - My 1 '97 - p111 [51-250]
Price, Nigel - *Decision and Discrete Mathematics*
    Choice - v34 - My '97 - p1536 [51-250]
Price, Pamela G - *Kingship and Political Practice in Colonial India*
    Choice - v34 - Ap '97 - p1395 [51-250]
Price, Paxton P - *Mesilla Valley Pioneers 1823-1912*
    WHQ - v27 - Win '96 - p548 [1-50]
Price, Reynolds - *The Collected Poems*
    y BL - v93 - My 1 '97 - p1475 [51-250]
    LJ - v122 - Ap 1 '97 - p98 [51-250]
    Good Hearts
    South CR - v28 - Spr '96 - p78+ [501+]
    The Promise of Rest
    NYTBR - v101 - N 17 '96 - p40 [51-250]
    PW - v243 - S 30 '96 - p79 [1-50]
    Three Gospels
    Bks & Cult - v2 - S '96 - p21+ [501+]
    LATBR - D 29 '96 - p5 [51-250]
    PW - v243 - N 4 '96 - p46+ [1-50]
    Trib Bks - My 18 '97 - p8 [1-50]
    W&I - v11 - S '96 - p280+ [501+]
Price, Richard - *Augustine*
    TES - F 21 '97 - p7* [1-50]
Price, Richard, 1941- - *Equatoria*
    JMH - v68 - S '96 - p617+ [501+]
Price, Rumi Kato - *Social Psychiatry across Cultures*
    Readings - v11 - S '96 - p22+ [51-250]
Price, Susan - *Horror Stories (Illus. by Harry Horse)*
    y CLW - v66 - Je '96 - p54+ [251-500]
Price, Susanna - *Click! Fun with Photography*
    c Sch Lib - v44 - Ag '96 - p125 [51-250]
Price Caps for Telecommunications
    J Gov Info - v23 - S '96 - p675 [51-250]
Price Waterhouse (Firm). Change Integration Team -
    The Paradox Principles
    Bus Bk R - v13 - 3 '96 - p40+ [501+]
The Price Waterhouse Guide to TIN Compliance. 1996-1997 Ed.
    r R&R Bk N - v12 - F '97 - p65 [51-250]
Priceman, Marjorie - *How to Make an Apple Pie and See the World (Illus. by Marjorie Priceman)*
    c Inst - v106 - O '96 - p93 [1-50]
    c PW - v243 - O 21 '96 - p85 [1-50]
Prices and Financial Statistics in the ESCWA Region. 13th Ed.
    r ARBA - v28 - '97 - p95 [51-250]
    r R&R Bk N - v12 - F '97 - p47 [51-250]
Prichard, Caradog - *One Moonlit Night*
    BL - v93 - F 1 '97 - p926 [51-250]
    BW - v27 - Mr 30 '97 - p3 [501+]
    KR - v65 - Ja 1 '97 - p20 [51-250]
    PW - v244 - Ja 20 '97 - p396 [51-250]
Prichard, E - *Trace Analysis*
    SciTech - v20 - S '96 - p16 [51-250]
Prickett, Stephen - *Origins of Narrative*
    Choice - v34 - F '97 - p960 [51-250]
    TLS - Ag 30 '96 - p32 [251-500]
Priddy, Laurance L - *Winning Passion*
    Aethlon - v13 - Spr '96 - p201+ [501+]

Priddy, Roger - *Baby's Book of the Body*
    c ECEJ - v24 - Win '96 - p108 [51-250]
    c HB Guide - v8 - Spr '97 - p15 [51-250]
    c SLJ - v42 - Ag '96 - p140 [51-250]
    My Big Book of Everything
    c BL - v93 - D 15 '96 - p730 [51-250]
    c HB Guide - v8 - Spr '97 - p15 [51-250]
    c PW - v243 - N 11 '96 - p77 [51-250]
    c SLJ - v43 - Ja '97 - p107+ [51-250]
Prideaux, James - *Knowing Hepburn and Other Curious Experiences*
    Ent W - N 8 '96 - p62 [51-250]
    KR - v64 - S 15 '96 - p1383+ [251-500]
    LJ - v121 - N 1 '96 - p69+ [51-250]
    PW - v243 - S 16 '96 - p61+ [51-250]
Pridgen, William - *Night of the Dragon's Blood*
    PW - v244 - F 17 '97 - p212 [51-250]
Priest, Christopher - *The Prestige*
    BW - v26 - O 27 '96 - p4 [501+]
    Ent W - N 1 '96 - p65 [51-250]
    LJ - v121 - S 15 '96 - p97 [51-250]
    Necro - Win '97 - p14+ [501+]
    PW - v243 - Jl 22 '96 - p226 [51-250]
Priest, Joan - *Sir Harry Gibbs: Without Fear or Favour*
    Aust Bk R - F '97 - p19 [501+]
Priest, John Michael - *Nowhere to Run*
    JSH - v62 - N '96 - p822+ [251-500]
Priest, Robert - *Knights of the Endless Day (Illus. by Vic Vaccaro)*
    y Can CL - v22 - Sum '96 - p87+ [51-250]
Priestley, David T - *Memory and History*
    R&R Bk N - v11 - D '96 - p6 [51-250]
Priestley, M J N - *Seismic Design and Retrofit of Bridges*
    Choice - v34 - S '96 - p160 [51-250]
Prigogine, I - *Polymeric Systems*
    SciTech - v20 - S '96 - p16 [51-250]
Prill, David - *Serial Killer Days*
    Necro - Fall '96 - p1+ [501+]
    The Unnatural
    Necro - Fall '96 - p1+ [501+]
Primack, Richard B - *Ecology, Conservation, and Management of Southeast Asian Rainforests*
    Env - v38 - N '96 - p30+ [51-250]
The Primary Assembly File
    TES - Mr 21 '97 - p27* [251-500]
Primeau, Ronald - *Romance of the Road*
    Choice - v34 - N '96 - p459 [51-250]
    R&R Bk N - v11 - N '96 - p72 [51-250]
Prince, Betty - *High Performance Memories*
    SciTech - v21 - Mr '97 - p93 [51-250]
Prince, Maggie - *Here Comes a Candle to Light You to Bed*
    y JB - v60 - O '96 - p205+ [251-500]
    y Obs - v54 - O 13 '96 - p18* [51-250]
    y Sch Lib - v44 - N '96 - p171+ [51-250]
    c TES - S 13 '96 - p7* [501+]
    Pulling the Plug on the Universe
    c Bks Keeps - v100 - S '96 - p13 [51-250]
Princeau, Gerard M - *Le Ravin*
    BL - v93 - Ja '97 - p827 [1-50]
Princeton Arts Review
    p Sm Pr R - v29 - F '97 - p23 [51-250]
The Princeton Review College Advisor. 1997 Ed. Electronic Media Version
    yr Kliatt - v30 - N '96 - p34 [51-250]
The Princeton Review Guide to Your Career. 1997 Ed.
    r B Ent - v27 - N '96 - p62 [51-250]
The Princeton Review Student Access Guide to the Best Business Schools. 1996 Ed.
    yr ARBA - v28 - '97 - p84+ [251-500]
The Princeton Review Student Advantage Guide to Summer Programs. 1997 Ed.
    yr Kliatt - v31 - Mr '97 - p27 [51-250]
Princeton University. Art Museum - *Greek Sculpture in the Art Museum, Princeton University*
    Rel St Rev - v23 - Ja '97 - p61 [51-250]
Pring, George W - *SLAPPs: Getting Sued for Speaking Out*
    Choice - v34 - O '96 - p362 [51-250]
    JMCQ - v73 - Aut '96 - p766+ [501+]
Pringle, David - *Imaginary People. 2nd Ed.*
    r BL - v93 - Ja '97 - p894 [251-500]
    St. James Guide to Fantasy Writers
    r ARBA - v28 - '97 - p434 [51-250]
    r RQ - v36 - Win '96 - p304+ [251-500]
    yr VOYA - v19 - O '96 - p244 [251-500]
    The Ultimate Guide to Science Fiction. 2nd Ed.
    r ARBA - v28 - '97 - p434 [51-250]
    r RQ - v36 - Win '96 - p224+ [51-250]
Pringle, Heather - *In Search of Ancient North America*
    BW - v26 - S 1 '96 - p4 [251-500]

Pringle, Keith - *Men, Masculinities and Social Welfare*
    Choice - v34 - N '96 - p547 [51-250]
Pringle, Laurence - *Dolphin Man (Illus. by Randall S Wells)*
    c LA - v73 - O '96 - p437+ [51-250]
    An Extraordinary Life (Illus. by Bob Marstall)
    c BL - v93 - Mr 15 '97 - p1239 [51-250]
    c CCB-B - v50 - My '97 - p333+ [51-250]
    c HB - v73 - My '97 - p344 [51-250]
    c KR - v65 - F 15 '97 - p304 [51-250]
    Fire in the Forest (Illus. by Bob Marstall)
    c LA - v73 - O '96 - p443 [251-500]
    Smoking: A Risky Business
    c BL - v93 - D 1 '96 - p660 [51-250]
    c HB Guide - v8 - Spr '97 - p96 [51-250]
    c KR - v64 - O 1 '96 - p1472 [51-250]
    c SLJ - v43 - Ja '97 - p132+ [51-250]
    c Trib Bks - F 9 '97 - p7 [51-250]
    Taking Care of the Earth (Illus. by Bobbie Moore)
    c HB Guide - v7 - Fall '96 - p317 [51-250]
Prins, Harald E L - *The Mi'kmaq: Resistance, Accommodation, and Cultural Survival*
    Choice - v34 - My '97 - p1542 [51-250]
Prinz, Christopher - *Cohabiting, Married, or Single*
    R&R Bk N - v11 - N '96 - p41 [51-250]
Prinzivalli, Emanuela - *Omelie Sui Salmi*
    Rel St Rev - v22 - O '96 - p301+ [501+]
Prinzler, Hans Helmut - *Chronik Des Deutschen Films 1895-1994*
    Ger Q - v69 - Sum '96 - p343+ [501+]
Prior, Lesley - *Buddhism*
    c TES - O 4 '96 - p16* [251-500]
    Sikhism
    c TES - O 4 '96 - p16* [251-500]
Prior, Lindsay - *The Social Organization of Mental Illness*
    SF - v75 - S '96 - p393+ [251-500]
Prior, Michael - *Jesus the Liberator*
    Rel St Rev - v23 - Ap '97 - p183 [51-250]
    TT - v53 - O '96 - p430 [51-250]
Prior, Natalie Jane - *West End Shuffle*
    y Aust Bk R - Je '96 - p60+ [501+]
Prior, Robin - *Passchendaele: The Untold Story*
    Choice - v34 - D '96 - p672 [51-250]
    J Mil H - v61 - Ap '97 - p390+ [501+]
    KR - v64 - S 1 '96 - p1304+ [251-500]
    Lon R Bks - v18 - Jl 18 '96 - p12+ [501+]
    Mar Crp G - v81 - Mr '97 - p72+ [501+]
    Spec - v277 - N 23 '96 - p46 [51-250]
Prior, Sandra Pierson - *The Fayre Formez of the Pearl Poet*
    Choice - v34 - My '97 - p1498 [51-250]
Prisco, Michele - *Il Pellicano Di Pietra*
    BL - v93 - D 1 '96 - p644 [1-50]
Prison Life
    p Utne R - Jl '96 - p118+ [51-250]
Pritchard, Evan T - *No Word for Time*
    PW - v244 - Ap 28 '97 - p67 [1-50]
Pritchard, James - *Anatomy of a Naval Disaster*
    J Mil H - v61 - Ap '97 - p368+ [501+]
    W&M Q - v54 - Ap '97 - p428+ [501+]
Pritchard, Michael S - *Reasonable Children*
    Choice - v34 - Ap '97 - p1391 [51-250]
    PW - v243 - N 11 '96 - p70 [51-250]
Pritchard, Robert - *Economic Development, Foreign Investment, and the Law*
    R&R Bk N - v11 - D '96 - p51 [51-250]
Pritchard, William H - *English Papers*
    Sew R - v104 - O '96 - p692+ [501+]
Privat, John Pierre - *The Privats: Lore, Legends and Facts 1600-1995*
    EGH - v50 - N '96 - p195 [51-250]
Prize Stories 1996
    SFR - v21 - Jl '96 - p39 [501+]
Pro Football Guide. 1996 Ed.
    r ARBA - v28 - '97 - p298+ [51-250]
Pro Sports Halls of Fame. Vols. 1-8
    y BL - v93 - My 1 '97 - p1534 [251-500]
Probable Cause
    p Sm Pr R - v28 - Je '96 - p17 [51-250]
Probate Death Records, Wood County, Ohio. Vol. 1
    r EGH - v50 - N '96 - p180 [51-250]
Probert, Ian - *Internet Spy*
    y CLW - v67 - S '96 - p57 [51-250]
Probst, Pierre - *Caroline En Russie*
    c BL - v93 - N 1 '96 - p500 [1-50]
Procacci, Giuliano - *Machiavelli Nella Cultura Europea Dell'eta Moderna*
    Choice - v34 - D '96 - p567 [1-50]
Procassini, Andrew A - *Competitors in Alliance*
    AAPSS-A - v549 - Ja '97 - p210+ [251-500]

Proceedings: 11th Annual Knowledge-Based Software Engineering Conference
    SciTech - v21 - Mr '97 - p8 [51-250]
Proceedings 1996 Symposium on Logic in Computer Science
    SciTech - v20 - D '96 - p13 [51-250]
Proceedings of the 2nd International Symposium on Parallel Architectures, Algorithms, and Networks (ISPAN)
    SciTech - v20 - D '96 - p7 [51-250]
Proceedings of the 4th International Workshop on Parallel and Distributed Real-Time Systems, April 15-16, 1996, Honolulu, Hawaii
    SciTech - v20 - N '96 - p7 [1-50]
Proceedings of the 4th Israeli Symposium on the Theory of Computing and Systems
    SciTech - v20 - N '96 - p6 [51-250]
Proceedings of the 15th Symposium on Reliable Distributed Systems
    SciTech - v21 - Mr '97 - p5 [51-250]
Proceedings of the 1995 Total Life Cycle Conference
    SciTech - v20 - D '96 - p80 [51-250]
Proceedings of the 1996 Annual Symposium on Foundations of Computer Science
    SciTech - v21 - Mr '97 - p5 [51-250]
Proceedings of the 1996 Conference on Parallel Architectures and Compilation Techniques
    SciTech - v21 - Mr '97 - p5 [51-250]
Proceedings of the 1996 IEEE/ASME Joint Railroad Conference
    SciTech - v20 - N '96 - p68 [51-250]
Proceedings of the 1997 Annual ACM-SIAM Symposium on Discrete Algorithms
    SciTech - v21 - Mr '97 - p6 [51-250]
Proceedings of the Annual IEEE Symposium on Computer-Based Medical Systems (9th: 1996: Ann Arbor, MI)
    SciTech - v20 - S '96 - p27 [51-250]
Proceedings of the ASME Noise Control and Acoustics Division 1996
    SciTech - v21 - Mr '97 - p83 [51-250]
Proceedings of the Danish Institute at Athens I
    AJA - v100 - O '96 - p809+ [251-500]
Proceedings of the Fifth Biennial Conference of the International Society for Scientometrics and Informetrics
    LQ - v67 - Ja '97 - p93+ [501+]
Proceedings of the Fifth Workshop on Enabling Technologies
    SciTech - v20 - D '96 - p6 [51-250]
Proceedings of the IEEE Symposium on Parallel and Distributed Processing - Parallel and Distributed Processing
    SciTech - v21 - Mr '97 - p6 [51-250]
Proceedings of the Second Biennial Conference on Research in Colorado Plateau National Parks
    J Gov Info - v23 - S '96 - p570+ [51-250]
Proceedings of the Seventh Annual International Symposium on Information Storage and Processing Systems
    SciTech - v21 - Mr '97 - p5 [51-250]
Proceedings of the Third International Conference on Massively Parallel Processing Using Optical Interconnections
    SciTech - v21 - Mr '97 - p11 [51-250]
Prochaska, Frank - *Royal Bounty*
    HRNB - v25 - Win '97 - p66 [251-500]
Prochnau, William - *Once upon a Distant War*
    JMCQ - v73 - Aut '96 - p764+ [501+]
    LATBR - N 10 '96 - p15 [51-250]
    NYTBR - v101 - S 29 '96 - p32 [51-250]
  y SLJ - v42 - Ag '96 - p186 [51-250]
  y SLJ - v42 - S '96 - p242 [51-250]
Procter, Garry - *Asymmetric Synthesis*
    New Sci - v153 - Mr 1 '97 - p38+ [51-250]
Proctor, Claude O - *NTC's Multilingual Dictionary of American Sign Language*
    r ARBA - v28 - '97 - p400 [51-250]
Proctor, George W - *Before Honor*
    Roundup M - v3 - Ag '96 - p31+ [51-250]
    Blood of My Blood
  y Kliatt - v30 - S '96 - p13 [51-250]
    Roundup M - v4 - O '96 - p32 [251-500]
Proctor, Michael - *The Natural History of Pollination*
    Choice - v34 - N '96 - p483 [51-250]
Proctor, Nick H - *Proctor and Hughes' Chemical Hazards of the Workplace. 4th Ed.*
    r Choice - v34 - Ja '97 - p828 [51-250]

Proctor, Robert N - *Cancer Wars*
    AHR - v101 - O '96 - p1312+ [501+]
    Am Sci - v84 - N '96 - p616+ [501+]
    Isis - v87 - S '96 - p576+ [501+]
    J Am St - v30 - D '96 - p464+ [501+]
Proctor, Robert W - *Skill Acquisition and Human Performance*
    A J Psy - v109 - Win '96 - p645+ [501+]
Proctor, Samuel DeWitt - *The Substance of Things Hoped For (Proctor). Audio Version*
  y Kliatt - v30 - S '96 - p60 [51-250]
Proddow, Penny - *Diamonds: A Century of Spectacular Jewels*
    LJ - v121 - N 15 '96 - p59 [51-250]
Professional Guide to Diseases. 5th Ed.
    r BL - v93 - F 1 '97 - p958 [1-50]
Profile of Courts in Canada
    r J Gov Info - v23 - S '96 - p618 [51-250]
Profiles in Business and Management. Electronic Media Version
    r ARBA - v28 - '97 - p106 [251-500]
Profillidis, V A - *Railway Engineering*
    SciTech - v20 - D '96 - p71 [51-250]
Profils Des Principaux Groupes Religieux De Quebec
    J Gov Info - v23 - S '96 - p637+ [51-250]
Programme on Educational Building - *Redefining the Place to Learn*
    J Gov Info - v23 - S '96 - p675 [51-250]
Progress In Inorganic Chemistry. Vol. 45
    SciTech - v21 - Mr '97 - p29 [51-250]
Prohaszka, Marianne - *Reflections from the Dead*
    AJA - v100 - O '96 - p773+ [501+]
Project on Disney - *Inside the Mouse*
    J Am St - v30 - Ap '96 - p151+ [251-500]
Projections 3
    FQ - v49 - Fall '95 - p62 [251-500]
Projections 6
    Si & So - v6 - N '96 - p38 [51-250]
    TES - N 22 '96 - p8* [51-250]
Prokes, S M - *Surface/Interface and Stress Effects in Electronic Material Nanostructures*
    SciTech - v20 - D '96 - p78 [51-250]
Prokhoris, Sabine - *The Witch's Kitchen*
    TranslRevS - v2 - D '96 - p12 [51-250]
Prokopenko, Joseph - *Management for Privatization*
    J Gov Info - v23 - S '96 - p672 [51-250]
Prokurat, Michael - *Historical Dictionary of the Orthodox Church*
    r ARBA - v28 - '97 - p550+ [51-250]
    r Choice - v34 - Ap '97 - p1314 [251-500]
Pronzini, Bill - *1001 Midnights*
    r RQ - v36 - Win '96 - p223+ [51-250]
    Blue Lonesome (Ukena). Audio Version
  y Kliatt - v30 - N '96 - p36 [51-250]
    Hardboiled: An Anthology of American Crime Stories
    Books - v9 - S '95 - p18 [51-250]
    Sentinels
    Arm Det - v30 - Win '97 - p114+ [251-500]
    BL - v92 - Ag '96 - p1887 [51-250]
    NYTBR - v101 - S 29 '96 - p28 [51-250]
    Spadework
    Arm Det - v30 - Win '97 - p119 [251-500]
    A Wasteland of Strangers
    PW - v244 - My 12 '97 - p61 [51-250]
    With an Extreme Burning
    Arm Det - v29 - Sum '96 - p282 [51-250]
Propertius, Sextus - *The Poems (Lee)*
    TranslRevS - v2 - D '96 - p6 [51-250]
Prophetic Voices
    p Sm Pr R - v28 - Je '96 - p19 [51-250]
Proposed Recovery Plan for Snake River Salmon
    J Gov Info - v23 - S '96 - p571 [51-250]
Proposed Recovery Plan for Snake River Salmon: Summary
    J Gov Info - v23 - S '96 - p571 [51-250]
Prose, Francine - *The Angel's Mistake (Illus. by Mark Podwal)*
    c BL - v93 - Mr 1 '97 - p1168 [51-250]
    c PW - v244 - Ap 28 '97 - p76 [51-250]
    Dybbuk: A Story Made in Heaven (Illus. by Mark Podwal)
    c HB Guide - v7 - Fall '96 - p323 [51-250]
    Guided Tours of Hell
    BL - v93 - D 15 '96 - p709 [51-250]
    BW - v27 - Ja 12 '97 - p3+ [501+]
    KR - v64 - O 15 '96 - p1489+ [251-500]
    LJ - v121 - N 15 '96 - p91 [51-250]
    NL - v79 - D 16 '96 - p24+ [501+]
    NW - v129 - F 10 '97 - p66 [51-250]
    NY - v72 - F 10 '97 - p83 [51-250]
    NYTBR - v102 - Ja 12 '97 - p7 [501+]

    Hunters and Gatherers
    NYTBR - v102 - Ja 19 '97 - p28 [1-50]
    PW - v243 - N 11 '96 - p72 [1-50]
    Trib Bks - Mr 16 '97 - p8 [1-50]
Prosek, James - *Joe and Me*
    KR - v65 - My 1 '97 - p703+ [251-500]
    Trout: An Illustrated History
    NYTLa - v146 - D 2 '96 - pC16 [1-50]
Prosise, Jeff - *How Computer Graphics Work*
    SciTech - v20 - N '96 - p60 [51-250]
    Programming Windows 95 with MFC
    CBR - v14 - S '96 - p30 [1-50]
    SciTech - v20 - D '96 - p11 [1-50]
Prospect
    p Dis - v44 - Spr '97 - p103+ [501+]
    p TLS - Mr 7 '97 - p26 [501+]
The Prospects for Nuclear Power in the UK
    J Gov Info - v23 - S '96 - p646+ [51-250]
Pross, Addy - *Theoretical and Physical Principles of Organic Reactivity*
    J Chem Ed - v73 - Je '96 - pA137 [51-250]
Prosterman, Leslie - *Ordinary Life, Festival Days*
    J Am Cult - v19 - Spr '96 - p103+ [251-500]
Protein Kinesis
    SciTech - v20 - D '96 - p35 [51-250]
Prothero, Donald R - *Sedimentary Geology*
  y New Sci - v151 - S 28 '96 - p46 [501+]
    The Terrestrial Eocene-Oligocene Transition in North America
    Choice - v34 - Mr '97 - p1190 [51-250]
    SciTech - v20 - D '96 - p29 [51-250]
Prothero, Stephen - *The White Buddhist*
    Choice - v34 - N '96 - p476+ [51-250]
    Rel St Rev - v23 - Ap '97 - p203 [51-250]
Proudfoot, Lindsay J - *Urban Patronage and Social Authority*
    Albion - v28 - Fall '96 - p551+ [501+]
Proulx, Annie - *Cider: Making, Using and Enjoying Sweet and Hard Cider. 2nd Ed.*
    LJ - v122 - Ap 1 '97 - p64 [1-50]
Proulx, E Annie - *Accordion Crimes*
    Atl - v278 - Jl '96 - p109 [51-250]
    BL - v93 - Ja '97 - p761 [51-250]
    Bloom Rev - v16 - S '96 - p18+ [501+]
    BWatch - v17 - S '96 - p1 [51-250]
    Comw - v123 - D 6 '96 - p27+ [501+]
    LJ - v122 - Ja '97 - p50 [1-50]
    New R - v215 - O 7 '96 - p44+ [501+]
    NS - v125 - O 18 '96 - p48 [251-500]
    Obs - O 20 '96 - p17* [501+]
    PW - v243 - N 4 '96 - p38 [51-250]
    Salm - Win '97 - p220+ [501+]
    Spec - v277 - O 12 '96 - p48+ [501+]
    TES - N 15 '96 - p8* [251-500]
    TLS - O 4 '96 - p25 [501+]
    W&I - v11 - S '96 - p275+ [501+]
    Woman's J - N '96 - p12 [1-50]
    Wom R Bks - v13 - S '96 - p11 [501+]
    YR - v85 - Ja '97 - p144+ [501+]
    The Shipping News (Schraf). Audio Version
  y Kliatt - v30 - S '96 - p52 [51-250]
Proulx, Earl - *Yankee Magazine's Make It Last*
    LJ - v121 - D '96 - p140 [51-250]
    PW - v243 - D 2 '96 - p58 [51-250]
Proulx, Monique - *Sex of the Stars*
    Quill & Q - v62 - My '96 - p25 [251-500]
Prousis, Theophilus C - *Russian Society and the Greek Revolution*
    Slav R - v55 - Sum '96 - p480+ [501+]
Proust, Marcel - *A La Recherche Du Temps Perdu*
    MLN - v111 - S '96 - p760+ [501+]
    Remembrance of Things Past (Rowe). Vol. 1. Audio Version
    Obs - Mr 23 '97 - p16* [501+]
    Swann's Way (Jason). Audio Version
    Spec - v277 - N 30 '96 - p55 [51-250]
    Swann's Way (Callow). Audio Version
    Spec - v277 - N 30 '96 - p55 [51-250]
    Swann's Way (Rowe). Audio Version
    Spec - v277 - N 30 '96 - p55 [51-250]
    Swann's Way. Swann in Love (Jason). Audio Version
    BIC - v25 - O '96 - p33+ [501+]
    Within a Budding Grove (Jason). Audio Version
    BWatch - v18 - Mr '97 - p9 [1-50]
Prout, Curtis - *Demand and Get the Best Health Care for You*
    BL - v93 - Ja '97 - p792 [51-250]
Provder, Theodore - *Film Formation in Waterborne Coatings*
    SciTech - v21 - Mr '97 - p97 [51-250]

Provensen, Alice - *The Glorious Flight*
  c New Ad - v9 - Fall '96 - p267+ [501+]
  My Fellow Americans
  c RT - v50 - O '96 - p154 [51-250]
Provine, Dorothy S - *District of Columbia Free Negro Registers 1821-1861. Vols. 1-2*
  r BW - v27 - Mr 23 '97 - p12 [51-250]
Prowell, Sandra West - *When Wallflowers Die*
  Arm Det - v29 - Fall '96 - p499 [251-500]
  BWatch - v17 - S '96 - p1 [51-250]
  Ent W - Ag 23 '96 - p119 [51-250]
  y SLJ - v43 - F '97 - p135 [51-250]
Prucha, Francis Paul - *American Indian Treaties*
  AHR - v101 - O '96 - p1273 [501+]
  Handbook for Research in American History. 2nd Ed.
  r ASInt - v34 - O '96 - p8 [51-250]
Prudhomme, Claude - *Strategie Missionnaire Du Saint-Siege Sous Leon XIII 1878-1903*
  r CHR - v82 - Jl '96 - p478+ [501+]
Prud'hon, Pierre-Paul - *The Language of the Body*
  Atl - v279 - Ja '97 - p98 [51-250]
  Bloom Rev - v16 - N '96 - p23 [51-250]
  LATBR - D 8 '96 - p14 [1-50]
  PW - v243 - S 23 '96 - p66 [51-250]
  TLS - Ag 30 '96 - p15 [1-50]
  WSJ-MW - v78 - D 5 '96 - pA18 [51-250]
Pruitt, Barbara - *A Christmas Wish*
  LJ - v121 - N 15 '96 - p50 [51-250]
Prunckun, Henry W, Jr. - *Shadow of Death*
  r ARBA - v28 - '97 - p225 [51-250]
Pruneti, Luigi - *Viking Explorers (Illus. by Claudia Saraceni)*
  c Ch BWatch - v7 - Ja '97 - p7 [1-50]
  c HB Guide - v8 - Spr '97 - p166 [51-250]
  c SLJ - v42 - D '96 - p132 [51-250]
Prunier, Gerard - *The Rwanda Crisis*
  JTWS - v13 - Spr '96 - p325+ [501+]
  NS - v125 - D 20 '96 - p116 [51-250]
Prunty, Wyatt - *Since the Noon Mail Stopped*
  PW - v244 - Ap 28 '97 - p73 [51-250]
Prus, Boleslaw - *The Doll*
  BW - v27 - Mr 23 '97 - p4 [501+]
  KR - v64 - D 1 '96 - p1704 [51-250]
  LJ - v122 - F 15 '97 - p166 [51-250]
  The Sins of Childhood and Other Stories
  BW - v27 - Mr 23 '97 - p4 [501+]
  KR - v64 - D 1 '96 - p1704 [51-250]
Prusiner, S B - *Prions Prions Prions*
  Sci - v273 - Ag 23 '96 - p1053 [51-250]
Prussin, Labelle - *African Nomadic Architecture*
  Wom R Bks - v13 - S '96 - p8+ [501+]
Pruter, Robert - *Doowop: The Chicago Scene*
  CAY - v17 - Fall '96 - p7 [51-250]
  Choice - v34 - N '96 - p471 [51-250]
Pruzanski, W - *Novel Molecular Approaches to Anti-Inflammatory Therapy*
  SciTech - v20 - N '96 - p55 [51-250]
Pry, Peter Vincent - *War Scare*
  y BL - v93 - Ap 1 '97 - p1272 [51-250]
  KR - v65 - Mr 1 '97 - p363 [51-250]
  LJ - v122 - Ap 1 '97 - p110+ [51-250]
  PW - v244 - Mr 17 '97 - p68+ [51-250]
Prychitko, David L - *Producer Cooperatives and Labor-Managed Systems. Vols. 1-2*
  JEL - v34 - S '96 - p1448 [51-250]
  R&R Bk N - v11 - D '96 - p29 [51-250]
Prymak, Thomas M - *Mykola Kostomarov: A Biography*
  Choice - v34 - O '96 - p341 [51-250]
Pryor, Bonnie - *The Dream Jar (Illus. by Mark Graham)*
  c Ch BWatch - v6 - My '96 - p3 [51-250]
  c HB Guide - v7 - Fall '96 - p271+ [51-250]
  c Smith - v27 - N '96 - p164 [1-50]
  Toenails, Tonsils, and Tornadoes (Illus. by Helen Cogancherry)
  c BL - v93 - My 15 '97 - p1576 [51-250]
  c KR - v65 - My 1 '97 - p725+ [51-250]
Pryor, Douglas W - *Unspeakable Acts*
  Choice - v34 - F '97 - p1044 [51-250]
Pryor, Frederic L - *Economic Evolution and Structure*
  Choice - v34 - O '96 - p331 [51-250]
  JEL - v34 - D '96 - p2123 [51-250]
Pryor, Gale - *Nursing Mother, Working Mother*
  BL - v93 - F 1 '97 - p917 [51-250]
  LJ - v122 - F 1 '97 - p100 [51-250]
  PW - v244 - Ja 6 '97 - p71 [51-250]
Prys-Roberts, Cedric - *International Practice of Anaesthesia. Vol. 1*
  SciTech - v21 - Mr '97 - p60 [51-250]
Prytherch, Ray - *Harrod's Librarians' Glossary. 8th Ed.*
  r ARBA - v28 - '97 - p237 [51-250]

Prywes, Moshe - *Prisoner of Hope*
  Choice - v34 - O '96 - p344 [51-250]
Psihoyos, Louie - *Hunting Dinosaurs*
  y Emerg Lib - v24 - S '96 - p24 [1-50]
  y SLJ - v42 - D '96 - p33 [1-50]
Ptak, Carol A - *MRP and Beyond*
  SciTech - v20 - D '96 - p85 [51-250]
Ptak, Diane Snyder - *The American Loyalist*
  r EGH - v50 - N '96 - p158+ [51-250]
Pu, Songling - *Liao Zhai Zhi Yi*
  BL - v93 - N 1 '96 - p484 [1-50]
Puaux, Francoise - *Architecture, Decor Et Cinema*
  FR - v70 - Mr '97 - p607+ [251-500]
Public Affairs Television (Firm) - *Talking About Genesis*
  Bloom Rev - v16 - N '96 - p9+ [501+]
Public Integrity Annual 1996
  PAR - v57 - Ja '97 - p92 [501+]
Public Interest Profiles 1996-1997
  r ARBA - v28 - '97 - p270 [251-500]
  r R&R Bk N - v11 - N '96 - p249 [51-250]
Public Investment Programme 1994-1996
  J Gov Info - v23 - S '96 - p661 [1-50]
Publishers, Distributors, and Wholesalers of the United States 1996-97. Vols. 1-2
  r ARBA - v28 - '97 - p250 [51-250]
Pucci, Idanna - *The Trials of Maria Barbella*
  NY - v73 - Ap 28 '97 - p227 [51-250]
  NYTBR - v102 - Ap 6 '97 - p32 [51-250]
  PW - v244 - F 24 '97 - p88 [1-50]
Puccini, Giacomo - *The Complete Puccini Libretti. Vols. 1-2*
  ON - v61 - D 14 '96 - p73+ [501+]
Puckett, David L - *John Calvin's Exegesis of the Old Testament*
  Theol St - v57 - S '96 - p568 [251-500]
Puckett, Robert H - *The United States and Northeast Asia*
  Pac A - v69 - Sum '96 - p265+ [501+]
Pudup, Mary Beth - *Appalachia in the Making*
  CS - v26 - Mr '97 - p197+ [501+]
  JSH - v63 - F '97 - p167+ [501+]
Puerto, Cecilia - *Latin American Women Artists, Kahlo and Look Who Else*
  r ARBA - v28 - '97 - p364+ [51-250]
  r Choice - v34 - F '97 - p948 [51-250]
  r R&R Bk N - v11 - N '96 - p60 [51-250]
Puette, William J - *Through Jaundiced Eyes*
  JC - v46 - Sum '96 - p197+ [501+]
Puffer, Sheila M - *Business and Management in Russia*
  JEL - v34 - D '96 - p2127 [51-250]
Pugh, Cedric - *Sustainability, the Environment and Urbanization*
  New Sci - v152 - O 26 '96 - p47 [51-250]
Pugh, Deborah - *I Have Arrived before My Words*
  BL - v93 - Ja '97 - p807 [51-250]
  BW - v27 - Ap 6 '97 - p11 [501+]
  KR - v64 - N 15 '96 - p1658 [251-500]
  LJ - v122 - Ja '97 - p112 [51-250]
  PW - v243 - D 2 '96 - p54+ [51-250]
Pugh, Derek S - *Writers on Organizations. 5th Ed.*
  R&R Bk N - v11 - N '96 - p38 [51-250]
Pugh, Dianne - *Fast Friends*
  KR - v64 - D 15 '96 - p1770 [51-250]
  LATBR - Ap 20 '97 - p13 [501+]
  PW - v243 - D 16 '96 - p46 [51-250]
Pugh, Emerson W - *Building IBM*
  T&C - v37 - Ap '96 - p385+ [501+]
Pugh, Michael - *Maritime Security and Peacekeeping*
  NWCR - v50 - Win '97 - p137+ [501+]
Pugh, Peter - *Thatcher for Beginners*
  Obs - Mr 2 '97 - p15* [501+]
Pugh, Ronnie - *Ernest Tubb: The Texas Troubadour*
  AB - v98 - D 9 '96 - p1994 [51-250]
  Choice - v34 - Ap '97 - p1348+ [51-250]
  Ent W - D 6 '96 - p58 [51-250]
  LJ - v121 - O 15 '96 - p61 [51-250]
  LJ - v121 - N 1 '96 - p42 [1-50]
  PW - v243 - O 14 '96 - p74 [51-250]
Pugin, Augustus Welby Northmore - *Pugin: A Gothic Passion*
  VS - v39 - Spr '96 - p457+ [501+]
Pugliese Carratelli, Giovanni - *The Greek World*
  LJ - v121 - D '96 - p88 [51-250]
  The Western Greeks
  NYRB - v43 - S 19 '96 - p44+ [501+]
  Obs - O 27 '96 - p17* [501+]
  TLS - N 29 '96 - p13 [51-250]
  TLS - N 29 '96 - p16 [1-50]
Puig, Jaume De - *Les Sources De La Pensee Philosophique De Raimond Sebond (Ramon Sibiuda)*
  Six Ct J - v27 - Fall '96 - p829+ [501+]

Puig, Manuel - *Heartbreak Tango*
  TranslRevS - v2 - D '96 - p6 [51-250]
Pujade-Renaud, Claude - *La Nuit La Neige*
  Econ - v340 - S 14 '96 - p14*+ [501+]
Puledda, Salvatore - *Interpretations of Humanism*
  PW - v244 - Ja 27 '97 - p87 [51-250]
Pulido, Laura - *Environmentalism and Economic Justice*
  AJS - v102 - Ja '97 - p1208+ [501+]
  WHQ - v27 - Win '96 - p524 [501+]
Pullein-Thompson, Christine - *Thundering Hooves (Illus. by Victor Ambrus)*
  c Bks Keeps - v100 - S '96 - p13 [51-250]
  c CLW - v67 - Mr '97 - p60 [51-250]
  c Sch Lib - v44 - N '96 - p151+ [51-250]
Pullman, Philip - *Clockwork or All Wound Up (Illus. by Peter Bailey)*
  y Bks Keeps - v100 - S '96 - p33 [51-250]
  c Bks Keeps - Mr '97 - p25 [51-250]
  c TES - N 8 '96 - p11* [251-500]
  The Firework-Maker's Daughter (Illus. by Nick Harris)
  c Bks Keeps - Ja '97 - p24 [51-250]
  The Golden Compass
  y BL - v93 - Ja '97 - p765 [1-50]
  y BL - v93 - Ap 1 '97 - p1294 [1-50]
  y BL - v93 - Ap 1 '97 - p1305 [1-50]
  c CSM - v88 - S 26 '96 - pB3+ [51-250]
  y Emerg Lib - v23 - My '96 - p43 [1-50]
  c HB Guide - v7 - Fall '96 - p296 [51-250]
  y JAAL - v40 - S '96 - p73 [51-250]
  y MFSF - v92 - Ja '97 - p19+ [501+]
  c PW - v243 - N 4 '96 - p49 [51-250]
  His Dark Materials
  c Bks Keeps - v100 - S '96 - p15 [251-500]
  Northern Lights
  c TES - Jl 19 '96 - p22 [501+]
  c TES - O 18 '96 - p12* [51-250]
  Thunderbolt's Waxwork
  c Bks Keeps - Ja '97 - p23 [51-250]
Pullum, Geoffrey K - *Phonetic Symbol Guide. 2nd Ed.*
  r ARBA - v28 - '97 - p375+ [51-250]
  r R&R Bk N - v11 - N '96 - p63 [51-250]
Pulman, Felicity - *Ghost Boy*
  c Magpies - v11 - My '96 - p44 [51-250]
Pultz, John - *Photography and the Body*
  BM - v139 - Ja '97 - p53 [251-500]
Pulver, Jeff - *The Internet Telephone Toolkit*
  CBR - v15 - Spr '97 - p5 [51-250]
  LJ - v121 - N 1 '96 - p104 [51-250]
  New Sci - v152 - N 30 '96 - p48 [51-250]
Pumphrey, Lela D - *Rethinking Management Accountability Systems Workshop, May 23, 1995*
  J Gov Info - v23 - S '96 - p605 [51-250]
Pumroy, Eric - *Research Guide to the Turner Movement in the United States*
  r ARBA - v28 - '97 - p154+ [251-500]
  r Choice - v34 - F '97 - p949 [51-250]
  R&R Bk N - v11 - D '96 - p21 [51-250]
Punchard, Lorraine - *Playtime Pottery and Porcelain from Europe and Asia*
  Ant & CM - v101 - D '96 - p31 [51-250]
Pundeff, Marin V - *Bulgaria in American Perspective*
  Slav R - v55 - Sum '96 - p464 [251-500]
Puniello, Francoise S - *Abstract Expressionist Women Painters*
  r AB - v99 - Mr 17 '97 - p870 [501+]
  r ARBA - v28 - '97 - p371 [51-250]
Punin, Nikolai - *O Tatline*
  Russ Rev - v55 - O '96 - p708+ [501+]
  Slav R - v55 - Fall '96 - p707+ [501+]
Punter, David - *The Literature of Terror. Vol. 1*
  Choice - v34 - N '96 - p459 [51-250]
Purcell, Deirdre - *Sky*
  PW - v244 - F 3 '97 - p100 [51-250]
Purcell, Susan Kaufman - *Europe and Latin America in the World Economy*
  HAHR - v77 - F '97 - p156+ [251-500]
Purcell-Gates, Victoria - *Other People's Words*
  ES - v27 - Sum '96 - p159+ [501+]
Purdy, Al - *Rooms for Rent in the Outer Planets*
  Quill & Q - v62 - N '96 - p40 [251-500]
Purdy, Carol - *Mrs. Merriwether's Musical Cat (Illus. by Petra Mathers)*
  c LA - v73 - S '96 - p353 [51-250]
Purdy, John Lloyd - *The Legacy of D'Arcy McNickle*
  AL - v69 - Mr '97 - p252 [51-250]
  WHQ - v28 - Spr '97 - p102 [1-50]
Purdy, Laura M - *Reproducing Persons*
  Choice - v34 - D '96 - p645 [51-250]
  Hast Cen R - v26 - S '96 - p41 [1-50]

Purdy, Susan G - *Let Them Eat Cake*
    BL - v93 - F 15 '97 - p989 [51-250]
    LJ - v122 - F 15 '97 - p158 [51-250]
Purich, Daniel L - *Contemporary Enzyme Kinetics and Mechanism. 2nd Ed.*
    SciTech - v20 - D '96 - p35 [51-250]
Purkis, Christine - *Sea Change*
   y Bks Keeps - v100 - S '96 - p17 [51-250]
   y JB - v60 - O '96 - p212 [51-250]
Purkis, Sally - *Investigating Local History*
   c Sch Lib - v44 - N '96 - p165 [51-250]
Purkiss, Diane - *The Witch in History*
    TLS - N 29 '96 - p16 [1-50]
Purpel, David E - *Beyond Liberation and Excellence*
    ES - v27 - Fall '96 - p242+ [501+]
Pursell, Carroll - *The Machine in America*
    BHR - v70 - Sum '96 - p275+ [501+]
    Pub Hist - v18 - Sum '96 - p76+ [501+]
Purser, Ann - *Spinster of the Parish*
    PW - v243 - D 30 '96 - p60 [1-50]
Purton, Michael - *Show-Me-How I Can Make Music*
   c SLJ - v42 - Ag '96 - p140 [51-250]
Purves, Alan C - *How Porcupines Make Love III*
    New Ad - v9 - Fall '96 - p309+ [501+]
Purves, Libby - *A Long Walk in Wintertime*
    Books - v10 - Je '96 - p17 [51-250]
Purvis, June - *Women's History*
    HRNB - v25 - Win '97 - p66 [251-500]
Purvis, Sally B - *The Stained Glass Ceiling*
    Intpr - v51 - Ja '97 - p108+ [251-500]
Purvis, Thomas L - *A Dictionary of American History*
   r ARBA - v28 - '97 - p193+ [251-500]
   Revolutionary America 1763 to 1800
   r ARBA - v28 - '97 - p184 [251-500]
    J Am St - v30 - Ag '96 - p342+ [501+]
The PUSH Guide to Which University 1997
   y TES - S 27 '96 - p8* [51-250]
The Pushcart Prize XX
    WLT - v70 - Sum '96 - p701+ [501+]
The Pushcart Prize XXI
    BL - v93 - Ja '97 - p822 [51-250]
    KR - v64 - S 15 '96 - p1373 [251-500]
    LJ - v121 - N 1 '96 - p68 [51-250]
    PW - v243 - S 23 '96 - p56 [51-250]
Pushkareva, Natalia - *Women in Russian History from the Tenth to the Twentieth Century*
    LJ - v122 - My 1 '97 - p121 [51-250]
Pushkin, Aleksandr Sergeevich - *The Bronze Horseman*
    Slav R - v55 - Sum '96 - p399+ [501+]
   The Tale of Tsar Saltan (Illus. by Gennady Spirin)
   y CCB-B - v50 - N '96 - p110+ [51-250]
   c HB Guide - v8 - Spr '97 - p104 [51-250]
   c KR - v64 - S 1 '96 - p1326 [51-250]
   c LATBR - D 8 '96 - p18 [1-50]
   c PW - v243 - S 16 '96 - p83 [51-250]
   c SLJ - v42 - O '96 - p116 [51-250]
Pustianaz, Marco - *Per Una Letteratura Giustificata*
    MLR - v92 - Ap '97 - p440+ [501+]
Puterman, Martin L - *Markov Decision Processes*
    SIAM Rev - v38 - D '96 - p689 [501+]
Putik, Jaroslav - *Der Mann Mit Dem Rasiermesser*
    WLT - v70 - Sum '96 - p725+ [501+]
Putnam, James - *Amazing Facts about Ancient Egypt*
   y Emerg Lib - v24 - S '96 - p26 [1-50]
Putnam, Michael C J - *Virgil's Aeneid*
    Class Out - v74 - Win '97 - p79+ [501+]
Putnam, Robert - *Making Democracy Work*
    NCR - v85 - Spr '96 - p63 [51-250]
Putney, Mary Jo - *River of Fire*
    PW - v243 - S 23 '96 - p74 [51-250]
   Shattered Rainbows
    LJ - v122 - F 15 '97 - p184 [51-250]
Putt-Putt and Pep
   c HB Guide - v7 - Fall '96 - p242+ [1-50]
Putten, Anton F P Van - *Electronic Measurement Systems. 2nd Ed.*
    SciTech - v21 - Mr '97 - p92 [51-250]
Putter, Ad - *An Introduction to the Gawain-Poet*
    Choice - v34 - Mr '97 - p1166 [51-250]
   Sir Gawain and the Green Knight and French Arthurian Romance
    Specu - v72 - Ja '97 - p213+ [501+]
Putterman, Louis - *The Economic Nature of the Firm*
    JEL - v34 - D '96 - p2026 [51-250]
Putz, Manfred, 1938- - *Nietzsche in American Literature and Thought*
    J Am St - v30 - Ag '96 - p303+ [251-500]
    Nine-C Lit - v50 - Mr '96 - p557 [1-50]
Putz, Martin - *Language Contact Language Conflict*
    MLJ - v80 - Fall '96 - p425+ [501+]

Puzo, Mario - *The Fortunate Pilgrim*
    PW - v244 - Mr 31 '97 - p68 [51-250]
   The Godfather (Mantegna). Audio Version
   y Kliatt - v30 - N '96 - p40 [51-250]
    LJ - v121 - D '96 - p170 [51-250]
   The Last Don
    CSM - v88 - S 19 '96 - p14 [51-250]
    Lon R Bks - v18 - O 17 '96 - p8+ [501+]
    NY - v72 - Ag 12 '96 - p73+ [501+]
Puzon, Bridget - *Women Religious and the Intellectual Life*
    RR - v55 - N '96 - p657+ [501+]
Pybus, Cassandra - *White Rajah*
    Aust Bk R - O '96 - p14+ [501+]
Pybus, Roger - *Safety Management*
    SciTech - v20 - S '96 - p46 [51-250]
Pycior, Helena M - *Creative Couples in the Sciences*
    Choice - v34 - O '96 - p300 [51-250]
    SB - v32 - O '96 - p200 [251-500]
Pye, Michael - *The Drowning Room*
    Ent W - Mr 14 '97 - p75 [51-250]
    NYTBR - v101 - D 8 '96 - p79 [1-50]
    NYTBR - v102 - Ap 6 '97 - p32 [51-250]
    PW - v244 - F 24 '97 - p88 [1-50]
    Trib Bks - F 23 '97 - p8 [1-50]
Pyke, Gillian - *Nea Nikomedeia. Vol. 1*
    AJA - v101 - Ja '97 - p172+ [501+]
Pyle, Ralph E - *Persistence and Change in the Protestant Establishment*
    R&R Bk N - v11 - D '96 - p39 [51-250]
Pym, Barbara - *Excellent Women (Stevenson). Audio Version*
   y Kliatt - v30 - N '96 - p40 [51-250]
   Some Tame Gazelle (McKenzie). Audio Version
    BL - v92 - Ag '96 - p1917 [51-250]
Pynchon, Thomas - *Mason and Dixon*
    NYTLa - v146 - Ap 29 '97 - pC11+ [501+]
    PW - v244 - Ap 14 '97 - p56 [251-500]
    Time - v149 - My 5 '97 - p98 [501+]
    Trib Bks - My 11 '97 - p1+ [501+]
    VV - v42 - My 6 '97 - p43+ [501+]
    WSJ-Cent - v99 - My 2 '97 - pA12 [501+]
Pyne, Kathleen - *Art and the Higher Life*
    AB - v99 - Mr 3 '97 - p693 [51-250]
    Choice - v34 - F '97 - p957 [51-250]
Pyne, Stephen J - *Introduction to Wildland Fire. 2nd Ed.*
    Choice - v34 - O '96 - p304 [51-250]
Pynn, Larry - *The Forgotten Trail*
    CG - v116 - N '96 - p83+ [501+]
Pynsent, Robert B - *The Literature of Nationalism*
    Choice - v34 - D '96 - p608 [51-250]
   Sex under Socialism
    MLR - v92 - Ja '97 - p270 [251-500]
Pyper, Andrew - *Kiss Me*
    Quill & Q - v62 - O '96 - p41 [251-500]
Pyta, Wolfram - *Gegen Hitler Und Fur Die Republik*
    JMH - v68 - S '96 - p629+ [501+]
The Pythagorean Golden Verses
    JR - v76 - O '96 - p616+ [501+]

Q R

Q-Zine: A Rocket to the Unknown
  p Sm Pr R - v28 - O '96 - p20 [51-250]
  p Sm Pr R - v28 - O '96 - p20 [51-250]
Qabbani, Nizar - *On Entering the Sea*
  WLT - v70 - Sum '96 - p756 [501+]
Qasim, Abd Al-Hakim - *The Seven Days of Man*
  TranslRevS - v2 - D '96 - p18+ [51-250]
  TranslRevS - v2 - D '96 - p18+ [51-250]
  WLT - v71 - Win '97 - p215+ [251-500]
Qayoumi, Mohammad - *Electrical Systems*
  R&R Bk N - v12 - F '97 - p98 [51-250]
Qian, Shie - *Joint Time-Frequency Analysis*
  SciTech - v20 - S '96 - p54 [51-250]
Qian, Zhaoming - *Orientalism and Modernism*
  J Am St - v30 - Ag '96 - p324+ [251-500]
Qiang, Zhai - *The Dragon, the Lion, and the Eagle*
  EHR - v111 - N '96 - p1355+ [251-500]
Qiao, Liang - *Mo Ri Zhi Men. Vols. 1-2*
  BL - v93 - My 1 '97 - p1484 [1-50]
Quadagno, Jill - *The Color of Welfare*
  SF - v75 - S '96 - p371+ [501+]
Quade, Quentin L - *Financing Education*
  Choice - v34 - Ap '97 - p1391 [51-250]
  JEL - v35 - Mr '97 - p231 [51-250]
Quaderni Dell' Istituto Italiano Di Cultura. New Ser., No. 1
  MLR - v91 - Jl '96 - p763+ [501+]
Quaderni Musicali Marchigiani
  p Notes - v53 - D '96 - p538+ [501+]
Quaill, Avril - *Marking Our Times*
  Choice - v34 - Ja '97 - p784 [51-250]
Qualey, Marsha - *Hometown*
  y Kliatt - v31 - My '97 - p9 [51-250]
  y PW - v244 - Ap 14 '97 - p77 [1-50]
Qualter, Anne - *Differentiated Primary Science*
  R&R Bk N - v11 - D '96 - p53 [51-250]
Quammen, David - *The Song of the Dodo*
  BioSci - v47 - F '97 - p124+ [501+]
  BL - v93 - D 1 '96 - p630 [1-50]
  BL - v93 - Ap 1 '97 - p1286 [1-50]
  Bloom Rev - v16 - S '96 - p17+ [501+]
  Choice - v34 - O '96 - p304 [51-250]
  Nature - v381 - My 16 '96 - p205+ [501+]
  NS - v125 - Ag 30 '96 - p45 [501+]
  NYTBR - v101 - D 8 '96 - p11 [51-250]
  NYTBR - v102 - Ap 13 '97 - p32 [51-250]
  Obs - S 1 '96 - p17* [501+]
  Queens Q - v103 - Fall '96 - p595+ [501+]
  y SB - v32 - Ag '96 - p174 [251-500]
  SciTech - v20 - S '96 - p20 [1-50]
  SFR - v21 - N '96 - p48 [1-50]
  Spec - v277 - S 14 '96 - p43+ [501+]
  TLS - F 21 '97 - p9 [501+]
  Trib Bks - Ap 20 '97 - p8 [501+]
Quandt, Richard E - *The Collected Essays of Richard E. Quandt. Vols. 1-2*
  Econ J - v106 - S '96 - p1465+ [501+]
Quant, Mary - *Ultimate Makeup and Beauty*
  y SLJ - v43 - F '97 - p138 [51-250]
Quantic, Diane Dufva - *The Nature of the Place*
  J Am St - v30 - Ag '96 - p286+ [501+]
  WAL - v31 - Win '97 - p400+ [251-500]
Quarrington, Paul - *Original Six*
  CF - v75 - D '96 - p37+ [501+]
  Mac - v109 - D 16 '96 - p72 [51-250]
  Quill & Q - v62 - Ag '96 - p35 [251-500]
Quarry West
  p Sm Pr R - v28 - Je '96 - p18 [251-500]
Quasthoff, Uta M - *Aspects of Oral Communication*
  Lang Soc - v25 - D '96 - p613+ [501+]

Quatrani, Terry - *Succeeding with the Booch and OMT Methods*
  SciTech - v20 - D '96 - p8 [51-250]
Quattlebaum, Mary - *In the Beginning (Illus. by Bryn Barnard)*
  c HB Guide - v7 - Fall '96 - p308 [1-50]
Jazz, Pizzazz, and the Silver Threads (Illus. by Robin Oz)
  c HB Guide - v7 - Fall '96 - p296 [1-50]
Jesus and the Children (Illus. by Bill Farnsworth)
  c HB Guide - v7 - Fall '96 - p308 [1-50]
The Magic Squad and the Dog of Great Potential (Illus. by Frank Remkiewicz)
  c BL - v93 - F 1 '97 - p942 [51-250]
  c CCB-B - v50 - F '97 - p220 [51-250]
  c HB - v73 - My '97 - p327 [51-250]
  c KR - v64 - N 15 '96 - p1673 [51-250]
Quayle, Marilyn Tucker - *The Campaign*
  NYTBR - v101 - Ap 7 '96 - p10 [501+]
Qubein, Nido R - *How to Be a Great Communicator in Person, on Paper and on the Podium*
  LJ - v121 - D '96 - p108 [51-250]
Que Es Que
  cr BL - v93 - Mr 1 '97 - p1196 [51-250]
Quebec (Province). Commission De Toponymie - *Noms Et Lieux De Quebec*
  r Names - v44 - Je '96 - p145+ [501+]
Queen, Carol - *Switch Hitters*
  HG&LRev - v3 - Fall '96 - p34+ [501+]
  Quill & Q - v62 - Jl '96 - p42 [501+]
Queen, Christopher S - *Engaged Buddhism*
  Choice - v34 - S '96 - p143 [51-250]
Queen, Edward L - *The Encyclopedia of American Religious History. Vols. 1-2*
  r ARBA - v28 - '97 - p537 [51-250]
  r Bks & Cult - v2 - N '96 - p38 [501+]
  r BL - v93 - Ja '97 - p769 [1-50]
  r LJ - v122 - Ap 15 '97 - p39+ [51-250]
  r Nine-C Lit - v51 - D '96 - p426 [51-250]
  r RQ - v36 - Fall '96 - p126+ [251-500]
Queen, J Allen - *Geography Smart Junior*
  y Kliatt - v31 - My '97 - p24 [51-250]
Queen, Sarah A - *From Chronicle to Canon*
  Rel St Rev - v23 - Ap '97 - p205 [51-250]
Queenan, Joe - *The Unkindest Cut*
  Obs - S 8 '96 - p15* [501+]
  Si & So - v6 - N '96 - p36 [1-50]
  Trib Bks - Mr 2 '97 - p8 [1-50]
Queer View Mirror
  Quill & Q - v62 - Jl '96 - p42 [501+]
Queer View Mirror 2
  Quill & Q - v63 - F '97 - p47 [251-500]
Queinnec, Christian - *Lisp in Small Pieces*
  Choice - v34 - Ap '97 - p1374 [51-250]
  SciTech - v20 - D '96 - p10 [51-250]
Queiros, Eca De - *The Maias*
  TranslRevS - v1 - My '95 - p27 [51-250]
The Yellow Sofa
  KR - v64 - O 1 '96 - p1419 [251-500]
  LJ - v122 - F 1 '97 - p112 [1-50]
  PW - v243 - O 14 '96 - p79 [251-500]
Quellmalz, Edys - *School-Based Reform*
  EL - v54 - O '96 - p92 [51-250]
Queneau, Raymond - *Chene Et Chien*
  MLR - v92 - Ja '97 - p204 [251-500]
Quest-Ritson, Charles - *The English Garden Abroad*
  CR - v269 - S '96 - p166 [51-250]
Quevedo, Francisco De - *Suenos Y Discursos*
  MLR - v91 - Jl '96 - p766+ [501+]
Suenos Y Discursos. Vols. 1-2
  MLR - v91 - Jl '96 - p766+ [501+]

Quibria, M G - *Critical Issues in Asian Development*
  Econ J - v106 - S '96 - p1482 [51-250]
Rural Poverty in Developing Asia. Vol. 2
  JEL - v34 - D '96 - p2111+ [51-250]
Quick, Amanda - *Affair*
  BL - v93 - Mr 1 '97 - p1069 [51-250]
  KR - v65 - Ap 1 '97 - p495 [251-500]
  LJ - v122 - Ap 1 '97 - p131 [51-250]
  PW - v244 - Ap 21 '97 - p58 [51-250]
  Trib Bks - My 11 '97 - p11 [51-250]
Mischief
  PW - v244 - Mr 31 '97 - p72 [1-50]
Quick Reference Atlas. Electronic Media Version
  cr Learning - v25 - Mr '97 - p70 [51-250]
Quigley, Christine - *The Corpse: A History*
  LJ - v122 - Mr 15 '97 - p81 [51-250]
  R&R Bk N - v12 - F '97 - p31 [51-250]
Quigley, Colin - *Music from the Heart*
  WestFolk - v55 - Spr '96 - p168+ [501+]
Quigley, Martin S - *First Century of Film*
  r ARBA - v28 - '97 - p508 [251-500]
Quignard, Pascal - *Rhetorique Speculative*
  WLT - v71 - Win '97 - p114 [251-500]
Quillec, Maurice - *Materials for Optoelectronics*
  SciTech - v20 - D '96 - p67 [51-250]
Quilted for Christmas. Bk. 3
  LJ - v121 - O 15 '96 - p56 [251-500]
Quinby, Lee - *Genealogy and Literature*
  AL - v68 - D '96 - p882 [51-250]
Quindlen, Anna - *Happily Ever After (Illus. by James Stevenson)*
  c BL - v93 - F 1 '97 - p942 [51-250]
  c KR - v65 - Ja 1 '97 - p62 [51-250]
  c PW - v244 - Ja 27 '97 - p107 [51-250]
  c SLJ - v43 - Mr '97 - p164 [51-250]
Quine, J R - *Extremal Riemann Surfaces*
  SciTech - v21 - Mr '97 - p16 [1-50]
Quine, W V - *From Stimulus to Science*
  CPR - v16 - O '96 - p367+ [501+]
Quiner, Krista - *Dominique Moceanu: A Gymnastics Sensation*
  c SLJ - v43 - Mr '97 - p206+ [51-250]
Quing, Lin - *Zur Fruhgeschichte Des Elektronenmikroskops*
  Isis - v88 - Mr '97 - p167 [501+]
Quinkert, Gerhard - *Aspects of Organic Chemistry: Structure*
  Choice - v34 - Ja '97 - p823 [51-250]
  SciTech - v20 - N '96 - p22 [51-250]
Quinlan, David - *Quinlan's Illustrated Directory of Film Character Actors*
  r ARBA - v28 - '97 - p505 [251-500]
Quinlan, Kathleen - *Anna Duncan: In the Footsteps of Isadora*
  Dance - v70 - N '96 - p78+ [501+]
Quinlan, Kieran - *Walker Percy: The Last Catholic Novelist*
  Choice - v34 - N '96 - p459+ [51-250]
  WLT - v71 - Win '97 - p160+ [501+]
Quinn, Arthur - *Hell with the Fire Out*
  BL - v93 - F 15 '97 - p1000 [51-250]
  KR - v65 - Ja 15 '97 - p127 [251-500]
  PW - v244 - F 24 '97 - p78+ [51-250]
Quinn, C Edward - *Roots of the Republic. Vols. 1-6*
  r ARBA - v28 - '97 - p189 [51-250]
  yr SLJ - v43 - F '97 - p132+ [51-250]
Quinn, D Michael - *The Mormon Hierarchy*
  LJ - v122 - Ap 1 '97 - p99 [51-250]
  PW - v244 - Mr 24 '97 - p76 [51-250]

Same-Sex Dynamics among Nineteenth-Century Americans
  BW - v26 - S 1 '96 - p13 [51-250]
  CC - v114 - Ja 15 '97 - p56+ [501+]
  Choice - v34 - Mr '97 - p1246 [51-250]
  PW - v243 - N 4 '96 - p47 [51-250]
  TLS - D 20 '96 - p30 [501+]
Quinn, Daniel - *The Story of B*
y BL - v93 - O 1 '96 - p292 [51-250]
  Econ - v341 - D 7 '96 - p6*+ [251-500]
  KR - v64 - S 15 '96 - p1349 [251-500]
  PW - v243 - O 7 '96 - p59 [51-250]
The Story of B (Heald). Audio Version
  BWatch - v18 - Mr '97 - p7 [1-50]
Quinn, Daniel P - *I Am Buddhist*
c SLJ - v43 - Ja '97 - p95+ [51-250]
Quinn, David B - *Sir Francis Drake as Seen by His Contemporaries*
  Sea H - Win '96 - p42 [51-250]
Quinn, Dennis J - *Peace Support Operations and the U.S. Military*
  RSR - v24 - 3 '96 - p44 [51-250]
Quinn, Julia - *Everything and the Moon*
  PW - v244 - F 24 '97 - p88 [51-250]
Quinn, Justin - *The 'O'o'a'a' Bird*
  Lon R Bks - v18 - Jl 18 '96 - p24+ [501+]
Quinn, Patricia O - *Attention Deficit Disorder*
  SciTech - v21 - Mr '97 - p65 [51-250]
The Putting on the Brakes Activity Book for Young People with ADHD
  Adoles - v31 - Win '96 - p995 [51-250]
Quinn, Patrick, 1957- - *Thick as Thieves*
y Kliatt - v30 - S '96 - p13 [51-250]
Quinn, Patrick J - *Recharting the Thirties*
  Choice - v34 - F '97 - p968 [51-250]
Quinn, Patrick J, 1946- - *The Great War and the Missing Muse*
  RES - v47 - Ag '96 - p447+ [501+]
Quinn, Paul J - *Titanic at Two A.M.*
  LJ - v122 - Ap 15 '97 - p105 [51-250]
Quinn, Robert E - *Deep Change*
  LJ - v121 - S 15 '96 - p78 [51-250]
Quinn, Susan - *Marie Curie: A Life*
  Am Sci - v84 - My '96 - p306+ [501+]
Quinn, Warren - *Morality and Action*
  Phil R - v105 - Ap '96 - p270+ [501+]
Quinn, William A - *Chaucer's Rehersynges*
  RES - v47 - N '96 - p562+ [501+]
Quinones, Ricardo J - *Foundation Sacrifice in Dante's Commedia*
  MLR - v91 - Jl '96 - p749+ [501+]
Quinones Keber, Eloise - *Chipping Away on Earth*
  HAHR - v76 - Ag '96 - p556+ [251-500]
Codex Telleriano-Remensis
  Six Ct J - v27 - Fall '96 - p950+ [501+]
Quint, David - *Epic and Empire*
  CLS - v33 - 3 '96 - p300+ [501+]
Quint, Michael D - *Environmental Impact of Chemicals*
  SciTech - v20 - N '96 - p37 [51-250]
Quintana, Leroy - *My Hair Turning Gray among Strangers*
  Prog - v60 - S '96 - p43+ [251-500]
Quinton, Ann - *Some Foul Play*
  BL - v93 - D 15 '96 - p713 [51-250]
  KR - v64 - N 1 '96 - p1568 [51-250]
Quintrell, Brian - *Charles I 1625-1640*
  HT - v46 - D '96 - p56 [251-500]
Quiri, Patricia Ryon - *The White House*
c HB Guide - v7 - Fall '96 - p385 [51-250]
c SLJ - v42 - Ag '96 - p159 [51-250]
Quirk, Anne - *Dancing with Great-Aunt Cornelia*
c PW - v244 - My 5 '97 - p209 [51-250]
Quirk, Charles F - *Sports and the Law*
y SLJ - v42 - O '96 - p166 [51-250]
Quirk, Lawrence J - *The Kennedys in Hollywood*
  BL - v92 - Ag '96 - p1850 [251-500]
  BW - v26 - S 22 '96 - p6+ [501+]
Paul Newman: The Unauthorized Biography
  LJ - v122 - Ap 15 '97 - p84 [51-250]
  PW - v244 - Mr 17 '97 - p68 [51-250]
Quisenberry, Anderson Chenault - *Revolutionary Soldiers in Kentucky*
r EGH - v50 - N '96 - p167 [51-250]
Qumsiyeh, Mazin B - *Mammals of the Holy Land*
  Choice - v34 - My '97 - p1526 [51-250]
Qunanbaev, Abai - *Book of Words*
  WLT - v71 - Win '97 - p231 [501+]
Quogan, Anthony - *Bodies in Motion*
  Quill & Q - v62 - Jl '96 - p53 [251-500]

Qureshi, Asif H - *The World Trade Organization*
  JEL - v34 - D '96 - p2080 [51-250]
  R&R Bk N - v11 - N '96 - p34 [51-250]
Quyen, Di - *Hoa Hong Nha Kin*
  BL - v93 - S 1 '96 - p70 [51-250]
Qvortrup, Jens - *Childhood Matters*
  CS - v25 - N '96 - p786+ [501+]
Raab, Elisabeth M - *And Peace Never Came*
  BIC - v26 - Mr '97 - p16+ [501+]
Raack, R C - *Stalin's Drive to the West 1938-1945*
  AHR - v102 - F '97 - p143+ [251-500]
  CEH - v29 - 2 '96 - p278+ [501+]
Ra'anan, Uri - *Russia: A Return to Imperialism?*
  Choice - v34 - S '96 - p206 [51-250]
  R&R Bk N - v11 - N '96 - p13 [51-250]
Raat, W Dirk - *Mexico's Sierra Tarahumara*
  Choice - v34 - F '97 - p1022 [51-250]
  For Aff - v76 - Mr '97 - p189 [51-250]
  R&R Bk N - v12 - F '97 - p27 [51-250]
Raban, Jonathan - *Bad Land*
  Aud - v99 - Mr '97 - p116+ [501+]
  BL - v93 - Ja '97 - p760 [1-50]
  BL - v93 - N 15 '96 - p568 [51-250]
  BW - v26 - D 1 '96 - p1+ [501+]
  Comw - v124 - Ap 11 '97 - p21+ [501+]
  CSM - v89 - F 5 '97 - p15 [501+]
  Econ - v341 - N 16 '96 - p7* [501+]
  KR - v64 - S 1 '96 - p1305 [251-500]
  LATBR - N 24 '96 - p4+ [501+]
  LJ - v121 - O 1 '96 - p110 [51-250]
  Lon R Bks - v18 - D 12 '96 - p25+ [501+]
  NS - v125 - O 25 '96 - p45 [501+]
  NYRB - v44 - F 6 '97 - p32+ [501+]
  NYTBR - v101 - N 10 '96 - p11 [501+]
  NYTBR - v101 - D 8 '96 - p11 [51-250]
  NYTLa - v146 - N 14 '96 - pC20 [501+]
  Obs - O 20 '96 - p16* [501+]
  PW - v243 - S 30 '96 - p66+ [51-250]
  Spec - v277 - O 19 '96 - p47 [251-500]
  Spec - v277 - N 23 '96 - p43 [1-50]
  Time - v148 - N 25 '96 - p118 [251-500]
  TLS - N 29 '96 - p13 [51-250]
  TLS - F 28 '97 - p6+ [501+]
Rabasa, George - *Glass Houses*
  Bloom Rev - v17 - Ja '97 - p15 [251-500]
  Choice - v34 - My '97 - p1498 [51-250]
  PW - v243 - S 9 '96 - p78 [51-250]
Rabate, Jean-Michel - *The Ghosts of Modernity*
  Choice - v34 - N '96 - p450 [51-250]
Rabb, Jane M - *Literature and Photography*
  Afterimage - v23 - Sum '96 - p22 [501+]
Rabe, Barry G - *Beyond NIMBY*
  Pol Stud J - v24 - Sum '96 - p334 [51-250]
Rabe, Susan A - *Faith, Art, and Politics at Saint-Riquier*
  AHR - v101 - O '96 - p1190+ [501+]
  CH - v65 - D '96 - p673+ [251-500]
Rabelais, Francois - *Gargantua*
  CML - v16 - Spr '96 - p265+ [501+]
Rabelais: Oeuvres Completes
  MLR - v91 - Jl '96 - p719+ [501+]
Rab-Gsal-Zla-Ba, Dis-Mgo Mkhyen-Brtse - *The Excellent Path to Enlightenment*
  Tric - v6 - Win '96 - p116 [1-50]
Rabie, Mohamed - *U.S.-PLO Dialogue*
  AAPSS-A - v546 - Jl '96 - p156+ [501+]
Rabin, Leah - *Rabin: Our Life, His Legacy*
y BL - v93 - Mr 15 '97 - p1203 [51-250]
  BW - v27 - Ap 6 '97 - p1+ [501+]
  KR - v65 - Mr 1 '97 - p364 [51-250]
  NYTBR - v102 - Ap 20 '97 - p22 [501+]
  PW - v244 - Mr 10 '97 - p56 [501+]
Rabin, Yitzhak - *Asher Ahavtah Et Yitshak*
  BL - v93 - Mr 1 '97 - p1115 [1-50]
Rodef Shalom Neome Ha-Shalom Shel Ha-Memshalah Yitshak Rabin
  BL - v93 - Mr 1 '97 - p1115 [1-50]
Rabinow, Paul - *Making PCR*
  Choice - v34 - N '96 - p482 [51-250]
  Sci - v274 - N 8 '96 - p934+ [51-250]
Rabinowitz, Anna - *At the Site of Inside Out*
  PW - v244 - Mr 31 '97 - p69 [51-250]
Rabinowitz, Nancy Sorkin - *Anxiety Veiled*
  CW - v90 - S '96 - p74+ [501+]
Rabinowitz, Noel - *Shockwave Power Solutions*
  SciTech - v20 - D '96 - p8 [51-250]
Rabinowitz, Paula - *They Must Be Represented*
  FQ - v49 - Sum '96 - p59+ [501+]
Rabinowitz, Richard - *The Spiritual Self in Everyday Life*
  Rel St Rev - v23 - Ap '97 - p135+ [501+]

Rabinowitz, Victor - *Unrepentant Leftist*
  LJ - v121 - O 1 '96 - p90+ [51-250]
  PW - v243 - N 4 '96 - p59 [51-250]
Raboteau, Albert J - *A Fire in the Bones*
  CC - v113 - O 16 '96 - p980+ [251-500]
  JR - v77 - Ap '97 - p303+ [501+]
Rabrenovic, Gordana - *Community Builders*
  Choice - v34 - N '96 - p547 [51-250]
Raby, Peter - *Bright Paradise*
  Nature - v383 - O 10 '96 - p491 [501+]
  Spec - v277 - S 28 '96 - p50 [501+]
  TLS - Ag 30 '96 - p26 [501+]
Raby, Rosalind Latiner - *Dimensions of the Community College*
  Choice - v34 - F '97 - p1013+ [51-250]
  R&R Bk N - v11 - N '96 - p55 [51-250]
Race, Phil - *500 Computing Tips for Teachers and Lecturers*
  TES - O 18 '96 - p43U [51-250]
  TES - Mr 14 '97 - p39U [501+]
Racey, Paul A - *Ecology, Evolution and Behavior of Bats*
  BioSci - v47 - Mr '97 - p188+ [501+]
Rachlin, Harvey - *Lucy's Bones, Sacred Stones, and Einstein's Brain*
  PW - v243 - O 21 '96 - p78 [1-50]
Rachlin, Nahid - *The Heart's Desire*
  ABR - v17 - Ag '96 - p16+ [501+]
Racina, Thom - *Snow Angel*
  Arm Det - v29 - Fall '96 - p468 [51-250]
  BL - v92 - Ag '96 - p1887+ [51-250]
Rackley, Virginia Ruth Waggoner - *Ten Sisters*
  BL - v93 - D 15 '96 - p697+ [51-250]
Racunovodstvo I Financije
p JEL - v34 - S '96 - p1506+ [51-250]
Raczynski, Dagmar - *Strategies to Combat Poverty in Latin America*
  JEL - v34 - S '96 - p1442+ [51-250]
  PSQ - v111 - Win '96 - p743+ [501+]
Radakovich, Anka - *Sexplorations: Journeys to the Erogenous Frontier*
  Ent W - Ap 4 '97 - p78 [51-250]
  KR - v65 - F 1 '97 - p205 [251-500]
  PW - v244 - Ja 20 '97 - p383+ [51-250]
Radbourne, Jennifer - *Arts Management*
  Aust Bk R - D '96 - p93 [1-50]
Radcliffe, David Hill - *Edmund Spenser: A Reception History*
  Choice - v34 - N '96 - p460 [51-250]
Radcliffe, Elizabeth - *Faith in Theory and Practice*
  Zygon - v31 - D '96 - p729+ [501+]
Radcliffe, Elsa J - *Gothic Novels of the Twentieth Century*
r RQ - v36 - Win '96 - p224 [51-250]
Radcliffe, Sarah A - *Viva: Women and Popular Protest in Latin America*
  Signs - v22 - Aut '96 - p237+ [501+]
Radcliffe, Theresa - *Cimru the Seal (Illus. by John Butler)*
c HB Guide - v8 - Spr '97 - p43 [51-250]
c JB - v60 - O '96 - p187 [51-250]
c Sch Lib - v44 - Ag '96 - p101 [51-250]
Raddall, Thomas H - *Courage in the Storm (Illus. by Are Gjesdal)*
c Can CL - v22 - Fall '96 - p131+ [51-250]
Radden, Jennifer - *Divided Minds and Successive Selves*
  Hast Cen R - v27 - Ja '97 - p47 [1-50]
Radder, Hans - *In and about the World*
  Choice - v34 - Ja '97 - p814 [51-250]
  R&R Bk N - v11 - D '96 - p67 [51-250]
Radding, Cynthia - *Entre El Desierto Y La Sierra*
  HAHR - v76 - Ag '96 - p560+ [501+]
Rader, Joanne - *Individualized Dementia Care*
  AJN - v96 - N '96 - p16D [51-250]
Radest, Howard B - *Humanism with a Human Face*
  Choice - v34 - D '96 - p693 [51-250]
  R&R Bk N - v11 - N '96 - p1 [51-250]
Radford, Derek - *Harry at the Garage (Illus. by Derek Radford)*
c ECEJ - v23 - Sum '96 - p221 [51-250]
Radicalism in Minnesota 1900-1960
r RQ - v35 - Sum '96 - p487 [51-250]
Radice, Giles - *What Needs to Change*
  NS & S - v9 - Ap 26 '96 - p29+ [501+]
Radin, Beryl A - *New Governance for Rural America*
  Choice - v34 - O '96 - p362 [51-250]
  Pol Stud J - v24 - Aut '96 - p515+ [501+]
Radin, Margaret Jane - *Contested Commodities*
  BW - v26 - D 8 '96 - p9 [51-250]
  Econ - v342 - F 15 '97 - p3*+ [501+]
  JEL - v35 - Mr '97 - p243 [51-250]
Radke, Linda Foster - *The Economical Guide to Self-Publishing*
  Quill & Q - v63 - Mr '97 - p73 [251-500]

Radner, Ephraim - *Inhabiting Unity*
   CLW - v66 - Je '96 - p33+ [501+]
   ER - v48 - O '96 - p528+ [501+]
Radner, Joan Newlon - *Feminist Messages*
   Signs - v22 - Win '97 - p491+ [501+]
Rado, Lisa - *Rereading Modernism*
   ELT - v39 - 4 '96 - p482+ [501+]
Rados, David L - *Marketing for Nonprofit Organizations.
2nd Ed.*
   Choice - v34 - O '96 - p327 [51-250]
Radosh, Ronald - *Divided They Fell*
   Bks & Cult - v2 - N '96 - p38 [251-500]
   BW - v26 - S 8 '96 - p4 [251-500]
   BW - v26 - D 8 '96 - p8 [1-50]
   Choice - v34 - D '96 - p691 [51-250]
   Nat - v264 - F 17 '97 - p30+ [501+]
   NYTBR - v101 - Ag 25 '96 - p12 [501+]
Radovich, Don - *Tony Richardson: A Bio-Bibliography*
  r ARBA - v28 - '97 - p501 [51-250]
Radstrom, Niklas - *Vad Du Vill*
   WLT - v70 - Sum '96 - p718+ [501+]
Radulski, John P - *Pleasure Paradises*
  r TCI - v30 - O '96 - p58 [1-50]
Radway, Richard - *Russia and the USSR 1900-95*
  y TES - S 6 '96 - pR6 [501+]
Radzinsky, Edvard - *Stalin: The First In-Depth Biography
Based on Explosive New Documents from Russia's
Secret Archives*
   LJ - v122 - Ja '97 - p50 [1-50]
   *Stalin: The First In-Depth Biography Based on
Explosive New Documents from Russia's Secret Archives
(McCallum). Audio Version*
  y Kliatt - v31 - Mr '97 - p50 [51-250]
   LJ - v122 - F 15 '97 - p115 [1-50]
Rae, Bob - *From Protest to Power*
   BIC - v25 - D '96 - p29+ [501+]
   CF - v75 - Mr '97 - p41+ [501+]
   Mac - v109 - O 28 '96 - p62+ [501+]
   Quill & Q - v62 - O '96 - p33 [251-500]
Rae, Colleen Mariah - *Movies in the Mind*
   LJ - v121 - O 15 '96 - p59 [51-250]
Rae, Noel - *Witnessing America*
   BW - v26 - N 24 '96 - p13 [51-250]
   PW - v243 - Jl 22 '96 - p220 [51-250]
Rae, Scott B - *Brave New Families*
   Ch Today - v41 - Ja 6 '97 - p52 [51-250]
Rae, Simon - *The Faber Book of Christmas*
   TLS - N 22 '96 - p14+ [501+]
Raeburn, D - *Airways Smooth Muscle: Modelling the
Asthmatic Response in Vivo*
   SciTech - v20 - N '96 - p46 [51-250]
   *Airways Smooth Muscle: Peptide Receptors, Ion
Channels, and Signal Transduction*
   SciTech - v20 - D '96 - p34 [51-250]
Raeburn, Paul - *The Last Harvest*
   NYRB - v44 - F 20 '97 - p30+ [501+]
Raeff, Marc - *Political Ideas and Institutions in Imperial
Russia*
   JMH - v68 - S '96 - p740+ [501+]
Rael, Elsa - *What Zeesie Saw on Delancey Street (Illus. by
Marjorie Priceman)*
  c BL - v93 - S 1 '96 - p144 [51-250]
  c BL - v93 - Ap 1 '97 - p1302 [1-50]
  c CBRS - v25 - F '97 - p78 [51-250]
  c CCB-B - v50 - D '96 - p149 [51-250]
  c HB - v72 - N '96 - p730+ [251-500]
  c HB Guide - v8 - Spr '97 - p43 [51-250]
  c KR - v64 - O 1 '96 - p1472 [51-250]
  c PW - v243 - O 21 '96 - p83 [51-250]
  c SLJ - v42 - D '96 - p103+ [51-250]
Rafael, Vicente L - *Discrepant Histories*
   Amerasia J - v22 - 3 '96 - p173+ [501+]
Rafenomanjato, Charlotte-Arrisoa - *Le Cinquieme Sceau*
   FR - v70 - D '96 - p356+ [501+]
Raff, Rudolf A - *The Shape of Life*
   Choice - v34 - N '96 - p482 [51-250]
   Sci - v273 - S 6 '96 - p1347 [501+]
   SciTech - v20 - S '96 - p19 [51-250]
Raffaelli, Tiziano - *Alfred Marshall's Lectures to Women*
   Econ J - v107 - Ja '97 - p247+ [501+]
Raffan, James - *Fire in the Bones*
   BIC - v25 - S '96 - p10+ [501+]
   CG - v116 - S '96 - p78+ [501+]
   KR - v65 - Ja 15 '97 - p127+ [251-500]
   PW - v244 - Ja 27 '97 - p90 [51-250]
Raffauf, Robert F - *Plant Alkaloids*
   SciTech - v20 - D '96 - p32 [51-250]

Raffelt, Georg G - *Stars as Laboratories for Fundamental
Physics*
   Choice - v34 - D '96 - p634 [51-250]
   Nature - v384 - N 14 '96 - p128 [51-250]
   Sci - v274 - N 1 '96 - p733+ [501+]
Raffer, Kunibert - *The Foreign Aid Business*
   Choice - v34 - Ja '97 - p846 [51-250]
   JEL - v35 - Mr '97 - p219+ [51-250]
Rafferty, Oliver P - *Catholicism in Ulster 1603-1983*
   Bks & Cult - v2 - Ja '96 - p11+ [501+]
   EHR - v112 - F '97 - p215+ [251-500]
Raffi - *Rise and Shine (Illus. by Eugenie Fernandes)*
  c BL - v93 - Ja '97 - p864 [251-500]
  c HB Guide - v8 - Spr '97 - p141 [51-250]
  c SLJ - v43 - Ja '97 - p108 [51-250]
Raffin, Deborah - *A Gift of Sharing*
   PW - v243 - S 2 '96 - p108 [51-250]
Raffo, Susan - *Queerly Classed*
   LJ - v122 - F 15 '97 - p152 [51-250]
Raftery, Judith Rosenberg - *Land of Fair Promise*
   J Urban H - v23 - N '96 - p113+ [501+]
Raftis, J A - *Peasant Economic Development within the
English Manorial System*
   Choice - v34 - My '97 - p1548 [51-250]
Ragan, James - *Lusions*
   LJ - v122 - Ap 1 '97 - p98 [51-250]
   PW - v244 - Ap 28 '97 - p72 [51-250]
Ragin, Charles C - *Constructing Social Research*
   SF - v75 - S '96 - p335+ [251-500]
Ragland, Bryce - *The Year 2000 Problem Solver*
  y SB - v33 - My '97 - p106 [51-250]
Raglus, Jeff - *Schnorky the Wave Puncher! (Illus. by Jeff
Raglus)*
  c HB Guide - v7 - Fall '96 - p272 [51-250]
  c SLJ - v42 - S '96 - p188 [51-250]
Ragon, Michel - *Les Coquelicots Sont Revenus*
   BL - v93 - Ja '97 - p827 [1-50]
Ragozin, Len - *The Odds Must Be Crazy*
   BL - v93 - My 15 '97 - p1556 [51-250]
Ragsdale, Bruce A - *A Planters' Republic*
   Choice - v34 - My '97 - p1548+ [51-250]
   W&M Q - v54 - Ap '97 - p434+ [501+]
Ragsdale, Katherine Hancock - *Boundary Wars*
   Cons - v17 - Win '96 - p31 [1-50]
Raguer, Hilari - *La Espada Y La Cruz*
   CHR - v82 - O '96 - p661+ [501+]
Ragussis, Michael - *Figures of Conversion*
   Albion - v28 - Sum '96 - p307+ [501+]
   JR - v77 - Ap '97 - p334+ [501+]
   Nine-C Lit - v51 - Mr '97 - p531+ [501+]
   VS - v39 - Spr '96 - p407+ [501+]
Raham, R Gary - *Explorations in Backyard Biology*
   SLMQ - v25 - Fall '96 - p66 [51-250]
Rahaman, Vashanti - *A Little Salmon for Witness (Illus.
by Sandra Speidel)*
  c KR - v65 - Ja 1 '97 - p62 [51-250]
  c PW - v244 - Ja 13 '97 - p75 [51-250]
  c SLJ - v43 - F '97 - p84 [51-250]
   O Christmas Tree (Illus. by Frane Lessac)
  c BL - v93 - S 1 '96 - p137 [51-250]
  c CBRS - v25 - O '96 - p17 [51-250]
  c CCB-B - v50 - N '96 - p111 [51-250]
  c HB Guide - v8 - Spr '97 - p44 [51-250]
  c KR - v64 - O 15 '96 - p1537+ [51-250]
  c NYTBR - v101 - D 22 '96 - p16 [1-50]
  c PW - v243 - S 30 '96 - p90 [51-250]
  c SLJ - v42 - O '96 - p39 [51-250]
   Read for Me, Mama (Illus. by Lori McElrath-Eslick)
  c BL - v93 - F 15 '97 - p1028+ [51-250]
  c CBRS - v25 - Mr '97 - p94 [51-250]
  c CCB-B - v50 - Mr '97 - p255+ [51-250]
  c KR - v65 - Ja 1 '97 - p63 [51-250]
Rahdert, Elizabeth - *Adolescent Drug Abuse*
   J Gov Info - v23 - S '96 - p548 [51-250]
Rahman, Anisur - *Fire and the Rose*
   WLT - v71 - Win '97 - p233 [251-500]
Rahman, Matiur - *Advances in Fluid Mechanics*
   SciTech - v20 - N '96 - p62 [51-250]
   Water Waves
   SIAM Rev - v39 - Mr '97 - p156+ [501+]
Rahman, Mushtaqur - *Divided Kashmir*
   Choice - v34 - S '96 - p183+ [51-250]
   MEJ - v50 - Aut '96 - p629 [51-250]
Rahn, Perry H - *Engineering Geology*
   SciTech - v20 - D '96 - p65 [51-250]
Rahnema, Ali - *Pioneers of Islamic Revival*
   Rel St Rev - v23 - Ap '97 - p200+ [51-250]
Rahner, Hugo - *Church and State in Early Christianity*
   CH - v66 - Mr '97 - p89+ [501+]
Rai, Milan - *Chomsky's Politics*
   RP - v59 - Spr '97 - p395+ [501+]

Raiche, Annabelle - *They Came to Teach*
   CHR - v82 - O '96 - p739+ [251-500]
Raichlen, Steven - *High-Flavor, Low-Fat Appetizers*
   BL - v93 - Mr 15 '97 - p1217 [251-500]
   High-Flavor, Low-Fat Desserts
   BL - v93 - Mr 15 '97 - p1217 [251-500]
Raiha, Victor - *K.G.B. A Aruncat In Aer Romania Cu
Complicitatea Unui Grup De Militari*
   BL - v93 - D 15 '96 - p714 [1-50]
Rail Transportation 1996
   SciTech - v21 - Mr '97 - p83 [51-250]
Railsback, Brian E - *Parallel Expeditions*
   AL - v68 - D '96 - p869+ [501+]
Raimond, Ernst - *The Westerbork Observatory,
Continuing Adventure in Radio Astronomy*
   SciTech - v21 - Mr '97 - p19 [51-250]
Raimundo, Daniel Efrain - *Habla El Coronel Orlando
Piedra*
   BL - v93 - Ap 1 '97 - p1284 [1-50]
Raina, V K - *Concrete Bridges*
   Choice - v34 - N '96 - p489 [51-250]
   SciTech - v20 - S '96 - p52 [51-250]
Raine, Craig - *Clay: Whereabouts Unknown*
   NS & S - v9 - My 17 '96 - p37 [51-250]
Raine, Jerry - *Smalltime*
   KR - v65 - Mr 15 '97 - p421 [51-250]
   NYTBR - v102 - Mr 30 '97 - p23 [51-250]
   PW - v244 - Mr 3 '97 - p67+ [51-250]
Rainer, Tristine - *Your Life as Story*
   BL - v93 - Ap 1 '97 - p1277 [51-250]
   LJ - v122 - Ap 15 '97 - p91 [51-250]
   PW - v244 - Ja 27 '97 - p86+ [51-250]
Raines, Rebecca Robbins - *Getting the Message Through*
   Choice - v34 - F '97 - p1026 [51-250]
   J Mil H - v61 - Ap '97 - p382+ [501+]
Raines, Robert - *A Time to Live*
   LJ - v122 - Mr 15 '97 - p77+ [51-250]
   PW - v244 - Ap 28 '97 - p67 [51-250]
Rainey, Buck - *The Reel Cowboy*
   LJ - v121 - S 15 '96 - p70 [51-250]
   R&R Bk N - v11 - D '96 - p61 [51-250]
Rainey, John Calvin - *The Thang That Ate My
Grandaddy's Dog*
   LJ - v122 - Ap 1 '97 - p131 [51-250]
   PW - v244 - Ap 21 '97 - p62 [51-250]
Rainey, Sue - *Creating Picturesque America*
   WHQ - v27 - Win '96 - p527+ [501+]
Rainier, Chris - *Where Masks Still Dance*
   BL - v93 - D 15 '96 - p696 [51-250]
   CSM - v89 - D 5 '96 - pB2 [51-250]
   NH - v106 - F '97 - p13 [1-50]
Rainis, Kenneth G - *Guide to Microlife*
  y BL - v93 - F 15 '97 - p1015 [51-250]
Raising Our Future
  r JAAL - v40 - S '96 - p78 [51-250]
Raitz, Karl B - *The Theater of Sport*
   J Am Cult - v19 - Sum '96 - p146 [501+]
Raizada, Mohan K - *Recent Advances in Cellular and
Molecular Aspects of Angiotensin Receptors*
   SciTech - v20 - S '96 - p23 [51-250]
Raizen, Senta A - *Technology Education in the Classroom*
   HER - v66 - Fall '96 - p691+ [501+]
Raizner, Albert E - *Topics in Clinical Cardiology*
   SciTech - v21 - Mr '97 - p57 [51-250]
Raj, A R Victor - *The Hindu Connection*
   Theol St - v57 - Je '96 - p389+ [251-500]
Rajan, Gita - *Postcolonial Discourse and Changing
Cultural Contexts*
   ELT - v39 - 4 '96 - p529 [51-250]
Rajan, Sudhir Chella - *The Enigma of Automobility*
   Choice - v34 - My '97 - p1567 [51-250]
Rajtar, Steve - *Hiking Trails, Eastern United States*
  r RQ - v35 - Sum '96 - p560 [251-500]
   Hiking Trails, Western United States
  r BL - v93 - Ja '97 - p896 [1-50]
Rakezic, Sasa - *Flock of Dreamers*
   BL - v93 - My 1 '97 - p1473 [51-250]
Rakodi, Carole - *Harare: Inheriting a Settler-Colonial
City*
   Choice - v34 - O '96 - p335+ [51-250]
Rakosi, Carl - *The Collected Poems of Carl Rakosi*
   J Am St - v30 - Ag '96 - p271+ [501+]
   Poems 1923-1941
   J Am St - v30 - Ag '96 - p271+ [501+]
Rakove, Jack N - *Original Meanings*
   Choice - v34 - O '96 - p362 [51-250]
   Lon R Bks - v19 - F 20 '97 - p26+ [501+]
   NYTBR - v101 - Jl 21 '96 - p20 [501+]
   Rapport - v19 - 4 '96 - p42 [251-500]
   W&M Q - v54 - Ap '97 - p444+ [501+]

Rakowski, Cathy A - *Contrapunto: The Informal Sector Debate in Latin America*
    EG - v72 - O '96 - p470+ [501+]
Raleigh, Michael - *The Riverview Murders*
    PW - v244 - My 12 '97 - p61 [51-250]
Raley, Harold C - *A Watch over Mortality*
    R&R Bk N - v12 - F '97 - p3 [51-250]
Rall, Ann P - *Directory of Services and Resources to the Asian Pacific American Community in the Metropolitan Washington Region*
    r J Gov Info - v23 - S '96 - p602 [51-250]
Ralling, Colin - *Media Guide to the New Parliament Constituencies*
    Econ - v342 - Mr 22 '97 - p106 [501+]
Ralston, Meredith L - *Nobody Wants to Hear Our Truth*
    NWSA Jnl - v8 - Fall '96 - p129+ [501+]
Ram, Haggay - *Myth and Mobilization in Revolutionary Iran*
    MEJ - v50 - Sum '96 - p431+ [501+]
Ramage, Douglas E - *Politics in Indonesia*
    Choice - v34 - D '96 - p683+ [51-250]
Ramamurti, Ravi - *Privatizing Monopolies*
    JEL - v34 - S '96 - p1453 [51-250]
Ramana, P Venkata - *Renewable Energy Development in India*
    JEL - v34 - S '96 - p1499+ [51-250]
Ramanujan, A K - *The Collected Poems of A.K. Ramanujan*
    Choice - v34 - S '96 - p121 [51-250]
    WLT - v70 - Sum '96 - p762 [501+]
Ramaty, R - *High Energy Solar Physics*
    SciTech - v20 - N '96 - p16 [51-250]
Rambeck, Richard - *Anfernee (Penny) Hardaway*
    c Ch BWatch - v6 - D '96 - p6+ [1-50]
    c HB Guide - v8 - Spr '97 - p145 [51-250]
    Dan Marino
    c Ch BWatch - v6 - D '96 - p6+ [1-50]
    c HB Guide - v8 - Spr '97 - p145 [51-250]
    Greg Maddux
    c Ch BWatch - v6 - D '96 - p6+ [1-50]
    c HB Guide - v8 - Spr '97 - p145 [51-250]
    Jackie Joyner-Kersee
    c Ch BWatch - v6 - D '96 - p6+ [1-50]
    c HB Guide - v8 - Spr '97 - p145 [51-250]
    Michael Jordan
    c Ch BWatch - v6 - D '96 - p6+ [1-50]
    c HB Guide - v8 - Spr '97 - p145 [51-250]
    Monica Seles
    c Ch BWatch - v6 - D '96 - p6+ [1-50]
    c HB Guide - v8 - Spr '97 - p145 [51-250]
    Pete Sampras
    c Ch BWatch - v6 - D '96 - p6+ [1-50]
    c HB Guide - v8 - Spr '97 - p145 [51-250]
    Steve Young
    c Ch BWatch - v6 - D '96 - p6+ [1-50]
    c HB Guide - v8 - Spr '97 - p145 [51-250]
Rambotham, Oliver - *Humanitarian Intervention in Contemporary Conflict*
    JPR - v34 - F '97 - p114 [251-500]
Ramesh, K T - *Structural Adjustment, World Trade and Third World Tourism*
    WorldV - v12 - Jl '96 - p18 [51-250]
Ramesh, S - *Venture Capital and the Indian Financial Sector*
    JEL - v34 - S '96 - p1437 [51-250]
Ramet, Sabrina Petra - *Social Currents in Eastern Europe. 2nd Ed.*
    Slav R - v55 - Sum '96 - p443+ [501+]
Ramirez, Santiago - *Mexican Studies in the History and Philosophy of Science*
    SciTech - v20 - D '96 - p3 [51-250]
Ramirez, Sergio - *Un Baile De Mascaras*
    BL - v93 - S 15 '96 - p227 [1-50]
Ramirez, Susan Elizabeth - *The World Upside Down*
    Choice - v34 - F '97 - p1022 [51-250]
Ramming, Cindy - *All Mothers Work*
    BL - v93 - D 15 '96 - p698 [51-250]
    PW - v243 - N 18 '96 - p73 [51-250]
Ramon, Shulamit - *Mental Health in Europe*
    SciTech - v20 - D '96 - p39 [51-250]
Ramondino, Fabrizia - *In Viaggio*
    WLT - v70 - Sum '96 - p676 [251-500]
Ramos, Manuel - *Blues for the Buffalo*
    y BL - v93 - My 1 '97 - p1483 [51-250]
    LJ - v122 - My 1 '97 - p143 [51-250]
    PW - v244 - Mr 31 '97 - p66 [51-250]
    The Last Client of Luis Montez
    Arm Det - v29 - Sum '96 - p363 [51-250]
    Rapport - v19 - 4 '96 - p29 [51-250]
Ramous, Mario - *Per Via Di Sguardo*
    TLS - Jl 19 '96 - p12 [501+]

Ramphele, Mamphela - *Across Boundaries*
    y BL - v93 - Ja '97 - p792 [51-250]
    KR - v65 - Ja 1 '97 - p47 [251-500]
    LJ - v122 - F 1 '97 - p90 [51-250]
Rampillon, Ute - *Lernen Leichter Machen*
    MLJ - v81 - Spr '97 - p132+ [501+]
Rampton, Ben - *Crossing: Language and Ethnicity among Adolescents*
    MLJ - v80 - Fall '96 - p426 [501+]
Ramras-Rauch, Gila - *Aharon Appelfeld: The Holocaust and Beyond*
    Rel St Rev - v22 - O '96 - p355 [51-250]
Ramsay, Jeff - *Historical Dictionary of Botswana. 3rd Ed.*
    r ARBA - v28 - '97 - p51+ [251-500]
Ramsay, Jim - *Write Your Own User Guide*
    BWatch - v17 - S '96 - p9 [51-250]
Ramsay, Meredith - *Community, Culture and Economic Development*
    APSR - v90 - D '96 - p920+ [501+]
Ramsay, Raylene L - *The French New Autobiographies*
    Biography - v19 - Fall '96 - p430 [1-50]
    Choice - v34 - O '96 - p286 [51-250]
Ramsay, William M - *Westminster Guide to the Books of the Bible*
    r Intpr - v50 - O '96 - p422 [51-250]
Ramsbotham, Oliver - *Humanitarian Intervention in Contemporary Conflict*
    Choice - v34 - D '96 - p687 [51-250]
Ramsdell, Kristin - *Happily Ever After*
    r RQ - v36 - Win '96 - p218 [51-250]
Ramsden, E N - *A-Level Chemistry Pass Books: London Board Examinations*
    y TES - Ja 3 '97 - pR12 [251-500]
    A-Level Chemistry Pass Books: Northern Board Examinations
    y TES - Ja 3 '97 - pR12 [251-500]
    Chemistry of the Environment
    y TES - Ja 3 '97 - pR12 [251-500]
Ramsey, Buck - *Christmas Waltz (Illus. by Janet Hurley)*
    c SLJ - v42 - O '96 - p39+ [51-250]
Ramsey, Dan - *101 Best Home Businesses*
    LJ - v122 - My 1 '97 - p53 [1-50]
    101 Best Weekend Businesses
    BL - v93 - Mr 1 '97 - p1098 [51-250]
    BWatch - v18 - F '97 - p3 [51-250]
    LJ - v122 - My 1 '97 - p53 [1-50]
    The Crafter's Guide to Pricing Your Work
    LJ - v122 - F 15 '97 - p133 [51-250]
Ramsey, Dave - *Financial Peace*
    BL - v93 - D 1 '96 - p618 [51-250]
    LJ - v122 - Ja '97 - p116 [51-250]
    Financial Peace (Ramsey). Audio Version
    LJ - v122 - F 15 '97 - p175 [51-250]
Ramsey, David - *Financial Peace (Ramsey). Audio Version*
    BWatch - v18 - Mr '97 - p6 [51-250]
Ramsey, Frances M R - *English Episcopal Acta. Vol. 10*
    Albion - v28 - Fall '96 - p463+ [501+]
Ramsey, Martha - *Where I Stopped*
    PW - v244 - My 12 '97 - p74 [1-50]
Ramshaw, Gail - *God beyond Gender*
    ER - v48 - Jl '96 - p419+ [501+]
Ramsland, Katherine - *The Anne Rice Reader*
    BL - v93 - F 15 '97 - p994 [51-250]
    PW - v244 - Ja 13 '97 - p67 [51-250]
Ramus, David - *Thief of Light*
    PW - v243 - D 2 '96 - p56 [1-50]
Ramzaev, P V - *Medical Consequences of the Chernobyl Nuclear Accident*
    Choice - v34 - S '96 - p163 [51-250]
Ran, Bin - *Modeling Dynamic Transportation Networks. 2nd Ed.*
    JEL - v35 - Mr '97 - p303 [51-250]
Rana, Pradumna B - *From Centrally Planned to Market Economies. Vol. 1*
    JEL - v34 - S '96 - p1492 [51-250]
Rancour-Laferriere, Daniel - *The Slave Soul of Russia*
    AHR - v101 - D '96 - p1581+ [501+]
    Russ Rev - v55 - O '96 - p729+ [501+]
Rancourt, James D - *Optical Thin Films*
    r SciTech - v20 - D '96 - p86 [51-250]
Rand, Erica - *Barbie's Queer Accessories*
    J Am St - v30 - Ap '96 - p171+ [501+]
Rand, Gloria - *Aloha, Salty! (Illus. by Ted Rand)*
    c HB Guide - v7 - Fall '96 - p272 [51-250]
    Willie Takes a Hike (Illus. by Ted Rand)
    c HB Guide - v7 - Fall '96 - p272 [51-250]
    c RT - v50 - My '97 - p682 [51-250]
    c Smith - v27 - N '96 - p165 [1-50]

Rand, Peter - *China Hands*
    HRNB - v25 - Fall '96 - p38 [251-500]
    PHR - v66 - F '97 - p140+ [501+]
Rand McNally and Company - *The World, Afghanistan to Zimbabwe*
    r ARBA - v28 - '97 - p174 [51-250]
    BL - v92 - Ag '96 - p1920 [51-250]
Randal, Jonathan C - *After Such Knowledge, What Forgiveness?*
    KR - v65 - Ap 1 '97 - p531 [251-500]
    PW - v244 - Ap 7 '97 - p79 [51-250]
Randall, Dale B J - *Winter Fruit*
    RMR - v50 - 2 '96 - p205+ [501+]
Randall, Fiona - *Palliative Care Ethics*
    MHR - v10 - Fall '96 - p64+ [501+]
Randall, Housk - *The Customized Body*
    NS - v125 - D 13 '96 - p47 [251-500]
Randall, Kenneth A - *Only the Echoes*
    Roundup M - v4 - Ap '97 - p23 [51-250]
    WHQ - v27 - Win '96 - p533+ [251-500]
Randall, Laura - *Changing Structure of Mexico*
    Choice - v34 - D '96 - p673 [51-250]
    JEL - v35 - Mr '97 - p286 [51-250]
    R&R Bk N - v11 - D '96 - p25 [51-250]
    Reforming Mexico's Agrarian Reform
    Choice - v34 - O '96 - p331 [51-250]
    JEL - v34 - D '96 - p2130+ [51-250]
Randall, Margaret - *Hunger's Table*
    BWatch - v18 - Mr '97 - p1 [1-50]
    LJ - v122 - F 1 '97 - p86 [51-250]
    The Price You Pay
    Ms - v7 - S '96 - p84 [251-500]
    Prog - v61 - Ja '97 - p37 [51-250]
    Wom R Bks - v14 - Ja '97 - p1+ [501+]
    Sandino's Daughter Revisited
    HAHR - v76 - N '96 - p803+ [501+]
Randall, Neil - *Guide to Netscape Navigator Gold*
    r CBR - v14 - S '96 - p29 [1-50]
    Using Microsoft FrontPage. Special Ed.
    TES - O 18 '96 - p41U [251-500]
Randall, Stephen J - *NAFTA in Transition*
    BIC - v25 - N '96 - p27 [501+]
Randall, William Lowell - *The Stories We Are*
    Rapport - v19 - 4 '96 - p37 [251-500]
Randel, Don Michael - *The Harvard Biographical Dictionary of Music*
    r AB - v98 - D 9 '96 - p2001 [51-250]
    r ARBA - v28 - '97 - p469 [251-500]
    yr BL - v93 - D 15 '96 - p749 [251-500]
    r Choice - v34 - Ap '97 - p1309 [51-250]
    r LJ - v121 - O 15 '96 - p50 [51-250]
    r M Ed J - v83 - Mr '97 - p43 [51-250]
    r PW - v243 - O 7 '96 - p58 [51-250]
    r R&R Bk N - v12 - F '97 - p69 [51-250]
    r TLS - N 1 '96 - p21 [501+]
Randi, James - *An Encyclopedia of Claims, Frauds, and Hoaxes of the Occult and Supernatural*
    r ARBA - v28 - '97 - p288 [51-250]
Randisi, Robert J - *For Crime Out Loud (Martin). Audio Version*
    Arm Det - v29 - Sum '96 - p355 [51-250]
    BL - v93 - N 1 '96 - p522 [51-250]
    How the West Was Read. Audio Version
    Quill & Q - v62 - Jl '96 - p52 [1-50]
    How the West Was Read (Kennedy). Audio Version
    BWatch - v17 - D '96 - p11 [1-50]
    Writing the Private Eye Novel
    LJ - v122 - My 1 '97 - p116 [51-250]
Randle, Kevin D - *The Randle Report*
    y BL - v93 - My 15 '97 - p1544 [51-250]
    PW - v244 - Ap 14 '97 - p68 [51-250]
Randle, Kristen D - *Only Alien on the Planet*
    y Emerg Lib - v24 - S '96 - p25 [1-50]
    y Emerg Lib - v24 - S '96 - p27 [1-50]
    y Kliatt - v31 - Ja '97 - p10 [51-250]
Rando, Daniela - *Una Chiesa Di Frontiera*
    CH - v65 - D '96 - p678+ [501+]
Randolph, Eleanor - *Waking the Tempests*
    Cu H - v95 - O '96 - p348 [501+]
    NL - v79 - Jl 15 '96 - p21 [501+]
Random House Compact Unabridged Dictionary. Special 2nd Ed. Book and Electronic Media Version
    r Choice - v34 - My '97 - p1479 [51-250]
Random House Concise Encyclopedia
    r ARBA - v28 - '97 - p25 [51-250]
Random House Unabridged Electronic Dictionary: Version 1.7 for Windows. Electronic Media Version
    r Choice - v34 - S '96 - p108 [251-500]
Random House Webster's College Dictionary. Newly Rev. and Updated Ed.
    r Choice - v34 - Mr '97 - p1142 [51-250]

Random House Webster's Unabridged Dictionary. Book
and Electronic Media Version
   r Choice - v34 - My '97 - p1479 [51-250]
Random House Webster's Unabridged Dictionary
CD-ROM Version 2.0. Electronic Media Version
   r PW - v244 - F 24 '97 - p37 [51-250]
Randsborg, Klavs - Hjortspring: Warfare and Sacrifice in
Early Europe
   Choice - v34 - Ja '97 - p839 [51-250]
Raney, Deborah - In the Still of the Night
   LJ - v122 - F 1 '97 - p68 [51-250]
Ranft, Patricia - Women and the Religious Life in
Premodern Europe
   Choice - v34 - S '96 - p146 [51-250]
   HRNB - v25 - Fall '96 - p24+ [501+]
   RR - v56 - Mr '97 - p221 [1-50]
   Six Ct J - v27 - Win '96 - p1200+ [501+]
Rangel, Paulo - Renata Leoa
   WLT - v70 - Sum '96 - p679 [501+]
Rangell, Leo - Psychoanalysis at the Political Border
   Readings - v11 - D '96 - p24 [51-250]
Ranger Rick
   cp Par Ch - v20 - O '96 - p15 [1-50]
Ranicki, A A - The Hauptvermutung Book
   SciTech - v21 - Mr '97 - p18 [51-250]
Ranieri, John J - Eric Voegelin and the Good Society
   APSR - v91 - Mr '97 - p177+ [501+]
   J Pol - v59 - F '97 - p282+ [501+]
Ranis, Peter - Argentine Workers
   HAHR - v76 - N '96 - p817+ [501+]
Class, Democracy, and Labor in Contemporary
Argentina. Rev. Ed.
   HAHR - v77 - My '97 - p356+ [251-500]
   JTWS - v13 - Fall '96 - p301+ [501+]
Rank, Mark Robert - Living on the Edge
   SSQ - v78 - Mr '97 - p245+ [501+]
Rank, Otto - A Psychology of Difference
   Choice - v34 - N '96 - p543 [51-250]
Rankin, Bob - Dr. Bob's Guide to the Internet
   CBR - v14 - N '96 - p35 [1-50]
Rankin, Charles E - Legacy: New Perspectives on the
Battle of the Little Bighorn
   Roundup M - v4 - Ap '97 - p29 [1-50]
Wallace Stegner: Man and Writer
   LATBR - D 1 '96 - p11 [251-500]
   WAL - v31 - Win '97 - p381+ [501+]
Rankin, Chris - Splendid Silk Ribbon Embroidery
   LJ - v122 - Ap 15 '97 - p79 [51-250]
Rankin, David - Tertullian and the Church
   CH - v65 - D '96 - p659+ [501+]
   CHR - v83 - Ja '97 - p170 [51-250]
   CPR - v16 - Ap '96 - p132+ [501+]
   Rel St Rev - v23 - Ap '97 - p151+ [51-250]
   Theol St - v57 - S '96 - p566+ [251-500]
Rankin, Ian - Black and Blue
   TLS - F 28 '97 - p22 [501+]
Let It Bleed
   y BL - v93 - D 1 '96 - p643 [51-250]
   KR - v64 - O 1 '96 - p1430+ [251-500]
   LJ - v121 - D '96 - p151 [51-250]
   NYTBR - v102 - Ja 5 '97 - p20 [51-250]
   PW - v243 - O 7 '96 - p64 [51-250]
   Trib Bks - Ja 5 '97 - p4 [51-250]
Rankin, Joan - Scaredy Cat (Illus. by Joan Rankin)
   c BL - v93 - S 15 '96 - p250 [51-250]
   c HB Guide - v8 - Spr '97 - p15 [51-250]
   c JB - v60 - D '96 - p239 [51-250]
   c KR - v64 - O 1 '96 - p1473 [51-250]
   c PW - v243 - O 14 '96 - p83 [51-250]
   c SLJ - v42 - N '96 - p91 [51-250]
   c TES - S 27 '96 - p12* [501+]
Rankin, Judy - Play Better Golf
   LJ - v121 - O 1 '96 - p53 [1-50]
Rankin, Laura - The Handmade Alphabet
   c PW - v243 - N 18 '96 - p78 [51-250]
Rankin, Robert - A Dog Called Demolition
   Obs - O 6 '96 - p18* [51-250]
Rankin, Susan - Music in the Medieval English Liturgy
   CH - v65 - S '96 - p487+ [501+]
Ranlet, Philip - Enemies of the Bay Colony
   W&M Q - v53 - Jl '96 - p649+ [501+]
Ransmayr, Christoph - The Dog King
   BL - v93 - Ap 1 '97 - p1282 [51-250]
   KR - v65 - Mr 1 '97 - p331+ [51-250]
   LJ - v122 - Ap 15 '97 - p120 [51-250]
   PW - v244 - F 24 '97 - p64 [51-250]
Morbus Kitahara
   WLT - v70 - Sum '96 - p684 [501+]
The Terrors of Ice and Darkness
   NYTBR - v101 - S 8 '96 - p36 [51-250]

Ransom, Bill - Burn: A Novel
   y Kliatt - v31 - Ja '97 - p14+ [51-250]
Ransom, Candice F - Fire in the Sky (Illus. by Shelly O
Hass)
   c BL - v93 - My 1 '97 - p1498 [51-250]
One Christmas Dawn (Illus. by Peter Fiore)
   c HB Guide - v8 - Spr '97 - p44 [51-250]
   c PW - v243 - S 30 '96 - p90 [51-250]
   c SLJ - v42 - O '96 - p40 [51-250]
   c Smith - v27 - N '96 - p173 [1-50]
When the Whippoorwill Calls (Illus. by Kimberley
Bulcken Root)
   c RT - v50 - O '96 - p152 [51-250]
Ransom, Daniel - Zone Soldiers
   y Kliatt - v31 - Mr '97 - p20 [51-250]
Ransom, Jane - Bye-Bye
   KR - v65 - Ap 1 '97 - p496 [251-500]
   PW - v244 - Ap 21 '97 - p61 [51-250]
Ransom, Teresa - Fanny Trollope: A Remarkable Life
   Nine-C Lit - v50 - Mr '96 - p557 [1-50]
Ransome, Arthur - Signaling from Mars
   Obs - Mr 30 '97 - p17* [501+]
We Didn't Mean to Go to Sea
   c Sea H - Aut '96 - p47 [51-250]
Ransone, Gary - The Contractor's Legal Kit
   FHB - Ag '96 - p136+ [251-500]
Rantala, M L - O.J. Unmasked
   Esq - v126 - N '96 - p65 [1-50]
Rao, K R - Techniques and Standards for Image, Video,
and Audio Coding
   SciTech - v20 - N '96 - p73 [51-250]
Rao, Ming - Integrated Distributed Intelligent Systems for
Engineering Design
   SciTech - v21 - Mr '97 - p72 [51-250]
Rao, Nirmala - Towards Welfare Pluralism
   R&R Bk N - v11 - N '96 - p50 [51-250]
Rao, R Raj - One Day I Locked My Flat in Soul City
   WLT - v71 - Win '97 - p225 [501+]
Raous, M - Contact Mechanics
   SIAM Rev - v38 - D '96 - p713 [51-250]
Rapaport, Era - Letters from Tel Mond Prison
   For Aff - v76 - Mr '97 - p196 [51-250]
   KR - v64 - S 15 '96 - p1384 [251-500]
   LATBR - Ja 19 '97 - p8+ [501+]
   LJ - v121 - O 1 '96 - p106 [51-250]
   Nat - v264 - Ap 21 '97 - p25+ [501+]
   PW - v243 - S 30 '96 - p70 [51-250]
Rapee, Ronald M - Current Controversies in the Anxiety
Disorders
   AJPsych - v154 - Ja '97 - p128 [251-500]
Raphael, Elaine - Daniel Boone: Frontier Hero
   c HB Guide - v7 - Fall '96 - p388 [51-250]
Raphael, Lev - Let's Get Criminal
   LJ - v121 - O 15 '96 - p112 [51-250]
Rapid Thermal and Integrated Processing V
   SciTech - v21 - Mr '97 - p91 [51-250]
Rapkin, David P - National Competitiveness in a Global
Economy
   CS - v25 - S '96 - p605+ [501+]
Rapley, Ralph - PCR Sequencing Protocols
   SciTech - v20 - D '96 - p35 [51-250]
Rapoport, Janis - After Paradise
   BIC - v26 - Mr '97 - p14+ [501+]
Rapoport, Paul - The Compositions of Vagn Holmboe
   FF - v19 - Jl '96 - p424+ [501+]
Rapoport, Ron - A Kind of Grace
   Aethlon - v13 - Fall '95 - p143+ [251-500]
   J Am Cult - v19 - Spr '96 - p110+ [501+]
Rapp, Adam - The Buffalo Tree
   y PW - v244 - Ap 7 '97 - p93 [51-250]
Missing the Piano
   y Kliatt - v30 - S '96 - p13 [51-250]
Rapp, Doris J - Is This Your Child's World?
   BL - v93 - S 1 '96 - p49 [51-250]
   LJ - v121 - N 1 '96 - p102 [51-250]
Rapp, Stan - The New Maximarketing
   Choice - v34 - S '96 - p174 [51-250]
Rappaport, D - The New King
   c RT - v50 - Mr '97 - p477 [51-250]
Rappaport, George David - Stability and Change in
Revolutionary Pennsylvania
   Choice - v34 - Ap '97 - p1406+ [51-250]
Rappaport, Susan S - Traveler's Guide to Art Museum
Exhibitions. 9th Ed.
   r LJ - v122 - Ap 1 '97 - p84 [51-250]
Rapping, Elayne - The Culture of Recovery
   CS - v25 - N '96 - p721+ [501+]
The Movie of the Week
   QJS - v83 - F '97 - p90+ [501+]

Rappole, John H - The Ecology of Migrant Birds
   Choice - v34 - S '96 - p156 [51-250]
   SB - v32 - O '96 - p201 [251-500]
Rappoport, Ken - Grant Hill
   y BL - v93 - Ja '97 - p840+ [251-500]
   y HB Guide - v8 - Spr '97 - p145 [51-250]
   c SLJ - v43 - Ja '97 - p133 [51-250]
Sports Great Wayne Gretzky
   c HB Guide - v7 - Fall '96 - p361 [51-250]
Rappoport, R - Cytokinesis in Animal Cells
   SciTech - v21 - Mr '97 - p36 [51-250]
Rapport, Nigel - The Prose and the Passion
   RES - v47 - Ag '96 - p445+ [501+]
Rapport Des Resultats Officiels Du Scrutin
   J Gov Info - v23 - S '96 - p638 [51-250]
Rare Breed
   p LJ - v122 - My 1 '97 - p43 [51-250]
Raritan
   p TLS - N 15 '96 - p27 [501+]
Raschka, Chris - The Blushful Hippopotamus (Illus. by
Chris Raschka)
   c CBRS - v25 - Win '97 - p65 [51-250]
   c CCB-B - v50 - D '96 - p149+ [51-250]
   c HB - v72 - S '96 - p585 [51-250]
   c HB Guide - v8 - Spr '97 - p44 [51-250]
   c SLJ - v42 - S '96 - p188+ [51-250]
Raschke, Carl A - Fire and Roses
   R&R Bk N - v12 - F '97 - p2 [51-250]
Rash, Wayne - Politics on the Nets
   BL - v93 - My 15 '97 - p1547 [51-250]
Rashed, Roshdi - Encyclopedia of the History of Arabic
Science. Vols. 1-3
   r Choice - v34 - D '96 - p589 [51-250]
   r LJ - v122 - Ap 15 '97 - p64 [51-250]
   r Nature - v383 - O 10 '96 - p492+ [501+]
   r SciTech - v20 - N '96 - p3 [51-250]
Rasheed, Sadig - Development Management in Africa
   JTWS - v13 - Spr '96 - p295+ [501+]
Rasiah, Rajah - Foreign Capital and Industrialization in
Malaysia
   Econ J - v107 - Ja '97 - p283 [251-500]
Raskin, Jeffrey B - Colonoscopy: Principles and
Techniques
   SciTech - v20 - N '96 - p48 [1-50]
Raskin, Jonah - For the Hell of It
   BL - v93 - N 15 '96 - p555 [51-250]
   BW - v27 - Ja 26 '97 - p3 [501+]
   CHE - v43 - Ja 10 '97 - pA18 [51-250]
   KR - v64 - O 15 '96 - p1517 [251-500]
   LATBR - F 9 '97 - p5 [501+]
   LJ - v121 - D '96 - p108 [51-250]
   Nat - v264 - Ja 6 '97 - p25+ [501+]
   NS - v126 - Mr 21 '97 - p55+ [501+]
   NYTBR - v102 - F 2 '97 - p14 [501+]
   PW - v243 - N 25 '96 - p63 [51-250]
Raskin, Valerie Davis - When Words Are Not Enough
   PW - v244 - Ap 21 '97 - p67 [51-250]
Rasmussen, Cecilia - Curbside L.A.
   LATBR - N 10 '96 - p15 [51-250]
Rasmussen, Eric - A Textual Companion to Doctor
Faustus
   RES - v48 - F '97 - p93+ [501+]
Rasmussen, Larry L - Earth Community, Earth Ethics
   BWatch - v17 - D '96 - p7 [51-250]
Rasmussen, R Kent - Mark Twain A to Z
   yr Kliatt - v31 - My '97 - p18 [51-250]
   r Nine-C Lit - v50 - Mr '96 - p557 [51-250]
   r WAL - v31 - Win '97 - p384+ [501+]
Rasmussen, Arne - The Church as Polis
   Theol St - v57 - D '96 - p771+ [501+]
Rasor, Eugene L - The Southwest Pacific Campaign
1941-1945
   cr ARBA - v28 - '97 - p210 [51-250]
   yr Choice - v34 - My '97 - p1479+ [51-250]
   r R&R Bk N - v12 - F '97 - p14 [51-250]
Rasputin, Valentin Grigor'evich - Siberia, Siberia
   Atl - v278 - Ag '96 - p94 [51-250]
   Choice - v34 - F '97 - p1020 [51-250]
   KR - v64 - My 1 '96 - p672 [251-500]
   R&R Bk N - v11 - D '96 - p10 [51-250]
Rassias, Themistocles M - Finite Sums Decompositions in
Mathematical Analysis
   SIAM Rev - v39 - Mr '97 - p157+ [501+]
Rasula, Jed - The American Poetry Wax Museum
   Sm Pr R - v28 - S '96 - p12 [501+]
Ratay, Robert T - Handbook of Temporary Structures in
Construction. 2nd Ed.
   SciTech - v20 - D '96 - p71 [51-250]

Ratcliff, Carter - *The Fate of a Gesture*
BL - v93 - D 1 '96 - p637+ [51-250]
KR - v64 - O 15 '96 - p1517 [251-500]
LJ - v122 - F 1 '97 - p78 [51-250]
NYTBR - v102 - F 16 '97 - p9 [501+]
NYTLa - v146 - D 17 '96 - pC22 [501+]
PW - v243 - N 4 '96 - p58+ [51-250]
Ratcliff, Richard E - *Research in Politics and Society.*
Vol. 5
CS - v25 - N '96 - p769+ [501+]
Ratcliff, Roger - *How to Meet the Right Man*
PW - v243 - S 30 '96 - p74 [51-250]
How to Meet the Right Woman
PW - v243 - S 30 '96 - p74 [51-250]
Ratcliffe, Krista - *Anglo-American Feminist Challenges to the Rhetorical Traditions*
QJS - v83 - My '97 - p247+ [501+]
Ratey, John J - *Neuropsychiatry of Personality Disorders*
AJPsych - v153 - S '96 - p1226+ [501+]
Shadow Syndromes
PW - v244 - Ja 6 '97 - p70 [51-250]
Rath, Sura P - *Flannery O'Connor: New Perspectives*
AL - v68 - S '96 - p666 [51-250]
Choice - v34 - S '96 - p125 [51-250]
Rathbone, Andy - *Multimedia and CD-ROMs for Dummies. 2nd Ed.*
Quill & Q - v62 - Ag '96 - p23 [51-250]
Rathbone, Dominic - *Economic Rationalism and Rural Society in Third-Century A.D. Egypt*
CW - v89 - Jl '96 - p504 [251-500]
Rathbone, Eliza E - *Impressionists on the Seine*
PW - v243 - O 7 '96 - p55 [51-250]
Rathbone, Michael J - *Oral Mucosal Drug Delivery*
SciTech - v20 - S '96 - p42 [51-250]
Rather, Dan - *The Camera Never Blinks*
Parameters - v26 - Win '96 - p148+ [501+]
Rathmann, Peggy - *Good Night, Gorilla*
c Ch BWatch - v6 - My '96 - p2 [1-50]
c ECEJ - v24 - Win '96 - p110 [51-250]
c HB Guide - v7 - Fall '96 - p243 [51-250]
Officer Buckle and Gloria (Illus. by Peggy Rathmann)
c Bkbird - v34 - Spr '96 - p52 [51-250]
c Emerg Lib - v23 - My '96 - p65 [51-250]
c HB - v73 - Mr '97 - p188 [1-50]
c Inst - v105 - My '96 - p68 [51-250]
c RT - v50 - O '96 - p158 [51-250]
c SLJ - v43 - Ja '97 - p37 [1-50]
Rathmell, Andrew - *Secret War in the Middle East*
MEJ - v50 - Sum '96 - p445+ [501+]
MEQ - v3 - S '96 - p86 [251-500]
Rathschmidt, Jack - *Rituals for Home and Parish*
CLW - v67 - Mr '97 - p35 [51-250]
Ratledge, David - *The Art and Science of CCD Astronomy*
Astron - v25 - My '97 - p114 [51-250]
Ratner, Buddy D - *Biomaterials Science*
SciTech - v20 - D '96 - p37 [51-250]
Ratte, Paul-Michel - *The Gathering of the Aspects*
BIC - v26 - Mr '97 - p40 [51-250]
Rattigan, Jama Kim - *The Woman in the Moon (Illus. by Carla Golembe)*
c BL - v93 - N 1 '96 - p494+ [51-250]
c CBRS - v25 - D '96 - p40+ [51-250]
c HB Guide - v8 - Spr '97 - p104 [51-250]
c KR - v64 - S 15 '96 - p1407 [51-250]
c PW - v243 - N 4 '96 - p75 [51-250]
c SLJ - v42 - D '96 - p116+ [51-250]
Rattue, James - *The Living Stream*
Albion - v28 - Fall '96 - p458+ [501+]
Ratushinskaya, Irina - *The Odessans*
NS & S - v9 - My 17 '96 - p40 [251-500]
Ratzsch, Delvin Lee - *The Battle of Beginnings*
Bks & Cult - v2 - My '96 - p30 [501+]
Rapport - v19 - 5 '96 - p46 [251-500]
Rau, Dana Meachen - *A Box Can Be Many Things (Illus. by Paige Billin-Frye)*
c BL - v93 - My 1 '97 - p1504 [51-250]
Raub, Patricia - *Yesterday's Stories*
JPC - v30 - Fall '96 - p221 [51-250]
Raucci, Richard - *Way Cool Web Sites*
c Ch BWatch - v7 - F '97 - p6 [1-50]
Rauchbauer, Otto - *The Edith Oenone Somerville Archive in Drishane*
r RES - v47 - N '96 - p634+ [501+]
Rausa, Federico - *L'Immagine Del Vincitore*
AJA - v101 - Ja '97 - p178+ [501+]
Rausch, David A - *Building Bridges*
Rel Ed - v91 - Fall '96 - p614 [1-50]
Rauscher, Freya - *Cruising Guide to Belize and Mexico's Caribbean Coast. 2nd Ed.*
Yacht - v181 - F '97 - p16 [1-50]

Rautio, Veli-Matti - *Die Bernstein-Debatte: Die Politische-Ideologischen Stromungen Und Die Parteiideologie In Der Sozialdemokratischen Partei Deutschlands 1898-1903*
EHR - v111 - N '96 - p1334+ [251-500]
Raux, Sophie - *Catalogue Des Dessins Francais Du XVIIIe Siecle Du Palais Des Beaus-Arts De Lille*
BM - v138 - Jl '96 - p470 [251-500]
Rauzon, Mark J - *Parrots*
c BL - v93 - Ja '97 - p854 [251-500]
c HB Guide - v8 - Spr '97 - p125 [1-50]
c SB - v33 - My '97 - p114 [51-250]
Seabirds
c BL - v93 - Ja '97 - p854 [251-500]
c HB Guide - v8 - Spr '97 - p125 [1-50]
c SB - v33 - My '97 - p114 [251-500]
Ravanipur, Moniru - *Satan's Stones*
MEJ - v51 - Win '97 - p153 [51-250]
TranslRevS - v2 - D '96 - p29+ [51-250]
Rave, Elizabeth J - *Ethical Decision Making in Therapy*
Readings - v11 - D '96 - p21 [51-250]
Ravel, Aviva - *Canadian Mosaic*
WLT - v70 - Sum '96 - p706 [251-500]
Ravel, Edeet - *Lovers: A Midrash*
Can Lit - Win '96 - p120+ [501+]
Raven, Margot Theis - *Angels in the Dust (Illus. by Roger Essley)*
c KR - v64 - D 15 '96 - p1803 [51-250]
c PW - v244 - Ja 20 '97 - p401+ [51-250]
c Trib Bks - F 9 '97 - p7 [51-250]
Raven, Peter H - *Biology. 4th Ed.*
SciTech - v20 - D '96 - p29 [51-250]
Raven, Sarah - *The Cutting Garden*
LJ - v122 - Ap 15 '97 - p106 [51-250]
Raven: A Journal of Vexillology
p Sm Pr R - v28 - Jl '96 - p29 [51-250]
Ravenel, Shannon - *Best of the South*
VQR - v73 - Win '97 - p23* [51-250]
Ravenhill, Philip L - *Dreams and Reverie*
BWatch - v17 - S '96 - p3 [51-250]
Ravens, David - *Luke and the Restoration of Israel*
Rel St Rev - v23 - Ap '97 - p183 [51-250]
Raver, Anne - *Deep in the Green*
Sew R - v104 - S '96 - p701+ [51-250]
Rav-Hon, Orna - *Firebird*
TranslRevS - v2 - D '96 - p27 [51-250]
Ravilious, James - *A Corner of England*
Spec - v278 - Ap 5 '97 - p37 [251-500]
Ravin, Ed - *Using and Managing UUCP. 2nd Ed.*
SciTech - v20 - D '96 - p7 [1-50]
Ravino, Owen - *Kids and Koins*
c Coin W - v37 - D 30 '96 - p22 [1-50]
Ravitch, Diane - *Debating the Future of American Education*
NASSP-B - v80 - N '96 - p117+ [501+]
National Standards in American Education
AAPSS-A - v550 - Mr '97 - p184+ [501+]
BusLR - v21 - 3 '96 - p198+ [501+]
Rawick, George - *From Sundown to Sunup*
RAH - v24 - D '96 - p712+ [501+]
Rawley, James A - *Abraham Lincoln and a Nation Worth Fighting For*
Choice - v34 - N '96 - p527+ [51-250]
Rawlings, Ellen - *The Murder Lover*
y Kliatt - v31 - Mr '97 - p12 [51-250]
Rawlings, Marjorie Kinnan - *Poems by Marjorie Kinnan Rawlings*
LJ - v122 - My 1 '97 - p108 [51-250]
Rawlins, C L - *Broken Country*
BL - v93 - S 15 '96 - p194 [51-250]
HMR - Spr '97 - p17 [501+]
LATBR - O 13 '96 - p6 [501+]
LJ - v121 - S 15 '96 - p91 [51-250]
NYTBR - v101 - D 1 '96 - p31+ [501+]
PW - v243 - S 16 '96 - p63+ [51-250]
Rawlins, Gregory J E - *Moths to the Flame*
BL - v93 - S 1 '96 - p34 [51-250]
Choice - v34 - F '97 - p999 [51-250]
LJ - v121 - O 1 '96 - p114 [51-250]
New Sci - v152 - O 5 '96 - p49 [51-250]
RP - v59 - Spr '97 - p414+ [501+]
SB - v32 - N '96 - p229 [51-250]
Slaves of the Machine
KR - v65 - My 1 '97 - p704 [251-500]
PW - v244 - Ap 28 '97 - p58 [51-250]
Rawlins, Paul - *No Lie like Love*
BL - v93 - N 1 '96 - p482 [51-250]
KR - v64 - O 15 '96 - p1490 [251-500]
LJ - v121 - N 15 '96 - p91 [51-250]
Rawls, John - *Political Liberalism*
PSR - v25 - '96 - p151+ [501+]

Rawls, Wilson - *Where the Red Fern Grows*
c Ch BWatch - v6 - N '96 - p7 [1-50]
c HMR - Win '96 - p45 [1-50]
y Kliatt - v30 - S '96 - p3 [1-50]
Rawlyk, George A - *The Canada Fire*
JR - v77 - Ja '97 - p142+ [501+]
Is Jesus Your Personal Saviour?
Ch Today - v41 - Ap 7 '97 - p44 [501+]
Rawn, Melanie - *The Golden Key*
y BL - v93 - S 1 '96 - p69 [51-250]
y VOYA - v19 - F '97 - p340 [251-500]
Rawnsley, Gary D - *Radio Diplomacy and Propaganda*
Choice - v34 - O '96 - p271 [51-250]
Rawnsley, Irene - *Hiding Out*
c Sch Lib - v44 - N '96 - p168 [51-250]
Raworth, Tom - *Clean and Well Lit*
PW - v243 - Jl 22 '96 - p238 [1-50]
Sulfur - Fall '96 - p139+ [501+]
Rawski, Thomas G - *Economics and the Historian*
Choice - v34 - N '96 - p512 [51-250]
JEL - v34 - D '96 - p2094 [251-500]
Rawson, Claude - *Satire and Sentiment 1660-1830*
Eight-C St - v30 - Fall '96 - p100+ [501+]
Rawson, Don C - *Russian Rightists and the Revolution of 1905*
Slav R - v55 - Sum '96 - p483+ [501+]
Rawson, Hugh - *Rawson's Dictionary of Euphemisms and Other Doubletalk. Rev. Ed.*
r ARBA - v28 - '97 - p381 [251-500]
Rawson, Jessica - *Chinese Jade from the Neolithic to the Qing*
Ch Rev Int - v3 - Fall '96 - p511+ [501+]
Mysteries of Ancient China
TLS - S 13 '96 - p18+ [501+]
Rawsthorn, Alice - *Yves Saint Laurent: A Biography*
BL - v93 - N 15 '96 - p548 [51-250]
Econ - v342 - Mr 15 '97 - p3*+ [501+]
Ent W - Ja 31 '97 - p54 [51-250]
KR - v64 - O 15 '96 - p1518 [251-500]
Lon R Bks - v19 - F 6 '97 - p21+ [501+]
NS - v125 - N 15 '96 - p47 [501+]
NYTBR - v102 - Ja 12 '97 - p14+ [501+]
PW - v243 - N 4 '96 - p58 [51-250]
Spec - v277 - N 30 '96 - p53+ [501+]
Ray, Arthur J - *I Have Lived Here since the World Began*
Beav - v76 - O '96 - p46 [51-250]
Beav - v76 - D '96 - p39+ [501+]
CG - v117 - Ja '97 - p80+ [501+]
Mac - v109 - D 9 '96 - p64 [1-50]
Quill & Q - v62 - S '96 - p68 [251-500]
Ray, C Claiborne - *The New York Times Book of Science Questions and Answers*
y BL - v93 - My 15 '97 - p1549 [51-250]
Ray, Delia - *A Nation Torn*
y Kliatt - v31 - Ja '97 - p26 [251-500]
Ray, Dorothy Jean - *A Legacy of Arctic Art*
Am Craft - v56 - O '96 - p52 [51-250]
BWatch - v17 - S '96 - p3 [51-250]
Choice - v34 - Mr '97 - p1153 [51-250]
LJ - v121 - O 1 '96 - p74 [51-250]
Ray, Francis - *Incognito*
LJ - v122 - F 15 '97 - p126 [51-250]
Ray, Helene - *Pas De Bruit Julie*
c BL - v93 - N 1 '96 - p500 [1-50]
Ray, Himanshu P - *The Winds of Change*
AHR - v101 - O '96 - p1261 [501+]
Ray, James Lee - *Democracy and International Conflict*
AAPSS-A - v550 - Mr '97 - p177+ [251-500]
APSR - v90 - S '96 - p703+ [501+]
PSQ - v111 - Fall '96 - p551+ [501+]
Ray, Jane - *Noah's Ark*
c Bks Keeps - Mr '97 - p7 [51-250]
The Twelve Dancing Princesses (Illus. by Jane Ray)
c BIC - v25 - D '96 - p37 [251-500]
c BL - v93 - O 1 '96 - p351 [51-250]
c CCB-B - v50 - Ja '97 - p171 [51-250]
c HB Guide - v8 - Spr '97 - p105 [51-250]
c PW - v243 - S 23 '96 - p75 [51-250]
c Sch Lib - v45 - F '97 - p20+ [51-250]
c SLJ - v42 - O '96 - p114 [51-250]
Ray, Larry J - *Social Theory and the Crisis of State Socialism*
JEL - v35 - Mr '97 - p291+ [51-250]
R&R Bk N - v11 - D '96 - p37 [51-250]
Ray, Man - *Man Ray's Celebrity Portraits*
LATBR - Mr 24 '96 - p11 [1-50]
Ray, Mary Lyn - *Mud (Illus. by Lauren Stringer)*
c HB Guide - v7 - Fall '96 - p272 [51-250]
Ray, Michael - *Creativity in Business*
Inc. - v18 - D '96 - p60 [251-500]

Ray, Reginald A - *Buddhist Saints in India*
   JAAR - v64 - Sum '96 - p425+ [501+]
Ray, Rita - *Read On*
   c TES - Jl 5 '96 - pR6 [501+]
   Telling Stories
   TES - D 13 '96 - p43 [51-250]
Ray, Robert H - *A George Herbert Companion*
   RES - v48 - F '97 - p103+ [501+]
Ray, Satjavit - *My Years with Apu*
   Obs - Mr 16 '97 - p18* [51-250]
Rayban, Chloe - *Love. In Cyberia*
   y Bks Keeps - Ja '97 - p27 [51-250]
   y Bks Keeps - Ja '97 - p27 [51-250]
   Virtual Sexual Reality
   y Bks Keeps - N '96 - p11 [51-250]
Raybon, Patricia - *My First White Friend*
   PW - v244 - My 12 '97 - p74 [1-50]
Rayburn, Alan - *Naming Canada*
   AAAGA - v86 - S '96 - p598+ [501+]
Raylor, Timothy - *Cavaliers, Clubs, and Literary Culture*
   EHR - v112 - F '97 - p196+ [501+]
   RES - v48 - F '97 - p104+ [501+]
Raymo, Chet - *The Soul of the Night*
   S&T - v93 - F '97 - p60 [51-250]
Raymond, Diana - *The Sea Family*
   Books - v11 - Ap '97 - p21 [51-250]
Raymond, Eric - *New Hacker's Dictionary. 3rd Ed.*
   r New Sci - v153 - Ja 4 '97 - p38 [1-50]
Raymond, Joad - *The Invention of the Newspaper*
   TLS - F 21 '97 - p26 [501+]
Raymond, Linda - *Rocking the Babies*
   SFR - v21 - Jl '96 - p48 [1-50]
Raymond, Susan U - *The Technology Link to Economic Development*
   R&R Bk N - v11 - N '96 - p26 [51-250]
Raymond Chandler's Philip Marlowe
   PW - v244 - Ap 28 '97 - p51 [51-250]
Rayner, Mary - *Mr. and Mrs. Pig's Evening Out*
   c HB - v73 - Mr '97 - p188 [1-50]
   Mrs. Pig Gets Cross
   c Bks Keeps - Mr '97 - p18 [51-250]
   Wicked William
   c Bks Keeps - Mr '97 - p18 [51-250]
Rayner, Shoo - *The Ginger Ninja--St. Felix for the Cup!*
   c Bks Keeps - N '96 - p8 [51-250]
   The Ginger Ninja--The Dance of the Apple Dumplings
   c Bks Keeps - N '96 - p8 [51-250]
Rayner-Canham, Geoffrey - *Descriptive Inorganic Chemistry*
   J Chem Ed - v73 - Ag '96 - pA174+ [501+]
Raza, M Ali - *Labor Relations and the Law*
   R&R Bk N - v12 - F '97 - p64 [51-250]
Raza, Moosa - *Of Nawabs and Nightingales and Other Episodes*
   WLT - v71 - Win '97 - p225+ [501+]
Razavi, Behzad - *Monolithic Phase-Locked Loops and Clock Recovery Circuits*
   r SciTech - v20 - D '96 - p78 [1-50]
Razgon, Lev - *True Stories*
   PW - v244 - Ap 21 '97 - p50 [51-250]
Razi, Zvi - *Medieval Society and the Manor Court*
   HT - v46 - O '96 - p56 [1-50]
Razin, Assaf - *Population Economics*
   Econ J - v106 - N '96 - p1812+ [501+]
Razin, Sergey V - *The Nuclear Matrix and Spatial Organization of Chromosomal DNA Domains*
   SB - v33 - My '97 - p105 [251-500]
Razzell, Peter - *The English Civil War. Vols. 1-2*
   Spec - v278 - F 8 '97 - p44 [501+]
   Essays in English Population History
   EHR - v111 - N '96 - p1295 [51-250]
Razzi, Jim - *Mighty Max and the Castle of Doom (Illus. by Bernat Serrat)*
   c HB Guide - v7 - Fall '96 - p272 [51-250]
   Polly Pocket's Pajama Party (Illus. by Emilie Kong)
   c HB Guide - v7 - Fall '96 - p272 [51-250]
RCRA Hazardous Waste Sourcedisk. Electronic Media Version
   Choice - v34 - My '97 - p1530 [51-250]
Rea, Paul W - *Canyon Interludes*
   PW - v244 - F 24 '97 - p79 [51-250]
Rea, Tony - *International Relations 1914-1995*
   y TES - Mr 28 '97 - p13* [501+]
Read, Alan - *The Fact of Blackness*
   Afterimage - v24 - Ja '97 - p23 [51-250]
   Bl S - v26 - Fall '96 - p105 [51-250]
   BWatch - v17 - D '96 - p5 [1-50]
   LJ - v122 - F 1 '97 - p76 [51-250]

Read, Christopher - *From Tsar to Soviets*
   Choice - v34 - S '96 - p188 [51-250]
   HRNB - v25 - Fall '96 - p35 [251-500]
   HT - v47 - Ja '97 - p58+ [501+]
Read, Donald - *The Age of Urban Democracy*
   HT - v47 - Mr '97 - p55 [251-500]
Read, Donald A - *Health Education*
   R&R Bk N - v12 - F '97 - p95 [1-50]
Read, Edward M - *Partners in Change*
   Fed Prob - v60 - S '96 - p85+ [501+]
Read, Peter - *The International Avant-Garde 1905-1924*
   L'Esprit - v36 - Fall '96 - p120 [251-500]
   Picasso Et Apollinaire
   MLR - v91 - O '96 - p1000 [251-500]
Read, Peter, 1945- - *Returning to Nothing*
   Aust Bk R - N '96 - p32 [501+]
Read, Phyllis J - *The Book of Women Firsts*
   r T&C - v38 - Ja '97 - p214+ [501+]
Read Up on It, Out of This World 1995
   r Bkbird - v34 - Spr '96 - p52 [1-50]
Read-Danahay, Deborah - *Education and Identity in Rural France*
   Choice - v34 - O '96 - p324 [51-250]
Reader, Ian - *Japanese Religions*
   JAAR - v64 - Fall '96 - p668+ [501+]
Reader, Lesley - *Bali and Lombok*
   r Quill & Q - v62 - S '96 - p22 [51-250]
Reader, Mary - *Book of One-Pot Cooking*
   BWatch - v18 - Mr '97 - p5 [51-250]
The Reader's Adviser on CD-ROM. Electronic Media Version
   r ARBA - v28 - '97 - p8+ [501+]
   r BL - v93 - N 1 '96 - p540 [251-500]
   r R&R Bk N - v11 - D '96 - p74 [51-250]
Reader's Digest - *The Bible through the Ages*
   PW - v244 - F 10 '97 - p81 [51-250]
Reader's Digest Association - *Foods That Harm, Foods That Heal*
   r BL - v93 - Ja '97 - p798 [51-250]
   r LJ - v122 - F 1 '97 - p72 [51-250]
   Reader's Digest New Complete Do-It-Yourself Manual. Rev. Ed.
   LJ - v122 - F 1 '97 - p52 [1-50]
Reader's Digest Book of Skills and Tools
   LJ - v122 - F 1 '97 - p52 [1-50]
Reader's Digest Complete Do-It-Yourself Guide. Electronic Media Version
   LJ - v122 - F 1 '97 - p53 [1-50]
   r LJ - v122 - My 1 '97 - p148 [51-250]
Reader's Digest New Fix-It-Yourself Manual
   LJ - v122 - F 1 '97 - p53 [1-50]
   PW - v243 - O 7 '96 - p72 [51-250]
Reader's Guide to Periodical Literature 1901-
   r ASInt - v34 - O '96 - p19 [1-50]
Readicker-Henderson, Lynn - *Adventure Guide to Coastal Alaska and the Inside Passage. 2nd Ed.*
   r BL - v93 - S 15 '96 - p210 [1-50]
Reading, Alison J - *Humid Tropical Environments*
   GJ - v162 - Jl '96 - p227 [251-500]
Reading, H G - *Sedimentary Environments. 3rd Ed.*
   SciTech - v21 - Mr '97 - p32 [51-250]
Readings, Bill - *Postmodernism across the Ages*
   MLR - v92 - Ja '97 - p152+ [501+]
   The University in Ruins
   Choice - v34 - Ja '97 - p850 [51-250]
   Econ - v341 - O 19 '96 - p5*+ [501+]
   Nature - v382 - Jl 18 '96 - p219+ [501+]
   New Sci - v151 - S 28 '96 - p48 [51-250]
   TLS - Ja 24 '97 - p9 [501+]
Readings on Equal Education. Vol. 13
   R&R Bk N - v11 - D '96 - p54 [51-250]
Ready, Steady, Read! Series
   c Magpies - v11 - Jl '96 - p28 [1-50]
Reagan, Charles E - *Paul Ricoeur: His Life and His Work*
   CC - v113 - S 25 '96 - p906+ [251-500]
   Choice - v34 - Ja '97 - p809 [51-250]
   LJ - v121 - S 15 '96 - p71 [51-250]
Reagan, Douglas P - *The Food Web of a Tropical Rain Forest*
   Choice - v34 - Ja '97 - p820 [51-250]
   SciTech - v20 - N '96 - p25 [51-250]
Reagan, Leslie J - *When Abortion Was a Crime*
   KR - v64 - N 1 '96 - p1590 [251-500]
   LJ - v121 - D '96 - p128 [51-250]
   PW - v243 - D 2 '96 - p48 [51-250]
Reagan, Michael - *Making Waves*
   BL - v92 - Ag '96 - p1851+ [251-500]
Reagin, Nancy R - *A German Women's Movement*
   AHR - v102 - F '97 - p125+ [501+]
   CEH - v29 - 2 '96 - p255+ [501+]

Reaka-Kudla, Marjorie L - *Biodiversity II*
   Choice - v34 - F '97 - p986 [51-250]
   LJ - v121 - N 1 '96 - p103 [51-250]
   New Sci - v153 - Mr 1 '97 - p46 [51-250]
   Sci - v275 - Ja 10 '97 - p175 [501+]
   SciTech - v21 - Mr '97 - p34 [1-50]
Real, Leslie A - *Behavioral Mechanisms in Evolutionary Ecology*
   Am Sci - v84 - N '96 - p609 [501+]
Real, Michael R - *Exploring Media Culture*
   R&R Bk N - v12 - F '97 - p75 [51-250]
Real, Terrence - *I Don't Want to Talk about It*
   BL - v93 - Ja '97 - p798 [51-250]
   KR - v64 - N 15 '96 - p1658 [251-500]
   NYTBR - v102 - F 16 '97 - p24 [501+]
   PW - v243 - N 4 '96 - p53 [51-250]
Real Crime Book Digest
   p Arm Det - v29 - Sum '96 - p322 [1-50]
Real-Time Technology and Applications Symposium (1996: Brookline, MA) - *1996 IEEE Real-Time Technology and Applications Symposium*
   SciTech - v20 - N '96 - p7 [1-50]
REAL: Yearbook of Research in English and American Literature. Vol. 11
   Nine-C Lit - v51 - D '96 - p421+ [51-250]
The Reality of Aid 1996
   Env - v39 - Mr '97 - p26 [51-250]
Reaman, Micki - *Present Tense*
   BL - v93 - Ja '97 - p807 [51-250]
   LJ - v122 - Ja '97 - p99+ [51-250]
   Ms - v7 - Ja '97 - p82 [1-50]
   PW - v244 - Ja 20 '97 - p395 [51-250]
Reaney, James - *The Box Social and Other Stories*
   WLT - v70 - Aut '96 - p960 [501+]
Reaney, P H - *A Dictionary of English Surnames. 3rd Ed.*
   r Names - v44 - Je '96 - p126+ [501+]
Reardon, Bernard M G - *Religious Thought in the Victorian Age. 2nd Ed.*
   CR - v268 - Je '96 - p334 [51-250]
Reardon, Betty - *Educating for Human Dignity*
   EL - v54 - D '96 - p92 [51-250]
Reardon, Colleen - *Agostino Agazzari and Music at Siena Cathedral 1597-1641*
   Ren Q - v49 - Aut '96 - p685+ [501+]
Reardon, David C - *Making Abortion Rare*
   Rapport - v19 - 6 '96 - p32 [251-500]
Rearick, Charles - *The French in Love and War*
   LJ - v122 - My 1 '97 - p121 [51-250]
   PW - v244 - My 12 '97 - p64 [51-250]
Reasoner, Charles - *Color Crunch!*
   c HB Guide - v7 - Fall '96 - p243 [51-250]
   Who Drives This? (Illus. by Charles Reasoner)
   c Ch BWatch - v6 - My '96 - p2 [51-250]
   c HB Guide - v7 - Fall '96 - p243 [51-250]
   c SLJ - v42 - Ag '96 - p128 [51-250]
   Who Plays This Sport? (Illus. by Charles Reasoner)
   c Ch BWatch - v6 - O '96 - p6 [51-250]
   Who Pretends? (Illus. by Charles Reasoner)
   c Ch BWatch - v6 - My '96 - p2 [51-250]
   c HB Guide - v7 - Fall '96 - p243 [51-250]
   c SLJ - v42 - Ag '96 - p128 [51-250]
   Whose Tale Is This? (Illus. by Charles Reasoner)
   c Ch BWatch - v6 - O '96 - p6 [51-250]
Reaver, Chap - *Bill*
   c SLJ - v43 - Ja '97 - p37 [1-50]
Reay, Barry - *Microhistories: Demography, Society and Culture in Rural England 1800-1930*
   Choice - v34 - My '97 - p1559 [51-250]
Rebello, Stephen - *The Art of Hercules*
   y BL - v93 - My 15 '97 - p1555 [51-250]
   PW - v244 - Ap 28 '97 - p68 [1-50]
Reber, Arthur S - *The New Gambler's Bible*
   BL - v93 - S 1 '96 - p55 [51-250]
Rebhorn, Wayne A - *The Emperor of Men's Minds*
   MP - v94 - N '96 - p214+ [501+]
Rebick, Judy - *Politically Speaking*
   CF - v75 - Mr '97 - p38+ [501+]
   Quill & Q - v62 - N '96 - p36 [251-500]
Rebillard, Eric - *In Hora Mortis*
   AHR - v101 - D '96 - p1528 [501+]
   CHR - v82 - O '96 - p681+ [501+]
REBO Studio - *Guide to High Definition Video Production*
   R&R Bk N - v11 - N '96 - p66 [1-50]
Rebolledo, Francisco - *Rasero*
   HR - v49 - Sum '96 - p316+ [501+]
Rebolledo, Tey Diana - *Women Singing in the Snow*
   WAL - v31 - Win '97 - p406+ [251-500]
Rebora, Carrie - *John Singleton Copley in America*
   CR - v268 - Je '96 - p329+ [251-500]

Recent Advances in Solids/Structures and Applications of Metallic Materials 1996
SciTech - v21 - Mr '97 - p79 [51-250]
Recent Developments in Alcoholism. Vol. 12
AJPsych - v153 - Ag '96 - p1105+ [501+]
Rechenmacher, Hans - *Jungfrau, Tochter Babel*
Rel St Rev - v23 - Ap '97 - p166 [51-250]
Rechy, John - *Our Lady of Babylon*
KR - v64 - My 1 '96 - p629+ [251-500]
LATBR - Ag 18 '96 - p8 [501+]
NYTBR - v101 - S 15 '96 - p30 [51-250]
Recio, Belinda - *The Essence of Blue*
LJ - v122 - Ja '97 - p95 [51-250]
The Essence of Red
LJ - v122 - Ja '97 - p95 [51-250]
Reckenfelderbaumer, Alfred - *Medizin Und Wissenschaftstheorie*
Isis - v88 - Mr '97 - p166+ [501+]
Reckert, Stephen - *Beyond Chrysanthemums*
Comp L - v48 - Fall '96 - p368+ [501+]
MLR - v91 - Jl '96 - p685+ [501+]
Recommendations for the Primary Prevention of Cancer
J Gov Info - v23 - S '96 - p634 [51-250]
Recommended Reference Books for Small and Medium-Sized Libraries and Media Centers 1996
r SLJ - v42 - S '96 - p112 [1-50]
r SLMQ - v25 - Fall '96 - p62 [51-250]
Records of the 1996 IEEE International Workshop on Memory Technology, Design and Testing
SciTech - v20 - D '96 - p10 [51-250]
Recueil De Farces 1450-1550. Vol. 9
MLR - v92 - Ap '97 - p461 [251-500]
Recueil Des Actes De Louis VI, Roi De France 1108-1137. Vols. 1-4
CHR - v82 - Jl '96 - p539+ [501+]
The Red Book. Electronic Media Version
r LAR - v98 - D '96 - p650 [51-250]
The Red Cedar Review
p Sm Pr R - v28 - S '96 - p13 [51-250]
Red Pepper
p Dis - v44 - Spr '97 - p103+ [501+]
Redberg, Rita F - *You Can Be a Woman Cardiologist (Illus. by David Katz)*
c SLJ - v42 - S '96 - p219+ [51-250]
Redclift, Michael - *Social Theory and the Global Environment*
EG - v72 - O '96 - p473+ [501+]
The Sociology of the Environment. Vols. 1-3
CS - v25 - S '96 - p709+ [501+]
Redd, Louise - *Playing the Bones*
Bloom Rev - v16 - N '96 - p27 [51-250]
LJ - v121 - N 15 '96 - p116 [51-250]
Reddell, Rayford Clayton - *A Year in the Life of a Rose*
BL - v93 - N 1 '96 - p470+ [51-250]
LJ - v121 - N 15 '96 - p80 [51-250]
PW - v243 - O 7 '96 - p70 [51-250]
Reddick, John - *Georg Buchner: The Shattered Whole*
MLN - v112 - Ap '97 - p470+ [501+]
Redding, Gordon - *International Cultural Differences*
Per Psy - v50 - Spr '97 - p243+ [501+]
Redding, Paul - *Hegel's Hermeneutics*
Choice - v34 - N '96 - p473 [51-250]
CPR - v16 - D '96 - p433+ [501+]
Rel St Rev - v23 - Ap '97 - p151 [51-250]
Reddix, Valerie - *Dragon Kite of the Autumn Moon (Illus. by Jean Tseng)*
c Inst - v106 - S '96 - p87 [1-50]
Reddy, Allan C - *A Macro Perspective on Technology Transfer*
SciTech - v20 - N '96 - p59 [51-250]
Reddy, Maureen T - *Crossing the Color Line*
Wom R Bks - v14 - Ja '97 - p6+ [501+]
Everyday Acts against Racism
Choice - v34 - Mr '97 - p1244 [51-250]
LJ - v121 - N 15 '96 - p82 [51-250]
Redekop, Calvin - *Mennonite Entrepreneurs*
AJS - v102 - Jl '96 - p310+ [501+]
CS - v25 - S '96 - p670+ [501+]
Reden, Sitta Von - *Exchange in Ancient Greece*
AJA - v101 - Ja '97 - p175+ [501+]
Rel St Rev - v23 - Ja '97 - p60 [1-50]
Reder, Peter - *Assessment of Parenting*
Choice - v34 - N '96 - p540 [51-250]
Redfern, Angela - *Practical Ways to Teach Phonics*
Sch Lib - v44 - Ag '96 - p131 [51-250]
Redfern, Darren - *The Maple Handbook: Maple V Release 4*
r JEL - v34 - S '96 - p1410 [51-250]
Redfern, Walter - *Michel Tournier: Le Coq De Bruyere*
L'Esprit - v36 - Win '96 - p104+ [251-500]
TLS - Ja 10 '97 - p22 [501+]

Redfield, James - *The Celestine Prophecy*
Atl - v278 - Jl '96 - p103+ [501+]
CSM - v88 - S 19 '96 - p14 [51-250]
CSM - v88 - N 14 '96 - p14 [51-250]
Econ - v341 - D 7 '96 - p6*+ [251-500]
The Tenth Insight
CSM - v88 - S 19 '96 - p14 [51-250]
Ent W - D 27 '96 - p143 [1-50]
Mag Bl - Mr '97 - p57 [51-250]
The Tenth Insight (Sarandon). Audio Version
BWatch - v18 - Mr '97 - p8 [1-50]
Quill & Q - v62 - S '96 - p71 [51-250]
Redfield, Marc - *Phantom Formations*
Choice - v34 - My '97 - p1503 [51-250]
Redford, Bruce - *Venice and the Grand Tour*
LJ - v121 - N 1 '96 - p90 [51-250]
Spec - v277 - N 23 '96 - p50 [501+]
TLS - N 22 '96 - p18+ [501+]
WSJ-MW - v78 - D 16 '96 - pA14 [501+]
Redgrove, Peter - *Assembling a Ghost*
Obs - O 27 '96 - p18* [251-500]
Redhill, Michael - *Lake Nora Arms*
Can Lit - Win '96 - p189+ [501+]
Rediger, Pat - *Great African Americans in Business*
c BL - v93 - S 15 '96 - p235+ [51-250]
c Ch BWatch - v6 - S '96 - p8 [1-50]
c HB Guide - v7 - Fall '96 - p376 [51-250]
c SLJ - v42 - Ag '96 - p159 [51-250]
Great African Americans in Civil Rights
c BL - v93 - S 15 '96 - p235+ [51-250]
c Ch BWatch - v6 - S '96 - p8 [1-50]
c HB Guide - v7 - Fall '96 - p376 [51-250]
c SLJ - v42 - Ag '96 - p159 [51-250]
Great African Americans in Entertainment
c Ch BWatch - v6 - S '96 - p8 [1-50]
c HB Guide - v7 - Fall '96 - p376 [51-250]
Great African Americans in Literature
c Ch BWatch - v6 - S '96 - p8 [1-50]
c HB Guide - v7 - Fall '96 - p376 [51-250]
c SLJ - v42 - Ag '96 - p159 [51-250]
Great African Americans in Music
c Ch BWatch - v6 - S '96 - p8 [1-50]
c HB Guide - v7 - Fall '96 - p376 [51-250]
Great African Americans in Sports
c Ch BWatch - v6 - S '96 - p8 [1-50]
c HB Guide - v7 - Fall '96 - p362 [51-250]
Rediniotis, Othon K - *Proceedings of the ASME Fluids Engineering Division*
SciTech - v21 - Mr '97 - p75 [51-250]
Redmann, J M - *The Intersection of Law and Desire*
PW - v244 - Ja 27 '97 - p103 [1-50]
Redmon, Anne - *The Head of Dionysos*
TLS - F 21 '97 - p23 [251-500]
Redmond, Don - *Number Theory*
SciTech - v20 - S '96 - p9 [51-250]
Redmond, Elsa M - *Tribal and Chiefly Warfare in South America*
LA Ant - v7 - Je '96 - p165+ [501+]
Redmond, H Paul - *Essential Surgical Immunology*
SciTech - v20 - N '96 - p45 [51-250]
Redmond, Layne - *When the Drummers Were Women*
BL - v93 - My 1 '97 - p1463 [51-250]
LJ - v122 - My 1 '97 - p106 [51-250]
Redmond, Tony - *Microsoft Exchange Server*
SciTech - v21 - Mr '97 - p11 [1-50]
Redondo, Gonzalo - *Historia De La Iglesia En Espana 1931-1939. Vols. 1-2*
r CHR - v82 - O '96 - p661+ [501+]
Redonnet, Marie - *Forever Valley*
TranslRevS - v1 - My '95 - p21 [51-250]
Hotel Splendid
TranslRevS - v1 - My '95 - p21 [51-250]
Nevermore
BW - v26 - D 22 '96 - p9 [51-250]
TranslRevS - v2 - D '96 - p24 [51-250]
Rose Mellie Rose
TranslRevS - v1 - My '95 - p21 [51-250]
Redpath, James - *The Roving Editor*
AL - v68 - D '96 - p877 [1-50]
Nine-C Lit - v51 - D '96 - p426 [51-250]
Reducing Earthquake Losses
J Gov Info - v23 - S '96 - p555 [1-50]
Redwood, John - *Reason, Ridicule and Religion*
CR - v269 - O '96 - p223 [51-250]
Reece, Erik Anderson - *A Balance of Quinces*
BWatch - v17 - D '96 - p7 [51-250]
Reece, Maynard - *The Upland Bird Art of Maynard Reece*
KR - v65 - Mr 1 '97 - p372 [51-250]
Reece, William O - *Physiology of Domestic Animals. 2nd Ed.*
SciTech - v21 - Mr '97 - p70 [51-250]

Reed, Barry - *The Deception*
KR - v65 - Mr 1 '97 - p332 [51-250]
PW - v244 - Mr 3 '97 - p63 [51-250]
The Indictment (Lane). Audio Version
y Kliatt - v30 - S '96 - p48 [51-250]
Reed, Christopher - *Not at Home*
Choice - v34 - Ja '97 - p785 [51-250]
Reed, Cleota - *Henry Chapman Mercer and the Moravian Pottery and Tile Works*
R&R Bk N - v11 - D '96 - p58 [51-250]
Reed, David Wm. - *A Grower's Guide to Water, Media, and Nutrition for Greenhouse Crops*
SciTech - v20 - N '96 - p57 [51-250]
Reed, Edward S - *The Necessity of Experience*
Choice - v34 - F '97 - p1041 [51-250]
LJ - v121 - N 1 '96 - p70 [51-250]
Reed, Eli - *Black in America*
BW - v27 - Ap 13 '97 - p13 [51-250]
LJ - v121 - N 1 '96 - p80 [1-50]
Reed, Fred - *Civil War Encased Stamps*
Coin W - v37 - O 21 '96 - p78 [51-250]
Reed, Germaine M - *Crusading for Chemistry*
AHR - v101 - D '96 - p1632 [501+]
Reed, Ishmael - *Japanese by Spring*
BW - v26 - S 22 '96 - p12 [51-250]
NYTBR - v101 - S 1 '96 - p24 [51-250]
MultiAmerica: Essays on Cultural Wars and Cultural Peace
y BL - v93 - F 15 '97 - p980 [251-500]
KR - v65 - Ja 1 '97 - p47+ [251-500]
LJ - v122 - Mr 15 '97 - p78+ [51-250]
Mumbo Jumbo
NYTBR - v101 - S 1 '96 - p24 [1-50]
Reed, John R - *Dickens and Thackeray*
Clio - v25 - Sum '96 - p459+ [501+]
Nine-C Lit - v51 - S '96 - p260+ [501+]
Reed, John Shelton - *Glorious Battle*
Choice - v34 - D '96 - p629+ [51-250]
Nat R - v48 - D 31 '96 - p51+ [501+]
Reed, Kenneth - *Data Network Handbook*
r Choice - v34 - Mr '97 - p1196 [51-250]
r SciTech - v20 - D '96 - p3 [51-250]
Reed, Mark - *Produced Water 2*
SciTech - v21 - Mr '97 - p94 [51-250]
Reed, Merl E - *Seedtime for the Modern Civil Rights Movement*
AHR - v101 - O '96 - p1299+ [501+]
Reed, Nicholas - *One in a Million (Illus. by Chum McLeod)*
c Quill & Q - v62 - Ag '96 - p42 [251-500]
Reed, Peter - *The Vonnegut Chronicles*
R&R Bk N - v12 - F '97 - p90 [51-250]
Reed, Philip - *Bird Dog*
LJ - v122 - My 1 '97 - p143 [51-250]
PW - v244 - Ap 28 '97 - p49 [51-250]
On Mahler and Britten
Notes - v53 - S '96 - p78+ [501+]
Reed, Ralph - *Active Faith*
Bks & Cult - v2 - N '96 - p20+ [501+]
BW - v26 - Jl 7 '96 - p5 [501+]
CC - v113 - Ag 28 '96 - p812+ [501+]
Nat R - v48 - O 14 '96 - p85+ [501+]
Reason - v28 - O '96 - p58+ [501+]
Active Faith (Reed). Audio Version
BL - v93 - N 15 '96 - p604 [51-250]
How Christians Are Changing the Soul of American Politics
Comw - v123 - S 27 '96 - p23+ [501+]
Reed, Richard K - *Prophets of Agroforestry*
Cont Pac - v9 - Spr '97 - p262+ [501+]
Reed, Robert - *An Exaltation of Larks*
Analog - v116 - Jl '96 - p273+ [251-500]
Rapport - v19 - 4 '96 - p28 [251-500]
Guest of Honor (Bruce). Audio Version
BL - v93 - D 15 '96 - p740 [51-250]
Reed, Sally Gardner - *Creating the Future*
LAR - v99 - F '97 - p104 [51-250]
Reed, T J - *Goethe*
Utne R - My '96 - p18 [51-250]
Reed, T V - *Fifteen Jugglers, Five Believers*
Col Lit - v23 - Je '96 - p171+ [501+]
Reed, Thomas F - *The Sky Never Changes*
Bloom Rev - v16 - N '96 - p10 [51-250]
Choice - v34 - Ap '97 - p1400+ [51-250]
ILR - v135 - 5 '96 - p596 [51-250]
JEL - v35 - Mr '97 - p241 [51-250]
WorldV - v12 - O '96 - p10 [51-250]
Reeder, Carolyn - *Across the Lines*
c BL - v93 - Ap 1 '97 - p1331 [251-500]
c KR - v65 - Mr 15 '97 - p467 [51-250]

Reeder, Ellen D - *Pandora: Women in Classical Greece*
  Class Out - v74 - Win '97 - p83 [501+]
  Sculpt R - v45 - Ag '96 - p35 [501+]
Reeder, John P - *Killing and Saving*
  Choice - v34 - O '96 - p295 [51-250]
Reed-Gilbert, Kerry - *Black Woman, Black Life*
  Aust Bk R - D '96 - p73 [501+]
Reef, Catherine - *John Steinbeck*
  y BL - v93 - Ap 1 '97 - p1305 [1-50]
  y Ch BWatch - v6 - Jl '96 - p3+ [51-250]
  y CLW - v67 - D '96 - p63+ [51-250]
  c HB - v72 - S '96 - p624 [51-250]
  y HB Guide - v7 - Fall '96 - p374 [51-250]
Reeman, Douglas - *A Dawn like Thunder*
  Books - v10 - Je '96 - p22 [1-50]
Reenen, Pieter Th. Van - *Studies in Stemmatology*
  R&R Bk N - v11 - N '96 - p79 [51-250]
Rees, Alan M - *Consumer Health Information Source Book. 4th Ed.*
  r BL - v93 - F 1 '97 - p956 [1-50]
  Consumer Health U.S.A. 2nd Ed.
  r BL - v93 - F 1 '97 - p956 [1-50]
Rees, Celia - *Blood Sinister*
  y Sch Lib - v45 - F '97 - p49 [51-250]
Rees, Dafydd - *DK Encyclopedia of Rock Stars*
  r ARBA - v28 - '97 - p493 [251-500]
  r BL - v93 - Mr 1 '97 - p1188 [251-500]
  yr Kliatt - v31 - Mr '97 - p27 [251-500]
  r LJ - v122 - F 1 '97 - p74 [51-250]
  r PW - v243 - O 7 '96 - p68 [51-250]
Rees, E A - *Stalinism and Soviet Rail Transport 1928-41*
  AHR - v101 - O '96 - p1250 [501+]
Rees, G Wyn - *Anglo-American Approaches to Alliance Security 1955-60*
  R&R Bk N - v11 - N '96 - p18 [51-250]
Rees, Joseph V - *Hostages of Each Other*
  Nature - v383 - O 24 '96 - p682 [1-50]
Rees, Martin - *Before the Beginning*
  Nature - v385 - F 27 '97 - p786 [501+]
Rees, Mary - *Ten in a Bed*
  c BL - v93 - Ap 1 '97 - p1341 [1-50]
Rees, Nigel - *Brewer's Quotations*
  r CR - v269 - Ag '96 - p112 [51-250]
Rees, Owen - *Polyphony in Portugal c. 1530-c. 1620*
  Notes - v53 - S '96 - p65+ [501+]
Rees, Roberta - *Eyes Like Pigeons*
  Can Lit - Win '96 - p167+ [501+]
Rees, Yvonne - *Stained Glass and Ceramics*
  LJ - v121 - O 15 '96 - p57 [51-250]
Reese, Colleen L - *Prudence of Plymouth Plantation*
  c Ch BWatch - v6 - Jl '96 - p2 [1-50]
Reese, Judy S - *Recasting Social Values in the Work of Virginia Woolf*
  Choice - v34 - S '96 - p129 [51-250]
Reese, Roger R - *Stalin's Reluctant Soldiers*
  Choice - v34 - Ja '97 - p858 [51-250]
  J Mil H - v61 - Ap '97 - p394+ [501+]
Reese, Terence - *Learn Bridge in Five Days*
  y Ch BWatch - v7 - F '97 - p8 [1-50]
Reese, Thomas J - *Inside the Vatican*
  Am - v176 - Ja 18 '97 - p23 [501+]
  BL - v93 - D 15 '96 - p694+ [51-250]
  BW - v27 - Ja 19 '97 - p13 [51-250]
  CC - v114 - F 19 '97 - p200+ [501+]
  Choice - v34 - My '97 - p1516+ [51-250]
  Comw - v123 - D 6 '96 - p14+ [501+]
  Econ - v342 - Mr 15 '97 - p7* [501+]
  LJ - v121 - N 1 '96 - p72 [51-250]
  NL - v79 - D 16 '96 - p35+ [501+]
  NYTBR - v102 - Mr 2 '97 - p22 [501+]
  Wil Q - v21 - Win '97 - p100+ [251-500]
Reese, William J - *The Origins of the American High School*
  AHR - v102 - F '97 - p164 [501+]
  JIH - v27 - Win '97 - p549+ [501+]
  JSH - v63 - F '97 - p162+ [501+]
  J Soc H - v30 - Fall '96 - p264+ [501+]
Reese, William L - *Dictionary of Philosophy and Religion. New and Enl. Ed.*
  r Choice - v34 - F '97 - p949 [51-250]
Reetz, Marianne - *Professional Periodicals in International Children's Literature. 3rd Rev. Ed.*
  r ChLAQ - v20 - Fall '95 - p99
Reeve, Tim - *Action Robots (Illus. by Gavin MacLeod)*
  c HB Guide - v7 - Fall '96 - p351 [1-50]
Reeves, Byron - *The Media Equation*
  BW - v27 - Ja 12 '97 - p13 [51-250]
  Choice - v34 - Mr '97 - p1154+ [51-250]
  LATBR - D 1 '96 - p4 [501+]
  New Sci - v153 - Ja 18 '97 - p40 [251-500]

Reeves, Catherine - *The True World*
  Aust Bk R - Je '96 - p67 [1-50]
Reeves, Geoffrey D - *Earth's Trapped Particle Environment*
  SciTech - v21 - Mr '97 - p19 [51-250]
Reeves, Geoffrey W, 1945- - *Communications and the Third World*
  JC - v46 - Sum '96 - p183+ [501+]
Reeves, Nicholas - *The Complete Valley of the Kings*
  HT - v46 - O '96 - p55 [1-50]
  Nature - v386 - Ap 17 '97 - p669 [51-250]
Reeves, Nigel - *Linguistic Auditing*
  R&R Bk N - v11 - N '96 - p30 [51-250]
Reeves, Richard - *Family Travels*
  BL - v93 - Mr 1 '97 - p1107 [51-250]
  KR - v65 - Ja 1 '97 - p48 [251-500]
  LJ - v122 - F 15 '97 - p154 [51-250]
  PW - v244 - Ja 20 '97 - p386+ [51-250]
Reeves, Sue - *Country Rag Crafts*
  BL - v93 - F 15 '97 - p993 [51-250]
  LJ - v122 - F 15 '97 - p133 [51-250]
Reeves, Thomas C - *The Empty Church*
  BW - v26 - O 20 '96 - p5 [501+]
  Choice - v34 - F '97 - p980+ [51-250]
  KR - v64 - Ag 15 '96 - p1221 [251-500]
  LJ - v121 - N 1 '96 - p72 [51-250]
  Nat R - v48 - D 31 '96 - p49+ [501+]
  WSJ-Cent - v99 - Ja 3 '97 - pA6 [501+]
Reference and Price Guide for MicroTrains N Scale Rolling Stock
  r Model R - v64 - My '97 - p49+ [51-250]
Reference Books Bulletin 1994-1995
  r ARBA - v28 - '97 - p9 [251-500]
Reference Books Bulletin 1995-1996
  r BL - v93 - F 15 '97 - p1042 [1-50]
Reference Books for Children's Collections. 3rd Ed.
  r BL - v93 - N 1 '96 - p538 [1-50]
  r SLJ - v43 - Mr '97 - p119 [51-250]
Reference Reviews Europe Annual 1995
  r Choice - v34 - My '97 - p1480 [251-500]
Refugees, Immigration and Gender
  J Gov Info - v23 - S '96 - p618 [51-250]
Regan, Dian Curtis - *Daddies (Illus. by Mary Morgan)*
  c HB Guide - v7 - Fall '96 - p243 [51-250]
  Mommies (Illus. by Mary Morgan)
  c HB Guide - v7 - Fall '96 - p243 [51-250]
  Monsters in Cyberspace (Illus. by Melissa Sweet)
  c KR - v65 - My 1 '97 - p726 [51-250]
Regan, Geoffrey - *Blue on Blue*
  NWCR - v50 - Win '97 - p148+ [501+]
  Fight or Flight
  y Kliatt - v30 - S '96 - p34 [51-250]
Regan, Patrick - *Mary Engelbreit: The Art and the Artist*
  BL - v93 - N 1 '96 - p472 [51-250]
  BW - v27 - Ja 12 '97 - p8 [501+]
Regan, Priscilla M - *Legislating Privacy*
  J Gov Info - v23 - Jl '96 - p531+ [501+]
Regehr, T D - *Mennonites in Canada 1939-1970*
  Choice - v34 - Mr '97 - p1229 [51-250]
Regel, Pat - *The Houseplant Survival Guide*
  PW - v244 - Mr 24 '97 - p79 [51-250]
Regeneration Quarterly
  p Utne R - S '96 - p98+ [251-500]
Regens, James L - *The Economic Realities of Political Reform*
  Choice - v34 - O '96 - p362 [251-500]
  JEL - v34 - D '96 - p2030 [51-250]
Reger, Guido - *Organisation of Science and Technology at the Watershed*
  JEL - v34 - D '96 - p2117+ [51-250]
Reger, James P - *Life in the South during the Civil War*
  y SLJ - v43 - Mr '97 - p207 [51-250]
Regester, Seeley - *The Dead Letter*
  Arm Det - v30 - Win '97 - p39 [251-500]
Regier, Terry - *The Human Semantic Potential*
  R&R Bk N - v12 - F '97 - p75 [51-250]
Reginald, Robert - *Science Fiction and Fantasy Literature 1975-1991*
  r RQ - v36 - Win '96 - p218 [51-250]
The Regional Dimension of Unemployment in Transition Countries
  J Gov Info - v23 - S '96 - p675 [51-250]
Regional Theatre Directory 1996-97
  r ARBA - v28 - '97 - p524 [251-500]
Regionalism and the World Trading System
  J Gov Info - v23 - S '96 - p690 [51-250]
Regis, Ed - *Virus Ground Zero*
  BW - v27 - Ja 19 '97 - p1+ [501+]
  LJ - v121 - O 15 '96 - p88 [51-250]
  NYTBR - v101 - N 3 '96 - p30 [501+]
  y SLJ - v43 - Mr '97 - p218 [51-250]

Regis, Pamela - *Describing Early America*
  ASInt - v34 - O '96 - p103+ [501+]
Reglero De La Fuente, Carlos M - *Los Senorios De Los Montes De Torozos*
  Specu - v71 - Jl '96 - p758+ [501+]
Regnery, Henery - *A Few Reasonable Words*
  Univ Bkmn - v36 - Fall '96 - p3+ [501+]
Regnier, Victor - *Assisted Living for the Aged and Frail*
  Soc Ser R - v71 - Mr '97 - p168 [1-50]
Regosin, Richard L - *Montaigne's Unruly Brood*
  Choice - v34 - S '96 - p133 [51-250]
  R&R Bk N - v11 - N '96 - p68 [51-250]
Reh, Vincent - *Railroad Radio*
  SciTech - v21 - Mr '97 - p89 [1-50]
Rehmann, Ruth - *The Man in the Pulpit*
  KR - v65 - Ja 1 '97 - p20 [51-250]
Reiber, Johan H C - *Cardiovascular Imaging*
  SciTech - v20 - N '96 - p46 [51-250]
Reibetanz, John - *Morning Watch*
  BIC - v25 - S '96 - p21+ [501+]
Reich, Bernard - *An Historical Encyclopedia of the Arab-Israeli Conflict*
  r ARBA - v28 - '97 - p207 [51-250]
  r J Mil H - v61 - Ja '97 - p201+ [251-500]
  r MEJ - v50 - Sum '96 - p450+ [51-250]
  r MEQ - v3 - D '96 - p84+ [51-250]
  Securing the Covenant
  MEJ - v50 - Sum '96 - p440+ [501+]
Reich, Cary - *The Life of Nelson A. Rockefeller: Worlds to Conquer 1908-1958*
  BL - v93 - O 1 '96 - p320 [51-250]
  BW - v26 - D 1 '96 - p1+ [501+]
  Choice - v34 - Ap '97 - p1407 [51-250]
  KR - v64 - S 1 '96 - p1305+ [251-500]
  LJ - v122 - Ja '97 - p50 [1-50]
  LJ - v121 - O 1 '96 - p92 [51-250]
  NY - v72 - Ja 6 '97 - p69+ [501+]
  NYTBR - v101 - N 3 '96 - p10+ [501+]
  NYTBR - v101 - D 8 '96 - p11 [51-250]
  PW - v243 - S 2 '96 - p99 [251-500]
  PW - v243 - N 4 '96 - p46 [1-50]
  WSJ-MW - v78 - O 31 '96 - pA20 [501+]
Reich, Charles A - *Opposing the System*
  Am - v174 - My 25 '96 - p31+ [251-500]
  HLR - v110 - D '96 - p562 [51-250]
  Rapport - v19 - 5 '96 - p45 [251-500]
Reich, Lee - *The Pruning Book*
  LJ - v122 - My 1 '97 - p130 [51-250]
Reich, Robert B - *Locked in the Cabinet*
  Bus W - Ap 21 '97 - p22 [501+]
  NYTLa - v146 - Ap 30 '97 - pC16 [501+]
  Locked in the Cabinet (Reich). Audio Version
  PW - v244 - My 5 '97 - p41 [51-250]
Reichart, Thomas - *Stadte Ohne Wettbewerb*
  GJ - v162 - Jl '96 - p229+ [251-500]
Reichel, Elias - *Atlas of Indocyanine Green Angiography*
  r SciTech - v20 - S '96 - p39 [51-250]
Reichenberg-Ullman, Judyth - *Ritalin-Free Kids*
  LJ - v121 - N 1 '96 - p102 [51-250]
Reichert, Mickey Zucker - *Beyond Ragnarok*
  y Kliatt - v30 - N '96 - p16 [51-250]
Reichheld, Frederick F - *The Loyalty Effect*
  Bus Bk R - v13 - 3 '96 - p28+ [501+]
  LJ - v122 - Mr 15 '97 - p36 [1-50]
  The Quest for Loyalty
  BL - v93 - N 1 '96 - p466 [51-250]
  HR Mag - v42 - F '97 - p124 [51-250]
Reichman, Judith - *I'm Too Young to Get Old*
  BL - v92 - Ag '96 - p1869 [51-250]
Reichmanis, Elsa - *Microelectronics Technology*
  SciTech - v20 - N '96 - p75 [51-250]
Reid, Angus - *Shakedown: How the New Economy Is Changing Our Lives*
  CF - v75 - D '96 - p39+ [501+]
  Quill & Q - v62 - N '96 - p37 [251-500]
Reid, Brian Holden - *The Origins of the American Civil War*
  HT - v46 - O '96 - p58 [1-50]
Reid, Christopher - *Expanded Universes*
  Lon R Bks - v18 - N 28 '96 - p25+ [501+]
  Obs - S 15 '96 - p15* [501+]
  Obs - D 1 '96 - p16* [1-50]
  Obs - D 1 '96 - p17* [51-250]
  TLS - D 20 '96 - p25 [501+]
Reid, Constance - *Hilbert*
  JEL - v34 - D '96 - p2015 [1-50]
  Julia: A Life in Mathematics
  Choice - v34 - My '97 - p1537 [51-250]
  New Sci - v153 - F 15 '97 - p42 [51-250]
  SciTech - v21 - Mr '97 - p4 [1-50]

Reid, Elizabeth - *HIV and AIDS*
WorldV - v12 - O '96 - p6 [251-500]
Reid, Eric - *Biofluid Assay for Peptide-Related and Other Drugs*
SciTech - v20 - D '96 - p55 [51-250]
Reid, Francis - *The Stage Lighting Handbook. 5th Ed.*
TCI - v30 - O '96 - p55 [1-50]
Reid, Gayla - *To Be There with You*
Aust Bk R - N '96 - p51+ [501+]
Reid, James H - *Narration and Description in the French Realist Novel*
FR - v70 - D '96 - p328+ [501+]
Reid, Jefferson - *The Archaeology of Ancient Arizona*
Sci - v275 - Mr 7 '97 - p1439 [1-50]
Reid, Jennifer - *Myth, Symbol, and Colonial Encounter*
Can Hist R - v78 - Mr '97 - p165+ [501+]
Reid, John Phillip - *Constitutional History of the American Revolution. Abridged Ed.*
IndRev - v1 - Spr '96 - p132+ [501+]
Reid, Judith Prowse - *Genealogical Research in England's Public Record Office*
r ARBA - v28 - '97 - p166 [51-250]
r BL - v92 - Ag '96 - p1925 [251-500]
r Choice - v34 - N '96 - p435 [51-250]
LJ - v122 - Ja '97 - p112 [51-250]
Reid, Lori - *The Art of Hand Reading*
y BL - v93 - Ap 1 '97 - p1308 [1-50]
y SLJ - v43 - Mr '97 - p218 [51-250]
The Monkey. Chinese Horoscopes for Lovers
Horoscope - v62 - Ag '96 - p40+ [251-500]
Reid, Michaela - *Ask Sir James*
CR - v269 - N '96 - p278 [51-250]
Reid, Miles - *Undergraduate Commutative Algebra*
y New Sci - v151 - S 28 '96 - p44+ [501+]
Reid, Nancy - *Famous Friends of the Wolf Cookbook*
BWatch - v17 - D '96 - p10 [51-250]
Reid, Panthea - *Art and Affection*
BL - v93 - N 15 '96 - p566 [51-250]
KR - v64 - S 1 '96 - p1306 [251-500]
LJ - v121 - S 15 '96 - p69 [51-250]
PW - v243 - O 14 '96 - p71 [51-250]
Reid, Rob - *Wave Goodbye (Illus. by Lorraine Williams)*
c HB Guide - v7 - Fall '96 - p243 [51-250]
Reid, Robert - *Architects of the Web*
BL - v93 - My 1 '97 - p1468 [51-250]
KR - v65 - Mr 1 '97 - p364 [51-250]
PW - v244 - Mr 31 '97 - p58 [1-50]
Reid, Robert H - *Corazon Aquino and the Brushfire Revolution*
PSQ - v111 - Win '96 - p714+ [501+]
Reid, Thomas - *Thomas Reid on the Animate Creation*
Choice - v34 - S '96 - p150 [51-250]
Reider, Katja - *Snail Started It! (Illus. by Angeli Von Roehl)*
c CBRS - v25 - Ap '97 - p100 [51-250]
Reid-Merrit, Patricia - *Sister Power*
LJ - v121 - N 1 '96 - p86 [1-50]
Reidy, Hannah - *Capers (Illus. by Clare Mackie)*
c Sch Lib - v44 - N '96 - p147 [51-250]
Colours (Illus. by Clare Mackie)
c Sch Lib - v44 - N '96 - p147 [51-250]
Contrasts (Illus. by Clare Mackie)
c Sch Lib - v44 - N '96 - p147 [51-250]
Counting (Illus. by Clare Mackie)
c Sch Lib - v44 - N '96 - p147 [51-250]
Crazy Creature Capers (Illus. by Clare Mackie)
c HB Guide - v8 - Spr '97 - p15 [51-250]
c PW - v243 - S 16 '96 - p85 [51-250]
c SLJ - v43 - F '97 - p96 [51-250]
c TES - Mr 28 '97 - p11* [51-250]
Crazy Creature Contrasts (Illus. by Clare Mackie)
c HB Guide - v8 - Spr '97 - p15 [51-250]
c PW - v243 - S 16 '96 - p85 [51-250]
c SLJ - v43 - F '97 - p96 [51-250]
c TES - Mr 28 '97 - p11* [51-250]
Reidy, Sue - *The Visitation*
Woman's J - S '96 - p10 [51-250]
Reif, Heinz - *Die Verspatete Stadt. Pts. 1-2*
AHR - v101 - O '96 - p1232+ [501+]
Reife, Abraham - *Environmental Chemistry of Dyes and Pigments*
Choice - v34 - Ja '97 - p822 [51-250]
Reifenberg, Bernd - *Lessing Und Die Bibliothek*
Lib - v18 - Je '96 - p169+ [51-250]
Reiffenstuhl, Gunther - *Vaginal Operations. 2nd Ed.*
r SciTech - v20 - S '96 - p40 [51-250]
Reiger, George - *The Striped Bass Chronicles*
KR - v65 - Mr 1 '97 - p365 [51-250]
PW - v244 - Mr 24 '97 - p71 [51-250]

Reijnders, Lucas - *Environmentally Improved Production Processes and Products*
SciTech - v20 - N '96 - p81 [51-250]
Reill, Peter Hanns - *Encyclopedia of the Enlightenment*
r ARBA - v28 - '97 - p215 [51-250]
r Choice - v34 - N '96 - p428 [51-250]
Reilly, Catherine W - *Late Victorian Poetry 1880-1899*
r RES - v47 - Ag '96 - p460 [251-500]
Reilly, Edward C - *Jim Harrison*
Bloom Rev - v17 - Ja '97 - p17 [51-250]
Reilly, John - *Rapid Prototyping*
CBR - v14 - Jl '96 - p25 [1-50]
Reilly, Maria - *Now That I Am Old*
CLW - v67 - D '96 - p45+ [51-250]
Reilly, Rick - *Missing Links*
KR - v64 - My 1 '96 - p630 [251-500]
LATBR - My 26 '96 - p11 [51-250]
Reimann, Katya - *Wind from a Foreign Sky*
MFSF - v92 - Mr '97 - p36 [51-250]
Reinagle, Damon J - *Draw Alien Fantasies (Illus. by Damon J Reinagle)*
c BL - v93 - D 15 '96 - p722+ [51-250]
c Par Ch - v20 - N '96 - p8 [51-250]
c SLJ - v43 - Mr '97 - p207 [51-250]
Reinelt, Janelle - *After Brecht*
Theat J - v48 - D '96 - p525+ [501+]
Crucibles of Crisis
Choice - v34 - F '97 - p976 [51-250]
Reiner, Annie - *The History of Christmas (Illus. by Annie Reiner). Book and Audio Version*
c SLJ - v42 - O '96 - p40 [51-250]
This Nervous Breakdown Is Driving Me Crazy
KR - v64 - My 1 '96 - p630 [251-500]
LATBR - S 1 '96 - p10 [51-250]
Reiner, Robert - *Policing. Vols. 1-2*
R&R Bk N - v12 - F '97 - p57 [51-250]
Reinert, Paul - *Seasons of Change*
Am - v176 - Mr 22 '97 - p30+ [51-250]
Reinhardt, Peter A - *Pollution Prevention and Waste Minimization in Laboratories*
Choice - v34 - F '97 - p995 [51-250]
Reinhardt, Wolfgang - *Das Wachstum Des Gottesvolkes*
Rel St Rev - v23 - Ja '97 - p72 [51-250]
Reinhart, A Kevin - *Before Revelation*
JR - v77 - Ja '97 - p185+ [501+]
Rel St Rev - v23 - Ja '97 - p3+ [501+]
Rel St Rev - v23 - Ja '97 - p11+ [501+]
Reinharz, Peter - *Killer Kids, Bad Law*
PW - v243 - S 23 '96 - p65 [51-250]
Reinhold, Barbara Bailey - *Toxic Work*
LJ - v122 - Mr 15 '97 - p37 [1-50]
Reinicke, Wolfgang H - *Banking, Politics and Global Finance*
Econ J - v106 - N '96 - p1839 [51-250]
Reinken, Patrick - *Judgment Day*
Arm Det - v29 - Fall '96 - p501+ [251-500]
Reinmuth, Dean - *Tension-Free Golf*
LJ - v121 - O 1 '96 - p53 [1-50]
Reis, Carlos - *Towards a Semiotics of Ideology*
Poetics T - v18 - Spr '97 - p134+ [501+]
Reis, Jaime - *International Monetary Systems in Historical Perspective*
JEH - v57 - Mr '97 - p264+ [501+]
Reis, John C - *Environmental Control in Petroleum Engineering*
SciTech - v20 - N '96 - p67 [51-250]
Reiser, Howard - *Muggsy Bogues: Tall on Talent*
c HB Guide - v7 - Fall '96 - p359 [1-50]
Reiser, Lynn - *Any Kind of Dog. Book and Audio Version*
c SLJ - v43 - F '97 - p70 [51-250]
Beach Feet (Illus. by Lynn Reiser)
c HB Guide - v7 - Fall '96 - p272 [51-250]
Best Friends Think Alike (Illus. by Lynn Reiser)
c HB - v73 - Mr '97 - p194+ [251-500]
c KR - v65 - My 1 '97 - p726 [51-250]
Reisfeld, Randi - *This Is the Sound!*
y VOYA - v19 - D '96 - p289+ [251-500]
Reisman, David - *Anthony Crosland: The Mixed Economy*
NS - v126 - F 28 '97 - p44+ [501+]
TLS - Ap 11 '97 - p3+ [501+]
Crosland's Future
NS - v126 - F 28 '97 - p44+ [501+]
TLS - Ap 11 '97 - p3+ [501+]
Reisman, George - *Capitalism: A Treatise on Economics*
PW - v243 - N 18 '96 - p57 [51-250]
Reisman, Rose - *Rose Reisman's Enlightened Kitchen*
Quill & Q - v62 - Ag '96 - p30 [51-250]
Reiss, Bob - *Purgatory Road*
Arm Det - v29 - Sum '96 - p377 [251-500]
Reiss, Eric L - *The Compleat Talking Machine. 2nd Ed.*
r Ant & CM - v101 - Ag '96 - p18 [1-50]

Reiss, James - *The Parable of Fire*
ABR - v17 - Ag '96 - p16+ [501+]
Reiss, Johanna - *The Upstairs Room*
New Ad - v9 - Fall '96 - p297+ [501+]
Reiss, Kathryn - *Dreadful Sorry*
y Kliatt - v31 - Mr '97 - p20 [51-250]
Reiss, Michael J - *Improving Nature?*
BL - v93 - S 1 '96 - p51 [51-250]
Sci - v274 - N 15 '96 - p1147+ [501+]
Reiss, Steven A - *Sport in Industrial America 1850-1920*
Aethlon - v13 - Spr '96 - p203 [251-500]
Reissner, Eric - *Selected Works in Applied Mechanics and Mathematics*
SIAM Rev - v39 - Mr '97 - p176+ [51-250]
Reitano, Joanne - *The Tariff Question in the Gilded Age*
AHR - v101 - O '96 - p1291+ [251-500]
Reiter, Andrea - *Auf Dass Sie Entsteigen Der Dunkelheit*
MLR - v92 - Ja '97 - p250+ [501+]
Reiter, Frederick J - *They Built Utopia*
CHR - v83 - Ja '97 - p154+ [251-500]
Reiter, Thomas - *Crossovers*
PS - v70 - Fall '96 - p195+ [501+]
Reiter, Yitzhak - *Islamic Endowments in Jerusalem under British Mandate*
Choice - v34 - My '97 - p1570 [51-250]
Reith, Maarten E A - *Neurotransmitter Transporters*
SciTech - v21 - Mr '97 - p40 [51-250]
Reitz, Elizabeth J - *Case Studies in Environmental Archaeology*
Choice - v34 - Mr '97 - p1201 [51-250]
R&R Bk N - v11 - N '96 - p8 [51-250]
Rekela, George - *Sports Great Anfernee Hardaway*
c HB Guide - v7 - Fall '96 - p361 [51-250]
Relbstein, Janet - *Love Life*
Woman's J - Ap '97 - p18 [1-50]
Relf, Patricia - *Tonka Big Book of Trucks (Illus. by Tom LaPadula)*
c BL - v93 - O 1 '96 - p355+ [51-250]
c SLJ - v42 - S '96 - p200 [51-250]
Religion for Today
y TES - Mr 21 '97 - p27* [51-250]
Relihan, Constance C - *Framing Elizabethan Fictions*
Choice - v34 - My '97 - p1495 [51-250]
Remarque, Erich Maria - *All Quiet on the Western Front*
CR - v269 - O '96 - p223 [51-250]
CSM - v89 - D 11 '96 - p15 [251-500]
LJ - v121 - N 15 '96 - p93 [1-50]
Remboldt, Carole - *Respect and Protect*
R&R Bk N - v11 - N '96 - p56 [51-250]
Remen, Rachel Naomi - *Kitchen Table Wisdom*
BL - v92 - Ag '96 - p1869 [51-250]
Bloom Rev - v16 - N '96 - p14 [51-250]
Kitchen Table Wisdom (Remen). Audio Version
BL - v93 - F 15 '97 - p1038 [51-250]
Remensnyder, Amy G - *Remembering Kings Past*
HRNB - v25 - Fall '96 - p25 [251-500]
Remer, Gary - *Humanism and the Rhetoric of Toleration*
Choice - v34 - O '96 - p263+ [51-250]
Remer, Rosalind - *Printers and Men of Capital*
W&M Q - v54 - Ap '97 - p457+ [501+]
Remick, Jerry - *A Checklist of Countries Currently Issuing Their Own Paper Money*
r Coin W - v38 - Ap 28 '97 - p18 [51-250]
Remington, W Craig - *The Atlas of Alabama Counties*
r J Gov Info - v23 - S '96 - p577 [51-250]
Remnick, David - *The Devil Problem and Other True Stories*
BL - v92 - Ag '96 - p1875 [51-250]
BW - v26 - S 1 '96 - p13 [51-250]
Ent W - S 27 '96 - p74 [51-250]
LATBR - N 17 '96 - p14 [51-250]
NY - v72 - D 16 '96 - p109 [51-250]
NYTBR - v101 - S 8 '96 - p22 [51-250]
Resurrection: The Struggle for a New Russia
BL - v93 - F 1 '97 - p924 [51-250]
Bus W - Mr 17 '97 - p14+ [501+]
Econ - v342 - Mr 8 '97 - p100 [501+]
For Aff - v76 - My '97 - p138+ [51-250]
KR - v65 - Ja 15 '97 - p128 [251-500]
LATBR - Mr 9 '97 - p9 [501+]
LJ - v122 - F 15 '97 - p149 [51-250]
NL - v80 - Mr 10 '97 - p18+ [501+]
NYTBR - v102 - Mr 16 '97 - p7 [501+]
NYTLa - v146 - Mr 17 '97 - pC16 [501+]
PW - v244 - Ja 13 '97 - p59 [51-250]
Time - v149 - Mr 31 '97 - p82+ [251-500]
Trib Bks - My 25 '97 - p3 [501+]
WSJ-Cent - v99 - Mr 13 '97 - pA12 [501+]
Remski, Matthew - *Dying for Veronica*
Quill & Q - v63 - F '97 - p49 [251-500]

Renard, John - *Seven Doors to Islam*
  Choice - v34 - N '96 - p477 [51-250]
Renard, Ronald D - *The Burmese Connection*
  Pac A - v69 - Sum '96 - p286+ [501+]
Renardy, Yuriko Y - *Advances in Multi-Fluid Flows*
  SciTech - v20 - D '96 - p23 [51-250]
Renaudot, Patrick - *CX*
  BL - v93 - Ja '97 - p827 [1-50]
Renault, Mary - *The King Must Die*
  y SLJ - v42 - N '96 - p39 [1-50]
  The Last of the Wine
  y SLJ - v42 - N '96 - p39 [1-50]
Rendall, Steven - *Distinguo: Reading Montaigne Differently*
  Six Ct J - v27 - Win '96 - p1173+ [501+]
Rendell, Ruth - *Blood Lines*
  Books - v9 - S '95 - p22 [1-50]
  Blood Lines (Anthony). Audio Version
  Arm Det - v30 - Win '97 - p81 [51-250]
  LJ - v121 - N 1 '96 - p120 [51-250]
  The Keys to the Street
  BL - v92 - Ag '96 - p1856 [251-500]
  Nat R - v48 - D 23 '96 - p56+ [51-250]
  NS - v125 - S 6 '96 - p47+ [501+]
  NYTBR - v101 - O 13 '96 - p29 [51-250]
  Rapport - v19 - 6 '96 - p21 [251-500]
  y SLJ - v43 - Mr '97 - p216 [51-250]
  Spec - v277 - S 21 '96 - p48 [251-500]
  TLS - S 6 '96 - p22 [501+]
  Woman's J - O '96 - p12 [1-50]
  WSJ-MW - v78 - O 15 '96 - pA18 [51-250]
  The Reason Why
  Rapport - v19 - 4 '96 - p32 [251-500]
  Simisola
  Arm Det - v30 - Win '97 - p19 [51-250]
  Simisola (Peters). Audio Version
  y Kliatt - v31 - Ja '97 - p45+ [51-250]
  The Veiled One (Wilding). Audio Version
  y Kliatt - v30 - N '96 - p46 [51-250]
Rendle-Short, Francesca - *Imago*
  Aust Bk R - Je '96 - p45+ [501+]
Rendon, Marcie R - *Powwow Summer (Illus. by Cheryl Walsh Bellville)*
  c HB Guide - v8 - Spr '97 - p178 [51-250]
  c SLJ - v42 - O '96 - p138+ [51-250]
Reneaux, J J - *Cajun Fairy Tales. Audio Version*
  c Ch BWatch - v6 - My '96 - p6 [1-50]
  Why Alligator Hates Dog (Illus. by Donnie Lee Green)
  c RT - v50 - O '96 - p156 [51-250]
Renehan, Edward J - *Science on the Web*
  r Choice - v34 - Mr '97 - p1180 [51-250]
Renewal
  p Dis - v44 - Spr '97 - p103+ [501+]
Renewing Our Energy Future
  J Gov Info - v23 - S '96 - p556 [51-250]
Renfrew, John W - *Aggression and Its Causes*
  Choice - v34 - Ja '97 - p880 [51-250]
Rengert, George F - *The Geography of Illegal Drugs*
  Choice - v34 - D '96 - p696 [51-250]
  R&R Bk N - v11 - N '96 - p44 [51-250]
Rengger, N J - *Political Theory, Modernity, and Postmodernity*
  AJS - v102 - N '96 - p867+ [501+]
  APSR - v91 - Mr '97 - p178+ [501+]
Renino, Christopher - *The Way Home Is Longer*
  PW - v244 - Ap 28 '97 - p50 [251-500]
Renker, Elizabeth - *Strike through the Mask*
  Choice - v34 - D '96 - p616 [51-250]
  R&R Bk N - v11 - N '96 - p72 [51-250]
  TLS - Ja 10 '97 - p3+ [501+]
Renne, Tanya - *Ana's Land*
  Cons - v17 - Win '96 - p31 [1-50]
  R&R Bk N - v12 - F '97 - p54 [51-250]
Renner, Michael - *Fighting for Survival*
  BioSci - v47 - F '97 - p126 [51-250]
  Choice - v34 - Mr '97 - p1200 [51-250]
  Econ - v342 - F 15 '97 - p7* [51-250]
Rennie, Bryan S - *Reconstructing Eliade*
  CC - v113 - D 4 '96 - p1209 [51-250]
  R&R Bk N - v12 - F '97 - p8 [51-250]
Rennie, Neil - *Far-Fetched Facts*
  Choice - v34 - O '96 - p273 [51-250]
  Lon R Bks - v18 - O 31 '96 - p12+ [501+]
  Nine-C Lit - v51 - D '96 - p426 [1-50]
  VQR - v72 - Aut '96 - p140* [51-250]
Reno, Dawn E - *The Encyclopedia of Black Collectibles*
  r Ant & CM - v101 - Ag '96 - p18 [1-50]
Reno, Frank D - *The Historic King Arthur*
  R&R Bk N - v11 - D '96 - p8 [51-250]
Reno, Russell Ronald - *The Ordinary Transformed*
  Theol St - v58 - Mr '97 - p173+ [51-250]

Reno, William - *Corruption and State Politics in Sierra Leone*
  JIH - v27 - Win '97 - p563+ [251-500]
Renouard, Phillipe - *Repertoire Des Imprimeurs Parisiens Libraires Et Fondeurs De Caracteres Au XVIIe Siecle*
  BC - v45 - Sum '96 - p277 [251-500]
Renov, Michael - *Resolutions: Contemporary Video Practices*
  Afterimage - v24 - N '96 - p4 [1-50]
Rensberger, Boyce - *Life Itself*
  BW - v27 - Ap 13 '97 - p4 [501+]
  NYTBR - v102 - F 23 '97 - p8 [501+]
Rensberger, Susan - *A Multicultural Portrait of the Great Depression*
  y HB Guide - v7 - Fall '96 - p388 [51-250]
Rense, Paige - *Manor House*
  KR - v65 - Mr 1 '97 - p338+ [51-250]
  LJ - v122 - Mr 15 '97 - p91 [51-250]
  PW - v244 - F 24 '97 - p67 [51-250]
Renshon, Stanley A - *High Hopes*
  Pres SQ - v27 - Win '97 - p153+ [501+]
  Rapport - v19 - 6 '96 - p32 [251-500]
Renstrom, Peter G - *Constitutional Law and Young Adults*
  yr BL - v93 - Mr 1 '97 - p1154 [51-250]
Renton, Alice - *Winter Butterfly*
  Woman's J - v13 - p13 [51-250]
Rentoul, John - *Tony Blair*
  Books - v9 - S '95 - p24 [1-50]
Rentschler, Eric - *The Ministry of Illusion*
  Choice - v34 - Mr '97 - p1170+ [251-500]
  LJ - v121 - S 15 '96 - p70 [51-250]
Rentz, D C F - *Grasshopper Country*
  Choice - v34 - My '97 - p1523+ [51-250]
  r SciTech - v21 - Mr '97 - p38 [51-250]
Renversez, Francoise - *Elements D'Analyse Monetaire. 3rd Ed.*
  JEL - v34 - D '96 - p2052 [51-250]
Renwick, Robin - *Fighting with Allies*
  BW - v26 - Jl 14 '96 - p8+ [501+]
  BW - v26 - D 8 '96 - p7 [51-250]
  Choice - v34 - D '96 - p664 [51-250]
  For Aff - v75 - S '96 - p145 [51-250]
  Spec - v277 - N 2 '96 - p49 [501+]
  Spec - v277 - N 16 '96 - p44 [1-50]
  TLS - N 15 '96 - p6+ [501+]
Renwick, William - *Analyzing Fugue*
  Notes - v53 - S '96 - p93+ [501+]
Repchuk, Caroline - *The Glitter Dragon (Illus. by Colin Maclean)*
  c HB Guide - v7 - Fall '96 - p272 [1-50]
  My Little Supermarket (Illus. by Claire Henley)
  c PW - v244 - F 10 '97 - p85 [51-250]
Repertoire Des Etudes, Enquetes Et Seminaires Socio-Economiques Sur Le Benin 1988-1993
  r J Gov Info - v23 - S '96 - p656 [1-50]
Repetto, Robert - *Pesticides and the Immune System*
  BioSci - v46 - O '96 - p721+ [51-250]
Report of the American Workforce
  J Gov Info - v23 - S '96 - p551 [51-250]
Report of the Board of Banking Supervision Inquiry into the Circumstances of the Collapse of Barings
  J Gov Info - v23 - S '96 - p647 [51-250]
Report of the Commission Nationale Sur L'Avenir Du Quebec
  J Gov Info - v23 - S '96 - p638+ [51-250]
Report of the Efficiency Review Team, Correctional Services Division, Department of Justice
  J Gov Info - v23 - S '96 - p624+ [51-250]
Report of the Health Crisis Task Force
  J Gov Info - v23 - S '96 - p605 [51-250]
Report of the Joint Interim Study Committee on Violence Prevention
  J Gov Info - v23 - S '96 - p592 [51-250]
Report on Effects of Aircraft Overflights on the National Park System
  J Gov Info - v23 - S '96 - p549 [51-250]
Report on Object Analysis and Design 1994-1996. Electronic Media Version
  SciTech - v20 - N '96 - p8 [1-50]
Report on Public Consultation
  J Gov Info - v23 - S '96 - p619 [51-250]
Report to the Minister of Health (Urban Health Planning Partnership Committee, Canada)
  J Gov Info - v23 - S '96 - p629 [51-250]
Report to the Minister of Presidential Affairs and Public Administration on the General Election 1994 (Botswana)
  J Gov Info - v23 - S '96 - p656 [1-50]
Reps, John W - *Cities of the Mississippi*
  PHR - v65 - N '96 - p669+ [501+]

Repstad, Pal - *Religion and Modernity*
  R&R Bk N - v12 - F '97 - p9 [51-250]
Rescher, Nicholas - *Process Metaphysics*
  IPQ - v37 - Je '97 - p250+ [501+]
  R&R Bk N - v12 - F '97 - p4 [51-250]
Research Centre for Education and the Labour Market - *The Labour Market by Education and Occupation to 2000*
  JEL - v35 - Mr '97 - p238+ [51-250]
Research in Domestic and International Agribusiness Management. Vol. 12
  JEL - v34 - D '96 - p2129 [51-250]
Research in Experimental Economics. Vol. 6
  JEL - v35 - Mr '97 - p198 [51-250]
Research in Finance. 2nd Suppl.
  JEL - v34 - D '96 - p2053 [51-250]
Research in Finance. Vol. 13
  JEL - v34 - S '96 - p1435 [51-250]
Research in Organizational Behavior. Vol. 18
  JEL - v34 - S '96 - p1452+ [51-250]
Research in Personnel and Human Resources Management. Vol. 14
  JEL - v34 - D '96 - p2090 [51-250]
Research in the History of Economic Thought and Methodology. Vol.14
  JEL - v34 - D '96 - p2010 [51-250]
Research in the History of Economic Thought and Methodology: Archival Supplement 5
  JEL - v34 - S '96 - p1408 [51-250]
Research Services Directory 1995
  r ARBA - v28 - '97 - p85 [251-500]
Residual Stresses in Design, Fabrication, Assessment and Repair
  SciTech - v20 - N '96 - p83 [51-250]
Reskin, Barbara - *Women and Men at Work*
  SF - v75 - S '96 - p387+ [251-500]
Resnick, Mike - *The Widowmaker*
  y Kliatt - v30 - N '96 - p16 [51-250]
Resource Links
  p LJ - v122 - Ja '97 - p158 [51-250]
Resources for Elders with Disabilities. 3rd Ed.
  r ARBA - v28 - '97 - p306 [51-250]
Resources for People with Disabilities and Chronic Conditions. 3rd Ed.
  r ARBA - v28 - '97 - p306 [51-250]
Ressler, Robert K - *I Have Lived in the Monster*
  BL - v93 - My 1 '97 - p1466 [51-250]
Ressler, Sandy - *The Art of Electronic Publishing*
  BYTE - v22 - Mr '97 - p34 [51-250]
  CBR - v14 - N 14 '96 - p34 [51-250]
  SciTech - v21 - Mr '97 - p100 [51-250]
Restad, Penne L - *Christmas in America*
  AHR - v102 - F '97 - p161+ [501+]
  J Am St - v30 - D '96 - p488+ [251-500]
Restak, Richard - *Brainscapes: An Introduction to What Neuroscience Has Learned about the Structure, Function, and Abilities of the Brain*
  BWatch - v17 - N '96 - p3 [51-250]
  PW - v243 - S 9 '96 - p81 [1-50]
Retallack, Joan - *Afterimages*
  PS - v70 - Fall '96 - p175+ [501+]
  Musicage: Cage Muses on Words, Art, Music
  TLS - Ja 17 '97 - p9 [501+]
Rettenmund, Matthew - *Totally Awesome 80s*
  PW - v243 - O 7 '96 - p68 [51-250]
Rettie, Dwight F - *Our National Park System*
  Pub Hist - v18 - Sum '96 - p80+ [501+]
Reuben, Julie A - *The Making of the Modern University*
  Choice - v34 - Mr '97 - p1213 [51-250]
  JEL - v35 - Mr '97 - p264 [51-250]
Reuben, Shelly - *Spent Matches*
  Arm Det - v29 - Fall '96 - p485 [251-500]
  NYTBR - v101 - Jl 21 '96 - p25 [51-250]
Reuscher, Jay - *A Concordance to the Critique of Pure Reason*
  r R&R Bk N - v11 - D '96 - p2 [51-250]
Reuter, Bjarne - *The Boys from St. Petri*
  c RT - v50 - F '97 - p424 [51-250]
Revel, Jacques - *Histories: French Constructions of the Past*
  TranslRevS - v2 - D '96 - p2+ [51-250]
Reviere, Susan L - *Memory of Childhood Trauma*
  Readings - v12 - Mr '97 - p25+ [51-250]
Review of Colombia's Agriculture and Rural Development Strategy
  JEL - v34 - D '96 - p2135 [51-250]
Review of Derivatives Research
  p JEL - v35 - Mr '97 - p310 [51-250]
Review of Progress in Quantitative Nondestructive Evaluation. Vol. 15, Pts. A-B
  SciTech - v20 - S '96 - p49 [51-250]

Review of Psychiatry. Vol. 15
SciTech - v20 - S '96 - p32 [51-250]
Review of Urban and Regional Development Studies
p JEL - v35 - Mr '97 - p310 [51-250]
Reviews in Computational Chemistry. Vol. 8
SciTech - v20 - N '96 - p21 [51-250]
Revill, Don - *Working Papers on Disaster Management*
LAR - v98 - Mr '96 - p162 [51-250]
LR - v45 - 5 '96 - p67+ [501+]
Revista De La Facultad De Ciencias Economicas
p JEL - v34 - D '96 - p2144 [51-250]
Revoyr, Nina - *The Necessary Hunger*
KR - v64 - D 1 '96 - p1698 [251-500]
LJ - v121 - D '96 - p147 [51-250]
PW - v244 - Ja 13 '97 - p55 [51-250]
Time - v149 - My 5 '97 - p101+ [501+]
Trib Bks - Mr 2 '97 - p6+ [501+]
Rewald, John - *Cezanne: A Biography. Rev. Ed.*
Art J - v55 - Win '96 - p95+ [501+]
The Paintings of Paul Cezanne. Vols. 1-2
r PW - v244 - Ja 13 '97 - p68 [51-250]
r WSJ-Cent - v99 - F 10 '97 - pA16 [501+]
Rex, John - *Ethnic Minorities in the Modern Nation State*
Choice - v34 - N '96 - p536 [51-250]
Rey, Margret - *Spotty (Illus. by H A Rey)*
c PW - v244 - Mr 31 '97 - p77 [1-50]
Rey, Roselyne - *The History of Pain*
Rel St Rev - v23 - Ja '97 - p42 [51-250]
Reybold, Laura - *Everything You Need to Know about the Dangers of Tatooing and Body Piercing*
y BL - v93 - Ap 1 '97 - p1308 [1-50]
Reyes, A T - *Archaic Cyprus*
AJA - v100 - Jl '96 - p617+ [501+]
Reyes, Alina - *Le Chien Qui Voulait Me Manger*
WLT - v70 - Aut '96 - p916 [501+]
Rey-Henningsen, Marisa - *The World of the Ploughwoman*
Folkl - v107 - '96 - p119 [501+]
Reymond, Lizelle - *To Live Within*
Parabola - v21 - Ag '96 - p102+ [501+]
Reynolds, Albert B - *Bluebells and Nuclear Energy*
SciTech - v20 - D '96 - p80 [1-50]
Reynolds, Barry - *Beyond Trout*
AB - v97 - Je 17 '96 - p2412 [51-250]
Reynolds, Blair - *The Relationship of Calvin to Process Theology as Seen through His Sermons*
Six Ct J - v27 - Fall '96 - p881+ [501+]
Reynolds, Brad - *The Story Knife*
BW - v27 - Ja 19 '97 - p12 [51-250]
y Kliatt - v31 - Mr '97 - p12+ [51-250]
Reynolds, Christopher A - *Papal Patronage and the Music of St. Peter's 1380-1513*
Notes - v53 - D '96 - p450+ [501+]
Six Ct J - v27 - Fall '96 - p938+ [501+]
Reynolds, David - *Allies at War*
EHR - v112 - F '97 - p266 [501+]
The Origins of the Cold War in Europe
EHR - v111 - S '96 - p1032+ [251-500]
Rich Relations
AHR - v101 - O '96 - p1306+ [501+]
Books - v10 - Je '96 - p21 [1-50]
Comw - v123 - D 6 '96 - p28+ [51-250]
J Am St - v30 - Ap '96 - p141+ [251-500]
Reynolds, David S - *Walt Whitman's America*
AHR - v102 - F '97 - p186+ [501+]
y Kliatt - v30 - S '96 - p27 [251-500]
Reynolds, Dee - *Symbolist Aesthetics and Early Abstract Art*
BM - v138 - S '96 - p615 [251-500]
MLR - v92 - Ap '97 - p475+ [251-500]
Reynolds, Dwight Fletcher - *Heroic Poets, Poetic Heroes*
WestFolk - v55 - Sum '96 - p250+ [501+]
Reynolds, Frank E - *Religion and Practical Reason*
JR - v77 - Ja '97 - p115+ [501+]
Reynolds, G W M - *The Mysteries of London*
TLS - Ag 30 '96 - p32 [251-500]
Reynolds, Graham - *The Early Paintings and Drawings of John Constable. Vols. 1-2*
Apo - v144 - D '96 - p69 [501+]
Choice - v34 - F '97 - p957 [51-250]
LJ - v121 - N 1 '96 - p66 [51-250]
NYTBR - v101 - D 8 '96 - p22 [51-250]
TLS - N 8 '96 - p16+ [501+]
Reynolds, Guy - *Willa Cather in Context*
Choice - v34 - O '96 - p280 [51-250]
Legacy - v14 - 1 '97 - p74 [51-250]
Reynolds, Henry - *Aboriginal Sovereignty*
Aust Bk R - O '96 - p16+ [501+]

Reynolds, John - *Andre Citroen: The Henry Ford of France*
BL - v93 - D 15 '96 - p699 [51-250]
KR - v64 - D 1 '96 - p1724 [251-500]
PW - v243 - N 18 '96 - p56 [51-250]
Reynolds, Lloyd George - *Trade Union Publications. Vols. 1-3*
r RQ - v36 - Fall '96 - p52+ [51-250]
Reynolds, Malvina - *Morningtown Ride (Illus. by Michael Leeman)*
c HB Guide - v8 - Spr '97 - p141 [1-50]
Reynolds, Marilyn - *But What about Me?*
y Cur R - v36 - Ja '97 - p13 [51-250]
y HB Guide - v8 - Spr '97 - p83 [51-250]
y LATBR - Ag 11 '96 - p11 [51-250]
y SLJ - v42 - O '96 - p148 [51-250]
y VOYA - v19 - F '97 - p332 [251-500]
Telling
y BL - v93 - Ap 1 '97 - p1310 [1-50]
y HB Guide - v7 - Fall '96 - p304 [51-250]
Reynolds, Marilynn - *Belle's Journey (Illus. by Stephen McCallum)*
c Can CL - v22 - Fall '96 - p132+ [501+]
Reynolds, Marion Lavender - *Hardin County, Illinois Deaths 1884-1919 and Notes from the Pleasant Hill Church Register*
EGH - v50 - N '96 - p166 [51-250]
Reynolds, Michael - *Hemingway: The 1930s*
BL - v93 - My 15 '97 - p1557 [51-250]
KR - v65 - Ap 1 '97 - p531+ [251-500]
LJ - v122 - Ap 15 '97 - p82 [51-250]
PW - v244 - Ap 14 '97 - p62 [51-250]
Reynolds, Noel B - *Three Discourses*
Sev Cent N - v54 - Fall '96 - p61+ [501+]
Reynolds, Pamela - *Traditional Healers and Childhood in Zimbabwe*
JTWS - v13 - Fall '96 - p280+ [501+]
Reynolds, Phillip L - *Marriage in the Western Church*
Rel St Rev - v23 - Ja '97 - p80 [51-250]
Reynolds, Richard - *Super Heroes*
JPC - v30 - Fall '96 - p221+ [51-250]
Reynolds, Roger E - *Law and Liturgy in the Latin Church 5th-12th Centuries*
CHR - v82 - O '96 - p686+ [251-500]
Reynolds, Sheri - *The Rapture of Canaan*
y Kliatt - v31 - Mr '97 - p14 [51-250]
Reynolds, Simon - *The Sex Revolts*
Notes - v53 - Mr '97 - p776+ [501+]
Reynolds, Susan - *Fiefs and Vassals*
JIH - v27 - Spr '97 - p655+ [501+]
Specu - v71 - O '96 - p998+ [501+]
Reynolds, Verne - *The Horn Handbook*
Choice - v34 - Ap '97 - p1349 [51-250]
Reynolds-Cornell, Regine - *International Colloquium Celebrating the 500th Anniversary of the Birth of Marguerite De Navarre*
FR - v70 - Mr '97 - p595+ [501+]
Six Ct J - v27 - Fall '96 - p929+ [501+]
Rey Rosa, Rodrigo - *El Aqua Quieta*
BL - v93 - S 15 '96 - p227 [1-50]
Dust on Her Tongue
TranslRevS - v1 - My '95 - p6 [1-50]
Rezac, Jan - *Ruze Pro Josefa Sudka 1896-1976*
BM - v139 - Ja '97 - p50+ [501+]
Rezendes, Paul - *Wetlands: The Web of Life*
y BL - v93 - N 15 '96 - p558 [51-250]
y BL - v93 - D 1 '96 - p664 [1-50]
BWatch - v17 - N '96 - p7 [51-250]
y Kliatt - v31 - Ja '97 - p29 [251-500]
LJ - v121 - N 15 '96 - p86 [51-250]
Rezits, Joseph - *Beloved Tyranna*
Am MT - v46 - F '97 - p66+ [501+]
Reznik, Semyon - *The Nazification of Russia*
LJ - v121 - O 1 '96 - p106 [51-250]
Rezun, Miron - *Science, Technology, and Ecopolitics in the USSR*
JEL - v34 - S '96 - p1485 [51-250]
Rezvani - *Doubles Stances Des Amants*
WLT - v70 - Sum '96 - p656+ [501+]
L'Enigme
WLT - v70 - Sum '96 - p652 [501+]
Rgyal-Sras Thogs-Med-Dpal Bzacn-Po-Dpal - *The Thirty Seven Practices of Bodhisattvas*
LJ - v122 - Ap 1 '97 - p99 [51-250]
PW - v244 - Mr 24 '97 - p74 [51-250]
Rheims, Maurice - *Les Forets D'Argent*
WLT - v70 - Sum '96 - p653+ [501+]
Rheingold, Howard - *The Virtual Community*
QJS - v83 - My '97 - p230+ [501+]

Rheingrover, Jean Sasso - *Veronica's First Year (Illus. by Kay Life)*
c CBRS - v25 - F '97 - p78 [1-50]
c CCB-B - v50 - D '96 - p150 [51-250]
c HB Guide - v8 - Spr '97 - p84 [51-250]
c SLJ - v42 - O '96 - p104 [51-250]
Rhines, Jesse Algeron - *Black Film, White Money*
Choice - v34 - D '96 - p623 [51-250]
Rhinesmith, Stephen H - *A Manager's Guide to Globalization. 2nd Ed*
Choice - v34 - N '96 - p504 [51-250]
Rhoades, Dennis K - *The Legacy of Vietnam Veterans and Their Families*
J Gov Info - v23 - S '96 - p550+ [1-50]
Rhoads, Robert A - *Democracy, Multiculturalism, and the Community College*
Choice - v34 - F '97 - p1013+ [51-250]
Rhode Island Jobs Outlook to 2000
r J Gov Info - v23 - S '96 - p593+ [51-250]
Rhodes, Ann - *Take Care*
Quill & Q - v63 - F '97 - p46 [501+]
Rhodes, Carolyn - *Building a European Polity?*
APSR - v91 - Mr '97 - p242+ [501+]
Rhodes, Christine P - *The Encyclopedia of Beer*
r LJ - v122 - Ap 1 '97 - p63 [1-50]
Rhodes, Dennis E - *Bookbindings and Other Bibliophily*
Lib - v18 - Je '96 - p162+ [501+]
Rhodes, Frank H T - *Geology*
DW - v26 - D 8 '96 - p4 [51-250]
Rhodes, Gary Don - *Lugosi: His Life in Films, on Stage, and in the Hearts of Horror Lovers*
LJ - v122 - Mr 15 '97 - p65 [51-250]
Rhodes, Ginger - *Trying to Get Some Dignity*
KR - v64 - S 1 '96 - p1306+ [251-500]
LJ - v121 - O 15 '96 - p78+ [51-250]
PW - v243 - S 9 '96 - p71+ [501+]
Rhodes, Martha - *At the Gate*
VQR - v72 - Aut '96 - p135* [51-250]
Rhodes, Martin - *The Regions and the New Europe*
GJ - v162 - N '96 - p335 [251-500]
JEL - v34 - S '96 - p1500+ [51-250]
Rhodes, Olin E - *Population Dynamics in Ecological Space and Time*
Choice - v34 - D '96 - p636 [51-250]
SciTech - v20 - S '96 - p18 [51-250]
Rhodes, Richard - *Dark Sun*
AAPSS-A - v547 - S '96 - p175+ [251-500]
Am Sci - v84 - S '96 - p507+ [501+]
Arm F&S - v23 - Win '96 - p301+ [251-500]
Historian - v58 - Sum '96 - p870+ [251-500]
NYTBR - v101 - S 1 '96 - p24 [1-50]
Dark Sun (Adams). Pts. 1-2. Audio Version
LJ - v121 - D '96 - p171 [51-250]
Deadly Feasts
BL - v93 - F 15 '97 - p970 [51-250]
Bus W - Mr 31 '97 - p19 [501+]
BW - v27 - Mr 23 '97 - p3 [501+]
KR - v65 - F 15 '97 - p283 [251-500]
LJ - v122 - Mr 15 '97 - p86 [51-250]
Nature - v386 - Ap 10 '97 - p565 [501+]
NY - v73 - Ap 14 '97 - p82+ [501+]
NYTBR - v102 - Mr 16 '97 - p9 [501+]
PW - v244 - F 10 '97 - p75 [51-250]
Trib Bks - My 18 '97 - p5 [501+]
WSJ-Cent - v99 - Mr 14 '97 - pA11 [501+]
How to Write
r Bloom Rev - v17 - Ja '97 - p15 [51-250]
Rhodes, Robin Francis - *Architecture and Meaning on the Athenian Acropolis*
AJA - v100 - Jl '96 - p601+ [501+]
Rel St Rev - v22 - O '96 - p345+ [51-250]
Rhodes, Royal W - *The Lion and the Cross*
VS - v39 - Spr '96 - p459+ [501+]
Rhodes, Tim - *AIDS, Drugs and Prevention*
Choice - v34 - F '97 - p995 [51-250]
Rhody, Kurt - *Rendezvous: Reliving the Fur Trade Era of 1825-1840*
LATBR - S 8 '96 - p11 [51-250]
Rhyne, George N - *The Supplement to The Modern Encyclopedia of Russian, Soviet, and Eurasian History. Vol. 1*
r ARBA - v28 - '97 - p215+ [51-250]
Rhys, Jean - *After Leaving, Mr. MacKenzie*
Trib Bks - Ap 6 '97 - p8 [1-50]
Quartet
Trib Bks - Ap 6 '97 - p8 [1-50]
Ri Ben Te Wu Zai Zhong Guo
BL - v93 - My 1 '97 - p1484 [1-50]

Riahi-Belkaoui, Ahmed - *Accounting, a Multiparadigmatic Science*
    Choice - v34 - Ja '97 - p842 [51-250]
    JEL - v35 - Mr '97 - p256+ [51-250]
    R&R Bk N - v11 - D '96 - p35 [51-250]
Multinationality and Firm Performance
    R&R Bk N - v12 - F '97 - p40 [1-50]
Rian, Edwin H - *The Presbyterian Conflict*
    CH - v65 - D '96 - p771+ [501+]
Ribas, Teresa - *Miremos Donde Voy*
    c BL - v93 - F 15 '97 - p1033 [1-50]
Miremos El Campo
    c BL - v93 - F 15 '97 - p1033 [1-50]
Miremos El Fin De Semana
    c BL - v93 - F 15 '97 - p1033 [1-50]
Miremos El Hipermercado
    c BL - v93 - F 15 '97 - p1033 [1-50]
Miremos La Casa
    c BL - v93 - F 15 '97 - p1033 [1-50]
Miremos La Ciudad
    c BL - v93 - F 15 '97 - p1033 [1-50]
Miremos La Fiesta
    c BL - v93 - F 15 '97 - p1033 [1-50]
Miremos Las Tiendas
    c BL - v93 - F 15 '97 - p1033 [1-50]
Ribeiro, Aileen - *The Art of Dress*
    Albion - v28 - Fall '96 - p498+ [501+]
    Eight-C St - v29 - Sum '96 - p438+ [501+]
    SDA - v4 - Spr '97 - p116+ [501+]
    TCI - v31 - F '97 - p54+ [501+]
    W&M Q - v54 - Ap '97 - p430+ [501+]
Ribowsky, Mark - *The Power and the Darkness*
    y BL - v93 - Ja '97 - p763 [1-50]
    BW - v26 - Jl 7 '96 - p1+ [501+]
    Choice - v34 - D '96 - p650 [51-250]
Ricapito, Joseph V - *Cervante's Novelas Ejemplares*
    Choice - v34 - D '96 - p620 [51-250]
Ricard, Matthieu - *Journey to Enlightenment*
    LJ - v122 - F 15 '97 - p132 [51-250]
    Tric - v6 - Win '96 - p117 [1-50]
Riccards, Michael P - *The Ferocious Engine of Democracy. Vols. 1-2*
    Historian - v59 - Win '97 - p441+ [501+]
Ricchiardi, Sherry - *Bosnia: The Struggle for Peace*
    c HB Guide - v7 - Fall '96 - p381 [51-250]
Ricchiuto, Steven R - *The Rate Reference Guide to the U.S. Treasury Market 1984-1995*
    r ARBA - v28 - '97 - p91+ [251-500]
Ricci, Carla - *Mary Magdalene and Many Others*
    Intpr - v50 - O '96 - p430+ [251-500]
Riccio, Barry D - *Walter Lippmann--Odyssey of a Liberal*
    JEL - v34 - S '96 - p1503 [51-250]
Ricciuti, Edward R - *Chaparral*
    c Ch BWatch - v6 - My '96 - p6 [51-250]
    c HB Guide - v7 - Fall '96 - p336 [51-250]
Desert
    c Ch BWatch - v6 - My '96 - p6 [51-250]
    c HB Guide - v7 - Fall '96 - p336 [51-250]
Grassland
    c Ch BWatch - v6 - My '96 - p6 [51-250]
    c HB Guide - v7 - Fall '96 - p336 [51-250]
Ocean
    c HB Guide - v7 - Fall '96 - p336 [51-250]
Rainforest
    c HB Guide - v7 - Fall '96 - p336 [51-250]
What on Earth Is a Hyrax?
    c Cur R - v36 - N '96 - p12 [51-250]
    c HB Guide - v8 - Spr '97 - p128 [51-250]
    c KR - v64 - N 15 '96 - p1673+ [51-250]
What on Earth Is a Pout?
    c HB Guide - v8 - Spr '97 - p124 [1-50]
    c SLJ - v43 - F '97 - p96 [51-250]
Wildlife Special Agent (Illus. by Stephen Carpenteri)
    c HB Guide - v8 - Spr '97 - p91 [51-250]
    c KR - v64 - N 15 '96 - p1674 [51-250]
    c SLJ - v43 - F '97 - p96+ [51-250]
Rice, Anne - *Interview with the Vampire*
    LJ - v122 - Ap 15 '97 - p125 [51-250]
    Trib Bks - Ap 27 '97 - p8 [1-50]
Memnoch the Devil
    NYTBR - v101 - S 15 '96 - p44 [51-250]
Servant of the Bones
    CSM - v88 - S 19 '96 - p14 [51-250]
    Ent W - D 27 '96 - p143 [51-250]
    KR - v64 - My 1 '96 - p631 [251-500]
    Necro - Win '97 - p11+ [501+]
    Rapport - v19 - 6 '96 - p22 [251-500]
Servant of the Bones (Cumpsty). Audio Version
    LJ - v121 - O 15 '96 - p102 [51-250]

Servant of the Bones (Prichard). Audio Version
    BWatch - v18 - Mr '97 - p6 [1-50]
    LJ - v122 - F 1 '97 - p127 [51-250]
Rice, Bebe Faas - *The Jungle*
    c Ch BWatch - v6 - Jl '96 - p5 [1-50]
The Vampire
    c Ch BWatch - v6 - My '96 - p7 [1-50]
Rice, Charles Owen - *Fighter with a Heart*
    Comw - v124 - D 14 '97 - p22 [251-500]
    OS - v33 - Mr '97 - p35 [51-250]
Rice, Chris - *Family History*
    c LATBR - v263 - S 29 '96 - p15 [51-250]
Rice, Earle - *The Attack on Pearl Harbor*
    y HB Guide - v8 - Spr '97 - p168 [51-250]
    y SLJ - v43 - F '97 - p123 [51-250]
The Battle of Belleau Wood
    y HB Guide - v7 - Fall '96 - p381 [51-250]
The Battle of Midway
    y HB Guide - v7 - Fall '96 - p381 [51-250]
The Nuremberg Trials
    y BL - v93 - Mr 15 '97 - p1235 [51-250]
    y SLJ - v43 - Mr '97 - p207 [51-250]
Rice, Eve - *Swim! (Illus. by Marisabina Russo)*
    c BL - v92 - Ag '96 - p1908 [51-250]
    c CCB-B - v50 - S '96 - p26 [51-250]
    c HB Guide - v8 - Spr '97 - p44 [51-250]
    c SLJ - v42 - S '96 - p189 [51-250]
Rice, F Philip - *Child and Adolescent Development*
    R&R Bk N - v12 - F '97 - p7 [1-50]
Rice, Graham - *The Gardener's Guide to Perennials*
    TES - Ag 23 '96 - p22 [51-250]
Hardy Perennials
    Hort - v74 - D '96 - p56 [251-500]
Planting Planner
    TES - Ag 23 '96 - p22 [1-50]
The Reader's Digest Complete Book of Perennials
    r Hort - v94 - Mr '97 - p80 [251-500]
Rice, James - *The Ghost of Pont Diable (Illus. by James Rice)*
    c HB Guide - v8 - Spr '97 - p74 [51-250]
    c SLJ - v43 - Mr '97 - p191 [51-250]
Trail Drive (Illus. by James Rice)
    c HB Guide - v8 - Spr '97 - p44 [1-50]
    c Roundup M - v4 - Ap '97 - p29 [1-50]
Rice, Jerry - *Rice (St. Martin's Press)*
    CSM - v89 - D 5 '96 - pB4 [51-250]
Rice, John Steadman - *A Disease of One's Own*
    Choice - v34 - S '96 - p216 [51-250]
    Readings - v11 - S '96 - p29 [51-250]
Rice, Luanne - *Home Fires (Reading). Audio Version*
    y Kliatt - v31 - Ja '97 - p41 [1-50]
Rice, Michael - *The Archaeology of the Arabian Gulf c.5000-323 B.C.*
    AJA - v100 - Jl '96 - p634+ [501+]
Rice, Scott - *Dark and Stormy Rides Again*
    LATBR - Ag 25 '96 - p11 [51-250]
Rice, Stanley D - *Proceedings of the Exxon Valdez Oil Spill Symposium*
    Sci - v274 - N 22 '96 - p1321 [1-50]
Rice, Tamara Talbot - *Tamara: Memoirs of St. Petersburg, Paris, Oxford and Byzantium*
    CR - v269 - N '96 - p280 [51-250]
    LJ - v122 - Mr 15 '97 - p70 [251-500]
    TLS - Jl 7 '96 - p28 [501+]
Rice, William - *Steak Lover's Cookbook*
    BL - v93 - Ja '97 - p801 [51-250]
    LJ - v122 - F 15 '97 - p158 [51-250]
    NYTBR - v101 - D 8 '96 - p71 [51-250]
    PW - v243 - D 2 '96 - p57 [51-250]
Ricerche E Studi - *International Financial Aggregates*
    r JEL - v35 - Mr '97 - p250 [51-250]
Rich, Adrienne - *Adrienne Rich: Selected Poems 1950-1995*
    ILS - v16 - Spr '97 - p35 [51-250]
Dark Fields of the Republic
    Nat - v263 - Ag 26 '96 - p25+ [501+]
    TLS - Ja 3 '97 - p27 [501+]
    WLT - v70 - Sum '96 - p697 [501+]
Diving into the Wreck
    LJ - v122 - Ap 1 '97 - p95 [1-50]
The Facts of a Doorframe
    LJ - v122 - Ap 1 '97 - p95 [1-50]
Rich, Alan - *American Pioneers*
    M Ed J - v83 - N '96 - p54 [1-50]
    TLS - Jl 7 '96 - p19 [501+]
Rich, Bruce - *Mortgaging the Earth*
    CS - v26 - Mr '97 - p185+ [501+]
    TLS - S 6 '96 - p27 [501+]
Rich, Carole - *Writing and Reporting News. 2nd Ed.*
    R&R Bk N - v11 - N '96 - p68 [51-250]

Rich, Chris - *Stained Glass Basics*
    LJ - v122 - F 15 '97 - p134 [51-250]
Rich, Diane Wiatt - *Old and Homeless--Double-Jeopardy*
    Soc Ser R - v71 - Mr '97 - p167 [1-50]
Rich, Doris L - *Amelia Earhart: A Biography*
    NYTBR - v102 - Mr 23 '97 - p28 [51-250]
Rich, Elizabeth H - *National Guide to Funding for Community Development*
    r ARBA - v28 - '97 - p316+ [251-500]
National Guide to Funding for the Environment and Animal Welfare. 3rd Ed.
    r Workbook - v21 - Win '96 - p177+ [251-500]
Rich, Joe - *Hartnett: Portrait of a Technocratic Brigand*
    Aust Bk R - D '96 - p19+ [501+]
Rich, John, 1944- - *War and Society in the Greek World*
    J Mil H - v60 - O '96 - p763+ [501+]
War and Society in the Roman World
    J Mil H - v60 - O '96 - p763+ [501+]
Rich, John Martin - *Theories of Moral Development. 2nd Ed.*
    Ethics - v107 - O '96 - p195+ [251-500]
Rich, Paul B - *State Power and Black Politics in South Africa 1912-51*
    HRNB - v25 - Win '97 - p84 [251-500]
Rich, Robert F - *Health Policy, Federalism, and the American States*
    Choice - v34 - My '97 - p1533 [51-250]
Rich, Wilbur C - *Black Mayors and School Politics*
    Choice - v34 - N '96 - p511+ [51-250]
The Politics of Minority Coalitions
    Choice - v34 - My '97 - p1578 [51-250]
Richan, Willard C - *Lobbying for Social Change. 2nd Ed.*
    Choice - v34 - O '96 - p363 [51-250]
Richard, Carl J - *The Founders and the Classics*
    QJS - v83 - F '97 - p125+ [501+]
Richard, Earl - *First and Second Thessalonians*
    BTB - v26 - Win '96 - p173+ [501+]
    Rel St Rev - v23 - Ap '97 - p186 [51-250]
Richard, Pablo - *Apocalypse*
    Am - v176 - Mr 8 '97 - p29+ [51-250]
Richard, Yann - *Shiite Islam*
    Theol St - v57 - D '96 - p773+ [501+]
Richards, Alan - *A Political Economy of the Middle East. 2nd Ed.*
    Choice - v34 - Mr '97 - p1210 [51-250]
    MEJ - v51 - Win '97 - p152 [51-250]
Richards, Barry - *Disciplines of Delight*
    JPC - v30 - Fall '96 - p222+ [501+]
Richards, Ben - *Throwing the House out of the Window*
    Obs - O 20 '96 - p18* [51-250]
Richards, Brooks - *Secret Flotillas*
    CR - v268 - Je '96 - p332+ [251-500]
    J Mil H - v61 - Ja '97 - p189+ [501+]
Richards, Chris - *Christianity. Pt. 1*
    TES - D 6 '96 - pR7 [501+]
Sikhism
    TES - D 6 '96 - pR7 [501+]
Richards, David, 1953- - *Masks of Difference*
    TLS - N 29 '96 - p16 [1-50]
Richards, David Adams - *Hockey Dreams*
    CF - v75 - D '96 - p37+ [501+]
    Mac - v109 - D 9 '96 - p64 [1-50]
    Mac - v109 - D 16 '96 - p71 [51-250]
    Quill & Q - v62 - N '96 - p39 [251-500]
Hope in the Desperate Hour
    Quill & Q - v62 - My '96 - p27 [501+]
Richards, David G - *Exploring the Divided Self*
    Choice - v34 - D '96 - p619 [51-250]
    R&R Bk N - v11 - N '96 - p75 [51-250]
Richards, Denis - *The Hardest Victory*
    Historian - v59 - Win '97 - p475+ [251-500]
Richards, Elizabeth - *Every Day*
    KR - v65 - F 1 '97 - p165+ [251-500]
    LJ - v122 - Mr 15 '97 - p91+ [251-500]
    PW - v244 - Ja 20 '97 - p390 [251-500]
Every Day (Hurt). Audio Version
    PW - v244 - Ap 7 '97 - p33+ [51-250]
Richards, Glyn - *Studies in Religion*
    Rel St - v32 - S '96 - p427+ [51-250]
Richards, James D - *Richards/Cox and Barbee*
    r EGH - v50 - N '96 - p195 [51-250]
Richards, Jo-Anne - *The Innocence of Roast Chicken*
    Obs - D 22 '96 - p17* [51-250]
Richards, Mary Haskin Parker - *Winter Quarters*
    Choice - v34 - D '96 - p680 [51-250]
    WHQ - v28 - Spr '97 - p103 [1-50]
Richards, Nancy Wilcox - *Farmer Joe Baby-Sits (Illus. by Werner Zimmerman)*
    c Quill & Q - v63 - Mr '97 - p77 [251-500]
Richards, Paul - *Fighting for the Rainforest*
    Lon R Bks - v19 - Mr 6 '97 - p20+ [501+]

Richards, Sandra L - *Ancient Songs Set Ablaze*
  Choice - v34 - F '97 - p961+ [51-250]
  Theat J - v49 - Mr '97 - p87+ [501+]
Richards, Tad - *The New Country Music Encyclopedia*
  r LJ - v121 - N 1 '96 - p41 [1-50]
Richards, Thomas, 1956- - *Zero Tolerance*
  BL - v93 - D 1 '96 - p642 [51-250]
  BW - v27 - Ja 5 '97 - p11+ [501+]
  KR - v64 - O 15 '96 - p1490 [251-500]
  LJ - v122 - Ja '97 - p150 [51-250]
  NYTBR - v102 - F 16 '97 - p18 [51-250]
  PW - v243 - N 11 '96 - p56 [51-250]
Richards, Thomas, 1962- - *At Work with Grotowski on Physical Actions*
  Theat J - v48 - D '96 - p521+ [501+]
Richards, Tim - *Letters to Francesca*
  Aust Bk R - Jl '96 - p46+ [501+]
Richardson, Alan - *Literature, Education, and Romanticism*
  Nine-C Lit - v50 - Mr '96 - p531+ [501+]
  RES - v48 - F '97 - p117+ [501+]
Richardson, Bill - *Bachelor Brothers' Bed and Breakfast*
  Bloom Rev - v16 - Jl '96 - p27 [501+]
  HG&LRev - v3 - Fall '96 - p50 [51-250]
Richardson, Brian - *Print Culture in Renaissance Italy*
  MP - v94 - N '96 - p218+ [501+]
  Ren Q - v49 - Win '96 - p857+ [501+]
Richardson, David A - *Sixteenth-Century British Nondramatic Writers: Third Series*
  r ARBA - v28 - '97 - p449+ [51-250]
Richardson, Dick - *Decisions and Diplomacy*
  EHR - v112 - Ap '97 - p530+ [501+]
Richardson, Doug, 1959- - *Dark Horse*
  BL - v93 - D 15 '96 - p693 [51-250]
  KR - v64 - D 1 '96 - p1698+ [251-500]
  LJ - v122 - Ja '97 - p150 [51-250]
  PW - v244 - Ja 13 '97 - p54+ [51-250]
Richardson, Douglas - *A Not Unsightly Building*
  Archiv - Fall '94 - p196+ [501+]
Richardson, Duncan - *Aim at Morning*
  Aust Bk R - S '96 - p53+ [501+]
Richardson, Elliot - *Reflections of a Radical Moderate*
  KR - v64 - My 1 '96 - p672 [251-500]
  Parameters - v27 - Spr '97 - p181+ [501+]
Richardson, Henry S - *Practical Reasoning about Final Ends*
  Ethics - v107 - O '96 - p143+ [501+]
Richardson, Ian - *Science Now!*
  TES - Ja 3 '97 - pR15 [251-500]
Richardson, J L - *Crisis Diplomacy*
  AHR - v101 - O '96 - p1186 [501+]
  JIH - v27 - Aut '96 - p293+ [501+]
Richardson, J S - *The Romans in Spain*
  Choice - v34 - F '97 - p1018 [51-250]
  TLS - F 14 '97 - p8 [501+]
Richardson, James, 1953- - *Willie Brown: A Biography*
  KR - v64 - S 15 '96 - p1384 [251-500]
  LATBR - N 3 '96 - p7+ [501+]
  LJ - v121 - N 1 '96 - p86 [1-50]
  LJ - v121 - N 15 '96 - p75 [51-250]
  Nat - v263 - N 25 '96 - p29+ [501+]
  NL - v80 - F 24 '97 - p16+ [501+]
Richardson, Jean - *Four Little Swans and a Prince (Illus. by Amanda Harvey)*
  c JB - v60 - D '96 - p259 [51-250]
  c Sch Lib - v45 - F '97 - p24 [51-250]
Richardson, John - *Old Growler's Last Match*
  c JB - v60 - O '96 - p187 [51-250]
  Ten Bears Go Marching
  c Ch BWatch - v6 - N '96 - p4 [1-50]

Richardson, John, 1924- - *A Life of Picasso. Vol. 2*
  Apo - v144 - D '96 - p13 [51-250]
  BW - v26 - D 22 '96 - p5 [501+]
  Econ - v342 - F 8 '97 - p91+ [501+]
  KR - v64 - S 15 '96 - p1385 [251-500]
  LJ - v122 - Ja '97 - p50 [51-250]
  LJ - v121 - O 15 '96 - p55 [51-250]
  Lon R Bks - v19 - Mr 6 '97 - p3+ [501+]
  NS - v125 - N 15 '96 - p45+ [501+]
  NYRB - v44 - F 6 '97 - p18+ [501+]
  NYTBR - v101 - N 17 '96 - p9+ [501+]
  NYTBR - v101 - D 8 '96 - p88 [1-50]
  NYTLa - v146 - N 8 '96 - pC31 [501+]
  Obs - D 1 '96 - p15* [501+]
  Obs - D 1 '96 - p16* [1-50]
  PW - v243 - S 16 '96 - p59 [51-250]
  PW - v243 - N 4 '96 - p46 [51-250]
  Spec - v277 - N 9 '96 - p52+ [501+]
  Spec - v277 - N 23 '96 - p44 [1-50]
  Time - v148 - D 2 '96 - p85 [501+]
  Time - v148 - D 23 '96 - p86 [51-250]
  TLS - N 8 '96 - p11+ [501+]
  WSJ-MW - v78 - N 13 '96 - pA20 [501+]
Richardson, John, 1951- - *Nietzsche's System*
  RM - v50 - D '96 - p420+ [501+]
Richardson, John H - *The Vipers' Club*
  LATBR - Ag 4 '96 - p10 [51-250]
  NY - v72 - D 23 '96 - p146 [51-250]
  Rapport - v19 - 6 '96 - p20 [251-500]
Richardson, John T E - *Working Memory and Human Cognition*
  Choice - v34 - F '97 - p1041 [51-250]
Richardson, John V, Jr. - *Knowledge-Based Systems for General Reference Work*
  LRTS - v40 - O '96 - p383+ [501+]
Richardson, Joy - *Looking at Pictures*
  c Books - v11 - Ap '97 - p24 [51-250]
  c TES - Mr 21 '97 - p10* [501+]
  Looking at Pictures (Illus. by Charlotte Voake)
  c KR - v65 - Ap 1 '97 - p560 [51-250]
  c PW - v244 - Mr 17 '97 - p85 [51-250]
Richardson, Judith Benet - *First Came the Owl*
  c CLW - v67 - D '96 - p57 [51-250]
  c HB - v72 - S '96 - p599 [51-250]
  c HB Guide - v8 - Spr '97 - p74 [51-250]
  y VOYA - v19 - O '96 - p212+ [251-500]
  Old Winter (Illus. by R W Alley)
  c BL - v93 - O 1 '96 - p359 [51-250]
  c CBRS - v25 - Ja '97 - p52 [51-250]
  c CCB-B - v50 - D '96 - p150 [51-250]
  c HB Guide - v8 - Spr '97 - p44 [51-250]
  c Par - v72 - F '97 - p149 [51-250]
  c SLJ - v42 - D '96 - p104 [51-250]
Richardson, Mary Ann - *Use of Neuroleptics in Children*
  Readings - v11 - S '96 - p25 [51-250]
Richardson, Peter, 1935- - *Herod: King of the Jews and Friend of the Romans*
  AB - v99 - Mr 24 '97 - p968 [501+]
  BL - v93 - N 15 '96 - p569 [51-250]
  CC - v114 - F 26 '97 - p229+ [251-500]
Richardson, Peter Tufts - *Four Spiritualities, Expressions of Self, Expressions of Spirit*
  BL - v93 - S 1 '96 - p40 [51-250]
Richardson, R C - *British Economic and Social History. 3rd Ed.*
  r ARBA - v28 - '97 - p202+ [51-250]
  r Choice - v34 - S '96 - p106 [51-250]
Richardson, Robert D - *Emerson: The Mind on Fire*
  AL - v68 - S '96 - p642+ [251-500]
  Bks & Cult - v2 - Mr '96 - p25+ [501+]
  NEQ - v69 - D '96 - p631+ [501+]
  Nine-C Lit - v51 - S '96 - p235+ [501+]
  NYTBR - v101 - O 27 '96 - p48 [51-250]
  RP - v58 - Sum '96 - p620+ [501+]
  Theol St - v57 - S '96 - p538+ [501+]
  Trib Bks - Ja 12 '97 - p2 [51-250]
Richardson, Ronny - *Professional's Guide to Robust Spreadsheets*
  R&R Bk N - v11 - D '96 - p34 [51-250]
Richardson, Roy - *Planning Primary Design and Technology*
  TES - N 29 '96 - p12* [501+]
Richardson, Samuel - *Pamela*
  Clio - v25 - Sum '96 - p393+ [501+]
Richardson, W Mark - *Religion and Science*
  Choice - v34 - Mr '97 - p1179+ [51-250]
  R&R Bk N - v11 - D '96 - p4 [51-250]

Richburg, Keith B - *Out of America*
  Am - v176 - Mr 22 '97 - p4 [501+]
  BW - v27 - Mr 2 '97 - p3+ [501+]
  LATBR - F 23 '97 - p7 [501+]
  Nat R - v49 - Ap 21 '97 - p74+ [501+]
  NYTBR - v102 - Mr 30 '97 - p9 [501+]
  NYTLa - v146 - F 17 '97 - p21 [501+]
  PW - v244 - F 17 '97 - p203+ [51-250]
  WSJ-Cent - v99 - F 6 '97 - pA12 [501+]
Riche, Pierre - *L'Enfance Au Moyen Age*
  Specu - v71 - O '96 - p1006+ [251-500]
Richelson, Jeffrey T - *The U.S. Intelligence Community. 3rd Ed.*
  Arm F&S - v23 - Win '96 - p313+ [501+]
Richemont, Enid - *The Dream Dog*
  c JB - v60 - D '96 - p259 [51-250]
  c Sch Lib - v44 - N '96 - p152 [51-250]
  The Stone That Grew (Illus. by Derek Brazell)
  c Sch Lib - v45 - F '97 - p34 [251-500]
Riches, John - *Matthew*
  Rel St Rev - v23 - Ap '97 - p179+ [251-500]
Richetti, John - *The Cambridge Companion to the Eighteenth-Century Novel*
  Choice - v34 - Ap '97 - p1333 [51-250]
  The Columbia History of the British Novel
  RES - v47 - Ag '96 - p454+ [501+]
Richey, William - *Blake's Altering Aesthetic*
  Choice - v34 - My '97 - p1499 [51-250]
Richie, Donald - *The Films of Akira Kurosawa. 3rd Ed.*
  LJ - v121 - O 15 '96 - p61 [51-250]
Richler, Mordecai - *Jacob Two-Two's First Spy Case (Illus. by Michael Chesworth)*
  c Ch Bk News - v19 - Spr '96 - p20+ [501+]
  c KR - v65 - Ap 1 '97 - p560 [51-250]
  c PW - v244 - Mr 17 '97 - p85 [1-50]
  This Year in Jerusalem
  Can Lit - Win '96 - p191+ [501+]
Richler, Nancy - *Throwaway Angels*
  BIC - v25 - N '96 - p36 [51-250]
  LJ - v121 - N 1 '96 - p111 [51-250]
  Quill & Q - v62 - O '96 - p31 [251-500]
Richman, Phyllis - *The Butter Did It*
  KR - v65 - Ap 1 '97 - p507+ [251-500]
  LJ - v122 - My 1 '97 - p144 [51-250]
  PW - v244 - Ap 7 '97 - p77 [51-250]
Richman, Phyllis C - *The Washington Post Dining Guide*
  r BW - v26 - D 29 '96 - p12 [51-250]
Richmond, Anthony H - *Global Apartheid*
  CS - v25 - S '96 - p593+ [501+]
Richmond, Colin - *The Paston Family in the Fifteenth Century. Vol. 2*
  TLS - Ja 17 '97 - p30 [501+]
Richmond, Peter - *My Father's War*
  KR - v64 - My 1 '96 - p672+ [251-500]
  LATBR - Jl 7 '96 - p4+ [501+]
Richmond, Sheldon - *Aesthetic Criteria*
  JAAC - v55 - Win '97 - p79+ [501+]
Richmond, Theo - *Konin: A Quest*
  NYTBR - v101 - S 8 '96 - p36 [1-50]
Richmond, Yale - *From Da to Yes*
  MLJ - v80 - Win '96 - p545+ [501+]
Richter, David H - *The Progress of Romance*
  Choice - v34 - Ja '97 - p797+ [51-250]
Richter, Gerhard - *The Daily Practice of Painting*
  ABR - v18 - D '96 - p14 [501+]
  Art J - v55 - Fall '96 - p89+ [501+]
  Stammheim
  Art J - v55 - Fall '96 - p89+ [501+]
Richter, James G - *Khrushchev's Double Bind*
  Russ Rev - v55 - O '96 - p720+ [501+]
Richter, Melvin - *The History of Political and Social Concepts*
  AJS - v102 - Jl '96 - p261+ [501+]
Richter, Michael - *The Formation of the Medieval West*
  AHR - v102 - F '97 - p95+ [501+]
  HT - v46 - Jl '96 - p55+ [501+]
  JIH - v27 - Aut '96 - p285+ [501+]
  Specu - v71 - O '96 - p1007+ [501+]
Richter, William L - *The ABC-CLIO Companion to American Reconstruction 1862-1877*
  r ARBA - v28 - '97 - p194 [51-250]
  r LJ - v122 - Mr 15 '97 - p58 [51-250]
  The ABC-CLIO Companion to Transportation in America
  r ARBA - v28 - '97 - p653 [51-250]
Rickards, Guy - *Hindemith, Hartmann, and Henze*
  M Ed J - v83 - N '96 - p54 [1-50]
  TLS - Jl 7 '96 - p19 [501+]
Ricklen, Neil - *Baby's Christmas*
  c PW - v243 - S 30 '96 - p93 [1-50]

Ricklin, Thomas - *Die Physica Und Der Liber De Causis Im 12 Jahrhundert*
    Isis - v88 - Mr '97 - p136 [501+]
Rickman, H - *Worlds in Interaction*
    SciTech - v20 - D '96 - p21 [51-250]
Ricks, Christopher - *Essays in Appreciation*
    Spec - v277 - N 16 '96 - p43 [1-50]
    TLS - N 29 '96 - p6+ [501+]
Ricoeur, Paul - *Figuring the Sacred*
    Choice - v34 - S '96 - p146 [51-250]
    Rel St - v32 - D '96 - p530 [51-250]
    Theol St - v57 - S '96 - p545+ [501+]
Riddel, Joseph N - *Purloined Letters*
    AL - v69 - Mr '97 - p209+ [501+]
    Nine-C Lit - v50 - Mr '96 - p557+ [51-250]
The Turning Word
    R&R Bk N - v12 - F '97 - p88 [51-250]
Riddell, John - *How to Grow Your Own Light Bulbs*
    Quill & Q - v62 - D '96 - p33 [251-500]
Riddell, Roger - *Aid in the 21st Century*
    JEL - v35 - Mr '97 - p220 [51-250]
Non-Governmental Organizations and Rural Poverty Alleviation
    Econ J - v107 - Ja '97 - p225+ [501+]
    JEL - v34 - S '96 - p1481 [51-250]
    PSQ - v111 - Win '96 - p744+ [501+]
Riddick, John F - *A Guide to Indian Manuscripts*
    JTWS - v13 - Fall '96 - p244+ [501+]
Riddle, Rita Sizemore - *Aluminum Balloons and Other Poems*
    Sm Pr R - v28 - D '96 - p4 [51-250]
Riddle, Tohby - *The Tip at the End of the Street (Illus. by Tohby Riddle)*
    c Aust Bk R - S '96 - p61+ [501+]
    c Magpies - v11 - Jl '96 - p8 [501+]
Rideout, Judi - *Wolf Walking*
    PW - v244 - My 5 '97 - p192 [1-50]
Rider, Janine - *The Writer's Book of Memory*
    Col Comp - v47 - O '96 - p441+ [51-250]
Ridgway, John - *The Road to Elizabeth*
    TES - Ag 23 '96 - p21 [51-250]
Ridgway, Judy - *Vegetarian Cookbook*
    Books - v9 - S '95 - p24 [1-50]
Riding, Laura - *A Selection of the Poems of Laura Riding*
    BL - v93 - F 15 '97 - p996 [51-250]
    BW - v27 - Ap 13 '97 - p12 [51-250]
    LJ - v122 - Ja '97 - p104 [51-250]
    PW - v244 - Ja 27 '97 - p95 [51-250]
Ridinger, Robert B Marks - *The Gay and Lesbian Movement*
    r ARBA - v28 - '97 - p309 [51-250]
    yr BL - v93 - My 1 '97 - p1528+ [251-500]
    r LJ - v122 - Ap 15 '97 - p72 [51-250]
Ridley, Aaron - *Music, Value, and the Passions*
    JAAC - v55 - Win '97 - p64+ [501+]
    Notes - v53 - S '96 - p95+ [51-250]
Ridley, D D - *Online Searching*
    New Sci - v152 - O 5 '96 - p49 [51-250]
    SciTech - v21 - Mr '97 - p100 [51-250]
Ridley, F F - *The Quango Debate*
    Lon R Bks - v18 - O 17 '96 - p10+ [501+]
Sleaze: Politicians, Private Interests and Public Raction
    Lon R Bks - v18 - O 17 '96 - p10+ [501+]
Ridley, Hugh - *Mann's Buddenbrooks and the Magic Mountain*
    MLR - v92 - Ja '97 - p245+ [501+]
Ridley, Jane - *The Young Disraeli*
    TES - Jl 5 '96 - p7* [51-250]
Ridley, John - *Stray Dogs*
    KR - v65 - Mr 15 '97 - p412 [251-500]
    PW - v244 - Mr 24 '97 - p58 [51-250]
Ridley, Mark - *Evolution. 2nd Ed.*
    R&R Bk N - v12 - F '97 - p94 [51-250]
Ridley, Matt - *Down to Earth II*
    New Sci - v152 - O 19 '96 - p47 [1-50]
The Origins of Virtue
    Econ - v341 - D 7 '96 - p5*+ [501+]
    KR - v65 - F 15 '97 - p283 [251-500]
    LATBR - Mr 30 '97 - p3 [501+]
    LJ - v122 - My 1 '97 - p135 [51-250]
    Nature - v383 - O 31 '96 - p785+ [501+]
    New Sci - v152 - O 19 '96 - p49 [251-500]
    NS - v125 - N 15 '96 - p48 [501+]
    PW - v244 - Mr 10 '97 - p60 [51-250]
    Spec - v278 - Ja 11 '97 - p32+ [501+]
    TLS - N 29 '96 - p3+ [501+]
    TLS - N 29 '96 - p13 [51-250]
    WSJ-Cent - v99 - Mr 26 '97 - pA17 [501+]
Ridley, Philip - *Meteorite Spoon*
    c TES - Jl 5 '96 - pR8 [51-250]

Ridley, Ronald T - *A Walking Guide to Melbourne's Monuments*
    Aust Bk R - O '96 - p69 [1-50]
Ridlon, Marci - *Sun through the Window*
    c CBRS - v25 - N '96 - p27 [51-250]
    c CLW - v67 - D '96 - p58 [51-250]
    c SLJ - v42 - O '96 - p139 [51-250]
Ridpath, Ian - *The Monthly Sky Guide. 4th Ed.*
    r Astron - v24 - N '96 - p103 [51-250]
    r SLMQ - v25 - Fall '96 - p66 [1-50]
Ridpath, Michael - *Trading Reality*
    BL - v93 - Mr 15 '97 - p1231 [51-250]
    KR - v64 - N 15 '96 - p1628 [251-500]
    LJ - v122 - Ja '97 - p150 [51-250]
    PW - v243 - D 16 '96 - p40 [51-250]
    Spec - v277 - D 14 '96 - p74+ [51-250]
    Woman's J - O '96 - p12 [1-50]
Riecken, Nancy - *Today Is the Day (Illus. by Catherine Stock)*
    c BL - v93 - S 15 '96 - p250 [51-250]
    c CCB-B - v50 - S '96 - p26 [51-250]
    c HB Guide - v8 - Spr '97 - p44 [51-250]
    c PW - v243 - Jl 22 '96 - p241 [51-250]
    c SLJ - v42 - Ag '96 - p128 [51-250]
Riedinger, Jeffrey M - *Agrarian Reform in the Philippines*
    Pac A - v69 - Sum '96 - p288+ [501+]
Rief, Linda - *All That Matters*
    EL - v54 - D '96 - p83 [51-250]
    ES - v27 - Sum '96 - p123+ [501+]
Riefe, Barbara - *Against All Odds*
    y BL - v93 - F 1 '97 - p926 [51-250]
    LJ - v121 - D '96 - p147 [51-250]
    PW - v243 - N 25 '96 - p58 [51-250]
Rieff, David - *Going to Miami*
    BW - v26 - D 15 '96 - p4 [1-50]
Los Angeles: Capital of the Third World
    BW - v26 - D 15 '96 - p4 [1-50]
Slaughterhouse: Bosnia and the Failure of the West
    NYTBR - v101 - S 1 '96 - p24 [1-50]
Riegert, Ray - *Hidden San Francisco and Northern California*
    r BWatch - v17 - N '96 - p12 [1-50]
Riehecky, Janet - *The Mystery of the Missing Money*
    c HB Guide - v7 - Fall '96 - p296 [51-250]
The Mystery of the UFO (Illus. by Lydia Halverson)
    c HB Guide - v7 - Fall '96 - p296 [51-250]
Television
    c Ch BWatch - v6 - My '96 - p6 [51-250]
    c HB Guide - v7 - Fall '96 - p349+ [51-250]
    c SB - v32 - Ag '96 - p177 [51-250]
    c SLJ - v42 - Ag '96 - p148+ [51-250]
Riehl, Nikolaus - *Stalin's Captive*
    SciTech - v20 - N '96 - p19 [51-250]
Riekse, R J - *Growing Older in America*
    Fam Relat - v46 - Ap '97 - p192 [501+]
Rieman, Timothy D - *The Complete Book of Shaker Furniture*
    r SDA - v4 - Spr '97 - p123+ [501+]
Riemer, John J - *Cataloging and Classification Standards and Rules*
    r RQ - v36 - Win '96 - p313+ [251-500]
    R&R Bk N - v11 - N '96 - p80 [51-250]
    r SLMQ - v25 - Fall '96 - p62 [51-250]
Riemer, Neal - *Creative Breakthroughs in Politics*
    Choice - v34 - Mr '97 - p1231+ [51-250]
    R&R Bk N - v11 - D '96 - p46 [51-250]
Let Justice Roll
    CC - v113 - N 20 '96 - p1179 [51-250]
Riera Ojeda, Oscar - *Hyper-Realistic: Computer Generated Architectural Renderings. Book and Electronic Media Version*
    Choice - v34 - Mr '97 - p1196 [51-250]
    SciTech - v20 - D '96 - p13 [51-250]
Ries, Rotraud - *Judisches Leben In Niedersachsen Im 15. Und 16. Jahrhundert*
    Six Ct J - v27 - Win '96 - p1057+ [501+]
Rieselman, Brian - *Dream Girl*
    y Kliatt - v31 - Mr '97 - p20+ [51-250]
Riess, Jonathan B - *The Renaissance Antichrist*
    Bks & Cult - v2 - My '96 - p9+ [501+]
    Six Ct J - v27 - Fall '96 - p910+ [51-250]
    Theol St - v57 - D '96 - p777+ [251-500]
Riew, C Keith - *Toughened Plastics II*
    SciTech - v21 - Mr '97 - p26 [51-250]
Rifkin, Bernard - *American Labor Sourcebook*
    r RQ - v36 - Fall '96 - p51 [51-250]
Rifkin, Jeremy - *Beyond Beef*
    Lon R Bks - v18 - S 5 '96 - p17+ [501+]
The End of Work
    YR - v84 - O '96 - p137+ [501+]

Rifkin, Ned - *Sean Scully: Twenty Years 1979-1995*
    ABR - v18 - D '96 - p13+ [501+]
Rigby, Peter - *African Images*
    BWatch - v17 - D '96 - p4+ [51-250]
Rigby, S H - *English Society in the Later Middle Ages*
    Albion - v28 - Fall '96 - p467+ [501+]
    HT - v47 - Ja '97 - p61 [501+]
    Specu - v71 - O '96 - p1010+ [501+]
Riggio, Anita - *Secret Signs (Illus. by Anita Riggio)*
    c CBRS - v25 - F '97 - p78 [51-250]
    c CCB-B - v50 - F '97 - p220 [51-250]
    c KR - v64 - D 15 '96 - p1803 [51-250]
    c SLJ - v43 - Mr '97 - p164 [51-250]
Riggs, Bob - *My Best Defense*
    c CCB-B - v50 - S '96 - p26+ [51-250]
    y Kliatt - v30 - N '96 - p10 [51-250]
    y SLJ - v42 - Ag '96 - p164 [51-250]
    y VOYA - v19 - O '96 - p213+ [51-250]
Riggs, Marcia Y - *Awake, Arise and Act*
    JR - v77 - Ja '97 - p166+ [501+]
Riggs, Sandy - *Circles (Illus. by Richard Maccabe)*
    c HB Guide - v8 - Spr '97 - p111 [51-250]
    c SLJ - v43 - F '97 - p97 [51-250]
Triangles (Illus. by Richard Maccabe)
    c Ch BWatch - v7 - Ja '97 - p3 [1-50]
    c HB Guide - v8 - Spr '97 - p111 [51-250]
    c SLJ - v43 - F '97 - p97 [51-250]
Righter, Robert W - *Wind Energy in America*
    Choice - v34 - O '96 - p312 [51-250]
    PHR - v66 - F '97 - p112+ [251-500]
    WHQ - v27 - Win '96 - p546 [251-500]
Rights of the Terminally Ill Act
    Quad - v40 - D '96 - p76+ [501+]
Rigoni Stern, Mario - *Le Stagioni Di Giacomo*
    WLT - v70 - Aut '96 - p935+ [501+]
Rihaczek, August W - *Principles of High-Resolution Radar*
    SciTech - v20 - N '96 - p74 [51-250]
Riis, Jacob A - *How the Other Half Lives*
    JEL - v35 - Mr '97 - p264 [51-250]
Rijksuniversiteit Te Groningen. Bibliotheek - *De Wereld Aan Boeken*
    Lib & Cul - v32 - Win '97 - p137 [251-500]
Rijpkema, Peter - *State Perfectionism and Personal Freedom*
    Ethics - v107 - O '96 - p178 [51-250]
Riley, Carroll L - *Rio Del Norte*
    HAHR - v76 - N '96 - p773 [251-500]
Riley, Chris - *The Killing Fields*
    BL - v93 - F 15 '97 - p999 [51-250]
    VV - v52 - Ja 28 '97 - p48+ [501+]
Riley, Glenda - *Building and Breaking Families in the American West*
    Choice - v34 - F '97 - p1045 [51-250]
The Life and Legacy of Annie Oakley
    Aethlon - v13 - Spr '96 - p217+ [251-500]
    Historian - v59 - Fall '96 - p155 [251-500]
Riley, Gregory J - *Resurrection Reconsidered*
    Intpr - v51 - Ja '97 - p98 [251-500]
    Rel St Rev - v23 - Ap '97 - p188 [51-250]
    Theol St - v57 - Mr '96 - p182+ [251-500]
Riley, James A - *The Negro Leagues*
    c Ch BWatch - v6 - O '96 - p5 [51-250]
    c HB Guide - v8 - Spr '97 - p146 [51-250]
    c SLJ - v43 - F '97 - p123 [51-250]
    c Trib Bks - Mr 30 '97 - p4+ [51-250]
Riley, Judith Merkle - *The Serpent Garden*
    PW - v244 - Ap 21 '97 - p69 [1-50]
Riley, Kevin Jack - *Snow Job?*
    For Aff - v75 - S '96 - p140 [51-250]
    VQR - v72 - Aut '96 - p135* [51-250]
Riley, Len - *Harlem*
    LJ - v121 - N 1 '96 - p84 [1-50]
Riley, Linda Capus - *Elephants Swim (Illus. by Steve Jenkins)*
    c RT - v50 - O '96 - p130 [1-50]
    c RT - v50 - Mr '97 - p496 [51-250]
Riley, Margaret - *The Guide to Internet Job Searching*
    r BWatch - v17 - N '96 - p12 [1-50]
    r Choice - v34 - Ja '97 - p774 [51-250]
    J Car P&E - v57 - Win '97 - p16+ [251-500]
    J Car P&E - v57 - Win '97 - p22 [51-250]
Riley, Michael O - *Oz and Beyond*
    PW - v244 - My 12 '97 - p64+ [51-250]
Riley, Robert R - *Steina and Woody Vasulka and Machine Media*
    Per A J - v18 - 3 '96 - p20+ [501+]
Riley, Sam G - *Biographical Dictionary of American Newspaper Columnists*
    r JMCQ - v73 - Aut '96 - p753+ [501+]

Riley, Terrence L - *Ship's Doctor*
    SciTech - v20 - N '96 - p49 [51-250]
Riley, William Bell - *The Antievolution Pamphlets of William Bell Riley*
    Isis - v88 - Mr '97 - p160+ [501+]
Rilke, Rainer Maria - *Sonette An Orpheus*
    CLS - v33 - 2 '96 - p141+ [501+]
    Uncollected Poems
    Lon R Bks - v18 - Ag 22 '96 - p8+ [501+]
Rill, Gerhard - *Furst Und Hof In Osterreich Von Den Habsburgischen Teilungsvertragen Bis Zur Schlacht Von Mohacs 1521/22 Bis 1526*
    EHR - v112 - F '97 - p185+ [501+]
Rima, Ingrid H - *The Classical Tradition in Economic Thought*
    Econ J - v106 - S '96 - p1464 [51-250]
    Labor Markets in a Global Economy
    JEL - v34 - S '96 - p1443 [51-250]
Rimanelli, Giose - *Moliseide: Songs and Ballads in the Molisan Dialect*
    TranslRevS - v1 - My '95 - p24+ [51-250]
Rimbaud 1891-1991
    FR - v70 - D '96 - p329+ [501+]
Rimler, Walter - *A Cole Porter Discography*
    r ARBA - v28 - '97 - p487 [51-250]
Rimmer, Harry - *The Antievolution Pamphlets of Harry Rimmer*
    Isis - v88 - Mr '97 - p160+ [501+]
Rimmer, Russell - *Income Distribution in a Corporate Economy*
    Econ J - v106 - S '96 - p1470 [51-250]
Rimmer, Steve - *Internet Graphics Toolkit*
    Quill & Q - v62 - Ag '96 - p23 [51-250]
Rimmerman, Craig A - *Gay Rights, Military Wrongs*
    BW - v26 - S 29 '96 - p12 [51-250]
    Choice - v34 - D '96 - p650 [51-250]
    R&R Bk N - v11 - D '96 - p72 [51-250]
Rimmon-Kenan, Shlomith - *A Glance beyond Doubt*
    TLS - F 14 '97 - p24 [251-500]
Rinaldi, Ann - *The Blue Door*
    c BL - v93 - N 1 '96 - p491 [51-250]
    y HB Guide - v8 - Spr '97 - p83 [51-250]
    y KR - v64 - Ag 15 '96 - p1241 [51-250]
    y SLJ - v42 - N '96 - p124+ [51-250]
    y VOYA - v19 - F '97 - p332 [251-500]
    Hang a Thousand Trees with Ribbons
    y BL - v93 - S 1 '96 - p119+ [51-250]
    y BL - v93 - Ap 1 '97 - p1294 [1-50]
    y CBRS - v25 - N '96 - p35 [51-250]
    c CSM - v88 - S 26 '96 - pB3 [51-250]
    y HB Guide - v8 - Spr '97 - p84 [51-250]
    y Kliatt - v31 - Ja '97 - p10 [51-250]
    y KR - v64 - O 15 '96 - p1538 [51-250]
    y SLJ - v42 - N '96 - p126 [51-250]
    y VOYA - v19 - D '96 - p273+ [251-500]
    In My Father's House
    y Kliatt - v30 - S '96 - p3 [1-50]
    Keep Smiling Through
    c HB Guide - v7 - Fall '96 - p297 [51-250]
    y Kliatt - v30 - S '96 - p13 [51-250]
    The Second Bend in the River
    c BL - v93 - F 15 '97 - p1016 [51-250]
    c CCB-B - v50 - Mr '97 - p256 [51-250]
    y KR - v65 - Ja 1 '97 - p63 [51-250]
    y PW - v244 - Ja 13 '97 - p76+ [51-250]
Rinderknecht, Carol - *A Checklist of American Imprints for 1845*
    r R&R Bk N - v12 - F '97 - p103 [51-250]
Rindisbacher, Hans J - *The Smell of Books*
    Ger Q - v69 - Spr '96 - p205+ [501+]
Ring, Elizabeth - *What Rot! (Illus. by Dwight Kuhn)*
    c HB Guide - v7 - Fall '96 - p338 [51-250]
    c SB - v33 - Mr '97 - p49+ [51-250]
Ring, Jim - *Erskine Childers*
    CR - v269 - Ag '96 - p99+ [501+]
    TLS - My 24 '96 - p32 [501+]
Ring, Trudy - *International Dictionary of Historic Places. Vols. 4-5*
    r ARBA - v28 - '97 - p212 [51-250]
    r R&R Bk N - v12 - F '97 - p12 [51-250]
Ringel, Faye - *New England's Gothic Literature*
    NEQ - v69 - D '96 - p683+ [501+]
Ringer, Fritz - *Fields of Knowledge*
    JMH - v69 - Mr '97 - p160+ [501+]

Ringgold, Faith - *Bonjour, Lonnie (Illus. by Faith Ringgold)*
    c BL - v93 - O 1 '96 - p359 [51-250]
    c CBRS - v25 - D '96 - p41 [51-250]
    c HB Guide - v8 - Spr '97 - p45 [51-250]
    c NYTBR - v102 - F 2 '97 - p18 [1-50]
    c Par Ch - v21 - Mr '97 - p8 [1-50]
    c PW - v243 - S 2 '96 - p130+ [51-250]
    c SLJ - v43 - Ja '97 - p89+ [51-250]
    My Dream of Martin Luther King
    c HB Guide - v7 - Fall '96 - p315 [51-250]
    Tar Beach
    c PW - v244 - Ja 13 '97 - p77 [1-50]
    We Flew over the Bridge
    y BL - v93 - D 15 '96 - p717 [1-50]
Ringis, Rita - *Elephants of Thailand in Myth, Art, and Reality*
    SciTech - v20 - D '96 - p33 [51-250]
Ringrose, David R - *Spain, Europe, and the Spanish Miracle 1700-1900*
    Choice - v34 - D '96 - p672 [51-250]
    HRNB - v25 - Win '97 - p78+ [251-500]
    TLS - Ja 3 '97 - p28 [501+]
    TLS - Ja 3 '97 - p28 [501+]
Rink, John - *The Practice of Performance*
    TLS - Ja 17 '97 - p8 [501+]
Rinkewich, Mindy - *The White beyond the Forest*
    TranslRevS - v1 - My '95 - p34 [1-50]
Rinpochc, Sogyal - *Tang Thu Song Chet*
    BL - v93 - My 15 '97 - p1568 [1-50]
Rinzler, Carol Ann - *Why Eve Doesn't Have an Adam's Apple*
    r ARBA - v28 - '97 - p601 [51-250]
    yr BL - v93 - S 1 '96 - p173 [51-250]
Riopelle, Jean-Paul - *Riopelle in Conversation*
    TranslRevS - v2 - D '96 - p10 [51-250]
Riordan, James - *Pinocchio (Illus. by Victor G Ambrus)*
    c Magpies - v11 - S '96 - p45 [1-50]
    Stone: A Biography of Oliver Stone
    Spec - v277 - N 2 '96 - p52 [501+]
    Stone: The Controversies, Excesses, and Exploits of a Radical Filmmaker
    Obs - O 20 '96 - p16* [501+]
    Stone: The Controversies, Excesses and Exploits of a Radical Filmmaker
    Si & So - v6 - N '96 - p36 [1-50]
Riordan, James, 1936- - *The Barefoot Book of Stories from the Sea (Illus. by Amanda Hall)*
    c Bks Keeps - Ja '97 - p8+ [501+]
    The Barnyard Band (Illus. by Charles Fuge)
    c Bks Keeps - N '96 - p7 [51-250]
    My G-r-r-r-reat Uncle Tiger (Illus. by Alex Ayliffe)
    c RT - v50 - O '96 - p134 [1-50]
    The Songs My Paddle Sings (Illus. by Michael Foreman)
    c Bks Keeps - v100 - S '96 - p32 [51-250]
    Stories from the Sea (Illus. by Amanda Hall)
    c HB Guide - v8 - Spr '97 - p100 [51-250]
    c PW - v243 - O 21 '96 - p85 [51-250]
    c TES - D 6 '96 - p16* [501+]
    Treasury of Irish Stories (Illus. by Ian Newsham)
    c CLW - v66 - Je '96 - p51+ [51-250]
Riordan, Rick - *Big Red Tequila*
    PW - v244 - Ap 28 '97 - p73 [51-250]
Riordon, Michael - *Out Our Way*
    Quill & Q - v62 - Jl '96 - p49 [251-500]
Rios, Francisco - *Teacher Thinking in Cultural Contexts*
    Choice - v34 - D '96 - p662 [51-250]
    Urban Ed - v32 - My '97 - p320+ [501+]
Rios, Julian - *Poundemonium*
    BL - v93 - D 15 '96 - p709 [51-250]
    KR - v65 - Ja 1 '97 - p20 [51-250]
    LJ - v121 - N 1 '96 - p108 [51-250]
    NYTBR - v102 - F 16 '97 - p18 [51-250]
    PW - v243 - N 25 '96 - p69 [51-250]
Rio-Sukan, Isabel Del - *La Duda Y Otros Apuntes Para Escribir Una Coleccion De Relatos*
    Hisp - v79 - D '96 - p826+ [501+]
Rioux, Helen - *Traductrice De Sentiments*
    WLT - v70 - Sum '96 - p654 [501+]
Ripken, Cal - *The Only Way I Know*
    y BL - v93 - Mr 15 '97 - p1203 [51-250]
    PW - v244 - Mr 17 '97 - p64 [51-250]
Ripley, Alexandra - *From Fields of Gold*
    Books - v11 - Ap '97 - p22 [51-250]
    A Love Divine
    BL - v92 - Ag '96 - p1856 [251-500]
Ripley, Ann - *Death of a Garden*
    KR - v64 - My '96 - p646 [51-250]
Ripley, B D - *Pattern Recognition and Neural Networks*
    Nature - v381 - My 16 '96 - p206 [51-250]

Ripley, Catherine - *Why Do Stars Twinkle? and Other Nighttime Questions (Illus. by Scot Ritchie)*
    c BL - v93 - D 1 '96 - p663 [51-250]
    c Ch Bk News - v20 - Win '97 - p29+ [51-250]
    c Quill & Q - v62 - S '96 - p74 [51-250]
    Why Is the Sky Blue? and Other Outdoor Questions (Illus. by Scot Ritchie)
    c Quill & Q - v63 - F '97 - p59 [251-500]
Ripley, Earle A - *Environmental Effects of Mining*
    Am Sci - v85 - Mr '97 - p185 [251-500]
    Env - v38 - N '96 - p31 [51-250]
Ripley, Mike - *Fresh Blood*
    Arm Det - v29 - Sum '96 - p348 [51-250]
    KR - v65 - F 15 '97 - p260 [51-250]
    NYTBR - v102 - Mr 30 '97 - p23 [51-250]
Ripley, Tim - *Air War Bosnia*
    A & S Sm - v11 - F '97 - p87 [1-50]
Ripley, W L - *Electric Country Roulette*
    BL - v93 - N 1 '96 - p483 [51-250]
    KR - v64 - S 1 '96 - p1278 [51-250]
    PW - v243 - S 9 '96 - p68 [51-250]
Rippin, Sally - *Fang Fang's Chinese New Year (Illus. by Sally Rippin)*
    c Magpies - v11 - S '96 - p29+ [51-250]
    Speak Chinese, Fang Fang (Illus. by Sally Rippin)
    c Magpies - v11 - S '96 - p29+ [51-250]
Ripple, Wilhelminia - *Halloween School Parties*
    PW - v243 - S 30 '96 - p86 [1-50]
Ripples, Jeff - *Florida: The Natural Wonders*
    PW - v244 - Ja 20 '97 - p390 [1-50]
Rippley, La Vern J - *German-Bohemians: The Quiet Immigrants*
    Ger Q - v70 - Win '97 - p74+ [501+]
    WHQ - v28 - Spr '97 - p91+ [251-500]
Rippon, Norman - *Improve Your Child's Spelling. Rev. Ed., Vols. 1-2*
    Quill & Q - v62 - O '96 - p50 [51-250]
Ripskis, Al Louis - *Cutting Loose*
    BWatch - v17 - N '96 - p7 [51-250]
Rise, Eric W - *The Martinsville Seven*
    Historian - v58 - Sum '96 - p871+ [251-500]
Rishel, James B - *HVAC Pump Handbook*
    r SciTech - v21 - Mr '97 - p84 [51-250]
Rising, James - *A Guide to the Identification and Natural History of the Sparrows of the United States and Canada*
    r New Sci - v152 - N 2 '96 - p48 [51-250]
Risk-Based Decision Making in Water Resources VII
    SciTech - v20 - D '96 - p67 [51-250]
Risk-Based Inservice Testing. Vol. 2
    SciTech - v20 - D '96 - p68 [51-250]
Risks to Students in School
    J Gov Info - v23 - S '96 - p557 [51-250]
Risse-Kappen, Thomas - *Cooperation among Democracies*
    J Pol - v58 - N '96 - p1258+ [501+]
Risset, Jacqueline - *The Translation Begins*
    TranslRevS - v2 - D '96 - p24 [51-250]
Rissinger, Matt - *Biggest Joke Book in the World*
    c BWatch - v6 - My '96 - p1 [1-50]
Rissler, Jane - *The Ecological Risks of Engineered Crops*
    Choice - v34 - D '96 - p637 [51-250]
    SB - v33 - Ja '97 - p10 [251-500]
Risso, Patricia - *Merchants and Faith*
    Pac A - v69 - Sum '96 - p254+ [501+]
Rist, John M - *Augustine: Ancient Thought Baptized*
    JR - v76 - O '96 - p626+ [501+]
    Phil R - v105 - Ja '96 - p110+ [501+]
Riste, T - *Physics of Biomaterials*
    SciTech - v20 - D '96 - p30 [51-250]
Ritchey, Tim - *Programming with Java! Beta 2.0*
    Quill & Q - v62 - My '96 - p20+ [501+]
Ritchie, Andrew - *Major Taylor: The Extraordinary Career of a Champion Bicycle Racer*
    Am Vis - v12 - F '97 - p28+ [51-250]
Ritchie, Daniel E - *Reconstructing Literature in an Ideological Age*
    Bks & Cult - v3 - Ja '97 - p38 [251-500]
    Choice - v34 - Ja '97 - p798 [51-250]
Ritchie, David - *Shipwrecks: An Encyclopedia of the World's Worst Disasters at Sea*
    r ARBA - v28 - '97 - p657 [51-250]
    yr SLJ - v43 - F '97 - p138 [51-250]
    Superquake; Why Earthquakes Occur and When the Big One Will Hit Southern California
    y Kliatt - v31 - Mr '97 - p5 [51-250]
Ritchie, G S - *The Admiralty Chart*
    GJ - v162 - Jl '96 - p237 [51-250]

Ritchie, Harry - *New Scottish Writing*
   Econ - v343 - Ap 26 '97 - p83+ [501+]
   NS - v125 - O 25 '96 - p46+ [501+]
   TLS - D 20 '96 - p22 [501+]
Ritchie, James A - *The Wagon Wars*
   BL - v93 - My 1 '97 - p1480 [51-250]
   PW - v244 - Mr 24 '97 - p61 [51-250]
Ritsos, Yannis - *Iconostasis of Anonymous Saints*
   TLS - O 25 '96 - p26 [501+]
Ritter, Adolf Martin - *Charisma Und Caritas*
   Rel St Rev - v23 - Ap '97 - p189 [51-250]
Ritter, Gerhard X - *Handbook of Computer Vision Algorithms in Image Algebra*
   Choice - v34 - Ap '97 - p1374 [51-250]
   SciTech - v20 - D '96 - p66 [51-250]
Ritter, Kathleen - *Righteous Religion*
   Cons - v17 - Win '96 - p31 [1-50]
Ritter, Lawrence S - *Leagues Apart (Illus. by Richard Merkin)*
   c RT - v50 - Mr '97 - p478+ [51-250]
Ritter, Michael E - *Earth Online*
   r Choice - v34 - My '97 - p1528 [51-250]
Ritter, Stefan - *Hercules In Der Romischen Kunst Von Den Anfangen Bis Augustus*
   Choice - v34 - D '96 - p566 [1-50]
Ritthaler, Shelly - *With Love, Amanda*
   y Kliatt - v31 - My '97 - p9 [51-250]
Ritts, Herb - *Herb Ritts: Work*
   LJ - v122 - Mr 15 '97 - p59 [51-250]
   WSJ-MW - v78 - D 5 '96 - pA18 [51-250]
Work
   VLS - Win '96 - p30+ [51-250]
Ritz, Hans - *Die Geschichte Vom Rotkappchen. 11th Ed.*
   Ger Q - v69 - Spr '96 - p213+ [501+]
Ritzer, George - *Expressing America*
   J Con A - v30 - Win '96 - p502+ [501+]
Ritzer, Mariann - *Once I Loved Him Madly*
   Sm Pr R - v29 - Ja '97 - p10 [501+]
Rius, Maria - *Let's Discover the Five Senses Series*
   c Inst - v106 - S '96 - p92 [1-50]
Rivard, David - *Wise Poison*
   y Kliatt - v31 - My '97 - p18+ [51-250]
   PW - v243 - N 25 '96 - p73 [51-250]
Rivard, Ken - *If She Could Take All These Men*
   BIC - v26 - Mr '97 - p13 [501+]
Rivas, Ivonne - *El Dueno De La Luz (Illus. by Irene Savino)*
   c SLJ - v42 - Ag '96 - p179 [51-250]
Rivele, Stephen J - *A Booke of Days*
   BL - v93 - F 15 '97 - p1005 [51-250]
   KR - v64 - D 15 '96 - p1763 [251-500]
   LJ - v122 - Ja '97 - p150 [51-250]
   PW - v243 - D 16 '96 - p41 [51-250]
River Hydraulics
   SciTech - v20 - D '96 - p68 [51-250]
Rivera, Daniel - *Private Sector Participation in the Water Supply and Wastewater Sector*
   JEL - v35 - Mr '97 - p252 [51-250]
Rivera-Batiz, Francisco - *Island Paradox*
   BWatch - v18 - F '97 - p12 [51-250]
Rivers, Caryl - *Slick Spins and Fractured Facts*
   r Choice - v34 - N '96 - p447 [51-250]
   CJR - v35 - Jl '96 - p58+ [501+]
   JMCQ - v73 - Win '96 - p1015+ [501+]
   Rapport - v19 - 5 '96 - p43 [251-500]
   SFR - v21 - Jl '96 - p37+ [501+]
Rivers, Francine - *The Atonement Child*
   y BL - v93 - Mr 1 '97 - p1111 [51-250]
   LJ - v122 - F 1 '97 - p68 [51-250]
Rivers, Frank - *The Way of the Owl*
   Rapport - v19 - 4 '96 - p18+ [501+]
Rivers, Glenn - *Those Who Love the Game*
   y BL - v93 - D 15 '96 - p717 [1-50]
Rivers, Joan - *Bouncing Back*
   BL - v93 - F 15 '97 - p971 [51-250]
   PW - v244 - F 10 '97 - p76 [51-250]
   VLS - Spr '97 - p16+ [501+]
Riviere, Francois - *In the Footsteps of Agatha Christie*
   PW - v244 - F 10 '97 - p71 [51-250]
Rix, Jamie - *Fearsome Tales for Fiendish Kids (Illus. by Ross Collins)*
   c Bks Keeps - Jl '96 - p11 [51-250]
   c Sch Lib - v44 - Ag '96 - p108 [51-250]
Johnny Casanova
   y Sch Lib - v44 - Ag '96 - p121 [51-250]
Rizzi, Silvio - *The Pasta Bible*
   BL - v93 - N 15 '96 - p560 [51-250]
Rizzi, Timothy - *Eagles of Fire*
   BL - v93 - S 1 '96 - p64 [51-250]
Rizzuto, Phil - *The October Twelve*
   Aethlon - v13 - Fall '95 - p177 [251-500]

RNA
   p Nature - v383 - S 5 '96 - p37 [251-500]
Ro, Ronin - *Gangsta: Merchandizing the Rhymes of Violence*
   BWatch - v17 - N '96 - p9 [51-250]
   KR - v64 - My 1 '96 - p673 [251-500]
Roach, Joseph - *Cities of the Dead*
   r Choice - v34 - N '96 - p442 [51-250]
Roach, Marilynne K - *In the Days of the Salem Witchcraft Trials*
   c HB Guide - v7 - Fall '96 - p388 [51-250]
Road Trip USA
   r BWatch - v17 - S '96 - p5 [51-250]
   LJ - v121 - O 15 '96 - p81 [51-250]
Roads, Curtis - *The Computer Music Tutorial*
   M Ed J - v83 - Jl '96 - p65 [51-250]
Roald Dahl's Book of Ghost Stories
   BW - v26 - O 27 '96 - p12 [51-250]
Robards, Karen - *Heartbreaker*
   BL - v93 - N 1 '96 - p459 [51-250]
   KR - v64 - N 1 '96 - p1559 [251-500]
   PW - v243 - N 11 '96 - p57 [51-250]
Robards, Martin F - *Running a Team for Disabled Children and Their Families*
   Adoles - v31 - Fall '96 - p755 [51-250]
Robayo Avendano, Juan Manuel - *Iglesia, Tierra, Y Credito En La Colonia*
   HAHR - v76 - Ag '96 - p561+ [501+]
Robb, Candace M - *The King's Bishop*
   KR - v64 - Ag '96 - p1192 [251-500]
   LJ - v121 - O 1 '96 - p131 [1-50]
   PW - v243 - S 23 '96 - p60 [51-250]
The Nun's Tale
   PW - v243 - S 23 '96 - p74 [1-50]
Robb, Carol S - *Equal Value*
   CC - v113 - D 4 '96 - p1210 [51-250]
   TT - v53 - Ja '97 - p570 [51-250]
Robb, Graham - *La Poesie De Baudelaire Et La Poesie Francaise 1838-1852*
   MLR - v92 - Ja '97 - p199 [251-500]
Unlocking Mallarme
   Choice - v34 - N '96 - p464+ [51-250]
   TLS - D 13 '96 - p11 [501+]
Robb, H Amanda - *Encyclopedia of American Family Names*
   r NGSQ - v84 - D '96 - p312+ [251-500]
Robb, Jackie - *Bat (Illus. by Karen Duncan)*
   c PW - v244 - Mr 10 '97 - p68 [51-250]
Brain Cell (Illus. by Karen Duncan)
   c KR - v65 - Mr 15 '97 - p470 [51-250]
   c PW - v244 - Mr 10 '97 - p68 [51-250]
Slug (Illus. by Karen Duncan)
   c PW - v244 - Mr 10 '97 - p68 [51-250]
Spider (Illus. by Karen Duncan)
   c PW - v244 - Mr 10 '97 - p68 [51-250]
Robb, Kevin - *Literacy and Paideia in Ancient Greece*
   Class Out - v74 - Win '97 - p79 [251-500]
   CPR - v16 - Ag '96 - p282+ [501+]
   QJS - v83 - F '97 - p120+ [501+]
Robb, Laura - *Music and Drum (Illus. by Debra Lill)*
   c BL - v93 - Ap 1 '97 - p1328+ [51-250]
   c CCB-B - v50 - My '97 - p334 [51-250]
   c KR - v65 - Mr 1 '97 - p386+ [51-250]
   c PW - v244 - Mr 31 '97 - p76+ [51-250]
Snuffles and Snouts (Illus. by Steven Kellogg)
   c Inst - v105 - My '96 - p70 [1-50]
   c LA - v73 - D '96 - p625 [51-250]
Robb, Peter - *Midnight in Sicily*
   Aust Bk R - F '97 - p6+ [501+]
Robbe-Grillet, Alain - *Angelique Ou L'Enchantement*
   FR - v70 - O '96 - p44+ [501+]
La Belle Captive
   FR - v70 - O '96 - p126+ [501+]
   PW - v243 - N 25 '96 - p70 [1-50]
   TranslRevS - v2 - D '96 - p24 [51-250]
Les Derniers Jours De Corinthe
   FR - v70 - O '96 - p44+ [501+]
   FR - v70 - D '96 - p231+ [501+]
Le Miroir Qui Revient
   FR - v70 - O '96 - p44+ [501+]
Robbin, Tony - *Engineering a New Architecture*
   Choice - v34 - S '96 - p114+ [51-250]
   New Sci - v151 - S 28 '96 - p48 [51-250]
   SciTech - v21 - Mr '97 - p79 [51-250]
Robbins, Anthony - *Unlimited Power*
   y BL - v93 - D 15 '96 - p691 [51-250]
   LJ - v122 - My 1 '97 - p126+ [51-250]
   PW - v243 - D 30 '96 - p48 [51-250]
Robbins, Barbara H - *Wolf Country I*
   c Ch BWatch - v6 - D '96 - p3 [51-250]

Robbins, Harold - *The Raiders*
   Books - v9 - S '95 - p27 [1-50]
Tycoon
   BL - v93 - D 15 '96 - p693 [51-250]
   KR - v64 - D 1 '96 - p1699 [251-500]
   LJ - v122 - Ja '97 - p150 [51-250]
   PW - v243 - D 16 '96 - p41 [51-250]
   Trib Bks - Mr 2 '97 - p4 [501+]
Robbins, John - *Reclaiming Our Health*
   LJ - v121 - S 15 '96 - p86 [51-250]
Robbins, Keith - *A Bibliography of British History 1914-1989*
   r Choice - v34 - Mr '97 - p1143 [51-250]
   r Lib - v19 - Mr '97 - p96+ [251-500]
Robbins, Ken - *Air*
   c LA - v73 - O '96 - p438+ [51-250]
Fire
   c HB Guide - v7 - Fall '96 - p333 [51-250]
Rodeo (Illus. by Ken Robbins)
   c CCB-B - v50 - D '96 - p151 [51-250]
   c HB Guide - v8 - Spr '97 - p146 [51-250]
   c KR - v64 - Ag 15 '96 - p1241 [51-250]
   c NYTBR - v101 - N 10 '96 - p42 [501+]
   c PW - v243 - S 2 '96 - p133 [51-250]
   c SLJ - v42 - O '96 - p116+ [51-250]
Robbins, Margaret - *Remote Access Essentials*
   CBR - v14 - S '96 - p31 [1-50]
Robbins, Maria - *Chocolates for Christmas*
   BL - v93 - S 15 '96 - p197 [51-250]
   LJ - v121 - O 15 '96 - p86 [51-250]
Robbins, Michael - *Conceiving of Personality*
   Choice - v34 - Ap '97 - p1420+ [51-250]
Robbins, Paul D - *Gene Therapy Protocols*
   SciTech - v21 - Mr '97 - p48 [51-250]
Robbins, Paul R - *Hallucinogens*
   y HB Guide - v7 - Fall '96 - p317+ [51-250]
Romantic Relationships
   Choice - v34 - Ap '97 - p1421 [51-250]
Robbins, Richard - *Sidelines Activist*
   Choice - v34 - My '97 - p1585 [51-250]
Robbins, Ruth - *Victorian Identities*
   ELT - v40 - 2 '97 - p255 [51-250]
   Nine-C Lit - v51 - S '96 - p276 [51-250]
Robbins, Trina - *The Great Women Superheroes*
   y BL - v93 - Ja '97 - p804 [51-250]
   LJ - v122 - Mr 15 '97 - p62 [51-250]
   Ms - v7 - Mr '97 - p83 [1-50]
   PW - v243 - D 2 '96 - p55 [51-250]
Robbins, Wendy H - *The Portable College Adviser*
   y HB Guide - v8 - Spr '97 - p94 [51-250]
   y SLJ - v42 - Ag '96 - p176 [51-250]
   y VOYA - v19 - O '96 - p238 [251-500]
Robeck, Cecil M, Jr. - *Prophecy in Carthage*
   CHR - v82 - Jl '96 - p494+ [501+]
Roberson, Susan L - *Emerson in His Sermons*
   AHR - v101 - O '96 - p1275+ [501+]
   AL - v68 - D '96 - p850+ [501+]
   NEQ - v69 - S '96 - p525+ [501+]
Robert, Jean-Claude - *Atlas Historique De Montreal*
   r Can Hist R - v77 - S '96 - p438+ [501+]
Robert E. Lee: Gentleman General/Ulysses S. Grant: Unlikely Hero. Electronic Media Version
   r LJ - v122 - Ja '97 - p164 [51-250]
Robertazzi, Chiara - *Africa 8th to 18th Century (Illus. by Giorgio Bacchin)*
   c HB Guide - v8 - Spr '97 - p170+ [51-250]
   y SLJ - v43 - F '97 - p114 [51-250]
Robertini, Luca - *Liber Miraculorum Sancte Fidis*
   Specu - v72 - Ja '97 - p214+ [501+]
Roberts, A Wayne - *Calculus: The Dynamics of Change*
   Choice - v34 - O '96 - p316 [51-250]
   Math T - v89 - O '96 - p606 [51-250]
Roberts, Andrew - *The Aachen Memorandum*
   Obs - O 20 '96 - p18* [51-250]
   Obs - D 15 '96 - p18* [51-250]
Roberts, Bethany - *Camel Caravan (Illus. by Cheryl Munro Taylor)*
   c Ch BWatch - v6 - My '96 - p3 [1-50]
   c HB Guide - v7 - Fall '96 - p243 [51-250]
   c New Ad - v9 - Fall '96 - p327+ [501+]
Cat Parade (Illus. by Diane Greenseid)
   c HB Guide - v8 - Spr '97 - p45 [51-250]
   c SLJ - v43 - Ja '97 - p90 [51-250]
Eleven Elephants Going Up! (Illus. by Minh Uong)
   c HB Guide - v8 - Spr '97 - p45 [51-250]
Monster Manners (Illus. by Andrew Glass)
   c HB Guide - v7 - Fall '96 - p272 [51-250]
A Mouse Told His Mother (Illus. by Maryjane Begin)
   c BL - v93 - Ap 1 '97 - p1339 [51-250]
   c KR - v65 - Ap 1 '97 - p561 [51-250]
   c PW - v244 - Mr 17 '97 - p82 [51-250]

Roberts, Bette B - *Anne Rice*
Ext - v37 - Sum '96 - p178+ [501+]
Roberts, Brad - *New Forces in the World Economy*
JEL - v34 - D '96 - p2039+ [51-250]
Order and Disorder after the Cold War
JEL - v34 - S '96 - p1424+ [51-250]
Weapons Proliferation and World Order
R&R Bk N - v11 - D '96 - p72 [51-250]
Roberts, Brian K - *Landscapes of Settlement*
GJ - v163 - Mr '97 - p100 [251-500]
Roberts, Bryan R - *The Sociology of Development. Vols. 1-2*
CS - v25 - S '96 - p709+ [501+]
Roberts, Charlotte - *The Archeology of Disease. 2nd Ed.*
Rel St Rev - v23 - Ja '97 - p64+ [51-250]
Roberts, Clayton - *The Logic of Historical Explanation*
Hist & T - v36 - F '97 - p110 [251-500]
Roberts, Daniel K - *Ocular Disease. 2nd Ed.*
r SciTech - v20 - S '96 - p39 [51-250]
Roberts, David, 1796-1864 - *Egypt: Yesterday and Today*
BL - v93 - Mr 1 '97 - p1108 [51-250]
BW - v26 - D 8 '96 - p10 [51-250]
The Holy Land
Am - v176 - Mr 8 '97 - p25+ [51-250]
Roberts, David, 1937- - *Reconstructing Theory*
Aust Bk R - Ag '96 - p21+ [501+]
Roberts, David, 1943- - *Escape Routes*
KR - v65 - F 1 '97 - p205 [251-500]
Roberts, Diane - *The Myth of Aunt Jemima*
MLR - v91 - O '96 - p984+ [501+]
Roberts, Elizabeth - *A Woman's Place*
HT - v46 - Ag '96 - p60 [51-250]
Women and Families
AHR - v101 - D '96 - p1546+ [251-500]
Women's Work 1840-1940
JEL - v34 - D '96 - p2100 [51-250]
Roberts, Gareth - *The Mirror of Alchemy*
LR - v45 - 7 '96 - p61+ [251-500]
The Romance of Crime
SF Chr - v18 - O '96 - p77+ [51-250]
Roberts, Garyn G - *Dick Tracy and American Culture*
JPC - v29 - Spr '96 - p248+ [51-250]
Roberts, Geoffrey - *The Soviet Union and the Origins of the Second World War*
HRNB - v25 - Fall '96 - p35 P [251-500]
Russ Rev - v56 - Ja '97 - p139+ [251-500]
Roberts, Gerald - *Gerard Manley Hopkins: A Literary Life*
VS - v39 - Spr '96 - p453+ [501+]
Roberts, Gillian - *The Mummers' Curse*
y BL - v92 - Ag '96 - p1888 [51-250]
y BL - v92 - Ag '96 - p1891 [1-50]
Rapport - v19 - 6 '96 - p24 [51-250]
Roberts, J C - *Paper Chemistry. 2nd Ed.*
Choice - v34 - O '96 - p311 [51-250]
Roberts, J M - *A History of Europe*
Econ - v341 - N 16 '96 - p3*+ [501+]
HT - v46 - O '96 - p56 [1-50]
LAR - v98 - D '96 - p650 [51-250]
Spec - v277 - N 23 '96 - p44 [1-50]
Spec - v278 - Ja 4 '97 - p33+ [501+]
TES - N 1 '96 - p7* [501+]
TLS - D 20 '96 - p3+ [501+]
Roberts, Jack L - *Oskar Schindler*
c HB Guide - v7 - Fall '96 - p370 [1-50]
Roberts, James N - *The Silver Coins of Medieval France 476-1610 A.D.*
Coin W - v38 - Ja 6 '97 - p98 [51-250]
Roberts, Janet Wier - *City Kids and City Critters!*
c SB - v32 - Ag '96 - p179+ [51-250]
Roberts, Jason - *Director 5 Demystified*
LJ - v121 - D '96 - p138 [51-250]
Roberts, Jean-Marc - *Affaires Personnelles*
BL - v93 - Ja '97 - p827 [1-50]
Roberts, Jennifer Tolbert - *Athens on Trial*
Ethics - v107 - O '96 - p181 [51-250]
Roberts, John Maddox - *The Ghosts of Saigon*
Arm Det - v29 - Fall '96 - p496 [251-500]
Roberts, John R - *New Perspectives on the Seventeenth-Century English Religious Lyric*
Ren & Ref - v19 - Fall '96 - p96+ [501+]
RES - v47 - N '96 - p588+ [501+]
Roberts, John W - *Putting Foreign Policy to Work*
JEL - v34 - S '96 - p1468 [51-250]
Roberts, Julian V - *Disproportionate Harm*
J Gov Info - v23 - S '96 - p612 [51-250]
Roberts, Kate - *Feet in Chains*
BWatch - v17 - D '96 - p6 [51-250]
Roberts, Ken - *Hiccup Champion of the World*
c Quill & Q - v62 - My '96 - p13 [501+]

Roberts, Kenneth - *Boon Island*
VQR - v72 - Aut '96 - p143* [1-50]
Roberts, Les - *Collision Bend*
y BL - v93 - S 1 '96 - p68 [51-250]
Roberts, Lillian M - *The Hand That Feeds You*
PW - v244 - My 5 '97 - p206 [51-250]
Riding for a Fall
PW - v243 - N 4 '96 - p71 [51-250]
Roberts, Lisa M - *How to Raise a Family and a Career under One Roof*
BWatch - v18 - F '97 - p3 [1-50]
Roberts, M L - *World's Weirdest Birds*
c SB - v32 - N '96 - p242 [51-250]
Roberts, M Susan - *Living without Procrastination*
BWatch - v17 - S '96 - p10+ [51-250]
Roberts, Martin - *Michel Tournier: Bricolage and Cultural Mythology*
FR - v70 - D '96 - p341+ [501+]
Roberts, Michael C - *Handbook of Pediatric Psychology. 2nd Ed.*
Adoles - v31 - Fall '96 - p755 [51-250]
Roberts, Michele - *Daughters of the House*
Critiq - v37 - Sum '96 - p243+ [501+]
Roberts, Monty - *The Man Who Listens to Horses*
Spec - v278 - Ja 11 '97 - p38 [501+]
TLS - D 6 '96 - p27 [501+]
Roberts, Nancy - *Blackbeard and Other Pirates of the Atlantic Coast*
CAY - v17 - Win '96 - p13 [51-250]
Haunted Houses. 2nd Ed.
CAY - v17 - Win '96 - p7 [51-250]
Roberts, Nora - *From the Heart*
LJ - v121 - N 15 '96 - p52 [51-250]
Holding the Dream
PW - v243 - N 25 '96 - p70 [51-250]
Holding the Dream (Burr). Audio Version
LJ - v122 - Mr 15 '97 - p102 [51-250]
Sanctuary
BL - v93 - Ja '97 - p780 [51-250]
KR - v65 - Ja 1 '97 - p17 [251-500]
LJ - v122 - F 1 '97 - p107 [51-250]
PW - v244 - F 3 '97 - p95 [51-250]
Trib Bks - My 11 '97 - p11 [51-250]
True Betrayals (Shansky). Audio Version
y Kliatt - v30 - S '96 - p54 [51-250]
Roberts, Paul, 1949- - *Images: The Piano Music of Claude Debussy*
Notes - v53 - Mr '97 - p805+ [501+]
Roberts, Paul Craig - *The Capitalist Revolution in Latin America*
Bus W - Mr 17 '97 - p17 [51-250]
WSJ-Cent - v99 - My 22 '97 - pA13 [501+]
The New Color Line
NY - v72 - N 25 '96 - p106+ [501+]
Roberts, Paul William - *Empire of the Soul*
KR - v64 - S 1 '96 - p1307 [251-500]
PW - v243 - S 2 '96 - p105 [51-250]
In Search of the Birth of Jesus
NYTBR - v101 - D 22 '96 - p20 [1-50]
Roberts, Penny - *A City in Conflict*
Choice - v34 - D '96 - p672 [51-250]
Roberts, Perri Lee - *Masolino Da Panicale*
Ren Q - v49 - Win '96 - p907+ [501+]
Roberts, Richard - *The Bank of England*
Albion - v28 - Fall '96 - p534+ [51-250]
JEH - v56 - D '96 - p934+ [501+]
Roberts, Robin, 1926- - *The Whiz Kids and the 1950 Pennant*
Choice - v34 - Ap '97 - p1378 [51-250]
Roberts, Robin, 1957- - *Anne McCaffrey: A Critical Companion*
CLW - v67 - Mr '97 - p50 [251-500]
SFS - v24 - Mr '97 - p176+ [501+]
SLMQ - v25 - Fall '96 - p66 [51-250]
Ladies First
y BL - v93 - N 1 '96 - p472 [51-250]
LJ - v121 - O 15 '96 - p61+ [51-250]
Roberts, Shawn - *After the Guns Fall Silent*
JPR - v33 - Ag '96 - p382 [51-250]
Roberts, Shelly - *Roberts' Rules of Lesbian Living*
Wom R Bks - v14 - Mr '97 - p6+ [501+]
Roberts, Stephen - *Radical Politicians and Poets in Early Victorian Britain*
EHR - v111 - N '96 - p1314 [251-500]
Roberts, Stephen K - *Evesham Borough Records of the Seventeenth Century 1605-1687*
r EHR - v112 - Ap '97 - p469+ [251-500]

Roberts, Tara - *Am I the Last Virgin?*
y BL - v93 - F 15 '97 - p1009 [51-250]
y CBRS - v25 - Mr '97 - p96 [1-50]
y CCB-B - v50 - F '97 - p220+ [51-250]
y HB - v73 - Mr '97 - p213 [51-250]
y Kliatt - v31 - Mr '97 - p28 [51-250]
y KR - v64 - D 1 '96 - p1740+ [51-250]
y PW - v243 - D 16 '96 - p60 [51-250]
y SLJ - v43 - F '97 - p123+ [51-250]
Roberts, Thomas - *Religion and Psychoactive Sacraments*
r Rel St Rev - v23 - Ap '97 - p150 [51-250]
Roberts, Wess - *Protect Your Achilles Heel*
PW - v244 - Ap 28 '97 - p67 [51-250]
Roberts, Willo Davis - *Nightmare*
y JAAL - v40 - D '96 - p317 [51-250]
Secrets at Hidden Valley
c BL - v93 - Mr 15 '97 - p1243 [51-250]
Twisted Summer
y Emerg Lib - v23 - My '96 - p43 [1-50]
y HB Guide - v7 - Fall '96 - p305 [51-250]
Robertson, Adele Crockett - *The Orchard*
PW - v243 - D 30 '96 - p64 [1-50]
The Orchard (Gallagher). Audio Version
y Kliatt - v31 - My '97 - p48 [51-250]
Robertson, Brenda - *Francis Armstrong of Ireland and His Descendants in America*
r EGH - v50 - N '96 - p192 [51-250]
Robertson, Brian - *Little Blues Book*
PW - v243 - O 21 '96 - p78 [1-50]
Robertson, Bruce Carlisle - *Raja Rammohan Ray: The Father of Modern India*
AHR - v102 - F '97 - p161 [251-500]
Historian - v59 - Win '97 - p451+ [501+]
Robertson, Carol E - *Musical Repercussions of 1492*
RA - v25 - 4 '96 - p225+ [501+]
Robertson, David, 1937- - *Real Matter*
PW - v244 - Ap 21 '97 - p56 [51-250]
PW - v244 - Ap 21 '97 - p56 [51-250]
Robertson, David, 1947- - *Primer on the Autonomic Nervous System*
SciTech - v21 - Mr '97 - p40 [51-250]
Robertson, Denise - *Daybreak*
Woman's J - Ja '97 - p13 [51-250]
Robertson, Don - *Accessing Transport Networks*
r SciTech - v20 - D '96 - p75 [51-250]
Robertson, Fiona - *Legitimate Histories*
MP - v94 - F '97 - p406+ [501+]
RES - v47 - Ag '96 - p428+ [501+]
Robertson, George - *FutureNatural: Nature, Science, Culture*
Choice - v34 - Ja '97 - p813 [51-250]
NS & S - v9 - Ap 26 '96 - p35 [1-50]
SciTech - v20 - N '96 - p25 [51-250]
Robertson, Ian - *Oasis: What's the Story?*
PW - v244 - My 12 '97 - p64 [51-250]
Robertson, Ian Ross - *The Tenant League of Prince Edward Island 1864-1867*
Choice - v34 - D '96 - p678 [51-250]
R&R Bk N - v11 - N '96 - p31 [51-250]
Robertson, Jack S - *Twentieth-Century Artists on Art. 2nd Enl. Ed.*
r BL - v93 - N 1 '96 - p540 [51-250]
r Choice - v34 - F '97 - p949 [51-250]
Robertson, James C - *The Casablanca Man*
J Pop F&TV - v24 - Spr '96 - p45 [501+]
Robertson, James D - *The Beer-Taster's Log*
r ARBA - v28 - '97 - p570 [251-500]
r LJ - v122 - Ap 1 '97 - p63 [1-50]
Robertson, James I - *Stonewall Jackson--The Man, the Soldier, the Legend*
KR - v65 - Ja 1 '97 - p48+ [251-500]
LJ - v122 - F 15 '97 - p142 [51-250]
Stonewall Jackson: The Man, the Soldier, the Legend
NYTBR - v102 - Mr 16 '97 - p23 [501+]
Stonewall Jackson--The Man, the Soldier, the Legend
PW - v244 - F 3 '97 - p86 [51-250]
Robertson, Jennifer - *Native and Newcomer*
Am Ethnol - v23 - N '96 - p912+ [501+]
Robertson, Joel C - *Natural Prozac*
BL - v93 - F 15 '97 - p986+ [51-250]
PW - v244 - Ja 6 '97 - p71 [51-250]
Robertson, Kirk - *Just Past Labor Day*
BL - v93 - N '96 - p476 [51-250]
Robertson, Linda - *Kwanzaa Fun (Illus. by Julia Pearson)*
c PW - v243 - S 30 '96 - p88 [1-50]
Robertson, Pamela - *Guilty Pleasures*
Choice - v34 - D '96 - p622+ [51-250]
Robertson, Pat - *The End of the Age*
HM - v293 - S '96 - p64+ [501+]
Robertson, Ritchie - *The Habsburg Legacy*
EHR - v111 - N '96 - p1324+ [251-500]

Robertson, Robin - *366 Simply Delicious Dairy-Free Recipes*
    BL - v93 - F 15 '97 - p989 [51-250]
    PW - v244 - F 3 '97 - p103 [51-250]
Robertson, Robin, 1955- - *A Painted Field*
    Obs - Mr 2 '97 - p18* [51-250]
Robertson, Wendy - *Cruelty Games*
    PW - v244 - Ap 28 '97 - p55 [1-50]
Robertson-Lorant, Laurie - *Melville: A Biography*
    Choice - v34 - D '96 - p616 [51-250]
    LATBR - D 15 '96 - p8 [501+]
    NEQ - v69 - D '96 - p645+ [501+]
    W&I - v11 - D '96 - p266+ [501+]
Robideau, Henri - *Flapjacks and Photographs*
    Beav - v77 - F '97 - p44+ [251-500]
Robidoux, Rejean - *Fonder Une Litterature Nationale*
    Can Lit - Win '96 - p127+ [501+]
Robillard, Douglas - *American Supernatural Fiction*
    Nine-C Lit - v51 - S '96 - p276 [51-250]
Robin, Peggy - *The Starfleet Academy Entrance Exam*
    SF Chr - v18 - O '96 - p82 [1-50]
Robin, Ron - *The Barbed-Wire College*
    AHR - v102 - F '97 - p211+ [251-500]
    RAH - v25 - Mr '97 - p121+ [501+]
Robinet, Harriette Gillem - *Washington City Is Burning*
    c BL - v93 - N 1 '96 - p501 [51-250]
    c CBRS - v25 - N '96 - p35+ [51-250]
    c CCB-B - v50 - D '96 - p151 [51-250]
    c HB Guide - v8 - Spr '97 - p74 [51-250]
    c NYTBR - v102 - F 2 '97 - p18 [1-50]
    c SLJ - v42 - N '96 - p110 [51-250]
Robinett, Richard W - *Quantum Mechanics*
    Choice - v34 - Mr '97 - p1199 [51-250]
    J Chem Ed - v74 - Mr '97 - p343 [501+]
Robins, Anna Gruetzner - *Walter Sickert: Drawings*
    Apo - v145 - F '97 - p59+ [501+]
    Spec - v277 - S 21 '96 - p56 [501+]
Robins, Deri - *Santa's Sackful of Best Christmas Ideas*
    c Bks Keeps - N '96 - p21 [1-50]
Robinson, A B - *Witch Hunt in the B.C. Woods*
    Quill & Q - v62 - Jl '96 - p49 [251-500]
Robinson, Andrew - *The Story of Writing*
    LAR - v98 - Ag '96 - p424 [51-250]
Robinson, Andy - *Grassroots Grants*
    ChrPhil - v8 - O 3 '96 - p44 [51-250]
    Workbook - v21 - Fall '96 - p132 [501+]
Robinson, Barbara - *Best School Year Ever*
    c Sch Lib - v44 - Ag '96 - p108 [51-250]
Robinson, Cedric J - *Black Movements in America*
    y BL - v93 - D 15 '96 - p707 [51-250]
    LJ - v122 - Ja '97 - p124+ [51-250]
Robinson, Charles M - *Shark of the Confederacy*
    NWCR - v49 - Aut '96 - p158+ [501+]
Robinson, Christopher - *Scandal in the Ink*
    MLR - v92 - Ja '97 - p209 [251-500]
Robinson, Dale - *The Definitive Andy Griffith Show Reference*
    r ARBA - v28 - '97 - p517 [51-250]
    r R&R Bk N - v11 - N '96 - p66 [51-250]
Robinson, Daniel N - *Wild Beasts and Idle Humours*
    Choice - v34 - Mr '97 - p1232 [51-250]
    LJ - v121 - N 15 '96 - p75 [51-250]
    Nat - v264 - Ja 6 '97 - p29+ [501+]
Robinson, Dave - *Ethics for Beginners*
    New Sci - v152 - O 12 '96 - p42 [1-50]
Robinson, David, 1930- - *From Peep Show to Palace*
    ASInt - v34 - O '96 - p96+ [251-500]
    Bloom Rev - v16 - S '96 - p31 [51-250]
Robinson, David, 1936- - *Beautiful Death*
    WSJ-MW - v78 - D 5 '96 - pA18 [51-250]
Robinson, David L - *Brain, Mind, and Behavior*
    Choice - v34 - N '96 - p544 [51-250]
Robinson, Douglas - *Translation and Taboo*
    TLS - S 6 '96 - p10 [501+]
    TranslRevS - v2 - D '96 - p14 [51-250]
Robinson, Eden - *Traplines: Stories*
    BL - v93 - O 1 '96 - p323 [51-250]
    KR - v64 - Ag 15 '96 - p1181+ [251-500]
    LJ - v121 - S 15 '96 - p100 [51-250]
    Mac - v109 - D 9 '96 - p68 [501+]
    NYTBR - v101 - N 24 '96 - p21 [501+]
    NYTBR - v101 - D 8 '96 - p84 [1-50]
    Quill & Q - v62 - O '96 - p41 [51-250]
    Trib Bks - My 25 '97 - p3 [251-500]
Robinson, Fay - *Great Snakes! (Illus. by Jean Day Zallinger)*
    c BL - v93 - N 15 '96 - p597 [51-250]
    Pilots Fly Planes
    c HB Guide - v8 - Spr '97 - p91 [51-250]

Where Did All the Dragons Go? (Illus. by Victor Lee)
    c BL - v93 - D 15 '96 - p734 [51-250]
    c HB Guide - v8 - Spr '97 - p45 [1-50]
    c SFR - v22 - Ja '97 - p47 [51-250]
Robinson, Forrest G - *The Cambridge Companion to Mark Twain*
    Nine-C Lit - v50 - Mr '96 - p558 [51-250]
    WAL - v31 - Win '97 - p384+ [501+]
Robinson, Francis - *The Cambridge Illustrated History of the Islamic World*
    r MEJ - v50 - Aut '96 - p624 [51-250]
    y SLJ - v43 - Mr '97 - p218 [51-250]
    TLS - Mr 21 '97 - p31 [501+]
Robinson, Frank, Jr. - *Coping Plus*
    Soc Ser R - v70 - D '96 - p667+ [51-250]
Robinson, Fred C - *The Editing of Old English*
    MLR - v92 - Ja '97 - p157+ [501+]
Robinson, Geoffrey, 1917- - *Hedingham Harvest Victorian Family Life in Rural England*
    CR - v270 - F '97 - p109 [51-250]
Robinson, Geoffrey, 1957- - *The Dark Side of Paradise*
    TLS - My 24 '96 - p30+ [501+]
Robinson, Henry Morton - *The Cardinal*
    Nat R - v48 - D 23 '96 - p54 [51-250]
Robinson, Ian - *Life and Death under High Technology Medicine*
    Hast Cen R - v26 - Jl '96 - p42 [1-50]
Robinson, James W - *Atomic Spectroscopy. 2nd Ed.*
    SciTech - v20 - N '96 - p21 [51-250]
Robinson, Jancis - *Jancis Robinson's Guide to Wine Grapes*
    LJ - v122 - Ap 1 '97 - p64 [1-50]
    Jancis Robinson's Wine Course
    PW - v243 - S 2 '96 - p124 [51-250]
    The Oxford Companion to Wine
    r LJ - v122 - Ap 1 '97 - p62 [1-50]
Robinson, Jane - *Angels of Albion*
    Spec - v277 - O 5 '96 - p54+ [501+]
Robinson, Jeffrey, 1945- - *The Hotel: Backstairs at the World's Most Exclusive Hotel*
    KR - v65 - Ap 1 '97 - p532 [251-500]
    PW - v244 - Mr 31 '97 - p52+ [501+]
    The Laundrymen: Inside Money Laundering, the World's Third-Largest Business
    For Aff - v76 - Mr '97 - p177 [51-250]
Robinson, Jill - *Star Country*
    Rapport - v19 - 6 '96 - p24 [251-500]
Robinson, John B - *Life in 2030*
    Choice - v34 - My '97 - p1584 [51-250]
Robinson, John P - *Time for Life*
    PW - v244 - My 12 '97 - p71 [51-250]
Robinson, Joyntyle Theresa - *Bearing Witness*
    LJ - v122 - Mr 15 '97 - p59 [51-250]
Robinson, Julia - *The Collected Works of Julia Robinson*
    SciTech - v20 - D '96 - p4 [51-250]
Robinson, Karen - *Rescue! True Life Survival Stories*
    c TES - O 18 '96 - p12* [51-250]
Robinson, Kim Stanley - *Blue Mars*
    KR - v64 - My 1 '96 - p650 [251-500]
    LJ - v122 - Ja '97 - p51 [1-50]
    PW - v243 - N 4 '96 - p42 [1-50]
    Reason - v28 - D '96 - p37 [51-250]
    Red Mars
    Ext - v38 - Spr '97 - p57+ [501+]
Robinson, Leah Ruth - *First Cut*
    BL - v93 - Ja '97 - p780 [51-250]
    KR - v65 - Ja 15 '97 - p91 [251-500]
    LJ - v122 - F 1 '97 - p108 [51-250]
    PW - v244 - F 17 '97 - p210 [51-250]
Robinson, Lee - *Gateway*
    y Ch BWatch - v6 - Jl '96 - p3 [51-250]
    c HB Guide - v7 - Fall '96 - p297 [51-250]
Robinson, Lillian S - *Modern Women Writers. Vols. 1-4*
    r ARBA - v28 - '97 - p418+ [251-500]
    r BL - v93 - N 1 '96 - p538+ [501+]
    r Choice - v34 - F '97 - p947 [51-250]
Robinson, Lynda S - *Eater of Souls*
    LJ - v122 - My 1 '97 - p144 [1-50]
    PW - v244 - Ap 7 '97 - p77 [51-250]
Robinson, Mansel - *Colonial Tongues*
    Can Lit - Spr '97 - p219+ [501+]
Robinson, Marc - *Altogether Elsewhere*
    Salm - Sum '96 - p182+ [501+]
Robinson, Neil - *Ideology and the Collapse of the Soviet System*
    Russ Rev - v56 - Ja '97 - p148 [501+]
Robinson, Nicholas K - *Edmund Burke: A Life in Caricature*
    LJ - v122 - Ja '97 - p110 [51-250]
    Obs - N 3 '96 - p15* [51-250]
    TLS - D 20 '96 - p7 [501+]

Robinson, Nigel - *Second Nature*
    y Sch Lib - v44 - N '96 - p172 [51-250]
Robinson, Patrick - *Nimitz Class*
    y BL - v93 - Mr 1 '97 - p1069 [51-250]
    Books - v11 - Ap '97 - p22 [51-250]
    KR - v65 - Ap 1 '97 - p496 [251-500]
    PW - v244 - Ap 14 '97 - p51 [51-250]
Robinson, Paul - *Ludwig Van Beethoven, Fidelio*
    Choice - v34 - My '97 - p1509 [51-250]
Robinson, Peter - *The Transcription of Primary Textual Sources Using SGML*
    Compt & H - v30 - 1 '96 - p97+ [501+]
Robinson, Peter, 1938- - *The American Horticultural Society Complete Guide to Water Gardening*
    LJ - v122 - My 1 '97 - p130 [51-250]
Robinson, Peter, 1950- - *Innocent Graves*
    Arm Det - v30 - Win '97 - p71 [51-250]
    Arm Det - v30 - Win '97 - p1950+ [251-500]
    y BL - v92 - Ag '96 - p1887 [51-250]
    y BL - v92 - Ag '96 - p1891 [1-50]
    NYTBR - v101 - S 8 '96 - p26 [51-250]
    PW - v243 - N 4 '96 - p40 [1-50]
Robinson, Peter, 1953- - *Liverpool Accents*
    TLS - O 4 '96 - p40 [251-500]
Robinson, Rachel - *Jackie Robinson: An Intimate Portrait*
    BW - v26 - D 15 '96 - p13 [51-250]
    CSM - v89 - D 5 '96 - pB4 [51-250]
    LATBR - S 22 '96 - p1+ [501+]
    LATBR - D 29 '96 - p9 [51-250]
    LJ - v121 - N 1 '96 - p80 [1-50]
    NYTBR - v101 - N 3 '96 - p18 [51-250]
    NYTLa - v146 - D 2 '96 - pC16 [1-50]
    PW - v243 - S 30 '96 - p72 [51-250]
    Through Jackie Robinson
    B Ent - v27 - F '97 - p215 [1-50]
Robinson, Raoul A - *Return to Resistance*
    Am Sci - v84 - N '96 - p606+ [501+]
    BioSci - v47 - Ap '97 - p254+ [501+]
Robinson, Ray, 1905-1982 - *On Top Down Under*
    Aust Bk R - D '96 - p31+ [501+]
Robinson, Ray, 1920- - *American Original*
    HRNB - v25 - Fall '96 - p43 [251-500]
Robinson, Robert - *Skip All That*
    Spec - v277 - N 9 '96 - p51 [501+]
    TLS - N 22 '96 - p8 [501+]
Robinson, Roxana - *Asking for Love*
    BL - v93 - Ap 1 '97 - p1285 [1-50]
    HR - v49 - Aut '96 - p483+ [501+]
Robinson, Sancia - *Mary Jane: Living through Anorexia and Bulimia Nervosa*
    Aust Bk R - N '96 - p66 [51-250]
Robinson, Sharon - *Stealing Home*
    BW - v26 - Jl 7 '96 - p1+ [501+]
    LATBR - S 22 '96 - p1+ [501+]
    LATBR - D 29 '96 - p9 [51-250]
    NYTBR - v101 - N 3 '96 - p18 [51-250]
    y SLJ - v42 - O '96 - p166 [51-250]
Robinson, Spider - *Callahan's Legacy*
    Analog - v117 - F '97 - p145+ [51-250]
    KR - v64 - Ag 15 '96 - p1196 [51-250]
    PW - v243 - S 16 '96 - p75 [51-250]
Robinson, Sue - *The Smart Shopper's Guide to the Best Buys for Kids*
    PW - v243 - N 18 '96 - p73 [51-250]
    Well Dazzled
    c Bks Keeps - N '96 - p11 [51-250]
Robinson, T A - *Aristotle in Outline*
    CPR - v16 - O '96 - p369+ [501+]
Robinson, Tim - *Setting Foot on the Shores of Connemara and Other Writings*
    PW - v244 - Mr 17 '97 - p64+ [51-250]
Robinson, Tony - *Musical Tales (Robinson). Audio Version*
    c Quill & Q - v62 - My '96 - p31 [1-50]
    Odysseus Goes through Hell (Illus. by Chris Smedley)
    c Bks Keeps - Ja '97 - p22+ [51-250]
    c TES - N 15 '96 - p7* [51-250]
    Odysseus Super Hero (Illus. by Chris Smedley)
    c Bks Keeps - Ja '97 - p22+ [51-250]
    c TES - N 15 '96 - p7* [51-250]
    Theseus Monster Killer (Illus. by Chris Smedley)
    c Bks Keeps - Ja '97 - p22+ [51-250]
    Theseus, Monster Killer! (Illus. by Chris Smedley)
    c Bks Keeps - Ja '97 - p22+ [51-250]
    Theseus, Monster-Killer! (Illus. by Chris Smedley)
    c TES - N 15 '96 - p7* [51-250]
Robinson, W Douglas - *Southern Illinois Birds*
    r SciTech - v20 - N '96 - p29 [51-250]

Robinson, William H - *Transformations in Cleveland Art 1796-1946*
   Am Craft - v56 - O '96 - p50+ [251-500]
   Choice - v34 - O '96 - p269 [51-250]
Robinson, William I - *Promoting Polyarchy*
   Choice - v34 - Ap '97 - p1415 [51-250]
Robishaw, Sue - *The Last Lamp*
   BWatch - v18 - F '97 - p4 [51-250]
Robisheaux, Thomas - *Rural Society and the Search for Order in Early Modern Germany*
   J Soc H - v30 - Win '96 - p503+ [501+]
Robitaille, David F - *TIMSS Monograph. No. 2*
   Math T - v89 - N '96 - p696 [251-500]
Robl, Gregory - *A Student's Guide to German American Genealogy*
   yr ARBA - v28 - '97 - p167+ [251-500]
   y SLJ - v43 - Ja '97 - p133 [51-250]
Robles, Emmanuel - *Camus, Frere De Soleil*
   WLT - v70 - Aut '96 - p917 [501+]
Robles Garcia, Nelly M - *Las Canteras De Mitla, Oaxaca*
   LA Ant - v7 - D '96 - p380 [501+]
Robshaw, Brandon - *The Boy with the Eggshell Skull*
   c TES - Mr 21 '97 - p11* [51-250]
Robson, Ian - *Active Galactic Nuclei*
   Choice - v34 - D '96 - p634+ [51-250]
   SciTech - v20 - S '96 - p13 [51-250]
Robson, John M - *Marriage or Celibacy?*
   Albion - v28 - Fall '96 - p517+ [501+]
Robson, Mike - *A Practical Guide to Business Process Re-Engineering*
   R&R Bk N - v11 - N '96 - p30 [51-250]
Robson, Roy R - *Old Believers in Modern Russia*
   Choice - v34 - S '96 - p188 [51-250]
Robson, Ruthann - *Gay Men, Lesbians, and the Law*
   y BL - v93 - S 15 '96 - p228+ [51-250]
   y HB Guide - v8 - Spr '97 - p94 [51-250]
   y SLJ - v42 - O '96 - p159 [51-250]
   y VOYA - v19 - F '97 - p353 [251-500]
Robson, Sue - *Education in Early Childhood*
   r TES - F 7 '97 - p12* [501+]
Roca, Nuria - *Cells, Genes, and Chromosomes (Illus. by Antonio Munoz Tenllado)*
   y HB Guide - v7 - Fall '96 - p338 [51-250]
   The Nervous System (Illus. by Antonio Munoz Tenllado)
   y HB Guide - v7 - Fall '96 - p348+ [51-250]
   The Respiratory System (Illus. by Antonio Munoz Tenllado)
   y HB Guide - v7 - Fall '96 - p348+ [51-250]
Rocca, Giancarlo - *Donne Religiose*
   CH - v65 - D '96 - p762+ [501+]
Rocek, Thomas R - *Navajo Multi-Household Social Units*
   Am Ant - v61 - O '96 - p806+ [501+]
Roche, Alex F - *Human Body Composition*
   Choice - v34 - O '96 - p303 [251-500]
Roche, Anthony - *Contemporary Irish Drama*
   Col Lit - v23 - O '96 - p163+ [501+]
Roche, Daniel - *The Culture of Clothing*
   EHR - v111 - N '96 - p1295+ [251-500]
   JMH - v68 - D '96 - p974+ [501+]
   Sev Cent N - v54 - Spr '96 - p26+ [501+]
Roche, Denis - *Loo-Loo, Boo, and Art You Can Do (Illus. by Denis Roche)*
   c BL - v93 - S 15 '96 - p244 [51-250]
   c CBRS - v25 - N '96 - p31+ [51-250]
   c CCB-B - v50 - S '96 - p27 [51-250]
   c HB Guide - v8 - Spr '97 - p135 [51-250]
   c LATBR - O 27 '96 - p11 [51-250]
   c SLJ - v42 - Ag '96 - p140+ [51-250]
   Ollie All Over (Illus. by Denis Roche)
   c KR - v65 - F 1 '97 - p227 [51-250]
   c PW - v244 - Ja 13 '97 - p77 [51-250]
   Only One Ollie (Illus. by Denis Roche)
   c PW - v244 - Ja 13 '97 - p77 [51-250]
Roche, Hannah - *Corey's Kite (Illus. by Pierre Pratt)*
   c BL - v93 - N 15 '96 - p595 [51-250]
   Karl's Kite (Illus. by Pierre Pratt)
   c Sch Lib - v44 - Ag '96 - p101 [51-250]
   My Dad's a Wizard! (Illus. by Chris Fisher)
   c Sch Lib - v44 - Ag '96 - p113 [51-250]
   My Grandma Is Great! (Illus. by Chris Fisher)
   c HB Guide - v8 - Spr '97 - p134 [51-250]
   c Sch Lib - v44 - N '96 - p147 [51-250]
   c SLJ - v43 - Ja '97 - p90 [51-250]
   c TES - Ja 31 '97 - pR7 [251-500]
   My Mum Is Magic! (Illus. by Chris Fisher)
   c Sch Lib - v44 - Ag '96 - p113 [51-250]
   My Sister Is Super! (Illus. by Chris Fisher)
   c HB Guide - v8 - Spr '97 - p134 [51-250]
   c Sch Lib - v44 - N '96 - p147 [51-250]
   c SLJ - v43 - Ja '97 - p90 [51-250]
   c TES - Ja 31 '97 - pR7 [251-500]

Pete's Puddles (Illus. by Pierre Pratt)
   c BL - v93 - N 15 '96 - p595 [51-250]
   c Sch Lib - v44 - Ag '96 - p101 [51-250]
Sandra's Sun Hat (Illus. by Pierre Pratt)
   c BL - v93 - N 15 '96 - p595 [51-250]
Suki's Sun Hat (Illus. by Pierre Pratt)
   c Sch Lib - v44 - Ag '96 - p101 [51-250]
Su's Snowgirl (Illus. by Pierre Pratt)
   c Sch Lib - v44 - Ag '96 - p101 [51-250]
Roche, Jorg - *Fur- Und Wider-Spruche*
   MLJ - v80 - Fall '96 - p420+ [501+]
Rochlin, Gene I - *Trapped in the Net*
   BL - v93 - My 15 '97 - p1547 [51-250]
   PW - v244 - Mr 24 '97 - p65+ [51-250]
Rochlitz, Rainer - *The Disenchantment of Art*
   Choice - v34 - O '96 - p295 [51-250]
Rochman, Hazel - *Against Borders*
   r RQ - v36 - Win '96 - p210 [51-250]
   Bearing Witness
   y Emerg Lib - v24 - S '96 - p23 [1-50]
   Leaving Home
   y BL - v93 - Ja '97 - p844 [251-500]
   y CCB-B - v50 - Mr '97 - p256+ [51-250]
   y HB - v73 - My '97 - p327+ [251-500]
   y HMR - Spr '97 - p31+ [501+]
   y KR - v65 - Ja 15 '97 - p145 [51-250]
   y PW - v244 - Ja 13 '97 - p77 [51-250]
   y SLJ - v43 - Mr '97 - p191+ [51-250]
Rochon, Louis-Philippe - *Economics in Crisis*
   Econ J - v107 - Ja '97 - p262 [51-250]
Rock, Howard B - *American Artisans*
   BHR - v70 - Sum '96 - p267+ [501+]
   ILRR - v50 - O '96 - p182+ [501+]
   JSH - v63 - F '97 - p145+ [501+]
Rock, Lois - *Festivals of the Christian Year*
   c TES - F 14 '97 - p16* [51-250]
   The Little Fir Tree's Busy for Christmas Book (Illus. by Cathy Baxter)
   c Bks Keeps - N '96 - p21 [1-50]
Rock, Maxine - *Kishina: A True Story of Gorilla Survival*
   c SB - v33 - Mr '97 - p52 [251-500]
   c SLJ - v42 - Ag '96 - p159 [51-250]
Rock, Peter - *This Is the Place*
   KR - v65 - F 15 '97 - p251 [251-500]
   PW - v244 - F 24 '97 - p64 [51-250]
Rockcastle, Mary Francois - *Rainy Lake*
   y Kliatt - v30 - S '96 - p13+ [51-250]
Rocke, Michael - *Forbidden Friendships*
   Advocate - D 24 '96 - p67+ [501+]
   Choice - v34 - Mr '97 - p1222+ [51-250]
   VV - v42 - Ja 21 '97 - p51 [501+]
Rockenwagner, Hans - *Rockenwagner*
   LJ - v122 - Mr 15 '97 - p84 [51-250]
   PW - v244 - F 17 '97 - p215 [51-250]
Rockett, Kevin - *The Irish Filmography*
   r ILS - v16 - Spr '97 - p35 [51-250]
   r Si & So - v6 - N '96 - p38 [51-250]
The Rockies (Insight Guides). New Ed.
   r BL - v93 - S 15 '96 - p210 [1-50]
Rocklin, Joanne - *For Your Eyes Only! (Illus. by Mark Todd)*
   c BL - v93 - Mr 1 '97 - p1165 [51-250]
   c CCB-B - v50 - Ap '97 - p292+ [51-250]
   c KR - v65 - Ja 15 '97 - p145 [51-250]
   c PW - v244 - F 24 '97 - p91+ [51-250]
   c SLJ - v43 - Mr '97 - p192 [51-250]
   One Hungry Cat (Illus. by Rowan Barnes-Murphy)
   c BL - v93 - My 1 '97 - p1504 [51-250]
Rockman, Alexis - *Concrete Jungle*
   PW - v244 - Ja 27 '97 - p93 [51-250]
Rockmore, Tom - *On Heidegger's Nazism and Philosophy*
   RM - v49 - Je '96 - p943+ [501+]
Rockwell, Anne F - *Big Boss (Illus. by Anne F Rockwell)*
   c HB Guide - v8 - Spr '97 - p59 [51-250]
   I Fly (Illus. by Annette Cable)
   c PW - v244 - Mr 31 '97 - p76 [51-250]
   Once upon a Time This Morning (Illus. by Sucie Stevenson)
   c BL - v93 - Ap 1 '97 - p1339 [51-250]
   c CCB-B - v50 - Ap '97 - p293 [51-250]
   c KR - v65 - Ja 15 '97 - p145 [51-250]
   c PW - v244 - Ja 6 '97 - p72 [51-250]
   c SLJ - v43 - Mr '97 - p164 [51-250]
   The One-Eyed Giant and Other Monsters from the Greek Myths
   c Ch BWatch - v6 - My '96 - p4 [1-50]
   One-Eyed Giant and Other Monsters from the Greek Myths
   c Emerg Lib - v24 - S '96 - p43+ [1-50]

The One-Eyed Giant and Other Monsters from the Greek Myths
   c HB Guide - v7 - Fall '96 - p323 [51-250]
Show and Tell Day (Illus. by Lizzy Rockwell)
   c BL - v93 - Ap 1 '97 - p1339 [51-250]
The Story Snail (Illus. by Theresa Smith)
   c BL - v93 - My 1 '97 - p1504 [51-250]
Sweet Potato Pie
   c BL - v92 - Ag '96 - p1910 [51-250]
Rockwell, Norman - *Willie Was Different (Illus. by Norman Rockwell)*
   c PW - v244 - Ap 28 '97 - p77 [1-50]
Rockwell, Paul Vincent - *Rewriting Resemblance in Medieval French Romance*
   Choice - v34 - O '96 - p286 [51-250]
Rockwood, Charles A - *Fractures in Children. 4th Ed., Vol. 3*
   r SciTech - v21 - Mr '97 - p60 [51-250]
Rodari, Gianni - *The Grammar of Fantasy*
   y Kliatt - v30 - N '96 - p18 [51-250]
Rodda, Emily - *Power and Glory (Illus. by Geoff Kelly)*
   c BL - v93 - Ja '97 - p768 [51-250]
   c HB Guide - v7 - Fall '96 - p272 [51-250]
   c Inst - v106 - O '96 - p68 [51-250]
   Rowan and the Travellers
   y Sch Lib - v44 - N '96 - p172 [51-250]
Rodden, Lois - *Profiles of Women*
   Horoscope - v63 - F '97 - p16+ [251-500]
Rodcd, Ruth - *Women in Islamic Biographical Collections from Ibn Sa'd to Who's Who*
   JTWS - v13 - Spr '96 - p376+ [501+]
Rodell, Susanna - *Dear Fred (Illus. by Kim Gamble)*
   c RT - v50 - N '96 - p254+ [51-250]
Roden, Claudia - *The Book of Jewish Food*
   BL - v93 - D 15 '96 - p702 [51-250]
   LJ - v121 - D '96 - p135 [51-250]
   PW - v243 - N 4 '96 - p73 [51-250]
Roden, Katie - *Farming (Illus. by James Field)*
   c Bks Keeps - Ja '97 - p26 [51-250]
   c HB Guide - v8 - Spr '97 - p133 [51-250]
   c Sch Lib - v45 - F '97 - p40 [51-250]
   c SLJ - v43 - Ja '97 - p133 [51-250]
   In the Footsteps of the Mummy
   c HB Guide - v7 - Fall '96 - p379+ [51-250]
   Plague
   c HB Guide - v8 - Spr '97 - p130 [51-250]
   c Learning - v25 - Mr '97 - p38 [1-50]
   Solving International Crime
   c BL - v93 - Ja '97 - p850+ [251-500]
   c HB Guide - v8 - Spr '97 - p96 [51-250]
   c SLJ - v43 - Ja '97 - p103+ [51-250]
Rodenbach, Georges - *L'Arbre*
   RMR - v50 - 2 '96 - p137+ [501+]
Roderick, Timothy - *Dark Moon Mysteries*
   BWatch - v17 - S '96 - p12 [51-250]
Roderus, Frank - *Potter's Fields*
   Roundup M - v4 - F '97 - p29+ [251-500]
Rodes, Montserrat - *Escrits En Blanc*
   WLT - v70 - Aut '96 - p940 [251-500]
Rodger, Elizabeth - *Caterpillar to Butterfly*
   c Ch BWatch - v6 - Jl '96 - p4 [1-50]
   Tadpole to Frog
   c Ch BWatch - v6 - Jl '96 - p4 [1-50]
Rodger, N A M - *Naval Power in the Twentieth Century*
   NWCR - v50 - Win '97 - p136+ [501+]
   The Wooden World
   Sea H - Win '96 - p46 [51-250]
Rodger, Richard - *A Consolidated Bibliography of Urban History*
   r Choice - v34 - My '97 - p1480 [51-250]
   r R&R Bk N - v12 - F '97 - p54 [51-250]
Rodgers, Bradley A - *Guardian of the Great Lakes*
   Choice - v34 - N '96 - p528 [51-250]
Rodgers, Eugene - *Flying High*
   A & S Sm - v11 - O '96 - p88 [1-50]
   BW - v27 - Ja 5 '97 - p6 [251-500]
   KR - v64 - S 15 '96 - p1385 [251-500]
   PW - v243 - N 4 '96 - p59+ [51-250]
Rodgers, Frank - *A Is for AAARGH!*
   c Sch Lib - v44 - Ag '96 - p96+ [501+]
   Bumps in the Night (Illus. by Philip Hopman)
   c Bks Keeps - Ja '97 - p20 [51-250]
   The Pirate and the Pig
   c Sch Lib - v44 - Ag '96 - p101 [51-250]
   Rattle and Hum, Robot Detectives
   c Sch Lib - v44 - N '96 - p152 [51-250]
   c TES - Jl 5 '96 - pR6 [1-50]
Rodgers, Harrell R, Jr. - *Poor Women, Poor Children. 3rd Ed.*
   JEL - v34 - D '96 - p2065 [51-250]

Rodgers, James A - *Rare and Endangered Biota of Florida. Vol. 5*
   Choice - v34 - F '97 - p990+ [51-250]
Rodgers, Joni - *Crazy for Trying*
   KR - v64 - S 1 '96 - p1263 [251-500]
   LJ - v121 - O 15 '96 - p91 [51-250]
   PW - v243 - S 30 '96 - p60+ [51-250]
Rodgers, Silvia - *In Red Saint, Pink Daughter*
   Spec - v277 - N 23 '96 - p46 [1-50]
Rodgers, Susan - *Telling Lives, Telling History*
   Biography - v19 - Fall '96 - p430 [1-50]
Rodgers, Terry - *The Library Paraprofessional*
   LJ - v122 - F 1 '97 - p114 [51-250]
Rodi, Robert - *Kept Boy*
   BL - v93 - N 1 '96 - p482 [51-250]
   KR - v64 - O 1 '96 - p1423 [251-500]
   LJ - v121 - N 1 '96 - p108 [51-250]
   PW - v243 - O 21 '96 - p71 [51-250]
Rodker, John - *Poems and Adolphe 1920*
   ELT - v40 - 2 '97 - p255 [51-250]
Rodman, Dennis - *Bad as I Wanna Be*
   PW - v244 - My 5 '97 - p206 [1-50]
   Walk on the Wild Side
   BL - v93 - My 15 '97 - p1542 [1-50]
Rodman, Edmon J - *Nomo: The Tornado Who Took America by Storm*
   c SLJ - v42 - Ag '96 - p160 [51-250]
   Safety City (Illus. by Roger DeKlerk)
   c PW - v243 - S 23 '96 - p77 [51-250]
Rodman, Gilbert B - *Elvis after Elvis*
   LJ - v121 - O 1 '96 - p80 [51-250]
   Nat - v263 - D 9 '96 - p29+ [501+]
   PW - v243 - S 16 '96 - p76 [51-250]
Rodman, Peter W - *America Adrift*
   For Aff - v75 - S '96 - p144+ [51-250]
Rodman, Richard - *The 17 Laws of Successful Investing*
   BL - v92 - Ag '96 - p1866 [51-250]
Rodman, Selden - *Geniuses and Other Eccentrics*
   PW - v244 - Mr 3 '97 - p61 [51-250]
Rodowsky, Colby - *Remembering Mog*
   y BL - v93 - Ap 1 '97 - p1305 [1-50]
   y HB Guide - v7 - Fall '96 - p305 [51-250]
   y HMR - Fall '96 - p38 [501+]
   y JAAL - v40 - S '96 - p71 [51-250]
Rodriguez, Ferdinand - *Principles of Polymer Systems. 4th Ed.*
   SciTech - v20 - S '96 - p59 [51-250]
Rodriguez, Ileana - *House/Garden/Nation: Space, Gender, Ethnicity in Post-Colonial Latin American Literature by Women*
   HAHR - v77 - F '97 - p86+ [251-500]
   Women, Guerillas, and Love
   Choice - v34 - F '97 - p971 [51-250]
Rodriguez, Jeanette - *Stories We Live*
   Rel St Rev - v23 - Ja '97 - p94 [51-250]
Rodriguez, Jesus Antonio - *Mayo Del 68*
   HAHR - v77 - F '97 - p83+ [501+]
Rodriguez, Luis J - *Always Running*
   y BL - v93 - D 15 '96 - p717 [1-50]
Rodriguez, Mario - *William Burke and Francisco De Miranda*
   EHR - v111 - N '96 - p1308+ [501+]
   HAHR - v76 - N '96 - p805+ [251-500]
Rodriguez, Robert - *Mad about Martha*
   Ent W - Ja 10 '97 - p52 [51-250]
   Rebel without a Crew
   Ent W - S 27 '96 - p75 [51-250]
   FIR - v47 - S '96 - p84 [251-500]
Rodriguez, Roberto - *Justice: A Question of Race*
   BL - v93 - My 15 '97 - p1547+ [51-250]
Rodriguez, Sylvia - *The Matachines Dance*
   Choice - v34 - Ap '97 - p1382 [51-250]
Rodriguez Aisa, Maria Luisa - *El Cardenal Goma Y La Guerra De Espana*
   CHR - v82 - O '96 - p661+ [501+]
Rodriguez Baquero, Luis Enrique - *Encomienda Y Vida Diaria Entre Los Indios De Muzo 1550-1620*
   HAHR - v76 - Ag '96 - p561+ [501+]
Rodriguez Monegal, Emir - *Lautreamont Austral*
   WLT - v71 - Win '97 - p236 [501+]
Rodriguez O, Jaime E - *Mexico in the Age of Democratic Revolutions 1750-1850*
   HAHR - v76 - Ag '96 - p574+ [501+]
   JTWS - v13 - Spr '96 - p351+ [501+]
Rodriguez Silva, Delfin - *Cronologia Martiana*
   BL - v93 - Ap 1 '97 - p1284 [1-50]
Rodwin, Lloyd - *Rethinking the Development Experience*
   Econ J - v107 - Ja '97 - p283 [251-500]
   JEL - v34 - S '96 - p1385+ [501+]
Roe, Byron P - *Particle Physics at the New Millennium*
   Phys Today - v49 - S '96 - p91+ [501+]

Roe, C F - *A Hidden Cause of Murder*
   Arm Det - v29 - Sum '96 - p367+ [251-500]
Roe, Emery - *Narrative Policy Analysis*
   APSR - v90 - S '96 - p657+ [501+]
   QJS - v82 - Ag '96 - p313+ [501+]
Roe, Mark J - *Strong Managers, Weak Owners*
   Econ J - v106 - N '96 - p1781+ [501+]
   NYRB - v44 - Ap 10 '97 - p38+ [501+]
Roe, Michael - *Australia, Britain, and Migration 1915-1940*
   Choice - v34 - O '96 - p337 [51-250]
Roehner, Bertrand M - *Theory of Markets*
   JEL - v34 - D '96 - p2026+ [51-250]
Roehr, M - *Biotechnology: A Multi-Volume Comprehensive Treatise. 2nd Ed., Vol. 6*
   SciTech - v21 - Mr '97 - p36 [51-250]
Roehr, Sabine - *A Primer on German Enlightenment*
   RM - v50 - S '96 - p174+ [501+]
Roelker, Nancy L - *One King, One Faith*
   Choice - v34 - N '96 - p520 [51-250]
   HRNB - v25 - Win '97 - p80 [251-500]
   Rel St Rev - v23 - Ap '97 - p192 [51-250]
   TLS - O 11 '96 - p30+ [501+]
Roell, Craig H - *Remember Goliad!*
   JSH - v62 - N '96 - p862 [51-250]
Roemer, John E - *Theories of Distributive Justice*
   Choice - v34 - O '96 - p331 [51-250]
   JEL - v34 - S '96 - p1414 [51-250]
Roessner, Michaela - *The Stars Dispose*
   KR - v65 - Mr 1 '97 - p341 [51-250]
   LJ - v122 - Ap 15 '97 - p124 [51-250]
   PW - v244 - Mr 31 '97 - p67 [51-250]
Roett, Riordan - *The Mexican Peso Crisis*
   Choice - v34 - Ja '97 - p846 [51-250]
   For Aff - v76 - Mr '97 - p188+ [51-250]
Roffey, Maureen - *A Crooked Man and Other Rhymes*
   c TES - N 29 '96 - p13* [51-250]
   Little Bo Peep and Other Rhymes
   c TES - N 29 '96 - p13* [51-250]
   Ten Little Teddy Bears
   c Books - v9 - S '95 - p26 [1-50]
Rogal, Samuel J - *A Companion to the Characters in the Fiction and Drama of W. Somerset Maugham*
   r ARBA - v28 - '97 - p456 [51-250]
   r Choice - v34 - N '96 - p435 [51-250]
   ELT - v40 - 1 '97 - p121+ [501+]
   An Index to the Biblical References, Parallels, and Allusions in the Poetry and Prose of John Milton
   r Six Ct J - v27 - Win '96 - p1165+ [501+]
   Sing Glory and Hallelujah!
   r ARBA - v28 - '97 - p495 [51-250]
Rogal, Stan - *What Passes for Love*
   BIC - v25 - N '96 - p15+ [501+]
Rogasky, Barbara - *The Golem: A Version (Illus. by Trina Schart Hyman)*
   c BL - v93 - O 1 '96 - p335 [251-500]
   c CBRS - v25 - O '96 - p23+ [51-250]
   c CCB-B - v50 - S '96 - p27+ [51-250]
   c CLW - v67 - D '96 - p62+ [501+]
   c HB Guide - v8 - Spr '97 - p74 [51-250]
   c KR - v64 - S 15 '96 - p1407 [51-250]
   c NYTBR - v101 - N 10 '96 - p44 [501+]
   y PW - v243 - O 21 '96 - p84+ [51-250]
   c SLJ - v42 - O '96 - p126 [51-250]
Roger, Jacques - *Buffon: A Life in Natural History*
   KR - v65 - My 1 '97 - p704+ [251-500]
   PW - v244 - My 12 '97 - p68 [51-250]
Rogers, Anne - *Mental Health Policy in Britain*
   SciTech - v20 - D '96 - p40 [51-250]
Rogers, Annie G - *A Shining Reflection*
   NYTBR - v102 - F 2 '97 - p28 [1-50]
Rogers, Arthur - *Bioethics in Europe*
   J Gov Info - v23 - S '96 - p664 [51-250]
Rogers, Bogart - *A Yankee Ace in the RAF*
   Choice - v34 - My '97 - p1564+ [51-250]
Rogers, Carole Garibaldi - *Poverty, Chastity, and Change*
   Am - v176 - Mr 29 '97 - p26+ [501+]
   BW - v26 - N 24 '96 - p4+ [501+]
   CLW - v67 - Mr '97 - p33 [501+]
   LJ - v121 - O 1 '96 - p85 [51-250]
   RR - v56 - Mr '97 - p221+ [1-50]
Rogers, Clifford J - *The Military Revolution Debate*
   J Mil H - v61 - Ja '97 - p152+ [501+]
Rogers, Colin D - *The Family Tree Detective*
   TES - Jl 26 '96 - pR6 [51-250]
Rogers, Daniel E - *Politics after Hitler*
   AHR - v101 - D '96 - p1571 [501+]
Rogers, Deborah D - *Ann Radcliffe: A Bio-Bibliography*
   r ARBA - v28 - '97 - p456+ [51-250]
   r Choice - v34 - S '96 - p106 [51-250]

Rogers, Everett M - *Diffusion of Innovations*
   Inc. - v18 - D '96 - p54 [251-500]
Rogers, Fred - *Dear Mister Rogers, Does It Ever Rain in Your Neighborhood?*
   CSM - v89 - Mr 13 '97 - p13 [251-500]
   Divorce (Illus. by Jim Judkis)
   c HB Guide - v7 - Fall '96 - p311 [51-250]
Rogers, G A J - *Locke's Philosophy*
   Sev Cent N - v54 - Fall '96 - p63 [501+]
Rogers, J Daniel - *Mississippian Communities and Households*
   Am Ant - v61 - O '96 - p805+ [501+]
Rogers, Jack - *Claiming the Center*
   CH - v66 - Mr '97 - p215+ [51-250]
   Rel St Rev - v22 - O '96 - p339 [51-250]
Rogers, James Steven - *The Early History of the Law of Bills and Notes*
   BHR - v70 - Sum '96 - p260+ [501+]
Rogers, James T - *Woodrow Wilson: Visionary for Peace*
   y BL - v93 - My 15 '97 - p1572 [51-250]
Rogers, Jane - *Promised Lands*
   KR - v65 - Ap 1 '97 - p496+ [251-500]
   LJ - v122 - Ap 1 '97 - p131 [51-250]
   PW - v244 - Mr 10 '97 - p49+ [51-250]
Rogers, Joel - *Works Councils*
   AJS - v102 - Ja '97 - p1205+ [501+]
   JEL - v34 - S '96 - p1448+ [51-250]
   JEL - v34 - D '96 - p1979+ [501+]
Rogers, Joey - *Object-Oriented Neural Networks in C++*
   SciTech - v21 - Mr '97 - p10 [51-250]
Rogers, John, 1961- - *The Matter of Revolution*
   Choice - v34 - D '96 - p617 [51-250]
   NY - v72 - Ja 6 '97 - p73 [51-250]
Rogers, John Headly - *British Short-Fiction Writers 1915-1945*
   r ARBA - v28 - '97 - p448 [251-500]
   r Choice - v34 - N '96 - p426 [51-250]
Rogers, Juliet - *A Field Guide to Joint Disease in Archaeology*
   Am Ant - v61 - Jl '96 - p630 [251-500]
Rogers, Katrina S - *Toward a Postpositivist World*
   R&R Bk N - v11 - N '96 - p46 [51-250]
Rogers, Linda - *Molly Brown Is Not a Clown (Illus. by Rick Van Krugel)*
   c Quill & Q - v62 - Jl '96 - p56+ [251-500]
Rogers, Mark C - *Textbook of Pediatric Intensive Care. 3rd Ed.*
   SciTech - v20 - N '96 - p52 [51-250]
Rogers, Michael D - *Business and the Environment*
   SciTech - v20 - N '96 - p2 [51-250]
Rogers, Pat - *Johnson and Boswell*
   Albion - v28 - Fall '96 - p495+ [501+]
   RES - v48 - F '97 - p114+ [501+]
   The Samuel Johnson Encyclopedia
   r ARBA - v28 - '97 - p455 [51-250]
   r Choice - v34 - D '96 - p594 [51-250]
   r LJ - v121 - O 15 '96 - p53 [51-250]
   r R&R Bk N - v11 - N '96 - p70 [51-250]
Rogers, Pattiann - *Firekeeper: New and Selected Poems*
   Poet - v169 - D '96 - p160+ [501+]
   PS - v70 - Fall '96 - p195+ [501+]
Rogers, Paul - *Cat's Kittens (Illus. by Sophy Williams)*
   c BL - v93 - F 15 '97 - p1029 [51-250]
   c JB - v60 - O '96 - p187+ [51-250]
   c KR - v64 - D 15 '96 - p1803 [51-250]
   c PW - v243 - D 30 '96 - p66+ [51-250]
   c Sch Lib - v44 - N '96 - p147 [51-250]
   c SLJ - v43 - Mr '97 - p164+ [51-250]
   Giant Pie (Illus. by Nick Schon)
   c TES - Mr 21 '97 - p9* [501+]
   A Letter to Granny (Illus. by John Prater)
   c Bks Keeps - N '96 - p8 [51-250]
Rogers, Paul T - *Saul's Book*
   PW - v243 - N 18 '96 - p70 [1-50]
Rogers, Rebecca - *Les Demoiselles De La Legion D'Honneur*
   JMH - v68 - D '96 - p997+ [501+]
Rogers, Richard - *Richard Rogers Partnership*
   TLS - D 20 '96 - p19 [501+]
Rogers, Robert F - *Destiny's Landfall*
   AHR - v101 - D '96 - p1603+ [501+]
   Cont Pac - v9 - Spr '97 - p275+ [501+]
Rogers, Rolf E - *Implementation of Total Quality Management*
   JEL - v34 - S '96 - p1461 [51-250]
Rogers, Ruth - *The Rogers Gray Italian Country Cookbook*
   SFR - v22 - Ja '97 - p48 [51-250]
Rogers, Susan Fox - *Another Wilderness*
   Aethlon - v13 - Fall '95 - p142+ [251-500]

Close Calls
> BL - v93 - N 1 '96 - p481 [51-250]
> KR - v64 - S 15 '96 - p1349+ [251-500]
> LJ - v121 - O 1 '96 - p129 [51-250]
> Ms - v7 - Ja '97 - p82 [1-50]
> PW - v243 - O 7 '96 - p61 [51-250]

Portraits of Love
> Advocate - F 18 '97 - p61 [51-250]

Rogers, Will - *The Papers of Will Rogers. Vol. 1*
> AL - v68 - D '96 - p878 [51-250]
> Choice - v34 - S '96 - p110 [51-250]
> WHQ - v27 - Win '96 - p549 [51-250]

Rogers, William Elford - *Interpreting Interpretation*
> MLR - v92 - Ja '97 - p147+ [501+]

Rogerson, Robert - *Escape from the City*
> Books - v10 - Je '96 - p21 [51-250]

Rogg, Carla S - *The Boarding School Guide*
> r ARBA - v28 - '97 - p137+ [51-250]

Rogge, A E - *The Historical Archaeology of Dam Construction Camps in Central Arizona. Vol. 1*
> Pub Hist - v18 - Fall '96 - p162+ [501+]

Raising Arizona's Dams
> Pub Hist - v18 - Fall '96 - p162+ [501+]
> T&C - v37 - Ap '96 - p358+ [501+]

Roggeri, Henri - *Tropical Freshwater Wetlands*
> SciTech - v20 - N '96 - p25 [51-250]

Rogin, Michael - *Blackface, White Noise*
> Choice - v34 - N '96 - p468 [51-250]
> KR - v64 - My 1 '96 - p673+ [251-500]
> Lon R Bks - v18 - Jl 18 '96 - p22+ [501+]
> Si & So - v6 - N '96 - p34 [51-250]
> Tikkun - v11 - N '96 - p67+ [501+]

Rogow, Debbie - *Get Real Comics (Illus. by Charley Parker)*
> yp JAAL - v40 - Mr '97 - p512 [1-50]

Rogozhin, Mikhail - *Supermodell V Luchakh Smerti*
> BL - v93 - O 1 '96 - p327 [1-50]

Rogozkin, Victor A - *Current Research in Sports Sciences*
> SciTech - v21 - Mr '97 - p59 [51-250]

Rohde, David - *Endgame: The Betrayal and Fall of Srebrenica, Europe's Worst Massacre since World War II*
> BL - v93 - My 1 '97 - p1476 [51-250]
> KR - v65 - Mr 15 '97 - p448 [251-500]
> LJ - v122 - My 1 '97 - p126 [51-250]
> PW - v244 - Mr 31 '97 - p50 [51-250]

Rohdie, Sam - *The Passion of Pier Paolo Pasolini*
> Choice - v34 - O '96 - p264 [51-250]
> TLS - My 24 '96 - p22+ [501+]

Rohl, John C G - *The Kaiser and His Court*
> HT - v46 - Jl '96 - p54+ [501+]
> NYRB - v43 - Je 6 '96 - p20+ [501+]

Wilhelm II: Die Jugend Des Kaisers 1859-1888
> CEH - v29 - 1 '96 - p134+ [501+]

Rohmer, Harriet - *How We Came to the Fifth World*
> c SS - v88 - Ja '97 - p29+ [501+]

The Invisible Hunters (Illus. by J Sam)
> c SS - v88 - Ja '97 - p29+ [501+]

Rohr, John A - *Founding Republics in France and America*
> J Pol - v59 - F '97 - p293+ [501+]

Rohr, Rene R J - *Sundials: History, Theory, and Practice*
> y Ch BWatch - v6 - D '96 - p2 [1-50]
> LATBR - O 20 '96 - p15 [51-250]
> LJ - v122 - Mr 15 '97 - p94 [1-50]

Rohr, Richard - *Enneagram II*
> RR - v55 - S '96 - p550+ [251-500]

Jesus' Plan for a New World
> OS - v32 - Jl '96 - p43 [51-250]

Job and the Mystery of Suffering
> CLW - v67 - D '96 - p41 [251-500]

Rohr, Werner - *Okkupation Und Kollaboration 1938-1945*
> EHR - v112 - F '97 - p265 [251-500]

Rohrbough, Linda - *Upgrade Your Own PC*
> LJ - v121 - N 1 '96 - p104 [51-250]

Rohrbough, Malcolm J - *Days of Gold*
> CHE - v43 - Ap 4 '97 - pA16 [51-250]
> LJ - v122 - My 1 '97 - p121 [51-250]

Rohrer, James R - *Keepers of the Covenant*
> AHR - v102 - F '97 - p175 [501+]
> JR - v77 - Ja '97 - p144+ [501+]
> W&M Q - v53 - O '96 - p840+ [501+]

Ro'i, Yaacov - *Muslim Eurasia*
> JPR - v33 - Ag '96 - p382+ [251-500]
> Slav R - v55 - Sum '96 - p497+ [501+]

Roig, Montserrat - *El Temps De Les Cireres*
> WLT - v70 - Aut '96 - p944 [251-500]

Roiphe, Anne - *Fruitful: A Real Mother in the Modern World*
> BL - v93 - Ja '97 - p757 [1-50]
> BL - v93 - S 15 '96 - p190 [51-250]
> KR - v64 - Ag 15 '96 - p1222 [251-500]
> NYTBR - v101 - O 13 '96 - p33 [501+]
> Obs - F 2 '97 - p17* [501+]
> PW - v243 - S 23 '96 - p69 [51-250]
> Utne R - N '96 - p89 [1-50]

Roiphe, Katie - *Last Night in Paradise*
> BL - v93 - Mr 15 '97 - p1208 [51-250]
> KR - v65 - Ja 15 '97 - p128 [251-500]
> LATBR - Mr 23 '97 - p4 [501+]
> LJ - v122 - Mr 15 '97 - p79 [51-250]
> PW - v244 - Ja 20 '97 - p387 [51-250]
> Utne R - Mr '97 - p84+ [51-250]
> VLS - Spr '97 - p10+ [501+]
> WSJ-Cent - v99 - Mr 12 '97 - pA16 [501+]

Roitberg, Yakov - *Elliptic Boundary Value Problems in the Spaces of Distributions*
> SciTech - v21 - Mr '97 - p4 [51-250]

Roitblat, Herbert L - *Comparative Approaches to Cognitive Science*
> Choice - v34 - N '96 - p542 [51-250]

Rojany, Lisa - *Code Blue in the Emergency Room*
> y Kliatt - v30 - N '96 - p10 [51-250]

Tell Me about When I Was a Baby
> c HB Guide - v7 - Fall '96 - p243 [1-50]

Rojas, Carlos - *The Garden of Janus*
> Choice - v34 - F '97 - p971 [51-250]

Rojas, Jose Antonio - *El Sembrador De Salud*
> y JAAL - v40 - S '96 - p77 [51-250]

Rojas, Reinaldo - *El Regimen De La Encomienda En Barquisimeto Colonial 1530-1810*
> HAHR - v76 - N '96 - p787+ [501+]

Rojas Rabiela, Teresa - *Agricultura Indigena, Pasado Y Presente*
> HAHR - v76 - Ag '96 - p551+ [251-500]

Presente, Pasado, Y Futuro De Las Chinampas
> HAHR - v77 - My '97 - p328+ [251-500]

Roland-Entwistle, Theodore - *More Errata (Illus. by Hemesh Alles)*
> c HB Guide - v7 - Fall '96 - p358 [1-50]

Roland Michel, Marianne - *Chardin*
> Lon R Bks - v18 - D 12 '96 - p8+ [501+]
> NYTBR - v101 - D 8 '96 - p85 [1-50]

Roleff, Tamara L - *Abortion*
> y BL - v93 - Ja '97 - p828 [251-500]
> y Kliatt - v31 - Mr '97 - p30 [51-250]

Gay Rights
> y BL - v93 - Ap 1 '97 - p1321 [51-250]
> y Kliatt - v31 - Mr '97 - p29+ [51-250]
> y SLJ - v43 - F '97 - p124 [51-250]

Genetics and Intelligence
> y Ch BWatch - v6 - Jl '96 - p2 [1-50]
> y VOYA - v19 - D '96 - p286+ [251-500]

Global Warming
> y Kliatt - v31 - Mr '97 - p30 [51-250]

The Legal System
> y Ch BWatch - v6 - My '96 - p5 [51-250]

Rolfe, Frederick G - *The Early Rolfe Settlers of New England. Vol. 1*
> NGSQ - v84 - S '96 - p229+ [251-500]

Rolfe, Gary - *Closing the Theory-Practice Gap*
> SciTech - v21 - Mr '97 - p69 [51-250]

Rolfe, Randy - *The Secrets of Successful Parents*
> PW - v244 - Ap 21 '97 - p68 [51-250]

Rolfs, Richard W - *The Sorcerer's Apprentice*
> Choice - v34 - N '96 - p520 [51-250]

Roll Call: The Newspaper of Capitol Hill
> p BL - v93 - N 15 '96 - p608 [1-50]

Rolland, Maria Theresia - *Sprachverarbeitung Durch Logotechnik*
> MLR - v92 - Ap '97 - p498+ [501+]

Roller, Sibel - *Handbook of Fat Replacers*
> Choice - v34 - My '97 - p1527 [51-250]

Rollin, Bernard E - *The Frankenstein Syndrome*
> Ethics - v107 - Ja '97 - p396 [51-250]

Rolling Stone (San Francisco, Calif.) - *Bruce Springsteen: The Rolling Stone Files*
> LJ - v121 - S 15 '96 - p70+ [51-250]

Madonna: The Rolling Stone Files
> y BL - v93 - My 1 '97 - p1473 [51-250]

Rollins, Charlemae Hill - *Christmas Gif' (Illus. by Ashley Bryan)*
> c BL - v93 - F 15 '97 - p1014 [1-50]

Rollins, Deborah - *Reference Sources for Children's and Young Adult Literature*
> r SLJ - v43 - F '97 - p43 [51-250]

Rollins, Ed - *Bare Knuckles and Back Rooms*
> BL - v93 - S 1 '96 - p29 [1-50]
> BW - v26 - S 15 '96 - p3+ [501+]
> Ent W - S 6 '96 - p70 [51-250]
> LATBR - Ag 11 '96 - p3 [501+]
> NYTBR - v101 - Ag 25 '96 - p11 [501+]
> PW - v244 - Mr 24 '97 - p81 [1-50]

Bare Knuckles and Back Rooms (Rollins). Audio Version
> PW - v243 - S 2 '96 - p47 [51-250]

Rollins, Judith - *All Is Never Said*
> JSH - v62 - N '96 - p839+ [251-500]

Rollins, Susan W - *Gender in Popular Culture*
> J Am Cult - v19 - Sum '96 - p146+ [251-500]
> JPC - v29 - Spr '96 - p250+ [251-500]

Rollinson, Neil - *A Spillage of Mercury*
> TLS - N 22 '96 - p31 [51-250]

Rolls, Eric - *Citizens: Flowers and the Wide Sea*
> Aust Bk R - D '96 - p11+ [501+]

Rollyson, Carl - *Rebecca West: A Life*
> BW - v26 - O 13 '96 - p6 [501+]
> Choice - v34 - Ap '97 - p1339 [51-250]
> LATBR - N 17 '96 - p6 [501+]
> NL - v80 - Ja 13 '97 - p16+ [501+]
> NYTBR - v101 - O 27 '96 - p28 [501+]
> WSJ-MW - v78 - N 21 '96 - pA20

Rebecca West: A Saga of the Century
> ASInt - v34 - O '96 - p113+ [501+]

Roloff, Jurgen - *Die Kirche Im Neuen Testament*
> Rel St Rev - v23 - Ap '97 - p188 [51-250]

Rolt, L T C - *Sleep No More*
> Necro - Sum '96 - p13+ [501+]

Rom, Mark C - *Public Spirit in the Thrift Tragedy*
> Choice - v34 - Ja '97 - p846+ [251-500]
> R&R Bk N - v12 - F '97 - p47 [51-250]

Roma, Thomas - *Come Sunday*
> LATBR - D 8 '96 - p9 [501+]
> NYTBR - v101 - S 15 '96 - p31 [51-250]

Romagnoli, Margaret - *Zuppa! A Tour of the Many Regions of Italy and Their Soups*
> LJ - v121 - D '96 - p136 [51-250]
> PW - v243 - O 21 '96 - p79 [51-250]

Romain, Effie - *Herbal Remedies in Pots*
> Quill & Q - v62 - Ag '96 - p32 [51-250]

Romain, Joseph - *The Wagner Whacker*
> c Quill & Q - v63 - Ja '97 - p39 [251-500]

Roman, Beverly - *The Insiders' Guide to Relocation*
> LJ - v121 - S 15 '96 - p85 [51-250]

Roman, Daniel - *Asi Era Cuba*
> BL - v93 - Ap 1 '97 - p1284 [1-50]

Roman, Eric - *Hungary and the Victor Powers 1945-1950*
> Choice - v34 - D '96 - p672 [51-250]
> R&R Bk N - v11 - N '96 - p12 [51-250]

Roman, James - *Love, Life, and a Dream*
> R&R Bk N - v12 - F '97 - p81 [51-250]

Roman, Steven - *Introduction to Coding and Information Theory*
> Choice - v34 - My '97 - p1537+ [51-250]

Romance Forever
> p LJ - v121 - D '96 - p158 [51-250]

Romanelli, Raffaele - *Storia Dello Stato Italiano Dall'Unita A Oggi*
> TLS - Jl 19 '96 - p6 [501+]

Romania In Lumea Sportului
> BL - v93 - D 15 '96 - p714 [1-50]

Romano, Dennis - *Housecraft and Statecraft*
> Choice - v34 - Ap '97 - p1398 [51-250]

Romano, Frank - *Digital Media*
> BWatch - v17 - S '96 - p9 [51-250]

Romano, Lalla - *Ho Sognato L'Ospedale*
> WLT - v70 - Sum '96 - p675+ [501+]

Romanowiczowa, Zofia - *Ruchome Schody*
> WLT - v71 - Win '97 - p183+ [501+]

Romanowski, Patricia - *The New Rolling Stone Encyclopedia of Rock and Roll. Completely Rev. and Updated Ed.*
> r Ant R - v54 - Sum '96 - p362 [251-500]

Romanowski, William D - *Pop Culture Wars*
> Bks & Cult - v3 - Ja '97 - p26 [501+]
> CC - v113 - N 20 '96 - p1134+ [501+]

The Romantic Movement 1995
> r ARBA - v28 - '97 - p407 [51-250]

Romantic Times Magazine
> p RQ - v36 - Win '96 - p227 [51-250]

Romanus, Melodus, Saint - *On the Life of Christ*
> Rel St Rev - v23 - Ja '97 - p80 [251-500]

Romascanu, Mihail G - *Tezaurul Roman Dela Moscova*
> BL - v93 - D 15 '96 - p714 [1-50]

Romberg, T M - *Signal Processing for Industrial Diagnostics*
> SciTech - v20 - D '96 - p59 [51-250]

Romdhane, Mohamed S Ben - *Quick-Turnaround ASIC Design in VHDL*
  SciTech - v20 - D '96 - p79 [51-250]
Romei, Francesca - *The Story of Sculpture (Illus. by Giacinto Gaudenzi)*
  c RT - v50 - D '96 - p343 [51-250]
Romeo, John T - *Phytochemical Diversity and Redundancy in Ecological Interactions*
  SciTech - v21 - Mr '97 - p37 [51-250]
Romeo and Juliet: Center Stage. Electronic Media Version
  y Kliatt - v30 - S '96 - p40 [51-250]
Romer, Joachim - *Culinaria*
  Mac - v109 - D 9 '96 - p66 [1-50]
Romero, Danny - *Calle 10*
  BL - v93 - S 15 '96 - p222 [51-250]
  BW - v26 - N 3 '96 - p8 [51-250]
  LATBR - S 1 '96 - p10 [51-250]
Romero, Mary - *Maid in the U.S.A.*
  J Am Cult - v18 - Win '95 - p104+ [251-500]
Romilly, Jacqueline De - *Alcibade, Ou Les Dangers De L'Ambition*
  TLS - N 29 '96 - p29 [501+]
  Rencontres Avec La Grece Antique
  Choice - v34 - D '96 - p566 [1-50]
  Choice - v34 - D '96 - p566 [1-50]
  Tragedies Grecques Au Fil Des Ans
  TLS - N 29 '96 - p29 [501+]
Romney, Catharine Cottam - *Letters of Catharine Cottam Romney, Plural Wife*
  CH - v65 - D '96 - p748+ [501+]
Romo, Harriet - *Latino High School Graduation*
  AJE - v105 - N '96 - p117+ [501+]
  Choice - v34 - S '96 - p180 [51-250]
  CS - v26 - Mr '97 - p210+ [501+]
  JAAL - v40 - N '96 - p238 [51-250]
Romski, Mary Ann - *Breaking the Speech Barrier*
  R&R Bk N - v11 - D '96 - p55 [51-250]
  SciTech - v20 - N '96 - p3 [51-250]
Romtvedt, David - *Windmill: Essays from Four Mile Ranch*
  LJ - v122 - Ap 15 '97 - p105 [51-250]
Ronald, Nick - *Grand Illusions*
  BL - v93 - Mr 15 '97 - p1219 [51-250]
Ronan, Clifford - *Antike Roman*
  Critm - v38 - Sum '96 - p490+ [251-500]
Ronan, Colin A - *Science Explained*
  y Kliatt - v30 - S '96 - p36 [51-250]
  The Universe Explained
  y Kliatt - v31 - Mr '97 - p33+ [51-250]
Ronan, Frank - *Lovely*
  TLS - N 8 '96 - p27 [501+]
Rondal, Jean A - *Down's Syndrome*
  SciTech - v20 - N '96 - p54 [51-250]
  Exceptional Language Development in Down Syndrome
  AJMR - v101 - S '96 - p206+ [501+]
Rondeel, H E - *Geology of Gas and Oil under the Netherlands*
  SciTech - v20 - D '96 - p81 [51-250]
Rondon, Javier - *The Absent-Minded Toad (Illus. by Marcela Cabrera)*
  c RT - v50 - F '97 - p425 [51-250]
Ronell, Avital - *Finitude's Score*
  Poetics T - v18 - Spr '97 - p132+ [501+]
Ronen, Ruth - *Possible Worlds in Literary Theory*
  MLN - v111 - D '96 - p1045+ [501+]
  MLR - v92 - Ja '97 - p142+ [501+]
Roney, John B - *The Inside of History*
  Hist & T - v35 - 3 '96 - p413 [251-500]
  Six Ct J - v27 - Win '96 - p1143+ [501+]
Ron-Feder-Amit, Galilah - *Lo Mekubelet*
  BL - v93 - Mr 1 '97 - p1115 [1-50]
Ronsvalle, John - *Behind the Stained Glass Windows*
  BL - v93 - S 15 '96 - p184 [51-250]
  ChrPhil - v9 - O 31 '96 - p67 [51-250]
  CSM - v89 - D 26 '96 - p12 [51-250]
Ronveaux, R - *Heun's Differential Equations*
  SIAM Rev - v39 - Mr '97 - p175 [51-250]
Roodenberg, Jacob - *The Ilipinar Excavations I*
  AJA - v100 - Jl '96 - p608+ [501+]
Roof, Wade Clark - *The Post-War Generation and Establishment Religion*
  CS - v26 - Mr '97 - p236+ [501+]
Rooks, Noliwe M - *Hair Raising*
  Choice - v34 - Ja '97 - p838 [51-250]
Room, Adrian - *African Placenames*
  r CAY - v16 - Fall '95 - p8 [51-250]
  r GJ - v162 - N '96 - p343 [51-250]
  r Names - v44 - Je '96 - p141+ [501+]
  An Alphabetical Guide to the Language of Name Studies
  r ARBA - v28 - '97 - p379 [251-500]

Brewer's Dictionary of Phrase and Fable. 15th Ed.
  r CR - v269 - D '96 - p335 [51-250]
Literally Entitled
  r ARBA - v28 - '97 - p410+ [51-250]
Placenames of Russia and the Former Soviet Union
  r ARBA - v28 - '97 - p175+ [51-250]
Who's Who in Classical Mythology
  r Choice - v34 - Ap '97 - p1314 [51-250]
Rooney, Frances - *Working Light*
  Choice - v34 - Ap '97 - p1326 [51-250]
Roop, Connie - *Pilgrim Voices (Illus. by Shelley Pritchett)*
  c RT - v50 - O '96 - p158 [51-250]
Roop, Peter - *The Buffalo Jump (Illus. by Bill Farnsworth)*
  c Bloom Rev - v16 - S '96 - p29 [51-250]
  c Ch BWatch - v6 - S '96 - p7 [51-250]
  c HB Guide - v8 - Spr '97 - p45 [51-250]
  c SLJ - v43 - F '97 - p84 [51-250]
  Westward, Ho, Ho, Ho! (Illus. by Anne Canevari Green)
  c BL - v93 - D 15 '96 - p723 [51-250]
  c HB Guide - v8 - Spr '97 - p175 [51-250]
  c SLJ - v43 - Ja '97 - p108 [51-250]
Roos, Jane Mayo - *Early Impressionism and the French State 1866-1874*
  Choice - v34 - F '97 - p958 [51-250]
Roos, Rein A - *The Forgotten Pollution*
  SciTech - v20 - N '96 - p67 [51-250]
Roose, Steven P - *Anxiety as Symptom and Signal*
  AJPsych - v153 - N '96 - p1501+ [501+]
Roosens, Laurent - *History of Photography. Vol. 3*
  r SciTech - v20 - D '96 - p84 [51-250]
Roosevelt, Anna - *Amazonian Indians from Prehistory to the Present*
  Am Sci - v84 - N '96 - p608 [501+]
  HAHR - v77 - F '97 - p100+ [501+]
Roosevelt, Elliott - *Murder at Midnight*
  BL - v93 - My 1 '97 - p1483 [51-250]
  KR - v65 - Mr 15 '97 - p421 [51-250]
  PW - v244 - Mr 24 '97 - p62 [51-250]
  Murder in the Chateau
  KR - v64 - My 1 '96 - p647 [51-250]
  PW - v243 - N 18 '96 - p70 [1-50]
Roosevelt, P R - *Life on the Russian Country Estate*
  HRNB - v25 - Fall '96 - p34 [251-500]
  HT - v46 - Jl '96 - p51 [51-250]
Roosevelt, Theodore - *A Bully Father (McDonough). Audio Version*
  BL - v93 - My 15 '97 - p1596 [51-250]
  y Kliatt - v31 - My '97 - p46 [51-250]
  Hunting Trips of a Ranchman. The Wilderness Hunter
  Esq - v126 - D '96 - p40 [1-50]
  LJ - v122 - Ja '97 - p155 [1-50]
Root, Deborah - *Cannibal Culture*
  Choice - v34 - S '96 - p115 [51-250]
  WHQ - v27 - Win '96 - p551 [51-250]
Root, Hilton L - *The Fountain of Privilege*
  EHR - v112 - Ap '97 - p488+ [501+]
  Small Countries, Big Lessons
  JEL - v35 - Mr '97 - p286 [51-250]
Root, Phyllis - *Aunt Nancy and Old Man Trouble (Illus. by David Parkins)*
  c HB - v72 - S '96 - p585+ [51-250]
  c HB Guide - v7 - Fall '96 - p272+ [51-250]
  c JB - v60 - D '96 - p239 [251-500]
  c LATBR - Jl 7 '96 - p11 [51-250]
  c Magpies - v11 - S '96 - p30 [51-250]
  c RT - v50 - Ap '97 - p593 [51-250]
  c Sch Lib - v44 - Ag '96 - p101 [51-250]
  c TES - Jl 5 '96 - pR2 [501+]
  Contrary Bear (Illus. by Laura Cornell)
  c HB Guide - v7 - Fall '96 - p273 [51-250]
  The Hungry Monster (Illus. by Sue Heap)
  c HB - v73 - Mr '97 - p195+ [51-250]
  c KR - v65 - Ja 1 '97 - p63 [51-250]
  Mrs. Potter's Pig (Illus. by Russell Ayto)
  c BL - v92 - Ag '96 - p1905 [51-250]
  c HB Guide - v7 - Fall '96 - p273 [1-50]
  c JB - v60 - D '96 - p240 [51-250]
  c Sch Lib - v44 - N '96 - p147 [51-250]
  One Windy Wednesday (Illus. by Helen Craig)
  c HB Guide - v8 - Spr '97 - p15 [51-250]
  c NY - v72 - N 18 '96 - p101 [1-50]
  c PW - v243 - N 4 '96 - p74 [51-250]
  c SLJ - v42 - N '96 - p91 [51-250]
  Rosie's Fiddle (Illus. by Kevin O'Malley)
  c CBRS - v25 - Ap '97 - p103 [51-250]
  c CCB-B - v50 - Ap '97 - p293+ [51-250]
  c KR - v65 - F 1 '97 - p227 [51-250]
  c PW - v244 - Ja 13 '97 - p75+ [51-250]

Rootes, David - *The Arctic (Illus. by Bryan Alexander)*
  c BL - v93 - N 15 '96 - p585 [51-250]
  c Ch BWatch - v6 - S '96 - p5 [1-50]
  c HB Guide - v8 - Spr '97 - p97 [51-250]
  c SLJ - v43 - Ja '97 - p106+ [51-250]
Roozeman, Fred - *Advances in Rapid Thermal and Integrated Processing*
  SciTech - v20 - D '96 - p77 [51-250]
Roper, Michael - *Masculinity and the British Organization Man since 1945*
  Socio R - v44 - N '96 - p746+ [501+]
Rorabaugh, C Britton - *Error Coding Cookbook*
  SciTech - v20 - N '96 - p8 [51-250]
Rorby, Ginny - *Dolphin Sky*
  c Ch BWatch - v6 - O '96 - p3 [51-250]
  c HB Guide - v7 - Fall '96 - p297 [51-250]
  c RT - v50 - Ap '97 - p591 [51-250]
Rorem, Ned - *Other Entertainment*
  BL - v92 - Ag '96 - p1873 [51-250]
  BW - v26 - Ag 25 '96 - p13 [51-250]
  FF - v20 - Ja '97 - p377+ [501+]
  LATBR - S 1 '96 - p6 [501+]
  NY - v72 - N 11 '96 - p119 [1-50]
  NYTBR - v101 - N 3 '96 - p18 [51-250]
  ON - v61 - D 14 '96 - p73 [251-500]
  TLS - Ja 17 '97 - p9 [501+]
Rorty, Richard - *Consequences of Pragmatism*
  PSR - v25 - '96 - p210+ [501+]
  Contingency, Irony and Solidarity
  PSR - v25 - '96 - p210+ [501+]
  Philosophy and the Mirror of Nature
  PSR - v25 - '96 - p244+ [501+]
Ros, Enrique - *Giron, La Verdadera Historia*
  BL - v93 - Ap 1 '97 - p1284 [1-50]
Rosa, Joseph G - *Wild Bill Hickok: The Man and His Myth*
  Roundup M - v4 - O '96 - p28 [251-500]
Rosa-Casanova, Sylvia - *Mama Provi and the Pot of Rice (Illus. by Robert Roth)*
  c BL - v93 - My 15 '97 - p1580+ [51-250]
  c KR - v65 - My 1 '97 - p726 [51-250]
  c PW - v244 - Ap 21 '97 - p72 [51-250]
Rosaforte, Tim - *Tiger Woods: The Makings of a Champion (Addison). Audio Version*
  BWatch - v18 - Mr '97 - p7 [1-50]
  PW - v244 - F 3 '97 - p43 [51-250]
Rosair, David - *Photographic Guide to the Shorebirds of the World*
  r RQ - v35 - Sum '96 - p563+ [251-500]
Rosales, F Arturo - *Chicano!*
  BWatch - v17 - S '96 - p10 [51-250]
Rosales, Melodye - *'Twas the Night b'fore Christmas (Illus. by Melodye Rosales)*
  c CBRS - v25 - N '96 - p27 [1-50]
  c CCB-B - v50 - N '96 - p111 [51-250]
  c Ch BWatch - v6 - D '96 - p1 [1-50]
  c HB Guide - v8 - Spr '97 - p153 [1-50]
  c PW - v243 - S 30 '96 - p89 [51-250]
  c SFR - v21 - N '96 - p47 [51-250]
  c SLJ - v42 - O '96 - p40 [51-250]
Rosati, Kitty Gurkin - *Heal Your Heart*
  BL - v93 - Ja '97 - p798+ [51-250]
Rosbottom, Betty - *American Favorites*
  LJ - v121 - D '96 - p136 [51-250]
  PW - v243 - S 16 '96 - p80 [51-250]
Roscoe, Patrick - *Love Is Starving for Itself*
  Essays CW - Spr '96 - p202 [501+]
Roscoe, Will - *Queer Spirits*
  HG&LRev - v3 - Fall '96 - p38+ [501+]
  The Zuni Man-Woman
  HG&LRev - v3 - Fall '96 - p38+ [501+]
Rose, Anne C - *Voices of the Marketplace*
  Bks & Cult - v2 - N '96 - p25+ [501+]
Rose, Brian A - *Jekyll and Hyde Adapted*
  Nine-C Lit - v51 - Mr '97 - p564 [51-250]
  R&R Bk N - v11 - N '96 - p70 [51-250]
Rose, Carol - *Spirits, Fairies, Gnomes, and Goblins*
  r ARBA - v28 - '97 - p498 [51-250]
  yr BL - v93 - My 1 '97 - p1534 [51-250]
  r LJ - v122 - Ap 15 '97 - p40 [51-250]
Rose, Colin - *Accelerated Learning for the 21st Century. Rev. Ed.*
  LJ - v122 - F 15 '97 - p150 [51-250]
Rose, Danis - *The Textual Diaries of James Joyce*
  ILS - v15 - Fall '96 - p13 [501+]
Rose, David - *In the Name of the Law*
  CR - v268 - Je '96 - p325+ [501+]
  Obs - Ja 19 '97 - p17* [251-500]
Rose, Emma - *Ballet Magic (Illus. by Jan Palmer)*
  c BL - v93 - D 15 '96 - p732 [1-50]
  c Ch BWatch - v6 - Jl '96 - p4 [1-50]

Rose, Francis - *Restitution and the Conflict of Laws*
  Law Q Rev - v113 - Ja '97 - p167+ [501+]
Rose, Gillian - *Feminism and Geography*
  AAAGA - v86 - S '96 - p610+ [501+]
  Signs - v22 - Win '97 - p456+ [501+]
Love's Work
  Obs - Mr 2 '97 - p18* [51-250]
Morning Becomes the Law
  Utne R - Ja '97 - p97 [1-50]
Rose, Gustav - *Humboldt's Travels in Siberia 1837-1842*
  RocksMiner - v71 - N '96 - p419+ [251-500]
Rose, H E - *A Course in Number Theory. 2nd Ed.*
  Math T - v89 - O '96 - p606 [51-250]
Rose, H J - *A Handbook of Greek Mythology*
  SLJ - v42 - N '96 - p39 [1-50]
Rose, Iain - *Children of Coal and Iron*
  c Sch Lib - v44 - N '96 - p175 [251-500]
The Union of 1707
  c Sch Lib - v44 - Ag '96 - p125 [51-250]
Rose, Ingrid - *The Lithographs of Prentiss Taylor*
  r AB - v99 - Mr 3 '97 - p694 [51-250]
  r Choice - v34 - S '96 - p115 [51-250]
Rose, Jacqueline - *States of Fantasy*
  Choice - v34 - Ja '97 - p798 [51-250]
Rose, Joanna - *Little Miss Strange*
  BL - v93 - F 15 '97 - p1005 [51-250]
  KR - v65 - F 1 '97 - p166 [251-500]
  LJ - v122 - Mr 15 '97 - p92 [51-250]
  Ms - v7 - Mr '97 - p83 [1-50]
  PW - v244 - F 3 '97 - p96 [51-250]
Rose, Joel - *Kill Kill Faster Faster*
  BL - v93 - Mr 1 '97 - p1112 [51-250]
  Books - v11 - Ap '97 - p23 [51-250]
  KR - v65 - Ja 15 '97 - p91 [251-500]
  PW - v244 - Mr 3 '97 - p64 [51-250]
  VV - v42 - Ap 29 '97 - p57 [501+]
Rose, Jon - *United States Postage Stamps of 1869*
  Am Phil - v110 - O '96 - p909 [251-500]
  Phil Lit R - v45 - '96 - p350+ [501+]
Rose, Lisle A - *The Ship That Held the Line*
  Choice - v34 - S '96 - p196 [51-250]
  NWCR - v49 - Aut '96 - p154+ [501+]
Rose, Malcolm - *The Alibi*
  c Bks Keeps - Jl '96 - p13 [251-250]
Rose, Marilyn Gaddis - *Translation Horizons beyond the Boundaries of Translation Spectrum*
  TranslRevS - v2 - '96 - p14 [51-250]
Rose, Mark - *Authors and Owners*
  EHR - v111 - S '96 - p991+ [501+]
Rose, Mark H, 1942- - *Cities of Light and Heat*
  AAPSS-A - v549 - Ja '97 - p199+ [501+]
  AHR - v102 - F '97 - p197 [251-500]
  Isis - v87 - S '96 - p573+ [501+]
  J Am St - v30 - D '96 - p489+ [251-500]
Rose, Martial - *Stories in Stone*
  CSM - v89 - Mr 26 '97 - p16 [501+]
Rose, Michael - *For the Record*
  Aust Bk R - D '96 - p75 [251-500]
Rose, Mike - *Possible Lives*
  Cng - v29 - Mr '97 - p54 [51-250]
  Col Comp - v47 - O '96 - p424+ [501+]
  y Kliatt - v31 - Ja '97 - p20 [251-500]
  Nat - v263 - O 28 '96 - p32+ [501+]
  PW - v243 - Jl 22 '96 - p235 [1-50]
Rose, Nancy E - *Workfare or Fair Work*
  AAPSS-A - v550 - Mr '97 - p185+ [501+]
  AJS - v102 - S '96 - p630+ [501+]
  CS - v26 - Ja '97 - p40+ [501+]
  ILRR - v50 - Ja '97 - p354+ [501+]
  NWSA Jnl - v8 - Fall '96 - p129+ [501+]
  Soc Ser R - v71 - Mr '97 - p146+ [501+]
Rose, Paul Lawrence - *Wagner: Race and Revolution*
  CR - v269 - N '96 - p280 [51-250]
Rose, Peter Q - *The Gardener's Guide to Growing Ivies*
  CSM - v89 - F 27 '97 - pB2 [1-50]
Rose, Richard - *Inheritance in Public Policy*
  Pol Stud J - v24 - Sum '96 - p311+ [501+]
Rose, Ron - *7 Things Kids Never Forget and How to Make the Most of Them*
  VOYA - v19 - F '97 - p318 [51-250]
Rose-Ackerman, Susan - *Controlling Environmental Policy*
  AAPSS-A - v550 - Mr '97 - p180+ [501+]
  HLR - v110 - O '96 - p560 [501+]
Roseberry, William - *Coffee, Society, and Power in Latin America*
  CS - v25 - S '96 - p600+ [501+]
  Historian - v59 - Win '97 - p442+ [251-500]
  JEH - v56 - D '96 - p947+ [501+]

Rosell, Rosendo - *Vida Y Milagros De La Farandula De Cuba*
  BL - v93 - Ap 1 '97 - p1284 [1-50]
Rosemergy, Jim - *A Closer Walk with God. Audio Version*
  BWatch - v18 - Mr '97 - p8 [1-50]
Rosemire, Adeline - *The 2-Ingredient Cook Book*
  BWatch - v17 - S '96 - p2 [51-250]
Rosen, Charles, 1927- - *The Classical Style. Expanded Ed.*
  LJ - v122 - Mr 15 '97 - p65+ [51-250]
The Romantic Generation
  JAAC - v54 - Fall '96 - p393+ [501+]
Rosen, Charley - *The House of Moses All-Stars*
  BL - v93 - D 15 '96 - p710 [51-250]
  HMR - Spr '97 - p44+ [501+]
  LJ - v121 - D '96 - p147 [51-250]
  NYTBR - v101 - D 15 '96 - p13 [501+]
  PW - v243 - N 4 '96 - p65 [51-250]
  TLS - Mr 7 '97 - p23 [501+]
  Trib Bks - Mr 2 '97 - p6+ [501+]
Rosen, Clifford J - *Osteoporosis: Diagnostic and Therapeutic Principles*
  SciTech - v20 - S '96 - p37 [51-250]
Rosen, Craig - *The Billboard Book of Number One Albums*
  r ARBA - v28 - '97 - p484 [51-250]
Rosen, David - *The Tao of Jung*
  BL - v93 - S 1 '96 - p35 [51-250]
  Choice - v34 - Mr '97 - p1243+ [51-250]
  LJ - v121 - S 15 '96 - p83 [51-250]
Rosen, Evan - *Personal Videoconferencing*
  R&R Bk N - v12 - F '97 - p46 [51-250]
Rosen, Fred, 1942- - *Free Trade and Economic Restructuring in Latin America*
  HAHR - v77 - F '97 - p154+ [501+]
Rosen, Fred S - *Case Studies in Immunology*
  SciTech - v20 - D '96 - p46 [51-250]
Rosen, Hugh - *Constructing Realities*
  Readings - v11 - S '96 - p26 [51-250]
  SciTech - v20 - N '96 - p42 [51-250]
Rosen, Isaac - *Manny*
  LJ - v121 - S 15 '96 - p97 [51-250]
Rosen, Jonathan - *Eve's Apple*
  BL - v93 - My 15 '97 - p1564 [51-250]
  KR - v65 - Ap 1 '97 - p497 [251-500]
  NYTLa - v146 - My 7 '97 - pC19 [501+]
  PW - v244 - Mr 31 '97 - p60 [51-250]
  WSJ-Cent - v99 - Ap 25 '97 - pA12 [501+]
Rosen, Joseph - *The Handbook of Investment Technology*
  R&R Bk N - v11 - D '96 - p36 [51-250]
Rosen, Laura Epstein - *When Someone You Love Is Depressed*
  BL - v93 - S 1 '96 - p51 [51-250]
  LJ - v121 - O 1 '96 - p108 [51-250]
Rosen, Leora N - *The Hostage Child*
  BL - v93 - S 1 '96 - p42 [51-250]
  Choice - v34 - Ja '97 - p884 [51-250]
  LJ - v121 - O 1 '96 - p104 [51-250]
  PW - v243 - Jl 22 '96 - p221 [51-250]
Rosen, Lucy - *High Performance through Communicating Information*
  y Cur R - v36 - N '96 - p13 [51-250]
  y SLJ - v43 - Mr '97 - p204 [51-250]
  y VOYA - v19 - F '97 - p348 [251-500]
Rosen, Michael - *On Voluntary Servitude*
  Choice - v34 - Ja '97 - p873 [51-250]
Rosen, Michael, 1946- - *The Best of Michael Rosen (Illus. by Quentin Blake)*
  c HB Guide - v7 - Fall '96 - p368 [51-250]
Michael Rosen's ABC (Illus. by Bee Willey)
  c HB Guide - v8 - Spr '97 - p154 [51-250]
  c PW - v244 - Mr 3 '97 - p77 [51-250]
  c SLJ - v43 - Mr '97 - p165 [51-250]
Mind Your Own Business (Illus. by Quentin Blake)
  c JB - v60 - D '96 - p259 [51-250]
This Is Our House (Illus. by Bob Graham)
  c BL - v93 - N 1 '96 - p510 [51-250]
  c HB Guide - v8 - Spr '97 - p45 [51-250]
  c JB - v60 - D '96 - p240 [51-250]
  c Magpies - v11 - S '96 - p16 [501+]
  c Sch Lib - v44 - N '96 - p147 [51-250]
We're Going on a Bear Hunt (Illus. by Helen Oxenbury)
  c TES - O 18 '96 - p12* [1-50]
Wouldn't You Like to Know (Illus. by Quentin Blake)
  c JB - v60 - D '96 - p259+ [51-250]
You Can't Catch Me! (Illus. by Quentin Blake)
  c JB - v60 - D '96 - p194 [51-250]
You Wait till I'm Older than You! (Illus. by Shoo Rayner)
  c Bks Keeps - v100 - S '96 - p33 [51-250]
You Wait till I'm Older than You (Illus. by Shoo Rayner)
  c Bks Keeps - Ja '97 - p25 [51-250]

You Wait till I'm Older than You! (Illus. by Shoo Rayner)
  c Sch Lib - v45 - F '97 - p43 [51-250]
  c TES - D 13 '96 - p32 [51-250]
The Zoo at Night (Illus. by Bee Willey)
  c TES - S 27 '96 - p12* [501+]
Rosen, Michael J - *Bonesy and Isabel (Illus. by James Ransome)*
  c RT - v50 - N '96 - p255 [51-250]
Fishing with Dad (Illus. by Will Shively)
  c Bloom Rev - v16 - Jl '96 - p27 [51-250]
Food Fight (Illus. by Michael J Rosen)
  c BL - v93 - O 1 '96 - p345 [51-250]
  c Bloom Rev - v16 - S '96 - p29 [51-250]
  c Ch BWatch - v6 - O '96 - p3 [1-50]
  c HB - v73 - Ja '97 - p74+ [51-250]
  c HB Guide - v8 - Spr '97 - p151 [51-250]
Greatest Table
  c Emerg Lib - v23 - My '96 - p45 [51-250]
The Heart Is Big Enough (Illus. by Matthew Valiquette)
  c BL - v93 - Mr 1 '97 - p1165 [51-250]
  c PW - v244 - Mr 17 '97 - p84 [51-250]
Purr--: Children's Book Illustrators Brag about Their Cats
  c HB Guide - v7 - Fall '96 - p346 [51-250]
  c RT - v50 - My '97 - p683 [51-250]
A School for Pompey Walker (Illus. by Aminah Brenda Lynn Robinson)
  c RT - v50 - O '96 - p152 [51-250]
Telling Things
  LJ - v122 - Mr 15 '97 - p66 [51-250]
Traveling in Notions
  PW - v243 - N 25 '96 - p73 [51-250]
Rosen, Nick - *The Net-Head Handbook*
  NS - v125 - S 13 '96 - p47+ [51-250]
Rosen, Norma - *Biblical Women Unbound*
  BL - v93 - O 1 '96 - p304 [501+]
  Choice - v34 - Mr '97 - p1178 [51-250]
  PW - v243 - N 11 '96 - p69 [51-250]
Rosen, Robert H - *Leading People*
  PW - v244 - F 24 '97 - p88 [1-50]
Rosen, Sidney - *Can You Catch a Falling Star? (Illus. by Dean Lindberg)*
  c HB Guide - v7 - Fall '96 - p331 [51-250]
Where's the Big Dipper? (Illus. by Dean Lindberg)
  c HB Guide - v7 - Fall '96 - p331 [51-250]
Rosen, Stanley - *The Mask of Enlightenment*
  Choice - v34 - Ja '97 - p809 [51-250]
  CPR - v16 - Ag '96 - p284+ [501+]
  RP - v59 - Win '97 - p158+ [501+]
Plato's Statesman
  APSR - v90 - S '96 - p638+ [501+]
  J Pol - v58 - N '96 - p1241+ [501+]
  RP - v58 - Sum '96 - p641+ [501+]
Rosen, Stephen Peter - *Societies and Military Power*
  Choice - v34 - Mr '97 - p1217 [51-250]
  For Aff - v76 - Mr '97 - p180 [51-250]
Rosen, Steven M - *Science, Paradox, and the Moebius Principle*
  JP - v60 - Mr '96 - p71+ [501+]
Rosenak, Chuck - *Contemporary American Folk Art*
  r ARBA - v28 - '97 - p360 [51-250]
  r Choice - v34 - O '96 - p258 [51-250]
Rosenau, Milton - *The PDMA Handbook of New Product Development*
  R&R Bk N - v12 - F '97 - p44 [51-250]
Rosenbaum, Alan S - *Is the Holocaust Unique?*
  Choice - v34 - N '96 - p518 [51-250]
  TLS - Mr 7 '97 - p3+ [501+]
Rosenbaum, Martin - *From Soapbox to Soundbite*
  NS - v126 - Mr 27 '97 - p56+ [501+]
  TLS - Ap 11 '97 - p36 [501+]
Rosenbaum, Paul R - *Observational Studies*
  SIAM Rev - v38 - S '96 - p529 [501+]
Rosenbaum, Richard B - *Clinical Neurology of Rheumatic Diseases*
  SciTech - v21 - Mr '97 - p52 [51-250]
Rosenbaum, S P - *The Bloomsbury Group. Rev. Ed.*
  ELT - v39 - 4 '96 - p529 [51-250]
Rosenbaum, Thane - *Elijah Visible*
  Tikkun - v11 - S '96 - p85+ [501+]
Rosenberg, Beth Carole - *Virginia Woolf and Samuel Johnson*
  ELT - v39 - 3 '96 - p380+ [501+]
  RMR - v50 - 2 '96 - p169+ [501+]
Rosenberg, Brian - *Little Dorrit's Shadows*
  Choice - v34 - N '96 - p460 [51-250]
  R&R Bk N - v11 - N '96 - p70 [51-250]
Rosenberg, David - *The Hidden Holmes*
  HLR - v110 - Ja '97 - p769+ [501+]

Rosenberg, David, 1943- - *Communion: Contemporary Writers Reveal the Bible in Their Lives*
    BL - v93 - Ja '97 - p808 [1-50]
    Comw - v123 - D 6 '96 - p22 [51-250]
Genesis: As It Is Written
    BW - v26 - D 8 '96 - p5 [501+]
    CSM - v88 - N 6 '96 - p12 [51-250]
Genesis: Contemporary Writers on Our First Stories
    Nat R - v48 - D 9 '96 - p61+ [501+]
Rosenberg, Donna - *Folklore, Myths, and Legends*
    LJ - v122 - Ja '97 - p100 [51-250]
Rosenberg, Ian M - *Protein Analysis and Purification*
    SciTech - v21 - Mr '97 - p42 [51-250]
Rosenberg, Jay F - *Beyond Formalism*
    Phil R - v105 - Ja '96 - p79+ [501+]
Rosenberg, Joel - *The Silver Stone*
    BL - v93 - S 15 '96 - p226 [51-250]
Rosenberg, Jonathan - *How Debuggers Work*
    BYTE - v22 - F '97 - p154 [51-250]
Rosenberg, Judy - *Rosie's Bakery All-Butter, Fresh Cream, Sugar-Packed, No-Holds-Barred Baking Book*
    y Kliatt - v31 - My '97 - p31 [51-250]
Rosie's Bakery Chocolate-Packed, Jam-Filled, Butter-Rich, No-Holds-Barred Cookie Book
    BL - v93 - Ja '97 - p801+ [51-250]
    BL - v93 - D 15 '96 - p702 [51-250]
    LJ - v121 - D '96 - p136 [51-250]
    PW - v243 - N 18 '96 - p71 [51-250]
Rosenberg, Liz - *The Carousel (Illus. by Jim LaMarche)*
    c Sch Lib - v44 - N '96 - p152 [51-250]
    c TES - S 6 '96 - p7* [501+]
Eli and Uncle Dawn (Illus. by Susan Gaber)
    c BL - v93 - My 15 '97 - p1581 [51-250]
    c CBRS - v25 - Mr '97 - p90 [51-250]
    c PW - v244 - F 3 '97 - p105 [51-250]
Grandmother and the Runaway Shadow (Illus. by Beth Peck)
    c HB Guide - v7 - Fall '96 - p273 [51-250]
Heart and Soul
    y HB - v72 - N '96 - p746 [51-250]
    y HB Guide - v7 - Fall '96 - p305 [51-250]
    y Kliatt - v30 - N '96 - p10 [51-250]
    y NYTBR - v101 - S 22 '96 - p28 [501+]
The Invisible Ladder
    y BL - v93 - S 15 '96 - p228 [51-250]
    y CCB-B - v50 - N '96 - p112 [51-250]
    y HB Guide - v8 - Spr '97 - p151 [51-250]
    y KR - v64 - O 1 '96 - p1473 [51-250]
    y SLJ - v43 - F '97 - p124 [51-250]
    y VOYA - v19 - F '97 - p348+ [251-500]
Moonbathing (Illus. by Stephen Lambert)
    c HB Guide - v8 - Spr '97 - p45 [51-250]
    c Par - v71 - D '96 - p252 [51-250]
    c SLJ - v42 - O '96 - p104 [51-250]
    c Smith - v27 - N '96 - p175 [1-50]
Rosenberg, Martin R - *Raphael and France*
    Six Ct J - v27 - Fall '96 - p908+ [501+]
Rosenberg, Marvin - *The Masks of Hamlet*
    RES - v48 - F '97 - p98+ [501+]
Rosenberg, Maxine B - *Mommy's in the Hospital Having a Baby (Illus. by Robert Maass)*
    c BL - v93 - Ap 1 '97 - p1336 [51-250]
    c KR - v65 - Ap 1 '97 - p561 [51-250]
    c PW - v244 - Mr 24 '97 - p85 [51-250]
Rosenberg, Nancy Taylor - *Abuse of Power*
    BL - v93 - D 1 '96 - p621 [51-250]
    KR - v64 - D 1 '96 - p1699+ [251-500]
    LJ - v122 - F 1 '97 - p108 [51-250]
    NYTBR - v102 - Ap 6 '97 - p21 [51-250]
    PW - v244 - Ja 6 '97 - p62 [51-250]
Abuse of Power (Crouse). Audio Version
    LJ - v122 - Ap 15 '97 - p136 [51-250]
Trial by Fire (Crouse). Audio Version
    y Kliatt - v30 - S '97 - p53+ [51-250]
Trial by Fire (Cassidy). Audio Version
    LJ - v121 - D '96 - p170+ [51-250]
Rosenberg, Neil V - *Transforming Tradition*
    JSH - v62 - N '96 - p843+ [501+]
    WestFolk - v55 - Spr '96 - p170+ [501+]
Rosenberg, Peter Michael - *Because It Makes My Heart Beat Faster*
    Books - v10 - Je '96 - p24 [51-250]
Daniel's Dream
    TLS - My 24 '96 - p26 [501+]
Rosenberg, Pierre - *Nicolas Poussin 1594-1665. Vols. 1-2*
    r BM - v138 - Jl '96 - p467+ [501+]
Nicolas Poussin: Masterpieces 1594-1665
    BM - v138 - S '96 - p614 [51-250]

Rosenberg, Robert - *House of Guilt*
    BL - v93 - S 1 '96 - p68 [51-250]
    KR - v64 - Ag 15 '96 - p1192 [51-250]
    NYTBR - v101 - O 27 '96 - p42 [51-250]
Rosenberg, Roy A - *The Veneration of Divine Justice*
    Rel St Rev - v23 - Ja '97 - p76 [51-250]
Rosenberg, Samuel N - *Chansons Des Trouveres*
    MLR - v92 - Ap '97 - p459+ [251-500]
Rosenberg, Stephen - *Guide to Financial Security*
    BWatch - v18 - F '97 - p2 [1-50]
Rosenberg, Tina - *The Haunted Land*
    BW - v26 - D 8 '96 - p7 [51-250]
Rosenberger, Nancy R - *Japanese Sense of Self*
    Am Ethnol - v23 - N '96 - p913+ [501+]
Rosenblatt, Joe - *The Voluptuous Gardener*
    Quill & Q - v63 - Ja '97 - p32+ [51-250]
Rosenblatt, Naomi H - *Wrestling with Angels*
    PW - v243 - S 2 '96 - p121 [1-50]
Rosenblatt, Paul C - *Multiracial Couples*
    Fam in Soc - v77 - N '96 - p591+ [501+]
    Fam Relat - v45 - O '96 - p480 [501+]
    Soc Ser R - v71 - Mr '97 - p165 [1-50]
Rosenblatt, Richard - *Troy Aikman*
    c HB Guide - v7 - Fall '96 - p359 [1-50]
Rosenblatt, Roger - *Coming Apart*
    BL - v93 - F 15 '97 - p981 [51-250]
    KR - v65 - F 1 '97 - p205+ [251-500]
    LJ - v122 - Ap 1 '97 - p108 [51-250]
    NYTBR - v102 - Ap 20 '97 - p21 [51-250]
    NYTLa - v146 - Ap 10 '97 - pC16 [501+]
    PW - v244 - F 10 '97 - p73 [51-250]
    Time - v149 - Ap 21 '97 - p118 [1-50]
    Trib Bks - Ap 27 '97 - p7 [501+]
    WSJ-Cent - v99 - Ap 15 '97 - pA16 [501+]
Life Itself
    Cons - v17 - Aut '96 - p35+ [501+]
Rosenbloom, David H - *Public Administration and Law. 2nd Ed.*
    R&R Bk N - v12 - F '97 - p65 [51-250]
Rosenbloom, Joseph - *The Little Giant Book of Jokes (Illus. by Sanford Hoffman)*
    c PW - v243 - D 2 '96 - p62 [51-250]
The Little Giant Book of Riddles (Illus. by Sanford Hoffman)
    c PW - v243 - D 2 '96 - p62 [51-250]
Rosenblum, Jonathon D - *Copper Crucible*
    AAPSS-A - v550 - Mr '97 - p197+ [251-500]
Rosenblum, Mary - *Synthesis and Other Virtual Realities*
    y BL - v92 - Ag '96 - p1889 [51-250]
    y BL - v92 - Ag '96 - p1891 [1-50]
    MFSF - v91 - S '96 - p37+ [251-500]
    y VOYA - v19 - D '96 - p281+ [251-500]
Rosenblum, Mort - *Olives: The Life and Lore of a Noble Fruit*
    BL - v93 - N 15 '96 - p558 [51-250]
    BW - v26 - D 29 '96 - p3+ [501+]
    KR - v64 - S 15 '96 - p1385+ [251-500]
    NYTLa - v146 - N 28 '96 - pC21 [501+]
    PW - v243 - O 7 '96 - p57 [51-250]
    Trib Bks - Ja 12 '97 - p3 [501+]
Rosenblum, Nancy - *A World History of Photography. 3rd Ed.*
    y Kliatt - v31 - My '97 - p30 [51-250]
Rosenbluth, Michael - *Treating Difficult Personality Disorders*
    SciTech - v21 - Mr '97 - p56 [51-250]
Rosenburg, John - *William Parker: Rebel without Rights*
    y HB Guide - v7 - Fall '96 - p305 [51-250]
Young George Washington
    y BL - v93 - F 15 '97 - p1019+ [51-250]
    c KR - v64 - D 15 '96 - p1803+ [51-250]
Rosendorfer, Herbert - *Absterbende Gemutlichkeit*
    WLT - v71 - Win '97 - p138 [251-500]
Roseneil, Sasha - *Disarming Patriarchy*
    CS - v25 - S '96 - p635+ [501+]
Rosenfeld, Dina - *The Very Best Book (Illus. by Vitaliy Romanenko)*
    c PW - v244 - F 24 '97 - p84 [51-250]
Rosenfeld, Isadore - *Dr. Rosenfeld's Guide to Alternative Medicine*
    BL - v93 - N 15 '96 - p558+ [51-250]
    LJ - v121 - D '96 - p134 [51-250]
    PW - v243 - D 2 '96 - p58 [51-250]
Rosenfeld, Jo Ann - *Women's Health in Primary Care*
    SciTech - v21 - Mr '97 - p48 [51-250]
Rosenfeld, Louis - *The Internet Compendium: Subject Guides to Health and Science Resources*
    r RQ - v35 - Sum '96 - p574+ [501+]
    r RQ - v36 - Win '96 - p301+ [501+]
    r SL - v87 - Sum '96 - p233+ [501+]

The Internet Compendium: Subject Guides to Humanities Resources
    r RQ - v35 - Sum '96 - p574+ [501+]
    r RQ - v36 - Win '96 - p301+ [501+]
    r SL - v87 - Sum '96 - p98 [51-250]
The Internet Compendium: Subject Guides to Social Sciences, Business and Law Resources
    r RQ - v35 - Sum '96 - p574+ [501+]
    r RQ - v36 - Win '96 - p301+ [501+]
Rosenfeld, Paul - *Impression Management in Organizations*
    Per Psy - v49 - Aut '96 - p721+ [501+]
Rosenfeld, Richard N - *American Aurora*
    BL - v93 - Mr 15 '97 - p1206 [51-250]
    KR - v65 - Mr 15 '97 - p454 [51-250]
    LJ - v122 - Ap 15 '97 - p98 [51-250]
    PW - v244 - F 3 '97 - p85 [51-250]
Rosengarten, David - *The Dean and DeLuca Cookbook*
    CSM - v89 - D 13 '96 - p10+ [51-250]
    LJ - v121 - O 15 '96 - p85 [51-250]
    NYTBR - v101 - D 8 '96 - p71 [51-250]
    PW - v243 - S 2 '96 - p123+ [51-250]
Rosengrant, Sandra F - *Focus on Russian. 2nd Ed.*
    MLJ - v81 - Spr '97 - p138+ [501+]
The Golden Age
    MLJ - v81 - Spr '97 - p139+ [251-500]
Rosenkranz, E Joshua - *Reason and Passion*
    LJ - v122 - Ap 15 '97 - p99+ [51-250]
    PW - v244 - F 24 '97 - p75 [51-250]
Rosenstiehl, Jean-Marc - *Etudes Coptes IV*
    Rel St Rev - v23 - Ja '97 - p77 [51-250]
Rosenstock, S X - *United Artists*
    Ant R - v54 - Fall '96 - p497+ [251-500]
    Choice - v34 - D '96 - p617 [51-250]
    YR - v84 - O '96 - p171+ [501+]
Rosenstone, Robert A - *Revisioning History*
    AHR - v101 - O '96 - p1175 [251-500]
Visions of the Past
    QJS - v83 - My '97 - p256+ [501+]
Rosenthal, Alan - *Drawing the Line*
    Choice - v34 - Ja '97 - p877 [51-250]
Objectif France
    FR - v70 - O '96 - p158+ [501+]
Rosenthal, Bernard - *Salem Story*
    Am Geneal - v71 - O '96 - p257 [251-500]
    EHR - v111 - S '96 - p987+ [251-500]
Rosenthal, Bernice Glatzer - *Nietzsche and Soviet Culture*
    AHR - v101 - O '96 - p1247 [501+]
    JMH - v68 - D '96 - p976+ [501+]
    Slav R - v55 - Sum '96 - p504+ [501+]
Rosenthal, Bianca - *Pathways to Paul Celan*
    Choice - v34 - S '96 - p132 [51-250]
Rosenthal, Ed - *Why Marijuana Should Be Legal*
    y BL - v93 - D 15 '96 - p698 [51-250]
Rosenthal, J William - *Spectacles and Other Vision Aids*
    AB - v99 - Mr 31 '97 - p1045+ [501+]
Rosenthal, Joel H - *Ethics and International Affairs*
    Ethics - v107 - O '96 - p179 [51-250]
Rosenthal, Joel Thomas - *Old Age in Late Medieval England*
    Choice - v34 - F '97 - p1020 [51-250]
    R&R Bk N - v11 - D '96 - p41 [51-250]
Rosenthal, Karen L - *Practical Exotic Animal Medicine*
    SciTech - v21 - Mr '97 - p70 [51-250]
Rosenthal, Ken S - *Mosby's USMLE Step 1 Reviews: Microbiology and Immunology*
    SciTech - v20 - S '96 - p24 [1-50]
Rosenthal, M L - *Running to Paradise*
    RES - v47 - N '96 - p623+ [501+]
Rosenthal, M Sara - *The Breast Sourcebook*
    r PW - v243 - N 4 '96 - p73 [51-250]
Rosenthal, Mark - *Abstraction in the Twentieth Century*
    Art Bull - v79 - Mr '97 - p164+ [501+]
    Choice - v34 - F '97 - p958 [51-250]
    LATBR - D 8 '96 - p28 [1-50]
Rosenthal, Nadine - *Speaking of Reading*
    EJ - v85 - N '96 - p125+ [501+]
Rosentraub, Mark S - *Major League Losers*
    Bus W - Mr 3 '97 - p13 [501+]
    KR - v64 - D 15 '96 - p1788 [251-500]
    LJ - v122 - Ja '97 - p116 [51-250]
    PW - v244 - Ja 6 '97 - p56 [51-250]
    Trib Bks - Mr 30 '97 - p1+ [501+]
Rosenus, Alan - *General M.G. Vallejo and the Advent of the Americans*
    HAHR - v77 - My '97 - p324 [251-500]
Rosenzweig, Mark R - *Biological Psychology*
    SB - v33 - Ja '97 - p9 [251-500]
    Sci - v274 - N 15 '96 - p1149 [1-50]
    SciTech - v20 - S '96 - p22 [51-250]

Rosenzweig, Michael L - *Species Diversity in Space and Time*
   Am Sci - v84 - S '96 - p499+ [501+]
Rosenzweig, Roy - *The Park and the People*
   J Urban H - v22 - Jl '96 - p649+ [501+]
Roser, Susan E - *Mayflower Deeds and Probates*
   Am Geneal - v71 - Jl '96 - p187+ [51-250]
   Mayflower Increasings. 2nd Ed.
   Am Geneal - v71 - Jl '96 - p187+ [51-250]
Roses, Lorraine Elena - *Harlem's Glory*
   Choice - v34 - Ap '97 - p1336 [51-250]
   LJ - v121 - S 15 '96 - p69 [51-250]
   PW - v243 - S 23 '96 - p67 [51-250]
Roses (Eyewitness Handbooks)
   r ARBA - v28 - '97 - p581 [51-250]
   SB - v32 - Ag '96 - p171 [51-250]
Rosetta, Lyliane - *Variability in Human Fertility*
   SB - v33 - Mr '97 - p40 [51-250]
Rosevear, Sylvia K - *Handbook of Obstetric Management*
   SciTech - v20 - N '96 - p52 [51-250]
Rosheim, Mark E - *Robot Evolution*
   Robotica - v14 - S '96 - p589 [251-500]
Roshi, Richard Dogo Moss - *Absentee Zen*
   Tric - v6 - Fall '96 - p142 [1-50]
Rosillo-Calle, Frank - *The Charcoal Dilemma*
   New Sci - v153 - F 15 '97 - p44 [51-250]
Rosing, Norbert - *The World of the Polar Bear (Illus. by Norbert Rosing)*
   CSM - v89 - D 5 '96 - pD3 [1-50]
   PW - v243 - O 21 '96 - p67 [51-250]
   c SB - v33 - Mr '97 - p52+ [51-250]
Rosman, Doreen - *From Catholic to Protestant*
   HT - v46 - O '96 - p56 [51-250]
Rosnay, Tatiana De - *Le Diner Des Ex*
   BL - v93 - Ja '97 - p827 [1-50]
Rosner, David - *Hives of Sickness*
   CS - v25 - S '96 - p697+ [501+]
Rosoff, Morton - *Vesicles*
   SciTech - v20 - S '96 - p43 [51-250]
Rosovsky, Nitza - *City of the Great King*
   Am - v176 - Mr 8 '97 - p25 [51-250]
   Lon R Bks - v18 - O 31 '96 - p16 [501+]
   NYTBR - v101 - D 8 '96 - p13+ [501+]
Rosow, La Vergne - *Light 'n Lively Reads for ESL, Adult, and Teen Readers*
   r Emerg Lib - v24 - S '96 - p42 [1-50]
   r JAAL - v40 - Mr '97 - p512 [51-250]
   r JOYS - v10 - Win '97 - p222+ [251-500]
   r SLJ - v42 - N '96 - p42 [51-250]
   r SLMQ - v25 - Fall '96 - p66 [51-250]
   r VOYA - v19 - F '97 - p362+ [251-500]
Ross, Alan Duncan - *The Medicine of ER*
   BL - v93 - S 1 '96 - p44 [51-250]
   Choice - v34 - Ap '97 - p1372 [51-250]
   LJ - v121 - O 15 '96 - p84 [51-250]
   PW - v243 - S 30 '96 - p74 [51-250]
Ross, Alec - *Coke Stop in Emo*
   BIC - v25 - S '96 - p10+ [501+]
Ross, Andrew - *A Vision Betrayed*
   CHR - v82 - O '96 - p746+ [501+]
   Ch Rev Int - v3 - Fall '96 - p514+ [501+]
   EHR - v112 - F '97 - p199+ [501+]
   J Ch St - v38 - Sum '96 - p664+ [251-500]
Ross, Andrew, 1956- - *The Chicago Gangster Theory of Life*
   ABR - v18 - D '96 - p8+ [501+]
   HR - v49 - Sum '96 - p323+ [501+]
   Tikkun - v11 - My '96 - p64+ [501+]
   No Respect
   HR - v49 - Sum '96 - p323+ [501+]
   Strange Weather
   HR - v49 - Sum '96 - p323+ [501+]
Ross, Anna - *Elmo's Lift-and-Peek around the Corner Book (Illus. by Joe Mathieu)*
   c HB Guide - v7 - Fall '96 - p244 [51-250]
Ross, C T F - *Finite Element Programs in Structural Engineering and Continuum Mechanics*
   Choice - v34 - O '96 - p312 [51-250]
   Mechanics of Solids
   SciTech - v20 - S '96 - p50 [51-250]
Ross, Calvin - *The Frugal Youth Cybrarian*
   Kliatt - v31 - My '97 - p26 [51-250]
Ross, Carl T F - *Finite Element Techniques in Structural Mechanics*
   Choice - v34 - Ap '97 - p1371 [51-250]
Ross, Carol - *Something to Draw On*
   TES - Mr 28 '97 - p7* [51-250]
Ross, Catherine Sheldrick - *Circles: Fun Ideas for Getting A-Round in Math*
   c BL - v93 - Ap 1 '97 - p1341 [1-50]

Ross, Charles L - *Editing D.H. Lawrence*
   Choice - v34 - D '96 - p612 [51-250]
   ELT - v40 - 1 '97 - p98+ [501+]
Ross, Clifford - *The World of Edward Gorey*
   Atl - v278 - D '96 - p124 [51-250]
   y BL - v93 - O 1 '96 - p315+ [51-250]
   Bloom Rev - v16 - N '96 - p25 [51-250]
   BW - v26 - D 8 '96 - p1+ [501+]
   NYTBR - v101 - S 1 '96 - p17 [251-500]
   NYTBR - v101 - D 8 '96 - p21 [51-250]
   Obs - S 15 '96 - p18* [1-50]
   VV - v41 - O 15 '96 - p45+ [501+]
Ross, Colin - *Satanic Ritual Abuse*
   Skeptic - v4 - 2 '96 - p101+ [501+]
Ross, Dana Fuller - *Westward (Erickson). Audio Version*
   y Kliatt - v30 - S '96 - p54 [51-250]
Ross, David - *Why We Got Chucked Out of the Inter-Schools Football Competition (Illus. by Jacqui Thomas)*
   c Bks Keeps - N '96 - p11 [51-250]
Ross, Diana - *Prickety Prackety (Illus. by Caroline Crossland)*
   c SLJ - v43 - Ja '97 - p90 [51-250]
Ross, Ellen - *Love and Toil*
   EHR - v111 - N '96 - p1336+ [501+]
   JWomHist - v8 - Fall '96 - p219+ [501+]
Ross, Gayle - *How Turtle's Back Was Cracked (Illus. by Murv Jacob)*
   c RT - v50 - O '96 - p152+ [51-250]
   The Legend of the Windigo (Illus. by Murv Jacob)
   c BL - v93 - S 15 '96 - p235 [51-250]
   c CCB-B - v50 - N '96 - p112+ [51-250]
   c Emerg Lib - v24 - Mr '97 - p64 [51-250]
   c HB Guide - v8 - Spr '97 - p105 [51-250]
   c KR - v64 - N 1 '96 - p1607 [51-250]
   c SLJ - v42 - N '96 - p100+ [51-250]
Ross, George - *Jacques Delors and European Integration*
   APSR - v90 - S '96 - p704+ [501+]
   JEL - v34 - S '96 - p1425 [51-250]
Ross, Ian Campbell - *Umbria: A Cultural History*
   CR - v269 - N '96 - p278 [51-250]
   Econ - v339 - My 18 '96 - p14* [251-500]
   TLS - Jl 19 '96 - p32 [251-500]
Ross, Jim - *Dear Oklahoma City, Get Well Soon*
   c HB Guide - v7 - Fall '96 - p388 [51-250]
Ross, John M - *Employment/Unemployment and Earnings Statistics*
   r ARBA - v28 - '97 - p117 [251-500]
   r Choice - v34 - F '97 - p949 [51-250]
   r ILR - v135 - 5 '96 - p596+ [51-250]
   R&R Bk N - v11 - D '96 - p31 [51-250]
Ross, Katherine Ball - *The Quiet Center*
   y BL - v93 - My 1 '97 - p1466 [51-250]
   KR - v65 - Ap 1 '97 - p540 [251-500]
   LJ - v122 - My 1 '97 - p104 [51-250]
Ross, Kathleen - *The Baroque Narrative of Carlos De Siguenza Y Gongora*
   HAHR - v76 - N '96 - p792+ [251-500]
   MLR - v91 - Jl '96 - p768+ [501+]
Ross, Kathy - *The Best Holiday Crafts Ever! (Illus. by Sharon Lane Holm)*
   c PW - v243 - S 9 '96 - p85 [51-250]
   Crafts for Easter (Illus. by Sharon Lane Holm)
   c HB Guide - v7 - Fall '96 - p354 [51-250]
   Crafts for Hanukkah (Illus. by Sharon Lane Holm)
   c BL - v93 - S 1 '96 - p134+ [51-250]
   c HB Guide - v8 - Spr '97 - p136 [51-250]
   Crafts for Kids Who Are Wild about Dinosaurs (Illus. by Sharon Lane Holm)
   c BL - v93 - F 1 '97 - p938 [51-250]
   c CBRS - v25 - Ap '97 - p104 [51-250]
   c PW - v243 - D 16 '96 - p61 [51-250]
   Crafts for Kids Who Are Wild about Outer Space (Illus. by Sharon Lane Holm)
   c BL - v93 - F 1 '97 - p938 [51-250]
   c CBRS - v25 - Ap '97 - p104 [51-250]
   c PW - v243 - D 16 '96 - p61 [51-250]
   Gifts to Make for Your Favorite Grownup (Illus. by Anne Canevari Green)
   c CCB-B - v50 - D '96 - p151+ [51-250]
   c HB Guide - v8 - Spr '97 - p136 [51-250]
   c PW - v243 - S 9 '96 - p85 [51-250]
   c SLJ - v42 - O '96 - p139 [51-250]
   The Jewish Holiday Craft Book (Illus. by Melinda Levine)
   c BL - v93 - Mr 1 '97 - p1168 [51-250]
Ross, Kent - *Cemetery Quilt (Illus. by Rosanne Kaloustian)*
   c LA - v73 - S '96 - p357 [51-250]
Ross, Kristin - *Fast Cars, Clean Bodies*
   FR - v70 - O '96 - p134+ [501+]

Ross, Leon T - *African American Almanac*
   r LJ - v122 - Ap 1 '97 - p84 [51-250]
Ross, Leslie - *Medieval Art*
   r ARBA - v28 - '97 - p367 [51-250]
   r BL - v93 - D 15 '96 - p745+ [251-500]
   r LJ - v121 - S 15 '96 - p54 [51-250]
   r R&R Bk N - v12 - F '97 - p72 [51-250]
Ross, Linda M - *Gastrointestinal Diseases and Disorders Sourcebook*
   i Choice - v34 - F '97 - p996 [51-250]
   r SciTech - v20 - N '96 - p48 [51-250]
Ross, M J - *Polar Pioneers*
   Can Lit - Win '96 - p156+ [501+]
   GJ - v163 - Mr '97 - p107 [51-250]
Ross, Michael - *Naissance Et Mort Des Entreprises En Europe XIXe-XXe Siecles*
   JIH - v27 - Spr '97 - p668+ [501+]
Ross, Michael Elsohn - *Cricketology (Illus. by Brian Grogan)*
   c HB Guide - v8 - Spr '97 - p122 [51-250]
   c SLJ - v42 - Ag '96 - p160 [51-250]
   Rolypolyology (Illus. by Brian Grogan)
   c HB Guide - v7 - Fall '96 - p342 [51-250]
   c SB - v33 - Ja '97 - p19 [51-250]
   Snailology (Illus. by Brian Grogan)
   c HB Guide - v8 - Spr '97 - p122 [51-250]
   c SLJ - v42 - Ag '96 - p160 [51-250]
   Wormology (Illus. by Brian Grogan)
   c HB Guide - v7 - Fall '96 - p342 [51-250]
   c SB - v33 - Ja '97 - p19+ [51-250]
Ross, Pat - *The Kinship of Women*
   PW - v244 - Ap 14 '97 - p68 [51-250]
   PW - v244 - Ap 28 '97 - p68 [51-250]
Ross, Ramon Royal - *Storyteller. 3rd Ed.*
   CCB-B - v50 - N '96 - p120 [51-250]
Ross, Richard - *A Day in Part 15*
   PW - v244 - My 12 '97 - p66 [51-250]
Ross, Robert S - *China, the United States, and the Soviet Union*
   Ch Rev Int - v3 - Fall '96 - p517+ [501+]
   Negotiating Cooperation
   J Pol - v58 - N '96 - p1256+ [501+]
   RP - v58 - Sum '96 - p661+ [501+]
Ross, Rupert - *Returning to the Teachings*
   Mac - v109 - O 7 '96 - p85+ [501+]
   Quill & Q - v62 - Ag '96 - p39 [251-500]
Ross, Steven T - *From Flintlock to Rifle*
   Choice - v34 - N '96 - p513 [51-250]
Ross, Stewart - *And Then... (Illus. by John Lobban)*
   c HB Guide - v8 - Spr '97 - p164 [51-250]
   c SLJ - v43 - Mr '97 - p207 [51-250]
   Conquerors and Explorers (Illus. by McRae Books)
   c HB Guide - v8 - Spr '97 - p163 [51-250]
   Greek Theatre
   y Sch Lib - v45 - F '97 - p52 [51-250]
   Knights (Illus. by McRae Books)
   c HB Guide - v7 - Fall '96 - p380 [51-250]
   The Original Olympics
   c Bks Keeps - v100 - S '96 - p20+ [51-250]
   y Sch Lib - v45 - F '97 - p52 [51-250]
   Pirates (Illus. by McRae Books)
   c Par Ch - v20 - O '96 - p25 [51-250]
   Secret Societies (Illus. by McRae Books)
   c HB Guide - v8 - Spr '97 - p96 [51-250]
   Witches (Illus. by McRae Books)
   c HB Guide - v7 - Fall '96 - p307 [51-250]
Ross, Stewart Halsey - *Propaganda for War*
   Choice - v34 - S '96 - p196+ [51-250]
Ross, Thomas - *Just Stories*
   Choice - v34 - Ja '97 - p877 [51-250]
Ross, Tom - *Irma, the Flying Bowling Ball (Illus. by Rex Barron)*
   c HB Guide - v8 - Spr '97 - p45 [51-250]
   c KR - v64 - Ag 15 '96 - p1241 [51-250]
   Irma the Flying Bowling Ball (Illus. by Rex Barron)
   c SLJ - v43 - Ja '97 - p90 [51-250]
Ross, Tony - *Bedtime (Illus. by Tony Ross)*
   c HB Guide - v7 - Fall '96 - p244 [51-250]
   I Want My Dinner
   c Bks Keeps - v100 - S '96 - p9 [51-250]
   c Books - v10 - Je '96 - p25 [51-250]
   c HB Guide - v7 - Fall '96 - p273 [51-250]
   c Magpies - v11 - S '96 - p45 [1-50]
   I Want My Potty
   c Books - v10 - Je '96 - p25 [51-250]
   Nicky
   c Books - v11 - Ap '97 - p24 [51-250]
   Pets (Illus. by Tony Ross)
   c HB Guide - v7 - Fall '96 - p244 [51-250]
   Shapes (Illus. by Tony Ross)
   c HB Guide - v7 - Fall '96 - p244 [51-250]

Weather (Illus. by Tony Ross)
  c HB Guide - v7 - Fall '96 - p244 [51-250]
Ross, William G - *A Muted Fury*
    Historian - v59 - Fall '96 - p156 [251-500]
    ILRR - v50 - Ap '97 - p538+ [501+]
Rossanet, Bertrand De - *Peacemaking and Peacekeeping in Yugoslavia*
    R&R Bk N - v11 - D '96 - p10 [1-50]
Rossel, Seymour - *Sefer Ha-Aggadah (Illus. by Judy Dick)*
  c SLJ - v43 - Mr '97 - p208 [51-250]
Rossel, Sven Hakon - *Christmas in Scandinavia*
    BWatch - v17 - D '96 - p2 [51-250]
    PW - v243 - S 23 '96 - p62 [51-250]
    TranslRevS - v2 - D '96 - p1 [51-250]
Rossellini, Isabella - *Some of Me*
    BL - v93 - Ap 1 '97 - p1267+ [51-250]
    KR - v65 - My 1 '97 - p712 [51-250]
    LJ - v122 - My 1 '97 - p106 [51-250]
    PW - v244 - My 12 '97 - p71 [51-250]
Rosselson, Leon - *Gordon and the Giantkillers (Illus. by Michael Reid)*
  c Sch Lib - v44 - N '96 - p152 [51-250]
Gordon Goes for Glory (Illus. by Michael Reid)
  c Sch Lib - v44 - Ag '96 - p105 [51-250]
Rosa and Her Singing Grandfather (Illus. by Marcia Sewall)
  c CCB-B - v50 - S '96 - p28 [51-250]
  c HB - v72 - S '96 - p599+ [51-250]
  c HB Guide - v7 - Fall '96 - p297 [51-250]
  c Inst - v106 - Ja '97 - p51+ [51-250]
Where's My Mum (Illus. by Priscilla Lamont)
  c Magpies - v11 - Jl '96 - p45 [1-50]
Rosser, Sue Vilhauer - *Women's Health--Missing from U.S. Medicine*
    Rel St Rev - v22 - O '96 - p342 [51-250]
    Signs - v22 - Win '97 - p488+ [501+]
Rossetti, Christina - *The Letters of Christina Rossetti. Vol. 1*
    LJ - v122 - Ap 1 '97 - p93 [51-250]
Poems
    Bloom Rev - v17 - Ja '97 - p17 [1-50]
Rossi, Agnes - *The Quick: A Novella and Stories*
    NYTBR - v101 - O 13 '96 - p32 [51-250]
Rossi, Giovanni Maria - *Finis Terrae*
    BL - v93 - D 1 '96 - p644 [51-250]
Rossi, Graciella - *Greening the Grassroots*
    ChrPhil - v8 - O 3 '96 - p44 [1-50]
Rossi, Marco - *Giovannino De Grassi: La Corte E La Cattedrale*
    BM - v138 - D '96 - p830+ [501+]
Rossi, Marielisa - *Il Libro Antico Dal XV, Al XIX Secolo*
    Lib - v19 - Mr '97 - p79+ [501+]
Rossi, Mario - *Roosevelt and the French*
    Pres SQ - v26 - Sum '96 - p905+ [251-500]
Rossi, Melissa - *Courtney Love: Queen of Noise*
  y Kliatt - v30 - S '96 - p27 [51-250]
Rossi, Renzo - *The Atlas of Human History. Vols. 1-6*
  cr ARBA - v28 - '97 - p208 [51-250]
  cr R&R Bk N - v11 - D '96 - p19 [51-250]
  cr SLJ - v42 - N '96 - p136 [51-250]
Civilizations of Asia
  y Sch Lib - v44 - Ag '96 - p125+ [51-250]
Civilizations of the Americas
  y Sch Lib - v44 - Ag '96 - p125+ [51-250]
Rossiiskii Gosudarstvennyi Arkhiv Ekonomiki - *Putevoditel'. Vol. 1*
    Russ Rev - v55 - O '96 - p692+ [501+]
Rossiiskii Tsentr Khraneniia I Izucheniia Dokumentov Noveishei Istorii - *Kratkii Putevoditel'*
    Russ Rev - v55 - O '96 - p692+ [501+]
Rossillon, Philippe - *Atlas De La Langue Francaise*
  r FR - v70 - O '96 - p152+ [501+]
Rossiter, Margaret W - *Women Scientists in America*
    HER - v66 - Win '96 - p858+ [501+]
    Isis - v87 - S '96 - p574+ [501+]
    TCR - v98 - Spr '97 - p537+ [501+]
Rossiter, Nan Parson - *Rugby and Rosie (Illus. by Nan Parson Rossiter)*
  c CCB-B - v50 - Mr '97 - p257 [51-250]
  c KR - v65 - Ja 1 '97 - p63+ [51-250]
  c PW - v244 - Ja 13 '97 - p75 [51-250]
  c SLJ - v43 - F '97 - p84 [51-250]
Rossiter, Sean - *Hockey the NHL Way*
  y BL - v93 - Ap 1 '97 - p1308 [1-50]
  c Quill & Q - v62 - N '96 - p44 [251-500]
Rosskopf, Walter J - *Diseases of Cage and Aviary Birds. 3rd Ed.*
    SciTech - v21 - Mr '97 - p71 [51-250]
Rossler, Mechtild - *Der Generalplan Ost*
    CEH - v29 - 2 '96 - p270+ [501+]

Rossman, Douglas Athon - *The Garter Snakes*
    BWatch - v17 - S '96 - p4 [51-250]
    Choice - v34 - Ja '97 - p822 [51-250]
    SciTech - v20 - N '96 - p29 [51-250]
Rosso, George Anthony, Jr. - *Blake's Prophetic Workshop*
    RES - v47 - Ag '96 - p425+ [501+]
Rossow, Lawrence F - *Search and Seizure in the Public Schools. 2nd Ed.*
    HER - v66 - Win '96 - p892 [51-250]
Rosteet, Betty Tyler - *Civil War Veterans of Old Imperial Calcasieu Parish, Louisiana*
    NGSQ - v84 - D '96 - p316 [251-500]
Rostenberg, Leona - *Old Books in the Old World*
    BC - v45 - Win '96 - p556+ [251-500]
Old Books, Rare Friends
    KR - v65 - My 1 '97 - p705 [251-500]
    PW - v244 - My 12 '97 - p65 [51-250]
Rostocki, Jozef M - *Echapper A Ma Tombe*
    WLT - v70 - Aut '96 - p989+ [501+]
Roston, Murray - *Victorian Contexts*
    TLS - D 6 '96 - p24 [51-250]
Rostvig, Maren-Sofie - *Configurations: A Topomorphical Approach to Renaissance Poetry*
    RES - v47 - N '96 - p574+ [501+]
Rosu, Anca - *The Metaphysics of Sound in Wallace Stevens*
    AL - v68 - D '96 - p868+ [251-500]
Roszak, Theodore - *The Memoirs of Elizabeth Frankenstein*
    Ent W - O 18 '96 - p75 [51-250]
Rota, Gian-Carlo - *Gian-Carlo Rota on Combinatorics*
    SciTech - v20 - N '96 - p5 [51-250]
Indiscrete Thoughts
    SciTech - v21 - Mr '97 - p4 [51-250]
Rotberg, Robert I - *From Massacres to Genocide*
    Choice - v34 - F '97 - p1031 [51-250]
    WorldV - v12 - O '96 - p6 [51-250]
Rotella, Bob - *Golf Is a Game of Confidence*
    LJ - v121 - O 1 '96 - p53 [1-50]
Rotello, Gabriel - *Sexual Ecology*
    Advocate - Ap 29 '97 - p72 [251-500]
    BL - v93 - Mr 15 '97 - p1209 [51-250]
    KR - v65 - F 15 '97 - p284 [251-500]
    LJ - v122 - Ap 1 '97 - p111 [51-250]
    PW - v244 - F 10 '97 - p74 [51-250]
    VV - v42 - Ap 15 '97 - p52+ [501+]
Rotem, Judith - *Distant Sisters*
    KR - v64 - O 1 '96 - p1451 [251-500]
Rotenberg, Mordechai - *The Yetzer: A Kabbalistic Psychology of Eroticism and Human Sexuality*
    LJ - v121 - D '96 - p126 [51-250]
Rotenberg, Robert - *Landscape and Power in Vienna*
    AHR - v102 - F '97 - p136+ [501+]
Roth, Anthony - *What Works for Whom?*
    Readings - v12 - Mr '97 - p6+ [501+]
    SciTech - v20 - D '96 - p45 [51-250]
Roth, Barry - *An Annotated Bibliography of Jane Austen Studies 1984-94*
  r ARBA - v28 - '97 - p452 [51-250]
  r Choice - v34 - F '97 - p949 [51-250]
  r Nine-C Lit - v51 - Mr '97 - p564 [51-250]
  r R&R Bk N - v12 - F '97 - p85 [51-250]
Roth, Diether - *Marchen Und Marchenforschung In Europa*
    Folkl - v107 - '96 - p124+ [501+]
Roth, Gerhard - *See*
    WLT - v70 - Aut '96 - p950 [501+]
Roth, Henry - *Mercy of a Rude Stream. Vol. 3*
    Nat - v263 - S 23 '96 - p25+ [501+]
    NYTBR - v101 - D 8 '96 - p80 [1-50]
    TLS - N 22 '96 - p22 [501+]
Roth, Henry, 1916- - *Violin Virtuosos*
    BL - v93 - Mr 15 '97 - p1218 [51-250]
  r BL - v93 - Mr 15 '97 - p1260+ [51-250]
    LJ - v122 - Mr 15 '97 - p66 [51-250]
Roth, John E - *American Elves*
  r LJ - v122 - Ap 15 '97 - p72+ [51-250]
Roth, John K - *American Diversity, American Identity*
  r Ant R - v54 - Sum '96 - p378+ [51-250]
Roth, Kathleen Bittner - *Celine: A Circle of Life*
    PW - v244 - Mr 31 '97 - p65 [51-250]
Roth, Klaus - *South Slavic Folk Culture*
  r Folkl - v107 - '96 - p115+ [51-250]
Roth, Ladislav E - *The Face of Venus*
    J Gov Info - v23 - S '96 - p552 [1-50]
Roth, Marty - *Foul and Fair Play*
    Col Lit - v23 - O '96 - p201+ [501+]
    Sew R - v104 - Jl '96 - pR71+ [501+]
Roth, Matthew W - *Platt Brothers and Company*
    JEH - v56 - D '96 - p956+ [501+]

Roth, Michael - *The Poetics of Resistance*
    R&R Bk N - v11 - N '96 - p3 [1-50]
Roth, Norman - *Conversos, Inquisition, and the Expulsion of the Jews from Spain*
    AHR - v102 - F '97 - p97+ [501+]
    CHR - v83 - Ja '97 - p97+ [501+]
Jews, Visigoths and Muslims in Medieval Spain
    CHR - v82 - Jl '96 - p507+ [501+]
    Specu - v71 - Jl '96 - p1012+ [501+]
Roth, Philip - *American Pastoral*
    BL - v93 - F 15 '97 - p971 [51-250]
    Ent W - My 16 '97 - p108 [51-250]
    KR - v65 - F 1 '97 - p166+ [251-500]
    LJ - v122 - F 15 '97 - p164 [51-250]
    NYTBR - v102 - Ap 20 '97 - p8 [501+]
    NYTLa - v146 - Ap 15 '97 - pC11+ [501+]
    PW - v244 - F 10 '97 - p67 [251-500]
    Time - v149 - Ap 28 '97 - p74 [501+]
    Trib Bks - My 18 '97 - p3 [501+]
    WSJ-Cent - v99 - Ap 22 '97 - pA20 [501+]
The Counterlife
    LJ - v122 - F 15 '97 - p166 [51-250]
Patrimony: A True Story
    LATBR - Ag 25 '96 - p11 [51-250]
Sabbath's Theater
    WLT - v70 - Sum '96 - p693+ [501+]
Roth, Sol - *The Jewish Idea of Culture*
    BL - v93 - D 1 '96 - p622 [51-250]
Roth, Susan L - *The Biggest Frog in Australia (Illus. by Susan L Roth)*
  c Emerg Lib - v23 - My '96 - p43 [1-50]
  c HB Guide - v7 - Fall '96 - p273 [51-250]
Brave Martha and the Dragon (Illus. by Susan L Roth)
  c BL - v92 - Ag '96 - p1903 [51-250]
  c HB Guide - v7 - Fall '96 - p323 [51-250]
  c SLJ - v42 - Ag '96 - p141 [51-250]
My Love for You (Illus. by Susan L Roth)
  c BL - v93 - F 1 '97 - p949 [51-250]
  c BL - v93 - Ap 1 '97 - p1341 [1-50]
  c KR - v64 - D 15 '96 - p1808 [51-250]
  c PW - v243 - D 30 '96 - p66 [51-250]
  c SLJ - v43 - F '97 - p84 [51-250]
Rothaus, Don P - *Canyons*
  c Ch BWatch - v6 - D '96 - p6 [1-50]
  c HB Guide - v8 - Spr '97 - p119 [51-250]
  c SLJ - v43 - Mr '97 - p180 [51-250]
Oceans
  c Ch BWatch - v6 - D '96 - p6 [1-50]
  c HB Guide - v8 - Spr '97 - p119 [51-250]
Rothaus, James R - *Baseball Jokes (Illus. by Viki Woodworth)*
  c HB Guide - v8 - Spr '97 - p143 [51-250]
Basketball Jokes (Illus. by Viki Woodworth)
  c HB Guide - v8 - Spr '97 - p143 [51-250]
Football Jokes (Illus. by Viki Woodworth)
  c HB Guide - v8 - Spr '97 - p143 [51-250]
Olympic Jokes (Illus. by Viki Woodworth)
  c HB Guide - v8 - Spr '97 - p143 [51-250]
Rothbard, Murray Newton - *An Austrian Perspective on the History of Economic Thought. Vols. 1-2*
    Econ J - v106 - S '96 - p1414+ [501+]
    JEL - v34 - S '96 - p1336+ [501+]
Rothbart, Harold A - *Mechanical Design Handbook*
    Choice - v34 - O '96 - p311 [51-250]
  r SB - v32 - N '96 - p233 [51-250]
Rothblatt, Donald N - *Metropolitan Governance*
    NCR - v85 - Spr '96 - p64 [51-250]
Rothblatt, Martine - *The Apartheid of Sex*
    Hum - v57 - Ja '97 - p43 [501+]
Rothblum, Esther D - *Preventing Heterosexism and Homophobia*
    R&R Bk N - v11 - D '96 - p40 [51-250]
Rothchild, Donald - *Ghana: The Political Economy of Recovery*
    WP - v49 - O '96 - p92+ [501+]
Rothenberg, Jerome - *Poems for the Millennium. Vol. 1*
    ABR - v18 - D '96 - p28+ [501+]
Seedings and Other Poems
    BL - v93 - S 15 '96 - p205 [51-250]
    LJ - v121 - O 1 '96 - p83 [51-250]
Rothenberg, Joan - *Inside-Out Grandma*
  c Emerg Lib - v23 - My '96 - p54+ [51-250]
Rothermund, Dietmar - *The Global Impact of the Great Depression 1929-1939*
    Choice - v34 - Ja '97 - p847 [51-250]
    JEL - v35 - Mr '97 - p260 [51-250]
Rothert, Steve - *Lessons Unlearned*
    WorldV - v12 - Jl '96 - p18 [51-250]
Rothgeb, John M - *Foreign Investment and Political Conflict in Developing Countries*
    R&R Bk N - v12 - F '97 - p49 [51-250]

Rothkopf, Michael M - *Standards and Practice of Homecare Therapeutics. 2nd Ed.*
SciTech - v21 - Mr '97 - p46 [51-250]
Rothman, Cynthia - *Under the Sea*
c SB - v33 - Ja '97 - p17 [51-250]
Rothman, David J - *Medicine and Western Civilization*
Hast Cen R - v26 - Mr '96 - p49 [1-50]
T&C - v38 - Ja '97 - p237+ [501+]
Rothman, Hal K - *I'll Never Fight Fire with My Bare Hands Again*
Pub Hist - v18 - Sum '96 - p83+ [501+]
Rothman, Juliet - *A Birthday Present for Daniel (Illus. by Louise Gish)*
c HB Guide - v8 - Spr '97 - p60 [51-250]
Rothman, Robert - *Measuring Up*
EL - v54 - O '96 - p90 [51-250]
Rothman, Sheila M - *Living in the Shadow of Death*
J Soc H - v30 - Fall '96 - p274+ [501+]
NEQ - v69 - S '96 - p516+ [501+]
PHR - v65 - Ag '96 - p482+ [251-500]
Queens Q - v103 - Sum '96 - p403+ [501+]
Rothmann, Ralf - *Knife Edge*
TranslRevS - v1 - My '95 - p22 [51-250]
Rothra, Elizabeth Ogren - *Florida's Pioneer Naturalist*
Isis - v87 - S '96 - p564+ [501+]
Rothschild, Fritz A - *Jewish Perspectives on Christianity*
MEJ - v51 - Win '97 - p154 [51-250]
Rothschild, Miriam - *The Rothschild Gardens*
PW - v244 - Mr 24 '97 - p72 [51-250]
Rothstein, Bo - *The Social Democratic State*
AJS - v102 - N '96 - p899+ [501+]
Choice - v34 - O '96 - p355 [51-250]
Rothstein, Michael - *Ace the Technical Interview*
CBR - v15 - Spr '97 - p1 [1-50]
Rothstein, Mikael - *Belief Transformations*
Choice - v34 - D '96 - p630 [1-50]
Rothwax, Harold J - *Guilty: The Collapse of Criminal Justice*
Rapport - v19 - 4 '96 - p42 [251-500]
Rothwell, J - *Computer Programming. 4th Ed.*
SciTech - v20 - S '96 - p5 [51-250]
Rothwell, William J - *Beyond Training and Development*
Choice - v34 - D '96 - p656 [51-250]
HR Mag - v41 - Ag '96 - p123+ [51-250]
Rotkirch, Anna - *Women's Voices in Russia Today*
R&R Bk N - v11 - N '96 - p42 [51-250]
Rotman, Leonard Ian - *Parallel Paths*
R&R Bk N - v12 - F '97 - p66 [51-250]
Rotner, Shelley - *Action Alphabet (Illus. by Shelley Rotner)*
c BL - v92 - Ag '96 - p1903 [51-250]
c HB Guide - v7 - Fall '96 - p326 [51-250]
c SLJ - v43 - Ja '97 - p108 [51-250]
Close, Closer, Closest (Illus. by Shelley Rotner)
c BL - v93 - Ap 1 '97 - p1336 [51-250]
c CCB-B - v50 - Ap '97 - p294 [51-250]
c HB - v73 - My '97 - p311 [51-250]
c KR - v65 - Mr 15 '97 - p467 [51-250]
Colors around Us (Illus. by Shelley Rotner)
c HB Guide - v8 - Spr '97 - p15 [51-250]
c PW - v243 - N 25 '96 - p77 [51-250]
Faces
c Emerg Lib - v24 - Mr '97 - p46 [51-250]
Hold the Anchovies! (Illus. by Shelley Rotner)
c BL - v93 - S 15 '96 - p244 [51-250]
c HB Guide - v8 - Spr '97 - p134 [51-250]
c SLJ - v42 - O '96 - p117 [51-250]
Lots of Moms (Illus. by Shelley Rotner)
c HB Guide - v7 - Fall '96 - p311 [1-50]
Rotstein, Nancy-Gay - *Shattering Glass*
BIC - v25 - O '96 - p40+ [251-500]
Rottenberg, Dan - *Middletown Jews*
KR - v65 - F 1 '97 - p206 [251-500]
Rotzoll, Kim B - *Advertising in Contemporary Society. 3rd Ed.*
Choice - v34 - My '97 - p1544 [51-250]
Roubaud, Jacques - *Poesie, Etcetera*
WLT - v70 - Sum '96 - p661 [501+]
Roudinesco, Elisabeth - *Jacques Lacan: His Life and Work*
BL - v93 - Mr 15 '97 - p1206+ [51-250]
KR - v65 - F 15 '97 - p284 [251-500]
LJ - v122 - Ap 15 '97 - p102 [51-250]
NYTBR - v102 - Ap 13 '97 - p12 [501+]
PW - v244 - Mr 3 '97 - p56 [51-250]
Roueche, Berton - *The Man Who Grew Two Breasts and Other True Tales of Medical Detection*
LATBR - Ag 11 '96 - p11 [51-250]
NY - v72 - D 16 '96 - p108 [51-250]
Rouget, Francois - *L'Apotheose D'Orphee*
FR - v70 - D '96 - p322+ [501+]

Rougeyron, Andre - *Agents for Escape*
HRNB - v25 - Win '97 - p89+ [251-500]
Roughgarden, Jonathan - *Theory of Population Genetics and Evolutionary Ecology*
SciTech - v20 - S '96 - p19 [51-250]
Roulson, Robert - *The Winding Road to West Egg*
J Am St - v30 - Ag '96 - p305+ [251-500]
Roundhill, Clare - *Landscapes (Illus. by Lindy Norton)*
c Bks Keeps - v100 - S '96 - p20 [51-250]
Rounds, Glen - *Once We Had a Horse (Illus. by Glen Rounds)*
c HB Guide - v7 - Fall '96 - p273 [51-250]
c KR - v64 - My 1 '96 - p692 [51-250]
c Par Ch - v20 - O '96 - p21 [1-50]
Rouny, E L - *Engineer Memoirs*
T&C - v38 - Ja '97 - p263+ [501+]
Rouse, Irvin - *The Tainos: Rise and Decline of the People Who Greeted Columbus*
JTWS - v13 - Fall '96 - p321+ [501+]
Rousmaniere, John - *A Bridge to Dialogue*
Rel Ed - v91 - Fall '96 - p614 [1-50]
Rousseau, Francois - *La Croix Et Le Scalpel. Vol. 2*
Can Hist R - v77 - S '96 - p444+ [501+]
Rousseau, Jean-Jacques - *Social Contract. Discourse on the Virtue Most Necessary for a Hero. Political Fragments. Geneva Manuscript*
TranslRevS - v1 - My '95 - p6 [51-250]
Rousseau, John J - *Jesus and His World*
r ARBA - v28 - '97 - p551 [51-250]
r CR - v269 - S '96 - p167 [51-250]
r Rel St Rev - v23 - Ja '97 - p67 [51-250]
Rousseau, Philip - *Basil of Caesarea*
CHR - v82 - Jl '96 - p497+ [501+]
Theol St - v57 - Je '96 - p344+ [501+]
Roussel, Eric - *Jean Monnet 1888-1979*
TLS - Jl 19 '96 - p31 [501+]
Rout, Paul - *Francis and Bonaventure*
TES - F 21 '97 - p7* [1-50]
Route One
p Sm Pr R - v28 - Jl '96 - p27 [51-250]
Routledge German Technical Dictionary. Vols. 1-2
r ARBA - v28 - '97 - p391 [251-500]
Roux, Alain - *Greves Et Politique A Shanghai*
Ch Rev Int - v3 - Fall '96 - p523+ [501+]
Roux, Jean-Paul - *Le Roi: Mythes Et Symboles*
Choice - v34 - D '96 - p565 [1-50]
Roux, Michel - *Sauces: Sweet and Savory, Classic and New*
BL - v93 - D 15 '96 - p702 [51-250]
Rouxeville, Annie - *Passport Pour La France. 2nd Ed.*
MLJ - v80 - Win '96 - p546+ [501+]
Rovere, Richard - *Howe and Hummel*
VQR - v73 - Win '97 - p34* [1-50]
Rowan, Carl T - *The Coming Race War in America*
B Ent - v27 - F '97 - p215 [1-50]
y BL - v93 - O 1 '96 - p290 [51-250]
BW - v26 - N 3 '96 - p4+ [501+]
LJ - v121 - N 1 '96 - p86 [1-50]
LJ - v121 - N 15 '96 - p71 [51-250]
PW - v243 - S 9 '96 - p71 [51-250]
Rowan, Frances Dugger - *The Dugger Family, Johnson County, Tennessee*
EGH - v50 - N '96 - p193 [51-250]
Rowan, John - *The Transpersonal: Psychotherapy and Counselling*
Rel St Rev - v23 - Ap '97 - p141+ [501+]
Rowan, Roy - *First Dogs*
KR - v65 - My 1 '97 - p712 [51-250]
Rowbotham, David - *The Ebony Gates*
Aust Bk R - N '96 - p55 [501+]
Rowbotham, Sheila - *Hidden from History*
HT - v46 - Ag '96 - p60 [51-250]
Rowe, Alan J - *Intelligent Information Systems*
Choice - v34 - Ja '97 - p832 [51-250]
R&R Bk N - v11 - D '96 - p27 [51-250]
Rowe, Chip - *The Book of Zines*
BL - v93 - My 15 '97 - p1543 [51-250]
PW - v244 - Ap 14 '97 - p68 [1-50]
Rowe, Doc - *Midwinter: An Education Resource Pack for the Winter Term on British Traditions*
Folkl - v107 - '96 - p123+ [251-500]
Plough Monday to Hocktide
Folkl - v107 - '96 - p123+ [251-500]
Rowe, John A - *Baby Crow*
c Bks Keeps - Jl '96 - p7 [51-250]
Can You Spot the Spotted Dog? (Illus. by John A Rowe)
c BL - v93 - N 1 '96 - p510 [51-250]
c CBRS - v25 - D '96 - p41 [1-50]
c HB Guide - v8 - Spr '97 - p15 [51-250]
c JB - v60 - O '96 - p188 [51-250]
c SLJ - v42 - D '96 - p104 [51-250]

Jack the Dog (Illus. by John A Rowe)
c Bks Keeps - N '96 - p7 [51-250]
c PW - v243 - D 2 '96 - p62 [1-50]
Peter Piglet (Illus. by John A Rowe)
c BL - v93 - D 1 '96 - p669 [51-250]
c HB Guide - v8 - Spr '97 - p45 [51-250]
c KR - v64 - S 1 '96 - p1327 [51-250]
c SLJ - v42 - N '96 - p91+ [51-250]
Rabbit Moon (Illus. by John A Rowe)
c PW - v244 - My 12 '97 - p77 [1-50]
Rowe, Kathleen - *The Unruly Woman*
FQ - v50 - Win '96 - p58+ [501+]
Rowe, Kenneth - *The Postal History and Markings of the Forwarding Agents*
Phil Lit R - v45 - 3 '96 - p256 [51-250]
Rowe, Noel - *The Pictorial Guide to the Living Primates*
r BL - v93 - Ap 1 '97 - p1357+ [251-500]
SciTech - v21 - Mr '97 - p38 [1-50]
Rowe, W W - *The Rabbit and the Tigerdile*
c Ch BWatch - v7 - F '97 - p2 [51-250]
Rowell, Andrew - *Green Backlash*
Econ - v342 - F 15 '97 - p7* [51-250]
LJ - v121 - D '96 - p139 [51-250]
Nature - v384 - N 28 '96 - p325+ [501+]
New Sci - v152 - O 5 '96 - p48 [501+]
Rowell, Christopher - *Uppark Restored*
Econ - v341 - O 12 '96 - p93+ [501+]
Rowell, Derek - *System Dynamics*
SciTech - v20 - D '96 - p60 [51-250]
Rowell, Galen - *Poles Apart*
GJ - v162 - Jl '96 - p238 [51-250]
ILN - Christmas '96 - p88 [51-250]
Rowell, Geoffrey - *The English Religious Tradition and the Genius of Anglicanism*
CH - v65 - S '96 - p549+ [501+]
Rowell, Roger M - *Paper and Composites from Agro-Based Resources*
SciTech - v21 - Mr '97 - p99 [51-250]
Rowell, S C - *Lithuania Ascending*
EHR - v111 - N '96 - p1254+ [501+]
Rowland, C K - *Politics and Judgment in Federal District Courts*
Choice - v34 - F '97 - p1037+ [51-250]
Rowland, Edna - *True Crime Astrology*
Horoscope - v63 - Ap '97 - p41+ [501+]
Rowland, Herbert - *The Eighteenth Century German Book Review*
Lib - v18 - Je '96 - p169 [51-250]
Rowland, Laura Joh - *Bundori: A Novel*
NYTBR - v101 - Ap 7 '96 - p23 [51-250]
Shinju
Quill & Q - v62 - O '96 - p30 [51-250]
The Way of the Traitor
KR - v65 - My 1 '97 - p683 [251-500]
LJ - v122 - My 1 '97 - p143 [51-250]
PW - v244 - My 12 '97 - p62 [51-250]
Rowland, Mary - *A Commonsense Guide to Mutual Funds*
WSJ-MW - v77 - S 19 '96 - pA16 [51-250]
Rowland, Mary Canaga - *As Long as Life*
Roundup M - v3 - Ag '96 - p27 [251-500]
Rowland, Thomas W - *Developmental Exercise Physiology*
Choice - v34 - D '96 - p645 [51-250]
SciTech - v20 - S '96 - p40 [51-250]
Rowlands, Betty - *A Hive of Bees*
BL - v93 - Ap 1 '97 - p1280 [51-250]
Rowlands, Ian H - *The Politics of Global Atmospheric Change*
APSR - v90 - S '96 - p695+ [501+]
GJ - v162 - N '96 - p343 [51-250]
Rowlands, John - *The Surnames of Wales*
r ARBA - v28 - '97 - p164 [51-250]
r BL - v93 - S 1 '96 - p166 [1-50]
Rowlandson, Jane - *Landowners and Tenants in Roman Egypt*
Choice - v34 - F '97 - p1018 [51-250]
Rowlett, Lori L - *Joshua and the Rhetoric of Violence*
BTB - v27 - Spr '97 - p28+ [501+]
Rowley, Charles K - *The Political Economy of the Minimal State*
Choice - v34 - N '96 - p536 [51-250]
JEL - v34 - D '96 - p2123 [51-250]
TLS - S 20 '96 - p3+ [501+]
Trade Protection in the United States
Econ J - v107 - Ja '97 - p270 [51-250]
Rowley, Christopher - *A Dragon at World's End*
y Kliatt - v31 - My '97 - p15 [51-250]
The Wizard and the Floating City
y Kliatt - v30 - S '96 - p20 [51-250]

Rowley, Jennifer - *The Basics of Information Systems. 2nd Ed.*
    LAR - v98 - Ag '96 - p424 [51-250]
Rowley, Peter - *The Chronicles of the Rowleys*
    TLS - S 20 '96 - p32 [51-250]
Rowley, Thomas D - *Rural Development Research*
    JEL - v34 - S '96 - p1502+ [51-250]
    Pol Stud J - v24 - Aut '96 - p515+ [501+]
Rowley, William D - *Reclaiming the Arid West*
    Choice - v34 - S '96 - p198 [51-250]
    PHR - v66 - F '97 - p115+ [251-500]
    WHQ - v27 - Win '96 - p525 [501+]
Rowlinson, William - *The Oxford Paperback French Dictionary and Grammar*
    r MLR - v92 - Ja '97 - p181+ [501+]
Rowntree, Kathleen - *Laurie and Claire (Thomas). Audio Version*
    y Kliatt - v30 - N '96 - p42 [51-250]
Rowse, A L - *My View of Shakespeare*
    TLS - N '96 - p16 [501+]
Rowson, Martin - *The Life and Opinions of Tristram Shandy, Gentleman*
    Spec - v278 - Mr 22 '97 - p40 [501+]
    TLS - D 27 '96 - p32 [251-500]
Rowson, Susanna - *Charlotte Temple*
    J Am Cult - v19 - Spr '96 - p43+ [501+]
Roy, Arundhati - *The God of Small Things*
    BL - v93 - My 1 '97 - p1480 [51-250]
    Ent W - My 16 '97 - p109 [51-250]
    FEER - v160 - Ap 24 '97 - p66+ [501+]
    KR - v65 - Mr 15 '97 - p412 [251-500]
    LJ - v122 - Ap 15 '97 - p120 [51-250]
    PW - v244 - Mr 3 '97 - p62 [51-250]
Roy, Beth - *Some Trouble with Cows*
    AAPSS-A - v548 - N '96 - p234+ [501+]
Roy, Claude - *Balthus*
    VLS - Win '96 - p21 [51-250]
Roy, Donald H - *The Reuniting of America*
    Choice - v34 - My '97 - p1567 [51-250]
Roy, Frederick Hampton - *Ocular Differential Diagnosis. 6th Ed.*
    r SciTech - v20 - D '96 - p50 [51-250]
Roy, Jacqueline - *A Daughter like Me*
    y JB - v60 - O '96 - p206 [51-250]
Roy, James - *Almost Wednesday*
    c Magpies - v11 - Jl '96 - p36 [51-250]
Roy, Jules - *Mort Au Champ D'Honneur*
    WLT - v71 - Win '97 - p106+ [251-500]
Roy, Kartik C - *Economic Development and Women in the World Community*
    JEL - v34 - S '96 - p1445 [51-250]
Roy, Olivier - *Afghanistan: From Holy War to Civil War*
    MEJ - v50 - Sum '96 - p427+ [501+]
    The Failure of Political Islam
    JTWS - v13 - Spr '96 - p233+ [501+]
Roy, Sara M - *The Gaza Strip*
    MEJ - v50 - Aut '96 - p601+ [501+]
    MEP - v4 - 4 '96 - p137+ [501+]
Roy, Tapti - *The Politics of a Popular Uprising*
    AHR - v102 - F '97 - p160+ [501+]
    Historian - v59 - Fall '96 - p174+ [251-500]
Royal, Robert - *Jacques Maritain and the Jews*
    CHR - v82 - O '96 - p672+ [501+]
    Reinventing the American People
    Am Ethnol - v24 - F '97 - p237+ [501+]
The Royal and Ancient Golfer's Handbook 1996
    Books - v10 - Je '96 - p21 [1-50]
Royce, Easton - *The Aliens Approach*
    c SLJ - v42 - D '96 - p124 [51-250]
Royce, Kenneth - *The Judas Trail*
    PW - v244 - Ap 28 '97 - p55 [51-250]
Roylance, David - *Mechanics of Materials*
    Phys Today - v49 - D '96 - p56 [501+]
Royle, Edward - *William Ellerby and James Pigott Pritchett*
    CH - v65 - S '96 - p513+ [501+]
Royle, Nicholas - *After Derrida*
    MLR - v92 - Ap '97 - p419+ [501+]
Royle, Nicholas, 1963- - *A Book of Two Halves*
    TLS - O 11 '96 - p27 [251-500]
    Counterparts
    Necro - Sum '96 - p19+ [501+]
    Saxophone Dreams
    TES - Ag 23 '96 - p27 [51-250]
    TLS - N 15 '96 - p25 [51-250]
Royle, Trevor - *Winds of Change*
    CR - v270 - F '97 - p107+ [501+]
    NS - v125 - D 20 '96 - p119 [501+]
    Spec - v277 - O 19 '96 - p48+ [501+]
Royston, Angela - *Fish (Illus. by Oxford Scientific Films)*
    c Sch Lib - v45 - F '97 - p40+ [51-250]

Where Do Babies Come From? (Illus. by Steve Gorton)
    c CBRS - v24 - Ag '96 - p161+ [51-250]
    c HB Guide - v7 - Fall '96 - p338 [51-250]
    c KR - v64 - My 1 '96 - p692 [51-250]
    c SLJ - v42 - Ag '96 - p141 [51-250]
Royston, Mike - *Parallel Poems*
    c Sch Lib - v44 - N '96 - p168 [51-250]
    Ways of Telling
    Sch Lib - v45 - F '97 - p55 [51-250]
Rozan, S J - *Mandarin Plaid*
    Arm Det - v29 - Fall '96 - p497+ [251-500]
    y BL - v93 - S 15 '96 - p225 [51-250]
Rozario, Diane - *The Immunization Resource Guide. 2nd Ed.*
    r ARBA - v28 - '97 - p609 [51-250]
Roze, Janis A - *Coral Snakes of the Americas*
    Choice - v34 - Ap '97 - p1366 [51-250]
    SciTech - v21 - Mr '97 - p38 [51-250]
Roze, Pascale - *Le Chasseur Zero*
    Spec - v278 - Ja 4 '97 - p37 [501+]
Rozell, Mark J - *God at the Grassroots*
    APSR - v91 - Mr '97 - p197 [501+]
    In Contempt of Congress
    Choice - v34 - Ja '97 - p787 [51-250]
    R&R Bk N - v11 - D '96 - p62 [51-250]
    The Press and the Bush Presidency
    Choice - v34 - F '97 - p1038 [51-250]
    R&R Bk N - v11 - D '96 - p16 [51-250]
    Second Coming
    Bks & Cult - v2 - N '96 - p20+ [501+]
    R&R Bk N - v11 - N '96 - p7 [1-50]
    VQR - v72 - Aut '96 - p134* [51-250]
Rozett, Martha Tuck - *Talking Back to Shakespeare*
    MLR - v91 - O '96 - p968+ [501+]
Rozin, Elisabeth - *The Universal Kitchen*
    BL - v93 - S 15 '96 - p198 [51-250]
    LJ - v121 - O 15 '96 - p85 [51-250]
Rozzo, Ugo - *Biblioteche Italiane Del Cinquecento Tra Riforma E Controriforma*
    Lib - v18 - D '96 - p363+ [51-250]
Ruan, Ming - *Deng Xiaoping: Chronicle of an Empire*
    Ch Rev Int - v4 - Spr '97 - p227+ [501+]
Ruane, Christine - *Gender, Class, and the Professionalization of Russian City Teachers 1860-1914*
    AHR - v101 - O '96 - p1246+ [501+]
    Historian - v59 - Fall '96 - p203+ [501+]
Ruane, Joseph - *The Dynamics of Conflict in Northern Ireland*
    For Aff - v76 - My '97 - p135+ [51-250]
Rubaie, Abd Al-Rahman Majid - *Al-Washm*
    WLT - v70 - Sum '96 - p754 [501+]
Rubalcaba, Jill - *A Place in the Sun*
    c BL - v93 - Ap 1 '97 - p1334 [51-250]
    c CBRS - v25 - Ap '97 - p104 [51-250]
    c KR - v65 - Ap 1 '97 - p561 [51-250]
    Saint Vitus' Dance
    y BL - v93 - Ja '97 - p846 [251-500]
    c CCB-B - v50 - N '96 - p113 [51-250]
    c HB Guide - v8 - Spr '97 - p74 [51-250]
    c KR - v64 - S 1 '96 - p1327 [51-250]
    y SLJ - v42 - S '96 - p228 [51-250]
Rubatzky, Vincent E - *World Vegetables. 2nd Ed.*
    New Sci - v153 - Mr 1 '97 - p46 [51-250]
Rubel, David - *The United States in the 19th Century*
    cr BL - v93 - N 1 '96 - p540 [51-250]
    cr KR - v64 - O 15 '96 - p1538 [51-250]
    cr SLJ - v42 - N '96 - p138 [51-250]
Rubel, Lee A - *Entire and Meromorphic Functions*
    Choice - v34 - O '96 - p319 [51-250]
Rubenfeld, M Gaie - *Critical Thinking in Nursing*
    AJN - v96 - D '96 - p16M [51-250]
Rubenson, Samuel - *The Letters of St. Antony*
    Rel St Rev - v22 - O '96 - p301+ [501+]
    Theol St - v58 - Mr '97 - p187 [251-500]
Rubenstein, Gillian - *Shinkei*
    c Magpies - v11 - My '96 - p30+ [501+]
    Skymaze
    c Magpies - v11 - My '96 - p30+ [501+]
    Space Demons
    c Magpies - v11 - My '96 - p30+ [501+]
Rubenstein, Jeffrey L - *The History of Sukkot in the Second Temple and Rabbinic Periods*
    Rel St Rev - v22 - O '96 - p353 [51-250]
Rubenstein, Joshua - *Tangled Loyalties*
    BW - v26 - S 15 '96 - p13 [51-250]
    Dis - v44 - Win '97 - p131+ [501+]
    Lon R Bks - v18 - D 12 '96 - p21 [501+]
    New R - v215 - S 16 '96 - p39+ [501+]
    NYTBR - v101 - Ag 25 '96 - p14+ [501+]
    TLS - O 4 '96 - p12+ [501+]

Rubenstein, William B - *The Rights of People Who Are HIV Positive*
    LJ - v122 - Ap 15 '97 - p98+ [51-250]
Ruber, Peter - *The Last Bookman. Rev. and Enlarged Ed.*
    Arm Det - v30 - Win '97 - p74 [251-500]
Rubik, Margarete - *The Novels of Mrs. Oliphant*
    VS - v39 - Win '96 - p248+ [501+]
Rubin, Alexis - *Scattered among the Nations*
    Rel Ed - v91 - Fall '96 - p607 [1-50]
Rubin, Arnold - *Marks of Civilization*
    JAAC - v54 - Fall '96 - p411 [251-500]
Rubin, Barnett R - *The Fragmentation of Afghanistan*
    CS - v25 - N '96 - p736+ [501+]
    Pac A - v69 - Sum '96 - p253+ [501+]
    The Search for Peace in Afghanistan
    JPR - v34 - F '97 - p109+ [251-500]
    MEJ - v50 - Sum '96 - p427+ [501+]
Rubin, Charles - *Managing Your Business with QuickBooks*
    CBR - v15 - Spr '97 - p3 [1-50]
Rubin, David C - *Memory in Oral Traditions*
    A J Psy - v110 - Spr '97 - p142+ [501+]
    Rel St Rev - v23 - Ja '97 - p42+ [51-250]
    Remembering our Past
    R&R Bk N - v11 - N '96 - p4 [51-250]
Rubin, Don - *The World Encyclopedia of Contemporary Theatre. Vol. 2*
    r BIC - v26 - F '97 - p20+ [501+]
    r Choice - v34 - O '96 - p260 [51-250]
    r R&R Bk N - v11 - N '96 - p66 [51-250]
Rubin, Donald L - *Composing Social Identity in Written Language*
    Lang Soc - v25 - D '96 - p623+ [501+]
Rubin, Eva Johanna - *Flip-Flap Theatre (Illus. by Eva Johanna Rubin)*
    c HB Guide - v8 - Spr '97 - p46 [51-250]
    c KR - v64 - N 15 '96 - p1678 [51-250]
    c PW - v243 - N 25 '96 - p77 [51-250]
Rubin, Harriet - *The Princessa: Machiavelli for Women*
    BL - v93 - Mr 15 '97 - p1211 [51-250]
    Fortune - v135 - Ap 14 '97 - p162 [501+]
    KR - v65 - F 1 '97 - p206+ [251-500]
    LJ - v122 - Mr 15 '97 - p79 [51-250]
    PW - v244 - Mr 24 '97 - p71+ [51-250]
Rubin, Harvey W - *Dictionary of Insurance Terms. 3rd Ed.*
    r ARBA - v28 - '97 - p98 [51-250]
Rubin, Herbert J - *Qualitative Interviewing*
    MLJ - v80 - Win '96 - p555+ [501+]
Rubin, Janet - *Drama and Music*
    Learning - v25 - S '96 - p55 [1-50]
Rubin, Jeffrey B - *Psychotherapy and Buddhism*
    R&R Bk N - v12 - F '97 - p9 [1-50]
Rubin, Julius H - *Religious Melancholy and Protestant Experience in America*
    Rel St Rev - v23 - Ap '97 - p135+ [501+]
Rubin, Lewis J - *Primary Pulmonary Hypertension*
    SciTech - v21 - Mr '97 - p57 [51-250]
Rubin, Lilian - *The Transcendent Child*
    Adoles - v31 - Win '96 - p995 [51-250]
Rubin, Louis Decimus - *The Heat of the Sun*
    Sew R - v104 - Jl '96 - p468+ [501+]
    A Writer's Companion
    r ARBA - v28 - '97 - p423+ [251-500]
    yr Kliatt - v31 - Mr '97 - p37 [51-250]
Rubin, Patricia Lee - *Giorgio Vasari: Art and History*
    Six Ct J - v27 - Fall '96 - p973+ [501+]
Rubin, Rebecca B - *Communication Research Measures*
    SSQ - v77 - Je '96 - p453+ [501+]
Rubin, Rhea Joyce - *Of a Certain Age*
    r RQ - v36 - Win '96 - p215+ [51-250]
Rubin, Stanley - *Medieval English Medicine*
    TES - D 27 '96 - p16 [1-50]
Rubin, Stephen C - *Cervical Cancer and Preinvasive Neoplasia*
    SciTech - v20 - S '96 - p29 [51-250]
Rubin, Susan Goldman - *Emily in Love*
    y BL - v93 - My 15 '97 - p1573+ [51-250]
    y CCB-B - v50 - Ap '97 - p294 [51-250]
    c KR - v65 - F 15 '97 - p305 [51-250]
Rubin, Uri - *The Eye of the Beholder*
    MEJ - v51 - Win '97 - p154 [51-250]
    Rel St Rev - v22 - O '96 - p356 [51-250]
Rubin, Vera - *Bright Galaxies, Dark Matters*
    New Sci - v153 - Mr 22 '97 - p45 [1-50]
Rubin, William - *Picasso and Portraiture*
    LATBR - D 8 '96 - p14 [51-250]
    NS - v125 - N 15 '96 - p45+ [501+]
    NYTLa - v146 - D 2 '96 - pC16 [51-250]
    Picasso Et Le Portrait
    BM - v139 - Ja '97 - p60+ [501+]

Rubin-Dorsky, Jeffrey - *People of the Book*
Choice - v34 - Ja '97 - p851 [51-250]
R&R Bk N - v11 - D '96 - p14 [51-250]
Rubinetti, Donald - *Cappy the Lonely Camel (Illus. by Lisa Chauncy Guida)*
c SLJ - v42 - N '96 - p92 [51-250]
Rubinstein, Erna F - *After the Holocaust*
Wom R Bks - v14 - O '96 - p12+ [501+]
Rubinstein, Gillian - *Annie's Brother's Suit and Other Stories*
y Aust Bk R - O '96 - p60 [501+]
Foxspell
c Bkbird - v34 - Spr '96 - p51 [51-250]
c CBRS - v25 - Win '97 - p70 [51-250]
y CCB-B - v50 - Ja '97 - p184 [51-250]
y HB - v72 - N '96 - p746+ [251-500]
y HB Guide - v8 - Spr '97 - p84 [51-250]
c KR - v64 - Ag 15 '96 - p1242 [51-250]
c NYTBR - v102 - Mr 30 '97 - p18 [1-50]
c SLJ - v42 - S '96 - p206 [51-250]
y VOYA - v19 - D '96 - p282 [251-500]
Galax-Arena
y Kliatt - v30 - S '96 - p4 [1-50]
y PW - v244 - F 10 '97 - p85 [1-50]
Sharon, Keep Your Hair On (Illus. by David Mackintosh)
c Aust Bk R - Je '96 - p63 [501+]
c Magpies - v11 - Jl '96 - p24 [51-250]
Witch Music and Other Stories
c Aust Bk R - O '96 - p60 [501+]
Rubinstein, Murray A - *The Other Taiwan*
Ch Rev Int - v3 - Fall '96 - p526+ [501+]
Rubinstein, Ruth P - *Dress Codes*
J Am Cult - v19 - Spr '96 - p104 [51-250]
Rubinstein, W D - *A History of the Jews in the English-Speaking World*
HT - v47 - F '97 - p58+ [501+]
Judaism in Australia
J Gov Info - v23 - S '96 - p652 [1-50]
Rubio, Mary Henley - *Harvesting Thistles*
Can Lit - Win '96 - p133+ [501+]
Ruble, Blair - *Money Sings*
Russ Rev - v55 - O '96 - p725+ [501+]
Ruby, Jay - *Secure the Shadow*
Afterimage - v23 - Sum '96 - p8+ [501+]
AHR - v101 - D '96 - p1608+ [501+]
Ruby, Jennifer - *Underwear*
c Sch Lib - v44 - N '96 - p175 [51-250]
y SLJ - v43 - Ja '97 - p133+ [51-250]
Ruby, Jurgen - *Maschinen Fur Die Massenfertigung*
T&C - v37 - O '96 - p848+ [501+]
Ruby, Lois - *Skin Deep*
y Kliatt - v30 - S '96 - p14 [51-250]
Ruby, Pascal - *Le Crepuscule Des Marges*
AJA - v100 - O '96 - p773+ [501+]
Ruby, Robert H - *John Slocum and the Indian Shaker Church*
Choice - v34 - F '97 - p1027 [51-250]
Roundup M - v4 - Ap '97 - p23+ [251-500]
Ruck, Carl A P - *The World of Classical Myth*
CW - v90 - S '96 - p73+ [251-500]
Ruck, Rob - *Sandlot Seasons*
Aethlon - v13 - Fall '95 - p171+ [251-500]
Rucka, Greg - *Keeper*
BWatch - v17 - S '96 - p1 [51-250]
KR - v64 - My 1 '96 - p631 [251-500]
Rucker, Rudy - *Freeware*
BL - v93 - My 1 '97 - p1483 [51-250]
KR - v65 - Mr 15 '97 - p423 [51-250]
Rud, Jeff - *Long Shot*
c Ch BWatch - v6 - D '96 - p2 [51-250]
y Quill & Q - v62 - S '96 - p70 [51-250]
Rudanko, Martti Juhani - *Prepositions and Complement Clauses*
R&R Bk N - v12 - F '97 - p78 [51-250]
Rudd, Gillian - *Managing Language in Piers Plowman*
MLR - v92 - Ap '97 - p430+ [501+]
RES - v47 - N '96 - p559+ [501+]
Ruden, Ronald A - *The Craving Brain*
BL - v93 - Mr 1 '97 - p1100+ [51-250]
Rudenstine, David - *The Day the Presses Stopped*
AS - v66 - Spr '97 - p294+ [501+]
BW - v26 - Ag 4 '96 - p4 [501+]
Choice - v34 - D '96 - p678 [51-250]
CJR - v35 - Jl '96 - p55+ [501+]
HRNB - v25 - Fall '96 - p15+ [251-500]
JMCQ - v73 - Aut '96 - p759 [501+]
Nat - v264 - Mr 24 '97 - p28+ [501+]
NYTBR - v102 - Ap 13 '97 - p15 [501+]
PW - v243 - N 4 '96 - p46 [1-50]
TLS - O 11 '96 - p11 [501+]

Ruderman, Anne Crippen - *The Pleasures of Virtue*
APSR - v90 - S '96 - p896 [51-250]
Nine-C Lit - v51 - S '96 - p276 [51-250]
RP - v58 - Fall '96 - p817+ [501+]
Ruderman, David B - *Jewish Thought and Scientific Discovery in Early Modern Europe*
Ren Q - v50 - Spr '97 - p337+ [501+]
Rudersdorf, Manfred - *Das Gluck Der Bettler*
EHR - v112 - Ap '97 - p492+ [501+]
Rudin, A James - *A Time to Speak*
Rel Ed - v91 - Fall '96 - p614 [1-50]
Rudin, Donald - *Omega 3 Oils*
BL - v93 - N 1 '96 - p470 [51-250]
Rudin, Ernst - *Tender Accents of Sound*
Choice - v34 - Ap '97 - p1339 [51-250]
Rudin, Walter - *The Way I Remember It*
SciTech - v21 - Mr '97 - p4 [1-50]
Rudison, Ron - *Where to Find the Best Soul Food, Blues and Jazz in the Southeast*
r CAY - v16 - Fall '95 - p9 [51-250]
Rudloff, Holger - *Pelzdamen: Weiblichkeitsbilder Bei Thomas Mann Und Leopold Von Sacher-Masoch*
MLR - v92 - Ap '97 - p516+ [501+]
Rudman, Carol - *Frames of Reference*
Bus Bk R - v13 - 3 '96 - p110+ [501+]
Rudman, Mark - *The Millennium Hotel*
Choice - v34 - Mr '97 - p1166 [51-250]
LJ - v121 - N 15 '96 - p65 [51-250]
VLS - Win '96 - p10+ [51-250]
Rudman, Masha - *Children's Literature. 3rd Ed.*
TCR - v97 - Sum '96 - p658+ [501+]
Rudman, Warren B - *Combat: Twelve Years in the U.S. Senate*
NYTBR - v101 - Ag 25 '96 - p18 [51-250]
Rudner, Barry - *My Friends That Rhyme with Orange (Illus. by Peggy Trabalka)*
c RT - v50 - O '96 - p137 [1-50]
Rudner, David West - *Caste and Capitalism in Colonial India*
AHR - v101 - D '96 - p1607 [501+]
Am Ethnol - v24 - F '97 - p255+ [501+]
Rudnick, Ursula - *Post-Shoa Religious Metaphors*
R&R Bk N - v11 - N '96 - p75 [51-250]
Rudnytsky, Peter L - *Transitional Objects and Potential Spaces*
Dal R - v75 - Spr '95 - p136+ [501+]
Rudoe, Judy - *Cartier 1900-1939*
Mag Antiq - v151 - Ap '97 - p510 [501+]
PW - v244 - Ap 28 '97 - p68 [51-250]
Rudoff, Alvin - *Societies in Space*
SciTech - v21 - Mr '97 - p94 [51-250]
Rudoff, Carol - *Allergy Products Directory 1995-1996; Allergy/Asthma Finding Help*
r BL - v93 - F 1 '97 - p958 [1-50]
Allergy Products Directory 1995/1996: Protecting Your Skin
r BL - v93 - F 1 '97 - p958 [1-50]
Asthma Resources Directory
r BL - v93 - F 1 '97 - p958 [1-50]
Controlling Your Environment
r BL - v93 - F 1 '97 - p958 [1-50]
Rudolph, Bonnie A - *Brief Collaborative Therapy*
SciTech - v20 - D '96 - p45 [51-250]
Rudolph, Donna Keyse - *Historical Dictionary of Venezuela. 2nd Ed., Rev., Enl., and Updated*
r Choice - v34 - Ap '97 - p1314 [501+]
r R&R Bk N - v12 - F '97 - p27 [51-250]
Rudolph, Frederick B - *Biotechnology: Science, Engineering, and Ethical Challenges for the Twenty-First Century*
Choice - v34 - Mr '97 - p1181+ [501+]
SciTech - v20 - S '96 - p59 [51-250]
Rudolph, L C - *Hoosier Faiths*
CC - v113 - Ag 28 '96 - p826 [51-250]
Rudolph, Nancy Lyn - *Paper Animal Masks from Northwest Tribal Tales*
c HB Guide - v7 - Fall '96 - p354+ [1-50]
Rudolph, Richard L - *The European Peasant Family and Society*
JIH - v27 - Win '97 - p506+ [501+]
Rudolph, Susanne Hoebert - *Transnational Religion and Fading States*
MEJ - v51 - Spr '97 - p312 [51-250]
Rudolph, Wolf - *A Golden Legacy*
Choice - v34 - Ja '97 - p785 [51-250]
Rudy, John G - *Wordsworth and the Zen Mind*
Choice - v34 - O '96 - p280+ [51-250]
Rudy, Kathy - *Beyond Pro-Life and Pro-Choice*
Choice - v34 - N '96 - p473+ [51-250]
Cons - v17 - Win '96 - p31 [1-50]
Wom R Bks - v14 - F '97 - p7+ [501+]

Rudy, Lisa Jo - *Ben Franklin Book of Easy Incredible Experiments (Illus. by Cheryl Kirk Noll)*
c TES - Jl 19 '96 - pR8 [51-250]
Rudy, Willis - *The Campus and a Nation in Crisis*
Choice - v34 - Ap '97 - p1392 [51-250]
Rue, Nancy N - *Abusive Relationships*
y SLJ - v43 - Ja '97 - p134 [51-250]
Rue, Wendy - *The Dollar Bill Knows No Sex*
BL - v93 - Mr 15 '97 - p1211 [51-250]
LJ - v122 - Ap 1 '97 - p104 [51-250]
PW - v244 - Ja 13 '97 - p63 [51-250]
Ruebel, James S - *Caesar and the Crisis of the Roman Aristocracy*
Class Out - v74 - Spr '97 - p120+ [501+]
Rueda Mendez, David - *Esclavitud Y Sociedad En La Provincia De Tunja, Siglo XVIII*
HAHR - v77 - My '97 - p311+ [501+]
Ruedy, John - *Islamism and Secularism in North Africa*
MEJ - v50 - Sum '96 - p455 [51-250]
Ruefle, Mary - *Cold Pluto*
ABR - v18 - O '96 - p30 [501+]
VQR - v72 - Aut '96 - p138* [51-250]
Ruel, Francine - *Mon Pere Et Moi*
y Can CL - v22 - Sum '96 - p105+ [501+]
Ruelle, David - *Chance and Chaos (Cosham). Audio Version*
BL - v93 - F 15 '97 - p1038 [51-250]
Rueschemeyer, Dietrich - *States, Social Knowledge, and the Origins of Modern Social Policies*
CS - v26 - Ja '97 - p37+ [501+]
J Pol - v59 - F '97 - p290+ [501+]
PSQ - v111 - Fall '96 - p559+ [501+]
Ruestow, Edward G - *The Microscope in the Dutch Republic*
Choice - v34 - F '97 - p984 [51-250]
Nature - v386 - Mr 13 '97 - p141 [501+]
Ruff, Allen - *We Called Each Other Comrade*
LJ - v122 - Ap 1 '97 - p93 [51-250]
Ruff, Matt - *Sewer, Gas and Electric*
BW - v27 - F 16 '97 - p4 [251-500]
Ent W - F 14 '97 - p56+ [51-250]
KR - v64 - N 1 '96 - p1560 [251-500]
LJ - v121 - N 15 '96 - p92 [51-250]
VV - v42 - F 11 '97 - p54 [501+]
Ruff, Shawn Stewart - *Go the Way Your Blood Beats*
BL - v92 - Ag '96 - p1881 [51-250]
Ruffin, M Holt - *The Post-Soviet Handbook*
r ARBA - v28 - '97 - p64 [51-250]
r Choice - v34 - '97 - p594 [51-250]
r LJ - v121 - N 1 '96 - p62 [51-250]
Ruffin, Paul - *Circling*
Sm Pr R - v29 - Ja '97 - p9 [501+]
Ruffo, Titta - *Ruffo: My Parabola*
Spec - v277 - O 26 '96 - p48 [501+]
TranslRevS - v2 - D '96 - p9+ [51-250]
Rugarli, Giampaolo - *Llinfinito Forse*
BL - v93 - D 1 '96 - p644 [1-50]
Rugeley, Terry - *Yucatan's Maya Peasantry and the Origins of the Caste War*
Choice - v34 - Mr '97 - p1226 [51-250]
Rugen, Samantha - *Getting a Life*
y Sch Lib - v45 - F '97 - p49 [51-250]
Ruggero, Ed - *Breaking Ranks*
PW - v243 - N 18 '96 - p70 [1-50]
Ruggie, John Gerard - *Winning the Peace*
Choice - v34 - F '97 - p1038 [51-250]
For Aff - v75 - S '96 - p143+ [51-250]
Ruggie, Mary - *Realignments in the Welfare State*
Choice - v34 - My '97 - p1535 [51-250]
SciTech - v21 - Mr '97 - p45 [51-250]
Ruggiero, Greg - *Critical Mass*
Workbook - v21 - Win '96 - p172+ [501+]
Ruggiero, Vincenzo - *Organized and Corporate Crime in Europe*
Choice - v34 - N '96 - p548 [51-250]
R&R Bk N - v12 - F '97 - p57 [51-250]
Ruggles, Clive L N - *Astronomies and Cultures*
Am Ant - v61 - Ap '96 - p424+ [51-250]
Rugman, Jonathan - *Ataturk's Children*
JPR - v34 - F '97 - p114+ [51-250]
Ruhlen, Merritt - *The Origin of Language*
Nature - v383 - O 24 '96 - p682 [1-50]
Ruhlman, Michael - *Boys Themselves*
LJ - v121 - O 1 '96 - p96+ [51-250]
NYTBR - v101 - S 29 '96 - p17 [501+]
Ruhmkorf, Peter - *Tabu I*
WLT - v70 - Sum '96 - p687+ [501+]
Ruigrok, Winfried - *The Logic of International Restructuring*
JEL - v35 - Mr '97 - p244+ [51-250]

Ruiz, Octavio Madigan - *Many Faces of Mexico*
    Workbook - v21 - Fall '96 - p126+ [251-500]
Ruiz, Teofilo F - *Crisis and Continuity*
    EHR - v111 - S '96 - p960 [251-500]
    Specu - v71 - O '96 - p1013+ [501+]
Ruiz-De-Medina, Juan - *Documentos Del Japon 1558-1562*
    r CHR - v83 - Ja '97 - p156+ [251-500]
Ruiz Silva, Carlos - *Don Alvaro O La Fuerza Del Sino*
    CML - v16 - Spr '96 - p203+ [501+]
Ruiz Zevallos, Augusto - *Psiquiatras Y Locos*
    HAHR - v77 - F '97 - p151 [251-500]
Rukeyser, Muriel - *The Life of Poetry*
    LJ - v122 - F 1 '97 - p112 [1-50]
    Nat - v264 - Ap 14 '97 - p30+ [501+]
    Prog - v61 - Ja '97 - p35+ [251-500]
    Wom R Bks - v14 - F '97 - p10 [501+]
Rukl, Antonin - *Atlas of the Moon*
    r Astron - v24 - N '96 - p102 [51-250]
Rulau, Russell - *Hard Times Tokens 1832-1844. 6th Ed.*
    r Coin W - v37 - D 9 '96 - p38+ [51-250]
Rule, Ann - *Dead by Sunset*
    y Kliatt - v30 - S '96 - p32 [51-250]
    A Fever in the Heart and Other True Cases
    LJ - v121 - N 1 '96 - p91 [51-250]
    PW - v243 - S 16 '96 - p78 [51-250]
Rule, Keith - *3D Graphics File Formats*
    SciTech - v21 - Mr '97 - p72 [51-250]
Rule, Wilma - *Russian Women in Politics and Society*
    Choice - v34 - Ap '97 - p1398 [51-250]
    R&R Bk N - v12 - F '97 - p54 [51-250]
Ruler, J A Van - *The Crisis of Causality*
    RM - v50 - S '96 - p177+ [501+]
Rumalshah, Mano - *Pakistan*
    y SLJ - v42 - O '96 - p45 [1-50]
Rumball, Donald - *Peter Munk: The Making of a Modern Tycoon*
    Quill & Q - v62 - O '96 - p36 [251-500]
Rumbaut, Ruben G - *California's Immigrant Children*
    HER - v66 - Fall '96 - p668+ [501+]
Rumble, Alexander R - *The Reign of Cnut*
    EHR - v111 - N '96 - p1236+ [251-500]
Rumer, Boris - *Central Asia in Transition*
    Choice - v34 - D '96 - p657 [51-250]
    JEL - v35 - Mr '97 - p292 [51-250]
    R&R Bk N - v11 - D '96 - p26 [51-250]
Rumford, James - *The Cloudmakers (Illus. by James Rumford)*
    c BL - v93 - S 15 '96 - p250 [51-250]
    c CBRS - v25 - S '96 - p8 [1-50]
    c HB Guide - v8 - Spr '97 - p46 [51-250]
    c Inst - v106 - N '96 - p24 [51-250]
    c SLJ - v42 - S '96 - p189 [51-250]
Rummel, Erika - *The Humanist-Scholastic Debate in the Renaissance and Reformation*
    AHR - v101 - D '96 - p1538+ [501+]
    CHR - v82 - Jl '96 - p562+ [501+]
    Rel St Rev - v23 - Ap '97 - p190+ [51-250]
    Ren Q - v50 - Spr '97 - p308+ [501+]
Rumrich, John P - *Milton Unbound*
    Choice - v34 - O '96 - p281 [51-250]
Rumsey, Barbara - *Hodgdon Shipbuilding and Mills*
    NEQ - v70 - Mr '97 - p170+ [501+]
Rumwell, Claudia - *Vascular Technology*
    SciTech - v20 - N '96 - p47 [51-250]
Rundell, James R - *The American Psychiatric Press Textbook of Consultation-Liaison Psychiatry*
    AJPsych - v154 - Ja '97 - p128+ [501+]
    SciTech - v20 - S '96 - p32 [51-250]
Rundell, Michael - *The Dictionary of Cricket*
    r Aethlon - v13 - Spr '96 - p228 [251-500]
Runge, Doris - *Grund Genug*
    WLT - v70 - Aut '96 - p954+ [501+]
Runia, David T - *Philo and the Church Fathers*
    Rel St Rev - v23 - Ja '97 - p78 [51-250]
Runnels, C N - *Artifact and Assemblage*
    AJA - v100 - O '96 - p810 [251-500]
Running, Thorpe - *The Critical Poem*
    Choice - v34 - N '96 - p465 [51-250]
Running a School--Legal Duties and Responsibilities. 1996/1997 Ed.
    TES - Ja 24 '97 - p11* [51-250]
Runyan, Timothy J - *To Die Gallantly*
    r J Mil H - v61 - Ap '97 - p401+ [501+]
Runyon, Randolph Paul - *Delia Webster and the Underground Railroad*
    Choice - v34 - Mr '97 - p1229 [51-250]
    VQR - v73 - Win '97 - p19* [51-250]

Ruokanen, Miikka - *The Catholic Doctrine of Non-Christian Religions According to the Second Vatican Council*
    Rel Ed - v91 - Fall '96 - p610+ [51-250]
Rupert, Jane E - *The African Mask*
    y SE - v60 - N '96 - p400+ [251-500]
Rupert, Mark - *Producing Hegemony*
    JEH - v56 - D '96 - p958+ [501+]
Rupesinghe, Kumar - *Internal Conflicts in South Asia*
    JPR - v33 - N '96 - p500 [251-500]
    WorldV - v12 - Jl '96 - p7 [51-250]
Rupke, Jorg - *Kalendar Und Offentlichkeit*
    Choice - v34 - D '96 - p566 [51-250]
Rupke, Nicolaas A - *Richard Owen: Victorian Naturalist*
    VS - v39 - Win '96 - p298+ [501+]
Rupp, Rebecca Ann - *Treasury of Barbie Doll Accessories 1961-1995*
    r Ant & CM - v101 - S '96 - p27 [51-250]
    Ant & CM - v101 - O '96 - p55 [51-250]
Ruppersburg, Hugh - *Georgia Voices*
    South CR - v29 - Fall '96 - p289+ [501+]
Ruppert, James - *Mediation in Contemporary Native American Fiction*
    AL - v68 - S '96 - p658+ [251-500]
    WAL - v31 - Sum '96 - p172+ [251-500]
    WHQ - v27 - Win '96 - p551 [51-250]
Ruppli, Michel - *The Decca Labels. Vols. 1-6*
    r ARBA - v28 - '97 - p472 [51-250]
Ruprecht, Louis A, Jr. - *Tragic Posture and Tragic Vision*
    Theol St - v58 - Mr '97 - p153+ [501+]
Rural Energy and Development
    JEL - v35 - Mr '97 - p301 [51-250]
Rury, John L - *Seeds of Crisis*
    J Urban H - v23 - N '96 - p113+ [501+]
Rusanov, A I - *Interfacial Tensiometry*
    SciTech - v21 - Mr '97 - p75 [51-250]
Rusch, Debbie - *Fuentes: Conversacion Y Gramatica*
    MLJ - v81 - Spr '97 - p146+ [501+]
Rusch, Frederik L - *A Jean Toomer Reader*
    J Am St - v30 - Ap '96 - p168+ [501+]
Rusch, Kristine Kathryn - *The Changeling*
    y Kliatt - v30 - S '96 - p20 [51-250]
    Star Wars: The New Rebellion
    y BL - v93 - O 1 '96 - p292 [51-250]
    LJ - v121 - N 15 '96 - p91 [51-250]
Ruse, Michael - *But Is It Science?*
    New Sci - v152 - N 30 '96 - p45 [51-250]
    Evolutionary Naturalism
    Skeptic - v4 - 4 '96 - p103+ [51-250]
    Monad to Man
    LJ - v121 - N 15 '96 - p86 [51-250]
    Nature - v385 - F 6 '97 - p497+ [501+]
    New Sci - v153 - Mr 15 '97 - p44 [251-500]
    Sci - v275 - Ja 24 '97 - p495+ [501+]
    Wil Q - v21 - Win '97 - p103+ [251-500]
Rush, Anne Kent - *The Modern Book of Stretching*
    LJ - v122 - Mr 15 '97 - p67 [51-250]
Rush, Caroline - *Levers (Illus. by Mike Gordon)*
    c Bks Keeps - Jl '96 - p22 [51-250]
    c HB Guide - v8 - Spr '97 - p131 [51-250]
    Pulleys (Illus. by Mike Gordon)
    c HB Guide - v8 - Spr '97 - p131 [51-250]
    c TES - Ja 31 '97 - pR7 [51-250]
    Slopes (Illus. by Mike Gordon)
    c HB Guide - v8 - Spr '97 - p131 [51-250]
    c TES - Ja 31 '97 - pR7 [51-250]
    Wheels and Cogs (Illus. by Mike Gordon)
    c Bks Keeps - Jl '96 - p22 [51-250]
    c HB Guide - v8 - Spr '97 - p131 [51-250]
Rush, John A - *Clinical Anthropology*
    R&R Bk N - v11 - D '96 - p20 [51-250]
Rush, Ken - *What about Emma? (Illus. by Ken Rush)*
    c BL - v93 - S 1 '96 - p144 [51-250]
    c HB Guide - v8 - Spr '97 - p46 [51-250]
    c SLJ - v42 - S '96 - p189 [51-250]
Rushdie, Salman - *Haroun and the Sea of Stories*
    c ChLAQ - v20 - Fall '95 - p100+ [501+]
    y Reason - v28 - D '96 - p39 [51-250]
    The Moor's Last Sigh
    BL - v93 - Ja '97 - p761 [1-50]
    HR - v49 - Sum '96 - p316+ [501+]
    LJ - v122 - Ja '97 - p50 [1-50]
    NYTBR - v101 - D 8 '96 - p11 [51-250]
    NYTBR - v102 - F 2 '97 - p28 [51-250]
    PW - v243 - N 4 '96 - p38 [51-250]
    PW - v243 - N 25 '96 - p70 [1-50]
    Tikkun - v11 - My '96 - p61+ [501+]
    Time - v148 - D 23 '96 - p86 [51-250]
    WLT - v70 - Sum '96 - p694+ [501+]

Rusher, William A - *The Ambiguous Legacy of the Enlightenment*
    Nat R - v48 - Je 3 '96 - p58 [51-250]
Rushford, Patricia H - *Betrayed*
    y VOYA - v19 - D '96 - p274 [51-250]
    The Jack and Jill Syndrome
    LJ - v121 - O 15 '96 - p78+ [51-250]
    Now I Lay Me Down to Sleep
    LJ - v122 - Ap 1 '97 - p80 [51-250]
Rushing, Janice Hocker - *Projecting the Shadow*
    QJS - v83 - F '97 - p110+ [501+]
Rushkoff, Douglas - *Children of Chaos*
    New Sci - v153 - F 22 '97 - p45 [51-250]
    Ecstasy Club
    KR - v65 - Ap 1 '97 - p497+ [251-500]
    PW - v244 - Mr 17 '97 - p75 [251-500]
    Playing the Future
    KR - v64 - My 1 '96 - p674 [251-500]
Rushton, A - *Solid-Liquid Filtration and Separation Technology*
    SciTech - v20 - N '96 - p67 [51-250]
Rushton, Rosie - *How Could You Do This to Me, Mum?*
    y Bks Keeps - Jl '96 - p12 [51-250]
    Poppy
    c JB - v60 - D '96 - p273+ [251-500]
    y Sch Lib - v45 - F '97 - p49 [51-250]
    Speak for Yourself!
    y Bks Keeps - Ja '97 - p27 [51-250]
    y Sch Lib - v45 - F '97 - p52 [51-250]
    You're My Best Friend--I Hate You
    y Bks Keeps - Ja '97 - p27 [51-250]
Rusiecki, Stephen M - *The Key to the Bulge*
    R&R Bk N - v11 - N '96 - p10 [51-250]
Rusinko, Susan - *Joe Orton*
    WLT - v70 - Sum '96 - p699 [251-500]
Rusk, David - *Cities without Suburbs*
    PAR - v57 - Ja '97 - p83+ [501+]
    Cities without Suburbs. 2nd Ed.
    NCR - v85 - Spr '96 - p64 [51-250]
Ruskin, John - *Ruskin's Letters in the Mikimoto Collection: A Facsimile Edition*
    RES - v47 - Ag '96 - p459+ [251-500]
Ruskin, Paul E - *Aging and Posttraumatic Stress Disorder*
    Choice - v34 - O '96 - p363 [51-250]
    Readings - v11 - S '96 - p29+ [51-250]
Russ, Joanna - *To Write like a Woman*
    Ext - v37 - Sum '96 - p189+ [501+]
    NAR - v281 - S '96 - p44+ [501+]
    NWSA Jnl - v8 - Fall '96 - p181+ [501+]
Russell, Adrian - *Information Technology for Parents*
    Sch Lib - v45 - F '97 - p55 [51-250]
    TES - Ja 3 '97 - p47U [251-500]
Russell, Alan - *Multiple Wounds*
    LATBR - O 13 '96 - p8 [51-250]
Russell, Barbara T - *Blue Lightning*
    c BL - v93 - F 15 '97 - p1024 [51-250]
    c CCB-B - v50 - F '97 - p221 [51-250]
    c HB - v73 - My '97 - p328 [251-500]
    c KR - v64 - N 15 '96 - p1674 [51-250]
    c SLJ - v43 - F '97 - p104 [51-250]
    Last Left Standing
    c BL - v93 - N 15 '96 - p589 [51-250]
    c CBRS - v25 - Win '97 - p70 [51-250]
    c Ch BWatch - v7 - Ja '97 - p4 [1-50]
    c Cur R - v36 - N '96 - p13 [51-250]
    c HB - v73 - Ja '97 - p67 [51-250]
    c HB Guide - v8 - Spr '97 - p74 [51-250]
    c KR - v64 - O 1 '96 - p1473 [51-250]
    c PW - v243 - N 11 '96 - p76+ [51-250]
    c SLJ - v42 - O '96 - p126 [51-250]
Russell, Bertrand - *Pacifism and Revolution 1916-18*
    R&R Bk N - v11 - N '96 - p2 [51-250]
    Prophecy and Dissent 1914-16
    R&R Bk N - v11 - N '96 - p2 [51-250]
    What I Believe (Hardiman). Audio Version
    BL - v93 - S 15 '96 - p264 [51-250]
    y Kliatt - v30 - S '96 - p26 [51-250]
Russell, Bruce L - *Jacob's Air*
    Aust Bk R - O '96 - p66 [51-250]
Russell, Carol Ann - *Silver Dollar*
    ABR - v18 - D '96 - p23 [501+]
Russell, Charles - *Trails Plowed Under*
    Roundup M - v4 - D '96 - p28+ [1-50]
Russell, Cheryl - *The Official Guide to Racial and Ethnic Diversity*
    r ACI - v9 - Spr '97 - p37 [501+]
    r ARBA - v28 - '97 - p150 [251-500]
    r Choice - v34 - Ja '97 - p774 [51-250]

Russell, Ching Yeung - *Lichee Tree (Illus. by Christopher Zhong-Yuan Zhang)*
  c BL - v93 - Mr 15 '97 - p1243 [51-250]
  c CCB-B - v50 - Ap '97 - p294+ [51-250]
Russell, Colin Archibald - *The Earth, Humanity, and God*
  Isis - v87 - S '96 - p531+ [501+]
  Edward Frankland: Chemistry, Controversy and Conspiracy in Victorian England
  Choice - v34 - F '97 - p992 [51-250]
  Nature - v383 - O 17 '96 - p591+ [501+]
Russell, Donna Valley - *Allegany and Garrett Counties, Maryland Genealogical Research Guide*
  EGH - v50 - N '96 - p170 [51-250]
Russell, Gillian - *The Theatres of War*
  Albion - v28 - Sum '96 - p319+ [501+]
Russell, Ginny - *Step by Step*
  c Quill & Q - v62 - Jl '96 - p56 [51-250]
Russell, Greg - *John Quincy Adams and the Public Virtues of Diplomacy*
  AHR - v101 - D '96 - p1647+ [501+]
Russell, Ian - *On This Delightful Morn*
  CAY - v16 - Fall '95 - p8 [51-250]
Russell, J P - *After the Quality Audit*
  R&R Bk N - v12 - F '97 - p38 [51-250]
Russell, J S - *Celestial Dogs*
  KR - v65 - Ja 15 '97 - p100 [51-250]
  PW - v244 - Ja 6 '97 - p68 [51-250]
  SF Chr - v18 - O '96 - p78 [51-250]
Russell, James - *Agency: Its Role in Mental Development*
  Choice - v34 - D '96 - p693 [51-250]
Russell, James C - *The Germanization of Early Medieval Christianity*
  CH - v66 - Mr '97 - p90+ [501+]
Russell, Janice - *Goldilocks (Illus. by Janice Russell)*
  c KR - v65 - Ja 1 '97 - p64 [51-250]
  c PW - v243 - D 9 '96 - p67 [51-250]
  c SLJ - v43 - Mr '97 - p180 [51-250]
Russell, Jay - *Burning Bright*
  Books - v11 - Ap '97 - p22 [51-250]
Russell, Jeffrey Burton - *A History of Heaven*
  KR - v65 - F 15 '97 - p285 [251-500]
  LJ - v122 - Ap 1 '97 - p99 [51-250]
  PW - v244 - F 24 '97 - p83 [51-250]
Russell, Jeffrey S - *Constructor Prequalification*
  SciTech - v20 - N '96 - p61 [51-250]
Russell, John, 1919- - *London*
  NYTBR - v102 - Ap 20 '97 - p32 [51-250]
  Obs - D 22 '96 - p18* [501+]
  PW - v243 - N 25 '96 - p70 [1-50]
Russell, John Malcolm - *From Nineveh to New York*
  KR - v65 - Ap 1 '97 - p532+ [251-500]
  PW - v244 - Mr 31 '97 - p54+ [51-250]
Russell, Judith - *The Story of Little Black Sambo*
  c HB Guide - v7 - Fall '96 - p273 [51-250]
Russell, Letty M - *Dictionary of Feminist Theologies*
  r ARBA - v28 - '97 - p536 [51-250]
  r BL - v92 - Ag '96 - p1922 [251-500]
  r Choice - v34 - Mr '97 - p1135 [51-250]
Russell, Mark, 1954- - *Out of Character*
  BL - v93 - D 1 '96 - p639 [51-250]
  PW - v243 - D 2 '96 - p54 [51-250]
Russell, Mary Doria - *The Sparrow*
  Am - v176 - Ja 4 '97 - p19+ [501+]
  BL - v93 - Ja '97 - p761 [1-50]
 y BL - v93 - S 1 '96 - p63 [51-250]
  BL - v93 - O 1 '96 - p304 [501+]
  BWatch - v17 - D '96 - p7 [51-250]
  Comw - v124 - F 28 '97 - p27+ [501+]
  CSM - v88 - N 13 '96 - p15 [251-500]
  Ent W - O 18 '96 - p71 [51-250]
  Ent W - D 27 '96 - p140 [51-250]
  NYTBR - v101 - D 15 '96 - p39 [501+]
  PW - v243 - S 9 '96 - p64 [51-250]
  SFR - v22 - Ja '97 - p48 [51-250]
  The Sparrow (Colacci). Audio Version
 y Kliatt - v31 - My '97 - p44 [51-250]
Russell, Norman L - *Suicide Charlie*
  JTWS - v13 - Spr '96 - p255+ [501+]
Russell, P E, 1913- - *Portugal, Spain, and the African Atlantic 1343-1490*
  HAHR - v77 - My '97 - p300+ [501+]
Russell, Paul - *Freedom and Moral Sentiment*
  CPR - v16 - O '96 - p371+ [501+]
Russell, Peter, 1921- - *The Elegies of Quintilius*
  Obs - Ja 12 '97 - p17* [251-500]
Russell, R B - *Tales from Tartarus*
  Necro - Sum '96 - p26 [251-500]
Russell, Ralph - *Hidden in the Lute*
  WLT - v70 - Sum '96 - p761+ [501+]
Russell, Raymond - *Utopia in Zion*
  AJS - v102 - N '96 - p905+ [501+]

Russell, Robert John - *Chaos and Complexity*
  Rel St - v32 - D '96 - p519+ [501+]
Russell, Sharman - *When the Land Was Young*
  SB - v32 - N '96 - p234 [251-500]
Russell, Sharon A - *Stephen King: A Critical Companion*
  SF Chr - v18 - O '96 - p81 [1-50]
  SFS - v24 - Mr '97 - p176+ [501+]
Russell, Sheila - *Collaborative School Self-Review*
  TES - N 15 '96 - p7* [51-250]
Russell, Steven - *Jewish Identity and Civilizing Processes*
  Choice - v34 - My '97 - p1585 [51-250]
Russian Federation
  JEL - v34 - D '96 - p2061 [51-250]
Russian Women's Shorter Fiction
  Choice - v34 - Ja '97 - p802+ [51-250]
  TLS - Ja 3 '97 - p23 [501+]
Russo, Albert - *Painting the Tower of Babel*
  WLT - v70 - Aut '96 - p965+ [501+]
  Zapinette Video
  WLT - v70 - Aut '96 - p910+ [501+]
Russo, David Anson - *Go for It! (Illus. by David Anson Russo)*
  c HB Guide - v8 - Spr '97 - p143 [51-250]
  c PW - v243 - S 23 '96 - p78 [51-250]
Russo, Elena - *Skeptical Selves*
  Choice - v34 - S '96 - p133+ [51-250]
  MLN - v111 - D '96 - p1041+ [501+]
Russo, Enzo - *Saluti Da Palermo*
  BL - v93 - D 1 '96 - p644 [1-50]
Russo, Marisabina - *Grandpa Abe (Illus. by Marisabina Russo)*
  c HB Guide - v7 - Fall '96 - p273 [51-250]
  Under the Table (Illus. by Marisabina Russo)
  c BL - v93 - Ap 1 '97 - p1339 [51-250]
  c CCB-B - v50 - My '97 - p334 [51-250]
Russo, Richard - *Straight Man*
  PW - v244 - My 12 '97 - p56 [51-250]
Russon, Anne E - *Reaching into Thought*
  Choice - v34 - Mr '97 - p1186 [51-250]
Russon, Jacqueline - *Making Faces*
  c Ch BWatch - v6 - Jl '96 - p1 [1-50]
Rust, Ezra Gardner - *The Music and Dance of the World's Religions*
  r ARBA - v28 - '97 - p495 [51-250]
  r Choice - v34 - Mr '97 - p1143 [501+]
  r R&R Bk N - v11 - D '96 - p55 [51-250]
Rustomji-Kerns, Roshni - *Living in America*
  J Am St - v30 - Ag '96 - p306+ [251-500]
Rutberg, Becky - *Mary Lincoln's Dressmaker*
 y BL - v93 - D 15 '96 - p717 [1-50]
Ruth, David E - *Inventing the Public Enemy*
  R&R Bk N - v11 - D '96 - p45 [51-250]
Rutheiser, Charles - *Imagineering Atlanta*
  BW - v27 - Ja 26 '97 - p11 [501+]
  JEL - v34 - D '96 - p2138 [51-250]
  Lon R Bks - v18 - S 5 '96 - p26+ [501+]
Rutherford, Donald, 1942- - *Leibniz and the Rational Order of Nature*
  CPR - v16 - Ag '96 - p287+ [501+]
  RM - v50 - D '96 - p421+ [501+]
  Routledge Dictionary of Economics
  r JEL - v34 - S '96 - p1404 [51-250]
Rutherford, R B - *The Art of Plato*
  RM - v50 - S '96 - p179+ [501+]
Rutherfurd, Edward - *London*
  BL - v93 - My 15 '97 - p1542 [51-250]
  KR - v65 - My 1 '97 - p678 [51-250]
Ruthner, Clemens - *Unheimliche Wiederkehr*
  MLR - v91 - Jl '96 - p793+ [501+]
Ruthven, Malise - *Freya Stark in Southern Arabia*
  MEJ - v50 - Sum '96 - p454 [51-250]
Rutland, Robert Allen - *A Boyhood in the Dust Bowl 1926-1934*
  WAL - v31 - Sum '96 - p178+ [251-500]
  WHQ - v27 - Win '96 - p548 [1-50]
  The Republicans: From Lincoln to Bush
 y BL - v93 - S 15 '96 - p187 [251-500]
  Bloom Rev - v16 - S '96 - p24 [51-250]
  BWatch - v17 - N '96 - p11+ [51-250]
  Choice - v34 - F '97 - p1038 [51-250]
  HT - v46 - O '96 - p59 [1-50]
  KR - v64 - Ag 15 '96 - p1222 [51-250]
Rutledge, D N - *Signal Treatment and Signal Analysis in NMR*
  SciTech - v21 - Mr '97 - p25 [51-250]
Rutman, Darrett P - *Small Worlds, Large Questions*
  JIH - v27 - Aut '96 - p331+ [51-250]
Rutman, Shereen - *Time to Tell Time*
  c Ch BWatch - v6 - O '96 - p6 [51-250]
Rutter, Michael - *Camping Made Easy*
  LJ - v122 - My 1 '97 - p111 [51-250]

Rutter, Peter - *Understanding and Preventing Sexual Harassment*
  PW - v243 - D 30 '96 - p64 [1-50]
Rutter, Virginia Beane - *Celebrating Girls*
  LJ - v121 - S 15 '96 - p88 [51-250]
  VOYA - v19 - F '97 - p363 [51-250]
Ruttley, Hilary Lewis - *Commercial Law in the Middle East*
  MEJ - v50 - Aut '96 - p629 [51-250]
Ruurs, Margriet - *Emma's Eggs (Illus. by Barbara Spurll)*
  c Quill & Q - v62 - Ag '96 - p42 [251-500]
  A Mountain Alphabet (Illus. by Andrew Kiss)
  c Emerg Lib - v24 - Mr '97 - p27 [1-50]
  c HB Guide - v8 - Spr '97 - p46 [51-250]
  c Quill & Q - v62 - D '96 - p37 [251-500]
  c SLJ - v43 - F '97 - p97+ [51-250]
Ruvalcaba, Carlos - *La Mariposa Bailarina (Illus. by Francisco N Mora)*
  c BL - v93 - My 1 '97 - p1506 [1-50]
Ruz, Mario Humberto - *Un Rostro Encubierto*
  HAHR - v76 - N '96 - p774+ [51-250]
Rwebangira, Magdalena K - *The Legal Status of Women and Poverty in Tanzania*
  WorldV - v13 - Ja '97 - p16 [51-250]
Ryall, Tom - *Alfred Hitchcock and the British Cinema*
  Si & So - v6 - N '96 - p38 [1-50]
Ryals, Clyde De L - *The Life of Robert Browning*
  VS - v39 - Aut '95 - p118+ [501+]
Ryan, Alan - *John Dewey and the High Tide of American Liberalism*
  AHR - v102 - F '97 - p206+ [251-500]
  Am - v174 - My 25 '96 - p29+ [501+]
  CR - v270 - Ja '97 - p51+ [501+]
  HT - v46 - O '96 - p59 [1-50]
  IPQ - v36 - S '96 - p371+ [501+]
  NS - v125 - N 22 '96 - p48 [501+]
  Obs - S 29 '96 - p16* [501+]
  PW - v244 - Ja 27 '97 - p103 [1-50]
  RAH - v25 - Mr '97 - p89+ [501+]
  Soc - v34 - Ja '97 - p90+ [501+]
  TES - O 25 '96 - p8* [501+]
  TLS - N 22 '96 - p3+ [501+]
  Trib Bks - Mr 23 '97 - p6 [1-50]
Ryan, Cheryl - *Sally Arnold*
  c HB Guide - v8 - Spr '97 - p46 [51-250]
Ryan, David - *U.S.-Sandinista Diplomatic Relations*
  R&R Bk N - v11 - N '96 - p18 [51-250]
Ryan, Donna F - *The Holocaust and the Jews of Marseille*
  Choice - v34 - Ap '97 - p1398+ [51-250]
Ryan, Frank - *Virus X*
 y BL - v93 - D 1 '96 - p633 [51-250]
  BW - v27 - Ja 19 '97 - p1+ [501+]
  KR - v64 - N 15 '96 - p1659 [251-500]
  LATBR - F 2 '97 - p4 [251-500]
  LJ - v122 - Ja '97 - p140 [51-250]
  New Sci - v153 - Mr 22 '97 - p46 [251-500]
  NYTBR - v102 - Mr 9 '97 - p22 [501+]
  PW - v243 - D 16 '96 - p50 [51-250]
Ryan, George - *Reclaiming Male Sexuality*
  BL - v93 - F 1 '97 - p917 [51-250]
  PW - v244 - Ja 27 '97 - p100 [51-250]
Ryan, Jake - *Strangers in Paradise*
  Choice - v34 - N '96 - p512 [51-250]
Ryan, Joan - *Little Girls in Pretty Boxes*
 y Emerg Lib - v24 - S '96 - p24 [1-50]
Ryan, John, 1941- - *Michael O'Meara's View from the Funny Farm*
  Aust Bk R - Ag '96 - p67 [1-50]
Ryan, John Augustine - *Economic Justice*
  BL - v93 - O 1 '96 - p308 [1-50]
Ryan, Kay - *Elephant Rocks*
  Ant R - v54 - Fall '96 - p496+ [251-500]
  NY - v72 - D 16 '96 - p108 [51-250]
Ryan, Margaret - *How to Write a Poem*
 y BL - v93 - F 1 '97 - p934+ [51-250]
 y HB Guide - v8 - Spr '97 - p149 [51-250]
 y SLJ - v43 - Ja '97 - p134 [51-250]
  The Littlest Dragon (Illus. by Jamie Smith)
  c Bks Keeps - Jl '96 - p11 [51-250]
  c Magpies - v11 - Jl '96 - p28 [51-250]
Ryan, Martin - *The Last Resort*
  CS - v25 - N '96 - p805+ [501+]
Ryan, Mary - *The Seduction of Mrs. Caine*
  Books - v11 - Ap '97 - p23 [51-250]
  Summer's End
  Books - v10 - Je '96 - p23 [51-250]
Ryan, Mary P - *Civic Wars*
  KR - v65 - Ap 1 '97 - p533 [251-500]

Ryan, Michael - *Secret Life*
  Bks & Cult - v3 - Ja '97 - p20+ [501+]
 y Kliatt - v30 - N '96 - p23 [51-250]
  LATBR - Ag 11 '96 - p11 [51-250]
  Lon R Bks - v18 - Jl 18 '96 - p19+ [501+]
  NYTBR - v101 - S 15 '96 - p44 [51-250]
Ryan, Michael J - *Your Future Career in Education*
 y BL - v93 - My 1 '97 - p1502 [1-50]
Ryan, Michael P - *Magmatic Systems*
  Am Sci - v84 - My '96 - p297+ [501+]
Ryan, Pam Munoz - *The Crayon Counting Book (Illus. by Frank Mazzola Jr.)*
 c CBRS - v25 - O '96 - p17 [51-250]
 c HB Guide - v8 - Spr '97 - p111 [51-250]
 c LATBR - O 27 '96 - p11 [51-250]
 c Learning - v25 - Ja '97 - p57 [1-50]
 The Flag We Love (Illus. by Ralph Masiello)
 c HB Guide - v7 - Fall '96 - p388 [51-250]
 A Pinky Is a Baby Mouse and Other Baby Animal Names (Illus. by Diane DeGroat)
 c KR - v65 - Mr 15 '97 - p468 [51-250]
Ryan, Robert P - *Toxicology Desk Reference. 3rd Ed., Vols. 1-3*
 r Choice - v34 - Ja '97 - p830 [251-500]
Ryan, Selwyn - *Entrepreneurship in the Caribbean*
  JEL - v34 - D '96 - p2092 [51-250]
Ryan, Simon - *The Cartographic Eye*
  Aust Bk R - D '96 - p10+ [501+]
Ryan, Steve - *Mystifying Math Puzzles*
 y Ch BWatch - v7 - F '97 - p8 [1-50]
 y Ch BWatch - v7 - F '97 - p8 [1-50]
Ryan, Steven - *Acute Paediatrics*
  SciTech - v21 - Mr '97 - p64 [51-250]
Ryan, Susan M - *Downloading Democracy*
  J Gov Info - v24 - Ja '97 - p77+ [501+]
Ryan, T Anthony - *Phosgene and Related Carbonyl Halides*
  SciTech - v20 - N '96 - p22 [51-250]
Ryan, Thomas P - *Modern Regression Methods*
  SciTech - v21 - Mr '97 - p15 [51-250]
Rybakov, Anatoli - *Dust and Ashes*
  W&I - v11 - S '96 - p243 [251-500]
  W&I - v11 - S '96 - p253+ [501+]
  WLT - v71 - Win '97 - p180 [501+]
Rybczynski, Witold - *City Life*
  NYTBR - v101 - D 15 '96 - p40 [1-50]
  PW - v243 - S 23 '96 - p73 [1-50]
Ryde, Roo - *Children's Rooms in a Weekend*
  Books - v10 - Je '96 - p24 [51-250]
Ryden, David K - *Representation in Crisis*
  Choice - v34 - D '96 - p691 [51-250]
  R&R Bk N - v11 - N '96 - p48 [51-250]
Ryden, Hope - *ABC of Crawlers and Flyers (Illus. by Hope Ryden)*
 c BL - v93 - S 15 '96 - p244 [51-250]
 c HB Guide - v8 - Spr '97 - p123 [51-250]
 c SLJ - v42 - O '96 - p117 [51-250]
Ryden, Kent C - *Mapping the Invisible Landscape*
  CAY - v16 - Fall '95 - p13 [51-250]
Ryder, Joanne - *Earth Dance (Illus. by Norman Gorbaty)*
 c HB Guide - v7 - Fall '96 - p368+ [51-250]
 c Inst - v106 - Mr '97 - p27 [51-250]
 c LA - v73 - D '96 - p621 [51-250]
 c RT - v50 - My '97 - p684 [51-250]
 Jaguar in the Rain Forest (Illus. by Michael Rothman)
 c HB Guide - v7 - Fall '96 - p273 [51-250]
 c New Ad - v9 - Fall '96 - p327+ [501+]
 c NYTBR - v101 - Ag 25 '96 - p23 [1-50]
 c RT - v50 - Ap '97 - p592+ [51-250]
 Night Gliders (Illus. by Melissa Bay Mathis)
 c HB Guide - v8 - Spr '97 - p46 [51-250]
 Shark in the Sea (Illus. by Michael Rothman)
 c BL - v93 - Mr 1 '97 - p1173 [51-250]
 c CCB-B - v50 - Ap '97 - p295 [51-250]
 Without Words (Illus. by Barbara Sonneborn)
 c RT - v50 - O '96 - p136 [1-50]
Ryder, Nora Leigh - *In the Wild (Illus. by Nora Leigh Ryder)*
 c KR - v65 - F 15 '97 - p305 [51-250]
Ryff, Carol D - *The Parental Experience in Midlife*
  LJ - v122 - Ja '97 - p126+ [51-250]
Rykwert, Joseph - *The Dancing Column*
  Choice - v34 - Ja '97 - p785 [51-250]
  Lon R Bks - v19 - Ap 3 '97 - p13 [501+]
  South CR - v29 - Fall '96 - p272+ [501+]
  TLS - N 8 '96 - p10 [501+]
  VLS - Win '96 - p11 [51-250]

Rylant, Cynthia - *The Bookshop Dog (Illus. by Cynthia Rylant)*
 c BL - v93 - S 1 '96 - p144+ [51-250]
 c HB Guide - v8 - Spr '97 - p46 [51-250]
 c SLJ - v42 - S '96 - p189+ [51-250]
 Dog Heaven (Illus. by Cynthia Rylant)
 c RT - v50 - O '96 - p156 [51-250]
 An Everyday Book (Illus. by Cynthia Rylant)
 c CBRS - v25 - Ap '97 - p100 [51-250]
 c PW - v244 - F 24 '97 - p93 [51-250]
 A Fine White Dust
 y JAAL - v40 - D '96 - p318 [51-250]
 Gooseberry Park (Illus. by Arthur Howard)
 c Emerg Lib - v24 - S '96 - p52 [51-250]
 c RT - v50 - N '96 - p245 [51-250]
 Henry and Mudge and the Happy Cat (Illus. by Sucie Stevenson)
 c SLJ - v43 - Ja '97 - p37 [1-50]
 Henry Y Mudge Con Barro Hasta El Rabo (Illus. by Sucie Stevenson)
 c BL - v93 - My 1 '97 - p1507 [1-50]
 Henry Y Mudge: El Primer Libro De Sus Aventuras (Illus. by Sucie Stevenson)
 c SLJ - v42 - Ag '96 - p179 [51-250]
 Margaret, Frank, and Andy
 c BL - v93 - Ja '97 - p854 [251-500]
 c HB Guide - v8 - Spr '97 - p149 [51-250]
 c SLJ - v42 - N '96 - p118 [51-250]
 Missing May
 c JOYS - v10 - Fall '96 - p46+ [501+]
 y Kliatt - v30 - S '96 - p4 [1-50]
 Missing May (Rogers). Audio Version
 c HB - v72 - S '96 - p566+ [501+]
 Mr. Putter and Tabby Fly the Plane (Illus. by Arthur Howard)
 c BL - v93 - Ap 1 '97 - p1334 [51-250]
 Mr. Putter and Tabby Pick the Pears (Illus. by Arthur Howard)
 c RT - v50 - Mr '97 - p496 [51-250]
 Mr. Putter and Tabby Row the Boat (Illus. by Arthur Howard)
 c BL - v93 - Ap 1 '97 - p1334 [51-250]
 The Old Woman Who Named Things (Illus. by Kathryn Brown)
 c Ch BWatch - v6 - My '96 - p5 [51-250]
 c HB Guide - v7 - Fall '96 - p274 [51-250]
 c RT - v50 - Ap '97 - p590+ [51-250]
 c SLJ - v42 - O '96 - p105 [51-250]
 Poppleton (Illus. by Mark Teague)
 c BL - v93 - F 1 '97 - p950 [51-250]
 c KR - v64 - D 15 '96 - p1804 [51-250]
 c PW - v243 - D 30 '96 - p67 [51-250]
 c SLJ - v43 - Mr '97 - p165 [51-250]
 The Van Gogh Cafe
 c RT - v50 - S '96 - p59 [51-250]
 The Whales (Illus. by Cynthia Rylant)
 c Emerg Lib - v24 - S '96 - p44 [1-50]
 c HB Guide - v7 - Fall '96 - p274 [51-250]
 c Par Ch - v20 - O '96 - p28 [1-50]
 c RT - v50 - Ap '97 - p593 [51-250]
Ryll, Wolfgang - *Litigation and Settlement in a Game with Incomplete Information*
  JEL - v35 - Mr '97 - p198+ [51-250]
Ryokan - *Great Fool*
  Choice - v34 - Ja '97 - p790 [51-250]
  Parabola - v22 - F '97 - p108+ [251-500]
  Tric - v6 - Win '96 - p116 [1-50]
Ryou, Daniel Hojoon - *Zephaniah's Oracles against the Nations*
  Rel St Rev - v23 - Ap '97 - p161+ [51-250]
Ryrie, William - *First World, Third World*
  JEL - v34 - D '96 - p2112 [51-250]
  R&R Bk N - v11 - N '96 - p25 [51-250]
  TLS - S 6 '96 - p27 [501+]
Ryskamp, Charles - *Art in the Frick Collection*
  LATBR - D 8 '96 - p29 [1-50]
  LJ - v122 - Ja '97 - p94 [51-250]
  NYTBR - v102 - Ap 6 '97 - p20 [51-250]
  Obs - D 1 '96 - p17* [51-250]
  WSJ-MW - v78 - D 5 '96 - pA18 [51-250]
Ryskamp, George R - *Finding Your Hispanic Roots*
 r BL - v93 - My 1 '97 - p1528 [51-250]
 A Student's Guide to Mexican American Genealogy
 yr SLJ - v43 - F '97 - p124 [51-250]
Rytcheu, Juri - *Die Suche Nach Der Letzten Zahl*
  WLT - v70 - Sum '96 - p723+ [501+]
Rzhevsky, Nicholas - *An Anthology of Russian Literature from Earliest Writings to Modern Fiction*
  R&R Bk N - v11 - N '96 - p64 [51-250]

S

Saare Gan Eden
   BL - v93 - Mr 1 '97 - p1115 [1-50]
Saari, Donald G - *Hamiltonian Dynamics and Celestial Mechanics*
   SciTech - v20 - D '96 - p19 [51-250]
Saari, Jon - *Ohio Short Fiction*
   Ant R - v55 - Spr '97 - p248 [51-250]
Saari, Peggy - *Prominent Women of the 20th Century. Vols. 1-4*
   cr ARBA - v28 - '97 - p14 [251-500]
Scientists: The Lives and Works of 150 Scientists. Vols. 1-3
   cr BL - v93 - Ap 1 '97 - p1358 [251-500]
Saarinen, Risto - *Weakness of the Will in Medieval Thought*
   Specu - v71 - Jl '96 - p759+ [501+]
Saastamoinen, Kari - *The Morality of the Fallen Man*
   AHR - v101 - O '96 - p1184+ [501+]
Saavedra, Pegerto - *La Vida Cotidiana En La Galicia Del Antiguo Regimen*
   AHR - v101 - D '96 - p1576 [501+]
Saba, Umberto - *Ernesto*
   MLR - v92 - Ap '97 - p486+ [501+]
Sabapathy, T K - *Modernity and Beyond*
   FEER - v159 - D 19 '96 - p52+ [501+]
Sabato, Larry J - *Dirty Little Secrets*
   Choice - v34 - O '96 - p363 [51-250]
   NYRB - v43 - Je 6 '96 - p11+ [501+]
Sabbagh, Suha - *Arab Women*
   MEJ - v50 - Aut '96 - p631+ [51-250]
   Wom R Bks - v14 - D '96 - p24+ [501+]
Sabbeth, Alex - *Rubber-Band Banjos and a Java Jive Bass*
   c BL - v93 - Mr 15 '97 - p1241 [51-250]
Saberhagen, Fred - *Dancing Bears (Ukena). Audio Version*
   BL - v93 - N 1 '96 - p522 [51-250]
A Sharpness on the Neck
   y BL - v93 - S 15 '96 - p226 [51-250]
   PW - v243 - S 16 '96 - p72 [51-250]
Saberi, Ali - *H2 Optimal Control*
   r SciTech - v20 - S '96 - p10 [51-250]
Sabin, Joseph - *Bibliotheca Americana. Vols. 1-29*
   r ASInt - v34 - O '96 - p10 [51-250]
Sabin, Roger - *Adult Comics*
   JC - v46 - Sum '96 - p201+ [501+]
   JPC - v29 - Spr '96 - p251+ [251-500]
Comics, Comix and the Graphic Novel
   BL - v93 - D 15 '96 - p704 [51-250]
   BW - v26 - D 22 '96 - p13 [51-250]
   LJ - v122 - Ap 1 '97 - p90 [51-250]
   Obs - N 24 '96 - p18* [501+]
Sabloff, Jeremy A - *Lowland Maya Civilization in the Eighth Century A.D.*
   HAHR - v77 - F '97 - p99+ [251-500]
Sabuda, Robert - *Arthur and the Sword (Illus. by Robert Sabuda)*
   c RT - v50 - O '96 - p136 [1-50]
The Christmas Alphabet
   c Bks Keeps - N '96 - p20 [51-250]
The Twelve Days of Christmas (Illus. by Robert Sabuda)
   c BL - v93 - Ja '97 - p768 [1-50]
   c BL - v93 - S 1 '96 - p138 [51-250]
   c Bloom Rev - v16 - N '96 - p29+ [51-250]
   c CCB-B - v50 - S '96 - p29+ [51-250]
   c CSM - v88 - N 21 '96 - pB4 [51-250]
   c HB - v72 - N '96 - p730 [51-250]
   c HB Guide - v8 - Spr '97 - p46 [51-250]
   c KR - v64 - S 1 '96 - p1327 [51-250]
   c NY - v72 - N 18 '96 - p101 [1-50]
   c PW - v243 - S 30 '96 - p88 [51-250]
   c SLJ - v42 - O '96 - p41 [51-250]

Sachar, Louis - *Sideways Arithmetic from Wayside School*
   c BL - v93 - Ap 1 '97 - p1342 [1-50]
Wayside School Gets a Little Stranger (Illus. by Joel Schick)
   c RT - v50 - O '96 - p138 [1-50]
Sachedina, Abdulaziz Abbulhussein - *The Just Ruler in Shiite Islam*
   Rel St Rev - v23 - Ja '97 - p3+ [501+]
Sachs, Carolyn E - *Gendered Fields*
   Am Sci - v85 - Ja '97 - p84 [501+]
   Choice - v34 - O '96 - p369 [51-250]
Sachs, Dan - *Emergency Room*
   y BL - v93 - S 15 '96 - p188 [51-250]
   Ent W - O 25 '96 - p108 [51-250]
   LJ - v121 - S 15 '96 - p86 [51-250]
Sachs, David H - *Guide to Kansas Architecture*
   R&R Bk N - v12 - F '97 - p72 [51-250]
Sachs, Joe - *Aristotle's Physics*
   Isis - v87 - D '96 - p716+ [501+]
Sachs, Judith - *Nature's Prozac*
   LJ - v122 - Mr 15 '97 - p81 [51-250]
   PW - v244 - Ja 6 '97 - p70 [51-250]
Sachs, Marilyn - *Another Day*
   c PW - v244 - My 5 '97 - p211 [51-250]
Sachs, Wolfgang - *The Development Dictionary*
   Am Ethnol - v23 - Ag '96 - p641+ [501+]
Sachs, Wulf - *Black Hamlet*
   Bl S - v26 - Fall '96 - p105+ [51-250]
   R&R Bk N - v11 - N '96 - p21 [51-250]
Sachwald, Frederique - *European Integration and Competitiveness*
   Econ J - v107 - Ja '97 - p278 [51-250]
Japanese Firms in Europe
   JEL - v34 - D '96 - p2046+ [51-250]
Sack, James J - *From Jacobite to Conservative*
   AHR - v101 - O '96 - p1205+ [501+]
   CH - v66 - Mr '97 - p142+ [501+]
   JMH - v68 - D '96 - p984+ [501+]
Sack, John - *Company C*
   y Kliatt - v30 - S '96 - p34 [1-50]
Sackett, Mike - *The Bog Spell*
   y Cur R - v36 - F '97 - p12 [51-250]
Sackett, Susan - *The Hollywood Reporter Book of Box Office Hits. Rev. Ed.*
   r ARBA - v28 - '97 - p514+ [51-250]
Sacks, David - *Encyclopedia of the Ancient Greek World*
   r ARBA - v28 - '97 - p205 [51-250]
Sacks, Jonathan - *The Politics of Hope*
   Spec - v278 - Mr 15 '97 - p36 [501+]
Sacks, Margaret - *Beyond Safe Boundaries*
   y SLJ - v43 - Mr '97 - p113 [1-50]
Sacks, Oliver - *An Anthropologist on Mars*
   Lon R Bks - v18 - O 17 '96 - p24+ [501+]
The Island of the Colorblind
   y BL - v93 - D 1 '96 - p618 [51-250]
   BW - v27 - Ja 19 '97 - p1+ [501+]
   Econ - v342 - Mr 15 '97 - p9*+ [501+]
   Ent W - F 14 '97 - p56 [51-250]
   KR - v64 - D 1 '96 - p1724 [251-500]
   LATBR - F 23 '97 - p4 [501+]
   LJ - v122 - Ja '97 - p140 [51-250]
   Mac - v110 - Ap 28 '97 - p62 [251-500]
   NY - v72 - F 10 '97 - p83 [51-250]
   NYRB - v44 - Mr 6 '97 - p15+ [501+]
   NYTBR - v102 - Ja 19 '97 - p7 [501+]
   NYTLa - v146 - Ja 9 '97 - pC18 [501+]
   PW - v243 - N 25 '96 - p63 [251-500]
The Island of the Colorblind (Sacks). Audio Version
   LJ - v122 - F 15 '97 - p176 [51-250]
   PW - v243 - D 2 '96 - p31 [51-250]

The Island of the Colour-Blind
   Lon R Bks - v18 - O 17 '96 - p24+ [501+]
   Nature - v385 - Ja 2 '97 - p34 [501+]
   New Sci - v152 - D 7 '96 - p48 [501+]
   Spec - v277 - N 2 '96 - p53+ [501+]
   TLS - N 29 '96 - p20 [501+]
Sacks, Peter - *Generation X Goes to College*
   Bks & Cult - v2 - S '96 - p38 [251-500]
Sacks, Peter M - *Woody Gwyn*
   A Art - v61 - Mr '97 - p100 [251-500]
Sacks, Terence J - *Careers in Medicine*
   y Kliatt - v31 - Ja '97 - p21+ [51-250]
Sackville-West, Vita - *English Country Houses*
   PW - v244 - Mr 24 '97 - p72 [1-50]
   TLS - D 27 '96 - p32 [251-500]
Sacramento Army Depot Reuse Plan
   J Gov Info - v23 - S '96 - p605+ [51-250]
Sa'dani, Izzat - *Basil Fi Uyun Al-Misriyin*
   MEQ - v3 - S '96 - p81 [251-500]
Sadavoy, Joel - *Comprehensive Review of Geriatric Psychiatry--II*
   SciTech - v20 - S '96 - p32 [51-250]
Sade, Marquis De - *The Crimes of Love*
   TLS - Ag 2 '96 - p3+ [501+]
   TranslRevS - v2 - D '96 - p24 [51-250]
Oeuvres II
   TLS - Ag 2 '96 - p3+ [501+]
La Philosophie Dans Le Boudoir
   SAQ - v95 - Fall '96 - p1009+ [501+]
Sadek, Paul C - *The HPLC Solvent Guide*
   SciTech - v20 - D '96 - p27 [51-250]
Sadgrove, Kit - *The Complete Guide to Business Risk Management*
   R&R Bk N - v12 - F '97 - p38 [51-250]
Sadie, Julie Anne - *The Norton/Grove Dictionary of Women Composers*
   r Notes - v53 - D '96 - p423+ [501+]
Sadie, Stanley - *The New Grove Book of Operas*
   Obs - D 22 '96 - p16* [501+]
Sadler, A E - *The Environment: Opposing Viewpoints*
   y Ch BWatch - v6 - My '96 - p5 [51-250]
Juvenile Crime
   y BL - v93 - F 1 '97 - p934 [51-250]
   y Kliatt - v31 - Mr '97 - p30 [51-250]
Urban Terrorism
   y Ch BWatch - v6 - Jl '96 - p2 [1-50]
   y SLJ - v42 - S '96 - p235+ [51-250]
Sadler, Kim Martin - *Atonement: The Million Man March*
   BW - v26 - N 17 '96 - p12 [51-250]
   BWatch - v17 - D '96 - p5 [51-250]
Sadler, Marilyn - *The Parakeet Girl (Illus. by Roger Bollen)*
   c BL - v93 - My 1 '97 - p1504+ [51-250]
Zenon: Girl of the 21st Century (Illus. by Roger Bollen)
   c Ch BWatch - v6 - N '96 - p7 [1-50]
   c HB Guide - v7 - Fall '96 - p274 [51-250]
Sadlier, Rosemary - *Tubman: Harriet Tubman and the Underground Railroad*
   c Ch Bk News - v20 - Win '97 - p31 [51-250]
   c Quill & Q - v63 - Mr '97 - p80+ [251-500]
Sadoulet, Elisabeth - *Quantitative Development Policy Analysis, with Diskettes*
   Econ J - v107 - Ja '97 - p284 [251-500]
Sadownick, Douglas - *Sex between Men*
   HG&LRev - v3 - Fall '96 - p33+ [501+]
Sadrin, Anny - *Parentage and Inheritance in the Novels of Charles Dickens*
   RES - v47 - N '96 - p614+ [501+]
Sadu, Itah - *Christopher Changes His Name (Illus. by Roy Condy)*
   c Quill & Q - v63 - Ja '97 - p38 [51-250]

Saenz, Benjamin Alire - *Dark and Perfect Angels*
WAL - v31 - Fall '96 - p285 [251-500]
The House of Forgetting
PW - v244 - My 12 '97 - p59+ [51-250]
Saenz Rovner, Eduardo - *Modernizacion Economica vs. Modernizacion Social*
HAHR - v76 - Ag '96 - p590+ [501+]
Safa, Helen I - *The Myth of the Male Breadwinner*
AAPSS-A - v547 - S '96 - p179+ [501+]
HAHR - v77 - F '97 - p169+ [501+]
Safarov, Yu - *The Asymptotic Distribution of Eigenvalues of Partial Differential Operators*
SciTech - v21 - Mr '97 - p16 [51-250]
Safdie, Moshe - *The City after the Automobile*
KR - v65 - Ap 1 '97 - p533+ [251-500]
PW - v244 - Ap 28 '97 - p58 [251-500]
Safer, Morley - *Flashbacks: On Returning to Vietnam*
Parameters - v26 - Win '96 - p148+ [501+]
Safford, Philip L - *Early Childhood Special Education*
AJMR - v101 - N '96 - p330+ [501+]
A History of Childhood and Disability
AJE - v105 - F '97 - p222+ [501+]
Safire, William - *Sleeper Spy*
PW - v244 - Mr 3 '97 - p72 [1-50]
Sagalyn, Raphael - *The Great American Web Book*
r LJ - v121 - O 1 '96 - p70 [51-250]
Sagan, Carl - *Billions and Billions*
KR - v65 - Ap 1 '97 - p534 [251-500]
PW - v244 - My 12 '97 - p69+ [51-250]
Comet. Rev. Ed.
S&T - v93 - F '97 - p58 [51-250]
The Demon-Haunted World
Analog - v116 - D '96 - p145+ [251-500]
Astron - v24 - S '96 - p98 [251-500]
Choice - v34 - S '96 - p150 [51-250]
NYRB - v44 - Ja 9 '97 - p28+ [501+]
NYTBR - v101 - Ap 7 '96 - p10 [501+]
NYTBR - v102 - Ap 13 '97 - p32 [51-250]
Sci - v273 - Jl 26 '96 - p442+ [501+]
Skeptic - v4 - 2 '96 - p108+ [251-500]
The Dragons of Eden
Reason - v28 - D '96 - p39 [251-500]
Pale Blue Dot
JAAR - v64 - Sum '96 - p459+ [501+]
S&T - v92 - S '96 - p54 [51-250]
Sagan, Leonard A - *Electric and Magnetic Fields*
Am Sci - v85 - Mr '97 - p193+ [501+]
Choice - v34 - Ja '97 - p830 [51-250]
Sagan, Miriam - *Malcolm X*
y BL - v93 - F 15 '97 - p1015 [51-250]
y SLJ - v43 - Mr '97 - p208 [51-250]
Sagan, Scott Douglas - *The Spread of Nuclear Weapons*
APSR - v91 - Mr '97 - p243+ [501+]
NWCR - v49 - Aut '96 - p139+ [501+]
Parameters - v26 - Aut '96 - p146+ [501+]
Sagawe, Thorsten - *Das Municipio In Mexiko Zwischen Tradition Und Modernisierung*
HAHR - v76 - N '96 - p800 [251-500]
Sage, Alison - *The Family Who Won a Million and Other Family Stories (Illus. by Tony Ross)*
c JB - v60 - O '96 - p194+ [51-250]
c TES - O 18 '96 - p12* [51-250]
The Hutchinson Treasury of Children's Literature
c Bks Keeps - Ja '97 - p8+ [501+]
Sage, Angie - *Ellie and the Wolves*
c Sch Lib - v44 - N '96 - p152 [51-250]
Ellie's Slugbucket
c Sch Lib - v44 - N '96 - p152 [51-250]
In My Home (Illus. by Angie Sage)
c KR - v64 - D 15 '96 - p1808 [51-250]
c PW - v243 - D 16 '96 - p60+ [51-250]
On the Move
c PW - v243 - D 16 '96 - p60+ [51-250]
Sage, Jacob L - *Practical Neurology of the Elderly*
SciTech - v20 - N '96 - p41 [51-250]
Sage Range Review
p Roundup M - v4 - F '97 - p37 [51-250]
Saggs, H W F - *Babylonians*
AJA - v100 - Jl '96 - p635+ [251-500]
Rel St Rev - v23 - Ap '97 - p164 [51-250]
Sagi, Avi - *Conversion to Judaism and the Meaning of Jewish Identity*
Rel St Rev - v22 - O '96 - p350 [51-250]
Religion and Morality
Rel St - v32 - S '96 - p424+ [501+]
Saha, Debabrata - *Gas Interactions in Nonferrous Metals Processing*
SciTech - v20 - N '96 - p64 [51-250]
Sahagun, Bernardino De - *Psalmodia Christiana*
TranslRevS - v1 - My '95 - p26 [51-250]

Sahgal, Manmohini Zutshi - *An Indian Freedom Fighter Recalls Her Life*
JTWS - v13 - Spr '96 - p267+ [251-500]
Sahlins, Marshall David - *How Natives Think*
Am Ethnol - v24 - F '97 - p261+ [501+]
Cont Pac - v8 - Fall '96 - p460+ [501+]
HAHR - v76 - N '96 - p763+ [251-500]
Pac A - v69 - Sum '96 - p297+ [501+]
W&M Q - v54 - Ja '97 - p253+ [501+]
Sahlins, Peter - *Forest Rites*
JMH - v68 - S '96 - p699+ [501+]
Sahn, David E - *Economic Reform and the Poor in Africa*
Choice - v34 - Mr '97 - p1207 [501+]
Sahnoun, Mohammed - *Somalia: The Missed Opportunities*
JTWS - v13 - Fall '96 - p283+ [501+]
Sahraoui, A E K - *Distributed Computer Control Systems 1995 (DCCS 95)*
SciTech - v20 - N '96 - p69 [51-250]
Sai, Yasutaka - *The Eight Core Values of the Japanese Businessman*
Per Psy - v50 - Spr '97 - p240+ [51-250]
Saich, Tony - *New Perspectives on the Chinese Communist Revolution*
Pac A - v69 - Fall '96 - p405+ [501+]
The Rise to Power of the Chinese Communist Party
Ch Rev Int - v4 - Spr '97 - p229+ [501+]
Said, Edward - *Culture and Imperialism*
QJS - v82 - N '96 - p402+ [501+]
Peace and Its Discontents
TLS - N 29 '96 - p15 [51-250]
Saidel, Rochelle G - *Never Too Late to Remember*
BL - v93 - S 15 '96 - p217 [51-250]
Choice - v34 - F '97 - p1027 [51-250]
LJ - v121 - O 1 '96 - p100 [51-250]
Saigal, Romesh - *Linear Programming*
SIAM Rev - v38 - D '96 - p711+ [501+]
Sainati, Robert A - *CAD of Microstrip Antennas for Wireless Applications*
SciTech - v20 - N '96 - p76 [51-250]
Sainsbury, Diane - *Gender, Equality, and Welfare States*
Choice - v34 - Ap '97 - p1412 [51-250]
Sainsbury, Keith - *Churchill and Roosevelt at War*
AHR - v101 - O '96 - p1213 [501+]
EHR - v111 - N '96 - p1346+ [251-500]
Sainsbury, Marian - *Primary English*
Sch Lib - v44 - Ag '96 - p131 [51-250]
SATs, the Inside Story
LAR - v99 - Mr '97 - p162 [251-500]
St. Bernard Church Records, Alpena, Michigan 1864-1925
r EGH - v50 - N '96 - p172 [51-250]
St. David's University College (Lampeter, Wales). Library - *Catalogue Des Ouvrages Du Fonds Francais 1601-1850, Conserves Dans La Founders' Library, Universite Du Pays De Galles, Lampeter*
r MLR - v92 - Ap '97 - p477+ [51-250]
St. Aubin De Teran, Lisa - *A Valley in Italy*
TES - D 27 '96 - p17 [51-250]
St. Clair, Barry - *Following Jesus*
y VOYA - v19 - F '97 - p320 [51-250]
Giving Away Your Faith
y VOYA - v19 - F '97 - p320 [51-250]
Influencing Your World
y VOYA - v19 - F '97 - p320 [51-250]
Making Jesus Lord
y VOYA - v19 - F '97 - p320 [51-250]
Moving toward Maturity
y VOYA - v19 - F '97 - p320 [51-250]
Spending Time Alone with God
y VOYA - v19 - F '97 - p320 [51-250]
St. Clair, Guy - *Entrepreneurial Librarianship*
LAR - v98 - D '96 - p651 [51-250]
LR - v45 - 8 '96 - p59+ [501+]
St. George, E A W - *Browning and Conversation*
VS - v39 - Aut '95 - p118+ [501+]
St. George, Judith - *To See with the Heart*
c CCB-B - v50 - S '96 - p31+ [51-250]
c HB Guide - v7 - Fall '96 - p374 [51-250]
y VOYA - v19 - D '96 - p290 [51-250]
Saint James, Synthia - *Sunday (Illus. by Synthia Saint James)*
c BL - v93 - N 15 '96 - p596 [51-250]
c CBRS - v25 - Win '97 - p65 [1-50]
c CCB-B - v50 - O '96 - p74 [51-250]
c HB Guide - v8 - Spr '97 - p15 [51-250]
c KR - v64 - Ag 15 '96 - p1242 [51-250]
c Par Ch - v20 - O '96 - p28 [1-50]
c SLJ - v43 - Ja '97 - p90 [51-250]
St. John, Liza - *Abby's Wish (Illus. by Michael Krone)*
c RT - v50 - O '96 - p136 [1-50]

St. John-Brooks, Caroline - *Mapping the Future*
TES - F 14 '97 - p8* [251-500]
St. Keeldare, Carmen - *Pulp Election*
Lon R Bks - v19 - Ja 23 '97 - p26+ [501+]
Saint-Leon, Arthur - *La Vivandiere Pas De Six*
Dance RJ - v28 - Fall '96 - p95+ [501+]
Saint-Pierre, Bernardin De - *Empsael Et Zoraide*
MLR - v91 - O '96 - p992+ [251-500]
St. Pierre, Meg - *My Buddhist Life*
TES - F 14 '97 - p16* [51-250]
St. Pierre, Stephanie - *Farm Day Fun (Illus. by Anne Kennedy)*
c HB Guide - v7 - Fall '96 - p244 [51-250]
To the Rescue! (Illus. by Patrick Merrell)
c HB Guide - v7 - Fall '96 - p244 [51-250]
Saisho, H - *Applications of Synchrotron Radiation to Materials Analysis*
SciTech - v21 - Mr '97 - p28 [51-250]
Sajauskas, Stasys - *Lietuvos Didziosios Kunigaikstystes Monetos*
r Coin W - v37 - O 7 '96 - p71 [1-50]
Lietvos Didziosios Kunigaikstystes Numizmatika
r Coin W - v37 - O 7 '96 - p71 [1-50]
Sak, Guven - *Public Policies Towards Financial Liberalization*
JEL - v34 - D '96 - p2053 [51-250]
Sakaiya, Taichi - *What Is Japan?*
TranslRevS - v1 - My '95 - p9 [51-250]
Sakashita, Noboru - *Optimum and Equilibrium for Regional Economies*
JEL - v34 - D '96 - p2136+ [51-250]
Sakenfeld, Katharine Doob - *Journeying with God*
Rel St Rev - v23 - Ap '97 - p165 [51-250]
Sakhnovich, Lev A - *Integral Equations with Difference Kernels on Finite Intervals*
SciTech - v20 - S '96 - p11 [51-250]
Sakkas, Dimitrios A - *The European Observatory for Small and Medium-Sized Enterprises*
JEL - v34 - S '96 - p1485 [51-250]
Saks, Claude M - *Strong Brew*
BL - v93 - Ja '97 - p794+ [51-250]
BWatch - v18 - F '97 - p1 [51-250]
Sakurai, Gail - *The Liberty Bell*
c HB Guide - v7 - Fall '96 - p384 [51-250]
c SLJ - v42 - Ag '96 - p150 [51-250]
Stephen Hawking: Understanding the Universe
c BL - v92 - Ag '96 - p1897 [51-250]
c HB Guide - v7 - Fall '96 - p371 [51-250]
c SB - v33 - My '97 - p115 [51-250]
c SLJ - v42 - S '96 - p220 [51-250]
Salabert, Juana - *Arde Lo Que Sera*
WLT - v71 - Win '97 - p120 [501+]
Sala Catala, Jose - *Ciencia Y Tecnica En La Metropolizacion De America*
HAHR - v77 - My '97 - p306+ [501+]
T&C - v38 - Ja '97 - p244+ [501+]
Salach, Cin - *Looking for a Soft Place to Land*
Trib Bks - Ap 20 '97 - p1+ [501+]
Salamon, Julie - *The Christmas Tree*
y BL - v93 - S 1 '96 - p30 [51-250]
CSM - v89 - D 19 '96 - p14 [51-250]
KR - v64 - S 1 '96 - p1270 [51-250]
LJ - v121 - S 15 '96 - p97+ [51-250]
NYTBR - v101 - D 8 '96 - p102 [51-250]
Time - v148 - N 18 '96 - p114 [1-50]
The Net of Dreams
BW - v26 - Jl 7 '96 - p9 [501+]
NYTBR - v101 - D 8 '96 - p89 [1-50]
Salamon, Lester M - *The Emerging Nonprofit Sector*
JEL - v35 - Mr '97 - p246+ [51-250]
Salamun, Tomaz - *The Four Questions of Melancholy*
PW - v244 - Ap 28 '97 - p70 [251-500]
Salas, Floyd - *Color of My Living Heart*
PW - v243 - S 30 '96 - p84 [1-50]
Salazar, Carles - *A Sentimental Economy*
Choice - v34 - F '97 - p1006+ [51-250]
Salazar, Philippe-Joseph - *Le Culte De La Voix Au XVIIe Siecle*
TLS - Ja 10 '97 - p23 [501+]
Salazar, Ruben - *Border Correspondent*
PHR - v66 - F '97 - p133+ [251-500]
Salby, Murry L - *Fundamentals of Atmospheric Physics*
Am Sci - v85 - Mr '97 - p185+ [501+]
SciTech - v20 - N '96 - p65 [51-250]
Saldanha, Ana - *Tres Semanas Com A Avo (Illus. by Cristina Malaquias)*
c Bkbird - v34 - Spr '96 - p53 [1-50]
Saldarini, Anthony J - *Matthew's Christian-Jewish Community*
JAAR - v64 - Sum '96 - p441+ [501+]

Pharisees, Scribes and Sadducees
  Rel Ed - v91 - Fall '96 - p605 [1-50]
Sale, June Solnit - *The Working Parents Handbook*
  Readings - v11 - D '96 - p23+ [51-250]
Sale, Kirkpatrick - *Rebels against the Future*
  New R - v214 - Je 10 '96 - p30+ [501+]
  YR - v84 - O '96 - p137+ [501+]
Saleh, Nabil - *The Qadi and the Fortune Teller*
  TLS - N 1 '96 - p25 [501+]
Salem, Jean - *Democrite: Grains De Poussiere Dans Un Rayon De Soleil*
  Isis - v87 - D '96 - p714+ [251-500]
Salem Press - *Psychology: An Introductory Bibliography*
  r ARBA - v28 - '97 - p283 [51-250]
  r Choice - v34 - F '97 - p948 [51-250]
  r R&R Bk N - v12 - F '97 - p5 [51-250]
  Recommended Reading
  r ARBA - v28 - '97 - p407 [251-500]
Sales, Roger - *Jane Austen and Representations of Regency England*
  RES - v47 - N '96 - p604+ [501+]
Sales, William W, Jr. - *From Civil Rights to Black Liberation*
  Bl S - v26 - Fall '96 - p83+ [501+]
Salessi, Jorge - *Medicos, Maleantes, Y Maricas*
  HAHR - v76 - N '96 - p813+ [501+]
Salies, G Hellenkemper - *Das Wrack: Die Antike Schiffsfund Von Mahdia. Vols. 1-2*
  AJA - v101 - Ja '97 - p182+ [501+]
Salifou, Andre - *Tels Peres, Tels Fils*
  BL - v93 - F 1 '97 - p930 [1-50]
Salih, Tayeb - *Bandarshah*
  TLS - N 1 '96 - p24 [501+]
Saline, Carol - *Mothers and Daughters*
  y BL - v93 - Mr 15 '97 - p1203 [51-250]
  KR - v65 - Ap 1 '97 - p544 [51-250]
  PW - v244 - Ap 28 '97 - p66+ [51-250]
Salinger, Adrienne - *In My Room*
  y Emerg Lib - v24 - S '96 - p26 [1-50]
Salinger, J D - *Hapworth 16, 1924*
  NYTLa - v146 - F 20 '97 - pC15+ [501+]
Salinger, Pierre - *P.S.: A Memoir*
  Trib Bks - Mr 16 '97 - p8 [1-50]
Salins, Peter D - *Assimilation, American Style*
  BW - v26 - D 15 '96 - p5 [501+]
  BWatch - v18 - Mr '97 - p1 [1-50]
  KR - v64 - N 1 '96 - p1591 [251-500]
  Pub Int - Spr '97 - p124+ [501+]
  Wil Q - v21 - Win '97 - p96 [251-500]
  WSJ-Cent - v99 - Ja 14 '97 - pA16 [501+]
Salisbury, David F - *Five Technologies for Educational Change*
  R&R Bk N - v11 - N '96 - p54 [1-50]
Salisbury, Graham - *Under the Blood-Red Sun (Woodman). Audio Version*
  c BL - v93 - Ap 1 '97 - p1314 [51-250]
  c HB - v72 - S '96 - p566+ [501+]
Salisbury, Jane - *Qualitative Studies in Education*
  R&R Bk N - v11 - N '96 - p54 [51-250]
Salitan, Lucille - *Virtuous Lives*
  Signs - v22 - Win '97 - p479+ [501+]
Salkeld, Audrey - *A Portrait of Leni Riefenstahl*
  CR - v270 - F '97 - p112 [51-250]
  TLS - S 13 '96 - p31 [501+]
Salkovskis, Paul M - *Frontiers of Cognitive Therapy*
  SB - v33 - Ja '97 - p9 [51-250]
  SciTech - v20 - D '96 - p45 [51-250]
Sallah, Tijan M - *New Poets of West Africa*
  WLT - v70 - Sum '96 - p746 [501+]
Sallee, Hyunjae Yee - *The Snowy Road and Other Stories*
  TranslRevS - v1 - My '95 - p4 [51-250]
Sallee, Wayne Allen - *With Wounds Still Wet*
  Sm Pr R - v29 - F '97 - p8 [51-250]
Salleh, Sirajuddin H - *Globalisation and the Asean Public Sector*
  Pac A - v69 - Fall '96 - p445+ [501+]
Sallenave, Daniele - *Les Trois Minutes Du Diable*
  FR - v70 - F '97 - p501+ [251-500]
Sallis, James - *Ash of Stars*
  Choice - v34 - D '96 - p610+ [51-250]
  SFS - v24 - Mr '97 - p154+ [501+]
  The Guitar in Jazz
  AB - v98 - D 9 '96 - p1996 [51-250]
  Bl S - v26 - Fall '96 - p106 [1-50]
  TLS - My 24 '96 - p36 [51-250]
  VQR - v72 - Aut '96 - p138* [51-250]
Sallis, John - *Stone*
  Ren Q - v50 - Spr '97 - p285+ [501+]
Sallis, Susan - *Water Under the Bridge*
  Books - v9 - S '95 - p24 [1-50]

Sallust - *The Histories (McGushin). Vol. 2*
  CW - v89 - Jl '96 - p519+ [51-250]
Salmansohn, Karen - *How to Succeed in Business Without a Penis*
  BL - v93 - O 1 '96 - p312 [51-250]
  Ent W - Ap 18 '97 - p61 [51-250]
  LJ - v121 - O 1 '96 - p95 [51-250]
  PW - v243 - S 2 '96 - p103+ [51-250]
  Wom R Bks - v14 - Ja '97 - p11+ [501+]
Salmi, Vexi - *Rantaravintola*
  WLT - v70 - Aut '96 - p995 [501+]
Salmon, Elon - *Titus*
  TLS - S 13 '96 - p25 [251-500]
Salmon, Keith G - *The Modern Spanish Economy*
  R&R Bk N - v11 - D '96 - p25 [51-250]
Salmon, Nicholas - *The William Morris Chronology*
  r TLS - N 1 '96 - p31 [51-250]
Salmon, Patrick - *Britain and Norway in the Second World War*
  JPR - v33 - Ag '96 - p383 [251-500]
Salmon, Sheila - *Power Up Your Library*
  BL - v93 - S 15 '96 - p254 [51-250]
  SLJ - v43 - F '97 - p43 [51-250]
Salmond, John A - *Gastonia 1929*
  CS - v26 - Ja '97 - p24+ [501+]
  Historian - v59 - Win '97 - p443+ [251-500]
  JSH - v63 - F '97 - p196+ [501+]
  My Mind Set on Freedom
  PW - v244 - Mr 31 '97 - p51 [51-250]
Salmond, Rachel - *Government Printing in New Zealand 1840 to 1843*
  BC - v44 - Win '95 - p488+ [51-250]
  Lib - v19 - Mr '97 - p88+ [501+]
Salokar, Rebecca Mae - *Women in Law*
  r ARBA - v28 - '97 - p219 [51-250]
  c BL - v93 - N 1 '96 - p542 [51-250]
  r Choice - v34 - Ap '97 - p1318 [51-250]
  r R&R Bk N - v12 - F '97 - p62 [51-250]
Salt Hill Journal
  p Sm Pr R - v28 - D '96 - p18 [51-250]
Salter, Anna - *Shiny Water*
  LJ - v122 - Ap 1 '97 - p131 [51-250]
Salter, David F - *Crashing the Old Boys' Network*
  Choice - v34 - Mr '97 - p1199 [51-250]
  PW - v243 - S 30 '96 - p71 [51-250]
Salter, Frank Kemp - *Emotions in Command*
  Skeptic - v4 - 2 '96 - p107+ [51-250]
Saltzberg, Barney - *Backyard Cowboy*
  c HB Guide - v7 - Fall '96 - p274 [1-50]
Saltzman, David - *The Jester Has Lost His Jingles (Illus. by David Saltzman)*
  c NYTBR - v101 - Ap 7 '96 - p21 [1-50]
Salutin, Rick - *The Age of Improv*
  Can Lit - Spr '97 - p242+ [501+]
Salvalaggio, Nantas - *Passione Dlinverno*
  BL - v93 - D 1 '96 - p644 [1-50]
Salvatore, Nick - *We All Got History*
  RAH - v25 - Mr '97 - p63+ [501+]
Salvatore, R A - *The Demon Awakens*
  y BL - v93 - My 1 '97 - p1483 [51-250]
  KR - v65 - Mr 15 '97 - p423 [51-250]
  LJ - v122 - Ap 15 '97 - p124 [51-250]
  PW - v244 - Ap 28 '97 - p55 [51-250]
  The Dragon King
  y BL - v93 - O 1 '96 - p326 [51-250]
  KR - v64 - S 1 '96 - p1282 [51-250]
  LJ - v121 - O 15 '96 - p93 [1-50]
  PW - v243 - O 21 '96 - p74+ [51-250]
  Luthien's Gamble
  y Kliatt - v31 - Mr '97 - p21 [51-250]
  y VOYA - v19 - O '96 - p220 [51-250]
Salvo Y Vela, Juan - *El Magico De Salermo Pedro De Vayalarde: Primera Y Segunda Partes*
  Hisp - v79 - D '96 - p793+ [501+]
Salwak, Dale - *Anne Tyler as Novelist*
  J Am St - v30 - Ag '96 - p323 [251-500]
Salway, Kate - *Collectors' Items*
  New Sci - v152 - D 14 '96 - p45 [51-250]
Salway, Peter - *The Oxford Illustrated History of Roman Britain*
  GJ - v162 - Jl '96 - p241 [51-250]
Salyer, Lucy E - *Laws Harsh as Tigers*
  PHR - v66 - F '97 - p111+ [501+]
  PSQ - v111 - Win '96 - p734+ [501+]
Salzman, Bernard - *The Handbook of Psychiatric Drugs. 2nd Ed.*
  r BL - v93 - F 1 '97 - p959 [1-50]
Salzman, Jack - *American Studies: An Annotated Bibliography. Vols. 1-3*
  r ASInt - v34 - O '96 - p6+ [251-500]

American Studies: An Annotated Bibliography 1984-1988
  r ASInt - v34 - O '96 - p6+ [51-250]
Encyclopedia of African-American Culture and History. Vols. 1-5
  r ARBA - v28 - '97 - p153+ [251-500]
  r BL - v93 - Ja '97 - p769 [1-50]
  r Bl S - v26 - Sum '96 - p67 [51-250]
  r Choice - v34 - S '96 - p95 [501+]
  r LJ - v122 - Ap 15 '97 - p37 [51-250]
  yr SLJ - v42 - Ag '96 - p183 [51-250]
Struggles in the Promised Land
  BL - v93 - F 15 '97 - p982 [51-250]
  KR - v65 - Ja 15 '97 - p129 [251-500]
  PW - v244 - F 24 '97 - p80 [1-50]
Salzman, Marian - *Going to the Net*
  c PW - v243 - N 25 '96 - p78 [51-250]
  Kids On-Line
  Adoles - v31 - Win '96 - p995 [51-250]
  The Ultimate On-Line Homework Helper
  c CSM - v88 - S 26 '96 - pB4 [51-250]
  y Kliatt - v31 - Ja '97 - p20+ [51-250]
Salzman, Mark - *Lost in Place*
  y BL - v93 - Ap 1 '97 - p1288 [1-50]
  y Kliatt - v30 - S '96 - p27 [51-250]
  NYTBR - v101 - S 15 '96 - p44 [51-250]
Salzman, Todd A - *Deontology and Teleology*
  Theol St - v57 - D '96 - p783+ [251-500]
Salzmann, Helmut - *Compact Projective Planes*
  Choice - v34 - Ap '97 - p1375 [51-250]
Samad, Syed Abdus - *People's Initiatives for Sustainable Development*
  WorldV - v12 - O '96 - p7+ [51-250]
Samalin, Samuel - *Secure UNIX*
  SB - v33 - Mr '97 - p36 [51-250]
  SciTech - v21 - Mr '97 - p9 [51-250]
Samara, Adel - *Women vs. Capital*
  WorldV - v13 - Ja '97 - p17 [251-500]
Samaranayake, Lakshman P - *Essential Microbiology for Dentistry*
  SciTech - v21 - Mr '97 - p43 [1-50]
Samaras, Zoe - *Montaigne: Espace, Voyage, Ecriture*
  Ren Q - v50 - Spr '97 - p252+ [501+]
Samarskii, A A - *Blow-Up in Quasilinear Parabolic Equations*
  SIAM Rev - v38 - D '96 - p692+ [501+]
Samartha, Stanley J - *Between Two Cultures*
  Rel St Rev - v23 - Ap '97 - p155 [51-250]
Samary, Catherine - *Yugoslavia Dismembered*
  CS - v25 - N '96 - p738+ [501+]
Samek, Stefanie - *A Cat's Christmas*
  NYTBR - v101 - D 8 '96 - p102 [1-50]
Sameroff, Arnold J - *The Five to Seven Year Shift*
  Choice - v34 - Ap '97 - p1419 [51-250]
  R&R Bk N - v12 - F '97 - p7 [51-250]
Samizdat
  p Dis - v44 - Spr '97 - p103+ [501+]
Sammataro, Robert F - *Development, Validation, and Application of Inelastic Methods for Structural Analysis and Design*
  SciTech - v21 - Mr '97 - p79 [51-250]
Sammon, Rick - *Creepy Crawlies in 3-D! (Illus. by David G Burder)*
  c HB Guide - v7 - Fall '96 - p342 [1-50]
  Under the Sea in 3-D!
  c HB Guide - v7 - Fall '96 - p338 [1-50]
Samona, Carmelo - *Brothers*
  TranslRevS - v1 - My '95 - p25 [51-250]
Sampiero, Dominique - *La Claire Audience*
  FR - v70 - Mr '97 - p621+ [251-500]
Sample, Tex - *White Soul*
  CC - v114 - Mr 19 '97 - p316+ [251-500]
Sampson, Anthony - *Company Man*
  New Sci - v151 - S 14 '96 - p44 [51-250]
Sampson, Geoffrey - *Evolutionary Language Understanding*
  Choice - v34 - Ja '97 - p788 [51-250]
Sampson, John - *Little Miss Magi*
  PW - v244 - Ap 14 '97 - p60 [51-250]
Sampson, Lisa - *Conquered Heart*
  BL - v93 - O 1 '96 - p304 [501+]
Sampson, Michael - *The Football That Won-- (Illus. by Ted Rand)*
  c CBRS - v24 - Ag '96 - p162 [51-250]
  c HB Guide - v8 - Spr '97 - p146 [51-250]
  c SLJ - v42 - O '96 - p105 [51-250]
  Star of the Circus (Illus. by Jose Aruego)
  c BL - v93 - Ap 1 '97 - p1339 [51-250]
  c CBRS - v25 - Ap '97 - p100+ [51-250]
  c SLJ - v43 - Mr '97 - p165+ [51-250]

Sampson, Richard - *Escape in America*
  W&M Q - v53 - Jl '96 - p668+ [501+]
Sams, Eric - *Shakespeare's Edward III*
  BL - v93 - S 15 '96 - p205 [51-250]
  Choice - v34 - F '97 - p968 [51-250]
  CR - v270 - F '97 - p108+ [251-500]
  NL - v79 - D 16 '96 - p32+ [501+]
  TLS - Ja 17 '97 - p3+ [501+]
Sams, Ferrol - *The Widow's Mite and Other Stories
(Guyer). Audio Version*
  y Kliatt - v30 - S '96 - p54 [51-250]
Sams, W Mitchell - *Principles and Practice of
Dermatology. 2nd Ed.*
  SciTech - v20 - N '96 - p54 [51-250]
Samsel, Jon - *The Multimedia Directory. 4th Ed.*
  r ARBA - v28 - '97 - p619 [51-250]
Samson, Fred B - *Prairie Conservation*
  Choice - v34 - F '97 - p988 [51-250]
Samson, Gloria Garrett - *The American Fund for Public
Service*
  Choice - v34 - S '96 - p198 [51-250]
Samson, Suzanne Marie - *Tumblebugs and Hairy Bears
(Illus. by Preston Neel)*
  c SB - v33 - Ja '97 - p20+ [251-500]
  c SLJ - v43 - Ja '97 - p108 [51-250]
Samuel, Ha-Nagid - *Selected Poems of Shmuel HaNagid*
  TranslRevS - v2 - D '96 - p27 [51-250]
Samuel, Claude - *Olivier Messiaen Music and Color*
  TranslRevS - v1 - My '95 - p12 [51-250]
Samuel, Lawrence R - *Pledging Allegiance*
  PW - v244 - My 12 '97 - p68 [251-500]
Samuel, Raphael - *Theatres of Memory. Vol. 1*
  BW - v26 - D 8 '96 - p6 [51-250]
  JMH - v68 - D '96 - p968+ [501+]
**Samuel Johnson: A Dictionary of the English Language.
Electronic Media Version**
  r LJ - v122 - My 1 '97 - p148 [51-250]
Samuels, Barbara G - *Your Reading. 1995-96 Ed.*
  r ARBA - v28 - '97 - p424 [251-500]
  r Emerg Lib - v23 - My '96 - p42 [1-50]
  yr JAAL - v40 - N '96 - p238 [51-250]
Samuels, Martin - *Command or Control?*
  Choice - v34 - S '96 - p188+ [51-250]
  J Mil H - v60 - O '96 - p778+ [251-500]
Samuels, Peggy - *Remembering the Maine*
  Historian - v59 - Fall '96 - p157 [251-500]
Samuels, Robert - *Mahler's Sixth Symphony*
  Notes - v53 - Mr '97 - p804+ [501+]
Samuels, Shirley - *Romances of the Republic*
  Choice - v34 - Ap '97 - p1339+ [51-250]
Samuels, Suzanne Uttaro - *Fetal Rights Women's Rights*
  J Pol - v59 - F '97 - p270+ [501+]
Samuels, Warren J - *American Economists of the Late
Twentieth Century*
  Choice - v34 - Ja '97 - p843 [51-250]
  JEL - v35 - Mr '97 - p189+ [51-250]
Samuelson, David W - *Panaflex User's Manual. 2nd Ed.*
  SciTech - v21 - Mr '97 - p98 [51-250]
Samuelson, Norbert Max - *Judaism and the Doctrine of
Creation*
  Cres - v60 - Christmas '96 - p32+ [501+]
  Rel St Rev - v23 - Ap '97 - p193 [51-250]
  Zygon - v32 - Mr '97 - p115+ [501+]
Samuelson, Robert J - *The Good Life and Its Discontents*
  Bks & Cult - v2 - N '96 - p38 [51-250]
  Bus W - v26 - D 16 '96 - p19 [51-250]
  BW - v26 - D 8 '96 - p8 [1-50]
  TLS - Ag 30 '96 - p10+ [501+]
Samway, Patrick H - *Walker Percy: A Life*
  BL - v93 - Mr 15 '97 - p1221 [51-250]
  KR - v65 - Mr 1 '97 - p365 [51-250]
  PW - v244 - Mr 24 '97 - p64+ [51-250]
  Trib Bks - My 25 '97 - p5 [501+]
San Antonio Museum of Art - *Greek Vases in the San
Antonio Museum of Art*
  Choice - v34 - My '97 - p1488 [51-250]
Sanborn, Robert - *How to Get a Job in New York City
and the Metropolitan Area*
  J Car P&E - v57 - Win '97 - p22 [51-250]
Sanborne, Mark - *Romania*
  y HB Guide - v7 - Fall '96 - p381 [51-250]
  y VOYA - v19 - O '96 - p238 [51-250]
Sancaktar, Erol - *Reliability, Stress Analysis, and Failure
Prevention Issues in Fastening and Joining, Composite
and Smart Structures, Numerical and SEA Methods*
  SciTech - v21 - Mr '97 - p76 [51-250]
Sanchez, George J - *Becoming Mexican American*
  Bks & Cult - v3 - Mr '97 - p39 [251-500]
  HAHR - v77 - F '97 - p92+ [501+]

Sanchez, Isidro - *Las Grandes Llanuras (Illus. by Luis
Rizo)*
  c SLJ - v42 - Ag '96 - p179 [51-250]
El Gusto (Illus. by Francisco Arredondo)
  c SLJ - v42 - Ag '96 - p179 [51-250]
El Oido (Illus. by Francisco Arredondo)
  c SLJ - v42 - Ag '96 - p179 [51-250]
El Olfato (Illus. by Francisco Arredondo)
  c SLJ - v42 - Ag '96 - p179 [51-250]
Plantas Del Mar (Illus. by Luis Rizo)
  c SLJ - v42 - Ag '96 - p179 [51-250]
Los Rios Y Los Lagos (Illus. by Luis Rizo)
  c SLJ - v42 - Ag '96 - p179 [51-250]
Las Selvas Misteriosas (Illus. by Luis Rizo)
  c SLJ - v42 - Ag '96 - p179 [51-250]
El Tacto (Illus. by Francisco Arredondo)
  c SLJ - v42 - Ag '96 - p179 [51-250]
La Vista (Illus. by Francisco Arredondo)
  c SLJ - v42 - Ag '96 - p179 [51-250]
Sanchez, Julio - *Solutions Handbook for PC
Programmers. 2nd Ed.*
  SciTech - v20 - S '96 - p7 [51-250]
Sanchez, Magdalena S - *Spanish Women in the Golden
Age*
  Choice - v34 - S '96 - p189 [51-250]
Sanchez, Sonia - *Does Your House Have Lions?*
  y BL - v93 - F 15 '97 - p996 [51-250]
  LJ - v122 - Ap 15 '97 - p85 [51-250]
  PW - v244 - F 24 '97 - p84+ [51-250]
Sanchez-Albornoz, Nicolas - *La Poblacion De America
Latina*
  HAHR - v76 - Ag '96 - p606+ [501+]
Sanchez Alonso, Blanca - *Las Causas De La Emigracion
Espanola 1880-1930*
  Choice - v34 - D '96 - p569 [1-50]
  Choice - v34 - D '96 - p569 [1-50]
Sanchez De Vercial, Clemente - *The Book of Tales by
A.B.C.*
  TranslRevS - v1 - My '95 - p32 [51-250]
Sanchez-Eppler, Karen - *Touching Liberty*
  Legacy - v13 - 2 '96 - p158+ [501+]
Sanchez Mariana, Manuel - *Bibliofilos Espanoles Desde
Sus Origenes Hasta Los Albores Del Siglo XX*
  Lib - v18 - S '96 - p273 [1-50]
Sanchez Vicario, Arantxa - *The Young Tennis Player*
  c HB Guide - v7 - Fall '96 - p362 [1-50]
  c Sch Lib - v44 - Ag '96 - p114 [51-250]
  y VOYA - v19 - O '96 - p238 [51-250]
Sancho, Ignatius - *The Letters of Ignatius Sancho*
  RES - v47 - N '96 - p595 [501+]
Sand, Faith Annette - *Prayers of Faith*
  Bloom Rev - v16 - N '96 - p14 [51-250]
Sand, Michael - *The Human Condition*
  Pet PM - v25 - Ap '97 - p8+ [51-250]
Sandage, Allan - *The Carnegie Atlas of Galaxies*
  r S&T - v92 - S '96 - p54 [51-250]
Sandak, Cass R - *The National Debt*
  c Ch BWatch - v6 - My '96 - p5 [1-50]
  c SLJ - v42 - Ag '96 - p153+ [51-250]
The United States
  c HB Guide - v8 - Spr '97 - p175 [51-250]
Sanday, Peggy Reeves - *A Woman Scorned*
  Wom R Bks - v14 - Mr '97 - p23+ [501+]
Sandberg, Ake - *Enriching Production*
  ILRR - v50 - Ja '97 - p359+ [501+]
Sandberg, Eve - *The Changing Politics of Non-
Government Organizations and African States*
  JTWS - v13 - Fall '96 - p261+ [501+]
Sandbrook, Richard - *The Politics of Africa's Economic
Recovery*
  WP - v49 - O '96 - p92+ [501+]
Sandeen, Eric J - *Picturing an Exhibition*
  AHR - v102 - F '97 - p218 [251-500]
  J Am St - v30 - S '96 - p465+ [501+]
Sandefur, Gary D - *Changing Numbers, Changing Needs*
  R&R Bk N - v12 - F '97 - p22 [51-250]
Sandel, Michael J - *Democracy's Discontent*
  AS - v65 - Aut '96 - p614+ [501+]
  BIC - v26 - Mr '97 - p27+ [501+]
  Bks & Cult - v3 - Ja '97 - p28+ [501+]
  CC - v113 - N 20 '96 - p1134+ [501+]
  CC - v113 - D 4 '96 - p1206+ [501+]
  Comw - v123 - N 22 '96 - p26+ [501+]
  Dis - v44 - Win '97 - p119+ [501+]
  Reason - v28 - F '97 - p59+ [501+]
  TLS - O 18 '96 - p14 [501+]
  W&I - v11 - Ag '96 - p254+ [501+]
Sandelin, Peter - *Vedhuggaren I Natten*
  WLT - v70 - Sum '96 - p719 [501+]
Sandeman, Anna - *Babies (Illus. by Ian Thompson)*
  c HB Guide - v7 - Fall '96 - p349 [51-250]

Blood (Illus. by Ian Thompson)
  c HB Guide - v7 - Fall '96 - p349 [51-250]
Brain (Illus. by Ian Thompson)
  c HB Guide - v8 - Spr '97 - p130 [1-50]
  c Sch Lib - v44 - N '96 - p165 [51-250]
  c SLJ - v43 - Ja '97 - p108 [51-250]
Skin, Teeth and Hair (Illus. by Ian Thompson)
  c HB Guide - v8 - Spr '97 - p130 [1-50]
  c Sch Lib - v44 - N '96 - p165 [51-250]
  c SLJ - v43 - Ja '97 - p108 [51-250]
Sander, Harald - *World Trade after the Uruguay Round*
  JEL - v34 - D '96 - p2044 [51-250]
Sander, Jochen - *Niederlandische Gemalde Im Stadel
1400-1550*
  Ren Q - v49 - Aut '96 - p682+ [501+]
Sander, William - *The Catholic Family*
  AAPSS-A - v546 - Jl '96 - p175+ [501+]
Sanders, Alan J K - *Historical Dictionary of Mongolia*
  r ARBA - v28 - '97 - p59 [51-250]
Sanders, Andrew - *The Short Oxford History of English
Literature. Rev. Ed.*
  yr Kliatt - v31 - Mr '97 - p22 [51-250]
Sanders, Barry, 1938- - *A Complex Fate*
  Choice - v34 - O '96 - p269 [51-250]
Sudden Glory
  Bks & Cult - v2 - Ja '96 - p4 [251-500]
Sanders, Cheryl J - *Saints in Exile*
  Bl S - v26 - Sum '96 - p67 [1-50]
  CC - v113 - N 13 '96 - p1122+ [501+]
Sanders, Dori - *Clover*
  y Kliatt - v30 - S '96 - p3 [1-50]
Sanders, E P - *Jesus and Judaism*
  Bks & Cult - v1 - N '95 - p3+ [501+]
Judaism: Practice and Belief 63 B.C.E.-66 C.E.
  Rel Ed - v91 - Fall '96 - p605 [1-50]
Sanders, Faye Sea - *Washington County, Kentucky Court
Order Book 1792-1800*
  EGH - v50 - N '96 - p169 [51-250]
Sanders, Joe - *Functions of the Fantastic*
  Ext - v37 - Fall '96 - p283+ [501+]
  SFS - v24 - Mr '97 - p166+ [501+]
Science Fiction Fandom
  Ext - v37 - Sum '96 - p172+ [501+]
  J Am Cult - v19 - Sum '96 - p147 [51-250]
Sanders, Joel - *Stud: Architectures of Masculinity*
  Esq - v126 - D '96 - p40 [1-50]
  LJ - v122 - F 1 '97 - p78 [51-250]
Sanders, John H - *The Economics of Agricultural
Technology in Semiarid Sub-Saharan Africa*
  Choice - v34 - S '96 - p177 [51-250]
  JEL - v34 - S '96 - p1495 [51-250]
Sanders, Lawrence - *McNally's Puzzle*
  Arm Det - v29 - Sum '96 - p374 [51-250]
Sanders, Leonard - *In the Valley of the Shadow*
  KR - v64 - My 1 '96 - p631+ [251-500]
Sanders, Pete - *AIDS*
  c Sch Lib - v45 - F '97 - p41 [51-250]
Bullying (Illus. by Mike Lacey)
  c HB Guide - v8 - Spr '97 - p96 [51-250]
  c KR - v64 - S 1 '96 - p1327+ [51-250]
  c SLJ - v43 - Mr '97 - p208 [51-250]
Child Abuse (Illus. by Mike Lacey)
  c HB Guide - v7 - Fall '96 - p317 [51-250]
  c SLJ - v42 - Ag '96 - p160 [51-250]
Depression and Mental Health
  c Sch Lib - v45 - F '97 - p41 [51-250]
Drugs (Illus. by Mike Lacey)
  c HB Guide - v7 - Fall '96 - p318 [51-250]
  c SLJ - v42 - Ag '96 - p160 [51-250]
People with Disabilities
  c Sch Lib - v44 - Ag '96 - p114 [51-250]
Smoking (Illus. by Mike Lacey)
  c HB Guide - v8 - Spr '97 - p96 [51-250]
  c SB - v33 - Ja '97 - p20 [251-500]
  c SLJ - v43 - Mr '97 - p208 [51-250]
Sanders, Ralph W - *Vintage Farm Tractors*
  BL - v93 - N 1 '96 - p468 [51-250]
Sanders, Ruth H - *Thirty Years of Computer Assisted
Language Instruction*
  MLJ - v81 - Spr '97 - p116+ [501+]
Sanders, Scott Russell - *Writing from the Center*
  Ken R - v18 - Sum '96 - p206+ [501+]
Sanderson, Elizabeth C - *Women and Work in Eighteenth-
Century Edinburgh*
  Choice - v34 - D '96 - p672+ [51-250]
Sanderson, Michael - *Education, Economic Change and
Society in England 1780-1870*
  JEL - v34 - D '96 - p2100 [51-250]
Sanderson, Michael J - *Homoplasy: The Recurrence of
Similarity in Evolution*
  SciTech - v21 - Mr '97 - p35 [51-250]

Sanderson, Peter - *Marvel Universe*
  y BL - v93 - Ja '97 - p804+ [51-250]
  y BL - v93 - Ap 1 '97 - p1308 [1-50]
     Bloom Rev - v17 - Ja '97 - p23 [51-250]
     BW - v26 - D 8 '96 - p13 [51-250]
     PW - v243 - S 30 '96 - p68 [51-250]
Sanderson, Ruth - *Papa Gatto (Illus. by Ruth Sanderson)*
  c Magpies - v11 - My '96 - p40 [51-250]
     Rose Red and Snow White (Illus. by Ruth Sanderson)
  c PW - v244 - Ap 14 '97 - p74 [51-250]
Sanderson, Stephen K - *Civilizations and World Systems*
     Hist & T - v35 - 3 '96 - p414 [251-500]
     JEH - v57 - Mr '97 - p262+ [501+]
     Social Transformations
     CS - v26 - Ja '97 - p47+ [501+]
     Hist & T - v36 - F '97 - p83+ [501+]
     SF - v75 - S '96 - p357+ [501+]
Sanderson, Warren C - *Population in Asia*
     J Gov Info - v23 - S '96 - p688 [51-250]
Sandford, Cedric - *Tax Compliance Costs*
     Econ J - v107 - Ja '97 - p275 [251-500]
Sandford, Christopher - *Kurt Cobain*
     Ent W - N 22 '96 - p131 [1-50]
     LATBR - N 10 '96 - p8 [501+]
Sandford, J C - *The Domestic Rabbit. 5th Ed.*
     SciTech - v20 - N '96 - p58 [51-250]
Sandford, John - *The Night Crew*
  y BL - v93 - Mr 1 '97 - p1069 [51-250]
     KR - v65 - F 15 '97 - p251 [251-500]
     LJ - v122 - Ap 1 '97 - p131 [51-250]
     PW - v244 - Mr 10 '97 - p49 [51-250]
     Trib Bks - Ap 20 '97 - p7 [51-250]
Sandiford, Keith A P - *Cricket and the Victorians*
     Albion - v28 - '96 - p713+ [501+]
     VS - v39 - Win '96 - p266+ [501+]
Sandison, Alan - *Robert Louis Stevenson and the Appearance of Modernism*
     Aust Bk R - N '96 - p29+ [501+]
     Nine-C Lit - v51 - Mr '97 - p564 [51-250]
     R&R Bk N - v11 - D '96 - p64 [51-250]
Sandler, Bernice Resnick - *The Chilly Classroom Climate*
     Choice - v34 - Ja '97 - p850 [51-250]
Sandler, Irving - *Art of the Postmodern Era*
     BL - v93 - N 15 '96 - p562 [251-500]
     Choice - v34 - Ap '97 - p1326 [51-250]
     LJ - v121 - N 1 '96 - p66 [51-250]
     WSJ-MW - v78 - D 5 '96 - pA18 [51-250]
Sandler, Martin W - *Civil War*
  c HB Guide - v7 - Fall '96 - p388+ [51-250]
  c Learning - v25 - N '96 - p82 [51-250]
     Immigrants
  c RT - v50 - D '96 - p340 [51-250]
  c RT - v50 - Mr '97 - p478 [51-250]
     Inventors
  c HB Guide - v7 - Fall '96 - p351 [51-250]
  c Learning - v25 - N '96 - p82 [51-250]
Sandler, Merton - *Migraine: Pharmacology and Genetics*
     SciTech - v20 - D '96 - p43 [51-250]
Sandler, Stanley R - *Polymer Syntheses. 2nd Ed., Vol. 3*
  r SciTech - v21 - Mr '97 - p30 [51-250]
Sandler, Todd - *The Economics of Defense*
     Econ J - v106 - S '96 - p1434+ [501+]
Sandlin, Tim - *Social Blunders*
     BW - v27 - Ap 13 '97 - p12 [51-250]
Sandman, Rochel - *As Big as an Egg (Illus. by Chana Zakashanskaya)*
  c Ch BWatch - v6 - S '96 - p7 [51-250]
Sandner, David - *The Fantastic Sublime*
     Choice - v34 - Mr '97 - p1166 [51-250]
Sandoval, Annette - *The Directory of Saints*
  r BL - v92 - Ag '96 - p1922 [1-50]
  r Choice - v34 - O '96 - p258 [51-250]
  r CLW - v67 - D '96 - p45 [251-500]
Sandoval, Dolores - *Be Patient, Abdul (Illus. by Dolores Sandoval)*
  c BL - v93 - S 15 '96 - p250 [51-250]
  c CBRS - v24 - Ag '96 - p165 [1-50]
  c HB Guide - v8 - Spr '97 - p46 [51-250]
  c SLJ - v42 - Ag '96 - p128 [51-250]
Sandoz, Mari - *The Christmas of the Phonograph Records*
     Roundup M - v4 - D '96 - p29 [1-50]
Sands, Bobby - *Bobby Sands: Writings from Prison*
     BL - v93 - My 15 '97 - p1557 [51-250]
Sandved, Kjell Bloch - *The Butterfly Alphabet (Illus. by Kjell Bloch Sandved)*
  c HB Guide - v7 - Fall '96 - p342 [51-250]
  c RT - v50 - Ap '97 - p591+ [51-250]
Sandywell, Barry - *The Beginnings of European Theorizing*
     R&R Bk N - v11 - N '96 - p38 [51-250]

     Presocratic Reflexivity
     R&R Bk N - v11 - D '96 - p1 [51-250]
Sanello, Frank - *Naked Instinct*
     BL - v93 - Mr 15 '97 - p1203 [51-250]
     PW - v244 - Mr 3 '97 - p60 [51-250]
     Spielberg: The Man, the Movies, the Mythology
     Econ - v339 - My 18 '96 - p13* [501+]
Sanfield, Steve - *The Girl Who Wanted a Song (Illus. by Stephen T Johnson)*
  c HB Guide - v8 - Spr '97 - p46 [51-250]
  c KR - v64 - O 1 '96 - p1474 [51-250]
  c PW - v243 - N 11 '96 - p74 [51-250]
  c Tric - v6 - Win '96 - p117 [1-50]
     The Great Turtle Drive (Illus. by Dirk Zimmer)
  c HB Guide - v7 - Fall '96 - p287 [51-250]
  c KR - v64 - My 1 '96 - p692 [51-250]
     Just Rewards (Illus. by Emily Lisker)
  c BL - v93 - O 1 '96 - p356 [51-250]
  c HB - v72 - N '96 - p753 [51-250]
  c HB Guide - v8 - Spr '97 - p105 [51-250]
  c SLJ - v42 - S '96 - p200 [51-250]
Sanford, John A - *Mystical Christianity*
     Rel St Rev - v22 - O '96 - p347 [501+]
Sanford, John B - *The People from Heaven*
     AL - v68 - S '96 - p669 [1-50]
     Nat - v263 - S 23 '96 - p30+ [501+]
     SFR - v21 - S '96 - p27+ [501+]
Sanford, Terry - *Outlive Your Enemies*
     SciTech - v21 - Mr '97 - p46 [1-50]
Sanford, William R - *Bill Pickett: African-American Rodeo Star*
  c KR - v64 - D 1 '96 - p1741 [51-250]
     Brigham Young: Pioneer and Mormon Leader
  c HB Guide - v8 - Spr '97 - p175 [1-50]
  c SLJ - v42 - S '96 - p220 [51-250]
  y VOYA - v19 - D '96 - p290 [51-250]
     Buffalo Bill Cody: Showman of the Wild West
  c HB Guide - v7 - Fall '96 - p389 [51-250]
     Calamity Jane: Frontier Original
  c HB Guide - v7 - Fall '96 - p389 [51-250]
     Chief Joseph: Nez Perce Warrior
  c Ch BWatch - v6 - Jl '96 - p7 [51-250]
     Crazy Horse: Sioux Warrior
  c Ch BWatch - v6 - Jl '96 - p7 [51-250]
     Davy Crockett: Defender of the Alamo
  c HB Guide - v7 - Fall '96 - p389 [51-250]
     Geronimo: Apache Warrior
  c Ch BWatch - v6 - Jl '96 - p7 [51-250]
     John C. Fremont: Soldier and Pathfinder
  c HB Guide - v7 - Fall '96 - p389 [51-250]
     Kit Carson: Frontier Scout
  c HB Guide - v7 - Fall '96 - p389 [51-250]
     Osceola: Seminole Warrior
  c Ch BWatch - v6 - Jl '96 - p7 [51-250]
     Quanah Parker: Comanche Warrior
  c Ch BWatch - v6 - Jl '96 - p7 [51-250]
     Red Cloud: Sioux Warrior
  c Ch BWatch - v6 - Jl '96 - p7 [51-250]
     Sacagawea: Native American Hero
  c SLJ - v43 - Mr '97 - p180 [51-250]
     Sam Houston: Texas Hero
  c HB Guide - v7 - Fall '96 - p389 [51-250]
     Sitting Bull: Sioux Warrior
  c Ch BWatch - v6 - Jl '96 - p7 [51-250]
     Zebulon Pike: Explorer of the Southwest
  c HB Guide - v8 - Spr '97 - p175 [1-50]
  c SLJ - v42 - S '96 - p220 [51-250]
Sang, Ye - *The Year the Dragon Came*
     Aust Bk R - Ag '96 - p10+ [501+]
Sanger, Clyde - *Malcolm MacDonald: Bringing an End to Empire*
     Beav - v76 - O '96 - p41+ [501+]
     Econ - v339 - My 18 '96 - p9*+ [501+]
Sanger, S L - *Working on the Bomb*
     Isis - v87 - D '96 - p753+ [501+]
Sangharakshita - *Buddhism for Today and Tomorrow*
     Tric - v6 - Win '96 - p116 [1-50]
Sangster, Joan - *Earning Respect*
     AHR - v102 - F '97 - p229 [501+]
Sangsue, Daniel - *La Parodie*
     MLR - v91 - O '96 - p1008 [251-500]
Sanitt, Nigel - *Science as a Questioning Process*
     Choice - v34 - F '97 - p981+ [51-250]
Sanjek, Russell - *Pennies from Heaven*
     Choice - v34 - Ap '97 - p1349 [51-250]
Sanjines, Jose - *Paseos En El Horizonte*
     WLT - v70 - Sum '96 - p668+ [501+]
San Juan, E - *The Philippine Temptation*
     Choice - v34 - N '96 - p451 [51-250]
     Smile of the Medusa
     Amerasia J - v22 - 2 '96 - p155+ [501+]

Sanneh, Lamin - *The Crown and the Turban*
     Choice - v34 - Ap '97 - p1357 [51-250]
Sano, Darrell - *Designing Large-Scale Web Sites*
     BL - v93 - S 15 '96 - p193 [501+]
     CBR - v14 - N '96 - p35 [51-250]
Sansen, Willy - *Analog Circuit Design*
     SciTech - v21 - Mr '97 - p91 [51-250]
Sansome, Rosemary - *Oxford Junior Dictionary. 3rd Rev. Ed.*
  cr Bks Keeps - v100 - S '96 - p22+ [501+]
     The Oxford Junior Dictionary. 3rd Rev. Ed.
  cr Books - v9 - S '95 - p26 [1-50]
San Souci, Robert D - *The Faithful Friend (Illus. by Brian Pinkney)*
  c RT - v50 - N '96 - p257 [51-250]
     The Hired Hand (Illus. by Jerry Pinkney)
  c BL - v93 - F 15 '97 - p1025 [51-250]
  y CCB-B - v50 - Ap '97 - p295 [51-250]
  c HB - v73 - My '97 - p335 [51-250]
  c PW - v244 - Ap 14 '97 - p75 [51-250]
     The House in the Sky (Illus. by Wil Clay)
  c HB Guide - v7 - Fall '96 - p324 [51-250]
     Los Huevos Parlantes (Illus. by Jerry Pinkney)
  c BL - v93 - My 1 '97 - p1507 [1-50]
  c SLJ - v42 - N '96 - p134 [51-250]
     Kate Shelley: Bound for Legend (Illus. by Max Ginsburg)
  c RT - v50 - S '96 - p57 [51-250]
  c RT - v50 - N '96 - p245 [51-250]
     Nicholas Pipe (Illus. by David Shannon)
  c PW - v244 - My 5 '97 - p209 [51-250]
     Pedro and the Monkey (Illus. by Michael Hays)
  c BL - v93 - S 1 '96 - p140 [51-250]
  c CCB-B - v50 - N '96 - p113+ [51-250]
  c Ch BWatch - v6 - S '96 - p7 [1-50]
  c Emerg Lib - v24 - Mr '97 - p45 [1-50]
  c HB Guide - v8 - Spr '97 - p105 [51-250]
  c LATBR - Ag 4 '96 - p11 [251-500]
  c SLJ - v42 - O '96 - p117 [51-250]
     The Red Heels (Illus. by Gary Kelley)
  c BL - v93 - S 1 '96 - p131+ [51-250]
  c CBRS - v25 - Ja '97 - p52 [51-250]
  y CCB-B - v50 - O '96 - p74 [51-250]
  c Ch BWatch - v6 - O '96 - p5 [1-50]
  c HB Guide - v8 - Spr '97 - p46+ [51-250]
  c LATBR - D 8 '96 - p18+ [1-50]
  c PW - v243 - Jl 22 '96 - p242 [51-250]
  c SLJ - v42 - O '96 - p105+ [51-250]
  c Smith - v27 - N '96 - p173 [1-50]
     Young Guinevere (Illus. by Jamichael Henterly)
  c PW - v243 - N 25 '96 - p78 [1-50]
     Young Guinevere (Leishman). Audio Version
  c BL - v93 - My 15 '97 - p1595 [51-250]
  c HB - v73 - My '97 - p357+ [501+]
     Young Lancelot (Illus. by Jamichael Henterly)
  c BL - v93 - N 15 '96 - p592 [51-250]
  c HB Guide - v8 - Spr '97 - p105 [51-250]
  c KR - v64 - N 15 '96 - p1674 [51-250]
  c PW - v243 - N 25 '96 - p77 [51-250]
  c SLJ - v42 - N '96 - p118 [51-250]
     Young Lancelot (Leishman). Audio Version
  c HB - v73 - My '97 - p357+ [501+]
  c HB - v73 - My '97 - p357+ [501+]
     Young Merlin (Leishman). Audio Version
  y HB - v73 - Ja '97 - p85+ [501+]
  y Kliatt - v31 - Ja '97 - p48 [51-250]
Santa Barbara Review
  p Sm Pr R - v29 - Ja '97 - p17 [51-250]
Santaeugenia Grau, Juan -
     Czechoslovakia--Revolutionary Stamps and Overprints 1944-1945
  r Phil Lit R - v46 - 1 '97 - p69+ [251-500]
Santamaria, Peggy - *High Performance through Self-Management*
  y Cur R - v36 - N '96 - p13 [51-250]
  y SLJ - v42 - Ag '96 - p168 [51-250]
Santana, Deborah Berman - *Kicking Off the Bootstraps*
     Choice - v34 - My '97 - p1560 [51-250]
Santaniello, Weaver - *Nietzsche, God and the Jews*
     JAAR - v65 - Spr '97 - p210+ [501+]
Santarelli, Enrico - *Finance and Technological Change*
     JEL - v34 - D '96 - p2118 [51-250]
Santarrita, Marcos - *Bahia Minha*
     WLT - v71 - Win '97 - p131+ [501+]
Santella, Andrew - *Jackie Robinson Breaks the Color Line*
  c HB Guide - v7 - Fall '96 - p362 [51-250]
  c SLJ - v42 - N '96 - p114 [51-250]
     Mo Vaughn: Big Mo
  c HB Guide - v7 - Fall '96 - p359 [1-50]

Santelli, Maurice - *Lewis Acids and Selectivity in Organic Synthesis*
    Choice - v34 - O '96 - p308 [51-250]
Santiago, Danny - *Famous All over Town*
  y BL - v93 - Ja '97 - p832 [51-250]
Santiago, Esmeralda - *America's Dream*
    Wom R Bks - v14 - Ja '97 - p22 [501+]
  El Sueno De America
    LJ - v122 - Ja '97 - p80 [51-250]
  When I Was Puerto Rican
  y BL - v93 - D 15 '96 - p717 [1-50]
Santiago, Soledad - *Streets of Fire*
    KR - v64 - My 1 '96 - p632 [251-500]
Santich, Barbara - *Looking for Flavour*
    Aust Bk R - N '96 - p21 [501+]
  Original Mediterranean Cuisine
    BWatch - v17 - D '96 - p9 [51-250]
Santideva - *A Guide to the Bodhisattva Way of Life*
    LJ - v122 - Ap 1 '97 - p99 [51-250]
    PW - v244 - F 24 '97 - p81 [51-250]
Santino, Jack - *New Old-Fashioned Ways*
    PW - v243 - N 4 '96 - p70 [51-250]
Santner, Eric L - *My Own Private Germany*
    TLS - O 4 '96 - p16 [501+]
Santoni, Pedro - *Mexicans at Arms*
    Choice - v34 - Ap '97 - p1401 [51-250]
Santoni, Ronald E - *Bad Faith, Good Faith, and Authenticity in Sartre's Early Philosophy*
    IPQ - v36 - S '96 - p367+ [501+]
SantoPietro, Nancy - *Feng Shui*
    BL - v93 - N 15 '96 - p552 [51-250]
Santos, Barbara - *The Maui Onion Cookbook*
    BWatch - v17 - N '96 - p1 [51-250]
Santos, Boaventura De Sousa - *Toward a New Common Sense*
    AJS - v102 - N '96 - p861+ [501+]
    CS - v26 - Mr '97 - p213+ [501+]
Santos, Helen - *Pepe's Dog (Illus. by Martin Salisbury)*
  c Bks Keeps - v100 - S '96 - p10 [51-250]
Santos, Rosario - *And We Sold the Rain*
    TLS - S 6 '96 - p23 [251-500]
Santos Febres, Mayra - *Urban Oracles*
    BL - v93 - My 1 '97 - p1480+ [501+]
    KR - v65 - Ap 1 '97 - p504 [51-250]
    PW - v244 - Mr 10 '97 - p49 [51-250]
Santos Torres, Jose - *El Bandolerismo En Espana*
    Choice - v34 - D '96 - p569 [1-50]
    Choice - v34 - D '96 - p569 [1-50]
Santucci, Robert M - *A Consumer's Guide to Home Improvement, Renovation, and Repair. Rev. Ed.*
    LJ - v122 - F 1 '97 - p52 [1-50]
Sap, J W - *Wegbereiders Der Revolutie*
    Six Ct J - v27 - Fall '96 - p959+ [501+]
Saperstein, Marc - *Moments of Crisis in Jewish-Christian Relations*
    Rel Ed - v91 - Fall '96 - p607 [1-50]
Sapolsky, Robert M - *The Trouble with Testosterone and Other Essays on the Biology of the Human Predicament*
    KR - v65 - F 15 '97 - p285 [251-500]
    LATBR - Ap 20 '97 - p5 [501+]
    LJ - v122 - Mr 15 '97 - p86 [51-250]
    PW - v244 - Mr 24 '97 - p70 [51-250]
Sapp, Allen - *I Heard the Drum*
    Quill & Q - v62 - O '96 - p38 [51-250]
Sapphire - *American Dreams*
    HG&LRev - v3 - Fall '96 - p43 [51-250]
    NYTBR - v101 - Jl 21 '96 - p28 [1-50]
  Push
    Advocate - Je 11 '96 - p59+ [501+]
    Ent W - Je 28 '96 - p98 [251-500]
    HG&LRev - v3 - Fall '96 - p37+ [501+]
    LATBR - Jl 7 '96 - p1+ [501+]
    LATBR - D 29 '96 - p5 [51-250]
    LJ - v121 - O 1 '96 - p48 [1-50]
    Lon R Bks - v19 - F 6 '97 - p25+ [501+]
    Obs - D 8 '96 - p17* [51-250]
    TLS - O 11 '96 - p24 [501+]
    VLS - Win '96 - p11 [51-250]
    Wom R Bks - v14 - N '96 - p1+ [501+]
Sappho's Lyre
    CW - v90 - S '96 - p70+ [251-500]
Saprykin, S J - *Ancient Farms and Land-Plots on the Khora of Khersonesos Taurike*
    AJA - v100 - O '96 - p792 [501+]
Saraiva, Arnaldo - *Fernando Pessoa: Poeta-Tradutor De Poetas*
    WLT - v71 - Win '97 - p132+ [251-500]
Saramago, Jose - *Cadernos De Lancarote: Diario III*
    WLT - v71 - Win '97 - p133 [501+]

The History of the Siege of Lisbon
    BL - v93 - Ap 1 '97 - p1282 [51-250]
    KR - v65 - Mr 15 '97 - p413 [251-500]
    LJ - v122 - Mr 15 '97 - p92 [51-250]
    PW - v244 - F 17 '97 - p208 [251-500]
Sarasohn, Lisa T - *Gassendi's Ethics*
    Choice - v34 - Ap '97 - p1353 [51-250]
Sarason, Seymour B - *Barometers of Change*
    Choice - v34 - N '96 - p479 [51-250]
  Parental Involvement and the Political Principle
    Cont Ed - v67 - Sum '96 - p254 [501+]
    TCR - v98 - Win '96 - p359+ [501+]
  Revisiting The Culture of the School and the Problem of Change
    Nat - v263 - O 28 '96 - p32+ [501+]
Sarat, Austin - *Divorce Lawyers and Their Clients*
    AJS - v102 - S '96 - p650+ [501+]
    CS - v26 - Mr '97 - p218+ [501+]
    J Pol - v59 - F '97 - p272+ [501+]
  Identities, Politics, and Rights
    Choice - v34 - N '96 - p534 [51-250]
  Legal Rights
    Choice - v34 - D '96 - p681 [51-250]
Sardi, Jan - *Shine: The Screenplay*
    Ent W - Mr 28 '97 - p61 [51-250]
    Lon R Bks - v19 - Ap 3 '97 - p30+ [501+]
Sarduy, Severo - *From Cuba with a Song*
    TranslRevS - v1 - My '95 - p32 [1-50]
Sareen, S K - *South Asian Love Poetry*
    WLT - v70 - Sum '96 - p760+ [501+]
Sarewitz, Daniel R - *Frontiers of Illusion*
    Am Sci - v85 - Ja '97 - p74+ [501+]
    Choice - v34 - D '96 - p632 [51-250]
    Sci - v273 - S 27 '96 - p1806+ [501+]
Sarfati, Sonia - *Les Voix Truquees (Illus. by Caroline Merola)*
  c Can CL - v22 - Sum '96 - p102+ [251-500]
Sargent, Pamela - *A Fury Scorned*
  y Kliatt - v31 - Mr '97 - p21 [51-250]
Sargentson, Carolyn - *Merchants and Luxury Markets*
    BM - v139 - Ja '97 - p46+ [501+]
Saricks, Joyce G - *Readers' Advisory Service in the Public Library*
  r RQ - v36 - Win '96 - p208 [51-250]
Sarin, Oleg - *Alien Wars*
    BL - v92 - Ag '96 - p1878 [51-250]
Sarjeant, William Antony S - *Geologists and the History of Geology. 2nd Suppl., Vol. 1*
  r ARBA - v28 - '97 - p636 [51-250]
  r SciTech - v20 - S '96 - p17 [51-250]
Sarkesian, Sam C - *Soldiers, Society, and National Security*
    Arm F&S - v23 - Fall '96 - p113+ [501+]
Sarkozi, Matyas - *Szinhaz Az Egesz Vilag*
    WLT - v70 - Sum '96 - p734+ [501+]
Sarlin, Janeen - *The New Meat Lover's Cookbook*
    BL - v93 - N 15 '96 - p560 [51-250]
    CSM - v89 - D 13 '96 - p11 [51-250]
    LJ - v121 - D '96 - p136 [51-250]
    PW - v243 - S 16 '96 - p78 [51-250]
Sarlo, Christopher A - *Poverty in Canada. 2nd Ed.*
    JEL - v34 - D '96 - p2065+ [51-250]
Sarma, R H - *Biological Structure and Dynamics. Vols. 1-2*
    SciTech - v20 - N '96 - p33 [51-250]
Sarma, Sankar Das - *Perspectives in Quantum Hall Effects*
    SciTech - v21 - Mr '97 - p24 [51-250]
Sarna, Jonathan D - *The Jews of Boston*
    NEQ - v69 - D '96 - p669+ [501+]
Sarno, Louis - *Bayaka: The Extraordinary Music of the Babenzele Pygmies*
    Teach Mus - v4 - O '96 - p56 [51-250]
Sarnowsky, Jurgen - *Die Wirtschaftsfuhrung Des Deutschen Ordens In Preussen 1382-1454*
    Specu - v72 - Ja '97 - p216+ [501+]
Saro Wiwa, Ken - *Lemona's Tale*
    Obs - Ja 19 '97 - p18* [51-250]
Saro-Wiwa, Ken - *A Month and a Day*
    LATBR - S 15 '96 - p11 [51-250]
Sarrantonio, Al - *Exile*
  y Kliatt - v30 - N '96 - p16 [51-250]
    SF Chr - v18 - O '96 - p79 [51-250]
Sarraute, Nathalie - *Ici*
    FR - v70 - F '97 - p502+ [501+]
    WLT - v70 - Sum '96 - p654+ [251-500]
  Oeuvres Completes
    Lon R Bks - v19 - F 20 '97 - p3+ [501+]
Sarre, Philip - *An Overcrowded World?*
    GJ - v163 - Mr '97 - p102+ [501+]

Sarris, Andrew - *The American Cinema*
    BW - v26 - O 6 '96 - p12 [51-250]
    LJ - v122 - Ja '97 - p155 [1-50]
Sarsfield, Mairuth - *No Crystal Stair*
  y Quill & Q - v63 - F '97 - p58 [1-50]
Sarti, Ron - *The Chronicles of Scar*
    SF Chr - v18 - O '96 - p76 [51-250]
Sarton, May - *Anger*
    NYTBR - v101 - O 13 '96 - p32 [51-250]
  At Eighty-Two
    PW - v244 - Mr 24 '97 - p81 [1-50]
  A Private Mythology
    NYTBR - v101 - O 13 '96 - p32 [51-250]
  Selected Letters. Vol. 1
    BL - v93 - My 15 '97 - p1557 [51-250]
    KR - v65 - Ap 1 '97 - p534+ [251-500]
    PW - v244 - Ap 28 '97 - p60+ [51-250]
Sartori, Leo - *Understanding Relativity*
    Choice - v34 - D '96 - p649 [51-250]
    Phys Today - v49 - D '96 - p58+ [501+]
Sartoris, David J - *Osteoporosis: Diagnosis and Treatment*
    SciTech - v20 - N '96 - p48 [51-250]
Sartre, Jean Paul - *Les Mouches*
    CML - v16 - Win '96 - p107+ [501+]
Sartre Studies International
  p MLR - v91 - O '96 - p1001+ [251-500]
Sarup, Madan - *Identity, Culture and the Postmodern World*
    Choice - v34 - Mr '97 - p1149 [51-250]
Sarver, Linda - *A Novel Approach to the Theatre*
  r LJ - v122 - Ap 1 '97 - p86 [51-250]
Sasanov, Catherine - *Traditions of Bread and Violence*
    Chel - 61 '96 - p125+ [501+]
    Choice - v34 - Ap '97 - p1340 [51-250]
Sasao, Tsutomu - *Representations of Discrete Functions*
    SciTech - v20 - N '96 - p75 [51-250]
The Saskatchewan Air Quality Task Force
    J Gov Info - v23 - S '96 - p641 [51-250]
Saslow, James - *The Medici Wedding of 1589*
    VQR - v72 - Aut '96 - p140* [51-250]
Sass, Edmund J - *Polio's Legacy*
    Choice - v34 - N '96 - p495 [51-250]
    SciTech - v20 - S '96 - p30 [51-250]
Sass, Louis A - *Madness and Modernism*
    Can Lit - Win '96 - p121+ [501+]
Sassaman, Kenneth E - *Archaeology of the Mid-Holocene Southeast*
    Choice - v34 - My '97 - p1540 [51-250]
Sasse, Hermann - *Scripture and the Church*
    CH - v66 - Mr '97 - p210+ [51-250]
Sassen, Saskia - *Losing Control?*
    Choice - v34 - F '97 - p1033 [51-250]
    JEL - v35 - Mr '97 - p216 [51-250]
Sasser, Charles W - *Smoke Jumpers*
  y Kliatt - v30 - S '96 - p32 [51-250]
Sasso, Sandy Eisenberg - *But God Remembered (Illus. by Bethanne Andersen)*
  c BL - v93 - O 1 '96 - p339 [1-50]
  A Prayer for the Earth (Illus. by Bethanne Andersen)
  c BL - v93 - F 15 '97 - p1029 [51-250]
  c KR - v65 - Ja 15 '97 - p146 [51-250]
  c PW - v244 - F 24 '97 - p83 [51-250]
Sasson, Theodore - *Crime Talk*
    AJS - v102 - S '96 - p642+ [501+]
    CS - v26 - Ja '97 - p85+ [501+]
Sassoon, Donald - *One Hundred Years of Socialism*
    NS - v125 - D 20 '96 - p117 [51-250]
    TLS - N 8 '96 - p21 [501+]
Sassower, Raphael - *Cultural Collisions*
    CPR - v16 - Ap '96 - p133+ [501+]
    Isis - v87 - S '96 - p582+ [501+]
Sateren, Shelley Swanson - *Canada: Star of the North*
  c HB Guide - v8 - Spr '97 - p175 [51-250]
  The Humane Societies
  c CCB-B - v50 - O '96 - p75 [51-250]
  c HB Guide - v8 - Spr '97 - p96 [51-250]
  c SLJ - v42 - N '96 - p118 [51-250]
Sathaye, Jayant A - *Greenhouse Gas Mitigation Assessment*
    SciTech - v20 - N '96 - p68 [51-250]
Sathre, Vivian - *Leroy Potts Meets the McCrooks (Illus. by Rowan Barnes-Murphy)*
  c BL - v93 - My 1 '97 - p1505 [51-250]
  c KR - v65 - Mr 15 '97 - p468 [51-250]
  Three Kind Mice (Illus. by Rodger Wilson)
  c CBRS - v25 - Mr '97 - p90 [1-50]
  c KR - v65 - F 1 '97 - p228 [51-250]
  c PW - v244 - F 10 '97 - p82 [51-250]
  c SLJ - v43 - Mr '97 - p166 [51-250]

Sathyamurthy, T V - *Region, Religion, Caste, Gender and Culture in Contemporary India*
    Choice - v34 - Ap '97 - p1412 [51-250]
Satie, Erik - *A Mammal's Notebook*
    LJ - v121 - O 15 '96 - p62 [51-250]
    TLS - Ja 10 '97 - p16 [501+]
Satin, Morton - *Food Irradiation. 2nd Ed.*
    SciTech - v20 - N '96 - p80 [51-250]
Satinover, Jeffrey - *Homosexuality and the Politics of Truth*
    Nat R - v48 - S 30 '96 - p66+ [501+]
Satlow, Michael L - *Tasting the Dish*
    Rel St Rev - v23 - Ja '97 - p88 [51-250]
Sato, Haruo - *Beautiful Town*
    Choice - v34 - My '97 - p1492 [51-250]
Sato, Ken-Ichi - *Advances in Transport Network Technologies*
    SciTech - v20 - D '96 - p76 [51-250]
Sato, Ryuzo - *Trade and Investment in the 1990s*
    JEL - v35 - Mr '97 - p214+ [51-250]
Sato, Shigeru - *War, Nationalism and Peasants*
    J Mil H - v61 - Ja '97 - p192+ [251-500]
Satoh, Akira - *Building in Britain*
    Albion - v28 - Sum '96 - p334+ [501+]
    JEH - v56 - D '96 - p936+ [501+]
Satpathy, Sumanyu - *Re-Viewing Reviewing*
    ELT - v39 - 4 '96 - p529+ [51-250]
Satter, David - *Age of Delirium*
    NL - v79 - Ag 12 '96 - p19+ [501+]
    NYTBR - v101 - S 8 '96 - p16 [501+]
    TLS - N 8 '96 - p22 [501+]
    VQR - v73 - Win '97 - p24* [51-250]
Satterfield, Barbara - *The Story Dance (Illus. by Fran Gregory)*
    c PW - v244 - My 5 '97 - p208 [51-250]
Satterfield, Charles N - *Heterogeneous Catalysis in Industrial Practice. 2nd Ed.*
    SciTech - v20 - D '96 - p82 [51-250]
Satterthwait, Walter - *Accustomed to the Dark*
    BL - v93 - N 15 '96 - p575 [51-250]
    BW - v26 - N 17 '96 - p6 [51-250]
    KR - v64 - S 15 '96 - p1358 [51-250]
    LJ - v121 - D '96 - p150+ [51-250]
    PW - v243 - S 9 '96 - p67 [51-250]
Escapade: A Mystery
    Arm Det - v30 - Win '97 - p19 [51-250]
Satterthwaite, David - *The Environment for Children*
    New Sci - v153 - F 15 '97 - p43 [51-250]
Satterthwaite, Philip E - *A Pathway into the Holy Scripture*
    Bks & Cult - v2 - Ja '96 - p30 [251-500]
Sattler, Helen Roney - *The Book of North American Owls (Illus. by Jean Day Zallinger)*
    c LA - v73 - O '96 - p440+ [251-500]
Saubin, Beatrice - *The Ordeal: My Ten Years in a Malaysian Prison*
    TranslRevS - v1 - My '95 - p11 [51-250]
Sauchenko, Jack P - *Canadian Municipal Trade Tokens and Related Issues Handbook. 1997 Ed.*
    r Coin W - v38 - F 24 '97 - p66 [51-250]
Sauer, Elizabeth - *Barbarous Dissonance and Images of Voice in Milton's Epics*
    Choice - v34 - Ap '97 - p1340 [51-250]
Sauers, Richard A - *A Succession of Honorable Victories*
    Choice - v34 - S '96 - p198 [51-250]
Saugier, Philippe - *The Ozone Project*
    J Gov Info - v23 - S '96 - p665 [51-250]
Saul, John - *Black Lightning*
    Books - v9 - S '95 - p22 [1-50]
    Rapport - v19 - 4 '96 - p26 [251-500]
Saul, John Ralston - *The Unconscious Civilization*
    BL - v93 - D 15 '96 - p698 [51-250]
    BW - v27 - F 2 '97 - p8 [501+]
    KR - v64 - N 1 '96 - p1591 [251-500]
    LJ - v121 - D '96 - p97+ [51-250]
    PW - v243 - D 2 '96 - p47+ [51-250]
    Utne R - Ja '97 - p96+ [51-250]
The Unconscious Civilization (Saul). Audio Version
    Quill & Q - v62 - My '96 - p31 [51-250]
Saul, Nigel - *Richard II*
    LJ - v122 - My 1 '97 - p116 [51-250]
    PW - v244 - My 5 '97 - p192 [51-250]
Saul, Norman E - *Concord and Conflict*
    HRNB - v25 - Fall '96 - p34 [251-500]
    TLS - O 11 '96 - p12 [501+]
Saul, Pauline - *Tracing Your Ancestors*
    r TES - Jl 26 '96 - pR6 [1-50]
Saunders, Alan - *George C. Marshall: A General for Peace*
    y HB Guide - v7 - Fall '96 - p374 [51-250]

Saunders, Anthony - *Universal Banking*
    Choice - v34 - S '96 - p177+ [51-250]
Saunders, Bonnie F - *The United States and Arab Nationalism*
    MEJ - v50 - Aut '96 - p610+ [51-250]
    MEP - v5 - 1 '97 - p202+ [501+]
Saunders, George - *CivilWarLand in Bad Decline*
    y Kliatt - v31 - My '97 - p15 [51-250]
CivilWarland in Bad Decline
    NYTBR - v101 - D 8 '96 - p79 [1-50]
    NYTBR - v102 - Mr 2 '97 - p28 [1-50]
Saunders, Graham - *A History of Brunei*
    AHR - v102 - F '97 - p158 [251-500]
    Historian - v58 - Sum '96 - p886+ [501+]
Saunders, Janet McGee - *Patient Confidentiality*
    SciTech - v20 - D '96 - p3 [51-250]
Saunders, Jean - *Journey's End*
    y BL - v93 - D 15 '96 - p710 [51-250]
    PW - v243 - D 2 '96 - p42 [51-250]
Saunders, Kate - *Eighteen Layers of Hell*
    TLS - N 22 '96 - p27 [501+]
Saunders, Kevin W - *Violence as Obscenity*
    Choice - v34 - N '96 - p539 [51-250]
Saunders, Lucy - *Cooking with Beer*
    PW - v243 - S 16 '96 - p80 [51-250]
Saunders, Max - *Ford Madox Ford: A Dual Life. Vol. 1*
    NYTBR - v101 - D 8 '96 - p87 [1-50]
Ford Madox Ford: A Dual Life. Vol. 2
    Choice - v34 - My '97 - p1499+ [51-250]
    Econ - v341 - N 23 '96 - p104 [251-500]
    Lon R Bks - v19 - F 6 '97 - p17+ [501+]
    Spec - v277 - N 16 '96 - p53+ [501+]
    TLS - N 1 '96 - p4+ [501+]
Ford Madox Ford: A Dual Life. Vols. 1-2
    NYRB - v44 - Ja 9 '97 - p23+ [501+]
Saunders, Peter - *Capitalism*
    JEL - v34 - S '96 - p1490 [51-250]
Saunders, Ray - *Blood Tells*
    KR - v64 - Ag 15 '96 - p1182 [251-500]
    PW - v243 - S 30 '96 - p61+ [51-250]
Saunders, Ross - *Outrageous Women, Outrageous God*
    CLW - v67 - Mr '97 - p31 [251-500]
Saunders, Stephen - *McGraw-Hill High-Speed LANs Handbook*
    CBR - v14 - N '96 - p38 [51-250]
Saunders, Steven - *Cross, Sword, and Lyre*
    AHR - v102 - F '97 - p136 [251-500]
    Notes - v53 - D '96 - p453 [501+]
Saunders, Susan - *The Curse of the Cat Mummy*
    c SLJ - v43 - Mr '97 - p166 [51-250]
The Ghost Who Ate Chocolate (Illus. by Jane Manning)
    c BL - v93 - D 15 '96 - p727 [51-250]
    c SLJ - v42 - N '96 - p92 [51-250]
The Haunted Skateboard (Illus. by Jane Manning)
    c BL - v93 - D 15 '96 - p727 [51-250]
    c SLJ - v42 - N '96 - p92 [51-250]
Saunders, Thomas - *Hollywood in Berlin*
    FQ - v49 - Fall '95 - p49+ [501+]
Sauron, Gilles - *Quis Deum?*
    AJA - v101 - Ja '97 - p185+ [501+]
Saussy, Carroll - *The Gift of Anger*
    Rel St Rev - v22 - O '96 - p336 [51-250]
Sauter, E G - *Nonlinear Optics*
    SciTech - v20 - D '96 - p24 [51-250]
Sautter, Hermann - *Economic Reforms in Latin America*
    HAHR - v76 - N '96 - p832+ [501+]
Indebtedness, Economic Reforms, and Poverty
    HAHR - v76 - N '96 - p832+ [501+]
Sautter, R Craig - *Inside the Wigwam*
    BL - v92 - Ag '96 - p1862+ [501+]
    Bloom Rev - v16 - S '96 - p24 [51-250]
Sauvain, Philip - *Key Themes of the Twentieth Century*
    y TES - Mr 28 '97 - p13* [501+]
Kings and Queens
    c Sch Lib - v44 - Ag '96 - p114 [51-250]
Mountains
    c BL - v93 - S 1 '96 - p124 [51-250]
    c HB Guide - v8 - Spr '97 - p163 [51-250]
    c Sch Lib - v44 - N '96 - p165 [251-500]
    c SLJ - v43 - Mr '97 - p208 [51-250]
Rivers and Valleys
    c HB Guide - v8 - Spr '97 - p163 [51-250]
    c SLJ - v43 - Mr '97 - p208 [51-250]
Saints
    c Sch Lib - v44 - Ag '96 - p114 [51-250]
Sauve, Pierre - *Investment Rules for the Global Economy*
    JEL - v35 - Mr '97 - p216+ [51-250]
Savage, Candace - *Bird Brains*
    AB - v97 - Je 17 '96 - p2397+ [51-250]

Cowgirls
    y BL - v93 - S 1 '96 - p59 [51-250]
    y BL - v93 - Ap 1 '97 - p1288 [1-50]
    CG - v116 - N '96 - p90 [51-250]
    LATBR - D 8 '96 - p5 [1-50]
    Obs - D 1 '96 - p18* [1-50]
    TLS - Ap 11 '97 - p28 [1-50]
Wild Cats, Lynx, Bobcats, Mountain Lions
    AB - v97 - Je 17 '96 - p2404 [51-250]
The World of the Wolf
    BL - v93 - D 1 '96 - p632 [51-250]
    PW - v243 - O 21 '96 - p68 [1-50]
    y SLJ - v43 - Mr '97 - p218 [51-250]
Savage, Deborah - *To Race a Dream*
    y Kliatt - v30 - N '96 - p10 [51-250]
Under a Different Sky
    y BL - v93 - Mr 15 '97 - p1239 [51-250]
    y KR - v65 - Mr 1 '97 - p387 [51-250]
    y PW - v244 - Mr 31 '97 - p76 [51-250]
Savage, Jeff - *Barry Bonds: Mr. Excitement*
    c Ch BWatch - v7 - F '97 - p7 [1-50]
    c SLJ - v43 - F '97 - p124 [51-250]
Deion Sanders: Star Athlete
    c HB Guide - v7 - Fall '96 - p361+ [51-250]
Demolition Derby
    c Ch BWatch - v6 - D '96 - p6 [1-50]
    c HB Guide - v8 - Spr '97 - p146 [51-250]
    c SLJ - v43 - F '97 - p98 [51-250]
Drag Racing
    c Ch BWatch - v6 - D '96 - p6 [1-50]
    c HB Guide - v8 - Spr '97 - p146 [51-250]
    c SLJ - v43 - F '97 - p124 [51-250]
Emmitt Smith: Star Running Back
    c HB Guide - v7 - Fall '96 - p361+ [51-250]
Gold Miners of the Wild West
    c CLW - v66 - Je '96 - p52 [251-500]
Grant Hill: Humble Hotshot
    c Ch BWatch - v7 - F '97 - p7 [1-50]
Julie Krone: Unstoppable Jockey
    c BL - v92 - Ag '96 - p1899 [51-250]
    c HB Guide - v8 - Spr '97 - p144 [51-250]
    c SLJ - v42 - S '96 - p217 [51-250]
Monster Trucks
    c Ch BWatch - v6 - D '96 - p6 [1-50]
    c SLJ - v43 - F '97 - p98 [51-250]
Mud Racing
    c Ch BWatch - v6 - D '96 - p6 [1-50]
    c HB Guide - v8 - Spr '97 - p146 [51-250]
    c SLJ - v43 - F '97 - p124 [51-250]
Pony Express Riders of the Wild West
    c CLW - v66 - Je '96 - p52 [251-500]
Supercross Motorcycle Racing
    c Ch BWatch - v6 - D '96 - p6 [1-50]
    c HB Guide - v8 - Spr '97 - p146 [51-250]
    c SLJ - v43 - F '97 - p124 [51-250]
Truck and Tractor Pullers
    c Ch BWatch - v6 - D '96 - p6 [1-50]
    c HB Guide - v8 - Spr '97 - p146 [51-250]
    c SLJ - v43 - F '97 - p98 [51-250]
Savage, Jon - *Time Travel*
    TLS - Ag 2 '96 - p14 [501+]
Savage, Mike - *Property, Bureaucracy and Culture*
    JEL - v35 - Mr '97 - p239 [51-250]
Savage, Robert C Woosnam - *1745: Charles Edward Stuart and the Jacobites*
    J Gov Info - v23 - S '96 - p647 [51-250]
Savage, Robert J, Jr. - *Irish Television*
    CR - v269 - N '96 - p270+ [501+]
Savage, Stephen - *Animals of the Desert*
    c BL - v93 - My 15 '97 - p1574 [51-250]
Animals of the Rain Forest
    c BL - v93 - My 15 '97 - p1574 [51-250]
Savageau, Cheryl - *Muskrat Will Be Swimming (Illus. by Robert Hynes)*
    c HB Guide - v8 - Spr '97 - p47 [51-250]
    c Nat Peop - v10 - Fall '96 - p79+ [501+]
    c SLJ - v42 - Ag '96 - p128+ [51-250]
    c Smith - v27 - N '96 - p173 [51-250]
Savage-Rumbaugh, Sue - *Kanzi: The Ape at the Brink of the Human Mind*
    NYTBR - v101 - D 1 '96 - p36 [51-250]
Savan, Leslie - *The Sponsored Life*
    J Am Cult - v19 - Spr '96 - p104 [51-250]
Savater, Fernando - *Idea De Nietzsche*
    Choice - v34 - D '96 - p566 [1-50]
Savel'yev, Alexsandr' G - *The Big Five*
    Parameters - v26 - Win '96 - p144+ [501+]
Save-Soderbergh, Torgny - *The Old Kingdom Cemetery at Hamara Dom*
    AJA - v101 - Ja '97 - p165+ [501+]

Savickas, Mark L - *Handbook of Career Counseling Theory and Practice*
    J Car P&E - v57 - Fall '96 - p19 [251-500]
    J Car P&E - v57 - Win '97 - p15+ [51-250]
Savigliano, Marta E - *Tango and the Political Economy of Passion*
    Col Lit - v23 - O '96 - p205+ [501+]
    TDR - v40 - Win '96 - p164+ [501+]
Saville, Carole - *Exotic Herbs*
    BL - v93 - Mr 15 '97 - p1217 [51-250]
    LJ - v122 - Mr 15 '97 - p80 [51-250]
Saville, Diana - *The Honey Makers*
    BL - v93 - Ja '97 - p822 [51-250]
    Books - v10 - Je '96 - p22 [1-50]
    KR - v64 - D 1 '96 - p1700 [251-500]
    PW - v244 - Ja 20 '97 - p395+ [51-250]
The Marriage Bed
    LJ - v121 - N 1 '96 - p132 [51-250]
Saving Biodiversity
    BioSci - v47 - Mr '97 - p195 [51-250]
Saving Places
    c Sch Lib - v44 - Ag '96 - p116 [51-250]
Saviotti, Paolo - *Technological Evolution, Variety and the Economy*
    JEL - v34 - D '96 - p2118 [51-250]
Technological Evolution, Variety, and the Economy
    R&R Bk N - v11 - N '96 - p24 [51-250]
Savitch, H V - *Regional Politics*
    Choice - v34 - F '97 - p1037 [51-250]
    NCR - v85 - Spr '96 - p64 [51-250]
    R&R Bk N - v11 - D '96 - p38 [51-250]
Savitt, William - *Global Development*
    r ARBA - v28 - '97 - p108 [251-500]
Savoie, Donald J - *Budgeting and the Management of Public Spending*
    JEL - v35 - Mr '97 - p227 [51-250]
    Pol Stud J - v24 - Sum '96 - p334 [51-250]
Savoie, Paul - *Amour Flou*
    FR - v70 - Mr '97 - p622 [251-500]
Savonarola, Girolamo - *Prison Meditations on Psalms 51 and 31*
    CH - v66 - Mr '97 - p193 [51-250]
    Ren Q - v49 - Win '96 - p860+ [501+]
Saw, Insawn - *Paul's Rhetoric in 1 Corinthians 15*
    Rel St Rev - v23 - Ja '97 - p73+ [51-250]
Sawada, Mitziko - *Tokyo Life, New York Dreams*
    Choice - v34 - Ap '97 - p1395 [51-250]
    JEL - v35 - Mr '97 - p264+ [51-250]
Sawday, Jonathan - *The Body Emblazoned*
    Six Ct J - v27 - Fall '96 - p918+ [501+]
Sawers, James R - *Process Industry Procedures and Training Manual*
    SciTech - v20 - S '96 - p46 [51-250]
Sawers, Larry - *The Other Argentina*
    HAHR - v76 - N '96 - p815+ [251-500]
Sawicki, Marianne - *Seeing the Lord*
    Rel St Rev - v22 - O '96 - p339 [51-250]
Sawicki, Stephen - *Animal Hospital*
    Ant R - v55 - Spr '97 - p234 [251-500]
    y BL - v93 - O 1 '96 - p312 [51-250]
    LJ - v121 - O 1 '96 - p114 [51-250]
Sawin, Martica - *Surrealism in Exile and the Beginning of the New York School*
    Art J - v56 - Spr '97 - p95+ [501+]
    L'Esprit - v36 - Win '96 - p98+ [251-500]
Sawislak, Karen - *Smoldering City*
    ASInt - v34 - O '96 - p119 [51-250]
    HRNB - v25 - Win '97 - p57+ [251-500]
Sawyer, Corinne Holt - *Murder Ole!*
    LJ - v122 - My 1 '97 - p144 [1-50]
    PW - v244 - Ap 21 '97 - p63 [51-250]
Sawyer, Donald T - *Electrochemistry for Chemists. 2nd Ed.*
    J Chem Ed - v73 - Je '96 - pA137 [51-250]
Sawyer, John F A - *The Fifth Gospel*
    Choice - v34 - N '96 - p477 [51-250]
Sawyer, John O - *A Manual of California Vegetation*
    Choice - v34 - N '96 - p483+ [51-250]
Sawyer, Linda C - *Polymer Microscopy. 2nd Ed.*
    Choice - v34 - Ja '97 - p823 [51-250]
Sawyer, Meryl - *Unforgettable*
    PW - v243 - D 16 '96 - p55 [51-250]
Sawyer, Ralph D - *The Art of the Warrior*
    PW - v243 - S 2 '96 - p127 [51-250]
Sawyer, Richard C - *To Make a Spotless Orange*
    R&R Bk N - v11 - D '96 - p70 [51-250]
Sawyer, Robert J - *Frameshift*
    KR - v65 - Mr 15 '97 - p424 [51-250]
    PW - v244 - Ap 21 '97 - p65 [51-250]
Starplex
    Quill & Q - v62 - O '96 - p42 [251-500]

The Terminal Experiment
    MFSF - v91 - O '96 - p61+ [501+]
Sawyer, Roger - *Spike Milligan: A Celebration*
    Books - v10 - Je '96 - p22 [1-50]
Sax, Richard - *Classic Home Desserts*
    SFR - v22 - Ja '97 - p48 [51-250]
Get in There and Cook
    PW - v244 - Ap 21 '97 - p66+ [51-250]
Saxon, Ro - *A Woman's Guide to Starting a Small Business*
    Aust Bk R - Je '96 - p67 [1-50]
Saxton, Josephine - *Gardening down a Rabbit Hole*
    TLS - N 1 '96 - p31 [51-250]
Saxton, Judith - *Harvest Moon*
    PW - v243 - N 25 '96 - p58 [51-250]
Saxton, Ruth - *Woolf and Lessing*
    RMR - v50 - 2 '96 - p169+ [501+]
Say, Allen - *Emma's Rug (Illus. by Allen Say)*
    c BL - v93 - O 1 '96 - p359+ [51-250]
    c CBRS - v25 - N '96 - p28 [1-50]
    c CCB-B - v50 - N '96 - p114 [51-250]
    c Ch BWatch - v6 - D '96 - p3 [51-250]
    c HB - v72 - S '96 - p587 [51-250]
    c HB Guide - v8 - Spr '97 - p47 [51-250]
    c KR - v64 - S 1 '96 - p1328 [51-250]
    c LATBR - D 8 '96 - p18 [51-250]
    c NYTBR - v102 - Ap 13 '97 - p27 [501+]
    c NYTLa - v146 - D 9 '96 - pC18 [51-250]
    c Par Ch - v20 - O '96 - p28 [51-250]
    c PW - v243 - S 9 '96 - p82 [51-250]
    c SLJ - v42 - S '96 - p190 [51-250]
Grandfather's Journey
    c Learning - v25 - Mr '97 - p54 [1-50]
    c New Ad - v9 - Fall '96 - p267+ [501+]
A River Dream
    c New Ad - v9 - Fall '96 - p309+ [501+]
Stranger in the Mirror (Illus. by Allen Say)
    c ECEJ - v23 - Sum '96 - p223 [51-250]
    c LA - v73 - S '96 - p355 [51-250]
Under the Cherry Blossom Tree (Illus. by Allen Say)
    c PW - v244 - F 24 '97 - p93 [51-250]
Sayavedra, Roberto - *El Domador De La Electricidad*
    y JAAL - v40 - S '96 - p77 [51-250]
Sayer, M D J - *Wrasse: Biology and Use in Aquaculture*
    SciTech - v20 - S '96 - p45 [51-250]
Sayer, Paul - *The God Child*
    Obs - O 27 '96 - p16* [1-50]
    TLS - O 25 '96 - p24 [501+]
Sayers, Dorothy L - *Busman's Honeymoon (Carmichael). Audio Version*
    LJ - v121 - O 1 '96 - p142 [51-250]
The Letters of Dorothy L. Sayers 1899-1936
    Arm Det - v29 - Sum '96 - p348 [251-500]
    VQR - v72 - Aut '96 - p124*+ [251-500]
Whose Body? (Case). Audio Version
    BL - v93 - Ja '97 - p879 [51-250]
Sayers, Valerie - *Brain Fever*
    CC - v113 - N 20 '96 - p1169 [51-250]
    NYTBR - v101 - D 8 '96 - p79 [1-50]
Sayler, James - *Presidents of the United States--Their Written Measure*
    r Choice - v34 - Ja '97 - p774 [51-250]
Saylor, Steven - *The House of the Vestals*
    PW - v244 - Ap 28 '97 - p53 [251-500]
A Murder on the Appian Way
    PW - v244 - Ap 14 '97 - p72 [1-50]
A Murder on the Appian Way (Harrison). Audio Version
    LJ - v121 - N 1 '96 - p121 [51-250]
Sayre, April Pulley - *Coral Reef*
    c Ch BWatch - v6 - D '96 - p6 [1-50]
    c SLJ - v43 - Ja '97 - p134+ [51-250]
If You Should Hear a Honey Guide (Illus. by S D Schindler)
    c RT - v50 - O '96 - p155 [51-250]
Lake and Pond
    c Ch BWatch - v6 - My '96 - p5 [1-50]
Ocean
    c Ch BWatch - v6 - D '96 - p6 [1-50]
    c SLJ - v43 - Ja '97 - p134+ [51-250]
River and Stream
    c Ch BWatch - v6 - My '96 - p5 [1-50]
Seashore
    c Ch BWatch - v6 - D '96 - p6 [1-50]
    c SB - v33 - Mr '97 - p50 [51-250]
    c SLJ - v43 - Ja '97 - p134+ [51-250]
Wetland
    c Ch BWatch - v6 - My '96 - p5 [1-50]
Sayre, James Kedzie - *North American Bird Folknames and Names*
    r Choice - v34 - O '96 - p307 [51-250]

Sayre, Kenneth M - *Plato's Literary Garden*
    Choice - v34 - S '96 - p142 [51-250]
Sayre, Nora - *Previous Convictions*
    Am - v175 - N 23 '96 - p27+ [501+]
    NYTBR - v101 - D 8 '96 - p92 [1-50]
Sixties Going on Seventies
    LATBR - Ag 4 '96 - p11 [51-250]
Saz, Sara M - *Strategies for Learning Spanish*
    MLJ - v81 - Spr '97 - p144+ [251-500]
SBC Communications - *American Images*
    BL - v93 - S 15 '96 - p198 [51-250]
    Choice - v34 - F '97 - p958 [51-250]
Sbragia, Albert - *Carlo Emilio Gadda and the Modern Macaronic*
    Choice - v34 - Ap '97 - p1344 [51-250]
Sbragia, Alberta M - *Debt Wish*
    Choice - v34 - Ja '97 - p847 [51-250]
    Pol Stud J - v24 - Aut '96 - p521 [51-250]
Scaasi, Arnold - *Scaasi: A Cut Above*
    LATBR - D 8 '96 - p30 [51-250]
    PW - v243 - O 14 '96 - p71 [51-250]
Scagell, Robin - *Space Explained*
    c BL - v93 - D 1 '96 - p658 [51-250]
    cr HB Guide - v8 - Spr '97 - p112 [51-250]
Scales, Peter C - *Growing Pains*
    Adoles - v31 - Win '96 - p996 [51-250]
Scalia, Antonin - *A Matter of Interpretation*
    ABA Jour - v83 - Ja '97 - p86 [501+]
    KR - v64 - N 1 '96 - p1592 [251-500]
    LJ - v122 - Ja '97 - p122+ [51-250]
    Nat - v264 - Ja 27 '97 - p25+ [501+]
    WSJ-Cent - v99 - F 4 '97 - pA17 [501+]
Scally, Robert James - *The End of Hidden Ireland*
    Albion - v28 - Sum '96 - p373+ [501+]
    Historian - v59 - Win '97 - p476+ [251-500]
    JIH - v27 - Aut '96 - p311+ [501+]
    J Soc H - v30 - Fall '96 - p299+ [501+]
Scalon, Cesare - *Produzione E Fruizione Del Libro Nel Basso Medioevo*
    Lib - v18 - D '96 - p361 [51-250]
Scamell, Ragnhild - *Buster's Echo (Illus. by Genevieve Webster)*
    c HB Guide - v7 - Fall '96 - p274 [51-250]
Who Likes Wolfie? (Illus. by Tim Warnes)
    c HB Guide - v7 - Fall '96 - p274 [51-250]
Scammell, G V - *The World Encompassed*
    Sea H - Aut '96 - p42 [51-250]
Scammell, Michael - *The Solzhenitsyn Files*
    Bks & Cult - v2 - Jl '96 - p6+ [501+]
    MA - v38 - Fall '96 - p398+ [501+]
Scanlan, Lawrence - *Heading Home*
    CF - v75 - D '96 - p42+ [501+]
    CG - v117 - Ja '97 - p74+ [501+]
Scanlon, Dick - *Does Freddy Dance*
    PW - v244 - Ja 27 '97 - p103 [1-50]
Scanlon, Jennifer - *American Women Historians 1700s-1990s*
    r ARBA - v28 - '97 - p190 [51-250]
    r BL - v93 - Ja '97 - p884 [51-250]
    r Choice - v34 - Ap '97 - p1314+ [51-250]
    r R&R Bk N - v12 - F '97 - p23 [51-250]
Scanlon, Larry - *Narrative, Authority, and Power*
    MLR - v92 - Ap '97 - p429+ [501+]
    RES - v47 - N '96 - p560+ [501+]
Scanlon, Thomas J - *Waiting for the Snow*
    BW - v27 - Mr 23 '97 - p8 [501+]
Scanlon, Tony - *A Mask of Stone*
    Aust Bk R - Je '96 - p52+ [501+]
Scannell, Vernon - *The Black and White Days*
    TLS - N 29 '96 - p11 [51-250]
Scanniello, Stephen - *A Year of Roses*
    BL - v93 - F 1 '97 - p917+ [51-250]
    PW - v244 - Ja 6 '97 - p69+ [51-250]
SCAR/IUCN Workshop on Antarctic Protected Areas (1992: Cambridge, England) - *Developing The Antarctic Protected Area System*
    GJ - v163 - Mr '97 - p106 [51-250]
Scarboro, Allen - *Living Witchcraft*
    J Am Cult - v18 - Win '95 - p101+ [251-500]
    J Am Cult - v19 - Spr '96 - p104+ [251-500]
Scarboro, Elizabeth - *Phoenix, Upside Down*
    c CBRS - v25 - S '96 - p8 [51-250]
    y Ch BWatch - v6 - O '96 - p3+ [51-250]
    c HB Guide - v8 - Spr '97 - p74 [51-250]
Scarborough, Elizabeth Ann - *Carol for Another Christmas*
    BWatch - v17 - D '96 - p2 [51-250]
    CC - v113 - D 11 '96 - p1233+ [51-250]
The Godmother
    y VOYA - v19 - D '96 - p266 [1-50]

The Godmother's Apprentice
  y Kliatt - v30 - N '96 - p16 [51-250]
  y VOYA - v19 - D '96 - p266 [1-50]
Scarborough, Kate - *My First Canadian Science Encyclopedia (Illus. by Teresa Foster)*
  cr BIC - v26 - Mr '97 - p33+ [251-500]
Scarborough, Sheryl - *Scary Howl of Fame*
  c Ch BWatch - v6 - My '96 - p7 [1-50]
Scarf, Maggie - *Intimate Worlds*
  Trib Bks - F 16 '97 - p8 [1-50]
Scarman, John - *Gardening with Old Roses*
  Hort - v94 - F '97 - p66 [251-500]
Scarre, Chris - *The Penguin Historical Atlas of Ancient Rome*
  r AJA - v101 - Ja '97 - p195+ [251-500]
Scarry, Richard - *Richard Scarry's Best Reading Program Ever. Electronic Media Version*
  c PW - v244 - Ja 27 '97 - p38 [51-250]
Richard Scarry's Pop-Up Colors (Illus. by Renee Jablow)
  c Ch BWatch - v6 - My '96 - p3 [51-250]
Richard Scarry's Pop-Up Numbers (Illus. by Renee Jablow)
  c Ch BWatch - v6 - My '96 - p3 [51-250]
Richard Scarry's Pop-Up Wheels (Illus. by Bruce Reifel)
  c PW - v244 - Mr 24 '97 - p85 [1-50]
Scavillo, Anthony - *Plaire Et Instruire*
  FR - v70 - Mr '97 - p637+ [501+]
Scavone, Daniel C - *Vampires*
  y SLJ - v42 - O '96 - p45 [1-50]
Schaaf, Fred - *Comet of the Century*
  Choice - v34 - My '97 - p1521+ [51-250]
  Nature - v386 - Mr 13 '97 - p140+ [501+]
  New Sci - v153 - Mr 22 '97 - p46 [1-50]
  NH - v106 - Mr '97 - p13 [1-50]
  S&T - v93 - F '97 - p56+ [501+]
Planetology: Comparing Other Worlds to Our Own
  y HB Guide - v8 - Spr '97 - p112 [51-250]
Schaap, Ella B - *Dutch Floral Tiles in the Golden Age and Their Botanical Prints*
  Am Craft - v56 - D '96 - p30 [51-250]
Schaap, James Calvin - *The Secrets of Barneveld Calvary*
  LJ - v122 - F 1 '97 - p68 [51-250]
Schabas, Ezra - *Sir Ernest MacMillan: The Importance of Being Canadian*
  Can Hist R - v77 - D '96 - p625+ [501+]
Schabas, William A - *The Death Penalty as Cruel Treatment and Torture*
  Choice - v34 - Mr '97 - p1232 [51-250]
  R&R Bk N - v12 - F '97 - p63 [51-250]
Schaberg, William H - *The Nietzsche Canon*
  r ARBA - v28 - '97 - p527 [51-250]
  CPR - v16 - Je '96 - p201+ [501+]
  r Lib - v19 - Mr '97 - p98 [51-250]
  Lon R Bks - v18 - S 19 '96 - p8+ [501+]
  r MLN - v111 - D '96 - p1022+ [501+]
  VQR - v72 - Aut '96 - p118* [501+]
Schachner, Judith Byron - *Willy and May (Illus. by Judith Byron Schachner)*
  c RT - v50 - N '96 - p258+ [51-250]
Schacht, Richard - *Making Sense of Nietzsche*
  RM - v50 - S '96 - p180+ [501+]
Schachter, A - *Le Sanctuaire Grec*
  CW - v89 - Jl '96 - p518+ [501+]
Schachter, Hindy Lauer - *Reinventing Government*
  Choice - v34 - My '97 - p1575 [51-250]
Schacter, Daniel L - *Memory Distortion*
  AJCH - v39 - Ja '97 - p227+ [501+]
  Choice - v34 - S '96 - p216 [51-250]
Searching for Memory
  Choice - v34 - D '96 - p693 [51-250]
  KR - v64 - My 1 '96 - p674 [251-500]
  NY - v72 - S 30 '96 - p87 [51-250]
  NYTBR - v101 - Jl 21 '96 - p12 [501+]
  NYTBR - v101 - D 8 '96 - p92 [1-50]
  Skeptic - v4 - 3 '96 - p107 [251-500]
Schad, John - *Dickens Refigured*
  Nine-C Lit - v51 - Mr '97 - p564 [51-250]
  R&R Bk N - v11 - N '96 - p70 [51-250]
Schade, Susan - *Toad Takes Off*
  c BL - v93 - My 1 '97 - p1505 [51-250]
Schade, Werner - *Kathe Kollwitz: Schmerz Und Schuld*
  BM - v138 - D '96 - p836 [51-250]
Schadler, Cherie D - *Welcome to Bayou Town! (Illus. by Ann Biedenharn Jones)*
  c HB Guide - v8 - Spr '97 - p47 [51-250]
Schadlich, Hans Joachim - *Mal Horen, Was Noch Kommt/Jetzt, Wo Alles Zu Spat Is*
  WLT - v71 - Win '97 - p138+ [501+]

Schaechter, Moselio - *In the Company of Mushrooms*
  BL - v93 - Ap 1 '97 - p1273 [51-250]
  CHE - v43 - Ap 25 '97 - pA17 [51-250]
  LJ - v122 - Ap 1 '97 - p119 [51-250]
  New Sci - v153 - Mr 8 '97 - p44 [51-250]
Schaefer, Carole Lexa - *The Squiggle (Illus. by Pierr Morgan)*
  c BL - v93 - Ja '97 - p768 [1-50]
  c BL - v93 - D 1 '96 - p653 [51-250]
  c BL - v93 - Ap 1 '97 - p1296 [1-50]
  c CCB-B - v50 - F '97 - p221+ [51-250]
  c HB Guide - v8 - Spr '97 - p47 [51-250]
  c KR - v64 - N 1 '96 - p1607 [51-250]
  c NYTBR - v102 - F 2 '97 - p18 [1-50]
  c PW - v243 - D 2 '96 - p59 [51-250]
  c SLJ - v42 - D '96 - p104+ [51-250]
Schaefer, Christina K - *The Center: A Guide to Genealogical Research in the National Capital Area*
  r ARBA - v28 - '97 - p166+ [51-250]
  r Choice - v34 - N '96 - p435+ [51-250]
  r NGSQ - v85 - Mr '97 - p73+ [501+]
Schaefer, Claudia - *Danger Zones*
  Choice - v34 - Mr '97 - p1169 [51-250]
Schaefer, Dennis - *Vintage Talk*
  LJ - v122 - Ap 1 '97 - p64 [1-50]
Schaefer, Jack - *Shane*
  J Am Cult - v19 - Spr '96 - p51+ [501+]
Schaefer, Stacy B - *People of the Peyote*
  Choice - v34 - Mr '97 - p1202 [51-250]
Schaefer, Ursula - *Schriftlichkeit Im Fruhen Mittelalter*
  MLR - v91 - Jl '96 - p682+ [501+]
Schaeffer, Frank - *Portofino: A Novel*
  y Kliatt - v31 - Ja '97 - p10 [51-250]
Schaeffer, Susan Fromberg - *The Golden Rope*
  KR - v64 - My 1 '96 - p632+ [251-500]
  LATBR - Ag 4 '96 - p10 [51-250]
  NYTBR - v101 - D 8 '96 - p80 [1-50]
  Rapport - v19 - 5 '96 - p37 [251-500]
Schafer, Christoph - *Das Simultaneum: Ein Staatskirchenrechtliches, Politisches Und Theologisches Problem Des Alten Reiches*
  CHR - v83 - Ja '97 - p109+ [251-500]
Schafer, Donald W - *Relieving Pain*
  AJCH - v39 - O '96 - p148+ [501+]
Schafer, Peter - *Gershom Scholem Zwischen Den Disziplinen*
  TLS - Jl 7 '96 - p10+ [501+]
Schaffer, Kay - *In the Wake of First Contact*
  TLS - Jl 19 '96 - p24 [501+]
Schaffer, William A - *ErgoWise: A Personal Guide to Making Your Workspace Comfortable and Safe*
  HR Mag - v41 - S '96 - p138 [51-250]
Schaffner, Bradley L - *Bibliography of the Soviet Union, Its Predecessors and Successors*
  r ARBA - v28 - '97 - p64+ [251-500]
Schaffner, Christina - *Cultural Functions of Translation*
  TranslRevS - v2 - D '96 - p13 [1-50]
Schagen, Sandie - *Financial Literacy in Adult Life*
  LAR - v98 - O '96 - p537 [1-50]
Sixth Form Options
  LAR - v99 - Ja '97 - p47 [1-50]
Schall, James V - *At the Limits of Political Philosophy*
  Choice - v34 - F '97 - p1034 [51-250]
  RP - v59 - Spr '97 - p381+ [501+]
Schalock, R L - *Outcome-Based Evaluation*
  AJMR - v101 - Ja '97 - p437+ [501+]
Schalow, Paul Gordon - *The Woman's Hand*
  Choice - v34 - Ap '97 - p1332 [51-250]
Schaltenbrand, Phil - *Stoneware of Southwestern Pennsylvania*
  JEL - v34 - S '96 - p1472 [51-250]
Schama, Simon - *Landscape and Memory*
  AHR - v101 - O '96 - p1178 [501+]
  HT - v46 - Ag '96 - p55+ [501+]
  Ken R - v19 - Win '97 - p153+ [501+]
  NYTBR - v102 - Ja 12 '97 - p32 [51-250]
  PW - v243 - S 30 '96 - p79 [1-50]
  Sew R - v104 - O '96 - pR81+ [501+]
Schami, Rafik - *The Crow Who Stood on His Beak (Illus. by Els Cools)*
  c HB Guide - v7 - Fall '96 - p274 [51-250]
  c JB - v60 - Ag '96 - p143 [51-250]
  c NYTBR - v101 - N 10 '96 - p51 [501+]
Damascus Nights
  TranslRevS - v1 - My '95 - p22 [1-50]

Fatima and the Dream Thief (Illus. by Els Cools)
  c BL - v93 - D 15 '96 - p734 [51-250]
  c CCB-B - v50 - F '97 - p222 [51-250]
  c HB Guide - v8 - Spr '97 - p47 [51-250]
  c KR - v64 - N 15 '96 - p1675 [51-250]
  c PW - v243 - D 2 '96 - p60 [51-250]
  c SLJ - v43 - Ja '97 - p90 [51-250]
Die Sehnsucht Fahrt Schwarz
  WLT - v70 - Aut '96 - p950+ [251-500]
Schamschula, Eleonore - *A Pioneer of American Folklore*
  Choice - v34 - Ap '97 - p1382 [51-250]
Schandorff, Esther Dech - *The Doctrine of the Holy Spirit. Vols. 1-2*
  r ARBA - v28 - '97 - p542 [51-250]
  r Choice - v34 - S '96 - p106 [51-250]
Schansberg, D Eric - *How Poor Government Policy Harms the Poor*
  Pol Stud J - v24 - Sum '96 - p334 [51-250]
Poor Policy
  ChrPhil - v8 - Je 13 '96 - p38 [51-250]
  JEL - v34 - D '96 - p2066 [51-250]
Schantz, Harvey L - *American Presidential Elections*
  Choice - v34 - N '96 - p536 [51-250]
Schaper, Joachim - *Eschatology in the Greek Psalter*
  Rel St Rev - v23 - Ap '97 - p195 [51-250]
Schaphorst, Richard - *Videoconferencing and Videotelephony*
  SciTech - v20 - N '96 - p10 [51-250]
Schapiro, Meyer - *Theory and Philosophy of Art*
  JAAC - v55 - Win '97 - p1+ [501+]
  JAAC - v55 - Win '97 - p16+ [501+]
Words, Script, and Pictures
  BL - v93 - S 15 '96 - p191 [51-250]
  New R - v215 - N 18 '96 - p42+ [501+]
Schar, Brigitte - *Esto No Pueder Ser! (Illus. by Jacky Gleich)*
  c BL - v93 - F 15 '97 - p1032 [1-50]
Scharf, Claus - *Katharina II, Deutschland, Und Die Deutschen*
  JMH - v69 - Mr '97 - p194+ [501+]
Scharf, Thomas - *International Perspectives on Community Care for Older People*
  R&R Bk N - v11 - D '96 - p43 [51-250]
Scharfen, John C - *The Dismal Battlefield*
  NWCR - v50 - Win '97 - p143+ [501+]
Scharff, Robert C - *Comte after Positivism*
  Isis - v87 - S '96 - p580+ [501+]
Scharfstein, Ben-Ami - *Amoral Politics*
  Ethics - v107 - O '96 - p182 [51-250]
Scharfstein, Sol - *Understanding Jewish History. Vol. 1*
  y BL - v93 - O 1 '96 - p333 [51-250]
  y SLJ - v43 - Ja '97 - p135 [51-250]
Scharlemann, Robert P - *The Reason of Following*
  Rel St Rev - v23 - Ja '97 - p32+ [501+]
Scharnhorst, Gary - *Bret Harte: A Bibliography*
  r Choice - v34 - O '96 - p258 [51-250]
Scharper, Stephen Bede - *Redeeming the Time*
  PW - v244 - My 12 '97 - p73 [51-250]
Schary, Philip B - *Managing the Global Supply Chain*
  JEL - v34 - S '96 - p1431 [51-250]
Schatt, Stan - *Understanding ATM*
  CBR - v14 - N '96 - p39 [51-250]
  SciTech - v20 - S '96 - p56 [51-250]
Schattkowsky, Ralph - *Deutschland Und Polen Von 1918/19 Bis 1925*
  Slav R - v55 - Sum '96 - p470 [251-500]
Schatzki, Thoedore R - *Social Practices*
  Choice - v34 - Mr '97 - p1176 [51-250]
Schaub, Diana J - *Erotic Liberalism*
  J Pol - v58 - Ag '96 - p895+ [501+]
  RP - v58 - Sum '96 - p629+ [501+]
Schauer, Frederick - *The Philosophy of Law*
  R&R Bk N - v11 - D '96 - p15 [51-250]
Schay, Geza - *Introduction to Linear Algebra*
  SciTech - v20 - D '96 - p15 [51-250]
Schebera, Jurgen - *Kurt Weill: An Illustrated Life*
  New R - v216 - Ja 27 '97 - p31+ [501+]
  TLS - S 13 '96 - p14+ [501+]
Schechter, Eric - *Handbook of Analysis and Its Foundations*
  SciTech - v21 - Mr '97 - p15 [51-250]
Schechter, Joel - *Satiric Impersonations*
  TDR - v40 - Fall '96 - p192+ [501+]
Scheck, Florian - *Electroweak and Strong Interactions. 2nd Ed.*
  Phys Today - v50 - F '97 - p67+ [501+]
Scheck, Ree S - *Costa Rica: A Natural Destination*
  r BL - v93 - S 15 '96 - p210 [1-50]
Schecter, Darrow - *Planets (Illus. by Tom LaPadula)*
  c SB - v32 - O '96 - p209 [51-250]

Schecter, Ellen - *The Big Idea (Illus. by Bob Dorsey)*
  c BL - v93 - Ja '97 - p862 [251-500]
  c HB Guide - v7 - Fall '96 - p297 [1-50]
The Pet-Sitters (Illus. by Bob Dorsey)
  c HB Guide - v8 - Spr '97 - p75 [1-50]
  c SLJ - v43 - Mr '97 - p162 [51-250]
Schecter, Stephen - *David and Jonathan*
  Quill & Q - v62 - Ag '96 - p36 [51-250]
Scheepers, Alfred - *A Survey of Bhuddist Thought*
  IPQ - v37 - Je '97 - p253 [51-250]
Scheese, Don - *Nature Writing*
  Choice - v34 - Ja '97 - p798 [51-250]
Scheffer, Victor B - *The Year of the Whale*
  Under Nat - v23 - 3 '96 - p29 [51-250]
Scheffler, Eben - *Suffering in Luke's Gospel*
  Rel St Rev - v23 - Ap '97 - p183 [51-250]
Scheffler, Ursel - *Rinaldo on the Run*
  c TES - N 22 '96 - p12* [51-250]
The Spy in the Attic (Illus. by Christa Unzner)
  c KR - v65 - Mr 1 '97 - p390 [51-250]
Schefter, James - *All Corvettes Are Red*
  BL - v93 - Ja '97 - p797 [51-250]
  KR - v64 - N 1 '96 - p1592 [251-500]
  LJ - v122 - Ja '97 - p140 [51-250]
  PW - v243 - N 18 '96 - p55 [51-250]
Schehr, Lawrence R - *Alcibiades at the Door*
  MLN - v111 - D '96 - p1059+ [251-500]
Scheible, Heinz - *Philipp Melanchthon: Eine Gestalt Der Reformationszeit*
  Six Ct J - v27 - Fall '96 - p869+ [501+]
Scheick, William J - *The Critical Response to H.G. Wells*
  Ext - v37 - Fall '96 - p279+ [501+]
Scheifele, Sigrid - *Projektionen Des Weiblichen*
  Ger Q - v69 - Spr '96 - p211+ [501+]
Scheifler, Robert W - *X Window System*
  R&R Bk N - v12 - F '97 - p92 [51-250]
Schein, Edgar - *Strategic Pragmatism*
  JEL - v34 - D '96 - p2085 [51-250]
Schein, Virginia E - *Working from the Margins*
  AAPSS-A - v550 - Mr '97 - p193+ [501+]
  ILRR - v50 - O '96 - p165+ [501+]
  NWSA Jnl - v8 - Sum '96 - p107+ [501+]
Scheinin, Martin - *International Human Rights Norms in the Nordic and Baltic Countries*
  R&R Bk N - v11 - D '96 - p52 [51-250]
Scheinin, Richard - *Field of Screams*
  Aethlon - v13 - Fall '95 - p179+ [251-500]
Schellenberg, James A - *Conflict Resolution*
  Choice - v34 - F '97 - p1045 [51-250]
  R&R Bk N - v12 - F '97 - p51 [51-250]
Scheller, Robert W - *Exemplum: Model-Book Drawings and the Practice of Artistic Transmission in the Middle Ages Ca. 900-Ca. 1470*
  Apo - v144 - O '96 - p59 [501+]
  r Specu - v72 - Ja '97 - p217+ [501+]
Schelling, Friedrich Wilhelm Joseph Von - *Schelling's Philosophy of Mythology and Revelation*
  Theol St - v58 - Mr '97 - p192+ [251-500]
Schemann, Hans - *German-English Dictionary of Idioms*
  r ARBA - v28 - '97 - p392 [51-250]
Schengili-Roberts, Keith - *The Advanced HTML Companion*
  r SciTech - v21 - Mr '97 - p8 [51-250]
Schenk, George - *Moss Gardening*
  BL - v93 - Ap 1 '97 - p1274 [51-250]
Schenk, Vladimir - *Earthquake Hazard and Risk*
  SciTech - v20 - D '96 - p28 [51-250]
Schenkel, Albert F - *The Rich Man and the Kingdom*
  JR - v77 - Ap '97 - p305+ [501+]
Schenkel, Michael - *Fortschritts- Und Modernitatskritik In Der DDR-Literatur*
  Ger Q - v69 - Fall '96 - p464+ [501+]
Schenker, Alexander M - *The Dawn of Slavic*
  Choice - v34 - D '96 - p621 [51-250]
  R&R Bk N - v11 - N '96 - p64 [51-250]
Scherbaum, Frank - *Of Poles and Zeros*
  SciTech - v20 - N '96 - p24 [51-250]
Scherer, Barrymore Laurence - *Bravo! A Guide to Opera for the Perplexed*
  y BL - v93 - D 1 '96 - p638 [51-250]
  LJ - v121 - N 15 '96 - p64 [51-250]
  PW - v243 - O 21 '96 - p66 [51-250]
Scherer, Frederic M - *Industry Structure, Strategy, and Public Policy*
  JEL - v34 - D '96 - p2081 [51-250]
Scherf, Beate D - *World Watch List for Domestic Animal Diversity. 2nd Ed.*
  r J Gov Info - v23 - S '96 - p671 [51-250]
Scherr, Barry J - *D.H. Lawrence's Response to Plato*
  R&R Bk N - v12 - F '97 - p86 [1-50]

Schertle, Alice - *Advice for a Frog (Illus. by Norman Green)*
  c LA - v73 - O '96 - p429 [51-250]
  c RT - v50 - O '96 - p157 [51-250]
Down the Road (Illus. by E B Lewis)
  c RT - v50 - S '96 - p58 [51-250]
Keepers (Illus. by Ted Rand)
  c CBRS - v25 - O '96 - p17 [51-250]
  c HB Guide - v8 - Spr '97 - p154 [51-250]
  c NYTBR - v102 - F 2 '97 - p18 [1-50]
  c SLJ - v42 - D '96 - p117 [51-250]
Scherzer, Julius - *Hydrocracking Science and Technology*
  SciTech - v20 - D '96 - p83 [51-250]
Schettino, John - *AppleScript Applications*
  SciTech - v21 - Mr '97 - p4 [51-250]
Schettkat, Ronald - *The Flow Analysis of Labour Markets*
  JEL - v35 - Mr '97 - p242 [51-250]
Scheub, Harold - *The Tongue Is Fire*
  NYTBR - v102 - Mr 2 '97 - p19 [51-250]
Scheuer, Larry - *Wabash County, Indiana Marriages 1835-1899*
  r EGH - v50 - N '96 - p166 [51-250]
Schevill, Margot Blum - *The Maya Textile Tradition*
  PW - v244 - Ap 21 '97 - p57 [51-250]
Schewe, Manfred - *Towards Drama as Method in the Foreign Language Classroom*
  MLJ - v80 - Fall '96 - p404+ [501+]
Schezen, Roberto - *Adolf Loos: Architecture 1903-1932*
  TLS - N 8 '96 - p32 [251-500]
Schianchi, Lucia Fornari - *I Farnese: Arte E Collezionismo*
  Choice - v34 - D '96 - p570 [1-50]
Schiavetti, Nicholas - *Evaluating Research in Communicative Disorders. 3rd Ed.*
  SciTech - v20 - D '96 - p44 [1-50]
Schiavo, Mary - *Flying Blind, Flying Safe*
  Bus W - Ap 14 '97 - p15+ [501+]
Schick, Eleanor - *My Navajo Sister (Illus. by Eleanor Schick)*
  c BL - v93 - D 1 '96 - p669 [51-250]
  c CBRS - v25 - F '97 - p78 [51-250]
  c HB Guide - v8 - Spr '97 - p47 [51-250]
  c SLJ - v42 - D '96 - p105 [51-250]
Schick, Friedrike - *Hegels Wissenschaft Der Logik*
  RM - v49 - Je '96 - p944+ [501+]
Schick, Kathy D - *Making Silent Stones*
  Reason - v28 - D '96 - p38 [51-250]
Schick, Robert D - *Classical Music Criticism*
  ON - v61 - O '96 - p66 [51-250]
  R&R Bk N - v11 - D '96 - p56 [51-250]
Schickel, Richard - *Clint Eastwood: A Biography*
  BL - v93 - N 1 '96 - p458 [51-250]
  Ent W - N 22 '96 - p127+ [501+]
  KR - v64 - O 1 '96 - p1451+ [251-500]
  LATBR - D 22 '96 - p4 [501+]
  LJ - v121 - O 15 '96 - p60+ [51-250]
  NYTBR - v101 - D 1 '96 - p11+ [501+]
  NYTLa - v146 - N 26 '96 - pC15 [501+]
  Obs - D 15 '96 - p16* [501+]
  PW - v243 - S 30 '96 - p68 [51-250]
  Spec - v278 - F 1 '97 - p31 [501+]
  Time - v148 - D 2 '96 - p89 [51-250]
Schickele, Peter - *The Definitive Biography of P.D.Q. Bach (Schickele). Audio Version*
  BL - v93 - Ja '97 - p879 [51-250]
  y Kliatt - v30 - N '96 - p38 [51-250]
  PW - v243 - S 2 '96 - p48 [51-250]
Schiebinger, Londa - *Nature's Body*
  Isis - v87 - D '96 - p730+ [501+]
Schiechtl, Hugo M - *Ground Bioengineering Techniques for Slope Protection and Erosion Control*
  SciTech - v21 - Mr '97 - p80 [51-250]
Schields, Gretchen - *Cantsee: The Cat Who Was the Color of the Carpet (Illus. by Gretchen Schields)*
  c HB Guide - v8 - Spr '97 - p60 [51-250]
  c KR - v64 - Ag 15 '96 - p1242 [51-250]
  c SLJ - v42 - O '96 - p40 [51-250]
Schiff, Benjamin N - *Refugees unto the Third Generation*
  MEJ - v50 - Sum '96 - p438+ [501+]
Schiff, James A - *Understanding Reynolds Price*
  BL - v93 - F 1 '97 - p921 [51-250]
Schiff, Michel - *The Memory of Water*
  TLS - N 8 '96 - p31 [501+]
Schiffer, Michael Brian - *Taking Charge*
  J Am Cult - v19 - Spr '96 - p112+ [501+]
  NYRB - v43 - N 28 '96 - p32+ [501+]
  T&C - v37 - Ap '96 - p379+ [501+]
Schiffer, Nancy N - *Silver Jewelry Designs*
  Ant & CM - v101 - F '97 - p33 [51-250]

Schiffman, Lawrence H - *Reclaiming the Dead Sea Scrolls*
  Rel St Rev - v22 - O '96 - p351 [51-250]
Schiffmann, Erich - *Yoga: The Spirit and Practice of Moving into Stillness*
  y BL - v93 - N 15 '96 - p552+ [51-250]
Schifftner, Kenneth C - *Wet Scrubbers. 2nd Ed.*
  SciTech - v20 - N '96 - p79 [51-250]
Schild, Georg - *Between Ideology and Realpolitik*
  Slav R - v55 - Sum '96 - p487+ [501+]
Schildkraut, Joseph - *Depression and the Spiritual in Modern Art*
  New Sci - v152 - O 19 '96 - p48 [1-50]
Schildt, Axel - *Moderne Zeiten*
  CEH - v29 - 2 '96 - p280+ [501+]
Schilit, W Keith - *Fitzroy Dearborn International Directory of Venture Capital Funds. 2nd Ed.*
  r ARBA - v28 - '97 - p90 [251-500]
  r Choice - v34 - Ap '97 - p1307 [51-250]
  r R&R Bk N - v12 - F '97 - p49 [51-250]
Schillebeeckx, Edward - *The Language of Faith*
  Theol St - v57 - Je '96 - p361+ [501+]
Schiller, Dan - *Theorizing Communication*
  Choice - v34 - F '97 - p959+ [51-250]
Schiller, David - *Aromatherapy for Mind and Body*
  Quill & Q - v62 - Ag '96 - p32 [51-250]
Schiller, Gerald A - *Deadly Dreams*
  KR - v64 - Ag 15 '96 - p1195 [51-250]
Schiller, Herbert M - *Sumter Is Avenged*
  Sm Pr R - v29 - Ja '97 - p4 [51-250]
Schiller, Lawrence - *American Tragedy*
  BL - v93 - N 1 '96 - p459 [1-50]
  BW - v26 - N 3 '96 - p5 [501+]
  CSM - v88 - N 7 '96 - p14 [51-250]
  Ent W - N 1 '96 - p64 [51-250]
  New R - v215 - D 9 '96 - p27+ [501+]
  NYTBR - v101 - N 10 '96 - p16+ [501+]
  NYTBR - v101 - D 8 '96 - p84 [1-50]
  NYTLa - v146 - O 16 '96 - pC17 [501+]
  WSJ-MW - v78 - O 24 '96 - pA16 [51-250]
Schilling, Sabine Maja - *Ewald Matare, Das Plastische Werk. 2nd Ed.*
  r BM - v138 - D '96 - p835 [501+]
Schilsky, Richard L - *Principles of Antineoplastic Drug Development and Pharmacology*
  SciTech - v20 - N '96 - p40 [51-250]
Schimel, Lawrence - *Food for Life--and Other Dish*
  Advocate - D 10 '96 - p81+ [251-500]
Schimmel, Annemarie - *Deciphering the Signs of God*
  JAAR - v64 - Fall '96 - p672+ [501+]
Islamic Names
  Names - v44 - Je '96 - p138+ [501+]
Schimpky, David - *Children's Clothing of the 1800s (Illus. by Barb Bedell)*
  c Can CL - v22 - Fall '96 - p115+ [501+]
Schindler, Anton Felix - *Beethoven as I Knew Him*
  M Ed J - v83 - Mr '97 - p43+ [51-250]
Schindler, Emilie - *Memorias*
  BL - v93 - Mr 15 '97 - p1232 [1-50]
Schindler, Esther - *The Computer Speech Book*
  Choice - v34 - O '96 - p316 [51-250]
Schindler, Stephan K - *Das Subjekt Als Kind*
  Ger Q - v69 - Fall '96 - p442+ [501+]
Schine, Cathleen - *The Birdhouse*
  Trib Bks - Ja 19 '97 - p8 [1-50]
The Love Letter
  NYTBR - v101 - Ag 25 '96 - p28 [51-250]
  SFR - v21 - N '96 - p48 [1-50]
Rameau's Niece
  SFR - v21 - S '96 - p48 [1-50]
Schinharl, Cornelia - *Vegetarian Cooking of the Mediterranean*
  y Kliatt - v31 - My '97 - p31 [51-250]
Schink, Christopher - *Color and Light for the Watercolor Painter*
  A Art - v60 - Jl '96 - p80 [51-250]
Schinto, Jeanne - *Show Me a Hero*
  Aethlon - v13 - Spr '96 - p198 [501+]
Virtually Now
  y Kliatt - v31 - Mr '97 - p21 [51-250]
  LJ - v121 - O 15 '96 - p92 [51-250]
  PW - v243 - O 14 '96 - p80 [51-250]
Schipperges, Heinrich - *Hildegard of Bingen: Healing and the Nature of the Cosmos*
  LJ - v122 - My 1 '97 - p110 [51-250]
  PW - v244 - My 12 '97 - p73 [51-250]
Schirmacher, Wolfgang - *German Essays on Science in the 19th Century*
  SciTech - v20 - D '96 - p3 [51-250]
  TranslRevS - v2 - D '96 - p2 [51-250]

German Essays on Science in the 20th Century
SciTech - v20 - D '96 - p22 [1-50]
TranslRevS - v2 - D '96 - p2 [51-250]
Schirmer, Lothar - *Marlon Brando: Portraits and Film Stills 1946-1995*
BL - v93 - S 1 '96 - p52 [251-500]
LATBR - S 22 '96 - p14 [51-250]
Schirmer, Peter - *Farms, Factories and Free Trade*
J Gov Info - v23 - S '96 - p584 [51-250]
Schiro, Michael - *Integrating Children's Literature and Mathematics in the Classroom*
Cur R - v36 - Ap '97 - p3* [51-250]
Schissel, Marvin J - *The Whole Tooth*
BL - v93 - F 1 '97 - p917 [51-250]
Schjeldahl, Peter - *Columns and Catalogues*
BM - v138 - O '96 - p700 [251-500]
Schlag, Evelyn - *Unsichtbare Frauen*
WLT - v70 - Sum '96 - p684+ [501+]
Schlag, Pierre - *Laying Down the Law*
Choice - v34 - My '97 - p1575 [51-250]
Schlagel, Richard H - *From Myth to Modern Mind. Vol. 1*
Rel St Rev - v23 - Ja '97 - p45 [51-250]
From Myth to Modern Mind. Vol. 2
SciTech - v20 - S '96 - p2 [51-250]
Schlam, Carl C - *The Metamorphoses of Apuleius*
CW - v89 - Jl '96 - p498+ [251-500]
Schlanger, Jeff - *Maija Grotell: Works Which Grow from Belief*
Am Craft - v56 - D '96 - p29 [51-250]
Ceram Mo - v44 - N '96 - p28 [51-250]
Schlapfer-Geiser, Susanne - *Scherenschnitte: Designs and Techniques for Traditional Papercutting*
BL - v93 - Ap 1 '97 - p1275+ [51-250]
Schlappi, Elizabeth - *Roy Acuff: The Smoky Mountain Boy. 2nd Ed.*
LJ - v121 - N 1 '96 - p42 [1-50]
Schlechty, Phillip C - *Inventing Better Schools*
H Sch M - v4 - Mr '97 - p56 [51-250]
LJ - v122 - Ap 1 '97 - p104 [51-250]
Schlee, Ann - *The Time in Aderra*
TLS - F 14 '97 - p23 [251-500]
Schlegel, Dorothea Von - *Florentin: Roman, Fragmente, Varianten*
Ger Q - v69 - Spr '96 - p144+ [501+]
Schlegel, Friedrich - *Uber Die Sprache Und Weisheit Der Indier*
Ger Q - v69 - Sum '96 - p260+ [501+]
Schlegel, John Henry - *American Legal Realism and Empirical Social Science*
AHR - v101 - O '96 - p1302+ [501+]
Schleichert, Elizabeth - *Marijuana*
y HB Guide - v7 - Fall '96 - p317+ [51-250]
Schleiermacher, Friedrich - *On Religion*
Rel St Rev - v22 - O '96 - p334+ [51-250]
On What Gives Value to Life
Rel St Rev - v23 - Ap '97 - p152+ [51-250]
Schleifer, Jay - *The Dangers of Hazing*
y SLJ - v43 - Ja '97 - p134 [51-250]
Daytona: Thunder at the Beach!
y Emerg Lib - v24 - S '96 - p26 [1-50]
A Student's Guide to Jewish American Genealogy
yr SLJ - v43 - Ja '97 - p135 [51-250]
Thunderbird: Ford's High Flier
y SLJ - v42 - O '96 - p45 [1-50]
Schleifer, Martha Furman - *Women Composers. Vol. 1*
r Choice - v34 - N '96 - p438+ [51-250]
r M Ed J - v83 - S '96 - p58 [51-250]
Women Composers. Vols. 1-2
r ARBA - v28 - '97 - p478+ [501+]
Schleimer, Robert P - *Inhaled Glucocorticoids in Asthma*
SciTech - v20 - D '96 - p46 [51-250]
Schlein, Miriam - *More than One (Illus. by Donald Crews)*
c BL - v93 - N 1 '96 - p505 [51-250]
c CCB-B - v50 - Ja '97 - p185 [51-250]
c HB Guide - v8 - Spr '97 - p111 [51-250]
c KR - v64 - S 15 '96 - p1407 [51-250]
c Learning - v25 - Ja '97 - p56 [1-50]
c PW - v243 - O 7 '96 - p75 [51-250]
c SLJ - v42 - D '96 - p117 [51-250]
The Puzzle of the Dinosaur-Bird (Illus. by Mark Hallett)
c HB - v73 - Ja '97 - p79 [51-250]
c HB Guide - v8 - Spr '97 - p115 [51-250]
c KR - v64 - N 1 '96 - p1607 [51-250]
c SLJ - v42 - S '96 - p220 [51-250]
Schleiner, Louise - *Tudor and Stuart Women Writers*
NAR - v281 - S '96 - p45+ [501+]
Ren & Ref - v20 - Win '96 - p87+ [501+]

Schleiner, Winfried - *Medical Ethics in the Renaissance*
Hast Cen R - v26 - Mr '96 - p49 [1-50]
Isis - v87 - D '96 - p722+ [501+]
Six Ct J - v27 - Win '96 - p1142+ [501+]
Schleissner, Margaret R - *Manuscript Sources of Medieval Medicine*
Isis - v87 - D '96 - p721+ [501+]
Schlenther, Elizabeth - *Reading Therapy for Children. Vol. 2*
r Sch Lib - v44 - N '96 - p178 [51-250]
Schlesinger, Chris - *License to Grill*
PW - v244 - Mr 24 '97 - p77 [51-250]
Schlesinger, Jacob M - *Shadow Shoguns*
Bus W - My 19 '97 - p18+ [501+]
KR - v65 - Mr 1 '97 - p366 [251-500]
LJ - v122 - My 1 '97 - p126 [51-250]
PW - v244 - Mr 31 '97 - p50+ [51-250]
Schlesinger, Sarah - *500 Low-Fat and Fat-Free Pasta, Rice, and Grain Recipes*
BL - v93 - Ja '97 - p802 [51-250]
LJ - v122 - F 15 '97 - p158+ [51-250]
PW - v243 - D 16 '96 - p57 [51-250]
Schlesinger, William H - *Biogeochemistry: An Analysis of Global Change. 2nd Ed.*
Nature - v386 - Ap 10 '97 - p567 [1-50]
Schlessinger, Bernard S - *The Who's Who of Nobel Prize Winners 1901-1995. 3rd Ed.*
r ARBA - v28 - '97 - p16 [51-250]
r Choice - v34 - D '96 - p596 [51-250]
r R&R Bk N - v11 - N '96 - p1 [51-250]
Schlessinger, Laura - *How Could You Do That?*
Skeptic - v4 - 2 '96 - p106 [501+]
Schlink, Bernhard - *Der Vorleser*
WLT - v70 - Aut '96 - p951 [501+]
Schlogel, Karl - *Der Grosse Exodus*
Slav R - v55 - Sum '96 - p495+ [251-500]
Schlossberg, Terry - *Not My Own*
Rel St Rev - v22 - O '96 - p341+ [51-250]
TT - v53 - O '96 - p394+ [251-500]
Schlosser, Johann Aloys - *Beethoven: The First Biography*
FF - v20 - S '96 - p471 [251-500]
Schluchter, Wolfgang - *Paradoxes of Modernity*
APSR - v90 - D '96 - p896+ [501+]
Choice - v34 - S '96 - p220 [51-250]
Hist & T - v36 - F '97 - p110+ [251-500]
Schlueter, June - *Two Gentlemen of Verona*
Choice - v34 - S '96 - p130 [51-250]
Schmalleger, Frank - *Criminal Justice. 2nd Ed.*
R&R Bk N - v12 - F '97 - p58 [51-250]
Criminal Justice Today. 4th Ed.
R&R Bk N - v12 - F '97 - p58 [51-250]
Schmaus, Warren - *Durkheim's Philosophy of Science and the Sociology of Knowledge*
Isis - v87 - D '96 - p743+ [251-500]
Schmeelk, John - *Elementary Analysis through Examples and Exercises*
Choice - v34 - N '96 - p496 [51-250]
Schmeling, Gareth - *The Novel in the Ancient World*
R&R Bk N - v12 - F '97 - p77 [51-250]
Schmid, Armin - *Lost in a Labyrinth of Red Tape*
KR - v64 - My 1 '96 - p675 [251-500]
TranslRevS - v2 - D '96 - p16+ [51-250]
Schmid, Eleonore - *The Squirrel and the Moon (Illus. by Eleonore Schmid)*
c Ch BWatch - v6 - Jl '96 - p4 [1-50]
c HB Guide - v7 - Fall '96 - p274+ [51-250]
c SLJ - v42 - S '96 - p190+ [51-250]
Schmid, Estella - *Anthology of Contemporary Kurdish Poetry*
WLT - v70 - Sum '96 - p753+ [501+]
Schmidgall, Gary - *The Stranger Wilde*
Nine-C Lit - v51 - D '96 - p415+ [501+]
Schmidheiny, Stephan - *Financing Change*
Econ - v339 - My 18 '96 - p12* [51-250]
Env - v39 - Mr '97 - p25 [251-500]
JEL - v34 - S '96 - p1435+ [51-250]
JEL - v34 - D '96 - p1974+ [501+]
Schmidlin, Thomas W - *Thunder in the Heartland*
Choice - v34 - F '97 - p1002 [51-250]
R&R Bk N - v12 - F '97 - p93 [1-50]
Schmidt, Alejandro - *El Astronomo Que Perdio La Nariz*
y JAAL - v40 - S '96 - p77 [51-250]
Schmidt, Alvin J - *The Menace of Multiculturalism*
y BL - v93 - F 15 '97 - p981+ [51-250]
WSJ-Cent - v99 - Mr 24 '97 - pA16 [501+]
Schmidt, Arno - *The Collected Stories of Arno Schmidt*
BL - v93 - N 1 '96 - p482 [51-250]
KR - v64 - N 15 '96 - p1632 [51-250]
NYTBR - v102 - Ja 26 '97 - p18 [51-250]

Schmidt, Carl B - *The Livrets of Jean-Baptiste Lully's Tragedies Lyriques*
r Notes - v53 - D '96 - p455+ [501+]
The Music of Francis Poulenc 1899-1963
r ARBA - v28 - '97 - p477 [51-250]
Notes - v53 - Mr '97 - p807+ [501+]
Schmidt, Christian - *Uncertainty in Economic Thought*
JEL - v34 - D '96 - p2013 [51-250]
Schmidt, Frederick W, Jr. - *A Still Small Voice*
CC - v113 - N 6 '96 - p1085+ [501+]
Theol St - v58 - Mr '97 - p197 [251-500]
Schmidt, Gary D - *The Sin Eater*
y BL - v93 - N 1 '96 - p491 [51-250]
y BL - v93 - Ap 1 '97 - p1294 [1-50]
c CBRS - v25 - Win '97 - p70+ [51-250]
y CCB-B - v50 - N '96 - p114 [51-250]
y HB Guide - v8 - Spr '97 - p84 [51-250]
c KR - v64 - S 1 '96 - p1328 [51-250]
c PW - v243 - O 14 '96 - p84 [51-250]
y SLJ - v43 - Ja '97 - p116 [51-250]
Schmidt, George - *Der Dreissigjahrige Krieg*
Six Ct J - v27 - Fall '96 - p795+ [501+]
Schmidt, J D - *Within the Human Realm*
Ch Rev Int - v3 - Fall '96 - p305+ [501+]
Schmidt, Klaus, 1943- - *Dynamical Systems of Algebraic Origin*
SIAM Rev - v39 - Mr '97 - p146+ [501+]
Schmidt, Klaus H - *Blurred Boundaries*
Nine-C Lit - v51 - Mr '97 - p564+ [51-250]
R&R Bk N - v12 - F '97 - p87 [51-250]
Schmidt, Leigh Eric - *Consumer Rites*
ACI - v8 - Fall '96 - p33+ [501+]
CH - v65 - D '96 - p791+ [501+]
RAH - v24 - D '96 - p668+ [501+]
Rel St Rev - v23 - Ja '97 - p93 [51-250]
Holy Fairs
JR - v77 - Ap '97 - p268+ [501+]
Schmidt, Michael - *Selected Poems 1972-1997*
Obs - Mr 2 '97 - p18* [51-250]
Schmidt, Nelly - *Victor Schoelcher Et L'Abolition De L'Esclavage*
EHR - v112 - F '97 - p232 [251-500]
Schmidt, Norman - *Super Paper Flyers Book and Kit*
c LATBR - v263 - S 29 '96 - p15 [51-250]
Schmidt, Paul, 1934- - *Meyerhold at Work*
Am Theat - v14 - Ja '97 - p74 [51-250]
TranslRevS - v2 - D '96 - p9 [51-250]
Schmidt, Paul Gerhard - *Die Frau In Der Renaissance*
Six Ct J - v27 - Fall '96 - p857+ [501+]
Schmidt, Peter R - *The Culture and Technology of African Iron Production*
Choice - v34 - O '96 - p322 [51-250]
Plundering Africa's Past
New Sci - v152 - D 21 '96 - p75 [51-250]
Schmidt, Stanley - *Aliens and Alien Societies*
MFSF - v91 - S '96 - p44+ [251-500]
Schmidt, Steve - *Shock Compression of Condensed Matter 1995. Pts. 1-2*
SciTech - v20 - D '96 - p62 [51-250]
Schmidt, Vivien A - *From State to Market?*
Choice - v34 - D '96 - p684 [51-250]
JEL - v35 - Mr '97 - p288 [51-250]
Schmidt, Werner - *Kokoschka Und Dresden*
BM - v139 - Ja '97 - p64+ [501+]
Schmidt-Dengler, Wendelin - *Literaturgeschichte Osterreich*
Ger Q - v69 - Sum '96 - p340+ [501+]
Schmidt-Krayer, Barbara - *Kontinuum Der Reflexion*
MLR - v91 - Jl '96 - p791+ [501+]
Schmidt-Nielsen, Knut - *Animal Physiology. 5th Ed.*
Nature - v386 - Ap 10 '97 - p567 [1-50]
Schmidtz, David - *Rational Choice and Moral Agency*
CPR - v16 - Ap '96 - p135+ [501+]
Schmiechen, Peter - *Christ the Reconciler*
CC - v113 - D 18 '96 - p1261 [51-250]
Schmiedebach, Heinz-Peter - *Robert Remak 1815-1865*
Isis - v87 - D '96 - p739 [501+]
Schmieder, Robert W - *Rocas Alijos*
SciTech - v20 - D '96 - p29 [51-250]
Schmitt, Carl - *The Concept of the Political*
TranslRevS - v2 - D '96 - p12+ [51-250]
The Leviathan in the State Theory of Thomas Hobbes
R&R Bk N - v12 - F '97 - p58 [1-50]
Schmitt, Evmarie - *Cezanne in Provence*
BM - v138 - S '96 - p612+ [501+]
Schmitt, Miriam - *Medieval Women Monastics*
RR - v56 - Ja '97 - p106 [51-250]
Schmitz, Andrew - *Regulation and Protectionism under GATT*
JEL - v34 - S '96 - p1495 [51-250]

Schmitz, Christopher J - *The Growth of Big Business in the United States and Western Europe 1850-1939*
  JEL - v34 - D '96 - p2106 [51-250]
Schmitz, Susanne - *Race and Gender Discrimination across Urban Labor Markets*
  R&R Bk N - v11 - D '96 - p30 [51-250]
Schmookler, Andrew Bard - *Living Posthumously*
  BL - v93 - Ja '97 - p799 [51-250]
  PW - v243 - N 25 '96 - p61 [51-250]
  Utne R - Ja '97 - p96 [1-50]
Schmugge, Ludwig - *Kirche, Kinder, Karrieren*
  AHR - v102 - F '97 - p98 [501+]
Schnapp, Alain - *The Discovery of the Past*
  KR - v65 - F 15 '97 - p285+ [251-500]
  Nature - v383 - O 31 '96 - p775 [51-250]
  NS - v125 - O 18 '96 - p42 [1-50]
  PW - v244 - F 24 '97 - p75 [51-250]
Schnapp, Jeffrey T - *Staging Fascism*
  Choice - v34 - F '97 - p976 [51-250]
Schnarr, Grant R - *Return to the Promised Land*
  PW - v244 - Mr 10 '97 - p62+ [51-250]
Schnauber, Cornelius - *Placido Domingo*
  PW - v244 - Ap 21 '97 - p53 [51-250]
Schneck, Marcus - *Your Backyard Wildlife Garden*
  LJ - v121 - D '96 - p66 [1-50]
Schneerson, Menachem M - *Torah Studies. Rev. Ed.*
  PW - v243 - S 30 '96 - p77 [51-250]
Schneider, A Gregory - *The Way of the Cross Leads Home*
  CHR - v83 - Ja '97 - p134+ [251-500]
Schneider, Antonie - *The Birthday Bear (Illus. by Uli Waas)*
  c HB Guide - v8 - Spr '97 - p60 [51-250]
  c SLJ - v42 - D '96 - p105 [51-250]
Schneider, Bart - *Race: An Anthology in the First Person*
  BL - v93 - Ja '97 - p808 [1-50]
  y BL - v93 - N 1 '96 - p463 [251-500]
  y Kliatt - v31 - My '97 - p20 [51-250]
  LJ - v122 - Ja '97 - p128 [51-250]
  PW - v243 - D 9 '96 - p53 [51-250]
Schneider, Beth E - *Women Resisting AIDS*
  CS - v26 - Ja '97 - p113+ [501+]
Schneider, Carl D - *Shame, Exposure, and Privacy*
  Bks & Cult - v2 - Mr '96 - p3+ [501+]
Schneider, Cathy Lisa - *Shantytown Protest in Pinochet's Chile*
  CS - v25 - N '96 - p766+ [501+]
Schneider, David M - *Schneider on Schneider*
  Am Ethnol - v24 - F '97 - p208+ [501+]
Schneider, Edward L - *Handbook of the Biology of Aging. 4th Ed.*
  SciTech - v20 - N '96 - p31 [51-250]
Schneider, Gerald - *Towards a New Europe*
  APSR - v90 - S '96 - p705+ [501+]
Schneider, Gertrude - *Exile and Destruction*
  Historian - v58 - Sum '96 - p917+ [251-500]
Schneider, Harry - *Schweizer Theologen Im Zarenreich 1700-1917*
  Slav R - v55 - Sum '96 - p481+ [501+]
Schneider, Ira - *Video Art*
  Afterimage - v24 - N '96 - p4 [1-50]
Schneider, Jane C - *Festival of the Poor*
  Choice - v34 - D '96 - p651 [51-250]
Schneider, Jeremy - *JavaScript for the World Wide Web*
  LJ - v122 - My 1 '97 - p132 [1-50]
Schneider, Jerome - *The Complete Guide to Offshore Money Havens*
  r Kiplinger - v51 - Ja '97 - p44+ [501+]
Schneider, Mark - *Boston Confronts Jim Crow 1890-1920*
  LJ - v122 - F 15 '97 - p147 [51-250]
  PW - v244 - Ap 7 '97 - p80+ [51-250]
Schneider, Matthew - *Original Ambivalence*
  Nine-C Lit - v51 - S '96 - p277 [51-250]
Schneider, Mical - *Between the Dragon and the Eagle*
  c BL - v93 - F 1 '97 - p942 [51-250]
  c CCB-B - v50 - Mr '97 - p257 [51-250]
  y KR - v65 - Ja 1 '97 - p64 [51-250]
Schneider, Michael - *J.A. Hobson*
  TLS - Ja 17 '97 - p28 [501+]
Schneider, Moti - *Fuzzy Expert Systems Tools*
  SciTech - v21 - Mr '97 - p9 [51-250]
Schneider, Paul - *The Adirondacks: A History of America's First Wilderness*
  KR - v65 - Mr 15 '97 - p448+ [251-500]
  LJ - v122 - My 1 '97 - p129 [51-250]
  PW - v244 - Ap 28 '97 - p63 [251-500]
Schneider, Paul G - *The Mystery of the Acts of John*
  Rel St Rev - v22 - O '96 - p351 [51-250]

Schneider, Peter - *Couplings*
  BL - v93 - S 15 '96 - p222 [51-250]
  LATBR - S 22 '96 - p2 [501+]
  LJ - v121 - N 1 '96 - p108 [51-250]
  NYTBR - v101 - S 22 '96 - p17 [501+]
Schneider, R M - *Add It, Dip It, Fix It*
  c Inst - v106 - Ag '96 - p42+ [1-50]
Schneider, Richard C - *African American History in the Press 1851-1899. Vols. 1-2*
  yr ARBA - v28 - '97 - p190 [51-250]
  r BL - v93 - Ja '97 - p880+ [251-500]
  r LJ - v121 - N 15 '96 - p72 [51-250]
Schneider, Richard J - *Approaches to Teaching Thoreau's Walden and Other Works*
  Nine-C Lit - v51 - Mr '97 - p565 [1-50]
Schneider, Robert, 1961- - *Brother of Sleep*
  Obs - N 24 '96 - p16* [51-250]
Schneider, Robert Alan - *The Ceremonial City*
  AHR - v101 - O '96 - p1219+ [501+]
  CH - v65 - D '96 - p723+ [501+]
  JMH - v68 - D '96 - p993+ [501+]
Schneider, Robert R - *Government and the Economy on the Amazon Frontier*
  J Gov Info - v23 - S '96 - p686 [51-250]
Schneider, Ronald M - *Brazil: Culture and Politics in a New Industrial Powerhouse*
  Choice - v34 - S '96 - p204 [51-250]
Schneider, Saundra K - *Flirting with Disaster*
  APSR - v90 - S '96 - p658+ [501+]
Schneider, Sherrie - *The Rules*
  Ent W - D 13 '96 - p70 [251-500]
Schneider, Stephen Henry - *Laboratory Earth*
  BL - v93 - D 1 '96 - p633 [51-250]
  BW - v27 - Mr 2 '97 - p8 [51-250]
  KR - v64 - O 15 '96 - p1518 [251-500]
  Nature - v386 - Mr 27 '97 - p345 [501+]
  New Sci - v153 - Ja 25 '97 - p44 [251-500]
  NYTBR - v102 - Ja 19 '97 - p11 [501+]
  PW - v243 - O 21 '96 - p61 [51-250]
  Spec - v277 - N 16 '96 - p56 [501+]
Schneiderman, Stuart - *Saving Face*
  Rapport - v19 - 4 '96 - p38 [51-250]
Schneir, Miriam - *The Vintage Book of Historical Feminism*
  Obs - S 1 '96 - p18* [51-250]
Schneirov, Matthew - *The Dream of a New Social Order*
  CS - v25 - S '96 - p690+ [501+]
  J Am Cult - v19 - Spr '96 - p105+ [501+]
Schnell, Izhak - *Arab Industrialization in Israel*
  MEJ - v51 - Spr '97 - p287+ [501+]
Schneller, Robert J - *A Quest for Glory*
  Choice - v34 - S '96 - p198 [51-250]
Schnerb-Lievre, Marion - *Somnium Viridarii. Vols. 1-2*
  Specu - v71 - O '96 - p1015+ [501+]
Schnitzler, Arthur - *Tagebuch 1920-1922*
  MLR - v91 - Jl '96 - p796+ [501+]
Schnoor, Jerald L - *Environmental Modeling*
  SciTech - v20 - D '96 - p69 [51-250]
Schnur, Steven - *Beyond Providence*
  y HB Guide - v7 - Fall '96 - p305 [51-250]
  y JAAL - v40 - S '96 - p70 [51-250]
  The Koufax Dilemma (Illus. by Meryl Treatner)
  c BL - v93 - Mr 15 '97 - p1243 [51-250]
  c CCB-B - v50 - My '97 - p334+ [51-250]
  c Trib Bks - Mr 30 '97 - p5 [51-250]
  The Tie Man's Miracle (Illus. by Stephen T Johnson)
  c RT - v50 - N '96 - p258 [51-250]
Schnurmacher, Thomas - *Canada Is Not a Real Country*
  Quill & Q - v63 - Ja '97 - p30 [51-250]
Schobinger, Jean-Pierre - *Die Philosophie Des 17. Jahrhunderts. Pt. 2, Vols. 1-2*
  r Isis - v87 - D '96 - p726+ [501+]
Schodt, Frederik L - *Dreamland Japan*
  BL - v93 - S 1 '96 - p54 [51-250]
Schoem, David - *Multicultural Teaching in the University*
  Fam Relat - v45 - O '96 - p478 [251-500]
Schoeman, Elna - *Mandela's Five Years of Freedom*
  r Choice - v34 - N '96 - p436 [501+]
Schoemperlen, Diane - *In the Language of Love*
  PW - v244 - Mr 31 '97 - p72 [1-50]
  Trib Bks - My 25 '97 - p8 [1-50]
Schoenbaum, David - *The German Question and Other German Questions*
  Econ - v341 - N 16 '96 - p8* [51-250]
  For Aff - v76 - Mr '97 - p186+ [51-250]
Schoenberg, Arnold - *Coherence, Counterpoint, Instrumentation, Instruction in Form*
  TranslRevS - v1 - My '95 - p22+ [51-250]
  The Musical Idea and the Logic, Technique, and Art of Its Presentation
  M Ed J - v83 - Jl '96 - p50+ [51-250]

Schoenberg, Wilfred P - *Jesuit Mission Presses in the Pacific Northwest*
  r CHR - v83 - Ja '97 - p170+ [51-250]
Schoenfeld, Alan H - *Mathematical Thinking and Problem Solving*
  Am Sci - v84 - My '96 - p302+ [501+]
Schoenfeld, Max - *Stalking the U-Boat*
  J Mil H - v61 - Ap '97 - p401+ [501+]
  T&C - v38 - Ja '97 - p262+ [501+]
Schoenhals, Michael - *China's Cultural Revolution 1966-1969*
  R&R Bk N - v12 - F '97 - p20 [51-250]
Schoenherr, John - *Rebel (Illus. by John Schoenherr)*
  c RT - v50 - O '96 - p155 [51-250]
Schoentjes, Pierre - *Claude Simon Par Correspondance*
  MLR - v91 - Jl '96 - p740+ [501+]
  Recherche De L'Ironie Et Ironie De La Recherche
  MLR - v91 - Jl '96 - p736+ [501+]
Schoeser, Mary - *International Textile Design*
  Surface DJ - v20 - Sum '96 - p33 [501+]
Schofer, Peter - *Autour De La Litterature*
  FR - v70 - O '96 - p156+ [501+]
Schofield, Janet Ward - *Computers and Classroom Culture*
  TCR - v98 - Win '96 - p346+ [501+]
Schofield, John - *Medieval Towns*
  EHR - v112 - Ap '97 - p448+ [501+]
Schofield, Victoria - *Kashmir in the Crossfire*
  Choice - v34 - Mr '97 - p1217 [51-250]
  CR - v270 - Ja '97 - p46+ [501+]
  LJ - v121 - D '96 - p123+ [51-250]
Scholastic Children's Dictionary
  cr BL - v93 - Ja '97 - p372+ [251-500]
  cr Learning - v25 - N '96 - p81 [51-250]
  cr Par Ch - v21 - Mr '97 - p5 [1-50]
  cr SLJ - v42 - N '96 - p138 [51-250]
Scholastic Update
  yp Par Ch - v20 - O '96 - p26 [1-50]
Scholastic's The Magic School Bus Explores the Human Body. Electronic Media Version
  c RQ - v35 - Sum '96 - p544+ [501+]
Scholastic's The Magic School Bus Explores the Solar System. Electronic Media Version
  c CLW - v66 - Je '96 - p57 [51-250]
Scholder, Amy - *Cookin' with Honey*
  Advocate - S 17 '96 - p60 [1-50]
  High Risk 2
  Quill & Q - v62 - Jl '96 - p42 [501+]
Scholem, Gershom - *Briefe. Vols. 1-2*
  TLS - Jl 7 '96 - p10+ [501+]
  Tagebucher Nebst Aufsatzen Und Entwurfen Bis 1923. Vol. 1
  TLS - Jl 7 '96 - p10+ [501+]
Scholes, Katherine - *Make Me an Idol*
  Aust Bk R - Ag '96 - p50 [501+]
Scholfield, Phil - *Quantifying Language*
  MLJ - v80 - Win '96 - p535+ [501+]
Scholl, Armin - *Balancing and Sequencing of Assembly Lines*
  JEL - v34 - D '96 - p2020 [51-250]
Scholl, Peter A - *Garrison Keillor*
  TLS - My 24 '96 - p36 [51-250]
Scholliers, Peter - *Wages, Manufacturers, and Workers in the Nineteenth Century Factory*
  R&R Bk N - v12 - F '97 - p40 [51-250]
Schollmeier, Paul - *Other Selves*
  RP - v58 - Sum '96 - p646+ [501+]
Scholtz, A H M - *Vatmaar: 'N Lewendagge Verhaal Van 'N Tyd Wat Nie Meer Is Nie*
  WLT - v70 - Sum '96 - p752 [251-500]
Scholtz, James C - *Video Acquisitions and Cataloging*
  LRTS - v40 - Jl '96 - p294+ [51-250]
Scholz, Christopher - *Fieldwork: A Geologist's Memoir of the Kalahari*
  KR - v65 - Ap 1 '97 - p535 [251-500]
  LJ - v122 - Ap 15 '97 - p114 [51-250]
Schomp, Virginia - *The Ancient Greeks*
  c HB Guide - v7 - Fall '96 - p378 [51-250]
  He Fought for Freedom
  c Ch BWatch - v7 - F '97 - p7 [1-50]
  c HB Guide - v8 - Spr '97 - p156 [51-250]
  c SLJ - v43 - F '97 - p98 [51-250]
  New York
  c Ch BWatch - v6 - D '96 - p6 [1-50]
  c HB Guide - v8 - Spr '97 - p172 [51-250]
  c SLJ - v43 - F '97 - p108 [51-250]
  Russia--New Freedoms, New Challenges
  c HB Guide - v7 - Fall '96 - p381+ [51-250]
Schon, Gunter - *Weltmunzkatalog 19. Jahrhundert. 13th Ed.*
  r Coin W - v37 - O 21 '96 - p33 [51-250]

Weltmunzkatalog 20. Jahrhundert. 1996 Ed.
  r Coin W - v37 - O 21 '96 - p33 [51-250]
Schon, Isabel - *Introduccion A La Literatura Infantil Y Juvenil*
    BL - v93 - D 15 '96 - p719 [51-250]
    Lect Y V - v18 - Mr '97 - p47 [501+]
Recommended Books in Spanish for Children and Young Adults 1991-1995
  r SLJ - v43 - Mr '97 - p115 [51-250]
Schonberg, Harold C - *The Lives of the Great Composers. 3rd Ed.*
    LJ - v122 - Ap 15 '97 - p84 [51-250]
Schonberger, Richard J - *World Class Manufacturing*
    Choice - v34 - O '96 - p327 [51-250]
Schonbohm, Jorg - *Two Armies and One Fatherland*
    CR - v269 - S '96 - p167 [51-250]
Schonborn, Christoph - *God's Human Face*
    Theol St - v57 - Mr '96 - p184 [251-500]
Schonscheck, Jonathan - *On Criminalization*
    Ethics - v107 - O '96 - p183 [51-250]
Schooling the Generations in the Politics of Prison
    Bl S - v26 - Sum '96 - p64 [1-50]
Schools, Communities, and the Arts
  r Learning - v25 - S '96 - p55 [1-50]
Schoom, Talitha - *Pyke Koch*
    BM - v138 - N '96 - p761 [251-500]
Schopen, Bernard - *The Iris Deception*
    BL - v93 - S 15 '96 - p225 [51-250]
    KR - v64 - Ag 15 '96 - p1193 [51-250]
    PW - v243 - S 9 '96 - p79 [51-250]
Schopenhauer, Arthur - *On the Basis of Morality*
    South HR - v30 - Fall '96 - p385+ [501+]
Schopler, Eric - *Behavioral Issues in Autism*
    AJMR - v101 - Jl '96 - p92+ [501+]
Schoppa, R Keith - *Blood Road*
    AHR - v102 - F '97 - p152+ [501+]
    Ch Rev Int - v4 - Spr '97 - p236+ [501+]
Schoppmann, Claudia - *Days of Masquerade*
    TLS - S 13 '96 - p32 [251-500]
    TranslRevS - v2 - D '96 - p10 [51-250]
    Wom R Bks - v14 - N '96 - p9+ [501+]
Schor, Esther - *Bearing the Dead*
    Albion - v28 - Sum '96 - p330+ [501+]
    MLR - v92 - Ap '97 - p456+ [501+]
    RES - v48 - F '97 - p116+ [501+]
    VS - v39 - Win '96 - p258+ [501+]
Schor, Juliet - *Capital, the State and Labour*
    Econ J - v107 - Ja '97 - p284 [51-250]
Schor, Mira - *Wet: On Painting, Feminism, and Art Culture*
    PW - v244 - F 24 '97 - p74 [51-250]
Schore, Allan N - *Affect Regulation and the Origin of the Self*
    Cont Ed - v68 - Fall '96 - p84 [251-500]
Schories, Pat - *Over under in the Garden (Illus. by Pat Schories)*
  c HB Guide - v7 - Fall '96 - p275 [51-250]
  c RT - v50 - Ap '97 - p592 [51-250]
Schork, R J - *Sacred Song from the Byzantine Pulpit*
    Rel St Rev - v23 - Ja '97 - p80 [251-500]
Schorr, Alan Edward - *Hispanic Resource Directory. 3rd Ed.*
  r ARBA - v28 - '97 - p156 [251-500]
Schott, James R - *Matrix Analysis for Statistics*
    SciTech - v21 - Mr '97 - p13 [51-250]
Schott, Jane A - *Will Rogers (Illus. by David Charles Brandon)*
  c HB Guide - v8 - Spr '97 - p160 [51-250]
Schott, Jeffrey J - *The Uruguay Round*
    Econ J - v107 - Ja '97 - p232+ [501+]
Schotter, Roni - *Captain Snap and the Children of Vinegar Lane (Illus. by Marcia Sewall)*
  c SLJ - v43 - Ja '97 - p37 [1-50]
Dreamland (Illus. by Kevin Hawkes)
  c HB Guide - v7 - Fall '96 - p275 [51-250]
  c Inst - v106 - O '96 - p66 [51-250]
  c NYTBR - v102 - Ap 13 '97 - p27 [501+]
  c Smith - v27 - N '96 - p171 [1-50]
Fruit and Vegetable Man
  c Emerg Lib - v23 - My '96 - p44+ [51-250]
Nothing Ever Happens on 90th Street (Illus. by Kyrsten Brooker)
  c BL - v93 - Mr 1 '97 - p1173+ [51-250]
  c KR - v65 - F 1 '97 - p228 [51-250]
  c PW - v244 - F 3 '97 - p106 [51-250]
  c SLJ - v43 - Mr '97 - p166+ [51-250]
Schottroff, Luise - *Lydia's Impatient Sisters*
    CC - v113 - S 11 '96 - p867+ [251-500]
    Choice - v34 - D '96 - p630 [1-50]
    Theol St - v57 - S '96 - p525+ [501+]

Schoultz, Lars - *Security, Democracy, and Development in U.S.-Latin American Relations*
    HAHR - v77 - My '97 - p361 [251-500]
Schrader, Alvin - *Fear of Words*
    LAR - v98 - Mr '96 - p163 [251-500]
Schrader, David E - *The Corporation as Anomaly*
    Dialogue - v35 - Spr '96 - p410+ [501+]
Schraepler, Hans-Albrecht - *Directory of International Organizations*
  r ARBA - v28 - '97 - p278 [251-500]
  r BL - v93 - S 1 '96 - p164+ [251-500]
  r Choice - v34 - D '96 - p594 [51-250]
  r R&R Bk N - v11 - N '96 - p51 [51-250]
Schraff, Anne - *American Heroes of Exploration and Flight*
  c HB Guide - v7 - Fall '96 - p376 [1-50]
Are We Moving to Mars? (Illus. by Michael Carroll)
  c Cur R - v36 - F '97 - p13 [51-250]
  c SLJ - v43 - F '97 - p98 [51-250]
Colin Powell: Soldier and Patriot
  y KR - v64 - D 1 '96 - p1741 [51-250]
  y SLJ - v43 - Mr '97 - p202 [51-250]
Schram, Sanford - *Words of Welfare*
    CS - v25 - S '96 - p615+ [501+]
    NWSA Jnl - v8 - Sum '96 - p107+ [501+]
    PSQ - v111 - Fall '96 - p541+ [501+]
    Soc Ser R - v71 - Mr '97 - p156+ [501+]
Schram, Stuart R - *Mao's Road to Power. Vol. 2*
    Ch Rev Int - v3 - Fall '96 - p528+ [501+]
Schramm, Brooks - *The Opponents of Third Isaiah*
    JR - v76 - O '96 - p614+ [501+]
Schramm, David N - *The Big Bang and Other Explosions in Nuclear and Particle Astrophysics*
    Sci - v275 - F 28 '97 - p1276 [1-50]
Schramm, Ingo - *Fitchers Blau*
    Econ - v341 - O 19 '96 - p16*+ [501+]
Schramm-Evans, Zoe - *A Phoenix Rising*
    Econ - v340 - S 14 '96 - p7*+ [501+]
Schrank, Bernice - *Irish Playwrights 1880-1995*
  r LJ - v121 - D '96 - p82 [51-250]
Sean O'Casey: A Research and Production Sourcebook
  r Choice - v34 - Ja '97 - p798 [51-250]
  r ILS - v16 - Spr '97 - p35 [1-50]
  r R&R Bk N - v11 - D '96 - p64 [51-250]
Schrecengost, Maity - *Researching People*
  cr Cur R - v36 - F '97 - p13 [51-250]
Schreckenberg, Heinz - *Die Christlichen Adversus-Judaeos-Texte Und Ihr Literarisches Und Historisches Umfeld 13.-20. Jh.*
  r Theol St - v57 - Mr '96 - p186 [251-500]
The Jews in Christian Art
    HT - v46 - O '96 - p55 [1-50]
Schrecker, Judie - *Santa's New Reindeer (Illus. by Dan Rodriguez)*
  c HB Guide - v8 - Spr '97 - p47 [51-250]
  c PW - v243 - S 30 '96 - p89 [51-250]
Schreiber, Boris - *Un Silence D'Environ Une Demiheure*
    Spec - v278 - Ja 4 '97 - p37 [501+]
Schreiber, Gayle - *Saints Alive*
    CLW - v67 - Mr '97 - p42 [51-250]
Schreiber, Le Anne - *Light Years*
    BL - v93 - S 15 '96 - p189 [51-250]
    BW - v26 - D 8 '96 - p6 [1-50]
    LATBR - S 8 '96 - p6+ [501+]
    LATBR - D 29 '96 - p10 [51-250]
    NYTBR - v101 - S 15 '96 - p14 [501+]
    NYTBR - v101 - D 8 '96 - p88 [1-50]
    Smith - v27 - O '96 - p142+ [501+]
    Wom R Bks - v14 - D '96 - p1+ [501+]
Midstream
    NYTBR - v101 - S 29 '96 - p32 [501+]
Schreiber, Mark - *Shocking Crimes of Postwar Japan*
    Arm Det - v30 - Win '97 - p118 [251-500]
Schreiner, Claus - *Flamenco: Gypsy Dance and Music from Andalusia*
    TranslRevS - v1 - My '95 - p2 [51-250]
Schreiner, Klaus - *Stadtregiment Und Burgerfreiheit*
    Six Ct J - v27 - Win '96 - p1223+ [501+]
Schreiner, Susan E - *Where Shall Wisdom Be Found?*
    JR - v76 - O '96 - p639+ [501+]
Schremmer, Eckart - *Steuern, Abgaben Und Dienste Vom Mittelalter Bis Zur Gegenwart*
    JEH - v56 - D '96 - p941+ [501+]
Schremp, Gerry - *Celebration of American Food*
    BWatch - v17 - D '96 - p9 [1-50]
Schrenck, Gilbert - *La Reception D'Agrippa D'Aubigne XVIe-XXe Siecles*
    MLR - v92 - Ap '97 - p466 [251-500]
Schreter, Robert K - *Allies and Adversaries*
    AJPsych - v154 - Ja '97 - p124+ [501+]

Schreuder, Robert - *The Bilingual Lexicon*
    MLJ - v80 - Fall '96 - p406+ [501+]
Schreyer, Alice D - *The History of Books*
  r ASInt - v34 - O '96 - p11+ [51-250]
Schriber, Mary Suzanne - *Telling Travels*
    Legacy - v13 - 2 '96 - p161+ [501+]
Schrieber, Markus - *Marranen in Madrid 1600-1670*
    EHR - v112 - Ap '97 - p470+ [501+]
Schrift, Alan D - *Nietzsche's French Legacy*
    CPR - v16 - D '96 - p435+ [501+]
Schriver, Joe M - *Human Behavior and the Social Environment*
    Soc Ser R - v70 - D '96 - p669 [51-250]
Schriver, Karen A - *Dynamics in Document Design*
    BYTE - v22 - Ap '97 - p38 [251-500]
Schrodinger, Erwin - *The Interpretation of Quantum Mechanics*
    Isis - v87 - S '96 - p570+ [501+]
Nature and the Greeks. Science and Humanism
    New Sci - v152 - O 26 '96 - p46 [51-250]
Schroeder, Alan - *Carolina Shout! (Illus. by Bernie Fuchs)*
  c LA - v73 - O '96 - p430 [51-250]
  c LA - v73 - D '96 - p619+ [51-250]
  c RT - v50 - O '96 - p153+ [51-250]
Lily and the Wooden Bowl (Illus. by Yoriko Ito)
  c PW - v244 - Ap 14 '97 - p77 [1-50]
Minty: A Story of Young Harriet Tubman (Illus. by Jerry Pinkney)
  c Bks Keeps - Mr '97 - p20 [51-250]
  c BL - v93 - Ap 1 '97 - p1302 [1-50]
  c CLW - v67 - D '96 - p62 [51-250]
  c HB - v72 - S '96 - p589+ [51-250]
  c HB Guide - v7 - Fall '96 - p389 [51-250]
  c RT - v50 - My '97 - p680 [51-250]
  c Sch Lib - v45 - F '97 - p34 [51-250]
  c S Liv - v31 - D '96 - p58 [51-250]
  c SLJ - v42 - D '96 - p44 [51-250]
  c Time - v148 - D 9 '96 - p79 [51-250]
Ragtime Tumpie (Illus. by Bernie Fuchs)
  c SLJ - v42 - D '96 - p44 [51-250]
Satchmo's Blues (Illus. by Floyd Cooper)
  c BL - v93 - S 15 '96 - p251 [251-500]
  c Emerg Lib - v24 - Mr '97 - p66 [1-50]
  c HB Guide - v8 - Spr '97 - p47 [51-250]
  c KR - v64 - O 1 '96 - p1474 [51-250]
  c LATBR - Ag 18 '96 - p15 [51-250]
  c NYTBR - v101 - D 8 '96 - p78 [501+]
  c PW - v243 - O 14 '96 - p84 [51-250]
  c SLJ - v42 - S '96 - p191 [51-250]
  c Smith - v27 - N '96 - p167 [1-50]
Satchmo's Blues (James). Audio Version
  c HB - v73 - My '97 - p357+ [501+]
Smoky Mountain Rose (Illus. by Brad Sneed)
  c BL - v93 - My 15 '97 - p1578 [51-250]
  c PW - v244 - My 12 '97 - p76 [51-250]
Schroeder, Christopher F - *Inside OrCAD*
    SciTech - v20 - S '96 - p56 [51-250]
Schroeder, Eric James - *Vietnam, We've All Been There*
    JTWS - v13 - Fall '96 - p211+ [501+]
Schroeder, Fred E H - *Front Yard America*
    CAY - v17 - Win '96 - p13 [51-250]
Schroeder, Joanne F - *Fun Puppet Skits for Schools and Libraries*
    Learning - v25 - S '96 - p55 [1-50]
Schroeder, Patricia R - *The Feminist Possibilities of Dramatic Realism*
    AL - v69 - Mr '97 - p250 [51-250]
    Choice - v34 - Ja '97 - p798 [51-250]
Schroeder, Ralph - *Possible Worlds*
    New Sci - v152 - N 16 '96 - p49 [51-250]
    SciTech - v20 - S '96 - p8 [51-250]
Schroeder, Russell - *Walt Disney: His Life in Pictures*
  c CCB-B - v50 - N '96 - p115 [51-250]
  c SLJ - v42 - O '96 - p140 [51-250]
Schroeder, Steven - *Virginia Woolf's Subject and the Subject of Ethics*
    Choice - v34 - N '96 - p460 [51-250]
Schrumpf, Fred - *Peer Mediation. Rev. Ed.*
    Adoles - v32 - Spr '97 - p248 [51-250]
Schubeler, Peter - *Participation and Partnership in Urban Infrastructure Management*
    JEL - v35 - D '96 - p2112 [51-250]
Schubert, Franz - *Schubert's Complete Song Texts. Vol. 1*
    Choice - v34 - Ja '97 - p806 [51-250]
Schubert, Ingrid - *Abracadabra*
  c CBRS - v25 - Ap '97 - p101 [51-250]
Schubert Kalsi, Marie-Luise - *Alexius Meinong's Elements of Ethics*
    R&R Bk N - v12 - F '97 - p3 [51-250]

Schubot, David B - *South Dakota Native American Youth Risk Behavior Survey Report 1994*
J Gov Info - v23 - S '96 - p595 [51-250]
Schuchter, Arnold - *Hawaii: Travel-Smart Trip Planner*
r BL - v93 - S 15 '96 - p210 [1-50]
Schudson, Michael - *The Power of News*
JC - v47 - Win '97 - p158+ [501+]
Schueler, G F - *Desire: Its Role in Practical Reason and the Explanation of Action*
RM - v50 - D '96 - p423+ [501+]
Schuett, Stacey - *Somewhere in the World Right Now*
c HB Guide - v7 - Fall '96 - p275 [1-50]
Schuetz-Miller, Mardith K - *Building and Builders in Hispanic California 1769-1850*
HAHR - v76 - Ag '96 - p539+ [251-500]
Schulberg, Budd - *The Harder They Fall*
NYTBR - v101 - Ap 7 '96 - p24
Schuler, Douglas - *New Community Networks*
LJ - v121 - O 1 '96 - p120 [51-250]
Participatory Design
A J Psy - v109 - Win '96 - p630+ [501+]
Schuler, Harold H - *Fort Sisseton*
r Roundup M - v4 - Ap '97 - p24 [251-500]
WHQ - v28 - Spr '97 - p103 [1-50]
Schuler, Kurt - *Should Developing Countries Have Central Banks?*
JEL - v35 - Mr '97 - p208 [51-250]
Schuler, Robert M - *Alchemical Poetry 1575-1700*
Six Ct J - v27 - Win '96 - p1140+ [501+]
Schulkin, Jay - *The Delicate Balance*
Hast Cen R - v27 - Ja '97 - p47 [1-50]
Schull, Joseph - *Rebellion*
Beav - v77 - F '97 - p47 [51-250]
Schuller, Gunther - *The Compleat Conductor*
BL - v93 - My 15 '97 - p1555 [51-250]
LJ - v122 - My 1 '97 - p106 [51-250]
Schuller, Robert - *If It's Going to Be, It's Up to Me*
PW - v244 - F 24 '97 - p82 [51-250]
Schullery, Paul - *Echoes from the Summit*
CSM - v88 - N 21 '96 - pB1 [1-50]
y Kliatt - v31 - Ja '97 - p29+ [251-500]
LATBR - Ag 11 '96 - p11 [51-250]
y SB - v33 - Ja '97 - p14 [51-250]
Mark of the Bear
Aud - v98 - N '96 - p136 [51-250]
y BL - v93 - D 1 '96 - p632 [51-250]
BWatch - v17 - D '96 - p4 [1-50]
PW - v243 - S 2 '96 - p108 [51-250]
SciTech - v20 - D '96 - p33 [51-250]
y SLJ - v43 - Ja '97 - p142 [51-250]
Shupton's Fancy
PW - v243 - S 23 '96 - p62 [51-250]
The Yellowstone Wolf
BL - v93 - N 15 '96 - p557 [251-500]
Choice - v34 - My '97 - p1526+ [51-250]
Schulman, Arlene - *Muhammad Ali: Champion*
c Ch BWatch - v6 - My '96 - p6 [51-250]
c HB Guide - v7 - Fall '96 - p363 [51-250]
The Prizefighters: An Intimate Look at Champions and Contenders
Aethlon - v13 - Spr '96 - p221+ [501+]
Schulman, Faye - *A Partisan's Memoir*
Wom R Bks - v14 - O '96 - p12+ [501+]
Schulman, Sarah - *Rat Bohemia*
BW - v26 - O 13 '96 - p12 [51-250]
NYTBR - v101 - D 29 '96 - p20 [1-50]
Obs - Mr 9 '97 - p18* [51-250]
Schulte, Regina - *The Village in Court*
CEH - v29 - 2 '96 - p247+ [501+]
EHR - v111 - N '96 - p1327+ [251-500]
Schulte Nordholt, Annelies - *Maurice Blanchot: L'Ecriture Comme Experience Du Dehors*
MLR - v91 - Jl '96 - p739+ [251-500]
Schulte Nordholt, J W - *The Myth of the West*
CLW - v66 - Je '96 - p43 [51-250]
Schultes, Richard Evans - *Ethnobotany: Evolution of a Discipline*
BioSci - v46 - O '96 - p713+ [501+]
Choice - v34 - S '96 - p154 [51-250]
Schulting, Rick J - *Mortuary Variability and Status Differentiation on the Columbia-Fraser Plateau*
Am Ant - v61 - Jl '96 - p630+ [51-250]
Schultz, April R - *Ethnicity on Parade*
AHR - v101 - D '96 - p1639+ [501+]
Am Q - v48 - D '96 - p716+ [501+]
Schultz, David A - *The Jurisprudential Vision of Justice Antonin Scalia*
APSR - v90 - D '96 - p921+ [501+]
Choice - v34 - S '96 - p212 [51-250]

Schultz, Duane - *Quantrill's War*
BL - v93 - S 15 '96 - p216 [51-250]
LATBR - N 17 '96 - p14 [251-500]
LJ - v121 - S 15 '96 - p76 [51-250]
PW - v243 - S 9 '96 - p74 [51-250]
VQR - v73 - Win '97 - p16* [51-250]
Schultz, Elizabeth A - *Unpainted to the Last*
NEQ - v69 - D '96 - p651+ [501+]
Schultz, James A - *The Knowledge of Childhood in the German Middle Ages 1100-1350*
Bkbird - v34 - Spr '96 - p57 [51-250]
Schultz, James Willard - *With the Indians in the Rockies*
y Can CL - v22 - Fall '96 - p117+ [501+]
Schultz, Johann - *Exposition of Kant's Critique of Pure Reason*
BIC - v25 - O '96 - p24+ [501+]
Schultz, Karla L - *The Idea of the Forest*
R&R Bk N - v12 - F '97 - p97 [51-250]
Schultz, Lois Massengale - *A Beginner's Guide to Copy Cataloging on OCLC/Prism*
LAR - v98 - O '96 - p537 [251-500]
Schultz, Robert - *The Madhouse Nudes*
KR - v65 - F 1 '97 - p167 [251-500]
LJ - v122 - Mr 15 '97 - p92 [51-250]
PW - v244 - F 17 '97 - p209 [51-250]
Schultz, Stanley G - *Molecular Biology of Membrane Transport Disorders*
SciTech - v20 - N '96 - p39 [51-250]
Schultz, T Paul - *Research in Population Economics. Vol. 8*
JEL - v34 - D '96 - p2069 [51-250]
Schulz, Charles M - *Sally's Christmas Miracle (Illus. by Charles M Schulz)*
c PW - v243 - S 30 '96 - p93 [1-50]
Snoopy's Christmas Tree (Illus. by Charles M Schulz)
c PW - v243 - S 30 '96 - p93 [1-50]
Trick or Treat, Great Pumpkin (Illus. by Charles M Schulz)
c LATBR - O 20 '96 - p8 [51-250]
c PW - v243 - S 30 '96 - p86 [51-250]
Schulz, Constance B - *Bust to Boom*
LJ - v121 - O 1 '96 - p72+ [51-250]
Schulz, Donald E - *Cuba and the Future*
HAHR - v76 - N '96 - p829+ [251-500]
Mexico Faces the 21st Century
APSR - v90 - S '96 - p681+ [501+]
Schulz, James H - *The Economics of Aging. 6th Ed.*
J Con A - v31 - Sum '97 - p181+ [501+]
Schulz, Mat - *Claim*
Aust Bk R - Ag '96 - p47+ [501+]
Schulz, Rockwell - *Innovating in Community Mental Health*
Soc Ser R - v70 - D '96 - p667 [51-250]
Schulze, Carl - *IFOR: Allied Forces in Bosnia*
LAR - v99 - Ja '97 - p47 [51-250]
Schulze, Hagen - *Kleine Deutsche Geschichte*
TLS - O 11 '96 - p7 [501+]
States, Nations, and Nationalism
Choice - v34 - D '96 - p673 [51-250]
HRNB - v25 - Win '97 - p72+ [251-500]
Schulze, Rainer - *Industrial Regions in Transformation*
EHR - v111 - S '96 - p1001 [251-500]
Schulze, Robin G - *The Web of Friendship*
AL - v69 - Mr '97 - p240 [251-500]
TLS - Ag 30 '96 - p28 [501+]
Schulzinger, Robert D - *A Time for War*
y BL - v93 - Mr 15 '97 - p1209 [51-250]
KR - v65 - Mr 1 '97 - p366 [51-250]
PW - v244 - Ap 7 '97 - p84 [51-250]
Schumacher, Julie - *The Body Is Water*
PW - v244 - Mr 17 '97 - p81 [1-50]
An Explanation for Chaos
BL - v93 - D 1 '96 - p642 [51-250]
KR - v64 - N 1 '96 - p1560 [251-500]
LJ - v122 - Ja '97 - p152 [51-250]
Ms - v7 - Ja '97 - p82 [1-50]
NYTBR - v102 - F 16 '97 - p18 [51-250]
PW - v243 - N 11 '96 - p56 [51-250]
y SLJ - v43 - Mr '97 - p216 [51-250]
Schumacher, Michael - *There but for Fortune*
Choice - v34 - F '97 - p975 [51-250]
LJ - v121 - S 15 '96 - p71 [51-250]
NYTBR - v101 - S 15 '96 - p31 [51-250]
Schumaker, John F - *Religion and Mental Health*
Rel St Rev - v23 - Ap '97 - p149 [51-250]
Schumaker, Ward - *Dance!*
c HB Guide - v7 - Fall '96 - p275 [51-250]
Sing a Song of Circus (Illus. by Ward Schumaker)
c KR - v65 - F 15 '97 - p305 [51-250]
c PW - v244 - Mr 31 '97 - p73+ [51-250]

Schuman, Michael - *Franklin D. Roosevelt: The Four-Term President*
c HB Guide - v7 - Fall '96 - p371 [51-250]
c SLJ - v42 - Ag '96 - p150+ [51-250]
Martin Luther King, Jr., Leader for Civil Rights
c HB Guide - v7 - Fall '96 - p373 [51-250]
c SLJ - v42 - D '96 - p134 [51-250]
Schuman, Michael A - *Harry S. Truman*
c KR - v65 - Ja 15 '97 - p146 [51-250]
Schumann, Dirk - *Bayerns Unternehmer In Gesellschaft Und Staat 1834-1914*
CEH - v29 - 2 '96 - p241+ [501+]
Schumann Studien
p Notes - v53 - D '96 - p539+ [501+]
Schupp, Ulrike - *Ordnung Und Bruch*
Ger Q - v69 - Spr '96 - p220+ [501+]
Schur, Maxine Rose - *The Circlemaker*
y Kliatt - v30 - S '96 - p14 [51-250]
The Marvelous Maze (Illus. by Patricia Dewitt-Grush)
c HB Guide - v7 - Fall '96 - p275 [51-250]
When I Left My Village (Illus. by Brian Pinkney)
c HB Guide - v7 - Fall '96 - p287 [51-250]
c RT - v50 - My '97 - p683 [51-250]
Schurer, Ernst - *Franz Jung: Leben Und Werk Eines Rebellen*
MLR - v91 - O '96 - p1049+ [251-500]
Schussler Fiorenza, Elisabeth - *Jesus: Miriam's Child, Sophia's Prophet*
JR - v77 - Ap '97 - p286+ [501+]
Rel St Rev - v22 - O '96 - p293+ [501+]
Rel St Rev - v22 - O '96 - p296+ [501+]
Theol St - v57 - Mr '96 - p167+ [501+]
Schuster, Beate - *Die Freien Frauen*
Six Ct J - v27 - Fall '96 - p833+ [501+]
Schuster, Carl - *Patterns That Connect*
PW - v243 - O 21 '96 - p67 [51-250]
Schuster, Hal - *The Making of Quantum Leap*
SF Chr - v18 - O '96 - p82 [1-50]
Schuster, Heinz Georg - *Deterministic Chaos. 3rd Ed.*
J Chem Ed - v73 - Je '96 - pA137 [1-50]
Schutt, Christine - *Nightwork*
TLS - N 29 '96 - p11 [51-250]
Schutt, Hans-Werner - *Eilhard Mitscherlich: Prince of Prussian Chemistry*
SciTech - v21 - Mr '97 - p26 [51-250]
Schutte, David - *Behind Locked Doors*
c Sch Lib - v44 - Ag '96 - p108 [51-250]
Danger, Keep Out
c Sch Lib - v44 - Ag '96 - p108 [51-250]
Wake Up, It's Midnight
c Sch Lib - v44 - Ag '96 - p108 [51-250]
Wild Woods, Dark Secret
c Sch Lib - v44 - Ag '96 - p108 [51-250]
Schutte, Margret - *Die Galleria Delle Carte Geografiche In Vatikan*
Art Bull - v79 - Mr '97 - p156+ [501+]
Schuttner, Scott - *Building and Designing Decks*
LJ - v122 - F 1 '97 - p53 [1-50]
Schutz, Albert J - *The Voices of Eden*
Cont Pac - v8 - Fall '96 - p463+ [501+]
Schutz, Alfred - *Collected Papers. Vol. 4*
JEL - v34 - D '96 - p2015 [51-250]
Schutze, Jim - *Bully: A True Story of High School Revenge*
PW - v243 - D 16 '96 - p46+ [51-250]
Bully: Does Anyone Deserve to Die?
y BL - v93 - F 15 '97 - p982 [51-250]
KR - v65 - Ja 15 '97 - p129 [251-500]
LJ - v121 - O 15 '96 - p76 [51-250]
NYTBR - v102 - Mr 23 '97 - p19 [51-250]
Schuyler, David - *Apostle of Taste*
NYTBR - v101 - D 8 '96 - p57 [51-250]
R&R Bk N - v11 - N '96 - p78 [51-250]
TLS - Mr 28 '97 - p16+ [501+]
Schuyler, George - *Ethiopian Stories*
Obs - S 1 '96 - p16* [501+]
Schuyler, James - *The Diary of James Schuyler*
NYTBR - v102 - Ap 20 '97 - p18 [501+]
PW - v244 - F 24 '97 - p80 [1-50]
Schwab, David - *Caribbean. 3rd Ed.*
r BL - v93 - S 15 '96 - p210 [1-50]
Schwab, Gabriele - *The Mirror and the Killer-Queen*
Choice - v34 - D '96 - p617 [51-250]
Schwab, Gerald - *OSS Agents in Hitler's Heartland*
R&R Bk N - v11 - N '96 - p10 [51-250]
Schwan, Fred - *Collecting Coins*
Coin W - v37 - O 7 '96 - p71 [51-250]
Collecting Paper Money
Coin W - v37 - O 7 '96 - p71 [51-250]

The Comprehensive Catalog of Military Payment Certificates
  r Coin W - v37 - D 9 '96 - p48 [51-250]
Schwanitz, Dietrich - *Der Campus*
    WLT - v70 - Aut '96 - p951+ [501+]
Schwanitz, Wolfgang - *Jenseits Der Legenden*
    MEJ - v51 - Win '97 - p153 [1-50]
Schwantes, Carlos A - *The Pacific Northwest. Rev. and Enl. Ed.*
    Roundup M - v4 - Ap '97 - p24 [51-250]
So Incredibly Idaho!
    R&R Bk N - v11 - D '96 - p17 [51-250]
Schwartau, Winn - *Complete Internet Business Toolkit*
    CBR - v14 - S '96 - p28 [51-250]
Schwartz, A Truman - *Chemistry in Context. 2nd Ed.*
    SciTech - v21 - Mr '97 - p28 [51-250]
Schwartz, Amy - *Annabelle Swift, Kindergartner. Book and Audio Version*
  c Ch BWatch - v6 - S '96 - p1 [51-250]
  c SLJ - v43 - F '97 - p70 [51-250]
Schwartz, Bernard - *A Book of Legal Lists*
    KR - v65 - F 1 '97 - p207 [251-500]
Decision: How the Supreme Court Decides Cases
    Choice - v34 - S '96 - p212 [51-250]
The Warren Court
    Choice - v34 - Mr '97 - p1242 [51-250]
Schwartz, Daniel R - *Studies in the Jewish Background of Christianity*
    Rel St Rev - v23 - Ja '97 - p76 [51-250]
Schwartz, Dannel I - *Finding Joy*
    BL - v93 - Ja '97 - p785 [51-250]
    BWatch - v18 - F '97 - p10 [51-250]
    PW - v244 - Ja 27 '97 - p97 [51-250]
Schwartz, David - *The Encyclopedia of TV Game Shows. 2nd Ed.*
  r ARBA - v28 - '97 - p508 [51-250]
  r RQ - v35 - Sum '96 - p555+ [251-500]
Schwartz, Edward - *NetActivism: How Citizens Use the Internet*
    LJ - v121 - O 1 '96 - p120 [1-50]
Schwartz, Evan I - *Webonomics: The Nine Essential Principles for Growing Your Business on the World Wide Web*
    LJ - v122 - Ap 15 '97 - p93+ [51-250]
    PW - v244 - Mr 3 '97 - p61 [51-250]
Schwartz, Felice N - *The Armchair Activist*
    BL - v92 - Ag '96 - p1864 [51-250]
Schwartz, Fernando - *El Desencuentro*
    LJ - v122 - Ja '97 - p80 [51-250]
Schwartz, Glenn M - *Archaeological Views from the Countryside*
    Rel St Rev - v23 - Ap '97 - p164 [51-250]
Schwartz, Harriet Berg - *When Artie Was Little (Illus. by Thomas B Allen)*
  c HB Guide - v7 - Fall '96 - p275 [51-250]
  c SLJ - v42 - Ag '96 - p129 [51-250]
Schwartz, Harvey J - *Psychodynamic Concepts in General Psychiatry*
    AJPsych - v153 - Ag '96 - p1102+ [501+]
Schwartz, Hillel - *The Culture of the Copy*
    BWatch - v18 - F '97 - p5 [51-250]
    HMR - Spr '97 - p10+ [501+]
    LATBR - Ja 12 '97 - p5 [501+]
    New Sci - v153 - Mr 8 '97 - p44 [501+]
    NYTBR - v102 - Ja 19 '97 - p20 [501+]
    Utne R - Mr '97 - p84 [1-50]
Schwartz, Howard - *Next Year in Jerusalem (Illus. by Neil Waldman)*
  c BL - v93 - O 1 '96 - p339 [1-50]
  c BW - v26 - Jl 7 '96 - p15 [51-250]
  c HB Guide - v7 - Fall '96 - p324 [51-250]
  c Smith - v27 - N '96 - p166 [1-50]
The Wonder Child and Other Jewish Fairy Tales (Illus. by Stephen Fieser)
  c BL - v93 - S 15 '96 - p236 [51-250]
  c CCB-B - v50 - F '97 - p222 [51-250]
  c HB Guide - v8 - Spr '97 - p105 [51-250]
  c NYTBR - v101 - D 8 '96 - p78 [1-50]
  c PW - v243 - O 21 '96 - p85 [1-50]
  c SLJ - v42 - S '96 - p220 [51-250]
Schwartz, Ira M - *Home-Based Services for Troubled Children*
    Fam in Soc - v78 - Mr '97 - p220+ [501+]
    Soc Ser R - v70 - S '96 - p501 [51-250]
Schwartz, Joel - *The New York Approach*
    J Urban H - v22 - Jl '96 - p665+ [501+]
Schwartz, Joseph M - *The Permanence of the Political*
    APSR - v90 - S '96 - p640+ [501+]
    CS - v26 - Ja '97 - p34+ [501+]
    Dis - v44 - Spr '97 - p119+ [501+]
    J Pol - v59 - F '97 - p288+ [501+]

Schwartz, Lynne Sharon - *The Fatigue Artist*
    NYTBR - v101 - Ag 25 '96 - p28 [1-50]
Ruined by Reading
    Bloom Rev - v17 - Ja '97 - p12 [251-500]
    LATBR - My 26 '96 - p1+ [501+]
    LATBR - D 29 '96 - p4 [51-250]
    Smith - v27 - D '96 - p137 [251-500]
Schwartz, Marion - *A History of Dogs in the Early Americas*
    KR - v65 - Ap 1 '97 - p535 [251-500]
Schwartz, Mark F - *Sexual Abuse and Eating Disorders*
    Choice - v34 - S '96 - p216 [51-250]
    Readings - v11 - S '96 - p24 [51-250]
Schwartz, Martin D - *Race, Gender, and Class in Criminology*
    R&R Bk N - v11 - D '96 - p44 [51-250]
Schwartz, Mel M - *Composite Materials. Vols. 1-2*
    SciTech - v21 - Mr '97 - p77 [51-250]
Schwartz, Mischa - *Broadband Integrated Networks*
    SciTech - v20 - S '96 - p54 [51-250]
Schwartz, Morrie - *Letting Go*
    BL - v92 - Ag '96 - p1864 [51-250]
Schwartz, Oded - *Preserving*
    BL - v93 - N 15 '96 - p560+ [51-250]
Schwartz, Perry - *Carolyn's Story*
  c HB Guide - v8 - Spr '97 - p90 [51-250]
Schwartz, Rachel E - *Wireless Communications in Developing Countries*
    R&R Bk N - v11 - N '96 - p34 [51-250]
Schwartz, Richard Alan - *The Cold War Reference Guide*
  r LJ - v122 - Mr 15 '97 - p58 [51-250]
Schwartz, Richard C - *Internal Family Systems Therapy*
    Fam Relat - v45 - Jl '96 - p355+ [251-500]
Schwartz, Richard S - *Fundamentals of Operative Dentistry*
    SciTech - v20 - D '96 - p54 [51-250]
Schwartz, Robert - *Vision: Variations on Some Berkeleian Themes*
    A J Psy - v109 - Fall '96 - p483+ [501+]
    Phil R - v105 - Ja '96 - p97+ [501+]
Schwartz, Steven - *Quicken 6 for Windows*
    LJ - v122 - My 1 '97 - p132 [1-50]
Schwartz, Stuart B - *Implicit Understandings*
    JIH - v27 - Win '97 - p481+ [501+]
Schwartzberg, Steven S - *The Crisis of Meaning*
    BL - v93 - N 1 '96 - p464 [51-250]
A Crisis of Meaning
    Choice - v34 - Ap '97 - p1373 [51-250]
The Crisis of Meaning
    KR - v64 - S 15 '96 - p1386 [251-500]
A Crisis of Meaning
    LATBR - N 24 '96 - p3 [501+]
The Crisis of Meaning
    PW - v243 - O 7 '96 - p56 [51-250]
A Crisis of Meaning
    SciTech - v21 - Mr '97 - p56 [51-250]
Schwartzman, David - *The Japanese Television Cartel*
    JEL - v34 - D '96 - p1988+ [501+]
Schwarz, Bill - *The Expansion of England*
    HT - v47 - F '97 - p58+ [501+]
Schwarz, Hans, 1939- - *Evil: A Historical and Theological Perspective*
    JR - v76 - O '96 - p659+ [501+]
True Faith in the True God
    CC - v113 - O 9 '96 - p945 [51-250]
Schwarz, Hans-Peter, 1934- - *Konrad Adenauer: A German Politician and Statesman in a Period of War, Revolution and Reconstruction*
    CR - v269 - Ag '96 - p111+ [51-250]
Schwarz, K Robert - *Minimalists*
    BW - v26 - D 8 '96 - p8 [51-250]
Schwarz, L D - *London in the Age of Industrialisation*
    JMH - v68 - D '96 - p986+ [501+]
    J Urban H - v22 - S '96 - p727+ [501+]
Schwarz, Philip J - *Slave Laws in Virginia*
    Choice - v34 - My '97 - p1565 [51-250]
Schwarz, Steven - *Visual QuickStart Guide to Internet Explorer for Windows 95/NT*
  r LJ - v122 - F 1 '97 - p102 [51-250]
Schwarz, Ted - *Trust No One*
    BL - v93 - Mr 15 '97 - p1223+ [51-250]
    KR - v65 - Mr 1 '97 - p366+ [51-250]
    LJ - v122 - Mr 15 '97 - p70 [51-250]
    PW - v244 - F 3 '97 - p86 [51-250]
Schwedler, Jillian - *Toward Civil Society in the Middle East?*
    MEJ - v50 - Sum '96 - p456 [51-250]
Schwehn, Mark R - *Exiles from Eden*
    Rel St Rev - v23 - Ja '97 - p35+ [501+]

Schweickart, David - *Against Capitalism*
    Choice - v34 - O '96 - p331 [51-250]
    For Aff - v75 - N '96 - p145 [51-250]
    JEL - v34 - S '96 - p1494 [51-250]
Schweid, Eliezer - *Democracy and Halakhah*
    Rel St Rev - v23 - Ap '97 - p127+ [501+]
Wrestling until Daybreak
    Rel St Rev - v23 - Ap '97 - p127+ [501+]
Schweiger-Dmi'el, Itzhak - *Hanna's Sabbath Dress (Illus. by Ora Eitan)*
  c BL - v93 - O 1 '96 - p338 [51-250]
  c CBRS - v25 - Win '97 - p65 [1-50]
  c HB - v73 - Ja '97 - p52+ [51-250]
  c HB Guide - v8 - Spr '97 - p48 [51-250]
  c NYTBR - v101 - D 8 '96 - p78 [1-50]
  c SLJ - v42 - N '96 - p92 [51-250]
Schweiker, William - *Responsibility and Christian Ethics*
    Ethics - v107 - Ja '97 - p404+ [51-250]
    JR - v77 - Ja '97 - p168+ [501+]
    Rel St Rev - v23 - Ap '97 - p157 [51-250]
    Theol St - v57 - S '96 - p558+ [501+]
    TT - v53 - Ja '97 - p568 [51-250]
Schweitzer, Albert - *Brothers in Spirit*
    Choice - v34 - Ja '97 - p830 [51-250]
Schweitzer, Darrell - *Mask of the Sorcerer*
    Necro - Sum '96 - p24+ [501+]
Schweitzer, Philip A - *Corrosion Engineering Handbook*
  r SciTech - v20 - D '96 - p63 [51-250]
Schweizer Briefmarken Katalog 1996
  r Am Phil - v110 - Jl '96 - p636 [501+]
Schweizerische Nationalbank Quartalsheft
  p JEL - v34 - S '96 - p1507 [51-250]
Schwenger, Peter - *Letter Bomb*
    J Am St - v30 - Ag '96 - p328+ [501+]
Schwieder, Dorothy - *Iowa: The Middle Land*
    Choice - v34 - O '96 - p351 [51-250]
Schwimmer, George - *The Search for David*
    Mag Bl - Mr '97 - p57 [51-250]
Schwin, Lawrence - *Decorating Old House Interiors*
    LJ - v122 - Ja '97 - p95 [51-250]
Schwindt, Richard - *Business Administration Reading Lists and Course Outlines. Vols. 1-20*
  r JEL - v34 - S '96 - p1405 [51-250]
Schwuger, Milan Johann - *Detergents in the Environment*
    SciTech - v20 - D '96 - p68 [51-250]
Sciabarra, Chris M - *Marx, Hayek, and Utopia*
    CPR - v16 - Ap '96 - p141+ [501+]
Scicolone, Michele - *A Fresh Taste of Italy*
    LJ - v122 - Mr 15 '97 - p82 [51-250]
    PW - v243 - D 16 '96 - p55 [51-250]
Science and Engineering Ethics
  p Nature - v383 - S 5 '96 - p42 [251-500]
Science and Technical Writing
  r BL - v93 - My 1 '97 - p1511 [1-50]
Science and Technology: A Purchase Guide for Libraries 1995
  r ARBA - v28 - '97 - p562 [51-250]
Science Fiction Research Association (1993: Reno, Nevada) - *Imaginative Futures*
    Ext - v37 - Sum '96 - p177+ [501+]
Science Fiction: The Illustrated Encyclopedia
  r Books - v9 - S '95 - p11 [1-50]
Science Fiction: The Multimedia Encyclopedia of Science Fiction. Electronic Media Version
  yr Kliatt - v30 - S '96 - p40+ [51-250]
Science Framework for the 1996 National Assessment of Educational Progress
    J Gov Info - v23 - S '96 - p545 [51-250]
Science Handbook for Students, Writers and Science Buffs
  y Cur R - v36 - N '96 - p13 [51-250]
Science Spectra: The International Magazine of Contemporary Scientific Thought
  p Nature - v383 - S 5 '96 - p38 [251-500]
Science Year 97
  cr SciTech - v21 - Mr '97 - p3 [1-50]
Scientific American Library: The Planets. Electronic Media Version
  r Am Sci - v84 - N '96 - p595+ [501+]
Scientific Basis for Nuclear Waste Management. Vol. 19
    SciTech - v20 - S '96 - p52 [51-250]
Scieszka, Jon - *The Book That Jack Wrote (Illus. by Jon Scieszka)*
  c Emerg Lib - v24 - S '96 - p45 [51-250]
Knights of the Kitchen Table (Illus. by Lane Smith)
  c SLJ - v42 - N '96 - p41 [1-50]

Math Curse (Illus. by Lane Smith)
c BL - v93 - Ap 1 '97 - p1342 [1-50]
y Emerg Lib - v24 - S '96 - p25 [1-50]
c Inst - v105 - My '96 - p71 [51-250]
c LA - v73 - O '96 - p431 [51-250]
c RT - v50 - O '96 - p137 [1-50]
c RT - v50 - O '96 - p158 [51-250]
*The Stinky Cheese Man and Other Fairly Stupid Tales
(Illus. by Lane Smith)*
c HB - v73 - Mr '97 - p189 [1-50]
c Inst - v105 - My '96 - p69 [51-250]
*The True Story of the Three Little Pigs (Illus. by Lane
Smith)*
c Par Ch - v20 - O '96 - p21 [51-250]
Tut, Tut (Illus. by Lane Smith)
c BL - v93 - O 1 '96 - p352 [51-250]
c HB Guide - v8 - Spr '97 - p75 [51-250]
**SciTech Reference PLUS 1995-1996. Electronic Media
Version**
r ARBA - v28 - '97 - p559+ [51-250]
Scitovsky, Tibor - *Economic Theory and Reality*
Econ J - v106 - S '96 - p1463 [51-250]
Sclove, Richard E - *Democracy and Technology*
AAPSS-A - v546 - Jl '96 - p176+ [501+]
APSR - v90 - S '96 - p659+ [501+]
CPR - v16 - Je '96 - p203+ [501+]
Ethics - v107 - Ja '97 - p364+ [501+]
Scobie, H M - *The Italian Economy in the 1990s*
JEL - v34 - D '96 - p2037+ [51-250]
Scofield, Gregory - *Native Canadiana*
Quill & Q - v62 - My '96 - p28 [501+]
Scola, Angelo - *Hans Urs Von Balthasar: A Theological
Style*
Rel St Rev - v23 - Ja '97 - p45+ [51-250]
Scolnicov, Hanna - *Woman's Theatrical Space*
Theat J - v48 - O '96 - p398+ [501+]
**SCOPE Workshop on Soil and Groundwater Pollution
(1994: Cesky Krumlov , Czech Republic)** -
*Proceedings of the SCOPE Workshop on Soil and
Groundwater Pollution*
SciTech - v20 - N '96 - p68 [51-250]
Scoppettone, Sandra - *Let's Face the Music and Die*
KR - v64 - My 1 '96 - p647 [51-250]
Scoppola, Pietro - *25 Aprile: Liberazione*
Choice - v34 - D '96 - p568 [1-50]
Score
p Sm Pr R - v28 - Je '96 - p13+ [501+]
Scorrano, Luigi - *Presenza Verbale Di Dante Nella
Letteratura Italiana Del Novecento*
MLR - v91 - O '96 - p1012+ [251-500]
Scorsese, Catherine - *Italianamerican: The Scorsese
Family Cookbook*
LJ - v121 - N 15 '96 - p82+ [51-250]
Italianamerican: The Scorsese Family Cookbook
PW - v243 - N 18 '96 - p73 [51-250]
Scot, Barbara J - *Prairie Reunion*
NYTBR - v102 - Mr 23 '97 - p28 [51-250]
Trib Bks - Mr 23 '97 - p6 [1-50]
Scotchie, Joseph - *The Vision of Richard Weaver*
Univ Bkmn - v36 - Win '96 - p25+ [501+]
Scotford, Jessica - *The Distaff Side*
Aust Bk R - N '96 - p66 [51-250]
Scott, Alison MacEwen - *Gender Segregation and Social
Change*
SF - v75 - D '96 - p765 [51-250]
Scott, Ann, 1930- - *Real Events Revisited*
New Sci - v152 - N 2 '96 - p47 [51-250]
Scott, Ann Herbert - *Brave as a Mountain Lion (Illus. by
Glo Coalson)*
c HB Guide - v7 - Fall '96 - p275 [51-250]
c RT - v50 - Ap '97 - p591 [51-250]
Cowboy Country (Illus. by Ted Lewin)
c Par Ch - v20 - O '96 - p21 [51-250]
Scott, Anne Firor - *The Southern Lady*
JSH - v63 - F '97 - p216+ [501+]
Scott, Bernard Brandon - *Hollywood Dreams and
Biblical Stories*
Intpr - v51 - Ja '97 - p102 [251-500]
*Reading New Testament Greek: Complete Word Lists
and Reader's Guide*
r Rel St Rev - v23 - Ja '97 - p66 [51-250]
Scott, Bonnie Kime - *Refiguring Modernism. Vols. 1-2*
ELT - v40 - 2 '97 - p221+ [501+]
Scott, Catherine V - *Gender and Development*
CS - v26 - Ja '97 - p50+ [501+]
Scott, Clive - *Reading the Rhythm*
FR - v70 - F '97 - p457+ [501+]
Scott, David Alexander - *Behind the G-String*
R&R Bk N - v12 - F '97 - p80 [1-50]
Scott, Drusilla - *Everyman Revived*
CPR - v16 - Je '96 - p206+ [501+]

Scott, Elaine - *Adventure in Space (Runger). Audio
Version*
c BL - v93 - N 15 '96 - p604 [51-250]
Movie Magic
y HB Guide - v7 - Fall '96 - p356 [51-250]
SF Chr - v18 - O '96 - p81 [1-50]
Movie Magic (Runger). Audio Version
y Kliatt - v31 - Ja '97 - p49 [51-250]
Safe in the Spotlight (Runger). Audio Version
c HB - v73 - My '97 - p357+ [501+]
Scott, Eleanor - *Randalls Round*
Necro - Fall '96 - p20+ [501+]
Scott, Elizabeth M - *Those of Little Note*
Am Ant - v61 - Ap '96 - p422+ [501+]
Scott, Evelyn - *The Wave*
Bloom Rev - v16 - S '96 - p28 [51-250]
Scott, Gary Thomas - *The Kappa Alpha Order 1865-1897*
JSH - v62 - N '96 - p862+ [51-250]
Scott, Gini Graham - *Can We Talk?*
PW - v243 - S 30 '96 - p72 [51-250]
Rapport - v19 - 6 '96 - p29 [251-500]
Scott, Gregory M - *Political Science*
R&R Bk N - v12 - F '97 - p58 [51-250]
Scott, H M - *The European Nobilities in the Seventeenth
and Eighteenth Centuries. Vol. 2*
CEH - v29 - 1 '96 - p122+ [501+]
Scott, Hal S - *Financing Capital Market Intermediaries in
East and Southeast Asia*
R&R Bk N - v11 - D '96 - p37 [51-250]
Scott, Hugh - *The Camera Obscura*
c Bks Keeps - N '96 - p9 [51-250]
y TES - Ap 4 '97 - p8* [251-500]
A Ghost Waiting
y TES - Ap 4 '97 - p8* [251-500]
The Ghosts of Ravens Crag
c JB - v60 - D '96 - p274 [51-250]
Scott, J Julius, Jr. - *Customs and Controversies*
Rel St Rev - v23 - Ap '97 - p174 [51-250]
Scott, James M - *Deciding to Intervene*
Choice - v34 - Mr '97 - p1236 [51-250]
For Aff - v76 - Mr '97 - p183+ [51-250]
Paul and the Nations
Rel St Rev - v23 - Ja '97 - p73 [51-250]
Scott, Jeffrey - *Does Your Child's World Scare You?*
PW - v244 - Ap 28 '97 - p69 [51-250]
Scott, Joan Wallach - *Only Paradoxes to Offer*
Choice - v34 - S '96 - p189 [51-250]
CPR - v16 - Ag '96 - p289+ [501+]
TLS - F 28 '97 - p31 [501+]
Scott, Joanna, 1960- - *The Closest Possible Union*
y Kliatt - v31 - My '97 - p9 [51-250]
NYTBR - v102 - Ja 19 '97 - p28 [1-50]
The Manikin
NYTBR - v101 - D 8 '96 - p80 [1-50]
Salm - Win '97 - p220+ [501+]
Scott, Joanna C, 1943- - *Charlie and the Children*
KR - v65 - F 1 '97 - p167+ [251-500]
PW - v244 - F 10 '97 - p69 [51-250]
Scott, John - *Stratification and Power*
Choice - v34 - D '96 - p696 [51-250]
Scott, John A, 1932- - *Dante's Political Purgatory*
Choice - v34 - O '96 - p285 [251-500]
Scott, John A, 1948- - *Before I Wake*
Aust Bk R - Jl '96 - p45+ [501+]
Meanjin - v55 - 3 '96 - p583+ [501+]
Scott, Jonathan - *Salvator Rosa: His Life and Times*
Apo - v144 - Ag '96 - p73 [501+]
Sev Cent N - v54 - Fall '96 - p77+ [501+]
Six Ct J - v27 - Win '96 - p1231+ [501+]
Scott, Katie - *The Rococo Interior*
Lon R Bks - v18 - D 12 '96 - p8+ [501+]
Scott, L V - *Conscription and the Attlee Governments*
EHR - v111 - S '96 - p1032 [51-250]
Scott, Leonard B - *Solemn Duty*
PW - v244 - Mr 24 '97 - p80 [51-250]
Scott, Macrina - *Picking the Right Bible Study Program*
r CLW - v67 - Mr '97 - p36+ [51-250]
Scott, Mary Ann - *Ear-Witness*
y Quill & Q - v63 - F '97 - p55 [251-500]
Scott, Melissa - *Dreaming Metal*
KR - v65 - My 1 '97 - p685 [51-250]
The Garden
y Kliatt - v31 - My '97 - p15 [51-250]
Night Sky Mine
Analog - v117 - Ap '97 - p147+ [501+]
y BL - v92 - Ag '96 - p1889 [51-250]
y BL - v92 - Ag '96 - p1891 [51-250]
LJ - v122 - Ja '97 - p51 [1-50]
PW - v243 - Jl 22 '96 - p230 [51-250]
Shadow Man
NYTBR - v102 - Ja 5 '97 - p28 [51-250]

Scott, Michael - *Gemini Game*
y Emerg Lib - v24 - S '96 - p27 [1-50]
Scott, Michael, 1959- - *October Moon*
y VOYA - v19 - O '96 - p202 [501+]
Scott, Michael M - *The Young Oxford Book of Ecology*
y HB Guide - v7 - Fall '96 - p338 [1-50]
yr Par Ch - v21 - Mr '97 - p5 [1-50]
Scott, Nathan A - *Visions of Presence in Modern
American Poetry*
MP - v94 - Ag '96 - p118+ [501+]
Scott, Paul - *Hot Off the Press*
Ceram Mo - v44 - N '96 - p26+ [251-500]
Scott, Raymond P W - *Chromatographic Detectors*
r SciTech - v20 - N '96 - p21 [51-250]
Scott, Richard - *Report of the Inquiry into the Export of
Defence Equipment and Dual-Use Goods to Iraq and
Related Prosecutions. Vols. 1-5*
J Gov Info - v23 - S '96 - p647 [51-250]
*The Scott Report and Its Appendices on CD-ROM.
Electronic Media Version*
TLS - F 28 '97 - p25+ [501+]
Scott, Robert A - *Cytochrome C: A Multidisciplinary
Approach*
SB - v32 - O '96 - p200+ [51-250]
Scott, Robert Falcon - *Last Journey (Fox). Audio Version*
Spec - v277 - N 30 '96 - p55 [51-250]
Scott, Ruth - *The Canadian Spelling Program 2.1*
c Quill & Q - v62 - O '96 - p50 [51-250]
Scott, T Kermit - *Augustine: His Thought in Context*
Rel St - v33 - Mr '97 - p133 [251-500]
Scott, Tom - *The German Peasants' War*
TranslRevS - v1 - My '95 - p73 [51-250]
Scott, V D - *Quantitative Electron-Probe Microanalysis.
2nd Ed.*
SciTech - v20 - N '96 - p22 [51-250]
Scott, W Richard - *Institutions and Organizations*
SF - v75 - S '96 - p342+ [501+]
Scott, Walter, Sir - *Ivanhoe (Hinds). Audio Version*
Obs - Ja 12 '97 - p18* [51-250]
Tales of a Grandfather
Choice - v34 - Ap '97 - p1340 [51-250]
Nine-C Lit - v51 - Mr '97 - p565 [51-250]
TLS - F 14 '97 - p24 [251-500]
Scott, Whitney - *Alternatives--Roads Less Travelled*
BL - v93 - My 15 '97 - p1556 [1-50]
Scott, Wilbur J - *The Politics of Readjustment*
SF - v75 - Mr '97 - p1128+ [251-500]
Scott, William E - *Principles of Wet End Chemistry. 2nd
Ed.*
SciTech - v20 - D '96 - p86 [51-250]
Scott 1996 Classic Specialized Catalogue
r Am Phil - v110 - Jl '96 - p635+ [501+]
The Scott Report
TLS - N 29 '96 - p14 [1-50]
**Scottish Universities Summer School in Physics (43rd:
1994: Dundee, Scotland)** - *The Determination of
Geophysical Parameters from Space*
SciTech - v20 - D '96 - p25 [51-250]
**Scottish Universities' Summer School in Physics (44th:
1994: Stirling, Scotland)** - *Quantum Dynamics of
Simple Systems*
SciTech - v20 - S '96 - p14 [51-250]
Scotto, Marion - *Fresco: Modern Tuscan Cooking for All
Seasons*
PW - v244 - Mr 3 '97 - p69 [51-250]
Scottoline, Lisa - *Legal Tender*
Ent W - N 8 '96 - p62 [51-250]
KR - v64 - S 1 '96 - p1278+ [51-250]
PW - v243 - S 9 '96 - p62 [51-250]
Running from the Law
Books - v10 - Je '96 - p10 [51-250]
PW - v243 - O 21 '96 - p79 [1-50]
Running from the Law (Rosenblat). Audio Version
BWatch - v18 - Mr '97 - p7 [1-50]
Scovil, Jeffrey A - *Photographing Minerals, Fossils and
Lapidary Materials*
RocksMiner - v71 - N '96 - p418 [501+]
*Photographing Minerals, Fossils, and Lapidary
Materials*
SciTech - v20 - S '96 - p61 [51-250]
Scriba, Albrecht - *Die Geschichte Des Motivkomplexes
Theophanie*
Rel St Rev - v23 - Ap '97 - p186 [51-250]
Scribner, Bob - *Germany: A New Social and Economic
History. Vol. 1*
JEH - v57 - Mr '97 - p210+ [501+]
*Popular Religion in Germany and Central Europe
1400-1800*
R&R Bk N - v11 - D '96 - p5 [51-250]
The Reformation in National Context
EHR - v112 - F '97 - p186+ [251-500]

Scribner, R W - *For the Sake of Simple Folk*
 Ren Q - v50 - Spr '97 - p299+ [501+]
Scribner's Best of the Fiction Workshops 1997
 BL - v93 - Mr 1 '97 - p1105+ [51-250]
 KR - v64 - D 15 '96 - p1755+ [251-500]
 LJ - v121 - D '96 - p150 [51-250]
 PW - v243 - D 16 '96 - p42+ [51-250]
Scrimger, Richard - *Crosstown*
 BIC - v25 - N '96 - p35 [51-250]
 CF - v75 - S '96 - p43+ [501+]
Scruton, Roger - *The Classical Vernacular*
 JAAC - v54 - Fall '96 - p395+ [501+]
 Dictionary of Political Thought
 r CR - v269 - N '96 - p277 [1-50]
 An Intelligent Person's Guide to Philosophy
 Spec - v277 - N 9 '96 - p50+ [501+]
 TES - N 29 '96 - p10* [501+]
Scrutton, Thomas Edward, Sir - *Scrutton on Charterparties and Bills of Lading. 20th Ed.*
 Law Q Rev - v113 - Ap '97 - p350+ [501+]
Scudamore, Beverly - *Worm Pie*
 c Quill & Q - v63 - Mr '97 - p81 [51-250]
Scull, Andrew - *Masters of Bedlam*
 Choice - v34 - My '97 - p1580 [51-250]
 Econ - v342 - Mr 15 '97 - p10* [501+]
 KR - v64 - N 1 '96 - p1593 [251-500]
 LATBR - Mr 30 '97 - p7 [501+]
 LJ - v121 - O 15 '96 - p79 [51-250]
 Lon R Bks - v19 - Mr 6 '97 - p29+ [501+]
 New Sci - v153 - F 1 '97 - p45 [51-250]
 PW - v243 - N 25 '96 - p65 [51-250]
 Spec - v278 - Mr 1 '97 - p33+ [501+]
 The Most Solitary of Afflictions
 JMH - v68 - D '96 - p982 [251-500]
Scully, D Eleanor - *Early French Cookery*
 FR - v70 - Mr '97 - p623+ [501+]
 VQR - v72 - Aut '96 - p138* [51-250]
Scully, Gerald W - *The Market Structure of Sports*
 AAPSS-A - v550 - Mr '97 - p198 [251-500]
Sculpture (Illus. by Jean-Philippe Chabot)
 c TES - Ag 23 '96 - p24 [51-250]
Scutt, Jocelynne A - *Growing Up Feminist*
 Aust Bk R - N '96 - p66 [51-250]
 Growing Up Feminist Too
 Aust Bk R - N '96 - p66 [51-250]
 Living Generously
 Aust Bk R - O '96 - p66 [51-250]
Seabird Specialist Group Workshop (1990: Hamilton, New Zealand) - *Seabirds on Islands*
 Choice - v34 - O '96 - p307+ [501+]
Seaborg, Glenn Theodore - *The Plutonium Story*
 Isis - v87 - D '96 - p753+ [501+]
 A Scientist Speaks Out
 Sci - v274 - D 13 '96 - p1848 [1-50]
Seaborn, Charles - *Underwater Wilderness*
 Nature - v385 - F 6 '97 - p497 [51-250]
 yr SB - v33 - My '97 - p107+ [51-250]
Seabrook, John - *Deeper: My Two-Year Odyssey in Cyberspace*
 BL - v93 - F 1 '97 - p916 [51-250]
 KR - v64 - D 1 '96 - p1725 [251-500]
 New Sci - v153 - Mr 8 '97 - p41 [501+]
 NS - v126 - Mr 7 '97 - p48 [501+]
 NYTBR - v102 - F 16 '97 - p23 [501+]
 NYTLa - v146 - F 13 '97 - pC27 [501+]
 Obs - Mr 9 '97 - p16* [501+]
 PW - v244 - Ja 6 '97 - p58 [51-250]
 Spec - v278 - Mr 8 '97 - p30 [501+]
 Time - v149 - F 10 '97 - p84 [251-500]
 Trib Bks - F 16 '97 - p5+ [501+]
Seabrook, Mike - *Max: The Life and Music of Peter Maxwell Davies*
 Notes - v53 - S '96 - p79+ [501+]
Seabrooke, Brenda - *Looking for Diamonds (Illus. by Nancy Mantha)*
 c RT - v50 - Mr '97 - p498 [51-250]
Seaford, Richard - *Reciprocity and Ritual*
 CW - v89 - Jl '96 - p499+ [251-500]
Seager, Frederic - *The Jewish Challenge*
 Obs - v54 - O 13 '96 - p15* [501+]
Seager, Richard Hughes - *The Dawn of Religious Pluralism*
 JAAR - v64 - Fall '96 - p662+ [501+]
 The World's Parliament of Religions
 AHR - v101 - O '96 - p1182+ [501+]
 Can Hist R - v78 - Je '97 - p159+ [501+]
Seago, Alex - *Burning the Box of Beautiful Things*
 AJS - v102 - Ja '97 - p1192+ [501+]
Seagraves, Anne - *Soiled Doves*
 Roundup M - v3 - Ag '96 - p27 [251-250]

Seal, Graham - *The Outlaw Legend*
 Aust Bk R - O '96 - p20 [501+]
Seal, Jeremy - *A Fez of the Heart*
 Bloom Rev - v16 - N '96 - p25 [501+]
 PW - v243 - N 4 '96 - p46 [51-250]
Seale, William - *The White House Garden*
 Hort - v94 - Mr '97 - p80 [51-250]
Sealts, Merton M, Jr. - *Beyond the Classroom*
 AL - v68 - N '96 - p662 [51-250]
 Nine-C Lit - v51 - S '96 - p277 [51-250]
Seaman, Alison - *My Christian Life*
 TES - F 14 '97 - p16* [51-250]
Seaman, Julian - *Fashion Illustration*
 LJ - v121 - N 15 '96 - p61 [51-250]
Search, Gay - *Old Garden, New Gardener*
 PW - v244 - Ap 7 '97 - p87+ [51-250]
Searcy, Margaret Zehmer - *Eyr the Hunter (Illus. by Joyce Haynes)*
 c HB Guide - v7 - Fall '96 - p287 [51-250]
Searle, G R - *Country before Party*
 Albion - v28 - Fall '96 - p527+ [501+]
 HRNB - v25 - Win '97 - p65+ [251-500]
 VS - v39 - Spr '96 - p449+ [501+]
Searle, John - *Rediscovery of the Mind*
 Zygon - v31 - D '96 - p735+ [501+]
Searles, P David - *A College for Appalachia*
 AHR - v102 - F '97 - p207+ [251-500]
 CAY - v16 - Fall '95 - p8 [51-250]
Sears, Barry - *Mastering the Zone*
 BL - v93 - Ja '97 - p777+ [51-250]
 PW - v244 - Ja 6 '97 - p71 [51-250]
 Mastering the Zone (Sears). Audio Version
 Quill & Q - v62 - D '96 - p31 [1-50]
Sears, David W - *Rural Development Strategies*
 Pol Stud J - v24 - Aut '96 - p515+ [501+]
Sears, Laurie J - *Fantasizing the Feminine in Indonesia*
 Choice - v34 - O '96 - p322+ [51-250]
 Shadows of Empire
 Choice - v34 - O '96 - p292 [51-250]
Sears, Richard D - *A Utopian Experiment in Kentucky*
 Choice - v34 - Ja '97 - p865 [51-250]
 R&R Bk N - v11 - D '96 - p17 [1-50]
Sears, Stephen W - *Chancellorsville*
 BW - v26 - N 17 '96 - p3+ [501+]
 Choice - v34 - Mr '97 - p1230 [51-250]
 KR - v64 - S 1 '96 - p1307+ [51-250]
 LJ - v122 - Ja '97 - p50 [1-50]
 LJ - v121 - O 15 '96 - p73+ [51-250]
 NYTBR - v101 - O 20 '96 - p28 [501+]
 PW - v243 - S 9 '96 - p70 [51-250]
 PW - v243 - N 4 '96 - p46 [51-250]
Sears, William - *Parenting the Fussy Baby and High-Need Child*
 BL - v93 - S 1 '96 - p49+ [51-250]
Seary, Michael - *So You Love to Draw (Illus. by Michel Bisson)*
 cr Quill & Q - v62 - O '96 - p48 [251-500]
Seaton, A V - *Tourism: The State of the Art*
 AAAGA - v86 - S '96 - p603+ [501+]
Seaton, Barbara A - *Annexins: Molecular Structure to Cell Function*
 SciTech - v20 - S '96 - p23 [51-250]
Seaton, James - *Cultural Conservatism, Political Liberalism*
 Choice - v34 - S '96 - p119 [51-250]
Seaton, Maureen - *Furious Cooking*
 BW - v26 - D 8 '96 - p8 [51-250]
Seattle, Chief - *Hermana Aguila, Hermano Cielo (Illus. by Susan Jeffers)*
 c SLJ - v42 - N '96 - p132 [51-250]
Seay, James - *Open Field, Understory*
 PW - v243 - D 30 '96 - p61 [251-250]
Sebald, W G - *The Emigrants*
 TranslRevS - v2 - D '96 - p26 [51-250]
Sebald, Winfried Georg - *The Emigrants*
 BW - v26 - D 15 '96 - p6 [501+]
 Choice - v34 - F '97 - p970 [51-250]
 HMR - Win '96 - p25+ [501+]
 KR - v64 - S 1 '96 - p1263+ [251-500]
 LATBR - O 27 '96 - p2 [501+]
 LATBR - D 29 '96 - p11 [1-50]
 LJ - v122 - Ap 15 '97 - p148 [51-250]
 New R - v215 - D 16 '96 - p33+ [501+]
 NY - v73 - Mr 10 '97 - p93 [51-250]
 NYTBR - v102 - Mr 30 '97 - p19 [501+]
 Spec - v277 - N 16 '96 - p42 [1-50]
 TLS - N 29 '96 - p11 [51-250]
 TLS - N 29 '96 - p15 [51-250]
 TranslRevS - v2 - D '96 - p26 [51-250]
 VLS - Win '96 - p11 [51-250]
 VV - v42 - Ja 14 '97 - p51+ [501+]

Sebanc, Mark - *Flight to Hollow Mountain*
 y BL - v93 - S 1 '96 - p65 [501+]
 PW - v243 - Jl 22 '96 - p232 [51-250]
Sebastiani, Mario - *The Notion of Equilibrium in the Keynesian Theory*
 Econ J - v107 - Ja '97 - p262 [251-500]
Sebba, Leslie - *Third Parties*
 Choice - v34 - Ja '97 - p884 [51-250]
Sebestyen, Ouida - *Out of Nowhere*
 c SLJ - v43 - Ja '97 - p37 [1-50]
 Words by Heart
 c PW - v244 - F 10 '97 - p85 [1-50]
Secada, Walter G - *New Directions for Equity in Mathematics Education*
 Math T - v89 - My '96 - p437 [501+]
Sechan, Olivier - *El Zorro (Illus. by Javier Zabala)*
 y BL - v93 - F 15 '97 - p1032 [1-50]
Sechi-Johnson, Patricia - *100 Greatest Manmade Wonders*
 c Sch Lib - v44 - N '96 - p175 [51-250]
Sechzer, Jeri A - *Women and Mental Health*
 SciTech - v20 - D '96 - p3 [51-250]
Secombe, Fred - *Goodbye Curate (Secombe). Audio Version*
 y Kliatt - v30 - S '96 - p48 [51-250]
Secondary Adjustments and Related Aspects of Transfer Pricing Corrections
 R&R Bk N - v11 - D '96 - p37 [51-250]
The Secondary Assembly File
 TES - Mr 21 '97 - p27* [251-500]
La Seconde Guerre Mondiale, Guide Des Sources Conserves En France 1939-1945
 r J Mil H - v61 - Ap '97 - p396+ [501+]
Secretan, Lance H K - *Reclaiming Higher Ground*
 LJ - v122 - My 1 '97 - p118 [51-250]
 PW - v244 - Mr 17 '97 - p73 [51-250]
Secrist-Schmedes, Barbara - *Wind Chamber Music*
 r ARBA - v28 - '97 - p483 [501+]
Sector Investing. 1996 Ed.
 WSJ-MW - v77 - S 19 '96 - pA16 [51-250]
Secunda, Victoria - *When Madness Comes Home*
 LJ - v122 - My 1 '97 - p127 [51-250]
 PW - v244 - Ap 14 '97 - p67 [51-250]
Sedaris, David - *Barrel Fever*
 SFR - v21 - S '96 - p48 [1-50]
 VV - v42 - Ja 7 '97 - p43+ [51-250]
 Naked
 Advocate - Mr 18 '97 - p76+ [501+]
 BL - v93 - F 15 '97 - p996 [51-250]
 Ent W - Mr 21 '97 - p68 [51-250]
 KR - v65 - Ja 15 '97 - p129+ [251-500]
 LJ - v122 - Ap 1 '97 - p93 [51-250]
 NYTBR - v102 - Mr 16 '97 - p10 [501+]
 PW - v244 - Ja 27 '97 - p88 [251-500]
 Naked (Sedaris). Audio Version
 PW - v244 - My 5 '97 - p40+ [51-250]
Seddom, Tom - *Atom Bomb*
 c HB Guide - v7 - Fall '96 - p381 [51-250]
Seddon, George - *A House, a Cottage and a Shop*
 Meanjin - v55 - 2 '96 - p216+ [501+]
 Searching for the Snowy
 Meanjin - v55 - 2 '96 - p216+ [501+]
 Swan Song
 Meanjin - v55 - 2 '96 - p216+ [501+]
Sedgwick, Dawn - *Art across the Curriculum*
 Sch Lib - v44 - N '96 - p178 [51-250]
Sedgwick, Peter R - *Nietzsche: A Critical Reader*
 Ethics - v107 - Ja '97 - p402+ [51-250]
Sedlar, Jean W - *East Central Europe in the Middle Ages 1000-1500*
 Slav R - v55 - Sum '96 - p436+ [501+]
 Specu - v71 - O '96 - p1019+ [501+]
Sed-Rajna, Gabrielle - *Jewish Art*
 BL - v93 - My 15 '97 - p1555 [51-250]
Sedriks, A John - *Corrosion of Stainless Steels. 2nd Ed.*
 Choice - v34 - Ja '97 - p826 [51-250]
Sedycias, Joao - *The Naturalistic Novel of the New World*
 Hisp - v79 - D '96 - p819+ [501+]
 Nine-C Lit - v51 - S '96 - p277 [51-250]
See, Carolyn - *Golden Days*
 NYTBR - v101 - O 27 '96 - p48 [1-50]
 SFR - v21 - N '96 - p20+ [501+]
See, Klaus Von - *Barbar, Germane, Arier*
 Ger Q - v69 - Sum '96 - p339+ [501+]
See, Lisa - *On Gold Mountain*
 y Kliatt - v31 - Ja '97 - p19 [251-500]
 LATBR - N 17 '96 - p14 [51-250]
 NYTBR - v101 - O 20 '96 - p36 [51-250]
 y SLJ - v42 - D '96 - p33 [1-50]
See: A Journal of Visual Culture
 p Utne R - Jl '96 - p118+ [51-250]

Seebacher, Jacques - *Victor Hugo Ou Le Calcul Des Profondeurs*
Poetics T - v18 - Spr '97 - p137+ [501+]

Seed, Patricia - *Ceremonies of Possession in Europe's Conquest of the New World 1492-1640*
HAHR - v77 - My '97 - p304+ [251-500]
Six Ct J - v27 - Win '96 - p1111+ [501+]
W&M Q - v53 - O '96 - p797+ [501+]

Seegers, Annette - *The Military in the Making of Modern South Africa*
Choice - v34 - N '96 - p531 [51-250]

Seeley, F F - *From the Heyday of the Superfluous Man to Chekhov*
MLR - v92 - Ja '97 - p262+ [251-500]

Seelig, Tina - *Incredible, Edible Science*
c Emerg Lib - v23 - My '96 - p45 [51-250]

Seely, John - *The Heinemann English Programme 4*
y TES - S 20 '96 - pR7 [501+]

Seelye, H Ned - *Between Cultures*
MLJ - v81 - Spr '97 - p123+ [501+]

Seeman, Mary V - *Gender and Psychopathology*
AJPsych - v153 - S '96 - p1224 [501+]

See-Paynton, Colin - *The Incisive Eye*
R&R Bk N - v11 - D '96 - p58 [51-250]

Seery, John E - *Political Theory for Mortals*
Choice - v34 - F '97 - p1034 [51-250]
RP - v59 - Spr '97 - p401+ [51-250]

Seff, Philip - *Our Fascinating Earth. Rev. Ed.*
y Kliatt - v30 - N '96 - p29 [51-250]
Petrified Lightning and More Amazing Stories from Our Fascinating Earth
y Kliatt - v31 - Ja '97 - p27 [51-250]
y SB - v33 - My '97 - p106 [51-250]

Sefton, Catherine - *The Skeleton Club*
c Sch Lib - v44 - Ag '96 - p96+ [501+]
Watch Out, Fred's About! (Illus. by C Crossland)
c JB - v60 - Ag '96 - p148 [51-250]
c TES - Jl 5 '96 - pR6 [1-50]

Sefton, James - *Reconciliation of National Income and Expenditure*
JEL - v34 - D '96 - p2032+ [51-250]

Segal, Charles - *Euripides and the Poetics of Sorrow*
CW - v90 - S '96 - p74+ [501+]
Sophocles' Tragic World
Class Out - v74 - Spr '97 - p120 [251-500]
Rel St Rev - v23 - Ja '97 - p62 [51-250]

Segal, Erich - *Oxford Readings in Aristophanes*
Choice - v34 - F '97 - p962+ [51-250]
TLS - F 14 '97 - p10 [501+]

Segal, Gerald - *Chinese Economic Reform*
JEL - v34 - D '96 - p2060 [51-250]
R&R Bk N - v11 - D '96 - p26 [51-250]
The World Affairs Companion. 5th Ed.
r CR - v270 - Ja '97 - p56 [51-250]

Segal, Howard P - *Future Imperfect*
J Am St - v30 - Ap '96 - p179+ [251-500]

Segal, Robert A - *Explaining and Interpreting Religion*
Rel St Rev - v22 - O '96 - p333 [51-250]

Segal, Ronald - *The Black Diaspora*
NYTBR - v101 - D 29 '96 - p20 [51-250]

Segal, Sheila - *Women of Valor*
y Ch BWatch - v6 - N '96 - p2+ [51-250]
y KR - v64 - N 1 '96 - p1607 [51-250]
y PW - v243 - N 25 '96 - p77+ [51-250]
c SLJ - v43 - Mr '97 - p208+ [51-250]

Segal, Suzanne - *Collision with the Infinite*
PW - v243 - O 14 '96 - p77 [51-250]

Segalen, Victor - *Oeuvres Completes. Vols. 1-2*
TLS - O 4 '96 - p6+ [501+]

Segalen, Vincent - *Voyages Au Pays Du Reel*
TLS - O 4 '96 - p6+ [501+]

Segall, Jeffrey - *Joyce in America*
ASInt - v34 - O '96 - p108+ [501+]

Segbers, Klaus - *Post-Soviet Puzzles. Vols. 1-4*
JPR - v33 - Ag '96 - p371+ [501+]

Segel, B W - *A Lie and a Libel*
AB - v99 - Mr 24 '97 - p969+ [501+]
PW - v243 - S 23 '96 - p73 [1-50]
TranslRevS - v2 - D '96 - p17 [51-250]

Segel, Binjamin W - *A Lie and a Libel*
TranslRevS - v2 - D '96 - p17 [51-250]

Segel, Harold B, 1930- - *Pinocchio's Progeny*
Theat J - v48 - D '96 - p522+ [501+]
Stranger in Our Midst
Choice - v34 - Ja '97 - p803 [51-250]

Segelod, Esbjorn - *Resource Allocation in Divisionalized Groups*
JEL - v34 - S '96 - p1438 [51-250]

Segen, J C - *The Dictionary of Modern Medicine*
r BL - v93 - F 1 '97 - p956 [1-50]

Seger, Linda - *When Women Call the Shots*
Choice - v34 - Ap '97 - p1346 [51-250]
KR - v64 - O 1 '96 - p1452 [251-500]
LJ - v121 - D '96 - p96+ [51-250]
PW - v243 - S 23 '96 - p66 [51-250]

Segil, Larraine D - *Intelligent Business Alliances*
BL - v92 - Ag '96 - p1866 [51-250]
Choice - v34 - Mr '97 - p1205+ [51-250]

Segovia, Fernando - *Reading from This Place. Vol. 2*
Rel St Rev - v23 - Ap '97 - p176+ [51-250]

Segre, Emilio - *A Mind Always in Motion*
Isis - v87 - D '96 - p695+ [501+]

Segre, M - *Iscrizioni Di Cos. Vols. 1-2*
AJA - v100 - Jl '96 - p622+ [501+]

Seib, Philip - *Headline Diplomacy*
Choice - v34 - Ap '97 - p1329 [51-250]

Seiber, James N - *Fumigants: Environmental Fate, Exposure, and Analysis*
SciTech - v21 - Mr '97 - p81 [51-250]

Seibert, Patricia - *Toad Overload (Illus. by Jan Davey Ellis)*
c HB Guide - v7 - Fall '96 - p342+ [51-250]
c Inst - v106 - Mr '97 - p28 [1-50]
c RT - v50 - My '97 - p685 [51-250]

Seibold, Eugen - *The Sea Floor. 3rd Ed.*
Choice - v34 - S '96 - p158 [51-250]

Seibold, J Otto - *Free Lunch (Illus. by J Otto Seibold)*
c BL - v93 - S 1 '96 - p145 [51-250]
c HB Guide - v8 - Spr '97 - p48 [51-250]
c KR - v64 - S 1 '96 - p1328 [51-250]
c NYTBR - v102 - Ja 19 '97 - p24 [1-50]
c PW - v243 - S 2 '96 - p129 [51-250]
c SLJ - v42 - N '96 - p92+ [51-250]
Mr. Lunch Takes a Plane Ride
c PW - v244 - Ja 27 '97 - p108 [1-50]

Seidenberg, Charlotte - *The Wildlife Garden*
LJ - v121 - D '96 - p66 [1-50]

Seidensticker, John - *Dangerous Animals*
y BL - v93 - Ap 1 '97 - p1306 [1-50]

Seidler, Victor J - *Unreasonable Men*
Socio R - v44 - N '96 - p746+ [501+]

Seidman, Shlomo - *Transgenic Xenopus*
SciTech - v21 - Mr '97 - p40 [51-250]

Seifer, Marc J - *Wizard: The Life and Times of Nikola Tesla*
BL - v93 - N 15 '96 - p558 [51-250]
BW - v26 - D 1 '96 - p8+ [501+]
Choice - v34 - My '97 - p1520 [51-250]
LJ - v121 - D '96 - p139 [51-250]

Seifert, Horst S H - *Tropical Animal Health*
SciTech - v20 - N '96 - p58 [51-250]

Seigel, Jerrold - *The Private Worlds of Marcel Duchamp*
Lon R Bks - v18 - N 28 '96 - p30+ [501+]
NYRB - v44 - Mr 27 '97 - p22+ [501+]

Seigfried, Charlene Haddock - *Pragmatism and Feminism*
R&R Bk N - v11 - N '96 - p2 [51-250]

Seikel, John A - *Anatomy and Physiology for Speech and Language*
SciTech - v21 - Mr '97 - p40 [51-250]

Seil, William B - *Sherlock Holmes and the Titanic Tragedy*
Arm Det - v30 - Win '97 - p41 [51-250]
Rapport - v19 - 5 '96 - p30 [251-500]

Seiler-Baldinger, Annemarie - *Textiles: A Classification of Techniques*
Am Ant - v61 - Jl '96 - p634 [51-250]

Seim, Turid Karlsen - *The Double Message*
J Ch St - v38 - Sum '96 - p668+ [251-500]
TT - v53 - O '96 - p423 [501+]

Seip, Hans Kristian - *Forestry for Human Development*
Choice - v34 - My '97 - p1525 [51-250]
SciTech - v20 - D '96 - p57 [51-250]

Seiple, Chris - *The U.S. Military NGO Relationship in Humanitarian Interventions*
Mar Crp G - v80 - S '96 - p94+ [501+]

Seismic Engineering 1996
SciTech - v20 - N '96 - p83 [51-250]

Seismic, Shock, and Vibration Isolation 1996
SciTech - v20 - N '96 - p83 [51-250]

Seitenfus, Ricardo - *Para Uma Nova Politica Externa Brasileira*
HAHR - v76 - N '96 - p823+ [501+]

Seitz, Frederick - *On the Frontier*
Isis - v87 - D '96 - p695+ [501+]

Seitz, John L - *Global Issues*
JTWS - v13 - Spr '96 - p398+ [501+]

Seitz, Sharon - *The Other Islands of New York City*
PW - v243 - Jl 22 '96 - p234 [51-250]

Seix, Victoria - *Crea Con Huevos*
c BL - v93 - F 15 '97 - p1032 [1-50]

Sekirinskii, S S - *Liberalizm V Rossii*
Russ Rev - v55 - O '96 - p715+ [251-500]

Sekyi-Otu, Ato - *Fanon's Dialectic of Experience*
Choice - v34 - My '97 - p1539+ [51-250]

Seland, Torrey - *Establishment Violence in Philo and Luke*
Rel St Rev - v22 - O '96 - p353 [51-250]

Selbourne, David - *The Principle of Duty*
RP - v58 - Sum '96 - p639+ [501+]
TES - D 27 '96 - p16 [51-250]

Selby, Jennifer - *Beach Bunny (Illus. by Jennifer Selby)*
c BL - v92 - Ag '96 - p1908+ [51-250]
c HB Guide - v7 - Fall '96 - p244 [51-250]
The Seed Bunny (Illus. by Jennifer Selby)
c CCB-B - v50 - Ap '97 - p296 [51-250]
c KR - v65 - F 15 '97 - p305 [51-250]
c PW - v244 - Mr 3 '97 - p75 [51-250]

Selcer, Richard F - *Hell's Half Acre*
Roundup M - v4 - Ap '97 - p25 [251-500]

Selden, Raman - *The Cambridge History of Literary Criticism. Vol. 8*
ELT - v39 - 4 '96 - p530 [51-250]

Seldin, Peter - *Successful Use of Teaching Portfolios*
MLJ - v80 - Win '96 - p536+ [501+]
The Teaching Portfolio
MLJ - v80 - Win '96 - p536+ [501+]

Seldon, Anthony - *Conservative Century*
HT - v46 - S '96 - p56+ [501+]
How Tory Governments Fall
BW - v26 - D 8 '96 - p7 [1-50]
TLS - D 27 '96 - p28 [501+]

Selenic, Slobodan - *Premeditated Murder*
KR - v65 - F 1 '97 - p171+ [51-250]
LJ - v122 - Ap 15 '97 - p120+ [51-250]
Obs - F 16 '97 - p18* [51-250]

Self, David - *The Broadly Christian Assembly Book*
TES - D 6 '96 - pR5 [251-500]
Fifty Stories for Assembly
c TES - Mr 21 '97 - p27* [51-250]
World Religions
TES - F 14 '97 - p16* [51-250]

Self, Will - *Grey Area and Other Stories*
NYTBR - v101 - D 8 '96 - p80 [1-50]
RCF - v16 - Fall '96 - p194+ [501+]
Trib Bks - Mr 16 '97 - p8 [1-50]
The Sweet Smell of Psychosis
Obs - Ja 12 '97 - p16* [251-500]
TLS - D 20 '96 - p24 [51-250]

Seligman, Joel - *The Transformation of Wall Street. Rev. Ed.*
R&R Bk N - v11 - N '96 - p37 [51-250]

Seligman, Kevin L - *Cutting for All!*
r AB - v99 - Mr 10 '97 - p795+ [501+]

Seligman, Linda - *Diagnosis and Treatment Planning in Counseling. 2nd Ed.*
SciTech - v20 - D '96 - p45 [51-250]

Seligmann, Linda J - *Between Reform and Revolution*
AHR - v102 - F '97 - p242 [251-500]
HAHR - v77 - My '97 - p344+ [251-500]

Seligson, Gerda M - *Greek for Reading*
CW - v89 - Jl '96 - p508+ [251-500]

Seligson, Mitchell A - *Elections and Democracy in Central America, Revisited*
HAHR - v76 - N '96 - p841+ [251-500]

Selimovic, Mesa - *Death and the Dervish*
BW - v26 - S 8 '96 - p12 [51-250]
TranslRevS - v2 - D '96 - p31 [51-250]

Sell, Alan P F - *Philosophical Idealism and Christian Belief*
CPR - v16 - Je '96 - p210+ [251-500]

Selleck, R J W - *James Kay-Shuttleworth: Journey of an Outsider*
EHR - v112 - F '97 - p230+ [251-500]

Sellers, M N S - *An Ethical Education*
Ethics - v107 - O '96 - p188 [51-250]

Sellers, Paul - *Alphabats*
c TES - Mr 28 '97 - p11* [51-250]

Sellers, Ronnie - *The Official Dog Codependents Handbook*
Dog Fan - v28 - Ja '97 - p39 [51-250]

Sellers, Susan - *Helene Cixous: Authorship, Autobiography and Love*
Choice - v34 - O '96 - p287 [51-250]
Instead of Full Stops
BL - v93 - Mr 15 '97 - p1221 [51-250]

Selles, Johanna M - *Methodists and Women's Education in Ontario 1836-1925*
R&R Bk N - v12 - F '97 - p68 [51-250]

Sellier, Marie - *Cezanne from A to Z*
  y HB Guide - v7 - Fall '96 - p356+ [51-250]
  c Sch Lib - v44 - Ag '96 - p114 [51-250]
  c TES - Ag 23 '96 - p24 [51-250]
  Chagall from A to Z
  y HB Guide - v8 - Spr '97 - p139 [51-250]
  c KR - v64 - N 15 '96 - p1678 [51-250]
  Matisse from A to Z
  c HB Guide - v7 - Fall '96 - p357 [51-250]
  c Sch Lib - v44 - Ag '96 - p114 [51-250]
  c TES - Ag 23 '96 - p24 [51-250]
Sells, Michael Anthony - *The Bridge Betrayed*
    BW - v26 - N 17 '96 - p5 [1-50]
    Choice - v34 - Mr '97 - p1223 [51-250]
    KR - v64 - S 1 '96 - p1308 [251-500]
    LATBR - N 10 '96 - p4+ [501+]
    LJ - v121 - O 1 '96 - p106 [51-250]
    New R - v215 - N 25 '96 - p31+ [501+]
  Early Islamic Mysticism
    Theol St - v58 - Mr '97 - p188 [251-500]
Selman, Paul - *Local Sustainability*
    Choice - v34 - My '97 - p1549 [51-250]
Selnow, Gary W - *Society's Impact on Television*
    JPC - v29 - Spr '96 - p252+ [251-500]
Selth, Jefferson P - *Ambition, Discrimination, and Censorship in Libraries*
    Lib & Cul - v32 - Win '97 - p148+ [501+]
Seltzer, Eric - *Four Pups and a Worm*
  c HB Guide - v8 - Spr '97 - p55 [51-250]
Seltzer, Richard - *The Alta Vista Search Revolution*
  r LJ - v122 - F 1 '97 - p102 [51-250]
Selvadurai, Shyam - *Funny Boy*
    BL - v93 - Ap 1 '97 - p1285 [1-50]
    LJ - v121 - O 1 '96 - p156 [51-250]
    Nat - v263 - S 30 '96 - p33+ [501+]
    PW - v244 - My 5 '97 - p206 [1-50]
    WLT - v70 - Aut '96 - p1036 [501+]
Selvanathan, E A - *Recent Developments in Applied Demand Analysis*
    JEL - v34 - D '96 - p2025 [51-250]
Selvidge, Marla J - *Notorious Voices*
    Choice - v34 - O '96 - p299 [51-250]
Selya, Mark - *Taipei*
    GJ - v163 - Mr '97 - p109 [51-250]
Selz, Peter - *Max Beckmann*
    BL - v92 - Ag '96 - p1873 [51-250]
    Choice - v34 - O '96 - p269 [51-250]
Selzer, Jack - *Kenneth Burke in Greenwich Village*
    BL - v93 - F 1 '97 - p921 [51-250]
    NYTBR - v102 - Ap 20 '97 - p21 [51-250]
    PW - v243 - D 16 '96 - p49 [51-250]
    TLS - Mr 7 '97 - p25 [501+]
Selzer, Richard - *Down from Troy (Gray). Audio Version*
  y Kliatt - v30 - S '96 - p56 [51-250]
  Taking the World in for Repairs (Gray). Audio Version
  y Kliatt - v31 - Ja '97 - p50 [51-250]
Selznick, Brian - *The Robot King (Illus. by Brian Selznick)*
  c Emerg Lib - v24 - S '96 - p51 [51-250]
Semboja, Joseph - *Service Provision under Stress in East Africa*
    JEL - v34 - D '96 - p2083+ [51-250]
Semen, Vasyl - *Bud'te Zdorovi*
    BL - v93 - N 15 '96 - p577 [1-50]
Semetko, Holli A - *Germany's Unity Election*
    Pub Op Q - v60 - Fall '96 - p461+ [501+]
Seminar on Acceptable Risks for Extreme Events in the Planning and Design of Major Infrastructure (1994: Sydney, Australia) - *Acceptable Risks for Major Infrastructure*
    SciTech - v20 - S '96 - p51 [51-250]
Seminar on Gas Contracting Principles and Practices (1995: Sinaia, Romania) - *Gas Contracting*
    R&R Bk N - v12 - F '97 - p42 [51-250]
Seminara, George - *Mugshots: Celebrities under Arrest*
    Obs - Ja 5 '97 - p16* [51-250]
Semiotics 1994
    R&R Bk N - v12 - F '97 - p76 [51-250]
Semmes, Clovis - *Racism, Health, and Post-Industrialism*
    Bl S - v26 - Sum '96 - p67 [51-250]
Sempowski, Martha L - *Mortuary Practices and Skeletal Remains at Teotihuacan*
    LA Ant - v7 - D '96 - p378+ [501+]
Semprun, Jorge - *La Escritura O La Vida*
    WLT - v71 - Win '97 - p236+ [501+]
  Literature or Life
    KR - v65 - Ja 15 '97 - p92 [251-500]
    LATBR - Mr 16 '97 - p7 [501+]
    LJ - v122 - F 1 '97 - p108 [51-250]
    NYTBR - v102 - Ap 6 '97 - p28 [501+]
    PW - v244 - Ja 13 '97 - p51 [51-250]

  The Long Voyage
    LATBR - Mr 16 '97 - p7 [501+]
    LJ - v122 - F 1 '97 - p112 [1-50]
Semro, Jennifer - *A Dolphin of Many Colors*
  c SLJ - v42 - D '96 - p124 [51-250]
Semyonova Tian-Shanskaia, Olga - *Village Life in Late Tsarist Russia*
    CAY - v17 - Win '96 - p13 [51-250]
    TranslRevS - v1 - My '95 - p11 [1-50]
Sen, Amartya Kumar - *Inequality Reexamined*
    NYRB - v43 - S 19 '96 - p40+ [501+]
Sen, Gita - *Power and Decision*
    Signs - v22 - Aut '96 - p227+ [501+]
Sen, Sunil Kumar - *Working Class Movements in India 1885-1975*
    AHR - v101 - O '96 - p1261+ [501+]
Senak, Mark S - *HIV, AIDS, and the Law*
    Advocate - Je 11 '96 - p58+ [501+]
    Choice - v34 - O '96 - p314 [51-250]
Senarclens, Pierre De - *From Yalta to the Iron Curtain*
    JPR - v33 - Ag '96 - p383+ [251-500]
Senator, Rochelle B - *Collaborations for Literacy*
    Emerg Lib - v23 - My '96 - p39 [251-500]
    JAAL - v40 - S '96 - p76+ [501+]
Sencion, Viriato - *They Forged the Signature of God*
    Bloom Rev - v16 - N '96 - p10 [251-500]
    NYTBR - v101 - D 22 '96 - p15 [51-250]
Sendak, Maurice - *Donde Viven Los Monstruos*
  c BL - v93 - My 1 '97 - p1507 [1-50]
  Nutshell Library
  c BW - v26 - D 8 '96 - p20 [51-250]
  Where the Wild Things Are
  c HB - v73 - Mr '97 - p187 [1-50]
Seneca, Lucius Annaeus - *Moral and Political Essays*
    Ethics - v107 - O '96 - p179+ [51-250]
  Seneca's Troades (Boyle)
  y CW - v90 - S '96 - p68+ [251-500]
  Thyestes (Heywood)
    CML - v16 - Win '96 - p119+ [501+]
Senf, Carol A - *The Critical Response to Bram Stoker*
    JPC - v30 - Fall '96 - p224 [51-250]
SenGupta, Gunja - *For God and Mammon*
    Choice - v34 - S '96 - p198+ [51-250]
    WHQ - v28 - Spr '97 - p75 [251-500]
Senior, Donald - *What Are They Saying about Matthew?. Rev. Ed.*
    Rel St Rev - v23 - Ap '97 - p182 [51-250]
Senior, W A - *Stephen R. Donaldson's Chronicles of Thomas Covenant*
    Ext - v37 - Fall '96 - p274+ [501+]
Senjen, Rye - *The Internet for Women*
    Aust Bk R - O '96 - p69 [1-50]
    Ms - v7 - Ja '97 - p80 [51-250]
    TES - O 18 '96 - p42U [501+]
Senkevitch, Judith - *Rural Libraries and Internetworking*
    LR - v45 - 7 '96 - p49+ [501+]
Senn, Alfred Erich - *Gorbachev's Failure in Lithuania*
    Slav R - v55 - Sum '96 - p474+ [501+]
Senn, Bryan - *Golden Horrors*
  r ARBA - v28 - '97 - p512 [51-250]
  r Choice - v34 - Ja '97 - p774+ [51-250]
  r LJ - v121 - O 15 '96 - p60 [51-250]
  r R&R Bk N - v11 - N '96 - p67 [51-250]
Sennett, Richard - *Flesh and Stone*
    HT - v47 - Ja '97 - p56+ [501+]
    J Soc H - v30 - Fall '96 - p292+ [501+]
    South HR - v30 - Fall '96 - p396+ [501+]
Senter, Ruth - *Have We Really Come a Long Way, Baby?*
    LJ - v122 - Mr 15 '97 - p67 [51-250]
Seow, C L - *A Grammar for Biblical Hebrew. Rev. Ed.*
    Rel St Rev - v23 - Ja '97 - p53+ [51-250]
  Homosexuality and Christian Community
    Intpr - v51 - Ap '97 - p197+ [501+]
    Rel St Rev - v23 - Ap '97 - p159 [501+]
    TT - v53 - Ja '97 - p508+ [501+]
Seppala, Juha - *Tunnetteko Tyypin?*
    WLT - v70 - Aut '96 - p995+ [251-500]
Sepper, Dennis L - *Descartes's Imagination*
    Isis - v88 - Mr '97 - p143+ [501+]
    RM - v50 - D '96 - p424+ [501+]
  Newton's Optical Writings
    Isis - v88 - Mr '97 - p146+ [501+]
Sepstrup, Preben - *TV I Kulturhistorisk Perspektiv 1954-1994*
    JC - v47 - Win '97 - p120+ [501+]
Sepulveda, Juan Gines De - *Obras Completas. Vol. 1, Bks. 1-5*
    Six Ct J - v27 - Fall '96 - p845+ [501+]
Sepulveda, Luis - *Full Circle*
    LJ - v122 - F 15 '97 - p154 [51-250]
    TLS - 1 '97 - p32 [251-500]

  Historia De Una Gaviota Y Del Gato Que Le Enseno A Volar
    LJ - v122 - Ja '97 - p80 [51-250]
  The Name of a Bullfighter
    NYTBR - v101 - O 13 '96 - p21 [51-250]
Sequeira, A - *Navier-Stokes Equations and Related Nonlinear Problems*
    SIAM Rev - v38 - D '96 - p714 [501+]
Serafin, Joan - *East-Central Europe in the 1990s*
    Slav R - v55 - Sum '96 - p438+ [501+]
Serageldin, Ismail - *Architecture of the Contemporary Mosque*
    MEJ - v51 - Spr '97 - p310 [51-250]
  The Self and the Other
    JEL - v35 - Mr '97 - p273 [51-250]
Serdarevic, Olivia N - *Refractive Surgery*
    SciTech - v21 - Mr '97 - p61 [51-250]
Sered, Susan Starr - *Priestess, Mother, Sacred Sister*
    Am Ethnol - v24 - F '97 - p218 [51-250]
Seren, Tony Curtis - *How Poets Work*
    TES - F 28 '97 - p7* [251-500]
Sereni, Clara - *Eppure*
    WLT - v70 - Sum '96 - p674 [251-500]
Sereni, Vittorio - *Poesie*
    TLS - Jl 19 '96 - p11 [501+]
  Scritture Private
    TLS - Jl 19 '96 - p11 [501+]
Sereny, Gitta - *Albert Speer: His Battle with Truth*
    Books - v9 - S '95 - p24 [1-50]
    NS - v125 - Ag 30 '96 - p44 [1-50]
    NYTBR - v102 - Mr 9 '97 - p28 [51-250]
    PW - v243 - S 30 '96 - p79 [1-50]
    Quad - v40 - Je '96 - p83+ [501+]
    TLS - N 29 '96 - p14 [51-250]
Serfozo, Mary - *There's a Square (Illus. by David A Carter)*
  c HB Guide - v7 - Fall '96 - p244 [51-250]
  What's What? (Illus. by Keiko Narahashi)
  c BL - v93 - O 1 '96 - p351 [51-250]
  c CCB-B - v50 - O '96 - p75 [51-250]
  c HB Guide - v8 - Spr '97 - p48 [51-250]
  c KR - v64 - Ag 15 '96 - p1242 [51-250]
  c NYTBR - v102 - Ja 19 '97 - p24 [251-500]
  c PW - v243 - S 2 '96 - p130 [51-250]
  c SLJ - v42 - O '96 - p106 [51-250]
  Who Wants One? (Illus. by Keiko Narahashi)
  c BL - v93 - Ap 1 '97 - p1341 [1-50]
Sergeant, Jack - *Deathtripping*
    Afterimage - v23 - Sum '96 - p23 [501+]
Sergiovanni, Thomas - *Building Community in Schools*
    HER - v66 - Win '96 - p853+ [501+]
Serim, Ferdi - *Net Learning*
    TES - O 18 '96 - p41U [51-250]
Serle, Geoffrey - *Robin Boyd: A Life*
    Aust Bk R - Ag '96 - p67 [1-50]
Serlio, Sebastiano - *Sebastiano Serlio on Architecture. Vol. 1, Bks. 1-5*
    Apo - v145 - Ja '97 - p62 [501+]
    Choice - v34 - F '97 - p958 [51-250]
    TLS - N 8 '96 - p10 [501+]
Sernine, Daniel - *Ludovic*
  y Can CL - v22 - Fall '96 - p139+ [501+]
Serotta, Edward - *Jews, Germany, Memory*
    Trib Bks - Ja 12 '97 - p6+ [51-250]
Serpell, James - *In the Company of Animals*
    New Sci - v152 - D 21 '96 - p68 [51-250]
Serrano, Juan - *Treasury of Spanish Love Poems, Quotations and Proverbs*
    TranslRevS - v2 - D '96 - p4 [1-50]
Serrano, Monica - *Rebuilding the State*
    JEL - v34 - D '96 - p2038 [51-250]
Serrano Alonso, Javier - *Bibliografia General De Ramon Del Valle-Inclan*
  r Hisp - v79 - D '96 - p794+ [501+]
Serratosa, Felix - *Organic Chemistry in Action. 2nd Ed.*
    SciTech - v21 - Mr '97 - p29 [51-250]
Serres, Michel - *Angels, a Modern Myth*
    Choice - v34 - O '96 - p295 [51-250]
Service, Robert - *Lenin: A Political Life. Vol. 3*
    AHR - v101 - O '96 - p1248+ [501+]
    HT - v47 - Ja '97 - p58+ [501+]
Servies, James A - *A Bibliography of Florida. Vol. 2*
  r ARBA - v28 - '97 - p47+ [251-500]
Servos, John W - *Physical Chemistry from Ostwald to Pauling*
    Nature - v383 - O 24 '96 - p682 [1-50]
Sesame Street
  cp Par Ch - v20 - O '96 - p15 [1-50]

Seshadri, Vijay - *Wild Kingdom*
  Choice - v34 - O '96 - p281 [51-250]
  HR - v49 - Aut '96 - p503+ [501+]
  NY - v72 - My 27 '96 - p132 [51-250]
  VQR - v72 - Aut '96 - p137*+ [51-250]
Sessions, George - *Deep Ecology for the 21st Century*
  PAR - v56 - S '96 - p495+ [501+]
Sessions, Roger - *Object Persistence*
  SciTech - v20 - S '96 - p5 [51-250]
Seth, Vikram - *Arion and the Dolphin (Illus. by Jane Ray)*
  c RT - v50 - N '96 - p256 [51-250]
Sethi, Robbie Clipper - *The Bride Wore Red*
  BW - v26 - S 8 '96 - p6 [501+]
Sethi, S Prakash - *Up against the Corporate Wall. 6th Ed.*
  R&R Bk N - v11 - D '96 - p28 [51-250]
Seton, Anya - *Dragonwyck*
  Nat R - v48 - D 23 '96 - p52+ [51-250]
  Katherine
  Nat R - v48 - D 23 '96 - p53 [51-250]
Setting the Stage for the Next Century
  J Gov Info - v23 - S '96 - p619 [51-250]
Settipane, Guy A - *Columbus and the New World*
  HAHR - v77 - My '97 - p305+ [251-500]
Settis, Salvatore - *I Greci: Storia Cultura Arte Societa.*
  Vol. 1
  r TLS - N 1 '96 - p8+ [501+]
Settle, Mary Lee - *Choices*
  Bloom Rev - v16 - N '96 - p27 [251-500]
  The Killing Ground
  VQR - v72 - Aut '96 - p143* [1-50]
  Know Nothing
  VQR - v72 - Aut '96 - p143* [1-50]
  O Beulah Land
  VQR - v72 - Aut '96 - p143* [1-50]
  Prisons
  VQR - v72 - Aut '96 - p143* [1-50]
  The Scapegoat
  VQR - v72 - Aut '96 - p143* [1-50]
Setzer, Claudia J - *Jewish Responses to Early Christians*
  J Ch St - v38 - Aut '96 - p908+ [251-500]
Seung, T K - *Plato Rediscovered*
  IPQ - v37 - Mr '97 - p124 [51-250]
  RP - v59 - Win '97 - p165+ [501+]
Seuss, Dr. - *Dr. Seuss's ABC. Electronic Media Version*
  c HB - v73 - Mr '97 - p219+ [501+]
  Foot Book
  c Ch BWatch - v7 - F '97 - p5 [1-50]
  Green Eggs and Ham. Electronic Media Version
  c BW - v26 - D 15 '96 - p11 [51-250]
  c HB - v73 - Mr '97 - p219+ [501+]
  c Par - v71 - D '96 - p260 [51-250]
  A Hatful of Seuss
  c PW - v244 - F 10 '97 - p85 [51-250]
  Mr. Brown Can Moo! Can You?
  c Ch BWatch - v7 - F '97 - p5 [1-50]
  My Many Colored Days (Illus. by Steve Johnson)
  c BL - v93 - N 1 '96 - p510 [51-250]
  c HB Guide - v8 - Spr '97 - p48 [51-250]
  c Inst - v106 - Ja '97 - p4* [1-50]
  c KR - v64 - Ag 15 '96 - p1246 [51-250]
  c LATBR - S 22 '96 - p15 [51-250]
  c NY - v72 - N 18 '96 - p102 [1-50]
  c Par - v71 - D '96 - p252 [51-250]
  c PW - v243 - Jl 22 '96 - p240+ [51-250]
  c SLJ - v42 - D '96 - p105+ [51-250]
  Oh, the Places You'll Go!
  c Inst - v105 - My '96 - p26 [51-250]
  Read and Learn with Dr. Seuss (Illus. by Dr. Seuss)
  c JB - v60 - D '96 - p260 [51-250]
  Seuss-Isms: Wise and Witty Prescriptions for Living from the Good Doctor
  c PW - v244 - Mr 17 '97 - p85 [51-250]
Sevastiades, Philemon D - *I Am Eastern Orthodox*
  c SLJ - v43 - F '97 - p88 [51-250]
  I Am Protestant
  c SLJ - v43 - F '97 - p88 [51-250]
  I Am Roman Catholic
  c SLJ - v42 - N '96 - p100 [51-250]
Sevenich-Bax, Elisabeth - *Israels Konfrontation Mit Den Letzten Boten Der Weisheit*
  Rel St Rev - v23 - Ja '97 - p71 [51-250]
Severance, John B - *Gandhi, Great Soul*
  y BL - v93 - F 15 '97 - p1013 [51-250]
  Gandhi: Great Soul
  c HB - v73 - My '97 - p344+ [51-250]
  c KR - v65 - Mr 1 '97 - p387 [51-250]
  Gandhi, Great Soul
  c PW - v244 - F 24 '97 - p92+ [51-250]
  Winston Churchill: Soldier, Statesman, Artist
  y Ch BWatch - v6 - Jl '96 - p3 [51-250]
  y HB Guide - v7 - Fall '96 - p374 [51-250]

Severe, Martin L - *The Comprehensive Listing of Artcraft Covers. 4th Ed.*
  r Am Phil - v110 - D '96 - p1086 [51-250]
Severens, Martha R - *Andrew Wyeth: America's Painter*
  A Art - v60 - O '96 - p80 [51-250]
  LJ - v121 - N 1 '96 - p66 [51-250]
Severin, Dorothy Sherman - *Witchcraft in Celestina*
  MLR - v92 - Ja '97 - p226+ [501+]
Severin, Tim - *The China Voyage*
  GJ - v162 - Jl '96 - p241+ [51-250]
  y Kliatt - v31 - Mr '97 - p33 [51-250]
Severson, Richard James - *The Confessions of Saint Augustine*
  r ARBA - v28 - '97 - p548 [51-250]
  r Choice - v34 - My '97 - p1481 [51-250]
Severus, Bishop of Malaga - *Severi Episcopi Malacitani (?) in Evangelia Libri XII*
  Specu - v72 - Ja '97 - p219+ [501+]
Sevin, Dieter - *Textstrategien In DDR-Prosawerken Zwischen Bau Und Durchbruch Der Berliner Mauer*
  MLR - v92 - Ap '97 - p533+ [501+]
Sewall, Marcia - *The Pilgrims of Plimoth (Illus. by Marcia Sewall)*
  c PW - v243 - O 7 '96 - p78 [1-50]
Seward, Desmond - *The War of the Roses*
  PW - v243 - N 11 '96 - p72 [1-50]
  The Wars of the Roses
  Albion - v28 - Win '96 - p679+ [501+]
  HRNB - v25 - Fall '96 - p18 [251-500]
  NY - v72 - Ag 12 '96 - p73 [51-250]
  Trib Bks - Ja 5 '97 - p2 [51-250]
Sewell, Anna - *Black Beauty (Illus. by Victor Ambrus)*
  c PW - v244 - My 12 '97 - p77 [51-250]
  Black Beauty (Illus. by Lucy Kemp-Welch)
  c PW - v244 - Mr 31 '97 - p77 [1-50]
  Black Beauty (Jarvis). Audio Version
  c TES - Jl 19 '96 - pR8 [51-250]
Sewell, Bill - *Food from the Place Below*
  Books - v10 - Je '96 - p25 [51-250]
Sewell, Marilyn - *Claiming the Spirit Within*
  y BL - v93 - N 1 '96 - p475 [51-250]
  Ms - v7 - N '96 - p82 [1-50]
Sewell, William H, Jr. - *A Rhetoric of Bourgeois Revolution*
  AHR - v101 - D '96 - p1555+ [501+]
  AJS - v102 - Jl '96 - p299+ [501+]
  CS - v26 - Mr '97 - p240+ [501+]
The Sex Box
  Ent W - D 13 '96 - p74 [51-250]
  VLS - Win '96 - p25+ [501+]
Sexson, Jeanne E - *Down but Not Out*
  LJ - v121 - N 1 '96 - p95 [51-250]
Sexton, Conor - *Newnes C++ Pocket Book. 2nd Ed.*
  New Sci - v153 - Mr 1 '97 - p46+ [501+]
  Newnes C Pocket Book. 2nd Ed.
  r SciTech - v20 - S '96 - p7 [1-50]
Sexton, Donal J - *Signals Intelligence in World War II*
  r ARBA - v28 - '97 - p253 [51-250]
  r Choice - v34 - Ja '97 - p775 [51-250]
  J Mil H - v61 - Ap '97 - p399+ [251-500]
  r R&R Bk N - v11 - N '96 - p11 [51-250]
Sexton, Margot - *The Twelve Days of Christmas (Illus. by Janis Jones)*
  c BIC - v25 - D '96 - p33+ [501+]
Sextus, Empiricus - *Contro Gli Etici*
  RM - v50 - S '96 - p182+ [501+]
Seybolt, Peter J - *Throwing the Emperor from His Horse*
  Choice - v34 - Mr '97 - p1217 [51-250]
  R&R Bk N - v12 - F '97 - p13 [51-250]
Seyd, Patrick - *Labour and Conservative Party Members 1990-92*
  r Choice - v34 - D '96 - p594+ [1-50]
  R&R Bk N - v11 - D '96 - p48 [51-250]
Seydor, Paul - *Peckinpah: The Western Films: A Reconsideration*
  Choice - v34 - Ap '97 - p1346 [51-250]
  Ent W - Mr 14 '97 - p74 [51-250]
  FIR - v48 - Ja '97 - p105 [501+]
Seymour, Bruce - *Lola Montez: A Life*
  ABR - v18 - O '96 - p11+ [501+]
  Choice - v34 - O '96 - p341+ [51-250]
  CR - v270 - Ja '97 - p48+ [251-500]
  Lon R Bks - v18 - N 14 '96 - p20+ [501+]
  Spec - v276 - My 25 '96 - p30 [501+]
  TLS - Jl 7 '96 - p27 [501+]
Seymour, Christopher - *Yakuza Diary*
  LATBR - S 1 '96 - p11 [51-250]
Seymour, David - *Chim: The Photographs of David Seymour*
  CSM - v89 - D 5 '96 - pB2+ [51-250]

Seymour, Elaine - *Talking about Leaving*
  Nature - v386 - Ap 10 '97 - p566+ [501+]
  SciTech - v21 - Mr '97 - p3 [51-250]
Seymour, Gene - *Jazz: The Great American Art*
  y Kliatt - v31 - Mr '97 - p35 [51-250]
Seymour, Gerald - *Killing Ground*
  KR - v65 - F 15 '97 - p251+ [251-500]
  PW - v244 - Mr 10 '97 - p49 [51-250]
Seymour, M C - *A Catalogue of Chaucer Manuscripts. Vol. 1*
  r RES - v48 - F '97 - p82+ [501+]
Seymour, Michael - *Une Nation Peut-Elle Se Donner La Constitution De Son Choix?*
  Dialogue - v35 - Fall '96 - p844+ [501+]
Seymour, Michel - *Pensee, Langage Et Communaute*
  Dialogue - v35 - Sum '96 - p641+ [501+]
Seymour, Randy - *Wildflowers of Mammoth Cave National Park*
  BL - v93 - Mr 15 '97 - p1212 [51-250]
Seymour, Tres - *Black Sky River (Illus. by Dan Andreasen)*
  c BL - v93 - N 15 '96 - p596 [51-250]
  c HB Guide - v8 - Spr '97 - p48 [51-250]
  c SLJ - v42 - S '96 - p191 [51-250]
  The Gulls of the Edmund Fitzgerald (Illus. by Tres Seymour)
  c HB Guide - v7 - Fall '96 - p275 [51-250]
Seymour-Smith, Martin - *Dictionary of Fictional Characters. Rev. Ed.*
  r RQ - v36 - Win '96 - p215 [51-250]
  World Authors 1900-1950. Vols. 1-4
  r ARBA - v28 - '97 - p408 [51-250]
Seyvos, Florence - *Les Apparitions*
  FR - v70 - F '97 - p503+ [501+]
Sfez, Lucien - *Dictionnaire Critique De La Communication. Vols. 1-2*
  r JC - v47 - Win '97 - p144+ [501+]
Sgard, Jean - *Vingt Etudes Sur Prevost D'Exiles*
  MLR - v92 - Ap '97 - p470+ [501+]
Sgorlon, Carlo - *Il Costruttore*
  BL - v93 - D 1 '96 - p644 [1-50]
  WLT - v70 - Aut '96 - p936 [251-500]
Shaara, Jeff - *Gods and Generals*
  KR - v64 - My 1 '96 - p633 [251-500]
  Mar Crp G - v80 - N '96 - p80 [501+]
  PW - v244 - Mr 31 '97 - p72 [1-50]
  Gods and Generals (Lang). Audio Version
  y Kliatt - v31 - Mr '97 - p48 [51-250]
  LJ - v121 - N 15 '96 - p104 [51-250]
Shabecoff, Philip - *A New Name for Peace*
  Choice - v34 - N '96 - p479 [51-250]
Shaber, Sarah R - *Simon Said*
  KR - v65 - F 15 '97 - p259 [51-250]
  LJ - v122 - Ap 1 '97 - p133 [51-250]
  PW - v244 - F 10 '97 - p70+ [51-250]
Shackel, Paul A - *Culture Change and the New Technology*
  Choice - v34 - F '97 - p1027 [51-250]
  R&R Bk N - v11 - D '96 - p16 [51-250]
  Sci - v275 - Ja 10 '97 - p175 [1-50]
Shackleton, George Green - *Thomas Jefferson's Travels in Europe 1784-1789*
  W&M Q - v53 - O '96 - p838+ [501+]
Shackleton, Viv - *Business Leadership*
  Per Psy - v49 - Aut '96 - p740+ [501+]
Shadle, Stanley F - *Andres Molina Enriques*
  HRNB - v25 - Fall '96 - p17 [501+]
Shadwick, William F - *Mechanics Day*
  SIAM Rev - v38 - S '96 - p545 [1-50]
Shafarman, Steven - *Awareness Heals*
  PW - v244 - Ap 7 '97 - p89 [51-250]
Shafer, Byron E - *Postwar Politics in the G-7*
  Choice - v34 - My '97 - p1570 [51-250]
  For Aff - v75 - N '96 - p147 [51-250]
  R&R Bk N - v12 - F '97 - p59 [1-50]
  The Two Majorities
  J Am St - v30 - D '96 - p478+ [251-500]
  J Pol - v59 - F '97 - p253+ [501+]
Shaffer, Butler - *The Restraint of Trade*
  Choice - v34 - Ap '97 - p1389 [51-250]
Shaffer, David R - *Developmental Psychology. 4th Ed.*
  Adoles - v31 - Win '96 - p996 [51-250]
Shaffer, Louise - *Talked to Death*
  BWatch - v17 - S '96 - p1 [1-50]
Shafir, Gershon - *Immigrants and Nationalists*
  APSR - v90 - S '96 - p682+ [501+]
  CS - v25 - N '96 - p746+ [501+]
Shafranske, Edward P - *Religion and the Clinical Practice of Psychology*
  R&R Bk N - v11 - D '96 - p2 [51-250]

Shafrir, Eleazar - *Lessons from Animal Diabetes*
  SciTech - v20 - D '96 - p57 [51-250]
Shah, Anwar - *Fiscal Incentives for Investment and Innovation*
  JEL - v34 - S '96 - p1439 [51-250]
Shah, Diane K - *High-Heel Blue*
  BL - v93 - Ja '97 - p825 [51-250]
  Ent W - D 13 '96 - p75 [51-250]
  KR - v64 - N 1 '96 - p1560+ [251-500]
  PW - v243 - N 11 '96 - p56 [51-250]
  Trib Bks - F 2 '97 - p4 [51-250]
Shah, Idries - *Learning How to Learn*
  BL - v93 - O 1 '96 - p308 [1-50]
Shah, Kumud - *The Quick after Work Indian Vegetarian Cookbook*
  Books - v11 - Ap '97 - p20 [1-50]
Shahak, Israel - *Jewish History, Jewish Religion*
  Lon R Bks - v18 - O 31 '96 - p16+ [501+]
Shaham, Nathan - *Bone to the Bone*
  TranslRevS - v1 - My '95 - p23 [51-250]
Shahan, Sherry - *Barnacles Eat with Their Feet*
  c HB Guide - v7 - Fall '96 - p338 [51-250]
  Dashing through the Snow
  c BL - v93 - Mr 1 '97 - p1158+ [51-250]
  c CBRS - v25 - Ap '97 - p106 [51-250]
  Wait until Dark
  c Ch BWatch - v6 - N '96 - p7 [1-50]
Shahar, Lucy - *Border Crossings*
  MLJ - v80 - Win '96 - p551+ [501+]
Shahar, Meir - *Unruly Gods*
  Choice - v34 - Mr '97 - p1217 [51-250]
Shahar, Shulamith - *Growing Old in the Middle Ages*
  HT - v46 - O '96 - p55 [51-250]
Shahid, Irfan - *Byzantium and the Arabs in the Sixth Century. Vol. 1, Pts. 1-2*
  CHR - v82 - Jl '96 - p503+ [501+]
Shahrukh Husain - *What Do We Know about Islam?* *(Illus. by Celia Hart)*
  c TES - F 14 '97 - p16* [51-250]
Shaidurov, V V - *Multigrid Methods for Finite Elements*
  SIAM Rev - v38 - S '96 - p542+ [501+]
Shain, Barry Alan - *The Myth of American Individualism*
  Bks & Cult - v2 - N '96 - p22+ [501+]
  J Am St - v30 - Ap '96 - p156+ [251-500]
  JR - v76 - O '96 - p666+ [501+]
  Theol St - v57 - Mr '96 - p173+ [501+]
  Univ Bkmn - v36 - Win '96 - p7+ [501+]
  W&M Q - v53 - Jl '96 - p670+ [501+]
Shainberg, Lawrence - *Ambivalent Zen*
  Tric - v6 - Win '96 - p99+ [501+]
Shakar, Alex - *City in Love*
  KR - v64 - S 15 '96 - p1350 [251-500]
  PW - v243 - S 30 '96 - p78+ [51-250]
Shaker, Sallama - *State, Society, and Privatization in Turkey 1979-1990*
  MEJ - v50 - Aut '96 - p605+ [501+]
A Shaker Hymnal
  Teach Mus - v4 - F '97 - p52 [51-250]
Shakespeare, Nicholas - *The Dancer Upstairs*
  BL - v93 - Ja '97 - p820 [51-250]
  KR - v64 - D 1 '96 - p1700 [251-500]
  LJ - v122 - Ja '97 - p150+ [51-250]
  NYTBR - v102 - Mr 16 '97 - p21 [51-250]
  PW - v243 - D 9 '96 - p60 [51-250]
Shakespeare, Tom - *The Sexual Politics of Disability*
  Obs - Mr 2 '97 - p18* [51-250]
Shakespeare, William - *Anthony and Cleopatra (Neill)*
  RES - v47 - N '96 - p587+ [501+]
  As You Like It (Brissenden)
  Shakes Q - v47 - Win '96 - p374+ [501+]
  Coriolanus
  Shakes Q - v47 - Fall '96 - p334+ [501+]
  An Excellent Conceited Tragedie of Romeo and Juliet
  Shakes Q - v47 - Fall '96 - p330+ [501+]
  The First Quarto of King Lear (Halio)
  RES - v47 - Ag '96 - p409+ [501+]
  Hamlet
  CLS - v33 - 1 '96 - p59+ [501+]
  Hamlet (Advanced Shakespeare)
  y Sch Lib - v44 - Ag '96 - p128 [51-250]
  Henry V (Evans)
  Shakes Q - v47 - Sum '96 - p160+ [501+]
  Henry V (Taylor)
  Shakes Q - v47 - Sum '96 - p132+ [501+]
  King Lear: A Parallel Text Edition (Weis)
  RES - v47 - Ag '96 - p409+ [501+]
  King Lear (Advanced Shakespeare)
  y Sch Lib - v44 - Ag '96 - p128 [51-250]
  Love's Labor's Lost (Evans)
  Shakes Q - v47 - Win '96 - p387+ [501+]

M. William Shak-speare, His True Chronicle Historie of the Life and Death of King Lear and His Three Daughters
  Shakes Q - v47 - Fall '96 - p330+ [501+]
Macbeth (Attica Cybernetics/BBC Education/HarperCollins). Electronic Media Version
  y Quill & Q - v62 - Ag '96 - p37 [501+]
Macbeth (Voyager). Electronic Media Version
  Theat J - v48 - D '96 - p529+ [501+]
The Most Excellent Historie of The Merchant of Venice
  Shakes Q - v47 - Fall '96 - p330+ [501+]
Much Ado about Nothing. Audio Version
  BL - v93 - N 1 '96 - p522 [51-250]
Multimedia Shakespeare. Electronic Media Version
  yr Kliatt - v31 - My '97 - p32 [51-250]
Othello (Ridley)
  Shakes Q - v47 - Fall '96 - p235+ [501+]
Othello (Muir)
  Shakes Q - v47 - Win '96 - p451+ [501+]
Othello
  YR - v85 - Ap '97 - p120+ [501+]
Richard II. Audio Version
  BL - v93 - F 15 '97 - p1038 [51-250]
Romeo and Juliet. Electronic Media Version
  y Quill & Q - v62 - Ag '96 - p37 [501+]
The Second Part of King Henry VI (Hattaway)
  Critm - v38 - Sum '96 - p367+ [501+]
Shakespeare Interactive: Romeo and Juliet. Electronic Media Version
  LJ - v122 - F 1 '97 - p118 [51-250]
A Shorter Shakespeare Series (Illus. by Cal Williams)
  c NY - v72 - N 18 '96 - p101 [1-50]
Speak the Speech
  VQR - v72 - Aut '96 - p142* [1-50]
The Taming of the Shrew (Morris)
  Shakes Q - v47 - Sum '96 - p109+ [501+]
Titus Andronicus
  Critm - v38 - Sum '96 - p383+ [501+]
The Tragedie of Anthonie, and Cleopatra
  Shakes Q - v47 - Fall '96 - p330+ [501+]
The Tragedy of Coriolanus (Parker)
  RES - v48 - F '97 - p100+ [501+]
The Tragoedie of Othello, the Moore of Venice
  Shakes Q - v47 - Fall '96 - p330+ [501+]
Troilus and Cressida
  JHI - v58 - Ap '97 - p331+ [501+]
Twelfe Night, or, What You Will
  Shakes Q - v47 - Fall '96 - p330+ [501+]
Shakespeare Survey 47
  RES - v48 - F '97 - p96+ [501+]
Shalant, Phyllis - *The Great Eye*
  c BL - v93 - N 1 '96 - p501 [51-250]
  y CBRS - v25 - Win '97 - p71 [51-250]
  c CCB-B - v50 - F '97 - p222+ [51-250]
  c HB Guide - v8 - Spr '97 - p75 [51-250]
  y KR - v64 - N 15 '96 - p1675 [51-250]
  y PW - v243 - N 18 '96 - p76 [51-250]
  c SLJ - v42 - N '96 - p110 [51-250]
Shaleen, Kenneth H - *Volume and Open Interest. Rev. Ed.*
  R&R Bk N - v11 - D '96 - p37 [51-250]
Shalhope, Robert E - *Bennington and the Green Mountain Boys*
  Choice - v34 - Ap '97 - p1407 [51-250]
  R&R Bk N - v12 - F '97 - p25 [51-250]
Shalin, Dmitri N - *Russian Culture at the Crossroads*
  WLT - v70 - Aut '96 - p984 [501+]
Shalit, Andrew - *The Dylan Reference Manual*
  r SciTech - v20 - D '96 - p9 [51-250]
Shallat, Todd - *Structures in the Stream*
  T&C - v37 - O '96 - p842+ [51-250]
Shambaugh, David - *China and Europe 1949-1995*
  For Aff - v75 - S '96 - p158 [51-250]
  Deng Xiaoping: Portrait of a Chinese Statesman
  APSR - v90 - S '96 - p683+ [501+]
  Greater China
  Ch Rev Int - v4 - Spr '97 - p244+ [501+]
Shamberg, Michael - *Guerrilla Television*
  Afterimage - v24 - N '96 - p4 [51-250]
Shamblin, Gwen - *The Weigh Down Diet*
  PW - v244 - F 24 '97 - p81+ [51-250]
Shamdasani, Sonu - *Speculations after Freud*
  Rel St Rev - v23 - Ap '97 - p150 [51-250]
Shames, Irving H - *Engineering Mechanics. 4th Ed.*
  SciTech - v20 - N '96 - p61 [51-250]
Shames, Laurence - *Tropical Depression*
  Arm Det - v29 - Sum '96 - p365 [251-500]

Virgin Heat
  BL - v93 - Ja '97 - p779 [51-250]
  KR - v64 - D 15 '96 - p1763+ [251-500]
  LJ - v122 - F 1 '97 - p110 [51-250]
  NYTBR - v102 - Ap 13 '97 - p24 [51-250]
  PW - v244 - F 3 '97 - p95 [51-250]
Shamir, Ronen - *Managing Legal Uncertainty*
  AHR - v102 - F '97 - p209+ [251-500]
  AJS - v102 - Jl '96 - p320+ [501+]
  APSR - v90 - D '96 - p922+ [501+]
  CS - v26 - Ja '97 - p81+ [501+]
Shammas, Namir C - *Mathematical Algorithms in Visual Basic for Scientists and Engineers*
  r SocSciComR - v14 - Fall '96 - p364+ [251-500]
Shampine, Lawrence F - *Fundamentals of Numerical Computing*
  Choice - v34 - F '97 - p1000 [51-250]
  SciTech - v20 - N '96 - p14 [51-250]
Shamsie, Jalal - *Troublesome Children*
  Adoles - v31 - Win '96 - p996+ [51-250]
Shan Fei Qing Hua
  BL - v93 - N 1 '96 - p484 [1-50]
Shand, Phyllis - *The Orchid House*
  BW - v27 - Ja 5 '97 - p12 [51-250]
Shandler, Nina - *Estrogen: The Natural Way*
  BL - v93 - My 15 '97 - p1553 [51-250]
  LJ - v122 - My 1 '97 - p133+ [51-250]
  PW - v244 - Ap 21 '97 - p67 [51-250]
Shand-Tucci, Douglass - *Ralph Adams Cram: Life and Architecture. Vol. 1*
  ASInt - v34 - O '96 - p93+ [501+]
Shane, Paul G - *What about America's Homeless Children?*
  Choice - v34 - F '97 - p1045 [51-250]
  R&R Bk N - v12 - F '97 - p56 [51-250]
Shane, Scott - *Dismantling Utopia*
  Historian - v59 - Fall '96 - p128+ [501+]
  IndRev - v1 - Spr '96 - p142+ [501+]
Shanefield, Daniel J - *Organic Additives and Ceramic Processing. 2nd Ed.*
  SciTech - v21 - Mr '97 - p97 [51-250]
Shange, Ntozake - *Sassafrass, Cypress, and Indigo*
  Bl S - v26 - Sum '96 - p67 [51-250]
Shangraw, Clarence F - *A Chorus of Colors*
  Ch Rev Int - v4 - Spr '97 - p247+ [501+]
Shankar, Ramamurti - *Basic Training in Mathematics*
  y New Sci - v151 - S 28 '96 - p44+ [501+]
Shankman, Sarah - *I Still Miss My Man but My Aim Is Getting Better*
  MFSF - v92 - F '97 - p39+ [251-500]
  Rapport - v19 - 5 '96 - p35 [251-500]
Shankman, Steven - *In Search of the Classic*
  Comp L - v48 - Fall '96 - p369+ [501+]
Shanks, Andrew - *Civil Society, Civil Religion*
  TLS - Mr 28 '97 - p9 [501+]
Shanks, Hershel - *Christianity and Rabbinic Judaism*
  Rel Ed - v91 - Fall '96 - p605 [1-50]
  Jerusalem: An Archeological Biography
  MEQ - v4 - Mr '97 - p75+ [501+]
Shanks, Lela Knox - *Your Name Is Hughes Hannibal Shanks*
  Choice - v34 - F '97 - p998 [51-250]
  LJ - v121 - O 1 '96 - p116 [51-250]
  PW - v243 - S 23 '96 - p64 [51-250]
  Readings - v12 - Mr '97 - p26 [51-250]
Shannon, Christopher - *Conspicuous Criticism*
  AAPSS-A - v550 - Mr '97 - p194+ [251-500]
  RAH - v25 - Mr '97 - p107+ [501+]
Shannon, David - *The Amazing Christmas Extravaganza* *(Illus. by David Shannon)*
  c Emerg Lib - v23 - My '96 - p55+ [51-250]
  c RT - v50 - N '96 - p258 [51-250]
Shannon, George - *Spring: A Haiku Story (Illus. by Malcah Zeldis)*
  c HB Guide - v7 - Fall '96 - p365 [51-250]
  c LA - v73 - D '96 - p624 [51-250]
  This Is the Bird (Illus. by David Soman)
  c BL - v93 - F 15 '97 - p1029+ [51-250]
  c CBRS - v25 - Ap '97 - p101 [51-250]
  c HMR - Spr '97 - p29 [501+]
  c KR - v65 - Mr 1 '97 - p387+ [51-250]
  Tomorrow's Alphabet (Illus. by Donald Crews)
  c BL - v93 - Ja '97 - p768 [1-50]
  c HB Guide - v7 - Fall '96 - p244 [51-250]
  c Inst - v42 - Ag '96 - p44 [51-250]
  c NYTBR - v102 - Mr 30 '97 - p18 [1-50]
  True Lies (Illus. by John O'Brien)
  c BL - v93 - My 15 '97 - p1574 [51-250]
  Unlived Affections
  y SLJ - v43 - Mr '97 - p113 [1-50]

Shannon, John - *The Concrete River*
  Arm Det - v29 - Sum '96 - p360+ [251-500]
Shannon, Magdaline W - *Jean Price-Mars, the Haitian Elite and the American Occupation 1915-1935*
  Choice - v34 - Ap '97 - p1401 [51-250]
Shannon, Mike - *Tales from the Dugout*
  LJ - v122 - F 1 '97 - p83 [1-50]
Shannon, Richard - *The Age of Salisbury 1881-1902*
  EHR - v112 - Ap '97 - p420+ [501+]
  TLS - My 24 '96 - p8+ [501+]
Shannon, Thomas A - *The Ethical Theory of John Duns Scotus*
  Theol St - v58 - Mr '97 - p198 [251-500]
Shannon, Tom - *The Invisible Crying Tree*
  TLS - Jl 19 '96 - p28 [501+]
Shannon, William T - *The Power Struggle*
  Rapport - v19 - 6 '96 - p29 [251-500]
Shanta, N - *La Voie Jaina*
  Rel St Rev - v23 - Ap '97 - p103+ [501+]
Shantideva - *The Way of the Bodhisattva*
  PW - v243 - D 16 '96 - p54 [51-250]
Shao, Kuo-kang - *Zhou Enlai and the Foundations of Chinese Foreign Policy*
  Choice - v34 - My '97 - p1570 [51-250]
Shapard, Robert - *Sudden Fiction (Continued)*
  LATBR - S 1 '96 - p6+ [501+]
Shapcott, Jo - *Emergency Kit*
  Obs - O 27 '96 - p15* [501+]
  TES - O 18 '96 - p7* [501+]
  TES - D 27 '96 - p16+ [1-50]
Shapin, Steven - *The Scientific Revolution*
  Choice - v34 - Ap '97 - p1360+ [51-250]
  KR - v64 - S 15 '96 - p1386+ [251-500]
  Lon R Bks - v19 - Ap 3 '97 - p24+ [501+]
  Nature - v385 - Ja 23 '97 - p312 [501+]
  New Sci - v152 - D 21 '96 - p70+ [501+]
  NYTBR - v101 - N 17 '96 - p28 [501+]
  Sci - v274 - N 15 '96 - p1148+ [501+]
  A Social History of Truth
  Bks & Cult - v2 - Ja '96 - p22+ [501+]
  JHI - v57 - O '96 - p725+ [501+]
  JMH - v69 - Mr '97 - p134+ [501+]
  J Soc H - v30 - Spr '97 - p760+ [501+]
  T&C - v38 - Ja '97 - p238+ [501+]
Shapiro, Alan - *The Last Happy Occasion*
  BW - v26 - O 13 '96 - p7+ [501+]
  LJ - v121 - O 1 '96 - p77 [51-250]
  NYTBR - v101 - O 27 '96 - p38 [51-250]
  PW - v243 - N 4 '96 - p46 [1-50]
  Mixed Company
  South R - v33 - Win '97 - p136+ [501+]
  VQR - v72 - Aut '96 - p136*+ [51-250]
  YR - v84 - O '96 - p162+ [501+]
Shapiro, Ann-Louise - *Breaking the Codes*
  Choice - v34 - N '96 - p521 [51-250]
  TLS - Ja 17 '97 - p33 [51-250]
Shapiro, Anna - *A Feast of Words*
  NY - v72 - N 11 '96 - p119 [51-250]
Shapiro, Barbara - *See No Evil*
  Arm Det - v29 - Fall '96 - p502 [51-250]
Shapiro, Barry M - *Revolutionary Justice in Paris 1789-1790*
  EHR - v112 - F '97 - p218+ [501+]
Shapiro, Bonnie - *What Children Bring to Light*
  TCR - v98 - Fall '96 - p182+ [501+]
Shapiro, Dani - *Picturing the Wreck*
  Ent W - Mr 21 '97 - p69 [1-50]
  NYTBR - v102 - Mr 2 '97 - p28 [1-50]
Shapiro, Eileen C - *Fad Surfing in the Boardroom*
  NS - v125 - D 20 '96 - p17 [51-250]
  Per Psy - v49 - Aut '96 - p752+ [501+]
Shapiro, Ester R - *Grief as a Family Process*
  Fam in Soc - v77 - S '96 - p451+ [501+]
Shapiro, Francine - *EMDR: The Breakthrough Therapy for Overcoming Anxiety, Stress, and Trauma*
  BL - v93 - Mr 1 '97 - p1101 [51-250]
  LJ - v122 - Ap 15 '97 - p102 [51-250]
  PW - v244 - Mr 3 '97 - p69+ [51-250]
Shapiro, Gary - *Earthwards: Robert Smithson and Art after Babel*
  Art J - v55 - Sum '96 - p95+ [501+]
Shapiro, Ian - *Abortion: The Supreme Court Decisions*
  Ethics - v107 - Ja '97 - p396+ [51-250]
  Democracy's Place
  Choice - v34 - Mr '97 - p1237+ [51-250]
  For Aff - v75 - S '96 - p134+ [51-250]
  Political Order
  R&R Bk N - v11 - N '96 - p47 [51-250]

Shapiro, Ivor - *What God Allows*
  CC - v113 - S 25 '96 - p907+ [501+]
  Comw - v124 - Mr 14 '97 - p17+ [501+]
  Nat - v262 - Je 17 '96 - p34 [251-500]
Shapiro, James - *Shakespeare and the Jews*
  Albion - v28 - Win '96 - p691+ [501+]
  Clio - v25 - Sum '96 - p464+ [501+]
  Six Ct J - v27 - Win '96 - p1118+ [501+]
  Tikkun - v12 - Ja '97 - p70+ [501+]
  Tikkun - v12 - Mr '97 - p64+ [501+]
  TLS - O 11 '96 - p29 [501+]
Shapiro, Larry S - *Affine Analysis of Image Sequences*
  Robotica - v14 - S '96 - p585+ [501+]
Shapiro, Lawrence E - *How to Raise a Child with a High EQ*
  BL - v93 - My 15 '97 - p1550 [51-250]
Shapiro, Lillian L - *Fiction for Youth. 3rd Ed.*
  yr RQ - v36 - Win '96 - p220 [51-250]
Shapiro, Marc - *The Anderson Files*
  Ent W - Ap 18 '97 - p62 [51-250]
Shapiro, Michael - *Gender in Play on the Shakespearean Stage*
  MLR - v92 - Ap '97 - p451+ [501+]
Shapiro, Michael J - *Challenging Boundaries*
  For Aff - v75 - S '96 - p137 [51-250]
Shapiro, Norman R - *A Flea in Her Rear, or, Ants in Her Pants and Other Vintage French Farces*
  TranslRevS - v1 - My '95 - p1 [51-250]
Shapiro, Robert, 1951- - *Germaine Tailleferre: A Bio-Bibliography*
  r Notes - v53 - D '96 - p474+ [501+]
Shapiro, Robert L - *The Search for Justice*
  ABA Jour - v82 - D '96 - p92+ [501+]
  Esq - v126 - N '96 - p65 [1-50]
  NYRB - v43 - Je 6 '96 - p7+ [501+]
Shapiro, Stewart - *Foundations without Foundationalism*
  Dialogue - v35 - Sum '96 - p624+ [501+]
Shapiro, Susan R - *The Male-to-Female Dictionary*
  Ent W - S 13 '96 - p127 [1-50]
  The Men Out There
  PW - v244 - Ja 6 '97 - p59+ [51-250]
  PW - v244 - Ja 13 '97 - p68 [51-250]
Shared Responsibilities in Higher Education
  J Gov Info - v23 - S '96 - p632 [51-250]
Sharer, Robert J - *Daily Life in Maya Civilization*
  R&R Bk N - v12 - F '97 - p27 [51-250]
  y SLJ - v43 - F '97 - p125 [51-250]
Sharff, Stefan - *The Art of Looking*
  TCI - v30 - O '96 - p57 [1-50]
Shargel, Lee - *Voice in the Mirror*
  PW - v244 - F 24 '97 - p69 [51-250]
Sharir, Micha - *Davenport-Schinzel Sequences and Their Geometric Applications*
  SIAM Rev - v38 - D '96 - p689+ [501+]
Sharkansky, Ira - *Governing Jerusalem*
  MEQ - v4 - Mr '97 - p75+ [501+]
  R&R Bk N - v11 - N '96 - p50 [51-250]
  TLS - Mr 7 '97 - p8+ [501+]
  Israel and Its Bible
  Choice - v34 - O '96 - p299 [51-250]
El-Sharkawy, Mohamed - *Digital Signal Processing Applications with Motorola's DSP56002 Processor*
  SciTech - v20 - D '96 - p75 [51-250]
Sharma, Arvind - *Hinduism for Our Times*
  Choice - v34 - My '97 - p1517 [51-250]
  Our Religions
  JAAR - v64 - Fall '96 - p659+ [501+]
  The Philosophy of Religion: A Buddhist Perspective
  CPR - v16 - Ag '96 - p292+ [501+]
  The Philosophy of Religion and Advaita Vedanta
  JR - v76 - O '96 - p664+ [501+]
Sharma, Elizabeth - *The Ingredients of Music*
  c Magpies - v11 - Jl '96 - p41 [51-250]
Sharma, Narendra P - *African Water Resources*
  JEL - v35 - Mr '97 - p297 [51-250]
Sharma, Renu - *In Situ Electron and Tunneling Microscopy of Dynamic Processes*
  SciTech - v20 - D '96 - p23 [51-250]
Sharma, Virendra Nath - *Sawai Jai Singh and His Astronomy*
  Isis - v88 - Mr '97 - p150+ [501+]
Sharmat, Marjorie Weinman - *Mitchell Is Moving (Illus. by Jose Aruego)*
  c HB Guide - v7 - Fall '96 - p284 [51-250]
  Nate the Great and the Crunchy Christmas (Illus. by Marc Simont)
  c BL - v93 - S 15 '96 - p253 [51-250]
  c HB Guide - v8 - Spr '97 - p56 [51-250]
  c PW - v243 - S 30 '96 - p93 [51-250]
  c SLJ - v42 - O '96 - p40 [51-250]

Sharon, Donna - *Great Careers for People Interested in Travel and Tourism*
  y SLJ - v42 - S '96 - p230 [51-250]
Sharoni, Simona - *Gender and the Israeli-Palestinian Conflict*
  CS - v25 - N '96 - p735+ [501+]
Sharp, Anne Wallace - *Gifts: Two Hospice Professionals Reveal Messages from These Passing On*
  BWatch - v17 - D '96 - p3 [1-50]
  Gifts: Two Hospice Professionals Reveal Messages from Those Passing On
  LJ - v121 - N 1 '96 - p95+ [51-250]
Sharp, Ian - *Songs and Rhymes*
  TES - D 13 '96 - p43 [51-250]
Sharp, J Michael - *Directory of Congressional Voting Scores and Interest Group Ratings. 2nd Ed., Vols. 1-2*
  r Choice - v34 - My '97 - p1578 [51-250]
Sharp, Jo - *Knitted Sweater Style*
  LJ - v122 - Ap 15 '97 - p78 [51-250]
Sharp, John A - *The Management of a Student Research Project. 2nd Ed.*
  TES - O 4 '96 - p7* [51-250]
Sharp, Joseph - *Living Our Dying*
  PW - v244 - Mr 31 '97 - p72 [1-50]
Sharp, Lyle C - *A Carpenter Genealogy*
  r EGH - v50 - N '96 - p193 [51-250]
Sharp, Mitchell - *Which Reminds Me*
  Can Hist R - v78 - Mr '97 - p120+ [501+]
Sharp, Paula - *Crows over a Wheatfield*
  Ms - v7 - S '96 - p84 [251-500]
  NYTBR - v101 - D 8 '96 - p79 [1-50]
  TLS - Ja 24 '97 - p22 [251-500]
Sharp, Peggy - *Sharing Your Good Ideas*
  Emerg Lib - v24 - S '96 - p40 [251-500]
Sharpe, James - *Instruments of Darkness*
  NS - v126 - Ja 10 '97 - p46 [501+]
Sharpe, Kevin - *Culture and Politics in Early Stuart England*
  South HR - v30 - Sum '96 - p293+ [501+]
  The Personal Rule of Charles I
  Sev Cent N - v54 - Fall '96 - p66 [51-250]
Sharpe, Mal - *Weird Rooms*
  BL - v93 - F 15 '97 - p993 [51-250]
Sharpe, Pamela - *Adapting to Capitalism*
  Choice - v34 - D '96 - p660 [51-250]
Sharpe, Tom - *Grantchester Grind*
  TES - Jl 19 '96 - pR6 [51-250]
  The Midden
  Obs - v54 - O 13 '96 - p18* [501+]
  Spec - v277 - S 21 '96 - p54+ [501+]
Sharpley, G D A - *Sorry I Didn't Quite Catch That...*
  TES - Mr 7 '97 - pR8 [51-250]
Sharratt, Michael - *Galileo: Decisive Innovator*
  JMH - v68 - S '96 - p657+ [501+]
  SB - v33 - Ja '97 - p11 [251-500]
Sharratt, Nick - *A Cheese and Tomato Spider (Illus. by Nick Sharratt)*
  c Bks Keeps - Mr '97 - p19 [51-250]
  c TES - N 29 '96 - p13* [1-50]
  Don't Put Your Finger in the Jelly, Nelly!
  c Bks Keeps - Jl '96 - p7 [51-250]
  I Went to the Zoopermarket
  c Bks Keeps - Jl '96 - p7 [51-250]
  c TES - Mr 28 '97 - p11* [51-250]
  Ketchup on Your Cornflakes? (Illus. by Nick Sharratt)
  c Bks Keeps - Jl '96 - p7 [51-250]
  c KR - v65 - My 1 '97 - p727 [51-250]
Sharrock, Alison - *Seduction and Repetition in Ovid's Ars Amatoria 2*
  Class Out - v74 - Win '97 - p80 [251-500]
  CW - v89 - Jl '96 - p507+ [251-500]
Shatner, William - *Delta Search*
  y BL - v93 - Ja '97 - p780 [51-250]
  LJ - v122 - F 15 '97 - p165 [51-250]
  PW - v244 - Ja 27 '97 - p81 [51-250]
  Star Trek Avenger
  PW - v244 - Ap 21 '97 - p64+ [51-250]
  Star Trek: Avenger
  PW - v244 - Ap 21 '97 - p64+ [51-250]
  Star Trek: The Return (Shatner). Audio Version
  y Kliatt - v30 - S '96 - p52 [51-250]
  Tek Kill
  BL - v93 - N 1 '96 - p459 [1-50]
  Tek Money
  BWatch - v18 - Mr '97 - p10 [1-50]
Shattuc, Jane M - *The Talking Cure*
  BL - v93 - Ja '97 - p805 [51-250]
  PW - v243 - D 16 '96 - p52 [51-250]

Shattuck, Roger - *Forbidden Knowledge*
  Am - v176 - F 8 '97 - p34+ [501+]
  BL - v93 - Ja '97 - p759 [1-50]
  BL - v93 - S 15 '96 - p204 [51-250]
  BW - v26 - N 10 '96 - p9 [501+]
  Choice - v34 - Mr '97 - p1148 [51-250]
  CSM - v88 - O 23 '96 - p15 [501+]
  LATBR - N 17 '96 - p14 [51-250]
  LJ - v121 - O 1 '96 - p77 [51-250]
  New R - v215 - N 4 '96 - p34+ [501+]
  NYTBR - v101 - O 27 '96 - p17 [501+]
  NYTLa - v146 - O 25 '96 - pC40 [501+]
  TLS - D 13 '96 - p4 [501+]
  Wil Q - v20 - Aut '96 - p86+ [501+]
  WSJ-MW - v77 - S 23 '96 - pA18 [501+]
Shatzmiller, Joseph - *Jews, Medicine, and Medieval Society*
  Isis - v87 - S '96 - p538+ [501+]
  JIH - v27 - Aut '96 - p288+ [501+]
Shatzmiller, Maya - *Labour in the Medieval Islamic World*
  AHR - v101 - O '96 - p1253+ [501+]
  JEH - v56 - S '96 - p729+ [501+]
Shaughnessy, Dan - *At Fenway*
  Choice - v34 - D '96 - p650 [51-250]
  Econ - v340 - S 14 '96 - p4*+ [501+]
Seeing Red
  Aethlon - v13 - Spr '96 - p209+ [501+]
Shaviro, Daniel N - *Do Deficits Matter?*
  KR - v65 - Mr 15 '97 - p449 [251-500]
  LJ - v122 - Mr 15 '97 - p71 [51-250]
Shaviro, Steven - *Doom Patrols*
  Books - v11 - Ap '97 - p21 [51-250]
  KR - v64 - N 1 '96 - p1593 [51-250]
  PW - v243 - N 25 '96 - p67 [51-250]
Shavit, David - *Hunger for the Printed Word*
  LJ - v122 - My 1 '97 - p121 [51-250]
Shaw, A G L - *A History of the Port Phillip District*
  Aust Bk R - S '96 - p14+ [501+]
Shaw, Andrea - *Seen That, Now What?*
  r BL - v92 - Ag '96 - p1926 [251-500]
Shaw, Bernard - *Bernard Shaw and Gabriel Pascal*
  Choice - v34 - F '97 - p968+ [51-250]
  ILS - v16 - Spr '97 - p35 [1-50]
  R&R Bk N - v12 - F '97 - p86 [51-250]
Bernard Shaw Theatrics
  ELT - v39 - 4 '96 - p501+ [501+]
Bernard Shaw's Book Reviews. Vol. 2
  Choice - v34 - Ap '97 - p1333 [51-250]
Pygmalion (L.A. Theatre Works). Audio Version
  BWatch - v17 - D '96 - p10 [51-250]
Unpublished Shaw
  Nine-C Lit - v51 - Mr '97 - p559 [51-250]
Shaw, Christine - *Julius II: The Warrior Pope*
  JR - v76 - O '96 - p638+ [501+]
Shaw, Connie - *Mary's Miracles and Prophecies*
  BWatch - v17 - N '96 - p5 [51-250]
Shaw, David - *Gerald Massey: Chartist, Poet, Radical and Freethinker*
  ELT - v40 - 1 '97 - p118+ [501+]
Shaw, David, 1943- - *The Pleasure Police*
  KR - v64 - My 1 '96 - p675 [251-500]
  Nat R - v48 - O 28 '96 - p74+ [501+]
  Reason - v28 - Ja '97 - p62+ [501+]
Shaw, Diana - *The Essential Vegetarian Cookbook*
  y BL - v93 - Mr 15 '97 - p1217 [51-250]
  PW - v244 - F 17 '97 - p214 [51-250]
Shaw, Donald - *Antonio Skarmeta and the Post Boom*
  MLR - v91 - Jl '96 - p773+ [251-500]
Shaw, Eric - *The Labour Party since 1945*
  Choice - v34 - S '96 - p204 [51-250]
Shaw, Eve - *Grandmother's Alphabet*
  c HB Guide - v8 - Spr '97 - p48 [51-250]
  c PW - v243 - O 14 '96 - p85 [51-250]
Shaw, Gregory - *Theurgy and the Soul*
  Rel St Rev - v23 - Ap '97 - p172 [51-250]
Shaw, J Thomas - *Pushkin: Poet and Man of Letters and His Prose*
  RMR - v50 - 2 '96 - p206+ [501+]
Pushkin's Poetics of the Unexpected
  MLR - v91 - Jl '96 - p812+ [501+]
Shaw, James C - *North from Texas*
  LJ - v121 - N 1 '96 - p112 [1-50]
Shaw, Joseph W - *Kommos I. Pt. 1*
  r AJA - v100 - O '96 - p785+ [501+]
Shaw, Judith - *Raising Low-Fat Kids in a High-Fat World*
  BL - v93 - Mr 15 '97 - p1214 [51-250]
  LJ - v122 - Mr 15 '97 - p81+ [51-250]
  PW - v244 - F 17 '97 - p215 [51-250]

Shaw, Lisa - *Telecommute! Go to Work without Leaving Home*
  LJ - v122 - My 1 '97 - p52 [1-50]
The Under 35 Guide to Starting and Running Your Business
  LJ - v122 - My 1 '97 - p53 [1-50]
Shaw, Mark - *Nicklaus*
  PW - v244 - My 5 '97 - p192 [51-250]
Shaw, Miranda - *Passionate Enlightenment*
  Historian - v58 - Sum '96 - p843 [51-250]
Shaw, Nancy - *Sheep Take a Hike (Illus. by Margo Apple)*
  c Par Ch - v20 - N '96 - p3 [51-250]
Shaw, Patrick W - *Willa Cather and the Art of Conflict*
  ASInt - v34 - O '96 - p111+ [501+]
Shaw, R Paul - *Financing Health Services through User Fees and Insurance*
  J Gov Info - v23 - S '96 - p685+ [51-250]
Shaw, Ralph R - *American Bibliography, a Preliminary Checklist 1801-1819. Vols. 1-22*
  r ASInt - v34 - O '96 - p9 [1-50]
Shaw, Randy - *The Activist's Handbook*
  Bloom Rev - v16 - S '96 - p25 [51-250]
  Choice - v34 - N '96 - p548 [51-250]
Shaw, Rebecca - *Village Matters*
  PW - v244 - Mr 31 '97 - p68 [1-50]
Shaw, Robert - *Hawaiian Quilt Masterpieces*
  LJ - v122 - Ap 15 '97 - p80 [51-250]
Shaw, Simon - *Dead for a Ducat*
  BL - v92 - Ag '96 - p1888 [51-250]
Shaw, Stephanie J - *What a Woman Ought to Be and to Do*
  Bl S - v26 - Fall '96 - p106 [51-250]
  CS - v26 - Mr '97 - p225+ [501+]
  JEL - v34 - S '96 - p1468 [51-250]
  R&R Bk N - v11 - N '96 - p32 [51-250]
  VQR - v73 - Win '97 - p8* [501+]
Shaw, Victor N - *Social Control in China*
  R&R Bk N - v11 - N '96 - p40 [51-250]
Shaw, W David - *Elegy and Paradox*
  Critm - v38 - Sum '96 - p473+ [501+]
Shaw 16
  ILS - v16 - Spr '97 - p35 [51-250]
Shawhan, Dorothy - *Lizzie*
  Rapport - v19 - 5 '96 - p38 [251-500]
Shaw-MacKinnon, Margaret - *Tiktala (Illus. by Laszlo Gal)*
  c Emerg Lib - v24 - Mr '97 - p27 [1-50]
  c HB Guide - v7 - Fall '96 - p275 [51-250]
Shawn, Wallace - *The Designated Mourner*
  PW - v243 - N 11 '96 - p60 [51-250]
Shawver, Margaret - *What's Wrong with Grandma? (Illus. by Jeffrey K Bagby)*
  c HB Guide - v8 - Spr '97 - p60 [51-250]
Shay, Jonathan - *Achilles in Vietnam*
  J Am Cult - v18 - Win '95 - p113+ [501+]
Shaykh, Hanan - *Beirut Blues*
  Econ - v342 - Mr 15 '97 - p15*+ [501+]
  y Kliatt - v31 - Ja '97 - p5 [51-250]
Women of Sand and Myrrh
  Econ - v342 - Mr 15 '97 - p15*+ [501+]
She, Colleen - *A Student's Guide to Chinese American Genealogy*
  yr ARBA - v28 - '97 - p167 [51-250]
  yr BWatch - v18 - Mr '97 - p3 [51-250]
Shea, Ann M - *The Irish Experience in New York City*
  r ARBA - v28 - '97 - p160+ [251-500]
Shea, Daniel M - *Campaign Craft*
  Choice - v34 - Ja '97 - p877 [51-250]
  R&R Bk N - v12 - F '97 - p60 [51-250]
Shea, George - *First Flight (Illus. by Don Bolognese)*
  c BL - v93 - N 15 '96 - p597 [51-250]
  c HB - v73 - Mr '97 - p214+ [51-250]
  c KR - v64 - D 15 '96 - p1804 [51-250]
  c SLJ - v43 - Ja '97 - p108+ [51-250]
Shea, John - *Macedonia and Greece*
  LJ - v122 - Ap 15 '97 - p101 [51-250]
Shea, Michael - *To Lie Abroad*
  Econ - v339 - My 18 '96 - p9* [251-500]
Shea, Pegi Deitz - *New Moon (Illus. by Cathryn Falwell)*
  c BL - v93 - Ja '97 - p870 [251-500]
  c CBRS - v25 - S '96 - p6 [51-250]
  c CLW - v67 - D '96 - p57 [51-250]
  c HB Guide - v8 - Spr '97 - p48 [51-250]
  c SLJ - v42 - O '96 - p106+ [51-250]
The Whispering Cloth (Illus. by Anita Riggio)
  c LA - v73 - O '96 - p432+ [51-250]
  c RT - v50 - N '96 - p244 [51-250]
  c RT - v50 - Mr '97 - p478 [51-250]
Shea, Suzanne Strempek - *Hoopi Shoopi Donna*
  y Kliatt - v31 - My '97 - p9+ [51-250]
  PW - v244 - Mr 31 '97 - p72 [1-50]

Shea, William H - *The Struggle over the Past*
  JAAR - v65 - Spr '97 - p196+ [501+]
Sheafer, Silvia Anne - *Aretha Franklin: Motown Superstar*
  y HB Guide - v8 - Spr '97 - p159 [51-250]
  y SLJ - v42 - S '96 - p236 [51-250]
Women in America's Wars
  c HB Guide - v7 - Fall '96 - p376 [1-50]
Sheahan, Robyn - *Original Sin*
  y Aust Bk R - N '96 - p58+ [501+]
Shearer, Alex - *Professor Sniff and the Lost Spring Breezes (Illus. by Tony Kenyon)*
  c Sch Lib - v44 - N '96 - p152 [51-250]
The Summer Sisters and the Dance Disaster (Illus. by Tony Kenyon)
  c Sch Lib - v44 - N '96 - p152 [51-250]
Wilmot and Chips
  c Bks Keeps - v100 - S '96 - p13 [51-250]
Shearer, Benjamin F - *Notable Women in the Life Sciences*
  r ARBA - v28 - '97 - p561 [51-250]
  yr BL - v93 - S 1 '96 - p168 [251-500]
  r Choice - v34 - D '96 - p634 [51-250]
  r CLW - v67 - Mr '97 - p45 [51-250]
  yr New Sci - v152 - D 7 '96 - p47 [51-250]
  r R&R Bk N - v11 - D '96 - p68 [51-250]
  r SciTech - v20 - S '96 - p18 [51-250]
  yr SLJ - v42 - N '96 - p138+ [51-250]
  yr VOYA - v19 - F '97 - p364+ [251-500]
Shearer, Cynthia - *The Wonder Book of the Air*
  LJ - v122 - My 1 '97 - p164 [51-250]
  Obs - O 27 '96 - p16* [51-250]
  PW - v244 - My 5 '97 - p206 [1-50]
Shearer, Kenneth D - *Guiding the Reader to the Next Book*
  CLW - v67 - Mr '97 - p47 [251-500]
  LJ - v121 - S 15 '96 - p104 [51-250]
  R&R Bk N - v12 - F '97 - p102 [51-250]
  SLMQ - v25 - Fall '96 - p62 [51-250]
Shearmur, Jeremy - *The Political Thought of Karl Popper*
  TLS - F 7 '97 - p4+ [501+]
Sheble, Mary Ann - *Serials to the Tenth Power*
  SLMQ - v25 - Fall '96 - p62 [51-250]
Sheck, Laurie - *The Willow Grove*
  NL - v79 - O 7 '96 - p16+ [501+]
  VQR - v73 - Win '97 - p28* [51-250]
Sheckley, Robert - *Draconian New York*
  Rapport - v19 - 5 '96 - p30 [51-250]
Soma Blues
  KR - v65 - F 1 '97 - p175 [51-250]
  LJ - v122 - Ja '97 - p153 [51-250]
  PW - v244 - Ja 27 '97 - p80 [51-250]
Shecter, Ben - *Great-Uncle Alfred Forgets (Illus. by Ben Shecter)*
  c HB Guide - v7 - Fall '96 - p275 [51-250]
  c LA - v73 - S '96 - p355+ [51-250]
Shecterle, Ross A - *The Theology of Revelation of Avery Dulles 1980-1994*
  Choice - v34 - N '96 - p477 [51-250]
Sheed, Wilfrid - *Max Jamison*
  Nat R - v48 - D 23 '96 - p55 [51-250]
Sheehan, George - *Going the Distance*
  Choice - v34 - S '96 - p163 [51-250]
  Comw - v124 - Ja 17 '97 - p24+ [501+]
Sheehan, Michael J - *The Balance of Power*
  Choice - v34 - S '96 - p208+ [51-250]
Sheehan, Michael M - *Marriage, Family, and Law in Medieval Europe*
  R&R Bk N - v11 - N '96 - p41 [51-250]
Sheehan, Neil - *A Bright Shining Lie*
  Parameters - v26 - Win '96 - p148+ [501+]
Sheehan, Peter W - *Hypnosis and Experience*
  SciTech - v20 - N '96 - p44 [51-250]
Sheehan, Richard G - *Keeping Score*
  Choice - v34 - Mr '97 - p1210 [51-250]
Sheehan, Sean - *Cambodia*
  c HB Guide - v7 - Fall '96 - p383 [1-50]
  y SLJ - v42 - S '96 - p235 [51-250]
Lebanon
  c Ch BWatch - v7 - Ja '97 - p3 [1-50]
Sheehan, William - *The Planet Mars*
  Astron - v25 - Ja '97 - p102 [501+]
  y BL - v93 - S 1 '96 - p48 [51-250]
  y BL - v93 - D 1 '96 - p664 [1-50]
  Choice - v34 - Mr '97 - p1181 [51-250]
  NH - v106 - Mr '97 - p13 [1-50]
  NYTBR - v102 - Ja 26 '97 - p19 [51-250]
  PW - v243 - S 9 '96 - p79 [51-250]
  S&T - v93 - Mr '97 - p65+ [501+]
Sheehy, Barry - *Winning the Race for Value*
  Choice - v34 - Mr '97 - p1206 [51-250]

Sheehy, Eugene P - *Guide to Reference Books. 10th Ed.*
  r ASInt - v34 - O '96 - p6 [51-250]
Sheehy, Gerard - *The Canon Law, Letter and Spirit*
    Theol St - v57 - D '96 - p780 [251-500]
Sheehy, Helen - *Eva Le Gallienne: A Biography*
    Am Theat - v13 - D '96 - p21 [1-50]
    Ant R - v55 - Spr '97 - p245+ [251-500]
    BL - v93 - O 1 '96 - p316 [51-250]
    BW - v26 - N 3 '96 - p6+ [501+]
    Choice - v34 - Mr '97 - p1173 [51-250]
    KR - v64 - Ag 15 '96 - p1222+ [251-500]
    LJ - v122 - Ja '97 - p102 [51-250]
    NYTBR - v101 - O 27 '96 - p7 [501+]
    NYTBR - v101 - D 8 '96 - p87 [1-50]
    PW - v243 - S 16 '96 - p61 [51-250]
    VV - v41 - D 24 '96 - p59+ [501+]
Sheets, Payson D - *Archaeology, Volcanism, and Remote Sensing in the Arenal Region*
    LA Ant - v7 - Mr '96 - p84+ [501+]
Sheets-Pyenson, Susan - *John William Dawson: Faith, Hope, and Science*
    Beav - v77 - F '97 - p40 [501+]
    Isis - v88 - Mr '97 - p151+ [501+]
Sheffer, Gabriel - *Moshe Sharett: Biography of a Political Moderate*
    For Aff - v76 - Mr '97 - p195+ [51-250]
Sheffer, Susannah - *A Sense of Self*
    HER - v66 - Fall '96 - p693+ [501+]
Sheffield, Charles - *The Billion Dollar Boy*
  y BL - v93 - Ap 1 '97 - p1283 [51-250]
    LJ - v121 - D '96 - p152 [51-250]
    PW - v244 - Mr 31 '97 - p68 [51-250]
  The Ganymede Club
    Analog - v116 - Jl '96 - p273+ [251-500]
  y Kliatt - v31 - Ja '97 - p16 [51-250]
  Higher Education
  y BL - v93 - Ja '97 - p763 [1-50]
    BYTE - v22 - Mr '97 - p148 [51-250]
    MFSF - v91 - O '96 - p65+ [51-250]
  y SLJ - v43 - F '97 - p135+ [51-250]
  y VOYA - v19 - O '96 - p220 [251-500]
  Tomorrow and Tomorrow
  y BL - v93 - Ja '97 - p826 [51-250]
    BW - v27 - F 23 '97 - p11 [251-500]
  y Kliatt - v31 - My '97 - p15+ [51-250]
    KR - v64 - N 1 '96 - p1570 [51-250]
    LJ - v121 - D '96 - p152 [51-250]
    PW - v243 - N 4 '96 - p68 [51-250]
Shefter, Martin - *Political Parties and the State*
    JIH - v27 - Aut '96 - p338+ [501+]
Shehadi, Fadlou - *Philosophies of Music in Medieval Islam*
    Choice - v34 - O '96 - p291 [51-250]
Shehu, Bashkim - *Le Dernier Voyage D'Ago Umeri*
    WLT - v71 - Win '97 - p196 [501+]
  Rrugetimi I Mbrame I Ago Ymerit
    WLT - v71 - Win '97 - p196 [501+]
Sheidlower, Jesse - *The F Word*
    Utne R - Jl '96 - p105+ [51-250]
Sheikh, Fazal - *A Sense of Common Ground*
    VV - v52 - Ja 28 '97 - p48+ [501+]
Sheikh, Javaid I - *Treating the Elderly*
    SciTech - v20 - N '96 - p42 [51-250]
Sheikh Al-Shabab, Omar - *Interpretation and the Language of Translation*
    TranslRevS - v2 - D '96 - p13 [51-250]
Sheindlin, Judy - *Don't Pee on My Leg and Tell Me It's Raining*
    PW - v244 - Ja 27 '97 - p103 [1-50]
Sheinin, David - *The Jewish Diaspora in Latin America*
    Choice - v34 - F '97 - p1022 [51-250]
    R&R Bk N - v11 - N '96 - p20 [51-250]
  The Organization of American States
    Parameters - v26 - Win '96 - p155 [1-50]
Shelby, Anne - *Homeplace*
  c CLW - v67 - Mr '97 - p15 [1-50]
  The Someday House (Illus. by Rosanne Litzinger)
  c HB Guide - v7 - Fall '96 - p275+ [51-250]
  c NYTBR - v101 - S 8 '96 - p28 [1-50]
Shelby, Philip - *Days of Drums*
    PW - v244 - F 17 '97 - p217 [1-50]
  Last Rights
  y BL - v93 - Mr 15 '97 - p1227 [51-250]
    KR - v64 - D 15 '96 - p1764 [251-500]
    LJ - v122 - Ja '97 - p151 [51-250]
    PW - v243 - D 9 '96 - p59 [51-250]
    Trib Bks - Mr 16 '97 - p6 [51-250]
Sheldahl, Terry K - *Eighteenth-Century Book-Keeping*
    R&R Bk N - v11 - N '96 - p35 [51-250]
Shelden, Michael - *Graham Greene: The Enemy Within*
    AS - v66 - Win '97 - p128+ [501+]

Sheldon, D R - *Achieving Accountability in Business and Government*
    R&R Bk N - v11 - D '96 - p35 [51-250]
Sheldon, Dyan - *My Brother Is a Superhero (Illus. by Derek Brazell)*
  c Bks Keeps - N '96 - p10 [51-250]
  c HB Guide - v7 - Fall '96 - p297 [51-250]
Sheldon, Elisabeth - *The Flamboyant Garden*
    BL - v93 - Ja '97 - p800 [51-250]
    PW - v243 - N 18 '96 - p72 [51-250]
Sheldon, Jonathon - *Surviving Debt*
    BL - v93 - S 15 '96 - p192 [51-250]
Sheldon, Kathleen - *Courtyards, Markets, City Streets*
    Choice - v34 - Mr '97 - p1214 [51-250]
Sheldon, Mary - *Raising My Titanic*
    PW - v243 - S 23 '96 - p57 [51-250]
Sheldon, Mary, 1955- - *The Santasaurus (Illus. by Bartt Warburton)*
  c SLJ - v42 - O '96 - p40+ [51-250]
Sheldon, Stephen H - *Evaluating Sleep in Infants and Children*
    SciTech - v21 - Mr '97 - p65 [51-250]
Sheldon, Tom - *Windows NT Web Server Handbook*
    CBR - v14 - S '96 - p30 [1-50]
Sheldrake, Philip - *Living between Worlds*
    RR - v55 - S '96 - p552 [51-250]
Sheldrake, Rupert - *Seven Experiments That Could Change the World*
  y Kliatt - v31 - Mr '97 - p34 [51-250]
Shell, Marc - *Art and Money*
    Art J - v55 - Sum '96 - p107 [501+]
    Rel St Rev - v23 - Ap '97 - p155 [51-250]
  Children of the Earth
    Col Lit - v23 - Je '96 - p171+ [501+]
Shell, Susan Meld - *The Embodiment of Reason*
    R&R Bk N - v11 - N '96 - p2 [51-250]
Shelley, Bryan - *Shelley and Scripture*
    JAAR - v64 - Fall '96 - p710+ [501+]
    RES - v47 - Ag '96 - p429+ [501+]
Shelley, Fred M - *Political Geography of the United States*
    JEL - v34 - D '96 - p2104 [51-250]
Shelley, Mary Wollstonecraft - *Frankenstein*
    RM - v95 - Sum '96 - p729+ [501+]
  The Frankenstein Notebooks. Vols. 1-2
    Choice - v34 - Mr '97 - p1167 [51-250]
    LJ - v121 - D '96 - p154 [51-250]
    R&R Bk N - v12 - F '97 - p86 [51-250]
    TLS - F 14 '97 - p24 [251-500]
  Frankenstein: The 1818 Text, Contexts, Nineteenth-Century Responses, Modern Criticism
    CR - v268 - Je '96 - p334 [51-250]
  The Last Man
    Nine-C Lit - v51 - Mr '97 - p565 [51-250]
  The Novels and Selected Works of Mary Shelley. Vols. 1-8
    Choice - v34 - Ja '97 - p798+ [51-250]
    TLS - N 29 '96 - p9 [501+]
  Selected Letters of Mary Wollstonecraft Shelley
    RES - v48 - F '97 - p122+ [501+]
Shelley, Percy Bysshe - *The Bodleian Shelley Manuscripts. Vol. 20*
    RES - v47 - N '96 - p609 [501+]
  Opere (Rognoni)
    TLS - Ja 3 '97 - p26 [501+]
    TLS - Ja 3 '97 - p26 [501+]
  Shelley's 1821-1822 Huntington Notebook
    R&R Bk N - v11 - N '96 - p70 [51-250]
Shelp, Earl E - *Secular Bioethics in Theological Perspective*
    SciTech - v20 - N '96 - p35 [51-250]
Shelter Provision and Employment Generation
    J Gov Info - v23 - S '96 - p681 [51-250]
Shelton, Connie - *Partnerships Can Kill*
    LJ - v122 - My 1 '97 - p144 [1-50]
    PW - v244 - F 24 '97 - p66+ [51-250]
Shelton, Hal T - *General Richard Montgomery and the American Revolution*
    EHR - v111 - N '96 - p1298 [51-250]
Shelton, Sandi Kahn - *You Might as Well Laugh*
    KR - v65 - F 1 '97 - p207 [251-500]
Shem, Samuel - *Mount Misery*
    BL - v93 - Ja '97 - p780 [51-250]
    KR - v65 - Ja 15 '97 - p92 [251-500]
    LJ - v122 - F 1 '97 - p108 [51-250]
    NYTBR - v102 - Ap 13 '97 - p14 [501+]
    PW - v244 - F 3 '97 - p94+ [51-250]

Shemie, Bonnie - *Houses of China (Illus. by Bonnie Shemie)*
  c BIC - v26 - Mr '97 - p33 [251-500]
  c HB Guide - v8 - Spr '97 - p139 [51-250]
  c Quill & Q - v62 - D '96 - p38 [251-500]
  c SLJ - v43 - F '97 - p125 [51-250]
Shen, Alexander - *Algorithms and Programming*
    Choice - v34 - Ap '97 - p1374 [51-250]
    SciTech - v21 - Mr '97 - p10 [51-250]
Shen, Raphael - *Ukraine's Economic Reform*
    Choice - v34 - Ap '97 - p1389+ [51-250]
    R&R Bk N - v11 - D '96 - p25 [51-250]
Shen, Susan - *Environmental and Economic Issues in Forestry*
    JEL - v34 - D '96 - p2134 [51-250]
Shen, Tsung-Wen - *Imperfect Paradise*
    Ch Rev Int - v4 - Spr '97 - p250+ [501+]
    FEER - v159 - N 7 '96 - p58 [501+]
    WLT - v70 - Aut '96 - p1029+ [501+]
Sheng, Andrew - *Bank Restructuring*
    JEL - v34 - S '96 - p1437 [51-250]
Shengold, Leonard - *Delusions of Everyday Life*
    Readings - v11 - D '96 - p25+ [51-250]
Shenk, David - *Data Smog*
    LJ - v122 - Ap 1 '97 - p115 [51-250]
    NYTBR - v102 - Ap 20 '97 - p11 [501+]
    PW - v244 - F 10 '97 - p74 [51-250]
Shenkin, Henry A - *Current Dilemmas in Medical-Care Rationing*
    SciTech - v20 - S '96 - p27 [1-50]
Shenoy, A V - *Thermoplastic Melt Rheology and Processing*
  r SciTech - v20 - D '96 - p84 [51-250]
Shenson, Howard - *The Complete Guide to Consulting Success. 2nd Ed.*
    BL - v93 - Ja '97 - p795 [51-250]
Shentalinsky, Vitaly - *Arrested Voices*
    Choice - v34 - Ja '97 - p803 [51-250]
    KR - v64 - My 1 '96 - p676 [251-500]
    New R - v216 - F 3 '97 - p34+ [501+]
    NL - v79 - Ag 12 '96 - p18+ [501+]
    NYRB - v43 - O 3 '96 - p4+ [501+]
    VQR - v73 - Win '97 - p12* [501+]
    W&I - v11 - D '96 - p276+ [501+]
Sheon, Robert P - *Soft Tissue Rheumatic Pain. 3rd Ed.*
    SciTech - v20 - S '96 - p37 [51-250]
Shepard, Aaron - *The Maiden of Northland (Illus. by Carol Schwartz)*
  c HB Guide - v7 - Fall '96 - p324 [51-250]
  c Parabola - v22 - F '97 - p94+ [251-500]
  Stories on Stage
    CAY - v16 - Fall '95 - p13 [51-250]
Shepard, Ernest H - *Eeyore's Gloomy Little Instruction Book (Illus. by Joan Powers)*
  c HB Guide - v7 - Fall '96 - p276 [1-50]
Shepard, Jim - *Batting against Castro*
    Ent W - Je 28 '96 - p101 [51-250]
    NYTBR - v101 - Jl 21 '96 - p8+ [501+]
    NYTBR - v101 - D 8 '96 - p76 [1-50]
  y SLJ - v42 - D '96 - p152 [51-250]
Shepard, Lansing - *The Smithsonian Guides to Natural America: The Northern Plains*
  y Kliatt - v31 - Ja '97 - p27 [51-250]
Shepard, Mary B - *Fun with Stained Glass*
  c Ch BWatch - v6 - D '96 - p5 [51-250]
Shepard, Neil T - *Practical Management of the Balance Disorder Patient*
    SciTech - v20 - N '96 - p51 [51-250]
Shepard, Paul - *The Only World We've Got*
    LATBR - S 15 '96 - p11 [251-500]
  Traces of an Omnivore
    BL - v93 - N 15 '96 - p555 [51-250]
    BL - v93 - D 1 '96 - p630 [1-50]
    KR - v64 - O 1 '96 - p1452+ [251-500]
    New Sci - v153 - F 8 '97 - p42 [51-250]
    Parabola - v22 - F '97 - p121 [1-50]
    PW - v243 - S 30 '96 - p68+ [51-250]
Shepard, R Bruce - *Deemed Unsuitable*
    Quill & Q - v62 - O '96 - p37 [251-500]
Shepard, Richard F - *The Paper's Papers*
    Choice - v34 - D '96 - p606 [51-250]
Shepard, Roy - *The Latest Epistle of Jim*
    BL - v93 - N 15 '96 - p571 [501+]
    KR - v64 - O 1 '96 - p1423 [501+]
    PW - v243 - O 21 '96 - p75 [501+]
Shepard, Sam - *Cruising Paradise*
    Spec - v277 - N 16 '96 - p51 [501+]
    TLS - N 22 '96 - p22 [501+]
    WLT - v71 - Win '97 - p152+ [251-500]
  Cruising Paradise (Shepard). Audio Version
  y Kliatt - v30 - N '96 - p47 [51-250]

Shepard, Steve - *A Murder of Crows*
 BW - v27 - F 2 '97 - p9 [501+]
 KR - v64 - O 15 '96 - p1491 [251-500]
 LJ - v121 - N 15 '96 - p90 [51-250]
 PW - v243 - N 4 '96 - p66 [51-250]
Shepardson, Donald E - *Rosa Luxemburg and the Noble Dream*
 R&R Bk N - v11 - D '96 - p45 [1-50]
Shephard, Amanda - *Gender and Authority in Sixteenth-Century England*
 MLR - v92 - Ap '97 - p444+ [501+]
Shephard, Marie Tennent - *Maria Montessori: Teacher of Teachers*
 c BL - v92 - Ag '96 - p1899 [51-250]
 y HB Guide - v8 - Spr '97 - p160 [51-250]
 c SLJ - v42 - S '96 - p220+ [51-250]
Shephard, Roy J - *The Health Consequences of Modernization*
 Choice - v34 - D '96 - p653 [51-250]
Shepherd, Christine - *I Could Do That!*
 y Sch Lib - v44 - Ag '96 - p126 [51-250]
Shepherd, Donna Walsh - *Tundra*
 c BL - v93 - F 1 '97 - p938 [51-250]
 c HB Guide - v8 - Spr '97 - p120 [51-250]
Shepherd, Reginald - *Angel, Interrupted*
 BL - v93 - N 15 '96 - p567 [51-250]
 Bloom Rev - v17 - Ja '97 - p20 [51-250]
Shepherd, Robert - *Enoch Powell*
 Lon R Bks - v19 - Ja 23 '97 - p8+ [501+]
 NS - v125 - O 25 '96 - p43+ [501+]
 Obs - D 15 '96 - p17* [501+]
 TLS - N 8 '96 - p40 [501+]
Iain Macleod
 Books - v9 - S '95 - p25 [1-50]
Shepherd, Sandy - *Myths and Legends from around the World*
 y Emerg Lib - v24 - S '96 - p26 [1-50]
Shepherd, Simon - *English Drama*
 Choice - v34 - O '96 - p282 [51-250]
Shepherd, Stella - *Embers of Death*
 KR - v64 - N 15 '96 - p1638 [51-250]
 LJ - v122 - Ja '97 - p153 [51-250]
Shepherd, Steven - *In Praise of Tomatoes*
 BL - v92 - Ag '96 - p1870+ [51-250]
 BW - v26 - S 1 '96 - p5+ [501+]
 LATBR - S 8 '96 - p10 [51-250]
Shepherd, Verene - *Engendering History*
 HAHR - v76 - N '96 - p845+ [251-500]
Sheppard, Don - *Destroyer Skipper*
 BL - v93 - N 1 '96 - p464 [51-250]
 LJ - v121 - N 1 '96 - p90 [51-250]
 PW - v243 - O 21 '96 - p68 [1-50]
Sheppard, Richard - *Avantgarde Und Arbeiterdichter In Den Hauptorganen Der Deutschen Linken 1917-1922*
 r Lib - v18 - Je '96 - p164+ [501+]
Sheppard, Walter Lee, Jr. - *Passengers and Ships Prior to 1684*
 r EGH - v50 - N '96 - p185 [51-250]
Sheppard's International Directory of Ephemera Dealers 1996
 r AB - v99 - Mr 10 '97 - p794+ [501+]
Sher, Antony - *Woza Shakespeare!*
 TLS - Ja 24 '97 - p19 [501+]
Sher, Barbara - *How to Live the Life You Love (Sher). Audio Version*
 BL - v93 - S 15 '96 - p264 [51-250]
I Could Do Anything If I Only Knew What It Was
 Books - v9 - S '95 - p24 [1-50]
Shere, Charles - *Thinking Sound Music*
 Choice - v34 - N '96 - p471 [51-250]
Sheridan, Jean - *Writing-across-the-Curriculum and the Academic Library*
 r JAAL - v40 - S '96 - p79 [51-250]
Sheridan, John V - *Living the Psalms*
 RR - v55 - N '96 - p661 [1-50]
Sheridan, Richard B - *Sugar and Slavery*
 HAHR - v76 - N '96 - p784+ [501+]
 JEL - v34 - D '96 - p2105 [51-250]
Sheridan, Thomas E - *Arizona: A History*
 HAHR - v76 - Ag '96 - p545+ [501+]
 WHQ - v27 - Win '96 - p535+ [251-500]
Sherif, Faruq - *A Guide to the Contents of the Qur'an*
 Rel St Rev - v23 - Ap '97 - p199 [51-250]
Sheriff, Abdul - *The History and Conservation of Zanzibar Stone Town*
 GJ - v162 - Jl '96 - p239 [51-250]
Sheriff, Carol - *The Artificial River*
 ILS - v15 - Fall '96 - p31 [51-250]
 KR - v64 - My 1 '96 - p676 [251-500]
 RAH - v25 - Mr '97 - p54+ [501+]
 VQR - v73 - Win '97 - p9* [51-250]

Sheriff, Mary D - *The Exceptional Woman*
 r Choice - v34 - N '96 - p446 [51-250]
 R&R Bk N - v11 - N '96 - p61 [51-250]
 Wom R Bks - v14 - Ja '97 - p9+ [501+]
Sheriff, Robert E - *Exploration Seismology. 2nd Ed.*
 y New Sci - v151 - S 28 '96 - p46 [501+]
Sheringham, Michael - *French Autobiography*
 Biography - v19 - Fall '96 - p437+ [501+]
Parisian Fields
 TLS - Ag 30 '96 - p31 [501+]
Sherlock, Margie - *Writing OpenVMS Alpha Device Drivers in C*
 R&R Bk N - v12 - F '97 - p93 [51-250]
Sherlock, Richard - *The Normative Constitution*
 Choice - v34 - S '96 - p212 [51-250]
Sherman, Aliza - *Working Together against Violence against Women*
 y SLJ - v43 - F '97 - p118 [51-250]
Sherman, Althea R - *Birds of an Iowa Dooryard*
 LJ - v122 - F 15 '97 - p166 [51-250]
Sherman, Ann - *Rules, Routines and Regimentation*
 TES - N 29 '96 - p10* [51-250]
Sherman, Arloc - *Wasting America's Future*
 HER - v66 - Win '96 - p886+ [501+]
Sherman, Bernard D - *Inside Early Music*
 LJ - v122 - My 1 '97 - p106 [51-250]
Sherman, Charlotte Watson - *Eli and the Swamp Man (Illus. by James Ransome)*
 c BL - v93 - S 1 '96 - p132 [51-250]
 c CBRS - v24 - Ag '96 - p165+ [51-250]
 c HB - v72 - S '96 - p600 [51-250]
 c HB Guide - v7 - Fall '96 - p297 [51-250]
Sherman, Claire Richter - *Imaging Aristotle*
 AHR - v101 - O '96 - p1194 [501+]
Sherman, Daniel J - *Museum Culture*
 Afterimage - v24 - N '96 - p14+ [501+]
 JAAC - v54 - Fall '96 - p412 [501+]
Sherman, Howard J - *Reinventing Marxism*
 Choice - v34 - S '96 - p209 [51-250]
 CS - v26 - Mr '97 - p253+ [501+]
 S&S - v61 - Sum '97 - p269+ [501+]
Sherman, Jason - *The Leage of Nathans*
 Quill & Q - v62 - Jl '96 - p47 [501+]
The Retreat
 Quill & Q - v62 - D '96 - p32 [501+]
Three in the Back, Two in the Head
 Can Lit - Spr '97 - p219+ [501+]
Sherman, Joel - *Nat Sherman's Passion for Cigars*
 BL - v93 - O 1 '96 - p309 [51-250]
Sherman, Josepha - *Trickster Tales (Illus. by David Boston)*
 c BW - v26 - S 1 '96 - p7 [251-500]
 c CAY - v17 - Win '96 - p7 [51-250]
 c HB Guide - v7 - Fall '96 - p324 [51-250]
 c Parabola - v21 - N '96 - p120 [1-50]
Sherman, Kenneth - *The Northeast Shelf Ecosystem*
 SciTech - v20 - N '96 - p25 [51-250]
Sherman, Moshe D - *Orthodox Judaism in America*
 r ARBA - v28 - '97 - p555 [51-250]
 r Choice - v34 - N '96 - p436 [51-250]
Sherman, Richard A - *Phantom Pain*
 SciTech - v21 - Mr '97 - p60 [51-250]
Sherman, Russell - *Piano Pieces*
 TLS - N 29 '96 - p11 [51-250]
Sherman, Stuart - *Telling Time*
 LJ - v122 - Ja '97 - p118 [51-250]
Sherman, Thomas Fairchild - *A Place on the Glacial Till*
 Sci - v275 - Ja 31 '97 - p625 [1-50]
 SciTech - v21 - Mr '97 - p32 [51-250]
Sherman, Vincent - *Studio Affairs*
 AB - v98 - D 9 '96 - p1997 [501+]
 BW - v27 - Ja 26 '97 - p13 [51-250]
 New R - v216 - Mr 10 '97 - p31 [251-500]
 NYTBR - v102 - F 2 '97 - p20 [51-250]
Sherman, William H - *John Dee: The Politics of Reading and Writing in the English Renaissance*
 BC - v45 - Aut '96 - p784+ [501+]
Shermer, Michael - *Why People Believe Weird Things*
 PW - v244 - Ap 28 '97 - p67 [51-250]
Shermis, Michael - *Introduction to Jewish-Christian Relations*
 Rel Ed - v91 - Fall '96 - p614 [51-250]
Jewish-Christian Relations
 r Rel Ed - v91 - Fall '96 - p618+ [1-50]
Sherover, Charles M - *Time, Freedom, and the Common Good*
 PSR - v25 - '96 - p244+ [501+]
Sherr, Lynn - *Susan B. Anthony Slept Here*
 r T&C - v38 - Ja '97 - p214+ [501+]
Sherrer, Quin - *Miracles Happen When You Pray*
 PW - v244 - My 12 '97 - p72+ [51-250]

Sherrill, Sarah B - *Carpets and Rugs of Europe and America*
 Am Craft - v56 - Ag '96 - p27 [1-50]
 Ant & CM - v101 - Jl '96 - p25 [1-50]
 LJ - v121 - S 15 '96 - p65 [51-250]
Sherrin, Ned - *The Oxford Dictionary of Humorous Quotations*
 r ARBA - v28 - '97 - p36 [51-250]
 r Choice - v34 - S '96 - p104 [51-250]
Scratch an Actor
 Spec - v277 - O 19 '96 - p51+ [501+]
 Spec - v277 - N 16 '96 - p43 [1-50]
Sherrin's Year
 Spec - v277 - N 23 '96 - p44 [1-50]
Sherriton, Jacalyn - *Corporate Culture/Team Culture*
 HR Mag - v41 - O '96 - p148 [51-250]
Sherrow, Victoria - *Bioethics and High-Tech Medicine*
 y BL - v92 - Ag '96 - p1893 [51-250]
 y VOYA - v19 - D '96 - p291 [51-250]
Censorship in Schools
 y BL - v93 - Ja '97 - p842 [251-500]
 y HB Guide - v8 - Spr '97 - p97 [51-250]
 y SLJ - v42 - D '96 - p149 [51-250]
Dropping Out
 y HB Guide - v7 - Fall '96 - p315 [51-250]
Encyclopedia of Women and Sports
 r ARBA - v28 - '97 - p294 [251-500]
 r LJ - v122 - Ja '97 - p91 [51-250]
Freedom of Worship
 c BL - v93 - My 15 '97 - p1574 [51-250]
Mental Illness
 y HB Guide - v7 - Fall '96 - p316 [51-250]
Sports Great Pete Sampras
 c HB Guide - v7 - Fall '96 - p361 [51-250]
Violence and the Media
 y HB Guide - v7 - Fall '96 - p317 [51-250]
Women and the Military
 r ARBA - v28 - '97 - p254 [51-250]
 yr BL - v93 - My 1 '97 - p1534 [251-500]
Sherry, Michael S - *In the Shadow of War*
 AAPSS-A - v547 - S '96 - p186+ [251-500]
 J Mil H - v61 - Ap '97 - p417+ [501+]
 PSQ - v111 - Fall '96 - p539+ [501+]
 RAH - v24 - S '96 - p537+ [501+]
Sherry, Norman - *The Life of Graham Greene. Vols. 1-2*
 AS - v66 - Win '97 - p128+ [501+]
Shershow, Scott Cutler - *Puppets and Popular Culture*
 Theat J - v48 - D '96 - p522+ [501+]
Sherwin, David - *Going Mad in Hollywood*
 Spec - v276 - My 11 '96 - p37+ [501+]
Sherwin-White, Susan - *From Samarkhand to Sardis*
 AHR - v101 - D '96 - p1525 [501+]
Sherwonit, Bill - *Alaska Ascents*
 y BL - v93 - S 1 '96 - p55 [51-250]
Sherwood, John Darrell - *Officers in Flight Suits*
 Choice - v34 - Mr '97 - p1181 [51-250]
Sherwood, Marika - *Pastor Daniels Ekarte and the African Churches Mission*
 Bl S - v26 - Fall '96 - p106 [51-250]
Sherwood, Yvonne - *The Prostitute and the Prophet*
 Rel St Rev - v23 - Ap '97 - p166+ [51-250]
She's Got the Blues
 CAY - v16 - Fall '95 - p9 [51-250]
Sheu, Phillip C Y - *Software Engineering and Environment*
 SciTech - v21 - Mr '97 - p6 [51-250]
Shevchenko, V N - *Qualitative Topics in Integer Linear Programming*
 SciTech - v21 - Mr '97 - p72 [51-250]
Shevelev, Raphael - *Liberating the Ghosts*
 y BL - v93 - Ap 1 '97 - p1288 [1-50]
Shevrin, Howard - *Conscious and Unconscious Processes*
 R&R Bk N - v11 - N '96 - p4 [51-250]
Shevrin, L N - *Semigroups and Their Subsemigroup Lattices*
 SciTech - v21 - Mr '97 - p13 [51-250]
Sheward, Robert - *A Home in Hastie Hollow*
 BIC - v25 - O '96 - p41 [51-250]
Shewmaker, Eugene F - *Shakespeare's Language*
 r ARBA - v28 - '97 - p457 [51-250]
 r R&R Bk N - v12 - F '97 - p85 [51-250]
Shewring, Margaret - *King Richard II*
 Choice - v34 - D '96 - p625 [51-250]
Shi, David E - *Facing Facts*
 RAH - v24 - S '96 - p454+ [501+]
Shibley, Mark A - *Resurgent Evangelicalism in the United States*
 Choice - v34 - Ap '97 - p1357 [51-250]
Shibusawa, Eiichi - *The Autobiography of Shibusawa Eiichi*
 EHR - v111 - N '96 - p1322+ [251-500]

Shichor, David - *Punishment for Profit*
    AAPSS-A - v548 - N '96 - p236+ [501+]
    Fed Prob - v60 - Je '96 - p83 [501+]
    Three Strikes and You're Out
    R&R Bk N - v11 - D '96 - p45 [51-250]
Shields, Carol - *Small Ceremonies and the Box Garden*
    NYTBR - v101 - D 8 '96 - p82 [1-50]
    The Stone Diaries (Bresnahan). Audio Version
    BL - v92 - Ag '96 - p1917 [51-250]
    LJ - v122 - F 15 '97 - p115 [1-50]
    The Stone Diaries (Shields). Audio Version
    y Kliatt - v30 - S '96 - p52 [51-250]
Shields, Carol Diggory - *I Wish My Brother Was a Dog*
    (Illus. by Paul Meisel)
    c Trib Bks - My 4 '97 - p6 [51-250]
    Lunch Money and Other Poems about School (Illus. by Paul Meisel)
    c Inst - v105 - My '96 - p71 [1-50]
    c RT - v50 - O '96 - p134 [1-50]
    c RT - v50 - O '96 - p157 [51-250]
Shields, David - *Remote*
    LATBR - Mr 17 '96 - p10 [51-250]
Shields, David Lyle - *The Color of Hunger*
    CS - v25 - S '96 - p619+ [501+]
Shields, David S - *Civil Tongues and Polite Letters in British America*
    LJ - v122 - My 1 '97 - p121+ [51-250]
Shields, Patrick M - *Improving Schools from the Bottom Up*
    J Gov Info - v23 - S '96 - p545 [51-250]
    Improving Schools from the Bottom Up: Summary Volume
    J Gov Info - v23 - S '96 - p545 [51-250]
Shields, Paul C - *The Ergodic Theory of Discrete Sample Paths*
    SciTech - v20 - N '96 - p14 [51-250]
Shields, Rob - *Cultures of Internet*
    JMCQ - v73 - Win '96 - p997+ [251-500]
Shiers, George - *Early Television*
    r Choice - v34 - My '97 - p1481 [51-250]
    r R&R Bk N - v12 - F '97 - p98 [51-250]
Shifflett, Crandall A - *Victorian America 1876 to 1913*
    r ARBA - v28 - '97 - p184+ [51-250]
    r R&R Bk N - v12 - F '97 - p23 [51-250]
Shigley, Joseph E - *Standard Handbook of Machine Design. 2nd Ed.*
    Choice - v34 - My '97 - p1530 [51-250]
    r SciTech - v20 - D '96 - p73 [51-250]
Shih, Chih-Yu - *State and Society in China's Political Economy*
    APSR - v90 - D '96 - p944+ [501+]
Shih, Nai-An - *The Broken Seals: Part One of the Marshes of Mount Liang*
    Ch Rev Int - v4 - Spr '97 - p116+ [501+]
Shikibu, Murasaki - *The Diary of Lady Murasaki*
    TranslRevS - v2 - D '96 - p8 [51-250]
Shikin, E V - *Some Questions of Differential Geometry in the Large*
    SciTech - v20 - N '96 - p15 [51-250]
Shikishi, Princess, Daughter of Goshirakawa, Emperor of Japan - *String of Beads*
    TranslRevS - v1 - My '95 - p25 [51-250]
Shillenn, James K - *Validation Practices for Biotechnology Products*
    SciTech - v20 - D '96 - p82 [51-250]
Shils, Edward - *Cambridge Women*
    AS - v65 - Aut '96 - p618+ [501+]
    Lon R Bks - v18 - S 5 '96 - p23+ [501+]
    Portraits: A Gallery of Intellectuals
    KR - v65 - Ap 1 '97 - p536 [251-500]
Shilson-Thomas, Annabel - *A First Puffin Picture Book of Stories from World Religions (Illus. by Barry Smith)*
    c Bks Keeps - v100 - S '96 - p9 [51-250]
    c JB - v60 - Ag '96 - p151+ [51-250]
    c Sch Lib - v44 - Ag '96 - p108+ [51-250]
Shim, Jae K - *Dictionary of Economics*
    r ARBA - v28 - '97 - p79 [51-250]
    Financial Management for Nonprofits
    Choice - v34 - My '97 - p1544 [51-250]
    Handbook of Budgeting for Nonprofit Organizations
    ChrPhil - v8 - Ag 8 '96 - p50 [51-250]
Shimada, Izumi - *Pampa Grande and the Mochica Culture*
    HAHR - v76 - Ag '96 - p554+ [501+]
    LA Ant - v7 - Mr '96 - p82+ [501+]
Shimkofsky, Wendy Ashton - *Brainstorm! (Illus. by Lois Lesynski)*
    c Quill & Q - v63 - Ja '97 - p40 [51-250]
Shimmin, Hugh - *Low Life and Moral Improvement in Mid-Victorian England*
    J Urban H - v23 - N '96 - p108+ [501+]

Shimokawa, Koichi - *The Japanese Automobile Industry*
    BHR - v70 - Sum '96 - p294+ [501+]
Shimomura, Tsutomu - *Takedown: The Pursuit and Capture of Kevin Mitnick, America's Most Wanted Computer Outlaw--By the Man Who Did It*
    Ent W - D 20 '96 - p71 [51-250]
    Takedown: The Pursuit and Capture of Kevin Mitnick, America's Most Wanted Computer Outlaw--By the Man Who Did it
    PW - v243 - N 4 '96 - p71 [1-50]
Shimoni, Gideon - *The Zionist Ideology*
    r AHR - v102 - F '97 - p145+ [501+]
Shin, Sun-Joo - *The Logical Status of Diagrams*
    CPR - v16 - Je '96 - p208+ [501+]
Shin, Y S - *Structures under Extreme Loading Conditions 1996*
    SciTech - v20 - D '96 - p85 [51-250]
Shinder, Jason - *Lights, Camera, Poetry!*
    Parnassus - v22 - 1 '97 - p154+ [501+]
    VQR - v72 - Aut '96 - p120* [51-250]
Shindler, Colin - *Hollywood in Crisis*
    Choice - v34 - My '97 - p1507 [51-250]
    Si & So - v6 - N '96 - p34+ [51-250]
    TES - Ag 2 '96 - pR6 [51-250]
    TLS - Ja 17 '97 - p6 [501+]
Shindo, Charles J - *Dust Bowl Migrants in the American Imagination*
    LJ - v122 - Ja '97 - p121 [51-250]
    PW - v244 - Ja 6 '97 - p59 [251-500]
Shiner, J S - *Entropy and Entropy Generation*
    SciTech - v20 - D '96 - p24 [51-250]
Shinn, George - *You Gotta Believe*
    Rapport - v19 - 4 '96 - p18+ [501+]
Shinn, Roger Lincoln - *The New Genetics*
    Choice - v34 - Ap '97 - p1364 [51-250]
Shinn, Sharon - *Archangel*
    y BL - v93 - Ja '97 - p763 [1-50]
    MFSF - v91 - S '96 - p40+ [251-500]
    Jovah's Angel
    KR - v65 - Ap 1 '97 - p510 [51-250]
Shinn, Thelma J - *Women Shapeshifters*
    Choice - v34 - Mr '97 - p1167+ [51-250]
    R&R Bk N - v12 - F '97 - p88 [51-250]
Shionoya, Yuichi - *Innovation in Technology, Industries, and Institutions*
    JEL - v34 - S '96 - p1387+ [501+]
    Schumpeter in the History of Ideas
    Econ J - v107 - Ja '97 - p263 [51-250]
The Ship Captain's Medical Guide. 21st Ed.
    r New Sci - v153 - F 22 '97 - p46 [1-50]
Shipley, Stan - *Bombardier Billy Wells*
    Aethlon - v13 - Spr '96 - p221+ [501+]
Shipley, Thorne - *Intersensory Origin of Mind*
    Choice - v34 - Ja '97 - p880 [51-250]
    SciTech - v20 - N '96 - p1 [51-250]
Shipp, Steve - *American Art Colonies 1850-1930*
    r ARBA - v28 - '97 - p367+ [51-250]
Shipton, Paul - *The Mighty Skink*
    c JB - v60 - D '96 - p274 [51-250]
    y Sch Lib - v45 - F '97 - p49 [51-250]
Shirar, Lynda - *Dissociative Children*
    Readings - v11 - D '96 - p29 [51-250]
Shires, Michael A - *The Future of Public Undergraduate Education in California*
    Cng - v28 - N '96 - p63 [51-250]
Shirey, Lynn M - *Latin American Writers*
    y BL - v93 - Mr 15 '97 - p1235 [51-250]
    y KR - v64 - N 1 '96 - p1608 [51-250]
Shirk, Stephen R - *Change Processes in Child Psychotherapy*
    SciTech - v20 - D '96 - p53 [51-250]
Shirk, Susan L - *Power and Prosperity*
    For Aff - v75 - S '96 - p159 [51-250]
Shirley, Aleda - *Long Distance*
    PW - v243 - S 30 '96 - p82 [51-250]
Shirley, Edward - *Know Thine Enemy*
    PW - v244 - Ap 28 '97 - p57+ [51-250]
Shirley, John - *Silicon Embrace*
    KR - v64 - O 1 '96 - p1433 [51-250]
    LJ - v121 - N 15 '96 - p92 [51-250]
Shirrefs, Mark - *Paul's World*
    c Sch Lib - v44 - Ag '96 - p109 [51-250]
    Riana's World
    c Sch Lib - v44 - Ag '96 - p109 [51-250]
Shiva, V A - *Arts and the Internet*
    BWatch - v18 - F '97 - p4+ [51-250]
    BWatch - v18 - Mr '97 - p3 [51-250]
    Ceram Mo - v45 - Mr '97 - p28+ [251-500]
Shiva, Vandana - *Biopiracy: The Plunder of Nature and Knowledge*
    PW - v244 - Mr 17 '97 - p73 [51-250]

Shiver, Chuck - *The Rape of the American Constitution*
    Rapport - v19 - 6 '96 - p30 [251-500]
Shlapentokh, Dmitry - *The French Revolution in Russian Intellectual Life 1865-1905*
    Choice - v34 - Mr '97 - p1223 [51-250]
    R&R Bk N - v12 - F '97 - p17 [51-250]
Shlomowitz, Ralph - *Mortality and Migration in the Modern World*
    R&R Bk N - v11 - N '96 - p25 [51-250]
Shlyakhov, Vladimir - *Dictionary of Russian Slang and Colloquial Expressions*
    r MLJ - v80 - Win '96 - p558+ [501+]
Shmueli, Uri - *Introduction to Crystallographic Statistics*
    Choice - v34 - S '96 - p157 [51-250]
Shnayerson, Michael - *The Car That Could*
    Barron's - v76 - O 28 '96 - p62 [501+]
    BL - v93 - S 1 '96 - p46 [51-250]
    Bus W - S 23 '96 - p16+ [501+]
    Bus W - D 16 '96 - p19+ [51-250]
    Fortune - v134 - O 28 '96 - p193+ [501+]
    LJ - v122 - Mr 15 '97 - p37 [1-50]
    NYRB - v43 - N 28 '96 - p32+ [501+]
    NYTBR - v101 - N 24 '96 - p19 [51-250]
Shneidman, Edwin S - *The Suicidal Mind*
    Readings - v12 - Mr '97 - p25 [51-250]
Shneidman, N N - *Russian Literature 1988-1994*
    r Russ Rev - v56 - Ja '97 - p136 [251-500]
Shoaf-Grubbs, Mary Margaret - *Discovering Calculus with the Graphing Calculator*
    Choice - v34 - N '96 - p496+ [51-250]
Shockley, B - *Engaging Families*
    Emerg Lib - v24 - S '96 - p42 [1-50]
Shoemaker, Bill - *Dark Horse*
    Arm Det - v29 - Sum '96 - p361 [251-500]
    LATBR - My 12 '96 - p11 [51-250]
Shoemaker, Donald Joseph - *International Handbook of Juvenile Justice*
    R&R Bk N - v11 - N '96 - p46 [51-250]
Shoemaker, Fred - *Extraordinary Golf*
    LJ - v121 - O 1 '96 - p53 [1-50]
Shoemaker, Nancy - *Negotiators of Change*
    J Soc H - v30 - Fall '96 - p254+ [501+]
    JWomHist - v8 - Fall '96 - p205+ [501+]
Shoenfeld, Oscar - *Some Remembered Words*
    PW - v243 - N 25 '96 - p67 [51-250]
Shogan, Robert - *Hard Bargain*
    AHR - v101 - D '96 - p1648+ [251-500]
    Historian - v58 - Sum '96 - p872+ [251-500]
Shohat, Ella - *Unthinking Eurocentrism*
    Can Lit - Win '96 - p199+ [501+]
Shohei, Ooka - *Taken Captive*
    NYTBR - v101 - S 1 '96 - p17 [51-250]
    y SLJ - v43 - F '97 - p138 [51-250]
Shokeid, Moshe - *A Gay Synagogue in New York*
    AJS - v102 - N '96 - p916+ [501+]
    Am Ethnol - v23 - N '96 - p932+ [501+]
Shokek, Shimon - *Repentance in Jewish Ethics*
    Rel St Rev - v23 - Ap '97 - p196 [51-250]
Sholem Aleichem - *Song of Songs*
    PW - v243 - S 23 '96 - p62 [51-250]
    Tevye the Dairyman (Bikel). Audio Version
    y Kliatt - v31 - Mr '97 - p46+ [51-250]
    y SLJ - v42 - O '96 - p79 [51-250]
Sholokhov, Mikhail Aleksandrovich - *Quiet Flows the Don*
    BW - v27 - Mr 23 '97 - p4+ [501+]
    KR - v64 - N 15 '96 - p1632 [51-250]
    LJ - v121 - N 1 '96 - p108+ [51-250]
    PW - v243 - N 11 '96 - p60 [51-250]
    TLS - S 6 '96 - p23 [1-50]
Shopping LA
    r TCI - v30 - O '96 - p59 [1-50]
Shoptaw, John - *On the Outside Looking Out*
    AL - v68 - S '96 - p655+ [251-500]
Shore, Bill - *Revolution of the Heart*
    y Kliatt - v31 - Ja '97 - p24+ [51-250]
Shore, Bradd - *Culture in Mind*
    Choice - v34 - N '96 - p501 [51-250]
Shore, Jane - *Music Minus One*
    HMR - Spr '97 - p38+ [501+]
    LJ - v121 - S 15 '96 - p72 [51-250]
    NYTBR - v102 - F 23 '97 - p16 [51-250]
    PW - v243 - Jl 22 '96 - p237 [51-250]
    Tikkun - v12 - Mr '97 - p73 [51-250]
Shore, Stephen - *The Velvet Years*
    LATBR - My 26 '96 - p4 [501+]
Shorney, David - *Protestant Nonconformity and Roman Catholicism*
    CH - v66 - Mr '97 - p207 [51-250]
Shorrock-Kelly, Kerry - *Words and Pictures*
    c Sch Lib - v44 - N '96 - p165 [51-250]

Short, Gary - *Flying over Sonny Liston*
  LJ - v121 - D '96 - p99 [51-250]
  WAL - v31 - Fall '96 - p283+ [251-500]
Short, Kathy Gnagey - *Creating Classrooms for Authors.*
  2nd Ed.
  New Ad - v9 - Fall '96 - p309+ [501+]
Short, Sharon Gwyn - *Angel's Bidding*
  Books - v9 - S '95 - p22 [1-50]
  Books - v9 - S '95 - p24 [1-50]
Short Story Criticism. Vols. 18-19
  r ARBA - v28 - '97 - p436 [51-250]
Short Story Criticism. Vols. 20-21
  r ARBA - v28 - '97 - p437 [51-250]
Shortell, Stephen M - *Essentials of Health Care*
  Management
  SciTech - v20 - N '96 - p38 [51-250]
Shorter, Edward - *A History of Psychiatry*
  BL - v93 - Ja '97 - p799+ [51-250]
  KR - v64 - D 1 '96 - p1725 [251-500]
  LJ - v122 - F 15 '97 - p150+ [51-250]
  Nature - v386 - Mr 27 '97 - p346 [501+]
  NYTBR - v102 - Mr 30 '97 - p17 [51-250]
  PW - v243 - N 25 '96 - p65 [51-250]
Shortland, Michael - *Hugh Miller and the Controversies*
  of Victorian Science
  Choice - v34 - My '97 - p1519+ [51-250]
  Telling Lives in Science
  Choice - v34 - Ap '97 - p1359 [51-250]
Shorto, Russell - *Gospel Truth*
  BL - v93 - F 15 '97 - p976 [51-250]
  KR - v65 - F 1 '97 - p208 [251-500]
  LJ - v122 - Mr 15 '97 - p67 [51-250]
Shortridge, James R - *Peopling the Plains*
  PHR - v65 - N '96 - p673+ [501+]
Shortt, Tim - *The Babe Ruth Ballet School (Illus. by Tim*
  Shortt)
  c CLW - v67 - Mr '97 - p52 [51-250]
  c KR - v64 - O 15 '96 - p1538 [51-250]
  c NW - v128 - D 2 '96 - p88 [1-50]
  c PW - v243 - O 21 '96 - p82 [51-250]
  c Quill & Q - v62 - N '96 - p46+ [251-500]
  c SLJ - v43 - Ja '97 - p90+ [51-250]
Shoshan, Boaz - *Popular Culture in Medieval Cairo*
  Specu - v71 - O '96 - p1021+ [501+]
Shoshani, Jeheskel - *The Proboscidea: Evolution and*
  Palaeoecology of Elephants and Their Relatives
  Sci - v276 - Ap 4 '97 - p46+ [501+]
Shott, James R - *Bathsheba*
  BL - v93 - S 1 '96 - p65 [501+]
  LJ - v122 - Ap 1 '97 - p80 [51-250]
Shotwell, R Allen - *An Introduction to Fiber Optics*
  SciTech - v20 - D '96 - p67 [1-50]
Shoup, Barbara - *Stranded in Harmony*
  y CCB-B - v50 - Ap '97 - p296 [51-250]
  y PW - v244 - My 12 '97 - p77 [51-250]
Shoureshi, R - *Engineering Systems*
  SciTech - v21 - Mr '97 - p84 [51-250]
Shover, Neal - *Great Pretenders*
  Choice - v34 - N '96 - p548 [51-250]
Showalter, Dennis E - *The Wars of Frederick the Great*
  HRNB - v25 - Fall '96 - p27 [251-500]
  J Mil H - v61 - Ja '97 - p157 [51-250]
Showalter, Elaine - *Hystories: Hysterical Epidemics and*
  Modern Culture
  KR - v65 - F 1 '97 - p208 [251-500]
  LJ - v122 - Ap 15 '97 - p103+ [51-250]
  PW - v244 - F 24 '97 - p74 [51-250]
  Scribbling Women
  Obs - F 16 '97 - p15* [501+]
  TLS - Mr 21 '97 - p24 [501+]
Showalter, R E - *Monotone Operators in Banach Space*
  and Nonlinear Partial Differential Equations
  SciTech - v21 - Mr '97 - p16 [51-250]
Showers, Paul - *Los Sonidos A Mi Alrededor (Illus. by*
  Aliki)
  c HB Guide - v8 - Spr '97 - p108 [51-250]
  c SLJ - v42 - N '96 - p134 [51-250]
Shraddhananda, Swami - *Seeing God Everywhere*
  PW - v243 - S 30 '96 - p76 [51-250]
Shrader, Charles R - *Communist Logistics in the Korean*
  War
  J Mil H - v61 - Ja '97 - p199+ [251-500]
  Mar Crp G - v80 - N '96 - p81+ [501+]
Shreedhar, Jaya - *Broadening the Front*
  WorldV - v12 - O '96 - p17 [51-250]
Shreeve, James - *The Neandertal Enigma*
  BWatch - v17 - N '96 - p6 [1-50]
  y Kliatt - v31 - Ja '97 - p29 [51-250]
  Lon R Bks - v18 - O 31 '96 - p36+ [501+]
  NYTBR - v101 - N 10 '96 - p68 [51-250]
  Trib Bks - Ja 12 '97 - p2 [1-50]

Shreve, Anita - *Resistance*
  NYTBR - v102 - F 16 '97 - p32 [1-50]
  Trib Bks - F 16 '97 - p8 [1-50]
  The Weight of Water
  y BL - v93 - Ja '97 - p822 [51-250]
  KR - v64 - O 15 '96 - p1491 [251-500]
  LATBR - Ja 19 '97 - p7 [501+]
  LJ - v121 - O 15 '96 - p91 [51-250]
  NYTBR - v102 - Ja 19 '97 - p30 [501+]
  PW - v243 - O 14 '96 - p61 [51-250]
  Trib Bks - Ja 19 '97 - p1+ [501+]
Shreve, Susan - *The Goalie*
  c BL - v93 - D 1 '96 - p666 [51-250]
  c CBRS - v25 - N '96 - p36 [51-250]
  c CCB-B - v50 - Ja '97 - p185 [51-250]
  c HB Guide - v8 - Spr '97 - p75 [51-250]
  c PW - v243 - N 18 '96 - p76 [51-250]
  c SLJ - v43 - F '97 - p106 [51-250]
  Outside the Law
  PW - v244 - Ap 28 '97 - p57 [51-250]
  Warts (Illus. by Gregg Thorkelson)
  c HB - v72 - N '96 - p740+ [51-250]
  c HB Guide - v8 - Spr '97 - p75 [51-250]
  c Par Ch - v21 - Mr '97 - p8 [1-50]
  Zoe and Columbo
  c Emerg Lib - v24 - S '96 - p51 [51-250]
Shrier, Diane K - *Sexual Harassment in the Workplace*
  and Academia
  Readings - v11 - D '96 - p27 [51-250]
Shriqui, Christian L - *Contemporary Issues in the*
  Treatment of Schizophrenia
  AJPsych - v153 - O '96 - p1359+ [501+]
Shriver, Donald W - *An Ethic for Enemies*
  Intpr - v50 - O '96 - p438+ [251-500]
  PSQ - v111 - Fall '96 - p558+ [501+]
  Theol St - v57 - Je '96 - p386 [251-500]
Shropshire, Kenneth L - *In Black and White*
  BW - v26 - Jl 7 '96 - p1+ [501+]
  Choice - v34 - F '97 - p1003 [51-250]
Shrubb, Peter - *Catastrophe of an Old Man*
  Aust Bk R - F '97 - p28+ [501+]
Shrubs and Climbers (Eyewitness Handbooks)
  r ARBA - v28 - '97 - p585 [51-250]
Shrum, Wesley - *Fringe and Fortune*
  Choice - v34 - D '96 - p604 [51-250]
  LJ - v122 - Ja '97 - p102 [51-250]
  Science, Technology, and Society in the Third World
  r T&C - v37 - O '96 - p861+ [501+]
Shteir, Ann B - *Cultivating Women, Cultivating Science*
  Choice - v34 - N '96 - p480 [51-250]
Shua, Ana Maria - *El Libro De Recuerdos*
  Hisp - v79 - D '96 - p827+ [251-500]
Shubin, Seymour - *Fury's Children*
  LJ - v122 - My 1 '97 - p143 [51-250]
Shuchter, Stephen R - *Biologically Informed*
  Psychotherapy for Depression
  AJPsych - v154 - Mr '97 - p433 [501+]
  SciTech - v20 - S '96 - p34 [51-250]
Shugar, Dana R - *Separatism and Women's Community*
  AL - v68 - S '96 - p657+ [251-500]
  NWSA Jnl - v8 - Sum '96 - p139+ [501+]
Shugar, Gershon J - *Chemical Technicians' Ready*
  Reference Handbook. 4th Ed.
  r SciTech - v20 - D '96 - p27 [51-250]
Shuger, Debora Kuller - *The Renaissance Bible*
  Rel St Rev - v23 - Ap '97 - p190 [51-250]
  Ren Q - v49 - Aut '96 - p640+ [501+]
  Sev Cent N - v54 - Fall '96 - p60 [501+]
Shukla, Ramesh - *The UAE: Formative Years 1965-75*
  MEP - v5 - 1 '97 - p198+ [501+]
Shukman, David - *Tomorrow's War*
  BW - v26 - Ag 18 '96 - p13 [51-250]
  Econ - v342 - Mr 15 '97 - p8* [51-250]
Shukman, Henry - *Savage Pilgrims*
  BL - v93 - My 1 '97 - p1475 [51-250]
  LJ - v122 - Ap 1 '97 - p113 [51-250]
  PW - v244 - Ap 21 '97 - p54 [51-250]
Shukshin, Vasily - *Stories from a Siberian Village*
  Choice - v34 - Mr '97 - p1170 [51-250]
  LATBR - O 27 '96 - p3 [501+]
  LATBR - D 29 '96 - p6 [51-250]
  LJ - v121 - O 15 '96 - p130 [51-250]
  NYTBR - v101 - D 29 '96 - p14 [51-250]
  PW - v243 - S 9 '96 - p78+ [51-250]
  TranslRevS - v2 - D '96 - p31 [51-250]
Shul, R J - *Compound Semiconductor Electronics and*
  Photonics
  SciTech - v21 - Mr '97 - p90 [51-250]
Shuler, Jay - *Had I the Wings*
  JSH - v62 - N '96 - p805+ [251-500]

Shuler, Linda Lay - *Let the Drum Speak*
  BW - v26 - O 6 '96 - p8 [51-250]
  Roundup M - v4 - Ap '97 - p28 [251-500]
Shulevitz, Uri - *The Golden Goose (Illus. by Uri Shulevitz)*
  c RT - v50 - O '96 - p133 [1-50]
Shulimson, Jack - *The Marine Corps' Search for a*
  Mission 1880-1898
  Pub Hist - v18 - Sum '96 - p64+ [501+]
Shull, Michael S - *Hollywood War Films 1937-1945*
  r ARBA - v28 - '97 - p512+ [251-500]
  r Choice - v34 - D '96 - p596 [51-250]
  r LJ - v121 - O 15 '96 - p62 [51-250]
  r R&R Bk N - v11 - N '96 - p10 [51-250]
Shullenberger, Bonnie - *A Time to Be Born*
  Nat R - v49 - F 24 '97 - p58 [51-250]
Shulman, Burton - *Safe House*
  KR - v64 - O 15 '96 - p1492 [51-250]
  PW - v243 - O 21 '96 - p76 [51-250]
Shulman, Martha Rose - *Mexican Light*
  BL - v93 - S 15 '96 - p198 [51-250]
  LJ - v121 - O 15 '96 - p85 [51-250]
  PW - v243 - S 16 '96 - p79 [51-250]
Shultis, J Kenneth - *Radiation Shielding*
  r SciTech - v20 - S '96 - p28 [51-250]
Shuman, Howard E - *The Constitution and National*
  Security
  RSR - v24 - 3 '96 - p43 [51-250]
Shumate, Nancy - *Crisis and Conversion in Apuleius'*
  Metamorphoses
  Choice - v34 - D '96 - p610 [51-250]
Shupe, Anson - *In the Name of All That's Holy*
  CS - v25 - S '96 - p665+ [501+]
Shur, Richard - *Countertransference Enactments*
  Time - v57 - S '96 - p426 [501+]
Shurden, Walter B - *Going for the Jugular*
  CC - v113 - N 6 '96 - p1092+ [51-250]
Shure, Robert - *The Story of Digby and Marie*
  PW - v244 - Ap 14 '97 - p57 [51-250]
Shurin, Aaron - *Unbound: A Book of AIDS*
  PW - v244 - Ja 6 '97 - p55 [51-250]
Shurkin, Joel - *Engines of the Mind*
  Nature - v383 - O 24 '96 - p682 [1-50]
  New Sci - v152 - O 26 '96 - p45 [51-250]
Shurtleff, Lawton L - *The Wood Duck and the Mandarin*
  Choice - v34 - F '97 - p991 [51-250]
  LJ - v121 - S 15 '96 - p91 [51-250]
  Nature - v385 - Ja 30 '97 - p405 [51-250]
  New Sci - v152 - N 2 '96 - p48 [51-250]
Shushan, Ronnie - *Desktop Publishing by Design. 4th Ed.*
  CBR - v15 - Spr '97 - p8 [51-250]
  R&R Bk N - v11 - D '96 - p73 [51-250]
Shusterman, Neal - *The Dark Side of Nowhere*
  y BL - v93 - Ap 1 '97 - p1322 [51-250]
  y KR - v65 - Mr 15 '97 - p468 [51-250]
  y PW - v244 - Mr 17 '97 - p84 [51-250]
  Mindquakes: Stories to Shatter Your Brain
  y BL - v93 - Ap 1 '97 - p1310 [1-50]
  Mindstorms: Stories to Blow Your Mind
  y Kliatt - v31 - Ja '97 - p16 [51-250]
  Scorpion Shards
  y HB Guide - v7 - Fall '96 - p305 [51-250]
  y Kliatt - v31 - Ja '97 - p10+ [51-250]
  y PW - v243 - N 18 '96 - p78 [51-250]
Shute, Alan H - *Richard Shute of Boston, Massachusetts*
  1631-1703 and Selected Progeny
  Am Geneal - v71 - Jl '96 - p189+ [251-500]
Shute, Jenefer - *Sex Crimes*
  Ent W - D 6 '96 - p59 [51-250]
  KR - v64 - Ag 15 '96 - p1182 [251-500]
  LJ - v121 - O 15 '96 - p91+ [51-250]
  LJ - v122 - F 1 '97 - p136 [51-250]
  PW - v243 - S 2 '96 - p108 [51-250]
  TLS - F 21 '97 - p23 [251-500]
Shute, Michael - *The Origins of Lonergan's Notion of*
  Dialectic of History
  Dialogue - v35 - Sum '96 - p633+ [501+]
Shuter, Jane - *Christabel Bielenberg and Nazi Germany*
  y HB Guide - v7 - Fall '96 - p381 [51-250]
  Helen Williams and the French Revolution
  y HB Guide - v7 - Fall '96 - p383 [51-250]
  Sarah Royce and the American West
  y HB Guide - v7 - Fall '96 - p390 [51-250]
Shutes, Jeanne - *The Worlds of P'otsunu*
  WHQ - v27 - Win '96 - p551 [1-50]
Shuttleworth, Sally - *Charlotte Bronte and Victorian*
  Psychology
  New Sci - v153 - F 1 '97 - p48 [501+]
Shvets, V B - *Reinforcement and Reconstruction of*
  Foundations
  SciTech - v20 - N '96 - p65 [51-250]

Shvidkovskii, D O - *The Empress and the Architect*
  Choice - v34 - D '96 - p604 [51-250]
  CSM - v88 - N 21 '96 - pB3 [51-250]
  LJ - v121 - O 15 '96 - p55+ [51-250]
  Spec - v277 - N 30 '96 - p58 [51-250]
  VLS - Win '96 - p22 [51-250]
  St. Petersburg: Architecture of the Tsars
  Choice - v34 - Mr '97 - p1153 [51-250]
  LJ - v122 - Mr 15 '97 - p60+ [51-250]
  Spec - v277 - N 23 '96 - p45 [51-250]
  Time - v148 - N 18 '96 - p109 [1-50]
Shwalb, David W - *Japanese Childrearing*
  R&R Bk N - v12 - F '97 - p52 [51-250]
  SB - v33 - Ja '97 - p6 [251-500]
Shwartz, Susan - *Shards of Empire*
  y VOYA - v19 - O '96 - p220+ [251-500]
  Sisters in Fantasy 2
  y Kliatt - v30 - S '96 - p20 [51-250]
  SF Chr - v18 - O '96 - p80 [1-50]
Shy, Oz - *Industrial Organization*
  JEL - v34 - S '96 - p1450+ [51-250]
Shyer, Marlene Fanta - *Not like Other Boys*
  LATBR - Jl 7 '96 - p10 [51-250]
  y SLJ - v42 - O '96 - p166 [51-250]
  y SLJ - v42 - D '96 - p33 [1-50]
Shyldkrot, Hava Bat-Zeev - *Tendances Recentes En Linguistique Francaise Et Generale*
  FR - v70 - F '97 - p480+ [501+]
Si Shi Nian Lai Zhong Guo Wen Xue
  BL - v93 - My 1 '97 - p1484 [1-50]
Sibelman, Simon P - *Silence in the Novels of Elie Wiesel*
  FR - v70 - F '97 - p479+ [251-500]
Sibley, Brian - *Shadowlands (Suchet). Audio Version*
  LJ - v121 - S 15 '96 - p115 [51-250]
Sibley, F Ray - *The Confederate Order of Battle. Vol. 1*
  PW - v243 - S 16 '96 - p65 [51-250]
Sicard, Patrice - *Diagrammes Medievaux Et Exegese Visuelle*
  Specu - v71 - Jl '96 - p761+ [501+]
Sichel, Werner - *Networks, Infrastructure, and the New Task for Regulation*
  JEL - v34 - S '96 - p1458 [51-250]
Sicher, Efraim - *Jews in Russian Literature after the October Revolution*
  New R - v216 - F 3 '97 - p34+ [501+]
Sichtermann, Hellmut - *Kulturgeschichte Der Klassischen Archaologie*
  TLS - D 13 '96 - p26+ [501+]
Sick, Helmut - *Birds of Brazil*
  AB - v97 - Je 17 '96 - p2400 [51-250]
Sicken, Bernhard - *Herrschaft Und Verfassungsstrukturen Im Nordwesten Des Reiches*
  Six Ct J - v27 - Fall '96 - p798+ [501+]
Sicular, Daniel T - *Scavengers, Recyclers, and Solutions for Solid Waste Management in Indonesia*
  JTWS - v13 - Spr '96 - p268+ [501+]
Sidahmed, Abdel Salam - *Islamic Fundamentalism*
  Choice - v34 - D '96 - p628+ [51-250]
  Cons - v17 - Win '96 - p31 [1-50]
Sidak, J Gregory - *Protecting Competition from the Postal Monopoly*
  R&R Bk N - v11 - D '96 - p32 [51-250]
Siddals, Mary McKenna - *Tell Me a Season (Illus. by Petra Mathers)*
  c BL - v93 - Ap 1 '97 - p1339 [51-250]
  c CBRS - v25 - Mr '97 - p90 [1-50]
  c KR - v65 - F 1 '97 - p228 [51-250]
  c PW - v244 - Ja 6 '97 - p72 [51-250]
Siddiqi, Muhammad Nejatullah - *Role of the State in the Economy*
  JEL - v35 - Mr '97 - p295 [51-250]
Siddle, Bruce K - *Sharpening the Warrior's Edge*
  Fed Prob - v60 - D '96 - p62 [501+]
Siddons, Anne Rivers - *Up Island*
  KR - v65 - Ap 1 '97 - p498 [251-500]
  PW - v244 - My 5 '97 - p194 [51-250]
  Trib Bks - My 25 '97 - p11 [51-250]
Side Show 1997
  PW - v243 - D 2 '96 - p53 [51-250]
Sider, Gerald M - *Lumbee Indian Histories*
  RA - v25 - 4 '96 - p275+ [501+]
Sider, Ronald J - *Genuine Christianity*
  Ch Today - v41 - Ja 6 '97 - p51 [51-250]
Sides, Marilyn - *The Island of the Mapmaker's Wife and Other Tales*
  NYTBR - v101 - S 8 '96 - p23 [51-250]
Sidey, Hugh - *Iowa: A Celebration of Land, People and Purpose*
  J Gov Info - v23 - S '96 - p583 [51-250]

Sidoli, Richard Camillo - *The Cooking of Parma*
  BL - v93 - F 15 '97 - p989 [51-250]
  BWatch - v18 - F '97 - p8 [51-250]
Sidwell, Keith - *Reading Medieval Latin*
  Rel St Rev - v23 - Ja '97 - p77 [51-250]
Sieben, Hermann Josef - *Katholische Konzilsidee Im 19. Und 20. Jahrhundert*
  r Theol St - v57 - Mr '96 - p152+ [501+]
Siebers, Tobin - *Heterotopia: Postmodern Utopia and the Body Politic*
  TDR - v40 - Fall '96 - p201 [51-250]
Siebert, Horst - *Locational Competition in the World Economy*
  Econ J - v107 - Ja '97 - p290 [51-250]
Siebert, Renate - *Secrets of Life and Death*
  LJ - v121 - O 15 '96 - p76+ [51-250]
  PW - v243 - S 30 '96 - p77+ [51-250]
  Spec - v278 - Ja 18 '97 - p30 [501+]
  Wom R Bks - v14 - Mr '97 - p11 [501+]
Siebzehner, Batia B - *La Universidad Americana Y La Ilustracion*
  HAHR - v77 - F '97 - p105+ [501+]
Un Siecle De Sculpture Anglaise
  BM - v138 - S '96 - p622+ [501+]
Sieg, Katrin - *Exiles, Eccentrics, Activists*
  Ger Q - v69 - Sum '96 - p362+ [501+]
Siegal, Aranka - *Upon the Head of the Goat (Moore). Audio Version*
  BL - v93 - My 15 '97 - p1596 [51-250]
  y Kliatt - v31 - Mr '97 - p51 [51-250]
Siegal, Harvey A - *Case Management and Substance Abuse Treatment*
  Readings - v11 - D '96 - p24 [51-250]
Siegal, Mordecai - *UC Davis Book of Horses*
  r BL - v93 - S 15 '96 - p285 [51-250]
Siegel, Allen M - *Heinz Kohut and the Psychology of the Self*
  R&R Bk N - v12 - F '97 - p5 [51-250]
Siegel, David S - *The Used Book Lover's Guide to the Pacific Coast States*
  r R&R Bk N - v12 - F '97 - p101 [1-50]
Siegel, Don - *A Siegel Film*
  TES - N 22 '96 - p8* [1-50]
Siegel, Dorothy Schainman - *Ann Richards: Politician, Feminist, Survivor*
  y CLW - v66 - Je '96 - p55 [51-250]
  c HB Guide - v7 - Fall '96 - p371 [51-250]
  y SLJ - v42 - O '96 - p159+ [51-250]
Siegel, Katherine A S - *Loans and Legitimacy*
  Choice - v34 - D '96 - p678 [51-250]
  R&R Bk N - v11 - D '96 - p14 [51-250]
Siegel, Lawrence M - *Least Restrictive Environment*
  H Sch M - v4 - S '96 - p49 [51-250]
Siegel, Robert Anthony - *All the Money in the World*
  KR - v65 - Mr 1 '97 - p332 [51-250]
  LJ - v122 - Ap 1 '97 - p131 [51-250]
  PW - v244 - Mr 31 '97 - p64 [51-250]
Siegel, Robert J - *Ultrasound Angioplasty*
  SciTech - v20 - D '96 - p50 [51-250]
Siegelbaum, Lewis H - *Making Workers Soviet*
  JIH - v27 - Win '97 - p535+ [501+]
Siegelson, Kim - *The Terrible, Wonderful Tellin' at Hog Hammock (Illus. by Eric Velasquez)*
  c CCB-B - v50 - S '96 - p29 [51-250]
  c HB Guide - v7 - Fall '96 - p297 [51-250]
  c SLJ - v42 - Ag '96 - p144+ [51-250]
Siegen-Smith, Nikki - *Songs for Survival (Illus. by Bernard Lodge)*
  c CCB-B - v50 - S '96 - p29+ [51-250]
  c HB Guide - v7 - Fall '96 - p365 [51-250]
  Welcome to the World
  c CBRS - v25 - D '96 - p41 [1-50]
  y CCB-B - v50 - D '96 - p152 [51-250]
  y HB Guide - v8 - Spr '97 - p151 [51-250]
  LATBR - D 8 '96 - p10 [51-250]
  y NYTBR - v102 - Mr 30 '97 - p18 [501+]
  y SLJ - v42 - O '96 - p160 [51-250]
Siegfried, Susan L - *The Art of Louis-Leopold Boilly*
  Apo - v144 - Ag '96 - p70 [501+]
  Eight-C St - v30 - Fall '96 - p97+ [501+]
Siegler, Robert - *Emerging Minds*
  New Sci - v153 - F 1 '97 - p46 [51-250]
Sieg's Montkatalog. 1997 Ed.
  r Coin W - v37 - N 4 '96 - p82 [51-250]
Siembieda, Kevin - *Coalition War Campaign*
  c Ch BWatch - v6 - S '96 - p4 [51-250]
  Dragons and Gods. 2nd Ed.
  c Ch BWatch - v7 - F '97 - p8 [1-50]
  Monsters and Animals. 2nd Ed.
  c Ch BWatch - v6 - O '96 - p2 [51-250]

Siemerling, Winfried - *Discoveries of the Other*
  MLR - v92 - Ja '97 - p149 [251-500]
Siems, Larry - *Between the Lines*
  HAHR - v77 - F '97 - p95+ [251-500]
Sienkewicz, Thomas J - *World Mythology*
  r ARBA - v28 - '97 - p499 [251-500]
  r Choice - v34 - Ap '97 - p1316 [51-250]
  r LJ - v122 - F 1 '97 - p74 [51-250]
Sienkiewicz, Henryk - *The Little Trilogy*
  WLT - v70 - Sum '96 - p728 [501+]
Sierakowiak, Dawid - *The Diary of Dawid Sierakowiak*
  Atl - v278 - N '96 - p120+ [251-500]
  y BL - v92 - Ag '96 - p1878 [51-250]
  BL - v92 - Ag '96 - p1890 [1-50]
  Choice - v34 - Mr '97 - p1223 [51-250]
Sierra, Judy - *Good Night, Dinosaurs (Illus. by Victoria Chess)*
  c Ch BWatch - v6 - My '96 - p3 [1-50]
  c HB Guide - v7 - Fall '96 - p369 [51-250]
  c Par - v71 - S '96 - p209 [51-250]
  The House That Drac Built (Illus. by Will Hillenbrand)
  c RT - v50 - O '96 - p133 [1-50]
  Multicultural Folktales for the Feltboard and Readers' Theater
  r BL - v93 - Mr 1 '97 - p1177 [51-250]
  r SS - v88 - Ja '97 - p29+ [501+]
  Nursery Tales around the World (Illus. by Stefano Vitale)
  c BL - v93 - Ap 1 '97 - p1306 [1-50]
  c HB Guide - v7 - Fall '96 - p324 [51-250]
  c Par Ch - v20 - O '96 - p28 [1-50]
  c PW - v243 - N 4 '96 - p48 [1-50]
  c RT - v50 - Ap '97 - p593 [51-250]
  Storytellers' Research Guide
  r BL - v93 - Mr 1 '97 - p1177 [51-250]
  Wiley and the Hairy Man (Illus. by Brian Pinkney)
  c HB Guide - v7 - Fall '96 - p324 [51-250]
  c Inst - v106 - Ja '97 - p54 [51-250]
  c Par - v71 - D '96 - p252 [51-250]
  c RT - v50 - Ap '97 - p595 [51-250]
Sierra I Fabra, Jordi - *Dando La Nota (Illus. by Federico Delicado)*
  c JAAL - v40 - S '96 - p78 [51-250]
  Noche De Paz...O Casi (Illus. by Federico Delicado)
  c JAAL - v40 - S '96 - p78 [51-250]
  Tres Dias Salvajes (Illus. by Federico Delicado)
  c JAAL - v40 - S '96 - p78 [51-250]
Sies, Mary Corbin - *Planning the Twentieth-Century American City*
  JEL - v34 - D '96 - p2104 [51-250]
  R&R Bk N - v11 - N '96 - p43 [51-250]
Sifakis, Carl - *Three Men on Third and Other Wacky Events from the World of Sports*
  y Kliatt - v30 - S '96 - p5 [1-50]
Sifonis, John G - *Corporation on a Tightrope*
  HR Mag - v41 - S '96 - p137 [501+]
  LJ - v122 - Mr 15 '97 - p36 [1-50]
Sigal, Gale - *Erotic Dawn-Songs of the Middle Ages*
  Choice - v34 - N '96 - p450 [51-250]
Sigel, Roberta S - *Ambition and Accommodation*
  Choice - v34 - N '96 - p548 [51-250]
Sight and Sound Film Review Volume: January 1994 to December 1994
  r ARBA - v28 - '97 - p517 [251-500]
Siginer, Dennis A - *Rheology and Fluid Mechanics of Nonlinear Materials 1996*
  SciTech - v21 - Mr '97 - p76 [51-250]
Sigler, William F - *Fishes of Utah*
  SciTech - v21 - Mr '97 - p38 [51-250]
Signol, Christian - *Les Vignes De Sainte Colombe*
  BL - v93 - Ja '97 - p827 [1-50]
Signorielli, Nancy - *Women in Communication*
  r Choice - v34 - Ap '97 - p1318 [51-250]
  r R&R Bk N - v12 - F '97 - p75 [51-250]
Signorile, Marc - *Musique Et Societe*
  Notes - v53 - S '96 - p67+ [501+]
Signorile, Michaelangelo - *Life Outside*
  PW - v244 - My 12 '97 - p71 [51-250]
Sigwart, Ulrich - *Handbook of Cardiovascular Interventions*
  SciTech - v20 - D '96 - p47 [51-250]
Sihler, Andrew L - *New Comparative Grammar of Greek and Latin*
  AJP - v117 - Win '96 - p670+ [501+]
Sikainga, Ahmad Alawad - *Slaves into Workers*
  Choice - v34 - Ja '97 - p852 [51-250]
  JEL - v34 - D '96 - p2100+ [51-250]
  MEJ - v50 - Aut '96 - p627 [51-250]
  R&R Bk N - v11 - D '96 - p31 [51-250]

Siker, Jeffrey S - *Scripture and Ethics*
  BL - v93 - N 1 '96 - p462 [51-250]
  Choice - v34 - My '97 - p1517 [51-250]
Sikes, Gini - *8 Ball Chicks*
  y BL - v93 - D 15 '96 - p698 [51-250]
  KR - v64 - O 15 '96 - p1519 [51-250]
  LJ - v121 - D '96 - p122 [51-250]
  Ms - v7 - Mr '97 - p82+ [251-500]
  PW - v243 - N 4 '96 - p53 [51-250]
  Trib Bks - My 11 '97 - p6 [501+]
Siklos, Pierre L - *Great Inflations of the 20th Century*
  Econ J - v106 - S '96 - p1471 [51-250]
Sikorski, Radek - *Full Circle*
  PW - v244 - Ap 28 '97 - p57 [251-500]
Sikorski, Trevor M - *Financial Liberalization in Developing Countries*
  R&R Bk N - v12 - F '97 - p28 [1-50]
Sikula, John - *Handbook of Research on Teacher Education. 2nd Ed.*
  r BL - v93 - N 15 '96 - p611 [251-500]
  r R&R Bk N - v11 - N '96 - p55 [51-250]
Silbaugh, Elizabeth - *Let's Play Cards! (Illus. by Jef Kaminsky)*
  c CCB-B - v50 - S '96 - p30 [51-250]
  c HB Guide - v8 - Spr '97 - p143 [51-250]
  c SLJ - v42 - O '96 - p118 [51-250]
Silber, Evelyn - *Gaudier-Brzeska: Life and Art*
  Choice - v34 - Ap '97 - p1326 [51-250]
  Obs - D 15 '96 - p15* [51 250]
Silber, Ilana Friedrich - *Virtuosity, Charisma, and Social Order*
  Specu - v72 - Ja '97 - p222+ [501+]
Silber, Laura - *Yugoslavia: Death of a Nation*
  NYTBR - v101 - D 8 '96 - p94 [1-50]
  NYTBR - v102 - Mr 9 '97 - p28 [51-250]
Silber, Nina - *Yankee Correspondence*
  HRNB - v25 - Win '97 - p59+ [501+]
  NEQ - v70 - Mr '97 - p175+ [501+]
Silberg, Jackie - *More Games to Play with Toddlers*
  Cur R - v36 - N '96 - p3* [51-250]
Silberman, Lauren - *Transforming Desire*
  MLR - v92 - Ap '97 - p447+ [501+]
Silberman, Marc - *German Cinema*
  AB - v98 - D 9 '96 - p1997 [1-50]
Silberman, Neil Asher - *The Hidden Scrolls*
  y Kliatt - v31 - Mr '97 - p28+ [51-250]
  NYTBR - v101 - D 22 '96 - p20 [51-250]
  A Prophet from amongst You
  Nat - v263 - N 11 '96 - p25+ [501+]
Silberston, Aubrey - *The Changing Industrial Map of Europe*
  JEL - v34 - S '96 - p1455+ [501+]
Silbert, Layle - *New York, New York*
  NYTBR - v101 - N 24 '96 - p18 [51-250]
  PW - v243 - Jl 22 '96 - p233+ [51-250]
Silcox, David P - *Painting Place*
  BIC - v26 - F '97 - p2+ [501+]
  Mac - v109 - D 9 '96 - p66 [1-50]
  Quill & Q - v62 - D '96 - p28 [501+]
  R&R Bk N - v12 - F '97 - p74 [51-250]
Silem, Ahmed - *Histoire De L'Analyse Economique*
  JEL - v34 - D '96 - p2010 [51-250]
  Lexique: Economie. 5th Ed.
  r JEL - v34 - D '96 - p2009 [51-250]
Silent Night (Illus. by Belinda Downes)
  c Bks Keeps - N '96 - p20 [1-50]
Silfvast, William T - *Laser Fundamentals*
  New Sci - v151 - S 28 '96 - p54+ [501+]
  Phys Today - v49 - D '96 - p53 [501+]
Silk, Jennifer C - *Hazard Communication Compliance Manual*
  R&R Bk N - v11 - N '96 - p53 [51-250]
Silk, Joseph - *A Short History of the Universe*
  S&T - v92 - S '96 - p53 [51-250]
Silk, Leonard - *Making Capitalism Work*
  Choice - v34 - My '97 - p1549+ [51-250]
  NYTBR - v101 - D 15 '96 - p42 [501+]
Silk, Mark - *Unsecular Media*
  CH - v65 - D '96 - p770+ [501+]
  JAAR - v64 - Win '96 - p853+ [501+]
  JMCQ - v73 - Win '96 - p1020+ [501+]
  Theol St - v57 - D '96 - p787+ [251-500]
Silkensen, Gregory M - *Windy Gap*
  Pub Hist - v18 - Sum '96 - p87+ [501+]
Silko, Leslie - *Yellow Woman and a Beauty of the Spirit*
  Ant R - v54 - Sum '96 - p364 [251-500]
  Bloom Rev - v16 - Jl '96 - p3+ [51-250]
  LATBR - Mr 17 '96 - p11 [51-250]
  Trib Bks - Mr 16 '97 - p8 [1-50]
  WAL - v31 - Sum '96 - p171+ [251-500]

Sill, Geoffrey M - *Walt Whitman of Mickle Street*
  ASInt - v34 - O '96 - p116+ [501+]
Sillick, Ardis - *400 Videos You've Got to Rent!*
  r LJ - v122 - F 1 '97 - p74 [51-250]
Sillitoe, Alan - *Collected Stories*
  BL - v93 - S 15 '96 - p222 [51-250]
  KR - v64 - S 1 '96 - p1268 [51-250]
  LJ - v121 - S 15 '96 - p100 [51-250]
  Leading the Blind
  Books - v9 - S '95 - p23 [1-50]
Sills, Judith - *Biting the Apple*
  Rapport - v19 - 5 '96 - p38 [251-500]
  Loving Men More, Needing Men Less
  PW - v244 - F 3 '97 - p100 [1-50]
Sills, Yole G - *The AIDS Pandemic*
  Soc - v33 - Jl '96 - p86+ [501+]
Silo - *Tales for Heart and Mind*
  TranslRevS - v1 - My '95 - p32 [51-250]
Siltanen, Janet - *Gender Inequality in the Labour Market*
  J Gov Info - v23 - S '96 - p671 [51-250]
Silva, Daniel - *The Unlikely Spy*
  y BL - v93 - Ja '97 - p824 [251-500]
  BW - v27 - F 2 '97 - p9 [501+]
  KR - v64 - N 1 '96 - p1561 [251-500]
  LJ - v121 - D '96 - p147 [51-250]
  NYTBR - v102 - F 9 '97 - p20 [251-500]
  NYTLa - v146 - Ja 8 '97 - pC14 [501+]
  PW - v243 - D 2 '96 - p42+ [51-250]
  Trib Bks - Ja 26 '97 - p3 [501+]
  The Unlikely Spy (Rees). Audio Version
  CSM - v89 - Mr 27 '97 - pB8 [51-250]
Silva, David B - *The Disappeared*
  Necro - Fall '96 - p27 [51-250]
Silva, Eduardo, 1950- - *The State and Capital in Chile*
  Choice - v34 - N '96 - p509 [51-250]
  R&R Bk N - v11 - N '96 - p27 [51-250]
Silva, Eduardo Da - *Prince of the People*
  HAHR - v76 - Ag '96 - p597+ [251-500]
Silva, Fred G - *Renal Biopsy Interpretation*
  SciTech - v20 - N '96 - p48 [51-250]
Silva, Penny - *A Dictionary of South African English on Historical Principles*
  r ARBA - v28 - '97 - p382 [251-500]
  r Choice - v34 - My '97 - p1473 [51-250]
  r Obs - S 8 '96 - p17* [501+]
Silva-Corvalan, Carmen - *Spanish in Four Continents*
  Hisp - v79 - S '96 - p469+ [501+]
Silvam, E B - *Good Enough Mothering?*
  Socio R - v45 - F 1 '97 - p174+ [501+]
Silvennoinen, Olli - *Signaling by the Hematopoietic Cytokine Receptors*
  SciTech - v21 - Mr '97 - p43 [51-250]
Silver, A David - *Quantum Companies II*
  r Bus Bk R - v13 - 4 '96 - p123+ [51-250]
Silver, Arnold - *Shortchangers: A Story of the Near Future*
  PW - v244 - Mr 31 '97 - p63 [51-250]
Silver, Cheryl Simon - *Toxics and Health*
  Env - v38 - D '96 - p25 [51-250]
Silver, Christopher - *The Separate City*
  AAPSS-A - v550 - Mr '97 - p186+ [501+]
  APSR - v90 - D '96 - p867+ [501+]
  JSH - v63 - F '97 - p203+ [501+]
  J Soc H - v30 - Spr '97 - p791+ [501+]
Silver, Donald M - *Woods (Illus. by Patricia J Wynne)*
  c HB Guide - v7 - Fall '96 - p338 [51-250]
Silver, Jim - *Thin Ice*
  Mac - v109 - D 16 '96 - p73 [51-250]
Silver, Larry - *Art in History*
  Art J - v55 - Sum '96 - p99+ [501+]
Silver, Maggie - *Who Lives Here? (Illus. by Maggie Silver)*
  c RT - v50 - O '96 - p131 [1-50]
Silver, Marc L - *Contested Terrain*
  SF - v75 - S '96 - p376+ [501+]
Silver, Morris - *Economic Structures of Antiquity*
  AHR - v101 - D '96 - p1524+ [251-500]
  Historian - v58 - Sum '96 - p918+ [251-500]
  JEH - v56 - D '96 - p929+ [501+]
Silver, Norman - *The Blue Horse (Illus. by Jilly Wilkinson)*
  y JB - v60 - O '96 - p206 [51-250]
  y Obs - v54 - O 13 '96 - p18* [51-250]
  c Sch Lib - v44 - N '96 - p152 [51-250]
Silver, Paul A - *Psychotropic Drug Use in the Medically Ill*
  r AJPsych - v154 - F '97 - p284+ [501+]
Silver Bells (Illus. by Gwynne Forster)
  LJ - v121 - N 15 '96 - p50 [51-250]
Silvera, Makeda - *The Other Woman*
  Can Lit - Win '96 - p185+ [501+]

Silverberg, Robert - *Reflections and Refractions*
  y BL - v93 - Ap 1 '97 - p1277 [51-250]
  KR - v65 - F 1 '97 - p209 [251-500]
  PW - v244 - Ja 27 '97 - p86 [51-250]
  Starborne
  BL - v93 - Ja '97 - p762 [1-50]
  MFSF - v91 - Ag '96 - p34 [51-250]
  New Sci - v152 - O 5 '96 - p50 [51-250]
  y VOYA - v19 - O '96 - p221 [251-500]
Silverblatt, Arthur - *Dictionary of Media Literacy*
  r LJ - v122 - Ap 15 '97 - p74 [51-250]
Silverman, Barton - *Capturing the Moment*
  NYTBR - v102 - F 2 '97 - p20 [251-500]
Silverman, David - *Interpreting Qualitative Data*
  MLJ - v81 - Spr '97 - p136 [501+]
Silverman, Erica - *Gittel's Hands (Illus. by Deborah Nourse Lattimore)*
  c HB Guide - v7 - Fall '96 - p276 [51-250]
  Mrs. Peachtree and the Eighth Avenue Cat
  c CLW - v67 - Mr '97 - p15 [1-50]
  Mrs. Peachtree's Bicycle (Illus. by Ellen Beier)
  c HB Guide - v7 - Fall '96 - p276 [51-250]
  c KR - v64 - My 1 '96 - p693 [51-250]
  c LATBR - Jl 7 '96 - p11 [51-250]
Silverman, Gary S - *Handbook of Grignard Reagents*
  SciTech - v20 - S '96 - p17 [51-250]
Silverman, Helaine - *Ancient Peruvian Art*
  r ARBA - v28 - '97 - p365 [51-250]
Silverman, Hugh J - *Textualities: Between Hermeneutics and Deconstruction*
  JAAC - v55 - Win '97 - p70+ [501+]
Silverman, Jan F - *Fine Needle Aspiration Cytology of the Thorax and Abdomen*
  SciTech - v20 - D '96 - p48 [51-250]
Silverman, Jerry - *Just Listen to This Song I'm Singing*
  c Ch BWatch - v6 - Jl '96 - p3 [51-250]
  c HB Guide - v7 - Fall '96 - p357 [51-250]
  c RT - v50 - My '97 - p680 [51-250]
  y VOYA - v19 - F '97 - p353+ [251-500]
  Work Songs
  CAY - v17 - Fall '96 - p1 [51-250]
Silverman, Kaja - *The Threshold of the Visible World*
  Afterimage - v24 - N '96 - p16 [51-250]
Silverman, Kenneth - *Houdini! The Career of Ehrich Weiss*
  BW - v27 - F 9 '97 - p13 [51-250]
  Choice - v34 - Mr '97 - p1170 [51-250]
  KR - v64 - S 1 '96 - p1308 [251-500]
  New R - v216 - F 17 '97 - p32+ [501+]
  NY - v72 - D 2 '96 - p115 [51-250]
  NYTBR - v101 - D 15 '96 - p14+ [501+]
  WSJ-MW - v78 - O 29 '96 - pA20 [501+]
Silverman, Morton M - *Suicide Prevention*
  Readings - v11 - D '96 - p25 [51-250]
Silverman, Paul M - *Imaging Handbook for House Officers*
  SciTech - v21 - Mr '97 - p49 [51-250]
Silverman, Stephen M - *Dancing on the Ceiling*
  BW - v26 - Jl 7 '96 - p8 [51-250]
  Dance - v71 - Ja '97 - p98 [51-250]
  FIR - v47 - Jl '96 - p116+ [501+]
Silverman, Sue William - *Because I Remember Terror, Father, I Remember You*
  BL - v93 - N '96 - p465 [51-250]
  KR - v64 - S 15 '96 - p1387 [251-500]
  Ms - v7 - N '96 - p82 [1-50]
Silverman, Wendy K - *Anxiety and Phobic Disorders*
  Readings - v11 - S '96 - p25+ [51-250]
  SciTech - v20 - S '96 - p41 [51-250]
Silverman, Willa Z - *The Notorious Life of Gyp*
  AHR - v101 - D '96 - p1559+ [501+]
  MLR - v92 - Ap '97 - p476 [251-500]
Silvers, Robert B - *Hidden Histories of Science*
  Nature - v385 - F 20 '97 - p693 [1-50]
  New Sci - v153 - Ja 4 '97 - p39 [1-50]
  NS - v126 - Ja 24 '97 - p46+ [501+]
  Obs - Mr 2 '97 - p18* [51-250]
  TES - F 7 '97 - p8* [51-250]
Silversides, Brock V - *Waiting for the Light*
  Beav - v76 - D '96 - p40 [501+]
Silverstein, Alan - *Alternatives to Assimilation*
  AHR - v101 - O '96 - p1269 [501+]
Silverstein, Alvin - *Asthma*
  y SB - v33 - Mr '97 - p46+ [51-250]
  Invertebrates
  c SB - v32 - Ag '96 - p180 [51-250]
  Monerans and Protists
  c SB - v32 - Ag '96 - p180 [51-250]
  The Sea Otter
  cr SB - v32 - N '96 - p248 [51-250]

Sickle Cell Anemia
c SLJ - v43 - F '97 - p125 [51-250]
Vertebrates
c SB - v32 - N '96 - p242+ [51-250]
Silverstein, Gordon - *Imbalance of Powers*
Choice - v34 - Mr '97 - p1241 [51-250]
For Aff - v76 - Mr '97 - p182 [51-250]
Silverstein, Helena - *Unleashing Rights*
Choice - v34 - Mr '97 - p1180 [51-250]
Silverstein, Herma - *Threads of Evidence*
y BL - v93 - D 1 '96 - p657 [51-250]
y Ch BWatch - v7 - Ja '97 - p2 [51-250]
y SB - v33 - Mr '97 - p44 [251-500]
y SLJ - v43 - F '97 - p125+ [51-250]
Silverstein, Shel - *Falling Up (Illus. by Shel Silverstein)*
c BL - v93 - Ja '97 - p766 [1-50]
y BL - v93 - Ap 1 '97 - p1308 [1-50]
c Emerg Lib - v24 - S '96 - p43 [1-50]
c HB - v72 - S '96 - p606 [51-250]
c HB Guide - v7 - Fall '96 - p369 [51-250]
c Inst - v106 - N '96 - p26 [1-50]
c KR - v64 - My 1 '96 - p693 [51-250]
c Par - v71 - D '96 - p254 [1-50]
c Par Ch - v20 - O '96 - p11 [1-50]
c PW - v243 - N 4 '96 - p49 [1-50]
Silverthorne, Judith - *The Secret of Sentinel Rock*
y BIC - v25 - N '96 - p33+ [501+]
y Can CL - v22 - Fall '96 - p125+ [501+]
c Quill & Q - v62 - Ag '96 - p41 [251-500]
Silvestein, Michael - *Natural Histories of Discourse*
R&R Bk N - v11 - N '96 - p62 [51-250]
Silvester, Christopher - *The Literary Companion to Parliament*
NS - v125 - N 22 '96 - p45 [501+]
Obs - D 29 '96 - p28 [501+]
Spec - v277 - O 26 '96 - p45+ [501+]
TLS - N 22 '96 - p30 [501+]
The Norton Book of Interviews
Rapport - v19 - 4 '96 - p39 [51-250]
Sew R - v104 - Jl '96 - p483+ [501+]
Silvester, Hans - *The Mediterranean Cat*
MFSF - v91 - S '96 - p38 [51-250]
Silvester, Peter P - *Finite Elements for Electrical Engineers. 3rd Ed.*
SB - v33 - Ja '97 - p9+ [251-500]
Silvey, Anita - *Children's Books and Their Creators*
r ARBA - v28 - '97 - p429 [251-500]
r JOYS - v9 - Sum '96 - p412+ [501+]
Silvis, Randall - *Dead Man Falling*
BL - v93 - S 1 '96 - p68+ [51-250]
PW - v243 - Jl 22 '96 - p229 [51-250]
An Occasional Hell
EJ - v85 - N '96 - p138 [251-500]
Silyn-Roberts, Heather - *Writing for Science*
New Sci - v153 - Mr 1 '97 - p46 [51-250]
Sim, Dorrith M - *In My Pocket (Illus. by Gerald Fitzgerald)*
c PW - v244 - Mr 17 '97 - p83 [51-250]
Sim, May - *The Crossroads of Norm and Nature*
Ethics - v107 - Ja '97 - p385 [51-250]
Sima, John Ross - *Clay Speaks to Us of God*
RR - v56 - Mr '97 - p217+ [51-250]
Sima, Vasile - *Algorithms for Linear-Quadratic Optimization*
SciTech - v20 - S '96 - p10 [51-250]
Simak, Clifford D - *Neighbor*
SF Chr - v18 - O '96 - p76 [51-250]
Over the River and through the Woods
Analog - v117 - F '97 - p145+ [51-250]
BW - v27 - Ja 26 '97 - p6 [251-500]
MFSF - v92 - Ja '97 - p18+ [251-500]
Over the River and through the Woods (Frakes). Audio Version
SF Chr - v18 - O '96 - p76 [51-250]
Sime, Ruth Lewin - *Lise Meitner: A Life in Physics*
Isis - v87 - D '96 - p746+ [501+]
LJ - v122 - Ja '97 - p50+ [51-250]
NYRB - v44 - F 20 '97 - p39+ [501+]
SciTech - v20 - S '96 - p15 [51-250]
Wom R Bks - v13 - S '96 - p5+ [501+]
Simek, Rudolf - *Heaven and Earth*
HT - v46 - O '96 - p55 [51-250]
Simenon, Georges - *The Patience of Maigret (Norgate). Audio Version*
y Kliatt - v31 - Ja '97 - p44 [51-250]
Simeti, Mary Taylor - *On Persephone's Island*
SFR - v21 - N '96 - p48 [1-50]
Simic, Charles - *Selected Poems 1963-1983*
LJ - v122 - Ap 1 '97 - p95 [1-50]

Walking the Black Cat
BL - v93 - O 1 '96 - p317 [51-250]
y Kliatt - v31 - My '97 - p19 [51-250]
LJ - v121 - N 1 '96 - p71+ [51-250]
NY - v72 - D 16 '96 - p109 [51-250]
PW - v243 - S 30 '96 - p82 [51-250]
PW - v243 - N 4 '96 - p47 [1-50]
The World Doesn't End
LJ - v122 - Ap 1 '97 - p95 [1-50]
Simionescu, Dan - *Scurta Istorie A Cartii Romanesti*
BL - v93 - D 15 '96 - p714 [1-50]
Simiu, Emil - *Wind Effects on Structures. 3rd Ed.*
Choice - v34 - Mr '97 - p1192 [51-250]
SciTech - v20 - N '96 - p65 [51-250]
Simkin, John E - *The Whole Story*
r Choice - v34 - Ja '97 - p775 [51-250]
Simmie, Lois - *No Cats Allowed (Illus. by Cynthia Nugent)*
c CBRS - v25 - F '97 - p78+ [51-250]
c KR - v64 - N 15 '96 - p1675 [51-250]
c Sch Lib - v44 - N '96 - p147 [51-250]
Secret Lives of Sgt. John Wilson
Beav - v76 - D '96 - p46 [51-250]
Simmons, Posy - *F-Freezing ABC*
c Ch BWatch - v6 - My '96 - p4 [1-50]
c HB Guide - v7 - Fall '96 - p276 [51-250]
Simmonds, Roy - *John Steinbeck: The War Years 1939-1945*
Choice - v34 - S '96 - p129+ [51-250]
Simmons, Beth A - *Who Adjusts?*
J Pol - v58 - Ag '96 - p931+ [501+]
Simmons, C H - *Plymouth Colony Records. Vol. 1*
r Am Geneal - v71 - Jl '96 - p186 [501+]
Simmons, Dan - *Endymion*
Bloom Rev - v16 - Jl '96 - p5 [501+]
BWatch - v18 - Mr '97 - p9 [1-50]
NYTBR - v101 - D 8 '96 - p94 [1-50]
Simmons, Harvey G - *The French National Front*
Choice - v34 - D '96 - p684 [51-250]
Simmons, Herbert - *Corner Boy*
BW - v26 - S 1 '96 - p12 [51-250]
Simmons, Ian - *The Environmental Impact of Later Mesolithic Cultures*
New Sci - v153 - F 15 '97 - p44 [51-250]
Simmons, John - *The Scientific 100*
r Astron - v25 - My '97 - p114 [51-250]
r Choice - v34 - My '97 - p1518+ [51-250]
r Nature - v385 - Ja 16 '97 - p215+ [501+]
Simmons, Michael Bland - *Arnobius of Sicca: Religious Conflict and Competition in the Age of Diocletian*
HRNB - v25 - Fall '96 - p42 [51-250]
Rel St Rev - v23 - Ap '97 - p189 [51-250]
Simmons, Pat - *Vietnam*
c Sch Lib - v44 - Ag '96 - p110 [51-250]
Simmons, R C - *British Imprints Relating to North America 1621-1760*
r ARBA - v28 - '97 - p21 [251-500]
r BC - v45 - Aut '96 - p393+ [51-250]
Simmons, Richard - *The Richard Simmons Farewell to Fat Cookbook*
PW - v243 - S 2 '96 - p125+ [51-250]
Simmons, William Mark - *One Foot in the Grave*
SF Chr - v18 - O '96 - p77 [51-250]
Simms, Anngret - *More Irish County Towns*
ILS - v15 - Fall '96 - p31 [1-50]
Simms, Bryan R - *Alban Berg: A Guide to Research*
r ARBA - v28 - '97 - p477 [51-250]
r Choice - v34 - Ap '97 - p1316 [51-250]
r R&R Bk N - v11 - D '96 - p55 [51-250]
Music of the Twentieth Century. 2nd Ed.
Choice - v34 - Ja '97 - p806 [51-250]
Simms, Margaret - *Economic Perspectives on Affirmative Action*
NY - v72 - N 25 '96 - p106+ [501+]
Simms, Phil - *Phil Simms on Passing*
y BL - v93 - S 1 '96 - p55 [51-250]
Simms, William Gilmore - *Border Beagles*
AL - v68 - S '96 - p877 [51-250]
Nine-C Lit - v51 - D '96 - p426+ [1-50]
Poetry and the Practical
AL - v69 - Mr '97 - p247 [51-250]
Choice - v34 - F '97 - p960+ [51-250]
Nine-C Lit - v51 - Mr '97 - p565+ [51-250]
Tales of the South
AL - v69 - Mr '97 - p247 [51-250]
Nine-C Lit - v51 - Mr '97 - p566 [51-250]
R&R Bk N - v11 - D '96 - p65 [51-250]
VQR - v73 - Win '97 - p23* [51-250]
Simo, Isabel-Clara - *Perfils Cruels*
WLT - v70 - Aut '96 - p940+ [251-500]

Simola, Robert - *Teaching in the Real World*
Kliatt - v30 - S '96 - p30 [51-250]
Learning - v25 - Mr '97 - p15 [51-250]
SLMQ - v25 - Fall '96 - p62 [51-250]
Simon, Alan R - *Workgroup Computing*
CBR - v14 - N '96 - p39 [1-50]
R&R Bk N - v11 - D '96 - p29 [51-250]
Simon, Andrew L - *Hydraulics. 4th Ed.*
SciTech - v20 - D '96 - p67 [51-250]
Simon, Art - *Dangerous Knowledge*
Choice - v34 - N '96 - p468+ [251-500]
Pres SQ - v26 - Sum '96 - p890+ [501+]
Simon, Beth - *Out of Nowhere, the Body's Shape*
Sm Pr R - v28 - D '96 - p8 [51-250]
Simon, Brian - *Henry Simon of Manchester*
TES - Ja 24 '97 - p8* [51-250]
The State and Educational Change
Albion - v28 - Sum '96 - p346+ [501+]
Simon, Caroline J - *The Disciplined Heart*
BL - v93 - F 15 '97 - p976 [51-250]
PW - v244 - Ja 27 '97 - p96 [51-250]
Simon, Charnan - *One Happy Classroom (Illus. by Rebecca McKillip Thornburgh)*
c BL - v93 - My 1 '97 - p1505 [51-250]
Sam the Garbage Hound (Illus. by Gary Bialke)
c HB Guide - v8 - Spr '97 - p21 [51-250]
Simon, Clea - *Mad House*
BL - v93 - Mr 1 '97 - p1095 [51-250]
KR - v64 - D 15 '96 - p1789 [251-500]
LJ - v122 - Ap 15 '97 - p101+ [51-250]
PW - v244 - Ja 6 '97 - p54 [51-250]
Trib Bks - Ap 27 '97 - p3+ [501+]
Simon, Francesca - *Cafe at the Edge of the Moon (Illus. by Keren Ludlow)*
c JB - v60 - D '96 - p240+ [51-250]
c TES - Mr 21 '97 - p9* [501+]
Spider School (Illus. by Peta Coplans)
c CBRS - v25 - N '96 - p28 [51-250]
c HB Guide - v8 - Spr '97 - p48 [51-250]
c JB - v60 - O '96 - p188 [51-250]
c Magpies - v11 - Jl '96 - p27 [51-250]
c PW - v243 - S 9 '96 - p83 [51-250]
c Sch Lib - v44 - Ag '96 - p100 [51-250]
c SLJ - v42 - S '96 - p191 [51-250]
The Topsy-Turvies (Illus. by Keren Ludlow)
c HB Guide - v7 - Fall '96 - p276 [51-250]
c KR - v64 - My 1 '96 - p693 [51-250]
What's That Noise? (Illus. by David Melling)
c Sch Lib - v44 - N '96 - p147+ [51-250]
Simon, Frank - *Veiled Threats*
BL - v93 - N 15 '96 - p571 [501+]
Simon, Fritz B - *My Psychosis, My Bicycle, and I*
Choice - v34 - D '96 - p693 [51-250]
Simon, Herbert Alexander - *Models of My Life*
JEL - v35 - Mr '97 - p190 [1-50]
Nature - v384 - D 19 '96 - p618 [1-50]
The Sciences of the Artificial. 3rd Ed.
LJ - v122 - Ja '97 - p138 [1-50]
New Sci - v153 - Mr 1 '97 - p45 [51-250]
Simon, Joanna - *Wine with Food*
LJ - v122 - Ap 1 '97 - p62 [1-50]
Simon, Joel - *Endangered Mexico*
KR - v65 - F 15 '97 - p286 [251-500]
PW - v244 - Mr 10 '97 - p57 [51-250]
Simon, John D - *Ultrafast Dynamics of Chemical Systems*
Am Sci - v84 - My '96 - p296 [501+]
Simon, Jonathan - *Poor Discipline*
Fed Prob - v60 - Je '96 - p83+ [501+]
Simon, Julia - *Mass Enlightenment*
APSR - v90 - D '96 - p897+ [501+]
Simon, Julian Lincoln - *The Economic Consequences of Immigration*
BW - v26 - D 15 '96 - p4 [1-50]
The State of Humanity
Quad - v40 - Je '96 - p79+ [501+]
Reason - v28 - D '96 - p44+ [251-500]
The Ultimate Resource 2
BW - v27 - Mr 30 '97 - p6 [501+]
Choice - v34 - Mr '97 - p1210 [51-250]
New Sci - v153 - Ja 4 '97 - p39 [1-50]
Sci - v274 - D 13 '96 - p1848 [1-50]
Simon, Larry J - *Iberia and the Mediterranean World of the Middle Ages. Vol. 1*
CHR - v82 - Jl '96 - p509+ [501+]
Simon, Leon - *Theorems on Regularity and Singularity of Energy Minimizing Maps*
SciTech - v20 - S '96 - p12 [51-250]
Simon, Linda - *William James Remembered*
AL - v68 - D '96 - p880 [51-250]
VQR - v72 - Aut '96 - p126* [51-250]

Simon, Marc T - *Your Intuition Is Wrong*
Math T - v90 - Mr '97 - p250 [51-250]
Simon, Neil - *Brighton Beach Memoirs*
y BL - v93 - Ja '97 - p832+ [1-50]
Rewrites: A Memoir
BL - v93 - S 1 '96 - p4+ [51-250]
BW - v26 - S 22 '96 - p3 [501+]
LATBR - v263 - S 29 '96 - p1+ [501+]
LATBR - D 29 '96 - p9 [51-250]
NYTBR - v101 - S 29 '96 - p13 [501+]
NYTLa - v146 - O 24 '96 - pC19 [501+]
Obs - Ja 5 '97 - p17* [51-250]
Rapport - v19 - 6 '96 - p33 [251-500]
TLS - Ja 17 '97 - p13 [501+]
Rewrites: A Memoir (Simon). Audio Version
CSM - v88 - O 31 '96 - pB4 [51-250]
LJ - v121 - D '96 - p169 [51-250]
Simon, Norma - *All Kinds of Families*
c Learning - v25 - Mr '97 - p54 [1-50]
The Story of Passover (Illus. by Erika Weihs)
c BL - v93 - F 1 '97 - p943 [51-250]
c KR - v64 - D 15 '96 - p1804 [51-250]
c PW - v244 - Ja 27 '97 - p97 [51-250]
c SLJ - v43 - Mr '97 - p180+ [51-250]
Simon, Reeva S - *Encyclopedia of the Modern Middle East. Vols. 1-4*
r ARBA - v28 - '97 - p71 [251-500]
yr BL - v93 - N 15 '96 - p605 [251-500]
r Choice - v34 - F '97 - p943 [51-250]
r LJ - v122 - Ap 15 '97 - p64+ [51-250]
r MEQ - v3 - D '96 - p79+ [501+]
r R&R Bk N - v11 - D '96 - p10 [51-250]
Simon, Rita J - *Neither Victim nor Enemy*
CS - v26 - Ja '97 - p19+ [501+]
Simon, Ronald G - *A Reference Guide for Botany and Horticulture*
r ARBA - v28 - '97 - p572 [51-250]
yr BL - v93 - Mr 1 '97 - p1198 [251-500]
r LJ - v121 - D '96 - p86 [51-250]
r SB - v33 - Mr '97 - p39+ [51-250]
Simon, Seymour - *The Heart: Our Circulatory System*
c BL - v93 - Ja '97 - p766 [1-50]
c CCB-B - v50 - O '96 - p75+ [51-250]
c HB - v72 - S '96 - p624 [51-250]
c HB Guide - v8 - Spr '97 - p131 [51-250]
c SLJ - v42 - Ag '96 - p160 [51-250]
Lightning
c BL - v93 - Mr 15 '97 - p1240 [51-250]
The On-Line Spaceman and Other Cases (Illus. by S D Schindler)
c BL - v93 - My 1 '97 - p1498 [51-250]
Ride the Wind (Illus. by Elsa Warnick)
c BL - v93 - Ap 1 '97 - p1332 [51-250]
c KR - v65 - F 15 '97 - p306 [51-250]
Sharks (Illus. by Seymour Simon)
c RT - v50 - O '96 - p137 [1-50]
Spring across America
c Ch BWatch - v6 - Jl '96 - p6 [51-250]
c HB Guide - v7 - Fall '96 - p338+ [51-250]
Strange Mysteries from around the World. Rev. Ed.
c BL - v93 - F 15 '97 - p1022 [51-250]
Wild Babies
c BL - v93 - Ja '97 - p864+ [251-500]
c KR - v65 - Ja 1 '97 - p64 [51-250]
c SLJ - v43 - F '97 - p98 [51-250]
Wildfires
c HB Guide - v7 - Fall '96 - p339 [51-250]
c SB - v32 - N '96 - p240+ [51-250]
Simon, Ted - *The Gypsy in Me*
KR - v65 - My 1 '97 - p705 [251-500]
PW - v244 - My 5 '97 - p186+ [51-250]
Simon, Thomas W - *Democracy and Social Injustice*
Fed Prob - v60 - Je '96 - p87+ [501+]
Simoncini, Giorgio - *Sopra I Porti Di Mare. Vols. 1-2*
Six Ct J - v27 - Win '96 - p1169+ [501+]
Simonds, Fred - *Network Security*
CBR - v14 - N '96 - p38+ [51-250]
Simonds, Merilyn - *The Convict Lover*
Mac - v109 - D 9 '96 - p64 [1-50]
Queens Q - v103 - Sum '96 - p415+ [501+]
Quill & Q - v63 - F '97 - p50 [51-250]
Simonds, Peggy Munoz - *Iconographic Research in English Renaissance Literature*
r Ren Q - v49 - Aut '96 - p644+ [501+]
Simone, Luisa - *Microsoft Publisher by Design. 3rd Ed.*
CBR - v14 - S '96 - p27 [1-50]
Simone, Sonia - *Stealing Midnight*
LJ - v121 - N 15 '96 - p52 [51-250]
Simone, T Abdou Maliqalim - *In Whose Image?*
JTWS - v13 - Spr '96 - p317+ [501+]

Simonelli, Maria Picchio - *Inferno III*
Specu - v71 - Jl '96 - p762+ [501+]
Simoni, Carlo - *Cartai E Stampatori A Toscolano*
Lib - v18 - D '96 - p364 [51-250]
Simonian, Lane - *Defending the Land of the Jaguar*
AHR - v102 - F '97 - p235+ [251-500]
Simonian, Ron - *Thanatos. Audio Version*
BWatch - v18 - Mr '97 - p9 [51-250]
Simonides, of Amorgos - *The New Simonides (Boedeker)*
TLS - F 14 '97 - p11+ [501+]
Simonnet, Michel - *Measures and Probabilities*
Choice - v34 - D '96 - p648 [51-250]
Simonoff, Jeffrey S - *Smoothing Methods in Statistics*
JEL - v35 - Mr '97 - p195 [51-250]
Simons, Anna - *The Company They Keep*
y BL - v93 - F 1 '97 - p913 [51-250]
BW - v27 - Mr 30 '97 - p13 [51-250]
KR - v65 - Ja 15 '97 - p130 [251-500]
PW - v244 - F 10 '97 - p77 [51-250]
Networks of Dissolution
Choice - v34 - S '96 - p204 [51-250]
Simons, F Estelle R - *Histamine and H1-Receptor Antagonists in Allergic Disease*
SciTech - v20 - S '96 - p43 [51-250]
Simons, G L - *Iraq: From Sumer to Saddam*
MEJ - v51 - Win '97 - p150 [51-250]
Korea: The Search for the Sovereignty
JTWS - v13 - Fall '96 - p230+ [501+]
Libya: The Struggle for Survival
MEJ - v51 - Win '97 - p151 [51-250]
Simons, Geoff - *The Scourging of Iraq*
Choice - v34 - F '97 - p1033 [51-250]
Simons, Margaret, 1960- - *The Truth Teller*
Aust Bk R - Je '96 - p43 [501+]
Simons, Margaret A - *Feminist Interpretations of Simone De Beauvoir*
NWSA Jnl - v8 - Fall '96 - p177+ [501+]
Simons, Michael - *Where We've Been*
TES - Mr 7 '97 - p8* [501+]
Simons, Moya - *Dead Worried!*
c Magpies - v11 - Jl '96 - p32 [51-250]
c TES - F 21 '97 - p8* [51-250]
Simons, Paullina - *Red Leaves*
y BL - v92 - Ag '96 - p1883 [51-250]
BL - v92 - Ag '96 - p1891 [1-50]
LATBR - S 22 '96 - p8 [51-250]
Simons, Robert G - *Competing Gospels*
Theol St - v57 - S '96 - p575+ [251-500]
Simons, Ronald L - *Understanding Differences between Divorced and Intact Families*
R&R Bk N - v11 - N '96 - p41 [51-250]
Simonsohn, Shlomo - *The Apostolic See and the Jews. Vols. 1-8*
r CHR - v83 - Ja '97 - p75+ [501+]
Simonson, Harold P - *Going Where I Have to Go*
WAL - v31 - Win '97 - p397+ [251-500]
Simonson, Louise - *I Hate Superman! (Illus. by Kevin Altieri)*
c HB Guide - v7 - Fall '96 - p276 [1-50]
c SF Chr - v18 - O '96 - p82 [1-50]
Simonson, Sheila - *Malarkey*
KR - v64 - D 15 '96 - p1770+ [51-250]
LJ - v122 - F 1 '97 - p111 [51-250]
PW - v243 - D 9 '96 - p63 [51-250]
Simonton, Dean Keith - *Greatness: Who Makes History and Why*
r Per Psy - v49 - Win '96 - p1028+ [501+]
Simony, Maggy - *The Traveler's Reading Guide. Rev. Ed.*
r RQ - v36 - Win '96 - p215 [51-250]
Simply the Best
c Sch Lib - v44 - N '96 - p152 [51-250]
Simpson, Alan - *Mastering WordPerfect 7 for Windows 95*
Quill & Q - v62 - N '96 - p31 [51-250]
Simpson, Alan K - *Right in the Old Gazoo*
y BL - v93 - N 1 '96 - p460 [51-250]
BW - v26 - F 16 '97 - p3+ [501+]
CJR - v35 - Mr '97 - p55+ [501+]
KR - v64 - O 15 '96 - p1519 [51-250]
LJ - v121 - N 1 '96 - p93 [51-250]
NYTBR - v102 - F 2 '97 - p11+ [501+]
PW - v243 - O 21 '96 - p60+ [51-250]
Simpson, Brooks D - *America's Civil War*
Choice - v34 - S '96 - p199 [51-250]
Let Us Have Peace
PW - v244 - F 3 '97 - p100 [1-50]
The Political Education of Henry Adams
ASInt - v34 - O '96 - p99+ [501+]
Choice - v34 - S '96 - p199 [51-250]
Simpson, Carol Mann - *Internet for Library Media Specialists*
CLW - v66 - Je '96 - p41 [51-250]

Simpson, Carolyn - *High Performance through Negotiation*
y Cur R - v36 - N '96 - p13 [51-250]
y SLJ - v42 - O '96 - p156 [51-250]
y VOYA - v19 - F '97 - p348 [251-500]
High Performance through Organizing Information
y BL - v92 - Ag '96 - p1893 [51-250]
y Cur R - v36 - N '96 - p13 [51-250]
y SLJ - v42 - Ag '96 - p176 [51-250]
y VOYA - v19 - F '97 - p348 [251-500]
Simpson, Christopher - *National Security Directives of the Reagan and Bush Administrations*
r J Gov Info - v24 - Ja '97 - p76+ [501+]
Simpson, David - *The Academic Postmodern and the Rule of Literature*
ELT - v39 - 4 '96 - p530 [51-250]
Romanticism, Nationalism, and the Revolt against Theory
MP - v94 - Ag '96 - p115+ [501+]
Simpson, Dorothy - *Close Her Eyes (Hardiman). Audio Version*
LJ - v121 - D '96 - p169 [51-250]
A Day for Dying
BWatch - v17 - S '96 - p1 [51-250]
NYTBR - v101 - Jl 21 '96 - p25 [51-250]
Puppet for a Corpse (Hardiman). Audio Version
BL - v93 - F 15 '97 - p1038 [51-250]
Simpson, Elizabeth - *The Spoils of War*
PW - v244 - Ap 28 '97 - p59 [51-250]
Simpson, Howard R - *The Paratroopers of the French Foreign Legion*
BL - v93 - F 1 '97 - p913 [51-250]
Simpson, James - *Spanish Agriculture*
JEL - v34 - D '96 - p2105+ [51-250]
Simpson, James B - *Simpson's Contemporary Quotations*
r BL - v93 - Ap 1 '97 - p1354+ [251-500]
Simpson, Jeffrey - *American Elegy*
BL - v93 - S 15 '96 - p217 [51-250]
BW - v26 - S 8 '96 - p3 [501+]
LJ - v121 - O 1 '96 - p92 [51-250]
Simpson, Joe - *This Game of Ghosts*
HM - v293 - Ag '96 - p64+ [501+]
Touching the Void. Audio Version
Obs - Mr 23 '97 - p16* [501+]
Simpson, Judith - *Ancient China*
c HB Guide - v7 - Fall '96 - p378 [51-250]
c Magpies - v11 - Jl '96 - p38 [51-250]
Mighty Dinosaurs
c BL - v93 - D 15 '96 - p728 [51-250]
c HB Guide - v8 - Spr '97 - p115 [51-250]
c SLJ - v42 - D '96 - p111 [51-250]
Simpson, Ken - *The Princeton Field Guide to the Birds of Australia. 5th Ed.*
r Choice - v34 - D '96 - p638 [51-250]
r TLS - S 6 '96 - p33 [251-500]
Simpson, Louis - *There You Are*
HR - v49 - Aut '96 - p513+ [501+]
Simpson, Mark - *Anti-Gay*
Lon R Bks - v19 - F 6 '97 - p24 [501+]
NS - v125 - O 18 '96 - p45 [251-500]
Obs - N 3 '96 - p16* [51-250]
Male Impersonators
Can Lit - Spr '97 - p221+ [501+]
Simpson, Mona - *A Regular Guy*
BL - v93 - Ag '96 - p1856 [251-500]
BW - v26 - O 6 '96 - p4 [501+]
LATBR - O 6 '96 - p2 [501+]
Lon R Bks - v19 - Ap 3 '97 - p22+ [501+]
NW - v128 - O 7 '96 - p78 [251-500]
NYTBR - v101 - O 27 '96 - p16 [501+]
NYTLa - v146 - O 15 '96 - pC15 [501+]
Obs - F 16 '97 - p15* [501+]
Time - v148 - N 4 '96 - p95 [251-500]
TLS - F 21 '97 - p21 [501+]
VV - v41 - O 15 '96 - p45+ [501+]
Simpson, O J - *I Want to Tell You*
NYRB - v43 - Je 6 '96 - p7+ [501+]
Simpson, William A - *From Image to Likeness*
BL - v93 - Mr 15 '97 - p1207 [51-250]
PW - v244 - Ja 27 '97 - p96 [51-250]
Simpson, William Brand - *Philosophy of a Concerned Academic*
JEL - v34 - D '96 - p2009 [51-250]
Sims, Michael - *Darwin's Orchestra*
y BL - v93 - Mr 1 '97 - p1106 [51-250]
LJ - v122 - F 15 '97 - p160 [51-250]
Sims, Pamela - *Awakening Brilliance*
Quill & Q - v62 - O '96 - p27 [501+]
Sims, Patsy - *Can Somebody Shout Amen!*
LJ - v122 - F 1 '97 - p112 [1-50]

The Klan. 2nd Ed.
  LJ - v122 - My 1 '97 - p145 [1-50]
  Nat - v264 - F 24 '97 - p28+ [501+]
Sims, Richard A - *Global to Local*
  SciTech - v20 - D '96 - p30 [51-250]
Simsic, Wayne - *Songs of Sunrise, Seeds of Prayer*
  CLW - v67 - D '96 - p45 [51-250]
Sinclair, Alison - *Blueheart*
  Quill & Q - v62 - N '96 - p42 [51-250]
The Deceived Husband
  MLR - v92 - Ap '97 - p410+ [501+]
Sinclair, April - *Ain't Gonna Be the Same Fool Twice*
  BW - v27 - Ja 26 '97 - p12 [51-250]
  Ent W - Ja 31 '97 - p55 [1-50]
  PW - v244 - Ja 27 '97 - p103 [1-50]
Sinclair, Clive - *The Lady with the Laptop*
  Obs - O 27 '96 - p16* [1-50]
  Obs - D 15 '96 - p15* [501+]
  Spec - v278 - Ja 18 '97 - p34 [501+]
  TLS - O 18 '96 - p23 [501+]
Sinclair, Frank Livingstone - *Is There a Sphygmomanometerist in the House?*
  TES - D 27 '96 - p22 [51-250]
Sinclair, Iain - *Conductors of Chaos*
  TLS - S 20 '96 - p27 [501+]
Lights Out for the Territory
  NS - v126 - Ja 17 '97 - p48 [501+]
  Obs - D 22 '96 - p18* [501+]
  Spec - v278 - F 8 '97 - p38 [501+]
  TLS - F 14 '97 - p30 [501+]
Sinclair, John - *Today's English Dictionary*
  r MLJ - v80 - Fall '96 - p414 [501+]
Sinclair, John, 1944- - *New Patterns in Global Television*
  Choice - v34 - Ja '97 - p787 [51-250]
Sinclair, Joseph T - *Intranets vs. Lotus Notes*
  CBR - v15 - Spr '97 - p3 [51-250]
  SciTech - v21 - Mr '97 - p88 [51-250]
Sindell, Cheryl - *Cooking without Recipes*
  LJ - v122 - Ap 1 '97 - p116 [51-250]
Singer, Amy - *Palestinian Peasants and Ottoman Officials*
  AHR - v102 - F '97 - p144+ [501+]
Singer, Beth J - *Operative Rights*
  IPQ - v36 - S '96 - p375+ [501+]
Singer, Beth Wolfensberger - *Lefty: A Handbook for Left-Handed Kids (Illus. by Jack Keely)*
  c PW - v244 - Ap 14 '97 - p77 [51-250]
Singer, George H S - *Redefining Family Support*
  Readings - v11 - S '96 - p30+ [51-250]
  Soc Ser R - v70 - S '96 - p503 [51-250]
Singer, Gilbert L - *Object Technology Strategies and Tactics*
  Choice - v34 - Ap '97 - p1374 [51-250]
  SciTech - v21 - Mr '97 - p12 [51-250]
Singer, Igor - *Interventional Electrophysiology*
  SciTech - v21 - Mr '97 - p57 [51-250]
Singer, Irving - *The Harmony of Nature and Spirit*
  LJ - v121 - O 1 '96 - p81 [51-250]
Singer, Isaac Bashevis - *The Estate (Waterman). Audio Version*
  y Kliatt - v30 - N '96 - p40 [51-250]
The Golem (Illus. by Uri Shulevitz)
  c PW - v243 - O 21 '96 - p85 [1-50]
In My Father's Court (Kandinsky). Audio Version
  y Kliatt - v30 - S '96 - p57 [51-250]
The Topsy-Turvy Emperor of China (Illus. by Julian Jusim)
  c HB Guide - v7 - Fall '96 - p288 [51-250]
Singer, Margaret Thaler - *Crazy Therapies*
  LJ - v121 - N 15 '96 - p76 [51-250]
  SciTech - v21 - Mr '97 - p53 [51-250]
Singer, Marilyn - *All We Needed to Say (Illus. by Lorna Clark)*
  c BL - v92 - Ag '96 - p1903 [51-250]
  c CBRS - v25 - Ja '97 - p59 [1-50]
  c CCB-B - v50 - S '96 - p30+ [51-250]
  c HB Guide - v8 - Spr '97 - p154 [51-250]
  c HMR - Win '96 - p47+ [501+]
  c PW - v243 - S 9 '96 - p83 [51-250]
  c SLJ - v42 - S '96 - p221 [51-250]
Deal with a Ghost
  c KR - v65 - My 1 '97 - p727 [51-250]
Singer, Mark - *Citizen K*
  CJR - v35 - Mr '97 - p56+ [501+]
  Ent W - D 20 '96 - p70 [51-250]
  KR - v64 - O 1 '96 - p1453 [251-500]
  LJ - v121 - My '96 - p91+ [51-250]
  Nat - v263 - D 2 '96 - p28+ [501+]
  NY - v72 - D 16 '96 - p108 [51-250]
  NYTBR - v101 - N 10 '96 - p10 [501+]
  PW - v243 - O 7 '96 - p52 [51-250]
  SFR - v22 - Ja '97 - p38+ [501+]

Singer, Nicky - *What She Wanted*
  Woman's J - S '96 - p10 [1-50]
Singer, Noel F - *Burmese Dance and Theatre*
  Choice - v34 - D '96 - p625 [51-250]
Singer, Peter - *How Are We to Live?*
  Ethics - v107 - Ja '97 - p344+ [501+]
Singerman, Diane - *Avenues of Participation*
  Am Ethnol - v23 - N '96 - p920+ [501+]
  APSR - v91 - Mr '97 - p222 [501+]
Development, Change, and Gender in Cairo
  MEJ - v50 - Aut '96 - p625 [51-250]
Singerman, Robert - *American Library Book Catalogues 1801-1875*
  r Choice - v34 - D '96 - p596 [51-250]
Indigenous Languages of the Americas
  r ARBA - v28 - '97 - p373+ [251-500]
  r R&R Bk N - v12 - F '97 - p79 [51-250]
Singh, Amritjit - *Memory, Narrative, and Identity*
  J Am St - v30 - Ap '96 - p147+ [251-500]
Singh, B R - *Natural Toxins 2*
  SciTech - v20 - S '96 - p24 [51-250]
Singh, Daman - *The Last Frontier*
  JEL - v35 - Mr '97 - p273 [51-250]
Singh, G - *F.R. Leavis: A Literary Biography*
  TES - Ag 23 '96 - p25 [501+]
Singh, Hanwant B - *Composition, Chemistry, and Climate of the Atmosphere*
  Choice - v34 - O '96 - p319 [51-250]
Singh, Harry - *UNIX for MVS Programmers*
  SciTech - v20 - D '96 - p11 [51-250]
Singh, Jacquelin - *Home to India*
  KR - v65 - Ap 1 '97 - p498+ [251-500]
Singh, Jasprit - *Quantum Mechanics*
  Choice - v34 - Ap '97 - p1377 [51-250]
  SciTech - v21 - Mr '97 - p21 [51-250]
Singh, Narindar - *The Keynesian Fallout*
  JEL - v35 - Mr '97 - p289 [51-250]
Singh, Nikky-Guninder Kaur - *The Feminine Principle in the Sikh Vision of the Transcendent*
  Wom R Bks - v13 - S '96 - p26+ [501+]
Singh, Prabhat K - *The Creative Contours of Ruskin Bond*
  Bkbird - v34 - Spr '96 - p57 [1-50]
Singh, Priyam - *Victims or Criminals?*
  Choice - v34 - Ja '97 - p884 [51-250]
Singh, R Paul - *Computer Applications in Food Technology*
  SciTech - v20 - N '96 - p80 [51-250]
Singh, Ravindra - *Elements of Survey Sampling*
  JEL - v35 - Mr '97 - p196 [51-250]
  SciTech - v21 - Mr '97 - p14 [51-250]
Singh, Saran - *Encyclopedia of the Coins of Malaysia, Singapore and Brunei. 2nd Ed.*
  r Coin W - v38 - Ap 21 '97 - p77 [51-250]
Singh, Vijay P - *Dam Breach Modeling Technology*
  SciTech - v20 - D '96 - p68 [51-250]
Kinematic Wave Modeling in Water Resources
  Choice - v34 - O '96 - p312 [51-250]
Singleton, David - *The Age Factor in Second Language Acquisition*
  MLJ - v81 - Spr '97 - p118+ [501+]
Singley, Carol J - *Edith Wharton: Matters of Mind and Spirit*
  ASInt - v34 - O '96 - p109+ [501+]
  J Am St - v30 - D '96 - p472+ [251-500]
Singman, Jeffrey L - *Daily Life in Chaucer's England*
  HRNB - v25 - Win '97 - p71 [251-500]
  J Am St - v30 - Ap '96 - p39+ [51-250]
Sinha, Debabrata - *Understanding in Human Context*
  R&R Bk N - v12 - F '97 - p1 [51-250]
Sinha, Mrinalini - *Colonial Masculinity*
  HT - v46 - Ag '96 - p56+ [501+]
Sinnott-Armstrong, Walter - *Moral Knowledge*
  Hast Cen R - v27 - Ja '97 - p42 [501+]
Sinotte, Barbara - *Arizona, Utah and New Mexico*
  r BL - v93 - S 15 '96 - p210 [1-50]
  r BWatch - v17 - S '96 - p5 [51-250]
New York and New Jersey. 1996 Ed.
  r BL - v93 - S 15 '96 - p210 [1-50]
  r BWatch - v17 - S '96 - p5 [51-250]
Sinoue, Gilbert - *Le Livre De Saphir*
  BL - v93 - Ja '97 - p827 [1-50]
Sipaz Report
  p WorldV - v12 - O '96 - p12 [51-250]
Sipe, A W Richard - *Sex, Priests, and Power*
  Bks & Cult - v1 - N '95 - p24+ [501+]
Sipe, Beth - *I Am Not Your Victim*
  Wom R Bks - v14 - Mr '97 - p18+ [501+]
Sipherd, Ray - *Dance of the Scarecrows*
  BL - v92 - Ag '96 - p1888 [51-250]
Siporin, Ona - *Stories to Gather All Those Lost*
  WAL - v31 - Sum '96 - p168+ [251-500]

Siracusa, Catherine - *The Peanut Butter Gang (Illus. by Catherine Siracusa)*
  c HB Guide - v7 - Fall '96 - p288 [51-250]
Sirageldin, Ismail - *Population and Development Transformations in the Arab World*
  JEL - v35 - Mr '97 - p273+ [51-250]
Sirat Sayf Ibn Dhi Yazan. English. Selections - *The Adventures of Sayf Ben Dhi Yazan*
  Choice - v34 - D '96 - p608 [51-250]
  TranslRevS - v2 - D '96 - p18 [51-250]
Sirch, Willow Ann - *Eco-Women: Protectors of the Earth*
  c Ch BWatch - v6 - Jl '96 - p1 [1-50]
  y Kliatt - v31 - Ja '97 - p29 [51-250]
Sire, H J A - *The Knights of Malta*
  EHR - v111 - S '96 - p1040 [51-250]
  Rel St Rev - v22 - O '96 - p349 [51-250]
  Specu - v71 - O '96 - p1022+ [501+]
Sirera, Rodolf - *Maror: Les Regles Del Genere*
  WLT - v70 - Aut '96 - p941 [251-500]
Sirett, Dawn - *The Really Amazing Animal Book (Illus. by Peter Anderson)*
  c HB Guide - v8 - Spr '97 - p120 [51-250]
  c KR - v64 - N 15 '96 - p1678 [51-250]
  c PW - v243 - D 9 '96 - p69 [51-250]
Sirica, Alphonse E - *Biliary and Pancreatic Ductal Epithelia*
  SciTech - v21 - Mr '97 - p58 [51-250]
Sirinelli, Jean-Francois - *Dictionnaire Historique De La Vie Politique Francaise Au XXe Siecle*
  r Choice - v34 - D '96 - p568 [1-50]
Sirius, R U - *Cyberpunk Handbook*
  NS - v125 - S 13 '96 - p48 [51-250]
Sirk, Douglas - *Sirk on Sirk*
  Obs - Mr 16 '97 - p18* [51-250]
Sirluck, Ernest - *First Generation*
  R&R Bk N - v11 - N '96 - p54 [51-250]
Sirof, Harriet - *Bring Back Yesterday*
  c CBRS - v25 - F '97 - p84 [51-250]
  y CCB-B - v50 - O '96 - p76 [51-250]
  y HB Guide - v8 - Spr '97 - p84 [51-250]
  c SLJ - v42 - O '96 - p126 [51-250]
  y VOYA - v19 - D '96 - p274 [251-500]
Sirowitz, Hal - *Mother Said*
  Bloom Rev - v16 - S '96 - p11 [501+]
Sirr, Peter - *The Ledger of Fruitful Exchange*
  ILS - v15 - Fall '96 - p10 [51-250]
  PW - v243 - D 30 '96 - p61 [51-250]
  TLS - S 27 '96 - p12 [501+]
Siry, Joseph M - *Unity Temple*
  Choice - v34 - Ap '97 - p1327 [51-250]
Sis, Peter - *Follow the Dream (Illus. by Peter Sis)*
  c Par Ch - v20 - N '96 - p3 [51-250]
Starry Messenger (Illus. by Peter Sis)
  c Astron - v25 - Ja '97 - p103 [51-250]
  c BL - v93 - Ap 1 '97 - p1302 [1-50]
  c BW - v26 - D 8 '96 - p19 [51-250]
  c CBRS - v25 - N '96 - p32 [51-250]
  c CCB-B - v50 - N '96 - p115 [51-250]
  c HB - v73 - Ja '97 - p79+ [51-250]
  c HB Guide - v8 - Spr '97 - p112 [51-250]
  c HMR - Win '96 - p48 [501+]
  c Inst - v106 - O '96 - p67 [1-50]
  c JB - v60 - D '96 - p260 [51-250]
  c KR - v64 - O 1 '96 - p1474 [51-250]
  c Nature - v383 - O 31 '96 - p777 [1-50]
  c NYTBR - v101 - N 10 '96 - p32 [501+]
  c NYTLa - v146 - D 9 '96 - pC18 [51-250]
  c PW - v243 - N 4 '96 - p76 [51-250]
  c SLJ - v42 - O '96 - p118 [51-250]
  c SLJ - v42 - D '96 - p32 [1-50]
  c TES - N 22 '96 - p10* [51-250]
  c Trib Bks - Ja 12 '97 - p5 [51-250]
Sisk, Timothy D - *Power Sharing and International Mediation in Ethnic Conflicts*
  For Aff - v75 - N '96 - p146+ [51-250]
Sisler, Janice Cale - *In Remembrance. Vol. 1*
  r EGH - v50 - N '96 - p191 [51-250]
Sisson, C H - *Selected Poems*
  NL - v79 - O 7 '96 - p16+ [501+]
  WLT - v71 - Win '97 - p166 [251-500]
Sisson, Mary Barr - *The Gathering Storm*
  c Ch BWatch - v6 - O '96 - p5 [51-250]
  y HB Guide - v8 - Spr '97 - p173 [51-250]
  y SLJ - v43 - F '97 - p110 [51-250]
Sistare, Christine T - *Punishment: Social Control and Coercion*
  R&R Bk N - v12 - F '97 - p63 [51-250]

Sisulu, Elinor - *The Day Gogo Went to Vote (Illus. by Sharon Wilson)*
  c BL - v93 - Ap 1 '97 - p1298 [1-50]
  c HB Guide - v7 - Fall '96 - p276 [51-250]
  c HMR - Fall '96 - p40 [501+]
  c Inst - v106 - S '96 - p54 [51-250]
  c JB - v60 - O '96 - p188+ [51-250]
  c NYTBR - v101 - S 8 '96 - p28 [1-50]
  c RT - v50 - My '97 - p682+ [51-250]
  c Smith - v27 - N '96 - p165 [1-50]
Sitaraman, Bhavani - *The Middleground: The American Public and the Abortion Debate*
     SF - v75 - S '96 - p386+ [251-500]
Sitarz, Daniel - *Divorce Yourself. 3rd Ed.*
  r BL - v93 - S 15 '96 - p280+ [251-500]
Sitney, P Adams - *Vital Crises in Italian Cinema*
     TLS - My 24 '96 - p22+ [501+]
Sitton, John F - *Recent Marxian Theory*
     Choice - v34 - Mr '97 - p1238 [51-250]
Sitton, Thad - *Backwoodsmen: Stockmen and Hunters along a Big Thicket River Valley*
     JSH - v62 - N '96 - p788+ [251-500]
Sittser, Gerald L - *A Grace Disguised*
     Ch Today - v41 - Mr 3 '97 - p46+ [501+]
Sitwell, Edith - *Selected Letters of Edith Sitwell*
     Spec - v278 - F 22 '97 - p27+ [501+]
     TLS - Mr 21 '97 - p4 [501+]
Sivanandan, A - *When Memory Dies*
     Obs - Ja 5 '97 - p16* [501+]
     TLS - F 14 '97 - p23 [501+]
Siverton, Howard - *Tales of the Old North Shore*
     Beav - v76 - O '96 - p42 [51-250]
Sivery, Gerard - *Louis VIII: Le Lion*
     AHR - v101 - O '96 - p1197+ [501+]
     EHR - v112 - Ap '97 - p440 [501+]
Sivia, D S - *Data Analysis*
     New Sci - v151 - S 28 '96 - p49 [251-500]
Sivin, Nathan - *Medicine, Philosophy and Religion in Ancient China*
     R&R Bk N - v12 - F '97 - p95 [51-250]
Six Generation Charts. Vol. 1
     EGH - v50 - N '96 - p187 [51-250]
Sixty Years of American Poetry
     PW - v243 - N 25 '96 - p73 [51-250]
Sizer, Theodore R - *Horace's Hope*
     BL - v93 - S 15 '96 - p188 [251-500]
     Choice - v34 - My '97 - p1551 [51-250]
     EL - v54 - D '96 - p83+ [251-500]
     NASSP-B - v81 - Ja '97 - p120+ [501+]
     NYTBR - v101 - S 29 '96 - p14+ [501+]
Sjoberg, Gunilla Paetau - *Felt: New Directions for an Ancient Craft*
     LJ - v122 - Ap 15 '97 - p78+ [51-250]
Sjoblom, Johan - *Emulsions and Emulsion Stability*
     Choice - v34 - N '96 - p486 [51-250]
Sjolin, Lennart - *Crystallographically Determined Structure of Some Biologically Important Macromolecules*
     SciTech - v20 - D '96 - p35 [51-250]
Skaggs, Donald - *Roger Williams' Dream for America*
     W&M Q - v53 - Jl '96 - p649+ [501+]
Skaggs, Jimmy M - *The Great Guano Rush*
     Historian - v59 - Fall '96 - p158 [251-500]
     JSH - v62 - N '96 - p806+ [251-500]
     T&C - v37 - Ap '96 - p363+ [501+]
Skak, Mette - *From Empire to Anarchy*
     R&R Bk N - v12 - F '97 - p17 [51-250]
Skal, David J - *Dark Carnival*
     J Pop F&TV - v24 - Win '97 - p186+ [501+]
V Is for Vampire
     BW - v26 - O 27 '96 - p12 [51-250]
  y VOYA - v19 - F '97 - p340 [51-250]
Skalnes, Tor - *The Politics of Economic Reform in Zimbabwe*
     TLS - Ja 3 '97 - p14+ [501+]
Skandalakis, Lee John - *Modern Hernia Repair. 2nd Ed.*
     SciTech - v20 - D '96 - p50 [51-250]
Skandera-Trombley, Laura E - *Mark Twain in the Company of Women*
     MLR - v91 - Jl '96 - p707+ [501+]
Skardhamar, Rune - *Virus Detection and Elimination*
     CBR - v14 - N '96 - p40 [1-50]
Skarmeta, Antonio - *Love-Fifteen*
     PW - v243 - S 23 '96 - p71 [251-250]
     TranslRevS - v2 - D '96 - p33 [251-250]
Love--Fifteen
     TranslRevS - v2 - D '96 - p33 [251-250]
Skeele, Linda - *Teaching Information Literacy Using Electronic Resources for Grades K-6*
     SLJ - v42 - S '96 - p136 [51-250]
     SLMQ - v25 - Fall '96 - p66 [51-250]

Skeggs, Douglas - *The Phoenix of Prague*
     KR - v64 - D 15 '96 - p1771 [51-250]
     LJ - v122 - F 1 '97 - p110+ [51-250]
     PW - v243 - D 9 '96 - p63 [51-250]
Skeldon, Ronald - *Emigration from Hong Kong*
     Ch Rev Int - v3 - Fall '96 - p530+ [501+]
Skelton, Douglas - *A Time to Kill*
     Arm Det - v29 - Fall '96 - p504+ [251-500]
Skene-Melvin, David - *Canadian Crime Fiction*
  r Quill & Q - v63 - Ja '97 - p32 [251-500]
Skibo, James M - *Expanding Archaeology*
     Am Ant - v61 - Jl '96 - p610+ [501+]
Skidell, Myrna Bigman - *The Main Idea, Reading to Learn*
     JAAL - v40 - Mr '97 - p506+ [501+]
Skidelsky, Robert - *The Road from Serfdom*
     Choice - v34 - O '96 - p359 [51-250]
The World after Communism
     CR - v269 - N '96 - p277 [1-50]
Skidmore, Clive - *Practical Ethics for Roman Gentlemen*
     TLS - F 14 '97 - p9 [501+]
Skidmore, David - *Reversing Course*
     For Aff - v75 - S '96 - p145+ [51-250]
Skidmore, Steve - *Introducing Systems Design. 2nd Ed.*
     SciTech - v20 - N '96 - p12 [51-250]
Skiftesvik, Joni - *Salli Koistisen Talviosta*
     WLT - v71 - Win '97 - p189+ [251-500]
Skilton, David - *Anthony Trollope and His Contemporaries*
     Nine-C Lit - v51 - Mr '97 - p566 [1-50]
Skinner, Andrew Stewart - *A System of Social Science. 2nd Ed.*
     JEL - v35 - Mr '97 - p193 [51-250]
Skinner, Arthur N - *The Death of a Confederate*
     LJ - v122 - Ja '97 - p119 [51-250]
Skinner, Patricia - *Family Power in Southern Italy*
     JIH - v27 - Spr '97 - p692+ [251-500]
Skinner, Quentin - *Reason and Rhetoric in the Philosophy of Hobbies*
     J Phil - v94 - F '97 - p94+ [501+]
Skinner, Robert E - *Skin Deep, Blood Red*
     BL - v93 - F 1 '97 - p929 [51-250]
     KR - v64 - N 1 '96 - p1568 [51-250]
     LJ - v122 - Ja '97 - p153 [51-250]
     PW - v243 - O 21 '96 - p73 [51-250]
Skipper, John - *Umpires: Classic Baseball Stories from the Men Who Made the Calls*
     LJ - v122 - F 1 '97 - p82 [1-50]
Skipwith, Joanna - *The Sitwells and the Arts of the 1920s and 1930s*
     NYTBR - v101 - O 27 '96 - p38 [251-500]
     PW - v243 - Jl 22 '96 - p234 [51-250]
     PW - v243 - S 2 '96 - p121 [51-250]
Sklar, Holly - *Chaos or Community*
     Workbook - v21 - Fall '96 - p123+ [501+]
Sklar, Morty - *Patchwork of Dreams*
     BL - v93 - S 1 '96 - p33 [1-50]
     Bloom Rev - v17 - Ja '97 - p12 [51-250]
Sklar, Robert - *Movie-Made America*
     CSM - v89 - D 6 '96 - p10 [51-250]
Sklepowich, Edward - *Death in the Palazzo*
     BL - v93 - Mr 15 '97 - p1231 [51-250]
     Ent W - Mr 21 '97 - p68 [51-250]
     KR - v65 - Ja 15 '97 - p100+ [51-250]
     LJ - v122 - F 1 '97 - p111 [1-50]
     NYTBR - v102 - Mr 2 '97 - p20 [51-250]
     PW - v243 - D 30 '96 - p57 [51-250]
Skloot, Floyd - *The Night-Side: Seven Years in the Kingdom of the Sick*
     Sew R - v104 - O '96 - pR90+ [501+]
Skocpol, Theda - *Boomerang: Clinton's Health Security Effort and the Turn against Government in U.S. Politics*
     BW - v26 - Ag 4 '96 - p13 [51-250]
     Choice - v34 - N '96 - p495 [51-250]
     CS - v26 - Mr '97 - p150+ [501+]
     Rapport - v19 - 5 '96 - p41 [251-500]
     Trib Bks - My 25 '97 - p8 [1-50]
Social Policy in the United States
     AAPSS-A - v546 - Jl '96 - p171+ [501+]
     J Soc H - v30 - Win '96 - p521+ [501+]
     Pub Hist - v19 - Win '97 - p106+ [501+]
     Soc Ser R - v70 - S '96 - p499 [51-250]
Social Revolutions in the Modern World
     APSR - v91 - Mr '97 - p222+ [501+]
     SF - v75 - Mr '97 - p1121+ [501+]
Skofield, James - *Detective Dinosaur (Illus. by R W Alley)*
  c BL - v92 - Ag '96 - p1910 [51-250]
  c HB Guide - v7 - Fall '96 - p285 [51-250]
  c SLJ - v42 - Ag '96 - p129 [51-250]
Skogen, Larry C - *Indian Depredation Claims 1796-1920*
     WHQ - v28 - Spr '97 - p78+ [501+]

Skogerboe, Eli - *Privatising the Public Interest*
     JC - v47 - Win '97 - p120+ [501+]
Skoggard, Ian A - *The Indigenous Dynamic in Taiwan's Postwar Development*
     R&R Bk N - v12 - F '97 - p44 [51-250]
Skoglund, Elizabeth R - *A Quiet Courage*
     LJ - v122 - Ap 15 '97 - p90 [51-250]
Skotnes, Andor - *American Working-Class History in Historical Journals 1961-1972*
  r RQ - v36 - Fall '96 - p56 [1-50]
Skoug, Kenneth N - *The United States and Cuba under Reagan and Shultz*
     Choice - v34 - N '96 - p533 [51-250]
Skran, Claudena M - *Refugees in Inter-War Europe*
     AHR - v101 - O '96 - p1201+ [501+]
     CS - v25 - S '96 - p594+ [501+]
Skrentny, John David - *The Ironies of Affirmative Action*
     AJS - v102 - Ja '97 - p1202+ [501+]
     APSR - v91 - Mr '97 - p197+ [501+]
     BI S - v26 - Fall '96 - p106 [1-50]
     Choice - v34 - My '97 - p1585 [51-250]
     JEL - v34 - D '96 - p2078 [51-250]
     NY - v72 - N 25 '96 - p106+ [501+]
Skrepcinski, Denice - *Cody Coyote Cooks! (Illus. by Lois Bergthold)*
  c SLJ - v42 - O '96 - p140 [51-250]
Skroder, John C - *Using the M68HC11 Microcontroller*
     SciTech - v20 - D '96 - p73 [51-250]
Skrypuch, Marsha Forchuk - *Silver Threads (Illus. by Michael Martchenko)*
  c Quill & Q - v62 - N '96 - p48 [251-500]
Skrzynecki, Peter - *The Cry of the Goldfinch*
     Aust Bk R - F '97 - p27+ [501+]
Skujenieks, Knuts - *Lidz Kailai Rokai*
     WLT - v71 - Win '97 - p194+ [501+]
Skurzynski, Gloria - *Waves: The Electromagnetic Universe*
  c BL - v93 - D 1 '96 - p660 [51-250]
  c HB - v73 - Ja '97 - p80 [51-250]
  c HB Guide - v8 - Spr '97 - p113 [51-250]
  c SLJ - v42 - N '96 - p115 [51-250]
Skutch, Alexander Frank - *Antbirds and Ovenbirds*
     AB - v97 - Je 17 '96 - p2400+ [51-250]
     Choice - v34 - O '96 - p308 [51-250]
Life of the Flycatcher
     BL - v93 - F 15 '97 - p985 [51-250]
The Minds of Birds
     Choice - v34 - N '96 - p484 [51-250]
     NYTBR - v101 - D 8 '96 - p89 [1-50]
Orioles, Blackbirds, and Their Kin
     AB - v97 - Je 17 '96 - p2400 [51-250]
     Choice - v34 - O '96 - p308 [51-250]
Skutnabb-Kangas, Tove - *Multilingualism for All*
     MLJ - v80 - Win '96 - p537+ [501+]
Skvorecky, Josef - *The Bride of Texas*
     NS - v125 - O 25 '96 - p48 [501+]
     NYRB - v43 - O 3 '96 - p12+ [501+]
     Sew R - v104 - Jl '96 - pR62+ [501+]
     Spec - v277 - O 12 '96 - p46 [501+]
     TLS - O 4 '96 - p25 [501+]
     WLT - v70 - Aut '96 - p988 [501+]
Headed for the Blues
     Choice - v34 - O '96 - p288 [51-250]
     NYRB - v43 - O 3 '96 - p12+ [501+]
     NYTBR - v101 - N 10 '96 - p53 [501+]
Nove Canterburske Povidky A Jine Pribehy
     WLT - v71 - Win '97 - p182+ [501+]
Povidky Z Rajskeho Udoli
     WLT - v70 - Aut '96 - p988+ [251-500]
The Tenor Saxophonist's Story
     KR - v64 - D 1 '96 - p1701 [251-500]
     LJ - v121 - D '96 - p147+ [51-250]
Skwiercz, Andrew L - *Index to the Records of the Wally-Mills-Zimmerman Funeral Home, Elkhart, Indiana April 1912-October 1988*
  r EGH - v50 - N '96 - p166+ [51-250]
Sky, Patrick - *Ryan's Mammoth Collection*
     CAY - v17 - Fall '96 - p1 [51-250]
Skye, Christina - *Key to Forever*
     PW - v244 - F 17 '97 - p217 [51-250]
Skyttner, Lars - *General Systems Theory*
     Choice - v34 - D '96 - p646 [51-250]
Slabey, Robert M - *The United States and Viet Nam from War to Peace*
     R&R Bk N - v12 - F '97 - p20 [51-250]
Slabolepszy, Paul - *Mooi Street and Other Moves*
     Theat J - v49 - Mr '97 - p85+ [501+]
Slack, Paul - *The English Poor Law 1531-1782*
     JEL - v34 - D '96 - p2101 [51-250]
Slack, Trevor - *Understanding Sport Organizations*
     R&R Bk N - v12 - F '97 - p32 [51-250]

Slade, Alexander L - *Library Services for Off-Campus and Distance Education*
r ARBA - v28 - '97 - p235 [51-250]
Slade, Carole - *St. Teresa of Avila: Author of a Heroic Life*
  CH - v65 - D '96 - p707+ [501+]
  CHR - v83 - Ja '97 - p102+ [501+]
  Ren Q - v50 - Spr '97 - p344+ [501+]
  Six Ct J - v27 - Fall '96 - p934+ [501+]
  Theol St - v57 - S '96 - p567+ [251-500]
Slaight, Craig - *New Plays from A.C.T.'s Young Conservatory. Vol. 2*
y Kliatt - v30 - S '96 - p24 [51-250]
y VOYA - v19 - D '96 - p288+ [251-500]
  Short Plays for Young Actors
y BL - v93 - S 15 '96 - p230 [51-250]
y Kliatt - v30 - S '96 - p24 [51-250]
Slap, Gail B - *Teenage Health Care*
y VOYA - v19 - D '96 - p256 [1-50]
Slapak, Orpa - *The Jews of India*
  Afterimage - v24 - Ja '97 - p23 [1-50]
Slate, Joseph - *Miss Bindergarten Gets Ready for Kindergarten (Illus. by Ashley Wolff)*
c BL - v92 - Ag '96 - p1906 [501+]
c CCB-B - v50 - S '96 - p31 [51-250]
c HB - v72 - S '96 - p587+ [501+]
c HB Guide - v8 - Spr '97 - p49 [51-250]
c Inst - v106 - N '96 - p35 [51-250]
c NYTBR - v102 - Ja 5 '97 - p22 [501+]
c SLJ - v42 - Ag '96 - p129 [51-250]
Slater, Dan - *The Dogs Who Saved Christmas Day*
c Dog Fan - v88 - N '96 - p33 [51-250]
Slater, John G - *Bertrand Russell*
  Dialogue - v36 - Win '97 - p207+ [501+]
Slater, Lauren - *Welcome to My Country*
  NS & S - v9 - My 17 '96 - p39 [251-500]
  Spec - v277 - S 7 '96 - p33 [501+]
  TLS - Ag 2 '96 - p13 [501+]
  Welcome to My Country (Slater). Audio Version
  BL - v93 - N 15 '96 - p604 [51-250]
Slater, Peter - *Storm: Short Stories*
  CR - v269 - N '96 - p273+ [251-500]
Slater, Robert - *Rabin of Israel*
  CR - v269 - S '96 - p159+ [251-500]
Slater, Suzanne - *The Lesbian Family Life Cycle*
  JMF - v58 - Ag '96 - p807+ [251-500]
Slater, Teddy - *Stay in Line*
c BL - v92 - Ag '96 - p1910 [51-250]
Slater, William J - *Roman Theater and Society*
  Choice - v34 - Ap '97 - p1350 [51-250]
Slatta, Richard W - *The Cowboy Encyclopedia*
r Obs - D 1 '96 - p18* [1-50]
Slatyer, Will - *The Speculative Strategist*
  R&R Bk N - v11 - N '96 - p37 [51-250]
Slaughter, Richard A - *The Knowledge Base of Futures Studies. Vols. 1-3*
  Fut - v30 - N '96 - p56 [501+]
Slaughter, Thomas P - *The Natures of John and William Bartram*
  LJ - v121 - S 15 '96 - p91 [51-250]
  New R - v215 - D 9 '96 - p42+ [501+]
  NYRB - v43 - O 17 '96 - p4+ [501+]
  PW - v243 - S 2 '96 - p101 [51-250]
Slaughter, William - *The Politics of My Heart*
  BWatch - v17 - S '96 - p9+ [51-250]
Slavianov, S Yu - *Asymptotic Solutions of the One-Dimensional Schrodinger Equation*
  SciTech - v20 - S '96 - p14 [51-250]
Slavik, Jan - *Fluorescene Microscopy and Fluorescent Probes*
  SciTech - v21 - Mr '97 - p34 [51-250]
Slavin, Bill - *The Stone Lion (Illus. by Bill Slavin)*
c BIC - v26 - F '97 - p33+ [251-500]
c Can CL - v22 - Fall '96 - p129 [51-250]
Slavin, Moriss - *The Hebertistes to the Guillotine*
  EHR - v112 - Ap '97 - p496+ [501+]
Slavin, Sarah - *U.S. Women's Interest Groups*
r ARBA - v28 - '97 - p336 [51-250]
r RQ - v36 - Fall '96 - p141 [251-500]
Slavitt, David R - *A Gift: The Life of Da Ponte*
  HR - v49 - Win '97 - p659+ [501+]
Slawski, Wolfgang - *The Friendship Trip (Illus. by Wolfgang Slawski)*
c HB Guide - v7 - Fall '96 - p276 [51-250]
c JB - v60 - Ag '96 - p144 [51-250]
c SLJ - v42 - Ag '96 - p129+ [51-250]
Slawson, W David - *Binding Promises*
  JEL - v34 - D '96 - p2079 [51-250]
Slay, Ben - *De-Monopolization and Competition Policy in Post-Communist Economies*
  JEL - v34 - S '96 - p1454 [51-250]

Slaybaugh, Douglas - *William I. Myers and the Modernization of American Agriculture*
  Choice - v34 - N '96 - p528 [51-250]
Slaymaker, Olav - *Steepland Geomorphology*
  GJ - v162 - N '96 - p336 [251-500]
Sleator, William - *Interstellar Pig*
y HB Guide - v7 - Fall '96 - p297 [51-250]
  The Night the Heads Came
y Ch BWatch - v6 - My '96 - p2 [51-250]
y Emerg Lib - v23 - My '96 - p43 [1-50]
y Emerg Lib - v24 - S '96 - p53 [51-250]
y HB Guide - v7 - Fall '96 - p305 [51-250]
y JAAL - v40 - S '96 - p73 [51-250]
y NYTBR - v101 - O 13 '96 - p26 [51-250]
  Oddballs
y Kliatt - v30 - S '96 - p4 [1-50]
Slee, Vergil N - *Health Care Terms. 3rd Comprehensive Ed.*
r ARBA - v28 - '97 - p601+ [51-250]
r BL - v93 - F 1 '97 - p956 [1-50]
r Choice - v34 - My '97 - p1481 [51-250]
r CLW - v67 - D '96 - p51 [251-500]
r SciTech - v20 - D '96 - p39 [51-250]
Sleem, Patty - *Back in Time*
  LJ - v122 - Ap 1 '97 - p80 [51-250]
  Second Time Around
  Rapport - v19 - 5 '96 - p34 [251-500]
Sleeper, C Freeman - *The Victorious Christ*
  Am - v176 - Mr 8 '97 - p29+ [51-250]
Sleeter, Christine E - *Multicultural Education as Social Activism*
  Choice - v34 - Ja '97 - p850 [51-250]
  R&R Bk N - v11 - N '96 - p57 [51-250]
Slemrod, Joel - *Taxing Ourselves*
  Econ - v341 - D 7 '96 - p9* [51-250]
  JEL - v35 - Mr '97 - p224+ [51-250]
  WSJ-MW - v78 - D 24 '96 - pA7 [501+]
Slesin, Suzanne - *Everyday Things*
  NYTLa - v146 - D 2 '96 - pC16 [1-50]
Sletyr, Uwe B - *Crystalline Bacterial Cell Surface Proteins*
  SciTech - v20 - N '96 - p34 [51-250]
Slezak, Ellen - *The Book Group Book*
r RQ - v36 - Win '96 - p221 [51-250]
Slezkine, Yuri - *Arctic Mirrors*
  EHR - v111 - N '96 - p1342+ [251-500]
Slide, Anthony - *Lois Weber: The Director Who Lost Her Way in History*
  Choice - v34 - F '97 - p973+ [51-250]
  R&R Bk N - v11 - D '96 - p62 [1-50]
  The Silent Feminists
  Choice - v34 - Ja '97 - p804 [51-250]
  Some Joe You Don't Know
r ARBA - v28 - '97 - p505+ [51-250]
Slier, Deborah - *Make a Joyful Sound (Illus. by Cornelius Van Wright)*
c HB Guide - v7 - Fall '96 - p365 [51-250]
c SLJ - v42 - O '96 - p117+ [51-250]
Slifer, Stephen D - *By the Numbers*
  R&R Bk N - v11 - N '96 - p26 [51-250]
Slights, William W E - *Ben Jonson and the Art of Secrecy*
  MLR - v91 - O '96 - p969+ [501+]
  RES - v48 - F '97 - p101+ [501+]
  TLS - Ja 31 '97 - p23 [501+]
Slinger, Joey - *Down and Dirty Birding*
  Quill & Q - v62 - My '96 - p30 [501+]
Slive, Seymour - *Dutch Painting 1600-1800*
  BM - v138 - N '96 - p758+ [501+]
Sloan, Annie - *Decorative Gilding*
y BL - v93 - F 1 '97 - p920 [51-250]
  LJ - v122 - Ja '97 - p94 [51-250]
  Decorative Paint Effects
  BL - v93 - F 1 '97 - p920 [51-250]
  LJ - v122 - Ja '97 - p94 [51-250]
Sloan, Bob - *Bliss*
  Arm Det - v30 - Win '97 - p105 [251-500]
  BL - v92 - Ag '96 - p1888 [51-250]
Sloan, Carolyn - *An Incredible Journey (Illus. by Simon Smith)*
c Sch Lib - v44 - N '96 - p165 [51-250]
Sloan, Douglas - *Faith and Knowledge*
  CH - v65 - S '96 - p554+ [501+]
  Cres - v59 - Sum '96 - p36+ [501+]
  J Ch St - v38 - Aut '96 - p922+ [501+]
  Rel St Rev - v23 - Ja '97 - p35+ [501+]
  TCR - v98 - Fall '96 - p178+ [501+]
Sloan, James Park - *Jerzy Kosinski: A Biography*
  ABR - v18 - O '96 - p12+ [501+]
  LATBR - My 12 '96 - p3+ [501+]

Sloat, Teri - *Sody Sallyratus (Illus. by Teri Sloat)*
c BL - v93 - D 15 '96 - p730 [51-250]
c KR - v64 - D 15 '96 - p1805 [51-250]
c PW - v243 - D 2 '96 - p60 [51-250]
c SLJ - v43 - Ja '97 - p109 [51-250]
Sloboder, Bea - *Candy Canes! (Illus. by Paige Billin-Frye)*
c PW - v243 - S 30 '96 - p93 [1-50]
  Candy Hearts! (Illus. by Paige Billin-Frye)
c PW - v243 - D 30 '96 - p68 [1-50]
Slocum, Jerry - *The Book of Ingenious and Diabolical Puzzles*
  Math T - v89 - My '96 - p434 [51-250]
  The Puzzle Arcade
c Learning - v25 - Ja '97 - p56 [1-50]
c PW - v243 - O 7 '96 - p78 [1-50]
Slocum, Perry D - *Water Gardening*
  Fine Gard - Mr '97 - p80 [251-500]
Slomp, Hans - *Between Bargaining and Politics*
  Choice - v34 - F '97 - p1008 [51-250]
  R&R Bk N - v12 - F '97 - p40 [51-250]
Slonimsky, Nicolas - *The Portable Baker's Biographical Dictionary of Musicians*
cr Teach Mus - v3 - Ap '96 - p69 [51-250]
Sloop, John M - *The Cultural Prison*
  R&R Bk N - v11 - D '96 - p45 [51-250]
Slotboom, Wendy - *King Snake (Illus. by John Manders)*
c CBRS - v25 - Mr '97 - p90+ [51-250]
c PW - v244 - Mr 10 '97 - p66 [51-250]
Slotten, Hugh Richard - *Patronage, Practice, and the Culture of American Science*
  AHR - v101 - O '96 - p1278 [501+]
Slouka, Mark - *War of the Worlds*
y Kliatt - v30 - S '96 - p37 [51-250]
  Nat R - v48 - O 14 '96 - p81+ [501+]
Slovo, Gillian - *Catnap*
  KR - v64 - O 15 '96 - p1499 [51-250]
  PW - v243 - O 14 '96 - p67 [51-250]
  Every Secret Thing
  Econ - v342 - Mr 1 '97 - p84 [501+]
  KR - v65 - Mr 1 '97 - p367 [51-250]
  NS - v126 - F 21 '97 - p48 [501+]
  Obs - F 23 '97 - p18* [501+]
  PW - v244 - Ap 7 '97 - p80 [51-250]
  Spec - v278 - F 22 '97 - p32 [501+]
Sloyan, Gerard S - *The Crucifixion of Jesus*
  Intpr - v51 - Ja '97 - p96+ [251-500]
  TT - v53 - O '96 - p430 [51-250]
Sluga, Hans - *Heidegger's Crisis*
  Ger Q - v69 - Spr '96 - p206+ [501+]
Sluman, Roelf - *CompuServe Quick Tour Guide to WinCIM*
  CBR - v14 - Jl '96 - p19 [1-50]
  Internet Made Easy
  CBR - v14 - Jl '96 - p21 [1-50]
Slung, Michele - *Fever: Sensual Stories by Women Writers*
  Quill & Q - v62 - Jl '96 - p42 [501+]
  Slow Hand
  Quill & Q - v62 - Jl '96 - p42 [501+]
Slutsky, Jeff - *The Toastmasters International Guide to Successful Speaking*
  BWatch - v18 - F '97 - p11 [51-250]
Slyder, Ingrid - *The Fabulous Flying Fandinis (Illus. by Ingrid Slyder)*
c BW - v26 - D 8 '96 - p23 [51-250]
c CBRS - v25 - Ja '97 - p53 [51-250]
c HB Guide - v8 - Spr '97 - p49 [51-250]
c PW - v243 - O 7 '96 - p75 [51-250]
c SLJ - v42 - S '96 - p192 [51-250]
Smail, David - *How to Survive without Psychotherapy*
  Obs - v54 - O 13 '96 - p17* [501+]
  TLS - Ja 3 '97 - p32 [51-250]
Smail, John - *The Origins of Middle-Class Culture*
  AHR - v101 - O '96 - p1206+ [501+]
  JEH - v56 - D '96 - p932+ [501+]
  JIH - v27 - Win '97 - p512+ [501+]
  JMH - v68 - D '96 - p978+ [501+]
  J Soc H - v30 - Spr '97 - p755+ [501+]
Small, Alison - *The Effects of HIV/AIDS on Farming Systems in Eastern Africa*
  J Gov Info - v23 - S '96 - p670 [51-250]
Small, David - *Fenwick's Suit (Illus. by David Small)*
c BL - v93 - S 15 '96 - p242 [51-250]
c CBRS - v25 - N '96 - p28 [51-250]
c CCB-B - v50 - O '96 - p76 [51-250]
c HB Guide - v8 - Spr '97 - p49 [51-250]
c KR - v64 - Ag 15 '96 - p1243 [51-250]
c PW - v243 - Jl 22 '96 - p240 [51-250]
c SLJ - v42 - S '96 - p192 [51-250]
  George Washington's Cows
c PW - v244 - F 17 '97 - p220 [1-50]

Small, David B - *Methods in the Mediterranean*
  Am Ant - v61 - Ap '96 - p433+ [501+]
Small, Helen - *Love's Madness*
  Choice - v34 - N '96 - p460 [51-250]
  Nine-C Lit - v51 - D '96 - p427 [51-250]
Small, Meredith - *Female Choices*
  Wom R Bks - v14 - F '97 - p1+ [501+]
A Small Treasury of Easter Poems and Prayers (Illus. by Susan Spellman)
  c PW - v244 - Mr 24 '97 - p76 [51-250]
Smallman, Basil - *The Piano Quartet and Quintet*
  Notes - v53 - D '96 - p468+ [501+]
Smalls, Irene - *Beginning School (Illus. by Toni Goffe)*
  c IIB Guide - v8 - Spr '97 - p49 [51-250]
  c SLJ - v42 - Ag '96 - p130 [51-250]
  Dawn and the Round-to-It
  c CLW - v67 - Mr '97 - p15 [1-50]
  Ebony Sea (Illus. by Jon Onye Lockard)
  c HB Guide - v7 - Fall '96 - p276 [51-250]
  Irene Jennie and the Christmas Masquerade (Illus. by Melodye Rosales)
  c BL - v93 - S 15 '96 - p251 [51-250]
  c CBRS - v25 - O '96 - p17 [51-250]
  c CCB-B - v50 - N '96 - p115+ [51-250]
  c HB Guide - v8 - Spr '97 - p49 [51-250]
  c PW - v243 - S 30 '96 - p91 [51-250]
  c SLJ - v42 - O '96 - p41 [51-250]
  Jenny Reen and the Jack Muh Lantern (Illus. by Keinyo White)
  c BL - v93 - S 1 '96 - p137 [51-250]
  c Bloom Rev - v17 - Ja '97 - p20 [51-250]
  c CBRS - v25 - S '96 - p8+ [51-250]
  c CCB-B - v50 - D '96 - p152 [51-250]
  c Ch BWatch - v6 - N '96 - p6+ [1-50]
  c HB Guide - v8 - Spr '97 - p49 [51-250]
  c PW - v243 - S 30 '96 - p85 [51-250]
  c SLJ - v42 - D '96 - p106 [51-250]
  Louise's Gift (Illus. by Colin Bootman)
  c HB Guide - v7 - Fall '96 - p276 [51-250]
  c Par - v71 - D '96 - p252 [51-250]
Smalzer, William R - *Write to Be Read*
  MLJ - v81 - Spr '97 - p126 [251-500]
Smart, Jeffrey - *Not Quite Straight*
  Aust Bk R - N '96 - p15 [501+]
Smart, Mary - *A Flight with Fame*
  Choice - v34 - D '96 - p604 [51-250]
Smart, Ninian - *Dimensions of the Sacred*
  Choice - v34 - F '97 - p981 [51-250]
  LJ - v121 - D '96 - p100 [51-250]
  NS & S - v9 - My 24 '96 - p40 [251-500]
  Smart Verse
  BWatch - v17 - N '96 - p9 [51-250]
Smart, William B - *Utah: A Portrait*
  WHQ - v28 - Spr '97 - p103 [1-50]
Smart Funds 1997
  r Quill & Q - v63 - Ja '97 - p24 [251-500]
Smax, Willy - *Jack Tractor (Illus. by Keren Ludlow)*
  c HB Guide - v7 - Fall '96 - p276+ [51-250]
Smedes, Lewis B - *Shame and Grace*
  Bks & Cult - v2 - Mr '96 - p3+ [501+]
Smedley, Jack - *The Journey Back*
  BWatch - v17 - S '96 - p10 [1-50]
Smedley-Weill, Anette - *Les Intendants De Louis XIV*
  TLS - Ja 3 '97 - p31 [501+]
Smee, Nicola - *Charlie's Choice (Illus. by Nicola Smee)*
  c Bks Keeps - Mr '97 - p18 [51-250]
Smelcer, John E - *Changing Seasons and Other Poems*
  WAL - v31 - Fall '96 - p277+ [51-250]
Smethurst, William - *The Archers: The True Story*
  Spec - v277 - S 28 '96 - p46 [501+]
Smiga, George M - *Pain and Polemic*
  Rel Ed - v91 - Fall '96 - p607 [1-50]
Smil, Vaclav - *Cycles of Life*
  Nature - v386 - Mr 6 '97 - p35+ [51-250]
  New Sci - v153 - Mr 15 '97 - p42 [51-250]
  Global Ecology
  AAAGA - v86 - S '96 - p583+ [501+]
Smiles, Sam - *The Image of Antiquity*
  AHR - v102 - F '97 - p104+ [501+]
  Rel St Rev - v23 - Ja '97 - p65 [51-250]
  VS - v39 - Win '96 - p283+ [501+]
Smiley, Jane - *Duplicate Keys*
  Obs - D 22 '96 - p18* [51-250]
  Moo
  LQ - v67 - Ja '97 - p88+ [501+]
Smiley, Marion - *Moral Responsibility and the Boundaries of Community*
  Hast Cen R - v27 - Ja '97 - p38+ [501+]
Smilor, Raymond W - *Leadership and Entrepreneurship*
  Choice - v34 - S '96 - p172 [51-250]

Smirnov, N N - *Elsevier's Dictionary of Fundamental and Applied Biology*
  r ARBA - v28 - '97 - p576+ [51-250]
  r SciTech - v20 - N '96 - p26 [51-250]
Smit, Tim - *The Lost Gardens of Heligan*
  Obs - Mr 30 '97 - p18* [501+]
Smith, A R - *Plant Hormone Signal Perception and Transduction*
  SciTech - v20 - D '96 - p31 [51-250]
Smith, Adam - *Adam Smith's Wealth of Nations*
  JEH - v56 - S '96 - p755+ [501+]
Smith, Adrian - *The New Statesman*
  Choice - v34 - S '96 - p117 [51-250]
  Lon R Bks - v18 - My 23 '96 - p18+ [501+]
Smith, Alan - *Russia and the World Economy*
  Econ J - v106 - N '96 - p1837 [51-250]
Smith, Alastair - *How Are Babies Made?*
  c Books - v11 - Ap '97 - p24 [51-250]
  How Do Your Senses Work?
  c Books - v11 - Ap '97 - p24 [51-250]
  The Usborne Big Book of Experiments
  c New Sci - v153 - Ja 25 '97 - p45 [1-50]
  The Usborne Big Book of Papercraft
  c Sch Lib - v44 - N '96 - p162 [51-250]
  What Happens to Your Food?
  c Books - v11 - Ap '97 - p24 [51-250]
Smith, Alison - *The Victorian Nude*
  HT - v46 - O '96 - p58 [1-50]
Smith, Angel - *Historical Dictionary of Spain*
  r ARBA - v28 - '97 - p206 [51-250]
  r Choice - v34 - F '97 - p949 [51-250]
  r R&R Bk N - v12 - F '97 - p17 [51-250]
Smith, Anna - *Julia Kristeva Readings of Exile and Estrangement*
  Obs - F 16 '97 - p18* [51-250]
Smith, Annick - *Big Bluestem*
  LJ - v121 - S 15 '96 - p91 [51-250]
  S Liv - v32 - Mr '97 - p62 [51-250]
Smith, Anthony - *The Free Life*
  Aethlon - v13 - Spr '96 - p214+ [501+]
Smith, Arthur, 1948- - *Orders of Affection*
  Ken R - v18 - Sum '96 - p191+ [501+]
  y Kliatt - v30 - S '96 - p24 [51-250]
Smith, Arthur E, Jr. - *Bibliography of Colorado Mining History*
  r RocksMiner - v71 - S '96 - p361 [51-250]
Smith, B C - *Understanding Third World Politics*
  Choice - v34 - N '96 - p536 [51-250]
  WorldV - v12 - Jl '96 - p10 [51-250]
Smith, Barbara, 1949, Dec., 12- - *The Women of Ben Jonson's Poetry*
  Sev Cent N - v54 - Fall '96 - p50 [501+]
Smith, Barbara Burnett - *Celebration in Purple Sage*
  KR - v64 - S 15 '96 - p1358 [51-250]
  PW - v243 - O 7 '96 - p65 [51-250]
Smith, Barry, Ph.D. - *The Cambridge Companion to Husserl*
  CPR - v16 - Ag '96 - p294+ [501+]
  Ethics - v107 - O '96 - p198 [51-250]
  IPQ - v36 - D '96 - p490+ [501+]
Smith, Barry F - *Domain Decomposition*
  SciTech - v20 - D '96 - p18 [51-250]
Smith, Bernard - *Poems 1938-1993*
  Aust Bk R - O '96 - p53+ [501+]
Smith, Bernard, 1916- - *Imagining the Pacific*
  JMH - v68 - S '96 - p617+ [501+]
Smith, Betty - *Maggie-Now*
  Nat R - v48 - D 23 '96 - p53+ [51-250]
Smith, Beverley - *A Year in Figure Skating*
  Mac - v109 - D 9 '96 - p66 [1-50]
Smith, Bill - *Star Wars: The Essential Guide to Vehicles and Vessels*
  c SF Chr - v18 - O '96 - p81+ [1-50]
  Star Wars: The Galactic Empire
  c Ch BWatch - v6 - My '96 - p1 [1-50]
  c HB Guide - v7 - Fall '96 - p277 [51-250]
  c SF Chr - v18 - O '96 - p81 [1-50]
  Star Wars: The Rebel Alliance
  c Ch BWatch - v6 - My '96 - p1 [1-50]
  c HB Guide - v7 - Fall '96 - p277 [51-250]
  c SF Chr - v18 - O '96 - p81 [1-50]
Smith, Bradley F - *Sharing Secrets with Stalin*
  Choice - v34 - F '97 - p1027 [51-250]
  J Mil H - v61 - Ap '97 - p397+ [501+]
  KR - v64 - S 1 '96 - p1309 [251-500]
  PW - v243 - S 30 '96 - p71+ [501+]
Smith, Brenda - *Egypt of the Pharaohs*
  y HB Guide - v7 - Fall '96 - p379 [51-250]
Smith, Brian K - *Classifying the Universe*
  JAAR - v64 - Win '96 - p863+ [501+]

Smith, Bryan John - *Protein Sequencing Protocols*
  SciTech - v21 - Mr '97 - p43 [51-250]
Smith, Bud - *Creating Web Pages for Dummies*
  BL - v93 - S 15 '96 - p193 [501+]
  Quill & Q - v62 - N '96 - p32 [51-250]
Smith, C Carter - *Bridging the Continent*
  y Kliatt - v31 - Mr '97 - p32 [51-250]
  The Conquest of the West
  y Kliatt - v31 - Mr '97 - p32 [51-250]
  Exploring the Frontier
  y Kliatt - v31 - Mr '97 - p32 [51-250]
  The Legendary Wild West
  y Kliatt - v31 - Mr '97 - p32 [51-250]
  Native Americans of the West
  y Kliatt - v31 - Mr '97 - p32 [51-250]
  The Riches of the West
  y Kliatt - v31 - Mr '97 - p32 [51-250]
Smith, C U M - *Elements of Molecular Neurobiology. 2nd Ed.*
  r SciTech - v20 - S '96 - p22 [1-50]
Smith, C W - *Hunter's Trap*
  BL - v93 - S 1 '96 - p64 [51-250]
  LJ - v121 - S 15 '96 - p98 [51-250]
  PW - v243 - S 16 '96 - p70 [51-250]
Smith, Carl - *Urban Disorder and the Shape of Belief*
  AHR - v101 - D '96 - p1637 [251-500]
  JIH - v27 - Spr '97 - p722+ [501+]
  RAH - v24 - S '96 - p442+ [501+]
Smith, Carol - *Friends for Life*
  LATBR - Jl 14 '96 - p6 [51-250]
Smith, Carolyn D - *In the Field. 2nd Ed.*
  R&R Bk N - v11 - N '96 - p22 [51-250]
Smith, Charles D - *Palestine and the Arab-Israeli Conflict. 3rd Ed.*
  MEJ - v50 - Sum '96 - p453 [51-250]
Smith, Charles V - *Dalkey, Society and Economy in a Small Medieval Irish Town*
  ILS - v16 - Spr '97 - p36 [1-50]
Smith, Charlie - *Before and After*
  ABR - v18 - O '96 - p22 [501+]
  Cheap Ticket to Heaven
  BL - v92 - Ag '96 - p1883 [51-250]
  LATBR - S 15 '96 - p10 [251-500]
  NYTBR - v101 - S 22 '96 - p20 [51-250]
Smith, Charlotte - *Letters of a Solitary Wanderer 1800*
  Nine-C Lit - v51 - S '96 - p277 [1-50]
Smith, Christian - *Resisting Reagan*
  Choice - v34 - N '96 - p533 [51-250]
  R&R Bk N - v11 - N '96 - p20 [1-50]
  WorldV - v12 - Jl '96 - p10 [51-250]
Smith, Christopher John - *Early Rome and Latium*
  Choice - v34 - N '96 - p514 [51-250]
Smith, Chuck - *The New Mexico State Constitution*
  r R&R Bk N - v11 - N '96 - p53 [1-50]
Smith, Clark Ashton - *The Book of Hyperborea*
  Necro - Fall '96 - p5+ [501+]
  Tales of Zothique
  Necro - Fall '96 - p5+ [501+]
Smith, Constance - *Art Marketing 101*
  A Art - v61 - Ap '97 - p80 [51-250]
  Ceram Mo - v45 - Ap '97 - p32+ [251-500]
Smith, Craig - *Giving by Industry. 1996-1997 Ed.*
  r ChrPhil - v9 - O 31 '96 - p67 [51-250]
Smith, Craig Allen - *The White House Speaks*
  AAPSS-A - v546 - Jl '96 - p155+ [501+]
  JC - v46 - Sum '96 - p176+ [501+]
Smith, Cynthia - *Noblesse Oblige*
  PW - v243 - O 14 '96 - p81 [51-250]
Smith, D J - *Prayers for the Dead Ventriloquist*
  WAL - v31 - Fall '96 - p272+ [51-250]
Smith, D Moody - *The Theology of the Gospel of John*
  Intpr - v51 - Ja '97 - p94+ [251-500]
Smith, Dale - *What the Parrot Told Alice (Illus. by John Bardwell)*
  c Ch BWatch - v6 - S '96 - p5 [51-250]
  y JB - v60 - O '96 - p207 [51-250]
  y VOYA - v19 - F '97 - p332 [251-500]
Smith, Darren L - *The Traveler's Sourcebook*
  r Choice - v34 - F '97 - p951 [51-250]
  r R&R Bk N - v11 - D '96 - p19 [51-250]
Smith, Dave, 1940- - *Disney A to Z*
  r BW - v26 - S 15 '96 - p13 [51-250]
  r Choice - v34 - Mr '97 - p775 [51-250]
  r LATBR - S 8 '96 - p10 [51-250]
  r LJ - v121 - N 15 '96 - p56 [51-250]
Smith, Dave, 1942- - *Floating on Solitude*
  NL - v79 - D 16 '96 - p30+ [501+]
Smith, Dave, 1950- - *Backcountry Bear Basics*
  y BL - v93 - My 1 '97 - p1469 [51-250]
Smith, David, 1944- - *The Dance of Siva*
  Choice - v34 - Ap '97 - p1357+ [51-250]

Smith, David A - *Third World Cities in Global Perspective*
  AJS - v102 - S '96 - p618+ [501+]
  Choice - v34 - S '96 - p182 [51-250]
  CS - v25 - S '96 - p609+ [501+]
Smith, David L, 1946- - *The Gods of Golf*
  KR - v64 - My 1 '96 - p633 [251-500]
Smith, David L, 1963- - *The Theatrical City*
  Albion - v28 - Sum '96 - p300+ [501+]
Smith, David Martyn - *The Practice of Silviculture. 9th Ed.*
  SciTech - v21 - Mr '97 - p70 [51-250]
Smith, David Michael - *English Episcopal Acta. Vol. 7*
  EHR - v111 - S '96 - p952+ [501+]
Smith, David R - *Realism and Invention in the Prints of Albrecht Durer*
  Ren Q - v50 - Spr '97 - p322+ [501+]
Smith, Dean Wesley - *Klingon. Audio Version*
  Quill & Q - v62 - Jl '96 - p52 [1-50]
  The Soldiers of Fear
  y Kliatt - v30 - N '96 - p12 [51-250]
Smith, Deborah - *A Place to Call Home*
  BL - v93 - My 15 '97 - p1542 [51-250]
Smith, Denis, 1932- - *Rogue Tory*
  Beav - v76 - Ag '96 - p42+ [501+]
Smith, Derek - *Frances Fairweather--Demon Striker!*
  c Bks Keeps - v100 - S '96 - p13 [51-250]
  c JB - v60 - Ag '96 - p160 [51-250]
  c Sch Lib - v44 - Ag '96 - p109 [51-250]
  Whistle up the Devil
  Arm Det - v30 - Win '97 - p41 [251-500]
Smith, Dodie - *The Hundred and One Dalmatians (Lumley). Audio Version*
  c Obs - Ja 12 '97 - p18* [51-250]
  I Capture the Castle
  TES - Jl 26 '96 - pR5 [51-250]
Smith, Edith K - *Captured Essence*
  Sm Pr R - v29 - F '97 - p10 [251-500]
Smith, Emmitt - *The Emmitt Zone*
  Aethlon - v13 - Spr '96 - p212+ [251-500]
Smith, Evans Lansing - *Ricorso and Revelation*
  Ger Q - v69 - Fall '96 - p436+ [501+]
Smith, F Todd - *The Caddo Indians*
  AHR - v102 - F '97 - p179+ [251-500]
  HAHR - v76 - N '96 - p775+ [501+]
  The Caddos, the Wichitas, and the United States 1846-1901
  Choice - v34 - My '97 - p1565 [51-250]
Smith, Faye McDonald - *Flight of the Blackbird*
  Bloom Rev - v17 - Ja '97 - p19 [1-50]
  CSM - v89 - Ja 13 '97 - p13 [251-500]
  KR - v64 - S 15 '96 - p1350+ [251-500]
  LJ - v121 - O 1 '96 - p128 [51-250]
  PW - v243 - O 7 '96 - p60 [51-250]
Smith, Fran Devereux - *First Horse*
  y Ch BWatch - v6 - S '96 - p6 [51-250]
Smith, Frank, 1927- - *Fatal Flaw*
  Arm Det - v29 - Fall '96 - p493 [51-250]
Smith, Frank, 1928- - *Between Hope and Havoc*
  Kliatt - v30 - S '96 - p30 [51-250]
Smith, G E Kidder - *Source Book of American Architecture*
  r Choice - v34 - Ja '97 - p775+ [51-250]
  r TCI - v30 - O '96 - p58+ [1-50]
Smith, George Patrick - *Legal and Healthcare Ethics for the Elderly*
  Readings - v11 - S '96 - p30 [51-250]
Smith, Giles - *Lost in Music*
  Books - v9 - S '95 - p23 [1-50]
  NS & S - v9 - My 24 '96 - p40 [1-50]
Smith, Graham - *Essex Airfields in the Second World War*
  A & S Sm - v11 - F '97 - p87 [1-50]
  Norfolk Airfields in the Second World War
  A & S Sm - v11 - F '97 - p87 [1-50]
  Suffolk Airfields in the Second World War
  A & S Sm - v11 - F '97 - p87 [1-50]
Smith, Graham W - *A Critical Review of the Aerial and Ground Surveys of Breeding Waterfowl in North America*
  J Gov Info - v23 - S '96 - p565 [51-250]
Smith, Grahame - *Charles Dickens: A Literary Life*
  Choice - v34 - S '96 - p130 [51-250]
  Nine-C Lit - v51 - D '96 - p427 [51-250]
Smith, Gregory Bruce - *Nietzsche, Heidegger, and the Transition to Postmodernity*
  APSR - v91 - Mr '97 - p179+ [501+]
Smith, Gregory C - *Strengthening Aging Families*
  Fam Relat - v45 - Jl '96 - p352+ [51-250]

Smith, Gregory White - *On a Street Called Easy, in a Cottage Called Joye*
  Ent W - Je 28 '96 - p100 [51-250]
  NYTBR - v101 - Jl 21 '96 - p18+ [51-250]
  PW - v244 - My 5 '97 - p206 [1-50]
Smith, Harmon L - *Where Two or Three Are Gathered*
  Theol St - v57 - D '96 - p785 [251-500]
Smith, Haywood - *Secrets in Satin*
  PW - v244 - Mr 10 '97 - p64 [51-250]
Smith, Hazel - *European Union Foreign Policy and Central America*
  HAHR - v77 - F '97 - p171+ [501+]
Smith, Hedrick - *Rethinking America*
  y Kliatt - v30 - N '96 - p26 [51-250]
  NYTBR - v101 - Jl 21 '96 - p28 [1-50]
Smith, Helmut Walser - *German Nationalism and Religious Conflict*
  AAPSS-A - v546 - Jl '96 - p166+ [501+]
  AHR - v101 - O '96 - p1236+ [501+]
  AJS - v102 - S '96 - p614+ [501+]
  CH - v65 - S '96 - p527+ [501+]
  Theol St - v57 - Je '96 - p357+ [501+]
Smith, Henry Nash - *Virgin Land*
  RAH - v24 - S '96 - p542+ [501+]
Smith, Holly S - *Adventuring in Indonesia*
  LJ - v122 - Ap 15 '97 - p105 [51-250]
Smith, Howard K - *Events Leading Up to My Death*
  Sew R - v104 - O '96 - p673+ [501+]
Smith, Huston - *The Illustrated World's Religions*
  r CLW - v67 - Mr '97 - p45 [51-250]
  One Nation under God
  Nat Peop - v9 - Sum '96 - p80+ [501+]
Smith, Iain R - *The Origins of the South African War 1899-1902*
  HRNB - v25 - Win '97 - p85 [501+]
Smith, J C, 1930- - *The Castration of Oedipus*
  Choice - v34 - N '96 - p544 [51-250]
Smith, J C, 1933- - *Structural Steel Design. 2nd Ed.*
  Choice - v34 - S '96 - p160 [51-250]
Smith, J Walker - *Rocking the Ages*
  LJ - v122 - Ap 15 '97 - p94 [51-250]
  PW - v244 - Ap 14 '97 - p67 [51-250]
Smith, Jack - *God and Mr. Gomez*
  PW - v244 - Ap 21 '97 - p69 [1-50]
  Wait for Me at the Bottom of the Pool
  KR - v65 - Ja 15 '97 - p130+ [251-500]
Smith, James F - *The Path to a Successful Retirement*
  BWatch - v18 - F '97 - p15 [51-250]
Smith, Jane Bandy - *Achieving a Curriculum-Based Library Media Center Program*
  Emerg Lib - v23 - My '96 - p38 [51-250]
Smith, Janna Malamud - *Private Matters*
  BL - v93 - My 15 '97 - p1544 [51-250]
  KR - v65 - Ap 1 '97 - p537 [251-500]
  PW - v244 - Ap 21 '97 - p55 [51-250]
Smith, Jay M - *The Culture of Merit*
  Choice - v34 - Ap '97 - p1399 [51-250]
Smith, Jean Edward - *John Marshall: Definer of a Nation*
  BL - v93 - N 15 '96 - p555 [51-250]
  KR - v64 - S 1 '96 - p1309 [251-500]
  LJ - v121 - N 1 '96 - p92 [51-250]
  New R - v216 - F 17 '97 - p38+ [501+]
  NY - v73 - Mr 10 '97 - p93 [51-250]
  NYTBR - v101 - D 1 '96 - p14 [501+]
  NYTBR - v101 - D 8 '96 - p88 [1-50]
  PW - v243 - S 30 '96 - p67 [51-250]
  WSJ-MW - v78 - D 10 '96 - pA20 [501+]
Smith, Jeff - *Bone. Vols. 1-2*
  VV - v42 - Ja 7 '97 - p43 [51-250]
Smith, Jeffrey Chipps - *German Sculpture of the Later Renaissance c. 1520-1580*
  CHR - v82 - O '96 - p701+ [501+]
  Ren Q - v49 - Aut '96 - p675+ [501+]
Smith, Jessie Carney - *Notable Black American Women. Bk. 2*
  yr ARBA - v28 - '97 - p18 [251-500]
  Powerful Black Women
  r BW - v27 - F 2 '97 - p12 [251-500]
Smith, Joan - *Hungry for You*
  NS - v125 - N 15 '96 - p46+ [501+]
  Obs - D 15 '96 - p18* [501+]
  TLS - D 13 '96 - p36 [501+]
Smith, Joan, 1938- - *A Christmas Gambol*
  LJ - v121 - N 15 '96 - p50 [51-250]
Smith, Joan, 1953- - *Misogynies*
  Obs - N 24 '96 - p18* [51-250]
Smith, Joel - *Understanding the Media*
  JMCQ - v73 - Win '96 - p1018+ [251-500]

Smith, John David - *Black Voices from Reconstruction 1865-1877*
  y BL - v93 - N 1 '96 - p485+ [51-250]
  Choice - v34 - Ap '97 - p1407 [51-250]
  y HB Guide - v8 - Spr '97 - p175 [51-250]
  y SLJ - v43 - F '97 - p126 [51-250]
Smith, John L - *The Johnny Cash Record Catalog*
  r J Am Cult - v19 - Sum '96 - p147+ [51-250]
Smith, Jonathan, 1960- - *Fact and Feeling*
  VS - v39 - Spr '96 - p435+ [501+]
Smith, Jonathan Z - *The HarperCollins Dictionary of Religion*
  r J Ch St - v38 - Aut '96 - p904+ [251-500]
  r Rel St Rev - v22 - O '96 - p333 [251-500]
Smith, Julie - *The Kindness of Strangers*
  Arm Det - v29 - Fall '96 - p493+ [251-500]
  BWatch - v17 - N '96 - p10 [51-250]
  LATBR - Ag 11 '96 - p8 [251-500]
  Rapport - v19 - 6 '96 - p23 [51-250]
Smith, Karen Patricia - *African-American Voices in Young Adult Literature*
  LR - v45 - 4 '96 - p63+ [251-500]
Smith, Kathleen E - *Remembering Stalin's Victims*
  Choice - v34 - N '96 - p521 [51-250]
  Nat - v263 - S 23 '96 - p32+ [501+]
  VQR - v72 - Aut '96 - p133* [51-250]
Smith, Kathryn Schneider - *Fifty Years of Building Community*
  Pub Hist - v18 - Fall '96 - p181+ [501+]
Smith, Kathy - *Kathy Smith's Fitness Makeover*
  Quill & Q - v62 - S '96 - p24+ [501+]
  Kathy Smith's Walkfit for a Better Body
  Quill & Q - v62 - D '96 - p24+ [501+]
Smith, Keith - *Environmental Hazards. 2nd Ed.*
  SciTech - v20 - N '96 - p2 [51-250]
Smith, Kevin - *Conflict over Convoys*
  J Mil H - v61 - Ap '97 - p403+ [251-500]
Smith, Kurt - *Math Logic Puzzles*
  c Ch BWatch - v6 - My '96 - p1 [1-50]
  c Math T - v89 - O '96 - p608 [51-250]
Smith, L J - *Secret Vampire*
  y BL - v92 - Ag '96 - p1896 [51-250]
Smith, Lacey Baldwin - *Fools, Martyrs, Traitors*
  BL - v93 - My 15 '97 - p1544 [51-250]
  KR - v65 - Ap 1 '97 - p537 [251-500]
  PW - v244 - Ap 14 '97 - p69 [51-250]
Smith, Lane - *Disney's James and the Giant Peach (Illus. by Karey Kirkpatrick)*
  c HB Guide - v7 - Fall '96 - p252 [1-50]
Smith, Laurence D - *B.F. Skinner and Behaviorism in American Culture*
  Choice - v34 - F '97 - p1039 [51-250]
Smith, Laurie - *Gall/Stones*
  BIC - v26 - F '97 - p35 [251-500]
Smith, Lee - *The Christmas Letters*
  BL - v93 - S 1 '96 - p30 [51-250]
  BWatch - v17 - D '96 - p1 [51-250]
  Ent W - D 13 '96 - p75 [51-250]
  KR - v64 - Ag 15 '96 - p1183 [251-500]
  NYTBR - v101 - D 8 '96 - p102 [1-50]
  S Liv - v31 - N '96 - p48 [51-250]
  Fair and Tender Ladies
  Critiq - v38 - Win '97 - p135+ [501+]
  Saving Grace
  y EJ - v85 - S '96 - p108+ [501+]
  Rel St Rev - v22 - O '96 - p344+ [51-250]
Smith, Lendon H - *How to Raise a Healthy Child*
  LJ - v121 - O 1 '96 - p118 [51-250]
  PW - v243 - S 16 '96 - p80 [51-250]
Smith, Leonard H, Jr. - *Vital Records of the Towns of Barnstable and Sandwich*
  r EGH - v50 - N '96 - p171 [51-250]
Smith, Les W - *Confession in the Novel*
  Choice - v34 - Ja '97 - p788 [51-250]
Smith, Lesley - *Women, the Book and the Godly*
  CH - v65 - D '96 - p687+ [501+]
Smith, Leslie - *Critical Readings on Piaget*
  Adoles - v32 - Spr '97 - p248 [51-250]
Smith, Linda, 1949- - *Wind Shifter*
  y Can CL - v22 - Sum '96 - p94 [251-500]
Smith, Linda C - *Geographic Information Systems and Libraries*
  A Lib - v27 - Ag '96 - p70 [51-250]
  LRTS - v41 - Ja '97 - p67+ [501+]
  Technical Services Management 1965-1990
  LAR - v98 - S '96 - p479 [51-250]
  LRTS - v40 - Jl '96 - p289+ [501+]
  RQ - v35 - Sum '96 - p575+ [251-500]
Smith, Linda Wasmer - *Of Mind and Body*
  y Kliatt - v31 - My '97 - p29 [251-500]

Smith, Lindsay - *Victorian Photography, Painting, and Poetry*
    Nine-C Lit - v51 - D '96 - p427 [51-250]
Smith, Lois M - *Sex and Revolution*
    Choice - v34 - S '96 - p190 [51-250]
Smith, Louis P F - *Farm Organizations in Ireland*
    ILS - v16 - Spr '97 - p36 [1-50]
Smith, Lucy - *Grooming and Stable Management*
  c Bks Keeps - N '96 - p14+ [51-250]
  c Sch Lib - v44 - N '96 - p163 [51-250]
Smith, Maggie - *Interiors Management*
  r R&R Bk N - v12 - F '97 - p98 [51-250]
Smith, Malcolm - *Ronsard and Du Bellay versus Beze*
    Ren Q - v50 - Spr '97 - p252+ [501+]
Smith, Margaret - *Margy Misunderstood*
  y Can CL - v22 - Fall '96 - p119+ [501+]
Smith, Margaret, 1884- - *Rabi'a the Mystic and Her Fellow Saints*
    TLS - Ja 10 '97 - p24+ [501+]
Smith, Margaret Charles, 1906- - *Listen to Me Good*
    Choice - v34 - Ja '97 - p865 [51-250]
    LJ - v121 - N 1 '96 - p102 [51-250]
Smith, Marion E, Jr. - *Function and Technology of Anasazi Ceramics from Black Mesa, Arizona*
    Am Ant - v61 - Ap '96 - p440+ [501+]
Smith, Marisa - *Women Playwrights*
    BL - v93 - N 15 '96 - p566 [51-250]
Smith, Mark - *Religion in Industrial Society*
    EHR - v112 - F '97 - p221+ [501+]
    JMH - v69 - Mr '97 - p140+ [501+]
Smith, Mark, 1956- - *Collecting and Using Public Library Statistics*
    R&R Bk N - v12 - F '97 - p101 [51-250]
Smith, Mark C - *Social Science in the Crucible*
    AHR - v102 - F '97 - p207 [501+]
    JEH - v57 - Mr '97 - p253+ [501+]
Smith, Martin Cruz - *Rose*
    Comw - v123 - D 6 '96 - p23+ [51-250]
    PW - v244 - My 12 '97 - p74 [1-50]
Smith, Martin J - *Time Release*
    PW - v244 - Ja 27 '97 - p102 [51-250]
Smith, Matthew - *The Men Who Murdered Marilyn*
    Obs - D 22 '96 - p16* [501+]
Smith, Maye - *Maye and Faye's Building and Loan*
    KR - v64 - D 15 '96 - p1789 [251-500]
    LJ - v122 - Mr 15 '97 - p71 [51-250]
    PW - v243 - D 16 '96 - p49+ [51-250]
Smith, Michael - *After the Darkness*
  y Bks Keeps - N '96 - p11 [51-250]
  y JB - v60 - O '96 - p212+ [251-500]
  y Sch Lib - v44 - N '96 - p172 [51-250]
The Moral Problem
    RM - v50 - S '96 - p184+ [501+]
Smith, Michael, 1943- - *Sanctuary Stories*
    Choice - v34 - Ja '97 - p799 [51-250]
Smith, Michael, 1952, May, 5- - *New Cloak, Old Dagger*
    TLS - Ja 17 '97 - p27 [501+]
Smith, Michael A - *Jeremiah: Terrorist Prophet*
    BL - v93 - Ap 1 '97 - p1269 [51-250]
    KR - v65 - F 15 '97 - p252 [251-500]
    LJ - v122 - Ap 1 '97 - p131 [51-250]
    PW - v244 - Mr 31 '97 - p64 [51-250]
Smith, Michael E - *The Aztecs*
  y BL - v93 - N 15 '96 - p569 [51-250]
    LJ - v121 - N 1 '96 - p90 [51-250]
Smith, Michael Marshall - *Spares*
    KR - v65 - Mr 15 '97 - p413 [251-500]
    LJ - v122 - F 15 '97 - p164 [51-250]
    PW - v244 - Mr 3 '97 - p63 [51-250]
Smith, Michael P - *Jazz Fest Memories*
    PW - v244 - Ap 28 '97 - p68 [51-250]
Smith, Michael Peter - *The Bubbling Cauldron*
    APSR - v90 - D '96 - p867+ [501+]
    CS - v25 - N '96 - p748+ [501+]
Smith, Michelle - *Gold: A Triple Champion's Story*
    PW - v244 - F 24 '97 - p75 [51-250]
Smith, Mickey C - *Studies in Pharmaceutical Economics*
    R&R Bk N - v12 - F '97 - p42 [51-250]
Smith, Miranda - *Eyewitness Living Earth*
  y BL - v93 - Ap 1 '97 - p1308 [1-50]
  y Sch Lib - v44 - Ag '96 - p125 [51-250]
  c SLJ - v42 - O '96 - p140 [51-250]
  y VOYA - v19 - F '97 - p354 [251-500]
Smith, Mitchell - *Sacrifice*
    BL - v93 - Ja '97 - p822 [51-250]
    KR - v64 - N 1 '96 - p1561+ [51-250]
    LJ - v121 - D '96 - p148 [51-250]
Smith, Murray - *Killing Time*
    Woman's J - O '96 - p12 [1-50]
Smith, Murray E G - *Invisible Leviathan*
    Can Lit - Win '96 - p195+ [501+]

Smith, Myron J - *Cloak and Dagger Fiction. 3rd Ed.*
  r RQ - v36 - Win '96 - p219 [51-250]
Sea Fiction Guide
  r RQ - v36 - Win '96 - p225+ [51-250]
War Story Guide
  r RQ - v36 - Win '96 - p225 [51-250]
Smith, Nelson - *Wilkie Collins to the Forefront*
    Nine-C Lit - v50 - Mr '96 - p558 [1-50]
Smith, Nigel, 1947- - *Medieval Monarchs*
  y Sch Lib - v44 - Ag '96 - p123 [51-250]
Sports (Illus. by James Field)
  c HB Guide - v8 - Spr '97 - p146 [51-250]
Smith, Nigel, 1958- - *Literature and Revolution in England 1640-1660*
    EHR - v111 - N '96 - p1285+ [251-500]
    Ren Q - v49 - Win '96 - p886+ [501+]
    RES - v47 - Ag '96 - p415+ [501+]
    South HR - v31 - Win '97 - p80+ [501+]
Smith, Page - *Democracy on Trial*
    Amerasia J - v22 - 3 '96 - p177+ [501+]
    Bks & Cult - v2 - N '96 - p30+ [501+]
    Pac A - v69 - Sum '96 - p304+ [501+]
    PHR - v65 - Ag '96 - p498+ [251-500]
Smith, Pamela - *WomanGifts: Biblical Models for Forming Church*
    CLW - v66 - Je '96 - p35 [51-250]
Smith, Pamela H - *The Business of Alchemy*
    EHR - v111 - N '96 - p1286+ [501+]
Smith, Patricia R - *Modern Collector's Dolls*
  r Ant & CM - v101 - Ja '97 - p44 [1-50]
Smith, Patrick - *Japan: A Reinterpretation*
    BL - v93 - Ap 1 '97 - p1279 [51-250]
    Bus W - My 19 '97 - p18+ [501+]
    KR - v65 - Mr 1 '97 - p367+ [51-250]
    LJ - v122 - Ap 1 '97 - p111 [51-250]
    PW - v244 - F 24 '97 - p72 [51-250]
Smith, Patti - *The Coral Sea*
    Prog - v61 - Ja '97 - p37 [51-250]
Smith, Paul, 1937- - *Disraeli: A Brief Life*
    Choice - v34 - My '97 - p1559 [51-250]
    HT - v46 - O '96 - p57 [1-50]
    Lon R Bks - v19 - Ja 23 '97 - p22+ [501+]
    TLS - O 18 '96 - p30 [501+]
Smith, Paul, 1963- - *Feminism and the Third Republic*
    Choice - v34 - Mr '97 - p1223 [51-250]
    TLS - Ja 3 '97 - p32 [51-250]
Smith, Paul A - *Rhetoric and Redaction in Trito-Isaiah*
    Rel St Rev - v23 - Ja '97 - p59 [51-250]
Smith, Paul Chaat - *Like a Hurricane*
    Choice - v34 - F '97 - p1027 [51-250]
Smith, Paul F - *Clinical Psychopharmacology*
    Readings - v11 - S '96 - p29 [51-250]
    SB - v32 - Ag '96 - p170 [51-250]
Smith, Paul Hubert - *Letters of Delegates to Congress 1774-1789. Vol. 21*
    EHR - v111 - N '96 - p1298+ [501+]
Smith, Paul Julian, 1960- - *Desire Unlimited*
    FQ - v49 - Fall '95 - p42+ [501+]
Smith, Peter H - *Latin America in Comparative Perspective*
    HAHR - v77 - My '97 - p364+ [501+]
Talons of the Eagle
    Choice - v34 - O '96 - p358 [51-250]
    TLS - F 7 '97 - p31 [501+]
Smith, Peter J, 1935, May, 5- - *The History of American Art Education*
    R&R Bk N - v11 - D '96 - p57 [51-250]
Smith, Peter J, 1959- - *A Good Family*
    BL - v93 - S 1 '96 - p64 [51-250]
    NYTBR - v101 - S 29 '96 - p29 [501+]
Smith, Quentin - *Time, Change and Freedom*
    CPR - v16 - Ag '96 - p297+ [501+]
Smith, Ray - *A Night at the Opera*
    Essays CW - Spr '96 - p206+ [501+]
Smith, Raymond T - *The Matrifocal Family*
    Bl S - v26 - Fall '96 - p106 [1-50]
Smith, Richard Candida - *Utopia and Dissent*
    Am Q - v48 - D '96 - p708+ [501+]
    WHQ - v27 - Win '96 - p539 [501+]
Smith, Richard D - *Bluegrass: An Informal Guide*
    CAY - v16 - Fall '95 - p8 [51-250]
Smith, Richard Norton - *Patriarch: George Washington and the New American Nation*
    PW - v244 - Ja 27 '97 - p103 [1-50]
    Trib Bks - F 16 '97 - p8 [1-50]
Smith, Robert, 1965- - *Derrida and Autobiography*
    Biography - v19 - Fall '96 - p430 [1-50]
    MLR - v92 - Ap '97 - p419+ [501+]
    MLR - v92 - Ap '97 - p419+ [501+]

Smith, Robert Barr - *Daltons! The Raid on Coffeyville, Kansas*
    Rapport - v19 - 5 '96 - p42 [251-500]
Smith, Robert C - *The Wounded Jung*
    Choice - v34 - N '96 - p544 [51-250]
Smith, Robert Charles - *We Have No Leaders*
    APSR - v90 - D '96 - p867+ [501+]
    Choice - v34 - Ap '97 - p1407 [51-250]
    R&R Bk N - v11 - D '96 - p15 [51-250]
Smith, Robert Kimmel - *Chocolate Fever (Wilson). Audio Version*
  c SLJ - v43 - Mr '97 - p142 [51-250]
Smith, Robert McClure - *The Seductions of Emily Dickinson*
    Choice - v34 - O '96 - p282 [51-250]
Smith, Roger, 1945- - *The Fontana History of the Human Sciences*
  r New Sci - v154 - My 3 '97 - p49 [51-250]
Smith, Roger, 1953, Apr., 4- - *Popular Physics and Astronomy*
  r ARBA - v28 - '97 - p640 [51-250]
  r Astron - v25 - Ja '97 - p103 [51-250]
  r Choice - v34 - F '97 - p950 [51-250]
  r R&R Bk N - v12 - F '97 - p93 [51-250]
Smith, Roger P - *Gynecology in Primary Care*
    SciTech - v21 - Mr '97 - p62 [51-250]
Smith, Roland - *Jaguar*
  c BL - v93 - My 15 '97 - p1576 [51-250]
Journey of the Red Wolf (Illus. by Roland Smith)
  c HB Guide - v7 - Fall '96 - p346 [51-250]
  c SB - v32 - O '96 - p212 [51-250]
Thunder Cave
  c RT - v50 - Mr '97 - p480+ [51-250]
Smith, Ron F - *Editing Today*
    R&R Bk N - v11 - N '96 - p68 [51-250]
Smith, Ronald L - *Cosby: The Life of a Comedy Legend*
    BL - v93 - F 1 '97 - p919 [51-250]
Smith, Ronn - *Nothing but the Truth*
  y Kliatt - v31 - My '97 - p19 [51-250]
  y PW - v244 - Mr 17 '97 - p85 [51-250]
Smith, Rosamond - *Double Delight*
    BL - v93 - Mr 1 '97 - p1069 [51-250]
    KR - v65 - My 1 '97 - p673 [251-500]
    LJ - v122 - Mr 15 '97 - p92 [51-250]
    PW - v244 - Ap 21 '97 - p58 [51-250]
You Can't Catch Me
    Arm Det - v29 - Fall '96 - p504 [51-250]
Smith, Rowland - *Julian's Gods*
    TLS - S 20 '96 - p30 [501+]
Smith, Roy C - *Global Banking*
    Choice - v34 - Ap '97 - p1390 [51-250]
Smith, Ruth - *Handel's Oratorios and Eighteenth-Century Thought*
    Eight-C St - v30 - Win '96 - p199+ [501+]
    Notes - v53 - D '96 - p459+ [501+]
Smith, S W - *Landscape Irrigation*
    SciTech - v21 - Mr '97 - p70 [1-50]
Smith, Sally Bedell - *Reflected Glory*
    BL - v93 - D 15 '96 - p707 [51-250]
    BW - v26 - N 3 '96 - p1+ [501+]
    BW - v26 - D 8 '96 - p6 [51-250]
    Econ - v342 - Ja 4 '97 - p82 [251-500]
    KR - v64 - S 1 '96 - p1310 [251-500]
    LJ - v121 - O 1 '96 - p92 [51-250]
    Nat - v263 - N 25 '96 - p31+ [501+]
    Nat R - v49 - F 10 '97 - p55+ [501+]
    NYTBR - v101 - N 10 '96 - p7 [501+]
    NYTBR - v101 - D 8 '96 - p92 [1-50]
    PW - v243 - S 16 '96 - p57+ [51-250]
    Time - v148 - N 11 '96 - p95+ [501+]
    WSJ-MW - v78 - N 4 '96 - pA17 [501+]
Smith, Sanderson M - *Agnesi to Zeno*
    Math T - v89 - D '96 - p780 [251-500]
Smith, Sarah - *The Knowledge of Water*
    Arm Det - v30 - Win '97 - p100+ [251-500]
    BL - v92 - Ag '96 - p1888 [51-250]
    Ent W - S 27 '96 - p75 [51-250]
    LATBR - S 22 '96 - p8 [51-250]
    NYTBR - v101 - S 8 '96 - p26 [51-250]
    NYTBR - v101 - D 8 '96 - p94 [1-50]
    Rapport - v19 - 6 '96 - p22 [251-500]
Smith, Sheila - *Two Generation Programs for Families in Poverty*
    Fam Relat - v45 - O '96 - p477+ [501+]
Smith, Sherwood - *Crown Duel*
  y PW - v244 - Mr 10 '97 - p67 [51-250]
Smith, Simon C - *British Relations with the Malay Rulers from Decentralization to Malayan Independence 1930-1957*
    AHR - v102 - F '97 - p113+ [501+]
    Albion - v28 - '96 - p747+ [501+]

Smith, Stanley E - *The Sacred Rules of Management*
    BL - v93 - Mr 15 '97 - p1211 [51-250]
Smith, Stephanie A - *Conceived by Liberty*
    Nine-C Lit - v51 - S '96 - p238+ [501+]
Smith, Stephen - *The Land of Miracles*
    Econ - v342 - F 15 '97 - p12* [501+]
    NS - v126 - Ja 17 '97 - p46+ [501+]
    Obs - Ja 12 '97 - p16* [501+]
Smith, Steven B - *Spinoza, Liberalism, and the Question of Jewish Identity*
    Wil Q - v21 - Spr '97 - p103 [251-500]
Smith, Steven D - *Foreordained Failure*
    Bks & Cult - v1 - N '95 - p5+ [501+]
Smith, Steven E - *Roy Fuller: A Bibliography*
    r R&R Bk N - v12 - F '97 - p86 [51-250]
Smith, Susan L - *The Power of Women*
    RMR - v50 - 2 '96 - p208+ [501+]
Smith, Tara - *Moral Rights and Political Freedom*
    APSR - v90 - D '96 - p898+ [501+]
Smith, Taylor - *The Best of Enemies*
    PW - v244 - Ap 14 '97 - p71 [51-250]
Smith, Teresa - *Education Divides*
    TES - D 27 '96 - p16 [1-50]
Smith, Terry - *Accounting for Growth*
    Econ - v340 - S 14 '96 - p9* [51-250]
Smith, Tim - *Hi, I'm Bob and I'm the Parent of a Teenager*
    VOYA - v19 - F '97 - p318 [51-250]
Smith, Tom - *Easy Target*
    KR - v64 - Ag 15 '96 - p1223 [251-500]
    LJ - v121 - S 15 '96 - p80+ [51-250]
    PW - v243 - S 2 '96 - p105+ [51-250]
Smith, Tony - *America's Mission*
    AAPSS-A - v546 - Jl '96 - p157+ [501+]
    SSQ - v77 - Je '96 - p464+ [501+]
Smith, V Kerry - *Estimating Economic Values for Nature*
    JEL - v34 - D '96 - p2134+ [51-250]
Smith, Virginia Llewellyn - *Henry James and the Real Thing*
    Nine-C Lit - v50 - Mr '96 - p558+ [51-250]
    RES - v47 - Ag '96 - p461 [251-500]
Smith, Warner - *Covert Warrior*
    LJ - v122 - Ja '97 - p121+ [51-250]
    PW - v243 - O 14 '96 - p73 [51-250]
Smith, Warren W - *Tibetan Nation*
    Choice - v34 - My '97 - p1555 [51-250]
    KR - v65 - Ja 1 '97 - p49 [251-500]
    R&R Bk N - v12 - F '97 - p20 [51-250]
Smith, Wendy - *Bubblegum Bother*
    c TES - Jl 5 '96 - pR6 [1-50]
    Sweetapple Farm
    c Bks Keeps - Mr '97 - p19 [51-250]
Smith, Wesley J - *Forced Exit*
    KR - v65 - My 1 '97 - p706 [251-500]
    PW - v244 - Ap 28 '97 - p56 [51-250]
Smith, Wilbur - *Birds of Prey*
    LJ - v122 - My 1 '97 - p141 [51-250]
    PW - v244 - My 12 '97 - p55 [51-250]
Smith, William B - *Introduction to Theoretical Organic Chemistry and Molecular Modeling*
    Choice - v34 - Ja '97 - p823 [51-250]
    SciTech - v20 - S '96 - p17 [51-250]
Smith, William C - *Democracy, Markets, and Structural Reform in Latin America*
    HAHR - v76 - Ag '96 - p609+ [501+]
Smith, William Jay - *The Sun Is Up (Illus. by Jane Chambless Wright)*
    c HB Guide - v8 - Spr '97 - p151 [51-250]
    c SLJ - v42 - D '96 - p117+ [51-250]
Smith, William R, Jr. - *Exchange Rates and Prices*
    JEL - v34 - S '96 - p1434 [51-250]
Smith, William Robertson - *Lectures on the Religion of the Semites*
    Rel St Rev - v23 - Ja '97 - p55 [51-250]
Smith and Hawken - *The Book of Outdoor Gardening*
    r NYTBR - v101 - D 8 '96 - p42 [51-250]
Smith-Ayala, Emilie - *Clouds on the Mountain (Illus. by Alice Priestley)*
    c Sch Lib - v44 - N '96 - p148 [251-500]
    Marisol and the Yellow Messenger
    c Emerg Lib - v24 - Mr '97 - p47 [51-250]
Smithers, Peter - *Adventures of a Gardener*
    Hort - v74 - O '96 - p75+ [501+]
Smithin, John - *Macroeconomic Policy and the Future of Capitalism*
    Choice - v34 - F '97 - p1013 [51-250]
    JEL - v35 - Mr '97 - p210 [51-250]
Smith-Levin, Judith - *Do Not Go Gently*
    PW - v243 - S 30 '96 - p81 [51-250]
Smith-Moran, Barbara - *Soul at Work*
    PW - v243 - D 16 '96 - p54 [51-250]

Smithson, Isaiah - *English Studies/Culture Studies*
    AL - v68 - D '96 - p881+ [51-250]
    Can Lit - Win '96 - p165+ [501+]
Smithson, Robert - *Robert Smithson: The Collected Writings*
    Art J - v55 - Sum '96 - p95+ [501+]
The Smithsonian Book of the First Ladies
    y BL - v93 - Ap 1 '97 - p1305 [1-50]
    y HB Guide - v7 - Fall '96 - p376 [51-250]
    c LATBR - Jl 14 '96 - p11 [51-250]
Smithsonian Institution. Traveling Exhibition Service - *Mexico: A Landscape Revisited*
    y JOYS - v9 - Sum '96 - p417 [51-250]
Smits, Alexander J - *Turbulent Shear Layers in Supersonic Flow*
    SciTech - v20 - D '96 - p80 [51-250]
Smock, David R - *African Conflict Resolution*
    For Aff - v75 - N '96 - p170+ [51-250]
    Perspectives on Pacifism
    MEJ - v50 - Sum '96 - p456 [51-250]
Smock, Frederick - *This Meadow of Time*
    ABR - v18 - O '96 - p19 [501+]
Smocovitis, Vassiliki Betty - *Unifying Biology*
    Choice - v34 - My '97 - p1524 [51-250]
Smolak, Linda - *The Developmental Psychopathology of Eating Disorders*
    Readings - v11 - D '96 - p29 [51-250]
Smolan, Rick - *24 Hours in Cyberspace*
    y BL - v93 - F 1 '97 - p916 [51-250]
    BW - v26 - D 1 '96 - p3+ [501+]
    CSM - v89 - D 5 '96 - pB1+ [51-250]
    LJ - v121 - N 1 '96 - p100 [51-250]
    Mac - v109 - D 9 '96 - p66 [1-50]
    NYTBR - v102 - Ja 19 '97 - p25 [501+]
    PW - v243 - S 9 '96 - p69 [51-250]
    Quill & Q - v63 - F '97 - p28 [51-250]
    Passage to Vietnam. Electronic Media Version
    Trib Bks - F 2 '97 - p7 [51-250]
Smolen, James J - *Cased Hole and Production Log Evaluation*
    SciTech - v20 - N '96 - p78 [51-250]
Smolensky, Paul - *Mathematical Perspectives on Neural Networks*
    Choice - v34 - Ja '97 - p832+ [51-250]
Smoley, Lewis M - *Gustav Mahler's Symphonies*
    r R&R Bk N - v12 - F '97 - p70 [51-250]
Smolin, Lee - *The Life of the Cosmos*
    KR - v65 - Ap 1 '97 - p537+ [251-500]
    NH - v106 - Mr '97 - p13 [1-50]
Smoller, Laura Ackerman - *History, Prophecy, and the Stars*
    CH - v66 - Mr '97 - p104+ [501+]
    CHR - v82 - Jl '96 - p555+ [251-500]
    JR - v76 - O '96 - p655+ [501+]
Smoodin, Eric - *Animating Culture*
    JPC - v29 - Spr '96 - p253+ [251-500]
Smorkaloff, Pamela Maria - *If I Could Write This in Fire*
    Bl S - v26 - Sum '96 - p55+ [501+]
Smothers, Mary Ann - *Journey through Kurdistan*
    MEJ - v51 - Spr '97 - p311 [51-250]
Smrekar, Claire - *The Impact of School Choice and Community*
    AJE - v104 - Ag '96 - p323+ [501+]
    Choice - v34 - O '96 - p333+ [51-250]
    CS - v26 - Mr '97 - p208+ [51-250]
Smrtisthal. English - *In the Absence of God*
    TranslRevS - v1 - My '95 - p13 [51-250]
Smucker, Barbara Claassen - *Garth and the Mermaid*
    y Can CL - v22 - Sum '96 - p89+ [501+]
    Selina and the Bear Paw Quilt (Illus. by Janet Wilson)
    c HB Guide - v7 - Fall '96 - p277 [51-250]
    Underground to Canada
    c New Ad - v9 - Fall '96 - p297+ [501+]
Smucker, Donovan E - *The Origins of Walter Rauschenbusch's Social Ethics*
    JAAR - v64 - Sum '96 - p450+ [501+]
Smulders, Sharon - *Christina Rossetti Revisited*
    Choice - v34 - S '96 - p130 [51-250]
Smulyan, Susan - *Selling Radio*
    CS - v25 - S '96 - p689+ [501+]
Smyer, Michael - *Older Adults' Decision-Making and the Law*
    Readings - v11 - S '96 - p30 [51-250]
Smylie, James H - *A Brief History of the Presbyterians*
    BL - v93 - N 1 '96 - p462 [51-250]
Smyth, Alfred P - *King Alfred the Great*
    HRNB - v25 - Win '97 - p72 [251-500]
    HT - v46 - D '96 - p58 [501+]
    J Mil H - v61 - Ap '97 - p363+ [501+]

Smyth, Craig Hugh - *The Early Years of Art History in the United States*
    BM - v139 - Ja '97 - p50 [501+]
Smyth, Iain - *Pirate Plunder's Treasure Hunt (Illus. by Iain Smyth)*
    c KR - v64 - S 1 '96 - p1332 [51-250]
    c PW - v243 - S 23 '96 - p78 [51-250]
Smyth, K - *A Guide to Information Sources and Resources for Economic Development*
    r LAR - v98 - S '96 - p480 [51-250]
Smyth, W Franklin - *Analytical Chemistry of Complex Matrices*
    SciTech - v20 - S '96 - p16 [51-250]
Smythe, Anne - *Islands (Illus. by Laszlo Gal)*
    c BL - v93 - D 1 '96 - p669+ [51-250]
    c CBRS - v25 - Win '97 - p66 [51-250]
    c Ch BWatch - v6 - S '96 - p7 [1-50]
    c Ch BWatch - v6 - N '96 - p6 [51-250]
    c HMR - Win '96 - p40+ [501+]
Smythe, William Ellsworth - *The Conquest of Arid America. 1st Ed.*
    WAL - v31 - Fall '96 - p213+ [501+]
    The Conquest of Arid America. 2nd Ed.
    WAL - v31 - Fall '96 - p213+ [501+]
Snape, Charles - *Puzzles, Mazes and Numbers*
    c Cur R - v36 - Ap '97 - p13 [51-250]
Snape, Juliet - *The Great Book of Picture Puzzles*
    c Bks Keeps - v100 - S '96 - p9 [51-250]
Snape, Robert - *Leisure and the Public Library*
    LQ - v66 - O '96 - p485+ [501+]
    LR - v45 - 5 '96 - p71+ [501+]
Snapp, J Russell - *John Stuart and the Struggle for Empire on the Southern Frontier*
    Choice - v34 - Ja '97 - p865 [51-250]
    R&R Bk N - v11 - D '96 - p16 [51-250]
Snay, Mitchell - *Gospel of Disunion*
    CH - v65 - S '96 - p516+ [251-500]
Snead, Sam - *Golf Begins at Forty*
    LJ - v121 - O 1 '96 - p54 [1-50]
Snedden, Robert - *Energy*
    c HB Guide - v7 - Fall '96 - p331 [51-250]
    c SB - v32 - Ag '96 - p176+ [51-250]
    Life
    c HB Guide - v7 - Fall '96 - p339 [51-250]
    c SB - v32 - Ag '96 - p180 [51-250]
    Space
    c HB Guide - v7 - Fall '96 - p331 [51-250]
    c SB - v32 - N '96 - p239 [51-250]
    Time
    c HB Guide - v7 - Fall '96 - p331 [51-250]
    c SB - v32 - N '96 - p239 [51-250]
    Yuck! A Big Book of Little Horrors
    y BL - v93 - Ap 1 '97 - p1308 [1-50]
    c HB Guide - v7 - Fall '96 - p329 [51-250]
    c Learning - v25 - Mr '97 - p38 [1-50]
    c Sch Lib - v44 - N '96 - p165 [251-500]
    c TES - S 20 '96 - p16* [51-250]
Sneddon, Pamela Shires - *Brothers and Sisters*
    y KR - v65 - Mr 1 '97 - p388 [51-250]
Sneh, Ephraim - *Ba-Ahariyut*
    BL - v93 - Mr 1 '97 - p1115 [1-50]
Snell, Cudore L - *Young Men in the Street*
    Soc Ser R - v71 - Mr '97 - p167+ [1-50]
Snell, Gordon - *Lottie's Letter (Illus. by Peter Bailey)*
    c Bks Keeps - Mr '97 - p18 [51-250]
Snell, James G - *The Citizen's Wage*
    Choice - v34 - D '96 - p696+ [51-250]
    JEL - v34 - D '96 - p2101 [51-250]
Snell, Ned - *Navigating the Microsoft Network*
    BYTE - v22 - Ja '97 - p147 [51-250]
Snelling, Dennis - *The Pacific Coast League*
    r ARBA - v28 - '97 - p295 [51-250]
Snelling, Lauraine - *A New Day Rising*
    BL - v93 - Ja '97 - p819 [51-250]
    LJ - v121 - N 1 '96 - p54 [51-250]
Sneve, Virginia Driving Hawk - *The Apaches (Illus. by Ronald Himler)*
    c BL - v93 - Ap 1 '97 - p1332 [51-250]
    The Cherokees (Illus. by Ronald Himler)
    c HB Guide - v7 - Fall '96 - p391 [51-250]
    The Cheyennes (Illus. by Ronald Himler)
    c HB Guide - v8 - Spr '97 - p178 [51-250]
    c KR - v64 - S 15 '96 - p1411 [51-250]
    c SLJ - v43 - F '97 - p98 [51-250]
    Completing the Circle
    CAY - v16 - Fall '95 - p8 [51-250]
    When Thunders Spoke
    y CAY - v16 - Fall '95 - p13 [51-250]
Snider, Don M - *U.S. Civil-Military Relations*
    APSR - v90 - S '96 - p706+ [501+]

Snider, Jerry - *A Magical Universe*
    PW - v244 - F 24 '97 - p81 [1-50]
Sniderman, Paul M - *The Clash of Rights*
    Choice - v34 - Ap '97 - p1416 [51-250]
    TLS - Ap 11 '97 - p8+ [501+]
Snoddy, Raymond - *Greenfinger: The Rise of Michael Green and Carlton Communications*
    Obs - v54 - O 13 '96 - p16* [501+]
Snodgrass, Chris - *Aubrey Beardsley: Dandy of the Grotesque*
    Critm - v38 - Sum '96 - p482+ [501+]
    ELT - v39 - 4 '96 - p474+ [501+]
Snodgrass, Jon - *Follow Your Career Star*
    J Car P&E - v57 - Win '97 - p15 [51-250]
Snodgrass, Mary Ellen - *Encyclopedia of Satirical Literature*
    yr ARBA - v28 - '97 - p411 [51-250]
Snodgrass, W D - *The Fuehrer Bunker*
    Agenda - v34 - Spr '96 - p112+ [501+]
    In Radical Pursuit
    Agenda - v34 - Spr '96 - p121+ [501+]
Snodin, Michael - *Ornament: A Social History since 1450*
    Choice - v34 - S '96 - p115+ [51-250]
Snooks, Graeme Donald - *The Dynamic Society*
    Choice - v34 - D '96 - p660 [51-250]
Snow, Alan - *The Truth about Cats (Illus. by Alan Snow)*
    c HB Guide - v7 - Fall '96 - p277 [51-250]
    c NYTBR - v101 - S 22 '96 - p28 [1-50]
Snow, Dale E - *Schelling and the End of Idealism*
    Choice - v34 - O '96 - p295 [51-250]
    R&R Bk N - v12 - F '97 - p3 [51-250]
Snow, Dean R - *The Iroquois*
    Can Hist R - v78 - Mr '97 - p164+ [251-500]
Snow, Donald M - *Beyond the Water's Edge*
    Choice - v34 - Mr '97 - p1236 [51-250]
Snow, Edgar - *Red Star Over China*
    FEER - Anniv '96 - p222 [501+]
Snow, Hank - *The Hank Snow Story*
    LJ - v121 - N 1 '96 - p42 [1-50]
Snow, Jack - *Spectral Snow*
    Necro - Fall '96 - p27+ [51-250]
Snow, Jonathan - *The Most Beautiful Christmas*
    PW - v243 - S 16 '96 - p68 [51-250]
    The Most Beautiful Gift (Wood). Audio Version
    BWatch - v17 - D '96 - p11 [1-50]
Snow, Nancy E - *In the Company of Others*
    Choice - v34 - Ja '97 - p809 [51-250]
    Hast Cen R - v26 - Jl '96 - p42 [1-50]
Snow, Pegeen - *Eat Your Peas, Louise*
    c New Ad - v9 - Fall '96 - p309+ [501+]
Snowden, Frank M - *Naples in the Time of Cholera 1884-1911*
    Choice - v34 - O '96 - p314 [51-250]
    TLS - Jl 19 '96 - p36 [501+]
Snowdon, Anthony Armstrong-Jones, Earl of - *Snowdon on Stage*
    Obs - F 2 '97 - p16* [51-250]
Snowling, Margaret - *Dyslexia, Speech and Language*
    r R&R Bk N - v11 - D '96 - p53 [51-250]
Snyder, Charles W - *Liberty and Morality*
    Albion - v28 - Fall '96 - p509+ [501+]
Snyder, Don J - *The Cliff Walk*
    KR - v65 - F 15 '97 - p286+ [251-500]
    LJ - v122 - My 1 '97 - p116 [51-250]
    PW - v244 - F 17 '97 - p200 [51-250]
Snyder, Douglas M - *The Mind and the Physical World*
    Choice - v34 - F '97 - p982 [51-250]
Snyder, Gary - *Mountains and Rivers without End*
    y BL - v93 - S 15 '96 - p205+ [51-250]
    LJ - v122 - Ap 1 '97 - p95 [1-50]
    New R - v216 - Mr 24 '97 - p38+ [501+]
    Parabola - v22 - F '97 - p100+ [251-500]
    PW - v243 - N 4 '96 - p47 [1-50]
    Tric - v6 - Spr '97 - p101+ [501+]
    Utne R - Mr '97 - p80+ [501+]
    No Nature
    LJ - v122 - Ap 1 '97 - p95 [1-50]
    A Place in Space
    Env - v38 - D '96 - p25 [51-250]
    Ken R - v18 - Sum '96 - p206+ [501+]
    New R - v216 - Mr 24 '97 - p38+ [501+]
    TLS - F 21 '97 - p12 [501+]
Snyder, Ilana - *Hypertext: The Electronic Labyrinth*
    Aust Bk R - S '96 - p18+ [501+]
Snyder, Jed C - *After Empire*
    MEJ - v50 - Sum '96 - p451 [51-250]
Snyder, Lawrence D - *German Poetry in Song*
    r ARBA - v28 - '97 - p472+ [251-500]
Snyder, Margaret - *Transforming Development*
    JEL - v35 - Mr '97 - p274 [51-250]

Snyder, Margaret C, 1929- - *African Women and Development*
    Wom R Bks - v14 - Ja '97 - p19+ [501+]
Snyder, Solomon H - *Drugs and the Brain*
    LJ - v121 - O 1 '96 - p132 [1-50]
Snyder, Tim - *Easy-to-Build Shelving and Storage*
    LJ - v121 - S 15 '96 - p92 [51-250]
Snyder, Zilpha Keatley - *The Gypsy Game*
    c BL - v93 - F 1 '97 - p942 [51-250]
    c CCB-B - v50 - F '97 - p223 [51-250]
    c HB - v73 - Mr '97 - p204 [51-250]
    c KR - v64 - N 15 '96 - p1675+ [51-250]
    c PW - v244 - Ja 20 '97 - p402+ [51-250]
    c SLJ - v43 - F '97 - p106 [51-250]
    The Trespassers
    y Ch BWatch - v7 - F '97 - p5+ [1-50]
Snyder-Grenier, Ellen M - *Brooklyn! An Illustrated History*
    Am - v175 - S 21 '96 - p36 [51-250]
    LATBR - Ag 25 '96 - p10 [51-250]
    LJ - v121 - O 1 '96 - p100 [51-250]
Snyderman, Nancy - *Dr. Nancy Snyderman's Guide to Good Health*
    PW - v243 - O 21 '96 - p78 [1-50]
So, Alvin Y - *East Asia and the World Economy*
    CS - v26 - Mr '97 - p187+ [501+]
Soane, John V N - *Fashionable Resort Regions*
    GJ - v162 - Jl '96 - p230 [251-500]
Soards, Marion L - *Scripture and Homosexuality*
    TT - v53 - Ja '97 - p508+ [501+]
Soares, Jo - *O Xango De Baker Street*
    WLT - v70 - Aut '96 - p941+ [501+]
Sobel, Brian M - *The Fighting Pattons*
    LJ - v122 - Ap 1 '97 - p102 [51-250]
    PW - v244 - Mr 17 '97 - p70 [251-500]
Sobel, Burton E - *Medical Management of Heart Disease*
    SciTech - v20 - S '96 - p35 [51-250]
Sobel, Dava - *Longitude: The True Story of a Lone Genius Who Solved the Greatest Scientific Problem of His Time*
    Beav - v76 - Ag '96 - p44 [501+]
    BL - v93 - Ap 1 '97 - p1286 [1-50]
    Econ - v341 - O 19 '96 - p13* [251-500]
    LATBR - O 13 '96 - p15 [51-250]
    Lon R Bks - v18 - O 31 '96 - p11+ [501+]
    Nature - v385 - Ja 23 '97 - p309+ [501+]
    NWCR - v49 - Aut '96 - p160+ [501+]
    NYTBR - v101 - O 20 '96 - p36 [1-50]
    Obs - Ag 18 '96 - p17* [501+]
    Obs - D 1 '96 - p16* [51-250]
    PW - v243 - S 9 '96 - p81 [1-50]
    SE - v60 - S '96 - p316 [251-500]
    Spec - v277 - N 23 '96 - p43 [1-50]
    y SLJ - v42 - D '96 - p33 [1-50]
    TES - D 27 '96 - p16 [1-50]
    TLS - O 11 '96 - p34 [501+]
    Longitude: The True Story of a Lone Genius Who Solved the Greatest Scientific Problem of His Time (Rintoul). Audio Version
    New Sci - v152 - D 21 '96 - p72 [1-50]
Sobel, Dean - *Anna and Bernhard Blume*
    Afterimage - v24 - S '96 - p12 [501+]
Sobelman, 'Annah - *The Tulip Sacrament*
    Ken R - v18 - Sum '96 - p191+ [501+]
    South R - v33 - Win '97 - p136+ [501+]
Sober, Elliott - *From a Biological Point of View*
    J Phil - v94 - Mr '97 - p160+ [501+]
Sobey, Ed - *Wrapper Rockets and Trombone Straws*
    c BL - v93 - Mr 1 '97 - p1159 [51-250]
Sobieszek, Robert A - *Ports of Entry*
    LJ - v121 - O 1 '96 - p76 [51-250]
Soble, Alan - *Sexual Investigations*
    Choice - v34 - Mr '97 - p1246+ [51-250]
    R&R Bk N - v11 - D '96 - p39 [51-250]
Sobo, Elisa J - *Choosing Unsafe Sex*
    CS - v26 - Ja '97 - p112+ [501+]
Sobol, Donald J - *Encyclopedia Brown and the Case of Pablo's Nose (Illus. by Eric Velasquez)*
    c BL - v93 - Ja '97 - p862 [251-500]
    c HB Guide - v8 - Spr '97 - p75 [51-250]
    c SLJ - v42 - N '96 - p110 [51-250]
Sobol, Richard - *Mayor: In the Company of Norman Rice, Mayor of Seattle*
    c HB Guide - v7 - Fall '96 - p315 [51-250]
Sobosan, Jeffrey G - *The Turn of the Millennium*
    CC - v113 - N 6 '96 - p1093 [51-250]
Sobran, Joseph - *Alias Shakespeare*
    PW - v244 - Mr 17 '97 - p66 [51-250]
    WSJ-Cent - v99 - My 1 '97 - pA16 [501+]
Sobrino, Jon - *The Principle of Mercy*
    TT - v53 - Ja '97 - p556+ [501+]

    Systematic Theology
    Rel St Rev - v23 - Ap '97 - p153+ [51-250]
Socarides, Charles W - *Work and Its Inhibitions*
    R&R Bk N - v12 - F '97 - p6 [51-250]
Social Indicators of Development 1996
    r JEL - v35 - Mr '97 - p275 [51-250]
Social Science Index 1974-
    r ASInt - v34 - O '96 - p20 [1-50]
Social Sciences Citation Index 1979-
    r ASInt - v34 - O '96 - p18 [1-50]
Social Trends 1970-1995. Electronic Media Version
    r J Gov Info - v23 - S '96 - p647 [51-250]
    r LAR - v99 - Mr '97 - p160 [51-250]
Social Watch
    p WorldV - v12 - O '96 - p12 [51-250]
Societat Catalana D'Economia. Vol. 12
    JEL - v35 - Mr '97 - p294 [51-250]
Society for Experimental Mechanics (U.S.) - *Handbook of Measurement of Residual Stresses*
    Choice - v34 - D '96 - p642 [51-250]
Society for Storytelling - *Directory of Storytellers*
    r LR - v45 - 4 '96 - p71+ [501+]
Socio-Economic Statistical Profiles of British Columbia Regions. 3rd Ed.
    r J Gov Info - v23 - S '96 - p627 [51-250]
Sockin, Brian Scott - *Treasury of Children's Folklore*
    c CAY - v17 - Fall '96 - p7 [51-250]
Socolow, R - *Industrial Ecology and Global Change*
    BioSci - v46 - O '96 - p701+ [501+]
Sodaro, Craig - *Ghost at the Globe*
    c SLJ - v42 - D '96 - p124 [51-250]
Soder, Roger - *Democracy, Education, and the Schools*
    APSR - v90 - S '96 - p660+ [501+]
    EL - v54 - S '96 - p87 [251-500]
Soderberg, Susan Cooke - *Lest We Forget*
    Historian - v58 - Sum '96 - p874 [251-500]
Sodergran, Edith - *Violet Twilights*
    TranslRevS - v1 - My '95 - p33 [1-50]
    TranslRevS - v9 - F '96 - p33 [51-250]
Soderholm, James - *Fantasy, Forgery, and the Byron Legend*
    TLS - D 6 '96 - p24 [51-250]
Soebers, Tobin - *Cold War Criticism and the Politics of Skepticism*
    Col Lit - v23 - Je '96 - p171+ [501+]
Soelle, Dorothee - *Theology for Skeptics*
    JR - v77 - Ap '97 - p313+ [501+]
    TT - v53 - Ja '97 - p563 [51-250]
Soendergaard, Henrik - *DR I TV-Konkurrencens Tidsalder*
    JC - v47 - Win '97 - p120+ [501+]
Sofer, Barbara - *Shalom, Haver*
    c BL - v92 - Ag '96 - p1905 [51-250]
    The Thirteenth Hour
    Arm Det - v30 - Win '97 - p116+ [501+]
    BL - v93 - O 1 '96 - p323 [51-250]
    BW - v27 - F 16 '97 - p4 [51-250]
    KR - v64 - S 1 '96 - p1264 [251-500]
    NYTBR - v102 - F 2 '97 - p22 [51-250]
    PW - v243 - O 7 '96 - p62 [251-500]
Sofer, Morry - *Guide for Translators*
    r RQ - v36 - Fall '96 - p129+ [501+]
    The Translator's Handbook
    r BL - v93 - O 1 '96 - p367 [1-50]
Soffer, Gail - *Husserl and the Question of Relativism*
    RM - v50 - S '96 - p185+ [501+]
Sofsky, Wolfgang - *The Order of Terror*
    AB - v99 - Mr 24 '97 - p964+ [501+]
    BL - v93 - N 15 '96 - p569 [51-250]
    KR - v64 - O 15 '96 - p1520 [251-500]
    LJ - v121 - D '96 - p119 [51-250]
    PW - v243 - N 4 '96 - p55 [51-250]
Softic, Elma - *Sarajevo Days, Sarajevo Nights*
    BIC - v25 - N '96 - p25+ [501+]
    BW - v26 - N 17 '96 - p5 [51-250]
    CSM - v88 - O 9 '96 - p13 [251-500]
    LJ - v121 - S 15 '96 - p82 [51-250]
    PW - v243 - S 9 '96 - p78 [51-250]
The Software Encyclopedia 1996. Vols. 1-2
    r SciTech - v20 - N '96 - p10 [51-250]
Sogrin, Vladimir V - *Politicheskaia Istoriia Sovremennoi Rossii 1985-1994*
    Slav R - v55 - Fall '96 - p694+ [501+]
Sohn, Mark F - *Mountain Country Cooking*
    LJ - v122 - F 15 '97 - p158 [51-250]
Sohn, Ned - *The Cost Management Redbook for Employee Relocation Home Sale Real Estate Transactions*
    HR Mag - v42 - Ja '97 - p148+ [51-250]
Soho Square Seven
    Obs - N 24 '96 - p17* [501+]

Soitos, Stephen F - *The Blues Detective*
    AL - v68 - D '96 - p873+ [501+]
    Bl S - v26 - Sum '96 - p67 [1-50]
    Choice - v34 - S '96 - p130 [51-250]
Sokol, B J - *Art and Illusion in The Winter's Tale*
    Shakes Q - v47 - Fall '96 - p352+ [501+]
Sokolow, Anna - *Ballade*
    Dance RJ - v28 - Fall '96 - p95+ [501+]
Sokolowski, Robert - *The God of Faith and Reason*
    CLW - v67 - D '96 - p40+ [251-500]
Sola, Michele - *Angela Weaves a Dream (Illus. by Jeffrey J Foxx)*
    c Trib Bks - Ap 13 '97 - p7 [51-250]
Solan, Lawrence M - *The Language of Judges*
    JC - v47 - Win '97 - p128+ [501+]
Solans, Conxita - *Industrial Applications of Microemulsions*
    SciTech - v21 - Mr '97 - p95 [51-250]
Solar Engineering 96
    SciTech - v20 - S '96 - p53 [51-250]
Solari, Hernan G - *Nonlinear Dynamics*
    SciTech - v21 - Mr '97 - p20 [51-250]
Soldatow, Sasha - *Jump Cuts*
    Aust Bk R - Ag '96 - p43+ [501+]
Sole, Robert - *La Mamelouka*
    TLS - N 29 '96 - p15 [51-250]
Soled, Debra E - *China: A Nation in Transition*
    Ch Rev Int - v3 - Fall '96 - p535+ [501+]
Soley, Lawrence C - *Leasing the Ivory Tower*
    QJS - v82 - N '96 - p402+ [501+]
A Solid Investment
    J Gov Info - v23 - S '96 - p559 [51-250]
Solin, Sabrina - *The Seventeen Guide to Sex and Your Body*
    y BL - v93 - O 1 '96 - p332 [51-250]
    y BL - v93 - Ap 1 '97 - p1308 [1-50]
    y CBRS - v25 - N '96 - p36 [1-50]
    c CCB-B - v50 - Ja '97 - p185+ [51-250]
    y HB Guide - v8 - Spr '97 - p90 [51-250]
    y Kliatt - v31 - Ja '97 - p22 [51-250]
    y KR - v64 - Ag 15 '96 - p1243 [51-250]
    y SLJ - v42 - N '96 - p130 [51-250]
Solingen, Etel - *Industrial Policy, Technology, and International Bargaining*
    JEL - v35 - Mr '97 - p252+ [51-250]
Solkin, David H - *Painting for Money*
    JEL - v34 - S '96 - p1468+ [51-250]
Sollamo, Raija - *Repetition of the Possessive Pronouns in the Septuagint*
    Rel St Rev - v23 - Ja '97 - p56+ [51-250]
Solle, Dorothee - *Creative Disobedience*
    JR - v77 - Ap '97 - p313+ [501+]
    Great Women of the Bible in Art and Literature
    Rel St Rev - v23 - Ap '97 - p161 [51-250]
Sollors, Werner - *The Return of Thematic Criticism*
    r Can Lit - Win '96 - p193+ [501+]
Solnit, Rebecca - *A Book of Migrations*
    KR - v65 - Ap 1 '97 - p538 [251-500]
    LJ - v122 - Ap 15 '97 - p105 [51-250]
    PW - v244 - Mr 10 '97 - p54 [51-250]
Solomita, Stephen - *Damaged Goods (Murdock). Audio Version*
    BL - v93 - N 1 '96 - p522 [51-250]
    y Kliatt - v31 - Ja '97 - p38 [51-250]
Solomon, Charles - *The Disney That Never Was*
    TLS - N 15 '96 - p21 [501+]
Solomon, Clara - *The Civil War Diary of Clara Solomon*
    HRNB - v25 - Fall '96 - p8+ [501+]
    JSH - v62 - N '96 - p814+ [251-500]
Solomon, David A - *Windows NT for Open VMS Professionals*
    SciTech - v20 - D '96 - p12 [51-250]
Solomon, Deborah - *Utopia Parkway*
    BL - v93 - F 15 '97 - p991 [51-250]
    KR - v64 - D 15 '96 - p1789+ [251-500]
    LJ - v122 - F 1 '97 - p78 [51-250]
    NYTBR - v102 - Mr 23 '97 - p11+ [501+]
    NYTLa - v146 - Mr 18 '97 - pC17 [501+]
    PW - v244 - Ja 13 '97 - p60 [51-250]
    Trib Bks - Mr 23 '97 - p1+ [501+]
    WSJ-Cent - v99 - Mr 19 '97 - pA16 [501+]
Solomon, Harry M - *The Rise of Robert Dodsley*
    r Choice - v34 - N '96 - p442 [51-250]
    TLS - F 14 '97 - p33 [501+]
Solomon, Jon - *Apollo: Origins and Influences*
    CAY - v16 - Fall '95 - p9 [51-250]
Solomon, Julie - *Proust: Lecture Du Narrataire*
    MLR - v91 - Jl '96 - p737+ [501+]
Solomon, Maynard - *Mozart: A Life*
    CR - v269 - O '96 - p222+ [51-250]
    Notes - v53 - Mr '97 - p761+ [501+]

Solomon, Norman - *Judaism: A Very Short Introduction*
    MEJ - v51 - Spr '97 - p313 [51-250]
Solomon, Robert - *The Transformation of the World Economy 1980-93*
    Econ J - v106 - S '96 - p1479+ [51-250]
    JEL - v34 - S '96 - p1395+ [501+]
Solomon, Robert C - *A Passion for Justice*
    Ethics - v107 - Ja '97 - p388 [51-250]
    A Passion for Wisdom
    y BL - v93 - Mr 15 '97 - p1207 [51-250]
    LJ - v122 - Ap 1 '97 - p97 [51-250]
    PW - v244 - Mr 24 '97 - p72 [51-250]
Solomon, Sandy - *Pears, Lake, Sun*
    Econ - v342 - Mr 29 '97 - p93 [51-250]
Solomon, Steven - *The Confidence Game*
    CS - v25 - S '96 - p603+ [501+]
Solomons, T W Graham - *Fundamentals of Organic Chemistry. 5th Ed.*
    SciTech - v20 - D '96 - p27 [51-250]
    Organic Chemistry. 6th Ed.
    J Chem Ed - v73 - D '96 - pA313 [501+]
Solomos, John - *Racism and Society*
    Choice - v34 - D '96 - p697 [51-250]
Solomou, Solomos - *Themes in Macroeconomic History*
    JEL - v35 - Mr '97 - p260 [51-250]
Solorzano, Carlos Jose - *Nosotros, Los Nicaraguenses*
    BL - v93 - S 15 '96 - p227 [1-50]
Solotareff, Gregoire - *Father Christmas (Illus. by Gregoire Solotareff)*
    c JB - v60 - D '96 - p260+ [51-250]
    The Secret Life of Santa Claus
    NYTBR - v101 - D 22 '96 - p14 [51-250]
Soloviev, Sergei M - *History of Russia. Vol. 10*
    Six Ct J - v27 - Win '96 - p1082+ [501+]
Solovyov, Vladimir - *Zhirnovsky: Russian Fascism and the Making of a Dictator*
    PSQ - v111 - Fall '96 - p550+ [501+]
Solow, Herbert F - *Inside Star Trek*
    KR - v64 - My 1 '96 - p677 [251-500]
    SF Chr - v18 - O '96 - p82 [1-50]
    Inside Star Trek (Solow). Audio Version
    Kliatt - v30 - N '96 - p49 [51-250]
Solso, Robert L - *The Science of the Mind*
    A J Psy - v109 - Win '96 - p649+ [501+]
    Readings - v11 - S '96 - p26 [51-250]
Solterer, Helen - *The Master and Minerva*
    AHR - v101 - O '96 - p1193+ [501+]
Solwitz, Sharon - *Blood and Milk*
    BL - v93 - My 1 '97 - p1479 [251-500]
    KR - v65 - Mr 15 '97 - p414 [251-500]
    LJ - v122 - Ap 15 '97 - p122 [51-250]
    PW - v244 - Ap 28 '97 - p48 [51-250]
Soly, Hugh - *Minderheden In Westeuropese Steden 16de-20ste Eeuw*
    JEH - v56 - S '96 - p718+ [501+]
Solzhenitsyn, Aleksandr Isaevich - *Invisible Allies*
    Am - v175 - N 16 '96 - p22+ [501+]
    Bks & Cult - v2 - Jl '96 - p6+ [501+]
    Obs - F 9 '97 - p18* [51-250]
    PW - v244 - Ap 21 '97 - p69 [1-50]
    PW - v244 - Ap 21 '97 - p69 [1-50]
    The Russian Question
    Bks & Cult - v2 - Jl '96 - p6+ [501+]
Somakian, Manoug J - *Empires in Conflict*
    HT - v47 - Ja '97 - p59 [501+]
    MEJ - v50 - Aut '96 - p596+ [501+]
Somekh, Bridget - *Using Information Technology Effectively in Teaching and Learning*
    TES - Mr 14 '97 - p39U [501+]
Somer, Mesa - *Night of the Five Aunties (Illus. by Kate Salley Palmer)*
    c HB Guide - v7 - Fall '96 - p277 [51-250]
Someren, Ayten - *Differential Diagnosis in Pathology*
    SciTech - v21 - Mr '97 - p69 [51-250]
Somers, Suzanne - *Suzanne Somers' Eat Great, Lose Weight*
    BL - v93 - D 1 '96 - p636 [51-250]
    LJ - v121 - D '96 - p134 [51-250]
    PW - v244 - Ja 6 '97 - p71 [51-250]
Somersall, Alan - *A Passion for Living*
    Rapport - v19 - 4 '96 - p43+ [501+]
Somerset, Anne - *Unnatural Murder*
    Books - v11 - Ap '97 - p20 [51-250]
    Spec - v278 - F 1 '97 - p35+ [501+]
    TLS - F 7 '97 - p33 [501+]
Somerset, J Alan B - *Records of Early English Drama: Shropshire. Vols. 1-2*
    MLR - v92 - Ap '97 - p438+ [501+]
    Specu - v72 - Ja '97 - p223+ [501+]

Somerset Fry, Plantagenet - *Castles of Britain and Ireland*
    HT - v46 - O '96 - p56 [1-50]
Somerville, Alexander - *Letters from Ireland during the Famine of 1847*
    VS - v39 - Win '96 - p205+ [501+]
Somerville, Louisa - *Animals in Art*
    c HB Guide - v8 - Spr '97 - p137 [51-250]
    c SLJ - v43 - Ja '97 - p130 [51-250]
Somerville, Richard - *The Forgiving Air*
    Choice - v34 - N '96 - p497 [51-250]
    For Aff - v75 - S '96 - p140 [51-250]
    y SB - v32 - Ag '96 - p172 [51-250]
    SciTech - v20 - S '96 - p15 [51-250]
Something about the Author. Vols. 81-85
    yr ARBA - v28 - '97 - p425 [51-250]
Somfai, Laszlo - *Bela Bartok: Composition, Concepts, and Autograph Sources*
    Choice - v34 - S '96 - p138 [51-250]
Somin, Ilya - *Stillborn Crusade*
    Choice - v34 - F '97 - p1020+ [51-250]
Sommer, Gerald - *Vom Sinn Aller Metaphorie Zur Funktion Komplexer Bildgestaltungen In Heimito Von Doderers Roman Die Strudlhofstiege*
    Ger Q - v69 - Spr '96 - p220+ [501+]
Sommerfelt, Aimee, 1892- - *Miriam*
    c New Ad - v9 - Fall '96 - p297+ [501+]
Sommerhoff, Gerd - *In and Out of Consciousness*
    New Sci - v153 - Ja 18 '97 - p38 [51-250]
Sommer-Mathis, Andrea - *Tu Felix Austria Nube*
    Notes - v53 - D '96 - p463+ [501+]
Sommers, Christina Hoff - *Who Stole Feminism?*
    Dialogue - v35 - Spr '96 - p327+ [501+]
Sommers, Laurie Kay - *Fiesta, Fe, Y Cultura*
    Am Ethnol - v23 - N '96 - p931+ [501+]
Sommers, Marilyn Sawyer - *Davis's Manual of Nursing Therapeutics for Diseases and Disorders*
    SciTech - v21 - Mr '97 - p69 [51-250]
Sommerville, C John - *The News Revolution in England*
    TLS - F 21 '97 - p26 [501+]
Somtow, S P - *Riverrun Trilogy*
    Sm Pr R - v29 - Ja '97 - p10 [51-250]
    Vanitas
    Rapport - v19 - 4 '96 - p27 [251-500]
Sonbol, Amira El Azhary - *Women, the Family, and Divorce Laws in Islamic History*
    MEJ - v50 - Aut '96 - p632 [51-250]
Sonder, Ben - *Gangs*
    y BL - v92 - Ag '96 - p1892 [51-250]
    y HB Guide - v7 - Fall '96 - p316 [51-250]
    y SLJ - v42 - Ag '96 - p168+ [51-250]
Sondhaus, Lawrence - *The Naval Policy of Austria-Hungary 1867-1918*
    EHR - v111 - S '96 - p1010+ [501+]
Sonenklar, Carol - *Bug Boy (Illus. by Betsy Lewin)*
    c BL - v93 - Ap 1 '97 - p1334 [51-250]
    c CCB-B - v50 - My '97 - p335 [51-250]
    c KR - v65 - Mr 1 '97 - p388 [51-250]
Sonenshein, Raphael - *Politics in Black and White*
    JEL - v35 - Mr '97 - p306 [51-250]
    PHR - v66 - F '97 - p99+ [501+]
Song, Cathy - *School Figures*
    South HR - v30 - Sum '96 - p297+ [501+]
Song Ni Qi Zhi Huo Wang Ba
    BL - v93 - My 1 '97 - p1484 [1-50]
Song Writer's Market 1997
    r CAY - v17 - Win '96 - p6 [51-250]
Sonn, Tamara - *Interpreting Islam*
    Choice - v34 - My '97 - p1517 [51-250]
Sonnenstuhl, William J - *Working Sober*
    CS - v26 - Mr '97 - p249+ [501+]
    JEL - v34 - S '96 - p1447 [51-250]
    Per Psy - v50 - Spr '97 - p193+ [501+]
Sonnert, Gerhard - *Gender Differences in Science Careers*
    CS - v25 - S '96 - p678+ [501+]
    Who Succeeds in Science?
    BioSci - v46 - D '96 - p874+ [501+]
    CS - v25 - S '96 - p678+ [501+]
Sonnevi, Goran - *A Child Is Not a Knife*
    TranslRevS - v1 - My '95 - p33 [51-250]
Sonora Review
    p Sm Pr R - v29 - Ja '97 - p19 [51-250]
    p Sm Pr R - v29 - F '97 - p23 [51-250]
Sontag, Frederick - *Wittgenstein and the Mystical*
    IPQ - v36 - S '96 - p377+ [501+]
    Rel St - v32 - D '96 - p531 [251-500]
    RM - v50 - S '96 - p188+ [501+]
Son Tung - *Bay Thu Nho*
    BL - v93 - S 1 '96 - p70 [51-250]

Sony Lab'ou Tansi - *Le Commencement Des Douleurs*
    WLT - v70 - Aut '96 - p1011+ [501+]
Soos, Troy - *Hunting a Detroit Tiger*
    KR - v65 - F 15 '97 - p259 [51-250]
    PW - v244 - Mr 24 '97 - p63 [51-250]
    Murder at Fenway Park
    Aethlon - v13 - Fall '95 - p140+ [251-500]
Soparkar, Nandit R - *Time-Constrained Transaction Management*
    SciTech - v21 - Mr '97 - p6 [51-250]
Soper, J Christopher - *Evangelical Christianity in the United States and Great Britain*
    JR - v77 - Ja '97 - p149+ [501+]
Sophocleous, Sophocles - *Icons of Cyprus 7th-20th Century*
    Specu - v71 - O '96 - p1024+ [501+]
Sorajbi, Richard - *Animal Minds and Human Morals*
    Nature - v385 - F 20 '97 - p693 [1-50]
Soranus, of Ephesus - *Soranus' Gynecology*
    CW - v89 - Jl '96 - p506 [51-250]
Sorbier, F - *Vincent Van Gogh (Illus. by Jean Philippe Chabot)*
    c JB - v60 - O '96 - p195 [51-250]
Soreff, Stephen M - *Handbook for the Treatment of the Seriously Mentally Ill*
    SciTech - v20 - N '96 - p43 [51-250]
Sorel, Claudette - *Mind Your Musical Manners. 3rd Ed.*
    Am MT - v46 - D '96 - p65 [1-50]
Sorell, Tom - *The Cambridge Companion to Hobbes*
    Choice - v34 - O '96 - p293 [51-250]
    CPR - v16 - O '96 - p374+ [501+]
    Sev Cent N - v54 - Fall '96 - p61+ [501+]
Sorensen, Aage B - *Social Theory and Social Policy*
    SF - v75 - Mr '97 - p1131+ [501+]
Sorensen, Elaine - *Comparable Worth*
    ILRR - v50 - Ja '97 - p358+ [501+]
Sorensen, Henri - *New Hope (Illus. by Henri Sorensen)*
    c RT - v50 - D '96 - p340 [51-250]
    Your First Step
    c BL - v92 - Ag '96 - p1909 [51-250]
    c HB Guide - v7 - Fall '96 - p244 [51-250]
Sorensen, Marilou - *Teaching with Children's Books*
    Emerg Lib - v23 - My '96 - p41 [251-500]
Sorensen, W Conner - *Brethren of the Net*
    Isis - v87 - S '96 - p563+ [501+]
    WHQ - v28 - Spr '97 - p104 [1-50]
Sorenson, John - *Disaster and Development in the Horn of Africa*
    JTWS - v13 - Fall '96 - p289+ [501+]
Sorenson, Leonard R - *Madison on the General Welfare of America*
    APSR - v90 - D '96 - p923+ [501+]
Soriano, Osvaldo - *La Hora Sin Sombra*
    WLT - v71 - Win '97 - p121 [501+]
Sorin, Gerald - *Tradition Transformed*
    PW - v244 - Mr 3 '97 - p56+ [51-250]
Sorkin, David - *Moses Mendelssohn and the Religious Enlightenment*
    Choice - v34 - N '96 - p474 [51-250]
Sorlin, Pierre - *Italian National Cinema 1896-1996*
    Si & So - v6 - N '96 - p35 [1-50]
Sorrell, Martin - *Elles: A Bilingual Anthology of Modern French Poetry by Women*
    MLR - v92 - Ja '97 - p208+ [501+]
    TLS - D 20 '96 - p26 [501+]
Sorrells, Walter - *Will to Murder*
    Arm Det - v29 - Sum '96 - p365 [251-500]
Sorrels, Roy - *The Alamo in American History*
    y BL - v93 - Mr 1 '97 - p1154+ [51-250]
    c HB Guide - v8 - Spr '97 - p176 [51-250]
    c KR - v64 - N 15 '96 - p1676 [51-250]
Sorrow, Barbara Head - *CD-ROM for Librarians and Educators. 2nd Ed.*
    r BL - v93 - D 15 '96 - p746 [251-500]
    r VOYA - v19 - F '97 - p363 [251-500]
Sorsby, Claudia - *Grammar 101*
    yr BWatch - v17 - S '96 - p9 [51-250]
    Spelling 101
    yr BWatch - v17 - S '96 - p9 [51-250]
    Writing 101
    yr BWatch - v17 - S '96 - p9 [51-250]
Sosa, Roberto - *El Llanto De Las Cosas*
    BL - v93 - S 15 '96 - p227 [1-50]
Soseki, Natsume - *Kojin*
    CLS - v33 - 1 '96 - p59+ [501+]
Sosinsky, Barrie - *The Web Page Recipe Book*
    CBR - v14 - N '96 - p37 [1-50]
    SciTech - v20 - D '96 - p12 [51-250]
Sosnoski, James J - *Modern Skeletons in Postmodern Closets*
    Choice - v34 - O '96 - p273 [51-250]

Token Professionals and Master Critics
    Col Comp - v47 - O '96 - p442 [51-250]
Sosnowski, David - *Rapture*
    NYTBR - v101 - N 17 '96 - p25 [51-250]
    Obs - D 22 '96 - p17* [51-250]
    Obs - Ja 26 '97 - p18* [51-250]
    PW - v243 - Jl 22 '96 - p227 [51-250]
Sotheby, Lionel - *Lionel Sotheby's Great War*
    KR - v65 - Ja 1 '97 - p49 [251-500]
Soto, Gary - *Boys at Work (Illus. by Robert Casilla)*
    c JOYS - v9 - Sum '96 - p417 [51-250]
    Chato's Kitchen (Illus. by Susan Guevara)
    c ECEJ - v24 - Spr '97 - p176 [51-250]
    c RT - v50 - F '97 - p426 [51-250]
    A Fire in My Hands
    y JAAL - v40 - D '96 - p319 [51-250]
    Jesse
    y SLJ - v42 - O '96 - p45 [1-50]
    Junior College
    LJ - v122 - My 1 '97 - p108 [51-250]
    PW - v244 - Ap 28 '97 - p73 [1-50]
    Novio Boy
    y PW - v244 - Mr 10 '97 - p69 [1-50]
    Off and Running (Illus. by Eric Velasquez)
    c BL - v93 - O 1 '96 - p352+ [51-250]
    c CCB-B - v50 - O '96 - p77 [51-250]
    c HB Guide - v8 - Spr '97 - p75 [51-250]
    c SLJ - v42 - S '96 - p206 [51-250]
    The Old Man and His Door (Illus. by Joe Cepeda)
    c CCB-B - v50 - S '96 - p31 [51-250]
    c HB Guide - v7 - Fall '96 - p277 [51-250]
    c LATBR - S 1 '96 - p11 [51-250]
    c New Ad - v9 - Fall '96 - p327+ [501+]
    Snapshots from the Wedding (Illus. by Stephanie Garcia)
    c BL - v93 - F 15 '97 - p1021 [51-250]
    c CCB-B - v50 - Ap '97 - p296+ [51-250]
    c KR - v65 - F 1 '97 - p228 [51-250]
    c PW - v244 - Ja 20 '97 - p401 [51-250]
    A Summer Life
    y BL - v93 - D 15 '96 - p717 [1-50]
    Summer on Wheels
    c RT - v50 - N '96 - p252+ [51-250]
Soto, Lourdes Diaz - *Language, Culture, and Power*
    Choice - v34 - My '97 - p1551 [51-250]
Sotte, Franco - *The Regional Dimension in Agricultural Economics and Policies*
    JEL - v34 - D '96 - p2131 [51-250]
Sottsass, Ettore - *Ceramics*
    Am Craft - v56 - O '96 - p51 [51-250]
Soucie, Gary - *Lenses and Prisms and Other Scientific Things*
    y New Sci - v153 - F 8 '97 - p46 [51-250]
Soucy, Robert - *French Fascism*
    AHR - v101 - O '96 - p1223+ [501+]
Souder, Jon A - *State Trust Lands*
    APSR - v91 - Mr '97 - p199 [501+]
    Pol Stud J - v24 - Sum '96 - p334 [1-50]
    WHQ - v28 - Spr '97 - p87+ [251-500]
Soufas, C Christopher - *Audience and Authority in the Modernist Theater of Federico Garcia Lorca*
    Choice - v34 - D '96 - p620+ [51-250]
    R&R Bk N - v11 - N '96 - p68 [1-50]
    VQR - v73 - Win '97 - p14* [51-250]
    WLT - v71 - Win '97 - p125+ [501+]
Souhami, Diana - *Mrs. Keppel and Her Daughter*
    CR - v269 - N '96 - p280 [51-250]
    NS & S - v9 - My 3 '96 - p37+ [251-500]
    PW - v244 - My 5 '97 - p185+ [51-250]
    Spec - v276 - My 11 '96 - p42 [251-500]
    TLS - My 24 '96 - p34 [501+]
Souhami, Jessica - *The Leopard's Drum (Illus. by Jessica Souhami)*
    c HB Guide - v7 - Fall '96 - p324 [1-50]
    c NYTBR - v101 - Ag 25 '96 - p23 [1-50]
    Old MacDonald
    c HB Guide - v7 - Fall '96 - p244 [1-50]
Soukhanov, Anne H - *Word Watch*
    y Kliatt - v30 - N '96 - p18+ [51-250]
Soukup, James E - *Alzheimer's Disease*
    SciTech - v20 - S '96 - p34 [51-250]
Soulen, R Kendall - *The God of Israel and Christian Theology*
    CC - v113 - N 6 '96 - p1089+ [51-250]
    Choice - v34 - D '96 - p630 [1-50]
    Rel St Rev - v23 - Ja '97 - p48 [51-250]
Soundings
    p Dis - v44 - Spr '97 - p103+ [501+]
A Source Book for the Community of Religions
    r Quill & Q - v62 - D '96 - p40 [51-250]
The Sourcebook of Federal Courts. 2nd Ed.
    r ARBA - v28 - '97 - p224+ [251-500]

The Sourcebook of State Public Records. 2nd Ed.
    r AJR - v18 - O '96 - p62 [501+]
Sources and Methods. 2nd Ed., Vol. 2
    r ARBA - v28 - '97 - p121 [51-250]
Sourkes, Barbara M - *Armfuls of Time*
    Hast Cen R - v27 - My '97 - p49 [1-50]
    Readings - v11 - S '96 - p8+ [501+]
Sourvinou-Inwood, Christiane - *Reading Greek Death*
    AJP - v117 - Win '96 - p645+ [501+]
Souster, Raymond - *Old Bank Notes*
    Can Lit - Win '96 - p145+ [501+]
Souter, Gavin - *A Torrent of Words*
    Quad - v40 - S '96 - p87+ [501+]
South, Coleman - *Jordan*
    c Ch BWatch - v7 - Ja '97 - p3 [1-50]
South, Stanley - *Pioneers in Historical Archaeology*
    Am Ant - v61 - Jl '96 - p613+ [501+]
South America, Central America, and the Caribbean 1997
    r ARBA - v28 - '97 - p68 [251-500]
South American Handbook 1997
    r WorldV - v13 - Ja '97 - p11 [251-500]
South Carolina Advisory Commission on Intergovernmental Relations - *Home Rule in South Carolina*
    J Gov Info - v23 - S '96 - p594 [51-250]
South Carolina Directory of Services for Women, Children and Families
    r J Gov Info - v23 - S '96 - p594 [51-250]
South King County Genealogical Society - *King County, Washington Deaths 1891-1907*
    r EGH - v50 - N '96 - p191 [51-250]
South Texas College of Law. Library. Special Collections - *Annotated Catalog, South Texas College of Law, Special Collections*
    r ARBA - v28 - '97 - p217 [1-50]
Southam, B C - *A Guide to the Selected Poems of T.S. Eliot*
    BW - v26 - S 1 '96 - p12 [51-250]
Southcott, Joanna - *A Dispute between the Woman and the Powers of Darkness 1802*
    Nine-C Lit - v51 - S '96 - p277+ [51-250]
Southeast Asian Art Today
    FEER - v159 - D 19 '96 - p52+ [501+]
Southern, David W - *John LaFarge and the Limits of Catholic Interracialism 1911-1963*
    R&R Bk N - v11 - D '96 - p6 [51-250]
Southern, Eileen - *African American Theater*
    Notes - v53 - D '96 - p622+ [501+]
    The Music of Black Americans. 3rd Ed.
    LJ - v122 - Ap 1 '97 - p96 [51-250]
Southern, Pat - *The Late Roman Army*
    HRNB - v25 - Win '97 - p88 [51-250]
Southern, R W - *Scholastic Humanism and the Unification of Europe. Vol. 1*
    Theol St - v57 - D '96 - p747+ [501+]
The Southern Quarterly
    p Sm Pr R - v28 - O '96 - p17+ [251-500]
Southgate, Beverley C - *Covetous of Truth*
    Rel St Rev - v23 - Ja '97 - p83 [51-250]
Southgate, Martha - *Another Way to Dance*
    y BL - v93 - D 1 '96 - p646 [51-250]
    y BL - v93 - Ap 1 '97 - p1294 [1-50]
    y CBRS - v25 - Win '97 - p71 [51-250]
    c CCB-B - v50 - Ja '97 - p186 [51-250]
    c Ch BWatch - v7 - Ja '97 - p4 [51-250]
    y HB Guide - v8 - Spr '97 - p84 [51-250]
    y JAAL - v40 - F '97 - p406+ [51-250]
    y KR - v64 - S 15 '96 - p1407+ [51-250]
    y PW - v243 - N 11 '96 - p77 [51-250]
    c SLJ - v42 - D '96 - p139 [51-250]
    y VOYA - v19 - O '96 - p214 [251-500]
Southwick, Charles H - *Global Ecology in Human Perspective*
    Choice - v34 - Ja '97 - p818+ [51-250]
Southworth, Michael - *Streets and the Shaping of Towns and Cities*
    R&R Bk N - v12 - F '97 - p98 [51-250]
    SB - v33 - My '97 - p105 [51-250]
Sou'wester
    p LMR - v15 - Fall '96 - p29+ [501+]
Souza, D M - *Hurricanes*
    c BL - v92 - Ag '96 - p1899 [51-250]
    c Ch BWatch - v6 - O '96 - p5+ [1-50]
    c Cur R - v36 - D '96 - p13 [51-250]
    c HB Guide - v8 - Spr '97 - p114 [51-250]
    c SLJ - v42 - N '96 - p118+ [51-250]
Souza, Raymond D - *Guillermo Cabrera Infante: Two Islands, Many Worlds*
    Choice - v34 - N '96 - p465 [51-250]

Sowa, Michael - *Sowa's Ark*
  Aud - v98 - N '96 - p136 [1-50]
  Spec - v277 - O 19 '96 - p55 [501+]
Sowell, Thomas - *Migrations and Cultures*
  Bks & Cult - v2 - S '96 - p18+ [501+]
  Choice - v34 - S '96 - p220 [51-250]
  Nat R - v48 - N 25 '96 - p65+ [501+]
  Pub Int - Fall '96 - p132+ [501+]
  The Vision of the Anointed
    IndRev - v1 - Spr '96 - p129+ [501+]
Sowerby, Robin - *The Classical Legacy in Renaissance Poetry*
  RES - v47 - N '96 - p572+ [501+]
Sowers, George F - *Building on Sinkholes*
  SciTech - v21 - Mr '97 - p80 [51-250]
Sowers, James R - *Endocrinology of the Vasculature*
  SciTech - v20 - S '96 - p36 [51-250]
Sowler, Sandie - *Asombrosos Animales Acorazados*
  c BL - v93 - F 15 '97 - p1032 [1-50]
Soyfer, Jura - *It's Up to Us!*
  Choice - v34 - My '97 - p1503 [51-250]
Soyfer, Valery N - *Triple-Helical Nucleic Acids*
  Nature - v385 - Ja 16 '97 - p218 [51-250]
Soyinka, Wole - *The Beatification of Area Boy*
  WLT - v70 - Sum '96 - p750+ [501+]
  The Open Sore of a Continent
    Am - v175 - S 21 '96 - p35 [51-250]
    BL - v93 - N 1 '96 - p475 [51-250]
    BW - v26 - N 10 '96 - p4 [501+]
    Choice - v34 - Mr '97 - p1234 [51-250]
    For Aff - v75 - N '96 - p139+ [501+]
    KR - v64 - My 1 '96 - p677 [251-500]
    NYTBR - v101 - D 8 '96 - p90 [1-50]
    Obs - Ja 19 '97 - p18* [501+]
    VLS - Win '96 - p11 [51-250]
Soysal, Yasemin Nuhoglu - *Limits of Citizenship*
  WP - v49 - O '96 - p130+ [501+]
Spaas, Lieve - *Robinson Crusoe*
  TLS - D 27 '96 - p23 [501+]
Space '96 (1996: Albuquerque, N.M.) - *Engineering, Construction, and Operations in Space V. Vols. 1-2*
  SciTech - v20 - D '96 - p81 [51-250]
Space Charge Dominated Beams and Applications of High Brightness Beams (1995: Bloomington, IN) - *Space Charge Dominated Beams and Applications of High Brightness Beams*
  SciTech - v20 - N '96 - p20 [51-250]
Space Safety and Rescue 1993
  SciTech - v20 - S '96 - p58 [51-250]
Space Technology
  c CLW - v66 - Je '96 - p53 [51-250]
  c HB Guide - v7 - Fall '96 - p352 [51-250]
Space Telescope Science Institute (U.S.) - *The Collision of Comet Shoemaker-Levy 9 and Jupiter*
  Choice - v34 - Ja '97 - p816 [51-250]
Spackman, W M - *Complete Fiction of W.M. Spackman*
  KR - v65 - Mr 1 '97 - p334 [51-250]
  LJ - v122 - Mr 15 '97 - p94 [51-250]
  PW - v244 - Mr 10 '97 - p51 [51-250]
Spacks, Patricia Ann Meyer - *Advocacy in the Classroom*
  LJ - v121 - N 15 '96 - p70 [51-250]
  PW - v243 - O 14 '96 - p68 [51-250]
Spada, James - *Streisand: Her Life*
  Ent W - S 13 '96 - p127 [51-250]
Spadafori, Gina - *Dogs for Dummies*
  r Dog Fan - v28 - Ja '97 - p38 [51-250]
  LJ - v121 - N 15 '96 - p80 [51-250]
Spadolini, Giovanni - *The Crisis of the Societies of the East and the Return to a Common Europe*
  Wil Q - v21 - Win '97 - p38 [1-50]
Spady, James G - *Twisted Tales*
  PMS - v19 - Fall '95 - p131+ [501+]
Spaeth, Barbette Stanley - *The Roman Goddess Ceres*
  Rel St Rev - v23 - Ja '97 - p65 [51-250]
Spahn, Mark - *The Kanji Dictionary*
  r ARBA - v28 - '97 - p395 [251-500]
  r Choice - v34 - S '96 - p106 [51-250]
Spahr, William J - *Zhukov: The Rise and Fall of a Great Captain*
  NWCR - v50 - Win '97 - p162+ [501+]
Spain, Daphne - *Balancing Act*
  Choice - v34 - Ja '97 - p884+ [51-250]
  JEL - v35 - Mr '97 - p236 [51-250]
  R&R Bk N - v11 - D '96 - p42 [51-250]
  Signs - v22 - Win '97 - p440+ [501+]
  Soc Ser R - v71 - Mr '97 - p164+ [1-50]
Spain (Eyewitness Travel Guides)
  r ARBA - v28 - '97 - p181 [251-500]

Spain. Sovereign (1479-1504: Ferdinand V and Isabella I) - *The Book of Privileges Issued to Christopher Columbus by King Fernando and Queen Isabel 1492-1502. Vol. 2*
  TranslRevS - v2 - D '96 - p15 [51-250]
Spainhour, Stephen - *Webmaster in a Nutshell*
  LJ - v122 - Ja '97 - p138 [1-50]
Spalanca, Carmelo - *De Regalpetra A Parigi*
  MLR - v91 - O '96 - p1013+ [501+]
Spalding, Andrea - *Finders Keepers*
  y Ch Bk News - v19 - Sum '96 - p30 [51-250]
Spalding, Matthew - *A Sacred Union of Citizens*
  LJ - v121 - O 1 '96 - p100 [51-250]
Spalding, Susan Eike - *Communities in Motion*
  ASInt - v34 - O '96 - p97+ [501+]
  CAY - v16 - Fall '95 - p10 [51-250]
Spalding, Thomas W - *The Premier See*
  CH - v65 - D '96 - p774+ [501+]
  St. Vincent De Paul of Baltimore
    CHR - v83 - Ja '97 - p137+ [251-500]
SPAN Connection
  p LJ - v122 - F 15 '97 - p167 [51-250]
Spanbauer, Scott - *The No B.S. Guide to Windows 95*
  BL - v92 - Ag '96 - p1868 [501+]
  CBR - v14 - N '96 - p39 [51-250]
Spangenburg, Ray - *Eleanor Roosevelt: A Passion to Improve*
  y KR - v64 - D 15 '96 - p1805 [51-250]
Spangle, Douglas - *Initial*
  Sm Pr R - v28 - N '96 - p12 [501+]
Spangler, David - *The Call*
  LJ - v121 - N 15 '96 - p66+ [51-250]
Spanier, Bonnie - *Im/Partial Science*
  NWSA Jnl - v8 - Fall '96 - p183+ [501+]
The Spanish Balance of Payments 1995
  JEL - v34 - D '96 - p2048 [51-250]
Spanish Women on the Threshold of the 21st Century
  J Gov Info - v23 - S '96 - p661 [1-50]
Spanos, William V - *The Errant Art of Moby-Dick*
  AL - v68 - S '96 - p644+ [251-500]
  J Am St - v30 - Ag '96 - p304+ [501+]
Sparer, Michael S - *Medicaid and the Limits of State Health Reform*
  AAPSS-A - v550 - Mr '97 - p187+ [501+]
  Choice - v34 - D '96 - p645+ [51-250]
Spark, Muriel - *Reality and Dreams*
  BL - v93 - Mr 1 '97 - p1112 [51-250]
  KR - v65 - Ja 15 '97 - p93 [51-250]
  LJ - v122 - F 15 '97 - p164 [51-250]
  Lon R Bks - v18 - N 14 '96 - p23+ [501+]
  NYTLa - v146 - My 16 '97 - pC29 [501+]
  Obs - S 15 '96 - p17* [501+]
  PW - v244 - Ja 27 '97 - p76 [51-250]
  Spec - v277 - S 14 '96 - p34+ [501+]
  TES - N 15 '96 - p8* [51-250]
  TLS - S 20 '96 - p22 [501+]
  TLS - N 29 '96 - p16 [1-50]
  Woman's J - N '96 - p12 [1-50]
Sparkie - *Jolly Old Santa Claus (Illus. by George Hinke)*
  c HB Guide - v8 - Spr '97 - p33 [51-250]
  c PW - v243 - S 30 '96 - p92 [51-250]
Sparks, Allister - *Tomorrow Is Another Country*
  CR - v270 - Ja '97 - p47+ [501+]
  JTWS - v13 - Spr '96 - p333+ [501+]
  LATBR - Ag 11 '96 - p11 [51-250]
Sparks, Beatrice - *Almost Lost*
  y VOYA - v19 - O '96 - p224 [51-250]
Sparks, Nicholas - *The Notebook*
  BL - v92 - Ag '96 - p1856 [251-500]
  CSM - v88 - N 14 '96 - p14 [51-250]
  CSM - v89 - D 19 '96 - p14 [51-250]
  CSM - v89 - Ja 16 '97 - p14 [51-250]
  CSM - v89 - F 20 '97 - p10 [51-250]
  CSM - v89 - Mr 20 '97 - p14 [51-250]
  LJ - v122 - Mr 15 '97 - p43 [1-50]
  PW - v243 - Jl 22 '96 - p224+ [51-250]
  Rapport - v19 - 6 '96 - p25 [251-500]
  The Notebook (Nelligan). Audio Version
    BWatch - v17 - D '96 - p11 [1-50]
    PW - v243 - N 4 '96 - p35 [51-250]
Sparks, Randy J - *On Jordan's Stormy Banks*
  JIH - v27 - Aut '96 - p334+ [251-500]
Sparks, Sheila M - *Nursing Diagnosis Pocket Manual*
  r ARBA - v28 - '97 - p615 [51-250]
Sparling, Ken - *Dad Says He Saw You at the Mall*
  BIC - v25 - O '96 - p40 [51-250]
Sparr, Pamela - *Mortgaging Women's Lives*
  NWSA Jnl - v8 - Sum '96 - p134+ [501+]

Sparrow, Bartholomew H - *From the Outside In*
  AJS - v102 - Ja '97 - p1180+ [501+]
  Choice - v34 - S '96 - p199 [51-250]
  HRNB - v25 - Fall '96 - p12+ [251-500]
  JEL - v34 - S '96 - p1470 [51-250]
  J Pol - v59 - F '97 - p255+ [501+]
Sparrow, Scott - *Blessed among Women*
  BL - v93 - D 1 '96 - p622+ [51-250]
  LJ - v121 - N 15 '96 - p66+ [51-250]
Sparschuh, Jens - *Der Zimmerspringbrunnen: Ein Heimatroman*
  WLT - v71 - Win '97 - p139 [501+]
Sparshott, Margaret - *Pain, Distress, and the Newborn Baby*
  SciTech - v21 - Mr '97 - p64 [51-250]
Spartacus: International Gay Guide 96-97
  r Quill & Q - v62 - S '96 - p24 [51-250]
Spatz, Chris - *Basic Statistics. 6th Ed.*
  SciTech - v20 - D '96 - p16 [51-250]
Spaulding, Amy E - *The Page as a Stage Set*
  LR - v45 - 4 '96 - p71+ [501+]
Spaulding, Jonathan - *Ansel Adams and the American Landscape*
  WHQ - v27 - Win '96 - p528+ [501+]
Spaziani, Maria Luisa - *Star of Free Will*
  Choice - v34 - O '96 - p287 [51-250]
  Sm Pr R - v28 - Jl '96 - p12 [51-250]
  TranslRevS - v2 - D '96 - p28 [51-250]
Speak, Dorothy - *Object of Your Love*
  CF - v75 - N '96 - p38+ [501+]
  Quill & Q - v62 - Ag '96 - p34 [251-500]
Speaks, Charles E - *Introduction to Sound. 2nd Ed.*
  SciTech - v20 - S '96 - p14 [51-250]
Spear, Frederick A - *Bibliographie Analytique Des Ecrits Relatifs A Voltaire 1966-1990*
  r MLR - v92 - Ap '97 - p468+ [501+]
Spear, Joanna - *Carter and Arms Sales*
  J Pol - v59 - F '97 - p313+ [501+]
Spear, Peta - *Sex Crimes*
  Aust Bk R - Je '96 - p45+ [501+]
Spear, Peter - *Return to Zork*
  Quill & Q - v62 - Ag '96 - p22 [501+]
Speare, Elizabeth George - *The Bronze Bow*
  c JOYS - v10 - Fall '96 - p46+ [501+]
  The Witch of Blackbird Pond
    c JOYS - v10 - Fall '96 - p46+ [501+]
Spearing, A C - *The Medieval Poet as Voyeur*
  MP - v94 - Ag '96 - p63+ [501+]
Spearing, Darwin - *Roadside Geology of Louisiana*
  Bloom Rev - v16 - Jl '96 - p25 [1-50]
Spearman, R Michael - *The Age of Migrating Ideas*
  BM - v138 - D '96 - p836 [1-50]
Spears, John R - *Captain Nathaniel Brown Palmer: An Old-Time Sailor of the Sea*
  Sea H - Sum '96 - p31 [51-250]
Spears, Monroe K - *One Writer's Reality*
  HR - v49 - Aut '96 - p491+ [501+]
Spears, Timothy B - *100 Years on the Road*
  AHR - v101 - O '96 - p1290 [251-500]
  BusLR - v21 - 3 '96 - p257 [51-250]
  T&C - v37 - Ap '96 - p784+ [501+]
Spear-Swerling, Louise - *Off Track*
  Choice - v34 - D '96 - p661+ [51-250]
Spechler, Jay W - *Reasonable Accommodation*
  Choice - v34 - S '96 - p174 [51-250]
  HR Mag - v41 - Ag '96 - p122 [51-250]
Specht, Jim - *More Than Graphs*
  y Math T - v89 - S '96 - p520 [251-500]
Special Libraries Association. Conference (87th: 1996: Boston, Mass.) - *Information Revolution*
  LHTN - Jl '96 - p22 [51-250]
Specialized Catalog of U.S. Non-Pictorial Waterfowl Stamps 1996
  r Am Phil - v110 - N '96 - p1038 [51-250]
Specialized Catalogue of U.S. Stamps 1996
  r Am Phil - v110 - Jl '96 - p634+ [501+]
Specialty Conference on Probabilistic Mechanics and Structural Reliability (7th: 1996: Worcester, Mass.) - *Probabilistic Mechanics and Structural Reliability*
  SciTech - v20 - D '96 - p64 [51-250]
Specialty Occupational Outlook: Trade and Technical. 1st Ed.
  yr ARBA - v28 - '97 - p121 [251-500]
Speck, Frank G - *Cherokee Dance and Drama*
  CAY - v16 - Fall '95 - p13 [51-250]
Speck, James S - *Epitaxial Oxide Thin Films II*
  SciTech - v20 - S '96 - p49 [51-250]
Speck, W A - *The Birth of Britain*
  EHR - v111 - N '96 - p1291+ [251-500]

Speed, Toby - *Two Cool Cows (Illus. by Barry Root)*
  c RT - v50 - O '96 - p131 [1-50]
Whoosh! Went the Wish (Illus. by Barry Root)
  c KR - v65 - My 1 '97 - p727 [51-250]
  c PW - v244 - Ap 21 '97 - p71 [51-250]
Speer, Andreas - *Die Entdeckte Natur*
   Choice - v34 - D '96 - p566 [1-50]
Speert, Harold - *Obstetric and Gynecologic Milestones Illustrated. 2nd Ed.*
   SciTech - v20 - D '96 - p51 [51-250]
Spegele, Roger D - *Political Realism in International Theory*
   Choice - v34 - Mr '97 - p1236 [51-250]
Spehr, Paul C - *American Film Personnel and Company Credits 1908-1920*
  r ARBA - v28 - '97 - p520 [51-250]
  r Choice - v34 - F '97 - p950 [51-250]
  r R&R Bk N - v11 - D '96 - p61 [51-250]
Speiser, Felix - *Ethnology of Vanuatu*
   Choice - v34 - My '97 - p1542 [51-250]
Speke, John Hanning - *Journal of the Discovery of the Source of the Nile*
   BWatch - v18 - F '97 - p2 [1-50]
   LJ - v122 - F 15 '97 - p166 [51-250]
Spellberg, D A - *Politics, Gender, and the Islamic Past*
   Rel St Rev - v23 - Ap '97 - p201 [51-250]
Spelling, Aaron - *Aaron Spelling: A Prime-Time Life*
   BL - v92 - Ag '96 - p1873 [51-250]
Aaron Spelling. A Prime-Time Life (Spelling). Audio Version
   PW - v243 - S 2 '96 - p48 [51-250]
Spellman, Lynne - *Substance and Separation in Aristotle*
   IPQ - v36 - S '96 - p365+ [501+]
Spelman, Cornelia - *After Charlotte's Mom Died (Illus. by Judith Friedman)*
  c HB Guide - v7 - Fall '96 - p277+ [51-250]
  c SLJ - v42 - Ag '96 - p130 [51-250]
Spence, Clark C - *The Northern Gold Fleet*
   Choice - v34 - D '96 - p634 [51-250]
Spence, Gerry - *The Making of a Country Lawyer*
   BL - v93 - S 1 '96 - p5 [51-250]
   KR - v64 - Ag 15 '96 - p1223+ [251-500]
   LATBR - O 20 '96 - p4 [501+]
   LJ - v121 - O 15 '96 - p68 [51-250]
The Making of a Country Lawyer. Audio Version
   BWatch - v17 - D '96 - p11 [1-50]
Spence, I G - *The Cavalry of Classical Greece*
   CW - v89 - Jl '96 - p510+ [251-500]
Spence, Jonathan D - *The Chinese Century*
  y BL - v93 - N 1 '96 - p480 [51-250]
   BWatch - v17 - D '96 - p8 [51-250]
   CSM - v89 - D 5 '96 - pB4 [51-250]
   FEER - v160 - Mr 13 '97 - p47+ [501+]
   HT - v46 - D '96 - p53 [51-250]
   KR - v64 - S 15 '96 - p1392 [51-250]
   LATBR - D 1 '96 - p2 [51-250]
   Mac - v109 - D 9 '96 - p66 [1-50]
   NYTBR - v101 - D 8 '96 - p26 [501+]
   Obs - D 22 '96 - p16* [501+]
   PW - v243 - S 9 '96 - p71 [51-250]
God's Chinese Son
   Am - v175 - Ag 17 '96 - p26 [501+]
   Bks & Cult - v2 - Jl '96 - p31 [251-500]
   FEER - v159 - N 14 '96 - p63 [501+]
   HRNB - v25 - Fall '96 - p37 [51-250]
   NS & S - v9 - My 24 '96 - p38 [251-500]
   NYTBR - v101 - D 8 '96 - p87 [1-50]
   NYTBR - v102 - Mr 23 '97 - p28 [51-250]
   PW - v243 - D 30 '96 - p64 [1-50]
   TLS - O 25 '96 - p4+ [501+]
Spence, Peter - *The Birth of Romantic Radicalism*
   Albion - v28 - '96 - p709+ [501+]
   R&R Bk N - v12 - F '97 - p60 [51-250]
Spencer, Anne - *The Memory Book (Illus. by Malcolm Cullen)*
  c Can CL - v22 - Fall '96 - p122+ [501+]
Spencer, Brent - *Are We Not Men?*
   BL - v93 - S 1 '96 - p64 [51-250]
   NYTBR - v101 - O 13 '96 - p21 [51-250]
   PW - v243 - Jl 22 '96 - p228 [51-250]
   VLS - Win '96 - p11+ [51-250]
   VV - v41 - S 10 '96 - p67 [501+]
Spencer, Charles - *Full Personal Service*
   TLS - D 13 '96 - p23 [51-250]
Spencer, Colin - *The Heretic's Feast*
   AHR - v102 - F '97 - p85+ [501+]
   VQR - v72 - Aut '96 - p143* [1-50]
Homosexuality: A History
   Books - v9 - S '95 - p23 [51-250]

Homosexuality in History
   KR - v64 - My 1 '96 - p677+ [251-500]
   VV - v41 - Ag 27 '96 - p57 [251-500]
Spencer, David E - *From Vietnam to El Salvador*
   R&R Bk N - v12 - F '97 - p100 [51-250]
Spencer, Donald D - *Great Men and Women of Computing*
  y Math T - v89 - O '96 - p606 [51-250]
Key Dates in Number Theory History from 10,529 B.C. to the Present
   Math T - v89 - My '96 - p437 [251-500]
Spencer, Frank - *History of Physical Anthropology. Vols. 1-2*
  r LJ - v122 - Mr 15 '97 - p54 [51-250]
Spencer, H Leith - *English Preaching in the Late Middle Ages*
   CH - v66 - Mr '97 - p107+ [501+]
   Specu - v71 - Jl '96 - p764+ [501+]
Spencer, John, 1925- - *The Art History Study Guide*
  y Sch Lib - v44 - Ag '96 - p127 [51-250]
   TES - S 13 '96 - pR10 [251-500]
Spencer, John B - *Quake City*
   KR - v65 - Mr 1 '97 - p340 [51-250]
   PW - v244 - Mr 10 '97 - p53 [51-250]
Spencer, Jon Michael - *The New Colored People*
   BL - v93 - My 1 '97 - p1476+ [51-250]
Re-Searching Black Music
   Choice - v34 - F '97 - p975 [51-250]
Sing a New Song
   JR - v76 - O '96 - p652+ [501+]
Spencer, Kenneth L - *OLE-Remote Automation Visual Basic 4*
   SciTech - v20 - S '96 - p6 [51-250]
Spencer, LaVyrle - *Small Town Girl*
   BL - v93 - D 1 '96 - p621 [51-250]
   CSM - v89 - F 20 '97 - p10 [51-250]
   CSM - v89 - Mr 20 '97 - p14 [51-250]
   KR - v64 - N 15 '96 - p1628+ [251-500]
   PW - v243 - D 9 '96 - p61 [51-250]
Spencer, Pam - *What Do Young Adults Read Next?. Vol. 1*
  yr RQ - v36 - Win '96 - p213 [51-250]
Spencer, Roger - *Horticultural Flora of South-Eastern Australia. Vol. 1*
   Choice - v34 - S '96 - p154+ [51-250]
Spencer, Scott - *Endless Love*
   VV - v42 - Ja 7 '97 - p41 [51-250]
Spencer, William, 1922- - *Iran: Land of the Peacock Throne*
  c Ch BWatch - v6 - D '96 - p6 [1-50]
  c HB Guide - v8 - Spr '97 - p169 [51-250]
Spencer, William Browning, 1946- - *Resume with Monsters*
   MFSF - v91 - O '96 - p58+ [501+]
Spencer-Churchill, Henrietta - *Classic Fabrics*
   Bloom Rev - v16 - N '96 - p25 [51-250]
   LJ - v122 - Ja '97 - p94+ [51-250]
Spender, Dale - *Nattering on the Net*
   Quill & Q - v62 - Ag '96 - p21 [251-500]
   TES - O 18 '96 - p42U [501+]
   Wom R Bks - v14 - N '96 - p17+ [501+]
Spengemann, William C - *A New World of Words*
   Sev Cent N - v54 - Spr '96 - p30+ [501+]
Nineteenth-Century American Poetry
   VQR - v73 - Win '97 - p34* [1-50]
Spenser Studies XI
   RES - v47 - N '96 - p580+ [501+]
Sperber, A M - *Bogart*
   KR - v65 - F 15 '97 - p287 [251-500]
   LATBR - Ap 6 '97 - p3 [501+]
   NYTBR - v102 - Ap 20 '97 - p7 [501+]
   NYTLa - v146 - Ap 17 '97 - pC20 [501+]
   PW - v244 - F 17 '97 - p202 [251-500]
Speregen, Devra - *The Wax Museum (Illus. by Donald Cook)*
  c SLJ - v42 - Ag '96 - p121 [51-250]
Sperelakis, Nicholas - *Cell Physiology Source Book*
   Choice - v34 - S '96 - p152 [51-250]
Spergel, Irving A - *The Youth Gang Problem*
   AJS - v102 - Jl '96 - p313+ [501+]
Spero, Simon - *The Bowles Collection of 18th-Century English and French Porcelain*
   Ceram Mo - v44 - S '96 - p28+ [251-500]
Speroff, Leon - *A Clinical Guide for Contraception. 2nd Ed.*
   SciTech - v20 - S '96 - p40 [1-50]
Sperry, Armstrong - *All Sail Set (Illus. by Armstrong Sperry)*
  c Sea H - Aut '96 - p47 [1-50]
Sperry, Len - *Aging in the Twenty-First Century*
   R&R Bk N - v11 - D '96 - p41 [51-250]

Psychopathology and Psychotherapy. 2nd Ed.
   SciTech - v20 - S '96 - p32 [51-250]
Psychopharmacology and Psychotherapy
   AJPsych - v153 - S '96 - p1227 [501+]
Treatment Outcomes in Psychotherapy and Psychiatric Interventions
   SciTech - v20 - N '96 - p43 [51-250]
Spessard, Gary O - *Organometallic Chemistry*
   SciTech - v20 - N '96 - p23 [51-250]
Spewack, Bella - *Streets: A Memoir of the Lower East Side*
   AL - v69 - Mr '97 - p248 [51-250]
   CLW - v67 - D '96 - p50 [51-250]
  y Kliatt - v30 - N '96 - p23 [51-250]
Spicer, Cindy - *Carolina Edens*
   Hort - v74 - Ag '96 - p69+ [251-500]
Spicer, Dorothy Gladys - *Yearbook of English Festivals*
  r JPC - v29 - Spr '96 - p258+ [251-500]
Spicer, Michael - *The Challenge from the East and the Rebirth of the West*
   KR - v64 - My 1 '96 - p678 [251-500]
Spicq, Ceslas - *Theological Lexicon of the New Testament. Vols. 1-3*
  r Intpr - v50 - O '96 - p422+ [251-500]
Spider Magazine - *The Year-Round Book of Fun Stuff (Illus. by Michael Chesworth)*
  c Ch BWatch - v6 - D '96 - p6 [51-250]
Spiegel, John - *Banking Redefined*
   Choice - v34 - O '96 - p331 [51-250]
Spiegel, Leonard - *Applied Structural Steel Design. 3rd Ed.*
   SciTech - v20 - D '96 - p65 [51-250]
Spiegel, Marjorie - *The Dreaded Comparison. Rev. and Expanded Ed.*
   LJ - v121 - N 15 '96 - p77+ [51-250]
   PW - v243 - S 30 '96 - p79 [51-250]
Spiegel, Maura - *The Grim Reader*
   PW - v244 - Mr 17 '97 - p72 [51-250]
Spiegelman, Annie - *Annie's Garden Journal*
   BL - v93 - O 1 '96 - p317 [51-250]
   LJ - v121 - N 1 '96 - p73+ [51-250]
   PW - v243 - S 9 '96 - p75 [51-250]
Spiegelman, Art - *The Complete Maus. Electronic Media Version*
   Trib Bks - F 2 '97 - p7 [51-250]
Spiegelman, Willard - *Majestic Indolence*
   Critm - v38 - Fall '96 - p648+ [501+]
   MP - v94 - F '97 - p399+ [501+]
   Sew R - v104 - Jl '96 - p483+ [501+]
Spiegl, Fritz - *Lives, Wives and Loves of the Great Composers*
   PW - v243 - O 7 '96 - p50 [51-250]
Musical Blunders and Other Musical Curiosities
   Spec - v277 - D 7 '96 - p54 [51-250]
Spieler, Marlena - *The Vegetarian Bistro*
   BL - v93 - My 15 '97 - p1553+ [51-250]
Spielman, Bethany - *Organ and Tissue Donation*
   AB - v99 - Mr 31 '97 - p1051+ [501+]
   Choice - v34 - My '97 - p1534+ [51-250]
Spier, Fred - *Religious Regimes in Peru*
   AHR - v101 - D '96 - p1661 [501+]
Spier, Peter - *Christmas! (Illus. by Peter Spier)*
  c TES - D 6 '96 - p16* [1-50]
Peter Spier's Rain
  c PW - v244 - Ap 7 '97 - p94 [1-50]
Spies, Gerty - *My Years in Theresienstadt*
   LJ - v122 - Ap 15 '97 - p98 [51-250]
   PW - v244 - Mr 31 '97 - p56 [51-250]
Spignesi, Stephen J - *The ER Companion*
   Ent W - Je 28 '96 - p96 [51-250]
The Gore Galore Quiz Book
   SF Chr - v18 - O '96 - p81 [1-50]
What's Your Friends I.Q.?
   Ent W - Je 28 '96 - p96+ [51-250]
What's Your Mad About You I.Q.?
   Ent W - Je 28 '96 - p96+ [51-250]
Spijker, W Van't - *Calvin: Erbe Und Auftrag*
   CH - v65 - S '96 - p483+ [501+]
The Ecclesiastical Offices in the Thought of Martin Bucer
   R&R Bk N - v12 - F '97 - p10 [51-250]
Spike, John T - *Angelico*
   PW - v244 - Mr 24 '97 - p72 [51-250]
Masaccio
   Atl - v278 - O '96 - p122 [51-250]
  r Choice - v34 - N '96 - p446 [51-250]
   Spec - v277 - S 21 '96 - p53+ [501+]
Spilka, Arnold - *Bumples, Fumdidlers, and Jelly Beans (Illus. by Arnold Spilka)*
  c HB Guide - v8 - Spr '97 - p154 [1-50]
  c SLJ - v43 - F '97 - p99 [51-250]

Spilka, Bernard - *The Psychology of Religion*
   R&R Bk N - v12 - F '97 - p8 [51-250]
Spilker, Bert - *Medical Dictionary in Six Languages*
   r ARBA - v28 - '97 - p606 [51-250]
Spillane, Mickey - *Black Alley*
   BL - v92 - Ag '96 - p1856+ [251-500]
   KR - v64 - S 1 '96 - p1279 [51-250]
   Nat R - v48 - D 23 '96 - p57 [1-50]
   NYTBR - v101 - N 17 '96 - p25 [51-250]
   PW - v243 - S 2 '96 - p116 [51-250]
   Black Alley (Keach). Audio Version
   PW - v243 - O 7 '96 - p32 [51-250]
Spiller, Robert E - *Literary History of the United States.*
4th Rev. Ed., Vols. 1-2
   r ASInt - v34 - O '96 - p8 [51-250]
Spinar, Zdenek V - *Life before Man. Rev. Ed.*
   y Kliatt - v30 - S '96 - p35+ [51-250]
   y SB - v32 - Ag '96 - p174 [51-250]
Spindler, Erica - *Fortune*
   PW - v244 - F 17 '97 - p217 [51-250]
The Spine (Coding Illustrated)
   r SciTech - v20 - N '96 - p50 [51-250]
Spinelli, Eileen - *Somebody Loves You, Mr. Hatch*
   c CLW - v67 - Mr '97 - p15 [1-50]
   Where Is the Night Train Going? (Illus. by Cyd Moore)
   c HB Guide - v7 - Fall '96 - p369 [51-250]
Spinelli, Jerry - *Crash*
   y BL - v93 - Ap 1 '97 - p1294 [1-50]
   y BW - v27 - Ja 12 '97 - p9 [251-500]
   y Emerg Lib - v23 - My '96 - p43 [1-50]
   c HB - v72 - S '96 - p600 [51-250]
   c HB Guide - v7 - Fall '96 - p297 [51-250]
   y JAAL - v40 - F '97 - p407 [51-250]
   c Learning - v25 - N '96 - p31 [51-250]
   c SLJ - v42 - D '96 - p32 [1-50]
   The Library Card
   c BL - v93 - F 1 '97 - p942 [51-250]
   c CBRS - v25 - Ap '97 - p107 [51-250]
   c CCB-B - v50 - Mr '97 - p257+ [51-250]
   c HB - v73 - Mr '97 - p204+ [251-500]
   c Par Ch - v21 - Mr '97 - p8 [1-50]
   c PW - v244 - F 10 '97 - p84 [51-250]
   c SLJ - v43 - Mr '97 - p192 [51-250]
   Maniac Magee
   c JOYS - v10 - Fall '96 - p92+ [501+]
Spinner, Jeff - *The Boundaries of Citizenship*
   RP - v59 - Win '97 - p127+ [501+]
Spinner, Stephanie - *Aliens for Dinner (Illus. by Steve Bjorkman)*
   c Sch Lib - v44 - Ag '96 - p107 [51-250]
   Born to Be Wild (Illus. by Steve Bjorkman)
   c KR - v65 - Ja 1 '97 - p68 [51-250]
   c SLJ - v43 - F '97 - p84+ [51-250]
   Gerbilitis (Illus. by Steve Bjorkman)
   c BL - v93 - Ja '97 - p862 [251-500]
   c SLJ - v42 - N '96 - p110 [51-250]
   Sing, Elvis, Sing! (Illus. by Steve Bjorkman)
   c BL - v93 - Ja '97 - p862 [251-500]
   c SLJ - v42 - N '96 - p110 [51-250]
Spinning Jenny
   p Sm Pr R - v28 - O '96 - p20 [51-250]
Spinoza, Benedictus De - *The Letters*
   Choice - v34 - S '96 - p142 [51-250]
Spires, Elizabeth - *With One White Wing (Illus. by Erik Blegvad)*
   c NYTBR - v101 - Ap 7 '96 - p21 [501+]
   Worldling
   Ken R - v18 - Sum '96 - p191+ [501+]
   Poet - v169 - F '97 - p295+ [501+]
Spires, Robert C - *Post-Totalitarian Spanish Fiction*
   Choice - v34 - Ja '97 - p802 [51-250]
   R&R Bk N - v11 - D '96 - p63 [51-250]
Spirn, Anne Whiston - *Frank Lloyd Wright: Designs for an American Landscape 1922-1932*
   r Choice - v34 - N '96 - p444 [51-250]
Spiro, Howard M - *Facing Death*
   Choice - v34 - D '96 - p644 [51-250]
   Hast Cen R - v27 - Ja '97 - p47 [51-250]
   y SB - v33 - Ja '97 - p12 [51-250]
Spiro, Melford - *Anthropological Other or Burmese Brother?*
   RA - v25 - 4 '96 - p241+ [501+]
Spiros, Dean - *Frank Thomas: Star First Baseman*
   c HB Guide - v8 - Spr '97 - p145 [51-250]
Spitler, Sue - *Skinny Comfort Foods*
   BWatch - v18 - F '97 - p8 [1-50]
Spitta, Silvia - *Between Two Waters*
   WLT - v70 - Aut '96 - p927+ [501+]
Spitz, Barry - *Mill Valley*
   BWatch - v18 - Mr '97 - p2 [51-250]

Spitz, Ellen Handler - *Museums of the Mind*
   JAAC - v55 - Win '97 - p72+ [501+]
Spitz, Lewis William - *Johann Sturm on Education*
   Six Ct J - v27 - Win '96 - p1120+ [501+]
Spitz, Luis - *Soaps and Detergents*
   SciTech - v21 - Mr '97 - p97 [51-250]
Spitzer, Quinn - *Heads, You Win!*
   BL - v93 - Mr 1 '97 - p1098 [51-250]
   Fortune - v135 - Mr 17 '97 - p150 [501+]
   LJ - v122 - Mr 15 '97 - p71 [51-250]
   PW - v243 - D 30 '96 - p44 [51-250]
Spitzer, Robert J - *Media and Public Policy*
   JPC - v29 - Spr '96 - p254+ [251-500]
   The Politics of Gun Control
   SSQ - v77 - Je '96 - p463+ [501+]
Spivack, Charlotte - *The Company of Camelot*
   J Am Cult - v19 - Sum '96 - p148+ [501+]
Spivak, Dawnine - *Grass Sandals (Illus. by Demi)*
   c BL - v93 - My 1 '97 - p1497 [51-250]
   c KR - v65 - Mr 15 '97 - p468+ [51-250]
   c PW - v244 - Ap 14 '97 - p75+ [51-250]
Spivak, Gayatri Chakravorty - *Outside in the Teaching Machine*
   Can Lit - Win '96 - p165+ [501+]
Spivey, J M - *An Introduction to Logic Programming through Prolog*
   SciTech - v20 - S '96 - p5 [51-250]
Spivey, Nigel - *Understanding Greek Sculpture*
   r Choice - v34 - N '96 - p446 [51-250]
   TLS - N 8 '96 - p33 [251-500]
Splichal, Slavko - *Media beyond Socialism*
   JC - v46 - Aut '96 - p171+ [501+]
Spodick, David H - *The Pericardium: A Comprehensive Textbook*
   SciTech - v21 - Mr '97 - p57 [51-250]
Spoelstra, Jon - *Ice to the Eskimos*
   PW - v244 - My 12 '97 - p67+ [51-250]
Spohn, Kate - *Dog and Cat Shake a Leg (Illus. by Kate Spohn)*
   c HB Guide - v7 - Fall '96 - p285 [1-50]
Spolsky, Ellen - *Gaps in Nature*
   Poetics T - v17 - Sum '96 - p262+ [501+]
   Summoning: Ideas of the Covenant and Interpretive Theory
   Poetics T - v18 - Spr '97 - p139+ [501+]
Sponenberg, Phillip D - *Equine Color Genetics*
   SciTech - v20 - D '96 - p57 [51-250]
Spong, John Shelby - *Liberating the Gospels*
   BL - v93 - S 1 '96 - p40 [51-250]
   LJ - v121 - S 15 '96 - p74 [51-250]
Sponholz, Melanie - *The Princeton Review College Companion*
   y Kliatt - v30 - S '96 - p29 [51-250]
Sponsel, Leslie E - *Tropical Deforestation*
   Choice - v34 - Mr '97 - p1185 [51-250]
   SciTech - v21 - Mr '97 - p70 [51-250]
Spoo, Robert - *James Joyce and the Language of History*
   PQ - v75 - Spr '96 - p259+ [501+]
   TLS - D 20 '96 - p12 [501+]
Spooner, A - *The Oxford School Thesaurus*
   yr JB - v60 - D '96 - p274+ [251-500]
Spooner, Michael - *Old Meshikee and the Little Crabs (Illus. by John Hart)*
   c HB Guide - v7 - Fall '96 - p324+ [51-250]
   c RT - v50 - My '97 - p685 [51-250]
Sport, Nigel - *Sport*
   c Sch Lib - v45 - F '97 - p41 [51-250]
The Sporting News Hockey Register. 1996-97 Ed.
   r ARBA - v28 - '97 - p299 [51-250]
The Sporting News Official Baseball Register. 1996 Ed.
   r ARBA - v28 - '97 - p296 [51-250]
The Sporting News Pro Football Register. 1996 Ed.
   r ARBA - v28 - '97 - p299 [51-250]
Sports Illustrated for Kids
   cp Par Ch - v20 - O '96 - p15 [1-50]
Sports Literate
   p Sm Pr R - v28 - N '96 - p18+ [251-500]
Sports People in the News 1996
   yr ARBA - v28 - '97 - p291+ [51-250]
Spoto, Donald - *Rebel: The Life and Legend of James Dean*
   Econ - v340 - Ag 24 '96 - p70 [251-500]
   Si & So - v6 - N '96 - p36 [1-50]
   TES - Ag 2 '96 - pR6 [1-50]
Spragg, Christopher J - *Fiber, Matrix, and Interface Properties*
   SciTech - v20 - D '96 - p63 [1-50]
Sprague, Michael W - *Using Visual Basic*
   R&R Bk N - v12 - F '97 - p92 [51-250]
Sprague, Robert L - *Stereotyped Movements*
   SciTech - v20 - N '96 - p45 [51-250]

Sprake, David - *Francoscope A La Mode*
   y TES - Ja 24 '97 - p12* [501+]
Spratt, John S - *Home Health Care*
   SciTech - v20 - D '96 - p39 [51-250]
Sprecher, Thomas - *Das Zauberberg-Symposium 1994 In Davos*
   Ger Q - v70 - Win '97 - p85+ [501+]
   MLR - v92 - Ap '97 - p519+ [501+]
Sprechman, Ellen Lew - *Seeing Women as Men*
   Nine-C Lit - v50 - Mr '96 - p559 [1-50]
Sprenkle, Douglas H - *Research Methods in Family Therapy*
   SciTech - v20 - N '96 - p43 [1-50]
Spretnak, Charlene - *The Resurgence of the Real*
   KR - v65 - Mr 15 '97 - p449+ [251-500]
   PW - v244 - Ap 28 '97 - p64+ [51-250]
Spring, Ira - *Lookouts: Firewatchers of the Cascades and Olympics. 2nd Ed.*
   r BL - v93 - S 15 '96 - p212 [1-50]
Spring, Joel - *The Intersection of Cultures*
   Cont Ed - v68 - Fall '96 - p85+ [251-500]
   Wheels in the Head
   ES - v27 - Fall '96 - p272+ [501+]
Spring, Justin - *Wolf Kahn*
   A Art - v60 - O '96 - p73+ [501+]
Spring, Michelle - *Running for Shelter*
   PW - v243 - Jl 22 '96 - p229+ [51-250]
Spring #4
   Sm Pr R - v28 - Jl '96 - p18 [51-250]
Spring Technical Conference of the ASME Internal Combustion Engine Division (1996: Youngstown, OH) - *Recent Developments on Engine Emissions. Vols. 1-3*
   SciTech - v20 - N '96 - p71 [51-250]
Springer, Claudia - *Electronic Eros*
   Film Cr - v21 - Fall '96 - p82+ [501+]
   NYTBR - v101 - O 27 '96 - p38 [51-250]
   SFS - v24 - Mr '97 - p124+ [501+]
   Wom R Bks - v13 - S '96 - p20+ [501+]
Springer, Melissa - *Breast Cancer Survivors*
   S Liv - v31 - O '96 - p108 [51-250]
   A Tribe of Warrior Women
   Ms - v7 - S '96 - p83 [1-50]
Springer, Nancy - *Fair Peril*
   KR - v64 - S 15 '96 - p1362 [51-250]
   PW - v243 - O 21 '96 - p76 [51-250]
   Secret Star
   y BL - v93 - Ap 1 '97 - p1322 [51-250]
   y KR - v65 - Ap 1 '97 - p561 [51-250]
Springford, Michael - *Electron*
   New Sci - v154 - My 3 '97 - p48 [501+]
Sprinkle, Robert Hunt - *Profession of Conscience*
   AHR - v101 - O '96 - p1181 [501+]
Sproles, George B - *Changing Appearances*
   JPC - v30 - Fall '96 - p224 [251-500]
Sprott, Duncan - *Our Lady of the Potatoes*
   Books - v9 - S '95 - p25 [1-50]
Sproul, R C - *Faith Alone*
   Ch Today - v40 - O 7 '96 - p54+ [501+]
   Ch Today - v40 - O 7 '96 - p55+ [501+]
Sproule, J Michael - *Channels of Propaganda*
   Rapport - v19 - 4 '96 - p36 [251-500]
Sproxton, Judy - *Violence and Religion*
   Rel St Rev - v23 - Ja '97 - p84 [51-250]
Spruill, Steven - *Daughter of Darkness*
   y BL - v93 - My 15 '97 - p1564 [51-250]
Sprung, Mervyn - *After Truth*
   RM - v49 - Je '96 - p947+ [251-500]
Sprunger, Keith L - *Trumpets from the Tower*
   CH - v65 - S '96 - p493+ [501+]
Spruyt, Hendrik - *The Sovereign State and Its Competitors*
   JIH - v27 - Win '97 - p504+ [501+]
   Specu - v71 - Jl '96 - p766+ [501+]
Spry, Jennifer - *Orlando's Sleep*
   PW - v244 - Ap 7 '97 - p87 [51-250]
Spudis, Paul D - *The Once and Future Moon*
   Astron - v25 - Ap '97 - p105 [51-250]
   y BL - v93 - N 1 '96 - p467+ [51-250]
   y BL - v93 - D 1 '96 - p664 [1-50]
   LJ - v121 - N 15 '96 - p86 [51-250]
   New Sci - v153 - F 22 '97 - p42 [51-250]
   NH - v106 - Mr '97 - p13 [1-50]
   PW - v243 - N 4 '96 - p61 [51-250]
Spufford, Francis - *I May Be Some Time*
   Lon R Bks - v18 - Jl 18 '96 - p10+ [501+]
Spufford, Margaret - *The World of Rural Dissenters 1520-1725*
   Albion - v28 - Fall '96 - p476+ [501+]
   JIH - v27 - Spr '97 - p673+ [501+]
   Sev Cent N - v54 - Spr '96 - p20+ [501+]

Spuler, David - *C++ and C Tools, Utilities, Libraries, and Resources*
 SciTech - v20 - D '96 - p9 [51-250]
Spurge, Lorraine - *Knowledge Exchange Business Encyclopedia Master Reference*
 r PW - v244 - Mr 17 '97 - p74 [51-250]
Spurr, Elizabeth - *The Long, Long Letter (Illus. by David Catrow)*
 c HB Guide - v7 - Fall '96 - p278 [51-250]
 c LATBR - My 26 '96 - p11 [51-250]
 c RT - v50 - Ap '97 - p595+ [51-250]
 c SLJ - v42 - Ag '96 - p130 [51-250]
 c Smith - v27 - N '96 - p168 [1-50]
Mama's Birthday Surprise (Illus. by Felipe Davalos)
 c BL - v93 - N 1 '96 - p501+ [51-250]
 c HB Guide - v8 - Spr '97 - p60 [51-250]
 c KR - v64 - Ag 15 '96 - p1243 [51-250]
 c SLJ - v42 - N '96 - p110+ [51-250]
Spyri, Johanna - *Heidi (Illus. by Jacques Rozier)*
 y HB Guide - v8 - Spr '97 - p84 [51-250]
 c SLJ - v43 - Mr '97 - p193 [51-250]
Heidi (Illus. by Jessie Willcox Smith)
 c HB Guide - v7 - Fall '96 - p297+ [51-250]
Heidi (McDonough). Audio Version
 y Kliatt - v31 - My '97 - p40 [51-250]
Heidi (Young Reader's Christian Library)
 c Ch BWatch - v6 - Jl '96 - p2 [1-50]
Spyropulos, Diana - *Cornelius and the Dog Star (Illus. by Ray Williams)*
 c Ch BWatch - v6 - S '96 - p8 [51-250]
Squire, Ann - *101 Questions and Answers about Backyard Wildlife (Illus. by Jennifer DiRubbio)*
 c BL - v93 - D 1 '96 - p660 [51-250]
 c HB Guide - v8 - Spr '97 - p120 [51-250]
 c KR - v64 - N 1 '96 - p1608 [51-250]
 c SLJ - v43 - Ja '97 - p109 [51-250]
Squire, Vernon A - *Moving Loads on Ice Plates*
 SciTech - v20 - S '96 - p50 [51-250]
Sreberny-Mohammadi, Annabelle - *Small Media, Big Revolution*
 Rel St Rev - v22 - O '96 - p357 [51-250]
Srebnick, Amy Gilman - *The Mysterious Death of Mary Rogers*
 Historian - v59 - Win '97 - p444+ [251-500]
 Lon R Bks - v18 - O 3 '96 - p26+ [501+]
Srebrnik, Henry - *London Jews and British Communism 1935-1945*
 S&S - v61 - Spr '97 - p140+ [501+]
Sreenivasan, Gopal - *The Limits of Lockean Rights in Property*
 APSR - v91 - Mr '97 - p180+ [501+]
 RM - v50 - D '96 - p426+ [501+]
Sreenivasan, Jyotsna - *Aruna's Journeys (Illus. by Merryl Winstein)*
 c PW - v243 - D 16 '96 - p60 [51-250]
Sri Lanka Handbook with the Maldives. 1st Ed.
 r BL - v93 - S 15 '96 - p210 [1-50]
Sridharan, Eswaran - *The Political Economy of Industrial Promotion*
 R&R Bk N - v11 - D '96 - p32 [1-50]
Sridharan, Kripa - *The ASEAN Region in India's Foreign Policy*
 Choice - v34 - N '96 - p533 [51-250]
 R&R Bk N - v12 - F '97 - p19 [51-250]
Srinivasan, K - *Regulating Reproduction in India's Population*
 Pac A - v69 - Fall '96 - p435+ [501+]
Srivastava, Aschok K - *Vanadium Compounds*
 SciTech - v20 - N '96 - p33 [51-250]
Srivastava, Jitendra P - *Biodiversity and Agricultural Intensification*
 JEL - v35 - Mr '97 - p297 [51-250]
Srivastava, Vivek - *Liberalization, Productivity and Competition*
 JEL - v35 - Mr '97 - p283 [51-250]
Srivatsa, Arun R - *Advances in Coatings Technologies for Corrosion and Wear Resistant Coatings*
 SciTech - v20 - N '96 - p80 [51-250]
SSADM for Handling Geographic Information
 GJ - v162 - Jl '96 - p242 [1-50]
Ssu-Ma, Chien - *The Grand Scribe's Records. Vols. 1, 7*
 Pac A - v69 - Sum '96 - p263+ [501+]
 Rel St Rev - v22 - O '96 - p359+ [51-250]
Staar, Richard F - *The New Military in Russia*
 For Aff - v75 - S '96 - p141 [51-250]
 Parameters - v26 - Win '96 - p160+ [501+]
Staats, Arthur W - *Behavior and Personality*
 Choice - v34 - F '97 - p1041 [51-250]
Stabenow, Dana - *Blood Will Tell*
 Arm Det - v29 - Fall '96 - p495 [251-500]

Breakup
 BL - v93 - My 15 '97 - p1567 [51-250]
 KR - v65 - My 1 '97 - p684 [251-500]
 PW - v244 - Ap 21 '97 - p64 [51-250]
Stabile, Donald R - *Work and Welfare*
 Choice - v34 - S '96 - p178 [51-250]
 JEH - v57 - Mr '97 - p258+ [501+]
 JEL - v34 - S '96 - p1406 [51-250]
Stabiner, Karen - *To Dance with the Devil*
 BL - v93 - Ap 1 '97 - p1272 [51-250]
 KR - v65 - Mr 15 '97 - p450 [251-500]
 LATBR - Ap 13 '97 - pD [501+]
 LJ - v122 - Ap 1 '97 - p116 [51-250]
 NYTBR - v102 - Ap 13 '97 - p8 [501+]
 PW - v244 - Ap 7 '97 - p83+ [51-250]
Stableford, Brian - *The Hunger and Ecstacy of Vampires*
 ABR - v18 - D '96 - p27 [501+]
Stacey, Cherylyn - *Gone to Maui*
 y Quill & Q - v62 - S '96 - p75 [251-500]
How Do You Spell Abducted?
 y BIC - v25 - O '96 - p31 [251-500]
 y Kliatt - v30 - N '96 - p11 [51-250]
 c SLJ - v42 - D '96 - p124 [51-250]
Stacey, Jackie - *Star Gazing*
 Signs - v22 - Aut '96 - p248+ [501+]
Stacey, Judith - *In the Name of the Family*
 Ms - v7 - Ja '97 - p82 [1-50]
 NYTBR - v101 - S 22 '96 - p27 [501+]
 Wom R Bks - v14 - Ja '97 - p10+ [501+]
Stacey, Ralph D - *Complexity and Creativity in Organizations*
 R&R Bk N - v11 - N '96 - p29 [51-250]
Stacey, Robin Chapman - *The Road to Judgement*
 EHR - v111 - N '96 - p1233+ [251-500]
Stacey, Susannah - *Bone Idle*
 Arm Det - v30 - Win '97 - p19 [51-250]
Stacey, William A - *The Violent Couple*
 SF - v75 - S '96 - p392+ [251-500]
Stachniak, Zbigniew - *Resolution Proof Systems*
 SciTech - v20 - D '96 - p14 [51-250]
Stack, Carol - *Call to Home*
 Choice - v34 - O '96 - p351+ [51-250]
 JSH - v63 - F '97 - p213 [251-500]
Stackhouse, Max L - *Christian Social Ethics in a Global Era*
 Rel St Rev - v22 - O '96 - p340+ [51-250]
On Moral Business
 Ch Today - v41 - F 3 '97 - p62+ [501+]
Stackpole, Michael A - *Bacta War*
 y Kliatt - v31 - My '97 - p16 [51-250]
Talion Revenant
 y BL - v93 - Mr 15 '97 - p1231 [51-250]
Stade, George - *British Writers. 3rd Suppl.*
 r ARBA - v28 - '97 - p449 [51-250]
Stadler, John - *The Cats of Mrs. Calamari (Illus. by John Stadler)*
 c BL - v93 - Mr 1 '97 - p1167 [51-250]
 c KR - v65 - Mr 1 '97 - p388 [51-250]
 c Par Ch - v21 - Mr '97 - p4 [1-50]
Ready, Set, Go! (Illus. by John Stadler)
 c BL - v93 - S 15 '96 - p253 [51-250]
 c HB Guide - v8 - Spr '97 - p56 [51-250]
 c SLJ - v42 - D '96 - p106 [51-250]
Stadler Genetics Symposium (21st: 1995: University of Missouri-Columbia) - *Genomes of Plants and Animals*
 SciTech - v20 - N '96 - p27 [51-250]
Stadtwald, Kurt - *Roman Popes and German Patriots*
 Six Ct J - v27 - Win '96 - p1132+ [501+]
Staels, Hilde - *Margaret Atwood's Novels*
 Can Lit - Spr '97 - p226+ [501+]
Stafford, Barbara Maria - *Artful Science*
 Skeptic - v3 - '95 - p103 [51-250]
Stafford, Charles - *The Roads of Chinese Childhood*
 AJS - v102 - Ja '97 - p1218+ [501+]
 Rel St Rev - v23 - Ap '97 - p205 [51-250]
Stafford, Fiona J - *The Last of the Race*
 Sev Cent N - v54 - Spr '96 - p3+ [501+]
Stafford, Peter G - *Psychedelics Encyclopedia. 3rd Ed.*
 r BL - v93 - F 1 '97 - p959 [51-250]
Stafford, Peter J - *Kaleidoscopic Tree Boas*
 Choice - v34 - N '96 - p485 [51-250]
 SciTech - v20 - S '96 - p20 [1-50]
Stafford, William - *Even in Quiet Places*
 HR - v49 - Win '97 - p659+ [501+]
 WAL - v31 - Fall '96 - p255+ [501+]
Stafford-Clark, David - *What Freud Really Said*
 LJ - v122 - Mr 15 '97 - p94 [1-50]
Stahl, Harriet K - *The Family of Johann Jacob Stahl, Sr. of Lehigh County, Pennsylvania*
 r EGH - v50 - N '96 - p195 [51-250]

Stahl, Hilda - *The White Pine Chronicles*
 y BL - v93 - Ja '97 - p819 [51-250]
Stahl, Jerry - *Permanent Midnight*
 PW - v244 - Mr 17 '97 - p81 [1-50]
Stahl, Peter W - *Archaeology in the Lowland American Tropics*
 Am Ant - v61 - O '96 - p810+ [501+]
Stahl, Saul - *Introductory Modern Algebra*
 SciTech - v21 - Mr '97 - p12 [51-250]
Stahl, Stephen M - *Essential Psychopharmacology*
 Readings - v12 - Mr '97 - p28 [51-250]
Staiger, Janet - *Bad Women*
 J Pop F&TV - v24 - Win '97 - p187+ [501+]
Stainer, Pauline - *The Wound-Dresser's Dream*
 Obs - S 29 '96 - p18* [51-250]
 y Sch Lib - v44 - N '96 - p176 [51-250]
 TLS - N 1 '96 - p22 [501+]
Staines, David - *Beyond the Provinces*
 BIC - v26 - F '97 - p21+ [501+]
 Can Lit - Spr '97 - p218+ [501+]
Stainforth, Gordon - *The Cullin: Great Mountain Ridge of Skye*
 GJ - v162 - Jl '96 - p236 [51-250]
Stainton, Robert J - *Philosophical Perspectives on Language*
 Choice - v34 - Ap '97 - p1353 [51-250]
 CPR - v16 - O '96 - p376+ [501+]
Stairs, William G - *Victorian Explorer*
 EHR - v112 - Ap '97 - p515+ [501+]
Stake, Robert E - *The Art of Case Study Research*
 MLJ - v80 - Win '96 - p556+ [501+]
Stakem, Patrick H - *A Practitioner's Guide to RISC Microprocessor Architecture*
 r SciTech - v20 - S '96 - p4 [51-250]
Stakes, Richard - *Meeting Special Needs in Mainstream Schools*
 TES - N 1 '96 - pR10 [251-500]
Stakhiv, IEvhen - *Kriz' Tiurmy, Pidpillia I Kordony*
 BL - v93 - N 15 '96 - p577 [1-50]
Stalcup, Brenda - *The Disabled*
 y Kliatt - v31 - Mr '97 - p29+ [51-250]
The Women's Rights Movement
 y Ch BWatch - v6 - My '96 - p5 [51-250]
 y SLJ - v42 - Ag '96 - p168 [51-250]
Staley, Jeffrey L - *Reading with a Passion*
 Rel St Rev - v22 - O '96 - p347 [51-250]
Staley, Katherine - *The Art of Short Selling*
 WSJ-Cent - v99 - My 12 '97 - pA12 [51-250]
Staley, Lynn - *Margery Kempe's Dissenting Fictions*
 MLR - v92 - Ap '97 - p434+ [501+]
 Specu - v71 - O '96 - p1027+ [501+]
Stalin, Joseph - *Stalin's Letters to Molotov 1925-1936*
 AHR - v101 - D '96 - p1585+ [501+]
 Historian - v59 - Win '97 - p468+ [251-500]
 NYRB - v44 - Mr 6 '97 - p6+ [501+]
 TLS - Ja 31 '97 - p6+ [501+]
Stallabrass, Julian - *Gargantua: Manufactured Mass Culture*
 Afterimage - v24 - Ja '97 - p23 [51-250]
 NS - v126 - Ja 24 '97 - p44+ [501+]
Stallings, Barbara - *Global Change, Regional Response*
 CS - v26 - Ja '97 - p54+ [501+]
 Econ J - v107 - Ja '97 - p271 [251-500]
Stallings, Joseph M - *Celebrating An Authentic Passover Seder*
 CLW - v67 - D '96 - p54 [251-500]
Stallings, Robert A - *Promoting Risk*
 SF - v75 - S '96 - p381+ [501+]
Stallings, William - *Data and Computer Communications. 5th Ed.*
 SciTech - v20 - D '96 - p76 [51-250]
Internet Protocols
 SciTech - v21 - Mr '97 - p88 [51-250]
Local and Metropolitan Area Networks. 5th Ed.
 SciTech - v20 - S '96 - p55 [51-250]
SNMP, SNMPv2, and RMON. 2nd Ed.
 SciTech - v20 - N '96 - p74 [51-250]
Stalls, Clay - *Possessing the Land*
 Choice - v34 - Ja '97 - p858 [51-250]
Stallwood, Veronica - *Oxford Mourning*
 Arm Det - v29 - Fall '96 - p484 [251-500]
Staltmane, V E - *Onomasticheskaya Leksikografiya*
 Names - v44 - Je '96 - p136+ [501+]
Stam, Allan C - *Win, Lose, or Draw*
 Choice - v34 - My '97 - p1575 [51-250]
Stam, Dagmar - *Cooking with Sara and Tommy*
 c Cur R - v35 - S '96 - p12 [51-250]
Gardening with Sara and Tommy
 c Cur R - v35 - S '96 - p12 [51-250]

Stamatis, D H - *Integrating QS-9000 with Your Automotive Quality System. 2nd Ed.*
    SciTech - v20 - N '96 - p77 [51-250]
Stamets, Paul - *Psilocybin Mushrooms of the World*
    r Choice - v34 - Ap '97 - p1365 [51-250]
Stamp, Daniel - *The Invisible Assembly Line*
    Per Psy - v49 - Aut '96 - p771+ [501+]
Stamp and Coin Mart
    p Am Phil - v110 - S '96 - p827+ [51-250]
Stamp Catalogue of Switzerland 1996
    r Am Phil - v110 - Ag '96 - p754 [51-250]
The Stamp Lover
    p Am Phil - v110 - S '96 - p828 [51-250]
Stamp Magazine
    p Am Phil - v110 - S '96 - p827 [51-250]
Stamp Yearbook 1996
    r Am Phil - v111 - F '97 - p163 [51-250]
Stampa, Gaspara - *Gaspara Stampa: Selected Poems*
    TranslRevS - v1 - My '95 - p25 [51-250]
Stampfle, Felice - *Netherlandish Drawings of the 15th and 16th Centuries and Flemish Drawings of the 17th and 18th Centuries in Pierpont Morgan Library*
    BM - v138 - Jl '96 - p465+ [501+]
Stancell, Steven - *Rap Whoz Who*
    r Choice - v34 - Ja '97 - p776 [51-250]
Standard and Poor's Insurance Company Ratings Guide. 1995 Ed.
    r ARBA - v28 - '97 - p98 [251-500]
Standard and Poor's SmallCap 600 Guide. 1996 Ed.
    r ARBA - v28 - '97 - p85+ [251-500]
Standard Catalogue of English and UK Coins 1066 to Date. 2nd Ed.
    r Coin W - v38 - Ja 13 '97 - p56 [51-250]
The Standard Periodical Directory 1997
    r ARBA - v28 - '97 - p34 [51-250]
Standard Postage Stamp Catalogue 1997. Vol. 1A
    r Am Phil - v110 - Jl '96 - p634 [501+]
Standards of Conduct in Public Life. Vols. 1-2
    J Gov Info - v23 - S '96 - p647+ [51-250]
Standifer, Leon C - *Binding Up the Wounds*
    KR - v65 - Ja 1 '97 - p50 [251-500]
Standiford, Les - *Deal on Ice*
    BW - v27 - F 16 '97 - p11 [51-250]
    KR - v64 - N 15 '96 - p1629 [251-500]
    LJ - v122 - F 1 '97 - p111 [1-50]
    PW - v243 - N 11 '96 - p55 [51-250]
Standiford, Natalie - *Astronauts Are Sleeping (Illus. by Allen Garns)*
    c CCB-B - v50 - F '97 - p223 [51-250]
    c HB Guide - v8 - Spr '97 - p49 [51-250]
    c Inst - v106 - O '96 - p68 [1-50]
    c KR - v64 - N 1 '96 - p1608 [51-250]
    c PW - v243 - N 25 '96 - p74 [51-250]
    c SLJ - v42 - D '96 - p106+ [51-250]
Bravest Dog Ever: The True Story of Balto
    c Bks Keeps - Jl '96 - p11 [51-250]
Standing, Guy - *Minimum Wages in Central and Eastern Europe*
    JEL - v34 - D '96 - p2073 [51-250]
Russian Unemployment and Enterprise Restructuring
    Choice - v34 - My '97 - p1550 [51-250]
Standish, Peter - *Hispanic Culture of Mexico, Central America, and the Caribbean*
    r ARBA - v28 - '97 - p161+ [51-250]
    r Choice - v34 - O '96 - p253 [51-250]
Standley, Ken - *From This High Place*
    PW - v243 - D 16 '96 - p53 [51-250]
Stanfield, James Ronald - *John Kenneth Galbraith*
    Choice - v34 - N '96 - p509 [51-250]
    JEL - v35 - Mr '97 - p193 [51-250]
    TLS - Ja 17 '97 - p28 [501+]
Stanford, Peter - *The Devil: A Biography*
    BL - v93 - O 1 '96 - p306 [51-250]
    CR - v269 - Ag '96 - p104+ [501+]
    LATBR - N 10 '96 - p5 [501+]
    LJ - v121 - S 15 '96 - p74 [51-250]
    NS & S - v9 - Ap 26 '96 - p37+ [251-500]
    PW - v243 - O 14 '96 - p76 [51-250]
    TES - F 21 '97 - p7* [51-250]
The Devil: A Biography. Audio Version
    BWatch - v18 - Mr '97 - p7 [1-50]
Stang, Mark - *Baseball by the Numbers. Vols. 1-2*
    r ARBA - v28 - '97 - p296+ [51-250]
Stange, Mary Zeiss - *Woman the Hunter*
    KR - v65 - Mr 15 '97 - p450+ [251-500]
    PW - v244 - Ap 7 '97 - p84+ [51-250]
Stanish, Charles - *Archaeological Research at Tumatumani, Juli, Peru*
    LA Ant - v7 - Je '96 - p168+ [501+]

Stanisic, Balsha R - *Synthesis of Power Distribution to Manage Signal Integrity in Mixed-Signal ICs*
    SciTech - v20 - D '96 - p79 [51-250]
Stanley, Autumn - *Mothers and Daughters of Invention*
    T&C - v38 - Ja '97 - p214+ [501+]
Stanley, Barbara H - *Research Ethics*
    Readings - v11 - D '96 - p21 [51-250]
Stanley, David - *South Pacific Handbook. 6th Ed.*
    r BL - v93 - S 15 '96 - p212 [51-250]
    r BWatch - v17 - S '96 - p5 [51-250]
Stanley, Diane - *Cleopatra (Illus. by Diane Stanley)*
    c SLJ - v42 - D '96 - p45 [51-250]
Elena
    c Ch BWatch - v6 - D '96 - p5 [1-50]
    c HB Guide - v7 - Fall '96 - p298 [51-250]
    c RT - v50 - My '97 - p683 [51-250]
Good Queen Bess (Illus. by Diane Stanley)
    c SLJ - v42 - D '96 - p45 [51-250]
Leonardo Da Vinci (Illus. by Diane Stanley)
    c BL - v93 - Ja '97 - p766 [1-50]
    c BL - v93 - S 15 '96 - p241 [51-250]
    c BL - v93 - Ap 1 '97 - p1302 [1-50]
    c CCB-B - v50 - S '96 - p32 [51-250]
    c CSM - v88 - N 21 '96 - pB4 [51-250]
    c HB - v73 - Ja '97 - p81+ [51-250]
    c HB Guide - v8 - Spr '97 - p139 [51-250]
    c NYTBR - v101 - D 8 '96 - p78 [501+]
    c PW - v243 - N 4 '96 - p49 [51-250]
    c SLJ - v42 - S '96 - p221 [51-250]
    c SLJ - v42 - D '96 - p32 [1-50]
Rumpelstiltskin's Daughter (Illus. by Diane Stanley)
    c BL - v93 - Mr 1 '97 - p1167 [51-250]
    c KR - v65 - F 15 '97 - p306 [51-250]
    c PW - v244 - F 17 '97 - p219 [51-250]
    c SLJ - v43 - Mr '97 - p167 [51-250]
Saving Sweetness (Illus. by G Brian Karas)
    c BL - v93 - Ja '97 - p768 [1-50]
    c BL - v93 - Ja '97 - p857 [51-250]
    c CBRS - v25 - F '97 - p79 [51-250]
    c CCB-B - v50 - N '96 - p116 [51-250]
    c CSM - v88 - S 26 '96 - pB1 [51-250]
    c HB - v72 - S '96 - p588+ [51-250]
    c HB Guide - v8 - Spr '97 - p49 [51-250]
    c NW - v128 - D 2 '96 - p86 [1-50]
    c PW - v243 - O 14 '96 - p83 [51-250]
    c SLJ - v42 - N '96 - p93 [51-250]
    c SLJ - v42 - D '96 - p32 [1-50]
    c Smith - v27 - N '96 - p166 [1-50]
The True Adventure of Daniel Hall (Illus. by Diane Stanley)
    c RT - v50 - S '96 - p57 [51-250]
    c RT - v50 - N '96 - p246 [51-250]
Stanley, Elizabeth - *The Deliverance of Dancing Bears*
    c Magpies - v11 - Jl '96 - p45 [1-50]
Stanley, Eric Gerald - *In the Foreground: Beowulf*
    MLR - v92 - Ja '97 - p159+ [501+]
    Specu - v71 - O '96 - p1029+ [501+]
Stanley, Fay - *The Last Princess (Illus. by Diane Stanley)*
    c SLJ - v42 - D '96 - p45 [51-250]
Stanley, G E - *The Day the Ants Got Really Mad (Illus. by Sal Murdocca)*
    c SLJ - v42 - Ag '96 - p130 [51-250]
Stanley, Gregory Kent - *The Rise and Fall of the Sportswoman*
    R&R Bk N - v12 - F '97 - p32 [51-250]
Stanley, Jerry - *Big Annie of Calumet*
    y BL - v93 - Ap 1 '97 - p1305 [1-50]
    c CLW - v67 - D '96 - p61+ [51-250]
    c HB - v72 - S '96 - p624+ [51-250]
    c HB Guide - v7 - Fall '96 - p315 [51-250]
    c NYTBR - v101 - Ag 25 '96 - p23 [51-250]
I Am an American
    y Ch BWatch - v6 - S '96 - p6 [51-250]
Stanley, John - *Creature Features*
    r PW - v244 - Ja 20 '97 - p390 [51-250]
Stanley, Malaika Rose - *Man Hunt*
    c Bks Keeps - Ja '97 - p22 [51-250]
    c Sch Lib - v45 - F '97 - p34 [51-250]
    c TES - N 22 '96 - p12* [51-250]
Stanley, Phyllis M - *American Environmental Heroes*
    c BL - v93 - S 1 '96 - p122 [51-250]
    c HB Guide - v7 - Fall '96 - p376 [1-50]
Stanley, Steven M - *Children of the Ice Age*
    LATBR - My 12 '96 - p1+ [501+]
    Nature - v383 - S 12 '96 - p137 [501+]
Stanley, Thomas J - *The Millionaire Next Door*
    Bus W - Ap 28 '97 - p16 [51-250]
    CSM - v89 - Ap 3 '97 - p14 [51-250]
Stanley, William - *The Protection Racket State*
    Choice - v34 - Ja '97 - p870 [51-250]
    WorldV - v12 - O '96 - p8+ [51-250]

Stanley Gibbons Stamp Catalogue: Middle East. 5th Ed.
    r Am Phil - v110 - D '96 - p1087 [51-250]
Stanley-Baker, Joan - *Old Masters Repainted*
    Ch Rev Int - v3 - Fall '96 - p538+ [51-250]
Stann, Kap - *Georgia Handbook. 2nd Ed.*
    r BL - v93 - S 15 '96 - p212 [1-50]
Stannard, Dorothy - *Bath and Surroundings*
    r BL - v93 - S 15 '96 - p210 [1-50]
Stannard, Russell - *Here I Am!*
    c Bks Keeps - Jl '96 - p28 [501+]
Letters to Uncle Albert
    c Bks Keeps - Jl '96 - p28 [501+]
    c New Sci - v153 - F 8 '97 - p46 [51-250]
    c Sch Lib - v44 - Ag '96 - p114 [51-250]
More Letters to Uncle Albert
    c Obs - Mr 30 '97 - p16* [501+]
Our Universe
    c Bks Keeps - Jl '96 - p28 [501+]
A Short History of God, Me and the Universe
    c Bks Keeps - Jl '96 - p28 [501+]
The Time and Space of Uncle Albert
    c Bks Keeps - Jl '96 - p28 [501+]
Uncle Albert and the Quantum Quest
    c Bks Keeps - Jl '96 - p28 [501+]
World of 1001 Mysteries
    c Bks Keeps - Jl '96 - p28 [501+]
Stanners, David - *Europe's Environment*
    Nature - v383 - S 12 '96 - p138 [501+]
Stans, Maurice H - *One of the President's Men*
    Pres SQ - v26 - Sum '96 - p898+ [501+]
Stansky, Peter - *London's Burning*
    JIH - v27 - Aut '96 - p307+ [501+]
On or about December 1910
    BW - v26 - N 3 '96 - p13 [51-250]
    Choice - v34 - Mr '97 - p1223+ [51-250]
    KR - v64 - Ag 15 '96 - p1224 [251-500]
    LJ - v121 - O 1 '96 - p77+ [51-250]
    NYTLa - v146 - N 29 '96 - pC36 [501+]
Stanton, Annette L - *The Psychology of Women's Health*
    Readings - v11 - S '96 - p22 [51-250]
Stanton, Eddie Allan - *The War Diaries of Eddie Allan Stanton*
    Aust Bk R - N '96 - p30+ [501+]
Stanton, Sarah - *Cambridge Paperback Guide to Theatre*
    yr Sch Lib - v44 - Ag '96 - p128 [51-250]
Stanway, Andrew - *The New Natural Family Doctor*
    Quill & Q - v62 - Ag '96 - p31 [51-250]
Stanway, Penny - *Nueva Guia Del Embarazo Y Cuidado Del Bebe*
    LJ - v122 - Ja '97 - p80 [51-250]
Stanzel, F K - *Intimate Enemies*
    RES - v47 - Ag '96 - p448+ [501+]
Stape, J H - *A Portrait in Letters*
    Nine-C Lit - v51 - Mr '97 - p566 [51-250]
Stapledon, Olaf - *An Olaf Stapledon Reader*
    BL - v93 - My 1 '97 - p1475 [51-250]
Staples, Suzanne Fisher - *Dangerous Skies*
    y BL - v93 - S 1 '96 - p128 [51-250]
    y BL - v93 - Ap 1 '97 - p1294 [1-50]
    c CBRS - v25 - Ja '97 - p59 [51-250]
    y CCB-B - v50 - O '96 - p77 [51-250]
    c HB - v73 - Ja '97 - p67+ [51-250]
    c HB Guide - v8 - Spr '97 - p75 [51-250]
    c NYTBR - v102 - F 16 '97 - p25 [51-250]
    y Par Ch - v20 - O '96 - p12 [1-50]
    c PW - v243 - N 4 '96 - p49 [51-250]
    y SLJ - v42 - O '96 - p148+ [51-250]
    y VOYA - v19 - D '96 - p274 [51-250]
Shabanu, Daughter of the Wind
    c JOYS - v10 - Fall '96 - p46+ [501+]
Staples, Walter - *In Search of Your True Self*
    Rapport - v19 - 6 '96 - p29 [251-500]
Stapleton, G P - *Institutional Shareholders and Corporate Governance*
    Econ - v340 - S 14 '96 - p9* [51-250]
Stapleton, Julia - *Englishness and the Study of Politics*
    EHR - v112 - F '97 - p262+ [501+]
Stapleton, M L - *Harmful Eloquence*
    Choice - v34 - N '96 - p452 [51-250]
Star, Susan Leigh - *Ecologies of Knowledge*
    CS - v25 - S '96 - p680+ [51-250]
Starck, Clemens - *Journeyman's Wages*
    Sm Pr R - v28 - Je '96 - p12 [251-500]
    WAL - v31 - Fall '96 - p271+ [251-500]
Starer, Robert - *The Music Teacher*
    KR - v65 - F 15 '97 - p252+ [51-250]
    NYTBR - v102 - Ap 13 '97 - p20 [51-250]
    PW - v244 - F 3 '97 - p95 [51-250]

Stares, Paul B - *Global Habit*
    Choice - v34 - O '96 - p358 [51-250]
    JEL - v34 - D '96 - p2081 [51-250]
    Pol Stud J - v24 - Sum '96 - p334 [51-250]
Stargardt, Nicholas - *The German Idea of Militarism*
    EHR - v111 - S '96 - p1008+ [251-500]
    HT - v46 - Jl '96 - p52+ [501+]
Starhawk - *Walking to Mercury*
    BL - v93 - D 15 '96 - p693 [51-250]
    KR - v65 - Ja 15 '97 - p93 [251-500]
    Ms - v7 - Mr '97 - p83 [251-500]
    PW - v244 - Ja 6 '97 - p65 [251-500]
Stark, Frank M - *Communicative Interaction, Power, and the State*
    Choice - v34 - Ja '97 - p838 [51-250]
    R&R Bk N - v11 - D '96 - p59 [51-250]
Stark, Oded - *Altruism and Beyond*
    JEL - v34 - D '96 - p1956+ [501+]
Stark, Rodney - *The Rise of Christianity*
    AJS - v102 - Ja '97 - p1163+ [501+]
    Am - v176 - Mr 8 '97 - p32 [51-250]
    CC - v113 - N 6 '96 - p1081+ [501+]
    Choice - v34 - O '96 - p299 [51-250]
    Comw - v124 - Mr 28 '97 - p27+ [501+]
Stark, Steven D - *Glued to the Set*
   y BL - v93 - My 1 '97 - p1473 [51-250]
    KR - v65 - Mr 15 '97 - p451 [251-500]
    LJ - v122 - My 1 '97 - p106 [51-250]
Stark, Suzanne J - *Female Tars*
    AB - v99 - Mr 17 '97 - p874+ [501+]
    R&R Bk N - v12 - F '97 - p101 [51-250]
    TLS - O 4 '96 - p34 [501+]
Stark, Ulf - *Mi Hermano Mayor (Illus. by Mati Lepp)*
    BL - v93 - F 15 '97 - p1032 [51-250]
Starke, Ruth - *Coming Out*
   y Aust Bk R - D '96 - p86+ [501+]
Starkell, Don - *Paddle to the Arctic*
    BIC - v25 - S '96 - p10+ [501+]
Starkey, Dinah - *Scholastic Atlas of Exploration*
   cr Inst - v106 - O '96 - p93 [1-50]
Starkie, Allan - *Fergie: Her Secret Life*
    BL - v93 - D 15 '96 - p690 [1-50]
    Ent W - D 13 '96 - p72 [251-500]
    NYTBR - v102 - Ja 5 '97 - p13+ [501+]
    Obs - D 1 '96 - p16* [251-250]
    Spec - v277 - N 23 '96 - p54+ [501+]
Starlanyl, Devin - *Fibromyalgia and Chronic Myofascial Pain Syndrome*
    LJ - v121 - S 15 '96 - p86+ [51-250]
Starlight 1
   y BL - v93 - S 1 '96 - p69 [51-250]
    BW - v26 - S 29 '96 - p11 [251-500]
    PW - v243 - S 2 '96 - p120 [51-250]
Starn, Orin - *The Peru Reader*
    HAHR - v76 - N '96 - p809 [251-500]
Starnes, Tanya - *Mad at Your Lawyer*
    LJ - v121 - O 15 '96 - p76 [51-250]
Starnes, Thomas C - *Der Teutsche Merkur*
    Lib - v18 - Je '96 - p169 [51-250]
    MLN - v112 - Ap '97 - p491+ [501+]
Starosta, Paul - *The Frog: Natural Acrobat (Illus. by Paul Starosta)*
   c SLJ - v43 - Ja '97 - p109 [51-250]
Starowieyski, Marek - *The Spirituality of Ancient Monasticism*
    CH - v66 - Mr '97 - p186 [51-250]
Starr, Kevin - *The Dream Endures*
    KR - v65 - F 1 '97 - p209 [251-500]
    LJ - v122 - My 1 '97 - p122 [51-250]
    NYTBR - v102 - Ap 20 '97 - p26 [501+]
    Endangered Dreams
    CAY - v17 - Win '96 - p7 [51-250]
    LATBR - D 29 '96 - p3 [51-250]
    PHR - v66 - F '97 - p127+ [501+]
    SE - v60 - S '96 - p302 [51-250]
    WAL - v31 - Sum '96 - p181+ [251-500]
Starr, Michael - *Art Carney: A Biography*
    BL - v93 - Ap 1 '97 - p1275 [51-250]
    KR - v65 - F 15 '97 - p287 [251-500]
    PW - v244 - Mr 17 '97 - p68 [51-250]
Starr, S Frederick - *Bamboula: The Life and Times of Louis Moreau Gottschalk*
    JPC - v30 - Fall '96 - p224+ [251-500]
Stars and Planets (Discoveries)
   c Magpies - v11 - Jl '96 - p38 [51-250]
Starting and Operating a Business in New York. 4th Ed.
    LJ - v122 - My 1 '97 - p52 [1-50]
Starting from Toys
    TES - F 14 '97 - p16* [51-250]
Stasheff, Christopher - *The Day the Magic Stopped*
    SF Chr - v18 - O '96 - p80 [1-50]

The Shaman
   y Kliatt - v30 - S '96 - p20 [51-250]
A Wizard in Peace
    LJ - v121 - S 15 '96 - p101 [51-250]
    PW - v243 - S 30 '96 - p66 [51-250]
Stasiulis, Daiva - *Unsettling Settler Societies*
    CS - v26 - Mr '97 - p164+ [501+]
Stasney, C Richard - *Atlas of Dynamic Laryngeal Pathology*
   r SciTech - v20 - D '96 - p51 [51-250]
State and Regional Associations of the United States. 8th Ed.
   r LJ - v122 - Ja '97 - p90 [51-250]
State (Comedy Group) - *State by State with the State*
   c Ent W - My 16 '97 - p108 [51-250]
State Legislative Sourcebook 1996
   r ARBA - v28 - '97 - p271 [51-250]
   r Choice - v34 - S '96 - p99 [51-250]
The State of Academic Freedom in Africa 1995
    WorldV - v13 - Ja '97 - p11+ [251-500]
The State of Canada's Climate
    J Gov Info - v23 - S '96 - p619+ [51-250]
State of the City 1995: Hartford, Conn.
   r J Gov Info - v23 - S '96 - p600 [51-250]
State of the World 1984-
   r CC - v113 - N 20 '96 - p1175 [51-250]
State of the World 1997
   r SB - v33 - My '97 - p101 [51-250]
State Solid Waste Management Plan 1995
    J Gov Info - v23 - S '96 - p591 [51-250]
Staten, Henry - *Eros in Mourning*
    MLN - v111 - D '96 - p1060+ [501+]
Staten, Vince - *Did Monkeys Invent the Monkey Wrench?*
    CSM - v88 - O 2 '96 - p15 [501+]
Stater, Victor L - *Noble Government*
    EHR - v112 - Ap '97 - p471+ [251-500]
States, Bert O - *Dreaming and Storytelling*
    CLS - v33 - 2 '96 - p218+ [501+]
The Pleasure of the Play
    MLR - v91 - Jl '96 - p712+ [501+]
Seeing in the Dark
    Obs - Mr 30 '97 - p15* [501+]
    Spec - v278 - Mr 22 '97 - p40+ [501+]
The Statesman's Year Book 1996-1997
   r BL - v92 - Ag '96 - p1919 [51-250]
Statham, Anne - *The Rise of Marginal Voices*
    Choice - v34 - Mr '97 - p1247 [51-250]
Statistical Handbook 1995: States of the Former USSR
   r JEL - v34 - S '96 - p1419+ [51-250]
Statistical Office of the European Communities - *Women and Men in the European Union*
    J Gov Info - v23 - S '96 - p670 [51-250]
Statistical Papers
   p JEL - v34 - S '96 - p1507 [51-250]
Statman, Daniel - *Moral Luck*
    Ethics - v107 - Ja '97 - p387+ [51-250]
Statt, Daniel - *Foreigners and Englishmen*
    AHR - v102 - F '97 - p103 [501+]
    JEH - v56 - S '96 - p711+ [501+]
    JIH - v27 - Spr '97 - p675+ [501+]
The Status of Black Atlanta 1993
    J Gov Info - v23 - S '96 - p606 [51-250]
The Status of Black Atlanta 1994
    J Gov Info - v23 - S '96 - p606 [51-250]
The Status of Black Atlanta 1995
    J Gov Info - v23 - S '96 - p606 [51-250]
Staub, Frank - *Children of Cuba (Illus. by Frank Staub)*
   c BL - v93 - D 1 '96 - p650+ [51-250]
   c HB Guide - v8 - Spr '97 - p178 [51-250]
   c SLJ - v43 - F '97 - p96 [51-250]
The Children of the Sierra Madre (Illus. by Frank Staub)
   c BL - v93 - O 1 '96 - p344 [51-250]
   c HB Guide - v8 - Spr '97 - p178 [51-250]
   c SLJ - v42 - Ag '96 - p160 [51-250]
Children of Yucatan (Illus. by Frank Staub)
   c BL - v93 - O 1 '96 - p344 [51-250]
   c CCB-B - v50 - N '96 - p116+ [51-250]
   c HB Guide - v8 - Spr '97 - p178 [51-250]
   c SLJ - v42 - O '96 - p140+ [51-250]
Stauber, John - *Toxic Sludge Is Good for You*
    JMCQ - v73 - Win '96 - p1017+ [251-500]
    Nat - v263 - N 18 '96 - p30+ [501+]
Staudohar, Paul D - *Baseball's Best Short Stories*
    PW - v244 - Mr 3 '97 - p72 [1-50]
Playing for Dollars. 3rd Ed.
    Choice - v34 - D '96 - p650 [51-250]
    JEL - v35 - Mr '97 - p241 [51-250]
Staunton, Irene - *Mothers of the Revolution*
    NWSA Jnl - v9 - Spr '97 - p1+ [501+]
Stavans, Ilan - *Art and Anger*
    Choice - v34 - F '97 - p971 [51-250]

The Hispanic Condition
   y JOYS - v9 - Sum '96 - p417+ [51-250]
Julio Cortazar: A Study of the Short Fiction
    Choice - v34 - S '96 - p134 [51-250]
New World
    KR - v64 - N 1 '96 - p1562 [251-500]
    LJ - v122 - Ja '97 - p152 [51-250]
The One-Handed Pianist and Other Stories
    ABR - v17 - Ag '96 - p17+ [501+]
    BW - v26 - Ag 4 '96 - p9 [501+]
Stave, Shirley A - *The Decline of the Goddess*
    ELT - v39 - 3 '96 - p357+ [501+]
Stave, Sondra Astor - *Achieving Racial Balance*
    AJE - v105 - F '97 - p227+ [501+]
Stavenhagen, Rodolfo - *Ethnic Conflicts and the Nation-State*
    Choice - v34 - Mr '97 - p1236 [51-250]
Stavreva, Kirilka - *Bulgaria*
   c Ch BWatch - v7 - Ja '97 - p3 [1-50]
Stavridis, Stelios - *Domestic Sources of Foreign Policy*
    R&R Bk N - v12 - F '97 - p28 [51-250]
Stay, Byron L - *Censorship*
   y BL - v93 - D 15 '96 - p715 [51-250]
   y Kliatt - v31 - Mr '97 - p30 [51-250]
Writing Center Perspectives
    Col Comp - v47 - O '96 - p442+ [51-250]
Stead, C K - *All Visitors Ashore*
    WLT - v70 - Aut '96 - p1034 [251-500]
Stead, Christopher - *Philosophy in Christian Antiquity*
    JR - v77 - Ap '97 - p307+ [501+]
Stead, W Edward - *Management for a Small Planet*
    Choice - v34 - N '96 - p504 [51-250]
Steadman, Ralph - *The Grapes of Ralph*
    LJ - v122 - Ap 1 '97 - p64 [1-50]
Steane, J B - *Singers of the Century*
   r Choice - v34 - Ja '97 - p776 [51-250]
    FF - v20 - S '96 - p473+ [501+]
    Spec - v277 - S 7 '96 - p33+ [501+]
Steane, John - *Oxfordshire*
    CR - v270 - Ja '97 - p56 [51-250]
Stearman, Kaye - *Gender Issues*
   y Sch Lib - v44 - Ag '96 - p126 [51-250]
Stearn, William T - *Botanical Latin. 4th Ed.*
   r Hort - v74 - D '96 - p61 [51-250]
Stearns, Michael - *A Nightmare's Dozen (Illus. by Michael Hussar)*
   y BL - v93 - Ja '97 - p844+ [251-500]
   y HB Guide - v8 - Spr '97 - p149 [51-250]
   y SLJ - v42 - D '96 - p139 [51-250]
A Starfarer's Dozen
   c New Ad - v9 - Fall '96 - p327+ [501+]
   y SF Chr - v18 - O '96 - p80 [1-50]
Stearns, Monteagle - *Talking to Strangers*
    Choice - v34 - S '96 - p212+ [51-250]
    JEL - v34 - S '96 - p1504 [51-250]
Stearns, Peter N - *The ABC-CLIO World History Companion to the Industrial Revolution*
   yr BL - v93 - S 1 '96 - p164 [251-500]
   r Choice - v34 - Ja '97 - p776 [51-250]
   r R&R Bk N - v11 - D '96 - p7 [51-250]
American Cool
    JIH - v27 - Aut '96 - p351+ [501+]
Fat History
    PW - v244 - Ap 21 '97 - p51 [251-250]
Stebbins, J Michael - *The Divine Initiative*
    Theol St - v57 - S '96 - p542+ [501+]
Stebbins, Robert A - *The Barbershop Singer*
    R&R Bk N - v11 - N '96 - p59 [51-250]
Stebbins, Robert C - *A Natural History of Amphibians*
    Am Sci - v85 - Ja '97 - p81+ [501+]
Stebenne, David L - *Arthur J. Goldberg: New Deal Liberal*
    ABA Jour - v82 - S '96 - p94 [501+]
    BW - v26 - Ag 25 '96 - p13 [51-250]
    Choice - v34 - D '96 - p679 [51-250]
    HRNB - v25 - Win '97 - p89 [251-500]
    NYTBR - v101 - O 27 '96 - p41 [501+]
Steckman, Elizabeth - *Silk Peony, Parade Dragon (Illus. by Carol Inouye)*
   c CBRS - v25 - F '97 - p79 [51-250]
   c KR - v65 - Ja 1 '97 - p65 [51-250]
   c SLJ - v43 - Mr '97 - p167+ [51-250]
Stedman, Jane W - *W.S. Gilbert: A Classic Victorian and His Theatre*
    AB - v98 - D 9 '96 - p1998+ [501+]
    Choice - v34 - F '97 - p975 [51-250]
    KR - v64 - O 1 '96 - p1453+ [251-500]
    LJ - v121 - N 1 '96 - p68+ [51-250]
    Nat R - v48 - D 23 '96 - p51+ [501+]
    NYTBR - v101 - D 8 '96 - p24 [501+]

Stedman, Stephen John - *South Africa*
JTWS - v13 - Spr '96 - p306+ [501+]
Steedly, Mary Margaret - *Hanging without a Rope*
Am Ethnol - v23 - Ag '96 - p650 [501+]
Steedman, Carolyn - *Strange Dislocations*
Albion - v28 - Sum '96 - p326+ [501+]
Bkbird - v34 - Spr '96 - p57 [1-50]
Critm - v39 - Win '97 - p126+ [501+]
Steedman, Ian - *Socialism and Marginalism in Economics 1870-1930*
Econ J - v106 - S '96 - p1465 [251-500]
Steedman, Mercedes - *Hard Lessons*
Can Hist R - v78 - Mr '97 - p108+ [501+]
Steedman, Scott - *The Egyptian News*
c Par Ch - v21 - Mr '97 - p8 [1-50]
c PW - v244 - Mr 31 '97 - p77 [51-250]
How Would You Survive as an American Indian? (Illus. by Mark Bergin)
c HB Guide - v7 - Fall '96 - p392 [51-250]
Pirates (Illus. by Nicholas Hewetson)
c HB Guide - v8 - Spr '97 - p164 [51-250]
Steel, Danielle - *Accident*
Books - v9 - S '95 - p24 [1-50]
Five Days in Paris
HMR - Spr '97 - p22+ [501+]
PW - v243 - D 2 '96 - p56 [1-50]
The Gift
y Emerg Lib - v24 - S '96 - p27 [1-50]
Lightning
Books - v9 - S '95 - p22 [1-50]
The Ranch
BL - v93 - Mr 15 '97 - p1205 [51-250]
KR - v65 - Mr 15 '97 - p414 [251-500]
LJ - v122 - Ap 15 '97 - p121 [51-250]
PW - v244 - Mr 17 '97 - p74 [51-250]
Silent Honor
CSM - v89 - D 19 '96 - p14 [51-250]
CSM - v89 - Ja 16 '97 - p14 [51-250]
KR - v64 - O 1 '96 - p1424 [251-500]
LJ - v121 - D '96 - p148 [51-250]
Silent Honor. Audio Version
BWatch - v18 - Mr '97 - p7 [1-50]
Steel, Dawn - *They Can Kill You, but They Can't Eat You*
FQ - v49 - Fall '95 - p65 [51-250]
Steel, Duncan - *Rogue Asteroids and Doomsday Comets*
Nat - v263 - O 28 '96 - p38+ [501+]
Phys Today - v50 - F '97 - p65+ [501+]
Steel, Edward M, Jr. - *The Court-Martial of Mother Jones*
JSH - v63 - F '97 - p191+ [501+]
Steel, Ronald - *Temptations of a Superpower*
JEL - v35 - Mr '97 - p211 [51-250]
Steel, Virginia - *The Future of Information Services*
LR - v45 - 4 '96 - p69+ [501+]
The Steel Market in 1995 and Prospects for 1996
r ARBA - v28 - '97 - p97 [51-250]
Steele, Allen - *All-American Alien Boy*
Analog - v117 - Ap '97 - p147+ [51-250]
Steele, David Ramsay - *From Marx to Mises*
Crit R - v10 - Sum '96 - p333+ [501+]
Steele, Ian K - *Warpaths, Invasions of North America*
J Am St - v30 - Ap '96 - p154+ [251-500]
Steele, J Michael - *Probability Theory and Combinatorial Optimization*
SciTech - v21 - Mr '97 - p14 [1-50]
Steele, Marshall K - *Sideline Help*
r VOYA - v19 - D '96 - p297 [51-250]
Steele, Mary - *Featherbys*
c BL - v93 - D 15 '96 - p727+ [51-250]
c PW - v243 - S 23 '96 - p77 [51-250]
Steele, Philip - *The Aztec News*
c PW - v244 - Mr 31 '97 - p77 [51-250]
Deserts
c HB Guide - v8 - Spr '97 - p163 [51-250]
c Sch Lib - v44 - N '96 - p165 [251-500]
c SLJ - v42 - S '96 - p221 [51-250]
Great Discoveries
c HB Guide - v7 - Fall '96 - p329 [51-250]
Islands
c BL - v93 - S 1 '96 - p124 [51-250]
c HB Guide - v8 - Spr '97 - p163 [51-250]
c SLJ - v42 - S '96 - p221 [51-250]
World of Festivals
c Emerg Lib - v24 - S '96 - p44 [1-50]
c Sch Lib - v44 - Ag '96 - p114 [51-250]
Steele, Thomas J - *Santos and Saints*
CH - v65 - S '96 - p546+ [251-500]
Steelesburg Homemakers Club - *Appalachian Heritage Cookbook*
BWatch - v18 - Mr '97 - p6 [51-250]

Steen, Edla Van - *Early Mourning*
BW - v26 - D 22 '96 - p9 [51-250]
KR - v64 - D 1 '96 - p1703 [51-250]
LJ - v121 - D '96 - p148 [51-250]
Steen, R Grant - *DNA and Destiny*
Choice - v34 - N '96 - p544 [51-250]
SB - v32 - N '96 - p231 [51-250]
Steen, Sara Jayne - *Ambrosia in an Earthern Vessel*
Ren Q - v49 - Win '96 - p877+ [501+]
Steer, Dugald - *Creepy Crawlies (Illus. by David Ansrey)*
c Ch BWatch - v6 - N '96 - p6 [1-50]
c PW - v243 - S 23 '96 - p78 [51-250]
Steer, John - *Atlas of Western Art*
r CLW - v66 - Je '96 - p38 [51-250]
Stefancic, Jean - *No Mercy*
Choice - v34 - F '97 - p1038 [51-250]
ChrPhil - v9 - Ja 9 '97 - p36 [51-250]
Nat - v264 - Ja 27 '97 - p28+ [501+]
Stefanescu, Domnita - *Cinci Ani Din Istoria Romaniei*
BL - v93 - D 15 '96 - p714 [1-50]
Steffe, Leslie P - *Constructivism in Education*
Math T - v89 - D '96 - p780+ [501+]
Theories of Mathematical Learning
SB - v33 - Mr '97 - p37+ [51-250]
Steffen, Albert - *Barrabas: Drama in Four Acts*
TranslRevS - v1 - My '95 - p23 [1-50]
Steffen, Lloyd - *Abortion: A Reader*
CC - v113 - N 6 '96 - p1089 [51-250]
Cons - v17 - Win '96 - p31 [1-50]
Life/Choice: The Theory of Just Abortion
Rel St Rev - v23 - Ap '97 - p160 [51-250]
Steffens, Bradley - *Censorship*
y HB Guide - v7 - Fall '96 - p316 [51-250]
Steffens, Henrich - *Was Ich Erlebte. Vols. 1-2*
Isis - v87 - S '96 - p557+ [501+]
Stefik, Mark - *Internet Dreams*
BYTE - v22 - Ja '97 - p34 [251-500]
LJ - v121 - F 1 '97 - p127 [51-250]
New Sci - v152 - N 30 '96 - p48 [51-250]
Stefoff, Rebecca - *Chameleon*
c BL - v93 - F 1 '97 - p944 [51-250]
c Ch BWatch - v7 - Ja '97 - p2 [51-250]
c HB Guide - v8 - Spr '97 - p124 [51-250]
c SLJ - v43 - Mr '97 - p181 [51-250]
Charles Darwin and the Evolution Revolution
y HB Guide - v7 - Fall '96 - p374+ [51-250]
y KR - v64 - My 1 '96 - p693+ [51-250]
y SLJ - v42 - S '96 - p236 [51-250]
Children of the Westward Trail
c HB Guide - v7 - Fall '96 - p389 [51-250]
Finding the Lost Cities
y BL - v93 - Mr 1 '97 - p1155 [51-250]
y CCB-B - v50 - Mr '97 - p258 [51-250]
y Cur R - v36 - Ja '97 - p13 [51-250]
y KR - v65 - Ja 1 '97 - p65 [51-250]
Giant Turtle
c Ch BWatch - v7 - Ja '97 - p2 [51-250]
c HB Guide - v8 - Spr '97 - p124 [51-250]
c SLJ - v43 - Mr '97 - p181 [51-250]
Herman Melville
y BL - v93 - D 15 '96 - p717 [1-50]
Mao Zedong: Founder of the People's Republic of China
y HB Guide - v7 - Fall '96 - p375 [51-250]
Octopus
c Ch BWatch - v7 - Ja '97 - p2 [51-250]
c HB Guide - v8 - Spr '97 - p123 [51-250]
c SLJ - v43 - Mr '97 - p181 [51-250]
Praying Mantis
c Ch BWatch - v7 - Ja '97 - p2 [51-250]
c HB Guide - v8 - Spr '97 - p123 [51-250]
c SLJ - v43 - Mr '97 - p181 [51-250]
Saddam Hussein: Absolute Ruler of Iraq
y BL - v93 - D 15 '96 - p717 [1-50]
Sea Horse
c BL - v93 - F 1 '97 - p944 [51-250]
c Ch BWatch - v7 - Ja '97 - p2 [51-250]
c HB Guide - v8 - Spr '97 - p124 [51-250]
c SLJ - v43 - Mr '97 - p181 [51-250]
Starfish
c Ch BWatch - v7 - Ja '97 - p2 [51-250]
c HB Guide - v8 - Spr '97 - p123 [51-250]
c SLJ - v43 - Mr '97 - p181 [51-250]
Stegeman, Michael - *Camille Saint-Saens and the French Solo Concerto from 1850 to 1920*
TranslRevS - v1 - My '95 - p12+ [51-250]
Stegenga, B - *Management of Temporomandibular Joint Degenerative Diseases*
SciTech - v20 - S '96 - p42 [51-250]

Steger, Will - *Over the Top of the World (Illus. by Will Steger)*
c CCB-B - v50 - F '97 - p223+ [51-250]
c KR - v65 - Ja 1 '97 - p65 [51-250]
Stegmaier, Mark Joseph - *Texas, New Mexico, and the Compromise of 1850*
HRNB - v25 - Win '97 - p60 [251-500]
PHR - v66 - F '97 - p104+ [501+]
R&R Bk N - v12 - F '97 - p26 [1-50]
WHQ - v27 - Win '96 - p537+ [501+]
Stegner, Page - *Call of the River*
BL - v93 - Ja '97 - p808 [1-50]
CSM - v88 - N 21 '96 - pB1 [1-50]
y Kliatt - v31 - Ja '97 - p29+ [251-500]
y SB - v33 - Ja '97 - p14 [51-250]
The Geography of Hope
BW - v26 - Jl 14 '96 - p12 [51-250]
LATBR - Jl 14 '96 - p11 [51-250]
LATBR - D 1 '96 - p11 [251-500]
Stegner, Wallace Earle - *Remembering Laughter*
Bloom Rev - v16 - N '96 - p22 [1-50]
LATBR - D 22 '96 - p6 [51-250]
LJ - v121 - S 15 '96 - p102 [51-250]
NYTBR - v101 - S 22 '96 - p40 [51-250]
A Shooting Star
LJ - v121 - S 15 '96 - p102 [51-250]
NYTBR - v101 - S 22 '96 - p40 [51-250]
Stehmann, Oliver - *Network Competition for European Telecommunications*
JEL - v34 - S '96 - p1458+ [51-250]
Steiber, Ellen - *Shapes*
y BL - v93 - Ap 1 '97 - p1310 [1-50]
Squeeze
y BL - v93 - Ap 1 '97 - p1310 [1-50]
Steidlmeier, Paul - *Strategic Management of the China Venture*
Pac A - v69 - Sum '96 - p255+ [251-500]
Steiert, Franz-Josef - *Die Weisheit Israels--Ein Fremdkorper Im Alten Testament*
Rel St Rev - v23 - Ap '97 - p163 [51-250]
Steig, William - *Amos and Boris*
c HMR - Win '96 - p45 [1-50]
Doctor De Soto
c HB - v73 - Mr '97 - p189 [1-50]
Grown-Ups Get to Do all the Driving (Illus. by William Steig)
c RT - v50 - O '96 - p133 [1-50]
Toby, Where Are You? (Illus. by Teryl Euvremer)
c BL - v93 - D 15 '96 - p734 [51-250]
c CBRS - v25 - F '97 - p79 [1-50]
c KR - v65 - Ja 1 '97 - p66 [51-250]
c PW - v243 - D 2 '96 - p59 [51-250]
c SLJ - v43 - Ja '97 - p91+ [51-250]
The Toy Brother (Illus. by William Steig)
c HB Guide - v7 - Fall '96 - p278 [51-250]
c Inst - v106 - O '96 - p66+ [51-250]
c LATBR - My 26 '96 - p11 [51-250]
c SLJ - v42 - D '96 - p32 [1-50]
c Smith - v27 - N '96 - p164+ [1-50]
Steiger, Brad - *Mother Mary Speaks to Us*
CLW - v67 - Mr '97 - p40 [51-250]
PW - v243 - S 30 '96 - p75 [51-250]
Steiger, Sherry Hansen - *Mysteries of Animal Intelligence*
y Emerg Lib - v24 - S '96 - p26 [1-50]
Steigerwald, David - *The Sixties and the End of Modern America*
Historian - v58 - Sum '96 - p875+ [501+]
HRNB - v25 - Fall '96 - p14 [501+]
Wilsonian Idealism in America
SSQ - v78 - Mr '97 - p242 [251-500]
Steil, Benn - *The European Equity Markets*
JEL - v34 - D '96 - p2054 [51-250]
Steil, Starr - *Picture Beaded Earrings for Beginners*
BWatch - v17 - S '96 - p11 [51-250]
Stein, Arlene - *Sex and Sensibility*
LJ - v122 - My 1 '97 - p128 [51-250]
Stein, Clarissa - *Billy Tea and Sand Ballet*
Aust Bk R - O '96 - p56+ [501+]
Stein, Deborah - *Poetry into Song*
Notes - v53 - Mr '97 - p816+ [501+]
Stein, Diane - *All Women Are Healers*
BWatch - v18 - Mr '97 - p11 [51-250]
Stein, Eugene - *Touch and Go*
KR - v65 - My 1 '97 - p674 [251-500]
PW - v244 - My 12 '97 - p55+ [251-250]
Stein, Georgina - *Designing and Making*
TES - D 13 '96 - p43 [51-250]
Stein, Gertrude - *How to Write*
RCF - v16 - Fall '96 - p203+ [251-500]

The Letters of Gertrude Stein and Thornton Wilder
  BW - v27 - F 23 '97 - p13 [51-250]
  Choice - v34 - Ap '97 - p1340 [51-250]
  HMR - Win '96 - p8+ [501+]
  KR - v64 - O 15 '96 - p1520 [51-250]
  LJ - v121 - O 15 '96 - p59 [51-250]
  NYTBR - v102 - Ja 12 '97 - p26 [501+]
  Obs - Mr 9 '97 - p18* [501+]
  PW - v243 - N 4 '96 - p53+ [51-250]
  Utne R - Mr '97 - p84 [1-50]
Stein, Gil - *Chiefdoms and Early States in the Near East*
  Am Ant - v61 - Ap '96 - p434+ [501+]
Stein, Gordon - *The Encyclopedia of the Paranormal*
 r ARBA - v28 - '97 - p287 [51-250]
 r Choice - v34 - O '96 - p250+ [51-250]
 r JP - v60 - S '96 - p259+ [501+]
 r Skeptic - v4 - 2 '96 - p109+ [251-500]
Stein, Harry - *Infinity's Child*
  BL - v93 - D 1 '96 - p621 [51-250]
  KR - v64 - D 1 '96 - p1701 [251-500]
  LJ - v122 - Ja '97 - p151 [51-250]
  PW - v243 - D 9 '96 - p60 [51-250]
  Trib Bks - Ja 19 '97 - p6 [51-250]
Stein, Herbert - *The Fiscal Revolution in America. 2nd Ed.*
  JEL - v34 - S '96 - p1465 [51-250]
Stein, Irving - *The Concept of Object as the Foundation of Physics*
  SciTech - v20 - D '96 - p23 [51-250]
Stein, Janice Gross - *We All Lost the Cold War*
  NWCR - v49 - Aut '96 - p147+ [501+]
Stein, Jerome L - *Fundamental Determinants of Exchange Rates*
  JEL - v34 - S '96 - p1433+ [51-250]
Stein, Jess - *Random House Webster's College Thesaurus. Rev. and Updated Ed.*
 r Choice - v34 - My '97 - p1479 [51-250]
Stein, John A - *Residential Treatment of Adolescents and Children*
  Soc Ser R - v70 - S '96 - p502 [51-250]
Stein, Kevin - *Private Poets, Worldly Acts*
  R&R Bk N - v12 - F '97 - p88 [51-250]
Stein, Lincoln D - *How to Set Up and Maintain a Web Site. 2nd Ed.*
  SciTech - v21 - Mr '97 - p88 [51-250]
Stein, Marvin - *Chronic Diseases*
  AJPsych - v154 - F '97 - p278+ [501+]
Stein, Murray B - *Social Phobia*
  AJPsych - v153 - N '96 - p1502 [501+]
Stein, Paul D - *Pulmonary Embolism*
  SciTech - v21 - Mr '97 - p58 [51-250]
Stein, R Conrad - *The Assassination of Martin Luther King, Jr.*
 c HB Guide - v8 - Spr '97 - p92 [51-250]
The Aztec Empire
 c HB Guide - v7 - Fall '96 - p378 [51-250]
The Boston Tea Party
 c HB Guide - v8 - Spr '97 - p172 [51-250]
Cairo
 c HB Guide - v8 - Spr '97 - p170 [1-50]
 c SLJ - v43 - F '97 - p118 [51-250]
London
 c HB Guide - v8 - Spr '97 - p169 [51-250]
 c SLJ - v42 - O '96 - p134 [51-250]
Mexico City
 c BL - v93 - N 1 '96 - p493 [51-250]
 c HB Guide - v8 - Spr '97 - p176 [1-50]
 c SLJ - v42 - S '96 - p217+ [51-250]
Paris
 c HB Guide - v8 - Spr '97 - p169 [51-250]
 c SLJ - v43 - F '97 - p126 [51-250]
Stein, Robert E, 1949- - *Re-Engineering the Manufacturing System*
  SciTech - v20 - N '96 - p81 [51-250]
Stein, Robert H, 1935- - *Jesus the Messiah*
  BL - v93 - N 1 '96 - p462 [51-250]
  PW - v243 - S 16 '96 - p67 [51-250]
Stein, Robert M - *Perpetuating the Pork Barrel*
  APSR - v90 - S '96 - p661 [501+]
  JEL - v34 - S '96 - p1415+ [51-250]
Stein, Sara Bonnett - *Noah's Garden*
  LJ - v121 - D '96 - p66 [1-50]
Planting Noah's Garden
  LJ - v122 - Ap 15 '97 - p106 [51-250]
  PW - v244 - Mr 24 '97 - p79 [51-250]
Stein, Sherman K - *Strength in Numbers*
  Choice - v34 - Ap '97 - p1376+ [51-250]
  New Sci - v153 - F 8 '97 - p44 [251-500]
 y SB - v33 - Ja '97 - p12 [51-250]
 y SciTech - v20 - D '96 - p14 [51-250]

Stein, Stephen J - *Jonathan Edwards's Writings*
  Choice - v34 - Mr '97 - p1177 [51-250]
Stein, William W - *A Peruvian Psychiatric Hospital*
  SciTech - v20 - S '96 - p32 [51-250]
Steinbach, Alice - *The Miss Dennis School of Writing and Other Lessons from a Woman's Life*
  AJR - v19 - Ap '97 - p53 [1-50]
  BL - v93 - S 15 '96 - p205 [51-250]
Steinbach, Meredith - *The Birth of the World as We Know It*
  KR - v64 - S 15 '96 - p1351 [251-500]
  LJ - v121 - O 15 '96 - p92 [51-250]
  PW - v243 - S 30 '96 - p60 [51-250]
  Trib Bks - Mr 2 '97 - p3+ [501+]
Steinbeck, John - *The Grapes of Wrath and Other Writings 1936-1941*
  AL - v69 - Mr '97 - p249 [51-250]
  BL - v93 - S 1 '96 - p33 [51-250]
Of Mice and Men. Electronic Media Version
 y SLJ - v42 - Ag '96 - p43+ [51-250]
The Pearl. The Red Pony. Electronic Media Version
 yr Kliatt - v30 - N '96 - p34 [51-250]
 y SLJ - v42 - N '96 - p52 [51-250]
Steinberg, Blema S - *Shame and Humiliation*
  Choice - v34 - N '96 - p539 [51-250]
  R&R Bk N - v12 - F '97 - p20 [51-250]
Steinberg, Janice - *Death-Fires Dance*
  Arm Det - v30 - Win '97 - p115+ [251-500]
Steinberg, Jonathan - *Midas Investing*
  BL - v93 - N 1 '96 - p466+ [51-250]
  LJ - v121 - N 15 '96 - p70 [51-250]
Steinberg, Laurence - *Beyond the Classroom*
  BL - v93 - Ja '97 - p757 [1-50]
  EL - v54 - O '96 - p88+ [501+]
Steinberg, Leo - *The Sexuality of Christ in Renaissance Art and in Modern Oblivion. 2nd Ed., Rev. and Expanded*
  CC - v114 - My 7 '97 - p457 [51-250]
  Lon R Bks - v19 - Ap 3 '97 - p11+ [501+]
Steinberg, Mark D - *The Fall of the Romanovs*
  AAPSS-A - v547 - S '96 - p181+ [501+]
Steinberg, Marlene - *Handbook for the Assessment of Dissociation*
  AJCH - v39 - O '96 - p154+ [501+]
Steinberg, Michael, 1928- - *The Symphony: A Listener's Guide*
  BW - v26 - D 8 '96 - p7+ [51-250]
Steinberg, Michael P - *Walter Benjamin and the Demands of History*
  HRNB - v25 - Win '97 - p90 [501+]
Steinberg, Neil - *The Alphabet of Modern Annoyances*
  BL - v93 - N 1 '96 - p475 [51-250]
  KR - v64 - O 1 '96 - p1454 [251-500]
  LJ - v121 - D '96 - p128 [51-250]
  PW - v243 - N 18 '96 - p59 [51-250]
Steinberg, Stephen - *Turning Back*
  CS - v26 - Mr '97 - p143+ [501+]
  CS - v26 - Mr '97 - p146+ [501+]
  J Soc H - v30 - Win '96 - p528+ [501+]
  SF - v75 - D '96 - p752+ [501+]
Steinberg, Theodore - *Slide Mountain*
  AHR - v101 - O '96 - p1304+ [251-500]
Steinberger, Kelvin - *Rapunzel (Illus. by Kelvin Steinberger)*
 c Magpies - v11 - Jl '96 - p32 [51-250]
Steinbring, Jack - *Rock Art Studies in the Americas*
  Am Ant - v62 - Ja '97 - p172+ [251-500]
Steinbrugge, Liselotte - *The Moral Sex*
  Historian - v59 - Win '97 - p477+ [251-500]
Steindl, Frank G - *Monetary Interpretations of the Great Depression*
  JEL - v34 - S '96 - p1407 [51-250]
  JEL - v35 - Mr '97 - p124+ [501+]
Steine, Kent - *Billy Devorss: The Classic Pin-Ups*
  BWatch - v18 - Mr '97 - p3 [1-50]
Steiner, Barbara A - *Desert Trip (Illus. by Ronald Himler)*
 c HB Guide - v7 - Fall '96 - p339 [51-250]
 c Inst - v106 - Mr '97 - p30 [1-50]
Spring Break
 y SLJ - v42 - D '96 - p140 [51-250]
Steiner, David - *Rethinking Democratic Education*
  RP - v59 - Win '97 - p127+ [501+]
Steiner, Deborah - *The Tyrant's Writ*
  CW - v89 - Jl '96 - p502+ [251-500]
Steiner, Erich - *The Chemistry Maths Book*
 r Choice - v34 - My '97 - p1528 [51-250]
Steiner, George - *No Passion Spent*
  New R - v215 - S 30 '96 - p32+ [501+]
  NYTBR - v101 - D 8 '96 - p90 [1-50]

Steiner, Hans - *Treating Adolescents*
  SciTech - v20 - N '96 - p52 [51-250]
Steiner, Henry J - *International Human Rights in Context*
  BW - v26 - D 8 '96 - p8+ [501+]
Steiner, Hillel - *An Essay on Rights*
  RM - v49 - Je '96 - p948+ [251-500]
Steiner, Kristian - *Strategies for International Legitimacy*
  MEJ - v51 - Spr '97 - p312 [51-250]
Steiner, Robert - *The Catastrophe*
  BW - v26 - N 17 '96 - p7 [501+]
  KR - v64 - My 1 '96 - p634 [251-500]
Steiner, Wendy - *The Scandal of Pleasure*
  Cres - v60 - Christmas '96 - p28+ [501+]
  Lon R Bks - v18 - My 23 '96 - p8+ [501+]
  NYTBR - v101 - D 8 '96 - p92 [1-50]
  Tikkun - v11 - N '96 - p70+ [501+]
Steingraber, Sandra - *Living Downstream*
  KR - v65 - My 1 '97 - p706 [251-500]
Steingrimsson, Sigurdur Orn - *Gottesmahl Und Lebensspende*
  Rel St Rev - v23 - Ja '97 - p59 [51-250]
Steinhart, Peter - *The Company of Wolves*
  LATBR - Ag 18 '96 - p15 [51-250]
  Soc - v33 - S '96 - p86+ [501+]
  Soc - v33 - S '96 - p86+ [501+]
Steinhauer, Lauren - *Macromedia Director 4 for Macs for Dummies*
  Quill & Q - v62 - Ag '96 - p23 [51-250]
Steinlauf, Michael C - *Bondage to the Dead*
  KR - v64 - D 15 '96 - p1790 [251-500]
Steinman, David - *The Safe Shopper's Bible*
 r BL - v93 - F 1 '97 - p958 [1-50]
Steinmetz, David Curtis - *Calvin in Context*
  Historian - v59 - Win '97 - p478+ [251-500]
  Intpr - v51 - Ap '97 - p189+ [501+]
  J Ch St - v38 - Sum '96 - p663 [251-500]
  Rel St Rev - v22 - O '96 - p349 [51-250]
  Ren Q - v50 - Spr '97 - p304+ [501+]
Steinmetz, George - *Regulating the Social*
  JMH - v68 - D '96 - p1021+ [501+]
Stejskal, Vladimir - *Kinematics and Dynamics of Machinery*
 r SciTech - v20 - S '96 - p52 [51-250]
Stella, Pietro - *Don Bosco: Religious Outlook and Spirituality*
  RR - v56 - Ja '97 - p107 [1-50]
Il Giansenismo In Italia. Vol. 2, Pt. 1
  CHR - v83 - Ja '97 - p110+ [251-500]
Stellbrink, Kuno K U - *Micromechanics of Composites*
  Choice - v34 - Ja '97 - p826 [51-250]
  SciTech - v20 - S '96 - p49 [51-250]
Stellino, Nick - *Nick Stellino's Mediterranean Flavors*
  LJ - v122 - Ap 15 '97 - p110 [51-250]
  PW - v244 - Mr 3 '97 - p69 [51-250]
Stelmach, Marjorie - *Night Drawings*
  ABR - v18 - O '96 - p29 [501+]
  Chel - 61 '96 - p134+ [501+]
Stemm, Antje Von - *Bertie and Gertie, Space Detectives! (Illus. by Antje Von Stemm)*
 c PW - v243 - S 23 '96 - p78 [51-250]
Stemp, Jane - *Waterbound*
 y BL - v92 - Ag '96 - p1896 [51-250]
 y CBRS - v25 - Ja '97 - p59+ [51-250]
 y CCB-B - v50 - D '96 - p153 [51-250]
 y HB Guide - v8 - Spr '97 - p84 [51-250]
 y KR - v64 - O 1 '96 - p1474+ [51-250]
 y PW - v243 - N 4 '96 - p78 [51-250]
 y SLJ - v42 - S '96 - p228 [51-250]
Stempel, Tom - *Storytellers to the Nation*
  AB - v98 - D 9 '96 - p2001+ [51-250]
  JMCQ - v73 - Win '96 - p1016+ [251-500]
Sten, Christopher - *Sounding the Whale*
  AL - v69 - Mr '97 - p249 [1-50]
The Weaver-God, He Weaves
  AL - v69 - Mr '97 - p218+ [251-500]
  Choice - v34 - O '96 - p282 [51-250]
  R&R Bk N - v12 - F '97 - p89 [51-250]
Stendahl, Krister - *Final Account*
  TT - v53 - O '96 - p396+ [501+]
Paul among Jews and Gentiles and Other Essays
  Rel Ed - v91 - Fall '96 - p605 [1-50]
Stendel, Ori - *The Arabs in Israel*
  Choice - v34 - Mr '97 - p1226 [51-250]
  R&R Bk N - v11 - D '96 - p11 [51-250]
Stendhal - *The Red and the Black*
  VV - v42 - Ja 7 '97 - p43 [51-250]
Stendhal Et La Hollande
  TLS - 1 '97 - p32 [251-500]
Stenerson, Jon - *Computer Numerical Control*
  SciTech - v20 - N '96 - p71 [1-50]

Stenflo, Jan Olof - *Solar Polarization*
  SciTech - v20 - S '96 - p13 [51-250]
Stenger, Victor J - *The Unconscious Quantum*
  SB - v32 - Ag '96 - p164 [51-250]
  Skeptic - v4 - 2 '96 - p109 [1-50]
  TLS - D 27 '96 - p30 [501+]
Stengers, Isabelle - *L'Effet Whitehead*
  RM - v50 - S '96 - p189+ [501+]
Stenmark, Mikael - *Rationality in Science, Religion, and Everyday Life*
  Choice - v34 - S '96 - p142 [51-250]
Stepan-Norris, Judith - *Talking Union*
  CS - v26 - Mr '97 - p165+ [501+]
Stephan, Alexander - *Im Visier Des FBI*
  Ger Q - v69 - Fall '96 - p456+ [501+]
  MLR - v92 - Ap '97 - p530+ [501+]
Stephan, Gunter - *Introduction into Capital Theory*
  JEL - v34 - D '96 - p2034 [51-250]
Stephan, Inge - *Unaufhorlich Lenz Gelesen...*
  MLR - v91 - Jl '96 - p784+ [501+]
Stephen, Herbert - *Who's Who of Victorian Cinema*
  r Choice - v34 - Mr '97 - p1144 [51-250]
Stephen, Leslie - *Selected Letters of Leslie Stephen. Vols. 1-2*
  Choice - v34 - Mr '97 - p1167 [51-250]
  TLS - F 14 '97 - p25 [501+]
Stephen, Margaret - *Schools in Victorian Times*
  c Bks Keeps - Ja '97 - p24 [51-250]
Stephen, Peter - *Simple Statistics for Library and Information Professionals*
  LR - v45 - 4 '96 - p66+ [251-500]
Stephens, Annabel K - *Assessing the Public Library Planning Process*
  LAR - v98 - Ag '96 - p427 [51-250]
Stephens, Anthony - *Heinrich Von Kleist: The Dramas and Stories*
  MLR - v91 - O '96 - p1043+ [501+]
Stephens, Brooks - *Talking Dollars and Making Sense*
  PW - v243 - O 7 '96 - p67 [51-250]
Stephens, Elaine C - *Learning about the Holocaust*
  r JOYS - v10 - Win '97 - p223 [251-500]
Stephens, George E - *A Voice of Thunder*
  LJ - v121 - N 1 '96 - p90+ [51-250]
Stephens, John, 1944- - *Language and Ideology in Children's Fiction*
  ChLAQ - v20 - Fall '95 - p140+ [501+]
Stephens, John Richard - *Vampires, Wine and Roses*
  y Kliatt - v31 - My '97 - p20 [51-250]
  PW - v244 - Ja 13 '97 - p67 [1-50]
Stephens, Michael L - *Gangster Films*
  r ARBA - v28 - '97 - p509 [51-250]
Stephens, Mitchell - *A History of News*
  AJR - v19 - Ap '97 - p53 [1-50]
Stephens, Philip - *Politics and the Pound*
  NS - v125 - D 20 '96 - p116 [1-50]
Stephens, Ronald D - *Safe Schools*
  Adoles - v31 - Win '96 - p997 [51-250]
Stephens, Sharon - *Children and the Politics of Culture*
  Bkbird - v34 - Spr '96 - p57 [51-250]
  CS - v25 - S '96 - p589+ [501+]
Stephenson, David A - *Metal Cutting Theory and Practice*
  r SciTech - v21 - Mr '97 - p85 [51-250]
Stephenson, John - *The Optimist*
  Aust Bk R - S '96 - p28+ [501+]
  Quad - v40 - O '96 - p81+ [501+]
Stephenson, Neal - *The Diamond Age*
  Books - v9 - S '95 - p22 [1-50]
  Reason - v28 - D '96 - p45 [51-250]
Stephenson, Peter H - *A Persistent Spirit*
  GJ - v163 - Mr '97 - p109 [51-250]
Stephenson, R H - *Goethe's Conception of Knowledge and Science*
  Isis - v87 - S '96 - p558+ [501+]
  MLR - v92 - Ja '97 - p243+ [251-500]
Steptoe, John - *Creativity (Illus. by E B Lewis)*
  c BL - v93 - F 15 '97 - p1030 [51-250]
  c CBRS - v25 - F '97 - p80 [51-250]
  c KR - v65 - F 1 '97 - p229 [51-250]
  c PW - v244 - Ja 13 '97 - p76 [51-250]
  Stevie
  c HB Guide - v8 - Spr '97 - p108 [1-50]
Sterba, James P - *Social and Political Philosophy*
  RM - v50 - S '96 - p192+ [501+]
Sterckx, Alan - *Collect Aircraft on Stamps. 1st Ed.*
  r Am Phil - v110 - O '96 - p910+ [501+]
Sterken, C - *Light Curves of Variable Stars*
  r Choice - v34 - My '97 - p1521 [51-250]
Sterling, Bruce - *Hollywood Kremlin (Williams). Audio Version*
  BL - v93 - D 15 '96 - p740 [51-250]

Holy Fire
  Analog - v117 - Mr '97 - p150+ [251-500]
  BIC - v25 - O '96 - p2+ [501+]
  BW - v26 - S 1 '96 - p11 [51-250]
  BWatch - v17 - N '96 - p8 [51-250]
  LJ - v122 - Ja '97 - p51 [1-50]
  LJ - v121 - S 15 '96 - p100 [51-250]
  NYTBR - v101 - D 29 '96 - p16 [51-250]
  VLS - Win '96 - p12 [51-250]
  y VOYA - v19 - F '97 - p340+ [251-500]
  VV - v41 - O 29 '96 - p64+ [501+]
Schismatrix Plus
  LJ - v121 - D '96 - p152 [1-50]
Sterling, Christopher H - *Commercial Air Transport Books*
  r Choice - v34 - Ap '97 - p1316 [51-250]
Sterling, Dorothy - *The Making of an Afro-American*
  Am Vis - v12 - F '97 - p29 [51-250]
Sterling, Joy - *A Cultivated Life*
  LJ - v122 - Ap 1 '97 - p64 [1-50]
Vintage Feasting
  LJ - v122 - Ap 1 '97 - p62 [1-50]
Sterling, Keir B - *Biographical Dictionary of American and Canadian Naturalists and Environmentalists*
  r BL - v93 - Ap 1 '97 - p1352 [501+]
  r LJ - v122 - F 15 '97 - p127 [51-250]
Sterling, Richard - *Travelers' Tales Food*
  r BL - v93 - S 15 '96 - p212 [1-50]
Sterling, Shirley - *My Name Is Seepeetza*
  c BL - v93 - Mr 1 '97 - p1155 [51-250]
  c CBRS - v25 - Ap '97 - p107 [51-250]
  c CCB-B - v50 - My '97 - p335+ [51-250]
  c HB - v73 - My '97 - p328+ [51-250]
  c PW - v244 - F 24 '97 - p92 [51-250]
Sterling and Francine Clark Art Institute - *The Clark: Selections from the Sterling and Francine Clark Art Institute*
  LJ - v121 - O 1 '96 - p74 [51-250]
  PW - v243 - Jl 22 '96 - p221 [51-250]
Stermer, Dugald, 1936- - *Vanishing Flora*
  GJ - v162 - Jl '96 - p241 [51-250]
Stern, Bonnie - *More Heartsmart Cooking*
  Quill & Q - v63 - Mr '97 - p20+ [501+]
Stern, Charlotte - *The Medieval Theater in Castile*
  Choice - v34 - Mr '97 - p1173 [51-250]
Stern, David - *Midrash and Theory*
  R&R Bk N - v11 - N '96 - p7 [51-250]
Stern, Ellen Norman - *Elie Wiesel: A Voice for Humanity*
  y HB Guide - v7 - Fall '96 - p375 [51-250]
Stern, Ellen Sue, 1954- - *Loving an Imperfect Man*
  PW - v244 - Ja 20 '97 - p389 [51-250]
Stern, Gerald - *Lucky Life*
  LJ - v122 - Ap 1 '97 - p95 [1-50]
Odd Mercy
  LJ - v122 - Ap 1 '97 - p95 [1-50]
Stern, Howard - *Howard Stern: Miss America*
  ABR - v17 - Ag '96 - p4+ [501+]
  ABR - v18 - O '96 - p6+ [501+]
Stern, J P - *The Dear Purchase*
  MLR - v92 - Ja '97 - p253+ [501+]
Stern, Jane - *Dog Eat Dog*
  BL - v93 - F 1 '97 - p916 [51-250]
  Econ - v342 - Ja 4 '97 - p82 [51-250]
  KR - v64 - O 15 '96 - p1521 [51-250]
  LJ - v122 - Ja '97 - p132 [51-250]
  Trib Bks - F 9 '97 - p1+ [501+]
Eat Your Way across the U.S.A.
  LJ - v122 - My 1 '97 - p129 [51-250]
Stern, Jerome - *Micro Fiction*
  LATBR - S 1 '96 - p6+ [501+]
Stern, Julian - *Homework and Study Support*
  TES - Ja 31 '97 - p8* [501+]
Stern, Ken - *50 Fabulous Places to Retire in America. 2nd Ed.*
  BWatch - v18 - Mr '97 - p1 [1-50]
Stern, Kenneth S - *A Force upon the Plain*
  CS - v26 - Ja '97 - p26+ [501+]
  Nat - v263 - O 28 '96 - p20+ [501+]
  Tikkun - v11 - My '96 - p56+ [501+]
Stern, Kingsley R - *Introductory Plant Biology. 7th Ed.*
  SciTech - v21 - Mr '97 - p37 [51-250]
Stern, Laura Ikins - *The Criminal Law System of Medieval and Renaissance Florence*
  Historian - v59 - Win '97 - p406+ [501+]
Stern, Lesley - *The Scorsese Connection*
  Choice - v34 - O '96 - p288+ [251-500]

Stern, Maggie - *The Missing Sunflowers (Illus. by Donna Ruff)*
  c BL - v93 - My 15 '97 - p1581 [51-250]
  c CBRS - v25 - Mr '97 - p91 [51-250]
  c CCB-B - v50 - Ap '97 - p297 [51-250]
  c KR - v65 - F 1 '97 - p229 [51-250]
  c PW - v244 - Ja 20 '97 - p402 [51-250]
Stern, Paul C - *Understanding Risk*
  New Sci - v153 - Mr 1 '97 - p49 [51-250]
  R&R Bk N - v11 - N '96 - p39 [51-250]
Stern, Peter A - *Sendero Luminoso*
  r ARBA - v28 - '97 - p225+ [51-250]
Stern, Philip Van Doren - *The Greatest Gift*
  BL - v93 - S 1 '96 - p33 [51-250]
Stern, Robert A M - *New York 1960*
  r TLS - N 8 '96 - p32 [51-250]
  Robert A.M. Stern Buildings
  PW - v243 - N 4 '96 - p61 [51-250]
Stern, Robert N - *The U.S. Labor Movement*
  r ARBA - v28 - '97 - p117+ [251-500]
  r BL - v93 - F 15 '97 - p1043 [251-500]
  r Choice - v34 - F '97 - p950 [51-250]
  JEL - v35 - Mr '97 - p241 [51-250]
  r R&R Bk N - v11 - D '96 - p31 [51-250]
Stern, Sacha - *Jewish Identity in Early Rabbinic Writings*
  Rel St Rev - v23 - Ap '97 - p196 [51-250]
Stern, Steve J - *The Secret History of Gender*
  HAHR - v77 - My '97 - p314+ [251-500]
  J Soc H - v30 - Fall '96 - p258+ [501+]
Stern, Steven B - *Stern's Guide to the Cruise Vacation. 6th Ed.*
  r ARBA - v28 - '97 - p657 [51-250]
Stern, Tracy - *Change of Heart*
  KR - v65 - F 15 '97 - p253 [251-500]
  PW - v244 - F 17 '97 - p208 [51-250]
  Trib Bks - My 11 '97 - p11 [51-250]
Sternberg, Martin L A - *Essential ASL*
  r ARBA - v28 - '97 - p400+ [251-500]
Sternberg, Robert - *The Sephardic Kitchen*
  LJ - v121 - S 15 '96 - p89 [51-250]
Sternberg, Robert J - *Successful Intelligence*
  BL - v93 - O 1 '96 - p293 [51-250]
Sterne, Jim - *World Wide Web Marketing*
  Quill & Q - v62 - My '96 - p22+ [501+]
Sternfeld, Janet - *Homework for Jews. 2nd, Rev. Ed.*
  Rel Ed - v91 - Fall '96 - p619 [1-50]
Sternfeld, Joel - *On This Site*
  BW - v27 - Mr 23 '97 - p12 [51-250]
Sternhell, Zeev - *The Birth of Fascist Ideology*
  EHR - v111 - S '96 - p1020+ [501+]
Sterrett, Andrew - *101 Careers in Mathematics*
  Choice - v34 - Mr '97 - p1196 [51-250]
  SB - v32 - N '96 - p229+ [51-250]
Sterritt, David - *The Films of Alfred Hitchcock*
  J Pop F&TV - v24 - Win '97 - p182 [501+]
Stetie, Salah - *Seize Paroles Voilees*
  WLT - v71 - Win '97 - p220 [51-250]
Un Suspens De Cristal
  WLT - v71 - Win '97 - p218 [501+]
Stetkevych, Jaroslav - *Muhammad and the Golden Bough*
  Choice - v34 - Ap '97 - p1331 [51-250]
Stetkevych, Suzanne Pinckney - *Reorientations/Arabic and Persian Poetry*
  TranslRevS - v1 - My '95 - p7 [51-250]
Stetson, Brad - *The Silent Subject*
  Nat R - v48 - O 14 '96 - p90 [51-250]
Stetson, Dorothy M - *Comparative State Feminism*
  AAPSS-A - v550 - Mr '97 - p195+ [251-500]
Stetson, Erlene - *Glorying in Tribulation*
  AHR - v101 - O '96 - p1282+ [251-500]
Steury, Donald P - *Intentions and Capabilities*
  For Aff - v75 - S '96 - p142 [51-250]
Steussy, Marti J - *Gardens in Babylon*
  Rel St Rev - v23 - Ja '97 - p86 [51-250]
Steven, Rob - *Japan and the New World Order*
  TLS - O 25 '96 - p6 [501+]
Stevens, Alan B - *Field Grown Cut Flowers*
  BL - v93 - F 1 '97 - p918 [51-250]
Stevens, Amanda - *A Man of Secrets*
  LJ - v121 - N 15 '96 - p50 [51-250]
Stevens, Anthony - *Evolutionary Psychiatry*
  Nature - v386 - Ap 3 '97 - p454+ [501+]
Private Myths
  TES - O 11 '96 - p8* [51-250]
Stevens, Ben - *Rolf Armstrong: The Dream Girls*
  BWatch - v18 - Mr '97 - p3 [1-50]
Stevens, C A - *Sailing on the Ice*
  PW - v243 - S 23 '96 - p61+ [51-250]
Stevens, C J - *Maine Mining Adventure*
  RocksMiner - v72 - Ja '97 - p68+ [251-500]

Stevens, Carla - *Lily and Miss Liberty (Illus. by Deborah Kogan Ray)*
  c Inst - v106 - S '96 - p55 [1-50]
Stevens, Carol Belkin - *Soldiers on the Steppe*
  AHR - v101 - O '96 - p1245+ [501+]
Stevens, David - *Roof Gardens, Balconies and Terraces*
  PW - v244 - My 5 '97 - p204 [51-250]
  The Ultimate Garden Book for North America
  r Fine Gard - Ja '97 - p68+ [251-500]
Stevens, Edward W, Jr. - *The Grammar of the Machine*
  AHR - v102 - F '97 - p164+ [251-500]
  AJE - v104 - Ag '96 - p335+ [501+]
  Historian v59 Win '97 p445+ [251-500]
  JIH - v27 - Spr '97 - p718+ [501+]
Stevens, Jan Romero - *Carlos and the Cornfield (Illus. by Jeanne Arnold)*
  c RT - v50 - F '97 - p426 [51-250]
  Carlos and the Skunk (Illus. by Jeanne Arnold)
  c BL - v93 - My 15 '97 - p1581 [51-250]
Stevens, Janet - *From Pictures to Words (Illus. by Janet Stevens)*
  c Inst - v106 - N '96 - p25 [51-250]
  c RT - v50 - S '96 - p55+ [51-250]
  Old Bag of Bones (Illus. by Janet Stevens)
  c Ch BWatch - v6 - My '96 - p4 [1-50]
  c HB Guide - v7 - Fall '96 - p325 [51-250]
  c RT - v50 - Ap '97 - p594+ [51-250]
  Tops and Bottoms (Illus. by Janet Stevens)
  c Inst - v105 - My '96 - p68 [1-50]
  c LATBR - Mr 24 '96 - p11 [51-250]
  c RT - v50 - O '96 - p135 [1-50]
  c RT - v50 - N '96 - p243+ [51-250]
Stevens, John A - *Encounters: Early Images of Canada's Aboriginal Peoples from the Library Collections of the Geological Survey of Canada*
  Beav - v77 - F '97 - p44 [251-500]
  CG - v117 - Mr '97 - p85 [51-250]
Stevens, Leonard A - *The Case of Roe v. Wade*
  y BL - v93 - Ja '97 - p765 [1-50]
  y BL - v93 - O 1 '96 - p351 [51-250]
  c Ch BWatch - v6 - N '96 - p2 [1-50]
  y HB Guide - v8 - Spr '97 - p94 [51-250]
  y KR - v64 - Ag 15 '96 - p1243+ [51-250]
  y SLJ - v43 - Ja '97 - p136 [51-250]
  y VOYA - v19 - D '96 - p291+ [251-500]
Stevens, Leonie - *Big Man's Barbie*
  Aust Bk R - D '96 - p63 [501+]
Stevens, Lewis - *Avian Biochemistry and Molecular Biology*
  Choice - v34 - N '96 - p485 [51-250]
Stevens, Maryanne - *Reconstructing the Christ Symbol*
  Rel St Rev - v23 - Ja '97 - p47 [51-250]
Stevens, Norman D - *Postcards in the Library*
  CLW - v66 - Je '96 - p44 [251-500]
  SLMQ - v24 - Sum '96 - p220 [51-250]
Stevens, Peter F - *The Development of Biological Systematics*
  Isis - v87 - S '96 - p552+ [501+]
Stevens, Roger - *The C++ Graphics Programming Handbook*
  SciTech - v21 - Mr '97 - p7 [51-250]
Stevens, Stuart - *Feeding Frenzy*
  KR - v65 - Ap 1 '97 - p538+ [251-500]
  LJ - v122 - My 1 '97 - p129 [51-250]
  PW - v244 - Mr 17 '97 - p61 [51-250]
Stevens, Wallace - *Letters of Wallace Stevens*
  LJ - v122 - My 1 '97 - p145 [1-50]
  PW - v243 - N 25 '96 - p70 [1-50]
Stevenson, Anne - *The Collected Poems of Anne Stevenson 1955-1995*
  Obs - S 29 '96 - p18* [51-250]
Stevenson, Brenda E - *Life in Black and White*
  AHR - v102 - F '97 - p189+ [501+]
  BW - v27 - F 2 '97 - p11 [501+]
  Choice - v34 - O '96 - p352 [51-250]
  HRNB - v25 - Win '97 - p61 [251-500]
  NYRB - v44 - F 20 '97 - p35+ [501+]
  y SLJ - v42 - S '96 - p242 [51-250]
Stevenson, David - *Armaments and the Coming of War*
  Choice - v34 - Mr '97 - p1224 [51-250]
Stevenson, Drew - *Terror on Cemetery Hill*
  c BL - v93 - S 1 '96 - p132 [51-250]
  c HB Guide - v8 - Spr '97 - p75 [51-250]
  c SLJ - v42 - S '96 - p206 [51-250]
Stevenson, Harvey - *Big, Scary Wolf*
  c PW - v244 - My 12 '97 - p75 [51-250]
Stevenson, Helen - *Windfall*
  Books - v10 - Je '96 - p13 [1-50]
Stevenson, James - *The Bones in the Cliff*
  c PW - v243 - D 9 '96 - p69 [1-50]
  c RT - v50 - S '96 - p55 [51-250]

Heat Wave at Mud Flat (Illus. by James Stevenson)
  c BL - v93 - My 15 '97 - p1581 [51-250]
I Meant to Tell You (Illus. by James Stevenson)
  c HB Guide - v7 - Fall '96 - p311 [51-250]
  c LATBR - Ag 4 '96 - p11 [251-500]
  c SLJ - v42 - Ag '96 - p141 [51-250]
  c Smith - v27 - My '96 - p170 [1-50]
Monty (Illus. by James Stevenson)
  c SLJ - v42 - Ag '96 - p179 [51-250]
The Oldest Elf (Illus. by James Stevenson)
  c BL - v93 - S '96 - p137+ [51-250]
  c CBRS - v25 - O '96 - p18 [51-250]
  c CCB-B - v50 - O '96 - p77+ [51-250]
  c HB Guide - v8 - Spr '97 - p49 [51-250]
  c KR - v64 - S 15 '96 - p1408 [51-250]
  c LATBR - N 10 '96 - p15 [51-250]
  c NYTBR - v101 - D 22 '96 - p16 [1-50]
  c PW - v243 - S 30 '96 - p92 [51-250]
  c SLJ - v42 - O '96 - p41 [51-250]
Sweet Corn Poems
  c LA - v73 - O '96 - p432 [51-250]
Yard Sale (Illus. by James Stevenson)
  c HB Guide - v7 - Fall '96 - p288 [51-250]
  c SLJ - v42 - D '96 - p32 [1-50]
Stevenson, James F - *Innovation in Polymer Processing*
  SciTech - v20 - N '96 - p81 [51-250]
Stevenson, Jonathan - *Losing Mogadishu*
  Arm F&S - v23 - Fall '96 - p128+ [501+]
  NWCR - v49 - Aut '96 - p135+ [501+]
  We Wrecked the Place
  y BL - v93 - N 15 '96 - p555 [51-250]
  BW - v27 - Ja 26 '97 - p4+ [501+]
  Choice - v34 - Mr '97 - p1224 [51-250]
  CSM - v89 - F 14 '97 - p14 [251-500]
  KR - v64 - S 15 '96 - p1387 [251-500]
  LATBR - Ja 12 '97 - p12 [501+]
  LJ - v121 - N 1 '96 - p93 [51-250]
  Nat - v264 - F 24 '97 - p25+ [501+]
  Nat R - v49 - F 10 '97 - p51+ [501+]
Stevenson, Patrick - *The German Language and the Real World*
  MLR - v92 - Ja '97 - p234+ [501+]
Stevenson, R Jan - *Algal Ecology*
  BioSci - v47 - Mr '97 - p191+ [501+]
Stevenson, Randall - *Scottish Theatre since the Seventies*
  TLS - D 13 '96 - p20 [501+]
Stevenson, Richard - *Chain of Fools*
  BL - v93 - N 1 '96 - p483 [51-250]
  BW - v26 - D 15 '96 - p10 [51-250]
  KR - v64 - S 1 '96 - p1279 [51-250]
Stevenson, Robert Louis - *The Bottle Imp (Illus. by Jacqueline Mair)*
  c HB Guide - v7 - Fall '96 - p298 [51-250]
  Catriona (Case). Audio Version
  y Kliatt - v30 - S '96 - p46 [51-250]
  Dr. Jekyll and Mr. Hyde. Travels with a Donkey (Case). Audio Version
  y Kliatt - v30 - S '96 - p48 [51-250]
  The Letters of Robert Louis Stevenson. Vols. 1-6
  Nine-C Lit - v50 - Mr '96 - p541+ [501+]
  The Letters of Robert Louis Stevenson. Vols. 1-8
  VQR - v73 - Win '97 - p175+ [501+]
  The Letters of Robert Louis Stevenson. Vols. 3-6
  ELT - v40 - '97 - p60+ [501+]
  Strange Case of Dr. Jekyll and Mr. Hyde
  ELT - v39 - 4 '96 - p412+ [501+]
  Treasure Island (Illus. by Francois Place)
  c Cres - v60 - Christmas '96 - p10+ [501+]
  y HB Guide - v7 - Fall '96 - p302 [51-250]
  c Magpies - v11 - S '96 - p39+ [501+]
  y NYTBR - v101 - S 22 '96 - p28 [1-50]
  c TES - Ja 31 '97 - p7* [501+]
  Treasure Island (Cummings). Audio Version
  c Ch BWatch - v7 - Ja '97 - p5 [1-50]
  Treasure Island (O'Herlihy). Audio Version
  c SLJ - v43 - Ja '97 - p71 [51-250]
Stevenson, Warren - *Romanticism and the Androgynous Sublime*
  Choice - v34 - Ja '97 - p799 [51-250]
Stevermer, Caroline - *River Rats*
  y Kliatt - v31 - Ja '97 - p16 [51-250]
Stevick, Robert D - *The Earliest Irish and English Bookarts*
  Albion - v28 - Win '96 - p657+ [501+]
Steward, Elizabeth Patrick - *Beginning Writers in the Zone of Proximal Development*
  Col Comp - v47 - O '96 - p443 [501+]
Steward, James Christian - *The New Child*
  Albion - v28 - Fall '96 - p507+ [501+]
Stewart, A T Q - *A Deeper Silence*
  Bks & Cult - v2 - Ja '96 - p11+ [501+]

Stewart, Carroll - *Ted's Travelling Circus*
  APH - v43 - Fall '96 - p64 [501+]
Stewart, Charles - *Demons and the Devil*
  CH - v65 - S '96 - p545+ [501+]
Stewart, Dianne - *Gift of the Sun (Illus. by Jude Daly)*
  c BL - v93 - S 1 '96 - p145 [51-250]
  c CBRS - v25 - Ja '97 - p53 [51-250]
  c CCB-B - v50 - D '96 - p153 [51-250]
  c HB - v72 - N '96 - p730+ [251-500]
  c HB Guide - v8 - Spr '97 - p50 [51-250]
  c JB - v60 - D '96 - p241 [51-250]
  c KR - v64 - Ag 15 '96 - p1244 [51-250]
  c PW - v243 - S 16 '96 - p83+ [51-250]
  c Sch Lib - v44 - N '96 - p148 [51-250]
  c SLJ - v42 - S '96 - p192+ [51-250]
  c Smith - v27 - N '96 - p169 [1-50]
Stewart, Douglas Ian - *After the Trees*
  HAHR - v76 - Ag '96 - p601+ [251-500]
Stewart, Edward - *Jury Double*
  PW - v243 - D 16 '96 - p55 [51-250]
Stewart, Elisabeth J - *Bimmi Finds a Cat (Illus. by James Ransome)*
  c CBRS - v25 - N '96 - p32 [1-50]
  c HB Guide - v8 - Spr '97 - p60 [51-250]
Stewart, Frances - *Adjustment and Poverty*
  JEL - v34 - D '96 - p2116 [51-250]
Stewart, Frank Henderson - *Honor*
  JIH - v27 - Aut '96 - p284 [501+]
Stewart, G W - *Afternotes on Numerical Analysis*
  Choice - v34 - O '96 - p319 [51-250]
  SIAM Rev - v39 - Mr '97 - p153 [501+]
Stewart, Gail B - *The Elderly*
  y HB Guide - v7 - Fall '96 - p317 [51-250]
  Gangs
  y BL - v93 - My 15 '97 - p1572 [51-250]
  c SLJ - v43 - Mr '97 - p209 [51-250]
  Gay and Lesbian Youth
  y BL - v93 - Mr 1 '97 - p1155 [51-250]
  The Homeless
  y HB Guide - v7 - Fall '96 - p317 [51-250]
  The New Deal
  y SE - v60 - S '96 - p304 [1-50]
  People with AIDS
  y HB Guide - v7 - Fall '96 - p317 [51-250]
  Teen Mothers
  y HB Guide - v7 - Fall '96 - p311 [51-250]
  Teen Runaways
  y BL - v93 - Mr 1 '97 - p1155 [51-250]
  Teens in Prison
  y BL - v93 - My 15 '97 - p1572 [51-250]
Stewart, Garrett - *Dear Reader*
  Choice - v34 - My '97 - p1500 [51-250]
  TLS - Mr 28 '97 - p24 [501+]
Stewart, Hilary - *Stone, Bone, Antler and Shell (Illus. by Hilary Stewart)*
  c SB - v32 - N '96 - p243 [51-250]
  y VOYA - v19 - F '97 - p354 [51-250]
Stewart, Ian - *From Here to Infinity. 3rd Ed.*
  Math T - v90 - Ja '97 - p70+ [251-500]
  SB - v32 - Ag '96 - p166 [51-250]
  Nature's Numbers
  y BL - v93 - Ap 1 '97 - p1342 [1-50]
  New Sci - v152 - N 9 '96 - p43 [1-50]
Stewart, J V - *Astrology: What's Really in the Stars*
  Astron - v25 - My '97 - p112+ [51-250]
  Choice - v34 - Ap '97 - p1421 [51-250]
Stewart, James B - *Blood Sport*
  Atl - v278 - O '96 - p114+ [501+]
  LATBR - Mr 24 '96 - p3 [501+]
  LATBR - D 29 '96 - p3 [51-250]
  NYTBR - v101 - D 8 '96 - p85 [1-50]
  NYTBR - v102 - Ap 6 '97 - p32 [51-250]
  PW - v244 - Ja 13 '97 - p73 [1-50]
Stewart, Jampa Mackenzie - *The Life of Gampopa*
  Tric - v6 - Fall '96 - p139+ [501+]
Stewart, John, 1952- - *The British Empire*
  r ARBA - v28 - '97 - p203 [51-250]
  r Choice - v34 - O '96 - p258 [51-250]
Stewart, John Robert - *Language as Articulate Contact*
  MLR - v92 - Ap '97 - p418+ [501+]
  MLR - v92 - Ap '97 - p418+ [501+]
  QJS - v83 - My '97 - p265+ [501+]
Stewart, John Robert, 1941- - *Beyond the Symbol Model*
  Choice - v34 - Mr '97 - p1155 [51-250]
  R&R Bk N - v12 - F '97 - p76 [51-250]
Stewart, Jon - *The Hegel Myths and Legends*
  R&R Bk N - v11 - N '96 - p2 [51-250]
Stewart, Katharine - *A School in the Hills*
  TES - D 27 '96 - p22 [51-250]
Stewart, Kathleen - *Nightflowers*
  Aust Bk R - S '96 - p32+ [501+]

A Space on the Side of the Road
  VQR - v72 - Aut '96 - p135* [51-250]
Stewart, Kathlyn M - *Palaeoecology and Palaeoenvironments of Late Cenozoic Mammals*
  Choice - v34 - N '96 - p487 [51-250]
  SciTech - v20 - S '96 - p18 [51-250]
Stewart, Ken - *The 1890's: Australian Literature and Literary Culture*
  Aust Bk R - O '96 - p24+ [501+]
Stewart, Marcia - *Leases and Rental Agreements*
  BL - v93 - F 1 '97 - p913 [51-250]
Stewart, Marjabelle Young - *The New Etiquette*
  PW - v244 - Ap 21 '97 - p69 [1-50]
Stewart, Mark - *Chris Zorich*
  c HB Guide - v8 - Spr '97 - p146+ [51-250]
Hakeem Olajuwon
  c HB Guide - v8 - Spr '97 - p146+ [51-250]
Joe Dumars
  c HB Guide - v8 - Spr '97 - p146+ [51-250]
Steve Young
  c HB Guide - v8 - Spr '97 - p146+ [51-250]
Stewart, Matthew - *The Truth about Everything*
  PW - v244 - Ja 13 '97 - p64 [51-250]
Stewart, Maureen - *All of Me*
  c Magpies - v11 - My '96 - p48 [51-250]
Stewart, Melville Y - *Philosophy of Religion*
  Hast Cen R - v26 - Jl '96 - p42 [1-50]
Stewart, Paul - *Clock of Doom*
  c Sch Lib - v45 - F '97 - p24 [51-250]
The Wakening
  c Bks Keeps - Ja '97 - p25 [51-250]
  c JB - v60 - D '96 - p261 [51-250]
  c Sch Lib - v45 - F '97 - p34 [51-250]
Stewart, R Michael - *Prehistoric Farmers of the Susquehanna Valley*
  Am Ant - v62 - Ja '97 - p156+ [501+]
Stewart, Richard W - *The English Ordnance Office 1585-1625*
  J Mil H - v61 - Ap '97 - p366+ [251-500]
Stewart, Robert J - *Religion and Society in Post-Emancipation Jamaica*
  CH - v66 - Mr '97 - p206 [51-250]
Stewart, Robin E - *New Faces (Illus. by Elspeth Lacey)*
  c Bkbird - v34 - Spr '96 - p51 [51-250]
Stewart, Sarah - *The Library (Illus. by David Small)*
  c RT - v50 - N '96 - p242 [51-250]
Stewart, Sean - *Clouds End*
  y BL - v92 - Ag '96 - p1889 [51-250]
  y BL - v92 - Ag '96 - p1891 [1-50]
  BWatch - v17 - N '96 - p8 [51-250]
  MFSF - v91 - D '96 - p97 [51-250]
  PW - v243 - Jl 22 '96 - p231 [51-250]
Stewart, Thomas A - *Intellectual Capital*
  LJ - v122 - Ap 15 '97 - p94 [51-250]
  PW - v244 - F 10 '97 - p73 [51-250]
Stewart, Whitney - *The 14th Dalai Lama: Spiritual Leader of Tibet*
  c Ch BWatch - v6 - My '96 - p6 [51-250]
  y HB Guide - v7 - Fall '96 - p375 [51-250]
  y VOYA - v19 - O '96 - p238 [51-250]
Aung San Suu Kyi: Fearless Voice of Burma
  y BL - v93 - Ap 1 '97 - p1321 [51-250]
  c KR - v65 - Ap 1 '97 - p562 [51-250]
Sir Edmund Hillary: To Everest and Beyond (Illus. by Anne B Keiser)
  y HB Guide - v8 - Spr '97 - p147 [51-250]
  c SLJ - v42 - S '96 - p221 [51-250]
Stewig, John - *Princess Florecita and the Iron Shoes (Illus. by K Wendy Popp)*
  c RT - v50 - S '96 - p52 [51-250]
Stiassny, Melanie L J - *Interrelationships of Fishes*
  Choice - v34 - Ap '97 - p1366 [51-250]
  SciTech - v21 - Mr '97 - p38 [51-250]
Stibbe, Mark W G - *John*
  Rel St Rev - v22 - O '96 - p347 [501+]
Stich, Stephen P - *Deconstructing the Mind*
  Choice - v34 - Ja '97 - p809 [51-250]
Stickland, Caroline - *The Darkening Leaf*
  KR - v64 - My 1 '96 - p634 [251-500]
Stickland, Paul - *Bedtime Bear*
  c PW - v244 - F 10 '97 - p85 [51-250]
Birthday Bear
  c PW - v244 - F 10 '97 - p85 [51-250]
Buddy Bear
  c PW - v244 - F 10 '97 - p85 [51-250]
Dinosaur Roar! (Illus. by Paul Stickland)
  c Bks Keeps - v100 - S '96 - p9 [51-250]
  c Obs - Mr 30 '97 - p17* [51-250]
  c PW - v244 - My 5 '97 - p211 [1-50]

Dinosaur Stomp! (Illus. by Paul Stickland)
  c BL - v93 - D 15 '96 - p732 [1-50]
  c HB Guide - v8 - Spr '97 - p15 [1-50]
  c KR - v64 - S 1 '96 - p1332 [51-250]
  c PW - v243 - O 7 '96 - p77 [51-250]
  c SLJ - v43 - F '97 - p85 [51-250]
Santa's Workshop (Illus. by Paul Stickland)
  c BIC - v25 - D '96 - p33+ [501+]
  c Bks Keeps - N '96 - p20 [1-50]
Share Bear
  c PW - v244 - F 10 '97 - p85 [51-250]
Swamp Stomp!
  c Bks Keeps - v100 - S '96 - p32 [51-250]
  c TES - N 29 '96 - p13* [51-250]
Stickler, Alfons M - *The Case for Clerical Celibacy*
  Rel St Rev - v23 - Ja '97 - p79+ [51-250]
Stickney, Brandon M - *All-American Monster*
  BL - v93 - S 1 '96 - p5 [51-250]
  PW - v243 - Jl 22 '96 - p224 [51-250]
Stickney, Doris - *Waterbugs and Dragonflies*
  c TES - N 22 '96 - p5* [51-250]
Stiebing, William H, Jr. - *Uncovering the Past*
  AJA - v100 - Jl '96 - p605 [501+]
Stiefel, Edward - *Transition Metal Sulfur Chemistry*
  SciTech - v21 - Mr '97 - p30 [51-250]
Stieglitz, Alfred - *Alfred Stieglitz at Lake George*
  Art J - v55 - Sum '96 - p105+ [501+]
Stienecker, David - *Addition (Illus. by Richard Maccabe)*
  c HB Guide - v7 - Fall '96 - p330 [1-50]
Division (Illus. by Richard Maccabe)
  c HB Guide - v7 - Fall '96 - p330 [1-50]
Fractions (Illus. by Richard Maccabe)
  c HB Guide - v7 - Fall '96 - p330 [1-50]
Multiplication (Illus. by Richard Maccabe)
  c HB Guide - v7 - Fall '96 - p330 [1-50]
Numbers (Illus. by Richard Maccabe)
  c HB Guide - v7 - Fall '96 - p330 [1-50]
Patterns (Illus. by Richard Maccabe)
  c Ch BWatch - v7 - Ja '97 - p3 [1-50]
  c HB Guide - v8 - Spr '97 - p111 [51-250]
  c SLJ - v43 - F '97 - p97 [51-250]
Polygons (Illus. by Richard Maccabe)
  c Ch BWatch - v7 - Ja '97 - p3 [1-50]
  c HB Guide - v8 - Spr '97 - p111 [51-250]
  c SLJ - v43 - F '97 - p97 [51-250]
Rectangles (Illus. by Richard Maccabe)
  c Ch BWatch - v7 - Ja '97 - p3 [1-50]
  c HB Guide - v8 - Spr '97 - p111 [51-250]
  c SLJ - v43 - F '97 - p97 [51-250]
Three-Dimensional Shapes (Illus. by Richard Maccabe)
  c Ch BWatch - v7 - Ja '97 - p3 [1-50]
  c HB Guide - v8 - Spr '97 - p111 [51-250]
  c SLJ - v43 - F '97 - p97 [51-250]
Stiff, Ruth - *Margaret Mee: Return to the Amazon*
  BWatch - v18 - Mr '97 - p3 [1-50]
Stigen, Terje - *Allegretto*
  WLT - v70 - Sum '96 - p714 [501+]
Stiles, David - *Storage Projects You Can Build*
  BWatch - v18 - F '97 - p1 [1-50]
Stiles, Kristine - *Theories and Documents of Contemporary Art*
  AB - v99 - Mr 3 '97 - p694 [51-250]
  Art Bull - v79 - Mr '97 - p164+ [501+]
Stiles, T J - *Robber Barons and Radicals*
  y LJ - v122 - Ap 1 '97 - p106 [51-250]
Stilgoe, John R - *Alongshore*
  Sew R - v104 - O '96 - p701+ [501+]
Still, James - *Jack and the Wonder Beans (Illus. by Margot Tomes)*
  c HB Guide - v8 - Spr '97 - p105 [51-250]
Still, John - *Asombrosos Escarabajos*
  c BL - v93 - F 15 '97 - p1032 [1-50]
Still, Judith, 1958- - *Textuality and Sexuality*
  MLR - v91 - Jl '96 - p686+ [501+]
Still, Judith Anne - *William Grant Still: A Bio-Bibliography*
  r ARBA - v28 - '97 - p478 [51-250]
  r Choice - v34 - F '97 - p950+ [51-250]
  r R&R Bk N - v11 - D '96 - p56 [51-250]
Stille, Alexander - *Excellent Cadavers*
  NYTBR - v101 - N 3 '96 - p28 [1-50]
Stiller, Brian C - *From the Tower of Babel to Parliament Hill*
  Quill & Q - v63 - Mr '97 - p72 [251-500]
Stillerman, Elaine - *The Encyclopedia of Bodywork*
  r ARBA - v28 - '97 - p613+ [51-250]
Stillie, Margaret - *Active Comprehension. Bks. 1-4*
  TES - Mr 14 '97 - p16* [251-500]
Stillinger, Jack - *Coleridge and Textual Instability*
  RES - v47 - N '96 - p603+ [501+]

Stillion, Judith M - *Suicide across the Life Span. 2nd Ed.*
  R&R Bk N - v11 - N '96 - p45 [51-250]
Stillman, Norman A - *Sephardi Religious Responses to Modernity*
  Choice - v34 - D '96 - p630 [1-50]
  Rel St Rev - v23 - Ap '97 - p197 [51-250]
Stillwell, Alexandra - *Cassell Illustrated Dictionary of Lacemaking*
  r BL - v93 - O 1 '96 - p316 [51-250]
  r LJ - v121 - D '96 - p91 [51-250]
Stillwell, John - *Sources of Hyperbolic Geometry*
  SciTech - v20 - N '96 - p15 [1-50]
Stillwell, Susan B - *Mosby's Critical Care Nursing Reference*
  r SciTech - v20 - S '96 - p44 [51-250]
Stilwell, Steven A - *What Mystery Do I Read Next?*
  r LJ - v122 - Ap 1 '97 - p86 [51-250]
Stimpson, Eddie, Jr. - *My Remembers*
  JSH - v62 - N '96 - p861 [1-50]
  y SLJ - v42 - Ag '96 - p186 [51-250]
Stimson, Joan - *Swim, Polar Bear, Swim! (Illus. by Meg Rutherford)*
  c JB - v60 - D '96 - p241 [51-250]
  c Sch Lib - v45 - F '97 - p22 [51-250]
Stinchcombe, Arthur L - *Sugar Island Slavery in the Age of Enlightenment*
  AAPSS-A - v549 - Ja '97 - p190+ [501+]
  JEH - v57 - Mr '97 - p235+ [501+]
  JEL - v34 - S '96 - p1469 [51-250]
  TLS - My 24 '96 - p16 [501+]
Stine, G Harry - *Halfway to Anywhere*
  A & S Sm - v11 - F '97 - p86 [501+]
  BYTE - v22 - F '97 - p154 [51-250]
  SciTech - v20 - D '96 - p81 [51-250]
Stine, Jean Marie - *Double Your Brain Power*
  LJ - v122 - My 1 '97 - p127 [51-250]
Stine, Karen E - *Principles of Toxicology*
  Choice - v34 - Mr '97 - p1193 [51-250]
  SciTech - v20 - D '96 - p40 [1-50]
Stine, Peter - *The Sixties*
  ABR - v18 - O '96 - p25+ [501+]
Stine, R L - *Attack of the Mutant. Audio Version*
  c BL - v93 - Mr 15 '97 - p1253 [51-250]
The Cuckoo Clock of Doom
  c RT - v50 - O '96 - p141 [1-50]
Goosebumps: Escape from Horrorland. Electronic Media Version
  c Par - v72 - F '97 - p155 [51-250]
Goosebumps Monster Edition. No. 1
  c RT - v50 - O '96 - p141 [1-50]
Goosebumps Series. Audio Version
  c SLJ - v43 - Mr '97 - p142 [51-250]
A Night in Terror Tower. Audio Version
  c BL - v93 - Mr 15 '97 - p1253 [51-250]
  c PW - v243 - S 30 '96 - p43 [51-250]
No Bajes Al Sotano!
  c SLJ - v42 - N '96 - p134 [51-250]
Piano Lessons Can be Murder
  c NY - v72 - N 18 '96 - p100+ [51-250]
R.L. Stine's Ghosts of Fear Street. Audio Version
  c PW - v244 - Ap 14 '97 - p32 [51-250]
A Shocker on Shock Street. Audio Version
  c BL - v93 - Mr 15 '97 - p1253 [51-250]
  y Kliatt - v31 - Ja '97 - p45 [51-250]
Stine, Robert - *Statistical Computing Environments for Social Research*
  R&R Bk N - v11 - D '96 - p22 [51-250]
Stine, Sharon - *Landscapes for Learning*
  Choice - v34 - My '97 - p1551+ [51-250]
Stiner, Mary C - *Honor among Thieves*
  Am Ant - v61 - O '96 - p815+ [501+]
Stinson, Russell - *Bach, the Orgelbuchlein*
  Choice - v34 - My '97 - p1510 [51-250]
Stipelman, Steven - *Illustrating Fashion--Concept to Creation*
  TCI - v30 - O '96 - p56 [51-250]
Stipp, Hermann-Josef - *Das Masoretische Und Alexandrinische Sondergut Des Jeremiabuches*
  Rel St Rev - v23 - Ja '97 - p59 [51-250]
Stirling, Jessica - *The Blue Evening Gone (Steafel). Audio Version*
  BWatch - v18 - Mr '97 - p8 [1-50]
The Marrying Kind
  KR - v64 - My 1 '96 - p634+ [251-500]
Stirling, S M - *The Chosen*
  y VOYA - v19 - D '96 - p282 [51-250]
The Ship Avenged
  KR - v64 - D 15 '96 - p1774 [51-250]
  PW - v244 - Ja 27 '97 - p82 [51-250]
Stirr, Thomas - *Miller's Bolt*
  PW - v244 - Mr 31 '97 - p62+ [51-250]

Stites, Richard - *Culture and Entertainment in Wartime Russia*
   CAY - v16 - Fall '95 - p10 [51-250]
Stith, Anthony - *Breaking the Glass Ceiling*
   LJ - v121 - N 1 '96 - p82 [1-50]
Stith, John E - *Reckoning Infinity*
   BL - v93 - Ap 1 '97 - p1283 [51-250]
   KR - v65 - F 1 '97 - p177+ [51-250]
   LJ - v122 - Mr 15 '97 - p93 [1-50]
   PW - v244 - Mr 31 '97 - p68 [51-250]
Stivender, Ed - *Still Catholic after All These Years*
   CAY - v17 - Fall '96 - p8 [51-250]
Stock, Brian - *Augustine the Reader*
   Choice - v34 - N '96 - p477 [51-250]
   Theol St - v57 - D '96 - p744+ [501+]
   TLS - Ag 30 '96 - p33 [501+]
Stock, Catherine McNicol - *Rural Radicals*
   CHE - v43 - N 1 '96 - pA20 [51-250]
   Choice - v34 - Mr '97 - p1230 [51-250]
   KR - v64 - Ag 15 '96 - p1224 [251-500]
   LJ - v121 - O 15 '96 - p74 [51-250]
   Nat - v263 - N 4 '96 - p27+ [501+]
   NYTBR - v101 - N 17 '96 - p20 [501+]
   PW - v243 - S 16 '96 - p63 [51-250]
Stock, Jonathan P J - *Musical Creativity in Twentieth-Century China*
   Choice - v34 - Ap '97 - p1349 [51-250]
   World Sound Matters
   TES - Ja 31 '97 - p17* [51-250]
Stock, Norman - *Buying Breakfast for My Kamikaze Pilot*
   PS - v70 - Win '96 - p182+ [501+]
Stock, Robert - *Africa South of the Sahara*
   GJ - v163 - Mr '97 - p94+ [501+]
Stockdale, Linda - *ABC Career Book for Girls (Illus. by John Schafer)*
   c SLJ - v43 - F '97 - p99 [51-250]
Stockdale, Melissa Kirschke - *Paul Miliukov and the Quest for a Liberal Russia 1880-1918*
   TLS - Ap 11 '97 - p13 [501+]
Stockdale, Susan - *Some Sleep Standing Up*
   c BL - v93 - S 1 '96 - p140 [51-250]
   c HB Guide - v7 - Fall '96 - p339 [1-50]
Stockenberg, Antoinette - *Dream a Little Dream*
   PW - v244 - My 5 '97 - p206 [51-250]
Stocking, George W - *After Tylor*
   AJS - v102 - N '96 - p911+ [501+]
   Am Sci - v85 - Mr '97 - p189 [501+]
   Choice - v34 - S '96 - p169 [51-250]
   Lon R Bks - v18 - My 23 '96 - p30 [501+]
   Romantic Motives
   Ant R - v54 - Sum '96 - p361+ [251-500]
Stockmans, Piet - *Piet Stockmans (Uitgeverij Lannoo)*
   Ceram Mo - v44 - N '96 - p27+ [51-250]
Stockton, Annis Boudinot - *Only for the Eye of a Friend*
   W&M Q - v53 - O '96 - p819+ [501+]
Stockton, Frank R - *The Queen's Museum and Other Fanciful Tales. Audio Version*
   c Ch BWatch - v7 - Ja '97 - p1 [1-50]
Stockton, Kathryn Bond - *God between Their Lips*
   VS - v39 - Aut '95 - p88+ [501+]
Stoddard, Alexandra - *The Art of the Possible*
   PW - v243 - S 23 '96 - p73 [1-50]
   Gracious Living in a New World
   PW - v243 - S 16 '96 - p65 [51-250]
Stoddard, Sandol - *What Are Roses For? (Illus. by Jacqueline Chwast)*
   c HB Guide - v7 - Fall '96 - p369 [51-250]
   c SLJ - v42 - D '96 - p107 [51-250]
Stoddard, Tom - *Turnaround: The Untold Story of Bear Bryant's First Year as Head Coach at Alabama*
   PW - v243 - S 2 '96 - p107 [51-250]
Stoeber, Michael - *Critical Reflections on the Paranormal*
   Choice - v34 - Mr '97 - p1242+ [51-250]
   New Sci - v152 - D 7 '96 - p48 [51-250]
   R&R Bk N - v12 - F '97 - p7 [51-250]
Stoehr, Shelley - *Wannabe*
   y CCB-B - v50 - Mr '97 - p258+ [51-250]
   y KR - v64 - N 1 '96 - p1608+ [51-250]
   y SLJ - v43 - Ja '97 - p116 [51-250]
   Weird on the Inside
   y Kliatt - v30 - S '96 - p14 [51-250]
Stoeke, Janet Morgan - *A Hat for Minerva Louise*
   c PW - v243 - D 30 '96 - p68 [1-50]
   Minerva Louise at School (Illus. by Janet Morgan Stoeke)
   c BL - v92 - Ag '96 - p1909 [51-250]
   c CCB-B - v50 - S '96 - p32 [51-250]
   c HB Guide - v8 - Spr '97 - p50 [51-250]
   c SLJ - v42 - Ag '96 - p130+ [51-250]

Stoichita, Victor Ieronim - *Visionary Experience in the Golden Age of Spanish Art*
   BM - v138 - Ag '96 - p552 [251-500]
   Choice - v34 - F '97 - p958 [51-250]
Stoil, Michael J - *Preventing Substance Abuse*
   r R&R Bk N - v12 - F '97 - p56 [1-50]
Stoker, Bram - *Dracula*
   Critm - v38 - Fall '96 - p607+ [501+]
   MLR - v92 - Ja '97 - p1+ [501+]
   Obs - Ap 6 '97 - p18* [51-250]
   Dracula (Illus. by Tudor Humphries)
   c PW - v244 - My 12 '97 - p77 [51-250]
   The Jewel of Seven Stars
   ELT - v39 - 3 '96 - p406 [51-250]
   Midnight Tales
   ELT - v39 - 4 '96 - p530 [51-250]
Stoker, Carol R - *Strategies for Mars*
   Choice - v34 - N '96 - p481 [51-250]
   Fut - v31 - Mr '97 - p50+ [251-500]
Stokes, Donald W - *The Complete Birdhouse Book*
   LJ - v121 - D '96 - p67 [1-50]
   Stokes Beginner's Guide to Birds: Eastern Region
   r Wildbird - v11 - F '97 - p38 [51-250]
   Stokes Beginner's Guide to Birds: Western Region
   r Wildbird - v11 - F '97 - p38 [51-250]
   Stokes Field Guide to Birds: Eastern Region
   r Wildbird - v10 - Ag '96 - p58+ [501+]
   Stokes Field Guide to Birds: Western Region
   r Wildbird - v10 - Ag '96 - p58+ [501+]
Stokes, Gale - *The Walls Came Tumbling Down*
   EHR - v111 - S '96 - p1037+ [251-500]
Stokes, John - *Oscar Wilde: Myths, Miracles, and Imitations*
   Choice - v34 - My '97 - p1500 [51-250]
Stokes, Melvyn - *The Market Revolution in America*
   Choice - v34 - N '96 - p508 [51-250]
Stokes, Penelope - *Picture Framing Made Easy*
   BL - v93 - F 1 '97 - p920 [51-250]
   LJ - v122 - F 15 '97 - p134 [51-250]
Stokes, Penelope J - *Till We Meet Again*
   LJ - v122 - Ap 1 '97 - p80 [51-250]
Stokesbury, James L - *A Short History of the Civil War*
   y SLJ - v42 - Ag '96 - p186 [51-250]
Stokesbury, Leon - *The Made Thing*
   S Liv - v31 - Jl '96 - p80 [51-250]
Stoklosa, Mitchell J - *Pharmaceutical Calculations. 10th Ed.*
   SciTech - v20 - N '96 - p56 [51-250]
Stokstad, Marilyn - *Art History*
   Art J - v55 - Sum '96 - p99+ [501+]
   Bloom Rev - v16 - N '96 - p23 [51-250]
Stolberg, Mary M - *Fighting Organized Crime*
   TLS - My 24 '96 - p36 [51-250]
Stolen, Kristi Anne - *The Decency of Inequality*
   R&R Bk N - v12 - F '97 - p30 [51-250]
Stoll, Clifford - *Silicon Snake Oil*
   Cont Ed - v68 - Win '97 - p148+ [501+]
   y Kliatt - v30 - S '96 - p37 [51-250]
   LQ - v66 - O '96 - p462+ [501+]
Stoller, David W - *Magnetic Resonance Imaging in Orthopaedics and Sports Medicine. 2nd Ed.*
   r SciTech - v21 - Mr '97 - p61 [1-50]
Stolley, Paul D - *Investigating Disease Patterns*
   AJPsych - v153 - N '96 - p1498+ [251-500]
Stolnitz, George J - *Social Aspects and Country Reviews of Population Aging*
   J Gov Info - v23 - S '96 - p679 [51-250]
Stolpe, Michael - *Technology and the Dynamics of Specialization in Open Economies*
   JEL - v34 - S '96 - p1485+ [51-250]
Stoltz, Paul - *Adversity Quotient*
   LJ - v122 - My 1 '97 - p127 [51-250]
Stoltzfus, Louise - *Amish Women*
   PW - v244 - Mr 3 '97 - p72 [1-50]
Stoltzfus, Nathan - *Resistance of the Heart*
   BL - v93 - N 15 '96 - p555 [51-250]
   Choice - v34 - Ap '97 - p1399 [51-250]
   KR - v64 - S 1 '96 - p1310 [51-250]
   LJ - v121 - O 1 '96 - p100+ [51-250]
   Obs - F 16 '97 - p17* [51-250]
   PW - v243 - S 16 '96 - p58+ [51-250]
Stolz, Dieter - *Vom Privaten Motivkomplex Zum Poetischen Weltentwurf*
   Ger Q - v69 - Spr '96 - p224+ [501+]
Stone, A J - *The Theory of Intermolecular Forces*
   SciTech - v21 - Mr '97 - p31 [51-250]
Stone, Abigail - *Recipes from the Dump*
   LJ - v121 - D '96 - p180 [51-250]
   PW - v243 - O 7 '96 - p1 [1-50]
Stone, Albert E - *Literary Aftershocks*
   J Am Cult - v19 - Sum '96 - p152+ [501+]

Stone, Allucquere Rosanne - *The War of Desire and Technology at the Close of the Mechanical Age*
   Afterimage - v24 - Ja '97 - p23 [1-50]
   QJS - v83 - My '97 - p230+ [501+]
   SocSciComR - v14 - Win '96 - p483+ [501+]
Stone, Bailey - *The Genesis of the French Revolution*
   EHR - v111 - N '96 - p1301+ [251-500]
Stone, Betsy - *Happily Ever After*
   PW - v244 - Ja 6 '97 - p71 [51-250]
Stone, Bob - *The Dating Dilemma*
   y VOYA - v19 - F '97 - p319 [51-250]
Stone, Bryan P - *Effective Faith*
   Rel St Rev - v23 - Ap '97 - p153 [51-250]
Stone, C J - *An Atlas of Seabird Distribution in North-West European Waters*
   r J Gov Info - v23 - S '96 - p643 [51-250]
Stone, Del, Jr. - *Dead Heat*
   LJ - v121 - N 15 '96 - p91 [51-250]
Stone, Desmond - *Alec Wilder in Spite of Himself*
   Choice - v34 - S '96 - p138 [51-250]
   NY - v72 - My 27 '96 - p131+ [501+]
Stone, Diane - *Capturing the Political Imagination*
   TLS - D 20 '96 - p28 [501+]
Stone, Ellen C - *Guide to the Ships Plans Collection at Mystic Seaport Museum*
   Sea H - Aut '96 - p46 [51-250]
Stone, Eric - *In a Heartbeat*
   KR - v64 - My 1 '96 - p647 [51-250]
Stone, Florence M - *The High-Value Manager*
   J Car P&E - v57 - Fall '96 - p16 [51-250]
Stone, Glenn Davis - *Settlement Ecology*
   Choice - v34 - My '97 - p1542 [51-250]
Stone, Glyn - *The Oldest Ally*
   Albion - v28 - Sum '96 - p353+ [501+]
   EHR - v112 - Ap '97 - p531+ [501+]
Stone, Harriet - *The Classical Model*
   Choice - v34 - F '97 - p971 [51-250]
Stone, Harry - *The Night Side of Dickens*
   RES - v47 - Ag '96 - p435+ [501+]
   Writing in the Shadow
   R&R Bk N - v11 - N '96 - p10 [51-250]
   TLS - N 15 '96 - p12 [251-500]
Stone, Howard W - *How to Think Theologically*
   CC - v114 - Mr 12 '97 - p275 [51-250]
Stone, Jon R - *Latin for the Illiterati*
   r LJ - v121 - D '96 - p86 [51-250]
Stone, Judith F, 1946- - *Sons of the Revolution*
   Choice - v34 - O '96 - p342 [51-250]
Stone, Judy, 1924- - *Eye on the World*
   PW - v244 - My 12 '97 - p65+ [51-250]
Stone, Julie - *Complementary Medicine and the Law*
   Hast Cen R - v26 - S '96 - p41 [1-50]
Stone, Lawrence - *Road to Divorce*
   Six Ct J - v27 - Fall '96 - p895+ [501+]
   Uncertain Unions and Broken Lives
   Six Ct J - v27 - Fall '96 - p895+ [501+]
Stone, Lyn - *The Wicked Truth*
   PW - v244 - F 24 '97 - p88 [51-250]
Stone, Marjorie - *Elizabeth Barrett Browning*
   RES - v48 - F '97 - p131+ [501+]
Stone, Michael, 1950- - *A Long Reach*
   BL - v93 - Ja '97 - p825 [51-250]
   KR - v64 - D 15 '96 - p1771 [51-250]
   LJ - v122 - Ja '97 - p152 [51-250]
   The Low End of Nowhere
   Arm Det - v29 - Fall '96 - p436 [51-250]
   PW - v244 - Ja 27 '97 - p103 [1-50]
Stone, Michael H, 1933- - *Healing the Mind*
   LJ - v121 - O 15 '96 - p79 [51-250]
Stone, Oliver - *A Child's Night Dream*
   Ent W - Ag 23 '96 - p117 [1-50]
Stone, Pat - *Real Gardener's True Confessions*
   BL - v93 - F 1 '97 - p918 [51-250]
Stone, Peter G - *The Presented Past*
   AJA - v100 - O '96 - p769+ [501+]
Stone, Philip - *Materials*
   y Sch Lib - v44 - N '96 - p175 [251-500]
Stone, Robert - *Bear and His Daughter*
   BL - v93 - Mr 1 '97 - p1112 [51-250]
   KR - v65 - F 1 '97 - p168 [251-500]
   LATBR - Ap 6 '97 - p2 [501+]
   LJ - v122 - F 1 '97 - p110 [51-250]
   NYTBR - v102 - Ap 20 '97 - p13 [501+]
   NYTLa - v146 - Ap 3 '97 - pC19 [501+]
   PW - v244 - F 3 '97 - p92+ [51-250]
   Trib Bks - Ap 27 '97 - p3+ [501+]
   Dog Soldiers
   SFR - v22 - Ja '97 - p48 [51-250]
Stone, Robert J - *Atlas of Skeletal Muscles. 2nd Ed.*
   r SciTech - v21 - Mr '97 - p39 [51-250]

Stone, Ruth - *Simplicity*
  BW - v26 - D 8 '96 - p8 [51-250]
Stone, Ted - *Alberta History along the Highway*
  r Beav - v77 - F '97 - p41 [51-250]
Stone, Tom - *April Ghoul's Day*
  c Ch BWatch - v6 - My '96 - p7 [1-50]
  Scream, Team!
  c Ch BWatch - v6 - Jl '96 - p5 [1-50]
  Tales to Scary to Tell at Camp
  y Ch BWatch - v6 - S '96 - p3+ [51-250]
Stone, Walter N - *Group Psychotherapy for People with*
  Chronic Mental Illness
  Readings - v11 - S '96 - p27 [51-250]
Stoner, Madeleine R - *The Civil Rights of Homeless*
  People
  Soc Ser R - v71 - Mr '97 - p160+ [501+]
Stones, Rob - *Sociological Reasoning*
  Choice - v34 - Ja '97 - p885 [51-250]
Stong, Phil - *State Fair*
  LJ - v121 - N 15 '96 - p93 [1-50]
Stoob, H - *Westfalischer Stadteatlas. Vols. 1-4*
  r J Urban H - v22 - S '96 - p739+ [501+]
Stoops, Erik D - *Dolphins*
  c BL - v93 - My 1 '97 - p1492 [51-250]
  c HB Guide - v8 - Spr '97 - p128 [51-250]
Stop the Violence
  r J Gov Info - v23 - S '96 - p629+ [51-250]
Stoppard, Michael - *A New Order for Gas in Europe?*
  En Jnl - v18 - 1 '97 - p134+ [501+]
Stoppard, Miriam - *The Breast Book*
  r BL - v93 - F 1 '97 - p959 [1-50]
  Conception, Pregnancy and Birth
  r BL - v93 - F 1 '97 - p960 [1-50]
Stoppard, Tom - *Arcadia*
  CML - v16 - Win '96 - p177+ [501+]
  Reason - v28 - D '96 - p44 [51-250]
Stoppleman, Monica - *Jewish*
  c HB Guide - v7 - Fall '96 - p308 [51-250]
Storace, Patricia - *Dinner with Persephone*
  Atl - v278 - N '96 - p121 [51-250]
  KR - v64 - Ag 15 '96 - p1225 [251-500]
  LJ - v122 - Ja '97 - p51 [51-250]
  NYRB - v43 - N 14 '96 - p14+ [501+]
  NYTBR - v101 - O 20 '96 - p9 [501+]
  NYTBR - v101 - D 8 '96 - p87 [1-50]
  Spec - v277 - N 16 '96 - p43 [1-50]
  VV - v41 - N 12 '96 - p86 [501+]
Storey, Gail Donohue - *God's Country Club*
  BL - v93 - S 1 '96 - p64+ [51-250]
Storey, Helen - *Fighting Fashion*
  Econ - v342 - Mr 15 '97 - p3*+ [501+]
Storey, John, 1950- - *Cultural Studies and the Study of*
  Popular Culture
  Si & So - v6 - N '96 - p35 [51-250]
Storey, M John, 1943- - *Taking Money out of Your*
  Corporation
  B Ent - v27 - N '96 - p34 [51-250]
Storey, William K - *Scientific Aspects of European*
  Expansion
  SciTech - v20 - S '96 - p2 [51-250]
Stork, David G - *HAL's Legacy*
  y BL - v93 - D 1 '96 - p633 [51-250]
  BWatch - v18 - Mr '97 - p10 [51-250]
  Choice - v34 - My '97 - p1535 [51-250]
  KR - v64 - N 15 '96 - p1659 [251-500]
  LJ - v121 - D '96 - p131 [51-250]
Storkey, Elaine - *The Search for Intimacy*
  CC - v113 - O 16 '96 - p982 [51-250]
Storlie, Erik Fraser - *Nothing on My Mind*
  BL - v93 - O 1 '96 - p307 [51-250]
  LJ - v121 - O 1 '96 - p85 [51-250]
  PW - v243 - O 21 '96 - p76 [51-250]
  Tric - v6 - Win '96 - p99+ [501+]
Storm, Theodor - *The Dykemaster*
  KR - v64 - N 15 '96 - p1632 [51-250]
  PW - v243 - D 2 '96 - p53 [51-250]
Storm Warning
  p Sm Pr R - v28 - N '96 - p18 [251-500]
Storme, Francoise - *Le Francais Des Affaires. 2nd Ed.*
  FR - v70 - O '96 - p160+ [501+]
Storr, Anthony - *Feet of Clay*
  BW - v26 - S 8 '96 - p11 [501+]
  Choice - v34 - Mr '97 - p1244 [51-250]
  Skeptic - v4 - '96 - p106 [51-250]
Storti, Craig - *Cross-Cultural Dialogues*
  MLJ - v80 - Win '96 - p544+ [501+]
Story, Dana - *The Shipbuilders of Essex*
  NEQ - v69 - D '96 - p662+ [501+]
  Sea H - Sum '96 - p29+ [251-500]
The Story of Flight
  c Books - v9 - S '95 - p26 [1-50]

Stothert, Karen E - *Un Sitio De Guangala Temprano En*
  El Suroeste Del Ecuador
  LA Ant - v7 - Mr '96 - p83+ [501+]
Stott, Jon C - *Native Americans in Children's Literature*
  r JOYS - v9 - Sum '96 - p411+ [251-500]
Stotz, Douglas F - *Neotropical Birds*
  r Choice - v34 - O '96 - p307 [51-250]
  SB - v32 - Ag '96 - p168 [251-500]
  SciTech - v20 - S '96 - p21 [51-250]
Stotzky, Irwin P - *Transition to Democracy in Latin*
  America
  HAHR - v76 - N '96 - p834+ [501+]
Stout, Daniel A - *Religion and Mass Media*
  r Choice - v34 - N '96 - p447+ [51-250]
  JMCQ - v73 - Aut '96 - p765+ [501+]
Stout, Glenn - *Jackie Robinson: Between the Baselines*
  LJ - v122 - F 1 '97 - p82 [1-50]
Stout, Harry S - *The Divine Dramatist*
  JR - v77 - Ap '97 - p268+ [501+]
Stout, Janis P - *Katherine Anne Porter: A Sense of the*
  Times
  AL - v68 - S '96 - p651+ [251-500]
Stout, Linda - *Bridging the Class Divide and Other*
  Lessons for Grassroots Organizing
  BL - v93 - F 1 '97 - p913+ [51-250]
Stout, Rex - *Black Orchids. Audio Version*
  BWatch - v17 - D '96 - p11 [1-50]
  The League of Frightened Men (Rubinek). Audio Version
  BWatch - v17 - D '96 - p11 [1-50]
  y Kliatt - v31 - My '97 - p42 [51-250]
  Quill & Q - v62 - Ag '96 - p37 [1-50]
Stout, Rick - *Internet Science, Research and Technology*
  Yellow Pages. Special Ed.
  r CBR - v14 - Jl '96 - p21 [1-50]
  Web Site Stats
  LJ - v122 - Ap 1 '97 - p118 [51-250]
  World Wide Web
  r CBR - v14 - S '96 - p30 [1-50]
Stout, Robert Joe - *They Still Play Baseball the Old Way*
  Aethlon - v13 - Fall '95 - p145+ [251-500]
Stout, Rowland - *Things That Happen Because They*
  Should
  Choice - v34 - My '97 - p1514 [501+]
Stovall, Tyler - *Paris Noir*
  BL - v93 - N 1 '96 - p480 [51-250]
  Bloom Rev - v17 - Ja '97 - p19 [51-250]
  BW - v27 - Ja 19 '97 - p4 [501+]
  Choice - v34 - Ap '97 - p1407+ [51-250]
  KR - v64 - O 1 '96 - p1454 [251-500]
  LJ - v121 - D '96 - p119 [51-250]
  LJ - v121 - N 1 '96 - p84 [1-50]
  Nat - v264 - Ja 13 '97 - p31+ [501+]
  PW - v243 - O 21 '96 - p62 [51-250]
Stover, Deb - *A Willing Spirit*
  PW - v243 - S 23 '96 - p74 [51-250]
Stover, John C - *Optical Scattering. 2nd Ed.*
  SciTech - v20 - D '96 - p24 [51-250]
Stover, Matthew Woodring - *Iron Dawn*
  LJ - v122 - Ap 15 '97 - p123 [51-250]
Stow, Jenny - *Following the Sun (Illus. by Jenny Stow)*
  c JB - v60 - D '96 - p241 [51-250]
  Sch Lib - v45 - F '97 - p22 [51-250]
Stowasser, Barbara Freyer - *Women in the Qur'an*
  Traditions, and Interpretation
  TLS - Ja 10 '97 - p24+ [501+]
Stowe, Harriet Beecher - *Oldtown Folks*
  AL - v69 - Mr '97 - p39+ [501+]
  Uncle Tom's Cabin
  CLS - v33 - 4 '96 - p350+ [501+]
Stowe, Rebecca - *The Shadow of Desire*
  KR - v64 - My 1 '96 - p635 [251-500]
  LATBR - Ag 11 '96 - p10 [51-250]
  LJ - v122 - F 1 '97 - p136 [51-250]
  NYTBR - v101 - Jl 21 '96 - p19 [51-250]
  PW - v244 - My 5 '97 - p206 [1-50]
Stowe, William W - *Going Abroad*
  AHR - v101 - O '96 - p1276+ [501+]
Stowers, Stanley K - *A Rereading of Romans*
  Intpr - v50 - O '96 - p431+ [501+]
Stoyan, Dietrich - *Stochastic Geometry and Its*
  Applications. 2nd Ed.
  SciTech - v20 - D '96 - p16 [51-250]
Stoyanov, Yuri - *The Hidden Tradition in Europe*
  CH - v66 - Mr '97 - p103+ [501+]
Stoye, John - *Marsigli's Europe 1680-1730*
  AHR - v101 - D '96 - p1578 [251-500]
Stoyle, Mark - *Loyalty and Locality*
  AHR - v102 - F '97 - p102+ [501+]
  EHR - v112 - Ap '97 - p472 [501+]
  HT - v46 - S '96 - p55+ [501+]

Straalen, N M Van - *Bioindicator Systems for Soil*
  Pollution
  SciTech - v20 - D '96 - p70 [51-250]
Straayer, Chris - *Deviant Eyes, Deviant Bodies*
  Afterimage - v24 - N '96 - p4 [1-50]
  Afterimage - v24 - Ja '97 - p22+ [51-250]
  Choice - v34 - F '97 - p974 [51-250]
  LJ - v122 - Ja '97 - p102 [51-250]
Strachan, Beth - *Mozambique, the Quest for Peace*
  r Choice - v34 - Ap '97 - p1316 [51-250]
Strachan, Ian - *Throwaways*
  y Books - v11 - Ap '97 - p24 [51-250]
  Which Way Is Home?
  y JB - v60 - O '96 - p207 [51-250]
  y Sch Lib - v44 - Ag '96 - p121 [51-250]
Strachan, Michael - *Esmond De Beer 1895-1990*
  CR - v269 - Ag '96 - p104 [251-500]
Strachan, Tom - *Human Molecular Genetics*
  Nature - v383 - O 24 '96 - p683+ [501+]
Stracher, Cameron - *The Laws of Return*
  BL - v93 - O 1 '96 - p323+ [51-250]
  KR - v64 - S 1 '96 - p1264+ [51-250]
  LJ - v121 - N 1 '96 - p109 [51-250]
  PW - v243 - S 9 '96 - p65 [251-500]
Strachota, Bob - *On Their Side*
  Inst - v105 - My '96 - p23 [51-250]
Stradley, Randy - *Aliens vs. Predator: War*
  p Quill & Q - v62 - Ag '96 - p26 [51-250]
Straffin, Philip D - *Game Theory and Strategy*
  SIAM Rev - v38 - D '96 - p698+ [501+]
Strafford CD-ROM. Electronic Media Version
  HT - v46 - D '96 - p49 [51-250]
Strahan, Jerry E - *Andrew Jackson Higgins and the Boats*
  That Won World War II
  T&C - v37 - O '96 - p858+ [501+]
Strahan, Lachlan - *Australia's China*
  Aust Bk R - Jl '96 - p28+ [501+]
  TLS - O 25 '96 - p11 [501+]
Strahinich, Helen - *The Holocaust: Understanding and*
  Remembering
  y BL - v93 - S 15 '96 - p230 [51-250]
  y HB Guide - v8 - Spr '97 - p167 [51-250]
  y SLJ - v42 - O '96 - p160 [51-250]
  y VOYA - v19 - O '96 - p239 [251-500]
Straight, Susan - *The Gettin Place*
  Atl - v278 - S '96 - p112+ [51-250]
  HMR - Fall '96 - p20+ [501+]
Strain, Mac B - *The Earth's Shifting Axis*
  SB - v33 - My '97 - p102 [251-500]
Straker, Anita - *Children Using Computers. 2nd Ed.*
  TES - Mr 14 '97 - p39U [501+]
  Mental Maths
  c TES - Ja 17 '97 - p14* [251-500]
Straley, John - *Death and the Language of Happiness*
  KR - v65 - Ap 1 '97 - p508 [51-250]
  LJ - v122 - Ap 1 '97 - p133 [51-250]
  PW - v244 - F 3 '97 - p98 [51-250]
  Trib Bks - My 4 '97 - p4 [51-250]
Stramel, James S - *How to Write a Philosophy Paper*
  CPR - v16 - Je '96 - p211+ [251-500]
Strand, Mark - *The Continuous Life*
  LJ - v122 - Ap 1 '97 - p95 [1-50]
  Selected Poems
  LJ - v122 - Ap 1 '97 - p95 [1-50]
Strand, Vibeke - *Novel Therapeutic Agents for the*
  Treatment of Autoimmune Diseases
  SciTech - v20 - D '96 - p46 [51-250]
Strange, Carolyn - *Toronto's Girl Problem*
  AHR - v101 - D '96 - p1653+ [501+]
  Can Hist R - v77 - S '96 - p425+ [501+]
  J Soc H - v30 - Fall '96 - p256+ [501+]
Strange, Craig - *Collector's Guide to Tinker Toys*
  r Ant & CM - v101 - D '96 - p32 [51-250]
  r BWatch - v17 - S '96 - p7 [1-50]
Strasburger, Victor C - *Adolescents and the Media*
  JMCQ - v73 - Aut '96 - p751 [501+]
  Getting Your Kids to Say No in the 90s When You Said
  Yes in the 60s
  VOYA - v19 - D '96 - p256 [1-50]
Strasser, Todd - *The Boys in the Band*
  y Kliatt - v30 - S '96 - p14 [51-250]
  Girl Gives Birth to Own Prom Date
  y BL - v93 - O 1 '96 - p344 [51-250]
  y HB Guide - v8 - Spr '97 - p84 [51-250]
  y LATBR - Ag 11 '96 - p11 [51-250]
  y SLJ - v42 - S '96 - p228 [51-250]

Hey Dad, Get a Life!
c   BL - v93 - F 15 '97 - p1024 [51-250]
c   CCB-B - v50 - Mr '97 - p259 [51-250]
c   KR - v64 - D 15 '96 - p1805 [51-250]
c   PW - v243 - D 2 '96 - p61 [51-250]
c   SLJ - v43 - Mr '97 - p193 [51-250]
How I Changed My Life
y   Emerg Lib - v24 - S '96 - p27 [1-50]
Strategic Appraisal 1996
APH - v43 - Win '96 - p63 [251-500]
Strategic Assessment 1996
For Aff - v76 - Mr '97 - p181 [51-250]
Strategic Research Corporation - *PC Magazine Network Buyer's Guide*
r   CBR - v15 - Spr '97 - p9 [1-50]
Strategies and Policies for Air Pollution Abatement: 1994 Major Review
J Gov Info - v23 - S '96 - p679 [51-250]
Strategies for Safer Communities in Prince Edward Island
J Gov Info - v23 - S '96 - p635 [51-250]
Strategies for Studying
y   BWatch - v17 - N '96 - p5 [51-250]
Stratford, Jenny - *The Bedford Inventories*
EHR - v111 - N '96 - p1257 [251-500]
Specu - v72 - Ja '97 - p226+ [501+]
Strathern, Andrew J - *Migration and Transformations*
Am Ethnol - v24 - F '97 - p265+ [501+]
Strathern, Marilyn - *Reproducing the Future*
RA - v25 - 3 '96 - p195+ [501+]
Strathern, Paul - *Aristotle in 90 Minutes*
CLW - v67 - Mr '97 - p48 [501+]
y   Kliatt - v31 - Mr '97 - p29 [51-250]
LJ - v121 - N 1 '96 - p70 [51-250]
Descartes in 90 Minutes
CLW - v67 - Mr '97 - p48 [501+]
y   Kliatt - v31 - Mr '97 - p29 [51-250]
LJ - v121 - N 1 '96 - p70 [51-250]
WSJ-Cent - v99 - Mr 18 '97 - pA20 [501+]
Kant in 90 Minutes
CLW - v67 - Mr '97 - p48 [501+]
y   Kliatt - v31 - Mr '97 - p29 [51-250]
LJ - v121 - N 1 '96 - p70 [51-250]
Nietzsche in 90 Minutes
CLW - v67 - Mr '97 - p48 [501+]
y   Kliatt - v31 - Mr '97 - p29 [51-250]
LJ - v121 - N 1 '96 - p70 [51-250]
Plato in 90 Minutes
CLW - v67 - Mr '97 - p48 [501+]
y   Kliatt - v31 - Mr '97 - p29 [51-250]
LJ - v121 - N 1 '96 - p70 [51-250]
Wittgenstein in 90 Minutes
CLW - v67 - Mr '97 - p48 [501+]
y   Kliatt - v31 - Mr '97 - p29 [51-250]
LJ - v121 - N 1 '96 - p70 [51-250]
Stratton, Beverly J - *Out of Eden*
Rel St Rev - v23 - Ja '97 - p57 [51-250]
Stratton, Dirk - *Ronald Johnson*
AL - v69 - Mr '97 - p251 [51-250]
Stratton, Elizabeth K - *Touching Spirit*
BL - v93 - O 1 '96 - p313 [51-250]
Mag Bl - Mr '97 - p57 [51-250]
PW - v243 - S 30 '96 - p73+ [51-250]
Stratton, Jon - *The Desirable Body*
Choice - v34 - F '97 - p1004 [51-250]
Stratton, Kathleen R - *Fetal Alcohol Syndrome*
Choice - v34 - Ja '97 - p827 [51-250]
Stratton, Suzanne L - *The Immaculate Conception in Spanish Art*
CHR - v82 - Jl '96 - p483+ [501+]
Stratton-Porter, Gene - *Coming through the Swamp*
Bloom Rev - v16 - Jl '96 - p20 [51-250]
Choice - v34 - S '96 - p149 [51-250]
Straub, Deborah Gillan - *African American Voices. Vols. 1-2*
yr   ARBA - v28 - '97 - p152 [51-250]
cr   SLJ - v43 - F '97 - p133 [51-250]
Voices of Multicultural America
r   ARBA - v28 - '97 - p442 [251-500]
r   RQ - v36 - Fall '96 - p142+ [501+]
Straub, Peter - *The Hellfire Club*
Arm Det - v29 - Sum '96 - p376 [251-500]
Straub, Richard E F - *David Aubert, Escripvain Et Clerc*
Specu - v71 - O '96 - p1032+ [501+]
Strauch, A Bruce - *Current Legal Issues in Publishing*
IRLA - v32 - Ag '96 - p11+ [51-250]
Strauch, Inge - *In Search of Dreams*
Readings - v11 - D '96 - p24+ [51-250]
R&R Bk N - v12 - F '97 - p7 [51-250]

Straus, Dorothea - *The Paper Trail*
KR - v65 - Ja 15 '97 - p131 [251-500]
LJ - v122 - Mr 15 '97 - p64 [51-250]
PW - v244 - Ja 27 '97 - p83 [51-250]
Straus, Lawrence Guy - *Humans at the End of the Ice Age*
Choice - v34 - F '97 - p1006 [51-250]
R&R Bk N - v11 - N '96 - p22 [51-250]
Straus, Murray A - *Beating the Devil Out of Them*
Adoles - v32 - Spr '97 - p248 [51-250]
JMF - v58 - N '96 - p1039+ [251-500]
SF - v75 - D '96 - p749+ [251-500]
Straus, Nina Pelikan - *Dostoevsky and the Woman Question*
Signs - v22 - Win '97 - p501+ [501+]
Strausbaugh, John - *E: Reflections on the Birth of the Elvis Faith*
Ent W - Ag 23 '96 - p118 [51-250]
Strausberg, Stephen F - *From Hills and Hollers*
J Gov Info - v23 - S '96 - p578 [51-250]
Strauss, Botho - *Couples, Passersby*
BL - v93 - N 15 '96 - p573 [51-250]
KR - v64 - O 1 '96 - p1424 [251-500]
NYTBR - v101 - D 29 '96 - p14 [51-250]
PW - v243 - N 4 '96 - p64+ [51-250]
Paare Passanten
Ger Q - v69 - Spr '96 - p181+ [501+]
The Young Man
Aut R - v34 - Sum '96 - p359 [251-500]
Strauss, Carol Ann - *Grandparents: An Annotated Bibliography on Roles, Rights, and Relationships*
r   Choice - v34 - Ap '97 - p1316 [51-250]
Strauss, Gerald - *Enacting the Reformation*
CEH - v29 - 1 '96 - p115+ [501+]
Strauss, Gwen - *Trail of Stones*
y   JAAL - v40 - D '96 - p320 [51-250]
y   VOYA - v19 - D '96 - p266 [1-50]
Strauss, Jennifer - *Judith Wright*
WLT - v70 - Aut '96 - p1026+ [501+]
Strauss, Mark L - *The Davidic Messiah in Luke-Acts*
Rel St Rev - v23 - Ap '97 - p184 [51-250]
Strauss, Peter J - *The Elder Law Handbook for Caregivers and Seniors*
r   BL - v93 - S 1 '96 - p42+ [51-250]
r   LJ - v121 - O 1 '96 - p70 [51-250]
Strauss, William - *The Fourth Turning*
BL - v93 - D 1 '96 - p618+ [51-250]
Fortune - v135 - F 3 '97 - p123 [501+]
KR - v65 - Ja 1 '97 - p50 [251-500]
NYTBR - v102 - Ja 26 '97 - p16 [501+]
PW - v244 - Ja 6 '97 - p60+ [51-250]
WSJ-Cent - v99 - Mr 31 '97 - pA12 [501+]
The Fourth Turning (Tilford). Audio Version
LJ - v122 - My 1 '97 - p156 [51-250]
Straw, Carole - *Gregory the Great: Perfection in Imperfection*
CH - v65 - S '96 - p455+ [501+]
Strawn, John - *Driving the Green*
Trib Bks - Mr 9 '97 - p8 [1-50]
Strawn, Martha A - *Alligators: A Prehistoric Presence in the American Landscape*
PW - v244 - Mr 17 '97 - p72 [51-250]
Strawson, Galen - *Mental Reality*
J Phil - v93 - Ag '96 - p421+ [501+]
Phil R - v105 - Ja '96 - p99+ [501+]
RM - v49 - Je '96 - p949+ [501+]
Stray, Christopher - *Grinders and Grammars*
TLS - Jl 19 '96 - p32 [251-500]
The Mushri-English Pronouncing Dictionary
r   TLS - N 22 '96 - p31 [251-500]
Strazzabosco, Jeanne - *High Performance through Dealing with Diversity*
y   BL - v92 - Ag '96 - p1893 [51-250]
y   Cur R - v36 - N '96 - p13 [51-250]
Learning about Determination from the Life of Gloria Estefan
c   SLJ - v42 - D '96 - p118 [51-250]
Learning about Dignity from the Life of Martin Luther King, Jr.
c   SLJ - v42 - D '96 - p132+ [51-250]
Learning about Forgiveness from the Life of Nelson Mandela
c   SLJ - v42 - N '96 - p101 [51-250]
Strecker, Georg - *The Johannine Letters*
Am - v176 - Mr 8 '97 - p29 [51-250]
Streeruwitz, Marlene - *Verführungen*
WLT - v70 - Aut '96 - p952 [251-500]
Streeten, Paul Patrick - *Thinking about Development*
JEL - v34 - D '96 - p2112 [51-250]
Streeter, Tal - *A Kite Journey through India*
NYTBR - v101 - D 8 '96 - p31 [51-250]

Streeter, Thomas - *Selling the Air*
Choice - v34 - N '96 - p499 [51-250]
JC - v47 - Win '97 - p153+ [51-250]
JEL - v34 - D '96 - p2088 [51-250]
R&R Bk N - v11 - N '96 - p33 [51-250]
Streetharan, Muthuthamby - *Cellular Digital Packet Data*
SciTech - v20 - N '96 - p73 [51-250]
Strege, John - *Tiger: A Biography of Tiger Woods*
PW - v244 - Ap 28 '97 - p60 [51-250]
Streicher, Bernard J - *Writing Handbook. 2nd Ed.*
r   CLW - v67 - Mr '97 - p45 [251-500]
Streifel, Shane S - *Review and Outlook for the World Oil Market*
J Gov Info - v23 - S '96 - p688+ [51-250]
Streitberger, W R - *Court Revels 1485-1559*
RES - v47 - N '96 - p568+ [501+]
Streitmatter, Rodger - *Mightier than the Sword*
KR - v65 - My 1 '97 - p707 [251-500]
Unspeakable: The Rise of the Gay and Lesbian Press in America
JMCQ - v73 - Win '96 - p1021+ [501+]
Streitwieser, Andrew - *A Lifetime of Synergy with Theory and Experiment*
SciTech - v21 - Mr '97 - p28 [51-250]
Strelka, Joseph P - *Im Takte Des Radetzkymarschs...Der Beamte Und Der Offizier In Der Osterreichischen Literatur*
Ger Q - v69 - Fall '96 - p447+ [501+]
Zwischen Wirklichkeit Und Traum
MLR - v92 - Ja '97 - p255+ [501+]
Stresser-Pean, Guy - *El Codice De Xicotepec*
HAHR - v77 - My '97 - p296+ [251-500]
Strete, Craig Kee - *How the Indians Bought the Farm (Illus. by Francisco X Mora)*
c   HB Guide - v7 - Fall '96 - p278 [51-250]
They Thought They Saw Him (Illus. by Jose Aruego)
c   HB Guide - v7 - Fall '96 - p278 [51-250]
Stretton, Hugh - *Public Goods, Public Enterprise, Public Choice*
RP - v58 - Fall '96 - p793+ [501+]
Streubert, Helen J - *Qualitative Research in Nursing*
AJN - v96 - N '96 - p16G [51-250]
Strickland, Brad - *The Hand of the Necromancer*
c   Ch BWatch - v6 - N '96 - p3 [51-250]
c   HB Guide - v8 - Spr '97 - p76 [51-250]
c   SLJ - v42 - S '96 - p206+ [51-250]
Strickland, Dorothy S - *Families: Poems Celebrating the African American Experience (Illus. by John Ward)*
c   BL - v93 - F 15 '97 - p1014 [1-50]
Strickland, Edward - *Minimalism: Origins*
Notes - v53 - S '96 - p77+ [501+]
Strickland, Jean - *Residents of the Mississippi Territory. Bk. 3*
EGH - v50 - N '96 - p172+ [51-250]
Strickland, Matthew - *War and Chivalry*
HT - v46 - O '96 - p55 [51-250]
Strickland, Michael R - *African-American Poets*
c   BL - v93 - F 15 '97 - p1016 [51-250]
c   HB Guide - v8 - Spr '97 - p161 [51-250]
y   KR - v64 - N 15 '96 - p1676 [51-250]
y   SLJ - v43 - Ja '97 - p136 [51-250]
Strickland, Stephanie - *True North*
BL - v93 - D 1 '96 - p640 [51-250]
Strickler, Dave - *Syndicated Comic Strips and Artists 1924-1995*
r   ARBA - v28 - '97 - p500 [251-500]
Strieber, Whitley - *The Secret School*
BL - v93 - N 15 '96 - p548 [51-250]
KR - v64 - N 15 '96 - p1659+ [251-500]
PW - v243 - N 4 '96 - p54 [51-250]
Stringer, Chris - *African Exodus*
Lon R Bks - v18 - O 31 '96 - p36+ [501+]
Nature - v384 - D 19 '96 - p618 [1-50]
New Sci - v152 - D 21 '96 - p68 [1-50]
Obs - D 1 '96 - p18* [51-250]
Stringer, Jenny - *The Oxford Companion to Twentieth-Century Literature in English*
r   AB - v99 - F 10 '97 - p416+ [501+]
r   BL - v93 - N 15 '96 - p612+ [251-500]
r   Choice - v34 - Ap '97 - p1312+ [51-250]
r   CR - v270 - F '97 - p102+ [501+]
yr   SLJ - v43 - F '97 - p133 [51-250]
r   TLS - N 1 '96 - p12+ [501+]
r   WSJ-MW - v78 - D 17 '96 - pA16 [251-500]
Strings
p   LJ - v122 - Mr 15 '97 - p95 [51-250]
Stritzler-Levine, Nina - *Josef Frank, Architect and Designer*
r   Choice - v34 - N '96 - p445 [51-250]
LJ - v121 - S 15 '96 - p64 [51-250]

Strobel, Lee - *God's Outrageous Claims*
  BL - v93 - Mr 1 '97 - p1067 [51-250]
  PW - v244 - Mr 24 '97 - p76 [51-250]
Strobel, Warren - *Late-Breaking Foreign Policy*
  PW - v244 - My 5 '97 - p191 [51-250]
Strobl, Gert R - *The Physics of Polymers*
  Choice - v34 - Ja '97 - p835 [51-250]
Strogat, Lev - *I Smekh, I Slezy*
  BL - v93 - O 1 '96 - p327 [1-50]
Stroik, Thomas S - *Minimalism, Scope, and VP Structure*
  R&R Bk N - v11 - N '96 - p63 [51-250]
Strom, Margot Stern - *Facing History and Ourselves*
  Rel Ed - v91 - Fall '96 - p619 [1-50]
Strom, Yale - *Quilted Landscape*
  c CBRS - v25 - D '96 - p48 [51-250]
  c CCB-B - v50 - F '97 - p224 [51-250]
  y HB Guide - v8 - Spr '97 - p90+ [51-250]
  c SLJ - v42 - D '96 - p134 [51-250]
Stromberg, Roland N - *Democracy: A Short, Analytical History*
  Choice - v34 - My '97 - p1575 [51-250]
  R&R Bk N - v11 - D '96 - p46 [51-250]
Stromstad, Triis - *Scandinavian Atlas of Historic Towns. Vols. 1-8*
  r J Urban H - v22 - S '96 - p739+ [501+]
Stronach, Neil - *Mountains*
  c BL - v93 - N 15 '96 - p585 [51-250]
  c Ch BWatch - v6 - S '96 - p5 [1-50]
  c HB Guide - v8 - Spr '97 - p97 [51-250]
  c SLJ - v42 - N '96 - p113 [51-250]
Strong, Ann Louise - *Transitions in Land and Housing*
  JEL - v35 - Mr '97 - p303 [51-250]
Strong, Dina - *Hosanna and Alleluia (Illus. by Donald Cook)*
  c PW - v244 - F 24 '97 - p83 [51-250]
Strong, Emory - *Seeking Western Waters*
  Bloom Rev - v16 - N '96 - p26 [251-500]
  WHQ - v27 - Win '96 - p547 [51-250]
Strong, Jeremy - *The Hundred-Mile-an-Hour Dog (Illus. by Nick Sharratt)*
  c Bks Keeps - Mr '97 - p23 [51-250]
  c Sch Lib - v45 - F '97 - p34 [51-250]
Strong, John S - *Moving to Market*
  JEL - v35 - Mr '97 - p292 [51-250]
Strong, M C - *The Great Rock Discography*
  r ARBA - v28 - '97 - p494+ [251-500]
Strong, Rowan - *Alexander Forbes of Brechin: The First Tractarian Bishop*
  AHR - v101 - D '96 - p1541+ [501+]
  Albion - v28 - Sum '96 - p333+ [501+]
  Historian - v59 - Fall '96 - p204+ [501+]
Strong, Roy - *Country Life 1897-1997*
  New Sci - v152 - O 19 '96 - p46 [51-250]
  Obs - v54 - O 13 '96 - p15* [501+]
  English Arcadia
  HT - v46 - O '96 - p58 [51-250]
  Spec - v277 - N 23 '96 - p44 [1-50]
  TLS - N 22 '96 - p12 [501+]
  The Story of Britain
  NS - v125 - S 20 '96 - p44+ [501+]
  Obs - S 29 '96 - p15* [501+]
  PW - v244 - My 12 '97 - p66 [51-250]
  Spec - v277 - S 14 '96 - p39+ [501+]
  TES - S 20 '96 - p8* [501+]
  TES - D 27 '96 - p17 [1-50]
  TLS - S 20 '96 - p31 [501+]
  The Tudor and Stuart Monarchy. Vol. 1
  Six Ct J - v27 - Fall '96 - p800 [501+]
Strong, Simon - *Whitewash: Pablo Escobar and the Cocaine Wars*
  Books - v9 - S '95 - p23 [51-250]
  Obs - Ag 25 '96 - p16* [51-250]
Strong, Stacie - *The Big Book of Noah's Ark*
  c Ch BWatch - v7 - F '97 - p5 [1-50]
Strong, Terence - *White Viper*
  Books - v10 - Je '96 - p22 [51-250]
Stroo, Eric - *Ultimate Office Book. 2nd Ed.*
  CBR - v14 - Jl '96 - p23 [51-250]
Stross, Randall E - *The Microsoft Way*
  BW - v26 - N 17 '96 - p11 [51-250]
  KR - v64 - S 15 '96 - p1388 [251-500]
  LJ - v121 - N 1 '96 - p76 [51-250]
  PW - v243 - O 14 '96 - p73 [51-250]
  WSJ-Cent - v99 - Ja 20 '97 - pA12 [251-500]
Strossen, Nadine - *Defending Pornography*
  TLS - Jl 19 '96 - p29 [501+]

Stroud, Bettye - *Down Home at Miss Dessa's (Illus. by Felicia Marshall)*
  c BL - v93 - D 15 '96 - p734 [51-250]
  c CBRS - v25 - Win '97 - p66 [51-250]
  c CCB-B - v50 - D '96 - p153+ [51-250]
  c Ch BWatch - v7 - F '97 - p3 [1-50]
  c HB Guide - v8 - Spr '97 - p50 [51-250]
  c KR - v64 - S 1 '96 - p1329 [51-250]
  c PW - v243 - S 16 '96 - p83 [51-250]
  c SLJ - v43 - Ja '97 - p92 [51-250]
Stroud, Gene S - *Labor History in the United States*
  r RQ - v36 - Fall '96 - p56 [1-50]
Stroud, Jonathan - *The Lost Treasure of Captain Blood (Illus. by Cathy Gale)*
  c HB Guide - v8 - Spr '97 - p143 [51-250]
  c SLJ - v43 - Ja '97 - p92 [51-250]
Stroud, Mark - *Matieres Premieres*
  y TES - Mr 7 '97 - pR8 [51-250]
Stroud, Matthew D - *The Play in the Mirror*
  Choice - v34 - O '96 - p287 [51-250]
Stroud, Virginia A - *The Path of the Quiet Elk*
  c HB Guide - v7 - Fall '96 - p309 [51-250]
Stroup, Alice - *A Company of Scientists*
  Ren Q - v50 - Spr '97 - p332+ [501+]
Strouthes, Daniel P - *Law and Politics*
  r ARBA - v28 - '97 - p220+ [51-250]
Strozier, Charles B - *Genocide, War, and Human Survival*
  Choice - v34 - N '96 - p512+ [51-250]
  For Aff - v75 - N '96 - p147 [51-250]
  Trauma and Self
  CC - v114 - Ja 15 '97 - p60+ [51-250]
Strube, Cordelia - *Teaching Pigs to Sing*
  BIC - v25 - O '96 - p42 [51-250]
  Quill & Q - v62 - My '96 - p26 [501+]
Strube, Penny - *Getting the Most from Literature Groups*
  Cur R - v36 - N '96 - p3* [51-250]
Strubel, Armand - *La Poetique De La Chasse Au Moyen Age*
  FR - v70 - D '96 - p320+ [501+]
Struble, John Warthen - *The History of American Classical Music*
  r ARBA - v28 - '97 - p484 [251-500]
Struck, Nancy - *Working Smarter from Home*
  LJ - v122 - My 1 '97 - p53 [1-50]
Structural Analysis in Microelectronics and Fiber Optics 1996
  SciTech - v21 - Mr '97 - p92 [51-250]
Structures under Shock and Impact IV
  SciTech - v20 - N '96 - p64 [51-250]
Strum, Phillipa - *Brandeis on Democracy*
  HLR - v110 - D '96 - p561 [51-250]
Struthers, Betsy - *Running Out of Time*
  Can Lit - Win '96 - p167+ [501+]
Struthers, James - *The Limits of Affluence*
  AHR - v101 - O '96 - p1318 [501+]
  r Can Hist R - v78 - Mr '97 - p125+ [501+]
Strutin, Michele - *The Smithsonian Guides to Natural America: The Great Lakes*
  r SciTech - v21 - Mr '97 - p34 [1-50]
Strutwolf, Holger - *Gnosis Als System*
  Rel St Rev - v22 - O '96 - p301+ [501+]
  Rel St Rev - v23 - Ja '97 - p76+ [51-250]
Struve, Walter - *Germans and Texans*
  Choice - v34 - F '97 - p1028 [51-250]
  JEL - v35 - Mr '97 - p265 [51-250]
Struyk, Raymond J - *Economic Restructuring of the Former Soviet Bloc*
  JEL - v34 - D '96 - p2140 [51-250]
Stryker, E De - *Plato's Apology of Socrates*
  AJP - v117 - Fall '96 - p487+
Stryker, Susan - *Gay by the Bay*
  PHR - v66 - F '97 - p122+ [251-500]
Strzepek, K M - *As Climate Changes*
  y New Sci - v151 - S 28 '96 - p50+ [501+]
Stuart, A M - *Dynamical Systems and Numerical Analysis*
  SciTech - v21 - Mr '97 - p14 [51-250]
Stuart, Alexander - *Life on Mars*
  Books - v10 - Je '96 - p21 [51-250]
Stuart, Andrea - *Showgirls*
  NS - v125 - O 18 '96 - p46 [251-500]
  Si & So - v6 - N '96 - p35 [51-250]
Stuart, Arabella, Lady - *The Letters of Lady Arabella Stuart*
  HT - v46 - Ag '96 - p60 [51-250]
Stuart, Chad - *The Ballymara Flood (Illus. by George Booth)*
  c HB Guide - v7 - Fall '96 - p278 [1-50]
Stuart, Chris - *Africa's Vanishing Wildlife*
  y BL - v93 - D 15 '96 - p700 [51-250]
  r LJ - v122 - Ja '97 - p91 [51-250]
  New Sci - v151 - S 21 '96 - p55 [51-250]

Stuart, Dabney - *Light Years*
  HR - v49 - Sum '96 - p341+ [501+]
  Long Gone
  PW - v243 - N 25 '96 - p72 [51-250]
  Second Sight
  South R - v32 - Aut '96 - p761+ [501+]
Stuart, Elizabeth - *Just Good Friends*
  Cons - v17 - Win '96 - p31 [1-50]
Stuart, Francis, 1902- - *Black List, Section H*
  Trib Bks - Mr 2 '97 - p8 [1-50]
  King David Dances
  KR - v65 - Ap 1 '97 - p503+ [51-250]
Stuart, Ian - *Politics in Performance*
  R&R Bk N - v12 - F '97 - p86 [51-250]
Stuart, Lettice - *Making the Move*
  PW - v244 - Mr 31 '97 - p58 [51-250]
Stuart, Sherman - *Telling Time*
  New Sci - v154 - My 3 '97 - p48 [51-250]
  Trib Bks - Ap 6 '97 - p7 [501+]
Stuart-Hamilton, Ian - *Dictionary of Developmental Psychology*
  r ARBA - v28 - '97 - p285 [51-250]
Stubblebine, Donald J - *Broadway Sheet Music*
  r ARBA - v28 - '97 - p487+ [51-250]
  r Choice - v34 - S '96 - p106+ [51-250]
Stubblefield, Harold W - *Adult Education in the American Experience*
  TCR - v98 - Fall '96 - p184+ [501+]
Stubbs, George - *George Stubbs 1724-1806*
  R&R Bk N - v12 - F '97 - p74 [1-50]
Stubbs, Jean - *Cuba*
  r ARBA - v28 - '97 - p69 [51-250]
  r R&R Bk N - v12 - F '97 - p27 [51-250]
Stuber, Gordon L - *Principles of Mobile Communication*
  SciTech - v20 - D '96 - p77 [51-250]
Stubley, Peter - *Authoring Multimedia*
  LAR - v98 - Mr '96 - p163 [51-250]
Stuckenbruch, Loren T - *Angel Veneration and Christology*
  Rel St Rev - v23 - Ap '97 - p186 [51-250]
Stuckey, Maggie - *Gardening from the Ground Up*
  BL - v93 - Mr 1 '97 - p1102 [51-250]
Stuckey, Mary E - *The Theory and Practice of Political Communication Research*
  APSR - v91 - Mr '97 - p199+ [501+]
  Choice - v34 - S '96 - p202 [51-250]
Studebaker, William - *Where the Morning Light's Still Blue*
  WAL - v31 - Win '97 - p391+ [251-500]
Studenski, Paul - *The Government of the Metropolitan Areas in the U.S.*
  NCR - v85 - Spr '96 - p63 [51-250]
Student Financial Services - *The Financial Aid Book. 2nd Ed.*
  yr Choice - v34 - N '96 - p428+ [51-250]
  yr Cur R - v35 - S '96 - p13 [51-250]
  The Government Financial Aid Book. 2nd Ed.
  yr Choice - v34 - N '96 - p428+ [51-250]
  yr Cur R - v35 - S '96 - p13 [51-250]
Student Reference Library. Electronic Media Version
  r LJ - v122 - My 1 '97 - p148 [51-250]
Student Services, Inc. - *The Complete Scholarship Book*
  yr BL - v93 - F 1 '97 - p962+ [251-500]
  yr LJ - v122 - Ap 1 '97 - p86 [51-250]
Student Writing and Research Center. Electronic Media Version
  y Kliatt - v31 - Ja '97 - p36 [251-500]
Studer, Basil - *Trinity and Incarnation*
  JAAR - v64 - Win '96 - p880+ [501+]
Studies in Bibliography. Vol. 48
  r RES - v48 - F '97 - p70+ [501+]
Studies in Bibliography. Vol. 49
  r AL - v68 - D '96 - p885 [1-50]
  r BC - v45 - Aut '96 - p389+ [51-250]
Studies in Eighteenth-Century Culture. Vol. 24
  Albion - v28 - Sum '96 - p316+ [501+]
Studies in Eighteenth-Century Culture. Vol. 25
  R&R Bk N - v12 - F '97 - p74 [51-250]
Studies in Newspaper and Periodical History 1994
  R&R Bk N - v11 - D '96 - p74 [51-250]
Studies in the American Renaissance 1995
  AL - v68 - S '96 - p664 [51-250]
  Nine-C Lit - v51 - D '96 - p425 [51-250]
Studies in Weird Fiction
  p SF Chr - v18 - O '96 - p83 [1-50]
Studies of High Temperature Superconductors. Vol. 18, Pt. 2
  SciTech - v21 - Mr '97 - p24 [51-250]
Studlar, Donley T - *Great Britain: Decline or Renewal?*
  Choice - v34 - O '96 - p355 [51-250]
  r Pol Stud J - v24 - Aut '96 - p521 [51-250]

Studlar, Gaylyn - *This Mad Masquerade*
  Choice - v34 - Ja '97 - p804 [51-250]
  R&R Bk N - v11 - D '96 - p61 [51-250]
Stueck, William - *The Korean War*
  AAPSS-A - v546 - Jl '96 - p158+ [501+]
  HRNB - v25 - Fall '96 - p39+ [251-500]
  Pac A - v69 - Fall '96 - p429+ [501+]
  PHR - v65 - N '96 - p695+ [251-500]
Stuefloten, D N - *Mexico Trilogy*
  BW - v26 - D 22 '96 - p9 [51-250]
Stuewe, Paul - *This Dark Embrace*
  BIC - v26 - F '97 - p36 [251-500]
  Quill & Q - v62 - O '96 - p32 [251-500]
Stuhlmacher, Peter - *How to Do Biblical Theology*
  Intpr - v51 - Ja '97 - p99+ [251-500]
  Paul's Letter to the Romans
  Intpr - v50 - O '96 - p432+ [251-500]
Stuhlmiller, Cynthia M - *Rescuers of Cypress*
  R&R Bk N - v12 - F '97 - p56 [51-250]
Stukel, Eileen Dowd - *Sharing Your Space*
  J Gov Info - v23 - S '96 - p594+ [51-250]
Stumm, Werner - *Aquatic Chemistry. 3rd Ed.*
  J Chem Ed - v73 - N '96 - pA277+ [501+]
Stump, Al - *Cobb: A Biography*
  Aethlon - v13 - Fall '95 - p173+ [251-500]
Stump, Philip H - *The Reforms of the Council of Constance 1414-1418*
  CHR - v82 - Jl '96 - p556+ [501+]
Sturdy, David J - *Science and Social Status*
  JIH - v27 - Spr '97 - p686+ [251-500]
Sturges, Jock - *Jock Sturges (Scalo)*
  LJ - v122 - F 1 '97 - p77 [51-250]
Sturges, Philemon - *Ten Flashing Fireflies (Illus. by Anna Vojtech)*
  c PW - v244 - F 17 '97 - p220 [1-50]
  What's That Sound, Woolly Bear? (Illus. by Joan Paley)
  c HB Guide - v7 - Fall '96 - p278 [51-250]
  c RT - v50 - Ap '97 - p591 [51-250]
  c SLJ - v42 - Ag '96 - p131 [51-250]
Sturgill, Claude C - *The Military History of the Third World since 1945*
  r JTWS - v13 - Spr '96 - p417+ [251-500]
Sturgis, Alexander - *Optical Illusions in Art*
  y BL - v93 - Ap 1 '97 - p1310 [1-50]
  c HB Guide - v7 - Fall '96 - p357 [51-250]
Sturken, Marita - *Tangled Memories*
  BL - v93 - F 15 '97 - p982 [51-250]
  NYTBR - v102 - Mr 2 '97 - p16 [501+]
Sturm, Chris Noonan - *Educator's World Wide Web Tourguide*
  Emerg Lib - v23 - My '96 - p39+ [51-250]
Sturm, Ernest - *Crebillon Fils, Ou La Science Du Desir*
  FR - v70 - D '96 - p326+ [501+]
Sturman, A P - *The Weather and Climate of Australia and New Zealand*
  Choice - v34 - My '97 - p1538 [51-250]
Sturrock, John - *The Oxford Guide to Contemporary Writing*
  r BL - v93 - Ja '97 - p898+ [51-250]
  Books - v10 - Je '96 - p24 [51-250]
  Choice - v34 - Mr '97 - p1156 [251-500]
  r CR - v269 - N '96 - p271+ [501+]
  r Obs - N 3 '96 - p18* [501+]
  r TLS - N 1 '96 - p12+ [501+]
Sturrock, June - *Heaven and Home*
  ELT - v39 - 4 '96 - p531 [51-250]
Stutson, Caroline - *By the Light of the Halloween Moon (Illus. by Kevin Hawkes)*
  c PW - v243 - S 30 '96 - p86 [1-50]
  Prairie Primer (Illus. by Susan Condie Lamb)
  c CBRS - v25 - D '96 - p41 [1-50]
  c HB Guide - v8 - Spr '97 - p50 [51-250]
  c KR - v64 - S 15 '96 - p1408 [51-250]
  c SLJ - v42 - O '96 - p107 [51-250]
  c Smith - v27 - N '96 - p170 [1-50]
Stwertka, Albert - *A Guide to the Elements*
  yr BL - v93 - D 1 '96 - p684+ [251-500]
  y Cur R - v36 - F '97 - p12 [51-250]
  yr HB Guide - v8 - Spr '97 - p113 [51-250]
  yr LJ - v121 - S 15 '96 - p60 [51-250]
  yr SLJ - v42 - N '96 - p139 [51-250]
Stwertka, Eve - *Twenty-Four Ways of Looking at Mary McCarthy*
  Choice - v34 - Ap '97 - p1341 [51-250]
Styan, J L - *The English Stage*
  Choice - v34 - Ap '97 - p1351 [51-250]
Stych, F S - *Boccaccio in English*
  r ARBA - v28 - '97 - p462 [51-250]
Styles, Morag - *Voices Off*
  Sch Lib - v44 - N '96 - p178 [251-500]
  TES - Jl 5 '96 - pR3 [501+]

Su, Hsiao-K'ang - *Yuan Si Zhong Sheng Sui*
  BL - v93 - My 1 '97 - p1484 [1-50]
Su, Kendall L - *Analog Filters*
  Choice - v34 - Ja '97 - p826 [51-250]
Su, Shih - *Selected Poems of Su Tung-Po*
  TranslRevS - v1 - My '95 - p16 [51-250]
Su, T'ung - *Raise the Red Lantern*
  y Kliatt - v31 - Mr '97 - p21+ [51-250]
  LATBR - D 22 '96 - p6 [51-250]
  NYTBR - v101 - N 17 '96 - p40 [51-250]
  Rice
  NYTBR - v101 - N 17 '96 - p40 [51-250]
Suarez, Juan A - *Bike Boys, Drag Queens and Superstars*
  Choice - v34 - S '96 - p136 [51-250]
Suarez, Margarita - *Comercio Y Fraude En El Peru Colonial*
  AHR - v102 - F '97 - p240+ [251-500]
  HAHR - v77 - My '97 - p318+ [251-500]
Suarez, Maria Luz - *Robinson Crusoe Revisited 1996*
  TLS - D 27 '96 - p23 [501+]
Suarez, Virgil - *Going Under*
  BW - v27 - Ja 19 '97 - p8 [251-500]
  KR - v64 - S 1 '96 - p1267 [51-250]
  LJ - v121 - S 15 '96 - p98 [51-250]
  Spared Angola
  PW - v244 - My 5 '97 - p189 [51-250]
Suarez-Orozco, Carola - *Transformations: Immigration, Family Life, and Achievement Motivation among Latino Adolescents*
  HER - v66 - Fall '96 - p668+ [501+]
Subak-Sharpe, Genell J - *The Columbia University College of Physicians and Surgeons Complete Home Medical Guide. 3rd Ed.*
  r BL - v93 - F 1 '97 - p957 [1-50]
Subbarao, Kalanidhi - *Selected Social Safety Net Programs in the Philippines*
  JEL - v34 - S '96 - p1443 [51-250]
Subbiah, S - *Protein Motions*
  SciTech - v20 - D '96 - p35 [51-250]
Subcellular Biochemistry. Vol. 26
  SciTech - v20 - D '96 - p20 [51-250]
Subcellular Biochemistry. Vol. 27
  SciTech - v21 - Mr '97 - p36 [51-250]
Sublett, Anne - *The Illustrated Rules of Softball (Illus. by Patrick Kelley)*
  c SLJ - v42 - Ag '96 - p158 [51-250]
Subrahmanyam, M B - *Finite Horizon H [Infinity] and Related Control Problems*
  SciTech - v20 - N '96 - p15 [51-250]
Subrahmanyam, Sanjay - *Merchant Networks in the Early Modern World*
  R&R Bk N - v11 - D '96 - p33 [51-250]
Subrahmanyam, Vedam - *Electric Drives*
  Choice - v34 - N '96 - p489 [51-250]
Subramanian, Lakshmi - *Indigenous Capital and Imperial Expansion*
  Choice - v34 - My '97 - p1555 [51-250]
Successful Gardening Journal
  r BWatch - v18 - F '97 - p11 [1-50]
Suchet, John - *The Last Master. Vol. 1*
  TLS - D 27 '96 - p21 [251-500]
Suchlicki, Jaime - *Mexico: From Montezuma to NAFTA, Chiapas, and Beyond*
  Soc - v34 - Mr '97 - p95+ [501+]
Suchocki, Marjorie Hewitt - *The Fall to Violence*
  TT - v53 - O '96 - p432 [51-250]
Suchoff, David - *Critical Theory and the Novel*
  VS - v39 - Win '96 - p281+ [501+]
Suddeth, J Allen - *Fight Directing for the Theatre*
  R&R Bk N - v11 - N '96 - p67 [1-50]
Sudo, Philip Toshio - *Zen Guitar*
  PW - v244 - Ja 13 '97 - p68+ [51-250]
Sue, Derald Wing - *A Theory of Multicultural Counseling and Therapy*
  SciTech - v20 - S '96 - p32 [51-250]
Suetonius - *Tiberius (Lindsay)*
  Class Out - v74 - Fall '96 - p44 [51-250]
Suffusion
  p LMR - v15 - Fall '96 - p44+ [51-250]
Suganami, Hidemi - *On the Causes of War*
  For Aff - v75 - S '96 - p136 [51-250]
  JPR - v33 - N '96 - p500+ [501+]
Sugar Mouth
  Aust Bk R - S '96 - p67+ [251-500]
Sugden, John - *Sir Francis Drake*
  Sea H - Win '96 - p42 [501+]
Suggs, Henry Lewis - *The Black Press in the Middle West 1865-1995*
  Bl S - v26 - Fall '96 - p106 [51-250]

Sugier, Claire - *Haiti Terre Cassee...Quinze Ans Dans La Campagne Haitienne*
  BL - v93 - F 1 '97 - p930 [1-50]
Sugiman, Pamela - *Labour's Dilemma*
  BusLR - v21 - 3 '96 - p257+ [251-500]
Sugunasiri, Suwanda - *The Whistling Thorn*
  BIC - v25 - S '96 - p7+ [501+]
Suid, Lawrence H - *Sailing on the Silver Screen*
  J Mil H - v60 - O '96 - p799+ [251-500]
  r R&R Bk N - v12 - F '97 - p81 [51-250]
Suino, Nicklaus - *Arts of Strength, Arts of Serenity*
  BWatch - v18 - F '97 - p9 [1-50]
Sui Sin Far - *Mrs. Spring Fragrance and Other Writings*
  Amerasia J - v22 - 3 '96 - p149+ [501+]
Suisman, Charles A - *Manhattan User's Guide*
  r LJ - v121 - O 15 '96 - p81 [51-250]
  r PW - v243 - S 16 '96 - p77+ [51-250]
Sukach, Jim - *Baffling Whodunit Puzzles (Illus. by Lucy Corvino)*
  c HB Guide - v7 - Fall '96 - p298 [51-250]
  Quick-Solve Whodunit Puzzles
  c Ch BWatch - v6 - My '96 - p1 [1-50]
Sukhwal, B L - *Political Geography*
  r Choice - v34 - Ap '97 - p1316+ [51-250]
Suleiman, Michael W - *U.S. Policy on Palestine*
  MEJ - v50 - Sum '96 - p447+ [501+]
Suleiman, Susan Rubin - *Budapest Diary*
  BL - v93 - O 1 '96 - p317 [51-250]
  Comw - v123 - D 6 '96 - p20 [51-250]
  TLS - Ja 17 '97 - p33 [51-250]
  Wom R Bks - v14 - D '96 - p21+ [501+]
Suleiman, Yasir - *Arabic Sociolinguistics*
  Lang Soc - v25 - S '96 - p481+ [501+]
Sullivan, Andrew - *Same-Sex Marriage, Pro and Con*
  LJ - v122 - Mr 15 '97 - p79 [51-250]
  PW - v244 - F 24 '97 - p73+ [51-250]
  Trib Bks - My 4 '97 - p8 [1-50]
  Virtually Normal
  HLR - v110 - Ja '97 - p684+ [501+]
  NYTBR - v101 - S 29 '96 - p32 [51-250]
  PW - v243 - S 30 '96 - p79 [1-50]
Sullivan, Arthur, Sir - *The Complete Annotated Gilbert and Sullivan*
  r AB - v98 - D 9 '96 - p1998 [501+]
  r Choice - v34 - Mr '97 - p1172 [51-250]
  CSM - v88 - N 21 '96 - pB3 [51-250]
  LJ - v121 - N 1 '96 - p68+ [51-250]
  r Nat R - v48 - D 23 '96 - p51+ [501+]
  r NYTBR - v101 - D 8 '96 - p24 [501+]
  r TLS - Ja 10 '97 - p17 [501+]
Sullivan, Barbara - *Gender, Politics and Citizenship in the 1990s*
  Aust Bk R - D '96 - p75 [51-250]
Sullivan, Caitlin - *Nearly Roadkill*
  Ent W - N 8 '96 - p63 [51-250]
Sullivan, Ceri - *Dismembered Rhetoric*
  Shakes Q - v47 - Fall '96 - p343+ [501+]
Sullivan, Charles - *Children of Promise*
  c BL - v93 - F 15 '97 - p1014 [1-50]
  y Kliatt - v30 - S '96 - p4 [51-250]
  Imaginary Animals
  c BW - v26 - D 29 '96 - p13 [51-250]
  c KR - v64 - D 1 '96 - p1741 [51-250]
  c NYTBR - v102 - F 2 '97 - p18 [501+]
  c PW - v243 - D 2 '96 - p62 [51-250]
  y SLJ - v43 - F '97 - p126 [51-250]
Sullivan, David - *The Westminster Corridor*
  EHR - v112 - F '97 - p158+ [251-500]
Sullivan, Dean A - *Early Innings*
  J Am Cult - v19 - Spr '96 - p113+ [501+]
Sullivan, Denis Joseph - *Private Voluntary Organizations in Egypt*
  MEJ - v51 - Spr '97 - p286+ [501+]
Sullivan, Edward J - *Latin American Art in the Twentieth Century*
  Choice - v34 - Ap '97 - p1325 [51-250]
  LJ - v122 - Mr 15 '97 - p60 [51-250]
  The Taft Museum
  Apo - v144 - Ag '96 - p72+ [501+]
Sullivan, Faith - *The Empress of One*
  y BL - v93 - S 15 '96 - p222 [51-250]
  BWatch - v17 - D '96 - p5+ [51-250]
  LJ - v121 - S 15 '96 - p98 [51-250]
Sullivan, Francis A - *Creative Fidelity*
  Am - v175 - S 21 '96 - p34 [51-250]
  CLW - v67 - D '96 - p40 [51-250]
  Theol St - v58 - Mr '97 - p178+ [501+]
Sullivan, Francis Patrick - *Credo and Other Poems*
  RR - v55 - N '96 - p660 [1-50]

Sullivan, George - *Black Artists in Photography 1840-1940*
  c BW - v27 - Ap 6 '97 - p8 [251-500]
  c Ch BWatch - v6 - O '96 - p5 [1-50]
  c Emerg Lib - v24 - Mr '97 - p66 [1-50]
  y HB Guide - v8 - Spr '97 - p139 [51-250]
  y SLJ - v42 - O '96 - p160 [51-250]
Glovemen: Twenty-Seven of Baseball's Greatest
  y BL - v93 - Ap 1 '97 - p1310 [1-50]
  c HB Guide - v7 - Fall '96 - p363 [51-250]
  c SLJ - v42 - Ag '96 - p160 [51-250]
Snowboarding: A Complete Guide for Beginners
  c BL - v93 - Ja '97 - p854 [251-500]
  c KR - v64 - D 15 '96 - p1805 [51-250]
  c SLJ - v43 - Mr '97 - p209 [51-250]
Sullivan, Gordon R - *Hope Is Not a Method*
  KR - v64 - O 1 '96 - p1455 [251-500]
  LJ - v121 - O 15 '96 - p69 [51-250]
Soldiers Serving the Nation
  J Gov Info - v23 - S '96 - p542 [51-250]
Sullivan, Helen - *Research Reports*
  y SLJ - v42 - S '96 - p236 [51-250]
Sullivan, Henry W, 1942- - *The Beatles with Lacan*
  Notes - v53 - D '96 - p489+ [501+]
Grotesque Purgatory
  Choice - v34 - F '97 - p971+ [51-250]
Sullivan, Jenny - *The Island of Summer*
  c Bks Keeps - v100 - S '96 - p13 [51-250]
  y Sch Lib - v44 - N '96 - p172 [51-250]
Sullivan, Lawrence R - *China since Tiananmen*
  Ch Rev Int - v4 - Spr '97 - p253+ [501+]
Sullivan, Margaret A - *Bruegel's Peasants*
  Ren Q - v49 - Aut '96 - p678+ [501+]
Sullivan, Marilyn D - *The New Home Buying Strategy*
  BWatch - v17 - N '96 - p8 [51-250]
Sullivan, Mark, 1874-1952 - *Our Times*
  y SLJ - v42 - Ag '96 - p186 [51-250]
Sullivan, Mark T - *The Purification Ceremony*
  BL - v93 - Mr 15 '97 - p1205 [51-250]
  KR - v65 - Ap 1 '97 - p499 [251-500]
  LJ - v122 - Ap 15 '97 - p121 [51-250]
  PW - v244 - Ap 28 '97 - p47 [251-500]
Sullivan, Mary C - *Catherine McAuley and the Tradition of Mercy*
  CH - v65 - D '96 - p729+ [501+]
  CHR - v83 - Ja '97 - p112+ [501+]
Sullivan, Michael, 1916- - *Art and Artists of Twentieth-Century China*
  Choice - v34 - Ap '97 - p1327 [51-250]
  FEER - v159 - D 19 '96 - p56 [251-500]
  LJ - v122 - F 15 '97 - p132 [51-250]
Sullivan, Michael J, 1941- - *Comparing State Politics*
  Choice - v34 - N '96 - p532 [51-250]
Sullivan, Michael John - *A Fatal Passion*
  BL - v93 - My 1 '97 - p1476 [251-500]
  KR - v65 - Ap 1 '97 - p539 [251-500]
  LJ - v122 - My 1 '97 - p116 [51-250]
  PW - v244 - Mr 31 '97 - p53 [251-250]
Sullivan, Michael John, 1960- - *Sports Great Barry Bonds*
  c CLW - v66 - Je '96 - p51 [51-250]
Sports Great Shaquille O'Neal
  c RT - v50 - O '96 - p143 [1-50]
Sullivan, Missy - *The Native American Look Book*
  c CBRS - v25 - O '96 - p24 [51-250]
  c HB Guide - v8 - Spr '97 - p139 [51-250]
  c Nat Peop - v10 - '97 - p78+ [501+]
Sullivan, Norma - *Masters and Managers*
  CS - v25 - S '96 - p646+ [501+]
Sullivan, Patricia - *Days of Hope*
  Choice - v34 - S '96 - p199 [51-250]
  HRNB - v25 - Fall '96 - p11 [501+]
  Nat - v263 - O 7 '96 - p27+ [501+]
Sullivan, Patricia Ann - *From the Margins to the Center*
  Choice - v34 - Ap '97 - p1329 [51-250]
Sullivan, Paul - *Keewatin*
  y Cur R - v35 - S '96 - p13 [51-250]
Legend of the North
  y Cur R - v35 - S '96 - p13 [51-250]
The Unforgiving Land
  y Cur R - v35 - S '96 - p13 [51-250]
Sullivan, Rob, 1967- - *Climbing Your Way to the Bottom*
  J Car P&E - v57 - Win '97 - p16+ [251-500]
Sullivan, Robert - *A Matter of Faith*
  Choice - v34 - Ja '97 - p799 [51-250]
  ILS - v16 - Spr '97 - p11+ [501+]
  R&R Bk N - v11 - D '96 - p64 [1-50]
Sullivan, Robert, 1940- - *The Small Business Start-Up Guide*
  LJ - v122 - My 1 '97 - p53 [1-50]

Sullivan, Robert, 1953- - *Flight of the Reindeer (Illus. by Glenn Wolff)*
  c Ch BWatch - v6 - D '96 - p1 [51-250]
  PW - v243 - S 23 '96 - p68 [51-250]
Flight of the Reindeer (Ritter). Audio Version
  c BWatch - v17 - D '96 - p2 [51-250]
Sullivan, Rosemary - *Shadow Maker*
  Can Lit - Spr '97 - p244+ [501+]
Sullivan, Silky - *Grandpa Was a Cowboy (Illus. by Bert Dodson)*
  c HB Guide - v7 - Fall '96 - p278 [51-250]
Sullivan, Vickie B - *Machiavelli's Three Romes*
  Choice - v34 - F '97 - p1034 [51-250]
  TLS - Ap 11 '97 - p30 [501+]
Sullivan, Walter - *A Time to Dance*
  Sew R - v104 - Jl '96 - p468+ [501+]
Sullivan, William - *The Secret of the Incas*
  VQR - v72 - Aut '96 - p117* [51-250]
Sullivan-Trainor, Michael - *Webmaster Strategies*
  LJ - v121 - D '96 - p138 [51-250]
Sulloway, Frank J - *Born to Rebel*
  Bus W - Ja 13 '96 - p22 [51-250]
  BW - v26 - D 1 '96 - p10 [501+]
  CHE - v43 - O 25 '96 - pA24 [51-250]
  Econ - v341 - D 7 '96 - p4*+ [501+]
  Nat R - v48 - D 9 '96 - p63+ [501+]
  Nature - v384 - N 14 '96 - p125+ [501+]
  New R - v215 - D 23 '96 - p29+ [501+]
  NS - v126 - Ja 10 '97 - p48 [501+]
  NYRB - v43 - N 14 '96 - p4+ [501+]
  NYTBR - v101 - O 20 '96 - p38 [501+]
  NYTBR - v101 - D 8 '96 - p85 [1-50]
  PW - v243 - O 21 '96 - p64 [51-250]
  Sci - v275 - Ja 31 '97 - p624+ [501+]
  Spec - v277 - N 9 '96 - p48 [501+]
  TLS - F 14 '97 - p26 [501+]
  Wil Q - v21 - Win '97 - p88+ [501+]
Sulock, Joseph M - *Cases in Financial Management. 2nd Ed.*
  R&R Bk N - v12 - F '97 - p48 [51-250]
Sulpher River Review
  p Sm Pr R - v28 - N '96 - p22 [51-250]
Sumich, James L - *An Introduction to the Biology of Marine Life. 6th Ed.*
  SciTech - v20 - N '96 - p25 [51-250]
Summ, G Harvey - *Brazilian Mosaic*
  HAHR - v77 - My '97 - p349+ [251-500]
Summary of Public Comments on the Inland Native Fish Strategy Environmental Assessment 1995
  J Gov Info - v23 - S '96 - p572 [51-250]
Summer, Lisa - *Music: The New Age Elixir*
  BWatch - v18 - F '97 - p8 [51-250]
  LJ - v122 - F 1 '97 - p81 [51-250]
  PW - v243 - O 21 '96 - p68 [1-50]
Summer, Robin Langley - *Great Cons and Con Artists*
  ACI - v7 - Fall '95 - p31 [501+]
Summer Theatre Directory 1996
  r ARBA - v28 - '97 - p525 [51-250]
Summerall, Pat - *Pat Summerall's Sports in America*
  KR - v64 - N 1 '96 - p1594 [251-500]
  PW - v243 - N 4 '96 - p56 [51-250]
Summerhayes, C P - *Oceanography: An Illustrated Guide*
  Nature - v385 - Ja 30 '97 - p408 [51-250]
Summers, Anne - *How to Find Source Materials*
  r LAR - v99 - Ja '97 - p50 [1-50]
Summers, Claude J - *The Gay and Lesbian Literary Heritage*
  r ARBA - v28 - '97 - p409 [251-500]
The Wit of Seventeenth-Century Poetry
  Ren Q - v49 - Win '96 - p881+ [501+]
Summers, Donna C S - *Quality*
  SciTech - v20 - D '96 - p85 [51-250]
Summers, Harry G, Jr. - *Historical Atlas of the Vietnam War*
  r APH - v44 - Spr '97 - p56+ [251-500]
  r ARBA - v28 - '97 - p199+ [51-250]
Summers, Judith - *Crime and Ravishment*
  Books - v10 - Je '96 - p10 [51-250]
  Books - v10 - Je '96 - p13 [1-50]
Summers, Ray - *Essentials of New Testament Greek. Rev. Ed.*
  Rel St Rev - v23 - Ja '97 - p66+ [251-500]
Summers, W Franklin - *Operas in One Act*
  LJ - v122 - Ja '97 - p102+ [51-250]
Summersett, John - *Going with the Weather*
  BWatch - v18 - Mr '97 - p1 [51-250]
Summit, Ginger - *The Complete Book of Gourd Craft*
  LJ - v121 - O 15 '96 - p57 [51-250]
Sumner, David E - *Graduate Programs in Journalism and Mass Communications*
  r Choice - v34 - Mr '97 - p1143+ [51-250]

Sumner, Gregory D - *Dwight Macdonald and the Politics Circle*
  BW - v26 - Ag 4 '96 - p13 [51-250]
  Choice - v34 - Ja '97 - p865 [51-250]
Sumner, L W - *Welfare, Happiness, and Ethics*
  Choice - v34 - My '97 - p1514 [51-250]
Sumner, Mark - *Dark Lies*
  y Kliatt - v31 - My '97 - p16 [51-250]
Devil's Engine
  y Kliatt - v31 - My '97 - p16 [51-250]
Devil's Tower
  y Kliatt - v31 - Mr '97 - p21 [51-250]
Night Terrors
  y Kliatt - v31 - My '97 - p16 [51-250]
Sumruld, William A - *Augustine and the Arians*
  CH - v65 - D '96 - p668+ [501+]
Sumser, John - *Morality and Social Order in Television Crime Drama*
  r Choice - v34 - N '96 - p448 [51-250]
Recruiters' Internet Survival Guide
  HR Mag - v41 - D '96 - p125 [51-250]
Sun, Cecile Chu-Chin - *Pearl from the Dragon's Mouth*
  Choice - v34 - N '96 - p451+ [51-250]
Sun, Chyng-Feng - *Cat and Cat-Face (Illus. by Lesley Liu)*
  c HB Guide - v7 - Fall '96 - p278 [1-50]
  c NYTBR - v101 - Ag 25 '96 - p23 [1-50]
Sun, Pin - *The Lost Art of War (Kelsey). Audio Version*
  LJ - v121 - N 1 '96 - p122 [51-250]
Sun Pin: Military Methods
  Ch Rev Int - v4 - Spr '97 - p233+ [501+]
Sun, Yan - *The Chinese Reassessment of Socialism 1976-1992*
  APSR - v91 - Mr '97 - p209+ [501+]
  RP - v58 - Sum '96 - p655+ [501+]
The Sun: A Magazine of Ideas
  p Sm Pr R - v28 - O '96 - p20 [51-250]
Sun Technical Publications - *Read Me First*
  CBR - v15 - Spr '97 - p10 [51-250]
Sunbeck, Deborah - *Infinity Walk*
  PW - v243 - S 9 '96 - p80 [51-250]
Sundaram, Rangarajan K - *A First Course in Optimization Theory*
  JEL - v35 - Mr '97 - p197 [51-250]
Sunderland, Lane V - *Popular Government and the Supreme Court*
  AAPSS-A - v549 - Ja '97 - p200+ [501+]
  APSR - v90 - D '96 - p924+ [501+]
Sundiata, I K - *From Slaving to Neoslavery*
  Bl S - v26 - Fall '96 - p106 [51-250]
  Choice - v34 - N '96 - p514 [51-250]
  JEL - v34 - D '96 - p2101+ [51-250]
Sundquist, Eric J - *Cultural Contexts for Ralph Ellison's Invisible Man*
  AL - v68 - S '96 - p668 [1-50]
To Wake the Nations
  Clio - v25 - Spr '96 - p313+ [501+]
Sunset Books - *Kitchens and Bathrooms*
  LJ - v122 - F 1 '97 - p53 [51-250]
Sunshine, Linda - *Bogus*
  c SLJ - v43 - Ja '97 - p92+ [51-250]
Sunstein, Cass R - *Free Markets and Social Justice*
  BL - v93 - F 15 '97 - p982 [51-250]
  NYTBR - v102 - F 9 '97 - p23 [501+]
Legal Reasoning and Political Conflict
  Choice - v34 - D '96 - p689 [51-250]
  NYTBR - v101 - S 8 '96 - p17+ [501+]
Sun-Tzu - *The Complete Art of War*
  Choice - v34 - D '96 - p689 [51-250]
  FEER - v159 - D 5 '96 - p58 [251-500]
  J Mil H - v61 - Ap '97 - p355+ [501+]
Super Senses (Snapshot)
  c Ch BWatch - v6 - D '96 - p8 [1-50]
  c PW - v243 - N 4 '96 - p78 [51-250]
Supervielle, Silvia Baron - *La Frontiere*
  WLT - v70 - Sum '96 - p655 [251-500]
Nouvelles Cantates
  WLT - v70 - Sum '96 - p657 [251-500]
Supica, Jim - *Standard Catalog of Smith and Wesson*
  r Ant & CM - v101 - D '96 - p32 [51-250]
Suplee, Curt - *Everyday Science Explained*
  y BL - v93 - D 1 '96 - p633 [51-250]
  BWatch - v18 - Mr '97 - p10 [51-250]
Supnick, Mark - *The Wonderful World of Cookie Jars*
  Ant & CM - v101 - F '97 - p33 [51-250]
Suppe, Frederick C - *Military Institutions on the Welsh Marches*
  AHR - v101 - D '96 - p1532 [251-500]
  EHR - v111 - N '96 - p1243+ [501+]
  Specu - v72 - Ja '97 - p203+ [501+]

Supramolecular Science
p Nature - v383 - S 5 '96 - p43 [251-500]
Supraner, Robyn - *Sam Sunday and the Mystery at the Ocean Beach Hotel (Illus. by Will Hillenbrand)*
c BL - v92 - Ag '96 - p1909 [51-250]
c CBRS - v25 - Ja '97 - p53 [51-250]
c CCB-B - v50 - S '96 - p33 [51-250]
c HB Guide - v8 - Spr '97 - p50 [51-250]
c PW - v243 - S 23 '96 - p75 [51-250]
c SLJ - v42 - O '96 - p107 [51-250]
The Supreme Court CD-ROM. Electronic Media Version
r Econ - v341 - D 7 '96 - p8* [51-250]
The Supreme Court Yearbook 1995-1996
r ARBA - v28 - '97 - p271+ [51-250]
Surappa, M K - *Inorganic Matrix Composites*
SciTech - v20 - N '96 - p63 [51-250]
Surat, Michele Maria - *Angel Child, Dragon Child*
c Learning - v25 - Mr '97 - p54 [1-50]
Suriyakumaran, C - *The Wealth of Poor Nations. 2nd Ed.*
JEL - v35 - Mr '97 - p274 [51-250]
Surles, Kathryn B - *The Health of Young Children in North Carolina*
J Gov Info - v23 - S '96 - p590 [51-250]
Surrey, John - *The British Electricity Experiment*
Lon R Bks - v19 - F 6 '97 - p10+ [501+]
Surtz, Ronald E - *Writing Women in Late Medieval and Early Modern Spain*
CHR - v82 - Jl '96 - p560+ [501+]
Rel St Rev - v23 - Ja '97 - p81 [51-250]
Ren Q - v50 - Spr '97 - p342+ [501+]
Specu - v72 - Ja '97 - p228+ [501+]
A Survey of Geographic Information Systems in Government 1994
GJ - v162 - Jl '96 - p242 [1-50]
Suryanarayana, C - *Processing and Properties of Nanocrystalline Materials*
SciTech - v20 - D '96 - p28 [51-250]
Suskin, Steven - *More Opening Nights on Broadway*
r LJ - v122 - Ap 15 '97 - p74 [51-250]
r TCI - v30 - O '96 - p59 [1-50]
Suskind, Patrick - *Maitre Mussard's Bequest*
New Sci - v152 - O 19 '96 - p49 [1-50]
Three Stories and a Reflection
Obs - N 10 '96 - p17* [501+]
TLS - N 22 '96 - p24 [501+]
Susser, Asher - *The Hashemites in the Modern Arab World*
MEJ - v50 - Sum '96 - p455 [51-250]
Sussex, Lucy - *The Scarlet Rider*
Aust Bk R - D '96 - p68+ [501+]
She's Fantastical
Arena - Ap '96 - p54+ [501+]
Susskind, Charles - *Heinrich Hertz: A Short Life*
Phys Today - v49 - S '96 - p90+ [501+]
Susskind, Lawrence - *Affordable Housing Mediation*
NCR - v85 - Spr '96 - p65 [51-250]
Dealing with an Angry Public
Choice - v34 - S '96 - p174 [51-250]
Susskind, Richard - *The Future of Law*
Lon R Bks - v18 - N 28 '96 - p16+ [501+]
Sussman, Elisabeth - *City of Ambition, Artists and New York*
LATBR - D 8 '96 - p7 [251-500]
Florine Stettheimer: Manhattan Fantastica
Art J - v55 - Sum '96 - p91+ [501+]
Nan Goldin: I'll Be Your Mirror
Afterimage - v24 - Ja '97 - p23 [1-50]
Econ - v341 - D 7 '96 - p15* [51-250]
NYTBR - v101 - D 8 '96 - p69+ [51-250]
VLS - Win '96 - p31 [251-500]
VV - v52 - Ja 28 '97 - p48+ [501+]
Sussman, Herbert - *Victorian Masculinities*
Art J - v55 - Win '96 - p88+ [501+]
RES - v48 - F '97 - p126+ [501+]
VS - v39 - Spr '96 - p471+ [501+]
Sussman, Paul - *Death by Spaghetti*
Spec - v277 - D 7 '96 - p54 [51-250]
Sustain: A Journal of Environmental and Sustainability Issues
p WorldV - v12 - Jl '96 - p12 [51-250]
Sustainable Transport
JEL - v34 - D '96 - p2090 [51-250]
Suster, Gerald - *Champions of the Ring*
PW - v244 - Mr 10 '97 - p55 [51-250]
Sutcliff, Rosemary - *Black Ships before Troy (Illus. by Alan Lee)*
y Kliatt - v30 - S '96 - p3 [1-50]
c RT - v50 - F '97 - p424 [51-250]
c SLJ - v42 - N '96 - p39 [1-50]

The Eagle of the Ninth
y SLJ - v42 - N '96 - p39 [1-50]
The Wanderings of Odysseus (Illus. by Alan Lee)
c BL - v93 - S 1 '96 - p124 [51-250]
c CCB-B - v50 - S '96 - p33 [51-250]
c HB Guide - v7 - Fall '96 - p325 [51-250]
c SLJ - v42 - N '96 - p39 [1-50]
c Smith - v27 - N '96 - p165 [1-50]
Sutcliffe, Andrea - *Numbers: How Many, How Far, How Long, How Much*
r BL - v93 - S 1 '96 - p169 [251-500]
r Choice - v34 - N '96 - p434 [51-250]
Sutcliffe, Anthony - *Paris: An Architectural History*
BW - v26 - D 29 '96 - p12 [51-250]
CR - v270 - F '97 - p110 [51-250]
PW - v243 - S 23 '96 - p73 [1-50]
Sutcliffe, Glyn - *Slide Collection Management in Libraries and Information Units*
LR - v45 - 7 '96 - p46+ [501+]
Sutcliffe, John - *Paint: Decorating with Water-Based Paints*
BL - v93 - Mr 1 '97 - p1100 [51-250]
PW - v244 - F 3 '97 - p104 [51-250]
Sutcliffe, Katherine - *Devotion*
PW - v243 - N 4 '96 - p42 [1-50]
Devotion (Reading). Audio Version
y Kliatt - v31 - Ja '97 - p40 [51-250]
Sutcliffe, Serena - *Champagne: The History and Character of the World's Most Celebrated Wine*
LJ - v122 - Ap 1 '97 - p62 [1-50]
Sutcliffe, Tom - *Believing in Opera*
LJ - v122 - My 1 '97 - p106 [51-250]
Obs - D 22 '96 - p16* [501+]
PW - v244 - Ja 27 '97 - p92 [251-500]
Spec - v278 - Ja 11 '97 - p32 [501+]
TES - Ja 10 '97 - p7* [501+]
TLS - Ja 3 '97 - p20 [501+]
Sutcliffe, William - *New Boy*
Obs - D 1 '96 - p17* [51-250]
Sutela, Pekka - *The Russian Economy in Crisis and Transition*
Slav R - v55 - Sum '96 - p499+ [501+]
Sutherland, Cherie - *Reborn in the Light*
Rel St Rev - v23 - Ap '97 - p141+ [501+]
Sutherland, Christine - *Enchantress: Marthe Bibesco and Her World*
KR - v64 - O 15 '96 - p1521 [251-500]
LJ - v121 - N 15 '96 - p68+ [51-250]
New R - v216 - F 24 '97 - p36+ [501+]
NYTBR - v102 - Ap 13 '97 - p21 [251-500]
Obs - Mr 23 '97 - p15* [501+]
PW - v243 - O 21 '96 - p61 [51-250]
Sutherland, Daniel E - *The Emergence of Total War*
LJ - v121 - N 15 '96 - p74 [51-250]
Seasons of War
RAH - v24 - D '96 - p613+ [501+]
Sutherland, Fraser - *Jonestown: A Poem*
BIC - v25 - S '96 - p12+ [501+]
Sutherland, John - *Is Heathcliff a Murderer?*
Econ - v341 - O 19 '96 - p15*+ [251-500]
Lon R Bks - v18 - S 19 '96 - p20+ [501+]
TES - Ag 2 '96 - p15 [51-250]
TLS - Jl 19 '96 - p25 [501+]
Victorian Fiction
Nine-C Lit - v51 - S '96 - p253+ [501+]
Sutherland, Laura - *The Best Bargain Family Vacations in the U.S.A.*
r LJ - v122 - F 15 '97 - p154 [51-250]
Sutherland, Richard L - *Handbook of Nonlinear Optics*
r SciTech - v20 - N '96 - p19 [51-250]
Sutherland, Robert - *If Two Are Dead*
c Quill & Q - v63 - Mr '97 - p80 [251-500]
Sutherland, Stuart - *The International Dictionary of Psychology. 2nd Ed.*
r Adoles - v31 - Win '96 - p997 [51-250]
r ARBA - v28 - '97 - p285+ [51-250]
r Choice - v34 - S '96 - p107 [51-250]
Sutherland, Titia - *Out of the Shadows (Bron). Audio Version*
y Kliatt - v31 - My '97 - p43 [51-250]
Sutherland, William J - *Ecological Census Techniques*
y New Sci - v151 - S 28 '96 - p50+ [501+]
From Individual Behaviour to Population Ecology
Choice - v34 - O '96 - p308 [51-250]
Sutherland, Zena - *Children and Books. 9th Ed.*
BL - v93 - Mr 1 '97 - p1177 [51-250]
Sutin, Jack - *Jack and Rochelle*
y Kliatt - v30 - N '96 - p23 [51-250]
VQR - v72 - Aut '96 - p124* [251-250]

Suto, Elizabeth - *INFORMIX Performance Tuning. 2nd Ed.*
SciTech - v21 - Mr '97 - p11 [51-250]
Sutphen, Joyce - *Straight Out of View*
Poet - v169 - D '96 - p158+ [501+]
Sutter, Robert G - *Shaping China's Future in World Affairs*
Choice - v34 - D '96 - p688 [51-250]
Cu H - v95 - S '96 - p292 [1-50]
Sutterlin, Ingmar - *Die Russische Abteilung Des Auswartigen Amtes In Der Weimarer Republik*
EHR - v112 - Ap '97 - p527+ [251-500]
Sutton, Adrian P - *Interfaces in Crystalline Materials*
Phys Today - v49 - S '96 - p88 [501+]
Sutton, Brett - *Public Library Planning*
LAR - v98 - Mr '96 - p164 [51-250]
Sutton, Brian - *A Century of Mycology*
Sci - v274 - N 22 '96 - p1321 [1-50]
Sutton, Clay - *How to Spot an Owl*
Wildbird - v10 - O '96 - p24 [51-250]
How to Spot Hawks and Eagles
Wildbird - v10 - O '96 - p24 [51-250]
Sutton, Geoffrey V - *Science for a Polite Society*
Bks & Cult - v2 - S '96 - p38 [251-500]
Isis - v87 - S '96 - p546+ [501+]
Sutton, John - *Psychic Pets*
c Books - v11 - Ap '97 - p24 [51-250]
Sutton, Leslie - *The History of the Faraday Society*
New Sci - v153 - Mr 1 '97 - p42 [51-250]
Sutton, Mark Q - *Archaeological Laboratory Methods*
r Am Ant - v62 - Ja '97 - p151+ [501+]
Sutton, Nina - *Bettelheim: A Life and a Legacy*
Ant R - v55 - Spr '97 - p234+ [251-500]
Choice - v34 - D '96 - p693+ [51-250]
NY - v73 - Mr 24 '97 - p76+ [501+]
Readings - v11 - S '96 - p13+ [501+]
Sutton, Robert Chester, R03 - *Human Existence and Theodicy*
JAAR - v64 - Win '96 - p901+ [501+]
Sutton, Sharon E - *Weaving a Tapestry of Resistance*
Choice - v34 - Mr '97 - p1213 [51-250]
R&R Bk N - v11 - N '96 - p57 [51-250]
Sutton, Walter - *Pound, Thayer, Watson and The Dial*
ELT - v39 - 3 '96 - p396+ [501+]
Suutari, Raymond K - *Business Strategy and Security Analysis*
Choice - v34 - S '96 - p178 [51-250]
Suvorov, Oleg - *Zhenskaia Filosofiia*
BL - v93 - O 1 '96 - p327 [1-50]
Al-Suwaidi, Jamal S - *Iran and the Gulf*
For Aff - v75 - N '96 - p164+ [51-250]
MEJ - v51 - Spr '97 - p311 [51-250]
MEP - v5 - 1 '97 - p195+ [501+]
Suykens, Johan A K - *Artificial Neural Networks for Modelling and Control of Non-Linear Systems*
SciTech - v20 - D '96 - p12 [51-250]
Suzanne, Claudia - *This Business of Books*
BWatch - v17 - S '96 - p9 [51-250]
Suzuki, David - *The Japan We Never Knew*
LJ - v122 - Mr 15 '97 - p79 [51-250]
Mac - v109 - D 30 '96 - p97 [251-500]
Suzumura, Kotaro - *Competition, Commitment, and Welfare*
Econ J - v106 - S '96 - p1437+ [501+]
JEL - v34 - S '96 - p1374+ [501+]
Svacha, Rostislav - *The Architecture of New Prague 1895-1945*
Slav R - v55 - Fall '96 - p668+ [501+]
Sveikauskas, Catherine - *The Impact of Trade on United States Employment*
JEL - v34 - S '96 - p1430 [51-250]
Svendsen, Elisabeth D - *The Story of Dusty (Illus. by Tom Morse-Brown)*
c Sch Lib - v45 - F '97 - p34 [51-250]
Svengalis, Kendall F - *The Legal Information Buyer's Guide and Reference Manual*
r SL - v87 - Sum '96 - p236 [251-500]
Svensson, Tommy - *On the Notion of Mental Illness*
Rel St Rev - v23 - Ja '97 - p43 [51-250]
SciTech - v20 - D '96 - p44 [51-250]
Svetlicic, Marjan - *The World Economy*
R&R Bk N - v11 - D '96 - p24 [51-250]
Svevo, Italo - *La Coscienza Di Zeng*
MLR - v91 - Jl '96 - p760+ [501+]
Svoboda, Jiri - *Hunters between East and West*
Choice - v34 - Ap '97 - p1382 [51-250]
R&R Bk N - v12 - F '97 - p30 [51-250]
Swaan, Bram De - *El Perseguidor De La Luz*
y JAAL - v40 - S '96 - p77 [51-250]

Swafford, Jan - *Charles Ives: A Life with Music*
    BW - v26 - D 8 '96 - p8 [51-250]
    Choice - v34 - D '96 - p624 [51-250]
    Econ - v341 - D 7 '96 - p12*+ [501+]
    LJ - v122 - Ja '97 - p51 [51-250]
    M Ed J - v83 - N '96 - p54 [51-250]
    NW - v128 - S 9 '96 - p74 [501+]
    NY - v72 - O 7 '96 - p96 [51-250]
    NYTBR - v101 - D 8 '96 - p85 [1-50]
    Spec - v277 - N 2 '96 - p44 [501+]
Swaim, Kathleen M - *Pilgrim's Progress, Puritan Progress*
    Ren Q - v49 - Win '96 - p876+ [501+]
Swain, Geoffrey - *The Origins of the Russian Civil War*
    HRNB - v25 - Fall '96 - p34+ [251-500]
    HRNB - v25 - Win '97 - p83+ [251-500]
Swain, Gwenyth - *The Road to Seneca Falls (Illus. by Mary O'Keefe Young)*
    c BL - v93 - F 15 '97 - p1022 [51-250]
    c HB Guide - v8 - Spr '97 - p161 [51-250]
    c SLJ - v43 - Mr '97 - p181+ [51-250]
Swain, Jon - *River of Time*
    NS & S - v9 - My 3 '96 - p37 [1-50]
Swain, Simon - *Hellenism and Empire*
    Choice - v34 - Ja '97 - p791 [51-250]
    Lon R Bks - v19 - Ja 23 '97 - p18+ [501+]
    TLS - N 1 '96 - p30 [501+]
Swaine, Dalway J - *Environmental Aspects of Trace Elements in Coal*
    SciTech - v20 - S '96 - p60 [51-250]
Swales, Erika - *The Poetics of Scepticism*
    MLR - v92 - Ap '97 - p511+ [501+]
Swales, John M - *Academic Writing for Graduate Students*
    Col Comp - v47 - O '96 - p443+ [51-250]
Swan, Gladys - *A Visit to Strangers*
    Sew R - v104 - Jl '96 - pR50+ [251-500]
Swan, Jennifer - *Sports Style Guide and Reference Manual*
    r ARBA - v28 - '97 - p349 [51-250]
    r BL - v93 - S 15 '96 - p285 [51-250]
    r BL - v93 - My 1 '97 - p1514 [1-50]
Swan, John - *The Rouge Mysteries*
    BIC - v26 - F '97 - p36 [51-250]
Swan, Susan - *Stupid Boys Are Good to Relax With*
    Quill & Q - v62 - S '96 - p66 [251-500]
Swan, Thomas - *The Cezanne Chase*
    BL - v93 - F 15 '97 - p1008 [51-250]
    KR - v65 - Ja 1 '97 - p18 [251-500]
    NYTBR - v102 - Mr 30 '97 - p23 [51-250]
    PW - v244 - F 3 '97 - p94 [51-250]
Swander, Mary - *Bloom and Blossom*
    BL - v93 - Mr 15 '97 - p1214 [51-250]
    LJ - v122 - Ap 1 '97 - p114 [51-250]
Swank, Walbrook - *Old Abe's Jokes*
    BWatch - v17 - N '96 - p11 [1-50]
Swann, Brian - *Coming to Light*
    WLT - v71 - Win '97 - p198 [501+]
    Wearing the Morning Star
    PW - v243 - S 30 '96 - p84 [51-250]
Swann, Ingo - *The Great Apparitions of Mary*
    y BL - v93 - O 1 '96 - p307 [51-250]
    LJ - v121 - N 15 '96 - p66+ [51-250]
    PW - v243 - S 30 '96 - p75 [51-250]
Swann, Julian - *Politics and the Parlement of Paris under Louis XV 1754-1774*
    Historian - v59 - Win '97 - p479+ [251-500]
Swann, William B - *Self-Traps: The Elusive Quest for Higher Self-Esteem*
    Choice - v34 - O '96 - p365 [51-250]
Swannell, John - *Twenty Years On*
    PW - v244 - F 3 '97 - p91 [51-250]
Swanson, Diane - *Buffalo Sunrise*
    c CLW - v67 - Mr '97 - p58 [51-250]
    c HB Guide - v7 - Fall '96 - p346 [51-250]
    Welcome to the World of Whales
    c Emerg Lib - v24 - Mr '97 - p28 [1-50]
    c Quill & Q - v62 - D '96 - p39 [251-500]
    Welcome to the World of Wolves
    c Quill & Q - v62 - D '96 - p39 [251-500]
Swanson, Doug J - *96 Tears*
    Arm Det - v30 - Win '97 - p114 [51-250]
    KR - v64 - S 1 '96 - p1279+ [51-250]
    NYTBR - v102 - F 2 '97 - p22 [51-250]
    PW - v243 - S 2 '96 - p116 [51-250]
Swanson, Jean - *By a Woman's Hand. 1st Ed.*
    r RQ - v36 - Win '96 - p217+ [51-250]
    By a Woman's Hand. 2nd Ed.
    Arm Det - v30 - Win '97 - p104 [251-500]
    yr Kliatt - v30 - N '96 - p19 [251-250]

Swanson, Jeffrey - *Echoes of the Call*
    Am Ethnol - v23 - N '96 - p929+ [501+]
    JR - v77 - Ja '97 - p152+ [501+]
Swanson, Philip - *The New Novel in Latin America*
    Choice - v34 - N '96 - p465+ [51-250]
Swanson, R N - *Religion and Devotion in Europe c. 1215-c. 1515*
    CH - v65 - D '96 - p692+ [501+]
    JR - v77 - Ap '97 - p297+ [501+]
    Theol St - v57 - S '96 - p535+ [501+]
Swanson, Roger M - *Becoming a Leader in Enrollment Services*
    C&U - v72 - Spr '97 - p25 [501+]
Swanson, Stevenson - *Chicago Days*
    Trib Bks - My 4 '97 - p5 [501+]
Swanson, Timothy M - *The Economics and Ecology of Biodiversity Decline*
    JEL - v34 - D '96 - p2002+ [501+]
Swanson-Natsues, Lyn - *Days of Adventure (Illus. by Joy Dunn Keenan)*
    c SLJ - v42 - Ag '96 - p131 [51-250]
Sward, Sharon - *You Are More than What You Weigh*
    y BWatch - v17 - S '96 - p11 [1-50]
Swartz, Clifford E - *Teaching Introductory Physics*
    SciTech - v21 - Mr '97 - p20 [51-250]
Swartzburg, Susan G - *Preserving Library Materials. 2nd Ed.*
    LR - v45 - 5 '96 - p65+ [501+]
Swasy, Alecia - *Changing Focus*
    BL - v93 - My 15 '97 - p1549 [51-250]
Swatland, Andrew - *The House of Lords in the Reign of Charles II*
    Choice - v34 - Mr '97 - p1224 [51-250]
Swatos, William H - *Politics and Religion in Central and Eastern Europe*
    CH - v65 - S '96 - p547+ [501+]
    Religion and Democracy in Latin America
    Parameters - v26 - Win '96 - p155 [1-50]
Swayne, Linda E - *The Physician Strategist*
    SciTech - v20 - N '96 - p36 [51-250]
Swayne, Martin - *The Blue Germ. Electronic Media Version*
    Analog - v117 - F '97 - p145+ [51-250]
Swaziland. Ministry of Economic Planning and Development. Economic Planning Office - *Development Plan 1995/96-1997/98*
    J Gov Info - v23 - S '96 - p661 [51-250]
Sweatman, Margaret - *Sam and Angie*
    Quill & Q - v62 - Ag '96 - p36 [251-500]
Swedberg, Richard - *Economic Sociology*
    CS - v25 - S '96 - p709+ [501+]
    JEL - v34 - D '96 - p2009 [51-250]
    R&R Bk N - v11 - D '96 - p37 [51-250]
    Explorations in Economic Sociology
    SF - v75 - S '96 - p365+ [251-500]
Swedenburg, Ted - *Memories of Revolt*
    CS - v26 - Mr '97 - p141+ [501+]
    MEJ - v50 - Aut '96 - p627 [51-250]
Sweel, Pat - *Troubled Waters*
    Books - v9 - S '95 - p24 [1-50]
Sweeney, Eamonn - *Waiting for the Healer*
    Obs - Mr 23 '97 - p18* [51-250]
Sweeney, Jacqueline - *Katie and the Night Noises. Book and Audio Version*
    c SLJ - v42 - Ag '96 - p63 [51-250]
Sweeney, Jerry K - *A Handbook of American Military History*
    r APH - v44 - Spr '97 - p54 [501+]
    r ARBA - v28 - '97 - p256+ [251-500]
    J Mil H - v61 - Ap '97 - p371+ [501+]
Sweeney, Joan - *Me on the Map (Illus. by Annette Cable)*
    c HB Guide - v7 - Fall '96 - p377 [51-250]
Sweeney, John J - *America Needs a Raise*
    BL - v93 - O 1 '96 - p311 [51-250]
    Bus W - S 9 '96 - p15 [501+]
    BW - v26 - S 22 '96 - p6+ [501+]
    Econ - v341 - O 19 '96 - p10*+ [501+]
    LJ - v121 - O 1 '96 - p95+ [51-250]
    Nat - v263 - N 25 '96 - p25+ [501+]
    NYTBR - v101 - O 13 '96 - p20+ [51-250]
Sweeney, Joyce - *Free Fall*
    y BL - v93 - Ap 1 '97 - p1310 [1-50]
    y HB Guide - v8 - Spr '97 - p84 [51-250]
    y KR - v64 - My 1 '96 - p694 [51-250]
    y SLJ - v42 - N '96 - p126 [51-250]
Sweeney, Julia - *God Said Ha*
    PW - v244 - Ap 28 '97 - p60 [51-250]
Sweeney, Patricia - *Women in Southern Literature*
    r RQ - v36 - Win '96 - p226 [51-250]
Sweet, Robert E - *Music Universe, Music Mind*
    LJ - v121 - O 15 '96 - p62 [51-250]

Sweeting, Adam W - *Reading Houses and Building Books*
    Choice - v34 - F '97 - p969 [51-250]
Sweetland, David - *C-Liners, Fairbanks-Morse's Consolidation Line of Locomotives*
    Model R - v64 - F '97 - p53 [251-500]
Sweetman, David - *Paul Gauguin: A Life*
    AB - v99 - Mr 3 '97 - p693 [51-250]
    CSM - v88 - O 16 '96 - p13 [51-250]
    A Tribal Fever
    TLS - Ag 2 '96 - p23 [251-500]
Sweetman, Jim - *The Courseware Guide to English Examinations at Key Stage 4*
    TES - F 28 '97 - pR7 [51-250]
Sweetman, John - *English Solutions*
    y TES - S 20 '96 - pR7 [51-250]
Sweet's Group - *Kitchen and Bath Source Book*
    r BWatch - v17 - N '96 - p8 [51-250]
Sweetser, Richard S - *The Fundamentals of Natural Gas Cooling*
    Choice - v34 - Ja '97 - p826 [51-250]
Swenson, Alan J - *Gods, Angels, and Narrators*
    MLR - v91 - O '96 - p1047+ [501+]
Swenson, Karen - *The Landlady in Bangkok*
    PS - v70 - Fall '96 - p197+ [501+]
Swenson, May - *May out West*
    WAL - v31 - Fall '96 - p270+ [251-500]
    Nature: Poems Old and New
    WAL - v31 - Fall '96 - p270+ [251-500]
Swerdlow, Amy - *Women Strike for Peace*
    Signs - v22 - Aut '96 - p237+ [501+]
Swetnam, Ford - *301*
    WAL - v31 - Win '97 - p413+ [51-250]
Swetz, Frank - *Learn from the Masters*
    y New Sci - v151 - S 28 '96 - p44+ [501+]
Swick, Marly A - *Paper Wings*
    KR - v64 - My 1 '96 - p635+ [251-500]
    NYTBR - v101 - S 8 '96 - p23 [251-500]
    TLS - Mr 28 '97 - p20 [501+]
Swidler, Leonard - *Toward a Catholic Constitution*
    BL - v93 - S 15 '96 - p185 [51-250]
Swietochowski, Tadeusz - *Russia and Azerbaijan*
    MEJ - v50 - Aut '96 - p615+ [501+]
    Slav R - v55 - Fall '96 - p698+ [501+]
Swift, Elaine K - *The Making of an American Senate*
    Choice - v34 - Mr '97 - p1242 [51-250]
Swift, Graham - *Last Orders*
    BL - v93 - Ap 1 '97 - p1285 [1-50]
    BW - v26 - D 8 '96 - p6 [1-50]
    CSM - v89 - F 27 '97 - pB1+ [501+]
    HR - v49 - Win '97 - p687+ [501+]
    LATBR - Jl 7 '96 - p6+ [501+]
    Nat R - v49 - Mr 10 '97 - p58 [51-250]
    NY - v72 - My 27 '96 - p132 [51-250]
    NYTBR - v101 - D 8 '96 - p80 [1-50]
    NYTBR - v102 - Mr 2 '97 - p28 [1-50]
    Obs - D 1 '96 - p16* [51-250]
    PW - v243 - N 4 '96 - p38 [51-250]
    W&I - v11 - O '96 - p285+ [501+]
    Woman's J - F '97 - p16 [1-50]
    Last Orders (Jayston). Audio Version
    BWatch - v18 - Mr '97 - p9 [1-50]
Swift, Karen J - *Manufacturing Bad Mothers*
    Fam in Soc - v77 - O '96 - p516+ [251-500]
Swigart, Edmund K - *An Emerson-Benson Saga*
    Am Geneal - v71 - O '96 - p255 [251-500]
Swinburne, Richard - *The Christian God*
    Theol St - v57 - Mr '96 - p163+ [501+]
    The Evolution of the Soul. Rev. Ed.
    Nature - v386 - Ap 10 '97 - p567 [51-250]
    Is There a God?
    Comw - v124 - Ja 31 '97 - p24+ [501+]
    Lon R Bks - v18 - O 3 '96 - p3+ [501+]
Swinburne, Stephen R - *Swallows in the Birdhouse (Illus. by Robin Brickman)*
    c HB Guide - v7 - Fall '96 - p344 [51-250]
Swindell, Simon R - *Sequence Data Analysis Guidebook*
    SciTech - v21 - Mr '97 - p42 [51-250]
Swindells, Robert - *Jacqueline Hyde (Illus. by A Rinaldi)*
    c JB - v60 - Ag '96 - p161 [51-250]
    c Sch Lib - v44 - Ag '96 - p109 [51-250]
    Last Bus (Illus. by Mark Edwards)
    c Bks Keeps - Ja '97 - p24 [51-250]
    c Sch Lib - v45 - F '97 - p22 [51-250]
    Stone Cold
    c Sch Lib - v44 - Ag '96 - p96+ [501+]
    World-Eater
    c Bks Keeps - v100 - S '96 - p16 [51-250]
Swinerton, E Nelson - *The National Guide to Educational Credit for Training Programs. 1996 Ed.*
    r R&R Bk N - v11 - D '96 - p55 [51-250]

Swinfen, Ann - *The Anniversary*
  Woman's J - S '96 - p10 [1-50]
Swir, Anna - *Talking to My Body*
  LATBR - v263 - S 29 '96 - p12 [501+]
  SFR - v21 - Jl '96 - p37 [251-500]
  TranslRevS - v2 - D '96 - p30 [51-250]
Swisher, Clarice - *Genetic Engineering*
  y HB Guide - v8 - Spr '97 - p120 [51-250]
  y SLJ - v43 - Ja '97 - p136 [51-250]
  y VOYA - v19 - D '96 - p292 [51-250]
  The Glorious Revolution
  c HB Guide - v7 - Fall '96 - p382 [51-250]
  Readings on John Steinbeck
  cr Ch BWatch - v6 - My '96 - p6 [1-50]
  yr Kliatt - v31 - Mr '97 - p22 [51-250]
  y SLJ - v42 - Ag '96 - p176 [51-250]
  Readings on Nathaniel Hawthorne
  cr Ch BWatch - v6 - My '96 - p6 [1-50]
  yr Kliatt - v31 - Mr '97 - p22 [51-250]
  y SLJ - v42 - Ag '96 - p176 [51-250]
  Readings on the Sonnets
  y BL - v93 - D 15 '96 - p720 [51-250]
  y SLJ - v43 - Ja '97 - p136 [51-250]
  Readings on the Tragedies of William Shakespeare
  y BL - v93 - N 15 '96 - p578+ [51-250]
  y Ch BWatch - v6 - Jl '96 - p2 [1-50]
  y Kliatt - v30 - N '96 - p18 [51-250]
  y SLJ - v42 - Ag '96 - p167+ [51-250]
Swisher, Karin L - *Single-Parent Families*
  y Kliatt - v31 - Mr '97 - p29 [51-250]
  The United Nations
  y Kliatt - v31 - Mr '97 - p29 [51-250]
Swisher, Valerie M - *Mastering Network Management*
  SciTech - v20 - N '96 - p74 [51-250]
Swiss, Deborah J - *Women Breaking Through*
  LJ - v122 - Mr 15 '97 - p37 [1-50]
Switten, Margaret L - *Music and Poetry in the Middle Ages*
  r Notes - v53 - Mr '97 - p784+ [501+]
  r Specu - v72 - Ja '97 - p142+ [501+]
Switzer, David K - *Coming Out as Parents*
  LJ - v121 - N 1 '96 - p94 [51-250]
Switzer, Ellen - *The Magic of Mozart (Illus. by Costas)*
  c LA - v73 - O '96 - p443+ [51-250]
Switzer, Jacqueline Vaughn - *Green Backlash*
  PW - v244 - F 24 '97 - p80 [1-50]
Switzer, Teri R - *Telecommuters: The Workforce of the Twenty-First Century*
  r LJ - v122 - My 1 '97 - p52 [1-50]
Swoboda, Jorg - *The Revolution of the Candles*
  CC - v113 - D 18 '96 - p1261 [51-250]
Swope, Sam - *The Araboolies of Liberty Street (Illus. by Barry Root)*
  c Par Ch - v20 - O '96 - p21 [51-250]
Sword, Elizabeth Hauge - *A Child's Anthology of Poetry*
  c BW - v26 - D 8 '96 - p20 [51-250]
Sword, Helen - *Engendering Inspiration*
  Choice - v34 - O '96 - p282 [51-250]
Sword, Keith - *Deportation and Exile*
  AHR - v101 - O '96 - p1244+ [501+]
  Slav R - v55 - Sum '96 - p473+ [501+]
Sword, Wiley - *Mountains Touched with Fire (Sevra). Audio Version*
  y Kliatt - v31 - My '97 - p47+ [51-250]
Sword and Sorceress XIII
  y Kliatt - v30 - N '96 - p12 [51-250]
Syal, Meera - *Anita and Me*
  BW - v27 - Ap 6 '97 - p9 [501+]
  KR - v65 - F 1 '97 - p168+ [251-500]
The Sycamore Review
  p Sm Pr R - v29 - Ja '97 - p19 [251-500]
Sydney (Eyewitness Travel Guides)
  r ARBA - v28 - '97 - p179 [51-250]
  r BL - v93 - S 15 '96 - p206 [1-50]
Syers, J K - *Soil Science and Sustainable Land Management in the Tropics*
  GJ - v162 - Jl '96 - p241 [51-250]
Sykes, Julie - *An Acorn for Tea (Illus. by Catherine Walters)*
  c TES - F 21 '97 - p16* [51-250]
  Hide and Narrow (Illus. by Catherine Walters)
  c TES - F 21 '97 - p16* [51-250]
  I Don't Want to Go to Bed! (Illus. by Tim Warnes)
  c Sch Lib - v44 - Ag '96 - p101 [51-250]
  Robbie Rabbit and the Little Ones (Illus. by Catherine Walters)
  c SLJ - v42 - Ag '96 - p131 [51-250]

Shhh! (Illus. by Tim Warnes)
  c CBRS - v25 - O '96 - p18 [51-250]
  c CCB-B - v50 - N '96 - p117 [51-250]
  c PW - v243 - S 30 '96 - p89 [51-250]
  c SLJ - v42 - O '96 - p41 [51-250]
  Squeak (Illus. by Catherine Walters)
  c TES - F 21 '97 - p16* [51-250]
  Sssh! (Illus. by Tim Warnes)
  c Bks Keeps - N '96 - p20 [51-250]
  This and That (Illus. by Tanya Linch)
  c HB Guide - v7 - Fall '96 - p278+ [51-250]
  c Sch Lib - v44 - Ag '96 - p101 [51-250]
Sykes, Peter - *A Primer to Mechanism in Organic Chemistry*
  J Chem Ed - v73 - D '96 - pA313+ [501+]
Syler, Allen B - *Clark County, Arkansas Obituaries and Death Notices 1914-1921*
  r EGH - v50 - N '96 - p162 [51-250]
Sylla, Richard - *Patterns of European Industrialization*
  BHR - v70 - Sum '96 - p284+ [501+]
Sylvester, David - *About Modern Art*
  Lon R Bks - v18 - S 5 '96 - p16 [501+]
  Spec - v277 - N 16 '96 - p43 [1-50]
  TLS - N 8 '96 - p14+ [501+]
  Francis Bacon
  TLS - Ag 2 '96 - p18+ [501+]
  Looking at Giacometti
  NYTBR - v101 - D 8 '96 - p88 [1-50]
Sylvester, Kathy - *Mommy Got Hurt*
  c Cur R - v35 - S '96 - p12 [51-250]
Syme, Ronald - *Anatolica: Studies in Strabo*
  AHR - v101 - D '96 - p1527+ [501+]
Symmetries in Science VIII
  SIAM Rev - v38 - D '96 - p714+ [51-250]
Symonds, Craig L - *Joseph E. Johnston: A Civil War Biography*
  Historian - v58 - Sum '96 - p876+ [501+]
  Stonewall of the West
  KR - v65 - F 15 '97 - p288 [251-500]
  LJ - v122 - Ap 1 '97 - p108 [51-250]
Symonds, Jimmy - *The Hunchback of Notre Dame (Illus. by Tony Smith)*
  c PW - v244 - My 12 '97 - p77 [51-250]
Symons, Ann - *Protecting the Right to Read*
  Emerg Lib - v24 - S '96 - p40 [51-250]
Symons, Julian - *Playing Happy Families (Shelley). Audio Version*
  BL - v92 - Ag '96 - p1917 [51-250]
  A Sort of Virtue
  TLS - N 29 '96 - p11 [1-50]
Symposium of Fundamentals and Applications of Microalloying Forging Steels (1996: Golden, Colorado) - *Fundamentals and Applications of Microalloying Forging Steels*
  SciTech - v20 - N '96 - p64 [51-250]
Symposium on AIDS, Drugs of Abuse, and the Neuroimmune Axix (3rd: 1995: San Diego, CA) - *AIDS, Drugs of Abuse, and the Neuroimmune Axis*
  SciTech - v20 - D '96 - p46 [51-250]
Symposium on Human Interaction with Complex Systems (3rd: 1996: Dayton, Ohio) - *Human Interaction with Complex Systems*
  SciTech - v20 - D '96 - p13 [1-50]
Symposium on the Ovary: Regulation, Dysfunction, and Treatment (1996: Florida) - *The Ovary: Regulation, Dysfunction, and Treatment*
  SciTech - v20 - D '96 - p52 [51-250]
Symposium Scenario Studies for the Rural Environment (1994: Wageningen, Netherlands) - *Scenario Studies for the Rural Environment*
  R&R Bk N - v12 - F '97 - p39 [51-250]
Symynkywicz, Jeffrey B - *1989: The Year the World Changed*
  y HB Guide - v7 - Fall '96 - p377+ [51-250]
  Germany: United Again
  y HB Guide - v7 - Fall '96 - p381 [51-250]
Synder, Bernadette McCarver - *Have You Seen an Elephant Sneeze?*
  c CLW - v67 - Mr '97 - p43 [51-250]
Syndergaard, Larry E - *English Translations of the Scandinavian Medieval Ballads*
  r TranslRevS - v2 - D '96 - p4+ [51-250]
Synge, J M - *Riders to the Sea. The Shadow of the Glen. The Tinker's Wedding. The Well of the Saints...*
  ELT - v39 - 4 '96 - p504+ [501+]
Sypher, Eileen - *Wisps of Violence*
  VS - v39 - Aut '95 - p81+ [501+]
Syrett, David - *The Defeat of the German U-Boats*
  EHR - v112 - F '97 - p266+ [501+]
  J Mil H - v61 - Ap '97 - p401+ [501+]

Szablya, Helen M - *The Fall of the Red Star*
  y HB Guide - v7 - Fall '96 - p305 [51-250]
Szabo, Corrine - *Sky Pioneer*
  c BL - v93 - F 15 '97 - p1022 [51-250]
  c CBRS - v25 - F '97 - p84 [51-250]
  c HB - v73 - My '97 - p345+ [51-250]
  c KR - v65 - F 1 '97 - p230 [51-250]
  c PW - v244 - F 10 '97 - p85 [1-50]
Szabo, Joe - *Cartoonometer: Taking the Pulse of the World's Cartoonists*
  JC - v46 - Sum '96 - p201+ [501+]
Szabo-Pelsoczi, M - *The Global Monetary System after the Fall of the Soviet Empire*
  Econ J - v107 - Ja '97 - p271+ [51-250]
Szarkowski, John - *Mr. Bristol's Barn*
  PW - v244 - Mr 17 '97 - p73+ [51-250]
Szarmach, Paul E - *Holy Men and Holy Women*
  R&R Bk N - v12 - F '97 - p84 [51-250]
Szasz, Thomas - *The Meaning of Mind*
  LJ - v121 - D '96 - p126 [51-250]
  PW - v243 - S 30 '96 - p73 [51-250]
Szczypiorski, Andrzej - *The Beautiful Mrs. Seidenman*
  Comw - v123 - D 6 '96 - p27+ [501+]
  Trib Bks - My 11 '97 - p8 [1-50]
  The Shadow Catcher
  y BL - v93 - Mr 15 '97 - p1227 [51-250]
  KR - v65 - F 1 '97 - p172 [51-250]
  PW - v244 - F 17 '97 - p211 [51-250]
  WSJ-Cent - v99 - Mr 20 '97 - pA14 [51-250]
Sze, Arthur - *Archipelago*
  Bloom Rev - v16 - Jl '96 - p13 [501+]
  WAL - v31 - Fall '96 - p267+ [501+]
Szechi, Daniel - *The Jacobites: Britain and Europe 1688-1788*
  EHR - v111 - S '96 - p990+ [501+]
Szekely, Istvan P - *Hungary: An Economy in Transition*
  Slav R - v55 - Fall '96 - p670+ [501+]
Szekeres, Cyndy - *I Love My Busy Book (Illus. by Cyndy Szekeres)*
  c BL - v93 - F 1 '97 - p949 [51-250]
  c CCB-B - v50 - Mr '97 - p259 [51-250]
  c KR - v65 - Ja 1 '97 - p66 [51-250]
  c PW - v244 - Ja 20 '97 - p400+ [51-250]
Szekessy, Tanja - *A Princess in Boxland (Illus. by Tanja Szekessy)*
  c HB Guide - v7 - Fall '96 - p279 [51-250]
Szewc, Piotr - *Annihilation*
  TranslRevS - v1 - My '95 - p27 [51-250]
Szirtes, George - *Selected Poems 1976-1996*
  Lon R Bks - v18 - Ag 22 '96 - p25+ [501+]
  TLS - Jl 7 '96 - p26 [501+]
Szold, Henrietta - *Lost Love*
  KR - v65 - Ap 1 '97 - p536 [251-500]
Szostak, Rick - *Technological Innovation and the Great Depression*
  JIH - v27 - Spr '97 - p728+ [251-500]
Szuchman, Mark D - *Revolution and Restoration*
  Historian - v59 - Fall '96 - p159 [51-250]
Szucs, Loretto Dennis - *Chicago and Cook County*
  r NGSQ - v84 - D '96 - p314+ [501+]
  Chicago and Cook County Sources
  r EGH - v50 - N '96 - p165+ [51-250]
  The Source: A Guidebook of American Genealogy. Rev. Ed.
  r BWatch - v18 - F '97 - p3+ [51-250]
Szulc, Tad - *Hoi Ky Duc Giao Hoang John Paul II*
  BL - v93 - My 15 '97 - p1568 [1-50]
  Pope John Paul II: The Biography
  y BL - v93 - D 15 '96 - p717 [1-50]
  Soc - v33 - Jl '96 - p91+ [501+]
Szumski, Bonnie - *Interracial America*
  y Ch BWatch - v6 - My '96 - p5 [51-250]
  Readings on Herman Melville
  y SLJ - v43 - Mr '97 - p209 [51-250]
Szuprowicz, Bohdan O - *Building a Multimedia Presence on the World Wide Web*
  SciTech - v20 - D '96 - p76 [51-250]
  Multimedia Tools for Managers
  HR Mag - v42 - F '97 - p124 [51-250]
Szuszczewicz, E P - *Visualization Techniques in Space and Atmospheric Sciences*
  J Gov Info - v23 - S '96 - p552 [51-250]
Szwarc, Michael - *Ionic Polymerization Fundamentals*
  Choice - v34 - D '96 - p640 [51-250]
  SciTech - v20 - N '96 - p22 [51-250]
Szycher, Michael - *Szycher's Dictionary of Medical Devices*
  r ARBA - v28 - '97 - p606+ [51-250]
Szymborska, Wislawa - *Sounds, Feelings, Thoughts*
  NYTBR - v102 - F 9 '97 - p32 [51-250]

T

Tabak, Daniel - *RISC Systems and Applications*
SciTech - v20 - S '96 - p4 [51-250]
Tabakoff, Boris - *Biological Aspects of Alcoholism*
r AJPsych - v153 - Ag '96 - p1105 [251-500]
Tabari - *The First Civil War*
MEJ - v50 - Sum '96 - p457 [51-250]
The History of Al-Tabari. Vols. 8, 16
MEJ - v51 - Spr '97 - p313 [51-250]
Tabb, William K - *The Postwar Japanese System*
AAPSS-A - v547 - S '96 - p176+ [501+]
Econ J - v107 - Ja '97 - p237+ [501+]
IndRev - v1 - Spr '97 - p618+ [501+]
JEL - v34 - S '96 - p1396+ [501+]
RP - v58 - Fall '96 - p854+ [501+]
Taber, Charles S - *Computational Modeling*
SocSciComR - v15 - Sum '97 - p225 [251-500]
Tabern, Peter - *Piratas En La Casa De Al Lado (Illus. by Korby Paul)*
c BL - v93 - F 15 '97 - p1032+ [51-250]
Taberski, Sharon - *Morning, Noon, and Night (Illus. by Nancy Doniger)*
c BL - v93 - D 15 '96 - p730 [51-250]
c HB Guide - v7 - Fall '96 - p365 [51-250]
Tabili, Laura - *We Ask for British Justice*
JMH - v68 - S '96 - p692+ [501+]
Tabor, Nancy - *A Taste of the Mexican Market*
c Cur R - v35 - S '96 - p13 [51-250]
Tabrah, Ruth M - *The Monk Who Dared*
Tric - v6 - Fall '96 - p135+ [501+]
Tabucchi, Antonio - *Declares Pereira*
Obs - D 1 '96 - p16* [51-250]
Pereira Declares
LATBR - v263 - S 29 '96 - p14+ [51-250]
NYTBR - v101 - Jl 21 '96 - p21 [501+]
RCF - v16 - Fall '96 - p187+ [251-500]
Sostiene Pereira
MLR - v92 - Ap '97 - p487+ [501+]
Tachibanaki, Toshiaki - *Wage Determination and Distribution in Japan*
JEL - v35 - Mr '97 - p239+ [51-250]
Tackach, James - *James Baldwin*
c HB Guide - v8 - Spr '97 - p157 [1-50]
y SLJ - v43 - F '97 - p123 [51-250]
Tackett, Timothy - *Becoming a Revolutionary*
Choice - v34 - N '96 - p521 [51-250]
HRNB - v25 - Fall '96 - p28 [251-500]
TLS - F 28 '97 - p30 [501+]
Tackling Racism and Xenophobia
J Gov Info - v23 - S '96 - p665 [51-250]
Tacou-Rumney, Laurence - *Peggy Guggenheim: A Collector's Album*
LATBR - Ag 18 '96 - p14 [51-250]
LJ - v121 - N 15 '96 - p60 [51-250]
Tada, Joni Eareckson - *Joni. 20th Anniversary Ed.*
BL - v93 - O 1 '96 - p308 [51-250]
Tadie, Jean-Yves - *Marcel Proust: Biographie*
TLS - O 4 '96 - p3+ [501+]
TLS - N 29 '96 - p14 [1-50]
Tadman, Michael - *Speculators and Slaves*
AB - v99 - F 17 '97 - p524+ [501+]
Taeuber, Cynthia M - *Statistical Handbook on Women in America. 2nd Ed.*
r ARBA - v28 - '97 - p338 [251-500]
r Choice - v34 - N '96 - p438 [51-250]
r R&R Bk N - v11 - N '96 - p42 [51-250]
Taft, Robert F - *Il 75 Anniversario Del Pontificio Istituto Orientale*
CHR - v82 - Jl '96 - p479+ [251-500]
Liturgy in Byzantium and Beyond
Rel St Rev - v23 - Ap '97 - p190 [51-250]

Tafuri, Nancy - *The Brass Ring (Illus. by Nancy Tafuri)*
c BL - v93 - O 1 '96 - p360 [51-250]
c CCB-B - v50 - O '96 - p78 [51-250]
c HB Guide - v8 - Spr '97 - p15 [51-250]
c SLJ - v42 - O '96 - p107+ [51-250]
Have You Seen My Duckling? (Illus. by Nancy Tafuri)
c HB Guide - v8 - Spr '97 - p16 [51-250]
Tagaut, Jean - *Odes A Pasithee*
Six Ct I - v27 - Fall '96 - p841+ [501+]
Tagliaferro, Laura - *La Magnificenza Privata*
BM - v138 - O '96 - p693+ [501+]
Tagore, Rabindranath - *The Post Office*
LATBR - N 24 '96 - p2 [51-250]
Tahan, Malba - *The Man Who Counted*
y BL - v93 - Ap 1 '97 - p1342 [1-50]
y Kliatt - v30 - S '96 - p4 [1-50]
Tahir, Baha' - *Aunt Safiyya and the Monastery*
CC - v113 - N 20 '96 - p1169 [51-250]
Choice - v34 - D '96 - p608 [51-250]
MEJ - v51 - Spr '97 - p299+ [501+]
TranslRevS - v2 - D '96 - p19 [51-250]
TranslRevS - v2 - D '96 - p19 [51-250]
WLT - v71 - Win '97 - p216+ [501+]
Tai, Ann T - *Software Performability*
SciTech - v21 - Mr '97 - p10 [51-250]
Tai, Ching - *Wang Shiwei and Wild Lilies*
TranslRevS - v1 - My '95 - p15 [51-250]
Taibbi, Robert - *Clinical Supervision*
Fam in Soc - v78 - Ja '97 - p108+ [501+]
Taibo, Paco Ignacio, II - *Return to the Same City*
LATBR - O 13 '96 - p8 [51-250]
NYTBR - v101 - S 29 '96 - p28 [51-250]
PW - v243 - Jl 22 '96 - p229 [51-250]
Taimni, K K - *Asia's Rural Cooperatives*
Pac A - v69 - Fall '96 - p398+ [501+]
Taitz, Emily - *Remarkable Jewish Women*
y BL - v93 - D 1 '96 - p646 [51-250]
y PW - v243 - N 25 '96 - p78 [1-50]
Taiwo, Olufemi - *Legal Naturalism*
Choice - v34 - S '96 - p209 [51-250]
Takacs, David - *The Idea of Biodiversity*
Nature - v385 - F 13 '97 - p591+ [501+]
New Sci - v153 - F 22 '97 - p45 [251-500]
NYTBR - v102 - Ja 12 '97 - p8 [51-250]
Takacs, Geza - *Hippocrene Concise Hungarian-English, English-Hungarian Dictionary*
r ARBA - v28 - '97 - p394 [251-500]
Takahashi, Patrick - *Ocean Thermal Energy Conversion*
Choice - v34 - N '96 - p489+ [51-250]
SciTech - v20 - S '96 - p54 [51-250]
Takahashi, Y - *Algorithms, Fractals, and Dynamics*
SciTech - v20 - S '96 - p12 [51-250]
Takamado, Princess - *Katie and the Dream-Eater (Illus. by Brian Wildsmith)*
c JB - v60 - D '96 - p233 [51-250]
c Sch Lib - v44 - N '96 - p148 [51-250]
c TES - Ja 31 '97 - pR7 [51-250]
Takamiya, Toshiyuki - *Treasures of the Keio University*
BC - v45 - Win '96 - p560+ [51-250]
Takayama, Sandi - *The Musubi Man (Illus. by Pat Hall)*
c HB Guide - v8 - Spr '97 - p105 [51-250]
Takezawa, Yasuko I - *Breaking the Silence*
Bks & Cult - v2 - N '96 - p30+ [501+]
CS - v25 - N '96 - p751+ [501+]
Tal, Israel - *Bitahon Leumi*
BL - v93 - Mr 1 '97 - p1115 [1-50]
Tal, Kali - *Worlds of Hurt*
Choice - v34 - N '96 - p450+ [51-250]

Talalay, Kathryn - *Composition in Black and White*
NYTBR - v101 - D 8 '96 - p85 [1-50]
Obs - S 1 '96 - p16* [501+]
Trib Bks - My 25 '97 - p8 [1-50]
Talarico, Ross - *Spreading the Word*
J Am St - v30 - Ap '96 - p180+ [501+]
Talaro, Kathleen P - *Foundations in Microbiology. 2nd Ed.*
SciTech - v20 - N '96 - p34 [51-250]
Talbert, Bart Rhett - *Maryland: The South's First Casualty*
Sm Pr R - v28 - Je '96 - p8 [51-250]
Talbert, Charles H - *Reading John*
Rel St Rev - v22 - O '96 - p346+ [501+]
Talbert, Marc - *Heart of a Jaguar*
y PW - v244 - Ap 28 '97 - p77 [1-50]
A Sunburned Prayer
c PW - v244 - Mr 10 '97 - p69 [1-50]
Talbot, Alice-Mary - *Holy Women of Byzantium*
TLS - Ja 10 '97 - p25 [501+]
Talbot, Bryan - *The Tale of One Bad Rat*
c Par Ch - v20 - N '96 - p11 [51-250]
Talbot, Colin - *The Zen Detective*
Arena - Ap '96 - p56 [501+]
Talbot, John - *Fairy Mischief*
c Sch Lib - v44 - Ag '96 - p101 [51-250]
It's for You
y Emerg Lib - v24 - S '96 - p26 [1-50]
Talbot, Vivian Linford - *David E. Jackson, Field Captain of the Rocky Mountain Fur Trade*
WHQ - v28 - Spr '97 - p101 [1-50]
Talbott, Hudson - *Amazon Diary (Illus. by Mark Greenberg)*
c CBRS - v25 - D '96 - p43 [51-250]
c CCB-B - v50 - Ja '97 - p186+ [51-250]
c Emerg Lib - v24 - Mr '97 - p46 [51-250]
c HB Guide - v8 - Spr '97 - p50 [51-250]
c KR - v64 - Ag 15 '96 - p1244 [51-250]
c Learning - v25 - N '96 - p29+ [51-250]
c NW - v128 - D 2 '96 - p88 [51-250]
c SLJ - v42 - S '96 - p208 [51-250]
Excalibur (Illus. by Hudson Talbott)
c BL - v93 - N 15 '96 - p585 [51-250]
c Cur R - v36 - D '96 - p13 [51-250]
c HB Guide - v8 - Spr '97 - p105 [51-250]
c PW - v243 - Jl 22 '96 - p240 [51-250]
c SLJ - v42 - S '96 - p221 [51-250]
Talebones
p SF Chr - v18 - O '96 - p83 [1-50]
Tales of Tears and Laughter
TranslRevS - v1 - My '95 - p4 [51-250]
Talhami, Ghada Hashem - *The Mobilization of Muslim Women in Egypt*
Choice - v34 - F '97 - p1045 [51-250]
Taliaferro, Charles - *Consciousness and the Mind of God*
Comw - v124 - Mr 28 '97 - p25+ [501+]
Taliaferro, John - *Charles M. Russell: The Life and Legend of America's Cowboy Artist*
Bloom Rev - v16 - N '96 - p23 [51-250]
Tall, Emily - *Let's Talk about Life*
MLJ - v81 - Spr '97 - p140+ [251-500]
Tallchief, Maria - *Maria Tallchief: America's Prima Ballerina*
y BL - v93 - Mr 1 '97 - p1103 [51-250]
KR - v65 - F 1 '97 - p209+ [251-500]
LJ - v122 - Ap 1 '97 - p96 [51-250]
NYTLa - v146 - Ap 22 '97 - pC14 [501+]
PW - v244 - Mr 10 '97 - p56 [51-250]
Trib Bks - My 11 '97 - p3 [501+]
WSJ-Cent - v99 - Ap 17 '97 - pA20 [501+]

Talleda, Miguel L - *Alpha 66 Y Su Historica Tarea*
BL - v93 - Ap 1 '97 - p1284 [1-50]
Talley, Nicholas J - *Clinical Examination. 3rd Ed.*
r SciTech - v21 - Mr '97 - p49 [1-50]
Tallis, Raymond - *Newton's Sleep*
SciTech - v20 - D '96 - p4 [51-250]
Tallmadge, John - *Meeting the Tree of Life*
BL - v93 - Mr 1 '97 - p1099 [51-250]
KR - v65 - Ja 1 '97 - p51 [251-500]
Talmage, Ellen - *Container Gardening for Kids (Illus. by Bruce Curtis)*
c BL - v92 - Ag '96 - p1899 [51-250]
c HB Guide - v8 - Spr '97 - p133 [51-250]
c SLJ - v42 - O '96 - p141 [51-250]
Talmage, F E - *Disputation and Dialogue*
Rel Ed - v91 - Fall '96 - p608 [51-250]
Talone, Patricia A - *Feeding the Dying*
SciTech - v21 - Mr '97 - p44 [51-250]
Tamaki, Norio - *Japanese Banking*
Choice - v34 - S '96 - p178 [51-250]
JEL - v34 - S '96 - p1466 [51-250]
TLS - O 25 '96 - p6 [501+]
Tamar, Erika - *Alphabet City Ballet*
c BL - v93 - S 15 '96 - p242 [51-250]
c CBRS - v25 - N '96 - p36 [51-250]
c CCB-B - v50 - Ja '97 - p187 [51-250]
c Dance - v70 - D '96 - p53 [1-50]
c HB Guide - v8 - Spr '97 - p76 [51-250]
c KR - v64 - S 1 '96 - p1329 [51-250]
c PW - v243 - N 11 '96 - p76 [51-250]
c SLJ - v43 - Mr '97 - p193+ [51-250]
The Garden of Happiness (Illus. by Barbara Lambase)
c HB Guide - v7 - Fall '96 - p279 [51-250]
Tamarkin, M - *Cecil Rhodes and the Cape Afrikaners*
Choice - v34 - My '97 - p1553 [51-250]
Econ - v341 - O 5 '96 - p80+ [501+]
R&R Bk N - v11 - D '96 - p12 [51-250]
Tamaro, Susanna - *Follow Your Heart*
LATBR - Ag 25 '96 - p11 [51-250]
Follow Your Heart (Plowright). Audio Version
y Kliatt - v31 - My '97 - p38 [51-250]
Tambiah, Stanley J - *Buddhism Betrayed?*
Am Ethnol - v23 - N '96 - p905+ [501+]
Leveling Crowds
Choice - v34 - My '97 - p1585 [51-250]
Tambini, Michael - *The Look of the Century*
r Am Craft - v57 - Ap '97 - p28 [1-50]
r ARBA - v28 - '97 - p362 [251-500]
BW - v26 - D 8 '96 - p11 [51-250]
Mac - v109 - D 9 '96 - p66 [1-50]
PW - v243 - O 21 '96 - p68 [51-250]
Terence Conran on Design
Mac - v109 - D 9 '96 - p66 [1-50]
Tambling, Jeremy - *Opera and the Culture of Fascism*
Choice - v34 - My '97 - p1510 [51-250]
ON - v61 - Ap 5 '97 - p53 [251-500]
Tamburello, Dennis E - *Union with Christ*
ER - v48 - Jl '96 - p418+ [501+]
Six Ct J - v27 - Fall '96 - p957+ [501+]
Tames, Richard - *Cover-Up: A Curious History of Clothes Uncovered (Illus. by Mark Draisey)*
c Magpies - v11 - S '96 - p41 [51-250]
Exploration into Japan
c BL - v92 - Ag '96 - p1897 [51-250]
c HB Guide - v7 - Fall '96 - p384 [51-250]
Food: Feast, Cooks, and Kitchens
cr Emerg Lib - v23 - My '96 - p44 [51-250]
History of Canals
c Sch Lib - v44 - N '96 - p166 [51-250]
c TES - N 8 '96 - p13* [501+]
Muslim
c HB Guide - v7 - Fall '96 - p308 [51-250]
Tamiozzo Goldmann, Silvana - *Lo Scapigliato In Archivio*
MLR - v91 - Jl '96 - p756+ [501+]
Tamiz, Mehrdad - *Multi-Objective Programming and Goal Programming*
JEL - v34 - D '96 - p2021+ [51-250]
Tan, Amy - *The Hundred Secret Senses*
Ent W - N 29 '96 - p85 [1-50]
y Kliatt - v31 - Ja '97 - p11 [51-250]
NYTBR - v101 - D 15 '96 - p40 [1-50]
PW - v243 - N 4 '96 - p71 [1-50]
WAL - v31 - Sum '96 - p170+ [251-500]
The Joy Luck Club
y BL - v93 - Ja '97 - p833 [1-50]
y TES - F 28 '97 - pR7 [501+]
Tan, C A - *Active Control of Vibration and Noise*
SciTech - v21 - Mr '97 - p74 [51-250]
Tan, Ed - *Emotion and the Structure of Narrative Film*
JC - v47 - Win '97 - p173+ [501+]

Tan, Sheri - *Seiji Ozawa*
c BL - v93 - My 1 '97 - p1492 [51-250]
Tan, Steven - *Hong Kong Coin and Paper Money Catalogue. 4th Ed.*
r Coin W - v38 - F 3 '97 - p72 [51-250]
Tanabe, George J, Jr. - *Myoe the Dreamkeeper*
Rel St Rev - v22 - O '96 - p313+ [501+]
Tanabe, Hiroki - *Functional Analytic Methods for Partial Differential Equations*
SciTech - v20 - D '96 - p18 [51-250]
Tanaka, C - *GABA: Receptors, Transporters, and Metabolism*
SciTech - v20 - S '96 - p23 [51-250]
Tanaka, Katsuto - *Time Series Analysis*
SciTech - v20 - D '96 - p17 [51-250]
Tanaka, Shelley - *Discovering the Iceman (Illus. by Laurie McGaw)*
c BIC - v25 - D '96 - p35 [251-500]
c CCB-B - v50 - My '97 - p336 [51-250]
c Quill & Q - v62 - N '96 - p44 [251-500]
I Was There
c Quill & Q - v63 - F '97 - p51 [51-250]
The Illustrated Father Goose (Illus. by Laurie McGaw)
c Sch Lib - v44 - Ag '96 - p101 [51-250]
On Board the Titanic (Illus. by Ken Marschall)
c BL - v93 - S 1 '96 - p132 [51-250]
y BL - v93 - Ap 1 '97 - p1310 [1-50]
c CBRS - v25 - D '96 - p48 [51-250]
c CCB-B - v50 - S '96 - p34 [51-250]
c HB Guide - v8 - Spr '97 - p76 [51-250]
c PW - v243 - S 9 '96 - p85 [51-250]
c SLJ - v42 - O '96 - p126+ [51-250]
Tanaka, Toshiyuki - *Hidden Horrors*
Aust Bk R - D '96 - p28 [501+]
BAS - v53 - Ja '97 - p62+ [501+]
Choice - v34 - Ja '97 - p854 [51-250]
VQR - v73 - Win '97 - p25* [501+]
Tanaka, Yukiko - *Contemporary Portraits of Japanese Women*
NWSA Jnl - v9 - Spr '97 - p117+ [501+]
Tandeter, Enrique - *Coercion and Market*
Historian - v59 - Fall '96 - p160+ [501+]
Tanenbaum, Andrew S - *Computer Networks. 3rd Ed.*
SciTech - v20 - S '96 - p55 [51-250]
Tanenbaum, Robert K - *Falsely Accused*
Arm Det - v30 - Win '97 - p71 [51-250]
BL - v93 - S 1 '96 - p69 [51-250]
Material Witness
Arm Det - v29 - Sum '96 - p338 [51-250]
Tanenbaum, Susie J - *Underground Harmonies*
Am Ethnol - v24 - F '97 - p235+ [51-250]
CS - v25 - S '96 - p686+ [501+]
Tanenhaus, Sam - *Whittaker Chambers: A Biography*
BL - v93 - F 1 '97 - p924 [51-250]
KR - v64 - D 1 '96 - p1725+ [251-500]
LJ - v122 - F 1 '97 - p90+ [51-250]
Nat - v264 - F 17 '97 - p27+ [501+]
Nat R - v49 - F 10 '97 - p49+ [501+]
New R - v216 - Ap 14 '97 - p38+ [501+]
NL - v80 - F 10 '97 - p15+ [501+]
NY - v73 - Mr 17 '97 - p112+ [501+]
NYTBR - v102 - Mr 9 '97 - p5 [501+]
NYTLa - v146 - F 18 '97 - pC16 [501+]
PW - v243 - D 16 '96 - p48 [251-500]
Time - v149 - Mr 10 '97 - p86 [501+]
Trib Bks - Mr 16 '97 - p3 [501+]
WSJ-Cent - v99 - F 20 '97 - pA18 [501+]
Tang, Haoming - *Kuang Dai Yi Cai. Vols. 1-6*
BL - v93 - N 1 '96 - p484 [1-50]
Tang, Joyce - *Women and Minorities in American Professions*
R&R Bk N - v12 - F '97 - p40 [51-250]
Tang, Qinghua - *Ru He Tou Zi*
BL - v93 - My 1 '97 - p1484 [1-50]
Tang, Xiaobing - *Global Space and the Nationalist Discourse of Modernity*
Choice - v34 - O '96 - p337 [51-250]
Ch Rev Int - v4 - Spr '97 - p29+ [501+]
Hist & T - v35 - 3 '96 - p414+ [251-500]
Tangeman, Michael - *Mexico at the Crossroads*
Workbook - v21 - Fall '96 - p139+ [501+]
Tangherlini, Timothy R - *Interpreting Legend*
WestFolk - v55 - Spr '96 - p172+ [501+]
Tangney, June Price - *Self-Conscious Emotions*
Soc Ser R - v70 - D '96 - p668 [51-250]
Taniguchi, Nancy J - *Necessary Fraud*
Choice - v34 - Ja '97 - p865+ [51-250]
Tanimori, Masahiro - *Handbook of Japanese Grammar*
MLJ - v80 - Fall '96 - p424+ [501+]
Tanizaki, Hisashi - *Nonlinear Filters. 2nd Ed.*
JEL - v35 - Mr '97 - p195 [51-250]

Tanizaki, Junichiro - *Seven Japanese Tales*
NYTBR - v102 - Ja 5 '97 - p28 [1-50]
Tankard, Judith B - *The Gardens of Ellen Biddle Shipman*
CSM - v89 - F 27 '97 - pB2 [251-500]
Tannacito, Dan J - *A Guide to Writing English as a Second Language*
r MLJ - v80 - Win '96 - p539+ [501+]
Tannen, Deborah - *Gender and Conversational Interaction*
NWSA Jnl - v8 - Sum '96 - p117+ [501+]
Gender and Discourse
NWSA Jnl - v8 - Sum '96 - p117+ [501+]
Talking from 9 to 5
NWSA Jnl - v8 - Sum '96 - p117+ [501+]
Tannen, Mary - *Loving Edith*
y Kliatt - v30 - S '96 - p14 [51-250]
Tanner, Albert - *Arbeitsame Patrioten--Wohlanstandige Damen*
AHR - v101 - D '96 - p1573+ [501+]
Tanner, John S - *Anxiety in Eden*
Ren Q - v49 - Aut '96 - p655+ [501+]
Tanner, Laura E - *Intimate Violence*
Critm - v38 - Fall '96 - p650+ [501+]
Tanner, Lee - *Images of Jazz*
BL - v93 - Ja '97 - p805 [51-250]
LATBR - D 8 '96 - p12 [51-250]
PW - v243 - O 21 '96 - p68 [51-250]
Tanner, Marcus - *Croatia: A Nation Forged in War*
KR - v65 - F 1 '97 - p210 [251-500]
LJ - v122 - F 15 '97 - p149 [51-250]
PW - v244 - Mr 17 '97 - p66+ [251-500]
Tanner, Marie - *The Last Descendant of Aeneas*
EHR - v111 - S '96 - p976+ [51-250]
Tanner, Michael - *Wagner*
Choice - v34 - Ap '97 - p1349 [51-250]
CR - v270 - Ja '97 - p56 [51-250]
LJ - v121 - S 15 '96 - p71 [51-250]
ON - v61 - O '96 - p65+ [501+]
TLS - Mr 7 '97 - p18+ [501+]
Tanner, Michael, 1956- - *The End of Welfare*
Choice - v34 - Mr '97 - p1247 [51-250]
Tanner, Rolf - *A Strong Showing*
Pac A - v69 - Fall '96 - p449+ [501+]
Tanner, Stephen L - *Ernest Haycox*
AL - v69 - Mr '97 - p250 [51-250]
Roundup M - v4 - F '97 - p26 [51-250]
Tanner, Suzy-Jane - *The Great Halloween Treat*
c PW - v243 - S 30 '96 - p85+ [51-250]
The Great Santa Surprise
c PW - v243 - S 30 '96 - p93 [1-50]
Tanner, Tony - *Henry James and the Art of Non-Fiction*
ELT - v39 - 4 '96 - p518+ [501+]
Tanous, Peter - *Investment Gurus*
BL - v93 - F 15 '97 - p984 [51-250]
LJ - v121 - D '96 - p112 [51-250]
PW - v243 - D 16 '96 - p51 [51-250]
Tanselle, G Thomas - *The Life and Work of Fredson Bowers*
Lib - v18 - S '96 - p269+ [501+]
Tansini, Raffaella - *I Ritratti Di Agrippina Maggiore*
AJA - v100 - O '96 - p797+ [501+]
Tansman, Alan - *The Writings of Koda Aya, a Japanese Literary Daughter*
MP - v94 - Ag '96 - p132+ [501+]
Tantillo, Leonard F - *Visions of New York State*
Sea H - Win '96 - p44+ [51-250]
Tanzi, Vito - *Taxation in an Integrating World*
Econ J - v107 - Ja '97 - p275+ [51-250]
Tao, Gang - *Adaptive Control of Systems with Actuator and Sensor Nonlinearities*
SciTech - v20 - S '96 - p53 [51-250]
Taormino, Tristan - *A Girl's Guide to Taking over the World*
PW - v244 - Ap 14 '97 - p68+ [51-250]
Tapert, Annette - *The Power of Style*
JPC - v30 - Fall '96 - p225+ [251-500]
Tapia, Orlando - *Solvent Effects and Chemical Reactivity*
SciTech - v21 - Mr '97 - p31 [51-250]
Tapley, Margaret - *Growing Camellias*
BL - v93 - O 1 '96 - p314 [51-250]
Tapley, Rebecca - *The Official Gamelan Java Directory*
r LJ - v121 - D '96 - p138 [51-250]
Tapon, Philippe - *A Parisian from Kansas*
BL - v93 - F 1 '97 - p926 [51-250]
KR - v65 - Ja 15 '97 - p94 [251-500]
LJ - v122 - F 1 '97 - p108 [51-250]
PW - v244 - Ja 6 '97 - p63 [51-250]
Tapori: A Children's Newsletter
cp HER - v66 - Win '96 - p881+ [501+]

Tapply, William G - *Close to the Bone*
BL - v93 - S 15 '96 - p225 [51-250]
KR - v64 - Ag 15 '96 - p1195 [51-250]
The Elements of Mystery Fiction
Arm Det - v29 - Fall '96 - p470 [51-250]
Arm Det - v29 - Fall '96 - p490+ [51-250]
TAPR Software Library. Vol. 1. Electronic Media Version
r SciTech - v20 - N '96 - p76 [51-250]
Taproot Reviews
p Sm Pr R - v28 - S '96 - p21 [251-500]
p Sm Pr R - v28 - O '96 - p14+ [501+]
p Sm Pr R - v28 - D '96 - p13+ [51-250]
Tapscott, Don - *The Digital Economy*
ACI - v9 - Spr '97 - p38+ [501+]
Fut - v31 - Mr '97 - p51 [251-500]
LJ - v122 - Mr 15 '97 - p37 [1-50]
WSJ-MW - v78 - N 5 '96 - pA20 [51-250]
Tapscott, Stephen - *Twentieth-Century Latin American Poetry*
Choice - v34 - F '97 - p972 [51-250]
PW - v243 - Jl 22 '96 - p237 [51-250]
TranslRevS - v2 - D '96 - p4 [51-250]
Tapson, Frank - *The Oxford Mathematics Study Dictionary*
yr TES - O 4 '96 - pR12 [51-250]
Tarabotti, Arcangela - *Che Le Donne Siano Della Spezie Degli Uomini*
MLR - v91 - Jl '96 - p752+ [501+]
Six Ct J - v27 - Fall '96 - p861+ [501+]
Taranovski, Theodore - *Reform in Modern Russian History*
Historian - v59 - Win '97 - p480+ [251-500]
Slav R - v55 - Sum '96 - p489+ [501+]
Tarantino, Quentin - *From Dusk Till Dawn*
TES - Ag 2 '96 - pR6 [1-50]
Taras, Raymond - *Consolidating Democracy in Poland*
PSQ - v111 - Win '96 - p723+ [501+]
Taraseiskey, Haim - *Power Hybrid Circuit Design and Manufacture*
SciTech - v20 - S '96 - p57 [51-250]
Tarbell, Ida Minerva - *More than a Muckraker*
JMCQ - v73 - Win '96 - p1007+ [251-500]
Tarcher, Martin - *Escape from Avarice*
Choice - v34 - My '97 - p1550 [51-250]
PW - v243 - N 25 '96 - p68 [51-250]
Tardiff, Joseph C - *Dictionary of Hispanic Biography*
r ARBA - v28 - '97 - p155 [51-250]
Tarkovskii, Andrei Arsen'evich - *Sculpting in Time*
Parnassus - v22 - 1 '97 - p185+ [501+]
Time within Time
TranslRevS - v1 - My '95 - p23 [51-250]
Tarling, Nicholas - *Britain, Southeast Asia and the Onset of the Pacific War*
Choice - v34 - Mr '97 - p1217 [51-250]
Tarlo, Emma - *Clothing Matters*
Choice - v34 - Ja '97 - p839+ [51-250]
R&R Bk N - v11 - D '96 - p20 [51-250]
TLS - N 1 '96 - p29 [501+]
Tarr, G Alan - *Constitutional Politics in the States*
APSR - v91 - Mr '97 - p200+ [501+]
Tarr, Judith - *King and Goddess*
y BL - v92 - Ag '96 - p1891 [1-50]
BW - v26 - N 10 '96 - p10 [251-500]
Queen of Swords
y BL - v93 - Ja '97 - p822 [51-250]
KR - v64 - D 15 '96 - p1764+ [251-500]
LJ - v122 - F 1 '97 - p108 [51-250]
PW - v244 - Ja '97 - p66+ [51-250]
Tarr, Rodger L - *Marjorie Kinnan Rawlings: A Descriptive Bibliography*
r AL - v69 - Mr '97 - p257 [51-250]
r ARBA - v28 - '97 - p445 [51-250]
r R&R Bk N - v11 - D '96 - p66 [51-250]
Tarrago, Rafael E - *Early U.S.-Hispanic Relations 1776-1860*
r HAHR - v76 - N '96 - p754+ [251-500]
Tarrant, John - *Perks and Parachutes*
BL - v93 - D 15 '96 - p699 [51-250]
Tarrant, Naomi - *The Development of Costume*
R&R Bk N - v11 - D '96 - p20 [51-250]
Tartt, Donna - *Secret History*
Spec - v277 - N 16 '96 - p44 [1-50]
Taruskin, Richard - *Defining Russia Musically*
LJ - v122 - My 1 '97 - p106 [51-250]
PW - v244 - Mr 31 '97 - p50 [51-250]

Stravinsky and the Russian Traditions. Vols. 1-2
New R - v215 - N 18 '96 - p34+ [501+]
NYTBR - v101 - D 8 '96 - p93 [1-50]
NYTLa - v146 - O 7 '96 - pC15 [501+]
Spec - v277 - N 16 '96 - p42 [1-50]
Spec - v277 - N 30 '96 - p44+ [501+]
TLS - S 13 '96 - p3+ [501+]
Text and Act
Notes - v53 - D '96 - p419+ [501+]
Taschek, Jennifer T - *The Artifacts of Dzibilchaltun, Yucatan, Mexico*
HAHR - v77 - My '97 - p295+ [251-500]
LA Ant - v7 - S '96 - p286+ [251-500]
Tashjian, Dickran - *A Boatload of Madmen*
AHR - v101 - D '96 - p1522+ [251-500]
Task Force on Archiving of Digital Information - *Preserving Digital Information*
LAR - v98 - D '96 - p652 [501+]
Tata Energy Research Institute - *Environmental Considerations and Options in Managing India's Long-Term Energy Strategy*
JEL - v34 - S '96 - p1500 [51-250]
Tatalovich, Raymond - *Nativism Reborn?*
J Am St - v30 - F '97 - p479+ [251-500]
MLJ - v80 - Win '96 - p540+ [501+]
Pol Stud J - v24 - Aut '96 - p521 [51-250]
Tatar, Maria - *Lustmord: Sexual Murder in Weimar Germany*
Historian - v59 - Fall '96 - p205+ [501+]
JIH - v27 - Aut '96 - p325+ [251-500]
Tate, Allen - *The Fathers*
Bloom Rev - v16 - S '96 - p28 [51-250]
Tate, C Neal - *The Global Expansion of Judicial Power*
APSR - v90 - S '96 - p684+ [501+]
Tate, Eleanora E - *Secret of Gumbo Grove*
y Ch BWatch - v7 - F '97 - p5 [1-50]
Tate, Eleanore E - *A Blessing in Disguise*
y Kliatt - v30 - N '96 - p11 [51-250]
Tate, Georges - *The Crusades and the Holy Land*
y Sch Lib - v44 - Ag '96 - p126 [51-250]
Tate, Linda - *A Southern Weave of Women*
Critiq - v37 - Sum '96 - p315+ [51-250]
Tate, Sonsyrea - *Little X*
y BL - v93 - Ja '97 - p785 [51-250]
BW - v27 - F 16 '97 - p8 [251-500]
KR - v64 - N 15 '96 - p1660 [251-500]
LJ - v122 - F 15 '97 - p142+ [51-250]
PW - v243 - D 16 '96 - p54 [51-250]
Tate, Suzanne - *Katie K. Whale (Illus. by James Melvin)*
c RT - v50 - O '96 - p134 [1-50]
Tate, William - *Developing Managerial Competence*
R&R Bk N - v12 - F '97 - p37 [51-250]
Tatelbaum, Linda - *Carrying Water as a Way of Life*
PW - v244 - F 10 '97 - p75 [51-250]
Tatham, David - *Winslow Homer in the Adirondacks*
AB - v99 - Mr 3 '97 - p693 [51-250]
Choice - v34 - Ja '97 - p785+ [51-250]
LATBR - Ag 18 '96 - p14 [51-250]
R&R Bk N - v12 - F '97 - p71 [51-250]
Tatham, James - *Evil Seed of the Father*
Aust Bk R - S '96 - p65 [501+]
Tatla, Darshan Singh - *Punjab*
r ARBA - v28 - '97 - p66 [251-500]
Tattersall, Ian - *The Fossil Trail*
New Sci - v153 - Mr 22 '97 - p44 [1-50]
Last Neanderthal
y BL - v93 - D 1 '96 - p664 [1-50]
Taub, Michael - *Israeli Holocaust Drama*
Choice - v34 - Ja '97 - p789 [51-250]
Taulbert, Clifton L - *Watching Our Crops Come In*
y BL - v93 - F 15 '97 - p1000 [51-250]
BW - v27 - F 9 '97 - p3+ [501+]
KR - v64 - D 1 '96 - p1726 [251-500]
LATBR - Ap 20 '97 - p14 [501+]
LJ - v122 - F 15 '97 - p143 [51-250]
PW - v243 - N 25 '96 - p62+ [51-250]
Tauranac, John - *The Empire State Building*
ASInt - v34 - O '96 - p93 [501+]
Taussig, Michael - *The Magic of the State*
Nat - v264 - Mr 17 '97 - p35+ [501+]
Tauxe, Caroline S - *Farms, Mines and Main Streets*
AAAGA - v86 - S '96 - p589+ [501+]
Tavalaro, Julia - *Look Up for Yes*
BL - v93 - Mr 1 '97 - p1095 [51-250]
KR - v65 - F 15 '97 - p288 [251-500]
LJ - v122 - F 1 '97 - p100 [51-250]
PW - v244 - Ja 27 '97 - p88 [51-250]
Tavard, George H - *The Thousand Faces of the Virgin Mary*
RR - v55 - N '96 - p654+ [501+]
Theol St - v58 - Mr '97 - p177+ [501+]

Tavarelli, Andrew - *Protection, Power and Display*
Am Ethnol - v23 - N '96 - p915+ [501+]
Tave, Stuart M - *Lovers, Clowns, and Fairies*
Comp L - v48 - Sum '96 - p296+ [501+]
Taveras, Juan M - *Neuroradiology. 3rd Ed.*
SciTech - v20 - N '96 - p41 [51-250]
Taverdet, Gerard - *Dictionnaire Historique Des Noms De Famille Romans: Actes Du Colloque IV (Dijon, 24-26 Septembre 1990)*
Names - v44 - Je '96 - p132+ [501+]
Tavernier-Courbin, Jacqueline - *The Call of the Wild*
EJ - v85 - S '96 - p98+ [501+]
Taves, Brian - *The Jules Verne Encyclopedia*
r ARBA - v28 - '97 - p435 [251-500]
r Choice - v34 - F '97 - p951 [51-250]
r LAR - v99 - F '97 - p101 [51-250]
Tawa, Nicholas - *American Composers and Their Public*
Notes - v53 - D '96 - p478+ [501+]
Tax, Meredith - *Families (Illus. by Marylin Hafner)*
c Inst - v106 - Ja '97 - p52 [1-50]
c PW - v243 - O 7 '96 - p78 [1-50]
Tayeb, Monir H - *The Management of a Multicultural Workforce*
Choice - v34 - My '97 - p1544 [51-250]
Tayler, Edward W - *Donne's Idea of a Woman*
Sev Cent N - v54 - Fall '96 - p48+ [501+]
Taylor, A - *A Child's Book of Irish Rhymes (Illus. by N Emoe)*
c IB - v60 - D '96 - p261+ [51-250]
Taylor, A G - *Soils, Sustainability and the Natural Heritage*
y New Sci - v151 - S 28 '96 - p50+ [501+]
Taylor, A J - *Archeological Investigations at the Loma Sandia Site 41LK28. Vols. 1-2*
Am Ant - v62 - Ja '97 - p160+ [501+]
Taylor, Ajibola - *Strengthening National Agricultural Research Systems in the Humid and Sub-Humid Zones of West and Central Africa*
JEL - v34 - D '96 - p2131 [51-250]
Taylor, Alan, 1955- - *William Cooper's Town*
AHR - v102 - F '97 - p175+ [501+]
ASInt - v34 - O '96 - p98+ [501+]
Beav - v77 - F '97 - p46+ [51-250]
JEH - v57 - Mr '97 - p246+ [501+]
NYRB - v43 - Ag 8 '96 - p36+ [501+]
NYTBR - v101 - S 22 '96 - p40 [51-250]
RAH - v25 - Mr '97 - p49+ [501+]
TLS - F 28 '97 - p8 [501+]
W&M Q - v53 - Jl '96 - p639+ [501+]
Taylor, Alan D, 1947- - *Mathematics and Politics*
SIAM Rev - v38 - D '96 - p698+ [501+]
Taylor, Alison S - *Simeon's Bride*
Arm Det - v30 - Win '97 - p111+ [251-500]
PW - v243 - Jl 22 '96 - p235 [51-250]
Taylor, Andrew - *The Mortal Sickness*
NYTBR - v101 - Jl 21 '96 - p25 [51-250]
Taylor, Barbara - *About Your Toys*
c LAR - v98 - N '96 - p594 [1-50]
c New Sci - v152 - D 14 '96 - p14 [51-250]
Animal Homes
c CBRS - v25 - D '96 - p44 [51-250]
c CLW - v67 - Mr '97 - p55 [51-250]
c HB Guide - v8 - Spr '97 - p120 [51-250]
c JB - v60 - D '96 - p262 [51-250]
c PW - v243 - N 4 '96 - p78 [51-250]
c SLJ - v42 - N '96 - p116 [51-250]
Arctic and Antarctic
y Emerg Lib - v24 - S '96 - p26 [1-50]
Atlas Visual De Las Aves (Illus. by Richard Orr)
cr BL - v93 - Mr 1 '97 - p1196 [51-250]
Butterflies and Moths
c Par Ch - v20 - O '96 - p25 [51-250]
Color and Light (Illus. by Peter Millard)
c Inst - v106 - Ja '97 - p4* [51-250]
Earth Explained
c KR - v65 - Mr 15 '97 - p469 [51-250]
I Wonder Why Zippers Have Teeth and Other Questions about Inventions
c HB Guide - v7 - Fall '96 - p351 [51-250]
Incredible Plants (Illus. by Geoff Brightling)
c KR - v65 - My 1 '97 - p727 [51-250]
Taylor, Benjamin - *Tales Out of School*
PW - v244 - Mr 17 '97 - p81 [1-50]
Taylor, Bob Pepperman - *America's Bachelor Uncle*
Choice - v34 - Mr '97 - p1168 [51-250]
LJ - v121 - D '96 - p124 [51-250]
Taylor, Bonnie B - *Education and the Law*
r ARBA - v28 - '97 - p221 [51-250]
Taylor, Brian C - *Setting the Gospel Free*
BL - v93 - O 1 '96 - p305 [51-250]
LJ - v121 - O 1 '96 - p86+ [51-250]

Taylor, Bron Raymond - *Ecological Resistance Movements*
  APSR - v90 - D '96 - p957+ [501+]
Taylor, Carol - *Last-Minute Christmas Gifts*
  LJ - v121 - O 15 '96 - p56 [51-250]
Taylor, Charles - *The Oxford Children's Book of Science*
  c BL - v93 - O 1 '96 - p346 [51-250]
  c Ch BWatch - v6 - Jl '96 - p7 [51-250]
  c HB Guide - v7 - Fall '96 - p329 [51-250]
  c SB - v32 - N '96 - p238 [51-250]
  y SLJ - v42 - Ag '96 - p176 [51-250]
  c Smith - v27 - N '96 - p169 [1-50]
Taylor, Charles, 1931- - *The Ethics of Authenticity*
  Quad - v40 - My '96 - p82+ [501+]
Taylor, Charles Alan - *Defining Science*
  Choice - v34 - Mr '97 - p1180 [51-250]
  R&R Bk N - v12 - F '97 - p91 [51-250]
Taylor, Charles R - *Marketing in Asia Pacific and Beyond*
  JEL - v34 - D '96 - p2093 [51-250]
Taylor, Charron E - *Stories to Sleep On (Illus. by Kelly Pulley)*
  c HB Guide - v7 - Fall '96 - p309 [1-50]
Taylor, Chris - *China, a Lonely Planet Travel Survival Kit. 5th Ed.*
  r BL - v93 - S 15 '96 - p210 [1-50]
Taylor, Chuck - *I Am Delighted That You Are Here*
  Sm Pr R - v28 - O '96 - p8+ [501+]
Taylor, Clare - *Women of the Anti-Slavery Movement*
  AHR - v101 - O '96 - p1282 [251-500]
Taylor, Clarence - *The Black Churches of Brooklyn*
  Bks & Cult - v1 - N '95 - p22+ [501+]
  Bl S - v26 - Sum '96 - p67 [1-50]
Taylor, Colin - *What Do We Know about Plains Indians?*
  c Bks Keeps - Mr '97 - p24 [51-250]
Taylor, Cora - *Julie*
  c Quill & Q - v62 - My '96 - p13 [501+]
Taylor, D J - *English Settlement*
  Obs - Ja 19 '97 - p18* [51-250]
Taylor, David, 1942- - *Practical Paediatric Ophthalmology*
  r SciTech - v21 - Mr '97 - p61 [51-250]
Taylor, David W, 1958- - *Flowering Plant Origin, Evolution and Phylogeny*
  Choice - v34 - Ja '97 - p820 [51-250]
Taylor, Debbie - *My Children, My Gold*
  CS - v26 - Ja '97 - p48+ [501+]
Taylor, Dennis - *Hardy's Literary Language and Victorian Philology*
  MP - v94 - N '96 - p256+ [501+]
  RES - v47 - Ag '96 - p437+ [501+]
Taylor, Diana - *Negotiating Performance*
  JPC - v30 - Fall '96 - p226+ [501+]
  TDR - v41 - Spr '97 - p155+ [501+]
  Theat J - v48 - O '96 - p387+ [501+]
Taylor, Don - *Directing Plays*
  TCI - v30 - O '96 - p55 [1-50]
Taylor, Drew Hayden - *Funny, You Don't Look Like One*
  Quill & Q - v62 - S '96 - p69 [251-500]
Taylor, Elisabeth Russell - *Present Fears*
  Obs - Ap 6 '97 - p18* [51-250]
Taylor, Emerson - *Graduates' Guide to Business Success*
  J Car P&E - v57 - Win '97 - p15+ [51-250]
Taylor, Eugene - *William James on Consciousness beyond the Margin*
  New Sci - v152 - O 26 '96 - p46 [501+]
  TLS - D 6 '96 - p6+ [501+]
Taylor, Gary - *Shakespeare Reshaped 1606-1623*
  MP - v94 - N '96 - p233+ [501+]
Taylor, George - *Imagination in Art*
  c HB Guide - v8 - Spr '97 - p137 [51-250]
  c SLJ - v43 - F '97 - p116 [51-250]
Taylor, Graham D - *A Concise History of Business in Canada*
  BHR - v70 - Aut '96 - p422+ [501+]
Taylor, Harriet Peck - *Brother Wolf (Illus. by Harriet Peck Taylor)*
  c BL - v93 - N 1 '96 - p505 [51-250]
  c Emerg Lib - v24 - Mr '97 - p64 [51-250]
  c HB Guide - v8 - Spr '97 - p105 [51-250]
  c SLJ - v42 - O '96 - p118 [51-250]
  Coyote Places the Stars
  c PW - v244 - My 5 '97 - p211 [1-50]
Taylor, Henry - *Understanding Fiction*
  BL - v93 - S 1 '96 - p57+ [51-250]
  LJ - v121 - N 1 '96 - p72 [51-250]
Taylor, Ian - *A Tale of Two Cities*
  Choice - v34 - Ja '97 - p858 [51-250]
Taylor, Insup - *Writing and Literacy in Chinese, Korean, and Japanese*
  JAAL - v40 - S '96 - p79 [51-250]

Taylor, James, 1947- - *The 500-Year Delta*
  BL - v93 - Ap 1 '97 - p1268 [51-250]
  PW - v244 - Mr 24 '97 - p70 [51-250]
Taylor, James, 1952- - *Smoke Proofs*
  Aust Bk R - S '96 - p54+ [501+]
Taylor, James R, 1928- - *The Vulnerable Fortress*
  Archiv - Fall '94 - p204+ [501+]
Taylor, Jane - *Weather in the Garden*
  Hort - v94 - F '97 - p64 [251-500]
  Spec - v277 - D 7 '96 - p55 [51-250]
Taylor, Jeff - *Tools of the Trade*
  Esq - v126 - D '96 - p40 [1-50]
  FHB - Ap '97 - p136 [251-500]
  NYTLa - v146 - N 11 '96 - pC14 [501+]
Taylor, Jeri - *Mosaic. Audio Version*
  Quill & Q - v62 - S '96 - p71 [1-50]
Taylor, Jill McLean - *Between Voice and Silence*
  AJS - v102 - N '96 - p883+ [501+]
  ES - v27 - Fall '96 - p253+ [501+]
Taylor, Jim - *Psychology of Dance*
  Dance RJ - v28 - Fall '96 - p89+ [501+]
Taylor, Joe - *Oldcat and Ms. Puss*
  PW - v244 - Ap 28 '97 - p50 [251-500]
Taylor, John, 1945- - *A Dream of England*
  VS - v39 - Spr '96 - p391+ [501+]
Taylor, John A, 1942- - *British Monarchy, English Church Establishment, and Civil Liberty*
  Choice - v34 - S '96 - p147 [51-250]
Taylor, John B - *Macroeconomic Policy in a World Economy*
  JEL - v34 - S '96 - p1355+ [501+]
Taylor, John McLellan - *Bloody Valverde*
  JSH - v62 - N '96 - p820+ [251-500]
Taylor, John Russell - *Hitch: The Life and Times of Alfred Hitchcock*
  LJ - v122 - F 15 '97 - p166 [51-250]
Taylor, Judy - *Beatrix Potter 1866-1943*
  RSR - v24 - 3 '96 - p23 [51-250]
  Beatrix Potter: Artist, Storyteller, and Countrywoman
  RSR - v24 - 3 '96 - p22+ [51-250]
  So Shall I Tell You a Story
  RSR - v24 - 3 '96 - p26+ [51-250]
Taylor, Kimberly Hayes - *Black Abolitionists and Freedom Fighters*
  y CLW - v67 - Mr '97 - p60 [251-500]
  y HB Guide - v8 - Spr '97 - p176 [51-250]
  y SLJ - v42 - O '96 - p160+ [51-250]
Taylor, Lance - *Reconciling Economic Reform and Sustainable Human Development*
  JEL - v35 - Mr '97 - p278+ [51-250]
Taylor, Marc - *A Touch of Classic Soul*
  y BL - v93 - N 15 '96 - p561+ [51-250]
  LJ - v121 - N 15 '96 - p64 [51-250]
Taylor, Mark Adams - *Prerequisites for Peace in the Middle East*
  J Gov Info - v23 - S '96 - p678+ [51-250]
Taylor, Mark S - *Internetwork Mobility*
  SciTech - v20 - D '96 - p75 [51-250]
Taylor, Mary - *Microsoft Internet Explorer 3.0 Frontrunner*
  LJ - v121 - N 1 '96 - p104 [51-250]
Taylor, Michael, 1946- - *Environmental Change*
  R&R Bk N - v11 - N '96 - p31 [51-250]
Taylor, Michael E - *Partial Differential Equations*
  Choice - v34 - D '96 - p648 [51-250]
Taylor, Michael John Haddrick - *Brassey's World Aircraft and Systems Directory 1996-97*
  r ARBA - v28 - '97 - p653+ [51-250]
  r A & S Sm - v11 - O '96 - p88 [1-50]
  r BL - v93 - Ja '97 - p769 [1-50]
Taylor, Michael Ray - *Cave Passages*
  BW - v26 - O 6 '96 - p9 [501+]
Taylor, Mildred D - *The Friendship*
  y HMR - Win '96 - p45 [1-50]
  The Road to Memphis (Thigpen). Audio Version
  BL - v93 - My 15 '97 - p1596 [51-250]
  Roll of Thunder, Hear My Cry
  c JOYS - v10 - Fall '96 - p35+ [51-250]
  c New Ad - v9 - Fall '96 - p297+ [501+]
  Roll of Thunder, Hear My Cry (Thigpen). Audio Version
  c Ch BWatch - v6 - My '96 - p6 [51-250]
  The Well: David's Story
  y Emerg Lib - v24 - S '96 - p27 [1-50]
  c LA - v73 - O '96 - p432 [51-250]
  c RT - v50 - N '96 - p246 [51-250]
  c RT - v50 - Mr '97 - p479 [51-250]
Taylor, Miles - *The Decline of British Radicalism 1847-1860*
  AHR - v101 - D '96 - p1543 [501+]
  Albion - v28 - Fall '96 - p518+ [501+]
  J Soc H - v30 - Fall '96 - p229+ [501+]

Taylor, Miriam S - *Anti-Judaism and Early Christian Identity*
  Theol St - v57 - Je '96 - p378+ [251-500]
Taylor, P J O - *A Companion to the Indian Mutiny of 1857*
  Obs - Ag 25 '96 - p15* [501+]
  TLS - Ja 10 '97 - p11 [501+]
Taylor, Patricia A - *Easy Care Native Plants*
  BL - v93 - N 1 '96 - p471 [51-250]
  LJ - v121 - N 1 '96 - p99 [51-250]
  PW - v243 - N 18 '96 - p72 [51-250]
Taylor, Patrick - *Only Wounded*
  BIC - v26 - Mr '97 - p37+ [501+]
  Quill & Q - v63 - Mr '97 - p71 [251-500]
Taylor, Paul - *After Andy*
  Meanjin - v55 - 2 '96 - p318+ [501+]
Taylor, Paul, 1963- - *Dutch Flower Painting 1600-1720*
  BM - v138 - N '96 - p759+ [501+]
  Sev Cent N - v54 - Fall '96 - p79+ [501+]
Taylor, Paul Beekman - *Chaucer's Chain of Love*
  Choice - v34 - My '97 - p1500 [51-250]
Taylor, Paul Michael - *Fragile Traditions*
  Am Ethnol - v23 - Ag '96 - p650+ [501+]
Taylor, Pete - *Christian County, Kentucky Newspaper Abstracts. Vols. 3-4*
  r EGH - v50 - N '96 - p168 [1-50]
  Trigg County 1880 Families
  EGH - v50 - N '96 - p168+ [51-250]
  Trigg County, Kentucky Newspaper Abstracts. Vol. 28
  r EGH - v50 - N '96 - p169 [51-250]
Taylor, Peter Hillsman - *The Old Forest and Other Stories*
  BW - v26 - S 15 '96 - p12 [51-250]
  A Woman of Means
  LATBR - O 6 '96 - p15 [51-250]
Taylor, Peter K - *Indentured to Liberty*
  JMH - v68 - S '96 - p726+ [501+]
Taylor, Richard, 1919- - *Restoring Pride*
  CPR - v16 - D '96 - p437+ [501+]
Taylor, Richard F, 1946- - *Handbook of Chemical and Biological Sensors*
  SciTech - v20 - N '96 - p79 [51-250]
Taylor, Robert A - *Rebel Storehouse*
  AHR - v101 - D '96 - p1627+ [501+]
  Historian - v59 - Fall '96 - p161 [251-500]
  JSH - v63 - F '97 - p176+ [501+]
Taylor, Robert M, Jr. - *Peopling Indiana*
  CAY - v17 - Win '96 - p8 [51-250]
Taylor, Rogan P - *Football and Its Fans*
  JPC - v29 - Spr '96 - p255+ [501+]
Taylor, Roger - *The Sun as a Star*
  New Sci - v152 - N 23 '96 - p47 [251-500]
Taylor, S J - *The Great Outsiders*
  NS & S - v9 - My 3 '96 - p41 [51-250]
Taylor, Scott - *Tarnished Brass*
  Quill & Q - v62 - O '96 - p39 [251-500]
Taylor, Sheila Ortiz - *Imaginary Parents*
  PW - v243 - N 25 '96 - p69 [51-250]
Taylor, Sheldon - *Darkening the Complexion of Canadian Society*
  y Quill & Q - v63 - F '97 - p58 [1-50]
Taylor, Stephen - *Shaka's Children*
  NYTBR - v101 - Jl 21 '96 - p24
Taylor, Terry - *Collector's Encyclopedia of Salt Glaze Stoneware*
  r Ant & CM - v101 - D '96 - p31 [51-250]
Taylor, Terry Lynn, 1955- - *The Alchemy of Prayer*
  LJ - v121 - O 1 '96 - p87 [51-250]
Taylor, Theodore - *The Bomb*
  y Emerg Lib - v23 - My '96 - p58 [51-250]
  y Emerg Lib - v24 - S '96 - p25 [51-250]
  c LA - v73 - O '96 - p429+ [51-250]
  y RT - v50 - Mr '97 - p480 [51-250]
  The Bomb (Guidall). Audio Version
  y BL - v93 - N 15 '96 - p604 [51-250]
  Rogue Wave and Other Red-Blooded Sea Stories
  y BL - v93 - N 1 '96 - p491 [51-250]
  y CCB-B - v50 - F '97 - p224+ [51-250]
  y HB Guide - v8 - Spr '97 - p84+ [51-250]
  y KR - v64 - O 15 '96 - p1539 [51-250]
  Walking Up a Rainbow
  y Kliatt - v30 - S '96 - p14 [51-250]
  The Weirdo
  c Bks Keeps - v100 - S '96 - p16 [51-250]
  y Kliatt - v30 - S '96 - p2 [1-50]
  The Weirdo (Guidall). Audio Version
  y SLJ - v42 - Ag '96 - p64+ [51-250]

Taylor, Timothy - *The Prehistory of Sex*
  BL - v93 - S 1 '96 - p43 [51-250]
  BW - v26 - S 8 '96 - p11 [501+]
  Ent W - O 4 '96 - p56 [51-250]
  Nature - v383 - O 24 '96 - p683 [501+]
  New Sci - v152 - O 5 '96 - p49 [251-500]
  NS - v125 - O 18 '96 - p42+ [501+]
  Obs - N 10 '96 - p18* [501+]
  Wom R Bks - v14 - F '97 - p1+ [501+]
Taylor, William B - *Magistrates of the Sacred*
  HRNB - v25 - Win '97 - p64 [251-500]
Taylor, William E - *A Shared Heritage*
  r Choice - v34 - N '96 - p446+ [51-250]
Taylor, William N - *Osteoporosis: Medical Blunders and Treatment Strategies*
  SciTech - v20 - N '96 - p48 [51-250]
Taylor, William O - *With Custer on the Little Bighorn*
  Atl - v278 - S '96 - p113 [51-250]
Taylor, William R - *Inventing Times Square*
  JEL - v34 - D '96 - p2107 [51-250]
  VQR - v72 - Aut '96 - p141* [1-50]
Taylor-Gerdes, Elizabeth - *Straight Up!*
  y Emerg Lib - v24 - S '96 - p26 [1-50]
Taylor-Hall, Mary Ann - *Come and Go, Molly Snow*
  y Kliatt - v30 - S '96 - p14+ [51-250]
  Sew R - v104 - Jl '96 - p476+ [501+]
Tchakerian, Vatche P - *Desert Aeolian Processes*
  GJ - v162 - N '96 - p336 [251-500]
Tchana, Katrin Hyman - *Oh, No, Toto! (Illus. by Colin Bootman)*
  c BL - v93 - Mr 1 '97 - p1174 [51-250]
  c CCB-B - v50 - Mr '97 - p259+ [51-250]
  c KR - v65 - Ja 15 '97 - p146 [51-250]
  c PW - v244 - F 10 '97 - p82 [51-250]
  c SLJ - v43 - Mr '97 - p168 [51-250]
Teachers and Technology
  J Gov Info - v23 - S '96 - p558 [51-250]
Teachers Guide to Cyberspace
  EL - v54 - S '96 - p106 [51-250]
  Inst - v106 - S '96 - p14 [51-250]
Teaching about the Holocaust
  r J Gov Info - v23 - S '96 - p554 [51-250]
Teaching for Justice in the Age of the Good Universities Guide
  Arena - Ag '96 - p52+ [501+]
Teaching Literature in Middle School
  New Ad - v9 - Fall '96 - p346 [51-250]
Teachings of the Tao
  PW - v244 - Ja 13 '97 - p71 [51-250]
Teaford, Jon C - *Cities of the Heartland*
  J Urban H - v23 - N '96 - p120+ [501+]
  T&C - v37 - Ap '96 - p368+ [501+]
  The Rough Road to Renaissance
  J Urban H - v22 - S '96 - p750+ [501+]
Teague, Mark - *How I Spent My Summer Vacation (Illus. by Mark Teague)*
  c HB Guide - v7 - Fall '96 - p279 [51-250]
  c Inst - v106 - N '96 - p26+ [51-250]
  The Secret Shortcut (Illus. by Mark Teague)
  c BL - v93 - S 15 '96 - p251 [51-250]
  c HB Guide - v8 - Spr '97 - p51 [51-250]
  c NY - v72 - N 18 '96 - p101 [1-50]
  c SLJ - v42 - N '96 - p93 [51-250]
Teahan, Sheila - *The Rhetorical Logic of Henry James*
  AL - v68 - D '96 - p858+ [501+]
  J Am St - v30 - D '96 - p492+ [251-500]
Teasdale, Wayne - *The Community of Religions*
  BL - v92 - Ag '96 - p1859 [51-250]
Tebbel, John - *America's Great Patriotic War with Spain*
  LJ - v121 - O 15 '96 - p74 [51-250]
  PW - v243 - S 9 '96 - p74 [51-250]
The Technological Reshaping of Metropolitan America
  J Gov Info - v23 - S '96 - p557 [51-250]
Tedeschi, Richard G - *Trauma and Transformation*
  Readings - v11 - S '96 - p24 [51-250]
Tedesco, Theresa - *Offside: The Battle for Control of Maple Leaf Gardens*
  Mac - v109 - D 16 '96 - p72+ [51-250]
  Quill & Q - v63 - Ja '97 - p31 [51-250]
Tedford, Sandra - *Chickasaw Nation, Indian Territory (Oklahoma) Marriage Book D*
  r EGH - v50 - N '96 - p183 [51-250]
Tedla, Ellini - *Sankofa: African Thought and Education*
  JNE - v64 - Fall '95 - p475+ [501+]
Tedlock, Barbara - *The Beautiful and the Dangerous*
  Am Ethnol - v24 - F '97 - p223+ [501+]
Tedlow, Richard S - *New and Improved*
  Econ - v339 - My 18 '96 - p4*+ [501+]
  JEL - v34 - S '96 - p1463 [51-250]
Teen Voices Magazine
  yp SLJ - v42 - N '96 - p36 [1-50]

Teeple, Gary - *Globalization and the Decline of Social Reform*
  Choice - v34 - S '96 - p220 [51-250]
Tefs, Wayne - *Due West*
  BIC - v25 - O '96 - p6+ [501+]
  Bloom Rev - v16 - Jl '96 - p27 [251-500]
Teicher, Beverly A - *Cancer Therapeutics*
  SciTech - v21 - Mr '97 - p51 [51-250]
Teichgraeber, Richard F - *Sublime Thoughts/Penny Wisdom*
  AHR - v101 - D '96 - p1622 [251-500]
  AL - v68 - S '96 - p641+ [251-500]
  ASInt - v34 - O '96 - p104+ [251-500]
Teichman, Judith A - *Privatization and Political Change in Mexico*
  Choice - v34 - Ja '97 - p847 [51-250]
  JEL - v35 - Mr '97 - p247 [51-250]
Teichroeb, Ruth - *Flowers on My Grave*
  Quill & Q - v63 - F '97 - p43 [251-500]
Teiser, Stephen - *The Scripture on the Ten Kings and the Making of Purgatory in Medieval Chinese Buddhism*
  Ch Rev Int - v4 - Spr '97 - p256+ [501+]
  JR - v77 - Ja '97 - p184+ [501+]
Teitelbaum, Jacob - *From Fatigued to Fantastic!*
  LJ - v121 - D '96 - p134 [51-250]
  PW - v243 - N 4 '96 - p72 [51-250]
Teitelbaum, Matthew - *Paterson Ewen*
  Mac - v109 - D 9 '96 - p66 [1-50]
Teitelbaum, Michael S - *Threatened Peoples, Threatened Borders*
  CS - v25 - S '96 - p594+ [501+]
Teiwes, Frederick C - *The Tragedy of Lin Biao*
  Choice - v34 - F '97 - p1018 [51-250]
Teiwes, Helga - *Hopi Basket Weaving*
  Choice - v34 - Ap '97 - p1408 [51-250]
  LJ - v121 - D '96 - p87+ [51-250]
Teixidor, Emili - *Corazon De Roble*
  y JAAL - v40 - S '96 - p78 [1-50]
Teja, Jesus F De La - *San Antonio De Bexar*
  AHR - v101 - D '96 - p1610 [251-500]
Tejdeep - *Caught in a Stampede*
  WLT - v71 - Win '97 - p226+ [501+]
Tejera, Victorino - *American Modern*
  Choice - v34 - Ap '97 - p1353+ [51-250]
Tekulsky, Matthew - *The Butterfly Garden*
  LJ - v121 - D '96 - p66 [1-50]
Telander, Rick - *In the Year of the Bull*
  BL - v93 - Ja '97 - p759 [1-50]
  y BL - v93 - N 1 '96 - p458 [51-250]
  PW - v243 - N 11 '96 - p67 [51-250]
Telecommunications Technology and Native Americans
  J Gov Info - v23 - S '96 - p558 [51-250]
Teleky, Richard - *Hungarian Rhapsodies*
  PW - v244 - My 5 '97 - p187 [51-250]
Teles, Steven Michael - *Whose Welfare?*
  Choice - v34 - F '97 - p1045 [51-250]
  Pol Stud J - v24 - Aut '96 - p522 [51-250]
Telesco, Patricia - *Seasons of the Sun*
  BWatch - v17 - N '96 - p2 [51-250]
Television Writers Guide. 4th Ed.
  r ARBA - v28 - '97 - p354 [51-250]
Telford, W R - *Mark*
  Rel St Rev - v23 - Ap '97 - p179+ [251-500]
Tellechea Idigoras, Jose Ignacio - *Ignatius of Loyola: The Pilgrim Saint*
  CHR - v82 - O '96 - p711+ [251-500]
Tellegen - *In N*
  TranslRevS - v2 - D '96 - p20+ [51-250]
Tellegen, Toon - *Als We Vlammen Waren*
  WLT - v71 - Win '97 - p168 [251-500]
  Misschien Wisten Zij Alles
  WLT - v70 - Sum '96 - p712 [501+]
Tellermann, Esther - *Pangeia*
  WLT - v71 - Win '97 - p109+ [251-500]
Telles, Matthew A - *Windows 95 API How-To*
  SciTech - v20 - N '96 - p10 [51-250]
Telo, Antonio Jose - *Os Acores E O Controlo Do Atlantico 1898-1948*
  J Mil H - v60 - O '96 - p786+ [501+]
  Portugal E A NATO
  J Mil H - v61 - Ap '97 - p412+ [251-500]
Telotte, J P - *Replications: A Robotic History of the Science Fiction Film*
  J Am St - v30 - D '96 - p500+ [251-500]
Teltser, Patrice A - *Evolutionary Archaeology*
  Am Ant - v61 - Ap '96 - p419+ [501+]
Tem, Steve Rasnic - *High Fantastic*
  Bloom Rev - v16 - S '96 - p16 [501+]
Temam, Roger - *Navier-Stokes Equations and Nonlinear Functional Analysis. 2nd Ed.*
  SIAM Rev - v38 - D '96 - p687+ [501+]

Temko, Florence - *Animals and Birds*
  c CBRS - v25 - N '96 - p36 [1-50]
  c Ch BWatch - v6 - D '96 - p6 [1-50]
  c HB Guide - v8 - Spr '97 - p136 [251-500]
  Planes and Other Flying Things
  c BL - v93 - Ja '97 - p854+ [251-500]
  c CBRS - v25 - N '96 - p36 [1-50]
  c CCB-B - v50 - Ja '97 - p187 [51-250]
  c Ch BWatch - v6 - D '96 - p6 [1-50]
  c HB Guide - v8 - Spr '97 - p136 [251-500]
  Traditional Crafts from Africa (Illus. by Diane Wolfe)
  c BL - v93 - S 1 '96 - p124 [51-250]
  c HB Guide - v8 - Spr '97 - p136 [51-250]
  c SLJ - v42 - O '96 - p141 [51-250]
  Traditional Crafts from Mexico and Central America (Illus. by Randall Gooch)
  c CCB-B - v50 - F '97 - p225 [51-250]
  c HB Guide - v8 - Spr '97 - p136 [51-250]
  c SLJ - v42 - D '96 - p134 [51-250]
Temple, Charles - *Cadillac (Illus. by Lynne Lockhart)*
  c NYTBR - v101 - Ap 7 '96 - p21 [1-50]
  Train (Illus. by Larry Johnson)
  c HB Guide - v7 - Fall '96 - p279 [51-250]
  c LA - v73 - D '96 - p620 [51-250]
Temple, Frances - *The Beduins' Gazelle*
  y Emerg Lib - v23 - My '96 - p43 [1-50]
  y HB Guide - v7 - Fall '96 - p305 [51-250]
  y NYTBR - v101 - O 13 '96 - p26 [1-50]
  The Beduin's Gazelle
  y VOYA - v19 - D '96 - p274 [51-250]
  Grab Hands and Run
  y SLJ - v42 - N '96 - p41 [1-50]
  The Ramsay Scallop
  y Kliatt - v30 - S '96 - p3 [1-50]
  Tonight, by Sea
  c PW - v244 - Ja 13 '97 - p77 [1-50]
  c RT - v50 - F '97 - p426+ [51-250]
  RT - v50 - Mr '97 - p478 [51-250]
Temple, Judy Nolte - *Open Spaces, City Places*
  CAY - v16 - Fall '95 - p9 [51-250]
Temple, Lou Jane - *Revenge of the Barbeque Queens*
  PW - v244 - Mr 10 '97 - p64 [51-250]
Temple, Peter - *Bad Debts*
  Aust Bk R - O '96 - p68 [501+]
Temple Foundation - *Who's Who in Theology and Science. 1996 Ed.*
  r ARBA - v28 - '97 - p535 [51-250]
Templeman, Corinne - *Mother Doesn't Know about Kissing*
  Aust Bk R - O '96 - p67 [51-250]
Templeton, Alice - *The Dream and the Dialogue*
  Col Lit - v23 - Je '96 - p190+ [501+]
Templin, Charlotte - *Feminism and the Politics of Literary Reputation*
  Col Lit - v23 - O '96 - p171+ [501+]
Tenaille, Marie - *Qui Est Mon Meilleur Ami*
  c BL - v93 - N 1 '96 - p500 [1-50]
Ten Boom, Corrie - *The Hiding Place*
  CSM - v89 - Ja 23 '97 - p12 [51-250]
Tench, Watkin - *1788: A Narrative of the Expedition to Botany Bay. A Complete Account of the Settlement at Port Jackson*
  Aust Bk R - N '96 - p19+ [501+]
  TLS - Ja 10 '97 - p32 [501+]
Tenenbaum, Barbara A - *Encyclopedia of Latin American History and Culture. Vols. 1-5*
  r ARBA - v28 - '97 - p162 [251-500]
  r BL - v93 - Ja '97 - p770 [1-50]
  r LJ - v122 - Ap 15 '97 - p39 [51-250]
  r RQ - v36 - Win '96 - p291+ [501+]
  yr SLJ - v42 - N '96 - p139 [51-250]
Tenenbaum, Frances - *Seashore Gardening*
  Hort - v94 - Mr '97 - p78 [51-250]
Teng, Wei - *Zang Hun*
  BL - v93 - My 1 '97 - p1484 [1-50]
Tennant, Agnita - *The Star and Other Korean Short Stories*
  KR - v64 - S 1 '96 - p1267 [51-250]
Tennant, Emma - *Emma in Love*
  Obs - S 29 '96 - p15* [501+]
Tennant, Roy - *Practical HTML*
  LJ - v121 - S 15 '96 - p104 [51-250]
  r RQ - v36 - Win '96 - p316+ [251-500]
Tennekes, H - *The Simple Science of Flight*
  Am Sci - v85 - Ja '97 - p80 [501+]
  A & S Sm - v11 - O '96 - p89+ [251-500]
  y SB - v32 - N '96 - p233+ [51-250]
  Sci - v274 - O 25 '96 - p523 [1-50]
  SciTech - v20 - S '96 - p58 [51-250]
Tenner, Arthur R - *Process Redesign*
  SciTech - v21 - Mr '97 - p2 [51-250]

Tenner, Edward - *Why Things Bite Back*
   BW - v26 - S 29 '96 - p8+ [501+]
   Choice - v34 - N '96 - p490 [51-250]
   For Aff - v76 - Mr '97 - p179 [51-250]
   Sci - v273 - Ag 23 '96 - p1052 [501+]
   SciTech - v20 - N '96 - p59 [51-250]
   SS - v88 - Ja '97 - p42+ [501+]
Tenorio-Trillo, Mauricio - *Mexico at the World's Fairs*
   Choice - v34 - Ap '97 - p1401 [51-250]
Tenquist, Alasdair - *Nigeria*
   c BL - v93 - Mr 1 '97 - p1158 [51-250]
   c HB Guide - v8 - Spr '97 - p171 [51-250]
Tenzin Gyatso, Dalai Lama XIV - *The Good Heart*
   BL - v93 - O 1 '96 - p307 [51-250]
   Tric - v6 - Spr '97 - p95+ [501+]
   Utne R - Ja '97 - p97+ [251-500]
Tepper, Sheri S - *Beauty*
   y VOYA - v19 - D '96 - p266 [1-50]
   The Family Tree
   KR - v65 - Mr 15 '97 - p424 [251-500]
   PW - v244 - Ap 21 '97 - p65 [51-250]
   Gibbon's Decline and Fall
   MFSF - v91 - O '96 - p60+ [251-500]
   New Sci - v152 - O 5 '96 - p50 [51-250]
Terada, Rei - *Derek Walcott's Poetry*
   AL - v69 - Mr '97 - p241+ [251-500]
Teraoka, Masami - *Paintings by Masami Teraoka*
   BW - v26 - S 8 '96 - p12 [51-250]
   BWatch - v18 - Mr '97 - p3 [51-250]
Terasawa, Jun - *Nominal Compounds in Old English*
   RES - v47 - N '96 - p552+ [501+]
Teres, Harvey M - *Renewing the Left*
   Choice - v34 - S '96 - p130 [51-250]
   RP - v59 - Win '97 - p151+ [501+]
Teresa, Mother - *No Greater Love*
   PW - v244 - Ja 13 '97 - p68 [51-250]
Terkel, Studs - *Coming of Age*
   CAY - v17 - Fall '96 - p8 [51-250]
   LATBR - v263 - S 29 '96 - p15 [51-250]
   NS - v126 - Mr 14 '97 - p46 [501+]
   NYTBR - v101 - N 24 '96 - p32 [51-250]
   The Good War
   Trib Bks - F 2 '97 - p8 [1-50]
   My American Century
   BL - v93 - My 1 '97 - p1459 [51-250]
Terkel, Susan Neiburg - *People Power*
   y BL - v92 - Ag '96 - p1894 [51-250]
   y HB Guide - v8 - Spr '97 - p94 [51-250]
   y SLJ - v42 - O '96 - p161 [51-250]
Terlaky, Tamas - *Interior Point Methods of Mathematical Programming*
   SciTech - v21 - Mr '97 - p17 [51-250]
Tern Moeng, Sao - *Shan-English Dictionary*
   r ARBA - v28 - '97 - p399+ [251-500]
Terplan, Kornel - *Effective Management of Local Area Networks. 2nd Ed.*
   CBR - v14 - N '96 - p38 [51-250]
   r SciTech - v20 - S '96 - p55 [51-250]
Terra Nova: Nature and Culture
   p Bloom Rev - v16 - Jl '96 - p17 [51-250]
   p E Mag - v8 - Mr '97 - p49 [51-250]
   p Utne R - Ja '97 - p98+ [501+]
TerraNova
   EL - v54 - D '96 - p88 [51-250]
Terranova, Jerry - *Antique Cigar Cutters and Lighters*
   Ant & CM - v101 - D '96 - p30 [1-50]
Terres, John K - *Songbirds in Your Garden*
   LJ - v121 - D '96 - p66 [1-50]
Terrien, Samuel - *The Iconography of Job through the Centuries*
   AB - v99 - Mr 3 '97 - p692 [51-250]
   The Magnificat: Musicians as Biblical Interpreters
   Intpr - v50 - O '96 - p436 [51-250]
Terriff, Terry - *The Nixon Administration and the Making of U.S. Nuclear Strategy*
   APSR - v90 - S '96 - p707+ [501+]
   Pres SQ - v26 - Sum '96 - p897 [501+]
Terry, Arthur - *Seventeenth-Century Spanish Poetry*
   MLR - v92 - Ja '97 - p228+ [501+]
   Ren Q - v49 - Aut '96 - p628+ [501+]
Terry, Jennifer - *Deviant Bodies*
   CS - v26 - Ja '97 - p107+ [501+]
Terry, Lawrence D - *The Leadership of Public Bureaucracies*
   Pol Stud J - v24 - Sum '96 - p335 [1-50]
Terry, R C - *Robert Louis Stevenson: Interviews and Recollections*
   Nine-C Lit - v51 - S '96 - p278 [51-250]
Terry, Roderick - *One Million Strong*
   y BL - v93 - D 15 '96 - p698 [51-250]

Terry, Roger - *Economic Insanity*
   Per Psy - v49 - Aut '96 - p736+ [501+]
Terzaghi, Karl - *Soil Mechanics in Engineering Practice. 3rd Ed.*
   Choice - v34 - S '96 - p160 [51-250]
Terzi, Antonio - *La Moglie Estatica*
   BL - v93 - D 1 '96 - p644 [1-50]
Tesar, Jenny E - *The New View Almanac (Illus. by David C Bell)*
   yr ARBA - v28 - '97 - p5+ [251-500]
   cr Ch BWatch - v6 - Jl '96 - p2 [51-250]
   yr RQ - v35 - Sum '96 - p561+ [251-500]
   cr SLJ - v42 - Ag '96 - p183 [51-250]
   What on Earth Is a Bustard?
   c HB Guide - v8 - Spr '97 - p125 [1-50]
   c SLJ - v43 - F '97 - p96 [51-250]
   What on Earth Is a Quokka?
   c HB Guide - v8 - Spr '97 - p128 [51-250]
   c SLJ - v43 - Mr '97 - p182 [51-250]
Tesche, Frederick M - *EMC Analysis Methods and Computational Models*
   SciTech - v21 - Mr '97 - p89 [51-250]
Teske, Paul - *Deregulating Freight Transportation*
   Choice - v34 - S '96 - p178 [51-250]
   JEH - v56 - D '96 - p961+ [501+]
   JEL - v34 - S '96 - p1459 [51-250]
Teskey, Gordon - *Allegory and Violence*
   Choice - v34 - My '97 - p1491 [51-250]
Tesler, Nancy - *Pink Balloons and Other Deadly Things*
   PW - v244 - Ap 28 '97 - p73 [51-250]
Tesniere, Marie-Helene - *Creating French Culture*
   Six Ct J - v27 - Fall '96 - p971+ [501+]
Tessin, Timothy - *Philosophy and the Grammar of Religious Belief*
   Rel St - v32 - D '96 - p523+ [501+]
Tessitore, Aristide - *Reading Aristotle's Ethics*
   Choice - v34 - N '96 - p474 [51-250]
   R&R Bk N - v11 - D '96 - p1 [51-250]
Tessitore, John - *The Hunt and the Feast*
   y BL - v93 - Ja '97 - p842 [251-500]
   y HB Guide - v8 - Spr '97 - p161 [51-250]
   y SLJ - v43 - Ja '97 - p136 [51-250]
Testa, Maria - *Dancing Pink Flamingos and Other Stories*
   y Emerg Lib - v24 - S '96 - p25 [1-50]
   y Emerg Lib - v24 - S '96 - p27 [1-50]
   Nine Candles (Illus. by Amanda Schaffer)
   c CCB-B - v50 - S '96 - p34 [51-250]
   c HB Guide - v8 - Spr '97 - p60 [51-250]
   c SLJ - v42 - S '96 - p193 [51-250]
   Someplace to Go (Illus. by Karen Ritz)
   c HB Guide - v7 - Fall '96 - p279 [51-250]
Tester, Keith - *The Inhuman Condition*
   CPR - v16 - Ap '96 - p146+ [501+]
Testerman, Joshua O - *Web Advertising and Marketing*
   BL - v93 - S 15 '96 - p193 [501+]
Tetreault, Mary Ann - *Women and Revolution in Africa, Asia, and the New World*
   CS - v26 - Ja '97 - p50+ [501+]
   HAHR - v77 - F '97 - p159+ [501+]
   J Pol - v58 - Ag '96 - p870+ [501+]
Tettman, Elizabeth - *The Scarlet Landscape*
   Books - v9 - S '95 - p25 [1-50]
Tetzchner, Stephen Von - *Augmentative and Alternative Communication*
   SciTech - v20 - D '96 - p44 [51-250]
Teubal, Morris - *Technological Infrastructure Policy*
   JEL - v34 - S '96 - p1486 [51-250]
   R&R Bk N - v11 - N '96 - p26 [51-250]
Teunissen, Jan Joost - *Can Currency Crises Be Prevented or Better Managed?*
   JEL - v35 - Mr '97 - p220 [51-250]
   Regionalism and the Global Economy
   JEL - v34 - S '96 - p1430 [51-250]
Teveth, Shabtai - *Ben-Gurion and the Holocaust*
   BL - v93 - S 1 '96 - p59 [51-250]
   KR - v64 - O 1 '96 - p1455 [251-500]
   New R - v216 - Mr 24 '97 - p42+ [501+]
   PW - v243 - O 7 '96 - p54 [251-500]
   Ben-Gurion's Spy
   For Aff - v75 - S '96 - p140+ [51-250]
   MEJ - v51 - Spr '97 - p288+ [501+]
   MEQ - v4 - Mr '97 - p85+ [251-500]
Texas Symposium on Relativistic Astrophysics (17th: 1994: Munich, Germany) - *Seventeenth Texas Symposium on Relativistic Astrophysics and Cosmology*
   SciTech - v20 - S '96 - p13 [51-250]
Textile Arts of India
   Choice - v34 - Ap '97 - p1327 [51-250]

Texto Y Espectaculo: Selected Proceedings of the Fourteenth Annual Golden Age Spanish Theatre Symposium
   Hisp - v79 - D '96 - p795+ [501+]
Textos En Contexto. Vols. 1-3
   Lect Y V - v17 - Je '96 - p39+ [501+]
Tezuka, Osamu - *Adolf: A Tale of the Twentieth Century*
   y VOYA - v19 - F '97 - p323 [251-500]
Thacker, Shelly - *His Forbidden Touch*
   PW - v244 - Mr 17 '97 - p80 [51-250]
Thackeray, Frank W - *Events That Changed the World in the Nineteenth Century*
   R&R Bk N - v11 - D '96 - p7 [51-250]
Thadani, Pushpa V - *Biological Mechanisms and Perinatal Exposure to Drugs*
   J Gov Info - v23 - S '96 - p548+ [51-250]
Thaddeus, Eva - *Steps of the Sun*
   PW - v244 - Mr 31 '97 - p64 [51-250]
Thaden, Barbara - *New Essays on the Maternal Voice in the Nineteenth Century*
   ELT - v39 - 4 '96 - p531 [51-250]
Thain, Colin - *The Treasury and Whitehall*
   APSR - v90 - D '96 - p945+ [501+]
   Econ J - v106 - S '96 - p1420+ [501+]
Thakur, Ramesh - *The United Nations at Fifty*
   R&R Bk N - v11 - D '96 - p49 [51-250]
Thakur, Shivesh C - *Religion and Social Justice*
   Choice - v34 - Ap '97 - p1358 [51-250]
Thampu, Valson - *Cross-Cultural Issues in AIDS*
   ER - v48 - O '96 - p527+ [501+]
Thandeka - *The Embodied Self*
   Rel St Rev - v23 - Ja '97 - p46 [51-250]
Tharlet, Eve - *Christmas Won't Wait*
   c Bloom Rev - v16 - N '96 - p29 [51-250]
Thatcher, Carol - *Below the Parapet*
   CR - v269 - O '96 - p224 [51-250]
   Lon R Bks - v18 - My 23 '96 - p15 [501+]
Thatcher, Robert W - *Developmental Neuroimaging*
   SciTech - v21 - Mr '97 - p40 [51-250]
Thau, Richard D - *Get It Together by 30 and Be Set for the Rest of Your Life*
   LJ - v122 - Ap 15 '97 - p94 [51-250]
Thayer, Nancy - *Belonging*
   PW - v243 - S 23 '96 - p74 [1-50]
Theall, Donald F, 1947- - *Beyond the Word*
   Choice - v34 - S '96 - p119 [51-250]
Theesen, Karen A - *The Handbook of Psychiatric Drug Therapy for Children and Adolescents*
   Readings - v11 - S '96 - p29 [51-250]
Theibault, John C - *German Villages in Crisis*
   CEH - v29 - 1 '96 - p116+ [501+]
   Six Ct J - v27 - Win '96 - p1151+ [501+]
Theil, Bernhard - *Germania Sacra. Vol. 4*
   EHR - v111 - N '96 - p1257+ [251-500]
Theil, Henri - *Studies in Global Econometrics*
   R&R Bk N - v12 - F '97 - p33 [51-250]
Theisen, Donna - *Angels of Emergency*
   y Kliatt - v30 - S '96 - p27 [51-250]
Theissen, Gerd - *The Shadow of the Galilean*
   Rel Ed - v91 - Fall '96 - p606 [1-50]
Thelen, David - *Becoming Citizens in the Age of Television*
   Choice - v34 - Mr '97 - p1242 [51-250]
   SFR - v21 - N '96 - p41 [251-500]
Thelwall, John - *The Politics of English Jacobinism*
   Critm - v38 - Fall '96 - p635+ [501+]
   Historian - v59 - Fall '96 - p181+ [501+]
Themerson, Stefan - *Bayamus. Cardinal Polatuo*
   KR - v65 - Ap 1 '97 - p503 [51-250]
Theobald, Marjorie - *Knowing Women*
   Aust Bk R - Je '96 - p15+ [501+]
   Choice - v34 - My '97 - p1552 [51-250]
Theobalds, Prue - *Cinderella (Illus. by Prue Theobalds)*
   c Bks Keeps - Mr '97 - p18 [51-250]
Theodosakis, Jason - *The Arthritis Cure*
   CSM - v89 - F 6 '97 - p14 [51-250]
   CSM - v89 - Mr 6 '97 - p14 [51-250]
   CSM - v89 - Ap 3 '97 - p14 [51-250]
Theoleptos, Metropolitan of Philadelphia - *The Life and Letters of Theoleptos of Philadelphia*
   Rel St Rev - v23 - Ja '97 - p80 [51-250]
Theone, Jess G - *Physician's Guide to Rare Diseases. 2nd Ed.*
   r BL - v93 - F 1 '97 - p958 [1-50]
Therese, De Lisieux, Saint - *The Poetry of Saint Therese of Lisieux*
   Am - v175 - O 26 '96 - p26+ [51-250]
   Am - v175 - N 2 '96 - p30+ [51-250]
   RR - v55 - N '96 - p660 [1-50]

Theriault, Luc F - *Confused? A Kid's Guide to the Internet's World Wide Web*
  c   Ch Bk News - v19 - Spr '96 - p21 [251-500]
Theriault, Reg - *How to Tell When You're Tired*
      NS - v125 - S 13 '96 - p48 [501+]
      PW - v243 - D 9 '96 - p66 [1-50]
Thernstrom, Stephan - *Harvard Encyclopedia of American Ethnic Groups*
  r   ASInt - v34 - O '96 - p8 [51-250]
Theroux, Alexander - *The Primary Colors*
      Bloom Rev - v16 - S '96 - p28 [51-250]
    The Secondary Colors
      BW - v26 - Jl 14 '96 - p4+ [501+]
    Three Wogs
      PW - v243 - D 9 '96 - p66 [1-50]
Theroux, Paul - *The Collected Stories*
      BL - v93 - My 15 '97 - p1542 [51-250]
      Obs - F 2 '97 - p16* [501+]
      Spec - v278 - Ja 18 '97 - p28+ [501+]
      TLS - Ja 31 '97 - p20 [501+]
    The Great Railway Bazaar
      TES - Ag 23 '96 - p21 [51-250]
    Kowloon Tong
      BL - v93 - Mr 1 '97 - p1069 [51-250]
      KR - v65 - Ap 1 '97 - p499 [251-500]
      PW - v244 - Ap 7 '97 - p70 [51-250]
      WSJ-Cent - v99 - My 21 '97 - pA12 [501+]
    The Mosquito Coast
  y   BL - v93 - Ja '97 - p833 [1-50]
    My Other Life
      Atl - v278 - N '96 - p122 [51-250]
      BW - v26 - S 22 '96 - p1+ [501+]
      CC - v113 - N 20 '96 - p1169 [51-250]
      Esq - v126 - S '96 - p184+ [501+]
      FEER - v159 - S 5 '96 - p46+ [501+]
      HMR - Win '96 - p18 [501+]
      LATBR - O 20 '96 - p6 [501+]
      NYTBR - v101 - S 15 '96 - p17 [501+]
      NYTBR - v101 - D 8 '96 - p82 [1-50]
      NYTLa - v146 - S 23 '96 - pC13 [501+]
      Rapport - v19 - 6 '96 - p25 [251-500]
      Time - v148 - S 23 '96 - p76+ [501+]
      WSJ-MW - v77 - S 13 '96 - pA10 [501+]
    My Other Life (Dukes). Audio Version
      PW - v243 - O 7 '96 - p32 [51-250]
    The Old Patagonian Express
      TES - Ag 23 '96 - p21 [51-250]
    The Pillars of Hercules
      CR - v269 - O '96 - p221+ [251-500]
      NYTBR - v101 - D 8 '96 - p92 [1-50]
      NYTBR - v102 - Ja 26 '97 - p28 [51-250]
      Trib Bks - Ja 12 '97 - p2 [51-250]
Theroux, Phyllis - *The Book of Eulogies*
      PW - v244 - Mr 17 '97 - p72 [51-250]
Thesiger, Wilfred - *The Danakil Diary*
      Spec - v277 - N 23 '96 - p51+ [501+]
      TLS - Ap 11 '97 - p29 [501+]
    My Kenya Days
      GJ - v162 - Jl '96 - p240 [51-250]
Thesing, William B - *Robinson Jeffers and a Galaxy of Writers*
      J Am St - v30 - Ap '96 - p157+ [501+]
      RMR - v50 - 2 '96 - p214+ [501+]
Thesman, Jean - *The Ornament Tree*
  y   BL - v93 - Ap 1 '97 - p1294 [1-50]
  y   Ch BWatch - v6 - My '96 - p2 [51-250]
  y   HB Guide - v7 - Fall '96 - p306 [51-250]
    The Rain Catchers
  y   SLJ - v43 - Mr '97 - p113 [1-50]
    Summerspell
  y   Emerg Lib - v24 - S '96 - p27 [1-50]
Theule, Frederic - *Alexander and His Times*
  y   HB Guide - v8 - Spr '97 - p165 [51-250]
  y   SLJ - v42 - D '96 - p140+ [51-250]
Thevet, Andre - *Portraits from the Age of Exploration*
      Ren Q - v49 - Aut '96 - p632+ [501+]
Thibodeau, Serge Patrice - *Le Quatuor De L'Errance Suivi De La Traversee Du Desert*
      WLT - v70 - Aut '96 - p914+ [251-500]
Thiede, Carsten Peter - *Eyewitness to Jesus*
      CLW - v67 - D '96 - p46 [251-500]
      Rapport - v19 - 4 '96 - p36 [251-500]
    Rekindling the Word
      Rel St Rev - v23 - Ja '97 - p70+ [51-250]
Thiel, P J J Van - *Framing in the Golden Age*
      BM - v138 - N '96 - p760 [51-250]
Thiele, Colin - *High Valley*
  c   Magpies - v11 - Jl '96 - p32 [51-250]
    Sun on the Stubble
      Aust Bk R - O '96 - p69 [1-50]

Thiele, Leslie Paul - *Timely Meditations*
      CPR - v16 - Ap '96 - p148+ [501+]
      J Pol - v59 - F '97 - p286+ [501+]
Thielman, Frank - *Paul and the Law*
      J Ch St - v38 - Sum '96 - p649 [251-500]
    Philippians
      Ch Today - v40 - N 11 '96 - p54+ [501+]
Thiemann, Ronald F - *Religion in Public Life*
      Bks & Cult - v2 - Jl '96 - p30 [251-500]
Thienel, Philip M - *Seven Story Mountain*
      JSH - v62 - N '96 - p860 [51-250]
Thiering, Barbara - *Jesus of the Apocalypse*
      Quill & Q - v62 - D '96 - p18 [51-250]
Thierry, Andre - *Histoire Universelle. Bk. 9*
      Six Ct J - v27 - Win '96 - p1137 [501+]
Thiesenhusen, William C - *Broken Promises*
      AAPSS-A - v548 - N '96 - p221+ [501+]
Thiessen, Del - *Bittersweet Destiny*
      Choice - v34 - N '96 - p544 [51-250]
Things That Grow (Snapshot Books)
  c   Ch BWatch - v6 - D '96 - p8 [1-50]
  c   PW - v243 - N 4 '96 - p78 [51-250]
Think Tank Directory. 1st Ed.
  r   ARBA - v28 - '97 - p281 [51-250]
Thiolier-Mejean, Suzanne - *La Poetique Des Troubadours*
      Specu - v72 - Ja '97 - p230+ [501+]
Third World Economics: Trends and Analysis
  p   WorldV - v13 - Ja '97 - p14 [51-250]
Third World Resurgence
  p   Utne R - Jl '96 - p118+ [51-250]
Third World Viewpoint
  p   Utne R - N '96 - p96+ [251-500]
Thirkell, Angela - *Miss Bunting*
      PW - v243 - S 16 '96 - p77 [51-250]
Thirkell, John - *Labor Relations and Political Change in Eastern Europe*
      ILRR - v50 - O '96 - p177+ [501+]
Thirlwall, A P - *The Economies of Growth and Development*
      Econ J - v106 - S '96 - p1482+ [51-250]
Thirteenth Century England V
      Albion - v28 - Fall '96 - p465 [251-500]
This Little Piggy (Illus. by Jane Manning)
  c   PW - v244 - Ap 28 '97 - p77 [51-250]
This Old House
  p   LJ - v122 - F 1 '97 - p53 [1-50]
Thiselton, Anthony C - *Interpreting God and the Postmodern Self*
      Rel St - v32 - S '96 - p428 [51-250]
Thody, Philip - *Barthes for Beginners*
      Obs - Ap 6 '97 - p18* [501+]
Thoene, Bodie - *Shiloh Autumn*
      BL - v93 - N 15 '96 - p571 [501+]
      LJ - v121 - N 1 '96 - p54 [51-250]
Thoene, Brock - *Hope Valley War*
      LJ - v121 - F 1 '97 - p68 [51-250]
Thoenen, Eugenia - *Health Risks*
      J Gov Info - v23 - S '96 - p596 [51-250]
Thole, Lou - *Forgotten Fields of America*
      A & S Sm - v11 - F '97 - p87 [1-50]
Thom, Mary - *Inside Ms.*
  y   BL - v93 - My 1 '97 - p1459 [51-250]
      KR - v65 - My 1 '97 - p707 [251-500]
      PW - v244 - My 12 '97 - p64 [51-250]
Thom, Paul - *The Logic of Essentialism*
      R&R Bk N - v11 - D '96 - p1 [51-250]
Thoma, Clemens - *Parable and Story in Judaism and Christianity*
      Rel Ed - v91 - Fall '96 - p614 [1-50]
    Understanding Scripture
      Rel Ed - v91 - Fall '96 - p606 [1-50]
Thomas, Aquinas, Saint - *Aquinas: Selected Philosophical Writings*
      IPQ - v36 - D '96 - p495+ [251-500]
    On Evil
      Rel St Rev - v22 - O '96 - p348 [51-250]
    The Ways of God
      RR - v55 - N '96 - p661 [1-50]
Thomas, Abigail - *An Actual Life*
      LJ - v122 - My 1 '97 - p164 [51-250]
  y   SLJ - v43 - Mr '97 - p216 [51-250]
Thomas, Alison - *Portraits of Women*
      NYRB - v44 - Mr 6 '97 - p24+ [501+]
Thomas, Allan - *New Song and Dance from the Central Pacific*
      R&R Bk N - v12 - F '97 - p32 [51-250]
Thomas, Anabel - *The Painter's Practice in Renaissance Tuscany*
      BM - v138 - O '96 - p691+ [501+]
      Choice - v34 - Ap '97 - p1327 [51-250]

Thomas, Andrew - *Virtual Help Desk*
      CBR - v14 - Jl '96 - p21 [1-50]
Thomas, Ann G - *The Women We Become*
      PW - v243 - O 21 '96 - p63 [51-250]
Thomas, Anna - *The New Vegetarian Epicure*
  y   Kliatt - v30 - S '96 - p38+ [51-250]
Thomas, Antony - *Rhodes: The Race for Africa*
      Econ - v341 - O 5 '96 - p80+ [501+]
      NS - v125 - D 20 '96 - p119 [501+]
      Obs - N 3 '96 - p17* [501+]
Thomas, Bernice L - *The Kress Legacy*
      BL - v93 - My 1 '97 - p1473+ [51-250]
Thomas, Brian - *The Return of the Native*
      ELT - v40 - 2 '97 - p247+ [501+]
Thomas, Brian J - *The Internet for Scientists and Engineers. 1996 Ed.*
      Choice - v34 - Mr '97 - p1196 [51-250]
      New Sci - v151 - S 28 '96 - p57 [51-250]
Thomas, Briony - *Nutrition in Primary Care*
      SciTech - v21 - Mr '97 - p67 [51-250]
Thomas, Brook - *Plessy v. Ferguson*
      Bl S - v26 - Fall '96 - p106 [51-250]
Thomas, Cecelia E - *The Caseys of the Strande, County Westmeath, Ireland, Canada, and the United States*
      NGSQ - v84 - S '96 - p227 [251-500]
Thomas, Charles Flint - *Art and Architecture in the Poetry of Robert Browning: Appendix A*
  r   Nine-C Lit - v51 - Mr '97 - p566 [51-250]
Thomas, Clara - *All My Sisters*
      Essays CW - Spr '96 - p60+ [501+]
Thomas, D E - *The Verilog Hardware Description Language. 3rd Ed.*
      SciTech - v20 - D '96 - p79 [51-250]
Thomas, D M - *Eating Pavlova*
      SFR - v21 - N '96 - p48 [1-50]
    Lady with a Laptop
      Ent W - Ag 23 '96 - p118 [51-250]
      NYTBR - v101 - Jl 21 '96 - p9 [501+]
Thomas, Dafydd - *Neurology--What Shall I Do?. 2nd Ed.*
      SciTech - v21 - Mr '97 - p52 [1-50]
Thomas, Dave - *SCTV: Behind the Scenes*
      Mac - v109 - D 9 '96 - p64 [1-50]
      Mac - v109 - D 23 '96 - p77+ [501+]
      Quill & Q - v62 - O '96 - p40 [251-500]
Thomas, Dawn C Gill - *Kai: A Mission for Her Village (Illus. by Vanessa Holley)*
  c   HB Guide - v8 - Spr '97 - p69 [51-250]
  c   SLJ - v43 - Mr '97 - p194 [51-250]
Thomas, Donald Serrell - *Lewis Carroll: A Portrait with Background*
      Econ - v340 - S 14 '96 - p6*+ [251-500]
Thomas, Downing A - *Music and the Origins of Language*
      Notes - v53 - D '96 - p486+ [501+]
Thomas, Edward - *Selected Letters*
      Choice - v34 - N '96 - p460+ [51-250]
      ELT - v40 - 1 '97 - p115+ [501+]
Thomas, Eliza - *The Road Home*
      PW - v244 - Ap 7 '97 - p78 [51-250]
Thomas, Elizabeth Marshall - *The Animal Wife (Muller). Audio Version*
      BWatch - v17 - D '96 - p10 [1-50]
    Certain Poor Shepherds
      CC - v113 - D 11 '96 - p1233 [51-250]
      KR - v64 - S 1 '96 - p1270 [51-250]
      LJ - v121 - S 15 '96 - p98 [51-250]
      NYTBR - v101 - D 8 '96 - p102 [51-250]
      PW - v243 - S 2 '96 - p108+ [51-250]
Thomas, Emory M - *Robert E. Lee: A Biography*
      AHR - v102 - F '97 - p192 [251-500]
      CR - v269 - Ag '96 - p108+ [501+]
      Historian - v59 - Fall '96 - p162 [251-500]
      JSH - v62 - N '96 - p809+ [501+]
      TLS - Jl 7 '96 - p36 [501+]
    Robert E. Lee: A Biography (Davidson). Audio Version
      BL - v93 - My 15 '97 - p1596 [51-250]
  y   Kliatt - v31 - My '97 - p48 [51-250]
Thomas, Eric - *Sarah's House*
  c   Ch BWatch - v7 - F '97 - p2 [51-250]
  c   PW - v243 - N 18 '96 - p77 [51-250]
Thomas, Evan - *Back from the Dead*
      BW - v27 - Ap 13 '97 - p13 [51-250]
    The Very Best Men
      NYTBR - v102 - F 23 '97 - p24 [51-250]
      PSQ - v111 - Fall '96 - p530+ [501+]
      PW - v243 - N 11 '96 - p72 [1-50]
Thomas, Frederic C - *Calcutta Poor*
      LJ - v122 - Ja '97 - p122 [51-250]
Thomas, Gail E - *Race and Ethnicity in America*
      SF - v75 - S '96 - p373+ [251-500]
Thomas, Gordon - *Enola Gay*
      LAR - v98 - Mr '96 - p163 [51-250]

Thomas, H Nigel - *How Loud Can the Village Cock Crow? and Other Stories*
  WLT - v71 - Win '97 - p209 [501+]
Thomas, Helen - *Dance, Modernity and Culture*
  TDR - v40 - Win '96 - p154+ [501+]
Thomas, Helmut - *Toxicology of Industrial Compounds*
  Choice - v34 - O '96 - p310 [51-250]
Thomas, Henry - *Living Biographies of Famous Rulers (May). Audio Version*
  LJ - v122 - Ja '97 - p170 [51-250]
Thomas, Herbert - *Human Origins*
  y SLJ - v42 - D '96 - p153 [51-250]
Thomas, Herbert, 1957- - *The Superlative Man*
  KR - v65 - My 1 '97 - p674 [251-500]
  PW - v244 - My 12 '97 - p56 [51-250]
Thomas, Hugh - *Conquest: Montezuma, Cortes, and the Fall of Old Mexico*
  Reason - v28 - D '96 - p37 [51-250]
  World History
  Econ - v341 - N 16 '96 - p3*+ [501+]
Thomas, Jane Resh - *Celebration! (Illus. by Raul Colon)*
  c BL - v93 - My 15 '97 - p1582 [51-250]
  Daddy Doesn't Have to Be a Giant Anymore (Illus. by Marcia Sewall)
  c CBRS - v25 - D '96 - p41 [1-50]
  c HB Guide - v8 - Spr '97 - p61 [51-250]
  c SLJ - v43 - Ja '97 - p93 [51-250]
  Scaredy Dog (Illus. by Marilyn Mets)
  c HB Guide - v8 - Spr '97 - p61 [51-250]
  c SLJ - v42 - N '96 - p93+ [51-250]
Thomas, John A - *Endocrine Methods*
  SciTech - v20 - N '96 - p31 [51-250]
Thomas, Joyce Carol - *Brown Honey in Broomwheat Tea*
  c CLW - v67 - Mr '97 - p15 [1-50]
  Brown Honey in Broomwheat Tea (Dee). Audio Version
  c BL - v93 - Ap 1 '97 - p1313 [1-50]
  Gingerbread Days (Illus. by Floyd Cooper)
  c LA - v73 - D '96 - p624 [51-250]
  c PW - v244 - Ja 27 '97 - p108 [1-50]
Thomas, Julian - *Time, Culture, and Identity*
  R&R Bk N - v12 - F '97 - p12 [51-250]
Thomas, June Manning - *Urban Planning and the African American Community*
  Choice - v34 - My '97 - p1585 [51-250]
Thomas, Keith - *Religion and the Decline of Magic*
  New Sci - v154 - My 3 '97 - p47 [1-50]
Thomas, Mark - *The Disintegration of the World Economy between the World Wars. Vols. 1-2*
  JEL - v34 - S '96 - p1474 [51-250]
Thomas, Michael M - *Baker's Dozen*
  BW - v26 - O 6 '96 - p5 [501+]
  NYTBR - v101 - O 20 '96 - p24 [501+]
Thomas, Naturi - *Uh-Oh! It's Mama's Birthday! (Illus. by Keinyo White)*
  c BL - v93 - F 15 '97 - p1030 [51-250]
  c HB - v73 - Mr '97 - p196 [51-250]
  c KR - v65 - Mr 1 '97 - p388+ [51-250]
Thomas, Nicholas - *Out of Time*
  Am Ethnol - v23 - Ag '96 - p640 [501+]
Thomas, Paul - *Dirty Laundry*
  Aust Bk R - O '96 - p68 [501+]
Thomas, Paul J - *Comets and the Origin and Evolution of Life*
  New Sci - v153 - Mr 8 '97 - p42 [1-50]
Thomas, Peter D G - *John Wilkes: A Friend to Liberty*
  Choice - v34 - Ap '97 - p1399 [51-250]
  TLS - O 18 '96 - p30 [501+]
Thomas, R Murray - *Classifying Reactions to Wrongdoing*
  Soc Ser R - v71 - Mr '97 - p166 [1-50]
Thomas, R Roosevelt - *Redefining Diversity*
  Choice - v34 - O '96 - p327 [51-250]
  J Car P&E - v57 - Win '97 - p20 [251-500]
Thomas, R S - *No Truce with the Furies*
  Agenda - v34 - Spr '96 - p173+ [501+]
  Obs - S 29 '96 - p18* [51-250]
  WLT - v70 - Aut '96 - p966 [501+]
Thomas, Raju G C - *Democracy, Security, and Development in India*
  R&R Bk N - v11 - N '96 - p50 [51-250]
Thomas, Randall - *Environmental Design*
  Choice - v34 - F '97 - p993 [51-250]
  New Sci - v151 - S 28 '96 - p48 [51-250]
Thomas, Randy Ann - *Where Do I Go from Here?*
  r J Gov Info - v23 - S '96 - p588 [51-250]

Thomas, Rob - *Rats Saw God*
  y BL - v93 - Ap 1 '97 - p1296 [1-50]
  y BL - v93 - Ap 1 '97 - p1310 [1-50]
  y Emerg Lib - v24 - S '96 - p54 [51-250]
  y HB Guide - v7 - Fall '96 - p306 [51-250]
  y HMR - Spr '97 - p31+ [501+]
  y SLJ - v42 - D '96 - p32 [1-50]
  Slave Day
  y CCB-B - v50 - Ap '97 - p297 [51-250]
  y KR - v65 - F 15 '97 - p306 [51-250]
  y PW - v244 - F 17 '97 - p220 [51-250]
Thomas, Robert David - *With Bleeding Footsteps*
  J Ch St - v38 - Sum '96 - p643+ [251-500]
Thomas, Roger - *On the Road around Normandy, Brittany, and the Loire Valley*
  r BL - v93 - S 15 '96 - p212 [1-50]
Thomas, Ruth - *Culpable*
  y JAAL - v40 - S '96 - p78 [51-250]
  Hideaway
  c Books - v9 - S '95 - p26 [1-50]
Thomas, S Bernard - *Season of High Adventure*
  Ch Rev Int - v4 - Spr '97 - p261+ [501+]
  FEER - v159 - N 28 '96 - p62+ [501+]
  PHR - v66 - F '97 - p139+ [251-500]
  R&R Bk N - v11 - N '96 - p68 [51-250]
  TLS - O 25 '96 - p10+ [501+]
Thomas, Sue - *Wild Women*
  Rapport - v19 - 4 '96 - p32 [251-500]
Thomas, Theodore N - *Women against Hitler*
  AHR - v101 - O '96 - p1237 [501+]
  J Ch St - v38 - Aut '96 - p911+ [251-500]
Thomas, V - *Winnie in Winter (Illus. by K Paul)*
  c JB - v60 - D '96 - p241+ [51-250]
Thomas, W Jenkyn - *The Welsh Fairy Book*
  Folkl - v107 - '96 - p121+ [501+]
  LJ - v122 - Ap 1 '97 - p134 [1-50]
Thomas, William H - *Life Worth Living*
  BL - v93 - S 15 '96 - p43 [51-250]
  LJ - v121 - O 1 '96 - p118 [51-250]
Thomas Cooper Library - *F. Scott Fitzgerald: Centenary Exhibition, September 24, 1896-September 24, 1996*
  BL - v93 - S 1 '96 - p33 [1-50]
Thomas De Chobham - *Sermones*
  Specu - v71 - Jl '96 - p768+ [501+]
Thomasma, David C - *Birth to Death*
  Choice - v34 - F '97 - p995 [51-250]
  Hast Cen R - v26 - S '96 - p41 [51-250]
Thomassie, Tynia - *Feliciana Feydra LeRoux (Illus. by Cat Bowman Smith)*
  c RT - v50 - N '96 - p257 [51-250]
  Mimi's Tutu (Illus. by Jan Spivey Gilchrist)
  c HB Guide - v7 - Fall '96 - p279 [51-250]
  c NY - v72 - N 18 '96 - p99 [51-250]
Thompson, Alice - *Justine*
  Obs - Ag 18 '96 - p16* [501+]
  TLS - Ag 30 '96 - p22+ [501+]
Thompson, Anthony C - *Minkowski Geometry*
  Choice - v34 - My '97 - p1538 [51-250]
  SciTech - v20 - D '96 - p20 [51-250]
Thompson, Antony Worrall - *Quisine*
  Books - v11 - Ap '97 - p21 [51-250]
Thompson, Bard - *Humanists and Reformers*
  CLW - v67 - D '96 - p40 [251-500]
  HRNB - v25 - Win '97 - p80 [251-500]
Thompson, Becky W - *A Hunger So Wide and So Deep*
  CS - v25 - S '96 - p693+ [501+]
  Names We Call Home
  Bl S - v26 - Fall '96 - p106+ [51-250]
Thompson, Brenda B - *Telecommuting Pluses and Pitfalls*
  LJ - v122 - My 1 '97 - p52 [1-50]
Thompson, Charles P - *Autobiographical Memory*
  Choice - v34 - S '96 - p213 [51-250]
Thompson, Colin - *The Haunted Suitcase*
  c Sch Lib - v45 - F '97 - p34 [51-250]
  How to Live Forever (Illus. by Colin Thompson)
  c Emerg Lib - v24 - S '96 - p43 [1-50]
  c HB Guide - v7 - Fall '96 - p279 [51-250]
  Looking for Atlantis (Illus. by Colin Thompson)
  The Paper Bag Prince (Illus. by Colin Thompson)
  c PW - v244 - Ap 7 '97 - p94 [1-50]
  The Tower to the Sun (Illus. by Colin Thompson)
  c KR - v65 - Mr 15 '97 - p469 [51-250]
  c PW - v244 - Mr 10 '97 - p65 [51-250]
  c Sch Lib - v45 - F '97 - p34 [51-250]
  c TES - Ja 17 '97 - p13* [51-250]
Thompson, Damian - *The End of Time*
  Econ - v341 - D 7 '96 - p6* [501+]
  NS - v125 - N 8 '96 - p44+ [501+]
  Spec - v277 - N 16 '96 - p46 [1-50]

Thompson, David - *Columbia Journals*
  GJ - v162 - Jl '96 - p237 [51-250]
Thompson, Dennis F - *Ethics in Congress*
  BusLR - v21 - 3 '96 - p258 [51-250]
  Ethics - v107 - O '96 - p161+ [501+]
  Hast Cen R - v26 - Jl '96 - p42 [1-50]
  J Pol - v58 - Ag '96 - p914+ [501+]
  Pol Stud J - v24 - Sum '96 - p335 [51-250]
Thompson, Dorothy Davis - *The Road Back*
  BL - v93 - S 15 '96 - p217 [51-250]
Thompson, E P - *Beyond the Frontier*
  NS - v126 - F 21 '97 - p45+ [501+]
  Customs in Common
  Folkl - v107 - '96 - p116 [501+]
Thompson, E V - *Ruddlemoor*
  Books - v10 - Je '96 - p25 [51-250]
Thompson, Edward K - *A Love Affair with Life and Smithsonian*
  Sew R - v104 - O '96 - p673+ [501+]
Thompson, Emma - *The Sense and Sensibility Screenplay and Diaries*
  W&I - v11 - S '96 - p261+ [501+]
Thompson, F M L - *Landowners, Capitalists and Entrepreneurs*
  EHR - v112 - F '97 - p224+ [251-500]
Thompson, Flora - *Lark Rise to Candleford (Dench). Audio Version*
  y Kliatt - v31 - Ja '97 - p42 [51-250]
Thompson, G R - *The Art of Authorial Presence*
  ASInt - v34 - O '96 - p115+ [501+]
Thompson, Gregory Lee - *The Passenger Train in the Motor Age*
  AHR - v101 - D '96 - p1634+ [501+]
  Pub Hist - v18 - Sum '96 - p75+ [501+]
Thompson, Helen Lester - *Sewing Tools and Trinkets*
  Ant & CM - v102 - Mr '97 - p33 [51-250]
Thompson, Henry O - *The Book of Jeremiah*
  r ARBA - v28 - '97 - p543 [51-250]
Thompson, Hilary - *Children's Voices in Atlantic Literature and Culture*
  Quill & Q - v62 - Jl '96 - p59 [251-500]
Thompson, Hunter S - *Fear and Loathing in Las Vegas and Other American Stories*
  Esq - v126 - D '96 - p40 [1-50]
  The Proud Highway
  KR - v65 - Ap 1 '97 - p539 [251-500]
  NW - v129 - My 19 '97 - p85 [501+]
  PW - v244 - Ap 21 '97 - p49 [51-250]
Thompson, I A A - *The Castilian Crisis of the Seventeenth Century*
  HAHR - v76 - Ag '96 - p622 [251-500]
  JMH - v68 - D '96 - p1012+ [501+]
Thompson, J P - *Collecting Black Memorabilia*
  Ant & CM - v101 - D '96 - p32 [1-50]
Thompson, Jack George - *Women in Celtic Law and Culture*
  Choice - v34 - F '97 - p1021 [51-250]
Thompson, James D - *Organizations in Action*
  Per Psy - v49 - Aut '96 - p776+ [501+]
Thompson, Jan - *Christian Festivals*
  c Sch Lib - v44 - Ag '96 - p112 [51-250]
Thompson, Jerry - *Confederate General of the West*
  Roundup M - v4 - D '96 - p22+ [51-250]
  WHQ - v27 - Win '96 - p549 [51-250]
Thompson, Jim - *Jim Thompson Omnibus*
  TLS - Ag 30 '96 - p29 [51-250]
Thompson, John B - *The Media and Modernity*
  Choice - v34 - S '96 - p117 [51-250]
  JC - v47 - Win '97 - p165+ [251-500]
Thompson, John Marcus - *Arthritis*
  SB - v33 - Mr '97 - p40+ [51-250]
Thompson, Jon - *Fiction, Crime, and Empire*
  VS - v39 - Aut '95 - p111+ [501+]
Thompson, Julian F - *Ghost Story*
  y CCB-B - v50 - Mr '97 - p260 [51-250]
  c KR - v65 - F 1 '97 - p229 [51-250]
  c PW - v244 - F 17 '97 - p220 [51-250]
  Shepherd
  y Kliatt - v30 - S '96 - p15 [51-250]
Thompson, Julie - *A Pirate's Life for Me! (Illus. by Patrick O'Brien)*
  c CBRS - v25 - D '96 - p43 [51-250]
  c Cur R - v36 - Ap '97 - p12 [51-250]
  c HB Guide - v8 - Spr '97 - p164 [51-250]
Thompson, Julius E - *The Black Press in Mississippi 1865-1985*
  J Am Cult - v18 - Win '95 - p99+ [501+]
Thompson, Kathleen - *New Jersey*
  c HB Guide - v7 - Fall '96 - p389 [51-250]

New York
c HB Guide - v7 - Fall '96 - p389 [51-250]
c SLJ - v42 - Ag '96 - p161 [51-250]
Pennsylvania
c HB Guide - v7 - Fall '96 - p389 [51-250]
c SLJ - v42 - Ag '96 - p161 [51-250]
Thompson, Kenneth W - *Fathers of International Thought*
JPR - v33 - N '96 - p501 [51-250]
Moral Dimensions of American Foreign Policy
J Ch St - v38 - Sum '96 - p670+ [251-500]
Schools of Thought in International Relations
R&R Bk N - v12 - F '97 - p61 [51-250]
Thompson, Linda - *The Teaching of Poetry*
JAAL - v40 - Mr '97 - p512 [1-50]
Sch Lib - v44 - Ag '96 - p131 [51-250]
Thompson, M M H - *The First Election*
Aust Bk R - Ag '96 - p67 [1-50]
Thompson, M W - *The Medieval Hall*
Albion - v28 - Fall '96 - p461+ [501+]
Thompson, Mark R - *The Anti-Marcos Struggle*
APSR - v90 - D '96 - p946+ [501+]
Pac A - v69 - Sum '96 - p291+ [501+]
PSQ - v111 - Win '96 - p714+ [501+]
Thompson, Mary - *Andy and His Yellow Frisbee (Illus. by Mary Thompson)*
c HB Guide - v8 - Spr '97 - p51 [51-250]
c SLJ - v43 - Ja '97 - p93 [51-250]
Gran's Bees (Illus. by Donna Peterson)
c HB Guide - v7 - Fall '96 - p279 [51-250]
Thompson, Michael S - *Books Change Lives*
JAAL - v40 - F '97 - p415 [51-250]
Thompson, N S - *Chaucer, Boccaccio, and the Debate of Love*
Choice - v34 - My '97 - p1500+ [51-250]
Thompson, Neil - *Ancient Greece*
c Sch Lib - v44 - N '96 - p166 [51-250]
Thompson, Nicola Diane - *Reviewing Sex*
Choice - v34 - O '96 - p282+ [51-250]
Nine-C Lit - v51 - Mr '97 - p566+ [51-250]
Thompson, Noel - *Political Economy and the Labour Party*
NS - v125 - S 6 '96 - p48 [501+]
TLS - Ja 3 '97 - p7+ [501+]
Thompson, Norma - *Herodotus and the Origins of the Political Community*
APSR - v90 - D '96 - p899+ [501+]
Hist & T - v35 - 3 '96 - p415 [251-500]
Thompson, Paul - *Issues in Evolutionary Ethics*
Skeptic - v4 - 2 '96 - p106+ [251-500]
Thompson, Robert J - *Television's Second Golden Age*
Choice - v34 - D '96 - p606 [51-250]
Thompson, Roger, 1933- - *Mobility and Migration*
AHR - v101 - O '96 - p1271+ [501+]
EHR - v111 - N '96 - p1279+ [251-500]
Thompson, Roger C, 1941- - *The Pacific Basin since 1945*
EHR - v111 - N '96 - p1357 [251-500]
Historian - v58 - Sum '96 - p929+ [501+]
Thompson, Roger C, 1944- - *Religion in Australia*
AHR - v101 - O '96 - p1264+ [501+]
Thompson, Roger R - *China's Local Councils in the Age of Constitutional Reform 1898-1911*
AHR - v102 - F '97 - p151+ [501+]
Thompson, Rupert - *Dreams of Leaving*
Obs - O 6 '96 - p18* [51-250]
The Insult
Obs - O 6 '96 - p18* [51-250]
Thompson, Ruth Plumly - *Captain Salt in Oz*
c Ch BWatch - v6 - Jl '96 - p3 [1-50]
Handy Mandy in Oz
c Ch BWatch - v6 - Jl '96 - p3 [1-50]
Thompson, Sharon - *Going All the Way*
CS - v25 - N '96 - p784+ [51-250]
J Am Cult - v19 - Sum '96 - p143+ [501+]
Thompson, Steven K - *Adaptive Sampling*
SciTech - v20 - S '96 - p9 [51-250]
Thompson, Stith - *A Folklorist's Progress*
CAY - v17 - Win '96 - p1 [51-250]
Thompson, Susan Conklin - *Elephants Are Wrinkly (Illus. by Thomas M Smucker)*
c SB - v33 - My '97 - p109+ [251-500]
Thompson, Susan Otis - *American Book Design and William Morris. 2nd Ed.*
R&R Bk N - v12 - F '97 - p101 [51-250]
Thompson, Tommy G - *Power to the People*
Rapport - v19 - 6 '96 - p35 [251-500]
Thompson, Tracy - *The Beast: A Journey through Depression*
y Kliatt - v31 - Ja '97 - p22 [51-250]
NYTBR - v102 - F 2 '97 - p28 [1-50]

Thompson, W Grant - *The Ulcer Story*
SciTech - v20 - D '96 - p48 [51-250]
Thompson, Wendy - *Alopecia Areata*
LJ - v121 - S 15 '96 - p88 [51-250]
Thompson, William - *The Contemporary Novel in France*
WLT - v70 - Sum '96 - p662+ [501+]
Thompson, William Irwin - *Coming into Being*
KR - v64 - My 1 '96 - p678+ [251-500]
Thompson, William M - *The Struggle for Theology's Soul*
Am - v176 - Mr 8 '97 - p30 [51-250]
Theol St - v57 - D '96 - p763+ [501+]
Thompson, William Norman - *Native American Issues*
r ARBA - v28 - '97 - p159 [51-250]
r Choice - v34 - Ap '97 - p1317+ [51-250]
r LJ - v121 - O 15 '96 - p53 [51-250]
r R&R Bk N - v12 - F '97 - p22 [51-250]
Thompson, Willie - *The Left in History*
NS - v126 - Mr 27 '97 - p52+ [501+]
Thomsen, Elizabeth - *Reference and Collection Development on the Internet*
CLW - v67 - Mr '97 - p46 [251-500]
R&R Bk N - v11 - N '96 - p80 [251-500]
SLJ - v42 - O '96 - p46 [51-250]
Thomsen, Jens Peter Frolund - *British Politics and Trade Unions in the 1980s*
R&R Bk N - v11 - N '96 - p32 [51-250]
Thomsen, Moritz - *My Two Wars*
A & S Sm - v11 - F '97 - p88 [251-500]
Thomson, Alistair - *ANZAC Memories*
J Mil H - v61 - Ja '97 - p179+ [251-500]
Thomson, Andrew - *Vincent D'Indy and His World*
TLS - Mr 7 '97 - p19 [501+]
Thomson, D B A - *Heaths and Moorlands*
J Gov Info - v23 - S '96 - p646 [51-250]
Thomson, David - *A Biographical Dictionary of Film. 3rd Ed.*
r FQ - v49 - Fall '95 - p65 [51-250]
Rosebud: The Story of Orson Welles
BL - v93 - Ja '97 - p758 [1-50]
BW - v26 - Ag 18 '96 - p3+ [501+]
Choice - v34 - D '96 - p623 [51-250]
Lon R Bks - v18 - O 3 '96 - p23+ [501+]
NYTBR - v101 - D 8 '96 - p92 [1-50]
Obs - O 6 '96 - p17* [501+]
Si & So - v6 - N '96 - p34 [51-250]
TLS - S 20 '96 - p20 [501+]
W&I - v11 - O '96 - p280+ [501+]
Thomson, Janice E - *Mercenaries, Pirates, and Sovereigns*
EHR - v111 - S '96 - p996+ [251-500]
Thomson, John Mansfield - *The Cambridge Companion to the Recorder*
r Notes - v53 - Mr '97 - p781+ [501+]
Thomson, Keith Stewart - *The Common but Less Frequent Loon and Other Essays*
LATBR - Ag 11 '96 - p11 [51-250]
Thomson, Maynard F - *Breaking Faith*
Arm Det - v30 - Win '97 - p113 [251-500]
KR - v64 - Ag 15 '96 - p1193 [51-250]
Thomson, Pat - *A Band of Joining-In Stories*
c Bks Keeps - N '96 - p8 [51-250]
Superpooch
c Magpies - v11 - Jl '96 - p28 [51-250]
Thomson, Peggy - *The Nine-Ton Cat*
c BL - v93 - Mr 15 '97 - p1240 [51-250]
c CBRS - v25 - Mr '97 - p96 [51-250]
c CCB-B - v50 - Ap '97 - p298 [51-250]
c HB - v73 - My '97 - p346 [51-250]
c KR - v65 - F 15 '97 - p306 [51-250]
c Par Ch - v21 - Mr '97 - p8 [1-50]
Thomson, Peter - *The Cambridge Companion to Brecht*
MLR - v92 - Ap '97 - p527+ [501+]
Thomson, Rosemarie Garland - *Extraordinary Bodies*
CHE - v43 - Mr 28 '97 - pA19 [51-250]
Freakery: Cultural Spectacles of the Extraordinary Body
Choice - v34 - Ap '97 - p1345 [51-250]
Thomson, Ross - *Learning and Technological Change*
Econ J - v106 - N '96 - p1850+ [251-500]
Thomson, Ruth - *The Inuit*
c HB Guide - v7 - Fall '96 - p390 [51-250]
c Sch Lib - v44 - Ag '96 - p112 [51-250]
The Rainforest Indians
c HB Guide - v7 - Fall '96 - p390 [51-250]
c Sch Lib - v44 - Ag '96 - p112 [51-250]
c SLJ - v42 - N '96 - p101 [51-250]
Thomson, Virgil - *Everbest Ever*
LATBR - S 22 '96 - p14 [51-250]

Thon, Melanie Rae - *First, Body*
BL - v93 - D 1 '96 - p642 [51-250]
KR - v64 - N 1 '96 - p1562+ [251-500]
LJ - v121 - D '96 - p150 [51-250]
NYTBR - v102 - F 16 '97 - p27 [501+]
PW - v243 - N 4 '96 - p62 [51-250]
Thondup, Tulku - *The Healing Power of Mind*
BL - v93 - S 15 '96 - p185 [51-250]
BWatch - v18 - F '97 - p10 [1-50]
The Masters of Meditation and Miracles
Tric - v6 - Spr '97 - p111+ [501+]
Thorbeck, Susanne - *Gender and Slum Culture in Urban Asia*
CS - v25 - S '96 - p646+ [501+]
Thore, Sten - *The Diversity, Complexity, and Evolution of High Tech-Capitalism*
JEL - v34 - S '96 - p1486 [51-250]
Thoreau, Henry David - *Walden*
LJ - v122 - Mr 15 '97 - p94 [51-250]
A Week on the Concord and Merrimack Rivers
Nine-C Lit - v51 - D '96 - p304+ [501+]
Thormahlen, Marianne - *T.S. Eliot at the Turn of the Century*
RES - v47 - N '96 - p627+ [501+]
Thorndike, John - *Another Way Home*
BW - v26 - Jl 7 '96 - p13 [51-250]
Thorndike-Barnhart Junior Dictionary. Rev. Ed.
cr SLJ - v42 - N '96 - p139 [51-250]
Thorne, John - *Serious Pig*
BL - v93 - N 15 '96 - p561 [51-250]
KR - v64 - S 1 '96 - p1311 [51-250]
LJ - v121 - N 15 '96 - p83 [51-250]
PW - v243 - O 21 '96 - p66 [51-250]
Thorne, Kip S - *Black Holes and Time Warps*
Skeptic - v3 - '95 - p100 [51-250]
Thorne, Nicola - *Repossession*
BL - v93 - Ja '97 - p826 [51-250]
PW - v243 - N 18 '96 - p63+ [51-250]
Trophy Wife (David). Audio Version
y Kliatt - v31 - Ja '97 - p47 [51-250]
Thorne, Sally E - *Nursing Praxis*
SciTech - v21 - Mr '97 - p69 [51-250]
Thorne-Thomsen, Kathleen - *Shaker Children*
c SLJ - v42 - Ag '96 - p161 [51-250]
Thornhill, Arthur H, III - *Six Circles, One Dewdrop*
HJAS - v56 - 2 '96 - p527+ [501+]
Thornhill, Jan - *Wild in the City (Illus. by Jan Thornhill)*
c BL - v93 - D 1 '96 - p663 [51-250]
c CBRS - v25 - S '96 - p6 [51-250]
c CCB-B - v50 - D '96 - p154 [51-250]
c HB Guide - v8 - Spr '97 - p51 [51-250]
c PW - v243 - O 7 '96 - p69 [51-250]
c SLJ - v42 - O '96 - p108 [51-250]
Thornhill, Teresa - *Sweet Tea with Cardamom*
Obs - Ja 26 '97 - p18* [51-250]
TLS - Ja 31 '97 - p29 [51-250]
Thornley, Diann - *Dominion's Reach*
KR - v65 - Ja 1 '97 - p28 [51-250]
LJ - v122 - Mr 15 '97 - p93 [1-50]
PW - v244 - F 24 '97 - p69 [51-250]
Thornley, Stew - *Emmitt Smith: Relentless Rusher*
c Ch BWatch - v7 - F '97 - p7 [1-50]
Sports Great Dennis Rodman
c HB Guide - v7 - Fall '96 - p361 [51-250]
Sports Great Reggie Miller
c HB Guide - v8 - Spr '97 - p143 [1-50]
Thornton, Arland - *Social Change and the Family in Taiwan*
CS - v26 - Ja '97 - p76+ [501+]
Thornton, Betsy - *The Cowboy Rides Away*
Arm Det - v29 - Fall '96 - p479 [251-500]
Thornton, Billy Bob - *Sling Blade*
Ent W - Mr 28 '97 - p61 [51-250]
Thornton, Bruce S - *Eros: The Myth of Ancient Greek Sexuality*
KR - v64 - D 1 '96 - p1726+ [251-500]
Obs - F 23 '97 - p15* [501+]
Thornton, Elizabeth - *The Bride's Bodyguard*
PW - v244 - F 3 '97 - p100 [51-250]
Dangerous to Hold
Arm Det - v29 - Fall '96 - p489 [251-500]
Thornton, Ian - *Krakatau: The Destruction and Reassembly of an Island Ecosystem*
y Kliatt - v31 - Mr '97 - p5+ [51-250]
Nature - v381 - My 16 '96 - p205+ [501+]
New Sci - v151 - S 21 '96 - p52 [501+]
SB - v32 - O '96 - p201 [51-250]
Sci - v274 - N 22 '96 - p1320 [501+]
TLS - F 21 '97 - p32 [501+]
Thornton, Kevin - *Tanks and Industry*
Pub Hist - v19 - Win '97 - p117+ [251-500]

Thornton, Lawrence - *Naming the Spirits*
  y Kliatt - v30 - N '96 - p11 [51-250]
Thornton, Sarah - *Club Cultures*
     AJS - v102 - N '96 - p927+ [501+]
     Socio R - v44 - N '96 - p778+ [501+]
Thornton, Tamara Plakins - *Handwriting in America*
     Choice - v34 - Ap '97 - p1408 [51-250]
     KR - v64 - O 15 '96 - p1522 [251-500]
     LJ - v121 - D '96 - p119 [51-250]
     NY - v72 - F 3 '97 - p79+ [501+]
     PW - v243 - N 25 '96 - p64+ [51-250]
Thornton, William - *Papers of William Thornton. Vol. 1*
     JSH - v63 - F '97 - p154+ [251-500]
Thornton, Willis - *Almanac for Americans*
  r JPC - v29 - Spr '96 - p258+ [51-250]
Thornton, Yvonne S - *Ditchdigger's Daughters*
  y Emerg Lib - v24 - S '96 - p24 [1-50]
Primary Care for the Obstetrician and Gynecologist
     SciTech - v21 - Mr '97 - p48 [51-250]
Woman to Woman
     BL - v93 - My 15 '97 - p1551 [51-250]
Thorp, Malcolm R - *Politics, Religion and Diplomacy in Early Modern Europe*
     CH - v65 - D '96 - p710+ [251-500]
     Historian - v59 - Win '97 - p481+ [51-250]
Thorp, Marilyn - *Designing and Making*
     TES - D 13 '96 - p43 [51-250]
Thorp, Nigel - *The Glory of the Page*
     AB - v99 - Mr 3 '97 - p685+ [501+]
Thorpe, Andrew - *A History of the British Labour Party*
     LJ - v122 - My 1 '97 - p122 [51-250]
Thorpe, Brian - *Quality Assurance in Construction. 2nd Ed.*
     SciTech - v20 - D '96 - p60 [51-250]
Thorpe, D R - *Alec Douglas-Home*
     Econ - v341 - N 30 '96 - p90 [501+]
     Lon R Bks - v18 - O 17 '96 - p12+ [501+]
     Obs - D 15 '96 - p17* [501+]
     Spec - v277 - O 26 '96 - p55+ [501+]
     TLS - N 8 '96 - p24 [501+]
Thorpe, Tony - *Young Citizen's Passport*
  y Sch Lib - v44 - Ag '96 - p126+ [51-250]
Thorson, John E - *River of Promise, River of Peril*
     AHR - v101 - O '96 - p1304 [251-500]
     SSQ - v77 - S '96 - p720+ [251-500]
A Thousand Years of Czech Culture
     Mag Antiq - v150 - D '96 - p760+ [501+]
     R&R Bk N - v12 - F '97 - p15 [51-250]
Threadgall, Colin - *Animal Families*
  c Bks Keeps - Jl '96 - p6 [51-250]
Animal Homes
  c Bks Keeps - Jl '96 - p6 [51-250]
Throne, James L - *Technology of Thermoforming*
     SciTech - v21 - Mr '97 - p97 [51-250]
Throop, Eugene F - *Lancaster County, Pennsylvania Divorces 1786-1832*
  r EGH - v50 - N '96 - p185 [51-250]
Through Indian Eyes
     Roundup M - v4 - O '96 - p28+ [51-250]
Thrower, Norman J W - *Maps and Civilization*
     Choice - v34 - S '96 - p182 [51-250]
Thrun, Sebastian - *Explanation-Based Neural Network Learning*
     SciTech - v21 - Mr '97 - p10 [51-250]
Thubron, Colin - *Distance*
     ILN - Christmas '96 - p90 [51-250]
     Obs - S 15 '96 - p15* [501+]
     Spec - v277 - S 21 '96 - p54 [51-250]
     TLS - S 20 '96 - p23 [501+]
     Woman's J - O '96 - p12 [51-250]
Thucydides - *The Landmark Thucydides*
     BW - v26 - S 22 '96 - p13 [51-250]
     J Mil H - v61 - Ap '97 - p358+ [501+]
  r LATBR - D 8 '96 - p8 [51-250]
     Mar Crp G - v81 - Ja '97 - p70 [501+]
  r R&R Bk N - v12 - F '97 - p16 [51-250]
Thue, Anniken - *Tone Vigeland*
     Am Craft - v56 - Ag '96 - p66 [1-50]
Thumser, Matthias - *Rom Und Der Romische Adel In Der Spaten Stauferzeit*
     AHR - v101 - O '96 - p1196+ [501+]
Thurber, James - *Writings and Drawings*
     BL - v93 - S 1 '96 - p57 [51-250]
     Bloom Rev - v16 - N '96 - p15 [51-250]
     BWatch - v17 - D '96 - p7 [51-250]
     Comw - v124 - F 28 '97 - p22+ [501+]
     LATBR - D 8 '96 - p8 [51-250]
     LJ - v121 - S 15 '96 - p69 [51-250]
     NYTBR - v101 - N 10 '96 - p57 [51-250]
     VLS - Win '96 - p28 [501+]

Thurber, James A - *Remaking Congress*
     APSR - v90 - D '96 - p925+ [501+]
     J Gov Info - v24 - Ja '97 - p67+ [501+]
Rivals for Power
     APSR - v91 - Mr '97 - p201+ [501+]
Thurlo, Aimee - *Death Walker*
     Arm Det - v29 - Sum '96 - p361+ [251-500]
  y SLJ - v43 - Mr '97 - p216+ [51-250]
Thurlow, Richard - *The Secret State*
     AHR - v102 - F '97 - p116 [251-500]
Thurm, Marian - *The Clairvoyant*
     KR - v65 - Ap 1 '97 - p500 [251-500]
     LJ - v122 - My 1 '97 - p141+ [51-250]
     PW - v244 - My 12 '97 - p58 [51-250]
Thurman, Robert A F - *Essential Tibetan Buddhism*
     Nat R - v48 - O 28 '96 - p73+ [501+]
Thurmon, John C - *Lumb and Jones' Veterinary Anesthesia. 3rd Ed.*
     SciTech - v20 - N '96 - p58 [51-250]
Thurmond, Amy S - *Gynecologic, Obstetric, and Breast Radiology*
     SciTech - v21 - Mr '97 - p63 [51-250]
Thurow, Lester C - *The Future of Capitalism*
     Bus Bk R - v13 - 4 '96 - p4+ [501+]
     CC - v113 - N 13 '96 - p1118+ [501+]
     For Aff - v75 - S '96 - p138 [251-500]
     Har Bus R - v74 - S '96 - p173+ [501+]
     LJ - v122 - Mr 15 '97 - p37 [1-50]
     PW - v244 - Mr 3 '97 - p72 [1-50]
     Quad - v40 - D '96 - p74+ [501+]
Thurston, Bonnie - *Reading Colossians, Ephesians and 2 Thessalonians*
     Rel St Rev - v23 - Ap '97 - p185 [51-250]
Thurston, Harry - *The World of the Shorebirds*
  y BL - v93 - D 1 '96 - p632 [51-250]
     PW - v243 - O 21 '96 - p68 [1-50]
  y SLJ - v43 - Mr '97 - p218 [51-250]
Thurston, John - *The Work of Words*
     R&R Bk N - v11 - N '96 - p71 [51-250]
Thurston, Mary Elizabeth - *The Lost History of the Canine Race*
     Choice - v34 - My '97 - p1526 [51-250]
     KR - v64 - O 1 '96 - p1456 [251-500]
Thurston, Robert W - *Life and Terror in Stalin's Russia 1934-1941*
     HRNB - v25 - Fall '96 - p35 [251-500]
     NL - v79 - Ag 12 '96 - p3+ [501+]
     VQR - v72 - Aut '96 - p117* [501+]
Thusing, Wilhelm - *Studien Zur Neutestament-Lichen Theologie*
     Rel St Rev - v23 - Ja '97 - p69 [51-250]
Thuyet Ngu - *Song Troi*
     BL - v93 - My 15 '97 - p1568 [1-50]
Thwaite, Ann - *Emily Tennyson: The Poet's Wife*
     Lon R Bks - v18 - N 28 '96 - p24 [501+]
     Spec - v277 - O 5 '96 - p49+ [501+]
     TLS - O 4 '96 - p32 [501+]
The Horse at Hilly Fields (Illus. by Elaine Mills)
  c JB - v60 - D '96 - p242 [51-250]
  c Sch Lib - v44 - N '96 - p148 [51-250]
Thybony, Scott - *Burntwater*
     KR - v65 - F 1 '97 - p210+ [251-500]
     PW - v244 - F 10 '97 - p74 [51-250]
Tiainen-Anttila, Kaija - *The Problem of Humanity*
     AHR - v101 - D '96 - p1518+ [501+]
Tian, Wenyi - *Chong Qing Feng Yun*
     BL - v93 - My 1 '97 - p1484 [1-50]
Zai Jian Cheng Du
     BL - v93 - My 1 '97 - p1484 [1-50]
Tiano, Olivier - *Ramses II and Egypt*
  y HB Guide - v8 - Spr '97 - p165 [51-250]
  y SLJ - v42 - D '96 - p148 [51-250]
Tiberghien, Gilles A - *Land Art*
     Art J - v55 - Sum '96 - p95+ [501+]
Tibor, Tom - *Implementing ISO 14000*
     Choice - v34 - Ap '97 - p1384 [51-250]
     SciTech - v21 - Mr '97 - p98 [51-250]
Tibullus - *Elegies II (Murgatroyd)*
     AJP - v117 - Fall '96 - p498+ [501+]
Tichenor, Bruce A - *Characterizing Sources of Indoor Air Pollution and Related Sink Effects*
     SciTech - v20 - D '96 - p70 [1-50]
Tichi, Cecelia - *High Lonesome*
     CAY - v17 - Win '96 - p8 [51-250]
     Col Lit - v23 - Je '96 - p177+ [501+]
     LJ - v121 - N 1 '96 - p42 [1-50]
Readin' Country Music
     J Am St - v30 - Ag '96 - p307+ [251-500]
The Tick Omnibus. Vol. 1
  y VOYA - v19 - O '96 - p203+ [51-250]

The Ticker Symbol Book. 1997 Ed.
  r Choice - v34 - F '97 - p950 [51-250]
Tickle, Phyllis - *God-Talk in America*
     KR - v65 - F 15 '97 - p288+ [251-500]
     LJ - v122 - Mr 15 '97 - p67 [51-250]
     PW - v244 - F 24 '97 - p81 [51-250]
Re-Discovering the Sacred
     RR - v56 - Ja '97 - p100+ [501+]
Tickoo, Makhan L - *Language and Culture in Multilingual Societies*
     MLJ - v80 - Fall '96 - p410+ [501+]
Reading and Writing
     MLJ - v80 - Win '96 - p541+ [501+]
Tidjani-Serpos, Noureini - *Bamikile*
     BL - v93 - F 1 '97 - p930 [1-50]
Tidwell, William A - *April '65*
     J Am Cult - v18 - Win '95 - p102 [51-250]
Tieger, Paul D - *Nurture by Nature*
     BL - v93 - My 1 '97 - p1470 [51-250]
Tieken-Boon Van Ostade, Ingrid - *The Two Versions of Malory's Morte D'Arthur*
     Lib - v19 - Mr '97 - p85+ [501+]
Tieleman, Teun - *Galen and Chrysippus on the Soul*
     R&R Bk N - v12 - F '97 - p2 [51-250]
Tien, Hung-Mao - *Taiwan's Electoral Politics and Democratic Transition*
     Ch Rev Int - v4 - Spr '97 - p265+ [501+]
Tienne, Andre De - *L'Analytique De La Representation Chez Peirce*
     CPR - v16 - Ag '96 - p251+ [501+]
Tiepolo, Giovanni Battista - *Giambattista Tiepolo 1696-1770*
     BM - v138 - D '96 - p848+ [501+]
     NYRB - v44 - F 6 '97 - p35+ [501+]
     PW - v244 - Ja 27 '97 - p93 [51-250]
Tierksy, Ronald - *France in the New Europe*
     FR - v70 - Mr '97 - p629+ [501+]
Tierney, William G - *Promotion and Tenure*
     Choice - v34 - F '97 - p1015 [51-250]
     R&R Bk N - v11 - D '96 - p53 [51-250]
Tierney-Tello, Mary Beth - *Allegories of Transgression and Transformation*
     R&R Bk N - v11 - N '96 - p69 [51-250]
     WLT - v71 - Win '97 - p237 [251-500]
Tiesdell, Steven - *Revitalizing Historic Urban Quarters*
     R&R Bk N - v11 - N '96 - p61 [51-250]
Tiffany, Daniel - *Radio Corpse*
     ELT - v40 - 1 '97 - p92+ [501+]
Tiffin, John - *In Search of the Virtual Class*
     Arena - O '96 - p51+ [501+]
Tiffin, Patricia M - *Watching Vanessa*
     LJ - v122 - Ja '97 - p151 [51-250]
     PW - v244 - Ja 6 '97 - p66 [51-250]
Tigchelaar, Eibert J C - *The Prophets of Old and the Day of the End*
     Rel St Rev - v23 - Ap '97 - p167 [51-250]
Tight, Malcolm - *Key Concepts in Adult Education and Training*
     Choice - v34 - Ap '97 - p1392 [251-500]
Tigler, Guido - *Il Portale Maggiore Di San Marco A Venezia*
     Specu - v72 - Ja '97 - p232+ [501+]
Tihanyi, Eva - *Saved by the Telling*
     BIC - v25 - S '96 - p25 [501+]
Tijerina, Andres - *Tejanos and Texas Under the Mexican Flag 1821-1836*
     HAHR - v76 - Ag '96 - p572+ [251-500]
Tikkun: A Bimonthly Jewish Critique of Politics, Culture and Society
  p TLS - N 15 '96 - p35 [501+]
Tilby, Michael - *Balzac*
     MLR - v92 - Ja '97 - p196+ [251-500]
Tildes, Phyllis Limbacher - *Animals: Black and White (Illus. by Phyllis Limbacher Tildes)*
  c Bloom Rev - v16 - S '96 - p29 [51-250]
  c CBRS - v25 - Win '97 - p66 [51-250]
  c HB Guide - v8 - Spr '97 - p120 [51-250]
  c SLJ - v43 - Ja '97 - p109 [51-250]
Calico Picks a Puppy
  c BL - v93 - N 1 '96 - p505 [51-250]
  c HB Guide - v8 - Spr '97 - p128 [51-250]
Tilghman, Benjamin R - *An Introduction to the Philosophy of Religion*
     South HR - v30 - Fall '96 - p379+ [501+]
Tilghman, Christopher - *Mason's Retreat*
     Bks & Cult - v2 - N '96 - p8+ [501+]
     LJ - v121 - O 1 '96 - p48 [1-50]
     LJ - v121 - O 1 '96 - p156 [51-250]
     NYTBR - v101 - D 8 '96 - p80 [1-50]
     PW - v243 - N 4 '96 - p38 [1-50]
  y SLJ - v42 - O '96 - p164 [51-250]

Mason's Retreat (Long). Audio Version
  BL - v93 - N 1 '96 - p522 [51-250]
Till, Geoffrey - *Seapower: Theory and Practice*
  NWCR - v50 - Win '97 - p134+ [501+]
Tillard, Francoise - *Fanny Mendelssohn*
  Notes - v53 - Mr '97 - p800+ [501+]
Tiller, Ruth - *Wishing (Illus. by Debrah Santini)*
  c HB Guide - v8 - Spr '97 - p51 [51-250]
Tiller, Veronica E Velarde - *Tiller's Guide to Indian Country*
  r JEL - v34 - S '96 - p1445 [51-250]
Tillery, Bill W - *Physical Science. 3rd Ed.*
  SciTech - v20 - N '96 - p4 [51-250]
Tilley, Terrence W - *Postmodern Theologies*
  Rel St Rev - v23 - Ap '97 - p155 [51-250]
  TT - v53 - Ja '97 - p550+ [501+]
The Wisdom of Religious Commitment
  Theol St - v58 - Mr '97 - p195 [251-500]
Tillinghast, Richard - *The Stonecutter's Hand*
  MQR - v35 - Fall '96 - p734+ [501+]
Tillis, Tracey - *Flashpoint*
  LJ - v122 - F 15 '97 - p126 [51-250]
Tillman, Barrett - *Hellcats: A Novel of War in the Pacific*
  A & S Sm - v11 - O '96 - p86+ [51-250]
Tillman, Hoyt Cleveland - *Ch'en Liang on Public Interest and the Law*
  Ch Rev Int - v4 - Spr '97 - p268+ [501+]
Tillmans, Wolfgang - *For When I'm Weak I'm Strong*
  LJ - v122 - Ja '97 - p92 [51-250]
  VLS - Win '96 - p31 [51-250]
Wolfgang Tillmans (Taschen)
  VLS - Win '96 - p31 [51-250]
Tilly, Charles - *Cities and the Rise of States in Europe A.D. 1000 to 1800*
  CS - v25 - N '96 - p773+ [501+]
Popular Contention in Great Britain 1758-1834
  AJS - v102 - Jl '96 - p301+ [501+]
  Albion - v28 - Sum '96 - p317+ [501+]
  APSR - v90 - D '96 - p874+ [501+]
  CS - v25 - N '96 - p755+ [501+]
  EHR - v112 - F '97 - p145+ [501+]
  J Pol - v58 - Ag '96 - p913+ [501+]
  J Soc H - v30 - Spr '97 - p741+ [501+]
  RP - v58 - Sum '96 - p652+ [501+]
Tilly, Chris - *Half a Job*
  AJS - v102 - N '96 - p895+ [501+]
  CS - v26 - Mr '97 - p223+ [501+]
  ILRR - v50 - Ap '97 - p531+ [501+]
  SF - v75 - D '96 - p765 [51-250]
Tilly, Richard - *European Economic Integration as a Challenge to Industry and Government*
  JEL - v34 - D '96 - p2044 [51-250]
Tilman, Rick - *The Intellectual Legacy of Thorstein Veblen*
  R&R Bk N - v12 - F '97 - p33 [51-250]
Tilney, Edmund - *The Flower of Friendship*
  Shakes Q - v47 - Fall '96 - p337+ [501+]
Tilton, Bill - *Drawing and Painting Animals*
  LJ - v122 - Mr 15 '97 - p63 [51-250]
Tilton, Mark - *Restrained Trade*
  JEL - v34 - S '96 - p1454 [51-250]
Tilton, Robert S - *Pocahontas: The Evolution of an American Narrative*
  AHR - v101 - O '96 - p1265+ [501+]
Timber Creek Review
  p Sm Pr R - v29 - F '97 - p16 [251-500]
Timberg, Robert - *The Nightingale's Song*
  APH - v43 - Win '96 - p62+ [251-500]
  Historian - v59 - Win '97 - p446+ [501+]
  NYTBR - v101 - S 29 '96 - p32 [51-250]
  PW - v243 - S 23 '96 - p73 [1-50]
A Time for Action
  J Gov Info - v23 - S '96 - p620 [51-250]
Time-Life Books - *The Alternative Advisor*
  BL - v93 - My 1 '97 - p1470 [501+]
  r PW - v244 - Ap 7 '97 - p89 [51-250]
Chancellorsville
  y BL - v93 - Ja '97 - p828 [251-500]
Christmas Is Cookies and Gingerbread and Spice Cake and Fudge and More
  BWatch - v17 - D '96 - p1 [51-250]
  PW - v243 - O 7 '96 - p71 [51-250]
The Medical Advisor
  r ARBA - v28 - '97 - p613 [51-250]
  r BL - v93 - S 1 '96 - p167+ [251-500]
  r BL - v93 - F 1 '97 - p957 [1-50]
  r LJ - v121 - O 1 '96 - p68 [51-250]
  r SB - v32 - N '96 - p233 [251-500]
Organic Vegetable Gardening
  SB - v32 - Ag '96 - p171 [251-500]

The Revolutionaries
  y BL - v93 - D 15 '96 - p720 [51-250]
  y SLJ - v43 - Ja '97 - p122 [51-250]
Shiloh
  y BL - v93 - Ja '97 - p828 [251-500]
War between Brothers
  y BL - v93 - D 15 '96 - p720 [51-250]
What Life Was like on the Banks of the Nile
  y BL - v93 - N 1 '96 - p490 [51-250]
  y SB - v33 - Mr '97 - p47 [51-250]
What Life Was Like on the Banks of the Nile
  y SLJ - v42 - D '96 - p148 [51-250]
Windows and Doors
  LJ - v121 - S 15 '96 - p92 [51-250]
Time Machine
  cp H Sch M - v4 - D '96 - p60 [51-250]
Time (Make It Work!)
  c TES - Jl 19 '96 - pR8 [51-250]
Time Out Budapest Guide
  r BL - v93 - S 15 '96 - p212 [1-50]
Time Out Film Guide. 5th Ed.
  r ARBA - v28 - '97 - p517+ [51-250]
  yr Kliatt - v31 - Mr '97 - p35+ [51-250]
Time Out New York Guide. 4th Ed.
  r BL - v93 - S 15 '96 - p212 [1-50]
Time Out Rome Guide. 2nd Ed.
  r BL - v93 - S 15 '96 - p212 [1-50]
Time Out San Francisco Guide
  r BL - v93 - S 15 '96 - p212 [1-50]
Timlin, Mark - *Find My Way Home*
  Books - v10 - Je '96 - p10 [51-250]
Paint It Black
  Books - v9 - S '95 - p19 [51-250]
  Books - v9 - S '95 - p22 [1-50]
Timm, Uwe - *Johannesnacht*
  Econ - v341 - O 19 '96 - p16*+ [501+]
Timmel, Carol Ann - *Tabitha: The Fabulous Flying Feline (Illus. by Laura Kelly)*
  c CBRS - v25 - N '96 - p28 [51-250]
  c HB Guide - v8 - Spr '97 - p51 [51-250]
  c KR - v64 - S 15 '96 - p1408 [51-250]
  c SLJ - v42 - N '96 - p94 [51-250]
Timmer, Doug A - *Paths to Homelessness*
  AAPSS-A - v546 - Jl '96 - p177+ [501+]
Timmins, Bret - *DirectDraw Programming*
  SciTech - v20 - N '96 - p60 [51-250]
Timmins, Nicholas - *The Five Giants*
  NS & S - v9 - Ap 26 '96 - p29 [1-50]
Timmins, Steve - *French Fun*
  MLJ - v81 - Spr '97 - p130 [251-500]
Timms, Edward - *Freud and the Child Woman*
  Ger Q - v69 - Sum '96 - p322+ [501+]
Timor-Tritschi, Ilan E - *Ultrasound and the Fallopian Tube*
  SciTech - v20 - D '96 - p51 [51-250]
Timpone, Anthony - *Men, Makeup and Monsters*
  y BL - v93 - O 1 '96 - p316 [51-250]
  LJ - v121 - S 15 '96 - p71 [51-250]
Tinasky, Wanda - *The Letters of Wanda Tinasky*
  RCF - v16 - Fall '96 - p206+ [501+]
Tindall, George Brown - *Natives and Newcomers*
  JIH - v27 - Win '97 - p543+ [251-500]
Tindall, William York - *A Reader's Guide to Finnegans Wake*
  VQR - v72 - Aut '96 - p142* [1-50]
Tinder, Glenn - *Tolerance and Community*
  APSR - v91 - Mr '97 - p170+ [501+]
  J Pol - v59 - F '97 - p277+ [501+]
  RP - v58 - Fall '96 - p826+ [501+]
Ting, Hsiao-Chi - *Maidenhome*
  WLT - v70 - Aut '96 - p1027+ [501+]
Tingay, Paul - *Wildest Africa*
  CSM - v89 - D 5 '96 - pB3 [51-250]
  LJ - v121 - D '96 - p139 [51-250]
  PW - v243 - N 4 '96 - p59 [51-250]
Tingley, Judith C - *Genderflex: Men and Women Speaking Each Other's Language at Work*
  NWSA Jnl - v8 - Sum '96 - p117+ [501+]
Tinker, George E - *Missionary Conquest*
  Rel St Rev - v23 - Ja '97 - p91+ [51-250]
Tinkham, Michael - *Introduction to Superconductivity*
  Phys Today - v49 - O '96 - p74 [501+]
Tinkle, Lon - *13 Days to Glory*
  Roundup M - v3 - Ag '96 - p27 [51-250]
Tinkle, Theresa - *Medieval Venuses and Cupids*
  Choice - v34 - N '96 - p461 [51-250]
Tinkler, Penny - *Constructing Girlhood*
  J Soc H - v30 - Win '96 - p539+ [501+]
  NWSA Jnl - v8 - Fall '96 - p144+ [501+]
  SF - v75 - S '96 - p388+ [251-500]

Tinsley, Bruce - *Mallard Fillmore...on the Stump*
  LATBR - O 27 '96 - p11 [51-250]
Tinsley, R C - *The Biology of Xenopus*
  Sci - v275 - Ja 31 '97 - p625 [1-50]
Tinterow, Gary - *Corot*
  BM - v138 - Jl '96 - p482+ [501+]
  Choice - v34 - F '97 - p958+ [51-250]
  LATBR - D 8 '96 - p14 [51-250]
  LJ - v122 - F 15 '97 - p132+ [51-250]
  PW - v243 - S 2 '96 - p106 [51-250]
  R&R Bk N - v12 - F '97 - p74 [51-250]
Tipitaka. Suttapitaka. Khuddakanikaya. Theragatha. English. Selections - *Songs of the Sons and Daughters of Buddha*
  BL - v93 - S 15 '96 - p185 [51-250]
Tipler, Frank J - *The Physics of Immortality*
  Skeptic - v3 - '95 - p100 [51-250]
Tipling, David - *Top Birding Spots in Britain and Ireland*
  r New Sci - v152 - N 2 '96 - p48 [51-250]
Tipper, Paul Andrew - *The Dream-Machine: Avian Imagery in Madame Bovary*
  FR - v70 - O '96 - p118 [251-500]
Tippett, Michael - *Tippett on Music*
  Notes - v53 - D '96 - p477+ [501+]
Tippett, Paul - *Teapots*
  r Ceram Mo - v44 - S '96 - p32 [51-250]
Tippette, Giles - *Heaven's Gold*
  PW - v243 - O 14 '96 - p65+ [51-250]
  Roundup M - v4 - F '97 - p30 [251-500]
Tipps, Betsy L - *Holocene Archeology near Squaw Butte, Canyonlands, National Park, Utah*
  J Gov Info - v23 - S '96 - p568 [51-250]
Tirado De Alonso, Irma - *Trade, Industrialization, and Integration in Twentieth-Century Central America*
  JEL - v35 - Mr '97 - p214+ [51-250]
  JTWS - v13 - Fall '96 - p315+ [501+]
Trade Issues in the Caribbean
  JEL - v35 - Mr '97 - p215 [51-250]
Tirion, Wil - *Bright Star Atlas 2000.0*
  r S&T - v92 - S '96 - p53 [51-250]
The Cambridge Star Atlas. 2nd Ed.
  r ARBA - v28 - '97 - p632 [51-250]
  r Astron - v24 - D '96 - p102 [51-250]
  yr BL - v93 - D 1 '96 - p684 [51-250]
  r Choice - v34 - F '97 - p985 [51-250]
  r New Sci - v152 - O 19 '96 - p47 [51-250]
Tirira, Jorge - *Forward Recoil Spectrometry*
  SciTech - v20 - D '96 - p25 [51-250]
Tirsch, Jessie - *A Taste of the Gulf Coast*
  BL - v93 - Mr 15 '97 - p1217 [51-250]
  PW - v244 - F 17 '97 - p214 [51-250]
Tisch, Sarah J - *Dilemmas of Development Assistance*
  JTWS - v13 - Spr '96 - p427+ [501+]
Tisma, Aleksandar - *Kapo*
  TranslRevS - v1 - My '95 - p28 [51-250]
Tismaneanu, Vladimir - *Political Culture and Civil Society in Russia and the New States of Eurasia*
  APSR - v90 - S '96 - p685+ [501+]
Tite, Colin G C - *The Manuscript Library of Sir Robert Cotton*
  BC - v45 - Sum '96 - p273+ [501+]
  EHR - v112 - F '97 - p198+ [501+]
  Sev Cent N - v54 - Fall '96 - p71 [251-500]
Titelman, Gregory Y - *Random House Dictionary of Popular Proverbs and Sayings*
  yr BL - v92 - Ag '96 - p1926 [251-500]
  yr BL - v93 - Ja '97 - p770 [1-50]
  yr Choice - v34 - N '96 - p438 [51-250]
  cr SLJ - v42 - N '96 - p139 [51-250]
Title, Elise - *Bleeding Hearts*
  Books - v10 - Je '96 - p10 [51-250]
  Books - v10 - Je '96 - p23 [51-250]
Titon, Jeff Todd - *Early Downhome Blues. 2nd Ed.*
  J Am St - v30 - Ap '96 - p135+ [251-500]
Tittel, Ed - *Computer Telephony*
  CBR - v14 - N '96 - p37 [51-250]
ISDN Networking Essentials
  CBR - v14 - S '96 - p30 [51-250]
Web Graphics Sourcebook
  r BYTE - v22 - Mr '97 - p34 [51-250]
Tittle, Charles R - *Control Balance*
  AJS - v102 - S '96 - p620+ [501+]
Tittle, Diana - *Welcome to Heights High*
  AAPSS-A - v549 - Ja '97 - p208 [251-500]
Titze, Hartmut - *Wachstum Und Differenzierung Der Deutschen Universitaten 1830-1945*
  Isis - v87 - S '96 - p529+ [501+]
Tizon, Hector - *The Man Who Came to a Village*
  TranslRevS - v1 - My '95 - p32+ [51-250]
Tkach, Daniel - *Visual Modeling Technique*
  SciTech - v20 - D '96 - p9 [51-250]

TLA Film and Video Guide 1996-1997
r   ARBA - v28 - '97 - p513 [51-250]

TMIN International Symposium on Amyotrophic Lateral Sclerosis (1995: Tokyo, Japan) - *Amyotrophic Lateral Sclerosis*
SciTech - v20 - D '96 - p43 [51-250]

To Turn the Tide: Newsletter for the World Council of Churches Climate Change Petition Campaign
p   WorldV - v12 - O '96 - p12+ [51-250]

Toaff, Ariel - *The Jews in Umbria. Vol. 1*
EHR - v112 - F '97 - p175+ [501+]
Love, Work, and Death
R&R Bk N - v11 - N '96 - p14 [51-250]

Tobacco and Health Network Directory 1996
r   ARBA - v28 - '97 - p603+ [51-250]

Tobias, Sheila - *Faces of Feminism*
LJ - v122 - F 15 '97 - p152 [51-250]
Ms - v7 - Mr '97 - p83 [1-50]
NYTBR - v102 - Mr 23 '97 - p12 [501+]

Tobin, Andrew B - *The Phospholipase C Pathway*
SciTech - v21 - Mr '97 - p42 [51-250]

Tobin, Frank - *Mechthild Von Magdeburg: A Medieval Mystic in Modern Eyes*
MLR - v92 - Ja '97 - p235+ [251-500]
Specu - v71 - Jl '96 - p770+ [501+]

Tobin, James, 1918- - *Essays in Economics: National and International*
JEL - v35 - Mr '97 - p204 [51-250]
Full Employment and Growth
BW - v26 - S 22 '96 - p11 [251-500]
R&R Bk N - v11 - N '96 - p26 [51-250]

Tobin, James, 1956- - *Ernie Pyle's War*
KR - v65 - Mr 15 '97 - p451+ [251-500]

Tobin, Lad - *Taking Stock*
Col Comp - v47 - D '96 - p619+ [51-250]

Tobin, Stephen - *The Cistercians: Monks and Monasteries of Europe*
BL - v93 - S 15 '96 - p201 [51-250]

Tocci, Christopher - *Applied MAPLE for Engineers and Scientists*
SciTech - v20 - N '96 - p61 [51-250]

Tocci, Ronald J - *Microprocessors and Microcomputers. 4th Ed.*
SciTech - v20 - D '96 - p7 [51-250]

Toczek, Nick - *Dragons (Illus. by Sally Townsend)*
c   Sch Lib - v44 - Ag '96 - p116 [51-250]

Toda, Kyoko - *Animal Faces (Illus. by Akira Satoh)*
c   HB Guide - v7 - Fall '96 - p339 [51-250]
c   SLJ - v42 - N '96 - p101+ [51-250]

Todaro, Michael P - *Reflections on Economic Development*
Econ J - v107 - Ja '97 - p284+ [251-500]

Todd, Charles - *A Test of Wills*
NYTBR - v101 - D 8 '96 - p94 [1-50]
PW - v243 - N 4 '96 - p40 [1-50]

Todd, Daniel - *Navies and Shipbuilding Industries*
Choice - v34 - My '97 - p1567 [51-250]
J Mil H - v61 - Ap '97 - p418+ [501+]
R&R Bk N - v11 - D '96 - p72 [51-250]

Todd, Dennis - *Imagining Monsters*
AJCH - v39 - Ja '97 - p228+ [501+]
Albion - v28 - Win '96 - p702+ [501+]
Critm - v39 - Win '97 - p135+ [501+]
Eight-C St - v30 - Spr '97 - p329+ [501+]

Todd, Douglas - *Brave Souls*
LJ - v122 - Ja '97 - p107 [51-250]
Quill & Q - v62 - D '96 - p19 [501+]

Todd, Helen - *Women at the Center*
Cu H - v95 - N '96 - p394 [501+]
R&R Bk N - v11 - N '96 - p36 [51-250]

Todd, Jan, 1947- - *Colonial Technology*
Choice - v34 - S '96 - p150 [51-250]

Todd, Janet M, 1942- - *Gender, Art and Death*
Signs - v22 - Win '97 - p469+ [501+]
The Secret Life of Aphra Behn
NS - v125 - D 6 '96 - p54+ [501+]
TLS - Ja 31 '97 - p23 [501+]

Todd, Olivier - *Albert Camus: Une Vie*
TLS - O 4 '96 - p4+ [501+]

Todd, Pamela - *Celebrating the Impressionist Table*
BL - v93 - My 15 '97 - p1554 [501+]

Todd, Richard - *Consuming Fictions*
NS - v125 - O 11 '96 - p44 [501+]
Spec - v277 - S 21 '96 - p55 [501+]
TLS - N 1 '96 - p27 [501+]

Toderi, Giuseppe - *Placchette, Secoli XV-XVIII Nel Museo Nazionale Del Bargello*
BM - v138 - D '96 - p832+ [501+]

Todeschi, Kevin J - *Twelve Lessons in Personal Spirituality*
LJ - v122 - Ja '97 - p107 [51-250]

Todorov, Tzvetan - *Facing the Extreme*
New R - v215 - O 28 '96 - p36+ [501+]
A French Tragedy
Choice - v34 - Ja '97 - p858 [51-250]
For Aff - v76 - Mr '97 - p187+ [51-250]
LJ - v121 - S 15 '96 - p81 [51-250]
NYTLa - v146 - S 18 '96 - pC19 [501+]

Toelken, Barre - *The Dynamics of Folklore. Rev. and Expanded Ed.*
CAY - v17 - Win '96 - p8 [51-250]
Morning Dew and Roses
WestFolk - v55 - Sum '96 - p255+ [501+]

Toer, Pramoedya Ananta - *Child of All Nations*
FEER - v159 - O 10 '96 - p55+ [501+]
Footsteps
FEER - v159 - O 10 '96 - p55+ [501+]
House of Glass
FEER - v159 - O 10 '96 - p55+ [501+]
This Earth of Mankind
FEER - v159 - O 10 '96 - p55+ [501+]

Toff, Nancy - *The Flute Book. 2nd Ed.*
r   Choice - v34 - F '97 - p975 [51-250]

Toffler, Alvin - *Creating a New Civilization*
Mar Crp G - v80 - O '96 - p74 [501+]
QJS - v83 - My '97 - p230+ [501+]
War and Anti-War
Mar Crp G - v80 - Ag '96 - p74 [501+]

Tofts, Hannah - *Fun to Make and Do*
c   TES - Jl 19 '96 - pR8 [51-250]

Toga, Arthur W - *Brain Mapping*
Nature - v385 - Ja 16 '97 - p218 [51-250]

Togan, Subidey - *The Economy of Turkey since Liberalization*
JEL - v34 - D '96 - p2044 [51-250]

Togawa, Masako - *Slow Fuse*
Arm Det - v29 - Sum '96 - p364+ [51-250]

Toht, David W - *Sodbuster (Illus. by Richard Erickson)*
c   HB Guide - v7 - Fall '96 - p386 [51-250]

Toibin, Colm - *The Kilfenora Teaboy*
ILS - v16 - Spr '97 - p35 [1-50]
The Sign of the Cross
NYTBR - v101 - O 20 '96 - p36 [1-50]
The Story of the Night
BL - v93 - My 15 '97 - p1564 [51-250]
KR - v65 - Ap 1 '97 - p500 [251-500]
Lon R Bks - v18 - O 3 '96 - p15 [501+]
NS - v125 - S 20 '96 - p48 [501+]
Obs - S 8 '96 - p18* [51-250]
PW - v244 - Ap 14 '97 - p53 [51-250]
Spec - v277 - S 21 '96 - p52 [501+]
Spec - v277 - N 23 '96 - p43 [51-250]
Spec - v277 - N 23 '96 - p46 [51-250]
Spec - v277 - N 30 '96 - p58 [51-250]
TLS - S 13 '96 - p25 [501+]

Tokareva, Viktoria - *Na Cherta Nam Chuzhie*
WLT - v71 - Win '97 - p177 [501+]

Tokenews
p   Coin W - v37 - O 14 '96 - p40 [1-50]

Tokes, Rudolf L - *Hungary's Negotiated Revolution*
Choice - v34 - My '97 - p1570 [51-250]
JEL - v35 - Mr '97 - p292 [51-250]
NYRB - v43 - N 14 '96 - p18+ [501+]

Toksvig, Sandi - *If I Didn't Have Elbows... (Illus. by David Melling)*
c   CBRS - v25 - S '96 - p9 [51-250]
c   CCB-B - v50 - D '96 - p154 [51-250]
c   HB Guide - v8 - Spr '97 - p131 [51-250]
c   New Sci - v152 - N 16 '96 - p54 [1-50]
c   Sch Lib - v45 - F '97 - p22 [51-250]
c   SLJ - v42 - N '96 - p102 [51-250]

Tokunaga, Suminori - *Landownership and Residential Land Use in Urban Economies*
JEL - v34 - S '96 - p1501 [51-250]

Tokyo: ANA's City Guide
r   FEER - v160 - Mr 27 '97 - p51+ [501+]

Tokyo (Insight Guides) 1991-
r   BL - v93 - S 15 '96 - p210 [1-50]

Tolan, John Victor - *Medieval Christian Perceptions of Islam*
CLW - v67 - D '96 - p39+ [251-500]
Petrus Alfonsi and His Medieval Readers
Rel St Rev - v22 - O '96 - p354 [51-250]
Specu - v72 - Ja '97 - p233+ [501+]

Tolan, Stephanie S - *Welcome to the Ark*
c   CBRS - v25 - Ja '97 - p60 [51-250]
y   CCB-B - v50 - N '96 - p117 [51-250]
y   Emerg Lib - v24 - Mr '97 - p54+ [51-250]
y   HB Guide - v8 - Spr '97 - p85 [51-250]
y   KR - v64 - Ag 15 '96 - p1244 [51-250]
y   SLJ - v42 - O '96 - p150 [51-250]

Toland, John - *Captured by History*
BL - v93 - My 1 '97 - p1459 [51-250]
PW - v244 - My 5 '97 - p184+ [51-250]

Tolchin, Susan J - *The Angry American*
y   BL - v93 - S 15 '96 - p187 [251-500]
Bloom Rev - v16 - S '96 - p24 [51-250]
Choice - v34 - F '97 - p1038 [51-250]

Toledano, Ehud - *Mitsrayim Be-Petah Ha-Idan Ha-Moderni*
BL - v93 - Mr 1 '97 - p1115 [1-50]

Tolhurst, Marilyn - *Home in the Blitz*
c   Bks Keeps - Ja '97 - p23+ [51-250]
c   Sch Lib - v45 - F '97 - p39 [51-250]
Victorian Factory
c   Bks Keeps - Ja '97 - p23+ [51-250]
c   Sch Lib - v45 - F '97 - p39 [51-250]

Tolhurst, Peter - *East Anglia*
TLS - Ja 3 '97 - p32 [51-250]

Toliver, Harold - *George Herbert's Christian Narrative*
Ren Q - v49 - Aut '96 - p642+ [501+]

Tolkien, J R R - *Lord of the Rings*
Ext - v38 - Spr '97 - p36+ [501+]
The Monsters and the Critics
TLS - F 21 '97 - p25 [501+]

Toll, Henry Wolcott - *An Analysis of Variability and Condition of Cavate Structures in Bandelier National Monument*
Am Ant - v62 - Ja '97 - p172 [251-500]
Soil, Water, Biology, and Belief in Prehistoric and Traditional Southwestern Agriculture
Am Ant - v61 - O '96 - p811+ [501+]

Tolley, Bruce - *Pastors and Parishioners in Wurttemberg during the Late Reformation 1581-1621*
AHR - v101 - O '96 - p1231 [501+]
JIH - v27 - Win '97 - p529+ [501+]
TLS - D 27 '96 - p32 [51-250]

Tolley, Rodney - *Transport Systems, Policy and Planning*
GJ - v163 - Mr '97 - p103 [251-500]

Tollifson, Joan - *Bare-Bones Meditation*
KR - v64 - Ag 15 '96 - p1225 [251-500]
Utne R - S '96 - p96 [251-500]

Tolnay, Stewart E - *A Festival of Violence*
AHR - v101 - D '96 - p1638+ [501+]
JSH - v62 - N '96 - p828+ [501+]

Tolstikov, Vladimir - *The Gold of Troy*
BL - v93 - S 1 '96 - p59+ [51-250]
NYRB - v43 - D 19 '96 - p15+ [501+]

Tolstoy, Leo, Graf - *Confession*
CR - v270 - F '97 - p109 [1-50]
Resurrection
CLS - v33 - 4 '96 - p350+ [501+]
Tolstoy's Diaries
LJ - v122 - Ja '97 - p98 [51-250]
What Is Art?
MLR - v92 - Ja '97 - p266+ [501+]

Toma, T L - *Border Dance*
Choice - v34 - Ap '97 - p1340+ [51-250]
KR - v64 - N 15 '96 - p1629+ [251-500]
NYTBR - v102 - Ja 26 '97 - p18 [51-250]
PW - v243 - N 4 '96 - p67 [51-250]

Tomajczyk, S F - *Dictionary of the Modern United States Military*
r   ARBA - v28 - '97 - p255 [251-500]
r   LJ - v122 - Ap 15 '97 - p40 [51-250]
r   RQ - v36 - Fall '96 - p125 [251-500]

Toman, James A - *Cleveland's Transit Vehicles*
SciTech - v21 - Mr '97 - p83 [51-250]
Horse Trails to Regional Rails
R&R Bk N - v12 - F '97 - p43 [51-250]

Tomas, Carmelo L - *Identifying Marine Diatoms and Dinoflagellates*
Choice - v34 - S '96 - p152 [51-250]

Tomaselli, Doris - *My First Stamp and Learn Book (Illus. by Cathy Beylon)*
c   PW - v243 - N 18 '96 - p77 [51-250]
Scary Sights and Funny Frights (Illus. by Nathan Young Jarvis)
c   LATBR - O 20 '96 - p8 [1-50]

Tomaselli-Maschovitis, Valerie - *Latin America on File*
r   BL - v93 - Ag '96 - p1920 [51-250]

Tomasi Di Lampedusa, Giuseppe - *The Leopard*
LATBR - D 29 '96 - p5 [51-250]

Tomasko, Robert M - *Go for Growth*
LJ - v122 - Mr 15 '97 - p36 [1-50]

Tomaskovic-Devey, Donald - *Gender and Racial Inequality at Work*
SF - v75 - D '96 - p757+ [501+]
SF - v75 - Mr '97 - p1133+ [501+]

Tomasky, Michael - *Left for Dead*
   BW - v26 - Ag 18 '96 - p4 [51-250]
   NY - v72 - N 25 '96 - p106+ [501+]
   Pub Int - Fall '96 - p116+ [501+]
Tomatis, Alfred A - *The Conscious Ear*
   MLJ - v80 - Win '96 - p542+ [501+]
Tomblin, Stephen G - *Ottawa and the Outer Provinces*
   Can Hist R - v78 - Mr '97 - p99+ [501+]
Tombs, Robert - *France 1814-1914*
   Spec - v278 - Mr 15 '97 - p37 [501+]
Tomczyk, Mary - *Shapes, Sizes and More Surprises!*
   (Illus. by Loretta Trezzo Braren)
   c SLJ - v42 - O '96 - p118+ [51-250]
Tomey, Ingrid - *The Queen of Dreamland*
   y BL - v93 - S 15 '96 - p233 [51-250]
   y CBRS - v25 - Win '97 - p71 [51-250]
   y CCB-B - v50 - O '96 - p78 [51-250]
   c HB - v73 - Ja '97 - p68+ [51-250]
   y HB Guide - v8 - Spr '97 - p85 [51-250]
   c KR - v64 - Ag 15 '96 - p1244+ [51-250]
   y LATBR - O 13 '96 - p15 [51-250]
   y SLJ - v42 - O '96 - p150 [51-250]
Tomiuk, J - *Transgenic Organisms*
   SciTech - v20 - S '96 - p19 [51-250]
Tomizza, Fulvio - *Alle Spalle Di Trieste*
   WLT - v70 - Aut '96 - p937+ [501+]
Tomjanovich, Rudy - *A Rocket at Heart*
   y BL - v93 - Ap 1 '97 - p1276 [51-250]
   KR - v65 - Mr 1 '97 - p368 [51-250]
   LJ - v122 - Ap 15 '97 - p87 [51-250]
   PW - v244 - F 24 '97 - p75 [51-250]
Tomkins, Calvin - *Duchamp*
   Obs - Mr 2 '97 - p17* [501+]
   Spec - v278 - Ap 5 '97 - p32+ [501+]
   Duchamp: A Biography
   AB - v99 - Mr 3 '97 - p693+ [51-250]
   BL - v93 - Ja '97 - p759 [1-50]
   BW - v26 - N 24 '96 - p1+ [501+]
   KR - v64 - S 15 '96 - p1388 [251-500]
   LATBR - N 24 '96 - p2 [501+]
   LJ - v121 - D '96 - p90 [51-250]
   LJ - v122 - Ja '97 - p51 [51-250]
   New R - v216 - Mr 10 '97 - p42+ [501+]
   NY - v72 - D 16 '96 - p108 [51-250]
   NYRB - v44 - Mr 27 '97 - p22+ [501+]
   NYTBR - v101 - D 1 '96 - p9 [501+]
   NYTBR - v101 - D 8 '96 - p87 [1-50]
   PW - v243 - S 16 '96 - p57 [51-250]
   PW - v243 - N 4 '96 - p46 [1-50]
   WSJ-MW - v78 - D 18 '96 - pA18 [501+]
Tomlinson, Charles - *Jubilation*
   HR - v49 - Aut '96 - p513+ [501+]
Tomlinson, Jim - *Government and the Enterprise since 1900*
   Albion - v28 - '96 - p728+ [501+]
Tomlinson, Joe - *The Ultimate Encyclopedia of Extreme Sports*
   r Econ - v341 - D 7 '96 - p16* [51-250]
Tomlinson, Richard - *From Mycenae to Constantinople*
   CW - v89 - Jl '96 - p513 [51-250]
Tomlinson, Theresa - *The Forestwife*
   c PW - v244 - Ap 28 '97 - p77 [1-50]
   Haunted House Blues (Illus. by G Floyd)
   c JB - v60 - O '96 - p195 [51-250]
Tommasi, Mariano - *The New Economics of Human Behavior*
   Econ J - v106 - N '96 - p1834 [51-250]
   JEH - v57 - Mr '97 - p259+ [501+]
   Soc Ser R - v70 - D '96 - p670 [51-250]
Tommasini, Anthony - *Virgil Thomson: Composer on the Aisle*
   KR - v65 - My 1 '97 - p708 [251-500]
   PW - v244 - My 12 '97 - p65 [51-250]
Tomnay, Susan - *The Essential Vegetarian Cookbook*
   Mac - v109 - D 9 '96 - p66 [1-50]
Tomocik, Joseph - *The American Garden Guides*
   Fine Gard - N '96 - p68 [51-250]
Tomorrow's Morning
   cp Par Ch - v20 - O '96 - p15 [1-50]
Tomory, David - *A Season in Heaven*
   TLS - O 18 '96 - p31 [51-250]
Tompert, Ann - *How Rabbit Lost His Tail (Illus. by Jacqueline Chwast)*
   c PW - v244 - Mr 24 '97 - p82+ [51-250]
   The Jade Horse, the Cricket, and the Peach Stone (Illus. by Winson Trang)
   c CBRS - v25 - S '96 - p9 [51-250]
   c HB Guide - v8 - Spr '97 - p51 [51-250]
   c PW - v243 - S 23 '96 - p76 [51-250]
   c SLJ - v42 - D '96 - p107 [51-250]

Tompkins, Jane - *A Life in School*
   Ant R - v55 - Spr '97 - p238 [251-500]
   BW - v27 - Ja 5 '97 - p3+ [501+]
   Comw - v123 - D 6 '96 - p20 [51-250]
   KR - v64 - S 15 '96 - p1388+ [251-500]
   NYTBR - v102 - Ap 6 '97 - p20 [51-250]
   PW - v243 - S 23 '96 - p66 [51-250]
Tompkins, Nancy - *Roe v. Wade*
   y BL - v93 - F 1 '97 - p935 [51-250]
   y HB Guide - v8 - Spr '97 - p93 [51-250]
   y SLJ - v43 - F '97 - p126 [51-250]
Tompkins, Peter - *The Secret Life of Nature*
   PW - v244 - My 5 '97 - p188+ [51-250]
Tompkins, Vincent - *American Decades 1900-1909*
   yr ARBA - v28 - '97 - p195 [51-250]
   American Decades 1910-1919
   yr ARBA - v28 - '97 - p195 [51-250]
Tompson, William J - *Khrushchev: A Political Life*
   AHR - v101 - O '96 - p1250+ [501+]
Tonchev, Vladimir - *Codes, Designs, and Geometry*
   SciTech - v21 - Mr '97 - p17 [51-250]
Tone, John Lawrence - *The Fatal Knot*
   EHR - v112 - Ap '97 - p498+ [501+]
   Historian - v58 - Sum '96 - p919+ [251-500]
   JMH - v68 - S '96 - p697+ [501+]
Toner, Barbara - *An Organised Woman*
   TLS - O 11 '96 - p27 [251-500]
Toner, James H - *True Faith and Allegiance*
   Soc - v33 - Jl '96 - p82+ [501+]
Toner, Jules J - *Spirit of Light or Darkness?*
   Am - v175 - N 2 '96 - p29 [51-250]
   What Is Your Will, O God?
   Am - v175 - N 2 '96 - p29 [51-250]
Toner, Michael - *Seeing the Light*
   Books - v11 - Ap '97 - p22 [51-250]
   NS - v126 - Ja 24 '97 - p45+ [251-500]
Tong, Benson - *Unsubmissive Women*
   Ch Rev Int - v3 - Fall '96 - p542+ [501+]
Tong, Keith S T - *Colloquial Cantonese*
   MLJ - v80 - Fall '96 - p407+ [251-500]
Tong, Rosemarie - *Feminist Approaches to Bioethics*
   SciTech - v21 - Mr '97 - p63 [51-250]
Tonge, Neil - *Tudor Times*
   TES - D 13 '96 - p43 [51-250]
Tongeren, F W Van - *Microsimulation Modelling of the Corporate Firm*
   JEL - v34 - S '96 - p1452 [51-250]
Tongerloo, Alois Van - *The Manichaean Nous*
   Rel St Rev - v23 - Ap '97 - p188+ [51-250]
Tonkin, Elizabeth - *Narrating Our Pasts*
   RA - v25 - 3 '96 - p215+ [501+]
Tonkinson, Carole - *Wake Up and Cook*
   BL - v93 - Ja '97 - p802 [51-250]
   PW - v244 - Ja 6 '97 - p71 [51-250]
Tonnessen, Diana - *50 Essential Things to Do When the Doctor Says It's Diabetes*
   BL - v92 - Ag '96 - p1870 [51-250]
Tonry, Michael - *Building a Safer Society*
   CS - v25 - S '96 - p666+ [501+]
   R&R Bk N - v11 - D '96 - p45 [51-250]
   Malign Neglect
   Bl S - v26 - Fall '96 - p75+ [501+]
   y Kliatt - v30 - S '96 - p32 [51-250]
Toobin, Jeffrey - *The Run of His Life*
   ABA Jour - v82 - D '96 - p92+ [501+]
   BL - v93 - O 1 '96 - p292 [1-50]
   BW - v26 - S 22 '96 - p3+ [501+]
   Ent W - S 20 '96 - p73 [51-250]
   Esq - v126 - N '96 - p65 [1-50]
   LATBR - S 8 '96 - p3 [501+]
   New R - v215 - D 9 '96 - p27+ [501+]
   NY - v72 - D 16 '96 - p107 [51-250]
   NYTBR - v101 - S 29 '96 - p12 [501+]
   NYTBR - v101 - D 8 '96 - p92 [1-50]
   NYTBR - v102 - Ap 20 '97 - p32 [51-250]
   NYTLa - v145 - S 10 '96 - pC14 [501+]
   TLS - N 29 '96 - p13+ [51-250]
   Trib Bks - Ap 27 '97 - p8 [1-50]
   WSJ-MW - v78 - O 24 '96 - pA16 [51-250]
Toobin, Jerome - *Agitato: A Romp through NYC's Music Scene (Toobin). Audio Version*
   LJ - v122 - My 1 '97 - p156 [51-250]
Toogood, Granville N - *The Inspired Executive*
   BL - v93 - My 1 '97 - p1468 [51-250]
Tooker, Elisabeth - *Lewis H. Morgan on Iroquois Material Culture*
   Am Ethnol - v24 - F '97 - p232+ [501+]
Tool, Marc R - *Pricing, Valuation and Systems*
   Econ J - v106 - S '96 - p1467 [51-250]
Toole, D H - *Moonlit Days and Nights*
   Essays CW - Spr '96 - p185+ [501+]

Tooley, James - *Education without the State*
   TES - Ja 31 '97 - p8* [251-500]
Tooley, Michael H - *Newnes Computer Engineer's Pocket Book. 4th Ed.*
   r SciTech - v20 - N '96 - p76 [51-250]
Toolis, Kevin - *Rebel Hearts*
   BL - v93 - Ja '97 - p760 [1-50]
Toombs, S Kay - *Chronic Illness*
   MHR - v10 - Fall '96 - p124+ [501+]
Toomer, Jean - *Jean Toomer: Selected Essays and Literary Criticism*
   Choice - v34 - My '97 - p1496 [51-250]
Toomey, Alice - *A World Bibliography of Bibliographies 1964-1974. Vols. 1-2*
   r ASInt - v34 - O '96 - p20 [1-50]
The Top Ten of Everything 1997
   y Kliatt - v31 - Ja '97 - p33 [51-250]
   y SLJ - v43 - Mr '97 - p218 [51-250]
Toplin, Robert Brent - *History by Hollywood*
   Choice - v34 - Ja '97 - p804 [51-250]
   Si & So - v6 - N '96 - p34 [51-250]
   VV - v41 - O 1 '96 - p39+ [251-500]
   Ken Burns's The Civil War
   HRNB - v25 - Win '97 - p58+ [501+]
   Trib Bks - My 18 '97 - p8 [1-50]
Topliss, Helen - *Modernism and Feminism*
   Aust Bk R - v - Ag '96 - p28+ [501+]
   Choice - v34 - Ap '97 - p1327 [51-250]
   Meanjin - v55 - 3 '96 - p473+ [501+]
Toporowski, Jan - *The Economics of Financial Markets and the 1987 Crash*
   Econ J - v106 - N '96 - p1839 [51-250]
Tordoir, Pieter P - *The Professional Knowledge Economy*
   JEL - v34 - S '96 - p1457 [51-250]
Torfs, Rik - *A Healthy Rivalry*
   Theol St - v57 - D '96 - p781+ [251-500]
Torgovnick, Marianna - *Primitive Passions*
   BL - v93 - D 15 '96 - p697 [51-250]
   LJ - v122 - Ap 15 '97 - p88 [51-250]
   PW - v244 - F 10 '97 - p73 [51-250]
Tornabene, Wanda - *La Cucina Siciliana Di Gangivecchio*
   BL - v93 - S 15 '96 - p198 [51-250]
   LJ - v121 - N 15 '96 - p83+ [51-250]
   PW - v243 - S 2 '96 - p122+ [51-250]
Tornqvist, Emil - *Between Stage and Screen*
   FQ - v50 - Win '96 - p47+ [501+]
Toropov, Brandon - *50 Biggest Baseball Myths*
   LJ - v122 - F 1 '97 - p83 [1-50]
   Last Minute Interview Tips
   BWatch - v17 - S '96 - p8 [51-250]
   Last Minute Job Search Tips
   BWatch - v17 - S '96 - p8 [51-250]
Torpey, John C - *Intellectuals, Socialism, and Dissent*
   AJS - v102 - N '96 - p901+ [501+]
   APSR - v90 - D '96 - p947+ [501+]
   CS - v26 - Mr '97 - p178+ [501+]
Torra, Joseph - *Gas Station*
   BL - v93 - S 15 '96 - p222+ [51-250]
   LATBR - N 3 '96 - p6 [501+]
   LJ - v122 - Mr 15 '97 - p112 [51-250]
   NYTBR - v102 - F 9 '97 - p20 [51-250]
   PW - v243 - N 4 '96 - p38 [51-250]
Torrado, Antonio - *O Mercador De Coisa Nenhuma (Illus. by Angela Melo)*
   c Bkbird - v34 - Spr '96 - p53 [1-50]
   Teatro As Tres Pancadas (Illus. by Joao Caetano)
   c Bkbird - v34 - Spr '96 - p53 [1-50]
Torrance, John - *Karl Marx's Theory of Ideas*
   AJS - v102 - Jl '96 - p263+ [501+]
Torrance, Robert M - *The Spiritual Quest*
   JAAR - v65 - Spr '97 - p212+ [501+]
   Rel St Rev - v23 - Ap '97 - p141+ [501+]
Torrance, Thomas F - *Divine Meaning*
   Theol St - v57 - D '96 - p743+ [501+]
   Trinitarian Perspectives
   Theol St - v57 - Mr '96 - p188+ [251-500]
Torre, Joe - *Chasing the Dream*
   NYTBR - v102 - Ap 20 '97 - p21 [51-250]
Torre-Bueno, Ava - *Peace after Abortion*
   Cons - v17 - Win '96 - p31 [1-50]
Torrell, Jean-Pierre - *Saint Thomas Aquinas. Vol. 1*
   Choice - v34 - Ap '97 - p1354 [51-250]
Torres, Carlos Alberto - *The Church, Society, and Hegemony*
   CH - v65 - D '96 - p780+ [251-500]
Torres, Daniel - *Tom (Illus. by Daniel Torres)*
   c HB Guide - v7 - Fall '96 - p279 [1-50]
   c LATBR - Mr 24 '96 - p11 [51-250]
   c SLJ - v42 - Ag '96 - p131+ [51-250]

Torres, Dominique - *Esclaves*
 BL - v93 - Ja '97 - p827 [1-50]
Torres, Laura - *Friendship Bracelets*
 c PW - v243 - O 7 '96 - p78 [51-250]
 Pipe Cleaners Gone Crazy
 c PW - v244 - Ap 7 '97 - p94 [51-250]
Torres, Leyla - *Saturday Sancocho (Illus. by Leyla Torres)*
 c RT - v50 - F '97 - p426 [51-250]
Torres, Luis - *Video Coding*
 SciTech - v20 - D '96 - p77 [51-250]
Torres, Olga Beatriz - *Memorias De Mi Viaje*
 HAHR - v76 - Ag '96 - p576+ [251-500]
Torreson, Rodney - *The Ripening of Pinstripes*
 BL - v93 - My 15 '97 - p1558 [51-250]
Torrey, E Fuller - *Out of the Shadows*
 KR - v64 - O 1 '96 - p1457 [251-500]
 LJ - v122 - F 1 '97 - p97 [51-250]
 NYTBR - v102 - Ja 19 '97 - p15 [501+]
Torrington, Derek - *Personnel Management. 3rd Ed.*
 R&R Bk N - v11 - D '96 - p35 [51-250]
Torrington, Jeff - *The Devil's Carousel*
 LJ - v122 - Ap 15 '97 - p121 [51-250]
Torruella I Casanas, Joan - *La Rima En La Lirica Medieval*
 Hisp - v79 - D '96 - p797+ [501+]
Tort, Patrick - *Dictionnaire Di Darwinisme Et De L'Evolution. Vols. 1-3*
 r Sci - v274 - D 20 '96 - p2032 [501+]
Tortora, Phyllis B - *Fairchild's Dictionary of Textiles. 7th Ed.*
 r TCI - v30 - O '96 - p56 [1-50]
Torvill, Jayne - *Torvill and Dean*
 Books - v9 - S '95 - p23 [51-250]
Tosches, Nick - *Country: The Twisted Roots of Rock 'n' Roll*
 PW - v243 - O 21 '96 - p78 [1-50]
Toth, Jennifer - *Orphans of the Living*
 y BL - v93 - My 15 '97 - p1548 [51-250]
 KR - v65 - Mr 1 '97 - p368 [51-250]
 LJ - v122 - My 1 '97 - p128 [51-250]
 PW - v244 - Mr 3 '97 - p54 [51-250]
Toth, Susan Allen - *England for All Seasons*
 LJ - v122 - Ap 15 '97 - p105 [51-250]
 PW - v243 - D 16 '96 - p47 [51-250]
Totman, Conrad - *The Lumber Industry in Early Modern Japan*
 Historian - v59 - Win '97 - p453+ [501+]
Totten, Herman L - *Culturally Diverse Library Collections for Youth*
 r CLW - v67 - Mr '97 - p47+ [51-250]
 r Emerg Lib - v24 - S '96 - p42 [1-50]
 r SLJ - v42 - N '96 - p42 [51-250]
 r SLMQ - v25 - Fall '96 - p66 [51-250]
Totten, Samuel - *Middle Level Education*
 r ARBA - v28 - '97 - p136+ [251-500]
 r Choice - v34 - N '96 - p434 [51-250]
Tougas, Gerald - *La Cle De Sol Et Autres Recits*
 FR - v70 - Mr '97 - p622+ [251-500]
Tough, Frank - *As Their Natural Resources Fail*
 Choice - v34 - D '96 - p679 [51-250]
 JEL - v34 - D '96 - p2102 [51-250]
Tougias, Michael - *Quiet Places of Massachusetts*
 r BL - v93 - S 15 '96 - p210 [1-50]
Toullelan, Pierre-Yves - *Missionnaires Au Quotidien A Tahiti*
 CHR - v83 - Ja '97 - p157+ [251-500]
Toumey, Christopher P - *Conjuring Science*
 Choice - v34 - F '97 - p982 [51-250]
 Nature - v384 - D 5 '96 - p423 [501+]
 New Sci - v152 - D 14 '96 - p46 [51-250]
 SB - v33 - Mr '97 - p36+ [251-500]
 Sci - v274 - N 1 '96 - p732+ [501+]
Touraine, Alain - *The Academic System in American Society*
 JEL - v35 - Mr '97 - p232 [51-250]
 Critique of Modernity
 AS - v66 - Spr '97 - p303+ [501+]
Tourism in Europe. 1995 Ed.
 J Gov Info - v23 - S '96 - p669 [51-250]
Tournavitou, Iphiyenia - *The Ivory Houses at Mycenae*
 AJA - v100 - Jl '96 - p615+ [501+]
Tourneur, Dina Kathelyn - *Marmouset Compte De Un A Dix*
 c BL - v93 - N 1 '96 - p500 [1-50]
Tournier, Michel - *Friday*
 PW - v244 - Mr 17 '97 - p81 [1-50]
 Le Miroir Des Idees
 FR - v70 - O '96 - p149+ [501+]
 The Ogre
 PW - v244 - Mr 17 '97 - p81 [1-50]

Tournikiotis, Panayotis - *The Parthenon and Its Impact in Modern Times*
 AJA - v100 - Jl '96 - p601+ [501+]
 Arch - v49 - S '96 - p80+ [501+]
 NYTBR - v101 - D 8 '96 - p54 [51-250]
Tournon, Andre - *En Sens Agile*
 MLR - v92 - Ja '97 - p187+ [251-500]
 Six Ct J - v27 - Fall '96 - p827+ [501+]
 Montaigne Et La Rhetorique
 Ren Q - v50 - Spr '97 - p252+ [501+]
 Or, Monnaie, Echange Dans La Culture De La Renaissance
 FR - v70 - Mr '97 - p593+ [501+]
Tourrenc, Philippe - *Relativity and Gravitation*
 Nature - v386 - Mr 13 '97 - p142 [51-250]
Toury, Gideon - *Descriptive Translation Studies and Beyond*
 TLS - S 6 '96 - p9+ [501+]
 TranslRev - 51 '96 - p50+ [501+]
Toussaint, Stephane - *Ilaria Del Carretto E Il Suo Monumento*
 Ren & Ref - v20 - Win '96 - p83+ [501+]
Toutenburg, Helge - *Experimental Design and Model Choice*
 JEL - v34 - D '96 - p2024 [51-250]
Tovar Pinzon, Hermes - *Convocatoria Al Poder Del Numero*
 HAHR - v77 - F '97 - p122+ [251-500]
Tovee, Martin J - *An Introduction to the Visual System*
 Choice - v34 - Mr '97 - p1183+ [51-250]
Tovell, Rosemarie - *A New Class of Art*
 CF - v75 - N '96 - p44+ [501+]
Toward Gender Equality
 J Gov Info - v23 - S '96 - p689 [51-250]
Towards Holistic Wellness
 J Gov Info - v23 - S '96 - p622 [51-250]
Tower, Edward - *Economics Reading Lists, Course Outlines, Exams, Puzzles and Problems. Vols. 1-25*
 r JEL - v34 - S '96 - p1405+ [251-500]
Towles, Louis P - *A World Turned Upside Down*
 Choice - v34 - My '97 - p1566 [51-250]
Town, Elke - *Video by Artists 2*
 Afterimage - v24 - N '96 - p4 [1-50]
The Towneley Plays. Vols. 1-2
 MLR - v92 - Ap '97 - p436+ [501+]
 RES - v47 - N '96 - p565+ [501+]
 Specu - v71 - O '96 - p1031+ [501+]
Towner, Ronald H - *The Archaeology of Navajo Origins*
 Choice - v34 - F '97 - p1004 [51-250]
 R&R Bk N - v11 - D '96 - p13 [51-250]
Townes, Emilie M - *In a Blaze of Glory*
 TT - v53 - Ja '97 - p536+ [501+]
Townley, Robert C - *Immunopharmacology of Allergic Diseases*
 SciTech - v20 - D '96 - p46 [51-250]
Townsend, Charles - *World's Most Perplexing Puzzles*
 c Ch BWatch - v6 - My '96 - p1 [1-50]
Townsend, Eileen - *Thine Is the Kingdom*
 Books - v10 - Je '96 - p23+ [51-250]
Townsend, Helen - *Turning Point*
 Aust Bk R - S '96 - p66 [251-500]
Townsend, Kim - *Manhood at Harvard*
 BW - v26 - N 3 '96 - p13 [51-250]
 Choice - v34 - Ja '97 - p866 [51-250]
 LJ - v121 - O 1 '96 - p102 [51-250]
 Nat R - v49 - Mr 10 '97 - p58 [251-500]
 NYTBR - v102 - Ja 5 '97 - p16+ [501+]
Townsend, Rhys F - *The East Side of the Agora*
 AJA - v100 - Jl '96 - p620+ [501+]
Townsend, Sue - *The Secret Diary of Adrian Mole, Age 13 3/4*
 y BL - v93 - Ja '97 - p833 [1-50]
Townshend, Jules - *The Politics of Marxism*
 Choice - v34 - Ja '97 - p873 [51-250]
Townson, Hazel - *Charlie the Champion Traveller (Illus. by Philippe Dupasquier)*
 c Bks Keeps - Mr '97 - p22 [51-250]
 Tale of the Terrible Teeth (Illus. by Russell Ayto)
 c Sch Lib - v45 - F '97 - p34+ [51-250]
Toye, Patricia - *Israel: Boundary Disputes with Arab Neighbors 1946-1964. Vols. 1-10*
 r MEJ - v51 - Win '97 - p149 [251-500]
Toynbee, J M C - *Animals in Roman Life and Art*
 y Kliatt - v31 - Mr '97 - p32+ [51-250]
Tozer, Edwin - *Strategic IS/IT Planning*
 CBR - v14 - N '96 - p34 [51-250]
Trabin, Tom - *The Computerization of Behavioral Healthcare*
 SciTech - v20 - N '96 - p42 [51-250]

Tracey, Liz - *So You Want to Be a Lesbian?*
 Prog - v61 - Ja '97 - p31 [251-500]
 Wom R Bks - v14 - Mr '97 - p6+ [501+]
Trachtenberg, Jeffrey A - *The Rain on Macy's Parade*
 BL - v93 - N 1 '96 - p467 [51-250]
 BW - v26 - N 17 '96 - p11+ [51-250]
 Ent W - D 20 '96 - p70 [51-250]
 Fortune - v134 - D 9 '96 - p219 [501+]
 KR - v64 - S 15 '96 - p1389 [251-500]
 LJ - v121 - N 1 '96 - p76 [51-250]
 NYTLa - v146 - N 18 '96 - pC14 [501+]
 PW - v243 - S 30 '96 - p67 [51-250]
 WSJ-MW - v78 - N 27 '96 - pA10 [501+]
 WSJ-MW - v78 - D 31 '96 - p17 [501+]
Trachtenberg, Peter - *Seven Tattoos*
 BL - v93 - Mr 15 '97 - p1209 [51-250]
 KR - v65 - Mr 1 '97 - p369 [51-250]
 LJ - v122 - Ap 15 '97 - p82 [51-250]
 PW - v244 - F 10 '97 - p71 [51-250]
Tracqui, Valerie - *Animal Babies*
 c SLJ - v42 - Ag '96 - p141 [51-250]
 Funny Faces
 c KR - v64 - D 15 '96 - p1806 [51-250]
 My Home Is the Desert
 c HB Guide - v7 - Fall '96 - p339 [1-50]
 My Home Is the Farm
 c HB Guide - v7 - Fall '96 - p339 [1-50]
 c SLJ - v42 - Ag '96 - p141 [51-250]
 My Home Is the Mountains
 c HB Guide - v7 - Fall '96 - p339 [1-50]
 My Home Is the Polar Regions
 c HB Guide - v7 - Fall '96 - p339 [1-50]
 My Home Is the Sea
 c HB Guide - v7 - Fall '96 - p339 [1-50]
Tractor (Snapshot Books)
 c Ch BWatch - v6 - D '96 - p8 [1-50]
Tracy, Brian - *Maximum Achievement*
 Rapport - v19 - 4 '96 - p18+ [501+]
Tracy, Charles - *Physical Processes*
 y Sch Lib - v44 - N '96 - p175 [251-500]
Tracy, David - *On Naming the Present*
 Rel St Rev - v23 - Ap '97 - p154 [51-250]
Tracy, Deborah - *CyberHound's Guide to People on the Internet*
 r BL - v93 - F 1 '97 - p963+ [251-500]
Tracy, James - *Direct Action*
 CC - v113 - D 18 '96 - p1261+ [51-250]
 Choice - v34 - Ja '97 - p866 [51-250]
 NYTBR - v101 - S 29 '96 - p25 [501+]
Tracy, Nicholas - *Nelson's Battles*
 Sea H - Win '96 - p43 [251-500]
Tracy, Paul E - *Continuity and Discontinuity in Criminal Careers*
 R&R Bk N - v12 - F '97 - p57 [1-50]
Tracy, Stephen V - *Athenian Democracy in Transition*
 AJA - v100 - O '96 - p811 [251-500]
Trade and Development Report 1996
 JEL - v35 - Mr '97 - p274 [51-250]
Traditions and Transitions
 EGH - v50 - N '96 - p154 [51-250]
Trafalgar Square (Holiday Geology Guides)
 New Sci - v153 - Mr 22 '97 - p47 [51-250]
Trahant, LeNora Begay - *The Success of the Navajo Arts and Crafts Enterprise (Illus. by Monty Roessel)*
 y HB Guide - v7 - Fall '96 - p313 [1-50]
Traill, Catharine Parr - *I Bless You in My Heart*
 Quill & Q - v63 - F '97 - p44 [251-500]
 TLS - Mr 21 '97 - p13 [251-500]
Traill, David A - *Schliemann of Troy*
 NYRB - v43 - D 19 '96 - p15+ [501+]
 VR - v84 - O '96 - p119+ [501+]
Traill, Nancy H - *Possible Worlds of the Fantastic*
 Choice - v34 - Ja '97 - p794+ [51-250]
 R&R Bk N - v11 - N '96 - p68 [51-250]
Training and Development Yearbook 1996/1997
 r Bus Bk R - v14 - 1 '97 - p123 [51-250]
Trainor, Luke - *British Imperialism and Australian Nationalism*
 AHR - v101 - D '96 - p1602+ [501+]
 EHR - v112 - F '97 - p247+ [501+]
 VS - v39 - Win '96 - p277+ [501+]
Trainor, Michael - *A Decent Boldness*
 Am Phil - v110 - S '96 - p844 [51-250]
Trainor, Richard H - *Black Country Elites*
 JMH - v69 - Mr '97 - p142+ [501+]
Traister, John E - *Electrical Wiring Design*
 Choice - v34 - F '97 - p995 [51-250]
Tramer, Andre - *Fast Elementary Processes in Chemical and Biological Systems*
 SciTech - v20 - S '96 - p15 [51-250]

Trammell, Mary Metzner - *The Reforming Power of the Scriptures*
  LJ - v122 - Mr 15 '97 - p67 [51-250]
Tran, Doan Nho - *Vet Xuoc Dau Doi*
  BL - v93 - S 1 '96 - p70 [51-250]
Tran, Gia Phung - *Trung Ky Dan Bjen 1908*
  BL - v93 - My 15 '97 - p1568 [1-50]
Tran, Hoai Huong - *The Official Guide to Household Spending. 3rd Ed.*
  r ARBA - v28 - '97 - p127 [251-500]
Tran, Mong Tu - *Cau Chuyen Cua La Phong*
  BL - v93 - S 1 '96 - p70 [51-250]
Tran, Quan Niem - *Nu Non Tren Nhanh Kho*
  BL - v93 - S 1 '96 - p70 [51-250]
Tran, Qui - *Long Tin Au My Day*
  BL - v93 - My 15 '97 - p1568 [1-50]
Tran, Thy Van - *Anh Hung Bat Mang*
  BL - v93 - My 15 '97 - p1568 [1-50]
Trance and Recalcitrance
  BC - v44 - Win '95 - p498 [51-250]
Trang, Chan - *Ve Bien Dong*
  BL - v93 - My 15 '97 - p1568 [1-50]
Transactions of the Canadian Numismatic Research Society. Vol. 32
  Coin W - v38 - F 3 '97 - p72 [1-50]
Transforming Libraries
  p LJ - v122 - Ap 15 '97 - p126 [51-250]
Transit
  p TLS - N 15 '96 - p27+ [501+]
The Transition from Work to Retirement
  J Gov Info - v23 - S '96 - p675+ [51-250]
Transnational Corporations
  p JEL - v35 - Mr '97 - p310 [51-250]
Transport and Storage of Radioactive Materials 1996
  SciTech - v20 - D '96 - p86 [51-250]
Transport Infrastructure in Central and Eastern European Countries
  J Gov Info - v23 - S '96 - p666 [51-250]
Transportation-Related Air Quality and Energy
  R&R Bk N - v12 - F '97 - p43 [1-50]
Transtromer, Tomas - *For the Living and the Dead*
  LATBR - My 12 '96 - p6 [251-500]
  Sorgegondolen
  WLT - v71 - Win '97 - p174 [501+]
Tranter, Jeff - *LINUX Multimedia Guide*
  LJ - v121 - N 1 '96 - p104 [51-250]
Tranter, N L - *British Population in the Twentieth Century*
  R&R Bk N - v11 - N '96 - p25 [1-50]
Tranter, Nigel - *Poetic Justice*
  PW - v244 - Mr 31 '97 - p68+ [1-50]
Trapani, Iza - *I'm a Little Teapot (Illus. by Iza Trapani)*
  c CBRS - v25 - S '96 - p6 [51-250]
  c HB Guide - v8 - Spr '97 - p141 [51-250]
Trapani, Margi - *Listen Up!*
  y Cur R - v36 - Ap '97 - p12 [51-250]
  Reality Check
  y Cur R - v36 - Ap '97 - p12 [51-250]
  Working Together against Gang Violence
  c SLJ - v43 - F '97 - p107+ [51-250]
Trapl, Milos - *Political Catholicism and the Czechoslovak People's Party in Czechoslovakia 1918-1938*
  Slav R - v55 - Sum '96 - p454+ [501+]
Trask, Kerry A - *Fire Within*
  AHR - v102 - F '97 - p192+ [251-500]
Trask, R L - *A Dictionary of Phonetics and Phonology*
  r ARBA - v28 - '97 - p377 [251-500]
Trasko, Mary - *Daring Do's*
  JPC - v30 - Fall '96 - p228+ [51-250]
Tratner, Michael - *Modernism and Mass Politics*
  TLS - Ag 30 '96 - p6 [501+]
Tratt, Jacqueline - *The Macmillan Government and Europe*
  Choice - v34 - Mr '97 - p1224 [51-250]
  Econ - v342 - F 15 '97 - p5*+ [501+]
  TLS - F 28 '97 - p14 [501+]
Traub, Valerie - *Desire and Anxiety*
  Queens Q - v103 - Win '96 - p807+ [501+]
Traubel, Horace - *With Walt Whitman in Camden. Vols. 8-9*
  LJ - v122 - Ap 15 '97 - p82 [51-250]
Traugott, Mark - *Repertoires and Cycles of Collective Action*
  JIH - v27 - Win '97 - p501+ [501+]
  Socio R - v45 - F 1 '97 - p147+ [501+]
Traupman, John C - *Latin Is Fun. Bk. 2*
  y Class Out - v74 - Spr '97 - p122+ [251-500]
Traveler's Tales Hong Kong
  r BL - v93 - S 15 '96 - p212 [1-50]

Travers, Bridget - *The Gale Encyclopedia of Science. Vols. 1-6*
  r ARBA - v28 - '97 - p563+ [51-250]
  yr BL - v93 - O 1 '96 - p368+ [51-250]
  r Choice - v34 - Ja '97 - p769 [51-250]
  r LJ - v121 - S 15 '96 - p54 [51-250]
Travers, Peter - *The Rolling Stone Film Reader*
  PW - v243 - N 4 '96 - p70 [51-250]
Travers, Will - *The Elephant Truck (Illus. by Lawrie Taylor)*
  c TES - F 21 '97 - p16* [51-250]
Traverso, Enzo - *The Jews and Germany*
  AHR - v101 - D '96 - p1569+ [501+]
  CEH - v29 - 2 '96 - p267+ [501+]
  TranslRevS - v2 - D '96 - p17 [51-250]
Travis, Brian E - *The SGML Implementation Guide*
  BYTE - v21 - S '96 - p34 [251-500]
Travis, Dempsey J - *The Louis Armstrong Odyssey*
  BL - v93 - F 15 '97 - p992 [51-250]
  LJ - v122 - Ap 15 '97 - p84 [51-250]
Travis-Bildahl, Sandra - *A Day in the Life of a Midshipman*
  c HB Guide - v8 - Spr '97 - p94 [51-250]
Travitsky, Betty S - *Attending to Women in Early Modern England*
  Ren Q - v49 - Win '96 - p898+ [501+]
Traylor, Ellen Gunderson - *Melchizedek*
  BL - v93 - Ja '97 - p819 [51-250]
  LJ - v122 - Ap 1 '97 - p80 [51-250]
Traynor, John - *The Struggle for Peace 1918-1989*
  y TES - Mr 28 '97 - p13* [501+]
Treacy, John M - *Las Chacras De Coporaque*
  AAAGA - v86 - D '96 - p786+ [501+]
  LA Ant - v7 - S '96 - p284+ [501+]
Treadgold, Warren - *Byzantium and Its Army 284-1081*
  J Mil H - v61 - Ap '97 - p360+ [501+]
Treadway, David C - *Dead Reckoning*
  BL - v92 - Ag '96 - p1858 [51-250]
  LATBR - O 6 '96 - p14 [51-250]
  LJ - v121 - O 1 '96 - p108 [51-250]
Treadway, Sandra Gioia - *Women of Mark*
  J Gov Info - v23 - S '96 - p596 [51-250]
  JSH - v62 - N '96 - p831+ [251-500]
Treadwell, Timothy - *Among Grizzlies*
  PW - v244 - Mr 17 '97 - p66 [51-250]
Treagust, David F - *Improving Teaching and Learning in Science and Mathematics*
  Math T - v89 - O '96 - p606+ [51-250]
Trease, Geoffrey - *Page to Jane Seymour (Illus. by Pauline Hazelwood)*
  c Bks Keeps - N '96 - p9+ [51-250]
  c Sch Lib - v44 - N '96 - p148 [51-250]
Treasure, G R R - *Mazarin: The Crisis of Absolutism in France*
  Choice - v34 - Ja '97 - p859 [51-250]
  HRNB - v25 - Win '97 - p91+ [501+]
  Rel St Rev - v23 - Ja '97 - p85 [51-250]
  R&R Bk N - v11 - N '96 - p12 [51-250]
  Six Ct J - v27 - Win '96 - p1193+ [501+]
  TLS - Ag 30 '96 - p27 [501+]
A Treasury of Prayers
  c JB - v60 - D '96 - p276 [51-250]
  c Sch Lib - v44 - N '96 - p166 [51-250]
Treasury of Wise Action
  c Ch BWatch - v6 - Jl '96 - p2 [51-250]
Treat, John Whittier - *Writing Ground Zero*
  Pac A - v69 - Fall '96 - p422+ [501+]
Treat, Rose - *The Seaweed Book*
  c Sch Lib - v44 - Ag '96 - p114 [51-250]
The Treatment of Dual Diagnosis
  J Gov Info - v23 - S '96 - p606+ [51-250]
Trebilcock, Michael J - *The Regulation of International Trade*
  Econ J - v107 - Ja '97 - p270+ [251-500]
Trechsel, Gail Andrews - *Pictured in My Mind*
  Choice - v34 - Mr '97 - p1153 [51-250]
Treckel, Paula A - *To Comfort the Heart*
  Choice - v34 - D '96 - p679 [51-250]
  HRNB - v25 - Win '97 - p63 [51-250]
Tredgold, Margaret H - *The Cucumber Girls and the Little Nurse*
  c Bkbird - v34 - Spr '96 - p54 [1-50]
Treese, Lorett - *Valley Forge*
  AHR - v101 - D '96 - p1620 [251-500]
Trefil, James - *Are We Unique?*
  KR - v65 - Ja 15 '97 - p131+ [251-500]
  LJ - v122 - Mr 15 '97 - p86 [51-250]
  PW - v244 - F 3 '97 - p86+ [51-250]

  The Edge of the Unknown
  y BL - v93 - S 15 '96 - p194 [51-250]
  y BL - v93 - D 1 '96 - p664 [1-50]
  BW - v26 - O 20 '96 - p8 [51-250]
  Choice - v34 - My '97 - p1519 [51-250]
  LJ - v121 - O 1 '96 - p122 [51-250]
  Nature - v384 - D 12 '96 - p528 [51-250]
  NYTBR - v101 - N 10 '96 - p57 [51-250]
  Skeptic - v4 - 4 '96 - p105+ [251-500]
Tregebov, Rhea - *Sasha and the Wind (Illus. by Helene Desputeaux)*
  c Quill & Q - v62 - O '96 - p47 [51-250]
Treib, Marc - *Sanctuaries of Spanish New Mexico*
  CH - v66 - Mr '97 - p203 [51-250]
Treip, Mindele Anne - *Allegorical Poetics and the Epic*
  CLS - v33 - 2 '96 - p198+ [501+]
  RES - v47 - N '96 - p573+ [501+]
Trejos S., Juan Diego - *La Lucha Contra La Pobreza En Costa Rica*
  BL - v93 - S 15 '96 - p227 [1-50]
Trela, D J - *Margaret Oliphant: Critical Essays on a Gentle Subversive*
  RES - v48 - F '97 - p130+ [501+]
  VS - v39 - Win '96 - p248+ [501+]
Tremaine, Jon - *Astrology and Predictions*
  c LATBR - Ag 25 '96 - p11 [51-250]
Tremaine, M David - *The Foot and Ankle Sourcebook*
  r ARBA - v28 - '97 - p609 [51-250]
Tremayne, Peter - *Shroud for the Archbishop*
  Arm Det - v30 - Win '97 - p102+ [251-500]
  KR - v64 - Ag 15 '96 - p1193+ [51-250]
Trembath, Don - *The Tuesday Cafe*
  y Ch Bk News - v20 - Win '97 - p30+ [51-250]
  y Kliatt - v30 - N '96 - p11 [51-250]
  y Quill & Q - v62 - My '96 - p34+ [501+]
  y SLJ - v42 - S '96 - p228+ [51-250]
  y VOYA - v19 - F '97 - p332+ [251-500]
Tremblay, Jean-Paul-Mederic - *Comme En Plein Jour*
  Ren & Ref - v20 - Win '96 - p89+ [501+]
Tremblay, Michel - *Marcel Pursued by the Hounds*
  Quill & Q - v62 - D '96 - p32 [501+]
Trembley, Elizabeth A - *Michael Crichton: A Critical Companion*
  y CLW - v67 - D '96 - p49 [251-500]
  Ext - v37 - Win '96 - p368+ [501+]
  SFS - v24 - Mr '97 - p176+ [501+]
  SLMQ - v24 - Sum '96 - p220 [51-250]
  VOYA - v19 - O '96 - p243+ [51-250]
Trends in Developing Economies 1996
  JEL - v35 - Mr '97 - p286 [51-250]
Trends in Educational Technology 1995
  Emerg Lib - v24 - Mr '97 - p42 [51-250]
Trends in Europe and North America 1995
  r ARBA - v28 - '97 - p326 [251-500]
The Trends Journal
  p LJ - v122 - F 15 '97 - p167 [51-250]
Trent, John - *Go the Distance*
  CC - v113 - O 9 '96 - p941+ [501+]
Trenter, Anna - *The Puffin Treasury of Children's Stories*
  c Bks Keeps - Ja '97 - p8+ [501+]
  The Viking Treasury of Children's Stories
  c PW - v244 - Ap 21 '97 - p73 [51-250]
Trenton, Patricia - *Independent Spirits*
  J Am Cult - v19 - Sum '96 - p160 [51-250]
  LATBR - D 8 '96 - p6 [51-250]
Treptow, Kurt W - *Historical Dictionary of Romania*
  r ARBA - v28 - '97 - p63 [251-500]
  r Choice - v34 - Ap '97 - p1318 [51-250]
  r R&R Bk N - v12 - F '97 - p18 [51-250]
Tresidder, Jody - *Hugh Grant: The Unauthorised Biography*
  Books - v10 - Je '96 - p [51-250]
Tresize, Percy - *Home of the Kadimakara People (Illus. by Percy Tresize)*
  c Aust Bk R - F '97 - p54+ [501+]
Treuer, David - *Little*
  Ent W - F 7 '97 - p65 [51-250]
  PW - v243 - D 9 '96 - p66 [51-250]
Trevelyan, Julian - *Indigo Days*
  TLS - N 15 '96 - p16 [501+]
Trevelyan, Raleigh - *The Companion Guide to Sicily*
  r TLS - Ap 11 '97 - p28 [51-250]
Trevino, A Javier - *The Sociology of Law*
  R&R Bk N - v11 - N '96 - p52 [51-250]
Trevor, Penelope - *Listening for Small Sounds*
  Aust Bk R - D '96 - p57 [501+]

Trevor, William - *After Rain*
BL - v92 - Ag '96 - p1857 [251-500]
BL - v93 - Ap 1 '97 - p1285 [1-50]
ILS - v16 - Spr '97 - p4 [501+]
LATBR - O 20 '96 - p2 [501+]
LATBR - D 29 '96 - p11 [1-50]
LJ - v121 - S 15 '96 - p100 [51-250]
NY - v72 - D 16 '96 - p108 [51-250]
NYRB - v44 - F 20 '97 - p19+ [501+]
NYTBR - v101 - O 20 '96 - p15 [501+]
NYTBR - v101 - D 8 '96 - p11 [51-250]
NYTLa - v146 - N 12 '96 - pC15 [501+]
Obs - N 10 '96 - p17* [501+]
Spec - v277 - O 5 '96 - p51+ [501+]
TLS - S 27 '96 - p23 [501+]
WSJ-MW - v77 - O 2 '96 - pA12 [501+]
Elizabeth Alone
NYTBR - v101 - D 29 '96 - p20 [51-250]
Felicia's Journey (Prebble). Audio Version
y Kliatt - v30 - S '96 - p48 [51-250]
Felicia's Journey (Hilder). Audio Version
y Kliatt - v31 - Ja '97 - p40 [51-250]
The Love Department
NYTBR - v101 - D 29 '96 - p20 [1-50]
Miss Gomez and the Brethren
KR - v65 - Mr 15 '97 - p414+ [251-500]
PW - v244 - Ap 14 '97 - p55 [51-250]
Trib Bks - My 11 '97 - p8 [1-50]
The Old Boys
NYTBR - v101 - D 29 '96 - p20 [51-250]
Two Lives
SFR - v21 - N '96 - p48 [1-50]
Trexler, Richard C - *Dependence in Context in Renaissance Florence*
Historian - v59 - Win '97 - p406+ [501+]
Ren Q - v49 - Aut '96 - p621+ [501+]
Gender Rhetorics
Ren Q - v49 - Win '96 - p895+ [501+]
Sex and Conquest
CS - v26 - Ja '97 - p46+ [501+]
HAHR - v77 - F '97 - p102+ [501+]
RP - v58 - Fall '96 - p819+ [501+]
Tri-quarterly (Northwester University)
p Sm Pr R - v28 - D '96 - p22 [51-250]
Tribble, Evelyn B - *Margins and Marginality*
Ren Q - v49 - Win '96 - p869+ [501+]
Tribe, Keith - *Strategies of Economic Order*
AHR - v101 - O '96 - p1239 [501+]
Econ J - v107 - Ja '97 - p248+ [501+]
JMH - v69 - Mr '97 - p175+ [501+]
Trible, Phyllis - *Feminist Approaches to the Bible*
Rel St Rev - v23 - Ap '97 - p170 [51-250]
Rhetorical Criticism
Intpr - v51 - Ja '97 - p84+ [251-500]
JR - v77 - Ja '97 - p122+ [501+]
Tribole, Evelyn - *Healthy Homestyle Desserts*
BL - v93 - S 15 '96 - p196 [51-250]
LJ - v121 - N 15 '96 - p84 [51-250]
PW - v243 - S 16 '96 - p79 [51-250]
Tricard, Louise Mead - *American Women's Track and Field*
r ARBA - v28 - '97 - p302 [251-500]
BL - v93 - D 15 '96 - p744+ [251-500]
Choice - v34 - F '97 - p1003 [51-250]
r R&R Bk N - v11 - N '96 - p23 [51-250]
Trice, Dawn Turner - *Only Twice I've Wished for Heaven*
BL - v93 - N 15 '96 - p573 [51-250]
KR - v64 - N 1 '96 - p1563 [251-500]
LJ - v121 - S 15 '96 - p98 [51-250]
NYTBR - v102 - F 23 '97 - p16 [51-250]
PW - v243 - N 4 '96 - p62 [51-250]
Trib Bks - F 23 '97 - p6+ [501+]
Tricomi, Albert H - *Reading Tudor-Stuart Texts through Cultural Historicism*
Choice - v34 - Mr '97 - p1168 [51-250]
Tricontinental Meeting of Hair Research Societies (1st: 1995: Brussels, Belgium) - *Hair Research for the Next Millennium*
SciTech - v20 - D '96 - p54 [51-250]
Triebs, Michaela - *Die Medizinische Fakultat Der Universitat Helmstedt 1576-1810*
r Lib - v18 - S '96 - p272 [51-250]
Trieste Conference on Chemical Evolution (4th: 1995: Trieste, Italy) - *Chemical Evolution—Physics of the Origin and Evolution of Life*
SciTech - v21 - Mr '97 - p35 [51-250]
Trigeorgis, Lenos - *Real Options*
JEL - v34 - D '96 - p2056 [51-250]
R&R Bk N - v12 - F '97 - p48 [1-50]

Trigg, George L - *Encyclopedia of Applied Physics. Vol. 16*
r SciTech - v20 - N '96 - p17 [51-250]
Encyclopedia of Applied Physics. Vols. 15-16
r ARBA - v28 - '97 - p638 [51-250]
Trigg, Liz - *The London Cookbook*
BL - v93 - Ja '97 - p802 [51-250]
Trigger, Bruce G - *The Cambridge History of the Native Peoples of the Americas. Vol. 1, Pts. 1-2*
Choice - v34 - My '97 - p1564 [51-250]
r LJ - v122 - My 1 '97 - p94 [51-250]
Early Civilizations
AJA - v101 - Ja '97 - p164 [501+]
Trigiano, Robert N - *Plant Tissue Culture Concepts and Laboratory Exercises*
SciTech - v20 - D '96 - p31 [51-250]
Trillin, Alice Stewart - *Dear Bruno (Illus. by Edward Koren)*
c HB Guide - v8 - Spr '97 - p131 [1-50]
y VOYA - v19 - O '96 - p239 [51-250]
Trillin, Calvin - *Messages from My Father*
BW - v26 - Jl 7 '96 - p9 [501+]
NY - v72 - D 16 '96 - p107 [51-250]
NYTBR - v101 - D 8 '96 - p89 [1-50]
Messages from My Father (Trillin). Audio Version
y Kliatt - v31 - Mr '97 - p49 [51-250]
Piece by Piece (Trillin). Audio Version
y Kliatt - v30 - N '96 - p50 [51-250]
Too Soon To Tell
LATBR - S 1 '96 - p11 [51-250]
Trimble, Judith - *Inge King: Sculptor*
Aust Bk R - Ag '96 - p27+ [501+]
Trimble, Michael R - *Biological Psychiatry. 2nd Ed.*
SciTech - v20 - N '96 - p41 [51-250]
Trimpey, Jack - *Rational Recovery*
LJ - v121 - O 15 '96 - p79 [51-250]
Tringham, Nigel J - *Charters of the Vicars Choral of York Minster*
EHR - v111 - N '96 - p1253+ [251-500]
Trinh, T Minh-Ha - *Framer Framed*
QJS - v82 - N '96 - p402+ [501+]
Trinkle, Dennis A - *The History Highway*
r BL - v93 - F 15 '97 - p974 [51-250]
r PW - v244 - Ja 6 '97 - p61+ [51-250]
Trioli, Virginia - *Generation F*
Aust Bk R - O '96 - p21+ [501+]
A Trip to the Moon
c Ch BWatch - v6 - My '96 - p3 [51-250]
Tripartite Meeting Improving Conditions of Employment and Work of Agricultural Wage Workers in Context of Economic Restructuring (1996: Geneva, Switz) - *Wage Workers in Agriculture*
ILR - v135 - S '96 - p600 [251-500]
Tripitaka. Sutrapitaka. Saddharmapundarikasutra. English - *The Lotus Sutra*
Ch Rev Int - v3 - Fall '96 - p559+ [501+]
Tripitaka. Sutrapitaka. Sukhavativyuha (Larger). English - *The Land of Bliss*
Parabola - v21 - N '96 - p120 [1-50]
Tric - v6 - Win '96 - p116 [1-50]
Tripolitis, Antonia - *Kassia: The Legend, the Woman, and Her Work*
CH - v66 - Mr '97 - p187 [51-250]
Tripp, Nathaniel - *Father, Soldier, Son*
BL - v93 - Ja '97 - p814 [51-250]
KR - v64 - D 15 '96 - p1790+ [251-500]
LJ - v122 - F 15 '97 - p143 [51-250]
NYTBR - v102 - F 2 '97 - p29 [501+]
PW - v244 - Ja 6 '97 - p57 [51-250]
Trib Bks - Ja 19 '97 - p7 [501+]
Trippi, Robert R - *Neural Networks in Finance and Investing. Rev. Ed.*
R&R Bk N - v11 - N '96 - p37 [51-250]
Triseliotis, John - *Foster Care*
Soc Ser R - v70 - S '96 - p501 [51-250]
Tristram, Fran - *Single Firing*
Ceram Mo - v44 - O '96 - p26+ [51-250]
Trivas, Irene - *Annie, Anya: A Month in Moscow*
c CLW - v67 - Mr '97 - p15 [1-50]
Trivedi, Harish - *Colonial Transactions*
Nine-C Lit - v51 - D '96 - p427 [51-250]
Trivers, Jonathan - *One Stop Marketing*
Choice - v34 - Mr '97 - p1206 [51-250]
Trivizas, Eugene - *The Three Little Wolves and the Big Bad Pig (Illus. by Helen Oxenbury)*
c PW - v244 - Ap 7 '97 - p94 [1-50]
c TES - O 18 '96 - p12* [51-250]
Trobaugh, Augusta - *Praise Jerusalem!*
LJ - v122 - F 1 '97 - p68 [51-250]
PW - v244 - Ap 14 '97 - p58+ [51-250]

Trocchi, Alexander - *Young Adam*
Obs - Ja 5 '97 - p18* [51-250]
TLS - N 15 '96 - p25 [251-500]
Trocheck, Kathy Hogan - *Crash Course*
KR - v65 - Ja 15 '97 - p101 [51-250]
PW - v244 - Ja 20 '97 - p397 [51-250]
Heart Trouble
y SLJ - v42 - O '96 - p164 [51-250]
Troesken, Werner - *Why Regulate Utilities?*
Choice - v34 - F '97 - p1013 [51-250]
Troester, Rod - *Jimmy Carter as Peacemaker*
Choice - v34 - Ja '97 - p877 [51-250]
R&R Bk N - v11 - N '96 - p19 [51-250]
Troll, Ray - *Raptors, Fossils, Fins and Fangs (Illus. by Ray Troll)*
c Ch BWatch - v6 - D '96 - p8 [1-50]
c HB Guide - v8 - Spr '97 - p115 [51-250]
c KR - v64 - S 1 '96 - p1329 [51-250]
c LATBR - Ag 18 '96 - p15 [51-250]
c PW - v243 - S 2 '96 - p133 [51-250]
c SFR - v22 - Ja '97 - p47 [51-250]
c SLJ - v42 - O '96 - p141 [51-250]
Trolley, Jack - *Juarez Justice*
KR - v64 - S 15 '96 - p1358+ [51-250]
LJ - v121 - O 1 '96 - p131 [51-250]
NYTBR - v101 - N 24 '96 - p26 [51-250]
PW - v243 - S 23 '96 - p58 [51-250]
Trollinger, William Vance, Jr. - *God's Empire*
CH - v65 - D '96 - p759+ [501+]
Trollope, Anthony - *Phineas Finn*
VV - v42 - Ja 7 '97 - p44 [251-500]
Trollope, Fanny - *Hargrave*
CR - v269 - Ag '96 - p112 [51-250]
The Vicar of Wrexhill
CR - v269 - D '96 - p333 [51-250]
Trollope, Joanna - *The Best of Friends*
TES - Jl 19 '96 - pR6 [51-250]
The Rector's Wife
LATBR - O 27 '96 - p11 [51-250]
A Spanish Lover
BL - v93 - F 1 '97 - p926 [51-250]
BW - v27 - Ja 12 '97 - p3 [501+]
KR - v64 - N 1 '96 - p1563 [251-500]
LJ - v121 - D '96 - p148 [51-250]
NY - v73 - Ap 7 '97 - p95 [51-250]
NYTBR - v102 - Ap 6 '97 - p21 [51-250]
PW - v243 - D 9 '96 - p59 [51-250]
Trib Bks - F 23 '97 - p3 [501+]
Trombetta, Vincenzo - *Storia Della Biblioteca Universitaria Di Napoli Dal Viceregno Spagnolo All'Unita D'Italia*
Lib - v19 - Mr '97 - p100 [1-50]
Trombly, Catherine A - *Occupational Therapy for Physical Dysfunction. 4th Ed.*
SciTech - v20 - N '96 - p56 [51-250]
Tromlitz, Johann George - *The Keyed Flute*
Choice - v34 - F '97 - p975+ [51-250]
Trompf, G W - *Payback: The Logic of Retribution in Melanesian Religions*
Am Ethnol - v23 - N '96 - p917+ [501+]
Trotman, Felicity - *Horse Stories*
c Sch Lib - v45 - F '97 - p36 [51-250]
Trott, Susan - *The Holy Man's Journey*
BL - v93 - Mr 15 '97 - p1227+ [51-250]
KR - v65 - F 15 '97 - p253 [51-250]
PW - v244 - F 24 '97 - p64 [51-250]
Trotta, Marcia - *Successful Staff Development*
LAR - v98 - N '96 - p595 [51-250]
Trotter, Charlie - *Charlie Trotter's Vegetables*
CSM - v89 - D 13 '96 - p10+ [51-250]
Trotter, Joe William - *From a Raw Deal to a New Deal?*
y Ch BWatch - v6 - My '96 - p5 [51-250]
Trotter, Robert T - *Multicultural AIDS Prevention Programs*
SciTech - v21 - Mr '97 - p46 [51-250]
Trottier, Maxine - *Pavlova's Gift (Illus. by Victoria Berdichevsky)*
c BIC - v26 - Mr '97 - p32+ [501+]
c Emerg Lib - v24 - Mr '97 - p27+ [1-50]
c Quill & Q - v62 - Ag '96 - p43+ [251-500]
The Tiny Kite of Eddie Wing (Illus. by Al Van Mil)
c BL - v93 - N 15 '96 - p596 [51-250]
c CBRS - v25 - Win '97 - p66 [51-250]
c HB Guide - v8 - Spr '97 - p51 [51-250]
c SLJ - v42 - D '96 - p107 [51-250]
Troughton, Joanna - *The Tiger Child (Illus. by Joanna Troughton)*
c Bks Keeps - Ja '97 - p19 [51-250]
c Sch Lib - v45 - F '97 - p22 [51-250]
Troupe, Quincy - *Avalanche*
Bl S - v26 - Fall '96 - p107 [1-50]

Trout, Andrew P - *City on the Seine*
   Choice - v34 - Ja '97 - p859 [51-250]
   HRNB - v25 - Win '97 - p79+ [251-500]
   R&R Bk N - v11 - N '96 - p12 [51-250]
Trout, Ed - *Historic Buildings of the Smokies*
   Pub Hist - v18 - Fall '96 - p156+ [501+]
Trout, Mike - *Off the Air*
   y VOYA - v19 - F '97 - p318 [51-250]
Trout, Robert J - *With Pen and Saber*
   JSH - v62 - N '96 - p812+ [251-500]
Trow, George W S - *Within the Context of No Context*
   LJ - v122 - Ap 1 '97 - p134 [1-50]
   NYTBR - v102 - Ap 6 '97 - p6 [501+]
Trowler, Paul - *Investigating Health, Welfare and Poverty. 2nd Ed.*
   y TES - F 21 '97 - p20* [251-500]
Troy, Gil - *Affairs of State*
   BL - v93 - D 15 '96 - p707 [51-250]
   BW - v27 - Ja 19 '97 - p3+ [501+]
   KR - v64 - D 1 '96 - p1727 [251-500]
   LJ - v122 - Ja '97 - p125 [51-250]
   NYTBR - v102 - F 2 '97 - p9 [501+]
   PW - v243 - N 11 '96 - p62 [51-250]
   See How They Ran
   Reason - v28 - D '96 - p43 [51-250]
Troy, Judy - *West of Venus*
   KR - v65 - Ap 1 '97 - p500+ [251-500]
   LJ - v122 - My 1 '97 - p142 [51-250]
   PW - v244 - Ap 14 '97 - p54 [51-250]
Troy, Patrick - *Australian Cities*
   Choice - v34 - N '96 - p514+ [51-250]
   GJ - v163 - Mr '97 - p109 [51-250]
Troy, Thomas F - *Wild Bill and Intrepid*
   BW - v26 - Jl 14 '96 - p1+ [501+]
   Choice - v34 - O '96 - p359+ [251-500]
Troyan, Scott D - *Textual Decorum*
   Specu - v71 - O '96 - p1033+ [501+]
Troyat, Henri - *Peter the Great (Kandinsky). Audio Version*
   y Kliatt - v30 - S '96 - p58 [51-250]
   Votre Tres Humble Et Tres Obeissant Serviteur
   BL - v93 - Ja '97 - p827 [1-50]
Troyer, Patricia - *Letters from Home*
   r BWatch - v17 - S '96 - p11 [51-250]
Troyna, Barry - *Racism in Children's Lives*
   JNE - v64 - Fall '95 - p484+ [501+]
Troy-Smith, Jean - *Called to Healing*
   R&R Bk N - v11 - N '96 - p6 [51-250]
Truant, Cynthia Maria - *The Rites of Labor*
   AHR - v101 - D '96 - p1554 [501+]
   JMH - v68 - D '96 - p995+ [501+]
   J Soc H - v30 - Win '96 - p523+ [501+]
Truax, Pamela Larson - *Market Smarter Not Harder*
   Choice - v34 - D '96 - p656 [51-250]
Trucillo, Luigi - *Navicelle*
   TLS - Jl 19 '96 - p12 [501+]
Trudeau, Noah Andre - *Voices of the 55th*
   Choice - v34 - O '96 - p352 [51-250]
Trudeau, Pierre Elliott - *Against the Current*
   BIC - v26 - F '97 - p28+ [51-250]
   Quill & Q - v62 - N '96 - p37 [251-500]
Trudell, Dennis - *Fragments in Us*
   BL - v93 - N 15 '96 - p567 [51-250]
   y Kliatt - v31 - My '97 - p19 [51-250]
   Full Court
   LATBR - O 13 '96 - p6+ [501+]
   LJ - v121 - S 15 '96 - p74 [51-250]
True, Dan - *What Do Women Want from Men?. Audio Version*
   BWatch - v18 - Mr '97 - p9 [51-250]
True Stories Series
   c Magpies - v11 - Jl '96 - p39 [1-50]
Trueb, Lucien F - *Die Chemischen Elemente*
   J Chem Ed - v74 - Mr '97 - p344+ [251-500]
Trueblood, Kathryn - *Homeground*
   Sm Pr R - v29 - Ja '97 - p5 [51-250]
Trueman, Carl R - *Luther's Legacy*
   Bks & Cult - v1 - N '95 - p30 [51-250]
   CH - v65 - S '96 - p479+ [501+]
   JR - v77 - Ja '97 - p140+ [501+]
   Rel St Rev - v23 - Ap '97 - p191 [51-250]
   Ren Q - v49 - Aut '96 - p639+ [501+]
Truffaut, Francois - *The Early Film Criticism of Francois Truffaut*
   TranslRevS - v1 - My '95 - p11 [51-250]
Truitt, Anne - *Prospect: The Journal of an Artist*
   BW - v26 - D 8 '96 - p6 [51-250]
   LATBR - D 29 '96 - p10 [51-250]
Trujillo, Stan - *Windows 95 Games Programming*
   CBR - v14 - Jl '96 - p24 [51-250]
   SciTech - v20 - N '96 - p10 [1-50]

Trulock, Alice Rains - *In the Hands of Providence (Parker). Audio Version*
   y Kliatt - v31 - My '97 - p47 [51-250]
Truman, Margaret - *First Ladies*
   y Kliatt - v30 - N '96 - p23+ [51-250]
   First Ladies (Caruso). Audio Version
   y Kliatt - v31 - Mr '97 - p48 [51-250]
   Murder at the National Gallery
   Rapport - v19 - 5 '96 - p28 [251-500]
   VQR - v73 - Win '97 - p24* [51-250]
   Murder in the House
   y BL - v93 - My 15 '97 - p1542 [51-250]
Trumble, Kelly - *Cat Mummies (Illus. by Laszlo Kubinyi)*
   c BL - v93 - S 15 '96 - p236 [51-250]
   c CBRS - v25 - D '96 - p43 [51-250]
   c CCB-B - v50 - O '96 - p78+ [51-250]
   c HB Guide - v8 - Spr '97 - p166+ [1-50]
   c SLJ - v42 - Ag '96 - p161 [51-250]
Trumbull, Robert - *The Raft (Parker). Audio Version*
   y Kliatt - v31 - Mr '97 - p50 [51-250]
Trungpa, Chogyam - *Dharma Art*
   PW - v243 - S 16 '96 - p66 [51-250]
Truscott, Lucian K - *Heart of War*
   y BL - v93 - Mr 15 '97 - p1205 [51-250]
   KR - v65 - Ap 1 '97 - p501 [251-500]
   LJ - v122 - Mr 15 '97 - p92 [51-250]
   PW - v244 - Mr 31 '97 - p58 [51-250]
Truss, Lynne - *Making the Cat Laugh*
   Woman's J - D '96 - p16 [1-50]
   Tennyson's Gift
   TES - Jl 26 '96 - p18 [251-500]
   TLS - Jl 19 '96 - p21 [501+]
   Woman's J - Ag '96 - p11 [51-250]
Trussler, Simon - *The Cambridge Illustrated History of British Theatre*
   RES - v48 - F '97 - p71+ [501+]
Trusted, Marjorie - *Spanish Sculpture*
   Apo - v145 - F '97 - p61 [501+]
Trynka, Paul - *Rock Hardware*
   y BL - v93 - Ja '97 - p804 [51-250]
   BWatch - v18 - F '97 - p8 [51-250]
   Choice - v34 - My '97 - p1509 [51-250]
   LJ - v122 - Mr 15 '97 - p65 [51-250]
Tryon, Leslie - *Albert's Ballgame*
   c HB Guide - v7 - Fall '96 - p280 [51-250]
Tryphon, Anastasia - *Piaget--Vygotsky*
   Choice - v34 - D '96 - p693 [51-250]
Tryster, Hillel - *Israel before Israel*
   Choice - v34 - Ja '97 - p804 [51-250]
   Si & So - v6 - N '96 - p35 [51-250]
   TES - Ag 2 '96 - pR6 [1-50]
Tsai, Shih-Shan Henry - *The Eunuchs in the Ming Dynasty*
   Ch Rev Int - v4 - Spr '97 - p271+ [501+]
Tsakunov, S V - *V Labirinte Doktriny*
   Slav R - v55 - Sum '96 - p490+ [501+]
Tsaloumas, Dimitris - *Six Improvisations on the River*
   WLT - v70 - Sum '96 - p758+ [501+]
   To Taxidi 1963-1992. Vols. 1-2
   WLT - v70 - Sum '96 - p741 [251-500]
Tsang, Ming W - *Hong Kong-Japanese Occupation and Mr. H. Da Luz*
   Am Phil - v110 - D '96 - p1088 [51-250]
Tsang, Steve Yui-Sang - *Documentary History of Hong Kong. Vol. 1*
   Ch Rev Int - v4 - Spr '97 - p275+ [501+]
   Pac A - v69 - Fall '96 - p409+ [501+]
Tsao, Kuan-Lung - *The Attic: Memoir of a Chinese Landlord's Son*
   Lon R Bks - v18 - My 23 '96 - p28+ [501+]
Tschichold, Jan - *The New Typography*
   JC - v46 - Sum '96 - p206 [251-500]
   TLS - S 20 '96 - p19 [501+]
Tschinag, Galsan - *Zwanzig Und Ein Tag*
   WLT - v70 - Sum '96 - p764+ [501+]
Tseng, Chi-Fen - *Testimony of a Confucian Woman*
   Ch Rev Int - v3 - Fall '96 - p598+ [501+]
Tseng, Gwyneth - *The Library and Information Professional's Guide to the Internet*
   LAR - v98 - Mr '96 - p162 [51-250]
Tsesis, Vladimir A - *Children, Parents, Lollipops*
   Rapport - v19 - 6 '96 - p32 [251-500]
Tshe-Rin-Dban-Rgyal, Mdo-Mkhar Zabs-Drun - *The Tale of the Incomparable Prince*
   NYTBR - v101 - D 8 '96 - p75 [501+]
   Tric - v6 - Spr '97 - p109+ [501+]
Tsiantis, John - *Countertransference in Psychoanalytic Psychotherapy with Children and Adolescents*
   SciTech - v21 - Mr '97 - p65 [51-250]

Tsiaras, Alexander - *BodyVoyage: A Three-Dimensional Tour of a Real Human Body*
   PW - v244 - Mr 24 '97 - p72 [51-250]
Tsing, Anna Lowenhaupt - *In the Realm of the Diamond Queen*
   Am Ethnol - v24 - F '97 - p258+ [501+]
Tsinganos, Kanaris C - *Solar and Astrophysical Magnetohydrodynamic Flows*
   SciTech - v20 - D '96 - p21 [51-250]
Tsipis, Constantinos A - *New Methods in Quantum Theory*
   SciTech - v20 - D '96 - p23 [51-250]
Tsirelson, V G - *Electron Density and Bonding in Crystals*
   SciTech - v20 - S '96 - p14 [51-250]
Tsoi, Edmund K M - *Abdominal Access in Open and Laparoscopic Surgery*
   r SciTech - v20 - D '96 - p49 [51-250]
Tsomo, Karma Lekshe - *Sisters in Solitude*
   R&R Bk N - v12 - F '97 - p9 [51-250]
Tsongas, Paul E - *Journey of Purpose*
   JEL - v34 - S '96 - p1504 [51-250]
Tsongkhapa Lobzang Drakpa - *Tsongkhapa's Six Yogas of Naropa*
   BL - v93 - O 1 '96 - p301 [51-250]
Tsonis, Panagiotis A - *Limb Regeneration*
   Choice - v34 - F '97 - p988 [51-250]
   Nature - v386 - Mr 13 '97 - p142 [51-250]
Tsosie, Dennison - *Spirit Visions*
   PW - v243 - D 16 '96 - p54 [51-250]
Tsouras, Peter G - *Warlords of the Ancient Americas: Central America*
   r BL - v93 - Ja '97 - p815 [51-250]
Tsuang, Ming T - *Textbook in Psychiatric Epidemiology*
   AJPsych - v153 - Ag '96 - p1103+ [501+]
Tsui, Chia-Chi - *Robust Control System Design*
   SciTech - v20 - N '96 - p70 [51-250]
Tsuji, Atsuo - *Studies in Accounting History*
   BusLR - v21 - 3 '96 - p259 [251-500]
Tsuji, Jiro - *Palladium Reagents and Catalysts*
   Choice - v34 - O '96 - p310 [51-250]
Tsuji, Shigebumi - *The Survey of Early Byzantine Sites in Oludeniz Area (Lycia, Turkey)*
   AJA - v100 - Jl '96 - p639 [251-500]
Tsujii, Takashi - *Niji No Misaki*
   Econ - v342 - F 15 '97 - p17*+ [501+]
Tsuru, Shigeto - *Japan's Capitalism*
   Econ J - v107 - Ja '97 - p237+ [501+]
   The Selected Essays of Shigeto Tsuru
   Econ J - v107 - Ja '97 - p285 [501+]
Tsushima, Yuko - *The Shooting Gallery*
   PW - v244 - Ap 21 '97 - p69 [1-50]
Tsvelik, Alexi M - *Quantum Field Theory in Condensed Matter Physics*
   Phys Today - v50 - F '97 - p66 [501+]
Tsytovich, Vadim N - *Lectures on Non-Linear Plasma Kinetics*
   Phys Today - v49 - Ag '96 - p65 [501+]
Tu, K N - *Advanced Metallization for Future ULSI*
   SciTech - v21 - Mr '97 - p91 [51-250]
Tu, Wei-Ming - *The Living Tree*
   Ch Rev Int - v4 - Spr '97 - p33+ [501+]
Tuana, Nancy - *The Less Noble Sex*
   JPC - v29 - Spr '96 - p257+ [501+]
Tubb, E C - *Pandora's Box*
   Analog - v117 - Mr '97 - p147+ [51-250]
   The Return
   Analog - v117 - Mr '97 - p147 [51-250]
   Temple of Death
   Analog - v117 - Mr '97 - p147+ [51-250]
Tubbs, James B, Jr. - *Christian Theology and Medical Ethics*
   Hast Cen R - v26 - S '96 - p41 [1-50]
Tuchman, Arleen Marcia - *Science, Medicine, and the State in Germany*
   JMH - v68 - S '96 - p727+ [501+]
Tuchman, Mitch - *Bauer: Classic American Pottery*
   Am Craft - v56 - Ag '96 - p26 [1-50]
Tuck, Jim - *McCarthyism and New York's Hearst Press*
   Historian - v58 - Sum '96 - p877+ [251-500]
Tuck, Lily - *The Woman Who Walked on Water*
   Trib Bks - Mr 23 '97 - p6 [1-50]
Tucker, Alan C - *Models That Work*
   Math T - v89 - O '96 - p608+ [51-250]
Tucker, Graham M - *Birds in Europe*
   r Choice - v34 - O '96 - p307+ [501+]
Tucker, Janet G - *Revolution Betrayed*
   Choice - v34 - N '96 - p466 [51-250]
Tucker, Karen B Westerfield - *The Sunday Service of the Methodists*
   CH - v66 - Mr '97 - p216+ [251-500]

Tucker, Kathy - *Do Cowboys Ride Bikes? (Illus. by Nadine Bernard Westcott)*
c   BL - v93 - Ap 1 '97 - p1339 [51-250]
c   KR - v65 - Mr 1 '97 - p389 [51-250]
Tucker, Lee - *The Small Hands of Slavery*
WorldV - v13 - Ja '97 - p10+ [251-500]
Tucker, Lori B - *Your Child with Arthritis*
SciTech - v20 - D '96 - p52 [51-250]
Tucker, Louis Leonard - *The Massachusetts Historical Society*
Choice - v34 - My '97 - p1565 [51-250]
NEQ - v70 - Mr '97 - p114+ [501+]
R&R Bk N - v12 - F '97 - p25 [1-50]
Tucker, Marcia - *A Labor of Love*
Am Craft - v56 - Ag '96 - p28 [1-50]
Tucker, Mary Evelyn - *Worldviews and Ecology*
J Ch St - v38 - Aut '96 - p927+ [501+]
Tucker, Naomi - *Bisexual Politics*
ABR - v18 - O '96 - p21 [501+]
Tucker, Paul Hayes - *Claude Monet: Life and Art*
BM - v138 - S '96 - p610+ [501+]
Tucker, Sian - *1 2 3 Count with Me*
c   PW - v243 - S 23 '96 - p77 [51-250]
One Two Three, Count with Me
c   TES - N 29 '96 - p13* [51-250]
Tucker, Spencer C - *The European Powers in the First World War*
r   ARBA - v28 - '97 - p212 [51-250]
r   Choice - v34 - N '96 - p428 [51-250]
r   J Mil H - v61 - Ja '97 - p174+ [251-500]
yr SLJ - v42 - N '96 - p139 [51-250]
yr VOYA - v19 - D '96 - p299 [251-500]
Injured Honor
Choice - v34 - D '96 - p679 [51-250]
J Mil H - v61 - Ja '97 - p163+ [251-500]
Tucker, Susan M - *Patient Care Standards. 6th Ed.*
r   SciTech - v20 - N '96 - p56 [51-250]
Tucker, Tanya - *Nickel Dreams*
BL - v93 - Mr 1 '97 - p1067 [51-250]
Ent W - Ap 4 '97 - p76+ [501+]
KR - v65 - F 15 '97 - p289 [251-500]
LJ - v122 - My 1 '97 - p107 [51-250]
PW - v244 - Mr 3 '97 - p60 [51-250]
Tucker, William, 1942- - *Progress and Privilege*
Reason - v28 - D '96 - p45 [51-250]
Tucker, William H, 1940- - *The Science and Politics of Racial Research*
J Am St - v30 - Ap '96 - p152+ [251-500]
Soc - v34 - Mr '97 - p78+ [501+]
Tuckerman, Diane - *The Best of Silk Painting*
LJ - v122 - Mr 15 '97 - p63 [51-250]
Tuckett, Christopher M - *Luke*
Rel St Rev - v23 - Ap '97 - p179+ [251-500]
Luke's Literary Achievement
Rel St Rev - v23 - Ap '97 - p184 [51-250]
Tudge, Colin - *The Day before Yesterday*
Lon R Bks - v18 - O 31 '96 - p36+ [501+]
Nature - v384 - D 5 '96 - p426 [1-50]
New Sci - v152 - N 23 '96 - p47 [51-250]
Obs - D 1 '96 - p18* [51-250]
The Time before History
LATBR - My 12 '96 - p8 [501+]
y   SB - v32 - Ag '96 - p174+ [251-500]
Tudor, Anthony - *Tudor's Soiree Musicale*
Dance RJ - v28 - Fall '96 - p95+ [251-500]
Tudor, Tasha - *A Time to Keep (Illus. by Tasha Tudor)*
c   HB Guide - v8 - Spr '97 - p51 [51-250]
Tufte, Edward R - *Visual Explanations*
BWatch - v18 - Mr '97 - p1 [51-250]
PW - v244 - Mr 31 '97 - p58 [51-250]
Sci - v275 - Mr 7 '97 - p1439 [1-50]
Tufts, Craig - *The National Wildlife Federation's Guide to Gardening for Wildlife*
LJ - v121 - D '96 - p66 [1-50]
Tuijnman, Albert C - *International Encyclopedia of Adult Education and Training. 2nd Ed.*
r   R&R Bk N - v11 - D '96 - p55 [51-250]
Tulard, Jean - *Dictionnaire Du Second Empire*
r   Choice - v34 - D '96 - p568 [1-50]
Tulchin, Joseph S - *The Consolidation of Democracy in Latin America*
JTWS - v13 - Fall '96 - p296+ [501+]
Is There a Transition to Democracy in El Salvador?
Parameters - v26 - Win '96 - p156 [1-50]
Tuller, David - *Cracks in the Iron Closet*
LJ - v121 - S 15 '96 - p85 [51-250]
NY - v72 - Ag 12 '96 - p73 [51-250]
Wom R Bks - v14 - F '97 - p12+ [501+]
Tulloch, Bobby - *Otters*
AB - v97 - Je 17 '96 - p2404 [1-50]

Tulloch, Richard - *Stage Fright!*
c   Aust Bk R - O '96 - p62 [501+]
Tully, James - *An Approach to Political Philosophy*
Dialogue - v35 - Fall '96 - p825+ [501+]
Strange Multiplicity
CPR - v16 - Je '96 - p213+ [501+]
Tully, Marianne - *Helping Students Revise Their Writing*
Inst - v106 - N '96 - p41 [1-50]
Tully, Mark - *The Heart of India*
CR - v270 - F '97 - p111 [1-50]
Obs - D 8 '96 - p18* [51-250]
Tully, Thomas N - *Ratite Management, Medicine, and Surgery*
SciTech - v20 - D '96 - p57 [51-250]
Tuna-Norlung, Yasemin - *Die Attisch-Schwarzfigurige Keramik Und Der Attische Keramikexport Nach Kleinasien*
AJA - v100 - Jl '96 - p637 [251-500]
Tung, Chieh-Yuan - *Master Tung's Western Chamber Romance*
TranslRevS - v1 - My '95 - p16 [51-250]
Tunisia's Global Integration and Sustainable Development
JEL - v35 - Mr '97 - p286+ [51-250]
Tunnell, Michael O - *The Children of Topaz*
c   CCB-B - v50 - S '96 - p34+ [51-250]
c   HB Guide - v8 - Spr '97 - p168 [51-250]
c   Par Ch - v20 - O '96 - p11 [1-50]
c   SLJ - v42 - Ag '96 - p161+ [51-250]
y   VOYA - v19 - D '96 - p292 [51-250]
Tunstall, Jeremy - *Newspaper Power*
Choice - v34 - Ap '97 - p1329 [51-250]
Lon R Bks - v18 - Jl 18 '96 - p13+ [501+]
Tunstrom, Goran - *Shimmer*
WLT - v71 - Win '97 - p174+ [501+]
Tuohy, Thomas - *Herculean Ferrara*
Apo - v144 - N '96 - p57+ [501+]
r   Choice - v34 - My '97 - p1559 [51-250]
Tuomela, Raimo - *The Importance of Us*
Choice - v34 - S '96 - p143 [51-250]
IPQ - v37 - Je '97 - p253 [1-50]
Tuoti, Frank X - *Why Not Be a Mystic?*
RR - v55 - S '96 - p540+ [501+]
Tupitsyn, Margarita - *The Soviet Photograph 1924-1937*
Choice - v34 - D '96 - p604 [51-250]
LJ - v121 - N 1 '96 - p64 [51-250]
Tupper, E Frank - *A Scandalous Providence*
TT - v53 - O '96 - p408+ [501+]
Tur, Evgeniya - *Antonina*
KR - v64 - N 15 '96 - p1633 [51-250]
Turabian, Kate L - *A Manual for Writers of Term Papers, Theses, and Dissertations. 6th Ed.*
r   ARBA - v28 - '97 - p348+ [51-250]
yr Kliatt - v30 - S '96 - p23 [51-250]
Turan, Guven - *101 Bir Dize*
WLT - v71 - Win '97 - p220 [251-500]
Toplu Siirler
WLT - v71 - Win '97 - p220 [251-500]
Turbak, Gary - *Grizzly Bears*
c   PW - v244 - My 5 '97 - p192 [51-250]
Pronghorn: Portrait of the American Antelope
AB - v97 - Je 17 '96 - p2404 [251-500]
Turbide, David A - *Why Systems Fail*
SciTech - v20 - S '96 - p63 [51-250]
Turcan, Robert - *The Cults of the Roman Empire*
Choice - v34 - My '97 - p1517 [51-250]
Turcotte, Elise - *The Sound of Living Things*
TranslRevS - v1 - My '95 - p21 [51-250]
Turcotte, Paul-Andre - *Intransigeance Ou Compromis*
CH - v65 - D '96 - p776+ [501+]
CHR - v82 - Jl '96 - p487+ [251-500]
Turfan, Barbara - *Emerging Democracies and Freedom of Information*
LR - v45 - 6 '96 - p70+ [501+]
Turgenev, Ivan - *Torrents of Spring*
LATBR - D 8 '96 - p8 [51-250]
Turgeon, Lynn - *Bastard Keynesianism*
Choice - v34 - Ja '97 - p847 [51-250]
JEL - v35 - Mr '97 - p210 [51-250]
R&R Bk N - v11 - D '96 - p22 [51-250]
The Search for Economics as a Science
r   ARBA - v28 - '97 - p76 [51-250]
r   Choice - v34 - My '97 - p1480 [51-250]
r   R&R Bk N - v12 - F '97 - p33 [51-250]
Turino, Thomas - *Moving Away from Silence*
RA - v25 - 4 '96 - p225+ [501+]
Turk, Ruth - *Ray Charles: Soul Man*
c   HB Guide - v7 - Fall '96 - p375 [51-250]
c   SLJ - v42 - Ag '96 - p162 [51-250]
Turkdogan, E T - *Fundamentals of Steelmaking*
Choice - v34 - D '96 - p643 [51-250]

Turkington, Carol - *The Brain Encyclopedia*
r   ARBA - v28 - '97 - p607 [51-250]
r   BL - v93 - S 15 '96 - p280 [251-500]
r   R&R Bk N - v12 - F '97 - p95 [51-250]
r   SciTech - v20 - D '96 - p35 [51-250]
The Home Health Guide to Poisons and Antidotes
r   BL - v93 - F 1 '97 - p957 [1-50]
Skin Deep
r   ARBA - v28 - '97 - p607 [51-250]
r   BL - v93 - F 1 '97 - p960 [1-50]
r   LJ - v122 - Ap 15 '97 - p40 [51-250]
r   RQ - v36 - Fall '96 - p137+ [251-500]
Turkle, Brinton - *Do Not Open*
c   HB - v73 - Mr '97 - p189 [1-50]
Turkle, Sherry - *Life on the Screen*
Lon R Bks - v18 - O 17 '96 - p27+ [501+]
Nat R - v48 - O 14 '96 - p81+ [501+]
Turks, Paul - *Philip Neri: The Fire of Joy*
TLS - F 7 '97 - p32 [251-500]
Turlea, Stelian - *Bomba Drogurilor*
BL - v93 - D 15 '96 - p714 [1-50]
Turley, James - *Compact Guide to Windows 95*
CBR - v14 - Jl '96 - p22 [1-50]
Windows NT Training Guide
SciTech - v21 - Mr '97 - p10 [51-250]
Turnauer, Andrew E - *Navigating the Mortgage Maze*
BL - v93 - N 1 '96 - p467 [51-250]
LJ - v121 - O 15 '96 - p69+ [51-250]
Turnberg, Wayne L - *Biohazardous Waste*
Env - v39 - Mr '97 - p25 [51-250]
Turnbull, Ann - *Deep Water (Illus. by Kenny McKendry)*
c   Bks Keeps - Ja '97 - p24 [51-250]
c   Sch Lib - v45 - F '97 - p22 [51-250]
c   TES - N 22 '96 - p12* [51-250]
Pigeon Summer
c   Magpies - v11 - Jl '96 - p45 [1-50]
Room for a Stranger
c   HB Guide - v7 - Fall '96 - p298 [51-250]
y   JB - v60 - Ag '96 - p161 [51-250]
c   RT - v50 - Ap '97 - p588+ [51-250]
y   Sch Lib - v44 - Ag '96 - p121 [51-250]
Turnbull, David - *Maps as Territories*
GJ - v162 - Jl '96 - p236 [51-250]
Turnbull, Malcolm J - *Elusion Aforethought*
Aust Bk R - F '97 - p56+ [501+]
LJ - v121 - O 1 '96 - p78 [51-250]
Turnbull, Mark M - *Molecule-Based Magnetic Materials*
SciTech - v21 - Mr '97 - p32 [51-250]
Turnbull, Michael - *Mary Garden*
BL - v93 - Ja '97 - p805 [51-250]
Spec - v278 - Mr 8 '97 - p32+ [501+]
Turnbull, Walter - *Lift Every Voice*
PW - v244 - Ja 13 '97 - p73 [1-50]
Turner, Alan - *The Big Cats and Their Fossil Relatives*
y   BL - v93 - Mr 1 '97 - p1099 [51-250]
LJ - v122 - F 15 '97 - p160 [51-250]
Sci - v276 - My 9 '97 - p909+ [501+]
Turner, Ann - *Occupational Therapy and Physical Dysfunction. 4th Ed.*
SciTech - Mr '97 - p67 [51-250]
Turner, Ann Warren - *Mississippi Mud (Illus. by Robert J Blake)*
c   KR - v65 - My 1 '97 - p728 [51-250]
Shaker Hearts (Illus. by Wendell Minor)
c   BL - v93 - F 15 '97 - p1025 [51-250]
c   CBRS - v25 - F '97 - p79 [1-50]
c   KR - v64 - D 15 '96 - p1806 [51-250]
c   PW - v243 - D 16 '96 - p58 [51-250]
c   SLJ - v43 - Ja '97 - p109 [51-250]
c   Trib Bks - My 4 '97 - p6 [51-250]
Turner, Anne M - *Getting Political*
LJ - v122 - Ap 15 '97 - p126 [51-250]
Turner, Barbara J - *A Little Bit of Rob (Illus. by Marni Backer)*
c   HB Guide - v8 - Spr '97 - p51 [51-250]
c   SLJ - v42 - D '96 - p107+ [51-250]
Turner, Barrie Carson - *The Living Clarinet*
c   BL - v93 - D 15 '96 - p723+ [51-250]
c   BWatch - v18 - F '97 - p9 [51-250]
c   PW - v243 - N 18 '96 - p77+ [51-250]
The Living Flute
c   PW - v243 - N 18 '96 - p77+ [51-250]
The Living Piano
c   PW - v243 - N 18 '96 - p77+ [51-250]
The Living Violin
c   BL - v93 - D 15 '96 - p723+ [51-250]
c   KR - v64 - N 1 '96 - p1609 [51-250]
c   PW - v243 - N 18 '96 - p77+ [51-250]
c   SLJ - v42 - N '96 - p119 [51-250]
Turner, C J G - *Time and Temporal Structure in Chekhov*
MLR - v91 - Jl '96 - p813+ [251-500]

Turner, Christena L - *Japanese Workers in Protest*
    CS - v26 - Ja '97 - p43+ [501+]
Turner, Denys - *The Darkness of God*
    JR - v77 - Ap '97 - p309+ [501+]
    RM - v50 - S '96 - p193+ [501+]
    Theol St - v57 - D '96 - p749+ [501+]
  Eros and Allegory
    CH - v65 - D '96 - p680+ [501+]
    Theol St - v57 - S '96 - p533+ [501+]
Turner, Edith - *The Hands Feel It*
    Choice - v34 - F '97 - p1007 [51-250]
    VQR - v73 - Win '97 - p16* [51-250]
Turner, Francis J - *Differential Diagnosis and Treatment in Social Work. 4th Ed.*
    r Soc Ser R - v70 - D '96 - p668 [51-250]
Turner, Frank M - *Contesting Cultural Authority*
    CH - v66 - Mr '97 - p155+ [501+]
Turner, Fred - *Echoes of Combat*
    LJ - v121 - N 15 '96 - p74 [51-250]
    PW - v243 - O 21 '96 - p64 [51-250]
Turner, Frederick W - *When the Boys Came Back*
    BW - v26 - Jl 7 '96 - p1+ [501+]
    Choice - v34 - F '97 - p1003 [51-250]
    HRNB - v25 - Win '97 - p54+ [251-500]
  y SLJ - v43 - F '97 - p138 [51-250]
Turner, Garth - *2015: After the Boom*
    Quill & Q - v63 - Ja '97 - p26 [51-250]
Turner, Henry Ashby, Jr. - *Hitler's Thirty Days to Power, January 1933*
    For Aff - v76 - My '97 - p135 [51-250]
    KR - v64 - O 1 '96 - p1457 [251-500]
    LJ - v121 - D '96 - p118 [51-250]
    PW - v243 - O 21 '96 - p64+ [51-250]
    TLS - Ja 24 '97 - p28 [501+]
Turner, Ian - *Mathematical Modeling and Numerical Techniques in Drying Technology*
    SciTech - v20 - D '96 - p83 [51-250]
Turner, Ike - *Takin' Back My Name*
    Books - v9 - S '95 - p22+ [1-50]
Turner, J C - *The History and Science of Knots*
    New Sci - v153 - F 1 '97 - p42+ [501+]
Turner, Jack - *The Abstract Wild*
    KR - v64 - S 1 '96 - p1311 [51-250]
    Roundup M - v4 - Ap '97 - p29 [1-50]
Turner, Jane Shoaf - *The Dictionary of Art. Vols. 1-34*
    r Apo - v144 - D '96 - p10+ [501+]
    r BL - v93 - Ja '97 - p769 [51-250]
    r BL - v93 - D 15 '96 - p742 [501+]
    r Choice - v34 - Ja '97 - p761+ [501+]
    r LJ - v121 - S 15 '96 - p54 [251-500]
    r LJ - v122 - Ap 15 '97 - p37 [51-250]
    r Spec - v277 - N 9 '96 - p45+ [501+]
    r Spec - v277 - N 23 '96 - p44 [1-50]
    r TES - F 7 '97 - p7* [51-250]
    r Time - v148 - N 4 '96 - p93+ [501+]
    r TLS - N 1 '96 - p18+ [501+]
    r WSJ-MW - v77 - O 10 '96 - pA14 [501+]
Turner, Jeffrey S - *Encyclopedia of Relationships across the Lifespan*
    r ARBA - v28 - '97 - p286 [251-500]
    r Choice - v34 - S '96 - p107 [51-250]
Turner, John - *Macmillan*
    EHR - v111 - N '96 - p1356+ [251-500]
Turner, Jonathan H - *Macrodynamics: Toward a Theory on the Organization of Human Populations*
    AJS - v102 - Jl '96 - p276+ [501+]
Turner, Kay - *Between Us*
    Bloom Rev - v16 - N '96 - p20 [51-250]
    PW - v243 - S 23 '96 - p66 [51-250]
  Dear Sappho
    TLS - S 27 '96 - p32 [1-50]
Turner, Lisa - *Meals That Heal*
    LJ - v121 - O 15 '96 - p84 [51-250]
Turner, Mark - *The Literary Mind*
    BL - v92 - Ag '96 - p1875 [51-250]
Turner, Mary - *From Chattel Slaves to Wage Slaves*
    Bl S - v26 - Sum '96 - p67+ [1-50]
    HAHR - v77 - My '97 - p310+ [251-500]
    JEH - v56 - S '96 - p742+ [501+]
Turner, Megan Whalen - *The Thief*
    c BL - v93 - Ja '97 - p863 [251-500]
    y BL - v93 - Ap 1 '97 - p1296 [1-50]
    y BL - v93 - Ap 1 '97 - p1305 [51-250]
    c CBRS - v25 - D '96 - p48 [51-250]
    y CCB-B - v50 - N '96 - p117+ [51-250]
    y HB - v72 - N '96 - p747 [51-250]
    y HB Guide - v8 - Spr '97 - p85 [51-250]
    c NYTBR - v102 - Mr 2 '97 - p25 [1-50]
    c PW - v243 - O 21 '96 - p84 [51-250]
    y SLJ - v42 - O '96 - p150 [51-250]

Turner, Michael - *Kingsway*
    BIC - v25 - S '96 - p27 [501+]
Turner, Michael Edward - *After the Famine*
    Choice - v34 - Mr '97 - p1224 [51-250]
Turner, Patricia A - *Ceramic Uncles and Celluloid Mammies*
    Am Q - v48 - D '96 - p746 [51-250]
Turner, Paul V - *Joseph Ramee: International Architect of the Revolutionary Era*
    Choice - v34 - Ap '97 - p1327 [51-250]
Turner, Paul W - *Styrofoam Benchwork for Model Railroads*
    Model R - v64 - Ap '97 - p52 [51-250]
Turner, Peter - *New Zealand: A Lonely Planet Travel Survival Kit. 8th Ed.*
    r BL - v93 - S 15 '96 - p210 [1-50]
Turner, Priscilla - *The War between the Vowels and the Consonants (Illus. by Whitney Turner)*
    c BL - v93 - D 1 '96 - p670 [51-250]
    c CBRS - v25 - O '96 - p9 [51-250]
    c HB Guide - v8 - Spr '97 - p51 [51-250]
    c Inst - v106 - N '96 - p24 [51-250]
    c NY - v72 - N 18 '96 - p101 [1-50]
    c SLJ - v42 - O '96 - p108 [51-250]
Turner, R Steven - *In the Eye's Mind*
    AHR - v101 - O '96 - p1180+ [501+]
Turner, Ralph - *Jewelry in Europe and America*
    Am Craft - v56 - O '96 - p52 [51-250]
    TCI - v31 - F '97 - p56 [501+]
Turner, Ralph V - *King John*
    EHR - v111 - N '96 - p1247 [251-500]
Turner, Richard Brent - *Islam in the African-American Experience*
    LJ - v121 - N 1 '96 - p86 [1-50]
Turner, Robert Griffith, Jr. - *The Fire and the Rose*
    Readings - v11 - D '96 - p28+ [51-250]
Turner, Robyn Montana - *Texas Traditions*
    c HB Guide - v7 - Fall '96 - p389 [51-250]
Turner, Roger - *Euphorbias: A Gardeners' Guide*
    Choice - v34 - S '96 - p155 [51-250]
    Hort - v74 - D '96 - p60+ [51-250]
Turner, Ronald C - *README.1ST: SGML for Writers and Editors*
    BYTE - v21 - S '96 - p34 [251-500]
Turner, S - *The Day I Fell down the Toilet (Illus. by David Mostyn)*
    c Sch Lib - v45 - F '97 - p43 [51-250]
Turner, Stephen P - *The Social Theory of Practices*
    Hist & T - v36 - F '97 - p93+ [501+]
Turner, Steve - *Jack Kerouac, Angelheaded Hipster*
    Obs - N 24 '96 - p16* [501+]
Turner, Thomas M - *Fundamentals of Hydraulic Dredging. 2nd Ed.*
    SciTech - v20 - S '96 - p51 [51-250]
Turner, Victor - *Blazing the Trail*
    Am Ethnol - v23 - N '96 - p933+ [501+]
Turnley, David - *In Times of War and Peace*
    PW - v244 - F 17 '97 - p207 [51-250]
Turnock, John - *A History Little Known*
    TES - Ag 30 '96 - p32 [51-250]
Turow, Joseph - *Breaking Up America*
    KR - v65 - Ja 1 '97 - p51 [251-500]
    LJ - v122 - F 1 '97 - p92 [51-250]
    PW - v244 - F 10 '97 - p72 [51-250]
Turow, Scott - *Guilty as Charged*
    WSJ-MW - v78 - O 15 '96 - pA18 [51-250]
  Guilty as Charged (Kaye). Audio Version
    y Kliatt - v31 - My '97 - p38 [51-250]
  The Laws of Our Fathers
    BL - v93 - S 1 '96 - p31 [51-250]
    BW - v26 - O 13 '96 - p3 [501+]
    CSM - v88 - N 14 '96 - p14 [51-250]
    CSM - v89 - D 19 '96 - p14 [51-250]
    CSM - v89 - Ja 16 '97 - p14 [51-250]
    Ent W - O 25 '96 - p104+ [251-500]
    LATBR - O 20 '96 - p1+ [501+]
    LATBR - D 29 '96 - p6 [51-250]
    NY - v72 - O 14 '96 - p100 [1-50]
    NYTBR - v101 - O 13 '96 - p10 [501+]
    NYTLa - v146 - O 8 '96 - pC18 [501+]
    Obs - D 8 '96 - p18* [251-500]
    PW - v243 - Jl 22 '96 - p225 [51-250]
    PW - v243 - N 4 '96 - p38 [51-250]
    Spec - v277 - N 9 '96 - p49+ [251-500]
    Time - v148 - O 14 '96 - p90 [501+]
    TLS - N 29 '96 - p23 [501+]
    WSJ-MW - v78 - O 15 '96 - pA18 [51-250]
  The Laws of Our Fathers (Brown). Audio Version
    LJ - v122 - F 15 '97 - p115 [1-50]
    Trib Bks - F 2 '97 - p6 [51-250]

Turpin, Jennifer E - *Reinventing the Soviet Self*
    AJS - v102 - Jl '96 - p306+ [501+]
    CS - v26 - Ja '97 - p98+ [501+]
Turtledove, Harry - *Thessalonica*
    PW - v243 - D 2 '96 - p55+ [51-250]
  Worldwar: Striking the Balance
    BL - v93 - O 1 '96 - p326 [51-250]
    KR - v64 - O 1 '96 - p1434 [51-250]
    LJ - v121 - N 15 '96 - p92 [51-250]
    PW - v243 - N 18 '96 - p66 [51-250]
  Worldwar: Upsetting the Balance
    y VOYA - v19 - O '96 - p221+ [251-500]
Turton, Richard - *The Quantum Dot*
    Am Sci - v84 - S '96 - p497 [501+]
Turton, Trevor - *Object REXX for OS/2 Warp*
    SciTech - v20 - D '96 - p8 [1-50]
Turvey, Roger - *Wales and Britain in the Early Modern World c. 1500 - c. 1760*
    y Sch Lib - v44 - Ag '96 - p127 [51-250]
Turville-Petre, Thorlac - *England the Nation*
    Choice - v34 - N '96 - p461 [51-250]
Tusa, Ann - *The Last Division*
    KR - v65 - Mr 15 '97 - p452 [251-500]
    LJ - v122 - My 1 '97 - p122 [51-250]
    PW - v244 - Mr 31 '97 - p50 [51-250]
Tusa, Vincenzo - *I Sarcofagi Romani in Sicilia*
    r AJA - v101 - Ja '97 - p196+ [251-500]
Tusell, Javier - *Franco, Espana Y La II Guerra Mundial*
    Choice - v34 - D '96 - p569 [1-50]
Tushingham, A D - *Excavations in Jerusalem 1961-1967. Vol. 4*
    AJA - v101 - Ja '97 - p170+ [501+]
Tushman, Michael L - *Winning through Innovation*
    BL - v93 - D 15 '96 - p699 [51-250]
    LJ - v121 - D '96 - p112 [51-250]
Tuska, Jon - *Billy the Kid: His Life and Legend*
    J Am Cult - v18 - Win '95 - p102 [51-250]
  The Morrow Anthology of Great Western Short Stories
    y BL - v93 - F 15 '97 - p1004+ [51-250]
    KR - v65 - Ja 1 '97 - p19 [251-500]
    LJ - v121 - N 15 '96 - p91 [51-250]
    PW - v244 - Ja 13 '97 - p53 [51-250]
Tuskes, Paul M - *The Wild Silk Moths of North America*
    Choice - v34 - S '96 - p153 [51-250]
Tuten, Donald N - *Fuentes: Lectura Y Redaccion*
    MLJ - v81 - Spr '97 - p146+ [501+]
Tuten, Frederic - *The Adventures of Mao on the Long March*
    LJ - v122 - Ap 15 '97 - p125 [1-50]
    PW - v244 - F 17 '97 - p217 [1-50]
  Van Gogh's Bad Cafe
    BL - v93 - Mr 1 '97 - p1112+ [51-250]
    KR - v64 - D 15 '96 - p1765 [251-500]
    LATBR - Mr 23 '97 - p2 [501+]
    LJ - v122 - F 1 '97 - p108 [51-250]
    NYTBR - v102 - Mr 30 '97 - p16 [51-250]
    PW - v243 - D 2 '96 - p38 [51-250]
Tuttle, Craig A - *An Ounce of Preservation*
    NGSQ - v85 - Mr '97 - p71+ [251-500]
Tuttle, Dean W - *Self-Esteem and Adjusting with Blindness. 2nd Ed.*
    J Rehab RD - v34 - Ja '97 - p121+ [501+]
Tuttle, Lisa - *Panther in Argyll*
    c JB - v60 - O '96 - p207+ [251-500]
  The Pillow Friend
    BW - v26 - N 24 '96 - p6 [251-500]
    MFSF - v91 - O '96 - p62+ [251-500]
Tuttle, William M, Jr. - *Daddy's Gone to War*
    J Soc H - v30 - Spr '97 - p763+ [501+]
Tuttleton, James W - *Vital Signs*
    AL - v68 - D '96 - p880 [51-250]
    BW - v26 - Jl 7 '96 - p13 [51-250]
    HR - v49 - Win '97 - p695+ [501+]
    Nat R - v48 - O 14 '96 - p90 [51-250]
    TLS - Ja 3 '97 - p24 [501+]
Tutu, Desmond - *The Rainbow People of God*
    BW - v26 - S 22 '96 - p12 [51-250]
Tuyen, P D - *Wild Origami*
    c SLJ - v42 - D '96 - p134 [51-250]
Tuyen, Tap - *Hai Muoi Nam Nguoi Viet Tai Canada*
    BL - v93 - S 1 '96 - p70 [51-250]
Tveten, John - *Butterflies of Houston and Southeast Texas*
    r SciTech - v21 - Mr '97 - p38 [51-250]
Twain, Mark - *Adventures of Huckleberry Finn*
    Ant R - v54 - Sum '96 - p363+ [251-500]
    Atl - v278 - Ag '96 - p94 [51-250]
  Adventures of Huckleberry Finn (Graff)
    J Am St - v30 - D '96 - p499+ [501+]
  Adventures of Huckleberry Finn (Kaplan)
    LJ - v122 - Ap 15 '97 - p125 [51-250]
    TLS - Ja 3 '97 - p24 [251-500]

The Adventures of Huckleberry Finn (Keillor). Audio Version
  BL - v93 - Ja '97 - p879 [51-250]
y Kliatt - v31 - Mr '97 - p39 [51-250]
The Adventures of Tom Sawyer (Illus. by Claude Lapointe)
y HB Guide - v8 - Spr '97 - p84 [51-250]
c SLJ - v43 - Ja '97 - p116 [51-250]
Carnival of Crime. The Diamond Lens. Audio Version
c BL - v92 - Ag '96 - p1917 [51-250]
Life on the Mississippi
  AH - v47 - O '96 - p64+ [501+]
Mark My Words
  BW - v26 - N 24 '96 - p13 [51-250]
  LATBR - S 8 '96 - p10 [51-250]
Mark Twain: Letters from the Earth (Layne). Audio Version
  BL - v93 - My 15 '97 - p1596 [51-250]
Mark Twain's Letters. Vol. 4
  Nine-C Lit - v51 - S '96 - p278 [51-250]
Mark Twain's Library of Humor. Audio Version
  BL - v93 - My 15 '97 - p1596 [51-250]
The Oxford Mark Twain. Vols. 1-29
  CSM - v88 - N 21 '96 - pB2 [51-250]
  Ent W - Ja 24 '97 - p50 [251-500]
  LATBR - Ja 26 '97 - p3+ [501+]
  Obs - Ap 6 '97 - p15* [501+]
The Prince and the Pauper (Reiner). Audio Version
c SLJ - v42 - O '96 - p78 [51-250]
Roughing It
  Nine-C Lit - v51 - S '96 - p278 [1-50]
Tom Sawyer Abroad (Dietz). Audio Version
y Kliatt - v31 - Ja '97 - p47 [51-250]
Tweedale, Geoffrey - *Steel City*
  AHR - v102 - F '97 - p105+ [501+]
  Albion - v28 - Fall '96 - p512+ [501+]
  BHR - v70 - Sum '96 - p289+ [501+]
  JEH - v56 - S '96 - p715+ [501+]
Tweedie, Sandra - *Trading Partners*
  AHR - v102 - F '97 - p158+ [51-250]
Tweedy, James T - *Healthcare Hazard Control and Safety Management*
r SciTech - v21 - Mr '97 - p45 [51-250]
The Twelfth Mental Measurements Yearbook
r Per Psy - v49 - Win '96 - p1022+ [501+]
Twelve Days of Christmas (English Folk Song) - *The 12 Days of Christmas (Illus. by Linnea Asplind Riley)*
c Ch BWatch - v6 - D '96 - p1 [1-50]
Woodleigh Marx Hubbard's Twelve Days of Christmas (Illus. by Woodleigh Hubbard)
c KR - v64 - S 15 '96 - p1402 [51-250]
c PW - v243 - S 30 '96 - p88 [51-250]
c SLJ - v42 - O '96 - p41 [51-250]
Twentieth-Century Crime and Mystery Writers. 3rd Ed.
r RQ - v36 - Win '96 - p211 [51-250]
Twentieth-Century Literary Criticism. Vol. 58
r ARBA - v28 - '97 - p422 [51-250]
Twentieth-Century Literary Criticism. Vol. 61
r ARBA - v28 - '97 - p423 [51-250]
Twentieth-Century Literary Criticism. Vols. 59-60
r ARBA - v28 - '97 - p422+ [251-500]
Twentieth-Century Literary Criticism Annual Cumulative Title Index for 1996
r ARBA - v28 - '97 - p423 [51-250]
Twentieth-Century Romance and Historical Writers. 3rd Ed.
r RQ - v36 - Win '96 - p211 [51-250]
Twentieth-Century Science Fiction Writers. 3rd Ed.
r RQ - v36 - Win '96 - p212 [51-250]
Twentieth-Century Western Writers. 2nd Ed.
r RQ - v36 - Win '96 - p213 [51-250]
Twesigye, Emmanuel K - *African Religion, Philosophy, and Christianity in Logos-Christ*
  R&R Bk N - v12 - F '97 - p9 [51-250]
Twiggs, Dennis G - *Psychological and Spiritual Evolution*
  LJ - v121 - S 15 '96 - p83 [51-250]
Twinem, Neecy - *Changing Colors (Illus. by Neecy Twinem)*
c HB Guide - v8 - Spr '97 - p16 [51-250]
c SLJ - v42 - D '96 - p108 [51-250]
High in the Trees (Illus. by Neecy Twinem)
c HB Guide - v8 - Spr '97 - p16 [51-250]
c SLJ - v42 - D '96 - p108 [51-250]
Twining, Charles E - *George S. Long: Timber Statesman*
  PHR - v65 - Ag '96 - p494+ [251-500]
Twinn, M - *Pocket Bunny (Illus. by P Adams)*
c HB Guide - v7 - Fall '96 - p244+ [1-50]
Pocket Frog (Illus. by P Adams)
c HB Guide - v7 - Fall '96 - p244+ [1-50]
Pocket Kitten (Illus. by P Adams)
c HB Guide - v7 - Fall '96 - p244+ [1-50]

Pocket Puppy (Illus. by P Adams)
c HB Guide - v7 - Fall '96 - p244+ [1-50]
Twinn, Sheila - *Community Health Care Nursing*
  SciTech - v20 - N '96 - p57 [51-250]
Twiss, Sumner B - *Experience of the Sacred*
  JAAR - v64 - Fall '96 - p654+ [501+]
Twitchell, James B - *Adcult USA*
  Econ - v339 - My 18 '96 - p4*+ [501+]
  J Am St - v30 - Ag '96 - p338+ [251-500]
  PW - v244 - F 24 '97 - p88 [1-50]
Two-Minute Teddy Bear Tales (Gordon). Book and Audio Version
c TES - Jl 19 '96 - pR8 [51-250]
Tworzecki, Hubert - *Parties and Politics in Post-1989 Poland*
  Choice - v34 - D '96 - p684 [51-250]
Twum-Baah, K A - *Infant, Child, and Maternal Mortality Study in Ghana*
  J Gov Info - v23 - S '96 - p658 [1-50]
Ty, Eleanor - *Unisex'd Revolutionaries*
  Eight-C St - v29 - Sum '96 - p440+ [501+]
Tyack, David - *Tinkering toward Utopia*
  AJE - v104 - Ag '96 - p313+ [501+]
  HER - v66 - Fall '96 - p658+ [501+]
  J Am St - v30 - D '96 - p486+ [501+]
  TCR - v98 - Spr '97 - p567+ [501+]
Tyack, Geoffrey - *Sir James Pennethorne and the Making of Victorian London*
  J Urban H - v22 - S '96 - p727+ [501+]
  VS - v39 - Spr '96 - p443+ [501+]
Tyau, Kathleen - *A Little Too Much Is Enough*
  NYTBR - v101 - N 3 '96 - p28 [1-50]
  PW - v243 - S 30 '96 - p79 [1-50]
Tye, Joe - *Never Fear, Never Quit*
  KR - v65 - Mr 15 '97 - p415 [251-500]
  PW - v244 - Ap 14 '97 - p60 [51-250]
Tye, Michael - *Ten Problems of Consciousness*
  TLS - F 7 '97 - p25+ [501+]
Tyers, A G - *Colour Atlas of Ophthalmic Plastic Surgery*
r SciTech - v20 - S '96 - p39 [51-250]
Tyers, Jenny - *When It Is Night, When It Is Day*
c HB Guide - v7 - Fall '96 - p280 [51-250]
Tygiel, Jules - *The Jackie Robinson Reader*
  BL - v93 - D 1 '96 - p639 [51-250]
  KR - v64 - D 15 '96 - p1791 [251-500]
  LJ - v121 - N 15 '96 - p67 [51-250]
  PW - v244 - F 24 '97 - p78 [51-250]
Tyl, Noel - *Astrology of the Famed*
  Horoscope - v63 - Mr '97 - p6+ [501+]
Predictions for a New Millennium
  BL - v93 - S 1 '96 - p35 [51-250]
  Horoscope - v63 - Ja '97 - p42+ [501+]
Tyldesley, Barbara - *Muscles, Nerves, and Movement. 2nd Ed.*
  SciTech - v21 - Mr '97 - p40 [51-250]
Tyldesley, Joyce - *Hatchepsut: The Female Pharaoh*
  KR - v64 - O 15 '96 - p1522 [251-500]
  New Sci - v152 - D 21 '96 - p75 [51-250]
Tyler, Anne - *Ladder of Years*
  Obs - D 1 '96 - p16* [51-250]
  PW - v244 - Mr 24 '97 - p81 [1-50]
  Sew R - v104 - Jl '96 - p476+ [501+]
Ladder of Years (Critt). Audio Version
  BL - v92 - Ag '96 - p1917 [51-250]
Ladder of Years (Peiffer). Audio Version
y Kliatt - v31 - Mr '97 - p43 [51-250]
Ladder of Years (Critt). Audio Version
y Kliatt - v31 - Mr '97 - p43 [51-250]
Tyler, Carol - *Carol Tyler's Greatest Zits*
  BL - v93 - F 15 '97 - p992 [51-250]
Tyler, Pamela - *Silk Stockings and Ballot Boxes*
  Choice - v34 - S '96 - p200 [51-250]
  VQR - v72 - Aut '96 - p118* [51-250]
Tyler, Ron - *New Handbook of Texas. Vols. 1-6*
r LJ - v122 - Ap 15 '97 - p39 [51-250]
Tyman, J H P - *Synthetic and Natural Phenols*
  SciTech - v21 - Mr '97 - p30 [51-250]
Tynes, Sheryl R - *Turning Points in Social Security*
  Pol Stud J - v24 - Sum '96 - p335 [51-250]
  SF - v75 - Mr '97 - p1140+ [501+]
Typing Tutor 7. Electronic Media Version
y Kliatt - v30 - S '96 - p41 [51-250]
Tyre, Peg - *In the Midnight Hour*
  PW - v243 - O 14 '96 - p81 [1-50]
Tyree, Omar - *Flyy Girl*
  Bloom Rev - v17 - Ja '97 - p19 [1-50]
  LJ - v121 - S 15 '96 - p98 [51-250]
Tyrer, Nicola - *They Fought in the Fields*
  TLS - O 18 '96 - p32 [501+]
Tyrer, Peter - *Community Psychiatry in Action*
  AJPsych - v154 - Mr '97 - p429 [501+]

Tyrer, Polly - *Leith's Cooking for One or Two*
  Obs - Ja 19 '97 - p18* [251-500]
Tyrkus, Michael J - *Gay and Lesbian Biography*
yr BL - v93 - My 15 '97 - p1612+ [501+]
r LJ - v122 - My 1 '97 - p96 [51-250]
Tyrrell, Frances - *Woodland Christmas (Illus. by Frances Tyrrell)*
c BIC - v25 - D '96 - p33+ [501+]
c BL - v93 - S 1 '96 - p138 [51-250]
c Ch BWatch - v6 - D '96 - p1 [1-50]
c HB Guide - v8 - Spr '97 - p141 [51-250]
c PW - v243 - S 30 '96 - p92 [1-50]
c SLJ - v42 - O '96 - p41+ [51-250]
Tyrrell, R Emmett - *Boy Clinton*
  Nat R - v48 - D 31 '96 - p47+ [501+]
  NYTBR - v101 - S 8 '96 - p22 [51-250]
  TLS - F 14 '97 - p14 [501+]
  W&I - v11 - N '96 - p256+ [501+]
  WSJ-MW - v77 - S 10 '96 - pA20 [501+]
Tyson, James - *Chinese Awakenings*
  Ch Rev Int - v4 - Spr '97 - p196+ [501+]
  FEER - v159 - S 5 '96 - p46+ [501+]
Tyson, Kirk W M - *Competition in the 21st Century*
  Bus Bk R - v14 - 1 '97 - p16+ [501+]
  Choice - v34 - Mr '97 - p1206 [51-250]
Tyson, Neil De Grasse - *Universe Down to Earth*
  AB - v98 - O 28 '96 - p1428+ [501+]
Tyson, Peter - *Vincent Van Gogh: Artist*
y HB Guide - v7 - Fall '96 - p357 [51-250]
y SLJ - v42 - Ag '96 - p176+ [51-250]
Tyson, Salinda - *Wheel of Dreams*
y Kliatt - v31 - Ja '97 - p16 [51-250]
Tythacott, Louise - *Musical Instruments*
c Teach Mus - v3 - Ap '96 - p69 [51-250]
Tzannes, Robin - *Mookie Goes Fishing (Illus. by Korky Paul)*
c Magpies - v11 - S '96 - p45 [1-50]

U

Ubben, Gerald C - *The Principal: Creative Leadership for Effective Schools. 3rd Ed.*
   R&R Bk N - v11 - N '96 - p55 [51-250]
Uceda, Julia - *The Poetry of Julia Uceda*
   WLT - v70 - Aut '96 - p924+ [501+]
Uchida, Yoshiko - *The Bracelet (Illus. by Joanna Yardley)*
   c PW - v243 - N 25 '96 - p78 [1-50]
Ucko, Hans - *Common Roots, New Horizons*
   Rel Ed - v91 - Fall '96 - p614 [1-50]
Udall, Brady - *Letting Loose the Hounds*
   BL - v93 - Ja '97 - p822+ [51-250]
   Bloom Rev - v17 - Ja '97 - p15 [251-500]
   Ent W - D 20 '96 - p70+ [51-250]
   KR - v64 - N 1 '96 - p1564 [251-500]
   LJ - v122 - Ja '97 - p152 [51-250]
   NYTBR - v102 - Mr 2 '97 - p12 [501+]
   PW - v243 - N 18 '96 - p61 [51-250]
Udall, Sharyn R - *Contested Terrain*
   Choice - v34 - D '96 - p605 [51-250]
Udal'tsova, Nadezhda - *Zhizn' Russkoi Kubistki*
   Russ Rev - v55 - O '96 - p708+ [501+]
   Slav R - v55 - Fall '96 - p706+ [501+]
Udehn, Lars - *The Limits of Public Choice*
   IndRev - v1 - Spr '97 - p605+ [501+]
   JEL - v34 - D '96 - p2030 [51-250]
Uebe, Gotz - *World of Economic Models*
   r Econ J - v107 - Ja '97 - p266 [51-250]
   r R&R Bk N - v11 - N '96 - p24 [51-250]
Uebe, Ingrid - *Melinda and Nock and the Magic Spell (Illus. by Alex De Wolf)*
   c HB Guide - v7 - Fall '96 - p288 [51-250]
Ueberschar, Gerd R - *Der 20: Juli 1944*
   EHR - v111 - N '96 - p1349+ [251-500]
Ueda, Makoto - *Modern Japanese Tanka*
   BWatch - v17 - S '96 - p3 [51-250]
   Choice - v34 - Mr '97 - p1157 [51-250]
   TranslRevS - v2 - D '96 - p3 [51-250]
Ueda, Osamu - *Reliability and Degradation of III-V Optical Devices*
   SciTech - v20 - D '96 - p78 [51-250]
Uekert, Brenda K - *Rivers of Blood*
   SF - v75 - D '96 - p748+ [251-500]
Uelmen, Gerald F - *Lessons from the Trial*
   ABA Jour - v82 - D '96 - p92+ [501+]
   Esq - v126 - N '96 - p65 [1-50]
Uganda: The Challenge of Growth and Poverty Reduction
   JEL - v34 - S '96 - p1488+ [51-250]
Ugarte, Michael - *Madrid 1900*
   Choice - v34 - My '97 - p1505 [51-250]
Uglea, Constantin - *Liquid Chromatography of Oligomers*
   SciTech - v20 - N '96 - p23 [51-250]
Uglow, Jenny - *Elizabeth Gaskell: A Habit of Stories*
   Dal R - v75 - Spr '95 - p127+ [501+]
Ugresic, Dubravka - *Die Kultur Der Luge*
   TLS - N 29 '96 - p12 [51-250]
Ugwu-Oju, Dympna - *What Will My Mother Say*
   y BL - v93 - D 15 '96 - p717 [1-50]
The UK Stamp Shops Directory 1994-95
   r Am Phil - v110 - S '96 - p829 [51-250]
Ukrains'ka Brafika XI Pochatky XX St.
   Lib - v18 - D '96 - p365+ [51-250]
Ulaby, Fawwaz T - *Fundamentals of Applied Electromagnetics*
   SciTech - v21 - Mr '97 - p25 [1-50]
Ulisse: Il Mito E La Memoria
   TLS - N 29 '96 - p16 [51-250]
Ullman, Dana - *The Consumer's Guide to Homeopathy*
   r BL - v93 - F 1 '97 - p958 [1-50]

Ullman, David G - *The Mechanical Design Process. 2nd Ed.*
   SciTech - v21 - Mr '97 - p85 [51-250]
Ullman, Montague - *Appreciating Dreams*
   Readings - v11 - D '96 - p27 [51-250]
Ullman, Richard H - *The World and Yugoslavia's Wars*
   Choice - v34 - Mr '97 - p1236+ [51-250]
Ullman, Shimon - *High-Level Vision*
   Choice - v34 - Ja '97 - p880 [51-250]
   Nature - v384 - N 14 '96 - p127 [501+]
   Robotica - v15 - Mr '97 - p234 [501+]
Ulmer, Gregory - *Teletheory: Grammatology in the Age of Video*
   Art J - v54 - Win '95 - p102+ [501+]
Ulmer, Michael - *Canadiens Captains*
   Mac - v109 - D 16 '96 - p72 [1-50]
Ulrich, Dave - *Human Resource Champions*
   HR Mag - v41 - D '96 - p125 [51-250]
Ulrich, Eugene - *The Community of the Renewed Covenant*
   JR - v77 - Ap '97 - p285+ [501+]
Ulrich, Jorg - *Die Anfange Der Abendlandischen Rezeption Des Nizanums*
   CH - v65 - S '96 - p442+ [501+]
Ulrich's International Periodicals Directory 1932-
   r ASInt - v34 - O '96 - p15 [1-50]
Ulrich's International Periodicals Directory 1997. Vols. 1-5
   r ARBA - v28 - '97 - p34+ [251-500]
   r LJ - v122 - Ja '97 - p158 [1-50]
Ulrich's Plus. Electronic Media Version
   r LJ - v122 - Ja '97 - p158 [1-50]
The Ultimate Book of Cross-Sections
   y BL - v93 - D 1 '96 - p657 [51-250]
   c LATBR - D 22 '96 - p6 [51-250]
   c PW - v243 - N 25 '96 - p78 [51-250]
   y Sch Lib - v45 - F '97 - p52 [51-250]
The Ultimate Einstein. Electronic Media Version
   r Am Sci - v84 - N '96 - p596+ [501+]
   LJ - v122 - F 1 '97 - p118 [51-250]
The Ultimate Human Body 2.0. Electronic Media Version
   yr Kliatt - v31 - My '97 - p34 [51-250]
Ulven, Tor - *Stein Og Speil*
   WLT - v70 - Sum '96 - p714+ [501+]
Umana-Murray, Mirtha - *Three Generations of Chilean Cuisine*
   BL - v93 - N 15 '96 - p561 [51-250]
   BWatch - v18 - F '97 - p8 [51-250]
   LJ - v121 - D '96 - p136 [51-250]
Umansky, Kaye - *Cinderella (Illus. by Caroline Crossland)*
   c Sch Lib - v45 - F '97 - p43 [51-250]
   The Empty Suit of Armour (Illus. by Keren Ludlow)
   c Magpies - v11 - My '96 - p40 [51-250]
   c Magpies - v11 - Jl '96 - p28 [1-50]
   The Night I Was Chased by a Vampire (Illus. by Keren Ludlow)
   c Bks Keeps - v100 - S '96 - p10 [51-250]
   c Magpies - v11 - Jl '96 - p28 [1-50]
   Spooky Tales to Read Alone (Illus. by Keren Ludlow)
   c Magpies - v11 - Jl '96 - p28 [1-50]
Umansky, Lauri - *Motherhood Reconceived*
   Choice - v34 - Mr '97 - p1247 [51-250]
   Ms - v7 - N '96 - p80+ [501+]
   Nat - v263 - O 14 '96 - p29+ [501+]
Umble, Diane Zimmerman - *Holding the Line*
   Choice - v34 - F '97 - p1028 [51-250]
Umbreit, Mark S - *Mediating Interpersonal Conflicts*
   Fed Prob - v60 - Je '96 - p89 [251-500]

Umiker, William O - *The Empowered Laboratory Team*
   SciTech - v20 - D '96 - p40 [51-250]
Umland, Jean B - *General Chemistry. 2nd Ed.*
   J Chem Ed - v73 - O '96 - pA240 [501+]
Umland, Rebecca A - *The Use of Arthurian Legend in Hollywood Film*
   Choice - v34 - Mr '97 - p1171 [51-250]
   R&R Bk N - v12 - F '97 - p81 [51-250]
   SFS - v24 - Mr '97 - p181 [1-50]
Umland, Samuel J - *Philip K. Dick: Contemporary Critical Interpretations*
   Ext - v37 - Sum '96 - p185+ [501+]
Umnik, Sharon Dunn - *175 Easy-to-Do Christmas Crafts*
   c PW - v243 - S 30 '96 - p87 [51-250]
   c SLJ - v42 - O '96 - p42 [51-250]
   175 Easy-to-Do Thanksgiving Crafts
   c PW - v243 - S 30 '96 - p87 [51-250]
   c SLJ - v43 - Mr '97 - p182 [51-250]
Umphlett, Wiley Lee - *Creating the Big Game*
   Aethlon - v13 - Fall '95 - p148 [251-500]
The UN at 50
   R&R Bk N - v12 - F '97 - p62 [51-250]
Uncertainty '96 (1996: Madison, Wis.) - *Uncertainty in the Geologic Environment. Vols. 1-2*
   SciTech - v20 - D '96 - p65 [51-250]
UNCTAD Commodity Yearbook 1995
   r R&R Bk N - v11 - D '96 - p32 [51-250]
Underdown, David - *A Freeborn People*
   HT - v46 - O '96 - p56+ [1-50]
Underdown, Emma D - *Step 1 Exam*
   SciTech - v20 - S '96 - p26 [51-250]
Underdown, R B - *Aviation Law for Pilots. 9th Ed.*
   R&R Bk N - v12 - F '97 - p64 [51-250]
The Underground CD-ROM Handbook for the SAT. Electronic Media Version
   y BL - v93 - My 15 '97 - p1591 [51-250]
Underhill, Lois Beachy - *The Woman Who Ran for President*
   y Kliatt - v30 - N '96 - p24 [251-500]
Underhill, Philip T - *Naturally Occurring Radioactive Material*
   Choice - v34 - N '96 - p497 [51-250]
Understanding McLuhan. Electronic Media Version
   r LJ - v122 - My 1 '97 - p148 [51-250]
Understanding Opposites
   c PW - v244 - Mr 10 '97 - p67+ [1-50]
Understanding the Internet
   IRLA - v32 - Jl '96 - p11 [51-250]
   LHTN - Jl '96 - p22 [51-250]
Underwood, Dudley - *Mathematical Cranks*
   New Sci - v152 - N 2 '96 - p47 [51-250]
Underwood, Geoffrey - *Implicit Cognition*
   Choice - v34 - N '96 - p542 [51-250]
Underwood, Michael - *Cause of Death*
   Arm Det - v30 - Win '97 - p71 [51-250]
Underwood, Peter G - *Soft Systems Analysis and Its Application in Libraries, Information Services and Resources Centres*
   LAR - v99 - F '97 - p104 [51-250]
Undorf, Wolfgang - *Hogenskild Bielke's Library*
   BC - v45 - Aut '96 - p406+ [501+]
   Six Ct J - v27 - Fall '96 - p792+ [501+]
Ungar, Sanford J - *Fresh Blood*
   Am - v175 - O 12 '96 - p25+ [501+]
Unger, Harlow G - *Encyclopedia of American Education. Vols. 1-3*
   r ARBA - v28 - '97 - p133 [51-250]
   r BL - v93 - Ja '97 - p769 [1-50]
   r BL - v93 - N 15 '96 - p609+ [251-500]
   r LJ - v121 - S 15 '96 - p60 [51-250]

Unger, Peter - *Living High and Letting Die*
New R - v215 - O 14 '96 - p54+ [501+]
TLS - Ja 31 '97 - p26 [501+]

Ungheanu, Mihai - *Rastalmacirea Lui Tepes*
BL - v93 - D 15 '96 - p714 [1-50]

Ungs, Tim - *Shaquille O'Neal*
c HB Guide - v7 - Fall '96 - p360 [51-250]

Ungson, Gerardo R - *Korean Enterprise*
LJ - v122 - Ap 15 '97 - p94 [51-250]

Unicode Consortium - *The Unicode Standard, Version 2.0*
r SciTech - v21 - Mr '97 - p13 [51-250]

Uniform Commercial Law in the Twenty-First Century
J Gov Info - v23 - S '96 - p680 [51-250]

Union List of Serials in Libraries of the United States and Canada. 3rd Ed., Vols. 1-5
r ASInt - v34 - O '96 - p15 [1-50]

Union Pacific Modeler. Vol. 2
Model R - v63 - N '96 - p56 [51-250]

United Nations - *The United Nations and Apartheid 1948-1994*
J Gov Info - v23 - S '96 - p680+ [51-250]
The United Nations and Human Rights 1945-1995
J Gov Info - v23 - S '96 - p680+ [51-250]
J Gov Info - v24 - Ja '97 - p72+ [501+]
The United Nations and the Advancement of Women 1945-1995
J Gov Info - v23 - S '96 - p680 [51-250]
J Gov Info - v23 - S '96 - p731+ [501+]
WorldV - v12 - O '96 - p10 [251-500]

The United Nations and Cambodia 1991-1995
J Gov Info - v23 - S '96 - p680+ [51-250]

The United Nations and El Salvador 1990-1995
J Gov Info - v23 - S '96 - p680+ [51-250]

The United Nations and Mozambique 1992-1995
J Gov Info - v23 - S '96 - p680+ [51-250]
J Gov Info - v24 - Ja '97 - p58+ [501+]

The United Nations and Nuclear Non-Proliferation
J Gov Info - v23 - S '96 - p680+ [51-250]

The United Nations and Rwanda 1993-1996
R&R Bk N - v12 - F '97 - p55 [51-250]
WorldV - v13 - Ja '97 - p12 [251-500]

The United Nations and Somalia 1992-1996
J Gov Info - v23 - S '96 - p680+ [51-250]

The United Nations and the Advancement of Women 1945-1996. Rev. Ed.
R&R Bk N - v11 - D '96 - p41 [51-250]

The United Nations and the Iraq-Kuwait Conflict 1990-1996
J Gov Info - v23 - S '96 - p680+ [51-250]
r MEQ - v3 - D '96 - p86 [51-250]

United Nations Centre for Human Settlements - *An Urbanizing World*
Choice - v34 - Ap '97 - p1393 [51-250]

United Nations Commission on Science and Technology for Development. Gender Working Group - *Missing Links*
Choice - v34 - Ap '97 - p1359 [51-250]

United Nations Conference on Trade and Development - *Information Technology for Development*
R&R Bk N - v11 - N '96 - p33 [51-250]

United Nations. Dept. for Economic and Social Information and Policy Analysis. Population Division - *The Challenge of Urbanization*
r ARBA - v28 - '97 - p328 [51-250]
J Gov Info - v23 - S '96 - p676 [51-250]

United Nations. Dept. for Policy Coordination and Sustainable Development - *Women in a Changing Global Economy*
J Gov Info - v23 - Jl '96 - p530+ [501+]
Signs - v22 - Aut '96 - p222+ [501+]

United Nations. Dept. of Economic and Social Development - *Abortion Policies. Vol. 3*
r ARBA - v28 - '97 - p303 [251-500]
J Gov Info - v23 - S '96 - p676 [51-250]

The United Nations Disarmament Yearbook 1995
R&R Bk N - v12 - F '97 - p62 [51-250]

United Nations. Economic Commission for Europe - *Directory of the Steel Industry and the Environment*
r ARBA - v28 - '97 - p96 [51-250]
Energy Balances for Europe and North America 1992, 1993-2010
r ARBA - v28 - '97 - p646 [51-250]
Rehabilitation Engineering
J Gov Info - v23 - S '96 - p679 [51-250]
Trade Data Elements Directory. Vol. 3
r ARBA - v28 - '97 - p127 [251-500]

United Nations. Expert Group Meeting on International Migration Policies and the Status of Female Migrants (1990: San Miniato, Italy) - *International Migration Policies and the Status of Female Migrants*
J Gov Info - v23 - S '96 - p677+ [51-250]
J Gov Info - v23 - S '96 - p732+ [501+]

United Nations. General Assembly - *Resolutions Adopted by the General Assembly during the First Part of Its Fiftieth Session, from 19 September to 23 December 1995*
R&R Bk N - v11 - D '96 - p50 [51-250]

United Nations Research Institute for Social Development - *States of Disarray*
JPR - v34 - F '97 - p115 [251-500]

United Nations. Secretary-General - *From Nairobi to Beijing*
Signs - v22 - Aut '96 - p222+ [501+]

United Nations. Terminology Section - *English-Russian Economics Glossary*
r ARBA - v28 - '97 - p78 [51-250]
r R&R Bk N - v11 - D '96 - p22 [51-250]

United Nations Women's Indicators and Statistics CD-ROM Database (WISTAT): Version 3. Electronic Media Version
r J Gov Info - v23 - S '96 - p734+ [501+]

United States. Advisory Board on Child Abuse and Neglect - *A Nation's Shame*
J Gov Info - v23 - S '96 - p549 [51-250]

United States. Advisory Commission on Intergovernmental Relations - *Substate Regionalism and the Federal System*
NCR - v85 - Spr '96 - p63 [51-250]

United States. Advisory Committee on Human Radiation Experiments - *Advisory Committee on Human Radiation Experiments: Final Report*
Hast Cen R - v26 - S '96 - p34+ [501+]
J Gov Info - v23 - S '96 - p553 [51-250]
Final Report. Supplemental Vols. 1, 2, 2A
J Gov Info - v23 - S '96 - p553 [51-250]

The United States and the Use of Force in the Post-Cold War Era
NWCR - v49 - Aut '96 - p137+ [501+]

United States. Commission on Roles and Missions of the Armed Forces - *Directions for Defense*
J Gov Info - v23 - S '96 - p542 [51-250]

United States. Congress (1st: 1789-1791). House - *Debates in the House of Representatives. Vols. 1-5*
W&M Q - v53 - O '96 - p836+ [501+]

United States. Congress. Commission on Security and Cooperation in Europe - *Implementation of the Helsinki Accords: Bosnia's Second Winter under Siege*
RSR - v24 - 3 '96 - p46 [51-250]

United States. Congress. House. Committee on Armed Services - *Administration's Plan for Continued U.S. Military Participation in U.N. Operations in Somalia*
RSR - v24 - 3 '96 - p46+ [51-250]
Crisis in the Persian Gulf
RSR - v24 - 3 '96 - p47 [51-250]
The Impact of the Persian Gulf War and the Decline of the Soviet Union on How the United States Does Its Defense Business
RSR - v24 - 3 '96 - p47 [51-250]
The Link Between Force Structure and Manpower Requirements
RSR - v24 - 3 '96 - p47 [51-250]
The Policy Implications of U.S. Involvement in Bosnia
RSR - v24 - 3 '96 - p47+ [51-250]
Reinvestment of Defense Resources for Economic Growth
RSR - v24 - 3 '96 - p39 [51-250]
Reserve and Guard Effectiveness
RSR - v24 - 3 '96 - p39 [51-250]

United States. Congress. House. Committee on Armed Services. Defense Policy Panel - *Building a Defense That Works for the Post-Cold War World*
RSR - v24 - 3 '96 - p47 [51-250]
Future Nuclear Weapons Requirements
RSR - v24 - 3 '96 - p49 [51-250]

United States. Congress. House. Committee on Armed Services. Military Forces and Personnel Subcommittee - *An Assessment of the Bottom-Up Review*
RSR - v24 - 3 '96 - p43 [51-250]
Assessment of the Plan to Lift the Ban on Homosexuals in the Military
RSR - v24 - 3 '96 - p49 [51-250]
The Impact of Peacekeeping on Army Personnel Requirements
RSR - v24 - 3 '96 - p44+ [51-250]

United States. Congress. House. Committee on Foreign Affairs - *Challenges to U.S. Security in the 1990's*
RSR - v24 - 3 '96 - p48 [51-250]
U.S. Nuclear Policy
RSR - v24 - 3 '96 - p50 [51-250]
U.S. Post Cold War Foreign Policy
RSR - v24 - 3 '96 - p43+ [51-250]

United States. Congress. House. Committee on Government Operations. Legislation and National Security Subcommittee - *Government Secrecy after the Cold War*
RSR - v24 - 3 '96 - p42 [51-250]

United States. Congress. House. Committee on Science, Space, and Technology. Subcommittee on Technology, Environment, and Aviation - *Communications and Computer Surveillance, Privacy and Security*
RSR - v24 - 3 '96 - p42+ [51-250]

United States. Congress. Office of Technology Assessment - *After the Cold War*
RSR - v24 - 3 '96 - p39+ [51-250]

United States. Congress. Senate. Advisory Commission to Study the Consumer Price Index - *Final Report of the Advisory Commission to Study the Consumer Price Index*
NYRB - v44 - Mr 6 '97 - p19+ [501+]

United States. Congress. Senate. Committee on Armed Services - *Briefing on Results of the Nuclear Posture Review*
RSR - v24 - 3 '96 - p50 [51-250]

United States. Congress. Senate. Committee on Armed Services. Subcommittee on Coalition Defense and Reinforcing Forces - *International Peacekeeping and Peace Enforcement*
RSR - v24 - 3 '96 - p45 [51-250]

United States. Congress. Senate. Committee on Foreign Relations - *The Peace Powers Act (S.5) and the National Security Revitalization Act (H.R. 7)*
RSR - v24 - 3 '96 - p44 [51-250]
U.S. Participation in Somalia Peacekeeping
RSR - v24 - 3 '96 - p48 [51-250]

United States. Congress. Senate. Committee on Foreign Relations. Subcommittee on European Affairs - *The Future of NATO*
RSR - v24 - 3 '96 - p48 [51-250]

United States. Congress. Senate. Committee on Government Affairs - *Evaluation of the U.S. Strategic Nuclear Triad*
RSR - v24 - 3 '96 - p50 [51-250]

United States. Defense Base Closure and Realignment Commission - *Defense Base Closure and Realignment Commission: 1993 Report to the President*
RSR - v24 - 3 '96 - p45 [51-250]

U.S. Department of the Navy - *Fiscal Years 1992-1993 Report to the Congress*
RSR - v24 - 3 '96 - p39 [51-250]

U.S. Electric Industry Phone and Fax Directory 1996
r ARBA - v28 - '97 - p644 [51-250]

United States. Environmental Protection Agency. Office of Research and Development. Biosystems Technology Development Program - *Bioremediation of Hazardous Wastes*
J Gov Info - v23 - S '96 - p546 [51-250]

United States. General Accounting Office - *Bottom-Up Review*
RSR - v24 - 3 '96 - p44 [51-250]
DOD Force Mix Issues
RSR - v24 - 3 '96 - p40 [51-250]
EPA and the States
J Gov Info - v23 - S '96 - p566 [51-250]
National Security
RSR - v24 - 3 '96 - p48 [51-250]
Peace Operations
RSR - v24 - 3 '96 - p45 [51-250]

U.S. Global Trade Outlook 1995-2000
r Bus Bk R - v14 - 1 '97 - p124 [51-250]
J Gov Info - v23 - S '96 - p542 [51-250]

The United States Government Manual 1996/1997
r ARBA - v28 - '97 - p272 [51-250]

United States. Information Infrastructure Task Force. Working Group on Intellectual Property Rights - *Intellectual Property and the National Information Infrastructure*
J Gov Info - v23 - S '96 - p542 [51-250]

United States. Joint Chiefs of Staff - *Joint Operation Planning and Execution System. Vol. 1*
RSR - v24 - 3 '96 - p41 [51-250]
Joint Warfare of the Armed Forces of the United States. 2nd Ed.
RSR - v24 - 3 '96 - p41 [51-250]

Unified Action Armed Forces (UNAAF)
RSR - v24 - 3 '96 - p42 [1-50]
**United States. National Archives and Records
Administration** - *Guide to Federal Records in the
National Archives of the United States. Vols. 1-3*
r   Am Geneal - v71 - O '96 - p258 [251-500]
r   ASInt - v34 - O '96 - p10+ [51-250]
r   Choice - v34 - Mr '97 - p1144 [51-250]
r   LJ - v122 - Ja '97 - p89+ [51-250]
r   R&R Bk N - v12 - F '97 - p12 [51-250]
**United States. National Historical Publications and
Records Commission** - *Directory of Archives and
Manuscript Repositories in the United States. 2nd Ed.*
r   ASInt - v34 - O '96 - p11 [1-50]
**United States. National Park Service. Interagency
Resources Division** - *Study of Civil War Sites in the
Shenandoah Valley of Virginia*
Pub Hist - v18 - Fall '96 - p170+ [501+]
**United States. National Science and Technology Council.
Working Group on Emerging and Re-Emerging
Infectious Diseases** - *Infectious Disease*
J Gov Info - v23 - S '96 - p553 [51-250]
United States. Naval History Division - *Naval Documents
of the American Revolution. Vol. 10*
r   J Mil H - v61 - Ja '97 - p159+ [501+]
NEQ - v70 - Mr '97 - p158 [501+]
United States. Office of the Pardon Attorney - *Civil
Disabilities of Convicted Felons*
Fed Prob - v60 - D '96 - p65 [51-250]
U.S. Oil Import Vulnerability
RSR - v24 - 3 '96 - p40 [51-250]
United States. President - *The Presidents Speak*
r   JSH - v62 - N '96 - p856+ [51-250]
**United States. Presidential Commission on the
Assignment of Women in the Armed Forces** - *The
Presidential Commission on the Assignment of Women in
the Armed Forces*
RSR - v24 - 3 '96 - p49 [51-250]
U.S.-Russian Cooperation in Space
J Gov Info - v23 - S '96 - p557 [1-50]
**United States Special Operations Forces Posture
Statement 1994**
RSR - v24 - 3 '96 - p39 [51-250]
United States. USAF Scientific Advisory Board - *New
World Vistas. Vols. 1-14*
APH - v43 - Win '96 - p58+ [501+]
For Aff - v75 - S '96 - p142 [51-250]
**Universidad De Valencia. Biblioteca General E
Historica** - *Catalogo De Obras Impresas En El Siglo
XVI De La Biblioteca General E Historica De La
Universitat De Valencia. Vols. 1-2*
r   Lib - v18 - S '96 - p274 [1-50]
**Universidad Interamericana De Puerto
Rico/Aguadilla** - *El Impacto Del Humanismo En El
Nuevo Mundo*
Hisp - v79 - D '96 - p820+ [501+]
**University of Florida. College of Architecture. Accessible
Space Team** - *Accessible Design Review Guide*
BWatch - v17 - S '96 - p2+ [51-250]
**The University of Michigan Index to Labor Union
Periodicals 1960-**
r   RQ - v36 - Fall '96 - p54 [51-250]
**University of Pennsylvania Institute of Contemporary
Art** - *Video Art*
Afterimage - v24 - N '96 - p4 [1-50]
University Places. 1996 Ed.
y   TES - S 27 '96 - p8* [51-250]
Unknown Public
p   TLS - Mr 7 '97 - p28+ [501+]
Unlearning Violence
J Gov Info - v23 - S '96 - p586 [51-250]
Unrau, William E - *White Man's Wicked Water*
Choice - v34 - D '96 - p679 [51-250]
Unschuld, Paul U - *Learn to Read Chinese. Vols. 1-2*
Ch Rev Int - v4 - Spr '97 - p279+ [501+]
Unseld, Siegfried - *Goethe and His Publishers*
Choice - v34 - Mr '97 - p1168 [51-250]
KR - v64 - S 1 '96 - p1311+ [251-500]
LJ - v121 - O 15 '96 - p59 [51-250]
PW - v243 - S 23 '96 - p63 [51-250]

Unsworth, Barry - *After Hannibal*
BL - v93 - F 1 '97 - p927 [51-250]
Ent W - Mr 14 '97 - p74 [51-250]
KR - v64 - D 15 '96 - p1765 [251-500]
LATBR - Mr 9 '97 - p2 [501+]
LJ - v122 - F 1 '97 - p108+ [51-250]
Lon R Bks - v18 - D 12 '96 - p28 [501+]
NYTBR - v102 - Mr 9 '97 - p30 [501+]
Obs - S 1 '96 - p15* [501+]
TLS - Ag 30 '96 - p24 [501+]
Trib Bks - Mr 9 '97 - p4 [501+]
Woman's J - N '96 - p12 [1-50]
WSJ-Cent - v99 - F 25 '97 - pA20 [251-500]
The Hide
NYTBR - v101 - D 8 '96 - p80 [1-50]
VQR - v72 - Aut '96 - p131* [51-250]
Mooncranker's Gift
NYTBR - v101 - S 29 '96 - p32 [51-250]
Morality Play
LATBR - S 8 '96 - p11 [51-250]
NYTBR - v101 - S 29 '96 - p32 [51-250]
NYTBR - v101 - D 8 '96 - p82 [1-50]
Sew R - v104 - Jl '96 - p456+ [501+]
Morality Play (Maloney). Audio Version
BL - v93 - Mr 15 '97 - p1253 [51-250]
The Rage of the Vulture
SFR - v21 - Jl '96 - p48 [1-50]
Sacred Hunger
SFR - v21 - N '96 - p48 [1-50]
Unsworth, Tim - *I Am Your Brother Joseph*
PW - v244 - F 10 '97 - p80 [51-250]
Unterman, Alan - *The Jews*
BWatch - v18 - F '97 - p10 [51-250]
Unwin, David - *Mysteries of Prehistoric Life (Illus. by
Francis Phillipps)*
c   HB Guide - v8 - Spr '97 - p115 [51-250]
y   Sch Lib - v45 - F '97 - p52 [51-250]
c   SLJ - v43 - Ja '97 - p136 [51-250]
Upadhya, Kamleshwar - *High Temperature, High
Performance Materials for Rocket Engines and Space
Applications*
SciTech - v20 - N '96 - p77 [51-250]
Upadhyaya, G S - *Nature and Properties of Refractory
Carbides*
SciTech - v21 - Mr '97 - p91 [51-250]
Upchurch, Carl - *Convicted in the Womb*
y   BL - v92 - Ag '96 - p1878+ [51-250]
y   BL - v92 - Ag '96 - p1891 [1-50]
LJ - v121 - N 1 '96 - p86 [1-50]
Prog - v61 - Ja '97 - p38+ [501+]
**Updates/2000 Forecasts Edition Demographic 1995.
Electronic Media Version**
r   J Gov Info - v23 - Jl '96 - p526+ [501+]
Updike, John - *The Afterlife and Other Stories*
Sew R - v104 - Jl '96 - pR48+ [51-250]
Golf Dreams
LATBR - S 8 '96 - p6 [501+]
LJ - v121 - O 1 '96 - p54 [1-50]
NY - v72 - D 16 '96 - p109 [51-250]
NYTBR - v101 - N 10 '96 - p57 [251-500]
NYTLa - v146 - S 19 '96 - pC17 [501+]
TLS - N 22 '96 - p11 [501+]
Golf Dreams (Updike). Audio Version
LJ - v121 - O 1 '96 - p145 [51-250]
In the Beauty of the Lilies
Ant R - v54 - Sum '96 - p363 [251-500]
Bks & Cult - v2 - Jl '96 - p22+ [501+]
BL - v93 - Ja '97 - p762 [1-50]
Ent W - D 27 '96 - p142 [51-250]
Ent W - Mr 7 '97 - p61 [51-250]
NS & S - v9 - My 3 '96 - p37 [251-500]
NYTBR - v101 - D 8 '96 - p80 [1-50]
NYTBR - v102 - F 16 '97 - p32 [251-500]
PW - v243 - N 4 '96 - p40 [51-250]
PW - v243 - N 11 '96 - p71 [1-50]
RAH - v24 - S '96 - p448+ [501+]
Rel St Rev - v22 - O '96 - p345 [51-250]
Spec - v277 - N 16 '96 - p42 [1-50]
YR - v84 - O '96 - p151+ [501+]
Upgrading and Repairing PCs. 5th Ed.
SciTech - v20 - D '96 - p79 [51-250]
Upgrading and Repairing PCs. 6th Ed.
r   LJ - v121 - D '96 - p138 [51-250]
Upmeier, Harald - *Toeplitz Operators and Index Theory
in Several Complex Variables*
SciTech - v20 - S '96 - p10 [51-250]
Upton, Clive - *An Atlas of English Dialects*
r   ARBA - v28 - '97 - p386 [51-250]
r   Econ - v340 - S 28 '96 - p103 [501+]
Survey of English Dialects
r   RES - v47 - Ag '96 - p397+ [501+]

Upton, Graham - *Stresses in Special Educational Needs
Teachers*
TES - Ja 17 '97 - p9* [501+]
Upton, Lee - *Approximate Darling*
VQR - v73 - Win '97 - p28* [51-250]
Obsession and Release
Choice - v34 - Ja '97 - p799+ [51-250]
Upton, Roy - *Echinacea*
BWatch - v18 - Mr '97 - p1 [1-50]
Urban, Angel - *Concordantia In Patres Apostolicos. Vols.
1-2*
r   Rel St Rev - v23 - Ja '97 - p78 [51-250]
Urban, G R - *Diplomacy and Disillusion at the Court of
Margaret Thatcher*
Lon R Bks - v18 - N 28 '96 - p20 [501+]
Spec - v277 - S 28 '96 - p48 [501+]
TLS - N 8 '96 - p25 [501+]
Urban, Greg - *Metaphysical Community*
Choice - v34 - S '96 - p169+ [51-250]
Urban, Marek W - *Attenuated Total Reflectance
Spectroscopy of Polymers*
SciTech - v21 - Mr '97 - p30 [51-250]
Urban, Mark - *UK Eyes Alpha*
New Sci - v152 - N 9 '96 - p44 [51-250]
Obs - O 20 '96 - p15* [501+]
TLS - Ja 17 '97 - p27 [501+]
Urban, Otto M - *Moderni Revue 1894-1925*
BM - v139 - Ja '97 - p52+ [51-250]
Urban, William L - *The Baltic Crusade. 2nd Ed., Rev.
and Enlarged*
CHR - v82 - O '96 - p693+ [501+]
Urban Travel and Sustainable Development
J Gov Info - v23 - S '96 - p666 [51-250]
Urbanelli, Lora - *The Book Art of Lucien Pissarro*
PW - v244 - Mr 31 '97 - p58 [51-250]
Urbanska, Wanda - *Moving to a Small Town*
LATBR - v263 - S 29 '96 - p15 [51-250]
Urbanski, Marie Mitchell Olesen - *Margaret Fuller:
Visionary of the New Age*
Legacy - v13 - 2 '96 - p154+ [501+]
Urbina, Nicasio - *Sintaxis De Un Signo*
WLT - v71 - Win '97 - p123 [501+]
Urciuoli, Bonnie - *Exposing Prejudice*
Choice - v34 - N '96 - p548 [51-250]
Urdaneta, Maria Luisa - *Deleites De La Cocina
Mexicana*
BWatch - v18 - F '97 - p8 [51-250]
PW - v243 - O 7 '96 - p72 [51-250]
Ure, Jean - *The Children Next Door*
c   HB Guide - v7 - Fall '96 - p298 [51-250]
The Girl in the Blue Tunic
c   TES - Mr 7 '97 - p12* [51-250]
Has Anyone Seen this Girl?
y   Sch Lib - v44 - Ag '96 - p121 [51-250]
Night Fright
c   Bks Keeps - v100 - S '96 - p16 [51-250]
Skinny Melon and Me (Illus. by Chris Fisher)
c   Sch Lib - v44 - Ag '96 - p109 [51-250]
Whatever Happened to Katy-Jane?
c   JB - v60 - Ag '96 - p161 [51-250]
Urgo, Joseph R - *Willa Cather and the Myth of American
Migration*
AL - v69 - Mr '97 - p230+ [251-500]
J Am St - v30 - D '96 - p494 [251-500]
PHR - v66 - F '97 - p126+ [251-500]
Uribe, Maria Victoria - *Limpiar La Tierra*
HAHR - v77 - My '97 - p340+ [501+]
Uriona G.A., Martha - *Elsevier's Dictionary of Financial
and Economic Terms: Spanish-English and
English-Spanish*
r   ARBA - v28 - '97 - p78 [51-250]
r   R&R Bk N - v12 - F '97 - p46 [51-250]
Uriu, Robert M - *Troubled Industries*
Choice - v34 - D '96 - p660 [51-250]
JEL - v34 - D '96 - p2087 [51-250]
R&R Bk N - v11 - D '96 - p30 [1-50]
Url, Thomas - *Econometrics of Short and Unreliable Time
Series*
JEL - v34 - D '96 - p2020 [51-250]
Urman, Dan - *Ancient Synagogues. Vols. 1-2*
Rel St Rev - v23 - Ja '97 - p88 [51-250]
Urquhart, Brian - *A World in Need of Leadership*
Econ - v341 - O 19 '96 - p10* [251-500]
Urquhart, G M - *Veterinary Parasitology. 2nd Ed.*
SciTech - v21 - Mr '97 - p70 [51-250]
Urrea, Luis Alberto - *By the Lake of Sleeping Children*
Bloom Rev - v17 - Ja '97 - p5 [501+]
BW - v26 - D 15 '96 - p1+ [501+]
KR - v64 - S 1 '96 - p1312 [251-500]
PW - v243 - S 16 '96 - p75 [51-250]

The Fever of Being
    WAL - v31 - Fall '96 - p279 [251-500]
Ursini, Aldo - *Logic and Algebra*
    SciTech - v20 - N '96 - p5 [51-250]
Urwin, Derek W - *A Dictionary of European History and Politics 1945-1995*
    yr ARBA - v28 - '97 - p438 [51-250]
    r BL - v93 - O 1 '96 - p368 [251-500]
    r Choice - v34 - N '96 - p438 [51-250]
    r CR - v269 - S '96 - p166 [51-250]
Us (New York, N.Y.: 1985) - *Crazysexycool*
    CSM - v89 - D 5 '96 - pB4 [51-250]
Usborne, Cornelie - *The Politics of the Body in Weimar Germany*
    JMH - v68 - S '96 - p629+ [501+]
The Usborne Illustrated Atlas of the 20th Century
    cr Spec - v277 - D 14 '96 - p77 [1-50]
The Usborne Illustrated Encyclopaedia of Science and Technology
    cr TES - Jl 19 '96 - pR8 [51-250]
Uschan, Michael V - *A Multicultural Portrait of World War I*
    y HB Guide - v7 - Fall '96 - p381 [51-250]
Useem, Bert - *Resolution of Prison Riots*
    Choice - v34 - Mr '97 - p1247 [51-250]
Useem, Michael - *Investor Capitalism*
    Choice - v34 - O '96 - p327 [51-250]
Usher, Dan - *The Uneasy Case for Equalization Payments*
    JEL - v34 - D '96 - p2062 [51-250]
Usher, Graham - *Palestine in Crisis*
    JPR - v33 - N '96 - p501 [51-250]
Usherwood, Bob - *Rediscovering Public Library Management*
    LAR - v99 - Mr '97 - p160 [251-500]
Usilton, Larry W - *The Kings of Medieval England c.560-1485*
    r ARBA - v28 - '97 - p203 [51-250]
Usner, Don J - *Sabino's Map*
    Roundup M - v4 - D '96 - p23 [251-500]
USSC CD-ROM. Electronic Media Version
    r Econ - v341 - D 7 '96 - p8* [51-250]
Ussishkin, David - *The Village of Silwan*
    Rel St Rev - v23 - Ja '97 - p55+ [51-250]
Ustinov, Peter - *Add a Dash of Pity and Other Short Stories*
    PW - v243 - S 16 '96 - p71 [51-250]
Usunier, Jean-Claude - *Marketing across Cultures. 2nd Ed.*
    R&R Bk N - v11 - D '96 - p34 [51-250]
Utah (Frommer's Guides)
    r BL - v93 - S 15 '96 - p210 [1-50]
Utah Energy: Statistical Abstract. 5th Ed.
    r J Gov Info - v23 - S '96 - p595 [51-250]
Utter, Glenn H - *The Religious Right*
    r ARBA - v28 - '97 - p553 [51-250]
    yr SLJ - v42 - Ag '96 - p183 [51-250]
Utton, M A - *Market Dominance and Antitrust Policy*
    Econ J - v106 - N '96 - p1846 [251-500]
Utz, Curtis A - *Assault from the Sea*
    Pub Hist - v18 - Fall '96 - p180+ [251-500]
Uustulnd, Albert - *Kui Jumalad Nutsid*
    WLT - v71 - Win '97 - p187 [501+]
Uva, Richard H - *Weeds of the Northeast*
    r LJ - v122 - Ap 1 '97 - p114 [51-250]
Uviller, H Richard - *Virtual Justice*
    Choice - v34 - N '96 - p539+ [51-250]
    NL - v79 - Ag 12 '96 - p22+ [501+]
UXL Biographies. Electronic Media Version
    cr ARBA - v28 - '97 - p14+ [251-500]
    yr SLJ - v42 - O '96 - p60 [51-250]
Uzan, Marc - *The Financial System under Stress*
    JEL - v35 - Mr '97 - p220 [51-250]
Uziel, Meir - *Makom Katan Im Deby*
    BL - v93 - Mr 1 '97 - p1115 [1-50]
Uzukwu, Elochukwu E - *A Listening Church*
    CLW - v67 - Mr '97 - p31 [251-500]
    Rel St Rev - v23 - Ja '97 - p48 [51-250]
Uzumcuoglu, Ozhan - *General Equilibrium Approach to Financial Decisions*
    JEL - v34 - D '96 - p2054 [51-250]

V

Vacca, John - *VRML: Bringing Virtual Reality to the Internet*
  SciTech - v20 - N '96 - p60 [51-250]
Vaccari De Venturini, Letizia - *Sobre Gobernadores Y Residencias En La Provincia De Venezuela Siglos XVI, XVII, XVIII*
  HAHR - v76 - N '96 - p787+ [501+]
Vaccines 96 (Illus. by Maurice Sendak)
  SciTech - v20 - S '96 - p26 [51 250]
Vachss, Andrew - *Batman: The Ultimate Evil*
  y VOYA - v19 - O '96 - p203+ [251-500]
  False Allegations
    BL - v93 - S 1 '96 - p31 [51-250]
    KR - v64 - Ag 15 '96 - p1183 [251-500]
    PW - v243 - S 30 '96 - p59 [51-250]
  Footsteps of the Hawk
    PW - v243 - S 30 '96 - p79 [1-50]
Vaes, Alain - *29 Bump Street*
  c HB Guide - v8 - Spr '97 - p52 [51-250]
  c PW - v243 - S 2 '96 - p129 [51-250]
Vaeth, Kim - *Her Yes*
  PS - v70 - Fall '96 - p186+ [501+]
Vago, Steven - *Law and Society. 5th Ed.*
  R&R Bk N - v11 - D '96 - p50 [51-250]
Vaid, Urvashi - *Virtual Equality*
  HLR - v110 - Ja '97 - p684+ [501+]
  NWSA Jnl - v9 - Spr '97 - p115+ [501+]
  NYTBR - v101 - S 29 '96 - p32 [1-50]
Vail, John J - *Peace, Land, Bread*
  y HB Guide - v7 - Fall '96 - p383 [51-250]
Vail, Ken - *Jazz Milestones*
  r Choice - v34 - O '96 - p258+ [51-250]
Vail, Rachel - *Daring to Be Abigail*
  c HB Guide - v7 - Fall '96 - p298 [51-250]
  c SLJ - v42 - D '96 - p32 [1-50]
Vaill, Peter B - *Learning as Way of Being*
  HER - v67 - Spr '97 - p150+ [501+]
Vaiskopf, Mikhail - *Siuzhet Gogolia*
  Slav R - v55 - Fall '96 - p703+ [501+]
Vakakis, Alexander F - *Normal Modes and Localization in Nonlinear Systems*
  SciTech - v20 - N '96 - p61 [51-250]
Vakil, Ravi - *A Mathematical Mosaic (Illus. by Taisa Kelly)*
  y Math T - v89 - O '96 - p608 [51-250]
Vakkuri, Juha - *Rajahdyksen Pelko Ja Kaipuu, Nobel*
  WLT - v70 - Aut '96 - p996 [251-500]
Valade, Roger M, III - *The Essential Black Literature Guide*
  r Bloom Rev - v17 - Ja '97 - p20 [51-250]
  The Schomberg Center Guide to Black Literature from the Eighteenth Century to the Present
  r ARBA - v28 - '97 - p421+ [51-250]
Valat, Pierre-Marie - *Water*
  c HB Guide - v7 - Fall '96 - p333 [1-50]
Valauskas, Edward J - *The Internet for Teachers and School Library Media Specialists*
  Emerg Lib - v24 - Mr '97 - p40+ [501+]
  JOYS - v10 - Win '97 - p224 [251-500]
  Sch Lib - v44 - N '96 - p177 [251-500]
  SLJ - v43 - Mr '97 - p115 [51-250]
  The Internet Initiative
    LAR - v99 - F '97 - p103 [51-250]
Valdes, Alberto - *Surveillance of Agricultural Price and Trade Policies*
  r JEL - v34 - D '96 - p2131 [51-250]
Valdes, Guadalupe - *Con Respeto*
  Choice - v34 - Ja '97 - p851 [51-250]
  CS - v26 - Mr '97 - p209+ [501+]

Valdes, Juan Gabriel - *Pinochet's Economists*
  AAPSS-A - v547 - S '96 - p180+ [251-500]
  AHR - v102 - F '97 - p246+ [501+]
  Econ J - v107 - Ja '97 - p230+ [501+]
Valdes, Mario J - *La Interpretacion Abierta*
  WLT - v70 - Sum '96 - p771 [501+]
Valdes, Zoe - *La Nada Cotidiana*
  BL - v93 - Ap 1 '97 - p1284 [1-50]
  LJ v122 Ja '97 p80 [51 250]
  Te Di La Vida Entera
    LJ - v122 - Ja '97 - p80 [51-250]
  Yocandra in the Paradise of Nada
    BL - v93 - My 15 '97 - p1564 [51-250]
    LJ - v122 - Ap 1 '97 - p132 [51-250]
    PW - v244 - Ap 7 '97 - p72 [51-250]
Valduga, Patrizia - *Corsia Deglincurabili*
  TLS - Jl 19 '96 - p12 [501+]
Vale, Brian - *Independence or Death!*
  Choice - v34 - Ja '97 - p860 [51-250]
Vale, Geoffrey - *The Other War*
  BIC - v25 - N '96 - p35+ [51-250]
Vale, V - *Search and Destroy #1-6*
  LJ - v122 - F 1 '97 - p79 [251-500]
Valek, Miroslav - *The Ground beneath Our Feet*
  Obs - Mr 2 '97 - p18* [51-250]
Valencia, Mark J - *The Russian Far East in Transition*
  Slav R - v55 - Sum '96 - p498+ [501+]
Valensi, Lucette - *The Birth of the Despot*
  TranslRevS - v1 - My '95 - p11 [51-250]
Valenta, Barbara - *Pop-o-Mania: How to Create Your Own Pop-Ups*
  c HB - v73 - My '97 - p346 [51-250]
  c PW - v244 - Ap 21 '97 - p74 [51-250]
Valente, Joseph - *James Joyce and the Problem of Justice*
  ELT - v39 - 4 '96 - p507+ [501+]
Valente, Thomas W - *Network Models of the Diffusion of Innovations*
  JMCQ - v73 - Win '96 - p1008+ [501+]
Valentich, Mary - *Acting Assertively at Work*
  Per Psy - v50 - Spr '97 - p260+ [501+]
Valentine, Jean - *Growing Darkness, Growing Light*
  LJ - v122 - My 1 '97 - p109 [51-250]
  PW - v244 - Mr 31 '97 - p70+ [51-250]
Valentine, Mark - *Arthur Machen*
  ELT - v40 - 2 '97 - p190+ [501+]
Valentine, Tim - *Cognitive and Computational Aspects of Face Recognition*
  SciTech - v20 - N '96 - p1 [51-250]
  The Cognitive Psychology of Proper Names
    Choice - v34 - Ja '97 - p880 [51-250]
Valentine Delights
  LJ - v122 - F 15 '97 - p126 [51-250]
Valenze, Deborah M - *The First Industrial Woman*
  BHR - v70 - Aut '96 - p424+ [501+]
  EHR - v111 - N '96 - p1220+ [501+]
  T&C - v37 - O '96 - p834+ [501+]
Valera, Juan - *Pepita Jimenez*
  Hisp - v79 - S '96 - p400+ [501+]
Valette, Jean-Paul - *A Votre Tour!*
  MLJ - v81 - Spr '97 - p130+ [501+]
  Workbook and Laboratory Manual for Con Mucho Gusto. 4th Ed.
    Hisp - v79 - S '96 - p470+ [501+]
Valfre, Edward - *Backseat Buckaroo (Illus. by Edward Valfre)*
  c RT - v50 - D '96 - p344 [51-250]

Valgardson, W D - *Sarah and the People of Sand River (Illus. by Ian Wallace)*
  c BIC - v25 - O '96 - p30 [251-500]
  c BL - v93 - N 1 '96 - p496 [51-250]
  c CBRS - v25 - N '96 - p32 [51-250]
  c CCB-B - v50 - D '96 - p154+ [51-250]
  c Ch Bk News - v19 - Sum '96 - p21 [501+]
  c Emerg Lib - v24 - Mr '97 - p27 [1-50]
  y JAAL - v40 - Mr '97 - p510+ [251-500]
  c PW - v243 - S 23 '96 - p76 [51-250]
  c Quill & Q - v62 - O '96 - p43 [251-500]
  c Quill & Q - v63 - F '97 - p51 [51-250]
  c SLJ - v42 - D '96 - p108 [51-250]
Valins, Martin S - *Futurecare: New Directions in Planning Health and Care Environments*
  SciTech - v20 - N '96 - p37 [51-250]
Valkeapaa, Nils-Aslak - *Trekways of the Wind*
  TranslRevS - v1 - My '95 - p28 [51-250]
Valladao, Alfredo G A - *The Twenty-First Century Will Be American*
  CSM - v88 - O 9 '96 - p13 [501+]
  For Aff - v75 - N '96 - p153+ [51-250]
  JEL - v35 - Mr '97 - p289 [51-250]
  NS - v125 - S 20 '96 - p46+ [501+]
Vallance, Elizabeth - *Business Ethics at Work*
  CPR - v16 - D '96 - p439+ [501+]
  Ethics - v107 - O '96 - p186 [51-250]
Vallat, Jean-Pierre - *L'Italie Et Rome 218-31 av. J.-C.*
  Choice - v34 - D '96 - p566 [1-50]
Vallcorba, Jaume - *Noucentisme, Mediterraneisme I Classicisme*
  MLR - v91 - O '96 - p1019+ [501+]
Vallee, Eleanor - *My Vagabond Lover*
  Rapport - v19 - 6 '96 - p28 [251-500]
Vallone, Lynne - *Disciplines of Virtue*
  AHR - v101 - D '96 - p1520 [501+]
  AL - v69 - Mr '97 - p212+ [251-500]
  Albion - v28 - Sum '96 - p320+ [501+]
  Critm - v39 - Win '97 - p132+ [501+]
  NWSA Jnl - v8 - Fall '96 - p144+ [501+]
Valman, Bernard - *Children's Symptoms*
  r Books - v11 - Ap '97 - p20 [51-250]
Valmiki - *The Ramayana of Valmiki. Vol. 4*
  TranslRevS - v1 - My '95 - p28 [1-50]
Valone, James S - *Huguenot Politics 1601-1622*
  Rel St Rev - v23 - Ja '97 - p84 [51-250]
Valtinos, Thanassis - *Deep Blue Almost Black*
  PW - v244 - Ap 28 '97 - p49 [251-500]
Van Gogh (Illus. by Jean-Philippe Chabot)
  c TES - Ag 23 '96 - p24 [51-250]
Van Allsburg, Chris - *Mysteries of Harris Burdick*
  c BL - v93 - N 15 '96 - p581 [51-250]
  The Polar Express (Illus. by Chris Van Allsburg). Electronic Media Version
  c HB - v73 - Mr '97 - p219+ [51-250]
  The Polar Express (Illus. by Chris Van Allsburg)
  c New Ad - v9 - Fall '96 - p267+ [501+]
  The Stranger
  c HB - v73 - Mr '97 - p189 [1-50]
  The Widow's Broom (Illus. by Chris Van Allsburg)
  c CLW - v67 - Mr '97 - p15 [1-50]
Van Arsdale, Sarah - *Toward Amnesia*
  NYTBR - v102 - Mr 9 '97 - p28 [51-250]
Vanasse, Andre - *Le Pere Vaincu, La Meduse Et Les Fils Castres*
  Can Lit - Spr '97 - p209+ [501+]

Vanasse, Deb - *A Distant Enemy*
  y BL - v93 - Ja '97 - p846 [251-500]
  y CCB-B - v50 - Ap '97 - p298 [51-250]
  c KR - v64 - N 15 '96 - p1676 [51-250]
  c PW - v244 - Ja 13 '97 - p76 [51-250]
  c SLJ - v43 - Ja '97 - p116 [51-250]
Van Beek, Stephen D - *Post-Passage Politics*
  APSR - v90 - S '96 - p662 [501+]
Van Buren, Paul Mathews - *A Theology of the Jewish-Christian Reality. Pts. 1-3*
  Rel Ed - v91 - Fall '96 - p614+ [1-50]
Van Camp, Richard - *The Lesser Blessed*
  BIC - v26 - Mr '97 - p40 [51-250]
  Quill & Q - v62 - O '96 - p41 [251-500]
A Man Called Raven (Illus. by George Littlechild)
  c KR - v65 - Mr 15 '97 - p469 [51-250]
Vance, Jack - *The Demon Princes. Vol. 1*
  KR - v65 - Mr 1 '97 - p342 [51-250]
  LJ - v122 - Ap 15 '97 - p124 [51-250]
  PW - v244 - Ap 28 '97 - p55 [51-250]
Night Lamp
  Analog - v117 - Ap '97 - p147+ [251-500]
  y BL - v93 - S 15 '96 - p226 [51-250]
  BW - v27 - Ja 26 '97 - p6 [51-250]
  LJ - v121 - S 15 '96 - p101 [51-250]
  New Sci - v153 - Mr 15 '97 - p45 [51-250]
  NYTBR - v101 - N 3 '96 - p24 [51-250]
  PW - v243 - S 16 '96 - p74+ [51-250]
Vance, James E, Jr. - *The North American Railroad*
  J Am Cult - v19 - Sum '96 - p160+ [51-250]
  T&C - v37 - O '96 - p843+ [501+]
Vance, Michael - *Forbidden Adventures*
  R&R Bk N - v11 - D '96 - p73 [51-250]
Vance, Mike - *Break out of the Box*
  LJ - v122 - F 15 '97 - p144 [51-250]
  PW - v244 - Ja 6 '97 - p55 [51-250]
Think out of the Box
  J Car P&E - v57 - Fall '96 - p16 [51-250]
  Per Psy - v49 - Win '96 - p1036+ [501+]
Vance, Peggy - *The Mosaic Book*
  LJ - v121 - O 15 '96 - p57 [51-250]
Vance, Robert Lee - *Sin and Self-Consciousness in the Thought of Friedrich Schleiermacher*
  Rel St Rev - v22 - O '96 - p334 [51-250]
Vance, Zebulon Baird - *The Papers of Zebulon Baird Vance. Vol. 2*
  JSH - v62 - N '96 - p821+ [251-500]
Vancil, David - *The Homesick Patrol*
  ABR - v17 - Ag '96 - p21 [501+]
Vancil, Mark - *NBA at 50*
  y BL - v93 - O 1 '96 - p290 [51-250]
  LJ - v122 - F 1 '97 - p87 [51-250]
NBA Basketball Basics
  y Emerg Lib - v24 - S '96 - p26 [1-50]
NBA Basketball Offense Basics
  c BL - v93 - S 1 '96 - p124 [51-250]
  y BL - v93 - Ap 1 '97 - p1310 [1-50]
  c Ch BWatch - v6 - Jl '96 - p1 [1-50]
  c HB Guide - v7 - Fall '96 - p363 [51-250]
Vanclay, Frank - *Environmental and Social Impact Assessment*
  GJ - v163 - Mr '97 - p105 [51-250]
VanCleave, Janice Pratt - *Geometry for Every Kid*
  c BL - v93 - Ap 1 '97 - p1342 [1-50]
Janice VanCleave's 202 Oozing, Bubbling, Dripping and Bouncing Experiments
  c New Sci - v153 - Ja 25 '97 - p45 [51-250]
  c SLJ - v43 - F '97 - p126 [51-250]
Janice VanCleave's Guide to the Best Science Fair Projects
  c BL - v93 - Mr 15 '97 - p1241 [51-250]
  c PW - v243 - D 2 '96 - p62 [51-250]
Janice VanCleave's Oceans for Every Kid
  c Magpies - v11 - Jl '96 - p42 [51-250]
  c SB - v32 - O '96 - p210 [51-250]
Janice VanCleave's Plants
  c BL - v93 - F 15 '97 - p1023 [51-250]
  c SLJ - v43 - Mr '97 - p209+ [51-250]
Janice VanCleave's Play and Find Out about Nature
  c PW - v244 - Ap 14 '97 - p77 [51-250]
Janice VanCleave's Play and Find Out about Science
  c SLJ - v42 - O '96 - p119 [51-250]
Janice VanCleave's Rocks and Minerals (Illus. by Doris Ettlinger)
  c New Sci - v153 - Ja 25 '97 - p45 [51-250]
  c SB - v32 - N '96 - p240 [51-250]
Van Cleve, Barbara - *Hard Twist*
  Bloom Rev - v16 - Jl '96 - p11 [251-500]
Van Cott, Donna Lee - *Indigenous Peoples and Democracy in Latin America*
  APSR - v90 - S '96 - p686+ [501+]

Van Creveld, Martin L - *Air Power and Maneuver Warfare*
  J Mil H - v61 - Ap '97 - p392+ [501+]
Van Dam, Theo - *A Century of War Dates and More 1859-1959*
  r Am Phil - v111 - F '97 - p162 [51-250]
  Phil Lit R - v45 - '96 - p347 [51-250]
Van Deburg, William L - *Modern Black Nationalism*
  LJ - v121 - N 1 '96 - p84 [1-50]
  LJ - v121 - N 1 '96 - p90 [51-250]
Vandenabeele, Frieda - *Cypriote Stone Sculpture*
  AJA - v100 - O '96 - p789+ [501+]
Van Den Berghe, Pierre L - *The Quest for the Other*
  AAAGA - v86 - S '96 - p614+ [501+]
Van Den Toorn, Pieter C - *Music, Politics, and the Academy*
  Notes - v53 - Mr '97 - p753+ [501+]
Vander Elst, Philip - *C.S. Lewis*
  Choice - v34 - D '96 - p630 [1-50]
Vanderford, Marsha L - *The Silicone Breast Implant Story*
  SB - v33 - Mr '97 - p41 [51-250]
Vandergrift, Kay E - *Mosaics of Meaning*
  BL - v93 - S 15 '96 - p254 [51-250]
  Sch Lib - v45 - F '97 - p55 [51-250]
  VOYA - v19 - F '97 - p360 [51-250]
Vanderhaeghe, Guy - *The Englishman's Boy*
  BIC - v25 - N '96 - p4+ [501+]
  Bloom Rev - v17 - Ja '97 - p8 [501+]
  CF - v75 - Mr '97 - p43+ [501+]
  Mac - v109 - D 9 '96 - p64 [1-50]
  Quill & Q - v62 - S '96 - p66 [251-500]
  Quill & Q - v63 - F '97 - p50 [51-250]
Vanderhoek, Jack Y - *Frontiers in Bioaction Lipids*
  SciTech - v21 - Mr '97 - p50 [51-250]
VanderKam, James C - *Enoch: A Man for All Generations*
  Rel St Rev - v23 - Ap '97 - p193 [51-250]
Van Der Kolk, Bessel A - *Traumatic Stress*
  Choice - v34 - D '96 - p694 [51-250]
  Hast Cen R - v26 - S '96 - p41 [1-50]
  SciTech - v20 - S '96 - p34 [51-250]
Vander Laan, Ray - *Echoes of His Presence*
  Ch Today - v40 - N 11 '96 - p53 [51-250]
Van Der Linden, Peter - *Just Java*
  CBR - v14 - Jl '96 - p22 [51-250]
  SciTech - v20 - S '96 - p5 [51-250]
VanderMeer, Jeff - *Dradin, in Love*
  Analog - v116 - D '96 - p145+ [251-500]
  RCF - v16 - Fall '96 - p192+ [251-500]
Leviathan: Into the Gray
  SF Chr - v18 - O '96 - p80 [1-50]
Vandermeer, John - *Reconstructing Biology*
  Choice - v34 - O '96 - p304+ [51-250]
Vander Meulen, Jacob - *Building the B-29*
  BusLR - v21 - 3 '96 - p227+ [501+]
  Pub Hist - v19 - Win '97 - p118+ [501+]
Vanderplank, John - *Passion Flowers*
  Choice - v34 - My '97 - p1525 [51-250]
  CSM - v88 - N 21 '96 - pB3 [51-250]
Vanderpool, Harold Y - *The Ethics of Research Involving Human Subjects*
  Choice - v34 - D '96 - p644 [51-250]
  Hast Cen R - v26 - S '96 - p41 [51-250]
Van Der Poorten, A J - *Notes on Fermat's Last Theorem*
  Choice - v34 - N '96 - p497 [51-250]
  y Math T - v89 - O '96 - p609+ [51-250]
Van Der Post, Laurens - *The Admiral's Baby*
  BW - v27 - F 16 '97 - p1+ [51-250]
  Spec - v277 - O 19 '96 - p49+ [501+]
  Spec - v277 - N 16 '96 - p46 [1-50]
  TLS - Ja 31 '97 - p32 [501+]
Van Der Ryn, Sim - *Ecological Design*
  Choice - v34 - S '96 - p160 [51-250]
  Workbook - v21 - Fall '96 - p133+ [501+]
Vandervort, Bruce - *Victor Griffuelhes and French Syndicalism 1895-1922*
  Choice - v34 - My '97 - p1559 [51-250]
Vandervort, Don - *Home Magazine's How Your House Works*
  LJ - v122 - F 1 '97 - p52 [1-50]
Van Der Vyver, Marita - *Childish Things*
  y BL - v92 - Ag '96 - p1891 [1-50]
Vande Velde, Vivian - *Companions of the Night*
  y Ch BWatch - v6 - N '96 - p7 [1-50]
  y Emerg Lib - v24 - S '96 - p25 [1-50]
  y Emerg Lib - v24 - S '96 - p27 [1-50]
  y Kliatt - v31 - Ja '97 - p16 [51-250]
  y New Ad - v9 - Fall '96 - p327+ [501+]

Curses, Inc. and Other Stories
  y CCB-B - v50 - My '97 - p336 [51-250]
  y KR - v65 - F 15 '97 - p307 [51-250]
Dragon's Bait
  y Kliatt - v31 - My '97 - p16 [51-250]
Tales from the Brothers Grimm and the Sisters Weird (Illus. by Brad Weinman)
  c CAY - v17 - Win '96 - p8 [51-250]
  c Emerg Lib - v24 - S '96 - p46 [51-250]
  c Inst - v105 - My '96 - p69 [51-250]
Vandewalle, Dirk - *North Africa: Development and Reform in a Changing Global Economy*
  Choice - v34 - N '96 - p531 [51-250]
  For Aff - v76 - Mr '97 - p196 [51-250]
  MEJ - v50 - Aut '96 - p626 [51-250]
  R&R Bk N - v11 - N '96 - p28 [51-250]
Qadhafi's Libya 1969-1994
  MEP - v4 - 4 '96 - p149+ [501+]
Van De Walle, Dominique - *Public Spending and the Poor*
  Econ J - v107 - Ja '97 - p225+ [501+]
  JEL - v34 - S '96 - p1439+ [51-250]
Van De Wetering, Janwillem - *The Hollow-Eyed Angel*
  VQR - v73 - Win '97 - p23* [51-250]
VanDiver, Bradford B - *Roadside Geology of Vermont and New Hampshire*
  RocksMiner - v71 - Jl '96 - p281 [251-500]
Vandiver, Frank E - *Shadows of Vietnam*
  BL - v93 - My 15 '97 - p1560 [51-250]
  KR - v65 - Mr 1 '97 - p369 [51-250]
  PW - v244 - Ap 7 '97 - p84 [51-250]
Vandivier, Elizabeth Louise - *Business A to Z Source Finder*
  r ARBA - v28 - '97 - p75+ [51-250]
Van Doren, Carl - *Benjamin Franklin (Cullen). Audio Version*
  y Kliatt - v30 - S '96 - p56 [51-250]
Van Doren, Mark - *Liberal Education*
  ES - v27 - Fall '96 - p217+ [51-250]
Van Dover, Cindy - *The Octopus's Garden*
  BioSci - v47 - Mr '97 - p180+ [501+]
  y SLJ - v42 - S '96 - p242 [51-250]
Van Dover, J Kenneth - *The Critical Response to Raymond Chandler*
  Arm Det - v29 - Fall '96 - p470 [51-250]
  Sew R - v104 - Jl '96 - pR71+ [501+]
Van Dulmen, Richard - *Kultur Und Alltag In Der Fruhen Neuzeit. Vol. 3*
  CEH - v29 - 1 '96 - p120+ [501+]
Van Duyn, Mona - *If It Not Be I*
  LJ - v122 - Ap 1 '97 - p95 [1-50]
Van Duzer, Chet A - *Duality and Structure in the Iliad and Odyssey*
  R&R Bk N - v12 - F '97 - p77 [51-250]
Vandyck, William - *Punctuation Repair Kit (Illus. by David Farris)*
  y Sch Lib - v44 - N '96 - p175 [51-250]
Van Dyke, Fred - *Redeeming Creation*
  Rel St Rev - v22 - O '96 - p344 [51-250]
Van Dyke, Janice - *Captivating Cryptograms*
  c SLJ - v42 - Ag '96 - p162 [51-250]
Van Eck, Jamae - *Healing: Wilt Thou Be Made Whole?*
  BWatch - v17 - N '96 - p3 [1-50]
Van Eenwyk, John R - *Archetypes and Strange Attractors*
  BWatch - v18 - F '97 - p12 [51-250]
Vanegas, Jorge - *Computing in Civil Engineering*
  SciTech - v20 - D '96 - p60 [51-250]
Van Emden, Helmut Fritz - *Beyond Silent Spring*
  Choice - v34 - F '97 - p988 [51-250]
Van Emon, Jeanette M - *Environmental Immunochemical Methods*
  SciTech - v21 - Mr '97 - p41 [51-250]
Van Engen, John H - *The Past and Future of Medieval Studies*
  CHR - v82 - Jl '96 - p506+ [501+]
  Specu - v71 - Jl '96 - p686+ [501+]
Vaner, Semih - *La Turquie En Mouvement*
  MEJ - v50 - Sum '96 - p452+ [51-250]
Van Flandern, Tom - *Dark Matter, Missing Planets and New Comets*
  Skeptic - v3 - '95 - p102 [51-250]
Van Fleet, Matthew - *Fuzzy Yellow Ducklings*
  c ECEJ - v24 - Win '96 - p110+ [51-250]
Van Fraassen, Bas C - *Lois Et Symetrie*
  Dialogue - v36 - Win '97 - p203+ [501+]
Van Gelder, Lindsy - *The Girls Next Door*
  HG&LRev - v3 - Fall '96 - p45+ [501+]
  KR - v64 - My 1 '96 - p679 [251-500]
Van Gieson, Judith - *Hotshots: A Neil Hamel Mystery*
  Bloom Rev - v16 - N '96 - p26+ [501+]
  LATBR - Ag 11 '96 - p8 [51-250]

Van Hage, Mary An - *Little Green Thumbs (Illus. by Bettina Paterson)*
c   HB Guide - v7 - Fall '96 - p352 [51-250]
Van Hartesveldt, Fred R - *The Battles of the Somme 1916*
r   ARBA - v28 - '97 - p253 [51-250]
r   Choice - v34 - N '96 - p438 [51-250]
r   Parameters - v26 - Win '96 - p164 [51-250]
Van Hazinga, Cynthia - *The Old Farmer's Almanac Book of Garden Wisdom*
Fine Gard - Mr '97 - p76+ [251-500]
Van Hoff, Arthur - *Hooked on Java*
CBR - v14 - S '96 - p29 [1-50]
Quill & Q - v62 - My '96 - p20+ [501+]
Vanhole, Kamiel - *Overstekend Wild*
WLT - v71 - Win '97 - p169+ [251-500]
Van Horne, Winston A - *Global Convulsions*
Choice - v34 - My '97 - p1572 [51-250]
Vanin, Gabriele - *A Photographic Tour of the Universe*
y   BL - v93 - D 1 '96 - p629 [51-250]
Choice - v34 - Ap '97 - p1362 [51-250]
Van Inwagen, Peter - *God, Knowledge, and Mystery*
CPR - v16 - Je '96 - p218+ [501+]
Van Keuren, Frances Dodds - *Guide to Research in Classical Art and Mythology*
r   Class Out - v74 - Fall '96 - p42+ [501+]
Van Kley, Dale K - *The French Idea of Freedom*
EHR - v112 - Ap '97 - p493+ [501+]
The Religious Origins of the French Revolution
AI11 - v175 - S 21 '96 - p35+ [51-250]
Choice - v34 - Ja '97 - p859 [51-250]
TLS - O 11 '96 - p31+ [501+]
Van Laan, Nancy - *La Boda: A Mexican Wedding Celebration (Illus. by Andrea Arroyo)*
c   HB Guide - v7 - Fall '96 - p280 [51-250]
c   JB - v60 - D '96 - p242 [51-250]
In a Circle Long Ago (Illus. by Lisa Desimini)
c   ECEJ - v24 - Fall '96 - p39+ [51-250]
Sleep, Sleep, Sleep (Illus. by Holly Meade)
c   RT - v50 - F '97 - p425+ [51-250]
Van Leeuwen, Jean - *Across the Wide Dark Sea (Illus. by Thomas B Allen)*
c   Inst - v106 - S '96 - p53 [51-250]
c   RT - v50 - O '96 - p158 [51-250]
Amanda Pig, Schoolgirl (Illus. by Ann Schweninger)
c   HB - v73 - My '97 - p329 [51-250]
Blue Sky, Butterfly
c   Ch BWatch - v6 - S '96 - p5 [51-250]
c   HB Guide - v7 - Fall '96 - p298 [51-250]
Bound for Oregon
c   PW - v243 - N 18 '96 - p78 [51-250]
Los Cuentos Del Cerdito Oliver (Illus. by Arnold Lobel)
c   BL - v93 - My 1 '97 - p1507 [1-50]
A Fourth of July on the Plains (Illus. by Henri Sorensen)
c   BL - v93 - My 15 '97 - p1582 [51-250]
Van Lew, Elizabeth L - *A Yankee Spy in Richmond*
BL - v92 - Ag '96 - p1879 [51-250]
Van Lieven, Richard - *Love Shack*
Aust Bk R - O '96 - p67 [51-250]
Van Loan, Charles F - *Introduction to Scientific Computing*
SciTech - v20 - D '96 - p13 [51-250]
Van Maanen, John - *Representation in Ethnography*
CS - v25 - S '96 - p707+ [501+]
Van Meter, David A - *Necessary Evil*
PW - v243 - N 18 '96 - p70 [1-50]
PW - v243 - D 2 '96 - p56 [1-50]
VanMeter, Vandelia L - *America in Historical Fiction*
yr BL - v93 - My 1 '97 - p1516+ [251-500]
Vann, J Don - *Victorian Periodicals and Victorian Society*
Albion - v28 - Sum '96 - p335+ [501+]
Vann, Marvin J - *Shenandoah County, Virginia. Vol. 3*
r   EGH - v50 - N '96 - p191 [51-250]
Vannoy, Allyn R - *Against the Panzers*
R&R Bk N - v11 - D '96 - p17 [51-250]
Vannucci, Marcello - *Splendidi Palazzi Di Firenze*
Choice - v34 - Mr '97 - p570 [1-50]
Van Onselen, Charles - *The Seed Is Mine*
Bl S - v26 - Sum '96 - p67 [51-250]
Lon R Bks - v18 - D 12 '96 - p15+ [501+]
NS - v126 - F 28 '97 - p45+ [501+]
NYTBR - v101 - D 8 '96 - p92 [1-50]
NYTBR - v102 - Mr 16 '97 - p32 [51-250]
Spec - v278 - Ap 5 '97 - p36+ [501+]
Van Patten, James J - *The Culture of Higher Education*
Choice - v34 - N '96 - p512 [51-250]
Van Peebles, Melvin - *The Making of Sweet, Sweetback's Baadasssss Songs. New Ed., Collector's Ed.*
FQ - v49 - Fall '95 - p65+ [251-500]
Van Praagh, David - *Thailand's Struggle for Democracy*
Choice - v34 - O '96 - p355 [51-250]

Van Put, Ed - *The Beaverkill: The History of a River and Its People*
BL - v93 - N 1 '96 - p473 [51-250]
Van Raalte, Judy L - *Exploring Sport and Exercise Psychology*
Choice - v34 - Mr '97 - p1199 [51-250]
Van Rensselaer, Mrs. Schuyler - *Accents as Well as Broad Effects*
Choice - v34 - D '96 - p605 [51-250]
NYTBR - v101 - D 8 '96 - p57+ [51-250]
Van Riel, Rachel - *Opening the Book*
LAR - v98 - D '96 - p611 [51-250]
r   LAR - v99 - Mr '97 - p160 [51-250]
Van Riper, A Bowdoin - *Men among the Mammoths*
RA - v25 - 4 '96 - p265+ [501+]
Van Rose, Susanna - *Atlas Visual De La Tierra (Illus. by Richard Bonson)*
cr BL - v93 - Mr 1 '97 - p1196 [51-250]
Van Sant, Ann Jessie - *Eighteenth-Century Sensibility and the Novel*
MP - v94 - Ag '96 - p107+ [501+]
Vansant, Rhonda - *Cats, Dogs, and Classroom Pets*
c   Learning - v25 - S '96 - p90 [51-250]
Moths, Butterflies, Insects, and Spiders
c   Learning - v25 - S '96 - p90 [51-250]
Van Seters, John - *The Life of Moses*
Rel St Rev - v23 - Ja '97 - p22+ [501+]
Prologue to History
Rel St Rev - v23 - Ja '97 - p22+ [501+]
Van Sickle, Jan - *GPS for Land Surveyors*
SciTech - v20 - N '96 - p64 [51-250]
Van Slyck, Abigail Ayres - *Free to All*
ASInt - v34 - O '96 - p94+ [251-500]
J Am Cult - v19 - Sum '96 - p161 [51-250]
VQR - v72 - Aut '96 - p115* [51-250]
Van Staaveren, Jacob - *Interdiction in Southern Laos 1960-1968*
Pub Hist - v18 - Fall '96 - p178+ [501+]
VanStavern, Jan - *Richard Ronan*
AL - v69 - Mr '97 - p251 [51-250]
Van Straten, F T - *Hiera Kala*
AJA - v100 - Jl '96 - p619+ [501+]
Van Straten, Giorgio - *Corruzione*
Econ - v339 - My 18 '96 - p16*+ [501+]
Van Tassel, David D - *The Dictionary of Cleveland Biography*
r   ARBA - v28 - '97 - p49 [251-500]
r   Choice - v34 - F '97 - p942 [51-250]
The Encyclopedia of Cleveland History. 2nd Ed.
r   ARBA - v28 - '97 - p49 [251-500]
r   Choice - v34 - F '97 - p942 [51-250]
Van Vliet, Willem - *Affordable Housing and Urban Redevelopment in the United States*
R&R Bk N - v11 - D '96 - p71 [51-250]
Van Voris, Jacqueline - *Carrie Chapman Catt: A Public Life*
Bloom Rev - v16 - S '96 - p24+ [251-500]
Van Wagoner, Richard S - *Sidney Rigdon: A Portrait of Religious Excess*
CH - v66 - Mr '97 - p150+ [501+]
Van Wert, William F - *What's It All About?*
KR - v64 - My 1 '96 - p636 [251-500]
LJ - v122 - Ap 1 '97 - p156 [51-250]
Van West, Carla R - *Modeling Prehistoric Agricultural Productivity in Southwestern Colorado*
Am Ant - v61 - Ap '96 - p441+ [501+]
Van Wijk-Bos, Johanna W H - *Reimagining God*
TT - v53 - O '96 - p426 [51-250]
Van Winckel, Nance - *Quake: Stories*
KR - v65 - F 15 '97 - p254 [251-500]
PW - v244 - Mr 17 '97 - p78+ [51-250]
Van Wormer, Katherine - *Alcoholism Treatment*
Fed Prob - v60 - S '96 - p87+ [501+]
Soc Ser R - v70 - S '96 - p503 [51-250]
Van Wormer, Laura - *Jury Duty*
Rapport - v19 - 5 '96 - p38 [251-500]
Just for the Summer
BL - v93 - Ap 1 '97 - p1269 [51-250]
KR - v65 - Ap 1 '97 - p501+ [251-500]
PW - v244 - Ap 14 '97 - p52 [51-250]
Vanwyck, Wayne - *Pure Selling*
Quill & Q - v62 - N '96 - p40 [251-500]
Van Wyk, Gary N - *Basotho*
y   SLJ - v43 - Mr '97 - p197+ [51-250]
Vanysek, Petr - *Modern Techniques in Electroanalysis*
SciTech - v20 - D '96 - p27 [51-250]
Van Zandt, Eleanor - *A History of the United States through Art*
c   HB Guide - v7 - Fall '96 - p389 [51-250]
Vanzant, Iyanla - *The Value in the Valley*
PW - v243 - O 7 '96 - p69 [1-50]

Van Zanten, David - *Building Paris*
AHR - v102 - F '97 - p119+ [501+]
JMH - v68 - S '96 - p701+ [501+]
Van Zeller, Hubert - *Holiness: A Guide for Beginners*
PW - v244 - F 10 '97 - p79 [51-250]
Vaporis, Constantine Nomikos - *Breaking Barriers*
AHR - v101 - O '96 - p1259+ [501+]
HJAS - v56 - 2 '96 - p552+ [501+]
Varberg, Dale - *Calculus. 7th Ed.*
SciTech - v20 - D '96 - p17 [51-250]
Varchol, Douglas - *Multimedia Scriptwriting Workshop*
CBR - v15 - Spr '97 - p8 [1-50]
Vardey, Lucinda - *God in All Worlds*
Utne R - My '96 - p107+ [251-500]
Vardy, Peter - *Kierkegaard*
TES - F 21 '97 - p7* [1-50]
The Puzzle of Evil
Rel St Rev - v23 - Ap '97 - p151 [51-250]
The Puzzle of God
Rel St - v32 - S '96 - p428+ [51-250]
Vardys, Vytas Stanley - *Lithuania: The Rebel Nation*
Choice - v34 - My '97 - p1570 [51-250]
R&R Bk N - v12 - F '97 - p17 [51-250]
Vare, Ethlie Ann - *Mothers of Invention*
T&C - v38 - Ja '97 - p214+ [501+]
Varela, Francisco - *Sleeping, Dreaming and Dying*
LJ - v122 - My 1 '97 - p111 [51-250]
Varela, Leoncio - *El Templo Del Gato*
BL - v93 - S 15 '96 - p227 [1-50]
Varennes, Fernand De - *Language, Minorities and Human Rights*
R&R Bk N - v11 - D '96 - p50 [51-250]
Varentsov, I M - *Manganese Ores of Supergene Zone*
SciTech - v20 - N '96 - p24 [51-250]
Varga, Janos - *A Hungarian Quo Vadis*
EHR - v111 - S '96 - p1002+ [501+]
Vargas, Diego De - *To the Royal Crown Restored*
HAHR - v77 - F '97 - p107+ [251-500]
Vargas, Maria Eugenia - *Educacion E Ideologia*
HAHR - v77 - F '97 - p134+ [501+]
Vargas Llosa, Mario - *Contra Viento Y Marea*
TLS - N 29 '96 - p14 [1-50]
Death in the Andes
Am - v176 - Mr 1 '97 - p36+ [501+]
HR - v49 - Aut '96 - p483+ [501+]
NYTBR - v101 - D 8 '96 - p79 [1-50]
NYTBR - v102 - Ja 26 '97 - p28 [51-250]
PW - v244 - Ja 13 '97 - p73 [1-50]
Making Waves
BL - v93 - My 15 '97 - p1557 [51-250]
KR - v65 - Ap 1 '97 - p540 [251-500]
LJ - v122 - Ap 15 '97 - p82+ [51-250]
Obs - D 1 '96 - p16* [1-50]
PW - v244 - Ap 21 '97 - p49 [51-250]
Varhol, Peter D - *Essentials of Multimedia for Business*
R&R Bk N - v11 - D '96 - p27 [51-250]
Varian, Hal R - *Computational Economics and Finance*
JEL - v35 - Mr '97 - p198 [51-250]
Varias, Alexander - *Paris and the Anarchists*
LJ - v121 - D '96 - p120 [51-250]
Varisco, Daniel Martin - *Medieval Agriculture and Islamic Science*
AAAGA - v87 - Mr '97 - p186+ [501+]
Varley, Ann - *Disasters, Development and Environment*
GJ - v162 - Jl '96 - p238 [51-250]
Varley, Frederick H - *Portrait of an Artist*
Quill & Q - v63 - F '97 - p44 [51-250]
Varley, James F - *Lola Montez: The California Adventures of Europe's Notorious Courtesan*
WHQ - v27 - Win '96 - p533 [251-500]
Varley, Peter - *Frederick H. Varley*
Mac - v109 - D 9 '96 - p66 [1-50]
Varley, Susan - *Badger's Parting Gifts*
c   TES - N 22 '96 - p5* [1-50]
Varlow, Sally - *A Reader's Guide to Writers' Britain*
r   LJ - v122 - F 1 '97 - p98 [51-250]
Varma, Ved - *Managing Children with Problems*
TES - Ja 24 '97 - p108 [501+]
Varnedoe, Kirk - *Jasper Johns: A Retrospective*
BM - v139 - Ja '97 - p66+ [501+]
LATBR - D 8 '96 - p28+ [51-250]
NYRB - v43 - D 19 '96 - p61+ [501+]
Varnum, Robin - *Fencing with Words*
Col Comp - v47 - O '96 - p424+ [501+]
Varo, Francisco - *Los Cantos Del Siervo En La Exegesis Hispano-Hebrea*
Specu - v71 - Jl '96 - p771+ [501+]
Varshney, Ashutosh - *Democracy, Development, and the Countryside*
Historian - v59 - Win '97 - p454+ [501+]

Vartian, Armen R - *Legal Guide to Buying and Selling Art and Collectibles*
  r Coin W - v38 - Mr 24 '97 - p80 [51-250]
Vartio, Marja-Liisa - *Nuoruuden Kolmas Naytos*
  WLT - v71 - Win '97 - p190+ [501+]
Vasconcelos, Renato Silva De Mendonca E - *Travels of the Mind*
  LJ - v122 - Ap 15 '97 - p148 [51-250]
  PW - v243 - Jl 22 '96 - p231 [51-250]
Vaseghi, Saeed V - *Advanced Signal Processing and Digital Noise*
  SciTech - v20 - D '96 - p74 [51-250]
Vasey, Ruth - *The World according to Hollywood 1918-1939*
  BL - v93 - Mr 15 '97 - p1209 [51-250]
  PW - v244 - F 10 '97 - p79 [51-250]
Vasileva, Tatiana - *Hostage to War*
  c Bks Keeps - v100 - S '96 - p33 [51-250]
  y CCB-B - v50 - Ap '97 - p299+ [51-250]
  y HB - v73 - My '97 - p330 [251-500]
  y JB - v60 - O '96 - p208 [51-250]
  c KR - v65 - Ja 15 '97 - p146+ [51-250]
  y Sch Lib - v44 - N '96 - p172 [51-250]
Vasilleva, Larisa - *Skazki O Liubvi*
  BL - v93 - O 1 '96 - p327 [1-50]
Vasquez, Olga A - *Pushing Boundaries*
  HER - v67 - Spr '97 - p158+ [251-500]
Vasquez, Priscilla - *El SIDA Y El Trabajo*
  BL - v93 - S 15 '96 - p227 [1-50]
Vassall-Adams, Guy - *Rwanda: An Agenda for International Action*
  WorldV - v12 - O '96 - p18 [51-250]
Vassanji, M G - *The Book of Secrets*
  Trib Bks - F 16 '97 - p8 [1-50]
Vassilian, Hamo B - *Ethnic Cuisines*
  r ARBA - v28 - '97 - p570 [51-250]
Vassilikos, Vassilis - *And Dreams Are Dreams*
  BW - v26 - Jl 14 '96 - p6 [251-500]
  TLS - O 4 '96 - p36 [501+]
  WLT - v70 - Aut '96 - p1004 [251-500]
Vasso, Madame - *Fergie: The Very Private Life of the Duchess of York*
  Ent W - D 13 '96 - p72 [251-500]
  NYTBR - v102 - Ja 5 '97 - p13+ [501+]
Vasta, Ellie - *The Teeth Are Smiling*
  Aust Bk R - S '96 - p20+ [501+]
Vasulka, Steina - *Eigenwelt Der Apparate-Welt*
  Per A J - v18 - 3 '96 - p20+ [501+]
Vatikiotis, Michael R J - *Political Change in Southeast Asia*
  FEER - v159 - O 17 '96 - p68 [251-500]
Vatter, Terry - *Civic Mathematics*
  Math T - v90 - Mr '97 - p248 [51-250]
  y SLMQ - v25 - Fall '96 - p66 [51-250]
  VOYA - v19 - F '97 - p355+ [251-500]
Vaucher, Andrea R - *Muses from Chaos and Ash*
  TDR - v40 - Fall '96 - p201 [251-500]
Vauchez, Andre - *The Laity in the Middle Ages*
  TranslRevS - v1 - My '95 - p14 [51-250]
Vauclair, Jacques - *Animal Cognition*
  Choice - v34 - Ap '97 - p1421+ [51-250]
  New Sci - v151 - S 28 '96 - p52 [1-50]
  Sci - v275 - F 28 '97 - p1276 [1-50]
  SciTech - v20 - N '96 - p30 [51-250]
Vaughan, Alden T - *Roots of American Racism*
  JIH - v27 - Spr '97 - p712+ [501+]
  W&M Q - v53 - O '96 - p803+ [501+]
Vaughan, Christopher - *How Life Begins*
  Choice - v34 - S '96 - p156 [51-250]
Vaughan, Diane - *The Challenger Launch Decision*
  CS - v25 - N '96 - p727+ [501+]
  JMCQ - v73 - Aut '96 - p756+ [501+]
  NYTBR - v102 - Mr 9 '97 - p32 [51-250]
Vaughan, Emmett J - *Risk Management*
  R&R Bk N - v12 - F '97 - p38 [51-250]
Vaughan, Frank A - *Again to the Life of Eternity*
  Choice - v34 - N '96 - p461 [51-250]
Vaughan, Garth - *The Puck Starts Here*
  Mac - v109 - D 16 '96 - p73 [51-250]
  Quill & Q - v62 - N '96 - p38 [501+]
Vaughan, Marcia - *The Dancing Dragon (Illus. by Stanley Wong Hoo Foon)*
  c SLJ - v42 - D '96 - p108 [51-250]
  Snap! (Illus. by Sascha Hutchinson)
  c HB Guide - v7 - Fall '96 - p280 [51-250]
  Whistling Dixie (Illus. by Barry Moser)
  c LA - v73 - O '96 - p433 [51-250]
Vaughan, Miceal F - *Suche Werkis To Werche*
  MLR - v91 - Jl '96 - p691+ [501+]
Vaughan, Robert - *Blood on the Plains*
  Roundup M - v4 - Ap '97 - p28+ [51-250]

Vaughan, Susan C - *The Talking Cure*
  BL - v93 - Mr 15 '97 - p1214 [51-250]
  KR - v65 - F 1 '97 - p211 [251-500]
  PW - v244 - Mr 31 '97 - p57 [51-250]
Vaughan, Virginia Mason - *Othello: A Contextual History*
  RES - v48 - F '97 - p99+ [501+]
Vaughan, W E - *Landlords and Tenants in Mid-Victorian Ireland*
  EHR - v111 - S '96 - p1006+ [251-500]
  JMH - v68 - S '96 - p685+ [501+]
  VS - v39 - Spr '96 - p426+ [501+]
Vaughan-Nichols, Steven J - *Intranets*
  SciTech - v21 - Mr '97 - p88 [51-250]
Vaughan-Whitehead, Daniel - *Workers' Financial Participation*
  J Gov Info - v23 - S '96 - p672 [51-250]
Vaughn, Barbara Biggers - *Lick Creek Beckoned*
  NGSQ - v84 - D '96 - p311+ [251-500]
Vaughn, Robert - *Texas Glory*
  Roundup M - v4 - D '96 - p28 [51-250]
Vaughn, Sharon - *Focus Group Interviews in Education and Psychology*
  HER - v67 - Spr '97 - p159+ [501+]
Vaughn, Stephen - *Ronald Reagan in Hollywood*
  J Am Cult - v18 - Win '95 - p105 [251-500]
Vaughn, William R - *Hitchhiker's Guide to Visual Basic and SQL Server. 4th Ed.*
  CBR - v14 - S '96 - p31 [1-50]
  SciTech - v20 - N '96 - p8 [51-250]
Vause, Mikel - *The Peregrine Reader*
  y BL - v93 - Mr 1 '97 - p1105+ [51-250]
  KR - v65 - F 1 '97 - p211+ [51-250]
  PW - v244 - Mr 31 '97 - p63 [51-250]
Vaz, Mark Cotta - *The Secrets of Star Wars*
  SF Chr - v18 - O '96 - p82 [1-50]
Vazirani, Reetika - *White Elephants*
  VQR - v72 - Aut '96 - p135* [51-250]
Vaz-Oxlade, Gail - *The Money Tree Myth*
  c Quill & Q - v62 - S '96 - p76 [51-250]
Vazquez, Diego - *Growing through the Ugly*
  BL - v93 - F 15 '97 - p1005 [51-250]
  KR - v64 - D 15 '96 - p1766 [251-500]
  NYTBR - v102 - Mr 30 '97 - p16 [51-250]
  PW - v244 - Ja 13 '97 - p55 [51-250]
Vazquez, Josefina Zoraida - *De La Rebelion De Texas A La Guerra Del 47*
  HAHR - v76 - Ag '96 - p573+ [501+]
  La Fundacion Del Estado Mexicano 1821-1855
  HAHR - v77 - F '97 - p130+ [501+]
Vazquez, Maria Esther - *Borges: Esplendor Y Derrota*
  WLT - v70 - Aut '96 - p925 [251-500]
Vazquez Montalban, Manuel - *Murder in the Central Committee*
  TLS - Ag 2 '96 - p22 [501+]
  Off Side
  TLS - Ag 2 '96 - p22 [501+]
Vdall, Denis - *Journeys through Our Classrooms*
  Cur R - v36 - Ja '97 - p3* [51-250]
Vea, Alfredo, Jr. - *The Silver Cloud Cafe*
  KR - v64 - Ag 15 '96 - p1183+ [251-500]
Veblen, Thomas L - *The Ecology and Biogeography of Nothofagus Forests*
  Choice - v34 - S '96 - p154 [51-250]
Veblen, Thorstein - *Absentee Ownership*
  JEL - v35 - Mr '97 - p191 [51-250]
  The Engineers and the Price System
  Reason - v28 - D '96 - p37+ [51-250]
Vecchione, Glen - *Make-It-Yourself Fair Projects*
  y Ch BWatch - v7 - Ja '97 - p2 [51-250]
Veciana-Suarez, Ana - *The Chin Kiss King*
  LJ - v122 - Ap 15 '97 - p121 [51-250]
Vecsey, Christopher - *On the Padres' Trail*
  LJ - v121 - D '96 - p100+ [51-250]
Vedeckis, Wayne V - *Hormones and Cancer*
  SciTech - v20 - S '96 - p30 [51-250]
Vedral, Joyce L - *Definition*
  Quill & Q - v62 - D '96 - p24+ [501+]
  Eat to Trim
  BL - v93 - D 1 '96 - p636 [51-250]
  BWatch - v18 - Mr '97 - p5 [1-50]
  LJ - v121 - D '96 - p134 [51-250]
  The Fat-Burning Workout
  Quill & Q - v62 - D '96 - p24+ [501+]
Veenendaal, Augustus J, Jr. - *Slow Train to Paradise*
  JEL - v34 - S '96 - p1474+ [51-250]
Veer, Akky Van Der - *Grutte Wurden*
  WLT - v71 - Win '97 - p169 [251-500]
Veer, Peter Van Der - *Religious Nationalism*
  Historian - v58 - Sum '96 - p888 [251-500]
Veerman, David R - *On Eagle's Wings*
  CLW - v67 - D '96 - p54 [51-250]

Veeser, H Aram - *The New Historicism Reader*
  Clio - v25 - Sum '96 - p421+ [501+]
Vega, Ana Lydia - *True and False Romances*
  TranslRevS - v1 - My '95 - p33 [51-250]
Veitch, Tom - *Dark Empire*
  y Emerg Lib - v24 - S '96 - p27 [1-50]
Vekshin, N L - *Energy Transfer in Macromolecules*
  SciTech - v21 - Mr '97 - p41 [51-250]
Velarde, Veronica E - *American Indian Reservations and Trust Areas*
  r ARBA - v28 - '97 - p158+ [251-500]
Velasco, Sherry M - *Demons, Nausea, and Resistance in the Autobiography of Isabel De Jesus 1611-1682*
  Choice - v34 - S '96 - p134 [51-250]
Velde, Rink Van Der - *The Trap*
  BL - v93 - F 1 '97 - p927 [51-250]
  KR - v64 - D 1 '96 - p1703 [51-250]
  PW - v243 - N 25 '96 - p55+ [51-250]
Velde, Rudi A Te - *Participation and Substantiality in Thomas Aquinas*
  IPQ - v37 - Mr '97 - p101+ [501+]
Velecky, Lubor - *Aquinas' Five Arguments in the Summa Theologiae 1a 2, 3*
  RM - v50 - D '96 - p427+ [501+]
Velema, Wyger R E - *Enlightenment and Conservatism in the Dutch Republic*
  JMH - v68 - S '96 - p718+ [501+]
Velez-Ibanez, Carlos G - *Border Visions*
  Choice - v34 - My '97 - p1586 [51-250]
Velie, Alan R - *Native American Perspectives on Literature and History*
  AL - v68 - D '96 - p874+ [501+]
Vella, J - *Learning to Listen, Learning to Teach*
  AE - v46 - Sum '96 - p242+ [501+]
Vellacott, Jane - *Life and Living*
  y Sch Lib - v44 - N '96 - p175 [251-500]
Veller, Mikhail Iosifovich - *Legendy Nevskogo Prospekta*
  WLT - v71 - Win '97 - p177+ [501+]
  Prikliucheniia Maiora Zviagina
  WLT - v71 - Win '97 - p178+ [501+]
Velthoven, Willem - *Multimedia Graphics*
  Bloom Rev - v16 - N '96 - p24+ [51-250]
  PW - v243 - S 16 '96 - p66 [51-250]
Velthuijs, Max - *A Birthday Cake for Little Bear*
  c Bks Keeps - Jl '96 - p6 [51-250]
Venbrux, Eric - *A Death in the Tiwi Islands*
  Choice - v34 - N '96 - p501 [51-250]
Vence-Deza, Xavier - *Wealth from Diversity*
  JEL - v35 - Mr '97 - p281+ [51-250]
Venclova, Tomas - *Aleksander Wat: Life and Art of an Iconoclast*
  Choice - v34 - N '96 - p466+ [51-250]
  NYRB - v43 - N 28 '96 - p4+ [501+]
  NYTBR - v101 - S 8 '96 - p30 [501+]
  TLS - O 4 '96 - p38 [501+]
  WLT - v70 - Aut '96 - p990+ [501+]
Vendler, Helen - *The Breaking of Style*
  NYRB - v43 - N 28 '96 - p59+ [501+]
  South CR - v28 - Spr '96 - p280+ [501+]
  WLT - v70 - Sum '96 - p699+ [501+]
  The Given and the Made
  NYRB - v43 - N 28 '96 - p59+ [501+]
  South CR - v28 - Spr '96 - p280+ [501+]
  WLT - v70 - Sum '96 - p699+ [501+]
  Soul Says
  NYRB - v43 - N 28 '96 - p59+ [501+]
  WLT - v70 - Sum '96 - p700+ [501+]
Venedikian, Harry M - *Export-Import Financing. 4th Ed.*
  JEL - v34 - S '96 - p1430 [51-250]
Venezia, Mike - *Andy Warhol*
  c HB Guide - v8 - Spr '97 - p139 [51-250]
  Igor Stravinsky (Illus. by Mike Venezia)
  c HB Guide - v8 - Spr '97 - p161 [1-50]
  Ludwig Van Beethoven
  c BL - v93 - S 15 '96 - p244+ [51-250]
  c HB Guide - v7 - Fall '96 - p375 [51-250]
  Pierre Auguste Renoir (Illus. by Mike Venezia)
  c BL - v93 - S 15 '96 - p244+ [51-250]
  c HB Guide - v8 - Spr '97 - p139 [51-250]
  c SLJ - v42 - D '96 - p118 [51-250]
Venkateswaran, Snadhya - *Environment, Development and the Gender Gap*
  SSQ - v77 - D '96 - p935+ [501+]
Venning, Timothy - *Cromwellian Foreign Policy*
  AHR - v101 - D '96 - p1548+ [251-500]
  Six Ct J - v27 - Win '96 - p1196+ [501+]
Ventura, Michael - *The Death of Frank Sinatra*
  LATBR - O 6 '96 - p3 [501+]
Ventura, Piero - *Food: Its Evolution through the Ages (Illus. by Piero Ventura)*
  c Emerg Lib - v23 - My '96 - p44 [51-250]

Venturi, Robert - *Iconography and Electronics upon a Generic Architecture*
  NYTBR - v101 - D 8 '96 - p54 [251-500]
  R&R Bk N - v12 - F '97 - p72 [51-250]
Venuti, Lawrence - *The Translator's Invisibility*
  Comp L - v48 - Fall '96 - p359+ [501+]
  TLS - S 6 '96 - p8 [501+]
Venzon, Anne Cipriano - *The United States in the First World War*
  r J Mil H - v61 - Ap '97 - p391+ [251-500]
Vera, Yvonne - *Without a Name*
  WLT - v70 - Sum '96 - p752 [501+]
Verani, Hugo J - *De La Vanguardia A La Posmodernidad*
  BL - v93 - Mr 15 '97 - p1232 [1-50]
Verba, Sidney - *Voice and Equality*
  AAPSS-A - v547 - S '96 - p187+ [251-500]
  CS - v25 - N '96 - p763+ [501+]
  J Pol - v58 - N '96 - p1219+ [501+]
  PSQ - v111 - Win '96 - p706+ [501+]
  RP - v58 - Fall '96 - p832+ [501+]
Verbitsky, Horacio - *The Flight: Confessions of an Argentine Dirty Warrior*
  Nat - v263 - S 30 '96 - p30+ [501+]
  NY - v72 - S 23 '96 - p95 [501+]
  WorldV - v13 - Ja '97 - p7 [251-500]
Vercellin, Giorgio - *Istituzioni Del Mondo Musulmano*
  MEJ - v51 - Win '97 - p154 [51-250]
Verde, Tom - *Twentieth-Century Writers 1950-1990*
  y HB Guide - v7 - Fall '96 - p364 [51-250]
Verdelle, A J - *The Good Negress*
  NYTBR - v101 - Ap 7 '96 - p24 [1-50]
Verdery, Katherine - *What Was Socialism, and What Comes Next?*
  APSR - v91 - Mr '97 - p223+ [251-500]
  Choice - v34 - S '96 - p204 [51-250]
  CS - v26 - Mr '97 - p177+ [501+]
Verdet, J P - *Light*
  c Inst - v106 - S '96 - p87 [1-50]
Verdi, Giuseppe - *The Complete Verdi Libretti. Vols. 1-3*
  ON - v61 - D 14 '96 - p73+ [501+]
Verdier, Daniel - *Democracy and International Trade*
  IndRev - v1 - Spr '97 - p611+ [501+]
Verdoia, Ken - *Utah: The Struggle for Statehood*
  WHQ - v27 - Win '96 - p552 [1-50]
Verdon, Michel - *Keynes and the Classics*
  JEL - v35 - Mr '97 - p194 [51-250]
Verdonk, Peter - *Twentieth-Century Poetry*
  RES - v47 - Ag '96 - p456+ [501+]
Veress, Laura-Louise - *Clear the Line*
  TLS - Ja 10 '97 - p29 [251-500]
Verey, Rosemary - *Rosemary Verey's English Country Gardens*
  CSM - v89 - F 27 '97 - pB2 [51-250]
Verga, Giovanni - *I Malavoglia*
  TLS - Jl 19 '96 - p10 [501+]
Vergara, Camilo Jose - *The New American Ghetto*
  ASInt - v34 - O '96 - p118+ [501+]
  CS - v26 - Ja '97 - p58+ [501+]
  NYRB - v43 - O 31 '96 - p34+ [501+]
Verghese, Abraham - *My Own Country*
  SFR - v21 - Jl '96 - p48 [1-50]
  SSQ - v77 - D '96 - p932+ [501+]
Vergne, Elisa - *Les Volailles*
  BL - v93 - Ja '97 - p827 [1-50]
Verhaar, C H A - *On the Challenges of Unemployment in a Regional Europe*
  JEL - v34 - S '96 - p1449 [51-250]
Verhagen, H L E - *Agency in Private International Law*
  Law Q Rev - v113 - Ja '97 - p177+ [501+]
Verhey, Allen - *Religion and Medical Ethics*
  CC - v113 - N 20 '96 - p1157+ [501+]
  Hast Cen R - v26 - S '96 - p41 [51-250]
Verification 1995
  Parameters - v26 - Aut '96 - p146+ [501+]
Verification 1996
  R&R Bk N - v11 - D '96 - p49 [51-250]
Verma, Nirmal - *Such a Big Yearning and Other Stories*
  WLT - v71 - Win '97 - p227 [251-500]
Vermeij, Geerat - *Privileged Hands*
  BW - v26 - D 29 '96 - p8 [251-500]
  LJ - v121 - S 15 '96 - p91 [51-250]
  Nature - v384 - N 14 '96 - p126+ [501+]
  New Sci - v152 - O 5 '96 - p47 [51-250]
  NH - v105 - O '96 - p10+ [501+]
  NYTBR - v101 - N 10 '96 - p20 [501+]
  Sci - v276 - Ap 18 '97 - p370 [501+]
Vermeulen, Hans - *The Anthropology of Ethnicity*
  Am Ethnol - v23 - Ag '96 - p639+ [501+]
  Fieldwork and Footnotes
  Am Ethnol - v24 - F '97 - p243+ [501+]
  Isis - v87 - S '96 - p524+ [501+]

Vermigli, Pietro Martire - *The Peter Martyr Library. Vol. 1*
  Ren & Ref - v20 - Win '96 - p91+ [501+]
  The Peter Martyr Library. Vols. 1-2
  CH - v65 - S '96 - p482+ [501+]
Vermilye, Jerry - *The Complete Films of Audrey Hepburn*
  FIR - v47 - S '96 - p85 [251-500]
Vermorel, Fred - *Vivienne Westwood: Fashion, Perversity and the Sixties Laid Bare*
  BL - v93 - S 1 '96 - p53 [256]
  LJ - v121 - O 1 '96 - p76 [51-250]
  PW - v243 - Jl 22 '96 - p219 [251-500]
Verne, Jules - *20,000 Leagues Under the Sea (Illus. by Stephen Armes)*
  c Ch BWatch - v6 - D '96 - p5 [1-50]
  Around the World in Eighty Days (Illus. by James Prunier)
  y HB Guide - v7 - Fall '96 - p302 [51-250]
  y KR - v64 - My 1 '96 - p696 [1-50]
  c Magpies - v11 - S '96 - p39+ [501+]
  c TES - Ja 31 '97 - p7* [501+]
  From the Earth to the Moon
  Books - v9 - S '95 - p24 [251-500]
  Journey to the Centre of the Earth (Glover). Audio Version
  c Ch BWatch - v7 - Ja '97 - p5 [1-50]
  c TES - D 27 '96 - p27 [51-250]
  Paris in the Twentieth Century
  Atl - v279 - Ja '97 - p98 [51-250]
  BL - v93 - N 15 '96 - p576 [251-500]
  BW - v26 - D 15 '96 - p9+ [501+]
  CSM - v89 - F 27 '97 - pB1+ [501+]
  Ent W - Ja 10 '97 - p53 [51-250]
  Esq - v126 - D '96 - p40 [1-50]
  KR - v64 - O 15 '96 - p1492 [251-500]
  LATBR - D 15 '96 - p10 [501+]
  LJ - v121 - N 15 '96 - p90 [51-250]
  NYTBR - v102 - Ja 26 '97 - p4 [501+]
  NYTLa - v146 - D 27 '96 - pC39 [501+]
  PW - v243 - O 14 '96 - p63 [51-250]
  SFS - v24 - Mr '97 - p133+ [501+]
Vernede, R V - *The Enchanted Loom*
  KR - v64 - S 15 '96 - p1353 [51-250]
  PW - v243 - S 23 '96 - p61 [51-250]
Verney, Edmund Hope - *Vancouver Island Letters of Edmund Hope Verney 1862-65*
  Choice - v34 - D '96 - p679 [51-250]
  R&R Bk N - v11 - N '96 - p20 [51-250]
Vernon, James - *Politics and the People*
  J Soc H - v30 - Fall '96 - p229+ [501+]
Vernon, Lillian - *An Eye for Winners*
  LJ - v121 - N 15 '96 - p70 [51-250]
  PW - v243 - S 30 '96 - p73 [51-250]
Vernon, Paul - *Ethnic and Vernacular Music 1898-1960*
  r ARBA - v28 - '97 - p490 [251-500]
  r RQ - v36 - Win '96 - p295+ [501+]
Vernon, Roland - *Introducing Bach*
  c SLJ - v43 - Ja '97 - p136+ [51-250]
  Introducing Beethoven
  c HB Guide - v7 - Fall '96 - p375 [51-250]
  Introducing Chopin
  c JB - v60 - D '96 - p276 [1-50]
  Introducing Gershwin
  c Bks Keeps - Jl '96 - p23 [51-250]
  c HB Guide - v7 - Fall '96 - p375 [51-250]
  c Sch Lib - v44 - Ag '96 - p114 [51-250]
  c SLJ - v42 - S '96 - p221+ [51-250]
  Introducing Mozart
  c Bks Keeps - Jl '96 - p23 [51-250]
  c HB Guide - v7 - Fall '96 - p375 [51-250]
  c JB - v60 - Ag '96 - p162 [51-250]
  c Sch Lib - v44 - Ag '96 - p114 [51-250]
  c SLJ - v43 - Ja '97 - p136+ [51-250]
  Introducing Vivaldi
  y Sch Lib - v45 - F '97 - p52 [51-250]
Vernon-Wortzel, Heidi - *Strategic Management in the Global Economy. 3rd Ed.*
  R&R Bk N - v11 - D '96 - p28 [51-250]
Vernoy, Mark W - *Behavioral Statistics in Action. 2nd Ed.*
  R&R Bk N - v11 - D '96 - p2 [51-250]
Veroff, Joseph - *Marital Instability*
  CS - v25 - N '96 - p791+ [501+]
  JMF - v58 - N '96 - p1045+ [501+]
Veronico, Nicholas A - *Blue Angels--50 Years of Precision Flight*
  A & S Sm - v11 - O '96 - p86 [51-250]
Verrier, Suzanne - *Rosa Gallica*
  Hort - v74 - D '96 - p59 [51-250]

Verrilli, Michael J - *Thermomechanical Fatigue Behavior of Materials. Vol. 2*
  SciTech - v20 - D '96 - p64 [51-250]
Verronen, Maarit - *Pimeasta Maasta*
  WLT - v71 - Win '97 - p191 [501+]
Verschuur, Karel - *Handbook of Environmental Data on Organic Chemicals. 3rd Ed.*
  r ARBA - v28 - '97 - p630 [51-250]
  r Choice - v34 - Ja '97 - p823+ [51-250]
Verschuur, Gerrit L - *Hidden Attraction*
  New Sci - v152 - O 12 '96 - p43 [1-50]
  Impact! The Threat of Comets and Asteroids
  Choice - v34 - Ap '97 - p1362 [51-250]
  Nat - v263 - O 28 '96 - p38+ [501+]
  New Sci - v153 - Ja 25 '97 - p41 [501+]
  SciTech - v21 - Mr '97 - p19 [51-250]
Verschuur-Basse, Denyse - *Chinese Women Speak*
  Pac A - v69 - Fall '96 - p402 [251-500]
Verschuuren, Gerard M - *Life Scientists*
  Isis - v88 - Mr '97 - p170+ [501+]
Versenyi, Adam - *Theatre in Latin America*
  TDR - v41 - Spr '97 - p155+ [501+]
Versluis, Arthur - *American Transcendentalism and Asian Religions*
  Nine-C Lit - v50 - Mr '96 - p559 [51-250]
Verso, Jo - *Jo Verso's Cross Stitch Gifts for Children*
  CAY - v17 - Win '96 - p9 [51-250]
Verstraete, Larry - *Whose Bright Idea Was It?*
  o Quill & Q - v63 - Mr '97 - p81 [251-500]
Vertinskii, A - *Za Kulisami*
  BL - v93 - O 1 '96 - p327 [1-50]
Vertosick, Frank - *When the Air Hits Your Brain*
  New Sci - v152 - D 21 '96 - p68 [501+]
Veryan, Patricia - *Lanterns*
  KR - v64 - S 15 '96 - p1351+ [251-500]
  LJ - v122 - F 15 '97 - p184 [51-250]
  PW - v243 - S 16 '96 - p71 [51-250]
  y SLJ - v43 - Mr '97 - p217 [51-250]
Vestal, James E - *Planning for Change*
  Econ J - v106 - S '96 - p1423+ [251-500]
Vet, Co - *Tense and Aspect in Discourse*
  MLR - v92 - Ap '97 - p403+ [501+]
Vetere, Richard - *The Third Miracle*
  KR - v65 - My 1 '97 - p674+ [251-500]
  PW - v244 - My 5 '97 - p198 [251-500]
Vetock, Dennis J - *Lessons Learned*
  Parameters - v26 - Aut '96 - p152+ [501+]
Vetter, Lawrence C - *Never without Heroes*
  Mar Crp G - v81 - Ja '97 - p75 [501+]
Vetter, Matthias - *Antisemiten Und Bolschewiki*
  Slav R - v55 - Sum '96 - p468+ [501+]
Vezin, Annette - *Kandinsky and the Blue Rider*
  Atl - v278 - S '96 - p114 [251-500]
Viacava, Antonietta - *L'Atleta Di Fano*
  AJA - v101 - Ja '97 - p178+ [501+]
Vian, Boris - *L'Ecume Des Jours*
  FR - v70 - Mr '97 - p603+ [501+]
  Froth on the Daydream
  TLS - S 6 '96 - p23 [251-500]
Viana, Antonio Manuel Couto - *Versos De Palmo E Meio (Illus. by Helena Fernandes)*
  c Bkbird - v34 - Spr '96 - p53 [1-50]
Vicentino, Nicola - *Ancient Music Adapted to Modern Practice*
  Choice - v34 - Ap '97 - p1349 [51-250]
Vick, Helen Hughes - *Tag against Time*
  y Kliatt - v30 - N '96 - p16 [51-250]
  y SLJ - v42 - O '96 - p150 [51-250]
  y VOYA - v19 - F '97 - p341 [251-500]
Vickers, Brian - *Appropriating Shakespeare*
  CLS - v33 - 2 '96 - p201+ [501+]
  Queens Q - v103 - Win '96 - p807+ [501+]
Vickers, Daniel - *Farmers and Fishermen*
  JIH - v27 - Aut '96 - p328+ [501+]
  Sev Cent N - v54 - Spr '96 - p35+ [501+]
  T&C - v37 - Ap '96 - p353+ [501+]
Vickers, Douglas - *Economics and the Antagonism of Time*
  Econ J - v107 - Ja '97 - p219+ [501+]
  The Tyranny of the Market
  JEL - v34 - S '96 - p1408 [51-250]
Vickers, Hugo - *The Kiss: The Story of an Obsession*
  Spec - v277 - N 16 '96 - p50 [501+]
  Spec - v277 - N 23 '96 - p44 [51-250]
  Spec - v277 - N 23 '96 - p46 [1-50]
  TLS - N 22 '96 - p9 [501+]
  The Private World of the Duke and Duchess of Windsor
  BL - v93 - D 1 '96 - p640+ [51-250]
  CSM - v88 - N 21 '96 - pB2 [51-250]
Vickers, Miranda - *The Albanians: A Modern History*
  AHR - v101 - D '96 - p1581 [501+]

Victor, Cynthia - *The Secret*
    KR - v65 - My 1 '97 - p675 [251-500]
Victor, Sextus Aurelius - *Liber De Caesaribus (Bird)*
    CW - v89 - Jl '96 - p520 [51-250]
Victoria, Carlos - *La Travesia Secreta*
    BL - v93 - Ap 1 '97 - p1284 [1-50]
The Victoria History of the County of Essex. Vol. 9
    EHR - v112 - F '97 - p274+ [501+]
Victorov, S V - *Regional Satellite Oceanography*
    SciTech - v21 - Mr '97 - p2 [51-250]
Vida, Ginny - *The New Our Right to Love*
  r Advocate - Je 11 '96 - p60+ [501+]
Vida, Nina - *Between Sisters*
    Rapport - v19 - 4 '96 - p30 [251-500]
Vidal, Beatriz - *The Legend of El Dorado*
  c SS - v88 - Ja '97 - p29+ [501+]
Vidal, Gore - *Palimpsest: A Memoir*
    Dis - v43 - Fall '96 - p123+ [501+]
    LATBR - S 8 '96 - p11 [51-250]
    NYTBR - v101 - S 29 '96 - p32 [51-250]
    PW - v243 - Jl 22 '96 - p235 [1-50]
    WLT - v70 - Sum '96 - p704 [501+]
  The Season of Comfort
    TLS - Jl 7 '96 - p25 [251-500]
  United States: Essays 1952-1992
    Dis - v43 - Fall '96 - p123+ [501+]
    SFR - v21 - S '96 - p48 [51-250]
Vidal, John - *Counter Culture vs. Burger Culture*
    Obs - Ap 13 '97 - p15* [501+]
Vidal I Barraquer, Francesc - *Eglesia I Estat Durant La Segona Republica Espanyola 1931-1936. Vols. 1-4*
    CHR - v82 - O '96 - p661+ [501+]
Vidal-Naquet, Pierre - *The Jews: History, Memory, and the Present*
    Choice - v34 - O '96 - p342 [51-250]
    NYRB - v43 - O 31 '96 - p18+ [501+]
  Memoires. Vol. 1
    Choice - v34 - D '96 - p568 [1-50]
Video Librarian
  p LJ - v121 - N 15 '96 - p94 [51-250]
Videocassette Instructor's Manual with Script for Con Mucho Gusto
    Hisp - v79 - S '96 - p470+ [501+]
VideoHound's Complete Guide to Cult Flicks and Trash Pics
  r ARBA - v28 - '97 - p518 [51-250]
Videomaker
  p LJ - v122 - Ap 15 '97 - p127 [51-250]
Viders, Hillary - *Marine Conservation for the 21st Century*
    E Mag - v8 - Ja '97 - p49 [51-250]
La Vie De Saint Alexis (Hemming)
    MLR - v91 - Jl '96 - p718+ [501+]
Vieira, Alice - *O Coelho Branquinho E A Formico Rabica (Illus. by Joao Tinoco)*
  c Bkbird - v34 - Spr '96 - p53 [1-50]
Vieira, Nelson H - *Jewish Voices in Brazilian Literature*
    Choice - v34 - O '96 - p287 [51-250]
    WLT - v70 - Aut '96 - p942+ [501+]
De Vierplichte Tewerkstelling In Duitsland 1942-1945
    EHR - v111 - S '96 - p1025+ [501+]
Vierra, Bradley J - *Subsistence and Stone Tool Technology*
    Am Ant - v62 - Ja '97 - p167+ [501+]
Viertl, Reinhard - *Statistical Methods for Non-Precise Data*
    Choice - v34 - O '96 - p319 [51-250]
Viesca, Carlos - *El Evangelizador Empecinado*
  y JAAL - v40 - S '96 - p77 [51-250]
Viesti, Joe - *Celebrate! In South Asia (Illus. by Joe Viesti)*
  c BL - v93 - S 1 '96 - p124 [51-250]
  c CBRS - v24 - Ag '96 - p166 [51-250]
  c CCB-B - v50 - O '96 - p79 [51-250]
  c HB Guide - v8 - Spr '97 - p99 [51-250]
  c SLJ - v42 - S '96 - p222 [51-250]
  Celebrate! In Southeast Asia (Illus. by Joe Viesti)
  c BL - v93 - S 1 '96 - p124 [51-250]
  c CBRS - v24 - Ag '96 - p166 [51-250]
  c CCB-B - v50 - O '96 - p79 [51-250]
  c HB Guide - v8 - Spr '97 - p99 [51-250]
  c SLJ - v42 - S '96 - p222 [51-250]
Viewegh, Michal - *Bringing Up Girls in Bohemia*
    BL - v93 - Ja '97 - p823 [51-250]
    KR - v64 - D 1 '96 - p1703 [51-250]
Vigano, Valeria - *L'Ora Preferita Della Sera*
    WLT - v70 - Aut '96 - p939 [51-250]
Vigevani, Alberto - *Due Nomi Per Charlie*
    WLT - v70 - Aut '96 - p936+ [251-500]
Vigil, Angel - *The Corn Woman. Audio Version*
  y SLJ - v42 - Ag '96 - p65 [51-250]

Teatro! Hispanic Plays for Young People
    BL - v93 - Mr 1 '97 - p1159 [51-250]
    Cur R - v36 - Ja '97 - p3* [51-250]
Vigna, Judith - *I Live with Daddy*
  c Cur R - v36 - Ja '97 - p12 [51-250]
  A Safe Place
  c Cur R - v36 - Ja '97 - p12 [51-250]
Vigneras, Marie-France - *Representations L-Modulaires D'un Groupe Reductif P-Adique Avec 1-P*
    SciTech - v20 - S '96 - p9 [51-250]
Vigny, Alfred De - *Servitude and Grandeur of Arms*
    TLS - O 18 '96 - p29 [501+]
Viharo, William - *Love Stories Are Too Violent for Me*
    Arm Det - v29 - Fall '96 - p497 [51-250]
Vihman, Marilyn May - *Phonological Development*
    Choice - v34 - S '96 - p119+ [51-250]
Viinikainen, Antero - *Joen Kyla*
    WLT - v70 - Aut '96 - p996+ [501+]
Vikela, Eugenia - *Die Weihreliefs Aus Dem Athener Pankrates-Heiligtum Am Ilissos*
    AJA - v100 - Jl '96 - p621+ [501+]
Vila, Xavier - *Valle-Inclan and the Theatre*
    MLR - v91 - Jl '96 - p769+ [251-500]
    MP - v94 - F '97 - p409+ [501+]
Vilanilam, J V - *Science Communication and Development*
    JC - v46 - Sum '96 - p183+ [501+]
Vilarino, Manuel - *A Fotografia Na Arte Contemporanea*
    Afterimage - v24 - N '96 - p15 [251-500]
Vilas, Carlos M - *Between Earthquakes and Volcanoes*
    HAHR - v77 - My '97 - p333+ [501+]
    S&S - v61 - Sum '97 - p289+ [501+]
Vile, John R - *Encyclopedia of Constitutional Amendments, Proposed Amendments, and Amending Issues 1789-1995*
  yr ARBA - v28 - '97 - p269 [251-500]
  r BL - v93 - Ja '97 - p769+ [1-50]
  yr BL - v93 - D 1 '96 - p684 [251-500]
  r Choice - v34 - Mr '97 - p1144 [51-250]
  r LJ - v121 - N 15 '96 - p56 [51-250]
  r LJ - v122 - Ap 15 '97 - p40 [51-250]
  r R&R Bk N - v12 - F '97 - p65 [51-250]
  yr SLJ - v43 - F '97 - p133 [51-250]
Viles, Heather - *Coastal Problems*
  r GJ - v162 - Jl '96 - p226 [251-500]
Vilicich-Solomon, Tina - *Creepy Cookies (Illus. by Dianne O'Quinn Burke)*
  c LATBR - O 20 '96 - p8 [51-250]
Villa, Dana R - *Arendt and Heidegger*
    APSR - v90 - D '96 - p901+ [501+]
    J Pol - v59 - F '97 - p284+ [501+]
Villalba, Susana M - *Grandes Peliculas Del Cine Gay*
    BL - v93 - Mr 15 '97 - p1232 [51-250]
Villani, John - *The 100 Best Small Art Towns in America*
  r SFR - v21 - S '96 - p45 [51-250]
Villanueva, Enrique - *Truth and Rationality*
    CPR - v16 - Je '96 - p220+ [501+]
Villar, Antonio - *General Equilibrium with Increasing Returns*
    JEL - v35 - Mr '97 - p200 [51-250]
Villari, Rosario - *Baroque Personae*
    Six Ct J - v27 - Fall '96 - p941+ [501+]
    TranslRevS - v2 - D '96 - p15 [51-250]
Villasenor, Victor - *Wild Steps of Heaven*
  y Kliatt - v31 - My '97 - p10 [251-500]
  Wild Steps of Heaven (Hill). Audio Version
  y Kliatt - v31 - Ja '97 - p51 [51-250]
    LJ - v121 - O 1 '96 - p145 [51-250]
Villatoro, Marcos McPeek - *Walking to La Milpa*
    BL - v93 - S 15 '96 - p213 [51-250]
Villa-Vicencio, Charles - *Doing Ethics in Context*
    J Ch St - v38 - Sum '96 - p661 [251-500]
  The Spirit of Freedom
    Bks & Cult - v3 - Mr '97 - p38 [501+]
Villedieu, Madame De - *Selected Writings of Madame De Villedieu*
    MLR - v92 - Ja '97 - p189+ [251-500]
Villegas, Anna Tuttle - *All We Know of Heaven*
    BL - v93 - Ja '97 - p823 [51-250]
    KR - v64 - N 15 '96 - p1630 [251-500]
    LJ - v121 - D '96 - p148 [51-250]
    PW - v243 - D 16 '96 - p43 [51-250]
Villemagne, Maurice - *Cement Concrete Pavements*
    SciTech - v20 - N '96 - p65 [51-250]
Villeneuve, Jacques - *Villeneuve: My First Season in Formula 1*
    Quill & Q - v63 - F '97 - p45 [251-500]
Vinaver, Michel - *Theatre De Chambre*
    MLR - v92 - Ja '97 - p205+ [501+]
Vinay, Jean-Paul - *Comparative Stylistics of French and English*
    FR - v70 - D '96 - p360+ [501+]

Vincendeau, Ginette - *The Companion to French Cinema*
  r Si & So - v6 - N '96 - p36 [51-250]
  Encyclopedia of European Cinema
  r ARBA - v28 - '97 - p507+ [251-500]
Vincent, Gilbert Tapley - *Masterpieces of American Indian Art*
    New R - v216 - Ap 21 '97 - p28+ [501+]
Vincent, John A - *Inequality and Old Age*
    Socio R - v45 - My '97 - p325+ [501+]
Vincent, Nicholas - *Peter Des Roches: An Alien in English Politics 1205-1238*
    Choice - v34 - F '97 - p1021 [51-250]
    EHR - v112 - Ap '97 - p415+ [501+]
    TLS - S 6 '96 - p30 [501+]
Vincent, Thomas - *Index to Pre-1900 English Language Canadian Cultural and Literary Magazines. Electronic Media Version*
  r Archiv - Spr '96 - p254 [251-500]
Vincent, Victoria - *Great Careers for People Interested in the Past*
  y SLJ - v42 - S '96 - p230 [51-250]
Vine, Barbara - *The Brimstone Wedding*
    Nat R - v48 - D 23 '96 - p57 [51-250]
    Spec - v277 - S 7 '96 - p37 [51-250]
Vine, Richard P - *Wine Appreciation. 2nd Ed.*
    BL - v93 - F 15 '97 - p989 [51-250]
    LJ - v122 - Ap 1 '97 - p63 [1-50]
Vinen, Richard - *Bourgeois Politics in France 1945-1951*
    AHR - v101 - O '96 - p1226+ [501+]
    Historian - v59 - Win '97 - p482+ [251-500]
Vines, David - *North-South Linkages and International Macroeconomic Policy*
    Econ J - v107 - Ja '97 - p272 [251-500]
Viney, Michael - *A Year's Turning*
    TLS - D 6 '96 - p27 [501+]
Vinge, Joan D - *Catspaw*
    Ext - v37 - Sum '96 - p121+ [501+]
Vinh, Le Quang - *Defy the Death Spirit*
    Aust Bk R - Je '96 - p67 [1-50]
Vinovskis, Maris A - *Education, Society, and Economic Opportunity*
    AHR - v102 - F '97 - p166+ [501+]
    JIH - v27 - Spr '97 - p724+ [501+]
    J Soc H - v30 - Win '96 - p563+ [501+]
Vinton, Ken - *Alphabet Antics (Illus. by Ken Vinton)*
  c SLJ - v43 - Ja '97 - p138 [51-250]
Vinz, Mark - *Imagining Home*
    Bloom Rev - v16 - Jl '96 - p20 [51-250]
Vinz, Warren L - *Pulpit Politics*
    Choice - v34 - Ap '97 - p1358 [51-250]
Viola, Bill - *Reasons for Knocking at an Empty House*
    Afterimage - v24 - S '96 - p9+ [501+]
    Per A J - v18 - 3 '96 - p20+ [501+]
    TCI - v30 - O '96 - p58 [51-250]
Viola, Herman J - *Diplomats in Buckskins*
    Historian - v59 - Fall '96 - p163 [251-500]
  North American Indians (Illus. by Bryn Barnard)
  c SLJ - v43 - Mr '97 - p210 [51-250]
Viorst, Judith - *Alexander, Que De Ninguna Manera--Le Oyen?--Lo Dice En Serio!--Se Va A Mudar (Illus. by Robin Preiss Glasser)*
  c HB Guide - v7 - Fall '96 - p327 [1-50]
  c SLJ - v42 - Ag '96 - p179 [51-250]
  Alexander, Who's Not (Do You Hear Me? I Mean It!) Going to Move (Illus. by Robin Preiss Glasser)
  c RT - v50 - O '96 - p131 [1-50]
  Rosie and Michael
  c HMR - Win '96 - p45 [1-50]
  Sad Underwear and Other Complications (Illus. by Richard Hull)
  c Inst - v105 - My '96 - p71 [51-250]
Vira, Soma - *Checkmating Aliens*
    BWatch - v17 - S '96 - p7 [51-250]
  Good-Bye Alien God
    BWatch - v17 - S '96 - p7 [51-250]
  Lord Kito's Revenge
    BWatch - v17 - S '96 - p7 [51-250]
  Nikita's Shadows
    BWatch - v17 - S '96 - p7 [51-250]
Virden, Jenel - *Good-Bye, Piccadilly*
    BWatch - v17 - N '96 - p6 [51-250]
    Choice - v34 - D '96 - p680 [51-250]
    RAH - v25 - Mr '97 - p127+ [501+]
Virgil - *Vergil's Eclogues*
    Class Out - v74 - Spr '97 - p121+ [251-500]
    LJ - v122 - Ap 1 '97 - p93 [51-250]
  Virgil in English (Gransden)
    Agenda - v34 - Spr '96 - p182+ [501+]
    BW - v26 - D 8 '96 - p15 [51-250]
    TranslRevS - v2 - D '96 - p29 [51-250]

Virginia Company of London - *The Records of the Virginia Company of London. Vol. 4*
    EGH - v50 - N '96 - p188 [51-250]
Virginia Museum of Fine Arts - *Art of Late Rome and Byzantium in the Virginia Museum of Fine Arts*
    BM - v138 - Ag '96 - p551+ [251-500]
Virginia Writers' Project - *The Negro in Virginia*
    CAY - v17 - Win '96 - p13 [51-250]
Viroli, Maurizio - *For Love of Country*
    APSR - v90 - D '96 - p885+ [501+]
    Lon R Bks - v19 - Mr 6 '97 - p22+ [501+]
    RP - v59 - Win '97 - p141+ [501+]
Virtue, Doreen - *I'd Change My Life If I Had More Time*
    BWatch - v17 - S '96 - p7 [51-250]
Vischer, Hanns - *Across the Sahara from Tripoli to Bornu*
    GJ - v163 - Mr '97 - p108 [51-250]
Vischer, Lukas - *Histoire Du Christianisme En Suisse*
    CH - v66 - Mr '97 - p213 [51-250]
Viscusi, W Kip - *Economics of Regulation and Antitrust. 2nd Ed.*
    JEL - v34 - S '96 - p1454 [51-250]
Viscuso, Maurice J - *The OS/2 Warp Toolkit for Software Developers*
    SciTech - v20 - N '96 - p6 [51-250]
Visentini, Margherita Azzi - *La Villa In Italia*
    BM - v138 - O '96 - p691 [501+]
Vishaka - *Our Most Dear Friend*
    c   BL - v93 - O 1 '96 - p338+ [51-250]
    c   Ch BWatch - v7 - Ja '97 - p4 [1-50]
Visher, Emily B - *Therapy with Stepfamilies*
    SB - v32 - Ag '96 - p164 [51-250]
Visions International
    p   Sm Pr R - v28 - N '96 - p22 [51-250]
Visitor Profile Study
    J Gov Info - v23 - S '96 - p603 [51-250]
Visotzky, Burton L - *Fathers of the World*
    Rel St Rev - v22 - O '96 - p354 [51-250]
  The Genesis of Ethics
    BL - v93 - S 1 '96 - p38 [51-250]
    CSM - v88 - N 6 '96 - p12 [51-250]
    CSM - v89 - N 25 '96 - p12 [51-250]
    KR - v64 - Ag 15 '96 - p1226 [251-500]
    Nat R - v48 - D 9 '96 - p61+ [501+]
    SLJ - v42 - D '96 - p40+ [51-250]
Visser, Hans - *A Guide to International Monetary Economics*
    Econ J - v106 - N '96 - p1837+ [51-250]
Vissing, Yvonne M - *Out of Sight, Out of Mind*
    Choice - v34 - D '96 - p697 [51-250]
The Visual Dictionary of Human Anatomy
    cr Ch BWatch - v6 - S '96 - p5+ [1-50]
    yr SLJ - v42 - Ag '96 - p183 [51-250]
    yr VOYA - v19 - O '96 - p240 [251-500]
The Visual Food Encyclopedia
    r   BL - v93 - Mr 15 '97 - p1261 [51-250]
Visweswaran, Kamala - *Fictions of Feminist Ethnography*
    Can Lit - Win '96 - p125+ [501+]
Vitali, Julius - *The Fine Artist's Guide to Marketing and Self-Promotion*
    Ceram Mo - v44 - D '96 - p30+ [251-500]
    LJ - v121 - O 15 '96 - p55 [51-250]
Vitalis, Robert - *When Capitalists Collide*
    AHR - v101 - D '96 - p1589+ [501+]
Vitanza, Victor - *Negation, Subjectivity, and the History of Rhetoric*
    Choice - v34 - Ap '97 - p1329+ [51-250]
  Writing Histories of Rhetoric
    QJS - v83 - My '97 - p267+ [501+]
Vitberg, Alan K - *Marketing Health Care into the Twenty-First Century*
    JEL - v35 - Mr '97 - p229 [51-250]
    SciTech - v20 - N '96 - p36 [51-250]
Vitek, William - *Rooted in the Land*
    CC - v114 - Mr 5 '97 - p250+ [501+]
    LJ - v121 - O 1 '96 - p110+ [51-250]
Vitell, Bettina - *The World in a Bowl of Tea*
    LJ - v122 - Ap 15 '97 - p110 [51-250]
    PW - v244 - Mr 24 '97 - p77 [51-250]
Viti, Paolo - *Firenze E Il Concilio Del 1439. Vols. 1-2*
    EHR - v111 - N '96 - p1261+ [251-500]
Vitola, Denise - *Quantum Moon*
    y   Kliatt - v30 - N '96 - p16+ [51-250]
Vitt, Lois A - *Encyclopedia of Financial Gerontology*
    r   Choice - v34 - O '96 - p252 [51-250]
    r   JEL - v34 - D '96 - p2069 [51-250]
Vitti, Antonio - *Giuseppe De Santis and Postwar Italian Cinema*
    Choice - v34 - O '96 - p290 [51-250]
Vitti, James Alan - *A Little Piece of Paradise*
    BL - v93 - S 1 '96 - p65 [501+]

Vitullo-Martin, Julia - *Breaking Away*
    JEL - v34 - D '96 - p2138 [51-250]
Vivarelli, Marco - *The Economics of Technology and Employment*
    Econ J - v107 - Ja '97 - p239+ [501+]
Vivarelli, Roberto - *Storia Delle Origini Del Fascismo. Vols. 1-2*
    JMH - v68 - D '96 - p1008+ [501+]
Vizenor, Gerald - *Hotline Healers*
    KR - v65 - Mr 15 '97 - p415+ [251-500]
    LJ - v122 - Ap 15 '97 - p121 [51-250]
    PW - v244 - Mr 31 '97 - p62 [51-250]
Vizzard, William J - *In the Cross Fire*
    PW - v244 - F 17 '97 - p203 [51-250]
Vlach, Michael - *Back of the Big House*
    T&C - v37 - O '96 - p840+ [501+]
Vlak, J M - *Insect Cell Culture*
    SciTech - v21 - Mr '97 - p96 [51-250]
Vlanton, Elias - *Who Killed George Polk?*
    JMCQ - v73 - Aut '96 - p772+ [501+]
    NYTBR - v101 - Ap 7 '96 - p17 [501+]
Vlastos, Gregory - *Studies in Greek Philosophy. Vols. 1-2*
    CPR - v16 - O '96 - p378+ [501+]
    Ethics - v107 - O '96 - p197 [51-250]
Vlavianos, Haris - *Adieu*
    WLT - v70 - Aut '96 - p1003 [51-250]
Voake, Charlotte - *First Things First*
    c   Bks Keeps - Jl '96 - p6 [51-250]
  Ginger (Illus. by Charlotte Voake)
    c   BL - v93 - F 1 '97 - p949 [51-250]
    c   CCB-B - v50 - Ap '97 - p299 [51-250]
    c   KR - v65 - Ja 1 '97 - p66 [51-250]
    c   Obs - Mr 30 '97 - p17* [51-250]
    c   PW - v244 - Ja 13 '97 - p74 [51-250]
  Mr. Davies and the Baby (Illus. by Charlotte Voake)
    c   HB Guide - v7 - Fall '96 - p245 [51-250]
    c   JB - v60 - O '96 - p189 [51-250]
    c   Magpies - v11 - Jl '96 - p25 [51-250]
    c   Sch Lib - v44 - Ag '96 - p101+ [51-250]
Vocabulaire Trilingue Des Vehicules De Transport Routier
    r   ARBA - v28 - '97 - p108+ [251-500]
Voegelin, Eric - *On the Form of the American Mind*
    RP - v58 - Sum '96 - p625+ [501+]
Vogel, Arthur A - *Radical Christianity and the Flesh of Jesus*
    Intpr - v51 - Ap '97 - p218 [251-500]
Vogel, Brenda - *Down for the Count*
    LR - v45 - 7 '96 - p60+ [251-500]
Vogel, Carole Garbuny - *Shock Waves through Los Angeles*
    c   BL - v93 - O 1 '96 - p346 [51-250]
    c   HB Guide - v8 - Spr '97 - p97 [1-50]
    c   PW - v243 - O 7 '96 - p78 [51-250]
    c   SLJ - v42 - O '96 - p119 [51-250]
Vogel, Colin - *The Complete Horse Care Manual*
    r   RQ - v35 - Sum '96 - p550+ [251-500]
  An Illustrated Guide to Veterinary Care of the Horse
    SciTech - v20 - S '96 - p45 [1-50]
Vogel, David - *Kindred Strangers*
    JEL - v34 - D '96 - p2092+ [51-250]
  Trading Up
    JEL - v35 - Mr '97 - p143+ [501+]
Vogel, Lester I - *To See a Promised Land*
    J Am Cult - v18 - Win '95 - p112+ [251-500]
Vogel, Shawna - *Naked Earth*
    y   Kliatt - v30 - S '96 - p36 [51-250]
Vogel, Steven, 1940- - *Life in Moving Fluids. 2nd Ed., Rev. and Expanded*
    Nature - v385 - Ja 30 '97 - p408 [1-50]
Vogel, Steven, 1954- - *Against Nature*
    R&R Bk N - v11 - N '96 - p3 [51-250]
Vogel, Steven Kent - *Freer Markets, More Rules*
    For Aff - v75 - S '96 - p139+ [251-500]
    JEL - v35 - Mr '97 - p248 [51-250]
Vogelfanger, Isaac J - *Red Tempest*
    Choice - v34 - N '96 - p521 [51-250]
Vogelsong, Diana - *Landscape Architecture Sourcebook*
    r   BL - v93 - My 1 '97 - p1530+ [251-500]
Vogler, John - *The Environment and International Relations*
    Choice - v34 - O '96 - p356 [51-250]
  The Global Commons
    GJ - v163 - Mr '97 - p108 [51-250]
Vogt, Evon Z - *Fieldwork among the Maya*
    Am Ethnol - v24 - F '97 - p224+ [501+]
Vogt, Gregory L - *Asteroids, Comets, and Meteors*
    c   HB Guide - v7 - Fall '96 - p331 [51-250]
  Earth
    c   HB Guide - v7 - Fall '96 - p331 [51-250]

  The Sun
    c   HB Guide - v7 - Fall '96 - p331 [51-250]
Vogt, William - *Road to Survival*
    Reason - v28 - D '96 - p45 [51-250]
Voices Israel 1995
    p   Sm Pr R - v28 - Je '96 - p17+ [51-250]
Voices of Freedom
    J Gov Info - v23 - S '96 - p553+ [51-250]
Voices of Sibyls
    WLT - v71 - Win '97 - p181+ [501+]
Voiculescu, Dan-Virgil - *Free Probability Theory*
    SciTech - v21 - Mr '97 - p16 [51-250]
Voien, Steven - *Black Leopard*
    BL - v93 - Ja '97 - p823 [51-250]
    KR - v65 - F 1 '97 - p178 [1-50]
    NYTBR - v102 - Mr 30 '97 - p16 [51-250]
    PW - v244 - Ja 27 '97 - p79+ [251-500]
Voigt, Anna - *New Visions, New Perspectives*
    Aust Bk R - Ag '96 - p23+ [501+]
Voigt, Cynthia - *Bad Girls*
    c   HB Guide - v7 - Fall '96 - p298 [51-250]
    y   HMR - Win '96 - p45 [1-50]
    c   PW - v243 - N 4 '96 - p49 [51-250]
  Dicey's Song
    c   JOYS - v10 - Fall '96 - p35+ [501+]
  Homecoming
    y   Kliatt - v30 - S '96 - p4 [1-50]
  Izzy Willy-Nilly
    y   JAAL - v40 - D '96 - p318 [51-250]
  Seventeen against the Dealer
    y   SLJ - v43 - Mr '97 - p113 [1-50]
  Sons from Afar
    y   PW - v243 - S 23 '96 - p78 [51-250]
  When She Hollers
    y   SLJ - v43 - Mr '97 - p113 [1-50]
Voigt, Ellen Bryant - *Kyrie*
    Ant R - v54 - Sum '96 - p377 [251-500]
Vojtech, Anna - *Marushka and the Month Brothers (Illus. by Anna Vojtech)*
    c   CCB-B - v50 - Mr '97 - p260 [51-250]
    c   HB - v73 - Mr '97 - p207 [51-250]
    c   KR - v64 - S 15 '96 - p1408 [51-250]
    c   PW - v243 - N 11 '96 - p74 [51-250]
    c   SLJ - v42 - N '96 - p102 [51-250]
Volansky, Michele - *20 One-Act Plays from 20 Years of the Humana Festival*
    y   VOYA - v19 - O '96 - p239+ [251-500]
Volavkova, Hana - *I Never Saw Another Butterfly*
    SS - v87 - My '96 - p101+ [501+]
Volcanoes. Electronic Media Version
    r   LJ - v122 - Ap 15 '97 - p40 [1-50]
Vold, Jan Erik - *Kalenderdikt*
    WLT - v70 - Sum '96 - p715 [501+]
Volgyes, Ivan - *The Legacies of Communism in Eastern Europe*
    APSR - v90 - S '96 - p687+ [501+]
Volkel, Markus - *Romische Kardinalshaushalte Des 17. Jahrhunderts*
    EHR - v111 - S '96 - p985+ [251-500]
Volklein, Helmut - *Groups as Galois Groups*
    SciTech - v20 - D '96 - p16 [51-250]
Volkman, Karen - *Crash's Law*
    Chel - 61 '96 - p131+ [501+]
    Choice - v34 - D '96 - p617 [51-250]
    LATBR - Ap 13 '97 - pG [51-250]
Volkmar, Fred R - *Psychoses and Pervasive Developmental Disorders in Childhood and Adolescence*
    Readings - v11 - D '96 - p29 [51-250]
Volkmer, Jane Anne - *Song of the Chirimia*
    c   SS - v88 - Ja '97 - p29+ [501+]
Volkogonov, Dmitrii Antonovich - *Lenin: A New Biography*
    AJPsych - v153 - D '96 - p1643+ [501+]
  Lenin: Life and Legacy
    JPR - v33 - N '96 - p501+ [51-250]
  Seml Vozhdei. Vols. 1-2
    BL - v93 - O 1 '96 - p327 [1-50]
  Trotsky: The Eternal Revolutionary
    Choice - v34 - N '96 - p521 [51-250]
    NYTBR - v101 - D 8 '96 - p93 [1-50]
    RP - v59 - Win '97 - p178+ [51-250]
Volkov, Solomon - *St. Petersburg: A Cultural History*
    NYRB - v44 - F 20 '97 - p43+ [501+]
    Slav R - v55 - Fall '96 - p690+ [501+]
    Spec - v276 - My 25 '96 - p31+ [501+]
    Trib Bks - Mr 16 '97 - p8 [1-50]
Voll, John - *Islam: Continuity and Change in the Modern World. 2nd Ed.*
    Rel St Rev - v23 - Ap '97 - p201 [51-250]

Vollbracht, James - *Small Acts of Kindness (Illus. by Christopher Fay)*
c CLW - v67 - D '96 - p58 [51-250]
Vollenweider, Marie-Louise - *Camees Et Intailles. Vol. 1, Pts. 1-2*
AJA - v101 - Ja '97 - p180+ [501+]
Vollers, Maryanne - *Ghosts of Mississippi*
JSH - v62 - N '96 - p840+ [501+]
Vollmann, William T - *The Ice-Shirt*
Critiq - v38 - Fall '96 - p52+ [501+]
You Bright and Risen Angels
Critiq - v38 - Fall '96 - p12+ [501+]
Vollrath, Hanna - *Koln: Stadt Und Bistum In Kirche Und Reich Des Mittelalters*
EHR - v111 - S '96 - p954+ [251-500]
Volodine, Antoine - *Le Nom Des Singes*
FR - v70 - O '96 - p150+ [501+]
Le Port Interieur
WLT - v70 - Aut '96 - p912 [501+]
Volsky, Paula - *The Gates of Twilight*
y BL - v93 - Ja '97 - p764 [1-50]
y Kliatt - v31 - My '97 - p16 [51-250]
Voltaire - *The Age of Louis XIV*
Wil Q - v21 - Win '97 - p37 [51-250]
Candide (Mason)
MLR - v92 - Ja '97 - p193 [51-250]
The Complete Works of Voltaire. Vols. 3B-4
TLS - Ja 24 '97 - p24 [501+]
Letters Concerning the English Nation
MLR - v92 - Ap '97 - p468+ [501+]
Volterra, Virginia - *From Gesture to Language in Hearing and Deaf Children*
J Rehab RD - v33 - Jl '96 - p336 [51-250]
Von Allmen, Stewart - *Saint Vitus Dances Eternity*
SF Chr - v18 - O '96 - p81 [1-50]
Von Baeyer, Edwinna - *Garden Voices*
BIC - v25 - S '96 - p19+ [501+]
Hort - v74 - N '96 - p64 [251-500]
Von Bencke, Matthew J - *The Politics of Space*
Choice - v34 - Mr '97 - p1236 [51-250]
R&R Bk N - v12 - F '97 - p98 [51-250]
Von Braun, Joachim - *Agricultural Commercialization, Economic Development, and Nutrition*
Econ J - v107 - Ja '97 - p288+ [51-250]
Von Drehle, David - *Among the Lowest of the Dead*
Clio - v25 - Spr '96 - p301+ [501+]
Vonesh, Edward F - *Linear and Nonlinear Models for the Analysis of Repeated Measurements*
SciTech - v21 - Mr '97 - p15 [51-250]
Von Gal, Edwina - *Fresh Cuts*
LJ - v122 - Ap 1 '97 - p89 [51-250]
Von Hallberg, Robert - *Literary Intellectuals and the Dissolution of the State*
Choice - v34 - O '96 - p284 [51-250]
TranslRevS - v2 - D '96 - p11+ [51-250]
Von Hammerstein, Katharina - *Sophie Mereau-Brentano: Freiheit, Liebe, Weiblichkeit*
Ger Q - v69 - Fall '96 - p445+ [501+]
Von Hildebrand, Dietrich - *Memoiren Und Aufsatze Gegen Den Nationalsozialismus 1933-1938*
CHR - v82 - O '96 - p737+ [501+]
Von Hoffman, Alexander - *Local Attachments*
T&C - v37 - Ap '96 - p367+ [501+]
Von Konigslow, Andrea Wayne - *Would You Love Me? (Illus. by Andrea Wayne-Von-Konigslow)*
c Quill & Q - v63 - Ja '97 - p37 [1-50]
c Quill & Q - v63 - F '97 - p56 [251-500]
Von Kurowsky, Agnes - *Hemingway in Love and War*
LJ - v121 - N '96 - p112 [51-250]
PW - v243 - N 11 '96 - p72 [1-50]
Von Mehren, Joan - *Minerva and the Muse*
AHR - v101 - O '96 - p1276 [501+]
Von Mueffling, Dini - *The 50 Most Romantic Things Ever Done*
PW - v244 - Ja 20 '97 - p389 [51-250]
Von Rydingsvard, Ursula - *The Sculpture of Ursula Von Rydingsvard*
BL - v93 - D 1 '96 - p636+ [51-250]
Choice - v34 - Mr '97 - p1153+ [51-250]
PW - v243 - N 25 '96 - p67 [51-250]
Von Saldern, Adelheid Von - *Hauserleben: Zur Geschichte Stadtischen Arbeiterwohnens Vom Kaiserreich Bis Heute*
AHR - v102 - F '97 - p130+ [501+]
Von Thungen, Suzanne - *Die Frei Stehende Griechische Exedra*
AJA - v101 - Ja '97 - p181+ [501+]
Von Tunzelmann, G N - *Technology and Industrial Progress*
JEH - v57 - Mr '97 - p261+ [501+]

Vorderman, Carol - *How Math Works*
c BL - v93 - N 1 '96 - p497 [51-250]
c BL - v93 - Ap 1 '97 - p1342 [1-50]
c HB Guide - v8 - Spr '97 - p111 [51-250]
c LATBR - O 27 '96 - p11 [51-250]
How Mathematics Works
c TES - D 6 '96 - p22* [51-250]
Vos, Alvin - *Place and Displacement in the Renaissance*
Six Ct J - v27 - Fall '96 - p877+ [501+]
Vos, Ida - *Dancing on the Bridge of Avignon*
c RT - v50 - F '97 - p424 [51-250]
Vos, Rob - *Debt and Adjustment in the World Economy*
r JEL - v34 - D '96 - p1969+ [501+]
The Philippine Economy
Choice - v34 - N '96 - p509 [51-250]
Vosler, Nancy R - *New Approaches to Family Practice*
R&R Bk N - v12 - F '97 - p56 [51-250]
Vospominaniia O Mikhaile Zoshchenko
BL - v93 - O 1 '96 - p327 [1-50]
Vougiouklis, Thomas - *New Frontiers in Hyperstructures*
SciTech - v20 - N '96 - p13 [51-250]
Voulkos, Peter - *The Art of Peter Voulkos*
BM - v138 - D '96 - p836 [1-50]
Vowell, Sarah - *Radio On*
y BL - v93 - D 1 '96 - p638 [51-250]
KR - v64 - O 15 '96 - p1523 [51-250]
PW - v243 - D 9 '96 - p56 [51-250]
VV - v42 - Mr 11 '97 - p57 [501+]
Vowles, Jack - *Towards Consensus?*
APSR - v90 - D '96 - p948+ [501+]
Vox: Diccionario Esencial De Sinonimos Y Antonimos. Rev. Ed.
yr BL - v93 - Mr 1 '97 - p1196 [1-50]
Vox Spanish and English School Dictionary
cr BL - v93 - Mr 1 '97 - p1196 [51-250]
Voyages Series
c TES - Jl 5 '96 - pR6 [501+]
Voynick, Stephen M - *Climax: The History of Colorado's Climax Molybdenum Mine*
Choice - v34 - Ja '97 - p816 [51-250]
SciTech - v20 - N '96 - p77 [51-250]
Vrba, Elisabeth S - *Paleoclimate and Evolution*
Choice - v34 - Mr '97 - p1202 [51-250]
Nature - v383 - S 12 '96 - p137 [501+]
Vreeland, Susan - *What Love Sees (Stephens). Audio Version*
y Kliatt - v31 - My '97 - p48+ [51-250]
Vrettos, Athena - *Somatic Fictions*
Albion - v28 - Fall '96 - p514+ [501+]
Isis - v87 - D '96 - p740+ [501+]
Nine-C Lit - v51 - D '96 - p403+ [501+]
VS - v39 - Win '96 - p295+ [501+]
Vries, Anke De - *Bruises*
y BL - v93 - Ap 1 '97 - p1292 [1-50]
y BL - v93 - Ap 1 '97 - p1310 [1-50]
y Ch BWatch - v6 - Jl '96 - p3 [51-250]
y HB Guide - v7 - Fall '96 - p301 [51-250]
My Elephant Can Do Almost Anything (Illus. by Ilia Walraven)
c HB Guide - v7 - Fall '96 - p238 [51-250]
Vromen, Jack J - *Economic Evolution*
Econ J - v106 - N '96 - p1791+ [501+]
JEL - v34 - S '96 - p1419 [51-250]
Vu, Hung V - *Dynamic Systems*
SciTech - v21 - Mr '97 - p74 [51-250]
Vu, Huu San - *Dia Ly Bien Dong Voi Hoang Sa Va Truong Sa*
BL - v93 - S 1 '96 - p70 [51-250]
Vucinich, Wayne S - *Ivo Andric Revisited*
Choice - v34 - O '96 - p287+ [51-250]
WLT - v70 - Aut '96 - p991 [501+]
Vuillemin, Jules - *Necessity or Contingency*
CPR - v16 - Ag '96 - p299+ [501+]
Vulliamy, Clara - *Ellen and Penguin and the New Baby*
c Ch BWatch - v6 - My '96 - p5 [1-50]
c HB Guide - v7 - Fall '96 - p245 [1-50]
c JB - v60 - O '96 - p189 [51-250]
c Par - v71 - N '96 - p114 [1-50]
Good Night, Baby
c ECEJ - v24 - Win '96 - p108 [1-50]
c HB Guide - v7 - Fall '96 - p245 [51-250]
Wide Awake!
c HB Guide - v7 - Fall '96 - p245 [51-250]
Vulpe, Nicola - *Sealed in Struggle*
BIC - v25 - O '96 - p18+ [501+]
Vuong, Hong Sen - *Hon Nua Doi Hu*
BL - v93 - S 1 '96 - p70 [51-250]
Vuong-Riddick, Thuong - *Two Shores*
WLT - v70 - Aut '96 - p1036+ [501+]
Vurpas, Anne-Marie - *Le Parler Lyonnais*
FR - v70 - Mr '97 - p632+ [501+]

Vyas, R T - *Studies in Jaina Art and Iconography and Allied Subjects*
Rel St Rev - v23 - Ap '97 - p203 [51-250]
Vyner, Tim - *Dragon Mountain (Illus. by Tim Vyner)*
c JB - v60 - D '96 - p242+ [51-250]
c Sch Lib - v44 - N '96 - p147+ [51-250]

W

W., Bill - *A Simple Program*
Utne R - N '96 - p93+ [251-500]
Waal, F B M De - *Bonobo: The Forgotten Ape*
KR - v65 - Mr 1 '97 - p347 [51-250]
LJ - v122 - F 1 '97 - p103 [51-250]
New Sci - v153 - Mr 15 '97 - p41 [501+]
PW - v244 - Mr 17 '97 - p62 [51-250]
Good Natured
AJPsych - v153 - D '96 - p1648+ [501+]
NS & S - v9 - My 3 '96 - p39 [251-500]
NYTBR - v101 - D 8 '96 - p87 [1-50]
Sew R - v104 - O '96 - p665+ [501+]
TLS - S 6 '96 - p25+ [501+]
VLS - Win '96 - p12 [51-250]
Waarsenburg, Demetrius J - *The Northwest Necropolis of Satricum*
AJA - v100 - O '96 - p773+ [501+]
Waber, Bernard - *Do You See a Mouse? (Illus. by Bernard Waber)*
c PW - v243 - O 14 '96 - p85 [1-50]
Ira Sleeps Over
c HB - v73 - Mr '97 - p188 [1-50]
A Lion Named Shirley Williamson (Illus. by Bernard Waber)
c BL - v93 - S 1 '96 - p128 [51-250]
c CBRS - v25 - N '96 - p28 [51-250]
c HB Guide - v8 - Spr '97 - p52 [51-250]
c KR - v64 - S 15 '96 - p1409 [51-250]
c PW - v243 - S 23 '96 - p75+ [51-250]
c SLJ - v42 - D '96 - p108+ [51-250]
Lyle at the Office (Illus. by Bernard Waber)
c PW - v243 - O 14 '96 - p85 [1-50]
Waberi, Abdourahman A - *Cahier Nomade*
WLT - v70 - Aut '96 - p1013+ [501+]
Wach, Kenneth - *Salvador Dali: Masterpieces from the Collection of the Salvador Dali Museum*
BW - v26 - D 8 '96 - p10 [51-250]
PW - v243 - O 7 '96 - p52 [51-250]
Wachman, Alan M - *Taiwan: National Identity and Democratization*
Ch Rev Int - v3 - Fall '96 - p551+ [501+]
Pac A - v69 - Fall '96 - p411+ [501+]
Wachsmann, Konrad - *Building the Wooden House*
SciTech - v20 - N '96 - p69 [51-250]
Wachsmann, Shelley - *The Sea of Galilee Boat*
AJA - v100 - Jl '96 - p635+ [251-500]
Wachtel, Andrew Baruch - *An Obsession with History*
MP - v94 - N '96 - p267+ [501+]
Wachtel, Chuck - *Because We Are Here*
NYTBR - v101 - S 8 '96 - p22+ [51-250]
The Gates
NYTBR - v101 - N 17 '96 - p40 [51-250]
Wachtel, Klaus - *Der Byzantinische Text Der Katholischen Briefe*
Rel St Rev - v23 - Ja '97 - p75 [51-250]
Wachtler, Sol - *After the Madness*
BL - v93 - F 1 '97 - p906 [51-250]
Bus W - Ap 28 '97 - p13 [501+]
KR - v65 - F 1 '97 - p212 [251-500]
LATBR - Ap 20 '97 - p4 [501+]
NYTBR - v102 - Ap 13 '97 - p16 [501+]
NYTLa - v146 - Ap 21 '97 - pC13 [501+]
PW - v244 - F 3 '97 - p83 [51-250]
WSJ-Cent - v99 - Ap 11 '97 - pA16 [501+]
Wachtman, J B - *Mechanical Properties of Ceramics*
Choice - v34 - D '96 - p643 [51-250]
r SciTech - v20 - S '96 - p49 [51-250]
Wack, Amy - *Burning the Bracken*
BL - v93 - D 1 '96 - p639 [51-250]
Wacker, Peter O - *Land Use in Early New Jersey*
RAH - v24 - D '96 - p574+ [501+]

Wackernagel, Mathis - *Our Ecological Footprint*
Workbook - v21 - Win '96 - p179+ [501+]
Wackwitz, Stephan - *Walkers Gleichung*
WLT - v71 - Win '97 - p139+ [501+]
Wada, Junichiro - *The Japanese Election System*
JEL - v35 - Mr '97 - p203 [51-250]
Wada, Yoko - *Temptations from Ancrene Wisse. Vol. 1*
Specu - v72 - Ja '97 - p236+ [501+]
Waddell, Helen - *Beasts and Saints*
BL - v93 - O 1 '96 - p308 [51-250]
Waddell, Martin - *The Big Big Sea (Illus. by Jennifer Eachus)*
c Bks Keeps - N '96 - p8 [51-250]
Can't You Sleep, Little Bear? (Illus. by Barbara Firth)
c PW - v244 - F 10 '97 - p85 [1-50]
Cup Final Kid (Illus. by Jeff Cummins)
c Sch Lib - v45 - F '97 - p36 [51-250]
Farmer Duck (Illus. by Helen Oxenbury)
c Bks Keeps - Mr '97 - p7 [51-250]
c Par Ch - v20 - O '96 - p21 [51-250]
John Joe and the Big Hen (Illus. by Paul Howard)
c RT - v50 - N '96 - p254 [51-250]
The Kidnapping of Suzie Q
y HB Guide - v7 - Fall '96 - p306 [51-250]
y KR - v64 - My 1 '96 - p694 [51-250]
Let's Go Home, Little Bear (Illus. by Barbara Firth)
c PW - v244 - F 10 '97 - p85 [1-50]
Owl Babies (Illus. by Patrick Benson)
c Ch BWatch - v6 - N '96 - p6 [1-50]
c HB Guide - v8 - Spr '97 - p16 [51-250]
c PW - v243 - O 14 '96 - p85 [1-50]
The Pig in the Pond (Illus. by Jill Norton)
c SFR - v21 - Jl '96 - p47 [51-250]
Sailor Bear (Illus. by Virginia Austin)
c PW - v244 - F 10 '97 - p85 [1-50]
Small Bear Lost (Illus. by Virginia Austin)
c BL - v93 - S 15 '96 - p251 [51-250]
c Ch BWatch - v6 - S '96 - p1 [1-50]
c HB Guide - v8 - Spr '97 - p16 [51-250]
c JB - v60 - D '96 - p243 [51-250]
c SLJ - v42 - S '96 - p193 [51-250]
c TES - O 18 '96 - p12* [1-50]
Tango's Baby
y Bks Keeps - Jl '96 - p13 [51-250]
y Magpies - v11 - Jl '96 - p45 [1-50]
What Use Is a Moose? (Illus. by Arthur Robins)
c Ch BWatch - v6 - S '96 - p1 [1-50]
c HB Guide - v8 - Spr '97 - p52 [51-250]
c SLJ - v43 - Ja '97 - p93 [51-250]
When the Teddy Bears Came (Illus. by Penny Dale)
c Bks Keeps - Ja '97 - p19 [51-250]
You and Me, Little Bear (Illus. by Barbara Firth)
c BL - v93 - O 1 '96 - p360 [51-250]
c Ch BWatch - v6 - S '96 - p1 [1-50]
c HB Guide - v8 - Spr '97 - p16 [51-250]
c JB - v60 - D '96 - p243 [51-250]
c Sch Lib - v45 - F '97 - p22 [51-250]
c SLJ - v42 - N '96 - p94 [51-250]
c TES - O 18 '96 - p12* [51-250]
Waddell, Sasha - *New Swedish Style*
LJ - v122 - Ja '97 - p76 [51-250]
Waddell, Steve R - *United States Army Logistics*
Mar Crp G - v80 - N '96 - p81+ [51-250]
Waddington, Jeremy - *The Politics of Bargaining*
ILRR - v50 - Ja '97 - p346+ [501+]
Waddington, Patrick - *From the Russian Fugitive to the Ballad of Bulgarie*
Slav R - v55 - Sum '96 - p520+ [501+]
Ivan Turgenev and Britain
Slav R - v55 - Sum '96 - p520+ [501+]
TLS - O 4 '96 - p13 [501+]

Waddington, Raymond B - *The Expulsion of the Jews 1492 and After*
CH - v65 - S '96 - p488+ [501+]
EHR - v112 - F '97 - p182 [251-500]
HT - v46 - D '96 - p53+ [501+]
Ren Q - v50 - Spr '97 - p288+ [501+]
Wade, Jenny - *Changes of Mind*
Choice - v34 - S '96 - p216+ [51-250]
R&R Bk N - v12 - F '97 - p6 [51-250]
Wade, Jill - *Houses for All*
Can Hist R - v77 - D '96 - p648+ [501+]
Wade, Mary Dodson - *Guadalupe Quintanilla, Leader of the Hispanic Community*
c CLW - v66 - Je '96 - p49+ [251-500]
Wade, Michael G - *Sugar Dynasty*
BHR - v70 - Sum '96 - p269+ [501+]
JSH - v63 - F '97 - p155+ [501+]
Wade, Rahima C - *Community Service-Learning*
Adoles - v32 - Spr '97 - p248+ [51-250]
Wade, Richard C - *The Urban Frontier*
LJ - v122 - Ap 1 '97 - p134 [1-50]
Wade, Terence - *A Russian Grammar Workbook*
MLJ - v81 - Spr '97 - p141+ [501+]
Wade-Gayles, Gloria - *Father Songs*
PW - v244 - Ap 21 '97 - p51+ [51-250]
Rooted against the Wind
BL - v93 - O 1 '96 - p310 [51-250]
LJ - v121 - O 15 '96 - p80 [51-250]
Ms - v7 - N '96 - p82 [501+]
Wom R Bks - v14 - Ja '97 - p18+ [501+]
Wadia-Ells, Susan - *The Adoption Reader*
Bloom Rev - v16 - Jl '96 - p21 [51-250]
Wadsworth, Ginger - *Farewell Jimmy the Greek*
BWatch - v18 - F '97 - p1 [51-250]
PW - v243 - D 2 '96 - p46 [51-250]
John Burroughs: The Sage of Slabsides (Illus. by Ginger Wadsworth)
c BL - v93 - Mr 15 '97 - p1241 [51-250]
c CCB-B - v50 - My '97 - p336+ [51-250]
c KR - v65 - F 1 '97 - p229+ [51-250]
Laura Ingalls Wilder: Storyteller of the Prairie
c BL - v93 - Mr 1 '97 - p1159 [51-250]
c KR - v65 - F 15 '97 - p307 [51-250]
Rachel Carson: Voice for the Earth (Hughes). Audio Version
y Kliatt - v30 - S '96 - p59 [51-250]
Wadsworth Atheneum - *American Paintings before 1945 in the Wadsworth Atheneum. Vols. 1-2*
LJ - v122 - Ap 15 '97 - p78 [51-250]
Waehler, Charles A - *Bachelors: The Psychology of Men Who Haven't Married*
Choice - v34 - Ap '97 - p1422 [51-250]
PW - v243 - S 30 '96 - p69 [51-250]
Wagenbach, Klaus - *Kafka's Prague*
PW - v243 - O 7 '96 - p58 [51-250]
Wagenbaur, Thomas - *The Moment: A History, Typology and Theory of the Moment in Philosophy and Literature*
Ger Q - v69 - Sum '96 - p333+ [501+]
Wagener, Gerda - *A Mouse in the House! (Illus. by Uli Waas)*
c RT - v50 - O '96 - p134 [1-50]
Wagener, Hans - *Carl Zuckmayer Criticism*
MLR - v92 - Ap '97 - p526+ [501+]
Wager, Susan - *A Doctor's Guide to Therapeutic Touch*
PW - v243 - O 21 '96 - p80+ [51-250]
Wager, Walter - *The Spirit Team*
Arm Det - v29 - Fall '96 - p503 [51-250]
Wagman, Fredrica - *Mrs. Hornstein*
BL - v93 - Ap 1 '97 - p1269 [51-250]
KR - v65 - Mr 15 '97 - p416 [251-500]
PW - v244 - Ap 7 '97 - p75 [51-250]

Wagman, Morton - *Human Intellect and Cognitive Science*
   Choice - v34 - S '96 - p217 [51-250]
Wagner, Anne Middleton - *Three Artists (Three Women)*
   Choice - v34 - My '97 - p1488 [51-250]
   LJ - v122 - My 1 '97 - p101+ [51-250]
Wagner, Anthony - *Medieval Pageant*
   TLS - Ap 11 '97 - p32 [501+]
Wagner, Bruce - *I'm Losing You*
   BW - v26 - D 1 '96 - p6 [51-250]
   KR - v64 - My 1 '96 - p636 [251-500]
   LATBR - Ag 4 '96 - p6 [501+]
   NYTBR - v101 - D 8 '96 - p80 [1-50]
   SFR - v21 - Jl '96 - p5 [251-500]
   Time - v148 - O 7 '96 - p96+ [501+]
Wagner, Cheryl - *Hello Molly! (Illus. by Cheryl Roberts)*
  c HB Guide - v7 - Fall '96 - p258 [1-50]
Wagner, David H - *Fire Protection*
   R&R Bk N - v12 - F '97 - p98 [51-250]
Wagner, Hilory - *The New Parents' Sourcebook*
  r ARBA - v28 - '97 - p321 [51-250]
  r BL - v93 - O 1 '96 - p371 [51-250]
Wagner, Jennifer Ann - *A Moment's Monument*
   Nine-C Lit - v51 - S '96 - p278 [1-50]
Wagner, Jenny - *John Brown, Rose and the Midnight Cat (Illus. by Ron Brooks)*
  c Magpies - v11 - Jl '96 - p10+ [501+]
Wagner, Jordan Lee - *The Synagogue Survival Kit*
   LJ - v122 - F 15 '97 - p139 [51-250]
   PW - v244 - F 10 '97 - p80 [51-250]
Wagner, Karin - *International Productivity Differences*
   JEL - v35 - Mr '97 - p283 [51-250]
   SciTech - v20 - N '96 - p2 [51-250]
Wagner, Laurie - *Living Happily Ever After*
   PW - v243 - O 7 '96 - p68 [51-250]
Wagner, Patricia Jean - *The Bloomsbury Review Booklover's Guide*
  r LJ - v121 - D '96 - p82 [51-250]
   PW - v243 - O 14 '96 - p80 [51-250]
Wagner, Richard, 1813-1883 - *Actors and Singers*
   Notes - v53 - S '96 - p40+ [501+]
  Art and Politics
   Notes - v53 - S '96 - p40+ [501+]
  The Art-Work of the Future and Other Works
   Notes - v53 - S '96 - p40+ [501+]
  Jesus of Nazareth and Other Writings
   Notes - v53 - S '96 - p40+ [501+]
  Judaism in Music and Other Essays
   Notes - v53 - S '96 - p40+ [501+]
  Opera and Drama
   Notes - v53 - S '96 - p40+ [501+]
  Pilgrimage to Beethoven and Other Essays
   Notes - v53 - S '96 - p40+ [501+]
  Religion and Art
   Notes - v53 - S '96 - p40+ [501+]
Wagner, Richard, 1952- - *In Der Hand Der Frauen*
   WLT - v71 - Win '97 - p140 [501+]
Wagner, Ronald L - *The McGraw-Hill World Wide Web Training Manual*
   LJ - v122 - Ja '97 - p138 [51-250]
Wagner, William G - *Marriage, Property and Law in Late Imperial Russia*
   EHR - v112 - Ap '97 - p521+ [501+]
Wagner-Martin, Linda - *The Age of Innocence*
   AL - v69 - Mr '97 - p250+ [51-250]
  Favored Strangers
   AL - v68 - D '96 - p862+ [501+]
  New Essays on Go Down, Moses
   AL - v69 - Mr '97 - p255 [51-250]
   Choice - v34 - Mr '97 - p1165 [51-250]
Wagnleitner, Reinhold - *Coca-Colonization and the Cold War*
   Am Q - v48 - D '96 - p731+ [501+]
   CEH - v29 - 2 '96 - p281+ [501+]
Wagoner, David - *Walt Whitman Bathing*
   PW - v243 - Jl 22 '96 - p236 [51-250]
Wagoner, Phillip B - *Tidings of the King*
   TranslRevS - v1 - My '95 - p33 [51-250]
Wagoner, Robert H - *Fundamentals of Metal Forming*
   SciTech - v20 - D '96 - p63 [51-250]
Wagstaff, Patty - *Fire and Air*
   PW - v244 - Ap 21 '97 - p52 [51-250]
Wah, Fred - *Diamond Grill*
   Quill & Q - v62 - S '96 - p65 [251-500]
Wahid, Abu N M - *The Economy of Bangladesh*
   Choice - v34 - My '97 - p1547 [51-250]
   R&R Bk N - v12 - F '97 - p36 [51-250]
Wahl, Jan - *Once When the World Was Green (Illus. by Fabricio Vandenbroeck)*
  c Ch BWatch - v6 - My '96 - p3 [1-50]
  c HB Guide - v7 - Fall '96 - p280 [51-250]

Tailypo! (Illus. by Wil Clay)
  c PW - v243 - S 16 '96 - p85 [51-250]
Wahl, Nicholas - *La France Presidentielle*
   Choice - v34 - D '96 - p568+ [1-50]
Wahrman, Dror - *Imagining the Middle Class*
   AJS - v102 - Jl '96 - p305+ [501+]
   Albion - v28 - Sum '96 - p321+ [501+]
   J Soc H - v30 - Win '96 - p553+ [501+]
Wainscott, Ronald H - *The Emergence of the Modern American Theater 1914-1929*
   LJ - v122 - Ap 15 '97 - p84 [51-250]
   PW - v244 - F 3 '97 - p90 [51-250]
Wainscott, Tina - *Dreams of You*
   PW - v243 - S 2 '96 - p122 [51-250]
Wainstock, Dennis D - *The Decision to Drop the Atomic Bomb*
   Choice - v34 - N '96 - p528 [51-250]
Wainwright, Cherry L - *Myocardial Preconditioning*
   SciTech - v20 - S '96 - p36 [51-250]
Wainwright, J A - *Landscape and Desire*
   Can Lit - Win '96 - p189+ [501+]
Wainwright, William J - *Reason and the Heart*
   IPQ - v37 - Mr '97 - p104+ [501+]
   Rel St - v32 - D '96 - p513+ [501+]
   Theol St - v58 - Mr '97 - p199 [251-500]
Waiser, Bill - *Park Prisoners*
   Beav - v77 - F '97 - p41 [51-250]
   Can Hist R - v78 - Mr '97 - p130+ [501+]
   Choice - v34 - S '96 - p200 [51-250]
   WHQ - v28 - Spr '97 - p86+ [251-500]
Waite, Michael P - *Camp Windy Woods Series*
  c Ch BWatch - v6 - O '96 - p6 [51-250]
  Jojofu (Illus. by Yoriko Ito)
  c BL - v93 - N 15 '96 - p592 [51-250]
  c CBRS - v25 - D '96 - p43 [51-250]
  c CCB-B - v50 - O '96 - p79+ [51-250]
  c CSM - v88 - S 26 '96 - pB3 [51-250]
  c HB Guide - v8 - Spr '97 - p106 [51-250]
  c SLJ - v42 - O '96 - p108+ [51-250]
Waites, Elizabeth - *Trauma and Survival*
   HER - v66 - Win '96 - p884+ [501+]
Waitley, Denis - *Empires of the Mind*
   Rapport - v19 - 4 '96 - p18+ [501+]
  The New Dynamics of Goal Setting
   BL - v92 - Ag '96 - p1866 [51-250]
  The New Dynamics of Goal Setting (Waitley). Audio Version
   Quill & Q - v62 - Jl '96 - p52 [1-50]
Waitzman, Norman J - *The Cost of Birth Defects*
   JEL - v34 - D '96 - p2062 [51-250]
Wakefield, Ali - *Those Calculating Crows! (Illus. by Christy Hale)*
  c BL - v93 - N 15 '96 - p596 [51-250]
  c CBRS - v24 - Ag '96 - p162 [1-50]
  c HB Guide - v8 - Spr '97 - p52 [51-250]
  c SLJ - v42 - D '96 - p109 [51-250]
Wakefield, Dan - *Creating from the Spirit*
   Nat - v263 - D 23 '96 - p30+ [501+]
   PW - v244 - My 5 '97 - p206 [1-50]
   Rapport - v19 - 5 '96 - p45 [251-500]
   Utne R - S '96 - p92+ [501+]
  Expect a Miracle
   Nat - v263 - D 23 '96 - p30+ [501+]
  Expect a Miracle (Sevra). Audio Version
  y Kliatt - v30 - S '96 - p56+ [51-250]
  Expect a Miracle (Wakefield). Audio Version
  y Kliatt - v30 - N '96 - p48 [51-250]
  Returning: A Spiritual Journey
   Nat - v263 - D 23 '96 - p30+ [501+]
Wakefield, Robert S - *Mayflower Families in Progress*
   Am Geneal - v71 - Ap '96 - p125+ [501+]
Wakelin, Derek - *Immunity to Parasites. 2nd Ed.*
   Choice - v34 - Ap '97 - p1364 [51-250]
Wakelin, Michael - *J. Arthur Rank: The Man behind the Gong*
   Si & So - v6 - N '96 - p35 [1-50]
   TLS - S 6 '96 - p33 [251-500]
Wakelyn, Jon L - *Southern Pamphlets on Secession November 1860-April 1861*
   Choice - v34 - F '97 - p1027+ [51-250]
Wakeman, Frederic, Jr. - *Policing Shanghai 1927-1937*
   HJAS - v56 - 2 '96 - p479+ [501+]
Wakin, Edward - *Contemporary Political Leaders of the Middle East*
  y Ch BWatch - v6 - S '96 - p7 [51-250]
  y HB Guide - v7 - Fall '96 - p384 [51-250]
  How TV Changed America's Mind
  y HB Guide - v7 - Fall '96 - p307 [51-250]
Wakowski, Diane - *Emerald Ice*
   LJ - v122 - Ap 1 '97 - p95 [1-50]

Waks, Leonard J - *Technology's School*
   AJE - v105 - N '96 - p122+ [501+]
Walach, Harald - *Notitia Experimentalis Dei-- Erfahrungserkenntis Gottes*
   CH - v66 - Mr '97 - p99+ [501+]
Walch, Timothy - *Parish School*
   Am - v176 - Ja 18 '97 - p26+ [501+]
   Choice - v34 - S '96 - p181 [51-250]
Walcott, Charles E - *Governing the White House*
   Historian - v59 - Fall '96 - p164+ [501+]
   J Pol - v58 - Ag '96 - p879+ [501+]
Walcott, Derek - *The Bounty*
   LJ - v122 - Ap 15 '97 - p85 [51-250]
   NYRB - v44 - Mr 27 '97 - p18+ [501+]
  Conversations with Derek Walcott
   WLT - v71 - Win '97 - p208+ [501+]
  Omeros
   LJ - v122 - Ap 1 '97 - p94 [1-50]
Wald, Elissa - *Meeting the Master*
   KR - v64 - Ag 15 '96 - p1184 [251-500]
   VV - v41 - S 24 '96 - p43 [251-500]
Wald, Peter - *Yemen*
   TLS - D 27 '96 - p32 [51-250]
Wald, Priscilla - *Constituting Americans*
   AL - v68 - D '96 - p855+ [501+]
   J Am St - v30 - Ap '96 - p170 [251-500]
Waldbauer, Gilbert - *Insects through the Seasons*
   BL - v93 - D 1 '96 - p630 [1-50]
Walde, Klaus - *Convergence, Divergence and Changing Trade Patterns*
   JEL - v34 - D '96 - p2045 [51-250]
Walden, David - *How to Stay Awake during Anybody's Second Movement*
   PW - v243 - O 21 '96 - p78 [1-50]
Walden, Gale Renee - *Same Blue Chevy*
   RCF - v16 - Fall '96 - p205+ [251-500]
Walden, George - *We Should Know Better*
   Lon R Bks - v18 - O 3 '96 - p9+ [501+]
   NS - v125 - S 13 '96 - p44+ [501+]
   Obs - S 29 '96 - p16* [501+]
   TES - S 20 '96 - p7* [501+]
   TLS - O 25 '96 - p29 [501+]
Walden, Graham R - *Polling and Survey Research Methods 1935-1979*
  r ARBA - v28 - '97 - p43 [251-500]
  r Choice - v34 - Ap '97 - p1318 [51-250]
  r R&R Bk N - v12 - F '97 - p51 [51-250]
Walden, Gregory S - *On Best Behavior*
   Choice - v34 - N '96 - p540 [51-250]
Walder, Andrew G - *The Waning of the Communist State*
   APSR - v90 - D '96 - p949+ [501+]
Waldherr, Kris - *The Book of Goddesses*
  c Bloom Rev - v16 - Jl '96 - p27 [51-250]
  c HB Guide - v7 - Fall '96 - p325 [51-250]
Waldie, D J - *Holy Land*
   HMR - Spr '97 - p6+ [501+]
   LATBR - Ag 25 '96 - p4 [501+]
   NY - v72 - S 9 '96 - p91 [51-250]
   NYTBR - v102 - Ja 19 '97 - p19 [51-250]
Waldie, Doug - *A House Divided*
   Quill & Q - v62 - O '96 - p37 [251-500]
Waldie, Scott - *Travers Corners*
   BL - v93 - Mr 15 '97 - p1228 [51-250]
   KR - v65 - Mr 1 '97 - p333 [51-250]
   LJ - v122 - Ap 1 '97 - p132 [51-250]
   PW - v244 - Ap 21 '97 - p62 [51-250]
Waldinger, Roger - *Still the Promised City?*
   BW - v26 - D 15 '96 - p5 [501+]
   Choice - v34 - Ja '97 - p885 [51-250]
   JEL - v35 - Mr '97 - p302 [51-250]
   WSJ-MW - v77 - S 3 '96 - pA13 [501+]
Waldman, Anne - *Iovis: All Is Full of Love. Vol. 2*
   PW - v243 - D 30 '96 - p60+ [51-250]
Waldman, Diane - *Ellsworth Kelly: A Retrospective*
   BM - v139 - Ja '97 - p68 [501+]
   LATBR - D 8 '96 - p29 [51-250]
Waldman, Harry - *Hollywood and the Foreign Touch*
  r ARBA - v28 - '97 - p506 [51-250]
  r LJ - v122 - F 1 '97 - p81 [51-250]
Waldman, Neil - *The Golden City*
  c LA - v73 - O '96 - p441 [51-250]
  The Never-Ending Greenness (Illus. by Neil Waldman)
  c BL - v93 - Mr 1 '97 - p1174 [51-250]
  c CBRS - v25 - Ap '97 - p104 [51-250]
  c PW - v244 - F 3 '97 - p107 [51-250]

Waldmeir, Patti - *Anatomy of a Miracle*
    BL - v93 - F 15 '97 - p1000+ [51-250]
    Econ - v342 - Mr 1 '97 - p84 [501+]
    KR - v65 - Ja 15 '97 - p132 [251-500]
    LATBR - Ap 6 '97 - p9 [501+]
    NYTBR - v102 - Ap 6 '97 - p18+ [501+]
    PW - v243 - D 30 '96 - p44 [251-500]
Waldram, James B - *Aboriginal Health in Canada*
    Can Hist R - v78 - Mr '97 - p103+ [501+]
Waldren, Jacqueline - *Insiders and Outsiders*
    Choice - v34 - Ja '97 - p840 [51-250]
Waldron, Arthur - *From War to Nationalism*
    Choice - v34 - O '96 - p337 [51-250]
    Ch Rev Int - v3 - Fall '96 - p552+ [501+]
Waldron, Jan L - *In the Country of Men*
    BL - v93 - My 15 '97 - p1548 [51-250]
    KR - v65 - Ap 1 '97 - p540+ [251-500]
    PW - v244 - Mr 31 '97 - p55 [51-250]
Waldron, Jeremy - *Liberal Rights*
    Dialogue - v35 - Sum '96 - p631+ [501+]
Waldron, Mary - *Lactilla, Milkwoman of Clifton*
    Choice - v34 - F '97 - p969 [51-250]
    TLS - D 27 '96 - p23 [501+]
Waldron, Robert - *The Bold and the Beautiful*
    BL - v93 - N 15 '96 - p548 [1-50]
Waldrop, Rosmarie - *Another Language*
    PW - v244 - Ap 28 '97 - p70+ [51-250]
Waldrup, Carole Chandler - *The Vice Presidents*
    r ΛRBΛ - v28 - '97 - p267 [51-250]
    yr BL - v93 - D 1 '96 - p686 [251-500]
Wale, Carole - *At Home*
    c Sch Lib - v44 - N '96 - p166 [51-250]
    Near Water
    c Bks Keeps - Mr '97 - p22 [251-500]
    On the Road
    c Sch Lib - v44 - N '96 - p166 [51-250]
    On Your Own
    c Bks Keeps - Mr '97 - p22 [251-500]
Wales, Katie - *Personal Pronouns in Present-Day English*
    Choice - v34 - My '97 - p1492 [51-250]
Waley, Daniel Philip - *Siena and the Sienese in the Thirteenth Century*
    J Urban H - v23 - Ja '97 - p240+ [501+]
Walford, Rex - *Challenging Times*
    GJ - v162 - N '96 - p342 [51-250]
Walford's Guide to Reference Material. 7th Ed., Vol. 1
    r ARBA - v28 - '97 - p560 [51-250]
Walicki, Andrzej - *Marxism and the Leap to the Kingdom of Freedom*
    AHR - v101 - O '96 - p1251+ [501+]
    Russ Rev - v55 - O '96 - p716+ [251-500]
Walker, Alan, 1930- - *Franz Liszt. Vol. 3*
    BW - v26 - D 8 '96 - p8 [51-250]
    NYRB - v43 - N 28 '96 - p35+ [501+]
    W&I - v11 - S '96 - p285+ [501+]
Walker, Alan, 1938- - *The Wisdom of the Bones*
    Choice - v34 - O '96 - p324 [51-250]
    Lon R Bks - v18 - O 31 '96 - p36+ [501+]
    Sew R - v104 - O '96 - p665+ [501+]
    VQR - v72 - Aut '96 - p139* [51-250]
Walker, Alice - *Alice Walker Banned*
    BL - v92 - Ag '96 - p1875+ [51-250]
    BWatch - v17 - N '96 - p9 [51-250]
    Anything We Love Can Be Saved
    y BL - v93 - Mr 1 '97 - p1067 [51-250]
    KR - v65 - F 15 '97 - p289+ [251-500]
    LJ - v122 - My 1 '97 - p104+ [51-250]
    PW - v244 - F 24 '97 - p77 [51-250]
    The Same River Twice
    Advocate - Ja 21 '97 - p94 [1-50]
    PW - v243 - N 25 '96 - p70 [1-50]
    Woman's J - D '96 - p16 [1-50]
Walker, Andre - *Andre Talks Hair!*
    y BL - v93 - My 1 '97 - p1469+ [51-250]
Walker, Ann - *To the Heart of Spain*
    BL - v93 - N 15 '96 - p561 [51-250]
    PW - v243 - N 4 '96 - p72 [51-250]
Walker, Anthony - *Project Management in Construction. 3rd Ed.*
    SciTech - v20 - D '96 - p3 [51-250]
Walker, B H - *Global Change and Terrestrial Ecosystems*
    Choice - v34 - My '97 - p1522 [51-250]
Walker, Barbara - *Out of the Ordinary*
    CAY - v17 - Win '96 - p9 [51-250]
Walker, Bob - *The Cats' House*
    BL - v93 - O 1 '96 - p313 [51-250]
    LJ - v121 - S 15 '96 - p66 [51-250]
Walker, Bonnie L - *Injury Prevention for Young Children*
    r ARBA - v28 - '97 - p322 [51-250]
Walker, Brian - *Dancing to History's Tune*
    TLS - S 27 '96 - p5+ [501+]

Walker, C H - *Principles of Ecotoxicology*
    Choice - v34 - D '96 - p636 [51-250]
Walker, Christopher - *Astronomy before the Telescope*
    r New Sci - v152 - N 2 '96 - p45 [51-250]
Walker, Dava - *Puzzles (Illus. by Cornelius Van Wright)*
    c CCB-B - v50 - Mr '97 - p261 [51-250]
Walker, David H - *Outrage and Insight*
    MLR - v91 - O '96 - p1004 [251-500]
Walker, David J - *Half the Truth*
    BL - v93 - N 1 '96 - p483 [51-250]
    KR - v64 - S 15 '96 - p1359 [51-250]
    PW - v243 - S 30 '96 - p65 [51-250]
Walker, Donald - *Welfare Economics and the Theory of Economic Policy*
    Econ J - v107 - Ja '97 - p276 [51-250]
Walker, Elizabeth - *The Snow Tree*
    Books - v9 - S '95 - p25 [1-50]
Walker, Fiona - *Kiss Chase*
    Books - v10 - Je '96 - p12 [1-50]
Walker, Garthine - *Women, Crime and the Courts in Early Modern England*
    EHR - v111 - S '96 - p983 [51-250]
Walker, George F - *Shared Anxiety*
    Can Lit - Spr '97 - p229+ [501+]
Walker, Greg - *Persuasive Fictions*
    r Choice - v34 - N '96 - p442 [51-250]
    HT - v47 - F '97 - p59+ [501+]
Walker, Ian R - *Faith and Belief*
    Rel St - v32 - S '96 - p429 [51-250]
    Rel St Rev - v22 - O '96 - p339 [51-250]
Walker, Jack M - *Handbook of Manufacturing Engineering*
    SciTech - v20 - N '96 - p81 [51-250]
Walker, Jacqueline - *The Subtropical Garden*
    BL - v93 - S 15 '96 - p195 [51-250]
Walker, James R - *The Remote Control in the New Age of Television*
    JPC - v29 - Spr '96 - p259+ [51-250]
Walker, James S - *Fast Fourier Transforms. 2nd Ed.*
    SciTech - v20 - O '96 - p18 [51-250]
Walker, Jane - *Ten Little Penguins (Illus. by Jane Walker)*
    c RT - v50 - O '96 - p131 [1-50]
Walker, Jay - *The Leno Wit*
    y BL - v93 - F 1 '97 - p919+ [51-250]
    KR - v64 - N 15 '96 - p1660+ [251-500]
    PW - v243 - N 11 '96 - p61 [51-250]
Walker, John, 1906- - *National Gallery of Art, Washington. New and Rev. Ed.*
    CR - v268 - Je '96 - p329+ [251-500]
Walker, John M, 1948- - *The Protein Protocols Handbook*
    SciTech - v20 - N '96 - p33 [51-250]
Walker, Keith M - *Applied Mechanics for Engineering Technology. 5th Ed.*
    SciTech - v20 - D '96 - p61 [51-250]
Walker, Kim - *Women Writers of the English Renaissance*
    Choice - v34 - F '97 - p970 [51-250]
Walker, Mark - *Nazi Science*
    TLS - N 22 '96 - p28 [501+]
Walker, Martin - *The President We Deserve*
    BW - v26 - S 29 '96 - p7 [501+]
    BW - v26 - D 8 '96 - p8 [1-50]
    NYTBR - v101 - S 22 '96 - p14 [501+]
    Pres SQ - v27 - Win '97 - p153+ [501+]
Walker, Mary Willis - *The Red Scream (Critt). Audio Version*
    y Kliatt - v30 - S '96 - p51 [51-250]
    Under the Beetle's Cellar (Fields). Audio Version
    LJ - v121 - D '96 - p171 [51-250]
    LJ - v122 - F 15 '97 - p115 [51-250]
    Zero at the Bone
    PW - v244 - Mr 17 '97 - p81 [1-50]
Walker, Mike - *Steam Powered Video's Comprehensive Railroad Atlas of North America: Great Lakes West Including Chicago and St. Louis*
    r SciTech - v21 - Mr '97 - p83 [1-50]
Walker, Mildred - *Dr. Norton's Wife*
    LJ - v121 - O 1 '96 - p132 [1-50]
    Unless the Wind Turns
    LJ - v121 - O 1 '96 - p132 [1-50]
Walker, Nancy A - *The Disobedient Writer*
    Legacy - v14 - 1 '97 - p66+ [501+]
Walker, Patricia Hinton - *Blueprint for Use of Nursing Models, Education, Research, Practice and Administration*
    SciTech - v20 - D '96 - p56 [1-50]
Walker, Paul Robert - *Little Folk (Illus. by James Bernardin)*
    c BL - v93 - Mr 15 '97 - p1246 [51-250]
    c PW - v244 - Mr 10 '97 - p69 [51-250]

Walker, Peter, 1932- - *Invisible Gardens*
    AAAGA - v86 - S '96 - p593+ [501+]
Walker, Peter, 1942- - *Baby Massage*
    BL - v93 - S 1 '96 - p51 [51-250]
Walker, Richard - *The Family Guide to Sex and Relationships*
    y LJ - v122 - F 15 '97 - p156 [51-250]
Walker, Robert H - *American Studies*
    r ASInt - v34 - O '96 - p7 [51-250]
Walker, Robert Martin - *Politically Correct Parables*
    CC - v113 - O 9 '96 - p945 [51-250]
Walker, Robert N - *Psychology of the Youthful Offender. 3rd Ed.*
    Adoles - v31 - Win '96 - p997 [51-250]
Walker, Sage - *Whiteout*
    BWatch - v17 - N '96 - p8 [1-50]
    MFSF - v91 - S '96 - p46 [51-250]
Walker, Sally M - *Earthquakes*
    c HB Guide - v7 - Fall '96 - p333 [1-50]
    Rhinos (Illus. by Gerry Ellis)
    c BL - v93 - D 1 '96 - p660 [51-250]
    cr Ch BWatch - v6 - N '96 - p7 [1-50]
    c HB Guide - v8 - Spr '97 - p128 [51-250]
    c SLJ - v42 - D '96 - p134 [51-250]
Walker, Susan - *Greek and Roman Portraits*
    AJA - v100 - O '96 - p795 [501+]
Walker, Sydney - *A Dose of Sanity*
    Choice - v34 - O '96 - p315 [51-250]
Walker, T J - *Colorado: A Newcomer's Manual*
    Bloom Rev - v16 - Jl '96 - p16+ [51-250]
Walker, Vanessa Siddle - *Their Highest Potential*
    Bl S - v26 - Fall '96 - p107 [51-250]
Walker, William - *Locke, Literary Criticism, and Philosophy*
    JAAC - v54 - Fall '96 - p391+ [501+]
Walker, William A - *Five-Minute Chillers (Illus. by Brian Dow)*
    c Ch BWatch - v6 - My '96 - p7 [1-50]
    c SLJ - v42 - N '96 - p111 [1-50]
Walker, William O, II - *Drugs in the Western Hemisphere*
    Parameters - v26 - Win '96 - p157 [1-50]
The Walker Book of First Rhymes
    c JB - v60 - D '96 - p262 [51-250]
Walker-Moffat, Wendy - *The Other Side of the Asian American Success Story*
    Cont Ed - v67 - Sum '96 - p254+ [251-500]
Walker's Manual of Unlisted Stocks 1996
    r Choice - v34 - Mr '97 - p1144 [51-250]
    r LJ - v121 - D '96 - p86 [51-250]
    r R&R Bk N - v12 - F '97 - p49 [51-250]
Walkowitz, Judith R - *City of Dreadful Delight*
    J Urban H - v23 - Ja '97 - p231+ [501+]
Walkowski, Paul J - *From Trial Court to United States Court*
    PW - v243 - Jl 22 '96 - p224 [51-250]
Wall, Alan - *Bless the Thief*
    Books - v11 - Ap '97 - p22 [51-250]
    Obs - Ja 19 '97 - p15* [51-250]
    Obs - Ja 19 '97 - p18* [51-250]
    Spec - v278 - Ja 18 '97 - p29 [501+]
    TLS - Ja 24 '97 - p23 [501+]
Wall, Helena M - *Fierce Communion*
    Rel St Rev - v22 - O '96 - p357 [51-250]
Wall, Larry - *Programming Perl. 2nd Ed.*
    BYTE - v22 - F '97 - p34 [51-250]
    LJ - v121 - D '96 - p138 [51-250]
Wall, Nancy - *Nuffield-BP Business and Economics for GCSE*
    y TES - Ap 4 '97 - pR4 [501+]
Wall, Peter - *Media Stories for GCSE*
    y TES - Ap 4 '97 - p15* [51-250]
Wall, Richard - *A Dictionary and Glossary for the Irish Literary Revival*
    r Choice - v34 - D '96 - p596 [51-250]
    r ELT - v40 - 1 '97 - p127 [51-250]
    r ILS - v15 - Fall '96 - p31 [51-250]
Wall, Steve - *Shadowcatchers: A Journey in Search of the Teachings of Native American Elders (Toms). Audio Version*
    BL - v93 - N 15 '96 - p603+ [51-250]
    LJ - v121 - O 15 '96 - p101 [51-250]
Wall Street Journal (Firm). Personal-Finance Staff - *The Wall Street Journal Lifetime Guide to Money*
    BL - v93 - N 15 '96 - p548 [51-250]
    LJ - v122 - Ja '97 - p116 [51-250]
    PW - v243 - N 18 '96 - p54 [51-250]
Wall Street's Picks for 1997
    BL - v93 - D 1 '96 - p627 [51-250]

Wallace, B Alan - *Choosing Reality*
    Choice - v34 - N '96 - p497 [51-250]
    Parabola - v21 - Ag '96 - p120 [1-50]
Wallace, Barbara Brooks - *Cousins in the Castle*
    c HB Guide - v7 - Fall '96 - p298 [51-250]
Wallace, Barbara C - *Adult Children of Dysfunctional Families*
    Choice - v34 - Ap '97 - p1422 [51-250]
    SciTech - v21 - Mr '97 - p53 [51-250]
Wallace, Bill - *Journey into Terror*
    c SLJ - v43 - F '97 - p106 [51-250]
Wallace, David - *Environmental Policy and Industrial Innovation*
    Nature - v383 - S 12 '96 - p138 [501+]
Wallace, David Foster - *Infinite Jest*
    Ant R - v54 - Fall '96 - p491 [251-500]
    Critiq - v38 - Fall '96 - p12+ [501+]
    LATBR - D 29 '96 - p8 [51-250]
    Lon R Bks - v18 - Jl 18 '96 - p14+ [501+]
    NYTBR - v101 - D 8 '96 - p80 [1-50]
    NYTBR - v102 - F 16 '97 - p32 [51-250]
    PW - v243 - N 4 '96 - p40 [51-250]
    PW - v244 - Ja 27 '97 - p103 [1-50]
    Time - v148 - D 23 '96 - p86 [51-250]
    Trib Bks - F 16 '97 - p8 [1-50]
    VLS - Win '96 - p12 [51-250]
A Supposedly Fun Thing I'll Never Do Again
    Ant R - v55 - Spr '97 - p249 [51-250]
    BL - v93 - F 15 '97 - p996 [51-250]
    BW - v27 - F 2 '97 - p13 [51-250]
    Ent W - Mr 7 '97 - p60 [51-250]
    KR - v64 - D 15 '96 - p1791+ [251-500]
    LJ - v122 - Ja '97 - p100 [51-250]
    NW - v129 - F 17 '97 - p63 [251-500]
    NYTBR - v102 - Mr 16 '97 - p11 [501+]
    NYTLa - v146 - F 4 '97 - pC15 [501+]
    PW - v243 - D 30 '96 - p47 [251-500]
    Time - v149 - Ap 14 '97 - p89+ [501+]
    Trib Bks - Mr 9 '97 - p1+ [501+]
Wallace, David Rains - *Adventuring in Central America*
    r Workbook - v21 - Fall '96 - p143+ [251-500]
Wallace, Helen - *Policy-Making in the European Union. 3rd Ed.*
    Choice - v34 - Ap '97 - p1415 [51-250]
    CR - v269 - O '96 - p216+ [501+]
Wallace, Ian - *Hansel and Gretel (Illus. by Ian Wallace)*
    c Can CL - v22 - Fall '96 - p132+ [501+]
    c Ch BWatch - v6 - My '96 - p4 [51-250]
Wallace, James, 1947- - *Overdrive: Bill Gates and the Race to Control Cyberspace*
    BL - v93 - My 15 '97 - p1542 [51-250]
Wallace, James D, 1937- - *Ethical Norms, Particular Cases*
    Choice - v34 - Ap '97 - p1354 [51-250]
Wallace, John - *Building a House with Mr. Bumble (Illus. by John Wallace)*
    c KR - v65 - Ja 1 '97 - p66+ [51-250]
    c TES - Mr 28 '97 - p11* [51-250]
Dressing Up with Mr. Bumble
    c Obs - Mr 30 '97 - p17* [51-250]
    c TES - Mr 28 '97 - p11* [51-250]
Little Bean's Friend (Illus. by John Wallace)
    c JB - v60 - D '96 - p243 [51-250]
    c TES - Mr 21 '97 - p9* [501+]
Wallace, Jonathan - *Sex, Laws, and Cyberspace*
    BYTE - v21 - O '96 - p38 [51-250]
    SciTech - v20 - N '96 - p3 [1-50]
Wallace, Joseph E - *The Baseball Anthology*
    Aethlon - v13 - Fall '95 - p170+ [251-500]
Wallace, Karen - *Imagine You Are a Crocodile (Illus. by Mike Bostock)*
    c BL - v93 - My 1 '97 - p1497 [51-250]
    c Sch Lib - v45 - F '97 - p22 [51-250]
Imagine You Are a Tiger (Illus. by Peter Melnyczuk)
    c Bks Keeps - Jl '96 - p9+ [51-250]
    c BL - v93 - D 1 '96 - p663 [51-250]
    c HB Guide - v8 - Spr '97 - p52 [51-250]
Wallace, Mark - *The Lawless Man*
    Sm Pr R - v28 - S '96 - p8 [51-250]
Wallace, Mark I - *Fragments of the Spirit*
    Choice - v34 - O '96 - p299 [51-250]
    Rel St Rev - v23 - Ap '97 - p154+ [51-250]
Wallace, Mary - *I Can Make Costumes*
    c Quill & Q - v62 - O '96 - p48+ [251-500]
I Can Make Jewelry
    c Quill & Q - v63 - Mr '97 - p81+ [251-500]
I Can Make Nature Crafts
    c Ch BWatch - v6 - Jl '96 - p2 [1-50]
    c Quill & Q - v62 - My '96 - p36 [251-500]

Wallace, Mike - *Mickey Mouse History and Other Essays on American Memory*
    Choice - v34 - N '96 - p528 [51-250]
Wallace, Patricia Ward - *Politics of Conscience*
    NEQ - v69 - S '96 - p511+ [501+]
Wallace, Peter G - *Communities and Conflict in Early Modern Colmar 1575-1730*
    AHR - v101 - O '96 - p1232 [501+]
    CEH - v29 - 1 '96 - p118+ [501+]
Wallace, Philip R - *Paradox Lost*
    Choice - v34 - N '96 - p498 [51-250]
Wallace, R Jay - *Responsibility and the Moral Sentiments*
    J Phil - v93 - N '96 - p574+ [501+]
Wallace, Rich - *Wrestling Sturbridge*
    y BL - v93 - S 1 '96 - p128 [51-250]
    y BL - v93 - Ap 1 '97 - p1296 [1-50]
    y BL - v93 - Ap 1 '97 - p1310 [51-250]
    y HB - v72 - N '96 - p747+ [51-250]
    y HB Guide - v7 - Fall '96 - p306 [51-250]
    y HMR - Spr '97 - p31+ [501+]
    y JAAL - v40 - F '97 - p409 [51-250]
    y LATBR - S 15 '96 - p11 [51-250]
    y NY - v72 - N 18 '96 - p102 [51-250]
    y SLJ - v42 - O '96 - p150 [51-250]
Wallace, Robert K - *Melville and Turner*
    Comp L - v49 - Win '97 - p94+ [501+]
Wallace, Shelagh - *The TV Book (Illus. by Lorraine Tuson)*
    c BL - v93 - F 1 '97 - p938 [51-250]
    c Ch Bk News - v20 - Win '97 - p31 [51-250]
    c Emerg Lib - v24 - Mr '97 - p28 [1-50]
Wallace, Susan Helen - *Call Me Little Theresa*
    c CLW - v67 - D '96 - p45 [51-250]
Wallace, Valerie - *Mrs. Alexander: A Life of the Hymn Writer*
    CH - v65 - S '96 - p522+ [501+]
Wallace, Virginia - *School News Shows*
    y SLMQ - v25 - Fall '96 - p66 [51-250]
Wallace, William - *Why Vote Liberal Democrat?*
    Econ - v342 - Mr 22 '97 - p106 [501+]
    NS - v126 - Mr 27 '97 - p51+ [501+]
    TES - F 28 '97 - p8* [501+]
    TLS - F 21 '97 - p27+ [501+]
Wallach, Amei - *Ilya Kabakov: The Man Who Never Threw Anything Away*
    Choice - v34 - S '96 - p116 [51-250]
Wallach, Anne Tolstoi - *Trials*
    BL - v93 - S 15 '96 - p180 [51-250]
    KR - v64 - S 1 '96 - p1265 [51-250]
    LJ - v121 - O 15 '96 - p92 [51-250]
    NYTBR - v102 - Ja 12 '97 - p21 [251-500]
    PW - v243 - S 23 '96 - p57 [51-250]
Wallach, Bret - *Losing Asia*
    SSQ - v77 - D '96 - p937+ [501+]
Wallach, Glenn - *Obedient Sons*
    PW - v243 - D 9 '96 - p57 [51-250]
Wallach, Janet - *Desert Queen*
    BL - v93 - S 1 '96 - p59 [51-250]
    BW - v26 - Ag 25 '96 - p7 [501+]
    CSM - v89 - Mr 12 '97 - p13 [251-500]
    LATBR - N 3 '96 - p4+ [501+]
    NY - v72 - S 30 '96 - p82+ [501+]
    NYTBR - v101 - S 8 '96 - p32 [501+]
    NYTBR - v101 - D 8 '96 - p85 [1-50]
    TLS - Ja 31 '97 - p28 [501+]
Walle, Heinrich - *Die Tragodie Des Oberleutnants Zur See Oskar Kusch*
    J Mil H - v61 - Ap '97 - p401+ [501+]
Wallenfeldt, E C - *The Six-Minute Fraternity*
    Aethlon - v13 - Spr '96 - p223+ [251-500]
Waller, Derek - *The Pundits: British Exploration of Tibet and Central Asia*
    Pac A - v69 - Fall '96 - p443+ [501+]
Waller, Gary - *Edmund Spenser: A Literary Life*
    RES - v47 - N '96 - p580+ [501+]
The Sidney Family Romance
    Ren Q - v49 - Aut '96 - p667+ [501+]
Waller, George R - *Saponins Used in Food and Agriculture*
    SciTech - v21 - Mr '97 - p70 [51-250]
Saponins Used in Traditional and Modern Medicine
    SciTech - v21 - Mr '97 - p67 [51-250]
Waller, Gregory A - *Main Street Amusements*
    AHR - v102 - F '97 - p197+ [501+]
    JSH - v63 - F '97 - p190+ [501+]
Waller, J Michael - *Secret Empire*
    Russ Rev - v56 - Ja '97 - p149 [501+]
Waller, Jenny - *The T.Q.M. Toolkit*
    r R&R Bk N - v11 - N '96 - p30 [51-250]
Waller, John H - *The Unseen War in Europe*
    NYRB - v44 - Ja 9 '97 - p49+ [501+]

Waller, Robert James - *Puerto Vallarta Squeeze*
    Ent W - D 13 '96 - p75 [1-50]
Waller, Ruth - *The Leaping Llama Carpet*
    c Sch Lib - v44 - N '96 - p148 [51-250]
Wallerstein, Immanuel - *After Liberalism*
    NYTBR - v101 - S 1 '96 - p17 [51-250]
    SF - v75 - S '96 - p341+ [251-500]
Open the Social Sciences
    SF - v75 - D '96 - p765 [51-250]
    Soc - v34 - Ja '97 - p73+ [501+]
    Soc - v34 - Ja '97 - p78+ [501+]
    TLS - Ja 24 '97 - p11 [501+]
Wallerstein, Judith S - *The Good Marriage*
    NYTBR - v101 - N 10 '96 - p68 [51-250]
    PW - v243 - S 23 '96 - p73 [1-50]
Surviving the Breakup
    Trib Bks - Ja 19 '97 - p8 [1-50]
Wallgren, Anders - *Graphing Statistics and Data*
    R&R Bk N - v11 - N '96 - p24 [51-250]
Walling, Linda Lucas - *Information Services for People with Developmental Disabilities*
    LAR - v99 - F '97 - p101 [51-250]
Wallington, Neil - *Firefighters*
    c Ch BWatch - v6 - Jl '96 - p6 [51-250]
Wallis, Ian G - *The Faith of Jesus Christ in Early Christian Traditions*
    CH - v65 - D '96 - p658+ [501+]
    Rel St Rev - v23 - Ap '97 - p178+ [51-250]
Wallis, Jim - *Who Speaks for God?*
    Bks & Cult - v2 - N '96 - p20+ [501+]
    BL - v93 - S 15 '96 - p185 [51-250]
    KR - v64 - Ag 15 '96 - p1226 [251-500]
    LJ - v121 - S 15 '96 - p74 [51-250]
    PW - v243 - S 2 '96 - p126+ [51-250]
Wallis, P J - *Book Subscription Lists*
    r LAR - v98 - Jl '96 - p369 [51-250]
Wallis, Velma - *Bird Girl and the Man Who Followed the Sun*
    BL - v93 - N 15 '96 - p555 [51-250]
    Bloom Rev - v17 - Ja '97 - p13 [51-250]
    LJ - v122 - F 1 '97 - p88 [51-250]
    Rapport - v19 - 6 '96 - p23 [251-500]
Two Old Women (Means). Audio Version
    BL - v93 - N 15 '96 - p603+ [51-250]
    y SLJ - v42 - D '96 - p73 [51-250]
Wallis, W D - *Computational and Constructive Design Theory*
    SciTech - v20 - S '96 - p9 [51-250]
Wallman, Sandra - *Kampala Women Getting By*
    Choice - v34 - Ap '97 - p1382 [51-250]
    R&R Bk N - v12 - F '97 - p95 [51-250]
Wallner, Alexandra - *An Alcott Family Christmas (Illus. by Alexandra Wallner)*
    c BL - v93 - S 1 '96 - p138 [51-250]
    c HB Guide - v8 - Spr '97 - p52 [51-250]
    c PW - v243 - S 30 '96 - p91 [51-250]
    c SLJ - v42 - O '96 - p42 [51-250]
Beatrix Potter (Illus. by Alexandra Wallner)
    c RSR - v24 - 3 '96 - p26 [51-250]
    c RT - v50 - N '96 - p242 [51-250]
    c SLJ - v42 - O '96 - p45 [51-250]
The First Air Voyage in the United States
    c HB Guide - v7 - Fall '96 - p375 [51-250]
Jingle Bells (Illus. by Alexandra Wallner)
    c Ch BWatch - v6 - D '96 - p1 [1-50]
    c PW - v243 - S 30 '96 - p93 [1-50]
Silent Night (Illus. by Alexandra Wallner)
    c Ch BWatch - v6 - D '96 - p1 [1-50]
    c PW - v243 - S 30 '96 - p93 [1-50]
Walls, Andrew F - *The Missionary Movement in Christian History*
    Bks & Cult - v2 - N '96 - p6+ [501+]
Walls, Laura Dassow - *Seeing New Worlds*
    AB - v97 - Je 17 '96 - p2407+ [501+]
    AL - v69 - Mr '97 - p215+ [251-500]
    Isis - v87 - D '96 - p741+ [501+]
Walls, Peter - *Music in the English Courtly Masque 1604-1640*
    Choice - v34 - Ja '97 - p807 [51-250]
    TLS - N 29 '96 - p18+ [501+]
Wallwork, Ernest - *Psychoanalysis and Ethics*
    JR - v77 - Ap '97 - p278+ [501+]
Walpole, Brenda - *Hearing (Illus. by Barrie Watts)*
    c Cur R - v36 - N '96 - p12 [51-250]
    c HB Guide - v8 - Spr '97 - p131 [51-250]
    c SLJ - v43 - Mr '97 - p182 [51-250]
I Wonder Why the Sun Rises and Other Questions about Time and Seasons
    c HB Guide - v7 - Fall '96 - p339 [51-250]
Looking (Illus. by Barrie Watts)
    c JB - v60 - O '96 - p195 [51-250]

Seeing (Illus. by Barrie Watts)
 c Cur R - v36 - N '96 - p12 [51-250]
 c HB Guide - v8 - Spr '97 - p131 [51-250]
 c SLJ - v43 - Mr '97 - p182 [51-250]
Smell and Taste (Illus. by Barrie Watts)
 c Cur R - v36 - N '96 - p12 [51-250]
 c HB Guide - v8 - Spr '97 - p131 [51-250]
 c SLJ - v43 - Mr '97 - p182 [51-250]
Touch (Illus. by Barrie Watts)
 c Cur R - v36 - N '96 - p12 [51-250]
 c HB Guide - v8 - Spr '97 - p131 [51-250]
 c JB - v60 - O '96 - p195 [51-250]
 c SLJ - v43 - Mr '97 - p182 [51-250]
Walrand, Jean - *High-Performance Communication Networks*
    SciTech - v21 - Mr '97 - p88 [51-250]
Walsch, Neale Donald - *Conversations with God. Bk. 1*
    CSM - v89 - Ja 23 '97 - p12 [51-250]
Conversations with God. Bk. 2
    PW - v244 - Ap 28 '97 - p69 [51-250]
Conversations with God (Walsch). Bk. 1. Audio Version
    Mag BI - Mr '97 - p62 [51-250]
    PW - v243 - D 2 '96 - p31 [51-250]
Walsdorf, John J - *Julian Symons: A Bibliography*
 r TLS - Ap 11 '97 - p33 [251-500]
Julian Symons Remembered
    TLS - N 1 '96 - p31 [51-250]
Walser, Martin - *Finks Krieg*
    TLS - Ja 10 '97 - p22 [501+]
    WLT - v71 - Win '97 - p140+ [501+]
Kaschmir In Parching
    WLT - v70 - Sum '96 - p685 [251-500]
Walsh, Aaron E - *Foundations of Java Programming for the World Wide Web*
    LJ - v121 - D '96 - p138 [51-250]
Walsh, Anthony - *Biosociology: An Emerging Paradigm*
    SF - v75 - S '96 - p351+ [501+]
Walsh, Ben - *GCSE Modern World History*
 y TES - S 6 '96 - pR7 [501+]
GCSE Modern World History Teacher's Resource Book
    TES - Mr 28 '97 - p13* [501+]
Walsh, Caroline - *The Little Book of Cats (Illus. by Lorna Hussey)*
 c HB Guide - v7 - Fall '96 - p365+ [51-250]
The Little Book of Christmas (Illus. by Sophie Allsopp)
 c Bks Keeps - N '96 - p19 [1-50]
 c HB Guide - v8 - Spr '97 - p149 [51-250]
 c PW - v243 - S 30 '96 - p92 [1-50]
The Little Book of Dogs (Illus. by Valerie Greeley)
 c HB Guide - v7 - Fall '96 - p365+ [51-250]
 c JB - v60 - O '96 - p195+ [51-250]
Walsh, Ellen Stoll - *Mouse Count*
 c HB Guide - v7 - Fall '96 - p245 [1-50]
Mouse Paint
 c HB Guide - v7 - Fall '96 - p245 [1-50]
 c Inst - v106 - Ja '97 - p4* [1-50]
Salta Y Brinca (Illus. by Ellen Stoll Walsh)
 c BL - v93 - My 1 '97 - p1507 [1-50]
Samantha (Illus. by Ellen Stoll Walsh)
 c HB Guide - v7 - Fall '96 - p280 [51-250]
Walsh, Elsa - *Divided Lives*
 y Kliatt - v31 - Ja '97 - p19+ [251-500]
Walsh, Frank - *Sin and Censorship*
    CC - v113 - Ag 28 '96 - p821+ [501+]
    Choice - v34 - S '96 - p136 [51-250]
    Comw - v123 - O 25 '96 - p22+ [501+]
    New R - v215 - S 9 '96 - p47+ [501+]
    NS & S - v9 - Ap 26 '96 - p36+ [251-500]
    NYTBR - v102 - Ja 12 '97 - p28 [501+]
    RP - v59 - Win '97 - p153+ [501+]
    VQR - v72 - Aut '96 - p133* [51-250]
Walsh, Jerome T - *1 Kings*
    Am - v176 - Mr 8 '97 - p24 [51-250]
Walsh, Jim - *Everything You Need to Know about College Sports Recruiting*
    LJ - v122 - Ja '97 - p117 [51-250]
Walsh, John - *Jan Steen: The Drawing Lesson*
    NYTBR - v101 - D 8 '96 - p22 [51-250]
Walsh, John Evangelist - *Unraveling Piltdown*
    BL - v93 - S 1 '96 - p48 [51-250]
    BW - v26 - S 29 '96 - p9 [501+]
    LATBR - S 22 '96 - p3+ [501+]
    LJ - v122 - Ja '97 - p51 [51-250]
    New Sci - v152 - N 23 '96 - p45 [51-250]
    NYRB - v44 - F 6 '97 - p23+ [501+]
    NYTLa - v145 - S 11 '96 - pC17 [501+]
Walsh, Julia Montgomery - *Risks and Rewards*
    BW - v26 - S 15 '96 - p12 [51-250]
Walsh, Kenneth T - *Feeding the Beast*
    Choice - v34 - N '96 - p540 [51-250]

Walsh, Kieron - *Public Services and Market Mechanisms*
    Soc Ser R - v71 - Mr '97 - p167 [1-50]
Walsh, Lawrence - *They Would Never Be Friends*
 y VOYA - v19 - F '97 - p333 [251-500]
Walsh, Maria Elena - *Manuelita (Illus. by Sara Facio)*
 c SLJ - v42 - N '96 - p134 [51-250]
Walsh, Marrie - *An Irish Country Childhood*
    KR - v65 - Ja 15 '97 - p132 [51-250]
    LJ - v122 - Ja '97 - p110 [51-250]
    PW - v244 - F 17 '97 - p206 [51-250]
Walsh, Mary Roth - *Women, Men, and Gender*
    BL - v93 - O 1 '96 - p310 [51-250]
Walsh, Meeka - *The Garden of Earthly Intimacies*
    Quill & Q - v62 - D '96 - p34 [251-500]
Walsh, Mel - *Guerrilla Cooking*
    BL - v93 - S 15 '96 - p198 [51-250]
Walsh, Melanie - *Do Pigs Have Stripes? (Illus. by Melanie Walsh)*
 c HB Guide - v7 - Fall '96 - p245 [51-250]
 c Par - v71 - D '96 - p251 [1-50]
 c Par Ch - v20 - O '96 - p28 [51-250]
Walsh, Michael - *Exchange Alley*
    LJ - v122 - Ap 15 '97 - p121 [51-250]
    LJ - v122 - My 1 '97 - p142 [51-250]
Walsh, Micheline Kerney - *An Exile of Ireland*
    CHR - v83 - Ja '97 - p172 [51-250]
Walsh, Richard - *Novel Arguments*
    J Am St - v30 - Ag '96 - p332+ [251-500]
Walsh, Vivian - *Rationality, Allocation, and Reproduction*
    JEL - v35 - Mr '97 - p200 [51-250]
Walsham, Alexandra - *Church Papists*
    EHR - v111 - S '96 - p978+ [251-500]
Walt, Stephen M - *Revolution and War*
    BAS - v52 - S '96 - p60+ [501+]
Walter, James - *Tunnel Vision*
    Aust Bk R - F '97 - p14+ [501+]
Walter, Mildred Pitts - *Second Daughter*
 y Ch BWatch - v6 - My '96 - p5 [51-250]
 y Emerg Lib - v23 - My '96 - p43 [1-50]
 y HB Guide - v7 - Fall '96 - p306 [51-250]
Walter, Tony - *The Eclipse of Eternity*
    R&R Bk N - v11 - N '96 - p6 [51-250]
Walter, Virginia A - *Output Measures and More*
    Adoles - v32 - Spr '97 - p249 [51-250]
    LAR - v98 - Je '96 - p318 [51-250]
Walters, Celeste - *The Killing of Mud-Eye*
 y Aust Bk R - F '97 - p53 [501+]
Who's Who at the Zoo (Illus. by Patricia Mullins)
 c Magpies - v11 - Jl '96 - p37 [51-250]
Walters, Eric - *Stars*
 y Quill & Q - v62 - My '96 - p35 [501+]
Walters, Eugene - *The Smithsonian Guides to Natural America: The Mid-Atlantic States*
 yr Kliatt - v31 - Mr '97 - p33 [251-500]
Walters, Glen - *Escaping the Journey to Nowhere*
    Soc Ser R - v70 - S '96 - p491+ [501+]
Walters, Gregory J - *Human Rights in Theory and Practice*
 r LAR - v98 - Ag '96 - p428 [51-250]
Walters, James W - *Choosing Who's to Live*
    Choice - v34 - Mr '97 - p1192 [51-250]
    SB - v33 - Ja '97 - p5 [251-500]
Walters, John R - *Perfection in New Testament Theology*
    Rel St Rev - v23 - Ja '97 - p69 [51-250]
Walters, Lori J - *Lancelot and Guinevere*
    Choice - v34 - N '96 - p450 [51-250]
    R&R Bk N - v11 - N '96 - p66 [51-250]
Walters, Minette - *The Dark Room*
    LJ - v122 - My 1 '97 - p164 [51-250]
    NYTBR - v101 - Ap 7 '96 - p23 [51-250]
The Dark Room (Merlington). Audio Version
 y Kliatt - v31 - My '97 - p36 [51-250]
The Echo
 y BL - v93 - F 1 '97 - p907 [51-250]
    KR - v65 - Ja 15 '97 - p101 [51-250]
    NYTBR - v102 - Mr 16 '97 - p28 [51-250]
    PW - v244 - F 3 '97 - p93 [51-250]
    Spec - v278 - Ap 5 '97 - p38 [251-500]
    TLS - Mr 7 '97 - p21 [251-500]
    Trib Bks - Mr 2 '97 - p6 [51-250]
    Woman's J - F '97 - p16 [1-50]
Walters, Suzanna Danuta - *Material Girls*
    CS - v25 - N '96 - p818+ [251-500]
Walters Art Gallery (Baltimore, Md.) - *Medieval and Renaissance Manuscripts in the Walters Art Gallery. Vol. 2*
    BC - v45 - Sum '96 - p270+ [501+]
 r BM - v138 - Jl '96 - p469 [251-500]
Walth, Brent - *Fire at Eden's Gate*
    AHR - v102 - F '97 - p221+ [501+]

Waltham, John - *The Register of John Waltham, Bishop of Salisbury 1388-1395*
    EHR - v112 - Ap '97 - p447+ [501+]
Walther, Robert R - *Dermatology and Person-Threatening Illness*
    SciTech - v21 - Mr '97 - p66 [51-250]
Walther, Wiebke - *Women in Islam*
    Rel St Rev - v23 - Ap '97 - p201 [51-250]
Walton, Anthony - *Mississippi: An American Journey*
    Bl S - v26 - Sum '96 - p68 [51-250]
    Comw - v123 - My 17 '96 - p20+ [501+]
    NYTBR - v101 - D 8 '96 - p89 [1-50]
    PW - v244 - Ja 27 '97 - p103 [1-50]
Walton, Bill - *Nothing but Net*
    Aethlon - v13 - Fall '95 - p158+ [251-500]
Walton, Christine - *Critical Social Literacies*
    Aust Bk R - S '96 - p67 [251-500]
Walton, Douglas - *Argument Structure*
    R&R Bk N - v11 - D '96 - p2 [51-250]
Arguments from Ignorance
    Choice - v34 - O '96 - p295 [51-250]
Walton, Frank E - *Once They Were Eagles*
    VQR - v73 - Win '97 - p34* [1-50]
Walton, Izaak - *The Complete Angler*
    LJ - v122 - F 1 '97 - p112 [51-250]
Walton, J Michael, 1939- - *Menander and the Making of Comedy*
    Class Out - v74 - Win '97 - p76+ [501+]
Walton, John - *NVQ Handbook*
    TES - F 28 '97 - p32 [251-500]
Walton, John, 1937- - *Free Markets and Food Riots*
    APSR - v90 - S '96 - p708+ [501+]
    GJ - v162 - N '96 - p340 [51-250]
    JPR - v33 - Ag '96 - p384 [51-250]
Walton, John Nicholas - *Oxford Companion to Medicine*
 r BL - v93 - F 1 '97 - p957+ [51-250]
Walton, Mary - *Car: A Drama of the American Workplace*
    KR - v65 - Mr 15 '97 - p452 [251-500]
    PW - v244 - Ap 28 '97 - p64 [251-500]
Walton, Peter J - *Country Studies in International Accounting: Europe*
    JEL - v35 - Mr '97 - p257 [51-250]
    R&R Bk N - v11 - D '96 - p35 [51-250]
Walton, Priscilla L - *Patriarchal Desire and Victorian Discourse*
    VS - v39 - Spr '96 - p431+ [501+]
Walton, Richard E - *Strategic Negotiations*
    ILRR - v50 - Ap '97 - p511+ [251-500]
Walton, Rick - *How Many, How Many, How Many (Illus. by Cynthia Jabar)*
 c CLW - v67 - Mr '97 - p15 [1-50]
What to Do When a Bug Climbs in Your Mouth and Other Poems to Drive You Buggy (Illus. by Nancy Carlson)
 c RT - v50 - O '96 - p155 [51-250]
You Don't Always Get What You Hope For (Illus. by Heidi Stetson Mario)
 c SLJ - v42 - N '96 - p94+ [51-250]
Walton, Stuart - *The World Encyclopedia of Wine*
 r BL - v93 - N 15 '96 - p561 [51-250]
Walton, Whitney - *France at the Crystal Palace*
    JMH - v68 - S '96 - p703+ [501+]
Walton, William C - *Aquifer Test Analysis with Windows Software*
    SciTech - v21 - Mr '97 - p1 [51-250]
Waltz, David L - *Natural and Artificial Parallel Computation*
    SIAM Rev - v39 - Mr '97 - p175 [251-500]
Waltz, Susan E - *Human Rights and Reform*
    APSR - v90 - S '96 - p709+ [501+]
    MEJ - v50 - Sum '96 - p442+ [501+]
Waluchow, W J - *Free Expression*
    CPR - v16 - O '96 - p382+ [501+]
Walvin, James - *Questioning Slavery*
    HT - v46 - O '96 - p58+ [1-50]
Walz, D - *Bioelectrochemistry of Cells and Tissues*
    SciTech - v21 - Mr '97 - p41 [51-250]
Walz, Guido - *Asymptotics and Extrapolation*
    SciTech - v20 - N '96 - p14 [51-250]
Walzer, Kevin - *Living in Cincinnati*
    Sm Pr R - v28 - D '96 - p8 [251-500]
Walzer, Michael - *On Toleration*
    KR - v65 - Ap 1 '97 - p541 [251-500]
    PW - v244 - Ap 21 '97 - p55 [51-250]
Walzer, Norman - *Community Strategic Visioning Programs*
    R&R Bk N - v12 - F '97 - p52 [51-250]
Wambaugh, Joseph - *Floaters*
    PW - v244 - Mr 24 '97 - p81 [1-50]

Floaters (McLarty). Audio Version
   Arm Det - v30 - Win '97 - p81 [51-250]
Wamsley, Gary L - *Refounding Democratic Public Administration*
   Choice - v34 - Mr '97 - p1241 [51-250]
   R&R Bk N - v11 - N '96 - p48 [51-250]
Wanasz-Bialasiewicz, Ewa - *Beginner's Polish*
   MLJ - v80 - Fall '96 - p427+ [251-500]
Wand, Ian - *Computing Tomorrow*
   Choice - v34 - Ap '97 - p1373 [51-250]
   New Sci - v152 - O 19 '96 - p49 [51-250]
   SciTech - v20 - D '96 - p6 [51-250]
Wandel, Lee Palmer - *Voracious Idols and Violent Hands*
   Bks & Cult - v1 - N '95 - p30 [51-250]
   CH - v65 - D '96 - p693+ [501+]
   CHR - v82 - O '96 - p703+ [501+]
   JMH - v68 - D '96 - p1017+ [501+]
   Rel St Rev - v23 - Ja '97 - p81+ [51-250]
Wander, W Thomas - *The Diffusion of Advanced Weaponry*
   Parameters - v26 - Aut '96 - p146+ [501+]
Wandrei, Howard - *The Last Pin*
   PW - v243 - N 4 '96 - p67 [51-250]
Wanegffelen, T - *La France Et Les Francais XIVe-Milieu-XVIe Siecles*
   Rel St Rev - v23 - Ja '97 - p84 [51-250]
Wang, An-I - *Shang Xin*
   BL - v93 - My 1 '97 - p1484 [1-50]
Wang, C C - *Radiation Therapy for Head and Neck Neoplasms. 3rd Ed.*
   SciTech - v21 - Mr '97 - p51 [51-250]
Wang, Chien-Wei - *Managing Arms in Peace Processes: Cambodia*
   R&R Bk N - v12 - F '97 - p21 [1-50]
Wang, Chih-Hung - *Yi Ge Tai Wan Xiao Liu Xue Sheng Dao Ha Fo Zhi Lu*
   BL - v93 - My 1 '97 - p1484 [1-50]
Wang, Doris Yi-Hsin - *Productivity Analysis*
   JEL - v34 - S '96 - p1411+ [51-250]
Wang, Enbao - *Hong Kong 1997*
   Choice - v34 - O '96 - p355+ [51-250]
   FEER - v159 - D 12 '96 - p52+ [501+]
Wang, Gungwu - *Global History and Migrations*
   R&R Bk N - v12 - F '97 - p13 [51-250]
Hong Kong's Transition
   JEL - v34 - S '96 - p1490+ [51-250]
   WorldV - v12 - Jl '96 - p6+ [51-250]
Wang, Jen - *Mechanics Problems in Geodynamics. Pt. 1*
   SciTech - v20 - S '96 - p18 [1-50]
Wang, Jing - *High Culture Fever*
   CHE - v43 - O 4 '96 - pA18 [51-250]
   Choice - v34 - Mr '97 - p1217 [51-250]
Wang, Li-Xin - *A Course in Fuzzy Systems and Control*
   SciTech - v20 - D '96 - p12 [1-50]
Wang, Margaret C - *Handbook of Special and Remedial Education. 2nd Ed.*
   Choice - v34 - N '96 - p510 [51-250]
Wang, Ping - *Foreign Devil*
   BL - v93 - S 1 '96 - p63 [51-250]
   Ms - v7 - N '96 - p82+ [251-500]
Wang, Shaoguang - *Failure of Charisma*
   AJS - v102 - S '96 - p609+ [501+]
Wang, Shap - *Di Si Zhi Yan Jing Kan Zhong Guo*
   BL - v93 - N 1 '96 - p484 [1-50]
Wang, Shi-Ch'un - *Qian Shan Du Xing*
   BL - v93 - My 1 '97 - p1484 [1-50]
Wang, Shuo - *Playing for Thrills*
   KR - v65 - Ja 1 '97 - p26 [51-250]
   LJ - v122 - Ja '97 - p153 [51-250]
   PW - v243 - D 2 '96 - p43 [51-250]
Wang, T L - *Embryogenesis: The Generation of a Plant*
   Choice - v34 - Ja '97 - p818 [51-250]
Wang, Tao - *Exploration into China*
 c HB Guide - v7 - Fall '96 - p384 [51-250]
Wang, Thomas C - *Plan and Section Drawing. 2nd Ed.*
   LJ - v121 - N 15 '96 - p60+ [51-250]
Wang, Wen-Hsing - *Family Catastrophe*
   Ch Rev Int - v4 - Spr '97 - p281+ [501+]
Wang, Wun-Cheng - *Volatile Organic Compounds (VOCs) in the Environment*
   SciTech - v20 - D '96 - p68 [51-250]
Wang, X F - *Fluorescence Imaging Spectroscopy and Microscopy*
   Choice - v34 - Ja '97 - p822+ [51-250]
   SciTech - v20 - N '96 - p21 [51-250]
Wang, Yao - *Multimedia Communications and Video Coding*
   SciTech - v20 - N '96 - p7 [51-250]
Wang, Yung-Chun - *Investment in China*
   LJ - v121 - D '96 - p112 [51-250]

Wanger, Jack - *Pulmonary Function Testing. 2nd Ed.*
   SciTech - v20 - N '96 - p47 [51-250]
Wanger, Ralph - *A Zebra in Lion Country*
   LJ - v122 - Ap 15 '97 - p94 [51-250]
Wangerin, Walter - *Probity Jones and the Fear Not Angel (Illus. by Tim Ladwig)*
 c BL - v93 - D 15 '96 - p734 [51-250]
 c CC - v113 - D 11 '96 - p1234 [51-250]
 c HB Guide - v8 - Spr '97 - p52 [51-250]
 c PW - v243 - S 30 '96 - p92 [51-250]
 c PW - v243 - N 4 '96 - p47 [51-250]
Thistle (Illus. by Bryna Waldman)
 c HB Guide - v8 - Spr '97 - p61 [51-250]
Wangford, Hank - *Lost Cowboys*
   Obs - D 1 '96 - p18* [1-50]
Wank, Solomon - *Aus Dem Nachlass Aehrenthal. Pts. 1-2*
   JMH - v68 - D '96 - p1025+ [501+]
   Slav R - v55 - Sum '96 - p451+ [501+]
Wanner, Adrian - *Baudelaire in Russia*
   Choice - v34 - N '96 - p466 [51-250]
Wansell, Geoffrey - *Cary Grant: Dark Angel*
   NYTBR - v102 - Ap 13 '97 - p21 [1-50]
   PW - v244 - Ap 14 '97 - p66 [51-250]
An Evil Love
   Obs - S 29 '96 - p17* [501+]
Terence Rattigan: A Biography
   PW - v244 - Mr 17 '97 - p61 [51-250]
Waplington, Nick - *The Wedding: New Pictures from the Continuing Living Room Series*
   Afterimage - v24 - Ja '97 - p23 [1-50]
   NYTBR - v101 - S 22 '96 - p24 [51-250]
Wapner, Paul Kevin - *Environmental Activism and World Civic Politics*
   R&R Bk N - v12 - F '97 - p29 [1-50]
   SSQ - v78 - Mr '97 - p240+ [501+]
   WorldV - v12 - Jl '96 - p6 [51-250]
The War in Vietnam. Electronic Media Version
   Econ - v339 - My 18 '96 - p10*+ [251-500]
War Literature and the Arts
 p LMR - v15 - Win '96 - p28+ [501+]
Warbrick, Sarah - *Bendy*
 c Sch Lib - v44 - Ag '96 - p114 [51-250]
Squashy
 c Sch Lib - v44 - Ag '96 - p114 [51-250]
Sticky
 c Sch Lib - v44 - Ag '96 - p114 [51-250]
Warburg, Aby - *Images from the Region of the Pueblo Indians of North America*
   New R - v216 - Mr 24 '97 - p30+ [501+]
   WHQ - v28 - Spr '97 - p101 [1-50]
Warburton, Nick - *Ackford's Monster*
 c JB - v60 - Ag '96 - p162 [51-250]
 c Magpies - v11 - Jl '96 - p36 [51-250]
Dennis Dipp on Gilbert's Pond (Illus. by Arthur Robins)
 c JB - v60 - O '96 - p196 [51-250]
Warburton, Nigel - *Thinking from A-Z*
   R&R Bk N - v12 - F '97 - p4 [51-250]
Ward, Andrew - *Our Bones Are Scattered*
   CSM - v89 - Ja 30 '97 - pB1+ [501+]
   HRNB - v25 - Win '97 - p87 [251-500]
   Obs - Ag 25 '96 - p15* [501+]
   TLS - Ja 10 '97 - p11 [501+]
Ward, Ann - *Peter Rabbit and Friends Study Guide*
 c RSR - v24 - 3 '96 - p26 [51-250]
Ward, Brenda - *Counting on Angels (Illus. by Sandra Salzillo Shields)*
 c HB Guide - v7 - Fall '96 - p280 [51-250]
Ward, Christine - *Listening and Performing*
   TES - D 13 '96 - p43 [51-250]
Ward, Christopher - *Imperial Panama*
   HAHR - v77 - My '97 - p315 [251-500]
Ward, Geoffrey C - *Baseball: An Illustrated History*
   Aethlon - v13 - Fall '95 - p170+ [251-500]
 y Kliatt - v30 - N '96 - p31 [51-250]
Closest Companion
   SE - v60 - S '96 - p302 [51-250]
The West (Ward). Audio Version
   LJ - v121 - N 1 '96 - p122 [51-250]
The West: An Illustrated History
   Aud - v98 - S '96 - p110+ [501+]
   Bloom Rev - v16 - S '96 - p26+ [501+]
   HT - v47 - Ja '97 - p60 [51-250]
   KR - v64 - Ag 15 '96 - p1228 [51-250]
   LATBR - S 15 '96 - p1+ [501+]
   Obs - D 1 '96 - p18* [1-50]
   SFR - v21 - N '96 - p32 [501+]
   S Liv - v31 - O '96 - p108 [51-250]
   TES - D 6 '96 - p6* [501+]
Ward, Graham - *Barth, Derrida and the Language of Theology*
   CC - v113 - S 11 '96 - p870+ [251-500]

Ward, Ian - *Law and Literature*
   ABR - v17 - Ag '96 - p21+ [501+]
   TLS - Jl 19 '97 - p25 [501+]
Ward, James A - *The Fall of the Packard Motor Company*
   JEH - v56 - S '96 - p751+ [501+]
Ward, James F - *Heidegger's Political Thinking*
   Ethics - v107 - O '96 - p191 [251-500]
Ward, Jerry W - *Trouble the Water*
   BW - v27 - Ja 19 '97 - p12 [251-500]
 y Kliatt - v31 - Mr '97 - p24 [51-250]
Ward, John - *Principles of Information Systems Management*
   LR - v45 - 7 '96 - p65 [251-500]
Ward, John Powell - *Genesis*
   BL - v93 - Ja '97 - p810 [51-250]
Ward, Keith - *God, Chance and Necessity*
   BL - v93 - Mr 1 '97 - p1071 [51-250]
   Choice - v34 - My '97 - p1517 [51-250]
   LJ - v122 - F 15 '97 - p139 [51-250]
   PW - v244 - Mr 10 '97 - p63+ [51-250]
   TLS - F 7 '97 - p27 [501+]
Religion and Creation
   Choice - v34 - D '96 - p630+ [51-250]
   Rel St Rev - v23 - Ap '97 - p154 [51-250]
Religion and Revelation
   Rel St - v32 - S '96 - p417+ [501+]
Ward, Martha - *Pissarro, Neo-Impressionism, and the Spaces of the Avant-Garde*
 r Choice - v34 - N '96 - p447 [51-250]
Ward, Peter Douglas - *The Call of Distant Mammoths*
   LJ - v122 - Ap 1 '97 - p119 [51-250]
   PW - v244 - Mr 17 '97 - p71 [51-250]
The End of Evolution
   TLS - S 6 '96 - p29 [501+]
Ward, Philip - *Contemporary Designer Bookbinders*
 r LAR - v98 - O '96 - p537 [51-250]
Ward, Richard I - *Beechcraft Twin Bonanza*
   FSM - v15 - Ja '97 - p29+ [1-50]
Ward, Robert - *Shedding Skin*
   NYTBR - v101 - Ap 7 '96 - p24 [1-50]
Ward, Robin - *Echoes of Empire*
   Quill & Q - v63 - Ja '97 - p32 [251-500]
Ward, Steven C - *Reconfiguring Truth*
   Choice - v34 - My '97 - p1514 [51-250]
Ward, Tim - *Arousing the Goddess*
   Quill & Q - v62 - My '96 - p26 [251-500]
Ward, W R - *Parson and Parish in Eighteenth-Century Hampshire*
   EHR - v112 - F '97 - p212+ [501+]
Parson and Parish in Eighteenth-Century Surrey
   EHR - v112 - F '97 - p212+ [501+]
The Protestant Evangelical Awakening
   JR - v77 - Ap '97 - p268+ [501+]
Warde, John - *The Healthy Home Handbook*
   BL - v93 - F 1 '97 - p916 [51-250]
The New York Times Season-by-Season Guide to Home Maintenance
 r LJ - v122 - F 1 '97 - p52 [1-50]
Wardin, Albert W - *Baptists around the World*
 r CH - v65 - D '96 - p783+ [501+]
Evangelical Sectarianism in the Russian Empire and the USSR
 r ARBA - v28 - '97 - p534 [51-250]
Wardlaw, Lee - *101 Ways to Bug Your Parents*
 c BL - v93 - O 1 '96 - p353 [51-250]
 c CCB-B - v50 - N '96 - p118 [51-250]
 c HB Guide - v8 - Spr '97 - p76 [51-250]
 c KR - v64 - O 1 '96 - p1475 [51-250]
 c SLJ - v42 - O '96 - p128 [51-250]
Punia and the King of Sharks (Illus. by Felipe Davalos)
 c BL - v93 - D 1 '96 - p667+ [51-250]
 c CCB-B - v50 - F '97 - p225 [51-250]
 c Ch BWatch - v7 - F '97 - p3 [1-50]
 c KR - v64 - D 15 '96 - p1806 [51-250]
 c PW - v243 - D 9 '96 - p68 [51-250]
 c SLJ - v43 - Ja '97 - p109+ [51-250]
Wardley, Rachel - *Usborne First Dictionary*
 cr Bks Keeps - v100 - S '96 - p22+ [501+]
Wardlow, Daniel L - *Gays, Lesbians, and Consumer Behavior*
   JEL - v34 - D '96 - p2025 [51-250]
   R&R Bk N - v11 - D '96 - p34 [51-250]
Wardrop, Daneen - *Emily Dickinson's Gothic*
   Choice - v34 - Ja '97 - p800 [51-250]
   Nine-C Lit - v51 - Mr '97 - p567 [1-50]
Wardwell, Allen - *Tangible Visions*
   Atl - v278 - Ag '96 - p94 [51-250]
Ware, Ann Patrick - *Naming Our Truth*
   RR - v55 - S '96 - p542+ [501+]

Ware, Cheryl - *Sea Monkey Summer*
 c HB Guide - v7 - Fall '96 - p298 [51-250]
 y NY - v72 - N 18 '96 - p102 [1-50]
Ware, Derek - *Stunt Performers*
 c Ch BWatch - v6 - Jl '96 - p6 [51-250]
Ware, Mark E - *Handbook of Demonstrations and Activities in the Teaching of Psychology. Vols. 1-3*
 SB - v32 - O '96 - p196+ [51-250]
Ware, Shirley Gerald - *The Final Goodbye*
 y Kliatt - v30 - S '96 - p27 [51-250]
Wargo, John - *Our Children's Toxic Legacy*
 Am Sci - v85 - Mr '97 - p195+ [501+]
 BL - v93 - S 1 '96 - p33 [51-250]
 BW - v26 - D 29 '96 - p8 [51-250]
 Choice - v34 - F '97 - p998 [51-250]
 LATBR - N 10 '96 - p8 [501+]
 LJ - v122 - Ja '97 - p123 [51-250]
 New Sci - v153 - F 8 '97 - p44 [251-500]
 NH - v106 - F '97 - p13 [1-50]
 NYRB - v44 - F 20 '97 - p30+ [501+]
 Sci - v274 - O 4 '96 - p61+ [501+]
Warhus, Mark - *Another America*
 KR - v65 - Mr 1 '97 - p369+ [51-250]
 LJ - v122 - My 1 '97 - p122 [51-250]
Waring, Robert - *Totally Unauthorized Guide to Doom II*
 Quill & Q - v62 - Ag '96 - p22 [501+]
Warkentin, Erwin J - *Unpublishable Works*
 Choice - v34 - My '97 - p1503 [51-250]
Warlick, Ashley - *The Distance from the Heart of Things*
 Choice - v34 - S '96 - p130 [51-250]
 LJ - v121 - O 1 '96 - p48 [1-50]
 NYTBR - v101 - S 22 '96 - p36 [501+]
 Rapport - v19 - 4 '96 - p25 [51-250]
 y SLJ - v42 - Ag '96 - p185 [51-250]
 Trib Bks - My 25 '97 - p8 [1-50]
Warloe, Constance - *I've Always Meant to Tell You*
 KR - v65 - Mr 1 '97 - p370 [51-250]
 LJ - v122 - Ap 15 '97 - p81 [51-250]
Warlow, Charles - *Stroke: A Practical Guide to Management*
 SciTech - v21 - Mr '97 - p52 [51-250]
Warme, Lars G - *A History of Swedish Literature*
 AB - v98 - D 2 '96 - p1924 [251-500]
 Choice - v34 - Ja '97 - p801 [51-250]
 TLS - N 29 '96 - p25 [501+]
Warn, Emily - *The Novice Insomniac*
 Parabola - v22 - F '97 - p114+ [251-500]
 PW - v243 - Jl 22 '96 - p237 [51-250]
Warnatz, J - *Combustion: Physical and Chemical Fundamentals, Modelling and Simulation, Experiments, Pollutant Formation*
 Choice - v34 - O '96 - p310 [51-250]
Warneford, F E - *Star Chamber Suits of John and Thomas Warneford*
 EHR - v111 - S '96 - p973+ [251-500]
Warneke, Sara - *Images of the Educational Traveller in Early Modern England*
 Ren Q - v49 - Aut '96 - p645+ [501+]
Warner, Alan - *Morvern Callar*
 BL - v93 - F 15 '97 - p1005 [51-250]
 Econ - v343 - Ap 26 '97 - p83+ [501+]
 KR - v65 - Ja 1 '97 - p18 [251-500]
 LJ - v122 - F 1 '97 - p109 [51-250]
 PW - v244 - Ja 27 '97 - p76+ [51-250]
 These Demented Lands
 NS - v126 - Ap 25 '97 - p54 [501+]
 Obs - Mr 23 '97 - p17* [501+]
Warner, Brian - *Cataclysmic Variable Stars*
 Phys Today - v49 - N '96 - p88+ [501+]
Warner, Deborah Jean - *Alvan Clark and Sons*
 S&T - v92 - O '96 - p55+ [501+]
Warner, Elizabeth - *Heroes, Monsters, and Other Worlds from Russian Mythology (Illus. by Alexander Koshkin)*
 y HB Guide - v7 - Fall '96 - p325 [51-250]
Warner, Jack - *The Unauthorized Teacher's Survival Guide*
 Rapport - v19 - 4 '96 - p42 [251-500]
Warner, Malcolm - *International Encyclopedia of Business and Management. Vols. 1-6*
 r BL - v93 - N 15 '96 - p606+ [251-500]
 r Choice - v34 - F '97 - p946 [51-250]
 r LAR - v98 - Ag '96 - p424 [251-500]
 The Management of Human Resources in Chinese Industry
 ILRR - v50 - Ap '97 - p533+ [501+]
Warner, Malcolm, 1953- - *The Victorians: British Painting 1837-1901*
 LJ - v122 - Ap 15 '97 - p78 [51-250]
Warner, Marina - *Alone of All Her Sex*
 HR - v49 - Sum '96 - p309+ [501+]

From the Beast to the Blonde
 HR - v49 - Sum '96 - p309+ [501+]
 NYTBR - v101 - D 29 '96 - p20 [1-50]
Six Myths of Our Time
 Rel St Rev - v22 - O '96 - p344 [51-250]
Wonder Tales
 KR - v64 - S 1 '96 - p1267 [51-250]
 LJ - v121 - O 1 '96 - p78 [51-250]
 Parabola - v22 - F '97 - p120 [1-50]
 PW - v243 - S 2 '96 - p111+ [51-250]
Warner, Michael - *Changing Witness*
 CHR - v83 - Ja '97 - p146+ [251-500]
 RP - v59 - Spr '97 - p377+ [501+]
Warner, Rachel - *Refugees*
 y Sch Lib - v44 - Ag '96 - p127 [51-250]
Warner, Ralph - *Get a Life*
 BL - v92 - Ag '96 - p1866 [51-250]
Warner, Richard - *Alternatives to the Hospital for Acute Psychiatric Treatment*
 J ClinPsyc - v57 - Ag '96 - p375+ [501+]
Warner, Roger - *Back Fire: The CIA's Secret War in Laos and Its Link to the War in Vietnam*
 Arm F&S - v22 - Sum '96 - p643+ [501+]
 NS & S - v9 - My 3 '96 - p36+ [501+]
 Pac A - v69 - Sum '96 - p284+ [501+]
 Shooting at the Moon
 NYTBR - v102 - Mr 16 '97 - p18 [501+]
 WorldV - v13 - Ja '97 - p10 [251-500]
Warner, Sally - *Ellie and the Bunheads*
 c PW - v244 - Ap 14 '97 - p76 [51-250]
 Some Friend
 c CCB-B - v50 - S '96 - p35 [51-250]
 c HB Guide - v7 - Fall '96 - p298 [51-250]
 c KR - v64 - My 1 '96 - p694 [51-250]
Warner, Simon - *Rockspeak: The Language of Rock and Pop*
 r BL - v93 - S 15 '96 - p284+ [51-250]
Warnke, Georgia - *Justice and Interpretation*
 JC - v47 - Win '97 - p128+ [501+]
Warnock, Ian - *Manufacturing and Business Excellence*
 r R&R Bk N - v11 - D '96 - p71 [51-250]
Warr, Michael - *Coloured Pencils for All*
 y BL - v93 - Mr 15 '97 - p1219 [51-250]
 LJ - v122 - Mr 15 '97 - p63 [51-250]
Warr, Peter G - *Thailand's Macroeconomic Miracle*
 Choice - v34 - Ap '97 - p1390 [51-250]
Warren, Alan - *This Is a Thriller*
 r ARBA - v28 - '97 - p518 [51-250]
 R&R Bk N - v12 - F '97 - p81 [51-250]
Warren, Andrea - *Everybody's Doing It*
 VOYA - v19 - D '96 - p256 [1-50]
 Orphan Train Rider
 c BL - v93 - Ap 1 '97 - p1302 [1-50]
 c CCB-B - v50 - S '96 - p35 [51-250]
 c HB Guide - v8 - Spr '97 - p176 [51-250]
 c RT - v50 - My '97 - p682 [51-250]
 c SLJ - v42 - Ag '96 - p162 [51-250]
 c SLJ - v42 - D '96 - p32 [1-50]
Warren, Ann - *Dust for Dinner (Illus. by Robert Barrett)*
 c RT - v50 - D '96 - p344 [51-250]
 Rosemary's Witch
 c SLJ - v42 - N '96 - p41 [1-50]
Warren, Austin - *Becoming What One Is*
 Sew R - v104 - O '96 - p692+ [501+]
Warren, Betsy - *Moses Austin and Stephen F. Austin*
 c HB Guide - v8 - Spr '97 - p162 [51-250]
Warren, Charles - *Beyond Document*
 Choice - v34 - N '96 - p467 [51-250]
Warren, Donald - *Radio Priest*
 BW - v26 - Ag 4 '96 - p4 [501+]
 KR - v64 - My 1 '96 - p680 [251-500]
 NYTBR - v101 - Ag 25 '96 - p20 [501+]
Warren, Elizabeth V - *Glorious American Quilts*
 Am Craft - v56 - D '96 - p33 [51-250]
Warren, Ernst - *Presenting ActiveX*
 New Sci - v153 - Ja 18 '97 - p41 [51-250]
Warren, Garry W - *EPD Congress 1996*
 SciTech - v20 - D '96 - p82 [51-250]
Warren, Gretchen Ward - *The Art of Teaching Ballet*
 Choice - v34 - My '97 - p1511 [51-250]
 LJ - v121 - D '96 - p97 [51-250]
Warren, James A - *Cold War*
 y BL - v93 - Ja '97 - p857 [51-250]
 y CCB-B - v50 - F '97 - p225+ [51-250]
 y HB Guide - v8 - Spr '97 - p168 [51-250]
 y SLJ - v42 - O '96 - p161 [51-250]
Warren, Karen J - *Bringing Peace Home*
 Choice - v34 - My '97 - p1566 [51-250]
Warren, Kenneth - *Triumphant Capitalism*
 Choice - v34 - F '97 - p1009 [51-250]

Warren, Larry - *Left at East Gate*
 PW - v244 - Ap 14 '97 - p68 [51-250]
Warren, Lynne - *Art in Chicago 1945-1995*
 BL - v93 - Ja '97 - p758 [1-50]
 BL - v93 - D 1 '96 - p637 [51-250]
 Choice - v34 - Ap '97 - p1324 [51-250]
Warren, Patricia - *British Film Studios*
 r ARBA - v28 - '97 - p519 [51-250]
Warren, Paul - *Caleb Beldragon's Chronicle of the Three Counties*
 c HB Guide - v8 - Spr '97 - p76 [51-250]
 Muffin Pigdoom and the Keeper
 c HB Guide - v7 - Fall '96 - p280 [51-250]
Warren, Preston - *Out of the Wilderness*
 Dialogue - v35 - Sum '96 - p628+ [51-250]
Warren, Raymond - *Opera Workshop*
 Notes - v53 - D '96 - p480 [501+]
Warren, Rebecca Lowe - *The Scientist within You. Vol. 1, Rev. Ed.*
 c SLMQ - v24 - Sum '96 - p222 [51-250]
 The Scientist within You. Vol. 1, Rev. Ed.; Vol. 2
 yr JAAL - v40 - D '96 - p328 [51-250]
Warren, Robert Penn - *All the King's Men*
 Am - v175 - D 28 '96 - p26+ [501+]
Warrick, R A - *The Implications of Climate and Sea-Level Change for Bangladesh*
 SciTech - v21 - Mr '97 - p26 [51-250]
Warrington, Freda - *Dark Cathedral*
 Books - v10 - Je '96 - p24 [51-250]
Warry, John - *Warfare in the Classical World*
 r Class Out - v74 - Fall '96 - p42 [251-500]
Warschauer, Mark - *E-Mail for English Teaching*
 MLJ - v81 - Spr '97 - p126+ [501+]
 Virtual Connections
 MLJ - v81 - Spr '97 - p119+ [501+]
Warshaw, Shirley Anne - *Powersharing: White House-Cabinet Relations in the Modern Presidency*
 APSR - v91 - Mr '97 - p202+ [501+]
 Choice - v34 - D '96 - p691 [51-250]
 Pres SQ - v27 - Win '97 - p174+ [501+]
Wartell, Matthew L - *Blood of Our Children*
 y Ch BWatch - v6 - Jl '96 - p1 [51-250]
Warton, Thomas - *The Correspondence of Thomas Warton*
 Lon R Bks - v18 - S 19 '96 - p19 [501+]
Wartski, Maureen - *Candle in the Wind*
 y CLW - v66 - Je '96 - p54 [51-250]
 Runaway
 y Kliatt - v31 - My '97 - p10 [51-250]
Warwick, Kevin - *March of the Machines*
 NS - v126 - Ap 25 '97 - p50 [501+]
Warwick, Paul V - *Government Survival in Parliamentary Democracies*
 APSR - v90 - S '96 - p689+ [501+]
 J Pol - v58 - N '96 - p1244+ [501+]
Warwick, Robert T - *Using OCLC under PRISM*
 LJ - v122 - My 1 '97 - p146 [51-250]
Wasafiri
 p LMR - v15 - Win '96 - p33+ [501+]
Wasby, Stephen L - *Race Relations Litigation in an Age of Complexity*
 APSR - v91 - Mr '97 - p203+ [501+]
 J Pol - v58 - N '96 - p1224+ [501+]
 JSH - v63 - F '97 - p204 [501+]
 R&R Bk N - v11 - D '96 - p52 [51-250]
Waschescio, Petra - *Vernunftkritik und Patriarchatskritik*
 Ger Q - v70 - Win '97 - p92+ [501+]
Waselkov, Gregory A - *William Bartram on the Southeastern Indians*
 JSH - v63 - F '97 - p148+ [501+]
Washabaugh, William - *Flamenco: Passion, Politics and Popular Culture*
 TLS - Ja 31 '97 - p29 [251-500]
Washburn, David E - *The Multicultural Education Directory*
 r BL - v93 - Mr 15 '97 - p1258+ [51-250]
 r BWatch - v18 - F '97 - p9 [51-250]
 r Choice - v34 - My '97 - p1481 [51-250]
 Multicultural Education in the U.S.
 BWatch - v18 - F '97 - p9 [51-250]
Washburn, James - *The Piedmont Conspiracy*
 PW - v243 - N 4 '96 - p65+ [51-250]
Washburn, Katharine - *Dumbing Down*
 BL - v93 - Ja '97 - p808 [1-50]
 CAY - v17 - Win '96 - p9 [51-250]
 HMR - Fall '96 - p8+ [501+]
 NS - v126 - Ja 10 '97 - p47+ [501+]
 Obs - Ja 26 '97 - p16* [501+]
 TES - F 14 '97 - p8* [501+]
 TLS - F 14 '97 - p15 [501+]

Washburn, Michael - *The Ego and the Dynamic Ground. 2nd Ed., Rev.*
  Rel St Rev - v22 - O '96 - p334 [51-250]
Washburne, Carolyn Kott - *Drug Abuse*
  y HB Guide - v7 - Fall '96 - p318 [1-50]
Washington, Donna L - *The Story of Kwanzaa (Illus. by Stephen Taylor)*
  c BL - v93 - S 1 '96 - p138 [51-250]
  c CBRS - v25 - O '96 - p20 [51-250]
  c HB Guide - v8 - Spr '97 - p99 [51-250]
  c KR - v64 - S 15 '96 - p1409 [51-250]
  c PW - v243 - S 30 '96 - p88 [51-250]
  c SFR - v21 - N '96 - p47 [1-50]
  c SLJ - v42 - O '96 - p42 [51-250]
Washington, George - *The Papers of George Washington*
  R&R Bk N - v12 - F '97 - p24 [1-50]
The Papers of George Washington: Colonial Series. Vols. 7-10
  JSH - v62 - N '96 - p795+ [501+]
Rules of Civility
  BL - v93 - Mr 15 '97 - p1209 [51-250]
  Nat R - v49 - Ap 21 '97 - p78 [51-250]
  Spec - v278 - F 15 '97 - p20 [501+]
Writings
  LATBR - F 23 '97 - p3 [501+]
  LJ - v122 - Ap 1 '97 - p134 [1-50]
  PW - v244 - Ja 13 '97 - p65+ [51-250]
Washington, Jerome - *Iron House*
  WAL - v31 - Sum '96 - p180+ [251-500]
Iron House (Washington). Audio Version
  BL - v93 - N 15 '96 - p603+ [51-250]
  Bloom Rev - v16 - S '96 - p21 [1-50]
  y Kliatt - v31 - Ja '97 - p49 [51-250]
Washington, Peter - *Madame Blavatsky's Baboon*
  New Sci - v153 - F 1 '97 - p48 [51-250]
  NYRB - v43 - S 19 '96 - p26+ [501+]
  NYRB - v43 - O 3 '96 - p38+ [501+]
Washington 96
  r R&R Bk N - v11 - N '96 - p1 [51-250]
The Washington Almanac of International Trade and Business 1995/96
  r ARBA - v28 - '97 - p109 [251-500]
  r Choice - v34 - O '96 - p259 [51-250]
Washington Representatives 1996
  r R&R Bk N - v11 - D '96 - p45 [51-250]
Washington State Association for Supervision and Curriculum Development - *R and R for American Schools*
  EL - v54 - S '96 - p106 [51-250]
Washington University (St. Louis, MO) - *The John Max Wulfing Collection in Washington University. Vol. 3*
  r ARBA - v28 - '97 - p358+ [51-250]
Wasko, Janet - *Hollywood in the Information Age*
  FQ - v49 - Sum '96 - p46+ [501+]
Waskow, Arthur - *Down to Earth Judaism*
  Tikkun - v11 - Jl '96 - p71+ [501+]
Godwrestling: Round 2
  Tikkun - v11 - Jl '96 - p71+ [501+]
Wasley, Patricia A - *Stirring the Chalkdust*
  EL - v54 - S '96 - p88 [251-500]
Wasman, Ann - *Best Kept Secrets*
  Emerg Lib - v24 - Mr '97 - p39 [51-250]
  Sch Lib - v45 - F '97 - p55 [51-250]
Wason, Paul K - *The Archaeology of Rank*
  Am Ant - v61 - Ap '96 - p423+ [501+]
Wasserman, Harriet - *Handsome Is*
  PW - v244 - Ap 28 '97 - p60 [251-500]
Wasserman, Pamela - *People and the Planet*
  c SB - v33 - My '97 - p109 [251-500]
Wasserman, Renata R Mautner - *Exotic Nations*
  CLS - v33 - 4 '96 - p423+ [501+]
  Col Lit - v23 - Je '96 - p197+ [501+]
Wasserman, Stanley - *Social Network Analysis*
  Am Ethnol - v24 - F '97 - p219+ [501+]
Wassermann, Selma - *The New Teaching Elementary Science*
  Cur R - v35 - S '96 - p3* [51-250]
Wasserstein, David J - *The Caliphate in the West*
  J Ch St - v38 - Sum '96 - p661+ [251-500]
Wasserstein, Wendy - *Pamela's First Musical (Illus. by Andrew Jackness)*
  c Am Theat - v13 - D '96 - p20 [1-50]
  c HB Guide - v7 - Fall '96 - p288 [51-250]
Wasserstrom, Steven M - *Between Muslim and Jew*
  Rel St Rev - v23 - Ap '97 - p199 [51-250]
Wassmo, Herbjorg - *The House with the Blind Glass Windows*
  TranslRevS - v1 - My '95 - p6 [51-250]
Wastberg, Per - *Fortojningar*
  WLT v71 Win '97 p175 [251-500]

Waswo, Richard - *The Founding Legend of Western Civilization*
  LJ - v122 - My 1 '97 - p122 [51-250]
Watanabe, Sylvia - *Into the Fire*
  Sm Pr R - v28 - O '96 - p9 [51-250]
Water, the Source of Life
  c HB Guide - v7 - Fall '96 - p333 [51-250]
Waterbeemd, Han Van De - *Structure-Property Correlations in Drug Research*
  SciTech - v20 - N '96 - p56 [51-250]
Waterhouse, Debra - *Like Mother, Like Daughter*
  BL - v93 - Ja '97 - p800 [51-250]
  LJ - v121 - D '96 - p134+ [51-250]
  PW - v243 - N 11 '96 - p64+ [51-250]
Waterhouse, Jane - *Graven Images*
  Arm Det - v30 - Win '97 - p19+ [51-250]
Waterhouse, Keith - *Good Grief*
  Spec - v278 - Mr 15 '97 - p40 [501+]
Waterlow, Julia - *The Atlantic Ocean*
  c SB - v33 - Mr '97 - p49 [51-250]
Grasslands
  c HB Guide - v8 - Spr '97 - p118 [51-250]
  c Magpies - v11 - Jl '96 - p38 [1-50]
  c SB - v33 - Mr '97 - p50 [251-500]
Islands
  c Magpies - v11 - Jl '96 - p38 [1-50]
Waterman, A M C - *Religion, Economics, and Revolution*
  CH - v66 - Mr '97 - p144+ [501+]
Waters, Alice - *Chez Panisse Vegetables*
  Hort - v74 - D '96 - p61 [51-250]
  PW - v243 - N 4 '96 - p47 [1-50]
  Quill & Q - v62 - Ag '96 - p30 [51-250]
Waters, Annie - *Glimmer*
  y BL - v93 - My 1 '97 - p1481 [51-250]
  KR - v65 - Ap 1 '97 - p502 [251-500]
  LJ - v122 - My 1 '97 - p142 [51-250]
  PW - v244 - Ap 14 '97 - p53 [51-250]
Waters, Fiona - *Glitter When You Jump (Illus. by Amanda Harvey)*
  c Sch Lib - v44 - Ag '96 - p116 [51-250]
  c TES - N 8 '96 - p10* [501+]
The Poetry Book (Illus. by Caroline Crossland)
  c JB - v60 - D '96 - p276 [51-250]
  c Sch Lib - v45 - F '97 - p43+ [51-250]
  c TES - N 8 '96 - p10* [501+]
Waters, John - *Race of Angels*
  Notes - v53 - D '96 - p483+ [501+]
Waters, Kate - *On the Mayflower (Illus. by Russ Kendall)*
  c BL - v93 - O 1 '96 - p346 [51-250]
  c HB Guide - v8 - Spr '97 - p52 [51-250]
  c SLJ - v42 - O '96 - p109 [51-250]
Tapenum's Day (Illus. by Russ Kendall)
  c HB Guide - v7 - Fall '96 - p392 [51-250]
Waters, Malcolm - *Daniel Bell*
  Choice - v34 - S '96 - p220 [51-250]
  JEL - v35 - Mr '97 - p306 [51-250]
  Socio R - v44 - N '96 - p769+ [501+]
Waters, Malcolm, 1946- - *Globalization*
  CS - v25 - S '96 - p585+ [501+]
Waters, Michael - *Green Ash, Red Maple, Black Gum*
  PW - v244 - F 24 '97 - p85 [51-250]
Waters, T F - *Fundamentals of Manufacturing for Engineers*
  Choice - v34 - Ja '97 - p827 [51-250]
Watkin, Absalom - *The Diaries of Absalom Watkin*
  EHR - v111 - S '96 - p1001+ [251-500]
Watkin, Barry - *Exploring Pastel with Barry Watkin*
  LJ - v122 - Mr 15 '97 - p62 [51-250]
Watkin, David - *Sir John Soane: Enlightenment Thought and the Royal Academy Lectures*
  Apo - v144 - D '96 - p68 [51-250]
  Choice - v34 - Mr '97 - p1154 [51-250]
  LJ - v122 - Ja '97 - p94 [51-250]
  Obs - D 1 '96 - p17* [1-50]
  TLS - N 8 '96 - p7+ [501+]
Watkins, Bonnie - *In the Company of Women*
  BWatch - v17 - N '96 - p6 [51-250]
  LJ - v121 - S 15 '96 - p84 [51-250]
Watkins, Calvert - *How to Kill a Dragon*
  Class Out - v74 - Spr '97 - p123 [501+]
Watkins, Daniel P - *A Materialist Critique of English Romantic Drama*
  RES - v47 - N '96 - p599+ [501+]
  South HR - v30 - Sum '96 - p290+ [501+]
Sexual Power in British Romantic Poetry
  Choice - v34 - D '96 - p617 [51-250]
  Nine-C Lit - v51 - Mr '97 - p567 [51-250]
Watkins, Graham - *Interception*
  KR - v65 - F 15 '97 - p254 [251-500]
  PW - v244 - Mr 3 '97 - p65 [51-250]
  Trib Bks - Mr 16 '97 - p6 [51-250]

Watkins, James - *Death and Beyond*
  y VOYA - v19 - F '97 - p319 [51-250]
Watkins, Joanne C - *Spirited Women*
  Choice - v34 - Ja '97 - p840 [51-250]
Watkins, John - *The Specter of Dido*
  Comp L - v49 - Win '97 - p90+ [501+]
  Six Ct J - v27 - Fall '96 - p969+ [501+]
Watkins, Marilyn P - *Rural Democracy*
  PHR - v66 - F '97 - p119+ [501+]
  WHQ - v28 - Spr '97 - p93+ [251-500]
Watkins, Paul - *Archangel*
  y Kliatt - v31 - My '97 - p10 [51-250]
  Obs - S 1 '96 - p18* [51-250]
Calm at Sunset, Calm at Dawn
  NYTBR - v102 - Ja 5 '97 - p28 [51-250]
Watkins, Sherrin - *Green Snake Ceremony (Illus. by Kim Doner)*
  c HB Guide - v7 - Fall '96 - p280 [51-250]
  c SLJ - v42 - D '96 - p109 [51-250]
Watkins, Susan - *Jane Austen in Style*
  CR - v269 - D '96 - p334 [1-50]
Watkins, Susan Cotts - *After Ellis Island*
  JIH - v27 - Aut '96 - p352+ [251-500]
Watkins, T H - *The Great Depression*
  y SE - v60 - S '96 - p303 [1-50]
Watkins, William John - *Cosmic Thunder*
  Analog - v117 - Ap '97 - p147+ [251-500]
Watkinson, Anthony - *Interventional Radiology*
  SciTech - v20 - N '96 - p49 [51-250]
Watkinson, John - *Television Fundamentals*
  SciTech - v20 - N '96 - p74 [51-250]
Watkins-Owens, Irma - *Blood Relations*
  Bl S - v26 - Fall '96 - p107 [51-250]
  Choice - v34 - O '96 - p352 [51-250]
Watkiss, Leslie - *The Waltham Chronicle*
  Albion - v28 - Win '96 - p662+ [501+]
  EHR - v112 - F '97 - p161+ [501+]
  Specu - v72 - Ja '97 - p237+ [501+]
Watnik, Webster - *Child Custody Made Simple*
  LJ - v122 - My 1 '97 - p123 [51-250]
Watring, Anna Miller - *Civil War Burials in Baltimore's Loudon Park Cemetery*
  r EGH - v50 - N '96 - p170 [51-250]
Watson, Alan - *Jesus the Jew*
  Rel St Rev - v23 - Ja '97 - p70 [51-250]
Watson, Alan D - *Onslow County*
  Pub Hist - v18 - Fall '96 - p160+ [501+]
Watson, Benjamin - *Taylor's Guide to Heirloom Vegetables*
  r ARBA - v28 - '97 - p573 [51-250]
Watson, Brad - *Last Days of the Dog-Men*
  Books - v11 - Ap '97 - p22 [51-250]
  Choice - v34 - O '96 - p283 [51-250]
  Dog Fan - v28 - Ja '97 - p36 [51-250]
  LATBR - Jl 7 '96 - p11 [51-250]
  NYTBR - v101 - D 8 '96 - p80 [1-50]
  SFR - v21 - Jl '96 - p4 [251-500]
  S Liv - v31 - Jl '96 - p80 [51-250]
Watson, Bruce Allen - *Desert Battle*
  MEJ - v50 - Aut '96 - p613+ [501+]
Watson, Carol - *Christian*
  c Sch Lib - v44 - N '96 - p166 [51-250]
  c TES - F 14 '97 - p16* [51-250]
First Bible Stories (Illus. by Kim Woolley)
  c HB Guide - v7 - Fall '96 - p309 [51-250]
Watson, Charles S - *From Nationalism to Secessionism*
  JSH - v63 - F '97 - p171+ [501+]
Watson, David - *Self-Directed Behavior*
  r BWatch - v18 - F '97 - p11 [51-250]
Watson, Derek - *Molotov and Soviet Government*
  r Choice - v34 - Mr '97 - p1225 [51-250]
  R&R Bk N - v12 - F '97 - p61 [1-50]
Watson, Donald - *A Dictionary of Mind and Body*
  r Choice - v34 - Ja '97 - p776 [51-250]
Watson, Douglas J - *The Politics of Redistributing Urban Aid*
  Pol Stud J - v24 - Sum '96 - p327+ [501+]
Watson, Elizabeth See - *Achille Bocchi and the Emblem Book as Symbolic Form*
  MLR - v92 - Ap '97 - p442+ [501+]
  Ren Q - v49 - Aut '96 - p673+ [501+]
  Ren & Ref - v19 - Fall '96 - p88+ [501+]
Watson, Esther - *Talking to Angels*
  c HB Guide - v7 - Fall '96 - p349 [1-50]
Watson, Francis - *Text, Church and World*
  Theol St - v57 - S '96 - p522+ [501+]
Watson, George, 1927- - *Lord Acton's History of Liberty*
  EHR - v111 - N '96 - p1331+ [251-500]
Watson, George J - *Irish Identity and the Literary Revival. 2nd Ed.*
  Col Lit - v23 - O '96 - p163+ [501+]

Watson, George L - *Shaping America*
PSQ - v111 - Fall '96 - p545 [501+]

Watson, Hugh J - *Building Executive Information Systems and Other Decision Support Applications*
SciTech - v21 - Mr '97 - p72 [51-250]

Watson, Ian - *Catawba Indian Genealogy*
Am Geneal - v71 - Jl '96 - p190+ [501+]
NGSQ - v84 - S '96 - p224+ [251-500]

Watson, Ian, 1943- - *Slow Birds (Bond). Audio Version*
BL - v93 - D 15 '96 - p740 [51-250]

Watson, James, Chief - *Walking Point*
y BL - v93 - Mr 15 '97 - p1209 [51-250]
LJ - v122 - Ap 1 '97 - p108 [51-250]

Watson, James, 1936- - *A Dictionary of Communication and Media Studies. 4th Ed.*
r LJ - v122 - Ap 15 '97 - p74 [51-250]

Watson, James D, 1928- - *The Double Helix*
Nature - v386 - Mr 27 '97 - p344+ [501+]

Watson, Janet C E - *Lexicon of Arabic Horse Terminology*
r R&R Bk N - v11 - D '96 - p70 [51-250]

Watson, Larry - *Justice*
WAL - v31 - Sum '96 - p178 [251-500]
Justice (Bridges). Audio Version
y Kliatt - v31 - Ja '97 - p42 [51-250]
LJ - v121 - N 15 '96 - p104+ [51-250]
Montana 1948
Books - v9 - S '95 - p22 [1-50]
White Crosses
BL - v93 - My 15 '97 - p1564 [51-250]
PW - v244 - My 5 '97 - p196 [51-250]

Watson, Lyall - *Dark Nature*
Choice - v34 - S '96 - p217 [51-250]
Nat R - v48 - S 2 '96 - p92+ [501+]
Warriors, Warthogs, and Wisdom (Illus. by Keith West)
c PW - v244 - Mr 10 '97 - p67 [51-250]

Watson, Mark - *Programming Intelligent Agents for the Internet*
BYTE - v21 - D '96 - p34 [51-250]
SciTech - v20 - S '96 - p56 [51-250]

Watson, Mary - *The Butterfly Seeds (Illus. by Mary Watson)*
c RT - v50 - D '96 - p340 [51-250]

Watson, Nancy Dingman - *Tommy's Mommy's Fish (Illus. by Thomas Aldren Dingman Watson)*
c HB Guide - v7 - Fall '96 - p280 [51-250]
c New Ad - v9 - Fall '96 - p327+ [501+]

Watson, Nicola - *Revolution and the Form of the British Novel 1790-1825*
Eight-C St - v29 - Sum '96 - p440+ [501+]

Watson, Paul - *Ocean Warrior*
SB - v32 - Ag '96 - p164+ [51-250]

Watson, Peter - *Capo*
PW - v244 - Ja 13 '97 - p56+ [51-250]

Watson, Robert N - *The Rest Is Silence*
MLR - v92 - Ap '97 - p452+ [501+]
RES - v48 - F '97 - p89+ [501+]
Sev Cent N - v54 - Fall '96 - p56+ [501+]

Watson, Robert P - *Latin America and the Caribbean in Transition*
JTWS - v13 - Spr '96 - p343+ [251-500]

Watson, Robert T - *Climate Change 1995: Impacts, Adaptations and Mitigation of Climate Change*
JEL - v35 - Mr '97 - p300 [51-250]

Watson, Ron - *A Sacred Heart*
WAL - v31 - Win '97 - p413+ [51-250]

Watson, Sophie - *Postmodern Cities and Spaces*
GJ - v162 - Jl '96 - p228+ [251-500]

Watson, Steven - *The Birth of the Beat Generation*
WAL - v31 - Sum '96 - p185 [251-500]
The Harlem Renaissance
LATBR - S 22 '96 - p15 [51-250]

Watson, Thomas - *The Complete Works of Thomas Watson 1556-1592. Vols. 1-2*
Choice - v34 - My '97 - p1494 [51-250]

Watson, Tony J - *Sociology, Work and Industry. 3rd Ed.*
JEL - v35 - Mr '97 - p190 [51-250]

Watson, Victor - *Talking Pictures*
Sch Lib - v44 - Ag '96 - p131 [51-250]
TES - Jl 5 '96 - pR2 [501+]

Watson, Wallace Steadman - *Understanding Rainer Werner Fassbinder*
Choice - v34 - O '96 - p290 [51-250]
R&R Bk N - v11 - N '96 - p67 [51-250]

Watson, William, 1917- - *The Arts of China to AD 900*
BM - v138 - D '96 - p829 [501+]

Watson, William, 1931- - *The Knight on the Bridge*
PW - v243 - S 2 '96 - p120 [51-250]

Watsuji, Tetsuro - *Watsuji Tetsuro's Rinrigaku*
R&R Bk N - v12 - F '97 - p8 [51-250]

Watt, Ben - *Patient: The True Story of a Rare Illness*
KR - v65 - F 1 '97 - p212+ [251-500]
New Sci - v153 - F 22 '97 - p46 [51-250]
PW - v244 - F 3 '97 - p89 [51-250]
VLS - Spr '97 - p8 [501+]

Watt, Ian - *Myths of Modern Individualism*
HR - v49 - Win '97 - p675+ [501+]
Rel St Rev - v23 - Ja '97 - p52 [51-250]
RMR - v50 - 2 '96 - p210+ [501+]

Watt, Laura - *Carry Me Back*
BL - v93 - F 1 '97 - p927 [51-250]
PW - v243 - D 16 '96 - p43+ [51-250]

Watten, Barrett - *Frame 1971-1990*
PW - v244 - F 24 '97 - p85+ [51-250]

Watters, G Thomas - *A Guide to the Freshwater Mussels of Ohio. Rev. 3rd Ed.*
r J Gov Info - v23 - S '96 - p591 [51-250]

Watters, Thomas R - *Planets: A Smithsonian Guide*
S&T - v92 - D '96 - p66 [51-250]

Watterson, Bill - *It's a Magical World*
BWatch - v17 - N '96 - p11 [51-250]

Watterson, Kathryn - *Women in Prison. Rev. Ed.*
Wom R Bks - v14 - O '96 - p19+ [501+]

Watt-Evans, Lawrence - *The Reign of the Brown Magician*
SF Chr - v18 - O '96 - p80 [51-250]

Wattison, Meredith - *Conversations of Love*
Aust Bk R - Je '96 - p50+ [501+]

Wattleton, Faye - *Life on the Line*
BW - v27 - Ja 5 '97 - p8 [501+]
Ent W - N 1 '96 - p62+ [501+]
LJ - v121 - N 1 '96 - p80 [1-50]
NY - v72 - F 10 '97 - p83 [51-250]
NYTBR - v101 - N 17 '96 - p30+ [501+]
Time - v148 - O 7 '96 - p99 [51-250]

Watton, Victor - *Religion and Life*
y TES - D 6 '96 - pR6 [251-500]

Watts, Barry D - *Clausewitzian Friction and Future War*
For Aff - v76 - Mr '97 - p179 [51-250]

Watts, Bernadette - *The Christmas Bird (Illus. by Bernadette Watts)*
c HB Guide - v8 - Spr '97 - p52 [51-250]
c PW - v243 - S 30 '96 - p91 [51-250]
c SLJ - v42 - O '96 - p42 [51-250]
Harvey Hare, Postman Extraordinaire (Illus. by Bernadette Watts)
c BL - v93 - Mr 15 '97 - p1247 [51-250]
c KR - v65 - F 15 '97 - p307 [51-250]
c PW - v244 - Ja 20 '97 - p401 [51-250]
c SLJ - v43 - Mr '97 - p168 [51-250]

Watts, Duncan - *Introducing the European Union*
y TES - F 21 '97 - p20* [501+]

Watts, George S - *The Bank of Canada*
Archiv - Fall '94 - p185+ [501+]

Watts, Irene N - *The Fish Princess (Illus. by Steve Mennie)*
c BIC - v26 - F '97 - p32 [501+]
c Ch BWatch - v6 - D '96 - p3 [51-250]
c Ch BWatch - v7 - F '97 - p3 [1-50]
c HB Guide - v8 - Spr '97 - p53 [51-250]
c SLJ - v43 - Mr '97 - p168+ [51-250]

Watts, Jerry Gafio - *Heroism and the Black Intellectual*
HR - v49 - Aut '96 - p497+ [501+]

Watts, John - *Henry VI and the Politics of Kingship*
Choice - v34 - F '97 - p1021 [51-250]
TLS - N 1 '96 - p28 [501+]

Watts, Larry L - *Romanian Cassandra*
Slav R - v55 - Fall '96 - p673+ [501+]

Watts, Leslie Fitzgerald - *Princess Stinky-Toes and the Brave Frog Robert (Illus. by Leslie Fitzgerald Watts)*
c Ch Bk News - v19 - Sum '96 - p29 [51-250]

Watts, Marjorie-Ann - *Crocodile Tears (Illus. by Joanna Walsh)*
c Bks Keeps - Mr '97 - p22+ [51-250]

Watts, Michael R - *The Dissenters. Vol. 2*
Bks & Cult - v2 - S '96 - p39 [51-250]

Watts, Thomas D - *International Handbook on Social Work Education*
r ARBA - v28 - '97 - p319 [251-500]
Soc Ser R - v70 - S '96 - p504 [51-250]

Watts, Timothy - *Steal Away*
BL - v93 - O 1 '96 - p325+ [51-250]
KR - v64 - S 1 '96 - p1265+ [251-500]
LJ - v122 - Ja '97 - p51 [1-50]
LJ - v121 - N 1 '96 - p110 [51-250]
NYTBR - v101 - N 24 '96 - p26 [51-250]
PW - v243 - N '96 - p40 [1-50]

Watts Miller, William - *Durkheim, Morals and Modernity*
Choice - v34 - F '97 - p979 [51-250]
R&R Bk N - v11 - D '96 - p37 [51-250]

Watzek, Georg - *Endosseous Implants*
SciTech - v21 - Mr '97 - p66 [51-250]

Waugh, Alexander - *Opera: A New Way of Listening*
BL - v93 - D 1 '96 - p638 [51-250]
LJ - v121 - N 15 '96 - p64 [51-250]
ON - v61 - Ja 11 '97 - p50 [51-250]
TES - Ja 10 '97 - p7* [501+]

Waugh, Charles G - *Supernatural Sleuths*
y Kliatt - v31 - Ja '97 - p16+ [51-250]

Waugh, Earle H - *Dissonant Worlds*
BWatch - v18 - F '97 - p9 [1-50]

Waugh, Evelyn - *Scoop (Cadell). Audio Version*
TES - D 27 '96 - p27 [51-250]
Vile Bodies
Comw - v123 - D 6 '96 - p21 [1-50]

Waugh, Sylvia - *Mennyms Alive*
c JB - v60 - D '96 - p276+ [51-250]
c Sch Lib - v44 - N '96 - p152+ [501+]
Mennyms Alone
c BL - v93 - S 15 '96 - p242+ [51-250]
c CCB-B - v50 - N '96 - p118 [51-250]
c HB - v73 - Ja '97 - p69 [51-250]
c HB Guide - v8 - Spr '97 - p76 [51-250]
y JB - v60 - O '96 - p208+ [51-250]
c SLJ - v42 - S '96 - p208 [51-250]
Mennyms under Siege
c HB Guide - v7 - Fall '96 - p299 [51-250]
c JB - v60 - D '96 - p276+ [51-250]
c PW - v244 - Mr 3 '97 - p77 [1-50]

Waugh, Thomas - *Hard to Imagine*
Advocate - Mr 4 '97 - p50 [51-250]
LJ - v121 - N 15 '96 - p78 [51-250]

Waukesha County Genealogical Society - *Obituary Index 1859 to 1920*
r EGH - v50 - N '96 - p192 [51-250]

Wauthier, Claude - *Quatre Presidents Et L'Afrique*
Choice - v34 - D '96 - p569 [1-50]

Wawro, Geoffrey - *The Austro-Prussian War*
Choice - v34 - Ja '97 - p859 [51-250]
J Mil H - v61 - Ja '97 - p168+ [251-500]
TLS - Mr 28 '97 - p27 [501+]

Wawrose, Susan C - *Griswold v. Connecticut*
y CCB-B - v50 - S '96 - p36 [51-250]
y HB Guide - v7 - Fall '96 - p315 [51-250]
y SLJ - v42 - S '96 - p236+ [51-250]
y VOYA - v19 - O '96 - p240 [51-250]

Wawrukiewicz, Anthony S - *U.S. International Postal Rates 1872-1996*
r Am Phil - v111 - F '97 - p162 [51-250]

Wawrykow, Joseph P - *God's Grace and Human Action*
Rel St Rev - v23 - Ap '97 - p152 [51-250]

Waxman, Barbara Frey - *Multicultural Literatures through Feminist/Poststructuralist Lenses*
TSWL - v15 - Fall '96 - p373+ [501+]

The Way of Silent Love
RR - v56 - Mr '97 - p220 [1-50]

The Way Science Works
c Ch BWatch - v6 - S '96 - p3 [51-250]

Wayland Atlas of Threatened Cultures
cr Bks Keeps - Mr '97 - p26 [51-250]
cr Sch Lib - v45 - F '97 - p41 [51-250]
cr TES - F 28 '97 - p21* [251-500]

Waylen, Georgina - *Gender in Third World Politics*
Choice - v34 - S '96 - p209 [51-250]
WorldV - v12 - Jl '96 - p6 [51-250]

Wayman, Tom - *I'll Be Right Back*
PW - v244 - Mr 31 '97 - p71 [1-50]

Wayne, Elizabeth - *Hindus*
TES - D 6 '96 - pR6 [251-500]

Wayne, Kathryn Ross - *Redefining Moral Education*
R&R Bk N - v11 - D '96 - p66 [51-250]

Wayner, Peter - *Disappearing Cryptography*
CBR - v14 - N '96 - p40 [51-250]
New Sci - v151 - S 14 '96 - p46 [51-250]

Weakley County, Tennessee Register Survey Books. Vol. 2
r EGH - v50 - N '96 - p187 [51-250]

Weaks, Mary Louise - *Southern Women's Writing*
AL - v68 - S '96 - p670 [51-250]
VQR - v72 - Aut '96 - p122* [501+]

Weale, Adrian - *Renegades: Hitler's Englishmen*
EHR - v111 - N '96 - p1347+ [251-500]

Weamys, Anna - *A Continuation of Sir Philip Sidney's Arcadia*
Six Ct J - v27 - Fall '96 - p902+ [501+]

Wear, Delese - *Women in Medical Education*
Choice - v34 - Mr '97 - p1194 [51-250]
SciTech - v20 - D '96 - p37 [51-250]

Wearne, Phillip - *Return of the Indian*
Choice - v34 - Mr '97 - p1230 [51-250]
TLS - F 7 '97 - p32 [251-500]
WorldV - v13 - Ja '97 - p10 [251-500]
Weatherall, David - *Science and the Quiet Art*
Hast Cen R - v26 - Jl '96 - p42 [1-50]
Weatherby, Harold L - *Mirrors of Celestial Grace*
Ren Q - v49 - Win '96 - p873+ [501+]
Sev Cent N - v54 - Spr '96 - p6+ [501+]
Weatherby, Mark Alan - *My Dinosaur (Illus. by Mark Alan Weatherby)*
c BL - v93 - Mr 1 '97 - p1174+ [51-250]
c CCB-B - v50 - My '97 - p337 [51-250]
c KR - v65 - Ja 1 '97 - p67 [51-250]
c PW - v243 - D 9 '96 - p67 [51-250]
c SLJ - v43 - Mr '97 - p169 [51-250]
Weatherford, Doris L - *Milestones: A Chronology of American Women's History*
r LJ - v122 - Ap 1 '97 - p86 [51-250]
Weatherford, Jack - *The History of Money*
Am - v176 - F 22 '97 - p2 [501+]
y BL - v93 - Ja '97 - p792 [51-250]
HMR - Spr '97 - p10 [51-250]
KR - v64 - N 15 '96 - p1661 [251-500]
LATBR - F 16 '97 - p12 [501+]
LJ - v122 - Ja '97 - p116+ [51-250]
PW - v243 - D 9 '96 - p52 [51-250]
Weatherill, Stephen - *Law and Integration in the European Union*
JEL - v34 - S '96 - p1450 [51-250]
Weatherly, Myra - *Inhalants*
y HB Guide - v8 - Spr '97 - p98 [51-250]
Weatherson, Michael A - *Hiram Johnson: Political Revivalist*
WHQ - v27 - Win '96 - p549 [51-250]
Weaver, Charles - *Hidden Logic Puzzles*
y BL - v93 - Ap 1 '97 - p1343 [1-50]
Weaver, Constance - *Teaching Grammar in Context*
Col Comp - v47 - D '96 - p620 [51-250]
Kliatt - v30 - N '96 - p25 [51-250]
Weaver, J T - *Mathematical Methods for Geo-Electromagnetic Induction*
SIAM Rev - v38 - D '96 - p697+ [501+]
Weaver, Jace - *Defending Mother Earth*
PW - v243 - S 30 '96 - p76 [51-250]
Weaver, John C - *Crimes, Constables, and Courts*
AHR - v101 - O '96 - p1316 [501+]
JIH - v27 - Win '97 - p554+ [251-500]
J Soc H - v30 - Win '96 - p530+ [501+]
Weaver, Marcia - *Empowering Employees through Basic Skills Training*
HR Mag - v41 - S '96 - p138+ [51-250]
Weaver, Mary C - *Tales as Tools*
CAY - v17 - Win '96 - p13 [51-250]
Weaver, Mary Jo - *Being Right*
J Ch St - v38 - Aut '96 - p902 [251-500]
Weaver, Michael - *The Lie*
BL - v93 - Mr 1 '97 - p1114 [51-250]
KR - v65 - F 1 '97 - p169 [251-500]
PW - v244 - F 17 '97 - p212 [51-250]
Trib Bks - Mr 16 '97 - p6 [51-250]
Weaver, Michael D - *A Second Infinity*
y Kliatt - v30 - S '96 - p20 [51-250]
Weaver, Rebecca Harden - *Divine Grace and Human Agency*
Rel St Rev - v22 - O '96 - p348 [51-250]
R&R Bk N - v11 - D '96 - p5 [51-250]
Theol St - v57 - D '96 - p746+ [501+]
Weaver, Richard L - *The Roswell Report*
J Gov Info - v23 - S '96 - p544 [51-250]
Weaver, Will - *Farm Team*
y Emerg Lib - v24 - S '96 - p26 [1-50]
Striking Out
y Kliatt - v30 - S '96 - p5 [1-50]
Weaver, William, 1923- - *A Legacy of Excellence*
PW - v244 - Mr 31 '97 - p53 [51-250]
Weaver, William Woys - *Heirloom Vegetable Gardening*
LJ - v122 - Ap 1 '97 - p114+ [51-250]
PW - v244 - Ap 7 '97 - p87 [51-250]
Web Bound
p LJ - v121 - D '96 - p158 [51-250]
Web Site Source Book 1996
r ARBA - v28 - '97 - p625 [51-250]
yr BL - v93 - S 1 '96 - p172+ [51-250]
r LJ - v121 - O 1 '96 - p70 [51-250]
r R&R Bk N - v11 - D '96 - p74 [51-250]
Webb, Cliff - *My Ancestors Were Londoners*
NGSQ - v84 - D '96 - p317 [51-250]
Webb, Cynthia - *No Daughter of the South*
LJ - v122 - Ap 1 '97 - p133 [51-250]

Webb, Dennis - *Greenberg's Guide to Marbles. 2nd Ed.*
r ARBA - v28 - '97 - p361 [51-250]
Webb, Don - *A Spell for the Fulfillment of Desire*
Chel - 61 '96 - p154+ [501+]
Webb, Elizabeth A - *Perspectives in Urban Ecology*
Workbook - v21 - Fall '96 - p145+ [501+]
Webb, James L A, Jr. - *Desert Frontier*
AHR - v102 - F '97 - p149 [251-500]
Webb, Kaye - *Family Tree*
c TES - O 18 '96 - p12* [51-250]
Webb, Laura - *Group Treatment for Adult Survivors of Abuse*
SciTech - v20 - N '96 - p45 [51-250]
Webb, Marion St. John (Adcock) - *Knock Three Times*
c Spec - v277 - D 14 '96 - p77 [51-250]
Webb, Michael C - *The Political Economy of Policy Coordination*
CS - v25 - S '96 - p605+ [501+]
J Pol - v58 - Ag '96 - p931+ [501+]
Webb, Nancy Boyd - *Social Work Practice with Children*
SB - v33 - My '97 - p101 [251-500]
Webb, Pamela A - *Hellenistic Architectural Sculpture*
Choice - v34 - Ap '97 - p1328 [51-250]
R&R Bk N - v12 - F '97 - p73 [51-250]
Webb, Patrick - *Famine and Food Security in Ethiopia*
GJ - v162 - Jl '96 - p239 [51-250]
Webb, Robyn - *Flavorful Seasons Cookbook*
BWatch - v18 - Mr '97 - p6 [51-250]
Webb, Stephen - *Palaeopathology of Aboriginal Australians*
Am Ant - v61 - O '96 - p814+ [501+]
Webb, Stephen Saunders - *Lord Churchill's Coup*
NEQ - v70 - Mr '97 - p150+ [501+]
RAH - v24 - S '96 - p389+ [501+]
W&M Q - v53 - O '96 - p809+ [501+]
Webb, Sylvia P - *Creating an Information Service. 3rd Ed.*
LAR - v99 - Mr '97 - p162 [1-50]
Webber, Christopher - *Finding Home*
PW - v243 - S 30 '96 - p75 [51-250]
Webber, Geoffrey - *North German Church Music in the Age of Buxtehude*
Choice - v34 - N '96 - p471 [51-250]
Webber, Mark - *The International Politics of Russia and the Successor States*
R&R Bk N - v11 - N '96 - p13 [51-250]
Russ Rev - v56 - Ja '97 - p146+ [501+]
Webber, Michael John - *The Golden Age Illusion*
Choice - v34 - Mr '97 - p1211 [51-250]
JEL - v35 - Mr '97 - p283+ [51-250]
R&R Bk N - v12 - F '97 - p34 [51-250]
Webber, Sabra J - *Fantasy or Ethnography?*
MEJ - v51 - Spr '97 - p314 [51-250]
Webber, Stephen E - *Solvents and Self-Organization of Polymers*
SciTech - v21 - Mr '97 - p30 [51-250]
Weber, Carl - *DramaContemporary: Germany*
R&R Bk N - v11 - D '96 - p66 [51-250]
Weber, Christoph - *Legati E Governatori Dello Stato Pontificio 1550-1809*
r CHR - v82 - O '96 - p696+ [251-500]
Weber, David - *Honor among Enemies*
y VOYA - v19 - D '96 - p282 [251-500]
Weber, Devra - *Dark Sweat, White Gold*
AHR - v101 - O '96 - p1298+ [501+]
Weber, Eugen Joseph - *The Hollow Years*
Historian - v59 - Win '97 - p483+ [251-500]
JMH - v68 - D '96 - p1001+ [501+]
Peasants into Frenchmen
LATBR - D 29 '96 - p6 [51-250]
Weber, Harold M - *Paper Bullets*
Sev Cent N - v54 - Fall '96 - p66+ [501+]
Weber, Janice - *Devil's Food*
Rapport - v19 - 4 '96 - p28 [51-250]
Weber, Max - *The Russian Revolutions*
CS - v25 - N '96 - p821+ [501+]
Slav R - v55 - Sum '96 - p485+ [501+]
Sociological Writings
TranslRevS - v2 - D '96 - p13 [51-250]
Weber, Nicholas Fox - *Patron Saints*
Dance - v71 - Ja '97 - p98 [51-250]
Weber, Retta Lou - *Lively Stones*
EGH - v50 - N '96 - p187+ [51-250]
Weber, Samuel - *Mass Mediauras*
MLN - v111 - D '96 - p1019+ [501+]
Weber, Sandra - *That's Funny, You Don't Look Like a Teacher!*
R&R Bk N - v11 - D '96 - p53 [51-250]
Weber, Walter J - *Process Dynamics in Environmental Systems*
Choice - v34 - S '96 - p160+ [51-250]

WebMaster
p LJ - v121 - O 15 '96 - p95 [51-250]
Webster, Alexander F C - *The Price of Prophecy. 2nd Ed.*
Bks & Cult - v2 - Mr '96 - p6+ [501+]
CH - v65 - S '96 - p548+ [501+]
ER - v48 - O '96 - p525+ [501+]
Webster, Barbara - *Beautiful Banners*
LJ - v122 - Ap 15 '97 - p79 [51-250]
Webster, Chris - *Writing to Communicate*
TES - D 13 '96 - p43 [51-250]
Webster, Donovan - *Aftermath: The Remnants of War*
BL - v93 - S 1 '96 - p43 [51-250]
BW - v26 - N 24 '96 - p13 [51-250]
NYTBR - v102 - Ja 12 '97 - p19 [501+]
Webster, Elizabeth - *Waiting for Katie*
BL - v93 - D 1 '96 - p642 [51-250]
PW - v243 - N 25 '96 - p58+ [51-250]
Webster, Graeme - *Skinning Time*
Aust Bk R - Je '96 - p52+ [501+]
Webster, John - *Barth's Ethics of Reconciliation*
Rel St Rev - v23 - Ap '97 - p153 [51-250]
Webster, Leila - *The Informal Sector and Microfinance Institutions in West Africa*
Choice - v34 - My '97 - p1547 [51-250]
World Bank Lending for Small Enterprises 1989-1993
JEL - v34 - D '96 - p2113 [51-250]
Webster, Richard - *Why Freud Was Wrong*
Comw - v123 - D 6 '96 - p20 [51-250]
Rel St Rev - v23 - Ap '97 - p150 [51-250]
Webster, T B L - *Monuments Illustrating New Comedy. 2nd Ed., Rev. and Enlarged, Vols. 1-2*
AJA - v101 - Ja '97 - p154+ [501+]
Webster's New American Dictionary
cr ARBA - v28 - '97 - p378+ [251-500]
Webster's New Biographical Dictionary. Electronic Media Version
yr SLJ - v42 - O '96 - p60 [51-250]
WEBTechniques
p LJ - v121 - O 15 '96 - p95 [51-250]
Wechsler, Lilla - *The Bernard Becker Collection in Ophthalmology*
r AB - v99 - Mr 31 '97 - p1052 [251-500]
Wecht, Cyril - *Grave Secrets*
y BL - v93 - S 15 '96 - p195 [51-250]
KR - v64 - S 1 '96 - p1312+ [251-500]
Weddle, David - *If They Move—Kill 'Em*
FQ - v49 - Fall '95 - p66 [251-500]
Obs - S 1 '96 - p18* [51-250]
Sam Peckinpah: If They Move, Kill 'Em
TES - N 22 '96 - p8* [51-250]
Weddle, Robert S - *Changing Tides*
JSH - v63 - F '97 - p144+ [501+]
WHQ - v28 - Spr '97 - p71+ [251-500]
Wedekind, Frank - *Spring's Awakening*
TranslRevS - v2 - D '96 - p26 [51-250]
Wedgwood, C V - *Montrose*
Sev Cent N - v54 - Spr '96 - p23+ [501+]
The Thirty Years War
BYTE - v21 - O '96 - p167+ [51-250]
Weed, Frank J - *Certainty of Justice*
CS - v25 - N '96 - p768+ [501+]
Weede, Erich - *Economic Development, Social Order, and World Politics*
CS - v26 - Ja '97 - p57+ [501+]
Weeden, Norman - *A Sierra Nevada Flora. 4th Ed.*
r BWatch - v17 - D '96 - p4 [1-50]
r Choice - v34 - Ap '97 - p1365+ [51-250]
Weekes, Don - *Ultimate Hockey Trivia*
c Quill & Q - v62 - D '96 - p37+ [251-500]
Weeks, Andrew - *Paracelsus: Speculative Theory and the Crisis of the Early Reformation*
Choice - v34 - Ap '97 - p1354 [51-250]
R&R Bk N - v12 - F '97 - p2 [51-250]
Weeks, Arthur R - *Fundamentals of Electronic Image Processing*
SciTech - v20 - D '96 - p66 [51-250]
Weeks, Christopher - *An Architectural History of Harford County, Maryland*
R&R Bk N - v11 - D '96 - p57 [51-250]
Weeks, G R - *The Marital-Relationship Therapy Casebook*
Fam Relat - v46 - Ja '97 - p95 [251-500]
Weeks, Kay D - *The Secretary of the Interior's Standards for the Treatment of Historic Properties*
J Gov Info - v23 - S '96 - p549 [1-50]
Weeks, Sarah - *Follow the Moon (Illus. by Suzanne Duranceau)*
c ECEJ - v23 - Sum '96 - p223 [51-250]
c RT - v50 - O '96 - p155 [51-250]

Noodles (Illus. by David Carter)
  c HB Guide - v7 - Fall '96 - p245 [51-250]
  c KR - v64 - My 1 '96 - p696 [1-50]
Weeks, Theodore R - *Nation and State in Late Imperial Russia*
  Choice - v34 - Mr '97 - p1225 [51-250]
Weeks, W William - *Beyond the Ark*
  Choice - v34 - Ap '97 - p1365 [51-250]
Weeks, William Earl - *Building the Continental Empire*
  y BL - v93 - N 15 '96 - p555+ [51-250]
  BWatch - v18 - F '97 - p2 [1-50]
  PW - v243 - O 14 '96 - p70 [51-250]
Weems, M L - *The Life of Washington*
  R&R Bk N - v11 - D '96 - p15 [51-250]
  VQR - v73 - Win '97 - p33* [1-50]
Weems, Renita J - *Battered Love*
  Intpr - v51 - Ap '97 - p200+ [251-500]
  OS - v32 - S '96 - p59 [51-250]
  TT - v53 - Ja '97 - p564 [51-250]
Weems, Robert E - *Black Business in the Black Metropolis*
  BHR - v70 - Aut '96 - p414+ [501+]
  Bl S - v26 - Fall '96 - p107 [1-50]
  Choice - v34 - O '96 - p327 [51-250]
  JEH - v57 - Mr '97 - p243+ [501+]
Wegar, Katarina - *Adoption, Identity, and Kinship*
  LJ - v122 - Ap 1 '97 - p112 [51-250]
Wege, David C - *Key Areas for Threatened Birds in the Neotropics*
  r Choice - v34 - O '96 - p307+ [501+]
Wegela, Karen Kissel - *How to Be a Help Instead of a Nuisance*
  Tric - v6 - Win '96 - p106+ [501+]
Wegener, Mark I - *Cruciformed: The Literary Impact of Mark's Story of Jesus and His Disciples*
  Intpr - v51 - Ja '97 - p92+ [251-500]
Wegener, Peter P - *The Peenemunde Wind Tunnels*
  Choice - v34 - F '97 - p984 [51-250]
  J Mil H - v61 - Ap '97 - p405+ [251-500]
  Nature - v383 - O 31 '96 - p779 [501+]
  New Sci - v152 - N 9 '96 - p42 [51-250]
  SB - v33 - Ja '97 - p10 [51-250]
  SciTech - v20 - D '96 - p87 [51-250]
Wegert, Karl H - *German Radicals Confront the Common People*
  JMH - v69 - Mr '97 - p176+ [501+]
Popular Culture, Crime, and Social Control in 18th-Century Wurttemberg
  AHR - v101 - D '96 - p1563+ [501+]
Weglyn, Michi Nishiura - *Years of Infamy. Updated Ed.*
  PW - v243 - O 7 '96 - p69 [1-50]
Wegman, William - *Wegman's Mother Goose (Illus. by William Wegman)*
  c NYTBR - v101 - N 24 '96 - p20 [1-50]
William Wegman's Farm Days (Illus. by William Wegman)
  c PW - v244 - Ap 14 '97 - p73 [51-250]
William Wegman's Mother Goose (Illus. by William Wegman)
  c HB Guide - v8 - Spr '97 - p107 [51-250]
  c KR - v64 - S 15 '96 - p1411 [51-250]
  c NW - v128 - D 2 '96 - p86 [1-50]
  c PW - v243 - Jl 22 '96 - p240 [51-250]
  c SLJ - v42 - O '96 - p119 [51-250]
Wehler, Hans-Ulrich - *Deutsche Gesellschaftsgeschichte. Vol. 3*
  CEH - v29 - 1 '96 - p107+ [501+]
Die Gegenwart Als Geschichte
  CEH - v29 - 1 '96 - p145+ [501+]
Wehner-Franco, Silke - *Deutsche Dienstmadchen In Amerika 1850-1914*
  AHR - v102 - F '97 - p199+ [251-500]
Wehrle, Josef - *Sprichwort Und Weisheit*
  Rel St Rev - v23 - Ap '97 - p163 [51-250]
Wei, Ching-Sheng - *The Courage to Stand Alone*
  BL - v93 - My 15 '97 - p1546 [51-250]
  KR - v65 - Mr 1 '97 - p370+ [51-250]
  LJ - v122 - Ap 1 '97 - p111 [51-250]
  NYTLa - v146 - My 12 '97 - pC11+ [501+]
Wei, Tzu-Yun - *Yi Ge Nu Ren De Bei Ju*
  BL - v93 - My 1 '97 - p1484 [1-50]
Weibel, Marguerite Crowley - *Choosing and Using Books with Adult New Readers*
  LJ - v122 - Ja '97 - p156 [51-250]
Weibull, Jorgen W - *Evolutionary Game Theory*
  Econ J - v107 - Ja '97 - p218+ [501+]
  JEL - v34 - D '96 - p1952+ [501+]
Weick, Karl E - *The Social Psychology of Organizing Inc.*
  r v18 - D '96 - p54 [251-500]
Weidenbach, Ronald P - *Freshwater Pond Life*
  r J Gov Info - v23 - S '96 - p581 [1-50]

Weidenbaum, Murray - *The Bamboo Network*
  Choice - v34 - S '96 - p178 [51-250]
  JEL - v34 - S '96 - p1493 [1-50]
Weidensaul, Scott - *Max Bonker and the Howling Thieves (Illus. by Bruce Van Patter)*
  c Ch BWatch - v6 - Jl '96 - p1 [1-50]
  c Ch BWatch - v6 - N '96 - p5 [51-250]
  c HB Guide - v8 - Spr '97 - p61 [51-250]
Raptors: The Birds of Prey
  yr Choice - v34 - Ap '97 - p776+ [51-250]
Weidner, Marsha - *Latter Days of the Law*
  Art Bull - v78 - S '96 - p556+ [501+]
Weigand, Phil C - *Evolucion De Una Civilizacion Prehispanica*
  LA Ant - v7 - Mr '96 - p88+ [501+]
Weigel, George - *Soul of the World*
  CLW - v67 - Mr '97 - p33+ [251-500]
  RP - v59 - Spr '97 - p377+ [501+]
Weigel, Van B - *Earth Cancer*
  JTWS - v13 - Spr '96 - p414+ [501+]
Weigert, Stephen L - *Religion and Guerrilla Warfare in Modern Africa*
  J Mil H - v60 - O '96 - p802+ [501+]
Weightman, Colin - *Theology in a Polanyian Universe*
  Theol St - v57 - Mr '96 - p155+ [501+]
Weightman, Simon - *Traveller's Literary Companion to the Indian Sub-Continent*
  TLS - O 4 '96 - p40 [251-500]
Weigl, Bruce - *Sweet Lorain*
  South R - v32 - Aut '96 - p761+ [501+]
Weigl, Michael - *Zefania Und Das Israel Der Armen*
  Rel St Rev - v23 - Ja '97 - p60 [51-250]
Weigle, Marta - *The Great Southwest of the Fred Harvey Company and the Santa Fe Railway*
  CAY - v17 - Fall '96 - p8 [51-250]
  Choice - v34 - O '96 - p347 [51-250]
  Roundup M - v4 - D '96 - p23 [51-250]
Two Guadalupes
  CAY - v16 - Fall '95 - p13 [51-250]
Weikel, William J - *Foundations of Mental Health Counseling. 2nd Ed.*
  SciTech - v21 - Mr '97 - p53 [51-250]
Weil, Andrew - *Eight Weeks to Optimum Health*
  BL - v93 - F 1 '97 - p906+ [51-250]
  CSM - v89 - Ap 3 '97 - p14 [51-250]
  LJ - v122 - Mr 15 '97 - p82 [51-250]
  PW - v244 - F 3 '97 - p102 [51-250]
Weil, Connie - *Health and Health Care in Latin America during the Lost Decade*
  RA - v25 - 4 '96 - p233+ [501+]
Weil, Robert - *Red Cat, White Cat*
  Choice - v34 - Ja '97 - p847 [51-250]
Weil, Sylvie - *Le Jardin De Dima*
  FR - v70 - D '96 - p357+ [251-500]
Weil-Bergougnoux, Michele - *Seminaire Robert Challe*
  MLR - v92 - Ja '97 - p192+ [251-500]
Weill, Kurt - *Speak Low (When You Speak Love)*
  AB - v98 - D 9 '96 - p2003+ [501+]
  Am Theat - v13 - D '96 - p21 [1-50]
  New R - v216 - Ja 27 '97 - p31+ [501+]
  NYTBR - v101 - D 8 '96 - p93 [1-50]
  TLS - S 13 '96 - p14+ [501+]
Weiller, Jean - *L'Economie Non Conformiste*
  Econ J - v106 - My '96 - p1818+ [501+]
Weimann, Gabriel - *The Influentials: People Who Influence People*
  Pub Op Q - v60 - Fall '96 - p468+ [501+]
Weimann, Robert - *Authority and Representation in Early Modern Discourse*
  TLS - Ag 30 '96 - p32 [251-500]
Weimer, Tonja Evetts - *Fingerplays and Action Chants. Vols. 1-2. Book and Audio Version*
  c CLW - v66 - Je '96 - p55+ [51-250]
Weinandy, Thomas G - *The Father's Spirit of Sonship*
  Theol St - v57 - Je '96 - p384 [251-500]
Weinberg, David H - *Between Tradition and Modernity*
  Choice - v34 - Mr '97 - p1225 [51-250]
  Rel St Rev - v23 - Ap '97 - p198 [51-250]
Weinberg, George - *Will Power!*
  BL - v93 - O 1 '96 - p293 [51-250]
  LJ - v121 - S 15 '96 - p84 [51-250]
Weinberg, Gerhard L - *Germany, Hitler, and World War II*
  CEH - v29 - 1 '96 - p141+ [501+]
  J Mil H - v61 - Ap '97 - p395+ [501+]
Weinberg, Horst D - *New Baby Owner's Manual*
  BWatch - v18 - F '97 - p6 [51-250]
Weinberg, Meyer - *Racism in Contemporary America*
  r ARBA - v28 - '97 - p151 [51-250]
  r Choice - v34 - N '96 - p438 [51-250]
  r R&R Bk N - v11 - D '96 - p74 [51-250]

Weinberg, Robert A - *Racing to the Beginning of the Road*
  Choice - v34 - D '96 - p636 [51-250]
  Nature - v383 - O 31 '96 - p777+ [501+]
  NYTBR - v101 - S 1 '96 - p13 [501+]
  NYTBR - v101 - D 8 '96 - p92 [1-50]
  Rapport - v19 - 5 '96 - p45 [251-500]
  Sci - v275 - Ja 3 '97 - p36 [501+]
  Trib Bks - Ja 19 '97 - p9 [1-50]
Weinberg, Steven - *The Quantum Theory of Fields. Vol. 2*
  Nature - v385 - Ja 23 '97 - p310+ [501+]
  New Sci - v152 - N 2 '96 - p44+ [501+]
  Phys Today - v50 - Ja '97 - p67+ [501+]
  SB - v33 - Mr '97 - p39 [251-500]
  Sci - v275 - F 14 '97 - p938+ [501+]
  SciTech - v21 - Mr '97 - p21 [51-250]
Weinberg, Winkler G - *No Germs Allowed!*
  r BL - v93 - F 1 '97 - p957 [1-50]
  Choice - v34 - Ja '97 - p830 [51-250]
Weinberger, Barbara - *The Best Police in the World*
  Albion - v28 - '96 - p731+ [501+]
Weinberger, Caspar - *The Next War*
  BW - v26 - D 1 '96 - p5 [501+]
  CSM - v89 - F 3 '97 - p12 [251-500]
  Econ - v342 - Mr 15 '97 - p8* [251-500]
  KR - v64 - O 1 '96 - p1458 [251-500]
  LJ - v121 - N 1 '96 - p93+ [51-250]
  NYTBR - v102 - Ja 5 '97 - p23 [501+]
  PW - v243 - O 14 '96 - p73 [51-250]
  WSJ-Cent - v99 - Mr 11 '97 - pA20 [501+]
Weinberger, Florence - *The Invisible Telling Its Shape*
  BL - v93 - F 1 '97 - p922 [51-250]
Weinberger, Norman - *You Just Don't Duct Tape a Baby*
  PW - v244 - F 3 '97 - p103 [51-250]
Weinbren, Daniel - *Generating Socialism*
  NS - v126 - Mr 27 '97 - p52+ [501+]
Weinbrot, Howard D - *Britannia's Issue*
  MLN - v111 - D '96 - p1050+ [501+]
Weiner, Deborah E B - *Architecture and Social Reform in Late-Victorian London*
  Albion - v28 - Sum '96 - p347+ [501+]
Weiner, Eric - *Deadline*
  c Ch BWatch - v6 - My '96 - p7 [1-50]
Weiner, James F - *The Lost Drum*
  Am Ethnol - v24 - F '97 - p263+ [501+]
  Choice - v34 - S '96 - p170 [51-250]
Weiner, Jonathan - *The Beak of the Finch*
  Reason - v28 - D '96 - p38 [51-250]
The Beak of the Finch (McDonough). Audio Version
  y Kliatt - v30 - S '96 - p55+ [51-250]
Weiner, Marc A - *Richard Wagner and the Anti-Semitic Imagination*
  Ger Q - v69 - Sum '96 - p337+ [501+]
  Notes - v53 - S '96 - p40+ [501+]
  Rel St Rev - v23 - Ap '97 - p198 [51-250]
  Salm - Fall '96 - p246+ [501+]
Weiner, Myron - *International Migration and Security*
  Arm F&S - v23 - Fall '96 - p133+ [501+]
Weiner, Richard - *Webster's New World Dictionary of Media and Communications. Rev. and Updated Ed.*
  r BL - v92 - Ag '96 - p1922 [1-50]
  r Choice - v34 - My '97 - p1481+ [51-250]
  r LJ - v122 - Ag 15 '97 - p74 [1-50]
  r R&R Bk N - v12 - F '97 - p75 [1-50]
  r TCI - v31 - F '97 - p55+ [501+]
Weiner, Steve - *The Museum of Love*
  Books - v9 - S '95 - p24 [1-50]
Weing, Siegfried - *The German Novella*
  MLR - v91 - Jl '96 - p806 [251-500]
Weingand, Darlene E - *Customer Service Excellence*
  LJ - v122 - Ag 15 '97 - p126 [51-250]
Weingarten, Henry - *Investing by the Stars*
  Horoscope - v62 - D '96 - p14+ [501+]
Weingarten, Jan - *Teach Yourself...Corel WordPerfect 7*
  Quill & Q - v62 - N '96 - p31 [51-250]
Weinhauer, Klaus - *Alltag Und Arbeitskampf Im Hamburger Hafen*
  AHR - v101 - O '96 - p1233+ [501+]
Weinman, Lynda - *Coloring Web Graphics*
  LJ - v122 - My 1 '97 - p132 [51-250]
Deconstructing Web Graphics
  LJ - v122 - My 1 '97 - p132 [51-250]
Designing Web Graphics. 2nd Ed.
  LJ - v122 - My 1 '97 - p132 [51-250]
Weinrib, Ernest Joseph - *The Idea of Private Law*
  CPR - v16 - Ag '96 - p302+ [501+]
  RM - v50 - Ap '97 - p194+ [251-500]
Weinroth, Michelle - *Reclaiming William Morris*
  Choice - v34 - Ap '97 - p1342 [51-250]

Weinstat, Hertzel - *Dear Rogue*
    AB - v98 - D 9 '96 - p1994 [51-250]
    ON - v61 - N '96 - p61 [251-500]
Weinstein, Arnold - *The Fiction of Relationship*
    CLS - v33 - 1 '96 - p125+ [501+]
Weinstein, Barbara - *For Social Peace in Brazil*
    Choice - v34 - My '97 - p1560 [51-250]
Weinstein, Bruce - *Ethical Issues in Pharmacy*
    Hast Cen R - v26 - Jl '96 - p42 [1-50]
Weinstein, Cindy - *The Literature of Labor and the Labors of Literature*
    AL - v68 - D '96 - p856+ [501+]
    J Am Chr - v30 - Ap '96 - p161+ [251-500]
    Nine-C Lit - v51 - S '96 - p256+ [501+]
Weinstein, Danny - *Ha-Barak*
    BL - v93 - Mr 1 '97 - p1115 [1-50]
Weinstein, Debra - *Rodent Angel*
    Nat - v263 - O 28 '96 - p56+ [501+]
Weinstein, Howard - *Revisitations*
    y VOYA - v19 - O '96 - p203+ [251-500]
Weinstein, Michael A - *Culture/Flesh: Explorations of Postcivilized Modernity*
    APSR - v90 - S '96 - p641 [501+]
    CPR - v16 - Ag '96 - p304+ [501+]
Weinstein, Philip M - *What Else but Love?*
    Choice - v34 - My '97 - p1501 [51-250]
Weinstein, Sanford - *Family beyond Family*
    Fam in Soc - v78 - Mr '97 - p219+ [501+]
Weinstein, Tilla - *An Introduction to Lorentz Surfaces*
    SciTech - v20 - D '96 - p22 [51-250]
Weinstock, Nicholas - *The Secret Love of Sons*
    KR - v65 - F 15 '97 - p290 [251-500]
    PW - v244 - F 3 '97 - p84 [51-250]
Weintraub, Linda - *Art on the Edge and Over*
    LJ - v121 - D '96 - p90 [51-250]
Weintraub, Neal - *Tricks of the Floor Trader*
    Barron's - v76 - S 2 '96 - p43 [51-250]
Weintraub, Sidney - *Integrating the Americas*
    HAHR - v76 - Ag '96 - p610+ [501+]
Weintraub, Stanley - *Albert: Uncrowned King*
    Spec - v278 - Mr 15 '97 - p38+ [501+]
    TLS - Mr 28 '97 - p11 [501+]
    The Last Great Victory
    y Kliatt - v31 - Ja '97 - p26 [51-250]
    PW - v243 - S 30 '96 - p79 [1-50]
    Shaw's People
    Choice - v34 - S '96 - p131 [51-250]
    ELT - v40 - 2 '97 - p203+ [501+]
    ILS - v16 - Spr '97 - p13 [501+]
    Uncrowned King
    BL - v93 - My 1 '97 - p1476 [251-500]
    PW - v244 - Ap 7 '97 - p78 [51-250]
    WSJ-Cent - v99 - My 23 '97 - pA16 [501+]
Weintraub, Steven H - *Differential Forms*
    SciTech - v20 - D '96 - p18 [1-50]
Weintraub, William - *City Unique*
    CG - v117 - Ja '97 - p78+ [501+]
    Mac - v110 - F 17 '97 - p75 [501+]
    Quill & Q - v62 - D '96 - p30 [501+]
    Quill & Q - v63 - F '97 - p50 [51-250]
Weir, Alison - *Children of England*
    CR - v269 - S '96 - p168 [51-250]
    NS & S - v9 - My 24 '96 - p37 [251-500]
    Obs - Mr 9 '97 - p18* [51-250]
    The Children of Henry VIII
    y BL - v93 - Ja '97 - p763 [1-50]
Weir, Allison - *Sacrificial Logics*
    CPR - v16 - Ag '96 - p305+ [501+]
Weir, B S - *Genetic Data Analysis II*
    Choice - v34 - D '96 - p636+ [51-250]
    SB - v32 - N '96 - p231 [51-250]
    SciTech - v20 - S '96 - p19 [51-250]
Weir, Bob - *Baru Bay: Australia*
    c Magpies - v11 - My '96 - p44 [51-250]
Weir, David - *Decadence and the Making of Modernism*
    ELT - v40 - 2 '97 - p210+ [501+]
    Rel St Rev - v23 - Ja '97 - p53 [51-250]
    James Joyce and the Art of Mediation
    Choice - v34 - My '97 - p1501 [51-250]
Weir, Jamie - *Imaging Atlas of Human Anatomy. Electronic Media Version*
    r SciTech - v20 - N '96 - p30 [51-250]
Weir, Liz - *Boom-Chicka-Boom (Illus. by Josip Lizatovic)*
    c Sch Lib - v45 - F '97 - p16 [51-250]
Weir, Robert E - *Beyond Labor's Veil*
    Choice - v34 - O '96 - p352 [51-250]
    HRNB - v25 - Win '97 - p58 [251-500]
    JEH - v57 - Mr '97 - p245+ [501+]
    JEL - v34 - D '96 - p2102 [51-250]
Weir, Robert F - *Physician-Assisted Suicide*
    LJ - v122 - My 1 '97 - p134 [51-250]

Weir, Ronald B - *The History of the Distillers Company 1877-1939*
    HRNB - v25 - Fall '96 - p22 [251-500]
    JEL - v34 - S '96 - p1456 [51-250]
Weir, Theresa - *American Dreamer*
    PW - v244 - Mr 31 '97 - p72 [51-250]
Weir, William - *A Well Regulated Militia*
    y BL - v93 - Mr 1 '97 - p1095 [51-250]
    PW - v243 - D 30 '96 - p46 [51-250]
Weirner, Lori S - *Be a Friend*
    c CLW - v67 - D '96 - p63 [51-250]
Weis, Margaret - *Fantastic Alice*
    SF Chr - v18 - Ap '96 - p80 [1-50]
    Legacy of the Darksword
    PW - v244 - My 12 '97 - p63 [51-250]
    Robot Blues
    LJ - v121 - N 15 '96 - p91 [51-250]
    Sentinels
    BL - v93 - N 15 '96 - p576 [51-250]
    KR - v64 - O 1 '96 - p1433+ [251-500]
    LJ - v121 - N 15 '96 - p91+ [51-250]
    PW - v243 - O 21 '96 - p75 [51-250]
Weis, W Michael - *Cold Warriors and Coups D'Etat*
    HAHR - v77 - My '97 - p363 [501+]
Weisberg, Chana - *The Crown of Creation*
    BL - v93 - Mr 1 '97 - p1071+ [51-250]
    LJ - v122 - Ap 15 '97 - p87 [51-250]
Weisberg, Herbert F - *Democracy's Feast*
    SSQ - v77 - Je '97 - p462+ [251-500]
    An Introduction to Survey Research, Polling, and Data Analysis. 3rd Ed.
    R&R Bk N - v11 - N '96 - p39 [51-250]
Weisberg, Jacob - *In Defense of Government*
    Choice - v34 - N '96 - p540 [51-250]
    Nat - v263 - O 28 '96 - p16+ [501+]
    Obs - D 1 '96 - p16* [1-50]
Weisberg, Richard H - *Vichy Law and the Holocaust in France*
    NYTLa - v146 - Mr 26 '97 - pC17 [501+]
Weisberg, Robert W - *What Is Creativity? (Lopez-Morillas). Audio Version*
    BL - v93 - F 15 '97 - p1038 [51-250]
Weiser, Alfons - *Die Gesellschaftliche Verantwortung Der Christen Nach Den Pastoralbriefen*
    Rel St Rev - v23 - Ja '97 - p75 [51-250]
Weisgall, Jonathan M - *Operation Crossroads*
    Pac A - v69 - Fall '96 - p453+ [501+]
Weishampel, David B - *Dinosaurs of the East Coast*
    Choice - v34 - Ja '97 - p824 [51-250]
    Nature - v384 - D 5 '96 - p426 [501+]
    SciTech - v20 - S '96 - p18 [1-50]
Weisheit, Eldon - *This Is the Baby (Illus. by Rick Incrocci)*
    c SLJ - v42 - O '96 - p42 [51-250]
Weisheit, Ralph A - *Crime and Policing in Rural and Small-Town America*
    J Gov Info - v23 - S '96 - p550 [51-250]
Weiss, Al - *Al Weiss's Official History of Karate in America*
    LJ - v121 - D '96 - p101 [51-250]
Weiss, Ann E - *Virtual Reality*
    y Ch BWatch - v6 - Jl '96 - p7 [1-50]
    c SB - v32 - Ag '96 - p176 [51-250]
    y VOYA - v19 - O '96 - p240 [51-250]
Weiss, Bernard G - *The Search for God's Law*
    Rel St Rev - v23 - Ja '97 - p11+ [501+]
Weiss, Bernard P - *I Am Jewish*
    c SLJ - v43 - F '97 - p88 [51-250]
Weiss, Brad - *The Making and Unmaking of the Haya Lived World*
    Choice - v34 - N '96 - p501+ [51-250]
Weiss, Brian L - *Only Love Is Real*
    Horoscope - v62 - Ag '96 - p42+ [501+]
    PW - v244 - F 17 '97 - p217 [1-50]
Weiss, Daniel Evan - *The Roaches Have No King*
    Obs - Ag 25 '96 - p18* [51-250]
    SFR - v21 - N '96 - p48 [1-50]
    The Swine's Wedding
    Ent W - N 29 '96 - p84 [51-250]
    KR - v64 - S 15 '96 - p1352 [251-500]
    PW - v243 - S 30 '96 - p75 [51-250]
Weiss, Ellen - *Color Me Criminal (Illus. by S M Taggart)*
    c BL - v93 - F 1 '97 - p941+ [51-250]
    c SLJ - v43 - F '97 - p85 [51-250]
    First Day at Day Care (Illus. by Nate Evans)
    c SLJ - v42 - Ag '96 - p122 [51-250]
    Where's Molly? (Illus. by Mary Collier)
    c HB Guide - v8 - Spr '97 - p53 [1-50]
Weiss, George David - *What a Wonderful World (Illus. by Ashley Bryan)*
    c LA - v73 - D '96 - p619 [51-250]

Weiss, Howard M - *Marine Animals of Southern New England and New York*
    r J Gov Info - v23 - S '96 - p580 [51-250]
Weiss, Jeffrey - *The Popular Culture of Modern Art*
    AHR - v101 - O '96 - p1222+ [501+]
    Art Bull - v78 - D '96 - p745+ [501+]
Weiss, John - *Economic Policy in Developing Countries*
    Econ J - v106 - N '96 - p1835 [251-500]
Weiss, Lawrence M - *Pathology of Lymph Nodes*
    SciTech - v20 - N '96 - p46 [51-250]
Weiss, Michael J - *Latitudes and Attitudes*
    J Am Cult - v19 - Spr '96 - p106+ [51-250]
Weiss, Peg - *Kandinsky and Old Russia*
    Art J - v55 - Fall '96 - p84+ [501+]
    Russ Rev - v56 - Ja '97 - p129+ [501+]
Weiss, Penny A - *Feminism and Community*
    NWSA Jnl - v8 - Sum '96 - p139+ [501+]
Weiss, Sabine - *Kurie Und Ortskirche*
    AHR - v101 - O '96 - p1192 [501+]
    EHR - v112 - Ap '97 - p452 [251-500]
    Specu - v71 - Jl '96 - p772+ [501+]
Weiss, Steve - *Allies in Conflict*
    Choice - v34 - My '97 - p1565 [51-250]
Weiss, Stuart L - *The President's Man*
    Choice - v34 - S '96 - p200 [51-250]
Weiss, Thomas Fischer - *Cellular Biophysics. Vols. 1-2*
    Choice - v34 - O '96 - p305 [51-250]
    Phys Today - v49 - D '96 - p54+ [501+]
    SciTech - v20 - N '96 - p28 [51-250]
Weiss, Thomas G - *Humanitarian Challenges and Intervention*
    R&R Bk N - v12 - F '97 - p55 [51-250]
Weiss, William R, Jr. - *The Catalog of Union Civil War Patriotic Covers*
    r Am Phil - v110 - D '96 - p1086+ [51-250]
Weissbach, Lee Shai - *The Synagogues of Kentucky*
    JSH - v62 - N '96 - p848+ [251-500]
Weissbourd, Richard - *The Vulnerable Child*
    Am - v175 - S 28 '96 - p35+ [501+]
    Comw - v123 - My 17 '96 - p18+ [501+]
    EL - v54 - O '96 - p88 [251-500]
    Fam in Soc - v77 - O '96 - p518+ [501+]
    SB - v32 - Ag '96 - p165 [51-250]
Weisser, Thomas - *Asian Trash Cinema*
    FQ - v49 - Fall '95 - p66+ [51-250]
Weissert, Carol S - *Governing Health*
    Choice - v34 - Mr '97 - p1194 [51-250]
    SciTech - v20 - D '96 - p38 [1-50]
Weisz, George - *The Medical Mandarins*
    AHR - v101 - D '96 - p1558+ [501+]
    Isis - v88 - Mr '97 - p153+ [501+]
    JMH - v68 - D '96 - p998+ [501+]
Weisz, Victor - *Vicky's Supermac*
    Obs - D 15 '96 - p17* [51-250]
Weisz, Virginia G - *Children and Adolescents in Need*
    Adoles - v32 - Spr '97 - p249 [51-250]
Weiten, Wayne - *Psychology: Themes and Variations. 3rd Ed.*
    R&R Bk N - v11 - D '96 - p2 [51-250]
Weitz, Margaret Collins - *Sisters in the Resistance*
    Wom R Bks - v14 - D '96 - p17+ [501+]
Weitzman, David - *Old Ironsides (Illus. by David Weitzman)*
    c BL - v93 - My 1 '97 - p1498 [51-250]
    c CBRS - v25 - Ap '97 - p107 [51-250]
    c HB - v73 - My '97 - p312 [51-250]
    c KR - v65 - F 15 '97 - p307+ [51-250]
Weitzman, David L - *Theater*
    y BL - v93 - F 1 '97 - p935 [51-250]
    c HB Guide - v8 - Spr '97 - p162 [51-250]
    c KR - v64 - O 15 '96 - p1539 [51-250]
    y SLJ - v42 - N '96 - p130 [51-250]
    y VOYA - v19 - D '96 - p294 [51-250]
Weitzman, Eben A - *Computer Programs for Qualitative Data Analysis*
    HER - v66 - Fall '96 - p686+ [501+]
Weitzman, Elizabeth - *Let's Talk about Foster Homes*
    c SLJ - v42 - D '96 - p130+ [51-250]
    Let's Talk about Living in a Blended Family
    c SLJ - v43 - Ja '97 - p103 [51-250]
    Let's Talk about Living with a Single Parent
    c SLJ - v43 - Ja '97 - p110 [51-250]
    Let's Talk about Smoking
    c SLJ - v43 - Ja '97 - p110 [51-250]
    Let's Talk about Staying in a Shelter
    c SLJ - v42 - D '96 - p118 [51-250]
    Let's Talk about When a Parent Dies
    c SLJ - v42 - D '96 - p118 [51-250]

Let's Talk about When Someone You Love Has Alzheimer's Disease
  c BL - v93 - Mr 1 '97 - p1168 [51-250]
  c SLJ - v42 - Ag '96 - p141 [51-250]
Let's Talk about Your Parents' Divorce
  c SLJ - v42 - D '96 - p130+ [51-250]
Weitzmann, Kurt - *Sailing with Byzantium from Europe to America*
  BC - v45 - Aut '96 - p386+ [251-500]
Weizmann, Daniel - *Take a Stand! (Illus. by Jack Keely)*
  c SLJ - v42 - D '96 - p134 [51-250]
Wekesser, Carol - *Pornography*
  y Kliatt - v31 - Mr '97 - p30 [51-250]
  y SLJ - v43 - F '97 - p112 [51-250]
Smoking
  y Kliatt - v31 - Mr '97 - p29+ [51-250]
  y SLJ - v43 - Mr '97 - p210 [51-250]
Welch, Claude E - *Protecting Human Rights in Africa*
  Africa T - v43 - 4 '96 - p423+ [501+]
  For Aff - v76 - Mr '97 - p200 [51-250]
  TLS - F 21 '97 - p3+ [501+]
Welch, Edwin - *Spiritual Pilgrim*
  Albion - v28 - Win '96 - p700+ [501+]
Welch, Evelyn S - *Art and Authority in Renaissance Milan*
  Apo - v144 - Ag '96 - p71+ [501+]
  Six Ct J - v27 - Win '96 - p1229+ [501+]
Welch, James - *Killing Custer*
  J Am St - v30 - Ag '96 - p301+ [501+]
Welch, John - *The Carmelite Way*
  RR - v56 - Mr '97 - p220+ [51-250]
Welch, Robert - *The Oxford Companion to Irish Literature*
  r Choice - v34 - S '96 - p104 [51-250]
  r CLW - v67 - D '96 - p49 [251-500]
  r CR - v269 - Ag '96 - p106+ [501+]
  r ILS - v15 - Fall '96 - p24+ [501+]
  r Nine-C Lit - v51 - D '96 - p428 [51-250]
  r Quad - v40 - S '96 - p84+ [501+]
  r WLT - v70 - Aut '96 - p1006+ [251-500]
Welch, Sheila Kelly - *A Horse for All Seasons*
  y Ch BWatch - v7 - F '97 - p5 [1-50]
Welch, Susan - *Crowning the Queen of Love*
  KR - v65 - Mr 15 '97 - p416 [251-500]
  PW - v244 - Mr 31 '97 - p63 [51-250]
Welch, Theodore F - *Libraries and Librarianship in Japan*
  LJ - v122 - Ap 15 '97 - p126 [51-250]
Welch, William C - *The Southern Heirloom Garden*
  Hort - v74 - Ag '96 - p65+ [501+]
Welchman, Jennifer - *Dewey's Ethical Thought*
  Ethics - v107 - O '96 - p193+ [51-250]
Welchman, John C - *Rethinking Borders*
  Afterimage - v24 - Ja '97 - p23 [51-250]
Welcome to the Catholic Church. Electronic Media Version
  r LJ - v122 - Mr 15 '97 - p97 [51-250]
Weldon, Fay - *Splitting*
  Books - v10 - Je '96 - p25 [51-250]
  LATBR - Jl 14 '96 - p11 [51-250]
Splitting (Hodge). Audio Version
  TLS - Ag 2 '96 - p24 [1-50]
Wicked Women
  BL - v93 - Ap 1 '97 - p1269 [51-250]
  KR - v65 - Mr 15 '97 - p417 [251-500]
  LJ - v122 - Ap 15 '97 - p123 [51-250]
  Obs - D 22 '96 - p18* [51-250]
  PW - v244 - Ap 7 '97 - p70 [51-250]
Worst Fears
  NYTBR - v101 - D 8 '96 - p84 [1-50]
  Obs - N 10 '96 - p18* [501+]
  Spec - v277 - N 2 '96 - p45+ [501+]
  TLS - N 1 '96 - p26 [51-250]
  WLT - v71 - Win '97 - p153 [251-500]
Worst Fears (Porter). Audio Version
  BWatch - v18 - Mr '97 - p7 [1-50]
Weldon, Michael J - *The Psychotronic Video Guide*
  r ARBA - v28 - '97 - p519 [251-500]
  r Ent W - N 29 '96 - p84+ [51-250]
  r Necro - Fall '96 - p26+ [251-500]
  r SF Chr - v18 - O '96 - p81 [51-250]
Welfeld, Joseph A - *Contracting with Managed Care Organizations*
  r SciTech - v21 - Mr '97 - p47 [51-250]
Welfens, Paul J J - *Economic Aspects of German Unification. 2nd Ed.*
  JEL - v34 - D '96 - p2120+ [51-250]
European Monetary Integration. 3rd Ed.
  JEL - v34 - D '96 - p2050 [51-250]
Welford, Sue - *The Shadow of August*
  y Magpies - v11 - Jl '96 - p36 [51-250]

Siren Song
  y Sch Lib - v44 - Ag '96 - p121 [51-250]
Welker, Michael - *God the Spirit*
  JR - v77 - Ap '97 - p317+ [501+]
  TT - v53 - O '96 - p380+ [501+]
Wellbery, David E - *The Specular Moment*
  Choice - v34 - Ja '97 - p801 [51-250]
Wellen, Edward - *Mind Slash (Auberjonois). Audio Version*
  SF Chr - v18 - O '96 - p76 [51-250]
Wellen, Richard - *Dilemmas in Liberal Democratic Thought since Max Weber*
  Choice - v34 - Ap '97 - p1417 [51-250]
  R&R Bk N - v12 - F '97 - p59 [51-250]
Wellens, Karel - *Economic Conflicts and Disputes before the World Court 1922-1995*
  R&R Bk N - v11 - D '96 - p50 [51-250]
Weller, Anthony - *The Garden of the Peacocks*
  BL - v93 - O 1 '96 - p324 [51-250]
  NYTBR - v101 - O 27 '96 - p24 [501+]
  PW - v243 - S 2 '96 - p112+ [51-250]
Weller, David - *Arctic and Antarctic*
  c Sch Lib - v44 - N '96 - p166 [51-250]
Weller, Frances Ward - *Madaket Millie (Illus. by Marcia Sewall)*
  c BL - v93 - Mr 15 '97 - p1247 [51-250]
  c CCB-B - v50 - Ap '97 - p300 [51-250]
  c KR - v65 - F 1 '97 - p230 [51-250]
  c PW - v244 - Ja 27 '97 - p105+ [51-250]
Matthew Wheelock's Wall
  c CLW - v67 - Mr '97 - p15 [1-50]
Wellershoff, Dieter - *Zikadengeschrei*
  WLT - v71 - Win '97 - p142 [501+]
Welles, Orson - *Les Bravades (Illus. by Orson Welles)*
  c NY - v72 - N 18 '96 - p102 [1-50]
Wellhofer, E Spencer - *Democracy, Capitalism, and Empire in Late Victorian Britain 1885-1910*
  Choice - v34 - F '97 - p1021 [51-250]
  R&R Bk N - v11 - D '96 - p8 [51-250]
Welling, Peter G - *The Drug Development Process*
  SciTech - v20 - D '96 - p54 [51-250]
Wellington, Craig - *Willis and the Echo (Illus. by Cheryl Lloyd)*
  c Aust Bk R - Jl '96 - p61+ [501+]
  c Magpies - v11 - Jl '96 - p26 [51-250]
Wellington, Monica - *Night House, Bright House (Illus. by Monica Wellington)*
  c BL - v93 - F 1 '97 - p949 [51-250]
  c KR - v64 - N 15 '96 - p1677 [51-250]
  c PW - v243 - D 16 '96 - p58 [51-250]
Wellman, Carl - *Real Rights*
  Ethics - v107 - O '96 - p151+ [501+]
Wellman, Sam - *Christopher Columbus*
  c Ch BWatch - v6 - Jl '96 - p2 [1-50]
Wellner, Alison Stein - *Who's Buying for the Home*
  r Choice - v34 - My '97 - p1482 [51-250]
Wells, Alison - *Subtraction (Illus. by Richard Maccabe)*
  c HB Guide - v7 - Fall '96 - p330 [1-50]
Wells, Amy Stuart - *Stepping over the Color Line*
  y BL - v93 - F 15 '97 - p982 [51-250]
Wells, Angus - *Exile's Challenge*
  y BL - v93 - N 15 '96 - p576 [51-250]
Wells, Carol - *Abstracts of Giles County, Tennessee*
  r EGH - v50 - N '96 - p186 [51-250]
Wells, Carol Wilcox - *Creative Bead Weaving*
  TCI - v30 - O '96 - p55 [1-50]
Wells, Charlotte Catherine - *Law and Citizenship in Early Modern France*
  AHR - v101 - O '96 - p1218+ [501+]
  Historian - v58 - Sum '96 - p920+ [501+]
  JHI - v57 - O '96 - p725+ [501+]
  Ren Q - v50 - Spr '97 - p291+ [501+]
  Six Ct J - v27 - Fall '96 - p863+ [501+]
Wells, D G - *You Are a Mathematician*
  y BL - v93 - Mr 15 '97 - p1212 [51-250]
  y BL - v93 - Ap 1 '97 - p1343 [1-50]
  LJ - v122 - Mr 15 '97 - p86 [51-250]
  PW - v244 - F 24 '97 - p80 [1-50]
Wells, Daniel A - *The Literary Index to American Magazines 1850-1900*
  r AL - v69 - Mr '97 - p256 [51-250]
  r ARBA - v28 - '97 - p438 [51-250]
  r BL - v93 - N 15 '96 - p612 [51-250]
  r Choice - v34 - Ja '97 - p777 [51-250]
  r Nine-C Lit - v51 - Mr '97 - p567+ [51-250]
  r R&R Bk N - v11 - N '96 - p71 [51-250]
Wells, David F - *God in the Wasteland*
  JR - v76 - O '96 - p683 [51-250]

Wells, Diana - *100 Flowers and How They Got Their Names*
  BL - v93 - N 1 '96 - p468 [51-250]
  LJ - v122 - F 15 '97 - p155 [51-250]
  PW - v244 - Mr 3 '97 - p70 [51-250]
Wells, Donald A - *An Encyclopedia of War and Ethics*
  r ARBA - v28 - '97 - p529 [251-500]
  r BL - v93 - S 15 '96 - p283 [251-500]
  r Choice - v34 - S '96 - p96+ [51-250]
Wells, Donna - *Biotechnology*
  c Ch BWatch - v6 - My '96 - p6 [51-250]
  c HB Guide - v7 - Fall '96 - p349 [51-250]
  c SB - v32 - Ag '96 - p181 [51-250]
  c SLJ - v42 - S '96 - p216 [51-250]
Wells, G A - *The Jesus Legend*
  HT - v46 - O '96 - p55 [1-50]
  LJ - v121 - D '96 - p101 [51-250]
Wells, H G - *The Invisible Man (Hardwicke). Audio Version*
  LJ - v122 - Mr 15 '97 - p103 [51-250]
The Island of Doctor Moreau
  Choice - v34 - N '96 - p461+ [251-500]
  LJ - v121 - O 1 '96 - p132 [1-50]
  SFS - v24 - Mr '97 - p109+ [501+]
  TLS - D 20 '96 - p10 [501+]
The Island of Doctor Moreau. Audio Version
  y Ch BWatch - v7 - Ja '97 - p5 [1-50]
The Time Machine
  Choice - v34 - N '96 - p461+ [251-500]
  SFS - v23 - N '96 - p363+ [501+]
  TLS - D 20 '96 - p10 [501+]
The Time Machine. Centennial Ed.
  TLS - D 20 '96 - p10 [501+]
Wells, John G - *Kiss Your Stockbroker Goodbye*
  BL - v93 - F 15 '97 - p984 [51-250]
  LJ - v122 - F 15 '97 - p144 [51-250]
Wells, Kenneth B - *Caring for Depression*
  SciTech - v20 - D '96 - p46 [51-250]
Wells, Lisa K - *LabVIEW for Everyone*
  SciTech - v20 - D '96 - p4 [51-250]
Wells, M Cyrene - *Literacies Lost*
  JAAL - v40 - D '96 - p328 [51-250]
  Readings - v11 - D '96 - p27 [51-250]
Wells, Mark K - *Courage and Air Warfare*
  J Mil H - v60 - O '96 - p793+ [251-500]
Wells, Miriam J - *Strawberry Fields*
  Choice - v34 - D '96 - p653+ [51-250]
  JEL - v34 - D '96 - p2076 [51-250]
Wells, Patricia - *Patricia Wells at Home in Provence*
  BL - v93 - S 15 '96 - p198 [51-250]
  CSM - v89 - D 13 '96 - p10 [51-250]
  LJ - v121 - O 15 '96 - p85 [51-250]
  NYTBR - v101 - D 8 '96 - p71 [51-250]
Wells, Paul - *Post-Keynesian Economic Theory*
  JEL - v34 - S '96 - p1419 [51-250]
Wells, Peter - *The New European Automobile Industry*
  EG - v72 - O '96 - p467+ [501+]
Wells, Robert E - *How Do You Lift a Lion? (Illus. by Robert E Wells)*
  c HB Guide - v8 - Spr '97 - p133 [51-250]
  c SLJ - v43 - Ja '97 - p110 [51-250]
Wells, Robin Headlam - *Elizabethan Mythologies*
  RES - v47 - N '96 - p575+ [501+]
Wells, Rosemary - *Bunny Cakes (Illus. by Rosemary Wells)*
  c BL - v93 - Ja '97 - p857 [251-500]
  c CCB-B - v50 - Mr '97 - p261 [51-250]
  c KR - v65 - Ja 1 '97 - p67 [51-250]
  c PW - v243 - N 25 '96 - p74 [51-250]
  c SLJ - v43 - Ja '97 - p94 [51-250]
Edward's First Day at School
  c TES - S 27 '96 - p12* [501+]
Edward's First Night Away
  c TES - S 27 '96 - p12* [501+]
Edward's First Swimming Party
  c TES - S 27 '96 - p12* [501+]
Jack and the Beanstalk (Illus. by Norman Messenger)
  c Books - v11 - Ap '97 - p24 [51-250]
The Language of Doves (Illus. by Greg Shed)
  c BL - v92 - Ag '96 - p1909 [51-250]
  c CBRS - v25 - D '96 - p43+ [51-250]
  c CCB-B - v50 - S '96 - p36 [51-250]
  c Ch BWatch - v6 - O '96 - p5 [51-250]
  c HB Guide - v8 - Spr '97 - p53 [51-250]
  c Par Ch - v21 - Mr '97 - p8 [1-50]
  c SLJ - v42 - S '96 - p193+ [51-250]
  c Smith - v27 - N '96 - p173 [1-50]
Lassie Come Home (Illus. by Susan Jeffers)
  c CLW - v66 - Je '96 - p48 [51-250]

Max and Ruby's Midas (Illus. by Rosemary Wells)
  c Inst - v105 - My '96 - p69+ [1-50]
  c RT - v50 - O '96 - p134 [1-50]
Max's Dragon Shirt
  c PW - v244 - Ja 27 '97 - p108 [1-50]
Max's First Word
  c HB - v73 - Mr '97 - p186 [1-50]
McDuff Moves In (Illus. by Susan Jeffers)
  c BL - v93 - Ap 1 '97 - p1331 [51-250]
  c CCB-B - v50 - Ap '97 - p300 [51-250]
  c KR - v65 - Mr 1 '97 - p389 [51-250]
  c PW - v244 - F 17 '97 - p218 [51-250]
Noisy Nora (Illus. by Rosemary Wells)
  c PW - v244 - Ap 7 '97 - p93 [1-50]
Wells, Ruth - *The Farmer and the Poor God (Illus. by
  Yoshi)*
  c Ch BWatch - v6 - My '96 - p4 [1-50]
  c HB Guide - v7 - Fall '96 - p325 [51-250]
Wells, Samuel F - *New European Orders 1919 and 1991*
  For Aff - v75 - N '96 - p157+ [51-250]
  JEL - v35 - Mr '97 - p265+ [51-250]
Wells, Stuart J - *From Sage to Artisan*
  HR Mag - v42 - Mr '97 - p134 [51-250]
  LJ - v122 - Mr 15 '97 - p72 [51-250]
Wells, Stuart W, III - *Comics Collectibles and Their
  Values*
  r BWatch - v17 - S '96 - p7 [51-250]
Wells, Susan - *Sweet Reason*
  Choice - v34 - D '96 - p606 [51-250]
Wells, Susan, 1956- - *Jerusalem: In the Shadow of Heaven*
  CSM - v89 - D 5 '96 - pB2+ [51-250]
Wells-Barnett, Ida B - *The Memphis Diary of Ida B.
  Wells*
  Am Vis - v12 - F '97 - p29 [51-250]
  Southern Horrors and Other Writings
  Choice - v34 - Mr '97 - p1230 [51-250]
Welsch, Roger - *Diggin' In and Piggin' Out*
  KR - v65 - Mr 1 '97 - p371 [51-250]
  PW - v244 - My 5 '97 - p205 [51-250]
Welsh, Alan H - *Aspects of Statistical Inference*
  SciTech - v20 - D '96 - p16 [51-250]
Welsh, Alexander - *Freud's Wishful Dream Book*
  MP - v94 - F '97 - p416+ [501+]
Welsh, Carol - *An Annotated Guide to The Chronicles of
  Oklahoma 1921-1994*
  r JSH - v62 - N '96 - p859 [51-250]
  r WHQ - v28 - Spr '97 - p103 [1-50]
Welsh, Irvine - *Ecstasy*
  BW - v26 - S 8 '96 - p1+ [501+]
  Ent W - S 6 '96 - p70 [51-250]
  LATBR - Ag 18 '96 - p1+ [501+]
  Spec - v276 - My 25 '96 - p28 [251-500]
  TLS - Jl 7 '96 - p23 [501+]
  Marabou Stork Nightmares
  AJPsych - v153 - D '96 - p1641+ [501+]
  PW - v244 - Ja 27 '97 - p103 [1-50]
  Trainspotting
  BW - v26 - S 8 '96 - p1+ [501+]
  LATBR - Ag 18 '96 - p1+ [501+]
  SFR - v21 - S '96 - p48 [51-250]
  TLS - N 29 '96 - p13 [51-250]
  VLS - Win '96 - p12 [51-250]
  VV - v42 - Ja 7 '97 - p43 [251-500]
Welsh, JoAnne P - *Chintz Ceramics*
  Ant & CM - v101 - D '96 - p31+ [51-250]
Welsh, John P - *The Music of Stuart Saunders Smith*
  M Ed J - v83 - N '96 - p54 [1-50]
  Notes - v53 - Mr '97 - p815+ [501+]
Welsh, Matt - *Running Linux. 2nd Ed.*
  LJ - v121 - N 1 '96 - p104 [51-250]
Welsh, Michael, 1942- - *Europe United?*
  Choice - v34 - Ja '97 - p870 [51-250]
  R&R Bk N - v11 - D '96 - p48 [51-250]
  TLS - Ja 3 '97 - p5+ [501+]
Welsh, Michael E - *Dunes and Dreams*
  Pub Hist - v18 - Fall '96 - p164+ [501+]
Welsh, Pat - *All My Edens*
  Hort - v74 - D '96 - p61+ [51-250]
Welsh, Wayne N - *Counties in Court*
  APSR - v90 - D '96 - p926+ [501+]
  CS - v26 - Ja '97 - p87+ [501+]
Welsh, William J - *Research Libraries*
  Lib & Cul - v32 - Win '97 - p149+ [501+]
Welt, Bernard - *Mythomania: Fantasies, Fables, and
  Sheer Lies in Contemporary American Popular Art*
  BW - v26 - S 1 '96 - p12 [51-250]
Welter, John - *I Want to Buy a Vowel*
  y BL - v93 - Ja '97 - p764 [1-50]
  y BL - v93 - S 1 '96 - p66 [51-250]
  y BL - v93 - Ap 1 '97 - p1296 [1-50]
  NYTBR - v101 - D 29 '96 - p14+ [51-250]

Welter, Matt - *Word of Mouth*
  Sm Pr R - v29 - Ja '97 - p10 [501+]
Weltner, Peter - *The Risk of His Music*
  KR - v65 - Ja 15 '97 - p94 [251-500]
  PW - v244 - F 10 '97 - p68+ [51-250]
Wen, Chihua - *The Red Mirror*
  Pac A - v69 - Fall '96 - p459+ [251-500]
  TLS - O 25 '96 - p8+ [501+]
Wen, P H - *Dynamic Fracture Mechanics*
  SciTech - v21 - Mr '97 - p76 [51-250]
Wendel, Charles B - *Business Buzzwords*
  r Bus Bk R - v13 - 3 '96 - p121+ [51-250]
Wendel, Ute - *Jesaja Und Jeremiah*
  Rel St Rev - v23 - Ap '97 - p166 [51-250]
Wendell, Susan - *The Rejected Body*
  Ms - v7 - N '96 - p82 [1-50]
Wenders, Wim - *The Act of Seeing*
  Obs - Mr 16 '97 - p17* [501+]
Wendling, Patricia A - *Adventures in Video*
  r ARBA - v28 - '97 - p145 [51-250]
  r Choice - v34 - O '96 - p259 [51-250]
Wendorf, Richard - *Sir Joshua Reynolds: The Painter in
  Society*
  Choice - v34 - Ap '97 - p1328 [51-250]
Wendt, Albert - *Black Rainbow*
  WLT - v71 - Win '97 - p232+ [501+]
Wendt, Lloyd M - *Dogs: A Historical Journey*
  Trib Bks - F 9 '97 - p1+ [501+]
Wenger, Beth S - *New York Jews and the Great
  Depression*
  Choice - v34 - Ap '97 - p1408 [51-250]
  LJ - v121 - D '96 - p120 [51-250]
  NL - v80 - Ja 13 '97 - p18+ [501+]
  Obs - Ja 12 '97 - p17* [501+]
  PW - v243 - N 11 '96 - p66 [51-250]
Wengert, Timothy J - *Telling the Churches' Stories*
  CH - v65 - D '96 - p788+ [501+]
  Rel St Rev - v22 - O '96 - p339+ [51-250]
  Six Ct J - v27 - Fall '96 - p843 [251-500]
Wenig, Laurin - *Forty Days of Grace*
  CLW - v67 - D '96 - p54 [51-250]
  RR - v56 - Ja '97 - p105 [51-250]
Wenig, Raymond - *Wireless LANs*
  CBR - v14 - N '96 - p39 [51-250]
Weninger, Brigitte - *Ragged Bear (Illus. by Alan Marks)*
  c HB Guide - v8 - Spr '97 - p53 [1-50]
  c KR - v64 - N 1 '96 - p1609 [51-250]
  c SLJ - v42 - D '96 - p109 [51-250]
  What Have You Done, Davy? (Illus. by Eve Tharlet)
  c HB Guide - v7 - Fall '96 - p280 [51-250]
  c JB - v60 - Ag '96 - p144 [51-250]
  Where Have You Gone, Davy? (Illus. by Eve Tharlet)
  c BL - v93 - D 1 '96 - p670 [51-250]
  c HB Guide - v8 - Spr '97 - p53 [51-250]
  c SLJ - v43 - Ja '97 - p94 [51-250]
  Will You Mind the Baby, Davy? (Illus. by Eve Tharlet)
  c BL - v93 - My 15 '97 - p1582 [51-250]
Weninger, Robert - *Framing a Novelist*
  Ger Q - v69 - Fall '96 - p461+ [501+]
  Literarische Konventionen
  Ger Q - v69 - Spr '96 - p202+ [501+]
Wenke, John Paul - *Melville's Muse*
  AL - v69 - Mr '97 - p217+ [251-500]
  Nine-C Lit - v51 - D '96 - p428 [1-50]
Wenner, Paul - *Garden Cuisine*
  BL - v93 - Mr 15 '97 - p1214 [51-250]
  LJ - v122 - Ap 15 '97 - p108+ [51-250]
Wennerstrom, Jack - *Leaning Sycamores*
  SciTech - v20 - S '96 - p18 [1-50]
Wenz, Peter S - *Nature's Keeper*
  Choice - v34 - F '97 - p982 [51-250]
Wenz, Philip S - *Adding to a House*
  LJ - v122 - F 1 '97 - p52 [1-50]
Wenzel, David - *Fairy Tales of the Brothers Grimm*
  y Par Ch - v20 - N '96 - p11 [1-50]
Wenzel, Siegfried - *Macaronic Sermons*
  EHR - v112 - F '97 - p176+ [501+]
  Specu - v71 - Jl '96 - p773+ [501+]
Wepman, Dennis - *The Struggle for Freedom*
  y HB Guide - v7 - Fall '96 - p389+ [51-250]
  y VOYA - v19 - O '96 - p240 [251-500]
Werbizky, George G - *Ostarbeiter Mail in World War II*
  Phil Lit R - v46 - 1 '97 - p74+ [51-250]
Werblowsky, R J Zwi - *The Oxford Dictionary of the
  Jewish Religion*
  r LJ - v122 - Ap 15 '97 - p70+ [51-250]
Werner, Emmy E - *Pioneer Children on the Journey West*
  AHR - v102 - F '97 - p182+ [251-500]
  TLS - Jl 19 '96 - p3+ [501+]
Werrell, Kenneth P - *Blankets of Fire*
  Choice - v34 - D '96 - p680 [51-250]

Wersba, Barbara - *Whistle Me Home*
  y BL - v93 - Ap 1 '97 - p1331 [51-250]
  y CBRS - v25 - Ap '97 - p107+ [51-250]
  y CCB-B - v50 - My '97 - p337 [51-250]
  y HB - v73 - My '97 - p330+ [51-250]
  y KR - v65 - Mr 1 '97 - p389 [51-250]
  y PW - v244 - Mr 24 '97 - p84 [51-250]
Wert, Jerry D - *Custer: The Controversial Life of George
  Armstrong Custer*
  y SLJ - v43 - Mr '97 - p218 [51-250]
Werth, James L - *Rational Suicide?*
  Readings - v11 - S '96 - p25 [51-250]
  R&R Bk N - v11 - N '96 - p77 [51-250]
Wertheim, Margaret - *Pythagoras' Trousers*
  Aust Bk R - Je '96 - p8+ [501+]
  Bks & Cult - v2 - S '96 - p11 [501+]
  Nature - v386 - Ap 3 '97 - p454 [51-250]
  New Sci - v153 - F 8 '97 - p43 [1-50]
  NS - v126 - Mr 7 '97 - p45 [501+]
  Obs - Mr 16 '97 - p17* [501+]
  Spec - v278 - Mr 1 '97 - p31 [501+]
Wertheimer, Alan - *Exploitation*
  Choice - v34 - Ja '97 - p880+ [51-250]
Wertheimer, Linda - *Listening to America*
  y Kliatt - v30 - S '96 - p34 [51-250]
  LATBR - Jl 7 '96 - p11 [51-250]
Wertsman, Vladimir F - *The Librarian's Companion. 2nd
  Ed.*
  r ARBA - v28 - '97 - p240 [51-250]
  r R&R Bk N - v12 - F '97 - p101 [51-250]
  What's Cooking in Multicultural America
  r ARBA - v28 - '97 - p571 [51-250]
Wertz, James R - *Reducing Space Mission Cost*
  SciTech - v21 - Mr '97 - p94 [51-250]
Wertz, Jay - *Smithsonian's Great Battles and Battlefields
  of the Civil War*
  r LJ - v122 - My 1 '97 - p129 [51-250]
Werup, Jacques - *Den Ofullbordade Himlen*
  WLT - v70 - Aut '96 - p981+ [501+]
Weschler, Lawrence - *Mr. Wilson's Cabinet of Wonder*
  BW - v27 - Ja 12 '97 - p12 [51-250]
  y Kliatt - v31 - Mr '97 - p37 [51-250]
  NYTBR - v102 - Mr 23 '97 - p28 [51-250]
  Trib Bks - F 2 '97 - p8 [1-50]
Wescott, Glenway - *The Grandmothers: A Family Portrait*
  R&R Bk N - v11 - N '96 - p73 [51-250]
Wesley, Mary - *An Imaginative Experience*
  SFR - v21 - N '96 - p48 [1-50]
  Part of the Furniture
  BL - v93 - Mr 1 '97 - p1113 [51-250]
  KR - v65 - F 1 '97 - p169+ [251-500]
  NS - v126 - F 14 '97 - p48 [501+]
  NYTBR - v102 - Ap 13 '97 - p17 [501+]
  PW - v244 - Ja 27 '97 - p75+ [251-500]
  Spec - v278 - F 8 '97 - p37+ [251-500]
  TLS - F 21 '97 - p23 [51-250]
Wesley, Valerie Wilson - *Freedom's Gifts (Illus. by
  Sharon Wilson)*
  c BL - v93 - My 1 '97 - p1498+ [51-250]
  c PW - v244 - Mr 31 '97 - p75 [51-250]
  Where Evil Sleeps
  Arm Det - v29 - Fall '96 - p499 [251-500]
  BW - v26 - Ag 18 '96 - p8 [51-250]
  Rapport - v19 - 6 '96 - p24 [51-250]
Wesman, Jane - *Dive Right In*
  PW - v244 - Mr 17 '97 - p81 [1-50]
Wesp, Clyde E - *Clinical Maps of Acute Care*
  SciTech - v20 - D '96 - p40 [51-250]
Wessel, John - *This Far, No Further*
  BL - v92 - Ag '96 - p1857 [251-500]
  NYTBR - v101 - O 27 '96 - p42 [51-250]
Wesseling, H L - *Divide and Rule*
  Choice - v34 - D '96 - p664 [51-250]
  R&R Bk N - v11 - D '96 - p12 [51-250]
Wesseling, Pieter, Dr. Ir. - *High Performance Computing
  in Fluid Dynamics*
  SciTech - v20 - N '96 - p16 [51-250]
Wesselman, Hank - *Spiritwalker (Tucker). Audio Version*
  y Kliatt - v30 - S '96 - p59 [51-250]
Wesselmann, Debbie Lee - *Trutor and the Balloonist*
  BL - v93 - My 15 '97 - p1564 [51-250]
  LJ - v122 - Ap 1 '97 - p132 [51-250]
  PW - v244 - Ap 7 '97 - p74 [51-250]
West, Carroll Van - *Tennessee's Historic Landscapes*
  r Pub Hist - v19 - Win '97 - p94+ [501+]
West, Chassie - *Loss of Innocence*
  PW - v244 - F 10 '97 - p81 [51-250]
West, Colin - *Buzz, Buzz, Buzz, Went Bumblebee*
  c HB Guide - v7 - Fall '96 - p245 [1-50]
  I Don't Care! Said the Bear
  c HB Guide - v7 - Fall '96 - p280+ [51-250]

Marmaduke the Magic Cat
  c Bks Keeps - v100 - S '96 - p10 [51-250]
West, Daphne - *Tanzit: A Bridge to Advanced Russian Language Studies*
  y TES - Mr 7 '97 - pR10 [51-250]
West, Delno C - *Braving the North Atlantic*
  c BL - v93 - D 15 '96 - p725 [51-250]
  c CCB-B - v50 - Ja '97 - p187+ [51-250]
  c HB Guide - v8 - Spr '97 - p163 [51-250]
  c SLJ - v42 - D '96 - p134+ [51-250]
West, Dorothy - *The Richer, the Poorer*
  y Kliatt - v30 - N '96 - p20 [51-250]
The Wedding
  LATBR - Mr 17 '96 - p11 [51-250]
West, Elliott - *Growing Up in Twentieth-Century America*
  r Choice - v34 - O '96 - p352+ [51-250]
  yr SLMQ - v25 - Fall '96 - p66 [51-250]
  r VOYA - v19 - D '96 - p301+ [51-250]
The Saloon on the Rocky Mountain Mining Frontier
  Obs - D 1 '96 - p18* [51-250]
  Roundup M - v4 - Ap '97 - p25 [51-250]
The Way to the West
  Bloom Rev - v16 - Jl '96 - p16 [51-250]
  PHR - v66 - F '97 - p102+ [51-250]
West, Frederick Hadleigh - *American Beginnings*
  Choice - v34 - Ap '97 - p1379 [51-250]
  Nature - v385 - Ja 9 '97 - p128+ [501+]
  New Sci - v153 - F 1 '97 - p46+ [501+]
West, James W - *The Betty Ford Center Book of Answers*
  y LJ - v122 - F 15 '97 - p151 [51-250]
West, John G - *The Politics of Revelation and Reason*
  AAPSS-A - v550 - Mr '97 - p188+ [251-500]
  Choice - v34 - N '96 - p477 [51-250]
  R&R Bk N - v11 - N '96 - p6 [1-50]
  W&M Q - v54 - Ap '97 - p454+ [501+]
West, Keith - *Raising Issues. Bks. 1-2*
  y Sch Lib - v44 - N '96 - p175 [51-250]
West, Linden - *Beyond Fragments*
  TES - Ja 24 '97 - p8* [51-250]
West, M L - *Ancient Greek Music*
  CW - v89 - Jl '96 - p493+ [251-500]
Greek Lyric Poetry
  CW - v90 - S '96 - p72+ [501+]
West, Mae - *Three Plays by Mae West*
  BL - v93 - Ja '97 - p806 [51-250]
  LJ - v122 - Ja '97 - p100 [51-250]
  PW - v243 - D 30 '96 - p52 [51-250]
West, Mark - *Trust Your Children*
  SLJ - v42 - S '96 - p112 [1-50]
West, Michael Lee - *American Pie*
  Ent W - S 13 '96 - p126+ [51-250]
  S Liv - v31 - N '96 - p48 [51-250]
West, Michelle - *Hunter's Death*
  y Kliatt - v30 - S '96 - p20+ [51-250]
  y VOYA - v19 - D '96 - p282 [51-250]
West, Morris - *Vanishing Point*
  Aust Bk R - S '96 - p31+ [501+]
A View from the Ridge
  Comw - v124 - Ap 11 '97 - p26+ [251-500]
  PW - v243 - S 30 '96 - p75+ [51-250]
West, Nathaniel - *A Cool Million. The Dream Life of Balso Snell*
  Trib Bks - Ja 12 '97 - p2 [1-50]
West, Nigel - *The Secret War for the Falklands*
  Books - v11 - Ap '97 - p20 [51-250]
  NS - v126 - Ja 17 '97 - p45 [501+]
West, Paul - *Sporting with Amaryllis*
  BL - v93 - N 1 '96 - p482 [51-250]
  KR - v64 - O 1 '96 - p1425 [251-500]
  LJ - v121 - N 15 '96 - p90 [51-250]
  NY - v72 - F 10 '97 - p83 [51-250]
  NYTBR - v102 - Ap 6 '97 - p14 [501+]
  PW - v243 - O 7 '96 - p59 [51-250]
West, Peter - *Fathers, Sons and Lovers*
  Aust Bk R - D '96 - p93 [1-50]
West, Rebecca - *Black Lamb and Grey Falcon*
  SFR - v21 - N '96 - p48 [1-50]
  VV - v41 - D 31 '96 - p47 [501+]
West, Robert - *Multiply Bonded Main Group Metals and Metalloids*
  SciTech - v20 - N '96 - p23 [51-250]
West, Robin - *My Very Own Birthday (Illus. by Jackie Urbanovic)*
  c HB Guide - v7 - Fall '96 - p353 [51-250]
My Very Own Mother's Day (Illus. by Jackie Urbanovic)
  c HB Guide - v7 - Fall '96 - p353 [51-250]
West, Shearer - *The Bulfinch Guide to Art History*
  r A Art - v61 - F '97 - p80 [501+]
  yr BL - v93 - N 15 '96 - p608 [251-500]
West Branch
  p Sm Pr R - v28 - D '96 - p18 [51-250]

West European Drawings of XVI-XX Centuries
  BM - v138 - O '96 - p695+ [501+]
Westall, Robert - *Blitzcat*
  y Kliatt - v30 - S '96 - p3 [1-50]
Blizzard
  y JB - v60 - D '96 - p279+ [251-500]
Cats Whispers and Tales (Illus. by Kate Aldous)
  c JB - v60 - O '96 - p209 [51-250]
  c Sch Lib - v44 - N '96 - p161 [51-250]
Cielo Negro Sobre Kuwait
  y JAAL - v40 - S '96 - p78 [51-250]
Gulf
  y BL - v93 - Ap 1 '97 - p1296 [1-50]
  y Emerg Lib - v24 - S '96 - p54 [51-250]
  y HB Guide - v7 - Fall '96 - p306 [51-250]
Harvest
  y JB - v60 - O '96 - p213 [51-250]
The Night Mare
  c Books - v9 - S '95 - p26 [1-50]
A Time of Fire
  c RT - v50 - F '97 - p422+ [51-250]
The Watch House
  y TES - Jl 5 '96 - pR8 [51-250]
Westberg, Daniel - *Right Practical Reason*
  Phil R - v105 - Ap '96 - p243+ [501+]
  Rel St Rev - v23 - Ap '97 - p152 [51-250]
Westbrook, Deeanne - *Ground Rules*
  Ant R - v54 - Fall '96 - p490+ [251-500]
Westbrook, Peter - *Harnessing Anger*
  y BL - v93 - My 15 '97 - p1555 [51-250]
  PW - v244 - Ap 28 '97 - p61 [51-250]
Westbrook, Robert - *Intimate Lies*
  Obs - F 9 '97 - p18* [51-250]
Westcott, Nadine Bernard - *I've Been Working on the Railroad*
  c HB Guide - v7 - Fall '96 - p357 [51-250]
Westen, C J Van - *Planning Estuaries*
  SciTech - v20 - D '96 - p2 [51-250]
Westerfield, Donald L - *War Powers*
  APSR - v91 - Mr '97 - p204+ [501+]
  Choice - v34 - O '96 - p363 [51-250]
Westerfield, H Bradford - *Inside CIA's Private World*
  Arm F&S - v23 - Win '96 - p310+ [501+]
  PSQ - v111 - Fall '96 - p530+ [501+]
Westerkamp, Marilyn J - *Triumph of the Laity*
  JR - v77 - Ap '97 - p268+ [501+]
Westerlund, David - *Questioning the Secular State*
  Choice - v34 - S '96 - p146 [51-250]
Westermann, Claus - *Roots of Wisdom*
  Intpr - v51 - Ja '97 - p83+ [251-500]
Westermann, John - *The Honor Farm*
  Arm Det - v30 - Win '97 - p109 [251-500]
  BL - v93 - O 1 '96 - p326 [51-250]
  KR - v64 - O 1 '96 - p1425 [251-500]
  LJ - v121 - N 1 '96 - p111 [51-250]
  PW - v243 - O 14 '96 - p64 [51-250]
Westermann, Mariet - *A Worldly Art*
  NYTBR - v101 - D 8 '96 - p22 [51-250]
Western Mail and South Wales Echo and Wales on Sunday on CD-Rom. Electronic Media Version
  r LAR - v98 - Je '96 - p321 [51-250]
Westfahl, Gary - *Cosmic Engineers*
  Ext - v37 - Win '96 - p364+ [501+]
Westfall, Patricia Tichenor - *Fowl Play*
  y BL - v93 - N 15 '96 - p575 [51-250]
  KR - v64 - S 15 '96 - p1359 [51-250]
  LJ - v121 - N 1 '96 - p111 [51-250]
  PW - v243 - S 23 '96 - p60 [51-250]
Westheider, James E - *Fighting on Two Fronts*
  BL - v93 - Mr 15 '97 - p1224 [51-250]
  LJ - v122 - Mr 15 '97 - p74+ [51-250]
Westheimer, Ruth K - *Heavenly Sex*
  LJ - v121 - D '96 - p126 [51-250]
The Value of Family
  BW - v26 - S 15 '96 - p13 [51-250]
Westlake, Donald E - *The Ax*
  LJ - v122 - My 1 '97 - p142 [51-250]
  PW - v244 - Ap 21 '97 - p64 [51-250]
The Hot Rock
  Nat R - v48 - D 23 '96 - p55 [51-250]
Murderous Schemes
  LJ - v121 - D '96 - p151 [51-250]
  WSJ-MW - v78 - D 9 '96 - pA12 [1-50]
Smoke
  Arm Det - v30 - Win '97 - p20 [51-250]
Smoke (Kramer). Audio Version
  y Kliatt - v30 - N '96 - p44 [51-250]
What's the Worst That Could Happen?
  BL - v92 - Ag '96 - p1857 [251-500]
  LJ - v121 - S 15 '96 - p101 [51-250]
  NYTBR - v101 - N 10 '96 - p62 [51-250]

Westlake, Martin - *The Council of the European Union*
  r RQ - v36 - Fall '96 - p124+ [501+]
Westling, Louise H - *The Green Breast of the New World*
  Choice - v34 - Ja '97 - p800 [51-250]
West-Meads, Zelda - *To Love, Honour and Betray*
  Books - v11 - Ap '97 - p21 [1-50]
Weston, Corinne Comstock - *The House of Lords and Ideological Politics*
  Historian - v59 - Win '97 - p484+ [501+]
Weston, Judith - *Directing Actors*
  BWatch - v17 - N '96 - p2 [51-250]
Weston, Kath - *Render Me, Gender Me*
  LJ - v122 - F 1 '97 - p98 [51-250]
  Wom R Bks - v14 - D '96 - p10+ [501+]
Weston, Martha - *Bad Baby Brother (Illus. by Martha Weston)*
  c KR - v65 - Ap 1 '97 - p562 [51-250]
Weston, Mary Ann - *Native Americans in the News*
  Choice - v34 - O '96 - p271 [251-500]
  JMCQ - v73 - Aut '96 - p761+ [501+]
Weston, Richard - *Modernism*
  Obs - O 20 '96 - p15* [501+]
  PW - v243 - S 30 '96 - p74 [51-250]
Weston, Ruth D - *Gothic Traditions and Narrative Techniques in the Fiction of Eudora Welty*
  J Am St - v30 - Ap '96 - p139+ [251-500]
Weston, William - *Masterworks in Lithography*
  BM - v138 - S '96 - p619+ [501+]
Westphal, Merold - *Becoming a Self*
  Choice - v34 - My '97 - p1518 [51-250]
Westphal, Sarah - *Textual Poetics of German Manuscripts 1300-1500*
  Ger Q - v69 - Fall '96 - p441+ [501+]
  Specu - v71 - O '96 - p1035+ [501+]
Westphal, Uwe - *Exil Ohne Ende*
  MLR - v91 - Jl '96 - p800+ [501+]
Westra, Haijo Jan - *The Berlin Commentary on Martianus Capella's De Nuptiis Philologiae Et Mercurii, Book 1*
  Specu - v72 - Ap '97 - p238+ [501+]
Westridge Young Writers Workshop - *Kids Explore America's Jewish Heritage*
  c Ch BWatch - v6 - S '96 - p8 [51-250]
  c Cur R - v36 - D '96 - p12 [51-250]
  c SLJ - v42 - N '96 - p119 [51-250]
Westrup, Hugh - *The Mammals*
  c HB Guide - v7 - Fall '96 - p333 [51-250]
Westwood, Chris - *Becoming Julia*
  c TES - Ap 4 '97 - p8* [51-250]
Virtual World
  c Bks Keeps - Mr '97 - p26 [51-250]
Wetherbe, James C - *The World on Time*
  BL - v93 - S 1 '96 - p46 [51-250]
Wetherell, W D - *Wherever That Great Heart May Be*
  HR - v49 - Aut '96 - p483+ [501+]
  LJ - v122 - Ja '97 - p184 [51-250]
  VQR - v72 - Aut '96 - p130* [51-250]
Wetsel, David - *Pascal and Disbelief*
  CH - v65 - S '96 - p499+ [501+]
  MLR - v91 - O '96 - p990+ [251-500]
  Rel St Rev - v23 - Ja '97 - p84+ [51-250]
  RM - v50 - D '96 - p428+ [501+]
  Theol St - v57 - Mr '96 - p148+ [501+]
Wetstein, Matthew E - *Abortion Rates in the United States*
  APSR - v91 - Mr '97 - p205+ [501+]
  Pol Stud J - v24 - Sum '96 - p321+ [501+]
  R&R Bk N - v12 - F '97 - p52 [51-250]
Wetterau, Bruce - *The Presidential Medal of Freedom*
  r BL - v93 - D 15 '96 - p750 [51-250]
  r Choice - v34 - Ap '97 - p1318 [51-250]
Wetterer, Margaret K - *Clyde Tombaugh and the Search for Planet X (Illus. by Laurie A Caple)*
  c BL - v93 - D 15 '96 - p725 [51-250]
  c HB Guide - v8 - Spr '97 - p112 [51-250]
  c SLJ - v43 - Ja '97 - p110 [51-250]
  c S&T - v93 - Ap '97 - p65 [51-250]
The Snow Walker (Illus. by Mary O'Keefe Young)
  c CCB-B - v50 - D '96 - p155 [51-250]
  c HB Guide - v7 - Fall '96 - p390 [51-250]
Wettre, Asa - *Old Swedish Quilts*
  Am Craft - v56 - Ag '96 - p62 [1-50]
Wetzel, David - *From the Berlin Museum to the Berlin Wall*
  HT - v46 - O '96 - p57 [1-50]
  R&R Bk N - v12 - F '97 - p16 [51-250]
Wetzel, Donald - *As I Walked Out One Evening*
  PW - v244 - Ap 28 '97 - p56 [51-250]
Wever, Grace - *Strategic Environmental Management*
  R&R Bk N - v11 - D '96 - p27 [51-250]
Wever, Kirsten - *Negotiating Competitiveness*
  ILRR - v50 - O '96 - p179+ [501+]

Weverka, Peter - *Quicken 6 for Windows for Busy People*
    CBR - v15 - Spr '97 - p3 [1-50]
    LJ - v122 - Ja '97 - p138 [1-50]
Wevers, John William - *Notes on the Greek Text of Deuteronomy*
    Rel St Rev - v23 - Ja '97 - p58 [51-250]
Wexler, Alice - *Mapping Fate*
    Nature - v385 - Ja 30 '97 - p408 [1-50]
    New Sci - v152 - D 21 '96 - p70 [1-50]
    PW - v243 - O 7 '96 - p69 [1-50]
Wexler, Jerome - *Everyday Mysteries*
    c RT - v50 - D '96 - p347 [51-250]
    Sundew Stranglers
    c RT - v50 - S '96 - p56 [51-250]
Wexler, John A - *The Complete Guide to the 1995 Doubled Die Cent Varieties*
    r Coin W - v37 - S 23 '96 - p16 [51-250]
Wexler, Madelin - *Dining in Style*
    r TCI - v30 - O '96 - p58 [1-50]
Wexler, Paul - *The Non-Jewish Origins of the Sephardic Jews*
    Choice - v34 - S '96 - p191 [51-250]
    R&R Bk N - v12 - F '97 - p19 [51-250]
Wexman, Virginia Wright - *Creating the Couple*
    J Film & Vid - v48 - Win '96 - p56+ [251-500]
Weyant, Robbin - *Identification of Unusual Pathogenic Gram-Negative Aerobic and Facultatively Anaerobic Bacteria. 2nd Ed.*
    r SciTech - v20 - N '96 - p35 [51-250]
Weyer, Johann - *Witches, Devils, and Doctors in the Renaissance*
    Historian - v58 - Sum '96 - p922+ [501+]
Weyl, Hermann - *Le Continu Et Autres Ecrits*
    Isis - v87 - D '96 - p744 [251-500]
Weyland, Kurt Gerhard - *Democracy without Equity*
    R&R Bk N - v12 - F '97 - p36 [51-250]
Wezeman, Phyllis Vos - *20 Prayer Lessons for Children*
    c CLW - v67 - Mr '97 - p44 [51-250]
Whaddaya Doin' in There?
    c PW - v243 - N 25 '96 - p78 [1-50]
Whalen, Charles J - *Political Economy for the 21st Century*
    JEL - v34 - S '96 - p1404 [51-250]
    JEL - v35 - Mr '97 - p121+ [501+]
Whalen, Mollie - *Counseling to End Violence against Women*
    Choice - v34 - O '96 - p369 [51-250]
    Readings - v12 - Mr '97 - p22 [51-250]
Whalen, Philip - *Canoeing Up Cabarga Creek*
    Tric - v6 - Fall '96 - p143+ [501+]
Whalen, Sharla - *Meet the Friends*
    c BL - v93 - My 15 '97 - p1576 [51-250]
Whaley, Emily - *Mrs. Whaley and Her Charleston Garden*
    BL - v93 - Mr 1 '97 - p1102 [51-250]
    KR - v65 - F 15 '97 - p290 [251-500]
    PW - v244 - F 17 '97 - p203 [51-250]
Wharton, Brooke - *The Writer Got Screwed (but Didn't Have to Go)*
    Emmy - v18 - O '96 - p50+ [51-250]
Wharton, Edith - *The Age of Innocence (Woodward).*
    Audio Version
    y Kliatt - v30 - S '96 - p42 [51-250]
    The Custom of the Country
    AL - v68 - D '96 - p765+ [501+]
    Ethan Frome (Osgood). Audio Version
    Books - v11 - Ap '97 - p19 [1-50]
    French Ways and Their Meaning
    PW - v244 - Mr 31 '97 - p57 [1-50]
    The Glimpses of the Moon
    Bloom Rev - v16 - Jl '96 - p27 [1-50]
    The House of Mirth
    RES - v47 - Ag '96 - p441+ [501+]
    The Reef (Underwood). Audio Version
    y Kliatt - v31 - Mr '97 - p44 [51-250]
    LJ - v121 - O 15 '96 - p102 [51-250]
    The Uncollected Critical Writings
    BL - v93 - F 1 '97 - p921 [51-250]
    KR - v64 - O 15 '96 - p1523 [251-500]
    LJ - v122 - Ja '97 - p100 [51-250]
    New R - v216 - Ja 20 '97 - p38+ [501+]
    NYTBR - v102 - F 16 '97 - p19 [51-250]
    PW - v243 - N 11 '96 - p62 [51-250]
Wharton, Lynda - *Natural Women's Health*
    Adoles - v32 - Spr '97 - p248+ [51-250]
    BWatch - v17 - N '96 - p3 [51-250]
Wharton, Thomas - *Icefields*
    BW - v26 - O 20 '96 - p7 [501+]
    NYTBR - v101 - O 13 '96 - p21 [51-250]
    Obs - Ja 19 '97 - p15* [51-250]
    TLS - Ja 10 '97 - p21 [501+]

Wharton, William - *Houseboat on the Seine*
    Atl - v278 - Jl '96 - p110 [51-250]
What Do I Read Next?. Electronic Media Version
    yr BL - v93 - F 1 '97 - p961 [501+]
What Do I Read Next? 1990-
    r RQ - v36 - Win '96 - p208+ [51-250]
What Is Enlightenment?
    p LJ - v122 - Mr 15 '97 - p95 [51-250]
What Makes Popcorn Pop?
    c Emerg Lib - v23 - My '96 - p45 [51-250]
What on Earth? Series
    c Cur R - v36 - N '96 - p12 [51-250]
What the Painter Sees
    c HB Guide - v7 - Fall '96 - p355 [51-250]
    c Sch Lib - v44 - Ag '96 - p114 [51-250]
    c TES - Ag 23 '96 - p24 [51-250]
What Your Travel Agent Knows That You Don't
    PW - v244 - F 17 '97 - p207 [1-50]
    Quill & Q - v63 - Mr '97 - p72+ [251-500]
Whatley, Bruce - *Detective Donut and the Wild Goose Chase*
    c PW - v244 - Ap 14 '97 - p74 [51-250]
    Tales from Grandad's Attic (Illus. by Bruce Whatley)
    c Magpies - v11 - My '96 - p38 [51-250]
Whayne, Jeannie - *Cultural Encounters in the Early South*
    JSH - v63 - F '97 - p140 [251-500]
Wheat, Carolyn - *Mean Streak*
    Arm Det - v29 - Fall '96 - p468 [1-50]
    Arm Det - v29 - Fall '96 - p483 [251-500]
    Where Nobody Dies
    BWatch - v17 - S '96 - p2 [51-250]
Wheatcroft, Andrew - *The Habsburgs: Embodying Empire*
    HRNB - v25 - Fall '96 - p27 [251-500]
Wheatcroft, Geoffrey - *The Controversy of Zion*
    BL - v93 - S 1 '96 - p43+ [51-250]
    Econ - v340 - S 14 '96 - p7* [251-500]
    For Aff - v76 - Mr '97 - p193 [51-250]
    LJ - v121 - O 15 '96 - p74+ [51-250]
    NYTBR - v101 - O 13 '96 - p8 [501+]
    NYTBR - v101 - D 8 '96 - p85 [1-50]
    PW - v243 - Jl 22 '96 - p223+ [51-250]
    Spec - v277 - N 16 '96 - p44 [1-50]
Wheathill, Anne - *A Handfull of Holesome (though Homelie) Hearbs 1584*
    Six Ct J - v27 - Fall '96 - p659+ [501+]
Wheatley, Margaret J - *Leadership and the New Science*
    PAR - v56 - S '96 - p495+ [501+]
    A Simpler Way
    BL - v92 - Ag '96 - p1852 [251-500]
Wheatley, Nigel - *Where to Watch Birds in Africa*
    r Wildbird - v10 - N '96 - p49 [51-250]
    Where to Watch Birds in South America
    r Wildbird - v10 - N '96 - p49 [51-250]
Wheaton, Elizabeth - *Myra Bradwell: First Woman Lawyer*
    y BL - v93 - Mr 1 '97 - p1155 [51-250]
    y KR - v64 - D 1 '96 - p1742 [51-250]
Wheelas, Jamie - *Wild Plum at Night*
    BL - v93 - N 1 '96 - p482 [51-250]
Wheeler, Brannon M - *Applying the Canon in Islam*
    R&R Bk N - v11 - D '96 - p43 [51-250]
Wheeler, Cindy - *The Emperor's Birthday Suit (Illus. by R W Alley)*
    c BL - v93 - S 15 '96 - p253 [51-250]
Wheeler, David A - *Software Inspection*
    SciTech - v20 - S '96 - p7 [51-250]
Wheeler, Gerald E - *Kinkaid of the Seventh Fleet*
    J Gov Info - v23 - S '96 - p543 [51-250]
    J Mil H - v60 - O '96 - p788 [251-500]
    R&R Bk N - v11 - D '96 - p72 [51-250]
Wheeler, Joe L - *Christmas in My Heart*
    y BL - v93 - N 15 '96 - p569 [51-250]
    Focus on the Family Presents Great Stories Remembered
    BL - v93 - Mr 1 '97 - p1111 [51-250]
Wheeler, Marjorie Spruill - *Votes for Women!*
    JSH - v63 - F '97 - p193+ [501+]
Wheeler, Michael - *Ruskin and Environment*
    Albion - v28 - Fall '96 - p521+ [501+]
Wheeler, Richard S - *Second Lives*
    BL - v93 - My 15 '97 - p1564+ [51-250]
    PW - v244 - Ap 28 '97 - p50 [51-250]
    Sierra: A Novel of the California Gold Rush
    y BL - v93 - S 1 '96 - p66 [51-250]
    Roundup M - v4 - O '96 - p33 [251-500]
Wheeler, Sara - *Terra Incognita*
    New Sci - v151 - S 21 '96 - p54 [501+]
    Obs - O 6 '96 - p18* [501+]
    TLS - D 13 '96 - p30 [501+]

Wheeler, Simon J - *Manual of Small Animal Neurology. 2nd Ed.*
    SciTech - v20 - S '96 - p45 [51-250]
Wheeler, Sondra Ely - *Wealth as Peril and Obligation*
    Intpr - v51 - Ap '97 - p206+ [251-500]
    TT - v53 - O '96 - p404+ [501+]
Wheeler, Susan - *Typesense: Making Sense of Type on the Computer*
    CBR - v14 - Jl '96 - p19+ [51-250]
Wheeler, Tony - *Bali and Lombok*
    r Quill & Q - v62 - S '96 - p22 [51-250]
Wheeless, Carl - *Landmarks of American Presidents*
    r ARBA - v28 - '97 - p179 [51-250]
    r Choice - v34 - S '96 - p107+ [51-250]
    r RQ - v36 - Fall '96 - p131+ [251-500]
Wheeless, Clifford R - *Atlas of Pelvic Surgery. 3rd Ed.*
    r SciTech - v21 - Mr '97 - p62 [51-250]
Wheelock, Arthur K - *Vermeer and the Art of Painting*
    Ren Q - v50 - Spr '97 - p329+ [501+]
    Sev Cent N - v54 - Spr '96 - p28 [501+]
    Six Ct J - v27 - Win '96 - p1237+ [501+]
Wheelwright, Jeff - *Degrees of Disaster*
    PW - v243 - S 23 '96 - p73 [1-50]
    SciTech - v21 - Mr '97 - p34 [1-50]
Whelan, Gloria - *The Indian School (Illus. by Gabriela Dellosso)*
    c CBRS - v25 - Ja '97 - p55 [51-250]
    c Ch BWatch - v6 - D '96 - p5 [51-250]
    c HB Guide - v8 - Spr '97 - p76 [51-250]
    c KR - v64 - S 15 '96 - p1409 [51-250]
    c PW - v243 - S 23 '96 - p77 [51-250]
    c SLJ - v42 - N '96 - p111 [51-250]
Whelan, Michael - *Living Strings*
    Comw - v123 - S 27 '96 - p29 [251-500]
Whelan, Richard - *Alfred Stieglitz: A Biography*
    Art J - v55 - Sum '96 - p105+ [501+]
Whelan, Robert J - *The Ecology of Fire*
    Am Sci - v85 - Mr '97 - p188+ [501+]
Where in the USA Is Carmen Sandiego?. Electronic Media Version
    c PW - v243 - N 25 '96 - p34+ [251-500]
Where's the Duckie? (Illus. by Stef De Reuver)
    c HB Guide - v7 - Fall '96 - p238 [51-250]
Whetstone
    p Sm Pr R - v28 - S '96 - p18 [51-250]
Whetung, James - *The Vision Seeker (Illus. by Paul Morin)*
    c BIC - v25 - D '96 - p35+ [251-500]
    c Emerg Lib - v24 - Mr '97 - p27 [1-50]
    c Quill & Q - v62 - Ag '96 - p43 [251-500]
Whigham, Frank - *Seizures of the Will in Early Modern English Drama*
    Choice - v34 - N '96 - p462 [51-250]
Whigham, Thomas L - *A Guide to Collections on Paraguay in the United States*
    r HAHR - v76 - N '96 - p753+ [501+]
Whinnom, Keith - *Medieval and Renaissance Spanish Literature*
    MLR - v92 - Ja '97 - p224+ [501+]
The Whirlwind War
    J Gov Info - v23 - S '96 - p542+ [1-50]
    Mar Crp G - v80 - O '96 - p76 [251-500]
    Pub Hist - v19 - Win '97 - p121+ [501+]
Whisenhunt, Donald W - *Poetry of the People*
    R&R Bk N - v11 - D '96 - p65 [51-250]
Whisler, Timothy R - *At the End of the Road*
    BHR - v70 - Sum '96 - p291+ [501+]
    JEH - v56 - D '96 - p939+ [501+]
Whisnant, David E - *Rascally Signs in Sacred Places*
    AHR - v102 - F '97 - p239+ [501+]
    WestFolk - v55 - Spr '96 - p174+ [501+]
Whistance-Smith, John Wallac - *Canadian Family On-Line*
    Quill & Q - v62 - My '96 - p21 [251-500]
Whistler, James McNeill - *Whistler on Art*
    Art J - v55 - Win '96 - p99+ [501+]
Whitaker, Craig - *Architecture and the American Dream*
    LJ - v121 - S 15 '96 - p65 [51-250]
    NYTLa - v146 - D 13 '96 - pC35 [501+]
Whitaker, John O - *National Audubon Society Field Guide to North American Mammals. Rev. Ed.*
    r ARBA - v28 - '97 - p589 [251-500]
    r Choice - v34 - O '96 - p259+ [51-250]
Whitaker, Ken - *Guide to Publishing User Manuals*
    CBR - v14 - S '96 - p27 [1-50]
Whitaker, Reg - *Cold War Canada*
    AHR - v101 - O '96 - p1318+ [501+]
    Can Hist R - v78 - Mr '97 - p139+ [501+]
Whitaker, Rogers E M - *All Aboard with E.M. Frimbo*
    Trib Bks - Ap 20 '97 - p8 [1-50]

Whitaker, William A - *White Male Applicant*
  y BL - v93 - F 15 '97 - p981 [51-250]
Whitbread, Ian K - *Greek Transport Amphorae*
    AJA - v101 - Ja '97 - p176+ [501+]
Whitburn, Joel - *The Billboard Book of Top 40 Albums. 3rd Ed.*
  r ARBA - v28 - '97 - p485 [51-250]
    The Billboard Book of Top 40 Hits. 6th Ed.
  r ARBA - v28 - '97 - p485 [251-500]
    Joel Whitburn's Top Pop Albums 1955-1996
  r ARBA - v28 - '97 - p488 [251-500]
    Joel Whitburn's Top R&B Singles 1942-1995
  r ARBA - v28 - '97 - p492 [51-250]
Whitcher, Susan - *Enchanter's Glass*
  c HB Guide - v7 - Fall '96 - p299 [51-250]
  c KR - v64 - My 1 '96 - p695 [51-250]
  y SF Chr - v18 - O '96 - p79 [51-250]
White, Alana J - *Sacagawea: Westward with Lewis and Clark*
  y KR - v65 - Ja 1 '97 - p67 [51-250]
White, Bailey - *Sleeping at the Starlight Motel and Other Adventures on the Way Back Home*
  y Kliatt - v30 - N '96 - p21 [51-250]
    LATBR - My 26 '96 - p11 [51-250]
White, Barbara Ehrlich - *Impressionists Side by Side*
    BL - v93 - N 1 '96 - p471+ [51-250]
    KR - v64 - Ag 15 '96 - p1228 [51-250]
    R&R Bk N - v12 - F '97 - p71 [51-250]
    WSJ-MW - v78 - D 5 '96 - pA18 [51-250]
White, Bebo - *HTML and the Art of Authoring for the World Wide Web*
    R&R Bk N - v11 - N '96 - p76 [51-250]
White, Brenda - *Library Materials Acquisitions*
    LAR - v98 - S '96 - p482 [51-250]
White, Bruce A - *PCR Cloning Protocols*
    SciTech - v21 - Mr '97 - p36 [51-250]
White, Carole Bess - *Made in Japan Ceramics Book II*
  r BWatch - v17 - S '96 - p7 [1-50]
White, Carolyn - *Whuppity Stoorie (Illus. by S D Schindler)*
  c PW - v244 - Ap 28 '97 - p74 [51-250]
White, Celeste - *The Natural Remedies for Common Ailments Handbook*
    BWatch - v17 - N '96 - p3 [51-250]
White, Christine A - *British and American Commercial Relations with Soviet Russia 1918-1924*
    Historian - v59 - Fall '96 - p211+ [501+]
White, Christine Schultz - *Now the Wolf Has Come*
    Roundup M - v3 - Ag '96 - p27+ [251-500]
    WHQ - v28 - Spr '97 - p76+ [251-500]
White, Christoper - *Anthony Van Dyck: Thomas Howard, the Earl of Arundel*
    BM - v138 - N '96 - p760 [251-500]
White, Curtis - *Anarcho-Hindu*
    Chel - 61 '96 - p154+ [501+]
White, David A - *News of the Plains and Rockies 1803-1865. Vol. 1*
    Roundup M - v4 - O '96 - p29 [251-500]
    WHQ - v28 - Spr '97 - p101 [1-50]
White, David C - *The Physiology and Biochemistry of Prokaryotes*
    BioSci - v46 - O '96 - p704 [501+]
White, Deborah Gray - *Let My People Go*
  y HB Guide - v7 - Fall '96 - p386 [51-250]
White, Donald W - *The American Century*
    Choice - v34 - My '97 - p1565 [51-250]
    For Aff - v76 - Mr '97 - p181+ [51-250]
    LJ - v121 - D '96 - p120 [51-250]
    PW - v243 - D 2 '96 - p49 [51-250]
White, E B - *Charlotte's Web (Illus. by Garth Williams)*
  c HMR - Win '96 - p45 [1-50]
  c JOYS - v10 - Fall '96 - p35+ [501+]
    Charlotte's Web (White). Audio Version
  c Trib Bks - F 2 '97 - p7 [1-50]
    White on White (White). Audio Version
    CSM - v89 - Ja 30 '97 - pB4 [51-250]
  y Kliatt - v31 - Mr '97 - p51 [51-250]
White, Edmund - *The Beautiful Room Is Empty*
    RCF - v16 - Fall '96 - p69+ [501+]
    A Boy's Own Story
    RCF - v16 - Fall '96 - p56+ [501+]
    The Burning Library
    Salm - Sum '96 - p208+ [501+]
    Caracole
    RCF - v16 - Fall '96 - p61+ [501+]
    The Darker Proof
    RCF - v16 - Fall '96 - p73+ [501+]
    Forgetting Elena
    RCF - v16 - Fall '96 - p31+ [501+]
    Mapplethorpe Altars
    Art J - v55 - Fall '96 - p99 [501+]

    Nocturnes for the King of Naples
    RCF - v16 - Fall '96 - p43+ [501+]
    States of Desire
    RCF - v16 - Fall '96 - p50+ [501+]
White, Ellen Emerson - *All Emergencies, Ring Super*
    PW - v244 - Ap 21 '97 - p64 [51-250]
    The Road Home
  y Emerg Lib - v24 - S '96 - p26 [1-50]
White, Eugene N - *Stock Market Crashes and Speculative Manias*
    JEL - v35 - Mr '97 - p261 [51-250]
White, Evelyn Davidson - *Choral Music by African American Composers. 2nd Ed.*
  r ARBA - v28 - '97 - p482 [51-250]
  r Choice - v34 - Mr '97 - p1144 [51-250]
White, G Edward - *Creating the National Pastime*
    Choice - v34 - S '96 - p166 [51-250]
    JEL - v34 - S '96 - p1475 [51-250]
    JIH - v27 - Spr '97 - p727+ [51-250]
    NYTBR - v101 - Ap 7 '96 - p11 [501+]
White, Gary - *Bassin' with the Best*
    BL - v93 - F 15 '97 - p994 [51-250]
White, Gillian - *The Beggar Bride*
    BL - v93 - Ap 1 '97 - p1282+ [51-250]
    KR - v65 - F 15 '97 - p255 [251-500]
    PW - v244 - Mr 24 '97 - p60+ [51-250]
White, Gloria - *Sunset and Santiago*
    LATBR - Ap 20 '97 - p13 [501+]
    PW - v243 - D 16 '96 - p55 [51-250]
White, Gordon - *In Search of Civil Society*
    JEL - v35 - Mr '97 - p292+ [51-250]
White, Graham - *Henry A. Wallace: His Search for a New World Order*
    AHR - v102 - F '97 - p211 [251-500]
    JSH - v62 - N '96 - p833+ [251-500]
White, Halbert - *Estimation, Inference and Specification Analysis*
    Econ J - v106 - S '96 - p1444+ [501+]
White, Harrison C - *Canvases and Careers*
    Socio R - v44 - N '96 - p772+ [501+]
White, Herbert S - *At the Crossroads*
    LR - v45 - 6 '96 - p65+ [251-500]
White, James, 1928- - *All Judgment Fled*
    Analog - v117 - Ap '97 - p147+ [51-250]
    LJ - v121 - N 1 '96 - p112 [1-50]
    Final Diagnosis
    KR - v65 - Mr 15 '97 - p424 [51-250]
    PW - v244 - Ap 28 '97 - p54 [51-250]
    The Galactic Gourmet
    Analog - v117 - Ja '97 - p141+ [51-250]
  y BL - v92 - Ag '96 - p1889 [51-250]
  y BL - v92 - Ag '96 - p1891 [1-50]
    BWatch - v17 - S '96 - p7 [51-250]
    MFSF - v92 - F '97 - p43+ [51-250]
    PW - v243 - Jl 22 '96 - p230 [51-250]
    The Watch Below
    Analog - v117 - Ap '97 - p147+ [51-250]
    LJ - v121 - N 1 '96 - p112 [1-50]
White, James Boyd, 1938- - *Acts of Hope*
    JC - v47 - Win '97 - p128+ [501+]
    Justice as Translation
    JC - v47 - Win '97 - p128+ [501+]
    This Book of Starres
    Ren Q - v49 - Win '96 - p894+ [501+]
White, James C - *Evaluating Climate Change Action Plans*
    R&R Bk N - v12 - F '97 - p29 [51-250]
White, James D, 1941- - *Karl Marx and the Intellectual Origins of Dialectical Materialism*
    Choice - v34 - Ap '97 - p1354 [51-250]
    The Russian Revolution 1917-1921
  r EHR - v111 - N '96 - p1338+ [251-500]
White, James F - *Roman Catholic Worship*
    CLW - v66 - Je '96 - p34 [51-250]
White, James Lindsay - *Rubber Processing*
    Choice - v34 - O '96 - p312 [51-250]
White, James W - *Ikki: Social Conflict and Political Protest in Early Modern Japan*
    APSR - v90 - D '96 - p874+ [501+]
    Pac A - v69 - Fall '96 - p426+ [501+]
White, Jeanne - *Weeding Out the Tears*
    KR - v65 - F 15 '97 - p291 [51-250]
    PW - v244 - Mr 10 '97 - p58 [51-250]
White, John H - *This Man Bernardin*
    CLW - v67 - D '96 - p36 [51-250]
White, Joseph - *Competing Solutions*
    AAPSS-A - v548 - N '96 - p231+ [501+]
    Pol Stud J - v24 - Sum '96 - p335 [51-250]
    Soc - v34 - Ja '97 - p80+ [501+]
White, Josh - *Designing 3D Graphics*
    SciTech - v20 - N '96 - p60 [51-250]

White, Kenton - *How to Publish Your Short and Long Fiction*
  r Choice - v34 - D '96 - p590 [51-250]
White, Kerry - *Australian Children's Fiction. Update 1996*
  r Magpies - v11 - Jl '96 - p15 [51-250]
White, Laurence B - *Math-a-Magic (Illus. by Ray Brockel)*
  c BL - v93 - Ap 1 '97 - p1342 [1-50]
White, Lawrence H - *Free Banking. Vols. 2-3*
    BusLR - v21 - 3 '96 - p213+ [501+]
White, Linda - *Too Many Pumpkins (Illus. by Megan Lloyd)*
  c BL - v93 - S 15 '96 - p252 [51-250]
  c CBRS - v25 - O '96 - p18 [1-50]
  c CCB-B - v50 - D '96 - p155 [51-250]
  c HB Guide - v8 - Spr '97 - p53 [51-250]
  c KR - v64 - S 1 '96 - p1330 [51-250]
  c SLJ - v42 - N '96 - p95 [51-250]
White, Mark J - *The Cuban Missile Crisis*
    PSQ - v111 - Fall '96 - p540+ [501+]
White, Martin S - *Gulf Logistics, Blackadder's War*
    Mar Crp G - v80 - N '96 - p81+ [501+]
White, Mel - *The Smithsonian Guides to Natural America: The South-Central States*
  y Kliatt - v30 - N '96 - p29 [51-250]
White, Michael - *The Science of the X-Files*
    New Sci - v152 - N 16 '96 - p52+ [501+]
    Obs - D 15 '96 - p16* [501+]
White, Michael C - *A Brother's Blood*
  y BL - v93 - O 1 '96 - p326 [51-250]
    KR - v64 - Ag 15 '96 - p1184+ [251-500]
    NYTBR - v101 - N 24 '96 - p26 [251-500]
    NYTBR - v101 - D 8 '96 - p94 [1-50]
    PW - v243 - S 9 '96 - p65 [51-250]
White, O Kendall, Jr. - *Religion in the Contemporary South*
    J Am Cult - v19 - Sum '96 - p149+ [501+]
White, Osmar - *Conquerors' Road*
    TLS - N 29 '96 - p14 [51-250]
White, Patricia - *Civic Virtues and Public Schooling*
    Choice - v34 - D '96 - p662 [51-250]
White, Patrick - *Letters*
    Choice - v34 - N '96 - p462 [51-250]
    NYTBR - v101 - Jl 21 '96 - p10+ [501+]
    PW - v243 - N 4 '96 - p46 [1-50]
    R&R Bk N - v11 - N '96 - p71 [1-50]
White, Peter - *It Pays to Play*
    Quill & Q - v63 - Mr '97 - p72 [51-250]
White, Randall P - *The Future of Leadership*
    BL - v93 - S 1 '96 - p46 [51-250]
White, Randy Wayne - *Captiva*
    Arm Det - v29 - Fall '96 - p479 [251-500]
    North of Havana
    KR - v65 - Mr 1 '97 - p339 [51-250]
    LJ - v122 - Ap 15 '97 - p121+ [51-250]
    PW - v244 - Mr 17 '97 - p77+ [51-250]
White, Richard - *The Organic Machine*
    PHR - v66 - F '97 - p109+ [251-500]
White, Ronald V - *New Ways in Teaching Writing*
    MLJ - v80 - Win '96 - p543+ [501+]
White, Ruth - *Belle Prater's Boy*
  y BL - v93 - Ap 1 '97 - p1296 [1-50]
  y BL - v93 - Ap 1 '97 - p1305 [1-50]
  c HB - v72 - S '96 - p601 [51-250]
  c HB Guide - v7 - Fall '96 - p299 [51-250]
  y NY - v72 - N 18 '96 - p102 [51-250]
  y NYTBR - v101 - O 27 '96 - p44 [501+]
  c PW - v243 - N 4 '96 - p49 [51-250]
  y SLJ - v42 - Je '96 - p32 [1-50]
  y SLJ - v43 - Mr '97 - p113 [1-50]
White, Sol - *History of Colored Baseball with Other Documents on the Early Black Games 1886-1936*
    Bl S - v26 - Fall '96 - p107 [51-250]
White, Stanford - *Stanford White: Letters to His Family*
    PW - v244 - Ap 28 '97 - p63 [251-500]
White, Stephen, 1945- - *Russia Goes Dry*
    Choice - v34 - N '96 - p522 [51-250]
White, Stephen K - *The Cambridge Companion to Habermas*
    CPR - v16 - Ap '96 - p151+ [501+]
    Ethics - v107 - Ja '97 - p369+ [501+]
    IPQ - v36 - D '96 - p498+ [501+]
White, Stephen Walsh - *Harm's Way*
    Arm Det - v29 - Fall '96 - p501 [251-500]
    Rapport - v19 - 4 '96 - p31 [251-500]

Remote Control
  BL - v93 - Ja '97 - p780 [51-250]
  KR - v65 - Ja 15 '97 - p94+ [251-500]
  LJ - v122 - Ja '97 - p151 [51-250]
  PW - v244 - Ja 20 '97 - p396 [51-250]
  Trib Bks - Ap 20 '97 - p7 [51-250]
Remote Control (Muller). Audio Version
  LJ - v122 - My 1 '97 - p154+ [51-250]
  PW - v244 - F 3 '97 - p42 [51-250]
White, Susan J - *Christian Worship and Technological
Change*
  ER - v49 - Ap '97 - p282+ [501+]
  JR - v77 - Ja '97 - p177+ [501+]
White, Suzanne - *Guide to Love*
  Horoscope - v62 - S '96 - p15 [251-500]
White, T H - *The Once and Future King*
  Analog - v117 - Ap '97 - p147+ [51-250]
White, Tekla N - *Missions of the San Francisco Bay Area*
  c BL - v93 - S 15 '96 - p236 [51-250]
  c HB Guide - v8 - Spr '97 - p172 [51-250]
  c SLJ - v42 - Ag '96 - p157+ [51-250]
White, Tiffany - *The 6'1 Grinch*
  LJ - v121 - N 15 '96 - p50 [51-250]
White, Timothy - *Music to My Ears*
  y BL - v93 - N 1 '96 - p472+ [51-250]
  LJ - v121 - O 15 '96 - p62 [51-250]
  PW - v243 - S 23 '96 - p63 [51-250]
The Nearest Faraway Place
  y Kliatt - v30 - S '96 - p27+ [51-250]
White Paper on Transport Policy (Namibia). Vol. 1
  J Gov Info - v23 - S '96 - p660 [1-50]
**White Plains Comprehensive Plan Management Group
(New York)** - *Comprehensive Plan*
  J Gov Info - v23 - S '96 - p601 [51-250]
The White Ravens 1995
  r ChLAQ - v20 - Fall '95 - p99 [1-50]
Whitebread, David - *Teaching and Learning in the Early
Years*
  r TES - F 7 '97 - p12* [501+]
Whitebrook, Joel - *Perversion and Utopia*
  AJS - v102 - Jl '96 - p265+ [501+]
Whitehead, B T - *Brags and Boasts*
  CR - v268 - Je '96 - p326+ [251-500]
Whitehead, Barbara Dafoe - *The Divorce Culture*
  BL - v93 - Ja '97 - p792+ [251-500]
  KR - v64 - N 15 '96 - p1661+ [251-500]
  LJ - v122 - F 15 '97 - p152 [51-250]
  New R - v216 - Ap 14 '97 - p30+ [501+]
  NYTBR - v102 - Ja 26 '97 - p21 [501+]
  Pub Int - Spr '97 - p115+ [501+]
  PW - v243 - D 2 '96 - p48 [51-250]
  Trib Bks - F 9 '97 - p6+ [501+]
  WSJ-Cent - v99 - Ja 21 '97 - pA12 [501+]
Whitehead, David - *From Political Architecture to
Stephanus Byzantius*
  Rel St Rev - v23 - Ja '97 - p60 [51-250]
Whitehead, Kim - *The Feminist Poetry Movement*
  Choice - v34 - My '97 - p1501 [51-250]
Whitehead, Laurence - *The International Dimensions of
Democratization*
  Choice - v34 - My '97 - p1574 [51-250]
  For Aff - v76 - My '97 - p124+ [51-250]
Whitehead, Marian - *The Development of Language and
Literacy*
  Sch Lib - v44 - N '96 - p178 [51-250]
Whitehead, Neil L - *Wolves from the Sea*
  Am Ant - v61 - Jl '96 - p615+ [501+]
  HAHR - v76 - Ag '96 - p552+ [251-500]
Whitehead, Ron - *I Will Not Bow Down*
  ABR - v18 - D '96 - p10+ [501+]
Whitehead, Sandra - *Lebanese Americans*
  yr Ch BWatch - v6 - O '96 - p5 [51-250]
  c HB Guide - v7 - Fall '96 - p312 [51-250]
Whitehorne, Joseph W A - *The Battle for Baltimore*
  BL - v93 - S 15 '96 - p217 [51-250]
Whitelam, Keith W - *The Invention of Ancient Israel*
  Choice - v34 - My '97 - p1561 [51-250]
  MEQ - v4 - Mr '97 - p75+ [501+]
  TLS - N 29 '96 - p11 [51-250]
Whitelaw, Billie - *Billie Whitelaw...Who He?*
  Books - v9 - S '95 - p23 [51-250]
  FIR - v47 - Jl '96 - p117 [501+]
Whitelaw, Nancy - *Nathaniel Hawthorne: American
Storyteller*
  y Ch BWatch - v7 - F '97 - p7 [1-50]
  y HB Guide - v8 - Spr '97 - p161 [51-250]
  y KR - v64 - S 1 '96 - p1330 [51-250]
  y SLJ - v43 - Mr '97 - p210 [51-250]
William Tecumseh Sherman: Defender and Destroyer
  y HB Guide - v7 - Fall '96 - p375 [51-250]
  y VOYA - v19 - O '96 - p241 [251-500]

Whiteley, Alma M - *The Teaching of Organizational
Behavior across Discipline and National Boundaries*
  JEL - v35 - Mr '97 - p190 [51-250]
Whiteley, Peter - *Lord North: The Prime Minister Who
Lost America*
  TLS - D 20 '96 - p8 [501+]
Whiteley, Richard - *Customer Centered Growth*
  Bus Bk R - v14 - 1 '97 - p84+ [501+]
  LJ - v122 - Mr 15 '97 - p36 [1-50]
Whiteman, David - *Communication in Congress*
  APSR - v90 - S '96 - p662+ [501+]
  J Pol - v59 - F '97 - p266+ [501+]
  PSQ - v111 - Win '96 - p707+ [501+]
Whiteman, Roberta Hill - *Philadelphia Flowers*
  Choice - v34 - S '96 - p131 [51-250]
White-Parks, Annette - *Sui Sin Far/Edith Maude Eaton*
  Amerasia J - v22 - 3 '96 - p149+ [501+]
Whiteread, Rachel - *Rachel Whiteread: Shedding Life*
  BM - v138 - D '96 - p837+ [501+]
Whites, LeeAnn - *The Civil War as a Crisis in Gender*
  HRNB - v25 - Fall '96 - p8 [501+]
  Wom R Bks - v14 - Mr '97 - p13+ [501+]
Whiteside, Abby - *Abby Whiteside on Piano Playing*
  LJ - v122 - My 1 '97 - p145 [51-250]
Whiteside, John, 1946- - *Flight of the Phoenix*
  BL - v93 - Ja '97 - p795 [51-250]
  PW - v243 - O 21 '96 - p77 [51-250]
Whiteside, Jonny - *Ramblin' Rose*
  KR - v65 - F 1 '97 - p213 [251-500]
Whitesides, Nigel - *Henry IV Part 1*
  c TES - F 7 '97 - p16* [51-250]
Macbeth
  c TES - F 7 '97 - p16* [51-250]
Romeo and Juliet
  c TES - F 7 '97 - p16* [51-250]
The Tempest
  c TES - F 7 '97 - p16* [51-250]
Whitestone, Heather - *Listening with My Heart*
  KR - v65 - My 1 '97 - p708 [251-500]
Whitfield, Emma - *Finishing Touches with Paint and
Paper*
  BL - v93 - Mr 15 '97 - p1219 [51-250]
Whitfield, Peter - *The Charting of the Oceans*
  r LJ - v122 - F 1 '97 - p75 [51-250]
The Mapping of the Heavens
  LR - v45 - 6 '96 - p60+ [251-500]
Whitfield, Roderick - *Dunhuang: Caves of the Singing
Sands*
  FEER - v160 - Ja 16 '97 - p38+ [501+]
Whitfield, Sarah - *Fauvism*
  LJ - v122 - Ap 15 '97 - p78 [51-250]
  NYTBR - v101 - D 8 '96 - p22 [251-500]
Whitfield, Stephen J - *The Culture of the Cold War. 2nd
Ed.*
  VQR - v72 - Aut '96 - p143* [1-50]
Whitin, Phyllis - *Sketching Stories, Stretching Minds*
  Kliatt - v31 - My '97 - p26 [51-250]
  SLJ - v42 - D '96 - p46 [51-250]
Whiting, Anthony - *The Never-Resting Mind*
  Choice - v34 - D '96 - p617 [51-250]
Whitley, David S - *A Guide to Rock Art Sites*
  r Nat Peop - v10 - '97 - p78+ [501+]
Whitley, M J - *Cruisers of World War Two*
  r ARBA - v28 - '97 - p259 [51-250]
  r Choice - v34 - S '96 - p108 [51-250]
Whitlock, Gillian - *Autographs: Contemporary Australian
Autobiography*
  Aust Bk R - D '96 - p93 [1-50]
Whitman, F H - *A Comparative Study of Old English
Metre*
  RES - v47 - N '96 - p552+ [501+]
Whitman, Jeffrey P - *The Power and Value of
Philosophical Skepticism*
  Choice - v34 - Ja '97 - p809+ [51-250]
Whitman, Sylvia - *Get Up and Go!*
  c Ch BWatch - v6 - S '96 - p5 [1-50]
  c HB Guide - v8 - Spr '97 - p176 [51-250]
  y SLJ - v42 - O '96 - p161 [51-250]
  y VOYA - v19 - F '97 - p354 [251-500]
Whitman, T Stephen - *The Price of Freedom*
  LJ - v122 - Ap 15 '97 - p98 [51-250]
Whitmer, John - *From Historian to Dissident*
  WHQ - v27 - Win '96 - p552 [51-250]
Whitmer, Peter - *The Inner Elvis*
  BW - v26 - Ag 4 '96 - p13 [51-250]
  LATBR - v263 - S 29 '96 - p4 [501+]
Whitmore, Harland William - *World Economy
Macroeconomics*
  R&R Bk N - v12 - F '97 - p43 [51-250]
Whitmore, Thomas - *Pleasant Weather Ratings*
  r BL - v93 - F 1 '97 - p966 [251-500]

Whitmyer, Margaret - *Fenton Art Glass*
  Ant & CM - v102 - Mr '97 - p33 [51-250]
Whitney, Ben - *Child Protection for Teachers and Schools*
  TES - Ag 30 '96 - p32 [501+]
Whitney, Brooks - *Jazz Up Your Jeans (Illus. by Geri
Strigenz Bourget)*
  c PW - v243 - S 9 '96 - p85 [51-250]
Whitney, Gordon G - *From Coastal Wilderness to Fruited
Plain*
  AHR - v101 - D '96 - p1618 [501+]
  JIH - v27 - Aut '96 - p326+ [501+]
  Nature - v384 - D 5 '96 - p426 [1-50]
  W&M Q - v53 - Jl '96 - p644+ [501+]
Whitney, Phyllis A - *Amethyst Dreams*
  BL - v93 - My 1 '97 - p1462 [51-250]
  KR - v65 - My 1 '97 - p675+ [251-500]
Snowfire (Harper). Audio Version
  BWatch - v18 - Mr '97 - p8 [1-50]
Whitney, Polly - *Until It Hurts*
  KR - v65 - Mr 1 '97 - p339 [51-250]
  PW - v244 - Mr 31 '97 - p66+ [51-250]
Whitson, Gene - *Handbook of Electrical Construction
Tools and Materials*
  Choice - v34 - N '96 - p490 [51-250]
Whitt, Margaret Earley - *Understanding Flannery
O'Connor*
  AL - v68 - D '96 - p871+ [501+]
Whittaker, David - *Mormon Americana*
  r CH - v66 - Mr '97 - p180+ [501+]
Whittaker, Lou - *Memoirs of a Mountain Guide*
  HM - v293 - Ag '96 - p64+ [501+]
Whittaker, Stella - *First Steps*
  J Gov Info - v23 - S '96 - p645 [51-250]
Whittell, Giles - *Central Asia*
  r FEER - v160 - Mr 27 '97 - p53 [501+]
Extreme Continental
  LJ - v121 - D '96 - p130 [51-250]
Whitten, David O - *Andrew Durnford: A Black Sugar
Planter in the Antebellum South. 2nd Ed.*
  JSH - v62 - N '96 - p804+ [251-500]
Whittier, Nancy - *Feminist Generations*
  CS - v26 - Ja '97 - p25+ [501+]
  NWSA Jnl - v8 - Fall '96 - p166+ [501+]
  SF - v75 - D '96 - p761+ [501+]
Whittier-Ferguson, John - *Framing Pieces*
  Choice - v34 - N '96 - p462 [51-250]
Whittle, Michael V - *Gait Analysis. 2nd Ed.*
  SciTech - v20 - N '96 - p32 [51-250]
Whittle, Peter - *Optimal Control*
  SciTech - v21 - Mr '97 - p84 [51-250]
Whittock, Martyn - *The Roman Empire*
  c HB Guide - v8 - Spr '97 - p165 [1-50]
  c SLJ - v42 - S '96 - p212 [51-250]
  y VOYA - v19 - D '96 - p285 [251-500]
Whitton, David - *Moliere: Don Juan*
  MLR - v91 - O '96 - p989+ [251-500]
Whittow, Mark - *The Making of Byzantium 600-1025*
  Choice - v34 - Mr '97 - p1216 [51-250]
Whitworth, John - *The Complete Poetical Works of
Phoebe Flood (Illus. by Lauren Child)*
  c Bks Keeps - Mr '97 - p23 [51-250]
Whitworth, Kathy - *Golf for Women*
  LJ - v121 - O 1 '96 - p53 [1-50]
**WHO Expert Committee on Biological Standardization:
Forty-Fifth Report**
  BioSci - v46 - O '96 - p722 [51-250]
Who Is Fourier?
  Math T - v89 - S '96 - p516+ [251-500]
Who Pays and When?
  J Gov Info - v23 - S '96 - p559 [51-250]
Who Was Who. Vol. 9
  r ARBA - v28 - '97 - p15 [51-250]
**Who Was Who in America. Vols. 1-12. Book and
Electronic Media Version**
  r ASInt - v34 - O '96 - p13 [51-250]
Wholesale and Retail Trade USA 1995
  r ARBA - v28 - '97 - p127+ [251-500]
  r Choice - v34 - D '96 - p596+ [51-250]
Wholey, Dennis - *The Miracle of Change*
  PW - v244 - Mr 17 '97 - p71 [51-250]
Who's Who 1897-1996. Electronic Media Version
  r HT - v46 - D '96 - p49 [51-250]
  yr Sch Lib - v45 - F '97 - p30 [251-500]
Who's Who in Finance and Industry 1996-1997
  r ARBA - v28 - '97 - p77+ [251-500]
Who's Who in Korean Literature
  r Choice - v34 - S '96 - p108 [51-250]
Who's Who in Labor 1946- (Dryden)
  r RQ - v36 - Fall '96 - p55 [51-250]
Who's Who in Labor (Arno)
  r RQ - v36 - Fall '96 - p55 [51-250]

Who's Who in Lebanon 1997-1998
r   MEJ - v51 - Win '97 - p149 [51-250]
r   R&R Bk N - v12 - F '97 - p18 [51-250]
Who's Who in Polish America 1996-1997
r   ARBA - v28 - '97 - p18 [51-250]
r   Choice - v34 - D '96 - p596 [51-250]
Who's Who in Science and Engineering 1996-1997
r   ARBA - v28 - '97 - p561 [51-250]
Who's Who in Science in Europe. 9th Ed., Vols. 1-2
r   ARBA - v28 - '97 - p561+ [51-250]
r   RQ - v36 - Win '96 - p306+ [251-500]
Who's Who in South African Politics. No. 5
r   ARBA - v28 - '97 - p275+ [51-250]
Who's Who in the Arab World 1997-1998
r   MEJ - v51 - Win '97 - p149 [51-250]
r   R&R Bk N - v12 - F '97 - p13 [51-250]
Who's Who in the New Testament
c   HB Guide - v7 - Fall '96 - p309+ [1-50]
Who's Who in the Old Testament
c   HB Guide - v7 - Fall '96 - p310 [1-50]
Who's Who in the South and Southwest 1995-1996
r   ARBA - v28 - '97 - p18+ [251-500]
Who's Who in the World 1996
r   ARBA - v28 - '97 - p15+ [251-500]
r   MEQ - v3 - D '96 - p86 [51-250]
Who's Who of Australian Children's Writers. 2nd Ed.
r   ARBA - v28 - '97 - p425+ [251-500]
r   Magpies - v11 - Jl '96 - p15 [251-500]
Whouley, Kate - *Manual on Bookselling. 5th Ed.*
Quill & Q - v62 - O '96 - p39 [251-500]
Why Do We Need Railways?. Seminar: Jan. 1995
J Gov Info - v23 - S '96 - p667 [51-250]
Whybrow, Ian - *Miss Wire and the Three Kind Mice*
(Illus. by Emma Chichester Clark)
c   TES - S 20 '96 - p16* [501+]
Whybrow, Peter C - *A Mood Apart*
BL - v93 - Mr 1 '97 - p1101+ [51-250]
KR - v65 - Ja 15 '97 - p133 [251-500]
PW - v244 - Ja 20 '97 - p386 [51-250]
Whymant, Robert - *Stalin's Spy*
FEER - v160 - F 27 '97 - p36 [251-500]
Obs - N 24 '96 - p16* [501+]
Spec - v277 - D 7 '96 - p46 [501+]
TLS - Ja 17 '97 - p26 [501+]
Whymper, Edward - *Scrambles amongst the Alps*
HM - v293 - Ag '96 - p64+ [501+]
Whyte, David - *The Heart Aroused (Whyte). Audio*
Version
Quill & Q - v62 - Ag '96 - p37 [251-500]
Whyte, Donald - *A Dictionary of Scottish Emigrants to*
Canada before Confederation. Vol. 2
r   NGSQ - v85 - Mr '97 - p74 [51-250]
Whyte, Ian D - *Scotland before the Industrial Revolution*
Albion - v28 - Sum '96 - p368+ [501+]
Whyte, Jack - *The Singing Sword*
PW - v243 - S 23 '96 - p61 [51-250]
The Skystone
y   Kliatt - v31 - Mr '97 - p14 [51-250]
Whyte, Peter - *Theophile Gautier, Conteur Fantastique Et*
Merveilleux
MLR - v92 - Ap '97 - p472+ [251-500]
Wians, William - *Aristotle's Philosophical Development*
IPQ - v37 - Je '97 - p236+ [501+]
Wiarda, Howard J - *Corporatism and Comparative*
Politics
Choice - v34 - Ap '97 - p1408+ [51-250]
R&R Bk N - v12 - F '97 - p59 [51-250]
Democracy and Its Discontents
APSR - v91 - Mr '97 - p244 [501+]
Choice - v34 - S '96 - p207 [51-250]
Parameters - v26 - Win '96 - p155 [1-50]
Iberia and Latin America
For Aff - v76 - My '97 - p138 [51-250]
Wice, Paul B - *Miranda v. Arizona*
y   HB Guide - v8 - Spr '97 - p94 [51-250]
y   SLJ - v42 - S '96 - p237 [51-250]
Wicharaya, Tamasak - *Simple Theory, Hard Reality*
CS - v26 - Mr '97 - p216+ [501+]
Wichegrod, Laurence - *Jolis Bijoux*
c   BL - v93 - N 1 '96 - p500 [1-50]
Wichers, Robert - *A Theory of Individual Behavior*
SciTech - v21 - Mr '97 - p2 [51-250]
Wick, David - *The Infamous Boundary*
Choice - v34 - Ap '97 - p1378 [51-250]
LJ - v121 - N 15 '96 - p86 [51-250]
WSJ-Cent - v99 - Ja 23 '97 - pA16 [501+]
Wick, Steve - *Heaven and Earth*
NYTBR - v102 - Ja 12 '97 - p24 [251-500]

Wick, Walter - *A Drop of Water (Illus. by Walter Wick)*
c   BL - v93 - F 1 '97 - p940 [51-250]
c   CCB-B - v50 - F '97 - p197+ [501+]
c   HB - v73 - Mr '97 - p215 [51-250]
c   KR - v65 - Ja 15 '97 - p147 [51-250]
c   SLJ - v43 - Mr '97 - p210 [51-250]
I Spy Picture Book Riddles Series
c   Inst - v106 - S '96 - p92 [1-50]
I Spy Spooky Night (Illus. by Walter Wick)
c   BL - v93 - S 15 '96 - p243 [51-250]
c   Ch BWatch - v7 - F '97 - p2 [1-50]
c   HB Guide - v8 - Spr '97 - p142 [1-50]
c   LATBR - O 20 '96 - p8 [51-250]
c   SLJ - v42 - S '96 - p199 [51-250]
Wickelgren, Ingrid - *Ramblin' Robots*
y   BL - v93 - N 15 '96 - p578 [51-250]
y   HB Guide - v8 - Spr '97 - p133 [51-250]
y   SLJ - v43 - Ja '97 - p138 [51-250]
Wickelgren, Wayne A - *How to Solve Mathematical*
Problems
Math T - v89 - S '96 - p514+ [51-250]
Wicker, Elmus - *The Banking Panics of the Great*
Depression
Choice - v34 - Ap '97 - p1390 [51-250]
Wicker, Richard Fenton, Jr. - *The Allen Family of*
England, Virginia, North Carolina, Tennessee,
Mississippi, Texas, and Illinois 1600-1995
NGSQ - v84 - S '96 - p225+ [501+]
Wicker, Tom - *Tragic Failure*
Atl - v279 - F '97 - p102+ [501+]
BW - v26 - S 1 '96 - p3+ [501+]
Econ - v341 - N 16 '96 - p6*+ [501+]
Utne R - S '96 - p93 [1-50]
Wickham, DeWayne - *Thinking Black*
y   SLJ - v43 - F '97 - p138 [51-250]
Woodholme: A Black Man's Story of Growing Up Alone
BW - v26 - S 29 '96 - p12 [51-250]
y   Kliatt - v30 - N '96 - p24 [51-250]
Wickham, Madeleine - *A Desirable Residence*
BL - v93 - Ja '97 - p823 [51-250]
KR - v64 - D 15 '96 - p1766 [251-500]
LJ - v121 - D '96 - p148 [51-250]
PW - v244 - Ja 20 '97 - p394 [51-250]
Wickings, Ruth - *Silly Heads (Illus. by Cathie*
Shuttleworth)
c   BL - v93 - D 15 '96 - p732 [1-50]
c   HB Guide - v7 - Fall '96 - p259 [51-250]
Wicks, Robert - *After 50*
PW - v244 - Mr 24 '97 - p76 [51-250]
Wicks, Stephen - *Warriors and Wildmen*
R&R Bk N - v12 - F '97 - p53 [51-250]
Wicks, Susan - *The Clever Daughter*
TLS - Ja 17 '97 - p23 [251-500]
Driving My Father
LATBR - Ag 18 '96 - p8 [501+]
Obs - F 23 '97 - p18* [51-250]
The Key
Obs - Ja 19 '97 - p15* [51-250]
TLS - Ja 17 '97 - p21 [501+]
Wickstrom, Polly Jeanne - *More Quizzes for Great*
Children's Books
SLMQ - v24 - Sum '96 - p222 [51-250]
Widdess, Richard - *The Ragas of Early Indian Music*
Choice - v34 - S '96 - p138 [51-250]
Widdicombe, Peter - *The Fatherhood of God from Origen*
to Athanasius
CH - v65 - D '96 - p662+ [501+]
Rel St Rev - v22 - O '96 - p301+ [501+]
Wideman, John Edgar - *The Cattle Killing*
Ant R - v55 - Spr '97 - p235+ [251-500]
BL - v92 - Ag '96 - p1857 [251-500]
BW - v26 - S 29 '96 - p5 [501+]
Nat - v263 - O 28 '96 - p58+ [501+]
NYRB - v44 - Mr 27 '97 - p39+ [501+]
NYTBR - v101 - N 3 '96 - p20 [501+]
PW - v243 - N 4 '96 - p40 [501+]
Fatheralong: A Meditation on Fathers and Sons, Race
and Society
Books - v9 - S '95 - p23 [51-250]
Obs - Ja 12 '97 - p18* [51-250]
The Stories of John Edgar Wideman
TLS - N 29 '96 - p14 [1-50]
Widner, Jennifer - *Economic Change and Political*
Liberalization in Sub-Saharan Africa
WP - v49 - O '96 - p92+ [501+]

Wiebe, Robert H - *Self-Rule: A Cultural History of*
American Democracy
Am - v175 - Jl 20 '96 - p26+ [501+]
Bks & Cult - v2 - My '96 - p24+ [501+]
BusLR - v21 - 3 '96 - p205+ [501+]
CS - v26 - Mr '97 - p172+ [501+]
Historian - v59 - Fall '96 - p165+ [251-500]
RP - v58 - Sum '96 - p617+ [501+]
Wiebe, Rudy - *River of Stone*
Can Lit - Spr '97 - p249+ [501+]
Wieck, Roger S - *Time Sanctified*
AB - v99 - Mr 3 '97 - p685+ [501+]
Wieczynski, Joseph L - *The Gorbachev Bibliography*
1985-1991
r   Choice - v34 - D '96 - p597 [51-250]
r   R&R Bk N - v11 - N '96 - p13 [51-250]
Wiedemann, Thomas - *Cicero and the End of the Roman*
Republic
CW - v89 - Jl '96 - p501+ [251-500]
Wiederhold, Gio - *Intelligent Integration of Information*
SciTech - v20 - D '96 - p59 [51-250]
Wiegand, Gayl H - *Models of Matter*
J Chem Ed - v73 - O '96 - pA243+ [501+]
Wiegand, Wayne A - *Irrepressible Reformer*
Choice - v34 - Mr '97 - p1148+ [251-500]
LAR - v98 - D '96 - p649 [51-250]
Wiegers, Karl E - *Creating a Software Engineering*
Culture
CBR   v15   Spr '97 - p10 [51-250]
SciTech - v21 - Mr '97 - p5 [51-250]
Wiegert, Stephen L - *Traditional Religion and Guerrilla*
Warfare in Modern Africa
Africa T - v44 - 1 '97 - p88+ [501+]
Wiegman, Robyn - *American Anatomies*
AHR - v102 - F '97 - p220+ [251-500]
AL - v68 - S '96 - p656+ [251-500]
J Am St - v30 - Ag '96 - p295+ [251-500]
Wiehe, Vernon R - *Working with Child Abuse and Neglect*
Choice - v34 - D '96 - p694 [51-250]
R&R Bk N - v11 - N '96 - p77 [51-250]
Wieland, Mitch - *Willy Slater's Lane*
BL - v93 - F 15 '97 - p1004 [51-250]
KR - v64 - N 15 '96 - p1630 [251-500]
NYTBR - v102 - F 23 '97 - p16 [51-250]
PW - v243 - N 25 '96 - p69 [251-500]
Wieland, Sandra - *Hearing the Internal Trauma*
SciTech - v21 - Mr '97 - p65 [51-250]
Wieler, Diana - *Ran Van*
y   Can CL - v22 - Sum '96 - p95 [251-500]
To the Mountains by Morning
c   Ch BWatch - v6 - Jl '96 - p4 [1-50]
Wiemar, Liza M - *Extraordinary Guidance*
LJ - v122 - My 1 '97 - p111 [51-250]
Wieneke, Connie - *Jackson Hole*
BWatch - v17 - S '96 - p5 [51-250]
Wiener, Daniel N - *B.F. Skinner: Benign Anarchist*
Choice - v34 - My '97 - p1580+ [51-250]
Wiener, Jon - *Professors, Politics and Pop*
JPC - v29 - Spr '96 - p260+ [251-500]
Wiener, Joshua M - *Persons with Disabilities*
JEL - v34 - S '96 - p1441+ [51-250]
Pol Stud J - v24 - Sum '96 - p335 [51-250]
Wiener, Margaret J - *Visible and Invisible Realms*
Am Ethnol - v24 - F '97 - p259+ [501+]
Wiener, Paul - *Patrick Ewing*
c   HB Guide - v7 - Fall '96 - p360 [51-250]
Wiener, Richard S - *An Object-Oriented Introduction to*
Computer Science Using Eiffel
SciTech - v20 - S '96 - p5 [51-250]
Wiener, Valerie - *Gang Free*
y   PW - v243 - S 23 '96 - p73 [1-50]
Wieners, Brad - *Reality Check*
Fut - v31 - Mr '97 - p50 [51-250]
Wiersema, Fred - *Customer Intimacy*
Bus Bk R - v14 - 1 '97 - p96+ [501+]
Customer Intimacy (Wiersema). Audio Version
LJ - v121 - S 15 '96 - p112 [51-250]
Wiese, Jan - *The Naked Madonna*
TLS - S 6 '96 - p23 [251-500]
Wiese, Jim - *Cosmic Science*
c   PW - v244 - Ap 14 '97 - p77 [51-250]
Detective Science (Illus. by Ed Shems)
c   SB - v32 - O '96 - p208 [51-250]
Spy Science (Illus. by Ed Shems)
y   SB - v33 - Mr '97 - p44 [51-250]
Wiesel, Elie - *All Rivers Run to the Sea*
NYTBR - v101 - D 8 '96 - p84 [1-50]
TLS - Jl 7 '96 - p12 [501+]
Memoirs A Deux Voix
Quad - v40 - D '96 - p79+ [501+]

The Night Trilogy
  SS - v87 - My '96 - p101+ [501+]
The Oath (Davidson). Audio Version
  LJ - v121 - O 1 '96 - p144 [51-250]
Wiesenthal, Simon - *The Sunflower: On the Possibilities and Limits of Forgiveness. Rev. and Expanded Ed., 2nd Ed.*
  LJ - v122 - Ap 1 '97 - p134 [51-250]
  PW - v244 - Ap 28 '97 - p66 [251-500]
Wiesner, David - *Tuesday*
  New Ad - v9 - Fall '96 - p267+ [501+]
Wiesner, Merry E - *Women and Gender in Early Modern Europe*
  Ren Q - v49 - Aut '96 - p668+ [501+]
Wiethoff, William E - *A Peculiar Humanism*
  VQR - v73 - Win '97 - p7* [1-50]
The Wife of Bath's Prologue on CD-ROM. Electronic Media Version
  LJ - v122 - F 15 '97 - p169 [51-250]
Wig
  p Workbook - v21 - Fall '96 - p146 [51-250]
Wigen, Karen - *The Making of a Japanese Periphery 1750-1920*
  AHR - v101 - O '96 - p1260+ [501+]
  HJAS - v56 - 2 '96 - p521+ [501+]
  JIH - v27 - Win '97 - p571+ [501+]
Wiget, Andrew - *Dictionary of Native American Literature*
  r WAL - v31 - Win '97 - p407+ [251-500]
  Handbook of Native American Literature
  BWatch - v17 - N '96 - p2 [51-250]
  yr VOYA - v19 - F '97 - p364 [251-500]
Wiggers, Raymond - *Geology Underfoot in Illinois*
  r SB - v33 - My '97 - p102+ [51-250]
Wiggins, David K - *Glory Bound*
  BL - v93 - Mr 1 '97 - p1104 [51-250]
  Sport in America
  Aethlon - v13 - Fall '95 - p147 [251-500]
Wiggins, Jerry S - *The Five-Factor Model of Personality*
  Choice - v34 - N '96 - p542 [51-250]
Wiggins, Marianne - *Eveless Den*
  NYTBR - v101 - S 29 '96 - p32 [51-250]
Wiggins, Martin - *Journeymen in Murder*
  Six Ct J - v27 - Win '96 - p1171+ [501+]
Wiggins, Stephen - *Global Dynamics, Phase Space Transport, Orbits Homoclinic to Resonances, and Applications*
  SIAM Rev - v38 - S '96 - p538+ [251-500]
Wiggins, VeraLee - *Wagons West*
  c Ch BWatch - v6 - Jl '96 - p2 [1-50]
Wigglesworth, Neil - *The Evolution of English Sport*
  R&R Bk N - v12 - F '97 - p31 [51-250]
Wightman, Alistair - *Karlowicz, Young Poland, and the Musical Fin-De-Siecle*
  R&R Bk N - v11 - N '96 - p58 [51-250]
Wigley, Mark - *White Walls, Designer Dresses*
  Choice - v34 - S '96 - p116 [51-250]
  R&R Bk N - v12 - F '97 - p73 [51-250]
  TLS - F 21 '97 - p20 [501+]
Wignall, Sydney - *Spy on the Roof of the World*
  KR - v65 - Ja 1 '97 - p52 [251-500]
  PW - v243 - D 30 '96 - p44+ [51-250]
Wigner, Eugene Paul - *The Collected Works of Eugene Paul Wigner. Pt. A, Vols. 1-2, 5; Pt. B, Vol. 6*
  Phys Today - v49 - O '96 - p65+ [501+]
Wigoder, Geoffrey - *The Holocaust. Vols. 1-4*
  yr BL - v93 - F 15 '97 - p1042 [51-250]
  r LJ - v122 - Mr 15 '97 - p54+ [51-250]
  New Encyclopedia of Zionism and Israel. Vols. 1-2
  r MEQ - v3 - D '96 - p85+ [51-250]
Wigzell, Faith - *Russian Writers on Russian Writers*
  MLR - v92 - Ja '97 - p261+ [251-500]
Wihl, Gary - *The Contingency of Theory*
  MLR - v92 - Ja '97 - p150+ [501+]
Wijers, Ralph Antoine Marie Joseph - *Evolutionary Processes in Binary Stars*
  SciTech - v20 - S '96 - p13 [51-250]
Wijnberg, K M - *Morphologic Behaviour of a Barred Coast Over a Period of Decades*
  GJ - v162 - N '96 - p341 [51-250]
Wijngaard, Juan - *The Nativity (Illus. by Juan Wijngaard)*
  c PW - v243 - S 30 '96 - p79 [51-250]
Wijnhoven, Joseph - *Nuntiaturberichte Aus Deutschland*
  CHR - v83 - Ja '97 - p107+ [251-500]
Wijsman, H J W - *Valerius Flaccus, Argonautica, Book V*
  R&R Bk N - v12 - F '97 - p78 [51-250]
Wijze, Louis De - *Only My Life*
  y BL - v93 - Ja '97 - p811+ [51-250]
  KR - v64 - D 1 '96 - p1713+ [251-500]
  PW - v243 - N 18 '96 - p53 [51-250]

Wikan, Unni - *Tomorrow, God Willing*
  BL - v92 - Ag '96 - p1864 [51-250]
  Choice - v34 - F '97 - p1007 [51-250]
  CSM - v89 - D 16 '96 - p13 [501+]
  CSM - v89 - D 19 '96 - p14 [501+]
Wikander, Ulla - *Protecting Women*
  JEH - v56 - D '96 - p964+ [501+]
  Soc Ser R - v71 - Mr '97 - p165 [1-50]
Wikler, Linda - *Alfonse, Where Are You?*
  c HB Guide - v7 - Fall '96 - p245 [51-250]
Wikler, Madeline - *Let's Have a Seder (Illus. by Miriam Sagasti)*
  c PW - v244 - Mr 24 '97 - p77 [51-250]
Wilber, Jessica - *Totally Private and Personal*
  y Kliatt - v31 - Mr '97 - p22 [51-250]
  y VOYA - v19 - F '97 - p354+ [251-500]
Wilber, Ken - *The Eye of Spirit*
  LJ - v122 - F 15 '97 - p139 [51-250]
  The Holographic Paradigm and Other Paradoxes
  PAR - v56 - S '96 - p495+ [501+]
Wilberforce, William - *A Practical View of Christianity*
  Bks & Cult - v2 - N '96 - p20+ [501+]
Wilborn, Thomas L - *How Northeast Asians View Their Security*
  RSR - v24 - 3 '96 - p49 [51-250]
Wilbur, C Martin - *China in My Life*
  R&R Bk N - v11 - N '96 - p15 [51-250]
Wilbur, Richard - *The Catbird's Song*
  KR - v65 - Mr 1 '97 - p371 [51-250]
  LJ - v122 - Ap 15 '97 - p83 [51-250]
  PW - v244 - F 10 '97 - p72 [51-250]
  A Game of Catch (Illus. by Barry Moser)
  c Trib Bks - Mr 30 '97 - p5 [51-250]
  New and Collected Poems
  LJ - v122 - Ap 1 '97 - p95 [1-50]
Wilbur, Sanford R - *If God Is God*
  BL - v93 - O 1 '96 - p304 [501+]
Wilbur, Todd - *Top Secret Restaurant Recipes*
  BL - v93 - Mr 15 '97 - p1217 [51-250]
  PW - v244 - My 5 '97 - p203 [51-250]
Wilcox, Brian - *Inspecting Schools*
  R&R Bk N - v11 - N '96 - p56 [51-250]
Wilcox, Catherine M - *Theology and Women's Ministry in Seventeenth-Century English Quakerism*
  CH - v65 - D '96 - p711+ [501+]
Wilcox, Charles F - *Experimental Organic Chemistry. 2nd Ed.*
  J Chem Ed - v73 - Ap '96 - pA92 [251-500]
Wilcox, Charlotte - *Powerhouse: Inside a Nuclear Power Plant (Illus. by Jerry Boucher)*
  c BL - v93 - O 1 '96 - p346+ [51-250]
  c HB Guide - v8 - Spr '97 - p133 [51-250]
  c SB - v32 - O '96 - p212 [51-250]
  c SLJ - v42 - S '96 - p222 [51-250]
Wilcox, Clyde - *Onward Christian Soldiers?*
  Choice - v34 - F '97 - p1038+ [51-250]
  Cons - v17 - Win '96 - p31 [1-50]
Wilcox, David C - *Perturbation Methods in the Computer Age*
  SIAM Rev - v38 - S '96 - p539+ [501+]
Wilcox, Derk Arend - *The Left Guide*
  r ARBA - v28 - '97 - p276+ [251-500]
  r BL - v93 - D 1 '96 - p685 [51-250]
  r Choice - v34 - Ap '97 - p1312 [51-250]
  r LJ - v122 - Mr '97 - p68+ [51-250]
Wilcox, James - *Modern Baptists*
  TLS - D 20 '96 - p24 [51-250]
  Woman's J - Ja '97 - p13 [1-50]
  North Gladiola
  Obs - Ap 13 '97 - p18* [51-250]
Wilcox, Jane - *Why Do We Celebrate That?*
  c HB Guide - v8 - Spr '97 - p99 [51-250]
  Why Do We Use That?
  c HB Guide - v8 - Spr '97 - p133 [51-250]
  c SLJ - v43 - Mr '97 - p198 [51-250]
Wilcox, John - *Masters of Battle*
  PW - v243 - S 16 '96 - p65 [1-50]
Wilcox, Jonathan, 1960- - *Iceland*
  c HB Guide - v7 - Fall '96 - p382 [1-50]
Wilcox, Kip - *Sweetness and Light*
  y Kliatt - v30 - N '96 - p30 [51-250]
Wilcox, Robert - *Wings of Fury*
  y BL - v93 - My 1 '97 - p1466 [51-250]
  KR - v65 - Ap 1 '97 - p541+ [251-500]
  LJ - v122 - Ap 15 '97 - p98 [51-250]
  PW - v244 - Ap 7 '97 - p83 [51-250]
Wilcox, Timothy - *Boudin to Dufy*
  Choice - v34 - D '96 - p600 [51-250]

Wilcox Paxton, Collin - *Papa's Angels*
  y BL - v93 - S 1 '96 - p30 [51-250]
  c BWatch - v17 - D '96 - p2 [51-250]
  y Ch BWatch - v6 - D '96 - p1 [1-50]
  c HB Guide - v8 - Spr '97 - p73 [51-250]
  c NYTBR - v101 - D 8 '96 - p102 [51-250]
  y PW - v243 - S 30 '96 - p93 [51-250]
  c S Liv - v31 - D '96 - p58 [51-250]
  c SLJ - v42 - O '96 - p39 [51-250]
Wild, Margaret - *Big Cat Dreaming (Illus. by Anne Spudvilas)*
  c Aust Bk R - Jl '96 - p61+ [501+]
  c Magpies - v11 - Jl '96 - p25 [51-250]
  The Midnight Gang (Illus. by Ann James)
  c Aust Bk R - D '96 - p91+ [501+]
  Old Pig (Illus. by Ron Brooks)
  c HB Guide - v7 - Fall '96 - p281 [51-250]
  c KR - v64 - My 1 '96 - p695 [51-250]
  c NY - v72 - N 18 '96 - p101 [1-50]
  c Sch Lib - v44 - Ag '96 - p102 [51-250]
  Toby
  c CLW - v67 - Mr '97 - p15 [1-50]
The Wild Life
  Aust Bk R - S '96 - p50 [501+]
Wild West Show
  SF Chr - v18 - O '96 - p82 [1-50]
Wildavsky, Aaron - *But Is It True?*
  Am Sci - v84 - S '96 - p491+ [501+]
  BioSci - v46 - O '96 - p707+ [501+]
  CS - v26 - Mr '97 - p203+ [501+]
  JPR - v33 - N '96 - p502 [51-250]
Wilde, Lady - *Ancient Legends of Ireland*
  CLW - v67 - D '96 - p49 [51-250]
Wilde, Jerry - *Anger Management in Schools*
  Adoles - v32 - Spr '97 - p250 [51-250]
Wilde, Oscar - *The Canterville Ghost (Illus. by Lisbeth Zwerger)*
  y BL - v93 - D 15 '96 - p722 [51-250]
  c HB Guide - v8 - Spr '97 - p76 [51-250]
  c PW - v243 - N 25 '96 - p77 [1-50]
  The Happy Prince (Illus. by Jane Ray)
  c Bks Keeps - Ja '97 - p20 [51-250]
  Plays, Prose Writings and Poems
  ELT - v40 - 2 '97 - p255 [1-50]
  Poems 1892
  Nine-C Lit - v51 - S '96 - p279 [51-250]
  The Star Child
  c TES - D 6 '96 - p16* [1-50]
  The Uncollected Oscar Wilde
  PW - v244 - Ja 6 '97 - p59 [51-250]
Wilde-Menozzi, Wallis - *Mother Tongue*
  PW - v244 - Ap 21 '97 - p51 [51-250]
Wildenstein, Alec - *Odilon Redon: Catalogue Raisonne De L'Oeuvre Peint Et Dessine. Vol. 2*
  r BM - v138 - S '96 - p613+ [501+]
Wildenstein, Daniel - *Monet: Catalogue Raisonne. Vols. 1-4*
  r ILN - Christmas '96 - p90 [51-250]
  Spec - v277 - D 14 '96 - p75+ [51-250]
Wilder, Amos N - *The Bible and the Literary Critic*
  CW - v89 - Jl '96 - p494+ [251-500]
Wilder, Cherry - *Signs of Life*
  y VOYA - v19 - O '96 - p222 [51-250]
Wilder, Effie Leland - *Over What Hill?*
  PW - v243 - S 23 '96 - p61 [51-250]
Wilder, Kathryn - *Walking the Twilight II*
  Bloom Rev - v16 - Jl '96 - p11 [501+]
Wilder, Laura Ingalls - *Going West (Illus. by Renee Graef)*
  c HB Guide - v8 - Spr '97 - p53 [51-250]
  Summertime in the Big Woods (Illus. by Renee Graef)
  c HB Guide - v7 - Fall '96 - p281 [1-50]
  Winter on the Farm (Illus. by Jody Wheeler)
  c HB Guide - v8 - Spr '97 - p53 [51-250]
Wilder, Thornton - *The Ides of March*
  y SLJ - v42 - N '96 - p39 [51-250]
Wildermann, Ansgar - *La Viste Des Eglises Du Diocese De Lausanne En 1453. Vols. 1-2*
  CHR - v82 - Jl '96 - p558+ [251-500]
Wilding, Michael - *Somewhere New*
  TLS - N 1 '96 - p24 [501+]
Wildlife Review and Fisheries Review. Electronic Media Version
  Choice - v34 - Mr '97 - p1186+ [501+]
Wildlife Worldwide. Electronic Media Version
  Choice - v34 - Mr '97 - p1186+ [501+]
Wildman, Stephanie M - *Privilege Revealed*
  R&R Bk N - v11 - N '96 - p40 [51-250]

Wildsmith, Brian - *Brian Wildsmith's Amazing World of Words (Illus. by Brian Wildsmith)*
  c CBRS - v25 - Mr '97 - p91 [51-250]
  c KR - v64 - D 15 '96 - p1806 [51-250]
  c PW - v244 - Ja 13 '97 - p75 [51-250]
  c Sch Lib - v45 - F '97 - p22 [51-250]
  c TES - Mr 28 '97 - p11* [51-250]
Brian Wildsmith's Puzzles
  c HB Guide - v7 - Fall '96 - p358 [1-50]
The Easter Story (Illus. by Brian Wildsmith)
  c HB Guide - v7 - Fall '96 - p310 [1-50]
Footprints in the Snow
  c TES - N 29 '96 - p13* [51-250]
Saint Francis (Illus. by Brian Wildsmith)
  c BL - v93 - O 1 '96 - p339 [1-50]
  c Ch BWatch - v6 - My '96 - p6 [51-250]
  c HB Guide - v7 - Fall '96 - p310 [51-250]
Tug, Tug
  c TES - N 29 '96 - p13* [51-250]
Wildwood, Chrissie - *Bloomsbury Encyclopedia of Aromatherapy*
  r Quill & Q - v62 - Ag '96 - p32 [51-250]
Wilen, Joan - *Garlic: Nature's Super Healer*
     BL - v93 - Mr 15 '97 - p1214 [51-250]
     PW - v244 - Ja 27 '97 - p102 [51-250]
Shoes in the Freezer, Beer in the Flower Bed and Other Down-Home Tips for House and Garden
     PW - v244 - Mr 24 '97 - p80 [51-250]
Wilentz, Gay - *Binding Cultures*
     Signs - v22 - Aut '96 - p243+ [501+]
Wiles, David - *The Masks of Menander*
     AJA - v101 - Ja '97 - p154+ [501+]
Wiles, Maurice - *Archetypal Heresy*
     Choice - v34 - Ap '97 - p1358 [51-250]
Christian Theology and Interfaith Dialogue
     Rel Ed - v91 - Fall '96 - p615 [1-50]
Wiley, Catherine - *Homemaking: Women Writers and the Politics and Poetics of Home*
     R&R Bk N - v11 - D '96 - p61 [51-250]
Wilford, Hugh - *The New York Intellectuals*
     J Am St - v30 - Ag '96 - p335+ [501+]
Wilhelm, Hans - *The Royal Raven*
  c HB Guide - v7 - Fall '96 - p281 [51-250]
Tyrone and the Swamp Gang
  c Sch Lib - v44 - N '96 - p146 [51-250]
Wilhelm, Hellmut - *Understanding the I Ching*
     Rel St Rev - v23 - Ap '97 - p203 [51-250]
Wilhelm, Kate - *Malice Prepense*
     Arm Det - v30 - Win '97 - p71 [51-250]
     Rapport - v19 - 5 '96 - p37 [501+]
Wilhelmsen, Alexandra - *La Formacion Del Pensamiento Politico Del Carlismo 1810-1875*
     CH - v65 - D '96 - p735+ [501+]
Wilhide, Elizabeth - *Traditional Country Style*
     LATBR - O 13 '96 - p14 [251-500]
Wilk, Chester A - *Medicine, Monopolies, and Malice*
     BL - v92 - Ag '96 - p1864+ [51-250]
Wilk, Christopher - *Western Furniture 1350 to the Present Day*
     Am Craft - v57 - Ap '97 - p28 [1-50]
     Spec - v277 - D 14 '96 - p76 [51-250]
Wilken, Robert L - *John Chrysostom and the Jews*
     Rel Ed - v91 - Fall '96 - p606 [1-50]
Judaism and the Early Christian Mind
     Rel Ed - v91 - Fall '96 - p606 [1-50]
Remembering the Christian Past
     Ch Today - v40 - D 9 '96 - p46+ [501+]
Wilker, Josh - *A.J. Foyt*
  c HB Guide - v7 - Fall '96 - p359 [51-250]
The Harlem Globetrotters
  c Ch BWatch - v6 - N '96 - p2 [51-250]
  c HB Guide - v8 - Spr '97 - p147 [51-250]
  c SLJ - v43 - Mr '97 - p210 [51-250]
Wilkes, Angela - *The Amazing Outdoor Activity Book*
  c Magpies - v11 - Jl '96 - p41 [51-250]
  c Sch Lib - v44 - N '96 - p166 [51-250]
  c TES - Jl 19 '96 - pR8 [51-250]
Dazzling Disguises and Clever Costumes
  c BL - v93 - O 1 '96 - p347 [51-250]
  c CCB-B - v50 - N '96 - p119 [51-250]
  c HB Guide - v8 - Spr '97 - p136 [51-250]
  c SLJ - v42 - D '96 - p135 [51-250]
Wilkes, G A - *A Dictionary of Australian Colloquialisms. 4th Ed.*
  r ARBA - v28 - '97 - p382 [51-250]
  r Choice - v34 - F '97 - p951 [51-250]
Wilkes, Maria D - *Little House in Brookfield (Illus. by Dan Andreasen)*
  c HB Guide - v7 - Fall '96 - p299 [1-50]
  c SLJ - v42 - Ag '96 - p148 [51-250]

Wilkes, Paul - *The Good Enough Catholic*
     Am - v176 - F 8 '97 - p35+ [501+]
     Comw - v124 - Mr 14 '97 - p17+ [501+]
     LJ - v121 - N 15 '96 - p67 [51-250]
     NYTBR - v101 - D 1 '96 - p22 [51-250]
Wilkes, Richard - *Bulmurn: A Swan River Nyoongar*
     Aust Bk R - Je '96 - p44 [501+]
     Choice - v34 - S '96 - p131 [51-250]
Wilkie, Bernard - *Creating Special Effects for TV and Video. 3rd Ed.*
     SciTech - v21 - Mr '97 - p98 [51-250]
Wilkin, Margaret - *Initial Teacher Training*
     R&R Bk N - v11 - N '96 - p55 [51-250]
Wilkins, Damien - *Little Masters*
     KR - v65 - My 1 '97 - p676 [251-500]
     PW - v244 - My 12 '97 - p58 [51-250]
Wilkins, Michael J - *Discipleship in the Ancient World and Matthew's Gospel. 2nd Ed.*
     Rel St Rev - v23 - Ap '97 - p182 [51-250]
Jesus under Fire
     Bks & Cult - v1 - N '95 - p3+ [501+]
     Rel St Rev - v23 - Ap '97 - p177+ [251-500]
Wilkins, Thurman - *John Muir: Apostle of Nature*
     PHR - v65 - N '96 - p680+ [501+]
     WAL - v31 - Win '97 - p399+ [251-500]
Wilkins, Verna Allette - *Toyin Fay (Illus. by Paul Hunt)*
  c Bks Keeps - N '96 - p7 [51-250]
Wilkinson, Alan G - *The Sculpture of Jacques Lipchitz. Vol. 1*
  r Choice - v34 - Ap '97 - p1328 [51-250]
Wilkinson, Anne - *Toys and Designs from the World of Beatrix Potter*
     RSR - v24 - 3 '96 - p25+ [51-250]
Wilkinson, Barry - *Computer Architecture. 2nd Ed.*
     SciTech - v20 - S '96 - p7 [51-250]
Wilkinson, Brenda - *The Civil Rights Movement*
     CC - v114 - F 5 '97 - p171+ [251-500]
Wilkinson, D Marion - *Not between Brothers*
     PW - v243 - N 11 '96 - p57+ [51-250]
Wilkinson, J Harvie, III - *One Nation Indivisible*
     PW - v244 - Mr 17 '97 - p63 [51-250]
Wilkinson, Myler - *The Dark Mirror*
     Choice - v34 - My '97 - p1501 [51-250]
Wilkinson, Pete - *Warrior: One Man's Environmental Crusade*
     PW - v243 - S 30 '96 - p69 [51-250]
Wilkinson, Philip - *A Celebration of Customs and Rituals of the World (Illus. by Robert Ingpen)*
  y HB Guide - v7 - Fall '96 - p318 [1-50]
Super Structures (Illus. by Andy Crawford)
  c BL - v93 - D 15 '96 - p725 [51-250]
  c CBRS - v25 - D '96 - p44 [51-250]
  c CLW - v67 - Mr '97 - p55 [51-250]
  c Emerg Lib - v24 - Mr '97 - p45 [1-50]
  c HB Guide - v8 - Spr '97 - p133 [51-250]
  c New Sci - v152 - D 14 '96 - p47 [1-50]
  c PW - v243 - N 4 '96 - p78 [51-250]
  c SLJ - v43 - F '97 - p111 [51-250]
Wilkinson, Rick - *Incredible Journeys*
  y Sch Lib - v45 - F '97 - p52 [51-250]
Wilkinson, T J - *Settlement Development in the North Jazira, Iraq*
     Am Ant - v61 - O '96 - p820 [501+]
Wilkinson, Tanya - *Persephone Returns*
     BL - v93 - N 1 '96 - p470 [51-250]
     LJ - v121 - N 15 '96 - p76 [51-250]
Wilkinson, Vanessa M - *Food Irradiation*
  r SciTech - v20 - N '96 - p80 [51-250]
Wilkomirski, Binjamin - *Fragments: Memories of a Wartime Childhood*
     BL - v92 - Ag '96 - p1879 [51-250]
  y BL - v93 - Ap 1 '97 - p1288 [1-50]
     Nat - v263 - O 28 '96 - p24+ [501+]
     NYTBR - v102 - Ja 12 '97 - p9 [501+]
     Tikkun - v12 - Mr '97 - p73 [51-250]
  y VOYA - v19 - F '97 - p355 [251-500]
     W&I - v12 - Ap '97 - p271+ [501+]
Wilks, Andrew F - *Intracellular Signal Transduction*
     SciTech - v21 - Mr '97 - p41 [51-250]
Willard, Charles Arthur - *Liberalism and the Problem of Knowledge*
     Choice - v34 - D '96 - p689 [51-250]
     VQR - v73 - Win '97 - p26* [51-250]
Willard, Frances E - *Writing Out My Heart*
     Nine-C Lit - v50 - Mr '96 - p559 [1-50]
Willard, Jim - *Ancestors: A Beginner's Guide to Family History and Genealogy*
  r LJ - v122 - Mr 15 '97 - p58 [51-250]

Willard, Nancy - *The Good-Night Blessing Book (Illus. by Nancy Willard)*
  c BL - v93 - O 1 '96 - p339 [51-250]
  c HB Guide - v8 - Spr '97 - p154 [51-250]
  c SLJ - v42 - O '96 - p119 [51-250]
The Magic Cornfield (Illus. by Nancy Willard)
  c KR - v65 - F 15 '97 - p308 [51-250]
  c PW - v244 - F 17 '97 - p219 [51-250]
Mountains of Quilt (Illus. by Tomie De Paola)
  c PW - v244 - My 12 '97 - p77 [1-50]
A Starlit Somersault Downhill (Illus. by Jerry Pinkney)
  c Par Ch - v20 - N '96 - p3 [51-250]
  c PW - v243 - S 23 '96 - p78 [51-250]
Swimming Lessons
     BL - v93 - Ja '97 - p759 [1-50]
     LJ - v121 - N 15 '96 - p65 [51-250]
     NYTBR - v102 - Ja 26 '97 - p18 [51-250]
     PW - v243 - S 30 '96 - p81 [51-250]
A Visit to William Blake's Inn (Illus. by Alice Provensen)
  c JOYS - v10 - Fall '96 - p35+ [501+]
Willard, Pat - *Pie Every Day*
     BL - v93 - Mr 15 '97 - p1217 [51-250]
     LJ - v122 - Ap 15 '97 - p110 [51-250]
Willard, Tom - *Buffalo Soldiers*
  y Kliatt - v31 - My '97 - p10 [51-250]
The Sable Doughboys
  y BL - v93 - F 15 '97 - p1005 [51-250]
     KR - v65 - Ja 1 '97 - p18+ [51-250]
     PW - v244 - Ja 27 '97 - p79 [51-250]
Willebrands, Johannes - *Church and Jewish People*
     Rel Ed - v91 - Fall '96 - p611 [51-250]
Willeford, Charles - *Miami Blues*
     Arm Det - v29 - Sum '96 - p358 [501+]
Willem, Michel - *Minimax Theorems*
     SciTech - v20 - N '96 - p17 [51-250]
Willemen, Paul - *Looks and Frictions*
     FQ - v49 - Fall '95 - p53+ [501+]
Willett, Cynthia - *Maternal Ethics and Other Slave Moralities*
     Bl S - v26 - Fall '96 - p107 [51-250]
Willett, Ralph - *The Naked City*
     Choice - v34 - S '96 - p131 [51-250]
     R&R Bk N - v11 - N '96 - p72 [51-250]
Willett, Robert L - *One Day of the Civil War*
     BL - v93 - N 15 '96 - p569 [51-250]
     PW - v243 - O 7 '96 - p54 [51-250]
Willett, Sabin - *The Deal*
     VQR - v72 - Aut '96 - p131* [51-250]
Willetts, David - *Why Vote Conservative?*
     Econ - v342 - Mr 22 '97 - p106 [501+]
     NS - v126 - Mr 27 '97 - p51+ [501+]
     TES - F 28 '97 - p8* [501+]
     TLS - F 21 '97 - p27+ [501+]
Willetts, Peter - *The Conscience of the World*
     JEL - v34 - D '96 - p2084 [51-250]
Willey, Gordon R - *Ceramics and Artifacts from Excavations in the Copan Residential Zone*
  r LA Ant - v7 - S '96 - p287 [501+]
Willey, Margaret - *Facing the Music*
  y BL - v93 - Ap 1 '97 - p1310 [1-50]
  y HB Guide - v7 - Fall '96 - p306 [51-250]
  y NY - v72 - N 18 '96 - p102 [51-250]
Willey, Ronald R - *Practical Design and Production of Optical Thin Films*
     SciTech - v20 - D '96 - p86 [51-250]
Willhoite, Michael - *Daddy's Wedding (Illus. by Michael Willhoite)*
  c CBRS - v24 - Ag '96 - p162 [51-250]
William, of Ockham - *A Letter to the Friars Minor and Other Writings*
     CHR - v83 - Ja '97 - p87+ [501+]
A Short Discourse on the Tyrannical Government
     CHR - v83 - Ja '97 - p87+ [501+]
William Little Symposium (1995: Stanford) - *From High-Temperature Superconductivity to Microminiature Refrigeration*
     SciTech - v20 - D '96 - p25 [51-250]
William Morris Revisited
     BM - v138 - Jl '96 - p471+ [501+]
Williams, A Susan - *The Penguin Book of Modern Fantasy by Women*
  y Kliatt - v31 - Mr '97 - p20 [51-250]
Williams, Ann, 1937- - *The English and the Norman Conquest*
     Albion - v28 - Fall '96 - p462+ [501+]
Williams, Anne - *Teaching Physical Education*
     TES - N 22 '96 - pR2 [51-250]
Williams, Anne, 1947- - *Art of Darkness*
     Critm - v38 - Fall '96 - p633+ [501+]
     VS - v39 - Spr '96 - p455+ [501+]

Williams, Antony - *Visual and Active Supervision*
Fam in Soc - v77 - O '96 - p517+ [501+]
Soc Ser R - v70 - S '96 - p504 [51-250]
Williams, Arlene - *Dragon Soup (Illus. by Sally J Smith)*
c HB Guide - v7 - Fall '96 - p281 [51-250]
c Smith - v27 - N '96 - p165 [1-50]
Williams, Bard - *The World Wide Web for Teachers*
Learning - v25 - S '96 - p49 [51-250]
Williams, Bernard - *La Fortune Morale*
Dialogue - v35 - Fall '96 - p842+ [501+]
Making Sense of Humanity and Other Philosophical Papers 1982-1993
CPR - v16 - Ag '96 - p231+ [501+]
IPQ - v36 - D '96 - p489+ [501+]
Shame and Necessity
CW - v89 - Jl '96 - p493 [251-500]
Williams, Betsy - *Potpourri and Fragrant Crafts*
BL - v93 - Ja '97 - p797 [51-250]
Williams, Brian - *Ancient China*
c HB Guide - v8 - Spr '97 - p167 [51-250]
c KR - v64 - N '96 - p1609 [51-250]
y SLJ - v43 - Mr '97 - p210+ [51-250]
Enciclopedia Visual: Ciencia Y Tecnologia
cr BL - v93 - Mr 1 '97 - p1196 [51-250]
Williams, Bruce A - *Democracy, Dialogue, and Environmental Disputes*
AAPSS-A - v549 - Ja '97 - p188+ [251-500]
J Pol - v58 - N '96 - p1228+ [501+]
Williams, C K - *The Vigil*
BL - v93 - D 1 '96 - p640 [51-250]
PW - v243 - N 25 '96 - p71 [51-250]
Williams, Carol Lynch - *Adeline Street*
c Ch BWatch - v6 - O '96 - p8 [51-250]
The True Colors of Caitlynne Jackson
y BL - v93 - Mr 1 '97 - p1155 [51-250]
c CBRS - v25 - Ap '97 - p108 [51-250]
y CCB-B - v50 - F '97 - p226 [51-250]
c KR - v64 - N 1 '96 - p1610 [51-250]
c PW - v243 - D 16 '96 - p60 [51-250]
c SLJ - v43 - F '97 - p106 [51-250]
Williams, Carol Traynor - *It's Time for My Story*
JPC - v29 - Spr '96 - p261+ [501+]
Williams, Charles, 1933- - *Bradman: An Australian Hero*
Lon R Bks - v18 - Ag 22 '96 - p22 [501+]
Quad - v40 - N '96 - p82+ [501+]
TLS - O 25 '96 - p30 [501+]
The Last Great Frenchman
BW - v27 - F 23 '97 - p12 [51-250]
Historian - v58 - Sum '96 - p923+ [501+]
Trib Bks - My 18 '97 - p8 [1-50]
Williams, Christine - *Fathers and Sons*
Aust Bk R - O '96 - p29 [501+]
Williams, Christine L - *Still a Man's World*
SF - v75 - D '96 - p756+ [501+]
Williams, Clarence G - *Reflections of the Dream 1975-1994*
Bl S - v26 - Fall '96 - p107 [1-50]
y Kliatt - v30 - N '96 - p26+ [51-250]
Williams, Colin - *Memorials of the Spanish Civil War*
TLS - Ag 2 '96 - p30 [501+]
Williams, Daniel H - *Ambrose of Milan and the End of the Arian-Nicene Conflicts*
JR - v77 - Ap '97 - p293+ [501+]
Rel St Rev - v23 - Ja '97 - p78+ [51-250]
Theol St - v58 - Mr '97 - p158+ [501+]
Williams, David - *Deformed Discourse*
Choice - v34 - My '97 - p1492 [51-250]
Williams, David, 1948, July, 7- - *Japan and the Enemies of Open Political Science*
Choice - v34 - S '96 - p204+ [51-250]
Williams, David Allen - *A Celebration of Humanism and Freethought*
Skeptic - v3 - '95 - p103 [51-250]
Williams, David B - *Transmission Electron Microscopy*
SciTech - v20 - D '96 - p62 [1-50]
Williams, David Brian - *Experiencing Music Technology*
Choice - v34 - S '96 - p138 [51-250]
M Ed J - v83 - Mr '97 - p42 [251-500]
Williams, Derek - *The Reach of Rome*
KR - v65 - My 1 '97 - p709 [51-250]
Williams, Diane - *The Stupefaction: Stories and a Novella*
RCF - v16 - Fall '96 - p186+ [251-500]
Williams, Donna - *Like Color to the Blind*
Wom R Bks - v14 - Mr '97 - p8+ [501+]
Williams, Eduardo - *Arqueologia Del Occidente De Mexico*
LA Ant - v7 - Mr '96 - p88+ [501+]
Williams, Edward B - *Rebel Brothers*
JSH - v63 - F '97 - p185+ [251-500]
Williams, Elizabeth A - *The Physical and the Moral*
EHR - v112 - F '97 - p223+ [501+]

Williams, Elizabeth Friar - *Voices of Feminist Therapy Readings*
Readings - v11 - D '96 - p21+ [51-250]
Williams, Eric B - *The Mirror and the Word*
MLR - v91 - Jl '96 - p794+ [501+]
Williams, Felicity - *Pocketful of Stars (Illus. by Michael Martchenko)*
c PW - v244 - Mr 24 '97 - p85 [51-250]
c Quill & Q - v63 - Mr '97 - p78+ [251-500]
Williams, Frederick - *Technology Transfer*
JC - v46 - Sum '96 - p183+ [501+]
Williams, G Melville - *Atlas of Aortic Surgery*
r SciTech - v21 - Mr '97 - p61 [51-250]
Williams, Gene - *HyperCELL. Electronic Media Version*
SciTech - v21 - Mr '97 - p37 [51-250]
Williams, George C - *Adaptation and Natural Selection*
New Sci - v151 - S 28 '96 - p49 [1-50]
Plan and Purpose in Nature
Nature - v384 - D 12 '96 - p526+ [501+]
New Sci - v152 - D 7 '96 - p49 [251-500]
The Pony Fish's Glow and Other Clues to Plan and Purpose in Nature
KR - v65 - F 1 '97 - p213 [251-500]
PW - v244 - Mr 17 '97 - p72 [51-250]
Williams, George Ronald - *The Molecular Biology of Gaia*
SciTech - v21 - Mr '97 - p35 [51-250]
Williams, Gerhild Scholz - *Defining Dominion*
Choice - v34 - S '96 - p189 [51-250]
HRNB - v25 - Win '97 - p81 [501+]
Williams, Glen - *Filling the Gaps*
WorldV - v12 - Jl '96 - p18 [51-250]
Williams, Greg - *Younger than Springtime*
KR - v65 - F 1 '97 - p170 [251-500]
LJ - v122 - F 1 '97 - p109 [51-250]
PW - v244 - F 10 '97 - p66 [51-250]
Williams, Hank - *Hank Williams: The Complete Lyrics*
CAY - v17 - Win '96 - p10 [51-250]
Williams, James D - *Preparing to Teach Writing*
JAAL - v40 - F '97 - p411+ [501+]
Williams, Jane A - *The Authentic Jane Williams' Home School Market Guide*
r ARBA - v28 - '97 - p128 [251-500]
How to Stock a Home Library Inexpensively. 3rd Ed.
New Ad - v9 - Fall '96 - p346 [51-250]
Williams, Jean Kinney - *The Amish*
y BL - v93 - O 1 '96 - p333+ [51-250]
c CCB-B - v50 - F '97 - p226+ [51-250]
c HB Guide - v8 - Spr '97 - p88 [51-250]
y SLJ - v43 - Ja '97 - p138 [51-250]
The Mormons
y BL - v93 - O 1 '96 - p333+ [51-250]
c HB Guide - v8 - Spr '97 - p88 [51-250]
y SLJ - v43 - Ja '97 - p138 [51-250]
Williams, Jeanne - *Wind Water*
LJ - v122 - My 1 '97 - p142 [51-250]
PW - v244 - Ap 14 '97 - p55 [51-250]
Williams, Jeffery, 1920- - *First in the Field*
Beav - v76 - O '96 - p47+ [501+]
Can Hist R - v78 - Mr '97 - p129+ [251-500]
Williams, Jeffrey, 1953- - *Manipulation on Trial*
Econ J - v106 - N '96 - p1785+ [501+]
JEL - v35 - Mr '97 - p162+ [501+]
Williams, Jerry M - *Censorship and Art in Pre-Enlightenment Lima*
Hisp - v79 - S '96 - p460+ [501+]
Early Images of the Americas
HAHR - v77 - F '97 - p103+ [501+]
Williams, Joanna - *The Two-Headed Deer*
Choice - v34 - O '96 - p270 [51-250]
Williams, Joel F - *Other Followers of Jesus*
Rel St Rev - v23 - Ap '97 - p183 [51-250]
Williams, John, 1946- - *William Wordsworth: A Literary Life*
Choice - v34 - O '96 - p283 [51-250]
Nine-C Lit - v51 - D '96 - p428 [51-250]
Williams, John, 1948- - *Fiction as False Document*
Choice - v34 - My '97 - p1501 [51-250]
Williams, John A - *The Angry Ones*
BW - v26 - S 1 '96 - p12 [51-250]
LATBR - Ag 4 '96 - p11 [51-250]
Williams, John Delane - *Statistical Methods*
Choice - v34 - S '96 - p165 [51-250]
SciTech - v20 - S '96 - p10 [51-250]
Williams, John L - *Faithless*
Obs - Mr 23 '97 - p18* [51-250]
Williams, Jonathan, Dr. - *Money: A History*
y BL - v93 - Mr 15 '97 - p1210 [51-250]
PW - v244 - F 24 '97 - p71 [51-250]
Williams, Jonathan, 1960- - *Geographic Information from Space*
GJ - v162 - Jl '96 - p219+ [501+]

Williams, Karen, 1959- - *NightShade*
SF Chr - v18 - O '96 - p77 [51-250]
Williams, Karen Lynn - *Tap-Tap (Taylor). Book and Audio Version*
c SLJ - v42 - O '96 - p77 [51-250]
Williams, Kathleen - *Marriages of Amelia County, Virginia 1735-1815*
r EGH - v50 - N '96 - p190 [51-250]
Williams, Kathleen Broome - *Secret Weapon*
Choice - v34 - Ap '97 - p1361 [51-250]
Williams, Kay - *Stuart: The Life and Art of Stuart Sutcliffe*
TLS - N 22 '96 - p9 [501+]
Under an English Heaven
S&T - v93 - Ap '97 - p65 [51-250]
Williams, Keith - *Gran Webster's War*
c Sch Lib - v44 - Ag '96 - p116 [51-250]
Williams, L Patricia - *The Regulation of Private Schools in America*
J Gov Info - v23 - S '96 - p544 [51-250]
Williams, Laura - *The Christmas Story. The Story of the Wisemen. Book and Audio Version*
c BL - v92 - Ag '96 - p1916 [51-250]
Williams, Laura E - *Behind the Bedroom Wall (Illus. by A Nancy Goldstein)*
c BL - v92 - Ag '96 - p1900+ [51-250]
c CBRS - v24 - Ag '96 - p168 [51-250]
c Ch BWatch - v7 - F '97 - p5 [51-250]
c HB - v73 - Ja '97 - p69+ [51-250]
c HB Guide - v8 - Spr '97 - p76 [51-250]
c SLJ - v42 - S '96 - p208 [51-250]
The Long Silk Strand (Illus. by Grayce Bochak)
c RT - v50 - N '96 - p257 [51-250]
Williams, Laura Rice - *Practical Horticulture. 3rd Ed.*
SciTech - v20 - D '96 - p56 [51-250]
Williams, Lea E - *Servants of the People*
BL - v93 - F 15 '97 - p1001 [51-250]
LJ - v122 - F 1 '97 - p95 [51-250]
PW - v243 - N 4 '96 - p56 [51-250]
Williams, Leslie - *Night Wrestling*
LJ - v122 - Ja '97 - p107 [51-250]
Williams, Linda D - *La Viejecita Que No Le Tenia Miedo A Nada (Illus. by Megan Lloyd)*
c BL - v93 - My 1 '97 - p1507 [1-50]
Williams, Linda Ruth - *Sex in the Head*
Film Cr - v21 - Fall '96 - p95+ [501+]
Williams, Lloyd C - *Business Decisions, Human Choices*
J Car P&E - v57 - Win '97 - p20 [51-250]
R&R Bk N - v11 - D '96 - p26 [51-250]
Williams, Lou Falkner - *The Great South Carolina Ku Klux Klan Trials 1871-1872*
Choice - v34 - F '97 - p1028 [51-250]
Williams, Lucy Chase - *The Complete Films of Vincent Price*
r SF Chr - v18 - O '96 - p81 [51-250]
Williams, Marcia - *The Adventures of Robin Hood*
c Bks Keeps - Ja '97 - p20 [51-250]
y Emerg Lib - v24 - S '96 - p26 [1-50]
The Iliad and the Odyssey (Illus. by Marcia Williams)
c CCB-B - v50 - F '97 - p227 [51-250]
c Ch BWatch - v6 - D '96 - p3 [1-50]
c HB - v73 - Ja '97 - p82 [51-250]
c HB Guide - v8 - Spr '97 - p149 [51-250]
c KR - v64 - N 1 '96 - p1610 [51-250]
c PW - v243 - N 25 '96 - p75 [51-250]
c Spec - v277 - D 14 '96 - p77 [51-250]
c TES - N 15 '96 - p7* [51-250]
King Arthur and the Knights of the Round Table (Illus. by Marcia Williams)
c HB Guide - v8 - Spr '97 - p106 [51-250]
c Magpies - v11 - Jl '96 - p27 [51-250]
c RT - v50 - Ap '97 - p594 [51-250]
c Sch Lib - v44 - Ag '96 - p109 [51-250]
c SLJ - v42 - Ag '96 - p141 [51-250]
Sinbad the Sailor (Illus. by Marcia Williams)
c Magpies - v11 - My '96 - p53 [1-50]
Williams, Margery - *The Velveteen Rabbit (Illus. by Donna Green)*
c Ch BWatch - v6 - My '96 - p5 [51-250]
Williams, Marilyn Thornton - *Washing the Great Unwashed*
J Urban H - v22 - My '96 - p531+ [501+]
RAH - v24 - S '96 - p461+ [501+]
Williams, Marion V - *Liberalising a Regulated Banking System*
JEL - v35 - Mr '97 - p223 [51-250]
Williams, Mark - *Post-Colonial Literatures in English: Southeast Asia, New Zealand, and the Pacific 1970-1992*
r ARBA - v28 - '97 - p463 [251-500]
r Choice - v34 - Ja '97 - p770+ [51-250]
r R&R Bk N - v11 - D '96 - p63 [51-250]

Williams, Mark E - *The American Geriatrics Society's Complete Guide to Aging and Health*
  r BL - v93 - F 1 '97 - p957 [1-50]
Williams, Martin - *The Green Dragon*
  FEER - v159 - D 19 '96 - p58+ [501+]
Williams, Martin A J - *Interactions of Desertification and Climate*
  GJ - v163 - Mr '97 - p99 [251-500]
Williams, Mary E - *The Jury System*
  y Kliatt - v31 - Mr '97 - p29 [51-250]
Williams, Merryn - *Clare and Effie (Illus. by Bernice Carlill)*
  y JB - v60 - D '96 - p280 [51-250]
  y Sch Lib - v44 - N '96 - p172 [51-250]
Williams, Michael, 1935- - *Understanding Geographical and Environmental Education*
  Choice - v34 - S '96 - p181 [51-250]
  SB - v32 - Ag '96 - p166 [251-500]
Williams, Michael, 1962- - *The Genuine Half-Moon Kid*
  y Kliatt - v30 - N '96 - p11 [251-500]
  y PW - v243 - Jl 22 '96 - p243 [1-50]
Williams, Michael W - *The African American Encyclopedia. Vols. 7-8*
  r BL - v93 - N 1 '96 - p538 [51-250]
  r Choice - v34 - My '97 - p1471 [51-250]
  r LJ - v122 - Ja '97 - p82 [51-250]
  r R&R Bk N - v12 - F '97 - p23 [51-250]
  yr SLJ - v43 - F '97 - p132 [51-250]
Williams, Miller - *Points of Departure*
  HR - v49 - Win '97 - p659+ [501+]
Williams, Neville - *The Expanding World 1492 to 1762. 2nd Ed.*
  r Rel St Rev - v23 - Ja '97 - p82+ [51-250]
Williams, Nick - *How Birds Fly*
  c Ch BWatch - v7 - Ja '97 - p3 [1-50]
  c HB Guide - v8 - Spr '97 - p125 [1-50]
  c SB - v33 - My '97 - p114 [51-250]
  c SLJ - v43 - F '97 - p95 [51-250]
Williams, Nigel - *From Wimbledon to Waco*
  TES - Ag 2 '96 - p15 [51-250]
Stalking Fiona
  Spec - v278 - F 15 '97 - p27+ [501+]
  TLS - F 21 '97 - p22 [501+]
Williams, Patricia J - *The Alchemy of Race and Rights*
  HER - v66 - Win '96 - p848+ [501+]
The Rooster's Egg
  CPR - v16 - Je '96 - p223+ [501+]
  CS - v26 - Ja '97 - p22+ [501+]
  Prog - v61 - Ja '97 - p34 [251-500]
  Prog - v61 - Ja '97 - p37 [51-250]
  Trib Bks - Mr 2 '97 - p8 [1-50]
Williams, Paul, 1948- - *Watching the River Flow*
  BL - v93 - Ja '97 - p805 [51-250]
Williams, Penry - *The Later Tudors*
  HRNB - v25 - Fall '96 - p18+ [251-500]
Williams, Peter, 1937, Jan., 1- - *When the Giants Were Giants*
  Aethlon - v13 - Fall '95 - p174+ [251-500]
Williams, Peter F - *The Organ in Western Culture 750-1250*
  Specu - v71 - Jl '96 - p776+ [501+]
Williams, Philip Lee - *Jenny Dorset*
  BL - v93 - Mr 15 '97 - p1228 [51-250]
  PW - v244 - Mr 31 '97 - p63 [51-250]
Williams, R J P - *The Natural Selection of the Chemical Elements*
  Nature - v383 - S 26 '96 - p310+ [501+]
Williams, Raymond L - *The Postmodern Novel in Latin America*
  Hisp - v79 - S '96 - p461+ [501+]
The Writings of Carlos Fuentes
  y BWatch - v17 - S '96 - p3 [51-250]
  Choice - v34 - D '96 - p621 [51-250]
  TLS - N 1 '96 - p31 [51-250]
Williams, Robert H - *Joyful Trek*
  WHQ - v27 - Win '96 - p547+ [51-250]
Williams, Robert L - *How to Build Your Own Log Home for Less than $15,000*
  BL - v93 - Ja '97 - p797 [51-250]
Williams, Robin - *Garden Design*
  Hort - v74 - My '96 - p73+ [251-500]
Williams, Robin, 1953- - *Home Sweet Home Page*
  LJ - v121 - N 1 '96 - p104 [51-250]
Home Sweet Home Page and the Kitchen Sink
  LJ - v122 - My 1 '97 - p132 [51-250]
Williams, Robyn - *Normal Service Won't Be Resumed*
  Aust Bk R - N '96 - p45 [501+]
Williams, Ronald P - *Contemporary Extensile Exposures in Orthopaedic Surgery*
  SciTech - v21 - Mr '97 - p61 [51-250]

Williams, Sheila - *Intergalactic Mercenaries*
  LJ - v121 - O 15 '96 - p93 [51-250]
Williams, Sheridan - *UK Solar Eclipses from Year 1*
  S&T - v92 - N '96 - p60 [51-250]
Williams, Sherley Anne - *Working Cotton (Illus. by Carole Byard)*
  c PW - v244 - Ap 7 '97 - p94 [1-50]
Williams, Stanley - *Gangs and Drugs*
  c BL - v93 - F 15 '97 - p1018 [51-250]
  c PW - v243 - S 9 '96 - p85 [51-250]
Gangs and Self-Esteem
  c PW - v243 - S 9 '96 - p85 [51-250]
  c SLJ - v42 - D '96 - p118 [51-250]
Gangs and the Abuse of Power
  c PW - v243 - S 9 '96 - p85 [51-250]
  c SLJ - v43 - Ja '97 - p138 [51-250]
Gangs and Violence
  c PW - v243 - S 9 '96 - p85 [51-250]
Gangs and Wanting to Belong
  c PW - v243 - S 9 '96 - p85 [51-250]
  c SLJ - v43 - Ja '97 - p138 [51-250]
Gangs and Weapons
  c PW - v243 - S 9 '96 - p85 [51-250]
  c SLJ - v43 - Ja '97 - p138 [51-250]
Gangs and Your Friends
  c PW - v243 - S 9 '96 - p85 [51-250]
  c SLJ - v43 - Ja '97 - p138 [51-250]
Gangs and Your Neighborhood
  o PW - v243 - S 9 '96 - p85 [51-250]
  c SLJ - v43 - Ja '97 - p138 [51-250]
Williams, Stephen - *Invisible Darkness*
  Mac - v109 - S 9 '96 - p54 [501+]
  Quill & Q - v62 - O '96 - p39 [251-500]
Williams, Stephen, 1942- - *Theodosius: The Empire at Bay*
  AHR - v101 - O '96 - p1189+ [501+]
  CH - v65 - D '96 - p663+ [501+]
  CHR - v82 - Jl '96 - p500+ [501+]
Williams, Sue, 1948- - *I Went Walking (Illus. by Julie Vivas)*
  c HB Guide - v7 - Fall '96 - p246 [1-50]
Williams, Susan, 1948- - *Savory Suppers and Fashionable Feasts*
  VQR - v73 - Win '97 - p32* [51-250]
Williams, Suzanne - *Emily at School (Illus. by Abby Carter)*
  c HB - v73 - Ja '97 - p70+ [51-250]
  c HB Guide - v8 - Spr '97 - p61 [51-250]
  c KR - v64 - Ag 15 '96 - p1246 [51-250]
  c SLJ - v42 - D '96 - p109 [51-250]
Made in China (Illus. by Andrea Fong)
  c BL - v93 - F 1 '97 - p938+ [51-250]
  c CBRS - v25 - F '97 - p84 [51-250]
  c Ch BWatch - v7 - Ja '97 - p1 [51-250]
  c KR - v64 - D 15 '96 - p1807 [51-250]
  c PW - v243 - D 9 '96 - p69 [51-250]
My Dog Never Says Please (Illus. by Tedd Arnold)
  c KR - v65 - My 1 '97 - p728 [51-250]
  c PW - v244 - Ap 21 '97 - p71 [51-250]
Williams, Tad - *Otherland. Vol. 1*
  BL - v93 - O 1 '96 - p292 [51-250]
  KR - v64 - O 1 '96 - p1434 [51-250]
  LJ - v121 - N 15 '96 - p92 [51-250]
  New Sci - v153 - Mr 15 '97 - p45 [51-250]
Williams, Ted - *The Insightful Sportsman*
  AB - v97 - Je 17 '96 - p2412 [51-250]
  WAL - v31 - Win '97 - p418+ [501+]
Williams, Tennessee - *Tennessee Williams' Letters to Donald Windham 1940-1965*
  Bloom Rev - v16 - S '96 - p28+ [51-250]
Williams, Terrie - *The Personal Touch*
  Bl S - v26 - Sum '96 - p68 [51-250]
Williams, Tom - *Chinese Medicine*
  BWatch - v18 - Mr '97 - p1 [51-250]
Williams, Tony - *Hearths of Darkness*
  Choice - v34 - F '97 - p973 [51-250]
Williams, Trevor I - *Our Scientific Heritage*
  r Nature - v384 - D 12 '96 - p528 [51-250]
  New Sci - v153 - Ja 25 '97 - p43 [51-250]
Williams, Ursula M - *Adventures of the Little Wooden Horse. Audio Version*
  c Ch BWatch - v6 - O '96 - p2 [1-50]
Williams, Vergil L - *Dictionary of American Penology. Rev. Ed.*
  r ARBA - v28 - '97 - p227 [251-500]
Williams, Vernon J, Jr. - *Rethinking Race*
  AJS - v102 - N '96 - p909+ [501+]
  CS - v26 - Ja '97 - p115+ [501+]
  Isis - v88 - Mr '97 - p162+ [501+]

Williams, Walter Jon - *City on Fire*
  BW - v27 - F 23 '97 - p11 [251-500]
  KR - v64 - D 1 '96 - p1708 [51-250]
  LJ - v121 - D '96 - p152 [51-250]
  NYTBR - v102 - F 23 '97 - p20 [251-500]
  PW - v243 - D 30 '96 - p59 [51-250]
Williams, William A - *Twas Only an Irishman's Dream*
  ILS - v16 - Spr '97 - p36 [51-250]
Williams, William Carlos - *The Collected Stories of William Carlos Williams*
  BW - v26 - Ag 18 '96 - p12 [51-250]
  LJ - v121 - O 15 '96 - p94 [51-250]
Williams, William H - *Slavery and Freedom in Delaware 1639-1865*
  Choice - v34 - Ja '97 - p866 [51-250]
  R&R Bk N - v11 - N '96 - p18 [51-250]
Williams, Willie L - *Taking Back Our Streets*
  Rapport - v19 - 5 '96 - p39 [251-500]
Williams-Garcia, Rita - *Blue Tights*
  y PW - v243 - D 2 '96 - p62 [1-50]
Like Sisters on the Homefront
  y EJ - v85 - N '96 - p131 [251-500]
  y Emerg Lib - v24 - S '96 - p26 [1-50]
  y Emerg Lib - v24 - S '96 - p27 [1-50]
  y RT - v50 - Mr '97 - p480 [51-250]
Williamson, Alan - *Love and the Soul*
  MQR - v36 - Spr '97 - p368+ [501+]
Williamson, Chet - *Murder in Cormyr*
  MFSF - v92 - Mr '97 - p36 [51-250]
Williamson, Chilton - *The Immigration Mystique*
  Choice - v34 - N '96 - p540 [51-250]
  Nat R - v48 - N 25 '96 - p65+ [501+]
  NYTBR - v101 - S 1 '96 - p18 [501+]
Williamson, Clark M - *A Guest in the House of Israel*
  Rel Ed - v91 - Fall '96 - p615 [51-250]
Williamson, David, 1927- - *Brewer's British Royalty*
  r BL - v93 - My 1 '97 - p1520 [51-250]
Williamson, David, 1942- - *Heretic: Based on the Life of Derek Freeman*
  Aust Bk R - Ag '96 - p42+ [501+]
Williamson, David A, 1955- - *Job Satisfaction in Social Services*
  JEL - v34 - S '96 - p1447+ [51-250]
Williamson, Gene - *Chesapeake Conflict*
  EGH - v50 - N '96 - p170+ [51-250]
Williamson, Henry - *Tarka the Otter (Maloney). Audio Version*
  y Kliatt - v31 - Ja '97 - p50 [51-250]
Williamson, J W, 1944- - *Hillbillyland: What the Movies Did to the Mountains and What the Mountains Did to the Movies*
  J Am Cult - v19 - Spr '96 - p111+ [251-500]
Southern Mountaineers in Silent Films
  r JSH - v62 - N '96 - p863 [51-250]
Williamson, Jack - *The Black Sun*
  BW - v27 - Mr 30 '97 - p8 [251-500]
  KR - v64 - D 15 '96 - p1774 [51-250]
  LJ - v122 - F 15 '97 - p164 [51-250]
  NYTBR - v102 - Ap 6 '97 - p24 [51-250]
  PW - v244 - Ja 20 '97 - p399 [51-250]
Williamson, James R - *Federal Antitrust Policy during the Kennedy-Johnson Years*
  JEH - v56 - S '96 - p753+ [501+]
Williamson, Joel - *William Faulkner and Southern History*
  ASInt - v34 - O '96 - p107+ [501+]
Williamson, Kevin - *Children of Albion Rovers*
  Econ - v343 - Ap 26 '97 - p83+ [501+]
  NS - v125 - O 25 '96 - p46+ [501+]
  Obs - N 24 '96 - p17* [501+]
Williamson, Marianne - *Emma and Mommy Talk to God (Illus. by Julia Noonan)*
  c HB Guide - v7 - Fall '96 - p281 [1-50]
  c KR - v64 - My 1 '96 - p695 [51-250]
Williamson, Martha - *Touched by an Angel*
  y BL - v93 - F 1 '97 - p907 [51-250]
Williamson, Miryam Ehrlich - *Fibromyalgia: A Comprehensive Approach*
  Choice - v34 - Ja '97 - p830 [51-250]
  LJ - v121 - S 15 '96 - p86+ [51-250]
Williamson, Oliver E - *The Mechanisms of Governance*
  JEL - v34 - S '96 - p1412 [51-250]
Williamson, Penelope - *The Outsider*
  KR - v64 - My 1 '96 - p637 [251-500]
  LJ - v122 - Ja '97 - p184 [51-250]
  Roundup M - v4 - O '96 - p33 [51-250]
Williamson, Sarah, 1974- - *Stop, Look and Listen (Illus. by Loretta Trezzo Braren)*
  c Ch BWatch - v6 - N '96 - p2 [51-250]
  c PW - v243 - S 9 '96 - p84 [51-250]
  c SLJ - v42 - D '96 - p118 [51-250]

Williamson, Tom - *Polite Landscapes*
  Albion - v28 - Sum '96 - p309+ [501+]
Williams-Taylor, Helen Sue Young - *The Roots and Branches of Daniel Roman Young and Ann Maria Beck, Delaware County, Iowa 1755-1996*
  r EGH - v50 - N '96 - p195+ [51-250]
Willich, Stefan N - *Triggering of Acute Coronary Syndromes*
  SciTech - v20 - N '96 - p47 [51-250]
Willig, Sidney H - *Good Manufacturing Practices for Pharmaceuticals. 4th Ed.*
  SciTech - v20 - D '96 - p55 [51-250]
Willimon, William H - *The Abandoned Generation*
  Cng - v28 - Jl '96 - p63 [51-250]
  Cres - v59 - Sum '96 - p33+ [501+]
  Rel St Rev - v23 - Ja '97 - p49 [51-250]
Concise Encyclopedia of Preaching
  r Rel St Rev - v22 - O '96 - p336+ [51-250]
  r TT - v53 - O '96 - p388+ [501+]
Willinger, Faith - *Red, White and Greens*
  BL - v93 - S 15 '96 - p198 [51-250]
  LJ - v121 - S 15 '96 - p88 [51-250]
Willingham, Ralph - *Science Fiction and the Theatre*
  Ext - v37 - Sum '96 - p174+ [501+]
Willink, Roseann Sandoval - *Weaving a World*
  BL - v93 - Ja '97 - p806 [51-250]
  Choice - v34 - My '97 - p1566 [51-250]
Willinsky, John - *Empire of Words*
  MLR - v92 - Ja '97 - p156+ [501+]
Willis, A J - *Astrophysical and Laboratory Plasmas*
  SciTech - v20 - D '96 - p21 [51-250]
Willis, Carol - *Form Follows Finance*
  TLS - N 8 '96 - p4+ [501+]
Willis, Christine - *Organic Synthesis*
  New Sci - v153 - Mr 1 '97 - p38 [1-50]
Willis, Connie - *Bellwether*
  LJ - v121 - O 1 '96 - p156 [51-250]
  MFSF - v91 - Ag '96 - p22+ [501+]
Willis, Deborah - *Malevolent Nurture*
  Six Ct J - v27 - Fall '96 - p830+ [501+]
Willis, G G - *A History of Early Roman Liturgy to the Death of Pope Gregory the Great*
  CH - v65 - S '96 - p454+ [501+]
Willis, Geoffrey Grimshaw - *A History of Early Roman Liturgy to the Death of Pope Gregory the Great*
  CHR - v82 - Jl '96 - p491+ [251-500]
  Rel St Rev - v23 - Ja '97 - p81 [51-250]
Willis, H Lee - *Spatial Electric Load Forecasting*
  SciTech - v20 - N '96 - p71 [51-250]
Willis, Jean - *The Salt and Pepper Boys*
  c TES - Jl 5 '96 - pR8 [51-250]
Willis, Jeanne - *The Pet Person (Illus. by Tony Ross)*
  c HB Guide - v8 - Spr '97 - p53 [51-250]
  c JB - v60 - D '96 - p243+ [51-250]
  c Sch Lib - v44 - N '96 - p148 [51-250]
  c SLJ - v43 - Ja '97 - p94+ [51-250]
  c TES - Jl 5 '96 - pR2 [501+]
The Pink Hare (Illus. by Ken Brown)
  c Sch Lib - v45 - F '97 - p22 [51-250]
The Tale of Mucky Mabel (Illus. by Margaret Chamberlain)
  c TES - O 18 '96 - p12* [1-50]
Willis, Kay - *Are We Having Fun Yet?*
  PW - v244 - Ap 21 '97 - p67 [51-250]
Willis, Laura - *Calloway County, Kentucky Tax Lists 1835-1836*
  r EGH - v50 - N '96 - p167+ [1-50]
Trigg County, Kentucky Deeds. Vol. 1
  EGH - v50 - N '96 - p168 [1-50]
Willis, Marjorie Canfield - *Medical Terminology*
  SciTech - v20 - N '96 - p35 [51-250]
Willis, Meredith Sue - *Marco's Monster*
  c BL - v93 - N 15 '96 - p589 [51-250]
  c HB - v73 - Ja '97 - p71 [51-250]
  c HB Guide - v8 - Spr '97 - p76 [51-250]
  c SLJ - v43 - Ja '97 - p95 [51-250]
Willis, Nancy Carol - *The Robins in Your Backyard*
  c BL - v93 - Ja '97 - p866 [251-500]
  c Ch BWatch - v7 - Ja '97 - p2 [51-250]
Willis, Patricia - *Danger along the Ohio*
  c BL - v93 - My 1 '97 - p1499 [51-250]
  c CBRS - v25 - Mr '97 - p96 [51-250]
  c CCB-B - v50 - Ap '97 - p300+ [51-250]
  c KR - v65 - F 15 '97 - p308 [51-250]
Out of the Storm
  y Kliatt - v31 - Mr '97 - p14 [51-250]
Willis, Roy - *World Mythology*
  y Kliatt - v31 - Mr '97 - p24 [51-250]
Willis-Thomas, Deborah - *Picturing Us*
  Bl S - v26 - Fall '96 - p107+ [51-250]
  y Kliatt - v30 - S '96 - p30 [51-250]

Willman, Marianne - *The Mermaid's Song*
  PW - v244 - My 12 '97 - p74 [51-250]
Willmer, Colin - *Stomata. 2nd Ed.*
  Choice - v34 - O '96 - p306 [51-250]
Willmott, Glenn - *McLuhan, or Modernism in Reverse*
  Choice - v34 - Ap '97 - p1323 [51-250]
Willmott, H P - *Grave of a Dozen Schemes*
  Choice - v34 - S '96 - p189 [51-250]
Willms, Johannes - *Paris: Capital of Europe*
  LJ - v121 - S 15 '96 - p81 [51-250]
Willner-Pardo, Gina - *Hunting Grandma's Treasures (Illus. by Walter Lyon Krudop)*
  c HB Guide - v7 - Fall '96 - p288 [51-250]
  c LA - v73 - S '96 - p357+ [51-250]
Willow Springs
  p Sm Pr R - v28 - N '96 - p22 [51-250]
Wills, Charles A - *A Historical Album of Colorado*
  c HB Guide - v7 - Fall '96 - p390 [1-50]
A Historical Album of Georgia
  c HB Guide - v8 - Spr '97 - p176 [1-50]
A Historical Album of Michigan
  c HB Guide - v8 - Spr '97 - p176 [1-50]
A Historical Album of Ohio
  c HB Guide - v7 - Fall '96 - p390 [1-50]
A Historical Album of Pennsylvania
  c HB Guide - v7 - Fall '96 - p390 [1-50]
Wills, Christopher - *Plagues: Their Origin, History and Future*
  Spec - v276 - My 18 '96 - p36+ [501+]
Yellow Fever, Black Goddess
  BW - v27 - Ja 5 '97 - p9 [501+]
  Choice - v34 - Mr '97 - p1194 [51-250]
  E Mag - v8 - Mr '97 - p48 [51-250]
  LJ - v121 - S 15 '96 - p91+ [51-250]
  New Sci - v152 - O 12 '96 - p44 [251-500]
  NH - v106 - F '97 - p13 [1-50]
  PW - v243 - S 2 '96 - p102 [51-250]
  SB - v33 - Ja '97 - p9 [51-250]
Wills, Gale - *A Marriage of Convenience*
  AHR - v102 - F '97 - p228 [501+]
  Can Hist R - v77 - S '96 - p429+ [501+]
Wills, Garry - *Certain Trumpets*
  Mar Crp G - v80 - D '96 - p74 [501+]
John Wayne's America
  BL - v93 - D 15 '96 - p691 [51-250]
  BW - v27 - Mr 2 '97 - p3 [501+]
  Ent W - Mr 21 '97 - p68 [51-250]
  KR - v65 - Ja 15 '97 - p133 [251-500]
  LJ - v122 - F 15 '97 - p137 [51-250]
  Nat R - v49 - Ap 21 '97 - p75+ [501+]
  NY - v73 - Ap 7 '97 - p95 [251-500]
  NYTBR - v102 - Mr 23 '97 - p13+ [501+]
  NYTLa - v146 - F 25 '97 - pC14 [501+]
  PW - v244 - Ja 6 '97 - p54 [251-500]
  Time - v149 - Ap 7 '97 - p80 [251-500]
  Trib Bks - Mr 2 '97 - p1+ [501+]
  VV - v42 - Mr 18 '97 - p57 [501+]
John Wayne's America (Wills). Audio Version
  PW - v244 - Ap 7 '97 - p34 [51-250]
Wills, Gary - *Witches and Jesuits*
  Six Ct J - v27 - Fall '96 - p898+ [501+]
Wills, Gregory A - *Democratic Religion*
  Choice - v34 - My '97 - p1518 [51-250]
Wills, Lawrence M - *The Jewish Novel in the Ancient World*
  JR - v77 - Ap '97 - p350+ [501+]
Wills, Linda - *Reverse Engineering*
  SciTech - v21 - Mr '97 - p8 [51-250]
Wills, W H - *The Ancient Southwestern Community*
  Am Sci - v84 - N '96 - p609+ [501+]
Willson, A Leslie - *Contemporary German Fiction*
  Choice - v34 - Ja '97 - p800 [51-250]
Willson, Quentin - *The Ultimate Classic Car Book*
  y BL - v93 - Ap 1 '97 - p1310 [1-50]
Wilmer, Clive - *Selected Poems 1965-1993*
  WLT - v70 - Aut '96 - p970 [51-250]
Wilmer, Franke - *The Indigenous Voice in World Politics*
  SSQ - v77 - Je '96 - p445+ [501+]
Wilmeth, Don B - *Cambridge Guide to American Theatre. Updated Ed.*
  r ARBA - v28 - '97 - p524 [51-250]
Wilms, Wellford W - *Restoring Prosperity*
  Choice - v34 - Ja '97 - p842 [51-250]
  LATBR - S 1 '96 - p1+ [501+]
  LJ - v121 - O 1 '96 - p96 [51-250]
Wilner, Barry - *Dan Marino*
  c HB Guide - v7 - Fall '96 - p359 [1-50]
Swimming (Illus. by Art Seiden)
  c HB Guide - v7 - Fall '96 - p360 [1-50]

Wilson, A Jeyaratnam - *S.J.V. Chelvanayakam and the Crisis of Sri Lankan Tamil Nationalism 1947-1977*
  Pac A - v69 - Sum '96 - p277+ [251-500]
Wilson, A N - *Paul: The Mind of the Apostle*
  BW - v27 - Mr 30 '97 - p1+ [501+]
  KR - v65 - F 15 '97 - p291 [251-500]
  LJ - v122 - Ap 1 '97 - p99 [51-250]
  PW - v244 - Ap 28 '97 - p69+ [51-250]
  TLS - Mr 28 '97 - p3+ [501+]
The Vicar of Sorrows (Davidson). Audio Version
  y Kliatt - v31 - Ja '97 - p47 [51-250]
A Watch in the Night
  BL - v93 - N 15 '96 - p573 [51-250]
  LJ - v121 - S 15 '96 - p98+ [51-250]
  NYTBR - v101 - D 22 '96 - p15 [51-250]
  Obs - Ag 18 '96 - p19 [501+]
  Spec - v277 - N 16 '96 - p42 [1-50]
  Spec - v277 - N 23 '96 - p46 [1-50]
Wilson, Adrian - *Rethinking Social History*
  J Urban H - v23 - N '96 - p94+ [501+]
Wilson, Andrew J - *Irish America and the Ulster Conflict 1968-1995*
  ILS - v16 - Spr '97 - p31+ [501+]
  TLS - S 27 '96 - p8 [501+]
Wilson, April - *The Christmas Deer*
  c BIC - v25 - D '96 - p33+ [501+]
  c PW - v243 - S 30 '96 - p92 [1-50]
Wilson, Barbara - *Blue Windows*
  BL - v93 - Mr 1 '97 - p1092 [51-250]
  KR - v65 - Ja 15 '97 - p134 [251-500]
  NY - v73 - Ap 14 '97 - p85 [51-250]
  PW - v244 - F 10 '97 - p79 [51-250]
  Trib Bks - My 25 '97 - p5 [501+]
If You Had a Family
  BL - v93 - S 15 '96 - p223 [51-250]
  LJ - v121 - O 1 '96 - p128 [51-250]
Wilson, Bruce G - *Manuscripts and Government Records in the United Kingdom and Ireland Relating to Canada*
  Archiv - Fall '94 - p181+ [501+]
Wilson, Budge - *Harold and Harold (Illus. by Terry Roscoe)*
  c Ch Bk News - v19 - Spr '96 - p20 [251-500]
The Long Wait (Illus. by Eugenie Fernandes)
  c Quill & Q - v63 - Mr '97 - p79 [251-500]
Mothers and Other Strangers
  y CCB-B - v50 - S '96 - p36+ [51-250]
  y HB Guide - v7 - Fall '96 - p306 [51-250]
  y SLJ - v42 - S '96 - p230 [51-250]
  y VOYA - v19 - O '96 - p214 [251-500]
Wilson, Carol Shiner - *Re-Visioning Romanticism*
  NWSA Jnl - v8 - Sum '96 - p147+ [501+]
Wilson, Carter A - *Racism: From Slavery to Advanced Capitalism*
  BWatch - v17 - D '96 - p5 [1-50]
  Choice - v34 - F '97 - p1045 [51-250]
  R&R Bk N - v11 - D '96 - p14 [51-250]
Wilson, Catherine - *The Invisible World*
  AHR - v101 - D '96 - p1517+ [501+]
  Am Sci - v85 - Ja '97 - p90+ [501+]
  RM - v50 - S '96 - p195+ [501+]
Wilson, Charles E - *Computer Integrated Machine Design*
  SciTech - v20 - D '96 - p73 [51-250]
Wilson, Charles Reagan - *Judgment and Grace in Dixie*
  Comw - v123 - N 22 '96 - p24+ [501+]
  JSH - v63 - F '97 - p222+ [51-250]
Wilson, Charles West - *Westmoreland Glass*
  Ant & CM - v101 - D '96 - p32 [51-250]
Wilson, Chris - *The Myth of Santa Fe*
  BW - v27 - Ap 6 '97 - p12 [51-250]
  PW - v244 - Ja 20 '97 - p385 [51-250]
Wilson, Clint C, II - *Race, Multiculturalism, and the Media. 2nd Ed.*
  JMCQ - v73 - Win '96 - p1013+ [501+]
Wilson, Colin - *The Atlas of Holy Places and Sacred Sites*
  yr ARBA - v28 - '97 - p532 [51-250]
  r Choice - v34 - Ap '97 - p1318 [51-250]
  r ILN - Christmas '96 - p89 [51-250]
  r LJ - v122 - F 1 '97 - p75 [51-250]
Wilson, David - *Love and Nausea*
  Books - v9 - S '95 - p9 [251-500]
Wilson, David Henry - *Do Gerbils Go to Heaven? (Illus. by Axel Scheffler)*
  c Books - v10 - Je '96 - p25 [1-50]
Do Goldfish Play the Violin? (Illus. by Axel Scheffler)
  c Books - v10 - Je '96 - p25 [1-50]
Elephants Don't Sit on Cars (Illus. by Axel Scheffler)
  c Books - v10 - Je '96 - p25 [1-50]
How the Lion Lost His Lunch (Illus. by Axel Scheffler)
  c Books - v10 - Je '96 - p25 [1-50]

Please Keep off the Dinosaur (Crane). Pts. 1-2. Audio Version
  c BL - v93 - N 1 '96 - p522 [51-250]
Wilson, David L - *Great American West Collectibles*
    Ant & CM - v101 - D '96 - p30 [1-50]
Wilson, David O - *Coachman Rat*
  y VOYA - v19 - D '96 - p266 [1-50]
Wilson, Derek - *Hans Holbein: Portrait of an Unknown Man*
    Apo - v144 - D '96 - p70 [251-500]
    TLS - F 28 '97 - p20 [501+]
Wilson, Dick - *China the Big Tiger*
    FEER - v159 - S 26 '96 - p50+ [501+]
Wilson, Don E - *Bats in Question*
    PW - v244 - My 5 '97 - p192 [51-250]
Wilson, Edmund - *The American Earthquake*
    LJ - v121 - S 15 '96 - p102 [51-250]
From the Uncollected Edmund Wilson
    WLT - v70 - Sum '96 - p705+ [501+]
Wilson, Edward Osborne - *In Search of Nature*
  y BL - v93 - S 1 '96 - p35 [51-250]
    BL - v93 - D 1 '96 - p630 [1-50]
    BW - v26 - N 3 '96 - p13 [51-250]
    Choice - v34 - Ja '97 - p814 [51-250]
    LATBR - S 22 '96 - p3 [501+]
    LATBR - D 29 '96 - p4 [51-250]
    Nature - v384 - N 14 '96 - p126+ [501+]
    NH - v105 - S '96 - p11 [1-50]
    NYTBR - v101 - S 22 '96 - p24 [51-250]
  y SB - v32 - O '96 - p203 [251-500]
    Sci - v274 - N 1 '96 - p734 [51-250]
    Skeptic - v4 - 4 '96 - p104+ [251-500]
Naturalist
    Isis - v87 - S '96 - p521+ [501+]
    Nature - v385 - Ja 2 '97 - p36 [1-50]
    Sew R - v104 - O '96 - p665+ [501+]
Wilson, Elizabeth - *The Internet Roadmap for Educators*
    Emerg Lib - v24 - Mr '97 - p40+ [501+]
Wilson, Emma - *Sexuality and the Reading Encounter*
    Choice - v34 - Ja '97 - p802 [51-250]
Wilson, F M G - *A Strong Supporting Cast*
    EHR - v111 - S '96 - p1003+ [251-500]
Wilson, F Paul - *Deep as the Marrow*
  y BL - v93 - F 1 '97 - p927 [51-250]
    KR - v65 - Ja 15 '97 - p95 [251-500]
    LJ - v121 - D '96 - p148 [51-250]
    PW - v244 - F 17 '97 - p210 [251-500]
    Trib Bks - My 18 '97 - p6 [51-250]
Diagnosis: Terminal
    Arm Det - v29 - Fall '96 - p476+ [251-500]
    BWatch - v18 - F '97 - p4 [51-250]
    KR - v64 - My 1 '96 - p637 [251-500]
    Necro - Win '97 - p21+ [501+]
Mirage
  y BL - v93 - O 1 '96 - p324 [51-250]
    KR - v64 - Ag 15 '96 - p1185 [251-500]
    PW - v243 - O 7 '96 - p60 [51-250]
Mirage (Mettey). Audio Version
    PW - v244 - F 3 '97 - p42 [51-250]
Wilson, Gahan - *Gahan Wilson's The Ultimate Haunted House*
    Necro - Fall '96 - p28 [51-250]
Wilson, Gartii S - *A History of Shipbuilding and Naval Architecture in Canada*
    Pub Hist - v18 - Fall '96 - p174+ [501+]
Wilson, Glenn D - *Psychology for Performing Artists*
    Dance RJ - v28 - Fall '96 - p89+ [501+]
Wilson, Gregory V - *Parallel Programming Using C++*
    New Sci - v153 - Mr 1 '97 - p46+ [501+]
Practical Parallel Programming
    Choice - v34 - S '96 - p164+ [51-250]
Wilson, Henry S - *African Decolonization*
    EHR - v112 - Ap '97 - p544+ [251-500]
Wilson, Hugo - *The Encyclopedia of the Motorcycle*
  yr Emerg Lib - v24 - S '96 - p26 [1-50]
Wilson, J Christian - *Toward a Reassessment of the Shepherd of Hermas*
    Rel St Rev - v23 - Ja '97 - p78 [51-250]
Wilson, J Holton - *Economics. 4th Ed.*
    R&R Bk N - v12 - F '97 - p33 [51-250]
Wilson, Jacqueline - *Bad Girls (Illus. by Nick Sharratt)*
  c JB - v60 - Ag '96 - p152 [51-250]
Beauty and the Beast (Illus. by Peter Kavanagh)
  c Sch Lib - v45 - F '97 - p43 [51-250]
The Bed and Breakfast Star
  c RT - v50 - F '97 - p423 [51-250]
Connie and the Water Babies (Illus. by Georgien Overwater)
  c Bks Keeps - Mr '97 - p22 [51-250]
  c Sch Lib - v45 - F '97 - p36 [51-250]

Double Act (Illus. by Nick Sharratt)
  c Bks Keeps - v100 - S '96 - p13 [51-250]
  c Magpies - v11 - S '96 - p45 [1-50]
Elsa, Star of the Shelter! (Illus. by Nick Sharratt)
  c HB Guide - v7 - Fall '96 - p299 [51-250]
Mr. Cool (Illus. by Stephen Lewis)
  c TES - S 20 '96 - p16* [501+]
The Suitcase Kid (Illus. by Nick Sharratt)
  c Bks Keeps - Mr '97 - p16 [51-250]
Wilson, James, 1779- - *Biography of the Blind*
    LJ - v121 - N 1 '96 - p112 [51-250]
Wilson, James Q - *Moral Judgment*
    CHE - v43 - My 2 '97 - pA18 [51-250]
    KR - v65 - Mr 15 '97 - p452+ [251-500]
    LJ - v122 - Ap 1 '97 - p109 [51-250]
    WSJ-Cent - v99 - Ap 24 '97 - pA16 [501+]
Wilson, Janet - *The Ingenious Mr. Peale*
  c HB - v72 - N '96 - p762+ [51-250]
  c HB Guide - v7 - Fall '96 - p375 [51-250]
  y SLJ - v42 - D '96 - p32 [1-50]
Wilson, Jean - *The Archaeology of Shakespeare*
    Arch - v49 - N '96 - p76+ [501+]
    R&R Bk N - v11 - N '96 - p69 [51-250]
Wilson, John - *The Gazetteer of Scotland*
  r EGH - v50 - N '96 - p157 [51-250]
Wilson, John F - *British Business History 1720-1994*
    JEH - v57 - Mr '97 - p216+ [501+]
Wilson, John K - *The Myth of Political Correctness*
    CS - v25 - S '96 - p660+ [501+]
Wilson, John Morgan - *Simple Justice*
    Advocate - S 17 '96 - p60 [1-50]
    Arm Det - v30 - Win '97 - p40+ [251-500]
    BW - v26 - S 15 '96 - p6 [251-500]
Wilson, John P - *Islands in the Desert*
    PHR - v65 - Ag '96 - p475+ [251-500]
Wilson, Jonathan - *The Hiding Room*
    PW - v244 - My 12 '97 - p74 [1-50]
Wilson, Karen Ann - *Beware Sleeping Dogs*
    Arm Det - v29 - Fall '96 - p485+ [251-500]
Wilson, Kathleen - *The Sense of the People*
    Albion - v28 - Win '96 - p703+ [501+]
    JIH - v27 - Spr '97 - p678+ [501+]
    J Soc H - v30 - Spr '97 - p767+ [501+]
Wilson, Kathleen J W - *Ross and Wilson Anatomy and Physiology in Health and Illness. 8th Ed.*
  r SciTech - v20 - D '96 - p56 [51-250]
Wilson, Keith - *Channel Tunnel Visions 1850-1945*
    AHR - v101 - O '96 - p1211+ [501+]
    Albion - v28 - Sum '96 - p357+ [501+]
    EHR - v112 - Ap '97 - p516+ [501+]
    T&C - v37 - O '96 - p855+ [251-500]
Decisions for War 1914
    Historian - v59 - Win '97 - p486+ [501+]
Wilson, Lanford - *Collected Plays. Vol. 2*
    BL - v93 - Ja '97 - p807 [51-250]
    LJ - v122 - F 15 '97 - p136 [51-250]
Wilson, Linda - *Summer Spy*
  c Ch BWatch - v7 - Ja '97 - p4 [1-50]
Wilson, Liz - *Charming Cadavers*
    Choice - v34 - Ap '97 - p1358 [51-250]
Wilson, Logan - *The Academic Man*
    ES - v27 - Fall '96 - p236+ [501+]
Wilson, Lucile - *People Skills for Library Managers*
    SLJ - v42 - S '96 - p136 [51-250]
    SLMQ - v24 - Sum '96 - p220 [51-250]
Wilson, Lynn B - *Speaking to Power*
    Cont Pac - v9 - Spr '97 - p290+ [501+]
Wilson, Marvin R - *Our Father Abraham*
    Rel Ed - v91 - Fall '96 - p615 [1-50]
Wilson, Midge - *Divided Sisters*
    BW - v27 - F 2 '97 - p12 [51-250]
Wilson, Nancy Hope - *Becoming Felix*
  c CBRS - v25 - Win '97 - p72 [51-250]
  c CCB-B - v50 - Ja '97 - p188 [51-250]
  c HB Guide - v8 - Spr '97 - p77 [51-250]
  c KR - v64 - O 15 '96 - p1539 [51-250]
  c PW - v243 - O 7 '96 - p76 [51-250]
  c SLJ - v42 - O '96 - p128 [51-250]
  y VOYA - v19 - D '96 - p274+ [251-500]
Wilson, Paul, 1949- - *Instant Calm*
    New Sci - v152 - N 2 '96 - p44 [1-50]
Wilson, Paul, 1960- - *Days of Good Hope*
    Obs - Ja 12 '97 - p18* [51-250]
Wilson, Peter W - *Saudi Arabia: The Coming Storm*
    MEJ - v50 - Aut '96 - p604+ [501+]
Wilson, R L - *Ruger and His Guns*
    BL - v93 - N 15 '96 - p556 [51-250]
    LJ - v121 - N 1 '96 - p72 [51-250]
    PW - v243 - O 21 '96 - p68 [51-250]

Wilson, Raymond - *The Puffin Book of Classic Verse (Illus. by Diz Wallis)*
  c Sch Lib - v44 - Ag '96 - p116+ [51-250]
Wilson, Rich - *Racing a Ghost Ship*
  c BL - v93 - O 1 '96 - p347 [51-250]
  c HB - v73 - Ja '97 - p82* [51-250]
  c HB Guide - v8 - Spr '97 - p164 [51-250]
  c SLJ - v42 - N '96 - p119 [51-250]
Wilson, Richard - *Particles in Our Air*
    New Sci - v153 - Mr 1 '97 - p38 [1-50]
Wilson, Robert A, 1941- - *Character above All*
    PW - v243 - D 30 '96 - p64 [1-50]
Wilson, Robert Andrew - *Cartesian Psychology and Physical Minds*
    CPR - v16 - Je '96 - p227+ [501+]
Wilson, Robert F - *Management of Trauma. 2nd Ed.*
    SciTech - v20 - N '96 - p49 [51-250]
Wilson, Robert McLiam - *Eureka Street*
    Obs - S 1 '96 - p15* [501+]
    Spec - v277 - N 16 '96 - p42 [1-50]
Wilson, Robin Scott - *Paragons: Twelve Master Science Fiction Writers Ply Their Craft*
    SF Chr - v18 - O '96 - p80 [1-50]
    SFS - v23 - N '96 - p531+ [501+]
  y VOYA - v19 - O '96 - p236+ [251-500]
Those Who Can
    SF Chr - v18 - O '96 - p80 [1-50]
Wilson, Rodney - *Economic Development in the Middle East*
    Choice - v34 - S '96 - p179 [51-250]
    JEL - v34 - D '96 - p2113 [51-250]
Wilson, Rodney C - *Software Rx*
    SciTech - v21 - Mr '97 - p6 [51-250]
Wilson, Sam - *The Sierra Club Wetlands Reader*
    LATBR - Jl 14 '96 - p11 [51-250]
Wilson, Sarah - *Good Zap, Little Grog (Illus. by Susan Meddaugh)*
  c Bks Keeps - Ja '97 - p20 [51-250]
Wilson, Sharon R - *Approaches to Teaching Atwood's The Handmaid's Tale and Other Works*
    Choice - v34 - Ap '97 - p1332+ [51-250]
Wilson, Stewart - *Boeing B-17, B-29 and Lancaster*
    FSM - v15 - Ja '97 - p79 [1-50]
Wilson, Susan - *Beauty*
    MFSF - v91 - D '96 - p41+ [251-500]
    NYTBR - v101 - Jl 21 '96 - p13 [501+]
  y SLJ - v42 - N '96 - p140+ [51-250]
Wilson, Theo - *Headline Justice*
    KR - v64 - N 15 '96 - p1662 [251-500]
    LATBR - F 9 '97 - p3 [501+]
    LJ - v122 - F 1 '97 - p95 [51-250]
    PW - v243 - N 18 '96 - p56+ [51-250]
Wilson, Thomas, 1525-1581 - *The Art of Rhetoric*
    RES - v47 - N '96 - p578+ [501+]
Wilson, Thomas A - *Genealogy of the Way*
    AHR - v101 - O '96 - p1258+ [501+]
    Ch Rev Int - v3 - Fall '96 - p564+ [501+]
Wilson, Thomas A, 1938- - *Reaching for a Better Standard*
    TES - N 15 '96 - p7* [51-250]
Wilson, Thomas B - *Innovative Reward Systems for the Changing Workplace*
    BusLR - v21 - 3 '96 - p261+ [51-250]
Wilson, Thomas G - *Fundamentals of Periodontics*
    SciTech - v20 - N '96 - p54 [51-250]
Wilson, Trevor - *Diversity at Work*
    Quill & Q - v62 - My '96 - p29 [251-500]
Wilson, William, 1923- - *Dictionary of the United States Intelligence Services*
  r ARBA - v28 - '97 - p269 [51-250]
  r Choice - v34 - Mr '97 - p1145 [51-250]
  r R&R Bk N - v12 - F '97 - p59 [51-250]

Wilson, William Julius - *When Work Disappears*
  B Ent - v27 - F '97 - p215 [1-50]
  BL - v92 - Ag '96 - p1852 [251-500]
  BL - v93 - Ja '97 - p757 [1-50]
  Bus W - O 7 '96 - p20+ [501+]
  BW - v26 - Ag 25 '96 - p4 [501+]
  Choice - v34 - Mr '97 - p1247 [51-250]
  Comw - v123 - N 8 '96 - p21+ [501+]
  Econ - v341 - N 16 '96 - p6*+ [501+]
  LATBR - S 1 '96 - p1+ [501+]
  Nat R - v49 - Ja 27 '97 - p53+ [501+]
  New R - v215 - O 28 '96 - p32+ [501+]
  NYRB - v43 - N 28 '96 - p8+ [501+]
  NYTBR - v101 - S 29 '96 - p7 [501+]
  NYTBR - v101 - D 8 '96 - p94 [1-50]
  Pub Int - Fall '96 - p125+ [501+]
  TLS - Ja 24 '97 - p3+ [501+]
  VQR - v73 - Win '97 - p26* [51-250]
  W&I - v12 - Ja '97 - p284+ [501+]
  Wil Q - v20 - Aut '96 - p89+ [501+]
  WSJ-MW - v77 - S 3 '96 - pA13 [501+]
Wilson-Max, Ken - *Big Blue Engine (Illus. by Ken Wilson-Max)*
  c Bks Keeps - Ja '97 - p20 [251-500]
  c HB Guide - v8 - Spr '97 - p16 [51-250]
  c PW - v243 - N 11 '96 - p77 [51-250]
  c Spec - v277 - D 14 '96 - p77 [1-50]
Big Yellow Taxi
  c Ch BWatch - v6 - Jl '96 - p4 [1-50]
  c HB Guide - v7 - Fall '96 - p246 [1-50]
  c Par - v71 - S '96 - p209 [51-250]
Little Green Tow Truck (Illus. by Ken Wilson-Max)
  c Bks Keeps - Ja '97 - p20 [251-500]
  c PW - v244 - Ja 6 '97 - p74 [51-250]
  c Spec - v277 - D 14 '96 - p77 [1-50]
Little Red Plane (Illus. by Ken Wilson-Max)
  c RT - v50 - O '96 - p134 [1-50]
Wilson-Smith, Timothy - *Napoleon and His Artists*
  Books - v10 - Je '96 - p21 [51-250]
Wilton, Andrew - *Grand Tour*
  BM - v139 - Ja '97 - p57+ [501+]
  TLS - N 22 '96 - p18+ [501+]
Wiltse, David - *Blown Away*
  BL - v93 - S 15 '96 - p225 [51-250]
  KR - v64 - Ag 15 '96 - p1185+ [251-500]
Wimbush, Vincent L - *Asceticism*
  CH - v65 - D '96 - p786+ [501+]
  JR - v77 - Ja '97 - p131 [501+]
Wimme, Dick - *The Sandlot Game*
  PW - v244 - Mr 17 '97 - p74 [51-250]
Wimmel, Kenneth - *The Alluring Target*
  BWatch - v17 - S '96 - p6 [1-50]
  y SB - v33 - Mr '97 - p47 [51-250]
Win, May Kyi - *Historical Dictionary of Thailand*
  r Choice - v34 - N '96 - p434 [51-250]
Winanas, A D - *The Charles Bukowski Second Coming Years*
  Sm Pr R - v28 - S '96 - p8 [51-250]
Winawer, Sidney J - *Cancer Free*
  LJ - v122 - Ja '97 - p58 [51-250]
Winch, Ben - *My Boyfriend's Father*
  Aust Bk R - Jl '96 - p50+ [501+]
Winch, Donald - *Riches and Poverty*
  Choice - v34 - Ja '97 - p848 [51-250]
Winch, John - *The Old Man Who Loved to Sing*
  c HB Guide - v7 - Fall '96 - p281 [51-250]
The Old Woman Who Loved to Read (Illus. by John Winch)
  c BL - v93 - Mr 1 '97 - p1175 [51-250]
  c KR - v65 - F 15 '97 - p308 [51-250]
  c PW - v244 - F 10 '97 - p84 [51-250]
Winchell, Mark Royden - *Cleanth Brooks and the Rise of Modern Criticism*
  Choice - v34 - D '96 - p618 [51-250]
  NL - v79 - Ag 12 '96 - p24+ [501+]
  South CR - v29 - Fall '96 - p279+ [501+]
Winchester, Simon - *The River at the Center of the World*
  BL - v93 - N 1 '96 - p477 [51-250]
  FEER - v160 - Ap 3 '97 - p39 [501+]
  KR - v64 - S 1 '96 - p1313 [251-500]
  LJ - v121 - O 15 '96 - p81 [51-250]
  NYTBR - v101 - D 8 '96 - p31 [51-250]
  PW - v243 - S 16 '96 - p59 [51-250]
The River at the Centre of the World
  Obs - Mr 2 '97 - p16* [501+]
Wind, Gary G - *Applied Laparoscopic Anatomy*
  SciTech - v21 - Mr '97 - p39 [51-250]
Wind, Herbert Warren - *Following Through. Expanded Ed.*
  Aethlon - v13 - Spr '96 - p213+ [251-500]

Wind, James P - *American Congregations. Vols. 1-2*
  Bks & Cult - v1 - N '95 - p22+ [501+]
Windas, Tom - *An Introduction to Option-Adjusted Spread Analysis. Rev. Ed.*
  R&R Bk N - v11 - N '96 - p37 [51-250]
Windeatt, Barry - *English Mystics of the Middle Ages*
  MLR - v92 - Ap '97 - p434+ [501+]
Winder, Robert - *Hell for Leather*
  NS - v125 - N 29 '96 - p43+ [501+]
  TLS - D 6 '96 - p31 [501+]
Winderlin, Christine - *Candida-Related Complex*
  BL - v93 - N 15 '96 - p559 [51-250]
  LJ - v121 - D '96 - p135 [51-250]
Windham, Donald - *Emblems of Conduct*
  LATBR - S 22 '96 - p15 [51-250]
Windham, Sophie - *The Mermaid and Other Sea Poems (Illus. by Sophie Windham)*
  c HB Guide - v7 - Fall '96 - p366 [1-50]
  c RT - v50 - Ap '97 - p593 [51-250]
Windler, Renata - *Das Graberland Von Elgg Und Die Besiedlung Der Nordostschweiz Im 5.-7. Jh.*
  Specu - v71 - O '96 - p1036+ [501+]
Windley, Brian F - *The Evolving Continents*
  GJ - v163 - Mr '97 - p105 [51-250]
Windling, Terri - *The Armless Maiden and Other Tales for Childhood's Survivors*
  y VOYA - v19 - D '96 - p266 [1-50]
The Wood Wife
  KR - v64 - Ag 15 '96 - p1196 [51-250]
  LJ - v121 - O 15 '96 - p93 [51-250]
  MFSF - v91 - D '96 - p42+ [501+]
  PW - v243 - S 16 '96 - p74 [51-250]
  y VOYA - v19 - F '97 - p341+ [251-500]
Window, Carolin - *Dim*
  Aust Bk R - Je '96 - p47+ [501+]
Windschuttle, Keith - *The Killing of History. Rev. Ed.*
  Skeptic - v4 - 4 '96 - p97 [501+]
Windsor, Gerard - *Heaven Where the Bachelors Sit*
  Aust Bk R - O '96 - p30+ [501+]
Windsor, Patricia - *The Blooding*
  y BL - v93 - Ap 1 '97 - p1310 [1-50]
  y CCB-B - v50 - Ja '97 - p188 [51-250]
  y HB Guide - v8 - Spr '97 - p85 [51-250]
  y KR - v64 - O 1 '96 - p1475 [51-250]
  y SLJ - v42 - D '96 - p140 [51-250]
The House of Death
  y JB - v60 - O '96 - p213 [251-500]
  y Sch Lib - v44 - N '96 - p172 [51-250]
Wine, Sherwin - *Judaism beyond God*
  Choice - v34 - O '96 - p299 [51-250]
Wine Spectator
  p LJ - v122 - Ap 1 '97 - p63 [1-50]
Wine Spectator's Guide to Great Wine Values $10 and Under
  r LJ - v122 - Ap 1 '97 - p64 [1-50]
Wine Spectator's Ultimate Guide to Buying Wine. 5th Ed.
  r LJ - v122 - Ap 1 '97 - p62 [1-50]
Wineapple, Brenda - *Sister Brother*
  BW - v26 - Ag 4 '96 - p11 [501+]
  Spec - v276 - My 25 '96 - p27+ [501+]
Winebrenner, Susan - *Teaching Kids with Learning Difficulties in the Regular Classroom*
  Kliatt - v30 - N '96 - p25+ [51-250]
  Learning - v25 - Mr '97 - p71 [51-250]
Winecoff, Charles - *Split Image*
  BL - v92 - Ag '96 - p1873 [51-250]
  BW - v26 - O 20 '96 - p13 [51-250]
  Ent W - S 20 '96 - p69+ [501+]
  NYTBR - v101 - S 29 '96 - p21 [51-250]
Winegar, Norman - *The Clinician's Guide to Managed Behavioral Care*
  SB - v32 - Ag '96 - p166 [251-500]
Winegardner, Mark - *The Veracruz Blues*
  NYTBR - v101 - Ap 7 '96 - p14+ [501+]
  NYTBR - v101 - D 8 '96 - p84 [1-50]
  PW - v244 - F 24 '97 - p88 [1-50]
The Veracruz Blues. Audio Version
  y Kliatt - v31 - My '97 - p45 [51-250]
Winegarten, Ruthe - *Black Texas Women: A Sourcebook*
  Bl S - v26 - Fall '96 - p108 [51-250]
  r WHQ - v28 - Spr '97 - p104 [1-50]
Wineman, Aryeh - *Mystic Tales from the Zohar*
  LJ - v121 - Ap '96 - p100 [51-250]
Winfield, Richard Dien - *Law in Civil Society*
  Ethics - v107 - Ja '97 - p394+ [51-250]
  HLR - v110 - D '96 - p561 [51-250]
Stylistics: Rethinking the Artforms after Hegel
  R&R Bk N - v12 - F '97 - p8 [51-250]

Winfrey, Dorman H - *The Indian Papers of Texas and the Southwest 1825-1916. Vols. 1-5*
  WHQ - v28 - Spr '97 - p102 [1-50]
Winfrey, Elizabeth - *My So-Called Boyfriend*
  y SLJ - v42 - Ag '96 - p164 [51-250]
Winfrey, Oprah - *The Uncommon Wisdom of Oprah Winfrey*
  LJ - v121 - N 1 '96 - p82 [51-250]
  PW - v243 - D 2 '96 - p51 [51-250]
Wing, Alan M - *Hand and Brain*
  Choice - v34 - Ja '97 - p828 [51-250]
Wing, Natasha - *Jalapeno Bagels (Illus. by Robert Casilla)*
  c CBRS - v24 - Ag '96 - p162 [51-250]
  c HB Guide - v7 - Fall '96 - p281 [51-250]
  c Inst - v106 - Ja '97 - p53 [51-250]
Wing Short-Title Catalogue 1641-1700. Electronic Media Version
  r Choice - v34 - Ap '97 - p1321 [51-250]
Wingerath, Halina - *Studien Zur Darstellung Des Menschen In Der Minoischen Kunst Der Alteren Und Jungeren Palastzeit*
  AJA - v100 - O '96 - p810+ [251-500]
Wingler, Sharon B - *Travel Alone and Love It*
  BL - v93 - S 15 '96 - p212 [1-50]
Wingo, Lowdon - *The Governance of Metropolitan Regions*
  NCR - v85 - Spr '96 - p63 [51-250]
Wings, Mary - *She Came to the Castro*
  BL - v93 - Mr 1 '97 - p1114 [51-250]
  KR - v65 - F 1 '97 - p176 [51-250]
  PW - v244 - Ja 13 '97 - p57+ [51-250]
Winik, Jay - *On the Brink*
  Nat R - v48 - N 11 '96 - p62 [51-250]
Winik, Marion - *First Comes Love*
  NYTBR - v101 - D 8 '96 - p87 [1-50]
  PW - v244 - My 12 '97 - p74 [1-50]
First Comes Love (Winik). Audio Version
  y Kliatt - v30 - N '96 - p48+ [51-250]
Winkates, James E - *U.S. Foreign Policy in Transition*
  JTWS - v13 - Fall '96 - p344+ [501+]
Winkleman, Katherine K - *Police Patrol (Illus. by John S Winkleman)*
  c BL - v93 - Ja '97 - p866 [251-500]
  c CBRS - v25 - D '96 - p42 [51-250]
  c CCB-B - v50 - Ja '97 - p189 [51-250]
  c HB Guide - v8 - Spr '97 - p95 [51-250]
  c SLJ - v42 - D '96 - p118 [51-250]
Winkler, Gabriele - *Koriwns Biographie Des Mesrop Mastoc*
  CHR - v82 - Jl '96 - p501+ [501+]
Winkler, Hans - *Woodpeckers: An Identification Guide to the Woodpeckers of the World*
  r AB - v97 - Je 17 '96 - p2402 [51-250]
Winkler, Heinrich August - *Weimar 1918-1933*
  JMH - v68 - S '96 - p629+ [501+]
Winkler, Johann - *Oskar Kokoschka: Die Gemalde 1906-1929*
  BM - v139 - Ja '97 - p49+ [501+]
Winkler, Kathleen - *How to Risk-Proof Your Kids*
  VOYA - v19 - O '96 - p244 [251-500]
Winkler, Kathy - *Radiology*
  c Ch BWatch - v6 - My '96 - p6 [51-250]
  c HB Guide - v7 - Fall '96 - p349 [51-250]
  c SB - v32 - Ag '96 - p181 [51-250]
  c SLJ - v42 - S '96 - p216 [51-250]
Winkler, Markus - *Mythisches Denken Zwischen Romantik Und Realismus*
  Ger Q - v70 - Win '97 - p80+ [501+]
Winkler, Martin M - *Der Lateinische Eulenspiegel Des Loannes Nemius*
  Ren Q - v49 - Win '96 - p840+ [501+]
Winks, Robin W - *A History of Civilization. 9th Ed.*
  R&R Bk N - v11 - N '96 - p8 [51-250]
Winn, Christine M - *Box-Head Boy (Illus. by Christine M Winn)*
  c HB Guide - v7 - Fall '96 - p281 [51-250]
Clover's Secret (Illus. by Christine M Winn)
  c HB Guide - v7 - Fall '96 - p282 [51-250]
Monster Boy (Illus. by Christine M Winn)
  c HB Guide - v7 - Fall '96 - p282 [51-250]
Winn, Colette H - *The Dialogue in Early Modern France 1547-1630*
  Ren Q - v50 - Spr '97 - p295+ [501+]
Les Representations De L'Autre Du Moyen Age Au XVIIe Siecle
  Ren Q - v50 - Spr '97 - p252+ [501+]

Winner, Cherie - *The Sunflower Family (Illus. by Sherry Shahan)*
  c BL - v93 - O 1 '96 - p347+ [51-250]
  c Ch BWatch - v6 - O '96 - p5+ [1-50]
  c HB Guide - v8 - Spr '97 - p121 [51-250]
  c KR - v64 - Ag 15 '96 - p1245 [51-250]
  c SB - v33 - Mr '97 - p50+ [251-500]
  c SLJ - v42 - O '96 - p142 [51-250]
Winner, Ellen - *Gifted Children*
  Choice - v34 - N '96 - p500 [51-250]
Winner, Karen - *Divorced from Justice*
  Nat - v264 - Ja 6 '97 - p31+ [501+]
Winners and Losers
  TES - N 8 '96 - pR5 [251 500]
Winnick, Karen B - *Mr. Lincoln's Whiskers (Illus. by Karen B Winnick)*
  c BL - v93 - D 15 '96 - p734 [51-250]
  c CBRS - v25 - Ja '97 - p56 [51-250]
  c HB Guide - v8 - Spr '97 - p176 [51-250]
  c SLJ - v43 - Ja '97 - p110 [51-250]
  c Trib Bks - Ja 12 '97 - p5 [51-250]
Winnicott, D W - *Thinking about Children*
  Choice - v34 - Ja '97 - p881 [51-250]
  Readings - v12 - Mr '97 - p23 [51-250]
  SciTech - v21 - Mr '97 - p64 [51-250]
Winnie the Pooh's 1,2,3
  c Books - v9 - S '95 - p26 [1-50]
Winnie-the-Pooh's 1,2,3 (Illus. by Ernest H Shepard)
  c HB Guide - v8 - Spr '97 - p14 [51-250]
Winnie the Pooh's ABC
  c Books - v9 - S '95 - p26 [1-50]
Winnie-the-Pooh's Cookie Book (Illus. by Ernest H Shepard)
  c HB Guide - v8 - Spr '97 - p134 [51-250]
Winnie-the-Pooh's Picnic Cookbook (Illus. by Ernest H Shepard)
  c PW - v244 - Ap 21 '97 - p74 [51-250]
Winning Checkers for Kids
  c Ch BWatch - v6 - S '96 - p1 [51-250]
Winninge, Mikael - *Sinners and the Righteous*
  Rel St Rev - v23 - Ap '97 - p185 [51-250]
Winnipeg Development Agreement 1995-2000
  J Gov Info - v23 - S '96 - p630 [51-250]
Winokur, George - *The Natural History of Mania, Depression, and Schizophrenia*
  Readings - v11 - S '96 - p23 [51-250]
Winokur, Jon - *The Rich Are Different*
  Ent W - N 22 '96 - p130 [51-250]
Winokur, Mark - *American Laughter*
  Si & So - v6 - N '96 - p34 [51-250]
Winquist, Charles E - *Desiring Theology*
  Rel St Rev - v23 - Ja '97 - p32+ [501+]
  Theol St - v57 - Mr '96 - p188 [51-250]
Winrow, A P - *MCQs for the Paediatric MRCP Part 1*
  SciTech - v21 - Mr '97 - p63 [51-250]
Winship, Ian - *The Student's Guide to the Internet*
  LAR - v99 - F '97 - p103 [51-250]
Winship, Michael - *American Literary Publishing in the Mid-Nineteenth Century*
  BC - v45 - Win '96 - p572+ [501+]
  Bibliography of American Literature: A Selective Index
  r AL - v68 - S '96 - p667 [1-50]
  Bibliography of American Literature: Epitome
  r AL - v68 - S '96 - p666 [1-50]
Winship, Michael P - *Seers of God*
  RAH - v25 - Mr '97 - p25+ [501+]
  W&M Q - v54 - Ap '97 - p418+ [501+]
Winslow, Anne - *Women, Politics, and the United Nations*
  Cons - v17 - Win '96 - p31 [1-50]
Winslow, Barbara, 1945- - *Sylvia Pankhurst: Sexual Politics and Political Activism*
  Choice - v34 - D '96 - p673 [51-250]
Winslow, Barbara, 1947- - *Dance on a Sealskin (Illus. by Teri Sloat)*
  c LA - v73 - S '96 - p355 [51-250]
Winslow, Don - *The Death and Life of Bobby Z*
  BL - v93 - Mr 15 '97 - p1205 [51-250]
  KR - v65 - Mr 1 '97 - p333 [51-250]
  LJ - v122 - Ap 1 '97 - p132 [51-250]
  PW - v244 - Mr 24 '97 - p60 [51-250]
  The Death and Life of Bobby Z (Larson). Audio Version
  PW - v244 - My 5 '97 - p40 [51-250]
Winslow, R M - *Blood Substitutes*
  SciTech - v20 - N '96 - p54 [51-250]
Winston, Brian - *Claiming the Real*
  FQ - v50 - Win '96 - p49+ [501+]
Wintemute, Robert - *Sexual Orientation and Human Rights*
  Choice - v34 - S '96 - p213 [51-250]
Winter, Bruce - *Seek the Welfare of the City*
  JR - v76 - O '96 - p622 [251-500]

Winter, Douglas - *Dahlonega Mint Gold Coins 1838-1861*
  r Coin W - v38 - Ap 28 '97 - p18 [51-250]
  Type Two Double Eagles 1866-1876
  r Coin W - v38 - Ja 13 '97 - p56 [51-250]
Winter, Douglas E - *Revelations*
  PW - v244 - Ap 21 '97 - p64 [251-500]
Winter, J M - *The Great War and the Shaping of the 20th Century*
  BL - v93 - N 1 '96 - p480 [51-250]
  KR - v64 - S 15 '96 - p1392 [51-250]
  y LJ - v121 - O 1 '96 - p102 [51-250]
  PW - v243 - O 21 '96 - p63 [51-250]
  Spec - v277 - N 16 '96 - p44+ [1-50]
  Sites of Memory, Sites of Mourning
  J Mil H - v61 - Ja '97 - p180+ [251-500]
  Lon R Bks - v18 - S 19 '96 - p3+ [501+]
  TLS - Ja 10 '97 - p12 [501+]
Winter, James - *Democracy's Oxygen*
  Quill & Q - v62 - O '96 - p40 [251-500]
Winter, Jeanette - *Cowboy Charlie*
  c RT - v50 - O '96 - p156 [51-250]
  Josefina (Illus. by Jeanette Winter)
  c CBRS - v25 - N '96 - p29 [51-250]
  c CCB-B - v50 - O '96 - p80 [51-250]
  c HB Guide - v8 - Spr '97 - p54 [51-250]
  c KR - v64 - S 15 '96 - p1409 [51-250]
  c SLJ - v42 - O '96 - p109 [51-250]
Winter, Mary Jean - *Geometry Experiments*
  Math T - v89 - My '96 - p436 [251-500]
Winter, Richard - *Professional Competence and Higher Education*
  R&R Bk N - v11 - D '96 - p54 [51-250]
Winter, Robert - *Toward a Simpler Way of Life*
  LJ - v122 - My 1 '97 - p100+ [51-250]
Winterhalter, Daniel - *Solar Wind Eight*
  SciTech - v21 - Mr '97 - p26 [51-250]
Wintermute, Alan - *The French Portrait*
  BWatch - v17 - S '96 - p3 [1-50]
Winterowd, W Ross - *A Teacher's Introduction to Composition and the Rhetorical Tradition*
  Col Comp - v47 - D '96 - p620 [51-250]
Winters, Jeffrey A - *Power in Motion*
  Choice - v34 - O '96 - p331+ [51-250]
  FEER - v159 - O 24 '96 - p55 [251-500]
  J Pol - v59 - F '97 - p308+ [501+]
Winters, Kay - *Did You See What I Saw? (Illus. by Martha Weston)*
  c BL - v92 - Ag '96 - p1903 [51-250]
  c CCB-B - v50 - S '96 - p37 [51-250]
  c HB Guide - v8 - Spr '97 - p154 [51-250]
  c SLJ - v42 - O '96 - p119 [51-250]
Winters, L Alan - *Eastern Europe's International Trade*
  Slav R - v55 - Fall '96 - p663+ [501+]
Winters, Paul A - *America's Victims*
  y BL - v93 - D 15 '96 - p715 [51-250]
  y Ch BWatch - v6 - Jl '96 - p2 [1-50]
  y SLJ - v42 - N '96 - p130 [51-250]
  y VOYA - v19 - F '97 - p342 [251-500]
  The Death Penalty. 3rd Ed., Rev.
  y BL - v93 - Ja '97 - p828 [251-500]
  y Kliatt - v31 - Mr '97 - p30 [51-250]
  Teen Addiction
  y Kliatt - v31 - Mr '97 - p29+ [51-250]
  y LJ - v122 - F 15 '97 - p152 [51-250]
  y SLJ - v43 - Mr '97 - p212 [51-250]
  Voting Behavior
  y Ch BWatch - v6 - Jl '96 - p2 [1-50]
  y SLJ - v42 - Ag '96 - p177 [51-250]
  y VOYA - v19 - O '96 - p292+ [251-500]
Winterson, Jeanette - *Art Objects*
  PW - v244 - Ja 27 '97 - p103 [1-50]
  Gut Symmetries
  BL - v93 - Ap 1 '97 - p1283 [51-250]
  KR - v65 - F 15 '97 - p255 [251-500]
  LATBR - Ap 13 '97 - pH [501+]
  LJ - v122 - Ap 15 '97 - p122 [51-250]
  NS - v126 - Ja 10 '97 - p47 [501+]
  Obs - Ja 5 '97 - p15* [501+]
  PW - v244 - Mr 17 '97 - p76 [51-250]
  Spec - v278 - Ja 4 '97 - p27+ [501+]
  TES - F 14 '97 - p8* [51-250]
  TLS - Ja 3 '97 - p21 [501+]
  VV - v42 - Ap 22 '97 - p55 [501+]
  Oranges Are Not the Only Fruit
  Obs - Ja 5 '97 - p18* [51-250]
  Written on the Body
  Obs - Ja 5 '97 - p18* [51-250]
Winthrop, Elizabeth - *Bear and Roly-Poly (Illus. by Patience Brewster)*
  c Ch BWatch - v6 - My '96 - p4 [1-50]
  c HB Guide - v7 - Fall '96 - p282 [51-250]

  Castle in the Attic
  c BL - v93 - Ap 1 '97 - p1313 [1-50]
  The Little Humpbacked Horse (Illus. by Alexander Koshkin)
  c BL - v93 - Mr 1 '97 - p1159+ [51-250]
  c CCB-B - v50 - My '97 - p337+ [51-250]
  c KR - v65 - F 15 '97 - p309 [51-250]
  c PW - v244 - Ja 20 '97 - p402 [51-250]
Winthrop, John - *The Journal of John Winthrop 1630-1649*
  Am Geneal - v71 - O '96 - p254 [251-500]
Wintle, Justin - *Furious Interiors*
  Spec - v277 - N 23 '96 - p45 [1-50]
  Spec - v278 - F 8 '97 - p42+ [501+]
  TLS - D 27 '96 - p24 [501+]
Winton, Tim - *The Riders*
  NYTBR - v101 - S 8 '96 - p36 [51-250]
Wintz, Cary D - *African American Political Thought 1890-1930*
  WHQ - v27 - Win '96 - p523+ [501+]
  Analysis and Assessment 1940-1979
  R&R Bk N - v12 - F '97 - p87 [51-250]
  Analysis and Assessment 1980-1984
  R&R Bk N - v12 - F '97 - p87 [51-250]
  Black Writers Interpret the Harlem Renaissance
  R&R Bk N - v12 - F '97 - p87 [51-250]
  The Critics and the Harlem Renaissance
  R&R Bk N - v12 - F '97 - p87 [51-250]
  The Emergence of the Harlem Renaissance
  R&R Bk N - v12 - F '97 - p87 [51-250]
  The Politics and Aesthetics of New Negro Literature
  R&R Bk N - v12 - F '97 - p87 [51-250]
  Remembering the Harlem Renaissance
  R&R Bk N - v12 - F '97 - p87 [51-250]
Wirsing, Robert G - *India, Pakistan, and the Kashmir Dispute*
  Historian - v58 - Sum '96 - p888+ [501+]
Wirt, Sherwood Eliot - *Billy: A Personal Look at the World's Best-Loved Evangelist*
  BL - v93 - Mr 1 '97 - p1092 [51-250]
  LJ - v122 - Mr 15 '97 - p67 [51-250]
  PW - v244 - F 10 '97 - p80 [51-250]
Wirth, Niklaus - *Compiler Construction*
  Choice - v34 - Ap '97 - p1374 [51-250]
Wirth-Nesher, Hana - *City Codes*
  Choice - v34 - O '96 - p283 [51-250]
  New Essays on Call It Sleep
  AL - v69 - Mr '97 - p255 [51-250]
  What Is Jewish Literature?
  MLR - v92 - Ja '97 - p143+ [501+]
  Poetics T - v18 - Spr '97 - p141+ [501+]
Wirths, Claudine G - *Choosing a Career in Law Enforcement*
  y SLJ - v43 - Mr '97 - p196+ [51-250]
  Upgrade: The High-Tech Road to School Success
  Adoles - v32 - Spr '97 - p250 [51-250]
Wirtschafter, Elise Kimerling - *Structures of Society*
  EHR - v112 - Ap '97 - p521 [251-500]
  JMH - v68 - D '96 - p1034+ [501+]
Wise, Alan R - *Jet Age Flight Helmets*
  A & S Sm - v11 - F '97 - p87 [1-50]
  MiG Pilot
  A & S Sm - v11 - F '97 - p87 [1-50]
Wise, David - *Nightmover: How Aldrich Ames Sold the CIA to the KGB for $4.6 Million*
  NYTBR - v101 - S 8 '96 - p36 [51-250]
Wise, David A - *Advances in the Economics of Aging*
  JEL - v35 - Mr '97 - p236 [51-250]
  Studies in the Economics of Aging
  Econ J - v107 - Ja '97 - p278 [51-250]
Wise, Donald L - *Human Biomaterials Applications*
  SciTech - v20 - D '96 - p37 [51-250]
Wise, M Norton - *The Values of Precision*
  Isis - v87 - S '96 - p517+ [501+]
  T&C - v38 - Ja '97 - p259+ [501+]
  VS - v39 - Spr '96 - p439+ [501+]
Wise, Michael - *The Dead Sea Scrolls*
  LJ - v121 - D '96 - p101 [51-250]
Wise, Patricia S Yoder - *Leading and Managing in Nursing*
  AJN - v96 - D '96 - p16M+ [51-250]
Wise, William - *Perfect Pancakes if You Please (Illus. by Richard Egielski)*
  c BL - v93 - D 1 '96 - p670 [51-250]
  c KR - v64 - D 15 '96 - p1807 [51-250]
  c PW - v243 - D 9 '96 - p67+ [51-250]
  c SLJ - v43 - F '97 - p86 [51-250]
  Ten Sly Piranhas (Illus. by Victoria Chess)
  c BL - v93 - Ap 1 '97 - p1341 [1-50]
Wiseman, Adele - *Crackpot*
  Essays CW - Spr '96 - p15+ [501+]

The Sacrifice
　Essays CW - Spr '96 - p1+ [501+]
Wiseman, Christopher - *Remembering Mr. Fox*
　Can Lit - Win '96 - p187+ [501+]
Wiseman, Eva - *A Place Not Home*
　y JAAL - v40 - D '96 - p327 [251-500]
　y Quill & Q - v62 - My '96 - p35 [251-500]
Wiseman, John A - *Democracy and Political Change in Sub-Saharan Africa*
　Africa T - v43 - 4 '96 - p405+ [501+]
The New Struggle for Democracy in Africa
　APSR - v91 - Mr '97 - p224+ [501+]
　Choice - v34 - My '97 - p1570+ [51-250]
Wiseman, Stella - *Beetle (Illus. by Tim Hayward)*
　c PW - v244 - Ap 21 '97 - p73 [51-250]
Cockroach (Illus. by Tim Hayward)
　c PW - v244 - Ap 21 '97 - p73 [51-250]
Spider (Illus. by Tim Hayward)
　c PW - v244 - Ap 21 '97 - p73 [51-250]
Worm (Illus. by Tim Hayward)
　c PW - v244 - Ap 21 '97 - p73 [51-250]
Wiseman, T P - *Remus: A Roman Myth*
　HT - v46 - D '96 - p58+ [501+]
　Lon R Bks - v18 - My 23 '96 - p22+ [501+]
　Rel St Rev - v22 - O '96 - p346 [51-250]
Wishart, David - *Nero*
　TLS - D 27 '96 - p21 [251-500]
Wishart, David J - *An Unspeakable Sadness*
　AHR - v101 - D '96 - p1617+ [251-500]
　PHR - v65 - Ag '96 - p481+ [251-500]
Wisler, G Clifton - *Caleb's Choice*
　c BL - v92 - Ag '96 - p1896 [51-250]
　c CCB-B - v50 - S '96 - p37+ [51-250]
　c HB Guide - v8 - Spr '97 - p77 [51-250]
　y JAAL - v40 - F '97 - p407 [51-250]
　c SLJ - v42 - Ag '96 - p148 [51-250]
The Drummer Boy of Vicksburg
　c BL - v93 - D 1 '96 - p666 [51-250]
　c KR - v64 - N 15 '96 - p1677 [51-250]
　c Par Ch - v21 - Mr '97 - p8 [1-50]
　c SLJ - v43 - Mr '97 - p194 [51-250]
Wisniewski, Andrzej - *The Posing of Questions*
　R&R Bk N - v11 - N '96 - p3 [51-250]
Wisniewski, David - *Golem (Illus. by David Wisniewski)*
　c BL - v93 - Ja '97 - p766 [1-50]
　c BL - v93 - O 1 '96 - p335 [251-500]
　c BL - v93 - Ap 1 '97 - p1302 [1-50]
　c CCB-B - v50 - S '96 - p27+ [51-250]
　c Ch BWatch - v6 - O '96 - p4 [51-250]
　c CLW - v67 - Mr '97 - p60 [51-250]
　c HB - v73 - Mr '97 - p208 [251-500]
　c HB Guide - v8 - Spr '97 - p106 [51-250]
　c KR - v64 - S 15 '96 - p1410 [51-250]
　c NYTBR - v101 - N 10 '96 - p44 [501+]
　c PW - v243 - O 21 '96 - p83 [51-250]
　c SLJ - v42 - O '96 - p142 [51-250]
Rain Player
　c SS - v88 - Ja '97 - p29+ [501+]
Rain Player. Book and Audio Version
　c SLJ - v42 - O '96 - p77 [51-250]
Wisniewski, Debra J - *Antique and Collectible Buttons*
　Ant & CM - v102 - Ap '97 - p66 [51-250]
Wistow, Gerald - *Social Care Markets*
　R&R Bk N - v11 - D '96 - p43 [51-250]
Wiszniowska, Marta - *American Studies. Vol. 1*
　J Am St - v30 - Ag '96 - p288+ [251-500]
Witchel, Alex - *Girls Only*
　BL - v93 - N 15 '96 - p551 [51-250]
　KR - v64 - O 15 '96 - p1523+ [251-500]
　LATBR - F 9 '97 - p8 [501+]
　LJ - v121 - N 1 '96 - p74 [51-250]
　NYTBR - v102 - Ja 26 '97 - p13 [501+]
　NYTLa - v146 - Ja 29 '97 - pC15 [501+]
　Trib Bks - F 2 '97 - p3 [501+]
Witcover, Jules - *The Year the Dream Died*
　KR - v65 - My 1 '97 - p709 [251-500]
　PW - v244 - My 5 '97 - p185 [51-250]
Witcover, Paul - *Waking Beauty*
　PW - v244 - Ja 20 '97 - p398 [51-250]
Witham, Barry B - *Theatre in the United States. Vol. 1*
　Choice - v34 - Mr '97 - p1173 [51-250]
　Nine-C Lit - v51 - S '96 - p279 [51-250]
Witherington, Ben, III - *Conflict and Community in Corinth*
　Intpr - v51 - Ja '97 - p95+ [251-500]
History, Literature, and Society in the Book of Acts
　Rel St Rev - v23 - Ja '97 - p72 [51-250]
The Jesus Quest
　Bks & Cult - v1 - N '95 - p3+ [501+]
　Rel St Rev - v23 - Ja '97 - p71 [51-250]

Withers, John - *Developing Java Entertainment Applets*
　LJ - v122 - Ap 1 '97 - p118 [51-250]
Witherspoon, Gary - *Navajo Kinship and Marriage*
　BWatch - v18 - Mr '97 - p11 [51-250]
Witherup, Ronald D - *Conversion in the New Testament*
　Intpr - v51 - Ja '97 - p98+ [251-500]
A Liturgist's Guide to Inclusive Language
　Am - v176 - Mr 22 '97 - p28+ [51-250]
Withey, Lynne - *Grand Tours and Cooks' Tours*
　BL - v93 - D 15 '96 - p706 [51-250]
　BW - v27 - F 9 '97 - p4+ [501+]
　KR - v64 - N 15 '96 - p1662 [251-500]
　LATBR - F 16 '97 - p8 [501+]
　LJ - v122 - Ja '97 - p128 [51-250]
Grand Tours and Cook's Tours
　PW - v243 - D 9 '96 - p54+ [51-250]
Witkiewicz, Stanislaw Ignacy - *Insatiability*
　KR - v64 - My 1 '96 - p638 [51-250]
　New R - v215 - O 7 '96 - p40+ [501+]
　TranslRevS - v2 - D '96 - p30 [51-250]
Witkin, Georgia - *It Must Be That Time of the Month and Other Lies That Drive Women Crazy*
　PW - v243 - D 9 '96 - p66 [1-50]
Witkin, Joel-Peter - *Harm's Way*
　Afterimage - v23 - Sum '96 - p8+ [501+]
Witman, Kathleen L - *CDs, Super Glue, and Salsa. 2nd Ser., Vols. 1-2*
　yr ARBA - v28 - '97 - p95+ [51-250]
Witt, Barbara - *Pan Asian Express*
　PW - v243 - O 16 '96 - p55+ [51-250]
Wittberg, Patricia - *Pathways to Re-Creating Religious Communities*
　RR - v56 - Ja '97 - p103+ [501+]
The Rise and Decline of Catholic Religious Orders
　CHR - v82 - Jl '96 - p486+ [251-500]
　Theol St - v57 - Mr '96 - p179+ [501+]
Wittcoff, Harold A - *Industrial Organic Chemicals*
　Choice - v34 - S '96 - p157+ [51-250]
　SciTech - v20 - S '96 - p59 [51-250]
Witte, John - *Religious Human Rights in Global Perspective: Legal Perspectives*
　R&R Bk N - v12 - F '97 - p63 [51-250]
Religious Human Rights in Global Perspective: Religious Perspectives
　R&R Bk N - v12 - F '97 - p63 [51-250]
Witten, David - *Nineteenth-Century Piano Music*
　Choice - v34 - Ap '97 - p1348 [51-250]
　R&R Bk N - v12 - F '97 - p70 [51-250]
Wittenberg, Janice Strubbe - *The Rebellious Body*
　BWatch - v17 - D '96 - p4 [51-250]
　LJ - v121 - N 1 '96 - p102 [51-250]
Wittgenstein, Ludwig - *Ludwig Wittgenstein, Cambridge Letters*
　Choice - v34 - S '96 - p141 [51-250]
Wiener Ausgabe. Vols. 1-2
　Dialogue - v35 - Fall '96 - p777+ [501+]
Wittman, Donald A - *The Myth of Democratic Failure*
　AJS - v102 - Jl '96 - p284+ [501+]
　APSR - v90 - S '96 - p663+ [501+]
　HLR - v110 - D '96 - p561+ [51-250]
　IndRev - v1 - Spr '96 - p111+ [501+]
　JEL - v34 - D '96 - p1957+ [501+]
　J Pol - v59 - F '97 - p260+ [501+]
　RP - v58 - Sum '96 - p657+ [501+]
Wittman, Friedner D - *Monitoring Report: Berkeley Measure O Service Programs*
　J Gov Info - v23 - S '96 - p604 [51-250]
Wittstock, Uwe - *Leselust: Wie Unterhaltsam Ist Die Neue Deutsche Literatur?*
　Ger Q - v69 - Fall '96 - p459+ [501+]
Witzleben, J Lawrence - *Silk and Bamboo Music in Shanghai*
　Ch Rev Int - v3 - Fall '96 - p573+ [501+]
Wixforth, Harald - *Banken Und Schwerindustrie In Der Weimarer Republik*
　JMH - v69 - Mr '97 - p183+ [501+]
Wixson, Douglas - *Worker-Writer in America*
　MP - v94 - N '96 - p271+ [501+]
Wladimiroff, J W - *Ultrasound and the Fetal Heart*
　SciTech - v21 - Mr '97 - p63 [51-250]
Wodarski, John S - *Adolescent Substance Abuse*
　Adoles - v31 - Fall '96 - p755 [51-250]
Wodehouse, P G - *The Cat-Nappers (Davidson). Audio Version*
　y Kliatt - v31 - My '97 - p40+ [51-250]
Cocktail Time (Davidson). Audio Version
　LJ - v122 - Ap 15 '97 - p136+ [51-250]
Jeeves and the Feudal Spirit (Davidson). Audio Version
　y Kliatt - v30 - N '96 - p42 [51-250]
Jeeves in the Morning (Davidson). Audio Version
　y Kliatt - v31 - My '97 - p40+ [51-250]

Psmith in the City (Davidson). Audio Version
　y Kliatt - v30 - S '96 - p51 [51-250]
Psmith Journalist (Davidson). Audio Version
　y Kliatt - v30 - S '96 - p51 [51-250]
Uncle Fred in Springtime (Cecil). Audio Version
　LJ - v122 - F 15 '97 - p175 [51-250]
Wogaman, J Philip - *Christian Ethics*
　CH - v65 - S '96 - p562+ [501+]
Readings in Christian Ethics
　Rel St Rev - v23 - Ap '97 - p156 [51-250]
Wohl, Robert - *A Passion for Wings*
　JMH - v68 - S '96 - p669+ [501+]
　J Mil H - v60 - O '96 - p779+ [251-500]
　PW - v243 - O 7 '96 - p69 [1-50]
Wohlert, Torsten - *Iran: Die Pragmatische Republik Gottes?*
　MEJ - v51 - Win '97 - p150 [51-250]
Woideck, Carl - *Charlie Parker: His Music and Life*
　Choice - v34 - My '97 - p1510 [51-250]
　LJ - v121 - O 1 '96 - p81 [51-250]
Woirol, Gregory R - *The Technological Unemployment and Structural Unemployment Debates*
　Choice - v34 - D '96 - p660 [51-250]
　JEL - v35 - Mr '97 - p242+ [51-250]
　R&R Bk N - v11 - D '96 - p30 [51-250]
Wojciechowski, Susan - *The Christmas Miracle of Jonathan Toomey (Illus. by P J Lynch)*
　c Bks Keeps - v100 - S '96 - p15 [251-500]
　c Bks Keeps - N '96 - p21 [51-250]
　c Emerg Lib - v23 - My '96 - p55+ [251-500]
　c RT - v50 - N '96 - p242 [51-250]
　c RT - v50 - N '96 - p258 [51-250]
Wojciehowski, Dolora A - *Old Masters, New Subjects*
　Six Ct J - v27 - Win '96 - p1207+ [501+]
Wojnarowicz, David - *The Waterfront Journals*
　SFR - v21 - S '96 - p5 [251-500]
Wojtasik, Ted - *No Strange Fire*
　y BL - v93 - Ja '97 - p764 [1-50]
　y BL - v93 - O 1 '96 - p304 [501+]
　LJ - v122 - Ap 1 '97 - p80 [51-250]
Wojtowicz, Robert - *Lewis Mumford and American Modernism*
　Choice - v34 - Ap '97 - p1328 [51-250]
　TLS - N 8 '96 - p32 [251-500]
Wokler, Robert - *Rousseau*
　MLR - v91 - O '96 - p993+ [251-500]
Rousseau and Liberty
　APSR - v90 - D '96 - p897+ [501+]
Wolbers, Marian Frances - *Rider*
　BL - v93 - N 1 '96 - p482 [51-250]
　KR - v64 - O 1 '96 - p1426 [251-500]
　LJ - v121 - N 1 '96 - p109 [51-250]
　Ms - v7 - Ja '97 - p82 [1-50]
　PW - v243 - O 7 '96 - p62 [51-250]
Wolcott, Harry F - *The Art of Fieldwork*
　AJS - v102 - N '96 - p913+ [501+]
　ES - v27 - Fall '96 - p282+ [51-250]
Transforming Qualitative Data
　MLJ - v80 - Fall '96 - p405+ [501+]
Wolf, Alfred - *A Journey of Discovery*
　Rel Ed - v91 - Fall '96 - p619 [1-50]
Wolf, Alois - *Heldensage Und Epos*
　Specu - v72 - Ja '97 - p240+ [501+]
Wolf, Anthony - *Get Out of My Life, but First Could You Drive Me and Cheryl to the Mall?. Audio Version*
　BWatch - v18 - Mr '97 - p7 [1-50]
Wolf, Bernard - *HIV Positive (Illus. by Bernard Wolf)*
　c BL - v93 - Mr 15 '97 - p1240 [51-250]
　c CCB-B - v50 - My '97 - p338 [51-250]
　c PW - v244 - Ap 21 '97 - p72 [51-250]
Wolf, Burt - *Gatherings and Celebrations*
　BL - v93 - N 15 '96 - p548 [1-50]
Wolf, Christa - *Medea: Stimmen*
　TLS - O 4 '96 - p17 [501+]
　WLT - v71 - Win '97 - p142+ [501+]
Wolf, Dennie Palmer - *More than the Truth*
　Kliatt - v31 - My '97 - p26 [51-250]
Wolf, Diane L - *Feminist Dilemmas in Fieldwork*
　CS - v26 - Mr '97 - p254+ [501+]
Wolf, Donald E - *Big Dams and Other Dreams*
　BL - v93 - S 1 '96 - p46+ [51-250]
　R&R Bk N - v11 - D '96 - p32 [51-250]
Wolf, Fred Alan - *The Spiritual Universe*
　BL - v93 - N 15 '96 - p552 [51-250]
　KR - v64 - S 15 '96 - p1390 [251-500]
　LJ - v121 - O 1 '96 - p85 [51-250]
　New Sci - v152 - N 16 '96 - p48+ [501+]
Wolf, Gita - *Mala (Illus. by Annouchka Gravel Galouchko)*
　c BIC - v25 - O '96 - p31 [51-250]
　c Quill & Q - v62 - O '96 - p44 [251-500]

The Very Hungry Lion (Illus. by Indrapramit Roy)
c   BL - v93 - N 1 '96 - p506 [51-250]
c   CLW - v67 - D '96 - p63 [51-250]
c   KR - v64 - Ag 15 '96 - p1245 [51-250]
c   SLJ - v43 - Ja '97 - p110 [51-250]
Wolf, Jake - *Daddy, Could I Have an Elephant? (Illus. by Marylin Hafner)*
c   CBRS - v24 - Ag '96 - p163 [51-250]
c   CCB-B - v50 - O '96 - p80 [51-250]
c   HB Guide - v8 - Spr '97 - p54 [51-250]
c   SLJ - v42 - S '96 - p194 [51-250]
What You Do Is Easy, What I Do Is Hard (Illus. by Anna Dewdney)
c   BL - v93 - D 15 '96 - p734 [51-250]
c   CBRS - v25 - N '96 - p29 [51-250]
c   HB Guide - v8 - Spr '97 - p54 [51-250]
c   KR - v64 - O 15 '96 - p1539 [51-250]
c   PW - v243 - O 21 '96 - p83 [51-250]
c   SLJ - v42 - D '96 - p109+ [51-250]
Wolf, Jill - *A Victorian Christmas*
BWatch - v17 - D '96 - p2+ [51-250]
Wolf, Joan - *The Deception*
LJ - v121 - N 15 '96 - p52 [51-250]
PW - v243 - O 14 '96 - p81 [51-250]
The Guardian
PW - v244 - Mr 3 '97 - p71 [51-250]
Wolf, John P - *Finite-Element Modelling of Unbounded Media*
SciTech - v21 - Mr '97 - p16 [51-250]
Wolf, Lars Christian - *Resource Management for Distributed Multimedia Systems*
SciTech - v21 - Mr '97 - p6 [51-250]
Wolf, Leonard - *Dracula: The Connoisseur's Guide*
KR - v65 - Mr 1 '97 - p372 [51-250]
PW - v244 - F 17 '97 - p201 [51-250]
Horror: A Connoisseur's Guide to Literature and Film
r   RQ - v36 - Win '96 - p222 [51-250]
Wolf, Markus - *Man without a Face*
BL - v93 - My 15 '97 - p1539 [51-250]
WSJ-Cent - v99 - Je 2 '97 - pA20 [501+]
Wolf, Naomi - *Promiscuities: The Secret Struggle for Womanhood*
y   BL - v93 - My 1 '97 - p1459+ [51-250]
KR - v65 - My 1 '97 - p710 [251-500]
PW - v244 - My 5 '97 - p186 [51-250]
Wolf, Nelly - *Une Litterature Sans Histoire*
MLR - v92 - Ja '97 - p207 [251-500]
Wolf, Rachel R - *Splash 4*
LJ - v121 - N 15 '96 - p61 [51-250]
Wolf, Sharyn - *How to Stay Lovers for Life*
LJ - v122 - My 1 '97 - p127 [51-250]
Wolf Head Quarterly
p   Sm Pr R - v29 - Ja '97 - p22 [51-250]
Wolf-Devine, Celia - *Descartes on Seeing*
RM - v49 - Je '96 - p951+ [501+]
Wolfe, Alan - *Marginalized in the Middle*
BW - v26 - D 29 '96 - p13 [51-250]
LJ - v121 - O 1 '96 - p112 [51-250]
NYTBR - v101 - D 15 '96 - p28+ [501+]
Wolfe, Art - *1, 2, 3 Moose (Illus. by Art Wolfe)*
c   BL - v93 - N 1 '96 - p503 [51-250]
c   Ch BWatch - v6 - O '96 - p4 [1-50]
c   HB Guide - v8 - Spr '97 - p31 [51-250]
c   PW - v243 - S 9 '96 - p84 [51-250]
c   SLJ - v43 - Ja '97 - p83 [51-250]
Tribes
KR - v65 - Mr 15 '97 - p454 [51-250]
Wolfe, Charles - *The Devil's Box*
KR - v65 - F 1 '97 - p214 [251-500]
LJ - v122 - Ap 1 '97 - p96+ [51-250]
In Close Harmony
BL - v93 - N 1 '96 - p473 [51-250]
Wolfe, Christopher - *How to Read the Constitution*
Choice - v34 - Mr '97 - p1242 [51-250]
Wolfe, Gene - *Exodus from the Long Sun*
Analog - v117 - Mr '97 - p148 [251-500]
BL - v93 - O 1 '96 - p326 [51-250]
KR - v64 - S 15 '96 - p1362 [51-250]
LJ - v121 - O 15 '96 - p93 [1-50]
New Sci - v152 - N 23 '96 - p48 [51-250]
NYTBR - v101 - N 3 '96 - p24 [251-500]
NYTBR - v101 - D 8 '96 - p94 [1-50]
PW - v243 - O 7 '96 - p65 [51-250]
Wolfe, Gregory - *Malcolm Muggeridge: A Biography*
PW - v244 - Ap 14 '97 - p69 [51-250]
Quad - v40 - My '96 - p83+ [501+]
Wolfe, J Kevin - *The Fat-Free Junkfood Cookbook*
BL - v93 - Ja '97 - p802 [51-250]
PW - v243 - D 16 '96 - p57 [51-250]
Wolfe, Margaret Ripley - *Daughters of Canaan*
JSH - v63 - F '97 - p215+ [501+]

Wolfe, Marshall - *Elusive Development*
Choice - v34 - N '96 - p509 [51-250]
Wolfe, Mary Ellen - *Western Water Rights*
r   BWatch - v18 - F '97 - p1 [51-250]
Wolfe, Swain - *The Woman Who Lives in the Earth*
y   VOYA - v19 - F '97 - p342 [251-500]
Wolfe, William L - *Introduction to Infrared System Design*
SciTech - v20 - D '96 - p65 [51-250]
Wolff, Daniel - *You Send Me*
CAY - v17 - Fall '96 - p8 [51-250]
TPR - v17 - Fall '96 - p18+ [501+]
Wolff, Ferida - *A Weed Is a Seed (Illus. by Janet Pedersen)*
c   HB Guide - v7 - Fall '96 - p282 [51-250]
Wolff, Jana - *Secret Thoughts of an Adoptive Mother*
BL - v93 - Ja '97 - p792+ [251-500]
PW - v243 - D 9 '96 - p57+ [51-250]
Wolff, Janet - *Resident Alien*
CS - v25 - N '96 - p818+ [501+]
JAAC - v54 - Fall '96 - p412+ [501+]
Wolff, Larry - *Inventing Eastern Europe*
EHR - v112 - Ap '97 - p490+ [501+]
Russ Rev - v55 - O '96 - p713 [501+]
Wil Q - v21 - Win '97 - p37+ [51-250]
Wolff, Michael - *NetDoctor: Your Guide to Health and Medical Advice on the Internet and Online Services*
r   BL - v93 - F 1 '97 - p957 [1-50]
Netsci Fi:
LJ - v121 - D '96 - p138 [51-250]
Your Personal Netspy
LJ - v121 - D '96 - p138 [51-250]
Wolff, Patricia Rae - *The Toll-Bridge Troll (Illus. by Kimberly Bulcken Root)*
c   Inst - v105 - My '96 - p69 [1-50]
c   RT - v50 - O '96 - p135 [1-50]
Wolff, Rick - *Playing Better Baseball*
LJ - v122 - F 1 '97 - p83 [51-250]
Wolff, Theodore F - *Enrico Donati: Surrealism and Beyond*
PW - v243 - N 11 '96 - p66 [51-250]
Wolff, Tobias - *Back in the World*
BW - v26 - N 10 '96 - p12 [51-250]
LJ - v122 - Ja '97 - p155 [1-50]
NYTBR - v101 - N 24 '96 - p32 [51-250]
In Pharaoh's Army
Shen - v46 - Sum '96 - p95+ [501+]
The Night in Question
y   BL - v92 - Ag '96 - p1857 [251-500]
BL - v93 - Ap 1 '97 - p1285 [1-50]
BW - v27 - Ja 5 '97 - p4 [501+]
Ent W - N 1 '96 - p65 [51-250]
KR - v64 - Ag 15 '96 - p1186 [251-500]
LATBR - O 13 '96 - p2 [501+]
NS - v126 - Ja 17 '97 - p48 [501+]
NYTBR - v101 - N 3 '96 - p12 [501+]
NYTBR - v101 - D 8 '96 - p82 [1-50]
NYTLa - v146 - O 3 '96 - pC19 [501+]
Obs - D 15 '96 - p16* [501+]
PW - v243 - N 4 '96 - p40 [1-50]
TLS - N 15 '96 - p23 [501+]
VV - v42 - Ja 7 '97 - p44 [51-250]
The Night in Question (Wolff). Audio Version
LJ - v121 - D '96 - p170 [51-250]
This Boy's Life
y   BL - v93 - Ja '97 - p833 [1-50]
Wolff, Virginia Euwer - *Make Lemonade*
y   Bks Keeps - N '96 - p11 [51-250]
Wolffe, John - *God and Greater Britain*
J Ch St - v38 - Aut '96 - p910+ [251-500]
Wolfle, Gerhard Martin - *Die Wesenslogik In Hegels Wissenschaft Der Logic*
RM - v49 - Je '96 - p953+ [501+]
Wolford, Lisa - *Grotowski's Objective Drama Research*
Am Theat - v14 - Ja '97 - p74 [51-250]
Wolfram, Von Eschenbach - *Wolfram Von Eschenbach: Parzival. Vols. 1-2*
MLR - v91 - Jl '96 - p777+ [501+]
Wolfram, Stephen - *The Mathematica Book. 3rd Ed.*
New Sci - v151 - S 28 '96 - p44 [1-50]
SB - v32 - O '96 - p195 [51-250]
Wolfschmidt, Gudrun - *Milchstrasse, Nebel, Galaxien*
Isis - v87 - S '96 - p528 [251-500]
Wolfson, Elliot R - *Through a Speculum That Shines*
CH - v65 - S '96 - p470+ [501+]
Theol St - v57 - Mr '96 - p146+ [501+]
Wolfson, Evelyn - *Growing Up Indian (Illus. by William Sauts Bock)*
y   Kliatt - v31 - Mr '97 - p33 [51-250]

Wolfson, Margaret Olivia - *Marriage of the Rain Goddess (Illus. by Clifford Alexander Parms)*
c   BL - v92 - Ag '96 - p1899 [51-250]
c   Ch BWatch - v6 - Jl '96 - p7 [1-50]
c   HB Guide - v8 - Spr '97 - p106 [51-250]
c   Sch Lib - v44 - Ag '96 - p102 [51-250]
c   SLJ - v42 - Ag '96 - p141 [51-250]
Wolfson, Paulette S - *Mexico Environmental Report*
r   ARBA - v28 - '97 - p106+ [251-500]
Wolgast, Eike - *Hochstift Und Reformation*
Six Ct J - v27 - Fall '96 - p926+ [501+]
Wolin, Jeffrey A - *Written on Memory*
y   BL - v93 - Mr 15 '97 - p1223 [51-250]
y   Kliatt - v31 - My '97 - p23 [51-250]
PW - v244 - F 3 '97 - p91 [51-250]
Wolinsky, Ira - *Nutritional Concerns of Women*
Choice - v34 - F '97 - p997 [51-250]
Wolinsky, Stephen H - *The Way of the Human*
LJ - v121 - N 15 '96 - p76 [51-250]
Wolk, Gloria Grening - *Cash for the Final Days*
BWatch - v17 - N '96 - p4 [51-250]
LJ - v122 - F 1 '97 - p92+ [51-250]
Wolkstein, Diane - *Esther's Story (Illus. by Juan Wijngaard)*
c   BL - v93 - O 1 '96 - p339 [1-50]
c   Ch BWatch - v6 - My '96 - p3 [1-50]
c   HB Guide - v7 - Fall '96 - p310 [51-250]
White Wave (Illus. by Ed Young)
c   CBRS - v25 - S '96 - p6 [51-250]
c   HB Guide - v8 - Spr '97 - p106 [51-250]
c   KR - v64 - S 15 '96 - p1410 [51-250]
c   SLJ - v43 - Ja '97 - p110 [51-250]
Wollen, Roger - *Derek Jarman: A Portrait*
Obs - Ag 18 '96 - p18* [1-50]
Wollenberg, Jorg - *The German Public and the Persecution of Jews 1933-1945*
R&R Bk N - v11 - N '96 - p14 [1-50]
Wolman, Benjamin B - *The Encyclopedia of Psychiatry, Psychology, and Psychoanalysis*
r   ARBA - v28 - '97 - p616 [51-250]
r   Nature - v386 - Ap 17 '97 - p667+ [501+]
Wolman, William - *The Judas Economy*
KR - v65 - My 1 '97 - p710 [251-500]
Wolpert, Stanley - *Nehru: A Tryst with Destiny*
BL - v92 - Ag '96 - p1879 [51-250]
Choice - v34 - Ap '97 - p1395 [51-250]
Econ - v342 - Ja 18 '97 - p82 [251-500]
NS - v126 - Ja 31 '97 - p46+ [501+]
NYTBR - v101 - D 1 '96 - p22 [51-250]
Obs - Mr 2 '97 - p16* [501+]
Spec - v278 - Mr 8 '97 - p35+ [501+]
Wolpin, Kenneth I - *Empirical Methods for the Study of Labor Force Dynamics*
JEL - v34 - D '96 - p2076+ [51-250]
Wolpoff, Milford - *Race and Human Evolution*
BL - v93 - D 1 '96 - p633 [51-250]
BW - v26 - D 29 '96 - p1+ [501+]
KR - v64 - N 1 '96 - p1594 [251-500]
LJ - v121 - D '96 - p139+ [51-250]
Nature - v386 - Mr 27 '97 - p350 [501+]
New Sci - v153 - F 22 '97 - p42+ [501+]
NH - v106 - F '97 - p10+ [501+]
NYTBR - v102 - F 2 '97 - p19 [501+]
PW - v243 - D 2 '96 - p49 [51-250]
Wolter, John A - *Images of the World*
r   BL - v93 - N 1 '96 - p477 [51-250]
Choice - v34 - Ap '97 - p1393 [51-250]
r   KR - v64 - O 1 '96 - p1458 [251-500]
r   LATBR - D 8 '96 - p35 [51-250]
r   LJ - v121 - N 1 '96 - p60+ [51-250]
PW - v243 - S 30 '96 - p74 [51-250]
Wolters, Raymond - *Right Turn*
Choice - v34 - F '97 - p1039 [51-250]
Nat R - v48 - D 9 '96 - p70 [51-250]
Wolterstorff, Nicholas - *Divine Discourse*
CPR - v16 - D '96 - p441+ [501+]
IPQ - v37 - Mr '97 - p107+ [501+]
John Locke and the Ethics of Belief
Choice - v34 - S '96 - p143 [51-250]
CPR - v16 - D '96 - p444+ [501+]
Woltmann, Johanna - *Gertrud Kolmar: Leben Und Werk*
MLR - v92 - Ap '97 - p524+ [251-500]
Wolverton, B C - *Eco-Friendly Houseplants*
BL - v93 - Mr 1 '97 - p1102 [51-250]
Wolverton, Dave - *Lords of the Seventh Swarm*
KR - v64 - N 15 '96 - p1640 [51-250]
PW - v243 - D 9 '96 - p65 [51-250]
Wolverton, Terry - *Bailey's Beads*
BL - v93 - S 1 '96 - p66 [51-250]
Hers: Brilliant New Fiction by Lesbian Writers
Quill & Q - v62 - Jl '96 - p42 [501+]

Womack, Jack - *Ambient*
NYTBR - v102 - F 9 '97 - p32 [51-250]
Elvissey
NYTBR - v102 - F 9 '97 - p32 [1-50]
Let's Put the Future behind Us
TLS - F 7 '97 - p23 [501+]
Womack, James P - *Lean Thinking*
BL - v93 - S 1 '96 - p47 [51-250]
LJ - v122 - Mr 15 '97 - p36 [1-50]
PW - v243 - Jl 22 '96 - p220+ [51-250]
WSJ-MW - v78 - N 1 '96 - pA11 [501+]
Womack, Steven - *Chain of Fools*
Arm Det - v29 - Fall '96 - p496 [251-500]
Woman's Day (New York, N.Y.) - *The Woman's Day Book of Holiday Crafts*
BL - v93 - Ja '97 - p806 [51-250]
A Woman's Guide to Coping with Disability
r BL - v93 - F 1 '97 - p960 [1-50]
Women and Drugs
J Gov Info - v23 - S '96 - p665+ [51-250]
Women and Men in Europe and North America 1995
yr ARBA - v28 - '97 - p326+ [251-500]
Women Envision
p WorldV - v12 - Jl '96 - p12 [51-250]
Women in the Netherlands
r J Gov Info - v23 - S '96 - p660 [1-50]
Women: Looking beyond 2000
Signs - v22 - Aut '96 - p222+ [501+]
Women Playwrights 1995
PW - v243 - N 11 '96 - p60 [51-250]
Women Workers: An Annotated Bibliography 1983-94
r ARBA - v28 - '97 - p334 [51-250]
r J Gov Info - v23 - S '96 - p672 [51-250]
Women's Rights Project (Human Rights Watch) - *All Too Familiar*
NYRB - v44 - F 6 '97 - p8 [501+]
Women's Travel in Your Pocket. 16th Ed.
r Quill & Q - v62 - S '96 - p24 [51-250]
Wonders, Karen - *Habitat Dioramas*
Isis - v87 - D '96 - p760+ [501+]
Wondra, Ellen K - *Humanity Has Been a Holy Thing*
JAAR - v64 - Fall '96 - p688+ [501+]
Wong, Bernice Y L - *The ABCs of Learning Disabilities*
R&R Bk N - v11 - D '96 - p55 [51-250]
Wong, David T K - *Hong Kong Stories*
Obs - Ja 12 '97 - p15* [501+]
Wong, Jan - *Red China Blues*
BIC - v25 - S '96 - p15+ [501+]
CF - v75 - S '96 - p44+ [501+]
FEER - v159 - S 5 '96 - p46+ [501+]
Mac - v109 - D 9 '96 - p64 [1-50]
Quill & Q - v63 - F '97 - p51 [51-250]
Time - v148 - D 23 '96 - p86 [51-250]
Wong, Janet S - *A Suitcase of Seaweed and Other Poems (Illus. by Janet S Wong)*
c HB Guide - v7 - Fall '96 - p369 [51-250]
y SLJ - v42 - S '96 - p237 [51-250]
y VOYA - v19 - O '96 - p241+ [251-500]
Wong, Kar-Yiu - *International Trade in Goods and Factor Mobility*
JEL - v35 - Mr '97 - p144+ [501+]
Wong, Linda - *Social Change and Social Policy in Contemporary China*
R&R Bk N - v11 - D '96 - p39 [51-250]
Soc Ser R - v70 - D '96 - p665+ [501+]
Wong, Orrin N C - *Fantastic Modernity*
Nine-C Lit - v51 - D '96 - p428 [51-250]
Wong, Sau-Ling Cynthia - *Reading Asian American Literature*
Amerasia J - v22 - 3 '96 - p160+ [501+]
Wong, Shawn - *American Knees*
Amerasia J - v22 - 2 '96 - p166+ [501+]
LATBR - O 13 '96 - p15 [51-250]
Wonham, Henry B - *Criticism and the Color Line*
Choice - v34 - D '96 - p611+ [51-250]
Wood, A J - *Invasion of the Giant Bugs (Illus. by Wayne Anderson)*
c Ch BWatch - v6 - N '96 - p6 [51-250]
c Emerg Lib - v24 - Mr '97 - p45 [1-50]
c PW - v243 - S 23 '96 - p78 [51-250]
Journey to the Haunted Planet (Illus. by Wayne Anderson)
c RT - v50 - O '96 - p133 [1-50]
The Lion and the Mouse (Illus. by Ian Andrew)
c RT - v50 - Mr '97 - p496 [51-250]
Nicki Palin's Hidden Pictures
c HB Guide - v7 - Fall '96 - p339 [1-50]
Time for Christmas (Illus. by Tony Linsell)
c PW - v243 - S 30 '96 - p93 [1-50]

Wood, Audrey - *Bright and Early Thursday Evening (Illus. by Don Wood)*
c CBRS - v25 - O '96 - p20 [51-250]
c HB Guide - v8 - Spr '97 - p54 [51-250]
c HMR - Spr '97 - p30 [501+]
c KR - v64 - Ag 15 '96 - p1245 [51-250]
c PW - v243 - Jl 22 '96 - p242 [51-250]
c SLJ - v42 - O '96 - p109+ [51-250]
The Bunyans (Illus. by David Shannon)
c BL - v93 - S 15 '96 - p252 [51-250]
c BW - v26 - D 8 '96 - p19+ [51-250]
c CBRS - v25 - N '96 - p29 [51-250]
c CCB-B - v50 - Ja '97 - p189 [51-250]
c HB Guide - v8 - Spr '97 - p54 [51-250]
c Inst - v106 - Ja '97 - p54 [1-50]
c KR - v64 - S 1 '96 - p1330 [51-250]
c LATBR - N 10 '96 - p15 [51-250]
c PW - v243 - S 16 '96 - p82 [51-250]
c SLJ - v42 - D '96 - p32 [1-50]
c SLJ - v42 - D '96 - p110 [51-250]
c Smith - v27 - N '96 - p173 [1-50]
Elbert's Bad Word (Illus. by Audrey Wood)
c PW - v243 - O 7 '96 - p78 [51-250]
The Flying Dragon Room (Illus. by Mark Teague)
c HB Guide - v7 - Fall '96 - p282 [51-250]
c Inst - v106 - O '96 - p66 [51-250]
c Par - v71 - D '96 - p254 [51-250]
The Napping House (Illus. by Don Wood)
c HB Guide - v7 - Fall '96 - p282 [51-250]
The Red Racer (Illus. by Audrey Wood)
c BL - v93 - S 1 '96 - p145 [51-250]
c CBRS - v25 - D '96 - p42 [1-50]
c Ch BWatch - v7 - F '97 - p2 [1-50]
c HB Guide - v8 - Spr '97 - p54 [51-250]
c Par - v71 - D '96 - p252 [51-250]
c SLJ - v42 - S '96 - p194 [51-250]
Weird Parents
c Magpies - v11 - S '96 - p45 [1-50]
Wood, B Dan - *Bureaucratic Dynamics*
Pol Stud J - v24 - Aut '96 - p522 [51-250]
Wood, Barbara - *The Prophetess (Breck). Audio Version*
y Kliatt - v31 - Mr '97 - p44 [51-250]
Wood, Betty - *The Origins of American Slavery*
y BL - v93 - Ap 1 '97 - p1279 [51-250]
LJ - v122 - Mr 15 '97 - p75 [51-250]
PW - v244 - Mr 17 '97 - p67+ [51-250]
Women's Work, Men's Work
AHR - v101 - O '96 - p1280+ [501+]
Wood, Christopher - *Tissot: The Life and Work of Jacques Joseph Tissot 1846-1902*
CR - v269 - S '96 - p167 [51-250]
Wood, Damon - *Light Upgrades*
R&R Bk N - v12 - F '97 - p99 [51-250]
Wood, David - *The Christmas Story (Illus. by Asun Balzola)*
c Sch Lib - v45 - F '97 - p43 [51-250]
Wood, David F - *The Concord Museum*
Mag Antiq - v151 - Ja '97 - p30 [251-500]
Wood, Don - *Piggies (Illus. by Don Wood)*
c HB Guide - v7 - Fall '96 - p282 [51-250]
Wood, Donald N - *Post-Intellectualism and the Decline of Democracy*
Choice - v34 - Ap '97 - p1409 [51-250]
R&R Bk N - v11 - D '96 - p39 [51-250]
Wood, Douglas - *Northwoods Cradle Song (Illus. by Lisa Desimini)*
c ECEJ - v24 - Spr '97 - p174+ [51-250]
c Emerg Lib - v24 - S '96 - p43 [1-50]
c HB Guide - v7 - Fall '96 - p369 [51-250]
Old Turtle (Wood). Audio Version
c BL - v93 - Ap 1 '97 - p1314 [1-50]
The Windigo's Return (Illus. by Greg Couch)
c BL - v93 - S 15 '96 - p235 [51-250]
c CBRS - v25 - Ja '97 - p53 [51-250]
c CCB-B - v50 - N '96 - p112+ [51-250]
c Emerg Lib - v24 - Mr '97 - p64 [51-250]
c HB Guide - v8 - Spr '97 - p106 [51-250]
c PW - v243 - S 16 '96 - p82 [51-250]
c SLJ - v42 - N '96 - p102 [51-250]
Wood, Ellen Meiksins - *Democracy against Capitalism*
CPR - v16 - Ap '96 - p153+ [501+]
Ethics - v107 - O '96 - p190 [51-250]
Wood, Eric S - *Historical Britain*
r BL - v93 - S 1 '96 - p166 [51-250]
Wood, Frances - *Did Marco Polo Go to China?*
BW - v26 - O 13 '96 - p13 [51-250]
VV - v41 - N 12 '96 - p85 [501+]

Wood, Frances M - *Becoming Rosemary*
y BL - v93 - Ja '97 - p846 [251-500]
c CBRS - v25 - Ap '97 - p108 [51-250]
c CCB-B - v50 - My '97 - p338+ [51-250]
c KR - v64 - N 1 '96 - p1610 [51-250]
c PW - v243 - D 9 '96 - p69 [51-250]
c SLJ - v43 - F '97 - p106+ [51-250]
Wood, Gordon S - *Russian-American Dialogue on the American Revolution*
W&M Q - v54 - Ap '97 - p442+ [501+]
Wood, Gregory A - *A Guide to the Acadians in Maryland in the Eighteenth and Nineteenth Centuries*
NGSQ - v85 - Mr '97 - p60 [251-500]
Wood, Jakki - *Animal Hullabaloo (Illus. by Jakki Wood)*
c JB - v60 - Ag '96 - p144 [51-250]
Bumper to Bumper (Illus. by Jakki Wood)
c HB Guide - v7 - Fall '96 - p246 [51-250]
c JB - v60 - Ag '96 - p144 [51-250]
c Sch Lib - v44 - Ag '96 - p102 [51-250]
Wood, James B - *The King's Army*
Choice - v34 - Mr '97 - p1225 [51-250]
J Mil H - v61 - Ap '97 - p364+ [501+]
Wood, James N - *The Art Institute of Chicago*
LJ - v122 - F 1 '97 - p76 [51-250]
WSJ-MW - v78 - D 5 '96 - pA18 [1-50]
Wood, Jenny - *I Wonder Why Kangaroos Have Pouches and Other Questions about Baby Animals*
c HB Guide - v8 - Spr '97 - p116 [51-250]
c JB - v60 - O '96 - p196+ [51-250]
c Sch Lib - v44 - N '96 - p161+ [51-250]
Wood, John - *The Scenic Daguerreotype*
AB - v99 - F 24 '97 - p620+ [501+]
Wood, Julia T - *Communication Theories in Action*
R&R Bk N - v11 - N '96 - p62 [51-250]
Under-Studied Relationships
JMF - v58 - N '96 - p1041+ [251-500]
Wood, June Rae - *A Share of Freedom*
c SLJ - v43 - Mr '97 - p113 [1-50]
Wood, Liz - *Longman's Parent's Guides: Pre-School Choices and Nursery Education*
TES - Ja 31 '97 - p8* [501+]
Wood, Marcus - *Radical Satire and Print Culture 1790-1822*
MP - v94 - N '96 - p246+ [501+]
RES - v47 - N '96 - p597+ [501+]
Wood, Marilyn - *Frommer's Wonderful Weekends from New York City*
r BL - v93 - S 15 '96 - p210 [1-50]
Wood, Mary Elene - *The Writing on the Wall*
Can Lit - Win '96 - p137+ [501+]
Wood, Michele - *Going Back Home (Illus. by Michele Wood)*
c BL - v93 - S 15 '96 - p235 [51-250]
c CCB-B - v50 - D '96 - p125+ [501+]
c Ch BWatch - v7 - F '97 - p1 [51-250]
c HB Guide - v8 - Spr '97 - p138 [51-250]
c KR - v64 - S 1 '96 - p1323 [51-250]
c LATBR - S 1 '96 - p11 [51-250]
c PW - v243 - S 23 '96 - p76 [51-250]
Wood, N Lee - *Faraday's Orphans*
BL - v93 - My 15 '97 - p1567 [51-250]
KR - v65 - My 1 '97 - p685 [51-250]
New Sci - v153 - Mr 15 '97 - p45 [51-250]
Looking for the Mahdi
NYTBR - v101 - D 8 '96 - p94 [1-50]
Wood, Nancy - *The Girl Who Loved Coyotes (Illus. by Diana Bryer)*
c RT - v50 - N '96 - p255+ [51-250]
Shaman's Circle (Illus. by Frank Howell)
c HB Guide - v8 - Spr '97 - p154 [51-250]
y SLJ - v42 - S '96 - p237+ [51-250]
Wood, Neal - *Foundations of Political Economy*
AHR - v101 - O '96 - p1202 [501+]
EHR - v111 - N '96 - p1265+ [251-500]
Wood, Peter H - *Strange New Land*
y Ch BWatch - v6 - My '96 - p5 [51-250]
y HB Guide - v7 - Fall '96 - p386 [51-250]
Wood, Rebecca - *The Splendid Grain*
BL - v93 - D 15 '96 - p702 [51-250]
LJ - v122 - F 15 '97 - p157+ [51-250]
PW - v243 - N 4 '96 - p72 [51-250]
Wood, Richard - *History of Fairs and Markets*
c Sch Lib - v44 - N '96 - p166 [51-250]
c TES - N 8 '96 - p13* [501+]
History of Food and Cooking
c Sch Lib - v44 - Ag '96 - p114 [51-250]
c TES - N 8 '96 - p13* [501+]
Wood, Richard A - *Weather of U.S. Cities. 5th Ed.*
r ARBA - v28 - '97 - p634 [51-250]
Wood, Robert B - *Opportunities in Electrical Trades*
y Kliatt - v31 - Ja '97 - p21 [51-250]

Wood, Robert W - *Heat FUNdamentals (Illus. by Rick Brown)*
  c SB - v33 - My '97 - p110 [251-500]
Mechanics FUNdamentals (Illus. by Rick Brown)
  c SB - v33 - My '97 - p110 [251-500]
Wood, Sebastian - *The Wanderer of the Subconscious Realm*
  Aust Bk R - Je '96 - p67 [1-50]
Wood, Selina - *The Rainforest*
  c Sch Lib - v45 - F '97 - p37 [51-250]
Wood, Sharon - *Italian Women Writing*
  MLR - v92 - Ap '97 - p481+ [501+]
  MLR - v92 - Ap '97 - p481+ [501+]
Italian Women's Writing 1860-1994
  MLR - v92 - Ap '97 - p481+ [501+]
  MLR - v92 - Ap '97 - p481+ [501+]
Wood, Ted - *Ghosts of the Southwest (Illus. by Ted Wood)*
  c BL - v93 - Mr 1 '97 - p1160 [51-250]
  c CBRS - v25 - Ap '97 - p101 [51-250]
Iditarod Dream (Illus. by Ted Wood)
  c HB Guide - v7 - Fall '96 - p363 [51-250]
  c RT - v50 - My '97 - p685+ [51-250]
Wood, Thomas Fullenwider - *Connections: The Wood and Fullenwider Families in America*
  EGH - v50 - N '96 - p195 [51-250]
Wood, Tim - *The Incas*
  c Bks Keeps - N '96 - p15 [51-250]
  c HB Guide - v8 - Spr '97 - p167 [51-250]
  y SLJ - v43 - Mr '97 - p210+ [51-250]
Racing Drivers
  c Ch BWatch - v6 - Jl '96 - p6 [51-250]
Wood, Victoria - *Chunky: The Victoria Wood Omnibus*
  TLS - N 29 '96 - p32 [251-500]
Woodall, Brian - *Japan under Construction*
  Choice - v34 - O '96 - p356 [51-250]
  JEL - v34 - S '96 - p1456+ [51-250]
Woodall, Jack - *Total Quality in Information Systems and Technology*
  Choice - v34 - F '97 - p999 [51-250]
  R&R Bk N - v11 - D '96 - p27 [51-250]
Woodall, James - *The Man in the Mirror of the Book*
  Obs - Ja 12 '97 - p18* [51-250]
  TLS - Ag 2 '96 - p8 [501+]
Woodard, Cheryl - *Starting and Running a Successful Newsletter or Magazine*
  BWatch - v18 - Mr '97 - p12 [51-250]
Woodard, Michael D - *Black Entrepreneurs in America*
  BL - v93 - D 15 '96 - p699+ [51-250]
  LJ - v121 - N 1 '96 - p82 [1-50]
  PW - v243 - N 25 '96 - p62 [51-250]
Woodbridge, John D - *Revolt in Prerevolutionary France*
  AHR - v101 - D '96 - p1551+ [501+]
  CH - v65 - D '96 - p718+ [501+]
  JMH - v68 - D '96 - p992+ [501+]
Woodbridge, Mark E - *American Federation of Labor and Congress of Industrial Organizations Pamphlets 1889-1955*
  r RQ - v36 - Fall '96 - p52 [51-250]
Woodburn, John H - *Opportunities in Chemistry Careers*
  y Kliatt - v31 - Ja '97 - p21 [51-250]
Woodbury, Francine G - *Shade and Shadow*
  y Kliatt - v30 - S '96 - p22 [51-250]
  MFSF - v91 - D '96 - p91+ [501+]
Woodcock, Jim - *Using Z*
  SciTech - v20 - S '96 - p9 [51-250]
Woodcock, Nigel - *Geology and Environment in Britain and Ireland*
  GJ - v162 - Jl '96 - p236 [51-250]
Wooden, John - *Wooden: A Lifetime of Observations On and Off the Court*
  LJ - v122 - Ap 15 '97 - p87 [51-250]
  PW - v244 - F 24 '97 - p80 [1-50]
Wooden, Wayne S - *Rodeo in America*
  Choice - v34 - My '97 - p1539 [51-250]
Wooderson, Philip - *The Mincing Machine (Illus. by Dee Shulman)*
  c Sch Lib - v44 - Ag '96 - p107 [51-250]
Spooked
  c Magpies - v11 - S '96 - p45 [1-50]
Woodford, Arthur M - *Tonnacour: Life in Grosse Pointe and along the Shores of Lake St. Clair*
  CAY - v16 - Fall '95 - p10 [51-250]
Woodgate, Ralph W - *The Handbook of Machine Soldering. 3rd Ed.*
  SciTech - v20 - D '96 - p77 [51-250]
Woodham-Smith, Cecil - *Florence Nightingale 1820-1910*
  CR - v268 - Je '96 - p335 [51-250]
Woodhead, Henry - *Atlanta*
  y SLJ - v43 - Mr '97 - p218 [51-250]
Soldier Life
  y SLJ - v43 - Mr '97 - p218 [51-250]

Woodhead, Sally - *No Longer Dead to Me*
  Sch Lib - v44 - Ag '96 - p131 [51-250]
Woodhouse, Mary - *How to Make Your Airplane Last Forever*
  SB - v33 - Mr '97 - p41 [51-250]
Woodhouse, Sarah - *Other Lives*
  BL - v93 - F 1 '97 - p927 [51-250]
  KR - v64 - D 15 '96 - p1766+ [251-500]
  LJ - v122 - F 1 '97 - p109 [51-250]
  PW - v243 - D 30 '96 - p56 [251-500]
Woodhull, Winifred - *Transfigurations of the Maghreb*
  Can Lit - Win '96 - p140+ [501+]
Woodland, Dennis W - *Contemporary Plant Systematics. 2nd Ed.*
  SciTech - v21 - Mr '97 - p37 [51-250]
Woodman, Harold D - *New South--New Law*
  AHR - v101 - D '96 - p1629+ [501+]
  JEH - v56 - D '96 - p954+ [501+]
  JIH - v27 - Win '97 - p544+ [501+]
Woodman, Marion - *Dancing in the Flames*
  Bloom Rev - v16 - N '96 - p15 [501+]
Woodmansee, Martha - *The Author, Art, and the Market*
  Art J - v55 - Sum '96 - p107 [501+]
  Comp L - v48 - Fall '96 - p389+ [501+]
  Ger Q - v70 - Win '97 - p66+ [501+]
The Construction of Authorship
  MLR - v92 - Ja '97 - p140+ [501+]
Woodrell, Daniel - *Give Us a Kiss*
  Arm Det - v29 - Sum '96 - p375 [251-500]
  Bloom Rev - v16 - Jl '96 - p24 [501+]
  NYTBR - v101 - D 8 '96 - p80 [1-50]
  NYTBR - v102 - Ap 6 '97 - p32 [51-250]
  Rapport - v19 - 5 '96 - p30 [51-250]
  TLS - F 7 '97 - p23 [501+]
Woodruff, Elvira - *The Orphan of Ellis Island*
  c CCB-B - v50 - Mr '97 - p261+ [51-250]
  c KR - v65 - Ja 15 '97 - p147 [51-250]
Woodruff, Sandra - *Secrets of Fat-Free Italian Cooking*
  LJ - v122 - F 15 '97 - p158+ [51-250]
Woods, Bernard - *Communication, Technology, and the Development of People*
  JC - v46 - Sum '96 - p183+ [501+]
Woods, Donald - *Bolton Abbey*
  Spec - v277 - N 16 '96 - p42 [1-50]
Woods, Earl - *Training a Tiger*
  PW - v244 - Mr 17 '97 - p71+ [51-250]
Woods, Edward - *Introducing Grammar*
  MLJ - v81 - Spr '97 - p120 [251-500]
Woods, May - *Visions of Arcadia*
  BL - v93 - D 1 '96 - p636 [51-250]
Woods, Ngaire - *Explaining International Relations since 1945*
  Choice - v34 - Ap '97 - p1413 [51-250]
Woods, Paula L - *Merry Christmas, Baby*
  c BW - v26 - D 8 '96 - p12 [51-250]
  c S Liv - v31 - D '96 - p58 [51-250]
Woods, Randall Bennett - *Fulbright: A Biography*
  AHR - v102 - F '97 - p215+ [51-250]
  Historian - v59 - Win '97 - p447+ [251-500]
  JSH - v63 - F '97 - p206+ [501+]
Woods, Roger - *The Conservative Revolution in the Weimar Republic*
  Choice - v34 - N '96 - p522 [51-250]
  HRNB - v25 - Win '97 - p75+ [251-500]
  R&R Bk N - v11 - N '96 - p12 [51-250]
Woods, S E - *Self-Directed RRSPs*
  Quill & Q - v63 - Ja '97 - p26 [51-250]
Woods, Stuart - *Chiefs*
  SFR - v21 - N '96 - p48 [1-50]
Dirt
  BL - v92 - Ag '96 - p1857 [251-500]
  LATBR - N 10 '96 - p6 [51-250]
  LJ - v121 - S 15 '96 - p99 [51-250]
Under the Lake (Stechschulte). Audio Version
  BWatch - v17 - D '96 - p10 [1-50]
Woodside, Arch G - *Measuring the Effectiveness of Image and Linkage Advertising*
  Choice - v34 - F '97 - p1009 [51-250]
  R&R Bk N - v11 - D '96 - p35 [51-250]
Woodson, Jacqueline - *From the Notebooks of Melanin Sun*
  y Emerg Lib - v24 - S '96 - p26 [1-50]
  y RT - v50 - Mr '97 - p480 [51-250]
Maizon at Blue Hill
  y Kliatt - v30 - S '96 - p3 [1-50]
A Way out of No Way
  y BL - v93 - F 15 '97 - p1016 [51-250]
  y HB Guide - v8 - Spr '97 - p149 [51-250]
  c NYTBR - v102 - Ja 19 '97 - p24 [1-50]

Woodtor, Dee Parmer - *Big Meeting (Illus. by Dolores Johnson)*
  c BL - v93 - S 1 '96 - p145 [51-250]
  c CBRS - v24 - Ag '96 - p163 [51-250]
  c HB Guide - v8 - Spr '97 - p54 [51-250]
  c SLJ - v42 - S '96 - p194+ [51-250]
Woodward, Ann - *The Exile Way*
  PW - v243 - O 21 '96 - p78+ [51-250]
Woodward, Anthony - *Rome: Time and Eternity*
  HT - v47 - Ja '97 - p56+ [501+]
Woodward, Bob - *The Choice*
  Nat - v263 - S 9 '96 - p39+ [501+]
  NYRB - v43 - S 19 '96 - p14+ [501+]
  Pres SQ - v27 - Win '97 - p153+ [501+]
  SFR - v21 - S '96 - p20 [501+]
  TLS - S 20 '96 - p14+ [501+]
Woodward, David - *Catalogue of Watermarks in Italian Printed Maps ca 1540-1600*
  r R&R Bk N - v11 - D '96 - p19 [51-250]
Woodward, Donald - *Men at Work*
  AHR - v101 - D '96 - p1539+ [501+]
  Albion - v28 - Win '96 - p684+ [501+]
  Historian - v59 - Fall '96 - p208 [501+]
  JIH - v27 - Aut '96 - p300+ [251-500]
  Six Ct J - v27 - Win '96 - p1099+ [501+]
Woodward, Harold R, Jr. - *Defender of the Valley*
  Sm Pr R - v29 - F '97 - p10 [51-250]
Woodward, John - *Hawks and Falcons*
  c Ch BWatch - v7 - Ja '97 - p2+ [1-50]
  c HB Guide - v8 - Spr '97 - p126 [51-250]
  c SB - v33 - Mr '97 - p53 [51-250]
Kangaroos
  c Ch BWatch - v7 - Ja '97 - p2+ [1-50]
  c HB Guide - v8 - Spr '97 - p127 [51-250]
  c SB - v33 - Mr '97 - p53 [51-250]
  c SLJ - v43 - F '97 - p92 [51-250]
Seals
  c Ch BWatch - v7 - Ja '97 - p2+ [1-50]
  c HB Guide - v8 - Spr '97 - p127 [51-250]
  c SB - v33 - Mr '97 - p53 [51-250]
Woodward, Peter - *The Horn of Africa*
  Choice - v34 - F '97 - p1031 [51-250]
Woodward, Susan L - *Balkan Tragedy*
  AAPSS-A - v548 - N '96 - p220+ [251-500]
  J Pol - v58 - Ag '96 - p930+ [501+]
  Lon R Bks - v18 - My 23 '96 - p20+ [501+]
Socialist Unemployment
  APSR - v90 - D '96 - p951 [501+]
  JEH - v56 - S '96 - p723+ [501+]
Woodworth, Deborah - *Death of a Winter Shaker*
  PW - v244 - F 24 '97 - p87 [51-250]
Woodworth, Steven E - *The American Civil War*
  yr ARBA - v28 - '97 - p194+ [51-250]
  r BL - v93 - N 15 '96 - p607 [251-500]
Davis and Lee at War
  JSH - v63 - F '97 - p181+ [501+]
Woody, Robert Henley - *Legally Safe Mental Health Practice*
  SciTech - v20 - D '96 - p44 [1-50]
Woog, Adam - *Amelia Earhart*
  y SLJ - v43 - Mr '97 - p203 [51-250]
Duke Ellington
  c HB Guide - v7 - Fall '96 - p370 [1-50]
Elvis Presley
  c HB Guide - v8 - Spr '97 - p157 [1-50]
  y SLJ - v43 - Ja '97 - p138 [51-250]
Marilyn Monroe
  y HB Guide - v8 - Spr '97 - p96 [51-250]
  y SLJ - v43 - Mr '97 - p212 [51-250]
Suicide
  y HB Guide - v8 - Spr '97 - p95 [51-250]
Wooldridge, Adrian - *Measuring the Mind*
  AHR - v101 - O '96 - p1209+ [501+]
  EHR - v112 - F '97 - p259+ [501+]
Wooldridge, Connie Nordhielm - *Wicked Jack (Illus. by Will Hillenbrand)*
  c PW - v244 - F 24 '97 - p93 [1-50]
Wooldridge, E T - *Into the Jet Age*
  NWCR - v50 - Win '97 - p154+ [501+]
Woolf, Harry, Sir - *Access to Justice: Final Report to the Lord Chancellor on the Civil Justice System in England and Wales*
  Lon R Bks - v18 - N 28 '96 - p16+ [501+]
Woolf, Virginia - *A Room of One's Own (Atkins). Audio Version*
  y Kliatt - v30 - N '96 - p51 [51-250]
To the Lighthouse
  PQ - v75 - Win '96 - p109+ [501+]
  RMR - v50 - 2 '96 - p121+ [501+]
To the Lighthouse (Atkins). Audio Version
  TLS - Ag 2 '96 - p24 [501+]

Woolfe, Ray - *Handbook of Counselling Psychology*
SciTech - v21 - Mr '97 - p1 [51-250]
Woolfe, Sue - *Leaning towards Infinity*
KR - v65 - Ja 15 '97 - p95+ [251-500]
PW - v244 - F 24 '97 - p65 [51-250]
Woolford, John - *Robert Browning*
Choice - v34 - N '96 - p462 [51-250]
Woolrich, Cornell - *Waltz into Darkness*
BW - v27 - Ja 19 '97 - p12 [51-250]
Woolsey, Marijke - *Dear Mother*
Woman's J - F '97 - p16 [1-50]
Woolsey, Ronald C - *Migrants West*
LATBR - D 22 '96 - p1+ [501+]
Woolverton, John F - *The Education of Phillips Brooks*
CH - v65 - D '96 - p740+ [501+]
Nine-C Lit - v50 - Mr '96 - p559 [1-50]
Woolwich, Madlyn-Ann C - *The Art of Pastel Portraiture*
A Art - v60 - D '96 - p80 [51-250]
Woosley, Anne I - *Mimbres Mogollon Archaeology*
Choice - v34 - My '97 - p1542+ [51-250]
Wooten, Patty - *Compassionate Laughter*
BL - v92 - Ag '96 - p1870 [51-250]
Worboys, Anne - *Seasons of the Senses*
BL - v93 - Mr 15 '97 - p1228 [51-250]
Worboys, Michael - *GIS, a Computing Perspective*
SciTech - v20 - D '96 - p17 [51-250]
Worden, Blair - *The Sound of Virtue*
Lon R Bks - v19 - Ap 3 '97 - p26+ [501+]
TLS - F 7 '97 - p13 [501+]
Worden, J William - *Children and Grief*
SB - v33 - My '97 - p101 [251-500]
Worden, Nigel - *The Making of Modern South Africa*
EHR - v111 - S '96 - p1016+ [251-500]
Wordsworth, J B - *Software Engineering with B*
Choice - v34 - My '97 - p1535+ [51-250]
Wordsworth, William - *The Letters of William and Dorothy Wordsworth. Vol. 8*
RES - v47 - Ag '96 - p427+ [501+]
Work Related Abstracts 1973-
r RQ - v36 - Fall '96 - p53+ [51-250]
Workers' Health International Newsletter
p WorldV - v13 - Ja '97 - p14 [51-250]
Workman, Marjean Holmes - *Index to the History of Northwestern Ohio, History of Paulding County by Everett A. Budd, and Township and Personal Histories of Paulding County*
r EGH - v50 - N '96 - p180 [51-250]
Workman, W Thom - *Banking on Deception*
CF - v75 - Mr '97 - p46+ [501+]
The Social Origins of the Iran-Iraq War
MEJ - v50 - Sum '96 - p446+ [501+]
Works of John Ruskin. Electronic Media Version
HT - v46 - F 12 '97 - p48 [51-250]
Workshop on Mathematical Methods in Biomedical Image Analysis (1996: San Francisco, Calif.) - *Mathematical Methods in Biomedical Image Analysis*
SciTech - v20 - N '96 - p36 [51-250]
Workshop on Object-Oriented Real-Time Dependable Systems (2nd: 1996: Laguna Beach, Calif.) - *Proceedings of WORDS'96*
SciTech - v20 - S '96 - p3 [51-250]
Workshop on Operator Theory and Boundary Eigenvalue Problems (1993: Vienna, Austria) - *Operator Theory and Boundary Value Problems*
SIAM Rev - v38 - S '96 - p545 [1-50]
Workshop on Optimal Design and Control (1994: Blacksburg, Va.) - *Optimal Design and Control*
SciTech - v20 - N '96 - p69 [51-250]
Workshop on Parallel and Distributed Simulation (10th: 1996: Philadelphia, Penn.) - *Proceedings of the 10th Workshop on Parallel and Distributed Simulation*
SciTech - v20 - S '96 - p5 [51-250]
The World
p Sm Pr R - v28 - S '96 - p14 [51-250]
The World: A Third World Guide 1995/96
r Choice - v34 - S '96 - p108 [51-250]
World Academic Database. Electronic Media Version
r ARBA - v28 - '97 - p142+ [251-500]
The World Almanac and Book of Facts 1996
yr RQ - v35 - Sum '96 - p568+ [51-250]
The World Almanac for Kids 1997
cr CLW - v67 - D '96 - p59 [51-250]
cr PW - v243 - S 16 '96 - p85 [51-250]
The World Almanac Job Finder's Guide 1997
r ARBA - v28 - '97 - p121+ [251-500]
World Art
p SFR - v21 - S '96 - p45 [51-250]
World Bank - *Bosnia and Herzegovina*
JEL - v34 - D '96 - p2060+ [51-250]
Private Sector Development in Low-Income Countries
JEL - v34 - S '96 - p1481 [51-250]

The World Bank Annual Report 1996
JEL - v35 - Mr '97 - p275 [51-250]
The World Bank Glossary: English-Spanish, Spanish-English
r JEL - v34 - D '96 - p2009+ [51-250]
The World Bank Participation Sourcebook
JEL - v34 - S '96 - p1481 [51-250]
The World Bank Research Program 1996
r JEL - v35 - Mr '97 - p275 [51-250]
World Biographical Index. 2nd Ed. Electronic Media Version
r ARBA - v28 - '97 - p16+ [251-500]
The World Book Encyclopedia. 1996 Ed., Vols. 1-22
cr ARBA - v28 - '97 - p25+ [501+]
cr BL - v93 - S 15 '96 - p278+ [501+]
The World Book Encyclopedia of People and Places. Vols. 1-6
cr BL - v92 - Ag '96 - p1918 [51-250]
cr CLW - v67 - D '96 - p59 [251-500]
The World Book Encyclopedia of Science. Vols. 1-8
r BL - v93 - Mr 15 '97 - p1262 [251-500]
r SciTech - v21 - Mr '97 - p3 [51-250]
The World Book Health and Medical Annual 1997
cr SciTech - v21 - Mr '97 - p48 [1-50]
World Book, Inc. - *The World Book Atlas*
cr CLW - v67 - D '96 - p59 [51-250]
The World Book Multimedia Encyclopedia. Electronic Media Version
yr BL - v93 - N 1 '96 - p532 [501+]
The World Book/Rush-Presbyterian-St. Luke's Medical Center Medical Encyclopedia. Updated and Expanded 7th Ed.
r ARBA - v28 - '97 - p608 [251-500]
The World Competitiveness Yearbook 1996
r Choice - v34 - Mr '97 - p1145 [51-250]
World Conference on Sea Turtle Conservation (1979: Washington, D.C.) - *Biology and Conservation of Sea Turtles. Rev. Ed.*
Choice - v34 - F '97 - p989+ [51-250]
Sci - v274 - O 25 '96 - p523 [1-50]
SciTech - v20 - S '96 - p20 [51-250]
World Congress of Sexology (12th: 1995: Yokohama-Shi, Japan) - *Sexuality and Human Bonding*
R&R Bk N - v11 - D '96 - p39 [51-250]
World Council of Churches - *The Theology of the Churches and the Jewish People*
Rel Ed - v91 - Fall '96 - p611 [1-50]
World Debt Tables. Electronic Media Version
r WorldV - v12 - O '96 - p24 [51-250]
World Debt Tables 1996. Vols. 1-2
JEL - v34 - D '96 - p2050 [51-250]
World Development Report 1996
JEL - v35 - Mr '97 - p293 [51-250]
World Directory of Business Information Libraries. 2nd Ed.
r ARBA - v28 - '97 - p247 [51-250]
World Directory of Country Environmental Studies. 3rd Ed.
r ARBA - v28 - '97 - p649 [51-250]
r BioSci - v47 - Mr '97 - p195+ [51-250]
World Directory of Human Rights Research and Training Institutions. 3rd Ed.
r ARBA - v28 - '97 - p232 [51-250]
World Directory of Non-Official Statistical Sources
r Choice - v34 - Mr '97 - p951 [51-250]
World Directory of Trade and Business Associations
r ARBA - v28 - '97 - p87 [251-500]
World Directory of Trade and Business Journals
r ARBA - v28 - '97 - p87+ [251-500]
r Choice - v34 - Mr '97 - p1145 [51-250]
World Disasters Report 1995
GJ - v162 - Jl '96 - p242 [51-250]
World Economic and Social Survey 1996
R&R Bk N - v11 - D '96 - p24 [51-250]
The World Economic Factbook 1996/97
r R&R Bk N - v12 - F '97 - p34 [51-250]
World Employment 1995
J Gov Info - v23 - S '96 - p672 [51-250]
M Lab R - v119 - Jl '96 - p53+ [501+]
World Energy and Nuclear Directory. 3rd Ed., Vols. 1-2
r RQ - v36 - Fall '96 - p144+ [501+]
World Engineering Industries and Automation 1994-1996
r ARBA - v28 - '97 - p97 [51-250]
The World Factbook 1996-97
r ARBA - v28 - '97 - p45 [51-250]
The World Factbook 1997-98
yr BL - v92 - Ag '96 - p1919 [51-250]
World Guide to Religious and Spiritual Organizations. 1st Ed.
r Choice - v34 - D '96 - p597 [51-250]

World Guide to Religious and Spiritual Organizations 1996
r ARBA - v28 - '97 - p538 [51-250]
World Guide to Trade Associations. 4th Ed.
r ARBA - v28 - '97 - p88 [51-250]
World Health Organization - *Integration of Health Care Delivery*
JEL - v35 - Mr '97 - p229 [51-250]
The World Health Report 1995
J Gov Info - v23 - S '96 - p690 [51-250]
World Industrial Robots 1995
Robotica - v14 - S '96 - p589+ [251-500]
World Industrial Robots 1996
SciTech - v21 - Mr '97 - p99 [51-250]
World Letter
p Sm Pr R - v28 - N '96 - p13 [51-250]
World Marketing Data and Statistics 1996 on CD-ROM. Electronic Media Version
r ARBA - v28 - '97 - p128+ [251-500]
World Media Handbook. 1995 Ed.
r J Gov Info - v24 - Ja '97 - p69+ [251-500]
World Military and Social Expenditures 1996
Workbook - v21 - Win '96 - p171+ [251-500]
World Mining Environment Congress (1st: 1995: New Delhi, India) - *Mining Environment*
SciTech - v20 - N '96 - p67 [51-250]
The World of Weather
c Books - v9 - S '95 - p26 [1-50]
World Population Monitoring 1993
R&R Bk N - v11 - N '96 - p24 [51-250]
World Press Photo 1995
LATBR - Mr 17 '96 - p11 [1-50]
World Radio TV Handbook. 1996 Ed.
r ARBA - v28 - '97 - p356 [251-500]
World Resources 1994-1995
r J Gov Info - v23 - Jl '96 - p534+ [501+]
World Resources 1996-1997
r BioSci - v46 - N '96 - p790 [1-50]
SB - v32 - O '96 - p198 [501+]
World Resources 1996-1997 Data Diskette. Electronic Media Version
r BioSci - v46 - N '96 - p790 [1-50]
World Retail Directory and Sourcebook. 2nd Ed.
r ARBA - v28 - '97 - p106 [251-500]
World Statistics in Brief 1976-
r ARBA - v28 - '97 - p327 [251-500]
World Stock Exchange Fact Book. 1st Ed.
r ARBA - v28 - '97 - p92 [251-500]
World Surfactants Congress (4th: 1996: Barcelona, Spain) - *World Surfactants Congress. Vols. 1-4*
SciTech - v21 - Mr '97 - p97 [251-500]
World Survey of Economic Freedom 1995-1996
JEL - v34 - D '96 - p2128 [51-250]
The World Today
p WorldV - v12 - O '96 - p22 [51-250]
World Trade Almanac 1996-1997
r ARBA - v28 - '97 - p100 [251-500]
World Trade Almanac and the Dictionary of International Trade. 1997 Ed. Electronic Media Version
r ARBA - v28 - '97 - p100+ [251-500]
World Travel Guide 1996/97
r Choice - v34 - F '97 - p951+ [251-500]
World War II (News Multimedia). Electronic Media Version
yr Sch Lib - v45 - F '97 - p30 [251-500]
World War One (YITM). Electronic Media Version
yr HT - v46 - D '96 - p48 [251-500]
World War Two (YITM). Electronic Media Version
yr HT - v46 - D '96 - p48 [251-500]
The World Wide Web Journal
p LJ - v121 - O 15 '96 - p95 [51-250]
World Wide Web Yellow Pages. 1997 Ed.
r CBR - v15 - Spr '97 - p8 [1-50]
Worldmark Encyclopedia of the Nations. 8th Ed., Vols. 1-5
yr BL - v92 - Ag '96 - p1919 [51-250]
The World's Women 1995
J Gov Info - v23 - S '96 - p681 [51-250]
Worldwide Government Directory 1996
r BL - v92 - Ag '96 - p1920 [51-250]
Worldwide Offshore Contractors and Equipment Directory 1996
r ARBA - v28 - '97 - p644 [51-250]
Worley, Leslie J - *Hippeis: The Cavalry of Ancient Greece*
CW - v89 - Jl '96 - p510+ [251-500]

Wormell, Christopher - *What I Eat (Illus. by Christopher Wormell)*
  c HB Guide - v8 - Spr '97 - p16 [51-250]
  c JB - v60 - D '96 - p244 [51-250]
  c PW - v243 - O 14 '96 - p82 [51-250]
  c SLJ - v42 - N '96 - p102 [51-250]
  Where I Live (Illus. by Christopher Wormell)
  c HB - v72 - N '96 - p730+ [51-250]
  c HB Guide - v8 - Spr '97 - p16 [51-250]
  c PW - v243 - O 14 '96 - p82 [51-250]
  c SLJ - v42 - N '96 - p102 [51-250]
Wormell, Mary - *Hilda Hen's Scary Night (Illus. by Mary Wormell)*
  c BL - v93 - S 15 '96 - p252 [51-250]
  c HB Guide - v8 - Spr '97 - p16 [51-250]
  c JB - v60 - Ag '96 - p145 [51-250]
  c Sch Lib - v44 - Ag '96 - p102 [51-250]
  c SLJ - v42 - O '96 - p110 [51-250]
Wormser, Richard - *American Childhoods*
  y BL - v93 - S 15 '96 - p230 [51-250]
  y CCB-B - v50 - O '96 - p81 [51-250]
  c HB Guide - v8 - Spr '97 - p97 [51-250]
  y SLJ - v42 - S '96 - p238 [51-250]
  y VOYA - v19 - D '96 - p294 [251-500]
  Growing up in The Great Depression
  y SE - v60 - S '96 - p303 [51-250]
Woronoff, Denis - *Histoire De L'Industrie En France*
  JMH - v68 - D '96 - p990+ [501+]
Woronoff, Jon - *The Japanese Economic Crisis*
  Econ J - v107 - Ja '97 - p237+ [501+]
Woronov, Mary - *Swimming Underground*
  LATBR - My 26 '96 - p4 [501+]
Worrall, David - *Radical Culture*
  RES - v48 - F '97 - p119+ [501+]
Worsham, Fabian - *The Harlot's Child*
  South HR - v30 - Sum '96 - p300+ [501+]
Worsley, Giles - *Classical Architecture in Britain*
  South CR - v29 - Fall '96 - p272+ [501+]
Worsley, Richard - *Human Freedom and the Logic of Evil*
  Rel St - v33 - Mr '97 - p133+ [51-250]
  Theol St - v58 - Mr '97 - p195+ [251-500]
Worsnip, Michael - *Priest and Partisan*
  Choice - v34 - F '97 - p1017 [51-250]
Worth, John E - *The Struggle for the Georgia Coast*
  CHR - v83 - Ja '97 - p133+ [251-500]
  HAHR - v76 - Ag '96 - p570 [251-500]
  JSH - v62 - N '96 - p789+ [251-500]
Worth, Steven - *Blood Oath*
  Esq - v126 - N '96 - p65 [1-50]
Worth, Valerie - *All the Small Poems and Fourteen More*
  y Kliatt - v30 - N '96 - p19+ [51-250]
Worthing, Mark William - *God, Creation, and Contemporary Physics*
  CC - v113 - S 25 '96 - p913 [51-250]
  Theol St - v57 - D '96 - p762+ [501+]
Worthington, Curtis - *Literary Charleston*
  AB - v98 - S 9 '96 - p752 [501+]
Worthington, Diane Rossen - *The California Cook*
  y Kliatt - v30 - N '96 - p30 [51-250]
Worthington, Ian - *Ventures into Greek History*
  Rel St Rev - v23 - Ap '97 - p170 [51-250]
  Voice into Text
  Choice - v34 - D '96 - p610 [51-250]
Worthington, Julian - *The New Encyclopedia of Home Repair. Rev. and Updated Ed.*
  r BWatch - v17 - N '96 - p8 [51-250]
Wortman, Richard S - *Scenarios of Power. Vol. 1*
  JMH - v68 - D '96 - p1033+ [501+]
Wortman, William A - *A Guide to Serial Bibliographies for Modern Literatures. 2nd Ed.*
  r ARBA - v28 - '97 - p407+ [51-250]
  r BL - v93 - N 15 '96 - p610+ [251-500]
  r Choice - v34 - Ja '97 - p777 [51-250]
  r R&R Bk N - v11 - D '96 - p61 [51-250]
Worton, Michael - *Michel Tournier*
  TLS - Ja 10 '97 - p22 [501+]
Wosh, Peter J - *Spreading the Word*
  CH - v66 - Mr '97 - p153+ [501+]
Wotherspoon, Garry - *Gay and Lesbian Perspectives III*
  Aust Bk R - Jl '96 - p16+ [501+]
Wou, Odoric Y K - *Mobilizing the Masses*
  APSR - v91 - Mr '97 - p225+ [501+]
  Pac A - v69 - Sum '96 - p259+ [501+]
Woy, James B - *Encyclopedia of Business Information Sources: Supplement. 10th Ed.*
  r ARBA - v28 - '97 - p88 [51-250]
Woy, Joann - *Accessible Gardening*
  BL - v93 - F 15 '97 - p987 [51-250]
  PW - v244 - Ja 27 '97 - p100 [51-250]

Woyczynski, Wojbor A - *Distributions in the Physical and Engineering Sciences. Vol. 1*
  SciTech - v21 - Mr '97 - p16 [51-250]
Wragg, Ted - *Longman's Parent's Guides: Key Stages 1-3, GCSE and Key Stage 4*
  TES - Ja 31 '97 - p8* [501+]
Wrangham, Richard W - *Demonic Males*
  BL - v93 - O 1 '96 - p293 [51-250]
  BW - v26 - N 17 '96 - p1+ [501+]
  KR - v64 - Ag 15 '96 - p1227 [251-500]
  LJ - v121 - O 15 '96 - p88 [51-250]
  Nat R - v48 - N 11 '96 - p52+ [501+]
  Nature - v384 - N 7 '96 - p35+ [501+]
  NH - v105 - N '96 - p12+ [501+]
  NYTBR - v101 - O 27 '96 - p18+ [501+]
  NYTLa - v146 - O 10 '96 - pC26 [501+]
  VLS - Win '96 - p12 [51-250]
  Wil Q - v20 - Aut '96 - p95+ [251-500]
  Wom R Bks - v14 - F '97 - p1+ [501+]
Wray, David - *Extending Literacy*
  TES - Mr 21 '97 - p18* [251-500]
Wray, Matt - *White Trash*
  CHE - v43 - Mr 14 '97 - pA17 [51-250]
Wray, Ralph D - *Fundamentals of Human Relations*
  R&R Bk N - v12 - F '97 - p45 [51-250]
Wrede, Patricia C - *Book of Enchantments*
  y HB Guide - v7 - Fall '96 - p306 [51-250]
  y JAAL - v40 - S '96 - p72+ [51-250]
  Dealing with Dragons. Audio Version
  c BL - v93 - Mr 15 '97 - p1253 [51-250]
  c Emerg Lib - v24 - Mr '97 - p25 [51-250]
  y HB - v73 - Ja '97 - p85+ [501+]
  c SLJ - v43 - Mr '97 - p142 [51-250]
Wren, Christopher S - *Hacks*
  NYTBR - v101 - S 1 '96 - p7 [501+]
  NYTLa - v146 - O 4 '96 - pC33 [501+]
Wren, Gary - *The PGA Manual of Golf*
  LJ - v121 - O 1 '96 - p54 [1-50]
Wrenn, Lynette Boney - *Cinderella of the New South*
  AHR - v102 - F '97 - p196 [251-500]
  JSH - v62 - N '96 - p807+ [251-500]
Wresch, William - *Disconnected: Haves and Have-Nots in the Information Age*
  Choice - v34 - My '97 - p1536 [51-250]
  PW - v243 - S 23 '96 - p72 [51-250]
Wressell, Pat - *Regional Library Development--Where Next?*
  LAR - v99 - Ja '97 - p50 [251-500]
Wright, Adrian - *Foreign Country*
  LJ - v122 - Ja '97 - p100 [51-250]
Wright, Anne E - *New England: Travel-Smart Trip Planner*
  r BL - v93 - S 15 '96 - p210 [1-50]
Wright, Austin - *Disciples*
  KR - v65 - Ap 1 '97 - p502 [251-500]
  PW - v244 - Ap 7 '97 - p75 [51-250]
Wright, Betty Ren - *Haunted Summer*
  c Ch BWatch - v6 - N '96 - p3 [1-50]
  c Emerg Lib - v24 - S '96 - p51 [51-250]
  c HB Guide - v7 - Fall '96 - p299 [51-250]
  c KR - v64 - My 1 '96 - p695 [1-50]
  Nothing but Trouble (Illus. by Jacqueline Rogers)
  c RT - v50 - N '96 - p257 [51-250]
Wright, Bill - *The Texas Kickapoo*
  Roundup M - v4 - Ap '97 - p22 [251-500]
Wright, Bruce, 1918- - *Black Justice in a White World*
  LJ - v121 - N 1 '96 - p74 [51-250]
Wright, Bruce E - *Theory in the Practice of the Nicaraguan Revolution*
  APSR - v90 - D '96 - p941+ [501+]
  HAHR - v76 - N '96 - p804+ [501+]
Wright, Bruce Lanier - *Gothic Horror Movies*
  SF Chr - v18 - O '96 - p81 [51-250]
Wright, Carol - *Museums and Galleries of New York*
  r LJ - v121 - N 15 '96 - p79 [51-250]
Wright, Charles - *Black Zodiac*
  LJ - v122 - Ap 15 '97 - p85+ [51-250]
  Nat - v264 - Ap 14 '97 - p27+ [501+]
  PW - v244 - F 24 '97 - p84 [51-250]
  VV - v42 - Ap 29 '97 - p55 [501+]
  Chickamauga
  Salm - Sum '96 - p195+ [501+]
  South R - v33 - Win '97 - p136+ [501+]
  WLT - v70 - Aut '96 - p967 [251-500]
  Country Music
  LJ - v122 - Ap 1 '97 - p95 [1-50]
  The World of the Ten Thousand Things
  LJ - v122 - Ap 1 '97 - p95 [1-50]
Wright, Daniel - *Dear Elvis*
  LATBR - v263 - S 29 '96 - p4 [501+]

**Wright, David, 1943- ** - *Computers*
  c HB Guide - v7 - Fall '96 - p349+ [51-250]
Wright, David F - *Martin Bucer: Reforming Church and Community*
  CH - v66 - Mr '97 - p114+ [501+]
  CHR - v82 - O '96 - p708+ [501+]
  Ren & Ref - v20 - Win '96 - p91+ [501+]
Wright, David H - *The Vatican Vergil*
  CW - v89 - Jl '96 - p497 [251-500]
Wright, David K - *Arthur Ashe: Breaking the Color Barrier in Tennis*
  y HB Guide - v8 - Spr '97 - p147 [51-250]
  c SLJ - v42 - O '96 - p142 [51-250]
  John Lennon: The Beatles and Beyond
  y HB Guide - v8 - Spr '97 - p161 [51-250]
  y SLJ - v42 - D '96 - p149 [51-250]
  y VOYA - v19 - F '97 - p355 [251-500]
  A Multicultural Portrait of the Vietnam War
  y HB Guide - v7 - Fall '96 - p381 [51-250]
Wright, Eric - *Buried in Stone*
  Arm Det - v29 - Sum '96 - p359+ [251-500]
  VQR - v72 - Aut '96 - p130* [51-250]
  Death of a Sunday Writer
  BL - v93 - S 15 '96 - p225 [51-250]
  NYTBR - v101 - O 13 '96 - p29 [51-250]
  Quill & Q - v62 - O '96 - p32 [51-250]
Wright, Erik Olin - *Class Counts*
  Choice - v34 - My '97 - p1586 [51-250]
Wright, Esmond - *The American Dream*
  Choice - v34 - S '96 - p201 [51-250]
  CR - v269 - S '96 - p161+ [251-500]
  TLS - Jl 7 '96 - p30 [51-250]
  An Empire for Liberty
  TLS - Jl 7 '96 - p30 [51-250]
  The Search for Liberty
  HRNB - v25 - Win '97 - p63 [251-500]
  J Am St - v30 - D '96 - p468+ [251-500]
  TLS - Jl 7 '96 - p30 [501+]
Wright, Frank - *Two Lands on One Soil*
  Choice - v34 - O '96 - p342 [51-250]
  HRNB - v25 - Win '97 - p67+ [51-250]
  R&R Bk N - v11 - N '96 - p15 [51-250]
Wright, Ian G - *Assessment of Factors Affecting Boiler Tube Lifetime in Waste-Fired Steam Generators*
  SciTech - v20 - D '96 - p73 [51-250]
Wright, Jeni - *Sensational Soups*
  CSM - v89 - D 13 '96 - p11 [51-250]
Wright, Jim - *Balance of Power*
  Rapport - v19 - 5 '96 - p44 [251-500]
  VQR - v72 - Aut '96 - p760+ [501+]
Wright, John F R - *Transcaucasian Boundaries*
  R&R Bk N - v11 - N '96 - p13 [51-250]
Wright, Jonathan V - *Natural Hormone Replacement for Women over 45*
  PW - v244 - Ap 21 '97 - p67+ [51-250]
Wright, Keith C - *Computer-Related Technologies in Library Operations*
  LR - v45 - 6 '96 - p62+ [501+]
Wright, Kenneth W - *Textbook of Ophthalmology*
  SciTech - v21 - Mr '97 - p61 [51-250]
Wright, Laura - *Sources of London English*
  r ARBA - v28 - '97 - p382+ [251-500]
Wright, Laurali - *Strangers among Us*
  BL - v93 - N 15 '96 - p575 [51-250]
  KR - v64 - O 1 '96 - p1431 [51-250]
  LATBR - F 16 '97 - p10 [51-250]
  LJ - v121 - D '96 - p151 [51-250]
  NYTBR - v102 - Ja 5 '97 - p20 [51-250]
  PW - v243 - S 30 '96 - p64 [51-250]
  Quill & Q - v62 - O '96 - p32 [51-250]
Wright, Lesley - *Corporate Abuse*
  Quill & Q - v63 - Ja '97 - p29 [51-250]
Wright, M R - *Cosmology in Antiquity*
  Rel St Rev - v23 - Ja '97 - p64 [51-250]
Wright, Marshall D - *Nineteenth Century Baseball*
  r ARBA - v28 - '97 - p297 [51-250]
  r Choice - v34 - Ja '97 - p777 [51-250]
  R&R Bk N - v11 - D '96 - p21 [51-250]
Wright, Mike - *What They Didn't Teach You about the Civil War*
  LJ - v121 - N 1 '96 - p91 [51-250]
  PW - v243 - N 25 '96 - p67 [51-250]
Wright, Moorhead - *Morality and International Relations*
  R&R Bk N - v11 - D '96 - p49 [51-250]
Wright, N T - *Jesus and the Victory of God*
  Am - v176 - Mr 8 '97 - p26+ [51-250]
  The Lord and His Prayer
  BL - v93 - F 15 '97 - p976 [501+]
  The New Testament and the People of God
  Bks & Cult - v1 - N '95 - p3+ [501+]

Wright, Nancy Means - *Mad Season*
  Arm Det - v30 - Win '97 - p91 [51-250]
  KR - v64 - S 15 '96 - p1359+ [51-250]
  PW - v243 - S 30 '96 - p65 [51-250]
Wright, Patrick - *The Village That Died for England*
  CR - v269 - D '96 - p333 [1-50]
Wright, R Gerald - *National Parks and Protected Areas*
  SciTech - v21 - Mr '97 - p70 [51-250]
Wright, R K McGregor - *No Place for Sovereignty*
  BL - v93 - S 15 '96 - p182 [51-250]
Wright, Richard - *Eight Men*
  NYTBR - v102 - F 2 '97 - p28 [1-50]
Wright, Richard A - *In Defense of Prisons*
  AAPSS-A - v548 - N '96 - p236+ [501+]
Wright, Rita P - *Gender and Archaeology*
  Choice - v34 - Ap '97 - p1380 [51-250]
  R&R Bk N - v12 - F '97 - p30 [51-250]
Wright, Robert - *The Moral Animal*
  NS & S - v9 - Ap 26 '96 - p35 [1-50]
  VV - v42 - Ja 7 '97 - p42 [51-250]
Wright, Roberta Hughes - *Lay Down Body*
  NGSQ - v84 - D '96 - p307 [251-500]
Wright, Roger - *Latin and the Romance Languages in the Early Middle Ages*
  AB - v98 - Ag 19 '96 - p570+ [501+]
Wright, Russell O - *A Twentieth-Century History of United States Population*
  r R&R Bk N - v12 - F '97 - p34 [51-250]
Wright, Sally S - *Publish and Perish*
  NYTBR - v102 - Mr 30 '97 - p23 [51-250]
Wright, Scott - *Japan Encountered*
  LJ - v121 - S 15 '96 - p80 [51-250]
Wright, Stephen Caldwell - *On Gwendolyn Brooks*
  AL - v68 - D '96 - p881 [1-50]
Wright, Stephen J - *Primal-Dual Interior-Point Methods*
  SciTech - v21 - Mr '97 - p71 [51-250]
Wright, Susan - *The Tempest*
  y Kliatt - v31 - My '97 - p16 [51-250]
Wright, Susan, 1939- - *Molecular Politics*
  T&C - v37 - Ap '96 - p397+ [501+]
Wright, Susan Kimmel - *Dead Letters*
  c SLJ - v42 - S '96 - p208 [51-250]
Wright, Terence - *Elizabeth Gaskell: We Are Not Angels*
  Nine-C Lit - v51 - S '96 - p279 [1-50]
Wright, Timothy M - *Implant Wear*
  SciTech - v20 - S '96 - p39 [51-250]
Wright, Tom - *The Original Jesus*
  BL - v93 - Ja '97 - p784 [51-250]
  CC - v114 - My 7 '97 - p457 [51-250]
  LJ - v122 - F 1 '97 - p86 [51-250]
  What Saint Paul Really Said
  TLS - Mr 28 '97 - p3+ [501+]
Wright, Tony - *Socialisms: Old and New*
  Obs - S 29 '96 - p15* [501+]
  Why Vote Labour?
  Econ - v342 - Mr 22 '97 - p106 [501+]
  NS - v126 - Mr 27 '97 - p51+ [501+]
  TES - F 28 '97 - p8* [501+]
  TLS - F 21 '97 - p27+ [501+]
Wright, Wendy M - *A Retreat with Francis De Sales, Jane De Chantal and Aelred of Rievaulx*
  CLW - v67 - Mr '97 - p29 [251-500]
Wright, Wilbur - *Miracle at Kitty Hawk*
  LJ - v121 - O 1 '96 - p132 [1-50]
Wright, William E - *Austria 1938-1988*
  Historian - v59 - Fall '96 - p206+ [501+]
Wright-Frierson, Virginia - *A Desert Scrapbook (Illus. by Virginia Wright-Frierson)*
  c BL - v92 - Ag '96 - p1899 [51-250]
  c HB Guide - v7 - Fall '96 - p339 [51-250]
  c KR - v64 - My 1 '96 - p696 [51-250]
Wrightson, Patricia - *Shadows of Time*
  y Sch Lib - v44 - Ag '96 - p121 [51-250]
Wrigley, Chris - *A History of British Industrial Relations 1939-1979*
  Choice - v34 - O '96 - p334 [51-250]
  JEL - v34 - D '96 - p2102 [51-250]
  R&R Bk N - v11 - N '96 - p33 [51-250]
Wrigley, Christopher - *Kingship and State*
  Choice - v34 - D '96 - p664+ [51-250]
Wrigley, Owen - *The Politics of Deafness*
  R&R Bk N - v11 - N '96 - p44 [51-250]
Wrigley, Richard - *The Origins of French Art Criticism*
  JAAC - v54 - Fall '96 - p383+ [51-250]
Wrigley, Robert - *In the Bank of Beautiful Sins*
  Poet - v169 - D '96 - p163+ [501+]
  South R - v33 - Win '97 - p136+ [501+]
Writer's Digest - *Writer's Encyclopedia. 3rd Ed.*
  r ARBA - v28 - '97 - p346+ [51-250]

Writers Harvest 2
  BL - v93 - N 1 '96 - p475 [51-250]
  BW - v26 - D 1 '96 - p12 [51-250]
  KR - v64 - O 1 '96 - p1417 [251-500]
  PW - v243 - S 30 '96 - p78 [51-250]
Writer's Market 1997: The Electronic Edition. Electronic Media Version
  r LJ - v121 - N 15 '96 - p95+ [501+]
Writes of Passage: The Literary Journal for Teenagers
  yp SLJ - v42 - N '96 - p36 [1-50]
  yp Sm Pr R - v28 - D '96 - p16 [51-250]
The Writing Path 2
  Bloom Rev - v17 - Ja '97 - p17 [51-250]
Writings on American History 1902-1961
  r ASInt - v34 - O '96 - p17 [51-250]
Writings on American History: A Subject Bibliography of Articles 1962-1990
  r ASInt - v34 - O '96 - p17 [51-250]
Wrobel, Murray - *Elsevier's Dictionary of Plant Names in Latin, English, French, German, and Italian*
  r ARBA - v28 - '97 - p579+ [51-250]
Wroblewski, Donald - *Heat Transfer in Turbulent Flows*
  SciTech - v21 - Mr '97 - p22 [51-250]
Wroe, Ann - *A Fool and His Money*
  HRNB - v25 - Win '97 - p80+ [251-500]
Wroth, Mary, Lady - *The First Part of the Countess of Montgomery's Urania*
  Six Ct J - v27 - Fall '96 - p878+ [501+]
Wu, Duncan - *Romanticism: A Critical Reader*
  RES - v47 - Ag '96 - p424+ [501+]
  Romanticism: An Anthology
  RES - v47 - Ag '96 - p424+ [501+]
  Six Contemporary Dramatists
  RES - v48 - F '97 - p135+ [501+]
  Wordsworth's Reading 1800-1815
  Choice - v34 - F '97 - p970 [51-250]
  r Nine-C Lit - v51 - Mr '97 - p568 [51-250]
  TLS - S 6 '96 - p33 [251-500]
Wu, Hai-Min - *Huang Se De You Huo*
  BL - v93 - My 1 '97 - p1484 [1-50]
Wu, Harry - *Troublemaker: One Man's Crusade against China's Cruelty*
  BW - v26 - D 15 '96 - p3+ [501+]
  Econ - v341 - D 7 '96 - p7* [501+]
  KR - v64 - S 1 '96 - p1313 [251-500]
  LATBR - N 17 '96 - p3 [501+]
  LJ - v121 - O 1 '96 - p106+ [51-250]
  New R - v216 - Mr 10 '97 - p45+ [501+]
  NYRB - v43 - D 19 '96 - p50+ [501+]
  NYTBR - v101 - N 10 '96 - p24 [501+]
  PW - v243 - S 2 '96 - p100 [51-250]
  TLS - N 22 '96 - p27 [501+]
Wu, Jaushieh Joseph - *Taiwan's Democratization*
  AAPSS-A - v549 - Ja '97 - p191+ [501+]
Wu, Jiang - *Shi Nian De Lu*
  BL - v93 - N 1 '96 - p484 [1-50]
Wu, Norbert - *A City under the Sea*
  c Ch BWatch - v6 - My '96 - p4 [51-250]
  c HB Guide - v7 - Fall '96 - p339+ [51-250]
  c SB - v33 - Ja '97 - p25 [251-500]
Wu, Priscilla - *The Abacus Contest (Illus. by Hsiao-Chun Li)*
  c HB Guide - v7 - Fall '96 - p299 [51-250]
Wu, Yanrui - *Productive Performance in Chinese Enterprises*
  JEL - v34 - D '96 - p2127 [51-250]
Wu, Yenna - *The Lioness Roars*
  Choice - v34 - S '96 - p121 [51-250]
Wu Hung - *Monumentality in Early Chinese Art and Architecture*
  Choice - v34 - O '96 - p270 [51-250]
  Rel St Rev - v23 - Ap '97 - p204 [51-250]
  TLS - S 13 '96 - p18+ [501+]
Wuketits, Franz M - *Die Entdeckung Des Verhaltens*
  Isis - v87 - S '96 - p571+ [501+]
Wukovits, John F - *Barry Sanders*
  c HB Guide - v7 - Fall '96 - p359 [1-50]
  Jesse James
  c Ch BWatch - v7 - F '97 - p7 [1-50]
  c Ch BWatch - v7 - F '97 - p7 [1-50]
Wulf, Jessica - *Hunter's Bride*
  PW - v243 - O 21 '96 - p78 [51-250]
Wulffson, Don L - *Future Fright*
  y SLJ - v43 - Mr '97 - p194 [51-250]
  The Kid Who Invented the Popsicle and Other Surprising Stories about Inventions
  c BL - v93 - F 15 '97 - p1023 [51-250]
  c KR - v65 - Ja 15 '97 - p147 [51-250]
  c SLJ - v43 - Mr '97 - p212 [51-250]

Wullimann, Mario F - *Neuroanatomy of the Zebrafish Brain*
  r SciTech - v20 - S '96 - p20 [51-250]
Wullschlager, Jackie - *Inventing Wonderland*
  HB - v72 - N '96 - p763 [51-250]
Wunder, John R - *Constitutionalism and Native Americans 1903-1968*
  R&R Bk N - v12 - F '97 - p65 [51-250]
  The Indian Bill of Rights 1968
  R&R Bk N - v12 - F '97 - p65 [51-250]
  Law and the Great Plains
  WHQ - v28 - Spr '97 - p89+ [251-500]
  Native American Cultural and Religious Freedoms
  R&R Bk N - v12 - F '97 - p65 [51-250]
  Native American Law and Colonialism before 1776 to 1903
  R&R Bk N - v12 - F '97 - p65 [51-250]
  Native American Sovereignty
  R&R Bk N - v12 - F '97 - p65 [51-250]
  Recent Legal Issues for American Indians 1968 to the Present
  R&R Bk N - v12 - F '97 - p65 [51-250]
Wunderli, Stephen - *The Heartbeat of Halftime*
  y BL - v93 - O 1 '96 - p344 [51-250]
  y CCB-B - v50 - S '96 - p38 [51-250]
  c HB Guide - v7 - Fall '96 - p299 [51-250]
  y SLJ - v42 - N '96 - p126+ [51-250]
  y VOYA - v19 - O '96 - p214 [251-500]
Wunderlich, Gene - *Agricultural Landownership in Transitional Economies*
  JEL - v34 - S '96 - p1495+ [51-250]
Wunderlich, Gooloo S - *Nursing Staff in Hospitals and Nursing Homes*
  Choice - v34 - Ja '97 - p828 [51-250]
  SciTech - v20 - S '96 - p43 [51-250]
Wunderman, Lester - *Being Direct*
  BL - v93 - Ja '97 - p795 [51-250]
  KR - v64 - D 1 '96 - p1727+ [251-500]
  LJ - v122 - Ja '97 - p117 [51-250]
  PW - v243 - N 25 '96 - p63 [51-250]
Wunsch, Carl - *The Ocean Circulation Inverse Problem*
  Sci - v275 - F 21 '97 - p1076 [501+]
Wurbs, Ralph Allen - *Modeling and Analysis of Reservoir System Operations*
  SciTech - v20 - S '96 - p51 [51-250]
Wurgau, Rainer - *Der Scheidungsprozess Von Gottfried Kellers Mutter*
  MLR - v92 - Ap '97 - p512+ [501+]
Wurlitzer, Rudolph - *Nog*
  LJ - v121 - D '96 - p154 [1-50]
Wurth, Shirley - *Books for You. 11th Ed.*
  yr RQ - v36 - Win '96 - p220 [51-250]
Wurts, Janny - *That Way Lies Camelot*
  y VOYA - v19 - O '96 - p222 [51-250]
  Warhost of Vastmark
  Books - v9 - S '95 - p24 [1-50]
Wurzner, Hans - *Deutsche Literatur Im Exil In Den Niederlanden 1933-1940*
  MLR - v91 - O '96 - p1051+ [251-500]
Wuthnow, Robert - *Christianity and Civil Society*
  Bks & Cult - v2 - N '96 - p4 [51-250]
  Learning to Care
  Soc Ser R - v71 - Mr '97 - p150+ [501+]
  Poor Richard's Principle
  Bks & Cult - v2 - N '96 - p4 [1-50]
  BL - v93 - S 1 '96 - p47 [51-250]
  BW - v27 - Ja 19 '97 - p13 [51-250]
  Choice - v34 - Mr '97 - p1248 [51-250]
  ChrPhil - v8 - S 5 '96 - p46 [51-250]
  Comw - v123 - D 20 '96 - p16+ [501+]
  JEL - v35 - Mr '97 - p306 [51-250]
  LJ - v121 - N 1 '96 - p76 [51-250]
  NYTBR - v102 - Ja 5 '97 - p24 [501+]
  Producing the Sacred
  J Ch St - v38 - Aut '96 - p901 [251-500]
  Rethinking Materialism
  CS - v26 - Ja '97 - p93+ [501+]
Wuthrich, Lucas Heinrich - *Das Druckgraphische Werk Von Matthaeus Merian Der Altere. Vol. 3*
  BM - v138 - N '96 - p758 [501+]
Wyatt, Gary - *Spirit Faces*
  Am Craft - v56 - D '96 - p33 [51-250]
Wyatt, John - *Wordsworth and the Geologists*
  Nature - v384 - D 19 '96 - p617+ [501+]
  TLS - My 24 '96 - p7 [501+]
Wyatt, Judith - *Work Abuse*
  BL - v93 - D 1 '96 - p628 [51-250]
Wyatt, Robert E - *Dynamics of Molecules and Chemical Reactions*
  Choice - v34 - Mr '97 - p1187+ [51-250]
  SciTech - v20 - N '96 - p23 [51-250]

Wyckoff, William - *The Mountainous West*
   AAAGA - v87 - Mr '97 - p194+ [501+]
Wydra, Nancilee - *Feng Shui in the Garden*
   PW - v244 - My 5 '97 - p205 [51-250]
   Feng Shui: The Book of Cures
   BWatch - v17 - N '96 - p4 [51-250]
Wyeth, John, Jr. - *Diana Ross*
   y HB Guide - v7 - Fall '96 - p375+ [51-250]
Wyeth, Sharon Dennis - *Always My Dad*
   c Learning - v25 - Mr '97 - p54 [1-50]
   Ginger Brown: The Nobody Boy (Illus. by Cornelius Van Wright)
   c BL - v93 - My 1 '97 - p1505 [51-250]
   Ginger Brown: Too Many Houses (Illus. by Cornelius Van Wright)
   c CLW - v67 - Mr '97 - p52+ [51-250]
   c HB Guide - v7 - Fall '96 - p288 [51-250]
   The Human Shark
   y Ch BWatch - v6 - S '96 - p3 [1-50]
   In Deep Water
   y Ch BWatch - v6 - S '96 - p3 [1-50]
   The Winning Stroke
   c BL - v93 - S 1 '96 - p124+ [51-250]
   y Ch BWatch - v6 - S '96 - p3 [1-50]
Wyke-Smith, E A - *The Marvellous Land of Snergs*
   BW - v27 - Ja 26 '97 - p6 [51-250]
Wykham, Helen - *Ribstone Pippins*
   KR - v65 - F 15 '97 - p255+ [251-500]
   PW - v244 - F 17 '97 - p211 [51 250]
Wylen, Stephen M - *The Jews in the Time of Jesus*
   CLW - v67 - D '96 - p39 [251-500]
   Rel St Rev - v23 - Ja '97 - p87 [51-250]
Wylie, Betty Jane - *The Best Is Yet to Come*
   Quill & Q - v63 - Ja '97 - p27 [51-250]
   The Solo Chef
   Quill & Q - v63 - Mr '97 - p21 [51-250]
Wylie, David - *New Refrigerants for Air Conditioning and Refrigeration Systems*
   SciTech - v21 - Mr '97 - p96 [51-250]
Wylie, Laurence - *Les Francais. 2nd Ed.*
   FR - v70 - F '97 - p505+ [501+]
Wylie, Philip - *Generation of Vipers*
   LJ - v121 - D '96 - p154 [51-250]
Wyllie, Elaine - *The Treatment of Epilepsy. 2nd Ed.*
   r SciTech - v21 - Mr '97 - p52 [51-250]
Wyllie, Stephen - *A Flea in the Ear (Illus. by Ken Brown)*
   c HB Guide - v7 - Fall '96 - p282 [51-250]
   c RT - v50 - My '97 - p685 [51-250]
Wyman, David S - *The World Reacts to the Holocaust*
   r Choice - v34 - My '97 - p1567 [51-250]
   TLS - Mr 7 '97 - p4+ [501+]
Wymbs, Norman - *Ronald Reagan's Crusade*
   BW - v26 - S 8 '96 - p4+ [251-500]
Wyndham, Francis - *Bruce Chatwin: Photographs and Notebooks*
   Obs - F 9 '97 - p17* [51-250]
Wyndham, John - *The Day of the Triffids (West). Audio Version*
   LJ - v121 - O 15 '96 - p101 [51-250]
Wynn, Charles M - *The Five Biggest Ideas in Science*
   Choice - v34 - My '97 - p1519 [51-250]
   y LJ - v122 - Mr 15 '97 - p86 [51-250]
   New Sci - v153 - Ja 18 '97 - p38 [1-50]
   PW - v243 - D 30 '96 - p52 [51-250]
Wynne-Davies, Marion - *Women and Arthurian Literature*
   Choice - v34 - N '96 - p462 [51-250]
   TLS - S 6 '96 - p33 [251-500]
Wynne-Jones, Tim - *The Hunchback of Notre Dame (Illus. by Bill Slavin)*
   y BIC - v25 - O '96 - p32 [51-250]
   c Ch Bk News - v19 - Sum '96 - p29 [51-250]
   c Quill & Q - v62 - O '96 - p43+ [251-500]
   The Maestro
   y BL - v93 - Ja '97 - p765 [51-250]
   y BL - v93 - D 15 '96 - p724 [51-250]
   y CCB-B - v50 - O '96 - p81 [51-250]
   y HB Guide - v8 - Spr '97 - p85 [51-250]
   y KR - v64 - Ag 15 '96 - p1245 [51-250]
   y Par Ch - v21 - Mr '97 - p12 [1-50]
   c PW - v243 - O 14 '96 - p84+ [51-250]
   y SLJ - v43 - Ja '97 - p116+ [51-250]
   Mouse in the Manger (Illus. by Elaine Blier)
   c BIC - v25 - D '96 - p33+ [501+]
   Some of the Kinder Planets
   c LA - v73 - O '96 - p432 [51-250]
   c PW - v243 - N 25 '96 - p78 [1-50]
   c RT - v50 - O '96 - p155 [51-250]
Wynton, Marsalis - *Marsalis on Music*
   Bl S - v26 - Sum '96 - p68 [1-50]
Wynveen, Tim - *Angel Falls*
   Quill & Q - v63 - F '97 - p49 [251-500]

Wyrwicka, Wanda - *Imitation in Human and Animal Behavior*
   Choice - v34 - O '96 - p305 [51-250]
Wyse, Lois - *Friend to Friend*
   PW - v244 - Mr 17 '97 - p63 [51-250]
Wyss, Edith - *The Myth of Apollo and Marsyas in the Art of the Italian Renaissance*
   Six Ct J - v27 - Win '96 - p1211+ [501+]
Wyss, Thelma Hatch - *A Stranger Here*
   y Kliatt - v30 - S '96 - p22 [51-250]

X Y Z

Xenophon - *Hellenika II.3.11-IV.2.8 (Krentz)*
  Rel St Rev - v23 - Ja '97 - p61+ [51-250]
Xenotransplantation: Science, Ethics, and Public Policy
  SciTech - v20 - N '96 - p36 [51-250]
Xerces Society - *Butterfly Gardening*
  LJ - v121 - D '96 - p67 [1-50]
Xiang, Lanxin - *Recasting the Imperial Far East*
  AHR - v101 - O '96 - p1315 [501+]
  Ch Rev Int - v3 - Fall '96 - p575+ [501+]
Xiao, Jianguo - *Xiang Gang Gu Dai Shi*
  BL - v93 - N 1 '96 - p484 [1-50]
Xiaomeng, Liu - *Zhongguo Zhiqing Shidian*
  r Ch Rev Int - v4 - Spr '97 - p207+ [501+]
Xin, Shi - *Xue Shang*
  BL - v93 - N 1 '96 - p484 [1-50]
Xin, Y L - *Geometry of Harmonic Maps*
  SciTech - v20 - S '96 - p12 [51-250]
Xing Bie Bei Ju
  BL - v93 - N 1 '96 - p484 [1-50]
Xu, Bing - *Zhan: Tai Wan De Zui Hou Shi Ke*
  BL - v93 - N 1 '96 - p484 [1-50]
Xuan, Vu - *Co Ba Tra*
  BL - v93 - My 15 '97 - p1568 [1-50]
  Que Huong Yen Dau
  BL - v93 - My 15 '97 - p1568 [1-50]
Yaakov, Juliette - *Fiction Catalog. 13th Ed.*
  r ARBA - v28 - '97 - p432 [51-250]
  r RQ - v36 - Win '96 - p209 [51-250]
Yablonsky, Lewis - *Gangsters: Fifty Years of Madness, Drugs, and Death on the Streets of America*
  BL - v93 - Mr 1 '97 - p1095+ [51-250]
Yablonsky, Linda - *The Story of Junk*
  BL - v93 - Mr 15 '97 - p1228 [51-250]
  Ent W - Ap 18 '97 - p63 [51-250]
  KR - v65 - F 1 '97 - p170 [251-500]
  NYTLa - v146 - Ap 8 '97 - pC13 [501+]
  PW - v244 - F 3 '97 - p92 [51-250]
Yaccarino, Dan - *If I Had a Robot (Illus. by Dan Yaccarino)*
  c CBRS - v25 - Win '97 - p66+ [51-250]
  c CCB-B - v50 - S '96 - p38+ [51-250]
  c HB Guide - v8 - Spr '97 - p54 [51-250]
  c SLJ - v42 - S '96 - p195 [51-250]
  c Time - v148 - D 9 '96 - p78 [51-250]
Yack, Bernard - *Liberalism without Illusions*
  APSR - v90 - S '96 - p642 [501+]
  R&R Bk N - v11 - N '96 - p48 [51-250]
  TLS - My 24 '96 - p29 [501+]
Yaffee, Steven L - *Ecosystem Management in the United States*
  Choice - v34 - F '97 - p987 [51-250]
  SciTech - v20 - N '96 - p25 [51-250]
Yager, Jan - *Friendshifts: The Power of Friendship and How It Shapes Our Lives*
  LJ - v121 - N 15 '96 - p76 [51-250]
  PW - v243 - N 4 '96 - p58 [51-250]
Yager, Robert E - *Science/Technology/Society as Reform in Science Education*
  R&R Bk N - v12 - F '97 - p92 [51-250]
  SciTech - v20 - N '96 - p4 [51-250]
Yagyu, Genichiro - *The Soles of Your Feet (Illus. by Genichiro Yagyu)*
  c KR - v65 - Mr 15 '97 - p470 [51-250]
  c PW - v244 - Mr 10 '97 - p68 [51-250]
Yahnke, Robert E - *Aging in Literature*
  r RQ - v36 - Win '96 - p216 [51-250]
Yahp, Beth - *Nothing Interesting about Cross Street*
  y Aust Bk R - Je '96 - p62 [501+]
  y Magpies - v11 - Jl '96 - p36 [51-250]
Yahuda, Michael - *Hong Kong: China's Challenge*
  FEER - v159 - D 12 '96 - p52+ [501+]

Yai, Olabiyi Babalola - *Yoruba-English/English-Yoruba Concise Dictionary*
  r ARBA - v28 - '97 - p404 [51-250]
Yakobson, Helen - *Crossing Borders*
  Slav R - v55 - Sum '96 - p488 [251-500]
Yakovlev, Alexander - *The Fate of Marxism in Russia*
  TranslRevS - v1 - My '95 - p9 [51-250]
The Yale Guide to Children's Nutrition
  r LJ - v122 - F 15 '97 - p129 [51-250]
  PW - v244 - F 3 '97 - p103 [51-250]
Yalfani, Mehri - *Parastoo: Stories and Poems*
  BIC - v26 - F '97 - p11+ [501+]
Yalichev, Serge - *Mercenaries of the Ancient World*
  HT - v46 - O '96 - p55 [1-50]
Yalom, Irvin D - *Lying on the Couch*
  AJPsych - v153 - D '96 - p1642 [501+]
  BW - v26 - S 8 '96 - p7 [501+]
  NYTBR - v101 - S 22 '96 - p25 [51-250]
  Rapport - v19 - 6 '96 - p24 [251-500]
Yalom, Marilyn - *A History of the Breast*
  BL - v93 - F 1 '97 - p912 [51-250]
  BW - v27 - F 9 '97 - p1+ [501+]
  KR - v64 - D 15 '96 - p1792 [251-500]
  LATBR - F 16 '97 - p12 [501+]
  LJ - v122 - F 15 '97 - p147 [51-250]
  NYTBR - v102 - F 23 '97 - p4 [501+]
  PW - v243 - D 16 '96 - p47+ [51-250]
  Spec - v278 - Ap 5 '97 - p39 [501+]
  VLS - Spr '97 - p14+ [501+]
Yalpani, Manssur - *Biomedical Functions and Biotechnology of Natural and Artificial Polymers*
  SB - v33 - Mr '97 - p41 [51-250]
Yamaguchi, Hiroichi - *Understanding the Developing World*
  JEL - v35 - Mr '97 - p275+ [51-250]
Yamaguchi, Yoji - *Face of a Stranger*
  y Kliatt - v30 - S '96 - p15 [51-250]
Yamahata, Yosuke - *Nagasaki Journey*
  Afterimage - v23 - Sum '96 - p8+ [501+]
Yamamoto, Georgia - *Zen Zulu*
  Tric - v6 - Fall '96 - p142 [1-50]
Yamamoto, Sam - *Global Exporting from the U.S.A.*
  JEL - v34 - D '96 - p2088 [51-250]
Yamamoto, Tadashi - *Emerging Civil Society in the Asia Pacific Community*
  R&R Bk N - v11 - D '96 - p38 [51-250]
Yamanaka, Lois-Ann - *Blu's Hanging*
  KR - v65 - F 1 '97 - p171 [251-500]
  PW - v244 - F 24 '97 - p62 [51-250]
  Trib Bks - Ap 13 '97 - p1+ [501+]
  Wild Meat and the Bully Burgers
  Obs - D 8 '96 - p17* [51-250]
  PW - v244 - Mr 3 '97 - p72 [1-50]
Yamane, Linda - *Weaving a California Tradition (Illus. by Dugan Aguilar)*
  c BL - v93 - Ja '97 - p855 [251-500]
  c HB Guide - v8 - Spr '97 - p140 [51-250]
  c SLJ - v43 - F '97 - p99 [51-250]
Yamazaki, Moriichi - *A Pada Index and Reverse Pada Index to Early Jain Canons*
  r ARBA - v28 - '97 - p546 [51-250]
Yamazawa, Ippei - *Evolution of Asia-Pacific Economies*
  Econ J - v107 - Ja '97 - p272+ [51-250]
Yamba, C Bawa - *Permanent Pilgrims*
  Choice - v34 - N '96 - p502 [51-250]
Yamin, Rebecca - *Landscape Archaeology*
  R&R Bk N - v11 - D '96 - p6 [51-250]
Yan, Jiaqi - *Turbulent Decade*
  Choice - v34 - Ja '97 - p853+ [51-250]
  HRNB - v25 - Win '97 - p86+ [501+]

Yan, Yunxiang - *The Flow of Gifts*
  Am Ethnol - v23 - N '96 - p910+ [501+]
  Ch Rev Int - v4 - Spr '97 - p283+ [501+]
Yanagisawa, Eiji - *Color Atlas of Diagnostic Endoscopy in Otorhinolaryngology*
  r SciTech - v21 - Mr '97 - p62 [51-250]
Yancey, Diane - *Life in War-Torn Bosnia*
  y HB Guide - v7 - Fall '96 - p381 [51-250]
Yandell, Keith E - *The Epistemology of Religious Experience*
  JAAR - v64 - Fall '96 - p651+ [501+]
Yandrick, Rudy M - *Behavioral Risk Management*
  SciTech - v20 - N '96 - p48 [51-250]
Yaney, George - *The World of the Manager*
  AHR - v101 - O '96 - p1236 [501+]
Yanez, Maria-Paz - *La Historia: Inagotable Tematica Novelesca*
  Hisp - v79 - D '96 - p798+ [501+]
Yang, Belle - *Baba: A Return to China upon My Father's Shoulders*
  y Kliatt - v30 - S '96 - p28 [51-250]
  The Odyssey of a Manchurian
  KR - v64 - S 1 '96 - p1314 [251-500]
Yang, Dali L - *Calamity and Reform in China*
  Choice - v34 - D '96 - p684 [51-250]
  JEL - v34 - D '96 - p2125 [51-250]
Yang, Du - *Da Ni Zhuan*
  BL - v93 - N 1 '96 - p484 [1-50]
Yang, Haiqun - *Banking and Financial Control in Reforming Planned Economies*
  JEL - v34 - D '96 - p2127 [51-250]
Yang, Hsiung - *The Canon of Supreme Mystery*
  TranslRevS - v1 - My '95 - p16 [51-250]
Yang, Jeff - *Eastern Standard Time*
  y BL - v93 - My 1 '97 - p1466 [51-250]
  PW - v244 - Ap 28 '97 - p67 [51-250]
Yang, John - *Over the Door*
  NYTBR - v101 - S 8 '96 - p22 [51-250]
Yang, Jwing-Ming - *Arthritis: The Chinese Way of Healing and Prevention*
  BWatch - v17 - D '96 - p3 [51-250]
  The Essence of Shaolin White Crane
  BWatch - v17 - N '96 - p3 [51-250]
  Tai Chi Chuan Martial Applications
  BWatch - v18 - F '97 - p9 [1-50]
  Tai Chi Theory and Martial Power
  BWatch - v18 - F '97 - p9+ [1-50]
Yang, Mayfair Mei-Hui - *Gifts, Favors, and Banquets*
  Am Ethnol - v23 - N '96 - p910+ [501+]
Yang, Mu - *Chinese Musical Instruments*
  Ch Rev Int - v3 - Fall '96 - p579+ [501+]
Yang, Rae - *Spider Eaters*
  y BL - v93 - Ap 1 '97 - p1279 [51-250]
  KR - v65 - F 15 '97 - p291+ [251-500]
  LJ - v122 - Ap 15 '97 - p90+ [51-250]
  PW - v244 - Mr 3 '97 - p55 [51-250]
Yang, William - *Sadness*
  Aust Bk R - D '96 - p24 [501+]
Yannella, Philip R - *The Other Carl Sandburg*
  Bloom Rev - v17 - Ja '97 - p12 [51-250]
  Choice - v34 - Ap '97 - p1342 [51-250]
  LJ - v121 - N 1 '96 - p68 [51-250]
  NYTBR - v101 - O 27 '96 - p33 [501+]
Yannuzzi, Della A - *Zora Neale Hurston: Southern Storyteller*
  y BL - v93 - S 1 '96 - p116+ [51-250]
  c HB Guide - v7 - Fall '96 - p373 [51-250]
Yansane, Aguibou Y - *Development Strategies in Africa*
  R&R Bk N - v11 - D '96 - p26 [51-250]
Yao, Hsin-Chung - *Confucianism and Christianity*
  Choice - v34 - S '96 - p147 [51-250]

Yap, Tieng K - *High Performance Computational Methods for Biological Sequence Analysis*
SciTech - v20 - N '96 - p34 [51-250]
Yapi Kredi Economic Review
p   JEL - v35 - Mr '97 - p310+ [51-250]
Yapko, Michael D - *Breaking the Patterns of Depression*
PW - v244 - Ja 6 '97 - p70+ [51-250]
Essentials of Hypnosis
AJCH - v38 - Ap '96 - p300 [501+]
Yapp, M E - *The Near East since the First World War*
MEJ - v51 - Spr '97 - p312 [51-250]
Yaravintelimath, C R - *New Perspectives in Indian Literature in English*
WLT - v70 - Sum '96 - p767 [251-500]
Yarbro, Chelsea Quinn - *Mansions of Darkness*
BL - v92 - Ag '96 - p1884 [51-250]
PW - v243 - Jl 22 '96 - p230 [51-250]
Rapport - v19 - 6 '96 - p20 [251-500]
Writ in Blood
KR - v65 - My 1 '97 - p686 [51-250]
Yarbro-Bejarano, Yvonne - *Feminism and the Honor Plays of Lope De Vega*
MLR - v91 - Jl '96 - p765+ [501+]
Yarbrough, Camille - *The Little Tree Growin' in the Shade (Illus. by Tyrone Geter)*
c   HB - v72 - S '96 - p590 [51-250]
c   HB Guide - v7 - Fall '96 - p288 [51-250]
c   SLJ - v42 - Ag '96 - p148 [51-250]
Yarbrough, Tinsley E - *Judicial Enigma*
AHR - v101 - D '96 - p1628+ [501+]
Yardley, Herbert O - *The Education of a Poker Player*
Obs - D 1 '96 - p18* [51-250]
Yarnell, Judith - *Transformations of Circe*
Folkl - v107 - '96 - p117+ [501+]
Yarnold, Barbara M - *Abortion Politics in the Federal Courts*
APSR - v90 - S '96 - p664+ [501+]
Yaroslavksy, Leonid - *Fundamentals of Digital Optics*
SciTech - v20 - D '96 - p66 [51-250]
Yartz, Frank J - *Introduction to Modern Philosophy*
IPQ - v36 - D '96 - p503 [51-250]
Yarwood, A T - *Samuel Marsden: The Great Survivor*
Aust Bk R - Ag '96 - p67 [1-50]
Yarwood, Doreen - *The Architecture of Europe*
TCI - v30 - O '96 - p56 [1-50]
Yashima, Taro - *Crow Boy*
c   HMR - Win '96 - p45 [1-50]
Nino Cuervo
c   BL - v93 - My 1 '97 - p1507 [1-50]
Yasutomo, Dennis T - *The New Multilateralism in Japan's Foreign Policy*
PSQ - v111 - Win '96 - p704+ [501+]
Yate, Martin - *CareerSmarts: Jobs with a Future*
y   BL - v93 - Mr 1 '97 - p1098 [51-250]
yr Kliatt - v31 - My '97 - p24+ [51-250]
y   LJ - v122 - Ap 15 '97 - p94+ [51-250]
Yates, Brock - *The Critical Path*
BL - v92 - Ag '96 - p1866+ [51-250]
Fortune - v134 - O 28 '96 - p193+ [1-50]
LJ - v122 - Mr 15 '97 - p37 [1-50]
NYTBR - v101 - Ag 25 '96 - p18 [51-250]
Yates, Denise - *Making It Real*
Sch Lib - v44 - Ag '96 - p131 [51-250]
Yates, Irene - *From Birth to Death (Illus. by Graham Austin)*
c   JB - v60 - Ag '96 - p152 [51-250]
c   TES - F 21 '97 - p16* [51-250]
Writing Skills for Parents
Sch Lib - v45 - F '97 - p55 [51-250]
Yates, Michael - *Power on the Job*
S&S - v60 - Win '96 - p495+ [501+]
Yates, Nigel - *Religion and Society in Kent 1640-1914*
CH - v65 - S '96 - p526+ [501+]
EHR - v112 - Ap '97 - p486+ [501+]
Traffic and Politics
EHR - v112 - F '97 - p153+ [251-500]
Yates, Norris - *Gender and Genre*
RMR - v50 - 2 '96 - p212+ [501+]
Yates, Simon - *Against the Wall*
Obs - Ja 26 '97 - p18* [501+]
TLS - N 22 '96 - p13 [501+]
Yates, Timothy - *Christian Mission in the Twentieth Century*
JR - v76 - O '96 - p683 [51-250]
Yates, W E - *Theatre in Vienna*
Choice - v34 - My '97 - p1511 [51-250]
Yates, W Edgar - *Vom Schaffenden Zum Edierten Nestroy*
MLR - v92 - Ap '97 - p508+ [501+]
Yau, John - *Forbidden Entries*
BL - v93 - D 1 '96 - p640 [51-250]
PW - v243 - N 25 '96 - p71+ [51-250]

The United States of Jasper Johns
PW - v244 - Ap 7 '97 - p80 [51-250]
Yawn, Mike - *The Legacy Continues*
SciTech - v20 - D '96 - p11 [51-250]
Ye, Ting-Xing - *A Leaf in the Bitter Wind*
Quill & Q - v63 - Ja '97 - p13 [51-250]
Ye Jian Ying Zhuan
BL - v93 - My 1 '97 - p1484 [1-50]
Yeager, Dorian - *Ovation by Death*
Arm Det - v29 - Sum '96 - p369 [251-500]
Summer Will End
KR - v64 - O 15 '96 - p1500 [51-250]
PW - v243 - O 21 '96 - p74 [51-250]
Yeager, Selene - *The Complete Book of Alternative Nutrition*
PW - v244 - Ap 21 '97 - p68 [51-250]
Yeang, Ken - *Designing with Nature*
FHB - D '96 - p144 [251-500]
The Skyscraper Bioclimatically Considered
New Sci - v153 - Mr 22 '97 - p45 [251-500]
A Year Between. 2nd Ed.
y   TES - S 27 '96 - p8* [51-250]
The Year Book of Psychiatry and Applied Mental Health 1995
AJPsych - v154 - Ja '97 - p129 [501+]
Year Book of the Muslim World 1996
r   ARBA - v28 - '97 - p46 [251-500]
r   Choice - v34 - Mr '97 - p1145 [51-250]
Yearbook of Cell and Tissue Transplantation 1996-1997
SciTech - v20 - N '96 - p50 [51-250]
Yearbook of Labour Statistics 1995
r   ARBA - v28 - '97 - p121 [51-250]
The Yearbook of Langland Studies. Vols. 6-7
MLR - v91 - Jl '96 - p691+ [501+]
Yeargers, Edward K - *An Introduction to the Mathematics of Biology*
Choice - v34 - Mr '97 - p1184 [51-250]
JEL - v35 - Mr '97 - p306+ [51-250]
SciTech - v20 - N '96 - p26 [1-50]
Yearley, Steven - *Sociology, Environmentalism, Globalization*
Socio R - v45 - My '97 - p350+ [501+]
The Year's 25 Finest Crime and Mystery Stories. 5th Ed.
KR - v64 - S 1 '96 - p1280 [51-250]
LJ - v121 - O 1 '96 - p131 [1-50]
PW - v243 - S 9 '96 - p68+ [51-250]
The Year's Best Fantasy and Horror: Eighth Annual Collection
Necro - Sum '96 - p15+ [501+]
The Year's Best Fantasy and Horror: Ninth Annual Collection
MFSF - v91 - O '96 - p59+ [251-500]
The Year's Best Science Fiction: Thirteenth Annual Collection
BL - v92 - Ag '96 - p1889 [51-250]
Yeats, W B - *The Collected Letters of W.B. Yeats. Vol. 3*
RES - v47 - N '96 - p622+ [501+]
The Early Poetry. Vol. 2
TLS - S 27 '96 - p10+ [501+]
The Herne's Egg
RES - v47 - Ag '96 - p443 [501+]
Michael Robartes and the Dancer
TLS - S 27 '96 - p10+ [501+]
Poems 1895
RES - v47 - Ag '96 - p444 [501+]
The Wild Swans at Coole
TLS - S 27 '96 - p10+ [501+]
The Wind among the Reeds
RES - v47 - Ag '96 - p444 [501+]
The Winding Stair 1929
ILS - v15 - Fall '96 - p23 [501+]
TLS - S 27 '96 - p10+ [501+]
Yedidiah, Sam - *Centrifugal Pump Users Guidebook*
SciTech - v20 - N '96 - p71 [51-250]
Yee, Paul - *Breakaway*
y   BL - v93 - Mr 1 '97 - p1155+ [51-250]
y   HB - v73 - My '97 - p331 [51-250]
Ghost Train (Illus. by Harvey Chan)
c   BIC - v25 - N '96 - p31 [251-500]
c   BL - v93 - N 1 '96 - p502 [51-250]
c   Can CL - v22 - Fall '96 - p130+ [251-500]
c   CBRS - v25 - D '96 - p44 [51-250]
c   CCB-B - v50 - F '97 - p227+ [51-250]
c   Emerg Lib - v24 - Mr '97 - p27 [1-50]
y   JAAL - v40 - Mr '97 - p510 [251-500]
c   Quill & Q - v62 - Jl '96 - p57 [251-500]
c   Quill & Q - v63 - F '97 - p51 [51-250]
Struggle and Hope
c   Emerg Lib - v24 - Mr '97 - p28 [1-50]
c   Quill & Q - v62 - Jl '96 - p57+ [251-500]

Yee, Wong Herbert - *Fireman Small*
c   Par Ch - v20 - N '96 - p3 [51-250]
Mrs. Brown Went to Town
c   HB Guide - v7 - Fall '96 - p282 [51-250]
The Officers' Ball (Illus. by Wong Herbert Yee)
c   BL - v93 - Mr 15 '97 - p1247 [51-250]
c   KR - v65 - Mr 1 '97 - p390 [51-250]
c   PW - v244 - Mr 3 '97 - p74 [51-250]
Yeh, Chao-Pin - *Sensing, Modeling and Simulation in Emerging Electronic Packaging*
SciTech - v21 - Mr '97 - p90 [51-250]
Yeh, Wen-Hsin - *Provincial Passages*
Choice - v34 - D '96 - p666 [51-250]
R&R Bk N - v11 - N '96 - p15 [51-250]
Yehoshua, A B - *Open Heart*
BW - v26 - Jl 14 '96 - p7 [501+]
MHR - v10 - Fall '96 - p129+ [501+]
PW - v244 - Mr 24 '97 - p81 [1-50]
W&I - v12 - F '97 - p278+ [501+]
Yektai, Niki - *Bears at the Beach*
c   HB Guide - v7 - Fall '96 - p330 [51-250]
Yellin, Jean Fagan - *The Abolitionist Sisterhood*
Historian - v59 - Fall '96 - p166+ [501+]
Yelvington, Kevin A - *Producing Power*
HAHR - v77 - F '97 - p169+ [501+]
Yenawine, Philip - *Colors*
c   Inst - v106 - Ja '97 - p4* [1-50]
Yentis, Steven M - *Encyclopedia of Anesthesia Practice*
r   SciTech - v20 - S '96 - p38 [51-250]
Yeo, Eileen - *The Contest for Social Science*
TLS - D 13 '96 - p29 [501+]
Yeo, Richard - *Defining Science*
VS - v39 - Win '96 - p296+ [501+]
Yeoman, John - *The Do-It-Yourself House that Jack Built (Illus. by Quentin Blake)*
c   Emerg Lib - v24 - S '96 - p45 [51-250]
Yeoman, P M - *Orthopaedic Practice*
SciTech - v20 - S '96 - p39 [51-250]
Yeomans, William N - *7 Survival Skills for a Reengineered World*
BL - v93 - S 15 '96 - p192 [51-250]
PW - v243 - S 9 '96 - p75+ [51-250]
Yep, Laurence - *The Case of the Goblin Pearls*
c   BL - v93 - Ja '97 - p846+ [251-500]
c   CBRS - v25 - Ap '97 - p108 [51-250]
c   CCB-B - v50 - My '97 - p339 [51-250]
c   KR - v65 - Ja 15 '97 - p147+ [51-250]
c   PW - v243 - D 16 '96 - p59+ [51-250]
c   SLJ - v43 - Mr '97 - p194+ [51-250]
Dragon's Gate
c   JOYS - v10 - Fall '96 - p92+ [501+]
Hiroshima
c   RT - v50 - O '96 - p154 [51-250]
The Khan's Daughter (Illus. by Jean Tseng)
c   BL - v93 - F 1 '97 - p940 [51-250]
c   CCB-B - v50 - Mr '97 - p262 [51-250]
c   HB - v73 - Mr '97 - p208+ [51-250]
c   KR - v65 - Ja 1 '97 - p68 [51-250]
c   PW - v243 - D 16 '96 - p59 [51-250]
c   SLJ - v43 - F '97 - p99 [51-250]
Ribbons
c   Emerg Lib - v23 - My '96 - p43 [1-50]
c   HB Guide - v7 - Fall '96 - p299 [51-250]
Yepsen, Roger - *Apples*
LATBR - N 17 '96 - p2 [51-250]
Yergin, Daniel - *The Prize*
TLS - N 29 '96 - p14+ [51-250]
Yerxa, Leo - *A Fish Tale (Illus. by Leo Yerxa)*
c   CCB-B - v50 - S '96 - p39 [51-250]
Yesil, Magdalena - *Creating the Virtual Store*
LJ - v122 - Ap 1 '97 - p118 [51-250]
Yetiv, Steve A - *America and the Persian Gulf*
APSR - v90 - S '96 - p710+ [501+]
NWCR - v50 - Win '97 - p144+ [501+]
Yevtushenko, Yevgenii - *Strofy Veka*
BL - v93 - O 1 '96 - p327 [1-50]
Yezierska, Anzia - *Arrogant Beggar*
AL - v68 - S '96 - p669 [501+]
Tikkun - v12 - Ja '97 - p72+ [501+]
Salome of the Tenements
AL - v68 - S '96 - p669 [1-50]
Nat - v263 - S 23 '96 - p30+ [501+]
SFR - v21 - S '96 - p27+ [501+]
Yglesias, Jose - *The Guns in the Closet*
BL - v93 - S 1 '96 - p64 [51-250]
BWatch - v17 - D '96 - p8 [1-50]
KR - v64 - Ag 15 '96 - p1186 [251-500]
LJ - v121 - O 1 '96 - p128+ [51-250]
Obs - Mr 30 '97 - p17* [51-250]
PW - v243 - S 2 '96 - p120 [51-250]

The Old Gents
  BL - v93 - S 1 '96 - p64 [51-250]
  BWatch - v17 - D '96 - p8 [1-50]
  KR - v64 - Ag 15 '96 - p1187 [251-500]
  LJ - v121 - O 1 '96 - p128+ [51-250]
  PW - v243 - S 2 '96 - p114 [51-250]
Yglesias, Rafael - *Dr. Neruda's Cure for Evil*
  BW - v26 - Ag 4 '96 - p9 [501+]
  KR - v64 - My 1 '96 - p637+ [251-500]
  NYTBR - v101 - S 15 '96 - p37 [501+]
Yi, Gang - *Money, Banking, and Financial Markets in China*
  Ch Rev Int - v3 - Fall '96 - p582+ [501+]
  JEL - v34 - S '96 - p1391+ [501+]
Yi, Hyong-Gu - *The Korean Economy*
  JEL - v34 - S '96 - p1482 [51-250]
  R&R Bk N - v12 - F '97 - p37 [51-250]
Yi, Li - *Sha Ying*
  BL - v93 - My 1 '97 - p1484 [1-50]
Yi, Sin-Bom - *South Korea Environmental Report*
  R&R Bk N - v11 - N '96 - p21 [51-250]
  SciTech - v20 - S '96 - p2 [51-250]
Yin, An - *The Tectonic Evolution of Asia*
  SciTech - v20 - D '96 - p29 [51-250]
Yin, Y K - *Engineering Mechanics. Vols. 1-2*
  SciTech - v20 - D '96 - p60 [51-250]
Ying, Lung-An - *Infinite Element Methods*
  SIAM Rev - v38 - D '96 - p703+ [501+]
Yinger, John - *Closed Doors, Opportunities Lost*
  ACI - v8 - Fall '96 - p35+ [501+]
  AJS - v102 - N '96 - p891+ [501+]
  APSR - v90 - D '96 - p927+ [501+]
  CS - v26 - Mr '97 - p155+ [501+]
Yip, Wai-Lim - *Diffusion of Distances*
  CLS - v33 - 1 '96 - p123+ [501+]
Yishai, Yael - *Between the Flag and the Banner*
  For Aff - v76 - Mr '97 - p194 [51-250]
Yishu - Cheng Huan Ji
  BL - v93 - My 1 '97 - p1484 [1-50]
Ymansky, Kaye - *Pongwiffy and the Holiday of Doom. Audio Version*
  c Ch BWatch - v6 - O '96 - p3 [1-50]
Yochelson, John - *The Future of the U.S.-EU-Japan Triad*
  BusLR - v21 - 3 '96 - p263+ [251-500]
Yoder, Andrew R - *Shortwave Listening on the Road*
  r ARBA - v28 - '97 - p356 [51-250]
Yoder, Edwin M, Jr. - *Joe Alsop's Cold War*
  AHR - v102 - F '97 - p214+ [251-500]
Yoffie, David B - *Competing in the Age of Digital Convergence*
  BL - v93 - F 15 '97 - p983 [51-250]
Yogananda, Paramahansa - *Autobiography of a Yogi (Kingsley). Audio Version*
  Bloom Rev - v16 - N '96 - p16 [51-250]
  LJ - v122 - Ja '97 - p170 [51-250]
Yogi, Stan - *Highway 99*
  LJ - v121 - O 15 '96 - p81 [51-250]
Yohn, Susan M - *A Contest of Faiths*
  CH - v65 - D '96 - p751+ [501+]
  HAHR - v77 - F '97 - p127+ [501+]
  PHR - v65 - Ag '96 - p490+ [251-500]
Yolen, Jane - *The Ballad of the Pirate Queens (Illus. by David Shannon)*
  c RT - v50 - S '96 - p58 [51-250]
  c RT - v50 - O '96 - p136 [1-50]
Briar Rose
  y VOYA - v19 - D '96 - p266 [1-50]
Camelot (Illus. by Winslow Pels)
  c RT - v50 - S '96 - p59 [51-250]
The Devil's Arithmetic
  y New Ad - v9 - Fall '96 - p287+ [501+]
  y New Ad - v9 - Fall '96 - p297+ [501+]
The Devil's Arithmetic (Rosenblat). Audio Version
  y HB - v73 - Ja '97 - p85+ [501+]
Dove Isabeau (Illus. by Dennis Nolan)
  c PW - v244 - Mr 10 '97 - p69 [1-50]
Encounter (Illus. by David Shannon)
  c PW - v243 - S 23 '96 - p78 [51-250]
Encuentro (Illus. by David Shannon)
  c BL - v93 - My 1 '97 - p1506 [1-50]
Grandad Bill's Song (Illus. by Melissa Bay Mathis)
  c LA - v73 - S '96 - p357 [51-250]
Here There Be Angels (Illus. by David Wilgus)
  c HB Guide - v8 - Spr '97 - p77 [51-250]
  c SLJ - v42 - N '96 - p119 [51-250]
Here There Be Witches
  y Emerg Lib - v24 - S '96 - p27 [1-50]

Hobby: The Young Merlin Trilogy
  y BL - v93 - Ja '97 - p848 [251-500]
  c CLW - v67 - Mr '97 - p53 [251-500]
  c Emerg Lib - v24 - S '96 - p52 [51-250]
  c HB - v72 - N '96 - p741 [51-250]
  c HB Guide - v8 - Spr '97 - p77 [51-250]
  c SLJ - v42 - S '96 - p208 [51-250]
Jane Yolen's Old MacDonald Songbook
  c CLW - v67 - Mr '97 - p15 [1-50]
Letting Swift River Go (Illus. by Barbara Cooney)
  c Par Ch - v20 - O '96 - p21 [51-250]
Little Mouse and Elephant (Illus. by John Segal)
  c Ch BWatch - v6 - My '96 - p4 [1-50]
  c HB Guide - v7 - Fall '96 - p325 [51-250]
  c NYTBR - v101 - O 13 '96 - p26 [1-50]
Meet the Monsters (Illus. by Patricia Ludlow)
  c CBRS - v25 - N '96 - p33 [51-250]
  c HB Guide - v8 - Spr '97 - p54 [51-250]
  c SLJ - v42 - N '96 - p95 [51-250]
Merlin and the Dragons (Illus. by Li Ming)
  c Magpies - v11 - My '96 - p44 [251-500]
Merlin: The Young Merlin Trilogy
  c HB - v73 - My '97 - p331 [51-250]
Milk and Honey (Illus. by Louise August)
  c BL - v93 - O 1 '96 - p337 [51-250]
  c CCB-B - v50 - N '96 - p119 [51-250]
  c HB Guide - v8 - Spr '97 - p89 [51-250]
  c NYTBR - v101 - D 8 '96 - p78 [1-50]
  c SLJ - v42 - D '96 - p135 [51-250]
Mother Earth, Father Sky (Illus. by Jennifer Hewitson)
  y HB Guide - v7 - Fall '96 - p366 [51-250]
The Musicians of Bremen (Illus. by John Segal)
  c Ch BWatch - v6 - My '96 - p4 [1-50]
  c HB Guide - v7 - Fall '96 - p325 [51-250]
  c Par Ch - v20 - O '96 - p3 [51-250]
O Jerusalem (Illus. by John Thompson)
  c BL - v93 - O 1 '96 - p339 [1-50]
  c BL - v93 - Ap 1 '97 - p1306 [1-50]
  c HB Guide - v7 - Fall '96 - p369 [51-250]
  c RT - v50 - My '97 - p680 [51-250]
Once upon Ice and Other Frozen Poems (Illus. by Jason Stemple)
  c BL - v93 - F 1 '97 - p937 [51-250]
  c SLJ - v43 - Mr '97 - p212 [51-250]
Owl Moon
  c New Ad - v9 - Fall '96 - p267+ [501+]
Passager: The Young Merlin Trilogy
  c CLW - v67 - Mr '97 - p53 [251-500]
  c Emerg Lib - v24 - S '96 - p52 [51-250]
  c HB Guide - v7 - Fall '96 - p299 [51-250]
  y JAAL - v40 - N '96 - p232+ [51-250]
  y SF Chr - v18 - O '96 - p79 [51-250]
Sacred Places (Illus. by David Shannon)
  c BL - v93 - O 1 '96 - p337 [51-250]
  c CBRS - v25 - S '96 - p9+ [51-250]
  c Emerg Lib - v24 - Mr '97 - p47 [51-250]
  c HB Guide - v7 - Fall '96 - p369 [51-250]
Sea Watch (Illus. by Ted Lewin)
  c Emerg Lib - v24 - S '96 - p44 [1-50]
  c HB Guide - v7 - Fall '96 - p369 [51-250]
  c RT - v50 - Ap '97 - p593 [51-250]
Sing Noel (Illus. by Nancy Sippel Carpenter)
  c HB Guide - v8 - Spr '97 - p141 [51-250]
  c PW - v243 - S 30 '96 - p92 [1-50]
A Sip of Aesop (Illus. by Karen Barbour)
  c ECEJ - v24 - Fall '96 - p38 [51-250]
Sky Scrape/City Scape (Illus. by Ken Condon)
  c CBRS - v24 - Ag '96 - p166 [51-250]
  c HB Guide - v7 - Fall '96 - p366 [51-250]
Welcome to the Sea of Sand (Illus. by Laura Regan)
  c Emerg Lib - v24 - S '96 - p44 [1-50]
  c HB Guide - v7 - Fall '96 - p340 [1-50]
  c RT - v50 - Ap '97 - p593 [51-250]
  c SLJ - v42 - D '96 - p32 [1-50]
The Wild Hunt
  y Kliatt - v31 - My '97 - p16+ [51-250]
Wizard's Hall (Yolen). Audio Version
  c BL - v93 - My 15 '97 - p1595 [1-50]
  c Ch BWatch - v6 - My '96 - p6 [51-250]
Xanadu 2
  y Kliatt - v31 - Ja '97 - p18 [51-250]
Yolton, John W - *Perception and Reality*
  Choice - v34 - O '96 - p295+ [51-250]
  Isis - v88 - Mr '97 - p124+ [501+]
Yoo, Claire Jung Jin - *Hear Our Voices*
  r Bl S - v26 - Sum '96 - p68 [51-250]
Yoon, Jung-Huyn - *Popposites: A Lift, Pull, and Pop Book of Opposites*
  c CLW - v67 - D '96 - p59+ [51-250]
  c HB Guide - v7 - Fall '96 - p246 [51-250]
  c Par - v71 - D '96 - p251 [1-50]

Yoran, Shalom - *The Defiant: A True Story*
  y BL - v93 - S 1 '96 - p60 [51-250]
  LJ - v121 - S 15 '96 - p81 [51-250]
Yorinks, Arthur - *Frank and Joey Eat Lunch (Illus. by Maurice Sendak)*
  c CCB-B - v50 - F '97 - p228 [51-250]
  c HB - v73 - Ja '97 - p53 [51-250]
  c HB Guide - v8 - Spr '97 - p16 [51-250]
  c NYTBR - v101 - N 24 '96 - p20 [1-50]
Frank and Joey Go to Work (Illus. by Maurice Sendak)
  c CCB-B - v50 - F '97 - p228 [51-250]
  c HB - v73 - Ja '97 - p53 [51-250]
  c HB Guide - v8 - Spr '97 - p16 [51-250]
Hey, Al
  c New Ad - v9 - Fall '96 - p267+ [501+]
York, Lorraine M - *Various Atwoods*
  Can Lit - Spr '97 - p226+ [501+]
York, Neil Longley - *Neither Kingdom nor Nation*
  EHR - v111 - S '96 - p993 [251-500]
York, Sarah Mountbatten-Windsor, Duchess of - *Bright Lights (Illus. by Jacqueline Rogers)*
  c CCB-B - v50 - F '97 - p228+ [51-250]
  c HB Guide - v8 - Spr '97 - p65 [51-250]
  c PW - v243 - N 4 '96 - p77 [51-250]
  c SLJ - v43 - F '97 - p75 [51-250]
My Story
  BL - v93 - D 15 '96 - p690 [1-50]
  CSM - v89 - D 12 '96 - p14 [51-250]
  Ent W - D 13 '96 - p72 [251-500]
  NS - v125 - N 22 '96 - p44+ [501+]
  NYTBR - v102 - Ja 5 '97 - p13+ [501+]
  Spec - v277 - N 23 '96 - p54+ [501+]
My Story. Audio Version
  PW - v244 - Ja 6 '97 - p29+ [51-250]
The Royal Switch (Illus. by Jacqueline Rogers)
  c CCB-B - v50 - F '97 - p228+ [51-250]
  c HB Guide - v8 - Spr '97 - p65 [51-250]
  c KR - v64 - N 15 '96 - p1667+ [51-250]
  c PW - v243 - N 4 '96 - p77 [51-250]
  c SLJ - v43 - F '97 - p75 [51-250]
Yorke, Douglas A, Jr. - *Hitting the Road*
  AB - v99 - Mr 10 '97 - p793+ [501+]
Yorke, Ivor - *Television News. 3rd Ed.*
  R&R Bk N - v12 - F '97 - p82 [51-250]
Yorke, Margaret - *Serious Intent (Rodska). Audio Version*
  y Kliatt - v31 - My '97 - p44 [51-250]
Yoshie, Satoko - *Sari Dialect*
  MEJ - v51 - Spr '97 - p311 [51-250]
Yoshikawa, Hideo - *Science Has No National Borders*
  Isis - v87 - D '96 - p750 [251-500]
Yoshikawa, Hiroshi - *Macroeconomics and the Japanese Economy*
  JEL - v34 - S '96 - p1420 [51-250]
Yoshimoto, Banana - *Amrita*
  KR - v65 - My 1 '97 - p676+ [251-500]
Yoshimura, Akira - *Shipwrecks*
  KR - v64 - My 1 '96 - p638 [251-500]
  LATBR - Ag 11 '96 - p10 [51-250]
  NYTBR - v101 - S 22 '96 - p25 [51-250]
  W&I - v11 - O '96 - p276+ [501+]
  WLT - v71 - Win '97 - p230+ [251-500]
Zero Fighter
  J Mil H - v60 - O '96 - p790+ [251-500]
Yoshimura, Noboru - *Inside the Kaisha*
  NYTBR - v102 - Mr 16 '97 - p31 [501+]
  PW - v244 - F 17 '97 - p205+ [51-250]
Yoshino, Kosaku - *Cultural Nationalism in Contemporary Japan*
  Am Ethnol - v23 - N '96 - p911+ [501+]
  Pac A - v69 - Sum '96 - p267+ [501+]
Yoshitomi, Masaru - *Foreign Direct Investment in Japan*
  JEL - v34 - D '96 - p2047 [51-250]
Yoter Muzar Meha-Dimayon 6
  BL - v93 - Mr 1 '97 - p1115 [1-50]
Yotopoulos, Pan A - *Exchange Rate Parity for Trade and Development*
  JEL - v34 - D '96 - p2050+ [51-250]
Youcha, Geraldine - *Minding the Children*
  J Soc H - v30 - Fall '96 - p262+ [501+]
Youds, Bryn - *Susie Cooper: An Elegant Affair*
  Am Craft - v57 - F '97 - p31+ [501+]
  BL - v93 - N 15 '96 - p565 [51-250]
  Ceram Mo - v44 - D '96 - p28+ [251-500]
  LJ - v121 - N 1 '96 - p66 [51-250]
Youens, Susan - *Schubert's Poets and the Making of Lieder*
  Choice - v34 - Ap '97 - p1349+ [51-250]
  TLS - O 25 '96 - p18+ [501+]
Youm, Kyu Ho - *Press Law in South Korea*
  R&R Bk N - v11 - N '96 - p53 [1-50]

Youmans, Marly - *Catherwood*
LJ - v122 - Ja '97 - p184 [51-250]
PW - v244 - Ap 14 '97 - p72 [1-50]
y SLJ - v42 - N '96 - p141 [51-250]
Youmans, Vance Joseph - *The Plough and the Pen*
CH - v66 - Mr '97 - p209 [51-250]
Younes, Munther A - *Elementary Arabic*
MEJ - v51 - Win '97 - p152 [51-250]
Young, Alan - *Woke Me up This Morning*
LJ - v122 - Ap 15 '97 - p84 [51-250]
Young, Alan R - *The English Emblem Tradition*
Sev Cent N - v54 - Fall '96 - p67+ [501+]
Young, Alfred E - *Beyond the American Revolution*
SE - v61 - Mr '97 - p173+ [501+]
Young, Alison - *Imagining Crime*
AJS - v102 - N '96 - p929+ [501+]
Young, Allan - *The Harmony of Illusions*
AJS - v102 - S '96 - p654+ [501+]
Isis - v87 - S '96 - p579+ [501+]
TLS - S 27 '96 - p26 [501+]
Young, Allen M - *Lives Intertwined*
c HB Guide - v8 - Spr '97 - p120 [51-250]
c SB - v33 - My '97 - p110 [51-250]
Young, Andrew - *An Easy Burden*
y BL - v93 - S 1 '96 - p4 [51-250]
BW - v26 - N 3 '96 - p4 [501+]
Choice - v34 - F '97 - p1028 [51-250]
KR - v64 - S 1 '96 - p1314 [251-500]
LATBR - N 10 '96 - p3 [501+]
LATBR - D 29 '96 - p10 [51-250]
LJ - v121 - O 1 '96 - p92+ [51-250]
LJ - v121 - N 1 '96 - p82 [1-50]
NYRB - v43 - S 19 '96 - p61+ [501+]
NYTBR - v101 - N 10 '96 - p54 [501+]
PW - v243 - S 9 '96 - p69 [51-250]
WSJ-MW - v78 - N 6 '96 - pA18 [501+]
An Easy Burden (Young). Audio Version
CSM - v89 - Ja 30 '97 - pB4 [51-250]
Young, Ann R M - *Environmental Change in Australia since 1788*
Choice - v34 - D '96 - p637 [51-250]
Young, Arabella Hong - *Singing Professionally*
ON - v61 - Ja 11 '97 - p50 [251-500]
Young, Bard, 1941- - *The Snake of God*
PW - v243 - D 30 '96 - p57 [51-250]
Young, Brad - *Jesus the Jewish Theologian*
Rel St Rev - v23 - Ja '97 - p70 [51-250]
Young, Brian - *The Politics of Codification*
AHR - v101 - O '96 - p1316+ [501+]
Young, Carol - *Little Walrus Warning (Illus. by Walter Stuart). Book and Audio Version*
c Inst - v106 - N '96 - p7 [51-250]
Young, Charles H - *Into the Valley*
APH - v43 - Fall '96 - p68+ [501+]
Young, Chester Raymond - *Baptists on the American Frontier*
NGSQ - v84 - D '96 - p316+ [251-500]
Young, Crawford - *The African Colonial State in Comparative Perspective*
AHR - v101 - O '96 - p1257+ [501+]
Historian - v58 - Sum '96 - p853+ [251-500]
Young, David - *F.D. Maurice and Unitarianism*
CH - v66 - Mr '97 - p148+ [51-250]
Young, Davis A - *The Biblical Flood*
TT - v53 - O '96 - p401+ [501+]
Young, Donald F - *A Brief Introduction to Fluid Mechanics*
Choice - v34 - My '97 - p1530+ [51-250]
SciTech - v21 - Mr '97 - p75 [51-250]
Young, Ed - *Lon Po Po (Illus. by Ed Young)*
c New Ad - v9 - Fall '96 - p267+ [501+]
c Par Ch - v20 - O '96 - p21 [51-250]
Night Visitors (Illus. by Ed Young)
c RT - v50 - S '96 - p52 [51-250]
Voices of the Heart (Illus. by Ed Young)
c CBRS - v25 - F '97 - p80+ [51-250]
y CCB-B - v50 - Ap '97 - p301 [51-250]
c HB - v73 - My '97 - p347 [51-250]
c KR - v65 - Ja 15 '97 - p148 [51-250]
c Par Ch - v21 - Mr '97 - p4 [1-50]
c PW - v244 - F 24 '97 - p80 [1-50]
Young, Elspeth - *Third World in the First*
GJ - v162 - Jl '96 - p227+ [501+]
Young, Fred Douglas - *Richard M. Weaver 1910-1963*
New R - v214 - Je 17 '96 - p36+ [501+]
Young, G C - *An Australian Phanerozoic Timescale*
Choice - v34 - My '97 - p1528 [51-250]
Young, Gloryann Hawkins - *Indian Ancestors?*
EGH - v50 - N '96 - p159+ [51-250]

Young, J Bradford - *A Thematic Catalog of the Works of Robert Valentine*
Notes - v53 - S '96 - p69+ [501+]
Young, James P - *Reconsidering American Liberalism*
APSR - v90 - D '96 - p903+ [501+]
PSQ - v111 - Win '96 - p717+ [501+]
RP - v59 - Win '97 - p143+ [501+]
Young, John W - *Britain and European Unity 1945-1992*
EHR - v111 - S '96 - p1035+ [251-500]
Winston Churchill's Last Campaign
Choice - v34 - N '96 - p522 [51-250]
CR - v269 - Ag '96 - p103+ [501+]
EHR - v112 - F '97 - p147+ [501+]
HRNB - v25 - Win '97 - p64+ [501+]
Young, Katharine Galloway - *Bodylore*
JPC - v29 - Spr '96 - p263 [51-250]
Young, Kathryn A - *Kin, Commerce, Community*
W&M Q - v53 - Jl '96 - p656+ [501+]
Young, Kenneth Ray - *The General's General*
AHR - v101 - O '96 - p1288+ [501+]
Young, Laura S - *Bookbinding and Conservation by Hand*
Bloom Rev - v16 - N '96 - p22 [1-50]
Young, Louise - *The Unfinished Universe*
Reason - v28 - D '96 - p40+ [51-250]
Young, Malcolm P - *The Analysis of Cortical Connectivity*
SciTech - v20 - S '96 - p21 [51-250]
Young, Mary Eming - *Early Child Development*
JEL - v34 - S '96 - p1445+ [51-250]
Young, Michael K - *Trilateral Perspectives on International Legal Issues*
R&R Bk N - v11 - D '96 - p49 [51-250]
Young, Oran R - *Global Environmental Change and International Governance*
Choice - v34 - Ja '97 - p813 [51-250]
The International Political Economy and International Institutions. Vols. 1-2
JEL - v34 - D '96 - p2040 [51-250]
JPR - v34 - F '97 - p115 [251-500]
R&R Bk N - v11 - D '96 - p33 [51-250]
Young, Pamela Dickey - *Christ in a Post-Christian World*
Rel St Rev - v23 - Ap '97 - p155 [51-250]
Young, Percy M - *Elgar, Newman and the Dream of Gerontius*
CHR - v83 - Ja '97 - p118+ [251-500]
R&R Bk N - v12 - F '97 - p70 [51-250]
Young, Raymond A - *Cultivating Cooperation*
JSH - v62 - N '96 - p832+ [251-500]
Young, Richard G - *Paths of a Prodigal*
PW - v244 - Mr 10 '97 - p63 [51-250]
Young, Robert - *Encyclopedia of Family Health*
r Books - v9 - S '95 - p11 [251-500]
Young, Robert, 1927- - *Roscoe Fatty Arbuckle: A Bio-Bibliography*
r FQ - v49 - Fall '95 - p64+ [51-250]
Young, Robert, 1950- - *Colonial Desire*
AHR - v101 - D '96 - p1519+ [501+]
Albion - v28 - '96 - p750+ [501+]
Can Hist R - v78 - Mr '97 - p177+ [501+]
Young, Robert A - *Measuring Economic Benefits for Water Investments and Policies*
JEL - v35 - Mr '97 - p300 [51-250]
Young, Robert J, 1942- - *France and the Origins of the Second World War*
Choice - v34 - Ap '97 - p1399 [51-250]
Young, Ronder Thomas - *Moving Mama to Town*
c KR - v65 - Mr 15 '97 - p470 [51-250]
Young, Rosamond M - *Two Perfectly Marvellous Cats*
KR - v64 - Ag 15 '96 - p1227 [251-500]
Young, Scott T - *Managing Global Operations*
R&R Bk N - v11 - D '96 - p28 [51-250]
Young, Selina - *Adam Pig's Big Book*
Bks Keeps - Ja '97 - p19 [51-250]
c Bks Keeps - Ja '97 - p19 [51-250]
c Books - v9 - S '95 - p26 [1-50]
Adam Pig's Everything Fun Book (Illus. by Selina Young)
c HB Guide - v7 - Fall '96 - p246 [51-250]
c Smith - v27 - N '96 - p174 [1-50]
Big Dog and Little Dog Visit the Moon (Illus. by Selina Young)
c Bks Keeps - Jl '96 - p8 [51-250]
Young, Steve - *Steve Young: Forever Young (Illus. by Doug Keith)*
c HB Guide - v8 - Spr '97 - p147 [51-250]
Young, Sue - *Writing with Style*
c BL - v93 - Mr 1 '97 - p1160 [51-250]
Young, Susan - *Private Business and Economic Reform in China*
Ch Rev Int - v3 - Fall '96 - p588+ [501+]
Pac A - v69 - Fall '96 - p407+ [501+]

Young, William A - *The Rashaayda Bedouin*
JTWS - v13 - Fall '96 - p356+ [501+]
Young Adults Library Services Association - *Outstanding Books for the College Bound*
r A Lib - v27 - Ag '96 - p70 [1-50]
BL - v93 - S 15 '96 - p254 [51-250]
r Emerg Lib - v24 - Mr '97 - p42 [1-50]
yr Kliatt - v30 - N '96 - p17+ [51-250]
yr VOYA - v19 - F '97 - p362 [251-500]
Young Adults Library Services Association. Intellectual Freedom Committee - *Hit List: Frequently Challenged Books for Young Adults*
BL - v93 - S 15 '96 - p254 [51-250]
r Emerg Lib - v24 - Mr '97 - p40 [51-250]
r JOYS - v10 - Win '97 - p221+ [251-500]
yr Kliatt - v30 - N '96 - p17+ [51-250]
r VOYA - v19 - F '97 - p357 [51-250]
Young Person's Occupational Outlook Handbook
yr ARBA - v28 - '97 - p122 [501+]
Young Bear, Ray A - *Remnants of the First Earth*
KR - v64 - D 1 '96 - p1701+ [251-500]
LJ - v122 - Ja '97 - p151 [51-250]
PW - v243 - D 16 '96 - p44 [51-250]
Young Bear, Severt - *Standing in the Light*
y Kliatt - v30 - My '96 - p28 [51-250]
Youngblood, Shay - *Soul Kiss*
KR - v65 - Mr 15 '97 - p417 [251-500]
PW - v244 - Ap 14 '97 - p54 [51-250]
Young-Bruehl, Elisabeth - *The Anatomy of Prejudices*
Choice - v34 - O '96 - p365+ [51-250]
TLS - D 13 '96 - p28+ [501+]
Youngdahl, Kristi M - *The Arams of Idaho*
WHQ - v27 - Win '96 - p548 [1-50]
Younger, Alan - *Openings*
TES - F 14 '97 - p16* [51-250]
TES - Mr 21 '97 - p27* [51-250]
Younger, Paul - *The Home of Dancing Sivan*
JR - v77 - Ap '97 - p346+ [501+]
Pac A - v69 - Fall '96 - p442+ [501+]
Youngman, Henny - *Henny Youngman's BIG Book of Insults*
Am - v176 - Ap 19 '97 - p2 [501+]
Youngner, Stuart J - *Organ Transplantation*
Hast Cen R - v26 - Jl '96 - p42 [1-50]
Youngson, R M - *Medical Blunders*
TLS - Jl 19 '96 - p32 [251-500]
Medical Curiosities
New Sci - v154 - My 3 '97 - p48 [1-50]
The Royal Society of Medicine's Dictionary of Symptoms
r New Sci - v153 - F 22 '97 - p46 [51-250]
The Surgery Book
r BL - v93 - F 1 '97 - p957 [1-50]
Yount, John - *Toots in Solitude*
LJ - v121 - S 15 '96 - p102 [51-250]
NYTBR - v101 - Ap 7 '96 - p24 [1-50]
Yount, Lisa - *Antoni Van Leeuwenhoek: First to See Microscopic Life*
c HB Guide - v8 - Spr '97 - p155 [51-250]
c SB - v32 - N '96 - p241 [51-250]
c SLJ - v42 - D '96 - p135 [51-250]
Memory
y HB Guide - v7 - Fall '96 - p349 [51-250]
y SLJ - v42 - Ag '96 - p177 [51-250]
Twentieth-Century Women Scientists
y HB Guide - v7 - Fall '96 - p376 [51-250]
Yourcenar, Marguerite - *How Many Years*
TranslRevS - v2 - D '96 - p10 [51-250]
Trib Bks - F 16 '97 - p8 [251-500]
Yourdon, Edward - *Case Studies in Object-Oriented Analysis and Design*
Choice - v34 - Ja '97 - p833 [51-250]
SciTech - v20 - N '96 - p8 [51-250]
Rise and Resurrection of the American Programmer
BYTE - v21 - S '96 - p178 [51-250]
CBR - v14 - S '96 - p32 [1-50]
Choice - v34 - N '96 - p496 [51-250]
SciTech - v20 - N '96 - p7 [51-250]
Ypma, Herbert - *London Minimum*
LJ - v121 - S 15 '96 - p67+ [51-250]
Morocco Modern
VLS - Win '96 - p20 [51-250]
Pacific Island
LJ - v121 - S 15 '96 - p67+ [51-250]
Paris Flea Market
VLS - Win '96 - p20 [51-250]
Yrigoyen, Charles - *Historical Dictionary of Methodism*
r ARBA - v28 - '97 - p551 [51-250]
r Choice - v34 - F '97 - p952 [51-250]
r R&R Bk N - v12 - F '97 - p11 [51-250]

Yu, Boris - *Borel-Laplace Transform and Asymptotic Theory*
    SIAM Rev - v39 - Mr '97 - p159+ [501+]
Yu, Francis T S - *Optical Storage and Retrieval*
    SciTech - v20 - N '96 - p66 [51-250]
Yu, George W - *Critical Operative Maneuvers in Urologic Surgery*
    SciTech - v20 - S '96 - p38 [51-250]
Yu, Hua - *The Past and the Punishments*
    Choice - v34 - Ja '97 - p790 [51-250]
    Ch Rev Int - v4 - Spr '97 - p288+ [501+]
    NYTBR - v101 - O 27 '96 - p39 [251-500]
    TranslRevS - v2 - D '96 - p20 [51-250]
Yu, Maochun - *OSS in China*
    KR - v65 - Ja 15 '97 - p134 [251-500]
    LJ - v122 - F 15 '97 - p147 [51-250]
Yu, Pauline - *Voices of the Song Lyric in China*
    Ch Rev Int - v3 - Fall '96 - p589+ [501+]
Yu, Youcheng - *Wo Kan Ying Dai Er*
    BL - v93 - My 1 '97 - p1484 [1-50]
Yuan, Mei - *Censored by Confucius*
    Pac A - v69 - Fall '96 - p408+ [51-250]
I Don't Bow to Buddhas
    Parabola - v22 - F '97 - p120 [1-50]
Yuan, Susan - *Techniques and Equipment for Gathering Visitor Use Data on Recreation Sites*
    J Gov Info - v23 - S '96 - p573 [51-250]
Yuce, Ayse - *An Examination of an Emerging Stock Exchange*
    JEL - v34 - D '96 - p2054 [51-250]
Yudofsky, Stuart C - *Synopsis of Neuropsychiatry*
    AJPsych - v153 - S '96 - p1225+ [501+]
Yue, Charlotte - *Shoes: Their History in Words and Pictures (Illus. by David Yue)*
  c BL - v93 - Ap 1 '97 - p1332+ [51-250]
  c HB - v73 - My '97 - p347+ [51-250]
  c KR - v65 - F 15 '97 - p309 [51-250]
Yuh, Junku - *Underwater Robots*
    SciTech - v20 - D '96 - p72 [51-250]
Yumoto, Kazumi - *The Friends*
  c BL - v93 - Ap 1 '97 - p1302 [1-50]
  c CBRS - v25 - O '96 - p24 [1-50]
  c CCB-B - v50 - F '97 - p229 [51-250]
  c HB - v72 - N '96 - p741+ [51-250]
  c HB Guide - v8 - Spr '97 - p77 [51-250]
  c HMR - Win '96 - p39+ [501+]
  c KR - v64 - O 15 '96 - p1540 [51-250]
  c NYTBR - v102 - Mr 2 '97 - p25 [1-50]
  c PW - v243 - O 14 '96 - p84 [51-250]
  c SLJ - v42 - D '96 - p124+ [51-250]
Yung, Judy - *Unbound Feet*
    CS - v26 - Ja '97 - p21+ [501+]
    J Soc H - v30 - Spr '97 - p743+ [501+]
    PHR - v65 - N '96 - p671+ [251-500]
Yungblut, Laura Hunt - *Strangers Settled Here amongst Us*
    R&R Bk N - v11 - D '96 - p8 [1-50]
Yunghans, Penelope - *Prize Winners*
  c Ch BWatch - v6 - My '96 - p6 [51-250]
  y HB Guide - v7 - Fall '96 - p364 [51-250]
Yunis, Harvey - *Taming Democracy*
    Choice - v34 - S '96 - p209 [51-250]
Yunus, Mohammad - *Plant Response to Air Pollution*
    Choice - v34 - Ja '97 - p820 [51-250]
Yusuf, Shahid - *Developing the Nonfarm Sector in Bangladesh*
    JEL - v35 - Mr '97 - p276 [51-250]
Yuzna, Susan - *Her Slender Dress*
    Choice - v34 - Ap '97 - p1342 [51-250]
Zabalza Seguin, Ana - *Aldeas Y Campesinos En La Navarra Prepirenaica 1550-1817*
    HAHR - v76 - N '96 - p764+ [501+]
Zabar, Abbie - *A Growing Garden*
    PW - v243 - S 16 '96 - p63 [51-250]
Zabbia, Kim Howes - *Painted Diaries*
    LATBR - D 8 '96 - p11 [51-250]
    LJ - v121 - O 15 '96 - p84 [51-250]
Zabka, Thomas - *Faust II*
    Ger Q - v69 - Sum '96 - p352+ [501+]
Zaborowska, Magdalena J - *How We Found America*
    AHR - v102 - F '97 - p200+ [501+]
    NWSA Jnl - v9 - Spr '97 - p110+ [501+]
Zacarias, Agostinho - *The United Nations and International Peacekeeping*
    Choice - v34 - Ja '97 - p872 [51-250]
Zachary, Joseph L - *Introduction to Scientific Programming*
    Choice - v34 - Ap '97 - p1374+ [51-250]
Zachau, Reinhard K - *Heinrich Boll: Forty Years of Criticism*
    MLR - v91 - Jl '96 - p802+ [501+]

Zack, Arnold M - *Labor Agreement in Negotiation and Arbitration. 2nd Ed.*
    ILRR - v50 - Ap '97 - p513+ [501+]
Zack, Naomi - *American Mixed Race*
    Ethics - v107 - O '96 - p187+ [51-250]
Zacker, Craig - *Upgrading and Repairing Networks*
  r SciTech - v20 - D '96 - p76 [51-250]
Zackheim, Michele - *Violette's Embrace*
    BL - v92 - Ag '96 - p1884 [51-250]
    NYTBR - v101 - D 15 '96 - p25 [51-250]
Zafra Oropeza, Aurea - *Agustin Rivera Y Agustin De La Rosa Ante La Filosofia Novohispana*
    HAHR - v77 - F '97 - p128+ [501+]
Zagajewski, Adam - *Two Cities*
    TLS - N 29 '96 - p11 [51-250]
    TranslRevS - v2 - D '96 - p10 [51-250]
Zagano, Phyllis - *Ita Ford: Missionary Martyr*
    CLW - v67 - Mr '97 - p38 [51-250]
    Comw - v124 - Ap 11 '97 - p26 [251-500]
    RR - v56 - Ja '97 - p107 [1-50]
Zagat, Eugene H - *Zagat Survey: America's Best Meal Deals*
  r J Account - v182 - D '96 - p98+ [51-250]
Zagelbaum, Bruce M - *Sports Ophthalmology*
  r SciTech - v20 - D '96 - p50 [51-250]
Zahariadis, Nikolaos - *Markets, States, and Public Policy*
    J Pol - v58 - Ag '96 - p920+ [501+]
Zahavi, Amotz - *The Handicap Principle*
    BL - v93 - My 1 '97 - p1469 [251-500]
    LJ - v122 - Ap 15 '97 - p114 [51-250]
Zahavi, Eliahu - *Fatigue Design*
    Choice - v34 - F '97 - p995 [51-250]
Zahavi, Helen - *True Romance*
    Books - v9 - S '95 - p25 [1-50]
Zahler, Karen Gantz - *Superchefs: Signature Recipes from America's New Royalty*
    BL - v93 - S 15 '96 - p198 [51-250]
    CSM - v89 - D 13 '96 - p10+ [51-250]
    LJ - v121 - N 15 '96 - p84 [51-250]
    PW - v243 - O 7 '96 - p72 [51-250]
Zahn, Theodor - *Einleitung In Das Neue Testament*
    Rel St Rev - v23 - Ap '97 - p176 [51-250]
Zahran, Yasmine - *A Beggar at Damascus Gate*
    MEJ - v50 - Sum '96 - p454 [51-250]
    WLT - v71 - Win '97 - p213+ [501+]
Zaichkin, Jeanette - *Newborn Intensive Care*
    LJ - v122 - Ap 1 '97 - p116 [51-250]
Zaichkowsky, Judith Lynne - *Defending Your Brand against Imitation*
    J Con A - v30 - Win '96 - p505+ [501+]
Zaidi, Zafar H - *Protein Structure-Function Relationship*
    SciTech - v21 - Mr '97 - p42 [51-250]
Zaidman, Louise Bruit - *Religion in the Ancient Greek City*
    JAAR - v64 - Sum '96 - p438+ [501+]
Zajac, Edward E - *Political Economy of Fairness*
    Econ J - v106 - N '96 - p1840+ [251-500]
    JEL - v34 - D '96 - p1959+ [501+]
Zak, Monica - *Save My Rainforest*
  c TranslRevS - v1 - My '95 - p10 [51-250]
Zak, William F - *The Polis and the Divine Order*
    Rel St Rev - v23 - Ja '97 - p62 [51-250]
Zakarian, Beverly - *The Activist Cancer Patient*
    LJ - v122 - Ja '97 - p57 [51-250]
Zakheim, Dov S - *Flight of the Lavi*
    For Aff - v75 - N '96 - p150 [51-250]
    LJ - v121 - S 15 '96 - p82 [51-250]
Zakin, Richard - *Hand-Formed Ceramics*
    BWatch - v17 - S '96 - p3 [51-250]
    Ceram Mo - v44 - O '96 - p24 [51-250]
Zakowski, Connie - *The Insect Book*
  c BL - v93 - D 1 '96 - p660+ [51-250]
  c Ch BWatch - v7 - Ja '97 - p2 [51-250]
Zaky, Amr - *Tools and Environments for Parallel and Distributed Systems*
    SciTech - v20 - S '96 - p5 [51-250]
Zalben, Jane Breskin - *Beni's Family Cookbook for the Jewish Holidays (Illus. by Jane Breskin Zalben)*
  c BL - v93 - S 15 '96 - p236 [51-250]
  c BL - v93 - Ap 1 '97 - p1306 [51-250]
  c HB Guide - v8 - Spr '97 - p134 [51-250]
  c PW - v243 - O 14 '96 - p85 [51-250]
  c SLJ - v43 - F '97 - p126 [51-250]
Papa's Latkes (Illus. by Jane Breskin Zalben)
  c BL - v93 - S 1 '96 - p138 [51-250]
  c HB Guide - v8 - Spr '97 - p54 [51-250]
  c PW - v243 - S 30 '96 - p88 [1-50]
Unfinished Dreams
  y HB - v72 - S '96 - p603 [51-250]
  y HB Guide - v7 - Fall '96 - p306 [51-250]
  c NYTBR - v101 - S 8 '96 - p28 [1-50]

Zaleski, Carol - *The Life of the World to Come*
    CC - v113 - D 18 '96 - p1259 [251-500]
    Parabola - v21 - N '96 - p106+ [501+]
Zall, Paul M - *Abe Lincoln Laughing*
    J Am Cult - v18 - Win '95 - p102+ [51-250]
The Wit and Wisdom of the Founding Fathers
  y LJ - v121 - O 1 '96 - p102 [51-250]
Zallen, Doris Teichler - *Does It Run in the Family?*
    LJ - v122 - Ap 15 '97 - p109 [51-250]
Zaloga, Steven J - *Inside the Blue Berets*
    Parameters - v26 - Aut '96 - p158+ [501+]
Zalups, Rudolfs K - *Methods in Renal Toxicology*
    SciTech - v20 - D '96 - p48 [51-250]
Zamagni, Stefano - *The Economics of Altruism*
    Econ J - v107 - Ja '97 - p264 [251-500]
Zaman, Fakhar - *The Prisoner*
    KR - v64 - S 15 '96 - p1354 [51-250]
    MEJ - v51 - Win '97 - p153 [51-250]
    PW - v243 - S 30 '96 - p62 [51-250]
    TranslRevS - v2 - D '96 - p30 [51-250]
Zambelli, Paola - *Una Reincarnazione Di Pico Ai Tempi Di Pomponazzi*
    Ren Q - v49 - Aut '96 - p598+ [501+]
Zambrana, Ruth E - *Understanding Latino Families*
    CS - v25 - S '96 - p657+ [501+]
Zamfirescu, Ion - *Intalniri Cu Oameni, Intalniri Cu Viata*
    BL - v93 - D 15 '96 - p714 [1-50]
Zamir, Shamoon - *Dark Voices*
    AJS - v102 - Jl '96 - p267+ [501+]
Zamora, Lois Parkinson - *Magical Realism*
    RCF - v16 - Fall '96 - p204 [51-250]
    WLT - v70 - Sum '96 - p770 [501+]
Zamorano, Ana - *Let's Eat (Illus. by Julie Vivas)*
  c CCB-B - v50 - Ap '97 - p301+ [51-250]
  c KR - v65 - Ja 15 '97 - p148 [51-250]
  c PW - v244 - Ap 21 '97 - p70 [51-250]
Zamski, Eli - *Photoassimilate Distribution in Plants and Crops*
    SciTech - v20 - S '96 - p20 [51-250]
Zamyatin, Yevgeny - *We*
    Reason - v28 - D '96 - p40 [51-250]
Zanca, Kenneth J - *American Catholics and Slavery 1789-1866*
    J Ch St - v38 - Aut '96 - p919 [51-250]
Zancanella, Don - *Western Electric*
    KR - v64 - S 15 '96 - p1352 [251-500]
    LATBR - O 6 '96 - p14 [51-250]
    NYTBR - v102 - Mr 23 '97 - p18 [51-250]
    PW - v243 - O 7 '96 - p61 [51-250]
Zand, Janet - *Smart Medicine for a Healthier Child*
  r BL - v93 - F 1 '97 - p959 [1-50]
Zanden, J L Van - *The Economic Development of the Netherlands since 1870*
    JEL - v34 - S '96 - p1465 [51-250]
    R&R Bk N - v11 - D '96 - p25 [1-50]
Zander, Alvin - *Motives and Goals in Groups*
    JEL - v34 - D '96 - p2143 [51-250]
Zander, Randolph - *The Silver Rubles and Yefimoks of Romanov Russia 1654-1915*
    Coin W - v37 - D 16 '96 - p24 [51-250]
Zandy, Janet - *Liberating Memory*
    NWSA Jnl - v8 - Fall '96 - p159+ [501+]
Zang, David W - *Fleet Walker's Divided Heart*
    Aethlon - v13 - Fall '95 - p130+ [251-500]
    Historian - v59 - Fall '96 - p127 [51-250]
    J Am Cult - v19 - Spr '96 - p108+ [501+]
Zangenberg, Jurgen - *Samareia: Antike Quellen Zur Geschichte Und Kultur Der Samaritaner In Deutscher Ubersetzung*
    Rel St Rev - v23 - Ja '97 - p87 [51-250]
Zangger, Eberhard - *The Geoarchaeology of the Argolid*
    AJA - v100 - Jl '96 - p636+ [251-500]
Zangwill, Andrew - *Evolution of Expitaxial Structure and Morphology*
    SciTech - v20 - N '96 - p18 [51-250]
Zangwill, Israel - *The Big Bow Mystery*
    ELT - v40 - 1 '97 - p23+ [501+]
Zaniello, Tom - *Working Stiffs, Union Maids, Reds, and Riffraff*
  r ARBA - v28 - '97 - p520 [51-250]
  r JEL - v34 - D '96 - p2077 [51-250]
    Nat - v262 - Je 17 '96 - p28+ [501+]
Zanier, Claudio - *Where the Roads Met*
    Isis - v88 - Mr '97 - p130+ [51-250]
Zanjani, Sally - *A Mine of Her Own*
    LJ - v122 - Ap 1 '97 - p108 [51-250]
Zank, Neal S - *Measuring the Employment Effects of Regulation*
    Choice - v34 - F '97 - p1009 [51-250]
    JEL - v35 - Mr '97 - p248+ [51-250]
    R&R Bk N - v11 - D '96 - p30 [51-250]

Zanker, Graham - *The Heart of Achilles*
  CW - v89 - Jl '96 - p513 [51-250]
Zanker, Paul - *Pompeij: Stadtbild Und Wohngeschmack*
  Choice - v34 - D '96 - p566 [1-50]
Zann, Richard A - *The Zebra Finch*
  Choice - v34 - My '97 - p1527 [51-250]
Zanzanelli, Eletta - *Le Cinquecentine Della Biblioteca Panizzi*
  r Lib - v18 - D '96 - p363 [251-500]
Zapol, Warren M - *Nitric Oxide and the Lung*
  SciTech - v21 - Mr '97 - p57 [51-250]
Zarembka, Paul - *Latest Developments in Marxist Theory*
  JEL - v34 - D '96 - p2014 [51-250]
Zaretsky, Robert - *Nimes at War*
  AHR - v101 - O '96 - p1225+ [501+]
Zarrilli, Phillip B - *Acting (Re)considered*
  Theat J - v48 - O '96 - p400+ [501+]
Zartman, I William - *Collapsed States*
  Africa T - v43 - 4 '96 - p429+ [501+]
  CS - v25 - N '96 - p736+ [501+]
  J Pol - v58 - Ag '96 - p903+ [501+]
  Elusive Peace
  APSR - v90 - S '96 - p711+ [501+]
  Polity and Society in Contemporary North Africa
  JTWS - v13 - Spr '96 - p279+ [501+]
Zarzyski, Paul - *All This Way for the Short Ride*
  NYTBR - v102 - Mr 16 '97 - p21 [51-250]
  I Am Not a Cowboy
  Sm Pr R - v28 - Jl '96 - p12 [51-250]
  WAL - v31 - Fall '96 - p280 [51-250]
Zaslavsky, Claudia - *Fear of Math*
  y BL - v93 - Ap 1 '97 - p1343 [1-50]
  The Multicultural Math Classroom
  Learning - v25 - Ja '97 - p57 [1-50]
Zaslavsky, Nancy - *Meatless Mexican Home Cooking*
  BL - v93 - Mr 15 '97 - p1217 [51-250]
  LJ - v122 - Mr 15 '97 - p82 [51-250]
  PW - v244 - Mr 3 '97 - p70 [51-250]
Zasloff, Tela - *Restoring Vision*
  SciTech - v20 - S '96 - p39 [51-250]
Zastoupil, Lynn - *John Stuart Mill and India*
  VS - v39 - Win '96 - p237+ [501+]
Zayas, Marius De - *How, When, and Why Modern Art Came to New York*
  AB - v99 - Mr 3 '97 - p693 [51-250]
  Choice - v34 - Ja '97 - p786 [51-250]
  PW - v243 - S 30 '96 - p72 [51-250]
  R&R Bk N - v11 - D '96 - p57 [51-250]
Zayed, Ahmed I - *Handbook of Function and Generalized Function Transformations*
  r SciTech - v20 - S '96 - p10 [51-250]
Zbornik Radova
  p JEL - v34 - S '96 - p1507 [51-250]
Zealberg, Joseph J - *Comprehensive Emergency Mental Health Care*
  Readings - v12 - Mr '97 - p22 [51-250]
  SciTech - v20 - S '96 - p33 [51-250]
Zeanah, David W - *An Optimal Foraging Model of Hunter-Gatherer Land Use in the Carson Desert*
  Am Ant - v61 - Jl '96 - p632 [251-500]
Zebadua, Emilio - *Banqueros Y Revolucionarios*
  AHR - v101 - O '96 - p1320+ [501+]
  JEH - v56 - D '96 - p942+ [501+]
Zebala, John - *Medical School Admissions. 3rd Rev. Ed.*
  C&U - v72 - Fall '96 - p30 [501+]
  Medical School Admissions. 4th Rev. Ed.
  r BWatch - v17 - N '96 - p5 [1-50]
Zebiri, Kate - *Mahmud Shaltut and Islamic Modernism*
  JAAR - v64 - Win '96 - p870+ [501+]
  Rel St Rev - v23 - Ja '97 - p90 [51-250]
Zecchini, Salvatore - *Lessons from the Economic Transition*
  For Aff - v76 - My '97 - p127 [51-250]
Zech, Paul - *The Birds in Langfoots's Belfry*
  TranslRevS - v1 - My '95 - p23 [51-250]
Zedeno, Maria Nieves - *Sourcing Prehistoric Ceramics at Chodistaas Pueblo, Arizona*
  Am Ant - v61 - O '96 - p807+ [501+]
Zeeberg, Peter - *Tycho Brahes Urania Titani*
  Isis - v87 - S '96 - p542+ [501+]
Zeeland, Steven - *The Masculine Marine*
  Choice - v34 - Mr '97 - p1248 [51-250]
  R&R Bk N - v12 - F '97 - p101 [51-250]
Ze'evi, Dror - *An Ottoman Century*
  Choice - v34 - Ja '97 - p861 [51-250]
  R&R Bk N - v11 - D '96 - p10 [51-250]
Zegher, M Catherine De - *Inside the Visible*
  Choice - v34 - N '96 - p444+ [51-250]
  R&R Bk N - v11 - N '96 - p60 [51-250]
Zegura, Elizabeth Chesney - *Rabelais Revisited*
  MLR - v92 - Ja '97 - p188+ [501+]

Zeh, Frederick - *An Immigrant Soldier in the Mexican War*
  HAHR - v77 - My '97 - p324+ [251-500]
  Roundup M - v4 - O '96 - p29 [251-500]
  TranslRevS - v2 - D '96 - p10 [251-500]
  WHQ - v28 - Spr '97 - p73+ [251-500]
Zehr, Howard - *Doing Life*
  y BL - v93 - S 15 '96 - p191 [51-250]
  Fed Prob - v60 - D '96 - p62+ [251-500]
  OS - v32 - S '96 - p59 [51-250]
Zeidan, Joseph T - *Arab Women Novelists*
  MEJ - v50 - Aut '96 - p628 [51-250]
Zeider, Moshe - *Handbook of Coping*
  Readings - v12 - Mr '97 - p27 [51-250]
Zeinert, Karen - *The Amistad Slave Revolt and American Abolition*
  y KR - v65 - My 1 '97 - p728 [51-250]
  The Persian Empire
  c Ch BWatch - v7 - Ja '97 - p3 [1-50]
  c HB Guide - v8 - Spr '97 - p165 [51-250]
  y SLJ - v43 - Mr '97 - p212 [51-250]
  Those Remarkable Women of the American Revolution
  c BL - v93 - D 1 '96 - p654 [51-250]
  y Ch BWatch - v6 - D '96 - p6 [1-50]
  c HB Guide - v8 - Spr '97 - p176 [51-250]
  y SLJ - v43 - Mr '97 - p212 [51-250]
  Victims of Teen Violence
  y HB Guide - v7 - Fall '96 - p316+ [51-250]
Zeitgeist
  New Sci - v154 - My 3 '97 - p47 [1-50]
Zeitlin, Froma I - *Playing the Other*
  Rel St Rev - v23 - Ja '97 - p62 [51-250]
  R&R Bk N - v11 - N '96 - p63 [51-250]
  TLS - F 14 '97 - p10 [501+]
Zeitlin, Judith - *Historian of the Strange*
  Ch Rev Int - v4 - Spr '97 - p290+ [501+]
Zeitlin, Marilyn A - *Bill Viola: Venice Biennale 1995*
  Art J - v54 - Win '95 - p97+ [501+]
Zeitner, June Culp - *Gem and Lapidary Materials*
  Choice - v34 - Ja '97 - p824 [51-250]
  R&R Bk N - v11 - D '96 - p68 [51-250]
Zelaznik, Howard N - *Advances in Motor Learning and Control*
  R&R Bk N - v11 - D '96 - p3 [51-250]
Zelazny, Roger - *Forever After*
  SF Chr - v18 - O '96 - p80 [1-50]
  Hymn to the Sun
  SF Chr - v18 - O '96 - p82 [1-50]
  Knight of Shadows (Zelazny). Audio Version
  y Kliatt - v31 - My '97 - p41 [51-250]
  Unicorn Variation (Auberjonois). Audio Version
  SF Chr - v18 - O '96 - p76 [51-250]
  The Williamson Effect
  SF Chr - v18 - O '96 - p76 [51-250]
  y VOYA - v19 - O '96 - p222 [51-250]
Zeldin, Theodore - *An Intimate History of Humanity*
  MLR - v92 - Ap '97 - p414+ [501+]
Zelewsky, Alexander Von - *Stereochemistry of Coordination Compounds*
  Choice - v34 - D '96 - p640 [51-250]
  SciTech - v20 - S '96 - p17 [51-250]
Zelikow, Philip - *Germany Unified and Europe Transformed*
  AHR - v102 - F '97 - p132 [501+]
  APSR - v90 - S '96 - p712+ [501+]
Zelinka, Joseph - *Directory of Anti-Violence Activities in the Washington Metropolitan Area*
  r J Gov Info - v23 - S '96 - p601+ [51-250]
Zelinski, Ernie J - *The Joy of Not Working*
  BL - v93 - Mr 1 '97 - p1098 [51-250]
Zelizer, Barbie - *Covering the Body*
  J Am Cult - v18 - Win '95 - p105+ [51-250]
Zell, Fran - *A Multicultural Portrait of the American Revolution*
  y HB Guide - v7 - Fall '96 - p388 [51-250]
Zell, Hans M - *Publishing and Book Development in Sub-Saharan Africa*
  r ARBA - v28 - '97 - p249 [51-250]
  r Choice - v34 - O '96 - p260 [51-250]
  r LAR - v98 - Jl '96 - p371 [1-50]
Zell, Michael - *Industry in the Countryside*
  EHR - v111 - N '96 - p1268+ [501+]
Zeller, F C Duke - *Devil's Pact*
  BL - v93 - N 15 '96 - p556+ [51-250]
  KR - v64 - S 15 '96 - p1390+ [251-500]
  LJ - v121 - N 15 '96 - p74 [51-250]
  PW - v243 - O 7 '96 - p53 [51-250]
Zeller, Ludwig - *The Invisible Presence*
  LJ - v121 - D '96 - p98 [51-250]

Zellner, Arnold - *An Introduction to Bayesian Inference in Econometrics*
  JEL - v35 - Mr '97 - p195 [51-250]
  R&R Bk N - v12 - F '97 - p33 [51-250]
Zelman, Walter A - *The Changing Health Care Marketplace*
  SciTech - v21 - Mr '97 - p45 [51-250]
Zelnick, Bob - *Backfire: A Reporter's Look at Affirmative Action*
  BW - v26 - Ag 18 '96 - p6+ [501+]
  NY - v72 - N 25 '96 - p106+ [501+]
  NYTBR - v101 - O 13 '96 - p20 [51-250]
Zelnik, Reginald E - *Law and Disorder on the Narova River*
  AHR - v101 - D '96 - p1583+ [501+]
  Historian - v59 - Win '97 - p487+ [251-500]
  Russ Rev - v55 - O '96 - p714+ [501+]
Zemach, Harve - *Duffy and the Devil (Leishman). Audio Version*
  c BL - v93 - My 15 '97 - p1595 [1-50]
Zeman, Leos J - *Microfiltration and Ultrafiltration*
  SciTech - v20 - D '96 - p82 [51-250]
Zeman, Ludmila - *The Last Quest of Gilgamesh (Illus. by Ludmila Zeman)*
  c Can CL - v22 - Fall '96 - p132+ [501+]
Zembsch-Schreve, Guido - *Pierre Lalande: Special Agent*
  TLS - Ja 31 '97 - p27 [251-500]
Zemel, Carol - *Van Gogh's Progress*
  Trib Bks - Ja 26 '97 - p5 [501+]
Zemlinsky, Alexander - *Briefwechsel Mit Arnold Schonberg, Anton Webern, Alban Berg Und Franz Schreker*
  Notes - v53 - D '96 - p437+ [501+]
Zemsky, Jessica - *Capturing the Magic of Children in Your Paintings*
  LJ - v121 - N 15 '96 - p60 [51-250]
Zencey, Eric - *Panama*
  Books - v10 - Je '96 - p13 [51-250]
  Obs - S 8 '96 - p18* [51-250]
  Sew R - v104 - Jl '96 - p461+ [501+]
  Panama (Gaines). Audio Version
  y Kliatt - v30 - S '96 - p50+ [51-250]
Zenger, Erich - *A God of Vengeance?*
  Am - v176 - Mr 8 '97 - p24+ [51-250]
  Rel St Rev - v23 - Ap '97 - p167 [51-250]
Zenith, Richard - *113 Galician-Portuguese Troubadour Poems*
  TLS - S 20 '96 - p26 [501+]
Zenner, Markus - *Learning to Become Rational*
  JEL - v35 - Mr '97 - p204 [1-50]
Zeno, Susan M - *The Educator's Word Frequency Guide*
  r ARBA - v28 - '97 - p376 [51-250]
Zepada, Ray - *Dying for a Bargain*
  Sm Pr R - v29 - F '97 - p8 [51-250]
Zepeda, Raphael - *Buying a Cabin*
  WAL - v31 - Fall '96 - p275+ [251-500]
Zepezauer, Mark - *Take the Rich Off Welfare*
  BW - v26 - D 8 '96 - p8 [1-50]
Zephaniah, Benjamin - *Funky Chickens (Illus. by Point)*
  c Bks Keeps - Ja '97 - p22 [51-250]
  c TES - D 13 '96 - p32 [51-250]
  Propa Propaganda
  y Sch Lib - v45 - F '97 - p44 [51-250]
  Talking Turkeys
  c RT - v50 - F '97 - p424 [51-250]
Zephir, Flore - *Haitian Immigrants in Black America*
  Bl S - v26 - Fall '96 - p108 [51-250]
  Choice - v34 - O '96 - p369 [51-250]
Zerbe, G M - *Non-Retaliation in Early Jewish and New Testament Texts*
  Rel St Rev - v22 - O '96 - p353 [51-250]
Zerubavel, Yael - *Recovered Roots*
  AJS - v102 - Jl '96 - p303+ [501+]
Zetka, James R, Jr. - *Militancy, Market Dynamics, and Workplace Authority*
  SF - v75 - S '96 - p366+ [501+]
Zettel, Sarah - *Fool's War*
  NYTBR - v102 - Ap 6 '97 - p24 [51-250]
  PW - v244 - Mr 3 '97 - p71 [51-250]
  Reclamation
  y BL - v30 - S '96 - p22 [51-250]
  y VOYA - v19 - D '96 - p282+ [51-250]
Zeuschner, Robert B - *Edgar Rice Burroughs: The Exhaustive Scholar's and Collector's Descriptive Bibliography*
  r Choice - v34 - My '97 - p1472 [251-500]
  r LJ - v122 - Ja '97 - p84 [51-250]
Zevon, Susan - *Inside Architecture*
  PW - v244 - Ap 7 '97 - p89 [51-250]

Zha, Jianying - *China Pop*
  Ch Rev Int - v4 - Spr '97 - p293+ [501+]
  LATBR - Mr 17 '96 - p11 [51-250]
Zhai, Zhenming - *The Radical Choice and Moral Theory*
  Ethics - v107 - Ja '97 - p386+ [51-250]
Zhang, Dianwan - *Ci Xing Shi Dai*
  BL - v93 - N 1 '96 - p484 [1-50]
Zhang, Feng - *Ha Fo Xin Ying Lu*
  BL - v93 - N 1 '96 - p484 [1-50]
Zhang, Fuzhen - *Linear Algebra*
  Choice - v34 - Ap '97 - p1377 [51-250]
  SciTech - v20 - D '96 - p15 [51-250]
Zhang, H - *Automated Mathematical Induction*
  SciTech - v20 - D '96 - p13 [51-250]
Zhang, Hanzhi - *Feng Yu Qing*
  BL - v93 - My 1 '97 - p1484 [1-50]
Zhang, HongJiang - *Representation and Retrieval of Visual Media in Multimedia Systems*
  SciTech - v21 - Mr '97 - p6 [51-250]
Zhang, Hsiao Yang - *Shakespeare in China*
  Choice - v34 - O '96 - p274 [51-250]
Zhang, Mei Miranda - *Competitiveness in United States Grain Exports*
  JEL - v34 - S '96 - p1430 [51-250]
Zhang, Min - *Zi Ji De Gu Shi*
  BL - v93 - My 1 '97 - p1484 [1-50]
Zhang, Shu Guang - *Mao's Military Romanticism*
  For Aff - v76 - My '97 - p129 [51-250]
  HRNB - v25 - Fall '96 - p38 [251-500]
  J Mil H - v61 - Ja '97 - p197+ [501+]
  Mar Crp G - v80 - N '96 - p81+ [501+]
Zhang, Xiaoge Gregory - *Corrosion and Electrochemistry of Zinc*
  Choice - v34 - My '97 - p1532 [51-250]
  r SciTech - v20 - D '96 - p63 [51-250]
Zhang, Yingjin - *The City in Modern Chinese Literature and Film*
  Choice - v34 - D '96 - p600 [51-250]
Zhang, Zijing - *Wo De Jie Jie*
  BL - v93 - N 1 '96 - p484 [1-50]
Zhao, Lingxi - *Jiang Qing Chuan Qi De Yi Sheng*
  BL - v93 - N 1 '96 - p484 [1-50]
Zhao, Shilin - *Nei Zhan*
  BL - v93 - N 1 '96 - p484 [1-50]
Zhirinovsky, Vladimir - *My Struggle*
  BL - v92 - Ag '96 - p1879 [51-250]
Zhizhiashvili, Levan V - *Trigonometric Fourier Series and Their Conjugates*
  SciTech - v20 - D '96 - p19 [51-250]
Zholkovskii, A K - *Babel=Babel*
  Russ Rev - v56 - Ja '97 - p132+ [501+]
  Text Counter Text
  Russ Rev - v55 - O '96 - p702+ [501+]
Zhong Guo Kang Ri Zhan Zheng Duan Pian J Ing Cui
  BL - v93 - My 1 '97 - p1484 [1-50]
Zhong Guo Ke Yi Shuo Bu
  BL - v93 - My 1 '97 - p1484 [1-50]
Zhou, Kate Xiao - *How the Farmers Changed China*
  Choice - v34 - O '96 - p332 [51-250]
Zhou, Yu - *Gui Lai De Jun Dao*
  BL - v93 - N 1 '96 - p484 [1-50]
Zhu, Weizheng - *Yindiao Weiding De Chuantong*
  Ch Rev Int - v4 - Spr '97 - p51+ [501+]
Zhu, Yi - *Bu Yao Yue Hui Zhi Yao He Ka Fei*
  BL - v93 - N 1 '96 - p484 [1-50]
Zhu Ming Wai Jiao Jia Yan Jiang Jian Shang
  BL - v93 - My 1 '97 - p1484 [1-50]
Zhuk, A B - *The Illustrated Encyclopedia of Handguns*
  r ARBA - v28 - '97 - p360 [51-250]
Ziefert, Allison - *People of the Bible (Illus. by Letizia Galli)*
  c HB Guide - v8 - Spr '97 - p87 [1-50]
  c SLJ - v42 - D '96 - p118 [51-250]
Ziefert, Harriet - *Animals of the Bible (Illus. by Letizia Galli)*
  c HB Guide - v8 - Spr '97 - p87 [1-50]
  c SLJ - v42 - D '96 - p118 [51-250]
  Baby Buggy, Buggy Baby (Illus. by Richard Brown)
  c CCB-B - v50 - Ap '97 - p302 [51-250]
  c PW - v244 - Mr 10 '97 - p68 [51-250]
  Benjy Bear's Halloween (Illus. by Emilie Boon)
  c PW - v243 - S 30 '96 - p85 [51-250]
  Donde Esta Mi Huevo De Pascua? (Illus. by Richard Brown)
  c SLJ - v42 - Ag '96 - p179 [51-250]
  Henny-Penny (Illus. by Emily Bolam)
  c BL - v93 - N 15 '96 - p597 [51-250]
  c SLJ - v43 - Mr '97 - p169 [51-250]
  The Magic Porridge Pot (Illus. by Emily Bolam)
  c KR - v64 - D 15 '96 - p1807 [51-250]
  c SLJ - v43 - Mr '97 - p169 [51-250]

  Night Knight (Illus. by Richard Brown)
  c CCB-B - v50 - Ap '97 - p302 [51-250]
  c PW - v244 - Mr 10 '97 - p68 [51-250]
  The Princess and the Pea (Illus. by Emily Bolam)
  c HB Guide - v8 - Spr '97 - p56 [51-250]
  c SLJ - v42 - Ag '96 - p132 [51-250]
  The Turnip (Illus. by Laura Rader)
  c BL - v92 - Ag '96 - p1910 [51-250]
  c HB Guide - v8 - Spr '97 - p106 [1-50]
  c SLJ - v42 - Ag '96 - p132 [51-250]
  Two Little Witches (Illus. by Simms Taback)
  c BL - v93 - S 1 '96 - p138 [51-250]
  c HB Guide - v8 - Spr '97 - p16 [51-250]
  c PW - v243 - S 30 '96 - p85 [51-250]
  c Sch Lib - v45 - F '97 - p22 [51-250]
  c SLJ - v42 - D '96 - p110 [51-250]
  Wee G. (Illus. by Donald Saaf)
  c PW - v244 - Ap 28 '97 - p74 [51-250]
  What Rhymes with Eel? (Illus. by Rick Brown)
  c HB Guide - v7 - Fall '96 - p246 [51-250]
Zieger, Robert H - *The CIO 1935-1955*
  AHR - v101 - O '96 - p1300 [501+]
  JSH - v63 - F '97 - p197+ [501+]
  RAH - v24 - D '96 - p641+ [501+]
Ziegler, Catherine - *The Harmonious Garden*
  BL - v93 - S 1 '96 - p52 [51-250]
  PW - v243 - N 4 '96 - p47 [1-50]
Ziegler, Charles A - *Spying without Spies*
  AHR - v101 - O '96 - p1310+ [501+]
  T&C - v37 - Ap '96 - p391+ [501+]
Ziegler, Jean - *L'Or Du Maniema*
  BL - v93 - F 1 '97 - p930 [1-50]
Ziegler, Joanna E - *Sculpture of Compassion*
  BM - v138 - D '96 - p836 [51-250]
Ziegler, Philip - *London at War 1939-1945*
  Historian - v58 - Sum '96 - p924+ [251-500]
Ziegler, Sandra - *Understanding (Illus. by Mechelle Ann)*
  c HB Guide - v8 - Spr '97 - p86 [51-250]
Ziemer, Maryann - *Quaaludes*
  y KR - v64 - D 1 '96 - p1742 [51-250]
Ziesk, Edra - *Acceptable Losses*
  BL - v93 - F 1 '97 - p927 [51-250]
  KR - v64 - N 15 '96 - p1631 [251-500]
  NY - v72 - Ja 27 '97 - p76 [51-250]
  NYTBR - v102 - F 9 '97 - p20 [51-250]
  PW - v243 - D 30 '96 - p57 [51-250]
Zietz, Karyl Lynn - *The National Trust Guide to Great Opera Houses in America*
  PW - v243 - O 21 '96 - p77+ [51-250]
Zigal, Thomas - *Hardrock Stiff*
  BL - v93 - N 15 '96 - p575 [51-250]
  KR - v64 - O 1 '96 - p1431 [251-500]
  PW - v243 - S 30 '96 - p63+ [51-250]
  Into Thin Air
  WAL - v31 - Sum '96 - p177 [251-500]
Zilbergleit, A S - *Spectral Theory of Guided Waves*
  SciTech - v21 - Mr '97 - p25 [51-250]
Zilberman, Shimon - *The Compact Up-to-Date English-Hebrew Dictionary*
  r ARBA - v28 - '97 - p393 [51-250]
Zilboorg, Caroline - *Women's Firsts*
  r BL - v93 - Mr 15 '97 - p1261+ [51-250]
  r LJ - v122 - Ap 15 '97 - p74 [51-250]
Zilli, Luigia - *La Comedie A L'Epoque D'Henri II Et De Charles IX*
  FR - v70 - O '96 - p107+ [251-500]
  Ren Q - v49 - Aut '96 - p633+ [501+]
Zillmer, Eric A - *The Quest for the Nazi Personality*
  AHR - v102 - F '97 - p129+ [501+]
Zimany, Roland D - *Vehicle for God*
  Theol St - v57 - D '96 - p778 [251-500]
Zimbaro, Valerie P - *Encyclopedia of Apocalyptic Literature*
  yr ARBA - v28 - '97 - p411 [51-250]
Zimelman, Nathan - *How the Second Grade Got $8,205.50 to Visit the Statue of Liberty*
  c Inst - v106 - S '96 - p55 [1-50]
Zimmer, Michael - *Fandango*
  Roundup M - v3 - Ag '96 - p32 [251-500]
Zimmerman, Barry E - *Killer Germs*
  y Kliatt - v30 - N '96 - p29 [51-250]
  y SB - v32 - N '96 - p237 [51-250]
Zimmerman, Bonnie - *The New Lesbian Studies*
  LJ - v122 - Ap 15 '97 - p103 [51-250]
Zimmerman, Cynthia - *Taking the Stage*
  Can Lit - Win '96 - p183+ [501+]
Zimmerman, Dale A - *Birds of Kenya and Northern Tanzania*
  r Choice - v34 - Ja '97 - p822 [51-250]

Zimmerman, David - *Top Secret Exchange*
  Choice - v34 - D '96 - p664 [51-250]
  New Sci - v152 - N 23 '96 - p46 [51-250]
  Sci - v275 - Ja 17 '97 - p321 [501+]
  SciTech - v20 - N '96 - p1 [51-250]
Zimmerman, Jeffrey L - *If Problems Talked*
  SciTech - v20 - D '96 - p45 [51-250]
Zimmerman, Joseph F - *Interstate Relations*
  Choice - v34 - Ja '97 - p877 [51-250]
  R&R Bk N - v11 - N '96 - p49 [51-250]
Zimmerman, Mari West - *Take and Make Holy*
  CLW - v66 - Je '96 - p37 [51-250]
Zimmerman, Michael, 1953- - *Science, Nonscience, and Nonsense*
  AB - v98 - O 28 '96 - p1430 [251-500]
  Am Sci - v84 - N '96 - p617+ [501+]
  Tikkun - v11 - My '96 - p64+ [501+]
Zimmerman, Michael E, 1946- - *Contesting Earth's Future*
  EG - v72 - O '96 - p456+ [501+]
Zimmerman, Neal - *Home Office Design*
  BL - v93 - O 1 '96 - p316 [51-250]
  LJ - v121 - S 15 '96 - p65+ [51-250]
  LJ - v122 - My 1 '97 - p53 [1-50]
  PW - v243 - O 7 '96 - p72 [51-250]
Zimmerman, Robert - *Ba Ba Ha Ha*
  c Par - v71 - D '96 - p251 [1-50]
  Oooh Oooh Moo
  c Par - v71 - D '96 - p251 [1-50]
Zimmerman, T C Price - *Paolo Giovio: The Historian and the Crisis of Sixteenth-Century Italy*
  Six Ct J - v27 - Fall '96 - p912+ [501+]
Zimmerman, William - *Dog-Mas: Simple Truths from a Wise Pet*
  Dog Fan - v27 - N '96 - p24 [1-50]
Zimmermann, David R - *The Healthcare Customer Service Revolution*
  SciTech - v20 - N '96 - p35 [51-250]
Zimmermann, H J - *Fuzzy Set Theory. 3rd Ed.*
  SciTech - v20 - N '96 - p13 [51-250]
Zimmermann, Warren - *Origins of a Catastrophe*
  y BL - v93 - S 1 '96 - p60 [51-250]
  BW - v26 - N 17 '96 - p5 [501+]
  BW - v26 - D 8 '96 - p7 [501+]
  For Aff - v75 - N '96 - p161 [51-250]
  LATBR - N 10 '96 - p4+ [501+]
  NL - v79 - N 4 '96 - p16+ [501+]
  NYTBR - v101 - O 13 '96 - p22+ [501+]
  Obs - D 8 '96 - p16* [501+]
  Wil Q - v20 - Aut '96 - p100+ [251-500]
Zimring, Franklin E - *Incapacitation: Penal Confinement and the Restraint of Crime*
  Ethics - v107 - O '96 - p183+ [51-250]
Zimroth, Evan - *Gangsters*
  LATBR - D 15 '96 - p15 [51-250]
  LJ - v121 - S 15 '96 - p99 [51-250]
  NYTBR - v101 - O 13 '96 - p21 [51-250]
Zimunya, Musaemura B - *Nightshift and Other Stories*
  WLT - v70 - Aut '96 - p1019+ [251-500]
Zinck, J Alfred - *Soil Survey*
  J Gov Info - v23 - S '96 - p670+ [51-250]
Zindel, Paul - *The Doom Stone*
  y Ch BWatch - v6 - O '96 - p8 [51-250]
  y Emerg Lib - v23 - My '96 - p57+ [51-250]
  y Emerg Lib - v24 - S '96 - p27 [1-50]
  y Kliatt - v30 - N '96 - p17 [51-250]
  y Sch Lib - v44 - Ag '96 - p121+ [51-250]
  Loch (Guidall). Audio Version
  y SLJ - v43 - Ja '97 - p70 [51-250]
  The Pigman and Me
  y BL - v93 - D 15 '96 - p717 [1-50]
Zindell, David - *The Wild*
  BL - v92 - Ag '96 - p1889 [51-250]
  y Kliatt - v30 - N '96 - p17 [51-250]
Zingg, Paul J - *Runs, Hits and an Era*
  Aethlon - v13 - Fall '95 - p172+ [251-500]
Zinik, Zinovy - *One-Way Ticket*
  KR - v64 - O 15 '96 - p1492+ [251-500]
  LJ - v121 - N 1 '96 - p110 [51-250]
  NYTBR - v102 - Ja 5 '97 - p18 [51-250]
  PW - v243 - O 14 '96 - p66 [51-250]
Zinj
  p SLJ - v42 - D '96 - p48 [51-250]
Zinkevych, Osyp - *Ukraina*
  r BL - v93 - N 15 '96 - p577 [1-50]
Zinn, Walter J - *Complete Guide to Eyecare, Eyeglasses and Contact Lenses. 4th Ed.*
  r BL - v93 - F 1 '97 - p960 [1-50]
Zinnes, Harriet - *My, Haven't the Flowers Been?*
  Chel - 61 '96 - p148+ [501+]

Zinn-Justin, Jean - *Quantum Field Theory and Critical Phenomena. 3rd Ed.*
  SciTech - v21 - Mr '97 - p21 [51-250]
Ziokowski, Mariusz S - *Andes: Radiocarbon Database for Bolivia, Ecuador and Peru*
  r LA Ant - v7 - Je '96 - p175 [251-500]
Ziolkowski, Jan M - *Talking Animals*
  CLS - v33 - 2 '96 - p208+ [501+]
Ziolkowski, Thad - *Our Son the Arson*
  PW - v243 - Jl 22 '96 - p238 [1-50]
Ziolkowski, Theodore - *Virgil and the Moderns*
  CLS - v33 - 1 '96 - p136+ [501+]
  MP - v94 - Ag '96 - p60+ [501+]
Zion, Gene - *Harry, El Perrito Sucio (Illus. by Margaret Bloy Graham)*
  c HB Guide - v7 - Fall '96 - p327 [1-50]
  c SLJ - v42 - Ag '96 - p179 [51-250]
  Harry the Dirty Dog (Illus. by Margaret Bloy Graham)
  c HB - v73 - Mr '97 - p187 [1-50]
Zipes, Jack - *Creative Storytelling*
  Sch Lib - v45 - F '97 - p55 [51-250]
  The Trials and Tribulations of Little Red Riding Hood. 2nd Ed.
  Ger Q - v69 - Spr '96 - p213+ [501+]
Zipkowitz, Fay - *Reference Services for the Unserved*
  CLW - v67 - D '96 - p47 [251-500]
  RQ - v36 - Win '96 - p317 [251-500]
  SB - v32 - N '96 - p228 [251-500]
  SLMQ - v25 - Fall '96 - p62 [1-50]
Zipoli, Riccardo - *Bidel: Concordance and Lexical Repertories of 1000 Lines*
  r MEJ - v51 - Win '97 - p152 [51-250]
  Un Giardino Nella Voce
  MEJ - v51 - Win '97 - p153 [51-250]
Zipperer, Lori A - *The Health Care Almanac*
  r ARBA - v28 - '97 - p600+ [51-250]
Ziring, Lawrence - *International Relations. 5th Ed.*
  r ARBA - v28 - '97 - p279+ [251-500]
Zisquit, Linda - *Unopened Letters*
  PW - v244 - F 24 '97 - p86 [51-250]
Zitkala-Sa - *American Indian Stories*
  Legacy - v14 - 1 '97 - p25+ [501+]
Zito, Angela - *Body, Subject and Power in China*
  Ch Rev Int - v3 - Fall '96 - p601+ [501+]
Zlatohlavek, Martin - *Kresby Z Cremony 1500-1580*
  BM - v138 - Jl '96 - p470 [251-500]
Zobel, Jan - *Minding Her Own Business*
  LJ - v122 - Ja '97 - p117 [51-250]
Zobrist, George W - *Object-Oriented Simulation*
  SciTech - v20 - D '96 - p14 [51-250]
Zocchi, Chiara - *Olga*
  BL - v93 - D 1 '96 - p644 [1-50]
Zoehfeld, Kathleen Weidner - *Ladybug at Orchard Avenue (Komisar) (Illus. by Thomas Buchs). Book and Audio Version*
  c SLJ - v42 - N '96 - p72 [51-250]
Zografi, Vlad - *Omul Nou*
  BL - v93 - D 15 '96 - p714 [1-50]
Zohar, Danah - *The Quantum Society*
  PAR - v56 - S '96 - p491+ [501+]
Zohar, Rakefet - *Devek Shkedim*
  BL - v93 - Mr 1 '97 - p1115 [1-50]
Zola, Emile - *Correspondance. Vol. 9*
  FR - v70 - F '97 - p472+ [501+]
  Correspondance. Vol. 10
  FR - v70 - F '97 - p473+ [501+]
  MLR - v91 - Jl '96 - p732+ [501+]
  The Dreyfus Affair
  Choice - v34 - Ja '97 - p859 [51-250]
  LJ - v121 - S 15 '96 - p81 [51-250]
  Lon R Bks - v18 - S 5 '96 - p7+ [501+]
  R&R Bk N - v11 - N '96 - p12 [51-250]
  Germinal (Davidson). Audio Version
  LJ - v121 - O 15 '96 - p102 [51-250]
Zolbrod, Paul - *Reading the Voice*
  J Am Cult - v19 - Sum '96 - p150+ [501+]
Zollinger Postgraduate Course in Surgery (1st: 1995: Ohio State University) - *Current Concepts in Hepatobiliary and Pancreatic Surgery*
  SciTech - v20 - N '96 - p49 [51-250]
Zollo, Peter - *Wise Up to Teens*
  Adoles - v32 - Spr '97 - p250 [51-250]
Zolotnitsky, David - *Sergei Radlov: The Shakespearean Fate of a Soviet Director*
  Choice - v34 - O '96 - p292 [51-250]
Zolotow, Charlotte - *The Old Dog (Illus. by James Ransome)*
  c RT - O '96 - p131 [1-50]
  When the Wind Stops (Illus. by Stefano Vitale)
  c PW - v244 - F 10 '97 - p85 [1-50]

Who Is Ben? (Illus. by Kathryn Jacobi)
  c KR - v65 - My 1 '97 - p728 [51-250]
  c PW - v244 - Ap 14 '97 - p75 [51-250]
Zomaya, Albert Y - *Parallel and Distributed Computing Handbook*
  Choice - v34 - S '96 - p164 [51-250]
Zombeck, Martin V - *Handbook of Space Astronomy and Astrophysics. 2nd Ed.*
  r S&T - v92 - S '96 - p52+ [51-250]
Zomchick, John P - *Family and the Law in Eighteenth-Century Fiction*
  MLR - v91 - O '96 - p976+ [501+]
Zonabend, Francoise - *The Nuclear Peninsula*
  Am Ethnol - v24 - F '97 - p247 [501+]
Zonal Film Archives (Hamburg, Germany) - *Catalogue of Forbidden German Feature and Short Film Productions Held in Zonal Film Archives*
  r ARBA - v28 - '97 - p352 [251-500]
Zong, Chuanming - *Strange Phenomena in Convex and Discrete Geometry*
  Choice - v34 - My '97 - p1538 [51-250]
Zoom: Resources for Struggling Readers: Sets A-C
  c TES - F 28 '97 - pR6 [251-500]
Zophy, Jonathan W - *A Short History of Renaissance and Reformation Europe*
  Six Ct J - v27 - Win '96 - p1180+ [501+]
Zornack, Annemarie - *Das Meer Unter Meinem Kopfkissen*
  WLT - v70 - Sum '96 - p686+ [501+]
Zornberg, Avivah Gottlieb - *The Beginning of Desire*
  Comw - v124 - Mr 14 '97 - p28+ [501+]
  Nat R - v48 - D 9 '96 - p61+ [501+]
  Genesis: The Beginning of Desire
  JR - v76 - O '96 - p611+ [501+]
Zoroaster: Life and Work of the Forerunner in Persia. 2nd Ed.
  LJ - v122 - F 1 '97 - p87 [51-250]
Zoss, Joel - *Diamonds in the Rough*
  y Kliatt - v31 - Ja '97 - p33 [51-250]
Zraly, Kevin - *Windows on the World Complete Wine Course. Rev. Ed.*
  LJ - v122 - Ap 1 '97 - p63 [1-50]
  PW - v243 - S 2 '96 - p125 [51-250]
Zubatsky, David S - *Sourcebook for Jewish Genealogies and Family Histories. 2nd Ed.*
  r BL - v93 - Ja '97 - p900+ [251-500]
  Spanish, Catalan, and Galician Literary Authors of the Eighteenth and Nineteenth Centuries
  r Hisp - v79 - D '96 - p799 [501+]
Zubok, Vladislav - *Inside the Kremlin's Cold War*
  Choice - v34 - N '96 - p532 [51-250]
  HRNB - v25 - Win '97 - p83 [251-500]
  NL - v79 - Ag 12 '96 - p19+ [501+]
  NYTBR - v101 - S 22 '96 - p35 [501+]
  Obs - O 20 '96 - p15* [501+]
  TLS - N 8 '96 - p20 [501+]
  VQR - v72 - Aut '96 - p116* [51-250]
Zubrin, Robert - *The Case for Mars*
  Astron - v25 - F '97 - p102+ [501+]
  Choice - v34 - F '97 - p985+ [51-250]
  Econ - v342 - F 15 '97 - p14*+ [501+]
  KR - v64 - O 1 '96 - p1458+ [251-500]
  LJ - v121 - N 15 '96 - p86 [51-250]
  Nature - v383 - O 31 '96 - p780 [501+]
  NYTBR - v101 - D 15 '96 - p15 [501+]
  Obs - D 22 '96 - p15* [501+]
  PW - v243 - O 14 '96 - p75 [51-250]
  Reason - v28 - Ap '97 - p59+ [501+]
Zubro, Mark Richard - *Rust on the Razor*
  Arm Det - v30 - Win '97 - p93 [251-500]
Zuccato, Edoardo - *Coleridge in Italy*
  Obs - D 29 '96 - p27 [501+]
Zucchino, David - *Myth of the Welfare Queen*
  BL - v93 - Mr 15 '97 - p1210 [51-250]
  BW - v27 - Mr 23 '97 - p1+ [501+]
  KR - v65 - F 1 '97 - p214 [251-500]
  LJ - v122 - Ap 1 '97 - p113 [51-250]
  PW - v244 - Ja 27 '97 - p90 [51-250]
Zuck, Colleen - *Daily Word*
  PW - v244 - Ap 14 '97 - p71 [51-250]
Zucker, Arthur - *Introduction to the Philosophy of Science*
  SciTech - v20 - D '96 - p3 [51-250]
Zucker, Kenneth J - *Gender Identity Disorder and Psychosexual Problems in Children and Adolescents*
  Readings - v11 - S '96 - p28 [51-250]
Zucker, Norman L - *Desperate Crossings*
  Choice - v34 - Mr '97 - p1237 [51-250]
  R&R Bk N - v12 - F '97 - p61 [51-250]

Zucker, Stanley - *Kathinka Zitz-Halein and Female Activism in Mid-Nineteenth-Century Germany*
  Historian - v58 - Sum '96 - p925+ [501+]
Zuckerman, Ben - *The Origin and Evolution of the Universe*
  Astron - v24 - N '96 - p103 [51-250]
Zuckerman, Fredric S - *The Tsarist Secret Police in Russian Society 1880-1917*
  Choice - v34 - Ja '97 - p859 [51-250]
Zuckerman, Harriet - *Scientific Elite*
  Nature - v383 - O 24 '96 - p682 [1-50]
  SF - v75 - D '96 - p765 [1-50]
Zuckert, Catherine H - *Postmodern Platos*
  Choice - v34 - D '96 - p627 [51-250]
  RP - v59 - Win '97 - p162+ [501+]
Zuckert, Michael P - *Natural Rights and the New Republicanism*
  AAPSS-A - v546 - Jl '96 - p172+ [501+]
  Bks & Cult - v2 - N '96 - p22+ [501+]
  Dal R - v75 - Spr '95 - p114+ [501+]
  EHR - v112 - Ap '97 - p476+ [501+]
  JMH - v69 - Mr '97 - p122+ [501+]
Zuckmayer, Carl - *Der Hauptmann Von Kopenick*
  MLR - v91 - Jl '96 - p635+ [501+]
Zuczek, Richard - *State of Rebellion*
  Choice - v34 - My '97 - p1566 [51-250]
Zuidervaart, Huib J - *Speculatie, Wetenschap En Vernuft*
  Isis - v87 - D '96 - p732+ [501+]
Zukav, Gary - *The Dancing Wu Li Masters*
  Reason - v28 - D '96 - p41 [51-250]
Zukin, Sharon - *The Cultures of Cities*
  CS - v25 - N '96 - p782+ [501+]
Zukowski, Sharon - *Prelude to Death*
  Arm Det - v29 - Sum '96 - p374 [51-250]
Zulaika, Joseba - *Terror and Taboo*
  Choice - v34 - Ja '97 - p867 [51-250]
Zulawski, Ann - *They Eat from Their Labor*
  AHR - v102 - F '97 - p242+ [251-500]
Zunder, William - *Writing and the English Renaissance*
  Choice - v34 - F '97 - p970 [51-250]
Zuo, Qingwen - *Qin Ai De Bao Jun*
  BL - v93 - N 1 '96 - p484 [1-50]
Zuravleff, Mary Kay - *The Frequency of Souls*
  Books - v10 - Je '96 - p23 [51-250]
  BW - v26 - Ag 25 '96 - p11 [501+]
Zurcher, Arnold - *Struggle to Unite Europe*
  Wil Q - v21 - Win '97 - p38 [1-50]
Zurick, David - *Errant Journeys*
  AAAGA - v87 - Mr '97 - p189+ [501+]
Zurier, Rebecca - *Metropolitan Lives*
  Lon R Bks - v18 - O 3 '96 - p25 [501+]
Zur Meuhlen, Karl-Heinz - *Reformatorisches Profil*
  Six Ct J - v27 - Win '96 - p1225+ [501+]
Zvekic, Ugljesa - *Criminal Victimisation in the Developing World*
  CS - v25 - S '96 - p663+ [501+]
  J Gov Info - v23 - S '96 - p676+ [51-250]
Zvirin, Stephanie - *The Best Years of Their Lives. 2nd Ed.*
  BL - v93 - S 15 '96 - p254 [51-250]
Zwarg, Christina - *Feminist Conversations*
  AL - v68 - D '96 - p851+ [501+]
  MLR - v91 - O '96 - p983+ [501+]
  NEQ - v69 - O '96 - p640+ [501+]
Zweibel, Alan - *Bunny Bunny*
  Ent W - My 16 '97 - p109 [51-250]
Zweifel, Frances - *The Make-Something Club Is Back! (Illus. by Ann Schweninger)*
  c BL - v93 - F 1 '97 - p944 [51-250]
  c KR - v65 - F 15 '97 - p309 [51-250]
  c SLJ - v43 - Mr '97 - p182 [51-250]
Zweifel, Karyn - *Southern Vampires*
  y Emerg Lib - v24 - S '96 - p27 [1-50]
Zweig, David - *China's Brain Drain to the United States*
  Ch Rev Int - v4 - Spr '97 - p298+ [501+]
Zweig, Phillip L - *Wriston: Walter Wriston, Citibank, and the Rise and Fall of American Financial Supremacy*
  Bus Bk R - v13 - 3 '96 - p56+ [501+]
Zweizig, Douglas - *The Tell It! Manual*
  LAR - v98 - O '96 - p534 [251-500]
  RQ - v36 - Fall '96 - p158+ [251-500]
  SLMQ - v24 - Sum '96 - p220 [51-250]
Zwicker, Steven N - *Lines of Authority*
  Ren Q - v49 - Win '96 - p866+ [501+]
Zwicky, Jan - *Lyric Philosophy*
  Dialogue - v35 - Fall '96 - p847+ [501+]
Zwinger, Susan - *Still Wild, Always Wild*
  PW - v244 - F 17 '97 - p207 [51-250]

Zwiren, Scott - *God Head*
    ABR - v18 - D '96 - p16 [501+]
 y BL - v92 - Ag '96 - p1884 [51-250]
 y BL - v92 - Ag '96 - p1891 [1-50]
    KR - v64 - S 15 '96 - p1353 [251-500]
    LATBR - O 6 '96 - p14 [51-250]
    LJ - v121 - N 1 '96 - p109 [51-250]
    LJ - v122 - Mr 15 '97 - p43 [1-50]
    NYTBR - v101 - D 29 '96 - p14 [51-250]
    PW - v243 - O 7 '96 - p66 [51-250]
Zwirn, Jerrold - *Accessing U.S. Government Information.*
  Rev. and Expanded Ed.
 r ARBA - v28 - '97 - p29 [51-250]

A

c 1-2-3 Caterpillar — *Calino*
c 1 2 3 Count with Me — *Tucker, Sian*
c 1, 2, 3 Moose (Illus. by Art Wolfe) — *Wolfe, Art*
c 1, 2, 3 to the Zoo (Illus. by Eric Carle) — *Carle, Eric*
c 1, 2, 3 What Do You See? (Illus. by Susi Bohdal) — *Bohdal, Susi*
1-900-Dead — *Fennelly, Tony*
1 Enoch and Sirach — *Argall, Randal A*
1 Kings   *Walsh, Jerome T*
1 Peter — *Achtemeier, Paul J*
c 2 Cuddly Ducks
c 2 Cuddly Lambs
The 2-Ingredient Cook Book — *Rosemire, Adeline*
2 Skadespel — *Frostenson, Katarina*
2nd Collector Steiff Values — *Consalvi, Peter*
2nd Time Around — *Hardy, James Earl*
3-D Geometric Origami — *Gurkewitz, Rona*
c 3-D Kid — *Culbertson, Roger*
3 K: The Cosmic Microwave Background Radiation — *Partridge, R B*
c 3 Kids Dreamin' (Illus. by Dena Schutzer) — *England, Linda*
y 3 NBs of Julian Drew — *Deem, James M*
III-Nitride, SiC, and Diamond Materials for Electronic Devices — *Gaskill, D Kurt*
3 Plays — *Crowley, Mart*
p 3D Design
3D Graphics and VRML 2 — *Lemay, Laura*
3D Graphics File Formats — *Rule, Keith*
3D Studio Hollywood and Gaming Effects — *Carter, David, 1965-*
3I: Fifty Years Investing in Industry — *Coopey, R*
3rd Rock from the Sun — *Glouberman, Michael*
yr The 4 Routes to Entrepreneurial Success — *Miner, John B*
The 4th Course of Chicken Soup for the Soul — *Canfield, Jack*
V Centenario Do Livro Impresso Em Portugal 1487-1987
r The 5 Minute Clinical Consult for Dental Professionals — *Hupp, James R*
5S for Operators — *Hirano, Hiroyuki*
The 7 Habits of Highly Effective People — *Covey, Stephen R*
7 Survival Skills for a Reengineered World — *Yeomans, William N*
7 Things Kids Never Forget and How to Make the Most of Them — *Rose, Ron*
y 8 Ball Chicks — *Sikes, Gini*
The VIII Olympiad — *Phillips, Ellen*
8th IEEE Signal Processing Workshop on Statistical Signal and Array Processing — *IEEE SP Workshop on Statistical Signal and Array Processing (8th: 1996: Corfu, Greece)*
The 9 Steps to Financial Freedom — *Orman, Suze*
10-Minute Guide to Annual Reports and Prospectuses — *Gelb, Eric*
10 Steps to Home Ownership — *Glink, Ilyce R*
10 Women by Peter Lindbergh — *Lindbergh, Peter*
10 Women Who Helped Shape America — *Glasscock, Sarah*
10 Years of Dolce and Gabbana
The XI, XII, and XIII Olympiads — *Constable, George*
c The 11th Commandment
11th International Congress on Catalysis — *International Congress on Catalysis (11th: 1996: Baltimore, MD)*
c The 12 Days of Christmas (Illus. by Linnea Asplind Riley) — *Twelve Days of Christmas (English Folk Song)*

c 12 Petits Europeens — *Lambert, Nicole*
12 Views of Manet's Bar — *Collins, Bradford R*
13 Days to Glory — *Tinkle, Lon*
c The 13th Floor (Illus. by Peter Sis) — *Fleischman, Sid*
c The 13th Floor (Adamson). Audio Version — *Fleischman, Sid*
y The 14th Dalai Lama: Spiritual Leader of Tibet — *Stewart, Whitney*
14th IEEE VLSI Test Symposium — *IEEE VLSI Test Symposium (14th: 1996: Princeton, N.J.)*
The 17 Laws of Successful Investing — *Rodman, Richard*
18th Century France to Art of the Sixties — *Crow, Thomas*
Der 20: Juli 1944 — *Ueberschar, Gerd R*
The 20-Minute Gardener — *Christopher, Tom*
The 20-Minute Gardener (Christopher). Audio Version — *Christopher, Tom*
20-Minute One-Dish Gourmet — *Levin, Karen*
20 Most Asked Questions about the Amish and Mennonites — *Good, Merle*
y 20 One-Act Plays from 20 Years of the Humana Festival — *Volansky, Michele*
c 20 Prayer Lessons for Children — *Wezeman, Phyllis Vos*
c The 20th Century — *Deary, Terry*
y 20th Century: A Visual History — *Adams, Simon*
r The 20th-Century Art Book
20th Century Composers Series
20th-Century Italian Women Writers — *Amoia, Alba*
20th Fighter Group — *MacKay, Ron*
The 21st Century Nonprofit — *Firstenberg, Paul B*
The XXIII Olympiad — *Galford, Ellen*
24 Hours (Collective Effort)
y 24 Hours in Cyberspace — *Smolan, Rick*
c 24 Strange Little Animals (Illus. by Graham Percy) — *Percy, Graham*
25 and Under: Fiction — *Ketchin, Susan*
25 and Under: Photographers — *George, Alice Rose*
25 Aprile: Liberazione — *Scoppola, Pietro*
The 25th Anniversary of Czechoslovak Independence — *Kralicek, V J*
c 29 Bump Street — *Vaes, Alain*
30-Minute Vegetarian Recipes — *Gwynn, Mary*
r 30 Years of Regional Trends. Electronic Media Version
The 37th Mandala — *Laidlaw, Marc*
40 Ways to Raise a Nonracist Child — *Mathias, Barbara*
c La 42e Soeur De Bebert — *Duchesne, Christiane*
'48 — *Herbert, James*
50 Biggest Baseball Myths — *Toropov, Brandon*
50 Essential Things to Do When the Doctor Says It's Diabetes — *Tonnessen, Diana*
50 Fabulous Places to Retire in America. 2nd Ed. — *Stern, Ken*
The 50 Most Erotic Films of All Time — *McDonagh, Maitland*
The 50 Most Influential Women in American Law — *Berry, Dawn Bradley*
The 50 Most Romantic Things Ever Done — *Von Mueffling, Dini*
The 50-Year Dash — *Greene, Bob*
The 50-Year Dash (Greene). Audio Version — *Greene, Bob*
50 Years Is Enough — *Danaher, Kevin*
60 Second Chronic Pain Relief — *Lehndorff, Peter*
c 60 Super Simple Crafts (Illus. by Leo Abbett) — *Hebert, Holly*
c 60 Super Simple Magic Tricks (Illus. by Leo Abbett) — *McMaster, Shawn*

The 60s: Spiritual Awakening — *Ellwood, Robert S*
The 6'1 Grinch — *White, Tiffany*
64 Intruder — *Glading, Gregory T*
Il 75 Anniversario Del Pontificio Istituto Orientale — *Taft, Robert F*
75 Years of All-Time Favorites
The 77 Habits of Highly Ineffective Christians — *Fabry, Chris*
c 92 Queen's Road — *Case, Dianne*
96 Great Interview Questions to Ask before You Hire — *Falcone, Paul*
96 Tears — *Swanson, Doug J*
99 Poems in Translation — *Pinter, Harold*
100 and More Basic NMR Experiments — *Braun, Siegmar*
r The 100 Best Mutual Funds You Can Buy 1995
r The 100 Best Small Art Towns in America — *Villani, John*
100 Flowers and How They Got Their Names — *Wells, Diana*
c 100 Greatest Manmade Wonders — *Sechi-Johnson, Patricia*
c 100 Greatest Natural Wonders — *Cranfield, Ingrid*
c 100 Greatest Tyrants — *Langley, Andrew*
r 100 Masterpieces from the Vitra Design Museum Collection — *Design Museum Vitra*
y 100% Mathematical Proof — *Garnier, Rowan*
yr The 100 Most Popular Young Adult Authors — *Drew, Bernard A*
c 100 Nursery Rhymes (Francis). Book and Audio Version
yr 100 Research Topic Guides for Students — *Borne, Barbara Wood*
100 Simple Sauces for Today's Healthy Home Cooking — *Jerome, Carl*
The 100 Things Everyone Needs to Know about Australia — *Dale, David*
100 Ways to Motivate Yourself (Chandler). Audio Version — *Chandler, Steve*
100 Years at Mackinac — *Armour, David A*
100 Years on the Road — *Spears, Timothy B*
c 101 American English Idioms
101 Best Home Businesses — *Ramsey, Dan*
101 Best Weekend Businesses — *Ramsey, Dan*
101 Bir Dize — *Turan, Guven*
101 Businesses You Can Start on the Internet — *Janal, Daniel S*
101 Careers in Mathematics — *Sterrett, Andrew*
101 Home Office Success Secrets — *Kanarek, Lisa*
c 101 Optical Illusions (Illus. by Alex Pang) — *Jennings, Terry*
c 101 Questions and Answers about Backyard Wildlife (Illus. by Jennifer DiRubbio) — *Squire, Ann*
p The 101 Times
c 101 Ways to Bug Your Parents — *Wardlaw, Lee*
r The 105 Best Investments for the 21st Century — *Maturi, Richard J*
113 Galician-Portuguese Troubadour Poems — *Zenith, Richard*
y 160 Ways to Help the World — *Duper, Linda Leeb*
c 175 Easy-to-Do Christmas Crafts — *Umnik, Sharon Dunn*
c 175 Easy-to-Do Thanksgiving Crafts — *Umnik, Sharon Dunn*
y 200 Intriguing Chess Puzzles — *Greif, Martin*
c 263 Brain Busters — *Phillips, Louis*
277 Secrets Your Dog Wants You to Know — *Cooper, Paulette*
301 — *Swetnam, Ford*
r 303 CD-ROMs to Use in Your Library — *Dewey, Partick R*

The 365 Days of Christmas — *Byron, William J*
365 Foods Kids Love to Eat — *Ellison, Sheila*
365 More Ways to Cook Chicken — *Barnard, Melanie*
r 365 Ways-- — *Kerschner, Helen K*
366 Healthful Ways to Cook Leafy Greens — *Leahy, Linda Romanelli*
366 Simply Delicious Dairy-Free Recipes — *Robertson, Robin*
400 Lettres De Musiciens Au Musee Royal De Mariemont — *Haine, Malou*
r 400 Videos You've Got to Rent! — *Sillick, Ardis*
500 Anos Del Ensayo En Hispanoamerica — *Maree, Kathy*
500 Computing Tips for Teachers and Lecturers — *Race, Phil*
500 Flower and Animal Cross Stitch Designs — *Hasler, Julie*
500 Low-Fat and Fat-Free Pasta, Rice, and Grain Recipes — *Schlesinger, Sarah*
The 500-Year Delta — *Taylor, James, 1947-*
r 501 Hebrew Verbs — *Bolozky, Shmuel*
r 501 Portuguese Verbs — *Nitti, John*
c 53<1/2> Things That Changed the World (Illus. by David West) — *Parker, Steve*
r 989 Great Part-Time Jobs in Seattle — *Carlson, Linda*
996-1996 Ostarrichi-Osterreich — *Bruckmuller, Ernst*
The 1,000 Hour War — *McCain, Thomas A*
r 1001 Colorado Place Names — *Benson, Maxine*
1,001 Great Gifts — *Brody, Jane A*
1001 Guitar Tips and Tricks — *Jones, Andy*
r 1001 Hints and Tips for Your Garden
r 1001 Midnights — *Pronzini, Bill*
1003 Salt and Pepper Shakers — *Carey, Larry*
1650-1850: Ideas, Aesthetics, and Inquiries in the Early Modern Era. Vol. 2 — *Cope, Kevin L*
1745: Charles Edward Stuart and the Jacobites — *Savage, Robert C Woosnam*
1788: A Narrative of the Expedition to Botany Bay. A Complete Account of the Settlement at Port Jackson — *Tench, Watkin*
y 1812 (Hill). Audio Version — *Nevin, David*
1815: The Roads to Waterloo — *Dallas, Gregor*
c 1848: Year of Revolution — *Grant, R G*
r 1850 Census of North Central Arkansas — *McLane, Bobbie Jones*
The 1890's: Australian Literature and Literary Culture — *Stewart, Ken*
1910: The Emancipation of Dissonance — *Harrison, Thomas J*
1922: The Birth of Irish Democracy — *Garvin, Tom*
1939: The Lost World of the Fair — *Gelernter, David*
1946, L'Art De La Reconstruction — *Frechuret, M*
1988 — *McGahan, Andrew*
y 1989: The Year the World Changed — *Symynkywicz, Jeffrey B*
r The 1990-91 Gulf War — *Orgill, Andrew*
The 1990s Slump — *Baldassarri, Mario*
1996 Australian Software Engineering Conference — *Australian Software Engineering Conference (1996: Melbourne, Vic.)*
1996 IEEE Real-Time Technology and Applications Symposium — *Real-Time Technology and Applications Symposium (1996: Brookline, MA)*
r 2000 Postmarks of Prince Edward Island 1814-1995 — *Murray, G Douglas*
r 2000 Years of Disbelief — *Haught, James A*
2001: Filming the Future — *Bizony, Piers*
r 2001 French and English Idioms. 2nd Ed. — *Denoeu, Francois*
r 2001 Italian and English Idioms. 2nd Ed. — *Gobetti, Daniela*
r 2001 Japanese and English Idioms — *Akiyama, Nobuo*
2015: After the Boom — *Turner, Garth*
The 3,000 Mile Garden — *Land, Leslie*
y 3001: The Final Odyssey — *Clarke, Arthur C*
The 4300 4-8-2s — *Church, Robert J*
c 20,000 Leagues Under the Sea (Illus. by Stephen Armes) — *Verne, Jules*
A. Aubrey Bodine: Baltimore Pictorialist 1906-1970 — *Ewing, Kathleen M H*
p A. Bacus
A+ Certification Success Guide — *Parks, Sarah T*
A Coeur De Jour — *Boucher, Denise*
A Fotografia Na Arte Contemporanea — *Vilarino, Manuel*
A.G. Rizzoli: Architect of Magnificent Visions — *Hernandez, Jo Farb*
c A Is for AAARGH! — *Rodgers, Frank*
c A Is for Apple, W Is for Witch (Illus. by Capucine Mazille) — *Dexter, Catherine*

y A Is for Arctic (Illus. by Wayne Lynch) — *Lynch, Wayne*
c A Is for Asia (Illus. by Yumi Heo) — *Chin-Lee, Cynthia*
c A.J. Foyt — *Wilker, Josh*
A La Decouverte Du Petit Prince — *Brown, Anne Gassaway*
A La Recherche De L'Ordre Cosmique. Vols. 1-2 — *Aellen, Christian*
A La Recherche Du Temps Perdu — *Proust, Marcel*
A La Sombra De La Corona — *Hernandez, Mauro*
y A-Level Chemistry Pass Books: London Board Examinations — *Ramsden, E N*
y A-Level Chemistry Pass Books: Northern Board Examinations — *Ramsden, E N*
A.M. Klein: The Story of the Poet — *Pollock, Zailig*
c A My Name Is... (Illus. by Lynne Cravath) — *Lyne, Alice*
c A.N.T.I.D.O.T.E. — *Blackman, Malorie*
A.P. Giannini and the Bank of America — *Nash, Gerald D*
A.P. Giannini: Banker of America — *Bonadio, Felice A*
y A. Philip Randolph: Messenger for the Masses — *Patterson, Lillie A*
A. Philip Randolph, Pioneer of the Civil Rights Movement — *Pfeffer, Paula F*
A Propos De Clemence — *Etcherelli, Claire*
A.S. Byatt — *Kelly, Kathleen Coyne*
c The A to Z Beastly Jamboree (Illus. by Robert Bender) — *Bender, Robert*
The A-to-Z Book of Managing People — *Kaplan, Victoria*
A to Z of Britain — *Lambton, Lucinda*
A-Train: Memoirs of a Tuskegee Airman — *Dryden, Charles W*
A Votre Tour! — *Valette, Jean-Paul*
A.W.N. Pugin: Master of Gothic Revival — *Aldrich, Megan Brewster*
r A-Z Encyclopedia of Garden Plants — *Brickell, Christopher*
r A-Z of Authorship — *Methold, Ken*
r The A-Z of Horror Films — *Maxford, Howard*
The Aachen Memorandum — *Roberts, Andrew*
r AAL Picture Book Index. 3rd Ed. — *Hobson, Margaret*
y Aama in America — *Coburn, Broughton*
The Aardvark Is Ready for War — *Blinn, James W*
Aaron Douglas: Art, Race, and the Harlem Renaissance — *Kirschke, Amy Helene*
Aaron Spelling: A Prime-Time Life — *Spelling, Aaron*
Aaron Spelling: A Prime-Time Life (Spelling). Audio Version — *Spelling, Aaron*
c Aaron's Awful Allergies (Illus. by Eugenie Fernandes) — *Harrison, Troon*
The AARP: America's Most Powerful Lobby and the Clash of Generations — *Morris, Charles R*
r AASL Electronic Library. 1st Ed. Electronic Media Version
A=B — *Petkovsek, Marko*
The Abacus and the Sword — *Duus, Peter*
c The Abacus Contest (Illus. by Hsiao-Chun Li) — *Wu, Priscilla*
The Abandoned Generation — *Willimon, William H*
Abandoned in the Wasteland — *Minow, Newton N*
Abandonment of Settlements and Regions — *Cameron, Catherine M*
El Abanico Y La Cigarrera — *Denegri, Francesca*
El Abate Viscardo. Rev. Ed. — *Batllori, Miguel*
L'Abbaye Premontre Du Lac De Joux Des Origines Au XIVe Siecle — *Martinet, Claire*
L'Abbe De Choisy, Androgyne Et Mandarin — *Cruysse, Dirk Van Der*
Abbot Aelred Carlyle, Caldey Island, and the Anglo-Catholic Revival in England — *Kollar, Rene*
Abbreviating Ernie — *Lefcourt, Peter*
The Abbreviation of the Introduction to Astrology — *Abu Mashar*
c Abby (Illus. by Alan Marks) — *Hanel, Wolfram*
Abby Whiteside on Piano Playing — *Whiteside, Abby*
c Abby's Wish (Illus. by Michael Krone) — *St. John, Liza*
c ABC Career Book for Girls (Illus. by John Schafer) — *Stockdale, Linda*
r ABC Chinese-English Dictionary — *DeFrancis, John*
r The ABC-CLIO Companion to American Reconstruction 1862-1877 — *Richter, William L*
r The ABC-CLIO Companion to the Native American Rights Movement — *Grossman, Mark*
r The ABC-CLIO Companion to Transportation in America — *Richter, William L*

yr The ABC-CLIO World History Companion to the Industrial Revolution — *Stearns, Peter N*
The ABC Collection — *Gray, Lyn*
r ABC for Book Collectors. 7th Ed. — *Carter, John*
c ABC I Like Me! (Illus. by Nancy Carlson) — *Carlson, Nancy*
c ABC of Crawlers and Flyers (Illus. by Hope Ryden) — *Ryden, Hope*
c ABC Snake — *Calino*
c ABC Yummy (Illus. by Lisa Jahn-Clough) — *Jahn-Clough, Lisa*
L'ABCdaire Du Cinema Francais — *Guegan, Gerard*
ABCD...SGML — *Alschuler, Liora*
The ABCs of Learning Disabilities — *Wong, Bernice Y L*
ABCs of the Internet — *Crumlish, Christian*
r Abdominal Access in Open and Laparoscopic Surgery — *Tsoi, Edmund K M*
y The Abduction — *Newth, Mette*
c Abe Lincoln Goes to Washington 1837-1865 (Illus. by Cheryl Harness) — *Harness, Cheryl*
Abe Lincoln Laughing — *Zall, Paul M*
Abelian Functions — *Baker, H F*
Abelian Groups and Modules — *Arnold, David M*
c The Abenaki — *Landau, Elaine*
Abhandlungen Fur Die Kunde Des Morgenlandes — *Lohlker, Rudiger*
Abiding Courage — *Lemke-Santangelo, Gretchen*
y Abigail Adams: Witness to a Revolution — *Bober, Natalie*
c Abigail's Drum (Illus. by Robert Quackenbush) — *Minahan, John A*
c Abimbolu — *Jacoby, Jean*
r Abingdon Clergy Income Tax Guide. 1997 Ed.
Able Children in Ordinary Schools — *Eyre, Deborah*
Abolishing Death — *Masing-Delic, Irene*
The Abolition of Marriage — *Gallagher, Maggie*
The Abolitionist Sisterhood — *Yellin, Jean Fagan*
The Abolitionists and the South 1831-1861 — *Harrold, Stanley*
Aboriginal Health in Canada — *Waldram, James B*
Aboriginal Self-Government — *Macklem, Patrick*
Aboriginal Self-Government and Social Services: Final Report — *Durst, Douglas*
Aboriginal Sovereignty — *Reynolds, Henry*
Aborting Law — *Kellough, Gail*
y Abortion — *Roleff, Tamara L*
Abortion: A Reader — *Steffen, Lloyd*
yr Abortion: A Reference Handbook. 2nd Ed. — *Costa, Marie*
Abortion and Catholicism — *Jung, Patricia Beattie*
r Abortion and Reproductive Rights. Electronic Media Version
Abortion and the Politics of Motherhood — *Luker, Kristin*
Abortion and Unborn Human Life — *Lee, Patrick*
Abortion and Woman's Choice — *Petchesky, Rosalind Pollack*
y The Abortion Battle — *Lowenstein, Felicia*
Abortion: Between Freedom and Necessity — *Hadley, Janet*
Abortion in America — *Mohr, James C*
Abortion: Law, Choice and Morality — *Callahan, Daniel*
r Abortion Policies. Vol. 3 — *United Nations. Dept. of Economic and Social Development*
Abortion Politics in the Federal Courts — *Yarnold, Barbara M*
Abortion Rates in the United States — *Wetstein, Matthew E*
y Abortion: Rights, Options, and Choices — *Andryszewski, Tricia*
Abortion: The Supreme Court Decisions — *Shapiro, Ian*
About Desire and Other Poems — *Clark, Alison*
About Law — *Honore, Tony*
About Modern Art — *Sylvester, David*
About Schmidt — *Begley, Louis*
About Storytelling — *McKay, Helen*
c About Your Toys — *Taylor, Barbara*
About Yvonne — *Masini, Donna*
Above the Law — *Burnham, David*
Above the Tree Line — *Mangan, Kathy*
c Above the Treeline (Illus. by Dorothy Emerling) — *Cooper, Ann*
c Abracadabra — *Schubert, Ingrid*
y The Abracadabra Kid — *Fleischman, Sid*
c Abracadabra! The Ultimate Magic Kit
Abraham Joshua Heschel: Exploring His Life and Thought — *Merkle, John C*

Abraham Lincoln — *Charnwood, Godfrey Rathbone Benson, Baron*

Abraham Lincoln and a Nation Worth Fighting For — *Rawley, James A*

Abraham: Sign of Hope for Jews, Christians and Muslims — *Kuschel, Karl-Josef*

Abraham's Promise — *Jeyaretnam, Philip*

Abram Tertz and the Poetics of Crime — *Nepomnyashchy, Catherine Theimer*

c Abran Paso A Los Patitos (Illus. by Robert McCloskey) — *McCloskey, Robert*

Abroad: British Literary Traveling between the Wars — *Fussell, Paul*

Abschied Von Den Feinden — *Jirgl, Reinhard*

Abschied Von Jerusalem — *Mitgutsch, Waltraud Anna*

c A...B...Sea (Illus. by Christopher Hartley) — *Kalman, Bobbie*

An Absence of Light — *Lindsey, David L*

Absent at the Creation — *Lord, Christopher*

Absent Lord — *Babb, Lawrence A*

c The Absent-Minded Toad (Illus. by Marcela Cabrera) — *Rondon, Javier*

Absentee Ownership — *Veblen, Thorstein*

Absentee Zen — *Roshi, Richard Dogo Moss*

Absolut Book — *Lewis, Richard W*

The Absolute Chronology of the Aegean Early Bronze Age — *Manning, Sturt W*

Absolute Disaster — *Montgomery, Lee*

Absolute Magnitude — *Lupine, Warren*

Absolute Monarchy and the Stuart Constitution — *Burgess, Glenn*

Absolute Power — *Baldacci, David*

Absolute Power — *Goldman, William*

y Absolute Power (Guidall). Audio Version — *Baldacci, David*

Absolute Power (Heald). Audio Version — *Baldacci, David*

Absolute Power (Kramer). Audio Version — *Baldacci, David*

y Absolutely Normal Chaos — *Creech, Sharon*

Absolutely, Positively — *Krentz, Jayne Ann*

Absolutely Typical — *Mather, Victoria*

Absolutismus Und Offentlichkeit — *Gestrich, Andreas*

Absterbende Gemutlichkeit — *Rosendorfer, Herbert*

Abstract Algebra. 2nd Ed. — *Beachy, John A*

r Abstract Expressionist Women Painters — *Puniello, Francoise S*

r An Abstract of North Carolina Wills from about 1760 to about 1800 — *Olds, Fred A*

The Abstract Wild — *Turner, Jack*

Abstracting Craft — *McCullough, Malcolm*

Abstraction in the Twentieth Century — *Rosenthal, Mark*

r Abstracts of Giles County, Tennessee — *Wells, Carol*

r Abstracts of the Wills and Inventories of Bath County, Virginia 1791-1842 — *Bruns, Jean R*

c Abuela (Illus. by Elisa Kleven) — *Dorros, Arthur*

c Abuela's Weave — *Castaneda, Omar S*

The Abuse Excuse and Other Cop-Outs, Sob Stories, and Evasions of Responsibility — *Dershowitz, Alan M*

The Abuse of Diplomatic Privileges and Immunities — *Barker, J Craig*

Abuse of Power — *Rosenberg, Nancy Taylor*

Abuse of Power (Crouse). Audio Version — *Rosenberg, Nancy Taylor*

The Abusive Elder — *Jackson, Vera R*

y Abusive Relationships — *Rue, Nancy N*

yr Academic American Encyclopedia 1996. Vols. 1-21

Academic Freedom in Africa — *Diouf, Mamadou*

Academic Libraries — *McCabe, Gerard B*

r Academic Libraries as High-Tech Gateways — *Bazillion, Richard J*

The Academic Man — *Wilson, Logan*

The Academic Postmodern and the Rule of Literature — *Simpson, David*

yr Academic Press Dictionary of Science and Technology. Version 1.0. Electronic Media Version

The Academic System in American Society — *Touraine, Alain*

Academic Writing for Graduate Students — *Swales, John M*

The Academic's Handbook. 2nd Ed. — *Deneef, A Leigh*

Accelerated Learning for the 21st Century. Rev. Ed. — *Rose, Colin*

The Accelerating Organization — *Maira, Arun*

Accents as Well as Broad Effects — *Van Rensselaer, Mrs. Schuyler*

Acceptable Losses — *Ziesk, Edra*

Acceptable Risks for Major Infrastructure — *Seminar on Acceptable Risks for Extreme Events in the Planning and Design of Major Infrastructure (1994: Sydney, Australia)*

r Access New York Restaurants 96/97

r Access San Francisco Restaurants. 2nd Ed.

Access to Air Travel for People with Reduced Mobility

Access to B-ISDN via PONs — *Killat, Ulrich*

Access to Justice: Final Report to the Lord Chancellor on the Civil Justice System in England and Wales — *Woolf, Harry, Sir*

Accessible Design Review Guide — *University of Florida. College of Architecture. Accessible Space Team*

Accessible Gardening — *Woy, Joann*

Accessible Meetings in North Dakota

r Accessing Transport Networks — *Robertson, Don*

r Accessing U.S. Government Information. Rev. and Expanded Ed. — *Zwirn, Jerrold*

The Accession of Henry II in England — *Amt, Emilie*

Accident — *Steel, Danielle*

Accident and Design — *Hood, Christopher, 1947-*

Accident and Emergency. 3rd Ed. — *Brown, Anthony F T*

Accident Prevention on Board Ship at Sea and in Port. 2nd Rev. Ed. — *International Labour Office*

The Accidental Activist — *Gingrich, Candace*

Accidental Archaeologist — *Jennings, Jesse D*

An Accidental Autobiography — *Harrison, Barbara Grizzuti*

y Accidental Death — *Cassidy, Anne*

Accidental Grace — *Beveridge, Judith*

Accidental Justice — *Bell, Peter Alan*

An Accidental Shroud — *Eccles, Marjorie*

Accidentally, on Purpose — *Dornstein, Ken*

Accidents in North American Mountaineering 1995

y Accidents May Happen (Illus. by John O'Brien) — *Jones, Charlotte Foltz*

r Accomack County, Virginia Early Marriage Records. Vols. 1-2 — *Lyons, Sherry H*

An Accompaniment to Higher Mathematics — *Exner, George R*

The Accomplice — *Ironside, Elizabeth*

According to the Law — *Balle, Solvej*

Accordion Crimes — *Proulx, E Annie*

The Account: Alvar Nunez Cabeza De Vaca's Relacion — *Nunez Cabeza De Vaca, Alvar*

Account Roll of the Holy Trinity Priory, Dublin 1337-1346 — *Gillespie, Raymond*

Accountability in Human Resource Management — *Phillips, Jack J*

Accounting, a Multiparadigmatic Science — *Riahi-Belkaoui, Ahmed*

Accounting as Social and Institutional Practice — *Hopwood, Anthony G*

Accounting for Fundamentalisms — *Marty, Martin E*

Accounting for Growth — *Smith, Terry*

Accounting for Tastes — *Becker, Gary Stanley*

Accounting History Newsletter 1980-1989 and Accounting History 1989-1994 — *Carnegie, Garry D*

p Accounting Horizons

r Accredited Institutions of Postsecondary Education, Programs, Candidates 1995-96

Accuracy and Stability of Numerical Algorithms — *Higham, Nicholas J*

Accustomed to the Dark — *Satterthwait, Walter*

y Ace Any Test. 3rd Ed. — *Fry, Ronald W*

Ace in the Hole — *Botti, Timothy J*

Ace the Technical Interview — *Rothstein, Michael*

Ache Life History — *Hill, Kim*

Achieving a Curriculum-Based Library Media Center Program — *Smith, Jane Bandy*

Achieving Accountability in Business and Government — *Sheldon, D R*

Achieving Racial Balance — *Stave, Sondra Astor*

Achieving School Readiness — *Immroth, Barbara Froling*

Achieving Sustainable Development — *Dale, Ann*

Achieving the Competitive Edge — *Frigon, Normand L*

Achille Bocchi and the Emblem Book as Symbolic Form — *Watson, Elizabeth See*

Achilles in the Quantum Universe — *Morris, Richard*

Achilles in Vietnam — *Shay, Jonathan*

Achim Von Arnims Kunsttheorie Und Sein Roman Die Kronenwachter Im Kontext Ihrer Epoche — *Neuhold, Martin*

Acid — *Falco, Edward*

c Acid Rain — *Edmonds, Alex*

Ackermanthology! — *Ackerman, Forrest J*

c Ackford's Monster — *Warburton, Nick*

The Acmeist Movement in Russian Poetry — *Doherty, Justin*

The Acolyte — *Compton, David*

The Acolyte (Diamond). Audio Version — *Compton, David*

Os Acores E O Controlo Do Atlantico 1898-1948 — *Telo, Antonio Jose*

c An Acorn for Tea (Illus. by Catherine Walters) — *Sykes, Julie*

Acorna: The Unicorn Girl — *McCaffrey, Anne*

c The Acorn's Story (Illus. by Valerie Greeley) — *Greeley, Valerie*

Acoustic Wave Sensors — *Ballantine, D S*

Acoustical Imaging — *International Symposium on Acoustical Imaging (22nd: 1995: Florence, Italy)*

Acousto-Optics. 2nd Ed. — *Korpel, Adrian*

Acqua Alta — *Leon, Donna*

Acquired Motives — *Lovett, Sarah Poland*

y Acquired Motives (Crouse). Audio Version — *Lovett, Sarah Poland*

Acquired Taste — *Peterson, T Sarah*

Acquiring, Adapting and Developing Technologies — *Minami, Ryoshin*

An Acre of Time — *Jenkins, Phil*

r Acronyms, Initialisms and Abbreviations Dictionary 1997. Vol. 1, Pts. 1-3

Acropolis Restoration — *Economides, Richard*

y Across Boundaries — *Ramphele, Mamphela*

Across Fortune's Tracks — *Campbell, Walter E*

c Across the Columbia Plain — *Lewty, Peter J*

c Across the Lines — *Reeder, Carolyn*

y Across the Plains in the Donner Party — *Murphy, Virginia Reed*

Across the Sahara from Tripoli to Bornu — *Vischer, Hanns*

Across the West — *Madsen, David B*

Across the Western Ocean — *Finamore, Daniel*

c Across the Wide and Lonesome Prairie — *Gregory, Kristiana*

c Across the Wide Dark Sea (Illus. by Thomas B Allen) — *Van Leeuwen, Jean*

Acrylics: A Step-by-Step Guide to Acrylics Techniques — *Gair, Angela*

r ACSM's Handbook for the Team Physician — *Kibler, W Ben*

The Act Itself — *Bennett, Jonathan*

Act of Betrayal — *Buchanan, Edna*

Act of Betrayal (Burr). Audio Version — *Buchanan, Edna*

The Act of Bible Reading — *Dyck, Elmer*

The Act of Seeing — *Wenders, Wim*

Actes Du Colloque La Fontaine, De Chateau-Thierry A Vaux-Le-Vicomte. Pt. 2 — *Dandrey, Patrick*

Acting Assertively at Work — *Valentich, Mary*

Acting Male — *Bingham, Dennis*

Acting (Re)considered — *Zarrilli, Phillip B*

c Action Alphabet (Illus. by Shelley Rotner) — *Rotner, Shelley*

Action and Reflection in Teacher Education — *Harvard, Gareth*

Action Directe — *Dartnell, Michael Y*

c Action Rhymes (Illus. by Carol Thompson) — *Foster, John*

c Action Robots (Illus. by Gavin MacLeod) — *Reeve, Tim*

r Action Series and Sequels — *Drew, Bernard A*

yr Action! The Action Movie A-Z — *Julius, Marshall*

Actium and Augustus — *Gurval, Robert Alan*

Active Comprehension. Bks. 1-4 — *Stillie, Margaret*

Active Control of Vibration and Noise — *Tan, C A*

r Active Electronic Component Handbook. 2nd Ed. — *Harper, Charles A*

Active Faith — *Reed, Ralph*

Active Faith (Reed). Audio Version — *Reed, Ralph*

Active Galactic Nuclei — *Robson, Ian*

Active X Sourcebook — *Coombs, Ted*

Actively Seeking Work? — *King, Desmond*

The Activist Cancer Patient — *Zakarian, Beverly*

Activist Research Manual of Sources of Information on Corporations — *Draffan, George*

The Activist's Daughter — *Bache, Ellyn*

The Activist's Handbook — *Shaw, Randy*

Activities for Public Sector Training — *Griffiths, Mary*

Activity-Based Cost Management — *Cokins, Gary*

An Actor and His Time — *Gielgud, John*

Actors and Singers — *Wagner, Richard, 1813-1883*

The Actors in Europe's Foreign Policy — *Hill, Christopher, 1948-*

Actors Take Action — *O'Neil, Brian*

Acts — *Larkin, William J*

Acts of Conscience — *Barton, William*

Acts of Discovery — *Furtwangler, Albert*
Acts of Fiction — *Carpenter, Scott*
Acts of Hope — *White, James Boyd, 1938-*
Acts of Love — *Michael, Judith*
Acts of Narrative — *O'Neill, Patrick*
Acts of Revision — *Bedford, Martyn*
r The Acts of the Apostles — *Mills, Watson E*
Acts of War — *Clancy, Tom*
The Actual — *Bellow, Saul*
y An Actual Life — *Thomas, Abigail*
c Acuarelas — *Comella, M Angels*
Acupuncture in Clinical Practice — *Bai, Xinghua*
Acute Paediatrics — *Ryan, Steven*
Acute Respiratory Failure in Chronic Obstructive
    Pulmonary Disease — *Derenne, Jean-Philippe*
Ad Nota — *Bandini, Raffaello*
y Adam and Eve and Pinch-Me — *Johnston, Julie*
c Adam Pig's Big Book — *Young, Selina*
c Adam Pig's Everything Fun Book (Illus. by Selina
    Young) — *Young, Selina*
Adam Smith's System of Liberty, Wealth, and Virtue
    — *Fitzgibbons, Athol*
Adam Smith's Wealth of Nations — *Smith, Adam*
Adam's Dream — *McDonald, Peter, 1962-*
Adaptable Livelihoods — *Davies, Susanna*
Adaptation and Natural Selection — *Williams, George
    C*
Adapting PCs for Disabilities — *Lazzaro, Joseph J*
Adapting to Capitalism — *Sharpe, Pamela*
Adaptive Control of Systems with Actuator and
    Sensor Nonlinearities — *Tao, Gang*
Adaptive Sampling — *Thompson, Steven K*
c Ada's Pal (Illus. by Marguerite Casparian) — *Lyon,
    George Ella*
Adcult USA — *Twitchell, James B*
Add a Dash of Pity and Other Short Stories
    — *Ustinov, Peter*
c Add It, Dip It, Fix It — *Schneider, R M*
The Added Value of Geographical Information
    Systems in Public and Environmental Health
    — *Lepper, Marion J C De*
Addictive Behaviour — *Banner, Adrian*
Adding Cross to Crown — *Noll, Mark A*
Adding to a House — *Wenz, Philip S*
Addison Gallery of American Art — *Faxon, Susan*
r The Addison-Wesley Science Handbook — *Coleman,
    Gordon J*
c Addition (Illus. by Richard Maccabe) — *Stienecker,
    David*
Additions: Your Guide to Planning and Remodeling
    — *Caringer, Denise L*
Adela Pankhurst: The Wayward Suffragette
    1885-1961 — *Coleman, Verna*
Adele Intime — *Brochu, Andre*
Adelhelm Abbey — *Newlin, Nicholas Paul*
c Adeline Street — *Williams, Carol Lynch*
y Adem's Cross — *Mead, Alice*
Aden Arabie — *Nizan, Paul*
Adenauer and Kennedy — *Mayer, Frank A*
y Adiamante — *Modesitt, L E*
Adieu — *Vlavianos, Haris*
Adios A Mama — *Arenas, Reinaldo*
The Adirondacks: A History of America's First
    Wilderness — *Schneider, Paul*
The Adjunct Faculty Handbook — *Bianco-Mathis,
    Virginia*
Adjusted to Death — *Girdner, Jaqueline*
Adjustment and Poverty — *Stewart, Frances*
r The Adman in the Parlor — *Garvey, Ellen Gruber*
The Admen Move on Lhasa — *Heighton, Steven*
Administration's Plan for Continued U.S. Military
    Participation in U.N. Operations in Somalia
    — *United States. Congress. House. Committee on
    Armed Services*
The Admirable Crichton. Peter Pan. When Wendy
    Grew Up. What Every Woman Knows. Mary Rose
    — *Barrie, J M*
The Admiral's Baby — *Van Der Post, Laurens*
The Admiralty Chart — *Ritchie, G S*
Admiring Silence — *Gurnah, Abdulrazak*
Adolescence and Delinquency — *Emler, Nicholas*
Adolescence and Youth in Early Modern England
    — *Ben-Amos, Ilana Krausman*
Adolescence: Guiding Youth through the Perilous
    Ordeal — *Newton, Miller*
Adolescence: Opportunities and Challenges
    — *Cicchetti, Dante*
Adolescent Development, Psychopathology, and
    Treatment — *Bloch, H Spencer*
Adolescent Drug Abuse — *Rahdert, Elizabeth*
Adolescent Gambling — *Griffiths, Mark*

Adolescent Girls and Their Friends — *Griffiths,
    Vivienne*
Adolescent Health Care. 3rd Ed. — *Neinstein,
    Lawrence S*
The Adolescent Molester. 2nd Ed. — *Breer, William*
Adolescent Sex, Contraception, and Childbearing
    — *Moore, Kristin A*
Adolescent Substance Abuse — *Wodarski, John S*
Adolescent Vulnerability — *Mitchell, John J*
Adolescents after Divorce — *Buchanan, Christy M*
Adolescents and the Media — *Strasburger, Victor C*
Adolescents and Their Music — *Epstein, Jonathon S*
Adolescents, Work, and Family — *Mortimer, Jeylan T*
y Adolf: A Tale of the Twentieth Century — *Tezuka,
    Osamu*
Adolf Galland: The Authorised Biography — *Baker,
    David*
c Adolf Hitler — *Ayer, Eleanor H*
Adolf Hitler: Eine Politische Biographie — *Patzold,
    Kurt*
Adolf Loos: Architecture 1903-1932 — *Schezen,
    Roberto*
Adolf Schlatter: A Biography of Germany's Premier
    Biblical Theologian — *Neuer, Werner*
Adolph Menzel 1815-1905: Between Romanticism and
    Impressionism — *Menzel, Adolph*
Adon Ha-Selihot — *Avitov, Yaron*
Adoption, Identity, and Kinship — *Wegar, Katarina*
The Adoption Reader — *Wadia-Ells, Susan*
c Adorna Con Mosaico — *Feixenet, Anna*
Adrienne Ou La Liberte — *Detry, Robert*
Adrienne Rich: Selected Poems 1950-1995 — *Rich,
    Adrienne*
y Adrift: Seventy-Six Days Lost at Sea — *Callahan,
    Steven*
Ads That Put America on Wheels — *Dregni, Eric*
p Adsorption: Journal of the International Adsorption
    Society
Adult Attachment — *Feeney, Judith*
Adult Children of Dysfunctional Families — *Wallace,
    Barbara C*
Adult Comics — *Sabin, Roger*
Adult Education in the American Experience
    — *Stubblefield, Harold W*
Adult Foster Care for the Elderly. Vols. 1-2
    — *Folkemer, Donna*
Adult Literacy in Indiana — *Jenkins, Lynn B*
Adult Psychiatry — *Guze, Samuel B*
Adultery and Divorce in Calvin's Geneva — *Kingdon,
    Robert McCune*
Adultery and Grace — *Gaddy, C Welton*
Adults with Learning Disabilities — *Gregg, Noel*
Advance and Retreat — *Hood, John Bell*
Advanced Analysis on the Real Line — *Kannan, R*
y Advanced Biology Statistics — *Edmundson, Andrew*
y Advanced Biology Study Guide — *Clegg, C J*
Advanced Catalyst and Nanostructured Materials
    — *Moser, William R*
Advanced Computational Methods in Heat Transfer
    IV
Advanced Concepts in Adaptive Signal Processing
    — *Jenkins, W Kenneth*
Advanced Educational Technology — *Liao, Thomas T*
Advanced Golf — *Norman, Greg*
r The Advanced HTML Companion
    — *Schengili-Roberts, Keith*
Advanced Java — *Laffra, Chris*
Advanced Laser Processing of Materials — *Cheung,
    Jeff*
Advanced Materials — *Nicholas, Ted*
Advanced Materials for Vibro-Acoustic Applications
    — *Mantena, P R*
Advanced Metallization for Future ULSI — *Tu, K N*
Advanced Relational Programming — *Cacace, Filippo*
Advanced Signal Processing and Digital Noise
    — *Vaseghi, Saeed V*
Advanced Telecommunications in U.S. Public
    Elementary and Secondary Schools 1995
Advanced Tutorials for the Biomedical Sciences
    — *Pidgeon, Charles*
Advanced University Physics — *Palmer, Stuart B*
Advanced Visual Basic 4.0 Programming — *Holzner,
    Steven*
Advanced Visual C++ 4 — *Holzner, Steven*
Advances in Acoustic Microscopy. Vol. 2 — *Briggs,
    Andrew*
Advances in Applied Microeconomics. Vol. 6
Advances in Behavioral Economics. Vol. 3
Advances in Bioengineering 1996
Advances in Biometry — *Armitage, Peter*
Advances in Chemical Physics. Vol. 95

Advances in Chemical Physics. Vol. 96
Advances in Chemical Physics. Vol. 99
Advances in Coatings Technologies for Corrosion and
    Wear Resistant Coatings — *Srivatsa, Arun R*
Advances in Cognitive-Behavioral Therapy
    — *Dobson, Keith S*
Advances in Collection Development and Resource
    Management. Vol. 1
Advances in Cryogenic Engineering. Vol. 41, Pts. A-B
Advances in Energy Efficiency, Heat/Mass Transfer
    Enhancement — *Ohadi, M M*
Advances in Environmental Control Technology
    — *Cheremisinoff, Paul N*
Advances in Environmental Remote Sensing
    — *Danson, F M*
Advances in Failure Mechanism in Brittle Materials
    — *Clifton, R J*
Advances in Fluid Mechanics — *Rahman, Matiur*
Advances in Futures and Options Research. Vol. 8
Advances in Groundwater Pollution Control and
    Remediation — *Aral, M M*
Advances in Group Processes. Vol. 13
Advances in Heat and Mass Transfer in Biotechnology
    1996
Advances in Image Understanding — *Bowyer, Kevin*
Advances in International Accounting. Vol. 9
Advances in International Comparative Management.
    Vol. 11
r Advances in Interventional Neuroradiology and
    Intravascular Neurosurgery — *International
    Congress on Interventional Neuroradiology and
    Intravascular Neurosurgery (1995: Kyoto, Japan)*
Advances in Knowledge Discovery and Data Mining
    — *Fayyad, Usama M*
Advances in Morphometrics — *NATO Advanced Study
    Institute on Advances in Morphometrics (1993:
    Tuscany, Italy)*
Advances in Motor Learning and Control — *Zelaznik,
    Howard N*
Advances in Multi-Fluid Flows — *Renardy, Yuriko Y*
Advances in Nuclear Dynamics — *, 1959-*
Advances in Nuclear Dynamics 2
Advances in Processing and Pattern Analysis of
    Biological Signals — *Gath, Isak*
Advances in Rapid Thermal and Integrated Processing
    — *Roozeman, Fred*
Advances in Slow Sand and Alternative Biological
    Filtration — *Graham, Nigel*
Advances in Stochastic Modelling and Data Analysis
    — *Janssen, Jacques*
Advances in Taxation. Vol. 8
Advances in the Astronautical Sciences
    — *International Space Conference of Pacific Basin
    Societies (6th: 1995: Marina Del Rey, CA)*
Advances in the Economics of Aging — *Wise, David A*
Advances in the Neurobiology of Schizophrenia
    — *Boer, J A Den*
Advances in the Theory of Computation and
    Computational Mathematics. Vol. 1
Advances in the Use of NOAA AVHRR Data for Land
    Applications — *D'Souza, Giles*
Advances in Transport Network Technologies — *Sato,
    Ken-Ichi*
Advances in Turbulence VI
Advances in Working Capital Management. Vol. 3
Advancing Prescription Medicine Compliance
    — *Fincham, Jack E*
Advent and Lent Activities for Children — *Kielly,
    Shiela*
r Adventure Guide to Coastal Alaska and the Inside
    Passage. 2nd Ed. — *Readicker-Henderson, Lynn*
r Adventure Guide to Costa Rica. 3rd Ed. — *Pariser,
    Harry S*
r Adventure Guide to the Great Smoky Mountains
    — *Howard, Blair*
r Adventure Guide to the High Southwest. 2nd Ed.
    — *Cohen, Steve*
c Adventure in Space (Runger). Audio Version — *Scott,
    Elaine*
c Adventure in the Witch's House (Illus. by Susan
    Synarski) — *Gordon, Lynn*
The Adventure of the Dancing Men (Raleigh). Audio
    Version — *Doyle, Arthur Conan, Sir*
Adventurers and Prophets — *Churchill, Charles B*
Adventures in Ancient Egypt — *Goldbarth, Albert*
Adventures in Asian Tapas and Wild Sushi
    — *Hooper, Trevor*
Adventures in Capitalism — *Litt, Toby*
c Adventures in Color — *O'Neill, Mary*
Adventures in Fast Forward — *Nadeau, Kathleen G*
Adventures in Speech — *Forni, Pier Massimo*

r Adventures in Video — *Wendling, Patricia A*
Adventures of a Gardener — *Smithers, Peter*
Adventures of an Inventor — *Fraden, Jacob*
Adventures of Huckleberry Finn — *Twain, Mark*
Adventures of Huckleberry Finn (Graff) — *Twain, Mark*
Adventures of Huckleberry Finn (Kaplan) — *Twain, Mark*
y The Adventures of Huckleberry Finn (Keillor). Audio Version — *Twain, Mark*
The Adventures of Mao on the Long March — *Tuten, Frederic*
The Adventures of Meng and Ecker — *Britton, David*
c The Adventures of Odysseus (Illus. by Peter Malone) — *Philip, Neil*
c The Adventures of Peter Rabbit and Benjamin Bunny. Electronic Media Version — *Potter, Beatrix*
The Adventures of Pinocchio — *Collodi, Carlo*
c The Adventures of Pinocchio (Illus. by Fritz Kredel) — *Collodi, Carlo*
y The Adventures of Robin Hood — *Williams, Marcia*
The Adventures of Sayf Ben Dhi Yazan — *Jayyusi, Lena*
The Adventures of Sayf Ben Dhi Yazan — *Sirat Sayf Ibn Dhi Yazan. English. Selections*
c The Adventures of Sparrowboy (Illus. by Brian Pinkney) — *Pinkney, Brian*
The Adventures of Superman — *Lowther, George*
c Adventures of the Little Wooden Horse. Audio Version — *Williams, Ursula M*
y The Adventures of Tom Sawyer (Illus. by Claude Lapointe) — *Twain, Mark*
Adventures on the Freedom Road — *Levy, Bernard-Henri*
c Adventures with Atoms and Molecules — *Mebane, Robert C*
r Adventuring in Arizona. 2nd Ed. — *Annerino, John*
r Adventuring in British Columbia. 2nd Ed. — *Nanton, Isabel*
r Adventuring in Central America — *Wallace, David Rains*
Adventuring in Indonesia — *Smith, Holly S*
r Adventuring in the Pacific. 2nd Ed. — *Margolis, Susanna*
Adversaria: Literature and Law — *Hinz, Evelyn J*
Adversarios Admirables — *Guirao, Olga*
r Adverse Cutaneous Reactions to Medication — *Goldstein, Sanford M*
Adverse Reactions to HIV Vaccines
Adversity Quotient — *Stoltz, Paul*
Advertising and Culture — *Cross, Mary*
Advertising and Popular Culture — *Fowles, Jib*
Advertising from the Desktop — *Floyd, Elaine*
Advertising in Contemporary Society. 3rd Ed. — *Rotzoll, Kim B*
c Advice for a Frog (Illus. by Norman Green) — *Schertle, Alice*
Advisory Committee on Human Radiation Experiments: Final Report — *United States. Advisory Committee on Human Radiation Experiments*
Advocacy in the Classroom — *Spacks, Patricia Ann Meyer*
The Advocate's Devil — *Dershowitz, Alan M*
c Aekyung's Dream (Illus. by Min Paek) — *Paek, Min*
Aelfric's Prefaces — *Aelfric*
Aelfwine's Prayerbook — *Gunzel, Beate*
Aerial Plant Surface Microbiology — *Morris, Cindy E*
Aerobiology: Proceedings of the Pan-American Aerobiology Association — *Pan-American Aerobiology Association*
Aeronautical Information Manual/Federal Aviation Regulations 1997
Aerosol Inhalation, Recent Research Frontiers — *International Workshop on Aerosol Inhalation, Lung Transport, Deposition and the Relation to the Environment (1995: Warsaw, Poland)*
Aeschylus: Mythic Theatre, Political Voice — *Chioles, John*
Aeschylus: The Earlier Plays and Related Studies — *Conacher, D J*
c Aesop's Fables (Illus. by Heidi Holder) — *Aesop*
y Aesop's Fables (Kent). Audio Version — *Aesop*
The Aesthete in the City — *Carrier, David*
The Aesthetic Code of Don Ramon Del Valle-Inclan — *Flynn, Gerard*
Aesthetic Criteria — *Richmond, Sheldon*
Aesthetic Ideology — *De Man, Paul*
The Aesthetic Movement — *Lambourne, Lionel*
Aesthetic Theory — *Adorno, Theodor W*
Aesthetic Value — *Goldman, Alan H, 1945-*
Aesthetics and Ideology — *Levine, George*

Aesthetics in Feminist Perspective — *Hein, Hilde*
The Aesthetics of Disturbance — *Graver, David*
The Aesthetics of Environment — *Berleant, Arnold*
Affair — *Quick, Amanda*
An Affair of the Mind — *Hall, Laurie*
r L'Affaire Dreyfus De A a Z — *Drouin, Michel*
Affaires Personnelles — *Roberts, Jean-Marc*
Affairs of State — *Troy, Gil*
Affect, Object, and Character Structure — *Kissen, Morton*
Affect Regulation and the Origin of the Self — *Schore, Allan N*
Affine Analysis of Image Sequences — *Shapiro, Larry S*
r Affirmative Action — *Nordquist, Joan*
Affirmative Action and the Stalled Quest for Black Progress — *Drake, W Avon*
The Affirmative Action Debate — *Curry, George E*
The Affirmative Action Fraud — *Bolick, Clint*
r Affordable Bed and Breakfasts in Quebec 96-97
An Affordable Development? — *Avramovic, Mila*
Affordable Housing and Urban Redevelopment in the United States — *Van Vliet, Willem*
Affordable Housing Mediation — *Susskind, Lawrence*
c Afghanistan — *Ali, Sharifah Enayat*
c Afghanistan — *Foster, Leila Merrell*
Afghanistan: From Holy War to Civil War — *Roy, Olivier*
Afghanistan. The Soviet Union's Last War — *Galeotti, Mark*
Afloat — *Maupassant, Guy De*
Afoot and Alone — *Powers, Steven*
Afraid to Eat — *Berg, Frances M*
r Africa — *Bever, Edward*
y Africa 8th to 18th Century (Illus. by Giorgio Bacchin) — *Robertazzi, Chiara*
r Africa: A Guide to Reference Material — *McIlwaine, John*
Africa and the International System — *Clapham, Christopher*
c Africa Calling (Illus. by Kimberly M Adlerman) — *Adlerman, Dan*
Africa Can Compete! — *Biggs, Tyler*
r Africa in Literature for Children and Young Adults — *Khorana, Meena*
Africa in the Contemporary International Disorder — *Agonafer, Mulugeta*
Africa in World Politics. 2nd Ed. — *Harbeson, John W*
Africa Now — *Ellis, Stephen, 1953-*
cr Africa On File. Vols. 1-2
Africa on Film — *Cameron, Kenneth M*
Africa South of the Sahara — *Stock, Robert*
Africa: The Art of a Continent
Africa Wo/man Palava — *Ogunyemi, Chikwenye Okonjo*
r African Acronyms and Abbreviations — *Hall, David E*
African American Acculturation — *Landrine, Hope*
r African American Almanac — *Ross, Leon T*
African-American Christianity — *Johnson, Paul E*
yr The African American Encyclopedia. Vols. 7-8 — *Williams, Michael W*
The African American Heritage of Florida — *Colburn, David R*
yr African American History in the Press 1851-1899. Vols. 1-2 — *Schneider, Richard C*
African American Islam — *McCloud, Aminah Beverly*
r African American Music: A Chronology 1619-1995 — *Caldwell, Hansonia L*
African American Nationalist Literature of the 1960s — *Flowers, Sandra Hollin*
yr The African American Network — *Bunkley, Crawford B*
r African-American Orators — *Leeman, Richard W*
y African-American Poets — *Strickland, Michael R*
African-American Political Thought 1890-1930 — *Wintz, Cary D*
African-American Proverbs in Context — *Prahlad, Sw. Anand*
African American Psychology — *Burlew, A Kathleen Hoard*
r The African American Resource Guide to the Internet and Online Services — *Battle, Stafford L*
y The African-American Soldier from Crispus Attucks to Colin Powell — *Lanning, Michael Lee*
African-American Stories of Triumph over Adversity — *Coleman, Geraldine*
African American Theater — *Southern, Eileen*
r The African American Theatre Directory 1816-1960 — *Peterson, Bernard L*

African American Visual Aesthetics — *Driskell, David C*
yr African American Voices. Vols. 1-2 — *Straub, Deborah Gillan*
African-American Voices in Young Adult Literature — *Smith, Karen Patricia*
y African American Women in Congress — *Gill, LaVerne McCain*
African-American Women's Health and Social Issues — *Collins, Catherine Fisher*
yr The African-American Yellow Pages — *Biddle, Stanton F*
y African Americans — *Dudley, William*
y African Americans and Civil Rights from 1619 to the Present — *Levine, Michael L*
y African Americans and Jewish Americans — *Garza, Hedda*
African Americans and the Living Constitution — *Franklin, John Hope*
African-Americans at the Crossroads — *Lusane, Clarence*
African Americans in the Creek and Cherokee Nations 1830s to 1920s — *May, Katja*
c African-Americans in the Thirteen Colonies — *Kent, Deborah*
c African Animal Tales (Illus. by Cica Fittipaldi) — *Barbosa, Rogerio Andrade*
c African Animals — *Arnold, Caroline*
c African Animals ABC (Illus. by Philippa-Alys Browne) — *Browne, Philippa-Alys*
African Architecture — *Elleh, Nnamdi*
r The African Business Handbook. Vol. 3
The African Colonial State in Comparative Perspective — *Young, Crawford*
African Conflict Resolution — *Smock, David R*
African Crossroads — *Fowler, Ian*
African Decolonization — *Wilson, Henry S*
r African Development Indicators 1996
r African Ethnonyms — *Biebuyck, Daniel P*
African Exodus
African Exodus — *Stringer, Chris*
African Experiences of Cinema — *Bakari, Imruh*
African Francophone Writing — *Ibnlfassi, Laila*
African Greenhouse Gas Emission Inventories and Mitigation Options — *Fitzgerald, John F*
African Images — *Rigby, Peter*
An African in Paris — *Dadie, Bernard Binlin*
The African Inheritance — *Griffiths, Ieuan Ll.*
African Intellectual Heritage — *Asante, Molefi K*
African Market Women and Economic Power — *House-Midamba, Bessie*
y The African Mask — *Rupert, Jane E*
African Material Culture — *Arnoldi, Mary Jo*
African Nemesis — *Moorcraft, Paul L*
African Nomadic Architecture — *Prussin, Labelle*
African Oral Literature — *Okpewho, Isidore*
African Perspectives on Development — *Himmelstrand, Ulf*
r African Placenames — *Room, Adrian*
African Popular Theatre — *Kerr, David*
The African Quest for Freedom and Identity — *Bjornson, Richard*
African Religion, Philosophy, and Christianity in Logos-Christ — *Twesigye, Emmanuel K*
African Rhythm — *Agawu, Kofi*
r African Statistical Yearbook. 1992 Ed., Vol. 1, Pt. 2
African Studies and the Undergraduate Curriculum — *Alden, Patricia*
The African Synod — *Africa Faith and Justice Network*
African Water Resources — *Sharma, Narendra P*
African Women — *Mathabane, Mark*
African Women and Development — *Snyder, Margaret C, 1929-*
r African Writers. Vols. 1-2 — *Cox, C Brian*
y The Africans (Runger). Audio Version — *Lamb, David, 1940-*
Africans in Colonial Louisiana — *Hall, Gwendolyn Midlo*
Africa's Management in the 1990s and Beyond — *Dia, Mamadou*
yr Africa's Vanishing Wildlife — *Stuart, Chris*
L'Afrique Des Incertitudes — *Hugon, Philippe*
Afro-Argentine Discourse — *Lewis, Marvin A*
The Afro-Argentines of Buenos Aires 1800-1900 — *Andrews, George Reid*
Afro-Cuban Religious Experience — *Matibag, Eugenio*
Afrocentrism and World Politics — *Henderson, Errol Anthony*
After — *Bukiet, Melvin Jules*
After 50 — *Wicks, Robert*
After a Fashion — *Finkelstein, Joanne*

After All — *Moore, Mary Tyler*
After Andy — *Taylor, Paul*
After Auschwitz — *Bohm-Duchen, Monica*
After Brecht — *Reinelt, Janelle*
After Cancer — *Harpham, Wendy S*
y After Caroline — *Hooper, Kay*
c After Charlotte's Mom Died (Illus. by Judith Friedman) — *Spelman, Cornelia*
After Christianity — *Hampson, Daphne*
After Colonialism — *Prakash, Gyan*
After Death — *Miller, Sukie*
After Derrida — *Royle, Nicholas*
After Effects — *Aird, Catherine*
After Ellis Island — *Watkins, Susan Cotts*
After Empire — *Gorra, Michael*
After Empire — *Snyder, Jed C*
After Frost — *Lyman, Henry*
After God — *Cupitt, Don*
After Hannibal — *Unsworth, Barry*
After-Image: A Vicky Bauer Mystery — *Gom, Leona*
y After January — *Earls, Nick*
After Leaving, Mr. MacKenzie — *Rhys, Jean*
After Liberalism — *Wallerstein, Immanuel*
After Lives — *Harlow, Barbara*
After Midnight — *Davis, Susan Bluestein*
After Paradise — *Rapoport, Janis*
After Rain — *Trevor, William*
y After Shanghai — *McLeay, Alison*
After Socialism — *Abrahams, Ray*
After Success — *Pahl, Ray*
After Such Knowledge, What Forgiveness? — *Randal, Jonathan C*
After the Breakthrough — *Nowotny, Helga*
After the Cold War — *United States. Congress. Office of Technology Assessment*
y After the Darkness — *Smith, Michael*
After the End of Art — *Danto, Arthur C*
After the Fact — *Geertz, Clifford*
After the Fall — *Dirlik, Arif*
After the Famine — *Turner, Michael Edward*
After the Flood
After the Future — *Epstein, Mikhail N*
After the Guns Fall Silent — *Roberts, Shawn*
After the Holocaust — *Rubinstein, Erna F*
After the Madness — *Wachtler, Sol*
After the Quality Audit — *Russell, J P*
After the School Bell Rings — *Grant, Carl A*
After the Trees — *Stewart, Douglas Ian*
After the USSR — *Khazanov, Anatoly M*
After the Victorians — *Pedersen, Susan*
After the Wall — *Fisher, Marc*
y After the War — *Matas, Carol*
c After the War Was Over (Illus. by Michael Foreman) — *Foreman, Michael*
After Thought — *Bailey, James*
After Truth — *Sprung, Mervyn*
After Tylor — *Stocking, George W*
After Wounded Knee — *Lauderdale, John Vance*
p Afterglow of Creation — *Chown, Marcus*
p Afterimage
The Afterimage — *Levin, Phillis*
Afterimages — *Retallack, Joan*
Afterlife — *Monette, Paul*
The Afterlife and Other Stories — *Updike, John*
y Aftermath — *Burton, LeVar*
Aftermath (Burton). Audio Version — *Burton, LeVar*
The Aftermath: A Survivor's Odyssey through War-Torn Europe — *Lilienheim, Henry*
y The Aftermath: Living with the Holocaust — *Hass, Aaron*
The Aftermath of Defeat — *Andreopoulos, George J*
The Aftermath of Real Existing Socialism in Eastern Europe. Vol. 1 — *Hersh, Jacques*
Aftermath: The Remnants of War — *Webster, Donovan*
Aftermath: Travels in a Post-War World — *Mowat, Farley*
c Afternoon of the Elves — *Lisle, Janet Taylor*
c Afternoon of the Elves (Moore). Audio Version — *Lisle, Janet Taylor*
Afternotes on Numerical Analysis — *Stewart, G W*
The Aga Khan Rural Support Program: A Third Evaluation
Again to the Life of Eternity — *Vaughan, Frank A*
Against All Odds — *Allen, John C*
Against All Odds — *Nebauer, Alan*
y Against All Odds — *Riefe, Barbara*
r Against Borders — *Rochman, Hazel*
Against Capital Punishment — *Haines, Herbert H*
Against Capitalism — *Schweickart, David*
Against Nature — *Vogel, Steven, 1954-*

Against Rousseau — *Maistre, Joseph Marie, Comte De*
Against the Current — *Finlayson, Judith*
Against the Current — *Trudeau, Pierre Elliott*
Against the Death Penalty — *Mello, Michael*
Against the Gods — *Bernstein, Peter L*
Against the Imperial Judiciary — *Franck, Matthew J*
Against the Panzers — *Vannoy, Allyn R*
Against the Tide — *Irwin, Douglas A*
Against the Wall — *Yates, Simon*
Agatha Raisin and the Murderous Marriage — *Beaton, M C*
Agatha Raisin and the Potted Gardener — *Beaton, M C*
Age: A Novel — *Calisher, Hortense*
Age and Guile Beat Youth, Innocence, and a Bad Haircut — *O'Rourke, P J*
L'Age D'Or Des Ecoles De Chartres — *Jeauneau, Edouard*
The Age Factor in Second Language Acquisition — *Singleton, David*
The Age of Anxiety — *Dunant, Sarah*
y The Age of Augustus — *Nardo, Don*
The Age of Caricature — *Donald, Diana*
Age of Delirium — *Satter, David*
The Age of Discovery. Vol. 1 — *Hattendorf, John B*
The Age of Extremes — *Hobsbawm, Eric*
The Age of Heresy — *Buzan, Tony*
The Age of Heretics — *Kleiner, Art*
The Age of Improv — *Salutin, Rick*
The Age of Innocence — *Wagner-Martin, Linda*
y The Age of Innocence (Woodward). Audio Version — *Wharton, Edith*
The Age of Justinian — *Evans, J A S*
The Age of Louis XIV — *Voltaire*
The Age of Migrating Ideas — *Spearman, R Michael*
The Age of Migration — *Castles, Stephen*
The Age of Minerva. Vols. 1-2 — *Ilie, Paul*
y Age of Miracles (Peiffer). Audio Version — *Gilchrist, Ellen*
y The Age of Pericles — *Nardo, Don*
The Age of Salisbury 1881-1902 — *Shannon, Richard*
The Age of Terrorism and the International Political System — *Guelke, Adrian*
The Age of Transition — *Hopkins, Terence K*
The Age of Upheaval — *Brooks, David, 1947-*
The Age of Urban Democracy — *Read, Donald*
The Age of Wire and String — *Marcus, Ben*
Age of Wonders — *Hartwell, David G*
Agee: Selected Literary Documents — *Agee, James*
Agency in Private International Law — *Verhagen, H L E*
Agency: Its Role in Mental Development — *Russell, James*
Agenda for Africa's Economic Renewal — *Ndulu, Benno*
An Agenda for Development 1995 — *Boutros-Ghali, Boutros*
Agenda for Excellence 2 — *Peters, B Guy*
An Agent for the Duration — *Cairncross, John*
Agents for Escape — *Rougeyron, Andre*
Agents in My Brain — *Hannon, Bill*
Agents of Apocalypse — *De Bevoise, Ken*
Agents of Hope — *Capps, Donald*
Un Aggiornamento Et Son Eclipse — *Naud, Andre*
Aggregate Money Demand Functions — *Hoffman, Dennis L*
Aggression and Its Causes — *Renfrew, John W*
Aggressor — *Cook, Nick*
The Agile Investor — *Leeb, Stephen*
Aging and Old Age — *Posner, Richard A*
Aging and Posttraumatic Stress Disorder — *Ruskin, Paul E*
r Aging in Literature — *Yahnke, Robert E*
Aging in the Past — *Kertzer, David I*
Aging in the Twenty-First Century — *Sperry, Len*
y An Aging Population — *Cozic, Charles P*
The Agitated Mind of God — *Irvin, Dale T*
Agitato: A Romp through NYC's Music Scene (Toobin). Audio Version — *Toobin, Jerome*
Agnes Chase's First Book of Grasses. 4th Ed. — *Clark, Lynn G*
Agnesi to Zeno — *Smith, Sanderson M*
p Agni
Agogo Bells to Xylophone — *Cotton, Maggie*
Agony in the Garden — *Hannon, Howard*
The Agony of Education — *Feagin, Joe R*
The Agony of the Russian Idea — *McDaniel, Tim*
Agostino Agazzari and Music at Siena Cathedral 1597-1641 — *Reardon, Colleen*
Agrarian Reform in the Philippines — *Riedinger, Jeffrey M*

Agri-Food Quality — *Fenwick, G R*
Agricide: The Hidden Farm and Food Crisis That Affects Us All. 2nd Ed. — *Fox, Michael W*
Agricultura Indigena, Pasado Y Presente — *Rojas Rabiela, Teresa*
p Agricultural and Resource Economics Review
Agricultural Biotechnology and the Environment — *Krimsky, Sheldon*
Agricultural Chemicals and the Environment — *Hester, R E*
Agricultural Commercialization, Economic Development, and Nutrition — *Von Braun, Joachim*
Agricultural Competitiveness — *International Conference of Agricultural Economists (22nd: 1994: Harare, Zimbabwe)*
p Agricultural Economics
Agricultural Economics — *Peters, George H*
Agricultural Extension. 2nd Ed. — *Ban, A W Van Den*
Agricultural Growth in Indonesia — *Eng, Pierre Van Der*
Agricultural Instability in China 1931-1991 — *Kueh, Y Y*
Agricultural Landownership in Transitional Economies — *Wunderlich, Gene*
r The Agricultural Outlook. 1996 Ed.
Agricultural Policies, Markets and Trade in OECD Countries 1996. Vols. 1-2
Agricultural Policy and U.S.-Taiwan Trade — *Johnson, D Gale*
Agricultural Policy in Kenya — *Pearson, Scott*
Agricultural Production and Indian History — *Ludden, David*
Agricultural Reform in Russia — *Brooks, Karen*
Agricultural Revolution in England — *Overton, Mark*
Agriculture, Trade, and the Environment
Agriculture, Trade, and the Environment — *Bredahl, Maury E*
Agrippina: Sex, Power, and Politics in the Early Empire — *Barrett, Anthony A*
The Aguero Sisters — *Garcia, Cristina*
Agustin Rivera Y Agustin De La Rosa Ante La Filosofia Novohispana — *Zafra Oropeza, Aurea*
Aha! 10 Ways to Free Your Creative Spirit and Find Your Great Ideas — *Ayan, Jordan*
c Ahaiyute and Cloud Eater (Illus. by Marek Zawadzki) — *Hulpach, Vladimir*
Aharon Appelfeld: The Holocaust and Beyond — *Ramras-Rauch, Gila*
Ai Qing Nu Zi Lian Meng — *Cao, Youfang*
Aid and Power. 2nd Ed., Vol. 1 — *Mosley, Paul*
Aid in the 21st Century — *Riddell, Roger*
AIDS — *Hodgkinson, Neville*
c AIDS — *Sanders, Pete*
y AIDS: A Handbook for the Future — *LeVert, Marianne*
AIDS: A Moral Issue. 2nd Ed. — *Almond, Brenda*
AIDS and Behavior — *Auerbach, Judith D*
AIDS and HIV-Related Diseases — *Powell, Josh*
AIDS and People with Severe Mental Illness — *Cournos, Francine*
AIDS and STDs in Africa — *Green, Edward C*
AIDS and the Sleeping Church — *Hoffman, Patricia L*
AIDS, Communication, and Empowerment — *Myrick, Roger*
AIDS Crossing Borders — *Mishra, Shiraz I*
AIDS, Drugs and Prevention — *Rhodes, Tim*
AIDS, Drugs of Abuse, and the Neuroimmune Axis — *Symposium on AIDS, Drugs of Abuse, and the Neuroimmune Axis (3rd: 1995: San Diego, CA)*
AIDS Education — *Moore, Melinda K*
r AIDS Funding. 4th Ed.
AIDS in the UK — *Berridge, Virginia*
r AIDS in the World II — *Mann, Jonathan M*
r The AIDS Knowledge Base. 2nd Ed. — *Cohen, P T*
AIDS Narratives — *Kruger, Steven F*
The AIDS Pandemic — *Sills, Yole G*
c AIDS: Ten Stories of Courage — *Gonzales, Doreen*
y AIDS: What Does It Mean to You? — *Hyde, Margaret O*
L'Aigle — *Kadare, Ismail*
Aim at Morning — *Richardson, Duncan*
Aim High — *Johnson, Dave, 1963-*
The Aim of Laboratory Analyses of Ceramics in Archaeology — *Lindahl, Anders*
Aimee and Jaguar — *Fischer, Erica*
Aiming High
Aiming Higher — *Bollier, David*
Ain't Gonna Be the Same Fool Twice — *Sinclair, April*
Ain't No Makin' It — *MacLeod, Jay*

Ain't You Glad You Joined the Republicans?
— *Batchelor, John Calvin*
c Air — *Robbins, Ken*
Air, 24 Hours — *Eisenberg, Deborah*
y Air Alert — *Miller, Christina G*
Air-Bird in the Water — *Harding, Mildred Davis*
y The Air Down Here — *Alicea, Gil*
The Air National Guard and the American Military
Tradition — *Gross, Charles J*
Air Pollution IV
Air Pollution Control — *Hesketh, Howard E*
Air Pollution Modeling and Its Application XI
Air Power and Maneuver Warfare — *Van Creveld,
Martin L*
r Air Quality A to Z — *Bertorelli, Victoria*
Air Toxic Risk Assessment and Management — *Gratt,
Lawrence B*
Air Toxics — *Ganesan, Kumar*
Air War Bosnia — *Ripley, Tim*
Air War in the Persian Gulf — *Murray, Williamson*
Airborne Pulsed Doppler Radar. 2nd Ed. — *Morris,
Guy*
c Airborne: The Truimph and Struggle of Michael
Jordan — *Kornbluth, Jesse*
Aircraft Mishap Photography — *Panas, John*
Aircraft of the Chaco War 1928-1935 — *Hagedorn,
Dan*
Aircraft Safety — *Krause, Shari Stamford*
y Airframe — *Crichton, Michael*
y Airframe (Cassidy). Audio Version — *Crichton,
Michael*
Airmen without Portfolio — *Edwards, John Carver*
c The Airplane Alphabet Book (Illus. by Rob Bolster)
— *Pallotta, Jerry*
c Airplanes — *Holland, Gini*
Airport Infrastructure — *Kapur, Anil*
The Airport: Planes, People, Triumphs, and Disasters
at John F. Kennedy International — *Kaplan, James*
Airport Terminals. 2nd Ed. — *Blow, Christopher J*
Airways Smooth Muscle: Modelling the Asthmatic
Response in Vivo — *Raeburn, D*
Airways Smooth Muscle: Peptide Receptors, Ion
Channels, and Signal Transduction — *Raeburn, D*
AIX for Breakfast — *Houtz, Phillip*
Akum: The Magic of Dreams — *Chavez-Vasquez,
Gloria*
Al Borde Del Naufragio — *Montoya, Rodrigo*
Al Capp Remembered — *Caplin, Elliot*
Al Weiss's the Official History of Karate in America
— *Weiss, Al*
The Alabama and the Kearsarge — *Marvel, William*
c Alabaster's Song (Illus. by Michael Garland)
— *Lucado, Max*
Alada Mia — *Castro, Juana*
The Alamo: An Epic — *Lind, Michael*
y The Alamo in American History — *Sorrels, Roy*
y Alan Turing: The Architect of the Computer Age
— *Gottfried, Ted*
c Alanna: The First Adventure — *Pierce, Tamora*
y An Alarming History of Famous and Difficult!
Patients — *Gordon, Richard, 1921-*
Alarums and Excursions — *Marowitz, Charles*
An Alaska Anthology — *Haycox, Stephen W*
y Alaska Ascents — *Sherwonit, Bill*
c The Alaska Purchase — *Cohen, Daniel, 1936-*
The Alaska-Siberia Connection — *Hays, Otis, Jr.*
r Alban Berg: A Guide to Research — *Simms, Bryan R*
The Albanians: A Modern History — *Vickers,
Miranda*
Albanien: Stammesleben Zwischen Tradition Und
Moderne — *Eberhart, Helmut*
An Albany Trio — *Kennedy, William, 1928-*
Albert Camus: A Biography — *Lottman, Herbert R*
y Albert Camus: The Thinker, the Artist, the Man
— *Bronner, Stephen Eric*
Albert Camus: Une Vie — *Todd, Olivier*
y Albert Einstein — *Goldberg, Jake*
Albert Einstein: A Biography — *Folsing, Albrecht*
y Albert Einstein and the Frontiers of Physics
— *Bernstein, Jeremy*
Albert Einstein/Mileva Maric--the Love Letters
— *Einstein, Albert*
Albert Speer: His Battle with Truth — *Sereny, Gitta*
Albert: Uncrowned King — *Weintraub, Stanley*
r Alberta History along the Highway — *Stone, Ted*
Alberta's Petroleum Industry and the Conservation
Board — *Breen, David H*
Alberto Giacometti 1901-1966 — *Giacometti, Alberto*
Alberto Struzzi: Un Precursor Barroco Del
Capitalismo Liberal — *Echevarria Bacigalupe,
Miguel Angel*

Alberto Vargas: The Esquire Years
c Albert's Ballgame — *Tryon, Leslie*
Albion's Classicism — *Gent, Lucy*
Albrick's Gold — *LeVay, Simon*
Album Calvino — *Baranelli, Luca*
Alcestis and Other Plays (Davie) — *Euripides*
Alchemical Poetry 1575-1700 — *Schuler, Robert M*
The Alchemy of Prayer — *Taylor, Terry Lynn, 1955-*
The Alchemy of Race and Rights — *Williams, Patricia
J*
The Alchemy of the Heavens — *Croswell, Ken*
Alchi: Ladakh's Hidden Buddhist Sanctuary
— *Goepper, Roger*
Alcibade, Ou Les Dangers De L'Ambition — *Romilly,
Jacqueline De*
Alcibiades at the Door — *Schehr, Lawrence R*
Alcohol and Homicide — *Parker, Robert Nash*
Alcohol, Gender and Culture — *Gefou-Madianou,
Dimitra*
r Alcohol in the British Isles from Roman Times to 1996
— *Gutzke, David W*
Alcoholics Anonymous as a Mutual-Help Movement
— *Makela, Klaus*
Alcoholism Treatment — *Van Wormer, Katherine*
L'Alcool Du Silence — *Jourde, Pierre*
c An Alcott Family Christmas (Illus. by Alexandra
Wallner) — *Wallner, Alexandra*
Aldeas Y Campesinos En La Navarra Prepirenaica
1550-1817 — *Zabalza Seguin, Ana*
Aldo Leopold: A Fierce Green Fire — *Lorbiecki,
Marybeth*
The Aldo Moro Murder Case — *Drake, Richard*
Aldous Huxley and the Mysticism of Science — *Deery,
June*
Aldous Huxley's Hearst Essays — *Huxley, Aldous*
O Aldrabista — *Araujo, Carlos*
Aldus Manutius: Printer and Publisher of Renaissance
Venice — *Davies, Martin*
Ale, Beer, and Brewsters in England — *Bennett, Judith
M*
Alec Douglas-Home — *Thorpe, D R*
Alec Wilder in Spite of Himself — *Stone, Desmond*
Aleck Maury, Sportsman — *Gordon, Caroline*
Alector Ou Le Coq. Vols. 1-2 — *Aneau, Barthelemy*
Aleksander Wat: Life and Art of an Iconoclast
— *Venclova, Tomas*
Aleksandr Blok: A Life — *Berberova, Nina*
Aleksei Remizov: Issledovaniia I Materialy
— *Gracheva, A M*
Alessandro Magnasco 1667-1749 — *Magnasco,
Alessandro*
Alessandro Stradella 1639-1682 — *Gianturco, Carolyn*
c Aleta and the Queen (Illus. by Normand Cousineau)
— *Galloway, Priscilla*
Alexander — *Dodge, Theodore Ayrault*
y Alexander and His Times — *Theule, Frederic*
Alexander Forbes of Brechin: The First Tractarian
Bishop — *Strong, Rowan*
c Alexander Graham Bell (Illus. by Lesley Bisseker)
— *Fischel, Emma*
c Alexander Graham Bell — *Petrie, A Roy*
y Alexander Graham Bell: Making Connections
— *Pasachoff, Naomi*
Alexander Neil and the Last Shenandoah Valley
Campaign — *Neil, Alexander*
c Alexander, Que De Ninguna Manera--Le Oyen?--Lo
Dice En Serio!--Se Va A Mudar (Illus. by Robin
Preiss Glasser) — *Viorst, Judith*
Alexander Rodchenko: Photography 1924-1954
— *Lavrentiev, Aleksandr Nikolaevich*
y Alexander the Great — *Green, Robert*
Alexander the Great in the Literature of Medieval
Britain — *Bunt, Gerrit H V*
c Alexander, Who's Not (Do You Hear Me? I Mean It!)
Going to Move (Illus. by Robin Preiss Glasser)
— *Viorst, Judith*
c Alexia: A Tale for Advanced Children — *Kefala,
Antigone*
Alexius Meinong's Elements of Ethics — *Schubert
Kalsi, Marie-Luise*
Alfabetizacion Por Todos Y Para Todos
c Alfie's Feet — *Hughes, Shirley*
c Alfonse, Where Are You? — *Wikler, Linda*
c Alfred Fitzpatrick — *Morrison, James H*
Alfred Hitchcock and the British Cinema — *Ryall,
Tom*
Alfred Hitchcock: The Legacy of Victorianism
— *Cohen, Paula Marantz*
Alfred Marshall's Lectures to Women — *Raffaelli,
Tiziano*
Alfred Schnittke — *Ivashkin, Alexander*

Alfred Stieglitz: A Biography — *Whelan, Richard*
Alfred Stieglitz at Lake George — *Stieglitz, Alfred*
Alfred Stieglitz: Photographer — *Museum of Fine Arts,
Boston*
Alfred Stieglitz's Camera Notes — *Peterson, Christian
A*
c Alfred the Great (Illus. by Peter Kent) — *Matthews,
Andrew*
Alfredo Bryce Echenique: Para Que Duela Menos
— *Juristo, Juan Angel*
r Algae: An Introduction to Phycology — *Hoek, C Van
Den*
Algal Ecology — *Stevenson, R Jan*
r Algarve and Southern Portugal — *Anderson, Brian*
Algebra and Analysis — *International Centennial
Chebotarev Conference (1994: Kazan, Russia)*
Algebra Unplugged — *Amdahl, Kenn*
Algebraic 3-D Modeling — *Hartwig, Andreas*
Algebraic Geometry and Singularities — *Campillo,
Antonio*
An Algebraic Introduction to Complex Projective
Geometry. Vol. 1 — *Peskine, Christian*
Algebraic K-Theory — *Banaszak, Grzegorz*
Algebraic Riccati Equations — *Lancaster, Peter*
Algebraic Semantics of Imperative Programs
— *Goguen, Joseph A*
Algebraic Topology — *Barcelona Conference on
Algebraic Topology (1994: San Feliu De Guixols,
Spain)*
r Algeria. Rev. Ed. — *Lawless, Richard I*
Algeria: The Fundamentalist Challenge — *Ciment,
James*
Algeria: The Next Fundamentalist State? — *Fuller,
Graham E*
Algerie: Chronique D'Une Femme Dans La
Tourmante — *Fatiah*
Une Algerienne Debout — *Messaoudi, Khalida*
Algorithmic Number Theory. Vol. 1 — *Bach, Eric*
Algorithms and Programming — *Shen, Alexander*
Algorithms for Linear-Quadratic Optimization
— *Sima, Vasile*
Algorithms, Fractals, and Dynamics — *Takahashi, Y*
Algorithms in Algebraic Geometry and Applications
— *Gonzalez-Vega, Laureano*
c Ali, Child of the Desert (Illus. by Ted Lewin)
— *London, Jonathan*
Alias Frank Canton — *Dearment, Robert K*
Alias Grace — *Atwood, Margaret*
y Alias Grace (McGovern). Audio Version — *Atwood,
Margaret*
Alias Shakespeare — *Sobran, Joseph*
c The Alibi — *Rose, Malcolm*
y Alibi for a Witch (Langford). Audio Version
— *Ferrars, Elizabeth*
c Alice In-Between — *Naylor, Phyllis Reynolds*
c Alice in Lace — *Naylor, Phyllis Reynolds*
Alice in Wonderland. Electronic Media Version
— *Carroll, Lewis*
c Alice in Wonderland (Jameson). Audio Version
— *Carroll, Lewis*
Alice Walker Banned — *Walker, Alice*
c Alice's Adventures in Wonderland (Illus. by Angel
Dominguez) — *Carroll, Lewis*
Alice's Adventures in Wonderland. Electronic Media
Version — *Carroll, Lewis*
c Alice's World Record (Illus. by Alex De Wolf)
— *Kennemore, Tim*
c Alicia's Treasure — *Bertrand, Diane Gonzales*
c Alien — *Pipe, Jim*
Alien Agenda — *Marrs, Jim*
Alien Candor — *Codrescu, Andrei*
y Alien Game — *Dexter, Catherine*
Alien Impact — *Craft, Michael*
y Alien Invaders — *Collard, Sneed B*
Alien Nation — *Brimelow, Peter*
c Alien on the 99th Floor (Illus. by M Chatterton)
— *Nimmo, Jenny*
Alien Wars — *Sarin, Oleg*
Aliens and Alien Societies — *Schmidt, Stanley*
Aliens and Dissenters. 2nd Ed. — *Preston, William, Jr.*
c The Aliens Approach — *Royce, Easton*
Aliens: Colonial Marines Technical Manual
— *Brimmicombe-Wood, Lee*
c Aliens for Dinner (Illus. by Steve Bjorkman)
— *Spinner, Stephanie*
c Aliens Stole My Dad — *Coville, Bruce*
c Aliens to Earth — *Cooling, Wendy*
p Aliens vs. Predator: War — *Stradley, Randy*
Alif Baa — *Brustad, Kristen*
Alimentations, Traditions Et Developpements En
Afrique Intertropicale — *Devisch, Rene*

c Alison's Puppy — *Bauer, Marion Dane*

c Alison's Wings (Illus. by Roger Roth) — *Bauer, Marion Dane*

y Alistair MacLean's Red Alert (Hodson). Audio Version — *MacNeill, Alastair*

All Aboard with E.M. Frimbo — *Whitaker, Rogers E M*

All about Albumin — *Peters, Theodore, 1922-*

p All about Beer

c All about Deer (Illus. by Jim Arnosky) — *Arnosky, Jim*

c All about How Things Are Made (Illus. by Robert Byrd) — *Kain, Kathleen*

c All about Pets (Illus. by Yoshi Miyake) — *Kain, Kathleen*

All about Your Car — *Kline, David*

All-American Alien Boy — *Steele, Allen*

All-American Monster — *Stickney, Brandon M*

The All-American Skin Game — *Crouch, Stanley*

y All American Vegetarian — *Grunes, Barbara*

All-American Waves of Grain — *Grunes, Barbara*

All Are Witnesses — *Friesen, Delores*

All at Sea — *Harlan, Louis R*

All Corvettes Are Red — *Schefter, James*

All Emergencies, Ring Super — *White, Ellen Emerson*

All Fall Down — *Fox, Zachary Alan*

y All God's Children — *Butterfield, Fox*

All God's Children — *Eidson, Thomas*

All I Thought about was Baseball — *Humber, William*

All in It Together

All Is Never Said — *Rollins, Judith*

All Is True — *Furst, Lilian R*

All Judgment Fled — *White, James, 1928-*

c All Kinds of Families — *Simon, Norma*

All Madden — *Madden, John*

All Made of Tunes — *Burkholder, J Peter*

All Mothers Work — *Ramming, Cindy*

r The All Music Book of Hit Albums — *McAleer, Dave*

r The All Music Book of Hit Singles — *McAleer, Dave*

r All Music Guide. 2nd Ed. — *Erlewine, Michael*

r All Music Guide to the Blues — *Erlewine, Michael*

All Must Have Prizes — *Phillips, Melanie*

All My Edens — *Welsh, Pat*

All My Enemies — *Maitland, Barry*

All My Sins Are Relatives — *Penn, W S, 1949-*

All My Sisters — *Thomas, Clara*

c All of Me — *Stewart, Maureen*

All of This Music Belongs to the Nation — *Bindas, Kenneth J*

y All of Us — *Anderson, Patricia June*

All of Us — *Carver, Raymond*

All of Us Together — *Banks, Jeri*

All One Universe — *Anderson, Poul*

All over the Map — *Ayers, Edward L*

All Quiet on the Western Front — *Remarque, Erich Maria*

All Rivers Run to the Sea — *Wiesel, Elie*

All Roads Are Good

The All-Round Man — *Grainger, Percy*

c All Sail Set (Illus. by Armstrong Sperry) — *Sperry, Armstrong*

c All Saints, All Souls, and Halloween — *Chambers, Catherine*

All She Was Worth — *Miyabe, Miyuki*

All Souls — *Marias, Javier*

All Souls' Day — *Morris, Bill*

All Souls' Rising — *Bell, Madison Smartt*

All That Glitters — *Andrews, V C*

y All That Glitters — *Ferris, Jean*

All That Glitters — *Gapper, John*

All That Glitters — *Kennealy, Jerry*

All That I Was — *Austen, Eric*

All That Jazz — *Atkins, Ronald*

All That Matters — *Rief, Linda*

All That We Can Be — *Moskos, Charles C*

All the Dark Air — *Michael, Livi*

All the Days and Nights — *Maxwell, William, 1908-*

All the King's Men — *Warren, Robert Penn*

All the Modern Conveniences — *Ogle, Maureen*

All the Money in the World — *Siegel, Robert Anthony*

All the Nations under Heaven — *Binder, Frederick M*

c All the Places to Love (Illus. by Mike Wimmer) — *MacLachlan, Patricia*

All the Powerful Invisible Things — *Legler, Gretchen*

All the Presidents' Words — *Gelderman, Carol*

y All the Proud Ships — *Friend, Charles E*

y All the Small Poems and Fourteen More — *Worth, Valerie*

All the Way Home — *Clark, Geoffrey*

y All Things Decently and in Order and Other Writing on a Germans from Russia Heritage — *Boardman, Edna*

All This Way for the Short Ride — *Zarzyski, Paul*

y All Together Now — *Bridgers, Sue Ellen*

All Too Familiar — *Women's Rights Project (Human Rights Watch)*

All Too Human — *Klein, Edward*

y All U Can Eat — *Nargi, Lela*

All under Heaven — *Berthrong, John H*

All Visitors Ashore — *Stead, C K*

c All We Know of Heaven — *Bridgers, Sue Ellen*

All We Know of Heaven — *Villegas, Anna Tuttle*

c All We Needed to Say (Illus. by Lorna Clark) — *Singer, Marilyn*

The All White World of Children's Books and African American Children's Literature — *Osa, Osayimwense*

All Will Be Well — *Chilson, Richard*

All Women Are Healers — *Stein, Diane*

y All You Wanted to Know about Mathematics...but Were Afraid to Ask — *Lyons, Louis*

Alla Luce Della Luna — *Piasentini, Stefano*

y Allan Pinkerton: The Original Private Eye — *Josephson, Judith Pinkerton*

Alle Origini Della Francia Contemporanea — *Di Rienzo, Eugenio*

Alle Spalle Di Trieste — *Tomizza, Fulvio*

Allegany and Garrett Counties, Maryland Genealogical Research Guide — *Russell, Donna Valley*

The Allegorical Impulse in the Works of Julien Gracq — *Murphy, Carol J*

Allegorical Poetics and the Epic — *Treip, Mindele Anne*

Allegories of America — *Dolan, Frederick M*

Allegories of History — *Bahti, Timothy*

Allegories of Transgression and Transformation — *Tierney-Tello, Mary Beth*

Allegory and Violence — *Teskey, Gordon*

Allegory in America — *Madsen, Deborah L*

Allegretto — *Stigen, Terje*

Allegro — *Machlis, Joseph*

The Allen Family of England, Virginia, North Carolina, Tennessee, Mississippi, Texas, and Illinois 1600-1995 — *Wicker, Richard Fenton, Jr.*

r Allen Sapp: A Bio-Bibliography — *Green, Alan, 1962-*

Allen Tate and the Catholic Revival — *Huff, Peter A*

r Allergies A-Z — *Lipkowitz, Myron A*

r Allergy Products Directory 1995-1996; Allergy/Asthma Finding Help — *Rudoff, Carol*

r Allergy Products Directory 1995/1996: Protecting Your Skin — *Rudoff, Carol*

I Alli Kardhia — *Plaskovitis, Spyros*

The Alliance Revolution — *Gomes-Casseres, Benjamin*

Alliance within the Alliance — *Haglund, David G*

Allied and American Naval Operations in the European Theater, World War I — *Coletta, Paolo E*

Allies and Adversaries — *Schreter, Robert K*

Allies at War — *Reynolds, David*

c Allie's Basketball Dream (Illus. by Darryl Ligasan) — *Barber, Barbara E*

Allies in Conflict — *Weiss, Steve*

c Alligator in the Basement (Illus. by Kyle Corkum) — *Keeshan, Bob*

Alligators: A Prehistoric Presence in the American Landscape — *Strawn, Martha A*

y The Allisons: America's First Family of Stock-Car Racing — *Frank, Steven*

c Allison's Story (Illus. by Rebecca Dallinger) — *Lurie, Jon*

Allocating Federal Funds for Science and Technology — *National Research Council (U.S.). Committee on Criteria for Federal Support of Research and Development*

Allons-Nous Etre Heureux? — *Fleutiaux, Pierrette*

Allowing the Light — *Dalton, Mary*

r Alloy Digest 1952-1995. Electronic Media Version

r Alloy Finder: Version 2.0. Electronic Media Version

Allt Man Kan Onska Sig — *Lundberg, Ulla-Lena*

Alltag Und Arbeitskampf Im Hamburger Hafen — *Weinhauer, Klaus*

y The Alluring Target — *Wimmel, Kenneth*

Allyn Young: The Peripatetic Economist — *Blitch, Charles P*

Alma Mater — *Kluge, P F*

r Almanac for Americans — *Thornton, Willis*

An Almanac for Trebizond for the Year 1336 — *Mercier, Raymond*

r The Almanac of American Employers 1996-97

r The Almanac of British Politics 1983-

r The Almanac of Canadian Politics. 2nd Ed. — *Eagles, Munroe*

r The Almanac of European Politics 1995

Almodovar on Almodovar — *Almodovar, Pedro*

Almost Adam — *Popescu, Petru*

c Almost Famous Daisy! (Illus. by Richard Kidd) — *Kidd, Richard*

Almost Innocent — *Bosworth, Sheila*

The Almost Late Gordon Chater — *Chater, Gordon*

y Almost Lost — *Sparks, Beatrice*

Almost No Memory — *Davis, Lydia*

c Almost Wednesday — *Roy, James*

Alms and Vagabonds — *Goodwin, Janet R*

He Alo A He Alo — *Furrer, Roger MacPherson*

c Aloha, Salty! (Illus. by Ted Rand) — *Rand, Gloria*

y Alone among the Living — *Hoard, G Richard*

c Alone at Home (Illus. by Karin Littlewood) — *Althea*

Alone of All Her Sex — *Warner, Marina*

Alongshore — *Stilgoe, John R*

Alopecia Areata — *Thompson, Wendy*

Alpha 66 Y Su Historica Tarea — *Talleda, Miguel L*

The Alpha Males — *Dukelow, W Richard*

c Alphabats — *Sellers, Paul*

The Alphabet Abecedarium — *Firmage, Richard A*

c Alphabet Antics (Illus. by Ken Vinton) — *Vinton, Ken*

Alphabet Avenue — *Morice, David*

c Alphabet City (Illus. by Stephen T Johnson) — *Johnson, Stephen T*

c Alphabet City Ballet — *Tamar, Erika*

The Alphabet of Modern Annoyances — *Steinberg, Neil*

An Alphabet of Sweets — *Desaulniers, Maurice*

c Alphabet Songs (Illus. by David Pace). Book and Audio Version

r An Alphabetical Guide to the Language of Name Studies — *Room, Adrian*

Als We Vlammen Waren — *Tellegen, Toon*

Also a Mother — *Miller-McLemore, Bonnie J*

r Alsop's Tables. Vol. 2 — *Alsup, Jerry David*

Alsos — *Goudsmit, Samuel A*

r The Alta Vista Search Revolution — *Seltzer, Richard*

r Altante Storico Delle Citta Italiane. Vols. 1-9 — *Bocchi, F*

y Altars in the Street — *Chavis, Melody Ermachild*

Alte Armut Und Neues Burgertum — *Kuster, Thomas*

Der Alte Heratempel In Paestum Und Die Archaische Baukunst In Unteritalien — *Mertens, Dieter*

Alter Egos — *Cohen, David, 1946-*

Altered Fates — *Lyon, Jeff*

Altered State — *Collin, Matthew*

Altered States — *Brookner, Anita*

Alterities: Criticism, History, Representation — *Docherty, Thomas*

r The Alternative Advisor — *Time-Life Books*

Alternative Dispute Resolution in the Workplace — *McDermott, E Patrick*

c Alternative Energy Sources — *Chandler, Gary*

Alternative Fuels — *Lee, Sunggyu*

r Alternative Healing — *Fox, Arnold*

r Alternative Library Literature 1994/1995

r Alternative Literature — *Atton, Chris*

An Alternative Macroeconomic Theory — *King, J E*

r Alternative Medicine — *Burton Goldberg Group*

y Alternative Medicine — *Facklam, Howard*

p Alternative Medicine Digest

Alternative Modernity — *Feenberg, Andrew*

r Alternative Press Index 1969-

r Alternative Press Index 1991-June 1996. Electronic Media Version

yr Alternative Press Index 1995

r Alternative Realities — *George, Leonard*

Alternative Revenue Sources — *Burlingame, Dwight F*

Alternative Shakespeares. Vol. 2 — *Hawkes, Terence*

Alternatives--Roads Less Travelled — *Scott, Whitney*

Alternatives to Assimilation — *Silverstein, Alan*

Alternatives to the Hospital for Acute Psychiatric Treatment — *Warner, Richard*

r Alternatives to the Peace Corps. 7th Ed.

Altertumswissenschaft In Den 20er Jahren — *Flashar, Hellmut*

An Altogether Different Language — *Porter, Anne*

Altogether Elsewhere — *Robinson, Marc*

Altruism and Beyond — *Stark, Oded*

Aluminum Alloys for Packaging II — *Morris, James G*

Aluminum and Magnesium for Automotive Applications — *Bryant, J Daniel*

Aluminum Balloons and Other Poems — *Riddle, Rita Sizemore*

Alvan Clark and Sons — *Warner, Deborah Jean*

y Alvin Ailey: A Life in Dance — *Dunning, Jennifer*

y Alvin Journeyman — *Card, Orson Scott*

c Always My Dad — *Wyeth, Sharon Dennis*

c The Always Prayer Shawl (Illus. by Ted Lewin) — *Oberman, Sheldon*

y Always Running — *Rodriguez, Luis J*

Alzheimer Disease — *Becker, Robert*

Alzheimer's, a Love Story — *Davidson, Ann*

Alzheimer's: Answers to Hard Questions for Families — *Nelson, James Lindemann*

y Alzheimer's Disease — *Landau, Elaine*

Alzheimer's Disease — *Soukup, James E*

p Alzheimer's Research

Am Ban — *Ngo, Nguyen Dung*

Am Fost Si Cioplitor De Himere — *Popescu, Dumitru*

y Am I Black Enough for You? — *Boyd, Todd*

y Am I the Last Virgin? — *Roberts, Tara*

Am I Thin Enough Yet? — *Hesse-Biber, Sharlene*

Ama Del Espiritu — *Castellon, Blanca*

r AMA Style Guide for Business Writing — *American Management Association*

c Amanda Pig, Schoolgirl (Illus. by Ann Schweninger) — *Van Leeuwen, Jean*

Amanecer — *Aguirre, Rafael A*

Amaryllis — *Castle, Jayne*

The Amate Tradition — *Amith, Jonathan D*

p Amateur Astronomy

An Amateur's Guide to the Planet — *Belliveau, Jeannette*

c Amazing Bugs — *MacQuitty, Miranda*

c The Amazing Christmas Extravaganza (Illus. by David Shannon) — *Shannon, David*

c Amazing Dirt Book — *Bourgeois, Paulette*

y Amazing Facts about Ancient Egypt — *Putnam, James*

c Amazing Grace (Illus. by Janet Wilson) — *Granfield, Linda*

y Amazing Grace — *Kozol, Jonathan*

y The Amazing Life of Moe Berg — *Andryszewski, Tricia*

c An Amazing Machine (Illus. by John Shackell) — *Parsons, Alexandra*

c Amazing Mallika (Illus. by Itoko Maeno) — *Parkison, Jami*

c The Amazing Mr. Pleebus — *Abadzis, Nick*

c The Amazing Outdoor Activity Book — *Wilkes, Angela*

y The Amazing Pop-Up Grammar Book (Illus. by Kate Petty) — *Maizels, Jennie*

c The Amazing Zoo (Illus. by Nate Evans) — *Gilmour, H B*

Amazingly Easy Puppet Plays — *Anderson, Dee*

c Amazon ABC (Illus. by Tara Darling) — *Darling, Kathy*

c Amazon Alphabet (Illus. by Martin Jordan) — *Jordan, Martin*

c Amazon Boy — *Lewin, Ted*

c Amazon Diary (Illus. by Mark Greenberg) — *Talbott, Hudson*

y The Amazon Papers — *Keller, Beverly*

Amazonia: Man and Culture in a Counterfeit Paradise. Rev. Ed. — *Meggers, Betty Jane*

Amazonian Indians from Prehistory to the Present — *Roosevelt, Anna*

c Ambar En Cuarto Y Sin Su Amigo (Illus. by Tony Ross) — *Danziger, Paula*

Ambassador Frederic Sackett and the Collapse of the Weimar Republic 1930-1933 — *Burke, Bernard V*

The Ambassadors and America's Soviet Policy — *Mayers, David*

c Amber Brown Goes Fourth — *Danziger, Paula*

c Amber Brown Sees Red (Illus. by Tony Ross) — *Danziger, Paula*

c Amber Brown Wants Extra Credit (Illus. by Tony Ross) — *Danziger, Paula*

c The Amber Cat. Audio Version — *McKay, Hilary*

Amber: Window to the Past — *Grimaldi, David A*

Ambergris and Arrowheads — *Harmon, Anne N*

Ambient — *Womack, Jack*

L'Ambiguite Du Livre — *Buc, Philippe*

Ambiguity and Deterrence — *Baylis, John*

Ambiguous Angels — *Jagoe, Catherine*

Ambiguous Empowerment — *Chase, Susan E*

The Ambiguous Legacy of the Enlightenment — *Rusher, William A*

L'Ambitieuse — *Gallo, Max*

Ambition and Accommodation — *Sigel, Roberta S*

Ambition, Discrimination, and Censorship in Libraries — *Selth, Jefferson P*

Ambivalent Journey — *Jones, Richard C*

y The Ambivalent Magician — *Hawke, Simon*

Ambivalent Zen — *Shainberg, Lawrence*

Ambrose Bierce: Alone in Bad Company — *Morris, Roy*

Ambrose of Milan and the End of the Arian-Nicene Conflicts — *Williams, Daniel H*

Ambrose of Milan: Church and Court in a Christian Capital — *McLynn, Neil B*

r Ambrose's Chronology of World Leaders and Rulers

Ambrosia in an Earthern Vessel — *Steen, Sara Jayne*

c Amelia Bedelia (Illus. by Fritz Siebel) — *Parish, Peggy*

y Amelia Earhart — *Woog, Adam*

Amelia Earhart: A Biography — *Rich, Doris L*

c Amelia Writes Again (Illus. by Marissa Moss) — *Moss, Marissa*

c Amelia's Notebook — *Moss, Marissa*

The Amendments to the Constitution — *Anastalpo, George*

The Amerasia Spy Case — *Klehr, Harvey*

America Adrift — *Rodman, Peter W*

America/Americas — *Kenworthy, Eldon*

America and Egypt — *Holland, Matthew F*

America and Europe — *Gompert, David C*

America and Other Poems — *Bien, Jeff*

America and the Persian Gulf — *Yetiv, Steve A*

America and the Shaping of German Society 1945-1955 — *Ermath, M*

r America as Story — *Howard, Elizabeth Fitzgerald*

America at War since 1945 — *Donaldson, Gary A*

America by Rivers — *Palmer, Tim*

r America: History and Life 1965-

America in European Consciousness 1493-1750 — *Kupperman, Karen Ordahl*

yr America in Historical Fiction — *VanMeter, Vandelia L*

America in Passing — *Cartier-Bresson, Henri*

America in the World — *Hogan, Michael J*

c America in World War I — *Dolan, Edward F*

America Is Me — *Jackson, Kennell*

c America: My Land, Your Land, Our Land — *Nikola-Lisa, W*

America Needs a Raise — *Sweeney, John J*

America Off-Line — *Jacobs, A J*

America on Record — *Millard, A J*

America on Wheels — *Coffey, Frank*

America Online 3 for Macintosh — *Langer, Maria*

America Online 3 for Windows 95 — *Langer, Maria*

America Online for Busy People — *Einstein, David*

r America Preserved

America Unequal — *Danziger, Sheldon*

American Academia and the Survival of Marxist Ideas — *Fernandez-Morera, Dario*

The American Aerospace Industry — *Bilstein, Roger E*

American Anatomies — *Wiegman, Robyn*

r American and British Poetry — *Alexander, Harriet Semmes*

American and Catholic — *Crews, Clyde F*

American Architects and Texts — *Bonta, Juan Pablo*

r American Art Colonies 1850-1930 — *Shipp, Steve*

American Art Pottery — *Frelinghuysen, Alice Cooney*

American Artisans — *Rock, Howard B*

c American Astronomers — *Camp, Carole Ann*

American Aurora — *Rosenfeld, Richard N*

r American Autobiography 1945-1980 — *Briscoe, Mary Louise*

The American Bar Association Guide to Consumer Law

The American Barbershop — *Hunter, Mic*

r American Battlefields — *Cobb, Hubbard*

An American Beach for African Americans — *Phelts, Marsha Dean*

American Beginnings — *Baker, Emerson W*

American Beginnings — *West, Frederick Hadleigh*

r American Best Sellers — *Hinckley, Barbara*

r American Bibliography. Vols. 1-14 — *Evans, Charles*

r American Bibliography, a Preliminary Checklist 1801-1819. Vols. 1-22 — *Shaw, Ralph R*

r The American Bibliography of Slavic and East European Studies for 1993

American Book Design and William Morris. 2nd Ed. — *Thompson, Susan Otis*

r American Business Locations Directory. Vols. 1-5

American Cardiology — *Fye, W Bruce*

American Catholic Pacifism — *Klejment, Anne*

American Catholics and Slavery 1789-1866 — *Zanca, Kenneth J*

The American Century — *Cantor, Norman F*

The American Century — *White, Donald W*

r American Chemical Society Directory of Graduate Research 1995

American Childhood — *MacLeod, Anne Scott*

y American Childhoods — *Wormser, Richard*

The American Cinema — *Sarris, Andrew*

yr The American Civil War — *Woodworth, Steven E*

American Coin Treasures and Hoards — *Bowers, Q David*

American Colonial — *Garrett, Wendell*

American Color — *Manos, Constantine*

American Communication Research — *Dennis, Everette E*

American Composers and Their Public — *Tawa, Nicholas*

American Congregations. Vols. 1-2 — *Wind, James P*

American Constitutionalism — *Griffin, Stephen M*

American Contradictions — *Binder, Wolfgang*

American Cool — *Stearns, Peter N*

The American Corporation Today — *Kaysen, Carl*

The American County — *Menzel, Donald C*

American Crawl — *Allen, Paul*

American Culture between the Wars — *Kalaidjian, Walter*

American Dark Comedy — *Gehring, Wes D*

yr American Decades 1900-1909 — *Tompkins, Vincent*

yr American Decades 1910-1919 — *Tompkins, Vincent*

yr American Decades 1920-1929 — *Baughman, Judith S*

yr American Decades 1980-1989 — *Bondi, Victor*

r American Dietetic Association's Complete Food and Nutrition Guide — *Duyff, Roberta Larson*

y American Dinosaur Hunters — *Aaseng, Nathan*

American Discoveries — *Dudley, Ellen*

r American Diversity, American Identity — *Roth, John K*

r American Drama Criticism: Supplement IV to the Second Edition — *Daniel, LaNelle*

The American Dream — *Wright, Esmond*

The American Dream in Nineteenth-Century Quebec — *Major, Robert*

American Dreamer — *Weir, Theresa*

American Dreamers — *Canning, Peter*

American Dreaming — *Mahler, Sarah J*

American Dreams — *Sapphire*

The American Earthquake — *Wilson, Edmund*

American Economic Policy in the 1980s — *Feldstein, Martin*

American Economists of the Late Twentieth Century — *Samuels, Warren J*

American Elegy — *Simpson, Jeffrey*

American Elites — *Lerner, Robert*

r American Elves — *Roth, John E*

An American Emmaus — *Duffy, Regis A*

c American Environmental Heroes — *Stanley, Phyllis M*

American Exceptionalism — *Lipset, Seymour Martin*

American Expatriate Writing and the Paris Moment — *Pizer, Donald*

American Extremists — *George, John*

y American Eye — *Greenberg, Jan*

y American Eyes — *Carlson, Lori M*

y American Fairy Tales (Illus. by Michael McCurdy) — *Philip, Neil*

American Falls — *Batchelor, John Calvin*

c The American Family Farm (Illus. by George Ancona) — *Anderson, Joan*

The American Family Farm — *Halberstadt, Hans*

American Farms — *Hurt, R Douglas*

The American Father — *Mackey, Wade C*

American Favorites — *Rosbottom, Betty*

r American Federation of Labor and Congress of Industrial Organizations Pamphlets 1889-1955 — *Woodbridge, Mark E*

r American Federation of Labor: History, Encyclopedia, Reference Book. Vols. 1-3 — *American Federation of Labor*

American Fiction. Vol. 7

American Fiction and the Metaphysics of the Grotesque — *Meindl, Dieter*

r American Film Personnel and Company Credits 1908-1920 — *Spehr, Paul C*

yr American First Ladies — *Gould, Lewis L*

yr American Folklore — *Brunvand, Jan Harold*

American Folklore and the Mass Media — *Degh, Linda*

American Forces in Berlin — *Grathwol, Robert P*

American Foreign Policy — *Ikenberry, G John*

c The American Frontier — *Barr, Robert*

c American Frontier (Illus. by Mark Bergin) — *Macdonald, Fiona*

American Frontiers — *Nobles, Gregory H*

The American Fund for Public Service — *Samson, Gloria Garrett*

American Furniture of the 18th Century — *Greene, Jeffrey P*

The American Garden Guides — *Tomocik, Joseph*

American Gay — *Murray, Stephen O*

r The American Geriatrics Society's Complete Guide to Aging and Health — *Williams, Mark E*
cp American Girl
y American Gothic Tales — *Oates, Joyce Carol*
American Health Care Blues — *Miller, Irwin*
American Heart Association around the World Cookbook
American Heart Association Guide to Heart Attack Treatment — *American Heart Association*
American Heaven — *Chernoff, Maxine*
American Hegemony — *Brilmayer, Lea*
r American Heritage Dictionary of American Quotations — *Miner, Margaret*
The American Heritage New History of the Civil War — *Catton, Bruce*
yr The American Heritage Talking Dictionary. Electronic Media Version
c American Heritage: The History of the United States for Young People. Electronic Media Version
cr The American Heritage Thesaurus
y An American Hero — *Denenberg, Barry*
c American Heroes of Exploration and Flight — *Schraff, Anne*
American Higher Education — *Lucas, Christopher J*
yr The American Historical Association's Guide to Historical Literature. 3rd Ed., Vols. 1-2
y American History Smart Junior — *Alouf, James L*
The American Horticultural Society Complete Guide to Water Gardening — *Robinson, Peter, 1938-*
American Horticultural Society Pruning and Training
r American House Designs — *Culbertson, Margaret*
r The American Humanities Index for 1995. Pts. 1-2
American Images — *SBC Communications*
American Images of China 1931-1949 — *Jespersen, T Christopher*
American Images SBC Communications
American Indian Ballerinas — *Livingston, Lili Cockerille*
American Indian Ethnic Renewal — *Nagel, Joane*
c American Indian Festivals — *Miller, Jay*
c American Indian Foods — *Miller, Jay*
American Indian Persistence and Resurgence — *Kroeber, Karl*
yr American Indian Quotations — *Langer, Howard J*
r American Indian Reference and Resource Books for Children and Young Adults. 2nd Ed. — *Kuipers, Barbara J*
r American Indian Reservations and Trust Areas — *Velarde, Veronica E*
American Indian Stories — *Zitkala-Sa*
American Indian Treaties — *Prucha, Francis Paul*
American Intelligence and the German Resistance to Hitler — *Heideking, Jurgen*
c American Inventors of the Twentieth Century — *Jeffrey, Laura S*
American Iron 1607-1900 — *Gordon, Robert B*
The American Jew 1585-1990 — *Marcus, Jacob Rader*
r American Jewish Year Book 1996
yr The American Journals CD. Electronic Media Version
yr American Justice. Vols. 1-3
The American Kitchen 1700 to the Present — *Plante, Ellen M*
American Knees — *Wong, Shawn*
r American Labor History — *Hoerder, Dirk*
r American Labor History and Comparative Labor Movements — *McBrearty, James C*
American Labor in the Era of World War II — *Miller, Sally M*
The American Labor Movement 1955-1995 — *Galenson, Walter*
American Labor on Stage — *Duffy, Susan*
r The American Labor Press
r American Labor Sourcebook — *Rifkin, Bernard*
r American Labor Union Periodicals — *Naas, Bernard G*
r American Labor Unions' Constitutions and Proceedings 1836-
r American Labor Unions, What They Are and How They Work. 2nd Rev. Ed. — *Peterson, Florence*
r The American Labor Who's Who 1925-
r The American Labor Year Book. 1916-1932 Eds.
The American Landscape. Vols. 1-3 — *Clarke, Graham*
American Laughter — *Winokur, Mark*
American Legal Realism and Empirical Social Science — *Schlegel, John Henry*
y American Legends of Rock — *Knapp, Ron*
r American Library Book Catalogues 1801-1875 — *Singerman, Robert*
r American Library Resources — *Downs, Robert Bingham*

r American Library Resources: Supplement 1950-1961 — *Downs, Robert Bingham*
r American Library Resources: Supplement 1961-1970 — *Downs, Robert Bingham*
r American Library Resources: Supplement 1971-1980 — *Downs, Robert Bingham*
r American Limoges — *Limoges, Raymonde*
American Literary Publishing in the Mid-Nineteenth Century — *Winship, Michael*
American Literary Scholarship 1993
American Literary Scholarship 1994
r The American Loyalist — *Ptak, Diane Snyder*
American Magus Harry Smith — *Igliori, Paolo*
r American Medical Association Complete Guide to Women's Health — *Allison, Kathleen Cahill*
r American Medical Association Family Medical Guide. 3rd Ed. — *Clayman, Charles B*
r American Medical Association Manual of Style. 8th Ed.
American Medicine — *Good, Mary-Jo Delvecchio*
American Mennonites and the Great War 1914-1918 — *Homan, Gerlof D*
American Military Power
American Militias — *Abanes, Richard*
American Mixed Race — *Zack, Naomi*
American Modern — *Tejera, Victorino*
American Monroe — *Baty, S Paige*
The American Mosaic — *Carnevale, Anthony Patrick*
r American Musicians II — *Balliett, Whitney*
yr American Nature Writers. Vols. 1-2 — *Elder, John*
American Nature Writing 1997
r American Newspapers 1821-1936 — *Gregory, Winifred*
American Nomad — *Erickson, Steve*
American Original — *Robinson, Ray, 1920-*
American Owned Love — *Boswell, Robert*
American Paintings before 1945 in the Wadsworth Atheneum. Vols. 1-2 — *Wadsworth Atheneum*
American Pastoral — *Roth, Philip*
American Patriotism in a Global Society — *Craige, Betty Jean*
r The American Pharmaceutical Association Parent's Guide to Childhood Medications — *Peirce, Andrea*
American Photographs — *Foresta, Merry A*
American Photographs in Europe — *Nye, David E, 1946-*
American Pie — *West, Michael Lee*
American Pioneers — *Rich, Alan*
American Plastic — *Meikle, Jeffrey L*
American Poetry. Electronic Media Version — *Hollander, John*
The American Poetry Wax Museum — *Rasula, Jed*
American Policy and the Reconstruction of West Germany 1945-1955 — *Diefendorf, Jeffry M*
The American Popular Ballad of the Golden Era 1924-1950 — *Forte, Allen*
American Popular Culture — *Dean, John*
cr The American Presidency. Electronic Media Version
The American Presidency — *McDonald, Forrest*
American Presidential Elections — *Schantz, Harvey L*
An American Procession — *Kazin, Alfred*
American Psychiatric Association Practice Guidelines
American Psychiatric Press Review of Psychiatry. Vol. 15
The American Psychiatric Press Synopsis of Psychiatry — *Hales, Robert E*
The American Psychiatric Press Textbook of Consultation-Liaison Psychiatry — *Rundell, James R*
The American Psychiatric Press Textbook of Geriatric Psychiatry. 2nd Ed. — *Busse, Ewald W*
An American Quarter Century — *Davies, Philip John*
The American Quest for the Primitive Church — *Hughes, Richard T*
American Racing — *Burnside, Tom*
r American Reform and Reformers — *Miller, Randall M*
An American Requiem — *Carroll, James*
c The American Revolution — *Grant, R G*
y The American Revolution — *Lukes, Bonnie L*
The American Revolution in Indian Country — *Calloway, Colin G*
American Sacred Space — *Chidester, David*
y An American Safari (Illus. by Jim Brandenburg) — *Brandenburg, Jim*
American Satire — *Bakalar, Nicholas*
American Scripture — *Maier, Pauline*
An American Seafarer in the Age of Sail — *Burg, B R*
r American Song. 2nd Ed., Vols. 1-2 — *Bloom, Ken*
An American South — *Kein, Sybil*
r American Southwest Travel-Smart Trip Planner. 1st Ed.-
y American Sphinx — *Ellis, Joseph J*

American Splendor Presents Bob and Harv's Comics — *Pekar, Harvey*
American Standards of Living 1918-1988 — *Brown, Clair*
The American Street Gang — *Klein, Malcolm W*
American Studies — *Merlis, Mark*
r American Studies — *Walker, Robert H*
American Studies. Vol. 1 — *Wiszniowska, Marta*
r American Studies: An Annotated Bibliography. Vols. 1-3 — *Salzman, Jack*
r American Studies: An Annotated Bibliography 1984-1988 — *Salzman, Jack*
American Supernatural Fiction — *Robillard, Douglas*
r The American Synagogue — *Olitzky, Kerry M*
American Technological Sublime — *Nye, David E, 1946-*
American Theatre: A Chronicle of Comedy and Drama 1869-1914 — *Bordman, Gerald Martin*
r American Theatre: A Chronicle of Comedy and Drama 1914-1930 — *Bordman, Gerald Martin*
c American Too (Illus. by Ted Lewin) — *Bartone, Elisa*
American Trade Laws after the Uruguay Round — *Mastel, Greg*
American Trade Policy — *Krueger, Anne O*
American Trade Policy 1923-1995 — *Kaplan, Edward S*
American Tragedy — *Schiller, Lawrence*
American Transcendentalism and Asian Religions — *Versluis, Arthur*
American Treasures in the Library of Congress
American Visions — *Hughes, Robert*
p American Visions: The Magazine of Afro-American Culture
The American Welfare System — *Gensler, Howard*
The American West — *Arnold, James R*
The American West — *Brown, Dee Alexander*
r The American West in the Twentieth Century — *Etulain, Richard W*
American Wildlife and Plants — *Martin, Alexander C*
American Windsor Chairs — *Evans, Nancy Goyne*
American Woman — *Einarson, John, 1952-*
r The American Woman's Almanac — *Bernikow, Louise*
r American Women Historians 1700s-1990s — *Scanlon, Jennifer*
r American Women Writers. Vols. 1-5 — *Maniero, Lina*
American Women Writers and the Work of History 1790-1860 — *Baym, Nina*
American Women Writers to 1800 — *Harris, Sharon M*
r The American Women's Almanac — *Bernikow, Louise*
r American Women's Track and Field — *Tricard, Louise Mead*
r American Working Class History — *Neufeld, Maurice F*
r American Working-Class History in Historical Journals 1961-1972 — *Skotnes, Andor*
yr American Writers. 4th Suppl., Vols. 1-2
y American Writers of the 20th Century — *Bredeson, Carmen*
p American Writing
Americanism: Revolutionary Order and Societal Self-Interpretation in the American Republic — *Gebhardt, Jurgen*
The Americanization of West Virginia — *Hennen, John C*
Americans: A Collision of Histories — *Countryman, Edward*
Americans No More — *Geyer, Georgie Anne*
Americans View Crime and Justice — *Flanagan, Timothy J*
America's Alternative Religions — *Miller, Timothy*
America's Bachelor Uncle — *Taylor, Bob Pepperman*
America's Civil War — *Simpson, Brooks D*
r America's Corporate Families 1995. Vols. 1-3
America's Dream — *Santiago, Esmeralda*
America's Dumbest Criminals — *Butler, Daniel*
America's Eye — *Dalsimer, Adele M*
America's Foreign Policy in a Changing World — *Hartmann, Frederick H*
r America's Garden Book. Rev. Ed. — *Bush-Brown, Louise*
America's Great Patriotic War with Spain — *Tebbel, John*
The Americas in the Age of Revolution 1750-1850 — *Langley, Lester D*
The Americas in the Spanish World Order — *Muldoon, James*
America's Mission — *Smith, Tony*
America's Modernisms — *Lindberg, Kathryne V*
America's Music — *Oermann, Robert K*

America's New Economic Order — *Hodges, Donald Clark*

America's Prisoner — *Noriega, Manuel*

America's Pursuit of Precision Bombing 1910-1945 — *McFarland, Stephen L*

p The Americas Review

America's Secret War against Bolshevism — *Foglesong, David S*

r America's Top Jobs on CD-ROM. Electronic Media Version

y America's Victims — *Winters, Paul A*

r Die Amerikanische Besetzung Deutschlands — *Henke, Klaus-Dietmar*

L'Amerique Saigne — *Franketienne*

Amethyst Dreams — *Whitney, Phyllis A*

Amethyst--Geschichte, Eigenschaften, Fundorte — *Lieber, Werner*

Amhrain Choilm De Bhailis — *Denvir, Gearoid*

L'Amica Della Modellista — *Cerati, Carla*

c The Amish — *Israel, Fred L*

y The Amish — *Williams, Jean Kinney*

c An Amish Christmas (Illus. by Pamela Patrick) — *Ammon, Richard*

Amish Enterprise — *Kraybill, Donald B*

Amish Kinder Komforts — *Havig, Bettina*

Amish Women — *Stoltzfus, Louise*

y Amistad — *Pesci, David*

y The Amistad Slave Revolt and American Abolition Zeinert, Karen

Ammonoid Paleobiology — *Landman, Neil H*

Amnesiascope — *Erickson, Steve*

Among All These Dreamers — *Bulkeley, Kelly*

Among Grizzlies — *Treadwell, Timothy*

Among the Ginzburgs — *Pall, Ellen*

Among the Lowest of the Dead — *Von Drehle, David*

Among the White Moon Faces — *Lim, Shirley*

Among Warriors — *Logan, Pamela*

y Among Whales — *Payne, Roger*

Amor Di Libro — *Crisostomi, Paolo*

El Amor En Los Tiempos De Castro — *Eranova-Cruz, Florencio*

Amoral Politics — *Scharfstein, Ben-Ami*

L'Amore E Salvo — *Barbiellini Amidei, Gaspare*

c Amos and Boris — *Steig, William*

Amour Flou — *Savoie, Paul*

c Amphibians and Reptiles. Book and Electronic Media Version

The Amphibians and Reptiles of New Mexico — *Degenhardt, William G*

The Amphibians and Reptiles of the Yucatan Peninsula — *Lee, Julian C*

r Amphibians of Oregon, Washington, and British Columbia — *Corkran, Charlotte C*

Amphibious Assault Falklands — *Clapp, Michael*

Amputation: Surgical Practice and Patient Management — *Murdoch, G*

Amputations and Prosthetics — *May, Bella J*

Amrita — *Yoshimoto, Banana*

y Amsterdam Quest — *Allen, Judy*

The Amusements of the People and Other Papers — *Dickens, Charles*

c Amy Angel Goes Home — *Lathrop, Kathleen*

Amy Fay: America's Notable Woman of Music — *McCarthy, Margaret William*

y Amy Tan: Author of the Joy Luck Club — *Kramer, Barbara*

Amyotrophic Lateral Sclerosis — *TMIN International Symposium on Amyotrophic Lateral Sclerosis (1995: Tokyo, Japan)*

An 1000, An 2000, Sur Les Traces De Nos Peurs — *Duby, Georges*

An Einen Jungen Dichter — *Nolden, Thomas*

Ana Historic — *Marlatt, Daphne*

Anachronism — *Mateer, John*

Anacreon Redivivus — *O'Brien, John, 1954-*

p Anaerobe

Anais Nin: A Biography — *Bair, Deirdre*

The Analects of Confucius — *Confucius*

Analog Circuit Design — *Sansen, Willy*

Analog Filters — *Su, Kendall L*

Analysis — *Lieb, Elliott H*

Analysis and Assessment 1940-1979 — *Wintz, Cary D*

Analysis and Assessment 1980-1984 — *Wintz, Cary D*

Analysis and Computation — *Cheng, Franklin Y*

Analysis and Mechanics of Continuous Media — *Anh, N H*

Analysis, Design and Evaluation of Man-Machine Systems 1995

The Analysis of Cortical Connectivity — *Young, Malcolm P*

The Analysis of Hysteria. 2nd Ed. — *Merskey, Harold*

The Analysis of Inflation — *Metin, Kivilcim*

Analysis of Observed Chaotic Data — *Abarbanel, Henry D I*

Analysis of Status Indians in British Columbia. Vol. 3

r Analysis of Surfactants — *Hummel, Dietrich O*

An Analysis of Variability and Condition of Cavate Structures in Bandelier National Monument — *Toll, Henry Wolcott*

The Analyst in the Inner City — *Altman, Neil*

Analyst-Patient Interaction — *Fordham, Michael*

The Analyst's Preconscious — *Hamilton, Victoria*

Analytic Semigroups and Optimal Regularity in Parabolic Problems — *Lunardi, Alessandra*

Analytic Theism, Hartshorne, and the Concept of God — *Dombrowski, Daniel A*

Analytical Chemistry by Open Learning — *Morgan, Ed*

Analytical Chemistry of Complex Matrices — *Smyth, W Franklin*

r Analytical Index. Updated 6th Ed., Vols. 1-2 — *Porges, Amelia*

r Analytical Profiles of Drug Substances and Excipients. Vol. 24

Analytical Techniques for Foods and Agricultural Products — *Linden, G*

r Analytical Techniques in Telecommunications — *Mazda, Fraidoon*

L'Analytique De La Representation Chez Peirce — *Tienne, Andre De*

Analyzing Fugue — *Renwick, William*

c Ananse and the Golden Drum — *Abdallah, Mohammed Ben*

Ananse: The Web of Life in Africa — *Biggers, John*

Anarchist Voices — *Avrich, Paul*

Anarcho-Hindu — *White, Curtis*

The Anarchy of King Stephen's Reign — *King, Edmund*

Anarchy Online — *Platt, Charles*

Ana's Land — *Renne, Tanya*

The Anasazi of Mesa Verde and the Four Corners — *Ferguson, William M*

c Anastasia, Absolutely — *Lowry, Lois*

y Anastasia's Album — *Brewster, Hugh*

Anatolica: Studies in Strabo — *Syme, Ronald*

Anatolica: Studies in the Greek East in the 18th and 19th Centuries — *Clogg, Richard*

Anatomy and Physiology for Speech and Language — *Seikel, John A*

The Anatomy Lesson — *Morley, John David*

Anatomy of a Controversy — *Altholz, Josef L*

Anatomy of a Dictatorship — *Fulbrook, Mary*

The Anatomy of a Little War — *Bachrach, Bernard S*

Anatomy of a Miracle — *Waldmeir, Patti*

Anatomy of a Naval Disaster — *Pritchard, James*

Anatomy of a Splitting Borderline — *Muller, Rene J*

The Anatomy of an International Monetary Regime — *Gallarotti, Giulio M*

The Anatomy of Disgust — *Miller, William Ian*

The Anatomy of Melancholy — *Burton, Robert*

The Anatomy of Prejudices — *Young-Bruehl, Elisabeth*

Anatomy of Restlessness — *Chatwin, Bruce*

Anatomy of the Spirit — *Myss, Caroline*

Anatomy of Wonder 4 — *Barron, Neil*

r Ancestors Charts Preserving Yesterday for Tomorrow. Vols. 1-2 — *Manery, Phyllis J*

Ancestors — *Hove, Chenjerai*

r Ancestors: A Beginner's Guide to Family History and Genealogy — *Willard, Jim*

y Ancestral Passions — *Morell, Virginia*

Ancestral Prayers — *Gasquet, F A*

Anchoring Points for Corporate Directors — *Mueller, Robert Kirk*

Anchors against Change — *Murray, Shoon Kathleen*

The Ancien Regime — *Le Roy Ladurie, Emmanuel*

Ancient Akamas I — *Feifer, Jane*

Ancient Art from the Shumei Family Collection

Ancient Astronomers — *Aveni, Anthony F*

c Ancient China — *Michaelson, Carol*

c Ancient China — *Simpson, Judith*

y Ancient China — *Williams, Brian*

Ancient Concepts of Philosophy — *Jordan, William*

y Ancient Echoes — *Holdstock, Robert*

Ancient Egyptian Art. Electronic Media Version

c The Ancient Egyptian Facts of Life — *Morley, Jacqueline*

c Ancient Egyptian People — *McNeill, Sarah*

c Ancient Egyptian Places — *McNeill, Sarah*

c Ancient Egyptians (Illus. by John James) — *Kerr, Daisy*

c The Ancient Egyptians — *Marston, Elsa*

Ancient Epic Poetry — *Beye, Charles Rowan*

Ancient Farms and Land-Plots on the Khora of Khersonesos Taurike — *Saprykin, S J*

y Ancient Greece — *Martin, Thomas R*

c Ancient Greece — *Pearson, Anne*

c Ancient Greece — *Thompson, Neil*

Ancient Greek Music — *West, M L*

c The Ancient Greeks — *Freeman, Charles*

c The Ancient Greeks — *Schomp, Virginia*

Ancient Ireland — *O'Brien, Jacqueline*

Ancient Israelite Religion — *Niditch, Susan*

Ancient Jewelry and Archaeology — *Calinescu, Adriana*

An Ancient Jewish Christian Source on the History of Christianity — *Jones, F Stanley*

Ancient Legends of Ireland — *Wilde, Lady*

Ancient Magic and Ritual Power — *Meyer, Marvin*

y The Ancient Maya — *Galvin, Irene Flum*

Ancient Music Adapted to Modern Practice — *Vicentino, Nicola*

The Ancient Near East. Vols. 1-2 — *Kuhrt, Amelie*

r Ancient Near Eastern Art — *Collon, Dominique*

Ancient Nubia — *O'Connor, David B*

Ancient People of the Arctic — *McGhee, Robert*

Ancient Peoples and Landscapes — *Johnson, Eileen*

r Ancient Peruvian Art — *Silverman, Helaine*

Ancient Philosophy, Mystery, and Magic — *Kingsley, Peter*

Ancient Rhetorics for Contemporary Students — *Crowley, Sharon*

y The Ancient Romans — *Hinds, Kathryn*

c Ancient Romans (Illus. by John James) — *Kerr, Daisy*

c Ancient Romans (Illus. by Mark Bergin) — *Macdonald, Fiona*

y Ancient Rome — *Liberati, Annamaria*

Ancient Secrets — *Meier, Levi*

y Ancient Shores — *McDevitt, Jack*

Ancient Songs Set Ablaze — *Richards, Sandra L*

The Ancient Southwestern Community — *Wills, W H*

c The Ancient Splendor of Prehistoric Cahokia — *Denny, Sidney*

Ancient Synagogues. Vols. 1-2 — *Urman, Dan*

The Ancients and the Moderns — *Lilly, Reginald*

And Dreams Are Dreams — *Vassilikos, Vassilis*

And I, Francis — *Dunlap, Lauren*

...And I Never Learned to Yodel — *Harmon, Anne N*

And I Shall Dwell among Them — *Folberg, Neil*

And if You Play Golf, You're My Friend — *Penick, Harvey*

And One to Die On — *Haddam, Jane*

And Peace Never Came — *Raab, Elisabeth M*

And Still I Rise — *Angelou, Maya*

And Still I Rise (Angelou). Audio Version — *Angelou, Maya*

c And Still the Turtle Watched (Illus. by Barry Moser) — *MacGill-Callahan, Sheila*

And Still We Rise — *Hayes, Diana L*

And Suddenly Spring — *Szyper, Adam*

c And Sunday Makes Seven (Illus. by M Edwards) — *Baden, Robert*

y And the Animals Will Teach You — *Lasher, Margot*

And the Blood Cried Out — *Levy, Harlan*

c And the Earth Trembled (Illus. by Neil Waldman) — *Oppenheim, Shulamith Levey*

And the Poor Get Welfare — *Copeland, Warren R*

And the Waters Turned to Blood — *Barker, Rodney*

And the Waters Turned to Blood (Gaines). Audio Version — *Barker, Rodney*

c And Then... (Illus. by John Lobban) — *Ross, Stewart*

And We Sold the Rain — *Santos, Rosario*

And What Books Do You Read? — *Petersson, Irmtraud*

And Zen Some — *Banks, Daibo Bill*

The Andean Cocaine Industry — *Clawson, Patrick L*

Andean Ecology — *Knapp, Gregory*

Andean Lives — *Condori Mamani, Gregorio*

Der Andere Aufbruch — *Assel, Heinrich*

r Anders CD-ROM Guide. 2nd Ed.

The Anderson Files — *Shapiro, Marc*

r Anderson's Travel Companion — *Anderson, Sarah*

r Andes: Radiocarbon Database for Bolivia, Ecuador and Peru — *Ziokowski, Mariusz S*

c Uma Andorinha No Alpendre (Illus. by Manuel Mouta Faria) — *Perafita, Alexandre*

Andorra — *Cameron, Peter*

Andre Citroen: The Henry Ford of France — *Reynolds, John*

Andre Gide Dans Le Labyrinthe De La Mythotextualite — *Genova, Pamela Antonia*

Andre Malraux: A Biography — *Cate, Curtis*

Andre-Marie Ampere: Enlightenment and Electrodynamics — *Hofmann, James R*

y Andre Talks Hair! — *Walker, Andre*
Andreas and the Ambiguity of Courtly Love — *Cherchi, Paolo*
Andrei Platonov: Materialy Dlia Biografi 1899-1929 GG — *Langerak, Tomas*
Andres Molina Enriques — *Shadle, Stanley F*
Andrew Durnford: A Black Sugar Planter in the Antebellum South. 2nd Ed. — *Whitten, David O*
Andrew Jackson Higgins and the Boats That Won World War II — *Strahan, Jerry E*
Andrew Wyeth: A Secret Life — *Meryman, Richard*
Andrew Wyeth: America's Painter — *Severens, Martha R*
Android Epistemology — *Ford, Kenneth M*
Andromede — *Curtis, Jean-Louis*
Androtion and the Atthis — *Harding, Phillip*
c Andy and His Yellow Frisbee (Illus. by Mary Thompson) — *Thompson, Mary*
c Andy Warhol — *Venezia, Mike*
Die Anfange Der Abendlandischen Rezeption Des Nizanums — *Ulrich, Jorg*
c Anfernee Hardaway — *Daniels, Jeremy*
c Anfernee (Penny) Hardaway — *Rambeck, Richard*
Angel — *Guild, Nicholas*
Angel — *Kilworth, Garry*
The Angel and the Beehive — *Mauss, Armand L*
c The Angel and the Donkey (Illus. by Alexander Koshkin) — *Paterson, Katherine*
c Angel Child, Dragon Child — *Surat, Michele Maria*
The Angel Doll — *Bledsoe, Jerry*
c Angel Falls (Illus. by Martin Jordan) — *Jordan, Tanis*
Angel Falls — *Wynveen, Tim*
Angel Flying Too Close to the Ground — *Garrett, Annie*
Angel, Interrupted — *Shepherd, Reginald*
y Angel Kisses — *Bennett, Cherie*
c The Angel Knew Papa and the Dog — *McKelvey, Douglas Kaine*
y Angel Light (Dukes). Audio Version — *Greeley, Andrew M*
Angel Maker — *Maitland, Sara*
c Angel of God, What's Your Name? (Illus. by Joan Hutson) — *McNall, Rebecca*
The Angel of History — *Forche, Carolyn*
The Angel of Solitude — *Blais, Marie-Claire*
The Angel of Twickenham — *Bentley, Ursula*
Angel on Trial — *Kerl, Mary Ann*
Angel Veneration and Christology — *Stuckenbruch, Loren T*
y Angel Voice — *Bennett, Rodney*
Angel Walk — *Govier, Katherine*
c Angela and Diabola — *Banks, Lynne Reid*
c Angela from the Arctic (Illus. by Lawrence Migdale) — *Hoyt-Goldsmith, Diane*
c Angela Weaves a Dream (Illus. by Jeffrey J Foxx) — *Sola, Michele*
c Angela's Aliens — *Lisle, Janet Taylor*
y Angela's Ashes — *McCourt, Frank*
Angela's Ashes (McCourt). Audio Version — *McCourt, Frank*
Angelface and Amazing Grace — *Copeland, Lori*
p Angelflesh
Angelico — *Spike, John T*
Angelique Ou L'Enchantement — *Robbe-Grillet, Alain*
Angelo Gambiglioni, Giuresconsulto Aretino Del Quattrocento — *Maffei, Domenico*
Angels, a Modern Myth — *Serres, Michel*
r Angels A to Z — *Bunson, Matthew*
r Angels A to Z — *Lewis, James R*
Angels, Anarchists and Gods — *Felver, Christopher*
Angels (and Demons) — *Kreeft, Peter*
Angels and Insects (May). Audio Version — *Byatt, A S*
Angels and Wild Things — *Cech, John*
Angels Are Black and White — *Berkewicz, Ulla*
Angel's Bidding — *Short, Sharon Gwyn*
c Angels in the Dust (Illus. by Roger Essley) — *Raven, Margot Theis*
c The Angel's Mistake (Illus. by Mark Podwal) — *Prose, Francine*
Angels of Albion — *Robinson, Jane*
y Angels of Emergency — *Theisen, Donna*
Angels of the Universe — *Gudmundsson, Einar Mar*
Angels on Toast — *Powell, Dawn*
Angels Sing in Me. Audio Version — *Freeman, James*
Angels: Their Mission and Message — *Jaekle, Charles*
Angels Unawares — *McKenna, Megan*
y Angels Watching over Me — *McDaniel, Lurlene*
Angelspeake — *Mark, Barbara*
Anger — *Sarton, May*
Anger Management in Schools — *Wilde, Jerry*
The Anger of Achilles — *Muellner, Leonard*

Les Anges De Sodome — *Bensoussan, Albert*
Angevin England 1154-1258 — *Mortimer, Richard*
Angkor Wat — *Mannikka, Eleanor*
Anglia, Swiat I Gwiazdy — *Basista, Jakub*
Anglizismen-Worterbuch. Vol. 1 — *Carstensen, Broder*
Anglo-American Approaches to Alliance Security 1955-60 — *Rees, G Wyn*
Anglo-American Feminist Challenges to the Rhetorical Traditions — *Ratcliffe, Krista*
Anglo-American Interplay in Recent Drama — *Cohn, Ruby*
Anglo-American Relations in the Twentieth Century — *Dobson, Alan P*
Anglo-French Relations and Strategy on the Western Front 1914-18 — *Philpott, William James*
Anglo-German Studies — *Byrn, R M F*
Anglo-Irish: The Literary Imagination in a Hyphenated Culture — *Moynahan, Julian*
Anglo-Norman Medicine — *Hunt, Tony*
The Anglo-Saxon Chronicle (Swanton)
Anglo-Saxon Church Councils c.650-c.850 — *Cubitt, Catherine*
Anglo-Saxon Medicine — *Cameron, M L*
Anglo-Saxon Oxfordshire — *Blair, John*
Angola: Promises and Lies — *Maier, Karl*
y The Angry American — *Tolchin, Susan J*
The Angry Ones — *Williams, John A*
Angry White Men — *McClaran, Robbie*
The Anguish of the Jews. Rev. Ed. — *Flannery, Edward H*
c Angus Rides the Goods Train (Illus. by Chris Riddell) — *Durant, Alan*
Angus Wilson: A Biography — *Drabble, Margaret*
Anh Hung Bat Mang — *Tran, Thy Van*
c Animal Action ABC (Illus. by Art Wolfe) — *Pandell, Karen*
Animal Appetite — *Conant, Susan*
c Animal Athletes (Illus. by Frans Lanting) — *Lanting, Frans*
cr Animal Babies — *Craig, Claire*
c Animal Babies — *Tracqui, Valerie*
Animal Cell Technology — *Beuvery, E C*
Animal Cognition — *Vauclair, Jacques*
c Animal Crackers (Illus. by Jane Dyer) — *Dyer, Jane*
c Animal Dads (Illus. by Steve Jenkins) — *Collard, Sneed B*
Animal Dreams — *Kingsolver, Barbara*
c Animal Faces (Illus. by Akira Satoh) — *Toda, Kyoko*
c Animal Families — *Threadgall, Colin*
c Animal Families (Snapshot Books)
Animal Farm — *Orwell, George*
y Animal Farm (West). Audio Version — *Orwell, George*
c Animal Friends (Illus. by Anita Jeram) — *King-Smith, Dick*
c Animal Grossology (Illus. by Jack Keely) — *Branzei, Sylvia*
c Animal Habitats (Illus. by Adam Hook) — *Fitzsimmons, Cecilia*
c Animal Hideaways (Illus. by Halli Verrinder) — *Ganeri, Anita*
c Animal Homes — *Taylor, Barbara*
c Animal Homes — *Threadgall, Colin*
y Animal Hospital — *Sawicki, Stephen*
c Animal Hullabaloo (Illus. by Jakki Wood) — *Wood, Jakki*
y Animal Instinct — *Metzenthen, David*
c Animal Lingo (Illus. by Barbara Bustetter Falk) — *Conrad, Pam*
Animal Minds and Human Morals — *Sorabji, Richard*
An Animal of the Sixth Day — *Fargas, Laura*
p Animal People
Animal Physiology. 5th Ed. — *Schmidt-Nielsen, Knut*
Animal Planet — *Bradfield, Scott*
y Animal Rights — *Bloyd, Sunni*
y Animal Rights — *Harnack, Andrew*
Animal Rights. Rev. Ed. — *Achor, Amy Blount*
c Animal Senses — *Berger, Melvin*
c Animal Stories — *King-Smith, Dick*
c Animal Tales for Children — *Elaturoti, D F*
Animal Theology — *Linzey, Andrew*
Animal Triste — *Maron, Monika*
Animal Welfare and Human Values — *Preece, Rod*
The Animal Wife (Muller). Audio Version — *Thomas, Elizabeth Marshall*
The Animal World of the Pharaohs — *Houlihan, Patrick F*
c Animalia (Illus. by Graeme Base) — *Base, Graeme*
c Animals — *King, Penny, 1963-*
c Animals and Birds — *Temko, Florence*
Animals and Temperature — *Johnston, Ian A*

c Animals and Their World — *Morgan, Sally*
Animals and Women — *Adams, Carol J*
Animals as Teachers and Healers — *McElroy, Susan Chernak*
c Animals: Black and White (Illus. by Phyllis Limbacher Tildes) — *Tildes, Phyllis Limbacher*
c Animals in Art — *Somerville, Louisa*
Animals in Medieval French Manuscript Illumination — *Gathercole, Patricia M*
y Animals in Roman Life and Art — *Toynbee, J M C*
c Animals in Winter (Illus. by Helen K Davie) — *Bancroft, Henrietta*
c The Animals of Paradise (Illus. by Simon Trethewey) — *Durkee, Noura*
c Animals of the Bible (Illus. by Letizia Galli) — *Ziefert, Harriet*
c Animals of the Desert — *Savage, Stephen*
c Animals of the Rain Forest — *Savage, Stephen*
Animals, Property, and the Law — *Francione, Gary L*
c The Animals' Song (Illus. by Chris L Demarest) — *Harrison, David L*
c Animals That Ought to Be (Illus. by Leonard Baskin) — *Michelson, Richard*
y Animalwatch — *Dimijian, Greg*
c An Animated Alphabet (Illus. by Marie Angel) — *Angel, Marie*
The Animated Alphabet — *Demeude, Hugues*
Animating Calculus — *Packel, Ed*
Animating Culture — *Smoodin, Eric*
r Animation, Caricature, Gag and Political Cartoons in the United States and Canada — *Lent, John A*
c Animation Magic — *Hahn, Don*
r The Anime Movie Guide — *McCarthy, Helen*
Anioma: A Social History of the Western Igbo People — *Ohadike, Don C*
c Anisett Lundberg — *Duey, Kathleen*
Anita and Me — *Syal, Meera*
Ann Petry — *Holladay, Hilary*
r Ann Radcliffe: A Bio-Bibliography — *Rogers, Deborah D*
y Ann Richards: Politician, Feminist, Survivor — *Siegel, Dorothy Schainman*
Anna and Bernhard Blume — *Sobel, Dean*
Anna Duncan: In the Footsteps of Isadora — *Quinlan, Kathleen*
Anna IAroslavna-Koroleva Frantsii — *Fylypchak, Ivan*
c Annabel Again (Illus. by Megan Halsey) — *Boland, Janice*
c Annabelle Swift, Kindergartner. Book and Audio Version — *Schwartz, Amy*
Annam — *Bataille, Christophe*
Annapolis — *Martin, William, 1950-*
Anna's Story — *Donaghy, Bronwyn*
Anne Bogart: Viewpoints — *Dixon, Michael Bigelow*
Anne Bronte — *Frawley, Maria H*
c Anne Frank (Illus. by Helena Owen) — *Castor, Harriet*
c Anne Frank — *Katz, Sandor*
y Anne Frank Remembered — *Gies, Miep*
Anne McCaffrey: A Critical Companion — *Roberts, Robin, 1957-*
c Anne of Green Gables. Audio Version — *Montgomery, L M*
Anne Rice — *Roberts, Bette B*
The Anne Rice Reader — *Ramsland, Katherine*
Anne Tyler as Novelist — *Salwak, Dale*
L'Annee Balzacienne 1994
Les Annees Romantiques — *Julia, Isabelle*
Annette Messager — *Conkelton, Sheryl*
Annexins: Molecular Structure to Cell Function — *Seaton, Barbara A*
y Annie — *Armstrong, Luanne*
c Annie Angel (Illus. by S Jenkin-Pearce) — *Jenkin-Pearce, S*
c Annie, Anya: A Month in Moscow — *Trivas, Irene*
c Annie Bananie Moves to Barry Avenue (Illus. by Abby Carter) — *Komaiko, Leah*
y Annie John — *Kincaid, Jamaica*
c Annie Oakley (Carradine) (Illus. by Fred Warter). Book and Audio Version — *Kunstler, James H*
y Annie's Brother's Suit and Other Stories — *Rubinstein, Gillian*
Annie's Garden Journal — *Spiegelman, Annie*
c Annie's Promise — *Levitin, Sonia*
Annihilation — *Szewc, Piotr*
The Anniversary — *Canon, Rachel*
The Anniversary — *Swinfen, Ann*
c Anno's Counting House (Illus. by Mitsumasa Anno) — *Anno, Mitsumasa*
y Annotated Art — *Cumming, Robert*

The Annotated Baseball Stories of Ring Lardner 1914-1919 — *Lardner, Ring*

r An Annotated Bibliography of Hispanic Feminist Criticism — *Charnon-Deutsch, Lou*

r An Annotated Bibliography of Jane Austen Studies 1984-94 — *Roth, Barry*

r An Annotated Bibliography of Jazz Fiction and Jazz Fiction Criticism — *Albert, Richard N*

r Annotated Catalog, South Texas College of Law, Special Collections — *South Texas College of Law. Library. Special Collections*

r An Annotated Guide to The Chronicles of Oklahoma 1921-1994 — *Welsh, Carol*

The Annotated Lost World — *Doyle, Arthur Conan, Sir*

r Annotated Texts for Translation: English-French — *Adab, B J*

r Annotations: A Directory of Periodicals Listed in the Alternative Press Index 1996

r Annotations to William Faulkner's The Town — *Horton, Merrill*

Annoying the Victorians — *Kincaid, James R*

Annual '96: Fiction

Annual '96: Non Fiction

r Annual Bulletin of Statistics of World Trade in Steel 1995

r Annual Bulletin of Steel Statistics for Europe. Vol. 21

r Annual Bulletin of Trade in Chemical Products

r The Annual Register 1995

Annual Report 1994. Abridged Ed. — *Bank of Portugal*

Annual Report 1995 — *Bank of Spain*

Annual Review of Astronomy and Astro-Physics. Vol. 34

Annual Review of Cell and Development Biology. Vol. 12

Annual Review of Nursing Research. Vol. 13

Annual Review of Psychology. Vol. 47

Annual World Bank Conference on Development Economics 1995

El Ano Del Fuego — *Martin del Campo, David*

The Anomalist — *Huyghe, Patrick*

Anonymous Tip — *Farris, Michael*

O Anorthoghrafos Epighrafopios — *Apostolou, Spyros*

Another America — *Jadjor, Kofi Buenor*

Another America — *Warhus, Mark*

c Another Day — *Sachs, Marilyn*

Another Day, Another Town — *Dusty, Slim*

Another Jackie Robinson — *Hester, M L*

y Another Kind of Monday — *Coles, William E*

Another Language — *Waldrop, Rosmarie*

Another Nation — *O'Loughlin, Michael*

Another Spring Darkness — *Mahapatra, Anuradha*

Another Turn of the Crank — *Berry, Wendell*

Another Way Home — *Thorndike, John*

y Another Way to Dance — *Southgate, Martha*

Another Wilderness — *Rogers, Susan Fox*

Another You — *Beattie, Ann*

Ansel Adams: A Biography — *Alinder, Mary Street*

Ansel Adams and the American Landscape — *Spaulding, Jonathan*

The Answer: Including a Selection of Poems — *Juana Ines De La Cruz, Sister*

Answered Prayers — *Oktavec, Eileen*

Antarctic and Subantarctic Pycnogonida — *Child, C Allan*

Antarctica — *Caddy, Caroline*

Antarctica — *Lucas, Mike*

Antbirds and Ovenbirds — *Skutch, Alexander Frank*

c Antelope Woman — *Lacapa, Michael*

Antenna Design — *Monser, George J*

Antenna Engineering Using Physical Optics — *Diaz, Leo*

Antenna Theory. 2nd Ed. — *Balanis, Constantine A*

The Anther: Form, Function and Phylogeny — *D'Arcy, William G*

Anthologie De Chansons Mandingues (Cote D'Ivoire, Guinee, Mali) — *Mamadi, Kaba*

An Anthology of Chinese Literature — *Owen, Stephen*

Anthology of Contemporary Kurdish Poetry — *Schmid, Estella*

Anthology of Palestinian Literature — *Jayyusi, Salma Khadra*

An Anthology of Russian Literature from Earliest Writings to Modern Fiction — *Rzhevsky, Nicholas*

An Anthology of Vietnamese Poems — *Huynh, Sanh Thong*

Anthony and Cleopatra (Neill) — *Shakespeare, William*

c Anthony Ant's Treasure Hunt (Illus. by Graham Philpot) — *Philpot, Lorna*

Anthony Crosland: The Mixed Economy — *Reisman, David*

Anthony Eden: A Life and Reputation — *Dutton, David*

c Anthony Reynoso: Born to Rope — *Cooper, Martha*

c Anthony, the Perfect Monster (Illus. by Angelo DeCesare) — *DeCesare, Angelo*

Anthony Trollope and His Contemporaries — *Skilton, David*

Anthony Van Dyck: Thomas Howard, the Earl of Arundel — *White, Christopher*

The Anthropic Cosmological Principle — *Barrow, John D*

Anthropoid Origins — *Fleagle, John G*

Anthropological Approaches to the Study of Ethnomedicine — *Nichter, Mark*

The Anthropological Imagination in Latin American Literature — *Emery, Amy Fass*

Anthropological Other or Burmese Brother? — *Spiro, Melford*

Anthropologie Und Schauspielkunst — *Kosenina, Alexander*

An Anthropologist on Mars — *Sacks, Oliver*

Anthropology: A Student's Guide to Theory and Method — *Barrett, Stanley R*

Anthropology and the German Enlightenment — *Faull, Katherine M*

The Anthropology of Anger — *Monga, Celestin*

The Anthropology of Ethnicity — *Vermeulen, Hans*

The Anthropology of Europe — *Goddard, V*

The Anthropology of Self-Person and Myth in Africa — *Kigunga, Raphael*

Anthropology of the Self — *Morris, Brian*

Anthropology of Tourism — *Nash, Dennison*

The Anthropology of Wisdom Literature — *Kaufmann, Wanda Ostrowska*

Anthropometrica: A Textbook of Body Measurement for Sports and Health Courses — *Norton, Kevin*

Anti-Discriminatory Practice — *Millam, Rosalind*

Anti-Dumping and Anti-Trust Issues in Free-Trade Areas — *Marceau, Gabrielle Z*

The Anti-Egotist: Kingsley Amis, Man of Letters — *Fussell, Paul*

Anti-Gay — *Simpson, Mark*

Anti-Judaism and Early Christian Identity — *Taylor, Miriam S*

Anti-Judaism in Feminist Religious Writings — *Kellenbach, Katharina Von*

The Anti-Marcos Struggle — *Thompson, Mark R*

Anti-Semitic Stereotypes — *Felsenstein, Frank*

Anti-Semitism and Early Christianity — *Evans, Craig A*

r Anti-Semitism Worldwide 1995/6

Antibiotic Therapy in Urology — *Mulholland, S Grant*

r Antibiotics in Laboratory Medicine. 4th Ed. — *Lorian, Victor*

Antic Hay — *Huxley, Aldous*

Antichrist: Two Thousand Years of the Human Fascination with Evil — *McGinn, Bernard*

Anticipating Adolescence — *Gabriel, H Paul*

Anticipating China — *Hall, David L*

An Anticlassical Political-Economic Analysis — *Murakami, Yasusuke*

Anticompetitive Practices in Japan — *Kotabe, Masaaki*

Anticonvulsants in Mood Disorders — *Joffe, Russell T*

Antievolution before World War I — *Numbers, Ronald L*

The Antievolution Pamphlets of Harry Rimmer — *Rimmer, Harry*

The Antievolution Pamphlets of William Bell Riley — *Riley, William Bell*

The Antievolution Works of Arthur I. Brown — *Brown, Arthur I*

Antifeminism in the Academy — *Clark, VeVe*

Antifraternalism and Anticlericalism in the German Reformation — *Dipple, Geoffrey*

The Antigay Agenda — *Herman, Didi*

Antigen Presentation by Intestinal Epithelial Cells — *Kaiserlian, Dominique*

Antike Roman — *Ronan, Clifford*

p The Antioch Review

The Antiquarian and the Myth of Antiquity — *Jacks, Philip*

Antiquaries, Book Collectors and the Circles of Learning — *Myers, Robin*

L'Antiquario Felice Feliciano, Veronese — *Conto, Agostino*

Antique and Collectible Buttons — *Wisniewski, Debra J*

Antique Cigar Cutters and Lighters — *Terranova, Jerry*

The Antique Drums of War — *McRandle, James H*

Antiques from the Garden — *Morris, Alistair*

Les Antiquites Juives. Vol. 2 — *Josephus, Flavius*

Antiracism, Culture and Social Justice in Education — *Griffiths, Morwenna*

Antisemiten Und Bolschewiki — *Vetter, Matthias*

Antisemitism: Its History and Causes — *Lazare, Bernard*

L'Antiteodicea: Dio, Dei, Religione Nello Zibaldone Di Giacomo Leopardi — *Girolami, Patrizia*

Antiviral Chemotherapy 4

Antivirals in the Elderly — *Cooper, James W*

Antoine Laurent De Lavoisier 1743-1794 — *Poirier, Jean-Pierre*

Antoine Lavoisier: Science, Administration, and Revolution — *Donovan, Arthur*

Antologia De La Poesia Latinoamericana De Vanguardia 1916-1935 — *Grunfeld, Mihai G*

Anton Reiser — *Moritz, Karl Philipp*

Anton Von Webern — *Hayes, Malcolm*

Antoni Van Leeuwenhoek 1632-1723 — *Boutibonnes, Philippe*

c Antoni Van Leeuwenhoek: First to See Microscopic Life — *Yount, Lisa*

Antonin Artaud and the Modern Theater — *Plunka, Gene A*

Antonina — *Tur, Evgeniya*

Antonio Pellegrini 1675-1741 — *Knox, George*

Antonio Skarmeta and the Post Boom — *Shaw, Donald*

Antonio Torres Y La Politica Espanola Del Foreign Office 1940-1944 — *Nadal, Rafael*

Antonio Vivaldi: The Red Priest of Venice — *Heller, Karl*

Antonioni: The Poet of Images — *Arrowsmith, William*

c Antonio's Apprenticeship — *Morrison, Taylor*

c Ants (Illus. by William Munoz) — *Berman, Ruth*

The Ants — *Holldobler, Bert*

Ants on the Melon — *Adair, Virginia Hamilton*

Antwerp in the Age of Reformation — *Marnef, Guido*

y Anvil of the Sun — *Groell, Anne Lesley*

Anxiety and Phobic Disorders — *Silverman, Wendy K*

Anxiety as Symptom and Signal — *Roose, Steven P*

Anxiety in Eden — *Tanner, John S*

Anxiety Veiled — *Rabinowitz, Nancy Sorkin*

Anxious Masculinity in Early Modern England — *Breitenberg, Mark*

c Any Kind of Dog. Book and Audio Version — *Reiser, Lynn*

Anyone but You — *Crusie, Jennifer*

Anyone Can Draw — *Linney, Mark*

Anyplace but Here — *Bontemps, Arna*

Anything but Mexican — *Acuna, Rodolfo F*

Anything Considered — *Mayle, Peter*

Anything Considered (Curry). Audio Version — *Mayle, Peter*

y Anything We Love Can Be Saved — *Walker, Alice*

Anything Your Little Heart Desires — *Bosworth, Patricia*

cr Anytime Weather Everywhere — *Mogil, H Michael*

y Anywhere but Here — *Dueck, Adele*

The ANZAC Illusion — *Andrews, E M*

ANZAC Memories — *Thomson, Alistair*

Aotearoa and New Zealand — *Grey, Alan H*

y Apache Pass (Illus. by John Hurford) — *Holmas, Stig*

c The Apaches (Illus. by Ronald Himler) — *Sneve, Virginia Driving Hawk*

The Apartheid of Sex — *Rothblatt, Martine*

Apartheid's Genesis 1935-1962 — *Bonner, Philip*

Apartheid's Last Stand — *Alden, Chris*

An Apartment Called Freedom — *Algosaibi, Ghazi*

c Apes — *Horton, Casey*

Aphasia: A Pathophysiological Key to Memory Function and Volitional Naming — *Cohn, Robert*

The Aphrodite of Knidos and Her Successors — *Havelock, Christine Mitchell*

Aphrodite's Daughters — *Bonheim, Jalaja*

Apocalypse — *Richard, Pablo*

Apocalypse and Armada in Kyd's Spanish Tragedy — *Ardolino, Frank*

The Apocalypse in African-American Fiction — *Montgomery, Maxine Lavon*

Apocalypse in Oklahoma — *Hamm, Mark S*

The Apocalypse Watch — *Ludlum, Robert*

Apocalyptic Overtures — *Dellamora, Richard*

Apocalypticism in the Western Tradition — *McGinn, Bernard*

The Apocryphal Jesus — *Elliott, J K*

Apocryphal Tales — *Capek, Karel*

Title Index

Apollinaire and the International Avant-Garde
— Bohn, William

c Apollo 13 — Cole, Michael D

Apollo: Origins and Influences — Solomon, Jon

L'Apologie De Jerome Contre Rufin — Lardet, Pierre

Apoptosis and the Immune Response — Gregory, Christopher D

Apostle of Taste — Schuyler, David

r The Apostolic See and the Jews. Vols. 1-8 — Simonsohn, Shlomo

L'Apotheose D'Orphee — Rouget, Francois

The Apotheosis of Captain Cook — Obeyesekere, Gananath

Appalachia in the Making — Pudup, Mary Beth

Appalachia Inside Out. Vols. 1-2 — Higgs, Robert J

Appalachian Heritage Cookbook — Steelesburg Homemakers Club

Appalachian Images in Folk and Popular Culture. 2nd Ed. — McNeil, W K

Appalachian Mountain Religion — McCauley, Deborah Vansau

Apparatus — McKay, Don

Les Apparitions — Seyvos, Florence

The Apparition's Daybook — Pearson, K F

Appassionata — Cooper, Jilly

An Appeal in Favor of That Class of Americans Called Africans — Child, Lydia Maria Francis

The Apple Falls from the Apple Tree — Papanikolas, Helen

c The Apple Pie Tree (Illus. by Shari Halpern) — Hall, Zoe

Apples — Yepsen, Roger

c Apples and Oranges — Ash, Russell

Apples and Oranges — Daley, Todd M

c Apples, Bubbles, and Crystals (Illus. by Melody Sarecky) — Bennett, Andrea T

AppleScript Applications — Schettino, John

AppleTalk Network Services — Cougias, Dorian J

An Application Christmas — Matteson, Richard

Application-Specific Systems, Architectures and Processors 1996

Applications and Developments in New Engine Design and Components

Applications of Advanced Technologies in Transportation Engineering: Proceedings of the 4th International Conference, Capri, Italy, June 27-30, 1995 — American Society of Civil Engineers. Urban Transportation Division. Committee of Advanced Technology

Applications of Advanced Technology to Ash-Related Problems in Boilers — Baxter, L

Applications of Artificial Intelligence in Engineering XI

Applications of Counseling in Speech-Language Pathology and Audiology — Crowe, Thomas A

Applications of New Technology — Higginbotham, Jack

Applications of Synchrotron Radiation Techniques to Materials Science III

Applications of Synchrotron Radiation to Materials Analysis — Saisho, H

Applications on Advanced Architecture Computers — Astfalk, Greg

Applied Body Composition Assessment — Heyward, Vivian H

Applied Cost-Benefit Analysis — Brent, Robert J

Applied Cost Engineering. 3rd Ed. — Clark, Forrest D

p Applied Geography and Development

Applied Industrial Organization — Aiginger, Karl

Applied Laparoscopic Anatomy — Wind, Gary G

Applied MAPLE for Engineers and Scientists — Tocci, Christopher

Applied Mathematics. 2nd Ed. — Logan, J David

Applied Mathematics. 6th Ed. — Barnett, Raymond A

Applied Mechanics for Engineering Technology. 5th Ed. — Walker, Keith M

Applied Optics and Optoelectronics 1996 — Institute of Physics (Great Britain). Applied Optics Division. Divisional Conference (4th: 1996: Reading, England)

Applied Population Ecology — Gutierrez, Andrew Paul

Applied Principles of Horticultural Science — Brown, L V

Applied Software Measurement. 2nd Ed. — Jones, Capers

Applied Statistical Science I — Ahsanullah, M

Applied Stochastic Processes — Biswas, Suddhendu

Applied Structural Steel Design. 3rd Ed. — Spiegel, Leonard

Applied Surface Thermodynamics — Neumann, A W

Applied UNIX Programming. Vol. 2 — Kurani, Bharat

Applying the Canon in Islam — Wheeler, Brannon M

Appointment in May — Albert, Neil

Appraisal Procedures for Counselors and Helping Professionals. 3rd Ed. — Drummond, Robert J

Appreciating Dreams — Ullman, Montague

Apprehending the Criminal — Leps, Marie-Christine

The Apprentice — Libby, Lewis

Apprentice to Power — Morse, Jennifer

y The Apprenticeship of Lucas Whitaker — DeFelice, Cynthia C

The Apprenticeship Writings of Frank Norris 1896-1898 — Norris, Frank

An Approach to Political Philosophy — Tully, James

Approaches to Literature through Literary Form — Montgomery, Paula Kay

Approaches to New Testament Study — Porter, Stanley E

Approaches to Teaching Atwood's The Handmaid's Tale and Other Works — Wilson, Sharon R

Approaches to Teaching Bronte's Jane Eyre — Hoeveler, Diane Long

Approaches to Teaching Flaubert's Madame Bovary — Porter, Laurence M

Approaches to Teaching Montaigne's Essays — Henry, Patrick

Approaches to Teaching Thoreau's Walden and Other Works — Schneider, Richard J

Approaches to the Welfare State — Chatterjee, Pranab

Approaching Eye Level — Gornick, Vivian

The Approaching Fury — Oates, Stephen B

Approaching Hysteria — Micale, Mark S

Approches Du Concret — Picavet, Emmanuel

Appropriating Shakespeare — Vickers, Brian

Approximate Darling — Upton, Lee

April '65 — Tidwell, William A

c April: A Pueblo Storyteller (Illus. by Lawrence Migdale) — Hoyt-Goldsmith, Diane

c April Ghoul's Day — Stone, Tom

The APSAC Handbook on Child Maltreatment — Briere, John

Aptitude Revisited — Drew, David E

Apverstas Pasaulis — Meras, Icchokas

El Aqua Quieta — Rey Rosa, Rodrigo

r Aquatic and Wetland Plants of India — Cook, Christopher D K

Aquatic Chemistry. 3rd Ed. — Stumm, Werner

p Aquatic Geochemistry

Aquatic Systems Engineering — Escobal, P R

Aquatic Therapy Programming — Koury, Joanne M

Aqueous Polymeric Coatings for Pharmaceutical Dosage Forms. 2nd Ed. — McGinity, James W

Aquifer Test Analysis with Windows Software — Walton, William C

Aquinas and Empowerment — Harak, G Simon

Aquinas and the Jews — Hood, John Y B

Aquinas' Five Arguments in the Summa Theologiae 1a 2, 3 — Velecky, Lubor

Aquinas: Selected Philosophical Writings — Thomas, Aquinas, Saint

Aquinas's Theory of Natural Law — Lisska, Anthony J

The Ara Pacis Augustae and the Imagery of Abundance in Later Greek and Early Roman Imperial Art — Castriota, David

Arab Awakening and Islamic Revival — Kramer, Martin

Arab Industrialization in Israel — Schnell, Izhak

The Arab-Israeli Accords — Cotran, Eugene

r The Arab-Israeli Dispute — Peretz, Don

The Arab Middle East and the United States — Kaufman, Burton I

Arab Women — Sabbagh, Suha

Arab Women Novelists — Zeidan, Joseph T

Arabian Days and Nights — Mahfouz, Naguib

The Arabian Epic. Vols. 1-3 — Lyons, M C

c Arabian Nights (Illus. by Deborah Nourse Lattimore) — Lattimore, Deborah Nourse

Arabic Historical Thought in the Classical Period — Khalidi, Tarif

r Arabic Lithographed Books — Gacek, Adam

Arabic Short Stories

Arabic Sociolinguistics — Suleiman, Yasir

c The Araboolies of Liberty Street (Illus. by Barry Root) — Swope, Sam

The Arabs, Byzantium, and Islam — Bosworth, Clifford Edmund

The Arabs in Israel — Stendel, Ori

The Arakmbut: Mythology, Spirituality, and History in an Amazonian Community — Gray, Andrew

Aramaic Daniel and Greek Daniel — Meadowcroft, T J

Aramis or the Love of Technology — Latour, Bruno

The Arams of Idaho — Youngdahl, Kristi M

Arapaly — Kabdebo, Tamas

Arbeitsame Patrioten--Wohlanstandige Damen — Tanner, Albert

Arbeitsfelder Der Theaterwissenschaft — Fischer-Lichte, Erika

Arbol De La Vida — Bencastro, Mario

L'Arbre — Rodenbach, Georges

Un Arbre Voyageur — Etcherelli, Claire

Arc D'X — Erickson, Steve

Arcadia — Stoppard, Tom

An Arcadian Death — Jeffries, Roderic

Arcanum 17 — Breton, Andre

Archaeological Chemistry — Orna, Mary Virginia

Archaeological Chemistry — Pollard, A Mark

An Archaeological Guide to Northern Central America — Kelly, Joyce

r Archaeological Laboratory Methods — Sutton, Mark Q

Archaeological Research at Tumatumani, Juli, Peru — Stanish, Charles

Archaeological Views from the Countryside — Schwartz, Glenn M

Archaeologists and Aesthetes — Jenkins, Ian

c Archaeologists Dig for Clues (Illus. by Kate Duke) — Duke, Kate

Archaeology and Geographical Information Systems — Lock, Gary

Archaeology, History and Society in Galilee — Horsley, Richard A

Archaeology in the Lowland American Tropics — Stahl, Peter W

The Archaeology of Ancient Arizona — Reid, Jefferson

The Archaeology of CA-MNO-2122 — Arkush, Brooke S

The Archaeology of Death in the Ancient Near East — Campbell, Stuart

The Archaeology of Early Christianity — Frend, William H C

The Archaeology of Early Historic South Asia — Allchin, F R

The Archaeology of Navajo Origins — Towner, Ronald H

The Archaeology of Northeast China — Nelson, Sarah Milledge

The Archaeology of Rank — Wason, Paul K

The Archaeology of Shakespeare — Wilson, Jean

The Archaeology of Spanish and Mexican Colonialism in the American Southwest — Ayres, James E

The Archaeology of the Arabian Gulf c.5000-323 B.C. — Rice, Michael

Archaeology of the Mid-Holocene Southeast — Sassaman, Kenneth E

r Archaeology of the Mississippian Culture — Peregrine, Peter N

The Archaeology of Wealth — Gibb, James G

Archaeology, Volcanism, and Remote Sensing in the Arenal Region — Sheets, Payson D

Archaic Cyprus — Reyes, A T

Archaiologia on Archaic Greek Body Armour — Jarva, Eero

y Archangel — Shinn, Sharon

y Archangel — Watkins, Paul

Archaologie Und Seismologie — Frolich, Thomas

Archbishop Theodore: Commemorative Studies on His Life and Influence — Lapidge, Michael

Archeological Investigations at the Loma Sandia Site 41LK28. Vols. 1-2 — Taylor, A J

Archeologie Et Droit De L'Urbanisme En Europe — Jegouzo, Yves

The Archeology of Disease. 2nd Ed. — Roberts, Charlotte

The Archers: The True Story — Smethurst, William

Arches, Vaults, and Buttresses — Heyman, Jacques

The Archetypal Actions of Ritual — Humphrey, Caroline

Archetypal Dimensions of the Psyche — Franz, Marie-Louise Von

Archetypal Heresy — Wiles, Maurice

The Archetype of Pilgrimage — Clift, Jean Dalby

Archetypes and Strange Attractors — Van Eenwyk, John R

Archipelago — Sze, Arthur

The Architect of Desire — Lessard, Suzannah

The Architect: Reconstructing Her Practice — Hughes, Francesca

Architects of the Web — Reid, Robert

Architectural Graphics — Goldman, Glenn

An Architectural History of Harford County, Maryland — Weeks, Christopher

The Architectural History of Scotland — Howard, Deborah

An Architectural Life — *Keim, Kevin P*
Architectural Perspective Grids — *Chen, John S M*
Architecture after Modernism — *Ghirardo, Diane*
Architecture and Authority in Japan — *Coaldrake, William H*
Architecture and Feminism — *Coleman, Debra*
Architecture and Meaning on the Athenian Acropolis — *Rhodes, Robin Francis*
Architecture and Power in the Ancient Andes — *Moore, Jerry D*
Architecture and Social Reform in Late-Victorian London — *Weiner, Deborah E B*
Architecture and the American Dream — *Whitaker, Craig*
Architecture and the Sites of History — *Borden, Iain*
c Architecture Animals (Illus. by Steve Rosenthal) — *Crosbie, Michael J*
Architecture, Decor Et Cinema — *Puaux, Francoise*
Architecture for Dolls' Houses — *Percival, Joyce*
Architecture, Form, Space and Order. 2nd Ed. — *Ching, Frank D K*
Architecture in Italy 1400-1500 — *Heydenreich, Ludwig H*
Architecture in Italy 1500-1600 — *Lotz, Wolfgang*
Architecture in the Family Way — *Adams, Annmarie*
The Architecture of Computer Hardware Systems Software — *Englander, Irv*
The Architecture of Europe — *Yarwood, Doreen*
The Architecture of Frank Lloyd Wright — *Levine, Neil*
The Architecture of New Prague 1895-1945 — *Svacha, Rostislav*
Architecture of the Contemporary Mosque — *Serageldin, Ismail*
The Architecture of Vision — *Antonioni, Michelangelo*
Architectures of Excess: Cultural Life in the Information Age — *Collins, Jim*
Die Architektur Der Sepulturas-Region Von Copan In Honduras. Vols. 1-2 — *Hohmann, Hasso*
Architrenius (Wetherbee) — *Johannes, De Hauvilla*
Archival Strategies and Techniques — *Hill, Michael R*
Archival Theory, Records, and the Public — *Livelton, Trevor*
Archive Fever — *Derrida, Jacques*
y Archyology: The Long Lost Tales of Archy and Mehitable (Illus. by Ed Frascino) — *Marquis, Don*
c The Arctic (Illus. by Bryan Alexander) — *Rootes, David*
y Arctic and Antarctic — *Taylor, Barbara*
c Arctic and Antarctic — *Weller, David*
Arctic Artist — *Back, George*
c Arctic Babies (Illus. by Tara Darling) — *Darling, Kathy*
c Arctic Fives Arrive (Illus. by Holly Berry) — *Pinczes, Elinor J*
Arctic Mirrors — *Slezkine, Yuri*
c Arctic Peoples — *Haslam, Andrew*
c Arctic Tundra — *Fowler, Allan*
Arde Lo Que Sera — *Salabert, Juana*
c Are Genes Us? — *Cranor, Carl F*
Are Girls Necessary? — *Abraham, Julie*
Are Sweet Dreams Made of This? — *McCarthy, J*
Are There Alternatives? — *Panitch, Leo*
Are We Alone? — *Davies, P C W*
Are We Becoming Two Societies? — *Beach, Charles M*
Are We Having Fun Yet? — *Willis, Kay*
c Are We Moving to Mars? (Illus. by Michael Carroll) — *Schraff, Anne*
Are We Not Men? — *Harper, Phillip Brian*
Are We Not Men? — *Spencer, Brent*
Are We Unique? — *Trefil, James*
Are You Anybody? — *Dillman, Bradford*
Are You Somebody? — *O'Faolain, Nuala*
Arena of Lust — *Ardonne, Marcus*
Arendt and Heidegger — *Villa, Dana R*
y Aretha Franklin: Motown Superstar — *Sheafer, Silvia Anne*
r Argentina. 3rd Ed. — *Ball, Deirdre*
r Argentina Business — *Hinkelman, Edward G*
r Argentina Company Handbook. 1995/96 Ed.
Argentina, the United States and the Anti-Communist Crusade in Central America 1977-1984 — *Armony, Ariel C*
r Argentina, Uruguay and Paraguay. 2nd Ed. — *Bernhardson, Wayne*
Argentina's Lost Patrol — *Moyano, Maria Jose*
Argentine Jewish Theatre — *Glickman, Nora*
Argentine Workers — *Ranis, Peter*
y Argonautika: The Story of Jason and the Argonauts (Stevenson). Audio Version — *Apollonius, Rhodius*
Arguing about Sex — *Monti, Joseph*

Arguing about Slavery — *Miller, William Lee*
Argument and Evidence — *Phelan, Peter*
Argument Revisited — *Emmel, Barbara*
Argument Structure — *Walton, Douglas*
Arguments from Ignorance — *Walton, Douglas*
Arguments with Gravity — *Crummey, Michael*
Aria — *Edmonds, Lucinda*
Aria Appasionata — *Hastings, Juliet*
Arianism and Other Heresies — *Augustine, Saint, Bishop of Hippo*
c Arion and the Dolphin (Illus. by Jane Ray) — *Seth, Vikram*
Aristocracy, Antiquity, and History — *Kinneging, A A M*
The Aristocrat (Strassman). Audio Version — *Coulter, Catherine*
Aristocratic Government in the Age of Reform — *Mandler, Peter*
Aristocratic Violence and Holy War — *Bonner, Michael*
Aristotelian and Cartesian Logic at Harvard — *Morton, Charles*
The Aristotle Adventure — *Laughlin, Burgess*
Aristotle and Augustine on Freedom — *Chappell, T D J*
Aristotle and Mathematics — *Cleary, John J*
y Aristotle in 90 Minutes — *Strathern, Paul*
Aristotle in Outline — *Robinson, T A*
Aristotle, Kant, and the Stoics — *Engstrom, Stephen*
Aristotle on Nature and Incomplete Substance — *Cohen, Sheldon M*
Aristotle's Metaphysics, Theta 1-3 — *Heidegger, Martin*
Aristotle's Modal Logic — *Patterson, Richard, 1946-*
Aristotle's Philosophical Development — *Wians, William*
Aristotle's Physics — *Sachs, Joe*
Aristotle's Rhetoric — *Garver, Eugene*
Aristotle's Theory of Actuality — *Bechler, Zev*
Aristotle's Theory of Material Substance — *Freudenthal, Gad*
Arithmetic, Geometry, and Coding Theory — *International Conference on Arithmetic, Geometry and Coding Theory (1993: Luminy, France)*
Arizona: A History — *Sheridan, Thomas E*
Arizona Charter Schools Handbook
The Arizona Game — *Hammick, Georgina*
r Arizona Traveler's Handbook. 6th Ed.
r Arizona, Utah and New Mexico — *Sinotte, Barbara*
Arizona's Yesterdays — *Cady, John Henry*
c Ark in the Park (Illus. by Kerry Millard) — *Orr, Wendy*
r Arkansas History — *Dougan, Michael B*
Arkansas Odyssey — *Dougan, Michael B*
Arkansas: Three Novellas — *Leavitt, David*
p Arkeologjia: Materiale, Studime Dhe Informacione Arkeologjike
Arkhiv Noveishei Istorii Rossii. Vols. 1-3 — *Gosudarstvennyi Arkhiv Rossiiskoi Federatsii*
r ARL Statistics 1994-95
Armadillo Charm — *Cumpian, Carlos*
c Armadillo Ray (Illus. by Peggy Turley) — *Beifuss, John*
Armageddon: The Reality behind the Distortions, Myths, Lies and Illusions of World War II — *Ponting, Clive*
Armagh and the Royal Centres in Early Medieval Ireland — *Aitchison, N B*
Armaments and the Coming of War — *Stevenson, David*
y Los Armarios Negros — *Gisbert, Joan Manuel*
Armas Y Herramientas De Metal Prehispanicas En Bolivia — *Mayer, Eugen Friedrich*
The Armature of Conquest — *Pastor Bodmer, Beatriz*
The Armchair Activist — *Schwartz, Felice N*
p The Armchair Detective
Armed and Dangerous — *Buckland, Wendy*
Armed with Cameras — *Maslowski, Peter*
Armed with the Constitution — *Newton, Merlin Owen*
Armenia from the Stone Age to the Middle Ages — *Kalantar, Ashkharbek*
r Armenian (Eastern)-English Dictionary — *Baghdasarian, Louisa*
Armfuls of Time — *Sourkes, Barbara M*
Armies and Warfare in the Middle Ages — *Prestwich, Michael*
Arming against Hitler — *Kiesling, Eugenia C*
Arming Iraq — *Phythian, Mark*
Arming Japan — *Green, Michael J*
The Arming of Europe and the Making of the First World War — *Herrmann, David G*

Arming Our Allies
Armistice 1918 — *Lowry, Bullitt*
y The Armless Maiden and Other Tales for Childhood's Survivors — *Windling, Terri*
L'Armonia Impossibile — *Centi, Beatrice*
Armored Hearts — *Bottoms, David*
Arms and Technology Transfers — *Lodgaard, Sverre*
Arms, Armies and Fortifications in the Hundred Years War — *Curry, Anne, 1948-*
Arms Control — *Larsen, Jeffrey A*
Arms Control during the Pre-Nuclear Era — *Kaufman, Robert Gordon*
The Army and Politics in Argentina 1962-1973. Vol. 3 — *Potash, Robert A*
An Army for Empire — *Cosmas, Graham A*
The Army Medical Department 1865-1917 — *Gillett, Mary C*
y An Army of Angels — *Marcantel, Pamela*
Army Wives on the American Frontier — *Eales, Anne Bruner*
Arnaldo Segarizzi: Un Intellettuale Trentino A Venezia Avio 1872-Asolo 1924 — *Peghini, Mauro*
Arnhem 1944 — *Middlebrook, Martin*
c Arnie and the Skateboard Gang (Illus. by Nancy Carlson) — *Carlson, Nancy*
Arnobius of Sicca: Religious Conflict and Competition in the Age of Diocletian — *Simmons, Michael Bland*
Arnold Toynbee and the Western Tradition — *Perry, Marvin*
r Aroma and Flavor Lexicon for Sensory Evaluation — *Civille, Gail V*
An Aroma of Coffee — *Laferriere, Dany*
Aromatherapy for Mind and Body — *Schiller, David*
Around Manhattan Island and Other Maritime Tales of New York — *Cudahy, Brian J*
c Around the Pond (Illus. by Lindsay Barrett George) — *George, Lindsay Barrett*
c Around the World in a Hundred Years — *Fritz, Jean*
y Around the World in Eighty Days (Illus. by James Prunier) — *Verne, Jules*
y Around the World in Seventy-Nine Days — *Lewis, Cam*
Around the World on a Bicycle — *Birchmore, Fred*
Arousing Sensation — *Gilbert, Sylvie*
Arousing the Goddess — *Ward, Tim*
Arqueologia Del Occidente De Mexico — *Williams, Eduardo*
y El Arquitecto Del Cosmos — *Martinez, Rafael*
Arranged Marriage — *Divakaruni, Chitra Banerjee*
Arrested Voices — *Shentalinsky, Vitaly*
Arrhenius: From Ionic Theory to the Greenhouse Effect — *Crawford, Elisabeth*
y Arrogant Armies — *Perry, James M*
Arrogant Beggar — *Yezierska, Anzia*
p Arrows for Change: Women's and Gender Perspectives in Health Policies and Programmes
p Arrowsmith
Ars Et Musica In Liturgia — *Brouwer, Frans*
An Ars Legendi for Chaucer's Canterbury Tales — *Frese, Dolores Warwick*
p Ars Poetica
c Art — *Grimshaw, Caroline*
Art across the Curriculum — *Sedgwick, Dawn*
Art and Affection — *Reid, Panthea*
Art and Anger — *Stavans, Ilan*
Art and Architecture in Byzantium and Armenia — *Mathews, Thomas F*
r Art and Architecture in the Poetry of Robert Browning: Appendix A — *Thomas, Charles Flint*
The Art and Architecture of Islam 1250-1800 — *Blair, Sheila*
Art and Artists of Twentieth-Century China — *Sullivan, Michael, 1916-*
Art and Authority in Renaissance Milan — *Welch, Evelyn S*
Art and Context in Late Medieval English Narrative — *Edwards, Robert R*
The Art and Craft of Natural Dyeing — *Liles, J N*
The Art and History of Books — *Levarie, Norma*
Art and Illusion in The Winter's Tale — *Sokol, B J*
y Art and Inspirations — *McDowell, Ruth B*
Art and Magic in the Court of the Stuarts — *Hart, Vaughan*
Art and Money — *Shell, Marc*
Art and Nationalism in Colonial India 1850-1922 — *Mitter, Partha*
Art and Politics — *Wagner, Richard, 1813-1883*
The Art and Science of Assessment in Psychotherapy — *Mace, Chris*
The Art and Science of CCD Astronomy — *Ratledge, David*

The Art and Science of Cytopathology — *DeMay, Richard M*

The Art and Science of Leadership — *Nahavandi, Afsaneh*

Art and Spirituality in Counter-Reformation Rome — *Ostrow, Steven F*

Art and Surburbia — *McAuliffe, Chris*

Art and the French Commune — *Boime, Albert*

Art and the Higher Life — *Pyne, Kathleen*

Art and the Roman Viewer — *Elsner, Jas.*

Art and the Victorian Middle Class — *Macleod, Dianne Sachko*

Art Apart — *Pointon, Marcia*

Art as Language — *Hagberg, G L*

Art as Politics in the Third Reich — *Petropoulos, Jonathan*

yr The Art Book

Art Carney: A Biography — *Starr, Michael*

Art De La Lettre — *Bray, Bernard*

L'Art De Lire. 2nd Ed. — *Hope, Quentin M*

Art Deco Ceramics — *Hay, Jane*

Art Deco Painting — *Lucie-Smith, Edward*

Art Deco Sculpture and Metalware — *Edward, Alfred W*

Art Does (Not!) Exist — *Drexler, Rosalyn*

c Art Dog (Illus. by Thacher Hurd) — *Hurd, Thacher*

The Art Fair — *Lipsky, David*

Art for Art's Sake and Literary Life — *Bell-Villada, Gene H*

Art History — *Stokstad, Marilyn*

y The Art History Study Guide — *Spencer, John, 1925-*

Art History's History — *Minor, Vernon Hyde*

Art in Chicago 1945-1995 — *Warren, Lynne*

Art in History — *Silver, Larry*

Art in Renaissance Italy — *Paoletti, John T*

Art in the American South — *Delehanty, Randolph*

Art in the Frick Collection — *Ryskamp, Charles*

Art in the Roman Empire — *Grant, Michael, 1914-*

r Art Index 1929-

The Art Institute of Chicago — *Wood, James N*

Art into Ideas — *Morgan, Robert C*

Art Lessons — *Marquis, Alice Goldfarb*

Art Line Thought — *Mallin, Samuel B*

Art Marketing 101 — *Smith, Constance*

L'Art Metaphysique — *De Chirico, Giorgio*

L'Art Metrique De La Chanson De Geste — *Heinemann, Edward A*

Art Nouveau — *Howard, Jeremy*

Art Objects — *Winterson, Jeanette*

The Art of Abstracting. 2nd Ed. — *Cremmins, Edward T*

The Art of Acting in Antiquity — *Neiiendam, Klaus*

The Art of African Textiles — *Picton, John*

The Art of Albert Paley — *Lucie-Smith, Edward*

The Art of Authorial Presence — *Thompson, G R*

The Art of Bargaining — *Lebow, Richard Ned*

The Art of Becoming Human — *Mercer, Mary E*

The Art of Being Black — *Alexander, Claire E*

The Art of Breaking Glass — *Hall, Matthew*

The Art of Campaign Advertising — *Boynton, G R*

The Art of Case Study Research — *Stake, Robert E*

c The Art of Construction

Art of Darkness — *Williams, Anne, 1947-*

The Art of Deception (Capaldi). Audio Version — *Capaldi, Nicholas*

The Art of Devotion in the Late Middle Ages in Europe 1300-1500 — *Os, H W Van*

The Art of Dress — *Ashelford, Jane*

The Art of Dress — *Ribeiro, Aileen*

The Art of Drowning — *Collins, Billy*

The Art of Electronic Publishing — *Ressler, Sandy*

The Art of Eric Carle — *Carle, Eric*

The Art of Fieldwork — *Wolcott, Harry F*

The Art of Film Music — *Burt, George*

The Art of George Du Maurier — *Kelly, Richard Michael*

The Art of Gordon Bennett — *McLean, Ian*

y The Art of Hand Reading — *Reid, Lori*

y The Art of Hercules — *Rebello, Stephen*

The Art of Kamau Brathwaite — *Brown, Stewart, 1951-*

The Art of Kitchen Design — *Grey, Johnny*

Art of Late Rome and Byzantium in the Virginia Museum of Fine Arts — *Virginia Museum of Fine Arts*

The Art of Literary Biography — *Batchelor, John, 1942-*

The Art of Living Consciously — *Branden, Nathaniel*

The Art of Looking — *Sharff, Stefan*

The Art of Louis-Leopold Boilly — *Siegfried, Susan L*

y The Art of Making Comic Books (Illus. by Howard Bender) — *Pellowski, Michael*

The Art of Midwifery — *Marland, Hilary*

The Art of Mingling (Martinet). Audio Version — *Martinet, Jeanne*

The Art of Pastel Portraiture — *Woolwich, Madlyn-Ann C*

The Art of Peter Voulkos — *Voulkos, Peter*

The Art of Plato — *Rutherford, R B*

y The Art of Practicing — *Bruser, Madeline*

The Art of Prayer — *Jones, Timothy K, 1955-*

Art of Rapid Prototyping — *Isensee, Scott*

The Art of Reflection — *Meskimmon, Marsha*

The Art of Renaissance Rome 1400-1600 — *Partridge, Loren*

The Art of Resilience — *Orsborn, Carol*

The Art of Rhetoric — *Wilson, Thomas, 1525-1581*

The Art of Roman Britain — *Henig, Martin*

The Art of Rulership — *Ames, Roger T*

The Art of Short Selling — *Staley, Katherine*

The Art of Teaching Ballet — *Warren, Gretchen Ward*

c Art of the American Indian Frontier — *Detroit Institute of Arts*

r Art of the American Indian Frontier — *Penney, David W*

The Art of the Brontes — *Alexander, Christine*

The Art of the Crusaders in the Holy Land 1098-1187 — *Folda, Jaroslav*

Art of the Formal Garden — *Horst, Arend Jan Van Der*

The Art of the Funnies — *Harvey, Robert C*

The Art of the Impossible — *Havel, Vaclav*

The Art of the Possible — *Stoddard, Alexandra*

Art of the Postmodern Era — *Sandler, Irving*

Art of the Renaissance — *Jestaz, Bertrand*

The Art of the Saljuqs in Iran and Anatolia — *Hillenbrand, Robert*

The Art of the Warrior — *Sawyer, Ralph D*

The Art of Thomas Wilmer Dewing — *Hobbs, Susan*

The Art of Vegetarian Cooking — *Abensur, Nadine*

Art on My Mind — *Hooks, Bell*

Art on the Edge and Over — *Weintraub, Linda*

p Art Papers

c Art School (Illus. by Mick Manning) — *Manning, Mick*

Art since 1940 — *Fineberg, Jonathan*

L'Art Singulier De Jean Huber, Voir Voltaire — *Apgar, Garry*

Art, Surgery and Transplantation — *Calne, Roy Yorke*

r Art, Truth, and High Politics — *Powell, John*

Art without Boundaries — *Anderson, Jack*

The Art-Work of the Future and Other Works — *Wagner, Richard, 1813-1883*

Artaud and the Gnostic Drama — *Goodall, Jane*

El Arte Autobiografico En Cuba En El Siglo XIX — *Jimenez, Luis A*

Arte E Historia De Peru Antiguo — *Bonavia, Duccio*

Artful Histories — *McCooey, David*

The Artful Ribbon — *Kling, Candace*

Artful Science — *Stafford, Barbara Maria*

Arthritis — *Thompson, John Marcus*

Arthritis and Allied Conditions. 13th Ed., Vols. 1-2

The Arthritis Cure — *Theodosakis, Jason*

Arthritis: The Chinese Way of Healing and Prevention — *Yang, Jwing-Ming*

c Arthur and the Sword (Illus. by Robert Sabuda) — *Sabuda, Robert*

y Arthur Ashe: Breaking the Color Barrier in Tennis — *Wright, David K*

c Arthur Babysits (Illus. by Marc Brown) — *Brown, Marc*

c Arthur Babysits (Illus. by Marc Brown). Book and Audio Version — *Brown, Marc*

r Arthur Bliss: A Source Book — *Craggs, Stewart R*

c Arthur Goes to School (Illus. by Marc Brown) — *Brown, Marc*

c Arthur, High King of Britain (Illus. by Michael Foreman) — *Morpurgo, Michael*

Arthur J. Goldberg: New Deal Liberal — *Stebenne, David L*

Arthur M. Schlesinger, Jr. and the Ideological History of American Liberalism — *Depoe, Stephen P*

Arthur Machen — *Valentine, Mark*

c Arthur Meets the President (Brown) (Illus. by Marc Brown). Book and Audio Version — *Brown, Marc*

c Arthur Mini Play Book — *Brown, Marc*

Arthur Rackham: A Life with Illustrations — *Hamilton, James*

c Arthur Writes a Story (Illus. by Marc Brown) — *Brown, Marc*

c Arthur's Back to School Day (Illus. by Lillian Hoban) — *Hoban, Lillian*

Arthur's Dream — *Giffin, Michael*

c Arthur's New Puppy — *Brown, Marc*

c Arthur's Reading Race (Illus. by Marc Brown) — *Brown, Marc*

c Arthur's Reading Race. Electronic Media Version — *Brown, Marc*

c Arthur's Teacher Trouble. Electronic Media Version — *Brown, Marc*

Artibus: Kulturwissenschaft Und Deutsche Philologie Des Mittelalters Und Der Fruhen Neuzeit — *Fussel, Stephan*

r Articles in American Studies 1954-1968. Vols. 1-2 — *Cohen, Hennig*

Articulating Change in the Last Unknown — *Errington, Frederick K*

Articulation and Phonological Disorders. 2nd Ed. — *Bleile, Ken M*

Artifact and Assemblage — *Runnels, C N*

The Artifacts of Dzibilchaltun, Yucatan, Mexico — *Taschek, Jennifer T*

Artificial Intelligence — *Boden, Margaret A*

Artificial Intelligence and Scientific Method — *Gillies, Donald*

Artificial Intelligence in Design '96

Artificial Life — *Levy, Stephen*

Artificial Minds — *Franklin, Stan*

Artificial Neural Networks for Modelling and Control of Non-Linear Systems — *Suykens, Johan A K*

y Artificial Organs — *Presnall, Judith Janda*

The Artificial River — *Sheriff, Carol*

Artificial Self-Assembling Systems for Gene Delivery — *Felgner, Philip L*

Artillery Hell — *Johnson, Curt*

Artisans in the North Carolina Backcountry — *Lewis, Johanna Miller*

The Artist and the Emotional World — *Gedo, John E*

c Artist in Overalls — *Duggleby, John*

Artistic Relations — *Collier, Peter*

c Artistic Trickery — *Capek, Michael*

r Artists and Writers Colonies — *Bowler, Gail Hellund*

An Artist's Book of Inspiration — *Fitzgerald, Astrid*

Artists' Books — *Bury, Stephen, 1954-*

r Artists Communities

Artists/Hawaii — *Clarke, Joan*

Artists in Crime — *Cooper, John*

Artists in Dylan Thomas's Prose Works — *Mayer, Ann Elizabeth*

y Artist's Manual — *Gair, Angela*

c The Artist's Model (Illus. by Allison Barrows) — *Barrows, Allison*

Arts and Crafts of China — *Minick, Scott*

Arts and Crafts of India — *Cooper, Ilay*

Arts and Crafts of Morocco — *Jereb, James F*

r Arts and Humanities Citation Index 1981-

Arts and the Internet — *Shiva, V A*

r Arts in America. Vols. 1-4 — *Karpel, Bernard*

The Arts in the American Home 1890-1930 — *Foy, Jessica H*

Arts Management — *Radbourne, Jennifer*

The Arts of China to AD 900 — *Watson, William, 1917-*

Arts of Impoverishment — *Bersani, Leo*

Arts of Strength, Arts of Serenity — *Suino, Nicklaus*

p ArtWord Quarterly

Artwork of the Mind — *Murray, Mary M*

c Aru in the Solomon Islands (Illus. by Alain Cheneviere) — *Cheneviere, Alain*

Aru Onna No Shi — *Inoue, Yasushi*

Aruhat Boker Temimah — *Hendel, Yehudit*

c Aruna's Journeys (Illus. by Merryl Winstein) — *Sreenivasan, Jyotsna*

p Arx: World Journal of Prehistoric and Ancient Studies

Arztelexikon: Von Der Antike Bis Zum 20. Jahrhundert — *Eckart, Wolfgang U*

AS/400 Application Development Using COBOL/400 — *Kaplan, Gerald S*

AS/400 Application Development with VisualAge for Smalltalk — *Bitterer, Andreas*

c As Big as an Egg (Illus. by Chana Zakashanskaya) — *Sandman, Rochel*

As by Law Established — *Ford, Alan*

y As Climate Changes — *Strzepek, K M*

As Ding Saw Herbert Hoover — *Darling, Jay N*

As for Me and My Body — *Fraser, Keath*

As Francesca — *Baer, Martha*

As Good as a Yarn with You — *Ferrier, Carole*

As I Walked Out One Evening — *Auden, W H*

As I Walked Out One Evening — *Wetzel, Donald*

As If — *Morrison, Blake*
As If the Future Mattered — *Goodwin, Neva R*
As Long as Life — *Rowland, Mary Canaga*
As Long as Sarajevo Exists — *Kurspahic, Kemal*
c As Long as the Rivers Flow — *Allen, Paula Gunn*
c As Quiet as a Mouse — *Offen, Hilda*
As Seen on TV — *Marling, Karal Ann*
As She Climbed across the Table — *Lethem, Jonathan*
As She Likes It — *Gay, Penny*
As Their Natural Resources Fail — *Tough, Frank*
As Time Goes By... — *Frederick, Judith A*
As You Like It (Brissenden) — *Shakespeare, William*
y Asante — *Boateng, Faustine Ama*
y Asante: The Gold Coast — *Koslow, Philip*
The Ascent of Chiefs — *Pauketat, Timothy R*
The Ascent of Man — *Bronowski, Jacob*
Asceticism — *Wimbush, Vincent L*
Ascetics and Ambassadors of Christ — *Binns, John*
Ase Tin Porta Anihti — *Papathanasiou, Vana*
The ASEAN Region in India's Foreign Policy
— *Sridharan, Kripa*
Aseptic Pharmaceutical Manufacturing II — *Groves, Michael J*
y Ash — *Fraustino, Lisa*
Ash of Stars — *Sallis, James*
c Ashanti Festival — *Highlights for Children*
Asher Ahavtah Et Yitshak — *Rabin, Yitzhak*
The Ashes of a God. Electronic Media Version
— *Bain, F W*
Ashes of Glory — *Furgurson, Ernest B*
Ashes to Ashes — *Kluger, Richard*
Ashes to Easter — *Morneau, Robert*
Ashkenazi Jews in Mexico — *Cimet, Adina*
y Ashworth Hall — *Perry, Anne*
Asi Era Cuba — *Roman, Daniel*
Asia in Japan's Embrace — *Hatch, Walter*
Asia in the Making of Europe. Vol. 3, Bks. 1-4
— *Lach, Donald F*
p Asia Pacific Business Review
Asia-Pacific Economic Community? — *Dutta, M*
Asia-Pacific Economies — *Dutta, M*
The Asia-Pacific Economy — *Das, Dilip K*
The Asia Pacific Region in the Global Economy
— *Harris, Richard G*
Asia-Pacific Security — *Klintworth, Gary*
Asia: Who Pays for Growth? — *Lele, Jayant*
yr The Asian American Almanac — *Natividad, Irene*
yr Asian American Chronology — *Baron, Deborah G*
r Asian American Genealogical Sourcebook — *Byers, Paula K*
Asian American Women and Men — *Espiritu, Yen Le*
y Asian Americans — *Dudley, William*
r Asian Americans — *Nordquist, Joan*
Asian Economic Regimes. Pts. A-B — *Dutta, M*
Asian Economies in Transition — *Pomfret, Richard W T*
p Asian Journal of Women's Studies
r Asian Markets. 4th Ed.
Asian NIEs and the Global Economy — *Clark, Gordon L*
Asian Popular Culture — *Lent, John A*
Asian Security Handbook — *Carpenter, William M*
Asian Trash Cinema — *Weisser, Thomas*
Asian Voyages — *Dathorne, O R*
Asia's Deadly Triangle — *Calder, Kent E*
Asia's Rural Cooperatives — *Taimni, K K*
Die Asiatische Hydra — *Dettke, Barbara*
Ask Barbara — *De Angelis, Barbara*
Ask Dr. Mueller — *Mueller, Cookie*
Ask Ms. Class — *Ohanian, Susan*
Ask Sir James — *Reid, Michaela*
c Aska's Sea Creatures (Illus. by Warabe Aska)
— *Aska, Warabe*
Asking for Love — *Robinson, Roxana*
Asking for the Earth — *George, James*
Asking for the Moon — *Hill, Reginald*
Asking Questions — *Keating, H R F*
r ASM Handbook Comprehensive Index. Electronic Media Version
ASME Aerospace and Materials Divisions — *Chan, Wen S*
ASME Aerospace Division — *Chang, J C I*
ASME Dynamic Systems and Control Division
— *Danai, Kourosh*
ASME Heat Transfer Division. Vol. 3 — *Cheung, F B*
ASME Proceedings of the 31st National Heat Transfer Conference. Vol. 6
ASME Proceedings of the 31st National Heat Transfer Conference. Vols. 1-5, 7-8
c Asmir in Vienna — *Mattingley, Christobel*

c La Asombrosa Graciela (Illus. by Caroline Binch)
— *Hoffman, Mary*
c Asombrosos Animales Acorazados — *Sowler, Sandie*
c Asombrosos Escarabajos — *Still, John*
c Asombrosos Lobos, Perros Y Zorros — *Ling, Mary*
c Asombrosos Murcielagos — *Greenaway, Frank*
Aspects of British Calendar Customs — *Buckland, Theresa*
Aspects of Distribution of Wealth and Income
— *Papadimitriou, Dimitri B*
Aspects of Labour Market Behaviour — *Christofides, Louis N*
Aspects of Oral Communication — *Quasthoff, Uta M*
Aspects of Organic Chemistry: Structure — *Quinkert, Gerhard*
Aspects of Statistical Inference — *Welsh, Alan H*
Aspects of the Novelist — *Lavin, Audrey A P*
Asphalt-Concrete Water Barriers for Embankment Dams — *Creegan, Patrick J*
Asphalt Nation — *Kay, Jane Holtz*
Aspirations and Mentoring in an Academic Environment — *Maach, Mary Niles*
The Aspiring Manager's Survival Guide — *Johnson, Mike*
Asquith as War Leader — *Cassar, George H*
Assassin — *Hagberg, David*
The Assassin Legends — *Daftary, Farhad*
The Assassination of Jesse James by the Coward Robert Ford — *Hansen, Ron*
c The Assassination of Martin Luther King, Jr.
— *Stein, R Conrad*
The Assassination of the Black Male Image
— *Hutchinson, Earl Ofari*
Assassin's Apprentice — *Hobb, Robin*
Assassin's Quest — *Hobb, Robin*
Assault and Logistics — *Gibson, Charles Dana*
Assault from the Sea — *Utz, Curtis A*
The Assault on Equality — *Knapp, Peter*
The Assault on Parenthood — *Mack, Peter*
Assault on the Left — *Davis, James Kirkpatrick*
The Assault on Tony's — *O'Brien, John, 1960-*
Assembling a Ghost — *Redgrove, Peter*
Assembling and Repairing Personal Computers
— *Beeson, Dan L*
The Assembly of Listeners — *Carrithers, Michael*
Assessing Alcohol Problems — *Allen, John P*
Assessing Business Excellence — *Porter, L J*
Assessing Democracy Assistance — *Carothers, Thomas*
Assessing Educational Practices — *Becker, William E*
Assessing Individual Differences in Human Behavior
— *Lubinski, David*
Assessing Knowledge of Retirement Behavior
— *Hanushek, Eric A*
Assessing Object Relations Phenomena — *Kissen, Morton*
Assessing the Achievement of J.M. Synge — *Gonzalez, Alexander G*
Assessing the Public Library Planning Process
— *Stephens, Annabel K*
Assessing the Risks of Nuclear and Chemical Contamination in the Former Soviet Union — *Kirk, Elizabeth J*
Assessing What Professors Do — *Dilts, David A*
Assessment and Management of Central Auditory Processing Disorders in the Educational Setting
— *Bellis, Teri James*
Assessment of Communication and Language — *Cole, Kevin N*
Assessment of Factors Affecting Boiler Tube Lifetime in Waste-Fired Steam Generators — *Wright, Ian G*
Assessment of Parenting — *Reder, Peter*
An Assessment of the Bottom-Up Review — *United States. Congress. House. Committee on Armed Services. Military Forces and Personnel Subcommittee*
Assessment of the Plan to Lift the Ban on Homosexuals in the Military — *United States. Congress. House. Committee on Armed Services. Military Forces and Personnel Subcommittee*
Assessment Standards for School Mathematics
Assimilation, American Style — *Salins, Peter D*
Assisted Living for the Aged and Frail — *Regnier, Victor*
r The Associated Press Stylebook and Libel Manual. 6th Ed. — *Goldstein, Norm*
r Association of British Philatelic Societies Year Book and Directory 1995
r Associations Unlimited. Electronic Media Version
Assumed Name — *Piglia, Ricardo*
Assyrian Rulers of the Early First Millennia BC. Vol. 2 — *Grayson, A Kirk*

r The ASTD Training and Development Handbook. 4th Ed.
c Astercote (Tomelty). Audio Version — *Lively, Penelope*
The Asterisked Materials in the Greek Job — *Gentry, Peter John*
c Asterix and Obelix All at Sea — *Goscinny*
Asteroid: Earth Destroyer or New Frontier?
— *Barnes-Svarney, Patricia*
c Asteroids, Comets, and Meteors — *Marsh, Carole*
c Asteroids, Comets, and Meteors — *Vogt, Gregory L*
y Asthma — *Silverstein, Alvin*
r Asthma Resources Directory — *Rudoff, Carol*
r ASTM Standards on Color and Appearance Measurement. 5th Ed. — *American Society for Testing and Materials*
ASTM Standards on Electrical Protective Equipment for Workers. 10th Ed.
r ASTM Standards on Ground Water and Vadose Zone Investigations
ASTM Standards on Whole Building Functionality and Serviceability
The Astonished Heart — *Capon, Robert Farrar*
The Astrolabe of the Sea — *Nadir, Shams*
yr Astrology — *Costello, Darby*
c Astrology and Predictions — *Tremaine, Jon*
Astrology and the Seventeenth Century Mind
— *Geneva, Ann*
Astrology of the Famed   *Tyl, Noel*
Astrology: What's Really in the Stars — *Stewart, J V*
c Astronauts — *Burch, Jonathan*
c Astronauts Are Sleeping (Illus. by Allen Garns)
— *Standiford, Natalie*
The Astronomers — *Goldsmith, Donald*
r Astronomical Almanac. 1996 Ed.
Astronomical Instruments and Their Users
— *Chapman, Allan*
Astronomie Planetaire Au Moyen Age Latin
— *Poulle, Emmanuel*
Astronomies and Cultures — *Ruggles, Clive L N*
y El Astronomo Que Perdio La Nariz — *Schmidt, Alejandro*
Astronomy and Mathematics in Ancient China
— *Cullen, Christopher*
yr Astronomy and Space. Vols. 1-3 — *Engelbert, Phillis*
r Astronomy before the Telescope — *Walker, Christopher*
Astronomy Education — *Percy, John R*
y Astronomy Smart Junior — *Bentley, Michael L*
Astrophysical and Laboratory Plasmas — *Willis, A J*
y Asturias — *Caswell, Brian*
Asylum — *McGrath, Patrick*
y Asylum for Nightface — *Brooks, Bruce*
Asymmetric Synthesis — *Procter, Garry*
Asymptotic Analysis — *Kanwal, R P*
The Asymptotic Distribution of Eigenvalues of Partial Differential Operators — *Safarov, Yu*
Asymptotic Efficiency of Nonparametric Tests
— *Nikitin, Yakov*
Asymptotic Methods for Turbulent Shear Flows at High Reynolds Numbers — *IUTAM Symposium on Asymptotic Methods for Turbulent Shear Flows at High Reynolds Numbers (1995: Bochum, Germany)*
Asymptotic Solutions of the One-Dimensional Schrodinger Equation — *Slavianov, S Yu*
Asymptotics and Extrapolation — *Walz, Guido*
Asymptotics of Nonlinearities and Operator Equations
— *Krasnosel'skii, Alexander M*
At a Century's Ending — *Kennan, George F*
At Beck and Call — *O'Leary, Elizabeth L*
At Belleau Wood — *Asprey, Robert B*
At Century's End — *Gardels, Nathan P*
At Eighty-Two — *Sarton, May*
At Fenway — *Shaughnessy, Dan*
c At Grandpa's Sugar Bush (Illus. by Janet Wilson)
— *Carney, Margaret*
At His Side — *Pirozhkova, A N*
c At Home — *Wale, Carole*
y At Home in Mitford (McDonough). Audio Version
— *Karon, Jan*
At Home in the Universe — *Kauffman, Stuart*
At Home in the World — *Merton, Thomas*
At Home on the Stroll — *Highcrest, Alexandra*
At Large — *Freedman, David H*
y At Least This Place Sells T-Shirts — *Amend, Bill*
At Passages — *Palmer, Michael, 1943-*
At Risk — *Blaikie, Piers*
At the Border Called Hope — *Leddy, Mary Jo*
c At the Carnival (Illus. by Laura Rader) — *Hall, Kirsten*
At the City Limits of Fate — *Bishop, Michael*

At the Crossroads — White, Herbert S
At the Edge of the World — Bassie-Sweet, Karen
At the End of the Road — Whisler, Timothy R
At the Fringes of Science — Friedlander, Michael W
At the Front Line — Johnston, Mark
At the Gate — Rhodes, Martha
At the Heart of It — Harrington, Walt
At the Limits of Political Philosophy — Schall, James V
At the Margins of the Economy — Kovalainen, Anne
At the Picture Show — Fuller, Kathryn H
c At the Seashore — Hickman, Pamela M
c At the Shore (Illus. by Margaret Miller) — Miller, Margaret
At the Site of Inside Out — Rabinowitz, Anna
At the Still Point — Buckley, Carol
At Twilight in the Country — Hurtig, Mel
At War in the Shadow of Vietnam — Castle, Timothy N
At Women's Expense — Daniels, Cynthia R
y At Work — Central Office of Information
At Work with Grotowski on Physical Actions — Richards, Thomas, 1962-
Ataturk — Macfie, A L
Ataturk's Children — Rugman, Jonathan
Athanasius and Constantius — Barnes, Timothy D
Athanasius and the Politics of Asceticism — Brakke, David
Athena — Banville, John
Athena: A Biography — Hall, Lee
Athenian Democracy in Transition — Tracy, Stephen V
Athenian Religion — Parker, Robert, 1950-
Athenian Settlements of the Fourth Century B.C. — Cargill, Jack
Athens on Trial — Roberts, Jennifer Tolbert
y Athletes — Lindop, Laurie
Athletes and the American Hero Dilemma — Harris, Janet C
c Athletic Activities for Juniors — O'Neill, Jean
Atlanta — Gleason, David K
y Atlanta — Woodhead, Henry
Atlanta Region Outlook 1994 — Atlanta Regional Commission
c Atlanta: The Fastest Runner in the World (Illus. by Normand Cousineau) — Galloway, Priscilla
The Atlantic Frontier of the Thirteen Colonies and States — Price, Jacob M
c The Atlantic Ocean — Waterlow, Julia
The Atlantic Region to Confederation — Buckner, Phillip A
The Atlantic Vision — Eriksson, Gunnar
Atlantis — Doty, Mark
r Atlas De La Langue Francaise — Rossillon, Philippe
r Atlas Des Sites Du Proche Orient 14000-5700 BP
r Atlas for the Information Superhighway — Crispen, Patrick Douglas
r Atlas Historique De Montreal — Robert, Jean-Claude
r Atlas Linguae Gallicae — Billy, Pierre-Henri
r The Atlas of Alabama Counties — Remington, W Craig
r Atlas of American Agriculture — Pillsbury, Richard
r The Atlas of American Society — Andrews, Alice
cr Atlas of Animals — Delafosse, Claude
r Atlas of Aortic Surgery — Williams, G Melville
r Atlas of Colonial Waterbirds of North Carolina Estuaries 1993 — Parnell, James F
r Atlas of Colorectal Surgery — Keighley, Michael
cr Atlas of Countries (Illus. by Donald Grant) — Jeunesse Gallimard
r Atlas of Dynamic Laryngeal Pathology — Stasney, C Richard
r An Atlas of English Dialects — Upton, Clive
r Atlas of Fetal Surgery — Harrison, Michael R
r Atlas of Forensic Pathology — Jones, Nancy L
r An Atlas of Fullerenes — Fowler, Patrick W
r Atlas of Gastrointestinal Surgery. Vols. 1-2 — Etala, Emilio
r Atlas of General Surgery. 3rd Ed. — Carter, David
r Atlas of Historical County Boundaries: Connecticut, Maine, Massachusetts, Rhode Island — Long, John Hamilton
r Atlas of Historical County Boundaries: Kentucky — DenBoer, Gordon
yr The Atlas of Holy Places and Sacred Sites — Wilson, Colin
cr The Atlas of Human History. Vols. 1-6 — Rossi, Renzo
r Atlas of Indocyanine Green Angiography — Reichel, Elias
r An Atlas of Industrial Protest in Britain 1750-1990 — Charlesworth, Andrew

r Atlas of Invertebrate Anatomy — Anderson, D T
r Atlas of Laparoscopic Colon Surgery — Jacobs, Moises
r The Atlas of Literature
r Atlas of Mammography — Gamagami, Parvis
r Atlas of Medieval Europe — Mackay, Angus
r Atlas of Nevada Conifers — Charlet, David Alan
r Atlas of Pediatric Orthopaedic Surgery. 2nd Ed. — Morrissy, Raymond T
r Atlas of Pelvic Surgery. 3rd Ed. — Wheeless, Clifford R
cr Atlas of People (Illus. by Denise Millet) — Delafosse, Claude
cr Atlas of Plants (Illus. by Sylvaine Perols) — Delafosse, Claude
r An Atlas of Seabird Distribution in North-West European Waters — Stone, C J
r Atlas of Skeletal Muscles. 2nd Ed. — Stone, Robert J
r An Atlas of Social Indicators for the Upper Columbia River Basin — Machlis, Gary E
r Atlas of the Moon — Rukl, Antonin
yr Atlas of the Rain Forests — Lewington, Anna
r Atlas of the Twentieth Century — Overy, Richard
cr Atlas of Threatened Cultures — Mason, Paul
r An Atlas of U.S. Economy, Technology, and Growth
r Atlas of Western Art — Steer, John
yr Atlas of World History — Miles, Lisa
cr Atlas Visual De La Tierra (Illus. by Richard Bonson) — Van Rose, Susanna
cr Atlas Visual De Las Aves (Illus. by Richard Orr) — Taylor, Barbara
L'Atleta Di Fano — Viacava, Antonietta
ATM Network Performance — Kesidis, George
ATM Networks — Clark, Martin P
ATM: The Key to High-Speed Broadband Networking — Hines, I J
c Atom Bomb — Seddom, Tom
Atom Optics with Laser Light — Balykin, V I
Atomic Collision Processes and Laser Beam Interactions with Solids — Milosavljevic, M
Atomic, Molecular, and Optical Physics Handbook — Drake, Gordon W F
Atomic Processes in Plasmas — Osterheld, Albert L
Atomic Spectroscopy. 2nd Ed. — Robinson, James W
L'Atomo Fantasma — Ciardi, Marco
Atomtheorien Des Lateinischen Mittelalters — Pabst, Bernhard
y The Atonement Child — Rivers, Francine
Atonement: The Million Man March — Sadler, Kim Martin
r ATSDR's Toxicological Profiles on CD-ROM. Electronic Media Version
c Attack of the Mutant. Audio Version — Stine, R L
c Attack of the Slime Monster — Baker, Carin Greenberg
y Attack on Montreal (Illus. by Paul McCusker) — Berton, Pierre
y The Attack on Pearl Harbor — Rice, Earle
Attacks on the Freedom to Learn. 14th Ed.
Attending to Women in Early Modern England — Travitsky, Betty S
y Attention Deficit Disorder — Moragne, Wendy
Attention Deficit Disorder — Quinn, Patricia O
Attention Deficit/Hyperactivity Disorder — Cooper, Paul
The Attentive Listener — Haskell, Harry
Attenuated Total Reflectance Spectroscopy of Polymers — Urban, Marek W
Attic Document Reliefs — Lawton, Carol L
The Attic: Memoir of a Chinese Landlord's Son — Tsao, Kuan-Lung
Atticus — Hansen, Ron
Attila: The Man and His Image — Bauml, Franz H
y Attila's Treasure — Grundy, Stephan
Die Attisch-Schwarzfigurige Keramik Und Der Attische Keramikexport Nach Kleinasien — Tuna-Norlung, Yasemin
Attracting Birds and Butterflies — Ellis, Barbara
Attracting Terrific People — Glass, Lillian
r The Atwood-Coffee Catalogue of United States and Canadian Transportation Tokens — Coffee, John M, Jr.
Atypical Employment — Delsen, Lei
Atypical Infant Development. 2nd Ed. — Hanson, Marci J
Aubrey Beardsley: Dandy of the Grotesque — Snodgrass, Chris
Audacious Women — Bartholomew, Rebecca
Auden — Davenport-Hines, Richard
Audience and Authority in the Modernist Theater of Federico Garcia Lorca — Soufas, C Christopher

The Audience and Its Landscape — Hay, James
Audio Measurements — Crowhurst, Norman
p AudioFile
Audiologic Evaluation and Management and Speech Perception Assessment — Mendel, Lisa Lucks
r Audiologists' Desk Reference. Vol. 1 — Hall, James W, 1948-
r Audiology and Auditory Dysfunction — Mencher, George T
r Audiovisual Resources for Family Programming — Jordan, Barbara A
p Auditory Neuroscience
Audrey Hepburn — Paris, Barry
y Audrey Hepburn's Neck — Brown, Alan, 1950-
Auf Dass Sie Entsteigen Der Dunkelheit — Reiter, Andrea
Auf Dem Weg Ins Burgerleben — Budde, Gunilla-Friederike
Auf Schwarzen Listen — Lendvai, Paul
Aufenthalt In Einem Irren Haus — Novak, Helga M
Aufhebung Zur Eigentlichkeit — Geister, Philip
Aufklarung, Burgerliche Selbstserfahrung Und Die Erfindung Der Psychiatrie In Deutschland 1770-1850 — Kaufmann, Doris
Die Auflosung Der Disharmonien — Bong, Jorg
Aufstand Der Bilder — Paul, Gerhard
Augmentative and Alternative Communication — Tetzchner, Stephen Von
Augsburg In Der Fruhen Neuzeit — Bruning, Jochen
Augusta National and The Masters — Christian, Frank
Augustan Culture — Galinsky, Karl
r Auguste Poulet-Malassis — Oberle, Gerard
r Auguste Poulet-Malassis: L'Editeur De Baudelaire — Pichois, Claude
Augustine — Clark, Mary T
Augustine — Price, Richard
Augustine: Ancient Thought Baptized — Rist, John M
Augustine and the Arians — Sumruld, William A
Augustine and the Catechumenate — Harmless, William
Augustine and the Limits of Politics — Elshtain, Jean Bethke
Augustine: De Doctrina Christiana (Green) — Augustine, Saint, Bishop of Hippo
Augustine: His Thought in Context — Scott, T Kermit
Augustine the Reader — Stock, Brian
Augustine's World — Burt, Donald X
Augusto Di Setteprati — Bompieri, Franco
Augustus John: The New Biography — Holroyd, Michael
y Aung San Suu Kyi: Fearless Voice of Burma — Stewart, Whitney
c Aunt Chip and the Great Triple Creek Dam Affair (Illus. by Patricia Polacco) — Polacco, Patricia
Aunt Dimity's Good Deed — Atherton, Nancy
c Aunt Eater's Mystery Christmas — Cushman, Doug
c The Aunt in Our House (Illus. by David Soman) — Johnson, Angela
c Aunt Isabel Makes Trouble (Illus. by Kate Duke) — Duke, Kate
r Aunt Minnie's Atlas and Imaging-Specific Diagnosis — Ford, Kenneth L
c Aunt Nancy and Old Man Trouble (Illus. by David Parkins) — Root, Phyllis
Aunt Safiyya and the Monastery — Tahir, Baha'
Aurelia Followed by Sylvie — Nerval, Gerard De
Aureole — Maso, Carole
Auriculas: Their Care and Cultivation — Hyatt, Brenda
The Aurora: Sun-Earth Interactions — Bone, Neil
Aurul — Monda, Virgiliu
Aus Dem Nachlass Aehrenthal. Pts. 1-2 — Wank, Solomon
Auschwitz 1270 to the Present — Dwork, Deborah
Auschwitz: A Doctor's Story — Adelsberger, Lucie
Auschwitz and After — Delbo, Charlotte
Auschwitz and After — Kritzman, Lawrence D
Ausgewahlte Und Neue Schriften Zur Literaturgeschichte Und Zur Bedeutungsforschung — Ohly, Friedrich
The Austen Chamberlain Diary Letters — Chamberlain, Austen, Sir
r Austin Locations (Demographics and Forecasting Group, Austin, Texas)
c Australia — Keys, Jane
c Australia — Lowe, David
Australia: A Continent Revealed
r Australia: A Reader's Guide — Arnold, John
Australia, Britain, and Migration 1915-1940 — Roe, Michael

r Australia Business — *Nolan, James L*
r Australia Handbook
r Australia: The Rough Guide — *Daly, Margo*
Australia Unbuttoned — *Cue, Kerry*
The Australia-U.S. Trade and Investment Review
r Australian Air Mail Catalogue. 6th Ed. — *Eustis, Nelson*
cr The Australian Animal Atlas (Illus. by Marion Westmacott) — *Cronin, Leonard*
Australian Astronomers — *Bhathal, Ragbir*
r Australian Birds of Prey — *Olsen, Penny*
r Australian Children's Fiction. Update 1996 — *White, Kerry*
Australian Children's Literature — *Foster, John E*
Australian Cities — *Troy, Patrick*
Australian Cricket Anecdotes — *Haigh, Gideon*
Australian Economic Institutions since Federation — *Kenwood, Albert G*
Australian Lives — *Hughes, Robin*
Australian Love Stories — *Goldsworthy, Kerryn*
An Australian Phanerozoic Timescale — *Young, G C*
Australian Poetry — *Kane, Paul*
An Australian Son — *Matthews, Gordon*
The Australian Yarn — *Edwards, Ron*
Australia's China — *Strahan, Lachlan*
Australia's Trade Policies — *Pomfret, Richard W T*
Australia's War 1939-45 — *Beaumont, Joan*
Australia's Welfare and Services Assistance 1995
Austria 1938-1988 — *Wright, William E*
Austria and Other Margins — *Arens, Katherine*
An Austrian Perspective on the History of Economic Thought. Vols. 1-2 — *Rothbard, Murray Newton*
The Austrians: A Thousand-Year Odyssey — *Brook-Shepherd, Gordon*
The Austro-Prussian War — *Wawro, Geoffrey*
Auteur/Provocateur: The Films of Denys Arcand — *Loiselle, Andre*
Authentic Assessment in Action — *Darling-Hammond, Linda*
r The Authentic Jane Williams' Home School Market Guide — *Williams, Jane A*
Authenticating Culture in Imperial Japan — *Pincus, Leslie*
c Author: A True Story (Illus. by Helen Lester) — *Lester, Helen*
The Author, Art, and the Market — *Woodmansee, Martha*
Authoring Multimedia — *Stubley, Peter*
Authoritarian Populism in Malaysia — *Munro-Kua, Anne*
Authority and Autonomy in L'Entree D'Espagne — *Bradley-Cromey, Nancy*
Authority and Benevolence — *Leung, Joe C B*
Authority and Democracy — *McMahon, Christopher*
Authority and Desire — *Hiscock, Andrew*
Authority and Representation in Early Modern Discourse — *Weimann, Robert*
Authority and Sexuality in Early Modern Burgundy 1550-1730 — *Farr, James R*
Authority and the Sacred — *Brown, Peter Robert Lamont*
Authority: Construction and Corrosion — *Lincoln, Bruce*
Authority Figures — *Collins, Christopher*
Authors and Owners — *Rose, Mark*
An Author's Guide to Scholarly Publishing — *Derricourt, Robin*
Authorship as Alchemy — *Kropf, David Glenn*
Autism and the Crisis of Meaning — *Durig, Alexander*
The Auto-Biography of Luke Hansard — *Hansard, Luke*
Auto Opium — *Gartman, David*
Autobiographical Memory — *Thompson, Charles P*
Autobiography and Postmodernism — *Ashley, Kathleen*
Autobiography and the Existential Self — *Keefe, Terry*
Autobiography, Historiography, Rhetoric — *Donaldson-Evans, Mary*
Autobiography of a Generation — *Passerini, Luisa*
Autobiography of a Murderer — *Collins, Hugh*
Autobiography of a Yogi (Kingsley). Audio Version — *Yogananda, Paramahansa*
Autobiography of an Aspiring Saint — *Ferrazzi, Cecilia*
The Autobiography of an Ex-Colored Man (Gilmore). Audio Version — *Johnson, James Weldon*
The Autobiography of LeRoi Jones — *Baraka, Imamu Amiri*
The Autobiography of Methuselah. Electronic Media Version — *Bangs, John Kendrick*

y The Autobiography of My Mother — *Kincaid, Jamaica*
Autobiography of Red Cloud — *Allen, Charles Wesley*
The Autobiography of S.S. McClure — *Cather, Willa*
The Autobiography of Shibusawa Eiichi — *Shibusawa, Eiichi*
Autobiography of Walker Percy — *Dupuy, Edward J*
c El Autobus Magico En Tiempos De Los Dinosaurios (Illus. by Bruce Degen) — *Cole, Joanna*
AutoCAD Performance Tuning Toolkit — *Peterson, Michael Todd*
The Autocritique of Enlightenment — *Hulliung, Mark*
Autographs: Contemporary Australian Autobiography — *Whitlock, Gillian*
y Automated Alice (Illus. by Harry Trumbore) — *Noon, Jeff*
Automated Mathematical Induction — *Zhang, H*
Automated Specification-Based Software Testing — *Poston, Robert M*
Automatic Face and Gesture Recognition — *International Conference on Automatic Face and Gesture Recognition (2nd: 1996: Killington, VT)*
Automatic Performance Prediction of Parallel Programs — *Fahringer, Thomas*
Automatic Speech and Speaker Recognition — *Lee, Chin-Hui*
Automatic Teller — *Bird, Carmel*
Automation in the Laboratory — *Hurst, W Jeffrey*
Automotive Air-Conditioning Refrigerant Service Guide. 2nd Ed. — *Gott, Philip G*
r Automotive Lubricants Reference Book — *Caines, A J*
Autonomous Agents — *Mele, Alfred R*
p Autonomous Robots
Autopsy on an Empire — *Matlock, Jack F, Jr.*
L'Autorite De La Science — *Lurcat, Francois*
Autos, Smog, and Pollution Control — *Grant, Wyn*
Autour De La Litterature — *Schofer, Peter*
Autowork — *Asher, Robert*
c Autumn (Illus. by Kim Woolley) — *Baxter, Nicola*
Autumn Dancing — *Chandler, Adam*
Autumn Gospel — *Fischer, Kathleen*
The Autumn of the Gun — *Compton, Ralph*
The Autumn of the Middle Ages — *Huizinga, Johan*
c Autumn on the Farm — *Powell, Jillian*
L'Autunno Della Signora Waal — *Orengo, Nico*
Aux Origines Des Communes — *Dumont, Bruno*
Avalanche — *Troupe, Quincy*
The Avant-Garde in Exhibition — *Altshuler, Bruce*
r Avantgarde Und Arbeiterdichter In Den Hauptorganen Der Deutschen Linken 1917-1922 — *Sheppard, Richard*
Avasyaka-Studien: Introduction Generale Et Traductions — *Balbir, Nalini*
p Avec
L'Avenir N'est A Personne 1990-1992 — *Green, Julien*
c Las Aventuras De Maxi, El Perro Taxista (Illus. by Mark Buehner) — *Barraca, Debra*
Avenues of Participation — *Singerman, Diane*
c Avi — *Markham, Lois*
Avian Biochemistry and Molecular Biology — *Stevens, Lewis*
Avian Energetics and Nutritional Ecology — *Carey, Cynthia*
Aviation Law for Pilots. 9th Ed. — *Underdown, R B*
y Aviation: Reaching for the Sky — *Berliner, Don*
Avicenna and I — *Parvin, Manoucher*
Avoiding Nuclear Anarchy — *Allison, Graham T*
Awaiting Oblivion — *Blanchot, Maurice*
y Awake and Dreaming — *Pearson, Kit*
Awake, Arise and Act — *Riggs, Marcia Y*
The Awakening — *Chopin, Kate*
The Awakening (Ross). Audio Version — *Chopin, Kate*
y The Awakening and Selected Stories (Adler). Audio Version — *Chopin, Kate*
Awakening at Midlife — *Brehony, Kathleen*
Awakening Brilliance — *Sims, Pamela*
Awakening China — *Fitzgerald, John, 1951-*
The Awakening of the West — *Batchelor, Stephen*
Awakening the Sleeping Buddha — *Pema Donyo Nyinche, Tai Situpa XII*
Awakening to Zen — *Kapleau, Philip*
r The Awards Almanac 1996
Awareness Heals — *Shafarman, Steven*
Awareness: What It Is, What It Does — *Nunn, Chris*
Away from Home — *Brewster, Elizabeth*
Away with the Manger — *Fabry, Chris*
cr Awesome Almanac--New York — *Grabowski, John*
r Awesome Almanac--Ohio — *Benson, Marjorie*
cr Awesome Almanac--Texas — *Martin, Suzanne*
The Awkward Age — *James, Henry*

The Ax — *Westlake, Donald E*
Ayacucho, Goodbye. Moscow's Gold — *Ortega, Julio*
The Azerbaijani Turks — *Altstadt, Audrey L*
Aztec Autumn — *Jennings, Gary*
c The Aztec Empire — *Stein, R Conrad*
The Aztec Image of Self and Society — *Leon-Portilla, Miguel*
c The Aztec News — *Steele, Philip*
Aztec Warfare — *Hassig, Ross*
c The Aztecs — *Hewitt, Sally*
y The Aztecs — *Smith, Michael E*

B

The B-Book: Assigning Programs to Meanings — Abrial, Jean-Raymond

B Cells and Autoantibody Production in Autoimmune Diseases — Boitard, Christian

B.F. Skinner and Behaviorism in American Culture — Smith, Laurence D

B.F. Skinner: Benign Anarchist — Wiener, Daniel N

c B Is for Baby (Illus. by Steel Stillman) — Livingston, Myra Cohn

Ba-Ahariyut — Sneh, Ephraim

c Ba Ba Ha Ha — Zimmerman, Robert

Ba Chi Em Nha Ho Tong — Nguyen, Van Ly

Ba-Midrakhot — Leshem, Nurit

y Baba: A Return to China upon My Father's Shoulders — Yang, Belle

c Baba Yaga (Illus. by Katya Arnold) — Arnold, Katya

cr Babar's French and English Word Book — Brunhoff, Laurent

y Babcock — Cottonwood, Joe

Babe (Parker). Audio Version — Creamer, Robert W

c Babe and Other Pig Tales (Illus. by Mary Rayner) — King-Smith, Dick

The Babe in Boyland — Fabulous Sports Babe

The Babe in Red Stockings — Keene, Kerry

c The Babe Ruth Ballet School (Illus. by Tim Shortt) — Shortt, Tim

The Babe Signed My Shoe — Harwell, Ernie

Babe: The Life and Legend of Babe Didrikson Zaharias — Cayleff, Susan E

y Babe, the Sheep Pig (Thorne). Audio Version — King-Smith, Dick

Babel and Babylon — Hansen, Miriam

Babel Tower — Byatt, A S

y Babel Tower (Atkins). Audio Version — Byatt, A S

Babel=Babel — Zholkovskii, A K

c Babes in the Woods — Lynch, Chris

c Babies (Illus. by Michael Evans) — Baxter, Nicola

c Babies (Illus. by Ian Thompson) — Sandeman, Anna

Babies: History, Art and Folklore — Fontanel, Beatrice

c Baboon (Illus. by Georg Hallensleben) — Banks, Kate

The Baburnama: Memoirs of Babur, Prince and Emperor — Babur, Emperor of Hindustan

c Babushka's Mother Goose — Polacco, Patricia

c The Baby — Burningham, John

y The Baby and Fly Pie — Burgess, Melvin

The Baby and the Bathwater — Coltart, Nina

c Baby Angels — Cowen-Fletcher, Jane

y Baby Be-Bop — Block, Francesca Lia

c Baby Bear Comes Home (Illus. by Ian Newsham) — Lishak, Antony

c Baby Buggy, Buggy Baby (Illus. by Richard Brown) — Ziefert, Harriet

c Baby Bugs (Illus. by Tom Arma) — Arma, Tom

c Baby Bugs' Favorite Things

c Baby Bunny's Busy Day (Illus. by Carol Wood) — Chambers, Julie

Baby Cat-Face — Gifford, Barry

c Baby Crow — Rowe, John A

c Baby Duck and the Bad Eyeglasses (Illus. by Jill Barton) — Hest, Amy

c Baby Earth — Petit-Jean, Michele

c Baby Farm Animals — Johnson, B J

c Baby Friends — Johnson, B J

Baby Massage — Walker, Peter, 1942-

c The Baby Sister (Illus. by Tomie De Paola) — De Paola, Tomie

Baby Stuff — Lipper, Ari

c Baby Tweety

c The Baby Who Wouldn't Go to Bed (Illus. by Helen Cooper) — Cooper, Helen

cp Babybug

y Babylon Boyz — Mowry, Jess

Babylonians — Saggs, H W F

c Baby's Book of the Body — Priddy, Roger

c Baby's Breakfast (Illus. by Randy Cecil) — Poulsson, Emilie

c Baby's Christmas — Ricklen, Neil

c The Babysitter's Handbook (Illus. by J J Smith Moore) — Kuch, K D

Babywatching — Morris, Desmond

Bacchae (Seaford) — Euripides

Bach Khoa Meo Vat Can Biet — Doan, Van Hai

Bach, the Orgelbuchlein — Stinson, Russell

Bachelor Brothers' Bed and Breakfast — Richardson, Bill

Bachelors: The Psychology of Men Who Haven't Married — Waehler, Charles A

r The Back Door Guidebook 1997

Back Fire: The CIA's Secret War in Laos and Its Link to the War in Vietnam — Warner, Roger

Back from the Brink — Beckner, Steven K

Back from the Dead — Thomas, Evan

Back in Keith County — Janovy, John, Jr.

Back in the World — Wolff, Tobias

Back in Time — Sleem, Patty

y Back of Beyond — Ellis, Sarah

Back of the Big House — Vlach, Michael

Back on the Quality Track — Huddleston, Kathryn

Back to Freud's Texts — Grubrich-Simitis, Ilse

Back to Heaven — Chon, Sang-Byong

Back to Mandalay — Lewis, Norman

c Back to the Blue (Illus. by Ian Andrew) — McKenna, Virginia

c Back to the Cabin (Illus. by Ann Blades) — Blades, Ann

Back to the Front — O'Shea, Stephen

y Backcountry Bear Basics — Smith, Dave, 1950-

Backfire: A Reporter's Look at Affirmative Action — Zelnick, Bob

Background Factors of Juvenile Delinquency — Angenent, Huub

r Background to the ANZUS Pact — McIntyre, W David

Backing into the Future — Knox, Bernard

Backs in Motion — Maharam, Lewis G

c Backseat Buckaroo (Illus. by Edward Valfre) — Valfre, Edward

Backstory 3 — McGilligan, Patrick

Backward and Upward — Brooks, David

Backwards out of the Big World — Hyland, Paul

Backwoodsmen: Stockmen and Hunters along a Big Thicket River Valley — Sitton, Thad

c The Backyard — Collier, John

y The Backyard Bird-Lover's Guide — Mahnken, Jan

The Backyard Bird Watcher — Harrison, George H

cr Backyard Birds of Summer (Illus. by Carol Lerner) — Lerner, Carol

c Backyard Cowboy — Saltzberg, Barney

The Bacon Fancier — Isler, Alan

Bacon: Portraits and Self-Portraits — Borel, France

r Bacon's International Media Directory 1996

y Bacta War — Stackpole, Michael A

Bacteria and Antibacterial Agents — Mann, John

y Bad Angel — Benedict, Helen

Bad as I Wanna Be — Rodman, Dennis

Bad Attitude/s on Trial — Cossman, Brenda

c Bad Baby Brother (Illus. by Martha Weston) — Weston, Martha

y Bad Behaviour — Horniman, Joanne

Bad Blood — Gambaro, Griselda

Bad Boy — Brady, John

Bad Boy Bubby — De Heer, Rolf

Bad Boys — Lieberman, Carole

Bad Business — Hobbs, Dick

c The Bad Day ABC (Illus. by Hilda Offen) — Offen, Hilda

y The Bad Death of Eduard Delacroix — King, Stephen

Bad Debts — Temple, Peter

c Bad Dreams — Cooling, Wendy

Bad Eye Blues — Barrett, Neal

Bad Faith, Good Faith, and Authenticity in Sartre's Early Philosophy — Santoni, Ronald E

y Bad Girls — Voigt, Cynthia

c Bad Girls (Illus. by Nick Sharratt) — Wilson, Jacqueline

Bad Girls/Good Girls — Maglin, Nan Bauer

c The Bad Good Manners Book (Illus. by Babette Cole) — Cole, Babette

A Bad Hair Day — Dunbar, Sophie

Bad Intentions — Heller, Peter

Bad Intentions — Partridge, Norman

Bad Judgment — Kaplan, William

Bad Karma — Harper, Andrew

Bad Land — Raban, Jonathan

c The Bad-Luck Penny (Illus. by Horatio Elena) — O'Connor, Jane

A Bad Man — Elkin, Stanley

Bad Manners — Kellogg, Marne Davis

Bad Memory — Franklet, Duane

r Bad Movies We Love — Margulies, Edward

Bad Neighbors — Beck, Kathrine

y Bad News Travels Fast — Haywood, Gar Anthony

The Bad Samaritan (Graham). Audio Version — Barnard, Robert

Bad Seed — Johnston, Ian

The Bad Tempered Man (Dyskolos) — Menander, of Athens

Bad Vibes — Fuguet, Alberto

Bad Women — Staiger, Janet

y Badger on the Barge — Howker, Janni

c The Badger's Bath (Illus. by Mocl Butterworth) — Butterworth, Nick

c Badger's Bring Something Party (Illus. by Susan Varley) — Oram, Hiawyn

c Badger's Parting Gifts — Varley, Susan

Badlands — Fackler, Elizabeth

Badlands — Minhinnick, Robert

r Baer's 1996 Agricultural Almanac and Gardener's Guide

c Baffling Cryptograms — Moll, Louise B

c Baffling Whodunit Puzzles (Illus. by Lucy Corvino) — Sukach, Jim

Bag Men — Flood, John, 1962-

c The Bagthorpe Triangle — Cresswell, Helen

c Bagthorpes Besieged — Cresswell, Helen

r Bahamas — Bohlender, Sylvia

Bahia Minha — Santarrita, Marcos

Un Baile De Mascaras — Ramirez, Sergio

Bailey's Beads — Wolverton, Terry

Baize-Covered Table with Decanter — Makanin, Vladimir

Bajar Es Lo Peor — Enriquez, Mariana

El Bajo Cauca Antioqueno — Garcia, Clara Ines

Baked Goods Freshness — Hebeda, Ronald E

r Baker Encyclopedia of Bible Places — Bimson, John J

Baker's Choice — Fendel, Dan

Baker's Dozen — Thomas, Michael M

Baking with Julia — Greenspan, Dorie

y Baking without Fat — Mateljan, George

The Balance of Power — Sheehan, Michael J

Balance of Power — Wright, Jim

A Balance of Quinces — Reece, Erik Anderson

The Balanced Scorecard — Kaplan, Robert S

Balancing Act — *Bunkley, Anita R*
y Balancing Act — *Charbonnet, Gabrielle*
Balancing Act — *Lucas, Robin*
Balancing Act — *Morreim, E Haavi*
Balancing Act — *Spain, Daphne*
Balancing and Sequencing of Assembly Lines
   — *Scholl, Armin*
Balancing Juvenile Justice — *Guarino-Ghezzi, Susan*
Balancing on Air — *Fenton, Kate*
Balancing the Scales — *Miller, Kenton R*
The Baldwin Locomotive Works 1831-1915 — *Brown, John K*
r Bali and Lombok — *Reader, Lesley*
r Bali and Lombok — *Wheeler, Tony*
r Bali (Knopf Guides)
Bali Style — *Helmi, Rio*
Balinese Dance in Transition. 2nd Ed. — *Bandem, I Made*
Balkan Odyssey — *Owen, David, 1938-*
Balkan Tragedy — *Woodward, Susan L*
Balkany: Mezhdu Proshlym I Budushchim
r Ball Perennial Manual — *Nau, Jim*
Ball Pest and Disease Manual. 2nd Ed. — *Powell, Charles C*
c The Ballad of Dinosaur Bob (Hemingway). Book and Audio Version — *Joyce, William*
The Ballad of Gussie and Clyde — *Latham, Aaron*
y The Ballad of Lucy Whipple — *Cushman, Karen*
c The Ballad of the Pirate Queens (Illus. by David Shannon) — *Yolen, Jane*
Ballade — *Sokolow, Anna*
cr Ballet — *Castle, Kate*
c Ballet Magic (Illus. by Jan Palmer) — *Rose, Emma*
Balling the Jack — *Baldwin, Frank*
Ballistic Missile Defense in the Post-Cold War Era
   — *Denoon, David B H*
c Le Ballon Rouge — *Lamorisse, Albert*
c The Balloon Detectives (Illus. by Michael Bailey)
   — *Jones, Michael*
c Ballooning — *Perry, Phyllis J*
c The Ballot Box Battle (Illus. by Emily Arnold McCully) — *McCully, Emily Arnold*
c The Ballymara Flood (Illus. by George Booth)
   — *Stuart, Chad*
y Balook — *Anthony, Piers*
Balor of the Evil Eye — *Crenshaw, Nadine*
Balthus — *Klossowski De Rola, Stanislas*
Balthus — *Roy, Claude*
The Baltic Crusade. 2nd Ed., Rev. and Enlarged
   — *Urban, William L*
The Baltic Economies in Transition — *Lainela, Seija*
The Baltic States after Independence — *Norgaard, Ole*
The Baltic World 1772-1993 — *Kirby, David*
Baltimore Blues — *Lippman, Laura*
r Baltimore County Families 1659-1759 — *Barnes, Robert W*
Balzac — *Tilby, Michael*
Balzac, Oeuvres Completes — *Duchet, Claude*
The Bamboo Network — *Weidenbaum, Murray*
Bamboo Stone — *Minden, Karen*
Bamboula: The Life and Times of Louis Moreau Gottschalk — *Starr, S Frederick*
Bamikile — *Tidjani-Serpos, Noureini*
Banal Nationalism — *Billig, Michael*
The Banana Men — *Langley, Lester D*
Bananaville — *Lilliefors, Jim*
r Banco De Datos Filologicos Semiticos Noroccidentales. Pt. 1 — *Cunchillos, Jesus-Luis*
c A Band of Joining-In Stories — *Thomson, Pat*
The Band Played Dixie — *Cohodas, Nadine*
Bandarshah — *Salih, Tayeb*
Bande Et Sarabande — *Beckett, Samuel*
Bandelier: The Life and Adventures of Adolph Bandelier — *Lange, Charles H*
Bandits on the Information Superhighway — *Barrett, Daniel*
El Bandolerismo En Espana — *Santos Torres, Jose*
Bang the Drum Slowly — *Harris, Mark, 1922-*
Bangladesh: Reflections on the Water — *Novak, James J*
The Bangladesh Rural Advancement Committee's Credit Programs — *Khandker, Shahidur R*
Bangs, Crunches, Whimpers and Shrieks — *Earman, John*
Banishing Bureaucracy — *Osborne, David*
The Bank of Canada — *Watts, George S*
The Bank of England — *Roberts, Richard*
y The Bank of Fear (Guidall). Audio Version
   — *Ignatius, David*
Bank Restructuring — *Sheng, Andrew*

Banken Und Schwerindustrie In Der Weimarer Republik — *Wixforth, Harald*
The Banker — *Cheng, Nai-Shan*
The Bankers: The Next Generation — *Mayer, Martin*
Bankers with a Mission — *Kraske, Jochen*
Banking and Financial Control in Reforming Planned Economies — *Yang, Haiqun*
Banking, Currency, and Finance in Europe between the Wars — *Feinstein, Charles H*
Banking in an Unregulated Environment — *Doti, Lynne Pierson*
Banking on Deception — *Workman, W Thom*
The Banking Panics of the Great Depression
   — *Wicker, Elmus*
Banking, Politics and Global Finance — *Reinicke, Wolfgang H*
Banking Redefined — *Spiegel, John*
Banking Sector Development in Central and Eastern Europe — *Anderson, Ronald W*
Banks and Industrial Finance in Britain 1800-1939
   — *Collins, Michael, 1946-*
Banlieue Mon Amour — *Boishue, Jean De*
Banqueros Y Revolucionarios — *Zebadua, Emilio*
c The Banshee Train (Illus. by Ted Rose) — *Bodkin, Odds*
Baptism of Fire — *Cook, Robert*
r Baptismal Records of the Dutch Reformed Churches in the City of Groningen, Netherlands. Vols. 1-2
   — *McKey, JoAnn Riley*
Baptist Successionism — *McGoldrick, James Edward*
Baptists and Their Doctrines — *George, Timothy*
r Baptists around the World — *Wardin, Albert W*
Baptists on the American Frontier — *Young, Chester Raymond*
Baptized in Dirty Water — *McQuade, Joe*
Bar-20: The Life of Clarence E. Mulford, Creator of Hopalong Cassidy — *Nevins, Francis M, Jr.*
Ha-Barak — *Weinstein, Danny*
Barbar, Germane, Arier — *See, Klaus Von*
Barbara Frum: A Daughter's Memoir — *Frum, Linda*
y Barbara Jordan: Congresswoman, Lawyer, Educator
   — *Jeffrey, Laura S*
Barbarian Asia and the Greek Experience — *Georges, Pericles*
Barbarian Play — *Anderson, William Scovil, 1927-*
The Barbarism of Reason — *Horowitz, Asher*
The Barbarous Coast — *Macdonald, Ross*
Barbarous Dissonance and Images of Voice in Milton's Epics — *Sauer, Elizabeth*
The Barbed-Wire College — *Robin, Ron*
r Barbershop Collectibles
The Barbershop Singer — *Stebbins, Robert A*
r The Barbie Doll Years 1959-1995 — *Olds, Patrick C*
r Barbie Doll's Cousin Francie and Her Mod, Mod, Mod, Mod World of Fashion — *Blitman, Joe*
Le Barbier De Seville — *Beaumarchais, Pierre Augustin Caron De*
Barbie's Queer Accessories — *Rand, Erica*
The Barbury Hall Murders — *Naef, Adam*
Barcelona and Its Rulers 1096-1291 — *Bensch, Stephen P*
Bare-Bones Meditation — *Tollifson, Joan*
Bare Knuckles and Back Rooms — *Rollins, Ed*
Bare Knuckles and Back Rooms (Rollins). Audio Version — *Rollins, Ed*
c The Barefoot Book of Animal Tales from around the World (Illus. by Amanda Hall) — *Adler, Naomi*
c The Barefoot Book of Stories from the Sea (Illus. by Amanda Hall) — *Riordan, James, 1936-*
c Barefoot: Escape on the Underground Railroad (Illus. by Henry Cole) — *Edwards, Pamela Duncan*
Bargaining for Peace — *Gastrow, Peter*
Bargaining in Economic and Ethical Environments
   — *Klemisch-Ahlert, Marlies*
c Bark — *Chambers, Catherine*
c Barker's Crime (Illus. by Dick Gackenbach)
   — *Gackenbach, Dick*
Barking at Prozac — *McNichol, Tom*
c Barn (Illus. by Debby Atwell) — *Atwell, Debby*
c Barnacles Eat with Their Feet — *Shahan, Sherry*
Barnesbook — *Mac Low, Jackson*
Barney Google and Snuffy Smith — *De Beck, Billy*
r The Barnhart Concise Dictionary of Etymology
   — *Barnhart, Robert K*
c The Barnyard Band (Illus. by Charles Fuge)
   — *Riordan, James, 1936-*
c Barnyard Banter — *Fleming, Denise*
c Barnyard Dance — *Boynton, Sandra*
Barometers of Change — *Sarason, Seymour B*
r Baroque Art — *Earls, Irene*
Baroque D'Aube — *Brossard, Nicole*

The Baroque Narrative of Carlos De Siguenza Y Gongora — *Ross, Kathleen*
Baroque Personae — *Villari, Rosario*
Barrabas: Drama in Four Acts — *Steffen, Albert*
Barragan: The Complete Works — *Barragan, Luis*
y Barred from the Bar — *Garza, Hedda*
Barrel Fever — *Sedaris, David*
y A Barrel of Laughs, a Vale of Tears — *Feiffer, Jules*
Barren in the Promised Land — *May, Elaine Tyler*
Barricades and Borders. 2nd Ed. — *Gildea, Robert*
Barriers and Boundaries — *Greene, Liz*
Barriers and Bridges — *Jung, Heidrun*
Barriers to Conflict Resolution — *Arrow, Kenneth J*
Barriers to Information — *Harris, Roma M*
y Barrio Streets Carnival Dreams — *Carlson, Lori M*
Barrios and Borderlands — *Heyck, Denis Lynn*
cr Barron's Diccionario Juvenil Illustrado (Illus. by Gerald Chmielewski) — *Livesey, Rupert*
r Barron's EZ-101 Study Keys — *Baucum, Don*
c Barry Bonds: Mr. Excitement — *Savage, Jeff*
The Barry Diller Story — *Mair, George*
Barry Goldwater — *Goldberg, Robert Alan*
c Barry Sanders — *Wukovits, John F*
Barth, Derrida and the Language of Theology
   — *Ward, Graham*
Barthes for Beginners — *Thody, Philip*
Barthes: Mythologies — *Leak, Andrew*
Bartholomaei Coloniensis Ecloga Bucolici Carminis. Silva Carminum — *Meckelnborg, Christina*
Barth's Ethics of Reconciliation — *Webster, John*
r Bartlett's Roget's Thesaurus
Bartok: Concerto for Orchestra — *Cooper, David*
c Baru Bay: Australia — *Weir, Bob*
Base Christian Communities and Social Change in Brazil — *Hewitt, W E*
y Baseball: An Illustrated History — *Ward, Geoffrey C*
The Baseball Anthology — *Wallace, Joseph E*
r Baseball by the Numbers. Vols. 1-2 — *Stang, Mark*
Baseball Cat — *Allen, Garrison*
Baseball Economics — *Fizel, John*
r Baseball Guide. 1996 Ed.
c Baseball in the Barrios — *Horenstein, Henry*
c Baseball Jokes (Illus. by Viki Woodworth) — *Rothaus, James R*
Baseball with a Latin Beat — *Bjarkman, Peter C*
Baseball's Best Short Stories — *Staudohar, Paul D*
c Baseball's Funniest People (Illus. by Sanford Hoffman) — *Pellowski, Michael*
A Basement Seat to History — *Jurey, Philomena*
Basement Tectonics 11 — *Oncken, O*
Basic and Clinical Applications of Flow Cytometry
   — *Detroit Cancer Symposium (24th: 1992)*
Basic Biomechanics Explained — *Low, John*
y Basic Black — *Bates, Karen Grigsby*
Basic Chemistry. 7th Ed. — *Daub, G William*
Basic Colored Pencil Techniques — *Borgeson, Bet*
Basic Concepts of Synthetic Differential Geometry
   — *Lavendhomme, Rene*
c The Basic Five Food Groups — *Patten, Barbara J*
Basic Geological Mapping. 3rd Ed. — *Barnes, J W, 1921-*
Basic Issues of the History of Nutrition
   — *Guggenheim, K Y*
Basic Level — *Brubaker, Susan Howell*
Basic Pharmacology. 4th Ed. — *Foster, R W*
y Basic Physics. 2nd Ed. — *Kuhn, Karl F*
Basic Principles of Membrane Technology. 2nd Ed.
   — *Mulder, Marcel*
Basic Principles of Monastic Spirituality — *Merton, Thomas*
Basic Social Policy and Planning — *Burch, Hobart A*
Basic Statistics. 6th Ed. — *Spatz, Chris*
Basic Theory of Surface States — *Davison, Sydney G*
y Basic Training in Mathematics — *Shankar, Ramamurti*
The Basics of Information Systems. 2nd Ed.
   — *Rowley, Jennifer*
The Basics of Java Animation — *Burgess, Jay*
The Basics of Selection — *Bell, Graham*
Basil: An Herb Lover's Guide — *DeBaggio, Thomas*
Basil Fi Uyun Al-Misriyin — *Sa'dani, Izzat*
Basil of Caesarea — *Rousseau, Philip*
The Basilica of St. Francis in Assisi — *Lunghi, Elvio*
Basilides Und Seine Schule — *Lohr, Winrich Alfried*
Basis for Cancer Management — *Castagnetta, Luigi*
Il Basket D'Italia — *Patton, Jim*
c Basketball ABC — *Mayers, Florence Cassen*
c Basketball Jokes (Illus. by Viki Woodworth)
   — *Rothaus, James R*
c The Basketball Player (Illus. by Sheldon Cohen)
   — *Carrier, Roch*
y Basotho — *Van Wyk, Gary N*

The Bassanos: Venetian Musicians and Instrument Makers in England 1531-1665 — *Lasocki, David*
Bassin' with the Best — *White, Gary*
Basta! Land and the Zapatista Rebellion in Chiapas — *Collier, George A*
Bastard Keynesianism — *Turgeon, Lynn*
Il Bastardo Ovvero Gli Amori, I Travagli E Le Lacrime Di Don Emanuel Di Savoia — *Lagorio, Gina*
c Bat (Illus. by Richard Hewett) — *Arnold, Caroline*
c Bat (Illus. by Karen Duncan) — *Robb, Jackie*
c The Bat in the Boot (Illus. by Annie Cannon) — *Cannon, Annie*
c Bat Jamboree (Illus. by Melissa Sweet) — *Appelt, Kathi*
c Bat Mitzvah — *Goldin, Barbara Diamond*
c Batboy: An Inside Look at Spring Training (Illus. by Matthew Cavanaugh) — *Anderson, Joan*
Batching and Scheduling — *Jordan, Carsten*
r Bath and Surroundings — *Stannard, Dorothy*
Bathrooms — *Lee, Vinny*
Baths: Your Guide to Planning and Remodeling
Bathsheba — *Shott, James R*
Batman Collected — *Kidd, Chip*
c Batman: The Joker's Apprentice (Illus. by John Calmette) — *Dixon, Chuck*
y Batman: The Ultimate Evil — *Vachss, Andrew*
yp Batman: The Ultimate Evil. Bks. 1-2 — *Barrett, Neal*
p Batman vs. Predator II — *Moench, Doug*
c Bats — *Lovett, Sarah, 1953-*
Bats: Biology and Behaviour — *Altringham, John D*
Bats in Question — *Wilson, Don E*
c Bats: Swift Shadows in the Twilight (Illus. by Gail Kohler Opsahl) — *Cooper, Ann*
c Batter Up, Bailey Benson! — *Maifair, Linda Lee*
Battered Love — *Weems, Renita J*
y Batting against Castro — *Shepard, Jim*
Batting Cleanup, Bill Conlin — *Conlin, Bill*
Battle Eye — *Moyes, Norman B*
The Battle for Baltimore — *Whitehorne, Joseph W A*
The Battle for Christmas — *Nissenbaum, Stephen*
y The Battle for History — *Keegan, John*
The Battle for Hunger Hill — *Bolger, Daniel P*
The Battle for Investment Survival — *Loeb, Gerald*
The Battle for Merger — *Lee, Kuan Yew*
The Battle of Beginnings — *Ratzsch, Delvin Lee*
y The Battle of Belleau Wood — *Rice, Earle*
y The Battle of Gettysburg — *Corrick, James A*
y The Battle of Hastings — *Lace, William W*
y The Battle of Lake Erie (Illus. by Paul McCusker) — *Berton, Pierre*
The Battle of Leyte Gulf 23-26 October, 1944 — *Cutler, Thomas J*
y The Battle of Midway — *Rice, Earle*
The Battle of Tassafaronga — *Crenshaw, Russell*
c The Battle of the Alamo — *Bredeson, Carmen*
The Battle of the Books in Higher Education — *Casement, William*
r The Battle of the Centuries — *Freitag, Ruth S*
The Battle of the Frogs and Fairford's Flies — *Friedman, Jerome*
c The Battle of the Little Bighorn in American History — *Ferrell, Nancy Warren*
c The Battle of Waterloo — *Pietrusza, David*
y The Battle of Zama — *Nardo, Don*
Battle Tactics of the Western Front — *Griffith, Paddy*
Battleaxe — *Douglass, Sara*
Battlefields and Playgrounds — *Nyiri, Janos*
yr Battles: A Concise Dictionary — *Hogg, Ian V*
r The Battles of the Somme 1916 — *Van Hartesveldt, Fred R*
Battles on the Bench — *Cooper, Phillip J*
Battleship and Cruiser Aircraft of the United States Navy 1910-1949 — *Larkins, William T*
Battling Dragons — *Lehr, Susan*
Battling for Peace — *Peres, Shimon*
Battling Wall Street — *Gibson, Donald*
c Batwings and the Curtain of Night (Illus. by Mary GrandPre) — *Davol, Marguerite W*
Baudelaire and Intertextuality — *Evans, Margery A*
Baudelaire in Russia — *Wanner, Adrian*
Baudelaire: Individualism, Dandyism and the Philosophy of History — *Howells, Bernard*
Baudelaire, Les Fleurs Du Mal — *Baudelaire, Charles*
Baudelaire: Selected Poems from Les Fleurs Du Mal — *Baudelaire, Charles*
Bauer: Classic American Pottery — *Tuchman, Mitch*
Bauhaus: Crucible of Modernism — *Hochman, Elaine S*
The Bauhaus Idea and Bauhaus Politics — *Forgacs, Eva*

The Bay Shrimpers of Texas — *Maril, Robert Lee*
Bay Thu Nho — *Son Tung*
p Bay Windows
Bayaka: The Extraordinary Music of the Babenzele Pygmies — *Sarno, Louis*
Bayamus. Cardinal Polatuo — *Themerson, Stefan*
y Bayard Rustin: Behind the Scenes of the Civil Rights Movement — *Haskins, James*
y Bayard Rustin: Troubles I've Seen — *Anderson, Jervis*
Bayerns Unternehmer In Gesellschaft Und Staat 1834-1914 — *Schumann, Dirk*
Bayesian Analysis in Statistics and Econometrics — *Berry, Donald A*
Bayesian Approach to Interpreting Archaeological Data — *Buck, Caitlin E*
Bayesian Computational Methods and Applications — *Hill, R Carter*
Bayesian Data Analysis — *Gelman, A*
Bayesian Methods Applied to Time Series Data — *Fomby, Thomas B*
Bayesian Theory — *Bernardo, Jose M*
r Bazak Guide to Israel and Jordan 1996 1997
r BBC Music Magazine Top 1000 CDs Guide — *Levi, Erik*
yp BD — *Hares, Rod*
c Be a Friend — *Weirner, Lori S*
c Be Aware of Danger — *Gutman, Bill*
Be-Bop — *Gailly, Christian*
Be Faithful Unto Death — *Moricz, Zsigmond*
y Be Mine — *Dokey, Cameron*
c Be Patient, Abdul (Illus. by Dolores Sandoval) — *Sandoval, Dolores*
c Be Ready at Eight (Illus. by Cynthia Fisher) — *Parish, Peggy*
Be Strong for Me — *Adkins, Mark*
Be Strong for Me (Rubinstein). Audio Version — *Adkins, Mark*
c Be Well, Beware (Illus. by Jos. A Smith) — *Haas, Jessie*
c Be Your Own Astronomy Expert (Illus. by Nathalie Locoste) — *Cannat, Guillaume*
Be Your Own Home Decorator — *Guntlow, Pauline*
The Beach — *Garland, Alex*
The Beach (Page). Audio Version — *Garland, Alex*
c Beach Bunny (Illus. by Jennifer Selby) — *Selby, Jennifer*
c Beach Day — *Kruusval, Catarina*
c Beach Feet (Illus. by Lynn Reiser) — *Reiser, Lynn*
Beach Management — *Bird, Eric C F*
Beach Music. Audio Version — *Conroy, Pat*
y Beach Music (Marosz). Audio Version — *Conroy, Pat*
Beach of Dreams — *Bambaren, Sergio*
r Beacham's Encyclopedia of Popular Fiction. Vols. 1-11 — *Beetz, Kirk H*
Beachcombing for a Shipwrecked God — *Coomer, Joe*
y The Beacon — *Freireich, Valerie J*
The Beak of the Finch — *Weiner, Jonathan*
y The Beak of the Finch (McDonough). Audio Version — *Weiner, Jonathan*
Beam Dynamics and Technology Issues for U+U-Muons Colliders — *Gallardo, Juan C*
Beam Me Up, Scotty — *Doohan, James*
Beaming Sonny Home — *Pelletier, Cathie*
The Bean Trees — *Kingsolver, Barbara*
c Beanstalk — *Kingsland, Robin*
c The Bear (Illus. by Raymond Briggs) — *Briggs, Raymond*
c Bear (Illus. by Diana Magnuson) — *Caldwell, E K*
c The Bear — *Crewe, Sabrina*
Bear and His Daughter — *Stone, Robert*
c Bear and Roly-Poly (Illus. by Patience Brewster) — *Winthrop, Elizabeth*
c Bear at the Beach (Illus. by Clay Carmichael) — *Carmichael, Clay*
The Bear Flag — *Holland, Cecelia, 1943-*
c A Bear for Miguel (Illus. by Joan Sandin) — *Alphin, Elaine Marie*
Bear Man of Admiralty Island — *Howe, John R*
c The Bear Santa Claus Forgot (Illus. by Anna Kiernan) — *Kimpton, Diana*
c The Bear under the Stairs (Illus. by Helen Cooper) — *Cooper, Helen*
y The Bear Went over the Mountain — *Kotzwinkle, William*
The Bear Went over the Mountain (Prichard). Audio Version — *Kotzwinkle, William*
c The Bear Who Didn't Like Honey (Illus. by Odilon Moraes) — *Maitland, Barbara*
c Beardream (Illus. by Jill Kastner) — *Hobbs, Will*
The Beardstown Ladies' Guide to Smart Spending for Big Savings — *Beardstown Ladies' Investment Club*

The Beardstown Ladies' Stitch-in-Time Guide to Growing Your Nest Egg — *Beardstown Ladies' Investment Club*
c Bearhead: A Russian Folktale — *Kimmel, Eric A*
y Bearing an Hourglass (Guidall). Audio Version — *Anthony, Piers*
Bearing Meaning — *Kahn, Robbie Pfeufer*
Bearing Secrets — *Barre, Richard*
Bearing the Dead — *Schor, Esther*
Bearing Witness — *Martin, Augustine*
Bearing Witness — *Robinson, Joyntyle Theresa*
y Bearing Witness — *Rochman, Hazel*
c Bearobics: A Hip-Hop Counting Story (Illus. by Emily Bolam) — *Parker, Vic*
c Bears — *Horton, Casey*
Bears and Forebears — *Bond, Michael*
c Bears at the Beach — *Yektai, Niki*
c Bears at Work. Electronic Media Version
y Bears: Behavior, Ecology, Conservation — *Bauer, Erwin A*
c Bears Can't Fly — *Biro, Val*
y Bearstone — *Hobbs, Will*
y The Beast: A Journey through Depression — *Thompson, Tracy*
The Beast of Barbaresco — *Aspler, Tony*
c Beastly Banquet (Illus. by Tracy Gallup) — *Munsterberg, Peggy*
y The Beastly Book — *Hanson, Jeanne K*
c The Beastly Visits (Illus. by Mitra Modarressi) — *Modarressi, Mitra*
Beasts and Saints — *Waddell, Helen*
c The Beasts of Boggart Hollow (Illus. by Chris Fisher) — *Matthews, Andrew*
Beat Culture and the New America 1950-1965 — *Phillips, Lisa*
The Beat Experience. Electronic Media Version
Beat Generation — *McDarrah, Fred W*
c The Beat: Smokescreen — *Belbin, David*
Beat Stress — *Kenton, Leslie*
y Beat Voices — *Kherdian, David*
The Beaten Track — *Buzard, James*
The Beatification of Area Boy — *Soyinka, Wole*
y Beating Murphy's Law — *Berger, Bob*
Beating Plowshares into Swords — *Koistinen, Paul A C*
Beating the Devil Out of Them — *Straus, Murray A*
Beating the Field — *Lara, Brian*
Beating the Odds — *Levine, Arthur*
Beatitudes of Ice — *Crusz, Rienzi*
The Beatles — *Kozinn, Allan*
The Beatles. 2nd Rev. Ed. — *Davies, Hunter*
y The Beatles and the Sixties — *Assayas, Michka*
y The Beatles: The Music Was Never the Same — *Martin, Marvin*
The Beatles with Lacan — *Sullivan, Henry W, 1942-*
Beatrice Ojakangas' Light and Easy Baking — *Ojakangas, Beatrice*
Beatrix Potter — *MacDonald, Ruth K*
c Beatrix Potter (Illus. by Alexandra Wallner) — *Wallner, Alexandra*
c Beatrix Potter. Rev. Ed. — *Buchan, Elizabeth*
Beatrix Potter 1866-1943 — *Taylor, Judy*
Beatrix Potter: Artist, Storyteller, and Countrywoman — *Taylor, Judy*
The Beatrix Potter Knitting Book — *Menchini, Pat*
The Beatrix Potter Needlepoint Book — *Menchini, Pat*
r Beatrix Potter: The V and A Collection — *Hobbs, Anne Stevenson*
Beatrix Potter's Americans — *Potter, Beatrix*
Beatrix Potter's Art. Rev. Ed. — *Hobbs, Anne Stevenson*
r Beatrix Potter's Derwentwater. Rev. Ed. — *Bartlett, Wynne*
Beatrix Potter's Lakeland — *Davies, Hunter*
Beatrix Potter's Letters — *Potter, Beatrix*
Beaumarchais and the Theatre — *Howarth, William D*
The Beautiful and the Dangerous — *Tedlock, Barbara*
Beautiful Banners — *Webster, Barbara*
Beautiful Death — *Robinson, David, 1936-*
Beautiful Loot — *Akinsha, Konstantin*
The Beautiful Mrs. Seidenman — *Szczypiorski, Andrzej*
The Beautiful, Novel, and Strange — *Paulson, Ronald*
The Beautiful Room Is Empty — *White, Edmund*
The Beautiful Soul — *Norton, Robert Edward*
Beautiful Swift Fox — *Gish, Robert*
Beautiful Town — *Sato, Haruo*
y Beauty — *McKinley, Robin*
y Beauty — *Tepper, Sheri S*
y Beauty — *Wilson, Susan*
Beauty and Revolution in Science — *McAllister, James W*

Beauty and the Beast — *Liebregts, Peter*
c Beauty and the Beast (Illus. by James Mayhew)
  — *Pearce, Philippa*
c Beauty and the Beast (Illus. by Peter Kavanagh)
  — *Wilson, Jacqueline*
c Beauty and the Beast and Other Stories (Illus. by
  Louise Brierley) — *Geras, Adele*
c Beauty Lab — *Dawson, Mildred L*
The Beauty of Men — *Holleran, Andrew*
y The Beauty of the Beastly — *Angier, Natalie*
Beauty Queens on the Global Stage — *Cohen, Colleen
  Ballerino*
A Beauty That Hurts — *Lovell, W George*
y Beauty without Nature (Hillman). Audio Version
  — *Hillman, James*
The Beaverkill: The History of a River and Its People
  — *Van Put, Ed*
Bebop and Nothingness — *Davis, Francis*
Bebop to the Boolean Boogie — *Maxfield, Clive*
c Becassine Aux Ameriques — *Caumery*
c Becassine--Quand La Mer Monte — *Caumery*
Because I Remember Terror, Father, I Remember
  You — *Silverman, Sue William*
Because I Said So — *Longman, Cleaver*
Because I Wanted You — *Garrett, Annie*
Because It Gives Me Peace of Mind — *Pearson, Anne
  Mackenzie*
Because It Makes My Heart Beat Faster
  — *Rosenberg, Peter Michael*
Because They Wanted To — *Gaitskill, Mary*
Because We Are Here — *Wachtel, Chuck*
Beckett On and On... — *Oppenheim, Lois*
Beckett Writing Beckett — *Abbott, H Porter*
Beckon — *Conoley, Gillian*
Becoming a Grandmother — *Kitzinger, Sheila*
Becoming a Leader in Enrollment Services
  — *Swanson, Roger M*
Becoming a Physician — *Bonner, Thomas Neville*
Becoming a Revolutionary — *Tackett, Timothy*
Becoming a Self — *Westphal, Merold*
Becoming Canonical in American Poetry — *Morris,
  Timothy, 1959-*
Becoming Citizens in the Age of Television — *Thelen,
  David*
y Becoming Felix — *Wilson, Nancy Hope*
Becoming Gentlemen — *Guinier, Lani*
Becoming Gods — *Gilliland, Cazekiel*
Becoming Good, Becoming Holy — *O'Keefe, Mark*
c Becoming Julia — *Westwood, Chris*
Becoming Mae West — *Leider, Emily Wortis*
Becoming Mexican American — *Sanchez, George J*
Becoming Modern — *Burke, Carolyn*
Becoming National — *Eley, Geoff*
Becoming Native to This Place — *Jackson, Wes*
y Becoming Rosemary — *Wood, Frances M*
Becoming Southern — *Morris, Christopher*
Becoming the Parent You Want to Be — *Davis, Laura*
Becoming Tongan — *Morton, Helen*
Becoming What One Is — *Warren, Austin*
c Becoming Your Bird's Best Friend (Illus. by Anne
  Canevari Green) — *Gutman, Bill*
c Becoming Your Dog's Best Friend (Illus. by Anne
  Canevari Green) — *Gutman, Bill*
Bed and Breakfast — *Battle, Lois*
c The Bed and Breakfast Star — *Wilson, Jacqueline*
c Bed-Time Alphabet Stories — *Poortvliet, Rien*
The Bed-Trick in English Renaissance Drama
  — *Desens, Marliss C*
The Bedbugs' Night Dance and Other Hopi Sexual
  Tales — *Malotki, Ekkehart*
Bede and His World. Vols. 1-2
Bede: On the Tabernacle — *Bede, the Venerable, Saint*
r The Bedford Guide to Teaching Writing in the
  Disciplines — *Howard, Rebecca Moore*
The Bedford Inventories — *Stratford, Jenny*
Bedlam: An Anthology of Sleepless Nights — *Messer,
  Jane*
The Bedouin of Cyrenaica — *Peters, Emrys L*
The Bedouins and the Desert — *Jabbur, Jibrail S*
y The Bedspread — *Fair, Sylvia*
c Bedtime (Illus. by Tony Ross) — *Ross, Tony*
c Bedtime Bear — *Stickland, Paul*
c Bedtime, Everybody! — *Gerstein, Mordicai*
c Bedtime for Laura (Illus. by Renee Graef)
c A Bedtime Story (Illus. by Elivia Savadier) — *Fox,
  Mem*
y The Beduins' Gazelle — *Temple, Frances*
c The Bee — *Crewe, Sabrina*
c The Bee and the Dream (Illus. by Kaoru Ono)
  — *Long, Jan Freeman*
c The Bee Tree — *Polacco, Patricia*

Beechcraft Twin Bonanza — *Ward, Richard I*
y The Beekeeper's Apprentice — *King, Laurie R*
y The Beekeeper's Apprentice (Follows). Audio Version
  — *King, Laurie R*
Beeld En Zelfbeeld In De Nederlandse Kunst
  1550-1750 — *Falkenburg, Reindert Leonard*
Been Down So Long It Looks like Up to Me
  — *Farina, Richard*
Been There, Haven't Done That — *McCarthy, Tara*
y Been to Yesterdays (Illus. by Charlene Rendeiro)
  — *Hopkins, Lee Bennett*
Beer for Dummies — *Nachel, Marty*
r The Beer Lover's Rating Guide — *Klein, Bob*
r The Beer-Taster's Log — *Robertson, James D*
p Beer: The Magazine
c Bees (Illus. by Ute Fuhr) — *Delafosse, Claude*
Beethoven — *Kinderman, William*
Beethoven: A Man of His Word — *Altman, Gail S*
Beethoven and the Construction of Genius — *DeNora,
  Tia*
Beethoven as I Knew Him — *Schindler, Anton Felix*
r The Beethoven Compendium — *Cooper, Barry*
Beethoven Hero — *Burnham, Scott*
Beethoven in German Politics 1870-1989 — *Dennis,
  David B*
c Beethoven in Paradise — *O'Connor, Barbara*
Beethoven: Naissance Et Renaissance Des Derniers
  Quatuors. Vols. 1-2 — *Mahaim, Ivan*
Beethoven: Pastoral Symphony — *Jones, David Wyn*
Beethoven: The First Biography — *Schlosser, Johann
  Aloys*
Beethoven's Kiss — *Kopelson, Kevin*
c Beetle (Illus. by Lee Montgomery) — *Hawcock, David*
c Beetle (Illus. by Tim Hayward) — *Wiseman, Stella*
c Beetles — *Gerholdt, James*
Before and After — *Smith, Charlie*
Before Big Science — *Nye, Mary Jo*
Before Honor — *Proctor, George W*
Before I Wake — *Bowman, Eric*
Before I Wake — *Scott, John A, 1948-*
Before Night Falls — *Arenas, Reinaldo*
Before Night Falls — *Minatra, Mary Ann*
Before Photography — *Galassi, Peter*
Before Revelation — *Reinhart, A Kevin*
Before Science — *French, R K*
Before the Animation Begins — *Canemaker, John*
Before the Backbone — *Gee, Henry*
Before the Beginning — *Rees, Martin*
Before the Bomb — *Chappell, John D*
Before the Dawn — *Adams, Gerry*
Before the Famine Struck — *Murphy, Ignatius*
y Before the Gold Rush (Illus. by Paul McCusker)
  — *Berton, Pierre*
Before the Heroes Came — *Baughman, T H*
y Before the Storm (Heald). Audio Version
  — *Kube-McDowell, Michael P*
Before Their Time — *Kotlowitz, Robert*
Before Women Had Wings — *Fowler, Connie May*
Before Writing — *Kress, Gunther*
Before...12:01...and After — *Lupoff, Richard A*
Befriending: The American Samaritans — *Dickens,
  Monica*
Beg, Borrow or Starve? — *Hesketh, Anthony*
The Beggar and the Professor — *Le Roy Ladurie,
  Emmanuel*
A Beggar at Damascus Gate — *Zahran, Yasmine*
The Beggar Bride — *White, Gillian*
Beggars and Thieves — *Fleisher, Mark S*
Beggars Ride — *Kress, Nancy*
c The Beginners Bible for Toddlers (Illus. by Danny
  Brooks Dalby) — *Baker, Carolyn*
A Beginner's Guide to Copy Cataloging on
  OCLC/Prism — *Schultz, Lois Massengale*
A Beginner's New Testament Greek Grammar. New
  Ed., Rev. — *Kubo, Sakae*
Beginner's Polish — *Wanasz-Bialasiewicz, Ewa*
The Beginning and the End of Religion — *Lash,
  Nicholas*
c Beginning Basketball (Illus. by Andy King) — *Jensen,
  Julie*
c Beginning Hockey (Illus. by Andy King) — *Jensen,
  Julie*
y Beginning Life — *Flanagan, Geraldine Lux*
c Beginning Mountain Biking (Illus. by Andy King)
  — *Jensen, Julie*
The Beginning of Desire — *Zornberg, Avivah Gottlieb*
The Beginning of Heaven and Earth
The Beginning of the End — *Hagee, John*
The Beginning of the Gospel — *Collins, Adela Yarbro*
c Beginning School (Illus. by Toni Goffe) — *Smalls,
  Irene*

c Beginning Snowboarding (Illus. by Jimmy Clarke)
  — *Jensen, Julie*
Beginning Teaching in the Secondary School — *Dean,
  Joan*
Beginning Writers in the Zone of Proximal
  Development — *Steward, Elizabeth Patrick*
c Beginnings and Endings — *Pluckrose, Henry*
y Beginnings: From the First Nations to the Great
  Migration — *Jamieson, Marshall*
The Beginnings of European Theorizing — *Sandywell,
  Barry*
The Beginnings of Rome — *Cornell, T J*
Begrimed and Black — *Hood, Robert E*
Begstvo V Rossiiu — *Granin, Daniil*
Beguiled — *Borchardt, Alice*
Behavior and Personality — *Staats, Arthur W*
Behavioral Intervention for Young Children with
  Autism — *Maurice, Catherine*
Behavioral Issues in Autism — *Schopler, Eric*
Behavioral Mechanisms in Evolutionary Ecology
  — *Real, Leslie A*
r Behavioral Medicine Approaches to Cardiovascular
  Disease Prevention — *Orth-Gomer, Kristina*
Behavioral Neurology and Neuropsychology
  — *Feinberg, Todd E*
Behavioral Norms, Technological Progress, and
  Economic Dynamics — *Helmstadter, Ernst*
Behavioral Risk Management — *Yandrick, Rudy M*
Behavioral Statistics In Action. 2nd Ed. — *Vernoy,
  Mark W*
Behavioral Synthesis — *Knapp, David W*
Behavioural Ecology. 4th Ed. — *Krebs, J R*
Behavioural Ecology of Siberian and European Roe
  Deer — *Danilkin, A*
Behind a Mask — *Alcott, Louisa May*
Behind Blue Eyes — *Giuliano, Geoffrey*
Behind Closed Doors — *Hejaiej, Monia*
Behind Enemy Lines — *Muhammad, Askia*
c Behind Locked Doors — *Schutte, David*
Behind the Battle — *Bennett, Ralph*
c Behind the Bedroom Wall (Illus. by A Nancy
  Goldstein) — *Williams, Laura E*
Behind the Courtyard Door — *Hart, Ursula Kingsmill*
y Behind the Crystal Ball — *Aveni, Anthony F*
Behind the Facade — *Mackay, Sheila*
Behind the Frontier — *Mandell, Daniel R*
Behind the G-String — *Scott, David Alexander*
y Behind the Lines (Hill). Audio Version — *Griffin, W E
  B*
c Behind the Mask (Illus. by Ruth Heller) — *Heller,
  Ruth*
Behind the Myth of European Union — *Amin, Ash*
Behind the Oval Office — *Morris, Dick*
Behind the Red Line — *Human Rights Watch/Africa*
Behind the Scenes (Jones). Audio Version — *Keckley,
  Elizabeth*
c Behind the Scenes at the Airport (Illus. by Ingo Fast)
  — *Miller, Marilyn*
c Behind the Scenes at the Hospital (Illus. by Ingo Fast)
  — *Miller, Marilyn*
Behind the Scenes at the Local News — *Goald, Robert
  S*
Behind the Scenes at the Museum — *Atkinson, Kate*
c Behind the Scenes at the Shopping Mall (Illus. by Ingo
  Fast) — *Miller, Marilyn*
c Behind the Scenes at the TV News Studio (Illus. by
  Ingo Fast) — *Miller, Marilyn*
c Behind the Scenes Series
Behind the Stained Glass Windows — *Ronsvalle, John*
Behind the Wall — *Huff, Richard*
c Behind the Wheel — *Otfinoski, Steve*
Behind the Wheel at Chrysler — *Levin, Doron P*
Behold the Child — *Avery, Gillian*
Behold the Man — *McCormick, Scott, Jr.*
The Beholder — *Davies, Julian*
Bei Jing Jian Shi — *Fang, Biao*
Bei Yang Xiao Xiong Zhang Zuo Lin — *Dong, Yao*
c Beijing — *Kent, Deborah*
r Beijing — *Krucker, Franz-Josef*
c Bein' with You This Way (Illus. by Michael Bryant)
  — *Nikola-Lisa, W*
Being and Idea — *Armour, Leslie*
Being and the Between — *Desmond, William*
Being and Time — *Heidegger, Martin*
Being and Truth — *Langan, Thomas*
Being and Value — *Ferre, Frederick*
Being Brett — *Hobbie, Douglas*
y Being Different — *Brimner, Larry Dane*
Being Direct — *Wunderman, Lester*

Title Index

Being Good and Being Logical — *Forrester, James W*
c Being Me (Illus. by Teri Gower) — *Parsons, Alexandra*
Being Muslim the Bosnian Way — *Bringa, Tone*
Being Religious, American Style — *Lippy, Charles H*
Being Right — *Weaver, Mary Jo*
Being There — *Clark, Andy*
y Beirut Blues — *Shaykh, Hanan*
Bela Bartok — *Chalmers, Kenneth*
Bela Bartok: Composition, Concepts, and Autograph Sources — *Somfai, Laszlo*
Bela Bartok Studies in Ethnomusicology — *Bartok, Bela*
Bela Lugosi — *Edwards, Larry*
Belarus: From Soviet Rule to Nuclear Catastrophe — *Marples, David R*
Belated Travelers — *Behdad, Ali*
c Belching Hill (Illus. by Forest Rogers) — *Hamilton, Morse*
Belfast English and Standard English — *Henry, Alison*
Belfast Merchant Families in the Seventeenth Century — *Agnew, Jean*
The Belgian Economy in the Twentieth Century — *Mommen, Andre*
The Belgian Essays — *Bronte, Charlotte*
c Belgium — *Pateman, Robert*
Belief Transformations — *Rothstein, Mikael*
y Beliefs, Values and Traditions — *Lovelace, Ann*
Believers: A Novella and Stories — *Baxter, Charles*
Believers: A Novella and Stories — *Baxter, Charles, 1947-*
yr Believers: Spiritual Leaders of the World — *Goldman, Elizabeth*
Believing in Australia — *Carey, Hilary M*
Believing in Opera — *Sutcliffe, Tom*
Belisaire — *Marmontel, Jean-Francois*
c Belize — *Morrison, Marion*
The Bell Curve — *Herrnstein, Richard*
The Bell Curve Debate — *Jacoby, Russell*
The Bell Curve Wars — *Fraser, Steven*
The Bell Jar — *Plath, Sylvia*
The Bell Jar (McDormand). Audio Version — *Plath, Sylvia*
The Bell Jar (Shaw). Audio Version — *Plath, Sylvia*
The Bell Witch — *Monahan, Brent*
c Bella and the Beanstalk — *Ball, Brian*
Bella Combe Journal — *Gaston, Bill*
c Bella Goes to Sea — *Blathwayt, Benedict*
Bella Vita E Guerre Altrui Di Mr. Pyle, Gentiluomo — *Barbero, Alessandro*
c Bella's Big Adventure — *Blathwayt, Benedict*
La Belle Captive — *Robbe-Grillet, Alain*
Belle Du Seigneur — *Cohen, Albert*
y Belle Prater's Boy — *White, Ruth*
c Belle's Journey (Illus. by Stephen McCallum) — *Reynolds, Marilynn*
p Belles Lettres
Belleville, Ottawa, and Galesburg — *Carr, Kay J*
Bellocq: Photographs from Storyville, the Red-Light District of New Orleans — *Bellocq, E J*
p Bellowing Ark
y The Bells of Freedom — *Gilman, Dorothy*
The Bells of San Carlos and Other Stories — *Brand, Max*
Bellwether — *Willis, Connie*
c Belly Flop — *Gleitzman, Morris*
p Beloit Poetry Journal
Belonging — *Thayer, Nancy*
Belonging to the Army — *Mayer, Holly A*
y Beloved — *Morrison, Toni*
The Beloved Disciple — *Charlesworth, James H*
Beloved Tyranna — *Rezits, Joseph*
Below the Beltway — *Jackley, John L*
y Below the Convergence — *Gurney, Alan*
Below the Parapet — *Thatcher, Carol*
Beluga: A Farewell to Whales — *Beland, Pierre*
c Beluga Passage (Illus. by Jon Wieman) — *Lingemann, Linda*
Bely, Joyce, and Doblin — *Barta, Peter I*
Ben and Jerry's Double-Dip — *Cohen, Ben*
c Ben Franklin Book of Easy Incredible Experiments (Illus. by Cheryl Kirk Noll) — *Rudy, Lisa Jo*
Ben-Gurion and the Holocaust — *Teveth, Shabtai*
Ben-Gurion's Spy — *Teveth, Shabtai*
Ben Jonson and the Art of Secrecy — *Slights, William W E*
Ben Jonson, Authority, Criticism — *Dutton, Richard*
Benacerraf and His Critics — *Morton, Adam*
Benchmarks: Great Constitutional Controversies in the Supreme Court — *Eastland, Terry*

Benchmarks of Fairness for Health Care Reform — *Daniels, Norman*
The Bend for Home — *Healy, Dermot*
A Bend in the River — *Naipaul, V S*
Bending the Landscape — *Griffith, Nicola*
Bending with the Wind — *Avis, Nick*
c Bendy — *Warbrick, Sarah*
y Beneath Blue Waters (Illus. by Larry Madin) — *Kovacs, Deborah*
Beneath the Cross — *Diefendorf, Barbara B*
Beneath the North Atlantic — *Bird, Jonathan*
Benedictine Maledictions — *Little, Lester K*
The Benedictional of Aethelwold — *Deshman, Robert*
The Benefits of Famine — *Keen, David*
yr Benet's Reader's Encyclopedia. 4th Ed. — *Murphy, Bruce*
Beneventanum Troporum Corpus. Vols. 1-2 — *Planchart, Alejandro Enrique*
Bengal Divided — *Chatterji, Joya*
c The Benin Kingdom of West Africa — *Peffer-Engels, John*
y Benin: Lords of the River — *Koslow, Philip*
c Beni's Family Cookbook for the Jewish Holidays (Illus. by Jane Breskin Zalben) — *Zalben, Jane Breskin*
Benjamin Britten — *Oliver, Michael*
r Benjamin Britten: A Guide to Research — *Hodgson, Peter John*
Benjamin Disraeli Letters. Vol. 5 — *Disraeli, Benjamin, Earl of Beaconsfield*
y Benjamin Franklin (Cullen). Audio Version — *Van Doren, Carl*
Benjamin Franklin and His Enemies — *Middlekauff, Robert*
Benjamin Franklin, Politician — *Jennings, Francis*
Benjamin Franklin's Science — *Cohen, I Bernard*
Benjamin Franklin's The Art of Virtue — *Franklin, Benjamin, 1706-1790*
Benjamin Grabbed His Chicken and Ran — *Gordon, Fred Jay*
Benjamin Lincoln and the American Revolution — *Mattern, David B*
r Benjamin Rush, M.D.: A Bibliographic Guide — *Fox, Claire G*
Benjamin's Crossing — *Parini, Jay*
c Benjy: A Ferocious Fairy Tale (Illus. by Catharine O'Neill) — *O'Connor, Edwin*
c Benjy Bear's Halloween (Illus. by Emilie Boon) — *Ziefert, Harriet*
c Benni and Victoria (Illus. by Robert Sprouse) — *Aust, Patricia H*
Bennington and the Green Mountain Boys — *Shalhope, Robert E*
r Benny Goodman: Wrappin' It Up — *Connor, D Russell*
Benozzo Gozzoli — *Ahl, Diane Cole*
c Ben's Christmas Carol (Illus. by Ruth Brown) — *Forward, Toby*
Benson J. Lossing and Historical Writing in the United States 1830-1890 — *Mahan, Harold E*
r The Bent Guide to Gay/Lesbian Canada 1995/96
The Benthams in Russia 1780-1791 — *Christie, Ian R*
c Bently and Egg (Illus. by William Joyce) — *Joyce, William*
Bentonville: The Final Battle of Sherman and Johnston — *Hughes, Nathaniel Cheairs*
Beowulf — *Alexander, Michael*
Beowulf: A Student Edition — *Jack, George*
Beowulf and the Medieval Proverb Tradition — *Deskis, Susan E*
y Beowulf's Children — *Niven, Larry*
Bequest and Betrayal — *Miller, Nancy K*
The Berbers — *Brett, Michael*
Berbice Crossing — *Dabydeen, Cyril*
Bereft of Reason — *Halton, Eugene*
c The Berenstain Bears at the Teen Rock Cafe — *Berenstain, Stan*
c The Berenstain Bears Draw-It! — *Berenstain, Stan*
c The Berenstain Bears Fly-It! — *Berenstain, Stan*
c The Berenstain Bears in Big Bear City — *Berenstain, Stan*
c The Berenstain Bears in Maniac Mansion — *Berenstain, Stan*
Bergson: Thinking Backwards — *Moore, F C T*
The Beribboned Bomb — *Belton, Robert J*
Berlin Cabaret — *Jelavich, Peter*
The Berlin Commentary on Martianus Capella's De Nuptiis Philologiae Et Mercurii, Book 1 — *Westra, Haijo Jan*
Berlin in Focus — *Becker-Cantarino, Barbara*

The Berlin Jewish Community — *Lowenstein, Steven M*
c Berlioz the Bear — *Brett, Jan*
r The Berlitz Travellers Guide to Canada. 6th Ed.
r Bermuda by Air — *Cwiakala, Charles E*
r The Bernard Becker Collection in Ophthalmology — *Wechsler, Lilla*
Bernard Manning — *Margolis, Jonathan*
Bernard Meadows: Sculpture and Drawings — *Bowness, Alan*
Bernard Molitor 1775-1833 — *Leben, Ulrich*
Bernard of Clairvaux and the Shape of Monastic Thought — *Pranger, M B*
Bernard of Clairvaux: Between Cult and History — *Bredero, Adriaan Hendrik*
c Bernard on His Own — *Hoff, Syd*
Bernard Palissy: In Search of Earthly Paradise — *Amico, Leonard N*
Bernard Shaw and Gabriel Pascal — *Shaw, Bernard*
Bernard Shaw: The Ascent of the Superman — *Peters, Sally*
Bernard Shaw Theatrics — *Shaw, Bernard*
Bernard Shaw's Book Reviews. Vol. 2 — *Shaw, Bernard*
Bernard Shaw's Novels — *Dietrich, Richard Farr*
c Bernard's Bath (Illus. by Dominic Catalano) — *Goodman, Joan Elizabeth*
c Bernard's Prize (Illus. by Scoular Anderson) — *Cate, Dick*
Bernhard Gutmann: An American Impressionist — *North, Percy*
Bernhard Von Clairvaux: Rezeption Und Wirkung Im Mittelalter Und In Der Neuzeit — *Elm, Kaspar*
p Bernoulli: Official Journal of the Bernoulli Society for Mathematical Statistics and Probability
Die Bernstein-Debatte: Die Politische-Ideologischen Stromungen Und Die Parteiideologie In Der Sozialdemokratischen Partei Deutschlands 1898-1903 — *Rautio, Veli-Matti*
c Berries, Nuts and Seeds (Illus. by John F McGee) — *Burns, Diane L*
Bertha Von Suttner: A Life for Peace — *Hamann, Brigitte*
Berthold Schwarz: Chemie Und Waffentechnik Im 15. Jahrhundert — *Kramer, Gerhard W*
c Bertie and Gertie, Space Detectives! (Illus. by Antje Von Stemm) — *Stemm, Antje Von*
c Bertie at the Horse Show (Illus. by Elizabeth Alger) — *Alger, Elizabeth*
Bertrand Russell — *Slater, John G*
Bertrand Russell: The Spirit of Solitude — *Monk, Ray*
y Beryl Markham: Never Look Back — *Gourley, Catherine*
Beset by Contradictions — *Lawyers Committee for Human Rights (U.S.)*
Beside the Ocean of Time — *Brown, George Mackay*
Bessie Head: Thunder behind Her Ears — *Eilersen, Gillian Stead*
Bessie Smith Songbook
y Bess's Log Cabin Quilt — *Love, D Anne*
The Best 125 Meatless Mediterranean Dishes — *Geiskopf-Hadler, Susann*
The Best American Erotica 1996
y The Best American Essays 1996
Best American Gay Fiction 1996
The Best American Poetry 1996
The Best American Short Plays 1995-1996
The Best American Short Stories 1996
y The Best American Sports Writing 1996
Best Approximation by Linear Superpositions (Approximate Nomography) — *Khavinson, S Ya.*
r The Best Bargain Family Vacations in the U.S.A. — *Sutherland, Laura*
c The Best Batsman in the World — *Luckett, Dave*
r Best Books for Public Libraries — *Arozena, Steven*
yr Best Books for Senior High Readers — *Gillespie, John T, 1928-*
Best Bread Machine Recipes
c The Best Bug Parade (Illus. by Holly Keller) — *Murphy, Stuart J*
The Best Butler in the Business — *Jones, D B*
Best Canadian Stories 96
c The Best Children's Books in the World — *Preiss, Byron*
c The Best Christmas Present of All (Illus. by Catherine Walters) — *Jennings, Linda*
r The Best Directory of Recruiters. 4th Ed. — *Gove, Thomas P*
r The Best Directory of Recruiters On-Line — *Gove, Thomas P*
y The Best Ever Book of Ballet — *Castle, Kate*

The Best Families — *Mazzola, Anthony T*
c Best Friends — *Benton, Hope*
The Best Friends Approach to Alzheimer's Care
   — *Bell, Virginia*
y The Best Friends Book — *Erlbach, Arlene*
c Best Friends For Ever (Illus. by Derek Brazell)
   — *Cave, Kathryn*
c Best Friends Think Alike (Illus. by Lynn Reiser)
   — *Reiser, Lynn*
Best Gay Erotica 1996
Best Gay Erotica 1997
c The Best Holiday Crafts Ever! (Illus. by Sharon Lane
   Holm) — *Ross, Kathy*
The Best Home Businesses for the 90s. 2nd Ed., Rev.
   and Expanded — *Edwards, Paul, 1940-*
The Best Interests of the Child — *Goldstein, Joseph*
The Best Is Yet to Come — *Wylie, Betty Jane*
Best Kept Secrets — *Wasman, Ann*
Best Lesbian Erotica 1996
Best Lesbian Erotica 1997
y The Best Little Girl in the World — *Levenkron, Steven*
Best-Loved Recipes: Celebrating 75 Years of Great
   Baking
The Best Money Murder Can Buy — *McGaughey,
   Neil*
The Best New Horror 6
The Best New Horror 7
The Best New Science Fiction 1996
Best Nightmare on Earth — *Gold, Herbert*
Best of Booch — *Booch, Grady*
Best of Dee Brown's West — *Brown, Dee Alexander*
The Best of Dorothy Parker — *Parker, Dorothy*
Best of Enemies — *Corbett, Val*
The Best of Enemies — *Smith, Taylor*
The Best of Flair — *Cowles, Fleur*
The Best of Flower Painting — *Kipp, Kathryn*
The Best of Friends — *Trollope, Joanna*
The Best of Gerald Durrell — *Durrell, Gerald*
The Best of Helmut Newton — *Newton, Helmut*
The Best of Jayanta Mahapatra — *Mahapatra,
   Jayanta*
y The Best of Josh McDowell — *McDowell, Josh*
The Best of Ken Hubbard — *Hubbard, Ken*
c The Best of Michael Rosen (Illus. by Quentin Blake)
   — *Rosen, Michael, 1946-*
The Best of OPL II — *Berner, A*
The Best of Silk Painting — *Tuckerman, Diane*
The Best of Sports Afield — *Cassell, Jay*
The Best of Sports Illustrated
Best of the Best 1995
The Best of the Brownies' Book — *Johnson-Feelings,
   Dianne*
Best of the South — *Ravenel, Shannon*
The Best of What We Are — *Brentlinger, John*
Best of Young American Novelists
c The Best Older Sister (Illus. by Cornelius Van
   Wright) — *Choi, Sook Nyul*
The Best Plays of 1995-1996
The Best Police in the World — *Weinberger, Barbara*
Best Practices for Photovoltaic Household
   Electrification Programs — *Cabraal, Anil*
Best Practices Report
yr The Best Resources for College Choice and
   Admissions
c Best School Year Ever — *Robinson, Barbara*
y Best Seat in the House — *Lee, Spike*
c The Best Treasury of Stories for Children (Illus. by A
   Lewis)
c The Best Vacation Ever (Illus. by Nadine Bernard
   Westcott) — *Murphy, Stuart J*
r Best Wine Buys for $12 and Under — *Ensrud,
   Barbara*
The Best Writing on Writing. Vol. 2 — *Heffron, Jack*
The Best Years of Their Lives. 2nd Ed. — *Zvirin,
   Stephanie*
Bestseller — *Goldsmith, Olivia*
The Bethel Pike Pottery — *Griner, Ned H*
y Beth's Basic Bread Book — *Hensperger, Beth*
Betrachtungen Zum Skaz Bei N.S. Leskov and
   Dragoslav Mihailovic — *Hodel, Robert*
Betrayal (Beale). Audio Version — *Francis, Clare*
Betrayal by the Brain — *Goldstein, Jay A*
r Betrayal: Employee Relations at DuPont 1981-1994
   — *Dent, Edward E*
The Betrayal of Richard III — *Lamb, V B*
y Betrayal of Science and Reason — *Ehrlich, Paul R*
Betrayal of the Spirit — *Muster, Nori J*
Betrayal of Trust — *Colton, Matthew*
Betrayal Trauma — *Freyd, Jennifer J*
Betrayals — *Palliser, Charles*
y Betrayed — *Rushford, Patricia H*

Betrayed: A History of Presidential Failure to Protect
   Black Lives — *Hutchinson, Earl Ofari*
Betrayed Trust — *Lambert, John*
c Betsey's Birthday Surprise (Illus. by Lis Toft)
   — *Blackman, Malorie*
Betsi Larousse Ou L'Ineffable Ecceite De La Loutre
   — *Hamelin, Louis*
Bettelheim: A Life and a Legacy — *Sutton, Nina*
Better Bones, Better Body — *Brown, Susan E*
c The Better Brown Stories (Illus. by Fritz Wegner)
   — *Ahlberg, Allan*
r Better Buys for Business. Vols. 1-10
Better Ceramics through Chemistry VII
Better, Deeper, and More Enduring Brief Therapy
   — *Ellis, Albert*
Better Homes and Gardens Eat and Stay Slim
Better Homes and Gardens Step-by-Step Wiring
   — *Allen, Benjamin W*
c Better Not Get Wet, Jesse Bear (Illus. by Bruce
   Degen) — *Carlstrom, Nancy White*
Better Red — *Coiner, Constance*
Better than Life — *Pennac, Daniel*
c Betting on Forever (Illus. by John Quinn) — *Aronson,
   Billy*
c Betty and Bala and the Proper Big Pumpkin (Illus. by
   Noel Cristaudo) — *Berolah, Lorraine*
Betty and Me — *Hyde, Dudley*
Betty Crocker's Good and Easy Cookbook
   — *Crocker, Betty*
y The Betty Ford Center Book of Answers — *West,
   James W*
y The Between, a Novel — *Due, Tananarive*
y Between a Rock and a Hard Place — *Carter, Alden R*
Between Affluence and Rebellion — *Frolich, Margrit*
Between Bargaining and Politics — *Slomp, Hans*
Between Bench and Bedside — *Lowy, Ilana*
Between Borders — *Giroux, Henry A*
Between City and Suburb — *Gonen, Amiram*
Between Copernicus and Galileo — *Lattis, James M*
Between Cultures — *Seelye, H Ned*
c Between Earth and Sky (Illus. by Thomas Locker)
   — *Bruchac, Joseph*
Between Earth and Sky — *Osborn, Karen*
Between Earthquakes and Volcanoes — *Vilas, Carlos
   M*
Between Facts and Norms — *Habermas, Jurgen*
Between Families and the Sky — *Cumyn, Alan*
Between Friends — *Arendt, Hannah*
Between Friends — *Najemy, John M*
Between Gospel and Culture — *Hunsberger, George R*
Between Heaven and Earth — *Gire, Ken*
Between Hope and Havoc — *Smith, Frank, 1928-*
Between Hope and History — *Clinton, Bill*
Between Ideology and Realpolitik — *Schild, Georg*
Between Languages and Cultures — *Dingwaney,
   Anuradha*
Between Mars and Mammon — *Peers, Douglas M*
Between Muslim and Jew — *Wasserstrom, Steven M*
Between Principle and Practice — *Gillies, David*
Between Race and Culture — *Cheyette, Bryan*
Between Reform and Revolution — *Seligmann, Linda
   J*
Between Seasons and Science — *Faasse, Patricia*
Between Sisters — *Vida, Nina*
Between Stage and Screen — *Tornqvist, Emil*
Between the Dollar-Sterling Gold Points — *Officer,
   Lawrence H*
y Between the Dragon and the Eagle — *Schneider, Mical*
Between the Dreaming and the Coming True
   — *Benson, Robert*
Between the Eagle and the Sun — *Hassan, Ihab*
Between the Fields and the City — *Engel, Barbara
   Alpern*
Between the Flag and the Banner — *Yishai, Yael*
Between the Lines — *Siems, Larry*
Between the Sheets, in the Streets — *Holmlund, Chris*
Between the Wars — *Huxley, Aldous*
Between Therapist and Client. Rev. Ed. — *Kahn,
   Michael D*
Between Tradition and Modernity — *Weinberg, David
   H*
Between Two Cultures — *Gimpel, Charles*
Between Two Cultures — *Samartha, Stanley J*
Between Two Fires — *Hauptman, Laurence M*
Between Two Waters — *Spitta, Silvia*
Between Two Worlds — *Kafadar, Cemal*
Between Us — *Turner, Kay*
Between Voice and Silence — *Taylor, Jill McLean*
Between War and Peace — *Karsh, Efraim*
Between Worlds — *Freeman, David*
Between Worlds — *Lionni, Leo*

Beverley Minster Fasti — *McDermid, Richard T*
Beverly and Marigold — *Coleman, Val*
The Beverly Cleary Handbook — *Kelly, Joanne*
c Beware of Boys — *Blundell, Tony*
Beware Sleeping Dogs — *Wilson, Karen Ann*
Beyond a Christian Commonwealth — *Hanley, Mark
   Y*
Beyond a Mountain Valley — *Brown, Paula, 1925-*
Beyond Acceptance — *Griffin, Carolyn Welch*
Beyond Alliance — *Mansour, Camille*
Beyond Amber Waves of Grain — *Lasley, Paul*
Beyond Animal Rights — *Donovan, Josephine*
Beyond Beef — *Rifkin, Jeremy*
Beyond Beijing — *Chittister, Joan*
Beyond Black and White — *Marable, Manning*
Beyond Borders — *Austin, Mary Hunter*
Beyond Borders — *Collinson, Sarah*
Beyond Bounds — *Gish, Robert*
Beyond Burnout — *Cherniss, Cary*
Beyond Calculation — *Denning, Peter*
Beyond Capital — *Meszaros, Istvan*
Beyond Caring — *Chambliss, Daniel F*
Beyond Certainty — *Handy, Charles*
Beyond Chrysanthemums — *Reckert, Stephen*
Beyond Comfort Zones in Multiculturalism
   — *Jackson, Sandra*
Beyond Confrontation — *Hauss, Charles*
Beyond Cuba — *Einaudi, Luigi*
Beyond Discipline — *Kohn, Alfie*
Beyond Document — *Warren, Charles*
Beyond Don't — *Danica, Elly*
Beyond Eurocentrism — *Gran, Peter*
Beyond Feminism — *Murphy, Cornelius F, Jr.*
Beyond Formalism — *Rosenberg, Jay F*
Beyond Fragments — *West, Linden*
y Beyond Gay or Straight — *Clausen, Jan*
Beyond Growth — *Daly, Herman E*
Beyond HTML — *Harpinski, Richard*
Beyond Humanity — *Paul, Gregory S*
Beyond Ice, Beyond Death — *McCall, Thomas*
Beyond Identity Politics — *Anner, John*
Beyond Imagination — *Grafstein, Jerry S*
Beyond Individualism — *Crittenden, Jack*
Beyond Integration — *Bryant, Doris*
Beyond Labor's Veil — *Weir, Robert E*
Beyond Left and Right — *Giddens, Anthony*
Beyond Left and Right — *Horowitz, David A*
Beyond Liberation and Excellence — *Purpel, David E*
Beyond Memory — *Dorfman, Len*
Beyond Microfoundations — *Colander, David C*
Beyond Missionaries — *Hallum, Anne Motley*
Beyond NIMBY — *Rabe, Barry G*
Beyond Ontological Blackness — *Anderson, Victor*
Beyond Peace — *Bowker, Robert*
Beyond Piety — *Gilbert-Rolfe, Jeremy*
Beyond Praetorianism — *Millett, Richard L*
Beyond Prejudice — *Pluhar, Evelyn B*
Beyond Pro-Life and Pro-Choice — *Rudy, Kathy*
Beyond Progress — *De Santis, Hugh*
y Beyond Providence — *Schnur, Steven*
Beyond Queer — *Bawer, Bruce*
y Beyond Ragnarok — *Reichert, Mickey Zucker*
Beyond Recognition — *Pearson, Ridley*
Beyond Reengineering — *Hammer, Michael*
Beyond Representation — *Eldridge, Richard*
Beyond Rhetoric and Realism in Economics
   — *Boylan, Thomas A*
Beyond Rio — *Ahmed, Iftikhar*
y Beyond Safe Boundaries — *Sacks, Margaret*
Beyond Science — *Polkinghorne, John*
Beyond Silent Spring — *Van Emden, Helmut Fritz*
Beyond Sovereignty — *Elkins, David J*
Beyond Sovereignty — *Farer, Tom*
Beyond Star Trek — *Crimmins, Cathy*
Beyond Subsistence — *Duke, Philip*
Beyond Success — *Kuhn, James W*
Beyond Superstructuralism — *Harland, Richard*
Beyond Survival — *Bina, Cyrus*
Beyond Suspicion — *Chenetier, Marc*
Beyond the American Revolution — *Young, Alfred E*
Beyond the Ark — *Weeks, W William*
Beyond the Basilica — *Emmett, Chad F*
Beyond the Beyond — *Goldberg, Lee*
Beyond the Borders — *Howard, Robert E*
Beyond the Boundaries — *French, Jackie*
Beyond the Broker State — *Bean, Jonathan J*
y Beyond the Burning Time — *Lasky, Kathryn*
Beyond the Classroom — *Sealts, Merton M, Jr.*
Beyond the Classroom — *Steinberg, Laurence*
Beyond the Conscious Mind — *Blakeslee, Thomas R*
Beyond the Double Bind — *Jamieson, Kathleen Hall*

Beyond the East Asian Miracle — *Ohno, Izumi*
r Beyond the Fantastic — *Mosquera, Gerardo*
Beyond the Flower — *Chicago, Judy*
Beyond the Front Line — *Geraghty, Tony*
Beyond the Frontier — *Thompson, E P*
Beyond the Great Story — *Berkhofer, Robert F, Jr.*
Beyond the Great Wall — *Gaubatz, Piper Rae*
y Beyond the Hanging Wall — *Douglass, Sara*
r Beyond the Hill — *Borders, Rebecca*
Beyond the Horizon — *Darko, Amma*
Beyond the Liberal Consensus — *Morgan, Ivan W*
Beyond the Limits — *Allison, Stacy*
Beyond the Looking Glass — *Downs, Alan*
Beyond the Melting Pot — *Glazer, Nathan*
y Beyond the Mississippi — *Herb, Angela M*
Beyond the Moon Cookbook — *Callan, Ginny*
Beyond the Muse of Memory — *Lieberman, Laurence*
Beyond the Myths — *Phillips, Shelley*
Beyond the Next Wave — *Peters, Glen*
y Beyond the Orchid House — *Harris, Ruth Elwin*
Beyond the Pale — *Dykewomon, Elana*
Beyond the Printed Word — *Lochead, Richard*
Beyond the Provinces — *Staines, David*
c Beyond the Rainbow Warrior — *Morpurgo, Michael*
Beyond the Red Notebook — *Barone, Dennis*
Beyond the Rhetorical Presidency — *Medhurst, Martin J*
Beyond the Rodney King Story — *Ogletree, Charles J*
Beyond the Shroud — *Hautala, Rick*
Beyond the Stars — *Eisenstein, Sergei*
Beyond the Stars. Vol. 5 — *Loukides, Paul*
Beyond the Symbol Model — *Stewart, John Robert, 1941-*
Beyond the Third Dimension — *Banchoff, Thomas F*
Beyond the Visible Terrain — *Hagerty, Donald J*
Beyond the Warming — *Milne, Antony*
Beyond the Water's Edge — *Snow, Donald M*
y Beyond the Western Sea. Bk. 1 — *Avi*
y Beyond the Western Sea. Bk. 2 — *Avi*
y Beyond the Western Sea. Bks. 1-2 — *Avi*
Beyond the Whiteness of Whiteness — *Lazarre, Jane*
Beyond the Wild Blue — *Boyne, Walter J*
Beyond the Word — *Theall, Donald F, 1947-*
Beyond Top Secret — *Good, Timothy*
Beyond Tracking — *Pool, Harbison*
Beyond Training and Development — *Rothwell, William J*
Beyond Translation — *Becker, A L*
Beyond Trout — *Reynolds, Barry*
Beyond Uhura — *Nichols, Nichelle*
Beyond Urban Bias in Africa — *Becker, Charles M*
Beyond Westphalia? — *Lyons, Gene Martin*
c Beyond Worlds (Illus. by Patrick K Luzadder) — *Marsh, Valerie*
BFGoodrich: Tradition and Transformation 1870-1995 — *Blackford, Mansel G*
r The BFI Companion to Horror — *Newman, Kim*
r BFI Film and Television Handbook 1996
r BHA: Bibliography of the History of Art 1996. Electronic Media Version
r BHA: Bibliography of the History of Art: Subject Headings
r Bhutan — *Pommaret-Imaeda, Francoise*
The Bianchi of 1399 — *Bornstein, Daniel Ethan*
The Bible and the Literary Critic — *Wilder, Amos N*
The Bible: Authorised King James Version — *Bible. English. Authorized. 1997*
r Bible Baby Names — *Diamant, Anita*
The Bible for Children — *Bottigheimer, Ruth B*
The Bible in Modern Culture — *Harrisville, Roy A*
Bible Stories for Adults — *Morrow, James*
c Bible Stories: Old Testament — *Fidge, Louis*
The Bible through the Ages — *Reader's Digest*
Biblical Commentaries from the Canterbury School of Theodore and Hadrian — *Bischoff, Bernhard*
The Biblical Drama of Medieval Europe — *Muir, Lynette R*
r Biblical Epics — *Babington, Bruce*
Biblical Ethics and Homosexuality — *Brawley, Robert L*
The Biblical Flood — *Young, Davis A*
c Biblical Sites — *Bowsher, Julian*
Biblical Studies — *Boadt, Lawrence*
c Biblical Times (Illus. by Michael Welply) — *Mason, Antony*
Biblical Women Unbound — *Rosen, Norma*
p Biblio
Bibliofilos Espanoles Desde Sus Origenes Hasta Los Albores Del Siglo XX — *Sanchez Mariana, Manuel*
r Bibliografia General De Ramon Del Valle-Inclan — *Serrano Alonso, Javier*

r Bibliografie Van De Geschiedenis Van De Kartografie Van De Nederlanden — *Krogt, Peter Van Der*
r Bibliographia Kleschiana — *Otto, Karl F*
r Bibliographia Medica Hispanica 1475-1950. Vols. 2, 4, 8, 9 — *Lopez Pinero, Jose Maria*
r A Bibliographic Guide to the History of Computer Applications 1950-1990 — *Cortada, James W*
r Bibliographic Index 1938-
r A Bibliographical Guide to the Study of Western American Literature. 2nd Ed. — *Etulain, Richard W*
r Bibliographie Analytique Des Ecrits Relatifs A Voltaire 1966-1990 — *Spear, Frederick A*
r Bibliographie Courante Archivistique — *Nijssen, Rombout*
r Bibliographie Des Traites De Savoir-Vivre En Europe Du Moyen Age A Nos Jours. Vols. 1-2 — *Montandon, Alain*
r Bibliographies for Biblical Research. Vol. 3 — *Mills, Watson E*
r Bibliographies in American History — *Beers, Henry Putney*
r Bibliographies in American History 1942-1978 — *Beers, Henry Putney*
r A Bibliography for History, History Curatorship and Museums — *Kavanagh, Gaynor*
r A Bibliography of African Literatures — *Limb, Peter*
r A Bibliography of American Autobiographies — *Kaplan, Louis*
r A Bibliography of American Literature: A Selective Index — *Winship, Michael*
r Bibliography of American Literature: Epitome — *Winship, Michael*
r A Bibliography of Bertrand Russell. Vols. 1-3 — *Blackwell, Kenneth*
r A Bibliography of British History 1914-1989 — *Robbins, Keith*
r Bibliography of Colorado Mining History — *Smith, Arthur E, Jr.*
r A Bibliography of Florida. Vol. 2 — *Servies, James A*
r A Bibliography of Labor History in Newsfilm. Vols. 1-4 — *Fauss, Richard*
r A Bibliography of Oil and Gas Law and Policy 1984-1995 — *Christie, Katherine M*
r Bibliography of Printed Works on London History to 1939 — *Creaton, Heather*
r A Bibliography of Salon Criticism in Paris from the Ancien Regime to the Restoration 1699-1827 — *McWilliam, Neil*
r A Bibliography of Salon Criticism in Paris from the July Monarchy to the Second Republic 1831-1851 — *McWilliam, Neil*
r Bibliography of Science Fiction, Fantasy, and Horror 1960-1993 — *Pastourmatzi, Domna*
r Bibliography of Sources in Christianity and the Arts — *Kari, Daven Michael*
r A Bibliography of the Caribbean — *Goslinga, Marian*
r Bibliography of the Septuagint — *Dogniez, Cecile*
r Bibliography of the Soviet Union, Its Predecessors and Successors — *Schaffner, Bradley L*
r La Biblioteca Antica Dell'Osservatorio Ximeniano. Vols. 1-2 — *Guerrini, M*
r Biblioteca De Catalunya — *Mundo, Anscario M*
La Biblioteca Di Un Neoclassico — *Errani, Paola*
Biblioteche Italiane Del Cinquecento Tra Riforma E Controriforma — *Rozzo, Ugo*
r Bibliotheca Americana. Vols. 1-29 — *Sabin, Joseph*
r Bibliotheca Calviniana. Vol. 2 — *Peter, Rodolphe*
r Bibliotheca Lavoisieriana — *Beretta, Marco*
r Bibliotheque Et Etat — *Damien, Robert*
Biblische Theologie Als Hermeneutik — *Hubner, Hans*
r A Bibliography of Mineral Law and Policy 1984-1995 — *Christie, Katherine M*
Bicho Raro — *Ampuero, Fernando*
The Bickersteth Diaries 1914-1918 — *Bickersteth, John*
The Bicycle — *Dodge, Pryor*
c Bicycle Safety (Illus. by Penny Dann) — *Loewen, Nancy*
c Bicycling (Illus. by Art Seiden) — *Francis, John*
Bicycling to Utopia — *Day, Peter*
r Bidel: Concordance and Lexical Repertories of 1000 Lines — *Zipoli, Riccardo*
The Biferno Valley Survey — *Barker, Graeme*
c Big and Little (Illus. by Steve Jenkins) — *Jenkins, Steve*
c Big and Small — *Challoner, Jack*
c Big Animals (Ladybird First Explorers)
y Big Annie of Calumet — *Stanley, Jerry*
Big as Life — *Cooper, Rand Richards*
Big Babies — *Kiraly, Sherwood*
The Big Ballad Jamboree — *Davidson, Donald*

c Big Band Sound (Illus. by Andrea Shine) — *Diller, Harriet*
The Big Bang and Other Explosions in Nuclear and Particle Astrophysics — *Schramm, David N*
The Big Bang Never Happened — *Lerner, Eric J*
c The Big Bazoohley — *Carey, Peter*
Big Bets Gone Bad — *Jorion, Philippe*
c The Big Big Sea (Illus. by Jennifer Eachus) — *Waddell, Martin*
Big Blondes — *Echenoz, Jean*
c Big Blue Engine (Illus. by Ken Wilson-Max) — *Wilson-Max, Ken*
c Big Blue Whale (Illus. by Nick Maland) — *Davies, Nicola*
Big Bluestem — *Smith, Annick*
Big, Bold and Beautiful — *Hope, Jackqueline*
c Big Book of Animals — *Hanly, Sheila*
c The Big Book of Beautiful Babies — *Ellwand, David*
r The Big Book of Country Music — *Carlin, Richard*
r The Big Book of Library Grant Money 1996/97
c The Big Book of Nature Projects — *Children's School of Science (Woods Hole, Mass.)*
c The Big Book of Noah's Ark — *Strong, Stacie*
y Big Book of Weirdos — *Posey, Carl*
c Big Boss (Illus. by Anne F Rockwell) — *Rockwell, Anne F*
y The Big Bounce (Adams). Audio Version — *Leonard, Elmore*
The Big Bow Mystery — *Zangwill, Israel*
c Big Boy (Illus. by E B Lewis) — *Mollel, Tololwa M*
y The Big Break — *Hide, Louise*
c Big Brother Dustin (Illus. by Dan Young) — *Carter, Alden R*
c Big Bugs (Illus. by Andrew Tewson) — *Gribbin, Mary*
c Big Cat Dreaming (Illus. by Anne Spudvilas) — *Wild, Margaret*
y The Big Cats and Their Fossil Relatives — *Turner, Alan*
Big Dams and Other Dreams — *Wolf, Donald E*
c Big David, Little David (Illus. by Alan Daniel) — *Hinton, S E*
c Big Dog and Little Dog (Illus. by Dav Pilkey) — *Pilkey, Dav*
c Big Dog and Little Dog Going for a Walk (Illus. by Dav Pilkey) — *Pilkey, Dav*
c Big Dog and Little Dog Visit the Moon (Illus. by Selina Young) — *Young, Selina*
The Big Domino in the Sky and Other Atheistic Tales — *Martin, Michael, 1932, Feb., 2-*
c Big Egg — *Coxe, Molly*
r The Big Emerging Markets 1996
A Big-Enough God — *Maitland, Sara*
Big Fat Lies — *Gaesser, Glenn A*
c Big Fish, Little Fish — *Durant, Alan*
The Big Five — *Savel'yev, Alexsandr' G*
cr The Big Guide to Irish Children's Books — *Coghlan, Valerie*
c The Big Idea (Illus. by Bob Dorsey) — *Schecter, Ellen*
c The Big Katie Morag Storybook (Illus. by Mairi Hedderwick) — *Hedderwick, Mairi*
The Big Kiss — *Huggins, David*
Big Leagues — *Fox, Stephen*
c Big Little Lion (Illus. by Lillian Hoban) — *Hoban, Lillian*
c Big Little Otter (Illus. by Lillian Hoban) — *Hoban, Lillian*
c Big Machines — *Barton, Byron*
Big Man's Barbie — *Stevens, Leonie*
c Big Meeting (Illus. by Dolores Johnson) — *Woodtor, Dee Parmer*
Big Men, Small Boys and Politics in Ghana — *Nugent, Paul*
c Big Ocean Creatures (Illus. by Julian Baker) — *Gribbin, Mary*
Big Picture — *Everett, Percival*
The Big Picture — *Kennedy, Douglas*
Big Picture, Small Screen — *Hill, John*
c A Big Quiet House (Illus. by Susan Greenstein) — *Forest, Heather*
c The Big Red Bus (Illus. by William Benedict) — *Hindley, Judy*
Big Red Tequila — *Riordan, Rick*
c Big Rig — *Bingham, Caroline, 1962-*
c Big, Scary Wolf — *Stevenson, Harvey*
The Big Show — *Olbermann, Keith*
The Big Sky — *Guthrie, A B, Jr.*
Big Sky Country — *Melford, Michael*
The Big Sleep (Gould). Audio Version — *Chandler, Raymond*
c Big Squeak, Little Squeak (Illus. by Kevin O'Malley) — *Kraus, Robert*

Big Story — *Braestrup, Peter*
The Big Ten — *Garten, Jeffrey E*
Big-Time Shakespeare — *Bristol, Michael D*
c Big Trucks (Illus. by Julian Baker) — *Gribbin, Mary*
c The Big-Wide-Mouthed Toad-Frog and Other Stories (Illus. by Sue Williams) — *Medicott, Mary*
c Big Wind Coming! (Illus. by Cedric Lucas) — *English, Karen*
c Big Words for Little Scientists (Illus. by Bruce McNally) — *Albee, Sarah*
c Big Yellow Taxi — *Wilson-Max, Ken*
Bigger Economies, Smaller Governments — *Glade, William*
c The Biggest Animal on Land — *Fowler, Allan*
Biggest Elvis — *Kluge, P F*
c The Biggest Frog in Australia (Illus. by Susan L Roth) — *Roth, Susan L*
c The Biggest Horse I Ever Did See (Illus. by Claire Ewart) — *Couture, Susan Arkin*
c Biggest Joke Book in the World — *Rissinger, Matt*
Biggie and the Mangled Mortician — *Bell, Nancy*
Biggie and the Poisoned Politician — *Bell, Nancy*
y Bigmama Didn't Shop at Woolworth's — *Nash, Sunny*
Bij Gelegenheid — *Mulisch, Harry*
y Bijapur — *Dalkey, Kara*
Bike Boys, Drag Queens and Superstars — *Suarez, Juan A*
Bike Cult — *Perry, David B*
p Bike Culture Quarterly
c Biking: An Outdoor Adventure Handbook — *McManners, Hugh*
Bildkatalog Der Skulpturen Des Vatikanischen Museums. Vol. 1, Pts. 1-3
Biliary and Pancreatic Ductal Epithelia — *Sirica, Alphonse E*
Bilingual Education — *Moraes, Marcia*
The Bilingual Lexicon — *Schreuder, Robert*
c Bill — *Reaver, Chap*
Bill James' Guide to Baseball Managers from 1870 to Today — *James, Bill, 1949-*
c Bill Pickett: African-American Rodeo Star — *Sanford, William R*
c Bill Pickett: Rodeo-Ridin' Cowboy (Illus. by Brian Pinkney) — *Pinkney, Andrea Davis*
Bill Viola: Venice Biennale 1995 — *Zeitlin, Marilyn A*
r The Billboard Book of Number One Albums — *Rosen, Craig*
r The Billboard Book of Top 40 Albums. 3rd Ed. — *Whitburn, Joel*
r The Billboard Book of Top 40 Hits. 6th Ed. — *Whitburn, Joel*
r Billboard's Hottest Hot 100 Hits. Rev. Ed. — *Bronson, Fred*
Billie Holiday — *Nicholson, Stuart*
y Billie Holiday: The Tragedy and Triumph of Lady Day — *Gourse, Leslie*
Billie Whitelaw...Who He? — *Whitelaw, Billie*
y The Billion Dollar Boy — *Sheffield, Charles*
Billions and Billions — *Sagan, Carl*
Billy: A Personal Look at the World's Best-Loved Evangelist — *Wirt, Sherwood Eliot*
Billy and Girl — *Leby, Deborah*
c Billy and the Barglebogle (Illus. by Peter Utton) — *Camp, Lindsay*
y Billy and the Bearman — *Poulsen, David A*
c Billy Beast (Illus. by Arthur Robins) — *Anholt, Laurence*
Billy Devorss: The Classic Pin-Ups — *Steine, Kent*
Billy Gashade — *Estleman, Loren D*
Billy in Love — *Kotker, Norman*
c Billy Lazroe and the King of the Sea (Illus. by Michael Steirnagle) — *Kimmel, Eric A*
Billy Sunday — *Jones, Rod, 1953-*
Billy Tea and Sand Ballet — *Stein, Clarissa*
c Billy the Ghost and Me (Illus. by Roger Roth) — *Greer, Gery*
Billy the Kid: His Life and Legend — *Tuska, Jon*
Billy Wilder — *Dick, Bernard F*
c Billy's Boots (Illus. by Anthea Sieveking) — *MacKinnon, Debbie*
c Billy's Drift — *Ashton, Charles*
c Bimmi Finds a Cat (Illus. by James Ransome) — *Stewart, Elisabeth J*
c Bindi — *Fairbairn, John*
Binding Cultures — *Wilentz, Gay*
Binding Promises — *Slawson, W David*
Binding Up the Wounds — *Standifer, Leon C*
r Bing Crosby: A Bio-Bibliography — *Osterholm, J Roger*
c Bingleman's Midway (Illus. by Barry Moser) — *Ackerman, Karen*

Bioarchaeology of the Stillwater Marsh, Prehistoric Human Adaptation in the Western Great Basin — *Larsen, Clark Spencer*
Biochemical Mechanism in Heart Function — *Krause, Ernst-Georg*
Biochemical Oscillations and Cellular Rhythms — *Goldbeter, Albert*
Biochemistry — *Garrett, R*
Biochemistry and Disease — *Cohn, Robert M*
Biochemistry of Exercise IX — *International Biochemistry of Exercise Conference (9th: 1994: Aberdeen, Scotland)*
Biochemistry of Signal Transduction in Myocardium — *Lamers, Jos. M J*
Biochemistry of Smooth Muscle Contraction — *Barany, Michael*
y Biodiversity (Illus. by William Munoz) — *Patent, Dorothy Hinshaw*
Biodiversity II — *Reaka-Kudla, Marjorie L*
Biodiversity: A Biology of Numbers and Difference — *Gaston, Kevin J*
Biodiversity and Agricultural Intensification — *Srivastava, Jitendra P*
Biodiversity Conservation — *Perrings, Charles*
Biodiversity Conservation in Transboundary Protected Areas — *Breymeyer, A I*
Biodiversity Loss — *Perrings, Charles*
Bioelectrochemistry of Cells and Tissues — *Walz, D*
Bioengineering Approaches to Pulmonary Physiology and Medicine — *Khoo, Michael C K*
Bioethics: A Primer for Christians — *Meilaender, Gilbert*
y Bioethics and High-Tech Medicine — *Sherrow, Victoria*
Bioethics and the Future of Medicine — *Kilner, John F*
Bioethics in Europe — *Rogers, Arthur*
Biofluid Assay for Peptide-Related and Other Drugs — *Reid, Eric*
Biofunctional Membranes — *Butterfield, D Allan*
Biogenic Trace Gases — *Matson, P A*
Biogeochemistry: An Analysis of Global Change. 2nd Ed. — *Schlesinger, William H*
Biogeography of the Reptiles of South Asia — *Das, Indraneil*
The Biographer's Moustache — *Kingsley, Amis*
Biographia Literaria. Vols. 1-2 — *Coleridge, Samuel Taylor*
r Biographical Dictionary of American and Canadian Naturalists and Environmentalists — *Sterling, Keir B*
r Biographical Dictionary of American Labor — *Fink, Gary M*
r Biographical Dictionary of American Newspaper Columnists — *Riley, Sam G*
yr A Biographical Dictionary of Artists. Rev. Ed.
r Biographical Dictionary of European Labor Leaders. Vols. 1-2
r A Biographical Dictionary of Film. 3rd Ed. — *Thomson, David*
r Biographical Dictionary of the History of Technology — *Day, Lance*
r Biographical Dictionary of the United States Secretaries of the Treasury 1789-1995 — *Katz, Bernard S*
r Biographical Dictionary of Transcendentalism — *Mott, Wesley T*
r Biographical Dictionary of Twentieth-Century Philosophers — *Brown, Stuart*
yr Biographical Dictionary of World War II — *Boatner, Mark Mayo*
r The Biographical Dictionary of World War II Generals and Flag Officers — *Ancell, R Manning*
yr The Biographical Directory of Native American Painters — *Lester, Patrick D*
r A Biographical Handbook of Hispanics and United States Film — *Keller, Gary D*
r The Biographical History of Baseball — *Dewey, Donald*
r Biographical Index to Artists in Canada — *McMann, Evelyn De R*
Biographies of Books — *Barbour, James*
p Biography
r Biography and Genealogy Master Index. 2nd Ed., Vols. 1-8. Book and Electronic Media Version
r Biography Database 1680-1830. Electronic Media Version
Biography of the Blind — *Wilson, James, 1779-*
The Biography of Thomas Lang — *Buckley, J*
cr Biography Today: Profiles of People of Interest to Young Readers

cr Biography Today: Scientists and Inventors Series. Vol. 1
Biohazardous Waste — *Turnberg, Wayne L*
Bioindicator Systems for Soil Pollution — *Straalen, N M Van*
Bioinorganic Chemistry — *Kaim, Wolfgang*
Biological and Environmental Chemistry of DMSP and Related Sulfonium Compounds — *Kiene, Ronald P*
r Biological Aspects of Alcoholism — *Tabakoff, Boris*
y Biological Consequences of Global Climate Change — *Ennis, Christine A*
Biological Mechanisms and Perinatal Exposure to Drugs — *Thadani, Pushpa V*
Biological Membranes — *Merz, Kenneth M, Jr.*
Biological Psychiatry. 2nd Ed. — *Trimble, Michael R*
Biological Psychology — *Rosenzweig, Mark R*
Biological Reactive Intermediates V — *International Symposium on Biological Reactive Intermediates (5th: 1995: Munich, Germany)*
Biological Recording in the United Kingdom. Vols. 1-2 — *Burnett, John*
The Biological Standard of Living in Europe and America 1700-1900 — *Komlos, John*
The Biological Standard of Living on Three Continents — *Komlos, John*
Biological Structure and Dynamics. Vols. 1-2 — *Sarma, R H*
r The Biological Universe — *Dick, Steven J*
Biologically Based Technologies for Pest Control
Biologically Informed Psychotherapy for Depression — *Shuchter, Stephen R*
Biologists under Hitler — *Deichmann, Ute*
Biology. 4th Ed. — *Raven, Peter H*
Biology. 5th Ed. — *Mader, Sylvia S*
Biology and Conservation of Sea Turtles. Rev. Ed. — *World Conference on Sea Turtle Conservation (1979: Washington, D.C.)*
Biology and Physiology of the Blood-Brain Barrier — *Couraud, Pierre-Oliver*
Biology and Social Thought 1850-1914 — *Bowler, Peter J*
Biology and Society — *Matthen, Mohan*
Biology for Beginners — *McCord, Wilson*
The Biology of Disease Vectors — *Beaty, Barry J*
The Biology of Nitric Oxide. Pt. 5 — *International Meeting on the Biology of Nitric Oxide (4th: 1995: Amelia Island, FL)*
The Biology of Rocky Shores — *Little, Colin*
Biology of the Invertebrates. 3rd Ed. — *Pechenik, Jan A*
The Biology of Xenopus — *Tinsley, R C*
Biology Takes Form — *Nyhart, Lynn K*
Biomaterials Science — *Ratner, Buddy D*
Biomedical Applications of Spectroscopy — *Clark, R J H*
Biomedical Functions and Biotechnology of Natural and Artificial Polymers — *Yalpani, Manssur*
Biomimicry: Innovation Inspired by Nature — *Benyus, Janine M*
The Biophilia Hypothesis — *Kellert, Stephen R*
Biopiracy: The Plunder of Nature and Knowledge — *Shiva, Vandana*
Biopsy Diagnosis in Rheumatic Diseases — *Lie, J T*
Bioremediation of Hazardous Wastes — *United States. Environmental Protection Agency. Office of Research and Development. Biosystems Technology Development Program*
The BIOS Companion — *Croucher, Phil*
Biosensors: An Introduction — *Eggins, Brian R*
Biosociology: An Emerging Paradigm — *Walsh, Anthony*
p Biospectroscopy
Biostatistics: A Methodology for the Health Sciences — *Fisher, Lloyd D*
Biotechnical and Soil Bioengineering Slope Stabilization — *Gray, Donald H*
c Biotechnology — *Wells, Donna*
Biotechnology: A Laboratory Course. 2nd Ed. — *Becker, Jeffrey M*
Biotechnology: A Multi-Volume Comprehensive Treatise. 2nd Ed., Vol. 6 — *Roehr, M*
r Biotechnology Abstracts. Electronic Media Version
Biotechnology and Biopharmaceutical Manufacturing, Processing, and Preservation — *Avis, Kenneth E*
Biotechnology Regulation — *Miller, Henry I*
Biotechnology: Science, Engineering, and Ethical Challenges for the Twenty-First Century — *Rudolph, Frederick B*
Biotechnology Unzipped — *Grace, Eric S*

Title Index

Biotic Recovery from Mass Extinction Events — *Hart, M B*

Bird Brains — *Savage, Candace*

y Bird by Bird (Lamott). Audio Version — *Lamott, Anne*

Bird Dog — *Reed, Philip*

y Bird (Eyewitness Virtual Reality Series). Electronic Media Version

Bird Girl and the Man Who Followed the Sun — *Wallis, Velma*

y The Bird in the Waterfall — *Dennis, Jerry*

Bird-Self Accumulated — *Judson, Don*

Bird Song — *Catchpole, C K*

p Bird Watcher's Digest

r Birder's Dictionary — *Cox, Randall*

r A Birder's Guide to Florida. 4th Ed. — *Pranty, Bill*

p Birder's World

The Birdhouse — *Schine, Cathleen*

c Birdie's Lighthouse (Illus. by Kimberly Bulcken Root) — *Hopkinson, Deborah*

r Birding — *Forshaw, James Michael*

c Birdman — *Novak, Jiri Tibor*

p Birds and Blooms

c Birds Conquer the Sky (Illus. by Miriam Ferron) — *Llamas, Andreu*

r Birds in Europe — *Tucker, Graham M*

The Birds in Langfoots's Belfry — *Zech, Paul*

c Birds in the Bushes (Illus. by Ralph L Ramstad) — *Dunlap, Julie*

y Birds of a Feather — *Masson, Sophie*

Birds of an Iowa Dooryard — *Sherman, Althea R*

Birds of Brazil — *Sick, Helmut*

Birds of Britain and Europe — *Peterson, Roger Tory*

r Birds of Europe with North Africa and the Middle East — *Jonsson, Lars*

y Birds of Forest, Yard, and Thicket — *Eastman, John*

r The Birds of Greece — *Handrinos, George*

r Birds of Kenya and Northern Tanzania — *Zimmerman, Dale A*

r Birds of New Guinea — *Beehler, Bruce M*

y Birds of North America — *Grove, Noel*

Birds of Prey — *Lynn, Matthew*

Birds of Prey — *Smith, Wilbur*

Birds of the West Indies. 5th Ed. — *Bond, James*

r Birds to Watch 2 — *Collar, N J*

Birds without a Nest — *Matto De Turner, Clorinda*

Birdsong — *Faulks, Sebastian*

r Birnbaum's Canada 97

r Birnbaum's Disneyland — *Birnbaum, Stephen*

yr Birnbaum's United States 97

cr Birnbaum's Walt Disney World for Kids by Kids 1997 — *Passavant, Tom*

r Birnbaum's Walt Disney World without Kids 1997

Il Birraio Di Preston — *Camilleri, Andrea*

Birth and Human Evolution — *Abitbol, M Maurice*

Birth, Marriage and Death — *Cressy, David*

c The Birth of a Humpback Whale (Illus. by Pamela Johnson) — *Matero, Robert*

Birth of a Nation'hood — *Morrison, Toni*

c The Birth of a Whale (Illus. by Janet Skiles) — *Archambault, John*

Birth of a Worldview — *Doran, Robert*

The Birth of Absolutism — *Berce, Yves-Marie*

y The Birth of Black America — *Frank, Andrew*

The Birth of Britain — *Speck, W A*

The Birth of European Romanticism — *Isbell, John Claiborne*

The Birth of Fascist Ideology — *Sternhell, Zeev*

The Birth of Liberal Guilt in the English Novel — *Born, Daniel*

The Birth of Romantic Radicalism — *Spence, Peter*

The Birth of the Beat Generation — *Watson, Steven*

The Birth of the Despot — *Valensi, Lucette*

The Birth of the Museum — *Bennett, Tony*

The Birth of the World as We Know It — *Steinbach, Meredith*

The Birth of Whiteness — *Bernardi, Daniel*

Birth to Death — *Thomasma, David C*

c The Birthday Bear (Illus. by Uli Waas) — *Schneider, Antonie*

c Birthday Bear — *Stickland, Paul*

c A Birthday Cake for Little Bear — *Velthuijs, Max*

c Birthday Flowers — *Kruusval, Catarina*

c The Birthday Party (Illus. by Karin Littlewood) — *Althea*

c A Birthday Present for Daniel (Illus. by Louise Gish) — *Rothman, Juliet*

c Birthday Surprises — *Hurwitz, Johanna*

c The Birthday Swap (Illus. by Loretta Lopez) — *Lopez, Loretta*

c Birthdays! Celebrating Life around the World — *Feldman, Eve B*

Birthpangs of a Nation — *Collymore, George*

r Births, Deaths, and Marriages from El Paso Area Newspapers 1891-1895. Vol. 3 — *Beard, Jane A*

r Births, Deaths and Marriages on California's Mendocino Coast. Vol. 1 — *Lewis, Eugene M*

c Biscuit (Illus. by Pat Schories) — *Capucilli, Alyssa Satin*

c Biscuit Finds a Friend (Illus. by Pat Schories) — *Capucilli, Alyssa Satin*

Bisexual Politics — *Tucker, Naomi*

Bisexuality: The Psychology and Politics of an Invisible Minority — *Firestein, Beth A*

Bishop and Chapter in Twelfth-Century England — *Crosby, Everett U*

The Bishops' Wars — *Fissel, Mark Charles*

Bismarck and Mitteleuropa — *Hayes, Bascom Barry*

Bismuth-Based High-Temperature Superconductors — *Maeda, Hiroshi*

Bisphosphonate on Bones — *Bijvoet, O L M*

Bisphosphonates in Bone Disease. 2nd Ed. — *Fleisch, Herbert*

The Bisses of Valais — *Bratt, Guy*

Bit by Bit — *Gaster, Robin*

Bitahon Leumi — *Tal, Israel*

Biting My Tongue — *Astley, Neil*

Biting the Apple — *Sills, Judith*

Bitter Business — *Hartzmark, Gini*

Bitter Lake — *Harleman, Ann*

Bitter Peaches and Plums — *Jacobs, J Bruce*

Bitter Scent — *Bar-Zohar, Michael*

A Bitter Truth — *Cork, Richard*

Bittersweet Destiny — *Thiessen, Del*

Bittersweet Legacy — *Greenwood, Janette Thomas*

c Bitty Fish. Book and Audio Version — *DeRubertis, Barbara*

c Bizarre Beasts and Other Oddities of Nature — *Ganeri, Anita*

c Bizarre Insects — *Anderson, Margaret J*

Black! — *Cooper, Clarence, Jr.*

y Black Abolitionists and Freedom Fighters — *Taylor, Kimberly Hayes*

The Black Album — *Kureishi, Hanif*

Black Alley — *Spillane, Mickey*

Black Alley (Keach). Audio Version — *Spillane, Mickey*

Black and Blue — *Rankin, Ian*

c Black and British — *Bygott, David W*

Black and Catholic in Savannah, Georgia — *McDonogh, Gary W*

Black and Right — *Faryna, Stan*

c Black and White — *Macaulay, David*

Black and White — *Ownby, Ted*

The Black and White Days — *Scannell, Vernon*

y Black and White Sat Down Together — *Ovington, Mary White*

y Black Art and Culture in the 20th Century — *Powell, Richard J*

y Black Artists in Photography 1840-1940 — *Sullivan, George*

Black Athena — *Bernal, Martin*

Black Athena Revisited — *Lefkowitz, Mary R*

The Black Atlantic — *Gilroy, Paul*

Black Atlantic Writers of the 18th Century — *Potkay, Adam*

The Black Bard of North Carolina — *Horton, George Moses*

c Black Beauty (Illus. by Victor Ambrus) — *Sewell, Anna*

c Black Beauty (Illus. by Lucy Kemp-Welch) — *Sewell, Anna*

c Black Beauty (Jarvis). Audio Version — *Sewell, Anna*

y The Black Bonnet — *Bryant, Louella*

The Black Book — *Keays, Sara*

The Black Book — *Pamuk, Orhan*

The Black Book and the Mob — *Farrell, Ronald A*

Black Box — *Oz, Amos*

Black Business in the Black Metropolis — *Weems, Robert E*

The Black Churches of Brooklyn — *Taylor, Clarence*

Black Communications — *Dandy, Evelyn B*

Black Confederates and Afro-Yankees in Civil War Virginia — *Jordan, Ervin L, Jr.*

Black Corporate Executives — *Collins-Lowry, Sharon M*

A Black Corps D'Elite — *Hill, Richard*

Black Country Elites — *Trainor, Richard H*

y The Black Death — *Corzine, Phyllis*

The Black Death and Pastoral Leadership — *Dohar, William J*

y Black Diamond — *McKissack, Pat*

The Black Diaspora — *Segal, Ronald*

Black Dixie — *Beeth, Howard*

Black Dog of Fate — *Balakian, Peter*

c Black Elephant with a Brown Ear (in Alabama) (Illus. by Bill Traylor) — *Porte, Barbara Ann*

Black Elk's Religion — *Holler, Clyde*

Black England — *Gerzina, Gretchen*

Black Entrepreneurs in America — *Woodard, Michael D*

The Black Envelope — *Manea, Norman*

y Black Explorers — *Gombar, Christina*

c Black-Eyed Susan (Illus. by Emily Martindale) — *Armstrong, Jennifer*

Black Families. 3rd Ed. — *McAdoo, Harriette Pipes*

Black Film, White Money — *Rhines, Jesse Algeron*

Black Flames — *Pearlman, Daniel*

The Black Flower — *Bahr, Howard*

y Black Girl Talk — *Black Girl Talk Collective*

Black Haiti — *Niles, Blair*

Black Hamlet — *Sachs, Wulf*

r Black Heritage Sites — *Curtis, Nancy C*

yr Black Holes (Illus. by Luciano Corbella) — *Couper, Heather*

Black Holes — *Pickover, Clifford A*

Black Holes and Time Warps — *Thorne, Kip S*

y Black Horses for the King — *McCaffrey, Anne*

Black in America — *Reed, Eli*

The Black Infantry in the West 1869-1891 — *Fowler, Arlen L*

Black Intellectuals — *Banks, William M*

Black Jack McEwen: Political Gladiator — *Golding, Peter*

Black Jacks — *Bolster, W Jeffrey*

Black Justice in a White World — *Wright, Bruce, 1918-*

Black Labor White Wealth — *Anderson, Claude*

Black Lamb and Grey Falcon — *West, Rebecca*

y Black Legacy — *Katz, William Loren*

Black Leopard — *Voien, Steven*

Black Liberation — *Fredrickson, George M*

Black Liberation in Conservative America — *Marable, Manning*

Black Liberation/Red Scare — *Horne, Gerald*

Black Light — *Hunter, Stephen*

Black Light (Bridges). Audio Version — *Hunter, Stephen*

Black Lightning — *Saul, John*

r Black List, Section H — *Stuart, Francis, 1902-*

r Black Literature 1827-1940. Electronic Media Version

Black London — *Gerzina, Gretchen*

Black Looks — *Hooks, Bell*

Black Male Deviance — *Lemelle, Anthony J, Jr.*

Black Maps — *Jauss, David*

Black Mayors and School Politics — *Rich, Wilbur C*

The Black Middle Class — *Dennis, Rutledge M*

Black Money — *Macdonald, Ross*

Black Mountain — *Duberman, Martin*

y Black Movements in America — *Robinson, Cedric J*

y Black Narcissus (Blair). Audio Version — *Godden, Rumer*

Black Orchids. Audio Version — *Stout, Rex*

Black Out — *Lawton, John*

c The Black Pearl — *O'Dell, Scott*

The Black Pearl. Vol. 3

Black Power, White Blood — *Andrews, Lori*

The Black Press in Mississippi 1865-1985 — *Thompson, Julius E*

The Black Press in the Middle West 1865-1995 — *Suggs, Henry Lewis*

y Black Profiles in Courage — *Abdul-Jabbar, Kareem*

The Black Progress Question — *Burman, Stephen*

The Black Public Sphere — *Black Public Sphere Collective*

Black Rainbow — *Wendt, Albert*

The Black Reeds — *McMorris, Mark*

p Black Renaissance/Renaissance Noire

y Black Sails, White Sails — *Dubosarsky, Ursula*

Black Saints in a White Church — *Embry, Jessie L*

Black Savannah 1788-1864 — *Johnson, Whittington B*

Black-Scholes and Beyond — *Chriss, Neil A*

Black Sea — *Ascherson, Neal*

The Black Seminoles — *Porter, Kenneth W*

y Black Ships before Troy (Illus. by Alan Lee) — *Sutcliff, Rosemary*

Black Shoes and Blue Water — *Muir, Malcolm, Jr.*

c Black Sky River (Illus. by Dan Andreasen) — *Seymour, Tres*

Black Snow — *Bulgakov, Mikhail Afanas'evich*

Black Soldiers in Jim Crow Texas 1899-1917 — *Christian, Garna L*

The Black Soul — *O'Flaherty, Liam*

c The Black Stallion's Shadow — *Farley, Steven*

The Black Stork — *Pernick, Martin S*

yr The Black Student's Guide to Colleges. 4th Ed. — *Beckham, Barry*

yr The Black Student's Guide to Scholarships — *Beckham, Barry*

r Black Studies on CD-ROM. Electronic Media Version

Black Studies, Rap and the Academy — *Baker, Houston A, Jr.*

Black Sun — *Kristeva, Julia*

The Black Sun — *Williamson, Jack*

Black Swan, White Raven — *Datlow, Ellen*

y Black Taxi — *Hunter, Kendall*

y Black Teachers on Teaching — *Foster, Michele*

r Black Texas Women: A Sourcebook — *Winegarten, Ruthe*

Black Theatre, U.S.A. — *Hatch, James V*

y Black Thorn, White Rose — *Datlow, Ellen*

The Black Underclass — *Darity, William A, Jr., 1953-*

y Black Voices from Reconstruction 1865-1877 — *Smith, John David*

Black Water — *Allyn, Doug*

y Black Water — *Anderson, Rachel*

Black Wealth/White Wealth — *Oliver, Melvin L*

Black Wine — *Dorsey, Candas Jane*

Black Woman, Black Life — *Reed-Gilbert, Kerry*

Black Women and Slavery in the Americas — *Gaspar, David Barry*

Black Women as Cultural Readers — *Bobo, Jacqueline*

Black Women in the New World Order — *Hemmons, Willa Mae*

y Black Women Leaders of the Civil Rights Movement — *Allen, Zita*

Black Women Novelists and the Nationalist Aesthetic — *Dubey, Madhu*

Black Writers Interpret the Harlem Renaissance — *Wintz, Cary D*

Black Zodiac — *Wright, Charles*

Blackbeard and Other Pirates of the Atlantic Coast — *Roberts, Nancy*

Blacked Out — *Fordham, Signithia*

Blackface, White Noise — *Rogin, Michael*

r Blackfoot Dictionary of Stems, Roots, and Affixes. 2nd Ed. — *Frantz, Donald G*

y The Blackgod — *Keyes, J Gregory*

Blackrock — *Enright, Nick*

Blacks and Reds — *Hutchinson, Earl Ofari*

Blacks and Whites in Sao Paulo, Brazil 1888-1988 — *Andrews, George Reid*

c The Blacksmith and Devils — *Brusca, Maria Cristina*

Blackwater — *Ekman, Kerstin*

r The Blackwell Companion to Philosophy — *Bunnin, Nicholas*

r The Blackwell Dictionary of Evangelical Biography 1730-1860. Vols. 1-2 — *Lewis, Donald M*

r The Blackwell Dictionary of Neuropsychology — *Beaumont, J Graham*

r The Blackwell Dictionary of Sociology — *Johnson, Allan G*

r The Blackwell Encyclopedia of Writing Systems — *Coulmas, Florian*

r The Blackwell Encyclopedic Dictionary of Organizational Behavior — *Nicholson, Nigel*

r The Blackwell Guide to Recorded Contemporary Music — *Morton, Brian*

c Bladderworts: Trapdoors to Oblivion — *Gentle, Victor*

Blade Runner — *Jeter, K W*

Blade Runner 2 — *Jeter, K W*

The Blair Agenda — *Perryman, Mark*

The Blair Revelation — *Barratt Brown, Michael*

The Blair Revolution — *Mandelson, Peter*

Blaise Pascal: Mathematician, Physicist, and Thinker about God — *Adamson, Donald*

Blake — *Ackroyd, Peter*

Blake; or The Huts of America — *Delany, Martin R*

Blake's Altering Aesthetic — *Richey, William*

Blake's Prophetic Workshop — *Rosso, George Anthony, Jr.*

Blameless in Abaddon — *Morrow, James*

A Blanc Christmas — *Blanc, Raymond*

c The Blanket — *Burningham, John*

Blankets of Fire — *Werrell, Kenneth P*

Blasphemy — *Lawton, David*

Blasphemy: Verbal Offense against the Sacred, from Moses to Salman Rushdie — *Levy, Leonard W*

Der Blasse Hund — *Boll, Heinrich*

c Blast Off! (Illus. by Melissa Sweet) — *Hopkins, Lee Bennett*

c Blast Off! — *Nielsen, Lee Brattland*

Blast: Vortizismus — *Orchard, Karin*

p Blazin' Auralities

The Blazing Lights of the Sun — *Copioli, Rosita*

Blazing the Trail — *Turner, Victor*

Bleeding Hearts — *Title, Elise*

p Bleeding Velvet Octopus

y Bless the Beasts — *Haber, Karen*

Bless the Pure and Humble — *Malavis, Nicholas George*

Bless the Thief — *Wall, Alan*

Blessed among Women — *Sparrow, Scott*

Blessed Assurance — *Heriot, M Jean*

A Blessed Death — *Lachnit, Carroll*

Blessed Is the Fruit — *Antoni, Robert*

y A Blessing in Disguise — *Tate, Eleanore E*

The Blessing of the Animals — *Gonzalez, Philip*

A Blessing to Each Other — *Bernardin, Joseph Louis*

Blessings in Disguise — *Guinness, Alec*

Blighty: British Society in the Era of the Great War — *De Groot, Gerard J*

Blind Bitter Happiness — *Mars-Jones, Adam*

Blind Faith — *Pella, Judith*

Blind Messiah — *Krakofsky, Shel*

Blind Pursuit — *Jones, Matthew F*

Blind Spot — *Barrow, Adam*

The Blind Spot — *Hall, Austin*

The Blind Swimmer — *Lux, Thomas*

Blind Watchers of the Sky — *Kolb, Rocky*

The Blind Watchmaker — *Dawkins, Richard*

Blindsight — *Guibert, Herve*

c Blintzes for Blitzen (Illus. by Alice Io Oglesby) — *Okrend, Elise*

Bliss — *Sloan, Bob*

The Blithedale Romance — *Hawthorne, Nathaniel*

y Blitzcat — *Westall, Robert*

y Blizzard — *Francis, Matthew*

y Blizzard — *Westall, Robert*

y The Blizzard of '88 — *Cable, Mary*

Blizzard's Garden Woodwork — *Blizzard, Richard*

y The Block (Illus. by Romare Bearden) — *Hughes, Langston*

Blockade Diary — *Ginzburg, Lidiia*

r Blockbuster Entertainment Movies and Videos. Electronic Media Version

Der Blockierte Wohlfahrtsstaat — *Graser, Marcus*

p Block's Magazine

Blonde with Attitude — *Blackburn, Virginia*

Blondes in Venetian Paintings, the Nine-Banded Armadillo and Other Essays in Biochemistry — *Bloch, Konrad*

c Blood (Illus. by Ian Thompson) — *Sandeman, Anna*

Blood and Honor — *Griffin, W E B*

Blood and Iron — *Friedrich, Otto*

Blood and Milk — *Solwitz, Sharon*

Blood and Oil — *Farmanfarmaian, Manucher*

Blood and Rubles (Murdock). Audio Version — *Kaminsky, Stuart M*

Blood and Treasure — *Frazier, Donald S*

Blood and Volts — *Metzger, Th.*

Blood and Water — *Kurzman, Dan*

Blood Brothers — *Barnes, Steven*

c Blood Brothers — *Morgan, Jill*

Blood Cell Biochemistry. Vol. 7

r Blood Cells: A Practical Guide. 2nd Ed. — *Bain, Barbara J*

Blood Cinema — *Kinder, Marsha*

c Blood Circulation (Illus. by Luis Rizo) — *Llamas Ruiz, Andres*

The Blood Countess — *Codrescu, Andrei*

c Blood Dance — *Cooper, Louise*

A Blood-Dimmed Tide — *Elon, Amos*

y Blood-Feeding Bugs and Beasts — *Kite, L Patricia*

The Blood Is Wild — *MacCaskill, Bridget*

y Blood Lines — *Harrod-Eagles, Cynthia*

Blood Lines — *Rendell, Ruth*

Blood Lines (Anthony). Audio Version — *Rendell, Ruth*

Blood Muse — *Friesner, Esther*

Blood Oath — *Worth, Steven*

Blood of Heaven — *Myers, Bill*

y Blood of My Blood — *Proctor, George W*

y Blood of Our Children — *Wartell, Matthew L*

y Blood of the Fold — *Goodkind, Terry*

Blood of Your Sisters — *Peel, Colin D*

Blood on the Plains — *Vaughan, Robert*

Blood Pact and Other Stories — *Benedetti, Mario*

y Blood Red Sunset — *Ma, Bo*

y Blood Relations — *Lynch, Chris*

Blood Relations — *Watkins-Owens, Irma*

Blood Rites — *Ehrenreich, Barbara*

Blood Road — *Schoppa, R Keith*

Blood Season — *Berger, Phil*

y Blood Sinister — *Rees, Celia*

Blood Sisters — *McGrail, Anna*

Blood Sport — *Jones, Robert F*

Blood Sport — *Stewart, James B*

Blood Substitutes — *Winslow, R M*

Blood Tells — *Saunders, Ray*

y Blood Ties — *Brouwer, Sigmund*

Blood Wedding — *Garcia Lorca, Federico*

Blood Will Tell — *Stabenow, Dana*

y Bloodchild and Other Stories — *Butler, Octavia E*

Bloodhounds — *Lovesey, Peter*

y The Blooding — *Windsor, Patricia*

Bloodline of the Holy Grail — *Gardner, Laurence*

Bloodlines: Odyssey of a Native Daughter — *Hale, Janet Campbell*

Bloodstained Bridal Gown (McDonough). Audio Version — *Oates, Joyce Carol*

c Bloodsuckers — *Knapp, Ron*

Bloodsucking Fiends — *Moore, Christopher*

Bloodworth's Endocrine Pathology. 3rd Ed. — *Lechago, Juan*

The Bloody Ground (Morse). Audio Version — *Cornwell, Bernard*

y The Bloody Red Baron — *Newman, Kim*

Bloody Shame — *Garcia-Aguilera, Carolina*

Bloody Valverde — *Taylor, John McLellan*

y Bloody Waters — *Garcia-Aguilera, Carolina*

Bloom and Blossom — *Swander, Mary*

Bloomberg by Bloomberg — *Bloomberg, Michael*

p Bloomberg Personal

The Blooming of a Lotus — *Nhat Hanh, Thich*

Bloom's Morning — *Berger, Arthur Asa*

r Blooms of Bressingham Garden Plants — *Bloom, Alan*

r Bloomsbury Encyclopedia of Aromatherapy — *Wildwood, Chrissie*

The Bloomsbury Group. Rev. Ed. — *Rosenbaum, S P*

r The Bloomsbury Guide to Women's Literature — *Buck, Claire*

Bloomsbury Recalled — *Bell, Quentin*

p The Bloomsbury Review

r The Bloomsbury Review Booklover's Guide — *Wagner, Patricia Jean*

Blow the Trumpets, Loudly! — *Farlow-Schlerf, Sharrye*

Blow-Up in Quasilinear Parabolic Equations — *Samarskii, A A*

Blow Your House Down — *Barker, Pat*

Blown Away — *Wiltse, David*

Blowup for Nonlinear Hyperbolic Equations — *Alinhac, Serge*

c Blue (Illus. by Zul Mukhida) — *Bryant-Mole, Karen*

The Blue Afternoon — *Boyd, William*

c The Blue and the Gray (Illus. by Ned Bittinger) — *Bunting, Eve*

Blue and White Japan — *Katoh, Amy Sylvester*

Blue Angels--50 Years of Precision Flight — *Veronico, Nicholas A*

Blue Bamboo — *Dazai, Osamu*

The Blue Caterpillar and Other Essays — *Pickering, Sam*

Blue City — *Macdonald, Ross*

Blue Coffee — *Mitchell, Adrian*

y Blue Coyote — *Ketchum, Liza*

y The Blue Door — *Rinaldi, Ann*

The Blue Evening Gone (Steafel). Audio Version — *Stirling, Jessica*

The Blue-Eyed Tarokaja — *Keene, Donald*

Blue Flame — *Kriebel, Robert C*

The Blue Flower — *Fitzgerald, Penelope*

c Blue Frogs — *Campilonga, Margaret S*

Blue Genes — *McDermid, Val*

Blue Geopolitics — *Fisas Armengol, Vincenc*

The Blue Germ. Electronic Media Version — *Swayne, Martin*

The Blue Hammer — *Macdonald, Ross*

y The Blue Hammer (Parker). Audio Version — *Macdonald, Ross*

Blue Heaven — *Kagan, Elaine*

y The Blue Horse (Illus. by Jilly Wilkinson) — *Silver, Norman*

Blue Italian — *Ciresi, Rita*

yp Blue Jean Magazine: For Girls Who Dare

Blue Jelly — *Bull, Debby*

The Blue Laser Diode — *Nakamura, Shuji*

c Blue Lightning — *Russell, Barbara T*

Blue Limbo — *Green, Terence M*

y Blue Lonesome (Ukena). Audio Version — *Pronzini, Bill*

Blue Mars — *Robinson, Kim Stanley*

y Blue Mondays — *Grunberg, Arnon*

c The Blue Monster (Illus. by Christa Unzner)
— *Ostheeren, Ingrid*
Blue on Blue — *Regan, Geoffrey*
Blue Pastures — *Oliver, Mary*
Blue Rhythms — *Deffaa, Chip*
Blue Rooms — *Jerome, John*
c Blue Sky, Butterfly — *Van Leeuwen, Jean*
Blue Sky Dream — *Beers, David*
Blue Streak — *Dooling, Richard*
y Blue Tights — *Williams-Garcia, Rita*
y Blue Train to the Moon — *Hofmeyr, Dianne*
The Blue Wall — *Abel, Kenneth*
c Blue Whales — *Calambokidis, John*
Blue Windows — *Wilson, Barbara*
y Bluebeard's Egg — *Atwood, Margaret*
Bluebells and Nuclear Energy — *Reynolds, Albert B*
Blueberries: A Century of Research — *Gough, Robert E*
c Blueberry Eyes — *Beatty, Monica Driscoll*
y The Bluebird and the Sparrow (Haas). Audio Version
— *Oke, Janette*
Bluebloods and Rednecks — *Anderson, Charles D*
Bluegrass: An Informal Guide — *Smith, Richard D*
Bluegrass Breakdown — *Cantwell, Robert*
r Bluegrass Music Festival: 1996 Guide for U.S. and Canada
Blueheart — *Sinclair, Alison*
Blueprint 4 — *Pearce, David*
The Blueprint for Business Objects — *Fingar, Peter*
Blueprint for Use of Nursing Models, Education, Research, Practice and Administration — *Walker, Patricia Hinton*
Blues All around Me — *King, B B*
Blues and the Poetic Spirit. Rev. and Expanded Ed.
— *Garon, Paul*
The Blues Detective — *Soitos, Stephen F*
Blues for America — *Dowd, Douglas E*
y Blues for the Buffalo — *Ramos, Manuel*
Bluestown — *Becker, Geoffrey, 1959-*
c Bluewater Journal (Illus. by Loretta Krupinski)
— *Krupinski, Loretta*
Blumenfeld Photographs — *Ewing, William A*
Blurred Boundaries — *Nichols, Bill*
Blurred Boundaries — *Schmidt, Klaus H*
Blu's Hanging — *Yamanaka, Lois-Ann*
c The Blushful Hippopotamus (Illus. by Chris Raschka)
— *Raschka, Chris*
r BMA Family Health Encyclopedia. Electronic Media Version
c Bo Jackson — *Kramer, Jon*
The Board Member's Guide — *Bradner, Jeanne H*
r The Boarding School Guide — *Rogg, Carla S*
The Boardman Tasker Omnibus — *Boardman, Peter*
c Boas (Illus. by Dwight Kuhn) — *McDonald, Mary Ann*
c The Boat of Many Rooms (Illus. by Reg Cartwright)
— *Lewis, J Patrick*
Boat People — *Gardner, Mary*
A Boatload of Madmen — *Tashjian, Dickran*
Boats — *Jones, Dilwyn*
c Boats and Ships (Voyages of Discovery)
Bob Dylan: A Life in Stolen Moments — *Heylin, Clinton*
Bob Hope's Dear Prez, I Wanna Tell Ya! — *Hope, Bob*
y Bob Marley — *Dolan, Sean*
c Bob the Dog — *French, Vivian*
c The Bobbin Girl (Illus. by Emily Arnold McCully)
— *McCully, Emily Arnold*
Bobby Jones on Golf — *Jones, Robert Tyre*
Bobby Sands: Writings from Prison — *Sands, Bobby*
c Bobo's Magic Wishes. Book and Audio Version
— *Palazzo-Craig, Janet*
Bocaditos: The Little Dishes of Mexico — *Hearon, Reed*
r Boccaccio in English — *Stych, F S*
Boccaccio's Des Cleres Et Nobles Femmes — *Buettner, Brigitte*
c La Boda: A Mexican Wedding Celebration (Illus. by Andrea Arroyo) — *Van Laan, Nancy*
The Bodacious Kid — *Lynde, Stan*
Bodenlos — *Kirsch, Sarah*
y Bodies from the Past — *Place, Robin*
Bodies in Motion — *Quogan, Anthony*
Bodies in Pieces — *Harter, Deborah A*
Bodies of the Text — *Goellner, Ellen W*
Bodies of Water — *Cash, Rosanne*
The Bodleian Shelley Manuscripts. Vol. 20 — *Shelley, Percy Bysshe*
y The Body — *Colson, Charles*
Body Alchemy — *Cameron, Loren*
Body and Soul — *Hastings, Anne Stirling*

Body and Soul — *Petroff, Elizabeth Alvilda*
The Body and the City — *Pile, Steve*
The Body and the Self (Vance). Audio Version
— *Cole, Jonathan*
The Body and the Song — *Lombardi, Marilyn May*
y Body Count — *Bennett, William John*
The Body Emblazoned — *Sawday, Jonathan*
yr Body Facts — *Brewer, Sarah*
y The Body Farm (Reading). Audio Version
— *Cornwell, Patricia Daniels*
The Body in Late Capitalist America — *Lowe, Donald M*
The Body in Pieces — *Nochlin, Linda*
The Body in the Transept — *Dams, Jeanne M*
The Body Is Water — *Schumacher, Julie*
The Body Language — *Blake, Andrew*
The Body Mutinies — *Perillo, Lucia*
Body of Life — *Alexander, Elizabeth*
The Body of This Death — *Haver, William*
The Body: Photographs of the Human Form
— *Ewing, William A*
Body, Remember — *Fries, Kenny*
Body, Sex, and Pleasure — *Gudorf, Christine E*
The Body Shop — *Berlinski, David*
Body, Soul, and Bioethics — *Meilaender, Gilbert*
Body Speaking Words — *Harrell, Loree*
Body, Subject and Power in China — *Zito, Angela*
Body Trauma — *Page, David W*
Body Work — *Brooks, Peter*
Bodyguards: The World of VIP Protection
— *O'Connor, Richard*
Bodylore — *Young, Katharine Galloway*
The Body's Edge — *Lappe, Marc*
Bodyscape: Art, Modernity and the Ideal Figure
— *Mirzoeff, Nicholas*
BodyVoyage: A Three-Dimensional Tour of a Real Human Body — *Tsiaras, Alexander*
Boeing B-17, B-29 and Lancaster — *Wilson, Stewart*
Boeken In De Late Middeleeuwen — *Hermans, Jos. M M*
The Boer War — *Pakenham, Thomas, 1933-*
y The Bog Spell — *Sackett, Mike*
Bogart — *Sperber, A M*
Bogart: A Life in Hollywood — *Meyers, Jeffrey*
Bogart: In Search of My Father — *Bogart, Stephen Humphrey*
Bogart: In Search of My Father (Whitener). Audio Version — *Bogart, Stephen Humphrey*
y Bogeys and Bandits — *Gandt, Robert*
c The Boggart — *Cooper, Susan*
c The Boggart and the Monster — *Cooper, Susan*
c Bogus — *Sunshine, Linda*
Boheems Glas — *Hamelink, Jacques*
Bohmian Mechanics and Quantum Theory
— *Cushing, James T*
Boiardo's Orlando Innamorato — *Cavallo, Jo Ann*
y Boikie, You Better Believe It — *Hofmeyr, Dianne*
The Bold and the Beautiful — *Waldron, Robert*
Bold New World — *Knoke, William*
c Bolivia — *Pateman, Robert*
Bolivia and Coca — *Painter, James*
The Bolivian Diary of Ernesto Che Guevara
— *Guevara, Ernesto*
The Bolsheviks' German Gold Revisitd — *Lyandres, Semion*
Bolt from the Blue — *Miles, Sarah*
Bolton Abbey — *Woods, Donald*
p Bomb
The Bomb — *Harris, Frank*
y The Bomb — *Taylor, Theodore*
y The Bomb (Guidall). Audio Version — *Taylor, Theodore*
y Bomb Grade — *Freemantle, Brian*
c The Bomb in the Bessledorf Bus Depot — *Naylor, Phyllis Reynolds*
Bomba Drogurilor — *Turlea, Stelian*
Bomba: Tainy I Strasti Atomnoi Preispodnei
— *Pestov, Stanislav*
Bombardier Beetles and Fever Trees — *Agosta, William*
Bombardier Billy Wells — *Shipley, Stan*
Bombay: A Contemporary Account of Mumbai
— *Bjogani, Namas*
Bombay Talkie — *Meer, Ameena*
Bombora — *Bennett, Tegan*
Bonaventure Des Periers: Le Cymbalum Mundi Avec Un Dossier Et Des Textes D'Accompagnement
— *Delegue, Yves*
The Bond Markets of Developing East Asia — *Emery, Robert F*
Bondage to the Dead — *Steinlauf, Michael C*

Bonds and Bondage — *Moffit, Gisela*
r Bond's Franchise Guide. 1996 Ed.
Bonds of Affection — *Bodnar, John*
Bone. Vols. 1-2 — *Smith, Jeff*
y Bone Black — *Hooks, Bell*
y Bone Breath and the Vandals (Montbertrand). Audio Version — *Kehret, Peg*
c Bone Button Borscht — *Davis, Aubrey*
The Bone Collector — *Deaver, Jeff*
The Bone Collector (McCallum). Audio Version
— *Deaver, Jeff*
y The Bone Detectives (Illus. by Charlie Fellenbaum)
— *Jackson, Donna M*
Bone Idle — *Stacey, Susannah*
Bone Marrow Pathology. 2nd Ed. — *Bain, Barbara J*
Bone Metastasis — *Orr, F William*
Bone Morphogenetic Proteins — *Lindholm, T Sam*
Bone Palace Ballet — *Bukowski, Charles*
Bone to the Bone — *Shaham, Nathan*
c Bonechillers: Teacher Creature — *Haynes, B R*
Bones — *Carter, Keith*
c The Bones in the Cliff — *Stevenson, James*
The Bones of Berdichev — *Garrard, John*
y The Bones of Time — *Goonan, Kathleen Ann*
c Bonesy and Isabel (Illus. by James Ransome)
— *Rosen, Michael J*
Bonfire of the Humanities — *Marc, David*
Bong Sac Giai Nhan Tren Duong Bac Va Nam Tien
— *Le, Van*
Bonheur Mais Sur Quel Ton Le Dire — *Atlan, Liliane*
c Bonjour, Lonnie (Illus. by Faith Ringgold)
— *Ringgold, Faith*
c Bonnie's Blue House (Illus. by Kelly Asbury)
— *Asbury, Kelly*
The Bonny Dawn — *Cookson, Catherine*
c Bono and Nonno (Illus. by Judi Lanfredi) — *Levine, Arthur A*
Bonobo: The Forgotten Ape — *Waal, F B M De*
Les Bons Mots — *Ehrlich, Eugene*
r Bonsai in Your Home — *Lesniewicz, Paul*
r Bonsai Survival Manual — *Lewis, Colin*
c Boo! (Illus. by Colin McNaughton) — *McNaughton, Colin*
c Boo and Baa at Sea (Illus. by Olof Landstrom)
— *Landstrom, Olof*
c Boo and Baa in a Party Mood (Illus. by Olof Landstrom) — *Landstrom, Olof*
c Boo and Baa in Windy Weather (Illus. by Olof Landstrom) — *Landstrom, Olof*
c Boo and Baa on a Cleaning Spree — *Landstrom, Olof*
y The Book and the Sword — *Halivni, David Weiss*
The Book Art of Lucien Pissarro — *Urbanelli, Lora*
Book Blitz — *Gaughen, Barbara*
Book Collecting as One of the Fine Arts — *Franklin, Colin*
c The Book Cupboard
Book Discussions for Adults — *Balcom, Ted*
A Book for Midwives — *Klein, Susan*
r The Book Group Book — *Slezak, Ellen*
Book Illumination in the Middle Ages — *Pacht, Otto*
The Book Illustrations of Orlando Jewitt
— *Broomhead, Frank*
The Book in America — *Clement, Richard W*
The Book in the Islamic World — *Atiyeh, George N*
r Book Industry Trends 1995
r Book Lover's Guide to the Internet — *Morris, Evan*
The Book of African-American Women — *Bolden, Tonya*
The Book of American Traditions — *Jenkins, Emyl*
The Book of American Values and Virtues — *Bruun, Erik A*
y The Book of Atrix Wolfe — *McKillip, Patricia A*
The Book of Bread — *Assire, Jerome*
The Book of Candy — *Dworkin, Susan*
The Book of Cerne — *Brown, Michelle P*
The Book of Chuang Tzu — *Chuang-Tzu*
The Book of Color — *Blackburn, Julia*
c Book of Colors — *Chardiet, Bernice*
The Book of Colour — *Blackburn, Julia*
The Book of David — *Eley, Beverley*
The Book of David — *Gelles, Richard J*
y Book of Enchantments — *Wrede, Patricia C*
r The Book of Ephesians — *Klein, William W*
The Book of Eulogies — *Theroux, Phyllis*
r The Book of European Forecasts. 2nd Ed.
The Book of Film Noir — *Cameron, Ian*
A Book of Folklore — *Baring-Gould, Sabine*
c The Book of Foolish Machinery (Illus. by Fred Winkowski) — *Pape, Donna Lugg*
c The Book of Goddesses — *Waldherr, Kris*

The Book of Hyperborea — *Smith, Clark Ashton*
The Book of Ingenious and Diabolical Puzzles
   — *Slocum, Jerry*
The Book of Intimate Grammar — *Grossman, David*
r The Book of Jeremiah — *Thompson, Henry O*
The Book of Jewish Food — *Roden, Claudia*
The Book of Jewish Wisdom — *Neusner, Jacob*
The Book of Job — *Beuken, W A M*
The Book of Job — *Bible. O.T. Job. English. Mitchell. 1992*
The Book of Knowledge — *Grumbach, Doris*
The Book of Lamentations — *Castellanos, Rosario*
A Book of Legal Lists — *Schwartz, Bernard*
The Book of Lies — *Kristof, Agota*
The Book of Light — *Clifton, Lucille*
r Book of Lists for Regulated Hazardous Substances 1996
A Book of Luminous Things — *Milosz, Czeslaw*
The Book of Margins — *Jabes, Edmond*
The Book of Medicines — *Hogan, Linda*
A Book of Memories — *Nadas, Peter*
The Book of Mercy — *Cambor, Kathleen*
A Book of Migrations — *Solnit, Rebecca*
The Book of Monsters — *Flynn, Keith*
Book of Moons — *Edghill, Rosemary*
c Book of Nonsense (Gielgud). Audio Version — *Lear, Edward*
c The Book of North American Owls (Illus. by Jean Day Zalllnger) — *Sattler, Helen Roney*
The Book of Numbers — *Conway, John H*
A Book of Object-Oriented Knowledge. 2nd Ed.
   — *Henderson-Sellers, Brian*
Book of One-Pot Cooking — *Reader, Mary*
r The Book of Outdoor Gardening — *Smith and Hawken*
The Book of Privileges Issued to Christopher Columbus by King Fernando and Queen Isabel 1492-1502. Vol. 2 — *Spain. Sovereign (1479-1504: Ferdinand V and Isabella I)*
r The Book of Revelation — *Muse, Robert L*
The Book of Reykjaholar — *Kalinke, Marianne E*
The Book of Ruth — *Hamilton, Jane*
The Book of Ruth (Winningham). Audio Version
   — *Hamilton, Jane*
A Book of Salvias — *Clebsch, Betsy*
The Book of Secrets — *Vassanji, M G*
The Book of Shadows — *Grace, C L*
y The Book of Shadows — *Nicholls, Stan*
c The Book of Slime (Illus. by Jan Davey Ellis)
   — *Jackson, Ellen*
The Book of Tales by A.B.C. — *Sanchez De Vercial, Clemente*
r The Book of Tequila — *Emmons, Bob*
c Book of the American Colonies (Illus. by D J Simison)
   — *Egger-Bovet, Howard*
c The Book of the Banshee — *Fine, Anne*
The Book of the Body Politic — *Christine, De Pisan*
The Book of the Spider — *Hillyard, Paul*
r The Book of the World — *Kartographisches Institut Bertelsmann*
A Book of Two Halves — *Royle, Nicholas, 1963-*
The Book of Uranus — *Negus, Joan*
r The Book of Visions — *Albery, Nicholas*
The Book of Westerns — *Cameron, Ian*
r The Book of Women Firsts — *Read, Phyllis J*
Book of Words — *Qunanbaev, Abai*
The Book of World-Famous Music. 4th Ed., Rev. and Enl. — *Fuld, James J*
r The Book of World Horoscopes. Rev. and Expanded Ed. — *Campion, Nicholas*
The Book of Yaak — *Bass, Rick*
The Book of Zines — *Rowe, Chip*
The Book Publishing Industry — *Greco, Albert N*
yr Book Scene...Especially for Teens. 4th Ed.
r Book Subscription Lists — *Wallis, P J*
The Book Talker. Vol. 2 — *Bodart, Joni Richards*
c The Book That Jack Wrote (Illus. by Jon Scieszka)
   — *Scieszka, Jon*
p Book Women: A Reader's Community for Those Who Love Women's Words
The Book Your Church Doesn't Want You to Read
   — *Leedom, Tim C*
Bookbinding and Conservation by Hand — *Young, Laura S*
Bookbindings and Other Bibliophily — *Rhodes, Dennis E*
A Booke of Days — *Rivele, Stephen J*
Booked for Murder — *McDermid, Val*
Booknotes: Writers and Their Stories from C-Span's Author Interviews — *Lamb, Brian*
Bookplay: 101 Creative Themes to Share with Young Children — *MacDonald, Margaret Read*

Books and Readers in the Early Church — *Gamble, Harry Y*
Books and Schools in the Italian Renaissance
   — *Grendler, Paul F*
Books Change Lives — *Thompson, Michael S*
Books for Colonial Readers — *Kirsop, Wallace*
yr Books for You. 11th Ed. — *Wurth, Shirley*
r Books in Print 1996-97. Vols. 1-9
The Books of Assumption of the Thirds of Benefices
   — *Kirk, James*
Books of Hours — *Backhouse, Janet*
Books of Hours and Their Owners — *Harthan, John*
Books of Passage — *Perkins, David*
r Books That Invite Talk, Wonder, and Play
   — *McClure, Amy A*
r Books to Build On — *Holdren, John*
Books to Enjoy 12-16 — *Cooling, Wendy*
r Books with Manuscript — *Alston, R C*
The Bookseller — *Cohen, Matt*
Bookshop. Electronic Media Version
c The Bookshop Dog (Illus. by Cynthia Rylant)
   — *Rylant, Cynthia*
c The Bookstore Mouse (Illus. by Gary Lippincott)
   — *Christian, Peggy*
r The BookTalker. Book and Electronic Media Version
r Booktalking the Award Winners 1993-1994
y Bookworms: Great Writers and Readers Celebrate Reading — *Furman, Laura*
c Boom, Baby, Boom! (Illus. by Patricia MacCarthy) — *Mahy, Margaret*
Boom Boom: The Life and Times of Bernard Geoffrion — *Geoffrion, Bernard*
Boom, Bust, and Echo — *Foot, David K*
c Boom-Chicka-Boom (Illus. by Josip Lizatovic)
   — *Weir, Liz*
c Boomer Goes to School (Illus. by Mary Whyte)
   — *McGeorge, Constance W*
Boomerang: Clinton's Health Security Effort and the Turn against Government in U.S. Politics
   — *Skocpol, Theda*
Boon Island — *Roberts, Kenneth*
Boost Energy — *Kenton, Leslie*
Boot: An L.A.P.D. Officer's Rookie Year — *Dunn, William*
Boots and Books — *Croucher, Trever*
c Bootsie Barker Ballerina (Illus. by G Brian Karas)
   — *Bottner, Barbara*
The Bordello Cookbook — *Foxworth, Jo*
Border Beagles — *Simms, William Gilmore*
Border Correspondent — *Salazar, Ruben*
Border Crossings — *Shahar, Lucy*
Border Cuates — *Kearny, Milo*
Border Dance — *Toma, T L*
p Border/Lines
Border Visions — *Velez-Ibanez, Carlos G*
Bordering on Chaos — *Oppenheimer, Andres*
Borderline Personality Disorder — *Horwitz, Leonard*
y Borderliners (Guidall). Audio Version — *Hoeg, Peter*
Borders of Chinese Civilization — *Howland, D R*
Bordersnakes — *Crumley, James*
Borderwork: Feminist Engagements with Comparative Literature — *Higonnet, Margaret R*
Bordism, Stable Homotopy, and Adams Spectral Sequences — *Kochman, Stanley O*
Borel-Laplace Transform and Asymptotic Theory
   — *Yu, Boris*
Borges: Esplendor Y Derrota — *Vazquez, Maria Esther*
Boris Eikhenbaum: Voices of a Russian Formalist
   — *Any, Carol*
Borland Delphi How-To — *Frerking, Gary*
Born at the Right Time — *Owram, Doug*
Born Gay — *Phillips, Jan, 1949-*
Born in Amazonia — *Dabydeen, Cyril*
Born in the Country — *Danbom, David B*
Born in the U.S.A. — *Cullen, Jim*
yr Born This Day — *Nowlan, Robert A*
Born to Be — *Gordon, Taylor*
c Born to Be Wild (Illus. by Steve Bjorkman)
   — *Spinner, Stephanie*
Born to Rebel — *Sulloway, Frank J*
r Born to Shop: Hong Kong. 6th Ed. — *Gershman, Suzy*
r Born to Shop: New York. 6th Ed. — *Gershman, Suzy*
r Borneo: Journey into the Tropical Rainforest. 2nd Ed.
   — *Muller, Kal*
Borneo Log — *Bevis, William W*
Borobudur — *Frederic, Louis*
The Borough — *Cannon, Michael*
c Borreguita and the Coyote (Illus. by Petra Mathers)
   — *Aardema, Verna*
Bose-Einstein Condensation — *Griffin, Allan*

Bosem Mar — *Bar-Zohar, Michael*
Bosnia: A Short History — *Malcolm, Noel*
Bosnia and Herzegovina — *World Bank*
c Bosnia: Can There Ever Be Peace? — *Flint, David*
c Bosnia: Civil War in Europe (Illus. by John Isaac)
   — *Isaac, John*
The Bosnia Elegies — *Oktenberg, Adrian*
Bosnia: Hope in the Ashes — *Manuel, David*
c Bosnia: The Struggle for Peace — *Ricchiardi, Sherry*
The Bosnian Muslims — *Friedman, Francine*
c The Bossy Gallito (Illus. by Lulu Delacre)
   — *Gonzalez, Lucia M*
Boston Confronts Jim Crow 1890-1920 — *Schneider, Mark*
The Boston Dog Lover's Companion. 1st Ed.
r Boston Facts and Figures. 1995 Ed.
The Boston Irish — *O'Connor, Thomas H*
Boston Marathon — *Derderian, Tom*
The Boston Mayor Who Became Truman's Secretary of Labor — *Lapomarda, Vincent A*
p Boston Review
c The Boston Tea Party — *O'Neill, Laurie A*
c The Boston Tea Party — *Stein, R Conrad*
Boswell: Citizen of the World, Man of Letters
   — *Lustig, Irma S*
The Botanical Gardens at the Huntington — *Houk, Walter*
r Botanical Latin. 4th Ed. — *Stearn, William T*
A Botanical Pioneer in South West China
   — *Handel-Mazzetti, Heinrich*
The Botanical World. 2nd Ed. — *Northington, David K*
Botany Bay Document — *Albiston, Jordie*
Both Ends of the Night — *Muller, Marcia*
c Both Sides of the Catflap (Illus. by Liz Pichou)
   — *Brownjohn, Sandy*
y Both Sides of Time — *Cooney, Caroline B*
y Botticelli's Bed and Breakfast — *Pienkowski, Jan*
c The Bottle Imp (Illus. by Jacqueline Mair)
   — *Stevenson, Robert Louis*
A Bottle in the Shade — *Levi, Peter*
Bottled Poetry — *Lapsley, James T*
The Bottom Line — *Amen, Karen*
Bottom Line Personal Book of Bests
c Bottom of the Ninth — *Gottlieb, Dale*
Bottom-Up Review — *United States. General Accounting Office*
The Bottomland — *Humes, Harry*
Boudin to Dufy — *Wilcox, Timothy*
p Boulevard
Boulevard Transportation — *Katz, Vincent*
Boulez and Mallarme — *Breatnach, Mary*
Bouncing Back — *Rivers, Joan*
c Bouncy Lamb — *Church, Caroline*
Bound and Determined — *Castiglia, Christopher*
Bound and Gagged — *Kipnis, Laura*
Bound by Our Constitution — *Hart, Vivien*
Bound Feet and Western Dress — *Chang, Pang-Mei Natasha*
y Bound for Glory — *Candaele, Kerry*
c Bound for Oregon — *Van Leeuwen, Jean*
Bound to Be Free — *Moser, Charles*
Bound upon a Wheel of Fire — *Dippel, John V H*
The Boundaries of Charity — *Newman, Martha G*
The Boundaries of Citizenship — *Spinner, Jeff*
The Boundaries of Faith — *Hirsh, John C*
The Boundaries of Modern Iran — *McLachlan, Keith*
The Boundaries of the State in Modern Britain
   — *Green, S J D*
Boundary Element Technology XI
Boundary Elements XVIII — *Brebbia, C A*
Boundary-Layer Meteorology--25th Anniversary Volume 1970-1995
Boundary Value Problems for Functional Differential Equations — *Henderson, Johnny*
Boundary Wars — *Ragsdale, Katherine Hancock*
The Boundary Waters Wilderness Ecosystem
   — *Heinselman, Miron*
Bounding Approaches to System Identification
   — *Milanese, Mario*
c Boundless Grace (Illus. by Caroline Binch)
   — *Hoffman, Mary*
Bountiful Island — *Damas, David*
The Bounty — *Walcott, Derek*
The Bourbaki Gambit — *Djerassi, Carl*
The Bourgeois Experience. Vol. 4 — *Gay, Peter*
Bourgeois Politics in France 1945-1951 — *Vinen, Richard*
Bourgeois Society in Nineteenth-Century Europe
   — *Kocka, Jurgen*

Title Index

Bovine Spongiform Encephalopathy (BSE) and Creutzfeldt-Jakob Disease (CJD): Recent Developments — *Great Britain. Parliament. House of Commons. Agriculture and Health Committees*

Bowering's B.C. — *Bowering, George*

r The Bowker Annual Library and Book Trade Almanac 1996

The Bowl of Night — *Edghill, Rosemary*

A Bowl of Warm Air — *Alvi, Moniza*

c Bowl Patrol! (Illus. by Marilyn Janovitz) — *Janovitz, Marilyn*

The Bowles Collection of 18th-Century English and French Porcelain — *Spero, Simon*

The Box: An Oral History of Television 1920-1961 — *Kisseloff, Jeff*

c A Box Can Be Many Things (Illus. by Paige Billin-Frye) — *Rau, Dana Meachen*

c Box-Head Boy (Illus. by Christine M Winn) — *Winn, Christine M*

A Box of Secret Thoughts — *Appleby, Stephen*

The Box Social and Other Stories — *Reaney, James*

Boxes and Chests — *Bridgewater, Alan*

y Boy — *Dahl, Roald*

y A Boy and His Bear — *Graham, Harriet*

Boy Clinton — *Tyrrell, R Emmett*

y Boy in Darkness (Illus. by P J Lynch) — *Peake, Mervyn Laurence*

The Boy in the Well — *Epstein, Daniel Mark*

c Boy Soup (Illus. by Loris Lesynski) — *Lesynski, Loris*

c The Boy Who Ate Around — *Drescher, Henrik*

c The Boy Who Ate Words (Illus. by Thierry Dedieu) — *Dedieu, Thierry*

c The Boy Who Longed for a Lift (Illus. by Brian Selznick) — *Farber, Norma*

c The Boy Who Loved Mammoths (Illus. by Richard Wehrman) — *Martin, Rafe*

y The Boy Who Went Away — *Gottlieb, Eli*

c The Boy Who Wouldn't Go to Bed (Illus. by Helen Cooper) — *Cooper, Helen*

c The Boy with the Eggshell Skull — *Robshaw, Brandon*

c The Boy with Two Shadows (Illus. by Jenny Williams) — *Mahy, Margaret*

A Boyhood in the Dust Bowl 1926-1934 — *Rutland, Robert Allen*

Boyopolis: Essays from Gay Eastern Europe — *Persky, Stan*

c Boys at Work (Illus. by Robert Casilla) — *Soto, Gary*

c The Boys from St. Petri — *Reuter, Bjarne*

y The Boys in the Band — *Strasser, Todd*

Boys like Us — *Merla, Patrick*

A Boy's Own Story — *White, Edmund*

The Boys: The Untold Story of 732 Young Concentration Camp Survivors — *Gilbert, Martin, 1936-*

Boys Themselves — *Ruhlman, Michael*

y Boys to Men — *Alan-Williams, Gregory*

The Boys: Triumph over Adversity — *Gilbert, Martin, 1936-*

y Boyz II Men — *Hardy, James Earl*

A Brace of Bloodhounds — *Lanier, Virginia*

c The Bracelet (Illus. by Joanna Yardley) — *Uchida, Yoshiko*

Bradman: An Australian Hero — *Williams, Charles, 1933-*

Bradshaw on the Family — *Bradshaw, John*

Brags and Boasts — *Whitehead, B T*

The Brahms-Keller Correspondence — *Brahms, Johannes*

Brahms, the Four Symphonies — *Frisch, Walter*

y The Brain — *Barmeier, Jim*

c Brain (Illus. by Ian Thompson) — *Sandeman, Anna*

c The Brain and Nervous System — *Parker, Steve*

c Brain Cell (Illus. by Karen Duncan) — *Robb, Jackie*

Brain Droppings — *Carlin, George*

r The Brain Encyclopedia — *Turkington, Carol*

Brain Fever — *Sayers, Valerie*

Brain Imaging in Psychiatry — *Lewis, Shon*

Brain Longevity — *Khalsa, Dharma Singh*

Brain Mapping — *Toga, Arthur W*

Brain Mechanisms and Psychotropic Drugs — *Baskysand, Andrius*

Brain, Mind, and Behavior — *Robinson, David L*

Brain Processes and Memory — *Ishikawa, K*

Brain Theory — *Aertsen, A*

Brainscapes: An Introduction to What Neuroscience Has Learned about the Structure, Function, and Abilities of the Brain — *Restak, Richard*

c Brainstorm! (Illus. by Lois Lesynski) — *Shimkofsky, Wendy Ashton*

Brainstyles: Change Your Life without Changing Who You Are — *Miller, Marlane*

Brakhage Scrapbook — *Brakhage, Stan*

Bram Stoker: A Biography of the Author of Dracula — *Belford, Barbara*

Brand New Cherry Flavor — *Grimson, Todd*

Brandeis on Democracy — *Strum, Phillipa*

Brandenburg — *Meade, Glenn*

r The Brandt History 1854-1994 — *Heck, Vera*

Braque: The Late Works — *Golding, John*

Brasilien Heute — *Briesemeister, Dietrich*

c Brass Button (Illus. by Susan Paradise) — *Dragonwagon, Crescent*

r Brass Music of Black Composers — *Horne, Aaron*

c The Brass Ring (Illus. by Nancy Tafuri) — *Tafuri, Nancy*

Brasseur and Eisler — *Brasseur, Isabelle*

r Brassey's Companion to the British Army — *Makepeace-Warne, Antony*

r Brassey's Encyclopedia of Military History and Biography

r Brassey's World Aircraft and Systems Directory 1996-97 — *Taylor, Michael John Haddrick*

Braudel — *Daix, Pierre*

c Les Bravades (Illus. by Orson Welles) — *Welles, Orson*

c Brave as a Mountain Lion (Illus. by Glo Coalson) — *Scott, Ann Herbert*

c Brave Bear and the Ghosts (Illus. by Charles Reasoner) — *Dominic, Gloria*

c Brave Bessie — *Fisher, Lillian*

c The Brave Little Bunny (Illus. by Catherine Walters) — *Jennings, Linda*

c The Brave Little Tailor (Illus. by Sergei Goloshapov) — *Grimm, Jacob*

c Brave Martha and the Dragon (Illus. by Susan L Roth) — *Roth, Susan L*

c Brave Mary (Illus. by Marilyn Mets) — *Brimner, Larry Dane*

Brave New Families — *Rae, Scott B*

Brave New Schools — *Kjos, Berit*

Brave New World — *Huxley, Aldous*

c The Brave Ones — *Kerins, Tony*

Brave Souls — *Todd, Douglas*

c Bravest Dog Ever: The True Story of Balto — *Standiford, Natalie*

c The Bravest Thing — *Napoli, Donna Jo*

Braving a New World — *Hopkins, MaryCarol*

y Braving the Elements — *Laskin, David*

y Braving the Frozen Frontier — *Johnson, Rebecca L*

c Braving the North Atlantic — *West, Delno C*

y Bravo! A Guide to Opera for the Perplexed — *Scherer, Barrymore Laurence*

c Bravo, Amelia Bedelia! (Illus. by Lynn Sweat) — *Parish, Herman*

y The Braxtons of Miracle Springs — *Phillips, Michael, 1946-*

c Brazil — *Morrison, Marion*

Brazil: Culture and Politics in a New Industrial Powerhouse — *Schneider, Ronald M*

c Brazil: Many Voices, Many Faces — *Galvin, Irene Flum*

The Brazilian Economy. 4th Ed. — *Baer, Werner*

r Brazilian Folk Narrative Scholarship — *MacGregor-Villarreal, Mary*

Brazilian Journal — *Page, P K*

Brazilian Legacies — *Levine, Robert M*

Brazilian Mosaic — *Summ, G Harvey*

The Brazilian Voter — *Mettenheim, Kurt Von*

Breach of Trust — *MacDougal, Bonnie*

y Breach the Watershed — *Niles, Douglas*

c Bread — *Powell, Jillian*

c Bread and Jam for Frances — *Hoban, Russell*

Bread and Roses — *Inglis, Dorothy*

Bread and the British Economy c.1770-1870 — *Petersen, Christian*

Break a Leg, Darlings — *Babson, Marian*

Break It Down — *Davis, Lydia*

Break out of the Box — *Vance, Mike*

y Break Those Chains at Last — *Frankel, Noralee*

y Breakaway — *Yee, Paul*

The Breakdown of Hierarchy — *Marlow, Eugene*

Breaking Away — *Vitullo-Martin, Julia*

y Breaking Barriers — *Archer, Jules*

Breaking Barriers — *Vaporis, Constantine Nomikos*

Breaking Bounds — *Erkkila, Betsy*

Breaking Eighty — *Eisenberg, Lee*

Breaking Faith — *Thomson, Maynard F*

y Breaking Free — *Gaeddert, Louann*

Breaking Free — *Noer, David M*

c Breaking into Print (Illus. by Bonnie Christensen) — *Krensky, Stephen*

The Breaking of Style — *Vendler, Helen*

Breaking Ranks — *Ruggero, Ed*

Breaking the Abortion Deadlock — *McDonagh, Eileen L*

Breaking the Codes — *Shapiro, Ann-Louise*

y Breaking the Fall — *Cadnum, Michael*

Breaking the Glass Ceiling — *Stith, Anthony*

Breaking the News — *Fallows, James*

Breaking the Patterns of Depression — *Yapko, Michael D*

Breaking the Silence — *Takezawa, Yasuko I*

Breaking the Speech Barrier — *Romski, Mary Ann*

Breaking the Ties That Bind — *Honey, Maureen*

Breaking Up America — *Turow, Joseph*

Breakup — *Stabenow, Dana*

r The Breast Book — *Stoppard, Miriam*

Breast Cancer — *Baron-Faust, Rita*

Breast Cancer — *Clorfene-Casten, Liane*

Breast Cancer Survivors — *Springer, Melissa*

r The Breast Sourcebook — *Rosenthal, M Sara*

Breath, Eyes and Memory — *Danticat, Edwidge*

y A Breath in May — *Hogan, Robyn*

c Breath of a Ghost — *Horrocks, Anita*

A Breath of Fresh Air — *James, Erica*

A Breath of Life — *Fishman, Sylvia Barack*

c Breath of the Dragon (Illus. by June Otani) — *Giles, Gail*

Breathe Something Nice — *Hammond, Emily*

The Breathing Book — *Farhi, Donna*

Breathing Each Other's Air — *McNeil, Florence*

y The Breathing Earth — *Massa, Renato*

Breathless: An Asthma Journal — *DeSalvo, Louise A*

Breathturn — *Celan, Paul*

Brecht Unbound — *Lyon, James K*

The Breezes — *O'Neill, Joseph*

c The Bremen Town Musicians (Illus. by Bernadette Watts) — *Grimm, Jacob*

Brendan Prairie — *O'Brien, Dan, 1947-*

c Brer Rabbit and Boss Lion (Glover) (Illus. by Bill Mayer). Book and Audio Version — *Kessler, Brad*

c Brer Rabbit and the Wonderful Tar Baby (Glover). Audio Version — *Harris, Joel Chandler*

Das Breslauer Schultheater Im 17. Und 18. Jahrhundert — *Gajek, Konrad*

r Bret Harte: A Bibliography — *Scharnhorst, Gary*

Brethren of the Net — *Sorensen, W Conner*

Brethren Society — *Bowman, Carl F*

Brett: A Portrait of Brett Whiteley by His Sister — *Hopkirk, Frannie*

The Bretton-Woods-GATT System — *Kirschner, Orin*

Breve Historia Economica De La Cuba Socialista — *Mesa-Lago, Carmelo*

Brew Chem 101 — *Janson, Lee W*

Brew Ware — *Lutzen, Karl F*

r Brewer's British Royalty — *Williamson, David, 1927-*

r Brewer's Cinema — *Law, Jonathan*

r Brewer's Dictionary of Phrase and Fable. 15th Ed. — *Room, Adrian*

r Brewer's Dictionary of Phrase and Fable. Centenary Ed. — *Brewer, Ebenezer Cobham*

r Brewer's Quotations — *Rees, Nigel*

Brewing Up a Storm — *Lathen, Emma*

c Brian Wildsmith's Amazing World of Words (Illus. by Brian Wildsmith) — *Wildsmith, Brian*

c Brian Wildsmith's Puzzles — *Wildsmith, Brian*

y Brian's Winter — *Paulsen, Gary*

Briar Rose — *Coover, Robert*

y Briar Rose — *Yolen, Jane*

y The Bride — *Atkins, D E*

The Bride of Texas — *Skvorecky, Josef*

The Bride Wore Red — *Sethi, Robbie Clipper*

The Bride's Bodyguard — *Thornton, Elizabeth*

A Bride's Passage — *Petroski, Catherine*

Bridge and Structure Estimating — *Nardon, J David*

The Bridge Betrayed — *Sells, Michael Anthony*

Bridge Builders — *National Research Council (U.S.). Office of International Affairs*

The Bridge of Lost Desire — *Delany, Samuel R*

Bridge on the River Kwai — *Boulle, Pierre*

A Bridge to Dialogue — *Rousmaniere, John*

c Bridge to Terabithia — *Paterson, Katherine*

c Bridge to Terabithia (Stechschulte). Audio Version — *Paterson, Katherine*

y A Bridge to Wiseman's Cove — *Moloney, James*

c Bridges — *Oxlade, Chris*

Bridges, Routers, Gateways — *Marney-Petix, V C*

Bridges to Cuba — *Behar, Ruth*

Bridges to Humanity — *Grindal, Bruce*

Bridget Jones's Diary — *Fielding, Helen*

Bridging Japanese/North American Differences — *Gudykunst, William B*

Bridging the Atlantic — *Perez De Mendiola, Marina*

Bridging the Class Divide and Other Lessons for Grassroots Organizing — *Stout, Linda*
y Bridging the Continent — *Smith, C Carter*
Bridging the Gap — *Five, Cora Lee*
Brief Calculus and Its Applications. 7th Ed. — *Goldstein, Larry J*
Brief Collaborative Therapy — *Rudolph, Bonnie A*
Brief Encounters — *Bourne, Stephen*
c A Brief History of Planet Earth — *Alper, Ann Fitzpatrick*
A Brief History of the Presbyterians — *Smylie, James H*
r A Brief History of the Town of Glocester, Rhode Island — *Perry, Elizabeth A*
y A Brief History of Time — *Hawking, Stephen*
A Brief Introduction to Fluid Mechanics — *Young, Donald F*
Brief Introduction to the Study of Theology with Reference to the Scientific Standpoint and the Catholic System — *Drey, Johann Sebastian*
Brief Landing on the Earth's Surface — *Brunk, Juanita*
A Brief Theology of Revelation — *Gunton, Colin E*
Brief Transit — *Gerard, David*
Briefe. Vols. 1-2 — *Scholem, Gershom*
Briefing on Results of the Nuclear Posture Review — *United States. Congress. Senate. Committee on Armed Services*
Briefwechsel Mit Arnold Schonberg, Anton Webern, Alban Berg Und Franz Schreker — *Zemlinsky, Alexander*
y Brigham Young: Pioneer and Mormon Leader — *Sanford, William R*
c Bright and Early Thursday Evening (Illus. by Don Wood) — *Wood, Audrey*
Bright Angel Time — *McPhee, Martha A*
c Bright Christmas (Illus. by Kate Kiesler) — *Clements, Andrew*
Bright College Years — *Matthews, Anne, 1957-*
c Bright Eyes and the Buffalo Hunt (Illus. by Laura Hughes) — *Hughes, Laura*
Bright Galaxies, Dark Matters — *Rubin, Vera*
Bright Knits for Kids — *Bliss, Debbie*
c Bright Lights (Illus. by Jacqueline Rogers) — *York, Sarah Mountbatten-Windsor, Duchess of*
y Bright Messengers — *Lee, Gentry*
Bright Orange for the Shroud (McGavin). Audio Version — *MacDonald, John D*
Bright Paradise — *Raby, Peter*
A Bright Shining Lie — *Sheehan, Neil*
r Bright Star Atlas 2000.0 — *Tirion, Wil*
y Brightness Reef — *Brin, David*
y Brighton Beach Memoirs — *Simon, Neil*
Brigid's Charge — *Lamb, Cynthia*
The Brilliance of Swedish Glass 1918-1939 — *Ostergard, Derek E*
Brilliant Stars — *Moore, Patrick*
The Brimstone Wedding — *Vine, Barbara*
y Bring Back Yesterday — *Sirof, Harriet*
c Bring 'Em Back Alive! — *Arnosky, Jim*
c Bring in the Holly (Illus. by Lisa Kopper) — *Causley, Charles*
Bringers of the Dawn (Marciniak). Audio Version — *Marciniak, Barbara*
Bringing Geographical Information Systems into Business — *Grimshaw, David J*
Bringing Health Care Online
Bringing in the Sheaves — *Higgs, Richard*
Bringing It Home — *Brown, Brenda Lea*
Bringing Peace Home — *Warren, Karen J*
Bringing the Mountain Home — *Campbell, SueEllen*
Bringing the Word to Life. Vol. 2 — *Kent, Michael R*
Bringing Up Girls in Bohemia — *Viewegh, Michal*
Briniskigas Pukes — *Kalnina, Laima*
Brink Road — *Ammons, A R*
Bristol and the Atlantic Trade in the Eighteenth Century — *Morgan, Kenneth*
Britain and America — *Englander, David*
Britain and European Union — *Beloff, Max Beloff, Baron*
Britain and European Unity 1945-1992 — *Young, John W*
Britain and Italy 1943-1949 — *Gat, Moshe*
Britain and Norway in the Second World War — *Salmon, Patrick*
Britain and Poland 1939-1943 — *Prazmowska, Anita J*
Britain and Suez — *Lucas, Scott*
Britain and the Congo Crisis 1960-63 — *James, Alan*
Britain and the Defeat of Napoleon 1807-1815 — *Muir, Rory*
Britain and the Last Tsar — *Neilson, Keith*

Britain and the Origins of Canadian Confederation 1837-67 — *Martin, Ged*
Britain Confronts the Stalin Revolution — *Morrell, Gordon W*
r Britain in Pictures — *Carney, Michael*
Britain in the 1970s — *Coopey, R*
Britain in the World Economy since 1880 — *Alford, B W E*
Britain, Japan, and Pearl Harbor — *Best, Anthony*
Britain on the Edge of Europe — *Chisholm, Michael*
Britain on Your Own — *Maroncelli, Dorothy*
Britain since 1939 — *Childs, David*
Britain, Southeast Asia and the Onset of the Pacific War — *Tarling, Nicholas*
Britain, the Cold War and Yugoslav Unity 1941-1949 — *Lane, Ann*
Britain, the United States and the Mediterranean War 1942-44 — *Jones, Matthew*
Britain's Economic Problem Revisited. 3rd Ed. — *Bacon, Robert*
Britain's Place in the World — *Milward, Alan S*
Britannia's Children — *Castle, Kathryn*
Britannia's Issue — *Weinbrot, Howard D*
r Britannica CD 2.0. Electronic Media Version
cr Britannica CD 97.0. Electronic Media Version
Britische Presse Und Nationalsozialistischer Kirchenkampf — *Huttner, Markus*
British and American Commercial Relations with Soviet Russia 1918-1924 — *White, Christine A*
British and American Responses to the Soviet Invasion of Afghanistan — *Grasselli, Gabriella*
r British Archives. 3rd Ed. — *Foster, Janet*
British Art Treasures from Russian Imperial Collections in the Hermitage — *Allen, Brian*
r The British Atlas of Historic Towns. Vols. 1-3 — *Lobel, M D*
British Business and Protection 1903-1932 — *Marrison, Andrew*
British Business History 1720-1994 — *Wilson, John F*
r British Children's Writers 1800-1880 — *Khorana, Meena*
r British Children's Writers 1914-1960 — *Hettinga, Donald R*
r British Children's Writers since 1960. 1st Ser. — *Hunt, Caroline C*
r The British Cinema Source Book — *Burrows, Elaine*
The British Cinematographer — *Petrie, Duncan*
British Columbia: A Natural History — *Cannings, Richard*
The British Communist Party and the Trade Unions 1933-45 — *Fishman, Nina*
British Cost Accounting 1887-1952 — *Boyns, Trevor*
British Counterinsurgency in the Post-Imperial Era — *Mockaitis, Thomas R*
British Dramatists — *Greene, Graham*
r British Economic and Social History. 3rd Ed. — *Richardson, R C*
British Economic Development since 1945 — *Booth, Alan, Ph.D.*
British Economic Performance 1945-1975 — *Alford, B W E*
The British Economy since 1945 — *Cairncross, Alec*
r British Elections and Parties Yearbook 1995
r The British Electorate 1963-1992 — *Crewe, Ivor*
The British Electricity Experiment — *Surrey, John*
r The British Empire — *Stewart, John, 1952-*
British Entry to the European Community under the Heath Government 1970-74 — *Lord, Christopher*
r British External Airmails Until 1934. 2nd Ed. — *Newall, Alexander S*
British Fighting Methods in the Great War — *Griffith, Paddy*
r British Film Studios — *Warren, Patricia*
British Foreign Policy during the Curzon Period 1919-24 — *Bennett, G H*
British Foreign Policy in an Age of Revolution 1783-1793 — *Black, Jeremy*
British High Politics and a Nationalist Ireland — *O'Callaghan, Margaret*
The British Housewife. Vol. 1 — *Bradley, Martha*
British Imperialism — *Cain, P J*
British Imperialism and Australian Nationalism — *Trainor, Luke*
r British Imprints Relating to North America 1621-1760 — *Simmons, R C*
The British in the Americas 1480-1815 — *McFarlane, Anthony*
The British Labour Party and the German Social Democrats 1900-1931 — *Berger, Stefan*
r The British Literacy Book Trade 1700-1820 — *Bracken, James K*

British Military Planning for the Defense of Germany — *Cornish, Paul*
British Military Spectacle — *Myerly, Scott Hughes*
British Monarchy, English Church Establishment, and Civil Liberty — *Taylor, John A, 1942-*
British Monetary Policy 1945-51 — *Howson, Susan*
The British Motor Industry — *Foreman-Peck, James*
British Multinational Banking 1830-1990 — *Jones, Geoffrey*
British Naval Documents 1204-1960 — *Hattendorf, John B*
British Non-Elite MPS 1715-1820 — *Christie, Ian R*
p The British Philatelic Bulletin
r British Playwrights 1880-1956 — *Demastes, William W*
r British Playwrights 1956-1995 — *Demastes, William W*
British Poetry 1900-50 — *Day, Gary*
British Poetry of the Nineteenth Century — *Gurney, Stephen*
British Politics and European Elections 1994 — *Butler, David*
British Politics and the Spirit of the Age — *Navari, Cornelia*
British Politics and Trade Unions in the 1980s — *Thomsen, Jens Peter Frolund*
British Population in the Twentieth Century — *Tranter, N L*
yr British Qualifications. 26th Ed.
The British Raj in India — *Burke, S M*
r British Reform Writers 1789-1832 — *Kelly, Gary*
British Relations with the Malay Rulers from Decentralization to Malayan Independence 1930-1957 — *Smith, Simon C*
r The British Secret Services — *Davies, Philip H J*
r British Short-Fiction Writers 1800-1880 — *Greenfield, John R*
r British Short-Fiction Writers 1880-1914 — *Naufftus, William F*
r British Short-Fiction Writers 1915-1945 — *Rogers, John Headly*
British Society since 1945 — *Marwick, Arthur*
r British Travel Writers 1837-1875 — *Brothers, Barbara, 1937-*
British Victory in Egypt 1801 — *Mackesy, Piers*
r British Women's History — *Hannam, June*
r British Writers. 3rd Suppl. — *Stade, George*
Broadband Integrated Networks — *Schwartz, Mischa*
Broadband Telecommunications Technology. 2nd Ed. — *Lee, Byeong Gi*
Broadcast News. 2nd Ed. — *Mayeux, Peter E*
Broadening the Front — *Shreedhar, Jaya*
The Broadly Christian Assembly Book — *Self, David*
y Broadway Costumes on a Budget — *Litherland, Janet*
r Broadway, Movie, TV, and Studio Cast Musicals on Record — *Lynch, Richard Chigley*
r Broadway Sheet Music — *Stubblebine, Donald J*
p The Brobdingnagian Times
Brock Biology of Microorganisms. 8th Ed. — *Madigan, Michael T*
c The Broken Blade — *Durbin, William*
Broken Brains or Wounded Hearts — *Colbert, Ty C*
c Broken Bridge — *Banks, Lynne Reid*
Broken Country — *Rawlins, C L*
Broken Covenant — *Arens, Moshe*
Broken Heartland — *Davidson, Osha Gray*
The Broken Hoe — *Iyam, David Uru*
Broken Ladders — *Osterman, Paul*
The Broken Mirror — *Phillips, Katharine A*
Broken Patterns — *Harris, Anita M*
Broken Promise — *Gross, James A*
The Broken Promise Land — *Muller, Marcia*
y The Broken Promise Land (Reed-Bahle). Audio Version — *Muller, Marcia*
y Broken Promises — *Baer, Judy*
Broken Promises — *Mills, Daniel Quinn*
Broken Promises — *Thiesenhusen, William C*
The Broken Seals: Part One of the Marshes of Mount Liang — *Shih, Nai-An*
The Broken Sword — *Cochran, Molly*
Broken Symmetry — *Citino, David*
Broken Symmetry — *Nambu, Y*
y The Broken Tusk (Illus. by Maniam Selven) — *Krishnaswami, Uma*
c The Broken Wheel — *Greenwood, Kerry*
Broken Windows — *Nolan, Patricia*
The Bronski House — *Marsden, Philip*
Bronte — *Hughes, Glyn*
y The Bronte Girls — *Kilworth, Garry*
The Brontes — *Barker, Juliet*
The Brontes: Interviews and Recollections — *Orel, Harold*
The Bronze Age of Southeast Asia — *Higham, Charles*

c The Bronze Bow — *Speare, Elizabeth George*
The Bronze Horseman — *Pushkin, Aleksandr Sergeevich*
The Bronze Screen — *Fregoso, Rosa Linda*
c The Bronze Trumpeter — *Nimmo, Jenny*
y A Brood of Vipers — *Clynes, Michael*
Brook Trout — *Karas, Nick*
Brooklyn! An Illustrated History — *Snyder-Grenier, Ellen M*
c The Brooklyn Bridge (Illus. by Alan Witschonke) — *Mann, Elizabeth*
Brother against Brother — *Halsey, Edmund*
c Brother Anansi and the Cattle Ranch (Illus. by S Von Mason) — *De Sauza, James*
y Brother, Can You Spare a Dime? — *Meltzer, Milton*
Brother Crow, Sister Corn — *Buchanan, Carol*
Brother of Sleep — *Schneider, Robert, 1961-*
c Brother Rabbit (Illus. by Jennifer Hewitson) — *Ho, Minfong*
c Brother Wolf (Illus. by Harriet Peck Taylor) — *Taylor, Harriet Peck*
A Brotherhood of Arms — *Davis, Sonny B*
A Brotherhood of Canons Serving God — *Lepine, David*
Brotherhoods and Secret Societies in Early and Mid-Qing China — *Ownby, David*
y Brotherman — *Boyd, Herb*
Brothers — *Bova, Ben*
Brothers — *Samona, Carmelo*
y Brothers and Sisters — *Sneddon, Pamela Shires*
y A Brother's Blood — *White, Michael C*
c The Brothers Grimm (Illus. by Michael Foreman) — *Grimm, Jacob*
Brothers in Spirit — *Schweitzer, Albert*
Brothers No More — *Buckley, William F*
y Brothers No More (Lawrence). Audio Version — *Buckley, William F*
c Brown Bear, Brown Bear, What Do You See? (Illus. by Eric Carle) — *Martin, Bill, 1916-*
The Brown Derby Restaurant — *Cobb, Sally Wright*
c Brown Honey in Broomwheat Tea — *Thomas, Joyce Carol*
c Brown Honey in Broomwheat Tea (Dee). Audio Version — *Thomas, Joyce Carol*
p The Brown Journal of World Affairs
c Brown Sunshine of Sawdust Valley (Illus. by Bonnie Shields) — *Henry, Marguerite*
Brown v. Board of Education — *Lagemann, Ellen Condliffe*
Browning and Conversation — *St. George, E A W*
Browning's Hatreds — *Karlin, Daniel*
Bruce Chatwin: Photographs and Notebooks — *Wyndham, Francis*
c Bruce Coville's Book of Monsters (Coville). Audio Version — *Coville, Bruce*
y Bruce Lee, Brandon Lee, and the Dragon's Curse — *Hoffman, Charles*
y Bruce Lee: The Tao of the Dragon Warrior — *Chunovic, Louis*
Bruce Nauman — *Benezra, Neal*
Bruce Springsteen: The Rolling Stone Files — *Rolling Stone (San Francisco, Calif.)*
c Bruce the Balding Moose (Illus. by Jonathan Allen) — *Mellor, Corinne*
Bruegel's Peasants — *Sullivan, Margaret A*
Bruise Theory — *Kenvin, Natalie*
y Bruises — *Vries, Anke De*
c La Bruja De Navidad (Illus. by Steven Kellogg) — *Kellogg, Steven*
y Bruno and the Crumhorn — *Dubosarsky, Ursula*
c Bruno Springs Up — *Daigneault, Sylvie*
c Bruno the Carpenter (Illus. by Lars Klinting) — *Klinting, Lars*
c Bruno the Tailor (Illus. by Lars Klinting) — *Klinting, Lars*
c Brush! Brush! Bunny — *Nann, Lizzie*
Brutal Bosses and Their Prey — *Hornstein, Harvey A*
Brutality and Benevolence — *Alves, Abel A*
r Bryan County, Oklahoma Cemeteries. Vols. 1-4
r Bryan County, Oklahoma Prestatehood Marriages July 1902-November 07 — *Ellis, Wanda M*
c Bryce Canyon National Park — *Petersen, David*
BSE: The Facts — *Ford, Brian*
Bu Yao Yue Hui Zhi Yao He Ka Fei — *Zhu, Yi*
c Bubbe and Gram (Illus. by Jane K Bynum) — *Hawxhurst, Joan C*
c Bubble Monkey — *Nann, Lizzie*
c Bubble Monster and Other Science Fun — *Falk, John*
c Bubble Trouble (Illus. by Elena Kuckarik) — *Packard, Mary*
c Bubblegum Bother — *Smith, Wendy*

The Bubbling Cauldron — *Smith, Michael Peter*
The Buchan Papers — *Jones, J D F*
Bucher Und Urkunden Aus Helmarshausen Und Corvey — *Hoffmann, Hartmut*
Buck Leonard, the Black Lou Gehrig — *Leonard, Buck*
Buck Naked — *Burditt, Joyce*
Buckeye Legends — *Katz, Michael Jay*
Bucking the Deficit — *Mackenzie, G Calvin*
Bucking the Sun — *Doig, Ivan*
Buckley: The Right Word — *Buckley, William F*
BuckyWorks: Buckminster Fuller's Ideas for Today — *Baldwin, J, 1933-*
Budapest and New York — *Bender, Thomas*
r Budapest and the Best of Hungary (Frommer's Guides)
Budapest Diary — *Suleiman, Susan Rubin*
The Budd Family — *Grant, Bruce*
c Buddha (Illus. by Demi) — *Demi*
The Buddha and the Christ — *Lefebure, L D*
The Buddha Image — *Krishan, Y*
c Buddha Stories (Illus. by Demi) — *Demi*
Buddhism — *Holmwood, Ruth*
c Buddhism — *Penney, Sue*
c Buddhism — *Prior, Lesley*
y Buddhism: A New Approach — *Clarke, Steve*
Buddhism and Bioethics — *Keown, Damien*
Buddhism and Interfaith Dialogue — *Abe, Masao*
Buddhism Betrayed? — *Tambiah, Stanley J*
Buddhism for Today and Tomorrow — *Sangharakshita*
Buddhism in Chinese Society — *Gernet, Jacques*
Buddhism in Practice — *Lopez, Donald S*
Buddhism without Beliefs — *Batchelor, Stephen*
c Buddhist — *Ganeri, Anita*
Buddhist Behavioral Codes and the Modern World — *Fu, Charles Wei-Hsun*
c Buddhist Festivals — *Erricker, Clive*
Buddhist Saints in India — *Ray, Reginald A*
Buddhist Woman on the Edge — *Dresser, Marianne*
c Buddy Bear — *Stickland, Paul*
y Buddy Concrackle's Amazing Adventure — *McMahan, Chris*
c Buddy Love — *Cooper, Ilene*
c Buddy: The First Seeing Eye Dog (Illus. by Don Bolognese) — *Moore, Eva*
c Budgee Budgee Cottontail (Illus. by Jo Mora) — *Mora, Jo*
Budget Deficits and Debt
Budgetary Decisions — *Kraan, Dirk-Jan*
Budgeting and the Management of Public Spending — *Savoie, Donald J*
Budgets and Markets — *Ilott, Terry*
Bud'te Zdorovi — *Semen, Vasyl*
La Buena Noticia Y Otros Cuentos — *Masliah, Leo*
Buenos Muchachos — *Mendoza, Elmer*
c Buffalo Bill Cody: Showman of the Wild West — *Sanford, William R*
y Buffalo Gals — *Miller, Brandon Marie*
c The Buffalo Jump (Illus. by Bill Farnsworth) — *Roop, Peter*
y Buffalo Nation — *Geist, Valerius*
Buffalo Palace — *Johnston, Terry C*
y Buffalo Soldiers — *Willard, Tom*
c Buffalo Sunrise — *Swanson, Diane*
y The Buffalo Tree — *Rapp, Adam*
The Buffet Book — *Peck, Carole*
Buffett: The Making of an American Capitalist — *Lowenstein, Roger*
Buffon: A Life in Natural History — *Roger, Jacques*
c Bug Boy (Illus. by Betsy Lewin) — *Sonenklar, Carol*
c Bug in a Rug (Illus. by Alan Tiegreen) — *Cole, Joanna*
y Bug Park — *Hogan, James P*
c Bugs at Play — *Carter, David A*
c Bugs at Work — *Carter, David A*
Bugs in the System — *Berenbaum, May R*
c Bugs on the Go — *Carter, David A*
c Bugs That Go Bump in the Night — *Carter, David A*
Build a World Wide Web Commerce Center — *Net.Genesis (Firm)*
Build, Operate, Transfer — *Levy, Sidney M*
Build Your Own Multimedia PC. 2nd Ed. — *Pilgrim, Aubrey*
Build Your Own Pentium Processor PC. 2nd Ed. — *Pilgrim, Aubrey*
r Building a Corporate Internet Strategy — *Maitra, Amit K*
Building a Defense That Works for the Post-Cold War World — *United States. Congress. House. Committee on Armed Services. Defense Policy Panel*

Building a Democratic Political Order — *Plotke, David*
Building a Dream — *Dunlop, Beth*
Building a European Polity? — *Rhodes, Carolyn*
c Building a House with Mr. Bumble (Illus. by John Wallace) — *Wallace, John*
Building a Multimedia Presence on the World Wide Web — *Szuprowicz, Bohdan O*
Building a New Boston — *O'Connor, Thomas H*
Building a Safer Society — *Tonry, Michael*
Building a Win-Win World — *Henderson, Hazel*
Building a Wood-Fired Oven for Bread and Pizza — *Jaine, Tom*
Building a Writing Community — *Freeman, Marcia S*
Building America — *Boyte, Harry C*
Building and Breaking Families in the American West — *Riley, Glenda*
Building and Builders in Hispanic California 1769-1850 — *Schuetz-Miller, Mardith K*
Building and Designing Decks — *Schuttner, Scott*
Building Bridges — *Rausch, David A*
Building Community in Schools — *Sergiovanni, Thomas*
Building Democratic Institutions — *Mainwaring, Scott*
Building Executive Information Systems and Other Decision Support Applications — *Watson, Hugh J*
Building IBM — *Pugh, Emerson W*
Building in Britain — *Satoh, Akira*
Building Maintenance Management — *Chanter, Barrie*
Building Microsoft Exchange Applications — *Krebs, Peter*
The Building of an Empire — *Larebo, Haile M*
Building of Faith — *Browne, John*
Building on Sinkholes — *Sowers, George F*
Building on Soft Soils
Building Paris — *Van Zanten, David*
Building Projects for the Home
Building Self-Esteem in At-Risk Youth — *Frank, Ivan Cecil*
The Building Stone Heritage of Leeds — *Dimes, Francis*
Building Successful Internet Businesses — *Elderbrock, David*
Building Sustainable Societies — *Pirages, Dennis C*
Building the B-29 — *Vander Meulen, Jacob*
c Building the Capital City — *Brill, Marlene Targ*
Building the Collective — *Dickerman, Leah*
y Building the Continental Empire — *Weeks, William Earl*
Building the Data Warehouse. 2nd Ed. — *Inmon, W H*
Building the Invisible Quality Corporation — *Maromonte, Kevin R*
Building the Learning Organization — *Marquardt, Michael J*
Building the Nineteenth Century — *Peters, Tom F*
Building the Service-Based Library Web Site — *Garlock, Kristen L*
Building the Third Sector — *Levy, Daniel C*
Building the Ultimate Dam — *Jackson, Donald C*
Building the Wooden House — *Wachsmann, Konrad*
Building Your Field of Dreams — *Morrissey, Mary Manin*
Building Your Own Website — *Peck, Susan B*
Buildings of County Antrim — *Brett, C E B*
r Bulbs for the Rock Garden — *Elliot, Jack*
r The Bulfinch Anatomy of Antique Furniture — *Forrest, Tim*
yr The Bulfinch Guide to Art History — *West, Shearer*
Bulgakov: The Novelist-Playwright — *Milne, Lesley*
c Bulgaria — *Stavreva, Kirilka*
Bulgaria in American Perspective — *Pundeff, Marin V*
The Bulgarian Economy in Transition — *Bristow, John A*
r Bulgarski Folklorni Prikazki — *Daskalova-Perkovska, L*
c The Bull and the Fire Truck (Illus. by R W Alley) — *Johnston, Tony*
y Bull Catcher — *Carter, Alden R*
y Bull Run — *Fleischman, Paul*
c Bull Run. Audio Version — *Fleischman, Paul*
c Bull Whackers to Whistle Punks — *Nelson, Sharlene*
Bullfight — *Marvin, Garry*
p Bullhead
c The Bullies (Illus. by Karin Littlewood) — *Althea*
c Bullies and Gangs — *Johnson, Julie*
Bullies and Victims — *Fried, SuEllen*
c The Bully — *Needle, Jan*
Bully: A True Story of High School Revenge — *Schutze, Jim*
y The Bully Coach — *Charbonnet, Gabrielle*
y Bully: Does Anyone Deserve to Die? — *Schutze, Jim*

A Bully Father — *Kerr, Joan Paterson*
y A Bully Father (McDonough). Audio Version
— *Roosevelt, Theodore*
y Bully for You, Teddy Roosevelt! — *Fritz, Jean*
c Bullying (Illus. by Mike Lacey) — *Sanders, Pete*
Bulmurn: A Swan River Nyoongar — *Wilkes, Richard*
c Bumper to Bumper (Illus. by Jakki Wood) — *Wood, Jakki*
c Bumples, Fumdidlers, and Jelly Beans (Illus. by Arnold Spilka) — *Spilka, Arnold*
Bumpo, Bill, and the Girls — *Conwell, Kent*
c Bumps in the Night (Illus. by Philip Hopman) — *Rodgers, Frank*
The Bum's Rush — *Ford, G M*
c Bun Bun's Birthday (Illus. by Mercer Mayer) — *Mayer, Mercer*
Bundori: A Novel — *Rowland, Laura Joh*
Bunker Man — *McLean, Duncan*
c Bunnies — *Potter, Beatrix*
Bunny Bunny — *Zweibel, Alan*
c Bunny Cakes (Illus. by Rosemary Wells) — *Wells, Rosemary*
c Bunny Riddles (Illus. by Nicole Rubel) — *Hall, Katy*
c Bunny's Tale (Illus. by Ernie Eldredge) — *Patrick, Ellen*
Bunting: The Shaping of His Verse — *Makin, Peter*
Bunuel — *Baxter, John*
c The Bunyans (Illus. by David Shannon) — *Wood, Audrey*
The Bunyaviridae — *Elliott, Richard M*
c Bunyips Don't! (Illus. by Kim Gamble) — *Odgers, Sally*
The Burden of Victory — *Kleine-Ahlbrandt, W Laird*
Burdens of History — *Burton, Antoinette*
Burdens of Proof in Modern Discourse — *Gaskins, Richard H*
The Burdens of Sister Margaret — *Harline, Craig*
Bureaucratic Dynamics — *Wood, B Dan*
Bureaucrats in Business
Burger Besonderer Art — *Janz, Oliver*
The Burgermeister's Daughter — *Ozment, Steven*
Burger's Daughter — *Gordimer, Nadine*
The Burglar in the Library — *Block, Lawrence*
r Burgundy — *Braunger, Manfred*
The Burial Brothers — *Mayle, Simon*
y Buried Alive — *Carey, Diane*
y Buried Alive (Illus. by Andrew Moore) — *Fletcher, Ralph*
y Buried Alive and Other True Stories Scarier than Fiction — *Pedersen, Ted*
Buried Caesars (Guidall). Audio Version — *Kaminsky, Stuart M*
Buried in Stone — *Wright, Eric*
Buried Lies — *Jacobsen, Peter*
Burkina Faso: Unsteady Statehood in West Africa — *Englebert, Pierre*
El Burlador De Sevilla Y Convidado De Piedra — *Molina, Tirso De*
Burma: The Politics of Constructive Engagement — *Bray, John*
The Burmese Connection — *Renard, Ronald D*
Burmese Dance and Theatre — *Singer, Noel F*
Burmese Days — *Orwell, George*
y Burn: A Novel — *Ransom, Bill*
r Burnham's Celestial Handbook. Vols. 1-3 — *Burnham, Robert*
Burning Angels — *Burke, James Lee*
Burning Bright — *Hampl, Patricia*
Burning Bright — *Russell, Jay*
Burning Down the House — *Baxter, Charles*
The Burning Ghats — *Mann, Paul*
The Burning House — *Ingram, Jay*
c Burning Issues — *Jones, Alan Frewin*
c Burning Issy — *Burgess, Melvin*
The Burning Library — *White, Edmund*
y The Burning Man — *Margolin, Phillip*
y The Burning Man (Scott). Audio Version — *Margolin, Phillip*
Burning the Box of Beautiful Things — *Seago, Alex*
Burning the Bracken — *Wack, Amy*
Burning the Flag — *Goldstein, Robert Justin*
Burning Your Boats — *Carter, Angela*
The Burnt Book — *Ouaknin, Marc-Alain*
Burnt Offerings — *Liu, Timothy*
c The Burnt Stick (Illus. by Mark Sofilas) — *Hill, Anthony*
c Burnt Toast on Davenport Street (Illus. by Tim Egan) — *Egan, Tim*
Burntwater — *Thybony, Scott*
r Burrelle's Media Directory. Vols. 1-5
r The Burroughs Cyclopaedia — *Brady, Clark A*

c Burt Dow, Deep-Water Man — *McCloskey, Robert*
Burt Lancaster: A Singular Man — *Karney, Robyn*
y Burton (Vance). Audio Version — *Farwell, Byron*
Burundi: Ethnic Conflict and Genocide — *Lemarchand, Rene*
Burundi: Ethnocide as Discourse and Practice — *Lemarchand, Rene*
y Bury Me Standing — *Fonseca, Isabel*
Burying Mao — *Baum, Richard, 1940-*
c Bus (Illus. by Chris L Demarest) — *Demarest, Chris L*
Bus Fare to Kentucky — *Davis, Skeeter*
Bus Ride to Justice — *Gray, Fred*
r Business A to Z Source Finder — *Vandivier, Elizabeth Louise*
r Business Administration Reading Lists and Course Outlines. Vols. 1-20 — *Schwindt, Richard*
Business and Accounting Ethics in Islam — *Gambling, Trevor*
Business and Democracy in Latin America — *Bartell, Ernest*
r Business and Economics Research Directory
y Business and Industry — *Oleksy, Walter*
Business and Law on the Internet — *Hance, Olivier*
Business and Macroeconomics — *Pass, Christopher*
Business and Management in Russia — *Puffer, Sheila M*
Business and Religion in the Age of New France 1600-1760 — *Bosher, J F*
Business and the Environment — *Rogers, Michael D*
Business and the State in International Relations — *Cox, Ronald L*
Business as a Calling — *Novak, Michael*
r Business Buzzwords — *Wendel, Charles B*
The Business Community of Seventeenth-Century England — *Grassby, Richard*
Business Cycle Theory — *Kydland, Finn E*
Business Cycles and Depressions — *Glasner, David*
Business Decisions, Human Choices — *Williams, Lloyd C*
Business Enterprise in Modern Britain from the Eighteenth to the Twentieth Century — *Kirby, Maurice W*
Business Ethics at Work — *Vallance, Elizabeth*
Business in British Columbia
Business Leadership — *Shackleton, Viv*
r The Business Library and How to Use It — *Maier, Ernest L*
Business Managers in Ancient Rome — *Aubert, Jean-Jacques*
The Business of Alchemy — *Smith, Pamela H*
The Business of Being an Artist — *Grant, Daniel*
The Business of Economics — *Kay, J A*
The Business of Higher Education — *Arzt, Noam H*
The Business of Talk — *Boden, Deirdre*
The Business of Wedding Photography — *Monteith, Ann*
r Business Organizations, Agencies, and Publications Directory. 8th Ed.
r Business Phone Book USA 1997
Business, Politics, and Cigarettes — *McGowan, Richard*
Business Process Change — *Grover, Varun*
p Business Publication Advertising Source
Business Research through Argument — *Metcalfe, Mike*
r Business Statistics of the United States. 1995 Ed.
Business Strategy and Security Analysis — *Suutari, Raymond K*
r Business Thesaurus — *De Vries, Mary Ann*
r Business Welsh — *Dery, Robert*
Busman's Honeymoon (Carmichael). Audio Version — *Sayers, Dorothy L*
r Bust Half Dollar Bibliomania — *Karoleff, Brad*
Bust to Boom — *Schulz, Constance B*
Le Buste Monetaire Des Empereurs Romains. Vols. 1-3 — *Bastien, Pierre*
Busted Scotch — *Kelman, James*
c Buster and the Black Hole — *Duffey, Betsy*
c Buster Gets Dressed — *Campbell, Rod*
c Buster's Echo (Illus. by Genevieve Webster) — *Scamell, Ragnhild*
c Busy at Day Care Head to Toe (Illus. by Jack Demuth) — *Demuth, Patricia Brennan*
c Busy Bugs, Lazy Bugs — *Carter, David A*
c A Busy Day at Mr. Kang's Grocery Store (Illus. by Christine Osinski) — *Flanagan, Alice K*
c Busy Lizzie — *Berry, Holly*
But Beautiful — *Dyer, Geoff*
y But Can the Phoenix Sing? — *Laird, Crista*
c But God Remembered (Illus. by Bethanne Andersen) — *Sasso, Sandy Eisenberg*

But I Love You Anyway — *Lewis, Sara*
But Is It Art? — *Felshin, Nina*
But Is It Science? — *Ruse, Michael*
But Is It True? — *Wildavsky, Aaron*
But She Said — *Fiorenza, Elisabeth Schussler*
y But That's Another Story — *Asher, Sandy*
y But What about Me? — *Reynolds, Marilyn*
But What If She Wants to Die? — *Delury, George E*
The Butcher's Wife and Other Stories — *Li, Ang*
Butter and Guns — *Kunz, Diane B*
The Butter Did It — *Richman, Phyllis*
c Butterflies — *Gerholdt, James*
c Butterflies and Bottlecaps (Illus. by Vladyana Krykorka) — *Clark, Eliza*
c Butterflies and Moths (Illus. by Dwight Kuhn) — *Pascoe, Elaine*
c Butterflies and Moths — *Taylor, Barbara*
c Butterflies, Bugs, and Worms — *Morgan, Sally*
r Butterflies of Houston and Southeast Texas — *Tveten, John*
Butterfly — *Butler, Gwendoline*
c The Butterfly (Illus. by Ann James) — *Carr, Roger Vaughan*
c The Butterfly — *Crewe, Sabrina*
c The Butterfly (Illus. by Helliadore) — *Delafosse, Claude*
c The Butterfly Alphabet (Illus. by Kjell Bloch Sandved) — *Sandved, Kjell Bloch*
c Butterfly Boy (Illus. by Gerardo Suzan) — *Kroll, Virginia*
The Butterfly Garden — *Tekulsky, Matthew*
Butterfly Gardening — *Xerces Society*
Butterfly Gardening for the South — *Ajilvsgi, Geyata*
Butterfly Gardens — *Lewis, Alcinda*
c The Butterfly Lion — *Morpurgo, Michael*
c The Butterfly Lion (Illus. by Christian Birmingham) — *Morpurgo, Michael*
Butterfly Lovers — *Foran, Charles*
c The Butterfly Seeds (Illus. by Mary Watson) — *Watson, Mary*
The Butterfly's Wing — *Foreman, Martin*
c Butterworts: Greasy Cups of Death — *Gentle, Victor*
Butun Eserleri — *Lav, Ercumend Behzad*
r A Buyer's and Enthusiast's Guide to Flying Eagle and Indian Cents — *Bowers, Q David*
Buying a Cabin — *Zepeda, Raphael*
Buying Breakfast for My Kamikaze Pilot — *Stock, Norman*
Buying Power — *Arase, David*
Buying the Best — *Clotfelter, Charles T*
c Buz (Illus. by Richard Egielski) — *Egielski, Richard*
c Buzz, Buzz, Buzz, Went Bumblebee — *West, Colin*
Buzz Cut — *Hall, Jim, 1947-*
y Buzz Cut (Muller). Audio Version — *Hall, Jim, 1947-*
y Buzz Cut (Patton). Audio Version — *Hall, Jim, 1947-*
y Buzz: The Science and Lore of Alcohol and Caffeine — *Braun, Stephen*
r By a Woman's Hand. 1st Ed. — *Swanson, Jean*
yr By a Woman's Hand. 2nd Ed. — *Swanson, Jean*
By Angels Driven — *Lippard, Chris*
By Force of Arms — *Nelson, James L*
By Honor Bound — *Morris, Alan*
By Philosophy and Empty Deceit — *Martin, Troy W*
By Salt Water — *Bourke, Angela*
By Southern Playwrights — *Dixon, Michael Bigelow*
By the Banks of the Neva — *Cross, Anthony*
By the Lake of Sleeping Children — *Urrea, Luis Alberto*
c By the Light of the Halloween Moon (Illus. by Kevin Hawkes) — *Stutson, Caroline*
By the Numbers — *Slifer, Stephen D*
By the River Piedra I Sat Down and Wept — *Coelho, Paulo*
By the Shores of Gitchee Gumee — *Janowitz, Tama*
Bye-Bye — *Ransom, Jane*
c Bye, Bye, Bali Kai — *Luger, Harriett Mandelay*
Bylines in Despair — *Liebovich, Louis W*
c Bypass — *Masters, Anthony*
Byrhtferth's Enchiridion (Baker) — *Byrhtferth*
Byrne: A Novel — *Burgess, Anthony*
Byrne's Wonderful World of Pool and Billiards — *Byrne, Robert*
Byron: The Flawed Angel — *Grosskurth, Phyllis*
The Byzantine and Early Islamic Near East. Vol. 3 — *Cameron, Averil*
Byzantine Figural Processional Crosses — *Cotsonis, John A*
The Byzantine Lady — *Nicol, Donald M*
Byzantine Magic — *Maguire, Henry*
Byzantine Scholars in Renaissance Italy — *Monfasani, John*

C

C*-Algebras by Example — *Davidson, Kenneth R*

C++ and C Tools, Utilities, Libraries, and Resources — *Spuler, David*

C/C++ Programmer's Guide — *Pappas, Chris H*

C for Scientists and Engineers — *Johnsonbaugh, Richard*

C++ Gems — *Lippman, Stanley B*

The C++ Graphics Programming Handbook — *Stevens, Roger*

C++ Interactive Course — *Lafore, Robert*

C Interfaces and Implementations — *Hanson, David R*

C.L.R. James on the Negro Question — *James, C L R*

C-Liners, Fairbanks-Morse's Consolidation Line of Locomotives — *Sweetland, David*

C Programming — *King, K N*

r C.R.I.S.: The Combined Retrospective Index Set to Journals in History 1838-1974. Vols. 1-11

r C.R.I.S.: The Combined Retrospective Index Set to Journals in Political Science 1886-1974. Vols. 1-8

r C.R.I.S.: The Combined Retrospective Index Set to Journals in Sociology 1895-1974. Vols. 1-6

C++ Report: The International Authority on C++ Development 1991-1995. Electronic Media Version

C.S. Lewis — *Vander Elst, Philip*

r C.S. Lewis: A Companion and Guide — *Hooper, Walter*

r C.S. Lewis Index — *Goffar, Janine*

C.S. Lewis, Mere Christian. 4th Ed. — *Lindskoog, Kathryn*

The C-Span Revolution — *Frantzich, Stephen*

The CA-Visual Objects Interface Handbook — *Mueller, John, 1958-*

A Cab Called Reliable — *Kim, Patti*

c La Cabalgata De Paul Revere (Illus. by Ted Rand) — *Longfellow, Henry Wadsworth*

Caballero — *Gonzalez, Jovita*

Cabaret McGonagall — *Herbert, W N*

c The Cabbage Patch Fib (Illus. by Keith McEwan) — *Jennings, Paul*

c The Cabbage Patch War (Illus. by Craig Smith) — *Jennings, Paul*

c Cabin 102 — *Garland, Sherry*

c The Cabinetmakers — *Fisher, Leonard Everett*

The Cabo Conference — *Locklin, Gerald*

Cabramatta/Cudmirrah — *Harrison, Jennifer*

Caciques and Their People — *Marcus, Joyce*

Cactus and Succulents — *Luebbermann, Mimi*

yr Cactus Country — *Murray, John A*

CAD Method for Industrial Assembly — *Delchambre, Alain*

CAD of Microstrip Antennas for Wireless Applications — *Sainati, Robert A*

Cadbury Castle, Somerset — *Alcock, Leslie*

c Caddie Woodlawn — *Brink, Carol Ryrie*

The Caddo Indians — *Smith, F Todd*

The Caddos, the Wichitas, and the United States 1846-1901 — *Smith, F Todd*

Cadernos De Lancarote: Diario III — *Saramago, Jose*

c Cadillac (Illus. by Lynne Lockhart) — *Temple, Charles*

Cadillac Jukebox — *Burke, James Lee*

y Cadillac Jukebox (Patton). Audio Version — *Burke, James Lee*

The Cadillac Kind — *Foss, Maureen*

The Cadillac of Six-By's — *Anselmo, Reverge*

p CADS

Caesar — *Meier, Christian*

y Caesar and Rome — *Bernard, Charlotte*

Caesar and the Crisis of the Roman Aristocracy — *Ruebel, James S*

Caesarius of Arles — *Klingshirn, William E*

Caesar's Coin Revisited — *Cromartie, Michael*

y Caesar's Conquest of Gaul — *Nardo, Don*

Caesar's Women — *McCullough, Colleen*

c Cafe at the Edge of the Moon (Illus. by Keren Ludlow) — *Simon, Francesca*

Cafe Europa — *Drakulic, Slavenka*

The Cafes of Paris — *Graf, Christine*

y Caffeine — *DeBenedette, Valerie*

r Cage Aquaculture. 2nd Ed. — *Beveridge, Malcolm C M*

The Cage of Age — *Bronk, William*

Cage of Night — *Gorman, Edward*

Cahier D'Un Retour Au Pays Natal — *Cesaire, Aime*

Cahier Nomade — *Waberi, Abdourahman A*

Cahiers Du Cinema. Vol. 3 — *Browne, Nick*

Cahiers Du Cinema. Vols. 1-2 — *Hillier, Jim*

Cahokia's Countryside — *Mehrer, Mark W*

Cain His Brother — *Perry, Anne*

c Cairo — *Stein, R Conrad*

Cajetan Et Luther En 1518. Vols. 1-2 — *Morerod, Charles*

Cajun and Creole Folktales — *Ancelet, Barry Jean*

c Cajun Fairy Tales. Audio Version — *Reneaux, J J*

c The Cajun Gingerbread Boy (Illus. by Berthe Amoss) — *Amoss, Berthe*

Calamity and Reform in China — *Yang, Dali L*

c Calamity Jane: Frontier Original — *Sanford, William R*

c Calculator Riddles (Illus. by Cynthia Fisher) — *Adler, David A*

Calculus. 7th Ed. — *Varberg, Dale*

y Calculus Lite — *Morgan, Frank*

Calculus: The Dynamics of Change — *Roberts, A Wayne*

The Calcutta Chromosome — *Ghosh, Amitav*

Calcutta Poor — *Thomas, Frederic C*

The Calderonian Stage — *Delgado Morales, Manuel*

r Caldwell County, Kentucky Vital Statistics--Births 1852-1910 — *Jerome, Brenda Joyce*

y Caleb (Illus. by Steven Woolman) — *Crew, Gary*

c Caleb Beldragon's Chronicle of the Three Counties — *Warren, Paul*

Caleb Williams — *Godwin, William*

y Caleb's Choice — *Wisler, G Clifton*

Calendar Year — *Agoos, Julie*

c Calendarbears: A Book of Months (Illus. by Michael Hague) — *Hague, Kathleen*

El Calendario Maya — *Cabrera, Edgar*

Calf's Head and Union Tale — *Green, Archie*

c Calico Picks a Puppy — *Tildes, Phyllis Limbacher*

c California — *Altman, Linda Jacobs*

The California Book of the Dead — *Farrington, Tim*

y The California Cook — *Worthington, Diane Rossen*

r California Environmental Law Handbook. 9th Ed. — *Monahan, Michael A*

California Fault — *Clarke, Thurston*

y The California Gold Rush — *Ito, Tom*

California Impressionists — *Landauer, Susan*

California in 1792 — *Cutter, Donald C*

r The California Locator. 1996 Ed.

California's Immigrant Children — *Rumbaut, Ruben G*

The Caliphate in the West — *Wasserstein, David J*

The Call — *Spangler, David*

Call and Response — *Hamer, Forrest*

Call for the Dead (Jayston). Audio Version — *Le Carre, John*

The Call from Algeria — *Malley, Robert*

r Call It Courage

c Call Me Ahnighito (Illus. by Richard Egielski) — *Conrad, Pam*

y Call Me Francis Tucket — *Paulsen, Gary*

c Call Me Francis Tucket (Jones). Audio Version — *Paulsen, Gary*

c Call Me Gretzky — *O'Conner, Jim*

c Call Me Little Theresa — *Wallace, Susan Helen*

c Call Mr. Vasquez, He'll Fix It! (Illus. by Christine Osinski) — *Flanagan, Alice K*

The Call of Distant Mammoths — *Ward, Peter Douglas*

The Call of Silent Love

Call of the Game — *Bender, Gary*

y Call of the River — *Stegner, Page*

y The Call of the Wild — *London, Jack*

y The Call of the Wild (Illus. by Philippe Munch) — *London, Jack*

The Call of the Wild — *Tavernier-Courbin, Jacqueline*

c The Call of the Wild (Hagon). Audio Version — *London, Jack*

c The Call of the Wild (Hootkins). Audio Version — *London, Jack*

c Call of the Wolves — *Berger, Melvin*

Call the Briefing! — *Fitzwater, Marlin*

Call to Home — *Stack, Carol*

A Call to Joy — *Kelly, Matthew*

The Call to Teach — *Hansen, David T*

r Callaham's Russian-English Dictionary of Science and Technology. 4th Ed. — *Callaham, Ludmilla Ignatiev*

Callahan's Legacy — *Robinson, Spider*

Callas: Images of a Legend — *Csampai, Attila*

Callaway Gardens — *Bender, Steve*

Calle 10 — *Romero, Danny*

Called to Healing — *Troy-Smith, Jean*

Called to Parish Ministry — *Dues, Greg*

c Callie and the Prince — *Johnson, Sylvia A*

c Callie Shaw, Stable Boy — *Alter, Judy*

The Calling of Katie Makanya — *McCord, Margaret*

Calling Out the Called — *Carson, Glenn Thomas*

c Calling the Doves (Illus. by Elly Simmons) — *Herrera, Juan Felipe*

Calling the Shots — *Bennis, Phyllis*

y Calling the Wind — *Major, Clarence*

c Calling Tracy — *Cherrington, Clare*

r Calloway County, Kentucky Tax Lists 1835-1836 — *Willis, Laura*

Calls from the Granite State — *Merrill, Richard*

The Callused Stick of Wanting — *Moreton, Romaine*

Calm at Sunset, Calm at Dawn — *Watkins, Paul*

Calvin: An Introduction to His Thought — *Parker, T H L*

Calvin and the Consolidation of the Genevan Reformation — *Naphy, William G*

Calvin and the Rhetoric of Piety — *Jones, Serene*

Calvin: Erbe Und Auftrag — *Spijker, W Van't*

Calvin in Context — *Steinmetz, David Curtis*

Calvinism in Europe 1540-1620 — *Pettegree, Andrew*

Calvinists and Libertines — *Kaplan, Benjamin J*

Calvino E Il Comico — *Clerici, Luca*

Calvin's Ecclesiastical Advice — *Calvin, Jean*

c Cam Jansen and the Ghostly Mystery (Illus. by Susanna Natti) — *Adler, David A*

Cam Thong De Voi Dau Kho. Vol. 2 — *Chu, Quang Minh*

c La Cama De Plumas De Agata (Illus. by Laura L Seeley) — *Deedy, Carmen Agra*

y Cambodia — *Sheehan, Sean*

c Cambodia--in Pictures — *Lerner Publications Company. Geography Dept.*

Cambodia: The Legacy and Lessons of UNTAC — *Findlay, Trevor*

The Cambria Forest — *Coffman, Taylor*

The Cambridge Ancient History. 2nd Ed., Vol. 6

The Cambridge Ancient History. 2nd Ed., Vol. 10
r Cambridge Astronomy Dictionary
r The Cambridge Atlas of Astronomy — Andouze, Jean
yr The Cambridge Biographical Dictionary — Crystal, David
The Cambridge Companion to American Realism and Naturalism — Pizer, Donald
The Cambridge Companion to Aquinas — Kretzmann, Norman
The Cambridge Companion to Bacon — Peltonen, Markku
The Cambridge Companion to Brecht — Thomson, Peter
The Cambridge Companion to Edith Wharton — Bell, Millicent
The Cambridge Companion to English Poetry, Donne to Marvell — Corns, Thomas N
The Cambridge Companion to Ernest Hemingway — Donaldson, Scott
The Cambridge Companion to Habermas — White, Stephen K
The Cambridge Companion to Henry David Thoreau — Myerson, Joel
The Cambridge Companion to Hobbes — Sorell, Tom
The Cambridge Companion to Husserl — Smith, Barry, Ph.D.
The Cambridge Companion to Leibniz — Jolley, Nicholas
The Cambridge Companion to Locke — Chappell, Vere
The Cambridge Companion to Mark Twain — Robinson, Forrest G
The Cambridge Companion to Medieval English Theatre — Beadle, Richard
r The Cambridge Companion to Spinoza — Garrett, Don
The Cambridge Companion to T.S. Eliot — Moody, A David
r The Cambridge Companion to the Bible — Kee, Howard Clark
r The Cambridge Companion to the Clarinet — Lawson, Colin
The Cambridge Companion to the Eighteenth-Century Novel — Richetti, John
r The Cambridge Companion to the Recorder — Thomson, John Mansfield
The Cambridge Companion to Walt Whitman — Greenspan, Ezra
r The Cambridge Dictionary of Philosophy — Audi, Robert
yr The Cambridge Dictionary of Scientists — Millar, David
The Cambridge Economic History of the United States. Vol. 1 — Engerman, Stanley L
r The Cambridge Encyclopedia of Australia — Bambrick, Susan
The Cambridge Encyclopedia of Language. 2nd Ed. — Crystal, David
r The Cambridge Encyclopedia of Russia and the Former Soviet Union. 2nd Ed. — Brown, Archie
r The Cambridge Gazetteer of the United States and Canada — Hobson, Archie
r Cambridge Guide to American Theatre. Updated Ed. — Wilmeth, Don B
r The Cambridge Guide to Theatre — Banham, Martin
The Cambridge History of American Literature. Vol. 2
r The Cambridge History of American Literature. Vol. 8
The Cambridge History of China. Vol. 6
r The Cambridge History of Latin America. Vol. 6, Pt. 1 — Bethell, Leslie
The Cambridge History of Latin America. Vol. 6, Pts. 1-2 — Bethell, Leslie
r The Cambridge History of Latin America. Vol. 11 — Bethell, Leslie
r The Cambridge History of Latin American Literature. Vols. 1-3 — Gonzalez Echevarria, Roberto
The Cambridge History of Literary Criticism. Vol. 8 — Selden, Raman
The Cambridge History of the English Language. Vol. 5 — Burchfield, Robert
r The Cambridge History of the Native Peoples of the Americas. Vol. 1, Pts. 1-2 — Trigger, Bruce G
yr The Cambridge Illustrated Atlas of Warfare: The Middle Ages — Hooper, Nicholas
yr Cambridge Illustrated Atlas, Warfare: Renaissance to Revolution 1492-1792 — Black, Jeremy
y The Cambridge Illustrated History of Archaeology — Bahn, Paul G

yr The Cambridge Illustrated History of Astronomy — Hoskin, Michael
The Cambridge Illustrated History of British Theatre — Trussler, Simon
yr The Cambridge Illustrated History of China — Ebrey, Patricia Buckley
The Cambridge Illustrated History of France — Jones, Colin
y The Cambridge Illustrated History of Germany — Kitchen, Martin
The Cambridge Illustrated History of Medicine — Porter, Roy
yr The Cambridge Illustrated History of the British Empire — Marshall, P J
yr The Cambridge Illustrated History of the Islamic World — Robinson, Francis
yr The Cambridge Paperback Guide to Literature in English — Ousby, Ian
yr Cambridge Paperback Guide to Theatre — Stanton, Sarah
Cambridge Reading
yr The Cambridge Star Atlas. 2nd Ed. — Tirion, Wil
r The Cambridge Survey of World Migration — Cohen, Robin
Cambridge Women — Shils, Edward
r The Cambridge World History of Human Disease — Kipple, Kenneth F
Camees Et Intailles. Vol. 1, Pts. 1-2 — Vollenweider, Marie-Louise
c Camel Caravan (Illus. by Cheryl Munro Taylor) — Roberts, Bethany
c Camelot (Illus. by Winslow Pels) — Yolen, Jane
The Camelot Caper — Peters, Elizabeth
The Camera Never Blinks — Rather, Dan
y The Camera Obscura — Scott, Hugh
c Cameron and Me (Illus. by Marilyn Mets) — Harris, Dorothy Joan
Camille Glenn's Old-Fashioned Christmas Cookbook — Glenn, Camille
Camille Saint-Saens and the French Solo Concerto from 1850 to 1920 — Stegeman, Michael
Caminemos Con Jesus — Goizueta, Roberto S
Camino Recorrido. Vols. 1-2; Vol. 3, Pts. 1-2 — Pinochet Ugarte, Augusto
El Camino: Walking to Santiago De Compostela — Hoinacki, Lee
The Camorra — Behan, Tom
c Camp Ghost-Away (Moore). Audio Version — Delton, Judy
c Camp Windy Woods Series — Waite, Michael P
The Campaign — Quayle, Marilyn Tucker
c Campaign Chronicles — Crane, Stephen
Campaign Craft — Shea, Daniel M
Campaign Dossier — John, J
A Campaign in New Mexico with Colonel Doniphan — Edwards, Frank S
The Campaign of 1812 in Russia — Clausewitz, Carl Von
La Campana Di Mezzanotte — Cassieri, Giuseppe
Campaneras: Voices from the Latin American Women's Movement — Kuppers, Gaby
Camping Made Easy — Rutter, Michael
Campos, Vigil, Barreras and Rubi Families of New Mexico — Jones, Patricia Clunn
The Campus and a Nation in Crisis — Rudy, Willis
Campus Architecture — Dober, Richard P
Der Campus — Schwanitz, Dietrich
r Campus-Free College Degrees. 7th Ed.
Campus Wars — Arthur, John
Campus Wars — Heineman, Kenneth J
Camus, Frere De Soleil — Robles, Emmanuel
Can Currency Crises Be Prevented or Better Managed? — Teunissen, Jan Joost
Can Democracies Fly in Space? — Kay, W D
Can Democracy Survive in Western Europe — Cortada, James N
Can Europe Work? — Hanson, Stephen E
c Can I Buy a Slice of Sky? — Nichols, Grace
c Can I Have a Stegosaurus, Mom? Can I? Please!? (Illus. by H B Lewis) — Grambling, Lois G
c Can I Help? (Illus. by Marilyn Janovitz) — Janovitz, Marilyn
Can Religion Be Explained Away? — Phillips, D Z
Can Somebody Shout Amen! — Sims, Patsy
Can South and Southern Africa Become Globally Competitive Economies? — Maasdorp, Gavin
Can the Free Market Pick Winners? — Davidson, Paul
Can We Afford to Grow Older? — Disney, Richard
c Can We Save Them? (Illus. by James M Needham) — Dobson, David

Can We Talk? — Scott, Gini Graham
c Can You Catch a Falling Star? (Illus. by Dean Lindberg) — Rosen, Sidney
c Can You Dance, Dalila? (Illus. by Nancy Carpenter) — Kroll, Virginia
Can You Drink the Cup? — Nouwen, Henri J M
Can You Hear, Bird — Ashbery, John
c Can You Jump like a Kangaroo? — Alborough, Jez
c Can You Peck like a Hen? — Alborough, Jez
c Can You Spot the Spotted Dog? (Illus. by John A Rowe) — Rowe, John A
c Can You Sue Your Parents for Malpractice? (Danziger). Audio Version — Danziger, Paula
Can Your Marriage Be a Friendship? — McDonald, Patrick
Canaan — Hill, Geoffrey
r Canada. 5th Ed., Rev. — Cunningham, Hillary
r Canada: A Travel Survival Guide — Lightbody, Mark
Canada and the Global Economy — Britton, John N H
Canada Dry — Noel, Jan
The Canada Fire — Rawlyk, George A
Canada from Afar — Davies, David Twiston
Canada Is Not a Real Country — Schnurmacher, Thomas
c Canada: Star of the North — Sateren, Shelley Swanson
Canada--UK Bilateral Trade and Investment Relations — Buckley, Peter J
r Canada Year Book 1997 on CD-ROM. Electronic Media Version
Canada's Origins — Ajzenstat, Janet
Canadian Archives in 1992
r The Canadian Bed and Breakfast Guide. 12th Ed. — Pantel, Gerda
r Canadian Crime Fiction — Skene-Melvin, David
The Canadian Demand for Household Furniture and Trends. 5th Ed. — McCormack, Thomas W
r The Canadian Encyclopedia Plus 1997. Electronic Media Version
Canadian Family On-Line — Whistance-Smith, John Wallac
Canadian Family Policies — Baker, Maureen
r Canadian Geographical Information Systems Source Book
r The Canadian Guide to Working and Living Overseas. 2nd Ed. — Hachey, Jean-Marc
Canadian History: A Reader's Guide. Vols. 1-2
r Canadian Internet Directory 1997
r Canadian Internet Handbook 1997
p Canadian Journal of Development Studies
Canadian Mosaic — Ravel, Aviva
r Canadian Municipal Trade Tokens and Related Issues Handbook. 1997 Ed. — Sauchenko, Jack P
r Canadian Reference Sources — Bond, Mary E
r Canadian Resident Abroad — Duncan, Garry R
r Canadian Sourcebook 1997
c The Canadian Spelling Program 2.1 — Scott, Ruth
The Canadian Way — Head, Ivan
r Canadian Who's Who 1996
The Canadian Women's Movement 1960-1990 — Fulford, Margaret
r Canadian Writers and Their Works: Fiction Series. Vol. 12 — Lecker, Robert
r Canadian Writers and Their Works: Poetry Series. Vol. 11 — Lecker, Robert
Canadiens Captains — Ulmer, Michael
The Canary Trainer — Meyer, Nicholas
Cancer and Faith — Carmody, John
Cancer and Self-Help — Chesler, Mark A
Cancer and the Family — Baider, Lea
The Cancer Book — Cooper, Geoffrey
Cancer Care in the Community — Hancock, Barry W
Cancer Care in the Hospital — Hancock, Barry W
Cancer Chemotherapy and Biological Response Modifiers Annual 16
Cancer De La Prostata — Marks, Sheldon
r The Cancer Dictionary — Altman, Roberta
Cancer Free — Winawer, Sidney J
Cancer from Beef — Marcus, Alan I
Cancer in Two Voices — Butler, Sandra
Cancer Medicine. 4th Ed., Vols. 1-2 — Holland, James F
Cancer Neutron Capture Therapy — Mishima, Yutaka
Cancer Pain Management — Parris, Winston C V
r Cancer Sourcebook for Women — Cook, Allan R
Cancer Therapeutics — Teicher, Beverly A
Cancer Wars — Proctor, Robert N
r Cancer: What Cutting-Edge Science Can Tell You and Your Doctor about the Causes and the Impact on Diagnosis and Treatment — McAllister, Robert
Candida-Related Complex — Winderlin, Christine

Candidate Images in Presidential Elections — *Hacker, Kenneth L*
Candidates in Conflict — *Benoit, William L*
Candide (Mason) — *Voltaire*
A Candle for a Corpse — *Granger, Ann*
y Candle in the Wind — *Wartski, Maureen*
c The Candlewick Book of Animal Tales
c The Candlewick Book of First Rhymes
c Candy Canes! (Illus. by Paige Billin-Frye) — *Sloboder, Bea*
c Candy Hearts! (Illus. by Paige Billin-Frye) — *Sloboder, Bea*
Candy Making for Beginners — *Fryatt, Evelyn Howe*
Candy Necklace — *Bedlent, Cal*
Cani E Lupi — *Lodoli, Marco*
Canine and Feline Geriatrics — *Davies, Mike*
Cannibal Culture — *Root, Deborah*
Cannibalism: From Sacrifice to Survival — *Askenasy, Hans*
The Canoe Rocks — *Hinckley, Ted C*
r Canoeing Canada's Northwest Territories — *McCreadie, Mary*
Canoeing Up Cabarga Creek — *Whalen, Philip*
The Canon Law, Letter and Spirit — *Sheehy, Gerard*
The Canon of Supreme Mystery — *Yang, Hsiung*
Die Canones Des Pseudo-Mesue — *Lieberknecht, Sieglinde*
c Can't You Sleep, Little Bear? (Illus. by Barbara Firth) — *Waddell, Martin*
Las Canteras De Mitla, Oaxaca — *Robles Garcia, Nelly M*
c The Canterbury Tales (Illus. by Victor G Ambrus) — *McCaughrean, Geraldine*
y The Canterville Ghost (Illus. by Lisbeth Zwerger) — *Wilde, Oscar*
Canticle for a Memory — *Arrivi, Francisco*
A Canticle for Leibowitz — *Miller, Walter M, Jr.*
Cantina: The Best of Casual Mexican Cooking — *Feniger, Susan*
Canto D'Amore — *Boehm, Gottfried*
Los Cantos Del Siervo En La Exegesis Hispano-Hebrea — *Varo, Francisco*
c Cantsee: The Cat Who Was the Color of the Carpet (Illus. by Gretchen Schields) — *Schields, Gretchen*
Canvases and Careers — *White, Harrison C*
Canyon De Chelly — *Hagerty, Donald J*
Canyon Interludes — *Rea, Paul W*
c Canyons — *Paulsen, Gary*
c Canyons — *Rothaus, Don P*
Canyons of the Colorado — *Holmes, Joseph*
Canyonvue — *Preston, Scott*
The Canzoniere or Rerum Vulgarium Fragmenta — *Petrarca, Francesco*
r Cap Guns — *Dundas, James L*
Capacitive Sensors — *Baxter, Larry K*
Capacity and Volition — *Courtenay, William J*
Cape Cod Radio Mystery Theater. Audio Version — *Oney, Steven Thomas*
Cape Cod Stories — *Miller, John, 1959-*
c Capers (Illus. by Clare Mackie) — *Reidy, Hannah*
Caperucita Roja Aprende A Escribir — *Ferreiro, E*
Capital. Vol. 3 — *Marx, Karl*
Capital Cities and Their Hinterlands in Early Modern Europe — *Clarke, Peter, 1942-*
Capital Control, Financial Regulation, and Industrial Policy in South Korea and Brazil — *Nembhard, Jessica Gordon*
Capital Controls, Exchange Rates, and Monetary Policy in the World Economy — *Edwards, Sebastian*
Capital Elites — *Jacob, Kathryn Allamong*
Capital Markets and Financial Intermediation — *Mayer, Colin*
Capital, Power, and Inequality in Latin America — *Halebsky, Sandor*
y Capital Punishment — *Gottfried, Ted*
Capital Punishment — *Hodgkinson, Peter*
Capital, the State and Labour — *Schor, Juliet*
p Capital Update
Capitalism — *Saunders, Peter*
Capitalism: A Treatise on Economics — *Reisman, George*
Capitalism from Within — *Howell, David L*
Capitalism in Context — *James, John A*
Capitalism with a Human Face — *Brittan, Samuel*
Capitalism with a Human Face — *Gay, William*
Capitalism with Morality — *Haslett, David W*
The Capitalist Revolution in Eastern Europe — *Csaba, Laszlo*
The Capitalist Revolution in Latin America — *Roberts, Paul Craig*
Capitol Cuisine — *Milliken, Diane*

A Capitol Idea?
Capitol Offense — *Mikulski, Barbara*
Capitula Generalia Cartusiae 1416-1442 — *De Grauwe, Jan*
Capo — *Watson, Peter*
Capone: The Man and His Era — *Bergreen, Laurence*
La Cappella Del Monte Tamaro — *Botta, Mario*
c Cappy the Lonely Camel (Illus. by Lisa Chauncy Guida) — *Rubinetti, Donald*
Capsules — *Ilton, Phil*
c Captain Abdul's Pirate School — *McNaughton, Colin*
Captain Corelli's Mandolin — *De Bernieres, Louis*
c Captain Daylight's Birthday Bash — *Mostyn, David*
Captain James Cook — *Hough, Richard*
Captain Lavender — *McGuckian, Medbh*
Captain Nathaniel Brown Palmer: An Old-Time Sailor of the Sea — *Spears, John R*
Captain Nemo — *Carbajal, Xavier Joseph*
Captain Paul Cuffe's Logs and Letters 1808-1817 — *Cuffe, Paul*
Captain Richardson: Mariner, Ranchero, and Founder of San Francisco — *Miller, Robert Ryal*
c Captain Salt in Oz — *Thompson, Ruth Plumly*
c Captain Snap and the Children of Vinegar Lane (Illus. by Marcia Sewall) — *Schotter, Roni*
Captain's Log — *Gross, Edward*
Captiva — *White, Randy Wayne*
c Captivating Cryptograms — *Van Dyke, Janice*
Captive Audience — *Henry, Paul, 1959-*
The Captive Republic — *McKenna, Mark*
The Capture of New Orleans 1862 — *Hearn, Chester G*
Captured by History — *Toland, John*
Captured by Texts — *Ebersole, Gary L*
Captured Essence — *Smith, Edith K*
Capturing Childhood Memories — *Morgan, Terri*
Capturing the Magic of Children in Your Paintings — *Zemsky, Jessica*
Capturing the Moment — *Silverman, Barton*
Capturing the Political Imagination — *Stone, Diane*
c The Car — *Paulsen, Gary*
Car: A Drama of the American Workplace — *Walton, Mary*
A Car Full of Songs — *Paxton, Tom*
Car Keys — *Ciullo, Peter A*
The Car That Could — *Shnayerson, Michael*
Car Wars — *Mantle, Jonathan*
La Cara Oculta De La Luna
y Carabas — *Masson, Sophie*
Caracole — *White, Edmund*
La Caracteristique Geometrique — *Leibniz, Gottfried Wilhelm, Freiherr Von*
The Carbohydrate Addict's Lifespan Program — *Heller, Richard F*
Carbon and Alloy Steels — *Davis, J R*
Carbon Dioxide, Populations, and Communities — *Korner, Christian*
Carbon Nanotubes — *Ebbesen, Thomas W*
Le Carcajou — *Clavel, Bernard*
Carcinogens and Anticarcinogens in the Human Diet — *National Research Council (U.S.). Committee on Comparative Toxicity of Naturally Occurring Carcinogens*
c Card Tricks (Illus. by Dave King) — *Eldin, Peter*
c Cardboard Boxes (Illus. by Sarah-Jane Neaves) — *Connor, Nikki*
El Cardenal Goma Y La Guerra De Espana — *Rodriguez Aisa, Maria Luisa*
Cardiac Pacing. 2nd Ed. — *Ellenbogen, Kenneth A*
Cardiac Radiology — *Miller, Stephen W*
Cardiac Stress Testing and Imaging — *Marwick, Thomas H*
The Cardiff Team — *Davenport, Guy*
Cardiganshire County History — *Davies, J L*
The Cardinal — *Robinson, Henry Morton*
Cardiovascular Imaging — *Reiber, Johan H C*
The Cards of the Gambler — *Kiely, Benedict*
c The Care and Feeding of Fish (Illus. by Sarajo Frieden) — *Frieden, Sarajo*
c The Care and Keeping of Friends (Illus. by Nadine Bernard Westcott)
Care, Autonomy, and Justice — *Clement, Grace*
Care, Gender, and Justice — *Bubeck, Diemut*
c Care of Henry (Illus. by Paul Howard) — *Fine, Anne*
Care of the Soul — *Moore, Thomas, 1940-*
y Career Basics — *Kuckkan, Kevin G*
The Career Chase — *Harkness, Helen Leslie*
Career Girls — *Ragshawe, Louise*
The Career Novelist — *Maass, Donald*
y Career Success for People with Physical Disabilities — *Kissane, Sharon F*

Career Success with Pets — *Barber, Kim*
Careering Along with Books — *Manley, K A*
Careers for Health Nuts — *Camenson, Blythe*
y Careers for Music Lovers and Other Tuneful Types — *Johnson, Jeff*
y Careers for Mystery Buffs and Other Snoops and Sleuths — *Camenson, Blythe*
y Careers in Horticulture and Botany — *Garner, Jerry*
y Careers in Medicine — *Sacks, Terence J*
Careers in Science and Engineering — *Committee on Science, Engineering, and Public Policy (U.S.)*
yr CareerSmarts: Jobs with a Future — *Yate, Martin*
r CareerXroads: The 1996 Directory to Jobs, Resumes and Career Management on the World Wide Web
Careless to Caring for Troubled Youth — *Krueger, Mark A*
Cargo of Lies — *Beeby, Dean*
r Caribbean. 3rd Ed. — *Schwab, David*
c The Caribbean and the Gulf of Mexico — *Morgan, Nina*
Caribbean Cooking — *DeMers, John*
c A Caribbean Counting Book (Illus. by Roberta Arenson) — *Charles, Faustin*
Caribbean Currents — *Manuel, Peter*
c A Caribbean Dozen (Illus. by Cathie Felstead) — *Agard, John*
Caribbean Hoops — *Mandle, Jay R*
Caribbean Immigrants — *Anderson, Wolseley*
The Caribbean Legion — *Ameringer, Charles D*
Caribbean Maritime Security — *Morris, Michael A*
r Caribbean: The Lesser Antilles — *Luntta, Karl*
c Caring (Illus. by Mechelle Ann) — *Moncure, Jane Belk*
Caring: An Essay in the Philosophy of Ethics — *Hooft, Stan Van*
Caring for Depression — *Wells, Kenneth B*
Caring for Patients — *Barbour, Allen B*
Caring for Perennials — *Macunovich, Janet*
Caring for the Alzheimer Patient. 3rd Ed. — *Dippel, Raye*
Caring for the Family Soul — *Dean, Amy E*
Caring for the Future — *Harrison, Paul*
Caring for the HIV/AIDS Caregiver — *Lynch, Vincent J*
r Caring for the Mind — *Hales, Dianne*
c Caring for Young — *Butler, Daphne*
r Caring for Your Adolescent Ages 12 to 21
r Caring for Your Baby and Young Child Birth to Age 5
Caring for Your Old House — *Kitchen, Judith L*
r Caring for Your School-Age Child Ages 5 to 12
Caring in an Unjust World — *Eaker-Rich, Deborah*
Caring: The Compassion and Wisdom of Nursing — *Brykczynska, Gosia*
Carl Andre, Sculptor 1996 — *Andre, Carl*
c Carl Caught a Flying Fish — *O'Malley, Kevin*
Carl Gustav Jung — *McLynn, Frank*
Carl Maria Von Weber Und Hector Berlioz — *Heidlberger, Frank*
Carl Rakosi: Man and Poet — *Heller, Michael, 1937-*
Carl Sagan and Immanuel Velikovsky — *Ginenthal, Charles*
Carl Schmitt and Leo Strauss — *Meier, Heinrich*
Carl Zuckmayer Criticism — *Wagener, Hans*
Carlo Emilio Gadda and the Modern Macaronic — *Sbragia, Albert*
c Carlos and Little Wolf (Illus. by Lesley Harker) — *Harker, Lesley*
c Carlos and the Cornfield (Illus. by Jeanne Arnold) — *Stevens, Jan Romero*
c Carlos and the Skunk (Illus. by Jeanne Arnold) — *Stevens, Jan Romero*
Carlos Lacerda, Brazilian Crusader. Vol. 2 — *Dulles, John W F*
The Carmelite Way — *Welch, John*
Carmilla — *Le Fanu, Joseph Sheridan*
Carmina — *Erigena, Johannes Scotus*
c Carmine the Crow (Illus. by Heidi Holder) — *Holder, Heidi*
Carn — *McCabe, Patrick*
Carnal Knowledge — *Lees, Sue*
Carnal Love — *Deluy, Henri*
The Carnal Prayer Mat — *Li, Yu*
Carnal Rhetoric — *Cable, Lana*
r The Carnegie Atlas of Galaxies — *Sandage, Allan*
Carnegie Libraries across America — *Jones, Theodore*
Les Carnets Du Cardinal Baudrillart 1914-1918 — *Christophe, Paul*
c Carnival (Illus. by Dan Yaccarino) — *Helldorfer, M C*
Carnival, Canboulay and Calypso — *Cowley, John*
Carnival Culture and the Soviet Modernist Novel — *Brandist, Craig*

Title Index

c Carnival of Crime. The Diamond Lens. Audio Version — *Twain, Mark*

Carnivore Behavior, Ecology, and Evolution. Vol. 2 — *Gittleman, John L*

c Carnivorous Mushrooms — *Gentle, Victor*

Carol for Another Christmas — *Scarborough, Elizabeth Ann*

Carol Tyler's Greatest Zits — *Tyler, Carol*

Carolan: The Life, Times and Music of an Irish Harper. Vols. 1-2 — *O'Sullivan, Donal*

Carolina Edens — *Spicer, Cindy*

y Carolina Moon — *McCorkle, Jill*

p The Carolina Quarterly

c Carolina Shout! (Illus. by Bernie Fuchs) — *Schroeder, Alan*

c Caroline En Russie — *Probst, Pierre*

c Carolyn's Story — *Schwartz, Perry*

c The Carousel (Illus. by Jim LaMarche) — *Rosenberg, Liz*

y The Carousel (Brown). Audio Version — *Plain, Belva*

r A Carpenter Genealogy — *Sharp, Lyle C*

The Carpenter's Apprentice — *Ariail, Dan*

Carpet of Silver — *Playford, Phillip*

Carpets and Rugs of Europe and America — *Sherrill, Sarah B*

Carriage of Justice — *Hammond, Gerald*

Carrie Chapman Catt: A Public Life — *Van Voris, Jacqueline*

Carry Me Back — *Watt, Laura*

Carry Me Home — *Del Vecchio, John M*

Carrying Water as a Way of Life — *Tatelbaum, Linda*

c Cars and Trucks and Other Vehicles (Illus. by Sophie Kniffke) — *Delafosse, Claude*

The Cars That Ate Bangkok — *Blenkinsop, Philip*

Carson Valley — *Barich, Bill*

Cartai E Stampatori A Toscolano — *Simoni, Carlo*

Cartas A Maria Regina — *Avila, Maria Regina*

Cartas A Ricardo — *Castellanos, Rosario*

Carte Decorate — *Gani, Michela*

r Carte Private Di Carlo Alfonso E Maria Nallino — *Baldinetti, Anna*

Cartea Plecarii — *Golopentia, Sanda*

Il Carteggio Indiretto Di Michelangelo. Vol. 2 — *Barocchi, P*

The Carter Administration and Vietnam — *Hurst, Steven*

Carter and Arms Sales — *Spear, Joanna*

Cartesian Psychology and Physical Minds — *Wilson, Robert Andrew*

Carthage: L'Histoire, Sa Trace Et Son Echo

Cartier 1900-1939 — *Rudoe, Judy*

The Cartographic Eye — *Ryan, Simon*

Cartographies of Danger — *Monmonier, Mark*

Cartography in the Traditional East and Southeast Asian Societies — *Harley, J B*

Cartography: Visualization of Spatial Data — *Kraak, Menno-Jan*

The Cartoon Guide to Genetics. Updated Ed. — *Gonick, Larry*

y The Cartoon Guide to the Environment — *Gonick, Larry*

c The Cartoonist — *Byars, Betsy*

Cartoonometer: Taking the Pulse of the World's Cartoonists — *Szabo, Joe*

Cartoons: One Hundred Years of Cinema Animation — *Bendazzi, Giannalberto*

cr Cartopedia: The Ultimate World Reference Atlas. Electronic Media Version

Les Cartulaires — *Guyotjeannin, Olivier*

Cartwheels on the Faultline — *Baer, Barbara L*

Caruso and the Art of Singing — *Fucito, Salvatore*

Carved Erosion — *Bening, Guy R*

Carved in Stone — *Drukier, Manny*

y Carving a Totem Pole (Illus. by Vickie Jensen) — *Jensen, Vickie*

Carving Masks — *Bridgewater, Alan*

Cary Grant: A Class Apart — *McCann, Graham*

Cary Grant: Dark Angel — *Wansell, Geoffrey*

La Casa De Los Espiritus — *Allende, Isabel*

The Casablanca Man — *Robertson, James C*

Casalinghe All'Inferno — *Giacobino, Margherita*

Cascadia: Inspired Gardening in the Pacific Northwest — *Lovejoy, Ann*

The Case against Immigration — *Beck, Roy*

The Case against the Global Economy — *Mander, Jerry*

The Case for Clerical Celibacy — *Stickler, Alfons M*

The Case for Freewill Theism — *Basinger, David*

The Case for Mars — *Zubrin, Robert*

The Case for Same-Sex Marriage — *Eskridge, William N*

The Case for Tenure — *Finkin, Matthew W*

The Case for Vegetarianism — *Hill, John Lawrence*

Case Management and Substance Abuse Treatment — *Siegal, Harvey A*

y The Case of Roe v. Wade — *Stevens, Leonard A*

c The Case of the Bashed-Up Bicycle — *Maifair, Linda Lee*

c The Case of the Goblin Pearls — *Yep, Laurence*

c The Case of the Missing Cutthroats — *George, Jean Craighead*

c The Case of the Nearsighted Neighbor — *Maifair, Linda Lee*

The Case of the Spotted Mice and Other Classic Essays on Science — *Medawar, Peter*

c The Case of the Wiggling Wig — *Hildick, E W*

Case Studies in Contracting and Organization — *Masten, Scott E*

Case Studies in Environmental Archaeology — *Reitz, Elizabeth J*

Case Studies in Human Ecology — *Bates, Daniel G*

Case Studies in Immunology — *Rosen, Fred S*

Case Studies in Nursing Case Management — *Blancett, Suzanne Smith*

Case Studies in Object-Oriented Analysis and Design — *Yourdon, Edward*

Case Studies in Opportunities for Libraries in Europe — *Brophy, Peter*

Case Studies in War-to-Peace Transition — *Colletta, Nat J*

y The Casebook of Forensic Detection — *Evans, Colin*

Cased Hole and Production Log Evaluation — *Smolen, James J*

Cases in Financial Management. 2nd Ed. — *Sulock, Joseph M*

c Casey in the Bath (Illus. by Chris L Demarest) — *DeFelice, Cynthia C*

Casey Stengel: A Splendid Baseball Life — *Bak, Richard*

Casey's Law — *Casey, Al*

c Casey's New Hat (Illus. by Margot Apple) — *Gardella, Tricia*

The Caseys of the Strande, County Westmeath, Ireland, Canada, and the United States — *Thomas, Cecelia E*

Cash, Crisis, and Corporate Governance — *Marklew, Victoria*

Cash Crop and Foodgrain Productivity in Senegal — *Kelly, Valerie*

Cash for the Final Days — *Wolk, Gloria Grening*

c Casimir Pulaski: Soldier on Horseback (Illus. by Larry Nolte) — *Collins, David R*

Casino — *Pileggi, Nicholas*

Casino and Other Stories — *Burnard, Bonnie*

Casino Lighting

c El Caso Del Forastero Hambriento (Illus. by Crosby Bonsall) — *Bonsall, Crosby*

yr Cass and Birnbaum's Guide to American Colleges. 17th Ed.

Cassatt: A Retrospective — *Mathews, Nancy Mowll*

r The Cassell Crossword Dictionary — *Kirkpatrick, Betty*

r Cassell Dictionary of Contemporary Quotations — *Andrews, Robert*

r Cassell Dictionary of Insulting Quotations — *Green, Jonathon*

r Cassell Illustrated Dictionary of Lacemaking — *Stillwell, Alexandra*

The Cassock and the Crown — *Monet, Jean*

y Cast in Stone — *Ford, G M*

Cast Irons — *Davis, J R*

Caste and Capitalism in Colonial India — *Rudner, David West*

Caste and Class — *Gordon, Fon Louise*

Caste, Nationalism and Communism in South India, Malabar 1900-1948 — *Menon, Dilip M*

The Castilian Crisis of the Seventeenth Century — *Thompson, I A A*

El Castillo De La Memoria — *Nolla, Olga*

c Casting a Spell and Other Poems (Illus. by Jane Ray) — *Huth, Angela*

Casting Her Own Shadow — *Black, Allida M*

Casting Her Own Shadow (Schraf). Audio Version — *Black, Allida M*

y Casting Off (Balcon). Audio Version — *Howard, Elizabeth Jane*

Castle Fantastic — *DeChancie, John*

Castle Garden — *Albert, Bill*

c Castle in the Attic — *Winthrop, Elizabeth*

The Castle of Indolence — *Disch, Thomas M*

The Castle of Lies — *Booker, Christopher*

c Castle Tales (Illus. by Stephen Cartwright) — *Amery, Heather*

Castle to Castle — *Celine, Louis-Ferdinand*

Castlereagh 1769-1822, Ou Le Defi A L'Europe De Napoleon — *D'Arjuzon, Antoine*

Castles Burning — *Denes, Magda*

Castles of Britain and Ireland — *Somerset Fry, Plantagenet*

The Castration of Oedipus — *Smith, J C, 1930-*

y Cat (Eyewitness Virtual Reality Series). Electronic Media Version

c Cat (Illus. by Brita Granstrom) — *Morley, Christine*

c Cat among the Cabbages (Illus. by Alison Bartlett) — *Bartlett, Alison*

c Cat and Cat-Face (Illus. by Lesley Liu) — *Sun, Chyng-Feng*

c Cat and Dog — *Coplans, Peta*

c Cat and Mouse (Illus. by Tomasz Bogacki) — *Bogacki, Tomasz*

Cat and Mouse — *Lane, Brian*

Cat and Mouse and Other Writings — *Grass, Gunter*

c The Cat and the Cook and Other Fables of Krylov (Illus. by Anita Lobel) — *Heins, Ethel*

y Cat Chaser (Adams). Audio Version — *Leonard, Elmore*

y Cat-Dogs and Other Tales of Horror — *Finnis, A*

Cat in a Flamingo Fedora — *Douglas, Carole Nelson*

c Cat Is Sleepy (Illus. by Satoshi Kitamura) — *Kitamura, Satoshi*

c Cat Mummies (Illus. by Laszlo Kubinyi) — *Trumble, Kelly*

y The Cat-Nappers (Davidson). Audio Version — *Wodehouse, P G*

A Cat on a Beach Blanket — *Adamson, Lydia*

Cat on the Edge — *Murphy, Shirley Rousseau*

c Cat Parade (Illus. by Diane Greenseid) — *Roberts, Bethany*

y Cat under Fire — *Murphy, Shirley Rousseau*

y A Cat under the Mistletoe — *Adamson, Lydia*

y The Cat Who Couldn't See in the Dark — *Padwee, Howard*

c The Cat Who Found His Way Home (Illus. by Michele Coxon) — *Coxon, Michele*

The Cat Who Said Cheese (Adams). Audio Version — *Braun, Lilian Jackson*

y The Cat Who Tailed a Thief — *Braun, Lilian Jackson*

Cat with an Emerald Eye — *Douglas, Carole Nelson*

r Cat World — *Morris, Desmond*

c Cat, You Better Come Home (Illus. by Steve Johnson) — *Keillor, Garrison*

Cataclysmic Variable Stars — *Warner, Brian*

Cataclysmic Variables and Related Objects — *International Astronomical Union. Colloquium (158th: 1995: Keele, Staffordshire)*

Catacombs — *McCusker, Paul*

r Catalago De Obras Impresas En El Siglo XVI De La Biblioteca General E Historica De La Universitat De Valencia. Vols. 1-2 — *Universidad De Valencia. Biblioteca General E Historica*

Catalan Nationalism — *Balcells, Albert*

Les Catalinaires — *Nothomb, Amelie*

r The Catalog of Catalogs V — *Palder, Edward*

r A Catalog of Music for the Cornett — *Collver, Michael*

r The Catalog of Union Civil War Patriotic Covers — *Weiss, William R, Jr.*

Catalogazione, Cooperazione, Servizi, Strumenti

Cataloging and Classification for Library Technicians — *Kao, Mary Liu*

r Cataloging and Classification Standards and Rules — *Riemer, John J*

r Catalogo Concordado De La Biblioteca De Hernando Colon. Vol. 1 — *Biblioteca Colombina*

r Catalogo De Los Pliegos Sueltos Poeticos Del Siglo XVII De La Biblioteca De Antonio Rodriguez Monino — *Campo, Victoria*

r Catalogo Della Biblioteca Di Scienze Carlo Vigano

r Catalogo Delle Edizioni Antiche Possedute Dalla Biblioteca Della Camera Dei Deputati Sec. XV-XVII — *Greco, Giorgio Del*

r Catalogue Des Dessins Francais Du XVIIIe Siecle Du Palais Des Beaus-Arts De Lille — *Raux, Sophie*

r Catalogue Des Ouvrages Du Fonds Francais 1601-1850, Conserves Dans La Founders' Library, Universite Du Pays De Galles, Lampeter — *St. David's University College (Lampeter, Wales). Library*

r Catalogue Du Fonds Musical De La Bibliotheque De Versailles — *Herlin, Denis*

r Catalogue of Books Printed in the German-Speaking Countries and of German Books Printed in Other Countries from 1601 to 1700 in the British Library. Vols. 1-5 — *British Library*

r A Catalogue of Chaucer Manuscripts. Vol. 1 — *Seymour, M C*

r Catalogue of Choral Music Arranged in Biblical Order. 2nd Ed. — *Laster, James*

r Catalogue of Forbidden German Feature and Short Film Productions Held in Zonal Film Archives — *Zonal Film Archives (Hamburg, Germany)*

A Catalogue of Manuscripts and Drawings in the General Library of the Natural History Museum, London — *Natural History Museum (London). General Library*

r Catalogue of Medieval and Renaissance Manuscripts in the Houghton Library, Harvard University. Vol. 1 — *Light, Laura*

r A Catalogue of the Fifteenth-Century Printed Books in the Harvard University Library. Vol. 4 — *Harvard University. Library*

r A Catalogue of the Lamps in the British Museum. Vol. 4 — *British Museum*

Catalogue of the Law Society's Mendham Collection — *Law Society (Great Britain)*

r Catalogue of the Manuscripts of Hereford Cathedral Library — *Mynors, R A B*

y The Catalogue of the Universe — *Mahy, Margaret*

A Catalogue of the Works of Ralph Vaughan Williams. 2nd Ed. — *Kennedy, Michael, 1926-*

r Catalogue of Watermarks in Italian Printed Maps ca 1540-1600 — *Woodward, David*

r Catalogue Switzerland/Liechtenstein, Campione and United Nations, Geneva 1996

r Catalogus Van De Pamfletten Aanwezig In De Bibliotheek Arnhem 1537-1795 — *Bibliotheek Arnhem*

Catalysis of Organic Reactions — *Malz, Russell E, Jr.*

Catalytic RNA — *Eckstein, Fritz*

Catapult — *Paral, Vladimir*

The Catastrophe — *Steiner, Robert*

Catastrophe of an Old Man — *Shrubb, Peter*

Catastrophic Politics — *Himelfarb, Richard*

Catawba Indian Genealogy — *Watson, Ian*

c Catbirds and Dogfish — *Most, Bernard*

The Catbird's Song — *Wilbur, Richard*

Catch: A Discovery of America — *Hartshorn, Nick*

Catch the Lightning — *Asaro, Catherine*

y Catch the Wave! — *Johnson, Kevin*

Catch Your Breath — *Auerbach, Jessica*

The Catcher Was a Spy — *Dawidoff, Nicholas*

Catching Babies — *Borst, Charlotte G*

Catching Sense — *Guthrie, Patricia*

The Catechism of the Catholic Church on Liturgy and Sacraments — *Joncas, Jan Michael*

The Catechism Yesterday and Today — *Marthaler, Berard L*

Categorical Topology — *Giuli, Eraldo*

c Caterina, the Clever Farm Girl (Illus. by Enzo Giannini) — *Peterson, Julienne*

Catering to Nobody (Rosenblat). Audio Version — *Davidson, Diane Mott*

c Caterpillar to Butterfly — *Rodger, Elizabeth*

c The Caterpillow Fight (Illus. by Jill Barton) — *McBratney, Sam*

y Catfantastic IV

The Cathedral: The Social and Architectural Dynamics of Construction — *Erlande-Brandenburg, Alain*

Cathedrals of the Spirit — *McLuhan, T C*

Cathedrals under Siege — *Lehmberg, Stanford E*

c Catherine and the Lion (Illus. by Clare Jarrett) — *Jarrett, Clare*

Catherine Booth: A Biography — *Green, Roger J*

y Catherine, Called Birdy — *Cushman, Karen*

y Catherine, Called Birdy (Maberly). Audio Version — *Cushman, Karen*

Catherine McAuley and the Tradition of Mercy — *Sullivan, Mary C*

Catherine of Siena: Vision through a Distant Eye — *Noffke, Suzanne*

y Catherwood — *Youmans, Marly*

Catholic and Reformed — *Milton, Anthony*

Catholic Devotion in Victorian England — *Heimann, Mary*

The Catholic Doctrine of Non-Christian Religions According to the Second Vatican Council — *Ruokanen, Miikka*

The Catholic Family — *Sander, William*

r Catholic Girlhood Narratives — *Evasdaughter, Elizabeth N*

The Catholic Imagination in American Literature — *Labrie, Ross*

The Catholic Philanthropic Tradition in America — *Oates, Mary J*

The Catholic Priesthood and the English Reformation — *Marshall, Peter*

Catholic Social Teaching as I Have Lived, Loathed and Loved It — *Land, Philip S*

Catholic Voices — *Campion, Ed*

Catholicism and Liberalism — *Douglass, R Bruce*

Catholicism in a Protestant Kingdom — *Leighton, C D A*

Catholicism in Ulster 1603-1983 — *Rafferty, Oliver P*

Catholicism, Liberalism, and Communitarianism — *Grasso, Kenneth L*

Catholics in Crisis — *Naughton, Jim*

Les Cathos — *Hanotel, Valerie*

c Cathy's Cake (Illus. by Anthea Sieveking) — *MacKinnon, Debbie*

r Cationic Polymerization — *Matyjaszewski, Krzysztof*

y The Catlike Canine. 2nd Ed. — *Henry, J David*

Catnap — *Slovo, Gillian*

p CATO Review of Business and Government

y Catriona (Case). Audio Version — *Stevenson, Robert Louis*

c Cats (Illus. by Gail Gibbons) — *Gibbons, Gail*

Cats Are Not Peas — *Gould, Laura*

A Cat's Christmas — *Samek, Stefanie*

c Cat's Colors (Illus. by Jane Cabrera) — *Cabrera, Jane*

c Cats, Dogs, and Classroom Pets — *Vansant, Rhonda*

y Cat's Eye — *Atwood, Margaret*

The Cats' House — *Walker, Bob*

c Cat's Kittens (Illus. by Sophy Williams) — *Rogers, Paul*

c Cats Love Christmas Too (Illus. by Isabelle Brent) — *Brent, Isabelle*

Cats of Any Color — *Lees, Gene*

c The Cats of Mrs. Calamari (Illus. by John Stadler) — *Stadler, John*

c Cats Sleep Anywhere (Illus. by Anne Mortimer) — *Farjeon, Eleanor*

c Cats' Whiskers — *McLean, Andrew*

c Cats Whispers and Tales (Illus. by Kate Aldous) — *Westall, Robert*

Catspaw — *Vinge, Joan D*

The Cattle Killing — *Wideman, John Edgar*

Cattle on a Thousand Hills — *Brown, C J*

Catullus: Advanced Placement Edition — *Bender, Henry V*

Cau Chuyen Cua La Phong — *Tran, Mong Tu*

Caught in a Stampede — *Tejdeep*

Caught in the Act — *McAdams, Dona Ann*

y Caught in the Crossfire — *Ousseimi, Maria*

Caught in the Middle — *Min, Pyong Gap*

Caught in the Net — *Bonanno, Alessandro*

Caught Inside — *Duane, Daniel*

y Caught Up in the Rapture — *Jackson, Sheneska*

Causal and Stochastic Elements in Business Cycles — *Aulin, Arvid*

Las Causas De La Emigracion Espanola 1880-1930 — *Sanchez Alonso, Blanca*

The Cause Lost — *Davis, William C*

Cause of Death — *Cornwell, Patricia Daniels*

Cause of Death — *Underwood, Michael*

y Cause of Death (Brown). Audio Version — *Cornwell, Patricia Daniels*

Causes and Consequences in International Relations — *Nicholson, Michael*

Causes and Control of Colorectal Cancer — *Kune, Gabriel A*

Causes of Growth and Stagnation in the World Economy — *Kaldor, Nicholas*

The Causes of Tropical Deforestation — *Brown, Katrina*

c Causing a Stink! — *Clayton, Caroline*

La Cavale: Memoire D'Albertine — *Lambert, Bernard*

y Cavaliers and Roundheads (Crossley). Audio Version — *Hibbert, Christopher*

Cavaliers, Clubs, and Literary Culture — *Raylor, Timothy*

The Cavalry of Classical Greece — *Spence, I G*

A Cavalryman's Story — *Howze, Hamilton H*

Cavan — *Gillespie, Raymond*

The Cave — *Matthews, Anne McLean*

The Cave beneath the Sea — *Clottes, Jean*

Cave Passages — *Taylor, Michael Ray*

The Cavell Reader — *Cavell, Stanley*

Caveman Politics — *Atkinson, Jay*

c Caves — *Morris, Neil*

Caves: Processes, Development and Management — *Gillieson, David*

Cavour — *Hearder, Harry*

Cay Dang Mui Doi — *Ho, Bieu Chanh*

Cay Tung Truoc Bao — *Hoang, Khoi Phong*

r Cayman Islands — *Boultbee, Paul G*

CCTV Surveillance — *Kruegle, Herman*

r CD Estimator 1996. Electronic Media Version

r The CD-ROM Directory 1996

r CD-ROM for Librarians and Educators. 2nd Ed. — *Sorrow, Barbara Head*

r CD-ROMs in Print 1995. Electronic Media Version

r CD-ROMs in Print 1996

CDMA for Wireless Personal Communications — *Prasad, Ramjee*

cDNA Library Protocols — *Cowell, Ian G*

yr CDs, Super Glue, and Salsa. 2nd Ser., Vols. 1-2 — *Witman, Kathleen L*

Cease Firing — *Johnston, Mary*

Ceausescu and the Securitate — *Deletant, Dennis*

Cecil B. DeMille and American Culture — *Higashi, Sumiko*

c Cecil Bunions and the Midnight Train (Illus. by Michael Paraskevas) — *Paraskevas, Betty*

Cecil Rhodes and the Cape Afrikaners — *Tamarkin, M*

Cecilia Bartoli: The Passion of Song — *Chernin, Kim*

Cecilia Payne-Gaposchkin: An Autobiography and Other Recollections. 2nd Ed. — *Gaposchkin, Cecilia Helena Payne*

Cecily Mary Barker and Her Art — *Laing, Jane*

c Cecily Small and the Rainy Day Adventure — *Mitchell, Cecily Harper*

r Cedar County Missouri 1870 Federal Census — *Looney, Janice Soutee*

y Cedar River Daydreams — *Baer, Judy*

c Celebrate! — *Hillel, Margot*

c Celebrate! In South Asia (Illus. by Joe Viesti) — *Viesti, Joe*

c Celebrate! In Southeast Asia (Illus. by Joe Viesti) — *Viesti, Joe*

c Celebrate the Spirit — *Dheensaw, Cleve*

The Celebrated Antiquary — *O Muraile, Nollaig*

Celebrating An Authentic Passover Seder — *Stallings, Joseph M*

Celebrating Children's Literature in Education — *Fox, Geoff*

c Celebrating Families (Illus. by Rosmarie Hausherr) — *Hausherr, Rosmarie*

Celebrating Florida — *Libby, Gary R*

Celebrating Girls — *Rutter, Virginia Beane*

c Celebrating Hanukkah (Illus. by Lawrence Migdale) — *Hoyt-Goldsmith, Diane*

Celebrating the Impressionist Table — *Todd, Pamela*

Celebrating the Saxophone — *Lindemeyer, Paul*

yr Celebrating Women in Mathematics and Science — *Cooney, Miriam P*

c Celebration! (Illus. by Raul Colon) — *Thomas, Jane Resh*

Celebration in Purple Sage — *Smith, Barbara Burnett*

Celebration in the Northwest — *Matute, Ana Maria*

Celebration of American Food — *Schremp, Gerry*

y A Celebration of Customs and Rituals of the World (Illus. by Robert Ingpen) — *Wilkinson, Philip*

A Celebration of Humanism and Freethought — *Williams, David Allen*

A Celebration of Marine Art

Celebrity Murders and Other Nefarious Deeds — *Haines, Max*

Celestial Dogs — *Russell, J S*

Celestial Encounters — *Diacu, Florin*

Celestial Matters — *Garfinkle, Richard*

Celestial Sirens — *Kendrick, Robert L*

The Celestine Prophecy — *Redfield, James*

The Celibacy Club — *Eidus, Janice*

Celibacy: Means of Control or Mandate of the Heart? — *Crosby, Michael H*

The Celibate — *Arditti, Michael*

c Celie and the Harvest Fiddler (Illus. by James E Ransome) — *Flournoy, Vanessa*

Celine: A Circle of Life — *Roth, Kathleen Bittner*

Cell Angel — *Elfyn, Menna*

Cell Physiology Source Book — *Sperelakis, Nicholas*

Cell Signalling — *Parker, P J*

Cellblock Visions — *Kornfeld, Phyllis*

Cellojaren — *Bernlef, J*

y Cells, Genes, and Chromosomes (Illus. by Antonio Munoz Tenllado) — *Roca, Nuria*

The Cells of the Body — *Harris, Henry*

Cells, Tissues, and Disease — *Majno, Guido*

Cellular Biophysics. Vols. 1-2 — *Weiss, Thomas Fischer*
Cellular Digital Packet Data — *Streetharan, Muthuthamby*
Cellular Mobile Systems Engineering — *Faruque, Saleh*
Celt and Greek — *Ellis, Peter Berresford*
Celtic Christian Spirituality — *Davies, Oliver*
Celtic Christianity — *Bamford, Christopher*
Celtic Cornwall — *Filbee, Marjorie*
y The Celtic Ring — *Larsson, Bjorn*
The Celtic World — *Green, Miranda J*
c The Celts — *Martell, Hazel Mary*
y The Celts of Northern Europe — *Hinds, Kathryn*
Cement Concrete Pavements — *Villemagne, Maurice*
A Cement of Blood — *Hall, Gregory*
r Cemeteries of the Dwight Mission, London and Scotia Areas of Pope County, Arkansas — *Ballard, James*
r Cemetery Inscriptions and Revolutionary, War of 1812, and Civil War Veterans of Bowdoin, Maine — *Bartlett, Charlene B*
Cemetery Murders — *Marcy, Jean*
c Cemetery Quilt (Illus. by Rosanne Kaloustian) — *Ross, Kent*
r Cemetery Records. Vol. 2 — *Gowdy, Catherine Lutes*
r Cemetery Records of the Township of Fort Ann, Washington County, NY — *Moore, Charles B*
p CEMS Business Review
Censored by Confucius — *Yuan, Mei*
Censored: The News That Didn't Make the News--and Why 1996
y Censorship — *Stay, Byron L*
y Censorship — *Steffens, Bradley*
Censorship and Art in Pre-Enlightenment Lima — *Williams, Jerry M*
y Censorship in Schools — *Sherrow, Victoria*
Censure Et Culture Sous L'Ancien Regime — *Minois, Georges*
Centaur of the North — *Mayo, Wendell*
The Centaur Pholus — *Alexander, Marianne*
The Centenary of a Paper on Slow Viscous Flow by the Physicist H.A. Lorentz — *Lorentz, H A*
r The Center: A Guide to Genealogical Research in the National Capital Area — *Schaefer, Christina K*
The Center for Bioethics and Human Dignity Presents Dignity and Dying — *Kilner, John F*
Centered in God — *Howard, Evan Drake*
A Central African Odyssey — *Cowen, William W*
Central America 1821-1871 — *Gudmundson, Lowell*
Central America and the Middle East — *Fernandez, Damian J*
Central and Eastern Europe — *Karp, Regina Cowen*
r Central Asia — *King, John*
r Central Asia — *Whittell, Giles*
Central Asia in Transition — *Rumer, Boris*
Central Asia since Independence — *Hunter, Shireen T*
Central Avenue--Its Rise and Fall 1890-C. 1955 — *Cox, Bette Yarbrough*
The Central Bank and the Financial System — *Goodhart, C A E*
Central Banking in Developing Countries — *Fry, Maxwell J*
Central Europe — *Johnson, Lonnie R*
Central Europe since 1945 — *Lewis, Paul G, 1945-*
r Central European Folk Music — *Bohlman, Philip Vilas*
Central Oregon — *Barnes, Christine*
Central to Excellence
The Centrality of Agriculture — *Duncan, Colin A M*
The Centrality of Jerusalem — *Poorthuis, Marcel*
Centralization Versus Pluralism — *Kindleberger, Charles P*
Centre and Circumference — *Kamijima, Kenkichi*
Centrifugal Pump Users Guidebook — *Yedidiah, Sam*
Centro Cooks — *Prevedello, Barbara*
Centuries' Ends, Narrative Means — *Newman, Robert*
y A Century of Automotive Style — *Lamm, Michael*
A Century of Cuban Writers in Florida — *Hospital, Carolina*
A Century of Mycology — *Sutton, Brian*
y Century of Struggle. Enl. Ed. — *Flexner, Eleanor*
Century of War — *Kolko, Gabriel*
r A Century of War Dates and More 1859-1959 — *Van Dam, Theo*
Cephalopod Behaviour — *Hanlon, Robert T*
Ceramic Production in the American Southwest — *Mills, Barbara K*
Ceramic Technology for Potters and Sculptors — *Cuff, Yvonne Hutchinson*
Ceramic Uncles and Celluloid Mammies — *Turner, Patricia A*

Ceramics — *Sottsass, Ettore*
r Ceramics and Artifacts from Excavations in the Copan Residential Zone — *Willey, Gordon R*
c Ceras — *Comella, M Angels*
The Cerebral Code — *Calvin, William H*
The Ceremonial City — *Schneider, Robert Alan*
A Ceremonial Death — *Oliphant, B J*
Ceremonial Songs — *Neruda, Pablo*
Ceremonies of Possession in Europe's Conquest of the New World 1492-1640 — *Seed, Patricia*
Cereus Blooms at Night — *Mootoo, Shani*
The Cerne Giant — *Castleden, Rodney*
y A Certain Justice (David). Audio Version — *Lescroart, John T*
Certain People and Other Stories — *Allen, Roberta*
Certain Poor Shepherds — *Thomas, Elizabeth Marshall*
A Certain Slant of Light — *Holman, David Marion*
Certain Trumpets — *Wills, Garry*
Certainty of Justice — *Weed, Frank J*
r Certification and Accreditation Programs Directory. 1st Ed.
Certified Tropical Timber and Consumer Behavior — *Brockmann, Karl Ludwig*
La Certosa Di Casotto. Vols. 1-2 — *Chiaberto, Silvio*
La Certosa Di Pavia. Vols. 1-2 — *Hogg, James*
Cervante's Novelas Ejemplares — *Ricapito, Joseph V*
Cervical Cancer and Preinvasive Neoplasia — *Rubin, Stephen C*
c Cesar Chavez — *Altman, Linda Jacobs*
y Cesar Chavez — *Conord, Bruce W*
y Cesar Chavez: Leader for Migrant Farm Workers — *Gonzales, Doreen*
C'Est Tout — *Duras, Marguerite*
C'Etait Toute Une Vie — *Bon, Francois*
Ceylon and the Dutch 1600-1800 — *Arasaratnam, Sinnappah*
Cezanne — *Cezanne, Paul*
Cezanne: A Biography. Rev. Ed. — *Rewald, John*
The Cezanne Chase — *Swan, Thomas*
y Cezanne from A to Z — *Sellier, Marie*
Cezanne in Provence — *Schmitt, Evmarie*
Cezanne: Landscape into Art — *Machotka, Pavel*
Cezanne Paintings — *Adriani, Gotz*
r The CFO Handbook. Rev. Ed. — *Haskins, Mark E*
CGI Programming on the World Wide Web — *Gundavaram, Shishir*
The Chaco War — *Farcau, Bruce W*
Las Chacras De Coporaque — *Treacy, John M*
Chagall: A Retrospective — *Baal-Teshuva, Jacob*
y Chagall from A to Z — *Sellier, Marie*
The Chain Gang — *McCord, Richard*
Chain of Evidence — *Pearson, Ridley*
Chain of Evidence. Audio Version — *Pearson, Ridley*
Chain of Fools — *Stevenson, Richard*
Chain of Fools — *Womack, Steven*
Chained Together — *Ottaway, David*
The Chains of Interdependence — *Krenn, Michael L*
y The Chains of Sarai Stone (Merlington). Audio Version — *Haseloff, Cynthia*
La Chair Et L'Ame — *Couton, Georges*
La Chair, Le Diable Et Le Confesseur — *Bechtel, Guy*
Chairman Mao Would Not Be Amused — *Goldblatt, Howard*
c The Challenge — *Edwards, Jay*
The Challenge and Promise of a Catholic University — *Hesburgh, Theodore M*
Challenge and Response — *Magyar, Karl P*
c Challenge at Second Base (Dietz). Audio Version — *Christopher, Matt*
The Challenge from the East and the Rebirth of the West — *Spicer, Michael*
The Challenge of Comparative Literature — *Guillen, Claudio*
The Challenge of Direct Democracy — *Johnston, Richard*
The Challenge of European Integration — *Abegaz, Berhanu*
y The Challenge of Immigration — *Cox, Vic*
The Challenge of Local Feminisms — *Basu, Amrita*
The Challenge of Periodization — *Besserman, Lawrence*
r The Challenge of Urbanization — *United Nations. Dept. for Economic and Social Information and Policy Analysis. Population Division*
A Challenge to C.S. Lewis — *Milward, Peter*
The Challenger Launch Decision — *Vaughan, Diane*
Challenges for the Former Soviet South — *Allison, Roy*
Challenges in Ceramic Product Development, Manufacture, and Commercialization — *Ghosh, A*
Challenges in Clinical Practice — *Pollack, Mark H*

The Challenges of Democratic Consolidation in Portugal — *Manuel, Paul Christopher*
Challenges to Social Security — *Midgley, James*
Challenges to U.S. Security in the 1990's — *United States. Congress. House. Committee on Foreign Affairs*
Challenging Boundaries — *Shapiro, Michael J*
Challenging Codes — *Melucci, Alberto*
y Challenging IQ Puzzles — *Carter, Philip*
Challenging Problems in Algebra — *Posamentier, Alfred S*
Challenging Problems in Geometry — *Posamentier, Alfred S*
Challenging the Growth Machine — *Ferman, Barbara*
Challenging the Orthodoxies — *Auty, Richard M*
Challenging the Secret Government — *Olmsted, Katherine S*
Challenging the State — *Grindle, Merilee S*
Challenging Times — *Walford, Rex*
The Chamber — *Grisham, John*
The Chamber (Beck). Audio Version — *Grisham, John*
Chamberlain, Germany and Japan 1933-4 — *Bell, Peter, 1949-*
r Chambers 21st Century Dictionary
r Chambers Biographical Dictionary of Women
cr Chambers Children's Illustrated Dictionary
cr Chambers Children's Pocket Dictionary
cr Chambers First Dictionary
cr Chambers Super-Mini Dictionary
c Chameleon — *Stefoff, Rebecca*
c Chameleon, on Location (Illus. by Tara Darling) — *Darling, Kathy*
Champagne: The History and Character of the World's Most Celebrated Wine — *Sutcliffe, Serena*
Champion Du Monde — *Lindon, Mathieu*
Champions of Charity — *Hutchinson, John F*
Champions of the Ring — *Suster, Gerald*
y Champions: Stories of Ten Remarkable Athletes (Illus. by Bernie Fuchs) — *Littlefield, Bill*
c Chancay and the Secret of Fire — *Charles, Donald*
Chance — *Parker, Robert B*
y Chance (Reynolds). Audio Version — *Parker, Robert B*
Chance and Chaos (Cosham). Audio Version — *Ruelle, David*
Chance, Culture and the Literary Text — *Kavanagh, Thomas M*
c A Chance to Make Good — *Grossman, James R*
The Chancellors: A History of the Chancellors of the Exchequer 1945-90 — *Dell, Edmund*
Chancellorsville — *Sears, Stephen W*
y Chancellorsville — *Time-Life Books*
Chancellorsville: The Battle and Its Aftermath — *Gallagher, Gary W*
Chancery Equity Records and Proceedings 1600-1800 — *Horwitz, Henry*
Chandler and Grant's Glaucoma. 4th Ed. — *Epstein, David L*
Change at Work — *Cappelli, Peter*
Change in British Society. 4th Ed. — *Halsey, A H*
Change of Heart — *Stern, Tracy*
Change Processes in Child Psychotherapy — *Shirk, Stephen R*
y Change the Game — *Hill, Grant*
Change Your Smile. 3rd Ed. — *Goldstein, Ronald E*
Change Your Standpoint, Change Your World — *Mills, Kenneth George*
The Changeling — *MacLeod, Alison*
The Changeling — *Middleton, Thomas*
y The Changeling — *Rusch, Kristine Kathryn*
Changes and Dreams — *Beagan, Glenda*
Changes in Land Use and Land Cover — *Meyer, William B*
Changes in the Roman Empire — *MacMullen, Ramsay*
Changes of Mind — *Wade, Jenny*
Changing Appearances — *Sproles, George B*
The Changing Capital Markets of East Asia — *Cao, Ky*
c Changing Childhoods
Changing Christian Paradigms and Their Implications for Modern Thought — *Knox, Crawford*
Changing College Classrooms — *Halpern, Diane F*
c Changing Colors (Illus. by Neecy Twinem) — *Twinem, Neecy*
Changing Differences — *Jeffreys-Jones, Rhodri*
Changing Enemies — *Annan, Noel*
The Changing Face of Jewish and Christian Worship in North America — *Bradshaw, Paul F*
Changing Fatherhood — *Dongen, Mirjam Van*
Changing Focus — *Swasy, Alecia*
Changing Health Care — *Jennings, Ken*
The Changing Health Care Marketplace — *Zelman, Walter A*

Changing HIV Risk Behavior — *Kelly, Jeffrey A*
The Changing Industrial Map of Europe
— *Silberston, Aubrey*
Changing Lives — *Committee on Women's Studies in Asia*
Changing Methods — *Burt, Sandra*
Changing Moods — *Parkinson, Brian*
Changing Nature's Course — *Becker, Gerhold K*
Changing Numbers, Changing Needs — *Sandefur, Gary D*
The Changing of the Guard — *Lasater, Martin L*
The Changing Political Economy of the Third World
— *Dorraj, Manochehr*
The Changing Politics of Non-Government Organizations and African States — *Sandberg, Eve*
Changing Primary Health Care — *Bryar, Rosamund*
Changing Roles of Women within the Christian Church in Canada — *Muir, Elizabeth Gillan*
The Changing Same — *McDowell, Deborah E*
Changing Seasons and Other Poems — *Smelcer, John E*
The Changing Seasons of Humor in Literature. 2nd Ed. — *Daemmrich, Ingrid G*
Changing States — *Ford, Glyn*
Changing Structure of Mexico — *Randall, Laura*
Changing the Boundaries — *Jiggins, Janice*
Changing the Bully Who Rules the World — *Bly, Carol*
Changing the Culture — *Fisher, Naomi D*
Changing the Educational Landscape — *Martin, Jane Roland*
Changing the Odds — *Lavin, David E*
Changing the Rules — *Dehue, Trudy*
Changing the Subject — *Black, Paul*
Changing the Subject — *Miller, Naomi J*
Changing the U.S. Health Care System — *Andersen, Ronald*
Changing Tides — *Weddle, Robert S*
Changing Trains — *Norris, Steven*
Changing Values in Medieval Scotland — *Gemmill, Elizabeth*
The Changing Voices of Europe — *Davies, Winifred V*
Changing Witness — *Warner, Michael*
Changing Woman — *Anderson, Karen*
y Changing Woman of the Apache — *Golston, Sydele E*
r Channel Islands — *Bell, Brian*
Channel-Surfing the Apocalypse — *Nash, Susan Smith*
Channel Tunnel Visions 1850-1945 — *Wilson, Keith*
Channel Zero — *Krekorian, Michael*
The Channeling Zone — *Brown, Michael F*
Channels of Propaganda — *Sproule, J Michael*
The Chansons De Geste in the Age of Romance
— *Kay, Sarah*
Chansons Des Trouveres — *Rosenberg, Samuel N*
c Chanting Rhymes (Illus. by Carol Thompson)
— *Foster, John*
c A Chanuka Story for Night Number 3 (Illus. by Harris Mandel) — *Pape, David Sholom*
Chaos and All That — *Liu, So-la*
Chaos and Complexity — *Russell, Robert John*
Chaos and the Changing Nature of Science and Medicine — *Conference on Chaos and the Changing Nature of Science and Medicine (1995: Mobile, AL)*
Chaos as Usual — *Lorenz, Juliane*
Chaos, Catastrophe, and Human Affairs — *Guastello, Stephen J*
Chaos in Gravitational N-Body Systems — *Muzzio, J C*
Chaos in the Cosmos — *Parker, Barry*
Chaos or Community — *Sklar, Holly*
Chaos Theory in Economics — *Dechert, W Davis*
Chaos Theory in the Social Sciences — *Kiel, L Douglas*
Chaosmos: Literature, Science, and Theory
— *Kuberski, Philip*
Chaotic Behavior of Deterministic Dissipative Systems
— *Marek, Milos*
Chaotic, Fractal, and Nonlinear Signal Processing
— *AIP Conference on Chaotic, Fractal, and Nonlinear Signal Processing (1995: Mystic, CT)*
c Chaparral — *Ricciuti, Edward R*
The Chapel of St. Anthony at the Santo and the Development of Venetian Renaissance Sculpture
— *McHam, Sarah Blake*
The Chaperonins — *Ellis, R John*
Character above All — *Wilson, Robert A, 1941-*
Character and Culture — *Babbitt, Irving*
Character and Personality in the Novels of William Faulkner — *Bockting, Ineke*
The Character of Our Communities — *Albrecht, Gloria*

Character Witness — *Forster, R A*
Characteristics of American Indian and Alaska Native Education — *Pavel, D Michael*
Characterization of Environmental Radiation and Radioactivity Near Albuquerque, New Mexico
— *Hostak, John Michael*
Characterizing Sources of Indoor Air Pollution and Related Sink Effects — *Tichenor, Bruce A*
y Characters from Pre-20th Century Novels
— *Campbell, Susie*
r Characters in 19th-Century Literature
r Characters in 20th-Century Literature. Bks. 1-2
The Characters of Love — *Boyt, Susie*
Characters on the Loose — *Kauffman, Janet*
The Charcoal Dilemma — *Rosillo-Calle, Frank*
Chardin — *Roland Michel, Marianne*
The Charge: Why the Light Brigade Was Lost
— *Adkin, Mark*
Charging Ahead — *Berger, John J*
Charisma Und Caritas — *Ritter, Adolf Martin*
r The Charismatic Movement. Vols. 1-2 — *Jones, Charles Edwin*
Charitable Knowledge — *Lawrence, Susan C*
The Charitable Nonprofits — *Bowen, William G*
Charity — *Callen, Paulette*
Charity — *Deighton, Len*
Charity and State in Late Renaissance Italy
— *Menning, Carol Bresnahan*
Charlemos Un Poco. 3rd Ed. — *Fernandez, Rosa*
Charles I 1625-1640 — *Quintrell, Brian*
Charles and Kathleen Norris — *Norris, Charles Gilman*
Charles and Ray Eames — *Kirkham, Pat*
c The Charles Barber Treatment — *Lloyd, Carole*
c Charles Barkley — *Dolan, Sean*
c Charles Barkley: Star Forward — *Knapp, Ron*
Charles Baudelaire Revisited — *Hyslop, Lois Boe*
The Charles Bukowski Second Coming Years
— *Winanas, A D*
r Charles Burchfield: An Annotated Bibliography
— *Makowski, Colleen Lahan*
y Charles Darwin: A Biography. Vol. 1 — *Browne, E J*
y Charles Darwin and the Evolution Revolution
— *Stefoff, Rebecca*
Charles Darwin's Letters — *Darwin, Charles*
Charles Dickens: A Literary Life — *Smith, Grahame*
r Charles Dickens on the Screen — *Pointer, Michael*
Charles Dickens: The Uses of Time — *Marlow, James E*
The Charles Dickens-Thomas Powell Vendetta
— *Moss, Carolyn*
Charles English: Macbeth
Charles G. Finney and the Spirit of American Evangelicalism — *Hambrick-Stowe, Charles E*
Charles Ives: A Life with Music — *Swafford, Jan*
Charles Ives and His World — *Burkholder, J Peter*
Charles Ives and the Classical Tradition — *Block, Geoffrey*
Charles Kuralt's America — *Kuralt, Charles*
Charles M. Russell: The Life and Legend of America's Cowboy Artist — *Taliaferro, John*
r Charles-Maurice De Talleyrand 1754-1838 — *Dwyer, Philip G*
Charles Murray and the Underclass — *Lister, Ruth*
c Charles of the Wild (Illus. by John Hassett)
— *Hassett, John*
Charles Rennie Mackintosh — *Kaplan, Wendy*
Charles Rennie Mackintosh 1868-1928 — *Fiell, Charlotte*
Charles Seeger: A Life in American Music
— *Pescatello, Ann M*
Charles Sumner — *Donald, David Herbert*
Charleston Kedding: A History of Kitchen Gardening
— *Campbell, Susan*
p The Charleston Report: Business Insights into the Library Market
c Charlie and Tess (Illus. by Catherine Walters)
— *Hall, Martin*
c Charlie and the Big Chill (Illus. by Chris Burke)
— *Henry, Lenny*
c Charlie and the Big Chill (Illus. by Chris Burke). Book and Audio Version — *Henry, Lenny*
Charlie and the Children — *Scott, Joanna C, 1943-*
c Charlie and the Chocolate Factory — *Dahl, Roald*
Charlie Boy — *Bargum, Johan*
Charlie Carrillo: Tradition and Soul — *Awalt, Barbe*
Charlie Chaplin and His Times — *Lynn, Kenneth S*
c Charlie Fait Du Sport — *Alen, Paule*
Charlie Parker and Thematic Improvisation
— *Martin, Henry*
Charlie Parker: His Music and Life — *Woideck, Carl*

c Charlie, Queen of the Desert (Illus. by Chris Burke)
— *Henry, Lenny*
c Charlie the Champion Traveller (Illus. by Philippe Dupasquier) — *Townson, Hazel*
c Charlie the Chicken — *Denchfield, Nick*
Charlie Trotter's Vegetables — *Trotter, Charlie*
c Charlie's Checklist (Illus. by Alison Bartlett)
— *Lerman, Rory S*
c Charlie's Choice (Illus. by Nicola Smee) — *Smee, Nicola*
Charlotte Bronte: A Passionate Life — *Gordon, Lyndall*
Charlotte Bronte and Victorian Psychology
— *Shuttleworth, Sally*
Charlotte Bronte's High Life in Verdopolis — *Bronte, Charlotte*
y Charlotte Bronte's Jane Eyre — *Bloom, Harold*
Charlotte Perkins Gilman: Her Progress toward Utopia with Selected Writings — *Kessler, Carol Farley*
c The Charlotte Stories (Illus. by Harvey Chan) — *Jam, Teddy*
Charlotte Temple — *Rowson, Susanna*
Charlotte Yonge — *Hayter, Alethea*
c Charlotte's Piggy Bank (Illus. by David McKee)
— *McKee, David*
c Charlotte's Web (Illus. by Garth Williams) — *White, E B*
c Charlotte's Web (White). Audio Version — *White, E B*
r The Charlton Price Guide to Canadian Clocks
— *Connell, James E*
Charmed — *Hart, Catherine*
Charming Cadavers — *Wilson, Liz*
r Charming Small Hotel Guide: Britain including Ireland. 6th Ed.
Charter Schools — *Nathan, Joe*
Charters and Custumals of the Abbey of Holy Trinity, Caen. Pt. 2
Charters of the Medieval Hospitals of Bury St. Edmunds — *Harper-Bill, Christopher*
Charters of the Redvers Family and the Earldom of Devon 1090-1217 — *Bearman, Robert*
Charters of the Vicars Choral of York Minster
— *Tringham, Nigel J*
r The Charting of the Oceans — *Whitfield, Peter*
r The Chartist Movement — *Ashton, Owen*
The Chase — *Alcott, Louisa May*
r Chase's 1997 Calendar of Events
r Chase's Sports Calendar of Events 1997
Chasing Cezanne — *Mayle, Peter*
Chasing Dirt — *Hoy, Suellen*
Chasing Grace — *Manning, Martha*
Chasing Hellhounds — *Hoffman, Marvin*
Chasing Progress in the Irish Republic — *Jacobsen, John Kurt*
y Chasing Redbird — *Creech, Sharon*
Chasing Shadows — *Gooding, Janda*
Chasing the Dragon — *Cox, Christopher R*
Chasing the Dream — *Hurt, Henry, III*
Chasing the Dream — *Torre, Joe*
Chasing the Sun — *Green, Jonathon*
Chasing the Tigers — *Hiebert, Murray*
Un Chasseur Dans L'Image — *Boucquey, Eliane*
Le Chasseur Zero — *Roze, Pascale*
y The Chatham School Affair — *Cook, Thomas H*
The Chatham School Affair (Guidall). Audio Version
— *Cook, Thomas H*
c Chato's Kitchen (Illus. by Susan Guevara) — *Soto, Gary*
c Chattanooga Sludge (Illus. by Molly Bang) — *Bang, Molly*
Chatterton — *Ackroyd, Peter*
c Chatting (Illus. by Shirley Hughes) — *Hughes, Shirley*
Chaucer and the Universe of Learning — *Astell, Ann W*
Chaucer at Work — *Brown, Peter, 1948-*
Chaucer, Boccaccio, and the Debate of Love
— *Thompson, N S*
Chaucer Yearbook. Vol. 2
Chaucerian Belief — *Hill, John M*
Chaucerian Realism — *Myles, Robert*
Chaucerian Theatricality — *Ganim, John M*
Chaucer's Chain of Love — *Taylor, Paul Beekman*
Chaucer's Ovidian Arts of Love — *Calabrese, Michael A*
yr Chaucer's Pilgrims — *Lambdin, Laura C*
Chaucer's Rehersynges — *Quinn, William A*
Chave's Memories — *Delgado, Maria Isabel*
Che Guevara: A Revolutionary Life — *Anderson, Jon Lee*

Che Le Donne Siano Della Spezie Degli Uomini — *Tarabotti, Arcangela*

Cheap and Easy Internet Access — *LeVitus, Bob*

Cheap Seats — *Campbell, James E*

Cheap Ticket to Heaven — *Smith, Charlie*

Cheap Wage Labour — *Muszynski, Alicja*

r The Cheapskate's Guide to Paris — *Emerson, Connie*

The Cheat of Words — *McCaffery, Steve*

Cheaters and Other Stories — *Albarelli, Dean*

r Cheatin' Hearts, Broken Dreams, and Stomped-On Love — *McMullan, Jim*

y Cheating Time — *Gosden, Roger*

Chechenskii Tranzit — *Barkovskii, V*

y Checkers — *Marsden, John*

Checking on Banks — *Khademian, Anne M*

r A Checklist of American Imprints for 1845 — *Rinderknecht, Carol*

r A Checklist of Contributions by William Makepeace Thackeray to Newspapers, Periodicals, Books, and Serial Part Issues 1828-1864 — *Harden, Edgar F*

r A Checklist of Countries Currently Issuing Their Own Paper Money — *Remick, Jerry*

r Checklist of Writings on American Music 1640-1992 — *Marco, Guy A*

Checkmating Aliens — *Vira, Soma*

c A Cheerful Note for Jack (Illus. by Arlene Boehm) — *Boehm, Arlene*

The Cheerio Killings — *Allyn, Doug*

c A Cheese and Tomato Spider (Illus. by Nick Sharratt) — *Sharratt, Nick*

Cheese Primer — *Jenkins, Steven W*

Cheevey: A Novel — *DiPego, Gerald*

y Cheevey: A Novel (Hall). Audio Version — *DiPego, Gerald*

Chekhov: A Life in Letters — *Chekhov, Anton*

Chekhov: Four Plays — *Chekhov, Anton*

Chekhov, the Complete Plays — *Chekhov, Anton*

Chekhov's Plays — *Gilman, Richard*

Chemical and Biochemical Sensing with Optical Fibers and Waveguides — *Boisde, Gilbert*

Chemical and Isotopic Groundwater Hydrology. 2nd Ed. — *Mazor, Emanuel*

Chemical Ecology — *Eisner, Thomas*

Chemical Engineering for Chemists — *Griskey, Richard G*

Chemical Evolution—Physics of the Origin and Evolution of Life — *Trieste Conference on Chemical Evolution (4th: 1995: Trieste, Italy)*

r Chemical Guide to the Internet — *Lee, C C*

p Chemical Intelligence

p The Chemical Intelligencer

The Chemical Physics of Fullerenes 10 (and 5) Years Later — *NATO Advanced Research Workshop on the Chemical Physics of Fullerenes 10 (and 5) Years Later (1995: Varenna, Italy)*

r Chemical Research Faculties

Chemical Sciences Graduate School Finder 1995-1996

Chemical Separations with Liquid Membranes — *Bartsch, Richard A*

Chemical Synthesis — *Chatgilialoglu, Chryssostomos*

r Chemical Technicians' Ready Reference Handbook. 4th Ed. — *Shugar, Gershon J*

Chemical Warfare Agents — *Marrs, Timothy C*

Chemical Waves and Patterns — *Kapral, Raymond*

Chemically Modified Surfaces — *Pesek, Joseph J*

Chemin D'Ecole — *Chamoiseau, Patrick*

Die Chemischen Elemente — *Trueb, Lucien F*

Chemistry and Chemical Reactivity. 3rd Ed. — *Kotz, John C*

Chemistry and Physics of Carbon. Vol. 25

r Chemistry Citation Index. Electronic Media Version

The Chemistry Classroom — *Herron, J Dudley*

y Chemistry: Concepts and Problems. 2nd Ed. — *Houk, Clifford C*

Chemistry for the Protection of the Environment 2 — *Pawlowski, Lucjan*

Chemistry in Context. 2nd Ed. — *Schwartz, A Truman*

r The Chemistry Maths Book — *Steiner, Erich*

The Chemistry of Conscious States — *Hobson, J Allan*

The Chemistry of Mind-Altering Drugs — *Perrine, Daniel M*

The Chemistry of Non-Sag Tungsten — *Bartha, Laszlo*

y Chemistry of the Environment — *Ramsden, E N*

Chemistry: The Central Science. 7th Ed. — *Brown, Theodore L*

Chemistry: The Study of Matter and Its Changes. 2nd Ed. — *Brady, James E*

Chemistry under Extreme and Non-Classical Conditions — *Eldik, Rudi Van*

r The Chemotherapy Source Book. 2nd Ed. — *Perry, Michael C*

The Chemotherapy Survival Guide — *McKay, Judith*

Ch'en Liang on Public Interest and the Law — *Tillman, Hoyt Cleveland*

Chene Et Chien — *Queneau, Raymond*

Cheng Huan Ji — *Yishu*

Chequers: The Prime Minister's Country House and Its History — *Major, Norma*

Les Chercheurs D'Os — *Djaout, Tahar*

Cherish Christ above All — *Dumm, Demetrius*

Cherishing Men from Afar — *Hevia, James L*

Cherokee Dance and Drama — *Speck, Frank G*

Cherokee Editor — *Boudinot, Elias*

Cherokee Messenger — *Bass, Althea*

The Cherokee Removal — *Perdue, Theda*

Cherokee Rose — *Alter, Judy*

c The Cherokees (Illus. by Ronald Himler) — *Sneve, Virginia Driving Hawk*

p Cherrypickers' News

r The Cherrypickers' Top 150 — *Fivaz, Bill*

c Cheshire Moon — *Butts, Nancy*

Chess among the Jews — *Keats, Victor*

c Chess for Children — *Nottingham, Ted*

y The Chess Garden — *Hansen, Brooks*

Chess: Its Origins — *Keats, Victor*

Chess, Jews and History — *Keats, Victor*

Chester Square — *Hernandez, Jaime*

Chestnut Mare, Beware — *Jaffe, Jody*

The Chevalier of Pensieri-Vani — *Fuller, Henry B*

Le Chevron — *Bergounioux, Pierre*

c The Cheyennes (Illus. by Ronald Himler) — *Sneve, Virginia Driving Hawk*

c The Cheyennes: People of the Plains — *Bonvillain, Nancy*

Chez Albert — *Baillie, Robert*

Chez Panisse Vegetables — *Waters, Alice*

c Chibi: A True Story from Japan (Illus. by June Otani) — *Brenner, Barbara*

r Chicago and Cook County — *Szucs, Loretto Dennis*

r Chicago and Cook County Sources — *Szucs, Loretto Dennis*

c Chicago and the Cat: The Family Reunion (Illus. by Robin Michal Koontz) — *Koontz, Robin Michal*

y Chicago Blues — *Deaver, Julie Reece*

r The Chicago Cubs Encyclopedia — *Holtzman, Jerome*

Chicago Days — *Swanson, Stevenson*

The Chicago Gangster Theory of Life — *Ross, Andrew, 1956-*

Chicago Hispanic Health Coalition

Chicago's War on Syphilis 1937-40 — *Poirier, Suzanne*

Chicana Creativity and Criticism — *Herrera-Sobek, Maria*

Chicanas/Chicanos at the Crossroads — *Maciel, David R*

Chicano! — *Rosales, F Arturo*

Chicano Graffiti and Murals — *Kim, Sojin*

The Chicano/Hispanic Image in American Film — *Berumen, Frank Javier Garcia*

Chicanos and Chicanas in Contemporary Society — *De Anda, Roberto Moreno*

c Chickadee Rescue — *Kittredge, Sonya*

Chickadees, Tits, Nuthatches and Treecreepers — *Harrap, Simon*

Chickamauga — *Wright, Charles*

r Chickasaw Nation, Indian Territory (Oklahoma) Marriage Book D — *Tedford, Sandra*

Chicken Dinners in One Pot — *Fallon, Peggy*

y The Chicken Doesn't Skate — *Korman, Gordon*

c Chicken Licken — *Allen, Jonathan*

The Chicken Parts Cookbook — *Pierce, Charles*

c The Chicken Sisters (Illus. by Sharleen Collicott) — *Numeroff, Laura Joffe*

c Chickie Riddles (Illus. by Thor Wickstrom) — *Hall, Katy*

c El Chico Karateka (Illus. by David Katzenstein) — *Morris, Ann*

Chief Engineer — *Green, Lorne*

The Chief Governors — *Brady, Ciaran*

c Chief Joseph: Nez Perce Warrior — *Sanford, William R*

y Chief Justice — *Cray, Ed*

The Chief Justiceship of Melville W. Fuller 1888-1910 — *Ely, James W, Jr.*

Chiefdoms and Early States in the Near East — *Stein, Gil*

Chiefs — *Woods, Stuart*

Un Chien Andalou, L'Age D'Or — *Murcia, Claude*

Le Chien Qui Voulait Me Manger — *Reyes, Alina*

Una Chiesa Di Frontiera — *Rando, Daniela*

The Chignecto Covenanters — *Hay, Eldon*

Chihuahua: Pictures from the Edge — *Hancock, Virgil*

c Child Abuse (Illus. by Mike Lacey) — *Sanders, Pete*

Child and Adolescent Development — *Rice, F Philip*

Child and Adolescent Psychiatry — *Parmelee, Dean X*

Child and Adolescent Psychiatry. 2nd Ed. — *Lewis, Melvin*

The Child and Adolescent Psychotherapy Treatment Planner — *Jongsma, Arthur E*

Child Care and Culture — *LeVine, Robert A*

Child Custody Made Simple — *Watnik, Webster*

A Child Is Not a Knife — *Sonnevi, Goran*

Child-Loving: The Erotic Child and Victorian Culture — *Kincaid, James R*

Child Maltreatment and Optimal Caregiving in Social Contexts — *Baumrind, Diana*

Child of All Nations — *Toer, Pramoedya Ananta*

Child of Mine — *Kline, Christina Baker*

Child of the Dawn — *Chopra, Gautama*

y Child of the Eagle — *Friesner, Esther*

c Child of the Wolves — *Hall, Elizabeth*

A Child on Her Mind — *Bergum, Vangie*

A Child Out of Alcatraz — *Ison, Tara*

Child Protection for Teachers and Schools — *Whitney, Ben*

Child Psychopathology — *Mash, Eric J*

Child Safety — *Gilham, Bill*

Child Safety on the Internet — *Classroom Connect*

The Child with a Spinal Cord Injury — *Betz, Randal R*

r Childhood and Children — *Bel Geddes, Joan*

Childhood and Society — *Erikson, Erik H*

y Childhood (Bygone Britian 1900-1970)

Childhood Matters — *Qvortrup, Jens*

Childhood Obsessive Compulsive Disorder — *Francis, Greta*

A Childhood: The Biography of a Place — *Crews, Harry*

Childhood Transformed — *Hopkins, Eric*

y Childish Things — *Van Der Vyver, Marita*

Children and Adolescents in Need — *Weisz, Virginia G*

Children and Books. 9th Ed. — *Sutherland, Zena*

Children and Childhood in Western Society since 1500 — *Cunningham, Hugh*

Children and Grief — *Worden, J William*

Children and Political Violence — *Cairns, Ed*

Children and the Internet — *Kehoe, Brendan*

Children and the Movies — *Jowett, Garth S*

Children and the Politics of Culture — *Stephens, Sharon*

The Children Bob Moses Led — *Heath, William*

p Children, Churches and Daddies

Children Doing Mathematics — *Nunes, Terezinha*

Children First — *Black, Maggie, 1945-*

Children, Health and the Social Order — *Mayall, Berry*

Children in Charge: The Child's Right to a Fair Hearing — *John, Mary*

Children in Charge: The Child's Right to Resources — *John, Mary*

Children in Court — *Mezey, Susan Gluck*

Children in Families at Risk — *Combrinck-Graham, Lee*

Children in Jeopardy — *Harris, Irving B*

y Children in the Holocaust and World War II — *Holliday, Laurel*

cr Children Just like Me — *Kindersley, Barnabas*

Children Learning to Read — *Itzkoff, Seymour W*

Children Making Books — *Johnson, Paul*

c The Children Next Door — *Ure, Jean*

Children of Albion Rovers — *Williamson, Kevin*

The Children of Amarid — *Coe, David B*

c Children of Asian America (Illus. by Gene H Mayeda) — *Asian American Coalition (Chicago, Ill.)*

The Children of Athena — *Loraux, Nicole*

c The Children of Bolivia — *Hermes, Jules*

Children of Cambodia's Killing Fields — *Dith Pran*

Children of Chaos — *Rushkoff, Douglas*

c Children of Coal and Iron — *Rose, Iain*

c Children of Cuba (Illus. by Frank Staub) — *Staub, Frank*

Children of England — *Weir, Alison*

y The Children of Henry VIII — *Weir, Alison*

Children of History — *Hayes, Patricia*

Children of Job — *Berger, Alan L*

Children of Peace — *McIntyre, W John*

y Children of Promise — *Sullivan, Charles*

c Children of Summer (Illus. by Marie LeGlatin Keis) — *Anderson, Margaret J*

Children of the Alley — *Mahfouz, Naguib*

Children of the Dark House — *Polk, Noel*

y Children of the Dust — *Lawrence, Louise*

c Children of the Earth (Illus. by Freddie Langeler) — *Langeler, Freddie*

Children of the Earth — *Shell, Marc*

c Children of the Ecuadorean Highlands — *Beirne, Barbara*

Children of the Empire — *Manthorpe, Victoria*

Children of the Fur Trade — *Jackson, John C*

Children of the Ice Age — *Stanley, Steven M*

y Children of the Jedi — *Hambly, Barbara*

c Children of the Longhouse — *Bruchac, Joseph*

y Children of the Mind — *Card, Orson Scott*

y Children of the Mind (Whitener). Audio Version — *Card, Orson Scott*

Children of the Night — *Naylor, Gloria*

c Children of the Philippines (Illus. by Elaine Little) — *Kinkade, Sheila*

y Children of the River — *Crew, Linda*

c The Children of the Sierra Madre (Illus. by Frank Staub) — *Staub, Frank*

c Children of the Stars (Illus. by Freddie Langeler) — *Langeler, Freddie*

Children of the Troubles — *Holliday, Laurel*

y Children of the Vampire. Abridged Ed. Audio Version — *Kalogridis, Jeanne*

y Children of the Vampire. Unabridged Ed. Audio Version — *Kalogridis, Jeanne*

c Children of the Westward Trail — *Stefoff, Rebecca*

The Children of Time — *Lestienne, Remy*

y The Children of Topaz — *Tunnell, Michael O*

c Children of Yucatan (Illus. by Frank Staub) — *Staub, Frank*

Children on the Move — *Doek, Jaap*

Children, Parents, and the Rise of the Novel — *Nelson, T G A*

Children, Parents, Lollipops — *Tsesis, Vladimir A*

Children, Race, and Power — *Markowitz, Gerald*

c Children Save the Rain Forest (Illus. by Dan L Perlman) — *Patent, Dorothy Hinshaw*

Children, Teachers and Schools in the History of British Columbia — *Barman, Jean*

Children: The Invisible Soldier — *Brett, Rachel*

Children Using Computers. 2nd Ed. — *Straker, Anita*

Children with Prenatal Drug Exposure — *Chandler, Lynette S*

r The Children's Aid Society of New York — *Inskeep, Carolee R*

c The Children's Book of Kwanzaa (Illus. by Dolores Johnson) — *Johnson, Dolores*

r Children's Books and Their Creators — *Silvey, Anita*

r Children's Books: Awards and Prizes. 1996 Ed.

r Children's Books of the Year 1996

c The Children's Classic Poetry Collection (Illus. by Cathie Shuttleworth) — *Baxter, Nicola*

c Children's Clothing of the 1800s (Illus. by Barb Bedell) — *Schimpky, David*

The Children's Kitchen Garden — *Brennan, Georgeanne*

Children's Literature — *Lesnik-Oberstein, Karin*

Children's Literature. 3rd Ed. — *Rudman, Masha P*

Children's Literature and Critical Theory — *May, Jill P*

Children's Literature Comes of Age — *Nikolajeva, Maria*

Children's Literature Research — *International Youth Library*

Children's Past Lives — *Bowman, Carol*

Children's Pleasures — *Burton, Anthony*

r Children's Rights — *Edmonds, Beverly C*

r Children's Rights — *Freeman, Michael*

Children's Rights Re-Visioned — *Ladd, Rosalind Ekman*

Children's Rooms in a Weekend — *Ryde, Roo*

r The Children's Song Index 1978-1993 — *Laughlin, Kay*

r Children's Symptoms — *Valman, Bernard*

Children's Understanding of Disability — *Lewis, Ann*

Children's Voices in Atlantic Literature and Culture — *Thompson, Hilary*

c A Child's Anthology of Poetry — *Sword, Elizabeth Hauge*

c A Child's Book of Irish Rhymes (Illus. by N Emoc) — *Taylor, A*

c A Child's Book of Play in Art — *Micklethwait, Lucy*

c A Child's Book of Prayer in Art — *Beckett, Wendy*

c A Child's Day (Illus. by Antoinette DeBiasi) — *Kalman, Bobbie*

c A Child's Good Morning Book (Illus. by Jean Charlot) — *Brown, Margaret Wise*

A Child's Night Dream — *Stone, Oliver*

The Child's Song — *Capps, Donald*

c Chile Fever (Illus. by Elizabeth King) — *King, Elizabeth*

Chile: The Great Transformation — *Martinez, Javier*

c Chile: Where the Land Ends — *Pickering, Marianne*

Chile's Free Market Miracle — *Collins, Joseph*

Chilkoot Trail — *Neufeld, David*

The Chill — *Macdonald, Ross*

The Chilly Classroom Climate — *Sandler, Bernice Resnick*

Chim: The Photographs of David Seymour — *Seymour, David*

c The Chimpanzee — *Crewe, Sabrina*

The Chin Kiss King — *Veciana-Suarez, Ana*

r China. 3rd Ed. — *Chan, Charis*

r China, a Lonely Planet Travel Survival Kit. 5th Ed. — *Taylor, Chris*

China: A Nation in Transition — *Soled, Debra E*

China after Deng Xiaoping — *Lam, Willy Wo-Lap*

China after Socialism — *McCormick, Barrett L*

China and Europe 1949-1995 — *Shambaugh, David*

China and Korea — *Lee, Chae-Jin*

China and the American Dream — *Madsen, Richard*

China at War 1901-1949 — *Dreyer, Edward L*

y China Dreams — *Maynard, Isabelle*

r China Environmental Report — *Gallagher, Michael G*

The China Factor in Modern Japanese Thought — *Li, Lincoln*

y The China Garden — *Berry, Liz*

China Hands — *Rand, Peter*

China in My Life — *Wilbur, C Martin*

China in the 1980s — *Breslin, Shaun*

China in the Information Age — *Mueller, Milton*

China in World History. 2nd Ed. — *Adshead, S A M*

China in World Politics — *Faust, John R*

China: Issues and Options in Greenhouse Gas Emissions Control — *Johnson, Todd M*

China Live — *Chinoy, Mike*

China: Macroeconomic Stability in a Decentralized Economy

China Men — *Kingston, Maxine Hong*

China, Modernisation and the Goal of Prosperity — *Hannan, Kate*

c China: Old Ways Meet New — *Kent, Deborah*

China Pop — *Zha, Jianying*

China Review 1995

China since the Cultural Revolution — *Chen, Jie*

China since Tiananmen — *Sullivan, Lawrence R*

China the Big Tiger — *Wilson, Dick*

China: The Many Facets of Demographic Change — *Goldstein, Alice*

China, the United States, and the Soviet Union — *Ross, Robert S*

y The China Voyage — *Severin, Tim*

China Voyager — *Haas, William J*

China Wakes — *Kristof, Nicholas D*

China's Arms Acquisitions from Abroad — *Gill, Bates*

China's Brain Drain to the United States — *Zweig, David*

China's Cultural Revolution 1966-1969 — *Schoenhals, Michael*

China's Economic Evolution — *Frantzen, Piet*

China's Economic Reform — *Kao, Shang-Chuan*

China's Energy Strategy — *Lin, Xiannuan*

China's Legalists — *Fu, Zhengyuan*

China's Local Councils in the Age of Constitutional Reform 1898-1911 — *Thompson, Roger R*

China's Media, Media's China — *Lee, Chin-Chuan*

China's Minority Cultures — *Mackerras, Colin*

China's Motor — *Gates, Hill*

China's Rise, Russia's Fall — *Nolan, Peter*

China's Road to the Korean War — *Chen, Jian*

c China's Tang Dynasty — *Millar, Heather*

China's Universities 1895-1995 — *Hayhoe, Ruth*

China's Warlords — *Bonavia, David*

Chinese Awakenings — *Tyson, James*

Chinese Brushstrokes — *Hutchison, Sandra*

y The Chinese Century — *Spence, Jonathan D*

Chinese Ceramics — *He, Li*

Chinese Checkers (Cassidy). Audio Version — *Doumani, Carol*

Chinese Civilization in the Making 1766-221 BC — *Li, Jun*

y The Chinese Cultural Revolution — *Pietrusza, David*

The Chinese Diaspora and Mainland China — *Lever-Tracy, Constance*

Chinese Economic Reform — *Segal, Gerald*

The Chinese Economy

Chinese Export Porcelain from the Museum of Anastacio Goncalves, Lisbon — *Matos, Maria Antonia Pinto De*

Chinese Families in the Post-Mao Era — *Davis, Deborah*

Chinese Fitness — *Liu, Qingshan*

Chinese Folktales — *Giskin, Howard*

Chinese Historical Microdemography — *Harrell, Stevan*

Chinese in Plain English — *De Mente, Boye*

Chinese Jade from the Neolithic to the Qing — *Rawson, Jessica*

c Chinese Jump Rope — *Johnson, Anne Akers*

Chinese Medicine — *Williams, Tom*

Chinese Musical Instruments — *Yang, Mu*

Chinese New Year — *Moyse, Sarah*

Chinese Propaganda Posters — *Landsberger, Stefan*

c The Chinese Puzzle — *Brouillet, Chrystine*

The Chinese Reassessment of Socialism 1976-1992 — *Sun, Yan*

Chinese Short Stories of the Twentieth Century — *Fang, Zhihua*

r Chinese Stamp Catalog Illustrated in Colors. 1996 Ed.

Chinese Views of Childhood — *Kinney, Anne Behnke*

The Chinese Way to Healing — *Cohen, Misha Ruth*

Chinese Women Speak — *Verschuur-Basse, Denyse*

Chintz Ceramics — *Welsh, JoAnne P*

Chipping Away on Earth — *Quinones Keber, Eloise*

Chirac President — *Bacque, Raphaelle*

Chirac's Challenge — *Keller, John T S*

Chiral Separations — *Ahuja, Satinder*

Chivalry in Twelfth-Century Germany — *Jackson, W H*

Chivalry Is Dead — *Kingsbury, Kate*

c The Chocolate-Covered-Cookie Tantrum (Illus. by Harvey Stevenson) — *Blumenthal, Deborah*

c Chocolate Fever (Wilson). Audio Version — *Smith, Robert Kimmel*

Chocolate for a Woman's Soul — *Allenbaugh, Kay*

Chocolate Kisses

Chocolate, Strawberry and Vanilla — *Funderburg, Anne Cooper*

c The Chocolate Wolf (Illus. by David Ray) — *Cohen, Barbara*

Chocolates for Christmas — *Robbins, Maria*

r Choctaw Census Blue County 1885

r Choctaw Census Kiamitia County 1885

r Choctaw Emigration Records 1831-1856. Vols. 1-2 — *Olsen, Monty*

Choctaw Genesis 1500-1700 — *Galloway, Patricia*

Choctaws and Missionaries in Mississippi 1818-1918 — *Kidwell, Clara Sue*

Choe Notes. 2nd Ed. — *Choe, Jae Y*

The Choice — *Woodward, Bob*

Choice and Democratic Order — *Graham, Bruce Desmond*

Choice Ayres, Songs, and Dialogues. Bks. 1-5

Choice, Growth and Development — *De Dios, Emmanuel S*

The Choice I Made — *Kelley, Maria Felicia*

A Choice of Coleridge's Verse — *Coleridge, Samuel Taylor*

A Choice of Evils — *Chand, Meira*

The Choice of the People? — *Best, Judith*

The Choice of the Private Trader — *Howard, David S*

Choices — *Settle, Mary Lee*

Choices and Change — *Dookeran, Winston C*

Choices in Healing — *Lerner, Michael, 1943, Oct., 10-*

Chokecherry — *Hawkins, Norma*

Cholera in Post-Revolutionary Paris — *Kudlick, Catherine Jean*

Cholesterol Testing and Treatment in Adults: Final Report

Chomsky for Beginners — *Maher, John C, 1951-*

Chomsky's Politics — *Rai, Milan*

Chondrules and the Protoplanetary Disk — *Hewins, R H*

Chong Qing Feng Yun — *Tian, Wenyi*

y Choosing a Career in Law Enforcement — *Wirths, Claudine G*

y Choosing a Career in the Restaurant Industry — *Beal, Eileen*

y Choosing a Career in Transportation — *McGlothlin, Bruce*

Choosing a Divorce Mediator — *Neumann, Diane*

Choosing and Using Books with Adult New Readers — *Weibel, Marguerite Crowley*

Choosing Auspicious Chinese Names. Rev. Ed. — *Lip, Evelyn*

Choosing Correctional Options That Work — *Harland, Alan T*

Choosing Democracy — *Campbell, Duane*
Choosing Reality — *Wallace, B Alan*
Choosing the Better Part — *Baar, Mirjam De*
Choosing the Chief — *Pierce, Roy*
Choosing to Lead — *Buchanan, Constance H*
Choosing Unsafe Sex — *Sobo, Elisa J*
Choosing Who's to Live — *Walters, James W*
c Chop, Simmer, Season (Illus. by Alexa Brandenberg)
   — *Brandenberg, Alexa*
Chopin at the Boundaries — *Kallberg, Jeffrey*
r Choral Music by African American Composers. 2nd
   Ed. — *White, Evelyn Davidson*
Choreographing History — *Foster, Susan Leigh*
Choreography and Narrative — *Foster, Susan Leigh*
A Chorus of Colors — *Shangraw, Clarence F*
A Chorus of Stones — *Griffin, Susan*
y The Chosen — *Stirling, S M*
The Chosen Primate — *Kuper, Adam*
c Chris Zorich — *Stewart, Mark*
Christ and the Spirit — *Colle, Ralph Del*
Christ Church, Philadelphia — *Gough, Deborah
   Mathias*
Christ in a Post-Christian World — *Young, Pamela
   Dickey*
Christ in Christian Tradition. Vol. 2, Pt. 4
   — *Grillmeier, Aloys*
Christ Is Risen — *Cotter, Theresa*
Christ, the Form of Beauty — *Murphy, Francesca
   Aran*
Christ the Reconciler — *Schmiechen, Peter*
y Christabel Bielenberg and Nazi Germany — *Shuter,
   Jane*
Christendom and Its Neighbours — *Nicolle, David*
The Christesen Romance — *Armstrong, Judith*
c Christian — *Watson, Carol*
Christian Antisemitism — *Nicholls, William*
Christian Confessions — *Campbell, Ted A*
r Christian County, Kentucky Newspaper Abstracts.
   Vols. 3-4 — *Taylor, Pete*
Christian Dior: The Man Who Made the World Look
   New — *Pochna, Marie-France*
Christian Doctrine in the Light of Michael Polanyi's
   Theory of Personal Knowledge — *Crewdson, Joan*
The Christian Effect on Jewish Life — *Hilton, Michael*
Christian Ethics — *Wogaman, J Philip*
Christian Ethics and Political Economy in North
   America — *Kroeker, P Travis*
Christian Faith and the Theological Life — *Cessario,
   Romanus*
Christian Fantasy from 1200 to the Present
   — *Manlove, Colin*
c Christian Festivals — *Thompson, Jan*
The Christian God — *Swinburne, Richard*
Christian Hermeneutics — *Fodor, James*
Christian Humanism — *Francis, Richard P*
The Christian Inscription at Pompeii — *Berry, Paul*
Christian-Jewish Dialogue — *Osten-Sacken, Peter Von
   Der*
Christian Lacroix: The Diary of a Collection
   — *Mauries, Patrick*
Christian Mission in the Twentieth Century — *Yates,
   Timothy*
Christian Mission--Jewish Mission — *Cohen, Martin*
A Christian Perspective on Political Thought — *Mott,
   Stephen Paul*
The Christian Philosopher — *Mather, Cotton*
Christian Plain Style — *Auksi, Peter*
Christian Science in the Age of Mary Baker Eddy
   — *Knee, Stuart E*
Christian Social Ethics in a Global Era — *Stackhouse,
   Max L*
Christian Souls and Chinese Spirits — *Constable,
   Nicole*
Christian Symbols — *Koch, Rudolf*
Christian Theology and Interfaith Dialogue — *Wiles,
   Maurice*
Christian Theology and Medical Ethics — *Tubbs,
   James B, Jr.*
The Christian Virtues in Medical Practice
   — *Pellegrino, Edmund D*
Christian Worship and Technological Change
   — *White, Susan J*
c Christianity — *McCreery, Elaine*
Christianity — *Moorcroft, Christine*
c Christianity — *Penney, Sue*
Christianity. Pt. 1 — *Richards, Chris*
Christianity. Pt. 2 — *Holmwood, Ruth*
yr Christianity: A Dictionary — *Keene, Michael*
Christianity and Civil Society — *Wuthnow, Robert*
Christianity and Classical Culture — *Pelikan, Jaroslav*

Christianity and Culture in the Crossfire — *Hoekema,
   David A*
Christianity and Democracy — *De Gruchy, John W*
Christianity and Hegemony — *Nederveen Pieterse, Jan*
Christianity and Rabbinic Judaism — *Shanks, Hershel*
Christianity and the Stranger — *Nichols, Francis W*
Christianity Comes to the Americas 1492-1776
   — *Lippy, Charles H*
Christianity: Essence, History and Future — *Kung,
   Hans*
Christianity for the Twenty-First Century — *Men,
   Aleksandr*
Christianity on Trial — *Chapman, Mark L*
Christians and Jews in the Twelfth-Century
   Renaissance — *Abulafia, Anna Sapir*
Christians and Jews Together — *Dawe, Donald G*
Christians and Muslims — *Goddard, Hugh*
c Christie and Company — *Page, Katherine Hall*
c Christie and Company down East — *Page, Katherine
   Hall*
c Christina Katerina and Fats and the Great
   Neighborhood War (Illus. by Stacey Schuett)
   — *Gauch, Patricia Lee*
Christina Rossetti: A Literary Biography — *Marsh,
   Jan*
Christina Rossetti: A Writer's Life — *Marsh, Jan*
Christina Rossetti Revisited — *Smulders, Sharon*
Christine — *King, Stephen*
Christine Brooke-Rose and Contemporary Fiction
   — *Birch, Sarah*
r Christine De Pizan: A Bibliographical Guide. 1st
   Suppl. — *Kennedy, Angus J*
r Die Christlichen Adversus-Judaeos-Texte Und Ihr
   Literarisches Und Historisches Umfeld 13.-20. Jh.
   — *Schreckenberg, Heinz*
c Christmas (Festival)
c Christmas! (Illus. by Peter Spier) — *Spier, Peter*
c Christmas All Over (Illus. by Ruth Hunter McAnespy)
   — *Bernardini, Robert*
c The Christmas Alphabet — *Sabuda, Robert*
Christmas: An Annual Treasury. Vol. 66
c Christmas and the New Year
c Christmas around the World (Illus. by Karen Dugan)
   — *Lankford, Mary D*
c The Christmas Bird (Illus. by Bernadette Watts)
   — *Watts, Bernadette*
The Christmas Box — *Evans, Richard Paul*
The Christmas Card — *Bowersock, William I*
c A Christmas Carol — *Dickens, Charles*
c A Christmas Carol (Illus. by Patrick Benson)
   — *Dickens, Charles*
c A Christmas Carol (Illus. by Quentin Blake)
   — *Dickens, Charles*
c A Christmas Carol (Illus. by Gustave Dore)
   — *Dickens, Charles*
c A Christmas Carol (Illus. by Carter Goodrich)
   — *Dickens, Charles*
c A Christmas Carol (Olivier). Audio Version
   — *Dickens, Charles*
c Christmas Crackered — *Plaisted, Caroline*
c Christmas Crafts — *Corwin, Judith Hoffman*
Christmas Day — *Durcan, Paul*
c The Christmas Deer — *Wilson, April*
Christmas Doughcrafts — *Bang, Elizabeth*
Christmas Elopement — *Eames, Anne*
c Christmas Fairy Tales (Illus. by Isabelle Brent)
   — *Philip, Neil*
A Christmas Gambol — *Smith, Joan, 1938-*
c Christmas Gif' (Illus. by Ashley Bryan) — *Rollins,
   Charlemae Hill*
Christmas in America — *Restad, Penne L*
Christmas in Calico — *Curtis, Jack*
c Christmas in Colonial and Early America
Christmas in Early America 1800-1900 — *Baur, John
   E*
y Christmas in My Heart — *Wheeler, Joe L*
Christmas in Scandinavia — *Rossel, Sven Hakon*
Christmas in the Good Old Days — *Foley, Daniel J*
Christmas Is Cookies and Gingerbread and Spice
   Cake and Fudge and More — *Time-Life Books*
Christmas Kisses
The Christmas Letters — *Smith, Lee*
c Christmas Lights (Illus. by Ann Fearrington)
   — *Fearrington, Ann*
Christmas Memories — *Greene, A C*
c A Christmas Memory (Illus. by Beth Peck) — *Capote,
   Truman*
A Christmas Miracle
c The Christmas Miracle of Jonathan Toomey (Illus. by
   P J Lynch) — *Wojciechowski, Susan*

c The Christmas Mouse (Illus. by Ruth Brown)
   — *Forward, Toby*
y The Christmas Mystery (Illus. by Rosemary Wells)
   — *Gaarder, Jostein*
The Christmas of the Phonograph Records — *Sandoz,
   Mari*
r Christmas on the American Frontier 1800-1900
   — *Baur, John E*
Christmas Pins, Past and Present — *Gallina, Jill*
c Christmas Poetry (Illus. by Annabel Spenceley)
   — *Hulll, Robert*
The Christmas Show — *Levin, Harriet*
c Christmas Stories for the Very Young (Illus. by Helen
   Cooper) — *Grindley, Sally*
c The Christmas Story (Illus. by Kay Chorao)
   — *Chorao, Kay*
c The Christmas Story (Illus. by Tim Wood)
   — *Clements, Andrew*
c The Christmas Story (Illus. by Asun Balzola)
   — *Wood, David*
c The Christmas Story from the Gospels of Matthew
   and Luke — *Bible. N.T. Matthew. English. Selections.
   1966. Authorized*
c The Christmas Story. The Story of the Wisemen. Book
   and Audio Version — *Williams, Laura*
y The Christmas Tree — *Salamon, Julie*
c Christmas Waltz (Illus. by Janet Hurley) — *Ramsey,
   Buck*
A Christmas Wish — *Pruitt, Barbara*
y Christmas with Anne and Other Holiday Stories
   — *Montgomery, L M*
Christmas with Eve — *Minger, Elda*
Christmas with Jinny Beyer — *Beyer, Jinny*
c Christmas with Teddy Bear (Illus. by Jacqueline
   McQuade) — *McQuade, Jacqueline*
c Christmas Won't Wait — *Tharlet, Eve*
Christology: A Biblical, Historical, and Systematic
   Study of Jesus — *O'Collins, Gerald*
Christology and Cosmology — *Lyman, J Rebecca*
c Christoph Wants a Party (Illus. by Winfried
   Opgenoorth) — *Lobe, Mira*
Christopher and His Kind — *Isherwood, Christopher*
c Christopher Changes His Name (Illus. by Roy Condy)
   — *Sadu, Itah*
c Christopher Columbus — *Wellman, Sam*
r Christopher Lee and Peter Cushing and Horror
   Cinema — *Miller, Mark A*
c Christopher the Holy Giant (Illus. by Tomie De Paola)
   — *De Paola, Tomie*
Christopher Wood — *Ingleby, Richard*
Christopher's Dream — *Bosnak, Robert*
Christopraxis: A Theology of Action — *Arens,
   Edmund*
Christ's Eucharistic Presence — *Jones, Paul H*
Christus Interpres — *Graumann, Thomas*
Chroma — *Jarman, Derek*
Chromatographic Analysis of Pharmaceuticals. 2nd
   Ed. — *Adamovics, John A*
r Chromatographic Detectors — *Scott, Raymond P W*
Chromium Picolinate — *Evans, Gary*
Chromosome 6 — *Cook, Robin*
Chromsome 6 (Gaines). Audio Version — *Cook, Robin*
Chronic Diseases — *Stein, Marvin*
Chronic Fatigue Syndrome — *Demitrack, Mark A*
Chronic Illness — *Toombs, S Kay*
Chronic Vigour — *Elder, Gregory P*
r A Chronicle of American Music 1700-1995 — *Hall,
   Charles J*
The Chronicle of John of Worcester. Vol. 2 — *John,
   of Worcester*
r A Chronicle of Pre-Telescopic Astronomy
   — *Hetherington, Barry*
yr Chronicle of the 20th Century. Electronic Media
   Version
yr Chronicle of the Olympics 1896-1996
r Chronicle of the World
yr Chronicle of the Year 1995
Chronicles of England, Scotland, and Ireland. Vol. 3
   — *Holinshed, Raphael*
The Chronicles of Scar — *Sarti, Ron*
Chronicles of the Frigate Macedonian 1809-1922
   — *De Kay, James Tertius*
The Chronicles of the Rowleys — *Rowley, Peter*
Chronik Des Deutschen Films 1895-1994 — *Prinzler,
   Hans Helmut*
Chronique Des Ayyoubides 602-658/1205-6-1259-60
   — *Makin, Jirjis Ibn Al-Amid*
Chroniques De Tanger Janvier 1994-Janvier 1995
   — *Mimouni, Rachid*
r A Chronology and Glossary of Propaganda in the
   United States — *Nelson, Richard Alan*

r Chronology of Women Worldwide — *Brakeman, Lynne*

c Chrysanthemum — *Henkes, Kevin*

Chu Ye Quan — *Ding, Wang*

c Chubbo's Pool (Illus. by Betsy Lewin) — *Lewin, Betsy*

c Chuck and Danielle (Illus. by Kees De Kiefte) — *Dickinson, Peter*

c Chuck and Danielle (Illus. by Robin Lawrie) — *Dickinson, Peter*

Chuck Reducks — *Jones, Chuck*

Chuffs: A Quitter's Guide to Smoking — *Karstedt, Mark J*

Chump Change — *Eddie, David*

Chunky: The Victoria Wood Omnibus — *Wood, Victoria*

Church and Age Unite! — *Appleby, R Scott*

Church and Community in Crisis — *Overman, J Andrew*

Church and Jewish People — *Willebrands, Johannes*

Church and Ministry in the Works of G.H. Tavard — *Alexander, Marc R*

Church and Society in Byzantium under the Commeni 1081-1261 — *Angold, Michael*

Church and Society in Documents 100-600 A.D. — *Hayes, Alan L*

Church and State in Bourbon Mexico — *Brading, D A*

Church and State in Early Christianity — *Rahner, Hugo*

Church and State in the Modern Era — *Maclear, J F*

The Church and the Churches — *Evans, G R*

The Church as Polis — *Rasmusson, Arne*

Church, Book, and Bishop — *Kaufman, Peter Iver*

Church, College, and Clergy — *Fraser, Brian J*

r Church History — *Bradley, James E*

The Church in Africa 1450-1950 — *Hastings, Adrian*

The Church of Dead Girls — *Dobyns, Stephen*

Church Papists — *Walsham, Alexandra*

The Church, Society, and Hegemony — *Torres, Carlos Alberto*

Church, State, and Religious Dissent — *Heinz, Daniel*

Church, State and Society 1760-1850 — *Gibson, William, 1959-*

Church Suppers and Potluck Dinners — *Chesman, Andrea*

Church Teaching Authority — *Boyle, John P*

The Church Triumphant — *Hinson, E Glenn*

r The Church Visible — *Noonan, James-Charles, Jr.*

Churchill and Roosevelt at War — *Sainsbury, Keith*

The Churchill War Papers. Vol. 2 — *Gilbert, Martin, 1936-*

Churchill's Grand Alliance — *Charmley, John*

Churchill's Secret War — *Denniston, Robin*

Chuyen Moi Chon Loc — *Duy, Lam*

Ci Xing Shi Dai — *Zhang, Dianwan*

r The CIA Insider's Dictionary of U.S. and Foreign Intelligence, Counterintelligence and Tradecraft — *Carl, Leo D*

Ciao, Don Camillo — *Guareschi, Giovanni*

Cicero and the End of the Roman Republic — *Wiedemann, Thomas*

Cicero: Pro P. Sulla Oratio — *Cicero, Marcus Tullius*

CICS Clients Unmasked — *DeSimoni, Guido*

c Cider Apples (Illus. by Sandy Nightingale) — *Nightingale, Sandy*

Cider: Making, Using and Enjoying Sweet and Hard Cider. 2nd Ed. — *Proulx, Annie*

y Cielo Negro Sobre Kuwait — *Westall, Robert*

Ciencia Y Censura — *Pardo Tomas, Jose*

Ciencia Y Tecnica En La Metropolizacion De America — *Sala Catala, Jose*

y El Cientifico De Sonrisa Contagiosa — *Chamizo, Jose Antonio*

The Cigar — *Conrad, Barnaby, III*

The Cigar in Art — *Conran, Terence*

y Cigarette Confidential — *Fahs, John*

The Cigarette Papers — *Glantz, Stanton A*

Cigarettes: What the Warning Label Doesn't Tell You — *Napier, Kristine*

Cimarron Jordan — *Braun, Matt*

Le Cimetiere De La Morale — *Jaccard, Roland*

c Cimru the Seal (Illus. by John Butler) — *Radcliffe, Theresa*

Cinci Ani Din Istoria Romaniei — *Stefanescu, Domnita*

c Cinder Edna — *Jackson, Ellen*

c Cinder-Elly (Illus. by G Brian Karas) — *Minters, Frances*

c Cinderboy (Illus. by Arthur Robins) — *Anholt, Laurence*

Cinderela Negra A Saga De Carolina Maria De Jesus — *Meihy, Jose Carlos Sebe Bom*

c Cinderella (Illus. by Gwen Tourret) — *Geras, Adele*

c Cinderella (Illus. by Prue Theobalds) — *Theobalds, Prue*

c Cinderella (Illus. by Caroline Crossland) — *Umansky, Kaye*

Cinderella of the New South — *Wrenn, Lynette Boney*

Cindy Crawford's Basic Face — *Crawford, Cindy*

Cinema and Spectatorship — *Mayne, Judith*

Cinema in Democratizing Germany — *Fehrenbach, Heide*

The Cinema of Isolation — *Norden, Martin*

The Cinema of Martin Scorsese — *Friedman, Lawrence S*

r Cinemania 96. Electronic Media Version

yr Cinemania 97. Electronic Media Version

Cinemas in Britain — *Gray, Richard, 1947-*

Cinemas of the Black Diaspora — *Martin, Michael T*

Cinematernity: Film, Motherhood, Genre — *Fischer, Lucy*

Cinquante Pseaumes De David Mis En Francoys Selon La Verite Hebraique — *Marot, Clement*

Le Cinquecentine Della Biblioteca Dell'Archivio Di Stato Di Roma — *Falcone, Giovanna*

r Le Cinquecentine Della Biblioteca Panizzi — *Zanzanelli, Eletta*

r Le Cinquecentine Della Biblioteca San Benedetto Di Seregno — *Motta, Giuseppe*

Le Cinquieme Sceau — *Rafenomanjato, Charlotte-Arrisoa*

The CIO 1935-1955 — *Zieger, Robert H*

p Circa Art Magazine

The Circle Dancers — *Der-Hovanessian, Diana*

Circle of Light — *Levendosky, Charles*

c Circle of Love — *Nixon, Joan Lowery*

Circle of One — *Fullilove, Eric James*

The Circle of Our Vision — *Pite, Ralph*

The Circle of Simplicity — *Andrews, Cecile*

c The Circle of Thanks (Illus. by Murv Jacob) — *Bruchac, Joseph*

Circle View — *Barkley, Brad*

y The Circlemaker — *Schur, Maxine Rose*

c Circles (Illus. by Richard Maccabe) — *Riggs, Sandy*

Circles: A Mathematical View — *Pedoe, Dan*

c Circles and Squares Everywhere! — *Grover, Max*

c Circles: Fun Ideas for Getting A-Round in Math — *Ross, Catherine Sheldrick*

y Circles of Stone — *Lambert, Joan Dahr*

Circling — *Ruffin, Paul*

cr Circling the Globe. Electronic Media Version

Circuit, Device, and Process Simulation — *Carey, G F*

Circuits: Engineering Concepts and Analysis of Linear Electric Circuits — *Carlson, A Bruce*

Circular Dichroism and the Conformational Analysis of Biomolecules — *Fasman, Gerald D*

La Circulation Des Nouvelles Au Moyen Age — *Balard, M*

y Circumstantial Evidence — *Earley, Pete*

Circumstellar Habitable Zones — *Doyle, Laurence R*

c Circuses: Under the Big Top — *Presnall, Judith Janda*

Ciro Fornaro

The Cistercians: Monks and Monasteries of Europe — *Tobin, Stephen*

r Citation World Atlas — *Hammond Incorporated*

Cite Et Territoire — *Clavel-Leveque, Monique*

Cities and the Rise of States in Europe A.D. 1000 to 1800 — *Tilly, Charles*

Cities and the Wealth of Nations — *Jacob, Jane*

Cities, Classes, and the Social Order — *Leeds, Anthony*

Cities in Our Future — *Geddes, Robert*

c Cities in the Sea (Illus. by Jackie Morris) — *Lewis, Sian*

Cities of Alexander the Great — *Fraser, P M*

Cities of Jiangnan in Late Imperial China — *Johnson, Linda Cooke*

Cities of Light and Heat — *Rose, Mark H, 1942-*

Cities of Memory — *Hinsey, Ellen*

Cities of Salt — *Munif, Abd Al-Rahman*

r Cities of the Dead — *Roach, Joseph*

Cities of the Heartland — *Teaford, Jon C*

Cities of the Mississippi — *Reps, John W*

Cities with Invisible Walls — *Chan, Kam Wing*

Cities without Suburbs — *Rusk, David*

Cities without Suburbs. 2nd Ed. — *Rusk, David*

Citistates: How Urban America Can Prosper in a Competitive World — *Peirce, Neal R*

Citizen and Subject — *Mamdani, Mahmood*

Citizen K — *Singer, Mark*

The Citizen of the World — *Goldsmith, Oliver*

Citizen Perot — *Posner, Gerald*

Citizen Science — *Irwin, Alan*

Citizen Sherman — *Fellman, Michael*

Citizen, State, and Social Welfare in Britain 1830-1990 — *Finlayson, Geoffrey*

Citizen Warriors — *Duncan, Stephen M*

The Citizen's Charter — *Great Britain. Prime Minister*

Citizens: Flowers and the Wide Sea — *Rolls, Eric*

The Citizen's Guide to Lobbying Congress — *DeKieffer, Donald E*

Citizens of the World — *Hancock, David*

Citizens, Politics, and Social Communication — *Huckfeldt, Robert*

The Citizen's Wage — *Snell, James G*

Citizens without Sovereignty — *Gordon, Daniel, 1961-*

Citizenship and Democratic Control in Contemporary Europe — *Einhorn, Barbara*

Citizenship in a Fragile World — *Dauenhauer, Bernard P*

Citizenship Today — *Bulmer, Martin*

La Citta Custodita — *Carlotto, Natascia*

La Citta E Gli Inganni — *Castellaneta, Carlo*

La Citta E La Rivoluzione — *Formica, Marina*

Una Citta Infetta — *Adorni-Braccesi, Simonetta*

The City after the Automobile — *Safdie, Moshe*

City and Spectacle in Medieval Europe — *Hanawalt, Barbara A*

The City and the Stars — *Clarke, Arthur C*

City at Sea — *Kaufmann, Yogi*

City Bankers 1890-1914 — *Cassis, Youssef*

The City Below — *Carroll, James*

City Building in America — *Orum, Anthony M*

City Center to Regional Mall — *Longstreth, Richard*

The City Churches of Sir Christopher Wren — *Jeffery, Paul*

City Codes — *Wirth-Nesher, Hana*

City Culture and the Madrigal at Venice — *Feldman, Martha*

The City in African American Literature — *Hakutani, Yoshinobu*

The City in Ancient Israel — *Fritz, Volkmar*

A City in Conflict — *Roberts, Penny*

City in Love — *Shakar, Alex*

The City in Modern Chinese Literature and Film — *Zhang, Yingjin*

The City in Which I Love You — *Lee, Li-Young*

y A City in Winter (Illus. by Chris Van Allsburg) — *Helprin, Mark*

c City Kids and City Critters! — *Roberts, Janet Wier*

City Kids, City Teachers — *Ayers, William*

City Life — *Rybczynski, Witold*

City Lights Pocket Poets Anthology — *Ferlinghetti, Lawrence*

City Lives — *Courtney, Cathy*

City Lives and City Forms — *Caulfield, Jon*

City of Ambition, Artists and New York — *Sussman, Elisabeth*

City of Bits — *Mitchell, William J*

City of Capital — *Carruthers, Bruce G*

The City of Collective Memory — *Boyer, M Christine*

City of Darkness, City of Light — *Piercy, Marge*

City of Diamond — *Emerson, Jane*

City of Dreadful Delight — *Walkowitz, Judith R*

City of Dreams — *Dick, Bernard F*

City of Dust — *Andrews, Gregg*

The City of Florence — *Lewis, R W B*

City of Memory and Other Poems — *Pacheco, Jose Emilio*

City of Stone — *Benvenisti, Meron*

City of the Century — *Miller, Donald L*

City of the Great King — *Rosovsky, Nitza*

City on Fire — *Williams, Walter Jon*

The City on the Edge of Forever — *Ellison, Harlan*

City on the Seine — *Trout, Andrew P*

City Poet — *Gooch, Brad*

r City Profiles USA 1996

r City-Smart Guidebook: Denver. 1st Ed.

City-States in the Global Economy — *Chiu, Stephen Wing-Kai*

City Terrace Field Manual — *Foster, Sesshu*

c A City under the Sea — *Wu, Norbert*

City Unique — *Weintraub, William*

y City within a City — *Krull, Kathleen*

The City without Women — *Duliani, Mario*

Cityports, Coastal Zones, and Regional Change — *Hoyle, Brian*

Cityscapes and Capital — *Pagano, Michael A*

The Civic Architecture of Paul Cret — *Grossman, Elizabeth Greenwell*

y Civic Mathematics — *Vatter, Terry*

Civic Politics in the Rome of Urban VIII — *Nussdorfer, Laurie*

The Civic Spectacle — *Flaumenhaft, Mera J*

Civic Virtues and Public Schooling — *White, Patricia*

Civic Wars — *Ryan, Mary P*
y A Civil Action — *Harr, Jonathan*
Civil Disabilities of Convicted Felons — *United States. Office of the Pardon Attorney*
Civil Justice Review
y Civil Rights — *Lucas, Eileen*
y The Civil Rights Movement — *Dudley, William*
The Civil Rights Movement — *Kasher, Steven*
The Civil Rights Movement — *Wilkinson, Brenda*
The Civil Rights of Homeless People — *Stoner, Madeleine R*
The Civil Service of Malaysia — *A H Ahmad Sarji*
The Civil Service System and Economic Development — *Kim, Hyung-Ki*
Civil Service Systems in Comparative Perspective — *Bekke, Hans*
Civil Society — *Hall, John A*
Civil Society, Civil Religion — *Shanks, Andrew*
Civil Society in the Middle East. Vol. 2 — *Norton, Augustus Richard*
Civil Society in the Middle East. Vols. 1-2 — *Norton, Augustus Richard*
Civil Tongues and Polite Letters in British America — *Shields, David S*
The Civil War — *Burns, Ken*
y A Civil War — *Feinstein, John*
c Civil War — *Sandler, Martin W*
Civil War and Restoration in the Three Stuart Kingdoms — *Ohlmeyer, Jane H*
The Civil War as a Crisis in Gender — *Whites, LeeAnn*
r Civil War Burials in Baltimore's Loudon Park Cemetery — *Watring, Anna Miller*
r The Civil War CD-ROM. Electronic Media Version
Civil War Command and Strategy — *Jones, Archer*
The Civil War Diary of Clara Solomon — *Solomon, Clara*
Civil War Encased Stamps — *Reed, Fred*
The Civil War in Apacheland — *Hand, Sergeant George*
r The Civil War in Books — *Eicher, David J*
The Civil War in Popular Culture — *Cullen, Jim*
Civil War Sites Advisory Commission Report on the Nation's Civil War Battlefields — *Civil War Sites Advisory Commission*
r The Civil War Trust's Official Guide to the Civil War Discovery Trail
Civil War Veterans of Old Imperial Calcasieu Parish, Louisiana — *Rosteet, Betty Tyler*
The Civil Wars in Britain and Ireland 1638-1651 — *Bennett, Martyn*
Civilian Pawns — *Human Rights Watch (Organization)*
The Civility of Indifference — *Bailey, F G*
Civilization and Black Progress — *Crummell, Alexander*
The Civilization of Europe in the Renaissance — *Hale, John*
Civilizations and World Systems — *Sanderson, Stephen K*
y Civilizations of Asia — *Rossi, Renzo*
y Civilizations of the Americas — *Rossi, Renzo*
yr Civilizations of the Ancient Near East. Vols. 1-4
The Civilized Tribes — *Bumpus, Jerry*
Civilizing Cyberspace — *Miller, Steven E*
Civilizing Rituals — *Duncan, Carol*
y CivilWarLand in Bad Decline — *Saunders, George*
Civis Zacensis, Epistola Cum Libello Ackerman Und Das Buchlein Ackerman. Vols. 1-2 — *Johannes, Von Tepl*
Claiborne of Virginia — *Dorman, John Frederick*
Claim — *Schulz, Mat*
A Claim to Land by the River — *Adams, Adrian*
Claiming a Continent — *Day, David, 1949-*
Claiming the Center — *Rogers, Jack*
Claiming the Real — *Winston, Brian*
y Claiming the Spirit Within — *Sewell, Marilyn*
The Claims of Common Sense — *Coates, John*
La Claire Audience — *Sampiero, Dominique*
Claire's Classic American Vegetarian Cooking — *Criscuolo, Claire*
The Clairmont Correspondence. Vols. 1-2 — *Clairmont, Clara Mary Jane*
The Clairvoyant — *Thurm, Marian*
Clambake: A History and Celebration of an American Tradition — *Neustadt, Kathy*
c Clams All Year — *Cocca-Leffler, Maryann*
The Clan — *Carroll, J R*
Clandestine Marriage in England 1580-1850 — *Outhwaite, R B*
Clanship to Crofters' War — *Devine, T M*
c Clara and the Hoodoo Man — *Partridge, Elizabeth*

y Clare and Effie (Illus. by Bernice Carlill) — *Williams, Merryn*
Clarembald of Arras as a Boethian Commentator — *Fortin, John R*
r Clark County, Arkansas Obituaries and Death Notices 1914-1921 — *Syler, Allen B*
r Clark County, Washington Cemeteries. Vols. 7-11 — *Clark County Genealogical Society*
r Clark County, Washington Marriages. Vols. 11-13 — *Clark County Genealogical Society*
r Clark County, Wisconsin Cemeteries. Vol. 1 — *Heath, Jim*
The Clark: Selections from the Sterling and Francine Clark Art Institute — *Sterling and Francine Clark Art Institute*
The Clash of Civilizations — *Burke, Victor Lee*
The Clash of Civilizations and the Remaking of World Order — *Huntington, Samuel P*
The Clash of Rights — *Sniderman, Paul M*
The Clash with Distant Cultures — *Payne, Richard J*
Clasicos Medicos Valencianos Del Siglo XVII — *Lopez Pinero, Jose Maria*
c Class Act (Illus. by Susan Slattery Burke) — *Jansen, John*
Class and Conservative Parties — *Gibson, Edward L*
Class and State in Ancient Regime France — *Parker, David, Ph.D.*
Class Counts — *Wright, Erik Olin*
Class, Democracy, and Labor in Contemporary Argentina. Rev. Ed. — *Ranis, Peter*
Class, Politics, and Ideology in the Iranian Revolution — *Moaddel, Mansoor*
Class, Power, and Agrarian Change — *Pincus, Jonathan*
Class Trip — *Carrere, Emmanuel*
Class Warfare — *Barlow, Maude*
La Classe De Neige — *Carrere, Emmanuel*
Classes Dominantes E Hegomonia Na Republica Velha — *Perissinotto, Renato M*
Classes, Estates, and Order in Early Modern Brittany — *Collins, James B*
Classic American Food without Fuss — *McCullough, Frances*
Classic Chemistry Demonstrations — *Lister, Ted*
y Classic Chilling Tales (Donovan). Vol. 2. Audio Version — *Poe, Edgar Allan*
Classic Fabrics — *Spencer-Churchill, Henrietta*
c Classic Fairy Tales to Read Aloud (Illus. by Jo Worth) — *Lewis, Naomi*
r The Classic FM Guide to Classical Music — *Nicholas, Jeremy*
The Classic French Cinema 1930-1960 — *Crisp, Colin*
The Classic Guide to Better Writing — *Flesch, Rudolf*
Classic Guitars of the '50s — *Bacon, Tony*
Classic Home Desserts — *Sax, Richard*
The Classic Italian Cookbook — *Della Croce, Julia*
c Classic Jump Rope Rhymes (Realworld Guides)
Classic Natchez — *Delehanty, Randolph*
c Classic Outdoor Games (Realworld Guides)
y Classic Poems — *Martin, Christopher*
Classic Quilts — *McKendry, Ruth*
c Classic Star Wars (Illus. by Isidre Mones) — *Alvarez, Cynthia*
Classic Writings on Instructional Technology — *Ely, Donald P*
Classical Architecture in Britain — *Worsley, Giles*
Classical Art in the Nicholson Museum, Sydney — *Cambitoglou, Alexander*
Classical Banach Spaces. Vols. 1-2 — *Lindenstrauss, Joram*
Classical Black Nationalism rvey — *Moses, Wilson Jeremiah*
Classical Cynicism — *Navia, Luis E*
Classical Economic Man — *Oakley, Allen*
Classical Economics, Public Expenditure and Growth — *Eltis, Walter*
The Classical Greek Reader — *Atchity, Kenneth John*
y The Classical Greeks — *Grant, Michael, 1914-*
Classical Hollywood Comedy — *Karnick, Kristine Brunovska*
Classical Humanism and Republicanism in English Political Thought 1570-1640 — *Peltonen, Markku*
Classical Imitation and Interpretation in Chaucer's Troilus — *Fleming, John V*
Classical Indian Metaphysics — *Phillips, Stephen H*
The Classical Legacy in Renaissance Poetry — *Sowerby, Robin*
Classical Liberalism — *Conway, David*
The Classical Model — *Stone, Harriet*
Classical Music and Postmodern Knowledge — *Kramer, Lawrence*

Classical Music Criticism — *Schick, Robert D*
Classical Nashville — *Kreyling, Christine*
c Classical Rome — *Clare, John D*
r Classical Singers of the Opera and Recital Stages — *Cowden, Robert H*
r Classical Studies — *Jenkins, Fred W*
The Classical Style. Expanded Ed. — *Rosen, Charles, 1927-*
Classical Theories of International Relations — *Clark, Ian*
The Classical Tradition in Economic Thought — *Rima, Ingrid H*
The Classical Vernacular — *Scruton, Roger*
y Classical Women Poets
Classics: A Very Short Introduction — *Beard, Mary*
Classics in Total Synthesis — *Nicolaou, K C*
The Classics of Catholic Spirituality — *Cameron, Peter John*
Classics of Children's Literature. 4th Ed. — *Griffith, John W*
The Classics of Judaism — *Neusner, Jacob*
Classics of Mathematics — *Calinger, Ronald*
Classification and Inventory of the World's Wetlands — *Finlayson, C Max*
r Classification Plus. Electronic Media Version
Classifying by Race — *Peterson, Paul E*
Classifying Reactions to Wrongdoing — *Thomas, R Murray*
Classifying the Universe — *Smith, Brian K*
Classism and Feminist Therapy — *Hill, Marcia*
c The Classroom at the End of the Hall (Illus. by Larry Di Fiori) — *Evans, Douglas*
y Claude Debussy: An Essential Guide to His Life and Work — *Brown, Jonathon, 1955-*
Claude McKay: Rebel Sojourner in the Harlem Renaissance — *Cooper, Wayne F*
c Claude Monet — *Harrison, Peter*
c Claude Monet — *Malam, John*
Claude Monet: Life and Art — *Tucker, Paul Hayes*
Claude Simon: Narrativities without Narrative — *Brewer, Maria Minich*
Claude Simon Par Correspondance — *Schoentjes, Pierre*
Claudia's Shadow — *Allen, Charlotte Vale*
Claudius — *Gass, Ken*
Clausewitz in English — *Bassford, Christopher*
Clausewitzian Friction and Future War — *Watts, Barry D*
Claves Del Espanol — *Dominguez, Pablo*
y The Claw — *Adams, Carmen*
Clay and Dough — *Burgess, Lynne*
Clay Birds — *Gunvaldsen Klaassen, Tonja*
c Clay Boy (Illus. by Jos. A Smith) — *Ginsburg, Mirra*
c Clay Hernandez, a Mexican American (Illus. by Lawrence Migdale) — *Hoyt-Goldsmith, Diane*
Clay Speaks to Us of God — *Sima, John Ross*
Clay Vessels — *McNamee, John*
Clay: Whereabouts Unknown — *Raine, Craig*
Clayoquot and Dissent — *Berman, Tzeporah*
Clay's Ark — *Butler, Octavia E*
La Cle De Sol Et Autres Recits — *Tougas, Gerald*
Clean and Well Lit — *Raworth, Tom*
c Clean House (Illus. by Yossi Abolafia) — *Haas, Jessie*
Clean Surplus — *Brief, Richard P*
Clean Water — *International Clean Water Conference (1995: La Jolla, Calif.)*
Clean Water, Clean Environment, 21st Century. Vols. 1-3
Cleaner Air Partnership — *Franz, Jennifer D*
Cleaning Recreation Sites — *Makel, William*
Cleansing the Fatherland — *Aly, Gotz*
Cleanth Brooks and the Rise of Modern Criticism — *Winchell, Mark Royden*
Clear the Line — *Veress, Laura-Louise*
Clear Waters Rising — *Crane, Nicholas*
Clearcut: A Novel of Bio-Consequences — *Hunger, Bill*
Cleared for Take-Off — *Bogarde, Dirk*
The Clearest Promises of God — *Davis, Thomas J*
c The Clearing: A Mystery — *Miller, Dorothy Reynolds*
Clearing for the Millennium — *Gaulden, Albert Clayton*
Cleft Lip and Palate. Vols. 1-2 — *Berkowitz, Samuel*
Cleisthenes the Athenian — *Leveque, Pierre*
Clematis as Companion Plants — *Fretwell, Barry*
r Clements' Encyclopedia of World Governments 1996-1997
Cleo — *Brody, Jean*
c Cleo and the Coyote (Illus. by Diana Bryer) — *Levy, Elizabeth*
y Cleopatra — *Green, Robert*

c Cleopatra (Illus. by Diane Stanley) — *Stanley, Diane*

y Cleopatra (Runger). Audio Version — *Grant, Michael, 1914-*

Le Clerge Du Grand Siecle En Ses Assemblees 1615-1717 — *Blet, Pierre*

Cleveland's Transit Vehicles — *Toman, James A*

The Clever Adulteress and Other Stories — *Granoff, Phyllis*

The Clever Daughter — *Wicks, Susan*

c Clever Duck (Illus. by Mike Terry) — *King-Smith, Dick*

Clever Girl — *Glyde, Tanya*

c Clever Kids Science: Ages 5-7

c Clever Kids Science: Ages 8-10

r Cliches — *Kirkpatrick, Betty*

c Click! A Book about Cameras and Taking Pictures — *Gibbons, Gail*

c Click! Fun with Photography — *Price, Susanna*

Clicking: 16 Trends to Future Fit Your Life, Your Work, and Your Business — *Popcorn, Faith*

Clicking: 16 Trends to Future Fit Your Life, Your Work, and Your Business. Audio Version — *Popcorn, Faith*

Clicking In — *Hershman-Leeson, Lynn*

Clicking In. Book and Electronic Media Version — *Hershman-Leeson, Lynn*

Client Access Token-Ring Connectivity — *Patterson, Chris*

Client-Centered and Experiental Psychotherapy — *Hutterer, Robert*

Client/Server Architecture. 2nd Ed. — *Berson, Alex*

The Cliff Walk — *Snyder, Don J*

c Clifford Barks! — *Bridwell, Norman*

Clifford (Geometric) Algebras with Applications to Physics, Mathematics, and Engineering — *Baylis, William E*

c Clifford's First Easter (Illus. by Norman Bridwell) — *Bridwell, Norman*

c Clifford's First Halloween (Illus. by Norman Bridwell) — *Bridwell, Norman*

Climate and Literature — *Perez, Janet*

Climate and the Affections — *Elsted, Crispin*

Climate Change — *Giambelluca, Thomas W*

Climate Change 1995: Economic and Social Dimensions of Climate Change — *Bruce, James P*

Climate Change 1995: Impacts, Adaptations and Mitigation of Climate Change — *Watson, Robert T*

Climate Change 1995: The Science of Climate Change — *Houghton, J T*

Climate Change, Acidification and Ozone — *Countryside Commission*

Climate, History and the Modern World. 2nd Ed. — *Lamb, H H*

Climate Research in the Netherlands

Climate since A.D. 1500 — *Bradley, R S*

Climax: The History of Colorado's Climax Molybdenum Mine — *Voynick, Stephen M*

y The Climb — *Hathorn, Libby*

Climb a Fallen Ladder — *Gordon, Rochelle H*

c Climb Away! — *Parks, Deborah*

The Climb of My Life — *Evans, Laura*

y Climb or Die — *Myers, Edward*

c Climb Your Family Tree (Illus. by Doug Keith) — *Depue, Anne*

r A Climber's Guide to the Teton Range. 3rd Ed. — *Ortenburger, Leigh N*

c Climbing Jacob's Ladder (Illus. by Ashley Bryan) — *Langstaff, John*

y Climbing Mount Improbable — *Dawkins, Richard*

r Climbing: The Complete Reference — *Child, Greg*

Climbing the Hill — *Foerstel, Karen*

Climbing Your Way to the Bottom — *Sullivan, Rob, 1967-*

p Clineaste

y The Clinic — *Kellerman, Jonathan*

The Clinic (Rubinstein). Audio Version — *Kellerman, Jonathan*

Clinical Anaesthesia — *Gwinnutt, Carl L*

Clinical and Experimental Pheochromocytoma. 2nd Ed. — *Manger, William Muir*

Clinical Anthropology — *Rush, John A*

Clinical Assessment and Management of Severe Personality Disorders — *Links, Paul S*

Clinical Biochemistry — *Marshall, William J*

Clinical Bioethics — *Drane, James F*

Clinical Decision Making and Treatment Planning in Osseointegration — *Engleman, Michael J*

Clinical Decision Making in Rehabilitation — *Basmajian, John V*

Clinical Diagnosis and Management of Alzheimer's Disease — *Gauthier, Serge*

r Clinical Examination. 3rd Ed. — *Talley, Nicholas J*

Clinical Examination of the Musculoskeletal System — *Buchanan, W Watson*

Clinical Gastroenterology in the Elderly — *Gelb, Alvin M*

A Clinical Guide for Contraception. 2nd Ed. — *Speroff, Leon*

Clinical Handbook of Couple Therapy — *Jacobson, Neil S*

Clinical Hematology and Fundamentals of Hemostasis. 3rd Ed. — *Harmening, Denise M*

Clinical Imaging. 3rd Ed. — *Eisenberg, Ronald L*

Clinical Management of Anxiety — *Boer, Johan A Den*

r Clinical Manual of Substance Abuse. 2nd Ed. — *Kinney, Jean*

Clinical Maps of Acute Care — *Wesp, Clyde E*

Clinical Neurology of Rheumatic Diseases — *Rosenbaum, Richard B*

Clinical Optics. 2nd Ed. — *Fannin, Troy E*

Clinical Pathways for Ambulatory Care Case Management — *Howe, Rufus S*

Clinical PET — *Bares, R*

Clinical Pharmacology of Cerebral Ischemia — *Horst, Gert J Ter*

Clinical Psychopharmacology — *Smith, Paul F*

Clinical Research in Pharmaceutical Development — *Bleidt, Barry*

Clinical Skills for Speech-Language Pathologists — *Goldberg, Stanley A*

Clinical Skills in Neurology — *Harrison, Michael J G*

Clinical Social Work — *Dorfman, Rachelle A*

Clinical Social Worker Misconduct — *Bullis, Ronald K*

Clinical Sociology — *Bruhn, John G*

Clinical Supervision — *Taibbi, Robert*

Clinical Surgery — *Cuschieri, Alfred*

Clinical Veterinary Toxicology — *Lorgue, G*

The Clinician's Guide to Managed Behavioral Care — *Winegar, Norman*

Clint Eastwood: A Biography — *Schickel, Richard*

Clint Eastwood, Film-Maker — *O'Brien, Daniel*

Clinton and Post-Cold War Defense — *Cimbala, Stephen J*

The Clinton Presidency — *Campbell, Colin*

The Clinton Presidency — *Denton, Robert E, Jr.*

Cliques, Coloring, and Satisfiability — *Johnson, David S*

r Cloak and Dagger Fiction. 3rd Ed. — *Smith, Myron J*

The Clock of Ages — *Medina, John J*

c Clock of Doom — *Stewart, Paul*

The Clockmaker. 1st-3rd Ser. — *Parker, George L*

y Clockwork or All Wound Up (Illus. by Peter Bailey) — *Pullman, Philip*

A Clockwork Orange (Burgess). Audio Version — *Burgess, Anthony*

The Cloister and the World — *Blair, John*

The Cloister Walk — *Norris, Kathleen*

y The Cloister Walk (Winger). Audio Version — *Norris, Kathleen*

The Cloisters Cross — *Parker, Elizabeth C*

Close Calls — *Rogers, Susan Fox*

c Close, Closer, Closest (Illus. by Shelley Rotner) — *Rotner, Shelley*

Close Cover before Striking — *Kuypers, Janet*

Close Encounters — *Isaacs, Ronald H*

Close Encounters of the Fourth Kind — *Bryan, C D B*

Close Her Eyes (Hardiman). Audio Version — *Simpson, Dorothy*

Close Quarters — *Curzon, Clare*

Close Relations — *Moggach, Deborah*

c A Close Shave — *Park, Nick*

Close Ties — *Cruikshank, Ken*

Close to the Bone — *Bolen, Jean Shinoda*

Close to the Bone — *Tapply, William G*

Close to the Bone (Bolen). Audio Version — *Bolen, Jean Shinoda*

Closed Doors, Opportunities Lost — *Yinger, John*

The Closed World — *Edwards, Paul N*

y Closely Akin to Murder — *Hess, Joan*

Closer and Closer Apart — *Lloyd, Rosemary*

y Closer, Closer — *May, Steve*

A Closer Walk with God. Audio Version — *Rosemergy, Jim*

Closest Companion — *Ward, Geoffrey C*

y The Closest Possible Union — *Scott, Joanna, 1960-*

The Closing of American Library Schools — *Ostler, Larry J*

Closing the Circle on the Splitting of the Atom

Closing the Shop — *Murphy, S T*

Closing the Theory-Practice Gap — *Rolfe, Gary*

Closing with the Enemy — *Doubler, Michael D*

Closure in International Politics — *Kroll, John A*

Closure Spaces and Logic — *Martin, Norman M*

Clotel or the President's Daughter — *Brown, William Wells*

Clothes and the Child — *Buck, Anne*

c Clothes and Uniforms — *Cox, Kath*

Clothes Make the Man — *Hotchkiss, Valerie R*

c Clothes (SnapShot)

Clothing Matters — *Tarlo, Emma*

Cloud Chamber — *Dorris, Michael*

Cloud Mountain — *Liu, Aimee*

Cloudhand, Clenched Fist — *Miller, Rhea*

c Cloudland (Illus. by John Burningham) — *Burningham, John*

c The Cloudmakers (Illus. by James Rumford) — *Rumford, James*

Clouds — *Aristophanes*

y Clouds End — *Stewart, Sean*

Clouds, Leaves, Waves — *Botts, Gregory*

c Clouds on the Mountain (Illus. by Alice Priestley) — *Smith-Ayala, Emilie*

y Cloud's Rider — *Cherryh, C J*

Clouds: The Biography of a Country House — *Dakers, Caroline*

c Cloudwalker: Contemporary Native American Stories (Illus. by Carson Waterman) — *Monture, Joel*

Cloudy in the West — *Kelton, Elmer*

Clough Williams-Ellis — *Jones, Jonah*

r Clover Newspaper Index: Clover Magazine Index. Electronic Media Version

c Clover's Secret (Illus. by Christine M Winn) — *Winn, Christine M*

c Clovis Crawfish and Bidon Box Turtle (Illus. by Scott R Blazek) — *Fontenot, Mary Alice*

c Clovis Ecrevisse Et Bidon Tortue Terrestre (Illus. by Scott R Blazek) — *Fontenot, Mary Alice*

c Clovis Ecrevisse Et L'Oiseau Orphelin (Illus. by Eric Vincent) — *Fontenot, Mary Alice*

c Clown (Illus. by Quentin Blake) — *Blake, Quentin*

The Club — *Brook, Stephen*

Club Cultures — *Thornton, Sarah*

The Club Dumas — *Perez-Reverte, Arturo*

r Cluefinder: A Dictionary of Crossword Clues — *Coleman, J A, 1920-*

c Clyde Tombaugh and the Search for Planet X (Illus. by Laurie A Caple) — *Wetterer, Margaret K*

r CNC Machining Handbook — *Madison, James G*

Co Ba Tra — *Xuan, Vu*

CO-Groups, Commutator Methods and Spectral Theory of N-Body Hamiltonians — *Amrein, Werner O*

Co-Integration, Error Correction, and the Econometric Analysis of Non-Stationary Data — *Banerjee, Anindya*

r Co-Op America's National Green Pages. 1996 Ed.

Co-Op America's National Green Pages. 1997 Ed.

Co-Op: The People's Business — *Birchall, Johnston*

Co-Opetition — *Brandenburger, Adam M*

y Coach: The Life of Paul Bear Bryant — *Dunnavant, Keith*

Coaching, Mentoring and Managing — *Hendricks, William*

Coaching Youth Volleyball. 2nd Ed. — *American Sport Education Program*

y Coachman Rat — *Wilson, David O*

Coal: Energy for the Future — *National Research Council (U.S.). Committee on the Strategic Assessment of the U.S. Department of Energy's Coal Program*

Coal Miner's Daughter — *Lynn, Loretta*

Coal Miners' Wives — *Giesen, Carol A B*

Coal: Resources, Properties, Utilization, Pollution — *Kural, Orhan Cevdet*

c Coalition War Campaign — *Siembieda, Kevin*

The Coast Guard Expands 1865-1915 — *King, Irving H*

The Coast of New England — *Patey, Stan*

Coastal Dynamics '95 — *International Conference on Coastal Research in Terms of Large Scale Experiments (1995: Gdansk, Poland)*

Coastal Environment — *International Conference on Environment Problems in Coastal Regions (1st: 1996)*

r Coastal Problems — *Viles, Heather*

y Coaster — *Duffey, Betsy*

The Coastline of Forgetting — *Choyce, Lesley*

c Coasts — *Cumming, David*

Coatings for High-Temperature Structural Materials — *National Research Council (U.S.) Committee on Coatings for High-Temperature Structural Materials*

Cobalt Blue — *Lykes, Dorothy Raitt*

Cobb: A Biography — *Stump, Al*

cp Cobblestone
Cobra! Bell Aircraft Corporation 1934-1946
— *Matthews, Birch*
c Cobras (Illus. by Dwight Kuhn) — *McDonald, Mary Ann*
y The Cobweb — *Bury, Stephen, 1959-*
Coca-Colonization and the Cold War — *Wagnleitner, Reinhold*
Cocaine Nights — *Ballard, J G*
Cochlear Implant Rehabilitation in Children and Adults — *Allum, Dianne J*
Cocina! — *Atkinson, Leland*
c Cock-a-Doodle-Doo (Illus. by Maureen Roffey)
c Cock-a-Doodle-Doo (Illus. by Steve Lavis) — *Lavis, Steve*
c Cock-a-Doodle-Moo! (Illus. by Bernard Most) — *Most, Bernard*
The Cockatoo's Life — *Bloem, Marion*
y The Cockatrice Boys — *Aiken, Joan*
c Cockcrow to Starlight (Illus. by Maggie Kneen) — *Godden, Rumer*
y Cocker Spaniel — *Fogle, Bruce*
Cocker Spaniels Today — *Caddy, Joyce*
Cockpit of Ideologies — *Grenville, Anthony*
c Cockroach (Illus. by Tim Hayward) — *Wiseman, Stella*
The Cockroach and Other Stories — *Liu, I-Ch'ang*
c Cockrow to Starlight (Illus. by Maggie Kneen) — *Godden, Rumer*
Cocktail Hour — *Brallier, Jess M*
Cocktail Time (Davidson). Audio Version — *Wodehouse, P G*
y Code Blue in the Emergency Room — *Rojany, Lisa*
Code Name Christiane Clouet — *Chevrillon, Claire*
Code-Name Downfall — *Allen, Thomas B*
y Code of Deception — *Ottley, Ted*
y Code of the Roadies — *Ottley, Ted*
The Codebreakers: The Story of Secret Writing. Rev. Ed. — *Kahn, David*
Codename Mule — *Parker, James E, 1942-*
Codes, Designs, and Geometry — *Tonchev, Vladimir*
Codex Borgia — *Codex Borgianus*
Codex Telleriano-Remensis — *Quinones Keber, Eloise*
El Codice De Xicotepec — *Stresser-Pean, Guy*
Codices Sangallenses — *Ochsenbein, Peter*
I Codici Latini Di Niccolo V — *Manfredi, Antonio*
Codiciaban La Tierra — *Martinez, Hildeberto*
c Cody and Quinn, Sitting in a Tree (Illus. by Nancy Poydar) — *Larson, Kirby*
c Cody Coyote Cooks! (Illus. by Lois Bergthold) — *Skrepcinski, Denice*
c O Coelho Branquinho E A Formico Rabica (Illus. by Joao Tinoco) — *Vieira, Alice*
Coercion and Market — *Tandeter, Enrique*
Coffee, Society, and Power in Latin America — *Roseberry, William*
p Coffeehouse Magazine
y Coffey on the Mile — *King, Stephen*
y Coffey's Hands — *King, Stephen*
The Coffin Tree — *Butler, Gwendoline*
Cognition: An Epistemological Inquiry — *Owens, Joseph*
Cognition within and between Organizations — *Meindl, James R*
Cognitive and Computational Aspects of Face Recognition — *Valentine, Tim*
Cognitive Aspects of Electronic Text Processing — *Oostendorp, Herre Van*
Cognitive Aspects of Human-Computer Interaction for Geographic Information Systems — *Nyerges, Timothy L*
Cognitive-Behavioral Therapy for Bipolar Disorder — *Basco, Monica Ramirez*
Cognitive Carpentry — *Pollock, John L*
Cognitive Ecology — *Friedman, Morton P*
Cognitive Planning — *Das, J P*
Cognitive Psychology in the Middle Ages — *Kemp, Simon*
The Cognitive Psychology of Proper Names — *Valentine, Tim*
Cohabiting, Married, or Single — *Prinz, Christopher*
Coherence and Quantum Optics VII
Coherence, Counterpoint, Instrumentation, Instruction in Form — *Schoenberg, Arnold*
Cohesion and Structure of Surfaces — *Binder, K*
Coin Locker Babies — *Murakami, Ryu*
c Coin Magic — *Klutz Press*
r Coin World Guide to U.S. Coins, Prices and Value Trends 1997
Coinage in the Roman Economy 300 B.C. to A.D. 700 — *Harl, Kenneth W*

r Coincraft's Standard Catalogue of English and United Kingdom Coins 1066 to Date. 2nd Ed.
Coins of New Brunswick — *Bird, Richard W*
Coke Stop in Emo — *Ross, Alec*
Colan En Cariay — *Gonzalez Vasquez, Fernando*
Colander — *McFee, Michael*
Colbert, Mercantilism, and the French Quest for Asian Trade — *Ames, Glenn J*
Cold Blood — *La Plante, Lynda*
Cold Blue Midnight — *Gorman, Edward*
Cold Case — *Barnes, Linda*
c Cold Climates — *Lye, Keith*
Cold Cold Heart — *Elliott, James*
Cold Gas at High Redshift — *Bremer, M N*
The Cold Heart of Capricorn — *Lawrence, Martha C*
Cold Mountain — *Frazier, Charles*
Cold Pluto — *Ruefle, Mary*
Cold Regions Engineering — *International Conference on Cold Regions Engineering (8th: 1996: University of Alaska Fairbanks)*
y Cold Sassy Tree — *Burns, Olive Ann*
Cold Shoulder — *La Plante, Lynda*
y Cold Shoulder Road — *Aiken, Joan*
Cold Snap — *Jones, Thom*
Cold War — *MacSkimming, Roy*
y Cold War — *Warren, James A*
y The Cold War and After — *Aylett, J F*
The Cold War and Soviet Insecurity — *Mastny, Vojtech*
The Cold War and the University — *Chomsky, Noam*
Cold War Canada — *Whitaker, Reg*
Cold War Criticism and the Politics of Skepticism — *Soebers, Tobin*
yr The Cold War Encyclopedia — *Parrish, Thomas*
r The Cold War Reference Guide — *Schwartz, Richard Alan*
Cold Warriors and Coups D'Etat — *Weis, W Michael*
Colder than Hell — *Owen, Joseph R*
r A Cole Porter Discography — *Rimler, Walter*
Coleridge and Textual Instability — *Stillinger, Jack*
Coleridge in Italy — *Zuccato, Edoardo*
Coleridge, Keats and Shelley — *Kitson, Peter J*
Coleridge: Selected Poems — *Coleridge, Samuel Taylor*
Coleridge: The Early Family Letters — *Coleridge, Samuel Taylor*
Coleridge's Later Poetry — *Paley, Morton D*
Coleridge's Philosophy — *Perkins, Mary Anne*
Coleridge's Submerged Politics — *Keane, Patrick J*
Colin Colahan: A Portrait — *Kinnane, Garry*
y Colin Powell: A Man of Quality — *Hughes, Libby*
y Colin Powell: Soldier and Patriot — *Schraff, Anne*
Collaboration in the Feminine — *Godard, Barbara*
Collaborations for Literacy — *Senator, Rochelle B*
Collaborative School Self-Review — *Russell, Sheila*
The Collapse of a Single-Party System — *Gill, Graeme*
The Collapse of Barings — *Fay, Stephen*
The Collapse of Soviet Military Power — *Bluth, Christoph*
The Collapse of the American Management Mystique — *Locke, Robert R*
The Collapse of the Democratic Presidential Majority — *Lawrence, David G*
The Collapse of the Soviet Empire — *Neimanis, George J*
Collapsed States — *Zartman, I William*
r Collect Aircraft on Stamps. 1st Ed. — *Sterckx, Alan*
Collected Earlier Poems — *Hecht, Anthony*
The Collected Essays of Ralph Ellison — *Ellison, Ralph*
The Collected Essays of Richard E. Quandt. Vols. 1-2 — *Quandt, Richard E*
The Collected Ghost Stories of E.F. Benson — *Benson, E F*
The Collected Letters of Antoni Van Leeuwenhoek. Vol. 13 — *Leeuwenhoek, Antoni Van*
The Collected Letters of George Gissing. Vol. 5 — *Gissing, George*
The Collected Letters of George Gissing. Vol. 7 — *Gissing, George*
The Collected Letters of George Gissing. Vol. 8 — *Gissing, George*
The Collected Letters of George Gissing. Vol. 9 — *Gissing, George*
The Collected Letters of W.B. Yeats. Vol. 3 — *Yeats, W B*
The Collected Letters of William Morris. Vols. 3-4 — *Morris, William, 1834-1896*
Collected Longer Poems — *Carruth, Hayden*
Collected Papers. Vol. 4 — *Schutz, Alfred*
The Collected Papers of Albert Einstein. Vol. 4 — *Einstein, Albert*

Collected Plays. Vol. 2 — *Foote, Horton*
Collected Plays. Vol. 2 — *Wilson, Lanford*
Collected Poems — *Boland, Eavan*
Collected Poems — *Bowers, Edgar*
Collected Poems — *Fuller, John*
Collected Poems — *Hayden, Robert*
Collected Poems — *Mallarme, Stephane*
Collected Poems — *Montague, John*
Collected Poems — *Norris, Leslie*
y The Collected Poems — *Price, Reynolds*
Collected Poems. Vol. 3 — *Gustafson, Ralph*
Collected Poems 1956-1994 — *Kinsella, Thomas*
Collected Poems and Prose — *Pinter, Harold*
c Collected Poems for Children (Illus. by John Lawrence) — *Causley, Charles*
The Collected Poems of A.K. Ramanujan — *Ramanujan, A K*
The Collected Poems of Anne Stevenson 1955-1995 — *Stevenson, Anne*
The Collected Poems of Carl Rakosi — *Rakosi, Carl*
The Collected Poems of John Ciardi — *Ciardi, John*
Collected Poems, Plays and Prose — *Frost, Robert*
The Collected Short Fiction of Bruce Jay Friedman — *Friedman, Bruce Jay*
Collected Short Stories — *Carey, Peter*
Collected Shorter Poems 1946-1991 — *Carruth, Hayden*
Collected Stories — *Barnes, Djuna*
Collected Stories — *Carey, Peter*
y The Collected Stories — *Cross, Amanda*
Collected Stories — *Nabokov, Vladimir Vladimirovich*
Collected Stories — *Norris, Leslie*
Collected Stories — *Sillitoe, Alan*
The Collected Stories — *Theroux, Paul*
The Collected Stories of Arno Schmidt — *Schmidt, Arno*
The Collected Stories of Evan S. Connell — *Connell, Evan S*
The Collected Stories of Mavis Gallant — *Gallant, Mavis*
The Collected Stories of William Carlos Williams — *Williams, William Carlos*
Collected Verse — *Beerbohm, Max*
Collected Works. Vols. 10, 14 — *Chesterton, G K*
The Collected Works of Abraham Cowley. Vol. 2, Pt. 1 — *Cowley, Abraham*
The Collected Works of Billy the Kid — *Ondaatje, Michael*
The Collected Works of Eugene Paul Wigner. Pt. A, Vols. 1-2, 5; Pt. B, Vol. 6 — *Wigner, Eugene Paul*
The Collected Works of Julia Robinson — *Robinson, Julia*
The Collected Works of Justice Holmes. Vols. 1-3 — *Holmes, Oliver Wendell*
The Collected Works of Lonergan. Vol. 6 — *Lonergan, Bernard F J*
The Collected Works of P.A.M. Dirac 1924-1948 — *Dirac, P A M*
Collected Works of W.M. Gorman. Vol. 1 — *Gorman, W M*
The Collected Writings of T.E. Hulme — *Hulme, T E*
Collectible American Coins — *Bressett, Kenneth*
Collectible Kay Finch — *Frick, Devin*
Collecting: An Unruly Passion — *Muesterberger, Werner*
r Collecting and Using Classic SLRs — *Matanle, Ivor*
Collecting and Using Public Library Statistics — *Smith, Mark, 1956-*
y Collecting Baseball Memorabilia — *Owens, Thomas S*
Collecting Black Memorabilia — *Thompson, J P*
Collecting Coins — *Schwan, Fred*
Collecting Occupied Japan with Values — *Parmer, Lynette*
Collecting Paper Money — *Schwan, Fred*
r Collecting Plastic Jewelry — *Lindenberger, Jan*
Collectins and Innate Immunity — *Ezekowitz, R Alan B*
Collection Management in the Electronic Age — *Boyarski, Jennie S*
r The Collection of Francis I — *Cox-Rearick, Janet*
r The Collection of the Nelson-Atkins Museum of Art — *Nelson-Atkins Museum of Art*
La Collection Sources Chretiennes — *Fouilloux, Etienne*
Collective Insecurity — *Cimbala, Stephen J*
The Collector (Wilby). Audio Version — *Fowles, John*
The Collector Collector — *Fischer, Tibor*
r The Collector's Encyclopedia of Brush-McCoy Pottery — *Huxford, Sharon*
r Collector's Encyclopedia of Salt Glaze Stoneware — *Taylor, Terry*

r Collector's Encyclopedia of the Dakota Potteries
— Dommel, Darlene Hurst

The Collector's Garden — Druse, Ken

r Collector's Guide to Celebrity Autographs — Baker, Mark Allen

r Collector's Guide to Tinker Toys — Strange, Craig

r Collector's Guide to TV Memorabilia 1960s and 1970s — Davis, Greg

r Collector's Guide to Vogue Dolls — Izen, Judith

r Collectors Guide to Yellow Ware — McAllister, Lisa S

Collectors' Items — Salway, Kate

y Colleen McCullough: A Critical Companion — DeMarr, Mary Jean

The College Aid Quandary — Gladieux, Lawrence E

r College Chemistry Faculties 1996

r College Degrees by Mail — Bear, John

A College for Appalachia — Searles, P David

The College of William and Mary. Vols. 1-2 — Godson, Susan H

r College Student's Guide to Merit and Other No-Need Funding 1996-1998

yr Colleges That Change Lives — Pope, Loren

r The Collegeville Pastoral Dictionary of Biblical Theology

The Collegiate Church of Wimborne Minster — Coulstock, Patricia H

yr Collier's Encyclopedia. 1996 Ed., Vols. 1-24

yr Collier's Encyclopedia 1996. 1996 Ed., Vols. 1-24

yr Collier's Encyclopedia on CD-ROM. Electronic Media Version

Collingwood Studies. Vols. 1-2

cr Collins Children's Encyclopedia

c Collins Christmas Treasury (Illus. by Ian Penney) — Nettell, Stephanie

cr Collins COBUILD English Dictionary. New Expanded Ed.

Collins COBUILD Key Words in the Media — Mascull, Bill

r Collins Electronic English Dictionary and Thesaurus V2.0. Electronic Media Version

r Collins Encyclopaedia of Scotland — Keay, John

c Collins Eyewitness Guides

cr Collins First Dictionary

cr Collins First Word Book

cr Collins French Dictionary on CD-Rom. Electronic Media Version

r Collins Nations of the World Atlas — Collins (Firm: London, England)

c Collins Nursery Rhymes. Audio Version

cr Collins Pocket Primary Dictionary

cr Collins School Dictionary

cr Collins Shorter School Dictionary

c Collins Songs and Rhymes. Audio Version

Collins, the Courts and the Colony — Nagle, J F

c Collins Yellow Storybooks

y Collision Bend — Roberts, Les

Collision Course — Harland, Bryce

The Collision of Comet Shoemaker-Levy 9 and Jupiter — Space Telescope Science Institute (U.S.)

Collision with the Infinite — Segal, Suzanne

Colloquial Cantonese — Tong, Keith S T

Colombia: The Genocidal Democracy — Giraldo, Javier

The Colombian Caribbean — Posada-Carbo, Eduardo

Colombia's Military and Brazil's Monarchy — Millington, Thomas

Colon Cancer and the Polyps Connection — Fisher, Stephen J, 1940-

r Colon, Rectum, and Anus — Boland, C Richard

Colonel Edward Saunderson: Land and Loyalty in Victorian Ireland — Jackson, Alvin

Colonial American Newspapers — Copeland, David A

Colonial and Postcolonial Literature — Boehmer, Elleke

c Colonial and Revolution Songbook — McNeil, Keith

Colonial Desire — Young, Robert, 1950-

Colonial Discourse/Postcolonial Theory — Barker, Francis

Colonial Masculinity — Sinha, Mrinalini

Colonial Psychiatry and the African Mind — McCulloch, Jock

Colonial Technology — Todd, Jan, 1947-

Colonial Tongues — Robinson, Mansel

Colonial Transactions — Trivedi, Harish

yr Colonial Wars of North America 1512-1763 — Gallay, Alan

A Colonial Woman's Bookshelf — Hayes, Kevin J

Colonialism and Development — Havinden, Michael

Colonialism and Its Forms of Knowledge — Cohn, Bernard S

Colonialism, Religion and Nationalism in Ireland — Kennedy, Liam, 1946-

Coloniality in the Cliff Swallow — Brown, Charles R

Colonialization of Islam — Malik, Jamal

Colonie Africane E Cultura Italiana Fra Ottocento E Novecento — Cerreti, Claudio

Colonising Egypt — Mitchell, Timothy

Colonization: A Global History — Ferro, Marc

Colonization, Violence, and Narration in White South African Writing — Jolly, Rosemary Jane

The Colonizer's Model of the World — Blaut, James M

Colonoscopy: Principles and Techniques — Raskin, Jeffrey B

c Color (Illus. by Ruth Heller) — Heller, Ruth

c Color and Light (Illus. by Peter Millard) — Taylor, Barbara

Color and Light for the Watercolor Painter — Schink, Christopher

Color and Light in Nature — Lynch, David K

r Color Atlas and Text of Clinical Medicine. 2nd Ed. — Forbes, Charles D

r Color Atlas of Diagnostic Endoscopy in Otorhinolaryngology — Yanagisawa, Eiji

r Color Atlas of Urologic Surgery — Cockett, Abraham T K

r Color Atlas/Text of Salivary Gland Tumor Pathology — Dardick, Irving

y Color-Blind: Seeing beyond Race in a Race-Obsessed World — Cose, Ellis

Color Class Identity — Arthur, John

y Color Conscious — Appiah, Anthony

c Color Crunch! — Reasoner, Charles

c Color Dance — Jonas, Ann

Color, Environment, and Human Response — Mahnke, Frank H

c Color Farm (Illus. by Lois Ehlert) — Ehlert, Lois

Color Lines — Kelly, Mike

c Color Me Criminal (Illus. by S M Taggart) — Weiss, Ellen

c A Color of His Own — Lionni, Leo

The Color of Hunger — Shields, David Lyle

Color of My Living Heart — Salas, Floyd

y The Color of Nature (Illus. by William Neill) — Murphy, Pat, 1955-

The Color of the Snow — Kremer, Rudiger

y The Color of Water — McBride, James

The Color of Water (Braugher). Audio Version — McBride, James

The Color of Welfare — Quadagno, Jill

r The Color of Words — Herbst, Phil

Color Technology for Electronic Imaging Devices — Kang, Henry R

Color Theory Made Easy — Ames, Jim

c Color Zoo (Illus. by Lois Ehlert) — Ehlert, Lois

Colorado: A Newcomer's Manual — Walker, T J

Colorado Cowboys — Marona, Christopher

r Colorado Handbook. 3rd Ed. — Metzger, Stephen

Colorado Medicaid Reform Study. Phase 2 — Barton, Phoebe Linsey

r Colorado Place Names — Bright, William

p The Colorado Review

Colored Contradictions — Elam, Harry Justin

Coloring Web Graphics — Weinman, Lynda

c Colors — Yenawine, Philip

c Colors around Us (Illus. by Shelley Rotner) — Rotner, Shelley

c Colors Everywhere (Illus. by Tana Hoban) — Hoban, Tana

The Colors of Violence — Kakar, Sudhir

The Colossian Syncretism — Arnold, Clinton E

Colour: Art and Science — Lamb, Trevor

r Colour Atlas of Ophthalmic Plastic Surgery — Tyers, A G

Colour Is the Suffering of Light — Green, Melissa

c Colour Me Crazy — Donkin, Andrew

The Colour of Sculpture 1840-1910

y Coloured Pencils for All — Warr, Michael

c Colours (Illus. by Clare Mackie) — Reidy, Hannah

The Colours of Light (Illus. by Richard Pare) — Ando, Tadao

Colours of the Rainbow — Mole, Sandra

Colt Rifles and Muskets from 1847 to 1870 — Houze, Herbert G

Colt: The Making of an American Legend — Hosley, William

The Columbia Anthology of Modern Chinese Literature — Lau, Joseph S M

The Columbia Anthology of Poetry of the American West — Deming, Alison Hawthorne

The Columbia Book of Civil War Poetry — Marius, Richard

r The Columbia Companion to British History — Gardiner, Juliet

r The Columbia Dictionary of Quotations. Electronic Media Version

yr The Columbia Encyclopedia on CD-ROM. Electronic Media Version

r The Columbia Granger's Index to Poetry in Collected and Selected Works — Frankovich, Nicholas

yr The Columbia Granger's World of Poetry. Electronic Media Version

The Columbia History of the British Novel — Richetti, John

Columbia Journals — Thompson, David

r The Columbia University College of Physicians and Surgeons Complete Home Medical Guide. 3rd Ed. — Subak-Sharpe, Genell J

r The Columbia World of Quotations. Electronic Media Version

Columbo: The Game Show Killer — Harrington, William

Columbo: The Glitter Murder — Harrington, William

Columbus and the New World — Settipane, Guy A

Columbus, Confrontation, Christianity — O'Keefe, Timothy J

Columbus Then and Now — Davidson, Miles H

Columns and Catalogues — Schjeldahl, Peter

Comanche Political History — Kavanagh, Thomas W

Il Comando — Carbone, Rocco

c Comb! Comb! Puppy — Nann, Lizzie

Combat: Twelve Years in the U.S. Senate — Rudman, Warren B

r Combined Membership List 1996-1997 — American Mathematical Society

r Combined Retrospective Index to Book Reviews in Humanities Journals 1802-1974. Vols. 1-10

r Combined Retrospective Index to Book Reviews in Scholarly Journals 1886-1974. Vols. 1-15

The Combing of History — Cohen, David William

Combining Work and Elder Care — Hoskins, Irene

Combustion: Physical and Chemical Fundamentals, Modelling and Simulation, Experiments, Pollutant Formation — Warnatz, J

y Come and Go, Molly Snow — Taylor-Hall, Mary Ann

c Come Away with Me — Lawlor, Laurie

c Come Back, Buster (Illus. by Catherine Walters) — Jennings, Linda

Come Back Dead — Faherty, Terence

c Come Sunday (Illus. by Michael Bryant) — Grimes, Nikki

Come Sunday — Roma, Thomas

y Come to Grief — Francis, Dick

y Come to Grief (Jones). Audio Version — Francis, Dick

Come to Me — Bloom, Amy

Come to Y(our) Senses — Lake, Bernard

Come with Me from Lebanon — Kerr, Ann Zwicker

c The Comeback Challenge (Illus. by Karen Meyer) — Christopher, Matt

La Comedie A L'Epoque D'Henri II Et De Charles IX — Zilli, Luigia

Comedy Central — Claro, Christopher

Comedy in the Pro Caelio — Geffcken, Katherine A

r Comedy in the Weimar Republic — Grange, William

Comenius: A Critical Reassessment of His Life and Work — Murphy, Daniel

Comerciantes, Arrieros, Y Peones — Boyle, Susan Calafate

El Comercio Libre En El Peru — Mazzeo, Cristina Ana

Comercio Y Fraude En El Peru Colonial — Suarez, Margarita

Comes the Millennium — Blake, Jack

Comet. Rev. Ed. — Sagan, Carl

The Comet Hale-Bopp Book — Hockey, Thomas

Comet of the Century — Schaaf, Fred

c Comets and Shooting Stars (Illus. by Paul Doherty) — Moore, Patrick

Comets and the Origin and Evolution of Life — Thomas, Paul J

c Comet's Nine Lives (Illus. by Jan Brett) — Brett, Jan

y Comfort Creek — McDonald, Joyce

Comfort Woman — Keller, Nora Okja

The Comfort Women — Hicks, George

The Comforting Whirlwind — McKibben, Bill

r Comic Art in Africa, Asia, Australia, and Latin America — Lent, John A

r Comic Art of Europe — Lent, John A

r Comic Books and Comic Strips in the United States — Lent, John A

y Comic Relief — *Gold, Todd*
r Comics Collectibles and Their Values — *Wells, Stuart W, III*
Comics, Comix and the Graphic Novel — *Sabin, Roger*
The Coming American Renaissance — *Moynihan, Michael*
Coming Apart — *Rosenblatt, Roger*
Coming Attractions 96
The Coming Conflict with China — *Bernstein, Richard*
The Coming Fin De Siecle — *Mestrovic, Stjepan G*
Coming from the Light — *Hinze, Sarah*
Coming Home — *Pilcher, Rosamunde*
y Coming Home (Peters). Audio Version — *Pilcher, Rosamunde*
Coming Home to America — *Osborn, Torie*
Coming in from the Cold
Coming into Being — *Thompson, William Irwin*
Coming into the Light — *Holmes, Janice*
Coming of Age — *Terkel, Studs*
y Coming of Age with Elephants — *Poole, Joyce*
The Coming of God — *Moltmann, Jurgen*
The Coming of Keynesianism to America — *Colander, David C*
The Coming of the King James Gospels — *Allen, Ward S*
The Coming of the Millennium — *Fasching, Darrell J*
The Coming of the Spanish Civil War. 2nd Ed. — *Preston, Paul*
y Coming Out — *Starke, Ruth*
Coming Out as Parents — *Switzer, David K*
The Coming Race War — *Delgado, Richard*
The Coming Race War? and Other Apocalyptic Tales of America after Affirmative Action and Welfare — *Delgado, Richard*
y The Coming Race War in America — *Rowan, Carl T*
The Coming Russian Boom — *Layard, P R G*
The Coming Shape of Organization — *Belbin, Meredith*
Coming through the Fire — *Lincoln, C Eric*
Coming through the Swamp — *Stratton-Porter, Gene*
Coming to America — *Daniels, Roger*
c Coming to America (Illus. by Susannah Ryan) — *Maestro, Betsy*
Coming to Light — *Swann, Brian*
Coming to Terms with the Soviet Regime — *Hardeman, Hilde*
y The Coming White Minority — *Maharidge, Dale*
The Comintern: A History of International Communism from Lenin to Stalin — *McDermott, Kevin*
Command or Control? — *Samuels, Martin*
r Command Performance, USA! — *Mackenzie, Harry*
Comme En Plein Jour — *Tremblay, Jean-Paul-Mederic*
r Commemorating Frostburg's Percy Cemetery — *Crosby, Anthony E, Jr.*
Commemorations: The Politics of National Identity — *Gillis, John R*
Le Commencement Des Douleurs — *Sony Lab'ou Tansi*
Commentaire Sur Le Cantique Des Cantiques — *Bresard, Luc*
Commentaire Sur S. Jean. Vol. 5 — *Blanc, Cecile*
p Commentary
Commentary and Ideology — *Parker, Deborah*
r Commercial Air Transport Books — *Sterling, Christopher H*
Commercial Competition and National Security — *Hofhansel, Claus*
Commercial Law in the Middle East — *Ruttley, Hilary Lewis*
Commercial Laws in the People's Republic of China — *Bachner, Bryan S*
A Commercialising Economy — *Britnell, R H*
Comminution 1994 — *European Symposium on Comminution (8th: 1994: Stockholm, Sweden)*
Commissions, Reports, Reforms, and Educational Policy — *Ginsberg, Rick*
y Committed to Memory — *Hollander, John*
The Commodore — *O'Brian, Patrick*
r Common Birds of East Africa — *Hosking, David*
The Common but Less Frequent Loon and Other Essays — *Thomson, Keith Stewart*
Common Carnage — *Dobyns, Stephen*
Common Clay — *Aldiss, Brian W*
Common Fire — *Daloz, Laurent A*
The Common Fisheries Policy — *Holden, Mike*
Common Ground — *Cowan, Andrew*
Common Knowledge — *McKemmish, Jan*
The Common Legal Past of Europe 1000-1800 — *Bellomo, Manilo*

A Common Life — *Laskin, David*
Common Places — *Boym, Svetlana*
Common Roots, New Horizons — *Ucko, Hans*
The Common Roots of Europe — *Geremek, Bronislaw*
Common Sense and a Little Fire — *Orleck, Annelise*
A Common Sense Theology — *Ellingsen, Mark*
Common Stocks and Uncommon Profits — *Fisher, Philip*
r Common Threads — *Heath, Alan*
Common Women — *Karras, Ruth Mazo*
A Commonsense Guide to Mutual Funds — *Rowland, Mary*
The Commonsense MBA (Astle). Audio Version — *Astle, Richard M*
r Commonsense Vegetable Gardening for the South — *Adams, William D*
Commonwealth of Toil — *Juravich, Tom*
Commonwealth or Empire? — *Odom, William E*
A Commotion in the Blood — *Hall, Stephen S*
Les Communautes Villageoises Dans Les Pays De Dalhem Et De Limbourg XVIe-XVIIe Siecle — *Dumont, Bruno*
Communicating for Change — *D'Aprix, Roger*
c Communicating Skills. 2nd Ed. — *Martin, Dave*
Communicating with Animals — *Myers, Arthur*
Communicating with Children and Adults — *Petrie, Pat*
c Communication (Illus. by Ed Dovey) — *Morris, Ting*
Communication and Computing for Distributed Multimedia Systems — *Lu, Guojun*
Communication and Group Decision Making. 2nd Ed. — *Hirokawa, Randy Y*
Communication and Social Influence Processes — *Berger, Charles R*
Communication Development and Disorders in African American Children — *Kamhi, Alan G*
Communication Disability and the Psychiatry of Old Age — *Bryan, Karen*
Communication in Congress — *Whiteman, David*
Communication in Eastern Europe — *Casmir, Fred L*
Communication in Latin America — *Cole, Richard R*
Communication in Mathematics, K-12 and Beyond — *Elliott, Portia C*
Communication in Personal Relationships across Cultures — *Gudykunst, William B*
Communication in the Jewish Diaspora — *Menache, Sophia*
Communication Research Measures — *Rubin, Rebecca B*
Communication, Technology, and the Development of People — *Woods, Bernard*
Communication Technology Update. 5th Ed. — *Grant, August E*
Communication Theories in Action — *Wood, Julia T*
Communication Theory — *Anderson, James A*
Communication Therapy — *Moseley, Mary June*
Communications and Computer Surveillance, Privacy and Security — *United States. Congress. House. Committee on Science, Space, and Technology. Subcommittee on Technology, Environment, and Aviation*
Communications and Power in Medieval Europe — *Leyser, Karl*
Communications and Power in Medieval Europe: The Carolingian and Ottoman Centuries — *Leyser, Karl*
Communications and Power in Medieval Europe: The Gregorian Revolution and Beyond — *Leyser, Karl*
Communications and the Third World — *Reeves, Geoffrey W, 1945-*
Communications Programming for Windows 95 — *Mirho, Charles A*
Communicative Interaction, Power, and the State — *Stark, Frank M*
r The Communicator's Handbook. 3rd Ed.
Communion: Contemporary Writers Reveal the Bible in Their Lives — *Rosenberg, David, 1943-*
A Communion of the Spirits — *Freeman, Roland L*
Communion with the Church and the Code of Canon Law — *Kaslyn, Robert J*
Communism: The Vanished Specter — *Pipes, Richard*
Communism's Collapse, Democracy's Demise? — *McFalls, Laurence H*
Communist Logistics in the Korean War — *Shrader, Charles R*
The Communist Road to Power in Vietnam. 2nd Ed. — *Duiker, William J*
Communitarian Ethics and Economics — *Kapur, Basant K*
The Communitarian Moment — *Clark, Christopher, 1953-*

Communities and Conflict in Early Modern Colmar 1575-1730 — *Wallace, Peter G*
Communities in Motion — *Spalding, Susan Eike*
Communities of Violence — *Nirenberg, David*
Community and Consent — *Nederman, Cary J*
Community Builders — *Rabrenovic, Gordana*
Community, Culture and Economic Development — *Ramsay, Meredith*
Community Health Care Nursing — *Twinn, Sheila*
Community Impact Evaluation — *Lichfield, Nathaniel*
Community Nutrition — *Frank-Spohrer, Gail C*
A Community of One — *Danahay, Martin A*
The Community of Religions — *Teasdale, Wayne*
The Community of Rights — *Gewirth, Alan*
Community of Suffering and Struggle — *Faue, Elizabeth*
The Community of the Renewed Covenant — *Ulrich, Eugene*
Community Oral Health — *Pine, Cynthia M*
Community Organizations in Latin America — *Navarro, Juan Carlos*
Community Psychiatry in Action — *Tyrer, Peter*
Community, Religion, Literature — *Brooks, Cleanth*
Community Service-Learning — *Wade, Rahima C*
Community Strategic Visioning Programs — *Walzer, Norman*
Community Supervision — *Del Carmen, Rolando V*
Commutative Ring Theory — *Cahen, Paul-Jean*
Commuting Stress — *Koslowsky, Meni*
c Como Crece Una Semilla (Illus. by Loretta Krupinski) — *Jordan, Helene J*
c Como Llueve, Guille! — *Elena, Horacio*
Compact Guide to Windows 95 — *Turley, James*
r The Compact Music Dictionary — *Bliss, Marilyn*
Compact Projective Planes — *Salzmann, Helmut*
r The Compact Up-to-Date English-Hebrew Dictionary — *Zilberman, Shimon*
r Companies International. Electronic Media Version
r Companion Encyclopedia of Asian Philosophy — *Carr, Brian*
r Companion Encyclopedia of Geography — *Douglas, Ian*
r Companion Encyclopedia of Theology — *Byrne, Peter*
r The Companion Guide to Sicily — *Trevelyan, Raleigh*
The Companion to 20th-Century Music — *Lebrecht, Norman*
A Companion to American Thought — *Fox, Richard Wightman*
r The Companion to British and Irish Cinema — *Caughie, John*
y A Companion to Chaucer's Canterbury Tales — *Hallissy, Margaret*
r The Companion to French Cinema — *Vincendeau, Ginette*
Companion to Grief — *Kelley, Patricia*
r The Companion to Italian Cinema — *Nowell-Smith, Geoffrey*
A Companion to Malory — *Archibald, Elizabeth*
r A Companion to Poe Studies — *Carlson, Eric W*
r A Companion to the Characters in the Fiction and Drama of W. Somerset Maugham — *Rogal, Samuel J*
r Companion to the Cosmos — *Gribbin, John*
A Companion to The Crying of Lot 49 — *Grant, J Kerry*
A Companion to the Indian Mutiny of 1857 — *Taylor, P J O*
A Companion Volume to Dr. Jay A. Goldstein's Betrayal by the Brain — *Courmel, Katie*
Companions for the Soul — *Hudson, Robert*
y Companions of the Night — *Vande Velde, Vivian*
y Company C — *Sack, John*
A Company Discovers Its Soul — *Green, Alan, 1931-*
Company Man — *Sampson, Anthony*
The Company of Camelot — *Spivack, Charlotte*
A Company of Scientists — *Stroup, Alice*
The Company of Wolves — *Steinhart, Peter*
The Company She Kept — *Eccles, Marjorie*
The Company They Keep — *Bukowski, William M*
y The Company They Keep — *Simons, Anna*
y The Company We Keep — *Chadwick, Douglas H*
The Company We Kept — *Kaye, Barbara*
Comparable Worth — *Sorensen, Elaine*
Comparative Analysis of Petroleum Exploration Contracts
Comparative Approaches to Cognitive Science — *Roitblat, Herbert L*
Comparative Asian Economies — *Kuark, John Y T*
Comparative Hemostasis in Vertebrates — *Lewis, Jessica H*

Comparative Indo-European Linguistics — *Beekes, Robert S P*

Comparative Literature in the Age of Multiculturalism — *Bernheimer, Charles*

Comparative National Development — *Kincaid, A Douglas*

r Comparative Neurobiology in Chiroptera. Vol. 1 — *Baron, Georg*

r The Comparative Russian-English Dictionary of Russian Proverbs and Sayings — *Mertvago, Peter*

Comparative State Feminism — *Stetson, Dorothy M*

A Comparative Study of Old English Metre — *Whitman, F H*

Comparative Stylistics of French and English — *Vinay, Jean-Paul*

Comparative Vertebrate Neuroanatomy — *Butler, Ann B*

Comparing Democracies — *LeDuc, Lawrence*

Comparing Environmental Risks — *Davies, J Clarence*

Comparing Government Activity — *Imbeau, Louis M*

Comparing Policy Networks — *Knoke, David*

Comparing State Polities — *Sullivan, Michael J, 1941-*

Comparisons in Policing — *Brodeur, Jean-Paul*

The Compass — *Morrissey, Stephen*

Compassion Fatigue — *Figley, Charles R*

Compassion: The Core Value That Animates Psychotherapy — *Lewin, Roger A*

c Compassion: Zach Lends a Hand (Illus. by Davis Henry) — *Canning, Shelagh*

Compassionate Laughter — *Wooten, Patty*

r Compendium of Human Settlements Statistics 1995

Compendium of Olfactory Research — *Gilbert, Avery N*

Compendium of Stone Fruit Diseases — *Ogawa, Joseph M*

Compensation for Regulatory Takings — *Miceli, Thomas J*

Compensation for Teams — *Gross, Steven E*

The Competent Head — *Jirasinghe, Dilum*

Competing Gospels — *Simons, Robert G*

Competing in the Age of Digital Convergence — *Yoffie, David B*

Competing in the Information Age — *Luftman, Jerry N*

Competing Solutions — *White, Joseph*

Competing through Technology and Manufacturing — *Kathuria, Sanjay*

Competition and Choice in Electricity — *Hunt, Sally*

Competition and Cooperation in Japanese Labour Markets — *Mosk, Carl*

Competition and Culture on Canada's Information Highway

Competition and Finance — *Dowd, Kevin*

Competition, Commitment, and Welfare — *Suzumura, Kotaro*

y Competition Fever — *Charbonnet, Gabrielle*

Competition in the 21st Century — *Tyson, Kirk W M*

Competition Policy — *Phlips, Louis*

Competition Policy and the Transformation of Central Europe — *Fingleton, John*

r Competitions: Maximizing Your Abilities — *Karnes, Frances A*

Competitive Frontiers — *Adler, Nancy J*

Competitive Governments — *Breton, Albert*

Competitive Intelligence — *Kahaner, Larry*

Competitive Strategy — *Porter, Michael*

Competitiveness: Forging Ahead

Competitiveness in United States Grain Exports — *Zhang, Mei Miranda*

Competitiveness, Subsidiarity, and Industrial Policy — *Devine, Pat*

Competitors in Alliance — *Procassini, Andrew A*

Compiler Construction — *Wirth, Niklaus*

r Complain, Complain, Complain — *Molson, Karen*

Complaint to the Lord — *Pollard, Leslie J*

y The Compleat Cockroach — *Gordon, David George*

The Compleat Conductor — *Schuller, Gunther*

r The Compleat Talking Machine. 2nd Ed. — *Reiss, Eric L*

Complementary Medicine and the Law — *Stone, Julie*

The Complete Angler — *Walton, Izaak*

r The Complete Annotated Gilbert and Sullivan — *Sullivan, Arthur, Sir*

The Complete Art of War — *Sun-Tzu*

The Complete Birdhouse Book — *Stokes, Donald W*

The Complete Book of Alternative Nutrition — *Yeager, Selene*

The Complete Book of Breast Care — *Lauersen, Niels H*

The Complete Book of Floorcloths — *Cooper, Kathy*

The Complete Book of Fruit — *Flowerdew, Bob*

The Complete Book of Gourd Craft — *Summit, Ginger*

y The Complete Book of Pregnancy and Childbirth. Rev. and Expanded Ed. — *Kitzinger, Sheila*

y The Complete Book of Sewing — *Cream, Penelope*

r The Complete Book of Shaker Furniture — *Rieman, Timothy D*

The Complete Breast Book — *Engel, June*

c The Complete Castle — *Denchfield, Nick*

Complete Computer Trainer — *Clothier, Paul*

Complete Conditioning for Baseball — *Murphy, Pat, 1958-*

The Complete Critical Prose — *Mandelstam, Osip*

The Complete Crumb. Vol. 12 — *Crumb, R*

cr The Complete Dog Book for Kids

The Complete Eldercare Planner — *Loverde, Joyce*

Complete Entrepreneur — *Peterson, Mark*

Complete Evangelism — *Maynard-Reid, Pedrito Uriah*

r The Complete Family Guide to Healthy Living — *Carroll, Stephen, Dr.*

Complete Fiction of W.M. Spackman — *Spackman, W M*

The Complete Films of Audrey Hepburn — *Vermilye, Jerry*

r The Complete Films of Vincent Price — *Williams, Lucy Chase*

r The Complete Games Trainers Play on CD-ROM. Electronic Media Version

The Complete Gospels. Rev. and Expanded Ed. — *Bible. N.T. Gospels. English. Scholars. 1994*

r The Complete Grants Sourcebook for Higher Education. 3rd Ed. — *Bauer, David G*

r Complete Guide to Amerian Bed and Breakfast. 4th Ed. — *Barnes, Rik*

A Complete Guide to Bird Feeding — *Dennis, John V*

The Complete Guide to Building and Outfitting an Office in Your Home — *Germer, Jerry*

The Complete Guide to Business Risk Management — *Sadgrove, Kit*

The Complete Guide to Chess — *Burgess, Graham*

The Complete Guide to Consulting Success. 2nd Ed. — *Shenson, Howard*

The Complete Guide to Eco-Friendly Design — *Evans, Poppy*

The Complete Guide to Experiential Psychotherapy — *Mahrer, Alvin R*

r Complete Guide to Eyecare, Eyeglasses and Contact Lenses. 4th Ed. — *Zinn, Walter J*

r The Complete Guide to Homeopathy — *Lockie, Andrew*

y A Complete Guide to Kissing — *Fisher, Nick*

r The Complete Guide to Lincoln Cents — *Lange, David W*

r The Complete Guide to Offshore Money Havens — *Schneider, Jerome*

The Complete Guide to Performance Appraisal — *Grote, Dick*

r The Complete Guide to Stationary Gas Engines — *Meincke, Mark*

r The Complete Guide to the 1995 Doubled Die Cent Varieties — *Wexler, John A*

The Complete Guide to World Mysticism — *Freke, Timothy*

r The Complete Hi$panic Media Directory 1996

r The Complete Home Health Advisor — *Elkins, Rita*

r The Complete Horse Care Manual — *Vogel, Colin*

r Complete Hostel Vacation Guide to England, Wales and Scotland

The Complete Idiot's Guide to Creating an HTML Web Page — *McFedries, Paul*

y The Complete Idiot's Guide to Dating — *Kuriansky, Judy*

The Complete Idiot's Guide to Multimedia — *Haskin, David*

The Complete Idiot's Guide to Windows 95 — *McFedries, Paul*

r The Complete Illustrated Holistic Herbal — *Hoffmann, David*

Complete Internet Business Toolkit — *Schwartau, Winn*

r Complete List of Reports Published by the British Library 1995

The Complete Manual of Wood Veneering — *Lincoln, William A*

r The Complete Marquis Who's Who on CD-ROM. Electronic Media Version

The Complete Maus. Electronic Media Version — *Spiegelman, Art*

The Complete Perfectionist — *Jimenez, Juan Ramon*

c The Complete Poetical Works of Phoebe Flood (Illus. by Lauren Child) — *Whitworth, John*

The Complete Poetical Works of Thomas Hardy. Vols. 4-5 — *Hardy, Thomas*

The Complete Puccini Libretti. Vols. 1-2 — *Puccini, Giacomo*

The Complete Quantum Leap Book — *Chunovic, Louis*

r The Complete Saving Source Catalog — *Potter, Michelle A*

yr The Complete Scholarship Book — *Student Services, Inc.*

Complete Short Stories — *Graves, Robert*

The Complete Short Stories. Vol. 1 — *Buchan, John*

The Complete Sourdough Cookbook for Camp, Trail, and Kitchen — *Holm, Don*

The Complete Stories — *Hurston, Zora Neale*

c The Complete Tales of Winnie-the-Pooh (Illus. by Ernest H Shepard) — *Milne, A A*

The Complete Theory Test for Cars and Motorcycles

The Complete Tracker — *McDougall, Len*

The Complete Valley of the Kings — *Reeves, Nicholas*

The Complete Verdi Libretti. Vols. 1-3 — *Verdi, Giuseppe*

Complete Works and Other Stories — *Monterroso, Augusto*

The Complete Works of Robert Browning. Vol. 6 — *Browning, Robert*

The Complete Works of Thomas Watson 1556-1592. Vols. 1-2 — *Watson, Thomas*

The Complete Works of Voltaire. Vols. 3B-4 — *Voltaire*

Completing the Circle — *Sneve, Virginia Driving Hawk*

A Complex Fate — *Sanders, Barry, 1938-*

Complex Problem Solving — *Frensch, Peter A*

p Complexity

Complexity and Creativity in Organizations — *Stacey, Ralph D*

Compliance Quantified — *Avenhaus, Rudolf*

Complications in Arterial Surgery — *Campbell, Bruce*

Complications in Diagnostic Imaging and Interventional Radiology. 3rd Ed. — *Ansell, George*

Complications of Colon and Rectal Surgery — *Hicks, Terry C*

Complicit Fictions — *Fujii, James A*

Component-Based Software Engineering — *Brown, Alan W*

The Composer's Handbook — *Cole, Bruce*

Composers on Music. 2nd Ed. — *Fisk, Josiah*

Composing for the Films — *Eisler, Hans*

Composing Social Identity in Written Language — *Rubin, Donald L*

Composing the Soul — *Parkes, Graham*

Composite Materials. Vols. 1-2 — *Schwartz, Mel M*

Composition, Chemistry, and Climate of the Atmosphere — *Singh, Hanwant B*

Composition in Black and White — *Talalay, Kathryn*

Composition in the Twenty-First Century — *Bloom, Lynn*

A Compositional Approach to Performance Modelling — *Hillston, Jane*

The Compositions of Vagn Holmboe — *Rapoport, Paul*

c Compost! Growing Gardens from Your Garbage (Illus. by Anca Hariton) — *Glaser, Linda*

Compound Semiconductor Electronics and Photonics — *Shul, R J*

Compound Semiconductors 1995

Comprehending Power in Christian Social Ethics — *Hinze, Christine Firer*

r A Comprehensive, Annotated Bibliography on Mahatma Gandhi. Vol. 1 — *Pandiri, Ananda M*

r A Comprehensive Annotated Book of Mormon Bibliography — *Parry, Donald W*

A Comprehensive Approach to Stereotactic Breast Biopsy — *Fjardo, Laurie L*

r The Comprehensive Catalog of Military Payment Certificates — *Schwan, Fred*

r Comprehensive Catalog of U.S. Paper Money. 6th Ed. — *Hessler, Gene*

r The Comprehensive Country Music Encyclopedia — *Country Music (New York, N.Y.)*

r Comprehensive Dictionary of Measurement and Control. 3rd Ed.

r Comprehensive Dissertation Index 1861-1972. Vols. 1-37

r Comprehensive Dissertation Index 1973-1982. Vols. 1-38

Comprehensive Emergency Mental Health Care — *Zealberg, Joseph J*

A Comprehensive Guide for Listing a Building in the National Register of Historic Places — *Greenberg, Gail*

A Comprehensive Guide to Attention Deficit Disorder in Adults — *Nadeau, Kathleen G*
r The Comprehensive Listing of Artcraft Covers. 4th Ed. — *Severe, Martin L*
Comprehensive Organometallic Chemistry II. Vols. 1-14
Comprehensive Plan — *White Plains Comprehensive Plan Management Group (New York)*
r Comprehensive Postanesthesia Care — *Brown, Morris*
Comprehensive Review of Geriatric Psychiatry--II — *Sadavoy, Joel*
r A Comprehensive Spanish Grammar — *Bruyne, Jacques De*
Comprehensive Supramolecular Chemistry. Vols. 1-11
Comprehensive Textbook of Psychiatry. 6th Ed., Vols. 1-2 — *Kaplan, Harold I*
Comprehensive Textbook of Thoracic Oncology — *Aisner, Joseph*
Compromising Traditions — *Hallett, J P*
cr Compton's Encyclopedia 1996. Vols. 1-26
yr Compton's Encyclopedia of American History. Electronic Media Version
cr Compton's Interactive Bible: New International Version. Electronic Media Version
yr Compton's Interactive Encyclopedia 1997. Electronic Media Version
yr Compton's Interactive World Atlas. Electronic Media Version
yr Compton's Reference Collection. Electronic Media Version
The Compulsion to Create — *Kavaler-Adler, Susan*
Compulsive Beauty — *Foster, Hal*
CompuServe Quick Tour Guide to WinCIM — *Sluman, Roelf*
Computation of Special Functions — *Chang, Shan-Chieh*
Computational and Constructive Design Theory — *Wallis, W D*
Computational Approaches to Novel Condensed Matter Systems — *Neilson, D*
Computational Complexity 11
Computational Differentiation — *Berz, Martin*
Computational Economics and Finance — *Varian, Hal R*
Computational Fluid Dynamics — *Lesieur, M*
Computational Intelligence PC Tools — *Eberhart, Russell C*
Computational Methods for Fluid Dynamics — *Ferziger, Joel H*
Computational Methods in Water Resources XI. Vols. 1-2 — *Aldama, A A*
Computational Modeling — *Taber, Charles S*
Computational Statistics in Climatology — *Polyak, Ilya*
y Computer: A History of the Information Machine — *Campbell-Kelly, Martin*
Computer Aided Design in Composite Material Technology — *International Conference on Computer Aided Design in Composite Material Technology (5th: 1996: Udine, Italy)*
Computer-Aided Qualitative Data Analysis — *Kelle, Udo*
Computer-Aided Transit Scheduling — *Daduna, Joachim R*
Computer Animation '95
Computer Applications in Food Technology — *Singh, R Paul*
Computer Architecture. 2nd Ed. — *Wilkinson, Barry*
Computer Assisted Analytical Spectroscopy — *Brown, Steven D*
Computer Assisted Radiology — *International Symposium on Computer and Communication Systems for Image Guided Diagnosis and Therapy (1996: Paris, France)*
Computer Conversations — *Jody, Marilyn*
Computer Design — *International Conference on Computer Design (1996: Austin, TX)*
r The Computer Desktop Encyclopedia — *Freedman, Alan*
r The Computer Desktop Encyclopedia. Electronic Media Version — *Freedman, Alan*
cr Computer Dictionary for Kids... — *Borman, Jami*
Computer Facial Animation — *Parke, Frederic I*
Computer Graphics. 2nd Ed. — *Hearn, Donald*
Computer Graphics International — *International Conference of the Computer Graphics Society (14th: 1996: Pohang, Korea)*
Computer Integrated Machine Design — *Wilson, Charles E*
p Computer Life

Computer Methods and Water Resources III — *Abousleiman, Y*
Computer Modelling of Seas and Coastal Regions — *International Conference on Computer Modelling of Seas and Coastal Regions (2nd: 1995: Cancun, Mexico)*
The Computer Music Tutorial — *Roads, Curtis*
Computer Networking and Scholarly Communication in the Twenty-First-Century University — *Harrison, Teresa M*
Computer Networks — *Hsu, John Y*
Computer Networks — *Peterson, Larry L*
Computer Networks. 3rd Ed. — *Tanenbaum, Andrew S*
Computer Numerical Control — *Stenerson, Jon*
Computer Numerical Control Programming — *Amic, Peter J*
c The Computer Nut — *Byars, Betsy*
Computer Pioneers — *Lee, J A N*
Computer Programming. 4th Ed. — *Rothwell, J*
Computer Programs for Qualitative Data Analysis — *Weitzman, Eben A*
Computer-Related Technologies in Library Operations — *Wright, Keith C*
yr Computer Resources for People with Disabilities. 2nd Ed., Fully Rev. — *Alliance for Technology Access*
Computer Security. 3rd Ed. — *Carroll, J M*
The Computer Security Foundations Workshop — *Computer Security Foundations Workshop*
Computer Simulation in Logistics — *Nersesian, Roy L*
Computer Simulation in Materials Science — *Kirchner, Helmut O*
Computer Simulation in Operations Management — *Klafehn, Keith*
Computer Simulations with Mathematica — *Gaylord, Richard J*
Computer Software and Applications Conference 1996
The Computer Speech Book — *Schindler, Esther*
Computer Technology 1996
Computer Technology and Social Issues — *Garson, G David*
Computer Telephony — *Tittel, Ed*
Computer Vision and Pattern Recognition — *IEEE Computer Society Conference on Computer Vision and Pattern Recognition (1996: San Francisco, CA)*
The Computerization of Behavioral Healthcare — *Trabin, Tom*
Computerized Control Systems in the Food Industry — *Mittal, Gauris S*
c Computers — *Hay, Carole*
c Computers — *Parker, Steve*
c Computers — *Wright, David, 1943-*
Computers and Classroom Culture — *Schofield, Janet Ward*
Computers in Railways V. Vols. 1-2 — *Allan, John J*
Computers in Small Bytes — *Joos, Irene*
Computers in the Classroom — *Gooden, Andrea R*
c Computers of the Future — *Darling, David*
Computing and Communications in the Extreme — *National Research Council (U.S.). Steering Committee, Workshop Series on High Performance Computing and Communications*
Computing for Site Managers — *Flowers, Robin*
Computing in Civil Engineering — *Vanegas, Jorge*
Computing Myths, Class Realities — *Hakken, David*
Computing Parliamentary History — *Phillips, John A, 1949-*
Computing Tomorrow — *Wand, Ian*
Comrade Criminal — *Handleman, Stephen*
Comrades and Enemies — *Lockman, Zachary*
Comte after Positivism — *Scharff, Robert C*
La Comunita Dei Lucchesi A Venezia — *Mola, Luca*
c Comus (Illus. by Trina Schart Hyman) — *Hodges, Margaret*
Con Che Soavita — *Fenlon, Iain*
Con Manh Ao Trang — *Dang, Duc*
Con Respeto — *Valdes, Guadalupe*
Conan and the Emerald Lotus — *Hocking, John C*
The Concealed Fancies — *Cavendish, Jane*
Conceived by Liberty — *Smith, Stephanie A*
Conceived Presences — *Falco, Raphael*
Conceived with Malice — *DeSalvo, Louise A*
Conceiving of Europe — *Musolff, Andreas*
Conceiving of Personality — *Robbins, Michael*
Conceiving the Embryo — *Evans, Donald*
Conceiving the New World Order — *Ginsburg, Faye D*
The Concept of Object as the Foundation of Physics — *Stein, Irving*
The Concept of the Political — *Schmitt, Carl*
Conception, Pregnancy, and Birth — *Niven, Catherine A*

r Conception, Pregnancy and Birth — *Stoppard, Miriam*
Concepts and Methods in Evolutionary Biology — *Brandon, Robert N*
Concepts in Human Geography — *Earle, Carville*
r Concepts in Physical Chemistry — *Atkins, P W*
Concepts of Chemical Dependency. 3rd Ed. — *Doweiko, Harold*
Concepts of Identity — *Hoffman, Katherine*
Concepts of Space in Greek Thought — *Algra, Keimpe*
Conceptual Foundations for Multidisciplinary Thinking — *Kline, S J*
Conceptual Foundations of Professional Nursing Practice. 2nd Ed. — *Creasia, Joan L*
Conceptual Schema and Relational Database Design. 2nd Ed. — *Halpin, Terry*
Conceptualizing the State — *Meadowcroft, James*
Concerning the Rites of Psychoanalysis — *Benvenuto, Bice*
Concert and Opera Halls — *Beranek, Leo*
Concert Music, Rock, and Jazz since 1945 — *Marvin, Elizabeth West*
r Concise Compendium of the World's Languages — *Campbell, George L*
r The Concise Conservative Encyclopedia — *Miner, Brad*
r A Concise Dictionary of Indian Philosophy. Rev. Ed. — *Grimes, John*
r Concise Dictionary of Library and Information Science — *Keenan, Stella*
yr Concise Encyclopedia Biology
r The Concise Encyclopedia of Food and Nutrition — *Ensmonger, Audrey*
r Concise Encyclopedia of Preaching — *Willimon, William H*
yr Concise Encyclopedia of Psychology. 2nd Ed. — *Corsini, Raymond J*
A Concise English-Russian Phrase Book — *Karras, Thomas*
Concise Guide to Neuropsychiatry and Behavioral Neurology — *Cummings, Jeffrey L*
r A Concise Historical Atlas of Eastern Europe — *Hupchick, Dennis P*
A Concise History of Business in Canada — *Taylor, Graham D*
A Concise History of the Early Church — *Brox, Norbert*
A Concise History of the Medieval Church — *Frank, Isnard Wilhelm*
A Concise History of the Middle East. 5th Ed. — *Goldschmidt, Arthur, Jr.*
y A Concise History of the Russian Revolution — *Pipes, Richard*
A Concise History of the University of Cambridge — *Leedham-Green, Elisabeth*
A Concise Introduction to Calculus — *Hsiang, W Y*
yr The Concise Oxford Companion to English Literature. Rev. Ed. — *Drabble, Margaret*
r The Concise Oxford Dictionary of Music. 4th Ed. — *Kennedy, Michael, 1926-*
r The Concise Oxford Russian Dictionary — *Howlett, Colin*
Concise Textbook of Clinical Psychiatry — *Kaplan, Harold I*
Concise Thermodynamics — *Dunning-Davies, Jeremy*
yr A Concise Ulster Dictionary — *Macafee, C I*
r Concise World Atlas
Concord and Conflict — *Saul, Norman E*
The Concord Museum — *Wood, David F*
r Concordance Latine Des Pseudepigraphes D'Ancien Testament — *Denis, A-M*
r A Concordance to the Complete Poems and Plays of T.S. Eliot — *Dawson, J L*
r A Concordance to the Critique of Pure Reason — *Reuscher, Jay*
Concordancias Del Poema Martin Fierro. Vols. 1-2 — *Dellepiane, Angela B*
r Concordantia In Patres Apostolicos. Vols. 1-2 — *Urban, Angel*
Concrete Bridges — *Raina, V K*
Concrete Candy — *Apollo, 1980-*
Concrete Jungle — *Rockman, Alexis*
The Concrete River — *Shannon, John*
The Concubine's Children — *Chong, Denise*
Concurrent Engineering — *Backhouse, Christopher J*
Concurrent Engineering Fundamentals. Vol. 2 — *Prasad, Biren*
Concurrent Programming in ERLANG. 2nd Ed. — *Armstrong, Joe*
Concurrent Programming in Java — *Lea, D*
Le Conditionnel Dans Le Discours Jouranlistique — *Haillet, Pierre*

Conditions for Civilized Politics — *Eide, Asbjorn*
Conditions for Direct Foreign Investments in the Baltic States — *Hoek, M Peter Van Der*
Conditions of Liberty — *Gellner, Ernest*
Condom Nation — *Panzer, Richard A*
y A Condor Brings the Sun — *McGahan, Jerry*
c The Condor Hoax — *Pageler, Elaine*
p The Condor Token Newsletter
Condorcet: Foundations of Social Choice and Political Theory — *Condorcet, Jean-Antoine-Nicolas De Caritat, Marquis De*
y The Conductor (Kohen). Audio Version — *Kennealy, Jerry*
y The Conductor (Lane). Audio Version — *Kennealy, Jerry*
Conductors of Chaos — *Sinclair, Iain*
The Confederados: Old South Immigrants in Brazil — *Dawsey, Cyrus B*
Confederate General of the West — *Thompson, Jerry*
The Confederate Housewife — *Moore, John Hammond*
The Confederate Order of Battle. Vol. 1 — *Sibley, F Ray*
Confederate Pathway to the Pacific — *Finch, L Boyd*
Confederate Treasure in Danville — *Carroll, J Frank*
Conference Record. Vols. 1-2 — *Asilomar Conference on Signals, Systems and Computers (29th: 1995: Pacific Grove, Ca.)*
Conference with the Dead   *Lamsley, Terry*
y Confess-O-Rama — *Koertge, Ron*
Confession — *Hahn, Susan*
Confession — *Tolstoy, Leo, Graf*
Confession in the Novel — *Smith, Les W*
The Confessions — *Augustine, Saint, Bishop of Hippo*
Confessions of a Spy — *Earley, Pete*
Confessions of a White House Ghost Writer — *Humes, James C*
Confessions of an Accidental Businessman — *Autry, James A*
Confessions of an Igloo Dweller — *Houston, James A*
Confessions of an Ivy League Bookie — *Alson, Peter*
r The Confessions of Saint Augustine — *Severson, Richard James*
The Confessions of Saint Augustine (Rotelle) — *Augustine, Saint, Bishop of Hippo*
The Confetti Bed — *Paige, Frances*
The Confetti Kid — *Lane, Robert*
c Confetti: Poems for Children (Illus. by Enrique O Sanchez) — *Mora, Pat*
The Confidence Course — *Anderson, Walter, 1944-*
Confidence, Credibility and Macroeconomic Policy — *Burdekin, Richard C K*
The Confidence Game — *Solomon, Steven*
The Confident Child — *Apter, Terri*
Configurable Distributed Systems — *International Conference on Configurable Distributed Systems (3rd: 1996: Annapolis, Maryland)*
Configuracion Textual De La Recopilacion Historial De Venezuela De Pedro De Aguado — *Navarro, Jose Maria*
Configurations: A Topomorphical Approach to Renaissance Poetry — *Rostvig, Maren-Sofie*
Configurations of Exile — *Kanaganayakam, Chelva*
Configuring CDE — *Fernandez, Charles*
Confirmation: Presbyterian Practices in Ecumenical Perspective — *Osmer, Richard Robert*
Confirmation: The Spiritual Wisdom That Has Shaped Our Lives — *Burns, Khephra*
Conflict and Change in Cuba — *Baloyra, Enrique A*
Conflict and Change in the Russian Industrial Enterprise — *Clarke, Simon*
Conflict and Chaos in Eastern Europe — *Hubchick, Dennis P*
Conflict and Community in Corinth — *Witherington, Ben, III*
Conflict and Harmony in Multi-Ethnic Societies — *Morris-Hale, Walter*
Conflict, Cooperation, and Justice — *Bunker, Barbara Benedict*
c Conflict in Art — *Gogerty, Clare*
Conflict in the Classroom. 5th Ed. — *Long, Nicholas J*
Conflict of Interest — *Lewis, Terry*
The Conflict of the Church and Synagogue — *Parkes, James*
Conflict over Convoys — *Smith, Kevin*
y Conflict Resolution — *Nathan, Amy*
Conflict Resolution — *Schellenberg, James A*
Conflicting Accounts — *Goldman, Kevin*
Conflicting Paths — *Graff, Harvey J*
Conflicting Visions of Reform — *Chrisman, Miriam Usher*
Conflicts about Class — *Lee, D J*

Conflicts and New Departures in World Society — *Bornschier, Volker*
Conflicts of Divided Nations — *Gu, Weiqun*
Conflicts of Interest — *Martel, John*
Conformal Differential Geometry and Its Generalizations — *Akivis, Maks A*
Conformal Quantum Field Theory in D-Dimensions — *Fradkin, Efim S*
p Confrontation
Confronting Crisis — *Moser, Caroline O N*
Confronting Death — *Moller, David Wendell*
Confronting Poverty — *Danziger, Sheldon*
Confronting Regional Challenges — *Donald G. Hagman Commemorative Conference (6th)*
Confronting Southern Poverty in the Great Depression — *Carlton, David L*
Confucian Statecraft and Korean Institutions — *Palais, James B*
Confucianism and Christianity — *Yao, Hsin-Chung*
c Confused? A Kid's Guide to the Internet's World Wide Web — *Theriault, Luc F*
Confusions in Christian Ethics — *Preston, Ronald H*
Congo Journey — *O'Hanlon, Redmond*
Congregation: The Journey Back to Church — *Dorsey, Gary*
Congregations in Conflict — *Hartman, Keith*
Congress and the Governance of the Nation's Capital — *Harris, Charles Wesley*
Congress and the Presidency — *Foley, Michael, 1948-*
Congress and the Rent-Seeking Society — *Parker, Glenn R*
Congress as Public Enemy — *Hibbing, John R*
y The Congress of the United States — *Kronenwetter, Michael*
A Congress of Wonders — *McClanahan, Ed*
Congressional Dynamics — *Jillson, Calvin*
Congressional Papers Management — *Phillips, Faye*
r Congressional Quarterly's Politics in America 1996. Book and Electronic Media Version
r Congressional Research Service Index 1916-1994 on CD-ROM. Electronic Media Version
The Congressional Yearbook 1994
Conjectures of a Guilty Bystander — *Merton, Thomas*
Conjesturas Sobre La Memoria De Mi Tribu — *Donoso, Jose*
Conjugate Gradient Type Methods for Ill-Posed Problems — *Hanke, Martin*
p Conjunctions
c The Conjure Woman (Illus. by Terea D Shaffer) — *Miller, William*
Conjuring Science — *Toumey, Christopher P*
Conjuring Tibet — *Painter, Charlotte*
p Connect: To the Fight against Discrimination and Racism
Connected Community — *Moffitt, Leonard C*
The Connected Family — *Papert, Seymour*
Connected Knowledge — *Cromer, Alan*
r Connecticut Career Guide
y A Connecticut Yankee in Criminal Court — *Heck, Peter J*
Connecting Kids and the Internet — *Benson, Allen C*
Connecting the Dots — *Kumin, Maxine*
Connection Community Content — *Canada. Information Highway Advisory Council*
Connectionism and the Philosophy of Psychology — *Horgan, Terence*
Connections in Steel Structures III — *Bjorhovde, Reidar*
Connections: The Wood and Fullenwider Families in America — *Wood, Thomas Fullenwider*
The Connective Edge — *Lipman-Blumen, Jean*
Connexity: How to Live in a Connected World — *Mulgan, Geoff*
c Connie and Bonnie's Birthday Blastoff — *Nelson, Ray*
c Connie and the Water Babies (Illus. by Georgien Overwater) — *Wilson, Jacqueline*
c Connie Came to Play (Illus. by Stephen Lambert) — *Paton Walsh, Jill*
Conor: A Biography of Conor Cruise O'Brien — *O'Brien, Conor Cruise*
Conor: An Anthology — *O'Brien, Conor Cruise*
Conoscere Per Governare — *Nubola, Cecilia*
Conquered Heart — *Sampson, Lisa*
The Conquerers of the New Kingdom of Granada — *Avellaneda Navas, Jose Ignacio*
c Conquerors and Explorers (Illus. by McRae Books) — *Ross, Stewart*
Conquerors' Road — *White, Osmar*
Conquest, Anarchy and Lordship — *Dalton, Paul*
Conquest and Colonisation — *Golding, Brian*
Conquest and Union — *Ellis, Steven G, 1950-*

Conquest: Montezuma, Cortes, and the Fall of Old Mexico — *Thomas, Hugh*
The Conquest of Arid America. 1st Ed. — *Smythe, William Ellsworth*
The Conquest of Arid America. 2nd Ed. — *Smythe, William Ellsworth*
The Conquest of Assyria — *Larsen, Mogens Trolle*
The Conquest of Jerusalem and the Third Crusade — *Edbury, Peter W*
y The Conquest of Mexico — *Lilley, Stephen R*
The Conquest of the Reich — *Neillands, Robin*
y The Conquest of the West — *Smith, C Carter*
Conquests and Historical Identities in California 1769-1936 — *Haas, Lisbeth*
Conquista Y Contraconquista — *Ortega, Julio*
Conscience and Power — *Garrett, Stephen A*
Conscience at War — *Linn, Ruth*
The Conscience of the World — *Willetts, Peter*
Conscious and Unconscious Processes — *Shevrin, Howard*
The Conscious Ear — *Tomatis, Alfred A*
A Conscious Life — *Cox, Fran*
The Conscious Mind — *Chalmers, David J*
Consciousness and Experience — *Lycan, William G*
Consciousness and the Brain (Lopez-Morillas). Audio Version — *Gazzaniga, Michael S*
Consciousness and the Mind of God — *Taliaferro, Charles*
Consciousness, Dreams, and Self — *Arden, John Boghosian*
Conscription and the Attlee Governments — *Scott, L V*
The Conscription Society — *Kasza, Gregory J*
Consequences of Pragmatism — *Rorty, Richard*
Consequences of Structural Adjustment — *LeFranc, Elsie*
Conservation and Biodiversity — *Dobson, Andrew P*
r Conservation and Environmentalism — *Paehlke, Robert*
Conservation and Management of Tropical Rainforests — *Bruenig, Eberhard F*
Conservation and Preservation in Small Libraries — *Hadgraft, Nicholas*
Conservation and the City — *Larkham, Peter J*
Conservation Book Repair — *BonaDea, Artemis*
Conservation of Great Plains Ecosystems — *Johnson, Stanley R*
Conservation-Tillage Systems for Cotton — *McClelland, Marilyn R*
Conservatism: An Anthology of Social and Political Thought from David Hume to the Present — *Muller, Jerry Z*
y The Conservative Agenda — *McCuen, Gary*
Conservative Century — *Seldon, Anthony*
Conservative Environmentalism — *Dunn, James R*
Conservative Management of Sports Injuries — *Hyde, Thomas E*
Conservative Realism — *Minogue, Kenneth*
The Conservative Revolution in the Weimar Republic — *Woods, Roger*
Conservative Systems and Quantum Chaos — *Bates, Larry M*
The Conservative Tradition in America — *Dunn, Charles W*
The Conservatives and British Society 1880-1990 — *Francis, Martin*
I Conservatori Della Virtu — *Groppi, Angela*
Conserving Culture — *Hufford, Mary*
y Conserving Rain Forests — *Banks, Martin*
Considerations on France — *Maistre, Joseph Marie, Comte De*
Consolation at Ground Zero — *Horvath, Brooke*
r A Consolidated Bibliography of Urban History — *Rodger, Richard*
Consolidating Democracy in Poland — *Taras, Raymond*
The Consolidation of Democracy in Latin America — *Tulchin, Joseph S*
Consorting with Saints — *McLaughlin, Megan*
Conspicuous Criticism — *Shannon, Christopher*
La Conspiracion De Los Idiotas — *Aguinis, Marcos*
The Conspiracy and Other Stories — *Kross, Joan*
A Conspiracy of Optimism — *Hirt, Paul W*
Constantinople and Its Hinterland — *Mango, Cyril*
Constantinople: City of the World's Desire 1453-1924 — *Mansel, Philip*
Constanze Mozart — *Gartner, Heinz*
Constellation — *Mulcahy, Greg*
Constituting Americans — *Wald, Priscilla*
Constituting Critique — *Goetschel, Willi*

The Constitution and National Security — *Shuman, Howard E*

The Constitution and the Conduct of American Foreign Policy — *Adler, David Gray*

The Constitution in the Courts — *Perry, Michael J*

The Constitution of Deliberative Democracy — *Nino, Carlos Santiago*

The Constitution of the Federal Republic of Germany — *Curry, David P*

y The Constitution of the United States — *Judson, Karen*

y Constitutional Amendments — *Feinberg, Barbara Silberdick*

Constitutional History of the American Revolution. Abridged Ed. — *Reid, John Phillip*

yr Constitutional Law and Young Adults — *Renstrom, Peter G*

Constitutional Policy and Change in Europe — *Hesse, Joachim Jens*

Constitutional Politics in the States — *Tarr, G Alan*

Constitutional Rights and Powers of the People — *Moore, Wayne D*

Constitutional Royalism and the Search for Settlement c. 1640-9 — *Aylmer, Gerald*

The Constitutional Thought of Thomas Jefferson — *Mayer, David N*

Constitutionalism and Native Americans 1903-1968 — *Wunder, John R*

Constitutions and National Identity — *Barron, Thomas J*

Constitutions and Political Theory — *Lane, Jan-Erik*

r Constitutions of the World — *Maddex, Robert L*

Constraints on the Success of Structural Adjustment Programmes in Africa — *Harvey, Charles, M A*

The Constructed Body — *Murphy, Julien S*

Constructing a Competitive Order — *Mercer, Helen*

Constructing Democracy — *Jelin, Elizabeth*

Constructing Girlhood — *Tinkler, Penny*

Constructing Identities — *Michael, Mike*

Constructing Panic — *Capps, Lisa*

Constructing Realities — *Rosen, Hugh*

Constructing School Success — *Mehan, Hugh*

Constructing Social Research — *Ragin, Charles C*

Constructing the Nation-State — *McNeely, Connie L*

La Construction De La Paix Ou Le Travail De Sisyphe — *Goyard-Fabre, Simone*

Construction Failure. 2nd Ed. — *Feld, Jacob*

Construction Insurance, Bonding, and Risk Management — *Palmer, William J, 1934-*

The Construction of Authorship — *Woodmansee, Martha*

The Construction of Cognitive Maps — *Portugali, Juval*

The Construction of Religious Boundaries — *Oberoi, Harjot*

Construction Safety — *Hinze, Jimmie W*

c Construction Zone (Illus. by Tana Hoban) — *Hoban, Tana*

Constructive Criticism — *Kreiswirth, Martin*

Constructive Therapies. Vol. 2 — *Hoyt, Michael F*

Constructivism in Education — *Steffe, Leslie P*

Constructor Prequalification — *Russell, Jeffrey S*

Construire Le Sens — *Boutet, Josiane*

r Consultants and Consulting Organizations Directory 1996 Supplement

Consumer Attitudes toward Credit Insurance — *Barron, John M*

r The Consumer Bible — *Green, Mark*

r Consumer Canada 1996

Consumer Culture — *Lury, Celia*

Consumer Culture and TV Programming — *Andersen, Robin*

Consumer Expenditures — *Lebergott, Stanley*

r Consumer Health Information Source Book. 4th Ed. — *Rees, Alan M*

r Consumer Health U.S.A. 2nd Ed. — *Rees, Alan M*

Consumer Involvement — *Laaksonen, Pirjo*

r Consumer Mexico 1996

r Consumer Protection and the Law — *Krohn, Lauren*

Consumer Rites — *Schmidt, Leigh Eric*

The Consumer Society — *Goodwin, Neva R*

r Consumer South Africa 1995

r Consumer USA 1996

y The Consumer's Good Chemical Guide — *Emsley, John*

A Consumer's Guide to Home Improvement, Renovation, and Repair. Rev. Ed. — *Santucci, Robert M*

r The Consumer's Guide to Homeopathy — *Ullman, Dana*

r Consumers Index to Product Evaluations and Information Sources, April-June 1996

r The Consumer's Medical Desk Reference — *Inlander, Charles B*

Consuming Angels — *Loeb, Lori Anne*

Consuming Fictions — *Houston, Gail Turley*

Consuming Fictions — *Todd, Richard*

Consumption and Identity at Work — *Du Gay, Paul*

Consumption in the Age of Affluence — *Fine, Ben*

The Consumption of Culture 1600-1800 — *Bermingham, Ann*

Contact Cards — *Carlsberg, Kim*

Contact Mechanics — *Raous, M*

Contacte Si Relatii Romano-Americane — *Comsa, Ioan*

Contacting Your Guardian Angel — *Levine, Joyce*

c Container Gardening for Kids (Illus. by Bruce Curtis) — *Talmage, Ellen*

The Container Revolution — *Hannes, Matt*

Containment Culture — *Nadel, Alan*

Contaminants and the Soil Environment in the Australasia-Pacific Region — *Australian-Pacific Conference on Contaminants and Soil Environment in the Australasia-Pacific Region (1st: 1996: Adelaide, S. Aust.)*

Contaminated Soil '95. Vols. 1-2

Contemplating Courts — *Epstein, Lee*

c Contemplating Your Bellybutton (Illus. by Tomoko Hasegawa) — *Nanao, Jun*

Contemplation and Action — *Gilchrist, Roberta*

The Contemplation of the World — *Maffesoli, Michel*

Contemplations of a Primal Mind — *Horn, Gabriel*

Contemplative Prayer — *Merton, Thomas*

r Contemporary American Folk Art — *Rosenak, Chuck*

Contemporary American Politics — *Grant, Alan*

Contemporary Art of Africa — *Magnin, Andre*

r Contemporary Artists. 4th Ed. — *Cerrito, Joann*

r Contemporary Australian Women 1996/97

r Contemporary Authors 1962-. Book and Electronic Media Version

Contemporary British Conservatism — *Ludlam, Steve*

Contemporary British Poetry — *Acheson, James*

The Contemporary Catholic School — *McLaughlin, Terence*

Contemporary China in the Post-Cold War Era — *Lin, Bih-Jaw*

Contemporary Coptic Nuns — *Doorn-Harder, Pieternella Van*

r Contemporary Counterfeit Capped Bust Half Dollars — *Davignon, Keith R*

The Contemporary Craft of Paper Mache — *Meyer, Helga*

r Contemporary Critical Theory — *Marshall, Donald G*

r Contemporary Designer Bookbinders — *Ward, Philip*

Contemporary Enzyme Kinetics and Mechanism. 2nd Ed. — *Purich, Daniel L*

Contemporary Extensile Exposures in Orthopaedic Surgery — *Williams, Ronald P*

Contemporary Feminist Fiction in Spain — *Davies, Catherine*

Contemporary French Cinema — *Austin, Guy*

Contemporary French Women Poets. Vol. 1 — *Bishop, Michael*

Contemporary French Women Poets. Vols. 1-2 — *Bishop, Michael*

r Contemporary Gay American Novelists — *Nelson, Emmanuel S*

Contemporary German Editorial Theory — *Gabler, Hans Walter*

Contemporary German Fiction — *Willson, A Leslie*

Contemporary German Legal Philosophy — *Herget, James E*

Contemporary Grandparenting — *Kornhaber, Arthur*

r The Contemporary History Handbook — *Brivati, Brian*

Contemporary Intellectual Assessment — *Flanagan, Dawn P*

Contemporary Irish Drama — *Roche, Anthony*

Contemporary Issues in Behavior Therapy — *Cautela, Joseph R*

Contemporary Issues in Breast Cancer — *Dow, Karen Hassey*

Contemporary Issues in Commercial Policy — *Kreinin, Mordechai E*

Contemporary Issues in the Treatment of Schizophrenia — *Shriqui, Christian L*

r Contemporary Italy — *Bull, Martin J*

The Contemporary Keyboardist — *Novello, John*

Contemporary Legend — *Bennett, Gillian*

r Contemporary Lesbian Writers of the United States — *Pollack, Sandra*

yr Contemporary Literary Criticism. Vols. 87-89

yr Contemporary Literary Criticism: Yearbook 1994

Contemporary Mathematical Physics — *Dobrushin, R L*

Contemporary Mexican Women Writers — *De Beer, Gabriella*

Contemporary Mormonism — *Cornwall, Marie*

Contemporary Music Education. 3rd Ed. — *Mark, Michael L*

Contemporary Nationalism in East Central Europe — *Latawski, Paul*

Contemporary Native American Architecture — *Krinsky, Carol Herselle*

Contemporary Norwegian Women's Writing — *Garton, Janet*

The Contemporary Novel in France — *Thompson, William*

Contemporary Painting in New Zealand — *Dunn, Michael*

r Contemporary Painting in Poland — *Noyce, Richard*

Contemporary Perspectives on Masculinity. 2nd Ed. — *Clatterbaugh, Kenneth C*

Contemporary Philosophy of Social Science — *Fay, Brian*

Contemporary Plant Systematics. 2nd Ed. — *Woodland, Dennis W*

Contemporary Plays By Women of Color — *Perkins, Kathy A*

y Contemporary Political Leaders of the Middle East — *Wakin, Edward*

r Contemporary Popular Writers — *Mote, Dave*

Contemporary Porcelain — *Lane, Peter*

Contemporary Portraits of Japanese Women — *Tanaka, Yukiko*

r The Contemporary Printed Literature of the English Counter-Reformation between 1558 and 1640. Vol. 2 — *Allison, A F*

r Contemporary Quotations in Black — *King, Anita*

r Contemporary Religious Ideas — *Lundin, G Edward*

Contemporary Short Stories from Central America — *Jaramillo Levi, Enrique*

r The Contemporary Spanish Novel — *Amell, Samuel*

Contemporary Television — *French, David*

Contemporary Theories and Practice in Education — *Bertrand, Yves*

Contemporary Urban Planning. 4th Ed. — *Levy, John M*

Contemporary Wicker Basketry — *Hoppe, Flo*

r Contemporary Women's Issues. Electronic Media Version

Contending Forces — *Hopkins, Pauline E*

Contending with Modernity — *Gleason, Philip*

The Content of America's Character — *Eberly, Don E*

Content of the Curriculum. 2nd Ed. — *Glatthorn, Allan A*

Contented among Strangers — *Pickle, Linda Schelbitzki*

The Contest for Social Science — *Yeo, Eileen*

Contest for the Heavens — *Jensen, Claus*

A Contest of Faiths — *Yohn, Susan M*

Contestable Markets Theory, Competition, and the United States Commercial Banking Industry — *Dickens, Ross N*

Contested Borders in the Caucasus — *Coppieters, Bruno*

Contested Boundaries — *Hall, Timothy D*

Contested Commodities — *Radin, Margaret Jane*

Contested Ground — *McGrath, Ann*

Contested Identities — *Kidd, Bruce*

Contested Meanings — *Gusfield, Joseph R*

Contested Terrain — *Silver, Marc L*

Contested Terrain — *Udall, Sharyn R*

Contesting Colonial Hegemony — *Engels, Dagmar*

Contesting Cultural Authority — *Turner, Frank M*

Contesting Cultural Rhetorics — *Marshall, Margaret J*

Contesting Earth's Future — *Zimmerman, Michael E, 1946-*

Contesting Tears — *Cavell, Stanley*

Context and Consciousness — *Nardi, Bonnie A*

Context North America — *La Bossiere, Camille R*

The Context of Casuistry — *Keenan, James F*

Contextual Media — *Barrett, Edward*

Continent — *Crace, Jim*

Continental and Postmodern Perspectives in the Philosophy of Science — *Babich, Babette E*

Continental Drift — *Houston, James D*

Continental Rifts — *Olsen, K H*

Contingency, Irony and Solidarity — *Rorty, Richard*

The Contingency of Theory — *Wihl, Gary*

Contingency Theory — *Itzkowitz, Gary*

Contingent Valuation and Endangered Species — Jakobsson, Kristin M

The Contingent Valuation of Environmental Resources — Bjornstad, David J

Le Continu Et Autres Ecrits — Weyl, Hermann

A Continuation of Sir Philip Sidney's Arcadia — Weamys, Anna

Continuing Bonds — Klass, Dennis

Continuing the Inquiry — Grose, Peter

Continuity and Discontinuity in Criminal Careers — Tracy, Paul E

Continuity and Disruption — Holden, Matthew

The Continuous Life — Strand, Mark

Continuum Percolation — Meester, Ronald

Contours of Continuity and Change — Nanda, Bikram Narayan

Contra Keynes and Cambridge — Hayek, Friedrich A Von

Contra Viento Y Marea — Vargas Llosa, Mario

Contraband — Foy, George

Contraception and Abortion in Nineteenth-Century America — Brodie, Janet Farrell

Contract and Economic Organisation — Campbell, David

Contract Ethics — Kahane, Howard

Contract Null and Void — Gores, Joe

r Contracting with Managed Care Organizations — Welfeld, Joseph A

Contractor and Client Relations to Assure Process Safety — Early, William F

The Contractor's Legal Kit — Ransone, Gary

r Contractual Correspondence for Architects and Project Managers. 3rd Ed. — Chappell, David

Contrails: A Boeing Salesman Reminisces — Bauer, Eugene E

Contrapunto: The Informal Sector Debate in Latin America — Rakowski, Cathy A

c Contrary Bear (Illus. by Laura Cornell) — Root, Phyllis

c Contrasts (Illus. by Clare Mackie) — Reidy, Hannah

The Contribution of People's Participation — Narayan-Parker, Deepa

Contributions to West Indian Herpetology — Powell, Robert

Contro Galileo — Bucciantini, Massimo

Contro Gli Etici — Sextus, Empiricus

Control and Dynamic Systems. Vol. 79

Control Balance — Tittle, Charles R

Control Engineering — Parr, E A

Control Flow Semantics — Bakker, J W De

Control, Information, and Technological Change — Flueckiger, Gerald E

Control of Bird Migration — Berthold, P

Control of Partial Differential Equations and Applications — Casas, Edwards

Control of Spacecraft and Aircraft — Bryson, Arthur E, Jr.

Control of Systems with Aftereffect — Kolmanovskii, Vladimir B

Control System Dynamics — Clark, Robert N

Controlling Environmental Policy — Rose-Ackerman, Susan

Controlling Human Heredity 1865 to Present — Paul, Diane B

Controlling Immigration — Cornelius, Wayne A

Controlling Laughter — Corbeill, Anthony

Controlling Your Class — McPhillimy, Bill

r Controlling Your Environment — Rudoff, Carol

Controversies in Ethics in Long-Term Care — Olson, Ellen

Controversies in Managed Mental Health Care — Lazarus, Arthur

Controversies in Media Ethics — Gordon, A David

Controversy, Conflict, and Compromise — Petersen, Keith C

The Controversy of Zion — Wheatcroft, Geoffrey

The Conundrum of Class — Burke, Martin J

The Convent of Pleasure — Cavendish, Margret

Le Conventum (Vers 1030) — Beech, George

Convergence — Green, Sharon

Convergence, Cohesion and Integration in the European Union — Leonardi, Robert

Convergence, Divergence and Changing Trade Patterns — Walde, Klaus

Converging Cultures — Fane, Diana

Converging Infrastructures — Branscomb, Lewis M

Converging Operations in the Study of Visual Selective Attention — Kramer, Arthur F

The Conversation Begins — Baker, Christina Looper

Conversation with Boulez — Boulez, Pierre

Conversational Arabic in 7 Days — Abu-Taleb, Samy

Conversations about Cancer — Auerbach, Michael

The Conversations at Curlow Creek — Malouf, David

Conversations in Bloomsbury — Anand, Mulk Raj

Conversations of Love — Wattison, Meredith

Conversations on the Uses of Science and Technology — Hackerman, Norman

Conversations with an Alzheimer's Patient — Hamilton, Heidi E

Conversations with and about Beckett — Gussow, Mel

Conversations with Boulez — Boulez, Pierre

Conversations with Derek Walcott — Walcott, Derek

Conversations with Dvora — Lieblich, Amia

Conversations with Fellini — Constantini, Costanzo

Conversations with God. Bk. 1 — Walsch, Neale Donald

Conversations with God. Bk. 2 — Walsch, Neale Donald

Conversations with God (Walsch). Bk. 1. Audio Version — Walsch, Neale Donald

Conversations with Kentucky Writers — Beattie, L Elisabeth

Conversations with Kostabi — Kostabi, Mark

Conversations with Madeleine Milhaud — Milhaud, Madeleine

Conversations with Maryse Conde — Conde, Maryse

Conversations with My Agent — Long, Rob

Conversations with Post Keynesians — King, J E

Conversations with the Sphinx — Klein, Etienne

Conversion and Utilization of Waste Materials — Khan, M Rashid

Conversion in the New Testament — Witherup, Ronald D

Conversion to Judaism and the Meaning of Jewish Identity — Sagi, Avi

Conversions and Visions in the Writings of African-American Women — Connor, Kimberly Rae

Conversos, Inquisition, and the Expulsion of the Jews from Spain — Roth, Norman

The Convict Lover — Simonds, Merilyn

Convict Maids — Oxley, Deborah

y Convicted in the Womb — Upchurch, Carl

Convocatoria Al Poder Del Numero — Tovar Pinzon, Hermes

Cook and Peary — Bryce, Robert M

Cook, Eat, Cha Cha Cha — Bellber, Philip

c Cookie Count and Bake (Illus. by Jane Kurisu) — Pearson, Debora

c Cookie Fun — Bastyra, Judy

c Cookies and Crutches (Moore). Audio Version — Delton, Judy

Cookin' with Honey — Scholder, Amy

Cooking and Canning with Mamma D'Amato — D'Amato, Antoinette

Cooking and Eating with Beer — LaFrance, Peter

Cooking Basics — Mallorca, Jacqueline

Cooking for Jack — Baratta, Tommy

Cooking for Life — Lehmann, Robert H

The Cooking of Parma — Sidoli, Richard Camillo

Cooking the Whole Foods Way — Pirello, Christina

Cooking under Cover — Griffith, Linda

Cooking under the Volcanoes — Lenten, Roelie

Cooking with Beer — Saunders, Lucy

c Cooking with Dad (Illus. by Paul Daviz) — Bastyra, Judy

c Cooking with Justin — Miller, Justin

c Cooking with Sara and Tommy — Stam, Dagmar

Cooking with Too Hot Tamales — Milliken, Mary Sue

y Cooking without Fat — Mateljan, George

Cooking without Recipes — Sindell, Cheryl

The Cook's Bible — Kimball, Christopher

r The Cook's Dictionary and Culinary Reference — Bartlett, Jonathan

c Cool Ali (Illus. by Nancy Poydar) — Poydar, Nancy

c Cool Cat — Mott, Evelyn Clarke

c The Cool Hot Rod and Other Electrifying Experiments on Energy and Matter — Doherty, Paul

Cool Memories II — Baudrillard, Jean

A Cool Million. The Dream Life of Balso Snell — West, Nathaniel

Cooperation among Democracies — Risse-Kappen, Thomas

Cooperation under Fire — Legro, Jeffrey W

Cooperative Information Systems — IFCIS International Conference Cooperative Information Systems (1st: 1996: Brussels, Belgium)

Cooperative Microeconomics — Moulin, Herve

The Cooperator's Dilemma — Lichbach, Mark Irving

r Cooper's Comprehensive Environmental Desk Reference — Cooper, Andre R

Coordination and Information — Lamoreaux, Naomi R

Cop Out — Dunlap, Susan

Copernico, Galilei E La Chiesa — Brandmuller, Walter

y Coping: A Young Woman's Guide to Breast Cancer Prevention — Eisenpreis, Bettijane

p Coping: Living with Cancer

Coping Plus — Robinson, Frank, Jr.

Coping with Austerity — Lustig, Nora

Coping with Capital Surges — Ffrench-Davis, Ricardo

Coping with Conflict after the Cold War — Kolodziej, Edward A

Coping with Financial Fragility and Systemic Risk — Benink, Harald A

Coping with Radiation Therapy — Cukier, Daniel

Copper Crucible — Rosenblum, Jonathon D

yr Cops, Crooks, and Criminologists — Axelrod, Alan

p Copy Editor

Copying and Duplicating. 2nd Ed. — Benson, Thomas A

Copying People — Francis, Daniel

Copyright in Further and Higher Education Libraries — Norman, Sandy

Copyright in Health Libraries — Norman, Sandy

Copyright in Industrial and Commercial Libraries — Norman, Sandy

Copyright in Public Libraries — Norman, Sandy

Copyright in School Libraries — Norman, Sandy

Copyright in Voluntary Sector Libraries — Norman, Sandy

Les Coquelicots Sont Revenus — Kagon, Michel

c Coral Reef — Cerullo, Mary M

c Coral Reef — Sayre, April Pulley

r Coral Reef Animals of the Indo-Pacific — Gosliner, Terrence

The Coral Sea — Smith, Patti

Coral Snakes of the Americas — Roze, Janis A

Corazon Aquino and the Brushfire Revolution — Reid, Robert H

y Corazon De Roble — Teixidor, Emili

La Corazza E La Spada — Giordano, Emilio

Le Corbeau — Poe, Edgar Allan

Corbie in the Carolingian Renaissance — Ganz, David

c Corduroy — Freeman, Don

c Corduroy's Birthday (Illus. by Lisa McCue) — Hennessy, B G

Core Java — Cornell, Gary

CorelDraw 7 for Windows 95/NT — Davis, Phyllis

c Corey in the Saddle — Bryant, Bonnie

c Corey's Kite (Illus. by Pierre Pratt) — Roche, Hannah

The Corinthian Body — Martin, Dale B

Coriolanus — Shakespeare, William

The Corn Laws. Vols. 1-2 — Kadish, Alon

The Corn Laws. Vols. 1-6 — Kadish, Alon

The Corn Laws. Vols. 3-6 — Kadish, Alon

y The Corn Woman. Audio Version — Vigil, Angel

c Cornelius and the Dog Star (Illus. by Ray Williams) — Spyropulos, Diana

Corner Boy — Simmons, Herbert

A Corner of England — Ravilious, James

Cornerstones of Peace — Brettschneider, Marla

The Cornish Trilogy — Davies, Robertson

Coronary Restenosis — Feuerstein, Giora Z

The Coroplastic Art of Ancient Cyprus. Vol. 4 — Karageorghis, Vassos

Corot — Tinterow, Gary

c Corot from A to Z — Larroche, Caroline

Corot in Italy — Galassi, Peter

Corot: Le Genie Du Trait, Estampes Et Dessins — Bouret, Claude

r Corporate 500. 13th Ed.

Corporate Abuse — Wright, Lesley

yr Corporate Affiliations PLUS, Spring/Summer 1995. Electronic Media Version

Corporate Bankruptcy — Bhandari, Jagdeep S

Corporate Comeback — Miles, Robert H

Corporate Crime — Pearce, Frank

r Corporate Crime Investigation — Bologna, Jack

Corporate Culture/Team Culture — Sherriton, Jacalyn

Corporate Decision-Making in Canada — Daniels, Ronald J

r The Corporate Directory of U.S. Public Companies. Electronic Media Version

r The Corporate Directory of U.S. Public Companies 1995

r The Corporate Directory of U.S. Public Companies 1996

Corporate Executions — Downs, Alan

Corporate Governance in Transitional Economies — Aoki, Masahiko

Corporate Governance of Public Enterprises in Transitional Economies — Pannier, Dominique

Corporate Intranet — Bernard, Ryan

Corporate Philanthropy — *Burlingame, Dwight F*

Corporate Power and the American Dream — *Labor Institute*

Corporate Responsibility in the Hebrew Bible — *Kaminsky, Joel S*

The Corporation as Anomaly — *Schrader, David E*

Corporation on a Tightrope — *Sifonis, John G*

Corporations Are Gonna Get Your Mama — *Danaher, Kevin*

Corporatism and Comparative Politics — *Wiarda, Howard J*

The Corps and the Shore — *Pilkey, Orrin H*

Corps Values — *Miller, Zell*

The Corpse: A History — *Quigley, Christine*

The Corpus in the Library — *MacLochlainn, Alf*

Corpus Inscriptionum Insularum Celticarum. Vol. 1 — *Macalister, Robert Alexander Stewart*

Corpus Linguistics — *McEnery, Tony*

The Corpus of Clandestine Literature in France 1769-1789 — *Darnton, Robert*

Corpus Processing for Lexical Acquisition — *Boguraev, Branimir*

Correggio Tradotto — *Mussini, Massimo*

Correlations in Rosenzweig and Levinas — *Gibbs, Robert*

Correspondance. Vol. 1 — *Bloch, Marc*

Correspondance. Vol. 9 — *Zola, Emile*

Correspondance. Vol. 10 — *Zola, Emile*

Correspondance De Giovanni Battista De Rossi Et De Louis Duchesne 1873-1894 — *Battista, Giovanni*

Correspondance De Martin Bucer. Vol. 3 — *Bucer, Martin*

Correspondance De Theodore De Beze. Vols. 17-18 — *Beze, Theodore De*

La Correspondance D'Eugene Fromentin. Vols. 1-2 — *Fromentin, Eugene*

Correspondence and Disquotation — *David, Marian*

Correspondence between Goethe and Schiller 1794-1805 — *Goethe, Johann Wolfgang Von*

Correspondence Generale 1774-1792 — *Constant, Benjamin*

The Correspondence of Adam Ferguson. Vols. 1-2 — *Ferguson, Adam*

The Correspondence of Alfred Marshall, Economist. Vol. 1 — *Marshall, Alfred*

The Correspondence of Alfred Marshall, Economist. Vols. 2-3 — *Marshall, Alfred*

The Correspondence of Charles Darwin. Vol. 9 — *Darwin, Charles*

The Correspondence of Edward Gordon Craig and Count Harry Kessler 1903-1937 — *Craig, Edward Gordon*

The Correspondence of Erasmus. Vol. 11 — *Erasmus, Desiderius*

The Correspondence of Henry Melchior Muhlenberg. Vol. 1 — *Muhlenberg, Henry Melchior*

The Correspondence of John Stuart Mill and Auguste Comte — *Mill, John Stuart*

The Correspondence of Northrop Frye and Helen Kemp 1932-1939. Vols. 1-2 — *Frye, Northrop*

The Correspondence of Shelby Foote and Walker Percy — *Foote, Shelby*

The Correspondence of Sigmund Freud and Sandor Ferenczi. Vol. 2 — *Freud, Sigmund*

The Correspondence of Thomas Hobbes. Vols. 1-2 — *Hobbes, Thomas*

The Correspondence of Thomas Warton — *Warton, Thomas*

The Correspondence of William James. Vol. 4 — *James, William*

Correspondence: Paul Celan and Nelly Sachs — *Celan, Paul*

Correspondent Colorings — *Post-Lauria, Sheila*

r Corrosion and Electrochemistry of Zinc — *Zhang, Xiaoge Gregory*

r Corrosion Engineering Handbook — *Schweitzer, Philip A*

Corrosion Mechanisms in Theory and Practice — *Marcus, P*

Corrosion of Reinforcement in Concrete Construction — *International Symposium on Corrosion of Reinforcement in Concrete Construction (4th: 1996: Cambridge, UK)*

Corrosion of Stainless Steels. 2nd Ed. — *Sedriks, A John*

Corrugated Shipping Containers. Rev. Ed. — *Maltenfort, George G*

y Corrupting Dr. Nice — *Kessel, John*

Corruption and State Politics in Sierra Leone — *Reno, William*

Corruzione — *Van Straten, Giorgio*

Il Corsaro E La Rosa — *Casati Modignani, Sveva*

Corsia Deglincurabili — *Valduga, Patrizia*

La Corte Del Granduca — *Fantoni, Marcello*

Las Cortes De Navarra Desde Su Incorporacion A La Corona De Castilla. Vols. 1-2 — *Garcia Bourrellier, Rocio*

p Cortext

r The Corvinus Press — *Nash, Paul W*

Corydon — *Gide, Andre*

Cosa IV — *Bruno, Vincent J*

Cosa Loro — *Andreotti, Giulio*

Cosby: The Life of a Comedy Legend — *Smith, Ronald L*

La Coscienza Di Zeng — *Svevo, Italo*

Cosi Fan Tutti — *Dibdin, Michael*

Cosi: The Screenplay — *Nowra, Louis*

Cosmic Engineers — *Westfahl, Gary*

c Cosmic Science — *Wiese, Jim*

Cosmic Thunder — *Watkins, William John*

Cosmology and Controversy — *Kragh, Helge*

Cosmology in Antiquity — *Wright, M R*

Cosmos, Bios, Theos — *Margenau, Henry*

Cosmos Crumbling — *Abzug, Robert H*

Cosmos in the Chaos — *Graham, Stephen R*

Cost-Benefit Analysis — *Nas, Tevfik F*

Cost-Benefit Analysis and Project Appraisal in Developing Countries — *Kirkpatrick, Colin*

Cost Management of Capital Projects — *Heinze, Kurt*

The Cost Management Redbook for Employee Relocation Home Sale Real Estate Transactions — *Sohn, Ned*

The Cost of Being Female — *Headlee, Sue*

The Cost of Birth Defects — *Waitzman, Norman J*

The Cost of Catholic Parishes and Schools — *Harris, Joseph Claude*

The Cost of Winning — *Cosgrove, Michael H*

c Costa Rica — *Foley, Erin*

r Costa Rica: A Natural Destination — *Scheck, Ree S*

r Costa Rica Handbook. 2nd Ed. — *Baker, Christopher P*

The Costly Consequences of Divorce — *Larson, David*

Il Costruttore — *Sgorlon, Carlo*

Costs and Effectiveness of Prostate Cancer Screening in Elderly Men

Costs, Benefits, and Farmer Adoption of Agro-Forestry — *Current, Dean*

Costumes for Your Cat — *Chang, Lynn*

c Cosy Christmas with Teddy Bear — *McQuade, Jacqueline*

c Cosy Moments with Teddy Bear — *McQuade, Jacqueline*

r Cote D'Ivoire — *Daniels, Morna*

c Cote D'Ivoire (Ivory Coast) — *Kummer, Patricia K*

A Cottage in Portugal — *Hewitt, Richard*

Cotton Is the Mother of Poverty — *Isaacman, Allen*

Cotton Production Prospects for the Next Decade — *Gillham, Fred E M*

r The Cougar Almanac — *Busch, Robert H*

c Cougar Cove (Illus. by David Powell) — *Lawson, Julie*

Coulomb Interactions in Nuclear and Atomic Few-Body Collisions — *Levin, Frank S*

Council and Context in Leonardo Boff's Ecclesiology — *Nordstokke, Kjell*

The Council of Ministers — *Hayes-Renshaw, Fiona*

r The Council of the European Union — *Westlake, Martin*

Counseling Clients with HIV Disease — *Hoffman, Mary Ann*

Counseling to End Violence against Women — *Whalen, Mollie*

Counselling for Managers — *MacLennan, Nigel*

Counselling in HIV Infection and AIDS. 2nd Ed. — *Green, John*

c Count! (Illus. by Denise Fleming) — *Fleming, Denise*

Count Me Out — *James, Russell*

Count Not the Dead — *Hadley, Michael L*

c Count Silvernose (Illus. by Omar Rayyan) — *Kimmel, Eric A*

c Count with Maisy (Illus. by Lucy Cousins) — *Cousins, Lucy*

Count Your Enemies — *Nathan, Paul*

c Count Your Way through Brazil (Illus. by Liz Brenner Dodson) — *Haskins, James*

c Count Your Way through France (Illus. by Andrea Shine) — *Haskins, James*

c Count Your Way through Greece (Illus. by Janice Lee Porter) — *Haskins, James*

c Count Your Way through Ireland (Illus. by Beth Wright) — *Haskins, James*

c Countdown (Illus. by David Higham) — *Fine, Anne*

y Countdown — *Mikaelsen, Ben*

Countdown: A History of Space Flight — *Heppenheimer, T A*

c Countdown to Christmas — *Argyle, Charlotte*

Counter Culture vs. Burger Culture — *Vidal, John*

The Counter Reformation — *Jones, Martin D W*

The Counter-Reformation in the Villages — *Forster, Marc R*

Counter-Revolution: The Second Civil War and Its Origins 1646-8 — *Ashton, Robert*

The Counterfeit Widow — *Mack, Dorothy*

The Counterlife — *Roth, Philip*

p Countermeasures

Counterparts — *Royle, Nicholas, 1963-*

Counterpoint: A Murder in Massachusetts Bay — *Press, Margaret*

p Counterpoise

Countertransference Enactments — *Shur, Richard*

Countertransference in Psychoanalytic Psychotherapy with Children and Adolescents — *Tsiantis, John*

Counties in Court — *Welsh, Wayne N*

c Counting (Illus. by Clare Mackie) — *Reidy, Hannah*

The Counting House — *Dabydeen, David*

c Counting Is for the Birds (Illus. by Frank Mazzola) — *Mazzola, Frank*

c Counting on Angels (Illus. by Sandra Salzillo Shields) — *Ward, Brenda*

Counting on the Latino Vote — *DeSipio, Louis*

c Counting Rhymes (Illus. by Carol Thompson) — *Foster, John*

cr Counting Wildflowers — *McMillan, Bruce*

Countries in Crisis: Hunger 1996

r Countries of the World and Their Leaders Yearbook 1996. Vols. 1-2

The Country Ahead of Us, the Country Behind — *Guterson, David*

The Country Ahead of Us, the Country Behind (Scott). Audio Version — *Guterson, David*

Country before Party — *Searle, G R*

Country, Class or Craft? — *Cronin, Maura*

p Country Connections: The Magazine of Alternatives

A Country Doctor's Notebook — *Bulgakov, Mikhail Afanas'evich*

Country Fabric Style — *Bird, Julia*

Country Foxes — *Kolb, Hugh*

Country House Life — *Gerard, Jessica*

The Country House Poem — *Fowler, Alastair*

The Country Houses of Northamptonshire — *Heward, John*

The Country I Remember — *Mason, David*

Country Life 1897-1997 — *Strong, Roy*

r Country Music — *Millard, Bob*

Country Music — *Wright, Charles*

Country Music Culture — *Ellison, Curtis W*

r The Country Music Lover's Guide to the U.S.A. — *Byron, Janet*

Country Music, USA — *Malone, Bill C*

r Country Music What's What — *Millard, Bob*

Country People in the New South — *Keith, Jeanette*

Country Rag Crafts — *Reeves, Sue*

The Country Reader — *Kingsbury, Paul*

r Country Studies — *Library of Congress. Federal Research Division*

Country Studies in International Accounting: Americas and the Far East — *Meek, Gary K*

Country Studies in International Accounting: Europe — *Walton, Peter J*

c Country Tales (Illus. by Amanda Harvey) — *Clark, Elizabeth*

r Country: The Music and the Musicians from the Beginnings to the '90s. Rev. Ed. — *Country Music Foundation*

Country: The Twisted Roots of Rock 'n' Roll — *Tosches, Nick*

r Country Walking

y A Country with No Name — *De Grazia, Sebastian*

The Country without a Post Office — *Agha, Shahid Ali*

r County and City Extra 1995

r County and City Extra 1996

r County Cork, Ireland — *Masterson, Josephine*

The Coup: Tactics in the Seizure of Power — *Farcau, Bruce W*

The Couple and Family in Managed Care — *Bagarozzi, Dennis A*

The Couple Who Became Each Other and Other Tales of a Master Hypnotherapist — *Calof, David L*

Couples: A Photographic Documentary of Gay and Lesbian Relationships — *Gettings, John*

Couples and Change — *Brothers, Barbara Jo, 1940-*

Couples: Building Bridges — *Brothers, Barbara Jo*

Couples, Passersby — *Strauss, Botho*

The Coupling Convention — *DuCille, Ann*
Couplings — *Schneider, Peter*
Courage — *Carter, Robert*
c Courage (Illus. by Mechelle Ann) — *Moncure, Jane Belk*
Courage and Air Warfare — *Wells, Mark K*
c Courage: Annie's Race (Illus. by Davis Henry) — *Canning, Shelagh*
c Courage in the Storm (Illus. by Are Gjesdal) — *Raddall, Thomas H*
Courage to Love — *Leckie, Will*
The Courage to Stand Alone — *Wei, Ching-Sheng*
Courage under Fire — *Duncan, Patrick Sheane*
The Courageous Followers — *Chaleff, Ira*
The Courier Air Travel Handbook. 6th Ed. — *Field, Mark I*
c La Couronne Du Roi Ludovic (Illus. by Isabelle Beaudin) — *Barrette, Johanne*
A Course in Digital Signal Processing — *Porat, Boaz*
A Course in Fuzzy Systems and Control — *Wang, Li-Xin*
y A Course in Group Theory — *Humphreys, J F*
A Course in Number Theory. 2nd Ed. — *Rose, H E*
A Course in Stochastic Processes — *Bosq, Denis*
The Course of Human History — *Goudsblom, Johan*
Course to Victory — *Coutts, Russell*
A Coursebook on Language Disorders in Children — *Hegde, M N*
The Courseware Guide to English Examinations at Key Stage 4 — *Sweetman, Jim*
The Court-Martial of Mother Jones — *Steel, Edward M, Jr.*
Court Masques — *Lindley, David, 1948-*
Court Patronage and Corruption in Early Stuart England — *Peck, Linda Levy*
Court Revels 1485-1559 — *Streitberger, W R*
Courting Saskatchewan — *Carpenter, David*
Courtly Dance of the Renaissance — *Caroso, Fabritio*
c Courtney — *Burningham, John*
y Courtney Love: Queen of Noise — *Rossi, Melissa*
The Courts, Crime and the Criminal Law in Ireland 1692-1760 — *Garnham, Neal*
Courts, Law, and Politics in Comparative Perspective — *Jacob, Herbert*
The Courts of Love — *Gilchrist, Ellen*
Courtship, Illegitimacy, and Marriage in Early Modern England — *Adair, Richard*
Courtyards, Markets, City Streets — *Sheldon, Kathleen*
c Cousin Ruth's Tooth (Illus. by Marjorie Priceman) — *MacDonald, Amy*
c Cousins in the Castle — *Wallace, Barbara Brooks*
Covalent Ceramics III — *Hepp, Aloysius F*
The Cove Shivering Club — *Curtin, Michael*
Covenant and Polity in Biblical Israel — *Elazar, Daniel Judah*
Covenant of Blood — *Hoffman, Lawrence A*
r Covenants Not to Compete. 2nd Ed. — *Malsberger, Brian M*
The Covenants with Earth and Rain — *Monaghan, John*
r Coventry Cathedral — *Campbell, Louise*
Cover Letters for Dummies — *Kennedy, Joyce Lain*
Cover Story — *Heller, Steven*
c Cover-Up: A Curious History of Clothes Uncovered (Illus. by Mark Draisey) — *Tames, Richard*
Covered Bridges of Vermont — *Barna, Ed*
Covered Wagon Women. Vol. 2 — *Holmes, Kenneth L*
Covered Wagon Women. Vol. 3 — *Holmes, Kenneth L*
Covering the 60's — *Lois, George*
Covering the Bases — *Cosgrove, Benedict*
Covering the Body — *Zelizer, Barbie*
Covering the Campus — *Baldwin, Patricia*
Covert Warrior — *Smith, Warner*
y Coverup — *Bennett, Jay*
Covetous of Truth — *Southgate, Beverley C*
Cow Country Cookbook — *Cushman, Dan*
Cowards — *Burgess, W A*
c Cowboy (Illus. by Richard Erickson) — *Klausmeier, Robert*
y Cowboy: An Album — *Granfield, Linda*
c Cowboy Charlie — *Winter, Jeanette*
c Cowboy Country (Illus. by Ted Lewin) — *Scott, Ann Herbert*
Cowboy Cuisine — *Montana, Monte, Jr.*
r The Cowboy Encyclopedia — *Slatta, Richard W*
c Cowboy Jess (Illus. by Lizzie Sanders) — *McCaughrean, Geraldine*
The Cowboy Rides Away — *Thornton, Betsy*
Cowboys and Kansas — *Hoy, Jim*
r Cowboys and the Wild West — *Cusic, Don*

c The Cowboy's Handbook — *Cody, Tod*
y Cowboys Have Always Been My Heroes — *Golenbock, Peter*
y Cowboys of the Sky — *Levi, Steven C*
c Cowboys: Roundup on an American Ranch (Illus. by George Ancona) — *Anderson, Joan*
y Cowgirls — *Savage, Candace*
c Cows Moo, Cars Toot (Illus. by Anthony Lewis) — *Crebbin, June*
Cowslips and Chainies — *Crowley, Elaine*
c Coyote and the Fire Stick (Illus. by Will Hillenbrand) — *Goldin, Barbara Diamond*
c Coyote and the Grasshoppers (Illus. by Charles Reasoner) — *Dominic, Gloria*
c Coyote in Love (Illus. by Mindy Dwyer) — *Dwyer, Mindy*
Coyote Medicine — *Mehl-Madrona, Lewis*
c Coyote Places the Stars — *Taylor, Harriet Peck*
Coyote Returns — *Hackler, Micah S*
Coyote v. Acme — *Frazier, Ian*
c Coyote Walks on Two Legs (Illus. by Floyd Cooper) — *Hausman, Gerald*
Coyotes I Have Known — *Duncklee, John*
p CPB Teacher's Digest
The Crab Nebula — *Chevillard, Eric*
p Crab Orchard Review
c Crack Another Yolk — *Foster, John*
Crack Cocaine, Crime, and Women — *Mahan, Sue*
Crack Hotel — *Hemmingson, Michael*
y The Crack in Everything — *Ostriker, Alicia*
A Crack in Forever — *Brewer, Jeannie*
Cracker: The Mad Woman in the Attic — *Mortimore, Jim*
Crackpot — *Wiseman, Adele*
Cracks in the Iron Closet — *Tuller, David*
Cradle of Splendor — *Anthony, Patricia*
The Craft and Art of Clay — *Peterson, Susan Harnly*
The Craft of Art — *Ladis, Andrew*
The Craft of Poetic Speech in Ancient Greece — *Calame, Claude*
A Crafter's Book of Santas — *Dierks, Leslie*
The Crafter's Guide to Pricing Your Work — *Ramsey, Dan*
Crafting a Life in Essay, Story, Poem — *Murray, Donald Morison*
The Crafting of Chaos — *Kuester, Hildegard*
Crafting Science — *Fujimura, Joan H*
Crafting the Third World — *Love, Joseph L*
c Crafts for Easter (Illus. by Sharon Lane Holm) — *Ross, Kathy*
c Crafts for Hanukkah (Illus. by Sharon Lane Holm) — *Ross, Kathy*
c Crafts for Kids Who Are Wild about Dinosaurs (Illus. by Sharon Lane Holm) — *Ross, Kathy*
c Crafts for Kids Who Are Wild about Outer Space (Illus. by Sharon Lane Holm) — *Ross, Kathy*
r Crafts Marketplace — *Manolis, Argie*
c Crafty Little Fingers (Illus. by Bettina Paterson) — *Mason, Lesley*
Cranial Guitar — *Kaufman, Bob*
c The Cranky Sun (Illus. by Lorenzo Mattotti) — *Kramsky, Jerry*
Crash — *Ballard, J G*
Crash — *Cronenberg, David*
y Crash — *Spinelli, Jerry*
Crash Course — *Trocheck, Kathy Hogan*
y Crash Landing — *Davidson, Nicole*
c The Crash of '29 and The New Deal — *Glassman, Bruce*
Crashing the Old Boys' Network — *Salter, David F*
Crash's Law — *Volkman, Karen*
The Craving Brain — *Ruden, Ronald A*
The Crawfish Book — *Pitre, Glen*
c Crawlies Creep — *Pelham, David*
cp Crayola Kids
c The Crayon Counting Book (Illus. by Frank Mazzola Jr.) — *Ryan, Pam Munoz*
c Crayons, Crafts, and Concepts — *Faggella, Kathy*
c Crazy Creature Capers (Illus. by Clare Mackie) — *Reidy, Hannah*
c Crazy Creature Contrasts (Illus. by Clare Mackie) — *Reidy, Hannah*
Crazy for Trying — *Rodgers, Joni*
Crazy Horse in Stillness — *Heyen, William*
c Crazy Horse: Sioux Warrior — *Sanford, William R*
y Crazy Horse: War Chief of the Oglala Sioux — *Goldman, Martin S*
c Crazy Lady! — *Conly, Jane Leslie*
Crazy Rhythm — *Garment, Leonard*
c The Crazy Shoe Shuffle (Illus. by Nick Sharratt) — *Cross, Gillian*

Crazy Therapies — *Singer, Margaret Thaler*
Crazy with Cotton — *Leone, Diana*
Crazysexycool — *Us (New York, N.Y.: 1985)*
r CRC Handbook of Laboratory Safety. 4th Ed. — *Furr, Keith A*
CRC Handbook of Tables for the Use of Order Statistics in Estimation — *Harter, H Leon*
yr CRC Standard Mathematical Tables and Formulae. 30th Ed.
CRC Standard Mathematical Tables and Formulae. 31st Ed.
c Crea Con Huevos — *Seix, Victoria*
The Cream of the Crop — *English, Allan D*
Create Your Own Stage Costumes — *Govier, Jacquie*
Creating a Family Garden — *Guinness, Bunny*
Creating a Garden — *Keen, Mary*
Creating a Home — *Merkel, Jeanean D*
Creating a New Civilization — *Toffler, Alvin*
Creating a Peaceable Kingdom — *Miller, Cynthia D*
Creating a Software Engineering Culture — *Wiegers, Karl E*
Creating an Information Service. 3rd Ed. — *Webb, Sylvia P*
Creating an Open Book Organization — *McCoy, Thomas J*
Creating Another Self — *Maio, Samuel*
Creating Boundaries — *Manzo, Kathryn A*
Creating Classrooms for Authors. 2nd Ed. — *Short, Kathy Gnagey*
Creating Connection — *Johnson, Susan M*
Creating French Culture — *Tesniere, Marie-Helene*
Creating from the Spirit — *Wakefield, Dan*
Creating GI Jane — *Meyer, Leisa D*
Creating Health. Audio Version — *Chopra, Deepak*
Creating Internet Entertainment — *Novak, Jeannie*
Creating Literature out of Life — *Alexander, Doris*
Creating Picturesque America — *Rainey, Sue*
Creating Public Value — *Moore, Mark H*
Creating Special Effects for TV and Video. 3rd Ed. — *Wilkie, Bernard*
Creating States — *Esterhammer, Angela*
Creating the Big Game — *Umphlett, Wiley Lee*
Creating the Child — *Evans, Donald*
Creating the Commonwealth — *Innes, Stephen*
Creating the Countryside — *DuPuis, E Melanie*
Creating the Couple — *Wexman, Virginia Wright*
Creating the Future — *Reed, Sally Gardner*
Creating the Modern South — *Flamming, Douglas*
Creating the National Pastime — *White, G Edward*
Creating the Virtual Store — *Yesil, Magdalena*
Creating Web Pages for Dummies — *Smith, Bud*
y Creating Your Own Support System — *Kreiner, Anna*
Creation and Christ — *Hildegard, Saint*
Creation and Evolution in the Early American Scientific Affiliation — *Kalthoff, Mark A*
Creation-Evolution Debates — *Numbers, Ronald L*
The Creation of Dr. B — *Pollak, Richard*
The Creation of History in Ancient Israel — *Brettler, Marc Zvi*
Creation of the Sacred — *Burkert, Walter*
Creationism in Twentieth Century America. Vols. 1-10
The Creationist Writing of Byron C. Nelson — *Nelson, Byron C*
Creation's Heartbeat — *Leonard, Linda Schierse*
Creation's Journey — *Hill, Tom*
y Creations of Fire — *Cobb, Cathy*
Creations of the Rainbow Serpent — *Helms, Mary*
Creative Applications — *Gelinas, Ayn*
Creative Bead Weaving — *Wells, Carol Wilcox*
Creative Breakthroughs in Politics — *Riemer, Neal*
The Creative Contours of Ruskin Bond — *Singh, Prabhat K*
Creative Couples in the Sciences — *Pycior, Helena M*
c Creative Crafts — *Butterfield, Moira*
Creative Crusader — *Juhnke, James C*
Creative Disobedience — *Solle, Dorothee*
Creative Experiences for Young Children. 2nd Ed. — *Chenfeld, Mimi Brodsky*
Creative Fidelity — *Sullivan, Francis A*
Creative Grace — *Dintaman, Stephen F*
Creative Individualism — *Lindsay, Peter*
cp Creative Kids
Creative Living Room Decorating
The Creative Monochrome Image — *Chamberlain, David*
The Creative Mystique — *Kavaler-Adler, Susan*
Creative Newspaper Design. 2nd Ed. — *Giles, Vic*
y Creative Nonfiction — *Gutkind, Lee*
Creative Puzzles of the World — *Delft, Pieter Van*
Creative Ritual: Combining Yoruba, Santeria, and Western Magic Traditions — *Healki, Thomas*

Creative Storytelling — *Zipes, Jack*
Creative Strategies for School Problems — *Durrant, Michael*
The Creative Use of Music in Group Therapy. 2nd Ed. — *Plach, Tom*
Creative Vegetable Gardening — *Larkcom, Joy*
Creative Window Treatments
Creative Women in Medieval and Early Modern Italy — *Matter, E Ann*
c Creativity (Illus. by E B Lewis) — *Steptoe, John*
Creativity: Flow and the Psychology of Discovery and Invention — *Csikszentmihalyi, Mihaly*
Creativity in Business — *Ray, Michael*
Creativity in Primary Science — *Frost, Jenny*
c Creature Features (Illus. by Steve Fricker) — *Ganeri, Anita*
r Creature Features — *Stanley, John*
c Creatures of the Past — *Fitzsimmons, Cecilia*
Crebillon Fils, Ou La Science Du Desir — *Sturm, Ernest*
y A Credible Threat — *Dawson, Janet*
Credit--Get It! — *Bock, Carl E*
Credit, Markets, and the Agrarian Economy of Colonial India — *Bose, Sugata*
Crediting Poetry — *Heaney, Seamus*
Credo — *Bragg, Melvyn*
Credo and Other Poems — *Sullivan, Francis Patrick*
c The Creek — *Newman, Shirlee P*
Creek Walk and Other Stories — *Giles, Molly*
c Creep and Chase — *Dowley, Ruth*
y Creep St. — *Marsden, John*
c Creep Show (Illus. by Jeff Spackman) — *Dussling, Jennifer*
c Creepe Hall — *Durant, Alan*
y Creepers — *Gray, Keith*
c A Creepy Company (Karpf). Audio Version — *Aiken, Joan*
c The Creepy Computer Mystery (Illus. by Denise Brunkus) — *Levy, Elizabeth*
c Creepy Cookies (Illus. by Jean Pidgeon) — *Curtis, Tracy*
c Creepy Cookies (Illus. by Dianne O'Quinn Burke) — *Vilicich-Solomon, Tina*
c Creepy Crawlies (Illus. by David Ansrey) — *Steer, Dugald*
c Creepy Crawlies in 3-D! (Illus. by David G Burder) — *Sammon, Rick*
c Creepy, Crawly Baby Bugs — *Markle, Sandra*
c Creepy, Crawly, Caterpillars (Illus. by Paul Facklam) — *Facklam, Margery*
c Creepy, Spooky Science (Illus. by Cecile Schoberle) — *Markle, Sandra*
Creole Folktales — *Chamoiseau, Patrick*
The Creole Mephistopheles — *Lieberman, Laurence*
Creoles of Color in the Bayou Country — *Brasseaux, Carl A*
Le Crepuscule Des Marges — *Ruby, Pascal*
Crescendo! A Thematic Approach to Intermediate Italian Language and Culture — *Italiano, Francesca*
The Crescent Obscured — *Allison, Robert J*
Cretaceous-Tertiary Mass Extinctions — *MacLeod, Norman*
Crews: Gang Members Talk to Maria Hinojosa — *Hinojosa, Maria*
cp Cricket
Cricket and the Victorians — *Sandiford, Keith A P*
c Cricket Never Does — *Livingston, Myra Cohn*
c Cricketology (Illus. by Brian Grogan) — *Ross, Michael Elsohn*
c The Cricket's Cage (Illus. by Stefan Czernecki) — *Czernecki, Stefan*
r Crime: An Encyclopedia — *Cyriax, Oliver*
Crime and Disrepute — *Hagan, John*
Crime and Economy
Crime and Justice in Nevada 1994
Crime and Mystery — *Keating, H R F*
Crime and Policing in Rural and Small-Town America — *Weisheit, Ralph A*
Crime and Public Policy — *Barlow, Hugh D*
Crime and Ravishment — *Summers, Judith*
Crime and the Criminal Justice System in Arizona
r Crime Fiction II. Vols. 1-2 — *Hubin, Allen J*
Crime Histories and Histories of Crime — *Emsley, Clive*
r Crime in America — *Durham, Jennifer L*
A Crime in the Neighborhood — *Berne, Suzanne*
Crime in the Public Mind — *Gaubatz, Kathryn Taylor*
Crime, Society and Law in Renaissance Italy — *Dean, Trevor*
Crime Talk — *Sasson, Theodore*
Crimes, Constables, and Courts — *Weaver, John C*

The Crimes of Love — *Sade, Marquis De*
r Crimes of Perception — *George, Leonard*
r Crimes of the Scene — *King, Nina*
Criminal Careers. Vols. 1-2 — *Greenberg, David F*
Criminal Churchmen in the Age of Edward III — *Aberth, John*
Criminal Justice — *Parker, Barbara*
Criminal Justice. 2nd Ed. — *Schmalleger, Frank*
Criminal Justice and Sentencing Policy — *Henham, Ralph J*
Criminal Justice Statistics — *Lurigio, Arthur J*
Criminal Justice Today. 4th Ed. — *Schmalleger, Frank*
The Criminal Law System of Medieval and Renaissance Florence — *Stern, Laura Ikins*
c Criminal Records (Illus. by Peter Viccars) — *Harvey, Anne*
Criminal Victimisation in the Developing World — *Zvekic, Ugljesa*
y Criminals — *Livesey, Margot*
Criminology: A Sociological Understanding — *Barkan, Steven E*
The Crimson Palace — *Briskin, Jacqueline*
c Crinkleroot's Guide to Knowing Butterflies and Moths — *Arnosky, Jim*
Cris Sur Le Bayou — *Ancelet, Barry Jean*
La Crise De L'Asile Politique En France — *Legoux, Luc*
Crises in U.S. Foreign Policy — *Hunt, Michael H*
Crisis — *Power, Jack*
Crisis and Commitment — *Accinelli, Robert*
Crisis and Continuity — *Ruiz, Teofilo F*
Crisis and Conversion in Apuleius' Metamorphoses — *Shumate, Nancy*
Crisis Bargaining and the State — *Peterson, Susan, 1961-*
Crisis Communications — *Fearn-Banks, Kathleen*
Crisis Diplomacy — *Richardson, J L*
Crisis in Christology — *Farmer, William R*
Crisis in the Academy — *Lucas, Christopher J*
Crisis in the Pacific — *Astor, Gerald*
Crisis in the Persian Gulf — *United States. Congress. House. Committee on Armed Services*
The Crisis of Causality — *Ruler, J A Van*
The Crisis of Conservatism — *Green, E H H*
The Crisis of Courtesy — *Carre, Jacques*
The Crisis of Meaning — *Schwartzberg, Steven S*
The Crisis of the Italian State — *McCarthy, Patrick*
The Crisis of the Societies of the East and the Return to a Common Europe — *Spadolini, Giovanni*
The Crisis of Vision in Modern Economic Thought — *Heilbroner, Robert*
Crisis Prevention, Confidence Building, and Reconciliation in South Asia — *Krepon, Michael L*
A Critic Writes — *Banham, Reyner*
The Critical 14 Years of Your Professional Life — *Dilenschneider, Robert L*
A Critical and Exegetical Commentary on the Acts of the Apostles 1 — *Barrett, C K*
Critical Care — *Dooling, Richard*
Critical Conditions — *Fairlamb, Horace L*
The Critical Double — *Gordon, Paul*
The Critical Editing of Music — *Grier, James*
A Critical Edition of George Buchanan's Baptistes and of Its Anonymous Seventeenth-Century Translation, Tyranicall-Government Anatomized — *Buchanan, George, 1506-1582*
A Critical Essay on Modern Macroeconomic Theory — *Hahn, Frank*
Critical Essays on Israeli Society, Religion, and Government. Vol. 4 — *Avruch, Kevin*
Critical Essays on John Donne — *Marotti, Arthur F*
Critical Ethnography in Educational Research — *Carspecken, Phil Francis*
Critical Events — *Das, Veena*
Critical Focus — *Coleman, A D*
The Critical Fortunes of a Romantic Novel — *Mahoney, Dennis F*
Critical Geopolitics — *O Tuathail, Gearoid*
r A Critical Guide to Management Training Videos and Selected Multimedia 1996 — *Ellet, William*
The Critical I — *Holland, Norman Norwood*
Critical Issues in Asian Development — *Quibria, M G*
Critical Issues in the Treatment of Schizophrenia — *Brunello, N*
y Critical Judgment (Gallagher). Audio Version — *Palmer, Michael, 1942-*
r Critical Legal Studies — *Bauman, Richard W*
Critical Legal Theory and the Challenge of Feminism — *Kramer, Matthew*
Critical Mass — *Ruggiero, Greg*

The Critical Mass in Collective Action — *Marwell, Gerald*
Critical Moments in Religious History — *Keulman, Kenneth*
Critical Operative Maneuvers in Urologic Surgery — *Yu, George W*
The Critical Path — *Yates, Brock*
Critical Perspectives on J.M. Coetzee — *Huggan, Graham*
The Critical Poem — *Running, Thorpe*
Critical Race Theory — *Crenshaw, Kimberle*
Critical Readings on Piaget — *Smith, Leslie*
Critical Realism — *Barnouw, Dagmar*
Critical Reflections on the Paranormal — *Stoeber, Michael*
Critical Regionalism and Cultural Studies — *Herr, Cheryl Temple*
r The Critical Response to Anais Nin — *Jason, Philip K*
The Critical Response to Bram Stoker — *Senf, Carol A*
The Critical Response to Dashiell Hammett — *Metress, Christopher*
The Critical Response to H.G. Wells — *Scheick, William J*
The Critical Response to Katherine Mansfield — *Pilditch, Jan*
The Critical Response to Raymond Chandler — *Van Dover, J Kenneth*
r The Critical Response to Tennessee Williams — *Crandell, George W*
A Critical Review of the Aerial and Ground Surveys of Breeding Waterfowl in North America — *Smith, Graham W*
Critical Social Literacies — *Walton, Christine*
Critical Social Theory — *Calhoun, Craig*
Critical Tales — *Lyons, John D*
Critical Terms for Art History — *Nelson, Robert S*
Critical Theory and the Novel — *Suchoff, David*
Critical Thinking in Nursing — *Rubenfeld, M Gaie*
Criticism and the Color Line — *Wonham, Henry B*
The Criticism of Didactic Poetry — *Dalzell, Alexander*
The Critics and the Harlem Renaissance — *Wintz, Cary D*
Critics on Trial — *O'Connell, Marvin R*
Critifiction: Postmodern Essays — *Federman, Raymond*
Critique, Action, and Liberation — *Marsh, James L*
Critique of Beckett Criticism — *Murphy, P J*
Critique of Modernity — *Touraine, Alain*
Critiques of God — *Angeles, Peter A*
c Critter Crackers (Illus. by Kathryn Barron) — *Barron, Kathryn*
Croatia: A Nation Forged in War — *Tanner, Marcus*
c Crocodile — *Newton, Jill*
c The Crocodile in the Piano — *Kenyon, Tony*
c Crocodile Tears (Illus. by Joanna Walsh) — *Watts, Marjorie-Ann*
La Croix Et Le Scalpel. Vol. 2 — *Rousseau, Francois*
y Cromwell (Peters). Audio Version — *Fraser, Antonia*
Cromwellian Foreign Policy — *Venning, Timothy*
Cromwell's Earl — *Ollard, Richard*
Cronologia Martiana — *Rodriguez Silva, Delfain*
Crook and Chase — *Crook, Lorianne*
y Crooked Little Heart — *Lamott, Anne*
The Crooked Man — *Davison, Philip*
A Crooked Man — *Lehmann-Haupt, Christopher*
c A Crooked Man and Other Rhymes — *Roffey, Maureen*
The Crooked Timber of Humanity — *Berlin, Isaiah*
c Croqu'sandwich--Super Et Geant — *Anargyros, Isabelle*
c Crosby (Illus. by Jonathan Green) — *Haseley, Dennis*
Crosland's Future — *Reisman, David*
The Cross and Human Transformation — *Brown, Alexandra R*
The Cross and the Pear Tree — *Perera, Victor*
The Cross and the Rising Sun. Vols. 1-2 — *Ion, A Hamish*
The Cross and the Serpent — *Griffiths, Nicholas*
Cross Channel — *Barnes, Julian*
Cross-Check — *Law, Janice*
Cross Country — *Poor, Alfred*
c Cross-Country Gallop — *Leitch, Patricia*
r Cross-Country Ski Tours: Washington's North Cascades. 2nd Ed. — *Kirkendall, Tom*
Cross-Cultural Business Negotiations — *Hendon, Donald W*
Cross-Cultural Dialogues — *Storti, Craig*
Cross-Cultural Issues in AIDS — *Thampu, Valson*
Cross-Cultural Reckonings — *Gelfant, Blanche H*

Cross-Cultural Roots of Minority Child Development
— *Greenfield, Patrick M*
Cross, Sword, and Lyre — *Saunders, Steven*
Crossfire Education — *Jordan, William A*
Crossing Borders — *Yakobson, Helen*
Crossing Boundaries — *Klein, Julie Thompson*
Crossing Brooklyn Ferry — *Fields, Jennie*
Crossing Cultures — *Bennett, Bruce*
Crossing Frontiers — *Achenbaum, W Andrew*
Crossing: Language and Ethnicity among Adolescents
— *Rampton, Ben*
Crossing Lines — *McGinn, Noel F*
Crossing over Jordan — *Brown, Linda Beatrice*
Crossing over the Line — *Langum, David J*
Crossing Rio Pecos — *Dearen, Patrick*
Crossing the Circle at the Holy Wells of Ireland
— *Brenneman, Walter L, Jr.*
Crossing the Color Line — *Reddy, Maureen T*
Crossing the Deadly Ground — *Jamieson, Perry D*
Crossing the Frontier — *Phillips, Sandra S*
Crossing the Line — *Finnegan, William*
Crossing the Moon — *Alden, Paulette Bates*
Crossing the Snow Bridge — *Lim-Wilson, Fatima*
Crossings: The Great Transatlantic Migrations
1870-1914 — *Nugent, Walter*
y Crossover — *Friedman, Michael Jan*
Crossover (Frakes). Audio Version — *Friedman,
Michael Ian*
Crossovers — *Reiter, Thomas*
The Crossroads of American History and Literature
— *Gura, Philip F*
The Crossroads of Justice — *Cohen, Esther*
The Crossroads of Norm and Nature — *Sim, May*
Crosstalk: Citizens, Candidates, and the Media in a
Presidential Campaign — *Just, Marion R*
Crosstown — *Scrimger, Richard*
c Crow Boy — *Yashima, Taro*
c The Crow Haunting — *Jarman, Julia*
c The Crow Who Stood on His Beak (Illus. by Els
Cools) — *Schami, Rafik*
Crown and Mitre — *Jacob, W M*
c Crown and Parliament — *Harris, Nathaniel*
The Crown and the Turban — *Sanneh, Lamin*
y Crown Duel — *Smith, Sherwood*
The Crown of Creation — *Weisberg, Chana*
y The Crown of Dalemark — *Jones, Diana Wynne*
y Crown of Shadows — *Friedman, C S*
y A Crown of Swords — *Jordan, Robert*
Crown Oklahoma — *Lehrer, Jim*
Crowning Achievements — *Arnoldi, Mary Jo*
Crowning Glory — *Grafman, Rafi*
Crowning the Queen of Love — *Welch, Susan*
Crowns of Glory, Tears of Blood — *Costa, Emilia
Viotti Da*
c A Crow's Journey (Illus. by David Cunningham)
— *Cunningham, David*
Crows over a Wheatfield — *Sharp, Paula*
Crucial Conversations — *Braham, Jeanne*
Crucial Issues in Teaching Social Studies K-12
— *Massialas, Byron G*
The Crucible CD-Rom. Electronic Media Version
Crucible of Empire — *Bradford, James C*
Crucible of Ideas — *Lipp, Solomon*
The Crucible of War 1939-1945 — *Greenhous,
Brereton*
The Crucible: Screenplay — *Miller, Arthur*
Crucibles of Crisis — *Reinelt, Janelle*
The Crucified Jew — *Cohn-Sherbok, Dan*
The Crucifixion of Jesus — *Sloyan, Gerard S*
Cruciformed: The Literary Impact of Mark's Story of
Jesus and His Disciples — *Wegener, Mark I*
Cruel as the Grave — *Armistead, John*
c The Cruelest Place on Earth — *Nicholson, John*
Cruelty Games — *Robertson, Wendy*
The Cruelty of Morning — *Bonner, Hilary*
r Cruisers of World War Two — *Whitley, M J*
Cruising Guide to Belize and Mexico's Caribbean
Coast. 2nd Ed. — *Rauscher, Freya*
Cruising Paradise — *Shepard, Sam*
y Cruising Paradise (Shepard). Audio Version
— *Shepard, Sam*
Cruising the Performative — *Case, Sue-Ellen*
y Crusade: The Untold Story of the Gulf War
(Riggenbach). Audio Version — *Atkinson, Rick*
Crusader Castles — *Kennedy, Hugh N*
Crusaders against Opium — *Lodwick, Kathleen L*
Crusaders and Heretics 12th-14th Centuries
— *Barber, Malcolm*
Crusaders in the Courts — *Greenberg, Jack*
y The Crusades — *Child, John*
y The Crusades and the Holy Land — *Tate, Georges*

The Crusades: Five Centuries of Holy Wars
— *Billings, Malcolm*
Crusading for Chemistry — *Reed, Germaine M*
y Cry Baby — *Karas, Phyllis*
y Cry Bloody Murder — *DePrince, Elaine*
A Cry for Self-Help — *Girdner, Jaqueline*
The Cry of Tamar — *Cooper-White, Pamela*
c Cry of the Benu Bird — *Greger, C Shana*
The Cry of the Goldfinch — *Skrzynecki, Peter*
The Cry of the Halidon — *Ludlum, Robert*
Cryogenic Engineering — *Flynn, Thomas M*
Cryogenic Two-Phase Flow — *Filina, N N*
Cryptography's Role in Securing the Information
Society — *Dam, Kenneth W*
The Crystal as a Supramolecular Entity — *Desiraju,
Gautam R*
A Crystal Diary — *Hucklenbroich, Frankie*
c The Crystal Garden — *Grove, Vicki*
Crystal Growth of Organic Materials — *Myerson,
Allan S*
Crystalline Bacterial Cell Surface Proteins — *Sletyr,
Uwe B*
Crystallographic Methods and Protocols — *Jones,
Christopher*
Crystallographically Determined Structure of Some
Biologically Important Macromolecules — *Sjolin,
Lennart*
Crystallography of Supramolecular Compounds
— *NATO Advanced Study Institute on
Crystallography of Supramolecular Compounds (1995:
Erice, Italy)*
r The CTD Pocket Guide. 1997 Ed.
Cu Frunzele In Vant — *Giurgiu, Eugen*
c Cuando Tengo Sueno (Illus. by Lynne Cherry)
— *Howard, Jane R*
Cuatro Nobles Titulados En Contienda Por La Tierra
— *Aguirre Beltran, Gonzalo*
The Cub-Hunting Season — *Ferris, Steve*
r Cuba — *Stubbs, Jean*
Cuba: Algunos Problemas De Su Historia — *Opatrny,
Josef*
Cuba and the Future — *Schulz, Donald E*
Cuba and the Night — *Iyer, Pico*
Cuba at a Crossroads — *Perez-Lopez, Jorge F*
y Cuba in Pictures — *Haverstock, Nathan A*
y The Cuban American Family Album — *Hoobler,
Dorothy*
Cuban Americans — *Olson, James Stuart*
The Cuban Missile Crisis — *Hilsman, Roger*
The Cuban Missile Crisis — *White, Mark J*
The Cuban Revolution — *Perez-Stable, Marifeli*
The Cuban Revolution in Crisis — *Fitzgerald, Frank T*
The Cuban Slave Market 1790-1880 — *Bergad, Laird
W*
Cuba's Second Economy — *Perez-Lopez, Jorge F*
The Cubist Poets in Paris — *Breunig, L C*
La Cucina Siciliana Di Gangivecchio — *Tornabene,
Wanda*
c Cuckoo: A Mexican Folktale (Illus. by Lois Ehlert)
— *Ehlert, Lois*
c The Cuckoo Clock — *Molesworth, Mrs.*
c The Cuckoo Clock of Doom — *Stine, R L*
y The Cuckoo's Child — *Freeman, Suzanne*
c The Cucumber Girls and the Little Nurse
— *Tredgold, Margaret H*
Cue the Elephant — *Nash, Knowlton*
Cuentos Completos — *Bryce Echenique, Alfredo*
Cuentos De Este Siglo — *Encinar, Angeles*
c Los Cuentos Del Cerdito Oliver (Illus. by Arnold
Lobel) — *Van Leeuwen, Jean*
Cuentos, Fabulas Y Lo Demas Es Silencio
— *Monterroso, Augusto*
Cuku Gramata — *Einfelds, Janis*
Cul-De-Sac — *Martin, David Lozell, 1946-*
Culinaria — *Romer, Joachim*
Culinary Arts and Sciences — *International
Conference on Culinary Arts and Sciences (1st: 1996:
London, England)*
The Cullin: Great Mountain Ridge of Skye
— *Stainforth, Gordon*
y Culpable — *Thomas, Ruth*
The Cult at the End of the World — *Kaplan, David E*
Cult Fiction — *Bloom, Clive*
Le Culte De La Voix Au XVIIe Siecle — *Salazar,
Philippe-Joseph*
A Cultivated Life — *Sterling, Joy*
Cultivating a Child's Imagination through Gardening
— *Jurenka, Nancy Allen*
Cultivating Congress — *Browne, William P*
Cultivating Cooperation — *Young, Raymond A*
Cultivating Crisis — *Murray, Douglass L*

Cultivating Customers — *Horn, Nancy E*
Cultivating Inner Peace — *Fleischman, Paul R*
Cultivating the Rosebuds — *Mihesuah, Devon A*
Cultivating Women, Cultivating Science — *Shteir, Ann
B*
The Cults of the Roman Empire — *Turcan, Robert*
Cultural Adaptation in the Workplace — *John,
Martha Tyler*
Cultural Aesthetics — *Fumerton, Patricia*
Cultural and Ethnic Diversity — *Fisher, Nancy L*
Cultural and Language Diversity and the Deaf
Experience — *Parsanis, Ila*
Cultural Anthropology and the Old Testament
— *Overholt, Thomas*
Cultural Artifacts and the Production of Meaning
— *Ezell, Margaret J M*
Cultural Capital — *Guillory, John*
Cultural Collisions — *Sassower, Raphael*
Cultural Combat — *Gullette, Margaret Morganroth*
Cultural Conservatism, Political Liberalism — *Seaton,
James*
Cultural Contexts for Ralph Ellison's Invisible Man
— *Sundquist, Eric J*
The Cultural Contradictions of Capitalism — *Bell,
Daniel*
The Cultural Contradictions of Motherhood — *Hays,
Sharon*
Cultural Contributions of Black Americans. Electronic
Media Version
Cultural Crusaders — *Passet, Joanne Ellen*
Cultural Diversity among Twentieth-Century Foragers
— *Kent, Susan*
Cultural Diversity, Educational Equity, and the
Transformation of Higher Education — *Benjamin,
Michael*
Cultural Economies Past and Present — *Halperin,
Rhoda H*
Cultural Encounters — *Clausen, Soren*
Cultural Encounters in the Early South — *Whayne,
Jeannie*
Cultural Encounters on China's Ethnic Frontiers
— *Harrell, Stevan*
The Cultural Front — *Denning, Michael*
Cultural Functions of Translation — *Schaffner,
Christina*
A Cultural History of the American Novel — *Minter,
David*
Cultural Interplay in the Eighth Century — *Netzer,
Nancy*
Cultural Landscape Report for Sagamore Hill
National Historic Site — *Bellavia, Regina M*
Cultural Liberalism in Australia — *Melleuish,
Gregory*
y Cultural Literacy (Whitener). Audio Version
— *Hirsch, E D*
The Cultural Meaning of Deafness — *Harris, Jennifer,
1954-*
Cultural Nationalism in Contemporary Japan
— *Yoshino, Kosaku*
Cultural Norms and National Security — *Katzenstein,
Peter J*
Cultural Politics and Education — *Apple, Michael W*
Cultural Politics at the Fin De Siecle — *Ledger, Sally*
Cultural Politics in Greater Romania — *Livezeanu,
Irina*
The Cultural Prison — *Sloop, John M*
The Cultural Production of the Educated Person
— *Levinson, Bradley A*
Cultural Psychology — *Cole, Michael, 1938-*
Cultural Realism — *Johnston, Alastair Iain*
Cultural Space and Theatrical Conventions in the
Works of Oduvaldo Vianna Filho — *Damasceno,
Leslie Hawkins*
Cultural Studies and the Study of Popular Culture
— *Storey, John, 1950-*
The Cultural Studies Reader — *During, Simon*
The Cultural World in Beowulf — *Hill, John M*
r Culturally Diverse Library Collections for Youth
— *Totten, Herman L*
Culture and Anarchy — *Arnold, Matthew*
Culture and Catastrophe — *Aschheim, Steven E*
Culture and Counterculture in Moroccan Politics
— *Entelis, John P*
Culture and Entertainment in Wartime Russia
— *Stites, Richard*
Culture and Gender in Nineteenth-Century Spain
— *Charnon-Deutsch, Lou*
Culture and Global Change — *Arizpe, Lourdes*
Culture and History in Eastern Europe — *Hubchick,
Dennis P*
Culture and Imperialism — *Said, Edward*

Culture and National Identity in Republican Rome
— Gruen, Erich S
Culture and Political Crisis in Vienna — Boyer, John W
Culture and Politics in Early Stuart England
— Sharpe, Kevin
The Culture and Technology of African Iron Production — Schmidt, Peter R
Culture and the Public Sphere — McGuigan, Jim
r Culture Briefings
Culture Change and the New Technology — Shackel, Paul A
Culture Clash — Goldberg, Steven
Culture, Conflict, and Communication in the Wildland-Urban Interface — Ewert, Allan W
Culture/Flesh: Explorations of Postcivilized Modernity
— Weinstein, Michael A
Culture, Health and Illness — Helman, Cecil
Culture in Action — Jacob, Mary Jane
Culture in Mind — Shore, Bradd
Culture Incarnate — Balzer, Marjorie Mandelstam
Culture, Modernity and Revolution — Kilminster, Richard
The Culture of Bible Belt Catholics — Anderson, Jon W
The Culture of Citizenship — Bridges, Thomas
The Culture of Civil War in Kyoto — Berry, Mary Elizabeth
The Culture of Clothing — Roche, Daniel
The Culture of Crime — LaMay, Craig L
The Culture of Education — Bruner, Jerome
The Culture of English Puritanism 1560-1700
— Durston, Christopher
The Culture of Forgetting — Manne, Robert
The Culture of Higher Education — Van Patten, James J
Culture of Honor — Nisbett, Richard E
The Culture of Korean Industry — Kim, Choong Soon
The Culture of Love — Kern, Stephen
The Culture of Merit — Smith, Jay M
The Culture of National Security — Katzenstein, Peter J
The Culture of Politics in Modern Kenya
— Haugerud, Angelique
The Culture of Possibility — Dooley, Edward
The Culture of Reading and the Teaching of English
— McCormick, Kathleen
The Culture of Recovery — Rapping, Elayne
Culture of Recovery, Culture of Denial Alcoholism among Men and Women Religious — King, Eleace
A Culture of Teaching — Bushnell, Rebecca W
The Culture of the Cold War. 2nd Ed. — Whitfield, Stephen J
The Culture of the Copy — Schwartz, Hillel
The Culture of the English People — Pounds, Norman John Greville
The Culture of Violence — Barker, Francis
The Culture of Wilderness — Knobloch, Frieda
Culture Policy and Management in the United Kingdom — Bennett, Oliver
Cultures and Societies in a Changing World
— Griswold, Wendy
Cultures in Conflict — Lewis, Bernard
Cultures in Flux — Frank, Stephen P
The Cultures of Cities — Zukin, Sharon
Cultures of Consumption — Mort, Frank
Cultures of Healing — Fancher, Robert T
Cultures of Internet — Shields, Rob
Cultures of Letters — Brodhead, Richard H
Cultures of Natural History — Jardine, N
Cultures of Print — Hall, David D
Cum Mor Taranii — Lacranjan, Ion
The Cummins Site Complex and Paleoindian Occupations in the Northwestern Lake Superior Region — Julig, Patrick J
Cung Dan Dang Do — Le, Thao Chuyen
The Cunning Man — Davies, Robertson
Il Cuore Indurito Del Faraone — Perrone, Lorenzo
c Cup Final Kid (Illus. by Jeff Cummins) — Waddell, Martin
The Cup of Wrath — Glazer, Mary
r Cupboard Love — Morton, Mark
c Cupid and Psyche (Illus. by K Y Craft) — Craft, M Charlotte
Cupid's Mistake — Harbaugh, Karen
La Cupula — Marquez-Sterling, Manuel
Curators of the Buddha — Lopez, Donald S
Curazao Y La Costa De Caracas — Aizpurua, Ramon
Curbing Population Growth — Harkavy, Oscar
Curbside L.A. — Rasmussen, Cecilia

y The Cure for Death by Lightning
— Anderson-Dargatz, Gail
Curing the Dutch Disease — Aarts, Leo J M
c Curious George ABC Adventure. Electronic Media Version
c Curious Kids Go to Preschool (Illus. by Ingrid Godon)
— Antoine, Heloise
The Curious Room — Carter, Angela
Curl Up and Die — Jorgensen, Christine T
Currency and Coercion — Kirshner, Jonathan
Currency Convertibility — Macedo, Jorge Braga De
The Current Account and Foreign Debt — Pitchford, John
r Current Biography 1940-
yr Current Biography on CD-ROM. Electronic Media Version
Current Concepts in Hepatobiliary and Pancreatic Surgery — Zollinger Postgraduate Course in Surgery (1st: 1995: Ohio State University)
Current Concepts in Primary and Revision Total Knee Arthroplasty — Insall, John N
Current Controversies in the Anxiety Disorders
— Rapee, Ronald M
Current Dilemmas in Medical-Care Rationing
— Shenkin, Henry A
Current Directions in Radiopharmaceutical Research and Development — Mather, Stephen J
Current Genitourinary Cancer Surgery. 2nd Ed.
— Crawford, E David
Current Issues and New Frontiers in Animal Research
— Bayne, Kathryn A L
Current Issues in Comparative Grammar — Freidin, Robert
Current Issues in International Trade. 2nd Ed.
— Greenaway, David
p Current Issues in Public Health
yr Current Issues SourceFile. Electronic Media Version
Current Legal Issues in Publishing — Strauch, A Bruce
p Current Opinion in Colloid and Interface Science
Current Perspectives on the Fetus as a Patient
— Chervenak, Frank A
Current Practice of Medicine 1996. Vols. 1-4
Current Psychotherapeutic Drugs — Klein, Donald F
Current Research in Phytolith Analysis — Pearsall, Deborah M
Current Research in Sports Sciences — Rogozkin, Victor A
Current Review of Laparoscopy. 2nd Ed. — Brooks, David C
Current Societal Concerns about Justice — Montada, Leo
Current Widowhood — Lopata, Helena Znaniecka
Currents of Change — Glantz, Michael H
Currents of Radicalism — Biagini, Eugenio F
Curriculum as Conversation — Applebee, Arthur N
Curriculum Development and Teaching Strategies for Gifted Learners. 2nd Ed. — Maker, C June
c Curriculum of Love (Illus. by Frank Riccio) — Daleo, Morgan Simone
Curriculum Related Assessment, Cummins and Bilingual Children — Cline, Tony
Curriculum: The Strategic Key to Schooling. 2nd Ed.
— Blair, Billie G
The Curry Book — McDermott, Nancie
c The Curse of the Cat Mummy — Saunders, Susan
c Curse of the Egyptian Mummy. Audio Version
— Hutchins, Pat
c The Curse of Tutankhamen — Landau, Elaine
Cursed — Duncan, Dave
y Curses, Inc. and Other Stories — Vande Velde, Vivian
Curtains — Hayes, Katy
y Curtis Piperfield's Biggest Fan — Fiedler, Lisa
Curzon — Gilmour, David
r Cushion Plants for the Rock Garden — Lowe, Duncan
c Custard Pie (Illus. by Jane Eccles) — Corbett, Pie
c Custard the Dragon and the Wicked Knight (Illus. by Lynn Munsinger) — Nash, Ogden
r Custer and the Battle of the Little Bighorn — Hatch, Thom
y Custer: The Controversial Life of George Armstrong Custer — Wert, Jerry D
Custodians of the Land — Maddox, Gregory
Custom, Culture and Community in the Later Middle Ages — Pettit, Thomas
The Custom of the Country — Wharton, Edith
Customer Centered Growth — Whiteley, Richard
Customer Intimacy — Wiersema, Fred
Customer Intimacy (Wiersema). Audio Version
— Wiersema, Fred
Customer Service Excellence — Weingand, Darlene E

The Customized Body — Randall, Housk
Customized Human Resource Planning — Duane, Michael J
Customs and Controversies — Scott, J Julius, Jr.
c Customs and Traditions (Illus. by Barbara Bedell)
— Kalman, Bobbie
Customs in Common — Thompson, E P
Cut to the Chase — Meade, Marion
Cut Your Losses! — O'Brien, Keith
Cutdown — Miller, John A
y Cutting-Edge Java Game Programming — Bartlett, Neil
r Cutting for All! — Seligman, Kevin L
Cutting for Sign — Langewiesche, William
The Cutting Garden — Raven, Sarah
Cutting Loose — Applewhite, Ashton
Cutting Loose — Ripskis, Al Louis
Cuttlefish Bones — Montale, Eugenio
CX — Renaudot, Patrick
Cyanide in My Shoe (Bishop). Audio Version
— Butler, Josephine
y Cybercats — Kilworth, Garry
CyberCities: Visual Perception in the Age of Electronic Communication — Boyer, M Christine
Cybercorp: The New Business Revolution — Martin, James
r CyberHound's Guide to Associations and Nonprofit Organizations on the Internet — Moran, Amanda M
r CyberHound's Guide to Companies on the Internet
— Mason, Wendy H
r CyberHound's Guide to Internet Databases
r CyberHound's Guide to Internet Discussion Groups
— Lewon, Paul
r CyberHound's Guide to Internet Libraries
r CyberHound's Guide to People on the Internet
— Tracy, Deborah
r CyberHound's Guide to Publications on the Internet
— Kahrs, Kristin
r CyberHound's Internet Guide to the Coolest Stuff Out There
Cyberpunk Handbook — Sirius, R U
Cybersex — Jones, Richard G
Cybersociety: Computer Mediated Communication and Community — Jones, Steven G
y Cybersong — Lewitt, S N
c Cyberspace Adventure — Dicks, Terrance
r The Cyberspace Lexicon — Cotton, Bob
r Cyberstocks: An Investor's Guide to Internet Companies — Chai, Alan
c CyberSurfer: The OWL Internet Guide for Kids (Illus. by Martha Newbigging) — Ahmad, Nyla
The Cybrarian's Guide to Developing Successful Internet Programs and Services — Kovacs, Michael
Cycles (Moon Poems) — Frazeur, Joyce
Cycles of Life — Smil, Vaclav
r Cycling Great Britain — Hughes, Tim
r Cycling Japan — Harrell, Bryan
r Cycling the Bush — Klinge, Sven
r Cycling the Mediterranean — Nasr, Kameel
r Cyclopedia of Literary Characters II. Vols. 1-4
— Magill, Frank Northen
Cynewulf: Basic Readings — Bjork, Robert E
Cynic Sage or Son of God? — Boyd, Gregory A
Cypriote Stone Sculpture — Vandenabeele, Frieda
r Cyprus. 1st Ed. — Braun, Ralph
r Cyprus. 2nd Ed. — Dubin, Marc S
r Cyprus. Rev. Ed. — Kitromilides, Paschalis M
Cyriax's Illustrated Manual of Orthopaedic Medicine. 2nd Ed. — Cyriax, J H
Cytochrome C: A Multidisciplinary Approach
— Scott, Robert A
Cytokine Yearbook. Vol. 1
p Cytokines and Molecular Therapy
Cytokines: Interleukins and Their Receptors
— Kurzrock, Razelle
Cytokines Produced by Polymorphonuclear Neutrophils — Cassatella, Marco A
Cytokinesis in Animal Cells — Rappoport, R
Cytopathology of the Breast — Masood, Shahla
The Czech and Slovak Republics — Leff, Carol Skalnik
Czechoslovakia between Stalin and Hitler — Lukes, Igor
r Czechoslovakia--Revolutionary Stamps and Overprints 1944-1945 — Santaeugenia Grau, Juan

D

D-Day, June 6, 1944 — *Ambrose, Stephen E*
y D.H. Lawrence (Peters). Audio Version — *Maddox, Brenda*
r D.H. Lawrence: A Reference Companion — *Poplawski, Paul*
D.H. Lawrence and Nine Women Writers — *Hamalian, Leo*
D.H. Lawrence: The Story of a Marriage — *Maddox, Brenda*
D.H. Lawrence: Triumph to Exile 1912-1922 — *Kinkead-Weekes, Mark*
D.H. Lawrence's Response to Plato — *Scherr, Barry J*
y The D-Poems of Jeremy Bloom — *Korman, Gordon*
D.W. Winnicott: A Biographical Portrait — *Kahr, Brett*
r The Da Capo Catalog of Classical Music Compositions — *Chwialkowski, Jerzy*
Da Dao Ge — *Fu, Jianwen*
Da Ni Zhuan — *Yang, Du*
Da Vinci's Bicycle — *Davenport, Guy*
Daar Komen Scherven Van — *Michiels, Ivo*
Dad Says He Saw You at the Mall — *Sparling, Ken*
Dada and Surrealist Film — *Kuenzli, Rudolf E*
c Daddies (Illus. by Mary Morgan) — *Regan, Dian Curtis*
c Daddy, Could I Have an Elephant? (Illus. by Marylin Hafner) — *Wolf, Jake*
c Daddy, Daddy Be There (Illus. by Floyd Cooper) — *Boyd, Candy Dawson*
c Daddy Doesn't Have to Be a Giant Anymore (Illus. by Marcia Sewall) — *Thomas, Jane Resh*
c Daddy, Would You Love Me — *Dijs, Carla*
Daddy's Gone to War — *Tuttle, William M, Jr.*
c Daddy's Wedding (Illus. by Michael Willhoite) — *Willhoite, Michael*
y El Dador — *Lowry, Lois*
Daemonic — *Laws, Stephen*
Daemonic Figures — *Lukacher, Ned*
Dafnis I Khloia Epokhi Kullta Lichnosti, Voliuntarizma I Zastoia — *Nagibin, IUrii*
c Daft Jack and the Bean Stack (Illus. by Arthur Robins) — *Anholt, Laurence*
p Daga Info
Dagdakiler — *Gursel, Kadri*
r Dahlonega Mint Gold Coins 1838-1861 — *Winter, Douglas*
Dahl's History of the Book. 3rd Ed. — *Katz, William A*
r Dahl's Law Dictionary: Spanish to English/English to Spanish. 2nd Ed. — *Dahl, Henry S*
c Dahomey: The Warrior Kings — *Koslow, Philip*
Daily Life in Chaucer's England — *Singman, Jeffrey L*
y Daily Life in Maya Civilization — *Sharer, Robert J*
Daily Life in the Inca Empire — *Malpass, Michael Andrew*
Daily Life in Victorian England — *Mitchell, Sally*
Daily Life of the Egyptian Gods — *Meeks, Dimitri*
The Daily Mail Centenary CD-ROM. Electronic Media Version
The Daily Practice of Painting — *Richter, Gerhard*
Daily Readings in Orthodox Spirituality — *Bouteneff, Peter*
The Daily Telegraph Second Book of Obituaries — *Massingberd, Hugh*
Daily Word — *Zuck, Colleen*
Daimonic Reality — *Harpur, Patrick*
y Dairy Queen Days — *Inman, Robert*
c Daisy (Illus. by Lynne Woodcock Cravath) — *Leverich, Kathleen*
c Daisy and the Girl Scouts (Illus. by Marie DeJohn) — *Brown, Fern G*

c Daisy Is a Mommy (Illus. by Lisa Kopper) — *Kopper, Lisa*
c Daisy Is a Mummy (Illus. by Lisa Kopper) — *Kopper, Lisa*
c Daisy Rabbit's Tree House — *Dale, Penny*
Dakota: A Spiritual Biography — *Norris, Kathleen*
c Dale Earnhardt — *Benson, Michael*
D'Alembert's Principle — *Crumey, Andrew*
Daley: Power and Presidential Politics — *Ciccone, F Richard*
Dali — *Ades, Dawn*
p Dalit International Newsletter
Dalkey, Society and Economy in a Small Medieval Irish Town — *Smith, Charles V*
Dallas Cowboys — *Guinn, Jeff*
Dallas: The Making of a Modern City — *Hill, Patricia Evridge*
Daltons! The Raid on Coffeyville, Kansas — *Smith, Robert Barr*
Dam Breach Modeling Technology — *Singh, Vijay P*
Damage Limitation or Crisis? — *Blackwill, Robert D*
Damage Mechanics — *Krajcinovic, Dusan*
y Damaged Goods (Murdock). Audio Version — *Solomita, Stephen*
Damascus Nights — *Schami, Rafik*
Dames Du XIIe Siecle. Vol. 1 — *Duby, Georges*
Damien Hirst: No Sense of Absolute Corruption
Damming the Danube — *Fitzmaurice, John*
The Damnation of Harold Frederic — *Bennett, Bridget*
Damnatur--Toleratur--Admittitur — *Plachta, Bodo*
Damned in Paradise — *Collins, Max Allan*
y Damned Strong Love — *Dijk, Lutz Van*
Damned to Fame — *Knowlson, James*
Dams and Rivers — *Collier, Michael*
Dan Gookin's Web Wambooli — *Gookin, Dan*
c Dan Marino — *Rambeck, Richard*
c Dan Marino — *Wilner, Barry*
Dan Stuart's Fistic Carnival — *Miletich, Leo N*
The Danakil Diary — *Thesiger, Wilfred*
c Dance! — *Schumaker, Ward*
Dance for the Dead — *Perry, Thomas*
y Dance for the Dead (Crouse). Audio Version — *Perry, Thomas*
Dance for Two — *Lightman, Alan*
The Dance Hall at Spring Hill and Other Stories — *Klassen, Duke*
Dance Kinesiology. 2nd Ed. — *Fitt, Sally Sevey*
Dance, Modernity and Culture — *Thomas, Helen*
Dance of Love — *Clephane, Ellen*
The Dance of Siva — *Smith, David, 1944-*
Dance of the Scarecrows — *Sipherd, Ray*
c Dance on a Sealskin (Illus. by Teri Sloat) — *Winslow, Barbara, 1947-*
Dance Real Slow — *Jaffe, Michael Grant*
Dance Script with Electric Ballerina — *Fulton, Alice*
A Dance with Death — *Anderson, Frank W*
c Dance with Me (Illus. by Megan Lloyd) — *Esbensen, Barbara Juster*
c Dance with Rosie (Illus. by Julie Durrell) — *Giff, Patricia Reilly*
r Dance Words — *Preston-Dunlop, Valerie*
y Dancer — *Peterson, Shelley*
The Dancer Upstairs — *Shakespeare, Nicholas*
r Dancers and Choreographers — *Getz, Leslie*
Dancers in the Sunset Sky — *Jones, Robert F*
The Dances of Africa — *Huet, Michel*
Dancing after Hours — *Dubus, Andre*
Dancing around the Volcano — *Kettelhack, Guy*
Dancing at the Rascal Fair — *Doig, Ivan*
c The Dancing Bear (Illus. by Christian Birmingham) — *Morpurgo, Michael*

Dancing Bears (Ukena). Audio Version — *Saberhagen, Fred*
The Dancing Column — *Rykwert, Joseph*
c The Dancing Dragon (Illus. by Stanley Wong Hoo Foon) — *Vaughan, Marcia*
y The Dancing Floor — *Michaels, Barbara*
c The Dancing Fox (Illus. by Mary K Okheena) — *Bierhorst, John*
Dancing in Limbo — *Pittman, Al*
Dancing in the Dark — *Donnell, David*
Dancing in the Dark (Guidall). Audio Version — *Kaminsky, Stuart M*
y Dancing in the Dark (Kohen). Audio Version — *Kaminsky, Stuart M*
Dancing in the Dark (Parker). Audio Version — *Kaminsky, Stuart M*
Dancing in the Flames — *Woodman, Marion*
Dancing in the Water of Life — *Merton, Thomas*
Dancing Modernism/Performing Politics — *Franko, Mark*
Dancing Naked — *Brandt, Di*
Dancing on Common Ground — *Meredith, Howard*
c Dancing on the Bridge of Avignon — *Vos, Ida*
Dancing on the Ceiling — *Silverman, Stephen M*
y Dancing Pink Flamingos and Other Stories — *Testa, Maria*
Dancing Queen — *Carver, Lisa*
c Dancing Rainbows — *Mott, Evelyn Clarke*
c The Dancing Skeleton (Illus. by Robert Andrew Parker) — *DeFelice, Cynthia C*
Dancing Spirits — *Fleurant, Gerdes*
Dancing the Code — *Leonard, Paul*
Dancing to a Black Man's Tune — *Curtis, Susan*
Dancing to History's Tune — *Walker, Brian*
c Dancing with Dziadziu (Illus. by Annika Nelson) — *Bartoletti, Susan Campbell*
Dancing with God — *Dosick, Wayne*
c Dancing with Great-Aunt Cornelia — *Quirk, Anne*
Dancing with Mister D — *Keizer, Bert*
Dancing with the Devil — *Limon, Jose E*
y Dancing with the Devil (Patton). Audio Version — *Barker, Rodney*
c Dancing with the Wind (Illus. by James Bernardin) — *Orser, Stanton*
The Dancing Wu Li Masters — *Zukav, Gary*
c Dandelions (Illus. by Greg Shed) — *Bunting, Eve*
Dandies and Desert Saints — *Adams, James Eli*
c Dando La Nota (Illus. by Federico Delicado) — *Sierra I Fabra, Jordi*
c Danger along the Ohio — *Willis, Patricia*
Danger and Opportunity — *Herring, Eric*
y Danger at the Fair — *Kehret, Peg*
y Danger Game — *Lawson, Julie*
c Danger, Keep Out — *Schutte, David*
Danger Wall May Fall — *Luria-Sukenick, Lynn*
y Danger Zone — *Klass, David*
Danger Zones — *Schaefer, Claudia*
y Dangerous Animals — *Seidensticker, John*
Dangerous Attachments — *Lovett, Sarah Poland*
Dangerous Dossiers — *Mitgang, Herbert*
Dangerous Earth — *Murck, Barbara W*
Dangerous Familiars — *Dolan, Frances E*
y Dangerous Ghosts — *Cohen, Daniel, 1936-*
A Dangerous Happiness — *Hucker, Hazel*
Dangerous Knowledge — *Simon, Art*
Dangerous Liaisons. Audio Version
The Dangerous Lives of Altar Boys — *Fuhrman, Chris*
A Dangerous Love — *Phillips, Michael R*
Dangerous Men — *Becker, Geoffrey, 1959-*
Dangerous Pilgrimages — *Bradbury, Malcolm*
y Dangerous Skies — *Staples, Suzanne Fisher*

Dangerous Talk and Strange Behavior — *Jansen, Sharon L*
Dangerous Temptation — *Mather, Anne*
Dangerous to Hold — *Thornton, Elizabeth*
Dangerous to Know — *Bradford, Barbara Taylor*
y The Dangers of Hazing — *Schleifer, Jay*
Daniel Bell — *Waters, Malcolm*
c Daniel Boone: Frontier Hero — *Raphael, Elaine*
Daniel's Dream — *Rosenberg, Peter Michael*
c Daniel's Duck (Illus. by Anthea Sieveking)
— *MacKinnon, Debbie*
c Daniel's Story — *Matas, Carol*
Danish Proverbs — *McDonald, Julie Jensen*
The Danish Revolution 1500-1800 — *Kjaergaard, Thorkild*
Danmark I Senmiddellalderen — *Ingesman, Per*
c Danny and the Dinosaur Go to Camp (Illus. by Syd Hoff) — *Hoff, Syd*
c Danny and the Sea of Darkness (Illus. by Stephen Player) — *Clayton, David*
c Danny's Duck (Illus. by Clara Vulliamy) — *Crebbin, June*
c Dans Mon Jardin — *Parmentelot, Elizabeth*
Dansk-Norsk Myntpris-Arbok 1995/6
Dante Alighieri's Divine Comedy. Vols. 1-2 — *Dante Alighieri*
Dante and the Middle Ages — *Barnes, John C*
Dante and the Mystical Tradition — *Botterill, Steven*
Dante E La Bella Scola Della Poesia — *Iannucci, Amilcare A*
Dante Gabriel Rossetti — *Ash, Russell*
Dante, Monarchia — *Dante Alighieri*
Dante Now — *Cachey, T J*
Dante's Christian Astrology — *Kay, Richard*
Dante's Disciples — *Crowther, Peter*
Dante's Hell (Ellis) — *Dante Alighieri*
Dante's Inferno (Musa) — *Dante Alighieri*
Dante's Interpretive Journey — *Franke, William*
Dante's Political Purgatory — *Scott, John A, 1932-*
Dao Chu Liu Qing — *Guan, Yuqian*
y The Darden Dilemma — *Cose, Ellis*
Daredevil: Predator's Smile — *Golden, Christopher*
Daring Diplomacy — *O'Clery, Conor*
Daring Do's — *Trasko, Mary*
c Daring to Be Abigail — *Vail, Rachel*
Dark and Perfect Angels — *Saenz, Benjamin Alire*
Dark and Stormy Rides Again — *Rice, Scott*
c Dark at the Foot of the Stairs (Illus. by Moira Kemp) — *Moore, Eileen*
c The Dark at the Top of the Stairs (Illus. by Ivan Bates) — *McBratney, Sam*
Dark Carnival — *Skal, David J*
Dark Cathedral — *Warrington, Freda*
A Dark Coffin — *Butler, Gwendoline*
c Dark Day, Light Night (Illus. by James Ransome) — *Carr, Jan*
Dark Debts — *Hall, Karen*
y Dark Debts (Heald). Audio Version — *Hall, Karen*
y Dark Empire — *Veitch, Tom*
Dark Fields of the Republic — *Rich, Adrienne*
y The Dark Garden — *Buffie, Margaret*
Dark Homecoming — *Lustbader, Eric*
Dark Horse — *Richardson, Doug, 1959-*
Dark Horse — *Shoemaker, Bill*
y The Dark Is Rising — *Cooper, Susan*
The Dark Island — *Conley, Robert J*
Dark Justice — *Farrington, Karen*
y Dark Lies — *Sumner, Mark*
Dark Love — *Collins, Nancy A*
Dark Matter, Missing Planets and New Comets — *Van Flandern, Tom*
The Dark Mirror — *Wilkinson, Myler*
Dark Moon — *Evanhoe, Ed*
Dark Moon Mysteries — *Roderick, Timothy*
Dark Nature — *Watson, Lyall*
A Dark Night's Dreaming — *Magistrale, Tony*
y Dark Odyssey — *Griffiths, Philip Jones*
Dark Prisms — *Lima, Robert*
Dark Rides — *McCormack, Derek*
Dark Road to Daylight — *Parker, Gary E*
The Dark Room — *Walters, Minette*
y The Dark Room (Merlington). Audio Version — *Walters, Minette*
The Dark Shore — *Lee, Adam*
The Dark Side of Humanity — *Parkin, Robert*
The Dark Side of Liberalism — *Hollinger, Robert*
y The Dark Side of Nowhere — *Shusterman, Neal*
The Dark Side of Paradise — *Robinson, Geoffrey, 1957-*
y The Dark Side of the Game (Green). Audio Version — *Green, Tim, 1963-*

Dark Songs — *Lieberman, Laurence*
c The Dark Stairs (Fairman). Audio Version — *Byars, Betsy*
y Dark Star — *Greenfield, Robert*
c Dark Starry Morning — *Patneaude, David*
Dark Sun — *Rhodes, Richard*
Dark Sun (Adams). Pts. 1-2. Audio Version — *Rhodes, Richard*
Dark Sweat, White Gold — *Weber, Devra*
Dark Terrors — *Jones, Stephen*
c Dark-Thirty: Southern Tales of the Supernatural — *McKissack, Pat*
The Dark Tunnel — *Macdonald, Ross*
Dark Voices — *Zamir, Shamoon*
Darke Hierogliphicks — *Linden, Stanton J*
y Darkenheight — *Niles, Douglas*
The Darkening Leaf — *Stickland, Caroline*
y Darkening the Complexion of Canadian Society — *Taylor, Sheldon*
y A Darker Magic — *Bedard, Michael*
The Darker Proof — *White, Edmund*
The Darker Side of the Renaissance — *Mignolo, Walter D*
The Darkest Days of the War — *Cozzens, Peter*
Darkest England — *Hope, Christopher*
y The Darkest Knight — *Anderson, Kevin J*
c Darkfright (Illus. by Jenny Stow) — *Huth, Holly Young*
y Darkness Be My Friend — *Marsden, John*
Darkness Moves — *Michaux, Henri*
The Darkness of God — *Turner, Denys*
The Darkness Starts Up Where You Stand — *Knight, Arthur Winfield*
Darkness, Take My Hand — *Lehane, Dennis*
y Darksaber — *Anderson, Kevin J*
Darnley: A Life of Henry Stuart, Lord Darnley, Consort of Mary Queen of Scots — *Bingham, Caroline, 1938-*
r The Dartmouth Atlas of Health Care
Darwin among the Machines — *Dyson, George B*
Darwin Et L'Apres-Darwin — *Gayon, Jean*
y Darwin in 90 Minutes — *Gribbin, John*
The Darwin Legend — *Moore, James R*
Darwin on Trial. 2nd Ed. — *Johnson, Phillip E*
Darwinian Impacts — *Oldroyd, D R*
Darwinism Evolving — *Depew, David J*
Darwinism, War and History — *Crook, Paul*
Darwin's Athletes — *Hoberman, John*
Darwin's Black Box — *Behe, Michael J*
Darwin's Dangerous Idea — *Dennett, Daniel C*
Darwin's Dreampond — *Goldschmidt, Tijs*
y Darwin's Orchestra — *Sims, Michael*
Das Cores Do Silencio — *Castro, Hebe Maria Mattos De*
c Dashing through the Snow — *Shahan, Sherry*
r Data Acquisition and Process Control Using Personal Computers — *Ozkul, Tarik*
Data Analysis — *Sivia, D S*
Data Analysis and Information Systems — *Bock, Hans-Hermann*
Data Analysis for Hyphenated Techniques — *Karjalainen, E J*
Data and Computer Communications. 5th Ed. — *Stallings, William*
Data and Image Compression. 4th Ed. — *Held, Gilbert*
Data Mining with Neural Networks — *Bigus, Joseph P*
r Data Network Handbook — *Reed, Kenneth*
Data Smog — *Shenk, David*
Data Structures and Program Design in C. 2nd Ed. — *Kruse, Robert L*
Data Trash — *Kroker, Arthur*
The Data Warehouse Challenge — *Brackett, Michael H*
The Data Warehouse Toolkit — *Kimball, Ralph*
Database and Expert Systems Applications — *Database and Expert Systems Applications Conference (7th: 1996: Zurich, Switzerland)*
Database Design and Programming for DB2/400 — *Conte, Paul*
Database Publishing on the Web and Intranets — *Lang, Curt*
Databases and Mobile Computing — *Barbara, Daniel*
Databases in Historical Research — *Harvey, Charles*
Databook on Mechanical and Thermophysical Properties of Particulate-Reinforced Ceramic Matrix Composites — *Campbell, Christian X*
Databook on Mechanical and Thermophysical Properties of Whisker-Reinforced Ceramic Matrix Composites — *Campbell, Christian X*
Date Rape — *Francis, Leslie*

y Dateline: Troy (Illus. by Gwen Frankfeldt) — *Fleischman, Paul*
y The Dating Dilemma — *Stone, Bob*
y Dating Violence — *Hicks, John*
Dating Your Mom — *Frazier, Ian*
Dau Vet Van Hoa Viet Nam Tren Bac My. Vols. 1-2 — *Pham, Quoc Bao*
The Daughter as Reader — *Cohen, Paula Marantz*
y A Daughter like Me — *Roy, Jacqueline*
y Daughter of Darkness — *Spruill, Steven*
y Daughter of Magic — *Brittain, C Dale*
y Daughter of Storms — *Cooper, Louise*
y Daughter of the Forest (Klein). Audio Version — *Munn, Vella*
Daughter of the Regiment — *Laurence, Mary Leefe*
c Daughter of the Sea — *Doherty, Berlie*
Daughters and Mothers (Illus. by Jayne Wexler) — *Cowen, Lauren*
Daughters of Canaan — *Wolfe, Margaret Ripley*
Daughters of Eve — *Lukens, Nancy*
Daughters of Palestine — *Kawar, Amal*
Daughters of Rahab — *Guider, Margaret Eletta*
Daughters of Self-Creation — *Eysturoy, Annie O*
r Daughters of the American Revolution: Lineage of Namaqua Chapter Members, Loveland, Colorado, January 8, 1914-October 31, 1994
Daughters of the Fifth Sun — *Milligan, Bryce*
Daughters of the Great Depression — *Hapke, Laura*
Daughters of the House — *Roberts, Michele*
c D'Aulaires' Book of Greek Myths. Audio Version — *D'Aulaire, Ingri*
y Dave Barry in Cyberspace — *Barry, Dave*
Dave Barry's Book of Bad Songs — *Barry, Dave*
Davenport-Schinzel Sequences and Their Geometric Applications — *Sharir, Micha*
c David and Goliath (Illus. by Scott Cameron) — *De Regniers, Beatrice Schenk*
c David and Goliath (Illus. by Douglas Fraser). Book and Audio Version — *Metaxas, Eric*
David and Jonathan — *Schecter, Stephen*
David Aubert, Escripvain Et Clerc — *Straub, Richard E F*
David Brinkley: 11 Presidents, 4 Wars, 22 Political Conventions, 1 Moon Landing, 3 Assassinations, 2,000 Weeks of News and Other Stuff on Television — *Brinkley, David*
y David Brinkley: A Memoir — *Brinkley, David*
y David Copperfield's Beyond Imagination — *Copperfield, David*
David Copperfield's Tales of the Impossible — *Copperfield, David*
David E. Jackson, Field Captain of the Rocky Mountain Fur Trade — *Talbot, Vivian Linford*
David E. Lilienthal: The Journey of an American Liberal — *Neuse, Steven M*
David Hare: Moral and Historical Perspectives — *Donesky, Finlay*
David Hockney — *Livingstone, Marco*
The David Hume Library — *Norton, David Fate*
David Jones: A Fusilier at the Front — *Hyne, Anthony*
David Jones: The Maker Unmade — *Miles, Jonathan*
David Le Marchand 1674-1726 — *Avery, Charles*
David Lean: A Biography — *Brownlow, Kevin*
y David Letterman — *Lefkowitz, Frances*
y David Letterman's Book of Top Ten Lists and Zesty Lo-Cal Chicken Recipes — *Letterman, David*
David Livingstone and the Victorian Encounter with Africa
David Mamet's Glengarry Glen Ross — *Kane, Leslie*
David to Corot — *Fogg Art Museum*
The Davidic Dynasty Tradition in Early Judaism — *Pomykala, Kenneth E*
The Davidic Messiah in Luke-Acts — *Strauss, Mark L*
c David's Flock of Sheep
c David's Story (Illus. by Benjamin Brink) — *Brink, Benjamin*
Davidson Et La Philosophie Du Langage — *Engel, Pascal*
c Davin — *Gordon, Dan, 1947-*
Davis and Lee at War — *Woodworth, Steven E*
y The Davis Cup Conspiracy — *Bickham, Jack M*
r Davis's Drug Guide for Nurses. 5th Ed. — *Deglin, Judith Hopfer*
Davis's Manual of Nursing Therapeutics for Diseases and Disorders — *Sommers, Marilyn Sawyer*
p Davka
c Davy Crockett: Defender of the Alamo — *Sanford, William R*
c Dawn and the Round-to-It — *Smalls, Irene*
A Dawn like Thunder — *Reeman, Douglas*
Dawn of Art — *Chauvet, Jean-Marie*

The Dawn of Peace in Europe — *Mandelbaum, Michael*

The Dawn of Religious Pluralism — *Seager, Richard Hughes*

The Dawn of Slavic — *Schenker, Alexander M*

y The Dawn Palace — *Hoover, H M*

Dawn Pearl — *Chadwick, Irene*

c A Day at Damp Camp (Illus. by Peter Catalanotto) — *Lyon, George Ella*

The Day before Yesterday — *Elliott, Michael*

The Day before Yesterday — *Tudge, Colin*

A Day for Dying — *Simpson, Dorothy*

c The Day Gogo Went to Vote (Illus. by Sharon Wilson) — *Sisulu, Elinor*

c The Day I Fell down the Toilet (Illus. by David Mostyn) — *Turner, S*

A Day in Part 15 — *Ross, Richard*

c A Day in the Life of a Midshipman — *Travis-Bildahl, Sandra*

A Day in the Life of India — *Cohen, David, 1955-*

A Day in the Life of the National Hockey League

c The Day of Ahmed's Secrets — *Heide, Florence Parry*

Day of Jubilee — *McNamara, Brooks*

y The Day of the Storm (Hunter). Audio Version — *Pilcher, Rosamunde*

y The Day of the Storm (Redgrave). Audio Version — *Pilcher, Rosamunde*

The Day of the Triffids (West). Audio Version *Wyndham, John*

y The Day That Elvis Came to Town — *Marino, Jan*

c The Day the Ants Got Really Mad (Illus. by Sal Murdocca) — *Stanley, G E*

c The Day the Daisies Danced (Illus. by Rex Barron) — *Lillegard, Dee*

The Day the Magic Stopped — *Stasheff, Christopher*

The Day the Presses Stopped — *Rudenstine, David*

The Day We Cut the Lavender — *Neville, Jill*

c The Day We Met You — *Koehler, Phoebe*

Daybreak — *Robertson, Denise*

Daydreams and Nightmares

Daylight. Audio Version — *Collins, Max Allan*

Daylight — *Feinstein, Elaine*

Daylight in Nightclub Inferno — *Lappin, Elena*

c The Days before Now (Illus. by Thomas B Allen) — *Blos, Joan W*

Days like Prose — *Parker, Alan Michael*

c Days of Adventure (Illus. by Joy Dunn Keenan) — *Swanson-Natsues, Lyn*

Days of Drums — *Shelby, Philip*

Days of Gold — *Rohrbough, Malcolm J*

Days of Good Hope — *Wilson, Paul, 1960-*

y Days of Grace — *Ashe, Arthur*

Days of Hope — *Sullivan, Patricia*

Days of Masquerade — *Schoppmann, Claudia*

The Days of Miracles and Wonders — *Louvish, Simon*

c Days of the Blackbird (Illus. by Tomie De Paola) — *De Paola, Tomie*

y Days of the Dead (Illus. by Christopher Knight) — *Lasky, Kathryn*

c A Day's Work (Illus. by Ronald Himler) — *Bunting, Eve*

y Daytona: Thunder at the Beach! — *Schleifer, Jay*

c Dazzling Disguises and Clever Costumes — *Wilkes, Angela*

y DC Versus Marvel/Marvel Versus DC — *Marz, Ron*

De Abditis Nonnullis Ac Mirandis Morborum Et Sanationum Causis — *Benivieni, Antonio*

De Bautizados A Fieles Difuntos — *Pescador, Juan Jose*

De Gaulle and the United States — *Paxton, Robert O*

De Gaulle and Twentieth-Century France — *Gough, Hugh*

De Gaulle: Statesmanship, Grandeur, and Modern Democracy — *Mahoney, Daniel J*

De La BBC A The Observer — *Nadal, Rafael*

De La Condition Humaine — *Garigue, Philippe*

De La Rebelion De Texas A La Guerra Del 47 — *Vazquez, Josefina Zoraida*

De La Uribe A Tlaxcala — *Garcia Duran, Mauricio*

De La Vanguardia A La Posmodernidad — *Verani, Hugo J*

De L'Allemagne, De La France — *Mitterand, Francois*

De Libris Compactis — *Malaguzzi, Francesco*

De L'Oppression A La Liberte — *Bozsoky, Paul G*

De Los Imperios A Las Naciones — *Annino, Antonio*

De Los Otros — *Carrier, Joseph*

De-Monopolization and Competition Policy in Post-Communist Economies — *Slay, Ben*

The De-Moralization of Society — *Himmelfarb, Gertrude*

c De Oro Y Esmeraldas (Illus. by Lulu Delacre) — *Delacre, Lulu*

De Quincey's Disciplines — *McDonagh, Josephine*

De Re Publica — *Cicero, Marcus Tullius*

De Regalpetra A Parigi — *Spalanca, Carmelo*

De Sommopere 1566. Le Miracle De Laon — *Postel, Guillaume*

De Toth on De Toth — *De Toth, Andre*

De Vulgari Eloquentia (Botterill) — *Dante Alighieri*

De Witt Clinton and the Rise of the People's Men — *Hanyan, Craig*

De Yalta A Vancouver — *Daremblum, Jaime*

Deactivation and Testing of Hydrocarbon-Processing Catalysts — *O'Connor, Paul*

Dead Again — *Gessen, Masha*

Dead Artists, Live Theories and Other Cultural Problems — *Aronowitz, Stanley*

Dead as a Dodo — *Langton, Jane*

y Dead Ball — *Gilbert, Thomas*

y Dead by Sunset — *Rule, Ann*

y Dead Cert (Prebble). Audio Version — *Francis, Dick*

Dead Folks — *Jackson, Jon A*

Dead for a Ducat — *Shaw, Simon*

Dead Game — *Harvey, James Neal*

Dead Glamorous — *Morin, Carole*

Dead Heat — *Stone, Del, Jr.*

The Dead Hollywood Moms Society — *Maracotta, Lindsay*

The Dead Horse Paint Company — *Emerson, Earl*

c Dead Letter — *Byars, Betsy*

The Dead Letter — *Regester, Seeley*

c Dead Letters — *Wright, Susan Kimmel*

c Dead Log Alive! — *Kittinger, Jo S*

Dead Man Falling — *Silvis, Randall*

A Dead Man out of Mind — *Charles, Kate*

y Dead Man's Sweetheart — *Linscott, Gillian*

Dead Men Do Tell Tales — *Maples, William R*

Dead Men Don't Dance — *Chittenden, Margaret*

The Dead of Winter — *Gosling, Paula*

The Dead of Winter — *Hall, Patricia*

Dead over Heels — *Harris, Charlaine*

Dead Reckoning — *Glavin, Terry*

Dead Reckoning — *LaTour, Susan*

Dead Reckoning — *Treadway, David C*

Dead Right — *Frum, David*

Dead Ringer — *Francome, John*

y Dead Ringer — *Hamley, Dennis*

c Dead Sailors Don't Bite (Illus. by Ann James) — *Fienberg, Anna*

The Dead Sea Poems — *Armitage, Simon*

c The Dead Sea Scrolls (Illus. by John Thompson) — *Cooper, Ilene*

The Dead Sea Scrolls — *Fisdel, Steven A*

The Dead Sea Scrolls — *Hanson, Kenneth*

The Dead Sea Scrolls — *Wise, Michael*

The Dead Sea Scrolls in English. 4th Ed., Rev. and Extended — *Dead Sea Scrolls. English*

The Dead Sea Scrolls on Microfiche

The Dead Sea Scrolls (Wise) — *Dead Sea Scrolls. English*

Dead Season — *Berlow, Alan*

Dead Silent — *Ferrigno, Robert*

Dead Snails Leave No Trails — *Nancarrow, Loren*

Dead Souls — *Gogol, Nikolai*

Dead Things — *Calder, Richard*

Dead to Rights — *Jance, J A*

Dead White Female — *Henderson, Lauren*

c Dead Worried! — *Simons, Moya*

c Deadline — *Weiner, Eric*

Deadline for Murder — *McDermid, Val*

Deadly Care — *Goldberg, Leonard S*

Deadly Dreams — *Schiller, Gerald A*

The Deadly Embrace — *Kass, Ilana*

Deadly Feasts — *Rhodes, Richard*

y Deadly Games — *Masters, Anthony*

Deadly Harvest — *Goldberg, Leonard S*

Deadly Impression — *Asen, Dennis*

A Deadly Judgment — *Bain, Donald*

Deadly Medicine — *Mancall, Peter C*

Deadly Obsession — *Ellis, Julie*

A Deadly Operation — *Goldberg, Marshall*

Deadly Partners — *Green, Christine*

Deadly Prospects — *Crosby, Virginia*

Deadly Pursuit (Addison). Audio Version — *Olsen, T V*

A Deadly Shade of Gold (McGavin). Audio Version — *MacDonald, John D*

Deadly Valentine (Reading). Audio Version — *Hart, Carolyn*

A Deadly Vineyard Holiday — *Craig, Philip R*

Deadly Waters — *Meehan, Christopher H*

Deadrush — *Navarro, Yvonne*

y The Deadwood Conspiracy — *Garretson, James D*

Deaf President Now! — *Christiansen, John B*

The Deal — *Willett, Sabin*

Deal on Ice — *Standiford, Les*

c Deal with a Ghost — *Singer, Marilyn*

Dealing with Aggression and Violence in Your Workplace — *Pantry, Sheila*

Dealing with an Angry Public — *Susskind, Lawrence*

c Dealing with Anger — *Johnston, Marianne*

c Dealing with Bullying — *Johnston, Marianne*

y Dealing with Dragons. Audio Version — *Wrede, Patricia C*

c Dealing with Fighting — *Johnston, Marianne*

c Dealing with Insults — *Johnston, Marianne*

c Dealing with Jealousy — *Croft, Priscilla*

Dealing with Risk — *Margolis, Howard*

c Dealing with Weapons at School and at Home — *Apel, Lorelei*

The Dealings of Daniel Kesserich — *Leiber, Fritz*

The Dean and DeLuca Cookbook — *Rosengarten, David*

y Dean Duffy — *Powell, Randy*

y Dean Duffy (Woodman). Audio Version — *Powell, Randy*

The Deanna Durbin Fairy Tale — *Mills, W E*

The Dean's List — *Chansky, Art*

The Dean's List — *Hassler, Jon*

y The Dean's Watch — *Goudge, Elizabeth*

y Dear Bruno (Illus. by Edward Koren) — *Trillin, Alice Stewart*

Dear Commissioner — *Coates, Ken*

Dear Diary — *Neubauer, Joan R*

Dear Digby — *Muske, Carol*

Dear Dr. Menninger — *Faulkner, Howard J*

Dear Dodie — *Grove, Valerie*

c Dear Elijah — *Bat-Ami, Miriam*

Dear Elvis — *Wright, Daniel*

c Dear Fred (Illus. by Kim Gamble) — *Rodell, Susanna*

c Dear Friend — *Bentley, Judith*

Dear Future — *D'Aguiar, Fred*

y Dear Great American Writers School — *Bunin, Sherry*

c Dear Hope...Love, Grandma — *Hurwitz, Hilda Abramson*

Dear Job Stressed — *Dempcy, Mary*

y Dear Judy, Did You Ever Like a Boy (Who Didn't Like You?) — *Baer, Judy*

y Dear Judy, What's It like at Your House? — *Baer, Judy*

Dear Kathleen, Dear Manning — *Clark, C M H*

c Dear Laura: Letters from Children to Laura Ingalls Wilder

Dear London — *Kurtz, Irma*

Dear Marian, Dear Hugh — *MacLennan, Hugh*

y Dear Michael — *Akagi, Cynthia G*

Dear Mister Rogers, Does It Ever Rain in Your Neighborhood? — *Rogers, Fred*

Dear Mother — *Woolsey, Marijke*

Dear Mr. Capote — *Lish, Gordon*

c Dear Mrs. Parks — *Parks, Rosa*

c Dear Mum, Don't Panic (Illus. by Stephen Lewis) — *Bradman, Tony*

c Dear Oklahoma City, Get Well Soon — *Ross, Jim*

c The Dear Old Briar-Patch (Norang). Audio Version — *Burgess, Thornton W*

c Dear Old Donegal (Illus. by John O'Brien) — *Graham, Steve*

c Dear Peter Rabbit (Illus. by Leslie Tryon) — *Ada, Alma Flor*

c Dear Peter Rabbit — *Potter, Beatrix*

The Dear Purchase — *Stern, J P*

Dear Reader — *Stewart, Garrett*

Dear Rogue — *Weinstat, Hertzel*

Dear Sappho — *Turner, Kay*

Dear Stranger — *Cameron, Stella*

c Dear Tooth Fairy (Illus. by Fran Thatcher) — *Mellentin, Kath*

Dear Uncle George — *Pound, Ezra*

Dear Writer. Rev. and Expanded Ed. — *Bird, Carmel*

Dear Writer, Dear Actress — *Chekhov, Anton Pavlovich*

Dear Zoe — *De Pree, Max*

Dearest Chums and Partners — *Harris, Joel Chandler*

Dearest Wilding — *Eastman, Yvette*

Dearing and Beyond — *Hodgson, Ann*

Death — *Fingarette, Herbert*

y Death and Beyond — *Watkins, James*

Death and Burial in Medieval England — *Daniell, Christopher*

Death and Deliverance — *Burleigh, Michael*

Death and Dying, Life and Living. 2nd Ed. — *Corr,
Charles A*
Death and Exile — *McCarthy, Justin*
The Death and Life of Bobby Z — *Winslow, Don*
The Death and Life of Bobby Z (Larson). Audio
Version — *Winslow, Don*
The Death and Life of Miguel De Cervantes
— *Marlowe, Stephen, 1928-*
The Death and Rebirth of American Radicalism
— *Aronowitz, Stanley*
Death and Representation — *Goodwin, Sarah Webster*
The Death and Resurrection of the Beloved Son
— *Levenson, Jon D*
Death and the Dervish — *Selimovic, Mesa*
Death and the Language of Happiness — *Straley, John*
Death and the Pregnant Virgin — *Haymon, S T*
Death and the Prince — *D'Avray, D L*
Death at Buckingham Palace — *Benison, C C*
Death at Rainy Mountain — *Medawar, Mardi Oakley*
y Death at the Dolphin (Saxon). Audio Version
— *Marsh, Ngaio*
Death at the Table — *Laurence, Janet*
Death at the Wheel — *Flora, Kate*
Death Blossoms — *Abu-Jamal, Mumia*
Death by Spaghetti — *Sussman, Paul*
Death Comes for Peter Pan — *Brady, Joan*
Death Comes in Yellow — *Karay, Felicja*
The Death Cycle Machine — *Mayerson, Charlotte*
Death Duty — *Kimball, Stephen*
Death, Ecstasy, and Other Worldly Journeys
— *Collins, John J*
Death-Fires Dance — *Steinberg, Janice*
Death in a Delphi Seminar — *Holland, Norman
Norwood*
Death in a Mood Indigo — *Mathews, Francine*
Death in Equality — *Ebersole, Lucinda*
Death in High Heels — *Brand, Christianna*
A Death in Jerusalem — *Marton, Kati*
Death in Little Tokyo — *Furutani, Dale*
Death in Lovers' Lane — *Hart, Carolyn*
Death in Milton's Poetry — *Daniel, Clay*
y Death in the Afternoon — *Chester, Kate*
Death in the Andes — *Vargas Llosa, Mario*
Death in the Metropolis — *Landers, John*
Death in the Palazzo — *Sklepowich, Edward*
A Death in the Tiwi Islands — *Venbrux, Eric*
Death in the Victorian Family — *Jalland, Pat*
A Death in Victory — *Bean, Gregory*
Death Is Now My Neighbor — *Dexter, Colin*
Death Is Now My Neighbor (Whately). Audio Version
— *Dexter, Colin*
Death Is Now My Neighbour — *Dexter, Colin*
The Death of a Confederate — *Skinner, Arthur N*
Death of a Garden — *Ripley, Ann*
Death of a Healing Woman — *Martin, Allana*
Death of a Hero — *Haymon, S T*
Death of a Macho Man — *Beaton, M C*
Death of a Sunday Writer — *Wright, Eric*
Death of a Winter Shaker — *Woodworth, Deborah*
y Death of an Adept — *Kurtz, Katherine*
Death of an Angel — *O'Marie, Carol Anne*
The Death of an Irish Sea Wolf — *Gill, Bartholomew*
The Death of Character — *Fuchs, Elinor*
The Death of Class — *Pakulski, Jan*
The Death of Competition — *Moore, James F*
The Death of Death — *Gillman, Neil*
The Death of Discourse — *Collins, Ronald K L*
The Death of Frank Sinatra — *Ventura, Michael*
The Death of Friends — *Nava, Michael*
The Death of Inflation — *Bootle, Roger*
The Death of Jesus — *Green, Joel B*
y The Death of Princes — *Peel, John*
The Death of Satan — *Delbanco, Andrew*
The Death of Socialism and Other Poems — *Mathews,
Robin*
The Death of Socrates and the Life of Philosophy
— *Ahrensdorf, Peter J*
Death of Somoza — *Alegria, Claribel*
The Death of Tarpons — *Edgerton, Leslie*
y The Death of Tecumseh (Illus. by Paul McCusker)
— *Berton, Pierre*
The Death of the Banker — *Chernow, Ron*
The Death of the Child Valerio Marcello — *King,
Margaret L*
Death of the Guilds — *Krause, Elliott A*
The Death of the Messiah. Vols. 1-2 — *Brown,
Raymond Edward*
Death on a Vineyard Beach — *Craig, Philip R*
y Death on the Mississippi — *Heck, Peter J*
y Death or Glory Boys — *Breslin, Theresa*
y The Death Penalty. 3rd Ed., Rev. — *Winters, Paul A*

The Death Penalty as Cruel Treatment and Torture
— *Schabas, William A*
The Death Penalty in America — *Bedau, Hugo A*
Death to Dust — *Iserson, Kenneth V*
Death to the Death of Poetry — *Hall, Donald, 1928-*
c Death Valley National Park — *Petersen, David*
y Death Walker — *Thurlo, Aimee*
y Death Walks Tonight — *Horowitz, Anthony*
c Death's Door — *Byars, Betsy*
Deathtripping — *Sergeant, Jack*
The Debate on Money in Europe — *Giovannini,
Alberto*
Debateable Land — *McWilliam, Candia*
Debates in the House of Representatives. Vols. 1-5
— *United States. Congress (1st: 1789-1791). House*
Debating Derrida — *Lucy, Niall*
Debating Revolutions — *Keddie, Nikki R*
Debating the Democratic Peace — *Brown, Michael E*
Debating the Future of American Education
— *Ravitch, Diane*
Debating the Future of Philosophy — *Habermas,
Jurgen*
Debbi Fields' Great American Desserts — *Fields,
Debbi*
Debord Est Mort, Le Che Aussi, Et Alors? — *Guegan,
Gerard*
Debrett's Tracing Your Ancestors
The Debris of Planets — *Doucet, Clive*
r Debt and Adjustment in the World Economy — *Vos,
Rob*
Debt Games — *Aggarwal, Vinod K*
Debt, Investment, Slaves — *Kilbourne, Richard
Holcombe, Jr.*
Debt of Honour — *Clancy, Tom*
The Debt to Pleasure — *Lanchester, John*
y The Debt to Pleasure (Ullett). Audio Version
— *Lanchester, John*
Debt Wish — *Sbragia, Alberta M*
Debugging and Performance Tuning for Parallel
Computing Systems — *Hayes, Ann H*
Decade of Betrayal — *Balderrama, Francisco E*
A Decade of Debate and Division — *Gardner, Robert
G*
Decade of Protest — *Martin, Susan*
Decadence and the Making of Modernism — *Weir,
David*
The Decalogue and a Human Future — *Lehmann,
Paul L*
r The Decca Labels. Vols. 1-6 — *Ruppli, Michel*
The Deceived Husband — *Sinclair, Alison*
The Decency of Inequality — *Stolen, Kristi Anne*
A Decent Boldness — *Trainor, Michael*
A Decent Proposal — *Evans, Donald*
The Decent Society — *Margalit, Avishai*
Decentralization of the Socialist State — *Bird, Richard
Miller*
The Deception — *Reed, Barry*
The Deception — *Wolf, Joan*
Deception on His Mind — *George, Elizabeth*
Deception Well — *Nagata, Linda*
Deciding to Be Legal — *Hagan, Jacqueline Maria*
Deciding to Intervene — *Scott, James M*
Deciphering the Balkan Enigma. 1st Rev. Ed.
— *Johnsen, William T*
Deciphering the Signs of God — *Schimmel, Annemarie*
Decision and Discrete Mathematics — *Price, Nigel*
Decision and Stress — *Broadbent, Donald E*
Decision: How the Supreme Court Decides Cases
— *Schwartz, Bernard*
Decision Making in Action — *Klein, Gary A*
Decision Making in Deng's China — *Hamrin, Carol
Lee*
Decision Making Structures — *Catalani, Mario S*
Decision Theory as Philosophy — *Kaplan, Mark*
The Decision to Drop the Atomic Bomb — *Wainstock,
Dennis D*
y The Decision to Use the Atomic Bomb and the
Architecture of an American Myth — *Alperovitz,
Gar*
Decisions and Diplomacy — *Richardson, Dick*
Decisions for War 1914 — *Wilson, Keith*
Decisive Force — *Hoffman, F G*
c Deck the Halls (Illus. by Iris Van Rynbach)
Declarations of Independence — *Hockenberry, John*
Declares Pereira — *Tabucchi, Antonio*
The Decline and Fall of Medieval Sicily — *Backman,
Clifford R*
The Decline and Fall of the American Empire
— *Bouza, Tony*
The Decline (and Fall?) of the Income Tax — *Graetz,
Michael J*

The Decline and Fall of the Soviet Empire
— *Coleman, Fred*
Decline and Growth in English Towns 1400-1640
— *Dyer, Alan*
The Decline of British Radicalism 1847-1860
— *Taylor, Miles*
The Decline of Deference — *Nevitte, Neil*
The Decline of Eastern Christianity under Islam
— *Bat Ye'or*
The Decline of Iranshahr — *Christensen, Peter*
The Decline of the Goddess — *Stave, Shirley A*
Decolonization and African Society — *Cooper,
Frederick*
Decolonization and Independence in Kenya 1940-93
— *Ogot, Bethwell A*
Decomposition, Combustion and Detonation
Chemistry of Energetic Materials — *Brill, Thomas B*
Deconstructing Apartheid Discourse — *Norval, Aletta
J*
Deconstructing the Mind — *Stich, Stephen P*
Deconstructing Web Graphics — *Weinman, Lynda*
Deconstruction and the Ethical Turn — *Baker, Peter*
Deconstruction and the Visual Arts — *Brunette, Peter*
Deconstruction in a Nutshell — *Caputo, John D*
Decorated Cloth in America — *Allen, Sue*
Decorating Eggs — *Pollak, Jane*
Decorating Entrances, Stairways and Landings
— *Berry, Susan*
Decorating in Blue and White — *Burgess, Lynda*
Decorating Old House Interiors — *Schwin, Lawrence*
The Decoration of the Royal Basilica of El Escorial
— *Mulcahy, Rosemarie*
y Decorative Gilding — *Sloan, Annie*
Decorative Ironwork — *Baur-Heinhold, Margarete*
Decorative Paint Effects — *Sloan, Annie*
The Decorative Tile in Architecture and Interiors
— *Herbert, Tony*
Decorative Walls — *Brand, Salli*
Decorum and Wit — *Fehl, Philipp P*
Decoupage — *Macchiavelli, M*
The Dedalus Book of Dutch Fantasy — *Huijing,
Richard*
The Dedalus Book of Polish Fantasy — *Powaga,
Wiesiek*
Dedication to Hunger — *Heywood, Leslie*
Deed of Gift — *Dalibard, Jill*
Deemed Unsuitable — *Shepard, R Bruce*
Deense Keramiek
y Deep as the Marrow — *Wilson, F Paul*
Deep as the Rivers — *Henke, Shirl*
y Deep Atlantic — *Ellis, Richard*
Deep Blue Almost Black — *Valtinos, Thanassis*
Deep Blues — *Palmer, Robert*
Deep Change — *Quinn, Robert E*
Deep Citizenship — *Clarke, Paul A B*
c Deep Doo-Doo — *Delaney, Michael*
Deep Ecology for the 21st Century — *Sessions, George*
The Deep End of the Ocean — *Mitchard, Jacquelyn*
y The Deep End of the Ocean (Cassidy). Audio Version
— *Mitchard, Jacquelyn*
y The Deep End of the Ocean (Ivey). Audio Version
— *Mitchard, Jacquelyn*
Deep in the Green — *Raver, Anne*
Deep River — *Endo, Shusaku*
A Deep Sense of Wrong — *Boissery, Beverley*
Deep Sightings and Rescue Missions — *Bambara, Toni
Cade*
Deep Space Nine — *Altman, Mark*
Deep Valley Malice — *Mitchell, Kirk*
c Deep Water (Illus. by Kenny McKendry) — *Turnbull,
Ann*
Deep Water Passage — *Linnea, Ann*
Deep Waters — *Krentz, Jayne Ann*
Deeper: My Two-Year Odyssey in Cyberspace
— *Seabrook, John*
A Deeper Silence — *Stewart, A T Q*
Deer: A Personal View — *Alcock, Ian*
The Deer Pasture — *Bass, Rick*
y Deerskin — *McKinley, Robin*
The Defeat of the German U-Boats — *Syrett, David*
The Defeat of the Mind — *Finkielkraut, Alain*
Defect Recognition and Image Processing in
Semiconductors 1995
Defence Doctrines and Conversion — *Moller, Bjorn*
A Defence of the Constitutions of Government of the
United States of America. Vols. 1-3 — *Adams, John,
1735-1826*
y Defend and Betray (Porter). Audio Version — *Perry,
Anne*
Defender of the Valley — *Woodward, Harold R, Jr.*
Defenders of God — *Lawrence, Bruce B*

Defenders of the Holy Land — *Phillips, Jonathan*
Defenders of the Race — *Efron, John M*
Defending Mexican Valor in Texas — *Navarro, Jose Antonio*
Defending Mother Earth — *Weaver, Jace*
Defending Our Lives — *Murphy-Milano, Susan*
Defending Pornography — *Strossen, Nadine*
Defending Rights — *Askin, Frank*
Defending the Faith — *Hart, D G*
Defending the Land of the Jaguar — *Simonian, Lane*
Defending Your Brand against Imitation — *Zaichkowsky, Judith Lynne*
Defense Base Closure and Realignment Commission: 1993 Report to the President — *United States. Defense Base Closure and Realignment Commission*
Defense Conversion — *Gansler, Jacques S*
Defense Industries in Latin American Countries — *Maldifassi, Jose O*
y The Defense Is Ready — *Abramson, Leslie*
The Defense Is Ready (Abramson). Audio Version — *Abramson, Leslie*
A Defense of Galileo, the Mathematician from Florence — *Campanella, Thomas*
A Defense of Poetry — *Fry, Paul H*
Defensor Minor. De Translatione Imperii — *Marsilius, of Padua*
Le Defi Des Langues — *Piron, Claude*
Defiance County — *Brandon, Jay*
y The Defiant: A True Story — *Yorun, Shalom*
Defining Dominion — *Williams, Gerhild Scholz*
Defining Jamaican Fiction — *Lalla, Barbara*
Defining Russia Musically — *Taruskin, Richard*
Defining Science — *Taylor, Charles Alan*
Defining Science — *Yeo, Richard*
Defining the Common Good — *Miller, Peter N*
Defining the Enemy — *Newman, Michael*
Defining Vision — *Brinkley, Joel*
Defining Women — *D'Acci, Julie*
Definition — *Vedral, Joyce L*
r The Definitive Andy Griffith Show Reference — *Robinson, Dale*
y The Definitive Biography of P.D.Q. Bach (Schickele). Audio Version — *Schickele, Peter*
r Definitive Country — *McCloud, Barry*
Defoe De-Attributions — *Furbank, P N*
Deformed Discourse — *Williams, David*
Defy the Death Spirit — *Vinh, Le Quang*
Defying Male Civilization — *Nash, Mary*
c Degas and the Little Dancer (Illus. by Laurence Anholt) — *Anholt, Laurence*
Degas as a Collector — *Dumas, Ann*
Degas: Beyond Impressionism — *Kendall, Richard*
Degas by Himself — *Degas, Edgar*
Degeneration, Culture and the Novel 1880-1940 — *Greenslade, William*
Degrees of Control — *Brown, David K*
Degrees of Disaster — *Wheelwright, Jeff*
The Degrees of Knowledge — *Maritain, Jacques*
Dehexing Sex — *Goscilo, Helena*
Dehumanizing the Vulnerable — *Brennan, William*
Dehydration of Foods — *Barbosa-Canovas, Gustavo V*
c Deion Sanders — *Chadwick, Bruce*
c Deion Sanders: Prime Time — *Harvey, Miles*
c Deion Sanders: Star Athlete — *Savage, Jeff*
Dekker and Heywood — *McLuskie, Kathleen E*
DeKok and Murder on the Menu — *Baantjer, A C*
Del Amor Y Otros Demonios — *Garcia Marquez, Gabriel*
Dela — *Brochu, Andre*
Delacroix Pastels — *Johnson, Lee*
Delaware Diary — *Dale, Frank*
r Delaware-English/English-Delaware Dictionary — *O'Meara, John*
Delegation of Nursing Activities — *Kane, Rosalie*
Deleites De La Cocina Mexicana — *Urdaneta, Maria Luisa*
Delia Webster and the Underground Railroad — *Runyon, Randolph Paul*
A Delicate Balance — *Albee, Edward*
The Delicate Balance — *Schulkin, Jay*
Les Delices De Nos Coeurs — *Gourdeau, Claire*
Delights for the Senses — *Ember, Ildiko*
c Delilah and the Dishwasher Dogs (Illus. by Ben Cort) — *Nimmo, Jenny*
c Delilah and the Dogspell (Illus. by Emma Chichester Clark) — *Nimmo, Jenny*
Delinquent Daughters — *Odem, Mary E*
El Delito Por Bailar El Chachacha — *Cabrera Infante, G*
y Deliver Us from Evie — *Kerr, M E*
Deliver Us from Evil — *Luber, Philip*

Deliverance Drive — *Ledbetter, Suzann*
c The Deliverance of Dancing Bears — *Stanley, Elizabeth*
c The Deliverers of Their Country (Illus. by Lisbeth Zwerger) — *Nesbit, E*
Delivrance Et Convivialite — *Mahias, Marie-Claude*
Delo IAkubovskogo. Tochny: Udar — *Belousov, Vladimir*
Delphi 2 — *Kellen, Vince*
Delphi Database Development — *Blue, Ted*
The Delta Factor — *Locke, Thomas*
y Delta Search — *Shatner, William*
A Delusion of Satan — *Hill, Frances*
Delusions of Everyday Life — *Shengold, Leonard*
The Deluxe Transitive Vampire — *Gordon, Karen Elizabeth*
c Dem Bones (Illus. by Bob Barner)
Demand and Get the Best Health Care for You — *Prout, Curtis*
y Demelza (Britton). Audio Version — *Graham, Winston*
r Dementia — *Burns, Alistair*
The Demise of Environmentalism in American Law — *Greve, Michael S*
Democracies and Foreign Policy — *Cohen, Bernard C*
Democracies of Unfreedom — *Mohan, Brij*
Democracy: A Short, Analytical History — *Stromberg, Roland N*
Democracy against Capitalism — *Wood, Ellen Meiksins*
Democracy and Arab Political Culture — *Kedourie, Elie*
Democracy and Authoritarianism in South Asia — *Jalal, Ayesha*
Democracy and Development in Africa — *Ake, Claude*
Democracy and Disagreement — *Gutmann, Amy*
Democracy and Efficiency in the Economic Enterprise — *Pagano, Ugo*
Democracy and Green Political Thought — *Doherty, Brian*
Democracy and Halakhah — *Schweid, Eliezer*
Democracy and International Conflict — *Ray, James Lee*
Democracy and International Trade — *Verdier, Daniel*
Democracy and Its Discontents — *Wiarda, Howard J*
Democracy and Political Change in Sub-Saharan Africa — *Wiseman, John A*
Democracy and Social Injustice — *Simon, Thomas W*
Democracy and Technology — *Sclove, Richard E*
Democracy and the Global Order — *Held, David*
Democracy and the Kingdom of God — *Kainz, Howard P*
Democracy by Other Means — *Buell, John*
Democracy, Capitalism, and Empire in Late Victorian Britain 1885-1910 — *Wellhofer, E Spencer*
Democracy, Development, and the Countryside — *Varshney, Ashutosh*
Democracy, Dialogue, and Environmental Disputes — *Williams, Bruce A*
Democracy, Education, and the Schools — *Soder, Roger*
Democracy from Below — *Koopmans, Ruud*
Democracy from Scratch — *Fish, M Steven*
Democracy: History, Theory, Practice — *Lakoff, Sanford*
Democracy Imposed — *Merritt, Richard L*
Democracy in Latin America — *Camp, Roderic Ai*
Democracy in Postwar Japan — *Kersten, Rikki*
Democracy, Markets, and Structural Reform in Latin America — *Smith, William C*
Democracy, Multiculturalism, and the Community College — *Rhoads, Robert A*
A Democracy of Despots — *Murray, Don, 1947-*
Democracy on Trial — *Smith, Page*
Democracy, Security, and Development in India — *Thomas, Raju G C*
Democracy, Sovereignty and the European Union — *Newman, Michael, 1946-*
Democracy without Equity — *Weyland, Kurt Gerhard*
Democracy's Discontent — *Sandel, Michael J*
Democracy's Feast — *Weisberg, Herbert F*
Democracy's Oxygen — *Winter, James*
Democracy's Place — *Shapiro, Ian*
Democratic Ideas and the British Labour Movement 1880-1914 — *Barrow, Logie*
Democratic Miners — *Blatz, Perry K*
Democratic Philosophy and the Politics of Knowledge — *Peterson, Richard T*
Democratic Reform and the Position of Women in Transitional Economies — *Moghadam, Valentine M*
Democratic Religion — *Wills, Gregory A*

Democratic Royalism — *Kuhn, William M*
Democratic Spain — *Gillespie, Richard*
Democratic Subjects — *Joyce, Patrick*
Democratic Temperament — *Miller, Joshua*
Democratic Transitions in Central America — *Dominguez, Jorge I*
Democraticon: For a Democratic Democracy — *Morina, Mimmo*
Les Democraties Antillaises En Crise — *Martin, Denis-Constant*
Democratisation Processes in Africa — *Chole, Eshetu*
Democratization and Social Settlements — *Nataf, Daniel*
Democratization and the Protection of Human Rights in Africa — *Ambrose, Brendalyn P*
Democratization in Russia — *Hahn, Jeffrey W*
Democratization Liberalization and Human Rights in the Third World — *Monshipouri, Mahmood*
Democratizing Mexico — *Dominguez, Jorge I*
Democrats under Siege in the Sunbelt Megastates — *Nelson, Albert J*
Democrite: Grains De Poussiere Dans Un Rayon De Soleil — *Salem, Jean*
r Demographic Yearbook 1994
Demography and Empire — *Lovell, W George*
The Demography of Famines — *Maharatna, Arup*
The Demography of Roman Egypt — *Bagnall, Roger S*
Les Demoiselles De La Legion D'Honneur — *Rogers, Rebecca*
Demokratie Und Menschenrechte In Der Arabischen Welt — *Jurgensen, Carsten*
The Demolished Man — *Bester, Alfred*
c Demolition Derby — *Savage, Jeff*
Demon and Other Tales — *Oates, Joyce Carol*
y The Demon Awakens — *Salvatore, R A*
The Demon-Haunted World — *Sagan, Carl*
c The Demon Headmaster Strikes Again — *Cross, Gillian*
The Demon Princes. Vol. 1 — *Vance, Jack*
Demonic Males — *Wrangham, Richard W*
Demonizing the Queen of Sheba — *Lassner, Jacob*
Demons and the Devil — *Stewart, Charles*
Demons Five, Exorcists Nothing — *Blatty, William Peter*
Demons, Nausea, and Resistance in the Autobiography of Isabel De Jesus 1611-1682 — *Velasco, Sherry M*
Die Demontage Deutscher Naturwissenschaftlicher Intelligenz Nach Dem 2. Weltkrieg — *Peltzer, Lilli*
p Demos
Demystifying ISO 9000 — *Paradis, Gerard W*
Demystifying Tibet — *Feigon, Lee*
y Den of the White Fox — *Namioka, Lensey*
Den Pessimismus Organisieren — *Dunker, Axel*
c Denali National Park and Preserve — *Petersen, David*
Deng Xiaoping: Chronicle of an Empire — *Ruan, Ming*
The Deng Xiaoping Era — *Meisner, Maurice*
Deng Xiaoping: Portrait of a Chinese Statesman — *Shambaugh, David*
Denial — *Ablow, Keith*
Denial — *Comfort, Bonnie*
Denial of the Soul — *Peck, M Scott*
Denmark in the Thirty Years' War 1618-1648 — *Lockhart, Paul Douglas*
Denne Gangen Horer Du Deg Selv. Vol. 2 — *Kiosterud, Erland*
c Dennis Dipp on Gilbert's Pond (Illus. by Arthur Robins) — *Warburton, Nick*
Density Functional Theory — *Gross, Eberhard K U*
Density Matrix Theory and Applications. 2nd Ed. — *Blum, Karl*
Dentin/Pulp Complex
The Denver Art Museum — *Harris, Neil*
The Denver Zoo — *Etter, Carolyn*
Deontology and Teleology — *Salzman, Todd A*
Depardieu — *Chutkow, Paul*
Depardieu: A Biography — *Chutkow, Paul*
The Department Store — *Lancaster, Bill*
Departures — *Cornell, Jennifer C*
Dependence Analysis — *Banerjee, Utpal*
Dependence in Context in Renaissance Florence — *Trexler, Richard C*
Dependency and Development — *Lewellen, Ted C*
The Dependent City Revisited — *Kantor, Paul*
The Depleted Self — *Capps, Donald*
Deportation and Exile — *Sword, Keith*
c Depression and Mental Health — *Sanders, Pete*
Depression and the Spiritual in Modern Art — *Schildkraut, Joseph*
y Derby Dugan's Depression Funnies — *De Haven, Tom*
Derby Magic — *Bolus, Jim*

Derechos Humanos De La Mujer — *Arango Durling, Virginia*

Deregulating Freight Transportation — *Teske, Paul*

Deregulating Telecommunications — *Higgins, Richard S*

Derek Jarman: A Portrait — *Wollen, Roger*

Derek Jarman: Dreams of England — *O'Pray, Michael*

Derek Walcott's Poetry — *Terada, Rei*

c Derek's Dog Days (Illus. by Chris L Demarest) — *Charlton, Nancy Lee*

y Derelict for Trade — *Norton, Andre*

Dereliction of Duty — *McMaster, H R*

Derivatives: A Comprehensive Resource for Options, Futures, Interest Rate Swaps, and Mortgage Securities — *Arditti, Fred D*

Dermatology and Person-Threatening Illness — *Walther, Robert R*

Dermatology Secrets — *Fitzpatrick, James E*

Le Dernier Des Aloukous — *Brival, Roland*

Le Dernier Voyage D'Ago Umeri — *Shehu, Bashkim*

La Derniere Repetition — *Jaumain, Claire*

Les Derniers Jours De Corinthe — *Robbe-Grillet, Alain*

Derrida and Autobiography — *Smith, Robert, 1965-*

Derrida and Wittgenstein — *Garver, Newton*

Derrida for Beginners — *Collins, Jeff*

Dersu the Trapper — *Arseniev, V K*

The Dervish Wars — *Neillands, Robin*

Derzhavna Zrada? — *Lapica, Rey*

Des Nobel Au Vatican — *Ladous, Regis*

Des Roles Et Missions De L'Universite — *Berleur, Jacques*

Los Desaffos Del Siglo XXI Desde America Latina — *Arias Sanchez, Oscar*

Descartes: An Intellectual Biography — *Gaukroger, Stephen*

Descartes and His Contemporaries — *Ariew, Roger*

Descartes Et L'Argumentation Philosophique

y Descartes in 90 Minutes — *Strathern, Paul*

Descartes on Seeing — *Wolf-Devine, Celia*

Descartes's Imagination — *Sepper, Dennis L*

The Descendant — *Dugdale, Joan*

Descendants De Chouans — *Bucher, Bernadette*

r Descendants of Jeremiah Mitchell of North Carolina (circa 1770-circa 1835) and Allied Families — *Horne, Ann Mitchell*

r Descendants of John Fogo and Mary Lambie — *Fogo, Rod*

Descendants of John Moore (Revolutionary War Soldier) and Mary Keller Moore — *Moore, Mack Arthur*

Descendants of Nicholas Humes of Massachusetts. Vol. 1 — *Humes, Charles Warren*

The Descendants of Richard Byrd (1818-189?) and (1) Rebecca Norman, and (2) Mary Jane Vinson — *Byrd, James*

Descendants of Salomon Bloch of Janowitz, Bohemia, and Baruch Wollman of Kempenin-Posen, Prussia — *Curran, Joan Ferris*

The Descent of Alette — *Notley, Alice*

The Descent of Love — *Bender, Bert*

The Descent to the Chariot — *Kuyt, Annelies*

Describing Early America — *Regis, Pamela*

Descripcion Geografica Y Estadistica Del Distrito De Cuernavaca 1826 — *Orellana, Ignacio*

Descripcion Geografica Y Estadistica Del Distrito De Tulacingo 1825 — *Ortega, Francisco*

r A Descriptive Catalogue of the Jorge Luis Borges Collection at the University of Virginia Library — *Lowenstein, C Jared*

Descriptive Inorganic Chemistry — *Rayner-Canham, Geoffrey*

Descriptive Psychology — *Brentano, Franz Clemens*

Descriptive Translation Studies and Beyond — *Toury, Gideon*

c Descubre El Colage — *Bohera, Carme*

c Desde El Principio — *Platt, Richard*

Desecrating the American Flag — *Goldstein, Robert Justin*

Desencanto Al Amanecer — *Palma, Milagros*

El Desencuentro — *Schwartz, Fernando*

c Desert — *Ricciuti, Edward R*

Desert Aeolian Processes — *Tchakerian, Vatche P*

c Desert Babies (Illus. by Tara Darling) — *Darling, Kathy*

Desert Battle — *Watson, Bruce Allen*

A Desert Bestiary — *McNamee, Gregory*

c Desert Birds — *Flanagan, Alice K*

Desert Capitalism — *Kopinak, Kathryn*

y Desert Danger (Montbertrand). Audio Version — *Kehret, Peg*

The Desert Fathers on Monastic Community — *Gould, Graham*

y Desert Fathers, Uranium Daughters — *Greger, Debora*

c The Desert Fox Family Book (Illus. by Hans Gerold Laukel) — *Laukel, Hans Gerold*

Desert Frontier — *Webb, James L A, Jr.*

c Desert Mammals — *Landau, Elaine*

A Desert of Pure Feeling — *Freeman, Judith*

y Desert Places — *Davidson, Robyn*

Desert Queen — *Wallach, Janet*

c A Desert Scrapbook (Illus. by Virginia Wright-Frierson) — *Wright-Frierson, Virginia*

The Desert Seen — *Friedlander, Lee*

Desert Songs — *Maier, John R*

c Desert Trip (Illus. by Ronald Himler) — *Steiner, Barbara A*

The Desert World — *Jouve, Pierre Jean*

Desertification in Developed Countries — *International Symposium and Workshop on Desertification in Developed Countries: Why Can't We Control It? (1994: Tuscon, Ariz.)*

Deserts — *Ferrari, Marco*

c Deserts (Illus. by Gail Gibbons) — *Gibbons, Gail*

c Deserts — *Jenkins, Martin*

c Deserts — *Murray, Peter, 1952, Sep., 9-*

c Deserts — *Steele, Philip*

c Deserts and Drylands — *Parker, Steve*

c Deserts (Wonders of Our World) — *Morris, Neil*

c Deserts (World's Top Ten) (Illus. by Vanessa Card) — *Morris, Neil*

Design and Color in Islamic Architecture — *Barry, Michael*

The Design and Management of Poverty Reduction Programs and Projects in Anglophone Africa — *Bamberger, Michael*

Design by Motley — *Mullin, Michael*

Design Criteria for Drill Rigs — *Chugh, C P*

Design Criteria for Lighting Interior Living Spaces

Design for Dying — *Leary, Timothy*

Design for Environment — *Fiksel, Joseph*

Design for Manufacturing and Assembly — *Billatos, Samir B*

Design for the Future of Health Care — *Bryan, Larry*

Design Fundamentals of High Temperature Composites, Intermetallics, and Metal-Ceramics Systems — *Lin, Ray Y*

Design Lines — *Chavis, William Muse*

Design, Monitoring and Evaluation of Technical Cooperation Programmes and Projects

The Design of Bibliographies — *Berger, Sidney E*

Design of Low-Voltage, Low-Power Operational Amplifier Cells — *Hogervorst, Ron*

Design of Sheet Pile Walls

Design Sense — *Blair, Linda*

Design, Writing, Research — *Lupton, Ellen*

The Designated Mourner — *Shawn, Wallace*

Designed and Signed — *Pina, Leslie*

Designer Techniques — *King, Kenneth D*

Designing 3D Graphics — *White, Josh*

r Designing and Conducting Health Surveys. 2nd Ed. — *Aday, Lu Ann*

Designing and Making — *Stein, Georgina*

Designing and Making — *Thorp, Marilyn*

Designing Great Beers — *Daniels, Ray*

Designing Hard Software — *Bennett, Douglas W*

Designing Information Technology in the Postmodern Age — *Coyne, Richard*

Designing Innovations in Industrial Logistics Modeling — *Kusiak, Andrew*

Designing Large-Scale Web Sites — *Sano, Darrell*

Designing Modernity — *Kaplan, Wendy*

Designing Qualitative Research. 2nd Ed. — *Marshall, Catherine*

Designing the Earth — *Bourdon, David*

Designing the Molecular World — *Ball, Philip*

Designing Web Graphics. 2nd Ed. — *Weinman, Lynda*

Designing with Nature — *Yeang, Ken*

Designs and Finite Geometries — *Jungnickel, Dieter*

Designs on Posterity — *Jones, Mark*

Designs within Disorder — *Barber, William J*

The Desirable Body — *Stratton, Jon*

A Desirable Residence — *Wickham, Madeleine*

Desire and Anxiety — *Traub, Valerie*

Desire and Duty — *Bader, Ted*

Desire for Society — *Furth, Hans G*

Desire in Language — *Kristeva, Julia*

Desire: Its Role in Practical Reason and the Explanation of Action — *Schueler, G F*

y Desire Lines — *Gantos, Jack*

Desire: Love Stories in Western Culture — *Belsey, Catherine*

Desire Unlimited — *Smith, Paul Julian, 1960-*

Desiring Italy — *Cahill, Susan*

Desiring Theology — *Winquist, Charles E*

Desktop Guide to Creating CL Commands — *Nelson, Lynn, 1957-*

Desktop Publishing by Design. 4th Ed. — *Shushan, Ronnie*

La Desobeissance: Histoire D'Un Mouvement Et D'Un Journal Clandestins — *Douzou, Laurent*

Despatch on War Operations 23rd February 1942 to 8th May 1945 — *Harris, Arthur T*

Desperado — *Brandewyne, Rebecca*

Desperadoes: A Novel — *Hansen, Ron*

Desperate Crossings — *Zucker, Norman L*

A Desperate Passion — *Caldicott, Helen*

y Desperation — *King, Stephen*

Desperation (King). Audio Version — *King, Stephen*

c D'Est En Quest — *Mathieu, Pierre*

Destination Zero — *Hamill, Sam*

c Destins (Illus. by Frederic Eibner) — *Laberge, Marc*

Destiny Not Defeat — *Desai, Meghnad*

The Destiny of Nathalie X and Other Stories — *Boyd, William*

Destiny's Landfall — *Rogers, Robert F*

Destiny's Road — *Niven, Larry*

Destroyer Skipper — *Sheppard, Don*

The Destruction of Art — *Gamboni, Dario*

Destructiones Modorum Significandi — *Kaczmarek, Ludger*

The Detached Retina — *Aldiss, Brian W*

r Detecting Women 2

Detecting Women 2 — *Heising, Willetta L*

Detective — *Hailey, Arthur*

c Detective Dinosaur (Illus. by R W Alley) — *Skofield, James*

c Detective Donut and the Wild Goose Chase — *Whatley, Bruce*

c Detective Science (Illus. by Ed Shems) — *Wiese, Jim*

Detergents in the Environment — *Schwuger, Milan Johann*

The Determinants and Effects of Work-Related Training in Britain — *Blundell, Richard*

The Determination of Geophysical Parameters from Space — *Scottish Universities Summer School in Physics (43rd: 1994: Dundee, Scotland)*

Determining Your Public Library's Future Size — *Brawner, Lee B*

Deterministic Chaos. 3rd Ed. — *Schuster, Heinz Georg*

The Detox Diet — *Haas, Elson S*

Detraditionalization — *Heelas, Paul*

Deur Die Oog Van 'N Naald — *Phosa, Matthews*

Os Deuses Mortos — *Bulhoes, Antonio*

Deuteronomy — *Mann, Thomas W*

Das Deutsche Buch — *Fabian, Bernhard*

Deutsche Dienstmadchen In Amerika 1850-1914 — *Wehner-Franco, Silke*

Deutsche Europapolitik — *Deubner, Christian*

Deutsche Gesellschaftsgeschichte. Vol. 3 — *Wehler, Hans-Ulrich*

Deutsche Karikaturen — *Lammel, Gisold*

Deutsche Literatur Im Exil In Den Niederlanden 1933-1940 — *Wurzner, Hans*

Deutsche Partikeln--Richtig Gebraucht? — *Helbig, Gerhard*

Das Deutsche Reich In Der Sudsee 1900-1921 — *Hiery, Hermann Joseph*

Die Deutsche Sachliteratur Des Mittelalters — *Crossgrove, William*

Deutsche Science Fiction 1870-1914 — *Innerhofer, Ronald*

Deutschland Und Der Westen Im 19. Und 20. Jahrhundert. Vols. 1-2

Deutschland Und Polen Von 1918/19 Bis 1925 — *Schattkowsky, Ralph*

Devek Shkedim — *Zohar, Rakefet*

Developing a Consensus for the Future — *CSIS U.S. China Policy Task Force*

Developing an Integrated Library Program — *Miller, Donna*

Developing and Managing Video Collections — *Mason-Robinson, Sally*

Developing CGI Applications with Perl — *Deep, John*

Developing English

Developing Java Entertainment Applets — *Withers, John*

Developing Managerial Competence — *Tate, William*

Developing Online Help for Windows 95 — *Boggan, Scott*

Developing Readers' Advisory Services — *McCook, Kathleen De La Pena*
Developing Second Generation Client/Server Applications — *Cashin, Jerry*
Developing SGML DTDs — *Maker, Eve*
Developing The Antarctic Protected Area System — *SCAR/IUCN Workshop on Antarctic Protected Areas (1992: Cambridge, England)*
y **Developing the Environment** — *Barrow, C J*
Developing the Nonfarm Sector in Bangladesh — *Yusuf, Shahid*
Developing the UN Register of Conventional Arms — *Chalmers, Malcolm*
Developing Visual Programming Applications Using Smalltalk — *Linderman, Michael*
p **Development**
Development among Africa's Migratory Pastoralists — *Majok, Aggrey Ayuen*
Development and Application of Computer Techniques in Environmental Studies V
Development and the Arts — *Franklin, Margery B*
Development, Change, and Gender in Cairo — *Singerman, Diane*
The Development Dictionary — *Sachs, Wolfgang*
Development Finance as Institution Building — *Krahnen, Jan Pieter*
Development for Exploitation — *Koponen, Juhani*
Development, Geography, and Economic Theory — *Krugman, Paul*
p **Development in Practice**
Development Macroeconomics — *Agenor, Pierre-Richard*
Development Management in Africa — *Rasheed, Sadig*
The Development of Biological Systematics — *Stevens, Peter F*
The Development of Cognitive Anthropology — *D'Andrade, Roy*
The Development of Costume — *Tarrant, Naomi*
Development of Education in the Kingdom of Saudi Arabia 1992-1994
The Development of Language and Literacy — *Whitehead, Marian*
The Development of Local Public Services 1650-1860 — *McKinney, Hannah J*
The Development of Military Thought — *Gat, Azar*
The Development of Swedish and Keynesian Macroeconomic Theory and Its Impact on Economic Policy — *Lundberg, Erik*
The Development of the French Economy 1750-1914 — *Heywood, Colin*
Development Plan 1995/96-1997/98 — *Swaziland. Ministry of Economic Planning and Development. Economic Planning Office*
Development Planning — *Dupont, Louis*
Development Policy of a Communist Government — *Mallick, Ross*
Development Strategies in Africa — *Yansane, Aguibou Y*
Development Studies — *Corbridge, Stuart*
Development, Validation, and Application of Inelastic Methods for Structural Analysis and Design — *Sammataro, Robert F*
Developmental Dyslexia — *Chase, Christopher H*
Developmental Exercise Physiology — *Rowland, Thomas W*
Developmental Neuroimaging — *Thatcher, Robert W*
Developmental Neuropsychiatry. Vols. 1-2 — *Harris, James C*
Developmental Psychology. 4th Ed. — *Shaffer, David R*
The Developmental Psychopathology of Eating Disorders — *Smolak, Linda*
Developmentally Based Psychotherapy — *Greenspan, Stanley I*
Developments around the Baltic and the North Sea in the Viking Age — *Ambrosiani, Bjorn*
r **Developments in Dementia and Functional Disorders in the Elderly** — *Levy, Raymond*
Developments in Local Government Finance — *Pola, Giancarlo*
Developments in Psychotherapy — *Dryden, Windy*
Devi: Goddesses of India — *Hawley, John Stratton*
Deviant Bodies — *Terry, Jennifer*
Deviant Eyes, Deviant Bodies — *Straayer, Chris*
Deviant Logic, Fuzzy Logic — *Haack, Susan*
Devices for Optoelectronics — *Leigh, Wallace B*
The Devil: A Biography — *Stanford, Peter*
The Devil: A Biography. Audio Version — *Stanford, Peter*
The Devil: A Mask without a Face — *Link, Luther*
The Devil at Noonday — *Dunnam, Maxie*

The Devil Himself — *Hughes, John*
Devil in a Blue Dress (Windfield). Audio Version — *Mosley, Walter*
The Devil in the New World — *Cervantes, Fernando*
The Devil Is an Ass — *Jonson, Ben*
The Devil Knows How to Ride — *Leslie, Edward E*
y **The Devil Latch** — *Hartnett, Sonya*
The Devil Problem and Other True Stories — *Remnick, David*
y **The Devil's Arithmetic** — *Yolen, Jane*
y **The Devil's Arithmetic (Rosenblat). Audio Version** — *Yolen, Jane*
The Devil's Birthday — *Powell, Geoffrey*
The Devil's Box — *Wolfe, Charles*
The Devil's Carousel — *Torrington, Jeff*
The Devil's Disciples — *Hoffer, Peter Charles*
y **Devil's Engine** — *Sumner, Mark*
Devil's Food — *Bruno, Anthony*
Devil's Food — *Weber, Janice*
The Devil's Footprint — *O'Reilly, Victor*
The Devil's Hunt — *Doherty, P C*
Devil's Pact — *Zeller, F C Duke*
The Devil's Red Nickel — *Greer, Robert O*
The Devil's Rights and the Redemption in the Literature of Medieval England — *Marx, C W*
y **Devil's Tower** — *Sumner, Mark*
Devil's Workshop — *Gallison, Kate*
The Devious Dr. Franklin, Colonial Agent — *Morgan, David T*
Devising Liberty — *Konig, David Thomas*
The Devonshire Collection of Italian Drawings. Vols. 1-4 — *Jaffe, Michael*
y **Devoted (Page). Audio Version** — *Borchardt, Alice*
Devotion — *Sutcliffe, Katherine*
y **Devotion (Reading). Audio Version** — *Sutcliffe, Katherine*
r **Dewey Decimal Classification. 2nd Ed., Rev. for DDC21** — *Chan, Lois Mai*
r **Dewey Decimal Classification and Relative Index. 21st Ed., Vols. 1-4** — *Dewey, Melvil*
c **The Dewey Decimal System** — *Fowler, Allan*
Dewey Defeats Truman — *Mallon, Thomas*
r **Dewey for Windows. Electronic Media Version**
Dewey's Ethical Thought — *Welchman, Jennifer*
Dewey's New Logic — *Burke, Tom*
Dexterity and Its Development — *Latash, Mark L*
Dhalgren — *Delany, Samuel R*
Dharma Art — *Trungpa, Chogyam*
Dharma Girl — *Cain, Chelsea*
Dhuoda, Ninth Century Mother and Theologian — *Mayeski, Marie Anne*
Di Logos Jorge Luis Borges-Ernesto Sabato — *Borges, Jorge Luis*
Di Serambi — *Brown, Iem*
Di Si Zhi Yan Jing Kan Zhong Guo — *Wang, Shap*
El Dia En Que Desaparecio Tia Marga (Illus. by Raul) — *Maar, Paul*
Dia Ly Bien Dong Voi Hoang Sa Va Truong Sa — *Vu, Huu San*
El Dia Menos Pensado — *Pico, Fernando*
y **Diabetes** — *Ferber, Elizabeth*
Diabetes — *Nathan, David M*
r **Diabetes A to Z. New Completely Rev. Ed.**
The Diabetes Annual. Vol. 10
Diabetes: Caring for Patients in the Community — *McDowell, Joan R S*
Diabetes Mellitus — *LeRoith, Derek*
Le Diable Au Couvent — *Garnot, Benoit*
c **La Diablesse and the Baby (Illus. by Marie Lafrance)** — *Keens-Douglas, Richardo*
Diabolical Designs — *Bendix, Deanna Marohn*
Diaghilev, Creator of the Ballets Russes — *Kodicek, Ann*
Diagnosing Unemployment — *Malinvaud, Edmond*
Diagnosis and Management of Male Sexual Dysfunction — *Mulcahy, John J*
Diagnosis and Management of Ovarian Disorders — *Altchek, Albert*
Diagnosis and Treatment of Chronic Depression — *Kocsis, James H*
Diagnosis and Treatment Planning in Counseling. 2nd Ed. — *Seligman, Linda*
Diagnosis: Terminal — *Wilson, F Paul*
r **Diagnostic and Statistical Manual of Mental Disorders. 4th Ed.**
Diagnostic Cytopathology — *Gray, Winifred*
Diagnostic Techniques for Semiconductor Materials Processing II — *Pang, Stella W*
Diagonales — *Poirot-Delpech, Bertrand*
Diagrammes Medievaux Et Exegese Visuelle — *Sicard, Patrice*

y **Dial a Ghost (Illus. by Kerstin Meyer)** — *Ibbotson, Eva*
c **The Dial Book of Animal Tales from around the World (Illus. by Amanda Hall)** — *Adler, Naomi*
r **Dial Up!. 1st Ed.**
r **The Dialect of Forth and Bargy, Co. Wexford, Ireland** — *Poole, Jacob*
Dialectic and Narrative in Aquinas — *Hibbs, Thomas S*
Dialectics in the Arts — *Cameron, Catherine M*
Dialectique Et Connaissance Dans La Sepmaine De Du Bartas — *Miernowski, Jan*
The Dialogics of Dissent in the English Novel — *Baldridge, Cates*
Dialogue Avec Alain Bosquet — *Kadare, Ismail*
The Dialogue in Early Modern France 1547-1630 — *Winn, Colette H*
Dialogue of Life — *McCahill, Bob*
Dialogue on the Government of Florence — *Guicciardini, Francesco*
Dialogue on the Infinity of Love — *D'Aragona, Tullia*
Dialogues across Civilizations — *Prazniak, Roxann*
The Dialogues of Plato (Allen). Vol. 3 — *Plato*
Dialogues with Zuni Potters — *Nahohai, Milford*
The Diamond Age — *Stephenson, Neal*
Diamond: Baseball Writings of Mark Harris — *Harris, Mark, 1922-*
Diamond Dreams — *Brunt, Stephen*
Diamond Grill *Wah, Fred*
Diamond Head — *Knief, Charles*
Diamond Slipper — *Feather, Jane*
Diamond Sutra — *Hester, Colin*
Diamonds: A Century of Spectacular Jewels — *Proddow, Penny*
Diamonds Forever — *Kinsella, W P*
y **Diamonds in the Rough** — *Zoss, Joel*
y **Diana Ross** — *Wyeth, John, Jr.*
Diana, the Goddess Who Hunts Alone — *Fuentes, Carlos*
Diana: The Lonely Princess — *Davies, Nicholas*
Diana Victrix — *Converse, Florence*
Diapause in the Crustacea — *Alekseev, Victor R*
Diaper Changes — *Farrisi, Theresa Rodriguez*
Diaries — *Clark, Alan*
Diaries. Vol. 1 — *Isherwood, Christopher*
y **Diaries and Letters** — *Flower, Celeste*
Diaries and Letters 1930-1964 — *Nicolson, Harold George, Sir*
The Diaries of Absalom Watkin — *Watkin, Absalom*
The Diaries of Charlotte Perkins Gilman. Vols. 1-2 — *Gilman, Charlotte Perkins*
The Diaries of Dawn Powell 1931-1965 — *Powell, Dawn*
Diario De Jerusalem En 1914-1919 — *Ballobar, Antonio De La Cierva Lewita, Conde De*
Diario Di Lo — *Pera, Pia*
Diary of a Humiliated Man — *Azua, Felix De*
Diary of a Left-Handed Birdwatcher — *Nathan, Leonard*
Diary of a Nobody (Hardiman). Audio Version — *Grossmith, George*
Diary of a Rose Lover — *Delbard, Henri*
Diary of a Wilderness Dweller — *Czajkowski, Chris*
y **The Diary of a Young Girl: The Definitive Edition** — *Frank, Anne*
Diary of an Emotional Idiot — *Estep, Maggie*
y **The Diary of Dawid Sierakowiak** — *Sierakowiak, Dawid*
The Diary of James Schuyler — *Schuyler, James*
The Diary of Lady Murasaki — *Shikibu, Murasaki*
The Diary of Mattie Spenser — *Dallas, Sandra*
The Diary of Samuel Pepys. Vols. 1-11 — *Pepys, Samuel*
The Diary of Sir Edward Walter Hamilton 1885-1906 — *Hamilton, Edward Walter, Sir*
A Diary of the Century — *Ellis, Edward Robb*
The Diary of William Maclay and Other Notes on Senate Debates — *Maclay, William*
c **Dias Festivos Y Celebraciones** — *Goring, Ruth*
c **Dia's Story Cloth (Illus. by Chue Cha)** — *Cha, Dia*
cr **Diccionario Didactico De Espanol**
yr **Diccionario Enciclopedico Salvat Cuatro. Vols. 1-4**
r **Diccionario Griego-Espanol. Vol. 4**
c **Dicey's Song** — *Voigt, Cynthia*
Dichotomy — *Little, Blake*
r **Dicionario Critico Da Literatura Infantil E Juvenil Brasiliera Seculos XIXe XX. 4th Rev. and Expanded Ed.** — *Coelho, Nelly Novaes*
Dick Clark's American Bandstand — *Clark, Dick*
Dick for a Day — *Giles, Fiona*

Title Index

c Dick King-Smith's Animal Friends (Illus. by Anita Jeram) — *King-Smith, Dick*
Dick Tracy and American Culture — *Roberts, Garyn G*
c Dick Whittington (Illus. by Lesley Bisseker) — *Matthews, Andrew*
Dickens and Thackeray — *Reed, John R*
Dickens and the Grown-Up Child — *Andrews, Malcolm*
Dickens' Fur Coat and Charlotte's Unanswered Letters — *Pool, Daniel*
Dicken's Journalism. Vol. 1 — *Dickens, Charles*
Dickens' Journalism. Vol. 2 — *Dickens, Charles*
Dickens Refigured — *Schad, John*
Dickens Studies Annual. Vol. 22
Dickens Studies Annual. Vol. 24
Dickinson and Audience — *Orzeck, Martin*
r Dickinson's American Historical Fiction. 5th Ed. — *Gerhardstein, Virginia Brokaw*
Dictee — *Cha, Theresa Hak Kyung*
r Dictionarius/Dictionnaire Latin-Francais De Firmin Le Ver (Merrilees) — *Firminus Verris*
r Dictionarul Personalitatilor Publice Si Politice 1992-1994
r A Dictionary and Glossary for the Irish Literary Revival — *Wall, Richard*
r Dictionary Catalog of the Collection of African American Literature in the Mildred F. Sawyer Library of Suffolk University — *Clark, Edward*
r The Dictionary of 19th Century British Book Illustrators and Caricaturists. Rev. Ed. — *Houfe, Simon*
r The Dictionary of 20th Century British Book Illustrators — *Horne, Alan*
r Dictionary of 1000 Spanish Proverbs with English Equivalents — *Mertvago, Peter*
r Dictionary of Afghan Wars, Revolutions, and Insurgencies — *Adamec, Ludwig W*
r Dictionary of American Biography. 1st Suppl.-
r Dictionary of American Biography. Vols. 1-21
r Dictionary of American Biography. Comprehensive Index: Complete through Supplement Ten
r Dictionary of American Children's Fiction 1990-1994 — *Helbig, Alethea*
r A Dictionary of American History — *Purvis, Thomas L*
yr Dictionary of American History Supplement. Vols. 1-2 — *Ferrell, Robert H*
r Dictionary of American Literary Characters
r Dictionary of American Naval Aviation Squadrons. Vol. 1 — *Grossnick, Roy A*
r Dictionary of American Penology. Rev. Ed. — *Williams, Vergil L*
r Dictionary of American Regional English. Vol. 3 — *Cassidy, Frederic G*
r A Dictionary of Anglo-Irish — *O Muirithe, Diarmaid*
r The Dictionary of Art. Vols. 1-34 — *Turner, Jane Shoaf*
r A Dictionary of Australian Colloquialisms. 4th Ed. — *Wilkes, G A*
r Dictionary of Automotive Engineering. 2nd Ed. — *Goodsell, Don*
r Dictionary of Belgian and Dutch Flower Painters Born between 1750 and 1880 — *Hostyn, Norbert*
r A Dictionary of Biblical Tradition in English Literature — *Jeffrey, David Lyle*
r Dictionary of Building Preservation — *Bucher, Ward*
yr Dictionary of Canine Terms — *Jackson, Frank*
yr Dictionary of Caribbean English Usage — *Allsopp, Richard*
r Dictionary of Christianity — *Cooper, J C*
r The Dictionary of Cleveland Biography — *Van Tassel, David D*
r A Dictionary of Communication and Media Studies. 4th Ed. — *Watson, James, 1936-*
yr Dictionary of Contemporary French Connectors — *Grieve, James*
r The Dictionary of Cricket — *Rundell, Michael*
r A Dictionary of Cultural and Critical Theory — *Payne, Michael*
r Dictionary of Dairy Terminology. 2nd Rev. Ed. — *International Dairy Federation*
r Dictionary of Developmental Psychology — *Stuart-Hamilton, Ian*
r Dictionary of Economics — *Shim, Jae K*
r Dictionary of Endocrinology and Related Biomedical Sciences — *Martin, Constance R*
r A Dictionary of English Surnames. 3rd Ed. — *Reaney, P H*
r The Dictionary of Environment and Sustainable Development — *Gilpin, Alan*

yr Dictionary of Ethics, Theology, and Society — *Clarke, Paul A B*
r A Dictionary of Euphemisms — *Holder, R W*
yr A Dictionary of European History and Politics 1945-1995 — *Urwin, Derek W*
r Dictionary of Feminist Theologies — *Russell, Letty M*
r Dictionary of Fictional Characters. Rev. Ed. — *Seymour-Smith, Martin*
r The Dictionary of Financial Risk Management — *Gastineau, Gary L*
r A Dictionary of Genetics. 5th Ed. — *King, Robert C*
r Dictionary of Glass — *Bray, Charles*
r The Dictionary of Global Culture — *Appiah, Anthony*
r Dictionary of Hispanic Biography — *Tardiff, Joseph C*
r Dictionary of Insurance Terms. 3rd Ed. — *Rubin, Harvey W*
r Dictionary of International Biography 1996
r Dictionary of International Business Terms — *Capela, John J*
r Dictionary of International Human Rights Law — *Gibson, John S*
r Dictionary of Irish Literature. Rev. and Expanded Ed., Vols. 1-2
r Dictionary of Islamic Architecture — *Petersen, Andrew*
r Dictionary of Italian Literature. Rev. and Expanded Ed. — *Bondanella, Peter*
r A Dictionary of Jewish Surnames from the Kingdom of Poland — *Beider, Alexander*
r A Dictionary of Judaism and Christianity — *Cohn-Sherbok, Dan*
yr Dictionary of Judaism in the Biblical Period 450 B.C.E. to 600 C.E. Vols. 1-2 — *Neusner, Jacob*
r Dictionary of Literary Biography. Vol. 1-
r Dictionary of Literary Biography Yearbook 1995
r Dictionary of Mechanical Engineering. 4th Ed. — *Nayler, G H F*
r Dictionary of Media Literacy — *Silverblatt, Arthur*
r A Dictionary of Military History — *Corvisier, Andre*
r A Dictionary of Mind and Body — *Watson, Donald*
r A Dictionary of Modern Legal Usage. 2nd Ed. — *Garner, Bryan*
r The Dictionary of Modern Medicine — *Segen, J C*
yr The Dictionary of Multimedia — *Hansen, Brad*
r The Dictionary of National Biography 1986-1990 — *Nicholls, C S*
r The Dictionary of National Biography on CD-ROM. Electronic Media Version
r Dictionary of Native American Literature — *Wiget, Andrew*
r Dictionary of Natural Resource Management — *Dunster, Julian*
r Dictionary of North Carolina Biography. Vols. 2-6 — *Powell, William S*
r Dictionary of Paper. 5th Ed. — *Kouris, Michael*
r A Dictionary of Philosophy. 3rd Ed. — *Lacey, A R*
r Dictionary of Philosophy and Religion. New and Enl. Ed. — *Reese, William L*
r A Dictionary of Phonetics and Phonology — *Trask, R L*
r Dictionary of Plant Toxins. Vol. 1 — *Harborne, Jeffrey B*
r Dictionary of Political Thought — *Scruton, Roger*
r Dictionary of Portuguese-African Civilization. Vol. 2 — *Nunez, Benjamin*
r Dictionary of Portuguese-African Civilization. Vols. 1-2 — *Nunez, Benjamin*
r Dictionary of Public Health Promotion and Education — *Modeste, Naomi N*
r Dictionary of Russian Personal Names — *Benson, Morton*
r Dictionary of Russian Slang and Colloquial Expressions — *Shlyakhov, Vladimir*
r A Dictionary of Scottish Emigrants to Canada before Confederation. Vol. 2 — *Whyte, Donald*
r A Dictionary of South African English on Historical Principles — *Silva, Penny*
r A Dictionary of Sports Injuries and Disorders — *Potparic, O*
r The Dictionary of Substances and Their Effects (DOSE). Electronic Media Version
yr Dictionary of Teleliteracy — *Bianculli, David*
r A Dictionary of the Bible — *Browning, W R F*
r Dictionary of the British Empire and Commonwealth — *Palmer, Alan Warwick*
r A Dictionary of the English Language on CD-ROM. Electronic Media Version — *Johnson, Samuel*
r The Dictionary of the First World War — *Pope, Stephen*
r Dictionary of the Middle East — *Hiro, Dilip*

r Dictionary of the Modern Politics of Southeast Asia — *Leifer, Michael*
r Dictionary of the Modern United States Military — *Tomajczyk, S F*
r Dictionary of the Turkic Languages — *Oztopcu, Kurtulus*
r Dictionary of the United States Intelligence Services — *Wilson, William, 1923-*
r Dictionary of Twentieth Century Culture — *Brosman, Catharine Savage*
r Dictionary of Word Origins — *Flavell, Linda*
r Dictionnaire Bilingue De L'Argot D'Aujourd'hui, Anglais-Francais-Francais-Anglais — *Brunet, Francois*
r Dictionnaire Critique De La Communication. Vols. 1-2 — *Sfez, Lucien*
r Dictionnaire Des Ecrivains Suisses D'Expression Francaise. Vols. 1-2 — *Nicollier, Alain*
r Dictionnaire Des Eglises De Paris — *Brunel, Georges*
r Dictionnaire Des Intellectuels Francais — *Julliard, Jacques*
r Dictionnaire Des Lettres Francaises — *Pauphilet, Albert*
r Dictionnaire Di Darwinisme Et De L'Evolution. Vols. 1-3 — *Tort, Patrick*
r Dictionnaire Du Second Empire — *Tulard, Jean*
r Dictionnaire Hachette Multimedia. Electronic Media Version
r Dictionnaire Historique De La Vie Politique Francaise Au XXe Siecle — *Sirinelli, Jean-Francois*
r Dictionnaire Historique Des Noms De Famille Romans: Actes Du 1er Colloque (Treves, 10-13 Decembre 1987) — *Kremer, Dieter*
Dictionnaire Historique Des Noms De Famille Romans: Actes Du Colloque IV (Dijon, 24-26 Septembre 1990) — *Taverdet, Gerard*
r Dictionnaire Raisonne De La Politesse Et Du Savoir-Vivre — *Montandon, Alain*
Did Marco Polo Go to China? — *Wood, Frances*
Did Monkeys Invent the Monkey Wrench? — *Staten, Vince*
c Did You Hear Wind Sing Your Name? (Illus. by Christopher Canyon) — *De Coteau Orie, Sandra*
c Did You See What I Saw? (Illus. by Martha Weston) — *Winters, Kay*
The Didache in Context — *Jefford, Clayton N*
Diderot on Art. Vols. 1-2 — *Diderot, Denis*
Diderot's La Religieuse — *Clarke-Evans, Christine*
c Die, Bug, Die! — *Martin, Les*
Die Rich — *Kaye, Barry*
y Diego Rivera: His Art, His Life — *Gonzales, Doreen*
Diesel Engine Combustion Processes
Diesel Modeler's Guide. Vol. 1
Diet 911 — *Bergman, Yolanda*
r Diet and Nutrition Sourcebook — *Harris, Dan R*
Diet-Behavior Relationships — *Christensen, Larry B*
Dietary Fats, Lipids, Hormones, and Tumorigenesis — *Heber, David*
Dietary Phytochemicals in Cancer Prevention and Treatment
The Dietitian's Guide to Vegetarian Diets — *Messina, Mark*
Dietrich Bonhoeffer Works. Vols. 2, 5 — *Bonhoeffer, Dietrich*
Difference and Cultures in Europe — *Camilleri, Carmel*
y The Difference: Discovering the Hidden Ways We Silence Girls — *Mann, Judy*
The Difference: Growing Up Female in America — *Mann, Judy*
Difference Unbound — *Metzidakis, Stamos*
Differences and Changes in Wage Structures — *Freeman, Richard B*
A Different Angle — *Morris, Holly*
c A Different Beat — *Boyd, Candy Dawson*
y A Different Kind of Courage — *Howard, Ellen*
Different Restorations — *Finzsch, Norbert*
Different Rules — *Buchanan, David*
y Different Voices — *Flynn, Warren*
Different Women Dancing — *Gash, Jonathan*
r Differential Diagnosis and Treatment in Social Work. 4th Ed. — *Turner, Francis J*
Differential Diagnosis in Pathology — *Someren, Ayten*
Differential Equations and Control Theory — *Deng, Z*
Differential Forms — *Weintraub, Steven H*
Differential Geometry and Its Applications — *Oprea, John*
Differentiated Primary Science — *Qualter, Anne*
The Difficult Wheel — *Adcock, Betty*
Difficulties of a Bridegroom — *Hughes, Ted*
Diffraction X-Ray Optics — *Erko, A I*

The Diffusion of Advanced Weaponry — *Wander, W Thomas*

The Diffusion of Classical Art in Antiquity — *Boardman, John*

Diffusion of Distances — *Yip, Wai-Lim*

Diffusion of Innovations — *Rogers, Everett M*

c Dig and Dug with Daisy (Illus. by Alex Wilson) — *Jenner, Caryn*

c Dig Hole, Soft Mole (Illus. by Laura Regan) — *Lesser, Carolyn*

Dig Your Well before You're Thirsty — *Mackay, Harvey*

c Digby (Illus. by Barbara J Phillips-Duke) — *Hazen, Barbara Shook*

Digerati: Encounters with the Cyber Elite — *Brockman, John*

Digest of Papers — *IEEE International Workshop on IDDQ Testing (1996: Washington, D.C.)*

c Digestion: Food at Work — *Patten, Barbara J*

Digestive Wellness — *Lipski, Elizabeth*

c Digger: The Story of a Mole in the Fall (Illus. by Kenneth Lilly) — *Potter, Tessa*

c Diggers and Dumpers (Illus. by Richard Chasemore) — *Atkinson, Mary*

c Diggers and Dumpers (Snapshot Books)

Diggin' In and Piggin' Out — *Welsch, Roger*

Digging — *Dowse, Sara*

Digging for Dollars — *Fagette, Paul*

Digging the Africanist Presence in American Performance — *Gottschild, Brenda Dixon*

Digging Up Butch and Sundance. Rev. Ed. — *Meadows, Anne*

c Diggory and the Boa Conductor (Illus. by Jacqueline East) — *Gregory, Philippa*

A Digit of the Moon. Electronic Media Version — *Bain, F W*

Digital and Analog Communication Systems. 5th Ed. — *Couch, Leon W*

Digital Baseband Transmission and Recording — *Bergmans, Jan W M*

Digital Beamforming in Wireless Communications — *Litva, John*

Digital Control Systems — *Paraskevopoulos, P N*

Digital Design Principles and Computer Architecture — *Karalis, Edward*

Digital Designing with Programmable Logic Devices — *Carter, John W*

The Digital Economy — *Tapscott, Don*

The Digital Estate — *Martin, Chuck, 1949-*

Digital Filmmaking — *Ohanian, Thomas A*

Digital Fundamentals. 6th Ed. — *Floyd, Thomas L*

Digital Image and Audio Communications — *Baron, Stanley N*

Digital Image Creation — *Kojima, Hisaka*

r The Digital Imaging Dictionary — *Farace, Joe*

Digital Libraries '94

y Digital Literacy — *Gilster, Paul*

Digital Media — *Romano, Frank*

Digital Media and Electronic Publishing — *Earnshaw, Rae*

The Digital Scribe — *Musgrave, James Ray*

Digital Signal Processing Applications with Motorola's DSP56002 Processor — *El-Sharkawy, Mohamed*

Digital Soldiers — *Dunnigan, James F*

Dignity — *Aristide, Jean-Bertrand*

The Dilbert Principle — *Adams, Scott*

The Dilbert Principle (Adams). Audio Version — *Adams, Scott*

The Dilemma of Einstein, Podolsky, and Rosen, 60 Years Later — *Mann, A*

The Dilemma of the Fetus — *Maynard-Moody, Steven*

Dilemmas in Liberal Democratic Thought since Max Weber — *Wellen, Richard*

The Dilemmas of Brief Psychotherapy — *Gustafson, James P*

Dilemmas of Development Assistance — *Tisch, Sarah J*

Dilemmas of Growth — *Dantwala, M L*

Dilemmas of International Trade — *Moon, Bruce R*

Dilemmas of the Dollar. 2nd Ed. — *Bergsten, C Fred*

Dillinger: The Untold Story — *Girardin, G Russell*

c Dilly and the Goody-Goody (Illus. by Susan Hellard) — *Bradman, Tony*

c Dilly and the Vampire (Illus. by Susan Hellard) — *Bradman, Tony*

Dim — *Window, Carolin*

Un Dimanche Apres-Midi Dans La Tete — *Maulpoix, Jean-Michel*

Dimension of the Americas — *Goldman, Shifra M*

Dimensions of a New Identity — *Erikson, Erik H*

Dimensions of Development with Emphasis on Africa — *Negash, Tekeste*

r Dimensions of Need — *Loftas, Tony*

Dimensions of Psychotherapy Supervision — *Haber, Russell*

Dimensions of the Community College — *Raby, Rosalind Latiner*

Dimensions of the Sacred — *Smart, Ninian*

Dimitri Hadzi

Le Diner Des Ex — *Rosnay, Tatiana De*

r Dining in Style — *Wexler, Madelin*

The Dinner Party — *Chicago, Judy*

Dinner with Persephone — *Storace, Patricia*

c A Dinosaur Ate My Homework — *Nelson, Ray*

The Dinosaur Club — *Heffernan, William*

c Dinosaur Dinner with a Slice of Alligator Pie (Illus. by Debbie Tilley) — *Lee, Dennis, 1939-*

Dinosaur Extinction and the End of an Era — *Archibald, J David*

c Dinosaur Fun File (Illus. by Barry Green) — *Hopwood, Clive*

c Dinosaur Ghosts (Illus. by Douglas Henderson) — *Gillette, J Lynett*

y Dinosaur in a Haystack — *Gould, Stephen Jay*

Dinosaur Lives — *Horner, John*

c Dinosaur Roar! (Illus. by Paul Stickland) — *Stickland, Paul*

c Dinosaur Stomp! (Illus. by Paul Stickland) — *Stickland, Paul*

c Dinosaur Worlds — *Lessem, Don*

c Dinosaurs — *Barton, Byron*

c The Dinosaurs — *Krueger, Robert*

c Dinosaurs and Other Prehistoric Animals — *Flugel, Maria*

c The Dinosaurs Are Back and It's All Your Fault, Edward! (Illus. by Niki Daly) — *Hartmann, Wendy*

Dinosaurs of the East Coast — *Weishampel, David B*

y Dinosaurs of the Flaming Cliffs — *Novacek, Michael*

c Dinosaurs Series (Child's World)

Dinotopia: Audio Adventure. Audio Version — *Gurney, James*

Dinotopia Lost — *Foster, Alan Dean*

y Dinotopia: The World Beneath. Audio Version — *Gurney, James*

Le Diocese D'Arras De 1093 Au Milieu Du XIVe Siecle. Vols. 1-2 — *Delmaire, Bernard*

Il Dipendente — *Nata, Sebastiano*

La Diplomacia Vaticana Y La Espana De Franco 1936-1945 — *Marquina Barrio, Antonio*

Diplomacy and Disillusion at the Court of Margaret Thatcher — *Urban, G R*

Diplomacy at the Highest Level — *Dunn, David H*

Diplomacy in the Former Soviet Republics — *Nichol, James P*

Diplomasi: Australia and Indonesia's Independence — *Dorling, Philip*

r Diplomatique Medievale — *Guyotjeannin, Olivier*

Diplomats in Buckskins — *Viola, Herman J*

c Dipper of Copper Creek (Illus. by Jean Craighead George) — *George, Jean Craighead*

Direct Action — *Tracy, James*

DirectDraw Programming — *Timmins, Bret*

Directed by Clint Eastwood — *Knapp, Laurence F*

Directed by Dorothy Arzner — *Mayne, Judith*

Directing Actors — *Weston, Judith*

Directing: Learn from the Masters — *Garnett, Tay*

Directing Plays — *Taylor, Don*

Direction of Cities — *Guinther, John*

y Directions. Bks. 1-2 — *Jones, David*

Directions for Defense — *United States. Commission on Roles and Missions of the Armed Forces*

Director 5 Demystified — *Roberts, Jason*

Director 5 for Macintosh — *Persidsky, Andre*

Director 5 for Windows — *Persidsky, Andre*

r Directors' and Officers' Liability 1995-

The Director's Cut — *Howell, Lis*

r Directory of African American Religious Bodies. 2nd Ed. — *Payne, Wardell J*

r Directory of African Media — *Adewale, Maja-Pearce*

r Directory of American Firms Operating in Foreign Countries. 14th Ed., Vols. 1-3

r A Directory of American Poets and Fiction Writers. 1995-1996 Ed.

r Directory of Anti-Violence Activities in the Washington Metropolitan Area — *Zelinka, Joseph*

r Directory of Archives and Manuscript Repositories in the United States. 2nd Ed. — *United States. National Historical Publications and Records Commission*

r A Directory of Cayuga County Residents Who Supported Publication of the History of Cayuga County, New York — *Meyer, Mary Keysor*

r Directory of Chemical Producers and Products. 2nd Ed., Vol. 1, Pt. 1

r Directory of College and University Librarians in Canada. 2nd Ed. — *Leckie, Gloria J*

yr Directory of College Cooperative Education Programs — *Hutcheson, Polly*

r Directory of Congressional Voting Scores and Interest Group Ratings. 2nd Ed., Vols. 1-2 — *Sharp, J Michael*

r The Directory of Corporate and Foundation Givers 1996. Vols. 1-2

r Directory of Designated Members 1996 — *Appraisal Institute (U.S.)*

r Directory of Electronic Journals, Newsletters, and Academic Discussion Lists. 6th Ed.

r A Directory of Environmental Electronic Mail Users in Eurasia. 4th Ed.

r The Directory of EU Information Sources 1995-1996

r Directory of European Research and Development 1997. Vols. 1-2

r Directory of Family Associations. 3rd Ed. — *Bentley, Elizabeth Petty*

r The Directory of Federal Jobs and Employers — *Krannich, Ronald L*

r Directory of Health and Social Services Databases — *Carmel, Simon*

r Directory of Health Grants

r Directory of International Organizations — *Schraepler, Hans-Albrecht*

r Directory of Japan Specialists and Japanese Studies Institutions in the United States and Canada. Vols. 1-3

r Directory of Japanese-Affiliated Companies in the EU 1996-97

r Directory of Labor Unions in the United States 1947-1953

r Directory of Library Automation. 1996 Ed.

r The Directory of MBAs: 1996/97 Academic Year

r Directory of National and International Law. 1955-1970 Eds.

r Directory of National Helplines 1996

r Directory of National Unions and Employee Associations. 1971-1979 Eds.

r Directory of Official Information. 1995/1997 Ed.

r The Directory of Overseas Catalogs 1997

r Directory of Power Plant Equipment and Processes 1996

r Directory of Research Grants 1996

r Directory of Research Grants 1997

r The Directory of Saints — *Sandoval, Annette*

r Directory of Services and Resources to the Asian Pacific American Community in the Metropolitan Washington Region — *Rall, Ann P*

r Directory of Social Service Grants — *Eckstein, Richard M*

r Directory of Storytellers — *Society for Storytelling*

r Directory of Texas Manufacturers. 1996 Ed., Vols. 1-2

r Directory of the Association for Library and Information Science Education 1995-96

r Directory of the Steel Industry and the Environment — *United Nations. Economic Commission for Europe*

r Directory of the World's Banks. 11th Ed.

r Directory of Theatre Training Programs. 5th Ed. — *Charles, Jill*

r Directory of Trade and Investment Related Organizations of Developing Countries and Areas in Asia and the Pacific. 7th Ed.

r Directory of U.S. Labor Organizations 1982-

y Dirge for a Doge — *Eyre, Elizabeth*

Dirichlet Forms and Stochastic Processes — *Ma, Zhi-Ming*

Dirt — *Woods, Stuart*

Dirt and Deity — *McIntyre, Ian*

The Dirt Doctor's Guide to Organic Gardening — *Garrett, J Howard*

Dirty Bird Blues — *Major, Clarence*

Dirty Laundry — *Thomas, Paul*

Dirty Little Secrets — *Sabato, Larry J*

Dirty Money — *Gilmore, William C*

c Dirty, Rotten, Dead? (Illus. by T Taylor Bruce) — *Emory, Jerry*

Dirty Tricks or Trump Cards — *Godson, Roy*

Disability and the Dilemmas of Education and Justice — *Christensen, Carol*

r Disability Evaluation — *Demeter, Stephen L*

c The Disability Rights Movement — *Kent, Deborah*

y The Disabled — *Stalcup, Brenda*

The Disabled God — *Eiesland, Nancy L*

Disabled Powers — *Howells, Robin*

The Disappearance of God — *Friedman, Richard Elliott*

Disappearances: A Map — *Nickerson, Sheila*

y The Disappearances of Madalena Grimaldi — *Day, Marele*
The Disappeared — *Silva, David B*
y The Disappearing American Farm — *Goldberg, Jake*
Disappearing Cryptography — *Wayner, Peter*
c Disappearing Lake (Illus. by Jon Van Zyle) — *Miller, Debbie S*
Disappearing Moon Cafe — *Lee, Sky*
Disarmed and Dangerous — *Polner, Murray*
Disarming Patriarchy — *Roseneil, Sasha*
Disaster and Development in the Horn of Africa — *Sorenson, John*
r Disaster and Recovery Planning — *Gustin, Joseph F*
y Disaster at Johnstown — *Dolson, Hildegarde*
Disaster Management in British Libraries — *Matthews, Graham*
Disaster Planning for Library and Information Service — *Ashman, John*
Disasters, Development and Environment — *Varley, Ann*
Discarded Legacy — *Boyd, Melba Joyce*
Discerning New Horizons — *Castner, Henry W*
The Discerning Reader — *Barratt, David*
Disciples — *Wright, Austin*
Disciples and Democracy — *Cromartie, Michael*
Discipleship in the Ancient World and Matthew's Gospel. 2nd Ed. — *Wilkins, Michael J*
Discipline and Experience — *Dear, Peter*
Discipline Made Easy — *Glavich, Mary Kathleen*
The Discipline of History and the History of Thought — *Lemon, M C*
The Disciplined Heart — *Simon, Caroline J*
Disciplined Hearts — *O'Nell, Theresa DeLeane*
Disciplines of Delight — *Richards, Barry*
Disciplines of Virtue — *Vallone, Lynne*
Disciplining Old Age — *Katz, Stephen*
Disco Biscuits — *Champion, Sarah*
Disconcerted Europe — *Moens, Alexander*
Disconnected: Haves and Have-Nots in the Information Age — *Wresch, William*
Discorso Storico Della Mia Vita Naturale E Civile Dal 1745 Al 1825 — *Ferroni, Pietro*
Le Discours Feminin De Marguerite Duras — *Anderson, Stephanie*
Discours Merveilleux De La Vie, Actions Et Deportements De Catherine De Medicis, Royne Mere — *Cazauran, Nicole*
Discourse Analysis of Biblical Literature — *Bodine, Walter R*
Discourse and Dominion in the Fourteenth Century — *Gellrich, Jesse M*
Discourse, Consciousness and Time — *Chafe, Wallace*
The Discourse of Enlightenment in Eighteenth-Century France — *Brewer, Daniel*
The Discourse of Negotiation — *Firth, Alan*
Discourse on History, Law, and Governance in the Public Career of John Selden 1610-1635 — *Christianson, Paul*
The Discourse on Terrorism — *Gold-Biss, Michael*
Discourse Variety in Contemporary French — *Coleman, James A*
The Discourses (Crick) — *Machiavelli, Niccolo*
Discourses of Jewish Identity in Twentieth Century France — *Astro, Alan*
Discourses of Martyrdom in English Literature 1563-1694 — *Knott, John R*
Discourses of Power — *Hindess, Barry*
Discourses of the Vanishing — *Ivy, Marilyn*
Discourses on Livy (Mansfield) — *Machiavelli, Niccolo*
Discourses on Violence — *Jabri, Vivienne*
y Discover America's Favorite Architects (Illus. by Joe Stites) — *Glenn, Patricia Brown*
Discover Romanian — *Botoman, Rodica*
c Discover the Seasons — *Iverson, Diane*
Discover the Universe. Book and Electronic Media Version
cr Discover the World Picture Atlas
Discover Your Voice — *Brown, Oren L*
Discoveries of the Other — *Siemerling, Winfried*
c Discoveries Series
y Discovering Advanced Mathematics: Pure Mathematics — *Francis, Bob*
Discovering and Restoring Antique Furniture — *Bennett, Michael*
r Discovering Antiques — *Knowles, Eric*
yr DISCovering Authors. Electronic Media Version
Discovering AutoCAD, Release 13 — *Dix, Mark*
yr DISCovering Biography. Electronic Media Version
Discovering Calculus with the Graphing Calculator — *Shoaf-Grubbs, Mary Margaret*

yr DISCovering Careers and Jobs Plus. Electronic Media Version
Discovering Columbus — *Chapman, Paul H*
yr Discovering Fossil Fishes — *Maisey, John G*
Discovering Molecular Genetics — *Miller, Jeffrey H*
r DISCovering Multicultural America. Electronic Media Version
yr DISCovering Science. Electronic Media Version
c Discovering Scottish Plants (Illus. by Fhiona Galloway) — *Paul, Heather*
r Discovering Spain. 2nd Ed. — *Casas, Penelope*
Discovering the Bible in the Non-Biblical World — *Kwok, Pui-Lan*
Discovering the Cosmos — *Bless, R C*
c Discovering the Iceman (Illus. by Laurie McGaw) — *Tanaka, Shelley*
Discovering the Possible — *Meldolesi, Luca*
Discovering the Women in Slavery — *Morton, Patricia*
yr DISCovering U.S. History. Electronic Media Version
yr DISCovering World History. Electronic Media Version
Discovering Your Career in Business — *Butler, Timothy*
y The Discovery — *Baer, Judy*
The Discovery and Conquest of Mexico 1517-1521 — *Diaz Del Castillo, Bernal*
y The Discovery of Dragons (Illus. by Graeme Base) — *Base, Graeme*
The Discovery of Heaven — *Mulisch, Harry*
The Discovery of Kepler's Laws — *Kozhamthadam, Job*
The Discovery of the Past — *Schnapp, Alain*
Discrepant Dislocations — *John, Mary E*
Discrepant Histories — *Rafael, Vicente L*
Discrete Gambling and Stochastic Games — *Maitra, Ashok P*
Discrete Hamiltonian Systems — *Ahlbrandt, Calvin D*
Discrete Mathematics. 4th Ed. — *Johnsonbaugh, Richard*
Discussion Starters — *Folse, Keith S*
Disease and Class — *Feldberg, Georgina D*
c Disease Fighters since 1950 — *Moser, Diane K*
y Disease: In Search of Remedy — *Marcuse, Peter M*
A Disease of One's Own — *Rice, John Steadman*
y Diseases: Finding the Cure — *Mulcahy, Robert*
Diseases of Cage and Aviary Birds. 3rd Ed. — *Rosskopf, Walter J*
Diseases of the Sinuses — *Gershwin, M Eric*
Disembodied Voices — *Monson, Craig A*
The Disenchanted Isle — *Dellheim, Charles*
The Disenchantment of Art — *Rochlitz, Rainer*
Disequilibria, Economic Reforms and Economic Policies — *Li, Xiaoming*
Disfarmer: 1939-1946 Heber Springs Portraits — *Disfarmer, Mike*
c Disguises and Surprises — *Llewellyn, Claire*
Dishonored — *Barrett, Maria*
Disintegrating Europe — *Hama, Noriko*
The Disintegration of the Soviet Union — *Fowkes, Ben*
The Disintegration of the World Economy between the World Wars. Vols. 1-2 — *Thomas, Mark*
Disintegration or Transformation — *McCarthy, Patrick*
Diskurs Und Konsens Im Prozess Theologischer Wahrheit — *Gruber, Franz*
The Dismal Battlefield — *Scharfen, John C*
Dismantling Desegregation — *Orfield, Gary*
Dismantling the Welfare State? — *Pierson, Paul*
Dismantling Utopia — *Shane, Scott*
Dismembered Rhetoric — *Sullivan, Ceri*
Dismembering the Male — *Bourke, Joanna*
r Disney A to Z — *Smith, Dave, 1940-*
The Disney That Never Was — *Solomon, Charles*
c Disney's 101 Dalmations — *Mazer, Anne*
c Disney's James and the Giant Peach (Illus. by Karey Kirkpatrick) — *Smith, Lane*
c Disney's Treasury of Children's Classics — *Ingoglia, Gina*
Disobedience — *Drinkard, Michael*
The Disobedient Writer — *Walker, Nancy A*
The Disorder of Love — *Connelly, Karen*
Disordered Materials and Interfaces — *Cummins, Herman Z*
Disorderly Women — *Juster, Susan*
Disorders of the Patellofemoral Joint. 3rd Ed. — *Fulkerson, John P*
y Dispatch from a Cold Country — *Cullen, Robert*
Dispatches — *Herr, Michael*
Dispatches from the Freud Wars — *Forrester, John*
Dispatches from the Poverty Line — *Capponi, Pat*

Displaced Homeless Adolescent Claimants for Social Security Payments — *Jordan, Alan*
The Disposable Work Force — *Moore, Thomas S*
Dispositions: A Debate — *Armstrong, D M*
Dispossession — *Brenchley, Chaz*
Disproportionate Harm — *Roberts, Julian V*
Disputatio Scholastica — *Palaeologus, Jacobus*
Disputation and Dialogue — *Talmage, F E*
A Dispute between the Woman and the Powers of Darkness 1802 — *Southcott, Joanna*
Disputed Questions in Theology and Philosophy of Religion — *Hick, John*
Disraeli: A Brief Life — *Smith, Paul, 1937-*
Disruption — *Appelbaum, David*
Disruption: Overturning Conventions and Shaking Up the Marketplace — *Dru, Jean-Marie*
The Dissemination of Music — *Lenneberg, Hans*
The Dissenters. Vol. 2 — *Watts, Michael R*
r Dissertation Abstracts. Electronic Media Version
r Dissertation Abstracts International 1938-
Dissociative Children — *Shirar, Lynda*
Dissolution: The Crisis of Communism and the End of East Germany — *Maier, Charles S*
Dissonant Worlds — *Waugh, Earle H*
The Distaff Side — *Scotford, Jessica*
Distance — *Thubron, Colin*
Distance Education for Language Teachers — *Howard, Ron*
y The Distance from the Heart of Things — *Warlick, Ashley*
r The Distance Learning Funding Sourcebook. 1996 Ed.
Distance Learning Technology and Applications — *Minoli, Daniel*
Distant Blood — *Abbott, Jeff*
Distant Desire — *Bakshi, Parminder*
A Distant Dream — *Graham, Margaret*
Distant Dreams — *Pella, Judith*
y A Distant Enemy — *Vanasse, Deb*
y Distant Fires — *Anderson, Scott*
Distant Friends and Intimate Strangers — *East, Charles*
A Distant Heritage — *Eldridge, Larry D*
Distant Sisters — *Rotem, Judith*
c The Distant Talking Drum (Illus. by F Lessac Honesdale) — *Olalleye, Isaac*
Distant Valor — *Moreau, C X*
yr Distinguished African American Scientists of the 20th Century — *Kessler, James H*
The Distinguished Guest — *Miller, Sue*
y The Distinguished Guest (Cassidy). Audio Version — *Miller, Sue*
Distinguo: Reading Montaigne Differently — *Rendall, Steven*
The Distorted Past — *Fontana, Joseph*
Distortion Theorems in Relation to Linear Integral Operators — *Komatsu, Yusaku*
Distress — *Egan, Greg*
Distress from Cleverness — *Griboyedov, Alexander S*
Distributed Computer Control Systems 1995 (DCCS 95) — *Sahraoui, A E K*
Distributed Computing Systems — *International Conference on Distributed Computing Systems (16th: 1996: Hong Kong)*
Distributed Feedback Laser Diodes — *Ghafouri-Shiraz, H*
Distributed Fuzzy Control of Multivariable Systems — *Gegov, Alexander*
Distributed Multimedia — *Agnew, Palmer*
Distributed Relational Database — *Podcameni, Silvio*
The Distribution of Wealth in Rural China — *McKinley, Terry*
Distributional Analysis of Tax Policy — *Bradford, David F*
Distributions in the Physical and Engineering Sciences. Vol. 1 — *Woyczynski, Wojbor A*
r District of Columbia Free Negro Registers 1821-1861. Vols. 1-2 — *Provine, Dorothy S*
The District of the Green Dragon — *Eckstein, Nicholas A*
p Disturbed Guillotine
Disturbing Pleasures — *Giroux, Henry A*
The Disunity of Science — *Galison, Peter*
y Ditchdigger's Daughters — *Thornton, Yvonne S*
The Diva's Mouth — *Leonardi, Susan J*
Divas Poemas — *Kraujiete, Aina*
y Dive — *Donovan, Stacey*
Dive Right In — *Wesman, Jane*
c Diver — *Church, Caroline*
Divergent Paths — *Egnal, Marc*
Divergent Realities — *Larson, Reed*
c Divers — *McDonald, Kendall*

Diverse Perspectives on Marxist Philosophy — *Luther, Sara F*
Diverse Practices — *Knight, Julia*
Diversification, Refocusing, and Economic Performance — *Markides, Constantinos C*
Diversity and Citizenship — *Jacobsohn, Gary Jeffrey*
Diversity and Complexity in Prehistoric Maritime Societies — *Bourque, Bruce J*
Diversity at Work — *Wilson, Trevor*
The Diversity, Complexity, and Evolution of High Tech-Capitalism — *Thore, Sten*
The Diversity Factor — *Cross, Elsie Y*
Diversity in Higher Education — *Musil, Caryn McTighe*
Diversity in Japanese Culture and Language — *Maher, John Christopher*
Diversity in Work Teams — *Jackson, Susan E*
Diversity Leadership — *Dreachslin, Janice L*
The Diversity Machine — *Lynch, Frederick R*
A Diversity of Women — *Parr, Joy*
c Divide and Ride (Illus. by George Ulrich) — *Murphy, Stuart J*
Divide and Rule — *Wesseling, H L*
Divided against Itself — *Hvinden, Bjorn*
Divided by Color — *Kinder, Donald R*
The Divided Democrats — *Mayer, William G*
Divided Kashmir — *Rahman, Mushtaqur*
y Divided Lives — *Walsh, Elsa*
Divided Loyalties — *Phelan, Craig*
Divided Minds and Successive Selves — *Radden, Jennifer*
Divided Nations — *Diez Medrano, Juan*
Divided Sisters — *Wilson, Midge*
Divided Sun — *Callon, Scott*
Divided They Fell — *Radosh, Ronald*
Dividing the Commons — *Peters, Pauline E*
y Dividing the Waters — *Postel, Sandra*
Divination, Mythology and Monarchy in Han China — *Loewe, Michael*
The Divine and the Demoniac — *Berkson, Carmel*
The Divine Comedy — *Dante Alighieri*
The Divine Comedy (Mandelbaum) — *Dante Alighieri*
The Divine Comedy of Dante Alighieri (Durling). Vol. 1 — *Dante Alighieri*
Divine Discourse — *Wolterstorff, Nicholas*
The Divine Dramatist — *Stout, Harry S*
Divine Energy — *Dorr, Donal*
Divine Enterprise — *McKean, Lise*
Divine Grace and Human Agency — *Weaver, Rebecca Harden*
Divine Immutability — *Dorner, Isaak August*
The Divine Initiative — *Stebbins, J Michael*
Divine Madness — *Jackowski, Karol*
The Divine Matrix — *Bracken, Joseph A*
Divine Meaning — *Torrance, Thomas F*
Divine Power — *Moonan, Lawrence*
Divine Will and the Mechanical Philosophy — *Osler, Margaret J*
y The Diviners — *McDowell, Robert*
Les Divines — *Boucher, Denise*
The Diving Bell and the Butterfly — *Bauby, Jean-Dominique*
y Diving In — *Cann, Kate*
Diving into the Wreck — *Rich, Adrienne*
c Division (Illus. by Richard Maccabe) — *Stienecker, David*
Division of Labor, Variability, Coordination, and the Theory of Firms and Markets — *Camacho, A*
c Divorce (Illus. by Jim Judkis) — *Rogers, Fred*
The Divorce Culture — *Whitehead, Barbara Dafoe*
Divorce Lawyers and Their Clients — *Sarat, Austin*
Le Divorce — *Johnson, Diane*
r Divorce Yourself. 3rd Ed. — *Sitarz, Daniel*
Divorced from Justice — *Winner, Karen*
c Diwali — *Marchant, Kerena*
Dixie Rising — *Applebome, Peter*
y Dixie Storms — *Hall, Barbara*
DIY Feminism — *Bail, Kathy*
DIY Futures — *Albery, Nicholas*
y Dizzy Gillespie and the Birth of Bebop — *Gourse, Leslie*
Djinn Rummy — *Holt, Tom*
Djuna: The Life and Work of Djuna Barnes — *Herring, Phillip*
yr DK Encyclopedia of Rock Stars — *Rees, Dafydd*
yr The DK Geography of the World
cr The DK Visual Timeline of the 20th Century — *Adams, Simon*
p The DLA Financial
c Dmitri the Astronaut (Illus. by Jon Agee) — *Agee, Jon*

DNA and Destiny — *Steen, R Grant*
DNA and RNA Cleavers and Chemotherapy of Cancer and Viral Diseases — *Meunier, Bernard*
DNA Based Computers — *DIMACS Workshop on DNA Based Computers (1995: Princeton University)*
The DNA Mystique — *Nelkin, Dorothy*
DNA Replication in Eukaryotic Cells — *DePamphilis, Melvin L*
r DNA Sequencing Strategies — *Ansorge, Wilehlm*
y Do Angels Sing the Blues? — *LeMieux, A C*
Do Campaigns Matter? — *Holbrook, Thomas M*
c Do Cowboys Ride Bikes? (Illus. by Nadine Bernard Westcott) — *Tucker, Kathy*
Do Deficits Matter? — *Shaviro, Daniel N*
c Do Gerbils Go to Heaven? (Illus. by Axel Scheffler) — *Wilson, David Henry*
c Do Goldfish Play the Violin? (Illus. by Axel Scheffler) — *Wilson, David Henry*
c The Do-It-Yourself House that Jack Built (Illus. by Quentin Blake) — *Yeoman, John*
Do-It-Yourself Housebuilding — *Nash, George*
r Do-It-Yourself Plumbing — *Alth, Max*
Do Lemmings Commit Suicide? — *Chitty, Dennis*
Do Not Go Gently — *Smith-Levin, Judith*
c Do Not Open — *Turkle, Brinton*
c Do Pigs Have Stripes? (Illus. by Melanie Walsh) — *Walsh, Melanie*
Do the Windows Open? — *Hecht, Julie*
Do They Grow out of It? — *Hechtman, Lily*
Do We Still Need Doctors? — *Lantos, John D*
Do You Remember? — *Mencken, H L*
c Do You See a Mouse? (Illus. by Bernard Waber) — *Waber, Bernard*
c Do You Want Fries with That? — *Godfrey, Martyn*
c Do You Want to Bet? — *Cushman, Jean*
Do Your Own Wiring — *Armpriester, K E*
Docklands in the Making — *Cox, Alan*
The Doctor-Activist: Physicians Fighting for Social Change — *Bassuk, Ellen L*
Dr. America — *Fisher, James T*
Dr. Bernstein's Diabetes Solution — *Bernstein, Richard K*
Dr. Bob Arnot's Program for Perfect Weight Control for Men and Women — *Arnot, Bob*
Dr. Bob's Guide to the Internet — *Rankin, Bob*
c Doctor De Soto — *Steig, William*
c Dr. Dog — *Cole, Babette*
Dr. Fulford's Touch of Life — *Fulford, Robert C*
Dr. Fulford's Touch of Life. Audio Version — *Fulford, Robert C*
y Dr. Jekyll and Mr. Hyde. Travels with a Donkey (Case). Audio Version — *Stevenson, Robert Louis*
c Dr. Jekyll, Orthodontist (Illus. by Jack E Davis) — *Greenburg, Dan*
Dr. Nancy Snyderman's Guide to Good Health — *Snyderman, Nancy*
Dr. Neruda's Cure for Evil — *Yglesias, Rafael*
Dr. Norton's Wife — *Walker, Mildred*
Dr. Richard Marrs' Fertility Book — *Marrs, Richard*
Dr. Rosenfeld's Guide to Alternative Medicine — *Rosenfeld, Isadore*
Dr. Seuss and Mr. Geisel — *Morgan, Judith*
c Dr. Seuss's ABC. Electronic Media Version — *Seuss, Dr.*
c Dr. Shivers' Carnival of Terror — *Katz, Fred E*
Dr. Strangelove's America — *Henriksen, Margot A*
r Dr. Susan Love's Breast Book. 2nd Ed. — *Love, Susan*
Dr. Susan Love's Hormone Book — *Love, Susan*
y The Doctor, the Murder, the Mystery — *D'Amato, Barbara*
r Dr. Tom Linden's Guide to Online Medicine — *Linden, Tom*
r Doctor Who Companions — *Howe, David J*
Doctor Zhivago — *Pasternak, Boris*
c The Doctors — *Fisher, Leonard Everett*
r The Doctors Book of Home Remedies for Women — *Prevention Magazine Health Books*
c The Doctor's Daughter (Illus. by Michael Charlton) — *Clarke, Norma*
A Doctor's Guide to Therapeutic Touch — *Wager, Susan*
c Doctors Help People — *Moses, Amy*
The Doctor's House — *Fagan, Cary*
Doctors of Conscience — *Joffe, Carole E*
r The Doctrine of the Holy Spirit. Vols. 1-2 — *Schandorff, Esther Dech*
Doctrines of Development — *Cowen, M P*
Document Delivery Services — *Mitchell, Eleanor*
Documenta Copernicana — *Copernicus, Nicolaus*
Documentary History of Hong Kong. Vol. 1 — *Tsang, Steve Yui-Sang*

Documentary History of the First Federal Congress of the United States of America. Vol. 14 — *De Pauw, Linda Grant*
I Documenti Diplomatici Italiani. 2nd Ser., Vols. 15-16 — *Italy. Commissione Per La Pubblicazione Dei Documenti Diplomatici*
I Documenti Diplomatici Italiani. 2nd Ser., Vols. 17-18 — *Italy. Commissione Per La Pubblicazione Dei Documenti Diplomatici*
I Documenti Diplomatici Italiani. 10th Ser., Vol. 1 — *Italy. Commissione Per La Pubblicazione Dei Documenti Diplomatici*
I Documenti Diplomatici Italiani. 10th Ser., Vol. 2 — *Italy. Commissione Per La Pubblicazione Dei Documenti Diplomatici*
r Documentos Del Japon 1558-1562 — *Ruiz-De-Medina, Juan*
r Documentos Para El Estudio De La Historia Del Libro En Zaragoza Entre 1501 Y 1521 — *Pedraza Gracia, Manuel Jose*
Documents Diplomatiques Francais Sur L'Histoire Du Bassin Des Carpates 1918-1932. Vol. 1 — *Adam, Magda*
Documents Diplomatiques Suisses 1848-1945 — *Imboden, Gabriel*
Documents for the Study of the Gospels. Rev. and Enlarged Ed. — *Cartlidge, David R*
Documents of the English Reformation — *Bray, Gerald*
Documents on British Policy Overseas. 1st Ser., Vol. 7
Documents on Canadian External Relations. Vols. 14-15 — *Mackenzie, Hector*
DOD Force Mix Issues — *United States. General Accounting Office*
De Doda Pjaserna I-IV 1989-1994 — *Noren, Lars*
The Dodge Collection of Eighteenth-Century French and English Art in the Detroit Institute of Arts — *Detroit Institute of Arts*
Dodoima: Tales of Oro — *Johnston, Elin*
r Dod's Parliamentary Companion 1996
Doers of the Word — *Peterson, Carla L*
y Does Anybody Know What Planet My Parents Are From? — *Johnson, Kevin*
Does Conquest Pay? — *Liberman, Peter*
Does Freddy Dance — *Scanlon, Dick*
Does It Run in the Family? — *Zallen, Doris Teichler*
Does It Show? — *Magrs, Paul*
Does My Child Need a Therapist? — *Alexander-Roberts, Colleen*
Does Training for the Disadvantaged Work? — *Orr, Larry L*
Does Wednesday Mean Mom's House or Dad's? — *Ackerman, Marc J*
Does Your Child's World Scare You? — *Scott, Jeffrey*
y Does Your House Have Lions? — *Sanchez, Sonia*
Does Your Project Have a Copyright Problem? — *Jensen, Mary Brandt*
c The Dog — *Burningham, John*
c Dog (Illus. by Brita Granstrom) — *Morley, Christine*
c Dog and Cat Shake a Leg (Illus. by Kate Spohn) — *Spohn, Kate*
c Dog Brain (Illus. by David Milgrim) — *Milgrim, David*
c Dog Breath — *Pilkey, Dav*
A Dog Called Demolition — *Rankin, Robert*
c Dog Dottington (Illus. by Margaret Chamberlain) — *Hendry, Diana*
Dog Eat Dog — *Berenson, Laurien*
Dog Eat Dog — *Bunker, Edward*
y Dog Eat Dog — *Lynch, Chris*
Dog Eat Dog — *Stern, Jane*
c Dog Heaven (Illus. by Cynthia Rylant) — *Rylant, Cynthia*
Dog Heroes — *Jones, Tim, 1942-*
y The Dog in the Freezer — *Mazer, Harry*
c Dog Is Thirsty (Illus. by Satoshi Kitamura) — *Kitamura, Satoshi*
The Dog King — *Ransmayr, Christoph*
Dog Love — *Garber, Marjorie*
Dog-Mas: Simple Truths from a Wise Pet — *Zimmerman, William*
Dog Music — *Duemer, Joseph*
c A Dog Named Sam (Illus. by G Brian Karas) — *Boland, Janice*
c Dog People (Illus. by Murv Jacob) — *Bruchac, Joseph*
Dog People — *Mazza, Cris*
c The Dog Show (Illus. by Margaret Wilson) — *Gray, Nigel*
Dog Soldiers — *Stone, Robert*
c Dog Training Projects for Young People — *McMains, Joel*

c The Dog Who Changed the World (Illus. by Alison Forsythe) — Leeson, Robert
c The Dog Who Cried Woof (Illus. by Nancy Coffelt) — Coffelt, Nancy
c The Dog Who Lost His Bob (Illus. by John Sandford) — McNeal, Tom
The Dog Who Loved Too Much — Dodman, Nicholas
y The Dog Who Loved Too Much (Dodman). Audio Version — Dodman, Nicholas
The Dog with the Chip in His Neck — Codrescu, Andrei
Dogbert's Top Secret Management Handbook — Adams, Scott
Dogless in Metchosin (Henry). Audio Version — Henry, Tom, 1961-
c Dogs (Illus. by Gail Gibbons) — Gibbons, Gail
Dogs: A Historical Journey — Wendt, Lloyd M
y Dog's Best Friend — Derr, Mark
c Dogs Don't Wear Glasses — Geoghegan, Adrienne
r Dogs for Dummies — Spadafori, Gina
c Dog's Journey (Illus. by Paul Howard) — Kemp, Gene
y A Dog's Life — Mayle, Peter
Dogs Never Lie about Love — Masson, J Moussaieff
c A Dog's Night before Christmas (Illus. by Shauna Mooney Kawasaki) — Carabine, Sue
The Dogs of Winter — Nunn, Kem
c The Dogs Who Saved Christmas Day — Slater, Dan
y Dogwolf — Carter, Alden R
Doin' Drugs — James, William H
Doing Battle — Fussell, Paul
Doing Brief Psychotherapy — Basch, Michael Franz
Doing Business with the Japanese — Goldman, Alan
Doing Documentary Work — Coles, Robert
Doing Ethics in Context — Villa-Vicencio, Charles
Doing It for Ourselves — Ballard, Donna
Doing Justice, Doing Gender — Martin, Susan Ehrlich
y Doing Life — Zehr, Howard
Doisneau Paris — Ollier, Brigitte
Dokhristiians'ki Viruvannia Ukrains'koho Narodu — Ilarion, Metropolitan of Winnipeg and Canada
The Doles: Unlimited Partners — Dole, Bob
The Doll — Prus, Boleslaw
r Doll Fashion Anthology and Price Guide. 5th Ed. — Mandeville, A Glen
The Dollar Bill Knows No Sex — Rue, Wendy
Dollar Signs — Morabito, Yvonne
Dollars for College Series
Dollars through the Doors — Germain, Richard N
The Dollmaker's Daughters — Padgett, Abigail
c The Doll's House — Anderson, Rachel
Dolor Y Alegria — LeVine, Sarah
y Dolores: The Alpine Years — Maurer-Alvarez, Pansy
y Dolphin Boy Blue — Arena, Felice
cp Dolphin Log
c Dolphin Man (Illus. by Randall S Wells) — Pringle, Laurence
c A Dolphin Named Bob (Illus. by Christine Herman Merrill) — George, Twig C
c A Dolphin of Many Colors — Semro, Jennifer
c Dolphin Sky — Rorby, Ginny
c Dolphin Treasure (Illus. by Jim Fowler) — Grover, Wayne
c Dolphins — Everts, Tammy
c Dolphins — Horton, Casey
c Dolphins — Stoops, Erik D
Dom Juan — Moliere
y El Domador De La Electricidad — Sayavedra, Roberto
Domain Decomposition — Smith, Barry F
y Dombey and Son (Davidson). Vols. 1-2. Audio Version — Dickens, Charles
y The Dome of the Rock — Nuseibeh, Said
Domestic and Divine — Kondoleon, Christine
Domestic Dangers — Gowing, Laura
Domestic Government — Mundy, Martha
The Domestic Rabbit. 5th Ed. — Sandford, J C
Domestic Sources of Foreign Policy — Stavridis, Stelios
r Domestic Violence — McCue, Margi Laird
The Domestication of Transcendence — Placher, William C
Domination and Resistance — Miller, Daniel
y Dominican Americans — Bandon, Alexandra
The Dominican Republic — Moya Pons, Frank
Il Dominio Del Cuore — Minore, Renato
Dominion: Can Nature and Culture Co-Exist? — Eldredge, Niles
p Dominion Review
Dominion's Reach — Thornley, Diann
c Dominique Moceanu: A Gymnastics Sensation — Quiner, Krista
c Domino Addition — Long, Lynette

The Domostroi: Rules for Russian Households in the Time of Ivan the Terrible — Pouncy, Carolyn Johnston
Don Alvaro O La Fuerza Del Sino — Ruiz Silva, Carlos
Don Bosco: Religious Outlook and Spirituality — Stella, Pietro
Don Quixote in Exile — Furst, Peter
Dona Juana — Hossfeld, Mok
r Donald Windham: A Bio-Bibliography — Kellner, Bruce
r The Doncaster Borough Courtier. Vol. 1
c Donde Esta Mi Huevo De Pascua? (Illus. by Richard Brown) — Ziefert, Harriet
Donde Van A Morir Los Elefantes — Donoso, Jose
c Donde Viven Los Monstruos — Sendak, Maurice
Done into Dance — Daly, Ann
Dong Co — Nguyen, Dinh Toan
The Dongan Paper 1683-1688. Pt. 2 — Christoph, Peter R
Donkey's Years — Higgins, Aidan
Donna Kooler's Glorious Needlepoint — Kooler, Donna
Donne and the Politics of Conscience in Early Modern England — Brown, Meg Lota
Donne Religiose — Rocca, Giancarlo
Donne's Idea of a Woman — Tayler, Edward W
Donnie Brasco (Pistone). Audio Version — Pistone, Joseph D
The Donor — Barnard, Christiaan
Dons and Workers — Goldman, Lawrence
Don't Block the Blessings — LaBelle, Patti
Don't Call It Night — Oz, Amos
c Don't Call Me Slob-O (Illus. by Bob Dorsey) — Orgel, Doris
y Don't Check Your Brains at the Door — McDowell, Josh
c Don't Dig So Deep, Nicholas! (Illus. by Gary Clement) — Harrison, Troon
Don't Erase Me — Ferrell, Carolyn
Don't Know Much about the Civil War — Davis, Kenneth C
Don't Know Much about the Civil War. Audio Version — Davis, Kenneth C
c Don't Laugh, Joe! (Illus. by Keiko Kasza) — Kasza, Keiko
c Don't Leave an Elephant to Go and Chase a Bird (Illus. by Ann Grifalconi) — Berry, James
Don't Leave Me This Way — Gott, Tedd
c Don't Let It Rain (Illus. by Jim Kavanagh) — Coppard, Yvonne
c Don't Panic — Posusta, Steven
Don't Pee on My Leg and Tell Me It's Raining — Sheindlin, Judy
c Don't Put Your Finger in the Jelly, Nelly! — Sharratt, Nick
y Don't Scream — Nixon, Joan Lowery
Don't Stand on the Grass — Finnie, Fleur
Don't Sweat the Small Stuff (Hall). Audio Version — Mantell, Michael R
Don't Talk to Strangers — Campbell, Bethany
y Don't Think Twice — Pennebaker, Ruth
r Don't Waste Your Time in the North Cascades — Copeland, Kathy
y Don't You Dare Read This, Mrs. Dunphrey — Haddix, Margaret Peterson
Doo-Dah! Stephen Foster and the Rise of American Popular Culture — Emerson, Ken
r Doody's Rating Service 1996
Doom Patrols — Shaviro, Steven
y The Doom Stone — Zindel, Paul
Doomed at the Start — Bartsch, William H
Doomsday Asteroid — Cox, Donald W
The Doomsters — Macdonald, Ross
Doonesbury Flashbacks. Electronic Media Version
y The Door in the Hedge — McKinley, Robin
y Door Number Three — O'Leary, Patrick, 1952-
Doors to Madame Marie — Meyers, Odette
Doowop: The Chicago Scene — Pruter, Robert
The Dopamine Receptors — Neve, Kim A
Dorfliche Gesellschaft Und Kriminalitat — Frank, Michael
Doria Shafik, Egyptian Feminist — Nelson, Cynthia
Dorinda's Taste of the Caribbean — Hafner, Dorinda
cr Dorling Kindersley Children's Illustrated Encyclopedia. 4th Rev. Ed.
r The Dorling Kindersley World Reference Atlas. 2nd American Ed. — Dorling Kindersley Publishing, Inc.
Dormition Et Assomption De Marie — Mimouni, Simon Claude
Dorothy Dandridge — Bogle, Donald

Dorothy Day: Arranged for Daily Reading — Day, Dorothy
y Dorothy Day: Friend to the Forgotten — Kent, Deborah
Dos Ensayos Sobre Jose Maria Arguedas — Galindo, Alberto Flores
Dos Testimonios Sobre Historia De Los Aprovechamientos Hidraulicos En Mexico — Arreguin Manon, Jose P
A Dose of Sanity — Walker, Sydney
Dossier Secreto — Andersen, Martin Edwin
Dossier: The Secret History of Armand Hammer — Epstein, Edward Jay
Dostoevskii and Britain — Leatherbarrow, W J
Dostoevsky and the Woman Question — Straus, Nina Pelikan
Dostoevsky: The Miraculous Years 1865-1871 — Frank, Joseph
D'Ou Surgi — Belanger, Marcel
The Double — Dostoyevsky, Fyodor
c Double Act (Illus. by Nick Sharratt) — Wilson, Jacqueline
Double Agent — Dickstein, Morris
p Double Bassist
y Double Birthday Trouble — Older, Effin
Double Dead — Hardwick, Gary
Double Deception — Barros, James
Double Delight — Smith, Rosamond
Double-Diffusive Convection — Brandt, Alan
r The Double Eagle Guide to Western State Parks. Vol. 1, 2nd Ed.; Vols. 2-6 — Preston, Tom
Double Edge — Etchison, Dennis
Double-Edged Sword — Drlica, Karl
Double Fighter Knight — Juutilainen, Eino Ilmari
The Double Flame — Paz, Octavio
The Double Helix — Watson, James D, 1928-
Double Lives — Koch, Stephen
The Double Message — Seim, Turid Karlsen
r Double Minorities of Spain — McNerney, Kathleen
c Double Play at Short — Christopher, Matt
Double Take — Coleman, Peter
The Double Tongue — Golding, William
c Double Trouble (Illus. by Lesley Harker) — Bruce, Lisa
Double Vision — Greenspon, Edward
Double Your Brain Power — Stine, Jean Marie
Doubled in Spades — Moody, Susan
Doubles Stances Des Amants — Rezvani
p DoubleTake
Doubling and Incest/Repetition and Revenge. Expanded Ed. — Irwin, John T
The Doubtful Strait — Cardenal, Ernesto
Douglas Duane. Electronic Media Version — Fawcett, Edgar
r Douglas Stewart: A Bibliography — Ballyn, Susan
c Dounia (Illus. by Natacha Karvoskaia) — Karvoskaia, Natacha
y Dove — Graham, Robin Lee
The Dove and the Rose — Herr, Ethel
c Dove Isabeau (Illus. by Dennis Nolan) — Yolen, Jane
r The Dow Jones Averages 1885-1995 — Pierce, Phyllis S
y The Dow Low Drop — Fisher, Roy
Down and Dirty Birding — Slinger, Joey
c The Down and Up Fall (Illus. by Gail Owens) — Hurwitz, Johanna
Down but Not Out — Sexson, Jeanne E
c Down by the River (Illus. by Caroline Binch) — Hallworth, Grace
Down by the River — O'Brien, Edna
Down for the Count — Vogel, Brenda
Down from Bureaucracy — Handler, Joel F
Down from Olympus — Marchand, Suzanne L
y Down from Troy (Gray). Audio Version — Selzer, Richard
c Down Home at Miss Dessa's (Illus. by Felicia Marshall) — Stroud, Bettye
Down in the Garden — Geddes, Anne
c Down on Casey's Farm (Illus. by Sandra Jordan) — Jordan, Sandra
Down on the Farm — Cochrane, Jean
Down the Asphalt Path — McShane, Clay
Down the Common — Baer, Ann
c Down the Road (Illus. by E B Lewis) — Schertle, Alice
Down to a Sunless Sea — Poyer, David
Down to Earth — Brennan, Georgeanne
Down to Earth — Faure, David
Down to Earth II — Ridley, Matt
Down to Earth Judaism — Waskow, Arthur
Down with Big Brother — Dobbs, Michael
Down with the Old Canoe — Biel, Steven

Downcast Eyes — *Jay, Martin*
Downhome: An Anthology of Southern Women Writers — *Mee, Susie*
Downloading Democracy — *Ryan, Susan M*
y Downriver — *Hobbs, Will*
Down's Syndrome — *Rondal, Jean A*
y Downsize This! — *Moore, Michael*
Downsize This! (Moore). Audio Version — *Moore, Michael*
Downsizing: Law and Practice — *Lipsig, Ethan*
Downtown, Inc. — *Frieden, Bernard J*
A Dozen Black Roses — *Collins, Nancy A*
DR I TV-Konkurrencens Tidsalder — *Soendergaard, Henrik*
Draconian New York — *Sheckley, Robert*
Dracula — *Stoker, Bram*
c Dracula (Illus. by Tudor Humphries) — *Stoker, Bram*
c Dracula Junior and the Fake Fangs (Illus. by Korky Paul) — *Bethlen, Julianna*
Dracula: The Connoisseur's Guide — *Wolf, Leonard*
Dracula: Truth and Terror. Electronic Media Version — *McNally, Raymond T*
Dradin, in Love — *VanderMeer, Jeff*
Draft High Peaks Wilderness Complex Unit Management Plan
c Drag Racing — *Savage, Jeff*
y The Dragon and the Djinn — *Dickson, Gordon R*
The Dragon and the Eagle — *Aldridge, A Owen*
y The Dragon and the Unicorn — *Attanasio, A A*
y A Dragon at World's End — *Rowley, Christopher*
Dragon Burning — *Gardner, Craig Shaw*
Dragon Circle — *Gardner, Craig Shaw*
y The Dragon King — *Salvatore, R A*
c Dragon Kite of the Autumn Moon (Illus. by Jean Tseng) — *Reddix, Valerie*
c Dragon Mountain (Illus. by Tim Vyner) — *Vyner, Tim*
c Dragon Naps (Illus. by Janet Street) — *Bertrand, Lynne*
c The Dragon of Brog (Illus. by Peter Kavanagh) — *Hood, Jean*
c The Dragon of Navy Pier (Illus. by Rachel Bass) — *Noble, Kate*
c Dragon Quest (Illus. by Jackie French Koller) — *Koller, Jackie French*
c Dragon Soup (Illus. by Sally J Smith) — *Williams, Arlene*
Dragon Strike — *Hawksley, Humphrey*
Dragon Teeth — *Hunt, E Howard*
The Dragon, the Lion, and the Eagle — *Qiang, Zhai*
c Dragon Tooth (Illus. by Cathryn Falwell) — *Falwell, Cathryn*
cp Dragonfly: A Magazine for Young Investigators
Dragonfly Beetle, Butterfly Bee — *Koch, Maryjo*
c Dragonfly Secret — *Gold, Carolyn J*
c Dragonquest (Illus. by Wayne Harris) — *Baillie, Allan*
c Dragons (Illus. by Sally Townsend) — *Toczek, Nick*
c Dragons and Gods. 2nd Ed. — *Siembieda, Kevin*
c Dragons and Monsters (Illus. by Alan Baker) — *Ganeri, Anita*
y Dragon's Bait — *Vande Velde, Vivian*
c The Dragon's Egg and Other Stories (Illus. by Wayne Anderson) — *Corbett, W J*
c Dragon's Gate — *Yep, Laurence*
The Dragons of Eden — *Sagan, Carl*
Dragons of God — *Coppola, Vincent*
c The Dragon's Tale and Other Animal Fables of the Chinese Zodiac (Illus. by Demi) — *Demi*
Dragons: The Modern Infestation — *Blanpied, Pamela Wharton*
y Dragonseye — *McCaffrey, Anne*
The Dragonstone — *McKiernan, Dennis L*
Dragonwyck — *Seton, Anya*
Drake and the Tudor Navy — *Corbett, Julian S*
The Drake Manuscript in the Pierpoint Morgan Library — *Drake Manuscript*
Drama and Music — *Rubin, Janet*
Drama in Early Tudor Britain 1485-1558 — *Norland, Howard B*
The Drama of Leadership — *Pitcher, Patricia C*
The Drama of the Gifted Child — *Miller, Alice*
DramaContemporary: Germany — *Weber, Carl*
Dramatic Approaches to Brief Therapy — *Gersie, Alida*
The Dramatic Art of David Storey — *Liebman, Herbert*
The Dramatic Criticism of Elizabeth Charlotte, Duchesse D'Orleans — *Brooks, W S*
Dramatic Discourse — *Herman, Vimala*
The Dramatic Monologue — *Howe, Elisabeth A*

The Dramatic Works in the Beaumont and Fletcher Canon. Vol. 9 — *Beaumont, Francis*
The Dramatic Works in the Beaumont and Fletcher Canon. Vol. 10 — *Beaumont, Francis*
Dramaworks — *Owens, Allan*
Drame — *Bojic, Veljko P*
c Draw Alien Fantasies (Illus. by Damon J Reinagle) — *Reinagle, Damon J*
c Draw Desert Animals (Illus. by D C DuBosque) — *DuBosque, D C*
c Draw! Grassland Animals (Illus. by D C Dubosque) — *Dubosque, D C*
y Drawing — *Dunn, Chris*
Drawing: A Step-by-Step Guide to Drawing Techniques — *Gair, Angela*
y Drawing and Painting — *Dunn, Chris*
Drawing and Painting Animals — *Tilton, Bill*
Drawing from Life — *Nugent, Frances*
Drawing on the Right Side of the Brain — *Edwards, Betty*
Drawing Out Your Soul — *Koff-Chapin, Deborah*
Drawing the Line — *Eisenberg, Carolyn Woods*
Drawing the Line — *Inada, Lawson Fusao*
Drawing the Line — *Rosenthal, Alan*
Drawings in Midwestern Collections. Vol. 1 — *Midwest Art History Society*
Drawn and Quartered — *Hess, Stephen*
Drawn from the Source — *Johnson, Eugene J*
Drawn with the Sword — *McPherson, James M*
The Dread of Difference — *Grant, Barry Keith*
The Dreaded Comparison. Rev. and Expanded Ed. — *Spiegel, Marjorie*
Dreadful Lies — *Bailey, Michele*
y Dreadful Sorry — *Reiss, Kathryn*
Dream a Little Dream — *Stockenberg, Antoinette*
Dream Analysis in Psychotherapy — *Gardner, Richard A*
The Dream and the Dialogue — *Templeton, Alice*
A Dream Betrayed — *Manera, Tony*
Dream Children — *Godwin, Gail*
Dream City Cinema — *Knight, Stephen*
Dream, Creativity, and Madness in Nineteenth-Century France — *James, Tony*
c The Dream Dog — *Richemont, Enid*
The Dream Endures — *Starr, Kevin*
y Dream Girl — *Rieselman, Brian*
c The Dream Jar (Illus. by Mark Graham) — *Pryor, Bonnie*
y The Dream Keeper and Other Poems (Illus. by J Brian Pinkney) — *Hughes, Langston*
Dream Lover — *Henley, Virginia*
The Dream-Machine: Avian Imagery in Madame Bovary — *Tipper, Paul Andrew*
The Dream Messenger — *Garfield, Patricia*
Dream Nation — *Gourgouris, Stathis*
Dream of a Falling Eagle — *Chesbro, George C*
The Dream of a New Social Order — *Schneirov, Matthew*
Dream of a Red Factory — *Kaple, Deborah A*
A Dream of England — *Taylor, John, 1945-*
Dream of Fair to Middling Women — *Beckett, Samuel*
Dream of Order — *Avena, Thomas*
The Dream of the Unified Field — *Graham, Jorie*
Dream On (Foxe-Tyler). Audio Version — *Foxe-Tyler, Cynthia*
Dream Revisionaries — *Lewes, Darby*
The Dream Seekers — *Irwin, Lee*
c Dream Team — *Blacker, Terence*
y Dream-Weaver — *Lawrence, Louise*
y Dream Weavers — *Collins, Paul*
Dreamcatcher — *McCall, Dinah*
A Dreamer for the People — *Buero Vallejo, Antonio*
The Dreamer of Dreams — *French, Sean*
y Dreamers — *Hunt, Angela Elwell*
Dreamhouse — *Habens, Alison*
The Dreamhunters of Corsica — *Carrington, Dorothy*
Dreaming and Other Involuntary Mentation — *Epstein, Arthur W*
Dreaming and Storytelling — *States, Bert O*
Dreaming in Urban Areas — *Bellear, Lisa*
Dreaming Metal — *Scott, Melissa*
Dreaming of Hitler — *Merkin, Daphne*
c Dreamland (Illus. by Kevin Hawkes) — *Schotter, Roni*
c Dreamland: A Lullaby (Illus. by Julia Noonan) — *Carpenter, Mary-Chapin*
Dreamland Japan — *Schodt, Frederik L*
Dreams and Reverie — *Ravenhill, Philip L*
Dreams and Wishes — *Cooper, Susan*
Dreams in Late Antiquity — *Miller, Patricia Cox*
Dreams of Chaos, Visions of Order — *Peterson, James, 1957-*

p Dreams of Decadence
c Dreams of Dolphins Dancing — *Bourque, Joan*
Dreams of Leaving — *Thompson, Rupert*
y The Dreams of Mairhe Mehan — *Armstrong, Jennifer*
Dreams of Millennium — *Kingwell, Mark*
Dreams of the Centaur — *Fontes, Montserrat*
Dreams of the Heart — *Chamorro, Violeta*
Dreams of You — *Wainscott, Tina*
y Dreamseeker's Road — *Deitz, Tom*
y Dreamskate — *Cash, Angela*
y Dreamweaver — *Lawrence, Louise*
Dreamweaver's Dilemma — *Bujold, Lois McMaster*
c The Dred Scott Case — *Fleischner, Jennifer*
Dred Scott's Advocate — *Kaufman, Kenneth C*
Dreiklassenwahlrecht Und Wahlkultur In Preussen 1867-1914 — *Kuhne, Thomas*
Dreiser's Russian Diary — *Dreiser, Theodore*
Der Dreissigjahrige Krieg — *Schmidt, George*
Drepturile Romanilor Asupra Basarabiei — *Crihan, Anton*
Dress and Ethnicity — *Eicher, Joanne B*
Dress Codes — *Rubinstein, Ruth P*
Dressed to Kill — *McInerney, Jay*
Dresses of Red and Gold — *Klein, Robin*
Dressing in Feathers — *Bird, S Elizabeth*
c Dressing Up with Mr. Bumble — *Wallace, John*
Le Dressoir Du Prince — *Crepin-Leblond, Thierry*
c Drew and the Bub Daddy Showdown (Illus. by Robb Armstrong) — *Armstrong, Robb*
The Dreyfus Affair — *Zola, Emile*
The Dreyfus Affair in French Society and Politics — *Cahm, Eric*
Dried Flowers — *Masera, M*
The Driftless Zone — *Harsch, Rick*
y A Drink before the War — *Lehane, Dennis*
Drinking: A Love Story — *Knapp, Caroline*
Drinking: A Love Story (Knapp). Audio Version — *Knapp, Caroline*
y Drive-By — *Ewing, Lynne*
The Drive for Self — *Hoffman, Edward*
Drive for Show, Putt for Dough — *Crump, Leon*
c Drive Your Car (Illus. by Tony Wells) — *Nilsen, Anna*
c Drive Your Tractor (Illus. by Tony Wells) — *Nilsen, Anna*
y Driver's Ed (Guidall). Audio Version — *Cooney, Caroline B*
y Driving Force — *Livingston, James D*
Driving My Father — *Wicks, Susan*
Driving the Amish — *Butterfield, Jim*
Driving the Green — *Strawn, John*
Driving under the Affluence — *Phillips, Julia*
Le Droit De Cuissage — *Boureau, Alain*
Le Droit De Cuissage — *Marie-Victoire, Louis*
Droit Du Travail. 5th Ed. — *Javilier, Jean-Claude*
c Drop Dead (Illus. by Babette Cole) — *Cole, Babette*
A Drop of Patience — *Kelly, William Melvin*
c A Drop of Water (Illus. by Walter Wick) — *Wick, Walter*
y Dropping Out — *Sherrow, Victoria*
Drought. Say What You Like — *Di Blasi, Debra*
Drover and the Designated Hitter — *Granger, Bill*
Drown — *Diaz, Junot*
The Drowner — *Drewe, Robert*
Drowning in Honey — *Hatfield, Kate*
The Drowning Pool — *Cooper, Natasha*
The Drowning Pool — *Macdonald, Ross*
The Drowning Room — *Pye, Michael*
Drucker on Asia — *Drucker, Peter Ferdinand*
Das Druckgraphische Werk Von Matthaeus Merian Der Altere. Vol. 3 — *Wuthrich, Lucas Heinrich*
y Drug Abuse — *Washburne, Carolyn Kott*
The Drug Development Process — *Welling, Peter G*
Drug-Induced Neurological Disorders — *Jain, K K*
Drug Lessons and Education Programs in Developing Countries — *Kirsch, Henry*
Drug Policy and Human Nature — *Bickel, Warren K*
Drug Testing in Hair — *Kintz, Pascal*
Drug Trafficking in the Americas — *Bagley, Bruce M*
Drug Treatment behind Bars — *Early, Kevin E*
Drug Use in Assisted Suicide and Euthanasia — *Battin, M Pabst*
Drug War Politics — *Bertram, Eva*
c Drugs (Illus. by Mike Lacey) — *Sanders, Pete*
Drugs Affecting Lipid Metabolism — *Gotto, A M*
c Drugs and Emotions — *Myers, Arthur*
Drugs and Narcotics in History — *Porter, Roy*
y Drugs and Sports — *Galas, Judith C*
Drugs and the Brain — *Snyder, Solomon H*
c Drugs and Violent Crime — *Miller, Maryann*
Drugs in Modern Society. 4th Ed. — *Carroll, Charles R*

Drugs in Ontario
Drugs in the Western Hemisphere — *Walker, William O, II*
y Drugs: Should They Be Legalized? — *Oliver, Marilyn Tower*
The Druid Source Book — *Matthews, John*
The Druids — *Lonigan, Paul R*
Drum and Stethoscope — *Bastien, Joseph W*
Drumblair: Memories of a Jamaican Childhood — *Manley, Rachel*
c The Drummer Boy of Vicksburg — *Wisler, G Clifton*
c Drummer Hoff (Illus. by Edward Emberley) — *Emberley, Barbara*
y Drummers of Jericho — *Meyers, Carolyn*
y Drums (Illus. by N C Wyeth) — *Boyd, James*
c Drums at Saratoga — *Banim, Lisa*
Drums of Autumn — *Gabaldon, Diana*
y Drums of Autumn (James). Audio Version — *Gabaldon, Diana*
y Drums of Change — *Oke, Janette*
Drumul Spre Damasc — *Leu, Corneliu*
y Drunken Master — *Maekawa, Takeshi*
c Dry Climates — *Lye, Keith*
Dry Fire — *Lewis, Catherine*
Dry Rain — *Fromm, Pete*
Drylands: Environmental Management and Development — *Beaumont, Peter*
DSM-IV Handbook of Differential Diagnosis — *First, Michael B*
The DSM-IV Personality Disorders — *Livesley, W John*
DSM-IV Primary Care Version — *American Psychiatric Association*
Du Plus Loin De L'Oubli — *Modiano, Patrick*
Du Silence — *Guillevic, Eugene*
The Dual Tradition — *Kinsella, Thomas*
Duality and Structure in the Iliad and Odyssey — *Van Duzer, Chet A*
r Dubester's U.S. Census Bibliography with SuDocs Class Numbers and Indexes — *Cook, Kevin L*
Dubious Conceptions — *Luker, Kristin*
y Dubliners — *Joyce, James*
y Dublines — *Donovan, Katie*
Duchamp — *Tomkins, Calvin*
Duchamp: A Biography — *Tomkins, Calvin*
The Duchamp Effect — *Buskirk, Martha*
y Duchamp (Faerna) — *Duchamp, Marcel*
The Duchess of Windsor — *Bloch, Michael*
The Duchess of York Uncensored — *Kortesis, Vasso*
The Duchovny Files — *Mitchell, P*
c The Duck and the Goat (Illus. by Maya Kennedy) — *Mamet, David*
c Duck, Duck, Goose? (Illus. by Katya Arnold) — *Arnold, Katya*
c Duck for Cover — *Jennings, Paul*
c A Duck in a Tree (Illus. by Jennifer A Loomis) — *Loomis, Jennifer A*
c Duck Is Dirty (Illus. by Satoshi Kitamura) — *Kitamura, Satoshi*
c Ducks Disappearing (Illus. by Tony Maddox) — *Naylor, Phyllis Reynolds*
The Dud Avocado — *Dundy, Elaine*
La Duda Y Otros Apuntes Para Escribir Una Coleccion De Relatos — *Rio-Sukan, Isabel Del*
Duden: Das Grosse Worterbuch Der Deutschen Sprache. 2nd Ed., Vols. 1-8 — *Droskowski, Gunther*
Dudley Moore — *Paskin, Barbara*
Due Diligence Techniques and Analysis — *Bing, Gordon*
Due Nomi Per Charlie — *Vigevani, Alberto*
Due West — *Tefs, Wayne*
Dueling: The Cult of Honor in Fin-De-Siecle Germany — *McAleer, Kevin*
c El Dueno De La Luz (Illus. by Irene Savino) — *Rivas, Ivonne*
c Duffy and the Devil (Leishman). Audio Version — *Zemach, Harve*
The Dugger Family, Johnson County, Tennessee — *Rowan, Frances Dugger*
c Duke Ellington — *Woog, Adam*
y Duke Ellington: Giant of Jazz — *Old, Wendie C*
c Duke the Dairy Delight Dog (Illus. by Lisa Campbell Ernst) — *Ernst, Lisa Campbell*
c The Dumb Bunnies (Illus. by Dav Pilkey) — *Denim, Sue*
c The Dumb Bunnies' Easter (Illus. by Dav Pilkey) — *Denim, Sue*
c The Dumb Bunnies Go to the Zoo (Illus. by Dav Pilkey) — *Denim, Sue*
Dumbing Down — *Washburn, Katharine*
Dumbocracy in America — *Brustein, Robert*

Dumbstruck — *Polain, Marcella*
c Dump Trucks and Diggers — *Crowther, Robert*
r The Dun and Bradstreet Regional Business Directory Disc. Electronic Media Version
r Dun and Bradstreet's Guide to Doing Business around the World — *Morrison, Terri*
D'Un Livre A L'Autre — *Lebel, Maurice*
r The Duncans, by George! — *Powell, Agnes D*
D'Une Rive A L'Autre — *Carbet, Marie-Magdeleine*
Dunes and Dreams — *Welsh, Michael E*
Dunhuang: Caves of the Singing Sands — *Whitfield, Roderick*
Duns Scotus, Metaphysician — *Frank, William A*
Duong Vao Dai Hoc Hoa Ky — *Bui, Tien Khoi*
Duplicate Keys — *Smiley, Jane*
Duplications and Other Stories — *Jaramillo Levi, Enrique*
Durability Analysis of Structural Composite Systems — *Cardon, Albert H*
Durable Tumblers — *Kenyon, Michael*
Durer to Matisse — *Nelson-Atkins Museum of Art*
Durkheim and Women — *Lehmann, Jennifer M*
Durkheim, Morals and Modernity — *Watts Miller, William*
Durkheim through the Lens of Aristotle — *Challenger, Douglas F*
Durkheim's Philosophy of Science and the Sociology of Knowledge — *Schmaus, Warren*
A Dusk of Idols and Other Stories — *Blish, James*
Dust and Ashes — *Rybakov, Anatoli*
y The Dust Bowl (Illus. by Karen Reczuch) — *Booth, David*
Dust Bowl Migrants in the American Imagination — *Shindo, Charles J*
Dust Disappears — *Oliver Labra, Carilda*
c Dust for Dinner (Illus. by Robert Barrett) — *Warren, Ann*
Dust on Her Tongue — *Rey Rosa, Rodrigo*
The Dust Rose like Smoke — *Gump, James O*
Dust to Dust — *Findley, Timothy*
Dust Tracks on a Road — *Hurston, Zora Neale*
Dusty and Self-Gravitational Plasmas in Space — *Bliokh, Paval*
p Dusty Dog Reviews
Dutch Farmer in the Missouri Valley — *Beltman, Brian W*
Dutch Floral Tiles in the Golden Age and Their Botanical Prints — *Schaap, Ella B*
Dutch Flower Painting 1600-1720 — *Taylor, Paul, 1963-*
r Dutch Modernism — *Langmead, Donald*
Dutch Painting 1600-1800 — *Slive, Seymour*
The Dutch Republic — *Israel, Jonathan*
Duty Free — *Pesman, Ros*
Dvanadstat' P'ies Bez Odniel Zibrani Dramatychni Tvory 1945-1989 — *Cholhan, Ilarion*
c The Dwarf Giant — *Lobel, Anita*
A Dwarf Kingdom — *Freeling, Nicolas*
c The Dwarf, the Giant, and the Unicorn (Illus. by Claire Ewart) — *Giblin, James Cross*
Dwelling Places — *Ferry, David*
Dwellings: A Spiritual History of the Living World — *Hogan, Linda*
Dwight D. Eisenhower and American Power — *Pickett, William B*
c Dwight D. Eisenhower, John F. Kennedy, Lyndon B. Johnson — *Lindop, Edmund*
Dwight Macdonald and the Politics Circle — *Sumner, Gregory D*
c Dybbuk: A Story Made in Heaven (Illus. by Mark Podwal) — *Prose, Francine*
The Dybbuk and Other Writings — *Ansky, S*
y Dyer's Thistle — *Balakian, Peter*
Dying for a Bargain — *Zepada, Ray*
Dying for Chocolate (Rosenblat). Audio Version — *Davidson, Diane Mott*
Dying for Veronica — *Remski, Matthew*
The Dying of the Trees — *Little, Charles E*
y Dying to Dance — *Davidson, Nicole*
Dying Well — *Byock, Ira*
Dying with Dignity — *Kung, Hans*
The Dykemaster — *Storm, Theodor*
Dylan Programming — *Feinberg, Neal*
r The Dylan Reference Manual — *Shalit, Andrew*
Dylan Thomas and His World — *Perkins, Derek*
Dynamic Alignment through Imagery — *Franklin, Eric N*
Dynamic Asset Pricing Theory — *Duffie, Darrell*
The Dynamic Cosmos — *Madsen, Mark S*
Dynamic Disequilibrium Modeling — *International Symposium in Economic Theory and Econometrics*

Dynamic Fracture Mechanics — *Wen, P H*
r The Dynamic Human. Electronic Media Version
The Dynamic Library Organizations in a Changing Environment — *Giesecke, Joan*
Dynamic Models of the Firm — *Blok, Mark W J*
A Dynamic of Hope — *MacGinley, Rosa*
Dynamic Patterns — *Kelso, Scott*
The Dynamic Society — *Snooks, Graeme Donald*
Dynamic Systems — *Vu, Hung V*
Dynamic Systems on Measure Chains — *Lakshmikantham, V*
Dynamical Evolution of Star Clusters — *International Astronomical Union. Symposium (174th: 1995: Tokyo, Japan)*
Dynamical Systems and Applications — *Agarwal, R P*
Dynamical Systems and Numerical Analysis — *Stuart, A M*
Dynamical Systems and Probabilistic Methods in Partial Differential Equations — *Deift, Percy*
Dynamical Systems of Algebraic Origin — *Schmidt, Klaus, 1943-*
Dynamics and Control of Structures in Space — *International Conference on Dynamics and Control of Structures in Space (3rd: 1996: Cranfield Institute of Technology)*
Dynamics and Income Distribution — *Adelman, Irma*
Dynamics and the Problem of Recognition in Biological Macromolecules — *Jardetzky, Oleg*
Dynamics, Ephemerides, and Astrometry of the Solar System — *International Astronomical Union. Symposium (172nd: 1995: Paris, France)*
Dynamics in Document Design — *Schriver, Karen A*
The Dynamics of American Ethnic, Religious, and Racial Group Life — *Perlmutter, Philip*
The Dynamics of Conflict in Northern Ireland — *Ruane, Joseph*
Dynamics of Exothermicity — *Bowen, J Ray*
The Dynamics of Folklore. Rev. and Expanded Ed. — *Toelken, Barre*
The Dynamics of Heat — *Fuchs, Hans U*
The Dynamics of Industrial Competition — *Baldwin, John R*
Dynamics of Marine Ecosystems. 2nd Ed. — *Mann, K H*
Dynamics of Modern Communication — *Flichy, Patrice*
Dynamics of Molecules and Chemical Reactions — *Wyatt, Robert E*
The Dynamics of Service — *Gutek, Barbara A*
Dynamics of Small Neural Populations — *Milton, John*
The Dynamics of Technical Innovation — *Duysters, Geert*
Dynamics of Weed Populations — *Cousens, Roger*
Les Dynamismes De La Recherche Au Quebec — *Mathieu, Jacques*
Dynasty and Empire in the Age of Augustus — *Kuttner, Ann L*
y Dyslexia — *Moragne, Wendy*
Dyslexia in Adults — *Nosek, Kathleen*
r Dyslexia, Speech and Language — *Snowling, Margaret*
The Dystopian Impulse in Modern Literature — *Booker, M Keith*
Dyvnyi Svit Ikon — *IArema, Volodymyr*

E

E. Coli 0157 — *Heersink, Mary*
E-Mail: A Practical Guide — *Collin, Simon*
E-Mail for English Teaching — *Warschauer, Mark*
E-Mail.This.Book.! — *Cartoon Bank, Inc.*
E. Ray Lankester and the Making of Modern British Biology — *Lester, Joseph*
E: Reflections on the Birth of the Elvis Faith — *Strausbaugh, John*
Each One Teach One — *Casanova, Ron*
c Each Orange Had Eight Slices (Illus. by Donald Crews) — *Giganti, Paul*
c Each Peach Pear Plum — *Ahlberg, Janet*
Each Thing We Know Is Changed Because We Know It and Other Poems — *Hearle, Kevin*
Eagle Adrift — *Lieber, Robert J*
The Eagle and the Crow — *Halikowska, Teresa*
The Eagle and the Peacock — *Chary, M Srinivas*
The Eagle and the Rose — *Altea, Rosemary*
c Eagle Boy (Illus. by Cara Moser) — *Hausman, Gerald*
c Eagle Dreams (Illus. by Ron Lightburn) — *McFarlane, Sheryl*
The Eagle in the Desert — *Head, William*
y The Eagle Kite — *Fox, Paula*
y The Eagle of the Ninth — *Sutcliff, Rosemary*
c Eagle Song (Illus. by Dan Andreasen) — *Bruchac, Joseph*
c Eagles — *Horton, Casey*
Eagles of Fire — *Rizzi, Timothy*
y Eagle's Plume — *Beans, Bruce E*
Eakins' Mistress — *Bradberry, James*
y The Ear, the Eye, and the Arm — *Farmer, Nancy*
c The Ear, the Eye, and the Arm (Guidall). Audio Version — *Farmer, Nancy*
y Ear-Witness — *Scott, Mary Ann*
Earl in the Yellow Shirt — *Daugharty, Janice*
y Earl Warren, Chief Justice for Social Change — *Herda, D J*
The Earliest Christian Heretics — *Hultgren, Arland J*
The Earliest Irish and English Bookarts — *Stevick, Robert D*
An Early Afterlife — *Pastan, Linda*
Early American Cookery — *Hale, Sarah Josepha*
r The Early American Sourcebook — *Lawliss, Chuck*
Early American Technology — *McGaw, Judith A*
r The Early Byzantine Churches of Cilicia and Isauria — *Hill, Stephen*
Early Cambridge Theatres — *Nelson, Alan H*
The Early Career of the Prophet Jeremiah — *Lundbom, Jack R*
Early Child Development — *Young, Mary Eming*
Early Childhood Special Education — *Safford, Philip L*
r Early Chinese Texts — *Loewe, Michael*
Early Christian Baptism and the Catechumenate — *Finn, Thomas M*
Early Christian Texts on Jews and Judaism — *MacLennan, Robert S*
Early Civilizations — *Trigger, Bruce G*
Early Creationist Journals — *Numbers, Ronald L*
Early Downhome Blues. 2nd Ed. — *Titon, Jeff Todd*
Early Embraces — *Elder, Lindsey*
The Early Film Criticism of Francois Truffaut — *Truffaut, Francois*
Early Formative Pottery of the Valley of Oaxaca — *Flannery, Kent V*
Early French Cookery — *Scully, D Eleanor*
Early French Feminisms 1830-1940 — *Gordon, Felicia*
Early Greek Political Thought from Homer to the Sophists — *Gagarin, Michael*
The Early History of the Law of Bills and Notes — *Rogers, James Steven*

Early Hunter-Gatherers of the California Coast — *Erlandson, Jon M*
Early Images of the Americas — *Williams, Jerry M*
Early Impressionism and the French State 1866-1874 — *Roos, Jane Mayo*
r Early Imprints in New Zealand Libraries
Early Innings — *Sullivan, Dean A*
Early Islamic Mysticism — *Sells, Michael Anthony*
The Early Journals and Letters of Fanny Burney. Vol. 3, Pt. 1 — *Burney, Fanny*
Early Judaism — *Jaffee, Martin S*
The Early Medieval Bible — *Gameson, Richard*
Early Medieval Georgian Monasteries in Historic Tao, Klarjet'i, and Savset'i — *Djobadze, Wachtang*
Early Medieval Ireland 400-1200 — *O Croinin, Daibhi*
r Early Metal Mining and Production — *Craddock, Paul T*
The Early Modern City 1450-1750 — *Friedrichs, Christopher R*
Early Modern Conceptions of Property — *Brewer, John*
Early Modern Democracy in the Grisons — *Head, Randolph C*
Early Modern Wales c. 1525-1640 — *Jones, J Gwynfor*
Early Mourning — *Steen, Edla Van*
The Early Novels of Naguib Mahfouz — *Moosa, Matti*
The Early Paintings and Drawings of John Constable. Vols. 1-2 — *Reynolds, Graham*
The Early Parties and Politics in Britain 1688-1832 — *Hill, Brian*
The Early Poetry. Vol. 2 — *Yeats, W B*
The Early Porcelain Kilns of Japan — *Impey, Oliver*
The Early Rolfe Settlers of New England. Vol. 1 — *Rolfe, Frederick G*
Early Rome and Latium — *Smith, Christopher John*
Early Science and the First Century of Physics at Union College 1795-1895 — *Pilcher, V Ennis*
Early Stages of Oxygen Precipitation in Silicon — *Jones, R*
The Early Stewart Kings — *Boardman, Stephen*
The Early Stuart Church 1603-1642 — *Fincham, Kenneth*
r Early Television — *Shiers, George*
An Early Toll-Road — *Broderick, David*
Early Tudor Government 1485-1558 — *Gunn, S J*
r Early U.S.-Hispanic Relations 1776-1860 — *Tarrago, Rafael E*
The Early Universe — *Johri, V B*
Early Vertebrates — *Janvier, Philippe*
Early Visitors to Haworth — *Lemon, Charles*
The Early Writings of Harold W. Clark and Frank Lewis Marsh — *Clark, Harold Willard*
The Early Years of Art History in the United States — *Smyth, Craig Hugh*
Earning Respect — *Sangster, Joan*
c Ears and the Secret Song (Illus. by William Geldart) — *Doney, Meryl*
c Earth — *Vogt, Gregory L*
y Earth Always Endures (Illus. by Edward S Curtis) — *Philip, Neil*
Earth Angel — *Obstfeld, Raymond*
The Earth Brokers — *Chatterjee, Pratap*
Earth Cancer — *Weigel, Van B*
Earth Community, Earth Ethics — *Rasmussen, Larry L*
c Earth Dance (Illus. by Norman Gorbaty) — *Ryder, Joanne*
y The Earth Dwellers — *Hoyt, Erich*
Earth Elegy — *Gibson, Margaret*
c Earth Explained — *Taylor, Barbara*

c Earth, Fire, Water, Air (Illus. by J Ray) — *Hoffman, Mary*
Earth First! — *Lee, Martha F*
c Earth-Friendly Outdoor Fun — *Pfiffner, George*
c The Earth Giant (Illus. by K Brown) — *Burgess, Melvin*
The Earth, Humanity, and God — *Russell, Colin Archibald*
The Earth Is Enough — *Middleton, Harry*
r Earth Online — *Ritter, Michael E*
Earth Prime — *Almon, Bert*
Earth Processes — *Basu, Asish*
Earth Science — *Conte, Donald J*
Earth Stories — *Aurelio, John R*
The Earth Strikes Back — *Chizmar, Richard*
Earth Summit Ethics — *Callicott, J Baird*
Earth Summit: The NGO Archives. Electronic Media Version
Earth: Then and Now. 3rd Ed. — *Montgomery, Carla W*
c The Earth under Sky Bear's Feet (Illus. by Thomas Locker) — *Bruchac, Joseph*
yr Earth Works — *Dwyer, Jim*
Earthcare: Women and the Environment — *Merchant, Carolyn*
Earthly Goods — *Hampson, Fen Osler*
The Earthly Paradise — *Lochman, Katharine A*
Earthquake Geotechnical Engineering. Vols. 1-3 — *International Conference on Earthquake Geotechnical Engineering (1st: 1995: Tokyo, Japan)*
Earthquake Hazard and Risk — *Schenk, Vladimir*
Earthquake Resistant Engineering Structures — *International Conference on Earthquake Resistant Engineering Structures (1st: 1996: Thessaloniki, Greece)*
c Earthquake Terror — *Kehret, Peg*
c Earthquakes — *Pope, Joyce*
c Earthquakes — *Walker, Sally M*
r Earthquakes and the Built Environment Index: 1984-July 1995. Electronic Media Version
c Earthquakes and Volcanoes — *Gribbin, John*
y Earthquakes and Volcanoes — *Gribbin, John*
c Earthquakes and Volcanoes (Illus. by Greg Harris) — *Merrians, Deborah*
Earth's Restless Surface — *Janson-Smith, Deirdre*
The Earth's Shifting Axis — *Strain, Mac B*
Earth's Trapped Particle Environment — *Reeves, Geoffrey D*
y Earthshine — *Nelson, Theresa*
y Earthsong — *Kelleher, Victor*
Earthstepper/The Ocean Is Very Shallow — *Motsapi, Seitlhamo*
Earthtalk: Communication Empowerment for Environmental Action — *Muir, Star A*
Earthwards: Robert Smithson and Art after Babel — *Shapiro, Gary*
c Earthworms (Illus. by Dwight Kuhn) — *Pascoe, Elaine*
r East and Northeast Africa Bibliography — *Blackhurst, Hector*
East Anglia — *Tolhurst, Peter*
East Asia and the World Economy — *So, Alvin Y*
The East Asian Miracle and Information Technology — *Hanna, Nagy*
East Asian Security — *Brown, Michael E*
East-Central Europe in the 1990s — *Serafin, Joan*
East Central Europe in the Middle Ages 1000-1500 — *Sedlar, Jean W*
East Coast Country — *Frost, Alan*
East German Dissidents and the Revolution of 1989 — *Joppke, Christian*

The East in the West — Goody, Jack
East Is East — Boyle, T Coraghessan
East Justice — Braverman, Melanie
East London for Mosley — Linehan, Thomas P
The East Side of the Agora — Townsend, Rhys F
y East Timor's Unfinished Struggle — Pinto, Constancio
y East to America — Kim, Elaine H
East-West Dialogue in Knowledge and Higher
    Education — Hayhoe, Ruth
East-West Technology Transfer — Bugliarello, George
c Easter Babies (Illus. by Roma Bishop) — Bishop,
    Roma
c The Easter Chicks (Illus. by Jackie Harland)
    — Harland, Jackie
c Easter Counting (Illus. by Roma Bishop) — Bishop,
    Roma
c Easter Egg Farm — Muhr, Ursula
c Easter Egg Hunt (Illus. by Roma Bishop) — Bishop,
    Roma
The Easter Mysteries — Bruteau, Beatrice
c The Easter Rising — Killeen, Richard
c The Easter Story (Illus. by Brian Wildsmith)
    — Wildsmith, Brian
c Easter Sunday (Illus. by Roma Bishop) — Bishop,
    Roma
c Easter Yolks (Illus. by R W Alley) — Hall, Katy
Eastern Asia — Mackerras, Colin
Eastern Body, Western Mind — Judith, Anodea
r Eastern Canada — Munn, Felicity
Eastern Destiny — March, G Patrick
r Eastern Europe and the Commonwealth of
    Independent States 1997
Eastern Europe's International Trade — Winters, L
    Alan
Eastern Old-Growth Forests — Davis, Mary Byrd
Eastern Orthodox Christianity — Clendenin, Daniel B
y Eastern Standard Time — Yang, Jeff
Eastern Sun, Winter Moon — Paulsen, Gary
y Eastern Wisdom — Littleton, C Scott
Easterns, Westerns, and Private Eyes — Klein,
    Marcus
Eastward toward Eve — Kolbenschlag, Madonna
y An Easy Burden — Young, Andrew
An Easy Burden (Young). Audio Version — Young,
    Andrew
Easy Care Native Plants — Taylor, Patricia A
Easy Garden Projects for All Seasons — Pleasant,
    Barbara
c Easy Math Puzzles (Illus. by Cynthia Fisher) — Adler,
    David A
Easy Meat — Harvey, John
Easy PC Astronomy — Duffett-Smith, Peter
c Easy Peasy! (Illus. by Tanya Linch) — Jennings, Linda
Easy Target — Smith, Tom
Easy-to-Build Shelving and Storage — Snyder, Tim
Easy Word Games — Furr, Jo
Eat and Stay Slim — Fuller, Kristi
Eat Fat — Klein, Richard
Eat Me — Jaivin, Linda
y Eat Right 4 Your Type — D'Adamo, Peter J
Eat to Trim — Vedral, Joyce L
c Eat Your Peas, Louise — Snow, Pegeen
Eat Your Way across the U.S.A. — Stern, Jane
Eater of Souls — Robinson, Lynda S
Eating Agendas — Maurer, Donna
Eating Fire and Drinking Water — Chai, Arlene J
c Eating Fractions — McMillan, Bruce
Eating Pavlova — Thomas, D M
c Eating the Alphabet — Ehlert, Lois
Eating Thin for Life — Fletcher, Anne M
Les Eaux Douces D'Europe — Peskine, Brigitte
L'Ebanisteria Genovese Del Settecento — Caimi,
    Lodovico Caumont
The Ebbs and Flows of Fortune — Head, David M
The Ebony Gates — Rowbotham, David
c Ebony Sea (Illus. by Jon Onye Lockard) — Smalls,
    Irene
The EC Member States and Immigration 1993
    — Marie, Claude-Valentin
Ecce Kosti — Augustine, Jane
Ecclesiastical Law — Hill, Mark
The Ecclesiastical Offices in the Thought of Martin
    Bucer — Spijker, W Van't
Ecclesiastical Silver Plate in Sixth Century Byzantium
    — Boyd, Susan A
Ecclesiological Impacts of the Principle of Subsidiarity
    — Leys, Ad
The Ecclesiology of Karl Rahner — Lennan, Richard
Echapper A Ma Tombe — Rostocki, Jozef M
Les Echelles Du Levant — Maalouf, Amin
Echinacea — Upton, Roy

y The Echo — Walters, Minette
Echo: Essays on Other Literatures — Pivato, Joseph
Echo House — Just, Ward
c The Echo in the Chimney (Illus. by Tony Kenyon)
    — McKay, Hilary
An Echo of Heaven — Oe, Kenzaburo
The Echo of War — Nicholas, Sian
Echoes — Binchy, Maeve
c Echoes for the Eye (Illus. by Helen K Davie)
    — Esbensen, Barbara Juster
y Echoes from the Holocaust — Kimmelman, Mira
    Ryczke
y Echoes from the Summit — Schullery, Paul
Echoes of an Autobiography — Mahfouz, Naguib
Echoes of Combat — Turner, Fred
Echoes of Desire — Dubrow, Heather
Echoes of Empire — Ward, Robin
Echoes of His Presence — Vander Laan, Ray
Echoes of the Call — Swanson, Jeffrey
Echoes of the Past, Epics of Dissent — Abelmann,
    Nancy
y Echohawk — Durrant, Lynda
Eclat De Sel — Germain, Sylvie
The Eclipse of Eternity — Walter, Tony
The Eclipse of Great Britain — Orde, Anne
The Eclipse of the State Mental Hospital — Dowdall,
    George W
Eclipses, Atmospheres, and Global Change
    — Mallama, Anthony
c Eclipses: Nature's Blackouts — Aronson, Billy
Eco-Friendly Houseplants — Wolverton, B C
y Eco-Women: Protectors of the Earth — Sirch, Willow
    Ann
The Ecocriticism Reader — Glotfelty, Cheryll
Ecofascism: Lessons from the German Experience
    — Biehl, Janet
Ecofeminism — Mies, Maria
Ecofeminism and the Sacred — Adams, Carol J
Ecofeminism, Women, Animals, Nature — Gaard,
    Greta
r Ecole De Barbizon — Fanica, Pierre-Olivier
L'Ecole Des Femmes — Moliere
The Ecolitan Enigma — Modesitt, L E
y Ecological Census Techniques — Sutherland, William J
Ecological Design — Van Der Ryn, Sim
Ecological Disaster — Feshbach, Murray
Ecological Economics — Faber, Malte Michael
Ecological Economics and Sustainable Development
    — Bergh, Jeroen C J M Van Den
An Ecological Guide to a North Temperate Garden
    — Beresford-Kroeger, Diana
Ecological Literary Criticism — Kroeber, Karl
Ecological Prospects — Chapple, Christopher Key
Ecological Relations in Historical Times — Butlin,
    Robin A
Ecological Resistance Movements — Taylor, Bron
    Raymond
The Ecological Risks of Engineered Crops — Rissler,
    Jane
Ecological Versatility and Community Ecology
    — MacNally, Ralph C
Ecologically Based Pest Management — National
    Research Council (U.S.). Committee on Pest and
    Pathogen Control
L'Ecologie Au Pouvoir — Boy, Daniel
Ecologies of Knowledge — Star, Susan Leigh
Ecologies of the Heart — Anderson, E N
Ecologies of Theater — Marranca, Bonnie
The Ecology and Biogeography of Nothofagus Forests
    — Veblen, Thomas L
Ecology and Conservation of Amphibians — Beebee,
    T J C
Ecology and Equity — Gadgil, Madhav
Ecology and Evolution in Anoxic Worlds — Fenchel,
    Tom
Ecology and Evolution of Acoustic Communication in
    Birds — Kroodsma, Donald E
Ecology and Liberation — Boff, Leonardo
The Ecology and Management of Non-Timber Forest
    Resources — Peters, Charles M
Ecology and Management of Tidal Marshes
    — Coultas, Charles L
Ecology and Religion — Kinsley, David
Ecology, Conservation, and Management of Southeast
    Asian Rainforests — Primack, Richard B
Ecology Control and Economic Development in East
    African History — Kjekshus, Helge
Ecology, Evolution and Behavior of Bats — Racey,
    Paul A
y Ecology: Individuals, Populations, and Communities.
    3rd Ed. — Begon, Michael

An Ecology of Communication — Altheide, David L
An Ecology of Embodied Interaction — Jarmon, Leslie
    Hope
The Ecology of Fire — Whelan, Robert J
The Ecology of Health — Chesworth, Jennifer
The Ecology of Migrant Birds — Rappole, John H
Ecology of the Southern Conifers — Enright, Neal J
Ecology of World Vegetation — Archibold, O W
Ecology, Sociopolitical Organization, and Cultural
    Change on the Southern Plains — Davis, Michael G
Ecomorphology of Fishes — Luczkovich, Joseph J
r Econoguide '97: Washington, D.C., Williamsburg,
    Busch Gardens, Richmond, and Other Area
    Attractions
Econometrics: Alchemy or Science? — Hendry, David
    F
Econometrics, Macroeconomics and Economic Policy
    — Christ, Carl F
The Econometrics of Panel Data. 2nd Ed. — Matyas,
    Laszlo
Econometrics of Short and Unreliable Time Series
    — Url, Thomas
Economic Analyses of Financial Crises
    — Levy-Livermore, Amnon
Economic Analysis and Moral Philosophy
    — Hausman, Daniel M
Economic Analysis of Institutions and Systems
    — Pejovich, Svetozar
p Economic and Financial Review
Economic and Industrial Performance in Europe
    — Coates, David
Economic and Monetary Union in Europe — Kenen,
    Peter B
An Economic and Social History of Gambling in
    Britain and the USA — Munting, Roger
An Economic and Social History of the Ottoman
    Empire 1300-1914 — Inalcik, Halil
r Economic and Social Progress in Latin America 1995
    Report
r Economic and Social Survey of Africa 1994-1995
An Economic Approach to the Analysis of the
    Monetary Sector and Balance of Payments
    Problems in Turkey — Civcir, Irfan
Economic Aspects of German Unification. 2nd Ed.
    — Welfens, Paul J J
Economic Change and Political Liberalization in Sub-
    Saharan Africa — Widner, Jennifer
Economic Change in Eastern Europe since 1918
    — Aldcroft, Derek H
Economic Choice Theory — Kagel, John H
r Economic Commission for Africa 1994-1995
Economic Conflicts and Disputes before the World
    Court 1922-1995 — Wellens, Karel
The Economic Consequences of Immigration
    — Simon, Julian Lincoln
Economic Decision-Making in a Changing World
    — Collenteur, G A
p Economic Design
Economic Development — Ezeala-Harrison, Fidelis
Economic Development and Women in the World
    Community — Roy, Kartik C
Economic Development, Foreign Investment, and the
    Law — Pritchard, Robert
Economic Development in the Middle East — Wilson,
    Rodney
The Economic Development of Japan 1868-1941
    — Macpherson, W J
The Economic Development of the Netherlands since
    1870 — Zanden, J L Van
Economic Development, Social Order, and World
    Politics — Weede, Erich
Economic Doctrine and Method — Clower, Robert W
Economic Dynamics. 3rd Ed., Completely Rev. and
    Enlarged — Gandolfo, Giancarlo
Economic Effects of Fundamental Tax Reform
    — Aaron, Henry J
Economic Efficiency and Social Justice — Bonner,
    John
The Economic Era of Health Care — Johnson, Everett
    A
The Economic Evaluation of Mental Health Care
    — Knapp, Martin
Economic Evolution — Vromen, Jack J
Economic Evolution and Structure — Pryor, Frederic
    L
Economic Forecasting — Kacapyr, Elia
The Economic Foundations of Government
    — Holcombe, Randall G
r Economic Freedom of the World 1975-1995
    — Gwartney, James
Economic Growth — Barro, Robert J

Economic Growth. Vols. 1-2 — *Grossman, Gene M*
Economic Growth in Europe since 1945 — *Crafts, Nicholas*
The Economic Growth of Singapore — *Huff, W G*
The Economic History of Britain since 1700. 2nd Ed., Vols. 1-3 — *Floud, Roderick*
r The Economic History of Latin America since Independence — *Bulmer-Thomas, Victor*
An Economic History of Russia 1856-1914 — *Mosse, W E*
Economic Ideas and Government Policy — *Cairncross, Alec*
The Economic Impact of New Firms in Post-Socialist Countries — *Brezinski, Horst*
The Economic Impact of the Welfare State and Social Wage — *Fazeli, Rafat*
Economic Impact Report: National Football League Franchise Opportunities
Economic Implications for Ireland of EMU — *Baker, Terry*
The Economic Implications of Climate Change in Britain — *Parry, Martin*
Economic Insanity — *Terry, Roger*
Economic Institutions, Markets and Competition — *Dallago, Bruno*
Economic Integration and Trade Liberalization in Southern Africa — *Holden, Merle*
Economic Interdependence and Innovative Activity — *DeBresson, Christian*
p The Economic Journal
Economic Justice — *Ryan, John Augustine*
The Economic Laws of Scientific Research — *Kealey, Terence*
y Economic Literacy — *De Rooy, Jacob*
Economic Modelling under the Applied General Equilibrium Approach — *Fossati, Amedeo*
The Economic Nature of the Firm — *Putterman, Louis*
The Economic Organization of East Asian Capitalism — *Orru, Marco*
Economic Perspectives on Affirmative Action — *Simms, Margaret*
Economic Policy and Stabilization in Latin America — *Nazmi, Nader*
Economic Policy and the Transition to Democracy — *Morales, Juan Antonio*
Economic Policy for Building Peace — *Boyce, James K*
Economic Policy in Developing Countries — *Weiss, John*
Economic Policy in the Carter Administration — *Campagna, Anthony S*
Economic Policy, Technology and Growth
Economic Politics — *Keech, William R*
Economic Rationalism and Rural Society in Third-Century A.D. Egypt — *Rathbone, Dominic*
The Economic Realities of Political Reform — *Regens, James L*
An Economic Record of Presidential Performance — *Carroll, Richard J*
Economic Reform and the Poor in Africa — *Sahn, David E*
Economic Reforms in Latin America — *Sautter, Hermann*
Economic Renewal Guide — *Kinsley, Michael J*
Economic Restructuring of the Former Soviet Bloc — *Struyk, Raymond J*
Economic Sociology — *Swedberg, Richard*
Economic Structures of Antiquity — *Silver, Morris*
r Economic Survey of Europe in 1995-1996
Economic Survey of Latin America and the Caribbean 1993. Vol. 2
Economic Theory and Reality — *Scitovsky, Tibor*
Economic Theory for Environmentalists — *Gowdy, John*
Economic Theory of Fuzzy Equilibria. 2nd Ed. — *Billot, Antoine*
Economic Transformation in Central Europe — *Portes, Richard*
Economic Transformation in Eastern Europe and East Asia — *Hax, Herbert*
The Economic Transformation of South China — *Lyons, Thomas P*
Economic Transition and Political Legitimacy in Post-Mao China — *Ch'en, Feng*
Economic Transition in Russia and the New States of Eurasia — *Kaminski, Bartlomiej*
Economic Value and Ways of Life — *Eriksson, Ralf*
The Economical Guide to Self-Publishing — *Radke, Linda Foster*
Economics. 4th Ed. — *Wilson, J Holton*
Economics and Discrimination. Vols. 1-2 — *Darity, William A, Jr., 1953-*

The Economics and Ecology of Biodiversity Decline — *Swanson, Timothy M*
Economics and Ethics? — *Groenewegen, Peter*
Economics and Politics of Energy — *Kursunoglu, Rehram N*
The Economics and Politics of the United States Oil Industry 1920-1990 — *Isser, Steve*
Economics and the Antagonism of Time — *Vickers, Douglas*
Economics and the Historian — *Rawski, Thomas G*
Economics as Literature — *Henderson, Willie*
Economics, Ecology, and the Roots of Western Faith — *Gottfried, Robert R*
Economics for a Civilized Society. Rev. Ed. — *Davidson, Greg*
Economics in Crisis — *Rochon, Louis-Philippe*
Economics in One Lesson (Riggenbach). Audio Version — *Hazlitt, Henry*
r The Economics Institute Guide to Graduate Study in Economics and Agricultural Economics in the United States of America and Canada. 9th Ed.
The Economics of Access Versus Ownership — *Kingma, Bruce R*
The Economics of Ageing — *Creedy, John*
The Economics of Aging. 6th Ed. — *Schulz, James H*
The Economics of Agricultural Technology in Semiarid Sub-Saharan Africa — *Sanders, John H*
The Economics of Altruism — *Zamagni, Stefano*
The Economics of Defense — *Sandler, Todd*
The Economics of Emancipation — *Butler, Kathleen Mary*
The Economics of Energy Security — *Bohi, Douglas R*
The Economics of Environmental Regulation — *Oates, Wallace E*
The Economics of Equal Opportunities — *Humphries, Jane*
The Economics of Financial Markets — *Houthakker, Hendrik S*
The Economics of Financial Markets and the 1987 Crash — *Toporowski, Jan*
The Economics of Information — *Kingma, Bruce R*
The Economics of Information in the Networked Environment — *Conference. Challenging Marketplace Solutions to Problems in the Economics of Information (1995: Washington, D.C.)*
Economics of Innovation — *Galizzi, Giovanni*
The Economics of International Security — *Chatterji, Manas*
The Economics of Joan Robinson — *Marcuzzo, Maria Cristina*
The Economics of Labour Migration — *Broeck, Julien Van Den*
The Economics of Leisure and Sport — *Cooke, Andrew*
The Economics of Life — *Becker, Gary Stanley*
The Economics of Localized Technological Change and Industrial Dynamics — *Antonelli, Cristiano*
The Economics of Offsets — *Martin, Stephen*
The Economics of Organised Crime — *Fiorentini, Gianluca*
The Economics of Power — *Eurich, S Amanda*
Economics of Regulation and Antitrust. 2nd Ed. — *Viscusi, W Kip*
The Economics of Seasonal Cycles — *Miron, Jeffrey A*
The Economics of Strategy — *Besanko, David*
The Economics of Sustainable Development — *Goldin, Ian*
The Economics of Technology and Employment — *Vivarelli, Marco*
The Economics of the Antitrust Process — *Coate, Malcolm B*
The Economics of the Business Firm — *Demsetz, Harold*
Economics of the Energy Industries. 2nd Ed. — *Peirce, William Spangar*
The Economics of the Family — *Folbre, Nancy*
The Economics of Third World Defense Expenditures — *Looney, Robert E*
The Economics of Time and Ignorance — *O'Driscoll, Gerald P*
The Economics of Training. Vols. 1-2 — *Ashenfelter, Orley C*
The Economics of Transition — *Lavigne, Marie*
The Economics of Violence in Latin America — *Chaffee, Wilber A, Jr.*
r Economics Reading Lists, Course Outlines, Exams, Puzzles and Problems. Vols. 1-25 — *Tower, Edward*
Economics, Society and Values — *Nankivell, Owen*
r Economics, Trade, and Development
L'Economie Non Conformiste — *Weiller, Jean*
Economies of Change — *Ginsburg, Michal Peled*

The Economies of Growth and Development — *Thirlwall, A P*
Economists Can Be Bad for Your Health — *Brockway, George P*
The Economy of Bangladesh — *Wahid, Abu N M*
The Economy of Ireland — *O'Hagan, J W*
The Economy of Literary Form — *Erickson, Lee*
The Economy of Turkey since Liberalization — *Togan, Subidey*
The Economy of Ulysses — *Osteen, Mark*
Economy without Walls — *Hamlin, Roger E*
Ecosystem Management in the United States — *Yaffee, Steven L*
Ecotheology: Voices from North and South — *Hallman, David*
Les Ecrits De L'Eau Suivi Les Sept Fenetres — *Jacob, Suzanne*
Ecrits Litteraires 1800-1813. Vols. 1-2 — *Constant, Benjamin*
Ecrits Politiques 1933-1966 — *Heidegger, Martin*
Ecstasy — *Welsh, Irvine*
Ecstasy Club — *Rushkoff, Douglas*
Ecstatic Naturalism — *Corrington, Robert S*
Ecstatic Occasions, Expedient Forms — *Lehman, David, 1948-*
L'Ecume Des Jours — *Vian, Boris*
Ecumenism 101 — *Motter, Alton M*
c Eddie's Monster (Illus. by Nicolas Van Pallandt) — *Abrams, Michael*
Eden Renewed — *Levi, Peter*
c Edgar Degas — *Meadows, Matthew*
Edgar Huntly — *Brown, Charles Brockden*
r Edgar Rice Burroughs: The Exhaustive Scholar's and Collector's Descriptive Bibliography — *Zeuschner, Robert B*
Edge — *Malroux, Claire*
Edge Effect — *McPherson, Sandra*
Edge of Empire — *Jacobs, Jane M*
Edge of the City — *Mahoney, Dan*
The Edge of the Crazies — *Harrison, Jamie*
Edge of the Knife — *Chevigny, Paul*
y The Edge of the Unknown — *Trefil, James*
Edges of Reality — *May, William D*
Edgeworks. Vol. 1 — *Ellison, Harlan*
Edgeworks. Vol. 2 — *Ellison, Harlan*
Edible France — *Christian, Glynn*
r Edicoes Aldinas Da Biblioteca Nacional, Seculos XV-XVI — *Instituto Da Biblioteca Nacional E Do Livro (Portugal)*
The Edifactory Prose of Kievan Rus'
The Edinburgh International Festival 1947-1996 — *Miller, Eileen*
Edison Laboratory. Vols. 1-2 — *Millard, A J*
The Edison Trait — *Palladino, Lucy Jo*
Edisto Revisited — *Powell, Padgett*
r The Edith Oenone Somerville Archive in Drishane — *Rauchbauer, Otto*
Edith Wharton: Art and Allusion — *Killoran, Helen*
Edith Wharton: Matters of Mind and Spirit — *Singley, Carol J*
Edith Wharton's Brave New Politics — *Bauer, Dale M*
Editing D.H. Lawrence — *Ross, Charles L*
The Editing of Old English — *Conference on the Editing of Old English Texts (1990: University of Manchester)*
The Editing of Old English — *Robinson, Fred C*
Editing Today — *Smith, Ron F*
r Le Edizioni Del XVI Secolo Nella Biblioteca Chelliana Di Grosseto — *Bosco, Anna*
c Edmund and Hillary (Illus. by Chris Jackson) — *Jackson, Chris*
Edmund Burke: A Life in Caricature — *Robinson, Nicholas K*
Edmund Spenser: A Literary Life — *Waller, Gary*
Edmund Spenser: A Reception History — *Radcliffe, David Hill*
Edmund Wilson: A Biography — *Meyers, Jeffrey*
Edo and Paris — *McClain, James L*
Edom, Israel's Brother and Antagonist — *Dicou, Bert*
Edouard Manet — *Perutz, Vivien*
Edouard Manet: Rebel in a Frock Coat — *Brombert, Beth Archer*
Edson — *Morrissey, Bill*
Educacion E Ideologia — *Vargas, Maria Eugenia*
Educating for Human Dignity — *Reardon, Betty*
Educating Hearts and Minds — *Lewis, Catherine C*
Educating Immigrant Children — *Glenn, Charles Leslie*
Educating Students in a Media-Saturated Culture — *Davies, John*
Educating the Able — *Montgomery, Diane*

Educating the Democratic Mind — *Parker, Walter C*
Educating Tomorrow's Valuable Citizen — *Burstyn, Joan N*
Education Achievements and School Efficiency in Rural Bangladesh — *Khandker, Shahidur R*
Education and Democratic Citizenship in America — *Nile, Norman H*
Education and Identity in Rural France — *Read-Danahay, Deborah*
Education and Technology — *Fisher, Charles*
r Education and the Law — *Taylor, Bonnie B*
y Education and Training — *Heaton, Tim*
Education as Contested Terrain — *Arnove, Robert F*
Education Divides — *Smith, Teresa*
Education, Economic Change and Society in England 1780-1870 — *Sanderson, Michael*
Education for Extinction — *Adams, David Wallace*
Education for Motherhood — *Arnup, Katherine*
Education for Shalom — *Cunningham, Philip A*
Education for Sustainability — *Huckle, John*
Education for the Nation — *Aldrich, Richard*
Education in a Research University — *Arrow, Kenneth J*
r Education in Early Childhood — *Robson, Sue*
Education Law — *McEwan, Vera*
The Education of a Poker Player — *Yardley, Herbert O*
The Education of a Soldier — *Mauck, Jeffrey*
The Education of a Speculator — *Niederhoffer, Victor*
The Education of a Woman — *Heilbrun, Carolyn G*
The Education of Phillips Brooks — *Woolverton, John F*
The Education of the Heart — *Moore, Thomas, 1940-*
Education Policy-Making in England and Wales 1895-1911 — *Daglish, Neil D*
The Education Racket — *Graham, Duncan*
Education, Society, and Economic Opportunity — *Vinovskis, Maris A*
r Education Sourcebook — *Gough, Jeanne*
Education, Training, and the Global Economy — *Ashton, David*
Education without the State — *Tooley, James*
Educational Advancement and Distributive Justice — *Kahane, Reuven*
p Educational Computing and Technology
Educational Development in the Small States of the Commonwealth — *Crocombe, Ron*
Educational Finance in Central Asia and Mongolia — *Kitaev, Igor*
yr The Educational Funding Guide — *Forrester, Susan*
yr Educational Grants Directory 1996/7
r Educational Media and Technology Yearbook 1995-1996
The Educational Process in Nursing Staff Development — *Alspach, JoAnn Grif*
The Educational Technology Handbook — *Hackbarth, Steven*
Educator's Companion to Children's Literature. Vol. 2 — *McElmeel, Sharron L*
r Educators Index of Free Materials 1995
Educator's Internet Companion — *Classroom Connect*
r Educators Internet Yellow Pages — *Place, Ron*
r The Educator's Word Frequency Guide — *Zeno, Susan M*
Educator's World Wide Web Tourguide — *Sturm, Chris Noonan*
Edward II — *Marlowe, Christopher*
c Edward and the Pirates (Illus. by David McPhail) — *McPhail, David*
Edward Bear Esq. — *Brown, Michele*
y Edward Elgar: An Essential Guide to His Life and Work — *Nice, David*
Edward Frankland: Chemistry, Controversy and Conspiracy in Victorian England — *Russell, Colin Archibald*
r Edward Hopper: A Catalogue Raisonne. Vols. 1-3. Electronic Media Version — *Levin, Gail*
Edward Hopper: An Intimate Biography — *Levin, Gail*
Edward James Lennox Builder of Toronto — *Litvak, Marilyn M*
Edward Kienholz 1954-1962 — *Hopps, Walter*
Edward Lear and the Critics — *Colley, Ann C*
Edward Stratemeyer and the Stratemeyer Syndicate — *Johnson, Deidre*
Edward Willis Redfield 1869-1965 — *Fletcher, J M W*
Edwardians: London Life and Letters 1901-1914 — *Paterson, John*
c Edward's First Day at School — *Wells, Rosemary*
c Edward's First Night Away — *Wells, Rosemary*
c Edward's First Swimming Party — *Wells, Rosemary*

Edwin Hubble: Mariner of the Nebulae — *Christianson, Gale E*
c Edwina the Emu (Illus. by Rod Clement) — *Knowles, Sheena*
c Eenie, Meenie, Manitoba (Illus. by Scot Ritchie) — *Heidbreder, Robert*
c Eeyore Has a Birthday (Illus. by Ernest H Shepard) — *Milne, A A*
c Eeyore's Gloomy Little Instruction Book (Illus. by Joan Powers) — *Shepard, Ernest H*
The Effect of Japanese Investment on the World Economy — *Hollerman, Leon*
Effect of Surface Coatings and Treatments on Wear — *Bahadur, Shyam*
Effective Faith — *Stone, Bryan P*
Effective Financial Planning for Library and Information Services — *McKay, Duncan*
r Effective Management of Local Area Networks. 2nd Ed. — *Terplan, Kornel*
r Effective Project Management through Applied Cost and Schedule Control — *Bent, James A*
Effective School District Leadership — *Leithwood, Kenneth*
Effective Teaching, Effective Learning — *Fairhurst, Alice M*
Effective User Support — *Bruton, Noel*
Effectiveness and Costs of Osteoporosis Screening and Hormone Replacement Therapy. Vols. 1-2
The Effectiveness of Early Intervention — *Guralnick, Michael J*
r The Effects of Drugs on the Fetus and Nursing Infant — *Friedman, J M*
The Effects of HIV/AIDS on Farming Systems in Eastern Africa — *Small, Alison*
Effects of Market Reform on Access to Food by Low-Income Households — *Jayne, T S*
Effeminate England — *Bristow, Joseph*
L'Effet Whitehead — *Stengers, Isabelle*
Effi Briest — *Fontane, Theodor*
Efficiency of Racetrack Betting Markets — *Hausch, Donald B*
Egalia's Daughters — *Brantenberg, Gerd*
The Egalitarian Moment — *Low, D A*
Egalite Et Partialite — *Nagel, Thomas*
c The Egg and I (Illus. by Francois Crozat) — *Chausse, Sylvie*
y Egghead — *May, Steve*
c Eggs — *Powell, Jillian*
c Eggs Mark the Spot — *Auch, Mary Jane*
Eglesia I Estat Durant La Segona Republica Espanyola 1931-1936. Vols. 1-4 — *Vidal I Barraquer, Francesc*
The Ego and the Dynamic Ground. 2nd Ed., Rev. — *Washburn, Michael*
Der Egoist — *Eisendle, Helmut*
c Egypt — *Arnold, Helen*
y Egypt: Antiquities from Above — *Bridges, Marilyn*
y Egypt, Greece, and Rome — *Freeman, Charles*
r Egypt (Handbooks of the World)
Egypt in Late Antiquity — *Bagnall, Roger S*
y Egypt in the Age of Pyramids — *Andreu, Guillemette*
Egypt, Islam and Democracy — *Ibrahim, Saad Eddin*
y Egypt of the Pharaohs — *Smith, Brenda*
Egypt: Yesterday and Today — *Roberts, David, 1796-1864*
L'Egypte Des Mamelouks — *Clot, Andre*
The Egyptian Economy — *Elkhafif, Mahmoud A T*
c The Egyptian News — *Steedman, Scott*
An Egyptian Satire about a Condemned Building
Egyptian Solar Religion in the New Kingdom — *Assmann, Jan*
c The Egyptians — *Allard, Denise*
c Egyptians — *Davies, Kath*
c The Egyptians — *Grant, Neil*
Les Egyptiennes — *Jacq, Christian*
Egyptomania: Egypt in Western Art 1730-1930 — *Humbert, Jean-Marcel*
Egyptomania: The Egyptian Revival — *Curl, James Steven*
Egypt's Road to Jerusalem — *Boutros-Ghali, Boutros*
Eigen-Sinn: Fabrikalltag, Arbeitererfahrungen Und Politik Vom Kaiserreich Bis In Den Faschismus — *Ludtke, Alf*
Eigenwelt Der Apparate-Welt — *Vasulka, Steina*
Eiger Dreams — *Krakauer, Jon*
The Eight Core Values of the Japanese Businessman — *Sai, Yasutaka*
c Eight Cousins — *Alcott, Louisa May*
Eight Easy Observing Projects for Amateur Astronomers — *Cortner, David*
Eight Men — *Wright, Richard*

Eight Months on Ghazzah Street — *Mantel, Hilary*
The Eight-Step Swing — *McLean, Jim*
Eight Weeks to Optimum Health — *Weil, Andrew*
Eighteen Layers of Hell — *Saunders, Kate*
Eighteenth-Century Aesthetics and the Reconstruction of Art — *Mattick, Paul, Jr.*
Eighteenth-Century Book-Keeping — *Sheldahl, Terry K*
Eighteenth-Century Furniture — *Edwards, Clive D*
The Eighteenth Century German Book Review — *Rowland, Herbert*
The Eighteenth-Century Hymn in England — *Davie, Donald*
Eighteenth-Century Music in Theory and Practice — *Parker, Mary Ann*
Eighteenth-Century Sensibility and the Novel — *Van Sant, Ann Jessie*
The Eighteenth Century Town — *Borsay, Peter*
The Eighth Day of Creation. Expanded Ed. — *Judson, Horace Freeland*
y Eighth Grade — *Lord, Christine*
Eighty Years — *Fruton, Joseph S*
Eilhard Mitscherlich: Prince of Prussian Chemistry — *Schutt, Hans-Werner*
Eine Elite Im Umbruch — *Meissner, Jochen*
Eingeordnete Freiheit — *Benjamins, Hendrik S*
Einleitung In Das Neue Testament — *Zahn, Theodor*
Einleitung In Die Targume Zum Pentateuch — *Glessmer, Uwe*
Einstein: A Life — *Brian, Denis*
r An Einstein Dictionary — *Kantha, Sachi Sri*
Einstein, History, and Other Passions — *Holton, Gerald James*
y Einstein in 90 Minutes — *Gribbin, John*
Einstein Lived Here — *Pais, Abraham*
Einstein's Bridge — *Cramer, John*
Einstein's Greatest Blunder? — *Goldsmith, Donald*
y Einstein's Wife — *Gabor, Andrea*
p EIPASCOPE
Eisenhower and the Mass Media — *Allen, Craig*
Eisenhower, Macmillan and the Problem of Nasser — *Ashton, Nigel John*
Eisenhower's New-Look National Security Policy 1953-61 — *Dockrill, Saki*
r EIT Review Manual — *Lindeburg, Michael R*
Either/Or. Pts. 1-2 — *Perkins, Robert L*
Either/Or: The Gospel or Neopaganism — *Braaten, Carl E*
Ejercito Y Milicias En El Mundo Colonial Americano — *Marchena Fernandez, Juan*
El Bronx — *Charyn, Jerome*
El Leah — *Lieblich, Amia*
The El Mozote Massacre — *Binford, Leigh*
y El Salvador — *Foley, Erin*
El Salvador in the Eighties — *Lungo, Mario*
El Salvador: Meeting the Challenge of Globalization
El Salvador's Civil War — *Byrne, Hugh*
Elasticity and Geomechanics — *Davis, R O*
Elasto-Impact and Friction in Dynamic Systems — *Ferri, Aldo*
c Elbert's Bad Word (Illus. by Audrey Wood) — *Wood, Audrey*
The Elbow in Sport — *Ellenbecker, Todd S*
r The Elder Law Handbook for Caregivers and Seniors — *Strauss, Peter J*
y The Elderly — *Stewart, Gail B*
The Elders: Seniority within Earliest Christianity — *Campbell, R Alastair*
c Eleanor (Illus. by Barbara Cooney) — *Cooney, Barbara*
c Eleanor. Hattie and the Wild Waves (Cooney). Audio Version — *Cooney, Barbara*
Eleanor of Castile: Queen and Society in Thirteenth-Century England — *Parsons, John Carmi*
r Eleanor Roosevelt: A Comprehensive Bibliography — *Edens, John A*
y Eleanor Roosevelt: A Life of Discovery — *Freedman, Russell*
y Eleanor Roosevelt: A Passion to Improve — *Spangenburg, Ray*
c Eleanora's Diary — *Parry, Caroline*
The Elect Nation — *Polizzotto, Lorenzo*
y Electing our Government — *Christian, Spencer*
r The Election: A Voter's Guide — *Linton, Martin*
Election Presidentielle Des 23 Avril Et 7 Mai 1995 — *Maus, Didier*
y Elections — *Majure, Janet*
Elections and Democracy in Central America, Revisited — *Seligson, Mitchell A*
Elections in Britain Today — *Leonard, Dick*
Elections in the French Revolution — *Crook, Malcolm*

Electoral Change Since 1945 — Norris, Pippa
c The Electoral College — Henry, Christopher
y The Electoral College Primer — Longley, Lawrence D
Electra: The Delphic Women — Greenwood, Kerry
Electric and Magnetic Fields — Sagan, Leonard A
Electric Circuit Analysis. 3rd Ed. — Johnson, David E
Electric Cooperatives
Electric Country Roulette — Ripley, W L
Electric Drives — Subrahmanyam, Vedam
Electric Drives and Their Controls — Crowder,
    Richard M
c Electric Full Stops
r Electric Power in Asia and the Pacific 1991 and 1992
r Electric Power Industry Yearbook 1996
r Electric Power Statistics Sourcebook. 3rd Ed.
Electrical, Optical, and Magnetic Properties of
    Organic Solid State Materials III
Electrical Power Distribution and Transmission
    — Faulkenberry, Luces M
Electrical Power Systems Quality — Dugan, Roger C
Electrical Systems — Qayoumi, Mohammad
Electrical Wiring Design — Traister, John E
Electrically Based Microstructural Characterization
    — Gerhardt, Rosario A
Electricity — Glendinning, Victoria
Electricity Transmission Pricing and Technology
    — Einhorn, Michael
Electroactive Polymer Electrochemistry. Pt. 2
    — Lyons, Michael E G
Electroanalytical Chemistry. Vol. 19
Electrochemistry for Chemists. 2nd Ed. — Sawyer,
    Donald T
Electromagnetic Fields — Blank, Martin
Electron — Springford, Michael
Electron Correlation in Molecules and Condensed
    Phases — March, N H
r Electron Cyclotron Resonance Ion Sources and ECR
    Plasmas — Geller, R
Electron Density and Bonding in Crystals
    — Tsirelson, V G
Electron Energy-Loss Spectroscopy in the Electron
    Microscope. 2nd Ed. — Egerton, R F
Electronic Capabilities of Federal Depository
    Libraries, Summer 1994 — MacGilvray, Marian W
Electronic Culture — Druckery, Timothy
Electronic Democracy — Browning, Graeme
Electronic Devices. 4th Ed. — Floyd, Thomas L
The Electronic Disturbance — Critical Arts Ensemble
Electronic Eros — Springer, Claudia
Electronic Highway Robbery — Carter, Mary E
Electronic Imaging Applications and Markets
    — Dailey, Franklyn E
Electronic Library and Visual Information Research--
    ELVIRA 2 — Collier, Mel
Electronic Measurement Systems. 2nd Ed. — Putten,
    Anton F P Van
Electronic Publishing and Libraries — Brown, David J
Electronic Publishing on CD-ROM — Cunningham,
    Steve
Electronic Searching of the Health Sciences Literature
Electronic Structure and Properties of Non-Transition
    Element Compounds — Korolkov, Dimitri V
Electronic Structure and Properties of Transition
    Metal Compounds — Bersuker, Isaac B
Electronic Surveillance in a Digital Age
Electronic Technology, Corporate Strategy, and World
    Transformation — Estabrooks, Maurice
The Electronic Word — Lanham, Richard A
Electroweak and Strong Interactions. 2nd Ed.
    — Scheck, Florian
Elegant Beading for Sewing Machine and Serger
    — Beck, Susan P
r Elegant Glassware of the Depression Era. 7th Ed.
    — Florence, Gene
Elegies — Egan, Desmond
Elegies II (Murgatroyd) — Tibullus
The Elegies of Quintilius — Russell, Peter, 1921-
Elegy and Paradox — Shaw, W David
r Element Speciation in Bioinorganic Chemistry
    — Caroli, Sergio
Elementary Analysis through Examples and Exercises
    — Schmeelk, John
Elementary Arabic — Younes, Munther A
cr Elementary Author/Illustrator Profiles
Elementary Differential Equations and Boundary
    Value Problems. 6th Ed. — Boyce, William E
The Elementary Forms of Religious Life — Durkheim,
    Emile
y Elementary Linear Algebra with DERIVE — Hill,
    Robert
r The Elementary School Library Collection. 20th Ed.

r The Elementary School Library Collection. 20th Ed.
    Electronic Media Version
Elementary Statistics for Geographers. 2nd Ed.
    — Burt, James E
Elements D'Analyse Monetaire. 3rd Ed. — Renversez,
    Francoise
Elements De La Geometrie De L'Infini — Fontenelle,
    M. De
cr Elements (Grolier). Vols. 1-15
The Elements of Academic Research — McCuen,
    Richard H
Elements of Controversy — Hacker, Barton C
The Elements of Expression — Plotnik, Arthur
Elements of Garden Design (Illus. by Lisa Brooks)
    — Eck, Joe
Elements of General, Organic, and Biological
    Chemistry. 9th Ed. — Holum, John R
Elements of Hypermedia Design — Gloor, Peter
The Elements of Language Curriculum — Brown,
    James D
Elements of Military Strategy — Jones, Archer
r Elements of Molecular Neurobiology. 2nd Ed.
    — Smith, C U M
The Elements of Mystery Fiction — Tapply, William G
Elements of Pattern Theory — Grenander, Ulf
The Elements of Social Scientific Thinking. 6th Ed.
    — Hoover, Kenneth
The Elements of Social Theory — Barnes, Barry
r The Elements of Style. Rev. Ed. — Calloway, Stephen
Elements of Survey Sampling — Singh, Ravindra
The Elements of Teaching — Banner, James M
Elements of the Theory of Structures — Heyman,
    Jacques
The Elements of Typographic Style. 2nd Ed.
    — Bringhurst, Robert
Elements of Web Design — DiNucci, Darcy
The Elements on Earth — Cox, P A
c Elena — Stanley, Diane
c Eleonora (Illus. by Britta Teckentrup) — Biebow,
    Natascha
c Elephant — Newton, Jill
c The Elephant at the Waldorf. Book and Audio
    Version — Miranda, Anne
Elephant Rocks — Ryan, Kay
c The Elephant Truck (Illus. by Lawrie Taylor)
    — Travers, Will
Elephant Winter — Echlin, Kim
c Elephants — Harman, Amanda
c Elephants Are Wrinkly (Illus. by Thomas M Smucker)
    — Thompson, Susan Conklin
c Elephants Don't Sit on Cars (Illus. by Axel Scheffler)
    — Wilson, David Henry
Elephants of Thailand in Myth, Art, and Reality
    — Ringis, Rita
c Elephants Swim (Illus. by Steve Jenkins) — Riley,
    Linda Capus
L'Elettore Sconosciuto — Calvi, Gabriele
Eletut. 3. Vol. 3 — Hatar, Gyozo
Eleutheria: A Play in Three Acts — Beckett, Samuel
Eleutheria (Minuit) — Beckett, Samuel
Eleutheria (Wright) — Beckett, Samuel
Elevated Temperature Coatings — Dahotre, Narendra
    B
Elevations--the Height of the Good in Rosenzweig and
    Levinas — Cohen, Richard A
Elevator Music — Lanza, Joseph
p Elevator World
L'Eleve Trouble — Lorrain, Francois-Guillaume
c Eleven Elephants Going Up! (Illus. by Minh Uong)
    — Roberts, Bethany
c Eleven Nature Tales (Illus. by Joe Shlichta)
    — DeSpain, Pleasant
The Eleventh Plague — Cole, Leonard A
Elgar, Newman and the Dream of Gerontius
    — Young, Percy M
c Eli and the Swamp Man (Illus. by James Ransome)
    — Sherman, Charlotte Watson
c Eli and Uncle Dawn (Illus. by Susan Gaber)
    — Rosenberg, Liz
Elianto — Benni, Stefano
c Elidor (Green). Audio Version — Garner, Alan
y Elie Wiesel: A Voice for Humanity — Stern, Ellen
    Norman
Elijah Visible — Rosenbaum, Thane
c Elijah's Tears (Illus. by Rossitza Skortcheva Penney)
    — Pearl, Sydelle
c Elisabeth (Illus. by Claire A Nivola) — Nivola, Claire
    A
Elisabeth Schwarzkopf — Jefferson, Alan
Elise Ou La Vraie Vie — Etcherelli, Claire
The Elite of the Elite — Barberis, Peter

Elites Ed Educazione Femminile Nell'Italia
    Dell'Ottocento — Franchini, Silvia
Elites, Enterprise and the Making of the British
    Overseas Empire 1688-1775 — Bowen, H V
c Elizabeth I (Illus. by Peter Kent) — Castor, Harriet
Elizabeth I — MacCaffrey, Wallace T
Elizabeth I: The Competition for Representation
    — Frye, Susan
Elizabeth I: War and Politics 1588-1603
    — MacCaffrey, Wallace T
Elizabeth: A Biography of Britain's Queen
    — Bradford, Sarah
Elizabeth Alone — Trevor, William
Elizabeth and Religion 1558-1603 — Doran, Susan
Elizabeth Barrett Browning — Stone, Marjorie
Elizabeth Barrett Browning: The Hope End Years
    — Dennis, Barbara
y Elizabeth Blackwell: A Doctor's Triumph — Kline,
    Nancy
Elizabeth Bowen (Harris). Audio Version — Bowen,
    Elizabeth
y Elizabeth Cary: Writer of Conscience — Brackett,
    Ginger Roberts
c Elizabeth Fry and the Forger's Daughter (Illus. by
    Amy Burch) — Apps, Roy
Elizabeth Gaskell: A Habit of Stories — Uglow, Jenny
Elizabeth Gaskell: We Are Not Angels — Wright,
    Terence
Elizabeth Robins 1862-1952 — Gates, Joanne E
Elizabeth Robins: Staging a Life 1862-1952 — John,
    Angela V
Elizabethan Mythologies — Wells, Robin Headlam
c Eliza's Dog (Illus. by Erica Thurston) — Hearne,
    Betsy
Elk: Behavior, Ecology, Conservation — Bauer, Erwin
    A
c Ella and the Naughty Lion (Illus. by Russell Ayto)
    — Cottringer, Anne
Ella Cantaba Boleros — Cabrera Infante, G
y Ella Enchanted — Levine, Gail Carson
Ella Fitzgerald 1917-1996 — Nicholson, Stuart
c Ella's Trip to the Museum — Clayton, Elaine
c Ellen and Penguin and the New Baby — Vulliamy,
    Clara
y Ellen Foster (Gibbons). Audio Version — Gibbons,
    Kaye
r Ellenhorn's Medical Toxicology. 2nd Ed. — Ellenhorn,
    Matthew J
Elles: A Bilingual Anthology of Modern French Poetry
    by Women — Sorrell, Martin
c Ellie and the Bunheads — Warner, Sally
c Ellie and the Wolves — Sage, Angie
c Ellie's Slugbucket — Sage, Angie
c Elliot Drives Away (Illus. by Jenny Williams)
    — Curtis, Matt
Elliott Carter: Collected Essays and Lectures
    1937-1995 — Carter, Elliott
Elliptic and Parabolic Methods in Geometry — Chow,
    Ben
Elliptic Boundary Value Problems in the Spaces of
    Distributions — Roitberg, Yakov
Ellsworth Kelly: A Retrospective — Waldman, Diane
c Elmer and Wilbur (Illus. by David McKee) — McKee,
    David
r Elmer's Price Guide to Toys. Vol. 2 — Duellman,
    Elmer
r Elmore County, Alabama Marriage Records
    1881-1893 — Muckleroy, D V
c Elmo's Lift-and-Peek around the Corner Book (Illus.
    by Joe Mathieu) — Ross, Anna
Elocuencia Espanola En Arte — Jimenez Paton,
    Bartolome
c Elsa, Star of the Shelter! (Illus. by Nick Sharratt)
    — Wilson, Jacqueline
r Elsevier's Dictionary of Computer Science and
    Mathematics in English, German, French, and
    Russian — Peeva, K
r Elsevier's Dictionary of Financial and Economic
    Terms: Spanish-English and English-Spanish
    — Uriona G.A., Martha
r Elsevier's Dictionary of Fundamental and Applied
    Biology — Smirnov, N N
r Elsevier's Dictionary of Plant Names in Latin, English,
    French, German, and Italian — Wrobel, Murray
r Elsevier's Dictionary of Science and Technology,
    English-Russian — Chakalov, G
Elsie Clews Parsons: Inventing Modern Life
    — Deacon, Desley
The Elsinore Appeal — Association of the Bar of the
    City of New York
r Elspeth Huxley: A Bibliography — Cross, Robert

Elusion Aforethought — *Turnbull, Malcolm J*
The Elusive Agenda — *Jahan, Rounaq*
Elusive Development — *Wolfe, Marshall*
Elusive Peace — *Zartman, I William*
Elvira: Transylvania 90210 — *Elvira*
Elvis after Elvis — *Rodman, Gilbert B*
y Elvis Presley — *Woog, Adam*
y Elvis Presley: The King of Rock 'n' Roll — *Daily, Robert*
c Elvis the Bulldozer (Illus. by Rick Meyerowitz) — *Meyerowitz, Rick*
r Elvis: The Ultimate Album Cover Book — *Dowling, Paul, 1945-*
Elvissey — *Womack, Jack*
The EM Algorithm and Extensions — *McLachlan, Geoffrey J*
The Emancipation of Prisoners — *Franke, Herman*
Embargo: Apartheid's Oil Secrets Revealed — *Hengeveld, R*
Embarrassment: Poise and Peril in Everyday Life — *Miller, Rowland S*
Embeddability in Graphs — *Liu, Yanpei*
Embedded Autonomy — *Evans, Peter B*
The Embedded Self — *Gerson, Mary-Joan*
y Ember from the Sun — *Canter, Mark*
Ember from the Sun (Bedard). Audio Version — *Canter, Mark*
Embers of Death — *Shepherd, Stella*
r Emblemata: Lyons 1550 — *Alciato, Andrea*
Emblems of Conduct — *Windham, Donald*
The Embodied Self — *Thandeka*
The Embodiment of Characters — *DeRitter, Jones*
The Embodiment of Reason — *Shell, Susan Meld*
Embodying Forgiveness — *Jones, L Gregory*
Embrace the Night — *Garland, Kit*
Embracing the Covenant — *Berkowitz, Allan L*
Embracing the Fire — *Boyd, Julia A*
The Embroidery Design Sourcebook — *Fairfield, Helen*
Embryogenesis: The Generation of a Plant — *Wang, T L*
EMC Analysis Methods and Computational Models — *Tesche, Frederick M*
EMDR: The Breakthrough Therapy for Overcoming Anxiety, Stress, and Trauma — *Shapiro, Francine*
EMD's SD60 Series — *Diesel Era*
c Emeka's Gift — *Onyefulu, Ifeoma*
c Emerald Blue (Illus. by Katherine Doyle) — *Linden, Anne Marie*
Emerald City — *Egan, Jennifer*
Emerald House Rising — *Kerr, Peg*
Emerald Ice — *Wakowski, Diane*
c Emerald Tree. Book and Audio Version — *Palazzo-Craig, Janet*
The Emergence of Japan's Foreign Aid Power — *Orr, Robert M, Jr.*
The Emergence of Pottery — *Barnett, William K*
The Emergence of Rus 750-1200 — *Franklin, Simon*
The Emergence of Stability in the Industrial City — *Hewitt, Martin*
The Emergence of Standard English — *Fisher, John H*
The Emergence of the Harlem Renaissance — *Wintz, Cary D*
The Emergence of the Modern American Theater 1914-1929 — *Wainscott, Ronald H*
The Emergence of Total War — *Sutherland, Daniel E*
c Emergencies (Illus. by Penny Dann) — *Loewen, Nancy*
Emergency and Confrontation — *Dennis, Peter*
Emergency and Disaster Planning Manual — *Kaplan, Laura G*
Emergency Incident Risk Management — *Kipp, Jonathan D*
Emergency Kit — *Shapcott, Jo*
Emergency Law in Ireland 1918-1925 — *Campbell, Colm*
y Emergency Room — *Sachs, Dan*
The Emerging Asian Bond Market — *Dalla, Ismail*
Emerging Civil Society in the Asia Pacific Community — *Yamamoto, Tadashi*
Emerging Democracies and Freedom of Information — *Turfan, Barbara*
Emerging Electronic Highways — *Bekkers, Victor*
Emerging Markets — *Keppler, Michael*
The Emerging Midwest — *Etcheson, Nicole*
Emerging Minds — *Siegler, Robert*
The Emerging New Order in Natural Gas — *De Vany, Arthur S*
The Emerging Nonprofit Sector — *Salamon, Lester M*
Emerging Organization Forms — *Hawdon, James*
Emerging Separation Technologies for Metals II — *Bautista, Renato G*

Emerging Viruses — *Horowitz, Leonard G*
Emeric Pressburger: The Life and Death of a Screenwriter — *Macdonald, Kevin*
Emerson among the Eccentrics — *Baker, Carlos*
Emerson and Power — *Lopez, Michael*
An Emerson-Benson Saga — *Swigart, Edmund K*
The Emerson Effect — *Newfield, Christopher*
Emerson in His Sermons — *Roberson, Susan L*
Emerson: The Mind on Fire — *Richardson, Robert D*
Emerson's Antislavery Writings — *Emerson, Ralph Waldo*
The Emigrants — *Sebald, W G*
The Emigrants — *Sebald, Winfried Georg*
Emigration from Hong Kong — *Skeldon, Ronald*
r Emil Brunner: A Bibliography — *McKim, Mark G*
Emile Combes — *Merle, Gabriel*
Emile Zola Centenary Colloquium 1893-1993 — *Emile Zola Centenary Colloquium (1993: London, England)*
Emiliano Zapata: Revolution and Betrayal in Mexico — *Brunk, Samuel*
c Emily and Alice (Illus. by Sucie Stevenson) — *Champion, Joyce*
c Emily at School (Illus. by Abby Carter) — *Williams, Suzanne*
Emily Bronte Re-Collects and Other Poems — *Newsom, Vera*
c Emily Bronte's Wuthering Heights — *Hiscott, Gillian*
Emily Dickinson: Daughter of Prophecy — *Doriani, Beth Maclay*
y Emily Dickinson: Selected Poems — *Dickinson, Emily*
y Emily Dickinson: Selected Poems (Clark). Audio Version — *Dickinson, Emily*
Emily Dickinson's Fascicles — *Oberhaus, Dorothy Huff*
Emily Dickinson's Gothic — *Wardrop, Daneen*
Emily Dickinson's Open Folios — *Dickinson, Emily*
y Emily in Love — *Rubin, Susan Goldman*
y Emily Post's Etiquette. 16th Ed. — *Post, Emily*
Emily Tennyson: The Poet's Wife — *Thwaite, Ann*
Eminent Georgians — *Halperin, John*
c Emitt Smith — *Hirshberg, Daniel*
Emma — *Austen, Jane*
Emma (Agutter). Audio Version — *Austen, Jane*
Emma (Keith). Audio Version — *Austen, Jane*
y Emma (Page). Audio Version — *Austen, Jane*
Emma (Scales). Audio Version — *Austen, Jane*
Emma (Shaw). Audio Version — *Austen, Jane*
Emma (Thompson). Audio Version — *Austen, Jane*
c Emma and Mommy Talk to God (Illus. by Julia Noonan) — *Williamson, Marianne*
y Emma Goldman — *Gay, Kathlyn*
Emma in Love — *Tennant, Emma*
y Emma Watson — *Aiken, Joan*
Emmanuel Levinas: The Genealogy of Ethics — *Llewelyn, John*
c Emma's Eggs (Illus. by Barbara Spurll) — *Ruurs, Margriet*
c Emma's Elephant — *Ellwand, David*
c Emma's Rug (Illus. by Allen Say) — *Say, Allen*
c Emmeline Pankhurst — *Pollard, Michael*
c Emmitt Smith: Relentless Rusher — *Thornley, Stew*
c Emmitt Smith: Star Running Back — *Savage, Jeff*
The Emmitt Zone — *Smith, Emmitt*
Emotion and the Structure of Narrative Film — *Tan, Ed*
Emotion, Disclosure, and Health — *Pennebaker, James W*
Emotion: Interdisciplinary Perspectives — *Kavanaugh, Robert D*
Emotional Blackmail — *Forward, Susan*
y The Emotional Brain — *LeDoux, Joseph*
Emotional Intelligence — *Goleman, Daniel*
The Emotional Jesus — *Breig, James*
Emotional Understanding — *Orange, Donna M*
Emotions in Asian Thought — *Marks, Joel*
Emotions in Command — *Salter, Frank Kemp*
Empathy: A Social Psychological Approach — *Davis, Mark H*
y Emperor Mage — *Pierce, Tamora*
The Emperor of Men's Minds — *Rebhorn, Wayne A*
c The Emperor Penguin's New Clothes (Illus. by Janet Perlman) — *Perlman, Janet*
c The Emperor's Birthday Suit (Illus. by R W Alley) — *Wheeler, Cindy*
c The Emperor's Gruckle Hound (Illus. by Chris Riddell) — *Cave, Kathryn*
c The Emperor's New Clothes (Illus. by Dorothee Duntze) — *Andersen, Hans Christian*
The Emperor's New Clothes — *Flannery, Kathryn T*
c The Emperor's New Clothes (Gielgud). Audio Version — *Andersen, Hans Christian*
The Emperor's Virtual Clothes — *Moore, Dinty W*

Empire Builder in the Texas Panhandle — *Carlson, Paul H*
Empire-Building and Empire-Builders — *Ingram, Edward*
L'Empire Du Livre — *Barbier, Frederic*
An Empire for Liberty — *Wright, Esmond*
The Empire God Built — *Foege, Alec*
An Empire Nowhere — *Knapp, Jeffrey*
Empire of Dreams — *Braschi, Giannina*
The Empire of Fashion — *Lipovetsky, Gilles*
The Empire of Kalman the Cripple — *Elberg, Yehuda*
y Empire of Light — *Perkowitz, Sidney*
An Empire of Schools — *Cutts, Robert L*
Empire of the Soul — *Roberts, Paul William*
The Empire of the Tetrarchs — *Corcoran, Simon*
Empire of Words — *Willinsky, John*
Empire or Republic — *Petras, James*
Empire State — *Bateman, Colin*
The Empire State Building — *Tauranac, John*
Empire: The British Imperial Experience from 1765 to the Present — *Judd, Denis*
Empire's End — *Keay, John*
Empires in Conflict — *Somakian, Manoug J*
y Empires Lost and Won — *Marrin, Albert*
Empires of the Mind — *Waitley, Denis*
Empirical Approaches to Literature and Aesthetics — *Kreuz, Roger J*
Empirical Foundations of Household Taxation — *Feldstein, Martin*
Empirical Methods for Artificial Intelligence — *Cohen, Paul R*
Empirical Methods for the Study of Labor Force Dynamics — *Wolpin, Kenneth I*
Empirical Studies in Institutional Change — *Alston, Lee J*
Empirically Based Assessment of Child and Adolescent Psychopathology. 2nd Ed. — *Achenbach, Thomas M*
p Emploi Plus
Employ Your PC. Vol. 1 — *Massie, Gabriele*
r Employee Benefits Desk Encyclopedia — *Kushner, Michael G*
r Employee Duty of Loyalty
r Employee Duty of Loyalty. 1996 Suppl.
Employee Turnover in the Public Sector — *Miller, Oscar, Jr.*
Employers' Prerogatives — *Nielsen, Ruth*
Employment and Technical Change in Europe — *Ducatel, Ken*
r Employment Relations Abstracts. 1952-1958 Eds.
Employment Relations and the Social Sciences — *Hills, Stephen M*
Employment Relations in a Changing World Economy — *Locke, Richard M*
Employment Training and Employment Action — *Payne, Joan*
r Employment/Unemployment and Earnings Statistics — *Ross, John M*
The Empowered Laboratory Team — *Umiker, William O*
Empowering Employees through Basic Skills Training — *Weaver, Marcia*
Empowering Ourselves and Transforming Schools — *Irwin, Judith Westphal*
Empowering Women — *Hay, Louise L*
Empowering You to Love Yourself — *Harrill, Suzanne E*
Empowerment Takes More than a Minute — *Blanchard, Kenneth H*
Empresariado Agricola Y Cambio Economico 1880-1936 — *Florencio Puntas, Antonio*
The Empress and the Architect — *Shvidkovskii, D O*
c The Empress and the Silkworm (Illus. by Lily Toy Hong) — *Hong, Lily Toy*
y The Empress of One — *Sullivan, Faith*
L'Emprise De La Nuit — *Pean, Stanley*
Empsael Et Zoraide — *Saint-Pierre, Bernardin De*
The Emptiness of Japanese Affluence — *McCormack, Gavan*
The Empty Bed — *Hadas, Rachel*
The Empty Church — *Reeves, Thomas C*
The Empty Cradle — *Marsh, Margaret*
c The Empty Suit of Armour (Illus. by Keren Ludlow) — *Umansky, Kaye*
EMU after Maastricht — *Currie, David*
Emulation: Making Artists for Revolutionary France — *Crow, Thomas*
Emulsions and Emulsion Stability — *Sjoblom, Johan*
Emyl Jenkins' Southern Hospitality — *Jenkins, Emyl*
En Quien Piensas Cuando Haces El Amor? — *Aridjis, Homero*

En Sens Agile — *Tournon, Andre*
En Toute Liberte — *Mitterrand, Danielle*
En Un Domingo De Mucha Luz — *Marti, Jose*
Enabling the Safe Use of Biotechnology — *Doyle, John J*
Enacting the Reformation — *Strauss, Gerald*
Enactments: American Modes and Psychohistorical Models — *Dervin, Daniel*
Enamels of Limoges 1100-1350
yr Encarta 97 Encyclopedia. Deluxe Ed. Electronic Media Version
cr Encarta 97 Encyclopedia. World English Ed. Electronic Media Version
r Encarta '97 World Atlas. Electronic Media Version
Enchanted — *Edmonds, Lucinda*
The Enchanted Loom — *Vernede, R V*
The Enchanted World of Sleep — *Lavie, Peretz*
Enchanter — *Douglass, Sara*
y Enchanter's Glass — *Whitcher, Susan*
c Enchantment in the Garden (Illus. by Shirley Hughes) — *Hughes, Shirley*
The Enchantment of Lily Dahl — *Hustvedt, Siri*
The Enchantment of Lily Dahl (Hustvedt). Audio Version — *Hustvedt, Siri*
The Enchantment of Sociology — *Flanagan, Kieran*
Enchantress: Marthe Bibesco and Her World — *Sutherland, Christine*
r Enciclopedia: Arte, Scienza E Letteratura — *Calvino, Italo*
cr Enciclopedia Visual: Ciencia Y Tecnologia — *Williams, Brian*
cr Enciclopedia Visual: El Planeta Tierra — *Allaby, Michael*
cr Enciclopedia Visual: El Universo — *Muirden, James*
cr Enciclopedia Visual: Historia Del Mundo — *Hills, Ken*
cr Enciclopedia Visual: Los Seres Vivos
cr Enciclopedia Visual: Paises Del Mundo
Enclosure Acts — *Burt, Richard*
Encomienda Politics in Early Colonial Guatemala 1524-1544 — *Kramer, Wendy*
Encomienda Y Vida Diaria Entre Los Indios De Muzo 1550-1620 — *Rodriguez Baquero, Luis Enrique*
c Encounter (Illus. by David Shannon) — *Yolen, Jane*
Encounter in the Pleiades — *Nichols, Preston*
y Encounter with Tiber — *Aldrin, Buzz*
Encountering Development — *Escobar, Arturo*
Encountering the Other(s) — *Brinker-Gabler, Gisela*
Encounters and Reflections — *Danto, Arthur C*
Encounters: Early Images of Canada's Aboriginal Peoples from the Library Collections of the Geological Survey of Canada — *Stevens, John A*
Encounters for Unity — *Kessler, Dianne*
Encounters in Magnetic Resonances — *Bloembergen, N*
Encounters with Kierkegaard — *Kirmmse, Bruce H*
Encouraging Reading — *Brown, Richard*
c Encuentro (Illus. by David Shannon) — *Yolen, Jane*
r The Encyclicals of John Paul II on CD ROM. Electronic Media Version — *John Paul II, Pope*
r Encyclopaedia of Sikh Religion and Culture — *Dogra, Ramesh Chander*
r The Encyclopedia Africana Dictionary of African Biography. Vol. 3 — *Ofosu-Appiah, L H*
yr Encyclopedia Americana 1996. Electronic Media Version
yr Encyclopedia Americana 1996. Vols. 1-30
r Encyclopedia Britannica CD 97. Electronic Media Version
c Encyclopedia Brown and the Case of Pablo's Nose (Illus. by Eric Velasquez) — *Sobol, Donald J*
yr Encyclopedia of African-American Culture and History. Vols. 1-5 — *Salzman, Jack*
r Encyclopedia of African-American Education — *Jones-Wilson, Faustine C*
r The Encyclopedia of African-American Heritage — *Altman, Susan*
yr Encyclopedia of Allegorical Literature — *Leeming, David Adams*
r The Encyclopedia of Alternative Medicine — *Jacobs, Jennifer*
r Encyclopedia of American Biography. 2nd Ed. — *Garraty, John A*
r Encyclopedia of American Education. Vols. 1-3 — *Unger, Harlow G*
r Encyclopedia of American Family Names — *Robb, H Amanda*
r Encyclopedia of American Prisons — *McShane, Marilyn D*
r The Encyclopedia of American Religions. 4th Ed. — *Melton, J Gordon*

r The Encyclopedia of American Religious History. Vols. 1-2 — *Queen, Edward L*
r Encyclopedia of Ancient Mesoamerica — *Bunson, Margaret*
r Encyclopedia of Anesthesia Practice — *Yentis, Steven M*
r Encyclopedia of Angels — *Guiley, Rosemary*
yr Encyclopedia of Apocalyptic Literature — *Zimbaro, Valerie P*
r Encyclopedia of Applied Physics. Vol. 16 — *Trigg, George L*
r Encyclopedia of Applied Physics. Vols. 15-16 — *Trigg, George L*
r Encyclopedia of Associations: National Organizations of the U.S. Electronic Media Version
r The Encyclopedia of Beer — *Rhodes, Christine P*
r Encyclopedia of Bioethics. Electronic Media Version
r Encyclopedia of Bioethics. Rev. Ed., Vols. 1-5
r The Encyclopedia of Black Collectibles — *Reno, Dawn E*
r The Encyclopedia of Bodywork — *Stillerman, Elaine*
r Encyclopedia of British Humorists. Vols. 1-2 — *Gale, Steven H*
r Encyclopedia of Business. Vols. 1-2 — *Maurer, John G*
r Encyclopedia of Business Information Sources: Supplement. 10th Ed. — *Woy, James B*
r Encyclopedia of Cancer. Vols. 1-3 — *Bertino, Joseph R*
r Encyclopedia of Chemical Processing and Design. Vol. 56 — *McKetta, John J*
r An Encyclopedia of Claims, Frauds, and Hoaxes of the Occult and Supernatural — *Randi, James*
r The Encyclopedia of Cleveland History. 2nd Ed. — *Van Tassel, David D*
r Encyclopedia of Climate and Weather. Vols. 1-2
r Encyclopedia of Common Natural Ingredients Used in Food, Drugs, and Cosmetics. 2nd Ed. — *Leung, Albert*
r Encyclopedia of Computer Science and Technology. Vol. 34, 19th Suppl.
yr Encyclopedia of Constitutional Amendments, Proposed Amendments, and Amending Issues 1789-1995 — *Vile, John R*
r Encyclopedia of Cosmology — *Hetherington, Norriss S*
r Encyclopedia of Cultural Anthropology. Vols. 1-4 — *Levinson, David*
r The Encyclopedia of Democracy. Vols. 1-4
r Encyclopedia of Designs for Quilting — *Miller, Phyllis D*
r Encyclopedia of Disability and Rehabilitation — *Dell Orto, Arthur E*
yr Encyclopedia of Drugs and Alcohol. Vols. 1-4 — *Jaffe, Jerome H*
r Encyclopedia of Early Christianity. 2nd Ed., Vols. 1-2 — *Ferguson, Everett*
yr Encyclopedia of Earth Sciences. Vols. 1-2
r Encyclopedia of Electronic Circuits. Vol. 6 — *Graf, Rudolf F*
r Encyclopedia of European Cinema — *Vincendeau, Ginette*
r Encyclopedia of Family Health — *Young, Robert*
r Encyclopedia of Feminist Literary Theory — *Kowaleski-Wallace, Elizabeth*
r Encyclopedia of Financial Gerontology — *Vitt, Lois A*
r The Encyclopedia of Flower Arranging — *Edwards, Susie*
yr Encyclopedia of Garbage — *Coffel, Steve*
r Encyclopedia of German Resistance to the Nazi Movement — *Benz, Wolfgang*
r Encyclopedia of Gerontology. Vols. 1-2 — *Birren, James E*
r Encyclopedia of Global Industries. 1st Ed.
r The Encyclopedia of Herbs and Their Uses — *Bown, Deni*
r Encyclopedia of Human Rights. 2nd Ed. — *Lawson, Edward*
yr The Encyclopedia of International Boundaries — *Biger, Gideon*
r Encyclopedia of Invasions and Conquests from Ancient Times to the Present — *Davis, Paul K*
r Encyclopedia of Islamic Law — *Bakhtiar, Laleh*
yr Encyclopedia of Latin American History and Culture. Vols. 1-5 — *Tenenbaum, Barbara A*
r Encyclopedia of Library and Information Science. Vol. 58
yr Encyclopedia of Life Sciences. Vols. 1-11
yr Encyclopedia of Literary Epics — *Jackson, Guida M*
r Encyclopedia of Marriage and the Family. Vols. 1-2 — *Levinson, David*
r Encyclopedia of Medical Media and Communications — *Kurian, George Thomas*

r The Encyclopedia of Medicinal Plants — *Chevallier, Andrew*
r Encyclopedia of Microcomputers. Vol. 18
r Encyclopedia of Molecular Biology and Molecular Medicine. Vol. 3 — *Meyers, Robert A*
r Encyclopedia of Molecular Biology and Molecular Medicine. Vols. 1-3 — *Meyers, Robert A*
r The Encyclopedia of Mythology — *Cotterell, Arthur*
r The Encyclopedia of Native American Biography — *Johansen, Bruce E*
r Encyclopedia of Native American Healing — *Lyon, William S*
r The Encyclopedia of New York City — *Jackson, Kenneth T*
r Encyclopedia of North American Eating and Drinking Traditions, Customs and Rituals — *Gay, Kathlyn*
r Encyclopedia of North American Indians — *Hoxie, Frederick E*
r The Encyclopedia of North American Indians. Vols. 1-11 — *Birchfield, D L*
r Encyclopedia of Nutritional Supplements — *Murray, Michael T*
r Encyclopedia of Occultism and Parapsychology. 4th Ed., Vols. 1-2 — *Melton, J Gordon*
r The Encyclopedia of Philosophy. Supplement
r Encyclopedia of Pinball. Vol. 1 — *Bueschel, Richard M*
r The Encyclopedia of Psychiatry, Psychology, and Psychoanalysis — *Wolman, Benjamin B*
r Encyclopedia of Relationships across the Lifespan — *Turner, Jeffrey S*
r Encyclopedia of Religion. Electronic Media Version — *Eliade, Mircea*
r The Encyclopedia of Revolutions and Revolutionaries
r Encyclopedia of Rhetoric and Composition — *Enos, Theresa*
yr Encyclopedia of Satirical Literature — *Snodgrass, Mary Ellen*
r Encyclopedia of Science Fiction — *Clute, John*
r Encyclopedia of Social and Cultural Anthropology — *Barnard, Alan*
r Encyclopedia of the American Constitution. Electronic Media Version
r Encyclopedia of the American Religious Experience. Vols. 1-3 — *Lippy, Charles H*
yr Encyclopedia of the American West. Vols. 1-4 — *Phillips, Charles*
r Encyclopedia of the Ancient Greek World — *Sacks, David*
r Encyclopedia of the Book. 2nd Ed. — *Glaister, Geoffrey Ashall*
r Encyclopedia of the Coins of Malaysia, Singapore and Brunei. 2nd Ed. — *Singh, Saran*
r Encyclopedia of the Enlightenment — *Reill, Peter Hanns*
r Encyclopedia of the First World. Vols. 1-2 — *Kurian, George Thomas*
yr Encyclopedia of the Future. Vols. 1-2 — *Kurian, George Thomas*
r Encyclopedia of the History of Arabic Science. Vols. 1-3 — *Rashed, Roshdi*
r An Encyclopedia of the History of Classical Archaeology. Vols. 1-2 — *De Grummond, Nancy Thomson*
r An Encyclopedia of the History of Technology — *McNeil, Ian*
r Encyclopedia of the Inter-American System — *Atkins, G Pope*
yr Encyclopedia of the McCarthy Era — *Klingaman, William K*
yr Encyclopedia of the Modern Middle East. Vols. 1-4 — *Simon, Reeva S*
yr The Encyclopedia of the Motorcycle — *Wilson, Hugo*
r The Encyclopedia of the Paranormal — *Stein, Gordon*
yr Encyclopedia of the Persian Gulf War — *Grossman, Mark*
yr Encyclopedia of the Reagan-Bush Years — *Levy, Peter B*
r The Encyclopedia of the Republican Party. The Encyclopedia of the Democratic Party. Vols. 1-4 — *Kurian, George Thomas*
r The Encyclopedia of the United Nations and International Agreements. 2nd Ed. — *Osmanczyk, Edmund Jan*
yr Encyclopedia of the United States in the Twentieth Century. Vols. 1-4 — *Kutler, Stanley I*
yr The Encyclopedia of the Victorian World — *Corey, Melinda*
r Encyclopedia of the Vietnam War — *Kutler, Stanley I*
r Encyclopedia of Transcendentalism — *Mott, Wesley T*
r The Encyclopedia of TV Game Shows. 2nd Ed. — *Schwartz, David*

r Encyclopedia of United States Army Insignia and Uniforms — *Emerson, William K*

r Encyclopedia of U.S. Biomedical Policy — *Blank, Robert H*

r Encyclopedia of U.S. Foreign Relations. Vols. 1-4 — *Jentleson, Bruce W*

r Encyclopedia of Values and Ethics — *Hester, Joseph P*

yr Encyclopedia of Vitamins, Minerals and Supplements — *Navarra, Tova*

r An Encyclopedia of War and Ethics — *Wells, Donald A*

r The Encyclopedia of Witches and Witchcraft — *Guiley, Rosemary*

r Encyclopedia of Women and Sports — *Sherrow, Victoria*

r Encyclopedia of Women in Religious Art — *Apostolos-Cappadona, Diane*

yr The Encyclopedia of Women's History in America — *Cullen-DuPont, Kathryn*

r Encyclopedia of Wonders. Vol. 1 — *Alban, Laureano*

r Encyclopedia of World Crime. Electronic Media Version

r Encyclopedia of World Cultures. Vols. 8-10

yr Encyclopedia of World Sport. Vols. 1-3 — *Levinson, David*

r Encyclopedia USA. Vol. 22 — *Lee, R Alton*

r Encyclopedia USA. Vol. 23 — *Lee, R Alton*

The End: Narration and Closure in the Cinema — *Neupert, Richard*

The End of a Primitive — *Himes, Chester*

The End of Affirmative Action — *McWhirter, Darien A*

The End of Affluence — *Madrick, Jeffrey*

The End of Alice — *Homes, A M*

The End of Capitalism (as We Knew It) — *Gibson-Graham, J K*

y The End of Days — *Paris, Erna*

The End of Desire — *Bialosky, Jill*

The End of Economics — *Perelman, Michael*

The End of Education — *Postman, Neil*

The End of Evolution — *Ward, Peter Douglas*

The End of Hidden Ireland — *Scally, Robert James*

The End of Our Small Town — *Hatzis, Dimitris*

The End of Racism — *D'Souza, Dinesh*

The End of Reform — *Brinkley, Alan*

The End of Roman Britain — *Jones, Michael E*

The End of Science — *Horgan, John*

y The End of Summer — *Lamb, John Lowry*

The End of Summer (James). Audio Version — *Pilcher, Rosamunde*

The End of the Age — *Robertson, Pat*

The End of the Age of Innocence — *Price, Alan*

The End of the Chinese Middle Ages — *Owen, Stephen*

End of the Drive — *L'Amour, Louis*

The End of the Future — *Gimpel, Jean*

The End of the Republican Era — *Lowi, Theodore J*

The End of the Story — *Davis, Lydia*

The End of the World — *Kortner, Ulrich H J*

The End of the World — *Leslie, John, 1940-*

The End of Time — *Thompson, Damian*

The End of Welfare — *Tanner, Michael, 1956-*

The End of Work — *Rifkin, Jeremy*

The End-User Revolution — *Biddiscombe, Richard*

The Endangered American Dream — *Luttwak, Edward N*

c Endangered Animals (Illus. by Carol Schwartz) — *McNulty, Faith*

c Endangered Birds! — *Burton, Bob*

Endangered Dreams — *Starr, Kevin*

c Endangered Environments! — *Burton, Bob*

c Endangered Mammals! — *Burton, Bob*

Endangered Mexico — *Simon, Joel*

c Endangered Sea Life! — *Burton, Bob*

The Endangered Self — *Fenn, Richard K*

y Endangered Species — *Barr, Nevada*

c Endangered Species — *Lovett, Sarah, 1953-*

Ende Des Grossenwahns — *Becker, Jurek*

c Endeavour Views the Earth — *Brown, Robert Alan, 1934-*

y Ender's Game — *Card, Orson Scott*

Endgame — *Beckett, Samuel*

Endgame: The Betrayal and Fall of Srebrenica, Europe's Worst Massacre since World War II — *Rohde, David*

Endgames: Questions in Late Modern Political Thought — *Gray, John, 1948-*

Ending a Career in the Auto Industry — *Hardy, Melissa A*

y Ending Affirmative Action — *Eastland, Terry*

Ending Auschwitz — *Ellis, Marc H*

The Ending of Epochs — *Brake, Laurel*

Ending the Explosion — *Hollingsworth, William G*

Ending the Stalemate — *Nenno, Mary K*

Endless Love — *Spencer, Scott*

y The Endless Steppe (Bresnahan). Audio Version — *Hautzig, Esther*

Endless Vow — *Nakagawa, Soen*

Endocrine Methods — *Thomas, John A*

Endocrinology of the Vasculature — *Sowers, James R*

Endosseous Implants — *Watzek, Georg*

The Ends of Philosophy — *Cahoone, Lawrence E*

The Ends of the Earth — *Kaplan, Robert D*

Ends of the Lyric — *Bahti, Timothy*

Endurance Athlete's Edge — *Evans, Marc*

The Enduring Covenant — *O'Hare, Padraic*

The Enduring Forests — *Kirk, Ruth*

Enduring the Most — *Costello, Francis J*

Endymion — *Lyly, John*

Endymion — *Simmons, Dan*

Enemies of Choice — *Merton, Andrew H*

Enemies of the Bay Colony — *Ranlet, Philip*

An Enemy of the State — *Lueders, Bill*

The Enemy Within — *Bond, Larry*

The Enemy Within — *Gould, Jay M*

The Enemy Within — *Jacobs, Steve*

y The Enemy Within (Purdham). Audio Version — *Bond, Larry*

y The Enemy You Killed — *McFarlane, Peter*

c Energy — *Snedden, Robert*

r Energy Analysis of 108 Industrial Processes — *Brown, Harry L*

Energy Anatomy (Myss). Audio Version — *Myss, Caroline*

y Energy and Change. Vols. 1-3 — *Boohan, Richard*

Energy and Environment — *International Conference on Energy and Environment (1995: Shanghai, China)*

Energy and Environment in the European Union — *Collier, Ute*

Energy and Environmental Challenges in Central Asia and the Caucasus — *Fifer, Sally Jo*

Energy Balances for Europe and North America 1992

r Energy Balances for Europe and North America 1992, 1993-2010 — *United Nations. Economic Commission for Europe*

The Energy Crisis — *Feldman, David Lewis*

Energy Demand in Five Major Asian Developing Countries — *Ishiguro, Masayasu*

Energy, Environment and the Economy — *Kleindorfer, Paul R*

Energy Planning and Policy — *Kleinpeter, Maxime*

r Energy Statistics Yearbook 1994

Energy Transfer in Macromolecules — *Vekshin, N L*

Energy Use, Air Pollution, and Environmental Policy in Krakow — *Adamson, Seabron*

Energy Watchers VII — *El Mallakh, Dorothea H*

L'Enfance Au Moyen Age — *Riche, Pierre*

c L'Enfant Et La Riviere (Illus. by E Jalabert-Edon) — *Bosco, Henri*

Enforcement at the EPA — *Mintz, Joel A*

Enforcing Normalcy — *Davis, Lennard J*

Enforcing the Law — *Hunter, Susan*

Engaged Buddhism — *Queen, Christopher S*

Engaging Families — *Shockley, W*

Engel Wider Willen — *Ortkemper, Hubert*

c Engelbert Joins the Circus (Illus. by Roberta Wilson) — *Paxton, Tom*

Engels Today — *Arthur, Christopher J*

Engendered Trope in Joyce's Dubliners — *Ingersoll, Earl G*

Engendering Business — *Kwolek-Folland, Angel*

Engendering History — *Shepherd, Verene*

Engendering Inspiration — *Sword, Helen*

Engendering Motherhood — *McMahon, Martha*

Engendering Slavic Literatures — *Chester, Pamela*

Engendering the Chinese Revolution — *Gilmartin, Christina Kelley*

Engendering Wealth and Well-Being — *Blumberg, Rae Lesser*

c Engine, Engine, Number Nine (Illus. by Paul Meisel) — *Calmenson, Stephanie*

The Engine of Reason, the Seat of the Soul — *Churchland, Paul M*

Engineer Memoirs — *Rouny, E L*

Engineered Organisms in Environmental Settings — *Levin, Morris A*

Engineering a New Architecture — *Robbin, Tony*

Engineering, Construction, and Operations in Space V. Vols. 1-2 — *Space '96 (1996: Albuquerque, N.M.)*

The Engineering Design Process. 2nd Ed. — *Ertas, Atila*

Engineering Drawings and Models Using AutoCAD Solid Modeling and Designer — *Kirkpatrick, James M*

Engineering Economy. 10th Ed. — *Degarmo, E Paul*

Engineering Geology — *Rahn, Perry H*

Engineering Materials 1. 2nd Ed. — *Ashby, Michael F*

Engineering Materials Technology. 3rd Ed. — *Jacobs, James A*

Engineering Mechanics. 4th Ed. — *Shames, Irving H*

Engineering Mechanics. 4th Ed., Vol. 1 — *Meriam, J L*

Engineering Mechanics. Vols. 1-2 — *Yin, Y K*

The Engineering of Sport — *International Conference on the Engineering of Sport (1st: 1996: Sheffield, UK)*

Engineering of/with Lipases — *Malcata, F Xavier*

Engineering Problem Solving with Matlab. 2nd Ed. — *Etter, Delores M*

Engineering Systems — *Shoureshi, R*

Engineering the F-4 Phantom II — *Bugos, Glenn E*

Engineers and Engineering — *Buchanan, R Angus*

The Engineers and the Price System — *Veblen, Thorstein*

Engineers of Dreams — *Petroski, Henry*

Engines of the Mind — *Shurkin, Joel*

r England. 2nd Ed. — *Andrews, Robert*

England and Normandy in the Middle Ages — *Bates, David*

England and the North — *Jansson, Maija*

England Arise! — *Fielding, Steven*

England for All Seasons — *Toth, Susan Allen*

England the Nation — *Turville-Petre, Thorlac*

England: Travels through an Unwrecked Landscape — *Green, Candida Lycett*

The English — *Elton, G R*

English and Communication for Colleges. 2nd Ed. — *Henson, Carol*

English and French Towns in Feudal Society — *Hilton, R H*

The English and the Norman Conquest — *Williams, Ann, 1937-*

English Arcadia — *Strong, Roy*

r English Castles — *Pettifer, Adrian*

English Cathedral Music in New York — *Ogasapian, John*

r English Catholic Books 1701-1800 — *Blom, Frans*

English Choral Practice 1400-1650 — *Moorhen, John*

The English Civil War. Vols. 1-2 — *Razzell, Peter*

English Comedy — *Cordner, Michael*

The English Conquest — *Higham, N J*

English Country Houses — *Sackville-West, Vita*

y English Creek — *Doig, Ivan*

English Drama — *Shepherd, Simon*

English Drama 1660-1700 — *Hughes, Derek*

The English Emblem Tradition — *Young, Alan R*

An English Empire — *Higham, N J*

English Episcopal Acta. Vol. 7 — *Smith, David Michael*

English Episcopal Acta. Vol. 10 — *Ramsey, Frances M R*

The English Fable — *Lewis, Jayne Elizabeth*

The English Faust Book — *Jones, John Henry*

The English Garden Abroad — *Quest-Ritson, Charles*

The English Gardener — *Cobbett, William*

The English Gentleman in Trade — *Grassby, Richard*

The English Hospital 1070-1570 — *Orme, Nicholas*

English Humanist Books — *Carlson, David R*

English in America — *Ohmann, Richard*

English Is Broken Here — *Fusco, Coco*

The English Language — *Hussey, Stanley*

r English Language Scholarship — *Gneuss, Helmut*

English Law in the Age of the Black Death 1348-1381 — *Palmer, Robert C, 1947-*

English Lessons and Other Stories — *Baldwin, Shauna Singh*

r English Maritime Books Printed before 1801 — *Adams, Thomas Randolph*

English Mystics of the Middle Ages — *Windeatt, Barry*

The English Nobility under Edward the Confessor — *Clarke, Peter A*

The English Ordnance Office 1585-1625 — *Stewart, Richard W*

English Papers — *Pritchard, William H*

The English Patient — *Minghella, Anthony*

The English Poets — *Cecil, David, Lord*

English Polemics at the Spanish Court — *Cresswell, Joseph*

The English Poor Law 1531-1782 — *Slack, Paul*

English Postcoloniality — *Mohanram, Radhika*

English Preaching in the Late Middle Ages — *Spencer, H Leith*

English Reformations — *Haigh, Christopher*

The English Religious Tradition and the Genius of Anglicanism — *Rowell, Geoffrey*

r English-Russian Economics Glossary — *United Nations. Terminology Section*

English Settlement — *Taylor, D J*

English Society in the Later Middle Ages — *Rigby, S H*

y English Solutions — *Sweetman, John*

r English-Spanish, Spanish-English Electrical and Computer Engineering Dictionary — *Kaplan, Steven M*

The English Stage — *Styan, J L*

English Studies/Culture Studies — *Smithson, Isaiah*

r English Translations of the Scandinavian Medieval Ballads — *Syndergaard, Larry E*

The English Tribe — *Haseler, Stephen*

English Verse (Penguin Classic). Vol. 1. Audio Version

English Weather — *Ferguson, Neil*

English Women's Poetry 1649-1714 — *Barash, Carol*

Englishe Akten Zur Geschichte Des Krimkriegs. Vol. 3 — *Baumgart, Winfried*

The Englishman's Boy — *Vanderhaeghe, Guy*

Englishmen and Jews — *Feldman, David, 1957-*

Englishness and the Study of Politics — *Stapleton, Julia*

Engraved Gems of the Carolingian Empire — *Kornbluth, Genevra Alisoun*

The Engraved Powder Horn — *Dresslar, Jim*

Enguerran De Marigny and the Church of Notre-Dame at Ecouis — *Gillerman, Dorothy*

Enhancing a New Design for Subject Access to Online Catalogs — *Drabenstott, Karen Markey*

Enhancing Communication: Making Your Case

Enhancing Communication: Teaching Technology

Enhancing Early Childhood Programs — *Besharov, Douglas J*

Enhancing External Communication: Managing Conflict

Enhancing Internal Communication: Building Effective Relationships

Enhancing Internal Communication: Using Negotiation to Resolve Conflict

Enhancing Professional Practice — *Danielson, Charlotte*

Enhancing the Safety and Soundness of the Canadian Financial System

y Enigma — *Harris, Robert, 1957-*

The Enigma of Automobility — *Rajan, Sudhir Chella*

The Enigma of Health — *Gadamer, Hans Georg*

The Enigma of the Mind — *Moravia, Sergio*

The Enigmatic Narrator — *Klawitter, George*

Enigmatiques — *Bancquart, Marie-Claire*

L'Enigme — *Rezvani*

Enjoying Wagner's Ring (Jenkins). Audio Version — *Jenkins, Speight*

Enlarging NATO — *Kugler, Richard L*

Enlightened Women — *Assiter, Alison*

The Enlightenment — *Im Hof, Ulrich*

Enlightenment and Conservatism in the Dutch Republic — *Velema, Wyger R E*

The Enlightenment's Fable — *Hundert, E J*

Enlightenment's Wake — *Gray, John, 1948-*

Ennead III. 6 — *Plotinus*

Enneagram II — *Rohr, Richard*

Enoch: A Man for All Generations — *VanderKam, James C*

Enoch Powell — *Shepherd, Robert*

Enola Gay — *Thomas, Gordon*

c The Enormous Snore (Illus. by Kevin Hawkes) — *Miller, M L*

Enough for One Lifetime — *Hermes, Matthew E*

Enough Is Enough — *Bertrand, Guy*

r Enquire Within — *Hyland, Sue*

Enquiry (Howard). Audio Version — *Francis, Dick*

An Enquiry Concerning the Intellectual and Moral Faculties, and Literature of Negroes — *Gregoire, Henri*

Enquiry Statistics — *Blake, Naomi*

Enriching Primary Mathematics with IT — *Ainley, Janet*

Enriching Production — *Sandberg, Ake*

Enrico Donati: Surrealism and Beyond — *Wolff, Theodore F*

De Ensamma Pojkarna — *Olsson, Mats*

Ensuring Competition — *Horstmann, Ignatius J*

ENT Secrets — *Jafek, Bruce W*

Entangled — *Peterson, Tracie*

Die Entdeckte Natur — *Speer, Andreas*

Die Entdeckung Des Verhaltens — *Wuketits, Franz M*

Enter Whining — *Drescher, Fran*

Enter Your House with Care — *Barber, Connie*

Enteric Infections and Immunity — *Paradise, Lois J*

Entering Adulthood — *Giarratano, Susan*

Entering the Circle — *Kharitidi, Olga*

Entering the Silence — *Merton, Thomas*

Enterprise and Labour — *Mathias, Peter*

Enterprise and Management — *Aldcroft, Derek H*

Enterprise and the Irish Economy — *Burke, Andrew E*

Enterprise One to One — *Peppers, Don*

Enterprise Zones — *Harrison, Taylor*

y Entertainment — *Oleksy, Walter*

r Entertainment Awards — *Franks, Don*

Enticed by the Light — *Beekman, Sharon*

Entire and Meromorphic Functions — *Rubel, Lee A*

Entitlements and the Elderly — *Moon, Marilyn*

Entre El Desierto Y La Sierra — *Radding, Cynthia*

Entre La Legitimidad Y La Violencia — *Palacios, Marco*

Entre Nation Et Jihad — *Carlier, Omar*

Entre Tu Nombre Y El Mar — *Perez Gonzalez, Domingo Julian*

Entrelazos — *Miranda, Julia*

Entrepreneurial Librarianship — *St. Clair, Guy*

Entrepreneurs, Institutions and Economic Change — *De Vecchi, Nicolo*

Entrepreneurship — *Lambing, Peggy*

Entrepreneurship and Business Culture — *Casson, Mark*

Entrepreneurship and the Market Process — *Harper, David A*

Entrepreneurship in the Caribbean — *Ryan, Selwyn*

Entretiens — *Cioran, E M*

Entropy and Entropy Generation — *Shiner, J S*

Entropy and the Magic Flute — *Morowitz, Harold J*

The Envelope Mill — *Harvey, Haila*

r Enveloping Algebras — *Dixmier, Jacques*

c Environment — *Bishop, Keith*

p Environment and Development Economics

Environment and Health in Central and Eastern Europe — *Hertzman, Clyde*

p Environment and History

The Environment and International Relations — *Vogler, John*

The Environment and NAFTA — *Johnson, Pierre Marc*

Environment and Resource Policies for the World Economy — *Cooper, Richard N*

r Environment and the Law — *Patton-Hulce, Vicki R*

Environment, Development, Agriculture — *Glaeser, Bernhard*

Environment, Development and the Gender Gap — *Venkateswaran, Snadhya*

The Environment for Children — *Satterthwaite, David*

Environment, Growth and Development — *Bartelmus, Peter*

The Environment of the British Isles — *Goudie, A S*

y The Environment: Opposing Viewpoints — *Sadler, A E*

Environmental Accounting — *Odum, Howard T*

Environmental Action in Eastern Europe — *Jancar-Webster, Barbara*

Environmental Activism and World Civic Politics — *Wapner, Paul Kevin*

Environmental and Economic Issues in Forestry — *Shen, Susan*

r Environmental and Health Atlas of Russia

Environmental and Resource Economics — *Fisher, Anthony C*

Environmental and Social Impact Assessment — *Vanclay, Frank*

Environmental and Workplace Safety — *O'Reilly, James T, 1947-*

Environmental Aspects of Trace Elements in Coal — *Swaine, Dalway J*

Environmental Biotechnology — *Moo-Young, Murray*

c Environmental Change — *Martin, Fred*

Environmental Change — *Taylor, Michael, 1946-*

Environmental Change in Australia since 1788 — *Young, Ann R M*

Environmental Chemistry — *Baird, Colin*

Environmental Chemistry. 2nd Ed. — *O'Neill, Peter*

Environmental Chemistry of Dyes and Pigments — *Reife, Abraham*

Environmental Compliance Handbook — *Bregman, Jacob I*

Environmental Considerations and Options in Managing India's Long-Term Energy Strategy — *Tata Energy Research Institute*

r Environmental Contaminant Reference Databook. Vols. 1-2 — *Prager, Jan C*

Environmental Contaminants in Wildlife — *Beyer, W Nelson*

Environmental Control in Petroleum Engineering — *Reis, John C*

Environmental Design — *Thomas, Randall*

Environmental Effects of Mining — *Ripley, Earle A*

Environmental Engineering Education and Training — *International Conference on Environmental Engineering Education and Training (1st: 1996: Southampton, UK)*

Environmental Geology. 7th Ed. — *Keller, Edward A*

Environmental Governance — *Hempel, Lamont C*

r Environmental Grantmaking Foundations 1996

Environmental Hazards. 2nd Ed. — *Smith, Keith*

Environmental Health Risks and Public Policy — *Bates, David V*

An Environmental History of the Little Applegate River Watershed, Jackson County, Oregon — *LaLande, Jeff*

The Environmental Imagination — *Buell, Lawrence*

Environmental Immunochemical Methods — *Van Emon, Jeanette M*

Environmental Impact Assessment: Training Resource Manual

Environmental Impact of Chemicals — *Quint, Michael D*

The Environmental Impact of Later Mesolithic Cultures — *Simmons, Ian*

Environmental Impact on the Airways — *Chretien, Jacques*

Environmental Impact Statements — *Kreske, Diori L*

Environmental Inequalities — *Hurley, Andrew*

r Environmental Issues and Sustainable Futures — *Marien, Michael*

Environmental Issues of Tourism and Recreation — *Mieczkowski, Z*

yr Environmental Justice — *Newton, David E*

Environmental Management — *Clarke, Regina*

r Environmental Management for Hotels. 2nd Ed. — *International Hotels Environment Initiatives (Firm)*

Environmental Management Tools on the Internet — *Katz, Michael*

Environmental Modeling — *Schnoor, Jerald L*

Environmental Policies in the Third World — *Dwivedi, O P*

Environmental Policy and Biodiversity — *Grumbine, R Edward*

Environmental Policy and Industrial Innovation — *Wallace, David*

Environmental Policy and Market Structure — *Carraro, Carlo*

Environmental Policy in Europe — *Leveque, Francois*

Environmental Policy Tools

Environmental Policy with Political and Economic Integration — *Braden, John B*

Environmental Politics in Poland — *Hicks, Barbara*

Environmental Practice in the Human Services — *Neugeboren, Bernard*

Environmental Pragmatism — *Light, Andrew*

Environmental Problems in the Shortage Economy — *Ahlander, Ann-Mari Satre*

The Environmental Promise of Democratic Deliberation — *Gundersen, Adolf G*

Environmental Protection and Economic Well-Being. 2nd Ed. — *Power, Thomas Michael*

r Environmental Racism and the Environmental Justice Movement — *Nordquist, Joan*

Environmental Racism in the City of Chicago — *Coursey, Don*

Environmental Sampling for Unknowns — *Hess, Kathleen*

y Environmental Science — *Jackson, A R W*

Environmental Science. 4th Ed. — *Cunningham, William P*

Environmental Science. 6th Ed. — *Miller, G Tyler*

Environmental Science and Engineering. 2nd Ed. — *Henry, J Glynn*

Environmental Site Investigation Guidance Manual — *American Society of Civil Engineers. Task Committee on Hazardous Waste Site Assessment Manual*

Environmental Sociology — *Hannigan, John A*

r Environmental Telephone Directory. 1996 Ed.

The Environmental Tradition — *Hawkes, Dean*

Environmental Values in American Culture — *Kempton, Willett*

Environmentalism and Economic Justice — *Pulido, Laura*

Environmentally Improved Production Processes and Products — *Reijnders, Lucas*

p Envision

Envisioning America — *Mancall, Peter C*

Envisioning Eastern Europe — *Kennedy, Michael D*

Envisioning Israel — *Gal, Allon*
Envisioning the New Adam — *Daly, Patricia Ellen Martin*
y Envol — *Bourdais, Daniele*
Envoy to Moscow — *Levin, Aryeh*
The Envy of Angels — *Jaeger, C Stephen*
The Envy of the World — *Carpenter, Humphrey, 1946-*
Enzymes for Carbohydrate Engineering — *Park, Kwan-Hwa*
Enzymes for Pulp and Paper Processing — *Jeffries, Thomas W*
Enzymology Primer for Recombinant DNA Technology — *Eun, Hyone-Myong*
EPA and the States — *United States. General Accounting Office*
EPA Environmental Assessment Sourcebook — *Boulding, Russell*
EPA Environmental Engineering Sourcebook — *Boulding, Russell*
EPA Office of Compliance Sector Notebook Project
EPD Congress 1996 — *Warren, Garry W*
Ephesians — *Kitchen, Martin, 1947-*
Epic and Empire — *Quint, David*
Epic Grandeur — *Mori, Masaki*
The Epic of Askia Mohammed — *Hale, Thomas A*
The Epic of Gilgamesh (Pasco). Audio Version — *Gilgamesh*
The Epic of Qayaq — *Oman, Lela Kiana*
Epic Reinvented — *Gibson, Mary Ellis*
Epic Romance — *Burrow, Colin*
Epicurus in Lycia — *Gordon, Pamela*
The Epidemic Streets — *Hardy, Anne*
Epidemics and Sickness in French Literature and Culture — *Lloyd, Christopher, 1945-*
Epidemiology of Sports Injuries — *Caine, Dennis J*
Epidemiology: The Logic of Modern Medicine — *Jenicek, Milos*
Epigrams. Vols. 1, 3 — *Martial*
Epigrams V — *Martial*
Epigraph — *Lish, Gordon*
Epikurs Garten — *Hahn, Ulla*
r Epilepsy and the Functional Anatomy of the Frontal Lobe — *Jasper, Herbert H*
Episcopal Women — *Prelinger, Catherine M*
Episodes of the Cuban Revolutionary War 1956-58 — *Guevara, Ernesto*
The Epistemology of Religious Experience — *Yandell, Keith E*
The Epistles to the Colossians and to Philemon — *Dunn, James D G*
Epistolario — *Enzinas, Francisco De*
Epistolario. Vol. 14, Pts. 1-2 — *Cavour, Camillo*
Epistolary Bodies — *Cook, Elizabeth Heckendorn*
Epistolary Responses — *Bower, Anne*
Epistres Familieres Et Invectives — *Crenne, Helisenne De*
Epitaph for American Labor — *Green, Max*
Epitaxial Oxide Thin Films II — *Speck, James S*
Epitope Mapping Protocols — *Morris, Glenn E*
r The EPM Licensing Letter Sourcebook. 1997 Ed.
Eppure — *Sereni, Clara*
L'Epuisant Desir De Ces Choses — *Camus, Renaud*
Equal Freedom — *Darwall, Stephen*
Equal Value — *Robb, Carol S*
Equality — *Franklin, Jane*
Equality in Community — *Dooley, Dolores*
r Equality State Almanac 1995
Equation for Evil — *Caputo, Philip*
Equations of State of Solids for Geophysics and Ceramic Science — *Anderson, Orson L*
Equatoria — *Price, Richard, 1941-*
c Equatorial Climates — *Lye, Keith*
Equilibrium Facility Location on Networks — *Miller, Tan C*
Equilibrium Versus Understanding — *Addleson, Mark*
Equine Color Genetics — *Sponenberg, Phillip D*
Equinox: Life, Love, and Falconry in the Great Outdoors — *O'Brien, Dan, 1947-*
Equity and the Law of Trusts in Ireland — *Delany, Hilary*
Equity, Efficiency and Growth — *Baldassarri, Mario*
The Equity Equation — *Davis, Cinda-Sue*
Equity Issues for Women in Archeology — *Nelson, Margaret Cecile*
Equivariant Homotopy and Cohomology Theory — *May, J Peter*
Equivocal Beings — *Johnson, Claudia L*
Equivocal Feminists — *Hunt, Karen*
The ER Companion — *Spignesi, Stephen J*
c The Era of the Dinosaurs (Illus. by Luis Rizo) — *Llamas, Andreu*

Erasme, Precepteur De L'Europe — *Margolin, Jean-Claude*
Erasmian Wit and Proverbial Wisdom — *Massing, Jean Michel*
Erasmus, Man of Letters — *Jardine, Lisa*
Erasmus on Women (Rummel) — *Erasmus, Desiderius*
Erasmus the Reformer — *Dickens, A G*
Erasmus, Utopia and the Jesuits — *Olin, John C*
Erasmus' Vision of the Church — *Pabel, Hilmar M*
Eretria, Fouilles Et Recherches VIII — *Ducrey, Pierre*
Die Erfindung Des Gemaldes — *Belting, Hans*
The Ergodic Theory of Discrete Sample Paths — *Shields, Paul C*
Ergodic Theory of Zd Actions — *Pollicott, Mark*
Ergodicity for Infinite Dimensional Systems — *Da Prato, Giuseppe*
ErgoWise: A Personal Guide to Making Your Workspace Comfortable and Safe — *Schaffer, William A*
c Eric and the Striped Horror (Illus. by Bridget MacKeith) — *Mitchelhill, Barbara*
r ERIC on CD-ROM. Electronic Media Version
Eric Voegelin and the Good Society — *Ranieri, John J*
Erich Wolfgang Korngold — *Duchen, Jessica*
c The Erie Canal — *Doherty, Craig A*
Erie Lackawanna — *Grant, H Roger*
Erik Estrada: My Road from Harlem to Hollywood — *Estrada, Erik*
Erinnerung An Brecht — *Mayer, Hans*
Erinnerungen — *Genscher, Hans Dietrich*
Eriophyoid Mites — *Lindquist, E E*
The Eritrean Struggle for Independence — *Iyob, Ruth*
Eriugena: East and West — *Internationales Eriugena-Colloquium (8th: 1991: Chicago, Ill., and Notre Dame, Ind.)*
Ernest Dowson 1867-1900 Et La Crise Fin De Siecle Anglaise — *Chardin, Jean-Jacques*
Ernest Haycox — *Tanner, Stephen L*
y Ernest Hemingway — *McDaniel, Melissa*
Ernest Hemingway Short Stories (Scourby). Audio Version — *Hemingway, Ernest*
Ernest Hemingway: The Oak Park Legacy — *Nagel, James*
y Ernest Hemingway's The Sun Also Rises — *Bloom, Harold*
Ernest Renan: In the Shadow of Faith — *Lee, David C J*
Ernest Tubb: The Texas Troubadour — *Pugh, Ronnie*
c Ernestine and Amanda — *Belton, Sandra*
Ernesto — *Saba, Umberto*
Ernie Pyle in the American Southwest — *Melzer, Richard*
Ernie Pyle's War — *Tobin, James, 1956-*
Ernst Junger and Germany — *Nevin, Thomas*
Ernst Ludwig Von Gerlach: Politisches Denken Und Handeln Eines Preussischen Altkonservativen. Vols. 1-2 — *Kraus, Hans-Christof*
Die Eroberung Von Fulek Durch Die Osmanen 1554 — *Kohbach, Markus*
Eros — *Bevilacqua, Alberto*
Eros — *Ferrer, Linda*
Eros and Allegory — *Turner, Denys*
Eros and Empire — *Higuera, Henry*
Eros and Evolution — *Michod, Richard E*
Eros Breaking Free — *Gilson, Anne Bathurst*
Eros En La Poesia De Miguel Hernandez — *Aggor, F Komla*
Eros in a Narcissistic Culture — *Ellis, Ralph D*
Eros in Mourning — *Staten, Henry*
Eros, Magic, and the Murder of Professor Culianu — *Anton, Ted*
The Eros of Everyday Life — *Griffin, Susan*
Eros: The Myth of Ancient Greek Sexuality — *Thornton, Bruce S*
Eros Unveiled — *Osborne, Catherine*
Erosion — *Graham, Jorie*
Erotic Dawn-Songs of the Middle Ages — *Sigal, Gale*
The Erotic in Sports — *Guttmann, Allen*
Erotic Justice — *Ellison, Marvin M*
Erotic Liberalism — *Schaub, Diana J*
Erotica I
Erotica II
Erotica III
Errands — *Guest, Judith*
The Errant Art of Moby-Dick — *Spanos, William V*
Errant Journeys — *Zurick, David*
Die Errichtung Des Bistums Arras 1093/1094 — *Kery, Lotte*
Error and the Growth of Experimental Knowledge — *Mayo, Deborah G*
Error Coding Cookbook — *Rorabaugh, C Britton*

The Error of Being — *Caraion, Ion*
Error of Judgement — *Dias, Dexter*
Error of Judgment — *Dias, Dexter*
The Error of My Ways — *Colless, Edward*
The Error of Our Ways — *Carkeet, David*
Erskine Caldwell: The Journey from Tobacco Road — *Miller, Dan B*
Erskine Childers — *Ring, Jim*
Das Erste Buch Der Konige — *Fritz, Volkmar*
Erzahlte Gesellschaft — *Auerochs, Bernd*
Erzahlungen — *Loggen, Karl Wilhelm*
c Es Hora (Illus. by Marilyn Janovitz) — *Janovitz, Marilyn*
y Esau — *Kerr, Philip*
Esbjerg, En La Costa Y Otros Cuentos — *Onetti, Juan Carlos*
Escanor: Roman Arthurien En Vers De La Fin Du XIIIe Siecle. Vols. 1-2 — *D'Amiens, Girart*
Escapade: A Mystery — *Satterthwait, Walter*
Escape — *Lambrianou, Chris*
y Escape — *Oldham, June*
The Escape Artist — *Chamberlain, Diane*
The Escape Artist — *Katz, Judith*
Escape from Avarice — *Tarcher, Martin*
Escape from Babel — *Miller, Scott D*
c Escape from Fire Mountain (Woodman). Audio Version — *Paulsen, Gary*
y Escape from Libby Prison — *Gindlesperger, James*
Escape from Management Hell — *Gilbreath, Robert D*
c Escape from Sarajevo — *Mattingley, Christobel*
Escape from the City — *Rogerson, Robert*
Escape Hatch. The Long Road Ahead — *Makanin, Vladimir*
Escape in America — *Sampson, Richard*
y Escape Key — *Coleman, Michael*
Escape Routes — *Roberts, David, 1943-*
Escape through the Balkans — *Grunbaum, Irene*
Escape Velocity — *Dery, Mark*
Escaping the Journey to Nowhere — *Walters, Glen*
c Los Escarabajos (Illus. by Estudio Marcel Socias) — *Julivert, Maria Angels*
Escardy Gap — *Crowther, Peter*
Eschatology in the Greek Psalter — *Schaper, Joachim*
Esclaves — *Torres, Dominique*
Esclavitud Y Sociedad En La Provincia De Tunja, Siglo XVIII — *Rueda Mendez, David*
Escriba Con Estilo! — *Gurney, David W*
Los Escribanos De Venezuela — *Avellan De Tamayo, Nieves*
Escrits En Blanc — *Rodes, Montserrat*
La Escritura O La Vida — *Semprun, Jorge*
ESD in Silicon Integrated Circuits — *Amerasekera, Ajith*
ESDA 1996. Vols. 1-9 — *European Joint Conference on Engineering Systems Design and Analysis (3rd: 1996: Montpellier, France)*
Eskimo Kissing — *Mosse, Kate*
Esmond De Beer 1895-1990 — *Strachan, Michael*
c ESP — *Landau, Elaine*
La Espada Y La Cruz — *Raguer, Hilari*
Espanol Iningun — *Brown, Sue*
p Esperantic Studies
El Esperpento Controlado — *Navascues, Javier De*
c El Espiritu De Tio Fernando (Illus. by Morella Fuenmayor) — *Levy, Janice*
Esquisses De Dialogues Philosophiques — *Boss, Gilbert*
Essai De Genetique Theatrale — *Forestier, Georges*
Essais Et Ecrits De Combat — *Bernanos, Georges*
r Essay and General Literature Index 1931-
An Essay on African Philosophical Thought. Rev. Ed. — *Gyekye, Kwame*
An Essay on Belief and Acceptance — *Cohen, L Jonathan*
An Essay on Rights — *Steiner, Hillel*
Essayism: Conrad, Musil and Pirandello — *Harrison, Thomas J*
The Essayistic Spirit — *Obaldia, Claire De*
Essays and Reviews and Travel Books in Prose and Verse — *Auden, W H*
Essays in Appreciation — *Ricks, Christopher*
Essays in Drama Therapy — *Landy, Robert J*
Essays in Economics: National and International — *Tobin, James, 1918-*
Essays in English Population History — *Razzell, Peter*
Essays in Indian History — *Habib, Irfan*
Essays in International Economics 1944-1994 — *Arndt, Heinz W*
Essays in Political Philosophy — *Collingwood, R G*
Essays in Semiotics — *Kristeva, Julia*

Essays in the History and Philosophy of Science — *Duhem, Pierre*

Essays in the History of Canadian Law. Vol. 5 — *Phillips, Jim*

Essays: Mainly Shakespearean — *Barton, Anne*

Essays of a Soviet Scientist — *Gol'danskii, Vitalii I*

Essays on African Writing 2 — *Gurnah, Abdulrazak*

Essays on Cuban History — *Perez, Louis A, Jr.*

Essays on Economics and Economists — *Coase, R H*

Essays on Medieval Music in Honor of David G. Hughes — *Boone, Graeme M*

Essays on Money, Banking, and Regulation — *Kool, Clemens*

Essays on Renaissance Literature. Vol. 1 — *Empson, William*

Essays on Skepticism, Relativism, and Ethics in the Zhuangzi — *Kjellber, Paul*

Essays on the Changing Images of the Southwest — *Francaviglia, Richard V*

Essays on the Early History of Plant Pathology and Mycology in Canada — *Estey, Ralph H*

Essays on the Nature of Art — *Deutsch, Eliot*

The Essence of Becker — *Becker, Gary Stanley*

The Essence of Blue — *Recio, Belinda*

The Essence of Parenting — *Johnson, Anne M*

The Essence of Red — *Recio, Belinda*

r Essence of Romance

The Essence of Shaolin White Crane — *Yang, Jwing-Ming*

r Essential ASL — *Sternberg, Martin L A*

r The Essential Black Literature Guide — *Valade, Roger M, III*

The Essential Book for Microsoft Office — *Bruck, Bill*

The Essential Book of Traditional Chinese Medicine. Vols. 1-2 — *Liu, Yen-Chih*

r The Essential Business Buyer's Guide — *Business Consumer Guide*

The Essential Carlstadt — *Karlstadt, Andreas Rudolff-Bodenstein Von*

Essential Chemistry — *Chang, Raymond*

Essential Clinical Pathology — *Parums, Dinah V*

Essential Endocrinology. 3rd Ed. — *Brook, Charles G D*

Essential English: Introductory Book. Bks. 1-4 — *Fidge, Louis*

yr Essential Facts and Figures

r Essential French Riviera — *Hopkins, Adam*

The Essential Gombrich — *Gombrich, E H*

The Essential Guide to Nature Walking in the United States — *Cook, Charles*

yr Essential History Dates — *Parsons, Martin*

Essential Java — *Manger, Jason*

The Essential Joseph Beuys — *Borer, Alain*

The Essential Kabbalah — *Matt, Daniel Chanan*

y The Essential Kabbalah (Asner). Audio Version — *Matt, Daniel Chanan*

Essential Microbiology for Dentistry — *Samaranayake, Lakshman P*

Essential Microeconomics for Public Policy Analysis — *Levy, John M*

The Essential Neoconservative Reader — *Gerson, Mark*

Essential Psychopharmacology — *Stahl, Stephen M*

The Essential Rosary — *Houselander, Caryll*

Essential Skiing — *Gordon, Herb*

y Essential Skills in Maths. Bks. 1-3 — *Newman, Graham*

Essential Surgical Immunology — *Redmond, H Paul*

Essential Tibetan Buddhism — *Thurman, Robert A F*

y The Essential Vegetarian Cookbook — *Shaw, Diana*

The Essential Vegetarian Cookbook — *Tomnay, Susan*

r Essential Wavelets for Statistical Applications and Data Analysis — *Ogden, R Todd*

Essentially Eggplant — *Kehayan, Nina*

Essentials of Buddhism — *Mizuno, Kogen*

Essentials of Cardiopulmonary Exercise Testing — *Myers, Jonathan*

Essentials of Chemistry. 2nd Ed. — *Burns, Ralph A*

Essentials of Clinical Anatomy. 2nd Ed. — *Ger, Ralph*

Essentials of Health Care Management — *Shortell, Stephen M*

Essentials of Hypnosis — *Yapko, Michael D*

Essentials of Multimedia for Business — *Varhol, Peter D*

Essentials of New Testament Greek. Rev. Ed. — *Summers, Ray*

Essentials of New Testament Greek: A Student's Guide. Rev. Ed. — *Cox, Steven L*

Essentials of Project and Systems Engineering Management — *Eisner, Howard*

Essentials of Safety and Health Management — *Lack, Richard W*

The Essex Aircraft Carriers — *Faltum, Andrew*

Essex Airfields in the Second World War — *Smith, Graham*

The Essex Genealogist. Vol. 2

r Essex Wills — *Emmison, F G*

Esszek — *Nadas, Peter*

y EST Marathon 1995

Establishing Exceptionalism — *Bushnell, Amy Turner*

Establishment Violence in Philo and Luke — *Seland, Torrey*

Estado Y Mercado — *Carmagnani, Marcello*

y The Estate (Waterman). Audio Version — *Singer, Isaac Bashevis*

r Estate Settlements in Blount County, Tennessee, Naming Heirs — *Dockter, Albert W*

The Estates General on Education 1995-1996

Esteem Enlivened by Desire — *Hagstrum, Jean H*

c Esther's Story (Illus. by Juan Wijngaard) — *Wolkstein, Diane*

Esthetics of the Moment — *Kavanagh, Thomas M*

L'Esthetique De Rabelais — *Demerson, Guy*

L'Esthetique De Voltaire — *Menant, Sylvain*

Estimating and Project Management for Building Contractors — *Kitchens, William Michael*

Estimating Economic Values for Nature — *Smith, V Kerry*

Estimation, Inference and Specification Analysis — *White, Halbert*

L'Estime Des Apparences — *Leibniz, Gottfried Wilhelm, Freiherr Von*

c Esto No Pueder Ser! (Illus. by Jacky Gleich) — *Schar, Brigitte*

Estonia and Russia, Estonians and Russians — *Olof Palme International Center*

La Estrella Que Cayo Una Noche En El Mar — *Alonso, Luis Ricardo*

Estrogen: The Natural Way — *Shandler, Nina*

L'Estuario — *Morazzoni, Marta*

Estudios Basicos De Derechos Humanos — *Almeida, Ileana*

L'Eta Di Savonarola — *D'Afflitto, Chiara*

L'Eta Di Savonarola — *Padovani, Serena*

Les Etats-Unis Et Leur Arriere-Cour — *Artaud, Denise*

c The Etch a Sketch Book

Etcherelli: Elise Ou La Vraie Vie — *Poole, Sara*

c The Etcher's Studio (Illus. by Arthur Geisert) — *Geisert, Arthur*

The Eternal — *Chadbourn, Mark*

Eternal Mexico — *Frerck, Robert*

y Eternity Road — *McDevitt, Jack*

Ethan Frome (Osgood). Audio Version — *Wharton, Edith*

Ethel: A Love Story — *Falkiner, Suzanne*

An Ethic for Enemies — *Shriver, Donald W*

Ethical Decision Making in Physical Activity Research — *Drowatzky, John N*

Ethical Decision Making in Therapy — *Rave, Elizabeth J*

Ethical Dilemmas — *Chirban, John T*

Ethical Dilemmas in Public Administration — *Pasquerella, Lynn*

The Ethical Dimensions of Financial Institutions and Markets — *Argandona, Antonio*

Ethical Dimensions of International Management — *Carroll, Stephen J, 1930-*

Ethical Dimensions of Leadership — *Kanungo, Rabindra N*

An Ethical Education — *Sellers, M N S*

Ethical Issues in Behavioral Research — *Kimmel, Allan J*

Ethical Issues in Pharmacy — *Weinstein, Bruce*

Ethical Issues in Suicide — *Battin, M Pabst*

Ethical Norms, Particular Cases — *Wallace, James D, 1937-*

The Ethical Primate — *Midgley, Mary*

Ethical Theories in Islam. 2nd Expanded Ed. — *Fakhry, Majid*

The Ethical Theory of John Duns Scotus — *Shannon, Thomas A*

The Ethical World of British MPs — *Mancuso, Maureen*

Ethics and Climate Change — *Coward, Harold*

Ethics and Economic Affairs — *Lewis, Alan*

Ethics and Economics. Vols. 1-2 — *Hamlin, Alan P*

Ethics and Epidemiology — *Coughlin, Steven S*

Ethics and International Affairs — *Rosenthal, Joel H*

Ethics and International Politics — *Bonanate, Luigi*

Ethics and National Defense — *Gaston, James C*

Ethics and Politics in the Hebrew Bible — *Knight, Douglas A*

Ethics and Rhetoric — *Innes, Doreen*

Ethics and Statecraft — *Nolan, Cathal J*

Ethics at the Bedside — *Culver, Charles M*

Ethics for Beginners — *Robinson, Dave*

Ethics in Business — *Childs, James M, Jr.*

Ethics in Business and Society — *Becker, Gerhold K*

Ethics in Congress — *Thompson, Dennis F*

Ethics in Early Buddhism — *Kalupahana, David J*

Ethics in International Relations — *Frost, Mervyn*

Ethics in Obstetrics and Gynecology — *McCullough, Laurence B*

Ethics, Killing and War — *Norman, Richard*

The Ethics of Accounting and Finance — *National Conference on Business Ethics (10th: 1994: Bentley College)*

The Ethics of Asking — *Elliott, Deni*

The Ethics of Authenticity — *Taylor, Charles, 1931-*

Ethics of Capitalism and Critique of Sociobiology — *Koslowski, Peter*

The Ethics of Collecting Cultural Property — *Messenger, Phyllis Mauch*

The Ethics of Liberal Democracy — *Churchill, Robert Paul*

The Ethics of Our Climate — *O'Neill, William R*

The Ethics of Policing — *Kleinig, John*

The Ethics of Reading in Manuscript Culture — *Dagenais, John*

The Ethics of Research Involving Human Subjects — *Vanderpool, Harold Y*

An Ethics of Sexual Difference — *Irigaray, Luce*

The Ethics of Suicide — *Cosculluela, Victor*

The Ethics of Travel — *Islam, Syed Manzuru*

The Ethics of War and Peace — *Christopher, Paul*

The Ethics of War and Peace — *Nardin, Terry*

Ethics on the Ark — *Norton, Bryan A*

Ethics, Politics, and Difference in Julia Kristeva's Writing — *Oliver, Kelly*

Ethics: Subjectivity and Truth — *Foucault, Michel*

Ethics, Theory and the Novel — *Parker, David, 1943-*

Ethics through Corporate Strategy — *Gilbert, Daniel R*

y Ethiopia — *Gish, Steven*

c Ethiopia — *Grunsell, Angela*

r Ethiopia — *Munro-Hay, Stuart*

Ethiopian Stories — *Schuyler, George*

Ethique Et Responsabilite--Paul Ricoeur — *Aeschlimann, Jean-Christopher*

r Ethnic and Vernacular Music 1898-1960 — *Vernon, Paul*

The Ethnic Canon — *Palumbo-Liu, David*

Ethnic Chicago — *Lindberg, Richard*

Ethnic Cleansing — *Bell-Fialkoff, Andrew*

Ethnic Conflict in the Post-Soviet World — *Drobizheva, Leokadia*

Ethnic Conflict in World Politics — *Gurr, Ted Robert*

Ethnic Conflicts and the Nation-State — *Stavenhagen, Rodolfo*

r Ethnic Cuisines — *Vassilian, Hamo B*

Ethnic Cultures in the 1920s in North America — *Binder, Wolfgang*

The Ethnic Eye — *Noriega, Chon A*

Ethnic Ironies — *De La Garza, Rodolfo O*

Ethnic Minorities in the Modern Nation State — *Rex, John*

y The Ethnic Moment — *Fetzer, Philip*

Ethnic Pride and Racial Prejudice in Victorian Cape Town — *Bickford-Smith, Vivian*

Ethnic Studies and Multiculturalism — *La Belle, Thomas J*

r Ethnic Studies in the United States — *Bataille, Gretchen M*

Ethnicity and Family Therapy. 2nd Ed. — *McGoldrick, Monica*

Ethnicity and Sport in North American History and Culture — *Eisen, George*

Ethnicity in the Mainstream — *Greenhill, Pauline*

Ethnicity, Markets, and Migration in the Andes — *Larson, Brooke*

Ethnicity on Parade — *Schultz, April R*

Ethnicity, Race, and Crime — *Hawkins, Darnell F*

Ethnobotany: Evolution of a Discipline — *Schultes, Richard Evans*

Ethnobotany: Principles and Applications — *Cotton, C M*

Ethnocultural Aspects of Posttraumatic Stress Disorder — *Marsella, Anthony J*

Ethnography, Linguistics, Narrative Inequality — *Hymes, Dell*

The Ethnography of Manners — *Bentley, Nancy, 1961-*

The Ethnology of Reading — *Boyarin, Jonathan*
Ethnology of Vanuatu — *Speiser, Felix*
Ethnomimesis — *Cantwell, Robert*
Ethnoregional Conflict in Democracies — *Newman, Saul*
Ethnoveterinary Research and Development — *McCorkle, Constance M*
The Ethos of Pluralization — *Connolly, William*
L'Etreinte Abhorree — *Berchtold, Jacques*
Etruscan Art — *Brendel, Otto J*
c ETs and UFOs — *Kettelkamp, Larry*
Etta Place: Her Life and Times with Butch Cassidy and the Sundance Kid — *Drago, Gail*
Etude Fur Adele Und Einen Hund — *Kern, Elfriede*
Etudes Coptes IV — *Rosenstiehl, Jean-Marc*
EU and US Banking in the 1990s — *Lewis, Alfred*
c Eugene Field: The Children's Poet — *Greene, Carol*
Eukaryotic DNA Replication — *Blow, J Julian*
Eukaryotic Gene Transcription — *Goodbourn, Stephen*
Eulogies — *Baraka, Imamu Amiri*
Eunuchs and Sacred Boundaries in Islamic Society — *Marmon, Shaun Elizabeth*
The Eunuchs in the Ming Dynasty — *Tsai, Shih-Shan Henry*
Euphorbias: A Gardeners' Guide — *Turner, Roger*
r The Eurail Guide to Train Travel in the New Europe 1996
r The Eurail Guide to World Train Travel 1996
Eureka Street — *Wilson, Robert McLiam*
Euripidean Polemic — *Croally, N T*
Euripides and the Poetics of Sorrow — *Segal, Charles*
Euro-DAC '95, European Design Automation Conference with Euro-VHDL — *European Design Automation Conference (1995: Brighton, England)*
Euro-DAC '96 European Design Automation Conference with Euro-VHDL and Exhibition — *European Design Automation Conference (1996: Geneva, Switzerland)*
Euromicro Workshop on Real-Time Systems — *Euromicro Workshop on Real-Time Systems (8th: 1996: L'Aquila, Italy)*
Europa — *Parks, Tim*
y Europa, Europa — *Perel, Shlomo*
r The Europa World Year Book 1996. Vols. 1-2
Europe: A History — *Davies, Norman*
Europe and America — *Kahler, Miles*
Europe and Latin America in the World Economy — *Purcell, Susan Kaufman*
Europe from the Balkans to the Urals — *Lukic, Reneo*
r Europe Info
Europe: Road to Unity — *Lewis, Flora*
Europe the European Way — *Gollattascheck, James F*
Europe--Toward 2001 — *Coffey, Peter*
Europe under Napoleon 1799-1815 — *Broers, Michael*
Europe United? — *Welsh, Michael, 1942-*
European Agriculture — *Gardner, Brian*
r The European Book World. Pt. 2. Electronic Media Version
The European City — *Benevolo, Leonardo*
European Clocks in the J. Paul Getty Museum — *J. Paul Getty Museum*
European Community Decision Making — *Bueno De Mesquita, Bruce*
European Consumer Guide to the Single Market. 1st Ed. — *European Commission*
r European Consumer Market Information. 2nd Ed. — *Brooke, Wendy*
The European Diaries of Richard Cobden 1846-1849 — *Cobden, Richard*
The European Discovery of America — *Morison, Samuel Eliot*
r European Drinks Marketing Directory 1995
European Economic Integration and Sustainable Development — *Barrass, Robert*
European Economic Integration as a Challenge to Industry and Government — *Tilly, Richard*
The European Economy 1750-1914 — *Aldcroft, Derek H*
The European Equity Markets — *Steil, Benn*
The European Experience of Declining Fertility 1850-1970 — *Gillis, John R*
r European Immigrant Women in the United States — *Litoff, Judy Barrett*
European Integration — *Calingaert, Michael*
European Integration and Competitiveness — *Sachwald, Frederique*
European Integration and Disintegration — *Bideleux, Robert*
European Integration and Regional Policy — *Fountas, Steve*

European Integration, Monetary Co-ordination and the Demand for Money — *Monticelli, Carlo*
p The European Journal of International Relations
p European Journal of Neurology: The Official Journal of the European Federation of Neurological Societies
p The European Legacy
r European Marketing Data and Statistics 1996
European Migrants — *Hoerder, Dirk*
European Migration in the Late Twentieth Century — *Fassmann, Heinz*
European Monetary Integration. 3rd Ed. — *Welfens, Paul J J*
European Monetary Union — *Davidson, Ian D*
The European Nobilities in the Seventeenth and Eighteenth Centuries. Vol. 2 — *Scott, H M*
The European Nobility 1400-1800 — *Dewald, Jonathan*
The European Observatory for Small and Medium-Sized Enterprises — *Sakkas, Dimitrios A*
r European Oilfield Service, Supply, and Manufacturers Directory 1996
The European Outthrust and Encounter — *Clough, Cecil H*
r European Paintings in the Metropolitan Museum of Art by Artists Born before 1865 — *Metropolitan Museum of Art (New York, NY)*
The European Peasant Family and Society — *Rudolph, Richard L*
yr The European Powers in the First World War — *Tucker, Spencer C*
r European Private Label Directory
European Proto-Industrialization — *Ogilvie, Sheilagh C*
European Readings of American Popular Culture — *Dean, John*
The European Reformations — *Lindberg, Carter*
r European Regional Incentives 1996-97
European Religion in the Age of Great Cities 1830-1930 — *McLeod, Hugh*
European Security in the 1990s — *Ghebali, Victor-Yves*
European Social Policy — *Leibfried, Stephan*
European Transport Trends and Infrastructural Needs
The European Union. 2nd Ed. — *Archer, Clive*
r The European Union Encyclopedia and Directory 1996
European Union Foreign Policy and Central America — *Smith, Hazel*
The European Union, the United Nations, and the Revival of Confederal Governance — *Lister, Frederick K*
The European Union's Common Foreign and Security Policy — *Cameron, Fraser*
European Warfare 1660-1815 — *Black, Jeremy*
The European Water Environment in a Period of Transformation — *Hassan, John*
European Women and Preindustrial Craft — *Hafter, Daryl M*
The Europeans (Bron). Audio Version — *James, Henry*
Europeans on the Move — *Canny, Nicholas*
Europe's Environment — *Clarke, Robin*
Europe's Environment — *Stanners, David*
r Europe's Medium-Sized Companies Directory
Europe's Population — *Hall, Ray*
Europe's Post-War Recovery — *Eichengreen, Barry*
Europe's Steppe Frontier — *McNeil, William*
The Eurosceptical Reader — *Holmes, Martin*
Euthanasia Examined — *Keown, John*
y Eva — *Dickinson, Peter*
Eva Le Gallienne: A Biography — *Sheehy, Helen*
Eva Peron — *Dujovne Ortiz, Alicia*
y Eva Peron (May). Audio Version — *Fraser, Nicholas*
Evadarea Tacuta — *Constante, Lena*
Evaluating and Assessing the Visual Arts in Education — *Boughton, Doug*
Evaluating Climate Change Action Plans — *White, James C*
Evaluating Health Risks — *Johansson, Per-Olov*
Evaluating Public Sector Research and Development — *Link, Albert N*
Evaluating Public Spending — *Pradhan, Sanjay*
Evaluating Research Articles from Start to Finish — *Girden, Ellen R*
Evaluating Research in Communicative Disorders. 3rd Ed. — *Schiavetti, Nicholas*
Evaluating Sleep in Infants and Children — *Sheldon, Stephen H*
Evaluating Training Programs — *Kirkpatrick, Donald*

Evaluating Women's Health Messages — *Parrott, Louiselle*
Evaluation and Treatment of Urinary Incontinence — *Blaivas, Jerry G*
Evaluation of Technical Assistance to Hungary — *Hughes, Kirsty*
Evaluation of the U.S. Strategic Nuclear Triad — *United States. Congress. Senate. Committee on Government Affairs*
Evaluation Results 1994
Evangelical Christianity in the United States and Great Britain — *Soper, J Christopher*
r Evangelical Dictionary of Biblical Theology — *Elwell, Walter A*
Evangelical Protestantism in Ulster Society 1740-1890 — *Hempton, David*
The Evangelical Rhetoric of Ramon Llull — *Johnston, Mark D*
r Evangelical Sectarianism in the Russian Empire and the USSR — *Wardin, Albert W*
An Evangelical Theology of Preaching — *English, Donald*
The Evangelical War against Slavery and Caste — *Howard, Victor B*
Evangelicals and Catholics Together — *Colson, Charles*
Evangelicals and Politics in Antebellum America — *Carwardine, Richard J*
Evangelicals at the Ballot Box — *Menendez, Albert J*
Evangelisches Kirchenlexikon — *Fahlbusch, Erwin*
Evangelism and Apostasy — *Bowen, Kurt*
y El Evangelizador Empecinado — *Viesca, Carlos*
L'Evangile Selon Matthieu — *Amphoux, Christian-Bernard*
Eve — *Finch, Annie*
Eveless Den — *Wiggins, Marianne*
y An Even Break — *Hite, Sid*
Even in Quiet Places — *Stafford, William*
Even Rage Will Rot — *Garcia, Carlos Ernesto*
y Even Stephen — *Hurwitz, Johanna*
Even the Wicked — *Block, Lawrence*
Even Yuppies Die — *Babson, Marian*
An Evening at the Garden of Allah — *Paulson, Don*
Evening Class — *Binchy, Maeve*
An Evening Performance — *Garrett, George P, 1929-*
Evening Train — *Levertov, Denise*
An Evening with the Messiah — *Jinks, Catherine*
Evenings and Avenues — *Dischell, Stuart*
Evenings on and off the Roof — *Crawford, Dorothy Lamb*
Event, Metaphor, Memory — *Amin, Shahid*
c The Eventful History of Three Blind Mice (Illus. by Winslow Homer)
Events Leading Up to My Death — *Smith, Howard K*
yr Events That Changed America in the Twentieth Century — *Findling, John E*
Events That Changed the World. Electronic Media Version — *Ingpen, Robert*
Events That Changed the World in the Nineteenth Century — *Thackeray, Frank W*
r The Ever-Changing Sky — *Kaler, James B*
c Ever Heard of an Aardwolf? (Illus. by Barry Moser) — *Moser, Madeline*
Everbest Ever — *Thomson, Virgil*
c Everett Anderson's Nine Month Long (Illus. by Ann Grifalconi) — *Clifton, Lucille*
p The Everglade Magazine
c Everglades (Illus. by Wendell Minor) — *George, Jean Craighead*
Everglades: The Ecosystem and Its Restoration — *Davis, Steven M*
p Evergreen Chronicles
The Everlasting Gospel — *Faupel, D William*
Evermore — *Perrick, Penny*
c Every Buddy Counts (Illus. by Fiona Dunbar) — *Murphy, Stuart J*
Every Day — *Richards, Elizabeth*
Every Day (Hurt). Audio Version — *Richards, Elizabeth*
Every Day a Visitor — *Abrons, Richard*
Every Inch a Soldier — *Head, William*
Every Man for Himself — *Bainbridge, Beryl*
Every Man Will Do His Duty — *King, Dean*
r Every Manager's Guide to Business Processes — *Keen, Peter G W*
c Every Monday in the Mailbox (Illus. by Jan Naimo Jones) — *Fox, Louisa*
Every Secret Thing — *Slovo, Gillian*
Every Shot I Take — *Love, Davis, III*
y Every Shut Eye Ain't Asleep — *Harper, Michael S*
y Every Substance Clothed — *Halme, Kathleen*

r Every Thing in Dickens — *Newlin, George*

Every Tub Must Sit on It's Own Bottom — *Plant, Deborah*

Every Wish Fulfilled — *James, Samantha*

Every Woman's Handbook for Preventing Cancer — *Altman, Roberta*

c Everybody Bakes Bread (Illus. by Peter J Thornton) — *Dooley, Norah*

Everybody Eats — *Mogelonsky, Marcia*

Everybody Is Sitting on the Curb — *Edelstein, Alan*

Everybody's Children — *Gormley, William T, Jr.*

Everybody's Children — *Gormley, William T*

Everybody's Comet — *Hale, Alan*

Everybody's Doing It — *Warren, Andrea*

Everyday Acts against Racism — *Reddy, Maureen T*

c An Everyday Book (Illus. by Cynthia Rylant) — *Rylant, Cynthia*

Everyday Cooking with Dr. Dean Ornish — *Ornish, Dean*

Everyday Forms of State Formation — *Joseph, Gilbert M*

Everyday Life in Medieval England — *Dyer, Christopher*

Everyday Life in the Muslim Middle East — *Bowen, Donna Lee*

c Everyday Machines (Illus. by John Kelly) — *Burnie, David*

c Everyday Mysteries — *Wexler, Jerome*

Everyday Mysticism — *Ciorra, Anthony J*

y Everyday Science Explained — *Suplee, Curt*

Everyday Things — *Slesin, Suzanne*

Everyman Revived — *Scott, Drusilla*

Everyone Has Roots — *Camp, Anthony*

r Everyone in Dickens. Vols. 1-3 — *Newlin, George*

Everyone Is Entitled to My Opinion — *Brinkley, David*

Everyone's Gone to the Moon — *Norman, Philip, 1943-*

r Everyone's Guide to Cancer Therapy. 2nd Ed. — *Dollinger, Malin*

r Everyone's Guide to Outpatient Surgery — *Macho, James*

Everyone's Guide to the Law — *Dranoff, Linda Silver*

Everyone's Money Book — *Goodman, Jordan E*

y Everything about Theatre! — *Lee, Robert L*

Everything and the Moon — *Quinn, Julia*

Everything as Divine — *Eckhart, Meister*

Everything but the Truth — *McPherson, Christopher*

r Everything Civil War — *Kope, Spencer*

Everything Elvis — *Mabes, Joni*

Everything for Sale — *Kuttner, Robert*

c Everything Happens on Mondays — *Davies, Nicola*

Everything to Gain — *Bradford, Barbara Taylor*

Everything You Always Wanted to Know about Sandy Berman but Were Afraid to Ask — *Dodge, Chris*

Everything You Ever Wanted to Know about AIDS, but Were Afraid to Ask — *Fowler, Bev*

y Everything You Need to Know about Asian American History — *Cao, Lan*

Everything You Need to Know about College Sports Recruiting — *Walsh, Jim*

r Everything You Need to Know about Diseases

r Everything You Need to Know about Medical Tests

r Everything You Need to Know about Medical Treatments

y Everything You Need to Know about Teen Marriage — *Ayer, Eleanor H*

y Everything You Need to Know about the Dangers of Tatooing and Body Piercing — *Reybold, Laura*

r Everything You Pretend to Know and Are Afraid Someone Will Ask — *Pugh, Lynette*

y Everywhere Faces Everywhere (Illus. by Reynold Ruffins) — *Berry, James*

r EveryWoman's Guide to Prescription and Nonprescription Drugs — *Cahill, Kathleen*

Eve's Apple — *Rosen, Jonathan*

r Evesham Borough Records of the Seventeenth Century 1605-1687 — *Roberts, Stephen K*

Evictions: Art and Spatial Politics — *Deutsche, Rosalyn*

Evidence Dismissed — *Lange, Tom*

Evidence of Guilt — *Jacobs, Jonnie*

Evil: A Historical and Theological Perspective — *Schwarz, Hans, 1939-*

Evil and Suffering in Jewish Philosophy — *Leaman, Oliver*

Evil and the Demonic — *Oppenheimer, Paul*

Evil Angels among Them — *Charles, Kate*

y Evil Encounter — *Levitin, Sonia*

Evil Incarnate — *Clark, Leigh*

Evil: Inside Human Cruelty and Violence — *Baumeister, Roy F*

An Evil Lost to View? — *Mills, Kenneth*

An Evil Love — *Wansell, Geoffrey*

Evil Seed of the Father — *Tatham, James*

Evil Sisters — *Dijkstra, Bram*

Evita: The Real Life of Eva Peron — *Fraser, Nicholas*

Evolucion De Una Civilizacion Prehispanica — *Weigand, Phil C*

c Evolution (Illus. by Ferron-Retana) — *Llamas Ruiz, Andres*

Evolution. 2nd Ed. — *Ridley, Mark*

Evolution and Ecology of Macaque Societies — *Fa, John E*

Evolution and Environment in Tropical America — *Jackson, Jeremy B C*

y The Evolution and Extinction of the Dinosaurs — *Fastovsky, David E*

Evolution and Literary Theory — *Carroll, Joseph*

y Evolution Isn't What It Used to Be — *Anderson, Walt*

The Evolution of Allure — *Hersey, George L*

The Evolution of Allure — *Hersey, George*

Evolution of Asia-Pacific Economies — *Yamazawa, Ippei*

The Evolution of British Social Policy and the Welfare State c. 1800-1993 — *Laybourn, Keith*

The Evolution of Communication — *Hauser, Marc D*

The Evolution of English Sport — *Wigglesworth, Neil*

Evolution of Epitaxial Structure and Morphology — *Zangwill, Andrew*

Evolution of Industrial Output of Russia — *Kafengauz, Lev Borisovich*

The Evolution of International Business — *Jones, Geoffrey*

Evolution of Social Insect Colonies — *Crozier, Ross H*

The Evolution of the Airline Industry — *Morrison, Steven A*

The Evolution of the Emotion-Processing Mind — *Langs, Robert*

The Evolution of the Sailing Navy 1509-1815 — *Harding, Richard*

The Evolution of the Soul. Rev. Ed. — *Swinburne, Richard*

The Evolution of U.S. Finance. Vols. 1-2 — *D'Arista, Jane W*

The Evolution of Useful Things — *Petroski, Henry*

Evolution, Order and Complexity — *Khalil, Elias L*

Evolution: The General Theory — *Laszlo, Ervin*

Evolutionary Algorithms in Management Applications — *Biethahn, Jorg*

Evolutionary Archaeology — *O'Brien, Michael J, 1950-*

Evolutionary Archaeology — *Teltser, Patrice A*

Evolutionary Biology. Vol. 29

Evolutionary Change and Heterochrony — *McNamara, Kenneth J*

Evolutionary Game Theory — *Weibull, Jorgen W*

Evolutionary Innovations — *McKelvey, Maureen D*

Evolutionary Language Understanding — *Sampson, Geoffrey*

Evolutionary Naturalism — *Ruse, Michael*

Evolutionary Paleobiology — *Jablonski, David*

Evolutionary Processes in Binary Stars — *Wijers, Ralph Antoine Marie Joseph*

Evolutionary Psychiatry — *Stevens, Anthony*

Evolutionary Search and the Job Shop — *Mattfeld, Dirk C*

The Evolutionist Economics of Leon Walras — *Jolink, Albert*

The Evolving Coast — *Davis, Richard A, Jr.*

Evolving Concepts in Gastrointestinal Motility — *Champion, Malcolm C*

The Evolving Continents — *Windley, Brian F*

The Evolving Pacific Power Structure — *Da Cunha, Derek*

The Evolving Self — *Csikszentmihalyi, Mihaly*

Evolving the Mind — *Cairns-Smith, A G*

Evolving Trends in the Dual Use of Satellites — *Alves, Pericles Gasparini*

r Ewald Matare, Das Plastische Werk. 2nd Ed. — *Schilling, Sabine Maja*

The Ex — *Lutz, John*

y The Ex (Griffin). Audio Version — *Lutz, John*

Ex Utero — *Foos, Laurie*

An Exaltation of Larks — *Reed, Robert*

y The Examination — *Bosse, Malcolm*

An Examination of an Emerging Stock Exchange — *Yuce, Ayse*

p Examiner (England 1808-)

y Examining the Media — *Connell, Barbara*

c Excalibur (Illus. by Hudson Talbott) — *Talbott, Hudson*

Excavations and Their Objects — *Barker, Steven*

Excavations at La Giostra — *Moltesen, Mette*

Excavations in Jerusalem 1961-1967. Vol. 4 — *Tushingham, A D*

Excel for Windows 95 for Busy People — *Mansfield, Ron*

Excellence in Ecology. Vol. 4

Excellent Cadavers — *Stille, Alexander*

An Excellent Conceited Tragedie of Romeo and Juliet — *Shakespeare, William*

The Excellent Path to Enlightenment — *Rab-Gsal-Zla-Ba, Dis-Mgo Mkhyen-Brtse*

The Excellent Trainer — *Kamp, Di*

y Excellent Women (Stevenson). Audio Version — *Pym, Barbara*

Exceptional Language Development in Down Syndrome — *Rondal, Jean A*

r The Exceptional Woman — *Sheriff, Mary D*

y Excession — *Banks, Iain M*

Exchange Alley — *Walsh, Michael*

Exchange in Ancient Greece — *Reden, Sitta Von*

r Exchange Rate Economics — *Isard, Peter*

Exchange Rate Parity for Trade and Development — *Yotopoulos, Pan A*

Exchange Rate Unions — *Kotilainen, Markku*

Exchange Rates and Prices — *Menon, Jayant*

Exchange Rates and Prices — *Smith, William R, Jr.*

Exchanges Within — *Pentland, John*

Exchanging Experiences of Technology Partnership

Exchanging Hats — *Bishop, Elizabeth*

Excitations in Liquid and Solid Helium — *Glyde, Henry R*

Excitatory Amino Acids and the Cerebral Cortex — *Conti, Fiorenzo*

Exclusion from School — *Blyth, Eric*

y Exclusive — *Brown, Sandra*

y Exclusive (Crosby). Audio Version — *Brown, Sandra*

The Excuse Factory — *Olson, Walter*

Executive Blues — *Meyer, G J*

Executive Orders — *Clancy, Tom*

Executive Orders (Herrmann). Audio Version — *Clancy, Tom*

The Executive Way — *Morrill, Calvin*

r An Exegetical Bibliography of the New Testament. Vol. 4 — *Gunter, Wagner*

r Exemplum: Model-Book Drawings and the Practice of Artistic Transmission in the Middle Ages Ca. 900-Ca. 1470 — *Scheller, Robert W*

Exercise Physiology. 4th Ed. — *McArdle, William D*

Exercise Programming for Older Adults — *Clark, Janie*

Exercises for Airplanes and Other Confined Spaces — *Diamond, Janet*

r The Exhaustive Concordance to the Greek New Testament — *Kohlenberger, John R, III*

An Exhibit Denied — *Harwit, Martin*

Exil--Asyl: Tatort Deutschland — *Muller, Henning*

Exil Ohne Ende — *Westphal, Uwe*

Exil Und Engagement — *Braun, Michael*

Exile — *Nelson, Blake*

y Exile — *Sarrantonio, Al*

Exile and Destruction — *Schneider, Gertrude*

Exile from Exile — *Berg, Nancy E*

An Exile of Ireland — *Walsh, Micheline Kerney*

Exile: The Sense of Alienation in Modern Russian Letters — *Patterson, David*

The Exile Way — *Woodward, Ann*

Exiles — *Caputo, Philip*

y Exile's Challenge — *Wells, Angus*

Exiles, Eccentrics, Activists — *Sieg, Katrin*

Exiles + Emigres — *Barron, Stephanie, 1950-*

Exiles from Eden — *Schwehn, Mark R*

y The Exiles in Love — *McKay, Hilary*

y Exile's Song — *Bradley, Marion Zimmer*

Existence in Black — *Gordon, Lewis R*

The Existential Pleasures of Engineering — *Florman, Samuel C*

Exit to Reality — *Forbes, Edith*

Exit with Honor — *Pemberton, William E*

Exito Latino — *Failde, Augusto*

Exits — *Houff, Richard D*

Exodus 11,1-13,16 Und Die Bedeutung Der Tragergruppen Fur Das Verstandnis Des Passa — *Ahuis, Ferdinand*

Exodus from the Long Sun — *Wolfe, Gene*

Exotic Brew — *Camporesi, Piero*

Exotic Herbs — *Saville, Carole*

c Exotic Invaders — *Lesinski, Jeanne M*

Exotic Nations — *Wasserman, Renata R Mautner*

Exoticism in Salammbo — *Hohl, Anne Mullen*

Expanded Universes — *Reid, Christopher*

Expanding Access to Financial Services in Latin America — *Basch, Miguel*

Expanding Archaeology — *Skibo, James M*

Expanding Export Markets — *Hammett, A L*

Expanding Partnerships in Conservation — *McNeely, Jeffrey A*

r The Expanding World 1492 to 1762. 2nd Ed. — *Williams, Neville*

The Expansion of England — *Schwarz, Bill*

Expansion of Trading Opportunities to the Year 2000 for Asia-Pacific Developing Countries

The Expansive Moment — *Goody, Jack*

Expect a Miracle — *Wakefield, Dan*

y Expect a Miracle (Sevra). Audio Version — *Wakefield, Dan*

y Expecting the Unexpected — *Jukes, Mavis*

r Expedition Guide. 3rd Ed. — *Keay, Wally*

Expendable — *Gardner, James Alan*

L'Experience Huguenote Au Nouveau Monde — *Lestringant, Frank*

The Experience of Nothingness — *Nisargadattam, Maharaj*

The Experience of Poverty — *Beck, Tony*

Experience of the Sacred — *Twiss, Sumner B*

The Experiences of Tiresias — *Loraux, Nicole*

Experiencing Abortion — *Kushner, Eve*

Experiencing HIV — *Adam, Barry D*

Experiencing Jesus — *O'Collins, Gerald*

Experiencing Lourdes — *Grosso, Stephen*

Experiencing Music Technology — *Williams, David Brian*

Experiencing Mystagogy — *Baumbach, Gerald F*

An Experiment in Love — *Mantel, Hilary*

y An Experiment in Love (Walter). Audio Version — *Mantel, Hilary*

Experiment-Research Methodology in Marketing — *Patzer, Gordon L*

c Experimenta Con La Electricidad (Illus. by Jon Barnes) — *Baker, Wendy*

Experimental and Molecular Approaches to Plant Biosystematics — *Hoch, Peter C*

Experimental Design and Model Choice — *Toutenburg, Helge*

Experimental Methods for Microgravity Materials Science — *International Conference on Experimental Methods for Microgravity Materials Science (7th: 1995: Las Vegas, NV)*

Experimental Organic Chemistry. 2nd Ed. — *Wilcox, Charles F*

Experimental Psychology. 4th Ed. — *Myers, Anne*

Experiments in Basic Chemistry. 4th Ed. — *Murov, Steven*

Experiments in Musical Intelligence — *Cope, David*

Experiments in Virtual Reality — *Harrison, David*

c Experiments with Senses — *Byles, Monica*

p The Experioddicist

Expert Consultations in Gynecological Cancers — *Markman, Maurie*

Experts and Politicians — *Finegold, Kenneth*

y Expiration Date — *Powers, Tim*

Explaining an Eclipse — *Goldin, Owen*

Explaining and Interpreting Religion — *Segal, Robert A*

Explaining Attitudes — *Baker, Lynne Rudder*

Explaining Auschwitz and Hiroshima — *Bosworth, R J B*

Explaining Economic Growth — *Lim, David*

Explaining Economic Policy Reversals — *Hood, Christopher, 1947-*

Explaining Family Interactions — *Fitzpatrick, Mary Anne*

Explaining International Relations since 1945 — *Woods, Ngaire*

Explaining Long-Term Economic Change — *Anderson, J L*

Explaining the Economic Performance of Nations — *Maddison, Angus*

Explaining the Reagan Years in Central America — *Brown, Jeremy M*

Explanation-Based Neural Network Learning — *Thrun, Sebastian*

y An Explanation for Chaos — *Schumacher, Julie*

Explanatory Style — *Buchanan, Gregory McClellan*

Explicit and Authentic Acts — *Kyvig, David E*

Exploitation — *Nielsen, Kai*

Exploitation — *Wertheimer, Alan*

y Exploitation of Children — *Ennew, Judith*

Les Explorateurs De L'Amerique Du Nord — *Litalien, Raymonde*

c Exploration into Australia — *Darian-Smith, Kate*

c Exploration into China — *Wang, Tao*

c Exploration into Japan — *Tames, Richard*

c Exploration into North America — *Asikinack, Bill*

y Exploration Seismology. 2nd Ed. — *Sheriff, Robert E*

Explorations in Backyard Biology — *Raham, R Gary*

Explorations in Cognitive Neuropsychology — *Parkin, Alan J*

Explorations in Economic Sociology — *Swedberg, Richard*

Explorations in Indexing and Abstracting — *O'Connor, Brian C*

Explorations in Metaphysics — *Clarke, W Norris*

Explorations in Strategy — *Gray, Colin S*

Explorations: My Quest for Adventure and Discovery under the Sea — *Ballard, Robert D*

c Explore the Wild — *Duncan, Beverly*

c Explorers — *Burns, Peggy*

c Explorers and Traders — *Millard, Anne*

The Explorers: From the Ancient World to the Present — *Novaresio, Paolo*

Explorers of Light — *Dowling, Claudia Glenn*

c Explorers of the Ancient World — *Brierley, Anthony*

Explorers of the Southern Sky — *Haynes, Raymond*

Exploring Baja by RV — *Peterson, Walt*

Exploring Diversity — *Brown, Jean E, 1945-*

Exploring General Equilibrium — *Black, Fischer*

Exploring Gogol — *Maguire, Robert A*

Exploring Jupiter — *Arroyo, Stephen*

Exploring Media Culture — *Real, Michael R*

c Exploring North America (Illus. by David Antram) — *Morley, Jacqueline*

Exploring Pastel with Barry Watkin — *Watkin, Barry*

yr Exploring Poetry. Electronic Media Version

Exploring Risk Communication — *Gutteling, Jan M*

Exploring Shape and Space — *Ebbutt, Sheila*

Exploring Shape and Space — *McKinnon, Leonie*

Exploring Sport and Exercise Psychology — *Van Raalte, Judy L*

Exploring/Teaching the Psychology of Women. 2nd Ed. — *Paludi, Michele Antoinette*

Exploring the Divided Self — *Richards, David G*

Exploring the Domain of Accident Law — *Dewees, Don*

y Exploring the Frontier — *Smith, C Carter*

Exploring the Gospel of John — *Culpepper, R Alan*

Exploring the IBM PC Power Series — *Hoskins, Jim*

Exploring the Identity and Vision of Jesus — *Perry, John Michael*

c Exploring the Rainforest — *Fredericks, Anthony D*

y Exploring the Solar System — *Booth, Nicholas*

Exploring the Underground Economy — *Pozo, Susan*

Exploring the Unknown. Vol. 1 — *Logsdon, John M*

Exploring the Unknown. Vol. 1 — *Longsdon, John M*

c Exploring the World (Illus. by Gerald Wood) — *Macdonald, Fiona*

Exploring the X-Ray Universe — *Charles, Philip A*

r Exploring Wine — *Koplan, Steven*

Exploring Workstation Applications with CDE and Motif — *Haramundanis, Katherine*

The Explosive World of Tatyana N. Tolstaya's Fiction — *Goscilo, Helena*

Export Dependence Versus the New Protectionism — *Fong, Glenn Randall*

r Export Financing and Insurance Vocabulary — *Johnston-Des Rochers, Janeen*

Export-Import Financing. 4th Ed. — *Venedikian, Harry M*

r Exporting to the USA and the Dictionary of International Trade. 1996-97 Ed. Electronic Media Version

Exposing Prejudice — *Urciuoli, Bonnie*

Expositio Et Quaestiones In Aristotelis De Anima — *Oresme, Nicolaus*

Exposition of Kant's Critique of Pure Reason — *Schultz, Johann*

Exposito Super Capitulum De Generatione Embrionis Canonis Avicennae Cum Quibusdam Quaestionibus — *Mondini De Leuciis*

Exposure — *Ball, Donna*

y Exposure — *Pineiro, R J*

Expressing America — *Ritzer, George*

The Expression of the Passions — *Montagu, Jennifer*

Expressive Details — *Dickinson, Duo*

Expressive Processes in Group Counseling — *Brown, Nina W*

Expulsion and the Nineteenth-Century Novel — *Heyns, Michiel*

The Expulsion of the Jews 1492 and After — *Waddington, Raymond B*

p Exquisite Corpse

Exquisite Corpse — *Brite, Poppy Z*

Exquisite Corpse — *Irwin, Robert*

Exquisite Specificity — *Cambrosio, Alberto*

Extending Literacy — *Wray, David*

Exteriors — *Ernaux, Annie*

Exterminate All the Brutes — *Lindqvist, Sven*

External Linkages and Growth in Small Economies — *McKee, David L*

External Manifestations of Systemic Infections — *Mandell, Gerald L*

The Extinction of Nation-States — *Khan, L Ali*

Extinction Rates — *Lawton, John H*

The Extra Mile — *Nivola, Pietro S*

Extra-Ordinary Human-Computer Interaction — *Edwards, Alistair D N*

Extracellular Regulators of Differentiation and Development — *Chapman, K*

Extragalactic Radio Sources — *International Astronomical Union. Symposium (175th: 1995: Bologna, Italy)*

Extraordinary Bodies — *Thomson, Rosemarie Garland*

Extraordinary Furniture — *Linley, David*

c The Extraordinary Gift (Illus. by Florence Langlois) — *Langlois, Florence*

Extraordinary Golf — *Shoemaker, Fred*

Extraordinary Guidance — *Wiemar, Liza M*

c An Extraordinary Life (Illus. by Bob Marstall) — *Pringle, Laurence*

c Extraordinary People with Disabilities — *Kent, Deborah*

Extraordinary Politics — *Euchner, Charles C*

y Extraordinary Young People — *Brill, Marlene Targ*

Extremal Riemann Surfaces — *Quine, J R*

Extreme Continental — *Whittell, Giles*

Extreme Denial — *Morrell, David*

y Extreme Faith — *Anderson, Neil T*

y Extreme Measures (Pankow). Audio Version — *Palmer, Michael, 1942-*

Extreme Prematurity — *Danish Council of Ethics*

c Extremely Weird Birds — *Lovett, Sarah, 1953-*

r Extremist Groups — *Builta, Jeffrey A*

An Eye for Winners — *Vernon, Lillian*

y The Eye in the Door (Firth). Audio Version — *Barker, Pat*

The Eye of Spirit — *Wilber, Ken*

The Eye of the Beholder — *Garland, Robert*

The Eye of the Beholder — *Rubin, Uri*

Eye of the Blackbird — *McFadden, Mary Ann*

c Eye of the Storm (Illus. by Warren Faidley) — *Kramer, Stephen*

The Eye of the World. Audio Version — *Jordan, Robert*

Eye on Nature — *Holmes, Judy*

Eye on the Flesh — *Boscagli, Maurizia*

Eye on the World — *Stone, Judy, 1924-*

Eye Priory Cartulary and Charters. Vol. 2 — *Eye Priory*

Eyeing the North Star — *Clarke, George Elliot*

Eyes Like Pigeons — *Rees, Roberta*

y Eyes of a Stranger — *Heisel, Sharon E*

y The Eyes of Light and Darkness — *Cat, Ivan*

Eyes of Love — *Kern, Stephen*

Eyes Right! — *Berlet, Chip*

Eyeshot — *Hightower, Lynn S*

yr The Eyewitness Atlas of the World. Rev. Ed. — *Dorling Kindersley, Inc.*

Eyewitness Bloody Sunday — *Mullan, Don*

c Eyewitness Books

cr Eyewitness Encyclopedia of Nature 2.0 Version. Electronic Media Version

yr Eyewitness Encyclopedia of Science 2.0. Electronic Media Version

yr Eyewitness Encyclopedia of Space and the Universe. Electronic Media Version

y Eyewitness Living Earth — *Smith, Miranda*

y Eyewitness to America — *Colbert, David*

Eyewitness to American History — *Crutchfield, James A*

y Eyewitness to Discovery — *Fagan, Brian M*

Eyewitness to Jesus — *Thiede, Carsten Peter*

Eyewitness to the Alamo — *Groneman, Bill*

cr Eyewitness Virtual Reality Cat. Electronic Media Version

c Eyr the Hunter (Illus. by Joyce Haynes) — *Searcy, Margaret Zehmer*

EZ-101 Study Keys — *Leff, Lawrence S*

c Ezra Jack Keats: A Biography with Illustrations — *Engel, Dean*

Ezra Pound and Senator Bronson Cutting — *Pound, Ezra*

**Ezra Pound, Popular Genres, and the Discourse of
   Culture** — *Coyle, Michael*

F

F.D. Maurice and Unitarianism — *Young, David*
c F-Freezing ABC — *Simmonds, Posy*
F. Holland Day: Selected Texts and Bibliography
— *Day, F Holland*
The F. John Barlow Mineral Collection
F.M. Dostojevskij: Die Grossen Romane Und
Erzahlungen — *Neuhauser, Rudolf*
F.R. Leavis: A Life in Criticism — *MacKillop, Ian*
F.R. Leavis: A Literary Biography — *Singh, G*
F. Scott Fitzgerald: Centenary Exhibition, September
24, 1896-September 24, 1996 — *Thomas Cooper
Library*
F. Scott Fitzgerald on Authorship — *Fitzgerald, F
Scott*
F. Scott Fitzgerald: The Princeton Years
— *Fitzgerald, F Scott*
The F Word — *Sheidlower, Jesse*
F.Y. Edgeworth: Writings in Probability, Statistics,
and Economics. Vols. 1-3 — *Edgeworth, Francis
Ysidro*
F2F — *Finch, Phillip*
F6F Hellcat — *Kinzey, Bert*
La Fabbrica Del Corpo — *Carlino, Andrea*
p La Fabbrica Del Libro
The Faber Book of Christmas — *Rae, Simon*
The Faber Book of Contemporary Stories about
Childhood — *Moore, Lorrie*
The Faber Book of Movie Verse — *French, Philip*
The Faber Book of Pop — *Kureishi, Hanif*
The Faber Book of Science — *Carey, John*
The Faber Book of War Poetry — *Baker, Kenneth*
c Fables Aesop Never Wrote — *Kraus, Robert*
Fables and Distances — *Haines, John*
Fables of Abundance — *Lears, T J Jackson*
Fables of Desire — *Geyer-Ryan, Helga*
The Fables of Reason — *Pearson, Roger*
c Fables of the Times Tables (Illus. by Dennis Nobel)
— *Kortright, Brigitte E*
The Fabric of Reality — *Deutsch, David*
y Fabric Painting — *Innes, Miranda*
r Fabric Reference — *Humphries, Mary*
The Fabrication of Labor — *Biernacki, Richard*
c Fabulous Faces — *Awan, Shaila*
c The Fabulous Flying Fandinis (Illus. by Ingrid Slyder)
— *Slyder, Ingrid*
c The Fabulous Four Skunks (Illus. by Bruce
Koscielniak) — *Fair, David*
y Fabulous Harbors — *Moorcock, Michael*
y The Face at the Window — *Alcock, Vivien*
c The Face at the Window (Illus. by Linda Saport)
— *Hanson, Regina*
A Face at the Window — *McFarland, Dennis*
Face Down in the Marrow-Bone Pie — *Emerson,
Kathy Lynn*
Face Forward — *Okwu, Julian C R*
y Face of a Stranger — *Yamaguchi, Yoji*
The Face of Fashion — *Craik, Jennifer*
The Face of Glory — *Anderson, William*
The Face of the Nation — *Fitzgerald, Keith*
The Face of Venus — *Roth, Ladislav E*
y The Face on the Milk Carton — *Cooney, Caroline B*
Faceless Killers — *Mankell, Henning*
c Faces — *Rotner, Shelley*
c Faces at the Window — *Fischel, Emma*
Faces in a Crowd — *Klee, Carol A*
Faces in the Clouds — *Guthrie, Stewart, 1941-*
Faces in the Crowd — *Giddins, Gary*
The Faces of Fantasy — *Perret, Patti*
Faces of Feminism — *Tobias, Sheila*
Faces of Labour — *McSmith, Andy*
Faces of Lebanon — *Harris, William W*

Faces of Poverty — *Berrick, Jill Duerr*
c Faces Only a Mother Could Love — *Dewey, Jennifer
Owings*
Facilitator's Guide to Participatory Decision Making
— *Kaner, Sam*
Facing Armageddon — *Cecil, Hugh*
y Facing Death — *Spiro, Howard M*
Facing Death and Finding Hope — *Longaker,
Christine*
Facing East — *Mathewes-Green, Frederica*
Facing Eden — *Nash, Steven A*
Facing Facts — *Shi, David E*
Facing Genocide — *African Rights (Organization)*
Facing History — *National Archives of Canada*
Facing History and Ourselves — *Strom, Margot Stern*
Facing Racism in Education. 2nd Ed.
— *Beauboeuf-Lafontant, Tamara*
Facing Shadows — *Jin, Ha*
Facing the Abusing God — *Blumenthal, David R*
Facing the Extreme — *Todorov, Tzvetan*
Facing the Lion — *Brown, Kurt*
Facing the Music — *Berger, Bruce*
Facing the Music — *Brown, Larry*
y Facing the Music — *Willey, Margaret*
Facing the Other — *Hand, Sean*
Facing the River — *Milosz, Czeslaw*
Facing the Technological Challenge — *Bhalla, A S*
Facing the Wrath — *Diamond, Sara*
Facing up to the American Dream — *Hochschild,
Jennifer L*
Facing West — *Perry, John Curtis*
Fact and Feeling — *Smith, Jonathan, 1960-*
The Fact of Blackness — *Read, Alan*
Factor Proportions, Trade, and Growth — *Findlay,
Ronald*
Factories of Death — *Harris, Sheldon H*
Factory Joker — *Bower, Susan*
The Factory Question and Industrial England
1830-1860 — *Gray, Robert Q*
r Facts about Britain 1945 to 1995. Electronic Media
Version — *Great Britain. Central Office of
Information*
r Facts about the Congress — *Christianson, Stephen G*
yr Facts about the Supreme Court of the United States
— *Paddock, Lisa*
Facts and Fancies — *Iannucci, Armando*
The Facts of a Doorframe — *Rich, Adrienne*
The Facts of Life — *Porter, Roy*
r Facts on File Encyclopedia of Black Women in
America. Vols. 1-11 — *Hine, Darlene Clark*
The Factsheet Five Zine Reader — *Friedman, R Seth*
Faculty at Work — *Blackburn, Robert T*
The Faculty of Useless Knowledge — *Dombrovsky,
Yury*
Faculty Work and Public Trust — *Fairweather, James
S*
Fad Surfing in the Boardroom — *Shapiro, Eileen C*
Fade Away — *Cooper, Harlan*
Faded Dreams — *Carnoy, Martin*
Failure and Forgiveness — *Gross, Karen*
The Failure of Agrarian Capitalism — *Koning, Niek*
Failure of Charisma — *Wang, Shaoguang*
The Failure of Economic Diplomacy — *Clavin,
Patricia*
The Failure of Marxism — *Campbell, David*
The Failure of Political Islam — *Roy, Olivier*
The Failure of U.S. Tax Policy — *Pollack, Sheldon D*
Fair and Tender Ladies — *Smith, Lee*
Fair Division — *Brams, Steven J*
Fair Employment Strategies in Human Resource
Management — *Barrett, Richard S*

Fair Girls and Gray Horses — *Josephine, Diana*
Fair Peril — *Springer, Nancy*
Fair Trade and Harmonization. Vol. 1 — *Bhagwati,
Jagdish N*
Fair Trade and Harmonization. Vol. 2 — *Bhagwati,
Jagdish N*
Fair Trade and Harmonization. Vols. 1-2 — *Bhagwati,
Jagdish N*
Fair Use — *Negativeland*
r Fairchild's Dictionary of Textiles. 7th Ed. — *Tortora,
Phyllis B*
c Fairies (Illus. by Freddie Langeler) — *Langeler,
Freddie*
Fairies: Real Encounters with Little People — *Bord,
Janet*
Fairness in Accounting — *Monti-Belkaoui, Janice*
Fairness in International Law and Institutions
— *Franck, Thomas M*
Fair's Fair — *Marley, Anne*
c Fairy Mischief — *Talbot, John*
Fairy Tales — *Ellis, Alice Thomas*
c Fairy Tales of Hans Christian Andersen (Illus. by
Isabelle Brent) — *Andersen, Hans Christian*
y The Fairy Tales of Hermann Hesse (Donovan). Audio
Version — *Hesse, Hermann*
c The Fairy Tales of London Town. Vol. 2 — *Mayne,
William*
c The Fairy Tales of London Town. Vols. 1-2 — *Mayne,
William*
y Fairy Tales of the Brothers Grimm — *Wenzel, David*
Fairyland — *McAuley, Paul J*
Fairytales in Reality — *Orum, Margo*
Faisons Le Point — *Harrington, Karen*
Faith Alone — *Sproul, R C*
Faith and Belief — *Walker, Ian R*
Faith and Credit — *George, Susan*
Faith and Fortune — *Bianco, Anthony*
Faith and Knowledge — *Sloan, Douglas*
c Faith and the Electric Dogs (Illus. by Patrick
Jennings) — *Jennings, Patrick*
Faith and Treason — *Fraser, Antonia*
Faith, Art, and Politics at Saint-Riquier — *Rabe,
Susan A*
Faith Fox — *Gardam, Jane, 1928-*
Faith, Freedom, and Rationality — *Jordan, Jeff*
Faith in Theory and Practice — *Radcliffe, Elizabeth*
Faith Matters — *Matthai, Sandra Higgins*
The Faith of a Physicist — *Polkinghorne, John*
The Faith of Jesus Christ in Early Christian
Traditions — *Wallis, Ian G*
Faith or Fear — *Abrams, Elliott*
A Faith That Loves the Earth — *Petty, Michael W*
Faith Thinking — *Hart, Trevor*
Faith Walkers — *Nassal, Joe*
Faith without Prejudice — *Fisher, Eugene J*
c The Faithful Friend (Illus. by Brian Pinkney) — *San
Souci, Robert D*
The Faithful Gardener — *Estes, Clarissa Pinkola*
The Faithful Gardener (Estes). Audio Version
— *Estes, Clarissa Pinkola*
Faithless — *Williams, John L*
Faktizitat Und Geltung — *Habermas, Jurgen*
The Falashas: A Short History of the Ethiopian Jews.
3rd Ed. — *Kessler, David*
Falconer and the Face of God — *Morson, Ian*
c The Falcon's Malteser — *Horowitz, Anthony*
c Falcons Nest on Skyscrapers (Illus. by Megan Lloyd)
— *Jenkins, Priscilla Belz*
r The Falkland Islands, South Georgia, and the South
Sandwich Islands — *Day, Alan*
The Falklands and the Dwarf — *Layman, Kit*

Fall — *Maristed, Kai*

The Fall and Rise of the Stately Home — *Mandler, Peter*

Fall Guys — *Fisher, Jim*

The Fall of Great Powers — *Nobel Symposium (87th: 1993: Tromso, Norway)*

The Fall of Kings and Princes — *Guerin, M Victoria*

The Fall of Sirius — *McCarthy, Wil*

The Fall of the Asante Empire — *Edgerton, Robert B*

The Fall of the House of Usher. The Phantom Island. Audio Version — *Poe, Edgar Allan*

The Fall of the Packard Motor Company — *Ward, James A*

y The Fall of the Red Star — *Szablya, Helen M*

The Fall of the Romanovs — *Steinberg, Mark D*

Fall on Your Knees — *MacDonald, Ann-Marie*

The Fall to Violence — *Suchocki, Marjorie Hewitt*

The Fall Upward — *Hodge, Dino*

y The Fallen Man — *Hillerman, Tony*

The Fallen Man (Guidall). Audio Version — *Hillerman, Tony*

The Fallen Man (Silverbird). Abridged Ed. Audio Version — *Hillerman, Tony*

Fallen Pillars — *Neff, Donald*

Falling Away — *Crewe, Candida*

The Falling Boy — *Long, David, 1948-*

Falling for Marilyn Monroe — *Carroll, Jock*

y Falling Free (Hanson). Audio Version — *Bujold, Lois McMaster*

y Falling in Love — *Duder, Tessa*

Falling through the Cracks — *Ayala, Victor*

y Falling Up (Illus. by Shel Silverstein) — *Silverstein, Shel*

The Fallon Pride — *O'Neal, Reagan*

y Fallout — *Lester, Jim*

False Allegations — *Vachss, Andrew*

False Dawn — *Levine, Paul*

c False Face — *Katz, Welwyn Wilton*

y False Friends — *Keene, Carolyn*

False Impressions — *Hoving, Thomas*

False Light — *Llewellyn, Caroline*

False Security — *Myers, Kenneth D*

False Witness — *Dias, Dexter*

Falsely Accused — *Tanenbaum, Robert K*

Fame and Folly — *Ozick, Cynthia*

The Fame Machine — *Donoghue, Frank*

Una Famiglia E Le Sue Ricordanze — *Ciappelli, Giovanni*

Familiar Heat — *Hood, Mary*

c Families — *Baxter, Nicola*

c Families (Illus. by Marylin Hafner) — *Tax, Meredith*

Families and Freedom — *Berlin, Ira*

Families and the Mental Health System for Children and Adolescents — *Heflinger, Craig Anne*

Families and Time — *Daly, Kerry J*

y The Families Book (Illus. by Stephen J Carrera) — *Erlbach, Arlene*

c Families: Can't Live with Them, Can't Live without Them! (Illus. by Carol Morley) — *Naik, Anita*

Families in Multicultural Perspective — *Ingoldsby, Bron B*

Families, Labour Markets, and Gender Roles — *Drew, Eileen P*

c Families: Poems Celebrating the African American Experience (Illus. by John Ward) — *Strickland, Dorothy S*

Familles Maghrebines De France — *Bouamama, Said*

Family Adventure Guide: Tennessee — *O'Brien, Tim*

r Family Adventures (Fodor Guides)

A Family Affair — *Lopo, Lisbet De Castro*

Family: American Writers Remember Their Own — *Fiffer, Sharon Sloan*

The Family and Family Relationships 1500-1900 — *O'Day, Rosemary*

Family and Future

Family and Gender among American Muslims — *Aswad, Barbara C*

Family and Human Development across Cultures — *Kagitcibasi, Cigdem*

Family and Social Change — *Janssens, Angelique*

Family and Society in the Works of Elizabeth Gaskell — *Pike, E Holly*

Family and the Law in Eighteenth-Century Fiction — *Zomchick, John P*

r Family Archive Viewer. Electronic Media Version

Family beyond Family — *Weinstein, Sanford*

Family Caregiving in an Aging Society — *Kane, Rosalie*

Family Caregiving in Mental Illness — *Lefley, Harriet P*

Family Catastrophe — *Wang, Wen-Hsing*

Family: Challenges for the Future

Family Connections — *Morgan, David H J, 1957-*

Family, Dependence, and the Origins of the Welfare State, Britain and France 1914-1945 — *Pedersen, Susan*

Family Diversity and Well-Being — *Acock, Alan C*

Family Fallout — *Landry, Dorothy Beaulieu*

c Family for Sale — *Clifford, Eth*

Family, Freedom and Faith — *Cooey, Paula M*

The Family Guide to Alternative Health Care — *Pietroni, Patrick*

Family Guide to Natural Therapies — *Beckham, Nancy*

y The Family Guide to Sex and Relationships — *Walker, Richard*

p The Family Handyman

A Family Heritage — *Fowke, Edith*

c Family History — *Rice, Chris*

r Family Homeopathy — *Callinan, Paul*

The Family in Bahia, Brazil 1870-1945 — *Borges, Dain*

Family Internet Companion

Family, Justice, and Delinquency — *Geiger, Brenda*

Family Life — *Luard, Elisabeth*

Family Literacy — *Benjamin, L Ann*

Family Man — *Coltrane, Scott*

The Family Markowitz — *Goodman, Allegra*

Family Mediation — *Irving, Howard H*

y The Family of Black America — *Cottman, Michael H*

The Family of Cats

r The Family of Johann Jacob Stahl, Sr. of Lehigh County, Pennsylvania — *Stahl, Harriet K*

The Family of Love in English Society 1550-1630 — *Marsh, Christopher W*

Family over the Life Course — *Beaujot, Roderic*

c The Family PC Guide to Homework — *Keizer, Gregg*

r The Family PC Software Buyer's Guide — *Carlson, Kurt*

Family Plots — *Heller, Dana*

Family Power in Southern Italy — *Skinner, Patricia*

Family Pride — *Beasley, Donna*

Family Resource Guide

Family-School Links — *Booth, Alan, 1935-*

Family Secrets — *Glaser, Sherry*

The Family Silver — *Krieger, Susan*

Family Skeletons — *MacPherson, Rett*

Family Structure in the Staffordshire Potteries 1840-1880 — *Dupree, Marguerite W*

Family Terrorists and Other Stories — *Nelson, Antonya*

Family Theories — *Klein, David M*

Family Therapy — *Carlson, Jon*

Family Therapy. 3rd Ed. — *Nichols, Michael P*

Family Therapy Sourcebook. 2nd Ed. — *Piercy, Fred P*

Family Ties — *Abbott, Mary*

Family Ties — *Logan, John R*

Family Tightrope — *Kibria, Nazli*

c Family Time (Illus. by Margaret Miller) — *Miller, Margaret*

Family Travels — *Reeves, Richard*

c A Family Treasury of Prayers

c Family Tree — *Ayres, Katherine*

The Family Tree — *Tepper, Sheri S*

c Family Tree — *Webb, Kaye*

The Family Tree Detective — *Rogers, Colin D*

The Family Trichodoridae — *Decraemer, W*

Family Values — *Bugeja, Michael J*

Family Values — *Constantine, K C*

y Family Violence — *Burby, Liza N*

Family Violence — *Kaplan, Sandra J*

A Family Wedding — *Benson, Angela*

A Family Weekend — *Fawcett, Patricia*

c The Family Who Won a Million and Other Family Stories (Illus. by Tony Ross) — *Sage, Alison*

r Family Wisdom — *Ginsberg, Susan*

Famine — *Komarnicki, Todd*

Famine and Food Security in Ethiopia — *Webb, Patrick*

The Famine Decade — *Killen, John*

The Famine Ships — *Laxton, Edward*

y Famous All over Town — *Santiago, Danny*

r Famous Animals of the States — *Buchanan, Paul D*

c Famous Artists Series

Famous Friends of the Wolf Cookbook — *Reid, Nancy*

c Famous Hispanic Americans — *Morey, Janet*

Famous Last Words — *Booth, Alison*

r Famous Lines — *Andrews, Robert*

Famous Long Ago — *Mungo, Ray*

c Famous People of Hispanic Heritage. Vol. 4 — *Marvis, Barbara J*

y Famous People of Hispanic Heritage. Vols. 4-6 — *Marvis, Barbara J*

Famous Spaceships of Fact and Fantasy. 2nd Ed.

Famous Writers Celebrate Motherhood with a Treasury of Short Stories, Essays and Poems — *O'Keefe, Claudia*

Fandango — *Zimmer, Michael*

y Fanfare for Earth — *McSween, Harry Y*

c Fang Fang's Chinese New Year (Illus. by Sally Rippin) — *Rippin, Sally*

c Fang, the Story of a Fox (Illus. by Kenneth Lilly) — *Potter, Tessa*

Fanny Mendelssohn — *Tillard, Francoise*

Fanny Stevenson: A Romance of Destiny — *Lapierre, Alexandra*

Fanny Trollope: A Remarkable Life — *Ransom, Teresa*

c Fanny's Dream (Illus. by Mark Buehner) — *Buehner, Caralyn*

Fanon and the Crisis of European Man — *Gordon, Lewis R*

Fanon's Dialectic of Experience — *Sekyi-Otu, Ato*

Fantasizing the Feminine in Indonesia — *Sears, Laurie J*

Fantastic Alice — *Weis, Margaret*

c The Fantastic Cutaway Book of Giant Machines (Illus. by Alex Pang) — *Kirkwood, Jon*

c The Fantastic Drawings of Danielle (Illus. by Barbara McClintock) — *McClintock, Barbara*

Fantastic Four — *Friedman, Michael Jan*

A Fantastic Journey — *Murray, Paul*

Fantastic Modernity — *Wong, Orrin N C*

The Fantastic Sublime — *Sandner, David*

Fantasy and Reality in History — *Loewenberg, Peter*

Fantasy Fiction and Wealth Myth — *Filmer-Davis, Kath*

Fantasy, Forgery, and the Byron Legend — *Soderholm, James*

r Fantasy Literature — *Barron, Neil*

Fantasy Literature in the Elementary Classroom — *Edinger, Monica*

Fantasy or Ethnography? — *Webber, Sabra J*

Le Fantome De L'Opera — *Leroux, Gaston*

Far Away and Never — *Campbell, Ramsey*

r The Far East and Australasia 1996

r The Far East and Australasia 1997

Far East Cafe — *Jue, Joyce*

Far-Fetched Facts — *Rennie, Neil*

y Far from Home — *Hardy, Charlotte*

y Far North — *Hobbs, Will*

Far Out in the New Age — *McConnell, Robert*

A Far Rockaway of the Heart — *Ferlinghetti, Lawrence*

The Far Side of the Dollar — *Macdonald, Ross*

Faraday's Orphans — *Wood, N Lee*

c The Faraway Drawer (Illus. by Andrea Shine) — *Diller, Harriet*

c Faraway Families (Illus. by Monisha Raja) — *Loredo, Betsy*

y Farewell, I'm Bound to Leave You — *Chappell, Fred*

Farewell Jimmy the Greek — *Wadsworth, Ginger*

y Farewell, John Barleycorn — *Hintz, Martin*

Farewell, Thunder Moon — *Brand, Max*

A Farewell to Arms? — *O'Prey, Kevin P*

Farewell to the Factory — *Milkman, Ruth*

Farewell to the Mockingbirds — *McEachin, James*

Farewell to the Twentieth Century — *Berton, Pierre*

c Les Farfeluches Autour Du Monde — *Gree, Alain*

c Les Farfeluches Jouent Avec Les Couleurs — *Gree, Alain*

Fargo — *Coen, Ethan*

c Farm (Illus. by Geoff Brightling) — *Halley, Ned B*

Farm and Factory — *Nelson, Daniel, 1941-*

Farm Animal Portraits — *Moncrieff, Elspeth*

c Farm Animals (Illus. by Heinrich Kita) — *Dudek, Isabella*

Farm Boys — *Fellows, Will*

c Farm Day Fun (Illus. by Anne Kennedy) — *St. Pierre, Stephanie*

y The Farm on Nippersink Creek — *May, Jim*

Farm Organizations in Ireland — *Smith, Louis P F*

c Farm Pops — *King, Dave*

c The Farm Summer 1942 — *Hall, Donald, 1928-*

y Farm Team — *Weaver, Will*

c The Farmer and the Poor God (Illus. by Yoshi) — *Wells, Ruth*

c Farmer Beans and the Dog with No Name — *Moffatt, Frank*

c Farmer Duck (Illus. by Helen Oxenbury) — *Waddell, Martin*

c Farmer Joe Baby-Sits (Illus. by Werner Zimmerman)
— Richards, Nancy Wilcox
Farmers' and Farm Workers' Movements — Mooney,
Patrick H
Farmers and Fishermen — Vickers, Daniel
p Farmer's Market
c Farmers' Market (Illus. by Paul Brett Johnson)
— Johnson, Paul Brett
c Farming (Illus. by Pat Cupples) — Drake, Jane
c Farming (Illus. by James Field) — Roden, Katie
Farming the Home Place — Matsumoto, Valerie J
Farms, Factories and Free Trade — Schirmer, Peter
Farms, Mines and Main Streets — Tauxe, Caroline S
c Farmworker's Friend — Collins, David R
c Farmyard Animals (Illus. by Paul Hess) — Hess, Paul
I Farnese: Arte E Collezionismo — Schianchi, Lucia
Fornari
c The Farolitos of Christmas (Illus. by Edward
Gonzales) — Anaya, Rudolfo
Farthest North — Holland, Clive
r Fasciculus Chemicus — Dee, Arthur
Fascination — Blair, Leona
y Fascism: A History — Eatwell, Roger
Fascism and Theatre — Berghaus, Gunter
Fascism: Past, Present, Future — Laqueur, Walter
r Fashion and Costume in American Popular Culture
— Oliver, Valerie Burnham
Fashion, Culture, and Identity — David, Fred
Fashion Design Illustration: Men — Ireland, Patrick
John
Fashion Illustration — Seaman, Julian
Fashion: Photography of the Nineties — Nickerson,
Camilla
Fashionable Resort Regions — Soane, John V N
Fashioning the Bourgeoisie — Perrot, Philippe
Fashions of the Roaring '20s — Laubner, Ellie
c Fast and Slow — Challoner, Jack
c Fast Break — Coldwell, Michael
Fast Cars, Clean Bodies — Ross, Kristin
p Fast Company
Fast Elementary Processes in Chemical and Biological
Systems — Tramer, Andre
Fast Forward — Greenfield, Lauren
Fast Forward — MacDonald, Scott B
Fast Forward — Mercer, Judy
The Fast Forward MBA in Business — O'Brien,
Virginia
Fast Fourier Transforms. 2nd Ed. — Walker, James S
Fast Friends — Pugh, Dianne
Fast, Fun, and Fabulous Quilts — Nelson, Suzanne
Fast Greens — Pipkin, Turk
Fast Polymerization Processes — Minsker, Karl S
r Fast Reference Facts. Electronic Media Version
y The Fastest Bowler in the World — Hardcastle,
Michael
The Fastest Kid on the Block — Glickman, Marty
Fat and Mean — Gordon, David M
The Fat-Burning Workout — Vedral, Joyce L
c The Fat Cat Sat on the Mat (Illus. by Nurit Karlin)
— Karlin, Nurit
Fat Chance — Cortopassi, Joan
y Fat Chance — Newman, Leslea
c Fat Charlie's Circus (Illus. by Marie-Louise Gay)
— Gay, Marie-Louise
Fat City — Gardner, Leonard
The Fat-Free Junkfood Cookbook — Wolfe, J Kevin
Fat History — Stearns, Peter N
Fat King, Lean Beggar — Carroll, William C
Fat Tuesday — Brown, Sandra
Fatal Analysis — Obler, Martin
Fatal Convictions — Geller, Shari
Fatal Convictions (Esterman). Audio Version
— Geller, Shari
The Fatal Cruise of the Argus — Dye, Ira
Fatal Elixir — DeAndrea, William L
The Fatal Englishman — Faulks, Sebastian
y Fatal Error — Dunmore, Helen
Fatal Flaw — Smith, Frank, 1927-
The Fatal Frontier — Gorman, Edward
Fatal Gift — Frase, H Michael
A Fatal Glass of Beer — Kaminsky, Stuart M
Fatal Glory — Chaffin, Tom
Fatal Justice — Potter, Jerry Allen
The Fatal Knot — Tone, John Lawrence
A Fatal Passion — Sullivan, Michael John
A Fatal Season — Colvin, Clare
Fatal Terrain — Brown, Dale
The Fatal Woman — Maxfield, James F
The Fate of a Gesture — Ratcliff, Carter
Fate of a Grasshopper — Chao
The Fate of Carmen — Gould, Evelyn

The Fate of Eloquence in the Age of Hume — Potkay,
Adam
The Fate of Marxism in Russia — Yakovlev, Alexander
The Fate of Place — Casey, Edward S
The Fate of the English Country House — Littlejohn,
David
y A Fate Totally Worse than Death — Fleischman, Paul
y The Fated Sky — Branford, Henrietta
A Fateful Choice — Lee, Rachel
Fateful Rendezvous — Ewing, Steve
Father and Son — Brown, Larry
Father Brown of the Church of Rome — Chesterton,
G K
Father-Child Relations — Hewlett, Barry S
c Father Christmas (Illus. by Gregoire Solotareff)
— Solotareff, Gregoire
Father Dancing — Papandreou, Nick
Father Elijah: An Apocalypse — O'Brien, Michael,
1948-
A Father for Christmas — Girard, Paula Tanner
Father Goose — Lishman, Bill
y Father Greg and the Homeboys — Fremon, Celeste
y Father Junipero Serra: Founder of California
Missions — Genet, Donna
Father Malachy's Miracle — Marshall, Bruce
Father Peter John De Smet: Jesuit in the West
— Carriker, Robert C
Father Ralph — O'Donovan, Gerald
Father, Soldier, Son — Tripp, Nathaniel
Father Songs — Wade-Gayles, Gloria
y Father Water, Mother Woods — Paulsen, Gary
Fatheralong: A Meditation on Fathers and Sons, Race
and Society — Wideman, John Edgar
Fatherhood — Parke, Ross D
Fatherhood: An Anthology of New Writing
— Howarth, Peter
Fatherhood: Contemporary Theory, Research, and
Social Policy — Marsiglio, William
The Fatherhood of God from Origen to Athanasius
— Widdicombe, Peter
Fatherhood Reclaimed — Burgess, Adrienne
Fathering the Nation — Castronovo, Russ
Fatherless America — Blankenthorn, David
The Fathers — Tate, Allen
Fathers: An Anthology — Guinness, Louise
Fathers and Divorce — Arendell, Terry
Fathers and Sons — Williams, Christine
Fathers as Primary Caregivers — Geiger, Brenda
The Father's Club — Katz, Jon
A Father's Kisses — Friedman, Bruce Jay
Fathers of International Thought — Thompson,
Kenneth W
Fathers of the World — Visotzky, Burton L
Fathers' Rights — Leving, Jeffrey M
Fathers, Sons, and Brothers — Lott, Bret
Fathers, Sons and Lovers — West, Peter
The Father's Spirit of Sonship — Weinandy, Thomas G
Fathoms — Alexander, Lucy
Fatigue and Fracture 1996. Vols. 1-2
Fatigue and Fracture of Ordered Intermetallic
Materials II
The Fatigue Artist — Schwartz, Lynne Sharon
r Fatigue Data Book — Henry, Scott D
Fatigue Design — Zahavi, Eliahu
Fatigue under Thermal and Mechanical Loading
— Bressers, J
c Fatima and the Dream Thief (Illus. by Els Cools)
— Schami, Rafik
Fatty Acid and Lipid Chemistry — Gunstone, F D
Faulkner and the Artist — Kartiganer, Donald M
y Fault Line — Marks, Graham
Fault Lines — Alexander, Meena
The Faun in the Garden — Barolsky, Paul
Faust II — Zabka, Thomas
Faust: Parts 1 and 2 — Goethe, Johann Wolfgang Von
Faust the Theologian — Pelikan, Jaroslav
Faust: Theater of the World — Brown, Jane K, 1943-
Faust-Variationen: Beitrage Zur Editionsgeschichte
Vom 16. Bis Zum 20. Jahrhundert — Henning,
Hans
c Faut-Il Croire A La Magie? (Illus. by Daniel
Sylvestre) — Desrosiers, Sylvie
Fauvism — Whitfield, Sarah
Favored Strangers — Wagner-Martin, Linda
c Favorite Norse Myths (Illus. by Troy Howell)
— Osborne, Mary Pope
c Favorite Songs of Japanese Children — Fukuda,
Hanaka
c Favourite Live Thing — Chapman, Jean
y Fax from Sarajevo — Kubert, Joe
Fay Weldon's Wicked Fictions — Barreca, Regina

The Fayre Formez of the Pearl Poet — Prior, Sandra
Pierson
y The FBI (Riggenbach). Audio Version — Kessler,
Ronald
The FBI's RACON — Hill, Robert A
The FDA Follies — Burkholz, Herbert
FDR and the Creation of the U.N. — Hoopes,
Townsend
FDR and the Holocaust — Newton, Verne
r FDR: Franklin Delano Roosevelt. Electronic Media
Version
c The FDR Way — Morris, Jeffrey
The FDR Years — Leuchtenburg, William Edward
FDR's Good Neighbor Policy — Pike, Fredrick B
Fear and Loathing in Las Vegas and Other American
Stories — Thompson, Hunter S
c The Fear Man — Halam, Ann
y A Fear of Heights — Newbery, Linda
y Fear of Math — Zaslavsky, Claudia
Fear of Physics — Krauss, Lawrence Maxwell
The Fear of Sinking — Kilmer, Paulette D
Fear of Wine — Brenner, Leslie
Fear of Words — Schrader, Alvin
Fearful Realities — Morash, Chris
Fearful Symmetry — Bills, Greg
Fearful Symmetry — Novick, Jack
Fearing the Dark — Bansak, Edward G
The Fearless Flyer — Hartman, Cherry
Fearless Wives and Frightened Shrews — Brauner,
Sigrid
c Fearsome Hunters of the Wild — Donnelly, Jane
c Fearsome Hunters of the Wild — Nicoll, David
c Fearsome Tales for Fiendish Kids (Illus. by Ross
Collins) — Rix, Jamie
c Feast for 10. Book and Audio Version — Falwell,
Cathryn
Feast for Life — Bartlett, Linda
A Feast of Words — Shapiro, Anna
Feasting on Herbs — Lawrence, Sue
Feather: A Child's Death and Life — Peters, Robert,
1924-
c The Feather-Bed Journey (Illus. by Stacey Schuett)
— Feder, Paula Kurzband
A Feather on the Breath of God — Nunez, Sigrid
Feather Reports — May, Derwent
c Featherbys — Steele, Mary
c Feathers and Fools (Illus. by Nicholas Wilton) — Fox,
Mem
Federal Antitrust Policy during the Kennedy-Johnson
Years — Williamson, James R
Federal Art and National Culture — Harris, Jonathan
The Federal Courts — Posner, Richard A
Federal Criminal Law Doctrines — Murchison,
Kenneth M
r Federal Employee's Almanac. 43rd Ed.
Federal Financial Support of Business
The Federal Impeachment Process — Gerhardt,
Michael J
Federal Information Policies in the 1990s — Hernon,
Peter
The Federal Judiciary and Institutional Change
— Barrow, Deborah J
The Federal Republic of Germany since 1949
— Larres, Klaus
Federal Taxation in America — Brownlee, W Elliot
Federalism and Rights — Katz, Ellis
Federico II: Immagine E Potere — Calo Mariani,
Maria Stella
c Federico Va A La Escuela (Illus. by Claudia Legnazzi)
— Montes, Graciela
c Federico Y El Mar (Illus. by Claudia Legnazzi)
— Montes, Graciela
c Fedge Makes a Wish! — Comanor, Jeffrey
Feeble-Minded in Our Midst — Noll, Steven
Feed Management in Intensive Aquaculture
— Goddard, Stephen, 1947-
Feeding a Hungry Planet — Lang, James
Feeding Frenzy — Stevens, Stuart
Feeding the Beast — Walsh, Kenneth T
Feeding the Dying — Talone, Patricia A
Feeding Your Allergic Child — Meyer, Elisa
Feel and Grow Rich — Milteer, Lee
Feel like Going Home — Guralnick, Peter
Feel No Fear — Karolyi, Bela
y Feeling Great — Bramwell, Vicky
Feelings — Birch, Charles
c Feelings for Little Children (Illus. by Mits Katayama)
— Crary, Elizabeth
y Feersum Endjinn — Banks, Iain M
Feet in Chains — Roberts, Kate
y Feet of Clay — Pratchett, Terry

Feet of Clay — *Storr, Anthony*

c Feliciana Feydra LeRoux (Illus. by Cat Bowman Smith) — *Thomassie, Tynia*

y Felicia's Journey (Prebble). Audio Version — *Trevor, William*

La Felicita Terrena — *Mozzi, Giulio*

Felicitation Volume in Honour of Prof. C. Suriyakumaran, Knight Commander of the Most Noble Order of the Crown of Thailand — *Gunawardena, Nalaka*

r Feline and Canine Infectious Diseases — *Gaskell, Rosalind M*

c Felix Activity Book (Illus. by George Ulrich) — *Nobleman, Tyler*

c Felix and the 400 Frogs — *Buller, Jon*

c Felix Explores Planet Earth — *Langen, Annette*

Felix: The Twisted Tale of the World's Most Famous Cat — *Canemaker, John*

c Feliz Navidad, Guille! — *Elena, Horacio*

Fellini's Films — *Burke, Frank*

Felt: New Directions for an Ancient Craft — *Sjoberg, Gunilla Paetau*

r The Female Body — *Prevention Magazine Health Books*

Female Choices — *Small, Meredith*

Female Control — *Eberhard, William G*

Female Education in the Age of Enlightenment. Vols. 1-6

y A Female Focus — *Horwitz, Margot F*

The Female Pelvic Floor — *Brubaker, Linda T*

Female Sexual Abuse of Children — *Elliott, Michele*

Female Tars — *Stark, Suzanne J*

The Female Thermometer — *Castle, Terry*

The Feminine Economy and Economic Man — *Burggraf, Shirley P*

Feminine Ingenuity — *Macdonald, Anne L*

The Feminine Principle in the Sikh Vision of the Transcendent — *Singh, Nikky-Guninder Kaur*

Femininmasculin — *Bernadac, Marie-Laure*

Feminism and Christian Ethics — *Parsons, Susan Frank*

Feminism and Community — *Friedman, Marilyn*

Feminism and Community — *Weiss, Penny A*

Feminism and Deconstruction — *Elam, Diane*

Feminism and Geography — *Rose, Gillian*

Feminism and Modern Jewish Theological Method — *Krafte-Jacobs, Lori*

r Feminism and Postmodern Theory — *Nordquist, Joan*

Feminism and Religion — *Gross, Rita M*

Feminism and Social Change — *Gottfried, Heidi*

Feminism and Sporting Bodies — *Hall, M Ann*

Feminism and the Honor Plays of Lope De Vega — *Yarbro-Bejarano, Yvonne*

Feminism and the Mastery of Nature — *Plumwood, Val*

Feminism and the Politics of Literary Reputation — *Templin, Charlotte*

Feminism and the Postmodern Impulse — *Michael, Magali Cornier*

Feminism and the Third Republic — *Smith, Paul, 1963-*

Feminism and Tradition in Aesthetics — *Brand, Peggy Zeglin*

Feminism Beside Itself — *Elam, Diane*

Feminism, Breasts and Breast-Feeding — *Carter, Pam*

Feminism in Action — *O'Barr, Jean F*

Feminism Is Not the Story of My Life — *Fox-Genovese, Elizabeth*

Feminism, Objectivity and Economics — *Nelson, Julie A*

Feminism/Postmodernism — *Nicholson, Linda J*

Feminism/Postmodernism/Development — *Marchand, Marianne*

Feminism under Fire — *Klein, Ellen R*

Feminisms and Pedagogies of Everyday Life — *Luke, Carmen*

Feminisms and the Self — *Griffiths, Morwenna*

Feminisms in the Cinema — *Pietropaolo, Laura*

Feminist Accused of Sexual Harassment — *Gallop, Jane*

Feminist Approaches to Bioethics — *Tong, Rosemarie*

Feminist Approaches to the Bible — *Trible, Phyllis*

A Feminist Clinician's Guide to the Memory Debate — *Contratto, Susan*

Feminist Contentions — *Benhabib, Seyla*

Feminist Conversations — *Zwarg, Christina*

Feminist Dilemmas in Fieldwork — *Wolf, Diane L*

Feminist Ferment — *Bolt, Christine*

Feminist Generations — *Whittier, Nancy*

Feminist Interpretations of G.W.F. Hegel — *Mills, Patricia Jagentowicz*

Feminist Interpretations of Hannah Arendt — *Honig, Bonnie*

Feminist Interpretations of Mary Wollstonecraft — *Falco, Maria*

Feminist Interpretations of Michel Foucault — *Hekman, Susan J*

Feminist Interpretations of Simone De Beauvoir — *Simons, Margaret A*

r Feminist Jurisprudence — *Holland, Francis Schmid*

Feminist Measures — *Keller, Lynn*

Feminist Messages — *Radner, Joan Newlon*

Feminist Perspective on Family Care — *Hooyman, Nancy R*

The Feminist Poetry Movement — *Whitehead, Kim*

The Feminist Possibilities of Dramatic Realism — *Schroeder, Patricia R*

The Feminist Question — *Martin, Francis*

Feminist Readings in Middle English Literature — *Evans, Ruth*

Feminist Theaters in the U.S.A. — *Canning, Charlotte*

Feminist Theory and the Study of Folklore — *Hollis, Susan Tower*

r Feminist Writers — *Kester-Shelton, Pamela*

Feminists, Islam, and Nation — *Badran, Margot*

The Feminization of Dr. Faustus — *Druxes, Helga*

La Femme A Rome — *Achard, Guy*

Une Femme Heureuse — *Chapsal, Madeleine*

Femmes D'Islam — *Benguigui, Yamina*

Les Femmes Et Le Marche Du Travail Urbain En Afrique Subsaharienne — *Lachaud, Jean-Pierre*

Fencing with Words — *Varnum, Robin*

Fenelon: Meditations on the Heart of God — *Fenelon, Francois De Salignac De La Mothe*

Fenelon: Talking with God — *Fenelon, Francois De Salignac De La Mothe*

Feng Ru Fei Tun — *Mo, Yan*

Feng Shui — *SantoPietro, Nancy*

Feng Shui for Today — *Lau, Kwan*

Feng Shui in the Garden — *Wydra, Nancilee*

Feng Shui: The Book of Cures — *Wydra, Nancilee*

Feng Yu Qing — *Zhang, Hanzhi*

Fenianism in Mid-Victorian Britain — *Newsinger, John*

Fenton Art Glass — *Whitmyer, Margaret*

c Fenwick's Suit (Illus. by David Small) — *Small, David*

Fergie: Her Secret Life — *Starkie, Allan*

Fergie: The Very Private Life of the Duchess of York — *Vasso, Madame*

c Fergus' Big Splash (Illus. by Tony Maddox) — *Maddox, Tony*

The Ferguson Affair — *Macdonald, Ross*

yp Ferguson's Off to College

Las Ferias De Castilla — *Ladero Quesada, Miguel-Angel*

Ferman's Devils — *Faust, Joe Clifford*

Fermat's Last Theorem — *Aczel, Amir D*

Fermentation — *J., Angelica*

Les Fermiers De L'Ile-De-France — *Moriceau, Jean-Marc*

Fernando Pessoa: Poeta-Tradutor De Poetas — *Saraiva, Arnaldo*

Fernando Pessoa: Voices of a Nomadic Soul — *Kotowicz, Zbigniew*

c Fernando's Gift — *Keister, Douglas*

c The Ferocious Beast (Illus. by Michael Paraskevas) — *Paraskevas, Betty*

The Ferocious Engine of Democracy. Vols. 1-2 — *Riccards, Michael P*

Ferranti-Packard: Pioneers in Canadian Electrical Manufacturing — *Ball, Norman R*

Ferroelectric Thin Films — *Paz De Araujo, Carlos*

Ferroelectric Thin Films V — *Desu, Seshu B*

Fertility and Faith — *McCarthy, Brendon*

Feste E Spettacoli Di Corte Nella Caserta Del Settecento — *Pascuzzi, Antonella*

The Festival of the Greasy Pole — *Depestre, Rene*

Festival of the Poor — *Schneider, Jane C*

A Festival of Violence — *Tolnay, Stewart E*

c Festivals (Illus. by Leonard Everett Fisher) — *Livingston, Myra Cohn*

c Festivals of the Christian Year — *Rock, Lois*

Fetal Alcohol Syndrome — *Stratton, Kathleen R*

Fetal Development — *Lecanuet, Jean-Pierre*

Fetal Positions — *Newman, Karen, 1949-*

Fetal Rights Women's Rights — *Samuels, Suzanne Uttaro*

c Fetch! (Illus. by G Pilbrow) — *Pilbrow, G*

c La Fete Est A L'Eau (Illus. by Gilles Tibo) — *Guillet, Jean-Pierre*

Fetes Urbaines En Italie A L'Epoque De La Renaissance, Verone, Florence, Sienne, Naples — *Plaisance, Michel*

Fetish Lives — *Jones, Gail*

Fettered for Life — *Blake, Lillie Devereux*

Feuding Allies — *Breuer, William B*

Feuding and Warfare — *Otterbein, Keith E*

Feuerbach and the Interpretation of Religion — *Harvey, Van A*

Feux Follets Et Champignons Nucleaires — *Charpak, Georges*

A Fever in the Heart and Other True Cases — *Rule, Ann*

The Fever of Being — *Urrea, Luis Alberto*

Fever Rising — *Ferguson, Maggie*

Fever: Sensual Stories by Women Writers — *Slung, Michele*

Fevered Lives — *Ott, Katherine*

The Few and the Many — *Carlton, Eric*

A Few Reasonable Words — *Regnery, Henery*

Few Returned — *Corti, Eugenio*

y Feynman's Lost Lecture — *Goodstein, David L*

A Fez of the Heart — *Seal, Jeremy*

p Fi

r Fiamminghi A Roma 1508-1608

Fiber, Matrix, and Interface Properties — *Spragg, Christopher J*

Fiber Optic Installations — *Chomycz, Bob*

Fiberarts Design Book V

Fibromyalgia: A Comprehensive Approach — *Williamson, Miryam Ehrlich*

Fibromyalgia and Chronic Myofascial Pain Syndrome — *Starlanyl, Devin*

The Fibromyalgia Handbook — *McIlwain, Harris H*

The Fickle Finger of Lady Death and Other Plays — *Morton, Carlos*

Fiction as False Document — *Williams, John, 1948-*

r Fiction Catalog. 13th Ed. — *Yaakov, Juliette*

Fiction, Crime, and Empire — *Thompson, Jon*

yr Fiction for Youth. 3rd Ed. — *Shapiro, Lillian L*

The Fiction of Paule Marshall — *Denniston, Dorothy Hamer*

The Fiction of Relationship — *Weinstein, Arnold*

Fictional Points of View — *Lamarque, Peter*

The Fictional Republic — *Nackenoff, Carol*

Fictions of Advice — *Ferster, Judith*

Fictions of Discourse — *O'Neill, Patrick*

Fictions of Feminist Ethnography — *Visweswaran, Kamala*

The Fictions of James Joyce and Wyndham Lewis — *Klein, Scott W*

Fictions of Loss in the Victorian Fin De Siecle — *Arata, Stephen*

Fictions of State — *Brantlinger, Patrick*

c The Fiddle Ribbon (Illus. by Francis Livingston) — *Lemieux, Margo*

c The Fiddler of the Northern Lights (Illus. by Leslie W Bowman) — *Kinsey-Warnock, Natalie*

Fidelity's World — *Henriques, Diana B*

Fiduciary Obligations and Joint Ventures — *Bean, Gerard M D*

Fie! Fie! Fi-Fi! — *Griffin, D D*

Fiefs and Vassals — *Reynolds, Susan*

y Fiela's Child — *Matthee, Dalene*

Field and Galois Theory — *Morandi, Patrick*

Field, Forest and Family — *Ireson, Carol J*

Field Grown Cut Flowers — *Stevens, Alan B*

A Field Guide to Butterflies of Texas — *Neck, Raymond W*

r A Field Guide to Common Animal Poisons — *Murphy, Michael J*

A Field Guide to Germs — *Biddle, Wayne*

A Field Guide to Hot Sauces — *Kaderabek, Todd*

A Field Guide to Joint Disease in Archaeology — *Rogers, Juliet*

The Field Guide to North American Males — *Ingall, Marjorie*

r A Field Guide to Rock Art Symbols of the Greater Southwest — *Patterson, Alex*

r A Field Guide to the Birds. Commemorative Ed. — *Peterson, Roger Tory*

r Field Guide to the Birds of the Middle East — *Porter, R F*

r A Field Guide to the Families and Genera of Woody Plants of Northwest South America (Colombia, Ecuador, Peru) — *Gentry, Alwyn H*

r A Field Guide to Trains of North America — *Foster, Gerald L*

The Field of Cultural Production — *Bourdieu, Pierre*

A Field of One's Own — *Agarwal, Bina*

Field of Screams — *Scheinin, Richard*

Field of Vision — *Knopp, Lisa*
yr A Field Trip to the Sky. Electronic Media Version
r Fielding's Borneo — *Pelton, Robert Young*
r Fielding's Thailand, Including Cambodia, Laos, Myanmar
Fields of Battle — *Keegan, John*
c Fields of Home (Illus. by Donald Teskey) — *Conlon-McKenna, Marita*
Fields of Knowledge — *Ringer, Fritz*
Fields of Vision — *Devereaux, Leslie*
Fields without Dreams — *Hanson, Victor Davis*
Fieldwork: A Geologist's Memoir of the Kalahari — *Scholz, Christopher*
Fieldwork among the Maya — *Vogt, Evon Z*
Fieldwork: An Expeditionary Learning Outward Bound Reader. Vol. 1 — *Cousins, Emily*
Fieldwork and Footnotes — *Vermeulen, Hans*
Fiennders Keepers — *Marsh, Jean*
Fierce Communion — *Wall, Helena M*
The Fierce Light — *Powell, Anne*
The Fiery Muse — *Degler, Teri*
y Fiery Vision — *Cox, Clinton*
c Fiesta! (Illus. by Rene King Moreno) — *Guy, Ginger Foglesong*
Fiesta, Fe, Y Cultura — *Sommers, Laurie Kay*
c Fiesta U.S.A. (Illus. by George Ancona) — *Ancona, George*
Fifteen Jugglers, Five Believers — *Reed, T V*
Fifteenth-Century Attitudes — *Horrox, Rosemary*
The Fifth Gospel — *Sawyer, John F A*
The Fifth Season — *Angel, George*
c Fifty Stories for Assembly — *Self, David*
Fifty Years at the Front — *Haverstock, Nathan A*
Fifty Years Later — *Oostindie, Gert*
Fifty Years of Building Community — *Smith, Kathryn Schneider*
r Fifty Years of Notable Books — *American Library Association. Reference and Adult Services Division. Notable Books Council*
Fifty Years on the Old Frontier as Cowboy, Hunter, Guide, Scout and Ranchman — *Cook, James H*
The Fifty Years War — *Crockatt, Richard*
Fight Club — *Palahniuk, Chuck*
Fight Directing for the Theatre — *Suddeth, J Allen*
The Fight for Canada — *Francis, Diane*
The Fight for Peace — *Mallie, Eamonn*
The Fight in the Fields — *Ferriss, Susan*
y Fight or Flight — *Regan, Geoffrey*
Fighter with a Heart — *Rice, Charles Owen*
Fighters from the Fringe — *Hall, Robert A*
Fighting Drug Abuse with Acupuncture — *Mitchell, Ellinor R*
Fighting Fashion — *Storey, Helen*
Fighting for Faith and Nation — *Mahmood, Cynthia Keppley*
Fighting for Jobs — *Nissen, Bruce*
Fighting for Life — *Casey, Robert P*
Fighting for Survival — *Renner, Michael*
Fighting for the Rainforest — *Richards, Paul*
Fighting for the Soul of Brazil — *Danaher, Kevin*
Fighting Forces, Writing Women — *Ouditt, Sharon*
Fighting on Two Fronts — *Westheider, James E*
Fighting Organized Crime — *Stolberg, Mary M*
The Fighting Pattons — *Sobel, Brian M*
A Fighting Retreat — *Neillands, Robin*
c Fighting Tackle — *Christopher, Matt*
Fighting Talk — *Brown, Colin*
Fighting Terrorism — *Netanyahu, Binyamin*
Fighting the Good Fight — *Hart, D G*
Fighting the Lamb's War — *Berrigan, Philip*
Fighting with Allies — *Renwick, Robin*
Fighting with Figures — *Great Britain. Central Statistical Office*
Fighting with the Soviets — *Conversino, Mark J*
A Fighting Withdrawal — *Ovenden, Keith*
Fighting Words — *Greenawalt, Kent*
The Fights — *Hoff, Charles*
Figur Und Raum — *Albrecht, V*
Figural Nodders — *Irtz, Hilma R*
Les Figurants — *Daeninckx, Didier*
The Figure of Joseph in Post-Biblical Jewish Literature — *Niehoff, Maren*
The Figured Wheel — *Pinsky, Robert*
Figures of Conversion — *Ragussis, Michael*
c The Figures of Julian Ashcraft (Illus. by Hans De Haas) — *Crew, Gary*
Figuring the Sacred — *Ricoeur, Paul*
File Under: Jeopardy — *Lacey, Sarah*
r Filipino Achievers in the USA and Canada — *Crisostomo, Isobelo T*
y Fill My Empty Heart — *Baer, Judy*

Les Filles De Marianne — *Bard, Christine*
Filling the Gaps — *Williams, Glen*
r Film Actors Guide 1997
r Film and Video on the Internet — *Deivert, Bert*
r The Film Anthologies Index — *Bowles, Stephen E*
Film Architecture — *Neumann, Dietrich*
Film at the Intersection of High and Mass Culture — *Coates, Paul*
Film at Wit's End — *Brakhage, Stan*
Film Biographies — *Brakhage, Stan*
Film Classics — *Frayling, Christopher*
r Film Composers Guide. 3rd Ed. — *Jacquet-Francillon, Vincent*
Film Design — *Giger, H R*
The Film Explainer — *Hofmann, Gert*
Film Formation in Waterborne Coatings — *Provder, Theodore*
Film Genre Reader II — *Grant, Barry Keith*
Film Music — *Meyers, Randall*
r Film Producers, Studios, Agents and Casting Directors Guide. 5th Ed.
r Film Writers Guide. 6th Ed.
Fil'mova Tvorchist' IAroslava Kulynycha
The Films of Akira Kurosawa. 3rd Ed. — *Richie, Donald*
The Films of Alfred Hitchcock — *Sterritt, David*
The Films of John Cassavetes — *Carney, Ray*
The Films of Luis Bunuel — *Evans, Peter William*
The Films of the Eighties — *Palmer, William J*
The Films of Woody Allen — *Girgus, Sam B*
Le Fils Naturel — *Diderot, Denis*
Fima — *Oz, Amos*
The Fin De Siecle Spirit — *Doyle, James*
Final Account — *Stendahl, Krister*
Final Arrangements — *Murray, Donna Huston*
The Final Bell — *Hunter, M S*
The Final Campaign — *Alexander, Joseph H*
Final Diagnosis — *White, James, 1928-*
Final Exam — *Bracey, Gerald W*
Final Exposure — *Jones, Lou*
y The Final Goodbye — *Ware, Shirley Gerald*
Final Jeopardy — *Fairstein, Linda*
y The Final Journey — *Pausewang, Gudrun*
The Final Judgement — *Easterman, Daniel*
The Final Judgement — *Patterson, Richard North*
y The Final Judgment — *Patterson, Richard North*
Final Report. Supplemental Vols. 1, 2, 2A — *United States. Advisory Committee on Human Radiation Experiments*
Final Report of the Advisory Commission to Study the Consumer Price Index — *United States. Congress. Senate. Advisory Commission to Study the Consumer Price Index*
Final Report of the Joint Executive-Legislative Task Force to Study Commercial Gaming Activities in Maryland — *Maryland. Joint Executive-Legislative Task Force to Study Commercial Gaming Activities in Maryland*
Final Rounds — *Dodson, James*
Final Solutions — *Lerner, Richard M*
The Final Superstition — *Daleiden, Joseph L*
Final Take — *Manthorne, Jackie*
Final Tour — *Heckler, Jonellen*
Final Victim — *Cannell, Stephen J*
Finance and Taxes for the Home-Based Business — *Lickson, Charles*
Finance and Technological Change — *Santarelli, Enrico*
Finance, Exchange Rates and Financial Liberalization — *Asikoglu, Yaman*
Finance, Investment and Macroeconomics — *Gordon, Myron J*
Finance Theory and Asset Pricing — *Milne, Frank*
yr The Financial Aid Book. 2nd Ed. — *Student Financial Services*
Financial Conglomerates — *Berghe, L Van Den*
Financial Decision-Making and Moral Responsibility — *Frowen, Stephen F*
Financial Deregulation and Integration in East Asia — *Ito, Takatoshi*
Financial, Economic and Social Trends 1985-1994
Financial Empowerment — *Brinckerhoff, Peter C*
Financial Factors and Corporate Investment — *Cho, Yong-Doo*
Financial Factors in Economic Stabilization and Growth — *Blejer, Mario I*
Financial Innovation, Banking and Monetary Aggregates — *Mullineux, Andrew*
Financial Integration, Corporate Governance, and the Performance of Multinational Companies — *Fukao, Mitsuhiro*

Financial Liberalization and Investment — *Gupta, Kanhaya L*
Financial Liberalization in Developing Countries — *Sikorski, Trevor M*
Financial Literacy in Adult Life — *Schagen, Sandie*
Financial Management for Nonprofits — *Shim, Jae K*
Financial Models and Simulation — *Chorafas, Dimitris N*
Financial Peace — *Ramsey, Dave*
Financial Peace (Ramsey). Audio Version — *Ramsey, Dave*
Financial Peace (Ramsey). Audio Version — *Ramsey, David*
Financial Planning for Nonprofit Organizations — *Blazek, Jody*
Financial Professional's Internet Guide — *Graves, John*
Financial Reform in Central and Eastern Europe — *Griffith-Jones, Stephany*
Financial Regulation in the Global Economy — *Herring, Richard J*
Financial Reporting by Multinationals — *Adams, Carol A*
Financial Repression and Economic Reform in China — *Li, Kui-Wai*
r Financial Resources for International Study. 2nd Ed. — *O'Sullivan, Marie*
Financial Services, Globalization and Domestic Policy Change — *Coleman, William D*
The Financial Services Revolution — *Kirsch, Clifford E*
The Financial System under Stress — *Uzan, Marc*
Financial Systems, Innovations and Development — *Bhatt, Vinayak V*
The Financial Times Guide to Marketing — *Ambler, Tim*
Financial Warnings — *Mulford, Charles W*
The Financially Independent Woman — *Lee, Barbara*
Financing Capital Market Intermediaries in East and Southeast Asia — *Scott, Hal S*
Financing Change — *Schmidheiny, Stephan*
y Financing College — *Davis, Kristin*
Financing Education — *Quade, Quentin L*
Financing Health Services through User Fees and Insurance — *Shaw, R Paul*
Financing Private Infrastructure — *Carter, Laurence*
Financing Regional Government in Britain — *Blow, Laura*
Financing the 1992 Election — *Alexander, Herbert E*
r Find a Space! — *Pain, Stephen*
Find a Victim — *Macdonald, Ross*
Find My Way Home — *Timlin, Mark*
y Finders Keepers — *Spalding, Andrea*
Finders: Poems — *Parson-Nesbitt, Julie*
Finding a Form — *Gass, William H*
c Finding a Job for Daddy (Illus. by Kay Life) — *Maslac, Evelyn Hughes*
Finding Art's Place — *Paley, Nicholas*
Finding Flow — *Csikszentmihalyi, Mihaly*
Finding God in All Things — *Himes, Michael J*
y Finding God in the Craziness of Life — *Mulhern, Kathy*
Finding God on the A Train — *Hamlin, Rick*
r Finding Help — *Giblin, Nan J*
Finding Her Voice — *Bufwack, Mary A*
Finding Home — *Webber, Christopher*
Finding Images Online — *Berinstein, Paula*
Finding It on the Internet. 2nd Ed. — *Gilster, Paul*
Finding Joy — *Schwartz, Dannel I*
y Finding Makeba — *Pate, Alexs D*
Finding Meaning in Dreams — *Domhoff, G William*
Finding Moon — *Hillerman, Tony*
y Finding My Father — *Hayes, Karen*
y Finding Our Way — *Abner, Allison*
Finding Philosophy in Social Science — *Bunge, Mario*
c Finding Providence (Illus. by James Watling) — *Avi*
Finding Serenity in the Age of Anxiety — *Gerzon, Robert*
c Finding Shelter — *Butler, Daphne*
Finding the Champion Within — *Jenner, Bruce*
Finding the God of Noah — *Davis, J David*
Finding the Landlord — *Lindskoog, Kathryn*
y Finding the Lost Cities — *Stefoff, Rebecca*
Finding the Trapdoor — *Hochschild, Adam*
Finding the Way Home — *Heiss, Gayle*
Finding True Love — *Kingma, Daphne Rose*
Finding What You Didn't Lose — *Fox, John, 1955-*
r Finding Your Hispanic Roots — *Ryskamp, George R*
Finding Your Writer's Voice — *Frank, Thaisa*
Findings from the Wildland Firefighters Human Factors Workshop

The Fine Art of California Indian Basketry — Bibby, Brian
r The Fine Art of Murder — Gorman, Edward
The Fine Art of the Tin Can — Hansson, Bobby
The Fine Artist's Guide to Marketing and Self-Promotion — Vitali, Julius
A Fine Balance — Mistry, Rohinton
The Fine Delight That Fathers Thought — Marucci, Franco
c Fine Feathered Friend (Illus. by Carol Walters) — Gavin, Jamila
p Fine Homebuilding
A Fine Italian Hand — Murray, William
c Fine Lines (Illus. by Michael Emery) — Heller, Ruth
Fine Machine Sewing — Ahles, Carol Laflin
Fine Needle Aspiration Biopsy of the Head and Neck — Powers, Celeste N
Fine Needle Aspiration Cytology of the Thorax and Abdomen — Silverman, Jan F
Fine Particles Science and Technology — Pelizzetti, Ezio
A Fine Romance — Mellencamp, Patricia
y A Fine White Dust — Rylant, Cynthia
The Finer Things — Joyce, Brenda
c Finger Rhymes (Illus. by Carol Thompson) — Foster, John
c Fingerplays and Action Chants. Vols. 1-2. Book and Audio Version — Weimer, Tonja Evetts
Finis Terrae — Rossi, Giovanni Maria
Finish Strong — Capen, Richard G, Jr.
Finishing Touches with Paint and Paper — Whitfield, Emma
Finite Element Approximation for Optimal Shape, Material and Topology Design. 2nd Ed. — Haslinger, J
The Finite Element Method in Heat Transfer Analysis — Lewis, R W
Finite-Element Modelling of Unbounded Media — Wolf, John P
Finite Element Programs in Structural Engineering and Continuum Mechanics — Ross, C T F
Finite Element Software for Microwave Engineering — Itoh, Tatsuo
Finite Element Techniques in Structural Mechanics — Ross, Carl T F
Finite Elements for Electrical Engineers. 3rd Ed. — Silvester, Peter P
Finite Horizon H [Infinity] and Related Control Problems — Subrahmanyam, M B
Finite Mathematics, Models, and Structure — Adams, William J
Finite Sums Decompositions in Mathematical Analysis — Rassias, Themistocles M
Finitely Additive Measures and Relaxations of Extremal Problems — Chentsov, A G
Finitude and Transcendence in the Platonic Dialogues — Hyland, Drew A
Finitude's Score — Ronell, Avital
Finks Krieg — Walser, Martin
c Finland — Lee, Tan Chung
Finnegans Wake — Joyce, James
Fins De Siecle — Briggs, Asa
Les Fins Dernieres Selon Origene — Crouzel, Henri
Finsler Geometry — Joint Summer Research Conference on Finsler Geometry (1995: Seattle, Wash.)
c The Fir Tree — Andersen, Hans Christian
c Fire — Robbins, Ken
Fire and Air — Wagstaff, Patty
y Fire and Fog — Day, Dianne
Fire and Roses — Raschke, Carl A
Fire and the Rose — Rahman, Anisur
The Fire and the Rose — Turner, Robert Griffith, Jr.
Fire at Eden's Gate — Walth, Brent
c Fire at the Triangle Factory (Illus. by Mary O'Keefe Young) — Littlefield, Holly
y Fire Dancer — Kelleher, Victor
c Fire Engine (Snapshot Books)
The Fire Fetched Down — Bradley, George
c Fire! Fire! Said Mrs. McGuire (Illus. by Richard Egielski) — Martin, Bill, 1916-
Fire from Heaven — Cox, Harvey
Fire in Ecosystems of Boreal Eurasia — Goldammer, Johann Georg
y A Fire in My Hands — Soto, Gary
Fire in the Andes — Menzel, Sewall H
A Fire in the Bones — Raboteau, Albert J
Fire in the Bones — Raffan, James
c Fire in the Forest (Illus. by Bob Marstall) — Pringle, Laurence
y Fire in the Hills — Myers, Anna
Fire in the Hole — Downing, Sybil

c Fire in the Mind — Johnson, George
c Fire in the Sky (Illus. by Shelly O Hass) — Ransom, Candice F
c Fire in the Wind — Levin, Betty
The Fire in These Ashes — Chittister, Joan
A Fire Is Burning, It Is in Me — Fukaya, Michiyo
The Fire Line — Ferguson, Trevor
Fire Margins — Norman, Lisanne
Fire Mountain — Medlin, William K
Fire of a Thousand Suns — Caron, George R
The Fire of Silence and Stillness — Harris, Paul
y Fire on Earth — Gribbin, John
Fire on the Earth — Barr, Kevin J
y The Fire Pony — Philbrick, Rodman
Fire Protection — Wagner, David H
y The Fire Rose — Lackey, Mercedes
y Fire Safety (Illus. by Penny Dann) — Loewen, Nancy
Fire, Salt, and Peace — Janzen, David
Fire This Time — Horne, Gerald
c Fire Trucks (Illus. by Hope Irvin Marston) — Marston, Hope Irvin
Fire Within — Trask, Kerry A
y Fireballs from Hell — Impey, Rose
y Firebird — Lackey, Mercedes
y Firebird — Rav-Hon, Orna
y Firebug — Gates, Susan
Fired Up! — Gill, Michael
c Firefighters — Wallington, Neil
c Firefighters Fight Fires — Greene, Carol
y Fireflies — Harlen, Johnathan
c Fireflies, Fireflies, Light My Way (Illus. by Linda Messier) — London, Jonathan
c Fireflies, Peach Pies, and Lullabies (Illus. by Nancy Cote) — Kroll, Virginia
y Firefly Summer — Belpre, Pura
c Firehouse Sal (Illus. by Ethel Gold) — Brimner, Larry Dane
Firekeeper: New and Selected Poems — Rogers, Pattiann
c Fireman Small — Yee, Wong Herbert
Firenze E Il Concilio Del 1439. Vols. 1-2 — Viti, Paolo
Firesong — Hone, Joseph
Firestar — Flynn, Michael F
y Firestorm — Barr, Nevada
c The Firework-Maker's Daughter (Illus. by Nick Harris) — Pullman, Philip
c Fireworks: The Science, the Art and the Magic (Illus. by Susan Kuklin) — Kuklin, Susan
A Firing Offense — Ignatius, David
A Firm Foundation — Olevianus, Caspar
Firm Objectives, Controls and Organization — Eliasson, Gunnar
Firms and Industrial Organization in Japan — Miwa, Yoshiro
The First $20 Million Is Always the Hardest — Bronson, Po
The First $20 Million Is Always the Hardest (Frye). Audio Version — Bronson, Po
First Aid and CPR. 3rd Ed. — National Safety Council
c The First Air Voyage in the United States — Wallner, Alexandra
The First American Frontier — Dunaway, Wilma A
First among Friends — Ingle, H Larry
c The First Amphibians (Illus. by Luis Rizo) — Llamas, Andreu
First and Second Peter, James, and Jude — Perkins, Pheme
First and Second Thessalonians — Richard, Earl
The First Angelinos — McCawley, William
c First Bible Stories (Illus. by Kim Woolley) — Watson, Carol
First, Body — Thon, Melanie Rae
First Book of Grasses — Chase, Agnes
y First Came the Owl — Richardson, Judith Benet
r First Century of Film — Quigley, Martin S
c First Children (Illus. by Katie Keller) — Leiner, Katherine
The First Christians in Their Social Worlds — Esler, Philip F
c The First Christmas (Illus. by Anna C Leplar) — Adams, Georgie
c The First Christmas (Illus. by Sue Ellen Brown) — Daniels, Patricia
The First Civil War — Tabari
First Comes Love — Winik, Marion
y First Comes Love (Winik). Audio Version — Winik, Marion
First Contact — Perry, Steve
A First Course in Fuzzy Logic — Nguyen, Hung T
A First Course in Optimization Theory — Sundaram, Rangarajan K

A First Course on Wavelets — Hernandez, Eugenio
First Cut — Robinson, Leah Ruth
y First Dawn — Moscoe, Mike
c First Day at Day Care (Illus. by Nate Evans) — Weiss, Ellen
cr A First Dictionary of Cultural Literacy. 2nd Ed., Rev. and Updated — Hirsch, E D
First Dogs — Rowan, Roy
The First Election — Thompson, M M H
c First Facts about the American Frontier (Illus. by Mark Bergin) — Macdonald, Fiona
c First Facts about the Ancient Egyptians (Illus. by Mark Bergin) — Morley, Jacqueline
c First Facts about the Ancient Romans (Illus. by Mark Bergin) — Macdonald, Fiona
c First Facts about the Vikings — Morley, Jacqueline
r First Facts of American Labor — Foner, Philip S
c First Farm Rhymes (Illus. by Lynn Adams)
c First Flight (Illus. by Don Bolognese) — Shea, George
The First Four Books of Poems — Merwin, W S
First Generation — Sirluck, Ernest
The First Generation of Electronic Records Archivists in the United States — Cox, Richard J
y First Generations — Berkin, Carol
The First Gift of Christmas — Evans, Richard Paul
r A First Glossary of Hiberno-English — Christensen, Lis
The First Helping Interview — Fine, Sara F
r The First Hollywood Musicals — Bradley, Edwin M
y First Horse — Smith, Fran Devereux
First Impression — Dalton, Margot
First Impressions. Vols. 5-6 — Dietzer, M'Lou
First in the Field — Williams, Jeffery, 1920-
The First Industrial Woman — Valenze, Deborah M
First Intermissions — Lee, M Owen
r The First International Credit Card Catalog 1997
The First International Lake Ladoga Symposium — International Lake Ladoga Symposium (1st: 1993: St. Petersburg, Russia)
First International Workshop on High-Level Programming Models and Supportive Environments — International Workshop on High-Level Programming Models and Supportive Environments (1st: 1996: Honolulu, HI)
y First King Shannara — Brooks, Terry
c First Ladies — Gormley, Beatrice
y First Ladies — Truman, Margaret
First Ladies. Expanded Ed. — Caroli, Betty Boyd
y First Ladies (Caruso). Audio Version — Truman, Margaret
First Light — Ackroyd, Peter
First Light. 1st Rev. Ed. — Preston, Richard
First Love — Oates, Joyce Carol
The First Man — Camus, Albert
The First Moderns — Everdell, William R
The First Mrs. Wordsworth — Baldwin, Michael
r First Name Reverse Dictionary — Navarro, Yvonne, 1957-
r First Names — Merry, Emma
The First Part of the Countess of Montgomery's Urania — Wroth, Mary, Lady
First Person Plural. Rev. Ed. — Braude, Stephen E
First Philharmonic — Ehrlich, Cyril
c A First Picture Book of Nursery Rhymes (Illus. by Elizabeth Harbour) — Harbour, Elizabeth
The First Polish Americans — Baker, T Lindsay
c First Pony (Illus. by M Rain) — Needham, Kate
First Principles of Typography — Morison, Stanley
c A First Puffin Picture Book of Stories from World Religions (Illus. by Barry Smith) — Shilson-Thomas, Annabel
The First Punic War — Lazenby, J F
The First Quarto of King Lear (Halio) — Shakespeare, William
The First R — Graves, Michael F
The First Sea Lords — Murfett, Malcolm H
c First, Second (Illus. by Marc Rosenthal) — Kharms, Daniil
c The First Snow (Illus. by David Christiana) — Christiana, David
First Steps — Whittaker, Stella
First Steps in Management — Morris, Beryl
The First Stone — Garner, Helen
c The First Story Ever Told (Illus. by Yoshi) — Jendresen, Erik
The First Strange Place — Bailey, Beth
y First Strike — Carey, Diane
The First Teenagers — Fowler, David
p First Things
c First Things First — Voake, Charlotte
First Things First in Child Labour — Bequele, Assefa

cr First Thousand Words
y The First Time. Vol. 2 — *Montpetit, Charles*
y The First Time. Vols. 1-2 — *Montpetit, Charles*
y The First-Time Gardener — *Barron, Pattie*
First Victim — *MacKinnon, Douglas*
First We Quit Our Jobs — *Abraham, Marilyn J*
The First Wives Club — *Goldsmith, Olivia*
The First Woman in the Republic — *Karcher, Carolyn L*
First World, Third World — *Ryrie, William*
The First World War — *Gilbert, Martin, 1936-*
The First World War — *Herwig, Holger H*
The First World War in British History — *Constantine, Stephen*
y The First Year of Nursing — *Finkelstein, Barbara*
The Fiscal Crisis of the States — *Gold, Steven D*
Fiscal Incentives for Investment and Innovation — *Shah, Anwar*
Fiscal Management in Russia
Fiscal Policy and Social Welfare — *Creedy, John*
The Fiscal Revolution in America. 2nd Ed. — *Stein, Herbert*
Fiscal Years 1992-1993 Report to the Congress — *U.S. Department of the Navy*
c Fish — *Powell, Jillian*
Fish and Shellfish — *Peterson, James*
c Fish Eyes (Illus. by Lois Ehlert) — *Ehlert, Lois*
c Fish (Illus. by Oxford Scientific Films) — *Royston, Angela*
c The Fish Princess (Illus. by Steve Mennie) — *Watts, Irene N*
Fish Show — *Delingpole, James*
p Fish Stories
c A Fish Tale (Illus. by Leo Yerxa) — *Yerxa, Leo*
Fishcamp: Life on an Alaskan Shore — *Lord, Nancy*
Fisheries Management in Crisis — *Crean, Kevin*
Fisheries Mismanagement — *Hannesson, Rognvaldur*
Fisheries Techniques. 2nd Ed. — *Murphy, Brian R*
A Fisherman of the Inland Sea — *Le Guin, Ursula K*
Fisherman's Hope — *Feintuch, David*
c Fishes (Illus. by Mary Sundstrom) — *Lovett, Sarah, 1953-*
Fishes, Crayfishes, and Crabs. Vols. 1-2 — *Pietsch, Theodore W*
r Fishes of Chesapeake Bay — *Murdy, Edward O*
Fishes of Utah — *Sigler, William F*
c Fishing for Trouble — *Dalrymple, T A*
c Fishing Sunday (Illus. by Barry Root) — *Johnston, Tony*
Fishing the Sloe-Black River — *McCann, Colum*
Fishing Villages in Tokugawa Japan — *Kalland, Arne*
c Fishing with Dad (Illus. by Will Shively) — *Rosen, Michael J*
yr The Fiske Guide to Colleges 1997
A Fist Full of Stories (and Articles) — *Lansdale, Joe R*
Fist Stick Knife Gun — *Canada, Geoffrey*
c Fit for Life (Illus. by John Shackell) — *Parsons, Alexandra*
Fitchers Blau — *Schramm, Ingo*
Fitness Aquatics — *Case, LeAnne*
Fitting Ends and Other Stories — *Chaon, Dan*
y Fitting In — *Bernardo, Anilu*
r Fitzroy Dearborn Directory of the World's Banks. 11th Ed.
r Fitzroy Dearborn International Directory of Venture Capital Funds. 2nd Ed. — *Schilit, W Keith*
Five Alarm Fire — *Borton, D B*
y The Five Biggest Ideas in Science — *Wynn, Charles M*
y The Five Books of Miriam — *Frankel, Ellen*
The Five Books of Moses — *Bible. O.T. Pentateuch. English. Fox. 1995*
Five by Feydeau — *Feydeau, Georges*
Five Cantos — *Ariosto, Lodovico*
c Five Children and It — *Nesbit, E*
Five Days in Paris — *Steel, Danielle*
Five Days of Bleeding — *Cruz, Ricardo Cortez*
Five Days to a Flatter Stomach — *Grenfell, Monica*
y Five Equations That Changed the World — *Guillen, Michael*
The Five-Factor Model of Personality — *Wiggins, Jerry S*
c Five Fall into Adventure. Book and Audio Version — *Blyton, Enid*
The Five Giants — *Timmins, Nicholas*
c Five Go Adventuring Again. Book and Audio Version — *Blyton, Enid*
c Five Go off to Camp. Book and Audio Version — *Blyton, Enid*
The Five Gospels — *Bible. N.T. Gospels. English. Scholars. 1993*

c Five Have Plenty of Fun. Book and Audio Version — *Blyton, Enid*
The Five Houses of Zen — *Cleary, Thomas*
Five Hundred Mathematical Challenges — *Barbeau, Edward J*
Five Lessons — *Hogan, Ben*
c Five Little Ducks (Story Web Series). Electronic Media Version
c Five Little Monkeys with Nothing to Do (Illus. by Eileen Christelow) — *Christelow, Eileen*
c Five Lost Chicks (Illus. by Kate Davies) — *Brett, Jane*
c Five-Minute Chillers (Illus. by Brian Dow) — *Walker, William A*
p Five Points
Five Rings over Seoul — *Pound, Richard W*
Five Screenplays — *Goldman, William*
c The Five Sisters (Illus. by Patricia MacCarthy) — *Mahy, Margaret*
Five Steps to Selecting the Best Alternative Medicine — *Morton, Mary*
Five Technologies for Educational Change — *Salisbury, David F*
r The Five Thomas Harrises of Isle of Wight County, Virginia — *Brayton, John A*
The Five to Seven Year Shift — *Sameroff, Arnold J*
Five Women — *Jaffe, Rona*
Five Years After — *Friedlander, Daniel*
Fix It Fast and Easy!. 2nd Rev. Ed. — *Haege, Glenn*
Fixed Income Mathematics. 3rd Ed. — *Fabozzi, Frank J*
Fixed Income Solutions — *Ho, Thomas S Y*
Fixing Broken Windows — *Kelling, George L*
c The Flag We Love (Illus. by Ralph Masiello) — *Ryan, Pam Munoz*
c Flags: Facts, Things to Make, Activities (Illus. by Raymond Turvey) — *Oxlade, Chris*
The Flamboyant Garden — *Sheldon, Elisabeth*
Flame of Love — *Pinnock, Clark H*
Flame Wars — *Dery, Mark*
Flamenco Deep Song — *Mitchell, Timothy J*
Flamenco: Gypsy Dance and Music from Andalusia — *Schreiner, Claus*
Flamenco: Passion, Politics and Popular Culture — *Washabaugh, William*
The Flaming Corsage — *Kennedy, William, 1928-*
y The Flaming Corsage (Kennedy). Audio Version — *Kennedy, William, 1928-*
Flaming Iguanas — *Lopez, Ericka*
c The Flamingos Are Tickled Pink (Illus. by Marshall Toomey) — *Lovitt, Chip*
The Flanders Panel — *Perez-Reverte, Arturo*
y Flanders Point — *Gordon, Jacquie*
Flannelboard Classic Tales — *Hicks, Doris Lynn*
Flannery O'Connor: New Perspectives — *Rath, Sura P*
Flapjacks and Photographs — *Robideau, Henri*
yr Flappers 2 Rappers — *Dalzell, Tom*
The Flash Effect — *Koperwas, Sam*
y Flash Fire — *Cooney, Caroline B*
A Flash of Red — *Harvey, Clay*
Flash! Splash! Crash! All at Sea with Cap'n Bob — *Maloney, Mike*
Flashbacks: On Returning to Vietnam — *Safer, Morley*
Flashpoint — *Hightower, Lynn S*
Flashpoint — *Tillis, Tracey*
c Flashy Fantastic Rain Forest Frogs (Illus. by Kendahl Jan Jubb) — *Patent, Dorothy Hinshaw*
Flat Tops Fire Management Area Guidebook for Prescribed Natural Fire Planning and Implementation — *Frary, Michael L*
Flatbush Odyssey — *Able, Allen*
c Flatfoot Fox and the Case of the Missing Schoolhouse (Illus. by Brian Lies) — *Clifford, Eth*
Flatheads and Spooneys — *Lund, Jens*
Flatland. 2nd Ed. — *Abbott, Edwin*
Flaubert in Egypt — *Flaubert, Gustave*
Flavor-Food Interactions — *McGorrin, Robert J*
Flavored Breads — *Miller, Mark Charles*
Flavorful Seasons Cookbook — *Webb, Robyn*
The Flavors of Modernity — *Biasin, Gian-Paolo*
Flavors of Puglia — *Jenkins, Nancy Harmon*
Flavors of the Riviera — *Andrews, Colman*
Flawless: The Ten-Week, Total-Image Method for Transforming Your Physique — *Paris, Bob*
A Flea in Her Rear, or, Ants in Her Pants and Other Vintage French Farces — *Shapiro, Norman R*
c A Flea in the Ear (Illus. by Ken Brown) — *Wyllie, Stephen*
y The Fleet of Stars — *Anderson, Poul*
Fleet Walker's Divided Heart — *Zang, David W*
Flemish Cities Explored. Rev. Ed. — *Blyth, Derek*

Flesh and Blood — *Cunningham, Michael*
Flesh and Bones — *Levine, Paul*
Flesh and Stone — *Miano, Mark*
Flesh and Stone — *Sennett, Richard*
Flesh and the Ideal — *Potts, Alex*
Flesh and the Word — *Preston, John*
Flesh and the Word 4
Flesh Peddlers and Warm Bodies — *Parker, Robert E*
Fleur De Pave — *Laine, Pascal*
Les Fleurs Du Mal — *Baudelaire, Charles*
Flexible Innovation — *Niosi, Jorge*
Flexible Pavements — *European Symposium EUROFLEX (1993: Lisbon, Portugal)*
Flickerbook — *Berg, Leila*
Flickering Shadows — *Kamau, Kwadwo Agymah*
Flickers: An Illustrated Celebration of 100 Years of Cinema — *Adair, Gilbert*
c Flight — *Burleigh, Robert*
y Flight #116 Is Down — *Cooney, Caroline B*
y Flight #116 Is Down (Guidall). Audio Version — *Cooney, Caroline B*
Flight among the Tombs — *Hecht, Anthony*
The Flight: Confessions of an Argentine Dirty Warrior — *Verbitsky, Horacio*
Flight from Honour — *Lyall, Gavin*
Flight from Neveryon — *Delany, Samuel R*
The Flight from Science and Reason — *Gross, Paul R*
Flight Management Systems — *Fishbein, Samuel B*
Flight of Passage — *Buck, Rinker*
Flight of the Blackbird — *Smith, Faye McDonald*
c Flight of the Golden Plover (Illus. by Daniel Van Zyle) — *Miller, Debbie S*
Flight of the Lavi — *Zakheim, Dov S*
Flight of the Phoenix — *Whiteside, John, 1946-*
The Flight of the Red Knot — *Harrington, Brian*
c Flight of the Reindeer (Illus. by Glenn Wolff) — *Sullivan, Robert, 1953-*
c Flight of the Reindeer (Ritter). Audio Version — *Sullivan, Robert, 1953-*
Flight Path — *Blais, Jan David*
Flight Paths of the Emperor — *Heighton, Steven*
y Flight to Hollow Mountain — *Sebanc, Mark*
A Flight with Fame — *Smart, Mary*
Flights in the Heavenlies — *Finney, Ernest J*
Flights of Fancy, Leaps of Faith — *Clark, Cindy Dell*
A Fling with a Demon Lover — *James, Kelvin Christopher*
c Flip-Flap — *Jenkins, Sandra*
c Flip-Flap Theatre (Illus. by Eva Johanna Rubin) — *Rubin, Eva Johanna*
y Flip-Flop Girl — *Paterson, Katherine*
Flip-Up Bulletin Boards — *Feldshuh, Muriel*
Flirting with Disaster — *Schneider, Saundra K*
Floaters — *Wambaugh, Joseph*
Floaters (McLarty). Audio Version — *Wambaugh, Joseph*
c Floating and Sinking — *Challoner, Jack*
c Floating Home (Illus. by Michael Rex) — *Getz, David*
Floating in My Mother's Palm — *Hegi, Ursula*
Floating on Solitude — *Smith, Dave, 1942-*
Flock of Dreamers — *Rakezic, Sasa*
c Flood (Illus. by Erick Ingraham) — *Calhoun, Mary*
c Flood Fish (Illus. by Sheldon Greenberg) — *Eversole, Robyn*
c Flood: Wrestling with the Mississippi — *Lauber, Patricia*
c Floods — *Armbruster, Ann*
c Floods — *Murray, Peter, 1952, Sep., 9-*
Floods across Europe — *Penning-Roswell, Edmund*
Floods of Fortune — *Goulding, Michael*
c Floppy Teddy Bear (Illus. by Karen Lee Baker) — *Lillie, Patricia*
Flora Britannica — *Mabey, Richard*
c Flora McDonnell's ABC — *McDonnell, Flora*
Flora Neotropica — *Luteyn, James L*
Floral Biology of Temperate Zone Fruit Trees and Small Fruits — *Nyeki, Jozsef*
Floral Style — *Lefferts, Vena*
Floreale and C. La Serie Che Non C'e Floral and Co. — *Filanci, Franco*
Florence: A Portrait — *Levey, Michael*
The Florence King Reader — *King, Florence*
Florence Nightingale 1820-1910 — *Woodham-Smith, Cecil*
Florence Nightingale in Egypt and Greece — *Nightingale, Florence*
Florentin: Roman, Fragmente, Varianten — *Schlegel, Dorothea Von*
Florida Cuban Heritage Trail
Florida in Poetry — *Jones, Jane Anderson*

Florida Indians and the Invasion from Europe — *Milanich, Jerald T*

r Florida (Insight Compact Guides)

The Florida Land Boom — *Frazer, William*

The Florida Negro — *McDonogh, Gary W*

Florida: The Natural Wonders — *Ripples, Jeff*

Florida's Geological History and Geological Resources — *Lane, Ed*

Florida's Pioneer Naturalist — *Rothra, Elizabeth Ogren*

Florine Stettheimer: Manhattan Fantastica — *Sussman, Elisabeth*

Flotsam and Jetsam — *Higgins, Aidan*

y Flour Babies — *Fine, Anne*

The Flour War — *Bouton, Cynthia A*

c Flow — *Goodhart, Pippa*

The Flow Analysis of Labour Markets — *Schettkat, Ronald*

Flow-Induced Vibration 1996

Flow Injection Atomic Absorption Spectrometry — *Fang, Zhaolun*

Flow Measurement Engineering Handbook. 3rd Ed. — *Miller, Richard W*

Flow My Tears, the Policeman Said — *Dick, Philip K*

Flow-of-Funds Analysis — *Dawson, John C*

The Flow of Gifts — *Yan, Yunxiang*

Flower and Hand — *Merwin, W S*

r The Flower Arranger's Encyclopedia of Preserving and Drying — *Foster, Maureen*

Flower Arranging European Styles — *Constable, Lyn*

c Flower Girl (Illus. by Paige Billin-Frye) — *Herman, Gail*

A Flower Much as Turkey — *Gunce, Ergin*

The Flower of Battle — *Cecil, Hugh*

The Flower of Friendship — *Tilney, Edmund*

y Flower Power — *McIntyre, Anne*

c Flower Street Friends (Illus. by Julie Douglas) — *Hendry, Diana*

c Flower, Why Do You Smell So Nice? (Illus. by Chiara Carrer) — *Grazzini, Francesca*

r Flowering, Fruiting and Foliage Vines — *Crandall, Chuck*

Flowering Plant Origin, Evolution and Phylogeny — *Taylor, David W, 1958-*

c Flowers (Illus. by Barrie Watts) — *Bryant-Mole, Karen*

y Flowers and Fables (Illus. by Rafal Olbinski) — *Gruen, John*

Flowers for Mei-Ling — *Lachs, Lorraine*

The Flowers of William Morris — *Baker, Derek W*

Flowers on My Grave — *Teichroeb, Ruth*

c Flowers on the Wall (Illus. by Miriam Nerlove) — *Nerlove, Miriam*

c Flowers, Trees, and Fruits — *Morgan, Sally*

Floyd Dell: The Life and Times of an American Rebel — *Clayton, Douglas*

Fluctuations and Order — *Millonas, Mark*

Flughunde — *Beyer, Marcel*

Fluid Dynamics for Physicists — *Faber, T E*

Fluid, Electrolyte, and Acid-Base Disorders. 2nd Ed. — *Arieff, Allen I*

Fluid Physics in Geology — *Furbish, David Jon*

Fluid Power Systems and Technology 1996

Fluid-Structure Interaction 1996

Fluids and Electrolytes. 4th Ed. — *Lee, Carla A B*

Fluorescence Imaging Spectroscopy and Microscopy — *Wang, X F*

Fluorescene Microscopy and Fluorescent Probes — *Slavik, Jan*

r The Flute Book. 2nd Ed. — *Toff, Nancy*

c Flute's Journey (Illus. by Lynne Cherry) — *Cherry, Lynne*

c Fly (Illus. by Lee Montgomery) — *Hawcock, David*

y Fly Away Home — *Hermes, Patricia*

Fly Away Home — *Kelman, Judith*

c Fly Eagle Fly (Illus. by Martine Gourbault) — *Pollard, Ian*

c A Fly in the Sky (Illus. by Kristin Joy Pratt) — *Pratt, Kristin Joy*

Fly Pushing — *Greenspan, Ralph J*

c Fly Traps! (Illus. by David Parkins) — *Jenkins, Martin*

c Fly with Me (Illus. by Jane Walker) — *Broome, Errol*

c Fly with the Birds (Illus. by Satoshi Katamura) — *Edwards, Richard*

y Flyers — *Hayes, Daniel*

Flying Blind — *Bryan, Sharon*

Flying Blind, Flying Safe — *Schiavo, Mary*

c The Flying Dragon Room (Illus. by Mark Teague) — *Wood, Audrey*

Flying High — *Rodgers, Eugene*

Flying Home and Other Stories — *Ellison, Ralph*

c Flying Machines (Illus. by Martin John) — *Arnold, Nick*

Flying Out with the Wounded — *Caston, Anne*

Flying over Sonny Liston — *Short, Gary*

c The Flying Trapeze (Illus. by Andrew McLean) — *Homes, Ruth*

Flynn: Whirlpool. Audio Version — *Brown, Lyle*

p Flyway

Flyy Girl — *Tyree, Omar*

Foamers — *Berson, Jon*

Focus — *Miller, Arthur*

Focus Group Interviews in Education and Psychology — *Vaughn, Sharon*

Focus on Russian. 2nd Ed. — *Rosengrant, Sandra F*

c Focus on the Child — *Elkin, Judith*

Focus on the Family Presents Great Stories Remembered — *Wheeler, Joe L*

Focus Your Business — *Brandt, Steven C*

Focusing-Oriented Psychotherapy — *Gendlin, Eugene T*

r Fodor's Canada 1997

r Fodor's Gay Guide to the USA — *Collins, Andrew*

r Fodor's South Africa. 1996 Ed. — *Barbour, Andrew*

c Fog Hounds. Wind Cat. Sea Mice (Illus. by Peter Bailey) — *Aiken, Joan*

Fokker: A Transatlantic Biography — *Dierikx, Marc*

The Folded Leaf — *Maxwell, William, 1908-*

p Folding and Design

Folens Information Technology: Key Stage 1 — *Lancaster, Lynn*

Folens Information Technology: Key Stage 2 — *Lancaster, Lynn*

Folie Et Rhetorique Dans La Sottie — *Dull, Olga Anna*

Folk Law — *Dundes Renteln, Alison*

Folk Legacies Revisited — *Cohen, David Steven*

Folk Lullabies of the World — *Cass-Beggs, Barbara*

Folk Roots and Mythic Wings in Sarah Orne Jewett and Toni Morrison — *Mobley, Marilyn Sanders*

c Folk Songs of Africa — *McLaughlin, Roberta*

r Folk Traditions of the Arab World. Vols. 1-2 — *El-Shamy, Hasan M*

Folklore, Myths, and Legends — *Rosenberg, Donna*

The Folklore of Birds — *Martin, Laura C*

A Folklorist's Progress — *Thompson, Stith*

Folktales of America. Vol. 4 — *Ainsworth, Catherine Harris*

Folktales of Newfoundland. Vols. 1-2 — *Halpert, Herbert*

Follow Me — *Griner, Paul*

Follow Me Home — *Hoffman, William, 1925-*

Follow That Bird! — *Oddie, Bill*

c Follow That Trash! (Illus. by Mavis Smith) — *Jacobs, Francine*

c Follow the Dream (Illus. by Peter Sis) — *Sis, Peter*

c Follow the Leader (Illus. by Miela Ford) — *Ford, Miela*

c Follow the Moon (Illus. by Suzanne Duranceau) — *Weeks, Sarah*

Follow the Rabbit Proof Fence — *Pilkington, Doris*

Follow Your Career Star — *Snodgrass, Jon*

Follow Your Heart — *Tamaro, Susanna*

y Follow Your Heart (Plowright). Audio Version — *Tamaro, Susanna*

Following a Lark — *Brown, George Mackay*

Following Ho Chi Minh — *Bui, Tin*

y Following Jesus — *St. Clair, Barry*

c Following My Own Footsteps — *Hahn, Mary Downing*

The Following Story — *Nooteboom, Cees*

r Following the Fugitive — *Deane, Bill*

c Following the Sun (Illus. by Jenny Stow) — *Stow, Jenny*

Following Through. Expanded Ed. — *Wind, Herbert Warren*

The Folly — *Chesney, Marion*

Le Fond De L'Etre Est Froid 1966-1992 — *Feyder, Vera*

Les Fondements Semantiques Du Discours Naturel — *Gardies, Jean-Louis*

Fonder Une Litterature Nationale — *Robidoux, Rejean*

r The Fontana History of the Human Sciences — *Smith, Roger, 1945-*

r Le Fonti Liturgiche A Stampa Della Biblioteca Musicale L. Feininger Presso Il Castello Del Buonconsiglio Di Trento. Vols. 1-2 — *Gozzi, Marco*

c Food (Snapshot)

c Food — *Cox, Kath*

c Food (Illus. by Sallie Alane Reason) — *Perham, Molly*

Food and Agrarian Orders in the World-Economy — *McMichael, Philip*

r Food and Beverage Market Place 1996

r Food and Drink in Literature — *Kiell, Norman*

c Food and Feasts in Ancient Greece — *Dawson, Imogen*

c Food and Feasts with the Vikings — *Martell, Hazel Mary*

Food Chemicals Codex. 4th Ed. — *Institute of Medicine (U.S.). Committee on Food Chemicals Codex*

cr Food: Feast, Cooks, and Kitchens — *Tames, Richard*

c Food Fight — *Bode, Janet*

c Food Fight (Illus. by Michael J Rosen) — *Rosen, Michael J*

Food Fights — *Bonnie, Fred*

Food for Life--and Other Dish — *Schimel, Lawrence*

Food from the Place Below — *Sewell, Bill*

Food in Russian History and Culture — *Glants, Musya*

r Food Irradiation — *Wilkinson, Vanessa M*

Food Irradiation. 2nd Ed. — *Satin, Morton*

c Food: Its Evolution through the Ages (Illus. by Piero Ventura) — *Ventura, Piero*

Food Lipids and Health — *McDonald, Richard E*

r Food Lover's Companion to France

r Food Lover's Companion to Italy

Food Processing Automation IV

r Food Proteins — *Nakai, S*

Food Safety and Quality Assurance. 2nd Ed. — *Hubbert, William T*

Food, the Body and the Self — *Lupton, Deborah*

Food: The Chemistry of its Components. 3rd Ed. — *Coultate, T P*

The Food Web of a Tropical Rain Forest — *Reagan, Douglas P*

Foods of Sicily and Sardinia and the Smaller Islands — *Bugialli, Giuliano*

r Foods That Harm, Foods That Heal — *Reader's Digest Association*

r Foods to Heal By — *Fox, Barry*

A Fool and His Money — *Wroe, Ann*

Fool Me Twice — *Levine, Paul*

y Fools for Scandal — *Lyons, Gene, 1943-*

Fools, Martyrs, Traitors — *Smith, Lacey Baldwin*

Fools' Names, Fools' Faces — *Ferguson, Andrew*

Fool's War — *Zettel, Sarah*

r The Foot and Ankle Sourcebook — *Tremaine, M David*

c Foot Book — *Seuss, Dr.*

A Foot in Both Worlds — *Baranosky, Edward*

y Football America — *Barber, Phil*

Football and Its Fans — *Taylor, Rogan P*

y Football Dreams — *Guy, David*

c Football Jokes (Illus. by Viki Woodworth) — *Rothaus, James R*

c The Football That Won-- (Illus. by Ted Rand) — *Sampson, Michael*

c Footprints in the Snow — *Wildsmith, Brian*

Footsteps — *McMahon, Katherine*

Footsteps — *Toer, Pramoedya Ananta*

Footsteps in the Jungle — *Maslow, Jonathan*

Footsteps of the Hawk — *Vachss, Andrew*

Footsucker — *Nicholson, Geoff*

For a Handful of Feathers — *De La Valdene, Guy*

For a Living — *Coles, Nicholas*

For a Modest God — *Ormsby, Eric*

y For All Time — *Kempthorne, Charley*

For All Who Love the Game — *Penick, Harvey*

y For Cause and Comrades — *McPherson, James M*

For Crime Out Loud (Martin). Audio Version — *Randisi, Robert J*

For Crying Out Loud — *Dujon, Diane*

For Fear of the Angels — *Pickstone, Charles*

For God and Country — *Lugg, Catherine A*

For God and Fatherland — *Burdick, Michael A*

For God and Glory — *Jeal, Tim*

For God and Mammon — *SenGupta, Gunja*

y For Home and Country — *Bolotin, Norman*

For Keeps — *Kael, Pauline*

y For Kicks (Gaminara). Audio Version — *Francis, Dick*

For Love (Reading). Audio Version — *Miller, Sue*

For Love of Country — *Cohen, Joshua*

For Love of Country — *Nussbaum, Martha Craven*

For Love of Country — *Viroli, Maurizio*

For Matters of Greater Moment — *Padberg, John W*

For Richer, for Poorer — *Kurz, Demie*

r For Sex Education, See Librarian — *Cornog, Martha*

For Social Peace in Brazil — *Weinstein, Barbara*

For the Blood Is the Life — *Crawford, F Marion*

For the Hell of It — *Raskin, Jonah*

c For the Life of Laetitia — *Hodge, Merle*

For the Living and the Dead — *Transtromer, Tomas*

For the Love of Perfection — *Arcilla, Rene Vincente*

Title Index

c For the Love of the Game (Illus. by Jan Spivey Gilchrist) — *Greenfield, Eloise*
For the President's Eyes Only — *Andrew, Christopher*
For the Record — *Rose, Michael*
For the Sake of Our Japanese Brethren — *Hayashi, Brian Masaru*
For the Sake of Simple Folk — *Scribner, R W*
For the Soul of the People — *Barnett, Victoria*
For the Union of Evangelical Christendom — *Guelzo, Allen C*
For When I'm Weak I'm Strong — *Tillmans, Wolfgang*
For Whom There Is No Room — *Egan, Eileen*
For You, Lili Marlene — *Peters, Robert, 1924-*
c For Your Eyes Only! (Illus. by Mark Todd) — *Rocklin, Joanne*
The Foraging Gourmet — *Lyle, Katie Letcher*
The Foraging Spectrum — *Kelly, Robert L*
Forbidden Acts — *Collins, Nancy A*
Forbidden Adventures — *Vance, Michael*
The Forbidden Best-Sellers of Pre-Revolutionary France — *Darnton, Robert*
Forbidden Entries — *Yau, John*
Forbidden Fires — *Anderson, Margaret C*
Forbidden Friendships — *Rocke, Michael*
Forbidden Fruit and Other Stories — *La Rosa, Pablo*
Forbidden Grounds — *Epstein, Richard Allen*
Forbidden Knowledge — *Shattuck, Roger*
The Forbidden Modern — *Gole, Nilufer*
Forbidden Relatives — *Ottenheimer, Martin*
Forbidden Signs — *Baynton, Douglas C*
Forbidden Texts — *Goulemot, Jean Marie*
Force and Geometry in Newton's Principia — *Gandt, Francois De*
Force and Touch Feedback for Virtual Reality — *Burdea, Grigore C*
The Force of Labour — *Berger, Stefan*
Force of Nature — *Hager, Thomas*
Force Recon Command — *Lee, Alex*
A Force upon the Plain — *Stern, Kenneth S*
Forced Exit — *Smith, Wesley J*
Forced Justice — *Armor, David J*
Forced Migration and Scientific Change — *Ash, Mitchell G*
y Ford — *Gould, William*
Ford Madox Ford: A Dual Life. Vol. 1 — *Saunders, Max*
Ford Madox Ford: A Dual Life. Vol. 2 — *Saunders, Max*
Ford Madox Ford: A Dual Life. Vols. 1-2 — *Saunders, Max*
y Forecasting the Future
Foregone Conclusions — *Bernstein, Michael Andre*
Foregone Conclusions — *Lebovic, James H*
The Foreign Aid Business — *Raffer, Kunibert*
Foreign Aid, Self-Reliance, and Economic Development in West Africa — *Olaniyan, R Omotayo*
Foreign Aid towards the Year 2000 — *Olav, Stokke*
Foreign Bodies — *Napier, A David*
Foreign Body — *Davies, Russell*
Foreign Capital and Industrialization in Malaysia — *Rasiah, Rajah*
Foreign Country — *Wright, Adrian*
Foreign Devil — *Wang, Ping*
Foreign Direct Investment and Multinational Enterprises — *Buckley, Peter J*
Foreign Direct Investment in Japan — *Yoshitomi, Masaru*
Foreign Direct Investment in Latin America — *Agosin, Manuel R*
Foreign Investment and Political Conflict in Developing Countries — *Rothgeb, John M*
Foreign Investment in Contemporary Russia — *Kuznetsov, Andrei*
The Foreign Language Classroom — *Haggstrom, Margaret Austin*
Foreign Language Learning — *Donato, Richard*
The Foreign Office and Foreign Policy 1919-1926 — *Maisel, Ephraim*
Foreign Policy Decision-Making — *Gallhofer, Irmtraud M*
p Foreign Policy in Focus
Foreign Trade in the Transition — *Kaminski, Bartlomiej*
The Foreign Worker and the German Labor Movement — *Kulczycki, John J*
Foreigners and Englishmen — *Statt, Daniel*
Forensic Assessment with the Millon Inventories — *McCann, Joseph T*
Foreordained Failure — *Smith, Steven D*

Forest Canopies — *Lowman, Margaret D*
Forest Dreams, Forest Nightmares — *Langston, Nancy*
c Forest Fire! — *Fraser, Mary Ann*
Forest Gardening — *Hart, Robert A De J*
Forest Insect and Disease Conditions in the United States 1994
Forest Insect Pests in Canada — *Armstrong, J A*
The Forest of Time and Other Stories — *Flynn, Michael F*
Forest Resource Economics and Finance — *Klemperer, W David*
Forest Resources Assessment 1990
Forest Rites — *Sahlins, Peter*
The Forest Service Program for Forest and Rangeland Resources
c Forest Tracks (Illus. by Janet Marshall) — *Duffy, Dee Dee*
The Forest Traveler — *Firkatian, Mari A*
c Forestry (Illus. by Pat Cupples) — *Drake, Jane*
Forestry for Human Development — *Seip, Hans Kristian*
c Forests — *Ganeri, Anita*
c The Forestwife — *Tomlinson, Theresa*
Les Forets D'Argent — *Rheims, Maurice*
y Forever — *Blume, Judy*
Forever After — *Zelazny, Roger*
c Forever Amber Brown (Illus. by Tony Ross) — *Danziger, Paula*
Forever, Erma — *Bombeck, Erma*
Forever Flying — *Hoover, R A*
Forever Valley — *Redonnet, Marie*
y Forged by Fire — *Draper, Sharon M*
Forged Correspondences — *Brady, Philip*
The Forged Feature — *Belitt, Ben*
Forged in Fury — *Elkins, Michael*
Forged in War — *Kimball, Warren F*
Forget Me Not — *Holm, Stef Ann*
Forgetting Elena — *White, Edmund*
Forgetting Whose We Are — *Keck, David*
Forging a Common Future — *Neusner, Jacob*
Forging Industrial Policy — *Dobbin, Frank*
The Forging of the Modern State — *Evans, Eric J*
y The Forgiving Air — *Somerville, Richard*
Forgiving the Boundaries — *Caesar, Terry*
The Forgotten Army — *Fay, Peter Ward*
The Forgotten Centuries — *Hudson, Charles*
The Forgotten Christians of Hangzhou — *Mungello, D E*
Forgotten Crisis — *Kaplan, Robert E*
Forgotten Fields of America — *Thole, Lou*
A Forgotten Offensive — *Goulter, Christina J M*
The Forgotten Pollinators — *Buchmann, Stephen L*
The Forgotten Pollution — *Roos, Rein A*
Forgotten Promise — *Kreuter, Gretchen V*
Forgotten Tragedy — *Jackson, Carlton*
The Forgotten Trail — *Pynn, Larry*
Forgotten Victims — *Bard, Mitchell G*
Fork Your Own Broncs. Audio Version — *L'Amour, Louis*
p Forkroads: A Journal of Ethnic-American Literature
Form Follows Finance — *Willis, Carol*
La Formacion Del Pensamiento Politico Del Carlismo 1810-1875 — *Wilhelmsen, Alexandra*
Formal Contributions to the Theory of Public Choice — *Black, Duncan*
Formal Ethics — *Gensler, Harry J*
Formal Introductions — *Gioia, Dana*
Formal Theory in Sociology — *Hage, Jerald*
Las Formas De Nuestras Voces — *Joysmith, Claire*
Format and Anxiety — *Goodman, Paul*
Format Integration and Its Effect on Cataloging, Training, and Systems — *Coyle, Karen*
La Formation De La Pratique Scientifique — *Licoppe, Christian*
La Formation Du Vocabulaire Scientifique Et Intellectual Dans Le Monde Grabe — *Jacquart, Danielle*
The Formation of the Book of the Twelve — *Jones, Barry Alan*
The Formation of the Christian Biblical Canon. Rev. and Expanded Ed. — *McDonald, Lee M*
The Formation of the English Common Law — *Hudson, John*
The Formation of the Medieval West — *Richter, Michael*
The Formation of the Parisian Bourgeoisie 1690-1830 — *Garrioch, David*
r Former Major League Teams — *Jones, Donald D*
Forming a Colonial Economy — *Butlin, N G*
Forming the Future — *O'Toole, Jack*
Forms and Meanings — *Chartier, Roger*

Forms of Disruption — *Donahue, Neil H*
Forms of Distance — *Pei-Tao*
Forms of Life and Following Rules — *Barry, Donald K*
Forms of Speech in Victorian Fiction — *Chapman, Raymond*
c Formula I Motor Racing Book
Formulation, Characterization, and Stability of Protein Drugs — *Pearlman, Rodney*
Formwork for Concrete Structures. 3rd Ed. — *Peurifoy, Robert L*
Formynderiets Teori — *Borg, Anders E*
Fornes: Theater in the Present Tense — *Moroff, Diane Lynn*
Forsaking Our Children — *Hagedorn, John M*
c Fort Biscuit (Illus. by Ann Kronheimer) — *Howarth, Lesley*
Fort Donelson's Legacy — *Cooling, Benjamin Franklin*
c Fort Life (Illus. by Tammy Everts) — *Kalman, Bobbie*
Fort Meade 1849-1900 — *Brown, Canter, Jr.*
r Fort Sisseton — *Schuler, Harold H*
Fortalecer La Familia — *Fuhrmann, Ingeburg*
Forties Fashion and the New Look — *McDowell, Colin*
Fortifications and the Synagogue — *Lambert, Phyllis*
Fortissimo! — *Bennett, Roy*
Fortojningar — *Wastberg, Per*
Fortran 90 for Engineers and Scientists — *Nyhoff, Larry*
Fortress-Churches of Languedoc — *Bonde, Sheila*
c Forts of Canada (Illus. by Don Kilby) — *Owens, Ann-Maureen*
Fortschritts- Und Modernitatskritik In Der DDR-Literatur — *Schenkel, Michael*
The Fortunate Fall — *Carter, Raphael*
The Fortunate Pilgrim — *Puzo, Mario*
Fortunate the Eyes That See — *Beck, Astrid B*
Fortune — *Spindler, Erica*
c A Fortune Branches Out (Mitchley). Audio Version — *Mahy, Margaret*
La Fortune D'Alexandrie — *Messadie, Gerald*
La Fortune Du Periple D'Hannon — *Mund-Dopchie, Monique*
La Fortune Morale — *Williams, Bernard*
c Fortune Telling — *Landau, Elaine*
Fortunes a Faire — *Manning, Catherine*
The Fortunes of the Courtier — *Burke, Peter*
Forty Days of Grace — *Wenig, Laurin*
Forty Lost Years — *O'Meara, Dan*
Forty New Ancient West Semitic Inscriptions — *Deutsch, R*
Forum on Research and Technology Advances in Digital Libraries — *Forum on Research and Technology Advances in Digital Libraries (3rd: 1996: Washington, DC)*
Forward Motion — *Menino, Holly*
Forward Recoil Spectrometry — *Tirira, Jorge*
Forward through the Rearview Mirror — *Benedetti, Paul*
r Fossil Atlas, Fishes — *Frickhinger, Karl Albert*
r Fossil Collector's Handbook — *Lichter, Gerhard*
The Fossil Trail — *Tattersall, Ian*
c Fossils and Bones — *Pirotta, Saviour*
Foster Care — *Triseliotis, John*
Foster Child — *Foster, Buddy*
Foster Parent Retention and Recruitment — *Mayers, Eileen*
Fostering: A Community Service Strategy for the Year 2000. Vols. 1-2
Fostering Continued Excellence in Adult Learning
Fostering Healing and Growth — *Edwards, Joyce*
Fostering Technological Dynamism
Fostering the Growth of High Ability — *Cropley, Arthur J*
Fostoria: Designer George Sakier — *Pina, Leslie*
Foucault and Literature — *During, Simon*
Foucault and Political Reason — *Barry, Andrew*
Foucault: Language to Infinity (Lopez-Morillas). Audio Version — *Foucault, Michel*
Foucault's Virginity — *Goldhill, Simon*
Foul and Fair Play — *Roth, Marty*
The Foul and the Fragrant — *Corbin, Alain*
Le Foulard Bleu — *Chapsal, Madeleine*
y Found — *Oldham, June*
The Found Generation — *Levine, Marilyn A*
Foundation — *Asimov, Isaac*
r The Foundation 1,000 1996/1997
r The Foundation Directory Supplement
Foundation Geography in Action. Bks. 1-3 — *Ashwell, Miranda*
The Foundation of Merit — *Ingraham, Patricia Wallace*

The Foundation Pit — *Platonov, Andrei Platonovich*
r Foundation Reporter 1997
Foundation Sacrifice in Dante's Commedia
   — *Quinones, Ricardo J*
yr Foundation Science to 14 — *Pople, Stephen*
Foundation's Fear — *Benford, Gregory*
Foundations for a New Democracy — *Alperson, Myra*
Foundations for Osteopathic Medicine
Foundations for Programming Languages — *Mitchell, J F*
Foundations for Programming Languages — *Mitchell, John C*
Foundations for the Future
Foundations in Microbiology. 2nd Ed. — *Talaro, Kathleen P*
Foundations of Animal Behavior — *Houck, Lynne D*
Foundations of Christian Music — *Foley, Edward*
Foundations of Corporate Success — *Kay, J A*
Foundations of Differential Geometry. Vol. 1
   — *Kobayashi, Shoshichi*
The Foundations of Econometric Analysis — *Hendry, David F*
Foundations of Electrical Engineering. 2nd Ed.
   — *Cogdell, J R*
Foundations of Electroheat — *Metaxas, A C*
Foundations of Futures Studies. Vol. 1 — *Bell, Wendell*
Foundations of Geomagnetism — *Backus, Georgia*
Foundations of International Macroeconomics
   — *Obstfeld, Maurice*
Foundations of Java Programming for the World Wide Web — *Walsh, Aaron E*
The Foundations of Knowledge — *McGrew, Timothy J*
Foundations of Linear Algebra — *Golan, Jonathan S*
Foundations of Liturgy — *Adam, Adolf*
Foundations of Low Vision — *Corn, A L*
Foundations of Mental Health Counseling. 2nd Ed.
   — *Weikel, William J*
Foundations of Political Economy — *Wood, Neal*
Foundations of Rehabilitation Teaching with Persons Who Are Blind or Visually Impaired — *Ponchillia, Paul E*
The Foundations of Socratic Ethics — *Gomez-Lobo, Alfonso*
Foundations of Understanding — *Newton, Natika*
Foundations without Foundationalism — *Shapiro, Stewart*
Founder: A Portrait of the First Rothschild and His Time — *Elon, Amos*
Founder: Meyer Amschel Rothschild and His Time
   — *Elon, Amos*
The Founders and the Classics — *Richard, Carl J*
The Founders of America — *Jennings, Francis*
yr Founders of Modern Nations — *Hamilton, Neil A, 1949-*
Founding Father — *Brookhiser, Richard*
The Founding Legend of Western Civilization
   — *Waswo, Richard*
Founding Mothers and Fathers — *Norton, Mary Beth*
Founding Republics in France and America — *Rohr, John A*
The Foundling: A Comedy. The Gamester: A Tragedy
   — *Moore, Edward*
Fount Christian Thinkers
Fountain House — *Flannery, Mary*
The Fountain of Privilege — *Root, Hilton L*
c Four Ancestors (Illus. by S S Burrus) — *Bruchac, Joseph*
r Four Centuries of American Furniture — *Fitzgerald, Oscar P*
y Four Corners — *Brown, Kenneth A*
The Four Cornerstones of Winning Golf — *Harmon, Claude*
Four Dreamers and Emily — *Davies, Stevie*
c Four Famished Foxes and Fosdyke (Illus. by Henry Cole) — *Edwards, Pamela Duncan*
Four Figures in Time — *Grossman, Patricia*
r Four French Symbolists — *Clement, Russell T*
Four Last Things — *Palmer, William, 1945-*
The Four Levers of Corporate Change — *Brill, Peter L*
c Four Little Swans and a Prince (Illus. by Amanda Harvey) — *Richardson, Jean*
The Four-Masted Barque Lawhill — *Edwards, Kenneth*
y Four Perfect Pebbles — *Perl, Lila*
The Four Pillars of Healing — *Galland, Leo*
c Four Pups and a Worm — *Seltzer, Eric*
Four Quartets — *Eliot, T S*
The Four Questions of Melancholy — *Salamun, Tomaz*
Four Restoration Marriage Plays — *Cordner, Michael*

c Four Seasons of Corn (Illus. by Joe Allen) — *Hunter, Sally M*
The Four Sonyas — *Paral, Vladimir*
Four Spiritualities, Expressions of Self, Expressions of Spirit — *Richardson, Peter Tufts*
Four-Star Desserts — *Luchetti, Emily*
Four Ways to Forgiveness — *Le Guin, Ursula K*
Fourier Integral Operators — *Duistermaat, J J*
Fourier-Related Transforms, Fast Algorithms, and Applications — *Ersoy, Okan K*
Fourteen Friends — *Lees-Milne, James*
The Fourth Discontinuity — *Mazlish, Bruce*
The Fourth Estate — *Archer, Jeffrey*
y The Fourth Estate (Jarvis). Audio Version — *Archer, Jeffrey*
Fourth International Conference on Computer Communications and Networks — *International Conference on Computer Communications and Networks (4th: 1995: Las Vegas, Nev.)*
c A Fourth of July on the Plains (Illus. by Henri Sorensen) — *Van Leeuwen, Jean*
y The Fourth Rome — *Drake, David*
The Fourth Turning — *Strauss, William*
The Fourth Turning (Tilford). Audio Version
   — *Strauss, William*
c Fowl Play — *Allen, Jonathan*
y Fowl Play — *Westfall, Patricia Tichenor*
c Fox (Illus. by Richard Hewett) — *Arnold, Caroline*
c Fox All Week — *Marshall, Edward*
c The Fox Gate and Other Stories (Illus. by William Geldart) — *Mayne, William*
c The Fox Maiden (Illus. by Tatsuro Kiuchi)
   — *Marston, Elsa*
Foxgloves and Hedgehog Days — *Blajan, Daniel*
y Foxspell — *Rubinstein, Gillian*
c Foxy Fox. Book and Audio Version — *DeRubertis, Barbara*
A Foxy Old Woman's Guide to Traveling Alone
   — *Ben-Lesser, Jay*
Fra Angelico at San Marco — *Hood, William*
Fra Angelico: The San Marco Frescoes
   — *Morachiello, Paolo*
Fractal Horizons — *Pickover, Clifford A*
Fractal Reviews in the Natural and Applied Sciences
   — *Novak, Miroslav M*
Fractals: Endlessly Repeated Geometrical Figures
   — *Lauwerier, Hans*
Fractals of Brain, Fractals of Mind — *Mac Cormac, Earl R*
c Fraction Fun (Illus. by Nancy Tobin) — *Adler, David A*
c Fractions (Illus. by Richard Maccabe) — *Stienecker, David*
Fractography of Glasses and Ceramics III
   — *Conference on the Fractography of Glasses and Ceramics (3rd: 1995: Alfred University)*
Fracture: Instability Dynamics, Scaling, and Ductile/Brittle Behavior — *Blumberg Selinger, Robin L*
Fracture Mechanics of Ceramics. Vols. 11-12
r Fractures in Children. 4th Ed., Vol. 3 — *Rockwood, Charles A*
Fragile Democracies — *Casper, Gretchen*
c The Fragile Frog (Illus. by John R Quinn) — *Mara, William P*
The Fragile Hour — *Laker, Rosalind*
Fragile Objects — *Gennes, Pierre-Gilles De*
Fragile Traditions — *Taylor, Paul Michael*
Fragile X Syndrome. 2nd Ed. — *Hagerman, Randi Jenssen*
The Fragility of Freedom — *Mitchell, Joshua*
The Fragmentation of Afghanistan — *Rubin, Barnett R*
The Fragmented World of the Social — *Honneth, Axel*
r Fragments from Hellenistic Jewish Authors. Vol. 3
   — *Holladay, Carl R*
y Fragments in Us — *Trudell, Dennis*
y Fragments: Memories of a Wartime Childhood
   — *Wilkomirski, Binjamin*
Fragments of Cities — *Bennett, Larry*
Fragments of Death, Fables of Identity — *Panourgia, Neni*
Fragments of the Spirit — *Wallace, Mark I*
Fragments: Portraits from the Inside — *De Toth, Andre*
Fragrance Bottle Masterpieces — *Ball, Joanne Dubbs*
Fragrance in Bloom — *Lovejoy, Ann*
The Fragrant Fire — *Jensen-Dudley, Claudia*
Frame 1971-1990 — *Watten, Barrett*
Frame Structures — *Howe, Susan*
Framer Framed — *Trinh, T Minh-Ha*
Frames and Resolvable Designs — *Furino, Steven*
Frames of Reference — *Rudman, Carol*

Frames of Referents — *Kruger-Robbins, Jill*
Frameshift — *Sawyer, Robert J*
The Framework of Systemic Organization
   — *Friedemann, Marie-Luise*
Framework Patterns — *Pree, Wolfgang*
Frameworks: Form, Function and Ornament in European Portrait Frames — *Mitchell, Paul*
Framing a Novelist — *Weninger, Robert*
Framing Anna Karenina — *Mandelker, Amy*
Framing Elizabethan Fictions — *Relihan, Constance C*
Framing History — *Carmichael, Virginia*
Framing in the Golden Age — *Thiel, P J J Van*
Framing Marginality — *Gunew, Sneja*
Framing Medieval Bodies — *Kay, Sarah*
Framing Pieces — *Whittier-Ferguson, John*
Framing Software Reuse — *Bassett, Paul G*
Framing the Margins — *Harper, Phillip Brian*
Framing Truths — *Kuester, Martin*
Le Francais Au Bureau — *Guilloton, Noelle*
Le Francais Des Affaires. 2nd Ed. — *Storme, Francoise*
Le Francais Langue Commune
Les Francais. 2nd Ed. — *Wylie, Laurence*
France 1814-1914 — *Tombs, Robert*
La France A L'Heure Allemande 1940-1944
   — *Burrin, Philippe*
France and Botany Bay — *Forster, Colin*
France and the Origins of the Second World War
   — *Young, Robert J, 1942-*
France at the Crystal Palace — *Walton, Whitney*
La France Et La Canada — *Prevost, Philippe*
La France Et Les Francais XIVe-Milieu-XVIe Siecles
   — *Waneggfelen, T*
France from the Air — *Philippe, Daniel*
France in the New Europe — *Tiersky, Ronald*
France in the Sixteenth Century — *Baumgartner, Frederic J*
La France Libre — *Cremieux-Brilhac, Jean-Louis*
La France Presidentielle — *Wahl, Nicholas*
France since 1945 — *Gildea, Robert*
France under the Germans — *Burrin, Philippe*
c Frances Fairweather--Demon Striker! — *Smith, Derek*
Francis and Bonaventure — *Rout, Paul*
r Francis Armstrong of Ireland and His Descendants in America — *Robertson, Brenda*
Francis Bacon — *Hergott, Fabrice*
Francis Bacon — *Sylvester, David*
Francis Bacon: Anatomy of an Enigma — *Peppiatt, Michael*
Francis Bacon: The History of a Character Assassination — *Mathews, Nieves*
Francis Bacon (Vickers) — *Bacon, Francis*
Francis Drake: The Lives of a Hero — *Cummins, John*
Francis Joseph — *Beller, Steven*
Francis Poulenc — *Ivry, Benjamin*
Francis Poulenc — *Mellers, Wilfrid*
c Francis, the Earthquake Dog (Illus. by Brooke Scudder) — *Enderle, Judith Ross*
Francisco Bayeu — *Anson Navarro, Arturo*
Francisco De Goya Y La Estampa De Su Epoca
Francisco De Rojas Zorrilla Y Agustin Moreto
   — *Mackenzie, Ann L*
Francisco Jose De Caldas: A Scientist at Work in Nueva Granada — *Appel, John Wilton*
Franco, Espana Y La II Guerra Mundial — *Tusell, Javier*
Francofonie Si Francofilie — *Craia, Sultana*
Francois-Auguste Ravier 1814-1895 — *Boyer-Thiollier, Christine*
Francois Mauriac Revisited — *O'Connell, David*
Francois Rabelais: Critical Assessments — *Carron, Jean-Claude*
Francois Truffaut — *Baecque, Antoine De*
Francophone African Women Writers — *D'Almeida, Irene Assiba*
y Francoscope A La Mode — *Sprake, David*
r Frank and Joe Turn Blue. 3rd Ed. — *Carpentieri, Tony*
c Frank and Joey Eat Lunch (Illus. by Maurice Sendak)
   — *Yorinks, Arthur*
c Frank and Joey Go to Work (Illus. by Maurice Sendak) — *Yorinks, Arthur*
Frank Capra: The Catastrophe of Success
   — *McBride, Joseph*
The Frank Lloyd Wright Companion. Electronic Media Version
r Frank Lloyd Wright: Designs for an American Landscape 1922-1932 — *Spirn, Anne Whiston*
y Frank Lloyd Wright: Maverick Architect — *Davis, Frances A*

Frank Lloyd Wright's Dana House — *Hoffmann, Donald*

The Frank Sinatra Reader — *Petkov, Steven*

c Frank Thomas: Power Hitter — *Gutman, Bill*

c Frank Thomas: Star First Baseman — *Spiros, Dean*

Frankenstein — *Shelley, Mary Wollstonecraft*

The Frankenstein Notebooks. Vols. 1-2 — *Shelley, Mary Wollstonecraft*

The Frankenstein Syndrome — *Rollin, Bernard E*

Frankenstein: The 1818 Text, Contexts, Nineteenth-Century Responses, Modern Criticism — *Shelley, Mary Wollstonecraft*

r Frankenthaler: A Catalogue Raisonne, Prints 1961-1994 — *Harrison, Pegram*

Franklin and Sterling Hill, New Jersey. Vols. 1-5, 1st-2nd Suppls. — *Dunn, Pete J*

c Franklin D. Roosevelt: The Four-Term President — *Schuman, Michael*

c Franklin's Bad Day (Illus. by Brenda Clark) — *Bourgeois, Paulette*

c Franklin's Halloween (Illus. by Brenda Clark) — *Bourgeois, Paulette*

c Franklin's School Play — *Bourgeois, Paulette*

Franklin's Tale — *Chaucer, Geoffrey*

Frankreich, Deutschland Und Europa Im 17. Und 18. Jahrhundert — *Malettke, Klaus*

r The Franks in the Aegean 1204-1500 — *Lock, Peter*

Franks, Moravians, and Magyars — *Bowlus, Charles R*

Franz Jung: Leben Und Werk Eines Rebellen — *Schurer, Ernst*

Franz Kafka, the Jewish Patient — *Gilman, Sander L*

Franz Liszt. Vol. 3 — *Walker, Alan, 1930-*

Franz Rosenzweig and Jehuda Halevi — *Galli, Barbara Ellen*

Franz Schreker 1878-1934 — *Hailey, Christopher*

Franz Schubert: A Biography — *McKay, Elizabeth Norman*

y Franz Schubert: An Essential Guide to His Life and Work — *Jackson, Stephen*

Franz Werfel and the Critics — *Michaels, Jennifer E*

Franz Werfel: Sein Weg In Den Roman — *Paulsen, Wolfgang*

Franz West: Proforma — *Badura-Triska, Eva*

The Fraser River — *Haig-Brown, Alan*

Die Frau In Der Renaissance — *Schmidt, Paul Gerhard*

y Fraud (Massey). Audio Version — *Brookner, Anita*

Frauds, Myths, and Mysteries — *Feder, Kenneth L*

Frauen: German Women Recall the Third Reich — *Owings, Alison*

Frauen Reisen — *Felden, Tamara*

Frauen Und Naturwissenschaften — *Hickel, Erika*

y The Freak — *Matas, Carol*

Freak Nights — *Folan, Ciaran*

Freak Show — *Hammer, Carl*

Freakery: Cultural Spectacles of the Extraordinary Body — *Thomson, Rosemarie Garland*

c The Freaky Beastie of Hill Road School — *Abadzis, Nick*

Freaky Deaky (Muller). Audio Version — *Leonard, Elmore*

The Fred Astaire and Ginger Rogers Murder Case — *Baxt, George*

r The Fred Waring Discography — *Kiefer, Peter T*

The Freddie Mercury Story — *Bret, David*

c Frederic Chopin — *Dineen, Jacqueline*

Frederic, Lord Leighton: Eminent Victorian Artist — *Ormond, Richard*

c Frederick — *Lionni, Leo*

Frederick III: Germany's Liberal Emperor — *Kollander, Patricia*

Frederick H. Varley — *Varley, Peter*

Free Advice, by the Advice Ladies — *Alkon, Amy*

Free Banking. Vols. 2-3 — *White, Lawrence H*

Free Books for All — *Bruce, Lorne*

Free City — *Darton, Eric*

Free Enterprise Moves East — *Henderson, Carter*

Free Expression — *Waluchow, W J*

y Free Fall — *Sweeney, Joyce*

The Free Life — *Smith, Anthony*

Free-Living Freshwater Protozoa — *Patterson, D J*

c Free Lunch (Illus. by J Otto Seibold) — *Seibold, J Otto*

A Free Man of Color — *Hambly, Barbara*

Free Markets and Food Riots — *Walton, John, 1937-*

Free Markets and Social Justice — *Sunstein, Cass R*

p Free Materials for Schools and Libraries

r Free Money for Small Businesses and Entrepreneurs. 4th Ed. — *Blum, Laurie*

r Free Money for the Arts. New Expanded, Rev. and Updated Ed. — *Blum, Laurie*

r Free Money from the Federal Government for Small Businesses and Entrepreneurs. 2nd Ed. — *Blum, Laurie*

Free Probability Theory — *Voiculescu, Dan-Virgil*

Free Radicals and Oxidative Stress — *Biochemical Society (Great Britain). Symposium (61st: 1994: University of Sussex)*

Free Radicals in Brain Physiology and Disorders — *Packer, Lester*

Free Reign — *Aubert, Rosemary*

Free Rein — *Breton, Andre*

The Free Society — *Pollock, Lansing*

Free Space — *Linaweaver, Brad*

Free Speech in the College Community — *O'Neil, Robert M*

Free Spirit in a Troubled World — *Phillips, John, 1914-1996*

Free Throw — *Amberry, Tom*

Free to All — *Van Slyck, Abigail Ayres*

y Free to Dream — *Osofsky, Audrey*

Free to Love — *Buckel, John*

Free Trade and Economic Restructuring in Latin America — *Rosen, Fred, 1942-*

y Free within Ourselves — *Jacques, Geoffrey*

The Free World — *Macdonald, J H*

y Free Your Mind — *Bass, Ellen*

A Freeborn People — *Underdown, David*

r Freedmen and Colored Marriage Records 1865-1890, Sumter County, Alabama — *Hester, Gwendolyn Lynette*

Freedom and Creation in Three Traditions — *Burrell, David B*

Freedom and Moral Sentiment — *Russell, Paul*

Freedom and Necessity — *Brust, Steven*

Freedom Betrayed — *Ledeen, Michael*

c Freedom Child of the Sea (Illus. by Julia Gukova) — *Keens-Douglas, Richardo*

Freedom Fighters of the United States Supreme Court — *Leahy, James E*

Freedom, Glorious Freedom — *McNeill, John J*

Freedom in Our Lifetime — *Lembede, Anton Muziwakhe*

Freedom in Rousseau's Political Philosophy — *Cullen, Daniel E*

c Freedom of Assembly — *King, David C*

Freedom of Information in Delaware — *Garrett, D*

r Freedom of Religion Decisions of the United States Supreme Court — *Harrison, Maureen*

r Freedom of Speech Decisions of the United States Supreme Court — *Harrison, Maureen*

r Freedom of the Press Decisions of the United States Supreme Court — *Harrison, Maureen*

c Freedom of Worship — *Sherrow, Victoria*

c The Freedom Riddle (Illus. by John Ward) — *Medearis, Angela Shelf*

y Freedom's Children — *Levine, Ellen*

y Freedom's Choice — *McCaffrey, Anne*

c Freedom's Fruit (Illus. by James Ransome) — *Hooks, William H*

c Freedom's Gifts (Illus. by Sharon Wilson) — *Wesley, Valerie Wilson*

Freedom's Landing — *McCaffrey, Anne*

Freedom's Law — *Dworkin, R M*

r Freedom's Lawmakers. Rev. Ed. — *Foner, Eric*

Freedom's Unfinished Revolution — *Friedheim, William*

Freeing the First Amendment — *Allen, David S*

Freeing the Hostages — *Moses, Russell Leigh*

Freer Markets, More Rules — *Vogel, Steven Kent*

Freeware — *Rucker, Rudy*

c Freeze a Crowd — *Jennings, Paul*

Freeze Frame — *Fienup-Riordan, Ann*

Die Frei Stehende Griechische Exedra — *Von Thungen, Suzanne*

Freie Richtungen — *Prahl, Roman*

Die Freien Frauen — *Schuster, Beate*

c Freight Train — *Crews, Donald*

Fremde: A Discourse — *Chiellino, Gino*

French Art: The Ancient Regime 1620-1775 — *Chastel, Andre*

French Autobiography — *Sheringham, Michael*

r French Cheeses — *Masui, Kazuko*

French Children of the Holocaust — *Klarsfeld, Serge*

The French Communist Party in the Fifth Republic — *Bell, David Scott*

French Constitution

The French Counterrevolutionary Theorist, Louis De Bonald 1754-1840 — *Klinck, David*

r The French Critical Reception of African-American Literature — *Fabre, Michel*

The French Descent into Renaissance Italy 1494-95 — *Abulafia, David*

The French Disease — *Keogh, Daire*

French Erotic Fiction — *Hughes, Alex*

French Essays on Shakespeare and His Contemporaries — *Maguin, Jean-Marie*

French Farmhouse Cookbook — *Loomis, Susan Herrmann*

French Fascism — *Soucy, Robert*

French Film Noir — *Bass, Robin*

r French Films 1945-1993 — *Biggs, Melissa E*

French Food, American Accent — *Ponzek, Debra*

French: From Dialect to Standard — *Lodge, R Anthony*

French Fun — *Timmins, Steve*

French Fur Traders and Voyaguers in the American West — *Hafen, LeRoy R*

The French Idea of Freedom — *Van Kley, Dale K*

French Impressionism — *Feist, Peter H*

The French in Love and War — *Rearick, Charles*

The French Letters of Godwyn Ainsley Ffrench — *Ffrench, Godwyn Ainsley*

French Literary Fascism — *Carroll, David*

The French Melting Pot — *Noiriel, Gerard*

French Music from the Enlightenment to Romanticism 1789-1830 — *Mongredien, Jean*

French National Cinema — *Hayward, Susan*

The French National Front — *Simmons, Harvey G*

The French New Autobiographies — *Ramsay, Raylene L*

French Organ Music — *Archbold, Lawrence*

French Politics 1774-1789 — *Hardman, John*

The French Portrait — *Wintermute, Alan*

The French Press in the Age of Enlightenment — *Censer, Jack R*

The French Renaissance in Prints, from the Bibliotheque Nationale De France

c The French Revolution — *Gilbert, Adrian*

The French Revolution in Russian Intellectual Life 1865-1905 — *Shlapentokh, Dmitry*

The French Revolutionary Wars 1787-1802 — *Blanning, T C W*

French River — *Harting, Toni*

The French School of Spirituality — *Deville, Raymond*

The French Secret Services — *Porch, Douglas*

French Tarts — *Dannenberg, Linda*

French Theater since 1968 — *Knapp, Bettina L*

The French Tradition and the Literature of Medieval England — *Calin, William*

A French Tragedy — *Todorov, Tzvetan*

French Ways and Their Meaning — *Wharton, Edith*

r French Women Playwrights of the Twentieth Century — *Beach, Cecilia*

French Women's Writing 1848-1994 — *Holmes, Diana*

Frenzy — *Everett, Percival*

Frequency Domain Filtering Strategies for Hybrid Optical Information Processing — *Chatwin, C R*

The Frequency of Souls — *Zuravleff, Mary Kay*

Fresco: Modern Tuscan Cooking for All Seasons — *Scotto, Marion*

p Fresh and Tasty: Women's Snowboarding

Fresh Blood — *Ripley, Mike*

Fresh Blood — *Ungar, Sanford J*

Fresh Cuts — *Von Gal, Edwina*

Fresh Peaches, Fireworks, and Guns — *Platt, Donald*

y A Fresh Start — *Ferry, Charles*

A Fresh Taste of Italy — *Scicolone, Michele*

Fresh Wind, Fresh Fire — *Cymbala, Jim*

y Freshman

y Freshmen

c The Freshwater Alphabet Book (Illus. by David Biedrzycki) — *Pallotta, Jerry*

Freshwater Ecosystems — *National Research Council (U.S.). Committee on Inland Aquatic Ecosystems*

The Freshwater Imperative — *Naiman, Robert J*

r Freshwater Pond Life — *Weidenbach, Ronald P*

Freud among the Philosophers — *Levy, Donald*

Freud and the Child Woman — *Timms, Edward*

Freud's Dora — *Mahony, Patrick J*

Freud's Paranoid Quest — *Farrell, John*

Freud's Wishful Dream Book — *Welsh, Alexander*

y Freya on the Wall — *Degens, T*

Freya Stark in Southern Arabia — *Ruthven, Malise*

A Friar's Joy — *Cronin, Kevin M*

The Friars: The Impact of the Early Mendicant Movement on Western Society — *Lawrence, C H*

Friction, Wear, Lubrication — *Ludema, Kenneth C*

Frid Och Fredloshet — *Breisch, Agneta*

y Frida Kahlo: Portrait of a Mexican Painter — *Cruz, Barbara C*
c Frida Maria — *Lattimore, Deborah Nourse*
Friday — *Tournier, Michel*
Friday (McQuay). Audio Version — *Heinlein, Robert A*
The Friday Book — *Barth, John*
Frieda Lawrence — *Jackson, Rosie*
Friedrich Nietzsche — *Holub, Robert C*
c The Friend — *Burningham, John*
c A Friend for Little Bear (Illus. by Harry Horse) — *Horse, Harry*
c A Friend for Tiger (Illus. by Laurence Henno) — *Bourguignon, Laurence*
Friend to Friend — *Wyse, Lois*
r The Friendly German-English Dictionary — *Bridgham, Fred*
Friendly Street New Poets Two — *Brooks, Anna*
Friendly Street Reader. No. 20 — *Dally, Judy*
Friendly Takeover — *Lieber, James B*
c Friends (Illus. by Michael Evans) — *Baxter, Nicola*
c The Friends — *Yumoto, Kazumi*
Friends, Brothers, and Informants — *Kumar, Nita*
Friends for Life — *Jonas, Susan*
Friends for Life — *Smith, Carol*
c Friends from the Other Side — *Anzaldua, Gloria*
The Friends of Freeland — *Leithauser, Brad*
Friends or Rivals? — *Armacost, Michael H*
y Friends to Die For — *Gibergu, June Sughrue*
c Friends to the Rescue (Illus. by Bob Dorsey) — *Orgel, Doris*
Friendshifts: The Power of Friendship and How It Shapes Our Lives — *Yager, Jan*
y The Friendship — *Taylor, Mildred D*
c Friendship Bracelets — *Torres, Laura*
Friendship East and West — *Leaman, Oliver*
c The Friendship Trip (Illus. by Wolfgang Slawski) — *Slawski, Wolfgang*
p Frieze
Frightening America's Elderly — *DiLorenzo, Thomas J*
c The Frightful Story of Harry Walfish (Illus. by Brian Floca) — *Floca, Brian*
c Frindle (Illus. by Brian Selznick) — *Clements, Andrew*
Fringe and Fortune — *Shrum, Wesley*
Fritz Lang: The Nature of the Beast — *McGilligan, Patrick*
Fritz London: A Scientific Biography — *Gavroglu, Kostas*
c The Frog — *Crewe, Sabrina*
The Frog — *Hawkes, John, 1925-*
Frog: A Novel — *Dixon, Stephen*
c Frog and Toad (Lobel). Audio Version — *Lobel, Arnold*
c Frog and Toad Together — *Lobel, Arnold*
Frog Math — *Kopp, Jaine*
c The Frog: Natural Acrobat (Illus. by Paul Starosta) — *Starosta, Paul*
c The Frog Princess of Pelham — *Conford, Ellen*
The Frog, the Prince, and the Problem of Men — *Dench, Geoff*
c The Frog Who Wanted to Be a Singer (Illus. by Cynthia Jabar) — *Goss, Linda*
c Froggy Goes to School (Illus. by Frank Remkiewicz) — *London, Jonathan*
c Froggy Learns to Swim (Illus. by Frank Remkiewicz) — *London, Jonathan*
Frogs — *Badger, David P*
c Frogs (Illus. by Mary Sundstrom) — *Lovett, Sarah, 1953-*
y Frogs in Pharaoh's Bed and Other Fun Devotions for Kids — *Pearson, Mary Rose*
c Frogs Jump (Illus. by Steven Kellogg) — *Brooks, Alan*
From a Biological Point of View — *Sober, Elliott*
From a Burning House. Audio Version — *Borger, Irene*
y From a Dark Sky — *Kelly, Orr*
From a Darkened Room — *Inman, Arthur Crew, 1845-*
From a Darkened Room — *Inman, Arthur Crew, 1895-*
From a Darkened Room — *Inman, Arthur, 1895-*
From a Native Son — *Churchill, Ward*
y From a Raw Deal to a New Deal? — *Trotter, Joe William*
From A to Z39.50 — *Michael, James J*
From Adjustment to Development in Africa — *Cornia, Giovanni Andrea*
cr From Afar to Zulu — *Haskins, James*
From Africa to America — *Piersen, William Dillon*
From Alpha to Omega — *Groton, Anne H*
From Anglo-Saxon to Early Middle English — *Godden, Malcolm*

c From Anne to Zach (Illus. by Michael Grejniec) — *Martin, Mary Jane*
From Arab Poet to Muslim Saint — *Homerin, Th. Emil*
From Art to Politics — *Edelman, Murray*
From Artisans to Paupers — *Green, David R, 1954-*
From Bad Policy to Chaos in Somalia — *Mubarak, Jamil Abdalla*
From Barbarians to New Men — *Dench, Emma*
From behind the Red Line — *Hartje, Tod*
From Belfast to Peking — *Porter, Francis Knowles*
From Belloc to Churchill — *Feske, Victor*
c From Birth to Death (Illus. by Graham Austin) — *Yates, Irene*
From Bishop to Witch — *Gentilcore, David*
From Bolshoi to Be'er Sheva, Scientists to Streetsweepers — *Galper, Allan S*
From Breviary to Liturgy of the Hours — *Campbell, Stanislaus*
From Brixton to Downing Street — *Junor, Penny*
c From Candle to Quartz Clock — *Ganeri, Anita*
From Cannibals to Radicals — *Celestin, Roger*
From Care to Action — *Holdgate, Martin W*
c From Caterpillar to Butterfly (Illus. by Bari Weissman) — *Heiligman, Deborah*
From Catholic to Protestant — *Rosman, Doreen*
From Centrally Planned to Market Economies. Vol. 1 — *Rana, Pradumna B*
From Chattel Slaves to Wage Slaves — *Turner, Mary*
From Chronicle to Canon — *Queen, Sarah A*
From Civil Rights to Black Liberation — *Sales, William W, Jr.*
From Coastal Wilderness to Fruited Plain — *Whitney, Gordon G*
From Colonization to Democracy — *Lester, Alan*
From Columbus to ConAgra — *Bonanno, Alessandro*
From Constantine to Julian — *Lieu, Samuel N C*
From Contamination to Defects, Faults, and Yield Loss — *Khare, Jitendra B*
From Court Jews to the Rothschilds — *Mann, Vivian B*
From Cover to Cover — *Horning, Kathleen T*
From Cuba with a Song — *Sarduy, Severo*
c From Cubit to Kilogram — *Ganeri, Anita*
From Da to Yes — *Richmond, Yale*
From Data to Knowledge — *Gaul, Wolfgang*
From Death to Life — *Chesnutt, Randall D*
From Dedekind to Godel — *Hintikka, Jaakko*
From Deluge to Discourse — *Porter, Deborah Lynn*
From Demagogue to Dixiecrat — *Feldman, Glenn*
From Downsizing to Recovery — *Knowdell, Richard L*
From Dusk Till Dawn — *Tarantino, Quentin*
From Empire to Anarchy — *Skak, Mette*
From Empire to International Commonwealth — *Lavin, Deborah*
y From Erdos to Kiev — *Honsberger, Ross*
From Eros to Gaia — *Dyson, Freeman*
From Eve to Esther — *Bronner, Leila Leah*
c From Far Away — *Munsch, Robert*
From Farmers to Pharaohs — *Bard, Kathryn A*
From Fatigued to Fantastic! — *Teitelbaum, Jacob*
From Faust to Strangelove — *Haynes, Roslynn D*
From Fields of Gold — *Ripley, Alexandra*
From Flintlock to Rifle — *Ross, Steven T*
From Freud's Consulting Room — *Hughes, Judith M*
From George Wallace to Newt Gingrich — *Carter, Dan T*
From Gesture to Language in Hearing and Deaf Children — *Volterra, Virginia*
From Globalism to Regionalism — *Cronin, Patrick M*
From Goldrush to Federation — *D'Aprano, Charles*
r From Grunts to Gigabytes — *Lacy, Dan*
c From Head to Toe (Illus. by Eric Carle) — *Carle, Eric*
From Here to Infinity. 3rd Ed. — *Stewart, Ian*
From High-Temperature Superconductivity to Microminiature Refrigeration — *William Little Symposium (1995: Stanford)*
From Hills and Hollers — *Strausberg, Stephen F*
From Hinton to Hamlet — *Herz, Sarah K*
From Historian to Dissident — *Whitmer, John*
From Hitler's Doorstep — *Dulles, Allen Welsh*
From Home and Abroad — *Burke, John J*
From Huntsville to Appomattox — *Coles, R T*
From Idolatry to Advertising — *Josephson, Susan G*
From Ignatius Loyola to John of the Cross — *O'Reilly, Terence*
From Image to Likeness — *Simpson, William A*
From India to the Planet Mars — *Flournoy, Theodore*
From Individual Behaviour to Population Ecology — *Sutherland, William J*

From Jacobite to Conservative — *Sack, James J*
From Jerusalem to the Edge of Heaven — *Elon, Ari*
From Kitchen to Market. 2nd Ed. — *Hall, Stephen F*
From Klein to Kristeva — *Doane, Janice*
From Leningrad to St. Petersburg — *Orttung, Robert W*
From Logic Programming to Prolog — *Apt, Krzysztof R*
From Lucy to Language — *Johanson, Donald C*
c From Lullaby to Lullaby (Illus. by Kathryn Brown) — *Geras, Adele*
From Madrid to Purgatory — *Eire, Carlos M N*
From Many, One — *Gabriele, Edward Francis*
From Maps to Metaphors — *Fisher, Robin*
From Marx to Mises — *Steele, David Ramsay*
From Massacres to Genocide — *Rotberg, Robert I*
From Media to Metaphor — *Atkins, Robert*
From Memories to Mental Illness — *Hall, William M*
From Memory to Written Record — *Clanchy, M T*
From Muslim Fortress to Christian Castle — *Glick, Thomas F*
From Mycenae to Constantinople — *Tomlinson, Richard*
From Myth to Modern Mind. Vol. 1 — *Schlagel, Richard H*
From Myth to Modern Mind. Vol. 2 — *Schlagel, Richard H*
From Nairobi to Beijing — *United Nations. Secretary-General*
From Nationalism to Secessionism — *Watson, Charles S*
From Nature — *Carper, Thomas*
r From Needmore to Prosperity — *Baker, Ronald L*
From Nineveh to New York — *Russell, John Malcolm*
From Noon to Starry Night — *Callow, Philip*
From Opportunity to Entitlement — *Davies, Gareth*
From Outlaw to Classic — *Golding, Alan*
From Parent to Child — *Behrman, Jere R*
From Pasture to Polis — *Langdon, Susan*
From Patriarch to Priest — *Kugler, Robert A*
From Peep Show to Palace — *Robinson, David, 1930-*
From Pentelicon to the Parthenon — *Korres, Manolis*
From People's War to People's Rule — *Lomperis, Timothy J*
From Personal Duties towards Personal Rights — *Monahan, Arthur P*
c From Pictures to Words (Illus. by Janet Stevens) — *Stevens, Janet*
From Plataea to Potidaea — *Badian, E*
From Political Architecture to Stephanus Byzantius — *Whitehead, David*
y From Polynomials to Sums of Squares — *Jackson, Terence*
From Post-Industrial to Post-Modern Society — *Kumar, Krishan*
y From Potter's Field — *Cornwell, Patricia Daniels*
From Promise to Performance — *Bauman, Robert P*
From Protest to Power — *Rae, Bob*
From Prussia with Love — *DeChancie, John*
From Renaissance Monarchy to Absolute Monarchy — *Major, J Russell*
From Renaissance to Revolution — *Benian, Silvia*
From Revolution to War — *Conge, Patrick J*
From Romance to Realism — *Cart, Michael*
From Russia to America with Love — *Govorchin, Gerald Gilbert*
From Sage to Artisan — *Wells, Stuart J*
From Salisbury to Major — *Evans, Brendan*
From Samarkhand to Sardis — *Sherwin-White, Susan*
From Scythia to Camelot — *Littleton, C Scott*
From Selma to Appomattox — *Laboda, Lawrence R*
From Slavery to Uncertain Freedom — *Finley, Randy*
From Slaving to Neoslavery — *Sundiata, I K*
c From Snowflakes to Sandcastles — *Owen, Annie*
From Soapbox to Soundbite — *Rosenbaum, Martin*
From State to Market? — *Schmidt, Vivien A*
From Stimulus to Science — *Quine, W V*
From Sundown to Sunup — *Rawick, George*
From Swing to Soul — *Barlow, William*
From Talking Chiefs to a Native Corporate Elite — *Mitchell, Marybelle*
From Test Tube to Patient. 2nd Ed. — *Cohn, Jeffrey P*
y From the Ashes — *Beckman, Pat Ramsey*
From the Ashes of Angels — *Collins, Andrew, 1957-*
From the Beast to the Blonde — *Warner, Marina*
From the Berlin Museum to the Berlin Wall — *Wetzel, David*
From the Earth to the Moon — *Verne, Jules*
From the Enemy's Point of View — *Castro, Eduardo Batalha Viveiros De*
From the Glittering World — *Morris, Irwin*

y From the Heart — *Miller, Lee*
From the Heart — *Roberts, Nora*
From the Heyday of the Superfluous Man to Chekhov — *Seeley, F F*
From the Holy Mountain — *Dalrymple, William*
From the Left Bank to the Mainstream — *McGuire, Patrick*
From the Margins of Hindu Marriage — *Harlin, Lindsey*
From the Margins to the Center — *Sullivan, Patricia Ann*
c From the Mixed-Up Files of Mrs. Basil E. Frankweiler — *Konigsburg, E L*
c From the Mouth of the Monster Eel (Illus. by Margo Vitarelli) — *Flood, Nancy Bohac*
y From the Notebooks of Melanin Sun — *Woodson, Jacqueline*
From the Other Side — *Gabaccia, Donna*
From the Other Side of the Century — *Messerli, Douglas*
From the Outside In — *Sparrow, Bartholomew H*
From the Perspective of the Self — *Brush, Craig B*
From the Polish Underground — *Bernhard, Michael*
From the Ruins of Colonialism — *Healy, Chris*
From the Russian Fugitive to the Ballad of Bulgarie — *Waddington, Patrick*
From the Shadows — *Gates, Robert M*
From the Shadows — *Gates, Robert Michael*
From the Top Down. Rev. Ed. — *Ellis, Susan J*
From the Tower of Babel to Parliament Hill — *Stiller, Brian C*
From the Uncollected Edmund Wilson — *Wilson, Edmund*
From the Wright Brothers to Top Gun — *Paris, Michael*
From This High Place — *Standley, Ken*
From Three Worlds — *Hogan, Ed*
From Time Immemorial — *Perry, Richard J*
y From Time to Time (Hecht). Audio Version — *Finney, Jack*
From Trial Court to United States Court — *Walkowski, Paul J*
From Tsar to Soviets — *Read, Christopher*
From Vagabond to Journalist — *Farnsworth, Robert M*
From Versailles to Maastricht — *Armstrong, J D, 1945-*
From Vietnam, Laos, and Cambodia — *Hein, Jeremy*
From Vietnam to El Salvador — *Spencer, David E*
From Virile Woman to WomanChrist — *Newman, Barbara*
From War to Nationalism — *Waldron, Arthur*
From Wimbledon to Waco — *Williams, Nigel*
From Xbase to Windows — *Booth, Joseph D*
From Yalta to the Iron Curtain — *Senarclens, Pierre De*
Fromental Halevy: His Life and Music 1799-1862 — *Jordan, Ruth*
r Frommer's Best Beach Vacations: The Mid-Atlantic from New York to Washington, D.C.
r Frommer's Canada. 9th Ed.
r Frommer's Montana and Wyoming
r Frommer's Nova Scotia, New Brunswick and Prince Edward Island
r Frommer's San Francisco by Night (Frommer's Guide). 1st Ed.
r Frommer's Wonderful Weekends from New York City — *Wood, Marilyn*
La Fronde — *Pernot, Michel*
Front Porch Tales — *Gulley, Philip*
c Front Runner — *Carroll, Jane*
Front Stage, Backstage — *Friedman, Raymond A*
Front Yard America — *Schroeder, Fred E H*
p Frontera
Frontier Development — *Adelman, Jeremy*
Frontier Doctor — *Horsman, Reginald*
Frontier Indiana — *Cayton, Andrew R L*
Frontier Settlement and Market Revolution — *Brooks, Charles E*
La Frontiere — *Supervielle, Silvia Baron*
La Frontiere Mexique-Etats-Unis — *Gachie-Pineda, Maryse*
Frontiers '96
Frontiers: Essays and Writings on Racism and Culture — *Philip, Marlene Nourbese*
Frontiers in Bioaction Lipids — *Vanderhoek, Jack Y*
Frontiers of Business Cycle Research — *Cooley, Thomas F*
Frontiers of Caribbean Literature in English — *Birbalsingh, Frank*
Frontiers of Cognitive Therapy — *Salkovskis, Paul M*

Frontiers of Complexity — *Coveney, Peter*
Frontiers of Developmental Psychopathology — *Lenzenweger, Mark F*
Frontiers of Heresy — *Monter, William*
Frontiers of Illusion — *Sarewitz, Daniel R*
Frontiers of Tax Reform — *Boskin, Michael J*
Frontiers of the Roman Empire — *Elton, Hugh*
The Frontiers of Women's Writing — *Georgi-Findlay, Brigitte*
Frontiers: Territory and State Formation in the Modern World — *Anderson, Malcolm*
Frontsoldaten: The German Soldier in World War II — *Fritz, Stephen G*
Frosts, Freezes and Fairs — *Currie, Ian*
Froth on the Daydream — *Vian, Boris*
Frozen and Refrigerated Doughs and Batters — *Kulp, Karel*
Frozen Desserts — *Liddell, Caroline*
A Frozen Woman — *Ernaux, Annie*
The Frugal Entrepreneur — *Lonier, Terri*
The Frugal Youth Cybrarian — *Ross, Calvin*
c Fruit (Illus. by Cecilia Fitzsimmons) — *Fitzsimmons, Cecilia*
c Fruit and Vegetable Man — *Schotter, Roni*
The Fruit of Devotion — *Falkenburg, Reindert Leonard*
Fruit of the Vine — *Durnbaugh, Donald F*
Fruitful: A Real Mother in the Modern World — *Roiphe, Anne*
Fruitful Encounters — *Brush, Stephen G*
Fruitful Sites — *Clunas, Craig*
y Fruiting Bodies and Other Fungi — *Lumley, Brian*
c Fruits: A Caribbean Counting Poem (Illus. by David Axtell) — *Bloom, Valerie*
Frustula Paleographica — *Pratesi, Alessandro*
r Fuchsias: The Complete Guide — *Goulding, Edwin*
Fuego De Marzo — *Mendicutti, Eduardo*
The Fuehrer Bunker — *Snodgrass, W D*
Fuel Cells and Their Applications — *Kordesch, Karl*
Fuentes: Conversacion Y Gramatica — *Rusch, Debbie*
Fuentes: Lectura Y Redaccion — *Tuten, Donald N*
r Fuentes Manuscritas Para La Historia De Iberoamerica — *Hilton, Sylvia L*
Die Fuggerkapelle Bei St. Anna In Augsburg — *Bushart, Bruno*
Fugitive Cultures — *Giroux, Henry A*
Fugitive from the Cubicle Police — *Adams, Scott*
Fugitive Images — *Petro, Patrice*
Fugitive Pieces — *Michaels, Anne*
Fugue — *Moore, Olive*
Fulbright: A Biography — *Woods, Randall Bennett*
Full Circle — *Coleman, Sheelagh*
Full Circle — *Sepulveda, Luis*
Full Circle — *Sikorski, Radek*
Full Court — *Trudell, Dennis*
Full Court Press — *Kessler, Lauren*
Full-Cycle Youth Evangelization — *Brennan, Patrick*
Full Disclosure — *Neil, Andrew*
Full Employment — *Grieve Smith, John*
Full Employment and Growth — *Tobin, James, 1918-*
Full Employment for Europe — *Coates, Ken*
Full Employment Regained? — *Meade, J E, 1907-*
Full Face — *Blatchford, Claire*
Full House — *Gould, Stephen Jay*
c Full Moon Stories (Illus. by Eagle Walking Turtle) — *Eagle Walking Turtle*
Full Personal Service — *Spencer, Charles*
y Full Steam Ahead — *Blumberg, Rhoda*
Full Sun — *Norris, Ken*
Fullalove — *Burn, Gordon*
Fumigants: Environmental Fate, Exposure, and Analysis — *Seiber, James N*
c Fun Factory (Illus. by Lyndsay Milne) — *Milne, Lyndsay*
c Fun for Ten Fingers (Illus. by Caroline Crossland) — *Hall, Pauline*
Fun Puppet Skits for Schools and Libraries — *Schroeder, Joanne F*
c Fun to Make and Do — *Tofts, Hannah*
c Fun with Materials (Illus. by Mike Gordon) — *Gordon, Maria*
c Fun with Stained Glass — *Shepard, Mary B*
c Fun with the Classics: A Christmas Carol (Porter). Audio Version — *Dickens, Charles*
Fun without Vulgarity — *Haill, Catherine*
Function and Technology of Anasazi Ceramics from Black Mesa, Arizona — *Smith, Marion E, Jr.*
The Function of Suffering in Philippians — *Bloomquist, L Gregory*
Functional Analysis — *Dierolf, Susanne*
Functional Analysis on the Eve of the 21st Century. Vol. 1 — *Gindikin, Simon*

Functional Analytic Methods for Partial Differential Equations — *Tanabe, Hiroki*
Functional Psychiatric Disorders of the Elderly — *Chiu, Edmond*
A Functional Theory of Cognition — *Anderson, Norman H*
Functions of the Fantastic — *Sanders, Joe*
Functions of Two Variables — *Dineen, Sean*
r Fund Raiser's Guide to Religious Philanthropy 1996
Fund Raising Realities Every Board Member Must Face — *Lansdowne, David*
La Fundacion Del Estado Mexicano 1821-1855 — *Vazquez, Josefina Zoraida*
Fundadores, Primeros Moradores, Y Familias Coloniales De Merida 1558-1810. Vol. 3 — *Picon-Parra, Roberto*
Fundamental and Applied Aspects of Animal Cell Cultivation — *Barford, J P*
Fundamental Astronomy. 2nd Ed. — *Karttunen, Hannu*
y Fundamental Basketball (Illus. by David Kyle) — *Klinzing, Jim*
The Fundamental Concepts of Metaphysics — *Heidegger, Martin*
Fundamental Determinants of Exchange Rates — *Stein, Jerome L*
c Fundamental Hockey (Illus. by Andy King) — *Foley, Mike*
Fundamental Method for Mallets. Bk. 1 — *Peters, Mitchell*
c Fundamental Mountain Biking (Illus. by Andy King) — *King, Andy*
Fundamental Neuroscience — *Haines, Duane E*
Fundamental Principles of Molecular Modeling — *Gans, Werner*
y Fundamental Snowboarding (Illus. by Jimmy Clarke) — *Lurie, Jon*
y Fundamental Soccer — *Coleman, Lori*
Fundamental Solutions for Differential Operators and Applications — *Kythe, Prem K*
Fundamental Tax Reform and Border Tax Adjustments — *Hufbauer, Gary Clyde*
Fundamental Toxicology for Chemists — *Duffus, John H*
The Fundamental Wisdom of the Middle Way — *Nagarjuna*
Fundamentalism, Mythos, and World Religions — *Nielsen, Niels C*
Fundamentalisms and Society — *Marty, Martin E*
Fundamentalisms and the State — *Marty, Martin E*
Fundamentalisms Comprehended — *Marty, Martin E*
Fundamentalisms Observed — *Marty, Martin E*
Fundamentals and Applications of Microalloying Forging Steels — *Symposium of Fundamentals and Applications of Microalloying Forging Steels (1996: Golden, Colorado)*
Fundamentals of Adsorption — *International Conference on Fundamentals of Adsorption (5th: 1995: Pacific Grove, CA)*
r Fundamentals of Aerospace Medicine. 2nd Ed. — *DeHart, Roy L*
Fundamentals of Applied Electromagnetics — *Ulaby, Fawwaz T*
Fundamentals of Artificial Neural Networks — *Hassoun, Mohamad H*
Fundamentals of Atmospheric Physics — *Salby, Murry L*
Fundamentals of Bidirectional Transmission over a Single Optical Fibre — *Deventer, M Oskar Van*
Fundamentals of Building Energy Dynamics — *Hunn, Bruce D*
Fundamentals of Chemistry. 2nd Ed. — *Burns, Ralph A*
Fundamentals of Clinical Practice — *Mengel, Mark B*
Fundamentals of Cognitive-Behavior Therapy — *Borcherdt, Bill*
Fundamentals of Complementary and Alternative Medicine — *Micozzi, Marc S*
Fundamentals of Digital Optics — *Yaroslavsky, Leonid*
Fundamentals of Electronic Image Processing — *Weeks, Arthur R*
Fundamentals of Entomology. 4th Ed. — *Elzinga, Richard J*
Fundamentals of Food Biotechnology — *Lee, B H*
Fundamentals of Force Planning. Vol. 2 — *Lloyd, Richmond M*
Fundamentals of Geology. 3rd Ed. — *Montgomery, Carla W*
Fundamentals of Human Relations — *Wray, Ralph D*
Fundamentals of Hydraulic Dredging. 2nd Ed. — *Turner, Thomas M*

Fundamentals of Hydraulic Engineering Systems. 3rd Ed. — *Hwang, Ned H C*

Fundamentals of Laser Diode Amplifiers — *Ghafouri-Shiraz, H*

Fundamentals of Manufacturing for Engineers — *Waters, T F*

Fundamentals of Marital Therapy — *Crane, D Russell*

Fundamentals of Metal Forming — *Wagoner, Robert H*

r**Fundamentals of Microwave Transmission Lines** — *Freeman, Jon C*

Fundamentals of Modern Manufacturing — *Grover, Mikell P*

The Fundamentals of Natural Gas Cooling — *Sweetser, Richard S*

Fundamentals of Number Theory — *LeVeque, William J*

Fundamentals of Numerical Computing — *Shampine, Lawrence F*

Fundamentals of Operative Dentistry — *Schwartz, Richard S*

Fundamentals of Organic Chemistry. 5th Ed. — *Solomons, T W Graham*

Fundamentals of Orthopedic Radiology — *McKinnis, Lynn N*

Fundamentals of Periodontics — *Wilson, Thomas G*

Fundamentals of Physics. 5th Ed. — *Halliday, David*

Fundamentals of Private Pensions. 7th Ed. — *McGill, Dan M*

Fundamentals of Soil Ecology — *Coleman, David C*

Fundamentals of Steelmaking — *Turkdogan, E T*

Fundamentals of Structural Mechanics — *Hjelmstad, Keith D*

r**Funding for United States Study. 2nd Ed.** — *O'Sullivan, Marie*

r**Funding Sources for Community and Economic Development 1996**

Funding the Modern American State 1941-1995 — *Brownlee, W Elliot*

The FundLine Advisor. 1997 Ed.

The Funeral Effigies of Westminster Abbey — *Harvey, Anthony*

Funerals for Horses — *Hyde, Catherine Ryan*

Fungal Disease — *Jacobs, Paul H*

Fungal Physiology. 2nd Ed. — *Griffin, David H*

r**Fungi on Rhododendron** — *Farr, David F*

yr**Funk and Wagnalls New Encyclopedia 1996. Vols. 1-29**

Funk Lore — *Baraka, Imamu Amiri*

Die Funktion Der Heilsarmeegeistlichen In Den Dramen Brechts — *Berger-Prossdorf, Tamara*

c**Funky Chickens (Illus. by Point)** — *Zephaniah, Benjamin*

c**Funny Bones and Other Body Parts (Illus. by Steve Fricker)** — *Ganeri, Anita*

Funny Boy — *Selvadurai, Shyam*

c**Funny Faces** — *Tracqui, Valerie*

c**Funny Farm (Illus. by Tom Arma)** — *Arma, Tom*

A Funny Time to Be Gay — *Karvoski, Ed, Jr.*

c**Funny Walks. Book and Audio Version** — *Hindley, Judy*

Funny, You Don't Look Like One — *Taylor, Drew Hayden*

Fur- Und Wider-Spruche — *Roche, Jorg*

La Furat De Fete Mari — *Baros, Aurel Maria*

Furious Cooking — *Seaton, Maureen*

Furious Interiors — *Wintle, Justin*

A Furious Place — *Hardie, Kerry*

y**Furman v. Georgia** — *Henson, Burt*

The Furniture Industry in China and Hong Kong — *Aktrin Research Institute*

c**The Furry Bedtime Book (Illus. by David McPhail)** — *Lundell, Margo*

Furst Und Hof In Osterreich Von Den Habsburgischen Teilungsvertragen Bis Zur Schlacht Von Mohacs 1521/22 Bis 1526 — *Rill, Gerhard*

Further and Higher Education Partnerships — *Abramson, Michael*

Further Lane — *Brady, James*

Furthering My Education — *Corbett, William*

y**A Fury Scorned** — *Sargent, Pamela*

Fury's Children — *Shubin, Seymour*

Fusewire — *Padel, Ruth*

El Futbol A Sol Y Sombra — *Galeano, Eduardo*

The Future Eaters — *Flannery, Tim*

y**Future Fright** — *Wulffson, Don L*

Future Global Capital Shortages — *Organisation for Economic Co-Operation and Development*

Future Imperfect — *Segal, Howard P*

Future Interventions with Battered Women and Their Families — *Edleson, Jeffrey L*

The Future Is Ours — *May, Graham H*

Future Legal Restraints on Arms Proliferation — *Dahlitz, Julie*

Future Libraries — *Bloch, R Howard*

Future Libraries — *Crawford, Walt*

Future Libraries, Future Catalogues — *Oddy, Pat*

y**Future Net** — *Greenberg, Martin Harry*

Future Nuclear Weapons Requirements — *United States. Congress. House. Committee on Armed Services. Defense Policy Panel*

The Future of Academic Freedom — *Menand, Louis*

The Future of Capitalism — *Thurow, Lester C*

The Future of Central Banking — *Capie, Forrest*

The Future of Copyright in a Digital Environment — *Hugenholz, D Bernt*

The Future of Employment Relations — *Beaumont, P B*

The Future of German Literature — *Bullivant, Keith*

The Future of Germanistik in the USA — *McCarthy, John A*

The Future of Governing — *Peters, B Guy*

The Future of Information Services — *Steel, Virginia*

The Future of Law — *Susskind, Richard*

The Future of Leadership — *White, Randall P*

The Future of Long-Term Care — *Binstock, Robert H*

The Future of NATO — *United States. Congress. Senate. Committee on Foreign Relations. Subcommittee on European Affairs*

The Future of Naval Operations in Alameda County

The Future of Our Land — *Fresco, Louise O*

The Future of Public Undergraduate Education in California — *Shires, Michael A*

The Future of Resource Sharing — *Baker, Shirley K*

The Future of Southern Letters — *Humphries, Jefferson*

The Future of the Canadian Broadcasting Corporation in the Multi-Channel Universe

The Future of the Family (Bradshaw). Audio Version — *Bradshaw, John*

The Future of the Humanities — *Kaufmann, Walter*

The Future of the Middle Ages — *Paden, William D*

The Future of the Pacific Rim — *Bundy, Barbara K*

The Future of the Race — *Gates, Henry Louis*

The Future of the Space Industry — *Handberg, Roger*

The Future of the U.S.-EU-Japan Triad — *Yochelson, John*

The Future of Tropical Savannas — *Ash, Andrew*

The Future of U.S.-Israel Strategic Cooperation — *Feldman, Shai*

The Future of War — *Friedman, George*

The Future of Warfare — *Alexander, Bevin*

The Future of Whole Language — *Church, Susan M*

The Future Population of the World — *Lutz, Wolfgang*

Future Training — *Pepitone, James S*

Future Visions

Futurecare: New Directions in Planning Health and Care Environments — *Valins, Martin S*

FutureNatural: Nature, Science, Culture — *Robertson, George*

Fuzziness in Database Management Systems — *Bosc, Patrick*

Fuzzy and Evidence Reasoning — *Lee, E Stanley*

Fuzzy Expert Systems Tools — *Schneider, Moti*

Fuzzy Logic — *Baldwin, J F*

Fuzzy Logic — *Patyra, M J*

Fuzzy Logic and Its Applications to Engineering, Information Sciences, and Intelligent Systems — *Bien, Z*

Fuzzy Logic for Business and Industry — *Cox, Earl D*

Fuzzy Modelling — *Pedrycz, Witold*

Fuzzy Set Theory — *Lowen, R*

Fuzzy Set Theory. 3rd Ed. — *Zimmermann, H J*

Fuzzy Sets, Fuzzy Logic, Fuzzy Methods with Applications — *Bandemer, Hans*

c**Fuzzy the Duckling** — *Buck, Gisela*

c**Fuzzy Yellow Ducklings** — *Van Fleet, Matthew*

G

r G.A. Henty 1832-1902 — *Newbolt, Peter*
G: A Novel — *Berger, John*
p G.F.W.: Golf for Women
G.K. Derman--Pervyi Direktor Moskovskogo Instituta — *Laynter, A I*
G.L.S. Shackle: The Dissenting Economist's Economist — *Ford, J L*
G.W.F. Hegel: The Philosophical System — *Kainz, Howard P*
GABA: Receptors, Transporters, and Metabolism — *Tanaka, C*
Gabriel Marcel's Theory of Religious Experience — *Cain, Seymour*
The Gadsden Times 1867-1871
Gaetano Gandolfi — *Maino, Donatello Biagi*
Gaff Topsails — *Kavanagh, Patrick*
r Gage Canadian Dictionary
c A Gaggle of Geese — *Browne, Philippa-Alys*
Gahan Wilson's The Ultimate Haunted House — *Wilson, Gahan*
Gahmurets Orientfahrt — *Noltze, Holger*
c Gail Devers — *Gutman, Bill*
The Gains from Trade and the Gains from Aid — *Kemp, Murray C*
Gait Analysis. 2nd Ed. — *Whittle, Michael V*
Gaite Parisienne — *Duteurtre, Benoit*
y The Galactic Gourmet — *White, James, 1928-*
Galatea 2.2 — *Powers, Richard, 1957-*
y Galax-Arena — *Rubinstein, Gillian*
Galaxies and Cosmology — *Combes, Francoise*
y Galaxy's Edge — *Hill, Douglas*
r Gale Directory of Publications and Broadcast Media 1990-. Book and Electronic Media Version
yr Gale Encyclopedia of Multicultural America. Vols. 1-2 — *Galens, Judy*
yr The Gale Encyclopedia of Psychology — *Gall, Susan*
yr The Gale Encyclopedia of Science. Vols. 1-6 — *Travers, Bridget*
Galen and Chrysippus on the Soul — *Tieleman, Teun*
yr Gale's Career Guidance System. Electronic Media Version
r Gale's Ready Reference Shelf. Electronic Media Version
Galilean Jewishness of Jesus — *Lee, Bernard J*
Galilee: History, Politics, People — *Horsley, Richard A*
The Galilee of Jesus — *Hennessy, Anne*
Galilei Vermisst Dantes Holle Und Bleibt An Den Massen Hangen — *Grunbein, Durs*
Galileo and the Church — *Feldhay, Rivka*
c Galileo: Astronomer and Physicist — *Hightower, Paul*
Galileo, Courtier — *Biagioli, Mario*
Galileo: Decisive Innovator — *Sharratt, Michael*
The Galitzin Quartets of Beethoven, Opp. 127, 132, 130 — *Chua, Daniel K L*
Gall/Stones — *Smith, Laurie*
La Galleria Delle Carte Geografiche In Vaticano — *Gambi, Lucio*
Die Galleria Delle Carte Geografiche In Vatikan — *Schutte, Margret*
A Gallery of Reflections — *Harries, Richard*
Gallery of Teddy Bears — *Hartman, Linda*
Gallium Nitride and Related Materials — *Ponce, F A*
y Gallows Hill — *Duncan, Lois*
y The Gallows Murders — *Clynes, Michael*
The Galton Case — *Macdonald, Ross*
The Gambler — *Dostoyevsky, Fyodor*
Gambler Way — *Gabriel, Kathryn*
Game and Economic Theory — *Hart, Sergiu*
c A Game of Catch (Illus. by Barry Moser) — *Wilbur, Richard*
The Game of Death in Ancient Rome — *Plass, Paul*

The Game of Forgetting — *Berrada, Mohamed*
The Game of Their Lives — *Douglas, Geoffrey*
y A Game of Thrones — *Martin, George R R*
The Game That Was — *Cahan, Richard*
Game Theory. 3rd Ed. — *Owen, Guillermo*
Game Theory and Strategy — *Straffin, Philip D*
Game without End — *Malamud Goti, Jaime E*
c Games — *Doney, Meryl*
Games for Infants — *Hall, Jim, 1947-*
c Games from Long Ago (Illus. by Barbara Bedell) — *Kalman, Bobbie*
The Games of Poetics — *Burke, Ruth*
Games Real Estate Agents Play — *Iversen, Theodore*
Gamma-Linolenic Acid — *International Symposium of GLA (1st: 1995: San Antonio, Tex.)*
Gamma Titanium Aluminides
En Gammal Karlek — *Jersild, P C*
y Gandhi: Father of a Nation — *Clement, Catherine*
y Gandhi, Great Soul — *Severance, John B*
Gandhi's Truth — *Erikson, Erik H*
y Gang Free — *Wiener, Valerie*
c Ganging Up — *Gibbons, Alan*
y Gangs — *Sonder, Ben*
y Gangs — *Stewart, Gail B*
yr Gangs: A Reference Handbook — *Kinnear, Karen L*
c Gangs and Drugs — *Williams, Stanley*
c Gangs and Self-Esteem — *Williams, Stanley*
c Gangs and the Abuse of Power — *Williams, Stanley*
c Gangs and Violence — *Williams, Stanley*
c Gangs and Wanting to Belong — *Williams, Stanley*
c Gangs and Weapons — *Williams, Stanley*
c Gangs and Your Friends — *Williams, Stanley*
c Gangs and Your Neighborhood — *Williams, Stanley*
Gangs in America. 2nd Ed. — *Huff, C Ronald*
Gangsta: Merchandizing the Rhymes of Violence — *Ro, Ronin*
r Gangster Films — *Stephens, Michael L*
The Gangster of Love — *Hagedorn, Jessica*
Gangsters — *Zimroth, Evan*
Gangsters: Fifty Years of Madness, Drugs, and Death on the Streets of America — *Yablonsky, Lewis*
Gant Ar Mareou-Bloaz — *Duval, Anjela*
y The Ganymede Club — *Sheffield, Charles*
Gao Bie Ge Ming — *Li, Tse-Hou*
y The Gap into Ruin — *Donaldson, Stephen R*
y The Gap Year Guidebook 1997/98
Gaps in Nature — *Spolsky, Ellen*
y Gaps in Stone Walls — *Neufeld, John*
Garbo: A Biography — *Paris, Barry*
Garcilaso De La Vega and the Italian Renaissance — *Heiple, Daniel L*
c Garden (Snapshot)
y The Garden — *Matas, Carol*
y The Garden — *Scott, Melissa*
A Garden Apart — *Haswell, Susan Olsen*
Garden Birds of America — *Harrison, George H*
Garden Butterflies of America — *Mikula, Rick*
The Garden Club and the Kumquat Campaign — *Kennedy, Des*
Garden Cuisine — *Wenner, Paul*
Garden Design — *Williams, Robin*
A Garden Folly — *Hern, Candice*
The Garden of Earthly Intimacies — *Walsh, Meeka*
The Garden of Eating — *Iggers, Jeremy*
c The Garden of Happiness (Illus. by Barbara Lambase) — *Tamar, Erika*
The Garden of Janus — *Rojas, Carlos*
Garden of Scandal — *Blake, Jennifer*
The Garden of the Peacocks — *Weller, Anthony*
The Garden Pack — *Phillips, Sue*

Garden Pavilions and the 18th Century French Court — *DeLorme, Eleanor*
The Garden Plot — *Borthwick, J S*
Garden State — *Moody, Rick*
The Garden Thrives — *Major, Clarence*
r Garden Trees (Eyewitness Handbooks)
The Garden Trellis — *Cook, Ferris*
The Garden Tutor — *Junkin, Angus*
Garden Voices — *Von Baeyer, Edwinna*
The Gardener's Book of Color — *Lawson, Andrew*
The Gardener's Book of Colour — *Lawson, Andrew*
The Gardener's Guide to Growing Hostas — *Grenfell, Diana*
The Gardener's Guide to Growing Ivies — *Rose, Peter Q*
The Gardener's Guide to Perennials — *Rice, Graham*
The Gardener's Son — *McCarthy, Cormac*
Gardener's World — *Fisher, Sue*
Gardening at Sissinghurst — *Lord, Tony*
Gardening down a Rabbit Hole — *Saxton, Josephine*
Gardening for Pleasure — *Buchan, Ursula*
Gardening from the Ground Up — *Stuckey, Maggie*
Gardening Hints and Tips — *Greenwood, Pippa*
Gardening in Iowa and Surrounding Areas — *Fowler, Veronica Lorson*
Gardening with Foliage Plants — *Clarke, Ethne*
Gardening with Old Roses — *Scarman, John*
c Gardening with Sara and Tommy — *Stam, Dagmar*
Gardens Are for People. 3rd Ed. — *Church, Thomas D*
Gardens in Babylon — *Steussy, Marti J*
The Gardens of Colonial Williamsburg — *Brinkley, M Kent*
The Gardens of Ellen Biddle Shipman — *Tankard, Judith B*
The Gardens of Light — *Maalouf, Amin*
Gardens of Revelation — *Beardsley, John*
The Gardens of Sallust and Other Writings — *Hocquard, Emmanuel*
Gardens of the National Trust — *Lacey, Stephen*
Gardens of the Sun — *Nottle, Trevor*
The Gardens of Versailles — *Andre, Pierre*
Les Gardiens Du Temple — *Kane, Cheikh Hamidou*
r Gardner Read: A Bio-Bibliography — *Dodd, Mary Ann*
Gardner's Art through the Ages. 10th Ed. — *Gardner, Helen*
Gargantua — *Rabelais, Francois*
Gargantua: Manufactured Mass Culture — *Stallabrass, Julian*
Gargarin and I — *Blanchard, Stephen*
The Garlic Ballads — *Mo, Yen*
Garlic: Nature's Super Healer — *Wilen, Joan*
Garrison Keillor — *Scholl, Peter A*
The Garter Snakes — *Rossman, Douglas Athon*
y Garth and the Mermaid — *Smucker, Barbara Claassen*
Garth Brooks: The Road out of Santa Fe — *O'Meilia, Matt*
Garth Turner's 1997 RRSP Guide
Gary Hill — *Bruce, Chris*
Gary in Your Pocket — *Fisher, Gary*
Gas and Oil in Northeast Asia — *Paik, Keun-Wook*
Gas Chromatography and Mass Spectrometry — *Kitson, Fulton G*
Gas Contracting — *Seminar on Gas Contracting Principles and Practices (1995: Sinaia, Romania)*
I Gas Di Mussolini — *Del Boca, Angelo*
Gas Interactions in Nonferrous Metals Processing — *Saha, Debabrata*
Gas Pipelines and the Emergence of America's Regulatory State — *Castaneda, Christopher J*
Gas Station — *Torra, Joseph*

The Gas Station in America — *Jakle, John A*
Gasoline Treasures — *Bruner, Mike*
c Gasp! (Illus. by Terry Denton) — *Denton, Terry*
Gasp! A Novel of Revenge — *Freudberg, Frank*
Gaspara Stampa: Selected Poems — *Stampa, Gaspara*
Gassendi's Ethics — *Sarasohn, Lisa T*
Gaston De Latour: The Revised Text — *Pater, Walter*
Gastonia 1929 — *Salmond, John A*
r Gastrointestinal Diseases and Disorders Sourcebook
    — *Ross, Linda M*
Gastrointestinal, Hepatobiliary, and Nutritional
    Physiology — *Chang, Eugene B*
The Gates — *Wachtel, Chuck*
The Gates of November — *Potok, Chaim*
c The Gates of the Wind (Illus. by Janet Stevens)
    — *Lasky, Kathryn*
y The Gates of Twilight — *Volsky, Paula*
y Gateway — *Robinson, Lee*
Gateway to the Promised Land — *Maffi, Mario*
Gather the Faces — *Gilroy, Beryl*
Gathered under Apostles — *Flegg, Columba Graham*
y A Gathering of Heroes — *Alan-Williams, Gregory*
A Gathering of Old Men — *Gaines, Ernest J*
y A Gathering of Old Men. Audio Version — *Gaines,
    Ernest J*
A Gathering of Saints — *Hyde, Christopher*
y A Gathering of Saints (Page). Audio Version — *Hyde,
    Christopher*
The Gathering of the Aspects — *Ratte, Paul-Michel*
y The Gathering Storm — *Davis, W E*
Gathering Storm — *Dees, Morris*
y The Gathering Storm — *Sisson, Mary Barr*
c Gathering the Sun (Illus. by Simon Silva) — *Ada,
    Alma Flor*
Gatherings and Celebrations — *Wolf, Burt*
c Gator or Croc? — *Fowler, Allan*
Gaudier-Brzeska: Life and Art — *Silber, Evelyn*
Gauguin's Intimate Journals — *Gauguin, Paul*
Gauguin's Skirt — *Eisenman, Stephen*
Gawain and Lady Green — *Crompton, Anne Eliot*
The Gay Agenda — *Nichols, Jack*
r The Gay Almanac — *National Museum and Archive of
    Lesbian and Gay History (U.S.)*
yr Gay and Lesbian Biography — *Tyrkus, Michael J*
r The Gay and Lesbian Handbook to New York City
    — *Laermer, Richard*
r The Gay and Lesbian Literary Heritage — *Summers,
    Claude J*
Gay and Lesbian Mental Health — *Alexander,
    Christopher J*
yr The Gay and Lesbian Movement — *Ridinger, Robert B
    Marks*
r Gay and Lesbian Online — *Dawson, Jeff*
Gay and Lesbian Perspectives III — *Wotherspoon,
    Garry*
Gay and Lesbian Politics — *Blasius, Mark*
Gay and Lesbian Rights — *Peddicord, Richard*
Gay and Lesbian Students — *Besner, Hilda F*
y Gay and Lesbian Youth — *Stewart, Gail B*
Gay by the Bay — *Stryker, Susan*
y Gay Men, Lesbians, and the Law — *Robson, Ruthann*
Gay New York — *Chauncey, George*
y Gay Rights — *Galas, Judith C*
y Gay Rights — *Roleff, Tamara L*
Gay Rights, Military Wrongs — *Rimmerman, Craig A*
A Gay Synagogue in New York — *Shokeid, Moshe*
r Gay USA — *Hobica, George*
Gays, Lesbians, and Consumer Behavior — *Wardlow,
    Daniel L*
Gaza: Legacy of Occupation--A Photographer's
    Journey — *Doughty, Dick*
The Gaza Strip — *Roy, Sara M*
Gazavat. Tsarskii Gnev — *Charskaia, Lidiia*
r The Gazetteer of Scotland — *Wilson, John*
y GCSE Modern World History — *Walsh, Ben*
GCSE Modern World History Teacher's Resource
    Book — *Walsh, Ben*
Gecko Tails — *Livingston, Carol*
Gedigte 1989-1995 — *Krog, Antjie*
Gegen Hitler Und Fur Die Republik — *Pyta, Wolfram*
Die Gegenwart Als Geschichte — *Wehler, Hans-Ulrich*
Gehalim Ba-Peh — *Dor, Moshe*
Geheime Staatspolizei — *Heuer, Hans-Joachim*
Gehennical Fire — *Newman, William R*
Gel Electrophoresis — *Martin, Robin*
The Gelfand Mathematical Seminars 1993-1995
    — *Gelfand, I M*
Gelignite Jack — *Davies, Paul*

Gem and Lapidary Materials — *Zeitner, June Culp*
Gemba Kaizen — *Imai, Masaaki*
Gemeindeburgetum Und Liberalismus In Baden
    1800-1850 — *Nolte, Paul*
y Gemini Game — *Scott, Michael*
Geminio Deshabitado — *Castillo, Amelia Del*
y Gems of Hubble — *Mitton, Jacqueline*
Gen X TV — *Owen, Robert*
Gender and Archaeology — *Wright, Rita P*
Gender and Assimilation in Modern Jewish History
    — *Hyman, Paula E*
Gender and Authority in Sixteenth-Century England
    — *Shephard, Amanda*
Gender and Career in Science and Engineering
    — *Evetts, Julia*
Gender and Class in Modern Europe — *Frader, Laura
    L*
Gender and Colonialism — *Foley, Timothy P*
Gender and Conversational Interaction — *Tannen,
    Deborah*
Gender and Crime — *Dobash, R Emerson*
Gender and Development — *Scott, Catherine V*
Gender and Development in the Arab World
    — *Khoury, Nabil F*
Gender and Discourse — *Tannen, Deborah*
Gender and Discourse in Victorian Literature and Art
    — *Harrison, Anthony H*
Gender and Economics — *Humphries, Jane*
Gender and Genre — *Yates, Norris*
Gender and Genre in Novels without End — *Felber,
    Lynette*
Gender and Genre in the Folklore of Middle India
    — *Flueckiger, Joyce Burkhalter*
Gender and Jim Crow — *Gilmore, Glenda Elizabeth*
Gender and National Identity — *Moghadam, Valentine
    M*
Gender and Psychopathology — *Seeman, Mary V*
Gender and Racial Inequality at Work
    — *Tomaskovic-Devey, Donald*
Gender and Romance in Chaucer's Canterbury Tales
    — *Crane, Susan*
Gender and Salvation — *Jaini, Padmanabh S*
Gender and Slum Culture in Urban Asia — *Thorbeck,
    Susanne*
Gender and the Gothic in the Fiction of Edith
    Wharton — *Fedorko, Kathy A*
Gender and the Israeli-Palestinian Conflict
    — *Sharoni, Simona*
Gender and the Politics of Social Reform in France
    1870-1914 — *Accampo, Elinor A*
Gender and War — *Damousi, Joy*
Gender, Art and Death — *Todd, Janet M, 1942-*
Gender Articulated — *Hall, Kira*
Gender Basics — *Minas, Anne*
Gender Blending — *Bullough, Bonnie*
Gender, Class, and Shelter — *Cromley, Elizabeth C*
Gender, Class, and the Professionalization of Russian
    City Teachers 1860-1914 — *Ruane, Christine*
Gender, Culture and Organizational Change — *Itzin,
    Catherine*
Gender Differences in Science Careers — *Sonnert,
    Gerhard*
Gender Dynamics in Congressional Elections — *Fox,
    Richard Logan*
Gender Equality and American Jews — *Hartman,
    Moshe*
Gender, Equality, and Welfare States — *Sainsbury,
    Diane*
Gender, Ethnicity, and Social Change on the Upper
    Slave Coast — *Greene, Sandra E*
Gender, Ethnicity, and the State — *Diaz-Cotto,
    Juanita*
Gender, Family, and Society — *Elliot, Faith Robertson*
y The Gender Gap in Schools — *Hanmer, Trudy J*
Gender, Genre, and the Romantic Poets — *Cox, Philip*
Gender, Identity, and Self-Esteem — *Anderson,
    Deborah Y*
Gender Identity Disorder and Psychosexual Problems
    in Children and Adolescents — *Zucker, Kenneth J*
Gender in Mystical and Occult Thought — *Gibbons, B
    J*
Gender in Play on the Shakespearean Stage
    — *Shapiro, Michael*
Gender in Popular Culture — *Rollins, Susan W*
Gender in Practice — *Hagan, John*
Gender in Third World Politics — *Waylen, Georgina*
Gender Inequality in the Labour Market — *Siltanen,
    Janet*
Gender Is Not a Synonym for Women — *Carver,
    Terrell*
y Gender Issues — *Stearman, Kaye*

Gender Issues in World Bank Lending — *Murphy,
    Josette L*
Gender, Lineage, and Ethnicity in Southern Africa
    — *Davison, Jean*
Gender Matters in Schools — *Darling, John*
The Gender of Modernity — *Felski, Rita*
Gender on the Market — *Kapchan, Deborah A*
The Gender Perspective — *Jeleff, Sophia*
Gender, Politics and Citizenship in the 1990s
    — *Sullivan, Barbara*
Gender Politics in Sudan — *Hale, Sondra*
Gender Power, Leadership, and Governance
    — *Duerst-Lahti, Georgia*
The Gender Question in Education — *Diller, Ann*
Gender Rhetorics — *Trexler, Richard C*
Gender Roles and Sexuality in Victorian Literature
    — *Parker, Christopher*
Gender Segregation and Social Change — *Scott,
    Alison MacEwen*
Gender Segregation in the Barbadian Labour Market
    1946 and 1980 — *Lynch, Roslyn*
Gender, Sex and Subordination in England 1500-1800
    — *Fletcher, Anthony*
Gender Shock — *Burke, Phyllis*
The Gender-Technology Relation — *Grint, Keith*
Gender Tracking in University Programs — *Gilbert,
    Sid*
Gender Trials — *Pierce, Jennifer L*
Gender, Work and Population in Sub-Saharan Africa
    — *Adepoju, Aderanti*
Gendered Fields — *Sachs, Carolyn E*
Gendered Modernisms — *Dickie, Margaret*
Gendered Moods — *Ettorre, Elizabeth*
The Gendered Object — *Kirkham, Pat*
Gendered Situations, Gendered Selves — *Howard,
    Judith A*
Gendered Work — *Adkins, Lisa*
Genderflex: Men and Women Speaking Each Other's
    Language at Work — *Tingley, Judith C*
Gendering Bodies/Performing Art — *Koritz, Amy*
Gendering the Middle East — *Kandiyoti, Deniz*
The Gene Bomb — *Comings, David E*
Gene Isolation and Mapping Protocols — *Boultwood,
    Jacqueline*
Gene Kelly: A Celebration — *Morley, Sheridan*
Gene Regulation and Fetal Development
    — *International Workshop on Fetal Genetic
    Pathology (3rd: 1993: Perugia, Italy)*
Gene Therapy in Cancer — *Brenner, Malcolm K*
Gene Therapy Protocols — *Robbins, Paul D*
The Gene Wars — *Cook-Degan, Robert*
r Genealogical Abstracts from Palmyra, Wayne County,
    New York Newspapers 1810-1854 — *Meyer, Mary
    Keysor*
r Genealogical and Local History Books in Print:
    Family History Volume. 5th Ed.
r Genealogical Research in England's Public Record
    Office — *Reid, Judith Prowse*
Genealogie Incredibili — *Bizzocchi, Roberto*
Genealogies of Conflict — *Greenstein, Ran*
Genealogy and Literature — *Quinby, Lee*
r Genealogy and Local History to 1900 — *Gilchrist, J
    Brian*
r The Genealogy Annual 1995
Genealogy as Pastime and Profession — *Jacobus,
    Donald Lines*
Genealogy: Helps, Hints, and Hope — *Heisey, John W*
The Genealogy of Disjunction — *Jennings, R E*
A Genealogy of Sovereignty — *Bartelson, Jens*
Genealogy of the Way — *Wilson, Thomas A*
r Genealogy Online. 2nd Ed. — *Crowe, Elizabeth Powell*
r General Bibliography for Music Research. 3rd Ed.
    — *Mixter, Keith E*
El General Charis Y La Pacificacion Del Mexico
    Postrevolucionario — *Cruz, Victor De La*
General Chemistry. 2nd Ed. — *Umland, Jean B*
General Equilibrium and Welfare — *Creedy, John*
General Equilibrium Approach to Financial Decisions
    — *Uzumcuoglu, Ozhan*
General Equilibrium Theory. Vols. 1-3 — *Debreu,
    Gerard*
General Equilibrium with Increasing Returns
    — *Villar, Antonio*
The General from America — *Nelson, Richard*
A General Introduction to the Semeiotic of Charles
    Sanders Peirce — *Liszka, James Jakob*
General Jose Cosme Urrea: His Life and Times
    1797-1849 — *Herring, Patricia Roche*
General M.G. Vallejo and the Advent of the
    Americans — *Rosenus, Alan*

The General Prologue. Vol. 2, Pts. A-B — *Chaucer, Geoffrey*
General Relativity — *Hall, G S*
General Richard Montgomery and the American Revolution — *Shelton, Hal T*
General Robert F. Hoke: Lee's Modest Warrior — *Barefoot, Daniel W*
General Statistics. 3rd Ed. — *Chase, Warren*
c The General Store — *Kalman, Bobbie*
General Systems Theory — *Skyttner, Lars*
General Theory of Relativity — *Dirac, P A M*
Generalist Social Work Practice — *Miley, Karla Krogsrud*
Der Generalplan Ost — *Rossler, Mechtild*
The General's General — *Young, Kenneth Ray*
yr Generals in Muddy Boots — *Cragg, Dan*
Generating Social Stratification — *Kerckhoff, Alan C*
Generating Socialism — *Weinbren, Daniel*
Generation F — *Trioli, Virginia*
Generation of Vipers — *Wylie, Philip*
Generation on Hold — *Cote, James E*
Generation Q — *Bernstein, Robin*
Generation to Generation — *Gersick, Kelin E*
Generation X — *Coupland, Douglas*
Generation X Goes to College — *Sacks, Peter*
Generations and the Challenge of Justice — *Lee, Daniel E*
Generative Fathering — *Hawkins, Alan J*
Generative Linguistics — *Newmeyer, Frederick J*
Genesis — *Bible. O.T. Genesis. English. Alter. 1996*
c Genesis (Illus. by Ed Young) — *Bible. O.T. Genesis. English. Young. 1995*
Genesis — *Ward, John Powell*
y Genesis: A Living Conversation — *Moyers, Bill D*
y Genesis: A Living Conversation (Patinkin). Audio Version — *Moyers, Bill D*
Genesis: A New Translation of the Classic Biblical Stories — *Bible. O.T. Genesis. English. Mitchell. 1996*
Genesis: As It Is Written — *Rosenberg, David, 1943-*
The Genesis Code — *Case, John*
Genesis: Contemporary Writers on Our First Stories — *Rosenberg, David, 1943-*
The Genesis of Chinese Communist Foreign Policy — *Hunt, Michael H*
The Genesis of Ethics — *Visotzky, Burton L*
The Genesis of the French Revolution — *Stone, Bailey*
Genesis of the Jet — *Golley, John*
Genesis: The Beginning of Desire — *Zornberg, Avivah Gottlieb*
Genesis: World of Myths and Patriarchs — *Feyerick, Ada*
Genetic Algorithms and Manufacturing Design — *Gen, Mitsuo*
Genetic Algorithms and Simulated Annealing — *Davies, Lawerence*
Genetic Analysis of Pathogenic Bacteria — *Maloy, Stanley R*
Genetic Connections — *Nelson-Anderson, Danette L*
Genetic Data Analysis II — *Weir, B S*
r Genetic Disorders Sourcebook — *Bellenir, Karen*
y Genetic Engineering — *Swisher, Clarice*
Genetic Engineering. Vol. 18
Genetics and Cancer Susceptibility — *International Conference on Carcinogenesis and Risk Assessment (8th: 1994: Austin, Tex.)*
y Genetics and Intelligence — *Roleff, Tamara L*
Genetics and the Manipulation of Life — *Holdrege, Craig*
The Genetics of Asthma — *Liggett, Stephen B*
y Genetics: Unlocking the Secrets of Life — *Aaseng, Nathan*
Geneva, Zurich, Basel — *Bouvier, Nicolas*
y Genial 2 — *Elston, Tony*
c The Genie in the Jar (Illus. by Chris Raschka) — *Giovanni, Nikki*
The Genie out of the Bottle — *Adelman, M A*
Genii of the River Niger — *Gibbal, Jean-Marie*
Genius and Lust — *Morella, Joseph*
A Genius for Letters — *Myers, Robin*
y The Genius of Alexander the Great — *Hammond, N G L*
y The Genius of Edison. Electronic Media Version
The Genius of the Jewish Joke — *Berger, Arthur Asa*
Genius: The Natural History of Creativity — *Eysenck, H J*
Geniuses and Other Eccentrics — *Rodman, Selden*
Genoa and the Genoese 958-1528 — *Epstein, Steven A*
Genocide after Emotion — *Mestrovic, Stjepan G*
Genocide and the Politics of Memory — *Hirsch, Herbert*
Genocide in Bosnia — *Cigar, Norman*

Genocide, War, and Human Survival — *Strozier, Charles B*
Genome Mapping in Plants — *Paterson, Andrew H*
p Genome Research
Genomes of Plants and Animals — *Stadler Genetics Symposium (21st: 1995: University of Missouri-Columbia)*
Genre and the New Rhetoric — *Freedman, Aviva*
Le Genre Des Memoires, Essai De Definition — *Bertaud, Madeleine*
Genre Knowledge in Disciplinary Communication — *Berkenkotter, Carol*
The Genre of Autobiography in Victorian Literature — *Machann, Clinton*
r Genreflecting: A Guide to Reading Interests in Genre Fiction. 4th Ed. — *Herald, Diana Tixier*
y Genres — *Barton, Geoff*
Genres in Dialogue — *Nightingale, Andrea Wilson*
A Gentile Account of Life in Utah's Dixie 1872-73 — *Kane, Elizabeth*
Gentility Recalled — *Anderson, Digby*
Gentle from the Night — *McKinney, Meagan*
Gentle Touch — *Hunt, Angela Elwell*
Gentlecare: Changing the Experience of Alzheimer's Disease in a Positive Way — *Jones, Moyra*
c Gentlehands (Woodman). Audio Version — *Kerr, M E*
c The Gentleman Outlaw and Me--Eli — *Hahn, Mary Downing*
A Gentleman Publisher's Commonplace Book — *Murray, John G*
Gentleman Spy — *Grose, Peter*
The Gentlemen at War — *Ingleton, Roy*
Gentlemen Bourgeois and Revolutionaries — *Cruz, Jesus*
The Gentry in England and Wales 1500-1700 — *Heal, Felicity*
Gents — *Collins, Warwick*
Genuine Christianity — *Sider, Ronald J*
y The Genuine Half-Moon Kid — *Williams, Michael, 1962-*
Geo-Space Urban Design — *Golany, Gideon S*
The Geoarchaeology of the Argolid — *Zangger, Eberhard*
Geochemistry. 2nd Ed. — *Brownlow, Arthur H*
Geochemistry of Organic Matter in River-Sea Systems — *Artemyev, V E*
Geodetic Network Analysis and Optimal Design — *Kuang, Shanlong*
Geoecology: An Evolutionary Approach — *Huggett, R J*
Geoff Hamilton's Private Paradise — *Hamilton, Geoff*
c Geoffrey Strangeways (Sacks). Audio Version — *Murphy, Jill*
Geographia Antiqua — *Biraschi, Anna Maria*
Geographic Information from Space — *Williams, Jonathan, 1960-*
Geographic Information Systems — *Bernhardsen, Tor*
Geographic Information Systems — *Martin, David, 1965-*
Geographic Information Systems and Libraries — *Smith, Linda C*
Geographical Information Systems and Dynamic Models — *Deursen, W P A Van*
Geographical Worlds — *Allen, John*
La Geographie Culturelle — *Claval, Paul*
c Geographunny: A Book of Global Riddles — *Gerberg, Mort*
cr Geography — *Bateman, Dick*
Geography and Air Transport — *Graham, Brian*
y Geography and Change — *Flint, David*
Geography and Empire — *Godlewska, Anne*
Geography and National Identity — *Hooson, David*
Geography and the Human Spirit — *Buttimer, Anne*
Geography in the School Grounds — *Hare, Ralph*
The Geography of Change in South Africa — *Lemon, Anthony*
The Geography of Finance — *Porteous, David J*
The Geography of Hope — *Stegner, Page*
The Geography of Illegal Drugs — *Rengert, George F*
y The Geography of the Earth — *Brooks, Susan*
A Geography of the European Union — *Nagle, Garrett*
Geography of the Heart — *Johnson, Fenton*
A Geography of the Welsh Language 1961-1991 — *Aitchson, John*
Geography: Realms, Regions, and Concepts. 8th Ed. — *De Blij, Harm J*
y Geography Smart Junior — *Queen, J Allen*
Geography Teachers' Handbook — *Bailey, Patrick*
A Geological Companion to Greece and the Aegean — *Higgins, Michael Denis*

r Geologists and the History of Geology. 2nd Suppl., Vol. 1 — *Sarjeant, William Antony S*
r The Geologist's Directory 1996
Geology — *Rhodes, Frank H T*
Geology and Environment in Britain and Ireland — *Woodcock, Nigel*
Geology and Scenery of Dorset — *Bird, E*
Geology and Seismic Stratigraphy of the Antarctic Margin — *Cooper, Alan K*
c Geology Crafts for Kids — *Anderson, Alan*
y The Geology of Fluvial Deposits — *Miall, Andrew D*
Geology of Gas and Oil under the Netherlands — *Rondeel, H E*
A Geology of School Reform — *Brouillette, Liane*
The Geology of Switzerland — *Hsu, Kenneth J*
Geology of the United States' Seafloor — *Gardner, James V*
r Geology Underfoot in Illinois — *Wiggers, Raymond*
y Geometric Measure Theory — *Morgan, Frank*
Geometric Scattering Theory — *Melrose, Richard B*
r Geometric Tomography — *Gardner, Richard J*
Geometrical Optics and Optical Design — *Mouroulis, Pantazis*
Geometry and Physics — *Andersen, Jorgen Ellegaard*
Geometry Experiments — *Winter, Mary Jean*
c Geometry for Every Kid — *VanCleave, Janice Pratt*
Geometry of Harmonic Maps — *Xin, Y L*
The Geometry of Love — *Cuccio, Joan Fay*
Geometry: Proceedings — *Indo-French Conference on Geometry (1989)*
Geometry, Topology and Quantization — *Bandyopadhyay, Pratul*
Geomorphology of Desert Dunes — *Lancaster, Nicholas*
yr Geopedia. Electronic Media Version
Geopolitical and Economic Changes in the Balkan Countries — *Gianaris, Nicholas V*
The Geopolitics of Energy Supply in the European Union in the 21st Century — *Pauwels, Jean-Pierre*
Georg Buchner — *Hauschild, Jan-Christoph*
Georg Buchner: The Shattered Whole — *Reddick, John*
c George and Martha — *Marshall, James*
y George Balanchine: American Ballet Master — *Kristy, Davida*
George Ball: Behind the Scenes in U.S. Foreign Policy — *Bill, James A*
George Berkeley: Idealism and the Man — *Berman, David*
George Bernard Shaw. Vols. 1-3 — *Holroyd, Michael*
George Bird Grinnell — *Evans, Robley*
r George Burns and Gracie Allen — *Clements, Cynthia*
George Bush and the Guardianship Presidency — *Mervin, David*
y George C. Marshall: A General for Peace — *Saunders, Alan*
George Cruikshank's Life, Times, and Art. Vol. 2 — *Patten, Robert L*
George Eastman: A Biography — *Brayer, Elizabeth*
George Eliot: A Life — *Ashton, Rosemary*
George Eliot: Voice of a Century — *Karl, Frederick R*
George F. Kennan and the Origins of Containment 1944-1946 — *Kennan, George F*
George Gissing's American Notebook — *Gissing, George*
r George Gordon: An Annotated Catalogue of His Scientific Correspondence — *Collie, Michael*
George Grant: A Biography — *Christian, William*
George Grant: Selected Letters — *Grant, George Parkin*
A George Herbert Companion — *Ray, Robert H*
George Herbert's Christian Narrative — *Toliver, Harold*
George MacDonald: Victorian Mythmaker — *Hein, Rolland*
George Mills — *Elkin, Stanley*
George Nelson: The Design of Modern Design — *Abercrombie, Stanley*
George Orwell: A Literary Life — *Davison, Peter Hobley*
George Rodrigue: A Cajun Artist — *Freundlich, Lawrence S*
George S. Long: Timber Statesman — *Twining, Charles E*
George Stubbs 1724-1806 — *Stubbs, George*
George Washington: A Biography — *Alden, John R*
c George Washington's Cows — *Small, David*
George Washington's Schooners — *Hearn, Chester G*
Georges De La Tour and His World — *Conisbee, Philip*

Georges Duhamel Et L'Idee De Civilisation — *Lafay, Arlette*

Georges Duhamel, Medecin-Ecrivain De Guerre

Georges Florovsky: Russian Intellectual and Orthodox Churchman — *Blane, Andrew*

c George's Gang in Trouble (Illus. by S Hellard) — *Cullimore, Stan*

George's Lair — *Bayley, John*

Georges Perec: A Life in Words — *Bellos, David*

r Georgia Handbook. 2nd Ed. — *Stann, Kap*

c Georgia O'Keeffe (Illus. by Rochelle Draper) — *Lowery, Linda*

Georgia Public Education Report Cards 1994-1995. Vols. 1-4

Georgia: Reform in the Food and Agriculture Sector

Georgia Voices — *Ruppersburg, Hugh*

Georgiade Plastic, Maxillofacial and Reconstructive Surgery. 3rd Ed. — *Georgiade, Gregory S*

Georgian: A Learner's Grammar — *Hewitt, George*

Gerald Massey: Chartist, Poet, Radical and Freethinker — *Shaw, David*

Gerald Vizenor: Writing in the Oral Tradition — *Blaeser, Kimberly*

c Geraldine First (Illus. by Holly Keller) — *Keller, Holly*

Gerard Manley Hopkins: A Literary Life — *Roberts, Gerald*

Gerard Manley Hopkins and Critical Discourse — *Hollahan, Eugene*

c Gerbilitis (Illus. by Steve Bjorkman) — *Spinner, Stephanie*

Gerechte Vermogensverteilung — *Losinger, Anton*

Gerhard Richter: 100 Bilder

Gerhard Richter: Painting in the Nineties

Geriatric Anesthesiology — *McLeskey, Charles H*

Geriatric Medicine. 2nd Ed. — *Jahnigen, Dennis*

Geriatric Secrets — *Forciea, Mary Ann*

Germaine De Stael Revisited — *Besser, Gretchen Rous*

r Germaine Tailleferre: A Bio-Bibliography — *Shapiro, Robert, 1951-*

yr The German American Family Album — *Hoobler, Dorothy*

r German-American Relations — *Krewson, Margrit B*

c The German Americans — *Galicich, Anne*

The German-Americans and World War II — *Holian, Timothy J*

German and American Art from Beuys and Warhol — *Beudert, Monique*

r German Baroque Writers 1580-1660 — *Hardin, James*

German-Bohemians: The Quiet Immigrants — *Rippley, La Vern J*

The German Book 1450-1750 — *Flood, John L*

The German Chancellors — *Klein, Hans*

German Cinema — *Silberman, Marc*

German Cooking — *Heberle, Marianna Olszweska*

r German-English Dictionary of Idioms — *Schemann, Hans*

German Epic Poetry — *Gentry, Francis G*

The German Episcopacy and the Implementation of the Decrees of the Fourth Lateran Council 1216-1245 — *Pixton, Paul B*

German Essays on Religion — *Oakes, Edward T*

German Essays on Science in the 19th Century — *Schirmacher, Wolfgang*

German Essays on Science in the 20th Century — *Schirmacher, Wolfgang*

The German Idea of Militarism — *Stargardt, Nicholas*

German-Jewish History in Modern Times. Vol. 1 — *Breuer, Mordechai*

The German Language and the Real World — *Stevenson, Patrick*

p German Monitor 30

German Monopolies Commission 1984-1993 — *Germany (West). Monopolkommission*

German Nationalism and Religious Conflict — *Smith, Helmut Walser*

German Notgeld — *Morris, Tudor*

The German Novella — *Weing, Siegfried*

The German Peasants' War — *Scott, Tom*

r German Poetry in Song — *Snyder, Lawrence D*

German Political Satires from the Reformation to the Second World War. Pt. 1, Vols. 1-2 — *Coupe, W A*

The German Public and the Persecution of Jews 1933-1945 — *Wollenberg, Jorg*

The German Question and Other German Questions — *Schoenbaum, David*

German Radicals Confront the Common People — *Wegert, Karl H*

German Realists in the Nineteenth Century — *Lukacs, Georg*

German Renaissance Prints 1490-1550 — *Bartrum, Giulia*

German Sculpture of the Later Renaissance c. 1520-1580 — *Smith, Jeffrey Chipps*

German Shepherd — *Fogle, Bruce*

German Social Democracy and the Rise of Nazism — *Harsch, Donna*

r German Theatre — *Patterson, Michael*

German Thought and Culture — *Hahn, Hans J*

German Villages in Crisis — *Theibault, John C*

r The German Way — *Flippo, Hyde*

German Women as Letter Writers 1750-1850 — *French, Lorely*

A German Women's Movement — *Reagin, Nancy R*

The German Workers and the Nazis — *Carsten, F L*

Germania E Santa Sede — *Fattorini, Emma*

Germania Judaica. Vol. 3, Pt. 2 — *Maimon, Arye*

Germania Sacra. Vol. 4 — *Theil, Bernhard*

The Germanic Hero — *Murdoch, Brian*

The Germanization of Early Medieval Christianity — *Russell, James C*

Germans and Texans — *Struve, Walter*

Germans in Britain since 1500 — *Panayi, Panikos*

The Germans: Power Struggles and the Development of Habitus in the Nineteenth and Twentieth Centuries — *Elias, Norbert*

Germans to the Front — *Large, David Clay*

Germany — *Finkelstein, Caroline*

Germany 1945 — *Barnouw, Dagmar*

Germany: A New Social and Economic History. Vol. 1 — *Scribner, Bob*

Germany after the First World War — *Bessel, Richard*

Germany and Europe — *Marsh, David*

Germany and Israel — *Lavy, George*

Germany from Napoleon to Bismarck 1800-1866 — *Nipperdey, Thomas*

Germany, Hitler, and World War II — *Weinberg, Gerhard L*

c Germany: In the Heartland of Europe — *Ayer, Eleanor H*

r Germany (Insight Guides)

Germany Unified and Europe Transformed — *Zelikow, Philip*

y Germany: United Again — *Symynkywicz, Jeffrey B*

Germany's Unity Election — *Semetko, Holli A*

Germinal (Davidson). Audio Version — *Zola, Emile*

c Germs! Germs! Germs! (Illus. by Steve Bjorkman) — *Katz, Bobbi*

c Geronimo: Apache Warrior — *Sanford, William R*

Gerontographics: Life-Stage Segmentation for Marketing Strategy Development — *Moschis, George P*

Gerry Anderson: The Authorised Biography — *Archer, Simon*

Gershom Scholem Zwischen Den Disziplinen — *Schafer, Peter*

c Gertie and the Bloop — *Jarman, Julia*

Gertrud Kolmar: Leben Und Werk — *Woltmann, Johanna*

c Gertrude Chandler Warner and the Boxcar Children (Illus. by Marie De John) — *Ellsworth, Mary Ellen*

The Gertrude Stein Awards in Innovative American Poetry 1994-1995

Gerushim, Ezrah Rishonah Mishpatit — *Boublil, Tsuriel*

Het Geschenk, De Maker — *Daalen, Maria Van*

Geschichte Der Buchillustration In Deutschland Das 16. Und 17. Jahrhundert. Vols. 1-2 — *Kunze, Horst*

Geschichte Der Deutschen Literatur Bis Zum Beginn Der Neuzeit. Rev. Ed., Vol. 1, Pts. 1-2; Vol. 2, Pt. 2 — *Heinzle, Joachim*

Geschichte Der Deutschen Literatur Von 1945 Bis Zur Gegenwart — *Barner, Wilfried*

Geschichte Des Christentums In Deutschland — *Nowak, Kurt*

Geschichte Des Kinderund Jugendtheaters Zwischen 1945 Und 1970 — *Doderer, Klaus*

Die Geschichte Des Motivkomplexes Theophanie — *Scriba, Albrecht*

Die Geschichte Vom Rotkappchen. 11th Ed. — *Ritz, Hans*

Geschichtsdenken Und Literarische Moderne — *Hey'l, Bettina*

Gesellschaft Fur Exilforschung. Vols. 1-3 — *Loewy, Ernst*

Die Gesellschaft Fur Schwerionenforschung — *Buchhaupt, Siegfried*

Die Gesellschaftliche Verantwortung Der Christen Nach Den Pastoralbriefen — *Weiser, Alfons*

Gesellschaftlicher Umbruch Und Historie Im Zeitgenossischen Drama Der Islamischen Welt — *Burgel, Johann Christoph*

Get a Financial Life (Kobliner). Audio Version — *Kobliner, Beth*

Get a Firmer Grip on Your Math — *Adams, William J*

Get a Good Night's Sleep — *Albert, Katherine*

Get a Grip on Your Math — *Adams, William J*

Get a Life — *Warner, Ralph*

Get a Life without Sacrificing Your Career — *Booher, Dianna*

c Get Back, Pimple! (Illus. by Point) — *Agard, John*

c Get Dressed, Santa! (Illus. by Tomie De Paola) — *De Paola, Tomie*

Get Fit — *Kenton, Leslie*

Get Hired! — *Green, Paul C*

Get in There and Cook — *Sax, Richard*

Get It Together by 30 and Be Set for the Rest of Your Life — *Thau, Richard D*

y Get It While It's Hot--or Not — *Hobbs, Valerie*

y Get Organized — *Fry, Ronald W*

Get Out of My Life, but First Could You Drive Me and Cheryl to the Mall?. Audio Version — *Wolf, Anthony*

yp Get Real Comics (Illus. by Charley Parker) — *Rogow, Debbie*

y Get Shorty (Mantegna). Audio Version — *Leonard, Elmore*

Get the Guests — *Davis, Walter A*

Get the Salt Out — *Gittleman, Ann Louise*

Get the Sugar Out — *Gittleman, Ann Louise*

c Get Up and Go! (Illus. by Diane Greenseid) — *Murphy, Stuart J*

y Get Up and Go! — *Whitman, Sylvia*

Get Your Share of Hidden Riches — *Carson, H Glenn*

p Getaways

Getraumte Taten — *Heftrich, Eckhard*

The Gettin Place — *Straight, Susan*

Getting a Job. 2nd Ed. — *Granovetter, Mark*

Getting a Life — *Ghazi, Polly*

y Getting a Life — *Rugen, Samantha*

c Getting Around — *Butler, Daphne*

Getting By — *Gringeri, Christina E*

Getting Down to Earth — *Costanza, Robert*

Getting Employees to Fall in Love with Your Company — *Harris, Jim, 1953-*

Getting Everyone on Board to Help Teenagers — *Fibkins, William L*

Getting High — *Hewitt, Paolo*

y Getting In — *Paul, Bill*

Getting into the Act — *Donkin, Ellen*

y Getting into the Game — *Greenberg, Judith E*

Getting into Your Customer's Head — *Davis, Kevin*

Getting It Right — *Barro, Robert J*

y Getting Lincoln's Goat — *Goldman, E M*

Getting Off Clean — *Murphy, Timothy*

Getting Over Getting Old — *Pogrebin, Letty Cottin*

Getting over Homer — *O'Donnell, Mark*

Getting Political — *Turner, Anne M*

Getting Prices Right — *Baker, Dean*

Getting Rid of Mr. Kitchen — *Higson, Charles*

Getting Specific — *Phelan, Shane*

Getting Started in Human Resource Management — *Bacarro, Joseph P*

Getting Started in Multimedia Design — *Olsen, Gary*

Getting the Boot — *Frei, Matt*

Getting the Message Through — *Raines, Rebecca Robbins*

Getting the Most from Literature Groups — *Strube, Penny*

Getting There — *Goddard, Stephen B*

c Getting Used to Harry (Illus. by Diane Palmisciano) — *Best, Cari*

c Getting Wired! (Illus. by Derek Brazell) — *James, Peter*

Getting Your Boss's Number and Many Other Ways to Use the Ennea Program at Work — *Goldberg, Michael*

Getting Your Kids to Say No in the 90s When You Said Yes in the 60s — *Strasburger, Victor C*

Getting Your S/NVQ — *Arundale, Justin*

c The Gettysburg Address (Illus. by Michael McCurdy) — *Lincoln, Abraham*

Geyser Life — *Hardy, Edward*

The Ghan: From Adelaide to Alice — *Downes, Jim*

Ghana Country Assistance Review — *Armstrong, Robert P*

c Ghana, Mali, Songhay — *Mann, Kenny*

Ghana: The Political Economy of Recovery — *Rothchild, Donald*

Ghana under PNDC Rule — *Gyimah-Boadi, E*

Ghana Vision 2020 — *Ghana. President (1981-: Rawlings)*
Al-Ghazali and the Ash'arite School — *Frank, R M*
Ghirlandaio's Daughter — *Hill, John Spencer*
The Ghost and the Darkness — *Goldman, William*
c Ghost at the Globe — *Sodaro, Craig*
c Ghost Boy — *Pulman, Felicity*
c The Ghost by the Sea — *Dunlop, Eileen*
y Ghost Canoe — *Hobbs, Will*
Ghost Dance — *Maso, Carole*
c The Ghost Dance (Illus. by Paul Morin) — *McLerran, Alice*
Ghost Dancing on the Cracker Circuit — *Brown, Rodger Lyle*
c The Ghost Dog (Illus. by Peter Dennis) — *Johnson, Pete*
Ghost Fleet — *Delgado, James P*
Ghost Grizzlies — *Petersen, David*
y Ghost Horses — *Hill, Pamela Smith*
Ghost Image — *Guibert, Herve*
c The Ghost in the Big Brass Bed (Moore). Audio Version — *Coville, Bruce*
c Ghost Knight — *Cascone, A G*
Ghost Movies II — *Haining, Peter*
c A Ghost Named Wanda (Illus. by Jack E Davis) — *Greenburg, Dan*
c Ghost Night (Illus. by Neil Johnson) — *Johnson, Neil*
p Ghost: Nocturnes — *Luke, Eric*
Ghost of a Chance — *Duchin, Peter*
y Ghost of a Chance — *Garland, Mark A*
c The Ghost of Grania O'Malley — *Morpurgo, Michael*
c The Ghost of Greyfriar's Bobby (Illus. by Ruth Brown) — *Brown, Ruth*
The Ghost of Major Pryor — *Honig, Donald*
c The Ghost of Nicholas Greebe (Illus. by S D Schindler) — *Johnston, Tony*
c The Ghost of Pont Diable (Illus. by James Rice) — *Rice, James*
c The Ghost of Uncle Arvie (Illus. by Simon Cooper) — *Creech, Sharon*
c The Ghost Pirate (Illus. by Brian Lee) — *Bethlen, Julianna*
The Ghost Road — *Barker, Pat*
y The Ghost Road (Crossley). Audio Version — *Barker, Pat*
Ghost Settlement on the Prairie — *Hickey, Joseph V*
y Ghost Shadow — *Franklin, Cheryl J*
y Ghost Story — *Thompson, Julian F*
Ghost-Town Tales of Oklahoma — *Etter, Jim Marion*
y Ghost Train — *Mowry, Jess*
The Ghost Train — *Ormsby, Frank*
y Ghost Train (Illus. by Harvey Chan) — *Yee, Paul*
Ghost Volcano — *Gilbert, Sandra M*
y A Ghost Waiting — *Scott, Hugh*
The Ghost Walker — *Coel, Margaret*
c The Ghost Who Ate Chocolate (Illus. by Jane Manning) — *Saunders, Susan*
Ghosting — *Preston, John, 1953-*
c Ghostlands — *Elboz, Stephen*
y Ghostlight — *Bradley, Marion Zimmer*
y Ghostly Haunts — *Morpurgo, Michael*
c Ghostly Warnings (Illus. by David Linn) — *Cohen, Daniel, 1936-*
The Ghosts of Berlin — *Ladd, Brian*
Ghosts of Mississippi — *Vollers, Maryanne*
The Ghosts of Modernity — *Rabate, Jean-Michel*
The Ghosts of N-Space — *Letts, Barry*
c The Ghosts of Ravens Crag — *Scott, Hugh*
The Ghosts of Saigon — *Roberts, John Maddox*
c Ghosts of the Southwest (Illus. by Ted Wood) — *Wood, Ted*
c The Ghosts' Trip to Loch Ness (Illus. by Jacques Duquennoy) — *Duquennoy, Jacques*
Giacometti: A Biography — *Lord, James*
Giacomo Puccini: L'Arte Internazionale Di Un Musicista Italiano — *Girardi, Michele*
Giambattista Tiepolo 1696-1770 — *Tiepolo, Giovanni Battista*
Giambologna, Narrator of the Catholic Reformation — *Gibbons, Mary Weitzel*
Gian-Carlo Rota on Combinatorics — *Rota, Gian-Carlo*
Il Giansenismo In Italia. Vol. 2, Pt. 1 — *Stella, Pietro*
c The Giant Baby (Illus. by Fritz Wegner) — *Ahlberg, Allan*
r The Giant Encyclopedia of Circle Time and Group Activities for Children 3 to 6 — *Charner, Kathy*
c Giant Pie (Illus. by Nick Schon) — *Rogers, Paul*
c The Giant That Sneezed (Illus. by Toni Goffe) — *Leach, Norman*
c Giant Turtle — *Stefoff, Rebecca*

r Giants: A Reference Guide from History, the Bible, and Recorded Legend — *DeLoach, Charles*
y The Giant's House — *McCracken, Elizabeth*
r Giants of Country Music — *Haislop, Neil*
Un Giardino Nella Voce — *Zipoli, Riccardo*
Gibbon's Decline and Fall — *Tepper, Sheri S*
p Gibbons Stamp Monthly
y Gideon's People — *Meyer, Carolyn*
Gideon's Torch — *Colson, Charles*
y The Gift — *Dickinson, Peter*
c The Gift (Illus. by Peter Perko) — *Kertes, Joseph*
y The Gift — *Steel, Danielle*
Gift and Mystery — *John Paul II, Pope*
Gift Giving — *Otnes, Cele*
c Gift Horse (Illus. by Jos. A Smith) — *Levin, Betty*
The Gift of Anger — *Saussy, Carroll*
The Gift of Death — *Derrida, Jacques*
The Gift of Fear — *De Becker, Gavin*
The Gift of Peace — *Bernardin, Joseph Louis*
The Gift of Prayer — *Kieling, Jared T*
A Gift of Sharing — *Raffin, Deborah*
Gift of the Red Bird — *D'Arcy, Paula*
c Gift of the Sun (Illus. by Jude Daly) — *Stewart, Dianne*
The Gift of Tongues — *Hamill, Sam*
The Gift of Trout — *Leeson, Ted*
A Gift: The Life of Da Ponte — *Slavitt, David R*
Gifted Children — *Winner, Ellen*
The Gifted Group in Later Maturity — *Holahan, Carole K*
y The Gifted Kids' Survival Guide. Rev., Expanded, and Updated Ed. — *Galbraith, Judy*
Gifting to People You Love — *Berg, Adriane*
c Gifts (Illus. by Barbara Reid) — *Bogart, Jo Ellen*
Gifts and Sorrows — *Pomian, Raphaelle*
Gifts, Favors, and Banquets — *Yang, Mayfair Mei-Hui*
Gifts of Earth — *Huyler, Stephen P*
The Gifts of the Body (Brown). Audio Version — *Brown, Rebecca*
The Gifts of the Child Christ and Other Stories and Fairy Tales. Rev. Ed. — *MacDonald, George*
Gifts of the Spirit — *Monroe, Dan L*
r Gifts That Save the Animals — *Berry, Ellen*
Gifts to Last — *Learning, Walter*
c Gifts to Make for Your Favorite Grownup (Illus. by Anne Canevari Green) — *Ross, Kathy*
Gifts: Two Hospice Professionals Reveal Messages from These Passing On — *Sharp, Anne Wallace*
Gifts: Two Hospice Professionals Reveal Messages from Those Passing On — *Sharp, Anne Wallace*
Gil Elvgren: The Wartime Pin-Ups — *Collins, Max Allan*
Gilbert and Sullivan — *Orel, Harold*
c Gilberto Y El Viento. Book and Audio Version — *Ets, Marie Hall*
Gilda's Disease — *Piver, M Steven*
The Gilded Cage — *Browne, Marshall*
Gilgamesh: A Rendering in English Verse — *Ferry, David*
Gilles Deleuze and the Question of Philosophy — *Goodchild, Philip*
y Gilroy's Ghost — *Gordon, John*
Gilt by Association — *Myers, Tamar*
c Ginger (Illus. by Charlotte Voake) — *Voake, Charlotte*
c Ginger Brown: The Nobody Boy (Illus. by Cornelius Van Wright) — *Wyeth, Sharon Dennis*
c Ginger Brown: Too Many Houses (Illus. by Cornelius Van Wright) — *Wyeth, Sharon Dennis*
c The Ginger Ninja--St. Felix for the Cup! — *Rayner, Shoo*
c The Ginger Ninja--The Dance of the Apple Dumplings — *Rayner, Shoo*
c Gingerbread Days (Illus. by Floyd Cooper) — *Thomas, Joyce Carol*
c The Gingerbread Man (Illus. by John A Rowe) —
c The Gingerbread Man. Electronic Media Version
c Ginkgo and Moon (Illus. by Lisa Mertins) — *Mertins, Lisa*
Ginkgo Biloba — *Murray, Frank*
Gio Pomodoro: Ornamenti 1954-1996 — *Centrodi, Giuliano*
Gioco E Giustizia Nell'Italia Di Comune — *Ortalli, Gherardo*
Il Gioco Segreto — *Garboli, Cesare*
Giordano Bruno and the Philosophy of the Ass — *Ordine, Nuccio*
Giorgio Vasari: Art and History — *Rubin, Patricia Lee*
Giorgione — *Anderson, Jaynie*
Giotto — *Flores D'Arcais, Francesca*

c Giotto and Medieval Art (Illus. by Sergio Ricciardi) — *Corrain, Lucia*
Giotto to Durer — *National Gallery (Great Britain)*
r Giovanni Gabrieli ca.1555-1612 — *Charteris, Richard*
Giovannino De Grassi: La Corte E La Cattedrale — *Rossi, Marco*
Giovanni's Gift — *Morrow, Bradford*
Giovanni's Gift (Muller). Audio Version — *Morrow, Bradford*
c Giraffe — *Newton, Jill*
The Giraffe — *Nimier, Marie*
c Giraffes (Illus. by John Lobban) — *Parker, Steve*
The Girard Reader — *Girard, Rene*
Girl by the Water — *Geddes, Gary*
y A Girl from Yamhill — *Cleary, Beverly*
y Girl Gives Birth to Own Prom Date — *Strasser, Todd*
y Girl Goddess #9 — *Block, Francesca Lia*
Girl Hurt — *Laino, E J Miller*
The Girl I Left Behind — *Endo, Shusaku*
c The Girl in the Blue Tunic — *Ure, Jean*
y A Girl Named Disaster — *Farmer, Nancy*
The Girl Next Door — *Ketchum, Jack*
Girl Power — *Carlip, Hillary*
y Girl Power — *Ellis, Patty*
The Girl Problem — *Alexander, Ruth M*
The Girl Wants To — *Crosbie, Lynn*
c The Girl Who Lived with the Bears (Illus. by Andrew Plewes) — *Goldin, Barbara Diamond*
c The Girl Who Loved Coyotes (Illus. by Diana Bryer) — *Wood, Nancy*
The Girl Who Remembered Snow — *Mathes, Charles*
c The Girl Who Wanted a Song (Illus. by Stephen T Johnson) — *Sanfield, Steve*
y The Girl with the Botticelli Eyes — *Lieberman, Herbert*
The Girl with the Brown Crayon — *Paley, Vivian Gussin*
Girls — *Busch, Frederick*
y Girls Are like Diamonds (Illus. by H Dell) — *Poulson, Joan*
y The Girls' Gang — *Impey, Rose*
c The Girls' Guide to Life (Illus. by Cynthia Jabar) — *Dee, Catherine*
A Girl's Guide to Taking over the World — *Taormino, Tristan*
cp Girls' Life
The Girls Next Door — *Van Gelder, Lindsy*
Girls of Alexandria — *Kharrat, Idwar*
Girls Only — *Witchel, Alex*
The Girl's Own — *Nelson, Claudia*
Girls' Schooling, Women's Autonomy, and Fertility Change in South Asia — *Jeffery, Roger*
y Girls Speak Out — *Johnston, Andrea*
c Girls to the Rescue
c Girls to the Rescue. No. 2
Girolamo Cardano: Philosoph, Naturforscher, Arzt — *Kessler, Eckhard*
Girolamo Tiraboschi: Mostra Documentario Bibliografica — *Barbolini, Anna Rosa Venturi*
Giron, La Verdadera Historia — *Ros, Enrique*
GIS, a Computing Perspective — *Worboys, Michael*
GIS: A Visual Approach — *Davis, Bruce E*
GIS and Environmental Modeling — *Goodchild, Michael F*
GIS Applications in Natural Resources 2 — *Heit, Michael*
c Gita Gets Lost (Illus. by Karin Littlewood) — *Althea*
c Gittel's Hands (Illus. by Deborah Nourse Lattimore) — *Silverman, Erica*
Giuseppe De Santis and Postwar Italian Cinema — *Vitti, Antonio*
c Give a Dog a Bone (Illus. by John Speirs) — *Cole, Joanna*
c Give Me Bach My Schubert (Illus. by Rick Dupre) — *Cleary, Brian P*
c Give Me Half! (Illus. by G Brian Karas) — *Murphy, Stuart J*
Give Us a Kiss — *Woodrell, Daniel*
c Give Yourself a Hug (Illus. by Kim Harley) — *Nichols, Grace*
The Given and the Made — *Vendler, Helen*
Given in Evidence — *Davies, Jonathan*
y The Giver — *Lowry, Lois*
y Giving Away Your Faith — *St. Clair, Barry*
r Giving by Industry. 1996-1997 Ed. — *Smith, Craig*
Giving: Charity and Philanthropy in History — *Bremner, Robert H*
Giving for Social Change — *Nagai, Althea K*
Giving Offense — *Coetzee, J M*
c The Gizmo Again (Illus. by Keith McEwan) — *Jennings, Paul*

The Glace Bay Miners' Museum — *Currie, Sheldon*
The Glace Bay Miners' Museum — *Lill, Wendy*
Glacial Geology — *Erickson, Jon*
Glad Morning Again — *Keon, Michael*
Gladiolus in Tropical Africa — *Goldblatt, Peter*
Gladly the Cross-Eyed Bear — *McBain, Ed*
Gladly the Cross-Eyed Bear (Heald). Audio Version
    — *McBain, Ed*
Gladstone — *Jenkins, Roy*
Gladstone 1875-1898 — *Matthew, H C G*
Gladstone: A Biography — *Jenkins, Roy*
Gladstone's Imperialism in Egypt — *Harrison, Robert T*
y Glaice: An Arbiter Tale — *Douglas, L Warren*
A Glance beyond Doubt — *Rimmon-Kenan, Shlomith*
Glasgow. Vol. 1 — *Devine, T M*
Glasgow: The Socio-Spatial Development of the City
    — *Pacione, Michael*
Glasnost and Soviet Television — *Paasilinna, Reino*
The Glass Air — *Page, P K*
Glass Art — *Layton, Peter*
Glass Houses — *Rabasa, George*
Glass, Irony and God — *Carson, Anne*
Glass, Paper, Beans — *Cohen, Leah Hager*
Glass, Paper, Beans. Audio Version — *Cohen, Leah Hager*
c The Glassmakers — *Fisher, Leonard Everett*
Glaucoma: A Colour Manual of Diagnosis and Treatment. 2nd Ed. — *Kanski, Jack J*
r Glendale Data Book
Glenn Gould: Selected Letters — *Gould, Glenn*
Glenn Gould: Some Portraits of the Artist as a Young Man — *Carroll, Jack*
Glenn Gould: The Ecstasy and Tragedy of Genius — *Ostwald, Peter*
y Glennis, Before and After — *Calvert, Patricia*
Gli Arabi E Noi — *Pirro, Vincenzo*
y Glimmer — *Waters, Annie*
Glimmering — *Hand, Elizabeth*
A Glimpse of Hell — *Forrest, Duncan*
Glimpses of Life in Victoria by a Resident — *Kerr, Frances*
The Glimpses of the Moon — *Wharton, Edith*
Glimpsing Reality — *Buckley, Paul*
c The Glitter Dragon (Illus. by Colin Maclean) — *Repchuk, Caroline*
c Glitter When You Jump (Illus. by Amanda Harvey) — *Waters, Fiona*
Global Apartheid — *Richmond, Anthony H*
Global Banking — *Smith, Roy C*
p Global Biodiversity: An International Forum on the Variety of Life on Earth...Research, Conservation and Wise Use
Global Biodiversity Assessment — *Heywood, V H*
Global Burnout — *Golembiewski, Robert T*
Global Change and Terrestrial Ecosystems — *Walker, B H*
Global Change, Regional Response — *Stallings, Barbara*
Global Civil Society and Global Environmental Governance — *Lipschutz, Ronnie D*
The Global Commons — *Vogler, John*
Global Communications
Global Competition and the Labour Market — *Driffield, Nigel L*
Global Competitiveness and Industrial Growth in Taiwan and the Philippines — *Kuo, Cheng-Tian*
Global Convulsions — *Van Horne, Winston A*
Global Dangers — *Lynn-Jones, Sean M*
Global Demographics — *Nichols, Judith E*
r Global Development — *Savitt, William*
The Global Dimension of Economic Evolution — *Dopfer, Kurt*
Global Dreams — *Barnet, Richard J*
Global Dynamics, Phase Space Transport, Orbits Homoclinic to Resonances, and Applications — *Wiggins, Stephen*
Global Ecology — *Smil, Vaclav*
Global Ecology in Human Perspective — *Southwick, Charles H*
Global Economic Prospects and the Developing Countries 1996
Global Emission Experiences
y Global Environmental Change — *Graves, Johnathan*
Global Environmental Change — *Hidore, John J*
Global Environmental Change and International Governance — *Young, Oran R*
The Global Environmental Movement. 2nd Ed. — *McCormick, John*
The Global Expansion of Judicial Power — *Tate, C Neal*

Global Exporting from the U.S.A. — *Yamamoto, Sam*
Global Finance — *Eng, Maximo V*
Global Gender Issues — *Peterson, V Spike*
Global Habit — *Stares, Paul B*
Global History and Migrations — *Wang, Gungwu*
The Global Human Genome Programme — *Organisation for Economic Co-Operation and Development*
Global Impact — *Odenwald, Sylvia B*
The Global Impact of the Great Depression 1929-1939 — *Rothermund, Dietmar*
The Global Information Society — *Martin, William J, 1938-*
Global Issues — *Seitz, John L*
Global Logistics and Strategy — *Leighton, Richard M*
Global Lorentzian Geometry. 2nd Ed. — *Beem, John K*
A Global Marketplace for Consumers
Global Migrants, Local Lives — *Gardner, Katy*
Global Minimization of Nonconvex Energy Functions — *Pardalos, P M*
The Global Monetary System after the Fall of the Soviet Empire — *Szabo-Pelsoczi, M*
Global Optimization. 3rd Ed. — *Horst, Reiner*
Global Optimization in Engineering Design — *Grossmann, Ignacio E*
Global Perspectives in Cross-Cultural and Cross-National Consumer Research — *Manrai, Lalita A*
The Global Politics of Power, Justice and Death — *Anderson, Peter J*
r Global Population Policy Data Base 1993
Global Portfolio Management for Institutional Investors — *Madura, Jeff*
The Global Positioning System and GIS — *Kennedy, Michael, 1939-*
Global Restructuring and Peripheral States — *Ould-Mey, Mohameden*
Global Space and the Nationalist Discourse of Modernity — *Tang, Xiaobing*
Global Tectonics — *Kearey, Philip*
Global to Local — *Sims, Richard A*
Global Unemployment — *Eatwell, John*
yr The Global Village Companion — *Levinson, David*
yr Global Voices, Global Visions — *Miller-Lachmann, Lyn*
Global Warming — *Brown, Paul*
y Global Warming — *Roleff, Tamara L*
Global Warming: Economic Dimensions and Policy Responses
A Global World? — *Anderson, J*
Globalisation and the Asean Public Sector — *Salleh, Sirajuddin H*
Globalization — *Waters, Malcolm, 1946-*
Globalization and Public Policy — *Gummett, Philip*
Globalization and the Decline of Social Reform — *Teeple, Gary*
Globalization: Critical Reflections — *Mittelman, James H*
Globalization in Question — *Hirst, Paul*
The Globalization of Capitalism in Third World Countries — *Maitra, Priyatosh*
Globalizing Capital — *Eichengreen, Barry*
The Globe Encircled and the World Revealed — *Lamb, Ursula*
La Gloire: The Roman Empire of Corneille and Racine — *Auchincloss, Louis*
Gloria's Gourmet Low-Fat Muffins — *Ambrosia, Gloria*
Glorious American Quilts — *Warren, Elizabeth V*
c Glorious Angels — *Myers, Walter Dean*
Glorious Battle — *Reed, John Shelton*
c The Glorious Flight — *Provensen, Alice*
Glorious Flowers — *Fell, Derek*
Glorious Gardens — *Heriteau, Jacqueline*
c The Glorious Revolution — *Swisher, Clarice*
Glory Bound — *Wiggins, David K*
yr Glory Days — *Adams, Janus*
y Glory Days and Other Stories — *Chan, Gillian*
y The Glory Field — *Myers, Walter Dean*
The Glory of the Page — *Thorp, Nigel*
The Glory of Van Gogh — *Heinich, Nathalie*
Glory Seekers — *Brandewyne, Rebecca*
c Glory Trail — *Maniatty, Taramesha*
Glorying in Tribulation — *Stetson, Erlene*
y Glory's People — *Coppel, Alfred*
Gloses A La Sorciere — *Frenaud, Andre*
Glosove Na Zheni
r A Glossary of Contemporary Literary Theory. 2nd Ed. — *Hawthorn, Jeremy*
r Glossary of HIV/AIDS-Related Terms
r Glossary of Insurance and Risk Management Terms. 6th Ed.

r A Glossary of Plastics Terminology in 5 Languages. 3rd Ed. — *Glenz, W*
r Glossary of Weather and Climate — *Geer, Ira W*
Glossed Books of the Bible and the Origins of the Parisian Booktrade — *De Hamel, Christopher*
c Glove Compartment Games — *Klutz Press*
y Glovemen: Twenty-Seven of Baseball's Greatest — *Sullivan, George*
c The Glow-in-the-Dark Book of Human Skeletons (Illus. by Kate Sweeney) — *Novak, Michael, 1968-*
Gluck: An Eighteenth-Century Portrait in Letters and Documents — *Howard, Patricia*
Das Gluck Der Bettler — *Rudersdorf, Manfred*
y Glued to the Set — *Stark, Steven D*
c Gluskabe and the Four Wishes (Illus. by Christine Nyburg Shrader) — *Bruchac, Joseph*
Gluttony: Ample Tales of Epicurean Excess — *Miller, John, 1959-*
Gnosis Als System — *Strutwolf, Holger*
The Gnostic Concept of Authority and the Nag Hammadi Documents — *Flory, Wayne Seelye*
The Gnostic Imagination — *Deutsch, Nathaniel*
Go Cat Go! — *Morrison, Craig*
Go, Cat, Go! — *Perkins, Carl*
Go Down, Moses — *Kinney, Arthur F*
c Go Figure, Gabriella Grant! — *Maifair, Linda Lee*
c Go for Goal (Dolphin Quids for Kids)
Go for Growth — *Tomasko, Robert M*
c Go for It! (Illus. by David Anson Russo) — *Russo, David Anson*
c Go Home, River (Illus. by Dianne Widom) — *Magdanz, James*
c Go In and Out the Window — *Fox, Dan*
Go Now — *Hell, Richard*
Go the Distance — *Trent, John*
Go the Way Your Blood Beats — *Ruff, Shawn Stewart*
c Go to Bed, Fred (Illus. by Lauren Attinello) — *Inches, Alison*
y Go West, Young Women! — *Karr, Kathleen*
y Goa — *Dalkey, Kara*
c The Goalie — *Shreve, Susan*
y The Goats — *Cole, Brock*
The Gobbler — *Edmondson, Adrian*
El Gobierno Barco — *Deas, Malcolm*
c The Goblin Companion (Illus. by Brian Froud) — *Jones, Terry*
c Goblins in the Castle (Illus. by Katherine Coville) — *Coville, Bruce*
God: A Biography — *Miles, Jack*
God and Caesar at the Rio Grande — *Cunningham, Hilary*
God and Government in an Age of Reason — *Nicholls, David*
God and Greater Britain — *Wolffe, John*
God and Humanity in Auschwitz — *Dietrich, Donald J*
God and Mr. Gomez — *Smith, Jack*
God and the Astronomers. 2nd Ed. — *Jastrow, Robert*
God and the Big Bang — *Matt, Daniel Chanan*
God and the Biologist — *Berry, R J*
God and the Holocaust — *Cohn-Sherbok, Dan*
God at the Grassroots — *Rozell, Mark J*
God Awaits You — *Chilson, Richard*
God between Their Lips — *Stockton, Kathryn Bond*
God beyond Gender — *Ramshaw, Gail*
God Bless John Wayne — *Friedman, Kinky*
c God Bless the Gargoyles (Illus. by Dav Pilkey) — *Pilkey, Dav*
God, Chance and Necessity — *Ward, Keith*
The God Child — *Sayer, Paul*
God, Cosmos, and Humankind — *Ladner, Gerhart B*
God, Creation, and Contemporary Physics — *Worthing, Mark William*
God, Creation, and Providence in the Thought of Jacob Arminius — *Muller, Richard A*
God Delights in You — *Meehan, Bridget Mary*
God Has Ninety-Nine Names — *Miller, Judith*
y God Head — *Zwiren, Scott*
The God Hypothesis — *Lewels, Joe*
God in All Worlds — *Vardey, Lucinda*
God in the Street — *Bergmann, Hans*
God in the Wasteland — *Wells, David F*
God in Us — *Freeman, Anthony*
God Is No Illusion — *Carmody, John, 1939-*
God, Knowledge, and Mystery — *Van Inwagen, Peter*
God, Mystery, Diversity — *Kaufman, Gordon D*
The God of Faith and Reason — *Sokolowski, Robert*
The God of Israel and Christian Theology — *Soulen, R Kendall*
The God of Peace — *Dear, John*
The God of Small Things — *Roy, Arundhati*
The God of the Machine — *Paterson, Isabel*

A God of Vengeance? — Zenger, Erich
God on the Internet — Kellner, Mark
God Owes Us Nothing — Kolakowski, Leszek
God, Reason, and Religions — Long, Eugene Thomas
God Said Ha — Sweeney, Julia
God Save the Queen! — Cannell, Dorothy
God-Talk in America — Tickle, Phyllis
God the Almighty — Bloesch, Donald
God the Spirit — Welker, Michael
The God We Never Knew — Borg, Marcus J
God with Us — Powell, Mark Allan
The God Within — Fackenheim, Emil L
God without the Supernatural — Forrest, Peter
The God You're Looking For — Hybels, Bill
The Goddess Affair — O'Donnell, Lillian
y Goddess of Cool — Jones, Carol
Goddess of the Americas — Castillo, Ana
y The Godfather (Mantegna). Audio Version — Puzo, Mario
The Godfather Legacy — Lebo, Harlan
y Godhanger — King-Smith, Dick
The Godless Constitution — Kramnick, Isaac
y The Godmother — Scarborough, Elizabeth Ann
Godmother Night — Pollack, Rachel
y The Godmother's Apprentice — Scarborough, Elizabeth Ann
Gods and Generals — Shaara, Jeff
y Gods and Generals (Lang). Audio Version — Shaara, Jeff
c The Gods and Goddesses of Olympus (Illus. by Aliki) — Aliki
r Gods and Heroes of Classical Antiquity — Aghion, Irene
Gods, Angels, and Narrators — Swenson, Alan J
God's Architect — O'Donovan, Donal
The Gods Are Thirsty — Lee, Tanith
God's Caress — Cohen, Charles Lloyd
God's Chinese Son — Spence, Jonathan D
God's Country Club — Storey, Gail Donohue
God's Empire — Trollinger, William Vance, Jr.
God's Fires — Anthony, Patricia
God's Gentle Rebels — Feldman, Christian
God's Government Begun — Hamm, Thomas D
God's Grace and Human Action — Wawrykow, Joseph P
God's Gym — Moore, Stephen D
God's Human Face — Schonborn, Christoph
Gods in the Global Village — Kurtz, Lester R
y God's Little Acre (Hammer). Audio Version — Caldwell, Erskine
c God's Mailbox (Illus. by Debbie Tilley) — Gellman, Marc
God's Mercy Endures Forever — Catholic Church. National Conference of Catholic Bishops. Bishops' Committee on the Liturgy
The Gods of Golf — Smith, David L, 1946-
Gods of Play — Aercke, Kristiaan P
God's Outrageous Claims — Strobel, Lee
A God's Own Tale — Kleeman, Terry F
God's Phallus and Other Problems for Men and Monotheism — Eilberg-Schwartz, Howard
God's Rascal — Hankins, Barry
God's Secret Formula — Plichta, Peter
God's Spirit — Muller-Fahrenholz, Geiko
God's Struggler — Middleton, Darren J N
God's Vitamin C for the Christmas Spirit — Miller, Kathy
c God's Week of Creation
God's Wrathful Children — Boesak, Willa
Godwrestling: Round 2 — Waskow, Arthur
Goebbels: Mastermind of the Third Reich — Irving, David
Goethe — Reed, T J
Goethe and His Publishers — Unseld, Siegfried
r Goethe in the History of Science. Vol. 1 — Amrine, Frederick
Goethe's Conception of Knowledge and Science — Stephenson, R H
Goethes Kantstudien — Molnar, Geza Von
c Goggle-Eyes — Fine, Anne
y Goin' Back to Memphis — Dickerson, James
Goin' to Kansas City — Pearson, Nathan W, Jr.
Going Abroad — Stowe, William W
Going against the Grain — Aaronsohn, Elizabeth
Going All the Way — Thompson, Sharon
c Going Back Home (Illus. by Michele Wood) — Wood, Michele
Going Comprehensive in England and Wales — Kerckhoff, Alan C
Going Crazy in Public — Emerson, Earl
Going Down — Belle, Jennifer

Going for Gold — Moodie, T Dunbar
Going for the Jugular — Shurden, Walter B
c Going Home (Illus. by David Diaz) — Bunting, Eve
Going Home — Lessing, Doris May
Going Into a Dark House — Gardam, Jane, 1928-
Going into Tax Court — Crouch, Holmes F
Going Local — Harrison, Jamie
Going Mad in Hollywood — Sherwin, David
Going Negative — Ansolabehere, Stephen
Going Out — Nasaw, David
Going Postal — Jaramillo, Stephan
Going the Distance — Sheehan, George
Going to Miami — Rieff, David
r Going to Salt Lake City to Do Family History Research. 3rd Ed. — Parker, J Carlyle
c Going to the Doctor (Illus. by Sam Ogden) — Brazelton, T Berry
c Going to the Fair — Causley, Charles
c Going to the Fair (Illus. by Sheena Lott) — McFarlane, Sheryl
c Going to the Net — Salzman, Marian
Going to the Sun — McManus, James
c Going to the Zoo (Illus. by Karen Lee Schmidt) — Paxton, Tom
Going Under — Suarez, Virgil
c Going West (Illus. by Renee Graef) — Wilder, Laura Ingalls
Going Where I Have to Go — Simonson, Harold P
y Going Where I'm Coming From — Mazer, Anne
Going with the Weather — Summersett, John
Gold: A Triple Champion's Story — Smith, Michelle
c The Gold at the End of the Rainbow (Illus. by Loek Koopmans) — Hanel, Wolfram
The Gold Bug Variations — Powers, Richard, 1957-
c The Gold Coin (Illus. by N Waldman) — Ada, Alma Flor
A Gold Miner's Daughter — Hacker, Shyrle Pedlar
c Gold Miners of the Wild West — Savage, Jeff
Gold Oder Rabenschwarz — Kellein, Sandra
The Gold of Troy — Tolstikov, Vladimir
y The Gold Rush — Ketchum, Liza
Gold Rush Desert Trails to San Diego and Los Angeles in 1849 — Ellis, George M
Gold Seeking — Goodman, David
Gold, Silver, and Bronze — Montagu, Jennifer
The Gold Standard — Koch, Kenneth
Gold Town — Cleary, Rita
The Goldberg Variations — Huston, Nancy
The Golden Age — Haak, Bob
The Golden Age — Rosengrant, Sandra F
The Golden Age Illusion — Webber, Michael John
The Golden Age of Dutch Manuscript Painting
The Golden Age of Promiscuity — Gooch, Brad
c The Golden Bird (Illus. by Isabelle Brent) — Philip, Neil
The Golden Bough. New Abridgement from the 2nd and 3rd Eds. — Frazer, James George, Sir
c The Golden City — Waldman, Neil
y The Golden Compass — Pullman, Philip
Golden Days — See, Carolyn
c The Golden Days of Greece — Coolidge, Olivia
Golden Fancy — Blake, Jennifer
c The Golden Flower (Illus. by Enrique O Sanchez) — Jaffe, Nina
c The Golden Flower. Book and Audio Version — Palazzo-Craig, Janet
c The Golden Goose (Illus. by Uri Shulevitz) — Shulevitz, Uri
c The Golden Hoard (Illus. by Bee Willey) — McCaughrean, Geraldine
r Golden Horrors — Senn, Bryan
y The Golden Key — Rawn, Melanie
A Golden Legacy — Rudolph, Wolf
The Golden Letters — Garab Dorje
Golden Mouth — Kelly, J N D
y The Golden Nineties — Mason, Lisa
The Golden Ocean — O'Brian, Patrick
Golden Palaces — Chaikin, Linda
y Golden Retriever — Fogle, Bruce
The Golden Rock — Hurst, Ronald
The Golden Rope — Schaeffer, Susan Fromberg
Golden Rule — Ferguson, Thomas
A Golden Sunbeam — Bender, Carrie
Golden Sunrise — Chesterman, Ross
c Golden Tales (Illus. by Lulu Delacre) — Delacre, Lulu
The Golden Yoke — French, Rebecca Redwood
c Goldie the Dollmaker — Goffstein, M B
c Goldilocks (Illus. by Janice Russell) — Russell, Janice
c Goldilocks and the Three Bears (Illus. by James Marshall) — Marshall, James

c Goldilocks and the Three Bears Told in Signed English (Illus. by Annie Lunsford) — Bornstein, Harry
c Goldilocks and the Three Hares — Petach, Heidi
r Goldmine Country Western Record and CD Guide — Heggeness, Fred
Goldratt's Theory of Constraints — Dettmer, H William
Goldsmith's Return — Blazes, Terry Richard
c The Golem (Illus. by Uri Shulevitz) — Singer, Isaac Bashevis
c Golem (Illus. by David Wisniewski) — Wisniewski, David
y The Golem: A Version (Illus. by Trina Schart Hyman) — Rogasky, Barbara
Golf Begins at Fifty — Player, Gary
Golf Begins at Forty — Snead, Sam
p Golf Digest
Golf Dreams — Updike, John
Golf Dreams (Updike). Audio Version — Updike, John
Golf for Women — Whitworth, Kathy
Golf Is a Game of Confidence — Rotella, Bob
p Golf Magazine
Golf My Way — Nicklaus, Jack
r Golf Resorts — Nicols, Jim
The Golfing Mind — Brown, Robert A, 1946-
Golf's Greatest Championship — Graubart, Julian I
The Golgotha Earthquake — Minear, Paul Sevier
Golly Gee It's Me! — Hodge, Charlie
Gone Fishin' — Mosley, Walter
Gone Fishing — Hordern, Michael
Gone the Sun — Groom, Winston
y Gone to Maui — Stacey, Cherylyn
y Gone Wild (Guidall). Audio Version — Hall, Jim, 1947-
Gongora and the Pyramus and Thisbe Myth from Ovid to Shakespeare — Garrison, David
c The Gooch Machine (Illus. by Tim Ellis) — Bagert, Brod
The Good Beer Book — Harper, Timothy
c The Good Book — Durant, Alan
y The Good Book — Gomes, Peter J
The Good Brother — Offutt, Chris
Good-Bye Alien God — Vira, Soma
c Good-bye, Curtis (Illus. by Marisabina Russo) — Henkes, Kevin
c Good-Bye, Papa (Illus. by Jennifer Eachus) — Leavy, Una
Good-Bye, Piccadilly — Virden, Jenel
The Good Cigar — Jeffers, H Paul
The Good City and the Good Life — Kemmis, Daniel
r The Good Detective's Guide to Library Research — Brown, Barbara J
The Good Enough Catholic — Wilkes, Paul
Good Enough Mothering? — Silvam, E B
Good Evening Mr. and Mrs. America, and All the Ships at Sea — Bausch, Richard
A Good Family — Smith, Peter J, 1959-
Good for Business — Jakubovich, Paul J
Good Friends Are Hard to Find — Frankel, Fred
Good Girl, Bad Girl — Ammons, Kevin
c Good Girl, Gracie Growler! — Offen, Hilda
Good Girls Go to Heaven, Bad Girls Go Everywhere — Ehrhardt, Jana U
Good Grief — Waterhouse, Keith
c The Good Guys of Baseball — Egan, Terry
Good Hair — Little, Benilde
The Good Heart — Tenzin Gyatso, Dalai Lama XIV
Good Hearts — Price, Reynolds
The Good Honeymoon Guide — Hone, Lucy
r The Good Hotel Guide: France 1997
Good Housekeeping Cook's Year
Good Intentions Make Bad News — Lichter, S Robert
Good Land — Bair, Bruce
y The Good Liar — Maguire, Gregory
A Good Life — Bradlee, Benjamin C
The Good Life and Its Discontents — Samuelson, Robert J
r The Good Life Guide to Sydney — Mountstephens, Tessa
A Good Looking Man — Moncur, Andrew
The Good Luck Book — Bechtel, Stefan
c Good Luck, Ronald Morgan! (Illus. by Susanna Natti) — Giff, Patricia Reilly
A Good Man's Love — Harris, Elizabeth
Good Manufacturing Practices for Pharmaceuticals. 4th Ed. — Willig, Sidney H
The Good Marriage — Wallerstein, Judith S
y Good Moon Rising — Garden, Nancy
Good Morning, Captain — Keeshan, Bob

c Good Morning, City (Illus. by William Low)
— *Moore, Elaine*
c Good Morning, Good Night — *Grejniec, Michael*
c Good Morning, Good Night — *O'Mara, Carmel*
Good Natured — *Waal, F B M De*
The Good Negress — *Verdelle, A J*
Good Neighborhoods — *Brower, Sidney*
Good News for Alienated Catholics — *Fehren, Henry*
Good News for Women — *Groothuis, Rebecca Merrill*
c Good Night, Baby — *Vulliamy, Clara*
c The Good-Night Blessing Book (Illus. by Nancy
Willard) — *Willard, Nancy*
c Good Night, Dinosaurs (Illus. by Victoria Chess)
— *Sierra, Judy*
c Good Night, Gorilla — *Rathmann, Peggy*
c Good Night Mr. Tom — *Magorian, Michelle*
c Good Night, Sleep Tight (Illus. by Adriano Gon)
— *Lively, Penelope*
c A Good Night's Sleep — *Fowler, Allan*
y The Good Old Days — *Gilbert, Thomas*
The Good Parsi — *Luhrmann, T M*
A Good Place to Live — *Pindell, Terry*
c Good Queen Bess (Illus. by Diane Stanley) — *Stanley,
Diane*
Good Reading. 23rd Ed.
The Good Ship — *Friel, Ian*
r The Good Skiing Guide 1997
The Good Society — *Galbraith, John Kenneth*
The Good Soldier — *Ford, Ford Madox*
Good Sons — *Constantine, K C*
The Good Times — *Baker, Russell*
The Good War — *Terkel, Studs*
y Good Wives (King). Audio Version — *Alcott, Louisa
May*
c Good Yontif (Illus. by Lynne Feldman) — *Blue, Rose*
c Good Zap, Little Grog (Illus. by Susan Meddaugh)
— *Wilson, Sarah*
Goodbye Again — *Dever, Edie*
y Goodbye Buffalo Sky — *Loveday, John*
y Goodbye Curate (Secombe). Audio Version
— *Secombe, Fred*
Goodbye, Descartes — *Devlin, Keith*
The Goodbye Look — *Macdonald, Ross*
Goodbye, Mr. Chips (Jarvis). Audio Version
— *Hilton, James*
Goodbye to Berlin (Cumming). Audio Version
— *Isherwood, Christopher*
Goodbye to Catholic Ireland — *Kenny, Mary*
Goodfellowe MP — *Dobbs, Michael*
c Goodnight Moon (Illus. by Clement Hurd) — *Brown,
Margaret Wise*
c Goodnight Moon: A 50th Anniversary Retrospective
(Illus. by Clement Hurd) — *Brown, Margaret Wise*
c Goody O'Grumpity (Illus. by Ashley Wolff) — *Brink,
Carol Ryrie*
c The Goof Who Invented Homework and Other School
Poems (Illus. by Denise Brunkus) — *Dakos, Kalli*
c Goose (Illus. by Molly Bang) — *Bang, Molly*
Goose in the Pond — *Fowler, Earlene*
c Gooseberry Park (Illus. by Arthur Howard) — *Rylant,
Cynthia*
c Goosebumps: Escape from Horrorland. Electronic
Media Version — *Stine, R L*
c Goosebumps Monster Edition. No. 1 — *Stine, R L*
c Goosebumps Series. Audio Version — *Stine, R L*
c The Goose's Tale (Illus. by Deborah Clearman)
— *Clearman, Deborah*
Gopher It! — *Cooper, Gail*
Gora Slut — *Hakanson, Bjorn*
r The Gorbachev Bibliography 1985-1991 — *Wieczynski,
Joseph L*
The Gorbachev Factor — *Brown, Archie*
Gorbachev's Failure in Lithuania — *Senn, Alfred
Erich*
c Gordon and the Giantkillers (Illus. by Michael Reid)
— *Rosselson, Leon*
c Gordon Goes for Glory (Illus. by Michael Reid)
— *Rosselson, Leon*
r Gordon Pape's 1997 Buyer's Guide to Mutual Funds
r Gordon Pape's 1997 Buyer's Guide to RRSP
c Gordon's Biscuit — *Millard, Kerry*
The Gore Galore Quiz Book — *Spignesi, Stephen J*
Gore Vidal: Writer against the Grain — *Parini, Jay*
c Gorillas: Gentle Giants of the Forest (Illus. by Bryn
Barnard) — *Milton, Joyce*
y Gorillas in the Mist — *Fossey, Dian*
Gorillas, Tea and Coffee — *Llewellyn, Kate*
Gospel — *Barnhardt, Wilton*
Gospel — *James, Bill, 1929-*
The Gospel according to John — *Brodie, Thomas L*

The Gospel according to Saint Mark — *Hooker,
Morna D*
The Gospel according to the Son — *Mailer, Norman*
Gospel Choirs — *Bell, Derrick*
The Gospel of Corax — *Park, Paul*
Gospel of Disunion — *Snay, Mitchell*
The Gospel of John — *Marrow, Stanley B*
The Gospel on Campus. 2nd Ed.
Gospel Truth — *Shorto, Russell*
The Gospels and Rabbinic Judaism — *Hilton, Michael*
Gospod Nad Vojskama — *Komanin, Zarko*
p Gospodarstvo Istre
Gossip — *Bram, Christopher*
c Gotcha! (Illus. by Kerry Argent) — *Jorgensen, Gail*
Gothic — *Botting, Fred*
Gothic Art — *Camille, Michael*
Gothic Horror Movies — *Wright, Bruce Lanier*
Gothic Images of Race in Nineteenth-Century Britain
— *Malchow, H L*
r Gothic Novels of the Twentieth Century — *Radcliffe,
Elsa J*
The Gothic Sublime — *Mishra, Vijay*
Gothic Traditions and Narrative Techniques in the
Fiction of Eudora Welty — *Weston, Ruth D*
The Gothic World of Anne Rice — *Hoppenstand, Gary*
Gott Eint--Trennt Christus? — *Augustin, George*
Der Gott Israels Und Die Volker — *Lohfink, Norbert*
Der Gottesknecht Bei Deutero-Jesaja — *Haag,
Herbert*
Gottesmahl Und Lebensspende — *Steingrimsson,
Sigurdur Orn*
Gottfried Semper: Architect of the Nineteenth
Century — *Mallgrave, Harry Francis*
Goud — *Geeraerts, Jef*
Gould: A Novel in Two Novels — *Dixon, Stephen*
La Gourmandise De Guillaume Apollinaire
— *Dormann, Genevieve*
Governance and Conflict in the Sudan 1985-1995
— *Kok, Peter N*
Governance and Politics in Africa — *Hyden, Goran*
Governance and Reform — *Lewis, John P*
Governance and Society in Colonial Mexico
— *Martin, Cheryl English*
Governance in Transition
The Governance of Metropolitan Regions — *Wingo,
Lowdon*
Governance of the Consuming Passions — *Hunt, Alan*
Governing China — *Lieberthal, Kenneth*
Governing Health — *Weissert, Carol S*
Governing Jerusalem — *Sharkansky, Ira*
Governing Prosperity — *Brown, Nicholas, 1961-*
Governing Rural England — *Eastwood, David*
Governing the New Europe — *Hayward, Jack*
Governing the White House — *Walcott, Charles E*
Government and Agriculture in Zimbabwe
— *Masters, William A*
Government and Politics in South Asia — *Baxter,
Craig*
Government and Society in Malaysia — *Crouch,
Harold*
Government and the Economy on the Amazon
Frontier — *Schneider, Robert R*
Government and the Enterprise since 1900
— *Tomlinson, Jim*
A Government as Good as Our People — *Oklahoma.
Governor's Commission on Government Performance*
r Government Assistance Almanac 1996-97
r The Government Directory of Addresses and
Telephone Numbers. 4th Ed.
The Government Factor — *Kaplar, Richard T*
yr The Government Financial Aid Book. 2nd Ed.
— *Student Financial Services*
Government Gay — *Hunter, Fred*
Government, Industry and Rearmament in Russia
1900-1914 — *Gatrell, Peter*
The Government Inspector — *Gogol, Nikolai*
Government Lawyers — *Clayton, Cornell W*
The Government of the Metropolitan Areas in the
U.S. — *Studenski, Paul*
Government Online in Canada — *Bourque, Pierre*
r Government Phone Book USA 1997
Government Printing in New Zealand 1840 to 1843
— *Salmond, Rachel*
Government Secrecy after the Cold War — *United
States. Congress. House. Committee on Government
Operations. Legislation and National Security
Subcommittee*
Government Structures in the U.S.A. and the
Sovereign States of the Former U.S.S.R. — *Hickey,
James E*

Government Survival in Parliamentary Democracies
— *Warwick, Paul V*
Government Versus the Market — *Middleton, Roger*
The Government We Choose
Governors and Settlers — *Francis, Mark*
Goya: 250 Aniversario — *Luna, Juan J*
GPS for Land Surveyors — *Van Sickle, Jan*
y Grab Hands and Run — *Temple, Frances*
Das Graberfeld Von Elgg Und Die Besiedlung Der
Nordostschweiz Im 5.-7. Jh. — *Windler, Renata*
Grace and Desolation — *Bentley, Sean*
Grace and Glory — *Leder, Jane Mersky*
Grace and Responsibility — *Cobb, John B, Jr.*
A Grace Disguised — *Sittser, Gerald L*
Grace Williams — *Boyd, Malcolm*
A Graceful Exit — *Basta, Lofty L*
Graceful Exits — *Blackman, Sushila*
Graceland: Going Home with Elvis — *Marling, Karal
Ann*
c Gracias, The Thanksgiving Turkey (Illus. by Joe
Cepeda) — *Cowley, Joy*
Gracious Living in a New World — *Stoddard,
Alexandra*
The Gracious Table — *Caselton, Margaret*
Grading the Teacher — *Jacobs, Nellie*
r Gradual Retirement in the OECD Countries
— *Delsen, Lei*
r Graduate Programs in Journalism and Mass
Communications — *Sumner, David E*
Graduates' Guide to Business Success — *Taylor,
Emerson*
r Graft-vs.-Host Disease. 2nd Ed. — *Ferrara, James L M*
Graham Greene: Friend and Brother — *Durano,
Leopoldo*
Graham Greene: The Enemy Within — *Shelden,
Michael*
Graham Greene: Three Lives — *Mockler, Anthony*
Graham Greene's Conradian Masterplot
— *Pendleton, Robert*
Graham Kerr's Swiftly Seasoned — *Kerr, Graham*
Grail — *Lawhead, Stephen R*
yr Grammar 101 — *Sorsby, Claudia*
The Grammar Book — *Bain, Elspeth*
A Grammar for Biblical Hebrew. Rev. Ed. — *Seow, C
L*
The Grammar of Discourse. 2nd Ed. — *Longacre,
Robert E*
y The Grammar of Fantasy — *Rodari, Gianni*
A Grammar of Responsibility — *Moran, Gabriel*
The Grammar of the Machine — *Stevens, Edward W,
Jr.*
y Grams, Her Boyfriend, My Family, and Me — *Derby,
Pat*
r Gran Canaria — *Koch, Hans-Peter*
c El Gran Granero Rojo (Illus. by Felicia Bond)
— *Brown, Margaret Wise*
El Gran Libro Ilustrado De Las Labores
c El Gran Negocio De Francisca (Illus. by Lillian
Hoban) — *Hoban, Russell*
c Gran Webster's War — *Williams, Keith*
Grand Coulee — *Pitzer, Paul C*
Grand Days — *Moorhouse, Frank*
Grand Expectations — *Patterson, James T*
A Grand Illusion? — *Judt, Tony*
Grand Illusions — *Ronald, Nick*
Grand Jury — *Friedman, Philip*
y Grand Jury (Rubinstein). Audio Version — *Friedman,
Philip*
Le Grand Livre Des Secrets — *Andries, Lise*
y Grand Mothers — *Giovanni, Nikki*
The Grand Ole Opry History of Country Music
— *Kingsbury, Paul*
The Grand Opera — *Plaut, Eric A*
Grand Promptness — *Mol, Pieter Laurens*
The Grand Scribe's Records. Vols. 1, 7 — *Ssu-Ma,
Chien*
p Grand Street
Grand Tour — *Wilton, Andrew*
Grand Tours and Cooks' Tours — *Withey, Lynne*
Grand Trunk Corporation — *Hofsommer, Don L*
c Grandad Bill's Song (Illus. by Melissa Bay Mathis)
— *Yolen, Jane*
c Granddaddy's Stars (Illus. by James Stevenson)
— *Griffith, Helen V*
c The Grandchildren of the Vikings — *Pitkanen, Matti A*
c Granddaddy's Gift (Illus. by Larry Johnson)
— *Mitchell, Margaree King*
La Grande Beune — *Michon, Pierre*
La Grande Pointe — *Matherne, Beverly*
Les Grandes Blondes — *Echenoz, Jean*

c Las Grandes Llanuras (Illus. by Luis Rizo)
— *Sanchez, Isidro*

Grandes Momentos De La Literatura Guatemalteca
— *Albizurez Palma, Francisco*

Grandes Peliculas Del Cine Gay — *Villalba, Susana M*

Grandfather: A Native American's Lifelong Search
for Truth and Harmony with Nature — *Brown,
Tom, 1950-*

c Grandfather and I (Illus. by Jan Ormerod)
— *Buckley, Helen E*

c Grandfather Twilight — *Berger, Barbara*

c Grandfather's Journey — *Say, Allen*

c Grandfather's Story (Illus. by Brenda Lena Fazio)
— *Fazio, Brenda Lena*

c Grandfather's Trolley (Illus. by Bruce McMillan)
— *McMillan, Bruce*

c Grandma Went to Market (Illus. by Bernard Lodge)
— *Blackstone, Stella*

c Grandma's Cat (Illus. by Marsha Lynn Winborn)
— *Ketteman, Helen*

c Grandma's Shoes (Illus. by Elivia Savadier)
— *Hathorn, Libby*

c Grandmother and the Runaway Shadow (Illus. by
Beth Peck) — *Rosenberg, Liz*

c Grandmother Bryant's Pocket (Illus. by Petra
Mathers) — *Martin, Jacqueline Briggs*

c Grandmother Spider Brings the Sun (Illus. by James
Bernardin) — *Keams, Geri*

The Grandmothers: A Family Portrait — *Wescott,
Glenway*

c Grandmother's Alphabet — *Shaw, Eve*

c Grandmother's Garden (Illus. by Raul Colon)
— *Archambault, John*

c Grandmother's Pigeon (Illus. by Jim LaMarche)
— *Erdrich, Louise*

c Grandpa Abe (Illus. by Marisabina Russo) — *Russo,
Marisabina*

c Grandpa Bear's Fantastic Scarf (Illus. by Gillian
Heal) — *Heal, Gillian*

c Grandpa Comes to Stay — *Lewis, Rob*

c Grandpa Takes Me to the Moon (Illus. by Barry Root)
— *Gaffney, Timothy R*

c Grandpa Toad's Secrets (Illus. by Keiko Kasza)
— *Kasza, Keiko*

c Grandpa Was a Cowboy (Illus. by Bert Dodson)
— *Sullivan, Silky*

r Grandparents: An Annotated Bibliography on Roles,
Rights, and Relationships — *Strauss, Carol Ann*

c Grandpa's Garden (Illus. by Karlyn Holman)
— *Darian, Shea*

c Grandpa's Indian Summer — *Gavin, Jamila*

c Grandpa's Visit (Illus. by Frances Clancy)
— *Keens-Douglas, Richardo*

Grands Decors Francais 1650-1800 — *Pons, Bruno*

p The Granite Review

Granite under Water — *Lohmann, Jeanne*

c Granny and the Desperadoes (Illus. by Steven
Kellogg) — *Parish, Peggy*

y Granny the Pag — *Bawden, Nina*

c Gran's Bees (Illus. by Donna Peterson) — *Thompson,
Mary*

y Grant Hill — *Rappoport, Ken*

y Grant Hill, a Biography — *Gutman, Bill*

c Grant Hill: Basketball's High Flier — *Gutman, Bill*

c Grant Hill: Humble Hotshot — *Savage, Jeff*

r Grant Seekers Guide. 4th Ed. — *Morris, James
McGrath*

Grant Us Courage — *Balm, Randall*

p Granta 54

p Granta 55

p Granta 56

The Granta Book of the Family — *Buford, Bill*

Grantchester Grind — *Sharpe, Tom*

r Grants and Awards Available to American Writers
1996-97

Grants for Education Support and Training — *Great
Britain. Dept. for Education and Employment*

Grants for Recreation, Sports and Athletics. 1994 Ed.

r Grants on Disc. Electronic Media Version

r The Grants Register 1997

r The Grantseeker's Handbook of Essential Internet
Sites — *DeAngelis, James*

The Grapes of Ralph — *Steadman, Ralph*

The Grapes of Wrath and Other Writings 1936-1941
— *Steinbeck, John*

p Graph

c The Graphic Alphabet (Illus. by David Pelletier)
— *Pelletier, David*

Graphic Java — *Geary, David*

Graphic Organizers — *Bromley, Karen D'Angelo*

Graphical Models — *Lauritzen, Steffen L*

y Graphics — *Dunn, Chris*

Graphics and GUIs with MATLAB — *Marchand,
Patrick*

Graphics and Web Page Design — *Lemay, Laura*

Graphing Statistics and Data — *Wallgren, Anders*

The Grass Harp — *Capote, Truman*

Grass Roots Politics in India — *Gould, Harold A*

c Grass Sandals (Illus. by Demi) — *Spivak, Dawnine*

The Grass Widow — *Holbrook, Teri*

c Grasses — *Chambers, Catherine*

r Grasshopper Country — *Rentz, D C F*

c Grasshoppers — *Gerholdt, James*

c Grassland — *Ricciuti, Edward R*

c Grassland Mammals — *Landau, Elaine*

Grassland: The History, Biology, Politics, and Promise
of the American Prairie — *Manning, Richard*

c Grasslands — *Waterlow, Julia*

Grassroot Horizons — *Morse, Richard*

Grassroots Grants — *Robinson, Andy*

Grassroots Leadership — *Mararike, C G*

Grave Exodus — *Cronin, Xavier A*

Grave Music — *Harrod-Eagles, Cynthia*

Grave of a Dozen Schemes — *Willmott, H P*

y Grave Secrets — *Wecht, Cyril*

y A Grave Talent (Bresnahan). Audio Version — *King,
Laurie R*

Graven Images — *Waterhouse, Jane*

c Graveyard Girl — *Myers, Anna*

Gravisca: Scavi Nel Santuario Greco 4 — *Boldrini,
Sabrina*

Gravitation and Inertia — *Ciufolini, Ignazio*

Gravity's Fatal Attraction — *Begelman, Mitchell C*

y Gray Matter — *Kennett, Shirley*

c Gray Rabbit's Odd One Out (Illus. by Alan Baker)
— *Baker, Alan*

y Grayheart — *Harper, Tara K*

r The Graying of America — *Kausler, Donald H*

r Grayson County, Texas Miscellaneous Wills and
Probates 1833-1923 — *Holder, Charlotte*

Graziers, Land Reform, and Political Conflict in
Ireland — *Jones, David Seth*

The Great Adventure — *Cruise, David*

c Great African Americans in Business — *Rediger, Pat*

c Great African Americans in Civil Rights — *Rediger,
Pat*

c Great African Americans in Entertainment
— *Rediger, Pat*

c Great African Americans in Literature — *Rediger,
Pat*

c Great African Americans in Music — *Rediger, Pat*

c Great African Americans in Sports — *Rediger, Pat*

The Great American — *Abella, Alex*

The Great American Blow-Up. Rev. Ed. — *Preston,
Ivan L*

y Great American Businesswomen — *Jeffrey, Laura S*

The Great American Deception — *Batra, Ravi*

c The Great American Elephant Chase — *Cross, Gillian*

Great American Food — *Palmer, Charlie*

The Great American Meat Book — *Ellis, Merle*

The Great American Outlaw — *Prassel, Frank
Richard*

Great American Railroad Stations — *Potter, Janet
Greenstein*

r The Great American Web Book — *Sagalyn, Raphael*

Great American West Collectibles — *Wilson, David L*

yr The Great American Wolf — *Hampton, Bruce*

Great American Writers (Asner). Audio Version
— *Carver, Raymond*

c The Great Antler Auction (Illus. by Michael J
Doolittle) — *Goodman, Susan E*

Great Ape Societies — *McGrew, William C*

y The Great Apes — *Leach, Michael*

y The Great Apparitions of Mary — *Swann, Ingo*

c Great-Aunt Martha (Illus. by Shelley Jackson)
— *Jones, Rebecca C*

y The Great Automatic Grammatizator and Other
Stories — *Dahl, Roald*

y Great Beginnings and Endings — *Ensign, Georgianne*

c The Great Blue Grump (Illus. by Kitty Macaulay)
— *Creighton, Jill*

c The Great Book of Picture Puzzles — *Snape, Juliet*

Great Books — *Denby, David*

yr Great Books for Girls — *Odean, Kathleen*

Great Books of the Christian Tradition and Other
Books Which Have Shaped Our World — *Glaspey,
Terry W*

c The Great Brain Is Back (Illus. by Diane DeGroat)
— *Fitzgerald, John D*

The Great Bridge — *McCullough, David*

c Great Britain — *Flint, David*

r Great Britain: Decline or Renewal? — *Studlar, Donley
T*

c Great Buildings — *Lynch, Anne*

Great Camps of the Adirondacks — *Kaiser, Harvey H*

The Great Canoes — *Neel, David*

The Great Canon Controversy — *Casement, William*

y Great Careers for People Fascinated by Government
and the Law — *Males, Anne Marie*

y Great Careers for People Interested in Art and Design
— *Bartlett, Gillian*

y Great Careers for People Interested in
Communications Technology — *Czerneda, Julie*

y Great Careers for People Interested in Food
— *Mason, Helen*

y Great Careers for People Interested in the Past
— *Vincent, Victoria*

y Great Careers for People Interested in Travel and
Tourism — *Sharon, Donna*

Great Carpets of the World — *Berinstain, Valerie*

c The Great Castle Mystery (Illus. by Steve Cox)
— *Denchfield, Nick*

The Great Chief Justice — *Hobson, Charles F*

Great Christian Thinkers — *Kung, Hans*

Great Cons and Con Artists — *Summer, Robin Langley*

y Great Courtroom Lawyers — *Calabro, Marian*

The Great Cruising Cookbook — *Payne, John C*

c Great Crystal Bear (Illus. by William Noonan)
— *Lesser, Carolyn*

r Great Dates in Islamic History

y The Great Depression — *Farrell, Jacqueline*

y The Great Depression — *Watkins, T H*

The Great Depression and the Culture of Abundance
— *Barnard, Rita*

The Great Dinosaur Extinction Controversy
— *Officer, Charles*

c Great Discoveries — *Steele, Philip*

The Great Disorder — *Feldman, Gerald D*

r The Great Encyclopedia of 19th-Century Major
League Baseball — *Nemec, David*

r Great Events. Vols. 1-3

r Great Events. Vols. 11-13

Great Excavations — *Elliott, Melinda*

Great Expectations. Audio Version — *Dickens,
Charles*

Great Explorations — *Bassett, Jan*

y The Great Eye — *Shalant, Phyllis*

y The Great Famine — *Jordan, William C*

y The Great Fire — *Murphy, Jim*

The Great Fires — *Gilbert, Jack*

The Great Flood of 1993 — *Changnon, Stanley A*

Great Fool — *Ryokan*

c The Great Frog Race and Other Poems (Illus. by Kate
Kiesler) — *George, Kristine O'Connell*

Great Gambles of the Civil War — *Katcher, Philip*

The Great Gatsby and Modern Times — *Berman,
Ronald*

c The Great Gilly Hopkins (Bresnahan). Audio Version
— *Paterson, Katherine*

c Great Girl Food (Illus. by Judy Pelikan)

c The Great Grammar Book — *Maizels, Jennie*

c The Great Grammar Book (Illus. by Jennie Maizels)
— *Petty, Kate*

c Great-Grandpa's in the Litter Box (Illus. by Jack E
Davis) — *Greenburg, Dan*

The Great Guano Rush — *Skaggs, Jimmy M*

c The Great Halloween Treat — *Tanner, Suzy-Jane*

y The Great House of Birds — *Hay, John*

y The Great Human Diasporas — *Cavalli-Sforza, L L*

Great Inflations of the 20th Century — *Siklos, Pierre
L*

y The Great Interactive Dream Machine — *Peck,
Richard*

The Great Irish Famine — *O Grada, Cormac*

The Great Irish Famine — *Poirteir, Cathal*

y The Great Iron Link — *Laughlin, Rosemary*

r Great Jewish Quotations — *Kolatch, Alfred J*

The Great Lakes — *Berton, Pierre*

Great Lakes Archaeology and Paleoecology
— *MacDonald, Robert I*

Great Lakes Bulk Carriers — *Devendorf, John F*

The Great Longing — *Moring, Marcel*

y The Great Machines — *Hedin, Robert*

y Great Men and Women of Computing — *Spencer,
Donald D*

The Great Migration Begins. Vols. 1-3 — *Anderson,
Robert Charles*

Great Moments in Science — *Haven, Kendall F*

y Great Names in Black College Sports — *Hunt, Donald*

Great Northern Railway 1945-1970 Photo Archive
— *Olsen, Byron D*

The Great Outsiders — *Taylor, S J*

Great Patchwork Collection — *Dahlstrom, Carol Field*
The Great Philosophers. Vol. 3 — *Jaspers, Karl*
The Great Philosophers. Vols. 3-4 — *Jaspers, Karl*
A Great Place to Die — *Connolly, Sean, 1943-*
y The Great Plains (Illus. by Luis Rizo) — *Llamas, Andreu*
The Great Powers and the End of the Ottoman Empire — *Kent, Marian*
The Great Pox — *Arrizabalaga, Jon*
Great Pretenders — *Shover, Neal*
The Great Pulp Heroes — *Hutchison, Don*
c The Great Pyramid (Illus. by Laura Lo Turco) — *Mann, Elizabeth*
The Great Railway Bazaar — *Theroux, Paul*
The Great Rebuildings of Tudor and Stuart England — *Platt, Colin*
c The Great Redwall Feast (Illus. by Christopher Denise) — *Jacques, Brian*
The Great Retreat — *Austin, Paul Britten*
r The Great Rock Discography — *Strong, M C*
c The Great Santa Surprise — *Tanner, Suzy-Jane*
The Great Shadow — *Goldfarb, Clifford S*
c The Great Skeleton Race — *Kermode, Mo*
c Great Snakes! (Illus. by Jean Day Zallinger) — *Robinson, Fay*
The Great South Carolina Ku Klux Klan Trials 1871-1872 — *Williams, Lou Falkner*
The Great Southwest of the Fred Harvey Company and the Santa Fe Railway   *Weigle, Marta*
The Great Speckled Bird — *Cornbleth, Catherine*
Great Time Coming — *Falkner, David*
y Great Time Coming (Davidson). Audio Version — *Falkner, David*
The Great Transformation — *Marsh, Robert M*
Great Travel Photography — *Hollenbeck, Cliff*
c The Great Turtle Drive (Illus. by Dirk Zimmer) — *Sanfield, Steve*
c Great-Uncle Alfred Forgets (Illus. by Ben Shecter) — *Shecter, Ben*
The Great Wall and the Empty Fortress — *Nathan, Andrew J*
The Great Wall in Ruins — *Chu, Godwin C*
The Great War and the Missing Muse — *Quinn, Patrick J, 1946-*
y The Great War and the Shaping of the 20th Century — *Winter, J M*
The Great Wave — *Fischer, David Hackett*
The Great Wheel — *Mariani, Paul*
c The Great White Man-Eating Shark (Illus. by Jonathan Allen) — *Mahy, Margaret*
Great White Sharks — *Klimley, A Peter*
Great Women of the Bible in Art and Literature — *Solle, Dorothee*
y The Great Women Superheroes — *Robbins, Trina*
c Great Writers and Kids Write Mystery Stories (Illus. by Gahan Wilson) — *Greenberg, Martin Harry*
Greater China — *Shambaugh, David*
Greater China and U.S. Foreign Policy — *Metzger, Thomas A*
Greater France — *Aldrich, Robert*
Greater Medieval Houses of England and Wales 1300-1500. Vol. 1 — *Emery, Anthony*
The Greatest Gift — *Stern, Philip Van Doren*
The Greatest Mystery in the World — *Mandino, Og*
c The Greatest Show off Earth — *Mahy, Margaret*
The Greatest Story Ever Told (Herrmann). Audio Version — *Oursler, Fulton*
c Greatest Table — *Rosen, Michael J*
r Greatness: Who Makes History and Why — *Simonton, Dean Keith*
r I Greci: Storia Cultura Arte Societa. Vol. 1 — *Settis, Salvatore*
The Greco-Persian Wars — *Green, Peter*
c Greece — *Allard, Denise*
Greece at the Crossroads — *Iatrides, John O*
Greece between East and West — *Kopcke, Gunter*
Greece in a Changing Europe — *Featherstone, Kevin*
yr Greek Americans — *Phillips, David*
Greek and Latin Literature of the Roman Empire — *Dihle, Albrecht*
Greek and Roman Portraits — *Walker, Susan*
The Greek Apocalypse of Baruch (3 Baruch) in Hellenistic Judaism and Early Christianity — *Harlow, Daniel C*
Greek Art. 4th Ed. — *Boardman, John*
Greek Bastardy in the Classical and Hellenistic Periods — *Ogden, Daniel*
A Greek Countryside — *Jameson, Michael H*
r A Greek-English Lexicon. Rev. and Augm. Throughout — *Liddell, Henry George*

r Greek-English Lexicon: Revised Supplement — *Glare, P G W*
Greek for Reading — *Seligson, Gerda M*
Greek in Jewish Palestine. Hellenism in Jewish Palestine — *Lieberman, Saul*
Greek Jewry in the Twentieth Century 1913-1983 — *Plaut, Joshua Eli*
Greek Law in Its Political Setting — *Foxhall, L*
Greek Lyric Poetry — *West, M L*
c The Greek News — *Powell, Anton*
The Greek Paradox — *Allison, Graham T*
Greek Poetry of the Imperial Period — *Hopkinson, Neil*
Greek Sanctuaries — *Marinatos, Nanno*
Greek Sculpture in the Art Museum, Princeton University — *Princeton University. Art Museum*
y A Greek Temple (Illus. by Fiona Macdonald) — *Macdonald, Fiona*
y Greek Theatre — *Ross, Stewart*
r Greek Tragedy on the American Stage — *Hartigan, Karelisa V*
Greek Transport Amphorae — *Whitbread, Ian K*
Greek Vases in the San Antonio Museum of Art — *San Antonio Museum of Art*
The Greek Vegetarian — *Kochilas, Diane*
The Greek World — *Pugliese Carratelli, Giovanni*
c The Greeks — *Allard, Denise*
c Greeks — *Davies, Kath*
c The Greeks — *Dineen, Jacqueline*
c Green — *Bryant-Mole, Karen*
p Green Anarchist
Green Ash, Red Maple, Black Gum — *Waters, Michael*
Green Backlash — *Rowell, Andrew*
Green Backlash — *Switzer, Jacqueline Vaughn*
The Green Breast of the New World — *Westling, Louise H*
Green Chemistry — *Anastas, Paul T*
r The Green Corporation — *Bhat, Vasanthakumar N*
Green Culture — *Herndl, Carl G*
y Green Dolphin Street — *Goudge, Elizabeth*
The Green Dragon — *Williams, Martin*
p Green Egg
c Green Eggs and Ham. Electronic Media Version — *Seuss, Dr.*
A Green Estate — *Feeley-Harnik, Gillian*
c The Green Frogs (Illus. by Yumi Heo) — *Heo, Yumi*
The Green Fuse — *Harte, John*
Green Guerrillas — *Collinson, Helen*
c The Green Hand (Illus. by Alex De Wolf) — *Krailing, Tessa*
Green Imperialism — *Grove, Richard H*
Green, Inc. — *Cairncross, Frances*
The Green Kitchen Handbook — *Berthold-Bond, Annie*
Green Lake — *Epperson, S K*
The Green Library — *Keefer, Janice Kulyk*
The Green Mile. Pts. 1-6 — *King, Stephen*
y Green Monkey Dreams — *Carmody, Isobelle*
Green Mountain Ghosts, Ghouls and Unsolved Mysteries — *Citro, Joseph A*
Green Nature/Human Nature — *Lewis, Charles A*
Green Networks — *Diani, Mario*
p Green: Personal Finance for the Unashamed
Green Places in Small Spaces — *Fischer, Kerwin*
Green Production — *Leff, Enrique*
The Green Rainbow — *Dalton, Russell J*
y Green Resistance — *Adams, Anna*
The Green Sea of Heaven — *Hafiz*
c Green Snake Ceremony (Illus. by Kim Doner) — *Watkins, Sherrin*
c Green Thumbs — *Carlson, Laurie M*
c The Green Truck Garden Giveaway (Illus. by Alec Gillman) — *Martin, Jacqueline Briggs*
Green Was the Earth on the Seventh Day — *Heyerdahl, Thor*
Green Witchcraft — *Moura, Ann*
r Greenberg's Guide to Marbles. 2nd Ed. — *Webb, Dennis*
Greenfinger: The Rise of Michael Green and Carlton Communications — *Snoddy, Raymond*
Greenhouse Gas Mitigation Assessment — *Sathaye, Jayant A*
Greening Environmental Policy — *Fischer, Frank*
The Greening of Faith — *Carroll, John E*
The Greening of Protestant Thought — *Fowler, Robert Booth, 1940-*
The Greening of Theology — *Bouma-Prediger, Steven*
r Greening the College Curriculum — *Collett, Jonathan*
Greening the GATT — *Esty, Daniel C*
Greening the Grassroots — *Rossi, Graciella*

Greenthieves — *Foster, Alan Dean*
c Greetings from America — *Nelson, Ray*
c Greetings from Sandy Beach (Illus. by Bob Graham) — *Graham, Bob*
c Greg Maddux — *Rambeck, Richard*
Gregor Mendel: The First Geneticist — *Orel, Vitezslav*
Gregor Von Tours 538-594 — *Heinzelmann, Martin*
c Gregory Cool (Illus. by Caroline Binch) — *Binch, Caroline*
Gregory the Great: Perfection in Imperfection — *Straw, Carole*
Greves Et Politique A Shanghai — *Roux, Alain*
The Grevillea Book. Vols. 1-3 — *Olde, Peter*
Grey Area and Other Stories — *Self, Will*
c Greyfriars Bobby — *Brown, Ruth*
c Greyfur, the Story of a Rabbit (Illus. by Kenneth Lilly) — *Potter, Tessa*
Greyhound to Wherever — *Imperato, Ayn*
y The Grid — *Kerr, Philip*
y The Grid (Spiner). Audio Version — *Kerr, Philip*
Gridiron — *Kerr, Philip*
Grief as a Family Process — *Shapiro, Ester R*
Grief Notes and Animal Dreams — *Munro, Jane Southwell*
Grievances, Remedies and the State. 2nd Ed. — *Birkinshaw, Patrick*
c Griffin's Castle — *Nimmo, Jenny*
The Grim Reader — *Spiegel, Maura*
Grinders and Grammars — *Siruy, Christopher*
Grindhouse: The Forbidden World of Adults Only Cinema — *Muller, Eddie*
The Gris-Gris Man — *Davis, Don*
y Griswold v. Connecticut — *Wawrose, Susan C*
c Grizzlies — *McDonald, Mary Ann*
c Grizzly Bears — *Turbak, Gary*
The Grizzly Bears of Yellowstone — *Craighead, John J*
y Grizzly Years — *Peacock, Doug*
The Groaning Board — *Meyers, Annette*
Groaning Tears — *Garrison, Elise P*
yr The Grolier Library of Environmental Concepts and Issues. Vols. 1-8 — *Aslett, Michael*
cr The Grolier Library of International Biographies. Vols. 1-10
r The Grolier Library of Science Biographies. Vols. 1-10
cr The Grolier Multimedia Encyclopedia 1996. Electronic Media Version
cr The Grolier Multimedia Encyclopedia 1997. Electronic Media Version
r Grolier Science Fiction. Electronic Media Version
cr The Grolier Student Encyclopedia of Science, Technology and the Environment. Vols. 1-11
y Groogleman — *Doyle, Debra*
c Grooming and Stable Management — *Smith, Lucy*
Grooming, Gossip, and the Evolution of Language — *Dunbar, Robin*
c Gross Anatomy — *Becker, Christine*
y Gross Grub — *Porter, Cheryl*
Grossbritannien, Das Scheitern Der EVG Und Der NATO-Beitritt Der Bundesrepublik Deutschland — *Jansen, Hans-Heinrich*
Der Grosse Exodus — *Schlogel, Karl*
Die Grosse Insel — *Byer, Doris*
Das Grossmahrische Reich — *Eggers, Martin*
y Grossology: The Science of Really Gross Things (Illus. by Jack Keely) — *Branzei, Sylvia*
r The Grosvenor Gallery — *Casteras, Susan P*
Grotesque Purgatory — *Sullivan, Henry W, 1942-*
Grotowski's Objective Drama Research — *Wolford, Lisa*
The Ground beneath Our Feet — *Valek, Miroslav*
Ground Bioengineering Techniques for Slope Protection and Erosion Control — *Schiechtl, Hugo M*
The Ground of Professional Ethics — *Koehn, Daryl*
Ground Rules — *Jaffe, Sherril*
Ground Rules — *Westbrook, Deeanne*
Ground Truth — *Pickles, John*
The Ground We Share — *Aitken, Robert*
Ground Zero — *Francke, Linda Bird*
y Ground Zero (Anderson). Audio Version — *Anderson, Kevin J*
Grounds of Natural Philosophy — *Newcastle, Margaret Cavendish*
GroundWork: New and Selected Poems of Don L. Lee/Haki R. Madhubuti from 1966-1996 — *Madhubuti, Haki R*
The Group of Seven — *Hill, Charles C*
c The Group of Seven and Tom Thomson — *Newlands, Anne*

Group Psychology and Political Theory — *Alford, C Fred*

Group Psychotherapy for People with Chronic Mental Illness — *Stone, Walter N*

Group Psychotherapy with Addicted Populations. 2nd Ed. — *Flores, Philip J*

Group Spiritual Direction — *Dougherty, Rose Mary*

Group Therapy for Schizophrenic Patients — *Kanas, Nick*

Group Treatment for Adult Survivors of Abuse — *Webb, Laura*

Group Work Practice in a Troubled Society — *Kurland, Roselle*

Groups as Galois Groups — *Volklein, Helmut*

Groups: Process and Practice. 5th Ed. — *Corey, Marianne Schneider*

Grow Old along with Me, the Best Is Yet to Be (Asner). Audio Version — *Martz, Sandra Haldeman*

Grow Young with HGH — *Klatz, Ronald*

A Grower's Guide to Water, Media, and Nutrition for Greenhouse Crops — *Reed, David Wm.*

Growing — *Morris, Jenny*

Growing a Girl — *Mackoff, Barbara*

Growing a Japanese Science City — *Dearing, James W*

Growing Artificial Societies — *Epstein, Joshua M*

r Growing Bulbs — *Mathew, Brian*

Growing Camellias — *Tapley, Margaret*

Growing Critical — *Morss, John R*

Growing Darkness, Growing Light — *Valentine, Jean*

A Growing Garden — *Zabar, Abbie*

r Growing Herbs — *Bown, Deni*

Growing in Wisdom, Age and Grace — *Bernardin, Joseph Louis*

Growing Miniature and Patio Roses — *Eagle, Dawn*

Growing Myself — *Handelsman, Judith*

Growing Old and Needing Care — *Chapman, Tom*

Growing Old in the Middle Ages — *Shahar, Shulamith*

c Growing Older — *Newson, Lesley*

Growing Older in America — *Riekse, R J*

Growing Out of the Plan — *Naughton, Barry*

Growing Pains — *Scales, Peter C*

y Growing Payne — *Larkin, John*

Growing Plants from Seed — *Kelly, John*

Growing through the Ugly — *Vazquez, Diego*

Growing Up — *Baker, Russell*

yr Growing Up — *Broude, Gwen J*

Growing Up African American in Catholic Schools — *Irvine, Jacqueline Jordan*

y Growing Up Black. Rev. Ed. — *David, Jay*

Growing Up Feminist — *Scutt, Jocelynne A*

Growing Up Feminist Too — *Scutt, Jocelynne A*

y Growing Up in Coal Country — *Bartoletti, Susan Campbell*

Growing Up in Europe — *Chisholm, Lynne*

Growing Up in Medieval London — *Hanawalt, Barbara A*

Growing Up in New York — *Leipzig, Arthur*

y Growing up in The Great Depression — *Wormser, Richard*

yr Growing Up in Twentieth-Century America — *West, Elliott*

Growing Up in Wales 1895-1939 — *Grenfell-Hill, Jeffrey*

y Growing Up Indian (Illus. by William Sauts Bock) — *Wolfson, Evelyn*

Growing Up Poor — *Davin, Anna*

y Growing Up Puerto Rican — *DeJesus, Joy L*

Growing Up Republican — *Beard, Patricia*

Growing Up Sad — *Cytryn, Leon*

Growing Up with Dick and Jane — *Kismaric, Carole*

Growing Up with My Grandfather — *Daniel, Clifton Truman*

Growing Your Business Online — *Hise, Phaedra*

Grown Men — *Mawe, S M*

c Grown-Ups Get to Do all the Driving (Illus. by William Steig) — *Steig, William*

Growth and Crisis in Cote D'Ivoire — *Berthelemy, Jean-Claude*

Growth and Crisis in the Spanish Economy 1940-93 — *Lieberman, Sima*

Growth and Development in Brazil — *Kinzo, Maria D'Alva G*

Growth and Economic Development — *Lombardini, Siro*

Growth in a Traditional Society — *Hoffman, Philip T*

The Growth of American Government — *Campbell, Ballard C*

The Growth of Big Business in the United States and Western Europe 1850-1939 — *Schmitz, Christopher J*

The Growth of Mysticism — *McGinn, Bernard*

The Growth of Nations — *Lewis, Mark*

y The Growth of the Mind — *Greenspan, Stanley I*

The Growth of Understanding — *Parker, Michael*

Growth, the Environment and the Distribution of Incomes — *Beckerman, Wilfred*

Growth Theories in Light of the East Asian Experience — *Ito, Takatoshi*

Growth Triumphant — *Easterlin, Richard A*

Growth with Stability — *Corry, Dan*

c Grumpers' Farm (Illus. by Penny Ives) — *Heiney, Paul*

c The Grumpy Shepherd and Other Christmas Plays — *Butler, Heather*

Grund Genug — *Runge, Doris*

c Gruntle Piggle Takes Off (Illus. by Johnny Wales) — *Little, Jean*

Grutte Wurden — *Veer, Akky Van Der*

The GSH Phenomenon — *Pressman, Alan H*

c Guadalupe Quintanilla, Leader of the Hispanic Community — *Wade, Mary Dodson*

y Guardate De Los Idus — *Gonzalez, Lola*

The Guardian — *Eidson, Bill*

The Guardian — *Wolf, Joan*

Guardian of the Great Lakes — *Rodgers, Bradley A*

Guardians of Marovo Lagoon — *Hviding, Edvard*

Guardians of the Parks — *Miles, John C*

y Guardians of Wildlife — *Chandler, Gary*

c A Guatemalan Family — *Malone, Michael, 1956-*

Guatemalan Journey — *Benz, Stephen Connely*

The Guatemalan Tax Reform — *Bahl, Roy*

Il Guerriero Di Agrigento — *Barbanera, Marcello*

Guerrilla Conflict before the Cold War — *Joes, Anthony James*

Guerrilla Cooking — *Walsh, Mel*

Guerrilla Marketing Online Weapons — *Levinson, Jay Conrad*

Guerrilla Marketing Weapons. Audio Version — *Levinson, Jay Conrad*

Guerrilla Television — *Shamberg, Michael*

r Guerrilla Warfare — *Joes, Anthony James*

The Guerrilla Wars of Central America — *Landau, Saul*

c Guess How Much I Love You (Illus. by Anita Jeram) — *McBratney, Sam*

The Guest — *Cory, Charlotte*

A Guest in the House of Israel — *Williamson, Clark M*

Guest of Honor (Bruce). Audio Version — *Reed, Robert*

Guest People — *Constable, Nicole*

Guests in Their Own House — *McEnroy, Carmel*

Guests without Grief — *Jhung, Paula*

Gui Lai De Jun Dao — *Zhou, Yu*

Guia Completa De Jardineria En Macetas — *Berry, Susan*

r Guia De Alojamiento En Casas Rurales De Espana 1996

Guia Para Viajeros Medievales (Oriente, Siglos XIII-XV) — *Guglielmi, Nilda*

Guide — *Cooper, Dennis*

Guide Des Aines. 3rd Ed. — *Dupont, Elaine*

r Guide for the Care and Use of Laboratory Animals — *Institute of Laboratory Animal Resources (U.S.). Committee on Care and Use of Laboratory Animals*

r Guide for Translators — *Sofer, Morry*

r A Guide to American Crime Films of the Forties and Fifties — *Langman, Larry*

r A Guide to America's Sex Laws — *Posner, Richard A*

r A Guide to Archives and Manuscripts in the United States — *Hamer, Philip M*

r Guide to Biblical Coins. 3rd Ed. — *Hendin, David*

r Guide to British Drama Explication. Vol. 1 — *Douglas, Krystan V*

A Guide to British Medieval Seals — *Harvey, P D A*

Guide to Career Success — *Hauter, Janet*

r Guide to Catalina — *Mallan, Chicki*

r A Guide to Children's Books about Asian Americans — *Blake, Barbara*

A Guide to China's Tax and Business Laws — *Gensler, Howard*

r Guide to Civil War Books — *Barbuto, Domenica M*

r Guide to Civil War Records — *McCawley, Patrick*

r A Guide to Collections on Paraguay in the United States — *Whigham, Thomas L*

r A Guide to Ethnic Health Collections in the United States — *Gibbs, Tyson*

r Guide to Federal Records in the National Archives of the United States. Vols. 1-3 — *United States. National Archives and Records Administration*

Guide to Financial Security — *Rosenberg, Stephen*

yr A Guide to Fossils — *Mayr, Helmut*

r Guide to Greater Washington D.C. Grantmakers. 2nd Ed.

A Guide to Helping Students Develop Their IEPs. Audio Version

Guide to High Definition Video Production — *REBO Studio*

r Guide to Impressionist Paris — *Lurie, Patty*

The Guide to Improve Your Credit — *Graham, Terry*

A Guide to Indian Manuscripts — *Riddick, John F*

r Guide to Information Resources in Ethnic Museum, Library, and Archival Collections in the United States — *Buttlar, Lois J*

r A Guide to Information Sources and Resources for Economic Development — *Smyth, K*

r Guide to Information Sources in the Botanical Sciences. 2nd Ed. — *Davis, Elisabeth B*

A Guide to International Monetary Economics — *Visser, Hans*

r The Guide to Internet Job Searching — *Riley, Margaret*

Guide to Kansas Architecture — *Sachs, David H*

r Guide to Legislative Information Technology — *Greenberg, Pam*

A Guide to Licensing Artwork — *Moore, Marilyn*

Guide to Local History and Genealogy Resources 1995 — *Doering, Anita Tylor*

Guide to Love — *White, Suzanne*

y Guide to Microlife — *Rainis, Kenneth G*

r The Guide to National Banking Law — *Levin, Jonathan L*

Guide to Netscape Navigator 2.0 — *Barnett, James*

r Guide to Netscape Navigator Gold — *Randall, Neil*

Guide to Networking — *Hadley, Joyce*

r Guide to Northeast Pacific Flatfishes Families Bothidae, Cynoglossidae, and Pleuronectidae — *Kramer, Donald E*

r Guide to Official Statistics. Electronic Media Version

Guide to Official Statistics — *Great Britain. Office for National Statistics*

A Guide to Poetry 0-13 — *Powling, Chris*

r A Guide to Popular Music Reference Books — *Haggerty, Gary*

Guide to Publishing User Manuals — *Whitaker, Ken*

r Guide to Reference Books. 10th Ed. — *Sheehy, Eugene P*

r Guide to Reference Books. 11th Ed. — *Balay, Robert*

r A Guide to Reference Books for Small and Medium-Sized Libraries 1984-1994 — *Dority, G Kim*

r Guide to Reference Books: Supplement to the Tenth Edition — *Balay, Robert*

A Guide to Remembering Japanese Characters — *Henshall, Kenneth G*

A Guide to Reproduction — *Pollard, Irina*

r Guide to Research in Classical Art and Mythology — *Van Keuren, Frances Dodds*

r A Guide to Rock Art Sites — *Whitley, David S*

r A Guide to Serial Bibliographies for Modern Literatures. 2nd Ed. — *Wortman, William A*

A Guide to Spiritual Discernment — *Job, Rueben P*

A Guide to the Acadians in Maryland in the Eighteenth and Nineteenth Centuries — *Wood, Gregory A*

A Guide to the Archives of the Ecclesiastical Province of British Columbia and Yukon — *Archivists of the Ecclesiastical Province of British Columbia and Yukon*

r A Guide to the Birds of Colombia — *Hilty, Steven L*

r A Guide to the Birds of the Galapagos Islands — *Castro, Isabel*

A Guide to the Bodhisattva Way of Life — *Santideva*

A Guide to the Contents of the Qur'an — *Sherif, Faruq*

r A Guide to the Early Reports of the Supreme Court of the United States — *Cohen, Morris L*

A Guide to the Economies in Transition — *Jeffries, Ian*

yr A Guide to the Elements — *Stwertka, Albert*

The Guide to the Federal Budget 1997

r A Guide to the Freshwater Mussels of Ohio. Rev. 3rd Ed. — *Watters, G Thomas*

A Guide to the Frogs and Toads of Belize — *Meyer, John R*

r A Guide to the Identification and Natural History of the Sparrows of the United States and Canada — *Rising, James*

r Guide to the Presidency. 2nd Ed., Vols. 1-2 — *Nelson, Michael*

A Guide to the Project Management Body of Knowledge. 1995 Ed.

r A Guide to the Reptiles and Frogs of the Perth Region — *Bush, Brian*

A Guide to the Sacraments — *Macquarrie, John*

r Guide to the Secular Poetry of T.S. Eliot — *Blalock, Susan E*

A Guide to the Selected Poems of T.S. Eliot — *Southam, B C*

Guide to the Ships Plans Collection at Mystic Seaport Museum — *Stone, Ellen C*

r A Guide to the Study of the United States of America — *Library of Congress. General Reference and Bibliography Division*

r A Guide to the Study of the United States of America. 1st Suppl. — *Library of Congress. General Reference and Bibliography Division*

r Guide to the Study of United States History Outside the U.S. 1945-1980. Vols. 1-5 — *Hanke, Lewis*

r Guide to the Top Southern California Companies

r A Guide to Tracing Your Donegal Ancestors — *Duffy, Godfrey F*

A Guide to Western Bird Feeding — *Dennis, John V*

y The Guide to Wooden Boats (Illus. by Benjamin Mendlowitz) — *Mendlowitz, Benjamin*

A Guide to Writing as an Engineer — *Beer, David F*

r A Guide to Writing English as a Second Language — *Tannacito, Dan J*

A Guidebook for Creating Three-Dimensional Theatre Art — *Carnaby, Ann J*

A Guidebook for the Jerusalem Pilgrimage in the Late Middle Ages — *Brefeld, Josephine*

Guidebook on Molecular Modeling in Drug Design — *Cohen. Claude*

A Guided Tour of Five Works by Plato. 2nd Ed. — *Biffle, Christopher*

Guided Tours of Hell — *Prose, Francine*

Guidelines for College Libraries. 5th Ed. — *Ennis, Kathy*

Guidelines for Use of Vapor Cloud Dispersion Models — *American Institute of Chemical Engineers. Center for Chemical Process Safety*

Guidelines for Writing Effective Operating and Maintenance Procedures

Guiding the Reader to the Next Book — *Shearer, Kenneth D*

r Guillaume De Machaut: A Guide to Research — *Earp, Lawrence*

Guillaume Postel Et Jean Boulaese

Guillermo Cabrera Infante: Two Islands, Many Worlds — *Souza, Raymond D*

Guilt — *Lescroart, John T*

Guilty as Charged — *Turow, Scott*

y Guilty as Charged (Kaye). Audio Version — *Turow, Scott*

Guilty as Sin — *Hoag, Tami*

Guilty Pleasures — *Cameron, Stella*

Guilty Pleasures — *Robertson, Pamela*

Guilty: The Collapse of Criminal Justice — *Rothwax, Harold J*

r Guinea — *Binns, Margaret*

The Guinea Pig — *Morales, Edmund*

r The Guinness Book of Names. 7th Ed. — *Dunkling, Leslie*

yr The Guinness Book of Records. 1997 Ed.

r The Guinness Book of World Records 1997

r The Guinness Encyclopedia. 2nd Ed.

r The Guinness Encyclopedia of Popular Music. 2nd Ed., Vols. 1-6 — *Larkin, Colin*

yr Guinness Multimedia Disc of Records. 1996 Ed. Electronic Media Version

The Guitar in Jazz — *Sallis, James*

The Gulag at War — *Bacon, Edwin*

y Gulf — *Westall, Robert*

Gulf Dreams — *Perez, Emma*

Gulf Logistics, Blackadder's War — *White, Martin S*

The Gulf War — *Cordesman, Anthony H*

The Gulf War and Mental Health — *Martin, James A*

The Gulf War Did Not Take Place — *Baudrillard, Jean*

Gullah Images — *Green, Jonathan, 1955-*

Gullah Statesman — *Miller, Edward A, Jr., 1927-*

c Gulliver in Lilliput (Illus. by Kimberly Bulcken Root) — *Hodges, Margaret*

Gulliver's Travels — *Knowles, Ronald*

c The Gulls of the Edmund Fitzgerald (Illus. by Tres Seymour) — *Seymour, Tres*

r Gun Control — *Kruschke, Earl R*

The Gun Seller — *Laurie, Hugh*

The Gunboat Philadelphia and the Defense of Lake Champlain in 1776 — *Lundeberg, Philip K*

Gunga Din Highway — *Chin, Frank*

The Gunpowder Plot — *Fraser, Antonia*

The Gunpowder Plot — *Haynes, Alan*

Guns and Boyhood in America — *Holden, Jonathan*

Guns, Crime, and Freedom — *LaPierre, Wayne*

Guns, Germs, and Steel — *Diamond, Jared*

The Guns in the Closet — *Yglesias, Jose*

Guns 'n' Rose — *Barrett, Robert G*

The Guns of Lattimer — *Novak, Michael*

The Guns of Victory — *Blackburn, George G*

Guns or Butter — *Bernstein, Irving*

Gurdjieff: Essays and Reflections on the Man and His Teaching — *Needleman, Jacob*

c Gus and Grandpa (Illus. by Catherine Stock) — *Mills, Claudia*

A Gust for Paradise — *McColley, Diane Kelsey*

Gustav Mahler. Vol. 2 — *La Grange, Henry-Louis De*

y Gustav Mahler: An Essential Guide to His Life and Work — *Haylock, Julian*

r Gustav Mahler's Symphonies — *Smoley, Lewis M*

Gustave Baumann: Nearer to Art — *Krause, Martin F*

c El Gusto (Illus. by Francisco Arredondo) — *Sanchez, Isidro*

Gut Symmetries — *Winterson, Jeanette*

The Gutenberg Elegies — *Birkerts, Sven*

The Gutenburg Bible — *Davies, Martin*

Gutes Geld — *Augustin, Ernst*

y Guts: Legendary Black Rodeo Cowboy Bill Pickett — *Johnson, Cecil*

r Gutsy Women — *Bend, Marybeth*

Guttuso — *Calvesi, Maurizio*

r Guy Davenport: A Descriptive Bibliography 1947-1995 — *Crane, Joan*

Guy De Maupassant: De L'Anecdote Au Conte Litteraire — *Haezewindt, Bernard P R*

Guy Debord — *Jappe, Anselm*

Gwendolyn MacEwen (Exile Editions). Vols. 1-2 — *McEwen, Gwendolyn*

c The Gym Day Winner (Illus. by Betsy Lewin) — *Maccarone, Grace*

y Gymnastics — *Gutman, Dan*

c Gymnastics (Illus. by Dwight Normile) — *Normile, Dwight*

Gymnastics Activities for Infants — *Hall, Jim, 1947-*

Gynaecological Symptoms in Primary Care — *Hammond, Robert*

Gynecologic Cancer Surgery — *Morrow, C Paul*

Gynecologic, Obstetric, and Breast Radiology — *Thurmond, Amy S*

Gynecologic Surgery — *Mann, William J, 1947-*

Gynecology in Primary Care — *Smith, Roger P*

Gynicide: Women in the Novels of William Styron — *Hadaller, David*

c Gynormous! (Illus. by Sally Gardner) — *Mitchell, Adrian*

c The Gypsy Game — *Snyder, Zilpha Keatley*

Gypsy Hearts — *Eversz, Robert M*

The Gypsy in Me — *Simon, Ted*

c The Gypsy Princess (Illus. by Phoebe Gilman) — *Gilman, Phoebe*

H

H.B. Morse: Customs Commissioner and Historian of China — *Fairbank, John King*
H.G.: The History of Mr. Wells — *Foot, Michael*
H.G. Wells and the Culminating Ape — *Kemp, Peter*
H.P. Lovecraft: A Life — *Joshi, S T*
r H2 Optimal Control — *Saberi, Ali*
p H2SO4
Ha Fo Xin Ying Lu — *Zhang, Feng*
Ha Noi Trong Mat Toi — *Pham, Xuan Dai*
La Habana — *Machover, Jacobo*
Habit of Blues — *Fitzgerald, Judith*
The Habit of Widowhood — *Barnard, Robert*
Habitat II and the Urban Economy — *Berghall, Pii Elina*
Habitat Creation — *Parker, D M*
Habitat Dioramas — *Wonders, Karen*
c Habitats Series
Habits of the Heart. Rev. Ed. — *Bellah, Robert N*
Habla El Coronel Orlando Piedra — *Raimundo, Daniel Efrain*
The Habsburg Legacy — *Robertson, Ritchie*
The Habsburg Monarchy 1618-1815 — *Ingrao, Charles W*
The Habsburgs: Embodying Empire — *Wheatcroft, Andrew*
Hacia Cortazar — *Alazraki, Jaime*
Hacia Una Democracia Participativa — *Fiallo, Amalio*
Hacia Una Historia Del Espacio En La Montana De Guerrero — *Dehouve, Daniele*
La Hacienda Publica Y La Politica Economica 1929-1958 — *Cardenas, Enrique*
Hacker's Guide to Visual Basic — *Montgomery, John*
Hacks — *Wren, Christopher S*
Had I the Wings — *Shuler, Jay*
Hadrian's Village and Its Legacy — *MacDonald, William L*
Hadron Spectroscopy and the Confinement Problem — *Bugg, D V*
r Haeger Potteries--Through the Years — *Dilley, David D*
Hagiographies: Histoire Internationale De La Litterature Hagiographique Latine Et Vernaculaire En Occident Des Origines A 1550. Vol. 1 — *Philippart, Guy*
Hai Muoi Nam Nguoi Viet Tai Canada — *Tuyen, Tap*
Haida Art — *MacDonald, George F*
Haight-Ashbury in the Sixties. Electronic Media Version
y Hail to the Chief — *Dallek, Robert*
Haim Nahum, a Sephardic Chief Rabbi in Politics 1892-1923 — *Benbassa, Esther*
y Hair: A Book of Braiding and Styles — *Johnson, Anne Akers*
y Hair of the Dog — *Davis, Brett*
Hair Raising — *Rooks, Noliwe M*
Hair Research for the Next Millennium — *Tricontinental Meeting of Hair Research Societies (1st: 1995: Brussels, Belgium)*
c The Hairy Book (Illus. by Jack Keely) — *Planet Dexter (Firm)*
Haiti: Dangerous Crossroads — *McFadyen, Deidre*
Haiti, History, and the Gods — *Dayan, Joan*
Haiti Terre Cassee...Quinze Ans Dans La Campagne Haitienne — *Sugier, Claire*
The Haitian Dilemma — *Preeg, Ernest H*
Haitian Immigrants in Black America — *Zephir, Flore*
The Hajj — *Peters, F E*
Hajj Paintings — *Parker, Ann*
c Hakeem Olajuwon — *Stewart, Mark*
Half a Job — *Tilly, Chris*
Half a Life — *Ciment, Jill*

Half a Revolution — *Gessen, Masha*
Half Finished Heaven — *Graham, William C*
c The Half-Mile Hat (Illus. by Bernard Lodge) — *Lodge, Bernard*
Half Moon Pocosin — *Johnson, Cherry L F*
Half the House — *Hoffman, Richard*
Half the Truth — *Walker, David J*
The Half You Don't Know — *Cameron, Peter*
Halfway Home — *Logue, Mary*
Halfway to Anywhere — *Stine, G Harry*
c El Hallazgo De Jamaica (Illus. by Anne Sibley O'Brien) — *Havill, Juanita*
y Halley in 90 Minutes — *Gribbin, John*
c The Hallo-Wiener (Illus. by Dav Pilkey) — *Pilkey, Dav*
Hallowed Ground — *Abramson, Rudy*
Halloween School Parties — *Ripple, Wilhelminia*
y The Halloween Tree (Illus. by Joseph Mugnaini) — *Bradbury, Ray*
The Halls of Justice — *Gruenfeld, Lee*
y The Halls of Justice (Whitener). Audio Version — *Gruenfeld, Lee*
Hallucinating Foucault — *Duncker, Patricia*
y Hallucinogens — *Robbins, Paul R*
Halon Replacements — *Miziolek, Andrzej W*
y HAL's Legacy — *Stork, David G*
Halting Degradation of Natural Resources — *Baland, Jean-Marie*
Hamiltonian Dynamics and Celestial Mechanics — *Saari, Donald G*
Hamilton's Blessing — *Gordon, John Steele*
r Hamito-Semitic Etymological Dictionary — *Orel, Vladimir E*
Hamlet — *Branagh, Kenneth*
Hamlet — *Shakespeare, William*
y Hamlet (Advanced Shakespeare) — *Shakespeare, William*
Hamlet's Perfection — *Kerrigan, William*
The Hamlyn Herb Book — *Boxer, Arabella*
The Hammer and the Sickle and the Washing Up — *Inglis, Amirah*
r Hammer Films — *Johnson, Tom*
p Hammers
yr Hammond Atlas of the 20th Century — *Hammond Incorporated*
r Hammond New Century World Atlas — *Hammond Incorporated*
Hammurabi's Code — *Kenney, Charles*
Hand and Brain — *Wing, Alan M*
A Hand at the Shutter — *King, Francis*
Hand-Formed Ceramics — *Zakin, Richard*
The Hand I Fan With — *Ansa, Tina McElroy*
y The Hand I Fan With (Ralph). Audio Version — *Ansa, Tina McElroy*
c The Hand-Me-Down Horse (Illus. by Joanna Yardley) — *Pomeranc, Marion Hess*
Hand of a Craftsman — *Acton, David*
Hand of God — *Burns, Jimmy*
c The Hand of the Necromancer — *Strickland, Brad*
The Hand That Feeds You — *Roberts, Lillian M*
Die Hand Vol Vere — *Breytenbach, Breyten*
c Handa's Surprise — *Browne, Eileen*
y Handbook for Catholic Youth — *Glavich, Mary Kathleen*
A Handbook for Interior Designers — *Gibbs, Jenny*
r The Handbook for No-Load Investors. 1996 Ed.
r Handbook for Research in American History. 2nd Ed. — *Prucha, Francis Paul*
Handbook for Self-Organized Learning — *Greif, Siegfried*

r Handbook for the 1997 Young Reader's Choice Awards
Handbook for the Assessment of Dissociation — *Steinberg, Marlene*
Handbook for the Heart — *Carlson, Richard*
Handbook for the International Treaties for the Protection of the Ozone Layer. 4th Ed.
Handbook for the Treatment of the Seriously Mentally Ill — *Soreff, Stephen M*
Handbook of Algebra. Vol. 1 — *Hazenwinkel, M*
r A Handbook of American Military History — *Sweeney, Jerry K*
Handbook of Analysis and Its Foundations — *Schechter, Eric*
r Handbook of Ancient Greek and Roman Coins — *Klawans, Zander H*
Handbook of Applied Cryptography — *Menezes, Alfred J*
r Handbook of Australian, New Zealand and Antarctic Birds. Vol. 3 — *Higgins, P J*
Handbook of Budgeting for Nonprofit Organizations — *Shim, Jae K*
Handbook of Cardiovascular Interventions — *Sigwart, Ulrich*
Handbook of Career Counseling Theory and Practice — *Savickas, Mark L*
r Handbook of Catholic Theology — *Beinert, Wolfgang*
Handbook of Chemical and Biological Sensors — *Taylor, Richard F, 1946-*
The Handbook of Commercial Mortgage-Backed Securities — *Fabozzi, Frank J*
Handbook of Computer Vision Algorithms in Image Algebra — *Ritter, Gerhard X*
yr A Handbook of Contemporary Fiction for Public Libraries and School Libraries — *Biagini, Mary K*
Handbook of Coping — *Zeider, Moshe*
Handbook of Corrosion Data. 2nd Ed. — *Craig, Bruce D*
Handbook of Counselling Psychology — *Woolfe, Ray*
r Handbook of Current Science and Technology. 2nd Ed. — *Bunch, Bryan*
Handbook of Demonstrations and Activities in the Teaching of Psychology. Vols. 1-3 — *Ware, Mark E*
Handbook of Developmental Disabilities — *Kurtz, Lisa A*
Handbook of Dissociation — *Michelson, Larry K*
Handbook of Diversity Issues in Health Psychology — *Kato, Pamela M*
r The Handbook of Education and Human Development — *Olson, David R*
r Handbook of Educational Psychology — *Berliner, David C*
Handbook of Electrical Construction Tools and Materials — *Whitson, Gene*
Handbook of Emotion, Adult Development, and Aging — *Magai, Carol*
r Handbook of Environmental Data on Organic Chemicals. 3rd Ed. — *Verschueren, Karel*
Handbook of Environmental Health and Safety. 3rd Ed., Vols. 1-2 — *Koren, Herman*
Handbook of Ethological Methods. 2nd Ed. — *Lehner, Philip N*
r Handbook of European Union. 2nd Rev. Ed. — *Moussis, Nicholas*
The Handbook of Experimental Economics — *Kagel, John H*
Handbook of Fat Replacers — *Roller, Sibel*
Handbook of Food Analysis. Vols. 1-2 — *Nollet, Leo M L*
r Handbook of Function and Generalized Function Transformations — *Zayed, Ahmed I*

Handbook of Functional Gastrointestinal Disorders — *Olden, Kevin W*

A Handbook of Greek Mythology — *Rose, H J*

Handbook of Grignard Reagents — *Silverman, Gary S*

Handbook of Hispanic Cultures in the United States. Vols. 1-4

The Handbook of Hospice Care — *Buckingham, Robert W*

Handbook of Human Factors Testing and Evaluation — *O'Brien, Thomas G*

The Handbook of Humor — *Buckman, Elcha Shain*

r Handbook of Image Processing Operators — *Klette, Reinhard*

Handbook of Individual Therapy — *Dryden, Windy*

Handbook of Infrared and Raman Spectra of Inorganic Compounds and Organic Salts. Vols. 1-4 — *Nyquist, Richard A*

Handbook of International Credit Management. 2nd Ed. — *Clarke, Brian W*

Handbook of International Economics. Vol. 3 — *Grossman, Gene M*

r Handbook of International Trade and Development Statistics 1994

Handbook of International Trade and Development Statistics 1995

The Handbook of Investment Technology — *Rosen, Joseph*

Handbook of Japanese Grammar — *Tanimori, Masahiro*

r Handbook of Labor Unions — *Peterson, Florence*

The Handbook of Landfill Operations — *Bolton, Neal*

r Handbook of Latin American Studies CD-ROM. Electronic Media Version

r Handbook of Leftist Guerrilla Groups in Latin America and the Caribbean — *Gross, Liza*

The Handbook of Machine Soldering. 3rd Ed. — *Woodgate, Ralph W*

Handbook of Manufacturing Engineering — *Walker, Jack M*

Handbook of Measurement of Residual Stresses — *Society for Experimental Mechanics (U.S.)*

Handbook of Metal Forming — *Lange, Kurt*

Handbook of Modern Sensors. 2nd Ed. — *Fraden, Jacob*

Handbook of Multicultural Counseling — *Ponterotto, Joseph G*

Handbook of Multiple Sclerosis. 2nd Ed. — *Cook, Stuart D*

Handbook of Muscle Disease — *Lane, Russell J M*

yr Handbook of Native American Literature — *Wiget, Andrew*

Handbook of Neurological Speech and Language Disorders — *Kirshner, Howard S*

r Handbook of Nonlinear Optics — *Sutherland, Richard L*

Handbook of Obstetric Management — *Rosevear, Sylvia K*

Handbook of Optical Fibers and Cables. 2nd Ed. — *Murata, Hiroshi*

r Handbook of Organic Chemistry — *Beyer, Hans*

r The Handbook of Over-the-Counter Drugs and Pharmacy Products — *Leber, Max*

r Handbook of Paint and Coating Raw Materials. Vols. 1-2 — *Ash, Michael*

Handbook of Parenting. Vol. 2 — *Bornstein, Marc H*

r Handbook of Parenting. Vol. 3 — *Bornstein, Marc H*

Handbook of Parenting. Vols. 3-4 — *Bornstein, Marc H*

Handbook of Pediatric Psychology. 2nd Ed. — *Roberts, Michael C*

r Handbook of Pharmaceutical Additives — *Ash, Michael*

r Handbook of Photosynthesis — *Pessarakli, Mohammad*

r Handbook of Physical Quantities — *Grigoriev, Igor S*

r Handbook of Plastic and Rubber Additives — *Ash, Michael*

The Handbook of Psychiatric Drug Therapy for Children and Adolescents — *Theesen, Karen A*

r The Handbook of Psychiatric Drugs. 2nd Ed. — *Salzman, Bernard*

Handbook of Pulping and Papermaking. 2nd Ed. — *Biermann, Christopher J*

Handbook of Qualitative Research — *Denzin, Norman K*

Handbook of Radiation and Scattering of Waves — *De Hoop, Adrianus T*

r Handbook of Research for Educational Communications and Technology — *Jonassen, David H*

Handbook of Research on Improving Student Achievement — *Cawelti, G*

Handbook of Research on Multicultural Education — *Banks, James A*

r Handbook of Research on Teacher Education. 2nd Ed. — *Sikula, John*

Handbook of Russian Affixes — *Cubberley, Paul*

Handbook of Self-Concept — *Bracken, Bruce A*

Handbook of Social Support and the Family — *Pierce, Gregory R*

Handbook of Solution-Focused Brief Therapy — *Miller, Scott D*

A Handbook of SOPs for Good Clinical Practice — *Maynard, Donald E*

r Handbook of Space Astronomy and Astrophysics. 2nd Ed. — *Zombeck, Martin V*

Handbook of Special and Remedial Education. 2nd Ed. — *Wang, Margaret C*

Handbook of Sports and Recreational Building Design. 2nd Ed., Vol. 3 — *John, Geraint*

Handbook of Subacute Health Care — *Griffin, Kathleen M*

Handbook of Sustainable Buildings — *Anink, David*

Handbook of Technology Management — *Gaynor, Gerard H*

Handbook of Temporary Structures in Construction. 2nd Ed. — *Ratay, Robert T*

Handbook of the Biology of Aging. 4th Ed. — *Schneider, Edward L*

r Handbook of the Birds of the World. Vol. 3 — *Hoyo, Josep Del*

Handbook of the Linguistic Atlas of the Middle and South Atlantic States — *Kretzschmar, William A*

Handbook of the Normal Distribution. 2nd Ed., Rev. and Expanded — *Patel, Jagdish K*

A Handbook of the Troubadours — *Akehurst, F R P*

Handbook of Twentieth-Century Literatures of India — *Natarajan, Nalini*

r Handbook of United States Coins 1997

r Handbook of Water Treatment Chemicals — *Ash, Michael*

Handbook on Continuous Fiber-Reinforced Ceramic Matrix Composites — *Lehman, Richard L*

Handbook on Discontinuously Reinforced Ceramic Matrix Composites — *Bowman, Keith J*

Handbook on Employment and the Elderly — *Crown, William H*

r Handbook on Ethnicity, Aging, and Mental Health — *Padgett, Deborah K*

r Handbook on Religious Liberty around the World — *Moreno, Pedro C*

r Handbook to Bach's Sacred Cantata Texts — *Bach, Johann Sebastian*

Handbuch Der Historischen Buchbestande In Deutschland. Vols. 14-15 — *Fabian, Bernhard*

Handbuch Der Historischen Buchbestande In Osterreich. Vols. 1-2 — *Fabian, Bernhard*

Handel and His Singers — *LaRue, C Steven*

Handel's Oratorios and Eighteenth-Century Thought — *Smith, Ruth*

c A Handful of Seeds (Illus. by Luis Garay) — *Hughes, Monica*

A Handfull of Holesome (though Homelie) Hearbs 1584 — *Wheathill, Anne*

The Handicap Principle — *Zahavi, Amotz*

c The Handmade Alphabet — *Rankin, Laura*

Handmade for Profit — *Brabec, Barbara*

The Handmaid of Desire — *L'Heureux, John*

The Handmaid's Tale — *Atwood, Margaret*

The Hands Feel It — *Turner, Edith*

c Hands-On Rocky Mountains — *Merrill, Yvonne Y*

Hands to the Spindle — *Marks, Paula Mitchell*

y Handsome Heroines — *Husain, Shahrukh*

Handsome Is — *Wasserman, Harriet*

Handwriting in America — *Thornton, Tamara Plakins*

Handy Dandy Reading Records K-3 — *Kinghorn, Harriet R*

c Handy Mandy in Oz — *Thompson, Ruth Plumly*

Hanemann — *Chwin, Stefan*

y Hang a Thousand Trees with Ribbons — *Rinaldi, Ann*

y Hang Loose — *Cargill, Linda*

Hanging Baskets — *Hendy, Jenny*

Hanging in Judgment — *Potter, Harry*

Hanging Judge — *Harrington, Fred Harvey*

p Hanging Loose

The Hanging Tree — *Gatrell, V A C*

Hanging without a Rope — *Steedly, Mary Margaret*

Hanh Trinh Mot Hat O — *Dang, Tran Huan*

The Hank Snow Story — *Snow, Hank*

y The Hank Wiescamp Story — *Holmes, Frank, 1947-*

Hank Williams: The Biography — *Escott, Colin*

Hank Williams: The Complete Lyrics — *Williams, Hank*

c Hannah and Jack (Illus. by Mary Morgan) — *Nethery, Mary*

Hannah Arendt and Leo Strauss — *Kielmansegg, Peter, Graf*

Hannah Arendt and the Jewish Question — *Bernstein, Richard J*

Hannah Arendt/Martin Heidegger — *Ettinger, Elzbieta*

Hannah Arendt: Twenty Years Later — *May, Larry*

Hannah More: A Critical Biography — *Ford, Charles Howard*

Hannah's Heirs — *Pollen, Daniel A*

c Hanna's Sabbath Dress (Illus. by Ora Eitan) — *Schweiger-Dmi'el, Itzhak*

Hannes Bok Drawings and Sketches — *Bok, Hannes*

c Hannibal — *Green, Robert*

Hannibal — *Leckie, Ross*

c Hans Christian Andersen's The Snow Queen (Illus. by Edward S Gazsi) — *Kennedy, Richard*

Hans Holbein: Portrait of an Unknown Man — *Wilson, Derek*

Hans Scharoun — *Blundell-Jones, Peter*

Hans Urs Von Balthasar: A Theological Style — *Scola, Angelo*

c Hansel and Gretel (Illus. by Ian Wallace) — *Wallace, Ian*

c Hanukkah Crafts — *Corwin, Judith Hoffman*

c Hanukkah Fun (Illus. by Catherine Ward) — *Bastyra, Judy*

c The Hanukkah Ghosts — *Penn, Malka*

c Happily Ever After (Illus. by James Stevenson) — *Quindlen, Anna*

r Happily Ever After — *Ramsdell, Kristin*

Happily Ever After — *Stone, Betsy*

The Happiness of Getting It Down Right — *O'Connor, Frank*

Happiness: Stories — *Agosin, Marjorie*

c Happy Adoption Day! (Illus. by Julie Paschkis) — *McCutcheon, John*

Happy Are the Oppressed — *Greeley, Andrew M*

c Happy Birth Day! (Illus. by Michael Emberley) — *Harris, Robie H*

c Happy Birthday! — *Bednarczyk, Angela*

c Happy Birthday, Danny and the Dinosaur! (Illus. by Syd Hoff) — *Hoff, Syd*

r Happy Birthdays Round the World — *Johnson, Lois S*

c Happy Days (Illus. by Margaret Miller) — *Miller, Margaret*

Happy Days 1880-1892 — *Mencken, H L*

y Happy Days, Uncle Sergio — *Garcia Ramis, Magali*

c Happy Families

Happy Is the Bride the Sun Shines On — *Jones, Leslie*

c Happy Mouseday — *King-Smith, Dick*

c Happy New Year! (Illus. by Durga Bernhard) — *Bernhard, Emery*

c Happy Old Birthday, Owl (Illus. by Sue Heap) — *Hendry, Diana*

c The Happy Prince (Illus. by Jane Ray) — *Wilde, Oscar*

Hapworth 16, 1924 — *Salinger, J D*

c Harald the Ruthless (Illus. by Leo Duranona) — *Hopkins, Andrea*

Harare: Inheriting a Settler-Colonial City — *Rakodi, Carole*

r Harbors and High Seas — *King, Dean*

Hard at It — *Adams, Anthony*

Hard Bargain — *Shogan, Robert*

Hard Bodies — *Jeffords, Susan*

Hard Curves — *Bell, Julie*

The Hard Disk Data Base — *Croucher, Phil*

The Hard Hand of War — *Grimsley, Mark*

Hard Labor — *Diamond, Susan L*

Hard Landing — *Petzinger, Thomas, Jr.*

Hard Lessons — *Steedman, Mercedes*

Hard Line — *Lewin, Michael Z*

Hard Questions, Heart Answers — *King, Bernice A*

y Hard Time — *Bode, Janet*

r Hard Times Tokens 1832-1844. 6th Ed. — *Rulau, Russell*

Hard to Imagine — *Waugh, Thomas*

Hard Twist — *Van Cleve, Barbara*

Hardboiled: An Anthology of American Crime Stories — *Pronzini, Bill*

The Harder They Fall — *Schulberg, Budd*

The Hardest Victory — *Richards, Denis*

Hardin County, Illinois Deaths 1884-1919 and Notes from the Pleasant Hill Church Register — *Reynolds, Marion Lavender*

Hardly Ever a Dull Moment — *Fisk, E K*

Hardrock Stiff — *Zigal, Thomas*

Hardware Component Modeling — *Berge, Jean-Michel*

Hardwired — *Chapman, Sally*
Hardy Perennials — *Rice, Graham*
Hardy's Literary Language and Victorian Philology — *Taylor, Dennis*
c The Hare and the Tortoise (Illus. by Carol Jones) — *Jones, Carol*
Hargrave — *Trollope, Fanny*
Harland's Half Acre — *Malouf, David*
y Harlem (Illus. by Christopher Myers) — *Myers, Walter Dean*
Harlem — *Riley, Len*
Harlem at War — *Brandt, Nat*
c The Harlem Globetrotters — *Wilker, Josh*
y The Harlem Renaissance — *Haskins, James*
The Harlem Renaissance — *Watson, Steven*
The Harlem Renaissance in Black and White — *Hutchinson, George*
Harlem's Glory — *Roses, Lorraine Elena*
The Harlequin Tea Set and Other Stories — *Christie, Agatha*
r Harley Hahn's Internet and Web Yellow Pages. 1997 Ed.
The Harlot by the Side of the Road — *Kirsch, Jonathan*
The Harlot's Child — *Worsham, Fabian*
Harm De Blij's Geography Book — *De Blij, Harm J*
Harmful Eloquence — *Stapleton, M L*
c Harmful to Your Health — *Gutman, Bill*
Harmless Souls — *Johnson, W J*
Harmonic Analysis and Applications — *Benedetto, John*
c Harmonica Night (Illus. by Alexi Natchev) — *Helldorfer, M C*
The Harmonious Garden — *Ziegler, Catherine*
Harmonious Tensions — *Martinson, Steven D*
p Harmony: Forum of the Symphony Orchestra Institute
r The Harmony Illustrated Encyclopedia of Country Music. 3rd Completely Rev. and Updated Ed. — *Cackett, Alan*
Harmony in Flesh and Black — *Nicholas, Kilmer*
Harmony in the Kitchen — *Glancy, Maida*
The Harmony of Illusions — *Young, Allan*
The Harmony of Nature and Spirit — *Singer, Irving*
Harmony of the World — *Baxter, Charles, 1947-*
Harm's Way — *White, Stephen Walsh*
Harm's Way — *Witkin, Joel-Peter*
y Harnessing Anger — *Westbrook, Peter*
c Harold and Harold (Illus. by Terry Roscoe) — *Wilson, Budge*
Harold Arlen: Rhythm, Rainbows, and Blues — *Jablonski, Edward*
r Harold Lloyd: A Bio-Bibliography — *D'Agostino, Annette M*
Harold Macmillan and Britain's World Role — *Aldous, Richard*
y Haroun and the Sea of Stories — *Rushdie, Salman*
r Harp Music Bibliography — *Palkovic, Mark*
c Harp Seal Pups (Illus. by Dan Guravich) — *Matthews, Downs*
r The HarperCollins Bible Dictionary
r The HarperCollins Dictionary of Religion — *Smith, Jonathan Z*
r The HarperCollins Encyclopedia of Catholicism
yr Harper's Pictorial History of the Civil War — *Guernsey, Alfred H*
Harping On — *Kizer, Carolyn*
c Harriet and the Promised Land (Illus. by Jacob Lawrence) — *Lawrence, Jacob*
y Harriet Chalmers Adams: Adventurer and Explorer — *Anema, Durlynn*
Harriet Jacobs and Incidents in the Life of a Slave Girl — *Garfield, Deborah M*
Harriet Martineau: The Poetics of Moralism — *Hunter, Shelagh*
y Harriet the Spy — *Fitzhugh, Louise*
c Harriet's Hare — *King-Smith, Dick*
c Harris and Me — *Paulsen, Gary*
r Harrod's Librarians' Glossary. 8th Ed. — *Prytherch, Ray*
c Harry at the Garage (Illus. by Derek Radford) — *Radford, Derek*
Harry Byrd of Virginia — *Heinemann, Ronald L*
Harry Callahan — *Greenough, Sarah*
The Harry Chronicles — *Pedrazas, Allan*
c Harry, El Perrito Sucio (Illus. by Margaret Bloy Graham) — *Zion, Gene*
Harry Pollitt — *Morgan, Kevin*
c Harry S. Truman — *Schuman, Michael A*
y Harry S. Truman (Runger). Audio Version — *Ferrell, Robert H*

Harry S. Truman and the Bomb — *Ferrell, Robert H*
Harry S. Truman and the War Scare of 1948 — *Kofsky, Frank*
c Harry the Dirty Dog (Illus. by Margaret Bloy Graham) — *Zion, Gene*
c Harry the Poisonous Centipede (Illus. by Tony Ross) — *Banks, Lynne Reid*
c Harry the Poisonous Centipede. Audio Version — *Banks, Lynne Reid*
c Harry the Superhero — *Powling, Chris*
c Harry's Aunt — *Lavelle, Sheila*
Harry's Bar — *Cipriani, Arrigo*
Hartnett: Portrait of a Technocratic Brigand — *Rich, Joe*
Hartung's Astronomical Objects for Southern Telescopes. 2nd Ed. — *Malin, David*
yr The Harvard Biographical Dictionary of Music — *Randel, Don Michael*
The Harvard Conference on the Internet and Society — *Harvard Conference on the Internet and Society (1996: Cambridge, Mass.)*
r Harvard Encyclopedia of American Ethnic Groups — *Thernstrom, Stephan*
r Harvard Guide to American History. Rev. Ed., Vols. 1-2 — *Freidel, Frank*
r The Harvard Guide to Women's Health — *Carlson, Karen J*
yr The Harvard Guide to Women's Health. Electronic Media Version — *Carlson, Karen J*
p The Harvard International Journal of Press/Politics
Harvard's Art Museums — *Harvard University. Art Museums*
y Harvest — *Westall, Robert*
y Harvest (Guidall). Audio Version — *Gerritsen, Tess*
c The Harvest Birds (Illus. by Enrique Flores) — *Lopez De Mariscal, Blanca*
Harvest Moon — *Saxton, Judith*
A Harvest of Technology — *Elmusa, Sharif*
c Harvest Year (Illus. by Alvis Upitis) — *Peterson, Cris*
Harvesting Minds — *Fox, Roy F*
Harvesting Mountains — *Gardella, Robert*
Harvesting the Edge — *Dutton, G F*
Harvesting Thistles — *Rubio, Mary Henley*
c Harvey and the Beast of Bodmin (Illus. by S Hellard) — *Dicks, Terrance*
c Harvey Hare, Postman Extraordinaire (Illus. by Bernadette Watts) — *Watts, Bernadette*
Harvey Penick's Little Red Book — *Penick, Harvey*
c Harvey's Wish (Illus. by Jean Pidgeon) — *Fitzgerald, Matthew*
y Has Anyone Seen this Girl? — *Ure, Jean*
The Hashemites in the Modern Arab World — *Susser, Asher*
Hasidism: Between Ecstacy and Magic — *Idel, Moshe*
Hasluck versus Coombs — *Partington, Geoffrey*
c Hasta La Vista, Blarney! (Illus. by S M Taggart) — *Peterson, Melissa*
c A Hat for Minerva Louise — *Stoeke, Janet Morgan*
The Hat of Victor Noir — *Mathews, Adrian*
Hat Ru Ba Mien — *Le, Van*
Hatchepsut: The Female Pharaoh — *Tyldesley, Joyce*
Hatchet Job — *Adams, Harold*
y Hatchet: Winter — *Paulsen, Gary*
Hatet — *Espmark, Kjell*
c A Hatful of Seuss — *Seuss, Dr.*
Hatreds: Racialized and Sexualized Conflicts in the 21st Century — *Eisenstein, Zillah*
c The Haunted Bike (Illus. by Blanche Sims) — *Herman, Gail*
c Haunted Horseback Holiday — *Hart, Alison*
The Haunted Hour — *Manson, Cynthia*
c Haunted House Blues (Illus. by G Floyd) — *Tomlinson, Theresa*
Haunted Houses. 2nd Ed. — *Roberts, Nancy*
Haunted Journeys — *Porter, Dennis*
The Haunted Land — *Rosenberg, Tina*
r Haunted Places. Rev. Ed. — *Hauck, Dennis William*
y Haunted School — *Masters, Anthony*
c The Haunted Skateboard (Illus. by Jane Manning) — *Saunders, Susan*
c The Haunted Suitcase — *Thompson, Colin*
c Haunted Summer — *Wright, Betty Ren*
Haunted Toronto — *Colombo, John Robert*
c The Haunting — *Apps, Roy*
c The Haunting of Hiram (Scales). Audio Version — *Ibbotson, Eva*
c The Haunting of Joey M'basa (Illus. by Bethan Matthews) — *Harris, Rosemary*
A Haunting Reverence — *Nerburn, Kent*
Hauntings: Popular Film and American Culture 1990-1992 — *Natoli, Joseph*

p Haunts
c Haunts: Five Hair-Raising Tales (Illus. by Trina Schart Hyman) — *Medearis, Angela Shelf*
Der Hauptmann Von Kopenick — *Zuckmayer, Carl*
The Hauptvermutung Book — *Ranicki, A A*
Hauserleben: Zur Geschichte Stadtischen Arbeiterwohnens Vom Kaiserreich Bis Heute — *Von Saldern, Adelheid Von*
Havana USA — *Garcia, Maria Cristina*
c Have a Heart! (Illus. by Marilyn Mets) — *McKay, Sharon*
y Have a Mega Memory (Illus. by Tony Smith) — *Hancock, Jonathan*
y Have No Fear — *Evers, Charles*
Have We Really Come a Long Way, Baby? — *Senter, Ruth*
c Have You Seen an Elephant Sneeze? — *Synder, Bernadette McCarver*
c Have You Seen Bugs? (Illus. by Ron Broda) — *Oppenheim, Joanne*
c Have You Seen My Duckling? (Illus. by Nancy Tafuri) — *Tafuri, Nancy*
Having It All/Having Enough — *Lee, Deborah*
The Having of Wonderful Ideas and Other Essays on Teaching and Learning — *Duckworth, Eleanor*
Having Our Say (Goldberg). Audio Version — *Delany, Sarah Louise*
Having Your Baby — *Hutcherson, Hilda*
r Hawaii: The Big Island Revealed — *Doughty, Andrew*
r Hawaii: Travel-Smart Trip Planner — *Schuchter, Arnold*
Hawaiian Quilt Masterpieces — *Shaw, Robert*
Hawk Flies Above — *Norton, Lisa Dale*
c Hawk Highway in the Sky (Illus. by Robert Kruidenier) — *Arnold, Caroline*
c Hawk Hill (Illus. by Sylvia Long) — *Gilbert, Suzie*
Hawk Moon — *Gorman, Edward*
y Hawk Moon — *MacGregor, Rob*
Hawk Woman Dancing with the Moon — *Lake, Tela Star Hawk*
Hawks — *Clark, William S*
c Hawks and Falcons — *Woodward, John*
c Hawkwood — *Guy, Jonathan*
Haydn, Mozart and the Viennese School 1740-1780 — *Heartz, Daniel*
Hayek: The Iron Cage of Liberty — *Gamble, Andrew*
Hayek's Social and Political Thought — *Kley, Roland*
The Haygoods of Columbus — *Haygood, Wil*
c The Hayloft (Illus. by K D Plum) — *Peters, Lisa Westberg*
Hazard Communication Compliance Manual — *Silk, Jennifer C*
Hazard Zones — *Maillard, Keith*
Hazardous Duty — *Hackworth, David H*
Hazardous Laboratory Chemicals Disposal Guide. 2nd Ed. — *Armour, Margaret-Ann*
Hazardous Materials Emergencies. 3rd Ed. — *Cashman, John R*
r Hazardous Materials Handbook — *Pohanish, Richard P*
r Hazardous Materials Reference Book Cross-Index — *Davis, Daniel J*
y Hazardous Waste Sites — *Kowalski, Kathiann M*
c Hazards at Home — *Gutman, Bill*
Hazel: A Life of Lady Lavery 1880-1935 — *McCoole, Sinead*
c He Fought for Freedom — *Schomp, Virginia*
He Leadeth Me — *Joseph-Gaudet, Frances*
y He Say, She Say — *Joe, Yolanda*
He Say, She Say. Audio Version — *Joe, Yolanda*
He Zhi Nu — *Ning, Tien-Pi*
Head Cook at Weddings and Funerals and Other Stories of Doukhobor Life — *Plotnikoff, Vi*
Head for the Web — *Mara, Mary Jane*
c A Head Full of Notions (Illus. by Lisa Harvey) — *Bowen, Andy Russell*
y Head Injuries — *Aaseng, Nathan*
The Head of Dionysos — *Redmon, Anne*
Headbanger — *Hamilton, Hugo*
Headed for the Blues — *Skvorecky, Josef*
Heading Home — *Scanlan, Lawrence*
Heading Inland — *Barker, Nicola*
y Headless and Other Stories — *Bliemann, Barbara*
Headline Diplomacy — *Seib, Philip*
Headline Justice — *Wilson, Theo*
Head's Legal Guide 1985-
Heads, You Win! — *Spitzer, Quinn*
Heal Your Heart — *Rosati, Kitty Gurkin*
The Healer Within — *Jahnke, Roger*
Healing Anger — *Bstan-Dzin-Rgya-Mtsho, Dalai Lama XIV*

The Healing Choice — *De Puy, Candace*
A Healing Family — *Oe, Kenzaburo*
Healing Hands — *Lofton, J Mack, Jr.*
y The Healing of Crossroads — *O'Donohoe, Nick*
c The Healing of Texas Jake — *Naylor, Phyllis Reynolds*
The Healing Power of Mind — *Thondup, Tulku*
Healing Powers — *Frohock, Fred M*
Healing the Downsized Organization — *Ambrose, Delorese*
Healing the Mind — *Stone, Michael H, 1933-*
Healing Traditions — *O'Connor, Bonnie Blair*
Healing: Wilt Thou Be Made Whole? — *Van Eck, Jamae*
Healing with Plants in the American and Mexican West — *Kay, Margarita Artschwager*
Healing Your Mind, Healing Your Heart. Audio Version — *Jackson, Christopher*
Health against Wealth — *Anders, George*
y Health and Fitness — *Barbour, Scott*
Health and Healing in Eighteenth-Century Germany — *Lindemann, Mary*
Health and Health Care in Latin America during the Lost Decade — *Weil, Connie*
Health and Safety/Risk Abstracts. Electronic Media Version
c Health and Safety (Time-Life)
Health and Societies — *Curtis, Sarah*
Health and Society in Twentieth-Century Britain — *Jones, Helen*
Health Aspects of Pregnancy and Childbirth — *Chandra, Anjani*
r The Health Care Almanac — *Zipperer, Lori A*
Health Care for Lesbians and Gay Men — *Peterson, K Jean*
Health Care in the United States — *Ayres, Stephen M*
Health Care Librarianship and Information Work — *Carmel, Michael*
Health Care Reform and the Battle for the Body Politic — *Beauchamp, Dan E*
r Health Care Software Sourcebook — *Ankrapp, Betty*
r Health Care Terms. 3rd Comprehensive Ed. — *Slee, Vergil N*
The Health Consequences of Modernization — *Shephard, Roy J*
p Health Economics
Health Economics — *Getzen, Thomas E*
Health Education — *Read, Donald A*
Health Effects of Exposure to Low-Level Ionizing Radiation — *Hendee, W R*
Health Effects of Hazardous Materials — *Ostler, Neal K*
The Health Gap — *Kitts, Jennifer*
r Health Industry QuickSource — *Cilurzo, Mary Jeanne*
Health Information--New Possibilities — *McSean, Tony*
Health Issues for Minority Adolescents — *Kagawa-Singer, Marjorie*
The Health of Manitoba's Children
The Health of Nations — *Iyun, B Folasade*
r Health of Native People of North America — *Gray, Sharon A*
The Health of Young Children in North Carolina — *Surles, Kathryn B*
r Health Online — *Ferguson, Tom*
Health Policy, Federalism, and the American States — *Rich, Robert F*
The Health Rationale for Family Planning
Health Resource Management Plan 1996-1999
y The Health Revolution — *Darling, David*
Health-Risk Behaviors Among Our Nation's Youth — *Adams, P F*
Health Risks — *Thoenen, Eugenia*
Health Sector Reform in Developing Countries — *Berman, Peter*
The Healthcare Customer Service Revolution — *Zimmermann, David R*
r Healthcare Design — *Mayberry, Sara O*
r Healthcare Hazard Control and Safety Management — *Tweedy, James T*
The Healthiest City — *Leavitt, Judith Walzer*
r Healthspeak: A Complete Dictionary of America's Health Care System — *Freudenheim, Ellen*
Healthy Cooking Deluxe. Electronic Media Version
Healthy Cooking for People Who Don't Have Time to Cook — *Jones, Jeanne*
The Healthy Home Handbook — *Warde, John*
Healthy Homestyle Desserts — *Tribole, Evelyn*
The Healthy House — *Baggs, Sydney*
Healthy Incentives — *McArthur, William*
Healthy Meals Fast
The Healthy Organization — *Newell, Susan*

A Healthy Rivalry — *Torfs, Rik*
Healthy Thai Cooking — *Owen, Sri*
The Healthy Woman — *Davis, Susan*
r Hear Our Voices — *Yoo, Claire Jung Jin*
r Hear the Word of the Lord — *Foxton, Rosemary*
c Hearing (Illus. by Francisco Arredondo) — *Llamas, Andreu*
c Hearing (Illus. by Barrie Watts) — *Walpole, Brenda*
Hearing the Internal Trauma — *Wieland, Sandra*
Hearing the Motet — *Pesce, Dolores*
The Hearing Trumpet — *Carrington, Leonora*
y Hearing Voices — *O'Neill, Judith*
Hearsay and Confrontation in Criminal Trials — *Choo, Andrew L-T*
c The Heart and Circulatory System — *Ballard, Carol*
Heart and Science — *Collins, Wilkie*
y Heart and Soul — *Rosenberg, Liz*
Heart and Soul of the Nation — *Heckler-Feltz, Cheryl*
The Heart and Stomach of a King — *Levin, Carole*
The Heart Aroused (Whyte). Audio Version — *Whyte, David*
A Heart at Leisure from Itself — *Prang, Margaret*
The Heart Can Be Filled Anywhere on Earth — *Holm, Bill*
r Heart Disease Diagnosis and Therapy — *Khan, M I Gabriel*
Heart Disease in Persons with Down Syndrome — *Marino, Bruno*
The Heart in Diabetes — *Chatham, John C*
c The Heart Is Big Enough (Illus. by Matthew Valiquette) — *Rosen, Michael J*
y The Heart Knows Something Different — *Desetta, Al*
The Heart of a Dog — *Bulgakov, Mikhail Afanas'evich*
y Heart of a Jaguar — *Talbert, Marc*
The Heart of Achilles — *Zanker, Graham*
The Heart of Altruism — *Monroe, Kristen Renwick*
Heart of Being — *Loori, John Daido*
The Heart of Conflict — *Muldoon, Brian*
Heart of Darkness — *Conrad, Joseph*
Heart of Hearts — *Dawe, Gerald*
The Heart of India — *Tully, Mark*
The Heart of Parenting — *Gottman, John*
The Heart of the Buddha's Teaching — *Nhat Hanh, Thich*
The Heart of the Game — *Hemphill, Paul*
The Heart of the Hills — *Fox, John, 1863-1919*
y Heart of War — *Truscott, Lucian K*
Heart of Whiteness — *Goodwin, June*
c The Heart: Our Circulatory System — *Simon, Seymour*
A Heart So White — *Marias, Javier*
y Heart Trouble — *Trocheck, Kathy Hogan*
y The Heartbeat of Halftime — *Wunderli, Stephen*
Heartbreak Tango — *Puig, Manuel*
y Heartbreaker — *Adams, Nick*
Heartbreaker — *Robards, Karen*
Heartburn — *Ephron, Nora*
Hearths of Darkness — *Williams, Tony*
The Heartland Chronicles — *Foley, Douglas E*
Heartland Excursions — *Nettl, Bruno*
Hearts and Bones — *Lawrence, Margaret*
Hearts and Minds — *Bibby, Michael*
Hearts and Minds — *Groves, Julian McAllister*
The Heart's Desire — *Rachlin, Nahid*
Heart's Journey in Winter — *Buchan, James*
y Hearts of Fire — *Battle, Kemp*
c Hearts of Gold — *Dinn, Sheila*
The Heart's Progress — *Bepko, Claudia*
Heartwood and Other Poems — *McEwen, R F*
c Hearty Har Har (Illus. by R W Alley) — *Hall, Katy*
p HEAT
c Heat and Cold (Illus. by Terry Hadler) — *Lafferty, Peter*
Heat and Lust — *Petropoulos, J C B*
c Heat FUNdamentals (Illus. by Rick Brown) — *Wood, Robert W*
y The Heat Is On — *Gelbspan, Ross*
Heat Lightning — *Cohen, Leah Hager*
The Heat of Arrivals — *Gonzales, Ray*
The Heat of the Sun — *Rubin, Louis Decimus*
Heat Transfer. 8th Ed. — *Holman, J P*
Heat Transfer, Houston 1996
Heat Transfer in Microgravity — *Gopinath, Ash*
Heat Transfer in Turbulent Flows — *Wroblewski, Donald*
Heat Treater's Guide — *Chandler, Harry*
Heat Wave — *Lively, Penelope*
c Heat Wave at Mud Flat (Illus. by James Stevenson) — *Stevenson, James*
The Heath Government 1970-1974 — *Ball, Stuart*
Heathcliff and the Great Hunger — *Eagleton, Terry*

Heathen Days 1890-1936 — *Mencken, H L*
c Heather (Illus. by Lynne Woodcock Cravath) — *Leverich, Kathleen*
Heaths and Moorlands — *Thomson, D B A*
c Heaven (Illus. by Nicholas Allan) — *Allan, Nicholas*
Heaven and Earth — *Simek, Rudolf*
Heaven and Earth — *Wick, Steve*
Heaven and Hell in Enlightenment England — *Almond, Philip C*
Heaven and Home — *Sturrock, June*
Heaven and the Flesh — *Hart, Clive*
Heaven Found — *Agee, M J*
y Heaven Help Us — *Bennett, Cherie*
Heaven of Animals — *Carter, Keith*
Heaven Stones — *Neruda, Pablo*
Heaven Where the Bachelors Sit — *Windsor, Gerard*
Heavenly Sex — *Westheimer, Ruth K*
c The Heavenly Zoo (Illus. by Monica Beisner) — *Lurie, Alison*
Heaven's Coast — *Doty, Mark*
Heaven's Gold — *Tippette, Giles*
Heaven's Prisoners (Hammer). Audio Version — *Burke, James Lee*
c Heavensbee (Illus. by Ronnie Rooney) — *Murphy, L A*
Heavy Justice — *Garrison, J Gregory*
Hebert: Les Fous De Bassan — *Noble, Peter*
The Hebertistes to the Guillotine — *Slavin, Moriss*
r The Hebrew and Aramaic Lexicon of the Old Testament, Vol. 2 — *Koehler, Ludwig*
Hebrew Bible or Old Testament — *Brooks, Roger*
The Hebrew Bible, the Old Testament, and Historical Criticism — *Levenson, Jon D*
Hebron Presbyterian Church
Hechiceria, Brujeria, E Inquisicion En El Nuevo Reino De Granada — *Ceballos Gomez, Diana Luz*
A Hedge Away — *Lombardo, Daniel*
Hedingham Harvest Victorian Family Life in Rural England — *Robinson, Geoffrey, 1917-*
Heeding the Voices of Our Ancestors — *Alfred, Gerald R*
The Hegel Myths and Legends — *Stewart, Jon*
Hegel on the Modern World — *Collins, Ardis B*
Hegel: Phenomenology and System — *Harris, H S*
Hegel's Dialectic of Desire and Recognition — *O'Neill, John*
Hegel's Hermeneutics — *Redding, Paul*
Hegel's Phenomenology — *Pinkard, Terry*
Hegel's Social Philosophy — *Hardimon, Michael O*
Hegels Wissenschaft Der Logik — *Schick, Friedrike*
The Hegemonic Male — *Almeida, Miguel Vale De*
Hegemonins Decennier — *Billing, Peter*
Hegemony to Empire — *Kallet-Marx, Robert*
Heidegger — *Cooper, David Edward*
Heidegger and Jaspers — *Olson, Alan M*
Heidegger, Dilthey, and the Crisis of Historicism — *Bambach, Charles R*
Heidegger Et Son Siecle — *Barash, Joseph Andrew*
Heidegger's Crisis — *Sluga, Hans*
Heidegger's Political Thinking — *Ward, James F*
Heidegger's Silence — *Lang, Berel*
c Heidi (Illus. by Loretta Krupinski) — *Krupinski, Loretta*
y Heidi (Illus. by Jacques Rozier) — *Spyri, Johanna*
c Heidi (Illus. by Jessie Willcox Smith) — *Spyri, Johanna*
y Heidi (McDonough). Audio Version — *Spyri, Johanna*
c Heidi (Young Reader's Christian Library) — *Spyri, Johanna*
y The Heinemann English Programme 4 — *Seely, John*
y Heinemann Modular Mathematics for London AS and A-Level: Mechanics 3
y Heinemann Modular Mathematics for London AS and A-Level: Pure Mathematics 3
Heinrich Boll: Forty Years of Criticism — *Zachau, Reinhard K*
Heinrich Hertz: A Short Life — *Susskind, Charles*
Heinrich Schneider, Bibliothekar Und Gelehrtet — *Hundhausen, Felicitas*
Heinrich Von Kleist: Die Familie Ghonorez/Die Familie Schroffenstein — *Kleist, Heinrich Von*
Heinrich Von Kleist: The Dramas and Stories — *Stephens, Anthony*
Heinz Kohut and the Psychology of the Self — *Siegel, Allen M*
Heirloom Vegetable Gardening — *Weaver, William Woys*
Heisenberg Probably Slept Here — *Brennan, Richard P*
Heiterkeit Ohne Grund — *Heise, Hans-Jurgen*
Helden Wie Wir — *Brussig, Thomas*
Heldensage Und Epos — *Wolf, Alois*

Title Index

Helen Garner — *Goldsworthy, Kerryn*

Helen of Troy and Her Shameless Phantom — *Austin, Norman*

y Helen Williams and the French Revolution — *Shuter, Jane*

Helene Cixous: Authorship, Autobiography and Love — *Sellers, Susan*

Helene (Dans Les Annees Profondes) — *Jouve, Pierre Jean*

Helicobacter Pylori — *Harris, A W*

Helicobacter Pylori — *Hunt, Richard H*

Helios Megistos — *Fauth, Wolfgang*

Hell-Bent for Music — *Hall, Wade*

y Hell Fighters — *Cooper, Michael L*

Hell for Leather — *Winder, Robert*

Hell with the Fire Out — *Quinn, Arthur*

Hellbent on Homicide — *Lovisi, Gary*

Hellboy — *Mignola, Mike*

Hellcats: A Novel of War in the Pacific — *Tillman, Barrett*

Hellenika II.3.11-IV.2.8 (Krentz) — *Xenophon*

Hellenism and Empire — *Swain, Simon*

Hellenism and Homosexuality in Victorian Oxford — *Dowling, Linda*

Hellenistic Architectural Sculpture — *Webb, Pamela A*

r Hellenistic Commentary to the New Testament — *Boring, M Eugene*

The Hellfire Club — *Straub, Peter*

Hellman and Hammett — *Mellen, Joan*

c Hello! Good-Bye! (Illus. by Aliki) — *Aliki*

Hello, He Lied and Other Truths from the Hollywood Trenches — *Obst, Lynda*

y Hello, I Lied — *Kerr, M E*

c Hello, Laura! (Illus. by Renee Graef) — *Graef, Renee*

c Hello Molly! (Illus. by Cheryl Roberts) — *Wagner, Cheryl*

c Hello, Poldy! — *Lavigne, Yves*

Hells Angels: Into the Abyss — *Lavigne, Yves*

Hell's Half Acre — *Selcer, Richard F*

Helmut Kohl — *Muller, Christian*

c Help! I'm a Hamster — *Bradman, Tony*

Help! I'm a Sunday School Teacher — *Johnston, Ray*

Help! I'm a Volunteer Youth Worker! — *Fields, Doug*

c Help! It's Halloween! (Illus. by Kathryn Mitter) — *Barkan, Joanne*

r Help! The Quick Guide to First Aid for Your Cat — *Bamberger, Michelle*

r Help Yourself — *Bucy, Douglas R*

yr Help Yourself — *Lewis, Erica-Lee*

Helping Families through Divorce — *Bogolub, Ellen B*

Helping Kids Get Organized

Helping Students Develop Their IEPs

Helping Students Revise Their Writing — *Tully, Marianne*

Helping Teenagers into Adulthood — *Holmes, George R*

Helping Teens in Crisis — *Neff, Miriam*

Helping Your College Student Succeed — *Harris, Marcia B*

Helvetia Sacra. Pt. 8, Vol. 1

Hematology: A Problem-Oriented Approach — *Gross, Samuel*

Hemingway in Love and War — *Von Kurowsky, Agnes*

Hemingway: The 1930s — *Reynolds, Michael*

Hemingway: The Postwar Years and the Posthumous Novels — *Burwell, Rose Marie*

Hemingway: The Toronto Years 1920-1924 — *Burrill, William*

Hemmed In — *Callaghy, Thomas M*

Hemp for Health — *Conrad, Chris*

r Hempstead County, Arkansas Marriages January 1, 1900 through December 31, 1912

r Hempstead County, Arkansas United States Census of 1830, 1840, 1850 and Tax Lists of 1828, 1829, 1830, 1831, 1832, 1839, 1841, 1842, 1847, 1848, 1849

c Hen Lake (Illus. by Mary Jane Auch) — *Auch, Mary Jane*

Hendrik Petrus Berlage: Thoughts on Style 1886-1909 — *Berlage, Hendrik Petrus*

Hengitys Yossa — *Nummi, Lassi*

c Henny-Penny (Illus. by Emily Bolam) — *Ziefert, Harriet*

Henny Youngman's BIG Book of Insults — *Youngman, Henny*

Henri IV, Le Roi Venge — *Castarede, Jean*

Henri Bergson and British Modernism — *Gillies, Mary Ann*

Henri Cartier-Bresson and the Artless Art — *Montier, Jean-Pierre*

Henri Laugier En Son Siecle — *Cremieux-Brilhac, Jean-Louis*

r Henri Matisse: A Guide to Research — *Bock-Weiss, Catherine C*

c Henrietta and the Big Sale (Illus. by John Farman) — *Cullimore, Stan*

Henriette D'Angleterre, Duchesse D'Orleans — *Duchene, Jacqueline*

Henrik Ibsen: A New Biography — *Ferguson, Robert*

c Henry IV Part 1 — *Whitesides, Nigel*

Henry V (Evans) — *Shakespeare, William*

Henry V (Taylor) — *Shakespeare, William*

Henry VI and the Politics of Kingship — *Watts, John*

Henry A. Wallace: His Search for a New World Order — *White, Graham*

c Henry and Horace Clean Up (Illus. by Gisela Durr) — *Mennel, Wolfgang*

c Henry and Mudge and the Happy Cat (Illus. by Sucie Stevenson) — *Rylant, Cynthia*

c Henry and Ribsy (Woodman). Audio Version — *Cleary, Beverly*

c Henry Bobbity Is Missing (Illus. by Ernie Eldredge) — *Childress, Mark*

Henry Brougham and His World — *Ford, Trowbridge H*

Henry Chapman Mercer and the Moravian Pottery and Tile Works — *Reed, Cleota*

Henry Clay and the American System — *Baxter, Maurice G*

Henry Darwin Rogers 1808-1866 — *Gerstner, Patsy*

Henry E. Huntington's Library of Libraries — *Dickinson, Donald C*

Henry Fielding's Novels and the Classical Tradition — *Mace, Nancy A*

Henry Ford: Mass Production, Modernism and Design — *Batchelor, Ray*

c Henry Ford Museum (Illus. by Wes Hardin) — *Hardin, Wes*

Henry Goulburn 1784-1856 — *Jenkins, Brian*

c Henry Higgins (Illus. by Louis Darling) — *Cleary, Beverly*

Henry James and the Art of Non-Fiction — *Tanner, Tony*

Henry James and the Ghostly — *Lustig, T J*

Henry James and the Real Thing — *Smith, Virginia Llewellyn*

Henry James and the Writing of Race and Nation — *Blair, Sara*

Henry James, Gertrude Stein, and the Biographical Act — *Caramello, Charles*

Henry James: The Contemporary Reviews — *Hayes, Kevin J*

Henry James: The Young Master — *Novick, Sheldon M*

Henry John Cody: An Outstanding Life — *Masters, D C*

Henry Miller: The Paris Years — *Brassai*

Henry Moore: From the Inside Out — *Allemand-Cosneau, Claud*

Henry Moore: Sculture, Disegni, Incisioni, Arazzi — *Moore, Henry, 1898-*

Henry Oian Flipper: West Point's First Black Graduate — *Eppinga, Jane*

Henry Parker and the English Civil War — *Mendle, Michael*

Henry Purcell — *Holman, Peter*

Henry Simon of Manchester — *Simon, Brian*

Henry Vaughan — *Davies, Stevie*

c Henry Y Mudge Con Barro Hasta El Rabo (Illus. by Sucie Stevenson) — *Rylant, Cynthia*

c Henry Y Mudge: El Primer Libro De Sus Aventuras (Illus. by Sucie Stevenson) — *Rylant, Cynthia*

c Henry's Ball — *Campbell, Rod*

Henry's Wars and Shakespeare's Laws — *Meron, Theodor*

The Henty Journals — *Peel, Lynnette J*

Hep-Cats, Narcs, and Pipe Dreams — *Jonnes, Jill*

Hepatic Metastases — *Morris, D L*

Hepatobiliary and Pancreatic Surgery. 5th Ed. — *Carter, David*

Her Little Majesty — *Erickson, Carolly*

Her Mother's Ashes and Other Stories by South Asian Women in Canada and the United States — *Aziz, Nurjehan*

y Her Own Rules — *Bradford, Barbara Taylor*

c Her Piano Sang (Illus. by Shelly O Haas) — *Allman, Barbara*

Her Slender Dress — *Yuzna, Susan*

y Her Stories (Illus. by Leo Dillon) — *Hamilton, Virginia*

y Her Story — *Merritt, Susan E*

y Her Story II — *Merritt, Susan E*

y Her Wild American Self — *Galang, M Evelina*

Her Yes — *Vaeth, Kim*

El Heraldo De Las Malas Noticias — *Machover, Jacobo*

The Herb Book — *Boxer, Arabella*

The Herb Garden — *Hillier, Malcolm*

Herb Ritts: Work — *Ritts, Herb*

Herbal Bonsai — *Bender, Richard W*

Herbal Remedies in Pots — *Romain, Effie*

c Herbert--Five Stories (Illus. by Patrick Benson) — *Cutler, Ivor*

c Herbert Richardson — *Masterson, Paul*

Herbs for Health and Healing — *Keville, Kathi*

Herbs for Magic and Ritual — *Moorey, Teresa*

Herbs for Your Health — *Foster, Steven*

Herbs to Relieve Headaches — *Hoffmann, David*

Herbs to Relieve Stress — *Hoffmann, David*

r Herculean Ferrara — *Tuohy, Thomas*

c Hercules (Illus. by Margaret Power) — *Noonan, Diana*

Hercules In Der Romischen Kunst Von Den Anfangen Bis Augustus — *Ritter, Stefan*

r Herder-Bibliographie 1977-1992 — *Kuhles, Doris*

Here a Captive Heart Busted — *Fulweiler, Howard W*

The Here and Now — *Cohen, Robert, 1957-*

Here and Now — *Leo, Vince*

Here and Nowhere Else — *Brox, Jane*

c Here Come the Aliens! (Illus. by Colin McNaughton) — *McNaughton, Colin*

y Here Comes a Candle to Light You to Bed — *Prince, Maggie*

c Here Comes the Snow (Illus. by Maxie Chambliss) — *Medearis, Angela Shelf*

Here Comes the Storyteller — *Hayes, Joe*

c Here I Am! — *Stannard, Russell*

c Here Is the Wetland (Illus. by Wayne McLoughlin) — *Dunphy, Madeleine*

Here, Kitty, Kitty — *Elze, Winifred*

Here Lies Henry — *MacIvor, Daniel*

c Here There Be Angels (Illus. by David Wilgus) — *Yolen, Jane*

y Here There Be Witches — *Yolen, Jane*

c Here We Are! (Illus. by Richard Fowler) — *Fowler, Richard*

Here We Are in Paradise — *Earley, Tony*

Here We Stand — *Boice, James Montgomery*

Herencia Y Patrimonio Familiar En La Castilla Del Antiguo Regimen 1650-1834 — *Garcia Fernandez, Maximo*

c Here's a Happy Elephant — *Hawkins, Colin*

c Here's a Happy Kitten — *Hawkins, Colin*

c Here's a Happy Pig — *Hawkins, Colin*

c Here's a Happy Puppy — *Hawkins, Colin*

c Here's How (Illus. by Laura Cornell) — *Grant, Robert M*

Heresy and Criticism — *Grant, Robert M*

Heresy and Literacy 1000-1530 — *Biller, Peter*

Heretic: Based on the Life of Derek Freeman — *Williamson, David, 1942-*

The Heretic's Feast — *Spencer, Colin*

r The Heretic's Handbook of Quotatons — *Bufe, Charles*

Heretics: The Other Side of Early Christianity — *Ludemann, Gerd*

Las Heridas De La Ciencia — *Peset Reig, Jose Luis*

The Heritage Crusade and the Spoils of History — *Lowenthal, David*

The Heritage of Central Asia — *Frye, Richard N*

The Heritage of Islam — *Callaway, Barbara*

c Herman and Marguerite (Illus. by Laura O'Callahan) — *O'Callahan, Jay*

y Herman Melville — *Stefoff, Rebecca*

Herman Melville: A Biography. Vol. 1 — *Parker, Hershel*

c Hermana Aguila, Hermano Cielo (Illus. by Susan Jeffers) — *Seattle, Chief*

Hermann Broch Und Die Demokratie — *Klinger, Monika*

r Hermann Sasse: A Bibliography — *Feuerhahn, Ronald R*

c El Hermano De Guille — *Elena, Horacio*

Hermeneutical Foundations of Hebrews — *Leschert, Dale F*

Hermeneutics Ancient and Modern — *Bruns, Gerald L*

Hermeneutics and the Study of History — *Dilthey, Wilhelm*

Hermits: The Insights of Solitude — *France, Peter*

c Hernando Cortes — *Lilley, Stephen R*

Hernando De Soto and the Indians of Florida — *Milanich, Jerald T*

The Herne's Egg — *Yeats, W B*

The Hero — *Le Nay, Louise*

y A Hero All His Life — *Mantle, Merlyn*

c The Hero and the Crown — *McKinley, Robin*

Un Hero De Passage — *Poivre D'Arvor, Patrick*

Hero Dogs — *Jones, Peter C*
y Hero of Lesser Causes — *Johnston, Julie*
c Hero Tales — *Jackson, Dave*
Herod: King of the Jews and Friend of the Romans — *Richardson, Peter, 1935-*
y Herod the Great — *Green, Robert*
Herodotus and the Origins of the Political Community — *Thompson, Norma*
c Heroes (Illus. by Dom Lee) — *Mochizuki, Ken*
Heroes and Adventures — *Massingberd, Hugh*
Heroes and Heroines in Medieval English Literature — *Carruthers, Leo*
Heroes: Embracing Your Role as Your Child's Hero — *Kraehmer, Steffen T*
y Heroes, Monsters, and Other Worlds from Russian Mythology (Illus. by Alexander Koshkin) — *Warner, Elizabeth*
r Heroes of Conscience — *Gay, Kathlyn*
Heroes of the Age — *Edwards, David B*
c Heroes of the Game — *Egan, Terry*
Heroes on Horseback — *Chasteen, John Charles*
Heroes' Twilight — *Bergonzi, Bernard*
The Heroic and Creative Meaning of Socialism — *Mariategui, Jose Carlos*
The Heroic Enterprise — *Hood, John M*
Heroic Legends of the North — *Haymes, Edward R*
y The Heroic Life of Al Capsella — *Clarke, Judith*
Heroic Poets, Poetic Heroes — *Reynolds, Dwight Fletcher*
Heroic Virtue, Comic Infidelity — *Polachek, Dora E*
Heroides--Select Epistles (Knox) — *Ovid*
r Heroines: A Bibliography of Women Series Characters in Mystery, Espionage, Action, Science Fiction, Fantasy, Horror, Western, Romance... — *Drew, Bernard A*
c Heroines: Great Women through the Ages (Illus. by Rebecca Hazell) — *Hazell, Rebecca*
Heroism and the Black Intellectual — *Watts, Jerry Gafio*
y Heroism in America — *Leinwand, Gerald*
Un Heros Tres Discrete — *Deniau, Jean-Francois*
Herotica 3
Herrschaft Gottes--Heute Oder Morgen? — *Giesen, Heinz*
Herrschaft, Kirche, Kultur — *Jenal, Georg*
Herrschaft Und Verfassungsstrukturen Im Nordwesten Des Reiches — *Sicken, Bernhard*
Hers: Brilliant New Fiction by Lesbian Writers — *Wolverton, Terry*
cr Herstory: Women Who Changed the World — *Ashby, Ruth*
He's Got the Time, Have You Got the Money? — *Lane, Wanda*
He's Got the Whole World in His Pants — *Edwards, Gavin*
c The Hessian's Secret Diary (Illus. by James Watling) — *Banim, Lisa*
Heterodox Economic Theories — *Moseley, Fred*
Heterogeneities: Race, Gender, Class, Nation, and State — *Ackermann, Robert John*
Heterogeneous Catalysis in Industrial Practice. 2nd Ed. — *Satterfield, Charles N*
Heterosexual Dictatorship — *Higgins, Patrick*
Heterosexual Plots and Lesbian Narratives — *Farwell, Marilyn R*
Heterostructure Epitaxy and Devices — *NATO Advanced Research Workshop on Heterostructure Epitaxy and Devices (1995: Smolenice Castle)*
Heterotopia: Postmodern Utopia and the Body Politic — *Siebers, Tobin*
Hetmans'kyi Skarb — *Mushketyk, IUrii*
Heun's Differential Equations — *Ronveaux, R*
Heures — *Argyridou-Peonidou, Elli*
y Las Heuronas De Don Santiago — *Leefmans, Alvarez*
Heute Neunzig Jahr — *Johnson, Uwe*
y Hexwood — *Jones, Diana Wynne*
c Hey, Al — *Yorinks, Arthur*
Hey, Cowboy, Wanna Get Lucky? — *Black, Baxter*
c Hey Dad, Get a Life! — *Strasser, Todd*
c Hey! I'm Reading! (Illus. by Sylvie Wickstrom) — *Miles, Betty*
Hey, Joe — *Neihart, Ben*
c Hey, New Kid! (Illus. by Ellen Thompson) — *Duffey, Betsy*
c Hey Willy, See the Pyramids (Illus. by Maira Kalman) — *Kalman, Maira*
Hi, I'm Bob and I'm the Parent of a Teenager — *Smith, Tim*
c Hiawatha (Illus. by Susan Jeffers) — *Longfellow, Henry Wadsworth*
Hibakusha Cinema — *Broderick, Mick*

Hibiscus Rouge — *Lancon, Daniel*
c Hiccup Champion of the World — *Roberts, Ken*
c Hiccups for Elephant (Illus. by Hans Wilhelm) — *Preller, James*
Hidatsa Suprasegmentals — *Bowers, Norman A*
Hidden Agenda — *Alers, Rochelle*
Hidden Agendas — *Lewis, Derek*
Hidden Americans — *Leaming, Hugo Prosper*
Hidden Attraction — *Verschuur, Gerrit L*
A Hidden Cause of Murder — *Roe, C F*
y Hidden Cities — *Kennedy, Roger G*
The Hidden Foundation — *James, David E*
Hidden Friends — *Carmelites of Indianapolis*
Hidden from History — *Rowbotham, Sheila*
Hidden Gold — *Frazee, Steve*
The Hidden Hand — *Pipes, Daniel*
Hidden Histories of Science — *Silvers, Robert B*
The Hidden History of the Human Race — *Cremo, Michael A*
The Hidden Holmes — *Rosenberg, David*
Hidden Horrors — *Tanaka, Toshiyuki*
Hidden in the Home — *Dangler, Jamie Faricellia*
Hidden in the Lute — *Russell, Ralph*
Hidden Latitudes — *Anderson, Alison*
The Hidden Law — *Hecht, Anthony*
Hidden Lives — *Forster, Margaret*
y Hidden Logic Puzzles — *Weaver, Charles*
c Hidden Music (Illus. by Gloria Kamen) — *Kamen, Gloria*
Hidden Order — *Friedman, David*
Hidden Order — *Holland, John*
r Hidden San Francisco and Northern California — *Riegert, Ray*
y The Hidden Scrolls — *Silberman, Neil Asher*
r Hidden Southwest. 3rd Ed. — *Harris, Richard, 1947-*
c Hidden Spirits (Illus. by Judy Larson) — *Kassirer, Sue*
Hidden Star — *Chaplin, Patrice*
The Hidden Target (Pacey). Audio Version — *MacInnes, Helen*
The Hidden Tradition in Europe — *Stoyanov, Yuri*
Hidden Wholeness — *Dash, Michael I N*
The Hidden Wiring — *Hennessy, Peter*
The Hidden Writer — *Johnson, Alexandra*
The Hide — *Unsworth, Barry*
c Hide and Narrow (Illus. by Catherine Walters) — *Sykes, Julie*
c Hide and Seek (Illus. by Dawn Apperley) — *Burns, Kate*
Hide and Seek — *Patterson, James*
y Hide and Seek — *Pausacker, Jenny*
c Hide and Seek with Anthony Ant — *Philpot, Lorna*
c Hide and Shriek! — *Dowling, Paul*
c Hideaway — *Thomas, Ruth*
Hiding My Candy — *Lady Chablis*
Hiding My Candy. Audio Version — *Lady Chablis*
c Hiding Out — *Rawnsley, Irene*
The Hiding Place — *Ten Boom, Corrie*
c Hiding Places (Illus. by Peter Melnyczuk) — *Dowley, Ruth*
The Hiding Room — *Wilson, Jonathan*
Hier — *Kristof, Agota*
Hiera Kala — *Van Straten, F T*
Hierarchy and Its Discontents — *Parish, Steven M*
Hierarchy Theory — *Ahl, Valerie*
Hieroglyphs and the Afterlife in Ancient Egypt — *Forman, Werner*
High and Low Moderns — *DiBattista, Maria*
High and Tight — *Klapisch, Bob*
High Art Down Home — *Plattner, Stuart*
High Churchmanship in the Church of England — *Hylson-Smith, Kenneth*
High Culture Fever — *Wang, Jing*
High Energy Solar Physics — *Ramaty, R*
High Fantastic — *Tem, Steve Rasnic*
High Fidelity — *Hornby, Nick*
High Fidelity (Carrington). Audio Version — *Hornby, Nick*
High-Flavor, Low-Fat Appetizers — *Raichlen, Steven*
High-Flavor, Low-Fat Desserts — *Raichlen, Steven*
High-Heel Blue — *Shah, Diane K*
High Hopes — *Renshon, Stanley A*
c High in the Sky and Making Tracks — *Parker, Steve*
c High in the Trees (Illus. by Neecy Twinem) — *Twinem, Neecy*
High Inflation — *Heymann, Daniel*
r High Interest-Easy Reading. 7th Ed. — *Phelan, Patricia*
High Latitudes — *Buchan, James*
High-Level Vision — *Ullman, Shimon*
High Life — *Macdougall, Lee*

High Lonesome — *Hannah, Barry*
High Lonesome — *Tichi, Cecelia*
High Noon on the Electronic Frontier — *Ludlow, Peter*
High Performance — *Post, Robert C*
High Performance Audio Power Amplifiers for Music Performance and Reproduction — *Duncan, Ben*
High Performance Cluster Configuration System Management — *Gursha, James E*
High-Performance Communication Networks — *Walrand, Jean*
High Performance Computational Methods for Biological Sequence Analysis — *Yap, Tieng K*
High Performance Computer Imaging — *Kabir, Ihtisham*
High Performance Computing — *Kuck, David J*
High Performance Computing in Fluid Dynamics — *Wesseling, Pieter, Dr. Ir.*
High Performance Liquid Chromatography — *Katz, Elena D*
High Performance Memories — *Prince, Betty*
y High-Performance Soccer — *Caligiuri, Paul*
y High Performance through Communicating Information — *Rosen, Lucy*
y High Performance through Dealing with Diversity — *Strazzabosco, Jeanne*
y High Performance through Effective Budgeting — *Hurwitz, Jane*
y High Performance through Effective Scheduling — *Hurwitz, Sue*
y High Performance through Leadership — *Parker, Julie F*
y High Performance through Negotiation — *Simpson, Carolyn*
y High Performance through Organizing Information — *Simpson, Carolyn*
y High Performance through Self-Management — *Santamaria, Peggy*
y High Performance through Teamwork — *Gartner, Robert*
y High Performance through Understanding Systems — *McGlothlin, Bruce*
The High Performance Vegetarian Cookbook — *Kleiner, Susan M*
High Power Lasers — *Kossowsky, Ram*
High Resolution Separation and Analysis of Biological Macromolecules. Pt. B — *Karger, Barry L*
High Risk 2 — *Scholder, Amy*
The High-Risk Society — *Mandel, Michael J*
yp High School Senior Magazine
yr High School Senior's Guide to Merit and Other No-Need Funding. 1st Ed.
High Society — *Mazzola, Anthony T*
High-Speed Europe
r High-Speed Networking for Multimedia Applications — *Effelsberg, Wolfgang*
r High Strangeness — *Clark, Jerome*
High Street — *Jacobs, Anna*
High-Tech Highways — *Pinkston, Elizabeth*
High-Tech Practice — *Farr, Cheryl*
r The High-Technology Editorial Guide and Stylebook — *Perdue, Lewis*
High Temperature, High Performance Materials for Rocket Engines and Space Applications — *Upadhya, Kamleshwar*
High Tide in Tucson — *Kingsolver, Barbara*
c High Valley — *Thiele, Colin*
The High-Value Manager — *Stone, Florence M*
High Velocity Neutron Stars and Gamma-Ray Bursts — *Conference on High Velocity Neutron Stars and Gamma-Ray Bursts (1995: La Jolla, CA)*
c High-Wire Henry (Illus. by Erick Ingraham) — *Calhoun, Mary*
Highcastle: A Remembrance — *Lem, Stanislaw*
r A Higher Branch of the Art — *Hamber, Anthony J*
The Higher Civil Service in the United States — *Huddleston, Mark W*
y Higher Education — *Sheffield, Charles*
Higher Education and Corporate Realities — *Brown, Philip, 1957-*
r The Higher Education Money Book for Women and Minorities. 1997 Ed.
Higher Education under Fire — *Berube, Michael*
Higher Engineering Mathematics. 2nd Ed. — *Bird, J O*
The Higher Learning in America — *Hutchins, Robert Maynard*
Higher Superstition — *Gross, Paul R*
c Highest, Longest, Deepest (Illus. by Gary Hincks) — *Malam, John*

A Highland Lady in France 1843-1845 — *Grant, Elizabeth*

r Highlander Polish-English/English-Highlander Polish Dictionary — *Gutt-Mostowy, Jan*

The Highlands of the Lowlands — *Graham, Elizabeth*

y Highlights from 19th-Century Novels — *Marsh, Linda*

Highway 99 — *Yogi, Stan*

Highway Engineering Handbook — *Brockenbrough, R L*

Highway Materials, Soils, and Concretes. 3rd Ed. — *Atkins, Harold N*

The Highwaymen: Warriors on the Information Superhighway — *Auletta, Ken*

Highways and Dancehalls — *Atkinson, Diana*

Highways to a War — *Koch, Christopher*

Hijacked: The True Story of the Heroes of Flight 705 — *Hirschman, Dave*

A Hiker's Guide to Art of the Canadian Rockies — *Christensen, Lisa*

r Hiking Trails, Eastern United States — *Rajtar, Steve*

r Hiking Trails, Western United States — *Rajtar, Steve*

c Hilary and the Lions (Illus. by Deborah Durland DeSaix) — *DeSaix, Frank*

Hilbert — *Reid, Constance*

Hilbert Transforms in Signal Processing — *Hahn, Stefan L*

c Hilda Hen's Scary Night (Illus. by Mary Wormell) — *Wormell, Mary*

c Hilda's Tea Party

Hildegard of Bingen: Healing and the Nature of the Cosmos — *Schipperges, Heinrich*

c Hill of Darkness — *Michael, Jan*

Hillbillyland: What the Movies Did to the Mountains and What the Mountains Did to the Movies — *Williamson, J W, 1944-*

c Hillel Builds a House (Illus. by Marilynn Barr) — *Lepon, Shoshana*

r The Hillel Guide to Jewish Life on Campus. 1996 Ed.

Himalaya Alpine-Style — *Fanshawe, Andy*

Himalayan Environment — *Messerli, Bruno*

Himself and Other Animals — *Hughes, David*

Hind — *Onnepalu, Tonu*

Hindemith, Hartmann, and Henze — *Rickards, Guy*

c Hindu — *Ganeri, Anita*

Hindu and Christian in South-East India — *Oddie, Geoffrey A*

The Hindu Connection — *Raj, A R Victor*

Hindu Scriptures — *Goodall, Dominic*

Hinduism — *Kadodwala, Dilip*

c Hinduism — *Moorcroft, Christine*

Hinduism for Our Times — *Sharma, Arvind*

Hindus — *Wayne, Elizabeth*

Hine Sight — *Hine, Darlene Clark*

Hinh Nhu La Tinh Yen — *Ali, Khanh*

Hints of His Mortality — *Borofka, David*

Hippeis: The Cavalry of Ancient Greece — *Worley, Leslie J*

Hippocrates Now! — *Parsons, Patricia*

r Hippocrene Concise Hungarian-English, English-Hungarian Dictionary — *Takacs, Geza*

r Hippocrene Concise Sanskrit-English Dictionary — *Apte, Vasudco Govind*

r Hippocrene Practical English-Yiddish, Yiddish-English Dictionary: Romanized. Expanded Ed. — *Gross, David C*

Hippolytus and the Roman Church in the Third Century — *Brent, Allen*

y The Hippopotamus Pool (Rosenblat). Audio Version — *Peters, Elizabeth*

c Hippos Go Berserk! (Illus. by Sandra Boynton) — *Boynton, Sandra*

Hiram Johnson: Political Revivalist — *Weatherson, Michael A*

The Hiram Key — *Knight, Christopher, 1950-*

y The Hired Hand (Illus. by Jerry Pinkney) — *San Souci, Robert D*

Hired Hands — *Danysk, Cecilia*

c Hiroshima — *Yep, Laurence*

y Hiroshima in America — *Lifton, Robert Jay*

Hiroshima in History and Memory — *Hogan, Michael J*

y Hiroshima Notes — *Oe, Kenzaburo*

Hirshhorn Museum and Sculpture Garden: 150 Works of Art — *Hirshhorn Museum and Sculpture Garden*

His — *Drake, Robert*

His Arms Are Full of Broken Things — *Parris, P B*

c His Dark Materials — *Pullman, Philip*

His Father's Son — *Churchill, Winston S*

His Forbidden Touch — *Thacker, Shelly*

His Holiness — *Bernstein, Carl*

y His Holiness (Hockenberry). Audio Version — *Bernstein, Carl*

His Name Is Ron — *Goldman Family*

y His Promised Land — *Parker, John P*

His Secret Life — *Berkowitz, Bob*

His Share of Glory — *Kornbluth, C M*

cr Hispanic American Chronology — *Kanellos, Nicholas*

r Hispanic American Genealogical Sourcebook — *Byers, Paula K*

Hispanic Catholic Culture in the U.S. — *Dolan, Jay P*

y The Hispanic Condition — *Stavans, Ilan*

r Hispanic Culture of Mexico, Central America, and the Caribbean — *Standish, Peter*

Hispanic Nation — *Fox, Geoffrey E*

r Hispanic Resource Directory. 3rd Ed. — *Schorr, Alan Edward*

r Hispanic Surnames and Family History — *Platt, Lyman D*

Hispanics and United States Film — *Keller, Gary D*

Histamine and H1-Receptor Antagonists in Allergic Disease — *Simons, F Estelle R*

Histoire De L'Alimentation — *Flandrin, Jean-Louis*

Histoire De L'Analyse Economique — *Silem, Ahmed*

Histoire De L'Eugenisme En France — *Carol, Anne*

Histoire De L'Industrie En France — *Woronoff, Denis*

Histoire De Tel Quel 1960-1982 — *Forest, Philippe*

L'Histoire Des Religions A-T-Elle Un Sens? — *Eliade, Mircea*

Histoire Du Christianisme, Des Origines A Nos Jours. Vol. 4 — *Mayeur, Jean Marie*

Histoire Du Christianisme En Suisse — *Vischer, Lukas*

Histoire Du Cinema Francais — *Jeancolas, Jean-Pierre*

Histoire D'Un Voyage En Terre De Bresil — *Lery, Jean De*

Histoire Et Historiens A Rome Dans L'Antiquite — *Cizek, Eugen*

L'Histoire Et Le Metier D'Historien En France 1945-1995 — *Bedarida, Francois*

Histoire Generale De L'Electricite En France. Vol. 2 — *Levy-Leboyer, Maurice*

Histoire Militaire De La France. Vol. 4

Histoire Naturelle Des Indes

Histoire Sociale De La Medecine (XVIIIe-XXe Siecles) — *Faure, Olivier*

Histoire Universelle. Bk. 9 — *Thierry, Andre*

Histopathology: A Color Atlas and Textbook — *Damjanov, Ivan*

Historia Da Politicia Exterior Do Brasil — *Cervo, Amado Luis*

Historia De Duobus Amantibus — *Pius II, Pope*

Historia De La Arquidiocesis De Bogota — *Mantilla R, Luis Carlos*

Historia De La Ciencia Al Pais Valencia — *Lopez Pinero, Jose Maria*

r Historia De La Iglesia En Espana 1931-1939. Vols. 1-2 — *Redondo, Gonzalo*

Historia De La Persecucion Religiosa En Espana 1936-1939 — *Moreno, Antonio Montero*

Historia De Las Sublevaciones Indias En La Tarahumara — *Neumann, Joseph*

Historia De Las Unidades De Riego — *Gomez Zepeda, Ignacio*

Historia De Una Gaviota Y Del Gato Que Le Enseno A Volar — *Sepulveda, Luis*

Historia General Del Peru. Vols. 1-10

La Historia: Inagotable Tematica Novelesca — *Yanez, Maria-Paz*

Historian of the Strange — *Zeitlin, Judith*

Historians and Race — *Cimbala, Paul*

Historians of the Christian Tradition — *Bauman, Michael*

Historias Del Kronen — *Manas, Jose Angel*

Historic Architecture in the Caribbean Islands — *Crain, Edward E*

Historic Buildings of the Smokies — *Trout, Ed*

r Historic Contact — *Grumet, Robert S*

r Historic Festivals — *Cantor, George*

The Historic King Arthur — *Reno, Frank D*

Historic Preservation — *Barthel, Diane*

r The Historic Railroad — *Norris, John R*

c A Historical Album of Colorado — *Wills, Charles A*

c A Historical Album of Georgia — *Wills, Charles A*

c A Historical Album of Michigan — *Wills, Charles A*

c A Historical Album of Ohio — *Wills, Charles A*

c A Historical Album of Pennsylvania — *Wills, Charles A*

An Historical and Historiographical Commentary on Suetonius' Life of C. Caligula — *Hurley, Donna W*

Historical and Philosophical Issues in the Conservation of Cultural Heritage — *Price, Nicholas Stanley*

The Historical Archaeology of Dam Construction Camps in Central Arizona. Vol. 1 — *Rogge, A E*

The Historical Archaeology of Dam Construction Camps in Central Arizona. Vol. 2A — *Ayres, James E*

The Historical Archaeology of Dam Construction Camps in Central Arizona. Vol. 2B — *Fenicle, Diane L*

The Historical Archaeology of Dam Construction Camps in Central Arizona. Vol. 2C — *Douglas, Diane L*

A Historical Archaeology of the Modern World — *Orser, Charles E*

r An Historical Atlas of Lincolnshire — *Bennett, Stewart*

r Historical Atlas of South-East Asia — *Pluvier, Jan M*

r The Historical Atlas of the Congresses of the Confederate States of America 1861-1865 — *Martis, Kenneth C*

yr Historical Atlas of the Earth — *Osborne, Roger*

r Historical Atlas of the Vietnam War — *Summers, Harry G, Jr.*

The Historical Boundaries between Bosnia, Croatia, Serbia — *Burdett, Anita L P*

r Historical Britain — *Wood, Eric S*

Historical Change and Human Rights — *Hufton, Olwen*

The Historical Christ and the Jesus of Faith — *Evans, C Stephen*

A Historical Commentary on Arrian's History of Alexander. Vol. 2 — *Bosworth, A B*

Historical Consciousness in the Early Republic — *Jones, H G*

r Historical Dictionary of Aid and Development Organizations — *Arnold, Guy*

r Historical Dictionary of Albania — *Hutchings, Raymond*

r Historical Dictionary of Botswana. 3rd Ed. — *Ramsay, Jeff*

r Historical Dictionary of Congo. 3rd Ed. — *Decalo, Samuel*

r Historical Dictionary of Feminism — *Boles, Janet K*

r Historical Dictionary of India — *Mansingh, Surjit*

r Historical Dictionary of Luxembourg — *Barteau, Harry C*

r Historical Dictionary of Mali. 3rd Ed. — *Imperato, Pascal James*

r Historical Dictionary of Mauritania. 2nd Ed. — *Pazzanita, Anthony G*

r Historical Dictionary of Methodism — *Yrigoyen, Charles*

r Historical Dictionary of Mongolia — *Sanders, Alan J K*

r Historical Dictionary of Multinational Peacekeeping — *Mays, Terry M*

r Historical Dictionary of New Zealand — *Jackson, Keith*

r Historical Dictionary of Organized Labor — *Docherty, James C*

r Historical Dictionary of Poland 966-1945 — *Lerski, George I*

r Historical Dictionary of Romania — *Treptow, Kurt W*

r Historical Dictionary of Saudi Arabia — *Peterson, J E*

r Historical Dictionary of Slovenia — *Plut-Pregelj, Leopoldina*

r Historical Dictionary of Spain — *Smith, Angel*

r Historical Dictionary of Stuart England 1603-1689 — *Fritze, Ronald H*

r Historical Dictionary of Syria — *Commins, David Dean*

r Historical Dictionary of Thailand — *Win, May Kyi*

r Historical Dictionary of the Civil Rights Movement — *Luker, Ralph E*

r Historical Dictionary of the Gulf Arab States — *Peck, Malcolm C*

r Historical Dictionary of the Modern Olympic Movement — *Findling, John E*

r Historical Dictionary of the Orthodox Church — *Prokurat, Michael*

r Historical Dictionary of the Spanish American War — *Dyal, Donald H*

r Historical Dictionary of Venezuela. 2nd Ed., Rev., Enl., and Updated — *Rudolph, Donna Keyse*

r Historical Encyclopedia of School Psychology — *Fagan, Thomas K*

r An Historical Encyclopedia of the Arab-Israeli Conflict — *Reich, Bernard*

r Historical Figures in Fiction — *Hartman, Donald K*

Historical Geography — *Butlin, Robin A*

The Historical Jesus — *Crossan, John Dominic*
Historical Perspectives on the Education of Black
    Children — *Morgan, Harry*
r Historical Publications 1994. Electronic Media Version
The Historical Society Murder Mystery — *Landrum,
    Graham*
r Historical Statistics 1960-1994
p Historical Studies in Industrial Relations
Historical Themes and Identity — *Lopez, Antoinette
    Sedillo*
Historicism in Russia — *Biriukova, Nina*
Historicizing Milton — *Knoppers, Laura Lunger*
The Histories (De Selincourt) — *Herodotus*
Histories: French Constructions of the Past — *Revel,
    Jacques*
The Histories (McGushin). Vol. 2 — *Sallust*
Historiographic Metafiction in Modern American and
    Canadian Literature — *Engler, Bernd*
Historiography of Europeans in Africa and Asia
    1450-1800 — *Disney, Anthony*
r Historische Stedenatlas Van Belgie. Vols. 1-3
    — *Leiding, O*
r The History, Ancestry and Descendants of Davis
    Billings 1826-1888 and His Wife Adelia Caroline
    Nichols 1830-1904 — *Dawson, Wayne E*
History and Belief — *Frykenberg, Robert Eric*
r History and Bibliography of American Newspapers
    1690-1820. Vols. 1-2 — *Brigham, Clarence S*
The History and Conservation of Zanzibar Stone
    Town — *Sheriff, Abdul*
A History and Ethnography of the Beothuk
    — *Marshall, Ingeborg*
The History and Geography of Human Genes
    — *Cavalli-Sforza, L L*
History and Literature in Contemporary Russia
    — *Marsh, Rosalind*
The History and Power of Writing — *Martin, Henri-
    Jean*
The History and Science of Knots — *Turner, J C*
History and Technology of Olive Oil in the Holy Land
    — *Frankel, Rafael*
History and the Idea of Progress — *Melzer, Arthur M*
History and the Shaping of Irish Protestantism
    — *Bowen, Desmond*
History and Utopia — *Cioran, E M*
History and Warfare in Renaissance Epic — *Murrin,
    Michael*
History as Rhetoric — *Carpenter, Ronald H*
History by Hollywood — *Toplin, Robert Brent*
History, Fiction, Verisimilitude — *Chinca, Mark*
r The History Highway — *Trinkle, Dennis A*
History in Three Keys — *Cohen, Paul A*
History KS1 — *Harnett, Penelope*
History KS2 — *Forrest, Martin*
History, Literature, and Society in the Book of Acts
    — *Witherington, Ben, III*
A History Little Known — *Turnock, John*
r The History of Accounting — *Chatfield, Michael*
The History of Al-Tabari. Vols. 8, 16 — *Tabari*
The History of Alta California — *Osio, Antonio Maria*
The History of American Art Education — *Smith,
    Peter J, 1935, May, 5-*
r The History of American Classical Music — *Struble,
    John Warthen*
A History of American Magazines. Vols. 1-5 — *Mott,
    Frank Luther*
A History of Ancient Egypt — *Grimal, Nicolas*
A History of Antarctica — *Martin, Stephen, 1951-*
History of Art. 5th Ed., Vols. 1-2 — *Janson, H W*
yr History of Art for Young People. 5th Ed. — *Janson, H
    W*
r History of Astronomy — *Lankford, John*
A History of Astronomy from 1890 to the Present
    — *Leverington, David*
r The History of Books — *Schreyer, Alice D*
A History of British Art
A History of British Industrial Relations 1939-1979
    — *Wrigley, Chris*
A History of Brixton — *Piper, Alan*
The History of Broadcasting in the United Kingdom.
    Vol. 5 — *Briggs, Asa*
r The History of Brown County, Ohio — *Beers, W H*
A History of Brunei — *Saunders, Graham*
c History of Canals — *Tames, Richard*
A History of Canterbury Cathedral — *Collinson,
    Patrick*
The History of Cartography. Vol. 2, Bk. 2 — *Harley,
    J B*
A History of Chemistry — *Bensaude-Vincent,
    Bernadette*

A History of Childhood and Disability — *Safford,
    Philip L*
A History of Chile 1808-1994 — *Collier, Simon*
A History of Christianity — *Chadwick, Owen*
A History of Christianity in Africa — *Isichei,
    Elizabeth*
c The History of Christmas (Illus. by Annie Reiner).
    Book and Audio Version — *Reiner, Annie*
A History of Civilization. 9th Ed. — *Winks, Robin W*
A History of Cloth Dolls — *Edwards, Linda*
History of Colored Baseball with Other Documents on
    the Early Black Games 1886-1936 — *White, Sol*
The History of Computers — *Freed, Les*
A History of Conservative Politics 1900-1996
    — *Charmley, John*
The History of Danish Dreams — *Hoeg, Peter*
The History of Decorative Arts. Vol. 1
The History of Decorative Arts. Vols. 2-3
A History of Dogs in the Early Americas — *Schwartz,
    Marion*
A History of Early Roman Liturgy to the Death of
    Pope Gregory the Great — *Willis, G G*
A History of Early Roman Liturgy to the Death of
    Pope Gregory the Great — *Willis, Geoffrey
    Grimshaw*
A History of East Africa 1592-1902 — *Beachey, R W*
A History of Enfield. Vols. 2-3 — *Pam, David Owen*
A History of English Field-Names — *Field, John*
The History of English Law — *Hudson, John*
A History of English Political Thought in the
    Nineteenth Century — *Francis, Mark*
A History of Europe — *Roberts, J M*
History of Europe in the Nineteenth Century
    — *Croce, Benedetto*
The History of Everyday Life — *Ludtke, Alf*
The History of Exercise and Sport Science
    — *Massengale, John D*
c History of Fairs and Markets — *Wood, Richard*
A History of Fascism 1914-1945 — *Payne, Stanley G*
History of Film — *Parkinson, David*
c History of Food and Cooking — *Wood, Richard*
c A History of France through Art — *Powell, Jillian*
A History of French Louisiana. Vol. 2 — *Giraud,
    Marcel*
A History of Game Theory. Vol. 1 — *Dimand, Mary
    Ann*
History of Geology. Vol. 1 — *Ellenberger, Francois*
The History of Germany since 1789 — *Mann, Golo*
A History of God — *Armstrong, Karen*
A History of Heaven — *Russell, Jeffrey Burton*
History of Hope, Maine — *Hardy, Anna Simpson*
A History of Horrors — *Meikle, Denis*
r A History of Humanity. Vol. 2 — *Dani, A H*
A History of Hypnotism — *Gauld, Alan*
A History of Illinois — *Ford, Thomas*
A History of Illuminated Manuscripts. 2nd Ed. — *De
    Hamel, Christopher*
History of Islamic Philosophy. Vols. 1-2 — *Nasr,
    Seyyed Hossein*
A History of Israelite Religion in the Old Testament
    Period. Vols. 1-2 — *Albertz, Rainer*
The History of Jerusalem — *Prawer, Joshua*
r History of Jewish Philosophy — *Frank, Daniel H*
A History of Keyboard Literature — *Gordon, Stewart,
    1930-*
The History of Lesbian Hair and Other Tales of Bent
    Life in a Straight World — *Dugger, Mary*
History of Libraries in the Western World. 4th Ed.
    — *Harris, Michael H*
c The History of Making Books — *Gallimard Jeunesse*
A History of Medicine in the Early U.S. Navy
    — *Langley, Harold D*
A History of Medieval Political Thought — *Canning,
    Joseph*
The History of Mental Symptoms — *Berrios, German
    E*
A History of Modern Europe — *Merriman, John*
A History of Modern Planetary Physics. Vols. 1-3
    — *Brush, Stephen G*
A History of Money — *Davies, Glyn*
y The History of Money — *Weatherford, Jack*
A History of Mountain Climbing — *Frison-Roche,
    Roger*
r The History of Natural History — *Bridson, Gavin*
History of New Paltz, New York and Its Old Families
    from 1678 to 1820. 2nd Ed. — *Le Fevre, Ralph*
History of New Testament Research. Vol. 1 — *Baird,
    William*
A History of News — *Stephens, Mitchell*
The History of Ophthalmology — *Albert, Daniel M*

History of Original Ideas and Basic Discoveries in
    Particle Physics — *Newman, Harvey B*
A History of Pagan Europe — *Jones, Prudence*
The History of Pain — *Rey, Roselyne*
History of Paradise — *Delumeau, Jean*
r History of Photography. Vol. 3 — *Roosens, Laurent*
r History of Physical Anthropology. Vols. 1-2
    — *Spencer, Frank*
The History of Political and Social Concepts
    — *Richter, Melvin*
The History of Political Theory and Other Essays
    — *Dunn, John, 1940-*
c The History of Printmaking
History of Programming Languages — *Gibson,
    Richard G*
A History of Psychiatry — *Shorter, Edward*
A History of Psychology — *Benjafield, John G*
The History of Radio Astronomy and the National
    Radio Astronomy Observatory — *Malphrus,
    Benjamin K*
A History of Reading — *Manguel, Alberto*
A History of Religion in Britain — *Gilley, Sheridan*
A History of Rome under the Emperors — *Mommsen,
    Theodor*
History of Russia. Vol. 10 — *Soloviev, Sergei M*
A History of Saint Luke's Episcopal Church
    Jacksonville, Alabama 1844-1994 — *Caldwell,
    Ronald J*
r History of Science in the United States — *Elliott,
    Clark A*
History of Sculpture
A History of Shipbuilding and Naval Architecture in
    Canada — *Wilson, Gartii S*
A History of Sixteenth-Century France 1483-1598
    — *Garrisson, Janine*
A History of Slovakia — *Kirschbaum, Stanislav J*
A History of Sociological Research Methods in
    America 1920-1960 — *Platt, Jennifer*
The History of Sukkot in the Second Temple and
    Rabbinic Periods — *Rubenstein, Jeffrey L*
A History of Swedish Literature — *Warme, Lars G*
The History of That Ingenious Gentleman Don
    Quijote De La Mancha — *Cervantes Saavedra,
    Miguel De*
The History of the 36th (Ulster) Division — *Falls,
    Cyril*
The History of the Armenian Genocide — *Dadrian,
    Vahakn N*
A History of the Breast — *Yalom, Marilyn*
A History of the British Cavalry 1816-1919. Vol. 8
    — *Anglesey, George Charles Henry Victor Paget,
    Marquis of*
r A History of the British Isles — *Black, Jeremy*
A History of the British Labour Party — *Thorpe,
    Andrew*
History of the Coal-Mining Industry in Ohio
    — *Crowell, Douglas L*
A History of the Confederate Navy — *Luraghi,
    Raimondo*
History of the Decline and Fall of the Roman Empire.
    Vols. 1-3 — *Gibbon, Edward*
A History of the Devil — *Messadie, Gerald*
The History of the Distillers Company 1877-1939
    — *Weir, Ronald B*
A History of the Dublin University Press 1734-1976
    — *Kinane, Vincent*
A History of the English Language — *Blake, N F*
A History of the Family. Vols. 1-2 — *Burguiere, Andre*
The History of the Faraday Society — *Sutton, Leslie*
A History of the Fleet Prison, London — *Brown,
    Roger Lee*
A History of the French Language through Texts
    — *Ayres-Bennett, Wendy*
A History of the Gypsies of Eastern Europe and
    Russia — *Crowe, David M*
A History of the Habsburg Empire — *Berenger, Jean*
History of the Hour — *Dohrn-Van Rossum, Gerhard*
y A History of the Jews (May). Audio Version
    — *Johnson, Paul, 1928-*
A History of the Jews in the English-Speaking World
    — *Rubinstein, W D*
A History of the Mont Pelerin Society — *Hartwell, R
    M*
A History of the Port Phillip District — *Shaw, A G L*
The History of the Reign of King Henry the Seventh
    — *Bacon, Francis*
History of the Roman Catholic Diocese of
    Steubenville, Ohio. Vol. 1 — *Brown, Francis F*
The History of the Siege of Lisbon — *Saramago, Jose*
The History of the Social-Democratic Federation
    — *Crick, Martin*

767

A History of the Timucua Indians and Missions
— *Hann, John H*
The History of the Unified Command Plan 1946-1993
— *Cole, Ronald H*
y A History of the United States — *Jenkins, Philip*
c A History of the United States through Art — *Van Zandt, Eleanor*
A History of the University in Europe. Vol. 2
History of the War of Independence. Vol. 1
— *Milstein, Uri*
History of the Western Highlands and Isles of Scotland from A.D. 1493 to A.D. 1625 — *Gregory, Donald*
A History of the Writings of Beatrix Potter. Rev. Ed.
— *Linder, Leslie*
c History of Toys and Games — *Chrisp, Peter*
A History of Ukraine — *Magocsi, Paul Robert*
History of Vatican II. Vol. 1 — *Alberigo, Giuseppe*
A History of Western Music — *Grout, Donald Jay*
A History of Women in the West. Vol. 4
History, Prophecy, and the Stars — *Smoller, Laura Ackerman*
c The History Puzzle — *Denman, Cherry*
y History Wars — *Linenthal, Edward T*
c History's Travellers and Explorers (Illus. by Chris Mould) — *Ardagh, Philip*
Hit and Run — *Griffin, Nancy*
y Hit and Run (McLarty). Audio Version — *Griffin, Nancy*
yr Hit List: Frequently Challenged Books for Children
— *Pistolis, Donna Reidy*
yr Hit List: Frequently Challenged Books for Young Adults — *Young Adults Library Services Association. Intellectual Freedom Committee*
Ha-Hitabdut: Miflagah Mevateret Al Shilton
— *Kaspit, Ben*
Hitch: The Life and Times of Alfred Hitchcock
— *Taylor, John Russell*
Hitchcock on Hitchcock — *Hitchcock, Alfred*
y The Hitchhiker's Guide to the Galaxy — *Adams, Douglas*
Hitchhiker's Guide to Visual Basic and SQL Server. 4th Ed. — *Vaughn, William R*
Hitler and the Occult — *Anderson, Ken*
Hitler as Philosophe — *Birken, Lawrence*
Hitler: Speeches and Proclamations 1932-1945. Vols. 1-2 — *Hitler, Adolph*
Hitler Versus Me — *Jack, Donald*
Hitler's Airwaves — *Bergmeier, Horst J P*
Hitler's Enforcers — *Lucas, James*
Hitler's Thirty Days to Power, January 1933
— *Turner, Henry Ashby, Jr.*
Hitler's U-Boat War — *Blair, Clay*
Hitler's Uranium Club — *Bernstein, Jeremy*
Hitler's Wahler — *Falter, Jurgen*
Hitlers Wien — *Hamann, Brigitte*
Hitler's Willing Executioners — *Goldhagen, Daniel Jonah*
Hitting into the Wind — *Meissner, Bill*
Hitting the Road — *Yorke, Douglas A, Jr.*
Hittite Diplomatic Texts — *Beckman, Gary*
The Hittites — *Macqueen, J G*
HIV, AIDS and Childbearing — *Faden, Ruth R*
r HIV/AIDS and HIV/AIDS-Related Terminology
— *Huber, Jeffrey T*
HIV, AIDS, and the Law — *Senak, Mark S*
HIV/AIDS and the Older Adult — *Nokes, Kathleen M*
r HIV/AIDS Community Information Services
— *Huber, Jeffrey T*
HIV and AIDS — *Reid, Elizabeth*
r HIV and AIDS Treatment Directory 1997
HIV Law — *Crockett, Paul Hampton*
c HIV Positive (Illus. by Bernard Wolf) — *Wolf, Bernard*
A Hive of Bees — *Rowlands, Betty*
Hives of Sickness — *Rosner, David*
Hiwassee: A Novel of the Civil War — *Price, Charles F*
Hjortspring: Warfare and Sacrifice in Early Europe
— *Randsborg, Klavs*
r HMO/PPO Directory 1996
Ho Sognato L'Ospedale — *Romano, Lalla*
Hoa Dia Nguc — *Nguyen, Chi Thien*
Hoa Hong Nha Kin — *Quyen, Di*
Hobbes and Christianity — *Cooke, Paul D*
r A Hobbes Dictionary — *Martinich, A P*
y Hobby: The Young Merlin Trilogy — *Yolen, Jane*
Hochgeehrter Herr Professor! — *Boltzmann, Ludwig*
Hochstift Und Reformation — *Wolgast, Eike*
Hockey Dreams — *Richards, David Adams*

c Hockey for Kids (Illus. by Bill Slavin) — *McFarlane, Brian*
r Hockey Guide. 1996-97 Ed.
Hockey Superstars Album 1986-
c Hockey Superstars: Amazing Forwards — *Duplacey, James*
c Hockey Superstars: Great Goalies — *Duplacey, James*
c Hockey Superstars: Top Rookies — *Duplacey, James*
Hockey Sur Glace — *LaSalle, Peter*
y Hockey the NHL Way — *Rossiter, Sean*
Hocus — *Burke, Jan*
Hodgdon Shipbuilding and Mills — *Rumsey, Barbara*
Hoe and Wage — *Cordell, Dennis D*
Der Hof Karls I Von England — *Asch, Ronald G*
Hoffer's Law of Natural Nutrition — *Hoffer, Abram*
c Hog-Eye — *Meddaugh, Susan*
A Hog Slaughtering Woman — *Marlatt, David*
Hogenskild Bielke's Library — *Undorf, Wolfgang*
Hogg — *Delany, Samuel R*
c Hogsel and Gruntel (Illus. by Liz Graham-Yooll)
— *King-Smith, Dick*
Hoi Ky Duc Giao Hoang John Paul II — *Szulc, Tad*
c The Hokey Pokey (Illus. by Sheila Hamanaka) — *La Prise, Larry*
c The Hokey Pokey and Other Party Rhymes
— *Augarde, Steve*
The Hoko River Archaeological Site Complex
— *Croes, Dale R*
c Hold Everything! — *Corbett, Sara*
y Hold Fast to Dreams — *Pinkney, Andrea Davis*
y Hold Fast Your Dreams (Illus. by Kimberly Colen)
— *Boyko, Carrie*
c Hold the Anchovies! (Illus. by Shelley Rotner)
— *Rotner, Shelley*
Hold the Press — *Hamilton, John Maxwell*
y Holding Me Here — *Conrad, Pam*
Holding My Own in No Man's Land — *Haskell, Molly*
Holding On — *Isay, David*
Holding Schools Accountable — *Ladd, Helen F*
Holding the Dream — *Roberts, Nora*
Holding the Dream (Burr). Audio Version — *Roberts, Nora*
Holding the Line — *Hermon, John*
Holding the Line — *Umble, Diane Zimmerman*
Holding Up a Mirror — *Glyn-Jones, Anne*
y A Hole in the Heart of the World — *Kaufman, Jonathan*
y Hole in the Water — *Kearney, Robert*
c Holes — *Fatus, Sophie*
Holes and Other Superficialities — *Casati, Roberto*
Holiday Hounds — *Loughlin, Laurie*
r Holidays and Festivals Index — *Henderson, Helene*
Holiness: A Guide for Beginners — *Van Zeller, Hubert*
Holiness in Words — *Kaplan, Edward K*
The Holiness of the Real — *Gutierrez, Donald*
Holland and the Dutch Republic in the Seventeenth Century — *Price, J L*
The Hollow-Eyed Angel — *Van De Wetering, Janwillem*
The Hollow Years — *Weber, Eugen Joseph*
r Hollywood and the Foreign Touch — *Waldman, Harry*
Hollywood Censored — *Black, Gregory D*
Hollywood Confidential — *Amende, Coral*
Hollywood Dreams and Biblical Stories — *Scott, Bernard Brandon*
Hollywood Gays — *Hadleigh, Boze*
Hollywood in Berlin — *Saunders, Thomas*
Hollywood in Crisis — *Shindler, Colin*
Hollywood in the Information Age — *Wasko, Janet*
Hollywood Kremlin (Williams). Audio Version
— *Sterling, Bruce*
Hollywood Kryptonite — *Kashner, Sam*
Hollywood, Mecca of the Movies — *Cendrars, Blaise*
Hollywood Memoirs — *Howard, Jean*
The Hollywood Posse — *Cary, Diana Serra*
r The Hollywood Reporter Book of Box Office Hits. Rev. Ed. — *Sackett, Susan*
Hollywood TV — *Anderson, Christopher*
r Hollywood War Films 1937-1945 — *Shull, Michael S*
Hollywood's America — *Powers, Stephen*
Hollywood's New Deal — *Muscio, Giuliana*
Holmes and Frankfurter — *Holmes, Oliver Wendell*
y Holmes for the Holidays — *Greenberg, Martin Harry*
yr The Holocaust. Vols. 1-4 — *Wigoder, Geoffrey*
The Holocaust and Strategic Bombing — *Markusen, Eric*
The Holocaust and the Jews of Marseille — *Ryan, Donna F*
The Holocaust and the Liberal Imagination
— *Kushner, Antony Robin Jeremy*
The Holocaust: Hoax or History? — *Kuttner, Paul*

The Holocaust in Historical Context. Vol. 1 — *Katz, Steven T*
The Holocaust in Latvia 1941-1944 — *Ezergailis, Andrew*
Holocaust Survivors' Mental Health — *Brink, T L*
y The Holocaust: Understanding and Remembering
— *Strahinich, Helen*
Holocene Archeology near Squaw Butte, Canyonlands, National Park, Utah — *Tipps, Betsy L*
Holographic Interferometry — *Kreis, Thomas*
The Holographic Paradigm and Other Paradoxes
— *Wilber, Ken*
A Holy Alliance? — *Miller, Eugene D*
Holy Aspic — *Marysmith, Joan*
Holy Bible: New Living Translation — *Bible. English. New Living Translation. 1996*
Holy Bible: The New Living Translation — *Bible. English. Living Translation. 1996*
The Holy Bible: With Illustrations from the Vatican Library — *Bible. English. New Revised Standard. 1995*
The Holy Book of the Beard — *Brenna, Duff*
Holy Days and Holidays — *Deems, Edward M*
Holy Fairs — *Schmidt, Leigh Eric*
y Holy Fire — *Sterling, Bruce*
The Holy Land — *Roberts, David, 1796-1864*
Holy Land — *Waldie, D J*
r The Holy Land: A Pilgrim's Guide to Israel, Jordan and the Sinai — *Freeman-Grenville, G S P*
The Holy Man's Journey — *Trott, Susan*
Holy Men and Holy Women — *Szarmach, Paul E*
Holy Root, Holy Branches — *Allen, Ronald J*
Holy Smoke — *Cabrera Infante, G*
The Holy Spirit and Christian Initiation in the East Syrian Tradition — *Chalassery, Joseph*
Holy Terror — *Brackett, D W*
Holy Women of Byzantium — *Talbot, Alice-Mary*
Homage to Horace — *Harrison, S J*
Homage to Robert Frost — *Brodsky, Joseph*
El Hombre, La Tierra, Y El Agua — *Kroeber, Clifton B*
y Home — *Fuller, Kimberly*
Home Again — *Hannah, Kristin*
Home and Work — *Nippert-Eng, Christena E*
The Home Based-Entrepreneur. 2nd Ed. — *Pinson, Linda*
Home-Based Interior Design Business — *DeWalt, Suzanne*
Home-Based Services for Troubled Children
— *Schwartz, Ira M*
Home Bistro — *Fussell, Betty*
The Home Brewer's Companion — *Papazian, Charlie*
c Home Child — *Haworth-Attard, Barbara*
Home: Chronicle of a North Country Life
— *Powning, Beth*
The Home Corner — *Garnett, Su*
Home Decorating with Fabric — *Parks, Carol*
The Home Decorator's Bible — *Parikh, Anoop*
The Home Environmental Checklist — *Davis, Andrew N*
Home Esteem Builders — *Borba, Michele*
Home Field — *Marshall, John Douglas*
y Home Fires (Reading). Audio Version — *Rice, Luanne*
A Home for the Heart — *Kasl, Charlotte Sophia*
Home from Nowhere — *Kunstler, James Howard*
Home from the Hill — *Humphrey, William*
The Home Guard — *Mackenzie, S P*
Home Health Care — *Spratt, John M*
r The Home Health Guide to Poisons and Antidotes
— *Turkington, Carol*
r Home Herbal — *Ody, Penelope*
Home Improvement 1-2-3
A Home in Hastie Hollow — *Sheward, Robert*
c Home in the Blitz — *Tolhurst, Marilyn*
Home Is the Hunter and Other Stories — *Files, Meg*
Home Landscapes — *Martin, Edward C, Jr.*
Home Magazine's How Your House Works
— *Vandervort, Don*
Home Medicine — *Crellin, John K*
The Home of Dancing Sivan — *Younger, Paul*
The Home of the Blizzard — *Mawson, Douglas*
c Home of the Kadimakara People (Illus. by Percy Tresize) — *Tresize, Percy*
The Home Office Book — *Paul, Donna*
Home Office Design — *Zimmerman, Neal*
c Home on the Bayou (Illus. by G Brian Karas)
— *Karas, G Brian*
Home on the Canal — *Kytle, Elizabeth*
Home Pool — *Lee, Philip*
Home Repair and Improvement. Vols. 1-24

Home Rule in South Carolina — *South Carolina Advisory Commission on Intergovernmental Relations*

c Home Safety (Illus. by Penny Dann) — *Loewen, Nancy*

Home-School Work in Multicultural Settings — *Bastiani, John*

c Home Sweet Home (Illus. by Ashley Wolff) — *Marzollo, Jean*

Home Sweet Home Page — *Williams, Robin, 1953-*

Home Sweet Home Page and the Kitchen Sink — *Williams, Robin, 1953-*

Home Team — *Danielson, Michael N*

Home to India — *Singh, Jacquelin*

Home to Work — *Boris, Eileen*

Home Was the Land of Morning Calm — *Kang, K Connie*

r Homebuying Made Easy. 2nd Ed. — *Gray, Douglas*

y Homecoming — *Voigt, Cynthia*

Homeground — *Trueblood, Kathryn*

Homegrown Lessons — *Pauly, Edward*

Homeland and Other Stories — *Kingsolver, Barbara*

Homeland and Other Stories (Kingsolver). Audio Version — *Kingsolver, Barbara*

y The Homeless — *Stewart, Gail B*

y Homeless Children — *Ayer, Eleanor H*

y The Homeless: Distinguishing between Fact and Opinion — *O'Neill, Teresa*

The Homeless of Ironweed — *Giamo, Benedict*

Homelessness and Mental Health — *Bhugra, Dinesh*

Homelessness in America — *Baumohl, Jim*

De L'Homelie Au Sermon — *Hamesse, Jacqueline*

Homelies Sur Les Juges — *Messie, Pierre*

Homely Girl, a Life and Other Stories — *Miller, Arthur*

y Homemade Lightning. 2nd Ed. — *Ford, R A*

Homemaking: Women Writers and the Politics and Poetics of Home — *Wiley, Catherine*

Homenagem A Alexandrino Severino — *Milleret, Margo*

c Homeplace — *Shelby, Anne*

Homer: His Art and His World — *Latacz, Joachim*

Homer in English — *Homer*

The Homeric Hymn to Demeter — *Foley, Helene P*

The Homeric Hymns (Shelmerdine)

Homeric Questions — *Nagy, Gregory*

c Homes — *Baxter, Nicola*

Homes — *Bryant-Mole, Karen*

Homesick — *Hanania, Tony*

The Homesick Patrol — *Vancil, David*

y Hometown — *Qualey, Marsha*

y Homeward Bound — *Bransby, Lawrence*

Homework and Study Support — *Stern, Julian*

Homework for Christians. 3rd, Rev. Ed. — *Fisher, Eugene J*

Homework for Jews. 2nd, Rev. Ed. — *Sternfeld, Janet*

Homeworking in the European Union

Homeworks: A Book of Tennessee Writers

Homicide: A Psychiatric Perspective — *Malmquist, Carl P*

Hommages Offerts A Maria Manoliu-Manea — *Lupu, Coman*

L'Homme-Dieu Ou Le Sens De La Vie — *Ferry, Luc*

L'Homme Du Livre — *Chraibi, Driss*

L'Homme Et La Secheresse — *Mainguet, Monique*

Un Homme Qui Dort — *Perec, Georges*

Homo Aestheticus — *Ferry, Luc*

Homo Economics — *Gluckman, Amy*

Homo Poeticus — *Kis, Danilo*

Homoplasy: The Recurrence of Similarity in Evolution — *Sanderson, Michael J*

Homos — *Bersani, Leo*

L'Homosexualite Dans L'Imaginaire De La Renaissance — *Poirier, Guy*

Homosexuality: A History — *Spencer, Colin*

Homosexuality and Biology — *Burr, Chandler*

Homosexuality and Christian Community — *Seow, C L*

y Homosexuality and Gay Rights — *McCuen, Gary E*

Homosexuality and the Politics of Truth — *Satinover, Jeffrey*

Homosexuality: Catholic Teaching and Pastoral Practice — *Coleman, Gerald D*

Homosexuality in History — *Spencer, Colin*

The Homosexual(ity) of Law — *Moran, Leslie*

Hon Nua Doi Hu — *Vuong, Hong Sen*

La Honda De David — *Llerena, Mario*

Honest to Jesus — *Funk, Robert Walter*

c Honest Tulio (Illus. by John Himmelman) — *Himmelman, John*

c Honesty: Zach's Tall Tale (Illus. by Davis Henry) — *Canning, Shelagh*

Honey, Honey, Miss Thang — *Pettiway, Leon E*

Honey, I Want to Start My Own Business — *Jaffe, Azriela*

c The Honey Makers (Illus. by Gail Gibbons) — *Gibbons, Gail*

The Honey Makers — *Saville, Diana*

c Honey Paw and Lightfoot (Illus. by Jon Van Zyle) — *London, Jonathan*

The Honeymoon Snaps — *Foulcher, John*

r Hong Kong — *Goncharoff, Nicko*

Hong Kong 1997 — *Wang, Enbao*

y Hong Kong Action Cinema — *Logan, Bey*

r Hong Kong and Macau — *Brown, Jules*

Hong Kong: China's Challenge — *Yahuda, Michael*

r Hong Kong Coin and Paper Money Catalogue. 4th Ed. — *Tan, Steven*

Hong Kong-Japanese Occupation and Mr. H. Da Luz — *Tsang, Ming W*

Hong Kong Stories — *Wong, David T K*

Hong Kong's Economic and Financial Future — *Luk, Y F*

Hong Kong's Transition — *Wang, Gungwu*

Hong Yan Nan Zi — *Li, Yuehua*

Hongergrond — *Malan, Lucas*

Honky Tonk Kat — *Kijewski, Karen*

Honor — *Stewart, Frank Henderson*

y Honor among Enemies — *Weber, David*

Honor among Thieves — *Stiner, Mary C*

Honor and Slavery — *Greenberg, Kenneth S*

y Honor Bright — *Platt, Randall Beth*

The Honor Farm — *Westermann, John*

Honor Thy Children — *Fumia, Molly*

y Honor to the Hills — *Charbonneau, Eileen*

Honorable Amendments — *Harper, Michael S*

The Honorable Thief — *Kirkland, Martha*

r Honore Daumier — *Laughton, Bruce*

Honour — *Decter, Ann*

y Honus and Me — *Gutman, Dan*

Honus Wagner: A Biography — *DeValeria, Dennis*

y Honus Wagner: A Biography (Esmo). Audio Version — *DeValeria, Dennis*

Honus Wagner: The Life of Baseball's Flying Dutchman — *Hittner, Arthur D*

Hood — *Donoghue, Emma*

Hooded Knights on the Niagara — *Lay, Shawn*

Hoofprints — *Crum, Laura*

Hooked on Java — *Van Hoff, Arthur*

The Hookmen — *Hillmer, Timothy*

Hooliganism: Crime, Culture and Power in St. Petersburg 1900-1914 — *Neuberger, Joan*

y Hoopi Shoopi Donna — *Shea, Suzanne Strempek*

Hoopla! Inside the Toronto Raptors' First Season — *Batten, Jack*

y HoopMania! The Jam-Packed Book of Basketball Trivia — *Herzog, Brad*

c Hooray! A Pinata! (Illus. by Elisa Kleven) — *Kleven, Elisa*

c Hooray for Me! (Illus. by Vera B Williams) — *Charlip, Remy*

c Hooray! It's Passover! (Illus. by John Himmelman) — *Kimmelman, Leslie*

Hoosier Faiths — *Rudolph, L C*

A Hoosier Holiday — *Dreiser, Theodore*

c Hoot (Illus. by Jane Hissey) — *Hissey, Jane*

r Hoover's Directory of Human Resources Executives 1996

Hoover's FBI. Audio Version — *DeLoach, Cartha D*

r Hoover's Guide to the Top Chicago Companies. 1st Ed.

r Hoover's Guide to the Top New York Companies. 1st Ed.

r Hoover's Handbook of American Business 1996. Vols. 1-2

r Hoover's Masterlist of Major Latin American Companies 1996-1997

r Hoover's Masterlist of Major U.S. Companies 1996-1997

p Hope

c Hope (Illus. by Randy Houk). Book and Audio Version — *Houk, Randy*

Hope and Deception in Conception Bay — *Cadigan, Sean T*

Hope and Glory — *Clarke, Peter, 1942-*

The Hope Chest — *Ahmad, Rukhsana*

Hope, Human and Wild — *McKibben, Bill*

Hope in Pastoral Care and Counseling — *Lester, Andrew D*

Hope in the Desperate Hour — *Richards, David Adams*

Hope Is Not a Method — *Sullivan, Gordon R*

Hope Is the Last to Die — *Birenbaum, Halina*

y Hope Mills — *Pierce, Constance*

Hope of Earth — *Anthony, Piers*

The Hope Slide. Little Sister — *MacLeod, Joan*

Hope: The Heart's Great Quest — *Aikman, David*

Hope Valley War — *Thoene, Brock*

Hope When You're Hurting — *Crabb, Larry*

Hopeful Journeys — *Fogleman, Aaron Spencer*

Hope's Cadillac — *Page, Patricia*

c Hope's Rainbow — *Marriott, Janice*

Hopi Basket Weaving — *Teiwes, Helga*

c Hopper's Treetop Adventure (Illus. by Marcus Pfister) — *Pfister, Marcus*

La Hora Sin Sombra — *Soriano, Osvaldo*

Horace: Behind the Public Poetry — *Lyne, R O A M*

Horace in English — *Horace*

Horace Made New — *Martindale, Charles*

Horace Odes I: Carpe Diem — *Horace*

Horace Walpole: The Great Outsider — *Mowl, Timothy*

Horace's Hope — *Sizer, Theodore R*

As Horas De Margarida De Cleves — *Marrow, James H*

Horizons One — *Hewitt, David*

Horizontal Woman — *Berger, Suzanne E*

Hormones and Cancer — *Vedeckis, Wayne V*

The Horn Handbook — *Reynolds, Verne*

The Horn of Africa — *Gurdon, Charles*

The Horn of Africa — *Woodward, Peter*

Horn of Darkness — *Cunningham, Carol*

The Horned Dinosaurs — *Dodson, Peter*

Hornet's Nest — *Cornwell, Patricia Daniels*

Hornet's Nest (Sarandon). Audio Version — *Cornwell, Patricia Daniels*

c Horns to Toes and in Between — *Boynton, Sandra*

Hornsby Hit One Over My Head — *Cataneo, David*

c Horrible Harry and the Dungeon (Illus. by Frank Remkiewicz) — *Kline, Suzy*

c Horrible Harry and the Green Slime (Heller). Audio Version — *Kline, Suzy*

c Horrible Harry in Room 2B (Heller). Audio Version — *Kline, Suzy*

r Horror: A Connoisseur's Guide to Literature and Film — *Wolf, Leonard*

Horror Hospital Unplugged — *Cooper, Dennis*

r Horror Literature — *Barron, Neil*

Horror Show — *Kihn, Greg*

y Horror Stories (Illus. by Harry Horse) — *Price, Susan*

y Horror Stories (Davenport). Audio Version — *Cuddon, J A*

cr Horrors: An Earthdawn Sourcebook

Horse and Stable Management. 2nd Ed. — *Brown, Jeremy Houghton*

c The Horse at Hilly Fields (Illus. by Elaine Mills) — *Thwaite, Ann*

Horse-Drawn Cabs and Omnibuses in Paris — *Papayanis, Nicholas*

y A Horse for All Seasons — *Welch, Sheila Kelly*

c Horse Stories — *Trotman, Felicity*

Horse Trails to Regional Rails — *Toman, James A*

The Horse Whisperer — *Evans, Nicholas*

The Horse Whisperer (Coyote). Audio Version — *Evans, Nicholas*

Horseman — *Nicol, Mike*

c Horsepower: The Wonder of Draft Horses (Illus. by Alvis Upitis) — *Peterson, Cris*

c Horses — *Everts, Tammy*

The Horses of San Marco and the Quadriga of the Lord — *Jacoff, Michael*

y Horses through Time — *Olsen, Sandra L*

y Horseshoes — *Boga, Steven*

Horst: Sixty Years of Photography — *Horst*

Horticultural Flora of South-Eastern Australia. Vol. 1 — *Spencer, Roger*

c Hosanna and Alleluia (Illus. by Donald Cook) — *Strong, Dina*

Hosea — *Landy, Francis*

Hospice: A Photographic Inquiry — *Goldberg, Jim, 1953-*

r Hospital and Physician Rate-Setting Systems — *Cromwell, Jerry*

Hospital Financing in Seven Countries

Hospital Time — *Hoffman, Amy*

The Hostage — *Dammaj, Zayd Muti*

c Hostage — *Myers, Edward*

The Hostage Child — *Rosen, Leora N*

y Hostage to War — *Vasileva, Tatiana*

Hostages of Each Other — *Rees, Joseph V*

r Hostelling USA 1996

Hostile Takeover — *Koopman, Douglas L*

Hot Air — *Kurtz, Howard*

c Hot Air (Illus. by Peter Bailey) — *Mole, John*

c Hot and Cold — *Challoner, Jack*

Hot Blood — *Englade, Ken*

Hot Carriers in Semiconductors — *Hess, Karl*
Hot Corner — *Phillips, Louis*
c Hot Dog — *Mott, Evelyn Clarke*
Hot Earth Cold Earth — *Berry, James*
c Hot Fudge Hero (Illus. by Diana Cain Bluthenthal)
  — *Brisson, Pat*
y Hot Heads, Warm Hearts, Cold Streets — *Foster,
  John*
c Hot Hippo (Illus. by Adrienne Kennaway) — *Hadithi,
  Mwenye*
Hot Licks — *Fleming, Lee*
Hot Off the Press — *Scott, Paul*
Hot Pantz — *Gautheir, Isabelle*
The Hot Rock — *Westlake, Donald E*
Hot Sand
y Hot Shot (Fields). Audio Version — *Phillips, Susan
  Elizabeth*
Hot Spots — *Cook, Diane*
Hot Type
The Hot Wired Dodo — *Chalker, Jack L*
y Hot Zone — *Preston, Richard*
Hotel America — *Lapham, Lewis H*
The Hotel: Backstairs at the World's Most Exclusive
  Hotel — *Robinson, Jeffrey, 1945-*
Hotel Bars and Lobbies — *Berens, Carol*
The Hotel Eden — *Carlson, Ron*
The Hotel in the Jungle — *Guerard, Albert J*
y Hotel Paradise — *Grimes, Martha*
Hotel Paradise (Jones). Audio Version — *Grimes,
  Martha*
Hotel Splendid — *Redonnet, Marie*
Hotels like Houses — *Hannah, Sophie*
Hotline Healers — *Vizenor, Gerald*
Hotshots: A Neil Hamel Mystery — *Van Gieson,
  Judith*
c The Hottest Boy Who Ever Lived (Illus. by Kim
  Gamble) — *Fienberg, Anna*
The Hottest State — *Hawke, Ethan*
Houdini! The Career of Ehrich Weiss — *Silverman,
  Kenneth*
c The Hound of the Baskervilles (Jones). Audio Version
  — *Doyle, Arthur Conan, Sir*
The Hour of Our Death — *Joseph, Alison*
The Hours of Simon De Varie — *Marrow, James H*
A House, a Cottage and a Shop — *Seddon, George*
y The House across the Cove — *Hall, Barbara*
House and Garden Samplers — *Jenkins, Mary*
House and Home — *Gunderson, Steve*
House Arrest — *Morris, Mary*
House as a Mirror of Self — *Marcus, Clare Cooper*
c A House by the River (Illus. by Cornelius Van
  Wright) — *Miller, William*
House Comfortable — *McMillan, Katharine Kaye*
y A House Divided. Electronic Media Version
y A House Divided — *Archer, Jules*
A House Divided — *Gerzon, Mark*
y A House Divided — *Martin, Vincent*
A House Divided — *Waldie, Doug*
c A House for Hermit Crab (Illus. by Mike Terry)
  — *Carle, Eric*
House/Garden/Nation: Space, Gender, Ethnicity in
  Post-Colonial Latin American Literature by Women
  — *Rodriguez, Ileana*
c The House in the Sky (Illus. by Wil Clay) — *San
  Souci, Robert D*
House Made of Dawn — *Momaday, N Scott*
y The House of Birds — *Jones, Jenny*
A House of Cards — *Bloom, John*
y The House of Death — *Windsor, Patricia*
y The House of Dies Drear (Thigpen). Audio Version
  — *Hamilton, Virginia*
House of Echoes — *Erskine, Barbara*
House of Eternity — *McDonald, John K*
The House of Fame — *Chaucer, Geoffrey*
The House of Forgetting — *Saenz, Benjamin Alire*
House of Glass — *Toer, Pramoedya Ananta*
House of Guilt — *Rosenberg, Robert*
House of Houses — *Mora, Pat*
House of Illusions — *Gedge, Pauline*
The House of Lords and Ideological Politics
  — *Weston, Corinne Comstock*
The House of Lords in the Reign of Charles II
  — *Swatland, Andrew*
The House of Mirth — *Wharton, Edith*
The House of Moses All-Stars — *Rosen, Charley*
House of Music — *Eagle, Chester*
r The House of Scribner 1846-1904 — *Delaney, John*
The House of the Vestals — *Saylor, Steven*
The House on Bloodhound Lane — *Lanier, Virginia*
The House on Brooke Street — *Bartlett, Neil, 1958-*
House on Fire — *Hamill, Denis*

The House on Nazareth Hill — *Campbell, Ramsey*
The House on the Borderland — *Hodgson, William
  Hope*
y The House on the Lagoon — *Ferre, Rosario*
A House on the Ocean, a House on the Bay — *Picano,
  Felice*
c House Pets (Illus. by Heinrich Kita) — *Dudek, Isabella*
c The House That Drac Built (Illus. by Will
  Hillenbrand) — *Sierra, Judy*
c The House That Jack Built (Illus. by Emily Bolam)
  — *Bolam, Emily*
y The House That Jack Built — *Masterton, Graham*
The House with the Blind Glass Windows — *Wassmo,
  Herbjorg*
Houseboat on the Seine — *Wharton, William*
Housecraft and Statecraft — *Romano, Dennis*
Household and Intrahousehold Impact of the Grameen
  Bank and Similar Targeted Credit Programs in
  Bangladesh — *Pitt, Mark M*
Household Composition in Latin America — *De Vos,
  Susan*
Households and Housing — *Clark, William A V*
Households: On the Moral Architecture of the
  Economy — *Booth, William James*
Housekeeping in a Dream — *Kasischke, Laura*
r The Houseplant Encyclopedia — *Jantra, Ingrid*
The Houseplant Survival Guide — *Regel, Pat*
Houses and Households — *Blanton, Richard E*
Houses for All — *Wade, Jill*
c Houses of China (Illus. by Bonnie Shemie) — *Shemie,
  Bonnie*
Housing for Seniors — *Porter, Douglas R*
c The Houston Astrodome — *Doherty, Craig A*
c How a Book Is Published — *Kalman, Bobbie*
How a People Die — *Fry, Alan*
c How a Plant Grows — *Kalman, Bobbie*
c How Anansi Captured Tiger's Stories (Illus. by Jenny
  Bent) — *Bent, Jenny*
c How Animals Communicate — *Kalman, Bobbie*
c How Are Babies Made? — *Smith, Alastair*
How Are We to Live? — *Singer, Peter*
c How Artists See Animals — *Carroll, Colleen*
c How Artists See People — *Carroll, Colleen*
c How Artists See the Elements — *Carroll, Colleen*
c How Bats See in the Dark — *Penny, Malcolm*
c How Bees Make Honey — *Chinery, Michael*
c How Birds Fly — *Williams, Nick*
How Brains Think — *Calvin, William H*
c How Can a Frozen Detective Stay Hot on the Trail?
  — *Bailey, Linda*
c How Can I Be a Detective if I Have to Baby-Sit?
  — *Bailey, Linda*
yr How Can You Tell if a Spider Is Dead? and More
  Moments of Science — *Glass, Don*
How Christians Are Changing the Soul of American
  Politics — *Reed, Ralph*
c How Come the Best Clues Are Always in the
  Garbage? — *Bailey, Linda*
How Computer Graphics Work — *Prosise, Jeff*
How Could You Do That? — *Schlessinger, Laura*
How Could You Do This to Me? — *Greer, Jane*
y How Could You Do This to Me, Mum? — *Rushton,
  Rosie*
How Crows Talk and Willows Walk — *Esarey, Gary*
How Culture Works — *Bohannan, Paul*
How Curious a Land — *Bryant, Jonathan M*
How Debuggers Work — *Rosenberg, Jonathan*
How Did They Do It? — *Baker, Christopher W*
c How Dinosaurs Came to Be — *Lauber, Patricia*
c How Do Airplanes Fly? (Illus. by Paul Babb)
  — *Berger, Melvin*
c How Do Animals Sleep? — *Berger, Melvin*
How Do Astronauts Scratch an Itch? — *Feldman,
  David, 1950-*
c How Do Birds Find Their Way? (Illus. by Paul
  Mirocha) — *Gans, Roma*
How Do We Know This? — *Harris, Jay M*
How Do We Know Who We Are? — *Ludwig, Arnold
  M*
c How Do You Lift a Lion? (Illus. by Robert E Wells)
  — *Wells, Robert E*
y How Do You Spell Abducted? — *Stacey, Cherylyn*
c How Do You Spell Geek? — *Peters, Julie Anne*
c How Do Your Senses Work? — *Smith, Alastair*
c How Does Your Garden Grow? (Illus. by Nathalie
  Locoste) — *Joly, Dominique*
How EC and World Bank Policies Are Destroying
  Agriculture and the Environment — *Bond, Jack W*
y How Far Do You Wanna Go? — *Dixon, Ramon*
How Far from Austerlitz? — *Horne, Alistair*

y How Far Would You Have Gotten If I Hadn't Called
  You Back? — *Hobbs, Valerie*
c How Fish Swim — *Bailey, Jill*
How Flowers Changed the World — *Eiseley, Loren*
How Good Do We Have to Be? — *Kushner, Harold S*
How Healthy Is Your Family Tree? — *Krause, Carol*
c How Humans Make Friends — *Leedy, Loreen*
How I Became Hettie Jones — *Jones, Hettie*
How I Came West and Why I Stayed — *Baker, Alison*
y How I Changed My Life — *Strasser, Todd*
How I Gave My Heart to the Restaurant Business
  — *Allison, Karen Hubert*
y How I Got Cultured — *Barber, Phyllis*
c How I Spent My Summer Vacation (Illus. by Mark
  Teague) — *Teague, Mark*
c How I Survived Being a Girl — *Draanen, Wendelin
  Van*
c How It Was with Dooms (Illus. by Xan Hopcraft)
  — *Hopcraft, Xan*
c How Jackrabbit Got His Very Long Ears — *Irbinskas,
  Karen*
c How Lama Saved the Day. Book and Audio Version
  — *Palazzo-Craig, Janet*
How Life Begins — *Vaughan, Christopher*
How Like a God — *Clough, Brenda W*
y How Long Does It Hurt? — *Mather, Cynthia L*
How Loud Can the Village Cock Crow? and Other
  Stories — *Thomas, H Nigel*
c How Many Days to America? — *Bunting, Eve*
c How Many Feet? How Many Tails? (Illus. by Lynn
  Adams) — *Burns, Marilyn*
c How Many, How Many, How Many (Illus. by Cynthia
  Jabar) — *Walton, Rick*
c How Many Miles to Jacksonville? (Illus. by Bart
  Forbes) — *Johnston, Tony*
How Many People Can the Earth Support? — *Cohen,
  Joel E*
How Many Years — *Yourcenar, Marguerite*
c How Math Works — *Vorderman, Carol*
c How Mathematics Works — *Vorderman, Carol*
c How Mr. Monkey Saw the Whole World (Illus. by
  Synthia Saint James) — *Myers, Walter Dean*
c How Much, How Many, How Far, How Heavy, How
  Long, How Tall Is 1000? (Illus. by Tracy Walker)
  — *Nolan, Helen*
How Multimedia Works — *Holsinger, Erik*
c How Music Came to the World (Illus. by C Ober)
  — *Ober, Hal*
How Natives Think — *Sahlins, Marshall David*
How Nature Works — *Bak, Per*
c How Night Came to Be. Book and Audio Version
  — *Palazzo-Craig, Janet*
How Northeast Asians View Their Security
  — *Wilborn, Thomas L*
How One of You Can Bring the Two of You Together
  — *Page, Susan*
c How Pizza Came to Queens (Illus. by Dayal Kaur
  Khalsa) — *Khalsa, Dayal Kaur*
c How Plants Grow — *Penny, Malcolm*
How Poets Work — *Seren, Tony Curtis*
How Poor Government Policy Harms the Poor
  — *Schansberg, D Eric*
How Porcupines Make Love III — *Purves, Alan C*
How Proust Can Change Your Life — *De Botton,
  Alain*
c How Rabbit Lost His Tail (Illus. by Jacqueline
  Chwast) — *Tompert, Ann*
How Right Is the Right? — *Frame, Randall L*
How Russia Became a Market Economy — *Aslund,
  Anders*
How Shall They Be Saved? — *Erickson, Millard J*
How Should One Live? — *Crisp, Roger*
y How Smudge Came (Illus. by Ron Lightburn)
  — *Gregory, Nan*
c How Snake Got His Hiss (Illus. by Mercedes
  McDonald) — *Davol, Marguerite W*
How Societies Change — *Chirot, Daniel*
c How Spiders Make Their Webs — *Bailey, Jill*
How Stella Got Her Groove Back — *McMillan, Terry*
c How Sweet the Sound (Illus. by Floyd Cooper)
  — *Hudson, Wade*
c How the Artists See the Weather — *Carroll, Colleen*
How the Cimarron River Got Its Name and Other
  Stories about Coffee — *Linck, Ernestine Sewell*
How the Farmers Changed China — *Zhou, Kate Xiao*
c How the Indians Bought the Farm (Illus. by Francisco
  X Mora) — *Strete, Craig Kee*
How the Irish Became White — *Ignatiev, Noel*
How the Irish Saved Civilization — *Cahill, Thomas*

How the Irish Saved Civilization (Donnelly). Audio Version — *Cahill, Thomas*

How the Leopard Changed Its Spots — *Goodwin, Brian*

c How the Lion Lost His Lunch (Illus. by Axel Scheffler) — *Wilson, David Henry*

How the Maya Built Their World — *Abrams, Elliott M*

c How the Ostrich Got Its Long Neck (Illus. by Marcia Brown) — *Aardema, Verna*

How the Other Half Lives — *Riis, Jacob A*

c How the Ox Star Fell from Heaven (Illus. by Lily Toy Hong) — *Hong, Lily Toy*

c How the Second Grade Got $8,205.50 to Visit the Statue of Liberty — *Zimelman, Nathan*

y How the Tiger Lost Its Stripes — *Meacham, Cory J*

How the West Was Read. Audio Version — *Randisi, Robert J*

How the West Was Read (Kennedy). Audio Version — *Randisi, Robert J*

c How the Wizard Came to Oz (Illus. by Donald Abbott) — *Abbott, Donald*

r How Therapists Diagnose — *Hamstra, Bruce*

c How Things Work — *Ardley, Neil*

y How Things Work — *Bloomfield, Louis A*

c How Things Work — *Graham, Ian, 1953-*

c How Things Work — *Porter, Alison*

How to Achieve ISO 9000 Registration Economically and Efficiently — *Naroola, Gurmeet*

How to Attract Birds. Rev. Ed. — *Dennis, John V*

How to Attract Hummingbirds and Butterflies — *Dennis, John V*

c How to Babysit an Orangutan (Illus. by Tara Darling) — *Darling, Tara*

How to Be a Black Belt in the Art of Life — *Gustafson, Jack*

How to Be a Fake Kreskin — *Kreskin*

How to Be a Great Communicator in Person, on Paper and on the Podium — *Qubein, Nido R*

How to Be a Help Instead of a Nuisance — *Wegela, Karen Kissel*

How to Be a Minister — *Kaufman, Gerald*

r How to Be a Perfect Stranger — *Magida, Arthur J*

How to Be a Perfect Stranger. Vol. 2 — *Magida, Arthur J*

How to Be a Successful Internet Consultant. 1st Ed. — *Keyes, Jessica*

c How to Be Cool in Junior School (Illus. by J Douglas) — *Duffey, Betsy*

How to Be Safe in an Unsafe World — *Bloomfield, Harold H*

How to Be the Person Successful Companies Fight to Keep — *Podesta, Connie*

How to Build a Theory in Cognitive Science — *Hardcastle, Valerie Gray*

How to Build Your Own Log Home for Less than $15,000 — *Williams, Robert L*

How to Buy a Diamond — *Cuellar, Fred*

r How to Buy Stocks Factory Direct and Save — *McCulla, L Cleaves, II*

How to Buy Technology Stocks — *Gianturco, Michael*

How to Conduct Organizational Surveys — *Edwards, Jack E*

How to Control Diabetes — *Alterman, Seymour L*

How to Cope with University Life — *Oni, Olusola O A*

c How to Count Crocodiles (Illus. by Emily Bolam) — *Mayo, Margaret*

How to Create Action, Fantasy, and Adventure Comics — *Alvarez, Tom*

How to Design and Implement a Results-Oriented Variable Pay System — *Belcher, John G, Jr.*

How to Do Biblical Theology — *Stuhlmacher, Peter*

How to Do Just About Everything

r How to Do Your Own Divorce without a Lawyer. Vol. 1 — *Anosike, Benji O*

How to Document Victims and Locate Survivors of the Holocaust — *Mokotoff, Gary*

y How to Draw Portraits in Colored Pencil from Photographs — *Hammond, Lee*

How to Eat Away Arthritis — *Aesoph, Lauri*

How to Find, Buy, Manage and Sell a Manufactured Home Community — *Allen, George*

r How to Find Source Materials — *Summers, Anne*

c How to Fly

How to Get a Job in New York City and the Metropolitan Area — *Sanborn, Robert*

How to Get Families More Involved in the Nursing Home — *LaBrake, Tammy*

How to Get Home — *Lott, Bret*

How to Get into the Top MBA Programs — *Montauk, Richard*

How to Grow Your Own Light Bulbs — *Riddell, John*

How to Have All the Answers when the Questions Keep Changing — *Ireland, Karin*

How to Hide Things in Public Places — *Fiery, Dennis*

How to Insure Your Income — *Merritt Publishing*

How to Keep Your Kids from Driving You Crazy — *Bender, Paula Stone*

How to Kill a Dragon — *Watkins, Calvert*

How to Learn the Alexander Technique. 3rd Ed. — *Conable, Barbara*

How to License Technology — *Megantz, Robert C*

How to Live Forever — *Clark, Stephen R L*

c How to Live Forever (Illus. by Colin Thompson) — *Thompson, Colin*

How to Live the Life You Love (Sher). Audio Version — *Sher, Barbara*

How to Love a Black Man — *Elmore, Ronn*

c How to Make an Apple Pie and See the World (Illus. by Marjorie Priceman) — *Priceman, Marjorie*

How to Make Clay Characters — *Carlson, Maureen*

c How to Make Holiday Pop-Ups (Illus. by Linda Hendry) — *Irvine, Joan*

How to Make Love to a Negro — *Laferriere, Dany*

How to Make Money Performing in Schools — *Heflick, David*

How to Make Your Airplane Last Forever — *Woodhouse, Mary*

How to Manage Stress for Success — *Geber, Sara Zeff*

r How to Market You and Your Book — *O'Connor, Richard F X*

How to Meet the Right Man — *Ratcliff, Roger*

How to Meet the Right Woman — *Ratcliff, Roger*

r How to Partner with Managed Care — *Browning, Charles H*

How to Pick Stocks — *Frailey, Fred W*

How to Plan Your Total Estate with a Will and Living Will, without the Lawyer's Fees — *Anosike, Benji O*

How to Play Your Best Golf All the Time — *Armour, Tommy*

y How to Prepare for the Advanced Placement Examination: AP U.S. Government and Politics — *Lader, Curt*

yr How to Prepare for the SAT II: Literature — *Myers-Schaffer, Christina*

How to Prepare Stuffings and Fillings — *Patten, Rena*

How to Profit from Flower and Herb Crafts — *Platt, Ellen Spector*

How to Properly Plan Your Total Estate with a Living Trust, without the Lawyer's Fees — *Anosike, Benji O*

r How to Publish Your Short and Long Fiction — *White, Kenton*

How to Quit Smoking without Gaining Weight — *Katahn, Martin*

How to Raise a Child with a High EQ — *Shapiro, Lawrence E*

How to Raise a Family and a Career under One Roof — *Roberts, Lisa M*

How to Raise a Healthy Child — *Smith, Lendon H*

y How to Read an Unwritten Language — *Graham, Philip, 1951-*

How to Read the Constitution — *Wolfe, Christopher*

How to Research — *Blaxter, Loraine*

r How to Research Congress — *Martin, Fenton S*

r How to Research the Presidency — *Martin, Fenton S*

How to Risk-Proof Your Kids — *Winkler, Kathleen*

c How to Rock Your Baby (Illus. by John Amoss) — *Fleming, Sibley*

How to Save the Underclass — *Marris, Robin*

How to Set Up and Maintain a Web Site. 2nd Ed. — *Stein, Lincoln D*

How to Sharpen Carving Tools — *Butz, Rick*

How to Solve Mathematical Problems — *Wickelgren, Wayne A*

c How to Sparkle at Alphabet Skills (Illus. by Kate Ford) — *Lawrence, Jo*

c How to Sparkle at Nursery Rhymes (Illus. by Kate Ford) — *Lawrence, Jo*

c How to Sparkle at Phonics (Illus. by Kate Ford) — *Lawrence, Jo*

c How to Sparkle at Prediction Skills (Illus. by Kate Ford) — *Lawrence, Jo*

c How to Speak Chimpanzee — *Brassey, Richard*

How to Spot an Owl — *Sutton, Clay*

How to Spot Hawks and Eagles — *Sutton, Clay*

How to Start a Home-Based Photography Business — *Oberrecht, Ken*

How to Start a Home-Based Secretarial Services Business. 2nd Ed. — *Melkin, Jan*

How to Start Your Own Private Investment Partnership — *Fiszel, Geoffrey L*

How to Stay Awake during Anybody's Second Movement — *Walden, David*

How to Stay Lovers for Life — *Wolf, Sharyn*

How to Stock a Home Library Inexpensively. 3rd Ed. — *Williams, Jane A*

y How to Study. 4th Ed. — *Fry, Ronald W*

How to Succeed in Business Without a Penis — *Salmansohn, Karen*

How to Succeed in Business without Being White — *Graves, Earl G*

How to Succeed in Cyberspace — *Haynes, Colin*

How to Survive without a Salary — *Long, Charles*

How to Survive without Psychotherapy — *Smail, David*

How to Talk So Kids Can Learn — *Faber, Adele*

r How to Teach about American Indians — *Harvey, Karen D*

How to Teach Nutrition to Kids — *Evers, Connie*

How to Tell When You're Tired — *Theriault, Reg*

How to Think about Statistics. 5th Ed. — *Phillips, John L, Jr.*

How to Think about War and Peace — *Adler, Mortimer J*

How to Think Like a CEO — *Benton, D A*

How to Think Like a CEO (Benton). Audio Version — *Benton, D A*

How to Think Theologically — *Stone, Howard W*

r How to Write — *Rhodes, Richard*

How to Write — *Stein, Gertrude*

How to Write a Family History — *FitzHugh, Terrick*

How to Write a Mystery — *Beinhart, Larry*

yr How to Write a News Article — *Kronenwetter, Michael*

How to Write a Philosophy Paper — *Stramel, James S*

y How to Write a Poem — *Ryan, Margaret*

How to Write and Publish a Scientific Paper — *Day, Robert A*

How to Write Crime — *Day, Marele*

c How to Write Really Badly (Illus. by Philippe Dupasquier) — *Fine, Anne*

c How to Write, Recite, and Delight in All Kinds of Poetry — *Hulme, Joy N*

How to Write the History of a Bank — *Fase, Martin M G*

How Tory Governments Fall — *Seldon, Anthony*

c How Turtle's Back Was Cracked (Illus. by Murv Jacob) — *Ross, Gayle*

y How TV Changed America's Mind — *Wakin, Edward*

c How Was I Born? (Illus. by Lennart Nilsson) — *Nilsson, Lennart*

c How We Came to the Fifth World — *Rohmer, Harriet*

How We Found America — *Zaborowska, Magdalena J*

How We Grieve — *Attig, Thomas*

How, When, and Why Modern Art Came to New York — *Zayas, Marius De*

How Wide the Divide? — *Blomberg, Craig L*

c How Would You Survive as an American Indian? (Illus. by Mark Bergin) — *Steedman, Scott*

c How Would You Survive in the American West? (Illus. by David Antram) — *Morley, Jacqueline*

c Howard and the Sitter Surprise (Illus. by Paul Meisel) — *Paton, Priscilla*

Howard Baker: Conciliator in an Age of Crisis — *Annis, J Lee, Jr.*

Howard Garrett's Plants for Texas. 1st Ed. — *Garrett, J Howard*

Howard Hawks: The Grey Fox of Hollywood — *McCarthy, Todd*

Howard Hughes: The Untold Story — *Brown, Peter Harry*

r Howard Keel: A Bio-Bibliography — *Leiby, Bruce R*

Howard Stern: King of All Media — *Colford, Paul D*

Howard Stern: King of All Media (Gould). Audio Version — *Colford, Paul D*

Howard Stern: Miss America — *Stern, Howard*

Howe and Hummel — *Rovere, Richard*

Howl and Other Poems — *Ginsberg, Allen*

The Howling Stones — *Foster, Alan Dean*

p Howlings: Wild Women of the West

The Hoydens and Mr. Dickens — *Palmer, William J, 1943-*

The HPLC Solvent Guide — *Sadek, Paul C*

Hryhorij Savyc Skovoroda — *Marshall, Richard H, Jr.*

HTML 3 How-To — *Kerven, David*

r HTML 3 Manual of Style — *Aronson, Larry*

HTML and the Art of Authoring for the World Wide Web — *White, Bebo*

r HTML for the World Wide Web — *Castro, Elizabeth*

HTML for the World Wide Web. 2nd Ed. — *Castro, Elizabeth*

HTML Publishing for Netscape. Windows Ed. — *Harris, Stuart*

r HTML Sourcebook. 2nd Ed. — *Graham, Ian S, 1955-*
Hua Ren Bang Pai — *Chen, Guolin*
Huang Se De You Huo — *Wu, Hai-Min*
Huang Tian Hou Tu — *Nan, Yujian*
Hubble: A New Window to the Universe — *Fischer, Daniel*
Hubble's Cosmology — *Hetherington, Norriss S*
y Hubble's Universe — *Goodwin, Simon*
Hubert Languet 1518-1581 — *Nicollier-De Weck, Beatrice*
r The Hudson River Guidebook — *Adams, Arthur G*
The Hudson through the Years — *Adams, Arthur G*
c Los Huevos Parlantes (Illus. by Jerry Pinkney) — *San Souci, Robert D*
Hugh Dalton — *Pimlott, Ben*
Hugh Gaitskell — *Brivati, Brian*
Hugh Grant: The Unauthorised Biography — *Tresidder, Jody*
r Hugh Johnson's Pocket Encyclopedia of Wine 1997
Hugh Miller and the Controversies of Victorian Science — *Shortland, Michael*
Hugh Primas and the Archpoet — *Adcock, Fleur*
Hugh Primas and the Archpoet — *Hugo Primas, Aurelianensis*
r Hughes, Hardee, McCumbee, Milligan Connection of the Carolinas — *Hughes, Virginia Hayden*
Hugo Black: A Biography — *Newman, Roger K*
Hugo Grotius, Ordinum Hollandiae Ac Westfrisiae Pietas — *Grotius, Hugo*
Hugo Grotius, Theologian — *Nellen, Henk J M*
Hugo L. Black: Cold Steel Warrior — *Ball, Howard*
Huguccio: The Life, Works, and Thought of a Twelfth-Century Jurist — *Muller, Wolfgang P*
Huguenot Politics 1601-1622 — *Valone, James S*
The Huguenots and French Opinion 1685-1787 — *Adams, Geoffrey*
y Huh Huh for Hollywood — *Doyle, Larry*
Human Action in Business — *Gasparski, Wojciech W*
yr Human Anatomy
r Human Anatomy. 3rd Ed. — *Gosling, J A*
Human Behavior and the Social Environment — *Schriver, Joe M*
Human Biology — *Benjamin, Clinton L*
Human Biology and Health Studies — *Givens, Peter*
Human Biology in Papua New Guinea — *Attenborough, Robert D*
The Human Biology of the English Village — *Harrison, G Ainsworth*
Human Biomaterials Applications — *Wise, Donald L*
cr The Human Body — *Ardley, Bridget*
c The Human Body — *Morgan, Sally*
y The Human Body — *Parker, Steve*
c The Human Body — *Perols, Sylvaine*
Human Body Composition — *Roche, Alex F*
Human Body on File: Physiology — *Diagram Group*
Human Capital, Employment and Bargaining — *Hart, Robert A*
Human Capital or Cultural Capital? — *Farkas, George*
Human Cell Culture Protocols — *Jones, Gareth E*
The Human Condition — *Sand, Michael*
The Human Cost of a Management Failure — *Allcorn, Seth*
Human Croquet — *Atkinson, Kate*
Human Development. 3rd Ed. — *Dacey, John S*
Human Development Report 1996
Human Diversity — *Lewontin, Richard*
r Human Embryology and Teratology. 2nd Ed. — *O'Rahilly, Ronan*
Human Error — *Casey, Tom*
Human Error Reduction and Safety Management. 3rd Ed. — *Petersen, Dan*
Human Evolution, Language and Mind — *Noble, William*
Human Existence and Theodicy — *Sutton, Robert Chester, R03*
The Human Face of the Urban Environment — *International Conference on Environmentally Sustainable Development (2nd: 1994: World Bank)*
The Human Factor
Human Factor Engineering and the Political Economy of African Development — *Adjibolosoo, Senyo B-S K*
The Human Factor in Developing Africa — *Adjibolosoo, Senyo B-S K*
Human Factors in Systems Engineering — *Chapanis, Alphonse*
Human Freedom and the Logic of Evil — *Worsley, Richard*
Human Gene Mapping 1995
Human Genetics — *Korf, Bruce R*
Human Genetics. 2nd Ed. — *Lewis, Ricki*

Human Genome Evolution — *Jackson, Michael S*
y The Human Genome Project — *Marshall, Elizabeth L*
The Human Genome Project and the Future of Health Care — *Murray, Thomas H, 1926-*
Human Genome Research and the Challenge of Contingent Future Persons — *Heller, Jan Christian*
Human Geography — *Agnew, John*
Human Geography — *Gregory, Derek*
The Human Geography of Ireland — *Johnson, James H*
Human History at the Crossroads — *Hausen, E*
r Human Impact on the Earth — *Meyer, William B*
Human Intellect and Cognitive Science — *Wagman, Morton*
Human Interaction with Complex Systems — *Ntuen, Celestine A*
Human Interaction with Complex Systems — *Symposium on Human Interaction with Complex Systems (3rd: 1996: Dayton, Ohio)*
y Human Interactions with Mrs. Gladys Furley, R.N. — *Jukes, Mavis*
Human Judgment and Social Policy — *Hammond, Kenneth R*
c The Human Machine
The Human Mind Explained — *Greenfield, Susan A*
Human Molecular Genetics — *Strachan, Tom*
The Human Nervous System. 5th Ed. — *Noback, Charles Robert*
Human Neuroanatomy. 9th Ed. — *Parent, Andre*
y Human Origins — *Thomas, Herbert*
y Human Prey — *Pierce, L D*
Human Protein Data — *Haeberli, Andre*
Human Reproduction, Emerging Technologies, and Conflicting Rights — *Blank, Robert H*
The Human Resource Challenge of International Joint Ventures — *Cyr, Dianne J*
Human Resource Champions — *Ulrich, Dave*
Human Resource Management — *Cowell, Noel M*
Human Resource Management Perspectives on TQM — *Knouse, Stephen B*
Human Resources — *Kemske, Floyd*
Human Resources and the Adjustment Process — *Paredes, Ricardo*
Human Resources in Latin America and the Caribbean — *Behrman, Jere R*
Human Rights and Gender
Human Rights and Reform — *Waltz, Susan E*
Human Rights and the Search for Community — *Howard, Rhoda E*
Human Rights in the United Kingdom — *Gordon, R J F*
Human Rights in the West Bank and Gaza — *Peleg, Ilan*
r Human Rights in Theory and Practice — *Walters, Gregory J*
Human Rights, Labor Rights, and International Trade — *Compa, Lance A*
Human Rights Watch World Report 1997
A Human Search — *Griffiths, Bede*
The Human Semantic Potential — *Regier, Terry*
y The Human Shark — *Wyeth, Sharon Dennis*
The Human Side of Enterprise — *McGregor, Douglas*
Human Spermatozoa in Assisted Reproduction. 2nd Ed. — *Acosta, Anibal A*
Human Tissue Monitoring and Specimen Banking — *Lee, Lester W*
Humana Festival '96
Humanature — *Goin, Peter*
Humane Medicine — *Little, Miles*
c The Humane Societies — *Sateren, Shelley Swanson*
Humanism and the Rhetoric of Toleration — *Remer, Gary*
Humanism with a Human Face — *Radest, Howard B*
L'Humanisme De Georges Duhamel — *Bourcier, Richard J*
The Humanist-Scholastic Debate in the Renaissance and Reformation — *Rummel, Erika*
r Humanistic Management by Teamwork — *Baldwin, David A*
Humanists and Reformers — *Thompson, Bard*
Humanitarian Challenges and Intervention — *Weiss, Thomas G*
Humanitarian Intervention in Contemporary Conflict — *Rambotham, Oliver*
Humanitarian Intervention in Contemporary Conflict — *Ramsbotham, Oliver*
The Humanities in Western Culture. 4th Ed. — *Lamm, Robert Carson*
r Humanities Index 1974-
Humanity Has Been a Holy Thing — *Wondra, Ellen K*

Humans at the End of the Ice Age — *Straus, Lawrence Guy*
Humans before Humanity — *Foley, Robert*
Humbolt's Travels in Siberia 1837-1842 — *Rose, Gustav*
y Humbug — *Martin, Les*
Humic and Fulvic Acids — *Gaffney, Jeffrey S*
Humic Substances in Terrestrial Ecosystems — *Piccolo, Alessandro*
Humid Tropical Environments — *Reading, Alison J*
The Humiliation of Sinners — *Mansfield, Mary C*
y Humming Whispers — *Johnson, Angela*
Hummingbird Gardens — *Newfield, Nancy L*
c The Hummingbird King (Illus. by F Davalos) — *Palacios, Argentina*
c The Humongous Book of Dinosaurs
r Humor in Irish Literature — *Nilsen, Don Lee Fred*
r Humor in Irish Literature — *Nilson, Don Lee Fred*
Humor of the Old Southwest. 3rd Ed. — *Cohen, Hennig*
r Humor Scholarship — *Nilson, Don Lee Fred*
Humphry Davy: Science and Power — *Knight, David*
Humpty Dumpty — *Knight, Damon*
c Humpty Dumpty (Illus. by Vuthy Kuon) — *Kuon, Vuthy*
c Humpty Dumpty and Other Nursery Rhymes (Illus. by Lucy Cousins) — *Cousins, Lucy*
y The Hunchback of Notre-Dame — *Hugo, Victor*
c The Hunchback of Notre Dame (Illus. by Tony Smith) — *Symonds, Jimmy*
y The Hunchback of Notre Dame (Illus. by Bill Slavin) — *Wynne-Jones, Tim*
c The Hundred and One Dalmatians (Lumley). Audio Version — *Smith, Dodie*
The Hundred Brothers — *Antrim, Donald*
The Hundred Fathom Curve — *Barr, John*
c The Hundred-Mile-an-Hour Dog (Illus. by Nick Sharratt) — *Strong, Jeremy*
y The Hundred Secret Senses — *Tan, Amy*
The Hundred Thousand Fools of God — *Levin, Theodore*
c The Hundredth Name (Illus. by Michael Hays) — *Oppenheim, Shulamith Levey*
Hungarian Folktales — *Palko, Zsuzsanna*
A Hungarian Quo Vadis — *Varga, Janos*
The Hungarian Revolution of 1956 — *Litvan, Gyorgy*
Hungarian Rhapsodies — *Teleky, Richard*
y Hungary — *Hill, Raymond*
Hungary: An Economy in Transition — *Szekely, Istvan P*
Hungary and the Victor Powers 1945-1950 — *Roman, Eric*
Hungary: Poverty and Social Transfers
Hungary: Structural Reforms for Sustainable Growth
Hungary's Negotiated Revolution — *Tokes, Rudolf L*
Hunger — *Hamsun, Knut*
The Hunger and Ecstacy of Vampires — *Stableford, Brian*
Hunger for the Printed Word — *Shavit, David*
Hunger Games — *Caesar, Adrian*
Hunger Point — *Medoff, Jillian*
A Hunger So Wide and So Deep — *Thompson, Becky W*
r The Hungerford Cartulary — *Kirby, John Lavan*
Hunger's Table — *Randall, Margaret*
c Hungry Animals (Illus. by Heather Collins) — *Hickman, Pamela M*
Hungry Eyes — *Hoffman, Barry*
y Hungry for Home — *Bowen, 'Asta*
Hungry for You — *Smith, Joan*
Hungry Ghosts — *Becker, Jasper*
Hungry Ghosts — *Johnson, S*
c The Hungry Monster (Illus. by Sue Heap) — *Root, Phyllis*
c The Hungry Otter (Illus. by Gavin Rowe) — *Ezra, Mark*
y The Hunt and the Feast — *Tessitore, John*
y The Hunt for Life on Mars — *Goldsmith, Donald*
The Hunt for the Heart — *Mahieu, Vincent*
The Hunt for the Whooping Cranes — *McCoy, J J*
y The Hunted — *Carter, Peter*
c The Hunter — *Geraghty, Paul*
Hunter-Gatherer Mortuary Practices during the Central Texas Archaic — *Bement, Leland C*
The Hunter Gracchus and Other Papers on Literature and Art — *Davenport, Guy*
c The Hunterman and the Crocodile (Illus. by Baba Wague Diakite) — *Diakite, Baba Wague*
Hunters and Collectors — *Griffiths, Tom*
Hunters and Gatherers — *Prose, Francine*
Hunters and Shooters — *Fawcett, Bill*

Hunters between East and West — Svoboda, Jiri

Hunter's Bride — Wulf, Jessica

y Hunter's Death — West, Michelle

A Hunter's Heart — Petersen, David

Hunter's Trap — Smith, C W

Huntin' and Shootin' — Bailey, Richard W

Hunting a Detroit Tiger — Soos, Troy

Hunting and Fishing for Sport — Hummel, Richard

y Hunting Dinosaurs — Psihoyos, Louie

Hunting down Home — McNeil, Jean

Hunting for Treasure — Castle, John

c Hunting Grandma's Treasures (Illus. by Walter Lyon Krudop) — Willner-Pardo, Gina

Hunting Trips of a Ranchman. The Wilderness Hunter — Roosevelt, Theodore

Huracan Corazon Del Cielo — Galich, Franz

The Hurdy-Gurdy in Eighteenth-Century France — Green, Robert A

Huron Paleoethnobotany — Monckton, Stephen G

y Hurricane — McCarthy, John

c Hurricanes — Souza, D M

y Hurricanes: Earth's Mightiest Storms — Lauber, Patricia

Hurrying toward Zion — Cherry, Conrad

A Hurting Business — Healy, Thomas

Hurting for More Territory — Garmon, John

Husbandry to Housewifery — Bourke, Joanna

c Hush! A Thai Lullaby (Illus. by Holly Meade) — Ho, Minfong

c Hush Little Baby (Illus. by Sylvia Long) — Long, Sylvia

Husserl and the Question of Relativism — Soffer, Gail

Hutchinson History Library. Electronic Media Version

r The Hutchinson Illustrated Encyclopedia of British History

cr Hutchinson Multimedia Encyclopedia 1995. Electronic Media Version

c The Hutchinson Treasury of Children's Literature — Sage, Alison

Hutterite Beginnings — Packull, Werner O

r Huxford's Collectible Advertising — Huxford, Sharon

r Huxford's Old Book Value Guide. 8th Ed.

Huxley: From Devil's Disciple to Evolution's High Priest — Desmond, Adrian J

Huxley: The Devil's Disciple — Desmond, Adrian J

c Huzzah Means Hooray — Carlson, Laurie M

r HVAC Controls — Gupton, Guy W

r HVAC Pump Handbook — Rishel, James B

Hvildarlaus Fero Inni Drauminn — Johannessen, Matthias

Hybrid: Bisexuals, Multiracials, and Other Misfits under American Law — Colker, Ruth

Hybrid Factory — Abo, Tetsuo

Hybrid Microelectronic Materials — Nair, K M

Hyde — Mahoney, Dan

r Hyde County North Carolina Record of Deeds A 1736-1762 — Norris, Allen Wilkinson Hart

Hyde Yesterdays — Harris, Morgan H

Hydrangeas: A Gardener's Guide — Lawson-Hall, Toni

Hydraulic Engineering Software VI — Blain, W R

Hydraulic Gates and Valves — Lewin, Jack

Hydraulics. 4th Ed. — Simon, Andrew L

Hydraulics for Engineering Technology — Johnson, James E

Hydrocracking Science and Technology — Scherzer, Julius

Hydroelectric Pumped Storage Technology — American Society of Civil Engineers. Task Committee on Pumped Storage

Hydrogels and Biodegradable Polymers for Bioapplications — National Meeting of the American Chemical Society (208th: 1994: Washington, DC)

Hydrogen Effects in Materials — International Conference on Effect of Hydrogen on the Behavior of Materials (5th: 1994: Moran, Wyo.)

Hydrogen Fuel for Surface Transporation — Norbeck, Joseph M

Hydroinformatics '96. Vols. 1-2 — Muller, Andreas

Hydrological Systems Analysis — Engelen, G B

Hydrology and Water Resources. Vols. 1-4 — International Conference on Hydrology and Water Resources (1993: New Delhi, India)

Hydrophilic Polymers — National Meeting of the American Chemical Society (206th: 1993: Chicago, IL)

Hydrotreating Technology for Pollution Control — Occelli, Mario L

Hymn to the Sun — Zelazny, Roger

Hymnology: A Collection of Source Readings — Music, David W

Hymns, Prayers, and Songs — Foster, John L, 1930-

Hypatia of Alexandria — Dzielska, Maria

Hyper-Realistic: Computer Generated Architectural Renderings. Book and Electronic Media Version — Riera Ojeda, Oscar

Hyper/Text/Theory — Landow, George P

HyperCELL. Electronic Media Version — Williams, Gene

Hyperion and the Hobbyhorse — Lindley, Arthur

Hypertension in Children — Feld, Leonard G

A Hypertext Approach to Information Skills — Creanor, L

Hypertext in Hypertext — Landow, George P

Hypertext: The Convergence of Contemporary Critical Theory and Technology — Landow, George P

Hypertext: The Electronic Labyrinth — Snyder, Ilana

Hypnosis: A Scientific Approach — Barber, Theodore X

Hypnosis and Experience — Sheehan, Peter W

r Hypnosis and Hypnotherapy with Children. 3rd Ed. — Olness, Karen

Hypnosis and Suggestion in the Treatment of Pain — Barber, Joseph

Hypnosis, Memory, and Behavior in Criminal Investigation — McConkey, Kevin M

Hypnotism Made Easy — Nimier, Marie

Hypoplastic Left Heart Syndrome — Jaworski, Anna Marie

Hystories: Hysterical Epidemics and Modern Culture — Showalter, Elaine

Title Index

I

I.A. Bunin I Russkaia Literatura XX Veka

c I Am a Little Hedgehog — *Crozat, Francois*

y I Am an American — *Stanley, Jerry*

y I Am an Artichoke — *Frank, Lucy*

c I Am an Astronaut (Illus. by Miriam Sagasti) — *Benjamin, Cynthia*

c I Am Angela — *Keller, Holly*

I Am Because We Are — *Hord, Fred Lee*

c I Am Buddhist — *Quinn, Daniel P*

I Am Dangerous — *Johnson, Greg*

I Am Delighted That You Are Here — *Taylor, Chuck*

c I Am Eastern Orthodox — *Sevastiades, Philemon D*

c I Am Hindu — *Aiyengar, Devi S*

c I Am Jewish — *Weiss, Bernard P*

c I Am Lavina Cumming (Caruso). Audio Version — *Lowell, Susan*

c I Am Me! (Illus. by Alexa Brandenberg) — *Brandenberg, Alexa*

c I Am Muslim — *Chalfonte, Jessica*

I Am My Body — *Moltmann-Wendel, Elisabeth*

I Am Not a Cowboy — *Zarzyski, Paul*

I Am Not Your Victim — *Sipe, Beth*

c I Am Protestant — *Sevastiades, Philemon D*

c I Am Roman Catholic — *Sevastiades, Philemon D*

c I Am Rosa Parks (Illus. by Wil Clay) — *Parks, Rosa*

c I Am Shinto — *Nomura, Noriko S*

I Am Spock — *Nimoy, Leonard*

y I Am the Darker Brother. Rev. Ed. (Illus. by Benny Andrews) — *Adoff, Arnold*

c I Am the Ice Worm — *Easley, Maryann*

c I Am the Mummy Heb-Nefert (Illus. by David Christiana) — *Bunting, Eve*

c I Am Water (Illus. by Judith Moffatt) — *Marzollo, Jean*

I Am Your Brother Joseph — *Unsworth, Tim*

I and Tao — *Herman, Jonathan R*

I Bless You in My Heart — *Traill, Catharine Parr*

I Bought It at Polk Bros — *Paden, Ann*

I Call to the Eye of the Mind — *Hyland, Sara*

I Came, I Saw, I Lost My Luggage — *Biddlecombe, Peter*

c I Can Cook (Illus. by Michael Evans) — *Bastyra, Judy*

c I Can Hear the Sun (Illus. by Patricia Polacco) — *Polacco, Patricia*

c I Can Make Costumes — *Wallace, Mary*

c I Can Make Jewelry — *Wallace, Mary*

c I Can Make Models (Illus. by Michael Evans) — *Campbell, Fiona*

c I Can Make Nature Crafts — *Wallace, Mary*

c I Can Move the Sea (Illus. by Jenny Fell) — *Clarke, Gillian*

I Capture the Castle — *Smith, Dodie*

The I Ching Handbook — *Hacker, Edward A*

I, Claudia — *Kleiner, Diana E E*

I Could Do Anything If I Only Knew What It Was — *Sher, Barbara*

y I Could Do That! — *Shepherd, Christine*

The I Could Eat Pasta Every Night Cookbook — *Kosoff, Susan*

y I Could Never Be So Lucky Again — *Doolittle, James H*

I.D.: How Heredity and Experience Make You Who You Are — *Gallagher, Winifred*

I Det Sedda — *Carpelan, Bo*

I Do! — *Luchetti, Cathy*

I Do Veils--So Can You — *Lynch, Claudia*

I Don't Bow to Buddhas — *Yuan, Mei*

c I Don't Care! Said the Bear — *West, Colin*

I Don't Know Why I Swallowed the Fly — *Maxwell, Jessica*

c I Don't Want to Go to Bed! (Illus. by Tim Warnes) — *Sykes, Julie*

c I Don't Want to Go to Camp (Illus. by Maryann Cocca-Leffler) — *Bunting, Eve*

I Don't Want to Talk about It — *Real, Terrence*

c I Dream of Murder — *Dexter, Catherine*

I Dreamed I Had a Girl in My Pocket — *Ewald, Wendy*

y I Feel a Little Jumpy around You — *Nye, Naomi Shihab*

I, Fellini — *Chandler, Charlotte*

c I Fly (Illus. by Annette Cable) — *Rockwell, Anne F*

c I Forgot! Said Troy (Illus. by Derek Brazell) — *Ashley, Bernard*

I Forgot to Wear Underwear on a Glass-Bottom Boat — *Fenton, Peter*

c I Gave Thomas Edison My Sandwich (Illus. by Donna Kae Nelson) — *Moore, Floyd C*

c I Go to Preschool — *Paterson, Bettina*

I Gotta Tell You — *Iacocca, Lee*

c I Had a Hippopotamus (Illus. by Hector Viveros Lee) — *Lee, Hector Viveros*

c I Hate Goodbyes! (Illus. by Mark Hick) — *Czaj, Kathleen C*

The I Hate Kathie Lee Gifford Book — *Blake, Gary*

c I Hate Superman! (Illus. by Kevin Altieri) — *Simonson, Louise*

c I Hate You! I Like You! (Illus. by Tomasz Bogacki) — *Bogacki, Tomasz*

I Have a Name — *Ignatow, David*

I Have Arrived before My Words — *Pugh, Deborah*

y I Have Lived a Thousand Years — *Bitton-Jackson, Livia*

I Have Lived Here since the World Began — *Ray, Arthur J*

I Have Lived in the Monster — *Ressler, Robert K*

I Have Tasted the Apple — *Crow, Mary*

c I Heal (Illus. by Cindy Karp) — *Marx, Trish*

I Heard God Laughing — *Ladinsky, Daniel*

I Heard the Drum — *Sapp, Allen*

The I in Science — *Brown, Judith R*

c I is for India (Illus. by Prodeepta Das) — *Das, Prodeepta*

c I Know an Old Lady (Illus. by G Brian Karas) — *Karas, G Brian*

c I Know an Old Lady Who Swallowed a Fly (Illus. by Glen Rounds)

c I Know What You Do When I Go to School (Illus. by Jennifer Mazzucco) — *Cannon, A E*

I Know Why the Caged Bird Sings — *Angelou, Maya*

c I Like It When... (Illus. by Mary Murphy) — *Murphy, Mary*

c I Live on a Raft — *Harasymowicz, Jerry*

c I Live with Daddy — *Vigna, Judith*

I Lived under Hitler — *Bannister, Sybil*

c I Love My Busy Book (Illus. by Cyndy Szekeres) — *Szekeres, Cyndy*

c I Love My Daddy Because... (Illus. by Ashley Wolff) — *Porter-Gaylord, Laurel*

c I Love My Mommy Because... (Illus. by Ashley Wolff) — *Porter-Gaylord, Laurel*

c I Love You, Mama, Any Time of Year (Illus. by Bruce Degen) — *Carlstrom, Nancy White*

c I Love You, Papa, in All Kinds of Weather (Illus. by Bruce Degen) — *Carlstrom, Nancy White*

c I Love You the Purplest (Illus. by Mary Whyte) — *Joosse, Barbara M*

I May Be Some Time — *Spufford, Francis*

c I Meant to Tell You (Illus. by James Stevenson) — *Stevenson, James*

I Met a Man Who Wasn't There — *Callaghan, Mary Rose*

c I Must Tell You Something — *Bo, Arno*

y I Never Came to You in White — *Farr, Judith*

I Never Saw Another Butterfly — *Volavkova, Hana*

c I Once Had a Pet Praying Mantis (Illus. by Robert A Dykstra) — *Gasparini, Leonard*

I Once Met — *Ingrams, Richard*

c I Pretend (Illus. by Heidi Goennel) — *Goennel, Heidi*

I Read It in the Wordless Book — *Carter, Betty Smartt*

c I Remember 121 — *Haskins, Francine*

I Remember Julia — *Carlson, Eric Stener*

I Rode with Jesse James — *Hackenberry, Charles*

I Saw a City Invincible — *Joseph, Gilbert M*

c I Say, I Play!

c I See a Sign (Illus. by Lars Klove) — *Klove, Lars*

c I See Animals Hiding (Illus. by Jim Arnosky) — *Arnosky, Jim*

I See by Your Outfit — *Lindmier, Tom*

c I See the Moon (Illus. by Debra Reid Jenkins) — *Appelt, Kathi*

y I See the Moon — *Christiansen, C B*

c I See the Moon (Illus. by Marcus Pfister) — *Pfister, Marcus*

c I See the Moon and the Moon Sees Me (Illus. by Peter Fiore) — *London, Jonathan*

c I See, You Saw (Illus. by Nurit Karlin) — *Karlin, Nurit*

I Shot Andy Warhol — *Harron, Mary*

I-Sight: The World of Rastafari — *Johnson-Hill, Jack A*

yr I Sing the Body Electronic — *Moody, Fred*

I Smekh, I Slezy — *Strogat, Lev*

c I Smell Honey (Illus. by Brian Pinkney) — *Pinkney, Andrea Davis*

c I Spy a Freight Train — *Micklethwait, Lucy*

c I Spy--Everything! — *Godon, Ingrid*

c I Spy Picture Book Riddles Series — *Wick, Walter*

c I Spy Spooky Night (Illus. by Walter Wick) — *Marzollo, Jean*

c I Spy Spooky Night (Illus. by Walter Wick) — *Wick, Walter*

I Still Miss My Man but My Aim Is Getting Better — *Shankman, Sarah*

c I Swim an Ocean in My Sleep (Illus. by Elivia Savadier) — *Farber, Norma*

I Tell You a Mystery — *Arnold, Johann Christoph*

c I Thought I Heard-- — *Baker, Alan*

c I Want My Dinner — *Ross, Tony*

c I Want My Potty — *Ross, Tony*

c I Want to Be a Clown — *Bulloch, Ivan*

c I Want to Be a Juggler — *Bulloch, Ivan*

c I Want to Be a Magician — *Bulloch, Ivan*

c I Want to Be an Acrobat — *Bulloch, Ivan*

c I Want to Be...a Veterinarian — *Maze, Stephanie*

c I Want to Be...an Astronaut — *Maze, Stephanie*

y I Want to Buy a Vowel — *Welter, John*

c I Want to Live — *McDaniel, Lurlene*

I Want to Tell You — *Simpson, O J*

I Want to Thank My Brain for Remembering Me — *Breslin, Jimmy*

y I Was a Teenage Professional Wrestler — *Lewin, Ted*

y I Was Amelia Earhart — *Mendelsohn, Jane*

c I Was Born about 10,000 Years Ago (Illus. by Steven Kellogg) — *Kellogg, Steven*

c I Was Dreaming to Come to America — *Lawler, Veronica*

y I Was Right on Time — *O'Neil, Buck*

I Was That Masked Man — *Moore, Clayton*

c I Was There — *Tanuka, Shelley*

I Was Wrong — *Bakker, Jim*

c I Went to the Zoopermarket — *Sharratt, Nick*
c I Went Walking (Illus. by Julie Vivas) — *Williams, Sue, 1948-*
I Who Have Never Known Men — *Harpman, Jacqueline*
I Will Not Bow Down — *Whitehead, Ron*
c I Wish My Brother Was a Dog (Illus. by Paul Meisel) — *Shields, Carol Diggory*
c I Wonder Why Kangaroos Have Pouches and Other Questions about Baby Animals — *Wood, Jenny*
c I Wonder Why Snakes Shed Their Skin and Other Questions about Reptiles — *O'Neill, Amanda*
c I Wonder Why the Dodo Is Dead and Other Questions about Extinct and Endangered Animals — *Charman, Andrew*
c I Wonder Why the Sun Rises and Other Questions about Time and Seasons — *Walpole, Brenda*
c I Wonder Why the Telephone Rings and Other Questions about Communication — *Mead, Richard*
c I Wonder Why Zippers Have Teeth and Other Questions about Inventions — *Taylor, Barbara*
I Write What I Like — *Biko, Steve*
The Iac Operon — *Muller-Hill, Benno*
Iain Macleod — *Shepherd, Robert*
IAk Zhyv Ukrains'kyi Narod — *Hrushevs'kyi, Mykhailo*
c Ian Beck's Picture Book (Illus. by Ian Beck) — *Beck, Ian*
Ian Fleming — *Lycett, Andrew*
c Ian Penney's Book of Fairy Tales — *Penney, Ian*
Iberia and Latin America — *Wiarda, Howard J*
Iberia and the Mediterranean World of the Middle Ages. Vol. 1 — *Simon, Larry J*
IBM AS/400. 6th Ed. — *Hoskins, Jim*
Ibn Battuta in Black Africa — *Hamdun, Said*
Ibn Sina and Mysticism. Pt. 4 — *Inati, Shams*
ICD-9-CM: International Classification of Diseases. 9th Revision, 5th Ed.
r ICD-9-CM: International Classification of Diseases, 9th Revision, Clinical Modification, Fifth Edition, Color Coded, Volumes 1, 2, and 3, 1997. Hospital Ed.
c Ice — *Naylor, Phyllis Reynolds*
The Ice-Age History of National Parks in the Rocky Mountains — *Elias, Scott A*
c Ice Country — *Cowan, Mary Morton*
An Ice Cream War (Wilby). Audio Version — *Boyd, William*
Ice Cube Sex — *Haberstroh, Jack*
The Ice-Shirt — *Vollmann, William T*
Ice to the Eskimos — *Spoelstra, Jon*
y Iceberg (Greenwood). Audio Version — *Cussler, Clive*
Icebound — *Koontz, Dean*
Icebreaker: The Autobiography of Rudy Galindo — *Galindo, Rudy*
Icefields — *Wharton, Thomas*
c Iceland — *Wilcox, Jonathan, 1960-*
r Iceland. Rev. Ed. — *McBride, Francis R*
Ich Bin...Nicht Ich — *Herzog, Madeleine*
Ich Habe Etwas Zu Sagen — *Bauschinger, Sigrid*
Ich Will Zeugnis Ablegen Bis Zum Letzten. Vols. 1-2 — *Klemperer, Victor*
Ich Wunschte So Gar Gelehrt Zu Werden — *Heuser, Magdalene*
Ici — *Sarraute, Nathalie*
ICIAM '95 — *International Congress on Industrial and Applied Mathematics (3rd: 1995: Hamburg, Germany)*
c Icky, Squishy Science (Illus. by Cecile Schoberle) — *Markle, Sandra*
y Icon — *Forsyth, Frederick*
y Icon (Lang). Audio Version — *Forsyth, Frederick*
p Icon Thoughtstyle Magazine
Iconografia Palestriniana — *Bianchi, Lino*
r Iconographic Research in English Renaissance Literature — *Simonds, Peggy Munoz*
Iconography and Electronics upon a Generic Architecture — *Venturi, Robert*
The Iconography of Job through the Centuries — *Terrien, Samuel*
Iconostasis of Anonymous Saints — *Ritsos, Yannis*
Icons of American Protestantism — *Morgan, David, 1957-*
Icons of Cyprus 7th-20th Century — *Sophocleous, Sophocles*
The ICU Therapeutics Handbook — *Marik, Paul Ellis*
I'd Change My Life If I Had More Time — *Virtue, Doreen*
I'd Kill for a Cookie — *Mitchell, Susan, Ph.D.*
c I'd Like to Be a Chemist
c I'd Like to Be a Meteorologist
c I'd Like to Be a Physicist

c I'd Like to Be a Zoologist
c Id-Ul-Fitr — *Marchant, Kerena*
Ida Lupino: A Biography — *Donati, William*
Idea De Nietzsche — *Savater, Fernando*
The Idea of a University — *Newman, John Henry*
The Idea of an Ethical Community — *Charvet, John*
The Idea of Biodiversity — *Takacs, David*
The Idea of Decline in Western History — *Herman, Arthur*
The Idea of Japan — *Littlewood, Ian*
The Idea of Private Law — *Weinrib, Ernest Joseph*
The Idea of Property in History and Modern Times — *Kolbert, Colin*
The Idea of the Forest — *Schultz, Karla L*
The Idea of the Union — *Foster, John Wilson*
The Ideal of Rationality — *Nathanson, Stephen*
The Ideal Real — *Davies, Paul*
Ideal Surroundings — *Morton, Suzanne*
Idealism and Liberal Education — *Freedman, James O*
Ideas and Forms of Tragedy from Aristotle to the Middle Ages — *Kelly, Henry Ansgar*
Ideas and Realities of Emotion — *Parkinson, Brian*
Ideas and Think Tanks in Contemporary Britain. Vol. 1 — *Kandiah, Michael David*
Ideas for Social Action — *Campolo, Anthony*
Ideas in God according to Saint Thomas Aquinas — *Boland, Vivian*
Ideas Into Books — *Derricourt, Robin*
r The Ideas That Changed the World. Electronic Media Version
The Ideas That Shaped Post-War Britain — *Marquand, David*
Die Idee Der Weiderholung In Peter Handkes Schriften — *Bonn, Klaus*
Identification and Character — *Kamler, Howard*
r Identification of Unusual Pathogenic Gram-Negative Aerobic and Facultatively Anaerobic Bacteria. 2nd Ed. — *Weyant, Robbin*
Identification Problems in the Social Sciences — *Manski, Charles F*
r Identifier Sources Et Citations — *Berlioz, Jacques*
Identifying Marine Diatoms and Dinoflagellates — *Tomas, Carmelo L*
Identities — *Appiah, Anthony*
Identities in North America — *Earle, Robert L*
Identities, Politics, and Rights — *Sarat, Austin*
Identity — *Harris, Henry*
Identity and Community — *Massey, Irving*
Identity and the Life Cycle — *Erikson, Erik H*
Identity, Culture and the Postmodern World — *Sarup, Madan*
Identity Designs — *Cerulo, Karen A*
Identity, Ideology and Conflict — *Cash, John Daniel*
Identity: Youth and Crisis — *Erikson, Erik H*
Ideological Profile of Twentieth-Century Italy — *Bobbio, Norberto*
Ideologies of the Raj — *Metcalf, Thomas R*
Ideology — *Hawkes, David*
Ideology. 2nd Ed. — *McLellan, David*
Ideology and the Collapse of the Soviet System — *Robinson, Neil*
Ideology of Obsession — *Baker, David*
y The Ides of March — *Wilder, Thornton*
r Idiom Savant — *Dunn, Jerry*
c Iditarod Dream (Illus. by Ted Wood) — *Wood, Ted*
c Idjhil (Illus. by Helen Bell) — *Bell, Helen*
Idle Curiosity — *Bergland, Martha*
Idle Hands — *Burnett, John, 1925-*
The Idler's Companion — *Hodgkinson, Tom*
Idlewild or Everything Is Subject to Change — *Lawson, Mark, 1962-*
Idoru — *Gibson, William, 1948-*
y Idoru (Sanders). Audio Version — *Gibson, William, 1948-*
IEEE Infocom '96. Vols. 1-3
IEEE Symposium on Information Visualization '96 — *IEEE Information Visualization Symposium (2nd: 1996: San Francisco, CA)*
r Iesna Lighting Ready Reference — *Murdoch, J*
c If... — *Perry, Sarah*
c If Anything Ever Goes Wrong at the Zoo (Illus. by Jane Dyer) — *Hendrick, Mary Jean*
c If Dogs Had Wings (Illus. by Chris L Demarest) — *Brimner, Larry Dane*
If God Is God — *Wilbur, Sanford R*
If He Hollers Let Him Go — *Himes, Chester*
If He Lived — *Fink, Jon Stephen*
If I Could Write This in Fire — *Smorkaloff, Pamela Maria*

c If I Didn't Have Elbows... (Illus. by David Melling) — *Toksvig, Sandi*
c If I Had a Dog — *Lum, Bernice*
c If I Had a Robot (Illus. by Dan Yaccarino) — *Yaccarino, Dan*
If I Should Die — *Edwards, Grace F*
If I Should Die — *Henry, Alexandra*
y If I Were a Carpenter — *Gaillard, Frye*
If I Were Me — *Blaise, Clark*
c If I Were Queen of the World (Illus. by Mark Graham) — *Hiatt, Fred*
If It Not Be I — *Van Duyn, Mona*
c If It Rains Again Tomorrow, Can We Go Home? — *O'Keefe, Frank*
If It's Going to Be, It's Up to Me — *Schuller, Robert*
c If My Dog Went on Vacation — *Lum, Bernice*
If Not Now — *Henry, Jeanne*
c If Only I Could Whistle Loudly! — *Mellen, Frank*
y If Only They Could Talk (Timothy). Audio Version — *Herriot, James*
If Problems Talked — *Zimmerman, Jeffrey L*
If She Could Take All These Men — *Rivard, Ken*
c If Somebody Lived Next Door (Illus. by Laura McGee) — *Hough, Libby*
If Symptoms Still Persist — *Dalrymple, Theodore*
c If the Dinosaurs Came Back (Illus. by Bernard Most) — *Most, Bernard*
If, Then — *Goldsworthy, Peter*
If These Walls Had Ears — *Morgan, James*
If They Move—Kill 'Em — *Weddle, David*
If This Was Happiness (Fields). Audio Version — *Leaming, Barbara*
c If Two Are Dead — *Sutherland, Robert*
If Two of Them Are Dead — *Cail, Carol*
If Wishes Were Horses — *Kinsella, W P*
If You Can Keep It — *Diamond, Michael*
If You Had a Family — *Wilson, Barbara*
If You Leave Me, Can I Come Too? — *Heimel, Cynthia*
If You Love Me — *Coffman, Elaine*
c If You Should Hear a Honey Guide (Illus. by S D Schindler) — *Sayre, April Pulley*
c If You Were a Bug (Illus. by Jack Graber) — *Bentley, Dawn*
c If You Were My Bunny (Illus. by David McPhail) — *McMullan, Kate*
c If You're Happy and You Know It — *Carter, David A*
c If You're Happy and You Know It — *Lodge, Jo*
If You've Seen One, You've Seen the Mall — *Kroes, Rob*
IFOR: Allied Forces in Bosnia — *Schulze, Carl*
IFOR on IFOR — *Murray, Rupert Wolfe*
Iglesia, Tierra, Y Credito En La Colonia — *Robayo Avendano, Juan Manuel*
Ignatius of Loyola: The Pilgrim Saint — *Tellechea Idigoras, Jose Ignacio*
Ignatius of Loyola: The Psychology of a Saint — *Meissner, W W*
Ignatius Sancho: An African Man of Letters — *King, Reyahn*
y Ignition — *Anderson, Kevin J*
The Ignored — *Little, Bentley*
Igor Stravinsky — *Oliver, Michael*
c Igor Stravinsky (Illus. by Mike Venezia) — *Venezia, Mike*
The Iguana — *Ortese, Anna Maria*
c Iguana Beach (Illus. by Lori Lohstoeter) — *Franklin, Kristine L*
Ihor Sovevyts'kyi — *Pavlyshyn, Stefaniia*
Ikki: Social Conflict and Political Protest in Early Modern Japan — *White, James W*
Il N'y A Plus De Chemin — *Brault, Jacques*
Il Y A 200 Ans Lavoisier — *Demeulenaere-Douyere, Christiane*
Ilaria Del Carretto E Il Suo Monumento — *Toussaint, Stephane*
L'Ile Des Gauchers — *Jardin, Alexandre*
L'Ile Et Une Nuit — *Maximin, Daniel*
Ilford Monochrome Darkroom Practice. 3rd Ed. — *Coote, Jack H*
The Iliad — *Homer*
The Iliad (Jacobi). Audio Version — *Homer*
The Iliad (Pope) — *Homer*
c The Iliad and the Odyssey (Illus. by Marcia Williams) — *Williams, Marcia*
c Iliana: A Winter Solstice Tale (Illus. by Tatjana Krizmanic) — *Fordham, Walter*
The Ilipinar Excavations I — *Roodenberg, Jacob*
I'll Always Have Paris — *Buchwald, Art*
I'll Be Right Back — *Wayman, Tom*
y I'll Be Seeing You — *McDaniel, Lurlene*

I'll Be with You in the Squeezing of a Lemon
— *David, Elizabeth*
I'll Be Your Mirror — *Goldin, Nan*
c I'll Catch the Moon (Illus. by Nina Crews) — *Crews, Nina*
Ill-Gotten Gains — *Katz, Leo*
I'll Never Fight Fire with My Bare Hands Again
— *Rothman, Hal K*
I'll Sing You Two-O — *Fraser, Anthea*
y Illegal Aliens — *Hauser, Pierre*
y Illegal Immigration — *Cozic, Charles P*
y Illegal Immigration — *Lee, Kathleen*
Illegal Tender — *Johnson, David R*
Illegitimacy and Social Structures — *Hendrix, Llewellyn*
Illegitimacy, Sex and Society — *Blaikie, Andrew*
Illegitimate Power — *Findlay, Alison*
r Illiana Ancestors. Vol. 5 — *Griffis, Joan A*
The Illicit Joyce of Postmodernism — *Dettmar, Kevin J H*
c Illinois — *Brill, Marlene Targ*
Illuminated and Decorated Medieval Manuscripts in the University Library, Utrecht — *Horst, K Van Der*
The Illuminated Book. Rev. Ed. — *Diringer, David*
Illuminated Books of the Middle Ages — *Calkins, Robert*
The Illuminated Manuscript — *Backhouse, Janet*
Illuminated Manuscripts of Medieval Spain
— *Mentre, Mireille*
Illuminated Poems — *Ginsberg, Allen*
Illuminating Video — *Fifer, Sally Jo*
Illumination in the Flatwoods — *Hutto, Joe*
Les Illuminations: Un Autre Lecteur? — *Piret, Pierre*
The Illusion of Trust — *DuBose, Edwin R*
L'Illusion Realiste — *Mitterand, Henri*
Illusions — *Dailey, Janet*
Illusions of Opportunity — *Ospina, Sonia*
The Illusions of Postmodernism — *Eagleton, Terry*
The Illustrated A Brief History of Time. Updated and Expanded Ed. — *Hawking, Stephen*
c The Illustrated Book of Myths, Tales and Legends of the World (Illus. by Nilesh Mistry) — *Philip, Neil*
cr The Illustrated Book of Questions and Answers
— *Langley, Andrew*
yr The Illustrated Book of Signs and Symbols
— *Bruce-Mitford, Miranda*
r The Illustrated Book of World Rankings. 4th Ed.
— *Kurian, George Thomas*
yr The Illustrated Dictionary of Constitutional Concepts
— *Maddex, Robert L*
r The Illustrated Encyclopedia of Essential Oils
— *Lawless, Julia*
r The Illustrated Encyclopedia of Handguns — *Zhuk, A B*
yr The Illustrated Encyclopedia of Musical Instruments
— *Dearling, Robert*
r The Illustrated Encyclopedia of World History
— *Heel, K Donker Van*
cr Illustrated Factopedia
c The Illustrated Father Goose (Illus. by Laurie McGaw) — *Tanaka, Shelley*
An Illustrated Guide to Attracting Birds — *Murphy, Daniel P*
yr An Illustrated Guide to Fossils — *Pellant, Chris*
The Illustrated Guide to the Bible — *Porter, J R*
An Illustrated Guide to Veterinary Care of the Horse
— *Vogel, Colin*
The Illustrated History of Canada. 2nd Rev. Ed.
— *Brown, Robert Craig*
r The Illustrated History of Country Music — *Carr, Patrick*
An Illustrated History of Eighteenth-Century Britain
— *Black, Jeremy*
An Illustrated History of Late Medieval England
— *Given-Wilson, Chris*
The Illustrated History of Magic. Rev. Ed.
— *Christopher, Milbourne*
y The Illustrated Life of Michael Collins — *Connolly, Colm*
c The Illustrated Rules of Ice Hockey — *Ayers, Tom*
c The Illustrated Rules of Inline Hockey (Illus. by Ned Butterfield) — *Mayo, Terry*
c The Illustrated Rules of Softball (Illus. by Patrick Kelley) — *Sublett, Anne*
r The Illustrated Werewolf Movie Guide — *Jones, Stephen*
r The Illustrated World's Religions — *Smith, Huston*
Illustrating Fashion--Concept to Creation
— *Stipelman, Steven*
r The Illustration of Robinson Crusoe 1719-1920
— *Blewett, David*

Illustrations of Political Economy. Vols. 1-9
— *Martineau, Harriet*
Illywhacker: A Novel — *Carey, Peter*
The ILO and the Netherlands — *Boonstra, Klara*
Ilya Kabakov: The Man Who Never Threw Anything Away — *Wallach, Amei*
c I'm a Baby, You're a Baby (Illus. by Lisa Kopper)
— *Kopper, Lisa*
c I'm a Big Brother (Illus. by Maxie Chambliss)
— *Cole, Joanna*
c I'm a Big Sister (Illus. by Maxie Chambliss) — *Cole, Joanna*
c I'm a Genius Vet (Illus. by David Hart) — *Page, Jason*
r I'm a Little Teapot — *Cobb, Jane*
c I'm a Little Teapot (Illus. by Iza Trapani) — *Trapani, Iza*
I'm Free, but It'll Cost You — *Coles, Kim*
c I'm Going to the Dentist (Illus. by Maxie Chambliss)
c I'm Going to the Doctor (Illus. by Maxie Chambliss)
c I'm in the Wedding Too (Illus. by Joanna Walsh)
— *Plaisted, Caroline*
I'm Losing You — *Wagner, Bruce*
I'm Not Crazy, I'm Just Not You — *Pearman, Roger R*
I'm Not Really Here — *Allen, Tim*
c I'm Not Scared — *Hannay, Lorraine*
I'm Only One Man — *Philbin, Regis*
c I'm Out of My Body...Please Leave a Message (Illus. by Jack E Davis) — *Greenburg, Dan*
Im/Partial Science — *Spanier, Bonnie*
y I'm Pregnant, Now What Do I Do? — *Buckingham, Robert W*
c I'm Sick of It! A Fishy Melodrama (Illus. by Vincent Bourgeau) — *Bourgeau, Vincent*
c I'm Sick of It! A Mouse's Reality Check (Illus. by Vincent Bourgeau) — *Bourgeau, Vincent*
Im Takte Des Radetzkymarschs...Der Beamte Und Der Offizier In Der Osterreichischen Literatur
— *Strelka, Joseph P*
c I'm the Real Santa Claus! (Illus. by Christa Unzner)
— *Ostheeren, Ingrid*
I'm Too Young to Get Old — *Reichman, Judith*
c I'm Tougher than Asthma! (Illus. by Dan Young)
— *Carter, Alden R*
Im Visier Des FBI — *Stephan, Alexander*
Image and Brain — *Kosslyn, Stephen M*
Image and Mind — *Currie, Gregory*
Image and Reality of the Israel-Palestine Conflict
— *Finkelstein, Norman G*
Image and Text — *Madland, Helga Stipa*
Image and Value in the Graeco-Roman World
— *Gordon, R L*
Image Management and Communication
— *International Conference on Image Management and Communication (4th: 1995: Oahu Island, Hawaii)*
Image Marketing — *Marconi, Joe*
The Image of America in Montaigne, Spenser, and Shakespeare — *Hamlin, William M*
The Image of Antiquity — *Smiles, Sam*
The Image of God — *Howe, Leroy T*
The Image of God the Father in Orthodox Theology and Iconography and Other Studies — *Bigham, Steven*
The Image of Man — *Mosse, George L*
An Image to Die For — *Phillips, Mike*
Imagen De John Keats — *Cortazar, Julio*
La Imagen De Los Negros En El Teatro Del Siglo De Oro — *Fra-Molinero, Baltasar*
La Imagen Romantica De Espana — *Calvo Serraller, Francisco*
Images Du Castor Canadien XVIe-XVIIIe — *Gagnon, Francois-Marc*
Images from the Region of the Pueblo Indians of North America — *Warburg, Aby*
Images in Ivory — *Barnet, Peter*
Images in Weather Forecasting — *Bader, M J*
Images: My Life in Film — *Bergman, Ingmar*
Images of Aging — *Featherstone, M*
Images of America
Images of Conversion in St. Augustine's Confessions
— *O'Connell, Robert J*
Images of Earth: A Teachers Guide to Remote Sensing in Geography at Key Stage 2 — *Barnett, Michael*
Images of Earth: A Teachers Guide to Remote Sensing in Geography at Key Stage 3 and GCSE
— *Barnett, Michael*
Images of Elvis Presley in American Culture 1977-1997 — *Plasketes, George*
Images of Excellence — *Janaway, Christopher*

Images of Invention — *Jeffares, A Norman*
Images of Jazz — *Tanner, Lee*
c Images of Nature — *Booth, David*
Images of Organization. 2nd Ed. — *Morgan, Gareth*
Images of the Algerian War — *Dine, Philip*
Images of the Educational Traveller in Early Modern England — *Warneke, Sara*
Images of the Greek Theatre — *Green, Richard*
Images of the Human — *Brown, Hunter*
Images of the Southern Writer — *Morrow, Mark*
Images of the Spirit — *Iturbide, Graciela*
r Images of the World — *Wolter, John A*
Les Images Ou Tableaux De Platte-Peinture. Vols. 1-2
— *De Vignere, Blaise*
Images, Reflections — *Alexander, Patrick*
Images That Injure — *Lester, Paul Martin*
Images: The Piano Music of Claude Debussy
— *Roberts, Paul, 1949-*
Les Imagiers De L'Orestie — *Knoepfler, Denis*
Imaginal Worlds — *Chittick, William C*
y Imaginary Animals — *Sullivan, Charles*
Imaginary Greece — *Buxton, Richard*
The Imaginary Jew — *Finkielkraut, Alain*
An Imaginary Life — *Malouf, David*
Imaginary Parents — *Taylor, Sheila Ortiz*
r Imaginary People. 2nd Ed. — *Pringle, David*
Imaginary Speeches — *Libanius*
The Imaginary War — *Oakes, Guy*
Imagination Engineering — *Birch, Paul*
c Imagination in Art — *Taylor, George*
The Imagination of Reference II — *Morot-Sir, Edouard*
Imagination, Understanding, and the Virtue of Liberality — *Norton, David L*
Imagination Verses — *Moxley, Jennifer*
The Imaginative Body — *Erskin, Aleda*
The Imaginative Claims of the Artist in Willa Cather's Fiction — *Peck, Demaree C*
An Imaginative Experience — *Wesley, Mary*
Imaginative Futures — *Science Fiction Research Association (1993: Reno, Nevada)*
Imagine the Angels of Bread — *Espada, Martin*
c Imagine You Are a Crocodile (Illus. by Mike Bostock)
— *Wallace, Karen*
c Imagine You Are a Tiger (Illus. by Peter Melnyczuk)
— *Wallace, Karen*
Imagined Worlds — *Dyson, Freeman*
Imagineering Atlanta — *Rutheiser, Charles*
Imaginer L'Eglise Catholique — *Lafont, Ghislain*
Imaging and Intervention in Cardiology — *Nienaber, Christoph A*
Imaging Aristotle — *Sherman, Claire Richter*
r Imaging Atlas of Human Anatomy. Electronic Media Version — *Weir, Jamie*
Imaging Handbook for House Officers — *Silverman, Paul M*
Imaging the Word. Vol. 3 — *Blain, Susan A*
Imagining America — *Elteren, Mel Van*
Imagining Characters — *Byatt, A S*
Imagining Crime — *Young, Alison*
Imagining Culture — *Hart, Jonathan*
Imagining Home — *Lemelle, Sidney*
Imagining Home — *Vinz, Mark*
Imagining Indians in the Southwest — *Dilworth, Leah*
Imagining Monsters — *Todd, Dennis*
Imagining Niagara — *McGreevy, Patrick V*
Imagining Reality — *Macdonald, Kevin*
Imagining Robert — *Neugeboren, Jay*
Imagining Rome — *Liversidge, Michael*
Imagining Scotland — *Gold, John R*
Imagining the Middle Class — *Wahrman, Dror*
Imagining the Pacific — *Smith, Bernard, 1916-*
Imagining Women — *Gernant, Karen*
Imaginings of Sand — *Brink, Andre*
Imago — *Rendle-Short, Francesca*
Imazighen: The Vanishing Traditions of Berber Women — *Courtney-Clarke, Margaret*
Imbalance of Powers — *Silverstein, Gordon*
To Imeroloyio Tou Ekmayiou — *Apostolou, Spyros*
IMF Programmes in Developing Countries — *Killick, Tony*
Imirce Ou La Fille De La Nature — *Laurens, Du*
y Imitate the Tiger — *Cheripko, Jan*
Imitating Art — *Ellis, David*
Imitation as Resistance — *Granqvist, Raoul*
Imitation in Human and Animal Behavior
— *Wyrwicka, Wanda*
Imitations Et Traduction De Cent Dix-huit Emblemes D'A Iciat — *Bouquet, Simon*
The Immaculate Conception in Spanish Art
— *Stratton, Suzanne L*

L'Immagine Del Vincitore — *Rausa, Federico*
Immanent Art — *Foley, John Miles*
Immediate Action — *McNab, Andy*
Immensites — *Germain, Sylvie*
Immersed in Technology — *Moser, Mary Anne*
Immigrant. Bk. 3 — *Nelson, Stanley*
Immigrant America. 2nd Ed. — *Portes, Alejandro*
r The Immigrant Labor Press in North America 1840s-
    1970s. Vols. 1-3 — *Hoerder, Dirk*
Immigrant Links to the Home Country — *Gould,
    David*
An Immigrant Soldier in the Mexican War — *Zeh,
    Frederick*
y The Immigrant Train and Other Stories — *Petesch,
    Natalie L M*
Immigrant Voices — *Dublin, Thomas, 1946-*
Immigrant Women and Integration
c Immigrants — *Sandler, Martin W*
Immigrants and Immigration Policy — *Duleep,
    Harriet Orcutt*
Immigrants and Nationalists — *Shafir, Gershon*
Immigrants, Markets, and States — *Hollifield, James
    F*
Immigrants Out! — *Perea, Juan F*
Immigration in America's Future — *Heer, David M*
The Immigration Mystique — *Williamson, Chilton*
r Immigration, Race and Ethnicity in Contemporary
    France — *Hargreaves, Alec G*
The Immigration Time-Bomb   *Lamm, Richard*
Immobile Dans Le Courant Du Fleuve — *Berger, Yves*
Immobilization of Enzymes and Cells — *Bickerstaff,
    Gordon F*
Immortal Love — *Petrushevskaya, Ludmilla*
Immortal Unicorn — *Beagle, Peter S*
Immortality — *Machon, Kirsty*
y The Immortals — *Hickman, Tracy*
y Immortelles: Memoir of a Will-o'-the-Wisp
    — *Marokvia, Mireille*
Immunity to Parasites. 2nd Ed. — *Wakelin, Derek*
r The Immunization Resource Guide. 2nd Ed.
    — *Rozario, Diane*
Immunoassay — *Diamandis, Eleftherios P*
Immunoassay Automation: An Updated Guide to
    Systems — *Chan, Daniel W*
Immunoassays for Residue Analysis — *Beier, Ross C*
Immunobiology and Pathogenesis of Persistent Virus
    Infections — *Mahy, Brian W J*
r Immunobiology Bookshelf on CD-ROM. Electronic
    Media Version
Immunochemistry in Practice. 3rd Ed. — *Johnstone,
    Alan*
Immunology: A Short Course. 3rd Ed. — *Benjamini,
    Eli*
Immunology of HIV Infection — *Gupta, Sudhir*
Immunology: Understanding the Immune System
    — *Elgert, Klaus D*
Immunopathology of Lung Disease — *Kradin, Richard
    L*
Immunopharmacology of Allergic Diseases
    — *Townley, Robert C*
Immunopharmacology Reviews. Vol. 2 — *Hadden,
    John W*
Immunotherapy of Malignant Melanoma — *Leong,
    Stanley P L*
The Impact of European Integration — *Kourvetaris,
    George A*
The Impact of Global Warming on Texas — *North,
    Gerald*
The Impact of Judicial-Selection Method on State-
    Supreme-Court Policy — *Pinello, Daniel R*
Impact of Managed Care on Psychodynamic
    Treatment — *Barron, James W*
The Impact of Peacekeeping on Army Personnel
    Requirements — *United States. Congress. House.
    Committee on Armed Services. Military Forces and
    Personnel Subcommittee*
The Impact of Population Growth on Well-Being in
    Developing Countries — *Ahlburg, Dennis A*
The Impact of Sanctions on Iraq — *Clark, Ramsey*
The Impact of School Choice and Community
    — *Smrekar, Claire*
The Impact of Technology on Library Instruction
    — *National LOEX Library Instruction Conference
    (21st: 1993: Racine, Wis.)*
Impact of the Arab-Israeli Wars on Language and
    Social Change in the Arab World — *Jassem, Zaidan
    Ali*
The Impact of the Persian Gulf War and the Decline
    of the Soviet Union on How the United States Does
    Its Defense Business — *United States. Congress.
    House. Committee on Armed Services*

The Impact of Trade on United States Employment
    — *Sveikauskas, Catherine*
The Impact of Values — *Deth, Jan W Van*
Impact! The Threat of Comets and Asteroids
    — *Verschuur, Gerrit L*
El Impacto Del Humanismo En El Nuevo Mundo
    — *Universidad Interamericana De Puerto Rico/
    Aguadilla*
Impacts of Antibiotic Resistant Bacteria
Impacts of National Technology Programmes
    — *Brown, Martin*
Impacts of the Early Cold War on the Formulation of
    U.S. Science Policy — *Golden, William T*
y Impeaching the President — *Morin, Isobel V*
The Imperative Future — *Barringer, Howard*
The Imperative of American Leadership
    — *Muravchik, Joshua*
Imperfect Paradise — *Shen, Tsung-Wen*
An Imperfect Spy (Mangan). Audio Version — *Cross,
    Amanda*
An Imperfect Union — *Baun, Michael J*
Imperial Carnival Glass — *O'Burns, Carl*
Imperial Diplomacy in the Era of Decolonization
    — *Hanes, W Travis*
The Imperial Dryden — *Kramer, David Bruce*
Imperial Encounters — *Doty, Roxanne Lynn*
Imperial Eyes — *Pratt, Mary Louise*
r Imperial Germany — *Chickering, Roger*
Imperial Germany 1871-1914 — *Berghahn, Volker*
r Imperial Glass Encyclopedia. Vol. 1 — *Measell, James*
Imperial Identities — *Lorcin, Patricia M E*
Imperial Leather — *McClintock, Anne*
Imperial London — *Port, M H*
The Imperial Metaphor — *Feuchtwang, Stephan*
Imperial Panama — *Ward, Christopher*
Imperial Panegyric in Statius — *Geyssen, John W*
Imperial Rivals — *Paine, Sarah C M*
Imperial Russia's Jewish Question 1855-1881 — *Klier,
    John Doyle*
The Imperial War Museum Book of the Somme
    — *Brown, Malcolm*
Imperialism and Its Contradictions — *Kiernan, V G*
Imperialism and Theatre — *Gainor, J Ellen*
Imperialism at Home — *Meyer, Susan, 1960-*
Imperiled Innocents — *Beisel, Nicola*
The Imperiled Red Cross and the Palestine-Eretz-
    Yisrael Conflict 1945-1952 — *Junod, Dominique-D*
Imperium Romanum — *Lintott, Andrew*
Impersonations: The Performance of Gender in
    Shakespeare's England — *Orgel, Stephen*
Implant Wear — *Wright, Timothy M*
The Implementation Challenge — *Hussey, D E*
Implementation of the Helsinki Accords: Bosnia's
    Second Winter under Siege — *United States.
    Congress. Commission on Security and Cooperation in
    Europe*
Implementation of Total Quality Management
    — *Rogers, Rolf E*
Implementing and Managing Client/Server Systems
    — *Cashin, Jerry*
Implementing Deregulation and Promoting Foreign
    Direct Investment in Africa — *Bachmann, Heinz*
Implementing ISO 14000 — *Tibor, Tom*
Implementing Mastery Learning. 2nd Ed. — *Guskey,
    Thomas R*
Implementing Projects for the Poor — *Carvalho,
    Soniya*
r Implementing S/NVQs in the Information and Library
    Sector — *Herzog, Juliet*
Implementing SAP R/3 — *Bancroft, Nancy H*
Implementing the New Community Care — *Lewis,
    Jane*
Implementing Town Planning — *Greed, Clara*
The Implications of Climate and Sea-Level Change for
    Bangladesh — *Warrick, R A*
The Implications of the Evolution of European
    Integration for UK Labour Markets — *Gold,
    Michael*
Implicit Cognition — *Underwood, Geoffrey*
Implicit Understandings — *Schwartz, Stuart B*
Impolite Learning — *Goldgar, Anne*
The Importance of Being a Wit — *Leach, Maria*
The Importance of Being Oscar — *MacLiammoir,
    Micheal*
The Importance of Living — *Lin, Yutang*
The Importance of Us — *Tuomela, Raimo*
r Important Bird Areas in the Middle East — *Evans, M
    I*
r Importers Manual USA and the Dictionary of
    International Trade. 1996-97 Ed. Electronic Media
    Version

Impossible Dreams — *Babbitt, Susan E*
An Impossible Life — *Black, David*
L'Impossible Marcel Proust — *Duchene, Roger*
Impossible Minds — *Aleksander, Igor*
Impossible Nation — *Conlogue, Ray*
Impostors in the Temple — *Anderson, Martin*
r Impresos Novohispanos 1808-1821 — *Garritz, Amalia*
Impressed and Incised Ceramics — *Minogue, Coll*
Impression Management in Organizations
    — *Rosenfeld, Paul*
Impressionist Masterpieces in American Museums
    — *Boardingham, Robert*
The Impressionist Print — *Melot, Michel*
Impressionists on the Seine — *Rathbone, Eliza E*
Impressionists Side by Side — *White, Barbara Ehrlich*
Impressions of Arabia — *Mauger, Thierry*
Les Imprimes Limousins 1788-1799 — *Cassan, Michel*
Improper Influence — *Gais, Thomas*
Improve Your Child's Spelling. Rev. Ed., Vols. 1-2
    — *Rippon, Norman*
Improving Economic and Social Cohesion in the
    European Community — *Mortensen, Jorgen*
Improving Fundraising with Technology — *Miller,
    James D*
Improving Intercultural Interactions — *Brislin,
    Richard W*
Improving Nature? — *Reiss, Michael J*
Improving Poor People — *Katz, Michael B*
Improving Schools from the Bottom Up — *Shields,
    Patrick M*
Improving Schools from the Bottom Up: Summary
    Volume — *Shields, Patrick M*
Improving Survey Questions — *Fowler, Floyd J, Jr.*
Improving Teaching and Learning in Science and
    Mathematics — *Treagust, David F*
Improving the Environment — *National Research
    Council (U.S.)*
Improving the Implementation of the Individuals with
    Disabilities Education Act
Improving the Prospects for Future International
    Peace Operations
Improving the Software Process through Process
    Definition and Modeling
Improving Women's Health in India
Impulsivity and Compulsivity — *Oldham, John M*
Impure Science — *Epstein, Steven*
In a Blaze of Glory — *Townes, Emilie M*
c In a Circle Long Ago (Illus. by Lisa Desimini) — *Van
    Laan, Nancy*
In a Closet Hidden — *Glasser, Leah Blatt*
c In a Creepy, Creepy Place and Other Scary Stories
    (Illus. by Kimberly Bulcken Root) — *Gorog, Judith*
y In a Different Light (Illus. by John McDonald)
    — *Meyer, Carolyn*
In a Generous Spirit — *Baker, Christina Looper*
In a Heartbeat — *Stone, Eric*
In a Land of Plenty — *Pears, Tim*
In a Pig's Ear — *Bryers, Paul*
In a Time of Violence — *Boland, Eavan*
In Adamless Eden — *Palmieri, Patricia Ann*
In Aedibus Aldi — *Angerhofer, Paul J*
In and about the World — *Radder, Hans*
In and Out of Consciousness — *Sommerhoff, Gerd*
In and Out of the Ghetto — *Hsia, R Po-chia*
In Another Place, Not Here — *Brand, Dionne*
In Awe — *Heim, Scott*
In Bed with an Elephant — *Kennedy, Ludovic*
In Bed with the Exotic Enemy — *Gioseffi, Daniela*
In Black and White — *Shropshire, Kenneth L*
In Close Harmony — *Wolfe, Charles*
In Confidence — *Dobrynin, Anatoly*
In Contact with the Gods? — *Delgado, Maria M*
In Contempt — *Darden, Christopher A*
y In Contempt (Darden). Audio Version — *Darden,
    Christopher A*
In Contempt of Congress — *Rozell, Mark J*
y In Control — *Kreiner, Anna*
y In Country — *Mason, Bobbie Ann*
c In Crack Willow Wood (Illus. by Ivan Bates)
    — *McBratney, Sam*
In Darkest Hollywood — *Davis, Peter, 1933-*
In Darwin's Wake — *Campbell, John, 1946-*
In Days Gone By — *Kirchner, Audrey Burie*
y In Deep Water — *Wyeth, Sharon Dennis*
y In Defense of Affirmative Action — *Bergmann,
    Barbara R*
In Defense of Decadent Europe. 2nd Ed. — *Aron,
    Raymond*
In Defense of Government — *Weisberg, Jacob*
In Defense of Humanism — *Etlin, Richard A*
In Defense of Marion — *Mencken, H L*

In Defense of Prisons — *Wright, Richard A*
In Defense of Single-Parent Families — *Dowd, Nancy E*
In Der Hand Der Frauen — *Wagner, Richard, 1952-*
c In Enzo's Splendid Gardens (Illus. by Patricia Polacco) — *Polacco, Patricia*
In Europe's Name — *Garton Ash, Timothy*
c In Flanders Fields (Illus. by Janet Wilson) — *Granfield, Linda*
c In Flight with David McPhail — *McPhail, David*
In Focus — *Naef, Weston*
c In for Winter, Out for Spring (Illus. by Jerry Pinkney) — *Adoff, Arnold*
In Front of the Children — *Bazalgette, Cary*
c In God's House — *Coles, Robert*
In Good Company — *Hauerwas, Stanley*
In Good Company — *Jasper, David*
In Great Haste — *Collins, Michael, 1890-1922*
In Harm's Way — *Bell, Martin*
In Harm's Way — *Coleman, Jules L*
y In Harm's Way (Bell). Audio Version — *Bell, Martin*
In Heaven as on Earth — *Peck, M Scott*
In Her Own Right — *Benderly, Beryl Lieff*
In Her Words — *Oden, Amy*
In His Own Write. A Spaniard in the Works — *Lennon, John*
In Honor Bound — *Dodson, DeAnna Julie*
In Hope of Liberty — *Horton, James Oliver*
In Hora Mortis — *Rebillard, Eric*
In Julia's Kitchen with Master Chefs — *Child, Julia*
y In Lane Three, Alex Archer — *Duder, Tessa*
The In-Law Survival Manual — *Horsley, Gloria Call*
In Light of India — *Paz, Octavio*
c In-Line Skating Basics (Illus. by Bruce Curtis) — *Millar, Cam*
In Memoriam to Postmodernism — *Amerika, Mark*
In Memory's Kitchen — *DeSilva, Cara*
c In My Family (Illus. by Carmen Lomas Garza) — *Lomas Garza, Carmen*
y In My Father's Court (Kandinsky). Audio Version — *Singer, Isaac Bashevis*
In My Father's Garden — *Chernin, Kim*
y In My Father's House — *Rinaldi, Ann*
c In My Home (Illus. by Angie Sage) — *Sage, Angie*
In My Own Words — *Peron, Eva*
c In My Pocket (Illus. by Gerald Fitzgerald) — *Sim, Dorrith M*
y In My Room — *Salinger, Adrienne*
In My World — *Logrippo, Ro*
In N — *Tellegen*
In Nonna's Kitchen — *Field, Carol*
In One House — *Aitken, Adam*
In Ordinary Time — *Bondi, Roberta C*
In Other Words — *Bialystok, Ellen*
In Other Words — *Cardinal, Marie*
In Other Words — *Manfull, Helen*
In Our Own Voices — *Keller, Rosemary Skinner*
In Our Own Voices — *Neely, Teresa*
In Our Own Words — *Boyd, Elza Dinwiddie*
In Our Own Words. 2nd Ed. — *Mylynarczyk, R*
In Our Time — *Fisher, Eugene J*
In Over Our Heads — *Kegan, Robert*
In Patagonia — *Chatwin, Bruce*
In Pharaoh's Army — *Wolff, Tobias*
In Place of the Forest — *Brookfield, Harold*
y In Praise of Our Fathers and Our Mothers — *Hudson, Wade*
In Praise of Tomatoes — *Shepherd, Steven*
In Public Houses — *Conroy, David W*
In Pursuit of Peace — *Bar-On, Mordechai*
In Pursuit of the English — *Lessing, Doris May*
In Pursuit of the Quality of Life — *Offer, Avner*
In Pursuit of the White House — *Mayer, William G*
In Quest of Mineral Wealth — *Craig, Alan K*
In Quest of the Sacred Baboon — *Kummer, Hans*
In Radical Pursuit — *Snodgrass, W D*
In Red Saint, Pink Daughter — *Rodgers, Silvia*
r In Remembrance. Vol. 1 — *Sisler, Janice Cale*
c In Rosa's Mexico (Illus. by Andrea Arroyo) — *Geeslin, Campbell*
In Search of a Calling — *Buford, Thomas O*
In Search of a New Left — *Laxer, James*
In Search of Ancient North America — *Pringle, Heather*
In Search of Churchill — *Gilbert, Martin, 1936-*
In Search of Civil Society — *White, Gordon*
In Search of Common Ground — *Erikson, Erik H*
In Search of Dreams — *Strauch, Inge*
In Search of Elvis — *Chadwick, Vernon*
In Search of Excellence — *Peters, Tom F*
In Search of Happiness — *Deayton, Angus*

In Search of Kinship — *Lambert, Page*
In Search of Mary — *Cunneen, Sally*
In Search of National Economic Success — *Kenworthy, Lane*
y In Search of Nature — *Wilson, Edward Osborne*
In Search of Planet Vulcan — *Baum, Richard, 1930-*
In Search of Respect — *Bourgois, Philippe*
In Search of Shambhala — *Brook, Elaine*
In Search of Steam Donkeys — *Johnson, Merv*
In Search of Sugihara — *Levine, Hillel*
In Search of Supervision — *Jacobs, Michael*
In Search of the Birth of Jesus — *Roberts, Paul William*
In Search of the Classic — *Shankman, Steven*
c In Search of the Grand Canyon — *Fraser, Mary Ann*
In Search of the Light. Rev. and Updated Ed. — *Blackmore, Susan J*
In Search of the Supernatural — *Kan, Pao*
In Search of the Swan Maiden — *Leavy, Barbara Fass*
In Search of the Ultimate Building Blocks — *Hooft, G 'T*
In Search of the Virtual Class — *Tiffin, John*
In Search of Your True Self — *Staples, Walter*
In Short — *Kitchen, Judith*
In/Sight: African Photographers 1940 to the Present
In Situ Electron and Tunneling Microscopy of Dynamic Processes — *Sharma, Renu*
In Situ Treatment Technology — *Nyer, Evan K*
y In Small Things Forgotten. Rev. and Expanded Ed. — *Deetz, James*
In Solitude for Company — *Auden, W H*
y In Sports, Money Talks — *Dolan, Edward F*
In Stalin's Shadow — *Khlevniuk, Oleg V*
In Subordination — *Kinnear, Mary*
In the Absence of God — *Smrtisthal. English*
In the Age of Mabo — *Attwood, Bain*
In the American West — *Avedon, Richard*
In the Bank of Beautiful Sins — *Wrigley, Robert*
In the Barrios — *Moore, Joan*
c In the Bathroom (Illus. by Geoff Dann) — *MacKinnon, Debbie*
In the Beauty of the Lilies — *Updike, John*
c In the Bedroom (Illus. by Geoff Dann) — *MacKinnon, Debbie*
In the Beginning — *Armstrong, Karen*
In the Beginning — *Dunne, Catherine*
In the Beginning — *Gribbin, John*
y In the Beginning — *Hamilton, Virginia*
c In the Beginning (Illus. by Katherine Janus Kahn) — *Levin, Miriam Ramsfelder*
c In the Beginning (Illus. by Bryn Barnard) — *Quattlebaum, Mary*
In the Beginning Was Love — *Kristeva, Julia*
In the Belly — *Gewanter, David*
In the Blood — *Jones, Steve*
In the Classroom — *Gerson, Mark*
In the Company of Animals — *Serpell, James*
In the Company of Children — *Hindley, Joanne*
In the Company of Giants — *Jager, Rama D*
In the Company of Mushrooms — *Schaechter, Moselio*
y In the Company of My Sisters — *Boyd, Julia A*
In the Company of Others — *Snow, Nancy E*
In the Company of Women — *Watkins, Bonnie*
In the Constellation of the Crab — *Brett, Doris*
y In the Country of Country — *Dawidoff, Nicholas*
In the Country of Men — *Waldron, Jan L*
In the Crevice of Time — *Jacobsen, Josephine*
In the Cross Fire — *Vizzard, William J*
In the Cut — *Moore, Susanna*
c In the Days of the Salem Witchcraft Trials — *Roach, Marilynne K*
In the Deep Midwinter — *Clark, Robert*
In the Dutch Mountains — *Notebeam, Cess*
In the Electric Mists of the Confederate Dead — *Burke, James Lee*
In the Eye's Mind — *Turner, R Steven*
In the Face of God — *Horton, Michael S*
p In the Family
In the Field. 2nd Ed. — *Smith, Carolyn D*
In the Footsteps of Agatha Christie — *Riviere, Francois*
c In the Footsteps of Dracula (Illus. by Francesca D'Ottavi) — *Pipe, Jim*
c In the Footsteps of Frankenstein (Illus. by Susanna Addario) — *Parker, Steve*
c In the Footsteps of the Mummy — *Roden, Katie*
c In the Footsteps of the Werewolf — *Pipe, Jim*
In the Foreground: Beowulf — *Stanley, Eric Gerald*
c In the Forest (Illus. by Dorothy Emerling) — *Cooper, Ann*
In the Fullness of Life — *Glavac, Cynthia*

c In the Garden (Illus. by Geoff Dann) — *MacKinnon, Debbie*
In the Garden of Desire — *Maltz, Wendy*
c In the Hand of the Goddess — *Pierce, Tamora*
y In the Hands of My Enemies — *Heide, Sigrid*
y In the Hands of Providence (Parker). Audio Version — *Trulock, Alice Rains*
c In the Heart of the Village (Illus. by Barbara Bash) — *Bash, Barbara*
In the Heat of the Day — *Anthony, Michael*
In the Hold — *Arsenijevic, Vladimir*
In the Hour of Signs — *Mahjoub, Jamal*
c In the Huddle with...Steve Young — *Christopher, Matt*
c In the Jungle (Illus. by Dawn Apperley) — *Burns, Kate*
c In the Kaiser's Clutch — *Karr, Kathleen*
c In the Kitchen (Illus. by Geoff Dann) — *MacKinnon, Debbie*
In the Land of Giants — *Bogues, Tyrone*
In the Land of Israel — *Oz, Amos*
In the Land of Nod — *Butler, Hubert*
In the Language of Love — *Schoemperlen, Diane*
In the Light of Italy — *Conisbee, Philip*
In the Memory of the Forest — *Powers, Charles T*
In the Middle — *Atwell, Nancie*
y In the Middle of the Night — *Cormier, Robert*
In the Middle of This Road We Call Our Life — *Jones, James W*
In the Midnight Hour — *Tyre, Peg*
In the Mountains of Morazan — *Macdonald, Mandy*
In the Name of All That's Holy — *Shupe, Anson*
In the Name of Elijah Muhammad — *Gardell, Mattias*
In the Name of Sorrow and Hope (Ben-Artzi Pelossof). Audio Version — *Ben-Artzi Pelossof, Noa*
In the Name of the Family — *Stacey, Judith*
In the Name of the Law — *Rose, David*
In the National Interest: 1996 Quadrennial Report on Human Rights and U.S. Foreign Policy — *Lawyers Committee for Human Rights (U.S.)*
c In the Ocean (Illus. by Dawn Apperley) — *Burns, Kate*
In the Ocean of Night — *Benford, Gregory*
In the Open — *Donohue, Timothy E*
In the Palm of Darkness — *Montero, Mayra*
In the Palm of Your Hand — *Kowit, Steve*
y In the Path of Lewis and Clark — *Lourie, Peter*
In the Presence of His Majesty — *Chambers, Oswald*
In the Presence of My Enemies — *Carnahan, Sumner*
In the Presence of the Enemy — *George, Elizabeth*
In the Presence of the Enemy (Peters). Audio Version — *George, Elizabeth*
In the Public Interest — *James, Gerald*
In the Quietness of My Aunt's House. Bad Blood — *Carroll, Joanne*
c In the Rain with Baby Duck (Illus. by Jill Barton) — *Hest, Amy*
In the Realm of the Diamond Queen — *Tsing, Anna Lowenhaupt*
In the Ring of Fire — *Houston, James D*
c In the Sand (Illus. by Dawn Apperley) — *Burns, Kate*
In the Season of the Daisies — *Phelan, Tom*
In the Service of Stalin — *Pike, David Wingeate*
In the Shadow of History — *Davidson, Andrew P*
In the Shadow of Islam — *Eberhardt, Isabelle*
In the Shadow of Lavoisier — *Crosland, Maurice*
In the Shadow of Polio — *Black, Kathryn*
In the Shadow of Prague — *Komenda-Soentgerath, Olly*
In the Shadow of the Giant — *Buchenau, Jurgen*
In the Shadow of the Han — *Holcombe, Charles*
y In the Shadow of the Holocaust — *Hass, Aaron*
In the Shadow of the Poorhouse — *Katz, Michael B*
In the Shadow of War — *Sherry, Michael S*
In the Sixties — *Connolly, Ray*
In the Skin of a Lion — *Ondaatje, Michael*
In the Slammer with Carol Smith — *Calisher, Hortense*
c In the Snow (Illus. by Dawn Apperley) — *Burns, Kate*
c In the Snow (Illus. by Lindsay Barrett George) — *George, Lindsay Barrett*
In the Soviet House of Culture — *Grant, Bruce, 1964-*
In the Still of the Night — *Raney, Deborah*
In the Street — *Levitt, Helen*
c In the Swim (Illus. by Douglas Florian) — *Florian, Douglas*
In the Theater of Consciousness — *Baars, Bernard J*
In the Theatre of Romanticism — *Carlson, Julie A*
In the Time of Cannibals — *Coplan, David B*
In the Time of the Americans — *Fromkin, David*
In the Tracks of African Predicament — *Irele, Dipo*
In the Trade of War — *Allan, James R*

In the Twilight Zone — *Black, Maggie, 1945-*
In the Unlikely Event of a Water Landing — *Noel, Christopher*
In the Valley of the Shadow — *Sanders, Leonard*
In the Wake of First Contact — *Schaffer, Kay*
In the War for Peace — *Hetzner, C N*
In the Weather of the Heart — *Monroe, Valerie*
In the Wheat — *Cingolani, Charles L*
c In the Wild (Illus. by Nora Leigh Ryder) — *Ryder, Nora Leigh*
In the Wilderness — *Barnes, Kim*
In the Year 1096 — *Chazan, Robert*
y In the Year of the Bull — *Telander, Rick*
In the Zone — *Perry, J Mitchell*
In the Zone — *Potterfield, Peter*
In Their Own Voices. Vols. 1-4. Audio Version
In Their Shoes — *Halsell, Grace*
y In These Girls, Hope Is a Muscle — *Blais, Madeleine*
In This Corner...! — *Heller, Peter*
In This Dark House — *Kehoe, Louise*
In This Sign Conquer — *Brand, Irene*
In Times of War and Peace — *Turnley, David*
In Transit — *Heller, Peter*
In Viaggio — *Ramondino, Fabrizia*
In Washington But Not of It — *Hofrenning, Daniel J B*
In Whose Image? — *Simone, T Abdou Maliqalim*
In Wolf's Clothing — *McCutcheon, Sandy*
In Your Dream — *Delaney, Gayle*
y In Your Dreams — *Neenan, Colin*
r In Your Pocket--Greek Islands — *Michelin Tyre Public Limited Company*
r In Your Pocket--New York — *Michelin Tyre Public Limited Company*
r In Your Pocket--Paris — *Michelin Tyre Public Limited Company*
r In Your Pocket--Prague — *Michelin Tyre Public Limited Company*
r In Your Pocket--Southern Spain — *Michelin Tyre Public Limited Company*
r In Your Pocket--the French Riviera — *Michelin Tyre Public Limited Company*
r In Your Pocket--Tuscany — *Michelin Tyre Public Limited Company*
Inagua: An Island Sojourn — *Klingel, Gilbert*
Inanna Hyper-Luminal — *Ferguson, V S*
Inappropriate Behaviour — *Mock, Irene*
Incapacitation: Penal Confinement and the Restraint of Crime — *Zimring, Franklin E*
y The Incas — *Wood, Tim*
L'Incendie De La Sainte-Victoire — *Fauconnier, Bernard*
Incentives: Motivation and the Economics of Information — *Campbell, Donald E*
Incerti Di Viaggio — *Pazzi, Roberto*
Incest, Drama and Nature's Law 1550-1700 — *McCabe, Richard A*
c Inch by Inch (Illus. by Ora Eitan) — *Mallett, David*
The Inchcape Bell. Did You Ever Send Your Wife to Camberwell? The Game of Speculation. The Lights o' London. The Middleman — *Fitzball, Edward*
r The Inchon Landing, Korea 1950 — *Edwards, Paul M*
Incidents in the Rue Laugier — *Brookner, Anita*
The Incisive Eye — *See-Paynton, Colin*
Incognito — *Ray, Francis*
Income Distribution in a Corporate Economy — *Rimmer, Russell*
Income Distribution in Australia — *Clare, Ross*
Income Distribution in OECD Countries
Income of the Population 55 or Older 1994
Incomes and the Welfare State — *Atkinson, A B*
The Incompleat Angler — *Engler, Jim*
Incompressible Flow. 2nd Ed. — *Panton, Ronald L*
Inconspicuous Consumption — *Lukas, Paul*
Incorporating Images — *Peucker, Brigitte*
Incorporations — *Crary, Jonathan*
Increasing Patient Satisfaction — *Messner, Roberta L*
Increasingly Safe and Successful Pregnancies — *International Congress on Pathophysiology of Pregnancy (27th: 1995: Quezon City, Philippines)*
c Incredible Comparisons — *Ash, Russell*
c Incredible Creatures — *Craig, Claire*
c Incredible Earth — *Clifford, Nick*
c Incredible, Edible Science — *Seelig, Tina*
c Incredible Explosions (Illus. by Stephen Biesty) — *Platt, Richard*
c The Incredible Human Body (Illus. by Mic Rolph) — *Balkwill, Fran*
c An Incredible Journey (Illus. by Simon Smith) — *Sloan, Carolyn*
c The Incredible Journey to the Centre of the Atom. The Incredible Journey to the Edge of the Universe

Incredible Journeys — *Marven, Nigel*
y Incredible Journeys — *Wilkinson, Rick*
c Incredible People — *Drimmer, Frederick*
c Incredible Plants (Illus. by Susanna Addario) — *Dow, Lesley*
c Incredible Plants (Illus. by Geoff Brightling) — *Taylor, Barbara*
c Incredibly Creepy Stories (Illus. by P Dennis) — *Bradman, T*
Incriminations: Guilty Women/Telling Stories — *McPherson, Karen S*
The Incumbent — *Bush, Clifton H*
r Incunaboli E Cinquecentine Della Provincia Dei Cappuccini Di Messina — *Lipari, Giuseppe*
r Incunaboli E Cinquecentine In Romagna — *Baldacchini, Lorenzo*
Indagine Sul Satanismo — *Introvigne, Massimo*
The Indebted Society — *Medoff, James*
Indebtedness, Economic Reforms, and Poverty — *Sautter, Hermann*
Indentured Labor in the Age of Imperialism 1834-1922 — *Northrup, David*
Indentured to Liberty — *Taylor, Peter K*
Independence Day — *Ford, Richard*
y Independence Day — *Molstad, Stephen*
Independence in Latin America — *Graham, Richard*
Independence in Spanish America — *Kinsbruner, Jay*
Independence or Death! — *Vale, Brian*
p The Independent American Indian Review
Independent Iraq — *Elliot, Matthew*
Independent People — *Laxness, Halldor*
p Independent Review: A Journal of Political Economy
An Independent Scholar in Twentieth Century America — *Bornet, Vaughn Davis*
Independent Spirit — *Butler, Hubert*
Independent Spirits — *Trenton, Patricia*
r The Independent Study Catalog. 6th Ed.
r The Independent Walker's Guide to France — *Booth, Frank*
r The Independent Walker's Guide to Great Britain — *Booth, Frank*
An Independent Woman — *Fast, Howard*
The Indestructible Book — *Connolly, W Kenneth*
p Index
r The Index of Antimicrobials — *Ash, Michael*
r Index of Certificates of Naturalization from the Board of Elections Lucas County, Ohio
r An Index of Civilisation — *Harvey, Ross*
r Index of Death Notices Appearing in the Cincinnati Commercial 1858-1899 — *Herbert, Jeffery G*
r Index of Economic Freedom. 1997 Ed.
r The Index of Middle English Prose. Handlists 9-10
p Index on Censorship
r An Index to American Jewish Historical Quarterly/ American Jewish History: Volumes 51-80. Vols. 1-2 — *American Jewish Historical Society*
r Index to American Photographic Collections. 3rd Ed. — *Eskind, Andrew H*
r Index to International Public Opinion 1994-1995
r Index to Labor Articles 1926-
r Index to Labor Periodicals 1926-
r Index to Marriage Notices in the Religious Herald 1828-1938
r Index to Marriage Notices in the Southern Churchman 1835-1941
r Index to Obituary Notices in the Religious Herald 1828-1938
r Index to Pre-1900 English Language Canadian Cultural and Literary Magazines. Electronic Media Version — *Vincent, Thomas*
r An Index to Short and Feature Film Reviews in the Moving Picture World — *D'Agostino, Annette M*
r An Index to the Biblical References, Parallels, and Allusions in the Poetry and Prose of John Milton — *Rogal, Samuel J*
r Index to the History of Northwestern Ohio, History of Paulding County by Everett A. Budd, and Township and Personal Histories of Paulding County — *Workman, Marjean Holmes*
r Index to the Records of the Wally-Mills-Zimmerman Funeral Home, Elkhart, Indiana April 1912-October 1988 — *Skwiercz, Andrew L*
c India — *Allard, Denise*
c India — *Howard, Dale E*
India: Economic Development and Opportunity — *Dreze, Jean*
y India in the Islamic Era and Southeast Asia 8th to 19th Century (Illus. by Giorgio Bacchin) — *Dolcini, Donatella*
India: Macroeconomics and Political Economy 1964-1991 — *Joshi, Vijay*

c India: One Nation, Many Traditions — *Cifarelli, Megan*
India, Pakistan, and the Kashmir Dispute — *Wirsing, Robert G*
India: Recent Economic Developments and Prospects
India Unveiled — *Arnett, Robert*
Indian Air Mails — *Brown, Jeffrey*
Indian Ancestors? — *Young, Gloryann Hawkins*
The Indian Bill of Rights 1968 — *Wunder, John R*
Indian Communism — *Mallick, Ross*
Indian Depredation Claims 1796-1920 — *Skogen, Larry C*
The Indian Face of God in Latin America — *Marzal, Manuel M*
Indian Freedom — *Casas, Bartolome De Las*
An Indian Freedom Fighter Recalls Her Life — *Sahgal, Manmohini Zutshi*
The Indian in Spanish America. Vol. 1 — *Himelblau, Jack J*
The Indian in Spanish America. Vol. 2 — *Himelblau, Jack J*
y Indian Killer — *Alexie, Sherman*
y Indian Killer (Alexie). Audio Version — *Alexie, Sherman*
The Indian Ocean — *McPherson, Kenneth*
The Indian Papers of Texas and the Southwest 1825-1916. Vols. 1-5 — *Winfrey, Dorman H*
Indian Sahib — *Anand, Sushila*
c The Indian School (Illus. by Gabriela Dellosso) — *Whelan, Gloria*
Indian Stream Republic — *Doan, Daniel*
r Indian Subcontinent
Indian Telegraphs 1851-1914 — *Patel, Ilyas*
Indian Territory and the United States 1866-1906 — *Burton, Jeffrey*
c Indian Treaties — *Gold, Susan Dudley*
r Indiana's Dedicated Nature Preserves
Indians and Anthropologists — *Deloria, Vine, Jr.*
Indians and Indian Agents — *Phillips, George Harwood*
Indians at Hampton Institute 1877-1923 — *Lindsey, Donal F*
Indians, Franciscans, and Spanish Colonization — *Jackson, Robert H*
Indians into Mexicans — *Frye, David*
India's Agony over Religion — *Larson, Gerald James*
India's Economic Reforms 1991-2001 — *Joshi, Vijay*
India's Family Welfare Program — *Measham, Anthony R*
c India's Gupta Dynasty — *Hinds, Kathryn*
y The Indictment (Lane). Audio Version — *Reed, Barry*
Indigenous Capital and Imperial Expansion — *Subramanian, Lakshmi*
The Indigenous Dynamic in Taiwan's Postwar Development — *Skoggard, Ian A*
p Indigenous Knowledge and Development Monitor
r Indigenous Languages of the Americas — *Singerman, Robert*
Indigenous Literature of Oceania — *Goetzfridt, Nicholas J*
Indigenous Peoples and Democracy in Latin America — *Van Cott, Donna Lee*
r Indigenous Peoples in International Law — *Anaya, S James*
Indigenous Responses to Western Christianity — *Kaplan, Steven*
The Indigenous Voice in World Politics — *Wilmer, Franke*
c Indigo and the Whale (Illus. by Geoffrey Patterson) — *Dunbar, Joyce*
Indigo Days — *Trevelyan, Julian*
Indigo Slam — *Crais, Robert*
y Indigo — *Garland, Sherry*
Indiscreet — *Balogh, Mary*
Indiscrete Thoughts — *Rota, Gian-Carlo*
An Indiscretion in the Life of an Heiress and Other Stories — *Dalziel, Pamela*
Individual and Social Responsibility — *Fuchs, Victor R*
Individual Choice and the Structures of History — *Mitchell, Harvey*
Individual Voices, Collective Visions — *Goetting, Ann*
Individualism and Community — *Peters, Michael, 1948-*
Individualism and Economic Order — *Hayek, Friedrich A Von*
Individualized Dementia Care — *Rader, Joanne*
Individuation in Scholasticism — *Gracia, Jorge J E*
p Indochina Interchange
c Indonesia — *Arnott, Susi*
r Indonesia Handbook — *Eliot, Joshua*

Indonesia: The Political Economy of Energy — Barnes, Philip

The Indonesian Economy since 1966 — Hill, Hal

Indoor Air and Human Health. 2nd Ed. — Gammage, Richard B

Indoor Air Pollution and Health — Bardana, Emil J

Indoor Air Quality — Bas, Ed

Indoor Plants — Courtier, Jane

Induced Innovation Theory and International Agricultural Development — Koppel, Bruce M

The Indus Saga and the Making of Pakistan — Ahsan, Aitzaz

The Indus Valley Civilisation — Bennett, Gill

Industrial and Commercial Power Systems Handbook — Prabhakara, F S

Industrial and Trade Cooperation in Eastern and Southern Africa — Kisanga, Eliawony J

Industrial Applications of Microemulsions — Solans, Conxita

r Industrial Commodity Statistics Yearbook 1994

Industrial Concentration and Economic Inequality — Casson, Mark

Industrial Ecology and Global Change — Socolow, R

Industrial Electronics — Kissell, Thomas E

Industrial Energy Conservation — Gottschalk, Charles M

Industrial Environmental Management — Daugherty, Jack E

Industrial Intelligent Control — Lu, Yung-Tsai

Industrial Mobility and Public Policy — Landwehr, Ulrich

Industrial Organic Chemicals — Wittcoff, Harold A

Industrial Organization — Shy, Oz

The Industrial Organization and Regulation of the Securities Industry — Lo, Andrew W

Industrial Park — Galvao, Patricia

Industrial Policy in Britain — Coates, David

Industrial Policy, Technology, and International Bargaining — Solingen, Etel

Industrial Regions in Transformation — Schulze, Rainer

Industrial Relations under Liberal Democracy — Adams, Roy J

Industrial Restructuring — Mathieu, Nicolas

r Industrial Solvents Handbook — Archer, Wesley L

Industrial Strength C++ — Henricson, Mats

Industrial Subsidies and Friction in World Trade — Behboodi, Rambod

Industrialisierung: Begriffe and Prozesse — Benad-Wagenhoff, Volker

Industrializing America — Licht, Walter

Industrieller Maschinenbau Im 19. Jahrhundert — Benad-Wagenhoff, Volker

Industry as a Player in the Political and Social Arena — Mahon, John F

Industry, Business and Society in Scotland since 1700 — Cummings, A J G

Industry in the Countryside — Zell, Michael

Industry in the Landscape 1700-1900 — Palmer, Marilyn

Industry Structure, Strategy, and Public Policy — Scherer, Frederic M

Inequality and Old Age — Vincent, John A

Inequality by Design — Fischer, Claude S

Inequality: Radical Institutionalist Views on Race, Gender, Class, and Nation — Dugger, William M

Inequality Reexamined — Sen, Amartya Kumar

Inescapable Decisions — Mechanic, David

Inevitable Illusions — Piattelli-Palmarini, Massimo

Infamous — Collins, Joan

The Infamous Boundary — Wick, David

Infant, Child, and Maternal Mortality Study in Ghana — Twum-Baah, K A

Infant Tongues — Goodenough, Elizabeth

Infanta — Belieu, Erin

Infants and Hearing — Hayes, Deborah

r Infection Control in the Child Care Center and Preschool. 3rd Ed. — Donowitz, Leigh G

Infectious Disease — Bannister, Barbara A

Infectious Disease — United States. National Science and Technology Council. Working Group on Emerging and Re-Emerging Infectious Diseases

The Infernal Diver — Bevan, John

The Infernal Machine — Hannant, Larry

Inferno III — Simonelli, Maria Picchio

The Inferno of Dante (Pinsky) — Dante Alighieri

Infidelities — Paschen, Elise

c Infield Hit — Dygard, Thomas J

Infinite-Dimensional Lie Groups — Omori, Hideki

Infinite Element Methods — Ying, Lung-An

Infinite in All Directions — Dyson, Freeman

Infinite Jest — Wallace, David Foster

Infinite Potential — Peat, F David

The Infinite Sea — Carver, Jeffrey A

Infinity Walk — Sunbeck, Deborah

Infinity's Child — Stein, Harry

Infinity's Shore — Brin, David

Inflatable Kayaking — Kuhne, Cecil

Inflation and Investment Controls in China — Huang, Yasheng

Inflation and Unemployment — Cencini, Alvaro

Inflation, Growth and Monetary Control — Bruno, Michael

Inflation Targets — Leiderman, Leonardo

The Inflationary Universe — Guth, Alan

Influence and Resistance in Nineteenth-Century English Poetry — Blank, G Kim

The Influence of Race and Racial Identity in Psychotherapy — Carter, Robert T

The Influencing Engine — Hayden, Richard

y Influencing Your World — St. Clair, Barry

The Influentials: People Who Influence People — Weimann, Gabriel

r Info New York. Electronic Media Version

Info-Rich--Info-Poor — Haywood, Trevor

yr Infopedia. Electronic Media Version

Informal Empire in Crisis — Atkins, Martyn

The Informal Sector and Microfinance Institutions in West Africa — Webster, Leila

The Informant — Grippando, James

The Informant (Naughton). Audio Version — Grippando, James

Informatica Y Humanidades — Marcos Marin, Francisco

r The Informatics Handbook — Fist, Stewart

The Information — Amis, Martin

Information Access and Delivery in Health Sciences Libraries — Lipscomb, Carolyn E

Information and Book Learning — Meek, Margaret

Information and Business Performance — Owens, Ian

Information and Frontiers — Lee, A D

Information and Measurement — Lesurf, J C G

Information and On-Line Data in Astronomy — Egret, Daniel

Information Architects — Graphis Press Corp.

Information Brokers — Johnson, Alice Jane Holland

Information Disclosure of the State-Related Universities

Information for Foreigners — Gambaro, Griselda

Information for Scotland II — MacKillop, Peigi

r Information Graphics — Harris, Robert L

r Information Please Almanac, Atlas, and Yearbook 1996

Information Retrieval and Hypertext — Agosti, Maristella

Information Revolution — Special Libraries Association. Conference (87th: 1996: Boston, Mass.)

Information Seeking — Johnson, J David

Information Seeking in Electronic Environments — Marchionini, Gary

Information Services for Innovative Organizations — Maguire, Carmel

Information Services for People with Developmental Disabilities — Walling, Linda Lucas

r Information Sources 1997

r Information Sources in Architecture and Construction. 2nd Ed. — Nurcombe, Valerie J

r Information Sources in Engineering. 3rd Ed. — Mildren, K W

r Information Sources in Environmental Protection — Eagle, Selwyn

r Information Sources in Finance and Banking — Lester, Ray

Information Space — Boisot, Max H

Information Superhighway

The Information Superhighway — Cameli, A P

y The Information Superhighway — Gay, Martin, 1950-

The Information Superhighway and Private Households — Brenner, Walter

Information Superhighways Revisited — Egan, Bruce L

Information System Development and Data Modeling — Hirschheim, Rudy

Information Tasks — Allen, Bryce L

Information Technologies and Social Orders — Couch, Carl J

Information Technologies for the Control of Money Laundering

Information Technology and Society — Heap, Nick

Information Technology as Business History — Cortada, James W

Information Technology for Development — United Nations Conference on Trade and Development

Information Technology for Parents — Russell, Adrian

Information Technology in the Hospitality Industry — Peacock, Martin

Information Technology Outsourcing Transactions — Halvey, John K

Informed Decisions — Murphy, Gerald P

The Informed Librarian

Informer 001 — Druzhnikov, Yuri

Informing Young Women — Farmer, Lesley S J

INFORMIX Performance Tuning. 2nd Ed. — Suto, Elizabeth

Infrared Detectors and Systems — Dereniak, Eustace L

An Infrastructure Initiative for Latin America and the Caribbean

Inge King: Sculptor — Trimble, Judith

y The Ingenious Mr. Peale — Wilson, Janet

Ingenious Pain — Miller, Andrew, 1961-

c Inger's Promise (Illus. by Andra Chase) — Parkison, Jami

Ingmar Bergman: The Art of Confession — Cohen, Hubert I

c The Ingredients of Music — Sharma, Elizabeth

Inhabiting Unity — Radner, Ephraim

y Inhalants — Weatherly, Myra

Inhalation Aerosols — Hickey, Anthony J

Inhaled Glucocorticoids in Asthma — Schleimer, Robert P

r Inherit the Alamo — Brear, Holly Beachley

y The Inheritance — Alcott, Louisa May

The Inheritance. Audio Version — Alcott, Louisa May

The Inheritance: How Three Families and America Moved from Roosevelt to Reagan and Beyond — Freedman, Samuel G

Inheritance in Public Policy — Rose, Richard

Inheritance of Light — Gonzalez, Ray

Inherited Rivalry — Cheng, Tun-Jen

Inherited Skin Disorders — Harper, John

y Inheritor — Cherryh, C J

The Inhuman Condition — Tester, Keith

The Inhuman Condition (Steele). Audio Version — Barker, Clive

The Inhuman Race — Cassuto, Leonard

Initial — Spangle, Douglas

Initial Teacher Training — Wilkin, Margaret

Injection in Pyrometallurgy — Howard Worner International Symposium on Injection in Pyrometallurgy (1996: Melbourne, Australia)

Injured Honor — Tucker, Spencer C

r Injury Prevention for Young Children — Walker, Bonnie L

Ink, Paper, Metal, Wood — Brown, Kathan

Ink Plum — Bickford, Maggie

c Inktomi and the Ducks and Other Assiniboin Trickster Stories (Evans). Audio Version — Evans, Ron

The Inn at Little Washington Cookbook — O'Connell, Patrick

r Inn Places. 9th Ed.

Inner Circle — McNab, Claire

y The Inner City Mother Goose (Illus. by David Diaz) — Merriam, Eve

The Inner Elvis — Whitmer, Peter

The Inner Jefferson — Burstein, Andrew

The Inner Life — Inayat Khan

The Inner Quarters — Ebrey, Patricia Buckley

The Inner Sanctum — Frey, Stephen W

The Inner Voice of Love — Nouwen, Henri J M

The Inner World of Abraham Lincoln — Burlingame, Michael

Der Innere Mensch — Heckel, Theo K

Innocence — Forster, Suzanne

Innocence Lost — Gowans, Christopher

The Innocence of Roast Chicken — Richards, Jo-Anne

Innocence, Power, and the Novels of John Hawkes — Ferrari, Rita

Innocence Undone — Martin, Kat

Innocent III: Studies on Papal Authority and Pastoral Care — Bolton, Brenda

y Innocent Blood — Dickey, Christopher

y Innocent Graves — Robinson, Peter, 1950-

An Innocent in Ireland — McFadden, David W

Innovating in Community Mental Health — Schulz, Rockwell

Innovation and Industry Evolution — Audretsch, David B

Innovation in Polymer Processing — Stevenson, James F

Innovation in Professional Education — *Boyatzis, Richard E*

Innovation in Technology, Industries, and Institutions — *Shionoya, Yuichi*

Innovation: Leadership Strategies for the Competitive Edge — *Kuczmarski, Thomas D*

Innovation Systems and Competitiveness — *Kuusi, Osmo*

The Innovation War — *Braun, Christoph-Friedrich Von*

An Innovative Economic Incentive Model for Improvement of the Working Environment in Europe — *Bailey, Stephen*

Innovative Reward Systems for the Changing Workplace — *Wilson, Thomas B*

The Innovators: The Engineering Pioneers Who Made America Modern — *Billington, David P*

yr An Inordinate Fondness for Beetles — *Evans, Arthur V*

Inorganic Matrix Composites — *Surappa, M K*

Inorganic Membranes for Separation and Reaction — *Hsieh, H P*

Inorganic Syntheses. Vol. 30

Input/Output in Parallel and Distributed Computer Systems — *Jain, Ravi*

Inquiry into Life. 8th Ed. — *Mader, Sylvia S*

p Inquisitor

L'Inquisizione E Gli Ebrei In Italia — *Luzzati, Michele*

Insanity as Redemption in Contemporary Fiction — *Lupack, Barbara T*

The Insanity of Normality — *Gruen, Arno*

Insatiability — *Witkiewicz, Stanislaw Ignacy*

r Inscribing the Daily — *Bunkers, Suzanne L*

Inscribing the Time — *Mallin, Eric S*

c The Insect Book — *Zakowski, Connie*

Insect Cell Culture — *Vlak, J M*

c Insect-Eating Plants — *Kite, L Patricia*

c Insects (Illus. by Barrie Watts) — *Bryant-Mole, Karen*

c Insects Are My Life (Illus. by Paul Brett Johnson) — *McDonald, Megan*

Insects through the Seasons — *Waldbauer, Gilbert*

Insecure Prosperity — *Morawska, Ewa*

L'Insecurite Linguistique Dans Les Communautes Francophones Peripheriques — *Francard, Michel*

Inside Agitators — *Eisenstein, Hester*

Inside American Philanthropy — *Nielsen, Waldemar A*

Inside an American Concentration Camp — *Nishimoto, Richard S*

Inside Architecture — *Gregotti, Vittorio*

Inside Architecture — *Zevon, Susan*

Inside ArcView — *Hutchinson, Scott*

Inside AutoCAD LT for Windows 95 — *Beall, Michael E*

Inside CIA's Private World — *Westerfield, H Bradford*

c Inside Collectible Card Games — *Owens, Thomas S*

Inside Daisy Clover — *Lambert, Gavin*

Inside Early Music — *Sherman, Bernard D*

Inside Edge — *Brennan, Christine*

Inside Hanoi's Secret Archives — *McConnell, Malcolm*

Inside Information — *Ewing, William A*

Inside Life — *Gorman, Greg*

Inside Managed Care — *Aronson, Jodi*

Inside Mexico — *Heusinkveld, Paula*

y Inside Ms. — *Thom, Mary*

The Inside of History — *Roney, John B*

Inside OrCAD — *Schroeder, Christopher F*

Inside Out — *Bernstein, Walter*

c Inside-Out Grandma — *Rothenberg, Joan*

c The Inside-Outside Book of Libraries (Illus. by Roxie Munro) — *Munro, Roxie*

r Inside Science Plus. Electronic Media Version

r Inside Sports World Series Factbook — *Cantor, George*

Inside Star Trek — *Solow, Herbert F*

Inside Star Trek (Solow). Audio Version — *Solow, Herbert F*

Inside Tap — *Feldman, Anita*

Inside the Arab World — *Field, Michael, 1949-*

Inside the Bestsellers — *Jenkins, Jerrold R*

Inside the Blue Berets — *Zaloga, Steven J*

Inside the Boardroom — *Bowen, William G*

yr Inside the Body (Illus. by Giuliano Fornari) — *Ganeri, Anita*

c Inside the Body — *Morgan, Sally*

Inside the Brain — *Kotulak, Ronald*

Inside the Concentration Camps — *Aroneanu, Eugene*

Inside the Drama-House — *Blackburn, Stuart*

Inside the Kaisha — *Yoshimura, Noboru*

Inside the Kremlin's Cold War — *Zubok, Vladislav*

Inside the Magic Kingdom — *Connellan, Tom*

Inside the Mouse — *Project on Disney*

y Inside the Privet Hedge — *Coyle, Neva*

Inside the Vatican — *Reese, Thomas J*

Inside the Visible — *Zegher, M Catherine De*

y Inside the Walls of Troy — *McLaren, Clemence*

Inside the War Cabinet — *Horner, David*

Inside the Wigwam — *Sautter, R Craig*

Inside the Writing Portfolio — *Jenkins, Carol Brennan*

Inside U.S.A.: 50th Anniversary Edition — *Gunther, John*

yp InsideOUT

Insider Lending — *Lamoreaux, Naomi R*

Insiders and Outsiders — *Waldren, Jacqueline*

The Insider's Guide to Buying a New or Used Car — *Leon, Burke*

r The Insiders' Guide to Greater Denver. 2nd Ed. — *Caruso, Laura*

The Insiders' Guide to Relocation — *Roman, Beverly*

Insidious Foes — *MacDonnell, Francis*

Insight and Responsibility — *Erikson, Erik H*

r Insight Compact Guides Dominican Republic — *Latzel, Monika*

The Insightful Sportsman — *Williams, Ted*

Insights into Teaching Mathematics — *Orton, Anthony*

Insights of Genius — *Miller, Arthur I*

r INSPEC List of Journals and Other Serial Sources 1996/7

Inspecting Schools — *Wilcox, Brian*

Inspecting Special Needs Provision in Schools — *Landy, Maria*

Inspection of Large Synchronous Machines — *Kerszenbaum, Isidor*

p Inspector

Inspector Ali — *Chraibi, Driss*

The Inspired Executive — *Toogood, Granville N*

Inspiring Commitment — *Mendes, Anthony*

Inspiring Reform

Instabilities and Nonequilibrium Structures V

Installation Art — *De Oliveira, Nicolas*

Instant Calm — *Wilson, Paul, 1949-*

The Instant Enemy — *Macdonald, Ross*

Instant HTML Web Page — *Ause, Wayne*

Instant Java — *Pew, John A*

Instant Java. 2nd Ed. — *Pew, John A*

Instant JavaScript — *Holman, Brian*

r Instat: International Statistics Sources. Vols. 1-2 — *Fleming, M C*

Instead of Full Stops — *Sellers, Susan*

The Institute of the Sisters of Mercy of the Americas — *Darcy, Catherine C*

Institution Arithmetique (Guillaumin) — *Boethius*

Institutional Analysis of Development Administration — *Foerster, Andreas*

Institutional and Entrepreneurial Leadership in the Brazilian Science and Technology Sector — *Holm-Nielsen, Lauritz*

The Institutional Economics of the International Economy — *Adams, John, 1938-*

Institutional Frameworks and Labor Market Performance — *Buttler, Friedrich*

Institutional Investors and Corporate Governance — *Brancato, Carolyn Kay*

Institutional Patronage in Post-Tridentine Rome — *O'Regan, Noel*

Institutional Shareholders and Corporate Governance — *Stapleton, G P*

Institutionen--Literarische Feindbilder? — *Banziger, Hans*

Institutions and Development Strategies — *Adelman, Irma*

Institutions and Organizations — *Scott, W Richard*

Institutions for Environmental Aid — *Keohane, Robert O*

Institutions, Inflation and Unemployment — *Amadeo, Edward J*

Instruction and the Learning Environment — *Keefe, James W*

Instructional Course Lectures. Vol. 44

Instructional Designs for Middle/Junior High School Band. Vols. 1-2 — *Garofalo, Robert Joseph*

Instructional Literature for Middle Level Band — *Kvet, Edward J*

Instructional Strategies for Secondary School Physical Education. 4th Ed. — *Harrison, Joyce*

r Instructions for Veterinary Clients. 3rd Ed. — *Erlewein, David L*

The Instructions of Gampopa — *Khenpo Karthar Rinpoche*

Instructions to the Cook. Audio Version — *Glassman, Bernard*

The Instructor — *Ireland, Ann*

Instruments and the Imagination — *Hankins, Thomas L*

Instruments of Darkness — *Sharpe, James*

The Insult — *Thompson, Rupert*

r Insurance Directory

Insurgency and Social Disorder in Guizhou — *Jenks, Robert D*

Insurgent Identities — *Gould, Roger V*

Insurrection and Revolution — *Perez, Gladys E Garcia*

Intalniri Cu Oameni, Intalniri Cu Viata — *Zamfirescu, Ion*

Integer-Valued Polynomials — *Cahen, Paul-Jean*

Integral Equations with Difference Kernels on Finite Intervals — *Sakhnovich, Lev A*

Integral Transformations, Operational Calculus, and Generalized Functions — *Buschman, R G*

The Integral Trees (Bottino). Audio Version — *Niven, Larry*

Integrated Active Antennas and Spatial Power Combining — *Navarro, Julio A*

Integrated Circuit Engineering — *Herbst, L J*

Integrated Colposcopy. 2nd Ed. — *Anderson, M C*

Integrated Distributed Intelligent Systems for Engineering Design — *Rao, Ming*

Integrated Health Care Delivery — *Brown, Montague*

Integrated Mental Health Care — *Falloon, Ian R H*

Integrated Mental Health Services — *Breakey, William R*

Integrated Principles of Zoology. 10th Ed. — *Hickman, Cleveland P*

Integrated Psychological Therapy for Schizophrenic Patients (IPT) — *Brenner, Hans D*

Integrating Children's Literature and Mathematics in the Classroom — *Schiro, Michael*

Integrating Computers into the Classroom — *O'Donnell, Edith*

Integrating Gender — *Hoskyns, Catherine*

Integrating QS-9000 with Your Automotive Quality System. 2nd Ed. — *Stamatis, D H*

Integrating Socially — *Hamston, Julie*

Integrating Southern Europe — *Holman, Otto*

Integrating the Americas — *Weintraub, Sidney*

Integrating Total Quality Management in a Library Setting — *Jurow, Susan*

Integrating UNIX and PC Network Operating Systems — *Lund, William*

Integration Algorithms and Classical Mechanics — *Marsden, Jerrold E*

Integration and Stabilization — *Macesich, George*

Integration of Health Care Delivery — *World Health Organization*

The Integration of the European Economy 1850-1913 — *Craig, Lee A*

The Integration of the World Economy 1850-1914. Vols. 1-2 — *Harley, C Knick*

Integration or Separation? — *Brooks, Roy L*

Integrative Approaches to Molecular Biology — *Collado-Vides, Julio*

Integrative Problem-Centered Therapy — *Pinsof, William M*

Integrative Treatment of Anxiety Disorders — *Ellison, James M*

y Integrity — *Carter, Stephen L*

Integrity of Structures and Fluid Systems, Hazardous Release Protection, Piping and Pipe Supports, and Pumps and Valves

Intellectual Capital — *Brooking, Annie*

Intellectual Capital — *Edvinsson, Leif*

Intellectual Capital — *Stewart, Thomas A*

r Intellectual Freedom Manual. 5th Ed. — *American Library Association. Office for Intellectual Freedom*

An Intellectual History of Liberalism — *Manent, Pierre*

The Intellectual Legacy of Thorstein Veblen — *Tilman, Rick*

Intellectual Odyssey — *Chamberlain, Neil W*

Intellectual Origins of Islamic Resurgence in the Modern Arab World — *Abu-Rabi, Ibrahim M*

Intellectual Property and the National Information Infrastructure — *United States. Information Infrastructure Task Force. Working Group on Intellectual Property Rights*

Intellectuals and Public Life — *Fink, Leon*

Intellectuals, Socialism, and Dissent — *Torpey, John C*

Un Intellectuel Avant La Lettre — *Bost, Hubert*

Intelligence — *Goldberg, Marshall*

Intelligence and Espionage in the Reign of Charles II 1660-1685 — *Marshall, Alan*

Intelligence De L'Anticommunisme — *Gremion, Pierre*

Intelligence Intervention in the Politics of Democratic States — *Bar-Joseph, Uri*

Intelligence Power in Peace and War — *Herman, Michael*

Intelligent Business Alliances — *Segil, Larraine D*

Intelligent Information Systems — *Rowe, Alan J*

Intelligent Integration of Information — *Wiederhold, Gio*

An Intelligent Person's Guide to Philosophy — *Scruton, Roger*

Les Intendants De Louis XIV — *Smedley-Weill, Anette*

Intending Death — *Beauchamp, Tom L*

Intensely Family — *Holly, Carol*

Intensity — *Koontz, Dean*

Intensive Care — *Mann, Thomas E*

The Intentional Family — *Doherty, William J*

Intentions and Capabilities — *Steury, Donald P*

The Inter-Relationship between Irrigation, Drainage, and the Environment in the Aral Sea Basin — *Bos, M G*

Interaction and Identity — *Mokros, Hartmut B*

Interaction between Functional Analysis, Harmonic Analysis, and Probability — *Kalton, Nigel*

Interactions between Sediments and Water — *International Symposium on Interactions between Sediments and Water (6th: 1993: Santa Barbara, Calif.)*

Interactions in Political Economy — *Pressman, Steven*

Interactions of Desertification and Climate — *Williams, Martin A J*

Interactions of Thought and Language in Old English Poetry — *Clemoes, Peter*

p Interactive

Interactive Ambulatory Medicine. Electronic Media Version — *Barker, L Randol*

Interactive Computer Animation — *Magnenat-Thalmann, Nadia*

Interactive Marketing — *Forest, Edward*

Interactive Marketing — *Molenaar, Cor*

Interactive Minds — *Baltes, Paul B*

r The Interactive Multimedia Sourcebook 1997

yr Interactive Periodic Table. Electronic Media Version

r Interactive Skeleton. Electronic Media Version

Interactive Technologies and the Social Studies — *Martorella, Peter H*

p InterActivity

Interception — *Watkins, Graham*

p Interconnect: For Grassroots Movement-Building and Sharing of Resources within the US-Latin America Solidarity Community

The Interconnected Universe — *Laszlo, Ervin*

Intercultural Communication at Work — *Clyne, Michael*

Intercultural Contacts in the Medieval Mediterranean — *Arbel, Benjamin*

The Intercultural Performance Reader — *Pavis, Patrice*

Interdiction in Southern Laos 1960-1968 — *Van Staaveren, Jacob*

r Interdisciplinary Undergraduate Programs. 2nd Ed. — *Edwards, Alan F*

Interest-Free Commercial Banking — *Gafoor, A L M Abdul*

Interest Groups and Education Reform — *DiConti, Veronica Donahue*

Interest Rate Dynamics, Derivatives Pricing, and Risk Management — *Chen, Lin*

Interested Parties — *Clines, David J A*

Interesting Times — *Pratchett, Terry*

r Interethnic Conflict and Political Change in the Former USSR — *Aklaey, Airat*

Interface Masque — *Lewitt, Shariann*

The Interface of Knots and Physics — *Kauffman, Louis H*

Interfaces in Crystalline Materials — *Sutton, Adrian P*

Interfacial Phenomena and Bioproducts — *Brash, John L*

Interfacial Tensiometry — *Rusanov, A I*

Interfaith Wedding Ceremonies — *Hawxhurst, Joan C*

Intergalactic Mercenaries — *Williams, Sheila*

Interieur — *Brakman, Willem*

Interior Design — *Graham, Philip, 1951-*

Interior Point Methods of Mathematical Programming — *Terlaky, Tamas*

r Interiors Management — *Smith, Maggie*

Interlibrary Loan Practices Handbook. 2nd Ed. — *Boucher, Virginia*

The Interloper — *Maharaj, Rabrindranath*

Intermediate Classical Dynamics with Applications to Beam Physics — *Michelotti, Leo*

Intermediate Sanctions for Women Offenders — *Intermediate Sanctions for Female Offenders Policy Group (Or.)*

Internal Conflicts in South Asia — *Rupesinghe, Kumar*

Internal Family Systems Therapy — *Schwartz, Richard C*

Internal Marketing — *Cahill, Dennis J*

International Accounting — *Nobes, Christopher*

r International Accounting, Financial Reporting, and Analysis — *Afterman, Allan B*

An International Accounting Practice Set — *Peterson, David R*

International Action against Racial Discrimination — *Banton, Michael*

The International Adoption Handbook — *Alperson, Myra*

International Approaches to Prevention in Mental Health and Human Services — *Hess, Robert E*

International Aspects of Irish Literature — *Furomoto, Toshi*

The International Avant-Garde 1905-1924 — *Read, Peter*

r International Bibliography of Business History — *Goodall, Francis*

r International Bibliography of Theatre 1992-1993

r International Biographical Directory of National Archivists, Documentalists, and Librarians — *Carroll, Frances L*

International Broadcasting Convention 1995

International Business and Europe in Transition — *Burton, Fred*

International Business Education Development — *Ahmed, Zafar U*

International Business Teaching — *Kaynak, Erdener*

International Capital Markets and American Economic Growth 1820-1914 — *Davis, Lance E*

International Colloquium Celebrating the 500th Anniversary of the Birth of Marguerite De Navarre — *Reynolds-Cornell, Regine*

International Commodity Prices, Macroeconomic Performance, and Politics in Sub-Saharan Africa — *Deaton, Angus S*

r International Companion Encyclopedia of Children's Literature — *Hunt, Peter*

International Comparisons of Electricity Regulation — *Gilbert, Richard J*

International Competitiveness and the Balance of Payments — *Dluhosch, Barbara*

The International Computer Software Industry — *Mowery, David C*

International Conference on Intelligent Systems in Process Engineering — *International Conference on Intelligent Systems in Process Engineering (1st: 1995: Snowmass, Colo.)*

International Cooperation on Competition Policy — *Australia Productivity Commission*

International Cultural Differences — *Redding, Gordon*

International Debt. Vols. 1-2 — *Bird, Graham*

International Debt Reexamined — *Cline, William R*

r International Dictionary of Historic Places. Vols. 4-5 — *Ring, Trudy*

r The International Dictionary of Psychology. 2nd Ed. — *Sutherland, Stuart*

r International Dictionary of Theatre. Vol. 3

The International Dimensions of Democratization — *Whitehead, Laurence*

The International Dimensions of Internal Conflict — *Brown, Michael E*

r The International Directory of Business Information Sources and Services 1996

r International Directory of Company Histories. Vols. 12-14

r International Directory of Educational Audiovisuals. Electronic Media Version

r The International Directory of Government. 2nd Ed.

International Economic Integration — *Lang, Franz Peter*

r The International Education Quotations Encyclopaedia — *Noble, Keith Allan*

r The International Encyclopaedic Dictionary of Numismatics — *Carlton, R Scott*

r International Encyclopedia of Adult Education and Training. 2nd Ed. — *Tuijnman, Albert C*

r International Encyclopedia of Business and Management. Vols. 1-6 — *Warner, Malcolm*

r International Encyclopedia of Horse Breeds — *Hendricks, Bonnie L*

r International Encyclopedia of Information and Library Science — *Feather, John*

r International Encyclopedia of Teaching and Teacher Education. 2nd Ed. — *Anderson, Lorin W*

r International Encyclopedia of Violin-Keyboard Sonatas and Composer Biographies. 2nd Ed. — *Pedigo, Alan*

p The International Executive

r International Financial Aggregates — *Ricerche E Studi*

International Financial Integration — *Marston, Richard C*

r The International Foundation Directory 1996

r International GIS Sourcebook 1994

International Handbook of Juvenile Justice — *Shoemaker, Donald Joseph*

International Handbook of Public Health — *Hurrelmann, Klaus*

International Handbook on Alcohol and Culture — *Heath, Dwight B*

r International Handbook on Social Work Education — *Watts, Thomas D*

International Harmonization of Accounting — *Nobes, Christopher*

International Human Rights in Context — *Steiner, Henry J*

International Human Rights Norms in the Nordic and Baltic Countries — *Scheinin, Martin*

r International Index to Music Periodicals. Electronic Media Version

r International Jobs. 4th Ed. — *Kocher, Eric*

International Joint Ventures — *Chatterjee, Kalyan*

p International Journal of Electronic Commerce

p International Journal of Forensic Document Examiners

p International Journal of Polymer Analysis and Characterization

The International Labor Organization — *Bartolomei De La Cruz, Hector G*

International Law and Ocean Use Management — *Juda, Lawrence*

International Law Decisions in National Courts — *Franck, Thomas M*

r The International Legalization Handbook

International Litigation and the Quest for Reasonableness — *Lowenfeld, Andreas F*

International Migration — *Macura, Miroslav*

International Migration and Security — *Weiner, Myron*

International Migration Policies and the Status of Female Migrants — *United Nations. Expert Group Meeting on International Migration Policies and the Status of Female Migrants (1990: San Miniato, Italy)*

International Monetary Economics — *McCallum, Bennett T*

The International Monetary System — *Kenen, Peter B*

International Monetary Systems in Historical Perspective — *Reis, Jaime*

r International Motion Picture Almanac 1996

International News and Foreign Correspondents — *Hess, Stephen*

International Offshore Engineering — *International Symposium on Offshore Engineering (9th: 1995: COPPE)*

International Organizations and Ethnic Conflict — *Esman, Milton J*

International Parallel Processing Symposium — *International Parallel Processing Symposium (10th: 1996: Honolulu, HI)*

International Peacekeeping and Peace Enforcement — *United States. Congress. Senate. Committee on Armed Services. Subcommittee on Coalition Defense and Reinforcing Forces*

International Perspectives on Child Abuse and Children's Testimony — *Bottoms, Bette L*

International Perspectives on Community Care for Older People — *Scharf, Thomas*

International Perspectives on the Yugoslav Conflict — *Danchev, Alex*

International Pipeline Conference 1996. Vols. 1-2 — *International Pipeline Conference (IPC'96) (1st: 1996: Calgary, Alberta, Canada)*

p International Policy Review

International Political Economy — *Cox, Robert W*

The International Political Economy and International Institutions. Vols. 1-2 — *Young, Oran R*

The International Politics of East Central Europe — *Hyde-Price, Adrian*

The International Politics of Russia and the Successor States — *Webber, Mark*

International Practice of Anaesthesia. Vol. 1 — *Prys-Roberts, Cedric*

International Problems of Economic Interdependence — *Baldassarri, Mario*

International Productivity Differences — *Wagner, Karin*

r International Relations. 5th Ed. — *Ziring, Lawrence*

y International Relations 1914-1995 — *Rea, Tony*

r International Relations Research Directory. 1st Ed.

International Responses to Traumatic Stress — *Danieli, Yael*

International Rights and Responsibilities for the Future — *Hunter, Kenneth W*

r International Stamp Dealers' Directory 1996

yr An International Student's Guide to Mexican Universities — *Adelman, Alan*

The International Style — *Hitchcock, Henry-Russell*

The International System Between New Integration and Neo-Protectionism — *Baldassarri, Mario*

r International Television and Video Almanac 1996

International Textile Design — *Schoeser, Mary*

r International Thesaurus of Refugee Terminology. 2nd Ed. — *Aitchison, Jean*

International Trade — *Landeck, Michael*

International Trade. Vols. 1-2 — *Neary, J Peter*

International Trade in Goods and Factor Mobility — *Wong, Kar-Yiu*

r International Trade Statistics Yearbook 1994. Vols. 1-2

International User Interfaces — *Del Galdo, Elisa M*

r The International Who's Who 1996-97

r International Who's Who in Music and Musician's Directory. Vol. 1, 15th Ed.; Vol. 2, 1st Ed.

r International Who's Who in Music and Musician's Directory. Vol. 2, 1st Ed.

International Workshop on Multi-Media Database Management Systems: Proceedings, August 14-16, 1996, Blue Mountain Lake, N.Y.

r International Yearbook of Industrial Statistics 1996

Internationales Cajkovskij-Symposium, Teubingen 1993 — *Kohlhase, Thomas*

Internationalism and Its Betrayal — *Ishay, Micheline R*

Internationalization and Domestic Politics — *Keohane, Robert O*

The Internationalization of Colonialism — *Kent, John*

y The Internet — *Cooper, Brian*

The Internet: A Guide for Chemists — *Bachrach, Stephen M*

The Internet and Instruction — *Barron, Ann E*

r The Internet and Library and Information Services — *Liu, Lewis-Guodo*

The Internet and the World Wide Web — *Kressin, Mark*

Internet Clear and Simple — *McBride, Peter*

r The Internet Compendium: Subject Guides to Health and Science Resources — *Rosenfeld, Louis*

r The Internet Compendium: Subject Guides to Humanities Resources — *Rosenfeld, Louis*

r The Internet Compendium: Subject Guides to Social Sciences, Business and Law Resources — *Rosenfeld, Louis*

Internet Digital Libraries — *Kessler, Jack*

Internet Dreams — *Stefik, Mark*

The Internet for Busy People. 1st Ed. — *Crumlish, Christian*

The Internet for Busy People. 2nd Ed. — *Crumlish, Christian*

Internet for Library Media Specialists — *Simpson, Carol Mann*

The Internet for Scientists and Engineers. 1996 Ed. — *Thomas, Brian J*

The Internet for Teachers and School Library Media Specialists — *Valauskas, Edward J*

The Internet for Windows 95 Made Simple — *McBride, Peter*

The Internet for Women — *Senjen, Rye*

Internet Graphics Toolkit — *Rimmer, Steve*

The Internet Initiative — *Valauskas, Edward J*

c The Internet Kids Yellow Pages. Special Ed. — *Polly, Jean Armour*

cr The Internet Kids Yellow Pages. Special Ed. — *Polly, Jean*

p Internet Life

Internet Made Easy — *Sluman, Roelf*

Internet Protocols — *Stallings, William*

p Internet Reference Services Quarterly

yr The Internet Research Guide — *Maloy, Timothy K*

r The Internet Resource Directory for K-12 Teachers and Librarians. 96/97 Ed.

The Internet Roadmap for Educators — *Wilson, Elizabeth*

The Internet Scares Me — *Boyd, John*

r Internet Science, Research and Technology Yellow Pages. Special Ed. — *Stout, Rick*

The Internet Searcher's Handbook — *Morville, Peter*

Internet Security for Business — *Bernstein, Terry*

y Internet Spy — *Probert, Ian*

The Internet Telephone Toolkit — *Pulver, Jeff*

r The Internet University — *Corrigan, Dan*

r The Internet Unleashed 1996

r The Internet Yellow Pages. 3rd Ed. — *Hahn, Harley*

Internetwork Mobility — *Taylor, Mark S*

Internetworking with TCP/IP. 2nd Ed., Vol. 3 — *Comer, Douglas E*

Interpersonal Diagnosis and Treatment of Personality Disorders. 2nd Ed. — *Benjamin, Lorna Smith*

Interplanetary Magnetohydrodynamics — *Burlaga, Leonard F*

Interplay: A Kind of Commonplace Book — *Enright, D J*

La Interpretacion Abierta — *Valdes, Mario J*

Interpretation and the Language of Translation — *Sheikh Al-Shabab, Omar*

Interpretation of Breast Biopsies. 3rd Ed. — *Carter, Darryl*

Interpretation of Geophysical Fields in Complicated Environments — *Khesin, Boris E*

The Interpretation of Quantum Mechanics — *Schrodinger, Erwin*

The Interpretations of Art — *Bornedal, Peter*

Interpretations of Humanism — *Puleda, Salvatore*

y The Interpreter: A Story of Two Worlds — *Moss, Robert*

Interpreting American Democracy in France — *Gray, Walter D*

Interpreting Arnauld — *Kremer, Elmar J*

Interpreting Astronomical Spectra — *Emerson, D*

Interpreting Early America — *Greene, Jack P*

Interpreting Environments — *Mugerauer, Robert*

Interpreting God and the Postmodern Self — *Thiselton, Anthony C*

Interpreting Goethe's Faust Today — *Brown, Jane K, 1943-*

Interpreting Interpretation — *Rogers, William Elford*

Interpreting Islam — *Sonn, Tamara*

Interpreting Ladies — *Gill, Pat*

Interpreting Legend — *Tangherlini, Timothy R*

Interpreting Nature — *Larson, James L*

Interpreting Objects and Collections — *Pearce, Susan M*

Interpreting Otherwise than Heidegger — *Manning, Robert John Sheffler*

Interpreting Qualitative Data — *Silverman, David*

Interpreting the Book of Acts — *Liefeld, Walter L*

Interpreting the New National Curriculum — *Andrews, Richard*

Interprocess Communications in UNIX — *Gray, John Shapley*

y Interracial America — *Szumski, Bonnie*

Interrelationships of Fishes — *Stiassny, Melanie L J*

An Interrupted Life. Letters from Westerbork — *Hillesum, Etty*

The Intersection of Cultures — *Spring, Joel*

The Intersection of Law and Desire — *Redmann, J M*

Intersensory Origin of Mind — *Shipley, Thorne*

Interstate — *Dixon, Stephen*

Interstate Relations — *Zimmerman, Joseph F*

y Interstellar Pig — *Sleator, William*

Intertemporal Production Frontiers — *Fare, Rolf*

Intertextualidad Generative En El Beso De La Mujer Arana, De Manuel Puig — *Gomez Lara, Ruben L*

Intertextuality: German Literature and Visual Art from the Renaissance to the Twentieth Century — *Hoesterey, Ingeborg*

Intertexuality and the Reading of Midrash — *Boyarin, Daniel*

Intervening with Drug-Involved Youth — *McCoy, Clyde B*

Intervention: The Use of American Military Force in the Post-Cold War World — *Haass, Richard N*

Interventional Breast Procedures — *Dershaw, D David*

Interventional Electrophysiology — *Singer, Igor*

Interventional Radiology — *Watkinson, Anthony*

Interventional Radiology. 3rd Ed., Vols. 1-2 — *Castaneda-Zuniga, Wilfrido R*

Interventions: Feminist Dialogues on Third World Women's Literature and Film — *Ghosh, Bishnupriya*

Interview with the Vampire — *Rice, Anne*

Interviewing and Salary Negotiation — *King, Julie*

Interviewing Elderly Relatives — *McLaughlin, Eve*

Interviewing in Depth — *Chirban, John T*

Interviews: An Introduction to Qualitative Research Interviewing — *Kvale, Steinar*

p Interweave Knits

Interwoven Destinies — *Cisneros, Henry G*

Interwoven Destinies — *Fisher, Eugene J*

Intimacy and Exclusion — *Herzog, Dagmar*

Intimacy and Terror — *Garros, Veronique*

The Intimacy Dance — *Berzon, Betty*

Intimacy with God — *Keating, Thomas*

Intimate Betrayal — *Hill, Donna*

The Intimate Critique — *Freedman, Diane P*

Intimate Enemies — *Benvenisti, Meron*

Intimate Enemies — *Stanzel, F K*

An Intimate History of Humanity — *Zeldin, Theodore*

The Intimate Hour — *Baur, Susan*

Intimate Lies — *Westbrook, Robert*

Intimate Relations — *Conrad, Margaret*

Intimate Strangers — *Mead, Juliette*

Intimate Violence — *Tanner, Laura E*

Intimate Worlds — *Scarf, Maggie*

y Into Africa — *Packer, Craig*

Into Battle — *Gilbert, Michael*

c Into Israel — *Massel, Norma*

Into Technology — *Bindon, Annette*

c Into the Castle (Illus. by John Bendall-Brunello) — *Crebbin, June*

c Into the Deep Forest with Henry David Thoreau (Illus. by Kate Kiesler) — *Murphy, Jim*

y Into the Fire — *Kelley, Robin D G*

Into the Fire — *Watanabe, Sylvia*

Into the Forest — *Hegland, Jean*

Into the Great Wide Open — *Canty, Kevin*

Into the Jet Age — *Wooldridge, E T*

y Into the Land of the Unicorns — *Coville, Bruce*

Into the Same River Twice — *Nevins, Francis M, Jr.*

c Into the Sea (Illus. by Alix Berenzy) — *Guiberson, Brenda Z*

r Into the Twilight Zone — *Lofficier, Randy*

Into the Valley — *Young, Charles H*

y Into the Wild — *Krakauer, Jon*

Into the Wilderness Dream — *Barclay, Donald A*

y Into the Wind — *Ferris, Jean*

c Into the Wind — *Otfinoski, Steve*

c Into the Woods (Illus. by Loretta Krupinski) — *Krupinski, Loretta*

y Into Thin Air — *Krakauer, Jon*

Into Thin Air — *Zigal, Thomas*

Intorno A Locatelli. Vols. 1-2 — *Dunning, Albert*

Intoxicated by My Illness — *Broyard, Anatole*

Intra-Abdominal Infections, Hepatitis, and Gastroenteritis — *Mandell, Gerald L*

Intra-Aortic Balloon Pump Therapy — *Maccioli, Gerald A*

Intracellular Signal Transduction — *Hidaka, Hiroyoshi*

Intracellular Signal Transduction — *Wilks, Andrew F*

Intranet Resource Kit — *Ambegaonkar, Prakash*

Intranets — *Vaughan-Nichols, Steven J*

Intranets vs. Lotus Notes — *Sinclair, Joseph T*

Intransigeance Ou Compromis — *Turcotte, Paul-Andre*

Intrarea In Casa

y An Intricate Weave — *Miller, Marlene*

Intrinsic Value — *Lemos, Noah M*

Introduccion A La Literatura Infantil Y Juvenil — *Schon, Isabel*

Introduccion Al Analisis Linguistico Del Discurso — *Jordan, Isolde*

Introduccion Al Estudio De Los Incunables — *Haebler, Konrad*

r Introducing and Managing Academic Library Automation Projects — *Head, John W*

r Introducing Applied Linguistics — *Carter, Ronald*

c Introducing Bach — *Vernon, Roland*

c Introducing Beethoven — *Vernon, Roland*

c Introducing Chopin — *Vernon, Roland*

y Introducing Comparative Government — *Davies, Alan*

c Introducing Gershwin — *Vernon, Roland*

Introducing Grammar — *Woods, Edward*

y Introducing International Politics — *Jones, Peter*

Introducing Microsoft FrontPage — *Lehto, Kerry A*

c Introducing Mozart — *Vernon, Roland*

Introducing Philosophy — *Phillips, D Z*

Introducing Systems Design. 2nd Ed. — *Skidmore, Steve*

y Introducing the European Union — *Watts, Duncan*

y Introducing Vivaldi — *Vernon, Roland*

Introduction A La Lexicologie Explicative Et Combinatoire — *Mel'cuk, Igor A*

Introduction A La Litterature Yiddish Ancienne — *Baumgarten, Jean*

Introduction A L'Histoire De L'Ecriture — *Gasparri, Francoise*

Introduction into Capital Theory — *Stephan, Gunter*

An Introduction to Aerospace Propulsion — *Archer, R Douglas*

An Introduction to AS/400 System Operations — *Gapen, Patrice*

Introduction to Audiology. 6th Ed. — *Martin, Frederick N*

An Introduction to Bayesian Inference in Econometrics — *Zellner, Arnold*

An Introduction to Bibliography for Literary Students — *McKerrow, Ronald B*

Introduction to Biophysical Methods for Protein and Nucleic Acid Research — *Glasel, Jay A*

Introduction to Chemistry. 7th Ed. — *Dickson, T R*

Introduction to Circulating Atmospheres — *James, Ian N*

An Introduction to Classical Korean Literature — *Kim, Kichung*

Introduction to Coding and Information Theory — *Roman, Steven*

Introduction to College Chemistry. 1st Ed. — *Driscoll, Jerry A*

Introduction to Combinatorics — *Erickson, Martin J*

An Introduction to Communications for the AS/400. 2nd Ed. — *Enck, John*

An Introduction to Composite Materials. 2nd Ed. — *Hull, D*

Introduction to Contemporary Social and Political Thinkers — *Irele, Dipo*

Introduction to Control System Technology. 5th Ed. — *Bateson, Robert N*

Introduction to Crystallographic Statistics — *Shmueli, Uri*

Introduction to Data Communications — *Hughes, Larry*

An Introduction to Dermatological Surgery — *Lawrence, Clifford M*

Introduction to Diagnostic Microbiology — *Delost, Maria Dannessa*

An Introduction to Difference Equations — *Elaydi, Saber N*

An Introduction to Distributed Algorithms — *Barbosa, Valmir C*

An Introduction to Dynamics of Colloids — *Dhont, Jan K G*

c An Introduction to Edgar Degas

Introduction to Electrical-Mechanical Drafting with CAD — *Bethune, James D*

An Introduction to Electromagnetic Wave Propagation and Antennas — *Cloude, Shane*

Introduction to Environmental Chemistry — *Bunce, Nigel*

y An Introduction to Experimental Physics — *Cooke, Colin*

Introduction to Fiber Optics — *Crisp, John*

An Introduction to Fiber Optics — *Shotwell, R Allen*

An Introduction to Film Studies — *Nelmes, Jill*

Introduction to Finite Elements in Engineering. 2nd Ed. — *Chandrupatla, Tirupathi R*

An Introduction to Formal Specification and Z. 2nd Ed. — *Potter, Ben*

Introduction to Fortran 90 for Engineers and Scientists — *Nyhoff, Larry*

An Introduction to Functional Analysis in Computational Mathematics — *Lebedev, Viacheslav Ivanovich*

Introduction to General, Organic, and Biological Chemistry. 4th Ed. — *Ouellette, Robert J*

An Introduction to Genetic Algorithms — *Mitchell, Melanie*

An Introduction to Geographic Information Systems 1994 — *Great Britain. Treasury. Central Computer and Telecommunications Agency*

Introduction to Health Sciences Librarianship — *Kellerman, Frank R*

Introduction to Hegel's Philosophy of History — *Hyppolite, Jean*

An Introduction to High-Performance Scientific Computing — *Fosdick, Lloyd D*

An Introduction to Hinduism — *Flood, Gavin*

Introduction to Human Disease. 4th Ed. — *Crowley, Leonard V*

An Introduction to Infinite-Dimensional Linear System Theory — *Curtain, R F*

Introduction to Infrared System Design — *Wolfe, William L*

r Introduction to International Organizations — *Louis-Jacques, Lyonette*

An Introduction to Italian Sculpture. 4th Ed., Vols. 1-3 — *Pope-Hennessy, John Wyndham, Sir*

Introduction to Jazz History. 4th Ed. — *Megill, Donald D*

Introduction to Jewish-Christian Relations — *Shermis, Michael*

Introduction to Linear Algebra — *Schay, Geza*

An Introduction to Logic Programming through Prolog — *Spivey, J M*

An Introduction to Lorentz Surfaces — *Weinstein, Tilla*

Introduction to Maple. 2nd Ed. — *Heck, Andre*

Introduction to Mechanics and Symmetry — *Marsden, Jerrold E*

An Introduction to Medieval Philosophy — *Martin, C J F*

An Introduction to Metal Matrix Composites — *Clyne, T W*

y Introduction to Mineral Exploration — *Evans, Anthony M*

Introduction to Modern Philosophy — *Yartz, Frank J*

Introduction to Molecular Dynamics and Chemical Kinetics — *Billing, G D*

Introduction to Motion Based Design — *Connor, Jerome J*

An Introduction to Neural Networks — *Anderson, James A*

Introduction to New Testament Textual Criticism. Rev. Ed. — *Greenlee, J Harold*

y Introduction to Nonlinear Science — *Nicolis, G*

An Introduction to Object-Oriented Programming. 2nd Ed. — *Budd, Timothy*

r Introduction to Optics and Lasers in Engineering — *Laufer, Gabriel*

An Introduction to Option-Adjusted Spread Analysis. Rev. Ed. — *Windas, Tom*

An Introduction to Parallel Computational Fluid Dynamics — *Pappetti, F*

Introduction to Perturbation Methods — *Holmes, M H*

Introduction to Philosophical Hermeneutics — *Grondin, Jean*

Introduction to Physical Oceanography — *Mellor, George L*

Introduction to Physical Oceanography. 2nd Ed — *Knauss, John A*

c An Introduction to Pieter Breugel

Introduction to Planetary Volcanism — *Mursky, Gregory*

An Introduction to Post-Colonial Theatre — *Crow, Brian*

Introduction to Practical Linear Programming — *Pannell, David J*

An Introduction to Psychological Tests and Scales — *Loewenthal, Kate Miriam*

Introduction to Psychopathology — *Lemma, Alessandra*

Introduction to Quantitative Analysis of Linguistic Survey Data — *Kretzschmar, William A*

An Introduction to Quantum Field Theory — *Peskin, Michael E*

An Introduction to Radio Astronomy — *Burke, Bernard F*

Introduction to Radio Propagation for Fixed and Mobile Communications — *Doble, John*

Introduction to Remote Sensing. 2nd Ed. — *Campbell, James B*

Introduction to Scientific Computing — *Van Loan, Charles F*

Introduction to Scientific Programming — *Zachary, Joseph L*

An Introduction to Shakespeare — *Hyland, Peter*

Introduction to Sound. 2nd Ed. — *Speaks, Charles E*

Introduction to Space Sciences and Spacecraft Applications — *Campbell, Bruce A*

Introduction to Spectral Theory — *Hislop, P D*

r An Introduction to Statistical Communication Theory — *Middleton, David*

Introduction to Statistical Quality Control. 3rd Ed. — *Montgomery, Douglas C*

An Introduction to Statistical Thermodynamics — *Gasser, Robert P H*

An Introduction to Stylistic Text Analysis — *Clark, Urszula*

Introduction to Superconductivity — *Tinkham, Michael*

An Introduction to Survey Research, Polling, and Data Analysis. 3rd Ed. — *Weisberg, Herbert F*

An Introduction to the Biology of Marine Life. 6th Ed. — *Sumich, James L*

An Introduction to the Bootstrap — *Efron, Bradley*

An Introduction to the Gawain-Poet — *Putter, Ad*

An Introduction to the History and Sources of Jewish Law — *Hecht, N S*

An Introduction to the History of Psychology. 3rd Ed. — *Hergenhahn, B R*

An Introduction to the History of the Institute of the Brothers of the Christian Schools — *Bedel, Henri*

An Introduction to the Mathematics of Biology — *Yeargers, Edward K*

An Introduction to the Nature and Functions of Language — *Jackson, Howard*

An Introduction to the Philosophy of Religion — *Tilghman, Benjamin R*

Introduction to the Philosophy of Science — *Zucker, Arthur*

Introduction to the Qualitative Theory of Dynamical Systems on Surfaces — *Aranson, S Kh.*

An Introduction to the Thought of Karl Popper — *Corvi, Roberta*

An Introduction to the UK Economy. 2nd Ed. — *Hare, Paul*

An Introduction to the Visual System — *Tovee, Martin J*

An Introduction to the World's Oceans. 5th Ed. — *Duxbury, Alyn C*

Introduction to Theoretical Organic Chemistry and Molecular Modeling — *Smith, William B*

Introduction to Thermodynamics and Heat Transfer — *Cengel, Yunus A*

Introduction to Time Series and Forecasting — *Brockwell, Peter J*

r Introduction to United States Government Information Sources. 5th Ed. — *Morehead, Joe*

An Introduction to Vygotsky — *Daniels, Harry*

Introduction to Wildland Fire. 2nd Ed. — *Pyne, Stephen J*

Introduction to X-Ray Powder Diffractometry — *Jenkins, Ron*

Introduction to Youth Ministry — *Dettoni, John M*

Introductory Circuit Analysis. 8th Ed. — *Boylestad, Robert L*

Introductory Computer Science — *Dewdney, A K*

Introductory Electronic Devices and Circuits. 4th Ed. — *Paynter, Robert T*

Introductory Electronic Devices and Circuits: Conventional Flow Version. 4th Ed. — *Paynter, Robert T*

Introductory Microbiology — *Heritage, J*

Introductory Modern Algebra — *Stahl, Saul*

Introductory Plant Biology. 7th Ed. — *Stern, Kingsley R*

Introduzione Alle Regole Alimentari Islamiche — *Francesca, Ersilia*

The Introspective Engineer — *Florman, Samuel C*

y The Intruder — *Baer, Judy*

The Intruder — *Blauner, Peter*

The Intruders — *Coonts, Stephen*

Intruders in the Play World — *Lalande, Roxanne Decker*

Intuition (Emery). Audio Version — *Emery, Marcia*

c The Inuit — *Thomson, Ruth*

Inuit Women Artists — *Leroux, Odette*

y The Invasion — *Applegate, Katherine*

y Invasion — *Cook, Robin*

c Invasion of the Giant Bugs (Illus. by Wayne Anderson) — *Wood, A J*

Inventaire Des Fonds Montaigne Conserves A Bordeaux — *Desgraves, Louis*

Invented Cities — *Domosh, Mona*

Inventing a Hero — *May, Glenn Anthony*

Inventing Better Schools — *Schlechty, Phillip C*

Inventing Eastern Europe — *Wolff, Larry*

Inventing Europe — *Delanty, Gerard*

Inventing Human Science — *Fox, Christopher*

Inventing Ireland — *Kiberd, Declan*

Inventing Kindergarten — *Brosterman, Norman*

Inventing Lesbian Cultures in America — *Lewin, Ellen*

Inventing Mark Twain — *Hoffman, Andrew*

Inventing Memory — *Jong, Erica*

Inventing Nations — *Pickett, Terry H*

Inventing New England — *Brown, Dona*

Inventing Ourselves Again — *Chan, Janis Fisher*

Inventing Reality — *Dolan, Therese*

Inventing the AIDS Virus — *Duesberg, Peter*

Inventing the American Primitive — *Carr, Helen*

Inventing the Modern Artist — *Burns, Sarah*

Inventing the Nonprofit Sector and Other Essays on Philanthropy, Voluntarism, and Nonprofit Organizations — *Hall, Peter Dobkin*

Inventing the Psychological — *Pfister, Joel*

Inventing the Public Enemy — *Ruth, David E*

Inventing the Southwest — *Howard, Kathleen L*

Inventing Times Square — *Taylor, William R*

Inventing Wonderland — *Wullschlager, Jackie*

Invention by Design — *Petroski, Henry*

The Invention of Ancient Israel — *Whitelam, Keith W*
The Invention of Heterosexuality — *Katz, Jonathan Ned*
The Invention of Politics in Colonial Malaya — *Milner, Anthony*
The Invention of Pornography — *Hunt, Lynn*
The Invention of Sodomy in Christian Theology — *Jordan, Mark D*
The Invention of the Modern Republic — *Fontana, Biancamaria*
The Invention of the Newspaper — *Raymond, Joad*
The Invention of the West — *GoGwilt, Christopher Lloyd*
The Invention That Changed the World — *Buderi, Robert*
Inventions of Difference — *Gasche, Rodolphe*
Inventions of the March Hare — *Eliot, T S*
c Inventors — *Burns, Peggy*
c Inventors — *Sandler, Martin W*
Inverse Problems in Geophysical Applications — *Engl, Heinz W*
p Invertebrate Neuroscience
c Invertebrates — *Silverstein, Alvin*
Invested in the Common Good — *Meeker-Lowry, Susan*
p Investigacion Economica
Investigating Disease Patterns — *Stolley, Paul D*
Investigating Geography — *Nagle, Garrett*
y Investigating Health, Welfare and Poverty. 2nd Ed. — *Trowler, Paul*
c Investigating Local History — *Purkis, Sally*
Investigating Modern Art — *Dawtrey, Liz*
Investigating Wildland Fire Entrapments — *Mangan, Richard*
c The Investigation of Murder (Illus. by Rob Shone) — *Lane, Brian*
Investigations by Order — *Donnely, J*
Investing by the Stars — *Weingarten, Henry*
Investing for Good — *Kinder, Peter*
Investing from Scratch — *Lowell, James*
Investing in People — *Beaulieu, Lionel*
Investing in Today's Joy, Tomorrow's Wealth
Investing On-Line — *Eckett, Stephen*
Investment. Vols. 1-2 — *Jorgenson, Dale Weldeau*
Investment Decision Making in the Private and Public Sectors — *Beenhakker, Henri L*
Investment Funds in Emerging Markets — *Carter, Laurence*
Investment Gurus — *Tanous, Peter*
Investment in China — *Wang, Yung-Chun*
Investment in Learning — *Bowen, Howard R*
Investment Opportunities in Russia and the CIS — *Dyker, David A*
Investment Rules for the Global Economy — *Sauve, Pierre*
Investor Capitalism — *Useem, Michael*
Invisible Allies — *Solzhenitsyn, Aleksandr Isaevich*
The Invisible Assembly Line — *Stamp, Daniel*
The Invisible Circus — *Egan, Jennifer*
The Invisible Country — *McAuley, Paul J*
Invisible Crises — *Gerbner, George*
The Invisible Crying Tree — *Shannon, Tom*
Invisible Darkness — *Williams, Stephen*
The Invisible Disability — *Accardo, Pasquale*
The Invisible Dragon — *Hickey, Dave*
The Invisible Drug — *Bailey, William Everett*
Invisible Gardens — *Walker, Peter, 1932-*
The Invisible God — *Corby, Paul*
c The Invisible Hunters (Illus. by J Sam) — *Rohmer, Harriet*
y The Invisible Ladder — *Rosenberg, Liz*
Invisible Leviathan — *Smith, Murray E G*
Invisible Lines of Connection — *Kushner, Lawrence*
Invisible Man — *Ellison, Ralph*
The Invisible Man (Hardwicke). Audio Version — *Wells, H G*
Invisible Power — *Haynes, Alan*
The Invisible Presence — *Zeller, Ludwig*
Invisible Republic — *Marcus, Greil*
c Invisible Stanley (Illus. by Steve Bjorkman) — *Brown, Jeff*
The Invisible Telling Its Shape — *Weinberger, Florence*
The Invisible World — *Wilson, Catherine*
p The Invisibles. Vol. 1 — *Morrison, Grant*
The Invisibles: A Tale of the Eunuchs of India — *Jaffrey, Zia*
An Invitation to Old English and Anglo-Saxon England — *Mitchell, Bruce, 1920-*
c Invitations to Cells — *Camp, Carole Ann*
c Invitations to Evolving — *Camp, Carole Ann*

c Invitations to Heredity — *Camp, Carole Ann*
c Invitations to Interdependence — *Camp, Carole Ann*
c Invitations to Life's Diversity — *Camp, Carole Ann*
c Invitations to the Matter-Energy Cycle — *Camp, Carole Ann*
Invulnerability: On Securing Happiness — *Luper, Steven*
The Inward Pilgrims — *Christensen, Bernhard*
Inwardness and Theater in the English Renaissance — *Maus, Katharine Eisaman*
Die Inzestgesetzgebung Der Merowingisch-Frankischen Konzilien 511-626/27 — *Mikat, Paul*
Io, Monna Lisa — *Pecci-Blunt, Donatella*
Ion Beam Modification of Materials — *International Conference on Ion Beam Modification of Materials (9th: 1995: Canberra, A.C.T.)*
Ion Channels — *Aidley, David J*
Ion Channels. Vol. 4
Ion Exchange Developments and Applications — *International Ion Exchange Conference (7th: 1996: Churchill College, Cambridge, UK)*
Ion-Solid Interactions for Materials Modification and Processing — *Poker, D B*
Ionic Polymerization Fundamentals — *Szwarc, Michael*
The Ionotropic Glutamate Receptors — *Monaghan, Daniel T*
Iovis: All Is Full of Love. Vol. 2 — *Waldman, Anne*
Iowa: A Celebration of Land, People and Purpose — *Sidey, Hugh*
r Iowa Merchant Trade Token Town Rarity List. 4th Ed. — *Hosek, George*
Iowa: The Middle Land — *Schwieder, Dorothy*
Iowa's Wild Places — *Kurtz, Carl*
Iphigenia: The Diary of a Young Lady Who Wrote Because She Was Bored — *Parra, Teresa De La*
IPv6: The New Internet Protocol — *Huitema, Christian*
Ira Gershwin: The Art of the Lyricist — *Furia, Philip*
c Ira Sleeps Over — *Waber, Bernard*
Iran and the Gulf — *Al-Suwaidi, Jamal S*
Iran and the Muslim World — *Keddie, Nikki R*
Iran: Die Pragmatische Republik Gottes? — *Wohlert, Torsten*
c Iran: Land of the Peacock Throne — *Spencer, William, 1922-*
The Iranian Constitutional Revolution 1906-1911 — *Afary, Janet*
Iranian Intellectuals and the West — *Boroujerdi, Mehrzad*
Iranian Military Power — *Eisenstadt, Michael*
The Iranians: Persia, Islam and the Soul of a Nation — *Mackey, Sandra*
Iraq: From Sumer to Saddam — *Simons, G L*
Iraq: The Search for National Identity — *Lukitz, Liora*
The Iraqi Aggression against Kuwait — *Danspeckgruber, Wolfgang F*
The Iraqi Invasion of Kuwait — *Musallam, Musallam Ali*
c Ireland — *Arnold, Helen*
Ireland — *Lange, Dorothea*
r Ireland (Insight Compact Guides)
Ireland: A New Economic History 1780-1939 — *O Grada, Cormac*
Ireland and Scotland in the Age of Revolution — *McFarland, E W*
Ireland and the Atlantic Heritage — *Evans, E Estyn*
Ireland and the Irish — *Ardagh, John*
Ireland and the Vatican — *Keogh, Dermot*
Ireland: Criminality, Land and the Law under Forster and Balfour — *O'Callaghan, Margaret*
Ireland Divided — *Hughes, Michael*
Ireland from Independence to Occupation 1641-1660 — *Ohlmeyer, Jane H*
Ireland's Women — *Donovan, Katie*
Irenaeus — *Minns, Denis*
c Irene Jennie and the Christmas Masquerade (Illus. by Melodye Rosales) — *Smalls, Irene*
Irene: Selected Writings of Irene Paull — *Paull, Irene*
Iridium — *Luxton, Steve*
The Iris Deception — *Schopen, Bernard*
Iris Murdoch and the Search for Human Goodness — *Antonaccio, Maria*
Irises: A Practical Gardening Guide — *Glasgow, Karen*
Irish Airmail 1919-1990 — *Murphy, William J*
r Irish Almanac and Yearbook of Facts 1997
Irish America and the Ulster Conflict 1968-1995 — *Wilson, Andrew J*
c The Irish Cinderlad (Illus. by Loretta Krupinski) — *Climo, Shirley*

The Irish Colony of Saskatchewan — *Coughlin, Jack*
An Irish Country Childhood — *Walsh, Marrie*
An Irish Empire? — *Jeffery, Keith*
The Irish Eros — *Marcus, David*
The Irish Experience. Rev. Ed. — *Hachey, Thomas E*
r The Irish Experience in New York City — *Shea, Ann M*
r The Irish Famine — *Kissane, Noel*
r The Irish Filmography — *Rockett, Kevin*
r Irish Government Publications — *Finnegan, Richard B*
The Irish Guards in the Great War — *Kipling, Rudyard*
Irish Hunger — *Hayden, Tom*
Irish Identity and the Literary Revival. 2nd Ed. — *Watson, George J*
Irish Illegals — *Corcoran, Mary P*
Irish Lace — *Greeley, Andrew M*
y Irish Magic II — *Llywelyn, Morgan*
The Irish Male at Home and Abroad — *O'Conner, Joseph*
Irish Peasant Society — *Connell, K H*
The Irish Penitentials and Their Significance for the Sacrament of Penance Today — *Connolly, Hugh*
r Irish Playwrights 1880-1995 — *Schrank, Bernice*
p The Irish Review
r The Irish Scientist. 1996 Ed.
Irish, Scottish and Border Melodies for Flatpicking Guitar — *Brennan, Bill*
Irish Television — *Savage, Robert J, Jr*
An Irish Theologian in Enlightenment France — *O'Connor, Thomas*
Irish Tin Whistle Book — *McCaskill, Mizzy*
Irish Urban Cultures — *Curtin, Chris*
Irish Voices from the Great War — *Dungan, Myles*
Irish Writers and Their Creative Process — *Genet, Jacqueline*
c Irma, the Flying Bowling Ball (Illus. by Rex Barron) — *Ross, Tom*
Iron Age Communities in Britain. 3rd Ed. — *Cunliffe, Barry*
Iron and Steel — *McKiven, Henry M, Jr.*
Iron Dawn — *Stover, Matthew Woodring*
c Iron Hans — *Heyer, Marilee*
Iron House — *Washington, Jerome*
y Iron House (Washington). Audio Version — *Washington, Jerome*
Iron Men, Wooden Women — *Creighton, Margaret S*
y The Iron Ring — *Alexander, Lloyd*
c The Iron Woman (Illus. by Barry Moser) — *Hughes, Ted*
c The Iron Woman (Hughes). Audio Version — *Hughes, Ted*
y Ironclaw: A Navy Carrier Pilot's Gulf War Experience — *Baldwin, Sherman*
c Ironfist Chinmi: Titles 1 to 12 — *Maekawa, Takeshi*
The Ironic Temper and the Comic Imagination — *Gurewitch, Morton*
The Ironies of Affirmative Action — *Skrentny, John David*
Der Ironiker Und Der Ideologe — *Bruntrager, Hubert*
y Ironman — *Crutcher, Chris*
y Ironman (Guidall). Audio Version — *Crutcher, Chris*
Irons in the Fire — *McPhee, John*
y The Irony of Free Speech — *Fiss, Owen M*
The Irony of Reform — *Mackenzie, G Calvin*
Irony's Edge — *Hutcheon, Linda, 1947-*
The Iroquois — *Snow, Dean R*
IRPTC Legal File 1994/1995. Vols. 1-2
Irradiation of Polymers — *National Meeting of the American Chemical Society (208th: 1994: Washington, DC)*
Irrationalite Individuelle Et Ordre Social — *Moessinger, Pierre*
Irrawaddy Tango — *Law-Yone, Wendy*
Irrepressible Reformer — *Wiegand, Wayne A*
y Irrepressible Spirit — *Kuklin, Susan*
r Irreverent Guides: Chicago
Irving Berlin: Songs from the Melting Pot — *Hamm, Charles*
r The Irwin Directory of Emerging Markets Brokers — *Lerner, William J*
The Irwin Handbook of Telecommunications. 3rd Ed. — *Green, James H*
Is Bank Lending Important for the Transmission of Monetary Policy? — *Peek, Joe*
Is Heathcliff a Murderer? — *Sutherland, John*
c Is It Rough? Is It Smooth? Is It Shiny? — *Hoban, Tana*
Is Jesus Unique? — *Cowdell, Scott*
Is Jesus Your Personal Saviour? — *Rawlyk, George A*

Is Long-Term Psychotherapy Unethical? — *Austad, Carol Shaw*
Is Religion Good for Your Health? — *Koenig, Harold G*
Is the Good Corporation Dead? — *Houck, John W*
Is the Holocaust Unique? — *Rosenbaum, Alan S*
Is There a God? — *Swinburne, Richard*
Is There a Sphygmomanometerist in the House? — *Sinclair, Frank Livingstone*
Is There a Transition to Democracy in El Salvador? — *Tulchin, Joseph S*
c Is There Room on the Bus? (Illus. by Hannah Giffard) — *Piers, Helen*
c Is There Room on the Feather Bed? (Illus. by Nadine Bernard Westcott) — *Gray, Libba Moore*
Is This Your Child's World? — *Rapp, Doris J*
r Isaac Asimov: An Annotated Bibliography of the Asimov Collection at Boston University — *Green, Scott E*
y Isaac Asimov's Utopia — *Allen, Roger MacBride*
y Isaac Asimov's Vampires — *Dozois, Gardner*
Isaac Bashevis Singer: A Life — *Hadda, Janet*
y Isaac Campion — *Howker, Janni*
Isaac Newton, Adventurer in Thought — *Hall, A Rupert*
y Isaac Newton and the Scientific Revolution — *Christianson, Gale E*
y Isaac Newton: The Greatest Scientist of All Time — *Anderson, Margaret J*
Isabel's Bed — *Lipman, Elinor*
y Isabel's Bed (Lipman). Audio Version — *Lipman, Elinor*
Isadora Duncan: The Dances — *Nahumck, Nadia Chilkovsky*
Isaiah 40-66 — *Hanson, Paul D*
Isaiah Berlin — *Gray, John, 1948-*
Isaiah: Spirit of Courage, Gift of Tears — *Berrigan, Dan*
Isaiah's Vision and the Family of God — *Darr, Katheryn Pfisterer*
c Isambard Kingdom Brunel — *Malam, John*
Isamu Noguchi/Rosanjin Kitaoji — *Ogawa, Kikuko*
Iscrizioni Di Cos. Vols. 1-2 — *Segre, M*
ISDN: Concepts, Facilities, and Services. 3rd Ed. — *Kessler, Gary C*
The ISDN Consultant — *Lee, Robert E*
ISDN Networking Essentials — *Tittel, Ed*
c Ishtar and Tammuz (Illus. by Christina Balit) — *Moore, C J*
Isidore De Peluse — *Evieux, Pierre*
Isis Regina, Zeus Sarapis — *Merkelbach, Reinhold*
c Isla (Illus. by Elisa Kleven) — *Dorros, Arthur*
Islam — *Le Pla, Frances*
c Islam — *Moorcroft, Christine*
Islam and Democracy — *Esposito, John L*
Islam and Human Rights. 2nd Ed. — *Mayer, Ann Elizabeth*
Islam and Identity in Eastern Indonesia — *Hitchcock, Michael*
Islam and the Abode of War — *Ayalon, David*
Islam and the Myth of Confrontation — *Halliday, Fred*
Islam and the West — *Lewis, Bernard*
Islam: Continuity and Change in the Modern World. 2nd Ed. — *Voll, John*
Islam in Anatolia after the Turkish Invasion — *Korprulu, Mehmed Fuad*
Islam in Revolution. 2nd Ed. — *Dekmejian, R Hrair*
Islam in the African-American Experience — *Turner, Richard Brent*
Islam in the Balkans — *Norris, Harry T*
Islam: Its Prophets, Peoples, Politics and Power — *Braswell, George W, Jr.*
Islam: The View from the Edge — *Bulliet, Richard W*
Islamic Architecture — *Hillenbrand, Robert*
Islamic Art in the Ashmolean. Pts. 1-2 — *Allan, J W*
Islamic Banking — *Al-Omar, Fuad*
The Islamic Baths of Palestine — *Dow, Martin*
The Islamic Concept of Belief in the 4th/10th Century — *Daiber, Hans*
Islamic Economic Systems — *Nomani, Farhad*
r Islamic Economics and Finance — *Khan, Javed Ahmad*
Islamic Endowments in Jerusalem under British Mandate — *Reiter, Yitzhak*
c Islamic Festivals — *Knight, Khadijah*
Islamic Fundamentalism — *Sidahmed, Abdel Salam*
Islamic Identity and the Struggle for Justice — *Barazangi, Nimat Hafez*
Islamic Legal Interpretation — *Masud, Muhammad Khalid*
Islamic Names — *Schimmel, Annemarie*

Islamic Politics in Palestine — *Milton-Edwards, Beverley*
The Islamic Threat — *Esposito, John L*
Islamic Urban Studies — *Haneda, Masahi*
Islamism and Secularism in North Africa — *Ruedy, John*
The Islamist Dilemma — *Guazzone, Laura*
c Island Alphabet — *Briggs, Kelly Paul*
An Island in the Lake of Fire — *Dalhouse, Mark Taylor*
The Island in the Mind — *Hall, Rodney*
Island in the Sky — *Bizony, Piers*
y An Island like You — *Ortiz Cofer, Judith*
y Island Magic — *Goudge, Elizabeth*
The Island of California — *Polk, Dora Beale*
The Island of Doctor Moreau — *Wells, H G*
y The Island of Doctor Moreau. Audio Version — *Wells, H G*
y The Island of Summer — *Sullivan, Jenny*
c Island of the Blue Dolphins — *O'Dell, Scott*
y The Island of the Colorblind — *Sacks, Oliver*
The Island of the Colorblind (Sacks). Audio Version — *Sacks, Oliver*
The Island of the Colour-Blind — *Sacks, Oliver*
The Island of the Day Before — *Eco, Umberto*
The Island of the Mapmaker's Wife and Other Tales — *Sides, Marilyn*
y An Island out of Time — *Horton, Tom*
Island Paradox — *Rivera-Batiz, Francisco*
The Island: Three Tales — *Herling, Gustaw*
c Islands (Illus. by Vanessa Card) — *Morris, Neil*
c Islands (Illus. by Laszlo Gal) — *Smythe, Anne*
c Islands — *Steele, Philip*
c Islands — *Waterlow, Julia*
Islands in Space and Time — *Campbell, David G*
Islands in the Desert — *Wilson, John P*
Islands in Time — *Patton, Mark*
The Isle of Joy — *Daugherty, Franklin*
The ISO 9000 Handbook. 3rd Ed. — *Peach, Robert W*
ISO 9000 Quality System Assessment Handbook — *Hoyle, David*
ISO 14000 Guide — *Cascio, Joseph*
ISO 14010 Environmental Auditing — *Kuhre, W Lee*
Isolationism Reconfigured — *Nordlinger, Eric*
Le Isole Fortunate — *Cachey, T J*
c Israel — *Allard, Denise*
Israel: A Traveler's Literary Companion — *Gluzman, Michael*
Israel and Its Bible — *Sharkansky, Ira*
Israel at the Polls 1992 — *Elazar, Daniel Judah*
Israel before Israel — *Tryster, Hillel*
r Israel: Boundary Disputes with Arab Neighbors 1946-1964. Vols. 1-10 — *Toye, Patricia*
Israel Construit Son Histoire — *De Pury, Albert*
Israel in Comparative Perspective — *Barnett, Michael N*
Israel in the Nineties — *Lazin, Frederick A*
Israel, Jordan, and the Peace Process — *Lukacs, Yehuda*
Israel on the Road to Peace — *Flamhaft, Ziva*
p Israel Studies
Israeli Holocaust Drama — *Taub, Michael*
Israeli-Palestinian Security — *Boutwell, Jeffrey*
r The Israeli Secret Services — *Clements, Frank A*
Israel's Best Defense — *Cohen, Eliezer*
Israel's Changing Society — *Goldscheider, Calvin*
Israels Konfrontation Mit Den Letzten Boten Der Weisheit — *Sevenich-Bax, Elisabeth*
Israels Letzter Psalm — *Gong, Alfred*
Issey Miyake — *Holborn, Mark*
Issue Update on Information Security and Privacy in Network Environments
Issues and Directions in Hydraulics — *Iowa Hydraulics Colloquium (1995: Iowa City, Iowa)*
p Issues in Accounting Education
Issues in Adolescent Sexuality — *Leeming, Frank C*
Issues in Evolutionary Ethics — *Thompson, Paul*
Issues in Feminist Film Criticism — *Erens, Patricia*
Issues in Librarianship 2 — *Hedges, G*
Istanbul 1900 — *Barillari, Diana*
r Istanbul (Essential Travel Guides)
Istituzioni Del Mondo Musulmano — *Vercellin, Giorgio*
Istoria Guvernelor Romaniei — *Neagoe, Stelian*
Istoria Romanilor Din Transilvania — *Nistor, Ioan Liviu*
IT across the Primary Curriculum — *Crompton, Rob*
It Came from Memphis — *Gordon, Robert, 1961-*
c It Came from Outer Space (Illus. by Carol Wright) — *Bradman, Tony*
It Came from the Drive-In — *Partridge, Norman*

It Comes from the People — *Hinsdale, Mary Ann*
c It Could Still Be a Lake — *Fowler, Allan*
c It Could Still Be a Worm — *Fowler, Allan*
c It Could Still Be Coral — *Fowler, Allan*
c The It-Doesn't-Matter Suit (Illus. by Rotraut Susanne Berner) — *Plath, Sylvia*
It Had to Be You — *Malouf, Melissa*
y It Had to Be You (Fields). Audio Version — *Phillips, Susan Elizabeth*
c It Happened in America (Illus. by Ib Ohlsson) — *Perl, Lila*
It Happened in Brooklyn — *Frommer, Myrna*
It Happened in the Catskills — *Frommer, Myrna*
IT in Primary Science — *Frost, Roger*
It Is So Ordered — *Burger, Warren E*
It Looked like For Ever — *Harris, Mark, 1922-*
c It Looks a Lot like Reindeer (Illus. by Rick Dupre) — *Cleary, Brian P*
It Looks at You — *Dixon, Wheeler Winston*
It Must Be That Time of the Month and Other Lies That Drive Women Crazy — *Witkin, Georgia*
It Never Snows in September — *Kershaw, Robert J*
It Pays to Play — *White, Peter*
y It Shouldn't Happen to a Vet (Timothy). Audio Version — *Herriot, James*
It Takes a Village and Other Lessons Children Teach Us — *Clinton, Hillary Rodham*
It Wasn't Pretty Folks, but Didn't We Have Fun? — *Polsgrove, Carol*
Ita Ford: Missionary Martyr — *Zagano, Phyllis*
Italia Quattrocentesca — *Fubini, Riccardo*
Italia: The Art of Living Italian Style — *Howard, Edmond*
L'Italia Tra Rivoluzione E Riforme 1831-1846
Italian Classics in One Pot — *Callen, Anna Teresa*
The Italian Economy in the 1990s — *Scobie, H M*
An Italian Education — *Parks, Tim*
Italian Foreign Policy — *Chabod, Federico*
Italian Industrialists from Liberalism to Fascism — *Adler, Franklin Hugh*
Italian Late-Medieval and Renaissance Drawing-Books from Giovannino De'Grassi to Palma Giovane — *Elen, Albert J*
Italian Maiolica and Incised Slipware at the Fitzwilliam Museum — *Poole, Julia E*
Italian National Cinema 1896-1996 — *Sorlin, Pierre*
Italian Neighbours — *Parks, Tim*
Italian Opera in Late Eighteenth-Century London. Vol. 1 — *Price, Curtis*
Italian Politics — *Katz, Richard S*
Italian Portfolio — *Colombo, Lanfranco*
y The Italian Renaissance — *Osman, Karen*
An Italian Renaissance Sextet — *Martines, Lauro*
The Italian Revolution — *Gilbert, Mark*
Italian Signs, American Streets — *Gardaphe, Fred L*
Italian Socialism — *Di Scala, Spencer*
The Italian South Atlantic Air Mail Service 1939-1941 — *Beith, Richard*
r The Italian Way — *Costantino, Mario*
Italian Women Poets of the Twentieth Century — *O'Brien, Catherine*
Italian Women Writers from the Renaissance to the Present — *Marotti, Maria Ornella*
Italian Women Writing — *Wood, Sharon*
Italian Women's Writing 1860-1994 — *Wood, Sharon*
Italianamerican: The Scorsese Family Cookbook — *Scorsese, Catherine*
Italians at the Court of Siam — *Ferri De Lazara, Leopoldo*
L'Italie Et Rome 218-31 av. J.-C. — *Vallat, Jean-Pierre*
Italienische Lyrik Des 20. Jahrhunderts — *Lentzen, Manfred*
Italienische Zeichnungen Des 16. Bis 18. Jahrhunderts — *Brink, Sonja*
Italinamerican: The Scorsese Family Cookbook — *Scorsese, Catherine*
Italo Svevo Scrittore Europeo — *Cacciaglia, Norberto*
c Italy — *Arnold, Helen*
r Italy. 3rd Ed. — *Belford, Ros*
Italy and the Wider World 1860-1960 — *Bosworth, R J B*
yr Italy (Eyewitness Travel Guides)
r Italy for the Gourmet Traveler — *Plotkin, Fred*
Italy in Mind — *Powers, Alice Leccese*
Italy since 1800 — *Absalom, Roger*
Italy: The Unfinished Revolution — *Frei, Matt*
Italy Today the Beautiful Cookbook — *De' Medici Stucchi, Lorenza*
r Iter Vaticanum Franciscanum — *Etzkorn, Girard J*

Itineraires De L'Ecriture Au Feminin — *Monicat, Benedicte*

r **ITP Nelson Canadian Dictionary of the English Language**

y **It's a Girl Thing (Illus. by Debbie Tilley)** — *Jukes, Mavis*

It's a Great Day to Fund-Raise! — *Poderis, Tony*

It's a Magical World — *Watterson, Bill*

y **It's a Matter of Trust** — *Byalick, Marcia*

c **It's a Spoon, Not a Shovel (Illus. by Mark Buehner)** — *Buehner, Caralyn*

It's about Our Health

It's about Time — *Hall, Fred M*

It's Alive! — *Cuozzo, Steven*

It's All Politics — *Durrenberger, E Paul*

IT's English

y **It's for You** — *Talbot, John*

c **It's Kwanzaa Time!** — *Goss, Linda*

c **It's like This Cat** — *Neville, Emily Cheney*

It's Murder Going Home — *Millhiser, Marlys*

c **It's My Birthday** — *Oxenbury, Helen*

It's Never Too Late — *Allen, Janet*

It's Not a Pretty Sight — *Haywood, Gar Anthony*

It's Not about a Salary... — *Cross, Brian*

c **It's Not Fair! (Illus. by Dominique Jolin)** — *Jolin, Dominique*

It's Not over Until You Win! — *Brown, Les, 1945-*

It's Not over Until You Win! (Brown). Audio Version — *Brown, Les, 1945-*

Its Quite an Education — *Boundy, Lynne*

c **It's Raining Cats and Dogs (Illus. by Bee Willey)** — *Corbett, Pie*

c **It's the Bear!** — *Aborough, Jez*

It's Time for My Story — *Williams, Carol Traynor*

It's Up to Us! — *Soyfer, Jura*

c **The Itsy Bitsy Spider and Other Hand Rhymes** — *Augarde, Steve*

c **Itty Bitty Kitty (Illus. by Jane Maday)** — *Keeshan, Bob*

IUTAM Symposium on Nonlinear Instability and Transition in Three-Dimensional Boundary Layers — *IUTAM Symposium on Nonlinear Instability and Transition in Three-Dimensional Boundary Layers (1995: Manchester, England)*

Iuzovka and Revolution. Vol. 2 — *Friedgut, Theodore H*

Iuzovka and Revolution. Vols. 1-2 — *Friedgut, Theodore H*

Ivan Albright — *Donnell, Courtney Graham*

c **Ivan and the Dynamos** — *Bowman, Crystal*

Ivan Turgenev and Britain — *Waddington, Patrick*

c **Ivana the Inventor** — *Burnard, Damon*

Ivanhoe (Hinds). Audio Version — *Scott, Walter, Sir*

I've Always Meant to Tell You — *Warloe, Constance*

y **I've Been Gone Far Too Long** — *Mulder, Monique Borgerhoff*

c **I've Been Working on the Railroad** — *Westcott, Nadine Bernard*

I've Got the Light of Freedom — *Payne, Charles M*

Ivo Andric Revisited — *Vucinich, Wayne S*

y **The Ivory Crocodile** — *Drew, Eileen, 1957-*

The Ivory Duchess — *Parr, Delia*

The Ivory Grin — *Macdonald, Ross*

The Ivory Houses at Mycenae — *Tournavitou, Iphiyenia*

Ivy League Autumns — *Goldstein, Richard*

Izbrannaia Proza. Vols. 1-2 — *Kharitonov, Mark*

Iznik: The Pottery of Ottoman Turkey — *Atasoy, Nurham*

y **Izzy Willy-Nilly** — *Voigt, Cynthia*

J

J.A. Hobson — *Schneider, Michael*

J. Arthur Rank: The Man behind the Gong — *Wakelin, Michael*

J.B. Oldham of Oldham's Hall 1882-1962 — *Charlesworth, Michael*

c J.J. versus the Baby-Sitter — *Himmelman, John*

J.M. Neale and the Quest for Sobornost — *Litvack, Leon*

The J. Paul Getty Museum — *Naef, Weston*

c J. Rooker, Manatee (Illus. by Paul Brent) — *Haley, Jan*

r J. Sheridan DeFanu: A Bio-Bibliography — *Crawford, Gary William*

J. William Fulbright and His Time — *Powell, Lee Riley*

Jack and Jackie — *Andersen, Christopher*

Jack and Jill — *Patterson, James, 1947-*

c Jack and Jill and Other Nursery Rhymes (Illus. by Lucy Cousins) — *Cousins, Lucy*

The Jack and Jill Syndrome — *Rushford, Patricia H*

y Jack and Rochelle — *Sutin, Jack*

c Jack and the Beanstalk (Illus. by Norman Messenger) — *Wells, Rosemary*

c Jack and the Wonder Beans (Illus. by Margot Tomes) — *Still, James*

Jack Hanna's Ultimate Guide to Pets — *Hanna, Jack*

Jack in Two Worlds — *McCarthy, William Bernard*

Jack Juggler and the Emperor's Whore — *Arden, John*

Jack Kerouac, Angelheaded Hipster — *Turner, Steve*

y A Jack Kerouac ROMnibus. Electronic Media Version — *Kerouac, Jack*

Jack Kerouac: Selected Letters 1940-1956 — *Kerouac, Jack*

Jack Nicklaus: My Story — *Nicklaus, Jack*

Jack Sheppard — *Buckstone, John Baldwin*

c Jack, Skinny Bones, and the Golden Pancakes (Illus. by Elise Primavera) — *Helldorfer, M C*

c Jack the Dog (Illus. by John A Rowe) — *Rowe, John A*

y Jack the Giant Killer — *De Lint, Charles*

y Jack the Ripper — *Geary, Rick*

r The Jack the Ripper A-Z — *Begg, Paul*

Jack the Ripper--First American Serial Killer — *Evans, Stewart*

c Jack Tractor (Illus. by Keren Ludlow) — *Smax, Willy*

Jackie by Josie — *Preston, Caroline*

c Jackie Joyner-Kersee — *Rambeck, Richard*

c Jackie Kennedy Onassis: Woman of Courage — *Anderson, Catherine Corley*

Jackie Robinson: An Intimate Portrait — *Robinson, Rachel*

Jackie Robinson: Between the Baselines — *Stout, Glenn*

c Jackie Robinson Breaks the Color Line — *Santella, Andrew*

The Jackie Robinson Reader — *Tygiel, Jules*

Jackie under My Skin — *Koestenbaum, Wayne*

c Jackrabbit (Illus. by Deborah Kogan Ray) — *London, Jonathan*

c Jacks around the World (Illus. by Karen Dugan) — *Lankford, Mary D*

y Jackson: A Novel — *Byrd, Max*

r Jackson County, Wisconsin Cemeteries. Vol. 1 — *Eddy, Sue*

Jackson Hole — *Wieneke, Connie*

Jackson Street and Other Soldier Stories — *Miller, John A*

The Jacksonian Promise — *Feller, Daniel*

Jackson's Dilemma — *Murdoch, Iris*

c Jacob Lawrence: American Scenes, American Struggles — *Howard, Nancy Shroyer*

Jacob the Liar — *Becker, Jurek*

c Jacob Two-Two's First Spy Case (Illus. by Michael Chesworth) — *Richler, Mordecai*

The Jacobites: Britain and Europe 1688-1788 — *Szechi, Daniel*

Jacob's Air — *Russell, Bruce L*

c Jacob's Best Sisters (Illus. by Joanne Fitzgerald) — *Jam, Teddy*

Jacob's Ladder — *BenShea, Noah*

Jacobus Hoogstraeten Gegen Johannes Reuchlin — *Peterse, Hans*

Jacopo Bassano and His Public — *Aikema, Bernard*

Jacqueline Bouvier: An Intimate Memoir — *Davis, John H*

c Jacqueline Hyde (Illus. by A Rinaldi) — *Swindells, Robert*

Jacqueline Kennedy Onassis: The Making of a First Lady — *Lowe, Jacques*

Jacques Chessex: Calvinism and the Text — *Bond, David J*

Jacques Delors and European Integration — *Ross, George*

Jacques Lacan: His Life and Work — *Roudinesco, Elisabeth*

Jacques Legardeur De Saint-Pierre: Officer, Gentleman, Entrepreneur — *Peyser, Joseph L*

Jacques Maritain and the Jews — *Royal, Robert*

c Jacques-Yves Cousteau: Exploring the Wonders of the Deep — *Markham, Lois*

y Jade and Iron (Illus. by Luis Garay) — *Aldana, Patricia*

c The Jade Horse, the Cricket, and the Peach Stone (Illus. by Winson Trang) — *Tompert, Ann*

The Jade Peony — *Choy, Wayson*

Jade Slash Laverna — *Montagnes, Anne*

Jaded — *Gaitano, Nick*

Jadid Al-Islam — *Patai, Raphael*

c Jaguar — *Smith, Roland*

The Jaguar and the Anteater — *Arcand, Bernard*

c Jaguar in the Rain Forest (Illus. by Michael Rothman) — *Ryder, Joanne*

Der Jahwist — *Levin, Christoph*

J'Ai Pas Ferme L'Oeil De L'Ete — *Koskas, Marco*

y Jaime Escalante: Sensational Teacher — *Byers, Ann*

c Jake Again (Illus. by Nick Butterworth) — *Butterworth, Annette*

c Jake--The Adventures of an Unusual Dog (Illus. by Nick Butterworth) — *Butterworth, Annette*

Jakob Michael Reinhold Lenz: Studien Zum Gesamtwerk — *Hill, David, 1943-*

Jalamanta: A Message from the Desert — *Anaya, Rudolfo*

c Jalapeno Bagels (Illus. by Robert Casilla) — *Wing, Natasha*

c Jamaica — *Barraclough, John*

r Jamaica (Essential Travel Guides)

c Jamaica Louise James (Illus. by Sheila White Samton) — *Hest, Amy*

c Jamaica Sandwich? (Illus. by Rick Dupre) — *Cleary, Brian P*

James I — *Brown, Michael*

James I — *Durston, Christopher*

James II and English Politics 1678-1688 — *Mullett, Michael*

r James A. Michener: A Bibliography — *Groseclose, David A*

c James and the Dinosaurs (Illus. by Bill Basso) — *Johnson, Doug*

c James and the Giant Peach (Illus. by Quentin Blake) — *Dahl, Roald*

c James and the Giant Peach (Illus. by Lane Smith) — *Dahl, Roald*

y James Baldwin — *Tackach, James*

y James Baldwin: Voice from Harlem — *Gottfried, Ted*

c James Balog's Animals A to Z — *Balog, James*

James Blish: A Dusk of Idols and Other Stories — *Lyall, Francis*

James Boswell's Life of Johnson. Vol. 1 — *Boswell, James*

James Boswell's Psychological Interpretations — *Newman, Donald J*

James Buchanan and the Political Crisis of the 1850s — *Birkner, Michael J*

y James Clavell: A Critical Companion — *Macdonald, Gina*

James Dobson's War on America — *Alexander-Moegerle, Gil*

y James Herriot's Favorite Dog Stories — *Herriot, James*

y James Herriot's Favorite Dog Stories (Timothy). Audio Version — *Herriot, James*

James J. Hill: Empire Builder of the Northwest — *Malone, Michael P*

r James Joyce A to Z — *Fargnoli, A Nicholas*

James Joyce and Nationalism — *Nolan, Emer*

James Joyce and the Art of Mediation — *Weir, David*

James Joyce and the Burden of Disease — *Ferris, Kathleen*

James Joyce and the Language of History — *Spoo, Robert*

James Joyce and the Problem of Justice — *Valente, Joseph*

James Joyce, Ulysses, and the Construction of Jewish Identity — *Davison, Neil R*

James Kay-Shuttleworth: Journey of an Outsider — *Selleck, R J W*

James Louis Petigru: Southern Conservative, Southern Dissenter — *Pease, William H*

r James Madison and the American Nation 1751-1836

y James McNair's Beans and Grains — *McNair, James*

James McNeill Whistler — *Dorment, Richard*

r James McNeill Whistler: Drawings, Pastels, and Watercolours — *MacDonald, Margaret F*

y James Printer: A Novel of Rebellion — *Jacobs, Paul Samuel*

James S. Coleman — *Clark, Jon*

James Smetham: Artist, Author, Pre-Raphaelite Associate — *Casteras, Susan P*

James Stewart: A Biography — *Dewey, Donald*

James, the Brother of Jesus — *Eisenman, Robert*

James Thurber: His Life and Times — *Kinney, Harrison*

James Wait Et Les Lunettes Noires — *Dorsinville, Max*

James Whale: A Biography — *Gatiss, Mark*

Jammin' at the Margins — *Gabbard, Krin*

Jan Messent's World of Embroidery — *Messent, Jan*

Jan Steen, Painter and Storyteller — *Chapman, H Perry*

Jan Steen: The Drawing Lesson — *Walsh, John*

Jan Van Goyen 1596-1656 — *Beck, Hans-Ulrich*

Jancis Robinson's Guide to Wine Grapes — *Robinson, Jancis*

Jancis Robinson's Wine Course — *Robinson, Jancis*

r The Jane Addams Papers — *Bryan, Mary Lynn McCree*

Jane and the Man of the Cloth — *Barron, Stephanie*

Jane and the Unpleasantness at Scargrave Manor — *Barron, Stephanie*

Jane Austen and Discourses of Feminism — *Looser, Devoney*
Jane Austen and Food — *Lane, Maggie*
Jane Austen and Representations of Regency England — *Sales, Roger*
Jane Austen and the Clergy — *Collins, Irene*
Jane Austen: Her Life — *Honan, Park*
Jane Austen in Style — *Watkins, Susan*
Jane Austen: Obstinate Heart — *Myer, Valerie Grosvenor*
Jane Austen's Business — *McMaster, Juliet*
Jane Austen's Christmas — *Hubert, Maria*
Jane Austen's Letters — *Austen, Jane*
Jane Brody's Allergy Fighter — *Brody, Jane E*
Jane Eyre — *Bronte, Charlotte*
Jane Fairfax — *Aiken, Joan*
Jane Fonda: Cooking for Healthy Living — *Fonda, Jane*
y Jane Goodall — *Pratt, Paula Bryant*
Jane Osborn — *D'Aunet, Leonie*
Jane Pepper's Garden — *Pepper, Jane*
c Jane Yolen's Old MacDonald Songbook — *Yolen, Jane*
r Jane's Aero-Engines — *Gunston, Bill*
r Jane's Air Traffic Control 1996-97
r Jane's Aircraft Upgrades 1996-97
r Jane's All the World's Aircraft 1996-97
r Jane's Armour and Artillery 1995-96
r Jane's Avionics 1996-97
r Jane's Electro-Optic Systems — *O'Leary, A P*
r Jane's Fighting Ships 1996-97
r Jane's Helicopter Markets and Systems — *Endres, Gunter*
r Jane's High-Speed Marine Transportation 1996-97
r Jane's International ABC Aerospace Directory 1996
r Jane's International Defence Directory 1997
r Jane's NBC Protection Equipment 1996-97
r Jane's Sentinel, the Unfair Advantage: Central America and the Caribbean. 1996 Ed.
r Jane's Space Directory 1995-96. Electronic Media Version
r Jane's Space Directory 1996-97
r Jane's Tank and Combat Vehicle Recognition Guide — *Foss, Christopher F*
yr Jane's Warship Recognition Guide — *Faulkner, Keith, 1940-*
Janet Campbell Hale — *Hale, Frederick*
c Janet's Thingamajigs (Illus. by DyAnne DiSalvo-Ryan) — *Cleary, Beverly*
c Janice VanCleave's 202 Oozing, Bubbling, Dripping and Bouncing Experiments — *VanCleave, Janice Pratt*
c Janice VanCleave's Guide to the Best Science Fair Projects — *VanCleave, Janice Pratt*
c Janice VanCleave's Oceans for Every Kid — *VanCleave, Janice Pratt*
c Janice VanCleave's Plants — *VanCleave, Janice Pratt*
c Janice VanCleave's Play and Find Out about Nature — *VanCleave, Janice Pratt*
c Janice VanCleave's Play and Find Out about Science — *VanCleave, Janice Pratt*
c Janice VanCleave's Rocks and Minerals (Illus. by Doris Ettlinger) — *VanCleave, Janice Pratt*
c Japan — *Bornoff, Nick*
c Japan: A Modern Land with Ancient Roots — *Galvin, Irene Flum*
Japan: A Reinterpretation — *Smith, Patrick*
Japan and Malaysian Development — *Jomo, K S*
Japan and the City of London — *Newall, Paul*
Japan and the Enemies of Open Political Science — *Williams, David, 1948, July, 7-*
r Japan and the Japanese — *Makino, Yasuko*
Japan and the New World Order — *Steven, Rob*
Japan and the World since 1868 — *Barnhart, Michael A*
Japan Encountered — *Wright, Scott*
r Japan Encyclopedia — *De Mente, Boye*
Japan in the International Financial System — *Iwami, Toru*
Japan in the Posthegemonic World — *Akaha, Tsuneo*
Japan, NAFTA and Europe — *Mason, T David*
Japan Swings — *McGregor, Richard*
Japan under Construction — *Woodall, Brian*
The Japan We Never Knew — *Suzuki, David*
Japan, Who Governs? — *Johnson, Chalmers*
The Japanese Advantage? — *Hunt, Brian*
yr The Japanese American Family Album — *Hoobler, Dorothy*
y Japanese-American Internment in American History — *Fremon, David K*
yr Japanese Americans — *Lee, Lauren*

The Japanese and Europe — *Conte-Helm, Marie*
The Japanese Automobile Industry — *Shimokawa, Koichi*
Japanese Banking — *Tamaki, Norio*
Japanese Business Information — *Clough, Ronald*
Japanese by Spring — *Reed, Ishmael*
Japanese Childrearing — *Shwalb, David W*
The Japanese Civil Service and Economic Development — *Kim, Hyung-Ki*
Japanese Classical Theater in Films — *McDonald, Keiko I*
Japanese Companies--British Factories — *McCormick, Brian*
Japanese Corrections — *Johnson, Elmer H*
The Japanese Economic Crisis — *Woronoff, Jon*
The Japanese Election System — *Wada, Junichiro*
r The Japanese Filmography — *Galbraith, Stuart*
Japanese Firms in Europe — *Sachwald, Frederique*
Japanese Garden Design — *Keane, Marc*
Japanese Industrialisation and the Asian Economy — *Latham, A J H*
Japanese Lessons — *Benjamin, Gail R*
The Japanese Main Bank System — *Aoki, Masahiko*
Japanese Modern — *Fraser, James*
r Japanese Psycholinguistics — *Kess, Joseph F*
Japanese Religions — *Reader, Ian*
Japanese Sense of Self — *Rosenberger, Nancy R*
Japanese Sentence Processing — *Mazuka, Reiko*
r Japanese Studies in Canada
r Japanese Studies in the United States, the 1990s
The Japanese Submarine Force and World War II — *Boyd, Carl*
The Japanese Television Cartel — *Schwartzman, David*
The Japanese Theatre — *Ortolani, Benito*
The Japanese Wartime Empire 1931-1945 — *Duus, Peter*
Japanese Women — *Fujimura-Fanselow, Kumiko*
Japanese Workers in Protest — *Turner, Christena L*
Japan's Capitalism — *Tsuru, Shigeto*
Japan's Computer and Communications Industry — *Fransman, Martin*
Japan's First Modern War — *Lone, Stewart*
Japan's Foreign Policy in the 1990s — *Drifte, Reinhard*
Japan's Golden Age — *Hickman, Money L*
Japan's Hidden Christians — *Harrington, Ann M*
r Japan's Hidden Hot Springs — *Neff, Robert*
Japan's Trade Policy — *Mikanagi, Yumiko*
p Jar of Fools. Pts. 1-2 — *Lutes, Jason*
c A Jar of Tiny Stars (Illus. by Andi MacLeod) — *Cullinan, Bernice E*
Le Jardin De Dima — *Weil, Sylvie*
c Jasmine Helps a Foal — *Bryant, Bonnie*
c Jasmine Trots Ahead — *Bryant, Bonnie*
Jasper Johns: A Retrospective — *Varnedoe, Kirk*
Jasper Johns: Privileged Information — *Johnston, Jill*
Java by Example. 1st Ed. — *Jackson, Jerry R*
Java by Example. 2nd Ed. — *Jackson, Jerry R*
Java Database Programming with JDBC — *Patel, Pratik*
Java Handbook — *Naughton, Patrick*
Java Language API Super Bible — *Groner, Daniel*
r Java Language Reference — *Grand, Mark*
r The Java Language Specification — *Gosling, James*
r Java Manual of Style — *Gurewich, Nathan*
Java Programming Basics — *Mangan, Mark*
p Java Report
Java Security — *McGraw, Gary*
Java Sourcebook — *Anuff, Ed*
Java Threads — *Oaks, Scott*
The Java Virtual Machine Specification — *Lindholm, Tim*
Java with Borland C++ — *Pappas, Chris H*
JavaScript Developer's Resource — *Husain, Kamran*
JavaScript Essentials — *Manger, Jason*
JavaScript for the World Wide Web — *Schneider, Jeremy*
JavaScript Sourcebook — *McComb, Gordon*
r JavaScript: The Definitive Guide. 2nd Ed. — *Flanagan, David*
Jawaharlal Nehru — *Nanda, B R*
p Jay's Journal of Anomalies
c Jazeera in the Sun (Illus. by Paul Howard) — *Bruce, Lisa*
The Jazz Age — *Fitzgerald, F Scott*
Jazz Fest Memories — *Smith, Michael P*
Jazz in American Culture — *Peretti, Burton W*
r Jazz Milestones — *Vail, Ken*
c Jazz, Pizzazz, and the Silver Threads (Illus. by Robin Oz) — *Quattlebaum, Mary*

r Jazz Research and Performance Materials. 2nd Ed. — *Meadows, Eddie S*
Jazz: The American Theme Song — *Collier, James Lincoln*
y Jazz: The Great American Art — *Seymour, Gene*
yr Jazz: The Rough Guide — *Carr, Ian*
r Jazz: The Ultimate Guide
c Jazz Up Your Jeans (Illus. by Geri Strigenz Bourget) — *Whitney, Brooks*
Jazz Veterans — *Deffaa, Chip*
c Je Lis Tu Lis — *Hameau, Marie-Anne*
Je Suis Cadien — *Arceneaux, Jean*
Je Suis Martiniquaise — *Capecia, Mayotte*
Jealous-Hearted Me — *Packer, Nancy Huddleston*
The Jealous Potter — *Levi-Strauss, Claude*
c Jean Craighead George — *Cary, Alice*
Jean Fautrier: Musee National Fernand Leger, Biot, 20 Juin - 15 Septembre 1996 Et Mucsarnok, Budapest, 15 Octobre - 10 Novembre 1996
Jean Girard: Musicien En Nouvelle-France, Bourges, 1696 - Montreal 1765 — *Gallat-Morin, Elisabeth*
Jean Howard's Hollywood — *Howard, Jean*
Jean-Jacques Rousseau in American Literature — *Dame, Frederick William*
Jean-Jacques: The Early Life and Work of Jean-Jacques Rousseau 1712-1754 — *Cranston, Maurice*
Jean Le Rond D'Alembert Philosophe — *Le Ru, Veronique*
Jean-Luc Godard's Hail Mary — *Locke, Meryl*
Jean Monnet 1888-1979 — *Roussel, Eric*
Jean-Paul Sartre and the Politics of Reason — *Dobson, Andrew*
Jean Price-Mars, the Haitian Elite and the American Occupation 1915-1935 — *Shannon, Magdaline W*
Jean Renoir: Projections of Paradise — *Bergan, Ronald*
Jean Rivard Ou L'Art De Reussir — *Major, Robert*
Jean-Roland Malet: Premier Historien Des Finances De La Monarchie Francaise — *Bonney, Margaret*
A Jean Toomer Reader — *Rusch, Frederik L*
Jean Toomer: Selected Essays and Literary Criticism — *Toomer, Jean*
Jed the Dead — *Foster, Alan Dean*
c Jedi Under Siege — *Anderson, Kevin J*
y Jeeves and the Feudal Spirit (Davidson). Audio Version — *Wodehouse, P G*
y Jeeves in the Morning (Davidson). Audio Version — *Wodehouse, P G*
Jeff Wall — *Duve, Thierry De*
Jefferson and Madison — *Banning, Lance*
Jefferson Davis: The Man and His Hour — *Davis, William C*
The Jeffersonian Dream — *Gates, Paul W*
Jeffrey Archer: Stranger than Fiction — *Crick, Michael*
Jekyll and Hyde Adapted — *Rose, Brian A*
c Jelly Beans for Sale (Illus. by Bruce McMillan) — *McMillan, Bruce*
c Jenius: The Amazing Guinea Pig (Illus. by Brian Floca) — *King-Smith, Dick*
c Jennifer Murdley's Toad (Coville). Audio Version — *Coville, Bruce*
y Jennifer's Secret — *Baer, Judy*
Jenny Dorset — *Williams, Philip Lee*
c Jenny Reen and the Jack Muh Lantern (Illus. by Keinyo White) — *Smalls, Irene*
Jenseits Der Legenden — *Schwanitz, Wolfgang*
Jeremiah: Terrorist Prophet — *Smith, Michael A*
y Jeremy Poldark (Britton). Audio Version — *Graham, Winston*
c Jeremy Thatcher, Dragon Hatcher (Coville). Audio Version — *Coville, Bruce*
y Jericho — *Hickman, Janet*
Jerome: After the Pagent — *Avena, Thomas*
Jersey Diners — *Genovese, Peter*
y Jerusalem — *Holland, Cecelia, 1943-*
Jerusalem: An Anthology of Jewish Canadian Poetry — *Mayne, Seymour*
Jerusalem: An Archeological Biography — *Shanks, Hershel*
The Jerusalem Continuations — *Grillo, Peter R*
Jerusalem in 3000 Years — *Gidal, Tim*
Jerusalem: In the Shadow of Heaven — *Wells, Susan, 1956-*
Jerusalem in the Twentieth Century — *Gilbert, Martin, 1936-*
Jerusalem: One City, Three Faiths — *Armstrong, Karen*
Jerusalem: One City, Three Faiths (Armstrong). Audio Version — *Armstrong, Karen*
Jerusalem: Rebirth of a City — *Gilbert, Martin, 1936-*

r The Jerusalem Report Five Year CD-ROM. Electronic Media Version
Jerusalem Today — *Karmi, Ghada*
Jerzy Kosinski: A Biography — *Sloan, James Park*
Jesaja Und Jeremiah — *Wendel, Ute*
y Jesse — *Soto, Gary*
c Jesse James — *Wukovits, John F*
Jesse James Was My Neighbor — *Croy, Homer*
Jesse: The Life and Pilgrimage of Jesse Jackson — *Frady, Marshall*
c Jessica (Illus. by Kevin Henkes) — *Henkes, Kevin*
c The Jester Has Lost His Jingles (Illus. by David Saltzman) — *Saltzman, David*
r Jesuit Mission Presses in the Pacific Northwest — *Schoenberg, Wilfred P*
Les Jesuites A La Renaissance — *Giard, Luce*
Jesus: An Unconventional Biography — *Duquesne, Jacques*
r Jesus and His World — *Rousseau, John J*
Jesus and Judaism — *Sanders, E P*
Jesus and Liberation — *Piar, Carlos R*
c Jesus and the Children (Illus. by Bill Farnsworth) — *Quattlebaum, Mary*
Jesus and the Dead Sea Scrolls — *Charlesworth, James H*
Jesus and the Holocaust — *Marcus, Joel*
Jesus and the Land — *Page, Charles R, II*
Jesus and the Other Names — *Knitter, Paul F*
Jesus and the Victory of God — *Wright, N T*
Jesus at 2000 — *Borg, Marcus J*
Jesus Christ and Christian Vision — *Ottati, Douglas F*
Jesus Christ in the Preaching of Calvin and Schleiermacher — *DeVries, Dawn*
c Jesus' Christmas Party — *Allan, Nicholas*
The Jesus Conspiracy — *Kersten, Holger*
Jesus in Contemporary Scholarship — *Borg, Marcus J*
Jesus' Jewishness — *Charlesworth, James H*
The Jesus Legend — *Wells, G A*
Jesus: Miriam's Child, Sophia's Prophet — *Schussler Fiorenza, Elisabeth*
Jesus of Nazareth and Other Writings — *Wagner, Richard, 1813-1883*
Jesus of Nazareth, Lord and Christ — *Green, Joel B*
Jesus of the Apocalypse — *Thiering, Barbara*
Jesus, Paul and the Law — *Dunn, James D G*
Jesus' Plan for a New World — *Rohr, Richard*
The Jesus Quest — *Witherington, Ben, III*
Jesus, Qumran, and the Vatican — *Betz, Otto*
Jesus, Son of God, Son of Mary, Immanuel — *Goergen, Donald J*
Jesus the Healer — *Davies, Stevan L*
Jesus the Jew — *Watson, Alan*
Jesus the Jewish Theologian — *Young, Brad*
Jesus the Liberator — *Prior, Michael*
Jesus the Messiah — *Stein, Robert H, 1935-*
Jesus the Pharisee — *Falk, Harvey*
Jesus the Wisdom of God — *Edwards, Denis*
Jesus under Fire — *Wilkins, Michael J*
Jesus within Judaism — *Charlesworth, James H*
Jesusgate — *Brown, Grayson Warren*
Die Jesusgeschichte Des Matthaus — *Luz, Ulrich*
Jet Age Flight Helmets — *Wise, Alan R*
c Jet Smoke and Dragon Fire — *Ashton, Charles*
c Jets (Illus. by Hans Jenssen) — *Jenssen, Hans*
c Jets Series
Le Jeu De La Vie Et De La Mort — *Dubuis, Pierre*
La Jeune Amante — *Montupet, Janine*
Une Jeunesse Francaise — *Pean, Pierre*
A Jew in Communist Prague. Vol. 1 — *Giardino, Vittorio*
The Jewel of Seven Stars — *Stoker, Bram*
The Jewellery of Roman Britain — *Johns, Catherine*
c Jewelry — *Doney, Meryl*
y Jewelry: A Practical Guide to Creative Crafts — *Innes, Miranda*
Jewelry in Europe and America — *Turner, Ralph*
c Jewish — *Stoppleman, Monica*
yr The Jewish American Family Album — *Hoobler, Dorothy*
Jewish and Christian Mysticism — *Cohn-Sherbok, Dan*
Jewish Art — *Sed-Rajna, Gabrielle*
Jewish Bridges — *Cohn, Michael*
The Jewish Challenge — *Seager, Frederic*
c The Jewish Children's Bible: Genesis (Illus. by Daniel Goldberg) — *Prenzlau, Sheryl*
Jewish-Christian Dialogue — *Novak, David*
r Jewish-Christian Relations — *Shermis, Michael*
The Jewish Chronicle †and Anglo-Jewry 1841-1991 — *Cesarani, David*
Jewish Days — *Klagsbrun, Francine*

The Jewish Diaspora in Latin America — *Sheinin, David*
r Jewish Entertainment Resource Directory — *Ginsburgh, Judy Caplan*
The Jewish Experience — *Cantor, Norman F*
r Jewish Heroes and Heroines of America — *Brody, Seymour*
Jewish History, Jewish Religion — *Shahak, Israel*
c The Jewish Holiday Craft Book (Illus. by Melinda Levine) — *Ross, Kathy*
r Jewish Holidays and Festivals — *Edidin, Ben M*
The Jewish Idea of Culture — *Roth, Sol*
Jewish Identity and Civilizing Processes — *Russell, Steven*
Jewish Identity in Early Rabbinic Writings — *Stern, Sacha*
Jewish Itineraries — *Brandes, Francesca*
Jewish Liberal Politics in Tsarist Russia 1900-1914 — *Gassenschmidt, Christoph*
Jewish Life in Renaissance Italy — *Bonfil, Roberto*
Jewish Liturgy — *Elbogen, Ismar*
The Jewish Manual — *Montefiore, Judith Cohen, Lady*
A Jewish Mother from Berlin. Susanna — *Kolmar, Gertrud*
The Jewish Novel in the Ancient World — *Wills, Lawrence M*
Jewish Perspectives on Christianity — *Rothschild, Fritz A*
Jewish Philosophers and Jewish Philosophy — *Fackenheim, Emil L*
Jewish Power — *Goldberg, J J*
p The Jewish Quarterly
The Jewish Religion — *Jacobs, Louis*
Jewish Responses to Early Christians — *Setzer, Claudia J*
Jewish Responses to Modernity — *Lederhendler, Eli*
Jewish Theology and Process Thought — *Lubarsky, Sandra B*
Jewish Thought and Scientific Discovery in Early Modern Europe — *Ruderman, David B*
Jewish Voices in Brazilian Literature — *Vieira, Nelson H*
The Jewish Wars — *Alexander, Edward*
Jewish Women in Greco-Roman Palestine — *Ilan, Tal*
Jewish Writers, German Literature — *Bahti, Timothy*
Jews — *Berkley, George E*
The Jews — *Unterman, Alan*
Jews, America — *Brenner, Frederic*
Jews and Blacks — *Lerner, Michael, 1943-*
Jews and Christians — *Harrelson, Walter*
Jews and Christians — *Klenicki, Leon*
Jews and Christians in Pursuit of Social Justice — *Falk, Randall M*
Jews and Gender — *Harrowitz, Nancy A*
The Jews and Germany — *Traverso, Enzo*
Jews and Revolution in Nineteenth-Century Russia — *Haberer, Erich*
Jews and the New American Scene — *Lipset, Seymour Martin*
Jews for Sale? — *Bauer, Yehuda*
Jews, Germany, Memory — *Serotta, Edward*
The Jews: History, Memory, and the Present — *Vidal-Naquet, Pierre*
The Jews in Christian Art — *Schreckenberg, Heinz*
The Jews in Nineteenth-Century France — *Graetz, Michael*
Jews in Russian Literature after the October Revolution — *Sicher, Efraim*
The Jews in the History of England 1485-1850 — *Katz, David S*
Jews in the Notarial Culture — *Burns, Robert I*
The Jews in the Time of Jesus — *Wylen, Stephen M*
Jews in Today's German Culture — *Gilman, Sander L*
The Jews in Umbria. Vol. 1 — *Toaff, Ariel*
Jews, Medicine, and Medieval Society — *Shatzmiller, Joseph*
The Jews of Boston — *Sarna, Jonathan D*
The Jews of Chicago — *Cutler, Irving*
The Jews of Egypt — *Modrzejewski, Joseph Meleze*
The Jews of Hungary — *Patai, Raphael*
The Jews of India — *Slapak, Orpa*
The Jews of Kurdistan — *Brauer, Erich*
The Jews of Moscow, Kiev and Minsk — *Brym, Robert J*
The Jews of the Balkans — *Benbassa, Esther*
The Jews of the Ottoman Empire — *Levy, Avigdor*
The Jews of the Republic — *Birnbaum, Pierre*
Jews on the Move — *Goldstein, Sidney*
Jews, Visigoths and Muslims in Medieval Spain — *Roth, Norman*
y JFK for a New Generation — *Hunt, Conover*

Ji Jian Suo Zhi. Vols. 1-2 — *Liu, Cui-Rong*
Jiang Gang Zhen Dang — *Bo, Yang*
Jiang Qing Chuan Qi De Yi Sheng — *Zhao, Lingxi*
The Jiangyin Mission Station — *Kessler, Lawrence D*
c Jig, Fig and Mrs. Pig (Illus. by Francesca Martin) — *Hansard, Peter*
Jiggers — *Bruce, Todd*
c Jigsaw Jackson (Illus. by Daniel San Souci) — *Birchman, David F*
Jihad in Classical and Modern Islam — *Peters, Rudolph*
Jihad vs. McWorld — *Barber, Benjamin R*
c Jill's Happy Un-Birthday — *Kaye, Marilyn*
c Jim Abbott — *Kramer, Jon*
c Jim Eisenreich — *Gutman, Bill*
Jim Fobel's Casseroles — *Fobel, Jim*
Jim Harrison — *Reilly, Edward C*
Jim Thompson Omnibus — *Thompson, Jim*
c Jimbo on Board the Nettie Quill (Illus. by Jeffrey Hurst) — *Harrison, Henry Ford*
y Jimi Hendrix — *Piccoli, Sean*
The Jimi Hendrix Experience — *Hopkins, Jerry*
Jimmie Rodgers: The Life and Times of America's Blue Yodeler — *Porterfield, Nolan*
c Jimmy (Jarvis). Audio Version — *Crompton, Richmal*
Jimmy and Rita — *Addonizio, Kim*
Jimmy Buffett: The Man from Margaritaville Revealed — *Eng, Steve*
y Jimmy Carter: A Comprehensive Biography from Plains to Post-Presidency — *Bourne, Peter G*
Jimmy Carter, American Moralist — *Morris, Kenneth E*
Jimmy Carter as Peacemaker — *Troester, Rod*
y Jimmy Carter: On the Road to Peace — *Lazo, Caroline*
Jimmy Durante: His Show Business Career — *Bakish, David*
c Jingle Babies (Illus. by Tom Arma) — *Arma, Tom*
Jingle Bell Baby — *Little, Kate*
c Jingle Bells (Illus. by Alexandra Wallner) — *Wallner, Alexandra*
c Jingo Django (Dufris). Audio Version — *Fleischman, Sid*
Jinnah Reinterpreted — *Khairi, Saad R*
y Jip: His Story — *Paterson, Katherine*
Jo Verso's Cross Stitch Gifts for Children — *Verso, Jo*
r Joan Baez: A Bio-Bibliography — *Fuss, Charles J*
Joan Lunden's Healthy Living — *Lunden, Joan*
Joan Mitchell — *Kertess, Klaus*
r Joan Robinson: A Bio-Bibliography — *Cicarelli, James*
Job Analysis Kit — *McIntire, Sandra*
Job and the Mystery of Suffering — *Rohr, Richard*
Job Creation and Destruction — *Davis, Steven J*
Job-Hunting on the Internet — *Bolles, Richard Nelson*
Job Interviews for Dummies — *Kennedy, Joyce Lain*
Job Satisfaction in Social Services — *Williamson, David A, 1955-*
Job Search. 2nd Ed. — *Dawson, Kenneth M*
The Jobless Future — *Aronowitz, Stanley*
Jobs and Skill Requirements for Entry-Level Workers
r Jobs in Paradise — *Maltzman, Jeffrey*
Jock Sturges (Scalo) — *Sturges, Jock*
Jocoserious Joyce — *Bell, Robert H*
Joe (Brown). Audio Version — *Brown, Larry*
Joe (Stechschulte). Audio Version — *Brown, Larry*
Joe Alsop's Cold War — *Yoder, Edwin M, Jr.*
y Joe and Marilyn (Estell). Audio Version — *Kahn, Roger*
Joe and Me — *Prosek, James*
c Joe Dumars — *Stewart, Mark*
Joe Orton — *Rusinko, Susan*
Joel — *Bible. O.T. Joel. English. Crenshaw. 1995*
r Joel Whitburn's Top Pop Albums 1955-1996 — *Whitburn, Joel*
r Joel Whitburn's Top R&B Singles 1942-1995 — *Whitburn, Joel*
Joen Kyla — *Viinikainen, Antero*
c Joey's Birthday Wish (Illus. by Victoria Vebell Bruck) — *Lambert, Matthew*
y The Joffrey Ballet — *Anawalt, Sasha*
Johann Christoph Gottsched 1700-1766 — *Mitchell, P M*
r Johann Gottfried Herder: Selected Early Works 1764-1767 — *Herder, Johann Gottfried*
Johann Gregorius Horoldt 1696-1775 Und Die Meissener Porzellan-Malerei — *Pietsch, Ulrich*
Johann Gutenberg: The Man and His Invention — *Kapr, Albert*

Johann Sebastian Bach as His World Knew Him — *Bettmann, Otto L*

Johann Sturm on Education — *Spitz, Lewis William*

Johann Wolfgang Goethe — *Jessing, Benedikt*

y Johanna — *Cooperstein, Claire*

y Johannes Brahms: An Essential Guide to His Life and Work — *Brown, Jonathon, 1955-*

Johannes Geiler Von Keysersberg Samtliche Werke. Bks. 1-3 — *Geiler Von Kaysersberg, Johann*

Johannesnacht — *Timm, Uwe*

The Johannine Letters — *Strecker, Georg*

The Johannine World — *Hawkin, David J*

John — *Stibbe, Mark W G*

y John Adams: A Life — *Ferling, John*

John Ash's Wine Country Cuisine. Electronic Media Version

John Bates Clark: The Making of a Neoclassical Economist — *Henry, John F*

John Betjeman: Letters. Vol. 2 — *Betjeman, John, Sir*

John Betjeman: Letters. Vols. 1-2 — *Betjeman, John, Sir*

c John Brown, Rose and the Midnight Cat (Illus. by Ron Brooks) — *Wagner, Jenny*

John Buchan's Collected Poems — *Buchan, John*

c John Burroughs: The Sage of Slabsides (Illus. by Ginger Wadsworth) — *Wadsworth, Ginger*

c John C. Fremont: Soldier and Pathfinder — *Sanford, William R*

John Calvin and John Owen on Mortification — *Gleason, Randall C*

John Calvin's Exegesis of the Old Testament — *Puckett, David L*

John Cardinal Krol and the Cultural Revolution — *Jones, E Michael*

John Chartres: Mystery Man of the Treaty — *Murphy, Brian P*

John Christian Bach: Mozart's Friend and Mentor — *Gartner, Heinz*

John Chrysostom and the Jews — *Wilken, Robert L*

John Clare by Himself — *Clare, John*

John Clare in Context — *Haughton, Hugh*

John Clavell 1601-43 — *Pafford, J H P*

r John Coltrane: A Discography and Musical Biography — *Fujioka, Yasuhiro*

John Courtney Murray and the Dilemma of Religious Toleration — *Pavlischek, Keith J*

John Deakin: Photographs — *Deakin, John*

John Deakin (Schirmer/Mosel) — *Deakin, John*

John Dee: The Politics of Reading and Writing in the English Renaissance — *Sherman, William H*

John Dewey: An Intellectual Portrait — *Hook, Sidney*

John Dewey and the High Tide of American Liberalism — *Ryan, Alan*

John Donne's Desire of More — *Hester, M Thomas*

John Dudley, Duke of Northumberland 1504-1553 — *Loades, D M*

John Everett Millais 1829-1896 — *Donovan, Claire*

y John F. Kennedy — *Pietrusza, David*

c John F. Kennedy: President of the New Frontier — *Cole, Michael D*

John Ford: Hollywood's Old Master — *Davis, Ronald L*

John Ford's Westerns — *Darby, William*

John Freeman of Norfolk County, Virginia — *Mosher, Merrill Hill*

John Gay: A Profession of Friendship — *Nokes, David*

John Goddard's Trout-Fishing Techniques — *Goddard, John*

A John Graves Reader — *Graves, John, 1920-*

John Guare. Vol. 1 — *Guare, John*

John Hedgecoe's Workbook of Photo Techniques — *Hedgecoe, John*

c John Henry — *Lester, Julius*

John Hittson: Cattle King on the Texas and Colorado Frontier — *Maddux, Vernon R*

c John Joe and the Big Hen (Illus. by Paul Howard) — *Waddell, Martin*

John Keane: Conflicts of Interest — *Lawson, Mark, 1962-*

John Kenneth Galbraith — *Stanfield, James Ronald*

John L. Sullivan and His America — *Isenberg, Michael T*

John LaFarge and the Limits of Catholic Interracialism 1911-1963 — *Southern, David W*

y John Lennon: The Beatles and Beyond — *Wright, David K*

John Locke and America — *Arneil, Barbara*

John Locke and the Ethics of Belief — *Wolterstorff, Nicholas*

John Locke: Resistance, Religion, and Responsibility — *Marshall, John, 1961-*

John M. Barber's Chesapeake — *Barber, John M*

John Marshall: Definer of a Nation — *Smith, Jean Edward*

r The John Max Wulfing Collection in Washington University. Vol. 3 — *Washington University (St. Louis, MO)*

John McGraw — *Alexander, Charles C*

John McPhee — *Pearson, Michael*

r The John Metcalf Papers — *Moore, Jean M*

John Millington Synge: A Biography — *Kiely, David M*

r John Milton: An Annotated Bibliography 1968-1988 — *Huckabay, Calvin*

John Muir — *Ito, Tom*

John Muir: Apostle of Nature — *Wilkins, Thurman*

John Muir: His Life and Letters and Other Writings — *Muir, John*

John Muir's Stickeen and the Lessons of Nature — *Limbaugh, Ronald H*

John of the Cross — *McGreal, Wilfrid*

John Quincy Adams and the Public Virtues of Diplomacy — *Russell, Greg*

John Ringo: The Gunfighter Who Never Was — *Burrows, Jack*

y John Saul: A Critical Companion — *Bail, Paul*

John Singleton Copley in America — *Rebora, Carrie*

John Sloan: Painter and Rebel — *Loughery, John*

John Slocum and the Indian Shaker Church — *Ruby, Robert H*

John Smyth's Congregation — *Coggins, James R*

y John Steinbeck — *Reef, Catherine*

y John Steinbeck: A Biography — *Parini, Jay*

r John Steinbeck: An Annotated Guide to Biographical Sources — *Harmon, Robert B*

John Steinbeck: The War Years 1939-1945 — *Simmonds, Roy*

John Stuart and the Struggle for Empire on the Southern Frontier — *Snapp, J Russell*

John Stuart Mill and India — *Zastoupil, Lynn*

John the Baptist: Prophet and Evangelist — *Kazmierski, Carl R*

John, the Son of Zebedee — *Culpepper, R Alan*

John Thornbury in Tennessee and Alabama — *Hill, Clara M*

John Wayne's America — *Wills, Garry*

John Wayne's America (Wills). Audio Version — *Wills, Garry*

John Wesley Hardin: Dark Angel of Texas — *Metz, Leon Claire*

John Wesley's Conception and Use of Scripture — *Jones, Scott J*

John Wilkes: A Friend to Liberty — *Thomas, Peter D G*

y John Wilkes Booth: A Sister's Memoir — *Clarke, Asia Booth*

John William Dawson: Faith, Hope, and Science — *Sheets-Pyenson, Susan*

c Johnny and the Bomb — *Pratchett, Terry*

y Johnny and the Bomb (Robinson). Audio Version — *Pratchett, Terry*

y Johnny Casanova — *Rix, Jamie*

r The Johnny Cash Record Catalog — *Smith, John L*

c Johnny Chesthair — *Lynch, Chris*

Johnny Critelli. The Knifemen — *Lentricchia, Frank*

y Johnny Hart's Heroes — *Metzenthen, David*

c Johnny Rides Again — *Muchmore, Jo Ann*

Johnny Rolf: Her Ceramics/Her Gouaches — *Marken, Amy Van*

y Johnny Voodoo — *Lane, Dakota*

c Johnny Wombat (Illus. by Craig Smith) — *Kelleher, Victor*

y Johns (Abrams) — *Johns, Jasper*

r Johns Hopkins Symptoms and Remedies — *Margolis, Simon*

John's Wife — *Coover, Robert*

Johnson and Boswell — *Rogers, Pat*

Johnson-Jahrbuch. Vol. 1

r The Johnson Mortuary Death Records 1904-1937

Johnson on Language — *Horgan, A D*

Joining the Entrepreneurial Elite — *Isachsen, Olaf*

r Joint Electronic Library on CD-ROM 1993

Joint Operation Planning and Execution System. Vol. 1 — *United States. Joint Chiefs of Staff*

Joint Review Committee Right-to-Work Study Final Report

Joint Time-Frequency Analysis — *Qian, Shie*

Joint Warfare of the Armed Forces of the United States. 2nd Ed. — *United States. Joint Chiefs of Staff*

c Jojofu (Illus. by Yoriko Ito) — *Waite, Michael P*

Jokapaivaista Aikaa — *Holappa, Pentti*

The Joke — *Kundera, Milan*

c Joke and Riddle Bonanza (Illus. by Sanford Hoffman) — *Pellowski, Michael*

c Jolis Bijoux — *Wichegrod, Laurence*

Jolly Old England — *Lucier, Armand Francis*

c Jolly Old Santa Claus (Illus. by George Hinke) — *Sparkie*

c The Jolly Pocket Postman — *Ahlberg, Janet*

Jonathan Belcher, Colonial Governor — *Batinski, Michael C*

Jonathan Carver's Travels through America 1766-1768 — *Carver, Jonathan*

Jonathan Edwards and the Catholic Vision of Salvation — *Morimoto, Anri*

A Jonathan Edwards Reader — *Edwards, Jonathan*

Jonathan Edwards, Religious Tradition, and American Culture — *Conforti, Joseph A*

Jonathan Edwards: The Miscellanies A-500 — *Edwards, Jonathan*

Jonathan Edwards's Writings — *Stein, Stephen J*

Jonathan Swift: The Irish Identity — *Mahony, Robert*

r Jones Family Genealogy — *Peck, Patricia D*

Jonestown — *Harris, Wilson*

Jonestown: A Poem — *Sutherland, Fraser*

Joni. 20th Anniversary Ed. — *Tada, Joni Eareckson*

Jonson and the Contexts of His Time — *Evans, Robert C*

c Jorah's Journal (Illus. by Judith Caseley) — *Caseley, Judith*

c Jordan — *South, Coleman*

Jordens Skygge — *Lokkeberg, Vibeke*

c Jordi's Star (Illus. by Susan Gaber) — *Ada, Alma Flor*

Jo's Girls — *McEwen, Christian*

Jose Donoso's House of Fiction — *Gonzalez Mandri, Flora*

Jose Luis Cuevas: El Monstruo Y El Monumento — *Moreno Villarreal, Jaime*

y Jose Marti: Cuban Patriot and Poet — *Goodnough, David*

r Josef Frank, Architect and Designer — *Stritzler-Levine, Nina*

Josef Muller-Brockmann, Designer — *Muller-Brockmann, Josef*

Josef Sudek — *Farova, Anna*

c Josefina (Illus. by Jeanette Winter) — *Winter, Jeanette*

Joseph II — *Blanning, T C W*

Joseph Andrews — *Fielding, Henry*

Joseph Banks and the English Enlightenment — *Gascoigne, John*

Joseph Chamberlain: Entrepreneur in Politics — *Marsh, Peter T*

Joseph Conrad and the Anthropological Dilemma — *Griffith, John W, 1964-*

Joseph De Maistre: An Intellectual Militant — *Lebrun, Richard A*

Joseph E. Johnston: A Civil War Biography — *Symonds, Craig L*

Joseph Losey: A Revenge on Life — *Caute, David*

y Joseph McCarthy: The Misuse of Political Power — *Cohen, Daniel, 1936-*

Joseph Perl's Revealer of Secrets — *Perl, Joseph*

Joseph Ramee: International Architect of the Revolutionary Era — *Turner, Paul V*

Joseph Scaliger: A Study in the History of Classical Scholarship. Vol. 2 — *Grafton, Anthony*

c Joseph's Coat of Colors

Josephus and Faith — *Lindsay, Dennis R*

Josephus: The Essential Works — *Josephus, Flavius*

Joshua — *Girzone, Joseph*

c Joshua and the Big Bad Blue Crabs (Illus. by Mary Barrett Brown) — *Childress, Mark*

Joshua and the Rhetoric of Violence — *Rowlett, Lori L*

c Jouanah: A Hmong Cinderella (Illus. by Anne Sibley O'Brien) — *Coburn, Jewell Reinhart*

p Journal Chretien Dedie A La Reine

Journal D'Un Athee Provisoire — *Lambersy, Werner*

y Journal of a Revolutionary War Woman — *Greenberg, Judith E*

Journal of a Visit to the Georgia Islands of St. Catherines, Green, Ossabaw, Sapelo, St. Simons, Jekyll, and Cumberland — *Bryan, Jonathan*

p Journal of Accounting, Auditing and Finance

p Journal of American Studies of Turkey

The Journal of Antonio Montoya — *Collignon, Rick*

The Journal of Beatrix Potter from 1881 to 1897. Rev. Ed. — *Potter, Beatrix*

p Journal of Biomedical Science

The Journal of Callie Wade — *Miller, Dawn*

p Journal of Customer Service in Marketing and Management: Innovations for Service, Quality and Value

p Journal of Economic Growth

p Journal of Energy Finance and Development
p Journal of HIV/AIDS Prevention and Education for Adolescents and Children
p Journal of Human Resource Costing and Accounting
p Journal of International and Comparative Economics
p Journal of Internet Cataloging
The Journal of Jean-Francois De Galaup De La Perouse 1785-1788. Vol. 1 — *La Perouse, Jean-Francois De Galaup, Comte De*
The Journal of John Winthrop 1630-1649 — *Winthrop, John*
c The Journal of Julia Singing Bear (Illus. by Adam Cvijanovic) — *Matthaei, Gay*
p Journal of Management Accounting Research
p Journal of Market-Focused Management
p Journal of Material Culture
p The Journal of Medieval and Early Modern Studies
p Journal of Molecular Medicine
p Journal of Poverty
p Journal of Public and International Affairs
p Journal of Real Estate Portfolio Management
p Journal of Synchrotron Radiation
Journal of the Discovery of the Source of the Nile — *Speke, John Hanning*
p Journal of the International Neuropsychological Society
Journal of the Waterloo Campaign — *Mercer, Cavalie*
p Journal of Undergraduate Sciences
Journalism: Selected Prose 1970-1995 — *Mahon, Derek*
The Journalist as Reformer — *Digby-Junger, Richard*
Journals 1987-1989 — *Powell, Anthony*
Journals Mid-Fifties 1954-1958 — *Ginsberg, Allen*
The Journals of Josiah Gorgas 1857-1878 — *Gorgas, Josiah*
The Journals of the Lewis and Clark Expedition. Vol. 9 — *Moulton, Gary E*
The Journals of the Lewis and Clark Expedition. Vol. 10 — *Moulton, Gary E*
The Journals of the Lewis and Clark Expedition. Vols. 5-9 — *Moulton, Gary E*
The Journey: A Spiritual Roadmap for Modern Christians — *Kreeft, Peter*
The Journey Back — *Smedley, Jack*
c Journey for Peace (Illus. by Ruben De Anda) — *Brill, Marlene Targ*
Journey from Anxiety to Freedom — *Feniger, Mani*
Journey from Hell — *Marino, Vinny*
The Journey Home — *Antler, Joyce*
The Journey Home — *Berman, Phillip L*
Journey into Darkness — *Douglas, John*
c Journey into Space (Illus. by Alex Pang) — *Langley, Andrew*
c Journey into Terror — *Wallace, Bill*
A Journey into the Deaf-World — *Lane, Harlan*
y The Journey of Diego Rivera — *Goldstein, Ernest*
A Journey of Discovery — *Wolf, Alfred*
Journey of Purpose — *Tsongas, Paul E*
Journey of the Heart — *Bartlett, Elizabeth Ann*
c Journey of the Nightly Jaguar (Illus. by Robert Roth) — *Albert, Burton*
c Journey of the Red Wolf (Illus. by Roland Smith) — *Smith, Roland*
Journey through Kurdistan — *Smothers, Mary Ann*
c Journey through Llandor — *Lawrence, Louise*
Journey to Enlightenment — *Ricard, Matthieu*
c Journey to Freedom (Illus. by Nick Mountain) — *McKenna, Virginia*
Journey to Ithaca — *Desai, Anita*
y Journey to Jo'burg — *Naidoo, Beverley*
Journey to Justice — *Cochran, Johnnie L, Jr.*
c Journey to Mount Shen — *Maekawa, Takeshi*
c Journey to Nowhere — *Auch, Mary Jane*
y Journey to Nowhere — *Baer, Judy*
c Journey to the Centre of the Earth (Glover). Audio Version — *Verne, Jules*
c Journey to the Haunted Planet (Illus. by Wayne Anderson) — *Wood, A J*
Journey to the Land of the Flies and Other Travels — *Buzzi, Aldo*
y A Journey to the New World — *Lasky, Kathryn*
A Journey to the Rivers — *Handke, Peter*
A Journey to the Western Islands of Scotland — *Boswell, James*
Journey to Vaja — *Naves, Elaine Kalman*
The Journey toward Ariel — *Hargrove, Nancy D*
Journey toward the Cradle of Mankind — *Gozzano, Guido*
A Journey with Elsa Cloud — *Hadley, Leila*
Journeying with God — *Sakenfeld, Katharine Doob*
Journeyman's Wages — *Starck, Clemens*

Journeymen in Murder — *Wiggins, Martin*
Journeys — *Heald, Chris*
y Journey's End — *Saunders, Jean*
c Journeys in Art — *Lewis, J D*
Journeys through Our Classrooms — *Vdall, Denis*
Jovah's Angel — *Shinn, Sharon*
c Joy (Illus. by Mechelle Ann) — *Moncure, Jane Belk*
Joy and Wonder in All God's Works — *Lloyd, Janet E*
c The Joy Boys (Illus. by Frank Remkiewicz) — *Byars, Betsy*
y The Joy Luck Club — *Tan, Amy*
The Joy of Being Awake — *Abad Fociolince, Hector Joaquin*
The Joy of Cooking — *Becker, Marion Rombauer*
y The Joy of Keeping Score — *Dickson, Paul*
The Joy of Living and Dying in Peace — *Bstan-Dzin-Rgya-Mtsho, Dalai Lama XIV*
The Joy of Not Working — *Zelinski, Ernie J*
The Joy of Opera — *Douglas, Nigel*
The Joy of Writing Sex — *Benedict, Elizabeth*
y Joy School — *Berg, Elizabeth*
c Joy to the World (Illus. by Christopher Gray) — *Greene, Carol*
Joyce and the Invention of Irish History — *Hofheinz, Thomas C*
Joyce and the Jews — *Nadel, Ira Bruce*
Joyce, Bakhtin, and the Literary Tradition — *Booker, M Keith*
Joyce, Decadence, and Emancipation — *Heller, Vivian*
Joyce in America — *Segall, Jeffrey*
Joyce in the Hibernian Metropolis — *Beja, Morris*
Joyce, Race, and Empire — *Cheng, Vincent J*
y Joycelyn Elders, M.D.: From Sharecropper's Daughter to Surgeon General of the United States of America — *Elders, Joycelyn*
Joyce's Iritis and the Irritated Text — *Gottfried, Roy*
Joyce's Waking Women — *Brivic, Sheldon*
The Joyful Journey — *Clairmont, Patsy*
Joyful Trek — *Williams, Robert H*
Joystick Nation — *Herz, J C*
Jozef Pilsudski 1867-1935 — *Garlicki, Andrzej*
Jua Kali Kenya — *King, Kenneth*
c Juan Bobo and the Pig — *Pitre, Felix*
The Juan Paez Hurtado Expedition of 1695 — *Colligan, John B*
Juana La Loca — *Barbera, Carmen*
Juarez — *Hamnett, Brian*
Juarez Justice — *Trolley, Jack*
Jubal: The Life and Times of General Jubal A. Early, C.S.A., Defender of the Lost Cause — *Osborne, Charles C*
Jubilation — *Tomlinson, Charles*
Jubilee Trail — *Bristow, Gwen*
Judaism — *Harris, Maureen*
c Judaism — *Penney, Sue*
yr Judaism: A Dictionary — *Forta, Arye*
Judaism: A Very Short Introduction — *Solomon, Norman*
Judaism and the Doctrine of Creation — *Samuelson, Norbert Max*
Judaism and the Early Christian Mind — *Wilken, Robert L*
Judaism beyond God — *Wine, Sherwin*
Judaism, Human Values and the Jewish State — *Leibowitz, Yeshayahu*
Judaism in a Secular Age — *Kogel, Renee*
Judaism in Australia — *Rubinstein, W D*
Judaism in Music and Other Essays — *Wagner, Richard, 1813-1883*
Judaism in Persia's Shadow — *Berquist, Jon L*
Judaism in the New Testament — *Chilton, Bruce*
Judaism: Practice and Belief 63 B.C.E.-66 C.E. — *Sanders, E P*
Judaisms and Their Messiahs at the Turn of the Christian Era — *Neusner, Jacob*
Judas: Betrayer or Friend of Jesus? — *Klassen, William*
The Judas Economy — *Wolman, William*
y The Judas Glass — *Cadnum, Michael*
The Judas Kiss — *Harris, Michael*
The Judas Trail — *Royce, Kenneth*
Jude the Obscure — *Hardy, Thomas*
Der Judenstaat — *Herzl, Theodor*
The Judge — *Martini, Steve*
y The Judge (Guidall). Audio Version — *Martini, Steve*
y The Judge (Tucci). Audio Version — *Martini, Steve*
Judging Rights — *McClure, Kirstie M*
Judging the State — *Newberg, Paula R*
Judgment and Grace in Dixie — *Wilson, Charles Reagan*

Judgment Day — *Reinken, Patrick*
The Judgment of Paris — *Damisch, Hubert*
Judicial Enigma — *Yarbrough, Tinsley E*
Judicial Politics since 1920 — *Griffith, J A G*
The Judicial Sector in Latin America and the Caribbean — *Dakolias, Maria*
Los Judios Del Reino De Navarra. Vol. 1 — *Carrasco, Juan*
Judisches Leben In Niedersachsen Im 15. Und 16. Jahrhundert — *Ries, Rotraud*
Judit--Eine Frau Im Spannungsfeld Von Autonomie Und Gottlicher Fuhrung — *Hellmann, Monika*
Judith Wright — *Strauss, Jennifer*
Judith's Pavilion — *Flitter, Marc*
Judy Cassab Diaries — *Cassab, Judy*
Jugement A Moscou — *Bukovskii, Vladimir Konstantinovich*
y The Juggler — *Morressy, John*
c Juggling with Jeremy (Illus. by Gus Clarke) — *D'Lacey, Chris*
Juifs De Hongrie 1825-1849 — *Horel, Catherine*
c Juke-Box Jive — *Hathorn, Libby*
Jules Verne: An Exploratory Biography — *Lottman, Herbert R*
r The Jules Verne Encyclopedia — *Taves, Brian*
Julia: A Life in Mathematics — *Reid, Constance*
Julia Kristeva Readings of Exile and Estrangement — *Smith, Anna*
Julia Margaret Cameron: Photographs from the J. Paul Getty Museum — *Cameron, Julia Margaret Pattle*
Julian of Norwich's Showings — *Baker, Denise Nowakowski*
y Julian Schwinger: The Physicist, the Teacher and the Man — *Ng, Jack*
r Julian Symons: A Bibliography — *Walsdorf, John J*
Julian Symons Remembered — *Walsdorf, John J*
Julian's Gods — *Smith, Rowland*
c Julie — *Taylor, Cora*
c Julie Krone — *Gutman, Bill*
c Julie Krone: Unstoppable Jockey — *Savage, Jeff*
Julie Taymor: Playing with Fire — *Blumenthal, Eileen*
c Juliet: A Secret Takes Flight, England 1339 (Illus. by Lynne Marshall) — *Kirwan, Anna*
Julio Cortazar: A Study of the Short Fiction — *Stavans, Ilan*
c Julius (Illus. by Dav Pilkey) — *Johnson, Angela*
Julius II: The Warrior Pope — *Shaw, Christine*
c Julius Caesar — *Green, Robert*
y Julius Caesar — *Nardo, Don*
y Julius Caesar (Runger). Audio Version — *Grant, Michael, 1914-*
Julius Knipl, Real Estate Photographer — *Katchor, Ben*
c Juma and the Honey Guide (Illus. by Nneka Bennett) — *Bernard, Robin*
The Jumanos: Hunters and Traders of the South Plains — *Hickerson, Nancy Parrott*
c The Jumbo Book of Nature Science (Illus. by Judie Shore) — *Hickman, Pamela M*
Jump at the Sun — *Lowe, John*
Jump Cuts — *Soldatow, Sasha*
The Jump-Off Creek — *Gloss, Molly*
c Jump Rope (Illus. by David Mostyn) — *Cary, Kate*
c Jump! The Adventures of Brer Rabbit (Illus. by Barry Moser) — *Parks, Van Dyke*
c Jump the World — *Pooley, Sarah*
Jumping Double Dutch — *Jenkins, Elaine Brown*
y Jumping Off to Freedom — *Bernardo, Anilu*
Jumpstart Tutorial for Microsoft Internet Explorer 3.0 — *Parker, Elisabeth*
c Junebug — *Mead, Alice*
Juneteenth Texas — *Abernethy, Francis Edward*
The Jung Cult — *Noll, Richard*
Jung in Context. 2nd Ed. — *Homans, Peter*
Der Junge Mit Den Blutigen Schuhen — *Forte, Dieter*
Jungfrau, Tochter Babel — *Rechenmacher, Hans*
c The Jungle — *Rice, Bebe Faas*
y The Jungle Book (Illus. by Christian Broutin) — *Kipling, Rudyard*
c Jungle Jack Hanna's Safari Adventure (Illus. by Rick A Prebeg) — *Hanna, Jack*
Jung's Advice to the Players — *Porterfield, Sally F*
c Junie B. Jones Loves Handsome Warren (Illus. by Denise Brunkus) — *Park, Barbara*
Junior College — *Soto, Gary*
c Junior Seau: High-Voltage Linebacker — *Morgan, Terri*
cr Junior Worldmark Encyclopedia of the Canadian Provinces — *Gall, Timothy L*

cr Junior Worldmark Encyclopedia of the Nations. Vols.
 1-9 — *Gall, Timothy L*
yr Junior Worldmark Encyclopedia of the States. Vols.
 1-4 — *Gall, Timothy L*
y Junk — *Burgess, Melvin*
c Junk Pile! (Illus. by Kimberly Bulcken Root)
 — *Borton, Lady*
y Jurassic Park — *Crichton, Michael*
 Jurassic Technolgies Revenant — *Crary, Jonathan*
 Jure Divino — *Defoe, Daniel*
 The Jurisprudential Vision of Justice Antonin Scalia
 — *Schultz, David A*
 Jury Double — *Stewart, Edward*
 Jury Duty — *Van Wormer, Laura*
 A Jury of Her Peers — *Korelitz, Jean Hanff*
y The Jury System — *Williams, Mary E*
 Jussi — *Bjorling, Anna-Lisa*
 Just a Range Ball in a Box of Titleists — *McCord,
 Gary*
 Just a Temp — *Henson, Kevin D*
y Just a Thought — *Francis, Dave*
 Just an Ordinary Day — *Jackson, Shirley*
c Just Another Ordinary Day (Illus. by Rod Clement)
 — *Clement, Rod*
 Just as I Am — *Graham, Billy*
 Just as We Were — *Mackintosh, Prudence*
 Just before Sunrise — *Neggers, Carla*
 Just Bones — *Denhart, Jeffrey*
 Just by Chance — *Page, Lynda*
c Just Dessert (Illus. by Polly Powell) — *Powell, Polly*
 Just Do It — *Katz, Donald*
 Just Environments — *Palmer, Joy A*
y Just Family — *Bolden, Tonya*
 Just for the Summer — *Van Wormer, Laura*
 Just Girls — *Finders, Margaret J*
 Just Good Friends — *Stuart, Elizabeth*
 Just-in-Time Accounting — *Bragg, Steven M*
 Just Java — *Van Der Linden, Peter*
c Just like New (Illus. by Karen Reczuch) — *Manson,
 Ainslie*
y Just Listen to This Song I'm Singing — *Silverman,
 Jerry*
c Just Look (Illus. by Tana Hoban) — *Hoban, Tana*
c Just Me and My Dad. Electronic Media Version
 — *Mayer, Mercer*
c Just Me and My Little Brother — *Mayer, Mercer*
c Just Me and My Mom. Electronic Media Version
 — *Mayer, Mercer*
 Just Once — *Landis, Jill Marie*
y Just One Flick of a Finger (Illus. by David Diaz)
 — *Lorbiecki, Marybeth*
 Just Past Labor Day — *Robertson, Kirk*
c Just Rewards (Illus. by Emily Lisker) — *Sanfield,
 Steve*
 The Just Ruler in Shiite Islam — *Sachedina, Abdulaziz
 Abbulhussein*
c Just So Stories (Illus. by Barry Moser) — *Kipling,
 Rudyard*
 The Just Society — *Paul, Ellen Frankel*
c Just Stay Put (Illus. by Gary Clement) — *Clement,
 Gary*
 Just Stories — *Ross, Thomas*
 Just the Fax, Ma'am — *O'Kane, Leslie*
 Just the Weigh You Are — *Jonas, Steven*
 Justice — *Watson, Larry*
y Justice (Bridges). Audio Version — *Watson, Larry*
 Justice: A Question of Race — *Rodriguez, Roberto*
 Justice All Their Own — *Egan, Ted*
 Justice and Christian Ethics — *Gardner, E Clinton*
 Justice and Generosity — *Laks, Andre*
 Justice and Health Care — *Grubb, Andrew*
 Justice and Interpretation — *Warnke, Georgia*
 Justice as Impartiality — *Barry, Brian*
 Justice as Translation — *White, James Boyd, 1938-*
 Justice for and by the Aboriginals — *Comitae De
 Consultation Sur L'Administration De La Justice En
 Milieu Autochtone (Quebec)*
c Justice for Emily — *Pfeffer, Susan Beth*
 Justice for Sale — *Berry, William A*
 Justice, Nature and the Geography of Difference
 — *Harvey, David*
 Justice Overruled — *Katz, Burton S*
 Justice Scalia and the Conservative Revival
 — *Brisbin, Richard*
 Justifying Ethics — *Gorecki, Jan*
 Justifying Language — *Mills, Kevin*
 Justine — *Thompson, Alice*
 Justinian — *Moorhead, John*
y Justyna's Narrative — *Draenger, Gusta Davidson*
y Juvenile Crime — *Sadler, A E*
 The Juvenile Justice System — *Clement, Mary*

 Juvenile Violence in a Winner-Loser Culture
 — *James, Oliver*

K

K-12 Resources on the Internet — *Junion-Metz, Gail*
y K.D. Lang — *Martinac, Paula*
K.G.B. A Aruncat In Aer Romania Cu Complicitatea Unui Grup De Militari — *Raiha, Victor*
KA — *Calasso, Roberto*
The Kabbalah of Envy — *Bonder, Nilton*
The Kabbalah of Money — *Bonder, Nilton*
Kabloona — *Poncins, Gontran De*
Kabloona in the Yellow Kayak — *Jason, Victoria*
Kabuki: Five Classic Plays
Kadotettu Puutarha — *Hamalainen, Helvi*
Kafeh Ham Ba-Boker
Kafka — *Mairowitz, David Zane*
Kafka: Gender, Class, and Race in the Letters and Fictions — *Boa, Elizabeth*
Kafka: Literatur Und Judentum — *Baioni, Guiliano*
Kafka, Love and Courage — *Hockaday, Mary*
Kafka Was the Rage — *Broyard, Anatole*
Kafka's Prague — *Wagenbach, Klaus*
y Kahless (Conway). Audio Version — *Friedman, Michael Jan*
c Kahtahah (Illus. by Rie Munoz) — *Paul, Frances Lackey*
c Kai, a Big Decision — *Posner, Mitch*
c Kai: A Mission for Her Village (Illus. by Vanessa Holley) — *Thomas, Dawn C Gill*
The Kaiser and His Court — *Rohl, John C G*
Kaiser Friedrich Barbarossa: Landesaubau--Aspekte Seiner Politik--Wirkung — *Engel, Evamaria*
p Kaleidoscope
y Kaleidoscope Century — *Barnes, John, 1957-*
Kaleidoscope Eyes — *DeRogatis, Jim*
A Kaleidoscope of Choices — *Holley, Beth*
Kaleidoscope of Play Therapy Stories — *Oe, Emily*
Kaleidoscopes and Quilts — *Nadelstern, Paula*
Kaleidoscopic Tree Boas — *Stafford, Peter J*
Kalendar Und Offentlichkeit — *Rupke, Jorg*
Kalenderdikt — *Vold, Jan Erik*
Kali's Child — *Kripal, Jeffrey J*
Kampala Women Getting By — *Wallman, Sandra*
Kan Nagur — *Kahana-Carmon, Amalia*
c Kancil and the Crocodiles (Illus. by Britta Teckentrup) — *Day, Noreha Yussof*
Kandinsky — *Hahl-Koch, Jelena*
Kandinsky and Old Russia — *Weiss, Peg*
Kandinsky and the Blue Rider — *Vezin, Annette*
Kandinsky: Compositions — *Dabrowski, Magdalena*
c The Kangaroo — *Crewe, Sabrina*
Kangaroo Notebook — *Abe, Kobo*
c Kangaroos — *Woodward, John*
c Kangaroos Have Joeys (Illus. by Philippa-Alys Browne) — *Browne, Philippa-Alys*
r The Kanji Dictionary — *Spahn, Mark*
p Kansas Quarterly/Arkansas Review
Kant after Duchamp — *Duve, Thierry De*
Kant and Political Philosophy — *Beiner, Ronald*
Kant and the Mind — *Brook, Andrew*
Kant Et Le Pouvoir De Juger — *Longuenesse, Beatrice*
y Kant in 90 Minutes — *Strathern, Paul*
Kantian Ethics Almost without Apology — *Baron, Marcia W*
Kant's Compatibilism — *Hudson, Hud*
Kant's Intuitionism — *Falkenstein, Lorne*
Kant's Methodology — *Bigger, Charles P*
Kant's Theory of Imagination — *Gibbons, Sarah L*
Kanzi: The Ape at the Brink of the Human Mind — *Savage-Rumbaugh, Sue*
r Kaplan and Sadock's Synopsis of Psychiatry. 7th Ed. — *Kaplan, Harold I*
Kapo — *Tisma, Aleksandar*

The Kappa Alpha Order 1865-1897 — *Scott, Gary Thomas*
Kapusta or Cabbage — *Choban, Jennie*
c Karate and Judo (Illus. by Art Seiden) — *Nardi, Thomas*
c Karate Boy (Illus. by David Katzenstein) — *Morris, Ann*
c The Karate Class Mystery (Illus. by Denise Brunkus) — *Levy, Elizabeth*
c Karate for Beginners — *Blot, Pierre*
Karen Horney: A Psychoanalyst's Search for Self-Understanding — *Paris, Bernard J*
Karen Kain: Movement Never Lies — *Kain, Karen*
Karl Barth's Critically Realistic Dialectical Theology — *McCormack, Bruce L*
Karl Gruber, Reden Und Documente 1945-1953 — *Gehler, Michael*
Karl Jaspers: Basic Philosophical Writings — *Jaspers, Karl*
Karl Mannheim and the Crisis of Liberalism — *Kettler, David*
Karl Marx and the Intellectual Origins of Dialectical Materialism — *White, James D, 1941-*
Karl Marx, Frederick Engels. Vol. 35 — *Marx, Karl*
Karl Marx's Theory of Ideas — *Torrance, John*
Karl Popper: Philosophy and Problems — *O'Hear, Anthony*
Karlowicz, Young Poland, and the Musical Fin-De-Siecle — *Wightman, Alistair*
c Karl's Kite (Illus. by Pierre Pratt) — *Roche, Hannah*
Karsh: A Sixty-Year Retrospective — *Karsh, Yousuf*
Die Kartause Aggsbach 1995
Die Kartauser Und Ihre Welt — *Hogg, James*
Kaschmir In Parching — *Walser, Martin*
Kashmir in the Crossfire — *Schofield, Victoria*
c Kashtanka (Illus. by Gennady Spirin) — *Chekhov, Anton*
Kasioraakkeli — *Envall, Markku*
Kassia: The Legend, the Woman, and Her Work — *Tripolitis, Antonia*
Kastratengesang: Hormonelle, Konstitutionelle Und Padagogische Aspekte — *Fritz, Hans*
Katalog Der Auslandischen Bildwerke Des Museums Der Bildenden Kunste In Budapest, IV.-XVIII. Jahrhundert. Vol. 3 — *Balogh, Jolan*
r Katalog Der Deutschen Luftpost. Pt. 8 — *Haberer, Erich*
r Katalog Metalnog Novca Jugoslavije 1700-1994 — *Mandic, Ranko*
Kate Burke Shoots the Old West — *Hurd, Jerrie*
Kate Field: Selected Letters — *Field, Kate*
c Kate Shelley: Bound for Legend (Illus. by Max Ginsburg) — *San Souci, Robert D*
Katharina II, Deutschland, Und Die Deutschen — *Scharf, Claus*
Kathe Kollwitz: Schmerz Und Schuld — *Schade, Werner*
Katherine — *Min, Anchee*
Katherine — *Seton, Anya*
Katherine Anne Porter: A Sense of the Times — *Stout, Janis P*
Katherine Anne Porter's Poetry — *Porter, Katherine Anne*
c Katherine Paterson — *Cary, Alice*
Kathinka Zitz-Halein and Female Activism in Mid-Nineteenth-Century Germany — *Zucker, Stanley*
Katholiken, Kirche Und Staat Als Problem Der Historie — *Hurten, Heinz*
r Katholische Konzilsidee Im 19. Und 20. Jahrhundert — *Sieben, Hermann Josef*

Katholische Vereine In Baden Und Wurttemberg 1848-1914 — *Halder, Winfrid*
Kathy Smith's Fitness Makeover — *Smith, Kathy*
Kathy Smith's Walkfit for a Better Body — *Smith, Kathy*
c Katie and the Dream-Eater (Illus. by Brian Wildsmith) — *Takamado, Princess*
c Katie and the Night Noises. Book and Audio Version — *Sweeney, Jacqueline*
c Katie K. Whale (Illus. by James Melvin) — *Tate, Suzanne*
Katie's Canon — *Cannon, Katie Geneva*
Katrapakian — *Fraghou-Kikilia, Ritsa*
Katutura: A Place Where We Stay — *Pendleton, Wade C*
c Katy Cat and Beaky Boo (Illus. by Lucy Cousins) — *Cousins, Lucy*
c Katya's Book of Mushrooms (Illus. by Katya Arnold) — *Arnold, Katya*
Ha-Kayits Shel Rina Oster — *Dankner, Amnon*
c Kayuktuk: An Arctic Quest (Illus. by Jon Van Zyle) — *Heinz, Brian J*
y Keanu Reeves — *Nickson, Chris*
Keating: The Inside Story — *Edwards, John, 1947-*
Keaton's Silent Shorts — *Oldham, Gabriella*
Kedoshim Be-Arvon Mugbal — *Bar-Moha, Josef*
p Keen SF
c Keep 'em Laughing (Illus. by Michael Chesworth) — *Phillips, Louis*
Keep It Simple, Stupid — *Goldsworthy, Peter*
y Keep Smiling Through — *Rinaldi, Ann*
Keep Still — *Bland, Eleanor Taylor*
Keep What You Earn — *Coxon, Terry*
c Keeper (Illus. by Keith West) — *Durrell, Gerald*
Keeper — *Rucka, Greg*
c Keeper for the Sea (Illus. by Peter M Fiore) — *Brady, Kimberley Smith*
Keeper of the King — *Bennett, Nigel*
c Keepers (Illus. by Ted Rand) — *Schertle, Alice*
Keepers of the Covenant — *Rohrer, James R*
Keepers of the Flame — *Kowalski, Theodore J*
y Keepers of the Kingdom — *Nichols, Michael*
c Keeping Cats — *Ashton, Jay*
Keeping Good Company — *Charkham, Jonathan*
Keeping Private Idaho — *Just, Rick*
c The Keeping Quilt — *Polacco, Patricia*
Keeping Score — *Sheehan, Richard G*
Keeping Together in Time — *McNeill, William H*
The Keepsake — *Gunn, Kirsty*
r Keesing's Record of World Events CD-ROM Full Archive 1960-1994. Electronic Media Version
y Keewatin — *Sullivan, Paul*
Kein Einig Volk — *Kaser-Leisibach, Ursula*
Keith County Journal — *Janovy, John, Jr.*
Keith Haring: Journals — *Haring, Keith*
c Kele's Secret (Illus. by Catherine Stock) — *Mollel, Tololwa M*
Kellogg's Six-Hour Day — *Hunnicutt, Benjamin Kline*
p Keltic Fringe
Ken Burns's The Civil War — *Toplin, Robert Brent*
c Ken Griffey Junior: All-Around All-Star — *Kramer, Barbara*
Ken Thomson: Canada's Enigmatic Billionaire — *Parsons, Vic*
Kennedy and Nixon — *Matthews, Christopher*
The Kennedy Persuasion — *Henggeler, Paul R*
The Kennedys in Hollywood — *Quirk, Lawrence J*
Kennedy's Paediatric Operative Dentistry. 4th Ed. — *Curzon, M E J*
Kenneth Burke and Contemporary European Thought — *Brock, Bernard L*

Kenneth Burke and the Scapegoat Process — *Carter, C Allen*

Kenneth Burke in Greenwich Village — *Selzer, Jack*

Kenneth Jay Lane: Faking It — *Lane, Kenneth Jay*

c Ken's Kitten (Illus. by Anthea Sieveking) — *MacKinnon, Debbie*

Kensho: The Heart of Zen — *Cleary, Thomas*

Kent at Law 1602 — *Knafla, Louis A*

r Kent Town Guides 1763-1900 — *Goulden, R J*

c Kente Colors (Illus. by John Ward) — *Chocolate, Deborah M Newton*

Kentucky Archaeology — *Lewis, R Barry*

c Kenya — *Arnold, Helen*

r Kenya. Rev. Ed. — *Coger, Dalvan*

The Kephalaia of the Teacher — *Kephalaia. English*

Kept Boy — *Rodi, Robert*

p The Kerf

y Keri — *Andrews, Jan*

p The Kerouac Connection

Kerouac's Ghost — *McGoogan, Ken*

y Kerry, a Teenage Mother — *Aitkens, Maggi*

Kerry Slides — *Muldoon, Paul, 1951-*

c Ketchup on Your Cornflakes? (Illus. by Nick Sharratt) — *Sharratt, Nick*

Kettle Broth to Gooseberry Fool — *Baker, Jenny*

Kevin McCloud's Complete Book of Paint and Decorative Techniques — *McCloud, Kevin*

Kew: The History of the Royal Botanic Gardens — *Desmond, Ray*

Kewpies and Beyond — *Armitage, Shelley*

The Key — *Wicks, Susan*

r Key Areas for Threatened Birds in the Neotropics — *Wege, David C*

Key Aspects of Caring for the Acutely Ill — *Funk, Sandra G*

Key Concepts in Adult Education and Training — *Tight, Malcolm*

r Key Concepts in Cinema Studies — *Hayward, Susan*

Key Concepts in Psychotherapy Integration — *Gold, Jerold R*

Key Dates in Number Theory History from 10,529 B.C. to the Present — *Spencer, Donald D*

r Key Guide to Electronic Resources: Engineering — *McBurney, Melissa*

r Key Guide to Electronic Resources: Language and Literature — *Kovacs, Diane K*

r Key Indicators of Developing Asian and Pacific Countries. Vol. 26

Key Issues in Women's Work — *Hakim, Catherine*

y Key Maths (Year 8)

r Key Organisations 96

Key Strategies: Music — *Biddle, Alan*

y Key Technologies for the 21st Century

y Key Themes of the Twentieth Century — *Sauvain, Philip*

Key to Forever — *Skye, Christina*

The Key to Newton's Dynamics — *Brackenridge, J Bruce*

The Key to the Asian Miracle — *Campos, Jose Edgardo*

The Key to the Bulge — *Rusiecki, Stephen M*

Key West Tales — *Hersey, John*

Key Witness — *Freedman, J F*

The Keyed Flute — *Tromlitz, Johann George*

Keynes and the Classics — *Verdon, Michel*

Keynes, Knowledge and Uncertainty — *Dow, Sheila C*

The Keynesian Fallout — *Singh, Narindar*

Keynes's Philosophical Development — *Davis, John Bryan*

Keynes's Uncertain Revolution — *Bateman, Bradley W*

Keys to the Garden — *Alcalay, Ammiel*

y The Keys to the Street — *Rendell, Ruth*

KGB I Vlast' — *Bobkov, Filipp*

c The Khan's Daughter (Illus. by Jean Tseng) — *Yep, Laurence*

y Khetho — *Bailey, Dennis*

Khrushchev: A Political Life — *Tompson, William J*

Khrushchev's Double Bind — *Richter, James G*

c Kia Tanisha (Illus. by Jan Spivey Gilchrist) — *Greenfield, Eloise*

c Kia Tanisha Drives Her Car (Illus. by Jan Spivey Gilchrist) — *Greenfield, Eloise*

Kibbutz Buchenwald — *Baumel, Judith Tydor*

c Kick, Pass, and Run (Illus. by Leonard Kessler) — *Kessler, Leonard*

Kicking Off the Bootstraps — *Santana, Deborah Berman*

Kicking the Pricks — *Jarman, Derek*

Kicking Your Kid Out of the Nest — *Black, Thom*

c The Kid Who Invented the Popsicle and Other Surprising Stories about Inventions — *Wulffson, Don L*

c The Kid Who Ran for President — *Gutman, Dan*

Kidding Ourselves — *Mahoney, Rhona*

c Kidnap at Denton Farm. Audio Version — *Crane, Andy*

The Kidnapped and the Ransomed — *Pickard, Kate E R*

The Kidnapping of Edgardo Mortara — *Kertzer, David I*

y The Kidnapping of Suzie Q — *Waddell, Martin*

The Kidnapping of the Painter Miro — *Hartel, Paul*

c Kids and Koins — *Ravino, Owen*

cr Kids and Science. Vols. 1-6 (Illus. by Len Rubenstein) — *Doris, Ellen*

c Kids Are Cookin' — *Brown, Karen, 1952, Feb., 2-*

y Kids at Work — *Freedman, Russell*

c Kids' Book of Wisdom — *Hudson, Cheryl*

c Kids Camp! — *Carlson, Laurie M*

c Kids Campfire Book — *Drake, Jane*

c Kids Canadian Bug Book — *Hickman, Pamela M*

c Kids Canadian Plant Book — *Hickman, Pamela M*

c The Kids' Catalog of Jewish Holidays — *Adler, David A*

Kids Country — *Lacome, Susie*

cp Kids Discover

c Kids Explore America's Jewish Heritage — *Westridge Young Writers Workshop*

c Kids Garden! — *Hart, Avery*

c The Kid's Guide to Money — *Otfinoski, Steve*

c A Kid's Guide to the Smithsonian (Illus. by Steven Rotblatt) — *Bay, Ann Phillips*

Kids On-Line — *Salzman, Marian*

c Kids Outdoors — *Logue, Victoria*

c Kids' Paper Airplane Book — *Blackburn, Ken*

Kids' Voices

y Kids Who Make a Difference — *Chandler, Gary*

c Kids with AIDS — *Forbes, Anna*

Kiep Phu Sinh — *Nguyen, Ngoc Nga*

Kierkegaard — *Vardy, Peter*

Kierkegaard and the Concept of Revelation — *Emmanuel, Steven M*

Kierkegaard as Religious Thinker — *Gouwens, David J*

Kierkegaard in Post-Modernity — *Matustik, Martin J*

Kiev: A Portrait 1800-1917 — *Hamm, Michael F*

Kiki's Memoirs — *Kiki*

The Kilfenora Teaboy — *Toibin, Colm*

Kill All the Lawyers? — *Kornstein, Daniel J*

Kill Kill Faster Faster — *Rose, Joel*

Kill Me Again — *Faherty, Terence*

Kill the Body, the Head Will Fall — *Denfeld, Rene*

Killed in the Fog — *DeAndrea, William L*

y Killer — *D'Amato, Barbara*

Killer among Us — *Fisher, Joseph C*

c Killer Asteroids — *Poynter, Margaret*

c Killer Boots — *Jenkins, Wendy*

Killer Calories — *McKevett, G A*

y Killer Germs — *Zimmerman, Barry E*

y A Killer in the House — *Carroll, J H*

Killer Kids, Bad Law — *Reinharz, Peter*

Killer Market — *Maron, Margaret*

y Killer on Campus — *Fox, James*

c Killer Plants and How to Grow Them (Illus. by Marjorie Crosby-Fairall) — *Cheers, Gordon*

Killeri Tulee — *Kylatasku, Jussi*

The Killer's Game — *Bonansinga, Jay R*

Killing and Saving — *Reeder, John P*

Killing Critics — *O'Connell, Carol*

y Killing Critics (Merlington). Audio Version — *O'Connell, Carol*

Killing Custer — *Welch, James*

The Killing Factory — *Parker, John, 1938-*

The Killing Fields — *Riley, Chris*

Killing Floor — *Child, Lee*

y Killing Floor (Hill). Audio Version — *Child, Lee*

The Killing Ground — *Settle, Mary Lee*

Killing Ground — *Seymour, Gerald*

A Killing in New Town — *Horsley, Kate*

y A Killing in Quail County — *Cole, Jameson*

y Killing Mr. Griffin — *Duncan, Lois*

The Killing of History. Rev. Ed. — *Windschuttle, Keith*

y The Killing of Mud-Eye — *Walters, Celeste*

The Killing of Robert F. Kennedy — *Moldea, Dan E*

The Killing of the Countryside — *Harvey, Graham*

y The Killing Season — *Corwin, Miles*

A Killing Shadow — *Crew, Randolph E*

A Killing Spring — *Bowen, Gail*

Killing the White Man's Indian — *Bordewich, Fergus M*

Killing Time — *Feyerabend, Paul*

The Killing Time — *Heuman, Gad*

Killing Time — *Martin, Scott C*

Killing Time — *Smith, Murray*

y Killjoy — *Forrest, Elizabeth*

Killoyle — *Boylan, Roger*

The Kiln — *McIlvanney, William*

y Kilo Option (Griffin). Audio Version — *Flannery, Sean*

Kimono: Fashioning Culture — *Dalby, Liza C*

Kin, Commerce, Community — *Young, Kathryn A*

y A Kind and Just Parent — *Ayers, William*

A Kind of Grace — *Rapoport, Ron*

A Kind of Life Imposed on Man — *Marshall, Paul A*

Die Kinder Der Toten — *Jelinek, Elfriede*

y The Kindling: A Novel — *Hernon, Peter, 1947-*

Kindling Does for Firewood — *King, Richard*

c Kindness (Illus. by Mechelle Ann) — *Moncure, Jane Belk*

y The Kindness of Strangers — *McIntyre, Mike*

The Kindness of Strangers — *Smith, Julie*

Kindred Strangers — *Vogel, David*

Kinds of Minds — *Dennett, Daniel C*

Kinematic Wave Modeling in Water Resources — *Singh, Vijay P*

r Kinematics and Dynamics of Machinery — *Stejskal, Vladimir*

p Kinesis

Kinfolks — *Lattany, Kristin Hunter*

King Alfred the Great — *Smyth, Alfred P*

King and Emperor — *Harrison, Harry*

y King and Goddess — *Tarr, Judith*

c King Arthur and the Knights of the Round Table (Illus. by Marcia Williams) — *Williams, Marcia*

c King Bobble (Illus. by Hans De Beer) — *Busser, Marianne*

c King Bob's New Clothes (Illus. by Christopher Santoro) — *DeLuise, Dom*

King Con — *Cannell, Stephen J*

r King County, Washington Deaths 1891-1907 — *South King County Genealogical Society*

King David Dances — *Stuart, Francis, 1902-*

King Death — *Platt, Colin*

King John — *Candido, Joseph*

King John — *Turner, Ralph V*

King Lear: A Parallel Text Edition (Weis) — *Shakespeare, William*

y King Lear (Advanced Shakespeare) — *Shakespeare, William*

c King Max the Last (Illus. by Linda Birch) — *King-Smith, Dick*

y The King Must Die — *Renault, Mary*

The King of Babylon Shall Not Come Against You — *Garrett, George P, 1929-*

King of Comedy — *Levy, Shawn*

c The King of Ireland's Son (Illus. by P J Lynch) — *Behan, Brendan*

The King of Swat — *McNeil, William F*

c King of the Dark Tower (Illus. by Peter Melnyczuk) — *Brown, Alan*

King of the Dead — *DeWeese, Gene*

King of the Mountain — *Fromm, Pete*

King of the Seven Dwarfs — *Oldfield, Homer R*

King of the World — *Beach, Milo Cleveland*

The King on the Road — *Gordon, Robert, 1961-*

King Richard II — *Shewring, Margaret*

c King Snake (Illus. by John Manders) — *Slotboom, Wendy*

King: The Bullitts of Seattle and Their Communications Empire — *Corr, O Casey*

King Tut's Private Eye — *Levin, Lee*

c The King with Dirty Feet and Other Stories (Illus. by Sue Williams) — *Medicott, Mary*

y Kingbird Highway — *Kaufman, Kenn*

The Kingdom of Afghanistan and the United States 1828-1973 — *Poullada, Leon B*

y The Kingdom of Benin in West Africa — *Millar, Heather*

The Kingdom of God and Human Society — *Barbour, Robin S*

The Kingdom of Heaven Is Like...a Doctor and a Patient — *Knighton, Douglas W*

The Kingdom of Individuals — *Bailey, F G*

The Kingdom of Matthias — *Johnson, Paul E*

Kingdom of Might — *Brakefield, Tom*

The Kingdom of Quito 1690-1830 — *Andrien, Kenneth J*

A Kingdom on Earth — *Phillips, Paul T*

Kingdom on Mount Cameroon — *Ardener, Edwin*

Kingdom on the Mississippi Revisited — *Launius, Roger D*

y Kingdoms of the Night — *Cole, Allan*
c The Kingfisher Book of Poems about Love — *McGough, Roger*
cr The Kingfisher First Dictionary — *Grisewood, John*
cr The Kingfisher First Encyclopedia — *Civardi, Anne*
cr Kingfisher I Wonder Why Encyclopedia
cr The Kingfisher Illustrated Children's Dictionary
cr The Kingfisher Illustrated Thesaurus. New and Rev. Ed. — *Beal, George*
cr The Kingfisher Young People's Book of Music — *Barber, Nicky*
y Kingfishers Catch Fire (Blair). Audio Version — *Godden, Rumer*
Kings and Connoisseurs — *Brown, Jonathan, 1939-*
Kings and Kingship in Medieval Europe — *Duggan, Anne J*
The Kings and Queens — *Baker, Kenneth*
c Kings and Queens — *Sauvain, Philip*
c Kings and Queens of Britain (Illus. by Rowan Barnes-Murphy) — *Barnes-Murphy, Frances*
The King's Army — *Wood, James B*
The King's Bedpost — *Aston, Margaret*
The King's Bishop — *Robb, Candace M*
A King's Commander — *Lambdin, Dewey*
y King's Dragon — *Elliott, Kate*
The King's English — *Amis, Kingsley*
c The King's Equal (Illus. by Vladimir Vagin) — *Paterson, Katherine*
c The King's Giraffe (Illus. by Stephan Poulin) — *Collier, Mary Jo*
r The Kings of Medieval England c.560-1485 — *Usilton, Larry W*
y Kings of the Klondike (Illus. by Paul McCusker) — *Berton, Pierre*
Kings Row — *Bellamann, Henry*
y The King's Shadow — *Alder, Elizabeth*
Kingship and Political Practice in Colonial India — *Price, Pamela G*
Kingship and State — *Wrigley, Christopher*
Kingsley Amis: A Biography — *Jacobs, Eric*
Kingsway — *Turner, Michael*
Kink — *Koja, Kathe*
Kink: An Autobiography — *Davies, Dave*
Kinkaid of the Seventh Fleet — *Wheeler, Gerald E*
Kinomythen 1920-1945 — *Bruns, Karin*
The Kinship of Women — *Ross, Pat*
Kinship with the Land — *Burns, E Bradford*
Kinski Uncut — *Kinski, Klaus*
c Kip: A Dog's Day (Illus. by Benedict Blathwayt) — *Blathwayt, Benedict*
c Kipper's Book of Counting — *Inkpen, Mick*
c Kipper's Book of Opposites — *Inkpen, Mick*
c Kipper's Book of Weather — *Inkpen, Mick*
c Kipper's Snowy Day (Illus. by Mick Inkpen) — *Inkpen, Mick*
c Kipton: Murder on Stage — *Fontenay, Charles L*
Die Kirche Im Neuen Testament — *Roloff, Jurgen*
Kirche, Kinder, Karrieren — *Schmugge, Ludwig*
Kirche Und Gesellschaft Im Heiligen Romischen Reich Des 15. Und 16. Jahrhunderts — *Boockmann, Hartmut*
Kirchenreform Und Sektenstiftung — *Holzem, Andreas*
c Kishina: A True Story of Gorilla Survival — *Rock, Maxine*
The Kiss — *Harrison, Kathryn*
Kiss and Tell — *De Botton, Alain*
Kiss Chase — *Walker, Fiona*
Kiss Me — *Pyper, Andrew*
The Kiss: The Story of an Obsession — *Vickers, Hugo*
Kiss Tomorrow Goodbye — *McCoy, Horace*
Kiss Your Stockbroker Goodbye — *Wells, John G*
c Kisses from Rosa (Illus. by Petra Mathers) — *Mathers, Petra*
y Kissing a Bone — *Dooley, Maura*
y Kissing the Witch — *Donoghue, Emma*
c Kit Carson: Frontier Scout — *Sanford, William R*
Al-Kitab Fii Taallum Al-Arabiyya. Pt. 1 — *Brustad, Kristen*
Kitaplar Kitabi — *Hizlan, Dogan*
r Kitchen and Bath Source Book — *Sweet's Group*
r Kitchen Antiques with Values — *Johnson, Frances*
Kitchen Conversations — *Goldstein, Joyce*
c Kitchen (SnapShot)
Kitchen Table Wisdom — *Remen, Rachel Naomi*
Kitchen Table Wisdom (Remen). Audio Version — *Remen, Rachel Naomi*
Kitchen Venom — *Hensher, Phillip*
Kitchens and Bathrooms — *Sunset Books*

Kitchens: The Culture of Restaurant Work — *Fine, Gary Alan*
c The Kite and Caitlin (Illus. by John Prater) — *McGough, Roger*
A Kite Journey through India — *Streeter, Tal*
c Kites: Twelve Easy-to-Make Fliers (Illus. by Linda Hendry) — *Dixon, Norma*
c Kitten in the Cold — *Daniels, Lucy*
c Kitten Training and Critters, Too! (Illus. by Darryl Bush) — *Peterson-Fleming, Judy*
c Kiyuktuk: Shadow without a Body (Illus. by Jon Van Zyle) — *Heinz, Brian J*
The Klan. 2nd Ed. — *Sims, Patsy*
Klatsch, Gerucht Und Wirklichkeit Bei Nathaniel Hawthorne — *Menzel, Manfred*
Klaus Moje: Glass — *Edwards, Geoffrey*
Kleber En Egypte 1798-1800. Vols. 3-4 — *Laurens, Jacques*
Kleffel, Kohnholdt, Gundermann
Kleine Deutsche Geschichte — *Schulze, Hagen*
Kleinkarierte Avantgarde — *Nenzel, Reinhard*
Klingon. Audio Version — *Smith, Dean Wesley*
y Klingon (Dorn). Audio Version — *Bader, Hilary*
y Klondyke Kate and Other Non-Fiction Texts — *Bleiman, Barbara*
c Klutz (Illus. by Henrik Drescher) — *Drescher, Henrik*
Knee Deep in Dishonour — *Norton-Taylor, Richard*
Knee Deep in Paradise — *Butler, Brett*
c Kneeknock Rise (Toren). Audio Version — *Babbitt, Natalie*
Knife Edge — *Rothmann, Ralf*
The Knight and Chivalry — *Barber, Richard*
y A Knight and His Castle. Rev. and Updated Ed. — *Oakeshott, Ewart*
y Knight of Shadows (Zelazny). Audio Version — *Zelazny, Roger*
The Knight of the Two Swords (Arthur)
The Knight on the Bridge — *Watson, William, 1931-*
A Knight to Remember — *Dodd, Christina*
c The Knight with the Lion (Illus. by John Howe) — *Howe, John, 1957-*
Knights — *Miller, Linda Lael*
c Knights (Illus. by McRae Books) — *Ross, Stewart*
Knights and Warhorses — *Ayton, Andrew*
c The Knight's Handbook — *Gravett, Christopher*
Knights in White Armour — *Bellamy, Christopher*
The Knight's Move — *Loder, James E*
The Knights of Malta — *Sire, H J A*
Knights of Spain, Warriors of the Sun — *Hudson, Charles*
y Knights of the Endless Day (Illus. by Vic Vaccaro) — *Priest, Robert*
c Knights of the Kitchen Table (Illus. by Lane Smith) — *Scieszka, Jon*
Knitted Sweater Style — *Sharp, Jo*
y Knitting in America — *Falick, Melanie D*
The Knitting Sutra — *Lydon, Susan Gordon*
Knitting Tips and Trade Secrets
y Knock-Off (Murdock). Audio Version — *Newman, Christopher*
c Knock Three Times — *Webb, Marion St. John (Adcock)*
Knossos: A Labyrinth of History — *Evely, Don*
Knot Theory and Its Applications — *Murasugi, Kunio*
Knots, Links, Braids and 3-Manifolds — *Prasolov, V V*
c Know about Mental Illness — *Hyde, Margaret O*
Know Life — *Petkovic, Danielle*
Know My Name — *Cleaver, Richard*
Know Nothing — *Settle, Mary Lee*
Know Thine Enemy — *Shirley, Edward*
Know Your Truth, Speak Your Truth, Live Your Truth — *Hannegan, Eileen R*
Knowing — *McMillan, Rosalyn*
Knowing and Being — *Mensch, James Richard*
Knowing Feeling — *Nathanson, Donald L*
Knowing Hepburn and Other Curious Experiences — *Prideaux, James*
Knowing Machines — *MacKenzie, Donald*
Knowing Women — *Theobald, Marjorie*
Knowledge and Persuasion in Economics — *McCloskey, Donald N*
Knowledge and Postmodernism in Historical Perspective — *Appleby, Joyce*
Knowledge and Practice in Mayotte — *Lambek, Michael*
Knowledge and Secrecy in an Aboriginal Religion — *Keen, Ian*
Knowledge and Social Practice in Medieval Damascus 1190-1350 — *Chamberlain, Michael*

Knowledge and the Scholarly Medical Traditions — *Bates, Don*
Knowledge as Culture — *McCarthy, E Doyle*
The Knowledge Base of Futures Studies. Vols. 1-3 — *Slaughter, Richard A*
Knowledge-Based Systems for General Reference Work — *Richardson, John V, Jr.*
Knowledge, Difference, and Power — *Goldberger, Nancy Rule*
r Knowledge Exchange Business Encyclopedia Master Reference — *Spurge, Lorraine*
cr The Knowledge Factory — *Edmonds, Alex*
c The Knowledge: Flaming Olympics — *Coleman, Michael*
Knowledge, Innovation and Economy — *Kwasnicki, Witold*
Knowledge of Angels — *Paton Walsh, Jill*
Knowledge of Angels (Scott). Audio Version — *Paton Walsh, Jill*
The Knowledge of Childhood in the German Middle Ages 1100-1350 — *Schultz, James A*
The Knowledge of Water — *Smith, Sarah*
Knowledge Painfully Acquired — *Lo, Chin-Shun*
The Known World — *Bogen, Don*
The Kobe Earthquake — *Brebbia, C A*
c Kodomo: Children of Japan — *Kuklin, Susan*
c Kofi and His Magic (Illus. by Margaret Courtney-Clarke) — *Angelou, Maya*
Kojin — *Soseki, Natsume*
Kokoschka Und Dresden — *Schmidt, Werner*
Koln: Stadt Und Bistum In Kirche Und Reich Des Mittelalters — *Vollrath, Hanna*
Die Kolner Handelsbeziehungen Im Spatmittelalter — *Hirschfelder, Gunther*
Der Koloss Neros — *Bergmann, Marianne*
Kommentar Zu Luthers Katechismen. Vol. 5 — *Peters, Albrecht*
r Kommos I. Pt. 1 — *Shaw, Joseph W*
c Komodo Dragon (Illus. by Tara Darling) — *Darling, Kathy*
c Komodo Dragons — *Maynard, Thane*
Komodo, the Living Dragon. Rev. Ed. — *Lutz, Richard L*
Komplekse Liv — *Liep, John*
Konfession Und Internationales System — *Graf, Holger Thomas*
Konfidenz — *Dorfman, Ariel*
c Kongi and Potgi (Illus. by Oki S Han) — *Han, Oki S*
y Kongo Ndongo — *Mann, Kenny*
Konin: A Quest — *Richmond, Theo*
Konrad Adenauer: A German Politician and Statesman in a Period of War, Revolution and Reconstruction — *Schwarz, Hans-Peter, 1934-*
Kontinuum Der Reflexion — *Schmidt-Krayer, Barbara*
Konzepte Von Elektrizitatsversorgung Und Elektrizitatswirtschaft — *Gilson, Norbert*
Kora and Ka — *H D*
Korea Remembered — *Cole, Charles F*
c Korea: The High and Beautiful Peninsula — *Collinwood, Dean Walter*
Korea: The Search for the Sovereignty — *Simons, G L*
Korea-United States Cooperation in the New World Order — *Bergsten, C Fred*
Korean Dynasty — *Kirk, Donald*
The Korean Economy — *Yi, Hyong-Gu*
Korean Enterprise — *Ungson, Gerardo R*
The Korean Management System — *Chang, Chan Sup*
r The Korean War — *Brune, Lester H*
y Korean War — *Gay, Kathlyn*
The Korean War — *Stueck, William*
Korea's Place in the Sun — *Cumings, Bruce*
Koriwns Biographie Des Mesrop Mastoc — *Winkler, Gabriele*
Korper/Kultur: Kalifornische Studien Zur Deutschen Moderne — *Kniesche, Thomas W*
Kostbare Illustrierte Bucher Des Sechzehnten Jahrhunderts In Der Stadtbibliothek Trier
c Kotik: The Baby Seal (Illus. by Fred Bruemmer) — *Delaunois, Angele*
c The Koufax Dilemma (Illus. by Meryl Treatner) — *Schnur, Steven*
Kowloon Tong — *Theroux, Paul*
Kozats'ki Stravy — *Mel'nychuk, IAroslav*
The KPT Bryce Book — *Kitchens, Susan A*
y Krakatau: The Destruction and Reassembly of an Island Ecosystem — *Thornton, Ian*
Krapp's Last Tape — *Beckett, Samuel*
Kratkii Putevoditel' — *Rossiiskii Tsentr Khraneniia I Izucheniia Dokumentov Noveishei Istorii*
r Kraus Family Genealogy — *Peck, Patricia D*
Kraven Images — *Isler, Alan*

Kreiseliana: About and around Georg Kreisel
— *Odifreddi, Piergiorgio*
Krekshuns — *Bolen, Dennis E*
Kremlin Capitalism — *Blasi, Joseph R*
The Kremlin's Agenda — *Galeotti, Mark*
Kresby Z Cremony 1500-1580 — *Zlatohlavek, Martin*
The Kress Legacy — *Thomas, Bernice L*
Der Kreuzzug Kaiser Heinrichs VI — *Naumann,*
Claudia
Krigsvintrar — *Friberg, Gosta*
Krik? Krak! — *Danticat, Edwidge*
Kriminalitat In Rom 1560-1585 — *Blastenbrei, Peter*
The Kristeva Reader — *Kristeva, Julia*
Kriz' Tiurmy, Pidpillia I Kordony — *Stakhiv, IEvhen*
Kronia O Velke Morave. Rev. Ed. — *Havlik, Lubomir*
E
Krymskaia Voina I Russko-Amerikanskie Otnosheniia
— *Ponomarev, V N*
Kuang Dai Yi Cai. Vols. 1-6 — *Tang, Haoming*
Kuca Mrtvih Mirisa — *Ognjenovic, Vida*
Kudriavyi Leitenant — *Murav'eva, Irina*
Kui Jumalad Nutsid — *Uustulnd, Albert*
c **The Kuia and the Spider** — *Grace, Patricia*
Kulap in Oz — *Barme, Scot*
A Kulcsfigura — *Dalos, Gyorgy*
Die Kultur Der Luge — *Ugresic, Dubravka*
Kultur Und Alltag In Der Fruhen Neuzeit. Vol. 3
— *Van Dulmen, Richard*
Kul'tura Ukralns'koho Narodu
Kulturgeschichte Der Klassischen Archaologie
— *Sichtermann, Hellmut*
Kulturprotestantismus Und Politik — *Hubinger,*
Gangolf
Kundalini: Empowering Human Evolution — *Krishna,*
Gopi
c **Kung-Fu Boy** — *Maekawa, Takeshi*
Kunst Des Sammelns — *Achilles-Syndram, Kathrin*
Die Kunste Und Die Wissenschaften Im Exil
1933-1945 — *Bohne, Edith*
The Kuomintang and the Democratization of Taiwan
— *Hood, Steven J*
Kuparitaivas — *Luoma, Heikki*
c **A Kurdish Family (Illus. by Rick Moncauskas)**
— *O'Connor, Karen, 1938-*
The Kurdish Nationalist Movement in the 1990s
— *Olson, Robert*
The Kurdish Struggle 1920-94 — *O'Ballance, Edgar*
Kurie Und Ortskirche — *Weiss, Sabine*
Kurt Cobain — *Sandford, Christopher*
Kurt Hahn's Schools and Legacy — *Hahn, Kurt*
Kurt Weill: An Illustrated Life — *Schebera, Jurgen*
r **Kuwait. Rev. Ed.** — *Clements, Frank A*
Kwaku, or, The Man Who Could Not Keep His
Mouth Shut — *Heath, Roy*
Kwanzaa and Me — *Paley, Vivian Gussin*
c **The Kwanzaa Contest (Illus. by Laurie Spencer)**
— *Moore, Miriam*
c **Kwanzaa Fun (Illus. by Julia Pearson)** — *Robertson,*
Linda
c **Kwanzaa Karamu (Illus. by Barbara Knutson)**
— *Brady, April A*
Kyrie — *Voigt, Ellen Bryant*

L

L Is for Lawless — *Grafton, Sue*

L Is for Lawless (Kaye). Audio Version — *Grafton, Sue*

c The La-Di-Da Hare (Illus. by Diana Cain Bluthenthal) — *Lewis, J Patrick*

La Fontaine's Bawdy — *La Fontaine, Jean De*

La Rochefoucauld and the Language of Unmasking in Seventeenth-Century France — *Clark, Henry C*

De La Terre Au Ciel — *Clavel-Leveque, Monique*

De Laatste Vrijheid — *Arion, Frank Martinus*

c The Lab Rats of Doctor Eclair (Illus. by John Bianchi) — *Bianchi, John*

Labor Agreement in Negotiation and Arbitration. 2nd Ed. — *Zack, Arnold M*

r The Labor Almanac — *Paradis, Adrian A*

Labor and Community — *Gonzalez, Gilbert G*

r Labor Conflict in the United States — *Filipelli, Ronald L*

Labor, Crafts and Commerce in Ancient Israel — *Aberbach, Moshe*

r Labor Fact Book. Vols. 1-17 — *Labor Research Association (U.S.)*

r Labor History Archives in the United States — *Leab, Daniel J*

r Labor History in the United States — *Stroud, Gene S*

r Labor in America

Labor Law, Industrial Relations and Employee Choice — *Block, Richard N*

Labor Markets in a Global Economy — *Rima, Ingrid H*

Labor Movements and Dictatorships — *Drake, Paul W*

A Labor of Love — *Tucker, Marcia*

r Labor-Personnel Index 1951-

Labor Relations and Political Change in Eastern Europe — *Thirkell, John*

Labor Relations and the Law — *Raza, M Ali*

Labor Shortages as America Approaches the Twenty-First Century — *Cohen, Malcolm S*

r Labor Unions — *Fink, Gary M*

The Labor Wars in Cordoba 1955-1976 — *Brennan, James P*

Laboratories of Virtue — *Meranze, Michael*

Laboratory Earth — *Schneider, Stephen Henry*

A Laboratory Guide to RNA — *Krieg, Paul A*

Laboratory Medicine and the Aging Process — *Knight, Joseph A*

Laboratory of Dreams — *Bowlt, John E*

The Laboratory Practice of Clinical Toxicology — *Berman, Eleanor*

r Labour and Conservative Party Members 1990-92 — *Seyd, Patrick*

Labour and Gold in Fiji — *Emberson-Bain, Atu*

Labour and Society in Britain and the USA. Vols. 1-2 — *Kirk, Neville*

p Labour Economics

p Labour File: A Monthly Journal of Labour and Economic Affairs

Labour Force Survey Report 1994

Labour in the Medieval Islamic World — *Shatzmiller, Maya*

The Labour Market by Education and Occupation to 2000 — *Research Centre for Education and the Labour Market*

The Labour Market in Africa — *Lachaud, Jean-Pierre*

The Labour Party since 1945 — *Jefferys, Kevin*

The Labour Party since 1945 — *Shaw, Eric*

Labour Relations in Transition — *Clarke, Simon*

Labour, Science and Technology in France 1500-1620 — *Heller, Henry*

Labour Statistics for a Market Economy — *Chernyshev, Igor*

Labour's Dilemma — *Sugiman, Pamela*

Labrador Odyssey — *Curwen, Eliot*

y Labrador Retriever — *Fogle, Bruce*

LabVIEW for Everyone — *Wells, Lisa K*

The Labyrinth — *Perry, S D*

The Labyrinth of Exile — *Pawel, Ernst*

The Labyrinth of Flames — *Evans, Chris*

The Labyrinths of Literacy — *Graff, Harvey J*

Labyrinths: Selected Stories and Other Writings — *Borges, Jorge Luis*

LaChapelle Land — *LaChapelle, David*

Lactilla, Milkwoman of Clifton — *Waldron, Mary*

The Lactose-Free Family Cookbook — *Main, Jan*

Ladder of Years — *Tyler, Anne*

y Ladder of Years (Critt). Audio Version — *Tyler, Anne*

c A Ladder to the Stars (Illus. by Prue Berthon) — *Greenway, Rosalynne*

y Ladies First — *Roberts, Robin, 1957-*

Ladies, Start Your Engines — *Nauen, Elinor*

Lady Chatterley's Lover — *Lawrence, D H*

c Lady Daisy (Lambert). Audio Version — *King-Smith, Dick*

Lady Gregory's Diaries 1892-1902 — *Gregory, Lady*

Lady in the Lake — *Foss, Jason*

y The Lady in the Tower (Jeater). Audio Version — *Plaidy, Jean*

Lady Mary Wortley Montagu and the Eighteenth-Century Familiar Letter — *Lowenthal, Cynthia J*

c Lady Muck (Illus. by Jonathan Heale) — *Mayne, William*

y Lady of Avalon — *Bradley, Marion Zimmer*

Lady of the Mist — *Hanchar, Peggy*

y Lady of the Trillium — *Bradley, Marion Zimmer*

The Lady Who Liked Clean Rest Rooms — *Donleavy, J P*

Lady with a Laptop — *Thomas, D M*

c The Lady with the Hat — *Orlev, Uri*

The Lady with the Laptop — *Sinclair, Clive*

A Lady without a Latitude — *Phelps, Susan*

cr Ladybird Dictionary (Illus. by Peter Massey)

The Ladybug — *Crewe, Sabrina*

c Ladybug at Orchard Avenue (Komisar) (Illus. by Thomas Buchs). Book and Audio Version — *Zoehfeld, Kathleen Weidner*

Ladybugs: A Teacher's Guide

y Ladyfingers and Nun's Tummies — *Barnette, Martha*

Ladylord — *Miller, Sasha*

Lady's Choice — *Lockwood, Karen*

Lafayette in Two Worlds — *Kramer, Lloyd*

c El Lago De La Luna — *Gantschev, Ivan*

The Lair — *Cave, Emma*

The Laity in the Middle Ages — *Vauchez, Andre*

c Lake and Pond — *Sayre, April Pulley*

c Lake Huron — *Armbruster, Ann*

c Lake Michigan — *Armbruster, Ann*

Lake Nora Arms — *Redhill, Michael*

c Lake Superior — *Armbruster, Ann*

Lake Superior Place Names — *Peters, Bernard C*

r Lake Township Cemetery, Wood County, Ohio — *Ohio Genealogical Society. Wood County Chapter*

Lambeaux — *Juliet, Charles*

Lament for the Makers — *Merwin, W S*

Laments — *Kochanowski, Jan*

The Lamp Shade Book — *Cusick, Dawn*

Lamps in the Whirlpool — *Krishnan, Rajam*

Lanark: A Life in 4 Books — *Gray, Alasdair*

r Lancaster County, Pennsylvania Divorces 1786-1832 — *Throop, Eugene F*

Lancelot and Guinevere — *Walters, Lori J*

The Lancelot-Grail Cycle — *Kibler, William W*

Land — *Pak, Kyong-Ni*

Land and Lordship — *Brunner, Otto*

Land and Popular Politics in Ireland — *Jordan, Donald E*

Land and Society in England 1750-1980 — *Mingay, G E*

Land Art — *Tiberghien, Gilles A*

y Land Girls — *Huth, Angela*

Land, Growth, and Politics — *DeGrove, John*

Land in Her Own Name — *Lindgren, H Elaine*

Land, Law, and Lordship in Anglo-Norman England — *Hudson, John*

Land Mosaics — *Forman, Richard T T*

The Land of Bliss — *Tripitaka. Sutrapitaka. Sukhavativyuha (Larger). English*

Land of Desire — *Leach, William*

A Land of Discord Always — *Mahaffie, Charles D, Jr.*

Land of Fair Promise — *Raftery, Judith Rosenberg*

The Land of Green Plums — *Muller, Herta*

The Land of Hunger — *Camporesi, Piero*

The Land of Lost Content — *Peel, Mark*

The Land of Milk and Honey — *Getty, Sarah*

The Land of Miracles — *Smith, Stephen*

Land of Opportunity — *Adler, William M*

Land of Rivers — *Mancall, Peter C*

Land of Women — *Bitel, Lisa M*

c Land Pacts — *Gold, Susan Dudley*

Land, Politics and Nationalism — *Bull, Philip*

Land Quality Indicators — *Pieri, Christian*

The Land Question in Zimbabwe — *Moyo, Sam*

Land Reborn — *Catton, Theodore*

Land Spirit Power — *Nemiroff, Diana*

Land to Light On — *Brand, Dionne*

Land Use in Early New Jersey — *Wacker, Peter O*

The Landed Estates of the Esterhazy Princes — *Gates-Coon, Rebecca*

Landform Systems — *Bishop, Victoria*

The Landlady in Bangkok — *Swenson, Karen*

Landlords and Haciendas in Modernizing Mexico — *Miller, Simon*

Landlords and Tenants in Mid-Victorian Ireland — *Vaughan, W E*

Landmark Essays on American Public Address — *Medhurst, Martin J*

Landmark Essays on Rhetorical Criticism — *Benson, Thomas W*

Landmark Essays on Writing Centers — *Murphy, Christina*

A Landmark in Accounting Theory — *Preinreich, Gabriel A D*

r The Landmark Thucydides — *Thucydides*

y Landmarks — *Marsh, Linda*

Landmarks: An Exploration of Great Rocks — *Craig, David*

y Landmarks in Mechanical Engineering — *American Society of Mechanical Engineers. History and Heritage Committee*

r Landmarks of American Presidents — *Wheeless, Carl*

Landowners and Tenants in Roman Egypt — *Rowlandson, Jane*

Landowners, Capitalists and Entrepreneurs — *Thompson, F M L*

Landownership and Residential Land Use in Urban Economies — *Tokunaga, Suminori*

Lands, Laws, and Gods — *Gargola, Daniel J*

Landscape and Desire — *Wainwright, J A*

Landscape and Memory — *Schama, Simon*

Landscape and Power in Vienna — *Rotenberg, Robert*

Landscape and Vegetation Ecology of the Kakadu Region, Northern Australia — *Finlayson, C Max*

Landscape Archaeology — *Yamin, Rebecca*
r Landscape Architecture Sourcebook — *Vogelsong, Diana*
Landscape Ecology Principles in Landscape Architecture and Land-Use Planning — *Dramstad, Wenche E*
Landscape Irrigation — *Smith, S W*
The Landscape of Belief — *Davis, John H, 1961-*
Landscape of the Heart — *Lyons, Stephen J*
Landscape over Zero — *Pei-Tao*
Landscape over Zero — *Pei-Tao, 1949-*
Landscape: Politics and Perspectives — *Bender, Barbara*
c Landscapes — *Delafosse, Claude*
c Landscapes — *King, Penny, 1963-*
c Landscapes (Illus. by Sallie Alane Reason) — *Perham, Molly*
c Landscapes (Illus. by Lindy Norton) — *Roundhill, Clare*
Landscapes for Learning — *Stine, Sharon*
Landscapes for the Homeless — *Hernandez, Anthony*
The Landscapes of Louis Remy Mignot — *Manthorne, Katherine E*
Landscapes of Resistance — *Byg, Barton*
Landscapes of Settlement — *Roberts, Brian K*
r Landscapes of South Ulster — *Duffy, P J*
Landscapes of the Interior — *Gayton, Don*
Landscaping for Wildlife — *Henderson, Carrol L*
Landscaping Makes Cents — *Dube, Richard*
Landslides: Glissements De Terrain — *International Symposium on Landslides (7th: 1996: Trondheim)*
Lanfranco Di Pavia E L'Europa Del Secolo XI — *D'Onofrio, Giulio*
Le Langage Dramatique De La Reine Morte — *Lancrey-Javal, Romain*
Langage Et Verite — *Ceard, Jean*
Langstaff: A Nineteenth-Century Medical Life — *Duffin, Jacalyn*
Language — *Everson, Stephen*
c Language — *Newson, Lesley*
Language and Communicative Practices — *Hanks, William F*
Language and Computers — *Barnbrook, Geoff*
Language and Culture in Multilingual Societies — *Tickoo, Makhan L*
Language and Human Behavior — *Bickerton, Derek*
Language and Ideology in Children's Fiction — *Stephens, John, 1944-*
Language and Learning for Robots — *Crangle, Colleen*
Language and Money in Rabelais — *Lavatori, Gerard Ponziano*
Language and Space — *Bloom, Paul*
Language and the Social Construction of Identity in Creole Situations — *Morgan, Marcyliena*
Language as Articulate Contact — *Stewart, John Robert*
Language as Discourse — *McCarthy, Michael*
Language Assessment in Action — *Brindley, Geoff*
y The Language Book — *Mayne, Andrew*
Language, Charisma, and Creativity — *Csordas, Thomas J*
Language Contact Language Conflict — *Putz, Martin*
Language, Culture, and Communication in Contemporary Europe — *Hoffmann, Charlotte*
Language, Culture, and Power — *Soto, Lourdes Diaz*
Language, Education and Society in a Changing World — *Hickey, Tina*
c Language Exercises — *Jones, Betty*
Language, Identity, and Social Division — *Ben-Rafael, Eliezer*
Language in the World — *Cresswell, M J*
Language, Learnability and Language Development — *Pinker, Steven*
Language, Mind and Art — *Jamieson, Dale*
Language, Minorities and Human Rights — *Varennes, Fernand De*
Language Minority Students in the Mainstream Classroom — *Carrasquillo, Angela L*
y The Language of Animals — *Hart, Stephen*
c The Language of Doves (Illus. by Greg Shed) — *Wells, Rosemary*
The Language of Empire — *MacDonald, Robert H*
The Language of Faith — *Schillebeeckx, Edward*
The Language of Judges — *Solan, Lawrence M*
The Language of Learning and the Language of Love — *Auden, W H*
The Language of Liberty 1660-1832 — *Clark, J C D*
r The Language of Middle English Literature — *Burnley, J D*

r The Language of Money 3. Expanded, Rev., Updated Ed. — *Carew, Edna*
The Language of Names — *Kaplan, Justin*
The Language of Old and Middle English Poetry — *Lester, G A*
The Language of Public Administration — *Farmer, David John*
y The Language of Reading — *Fitzgerald, Bernadette*
The Language of Sex — *Baldwin, John W*
The Language of the Body — *Prud'hon, Pierre-Paul*
Language Policies in English-Dominant Countries — *Herriman, Michael*
Language, Religion, and Ethnic Assertiveness — *Dharmadasa, K N O*
Language Teaching and Skill Learning — *Johnson, Keith*
Language the Unknown — *Kristeva, Julia*
The Language They Speak Is Things to Eat — *McFee, Michael*
Language, Thought, and Consciousness — *Carruthers, Peter*
Language through Play — *Henderson, Ann*
Language Understanding. 2nd Ed. — *Coulson, Mark*
The Language Web — *Aitchison, Jean*
Languages for the International Scientist — *Parker, Gabrielle*
Languages of Labor and Gender — *Canning, Kathleen*
The Languages of Psychoanalysis — *Gedo, John E*
r The Languages of the World. New Ed. — *Katzner, Kenneth*
Languages of Visuality — *Beate, Allert*
La Langue Maternelle — *Alexakis, Vassilis*
Les Langues De France — *Bonnemason, Jean*
Lantern Slides — *Bonham Carter, Violet*
y Lanterns — *Veryan, Patricia*
r Lao-English Dictionary — *Patterson, William L*
c Lao Lao of Dragon Mountain (Illus. by Francesca Pelizzoli) — *Bateson-Hill, Margaret*
Lao-Tzu's Taoteching — *Lao-Tzu*
c Laos--in Pictures — *Lerner Publications Company. Geography Dept.*
Lapham's Raiders — *Lapham, Robert*
The Lapland Journey — *Linnaeus, Carl*
Lapsit Services for the Very Young — *Ernst, Linda L*
c The Lapsnatcher (Illus. by Marissa Moss) — *Coville, Bruce*
Large Animals in Everyday Life — *Brenner, Wendy*
Large Clusters of Atoms and Molecules — *Martin, T P*
The Large Macaws — *Abramson, Joanne*
Large-Scale C++ — *Lakos, John*
Large-Scale Systems — *Jamshidi, Mohammad*
Large Scale Systems: Theory and Applications 1995. Vols. 1-2 — *IFAC/IFORS/IMAC Symposium Large Scale Systems (7th: 1995: London, England)*
The Large, the Small and the Human Mind — *Penrose, Roger*
The Largely Literary Legacy of the Late Leon Tolbert — *Kornberg, Grant*
r Larger Animals of East Africa — *Hosking, David*
y Lark Rise to Candleford (Dench). Audio Version — *Thompson, Flora*
Larkspur — *Garlock, Dorothy*
r The Larousse Desk Reference
r Larousse Dictionary of Literary Characters — *Goring, Rosemary*
r Larousse Dictionary of Science and Technology
r Larousse Dictionary of Women — *Parry, Melanie*
r Larousse Encyclopedia of Wine — *Foulkes, Christopher*
r Larousse English-Spanish, Spanish-English Dictionary. New Ed.
r Larousse Mini French-English, English-French Dictionary. New Ed.
r Larousse Mini German-English, English-German Dictionary. New Ed.
r Larousse Mini Italian-English, English-Italian Dictionary. New Ed.
r Larousse Mini Spanish-English, English-Spanish Dictionary. New Ed.
r Las Casas: In Search of the Poor of Jesus Christ — *Gutierrez, Gustavo*
Las Vegas: The Great American Playground — *McCracken, Robert D*
Laser Diagnostics for Combustion Temperature and Species. 2nd Ed. — *Eckbreth, Alan C*
Laser Fundamentals — *Silfvast, William T*
Laser Interaction and Related Plasma Phenomena. Pts. 1-2 — *International Conference on Laser Interaction and Related Plasma Phenomena (12th: 1995: Osaka, Japan)*

Laser Materials Processing — *Migliore, Leonard*
Laser Processing — *NATO Advanced Study Institute on Laser Processing: Surface Treatment and Film Deposition (1994: Sezimbra, Portugal)*
c Lasers — *Fox, Mary Virginia*
Lasers and Electro-Optics — *Davis, Christopher C*
c Lassie Come Home (Illus. by Susan Jeffers) — *Wells, Rosemary*
y Lasso the Moon — *Covington, Dennis*
y The Last Act Was Deadly and Other Stories (Rubinek). Audio Version — *Bankier, William*
The Last American Aristocrat — *Lankford, Nelson D*
The Last Appeal — *Blum, Bill*
The Last Arrow — *Canham, Marsha*
The Last Banner — *May, Peter, 1951, Feb., 2-*
The Last Best Thing — *Dillon, Patrick*
The Last Bookman. Rev. and Enlarged Ed. — *Ruber, Peter*
c Last Bus (Illus. by Mark Edwards) — *Swindells, Robert*
Last Call — *Mulisch, Harry*
Last Call: A Legacy of Madness
The Last Cannibals — *Basso, Ellen B*
Last Cavalier — *Porterfield, Nolan*
Last Chance for Eden — *Knight, Christopher*
Last Chants — *Matera, Lia*
Last Chapter and Worse — *Larson, Gary*
The Last Client of Luis Montez — *Ramos, Manuel*
The Last Closet — *Kissen, Rita M*
y Last Comes the Egg — *Duffy, Bruce*
The Last Coyote — *Connelly, Michael*
Last Dance at the Hotel Kempinski — *Hirsch, Robin*
The Last Days of Hitler — *Joachimsthaler, Anton*
The Last Days of Innocence — *Harries, Meirion*
Last Days of the Dog-Men — *Watson, Brad*
The Last Debate — *Lehrer, Jim*
The Last Descendant of Aeneas — *Tanner, Marie*
Last Dinner on the Titanic — *Archbold, Rick*
The Last Division — *Tusa, Ann*
The Last Don — *Puzo, Mario*
The Last Dust Storm — *McDaniel, Wilma Elizabeth*
The Last Enemy — *Longyear, Barry B*
y The Last Family (McRaney). Audio Version — *Miller, John Ramsey*
The Last Forbidden Kingdom, Mustang — *Marullo, Clara*
The Last Frontier — *Singh, Daman*
Last Gang in Town — *Gray, Marcus*
The Last Gift of Time — *Heilbrun, Carolyn G*
The Last Good Night — *Listfield, Emily*
The Last Great Frenchman — *Williams, Charles, 1933-*
y The Last Great Victory — *Weintraub, Stanley*
The Last Happy Occasion — *Shapiro, Alan*
The Last Harvest — *Raeburn, Paul*
c Last Hawaiian Queen — *Guzzetti, Paula*
The Last Hero — *Falkner, David*
The Last Hotel for Women — *Covington, Vicki*
The Last Inch — *Morris, Claud*
y The Last Integrationist (Morton). Audio Version — *Lamar, Jake*
The Last Jews of Cochin — *Katz, Nathan*
Last Journey (Fox). Audio Version — *Scott, Robert Falcon*
The Last Judgement — *Pears, Iain*
The Last Lamp — *Robishaw, Sue*
c Last Left Standing — *Russell, Barbara T*
The Last Machine — *Christie, Ian, 1945-*
The Last Man — *Shelley, Mary Wollstonecraft*
Last Man Out — *Parker, James E, Jr.*
c The Last Man's Reward — *Patneaude, David*
The Last Master. Vol. 1 — *Suchet, John*
Last-Minute Christmas Gifts — *Taylor, Carol*
Last Minute Interview Tips — *Toropov, Brandon*
Last Minute Job Search Tips — *Toropov, Brandon*
y Last Minute Study Tips — *Fry, Ronald W*
The Last Monopoly — *Hudgins, Edward L*
y Last Neanderthal — *Tattersall, Ian*
The Last New Land — *Mergler, Wayne*
Last Night in Paradise — *Roiphe, Katie*
Last Night in Rio — *Kaiser, Janice*
Last Night on Earth — *Jones, Bill T*
Last Night's Fun — *Carson, Ciaran*
c The Last Noo-Noo — *Murphy, Jill*
The Last of Deeds. Love in History — *McNamee, Eoin*
r Last of the Empires — *Keep, John L H*
The Last of the Race — *Stafford, Fiona J*
y The Last of the Savages — *McInerney, Jay*
y The Last of the Wine — *Renault, Mary*
Last Orders — *Swift, Graham*

Last Orders (Jayston). Audio Version — *Swift, Graham*
The Last Party — *Haden-Guest, Anthony*
The Last Party — *Mailer, Adele*
The Last Pin — *Wandrei, Howard*
y The Last Piper — *Cavanagh, Helen*
c The Last-Place Sports Poems of Jeremy Bloom — *Korman, Gordon*
The Last Plantation — *Njeri, Itabari*
The Last Poets on a Mission — *Oyewole, Abiodun*
c The Last Polar Bears (Illus. by Harry Horse) — *Horse, Harry*
Last Post — *Keay, John*
c The Last Princess (Illus. by Diane Stanley) — *Stanley, Fay*
c The Last Quest of Gilgamesh (Illus. by Ludmila Zeman) — *Zeman, Ludmila*
c The Last Rail (Illus. by Bill Farnsworth). Book and Audio Version — *Bailer, Darice*
y The Last Rainmaker — *Garland, Sherry*
The Last Ranch — *Bingham, Sam*
The Last Resort — *Max, Aggie*
The Last Resort — *Ryan, Martin*
Last Resorts — *Pattullo, Polly*
Last Rights — *Nerone, John C*
y Last Rights — *Shelby, Philip*
Last Rites — *Howarth, Glennys*
Last Rites and Resurrections. Vol. 1 — *Cox, Andy*
y The Last Safe Place on Earth — *Peck, Richard*
Last Seen — *Cohen, Matt*
Last Served? — *Patton, Cindy*
y The Last Shot — *Frey, Darcy*
The Last Six Million Seconds — *Burdett, John*
The Last Snow Leopard — *Kern, Gary*
The Last Stand — *Harris, David*
Last Stand in the Carolinas — *Bradley, Mark L*
Last Steps to Freedom — *Boyko, John*
c The Last Stronghold — *Luger, Harriett Mandelay*
y Last Sword of Power — *Gemmell, David*
The Last Thing He Wanted — *Didion, Joan*
The Last Time I Saw Mother — *Chai, Arlene J*
y The Last Trail — *Grey, Zane*
c The Last Train — *Lewis, Kim*
r The Last Voyage of El Nuevo Constante — *Pearson, Charles E*
The Last White Christmas — *Monchak, Ronald W*
The Last Witness — *Kestenberg, Judith S*
The Last Worthless Evening — *Dubus, Andre*
Last Year in Hong Kong — *Elegant, Robert*
The Lasting of the Mohicans — *Barker, Martin*
Laszlo Moholy-Nagy: Biographical Writings — *Kaplan, Louis*
Late Bloomers — *Gill, Brendan*
Late-Breaking Foreign Policy — *Strobel, Warren*
The Late Bronze Egyptian Garrison at Beth Shan. Vols. 1-2 — *James, Frances W*
The Late Child — *McMurtry, Larry*
The Late Devonian Mass Extinction — *McGhee, George R*
The Late Great Mexican Border — *Byrd, Bobby*
A Late Harvest — *McKane, William*
Late Imperial Culture — *De La Campa, Roman*
Late Payments — *Lewin, Michael Z*
Late Quarternary Chronology and Paleoclimates of the Eastern Mediterranean — *Bar-Yosef, Ofer*
The Late Roman Army — *Southern, Pat*
The Late Romances — *Pankey, Eric*
Late Seventeenth-Century Edinburgh — *Dingwall, Helen M*
r Late Victorian Poetry 1880-1899 — *Reilly, Catherine W*
Der Lateinische Eulenspiegel Des Loannes Nemius — *Winkler, Martin M*
Die Lateinische Evangelien-Motette Des 16. Jahrhunderts — *Krebs, Wolfgang*
Later Calvinism — *Graham, W Fred*
Later Ceramics in South-East Asia Sixteenth to Twentieth Centuries — *Harrisson, Barbara*
y Later Days at Highbury — *Austen-Leigh, Joan*
Later Families of Sanford-Springvale, Maine — *Boyle, Frederick R*
The Later Poetry of Charlotte Perkins Gilman — *Gilman, Charlotte Perkins*
The Later Tudors — *Williams, Penry*
The Lateran in 1600 — *Freiberg, Jack*
Latest Developments in Marxist Theory — *Zarembka, Paul*
The Latest Epistle of Jim — *Shepard, Roy*
Latifundium: Moral Economy and Material Life in a European Periphery — *Petrusewicz, Marta*
Latin America 1996

Latin America and the Caribbean
Latin America and the Caribbean in Transition — *Watson, Robert P*
Latin America Faces the Twenty-First Century — *Jonas, Susanne, 1941-*
Latin America in a New World — *Lowenthal, Abraham F*
Latin America in Comparative Perspective — *Smith, Peter H*
r Latin America on File — *Tomaselli-Maschovitis, Valerie*
Latin American Art in the Twentieth Century — *Sullivan, Edward J*
Latin American Civilization. 6th Ed., Rev. and Updated — *Keen, Benjamin*
r Latin American Classical Composers — *Ficher, Miguel*
c Latin American Folk Song — *McLaughlin, Roberta*
yr Latin American History on File — *Chapman, Victoria L*
Latin American Male Homosexualities — *Murray, Stephen O*
Latin American Revolutions 1808-1826 — *Lynch, John*
Latin American Spanish — *Lipski, John M*
Latin American Underdevelopment — *Park, James William*
r Latin American Women Artists, Kahlo and Look Who Else — *Puerto, Cecilia*
Latin-American Women Writers — *Jehenson, Myriam Yvonne*
y Latin American Writers — *Shirey, Lynn M*
Latin America's New Insertion in the World Economy — *Buitelaar, Ruud*
The Latin and German Etymachia — *Harris, Nigel*
The Latin and Greek Poems of Samuel Johnson — *Johnson, Samuel*
Latin and the Romance Languages in the Early Middle Ages — *Wright, Roger*
r Latin for the Illiterati — *Stone, Jon R*
y Latin Is Fun. Bk. 2 — *Traupman, John C*
p Latina
Latina Issues — *Lopez, Antoinette Sedillo*
Latina Politics, Latino Politics — *Hardy-Fanta, Carol*
r Latinas in the United States — *Nordquist, Joan*
Latino Employment, Labor Organizations, and Immigration — *Lopez, Antoinette Sedillo*
yr The Latino Encyclopedia. Vols. 1-6 — *Chabran, Richard*
Latino High School Graduation — *Romo, Harriett*
Latino Literacy — *De Varona, Frank*
y The Latino Reader — *Augenbraum, Harold*
y Latinos in Beisbol — *Cockcroft, James D*
r Latinos in English — *Augenbraum, Harold*
Latins Anonymous
Latitudes and Attitudes — *Weiss, Michael J*
Latitudinarianism in the Seventeenth-Century Church of England — *Griffin, Martin I J, Jr.*
The Latter Day Saints — *Kauffman, Ruth*
Latter Days of the Law — *Weidner, Marsha*
Latvia in Transition — *Dreifelds, Juris*
Laubhutte Davids Und Wolkensohn — *Nagele, Sabine*
The Laude in the Middle Ages
Lauderdale's Notes on Adam Smith's Wealth of Nations — *Lauderdale, James Maitland, Earl of*
Laughing at the Tao
The Laughing Hangman — *Marston, Edward*
Laughing on the Outside — *Knelman, Martin*
c Laughing Tomatoes (Illus. by Maya Christina Gonzalez) — *Alarcon, Francisco X*
Laughs, Luck...and Lucy — *Oppenheimer, Jess*
Laughter and Tears — *Bing, Elisabeth*
Laughter in the Dark — *Kalson, Albert E*
Laughter's Gentle Soul — *Altman, Billy*
Launching a Baby's Adoption — *Johnston, Patricia Irwin*
Launching a Business on the Web. 2nd Ed. — *Cook, David*
r Launching Democracy in South Africa — *Johnson, R W*
The Laundrymen: Inside Money Laundering, the World's Third-Largest Business — *Robinson, Jeffrey, 1945-*
c Laura Helps Pa (Illus. by Renee Graef) — *Graef, Renee*
c The Laura Ingalls Wilder Songbook (Illus. by Garth Williams) — *Garson, Eugenia*
c Laura Ingalls Wilder: Storyteller of the Prairie — *Wadsworth, Ginger*
Laura Lemay's Web Workshop — *Lemay, Laura*
Laura: Uncovering Gender and Genre in Wyatt, Donne, and Marvell — *Estrin, Barbara L*

c Laura's Garden (Illus. by Renee Graef) — *Graef, Renee*
Laure: The Collected Writings — *Laure*
p Laurel Review
Laurence Binyon: Poet, Scholar of East and West — *Hatcher, John*
Laurence Sterne Revisited — *Kraft, Elizabeth*
y Laurie and Claire (Thomas). Audio Version — *Rowntree, Kathleen*
Lautreamont Austral — *Rodriguez Monegal, Emir*
Lava — *Ball, Pamela*
The Lavender Vote — *Hertzog, Mark*
Lavish Self-Divisions — *Daly, Brenda*
Lavoisier: Chemist, Biologist, Economist — *Poirier, Jean-Pierre*
Lavoisier: Memoires D'Une Revolution — *Bensaude-Vincent, Bernadette*
Law and Citizenship in Early Modern France — *Wells, Charlotte Catherine*
Law and Disorder on the Narova River — *Zelnik, Reginald E*
Law and Economics of the Environment — *Eide, Erling*
Law and English Railway Capitalism 1825-1875 — *Kostal, R W*
Law and Family in Late Antiquity — *Grubbs, Judith Evans*
Law and Government in Medieval England and Normandy — *Garnett, George*
Law and Integration in the European Union — *Weatherill, Stephen*
Law and Literature — *Ward, Ian*
Law and Liturgy in the Latin Church 5th-12th Centuries — *Reynolds, Roger E*
Law and Local Society in Late Imperial China — *Allee, Mark A*
Law and Morality — *Dyzenhaus, David*
r Law and Politics — *Strouthes, Daniel P*
Law and Society. 5th Ed. — *Vago, Steven*
Law and Society in Byzantium 9th-12th Centuries — *Laiou, Angeliki E*
Law and the Emergence of Modern Dublin — *Osborough, W N*
Law and the Great Plains — *Wunder, John R*
Law and the Transformation of Aztec Culture 1500-1700 — *Kellogg, Susan*
Law and Truth — *Patterson, Dennis*
Law as Communication — *Nelken, David*
r Law Books and Serials in Print 1996. Vols. 1-3
Law in Civil Society — *Winfield, Richard Dien*
Law in Humanitarian Crises. Vols. 1-2
Law in the Sociological Enterprise — *McIntyre, Lisa J*
Law Librarianship — *Gasaway, Laura N*
r The Law Library Reference Shelf. 3rd Ed., Rev. — *Matthews, Elizabeth W*
Law, Magistracy, and Crime in Old Regime Paris 1735-1789. Vol. 1 — *Andrews, Richard Mowery*
Law-Making and Society in Late Elizabethan England — *Dean, David*
The Law of Enclosures — *Peck, Dale*
The Law of Love — *Esquivel, Laura*
The Law of Love (Arizmendi). Audio Version — *Esquivel, Laura*
The Law of Receivers of Companies. 2nd Ed. — *Lightman, Gavin*
The Law of Revenge — *Collins, Tess*
Law of the European Convention on Human Rights — *Harris, D J*
The Law of the International Criminal Tribunal for the Former Yugoslavia — *Bassiouni, M Cherif*
The Law of the Sea (United Nations)
r Law on the Net — *Evans, James*
Law, Power, and the Sovereign State — *Fowler, Michael Ross*
The Law Relating to Schools. 1995 Ed. — *Harris, Neville*
The Law School Book — *Hutchinson, Allan C*
Law, Society, and the State — *Knafla, Louis A*
Law, Space and the Geographies of Power — *Blomley, Nicholas K*
Law Stories — *Bellow, Gary*
Law, Violence and Community in Classical Athens — *Cohen, David*
Law, Writing, Meaning — *Nerhot, Patrick*
Lawful Revolution in Hungary 1989-94 — *Kiraly, Bela K*
The Lawless Man — *Wallace, Mark*
r Lawmaking and the Legislative Process — *Neal, Tommy*
The Lawn: A History of an American Obsession — *Jenkins, Virginia Scott*

Lawrence Durrell: The Mindscape — Pine, Richard
Lawrence of Arabia and American Culture
　— Hodson, Joel C
Laws and Explanation in the Social Sciences
　— McIntyre, Lee C
Laws and Order in Eighteenth-Century Chemistry
　— Duncan, Alistair
Law's Community — Cotterrell, Roger
Laws Harsh as Tigers — Salyer, Lucy E
The Laws of Our Fathers — Turow, Scott
The Laws of Our Fathers (Brown). Audio Version
　— Turow, Scott
The Laws of Return — Stracher, Cameron
The Laws of Spirit — Millman, Dan
The Laws of War — Howard, Michael
The Laws (Penguin) — Plato
Law's Stories — Brooks, Peter
Lawyerland — Joseph, Lawrence
Lawyers against Labor — Ernst, Daniel R
The Lawyer's Calling — Allegretti, Joseph G
Lay Down Body — Wright, Roberta Hughes
Layered Intrusions — Cawthorn, R Grant
Layered Materials for Structural Applications
　— Lewandowski, J J
Laying Down the Law — Schlag, Pierre
A Lazy Eye — Morrissy, Mary
c Lazy Jack (Illus. by Russell Ayto) — French, Vivian
Lead Us Not into Penn Station — Ducker, Bruce
Leader of the Band — Lees, Gene
The Leader of the Future — Hesselbein, Frances
Leader of the Pack — Baer, Nancy
Leadership and Entrepreneurship — Smilor, Raymond
　W
Leadership and the Job of the Executive — Barach,
　Jeffrey A
Leadership and the New Science — Wheatley,
　Margaret J
r Leadership Education 1996-1997. Vols. 1-2
The Leadership of Public Bureaucracies — Terry,
　Lawrence D
Leadership on Java — Antlov, Hans
Leadership Secrets of the Rogue Warrior (Marcinko).
　Audio Version — Marcinko, Richard
Leadership Skills for the Nurse Manager — Mott,
　Kathleen O'Sullivan
Leading and Managing in Nursing — Wise, Patricia S
　Yoder
Leading Change — Kotter, John P
Leading Kids to Books through Magic — Bauer,
　Caroline Feller
Leading Minds — Gardner, Howard
Leading on the Creative Edge — Firestien, Roger L
Leading People — Rosen, Robert H
Leading Sectors and World Powers — Modelski,
　George
Leading the Blind — Sillitoe, Alan
Leading to Change — Johnson, Susan Moore
y Leading with My Chin — Leno, Jay
Leading with My Chin (Leno). Audio Version
　— Leno, Jay
Leading Women — Cox, Eva
Leading Your Team — Leigh, Andrew
A Leaf in the Bitter Wind — Ye, Ting-Xing
c The Leaf Men and the Brave Good Bugs (Illus. by
　William Joyce) — Joyce, William
c Leafs vs. Canadiens — Duplacey, James
The Leage of Nathans — Sherman, Jason
The League of a Nation — Headon, David
y The League of Frightened Men (Rubinek). Audio
　Version — Stout, Rex
The League of Nations from 1919 to 1929
　— Ostrower, Gary B
c Leagues Apart (Illus. by Richard Merkin) — Ritter,
　Lawrence S
c Leah's Pony (Illus. by Michael Garland) — Friedrich,
　Elizabeth
p Leak CD Magazine
Leakage: The Bleeding of the American Economy
　— Powers, Treval C
Lean Thinking — Womack, James P
Leaning into the Future — Binney, George
Leaning into the Wind — Hasselstrom, Linda M
The Leaning Ivory Tower — Padilla, Raymond V
Leaning Sycamores — Wennerstrom, Jack
Leaning towards Infinity — Woolfe, Sue
y A Leap Ahead — Lowell, Melissa
Leap over a Wall — Peterson, Eugene H
c The Leaping Llama Carpet — Waller, Ruth
Leaps of Faith — Humphrey, Nicholas
c Learn about Colors
c Learn about Numbers

c Learn about Opposites
c Learn about Shapes
c Learn about Size
c Learn and Play in the Garden — Herd, Meg
y Learn Bridge in Five Days — Reese, Terence
c Learn French with Teddy Berlitz. Book and Audio
　Version
y Learn from the Masters — Swetz, Frank
c Learn Spanish with Teddy Berlitz. Book and Audio
　Version
y Learn to Play Blues — Marks, Anthony
Learn to Read Chinese. Vols. 1-2 — Unschuld, Paul U
Learn Visual Basic Now — Halvorson, Michael
Learn Visual C++ Now — Andrews, Mark
c Learn with Thomas — Awdry, Christopher
The Learned King — O'Callaghan, Joseph F
c Learning about Bravery from the Life of Harriet
　Tubman — Mosher, Kiki
c Learning about Dedication from the Life of Frederick
　Douglass — Marlowe, Sam
c Learning about Determination from the Life of Gloria
　Estefan — Strazzabosco, Jeanne
c Learning about Dignity from the Life of Martin
　Luther King, Jr. — Strazzabosco, Jeanne
c Learning about Fairness from the Life of Susan B.
　Anthony — Mosher, Kiki
c Learning about Forgiveness from the Life of Nelson
　Mandela — Strazzabosco, Jeanne
c Learning about Honesty from the Life of Abraham
　Lincoln — Mosher, Kiki
c Learning about Leadership from the Life of George
　Washington — Mosher, Kiki
r Learning about the Holocaust — Stephens, Elaine C
Learning Algorithms — Mars, Phil
Learning and Behavior. 2nd Ed. — Barker, Lewis M
Learning and Intelligence — Lapan, Maureen T
Learning and Teaching Genre — Freedman, Aviva
Learning and Teaching Therapy — Haley, Jay
Learning and Technological Change — Thomson, Ross
Learning as Way of Being — Vaill, Peter B
The Learning Curve — Mishne, Judith Marks
Learning from Data. 2nd Ed. — Glenberg, Arthur M
y Learning from the Dalai Lama (Illus. by John B
　Taylor) — Pandell, Karen
Learning from the Japanese — Nafziger, E Wayne
Learning from Things — Kingery, W David
The Learning Game — Barber, Michael
Learning GNU Emacs. 2nd Ed. — Cameron, Debra
Learning History in America — Kramer, Lloyd
y Learning How the Heart Beats — McCarthy, Claire
Learning How to Learn — Shah, Idries
Learning in Overdrive — Mitchell, Ruth
Learning, Language and Invention — Hackmann, W D
Learning Networks — Harasim, Linda
Learning the HP-UX Operating System
　— Poniatowski, Marty
Learning the Rules — Bigelow, Brian J
Learning through Play — Harpley, Avril
r Learning to Be Modern — Marshall, Byron K
Learning to Be Modern — McDonald, Gail
Learning to Become Rational — Zenner, Markus
Learning to Care — Wuthnow, Robert
Learning to Drive — Norwich, William
Learning to Listen, Learning to Teach — Vella, J
Learning to Speak — Clements, Keith
y Learning to Talk Bear — Cheek, Roland
Learning to Use the World Wide Web — Ackermann,
　Ernest
Learning to Work
Learning to Work — Grubb, W Norton
Learning Veterinary Terminology — McBride,
　Douglas A
Leases and Rental Agreements — Stewart, Marcia
Leasing in Emerging Markets — Carter, Laurence
Leasing the Ivory Tower — Soley, Lawrence C
The Least Developed Countries 1995 Report
The Least Developed Countries 1996 Report
y Least of These My Brethren — Baxter, Daniel J
Least Restrictive Environment — Siegel, Lawrence M
The Least You Need to Know — Martin, Lee
Leather Wings — Duckworth, Marilyn
Leave It to Me — Mukherjee, Bharati
Leaves from the Dry Tree — Levchev, Vladimir
Leaves of Mourning — Haverkamp, Anselm
Leaving a Doll's House — Bloom, Claire
Leaving England — Erickson, Charlotte
c Leaving for America — Bresnick-Perry, Roslyn
Leaving Home — Hall, Michael
y Leaving Home — Rochman, Hazel
Leaving Pipe Shop — McDowell, Deborah E
y The Leaving Summer — Harding, Donal

Leaving the Cave — Hutcheon, Pat Duffy
yr Lebanese Americans — Whitehead, Sandra
c Lebanon — Sheehan, Sean
Lebanon: A Shattered Country — Picard, Elizabeth
The Lebanon War — Abraham, A J
Das Leben Ist Eine Karawanserei — Ozdamar, Emine
　Sevgi
Leben Sammeln, Nicht Fragen Wozu Und Warum.
　Vols. 1-2 — Klemperer, Victor
Lecteur Et Lecture Dans L'Autobiographie Francaise
　Contemporaine — Jaccomard, Helene
Lecture Notes on Dermatology. 7th Ed.
　— Graham-Brown, Robin
Lecture Notes on Diseases of the Ear, Nose, and
　Throat. 8th Ed. — Bull, P D
Lecture Notes on Epidemiology and Public Health
　Medicine. 4th Ed. — Farmer, Richard
Lecture Notes on Obstetrics. 7th Ed. — Chamberlain,
　Geoffrey
Lectures D'Andre Gide — Debreuille, Jean-Yves
Lectures De La Fontaine — Brody, Jules
Lectures on Elliptic and Parabolic Equations in
　Holder Spaces — Krylov, N V
Lectures on Entire Functions — Levin, B IA.
Lectures on Finite Precision Computations
　— Chaitin-Chatelin, Francoise
Lectures on Natural Right and Political Science
　— Hegel, G W F
Lectures on Non-Linear Plasma Kinetics — Tsytovich,
　Vadim N
Lectures on Operator Theory and Its Applications
　— Lancaster, Peter
Lectures on Quantum Theory — Isham, C J
Lectures on the Mathematics of Finance — Karatzas,
　Ioannis
Lectures on the Religion of the Semites — Smith,
　William Robertson
The Ledger of Fruitful Exchange — Sirr, Peter
Ledoyt, a Novel — Emshwiller, Carol
Lee Bailey's the Way I Cook — Bailey, Lee
r Lee Krasner: A Catalogue Raisonne — Landau, Ellen
　G
y Lee Reconsidered — Nolan, Alan T
Lee the Soldier — Gallagher, Gary W
c Lee Trevino — Kramer, Jon
Lee vs. McClellan — Newell, Clayton R
Lee's Young Artillerist — Carmichael, Peter S
Leet's Christmas — Kirkland, Elithe Hamilton
Left at East Gate — Warren, Larry
Left for Dead — Tomasky, Michael
r The Left Guide — Wilcox, Derk Arend
The Left Hand of Darkness — Le Guin, Ursula K
The Left in History — Thompson, Willie
The Left in Search of a Center — Crozier, Michael
r The Left Index 1982-
r The Left Index 1995
Left Intellectuals and Popular Culture in Twentieth-
　Century America — Gorman, Paul R
Left Margins — Fitts, Karen
c Lefty: A Handbook for Left-Handed Kids (Illus. by
　Jack Keely) — Singer, Beth Wolfensberger
Legacies of Change — Campbell, John L
The Legacies of Communism in Eastern Europe
　— Volgyes, Ivan
Legacies of the Collapse of Marxism — Moore, John
　H
Legacies: Stories — Lawrence, Starling
The Legacy Continues — Yawn, Mike
r Legacy: General Aviation Highlights from 8 Decades
　of NACA/NASA Research. Electronic Media
　Version — Adkins, Susan L
Legacy: New Perspectives on the Battle of the Little
　Bighorn — Rankin, Charles E
Legacy of a Divided Nation — Hasan, Mushirul
The Legacy of Anomie Theory — Adler, Freda
A Legacy of Arctic Art — Ray, Dorothy Jean
The Legacy of D'Arcy McNickle — Purdy, John Lloyd
A Legacy of Excellence — Weaver, William, 1923-
Legacy of Light
A Legacy of Names — Borish, Elaine
The Legacy of Rome — Jenkyns, Richard
The Legacy of Rousseau — Orwin, Clifford
Legacy of the Darksword — Weis, Margaret
Legacy of the Diamond — Kane, Andrea
The Legacy of the French Revolution — Hancock,
　Ralph C
The Legacy of Tiananmen — Miles, James A R
The Legacy of Vietnam Veterans and Their Families
　— Rhoades, Dennis K
The Legacy of Woodrow Wilson — Esposito, David M
Legal Advocacy in the Roman World — Crook, J A

Legal and Healthcare Ethics for the Elderly — *Smith, George Patrick*

Legal and Moral Constraints on Low-Intensity Conflict — *Coll, Alberto R*

Legal Culture and the Legal Profession — *Friedman, Lawrence M*

The Legal Culture of Northern New Spain 1700-1810 — *Cutter, Charles R*

Legal Foundations of Capitalism — *Commons, John R*

r Legal Guide to Buying and Selling Art and Collectibles — *Vartian, Armen R*

r The Legal Information Buyer's Guide and Reference Manual — *Svengalis, Kendall F*

Legal Issues and the Internet. Vols. 1-2 — *Central Computer and Telecommunications Agency*

y Legal Lynching — *Jackson, Jesse*

Legal Malpractice and Other Claims against Your Lawyer — *Herskowitz, Suzan*

Legal Manual for Residential Construction — *Domel, August*

Legal Medicine in History — *Clark, Michael*

Legal Naturalism — *Taiwo, Olufemi*

Legal Reasoning and Political Conflict — *Sunstein, Cass R*

Legal Reelism — *Denvir, John*

r The Legal Researcher's Desk Reference 1996-97

Legal Rights — *Sarat, Austin*

The Legal Status of Women and Poverty in Tanzania — *Rwebangira, Magdalena K*

y The Legal System — *Roleff, Tamara L*

Legal Tender — *Scottoline, Lisa*

The Legal Theory of Ethical Positivism — *Campbell, Tom D*

Legally Safe Mental Health Practice — *Woody, Robert Henley*

r Legati E Governatori Dello Stato Pontificio 1550-1809 — *Weber, Christoph*

Legatura De Pregio In Valle D'Aosta — *Malaguzzi, Francesco*

The Legend of Danny Boy. Book and Audio Version

c The Legend of El Dorado — *Vidal, Beatriz*

The Legend of Light — *Hicok, Bob*

y The Legend of Mother Sarah — *Otomo, Katsuhiro*

The Legend of Muslim Spain. Vols. 1-2 — *Jayyusi, Salma Khadra*

c The Legend of Odysseus (Illus. by Peter Connolly) — *Connolly, Peter*

c The Legend of Red Horse Cavern (Woodman). Audio Version — *Paulsen, Gary*

c The Legend of Sleepy Hollow (Illus. by Michael Garland) — *Irving, Washington*

Legend of the Dead — *Hackler, Micah S*

y Legend of the North — *Sullivan, Paul*

The Legend of the Painted Horse — *Combs, Harry*

c The Legend of the Windigo (Illus. by Murv Jacob) — *Ross, Gayle*

The Legend of Thunder Moon — *Brand, Max*

The Legend of Tommy Morris — *Fisher, Anne Kinsman*

y The Legendary Wild West — *Smith, C Carter*

Legends: Legends of the Hockey Hall of Fame — *McKinley, Michael*

y Legends of Hockey — *McKinley, Michael*

c Legends of the Americas. Book and Electronic Media Version

Legendy Nevskogo Prospekta — *Veller, Mikhail Iosifovich*

Legionellae Control in Health Care Facilities — *Freije, Matthew R*

Legislating Privacy — *Regan, Priscilla M*

Legislations: The Politics of Deconstruction — *Bennington, Geoffrey*

Legislative Reference Services and Sources — *Low, Kathleen*

Legislative Term Limits — *Grofman, Bernard*

Legislatures and the New Democracies in Latin America — *Close, David*

Legitimate Histories — *Robertson, Fiona*

Leibniz and the Rational Order of Nature — *Rutherford, Donald, 1942-*

Leibniz: Determinist, Theist, Idealist — *Adams, Robert Merrihew*

Leid Soll Lehren — *Delvaux, Peter*

c Leif's Saga — *Hunt, Jonathan*

Leisure and Society in Colonial Brazzaville — *Martin, Phyllis M*

Leisure and the Public Library — *Snape, Robert*

Leisure in Later Life. 2nd Ed. — *Leitner, Michael J*

Leith's Cookery Bible — *Leith, Prue*

Leith's Cooking for One or Two — *Tyrer, Polly*

Lemaitre, Big Bang, and the Quantum Universe — *Heller, Michal*

Lemon-Aid: How to Buy a New Car (Edmonston). Audio Version — *Edmonston, Phil*

Lemona's Tale — *Saro Wiwa, Ken*

A Lender's Guide to Environmental Liability Management — *Missimer, Thomas M*

Lending for Electric Power in Sub-Saharan Africa — *Covarrubias, Alvaro J*

Lengua Madre — *Martinez, Demetria*

Lenin: A New Biography — *Volkogonov, Dmitrii Antonovich*

Lenin: A Political Life. Vol. 3 — *Service, Robert*

Lenin, Hegel, and Western Marxism — *Anderson, Kevin, 1948-*

Lenin: Life and Legacy — *Volkogonov, Dmitrii Antonovich*

Leninism: Political Economy as Pseudoscience — *Dovring, Folke*

y The Leno Wit — *Walker, Jay*

p Lenox Avenue: A Journal of Interartistic Inquiry

y Lenses and Prisms and Other Scientific Things — *Soucie, Gary*

Lenten Lunches — *Pilarczyk, Daniel E*

Leo Melamed: Escape to the Futures — *Melamed, Leo*

Leo Strauss and Judaism — *Novak, David*

Leo Strauss and Nietzsche — *Lampert, Laurence*

Leo Szilard: Science as a Mode of Being — *Grandy, David A*

c Leo the Magnificat (Illus. by Emily Arnold McCully) — *Martin, Ann M*

c Leon and Bob (Illus. by Simon James) — *James, Simon*

yr Leonard Maltin's Movie and Video Guide. 1997 Ed.

Leonard Nimoy's Primortals — *Perry, Steve*

r Leonardo Da Vinci. Electronic Media Version

c Leonardo Da Vinci (Illus. by Diane Stanley) — *Stanley, Diane*

Leonardo Da Vinci: A Singular Vision — *Clayton, Martin*

Leonardo Da Vinci's Sforza Monument Horse — *Ahl, Diane Cole*

Leonardo Sciascia — *Farrell, Joseph*

The Leopard — *Tomasi Di Lampedusa, Giuseppe*

c The Leopard Son — *Discovery Channel (Firm)*

c Leopards — *Harman, Amanda*

c The Leopard's Drum (Illus. by Jessica Souhami) — *Souhami, Jessica*

LEOS '94 Conference Proceedings. Vols. 1-2 — *Lasers and Electro-Optics Society (Institute of Electrical and Electronics Engineers). Meeting (7th: 1994: Boston, Mass.)*

r Leper Hospitals in Medieval Ireland — *Lee, Gerard A*

c A Leprechaun's St. Patrick's Day — *Blazek, Sarah Kirwan*

Lernen Leichter Machen — *Rampillon, Ute*

LeRoy Neiman on Safari — *Neiman, LeRoy*

c Leroy Potts Meets the McCrooks (Illus. by Rowan Barnes-Murphy) — *Sathre, Vivian*

c Leroy's Zoo (Illus. by Leroy Ramon Archuleta) — *Lowe, Warren*

r The Lesbian Almanac — *National Museum and Archive of Lesbian and Gay History (U.S.)*

Lesbian and Bisexual Fiction Writers — *Bloom, Harold*

Lesbian and Bisexual Identities — *Esterberg, Kristin G*

r Lesbian and Gay Liberation in Canada — *McLeod, Donald W*

Lesbian Art — *Ashburn, Elizabeth*

Lesbian Choices — *Card, Claudia*

The Lesbian Family Life Cycle — *Slater, Suzanne*

Lesbian Voices from Latin America — *Martinez, Elena M*

Lesbianism Made Easy — *Eisenbach, Helen*

r Lesbians in Print — *Gillon, Margaret*

Lese-Zeichen: Kognition, Medium Und Materialitat Im Leseprozess — *Gross, Sabine*

Leselust: Wie Unterhaltsam Ist Die Neue Deutsche Literatur? — *Wittstock, Uwe*

c Leslie's Story (Illus. by Martha McNey) — *McNey, Martha*

The Less Noble Sex — *Tuana, Nancy*

The Lesser Antilles in the Age of European Expansion — *Paquette, Robert L*

The Lesser Blessed — *Van Camp, Richard*

The Lesser Terror — *Parrish, Michael*

Lessing Und Die Bibliothek — *Reifenberg, Bernd*

The Lesson of This Century — *Popper, Karl Raimund, Sir*

Lessons from an Optical Illusion — *Hundert, Edward M*

Lessons from Animal Diabetes — *Shafrir, Eleazar*

Lessons from Privilege — *Powell, Arthur G*

Lessons from the Economic Transition — *Zecchini, Salvatore*

Lessons from the Trial — *Uelmen, Gerald F*

Lessons in Economic Policy for Eastern Europe from Latin America — *McMahon, Gary*

Lessons Learned — *Vetock, Dennis J*

Lessons of a Generation — *Adelman, Clifford*

The Lessons of Israel's Great Inflation — *Barkai, Haim*

r The Lessons of Modern War. Vol. 4 — *Cordesman, Anthony H*

Lessons Unlearned — *Rothert, Steve*

Lest Memory Cease — *Feingold, Henry L*

r Lest We Forget. Electronic Media Version

Lest We Forget — *Soderberg, Susan Cooke*

c Lester's Dog — *Hesse, Karen*

Let It Bleed — *Indiana, Gary*

y Let It Bleed — *Rankin, Ian*

Let Justice Roll — *Riemer, Neal*

Let Me Be the One — *Harvor, Elisabeth*

Let Me Count the Ways — *Bosley, Deborah*

Let My People Go — *Ewing, Preston*

y Let My People Go — *White, Deborah Gray*

y Let Nothing Disturb You — *Kirvan, John*

y Let One Hundred Flowers Bloom — *Jicai, Feng*

c Let Sleeping Bags Lie — *Jones, Judy*

Let the Cow Wander — *Myers, Michael W*

c Let the Drum Speak — *Shuler, Linda Lay*

c Let the Lynx Come In (Illus. by Patrick Benson) — *London, Jonathan*

Let the Magic Begin — *Crosby, Cathy Lee*

Let the Wind Speak — *Onetti, Juan Carlos*

Let Them Eat Cake — *Purdy, Susan G*

Let Us Have Peace — *Simpson, Brooks D*

Let Your Customers Do the Talking — *Cafferky, Michael E*

Lethal Frequencies — *Galvin, James*

y Lethal Genes — *Grant, Linda*

y A Lethal Involvement — *Egleton, Clive*

Lethal Ladies — *Collins, Barbara*

Lethal Legacy — *Dealler, Stephen*

Lethal Mercy — *Kraus, Harry Lee*

The Lethal Partner — *Page, Jake*

Lethal Statues — *Herndon, Nancy*

Letitia Baldrige's More than Manners! — *Baldrige, Letitia*

c Let's Build Airplanes and Rockets! (Illus. by Saundra Carmical) — *Millspaugh, Ben P*

c Let's Count It Out, Jesse Bear (Illus. by Bruce Degen) — *Carlstrom, Nancy White*

Let's Dance — *Hegarty, Frances*

c Let's Discover the Five Senses Series — *Rius, Maria*

c Let's Eat (Illus. by Julie Vivas) — *Zamorano, Ana*

Let's Face the Music and Die — *Scoppettone, Sandra*

Let's Get Criminal — *Raphael, Lev*

c Let's Go Home, Little Bear (Illus. by Barbara Firth) — *Waddell, Martin*

c Let's Go Rock Collecting (Illus. by Holly Keller) — *Gans, Roma*

c Let's Go Shopping (Snapshot)

c Let's Go Traveling in Mexico — *Krupp, Robin Rector*

c Let's Have a Seder (Illus. by Miriam Sagasti) — *Wikler, Madeline*

yr Let's Hear It for the Girls — *Bauermeister, Erica*

c Let's Look inside the Red Car — *Leslie, Amanda*

c Let's Look inside the Yellow Truck — *Leslie, Amanda*

p Let's Play

c Let's Play Cards! (Illus. by Jef Kaminsky) — *Silbaugh, Elizabeth*

c Let's Play Hide and Seek! (Illus. by Dara Goldman) — *Birney, Betty G*

Let's Put the Future behind Us — *Womack, Jack*

c Let's Rodeo! (Illus. by Robert Crum) — *Crum, Robert*

Let's Say Grace — *Hamma, Robert M*

c Let's Talk about Being Afraid — *Kreiner, Anna*

c Let's Talk about Drug Abuse — *Kreiner, Anna*

c Let's Talk about Foster Homes — *Weitzman, Elizabeth*

Let's Talk about Life — *Tall, Emily*

c Let's Talk about Living in a Blended Family — *Weitzman, Elizabeth*

c Let's Talk about Living with a Single Parent — *Weitzman, Elizabeth*

c Let's Talk about Smoking — *Weitzman, Elizabeth*

c Let's Talk about Staying in a Shelter — *Weitzman, Elizabeth*

c Let's Talk about When a Parent Dies — *Weitzman, Elizabeth*

c Let's Talk about When Someone You Love Has Alzheimer's Disease — *Weitzman, Elizabeth*

c Let's Talk about Your Parents' Divorce — *Weitzman, Elizabeth*

Let's Talk Turkey (About Japanese Turkeys) and Other Tales from The Asian Wall Street Journal — *Lehner, Urban C*

The Letter and the Spirit — *Chau, Wai-Shing*

Letter Bomb — *Schwenger, Peter*

The Letter of James — *Bible. N.T. James. English. Johnson. 1995*

A Letter of Mary — *King, Laurie R*

y A Letter of Mary (Follows). Audio Version — *King, Laurie R*

Letter to Daniel — *Keane, Fergal*

c A Letter to Granny (Illus. by John Prater) — *Rogers, Paul*

A Letter to the Friars Minor and Other Writings — *William, of Ockham*

Lettere A Stanislao Cannizzaro 1868-1872. Vols. 3-4 — *Cannizzaro, Stanislao*

c Lettering: Make Your Own Cards, Signs, Gifts and More (Illus. by Esperanca Melo) — *Lewis, Amanda*

Letters — *Barth, John*

The Letters — *Spinoza, Benedictus De*

Letters — *White, Patrick*

Letters and Charters of Gilbert Foliot — *Foliot, Gilbert*

Letters and Society in Fifteenth-Century Spain — *Deyermond, Alan*

c The Letters Are Lost! (Illus. by Lisa Campbell Ernst) — *Ernst, Lisa Campbell*

Letters Concerning the English Nation — *Voltaire*

Letters for Our Children — *Goode, Erica*

Letters from a Life. Vols. 1-2 — *Britten, Benjamin*

Letters from China — *Forbes, Robert Bennet*

Letters from Elko — *Preston, Scott*

r Letters from Home — *Troyer, Patricia*

Letters from Ireland during the Famine of 1847 — *Somerville, Alexander*

Letters from London 1990-5 — *Barnes, Julian*

Letters from Louisa — *Beaumont, Jeanette*

Letters from Tel Mond Prison — *Rapaport, Era*

Letters from the Avant-Garde — *Lupton, Ellen*

c Letters from the Grave — *Everett, Felicity*

y Letters from the Inside — *Marsden, John*

y Letters from the Light (Ryan). Audio Version — *Barker, Elsa*

y Letters from the Mountain — *Garland, Sherry*

Letters of a Solitary Wanderer 1800 — *Smith, Charlotte*

Letters of Catharine Cottam Romney, Plural Wife — *Romney, Catharine Cottam*

The Letters of Charlotte Bronte. Vol. 1 — *Bronte, Charlotte*

The Letters of Christina Rossetti. Vol. 1 — *Rossetti, Christina*

The Letters of Claudio Monteverdi — *Monteverdi, Claudio*

Letters of Delegates to Congress 1774-1789. Vol. 21 — *Smith, Paul Hubert*

The Letters of Dorothy L. Sayers 1899-1936 — *Sayers, Dorothy L*

Letters of Emma and Florence Hardy — *Hardy, Emma Lavinia Gifford*

The Letters of George Henry Lewes. Vols. 1-2 — *Lewes, George Henry*

The Letters of Gertrude Stein and Thornton Wilder — *Stein, Gertrude*

The Letters of Hildegard of Bingen — *Hildegard, Saint*

The Letters of Ignatius Sancho — *Sancho, Ignatius*

The Letters of John Bede Polding. Vols. 1-2 — *Polding, John Bede*

The Letters of Lady Arabella Stuart — *Stuart, Arabella, Lady*

The Letters of Matthew Arnold. Vol. 1 — *Arnold, Matthew*

The Letters of Nancy Mitford and Evelyn Waugh — *Mitford, Nancy*

Letters of Nichiren — *Nichiren*

Letters of Old Age. Vols. 1-2 — *Petrarca, Francesco*

The Letters of Ralph Waldo Emerson. Vols. 7-10 — *Emerson, Ralph Waldo*

The Letters of Robert Louis Stevenson. Vols. 1-6 — *Stevenson, Robert Louis*

The Letters of Robert Louis Stevenson. Vols. 1-8 — *Stevenson, Robert Louis*

The Letters of Robert Louis Stevenson. Vols. 3-6 — *Stevenson, Robert Louis*

The Letters of Rudyard Kipling. Vol. 3 — *Kipling, Rudyard*

The Letters of Saint Anselm of Canterbury. Vols. 1-3 — *Anselm, Saint, Archbishop of Canterbury*

The Letters of St. Antony — *Rubenson, Samuel*

Letters of the Queens of England 1100-1547 — *Crawford, Anne*

The Letters of Vincent Van Gogh — *Gogh, Vincent Van*

Letters of Wallace Stevens — *Stevens, Wallace*

The Letters of Wanda Tinasky — *Tinasky, Wanda*

The Letters of William and Dorothy Wordsworth. Vol. 8 — *Wordsworth, William*

Letters on Education — *Macaulay, Catharine*

Letters to America — *Daniels, Jim*

c Letters to Barbara — *Meter, Leo*

Letters to Beethoven and Other Correspondence. Vols. 1-3 — *Albrecht, Theodore*

Letters to Children from Beatrix Potter — *Potter, Beatrix*

Letters to Cristina — *Freire, Paulo*

Letters to Ellen — *Meilaender, Gilbert*

Letters to Francesca — *Richards, Tim*

y Letters to Julia — *Holmes, Barbara Ware*

c Letters to Uncle Albert — *Stannard, Russell*

Letting Go — *Schwartz, Morrie*

Letting Loose — *Leland, Christopher T*

Letting Loose the Hounds — *Udall, Brady*

c Letting Swift River Go (Illus. by Barbara Cooney) — *Yolen, Jane*

Lettres Algeriennes — *Boudjedra, Rachid*

Lettres Des Souverains Portugais A Charles Quint Et A L'Imperatrice 1528-1532

Leukocyte Recruitment in Inflammatory Disease — *Peltz, Gary*

y Level 4 — *McCormick, Joseph B*

Leveling Crowds — *Tambiah, Stanley J*

c Levers (Illus. by Mike Gordon) — *Rush, Caroline*

The Leviathan in the State Theory of Thomas Hobbes — *Schmitt, Carl*

Leviathan: Into the Gray — *VanderMeer, Jeff*

Levin's Mill — *Bobrowski, Johannes*

Leviticus: A Commentary — *Gerstenberger, Erhard*

Levy Processes — *Bertoin, Jean*

Lewis Acids and Selectivity in Organic Synthesis — *Santelli, Maurice*

y Lewis and Clark — *Bakeless, John*

y The Lewis and Clark Expedition — *Hall, Eleanor J*

Lewis Carroll: A Biography — *Cohen, Morton Norton*

Lewis Carroll: A Portrait with Background — *Thomas, Donald Serrell*

c Lewis Carroll's Jabberwocky (Illus. by Graeme Base) — *Carroll, Lewis*

Lewis Cass and the Politics of Moderation — *Klunder, Willard Carl*

Lewis H. Morgan on Iroquois Material Culture — *Tooker, Elisabeth*

Lewis Mumford and American Modernism — *Wojtowicz, Robert*

Lewis Mumford and Patrick Geddes — *Mumford, Lewis*

Lewis Mumford and the Ecological Region — *Luccarelli, Mark*

The Lewis Mumford Reader — *Mumford, Lewis*

Lex Et Evangelium — *Gummelt, Volker*

r Lexicographica Graeca — *Chadwick, John*

The Lexicon in Acquisition — *Clark, Eve*

r Lexicon of Arabic Horse Terminology — *Watson, Janet C E*

r Lexicon of Psychiatry, Neurology and the Neurosciences — *Ayd, Frank*

Lexikon Sozialistischer Literatur — *Barck, Simone*

Le Lexique De Charles D'Orleans Dans Les Rondeaux — *Galderisi, Claudio*

r Lexique: Economie. 5th Ed. — *Silem, Ahmed*

Lexiques-Grammaires Compares en Francais — *LaBelle, Jacques*

Leyes Palatinas — *Majorca (Kingdom). Sovereign (1324-1349: Jaime III)*

Lezioni Leopardiane — *Binni, Walter*

Li Ao: Buddhist, Taoist, or Neo-Confucian? — *Barrett, T H*

Li Da and Marxist Philosophy in China — *Knight, Nick*

Li-Ka-Shing: The Biography — *Chan, Anthony B*

Li Yong 1627-1705 and Epistemological Dimensions of Confucian Philosophy — *Birdwhistell, Anne D*

Les Liaisons Dangereuses — *Laclos, Choderlos De*

Liao Zhai Zhi Yi — *Pu, Songling*

y Liar — *Morris, Winifred*

The Liar's Club — *Karr, Mary*

Le Liban Et Les Derives Du Processus De Paix — *Kodmani-Darwish, Bassma*

Liber De Caesaribus (Bird) — *Victor, Sextus Aurelius*

Liber Gestorum Recentium — *Arnulf, Von Mailand*

Liber Miraculorum Sancte Fidis — *Robertini, Luca*

The Liberal Arts College Adapting to Change — *Bonvillian, Gary*

The Liberal Ascendancy 1830-1886 — *Jenkins, T A*

A Liberal Chronicle — *Pease, Joseph A*

Liberal Education — *Van Doren, Mark*

The Liberal Political Tradition — *Meadowcroft, James*

Liberal Rights — *Waldron, Jeremy*

The Liberal Self — *Donner, Wendy*

Liberalising a Regulated Banking System — *Williams, Marion V*

Liberalism. 2nd Ed. — *Gray, John, 1948-*

Liberalism and Community — *Kautz, Steven*

Liberalism and the Problem of Knowledge — *Willard, Charles Arthur*

Liberalism Divided — *Fiss, Owen M*

Liberalism without Illusions — *Yack, Bernard*

Liberalism's Crooked Circle — *Katznelson, Ira*

Liberalization in the Developing World — *Fernandez Jilberto, A E*

Liberalization, Productivity and Competition — *Srivastava, Vivek*

Liberalizm V Rossii — *Sekirinskii, S S*

The Liberated Enduser — *East, Harry*

Liberated Quiltmaking — *Marston, Gwen*

Liberating Conscience — *Patrick, Anne E*

Liberating Literature — *Lauret, Maria*

Liberating Memory — *Zandy, Janet*

y Liberating the Ghosts — *Shevelev, Raphael*

Liberating the Gospels — *Spong, John Shelby*

Liberation from Self — *Berofsky, Bernard*

Liberation: The Canadians in Europe — *McAndrew, Bill*

The Libertarian Reader — *Boaz, David*

Libertarianism: A Primer — *Boaz, David*

La Liberte Religieuse A Vatican II — *Gonnet, Dominique*

Liberty against the Law — *Hill, Christopher, 1912-*

Liberty and Morality — *Snyder, Charles W*

Liberty and Sexuality — *Garrow, David J*

c The Liberty Bell — *Sakurai, Gail*

y The Liberty Campaign (Longe). Audio Version — *Dee, Jonathan*

Liberty for the Twenty-First Century — *Machan, Tibor R*

Liberty, Property, and Privacy — *Keynes, Edward*

Liberty, Retrenchment and Reform — *Biagini, Eugenio F*

Liberty Square — *Forrest, Katherine V*

Libidinal Economy — *Lyotard, Jean-Francois*

Libido — *Hoffmann, Lis*

c The Librarian Who Measured the Earth (Illus. by Kevin Hawkes) — *Lasky, Kathryn*

r The Librarian's Companion. 2nd Ed. — *Wertsman, Vladimir F*

Librarianship and Information Work Worldwide 1994

Librarianship and Information Work Worldwide 1995

r Libraries and Copyright — *Gasaway, Laura N*

r Libraries and Culture: 25 Year Cumulative Index — *Anghelescu, Hermina G B*

Libraries and Librarianship in Japan — *Welch, Theodore F*

Libraries in a World of Cultural Change — *Greenhalgh, Liz*

Libraries in Africa — *Olden, Anthony*

Libraries in Post Primary Schools — *Library and Information Services Council (Northern Ireland)*

Libraries in Primary Schools — *Library and Information Services Council (Northern Ireland)*

r Libraries Unlimited Professional Collection CD 1995. Electronic Media Version

c The Library (Illus. by David Small) — *Stewart, Sarah*

Library and Information Plan for Leicestershire Working Party on Local Government Reorganisation

The Library and Information Professional's Guide to the Internet — *Tseng, Gwyneth*

Library Buildings, Equipment, and the ADA — *Cirillo, Susan E*

c The Library Card — *Spinelli, Jerry*

Library Instruction Revisited — *Martin, Lynne M*

r Library Literature 95

Library Materials Acquisitions — *White, Brenda*

c The Library of Congress — *Fowler, Allan*

Library of Congress Subject Headings. 3rd Ed. — *Chan, Lois Mai*

r Library of Congress Subject Headings. 19th Ed., Vols. 1-4 — *Library of Congress. Office for Subject Cataloging Policy*

r The Library of the Future. 4th Ed. Electronic Media Version

The Library of William Byrd of Westover — *Hayes, Kevin J*

The Library Paraprofessional — *Rodgers, Terry*

r Library Services for Off-Campus and Distance Education — *Slade, Alexander L*

Library: The Drama Within — *Griliches, Diane Asseo*

Il Libro Antico Dal XV, Al XIX Secolo — *Rossi, Marielisa*

El Libro De Recuerdos — *Shua, Ana Maria*

Libya Im 20. Jahrhundert — *Frank, Sabine*

c Libya--in Pictures — *Lerner Publications Company. Geography Dept.*

Libya: The Struggle for Survival — *Simons, G L*

Libya's Qaddafi — *El-Kikhia, Mansour O*

License to Grill — *Schlesinger, Chris*

A License to Steal — *Levy, Leonard W*

Licensed by Authority — *Burt, Richard*

Lich Su Ngan Nguoi Viet — *Nguyen, Sa*

c Lichee Tree (Illus. by Christopher Zhong-Yuan Zhang) — *Russell, Ching Yeung*

Lick Creek Beckoned — *Vaughn, Barbara Biggers*

Licking Our Wounds — *D'Haene, Elise*

Lidz Kailai Rokai — *Skujenieks, Knuts*

The Lie — *Weaver, Michael*

A Lie and a Libel — *Segel, B W*

A Lie and a Libel — *Segel, Binjamin W*

Lie Down with Dogs — *Gleiter, Jan*

The Lie of the Land — *Carter, Paul*

Lie Theory and Geometry — *Brylinski, J L*

Lieberman's Law. Audio Version — *Kaminsky, Stuart M*

r Liechtensteiner Briefmarkenkatalog 1995

The Lied: Mirror of Late Romanticism — *Kravitt, Edward F*

Le Lien — *Grainville, Patrick*

Lies! Lies!! Lies!!! — *Ford, Charles V*

Lies My Teacher Told Me — *Loewen, James W*

Lies of the Saints — *McGraw, Erin*

r Lietuvos Didziosios Kunigaikstystes Monetos — *Sajauskas, Stasys*

r Lietvos Didziosios Kunigaikstystes Numizmatika — *Sajauskas, Stasys*

Lieutenant Nun — *Erauso, Catalina De*

c Life — *Snedden, Robert*

Life after Head Injury — *Hubert, Jane*

Life after Life — *Parker, Tony*

Life after Lunch — *Harrison, Sarah*

Life after Politics — *Mulgan, Geoff*

Life after Television — *Gilder, George*

Life among the English — *Macaulay, Rose*

The Life and Art of Florine Stettheimer — *Bloemink, Barbara J*

The Life and Cuisine of Elvis Presley — *Adler, David, 1962-*

Life and Death — *Dworkin, Andrea*

Life and Death in Early Colonial Ecuador — *Newson, Linda A*

Life and Death in the Executive Fast Lane — *Kets De Vries, Manfred F R*

The Life and Death of a Rural American High School — *DeYoung, Alan J*

The Life and Death of Carolina Maria De Jesus — *Levine, Robert M*

y The Life and Death of Crazy Horse (Illus. by Amos Bad Heart Bull) — *Freedman, Russell*

The Life and Death of Industrial Languedoc 1700-1920 — *Johnson, Christopher H*

The Life and Death of Peter Sellers — *Lewis, Roger*

Life and Death under High Technology Medicine — *Robinson, Ian*

Life and Fate — *Grossman, Vassily*

Life and Holiness — *Merton, Thomas*

The Life and Legacy of Annie Oakley — *Riley, Glenda*

The Life and Legacy of Franz Xaver Hauser — *Jorgenson, Dale A*

The Life and Legacy of G.I. Taylor — *Batchelor, George*

The Life and Letters — *Feldman, Irving*

The Life and Letters of Theoleptos of Philadelphia — *Theoleptos, Metropolitan of Philadelphia*

y Life and Living — *Vellacott, Jane*

The Life and Opinions of Tristram Shandy, Gentleman — *Rowson, Martin*

Life and Terror in Stalin's Russia 1934-1941 — *Thurston, Robert W*

The Life and Times of John Trevisa, Medieval Scholar — *Fowler, David C*

c The Life and Times of the Honeybee — *Micucci, Charles*

c The Life and Times of the Peanut (Illus. by Charles Micucci) — *Micucci, Charles*

The Life and Work of Dennis Potter — *Gilbert, W Stephen*

The Life and Work of Fredson Bowers — *Tanselle, G Thomas*

The Life and Work of Harold Pinter — *Billington, Michael*

c Life around the Lake — *Presilla, Maricel E*

Life as We Know It — *Berube, Michael*

y Life at Small Scale — *Dusenbery, David B*

Life at the Crossroads — *Butt, Gerald*

Life at the Dakota — *Birmingham, Stephen*

y Life before Birth — *Nathanielsz, Peter W*

Life before Birth. 2nd Ed. — *England, Marjorie A*

Life before Death — *Frucht, Abby*

y Life before Man. Rev. Ed. — *Spinar, Zdenek V*

Life between Wars — *Patton, Robert H*

Life Briefs — *Hoggart, Simon*

Life/Choice: The Theory of Just Abortion — *Steffen, Lloyd*

The Life Cycle Completed — *Erikson, Erik H*

c Life Cycles of a Dozen Diverse Creatures — *Fleisher, Paul*

Life, Death and Aid — *Jean, Francois*

Life, Death, and the Law. Vols. 1-2 — *Keyes, W Noel*

Life Drawing — *Clark, Ronald*

y Life Happens — *McCoy, Kathy*

Life History and the Historical Moment — *Erikson, Erik H*

c The Life History of Life Histories (Illus. by Paxton Chadwick) — *Chadwick, Paxton*

Life in 2030 — *Robinson, John B*

Life in a Day — *Grumbach, Doris*

c Life in a Pond — *Fowler, Allan*

c Life in a Tide Pool — *Fowler, Allan*

Life in an Irish Country House — *Bence-Jones, Mark*

y Life in Ancient Greece — *Nardo, Don*

y Life in Black and White — *Stevenson, Brenda E*

Life in Double Time — *Lankford, Mike*

A Life in Letters — *Fitzgerald, F Scott*

Life in Moving Fluids. 2nd Ed., Rev. and Expanded — *Vogel, Steven, 1940-*

A Life in Ragtime — *Badger, Reid*

A Life in School — *Tompkins, Jane*

Life in the Balance — *Eisenberg, Mickey S*

c Life in the Coral Reef — *Kalman, Bobbie*

r Life in the Country House — *Durant, David N*

Life in the Gang — *Decker, Scott H*

Life in the Iron Mills and Other Stories — *Davis, Rebecca Harding*

Life in the Kornfield — *Lovullo, Sam*

y Life in the South during the Civil War — *Reger, James P*

Life in the World of Women — *Jakubowski, Maxim*

c Life in Tudor Times — *Counsell, Christine*

y Life in War-Torn Bosnia — *Yancey, Diane*

Life into Art — *Duncan, Doree*

Life Is Not a Rehearsal — *Brudnoy, David*

Life Itself — *Rensberger, Boyce*

Life Itself — *Rosenblatt, Roger*

Life Lines — *Bacon, Jean*

Life Lines — *Church, F Forrester*

y Life, Love, and Other Mysteries — *Jones, Denise*

c Life Magic — *Cooper, Melrose*

The Life Model of Social Work Practice. 2nd Ed. — *Germain, Carel B*

Life of a Poet — *Freedman, Ralph*

The Life of Charlotte Bronte — *Gaskell, Elizabeth*

The Life of Gampopa — *Stewart, Jampa Mackenzie*

The Life of God (As Told by Himself) — *Ferrucci, Franco*

The Life of Graham Greene. Vols. 1-2 — *Sherry, Norman*

The Life of Herbert Hoover. Vol. 3 — *Nash, George H*

The Life of Insects — *Pelevin, Viktor*

The Life of Ismail Ferik Pasha — *Galanaki, Rhea*

The Life of Jane Austen — *Halperin, John*

The Life of Jedidiah Morse — *Moss, Richard J*

c The Life of Jesus (Illus. by Lee Stinson) — *Billington, Rachel*

The Life of Joseph Conrad — *Batchelor, John, 1942-*

The Life of Knut Wicksell — *Gardlund, Torsten*

A Life of Matthew Arnold — *Murray, Nicholas*

The Life of Moses — *Van Seters, John*

The Life of Nelson A. Rockefeller: Worlds to Conquer 1908-1958 — *Reich, Cary*

A Life of Picasso. Vol. 2 — *Richardson, John, 1924-*

The Life of Poetry — *Rukeyser, Muriel*

The Life of Robert Browning — *Ryals, Clyde De L*

The Life of St. Edmund — *Paris, Matthew*

y The Life of Saint Nicholas — *Blechman, R O*

The Life of Stefan Banach — *Kaluza, Roman*

The Life of the Cosmos — *Smolin, Lee*

Life of the Flycatcher — *Skutch, Alexander Frank*

The Life of the Law — *Knight, Alfred H*

Life of the Party — *Fleener, Mary*

y The Life of the Skin — *Balin, Arthur K*

The Life of the Soul — *Julian, of Norwich*

The Life of the World to Come — *Zaleski, Carol*

The Life of Washington — *Weems, M L*

The Life of William Faulkner — *Gray, Richard J*

The Life of William Morris — *Mackail, J W*

y Life on a Medieval Pilgrimage — *Nardo, Don*

Life on a Mexican Ranch — *McKellar, Margaret Maud*

y Life on an Israeli Kibbutz — *Altman, Linda Jacobs*

c Life on Mars (Illus. by Peter McCarty) — *Getz, David*

Life on Mars — *Stuart, Alexander*

y Life on the Edge — *Dobson, James C*

A Life on the Edge — *Head, Wilson*

Life on the High Wire — *Camp, Martin*

Life on the Hyphen — *Perez Firmat, Gustavo*

Life on the Line — *Wattleton, Faye*

Life on the Mississippi — *Twain, Mark*

Life on the Russian Country Estate — *Roosevelt, P R*

Life on the Screen — *Turkle, Sherry*

Life Outside — *Signorile, Michaelangelo*

Life Prediction Methodology for Titanium Matrix Composites — *Johnson, W S*

Life Scientists — *Verschuuren, Gerard M*

c Life Starts in the Sea (Illus. by Luis Rizo) — *Llamas, Andreu*

Life Stories — *Linde, Charlotte*

Life Studies — *Lowell, Robert*

y Life Support — *Gordon, Suzanne*

Life Support — *Hahn, Michael P*

c A Life with Animals — *Ferber, Elizabeth*

Life with Gough — *Cohen, Barry, 1935, Apr., 4-*

Life without Father — *Popenoe, David*

Life without Parole — *Hassine, Victor*

Life without Principles — *Margolis, Joseph*

Life without Water — *Peacock, Nancy*

Life Work — *Hall, Donald, 1928-*

Life Worth Living — *Thomas, William H*

Lifebalance — *Eyre, Linda*

Lifecycles. Vol. 2 — *Orenstein, Debra*

The Lifeguard: Stories — *Morris, Mary*

Lifeline — *Boyle, Gerry*

Lifelines and Risks — *Cairns, Robert B*

Lifelong Learning — *Davies, W K*

A Lifelong Passion — *Nicholas II, Emperor of Russia*

Life's America — *Kozol, Wendy*

Life's Dominion — *Dworkin, R M*

Life's Golden Tree — *Kerth, Thomas*

Life's Grandeur — *Gould, Stephen Jay*

Life's Little Ironies — *Hardy, Thomas*

Life's Living toward Dying — *Guroian, Vigen*

Life's Splendid Drama — *Bowler, Peter J*

The Lifespan Development of Individuals — *Magnusson, David*

Lifestyle Stores — *Pegler, Martin*

A Lifetime Burning in Every Moment — *Kazin, Alfred*

Lifetime Data — *Jewell, Nicholas P*

A Lifetime of Synergy with Theory and Experiment — *Streitwieser, Andrew*

c Lift-and-Peek into Noah's Ark

Lift Every Voice — *Turnbull, Walter*

y Lift Off! — *Mullane, R Mike*

The Lifted Veil — *Eliot, George*

c Light — *Berger, Melvin*

c Light — *Verdet, J P*

Light and Color in the Outdoors — *Minnaert, M G J*

Light and Colour in Byzantine Art — *James, Liz*

c Light and Dark — *Challoner, Jack*

Light and Movement — *Mannoni, Laurent*

c Light and Sound (Illus. by Terry Hadler) — *Lafferty, Peter*

Light as an Energy Source and Information Carrier in Plant Physiology — *NATO Advanced Study Institute on Light as Energy Source and Information Carrier in Plant Photophysiology (1994: Volterra, Italy)*

r Light Curves of Variable Stars — *Sterken, C*

Light Fantastic — *Lahr, John*

c Light from the Yellow Star — *Fisch, Robert O*

Light in Flight or the Holodiagram — *Abramson, Nils H*

c A Light in Space (Illus. by Ruth Ohi) — *Orr, Wendy*

The Light in the Skull — *Glasser, Ronald*

y A Light in the Window (McDonough). Audio Version — *Karon, Jan*

Light Metals 1996 — *Hale, Wayne*

r Light 'n Lively Reads for ESL, Adult, and Teen Readers — *Rosow, La Vergne*
y The Light of Common Day — *Herman, John*
The Light of Other Days — *Lovell, Caroline Couper*
The Light of the Body — *Dunn, Stephen*
Light Revealing Architecture — *Millet, Marietta S*
Light Upgrades — *Wood, Damon*
Light Weight Alloys for Aerospace Applications — *Lee, Eui W*
Light Years — *Schreiber, Le Anne*
Light Years — *Stuart, Dabney*
The Lighted Path — *Henrique, Risha*
Lighten Up! — *Magee, Elaine*
Lighten Your Heart — *Cleary, William*
Lighthouse — *Parker, Tony*
y The Lighthouse at the End of the World — *Marlowe, Stephen, 1928-*
r Lighting Listings
Lighting Out for the Territory — *Fishkin, Shelley Fisher*
Lighting Techniques for Video Production — *LeTourneau, Tom*
Lightlike Submanifolds of Semi-Riemannian Manifolds and Applications — *Duggal, Krishan L*
c Lightning — *Murray, Peter, 1952, Sep., 9-*
c Lightning — *Simon, Seymour*
Lightning — *Steel, Danielle*
Lightning Song — *Nordan, Lewis*
Lightning Tree — *Kinsella, John*
Lights, Camera, Poetry! — *Shinder, Jason*
Lights, Camera, War — *Neuman, Johanna*
c Lights for Gita — *Gilmore, Rachna*
c Lights Out (Illus. by Susan Synarski) — *Gordon, Lynn*
c Lights Out! (Illus. by John Himmelman). Book and Audio Version — *Himmelman, John*
Lights Out for the Territory — *Sinclair, Iain*
c Lightsaber — *Anderson, Kevin J*
Ligne Directs — *Bldard-Gibson, Jacqueline*
Like a Film — *Murray, Timothy*
Like a Hurricane — *Smith, Paul Chaat*
cp Like a Mountain Series — *Chadwick, Paul*
c Like a Pebble in Your Shoe (Illus. by Beth Norling) — *Hunt, Nan*
Like a Summer Peach — *Farley, Blanche Flanders*
Like Color to the Blind — *Williams, Donna*
y Like Judgment Day — *D'Orso, Michael*
y Like Judgment Day (Davidson). Audio Version — *D'Orso, Michael*
Like Most Revelations — *Howard, Richard*
Like Mother, Like Daughter — *Waterhouse, Debra*
Like People in History — *Picano, Felice*
Like Plastic — *Flusfeder, David*
y Like Sisters on the Homefront — *Williams-Garcia, Rita*
Like Underground Water — *Koriyama, Naoshi*
Like Unto Like — *Bonner, Sherwood*
Like Whispers in the Wind — *Dysart, Norman*
Likelihood-Based Inference in Co-Integrated Vector Autoregressive Models — *Johansen, Soren*
Likely — *Coffman, Lisa*
c A Likely Place (Illus. by Edward Ardizzone) — *Fox, Paula*
Likely to Die — *Fairstein, Linda*
Likeness and Presence — *Belting, Hans*
Li'l Mama's Rules — *Jackson, Sheneska*
Lila Says
p Lilliput Review
c Lilly's Purple Plastic Purse (Illus. by Kevin Henkes) — *Henkes, Kevin*
c Lily and Me — *Aaron, Moses*
c Lily and Miss Liberty (Illus. by Deborah Kogan Ray) — *Stevens, Carla*
c Lily and the Wooden Bowl (Illus. by Yoriko Ito) — *Schroeder, Alan*
Lily Makes a Living — *Houbein, Lolo*
y Lily White — *Isaacs, Susan*
Lily White (Estabrook). Audio Version — *Isaacs, Susan*
c Lily's Crossing — *Giff, Patricia Reilly*
Limb Regeneration — *Tsonis, Panagiotis A*
Limba Pasarilor — *Plesu, Andrei*
Lime 5 — *Crutcher, Mark*
The Limerick Anthology — *Kemmy, Jim*
Limit Analysis of Solids and Structures — *Kamenjarzh, Jacov A*
r Limit Theorems of Probability Theory — *Petrov, Valentin V*
r The Limits of Affluence — *Struthers, James*

The Limits of Agrarian Radicalism — *Argersinger, Peter H*
Limits of Citizenship — *Soysal, Yasemin Nuhoglu*
The Limits of Dissent — *Halpern, Thomas*
The Limits of Lockean Rights in Property — *Sreenivasan, Gopal*
The Limits of Mercy — *Moore, John L*
The Limits of Moralizing — *Mikics, David*
The Limits of Participation — *Bremen, Riet Van*
The Limits of Public Choice — *Udehn, Lars*
The Limits of Racial Domination — *Cope, R Douglas*
The Limits of Settlement Growth — *Fletcher, Roland*
The Limits of Tolerance — *Curry, Ann, 1948-*
The Limits of Voice — *Lima, Luiz Costa*
Limits to Competition — *Group of Lisbon*
The Limnology, Climatology and Paleoclimatology of the East African Lakes — *Johnson, Thomas C*
Limpiar La Tierra — *Uribe, Maria Victoria*
Lincoln — *Donald, David Herbert*
y Lincoln: A Photobiography — *Freedman, Russell*
Lincoln, Land, and Labor 1809-60 — *Fraysse, Olivier*
c The Lincoln Memorial — *Kent, Deborah*
The Lincoln Persuasion — *Greenstone, J David*
c The Lincoln Way — *Morris, Jeffrey*
Lincoln's Abolitionist General — *Miller, Edward A, Jr., 1927-*
Lincoln's Admiral — *Duffy, James P*
Lincoln's Generals — *Boritt, Gabor*
Lincoln's Letters (Vail). Audio Version — *Lincoln, Abraham*
Lincoln's Prose (Vail). Audio Version — *Lincoln, Abraham*
Lincolnshire Airfields in the Second World War — *Otter, Patrick*
The Lindisfarne Gospels — *Backhouse, Janet*
The Line — *McGuire, Bob*
Line of Duty — *Lovelace, Merline*
A Lineage of Ragpluckers, Songpluckers, Elegiasts and Jewelers — *Goldbarth, Albert*
Linear Algebra — *Lax, Peter D*
Linear Algebra — *Zhang, Fuzhen*
Linear and Nonlinear Models for the Analysis of Repeated Measurements — *Vonesh, Edward F*
Linear and Quasilinear Parabolic Problems. Vol. 1 — *Amann, Herbert*
Linear Difference Equations with Discrete Transform Methods — *Jerri, Abdul J*
Linear Models — *Moser, Barry Kurt*
Linear Programming — *Panik, Michael J*
Linear Programming — *Saigal, Romesh*
Lineations — *Gray, Robert, 1945-*
Lines of Authority — *Zwicker, Steven N*
Lines of Country — *Andreae, Christopher*
Lines of Fate — *Kharitonov, Mark*
c Ling-Li and the Phoenix Fairy (Illus. by Zong-Zhou Wang) — *Greene, Ellin*
Lingua E Stile Di Giacomo Leopardi — *Convegno Internazionale Di Studi Leopardiani (8th: 1991: Recanari, Italy)*
Linguistic Auditing — *Reeves, Nigel*
Linguistic Ecology — *Muhlhausler, Peter*
The Linguistic Individual — *Johnstone, Barbara*
p Linguistics and Science Fiction
La Linguistique Appliquee Aujourd'hui — *Huot, Helene*
The Link Between Force Structure and Manpower Requirements — *United States. Congress. House. Committee on Armed Services*
Linnaeus: The Man and His Work — *Frangsmyr, Tore*
Linocuts of the Machine Age — *Coppel, Stephen*
Linoleum, Better Babies, and the Modern Farm Woman 1890-1930 — *Holt, Marilyn Irvin*
y Linus Pauling: A Life in Science and Politics — *Goertzel, Ted*
Linus Pauling in His Own Words — *Pauling, Linus*
LINUX Companion — *Komarinski, Mark*
LINUX Multimedia Guide — *Tranter, Jeff*
c Lion (Illus. by Richard Hewett) — *Arnold, Caroline*
The Lion and the Cross — *Rhodes, Royal W*
c The Lion and the Mouse (Illus. by Ian Andrew) — *Wood, A J*
c A Lion Named Shirley Williamson (Illus. by Bernard Waber) — *Waber, Bernard*
y The Lion Tamer's Daughter and Other Stories — *Dickinson, Peter*
c Lionel and Amelia (Illus. by Adrian Peguero) — *Peguero, Leone*
c Lionel and His Friends (Illus. by Susanna Natti) — *Krensky, Stephen*
Lionel Sotheby's Great War — *Sotheby, Lionel*
The Lioness in Bloom — *Kepner, Susan Fulop*

c Lioness Rampant — *Pierce, Tamora*
The Lioness Roars — *Wu, Yenna*
c Lions — *Harman, Amanda*
The Lions of the North — *Marston, Edward*
The Lion's Share — *Campbell, Robert*
c The Lion's Whiskers and Other Ethiopian Tales (Illus. by Helen Siegl) — *Ashabranner, Brent*
The Lip: A Biography of Leo Durocher — *Eskenazi, Gerald*
Lipid Second Messengers — *Bell, Robert M*
c Liplap's Wish (Illus. by Sylvia Long) — *London, Jonathan*
The Lipstick Proviso — *Lehrman, Karen*
Liquid- and Surface-Borne Particle Measurement Handbook — *Knapp, Julius Z*
Liquid Chromatography of Oligomers — *Uglea, Constantin*
Liquid Crystals for Advanced Technologies — *Bunning, Timothy J*
Liquid Detergents — *Lai, Kuo-Yann*
The Lira Da Braccio — *Jones, Sterling Scott*
Lire Le Regard — *Chenieux-Gendron, Jacqueline*
Lisa Fonssagrives, a Portrait — *Harrison, Martin*
Lise Meitner: A Life in Physics — *Sime, Ruth Lewin*
Lisippo: L'Arte E La Fortuna — *Moreno, Paolo*
Lisp in Small Pieces — *Queinnec, Christian*
LISREL Issues, Debates, and Strategies — *Hayduk, Leslie A*
r Lissauer's Encyclopedia of Popular Music in America 1888 to the Present. Vols. 1-3 — *Lissauer, Robert*
The List — *Martini, Steve*
Die List: Fruhe Erzahlungen — *Fleisser, Marieluise*
r A List of Pensioners of the War of 1812 (Vermont Claimants) — *Clark, Bryon N*
c Listen and Read Charles Dickens' A Christmas Carol (Hammond). Book and Audio Version — *Dickens, Charles*
c Listen and Read Edgar Allan Poe's The Tell-Tale Heart and Other Stories (Hammond). Book and Audio Version — *Poe, Edgar Allan*
c Listen and Read Emily Dickinson's Selected Poems (Seldes). Book and Audio Version — *Dickinson, Emily*
c Listen and Read James Joyce's Dubliners (Keating). Book and Audio Version — *Joyce, James*
c Listen and Read the Adventures of Peter Cottontail (Seldes). Book and Audio Version — *Burgess, Thornton W*
c Listen and Read The Ugly Duckling and Other Fairy Tales (Brill). Book and Audio Version — *Andersen, Hans Christian*
c Listen for the Bus (Illus. by John Godt) — *McMahon, Patricia*
Listen to Me — *Jampolsky, Gerald G*
Listen to Me Good — *Smith, Margaret Charles, 1906-*
y Listen to My Heart — *Applegate, Katherine*
y Listen to the Dark — *Henry, Maeve*
Listen to the Desert — *Mayers, Gregory*
c Listen to the Howl of the Wolf — *McCullough, Bill*
Listen Up — *Findlen, Barbara*
y Listen Up! — *Trapani, Margi*
Listening and Performing — *Ward, Christine*
A Listening Church — *Uzukwu, Elochukwu E*
Listening for God — *Carlson, Paula J*
Listening for Small Sounds — *Trevor, Penelope*
y Listening to America — *Wertheimer, Linda*
Listening to Children Think — *Hall, Nigel*
Listening to Movies — *Karlin, Fred*
Listening to Radio 1920-1950 — *Barfield, Ray*
Listening to Silences — *Hedges, Elaine*
Listening to the Orchestra — *Hill, Susan, 1942-*
Listening with My Heart — *Whitestone, Heather*
Liszt: Sonata in B Minor — *Hamilton, Kenneth*
The Lit De Justice — *Brown, Elizabeth A R*
Lite and Luscious Cuisine of India — *Gadia, Madhu*
Literacies Lost — *Wells, M Cyrene*
Literacy and Paideia in Ancient Greece — *Robb, Kevin*
Literacy and Power in the Ancient World — *Bowman, Alan K*
Literacy, Economy, and Society
Literacy, Emotion, and Authority — *Besnier, Niko*
Literacy Language and Community Publishing — *Mace, Jane*
Literacy, Power and Democracy in Mozambique — *Marshall, Judith*
Literacy Practices — *Baynham, Mike*
Literacy: Programs for Adults with Developmental Disabilities — *Giordano, Gerard*
r Literacy Techniques for Building Successful Readers and Writers

Literal Figures — *Luxon, Thomas H*
p Literal Latte
r Literally Entitled — *Room, Adrian*
Literarische Konventionen — *Weninger, Robert*
Literary Aftershocks — *Stone, Albert E*
Literary Aspects of Courtly Culture — *Maddox, Donald*
The Literary Bent — *Bloom, James D*
Literary Charleston — *Worthington, Curtis*
The Literary Companion to Gambling — *Davis-Goff, Annabel*
The Literary Companion to Parliament — *Silvester, Christopher*
r Literary-Critical Approaches to the Bible — *Minor, Mark*
The Literary Genres of Edmund Burke — *De Bruyn, Frans*
Literary History and the Challenge of Philology — *Lerer, Seth*
A Literary History of Cambridge. Rev. Ed. — *Chainey, Graham*
r Literary History of the United States. 4th Rev. Ed., Vols. 1-2 — *Spiller, Robert E*
Literary Imitation in the Italian Renaissance — *McLaughlin, Martin L*
r The Literary Index to American Magazines 1850-1900 — *Wells, Daniel A*
Literary Influence and African-American Writers — *Mishkin, Tracy*
The Literary Insomniac — *Cheney, Elyse*
Literary Intellectuals and the Dissolution of the State — *Von Hallberg, Robert*
Literary Inter-Relations — *Massoud, Mary*
Literary Interest — *Knapp, Steven*
r Literary Journalism — *Applegate, Edd*
r Literary Laurels. Kids' Ed. — *Carlson, Laura*
Literary Luxuries — *Bellamy, Joe David*
Literary Meaning — *Harris, Wendell V*
The Literary Mind — *Turner, Mark*
The Literary Reputation of Else Lasker-Schuler — *Jones, Calvin N*
Literary Symbiosis — *Cowart, David*
Literary Theory after Davidson — *Dasenbrock, Reed Way*
Literary Transmission and Authority — *Brady, Jennifer*
Literate Beginnings — *Jeffery, Debby Ann*
Literate Women and the French Revolution of 1789 — *Montfort, Catherine R*
Literati and Self-Re/presentation — *Huang, Martin W*
Literatur Und Drittes Reich — *Ketelsen, Uwe-K*
La Literatura Perdida De La Edad Media Castellana. Vol. 1 — *Deyermond, A D*
Literature against Philosophy, Plato to Derrida — *Edmundson, Mark*
Literature and Culture in Early Modern London — *Manley, Lawrence*
Literature and Culture in Modern Britain. Vol. 1 — *Bloom, Clive*
Literature and Humanitarian Reform in the Civil War Era — *Eiselein, Gregory*
Literature and Philosophy in Dialogue — *Gadamer, Hans Georg*
Literature and Photography — *Rabb, Jane M*
Literature and Revolution in England 1640-1660 — *Smith, Nigel, 1958-*
Literature and the Right in Postwar France — *Hewitt, Nicholas*
Literature as Social Action — *Currie, Pamela*
r Literature Criticism from 1400 to 1800. Vols. 28-29
r Literature Criticism from 1400 to 1800. Vols. 30-31
Literature, Education, and Romanticism — *Richardson, Alan*
r Literature for Children and Young Adults about Oceania — *Austin, Mary C*
Literature for Democracy — *Pradl, Gordon M*
r Literature for Today's Young Adults. 5th Ed. — *Donelson, Kenneth L*
Literature in Ireland — *MacDonagh, Thomas*
Literature in the Marketplace — *Jordan, John O*
r Literature of American Music III — *Marco, Guy A*
The Literature of Forestry and Agroforestry — *McDonald, Peter, 1952-*
The Literature of Labor and the Labors of Literature — *Weinstein, Cindy*
r The Literature of Music Bibliography — *Krummel, Donald William*
The Literature of Nationalism — *Pynsent, Robert B*
The Literature of Terror. Vol. 1 — *Punter, David*
r The Literature of the Nonprofit Sector. Vol. 7 — *McKenty, Elizabeth J*

The Literature of Travel in the Japanese Rediscovery of China 1862-1945 — *Fogel, Joshua A*
Literature or Life — *Semprun, Jorge*
Literature, Politics, and National Identity — *Hadfield, Andrew*
Literaturgeschichte Osterreich — *Schmidt-Dengler, Wendelin*
Lithium: Actions and Mechanisms — *El-Mallakh, Rif S*
r The Lithographs of Prentiss Taylor — *Rose, Ingrid*
Lithuania Ascending — *Rowell, S C*
Lithuania: The Rebel Nation — *Vardys, Vytas Stanley*
r Lithuanian Dictionary: English-Lithuanian, Lithuanian-English — *Piesarskas, Bronius*
Litigando En Washington — *Facio, Gonzalo J*
Litigation and Settlement in a Game with Incomplete Information — *Ryll, Wolfgang*
Litterature Et Societe — *Pelletier, Jacques*
Une Litterature Sans Histoire — *Wolf, Nelly*
Litteratures En Contexte — *Luce, Louise Fiber*
Littery Man — *Lowry, Richard S*
Little — *Treuer, David*
c Little Angels' Alphabet of Love (Illus. by Joan Walsh Anglund) — *Anglund, Joan Walsh*
c Little Bean's Friend (Illus. by John Wallace) — *Wallace, John*
c Little Bear Brushes His Teeth (Illus. by Vera Sobat) — *Langreuter, Jutta*
c Little Bear Goes to Kindergarten (Illus. by Vera Sobat) — *Langreuter, Jutta*
c Little Big Ears (Illus. by Martyn Colbeck) — *Moss, Cynthia*
c A Little Bit of Rob (Illus. by Marni Backer) — *Turner, Barbara J*
A Little Bit of Wisdom — *Axtell, Horace P*
Little Blues Book — *Robertson, Brian*
c Little Bo Peep and Other Rhymes — *Roffey, Maureen*
c The Little Boat (Illus. by Patrick Benson) — *Henderson, Kathy*
c The Little Book of Cats (Illus. by Lorna Hussey) — *Walsh, Caroline*
c The Little Book of Christmas (Illus. by Sophie Allsopp) — *Walsh, Caroline*
c The Little Book of Dogs (Illus. by Valerie Greeley) — *Walsh, Caroline*
A Little Book of Stars — *Gilheany, Sheila*
A Little Book on Love — *Needleman, Jacob*
Little Boy Blue — *Dee, Ed*
c Little Brother and Little Sister (Illus. by Bernadette Watts)
c Little Brown Bear Does Not Want to Eat (Illus. by Daniele Bour) — *Lebrun, Claude*
c Little Brown Bear Dresses Himself (Illus. by Daniele Bour) — *Lebrun, Claude*
c Little Brown Bear Goes on a Trip (Illus. by Daniele Bour) — *Lebrun, Claude*
c Little Brown Bear Helps His Mama (Illus. by Daniele Bour) — *Lebrun, Claude*
c Little Brown Bear Is Growing Up (Illus. by Daniele Bour) — *Lebrun, Claude*
c Little Brown Bear Takes a Bath (Illus. by Daniele Bour) — *Lebrun, Claude*
c Little Brown Bear Wants to Be Read To (Illus. by Daniele Bour) — *Lebrun, Claude*
c Little Bunny's Preschool Countdown (Illus. by Kathy Parkinson) — *Boelts, Maribeth*
c Little Caribou (Illus. by Sarah Fox-Davies) — *Fox-Davies, Sarah*
c The Little Chair (Illus. by Pauline Baynes) — *Godden, Rumer*
c Little Champ (Illus. by Jim Arnosky) — *Arnosky, Jim*
c Little Chicken Chicken (Illus. by Sue Heap) — *Martin, David, 1944-*
c Little Chick's Big Adventure — *Fowler, Richard*
c Little Clancy's New Drum (Illus. by Tony Kerins) — *Kerins, Tony*
c Little Cloud (Illus. by Eric Carle) — *Carle, Eric*
Little Dorrit's Shadows — *Rosenberg, Brian*
Little Dragons — *Bugeja, Michael J*
c Little Elephant Thunderfoot (Illus. by John Butler) — *Grindley, Sally*
c The Little Fir Tree's Busy for Christmas Book (Illus. by Cathy Baxter) — *Rock, Lois*
c The Little Flower King (Illus. by Kveta Pacovska) — *Pacovska, Kveta*
c Little Folk (Illus. by James Bernardin) — *Walker, Paul Robert*
c The Little Giant Book of Jokes (Illus. by Sanford Hoffman) — *Rosenbloom, Joseph*
c The Little Giant Book of Riddles (Illus. by Sanford Hoffman) — *Rosenbloom, Joseph*

c The Little Giant Encyclopedia of Puzzles — *Diagram Group*
Little Girls in Church — *Norris, Kathleen*
y Little Girls in Pretty Boxes — *Ryan, Joan*
c The Little Green Book — *Barber, Cicely Mary*
Little Green Man in Ireland — *Branham, Mary*
c Little Green Thumbs (Illus. by Bettina Paterson) — *Van Hage, Mary An*
c Little Green Tow Truck (Illus. by Ken Wilson-Max) — *Wilson-Max, Ken*
Little Havana Blues — *Poey, Delia*
The Little House — *Gregory, Philippa*
c Little House in Brookfield (Illus. by Dan Andreasen) — *Wilkes, Maria D*
c The Little Humpbacked Horse (Illus. by Alexander Koshkin) — *Winthrop, Elizabeth*
The Little Italy Cookbook — *Pace, Maria*
r Little-Known Museums in and around Paris — *Kaplan, Rachel*
c The Little Lame Prince and His Travelling Cloak — *Craik, Dinah Mulock*
c Little Lil and the Swing-Singing Sax (Illus. by Lisa Cohen) — *Gray, Libba Moore*
c The Little Lilac Book — *Barker, Cicely Mary*
c Little Magic Shop of Horrors — *Cascone, A G*
Little Man--What Now? — *Fallada, Hans*
Little Masters — *Wilkins, Damien*
Little Men (Herbert). Audio Version — *Alcott, Louisa May*
Little Miss Magi — *Sampson, John*
Little Miss Strange — *Rose, Joanna*
c Little Monster Did It! — *Cooper, Helen*
c Little Mouse and Elephant (Illus. by John Segal) — *Yolen, Jane*
r Little Oxford Dictionary of English Grammar
c The Little Painter of Sabana Grande — *Markun, Patricia Maloney*
y The Little PC Book. 2nd Ed. — *Magid, Lawrence J*
c The Little Pickpocket (Illus. by Avner Katz) — *Katz, Avner*
A Little Piece of Paradise — *Vitti, James Alan*
c Little Pig's Bouncy Ball — *Baron, Alan*
The Little Platoons — *Liebmann, George W*
c Little Polar Bear, Take Me Home! (Illus. by Hans De Beer) — *De Beer, Hans*
c The Little Prince and the Great Treasure Hunt — *Kavanagh, Peter*
y The Little Princes in the Tower — *Lace, William W*
y A Little Princess (Leishman). Audio Version — *Burnett, Frances Hodgson*
c Little Rabbit's First Word Book — *Baker, Alan*
c Little Red Cowboy Hat (Illus. by Randy Cecil) — *Lowell, Susan*
c The Little Red Hen (Illus. by Byron Barton) — *Barton, Byron*
c Little Red Hen (Illus. by Norman Messenger) — *Garner, Alan*
c Little Red Plane (Illus. by Ken Wilson-Max) — *Wilson-Max, Ken*
c Little Red Readers Series
c Little Red Riding Hood (Illus. by Lisa Campbell Ernst) — *Ernst, Lisa Campbell*
c Little Red Riding Hood (Illus. by Jonathan Langley) — *Langley, Jonathan*
c Little Red Riding Hood (Illus. by Mireille Levert) — *Levert, Mireille*
c Little Red Riding Hood (Illus. by Emma Chichester Clark) — *McBratney, Sam*
c The Little Reindeer (Illus. by Michael Foreman) — *Foreman, Michael*
c A Little Salmon for Witness (Illus. by Sandra Speidel) — *Rahaman, Vashanti*
c The Little Ships (Illus. by Michael Foreman) — *Borden, Louise*
The Little Sister — *Chandler, Raymond*
Little Sister — *Checkoway, Julie*
y Little Sister — *Dalkey, Kara*
c Little Sister's Bracelet (Illus. by Mercer Mayer) — *Mayer, Mercer*
The Little Team That Could — *Burroughs, Jeff*
c Little Theater (Illus. by Stef De Reuver)
A Little Too Much Is Enough — *Tyau, Kathleen*
c Little Town in the Ozarks (Illus. by David Gilleece) — *MacBride, Roger Lea*
The Little Town Where Time Stood Still — *Hrabal, Bohumil*
c The Little Tree Growin' in the Shade (Illus. by Tyrone Geter) — *Yarbrough, Camille*
The Little Trilogy — *Sienkiewicz, Henryk*
c Little Vampire's Diary — *Holleyman, Sonia*
c Little Walrus Warning (Illus. by Walter Stuart). Book and Audio Version — *Young, Carol*

c The Little White Hen (Illus. by Gillian McClure)
— *Pearce, Philippa*
c The Little White Horse — *Goudge, Elizabeth*
y Little Women — *Alcott, Louisa May*
c Little Women (Harper). Audio Version — *Alcott, Louisa May*
y Little Women (King). Audio Version — *Alcott, Louisa May*
y Little X — *Tate, Sonsyrea*
y A Little Yellow Dog — *Mosley, Walter*
A Little Yellow Dog (Winfield). Audio Version
— *Mosley, Walter*
c Littlejim's Dreams (Illus. by Thomas B Allen)
— *Houston, Gloria*
c The Littles Take a Trip — *Peterson, John*
c The Littlest Dragon (Illus. by Jamie Smith) — *Ryan, Margaret*
c The Littlest Duckling (Illus. by Ann Schweninger)
— *Herman, Gail*
c The Littlest Vaquero — *Liles, Maurine*
Liturgical Hermeneutics — *Nichols, Bridget*
Liturgies on the Holocaust — *Littell, Marcia Sachs*
A Liturgist's Guide to Inclusive Language
— *Witherup, Ronald D*
Liturgy and the Ecclesiastical History of Late Anglo-Saxon England — *Dumville, David N*
Liturgy in Byzantium and Beyond — *Taft, Robert F*
y Live a Little — *Neenan, Colin*
Live and Learn — *Middleton, Stanley*
Live at Five — *Haynes, David*
Live Better Longer — *Dispenza, Joseph*
Live Briefs — *Bell, Steve*
Live from Death Row — *Abu-Jamal, Mumia*
Live from the Battlefield — *Arnett, Peter*
Live Girls — *Nugent, Beth*
Live Large! — *Erdman, Cheri K*
Live Sex Acts — *Chapkis, Wendy*
The Lively Arts — *Kammen, Michael*
Lively Stones — *Weber, Retta Lou*
Liver and Biliary Diseases. 2nd Ed. — *Kaplowitz, Neil*
Liverpool Accents — *Robinson, Peter, 1953-*
c Lives and Legends of the Saints — *Armstrong, Carole*
yr Lives and Works in the Arts from the Renaissance to the 20th Century. Vols. 1-9
c Lives Intertwined — *Young, Allen M*
r Lives of North American Birds — *Kaufman, Kenn*
Lives of Promise — *Arnold, Karen D*
y Lives of the Artists (Illus. by Kathryn Hewitt)
— *Krull, Kathleen*
y Lives of the Artists (Brown). Audio Version — *Krull, Kathleen*
c Lives of the Athletes (Illus. by Kathryn Hewitt)
— *Krull, Kathleen*
Lives of the Bigamists — *Boyer, Richard*
The Lives of the Great Composers. 3rd Ed.
— *Schonberg, Harold C*
Lives of the Great Romantics. Vols. 1-3 — *Mullan, John*
The Lives of the Kings and Queens of England
— *Fraser, Antonia*
Lives of the Monster Dogs — *Bakis, Kirsten*
c Lives of the Musicians (Brown). Audio Version
— *Krull, Kathleen*
y Lives of the Writers (Brown). Audio Version — *Krull, Kathleen*
The Lives of Whales and Dolphins — *Connor, Richard C*
Lives of Women Public Schoolteachers — *Holmes, Madelyn*
The Lives to Come — *Kitcher, Philip*
c Lives Turned Upside Down — *Hubbard, Jim*
Lives, Wives and Loves of the Great Composers
— *Spiegl, Fritz*
y The Livewire Guide to Going, Being and Staying Veggie! — *Gellatley, Juliet*
Livia Oder Die Reise — *Donhauser, Michael*
Living and Dining in Medieval Paris
— *Crossley-Holland, Nicolle*
Living and Dying Well — *Petrinovich, Lewis*
Living and Learning — *Chase, Malcolm*
The Living and the Dead — *Hendrickson, Paul*
The Living and the Dead (Hendrickson). Audio Version — *Hendrickson, Paul*
Living Apart — *Berry, Ian*
Living Arrangements and Social Networks of Older Adults — *Knipscheer, C P M*
r Living Arrangements of Women and Their Children in Developing Countries
Living between Worlds — *Sheldrake, Philip*
Living Biographies of Famous Rulers (May). Audio Version — *Thomas, Henry*

Living Biographies of Great Scientists (May). Audio Version
Living Buddha, Living Christ — *Nhat Hanh, Thich*
c The Living Clarinet — *Turner, Barrie Carson*
y Living Dangerously — *Holland, Heinrich D*
Living Downstream — *Steingraber, Sandra*
The Living End — *Elkin, Stanley*
c The Living Environment. Vols. 1-6
Living Faith — *Carter, Jimmy*
The Living Flame of Love: Versions A and B — *John of the Cross, Saint*
c The Living Flute — *Turner, Barrie Carson*
Living Generously — *Scutt, Jocelynne A*
The Living God — *Lamm, Julia A*
Living Happily Ever After — *Wagner, Laurie*
Living High and Letting Die — *Unger, Peter*
Living History — *Herzog, Chaim*
Living in America — *Rustomji-Kerns, Roshni*
Living in Cincinnati — *Walzer, Kevin*
Living In, Living Out — *Clark-Lewis, Elizabeth*
Living in Paris — *Alvarez, Jose*
Living in the Resurrection — *Crunk, Tony*
Living in the Shadow of Death — *Rothman, Sheila M*
Living in the Spirit's Fire — *Hubanig, Alfred A*
y Living in Two Worlds — *Kosof, Anna*
Living inside Our Hope — *Lynd, Staughton*
Living Islam — *Ahmed, Akbar S*
Living It Up — *Finley, Karen*
Living Lean — *North, Larry*
Living Liberation in Hindu Thought — *Fort, Andrew O*
Living Life on Purpose — *Anderson, Greg*
Living like the Saints — *Pope, Liston*
Living Machines — *Jones, E Michael*
The Living of Maisie Ward — *Greene, Dana*
A Living of Words — *Albertine, Susan*
Living on the Boott — *Mrozowski, Stephen A*
Living on the Edge — *Rank, Mark Robert*
Living on the Fringe — *Finkelstein, Israel*
Living on the Front Line — *Pickard, Susan*
Living on the Lottery — *Davies, Hunter*
Living Our Dying — *Sharp, Joseph*
Living Our Stories, Telling Our Truths — *Franklin, V P*
c The Living Piano — *Turner, Barrie Carson*
Living Posthumously — *Schmookler, Andrew Bard*
Living Proof — *Harvey, John*
The Living Room — *Buchanan, George, 1948-*
Living Room Lectures — *Leibman, Nina C*
Living Somewhere between Estrogen and Death
— *Johnson, Barbara E*
The Living Stream — *Rattue, James*
Living Strings — *Whelan, Michael*
Living the Beatitudes — *L'Arche Daybreak Community*
Living the Psalms — *Sheridan, John V*
c Living Things (Illus. by Ray Boudreau) — *Mason, Adrienne*
The Living Tree — *Tu, Wei-Ming*
Living under Contract — *Little, Peter D*
c The Living Violin — *Turner, Barrie Carson*
A Living Wage for the Forgotten Man — *Paulsen, George E*
Living Water, Sealing Spirit — *Johnson, Maxwell E*
Living Well with HIV and AIDS — *Gifford, Allen*
Living Witchcraft — *Scarboro, Allen*
Living with Death — *Hennezel, Marie De*
Living with Defeat — *Burrin, Philippe*
Living with Ghosts — *Michel, Prince of Greece*
Living with God...in Good Times and Bad
— *Carmody, John, 1939-*
Living with Herbs — *Gardner, Jo Ann*
r Living with Low Vision. 4th Ed.
Living with Miracles — *Cowles, David*
c Living with My Stepfather Is Like Living with a Moose (Illus. by Blanche Sims) — *Bowdish, Lynea*
Living with One's Past — *Care, Norman S*
Living with the State — *Giles, Christopher*
Living without Procrastination — *Roberts, M Susan*
c The Living World (Illus. by Sue Barclay)
c Livingstone Mouse (Illus. by Henry Cole) — *Edwards, Pamela Duncan*
Le Livre De La Soeur — *Lejeune, Claire*
Le Livre De Saphir — *Sinoue, Gilbert*
Le Livre D'Enfance Et De Jeunesse En France
— *Glenisson, Jean*
Le Livre Du Duc Des Vrais Amans — *Christine, De Pisan*
r Livre Et Politique Au Bas-Canada 1791-1849
— *Gallichan, Gilles*

Le Livre Journal De La Fabrique Da La Chapelle Salviati A Saint-Marc De Florence 1579-1594
— *Jestaz, Bertrand*
r Les Livres Africains Pour La Jeunesse — *Laurentin, Marie*
r The Livrets of Jean-Baptiste Lully's Tragedies Lyriques — *Schmidt, Carl B*
Livy: Reconstructing Ancient Rome — *Miles, Gary B*
y Lizard — *Covington, Dennis*
Lizzie — *Shawhan, Dorothy*
c Lizzie Fights On (Illus. by James Mayhew)
— *Beresford, Elisabeth*
c Llaman A La Puerta. Book and Audio Version
— *Hutchins, Pat*
El Llanto De Las Cosas — *Sosa, Roberto*
r Llewellyn's 1997 Moon Sign Book
r Llewellyn's 1997 Sun Sign Book
Llinfinito Forse — *Rugarli, Giampaolo*
Lo Irremediable — *Kovadloff, Santiago*
Lo Mekubelet — *Ron-Feder-Amit, Galilah*
Lo Que Tu Madre No Te Dijo Y Tu Padre No Sabia
— *Gray, John, 1951-*
Loans and Legitimacy — *Siegel, Katherine A S*
Loaves and Fishes — *Blass, Virginia A*
c Loaves of Fun — *Harbison, Elizabeth M*
Lob Des Unsinns — *Menninghaus, Winfried*
Lobbying for Social Change. 2nd Ed. — *Richan, Willard C*
Lobbyists for Hire — *Moloney, Kevin*
c O Lobisomem (Illus. by Bayard Christ) — *Mota, Antonio*
c Lobster's Secret (Illus. by Jon Weiman). Book and Audio Version — *Hollenbeck, Kathleen M*
Local and Metropolitan Area Networks. 5th Ed.
— *Stallings, William*
Local and Regional Response to Global Pressure
— *Cossentino, Francesco*
Local Area Networking. 2nd Ed. — *Naugle, Matthew G*
Local Attachments — *Von Hoffman, Alexander*
Local Commons and Global Interdependence
— *Keohane, Robert O*
Local Computer Networks
Local Economic Development — *Blair, John P, 1947-*
Local Economic Development in Europe and the Americas — *Demaziere, Christophe*
Local Elites in Western Democracies — *Eldersveld, Samuel J*
Local Environmental Struggles — *Gould, Kenneth A*
r Local Government in Europe. Electronic Media Version
Local Government in Latin America — *Nickson, R Andrew*
Local Immunosuppression of Organ Transplants
— *Gruber, Scott A*
Local Justice in America — *Elster, Jon*
Local Markets and Regional Trade in Medieval Exeter
— *Kowaleski, Maryanne*
Local People — *Dittmer, John*
Local Rules — *Brandon, Jay*
Local Sustainability — *Selman, Paul*
Localized Damage IV
Locas — *Murray, Yxta Maya*
Location Economics — *Greenhut, Melvin L*
Location Portraiture — *McIntosh, William S*
Location, Scheduling, Design and Integer Programming — *Padberg, Manfred*
Locational Competition in the World Economy
— *Siebert, Horst*
y Loch (Guidall). Audio Version — *Zindel, Paul*
The Loch Ness Monster — *Campbell, Stueart*
Locke, Literary Criticism, and Philosophy — *Walker, William*
Locked in the Cabinet — *Reich, Robert B*
Locked in the Cabinet (Reich). Audio Version
— *Reich, Robert B*
y Locked in Time — *Duncan, Lois*
r Locked Room Murders and Other Impossible Crimes
— *Adey, Robert*
Locke's Philosophy — *Rogers, G A J*
c Locks, Crocs, and Skeeters — *Parker, Nancy Winslow*
Lockwood: A Western Story — *Paine, Lauran*
Locri Epizefiri IV — *Bagnasco, Marcella Barra*
La Locura De Fidel Castro — *Marin, Gustavo Adolfo*
p Locus: The Newspaper of the Science Fiction Field
Locusts at the Edge of Summer — *Balaban, John*
The Locusts Have No King — *Powell, Dawn*
Lodge in Vietnam — *Blair, Anne E*
The Lodger: The Arrest and Escape of Jack the Ripper — *Evans, Stewart*
Lofty Aims and Lowly Duties — *Jennings, Ruth*

c The Log Cabin Quilt (Illus. by Ronald Himler) — *Howard, Ellen*
Log Houses — *Christopher, Peter*
Logging the Globe — *Marchak, M Patricia*
Logic and Algebra — *Ursini, Aldo*
Logic and Computer Design Fundamentals — *Mano, M Morris*
Logic and Information — *Devlin, Keith*
Logic and Representation — *Moore, Robert C*
Logic-Based 0-1 Constraint Programming — *Barth, Peter*
The Logic of Essentialism — *Thom, Paul*
The Logic of Evil — *Brustein, William*
The Logic of Historical Explanation — *Roberts, Clayton*
The Logic of Imaginative Education — *McCleary, Dick*
The Logic of Incest — *Kunin, Seth Daniel*
The Logic of International Restructuring — *Ruigrok, Winfried*
Logic on the Track of Social Change — *Braybrooke, David*
Logic Synthesis and Verification Algorithms — *Hachtel, Gary D*
Logic Works Verilog Modeler — *Capilano Computing Systems, Ltd.*
Logical Frameworks for Truth and Abstraction — *Cantini, Andrea*
The Logical Status of Diagrams — *Shin, Sun-Joo*
Logics of Dislocation — *Barnes, Trevor J*
Logistics Systems Analysis. 2nd Ed. — *Daganzo, Carlos F*
Loie Fuller: Goddess of Light — *Current, Richard Nelson*
Lois Et Symetrie — *Van Fraassen, Bas C*
Lois Weber: The Director Who Lost Her Way in History — *Slide, Anthony*
Loitering with Intent. Vol. 1 — *O'Toole, Peter*
Loitering with Intent. Vol. 2 — *O'Toole, Peter*
Lola Montez: A Life — *Seymour, Bruce*
Lola Montez: The California Adventures of Europe's Notorious Courtesan — *Varley, James F*
Lolita (Irons). Audio Version — *Nabokov, Vladimir Vladimirovich*
c The Lollipop Witch (Illus. by Nick Sharratt) — *Hawkins, Elizabeth*
La Loma Del Angel — *Arenas, Reinaldo*
c Lon Po Po (Illus. by Ed Young) — *Young, Ed*
r London — *Creaton, Heather*
London — *Russell, John, 1919-*
London — *Rutherfurd, Edward*
c London — *Stein, R Conrad*
London: A Social History — *Porter, Roy*
London and the Invention of the Middle East — *Adelson, Roger*
London at War 1939-1945 — *Ziegler, Philip*
The London Cookbook — *Trigg, Liz*
London in Paint — *Galinov, Mireille*
London in the Age of Industrialisation — *Schwarz, L D*
London Jews and British Communism 1935-1945 — *Srebrnik, Henry*
London Minimum — *Ypma, Herbert*
p The London Philatelist
London's Burning — *Stansky, Peter*
London's Dreaded Visitation — *Champion, J A I*
London's Women Teachers — *Copelman, Dina Mira*
Lone Cowboy — *James, Will*
The Lone Man — *Atxaga, Bernardo*
The Lone Ranger and Tonto — *Lansdale, Joe R*
c Lone Wolf — *Franklin, Kristine L*
The Loneliest Road in America — *Parvin, Roy*
y Lonely Girl — *Baer, Judy*
Lonely Hearts of the Cosmos — *Overbye, Dennis*
c The Lonely Lioness and the Ostrich Chicks (Illus. by Yumi Heo) — *Aardema, Verna*
The Lonely Other — *George, Diane Hume*
The Lonely Planet Boy — *Hoskyns, Barney*
Lonely, Sad and Angry — *Ingersoll, Barbara D*
Lonesome Standard Time — *Jennings, Dana Andrew*
y The Long Affair — *O'Brien, Conor Cruise*
y Long after Midnight — *Johansen, Iris*
Long Ago God Spoke — *Holladay, William L*
Long Distance — *Shirley, Aleda*
Long Distance Calls — *Margoshes, Dave*
A Long Fatal Love Chase — *Alcott, Louisa May*
The Long Fuse — *Cook, Don*
Long Gone — *Stuart, Dabney*
Long Gone Lonesome Cowgirls — *Dean, Philip*
The Long Johns — *Bird, John*

c Long Live Music! (Illus. by Chats Peles (Group of Artists)) — *Chats Peles (Group of Artists)*
c The Long, Long Letter (Illus. by David Catrow) — *Spurr, Elizabeth*
The Long Night of White Chickens — *Goldman, Francisco*
y The Long Pale Corridor — *Benson, Judi*
A Long Rainy Season — *Lowitz, Leza*
A Long Reach — *Stone, Michael, 1950-*
The Long Roll — *Johnston, Mary*
y The Long Season of Rain — *Kim, Helen*
y Long Shot — *Rud, Jeff*
c The Long Silk Strand (Illus. by Grayce Bochak) — *Williams, Laura E*
c Long, Tall, Short and Hairy Poems (Illus. by Stephen Lewis) — *McBratney, Sam*
The Long-Term Care Nursing Assistant Training Manual. 2nd Ed. — *Anderson, Mary Ann*
Long-Term Climate Monitoring by the Global Climate Observing System — *Karl, Thomas R*
Long-Term Greedy — *Lindskoog, Nils*
Long-Term Studies of Vertebrate Communities — *Cody, Martin L*
Long-Term Treatments of Anxiety Disorders — *Mavissakalian, Matig R*
Long Time Gone — *Brent, William Lee*
Long Tin Au My Day — *Tran, Qui*
The Long Trail Home — *Dunham, Tracy*
Long Van Tu Cua Thien Day Song — *Buu, Sao*
The Long Voyage — *Semprun, Jorge*
c The Long Wait (Illus. by Eugenie Fernandes) — *Wilson, Budge*
A Long Walk in Wintertime — *Purves, Libby*
A Long Walk to Church — *Davis, Nathaniel*
y Long Walk to Freedom — *Mandela, Nelson*
The Long War — *Kutulas, Judy*
Long Waves of Capitalist Development. 2nd Rev. Ed. — *Mandel, Ernest*
A Long Way from Home — *Grygier, Pat Sandiford*
A Long Way from St. Louie — *McElroy, Colleen J*
Longer Views — *Delany, Samuel R*
y The Longest Memory — *D'Aguiar, Fred*
The Longest Shadow — *Hartman, Geoffrey H*
The Longest Shot — *Eisenberg, John*
The Longing — *Asher, Jane*
The Longing for Home — *Buechner, Frederick*
y Longitude: The True Story of a Lone Genius Who Solved the Greatest Scientific Problem of His Time — *Sobel, Dava*
Longitude: The True Story of a Lone Genius Who Solved the Greatest Scientific Problem of His Time (Rintoul). Audio Version — *Sobel, Dava*
Longlining — *Bjordal, Asmund*
The Longman Companion to Britain since 1945 — *Cook, Chris*
r The Longman Companion to the Tudor Age — *O'Day, Rosemary*
c The Longman Guide to English Usage — *Greenbaum, Sidney*
y Longman History Project Germany 1918-45 — *Brooman, Josh*
y Longman Homework Handbook — *Gardiner, Alan*
Longman's Parent's Guides: Key Stages 1-3, GCSE and Key Stage 4 — *Wragg, Ted*
Longman's Parent's Guides: Pre-School Choices and Nursery Education — *Wood, Liz*
Longstreet's Aide — *Cutrer, Thomas W*
Lontano Da Casa — *Ferrucci, Franco*
c Loo-Loo, Boo, and Art You Can Do (Illus. by Denis Roche) — *Roche, Denis*
Look at Me — *Brookner, Anita*
y Look at My Ugly Face! — *Halprin, Sara*
Look at the Evidence — *Clute, John*
c Look at the Moon (Illus. by Barbara Garrison) — *Garelick, May*
y Look for Me by Moonlight — *Hahn, Mary Downing*
Look Great — *Kenton, Leslie*
r A Look into Tokyo
r The Look-It-Up Guide to Washington Libraries and Archives — *Bergheim, Laura*
Look, Listen, Read — *Levi-Strauss, Claude*
r The Look of the Century — *Tambini, Michael*
c Look Once, Look Twice (Illus. by Janet Marshall) — *Marshall, Janet*
c Look Out, Cinder! (Illus. by Eugen Sopko) — *Lachner, Dorothea*
c Look to the North (Illus. by Lucia Washburn) — *George, Jean Craighead*
Look Up for Yes — *Tavalaro, Julia*
c Look What I've Got (Illus. by Anthony Browne) — *Browne, Anthony*

Look What They've Done to the Blues — *Blackaby, Mark*
c Looking (Illus. by Barrie Watts) — *Walpole, Brenda*
Looking After — *Daniel, John*
Looking after Cage Birds — *Alderson, David*
c Looking after Yourself — *Levete, Sarah*
Looking Ahead — *Hogg, Frank N*
cr Looking at Art. Vols. 1-12 — *Cooke, Tim*
Looking at Death — *Norfleet, Barbara P*
Looking at Giacometti — *Sylvester, David*
c Looking at Our Lives — *Carlisi, Karen*
Looking at Pictures — *Armstrong, John*
Looking at Pictures — *Clark, Kenneth*
c Looking at Pictures — *Richardson, Joy*
c Looking at Pictures (Illus. by Charlotte Voake) — *Richardson, Joy*
Looking at Shakespeare — *Kennedy, Dennis*
y Looking for a Rain God and Other Short Stories from Africa — *Gordon, Ian*
Looking for a Soft Place to Land — *Salach, Cin*
c Looking for Angels (Illus. by Leslie Baker) — *Gregory, Valiska*
c Looking for Atlantis (Illus. by Colin Thompson) — *Thompson, Colin*
c Looking for Cinderella (Illus. by Charlotte Dematons) — *Dematons, Charlotte*
c Looking for Diamonds (Illus. by Nancy Mantha) — *Seabrooke, Brenda*
Looking for Flavour — *Santich, Barbara*
Looking for George, Love and Death in Romania — *Drysdale, Helena*
c Looking for Juliette — *Lisle, Janet Taylor*
c Looking for Papito (Sacre). Audio Version
Looking for the Mahdi — *Wood, N Lee*
Looking for the Other Side — *Cohen, Sherry Suib*
Looking for Trouble — *De La Billiere, Peter, Sir*
c Looking into My Body (Illus. by Simone Able) — *Nelson, Nigel*
Looking Out — *Gere, David*
Looking through Glass — *Kesavan, Mukul*
r Lookouts: Firewatchers of the Cascades and Olympics. 2nd Ed. — *Spring, Ira*
Looks and Frictions — *Willemen, Paul*
The Loom of God — *Pickover, Clifford A*
Loomis's Essentials of Toxicology. 4th Ed. — *Loomis, Ted A*
Loons — *Lang, Aubrey*
The Looping Handbook — *Grant, Jim, 1942-*
Loose Change — *Fulker, Tina*
Loose Sugar — *Hillman, Brenda*
Loosestrife — *Dunn, Stephen, 1939-*
Lope Garcia De Salazar: El Primer Historiados De Bizkaia 1399-1476 — *Aguirre Gandarias, Sabino*
Lorca, Valle-Inclan Y Las Esteticas De La Disidencia — *Greenfield, Sumner*
Lorca's Drawings and Poems — *Cavanaugh, Cecelia J*
Lord Acton's History of Liberty — *Watson, George, 1927-*
The Lord and His Prayer — *Wright, N T*
The Lord and the General Din of the World — *Mead, Jane*
Lord Burlington 1694-1753. Vols. 1-2 — *Carre, Jacques*
Lord Byron's Strength — *Christensen, Jerome*
Lord Churchill's Coup — *Webb, Stephen Saunders*
Lord Curzon — *Goradia, Nayana*
Lord High Executioner — *Engel, Howard*
y Lord, I Haven't Talked to You since the Last Crisis, But... — *Peterson, Lorraine*
Lord Jim — *Conrad, Joseph*
Lord Kito's Revenge — *Vira, Soma*
Lord Lyndhurst: The Flexible Tory — *Lee, Dennis, 1943-*
Lord North: The Prime Minister Who Lost America — *Whiteley, Peter*
Lord of Dark Places — *Bennett, Hal*
c Lord of the Animals (Illus. by Fiona French) — *French, Fiona*
Lord of the Dark Lake — *Faust, Ron*
Lord of the Kongo — *Forbath, Peter*
Lord of the Kongo (Caulfield). Audio Version — *Forbath, Peter*
Lord of the Rings — *Tolkien, J R R*
Lord of the Vampires — *Kalogridis, Jeanne*
c Lord of the Winds (Illus. by Helen Ong) — *Pearson, Maggie*
Lord Savage — *Coughlin, Patricia*
Lords of All the World — *Pagden, Anthony*
Lords of Misrule — *Gill, James*

Lords of Parliament — *Davis, R W*

y Lords of Sipan (McDonough). Audio Version — *Kirkpatrick, Sidney D*

Lords of the Ascendancy — *James, Francis G*

Lords of the Lebanese Marches — *Gilsenan, Michael*

Lords of the Seventh Swarm — *Wolverton, Dave*

The Lords of the Valley — *Hanners, LaVerne*

Lordship and Community — *Oestmann, Cord*

Lorena — *Bean, Fred*

Lorenza's Pasta — *De' Medici Stucchi, Lorenza*

Lorenzo De Zavala: The Pragmatic Idealist — *Henson, Margaret Swett*

Lorenzo Il Magnifico — *Bullard, Melissa Meriam*

Lorenzo Il Magnifico E Il Suo Mondo — *Garfagnini, Gian Carlo*

Lorine Niedecker: Woman and Poet — *Penberthy, Jenny*

Los Alamos — *Kanon, Joseph*

Los Angeles: Capital of the Third World — *Rieff, David*

Lose Fat — *Kenton, Leslie*

The Loser — *Bernhard, Thomas*

c Losers, Inc. — *Mills, Claudia*

Losing Asia — *Wallach, Bret*

Losing Control? — *Sassen, Saskia*

y Losing Ground — *Dowie, Mark*

y Losing It — *Fraser, Laura*

Losing Mogadishu — *Stevenson, Jonathan*

Losing the Weight of the World — *Kramer, Jonathan*

Loss of Innocence — *West, Chassie*

r Loss Prevention in the Process Industries. 2nd Ed., Vols. 1-3 — *Lees, Frank P*

y The Lost — *Aycliffe, Jonathan*

c Lost (Illus. by Paul Brett Johnson) — *Johnson, Paul Brett*

y Lost and Found — *Baer, Judy*

Lost and Found — *Moorehead, Caroline*

Lost and Found Lovers — *Kalish, Nancy*

c Lost and Found Stories Jesus Told

The Lost Art of Healing — *Lown, Bernard*

The Lost Art of War (Kelsey). Audio Version — *Sun, Pin*

The Lost Artwork of Hollywood — *Basten, Fred E*

The Lost Birds of Paradise — *Fuller, Errol*

The Lost Brother — *Bennet, Rick*

c Lost Cat (Illus. by David Goldin) — *Hardy, Tad*

A Lost Cause — *Laham, Nicholas*

The Lost Chronicles of Terra Firma — *Aguilar, Rosario*

c Lost Cities — *Goldenstern, Joyce*

Lost Cities of the Ancient Southeast — *O'Connor, Mallory McCane*

The Lost City — *Ehrenhalt, Alan*

y Lost Civilisations — *Millard, Anne*

The Lost Coast — *Nightingale, Steven*

Lost Cowboys — *Wangford, Hank*

The Lost Day — *Clarke, Judith*

The Lost Drum — *Weiner, James F*

Lost Earth — *Callow, Philip*

The Lost Fortune of the Tsars — *Clarke, William*

Lost Futures — *Grossfeld, Stan*

The Lost Gardens of Heligan — *Smit, Tim*

Lost Gold and Silver Mines of the Southwest — *Conrotto, Eugene*

The Lost Gospel — *Mack, Burton L*

The Lost Gospel of the Earth — *Hayden, Tom*

The Lost Gospel Q — *Powelson, Mark*

The Lost Grizzlies — *Bass, Rick*

Lost Highway — *Currey, Richard*

Lost Highway — *Guralnick, Peter*

The Lost History of the Canine Race — *Thurston, Mary Elizabeth*

Lost in a Labyrinth of Red Tape — *Schmid, Armin*

Lost in Music — *Smith, Giles*

Lost in North America — *Gray, John, 1946-*

y Lost in Place — *Salzman, Mark*

Lost in the Alps — *Cosey, R Cosey*

Lost in the Funhouse — *Barth, John*

Lost in the Mirror — *Moskovitz, Richard A*

c Lost in the Tunnel of Time (Illus. by Michael Bryant) — *Draper, Sharon M*

Lost in Translation — *Hoffman, Eva*

r Lost Japan — *Kerr, Alex*

Lost Keys — *Jones, Seaborn*

Lost Landscapes and Failed Economies — *Power, Thomas Michael*

y Lost Laysen (Fellows). Audio Version — *Mitchell, Margaret*

Lost Legacy — *Bates, Irene M*

c The Lost Locket — *Keene, Carolyn*

The Lost Lore of a Man's Life — *Boyles, Denis*

Lost Love — *Szold, Henrietta*

The Lost Lunar Baedeker — *Loy, Mina*

The Lost May Day — *Peltola, Pekka*

y The Lost Mine — *Grant, Pamela*

The Lost Museum — *Feliciano, Hector*

The Lost Notebook — *Joyce, James*

Lost Plays of the Harlem Renaissance 1920-1940 — *Hatch, James V*

The Lost Prime Minister — *Nicholls, David*

Lost Prince — *Feuerbach, Paul Johann Anselm*

The Lost Province — *McCarthy, Thomas*

Lost Puritan — *Mariani, Paul*

Lost Russia — *Brumfield, William Craft*

The Lost Scrapbook — *Dara, Evan*

The Lost Steps — *Breton, Andre*

c Lost Summer — *Feuer, Elizabeth*

Lost Talent — *Hanson, Sandra L*

c Lost Tales (Illus. by Gleb Botkin) — *Botkin, Gleb*

c The Lost Treasure of Captain Blood (Illus. by Cathy Gale) — *Stroud, Jonathan*

The Lost Weekend — *Jackson, Charles*

Lost Women, Banished Souls — *Cohen, Garnett Kilberg*

Lost Words — *Manguel, Alberto*

The Lost World — *Crichton, Michael*

The Lost World. Audio Version — *Doyle, Arthur Conan, Sir*

Lost Wright — *Lind, Carla*

y The Lost Years of Merlin — *Barron, T A*

Lotion Bullwhip Giraffe — *Lin, Tan*

c Lotions, Potions and Slime — *Blake, Nancy*

c Lots of Moms (Illus. by Shelley Rotner) — *Rotner, Shelley*

y Lotta's Progress — *Johnston, Norma*

c Lottie's Letter (Illus. by Peter Bailey) — *Snell, Gordon*

Lotus Notes 4 Plain and Simple — *Clayton, Rubert*

c The Lotus Seed (Illus. by Tatsuro Kiuchi) — *Garland, Sherry*

The Lotus Sutra — *Tripitaka. Sutrapitaka. Saddharmapundarikasutra. English*

Lotus Word Pro 96 for Windows 3.1 — *Fingerman, Daniel*

Lotus Word Pro 96 for Windows 95 — *Fingerman, Daniel*

Lotusland: A Photographic Odyssey — *Gardener, Theodore Roosevelt*

Lotusland: A Photographic Odyssey — *Gardner, Theodore Roosevelt*

c Lou. Vol. 3 — *Nath, Nathalie*

c Lou Gehrig: The Luckiest Man (Illus. by Terry Widener) — *Adler, David A*

Lou Grant — *Daniel, Douglass K*

c Loud and Quiet — *Challoner, Jack*

The Loudspeaker Design Cookbook. 5th Ed. — *Dickason, Vance*

c Louella Mae, She's Run Away! (Illus. by Rosanne Litzinger) — *Alarcon, Karen Beaumont*

Louis VIII: Le Lion — *Sivery, Gerard*

Louis XII — *Baumgartner, Frederic J*

Louis XIV — *Petitfils, Jean-Christian*

Louis XIV and the French Monarchy — *Lossky, Andrew*

Louis XVI — *Hardman, John*

Louis-Antoine Dessaulles: Un Seigneur Liberal Et Anticlerical — *Lamonde, Yvan*

Louis Armstrong: A Cultural Legacy — *Miller, Marc H*

The Louis Armstrong Odyssey — *Travis, Dempsey J*

Louis Bouilhet: Lettres A Gustave Flaubert — *Bouilhet, Louis*

c Louis Braille (Illus. by Helena Owen) — *Potter, Tessa*

c Louis Braille: The Blind Boy Who Wanted to Read — *Fradin, Dennis Brindell*

y Louis Brandeis: The People's Justice — *Freedman, Suzanne*

y Louis Farrakhan and the Nation of Islam — *Haskins, James*

Louis Ginzberg: Keeper of the Law — *Ginzberg, Eli*

Louis Loucheur and the Shaping of Modern France 1916-1931 — *Carls, Stephen D*

Louis Massignon: The Crucible of Compassion — *Gude, Mary Louise*

Louisa May Alcott on Race, Sex, and Slavery — *Alcott, Louisa May*

Louisa May Alcott Unmasked — *Alcott, Louisa May*

Louisa S. McCord: Poems, Drama, Biography, Letters — *McCord, Louisa S*

Louise Bourgeois — *Bernadac, Marie-Laure*

c Louise the One and Only (Illus. by R W Alley) — *Koehler-Pentacoff, Elizabeth*

c Louise's Gift (Illus. by Colin Bootman) — *Smalls, Irene*

Louisiana and Quebec — *Hero, Alfred Olivier*

Louisiana Fever — *Donaldson, D J*

The Louisiana Native Guards — *Hollandsworth, James G, Jr.*

Louisiana Purchase — *Hotchner, A E*

Louisiana Real and Rustic — *Lagasse, Emeril*

Louisiana Toxics Release Inventory 1994

The Louisville Slugger Ultimate Book of Hitting — *Monteleone, John*

Loukoum: The Little Prince of Belleville — *Beyala, Calixthe*

r Le Louvre: The Palace and Its Paintings. Electronic Media Version

Love across the Color Line — *Hanley, Alice*

The Love Affair as a Work of Art — *Hofstadter, Dan*

A Love Affair with Life and Smithsonian — *Thompson, Edward K*

Love after the Riots — *Herrera, Juan Felipe*

Love, Again — *Lessing, Doris May*

Love and Betrayal — *Maddox, Muriel*

Love and Death and Other Disasters — *Levin, Jenifer*

Love and Friendship — *Bloom, Allan David*

Love and Houses — *Leimbach, Marti*

Love and Ideology in the Afternoon — *Mumford, Laura Stempel*

Love and Justice — *Niebuhr, Reinhold*

Love and Longing in Bombay — *Chandra, Vikram*

Love and Nausea — *Wilson, David*

Love and Saint Augustine — *Arendt, Hannah*

Love and the Soul — *Williamson, Alan*

Love and Theft — *Lott, Eric*

Love and Toil — *Ross, Ellen*

Love and War between the Signs — *Keehn, Amy*

Love between Men in English Literature — *Hammond, Paul*

Love between Women — *Brooten, Bernadette J*

Love beyond Life — *Martin, Joel*

The Love Charm — *Morsi, Pamela*

Love Cries — *Blazey, Peter*

Love: Daily Prayers for Virtue — *Koch, Carl*

c Love, David (Illus. by Dan Andreasen) — *Case, Dianne*

The Love Department — *Trevor, William*

A Love Divine — *Ripley, Alexandra*

Love Enter — *Kafka, Paul*

Love-Fifteen — *Skarmeta, Antonio*

A Love for All Seasons — *Domning, Denise*

Love for Sale — *Leslie, John, 1944-*

y Love, Ghosts and Nose Hair — *Herrick, Steven*

Love Had a Compass — *Lax, Robert*

Love in a Blue Time — *Kureishi, Hanif*

Love in Another Town — *Bradford, Barbara Taylor*

y Love. In Cyberia — *Rayban, Chloe*

y Love Invents Us — *Bloom, Amy*

Love Is Blind — *Heiferman, Marvin*

Love Is Starving for Itself — *Roscoe, Patrick*

Love Is the Crooked Thing — *Abbott, Lee K*

Love Junkie — *Plunket, Robert*

y Love Kills — *Gorman, Edward*

The Love Letter — *Schine, Cathleen*

c Love Letters (Illus. by Lisa Desimini) — *Adoff, Arnold*

Love Letters — *Alers, Rochelle*

Love Letters — *L'Engle, Madeleine*

Love Life — *Relbstein, Janet*

Love, Life, and a Dream — *Roman, James*

Love, Lucy — *Ball, Lucille*

Love Lyrics of Ancient Egypt

Love Me Forever — *Lindsey, Johanna*

Love Minus One and Other Stories — *Harrs, Norma*

The Love of the Last Tycoon — *Fitzgerald, F Scott*

y Love on the Net — *Clark, Margaret*

Love Passion Action — *Dowling, Eric*

y Love Poems — *Giovanni, Nikki*

Love, Sex, and Murder — *Cameron, Sue*

Love Shack — *Van Lieven, Richard*

The Love Song of J. Edgar Hoover — *Friedman, Kinky*

The Love Song of J. Edgar Hoover (Whitener). Audio Version — *Friedman, Kinky*

Love Songs of the Irish — *Healy, James N*

Love Stories Are Too Violent for Me — *Viharo, William*

Love Story Classics (Linton). Audio Version — *Linton, J P*

Love Thy Neighbor — *Maass, Peter*

y Love to Water My Soul — *Kirkpatrick, Jane*

Love to Write! — *Barden, Cindy*

Love Warps the Mind a Little — *Dufresne, John*

Love, Work, and Death — *Toaff, Ariel*

Love You to Bits and Pieces — *Helfgott, Gillian*
Love Your Work and Success Will Follow — *Hirsch, Arlene S*
Lovejoy: A Year in the Life of an Abortion Clinic — *Korn, Peter*
Lovely — *Ronan, Frank*
Loverboy — *Belsky, R G*
Loverboys: Stories — *Castillo, Ana*
Lovers: A Midrash — *Ravel, Edeet*
Lovers, Clowns, and Fairies — *Tave, Stuart M*
Lovers of Cinema — *Horak, Jan-Christopher*
Love's Labor's Lost (Evans) — *Shakespeare, William*
Love's Madness — *Small, Helen*
Love's Virtues — *Martin, Mike W*
Love's Work — *Rose, Gillian*
Lovesick — *Mastretta, Angeles*
Loving an Imperfect Man — *Stern, Ellen Sue, 1954-*
y Loving April — *Burgess, Melvin*
y Loving Edith — *Tannen, Mary*
Loving Men More, Needing Men Less — *Sills, Judith*
Loving Time — *Glass, Leslie*
Loving Wanda Beaver — *Baker, Alison*
Loving Work — *Price, Frank*
The Low End of Nowhere — *Stone, Michael, 1950-*
Low-Fat and Luscious Italian — *Fuller, Kristi*
The Low-Fat Jewish Cookbook — *Levy, Faye*
Low-Fat Soul — *Nash, Jonell*
Low-Fat Vegetarian Cooking — *Kreifzman, Sue*
Low Flow Anaesthesia — *Baum, Jan A*
The Low-Income Consumer — *Alwitt, Linda F*
Low-Income Housing and the State in the Eastern Caribbean — *Potter, Robert B*
Low Life and Moral Improvement in Mid-Victorian England — *Shimmin, Hugh*
Low Temperature and General Plasmas — *Milosavljevic, M*
Low Tide in the Desert — *Kranes, David*
Low Water Slack — *Bowling, Tim*
Lowland Maya Civilization in the Eighth Century A.D. — *Sabloff, Jeremy A*
c The Loyal Cat (Illus. by Aki Sogabe) — *Namioka, Lensey*
Loyal Letters — *Houwen, L A J R*
Loyalty and Locality — *Stoyle, Mark*
The Loyalty Effect — *Reichheld, Frederick F*
y LSD — *Littell, Mary Ann*
LSE: A History of the London School of Economics and Political Science 1895-1995 — *Dahrendorf, Ralf*
The LSU College of Engineering. Vol. 1 — *Frost, Dan R*
Lu Yuan Qing Shi — *Nie, Hualing*
Luba Conquers the World — *Hernandez, Gilbert*
Lucca 1430-1494 — *Bratchel, M E*
La Lucha Contra La Pobreza En Costa Rica — *Trejos S., Juan Diego*
Luci Del Nord — *Petti, Maria Rosario*
Lucian Freud (Bernard) — *Freud, Lucian*
Luciano Fabro — *Grenier, Catherine*
Luciano Pavarotti: The Myth of the Tenor — *Kesting, Jurgen*
Luciano's Luck (Macnee). Audio Version — *Higgins, Jack*
Lucien's Story — *Kroh, Aleksandra*
Lucio Fontana Retrospektive — *Messer, Thomas*
Luck: A Secular Faith — *Oates, Wayne E*
y Luck in the Shadows — *Flewelling, Lynn*
y The Luckiest Girl in the World — *Levenkron, Steven*
Lucky! — *Marjoribanks, Augustus*
A Lucky American Childhood — *Engle, Paul*
c Lucky Duck. Book and Audio Version — *DeRubertis, Barbara*
c Lucky Hares and Itchy Bears (Illus. by Evon Zerbetz) — *Ewing, Susan*
Lucky Life — *Stern, Gerald*
The Lucky Ones — *Mortman, Doris*
c Lucky Stars — *Adler, David A*
c Lucky's 24-Hour Garage (Illus. by Daniel Kirk) — *Kirk, Daniel*
y Lucretia Mott: A Guiding Light — *Bryant, Jennifer Fisher*
y Lucy and Her Times — *Picq, Pascal*
c Lucy and the Pirates (Illus. by Matilda Harrison) — *Petrie, Glen*
Lucy Hutchinson's Translation of Lucretius: De Rerum Natura — *Lucretius Carus, Titus*
Lucy Leighton's Journey — *Lyons, Genevieve*
Lucy on the West Coast and Other Lesbian Short Fiction — *Caschetta, Mary Beth*
Lucy's Bones, Sacred Stones, and Einstein's Brain — *Rachlin, Harvey*
c Lucy's Christmas — *Hall, Donald, 1928-*

c Lucy's Rabbit — *Northway, Jennifer*
c Lucy's Summer — *Hall, Donald, 1928-*
r Luddens' Adult Guide to Colleges and Universities — *Ludden, LaVerne L*
y Ludovic — *Sernine, Daniel*
Ludwig Bemelmans — *Eastman, Jacqueline Fisher*
c Ludwig Van Beethoven — *Venezia, Mike*
Ludwig Van Beethoven, Fidelio — *Robinson, Paul*
Ludwig Wittgenstein, Cambridge Letters — *Wittgenstein, Ludwig*
Ludwig Wittgenstein: Wiener Ausgabe — *Nedo, Michael*
Lugosi: His Life in Films, on Stage, and in the Hearts of Horror Lovers — *Rhodes, Gary Don*
Lukang: Commerce and Community in a Chinese City — *DeGlopper, Donald R*
Luke — *Tuckett, Christopher M*
Luke and the Restoration of Israel — *Ravens, David*
Luke's Literary Achievement — *Tuckett, Christopher M*
c Lullabyhullaballoo (Illus. by Mick Inkpen) — *Inkpen, Mick*
The Lulu Magnet — *Condon, Matthew*
Lumb and Jones' Veterinary Anesthesia. 3rd Ed. — *Thurmon, John C*
Lumbee Indian Histories — *Sider, Gerald M*
The Lumber Industry in Early Modern Japan — *Totman, Conrad*
c Lumberjack (Illus. by William Kurelek) — *Kurelek, William*
Lumiere! Les Freres Lumiere Et Le Japon 1895-1995 — *Koga, Futoshi*
The Luminous Image — *Husband, Timothy B*
Luna, Luna — *Marzan, Julio*
Lunar Perspectives — *Keefer, Michael*
Lunatics — *Denton, Bradley*
c Lunch Bunnies (Illus. by Marylin Hafner) — *Lasky, Kathryn*
c The Lunch Line (Illus. by Jerry Zimmerman) — *Nagel, Karen Berman*
c Lunch Money and Other Poems about School (Illus. by Paul Meisel) — *Shields, Carol Diggory*
c Lungs — *Parker, Steve*
c The Lungs and Respiratory System — *Parker, Steve*
The Lure of Neptune — *Philbin, Tobias R, III*
Lure of the Links — *Owen, David, 1955-*
y Lure of the Sea — *Brown, Joseph E*
Lurking Feminism — *Dyman, Jenni*
Lush Life — *Hajdu, David*
Lusions — *Ragan, James*
Lustmord: Sexual Murder in Weimar Germany — *Tatar, Maria*
Lustmord: The Writings and Artifacts of Murderers — *King, Brian*
Luther's Legacy — *Trueman, Carl R*
Luthers Theologie In Ihrer Historischen Entwicklung Und In Ihrem Systematischen Zusammenhang — *Lohse, Bernhard*
y Luthien's Gamble — *Salvatore, R A*
Lutyens and the Edwardians — *Brown, Jane, 1938-*
The Luxury of Exile — *Buss, Louis*
Lyapunov Matrix Equation in System Stability and Control — *Gajic, Zoran*
Lyautey and the French Conquest of Morocco — *Hoisington, William A, Jr.*
Lydia's Impatient Sisters — *Schottroff, Luise*
y The Lying Game — *Baker, Jennifer*
Lying on the Couch — *Yalom, Irvin D*
c Lyle at the Office (Illus. by Bernard Waber) — *Waber, Bernard*
r Lyme Disease — *Barbour, Alan G*
c Lyn St. James: Driven to Be First — *Olney, Ross Robert*
Lyndon Johnson Confronts the World — *Cohen, Warren I*
y Lyndon Johnson's War — *Hunt, Michael H*
Lyrebird Rising — *Davidson, Jim*
The Lyric Journey — *Cahill, James*
Lyric of the Circle Heart — *Eastlake, William*
Lyric Philosophy — *Zwicky, Jan*
Lyric Texts and Lyric Consciousness — *Miller, Paul Allen*
The Lyrical Lu Xun — *Kowallis, Jon Eugene*
r The Lyrics of the Trouveres — *Doss-Quinby, Eglal*
Lysozymes: Model Enzymes in Biochemistry and Biology — *Jolles, P*
Lytton Strachey: The New Biography — *Holroyd, Michael*

M

c The M & M's Brand Chocolate Candies Counting Board Book — *McGrath, Barbara Barbieri*

M and Other Poems — *Peck, John*

c M.C. Higgins the Great — *Hamilton, Virginia*

M.I.A., or, Mythmaking in America — *Franklin, H Bruce*

y M Is for Malice — *Grafton, Sue*

M. Tulli Ciceronis De Officiis (Winterbottom) *Cicero, Marcus Tullius*

M. William Shak-speare, His True Chronicle Historie of the Life and Death of King Lear and His Three Daughters — *Shakespeare, William*

The M68HC11 Microcontroller — *Kheir, Michael*

r Ma Bibliotheque Poetique — *Barbier, Jean-Paul*

c Ma Dear's Aprons (Illus. by Floyd Cooper) — *McKissack, Pat*

Ma Shi De Dong Yu — *Acheng*

Ma Vie A Belles Dents — *Carne, Marcel*

Ma Xiangbo and the Mind of Modern China 1840-1939 — *Hayhoe, Ruth*

Maakhal Taavah — *Levitan, Nadav*

p The Mac

Mac Bible Goodies Pack. Electronic Media Version — *Gavenda, Victor*

The Mac Web Server Book — *Bell, Mark R*

Macabre — *Laws, Stephen*

The Macao/Hong Kong Trip — *Locklin, Gerald*

Macaronic Sermons — *Wenzel, Siegfried*

MacArthur's Undercover War — *Breuer, William B*

Macau: The Imaginary City — *Porter, Jonathan*

y Macbeth — *Kliman, Bernice W*

c Macbeth — *Whitesides, Nigel*

y Macbeth (Attica Cybernetics/BBC Education/ HarperCollins). Electronic Media Version — *Shakespeare, William*

Macbeth (Voyager). Electronic Media Version — *Shakespeare, William*

Macedonia and Greece — *Shea, John*

The Macedonian Conflict — *Danforth, Loring M*

Machado De Assis and Feminism — *Lisboa, Maria Manuel*

Machiavelli and His Friends — *Machiavelli, Niccolo*

Machiavelli and the Discourse of Literature — *Ascoli, Albert Russell*

Machiavelli in Hell — *De Grazia, Sebastian*

Machiavelli, Leonardo, and the Science of Power — *Masters, Roger D*

Machiavelli Nella Cultura Europea Dell'eta Moderna — *Procacci, Giuliano*

The Machiavellian Moment — *Pocock, J G A*

Machiavellian Rhetoric — *Kahn, Victoria*

Machiavelli's The Prince — *Machiavelli, Niccolo*

Machiavelli's Three Romes — *Sullivan, Vickie B*

Machiavelli's Virtue — *Mansfield, Harvey C*

Machine — *Belleto, Rene*

The Machine in America — *Pursell, Carroll*

The Machine in the Nursery — *Baker, Jeffrey P*

Machine Learning and Statistics — *Nakhaeizadeh, G*

p The Machineel Journal

Machinery's Handbook Guide. 25th Ed. — *Amiss, John Milton*

c Machines — *Bryant-Mole, Karen*

c Machines (Illus. by George Fryer) — *Kerrod, Robin*

Machines and Economic Growth — *McPherson, Natalie*

Machines and Thought. Vols. 1-2 — *Millican, Peter*

Machos, Maricones, and Gays — *Lumsden, Ian*

Machos, Mistresses, Madonnas — *Melhuus, Marit*

r The Macintosh Bible. 6th Ed. — *Judson, Jeremy*

Mackintosh's Masterwork — *Buchanan, William*

Macmillan — *Turner, John*

yr Macmillan Color Atlas of the States — *Mattson, Mark T*

c Macmillan Early Science Big Books — *Berger, Melvin*

r Macmillan Encyclopedia of Earth Sciences. Vols. 1-2 — *Dasch, E Julius*

r Macmillan Encyclopedia of Physics. Vols. 1-4

The Macmillan Government and Europe — *Tratt, Jacqueline*

r The Macmillan World Atlas

Macnab's Backache. 3rd Ed. — *McCulloch, John A*

A Macro Perspective on Technology Transfer — *Reddy, Allan C*

Macrocycle Synthesis — *Parker, David, 1956-*

Macrodynamics: Toward a Theory on the Organization of Human Populations — *Turner, Jonathan H*

Macroeconometrics: Developments, Tensions, and Prospects — *Hoover, Kevin D*

Macroeconomic Crises, Policies, and Growth in Brazil 1964-90 — *Coes, Donald V*

The Macroeconomic Environment — *Ghatak, Subrata*

Macroeconomic Issues and Policies — *Hossain, Akhtar*

Macroeconomic Management in Southeast Asia's Transitional Economies — *Montes, Manuel F*

Macroeconomic Policy after the Conservative Era — *Epstein, Gerald A*

Macroeconomic Policy and the Future of Capitalism — *Smithin, John*

Macroeconomic Policy in a World Economy — *Taylor, John B*

Macroeconomics and Monetary Theory — *Desai, Meghnad*

Macroeconomics and the Japanese Economy — *Yoshikawa, Hiroshi*

Macroeconomics and the Market — *Matthews, Kent*

Macroeconomics: Theories and Policies. 5th Ed. — *Froyen, Richard T*

The Macroeconomy: Private Choices, Public Actions, and Aggregate Outcomes — *McElroy, Michael B*

Macromedia Director 4 for Macs for Dummies — *Steinhauer, Lauren*

Macromolecular Interactions in Food Technology — *Parris, Nicholas*

Mad about Martha — *Rodriguez, Robert*

y Mad about the Boy — *Hooper, Mary*

Mad about the Seventies — *Geissman, Grant*

The Mad Among Us — *Grob, Gerald N*

Mad Amos — *Foster, Alan Dean*

Mad as Hell — *Lupica, Mike*

Mad at Your Lawyer — *Starnes, Tanya*

Mad Cows — *Lette, Kathy*

Mad Dogs and Scotsmen — *Hammond, Gerald*

Mad House — *Simon, Clea*

The Mad King — *King, Greg*

A Mad, Mad, Mad, Mad World — *Kramer, Stanley*

Mad Princes of Renaissance Germany — *Midelfort, H C Erik*

Mad River — *Beatty, Jan*

Mad Season — *Wright, Nancy Means*

Mad to Be Normal — *Laing, R D*

A Mad World, My Masters and Other Plays — *Middleton, Thomas*

c Madaket Millie (Illus. by Marcia Sewall) — *Weller, Frances Ward*

Madaline: Love and Survival in Antebellum New Orleans — *Edwards, Madaline Selima*

Madam Foreman — *Cooley, Armanda*

c Madam Sizzers — *Garland, Sarah*

Madame Arnoul — *Pancrazi, Jean-Noel*

Madame Blavatsky's Baboon — *Washington, Peter*

c Madame Boskey's Fortune Telling Kit (Illus. by Dana Cooper) — *Hall, Kirsten*

Madame Bovary (Pickup). Audio Version — *Flaubert, Gustave*

c Madame Doubtfire — *Fine, Anne*

c Madame LaGrande and Her So High, to the Sky, Uproarious Pompadour (Illus. by S D Schindler) — *Fleming, Candace*

The Maddest Idea — *Nelson, James L*

Made for Each Other — *Lanner, Ronald M*

Made in America — *Bryson, Bill*

c Made in China (Illus. by Andrea Fong) — *Williams, Suzanne*

r Made in Japan Ceramics Book II — *White, Carole Bess*

The Made Thing — *Stokesbury, Leon*

r Madeira — *Lipps, Susanne*

Madeleine Delbrel: A Life beyond Boundaries — *Mann, Charles F*

Madeline: After the Fall of Usher — *Kiraly, Marie*

c Madeline European Adventure. Electronic Media Version

The Madhouse Nudes — *Schultz, Robert*

Madison on the General Welfare of America — *Sorenson, Leonard R*

r Madison Township, Williams County, Ohio Cemetery Records (Inclusive to August 1995)

Madly in Love — *Barnstone, Aliki*

Madness and Modernism — *Sass, Louis A*

Madness in America — *Gamwell, Lynn*

The Madness of Kings — *Green, Vivian Hubert Howard*

Madonna and Marilyn Ad Nausea — *Lifshin, Lyn*

Madonna Anno Domini — *Clover, Joshua*

Madonna Poems — *Lifshin, Lyn*

y Madonna: The Rolling Stone Files — *Rolling Stone (San Francisco, Calif.)*

La Madre Teresa — *Chawla, Navin*

Madrid 1900 — *Ugarte, Michael*

r Madrid 1996 — *Hayward, Vicky*

The Madrid Qumran Conference. Vols. 1-2 — *International Congress on the Dead Sea Scrolls (1991: Madrid, Spain)*

The Madwoman of the Sacred Heart — *Jodorowsky, Alexandro*

Maestri del Disegno Nelle Collezioni Di Palazzo Abatellis — *Abbate, Vincenzo*

y The Maestro — *Wynne-Jones, Tim*

Magazine Beach — *Gannett, Lewis*

The Magazine Publishing Industry — *Daly, Charles P*

Magazines for the Millions — *Damon-Moore, Helen*

Magdalena Sunderin — *Faschinger, Lilian*

Magdalena the Sinner — *Faschinger, Lilian*

The Magdalenes: Prostitution in the Nineteenth Century — *Mahood, Linda*

Maggie: A Girl of the Streets — *Crane, Stephen*

Maggie: A Girl of the Streets and Other New York Stories (Bregy). Audio Version — *Crane, Stephen*

Maggie-Now — *Smith, Betty*

The Maggody Militia — *Hess, Joan*

Magi: Quest for a Secret Tradition — *Gilbert, Adrian G*

y Magic and Perception (Illus. by Linda Eisenberg) — *Friedhoffer, Robert*

c The Magic Bat (Illus. by Don Weller) — *Griffin, Geoffrey*

c Magic Carpet — *Brisson, Pat*

c The Magic Cornfield (Illus. by Nancy Willard) — *Willard, Nancy*

c The Magic Costumes (Illus. by Tracey Morgan) — *Lehrer, Jamie*

c The Magic Crystal (Illus. by Peter Joyce) — *Maisner, Heather*

y The Magic Daughter — *Phillips, Jane*

c Magic Dogs of the Volcanoes (Illus. by E Simmons) — *Argueta, Manlio*

c The Magic Dreidels (Illus. by Katya Krenina) — *Kimmel, Eric A*

c Magic Easter Egg (Illus. by Ernie Eldredge) — *Patrick, Ellen*

c The Magic Fan — *Baker, Keith*

c The Magic Fountain by HRH Princess Gloriana (Illus. by Philip Hopman) — *McGough, Roger*

y The Magic Globe (Illus. by Alan Baron) — *Maisner, Heather*

The Magic Harvest — *Camporesi, Piero*

y The Magic Hourglass (Illus. by Peter Joyce) — *Maisner, Heather*

c The Magic Hummingbird (Illus. by Michael Lacapa) — *Malotki, Ekkehart*

c The Magic in the Mirror (Illus. by Tony Kenyon) — *McKay, Hilary*

y Magic Johnson: Champion with a Cause — *Greenberg, Keith Elliot*

c The Magic Maguey (Illus. by Elisa Kleven) — *Johnston, Tony*

The Magic Mirror — *Baeten, Elizabeth M*

c The Magic Moonberry Jump Ropes (Illus. by E B Lewis) — *Hru, Dakari*

The Magic Mountain — *Mann, Thomas*

The Magic Mountains — *Kennedy, Dane Keith*

c The Magic of Mozart (Illus. by Costas) — *Switzer, Ellen*

c The Magic of Spider Woman (Illus. by Shonto Begay) — *Duncan, Lois*

The Magic of the State — *Taussig, Michael*

c The Magic Peach. Book and Audio Version — *Palazzo-Craig, Janet*

c The Magic Porridge Pot (Illus. by Emily Bolam) — *Ziefert, Harriet*

Magic Realism — *Angulo, Maria-Elena*

c The Magic Saddle (Illus. by Patricia Mullins) — *Mattingley, Christobel*

c The Magic School Bus Explores in the Age of Dinosaurs. Electronic Media Version

c The Magic School Bus Explores Inside the Earth. Electronic Media Version — *Cole, Joanna*

c The Magic School Bus in the Time of the Dinosaur — *Cole, Joanna*

c The Magic School Bus inside a Beehive (Illus. by Bruce Degen) — *Cole, Joanna*

c The Magic School Bus Inside a Hurricane (Illus. by Bruce Degen) — *Cole, Joanna*

c The Magic Schoolbus Gets Eaten — *Cole, Joanna*

c The Magic Shoes. Book and Audio Version

c The Magic Squad and the Dog of Great Potential (Illus. by Frank Remkiewicz) — *Quattlebaum, Mary*

c The Magic Telescope (Illus. by Larry Salk) — *Paul, Richard*

The Magic Thread — *Idemon, Richard*

c The Magic Toy Box (Illus. by Rodney Peppe) — *Peppe, Rodney*

Magic, Witchcraft, and Religion. 3rd Ed. — *Lehmann, Arthur*

The Magic World behind the Curtain — *Menta, Ed*

A Magical Christmas — *Graham, Heather*

Magical Realism — *Zamora, Lois Parkinson*

A Magical Universe — *Snider, Jerry*

The Magician's Tale — *Hunt, David*

El Magico De Salermo Pedro De Vayalarde: Primera Y Segunda Partes — *Salvo Y Vela, Juan*

c Magid Fasts for Ramadan (Illus. by E B Lewis) — *Matthews, Mary*

r Magill's Cinema Annual 1995

r Magill's Guide to Science Fiction and Fantasy Literature. Vols. 1-4

yr Magill's Survey of World Literature. Vols. 1-2 — *Magill, Frank Northen*

Magistrates of the Sacred — *Taylor, William B*

Magmatic Systems — *Ryan, Michael P*

The Magnates — *Crosland, Susan*

p Magnet: Real Music Alternatives

The Magnetic Field of the Earth — *Merrill, Ronald T*

Magnetic Fluids and Applications Handbook — *Berkovski, B*

Magnetic Mountain — *Kotkin, Stephen*

Magnetic Resonance Imaging and Computed Tomography of the Head and Spine. 2nd Ed. — *Grossman, C Barrie*

r Magnetic Resonance Imaging in Orthopaedics and Sports Medicine. 2nd Ed. — *Stoller, David W*

Magnetic Resonance in Perspective — *Brey, Wallace S*

Magnetic Stratigraphy — *Opdyke, Neil D*

Magnetische Fiktionen — *Barkhoff, Jurgen*

Magnetism: A Supramolecular Function — *Kahn, Olivier*

Magnetodynamic Phenomena in the Solar Atmosphere — *International Astronomical Union. Colloquium (153rd: 1995: Makuhari, Japan)*

The Magnificat: Musicians as Biblical Interpreters — *Terrien, Samuel*

y The Magnificent Wilf — *Dickson, Gordon R*

La Magnificenza Privata — *Tagliaferro, Laura*

c The Magpie Song (Illus. by Dan Williams) — *Anholt, Laurence*

Magume, Ou Les Ombres Du Sentier — *Katihabwa, Sebastien*

y Mahalia Jackson: Queen of Gospel Song — *Gourse, Leslie*

Mahatma Gandhi: An Apostle of Applied Human Ecology — *Khosoo, T N*

Mahler's Sixth Symphony — *Samuels, Robert*

Mahmud Shaltut and Islamic Modernism — *Zebiri, Kate*

The Maias — *Queiros, Eca De*

Maid in the U.S.A. — *Romero, Mary*

Maid to Order in Hong Kong — *Constable, Nicole*

c The Maiden of Northland (Illus. by Carol Schwartz) — *Shepard, Aaron*

y Maiden Speech — *Brown, Eleanor*

y Maiden Voyage — *Bass, Cynthia*

Maiden Voyage — *O'Brien, Judith*

Maidenhome — *Ting, Hsiao-Chi*

Maija Grotell: Works Which Grow from Belief — *Schlanger, Jeff*

Mail — *Medwed, Mameve*

Mail It! — *McElhone, Alice*

Maillol (Flammarion/Musees Des Beaux-Arts)

The Maimie Papers — *Pinzer, Maimie*

Maimonides and Palamas on God — *Papademetriou, George C*

Maimonides and St. Thomas on the Limits of Reason — *Dobbs-Weinstein, Idit*

The Main Corpse — *Davidson, Diane Mott*

The Main Corpse (Rosenblat). Audio Version — *Davidson, Diane Mott*

Main Developments in Trade

The Main Idea, Reading to Learn — *Skidell, Myrna Bigman*

Main Justice — *McGee, Jim*

The Main Philosophical Writings and the Novel Allwill — *Jacobi, Friedrich Heinrich*

Main Street (Caruso). Audio Version — *Lewis, Sinclair*

Main Street Amusements — *Waller, Gregory A*

Main Street Revisited — *Francaviglia, Richard V*

Maine Mining Adventure — *Stevens, C J*

r Maine Sea Fisheries — *O'Leary, Wayne M*

Mainframe to Client/Server Migration — *Butler, Janet G*

Mainline — *Christian, Deborah*

y Mainstream Mathematics for GCSE — *Graham, Duncan*

Maintaining Cultures for Biotechnology and Industry — *Hunter-Cevera, Jennie C*

Maintaining Energy in a Global Context — *Martin, William F*

Maintaining Family Ties — *Palmer, Sally E*

Mais T'As Tout Pour Etre Heureuse! — *Buron, Nicole De*

Maistre Studies — *Lebrun, Richard A*

c Maisy's Colors (Illus. by Lucy Cousins) — *Cousins, Lucy*

Maitre Ling and Autres Histoires — *Ackerman, Al*

Maitre Mussard's Bequest — *Suskind, Patrick*

Les Maitres De La Parole Creole — *Confiant, Raphael*

y Maizon at Blue Hill — *Woodson, Jacqueline*

Majestic Indolence — *Spiegelman, Willard*

yr Major Authors on CD-ROM. Electronic Media Version

Major Biological Processes in European Tidal Estuaries — *Heip, C H R*

r Major Business Organisations of Eastern Europe and the Commonwealth of Independent States 1995/96

yr Major Characters in American Fiction

r Major Companies of Africa South of the Sahara 1996

r Major Companies of Central and Eastern Europe and the Commonwealth of Independent States 1996/97

r Major Companies of Latin America 1996

r Major Companies of the Arab World 1996/97

Major League Losers — *Rosentraub, Mark S*

The Major Plays of Nikolai Erdman — *Erdman, Nikolai*

The Major Powers of Northeast Asia — *Kwak, Tae-Hwan*

Major Problems in American Foreign Relations. 4th Ed., Vols. 1-2 — *Paterson, Thomas G*

Major Problems in the History of the Italian Renaissance — *Kohl, Benjamin G*

Major Taylor: The Extraordinary Career of a Champion Bicycle Racer — *Ritchie, Andrew*

Major Theories of Personality Disorder — *Clarkin, John F*

r Major U.S. Companies. 3rd Ed.

c Make a Christmas Memory — *Kammrath, Julaine*

y Make a Difference — *Foster, Henry W*

c Make a Joyful Sound (Illus. by Cornelius Van Wright) — *Slier, Deborah*

Make a Zine! — *Brent, Bill*

Make Believe — *Mordden, Ethan*

Make-Believe Town — *Mamet, David*

Make It Safe

c Make It Work! Sound — *Haslam, Andrew*

y Make-It-Yourself Fair Projects — *Vecchione, Glen*

y Make Lemonade — *Wolff, Virginia Euwer*

Make Me an Idol — *Scholes, Katherine*

c The Make-Something Club Is Back! (Illus. by Ann Schweninger) — *Zweifel, Frances*

Make the Connection — *Greene, Bob*

c Make Way for Dumb Bunnies (Illus. by Dav Pilkey) — *Denim, Sue*

Makeovers from the Budget Gardener — *Gilmer, Maureen*

Maker of Saints — *Davis, Thulani*

Makers and Takers — *Contoski, Edmund*

The Makers of Modern Economics. Vol. 2 — *Heertje, Arnold*

Makers of Modern Science. Vol. 9 — *Newton, David E*

r Makers of the Piano 1700-1820 — *Clinkscale, Martha Novak*

Makiko's Diary — *Nakano, Makiko*

Making a Difference — *Kamboureli, Smaro*

Making a Medical Living — *Digby, Anne*

Making a Social Body — *Poovey, Mary*

Making Abortion Rare — *Reardon, David C*

Making America/Making American Literature — *Lee, A Robert*

Making and Breaking Governments — *Laver, Michael*

Making and Molding Identity in Schools — *Davidson, Ann Locke*

The Making and Unmaking of the Haya Lived World — *Weiss, Brad*

Making Capitalism — *Janelli, Roger L*

Making Capitalism Work — *Silk, Leonard*

Making Cities Work — *Gilbert, Richard*

Making Cocoa for Kingsley Amis (Cope). Audio Version — *Cope, Wendy*

Making College Count — *O'Brien, Patrick S*

Making Communicative Language Teaching Happen — *Lee, James F*

Making Democracy Work — *Putnam, Robert*

y Making Documentary Films and Reality Videos — *Hampe, Barry*

Making Ends Meet — *Edin, Kathryn*

Making Ethnic Choices — *Leonard, Karen Isaksen*

c Making Faces — *Butterworth, Nick*

c Making Faces (Illus. by James Marsh) — *Forward, Toby*

c Making Faces — *Russon, Jacqueline*

Making Foreign Policy — *Briggs, Philip J*

Making Furniture in Preindustrial America — *Cooke, Edward S*

Making Gender — *Ortner, Sherry B*

Making Greeting Cards with Rubber Stamps — *McGraw, Mary Jo*

Making Heirloom Toys — *Makowicki, Jim*

y Making History — *Culpin, Christopher*

Making History — *Fry, Stephen*

Making Hypermedia Work — *DeRose, Steven J*

Making Intelligence Smarter — *Greenberg, Maurice R*

Making It Big — *Isenberg, Barbara*

Making It in Country Music — *Faragher, Scott*

Making It New — *Geldzahler, Henry*

Making It Real — *Lecker, Robert*

Making It Real — *Yates, Denise*

Making It through College — *Persaud, Rajen*

y Making Jesus Lord — *St. Clair, Barry*

Making Malcolm — *Dyson, Michael Eric*

Making Managed Care Work — *James, Genie*

Making Men — *Nauright, John*

Making Men Moral — *George, Robert*

Making Money with Boats — *Edwards, Fred*

Making Monsters — *Ofshe, Richard*

y Making Moral Choices — *Miller, Mark C*

y Making Mosaics — *Dierks, Leslie*
Making Movies — *Lumet, Sidney*
Making Movies Work — *Boorstin, Jon*
Making Muslim Space in North America and Europe
  — *Metcalf, Barbara Daly*
Making Nature, Shaping Culture — *Busch, Lawrence*
The Making of a Blockbuster — *Degeorge, Gail*
The Making of a Chinese City — *Clausen, Soren*
The Making of a Choreographer — *Genne, Beth*
The Making of a Conservative Environmentalist
  — *Durnil, Gordon K*
The Making of a Country Lawyer — *Spence, Gerry*
The Making of a Country Lawyer. Audio Version
  — *Spence, Gerry*
The Making of a Heretic — *Burrus, Virginia*
The Making of a Japanese Periphery 1750-1920
  — *Wigen, Karen*
The Making of a Jew — *Bronfman, Edgar M*
The Making of a New Indian Art — *Guha-Thakurta,
  Tapati*
The Making of a Quagmire — *Halberstam, David*
The Making of a Social Disease — *Barnes, David S*
The Making of a Spy — *Lunan, Gordon*
The Making of an Afro-American — *Sterling, Dorothy*
The Making of an American Senate — *Swift, Elaine K*
The Making of an Avant Garde — *Kauppi, Niilo*
The Making of an Enterprise — *Alden, Dauril*
The Making of Anti-Sexist Men — *Christian, Harry*
The Making of Byzantium 600-1025 — *Whittow, Mark*
The Making of Citizen Kane — *Carringer, Robert L*
The Making of Detente — *Nelson, Keith L*
The Making of Early Medieval India
  — *Chattopadhyaya, Brajadulal*
The Making of Economic Policy — *Dixit, Avinash K*
The Making of Europe — *Bartlett, Robert*
y The Making of Evita — *Parker, Alan, 1944-*
The Making of Fianna Fail Power in Ireland
  1923-1948 — *Dunphy, Richard*
The Making of Foreign Policy in Russia and the New
  States of Eurasia — *Dawisha, Adeed*
c The Making of Goodnight Moon — *Marcus, Leonard S*
The Making of Modern Irish History — *Boyce, David
  George*
The Making of Modern South Africa — *Worden, Nigel*
The Making of Modern Tibet. Rev. Ed. — *Grunfeld, A
  Tom*
The Making of New World Slavery — *Blackburn,
  Robin*
The Making of Peter Grimes. Vols. 1-2 — *Banks, Paul*
The Making of Portuguese Democracy — *Maxwell,
  Kenneth, 1941-*
The Making of Quantum Leap — *Schuster, Hal*
The Making of Rubens — *Alpers, Svetlana*
The Making of Sacagawea — *Kessler, Donna J*
The Making of Saudi Arabia 1916-1936 — *Kostiner,
  Joseph*
The Making of Strategy — *Murray, Williamson*
The Making of Sweet, Sweetback's Baadasssss Songs.
  New Ed., Collector's Ed. — *Van Peebles, Melvin*
The Making of Textual Culture — *Irvine, Martin*
The Making of the Australian National University
  1946-1996 — *Foster, S G*
The Making of the French Episcopate 1589-1661
  — *Bergin, Joseph*
The Making of the Hawthorne Subject — *Easton,
  Alison*
The Making of the Indian Working Class — *Bahl,
  Vinay*
The Making of the Modern University — *Reuben,
  Julie A*
The Making of the Professional Actor — *Cairns,
  Adrian*
The Making of the Wren Library, Trinity College,
  Cambridge — *McKitterick, David*
The Making of Victorian Sexual Attitudes — *Mason,
  Michael*
The Making of Victorian Sexuality — *Mason, Michael*
Making Our Voices Heard — *Mandate Review
  Committee, CBC, NFB, Telefilm (Canada)*
Making PCR — *Rabinow, Paul*
Making Peace with the 60s — *Burner, David*
Making Plastic-Laminate Countertops — *Kimball,
  Herrick*
Making Plays — *Nelson, Richard, 1950-*
Making Project Management Work for You
  — *MacLachlan, Liz*
Making Room — *O'Flaherty, Brendan*
Making Schools Work — *Hanushek, Eric A*
Making Science Pay — *Alston, Julian M*
Making Sense in Law — *Jackson, Bernard S*

Making Sense of a Changing Economy — *Nell,
  Edward J*
Making Sense of Humanity and Other Philosophical
  Papers 1982-1993 — *Williams, Bernard*
Making Sense of Humor (Green). Audio Version
  — *Green, Lila*
Making Sense of New Testament Theology — *Adam, A
  K M*
Making Sense of Nietzsche — *Schacht, Richard*
Making Sense of Research — *Hek, Gill*
Making Sense of Your Freedom — *Felt, James W*
Making Sense of Your Teenager — *Kutner, Lawrence*
Making Silent Stones — *Schick, Kathy D*
Making the American Home — *Motz, Marilyn Ferris*
Making the American Self — *Howe, Daniel Walker*
Making the Cat Laugh — *Truss, Lynne*
Making the Corn Belt — *Hudson, John C*
Making the Grade
Making the Majors — *Leifer, Eric Matheson*
Making the Modern Reader — *Benedict, Barbara M*
Making the Most of Bathrooms — *Haig, Catherine*
Making the Most of Bedrooms — *Howes, Karen*
Making the Most of New Technology — *Imhoff,
  Kathleen R T*
Making the Move — *Stuart, Lettice*
Making the Numbers Count — *Maskell, Brian H*
Making the Patient Your Partner — *Gordon, Thomas*
Making the Radiation Therapy Decision — *Brenner,
  David J*
Making the Russian Bomb — *Cochran, Thomas B*
Making the Team — *Morris, Timothy, 1959-*
Making Things Perfectly Queer — *Doty, Alexander*
Making Time with IT — *Freedman, Terry*
Making Vancouver — *McDonald, Robert A J*
Making Waves — *Huntington, Anna Seaton*
Making Waves — *Reagan, Michael*
Making Waves — *Vargas Llosa, Mario*
Making Workers Soviet — *Siegelbaum, Lewis H*
Making Your Own Biscotti and Dunking Delights
  — *Meilach, Dona*
Makom Katan Im Deby — *Uziel, Meir*
Mal Horen, Was Noch Kommt/Jetzt, Wo Alles Zu
  Spat Is — *Schadlich, Hans Joachim*
c Mala (Illus. by Annouchka Gravel Galouchko)
  — *Wolf, Gita*
Malarkey — *Simonson, Sheila*
I Malavoglia — *Verga, Giovanni*
Malawi Demographic and Health Survey 1992
The Malay Dilemma — *Mahathir Bin Mohamad*
Malay Peasants Coping with the World — *Koninck,
  Rodolphe De*
The Malayan Trilogy — *Burgess, Anthony*
r Malaysia and Singapore Handbook — *Eliot, Joshua*
Malcolm MacDonald: Bringing an End to Empire
  — *Sanger, Clyde*
Malcolm Muggeridge: A Biography — *Wolfe, Gregory*
y Malcolm X — *Sagan, Miriam*
y Malcolm X: By Any Means Necessary — *Myers,
  Walter Dean*
Male Aesthetic Surgery — *Marchac, Daniel*
Male Authors, Female Readers — *Bartlett, Anne Clark*
Male Authors, Female Subjects — *Oostrum, Duco Van*
The Male Body — *Caine, K Winston*
Male Call — *Auerbach, Jonathan*
Male Colors — *Leupp, Gary P*
The Male Dancer — *Burt, Ramsay*
r Male/Female Language. 2nd Ed. — *Key, Mary Ritchie*
Male Impersonators — *Simpson, Mark*
r Male Infertility from A to Z — *Hollanders, J M G*
Male Menopause — *Carruthers, Malcolm*
The Male Survivor — *Mendel, Matthew Parynik*
The Male-to-Female Dictionary — *Shapiro, Susan R*
Male Wiersze 1976-1994 — *Niemiec, Maciej*
Malemort — *Glissant, Edouard*
y Malevich (Faerna) — *Malevich, Kazimir*
Malevolent Nurture — *Willis, Deborah*
y Malice Aforethought (Montague). Audio Version
  — *Iles, Francis*
y Malice Domestic 5
Malice in Wonderland — *Perkins, John*
Malice Prepense — *Wilhelm, Kate*
y Malign Neglect — *Tonry, Michael*
Mallard Fillmore...on the Stump — *Tinsley, Bruce*
Mallarme: La Poetique Du Theatre Et L'Ecriture
  — *Alcolombre, Thierry*
Mallarme: Poesie Et Philosophie — *Campion, Pierre*
Malle on Malle — *Malle, Louis*
r Mallorca — *Albert, Kristiane*
Malta, Britain and the European Powers 1793-1815
  — *Gregory, Desmond*
y Malu's Wolf — *Craig, Ruth*

Mama Blanca's Memoirs — *Parra, Teresa De La*
c Mama, Let's Dance — *Hermes, Patricia*
Mama Might Be Better Off Dead — *Abraham, Laurie
  Kaye*
c Mama Provi and the Pot of Rice (Illus. by Robert
  Roth) — *Rosa-Casanova, Sylvia*
c Mama's Birthday Surprise (Illus. by Felipe Davalos)
  — *Spurr, Elizabeth*
y Mama's Girl — *Chambers, Veronica*
c Mama's Perfect Present (Illus. by Diane Goode)
  — *Goode, Diane*
La Mamelouka — *Sole, Robert*
c Mammals — *Creagh, Carson*
c The Mammals — *Westrup, Hugh*
c Mammals Dominate the Earth (Illus. by Carles
  Castellvi) — *Llamas, Andreu*
A Mammal's Notebook — *Satie, Erik*
r Mammals of Nevada — *Hall, E Raymond*
Mammals of the Holy Land — *Qumsiyeh, Mazin B*
y The Mammoth Book of Dracula — *Jones, Stephen*
r The Mammoth Book of Oddities — *O'Neil, Frank*
The Mammoth Book of Pulp Fiction — *Jakubowski,
  Maxim*
The Mammoth Book of Werewolves — *Jones, Stephen*
r The Mammoth Dictionary of Symbols — *Julien, Nadia*
Mammoth Hunt — *Blashford-Snell, John*
Mammy and Uncle Mose — *Goings, Kenneth W*
Mamur Zapt and the Camel of Destruction (Prebble).
  Audio Version — *Pearce, Michael*
c The Man — *Briggs, Raymond*
c A Man and His Camel — *Bertini, Jo*
Man and the Maritime Environment — *Fisher,
  Stephen*
Man and Wife — *Oakley, Ann*
The Man behind the Book — *Auchincloss, Louis*
The Man behind the Smile — *Abse, Leo*
c A Man Called Raven (Illus. by George Littlechild)
  — *Van Camp, Richard*
The Man-Eaters of Tsavo — *Patterson, J H*
A Man for All Connections — *Handler, Andrew*
The Man from God Knows Where — *Carroll, Denis*
y The Man from the Other Side — *Orlev, Uri*
c Man Hunt — *Stanley, Malaika Rose*
y The Man in the Box — *Moran, Thomas*
The Man in the High Castle — *Dick, Philip K*
c The Man in the Iron Mask. Audio Version — *Dumas,
  Alexandre*
The Man in the Mirror of the Book — *Woodall, James*
The Man in the Moon — *Barrow, Andrew*
The Man in the Moon — *Godwin, Francis*
c The Man in the Moon and the Hot Air Balloon
  — *Delamare, David*
The Man in the Moone — *Godwin, Francis*
The Man in the Pulpit — *Rehmann, Ruth*
The Man in the Scarlet Robe — *McAteer, Michael R*
The Man in the Shadows — *Krampner, Jon*
A Man Lay Dead — *Marsh, Ngaio*
Man-Made Medicine — *Moss, Kary L*
The Man Made of Words — *Momaday, N Scott*
A Man of Secrets — *Stevens, Amanda*
The Man of the House — *McCauley, Stephen*
Man of the People — *Hamby, Alonzo L*
The Man on the Spot — *Long, Roger D*
Man Ray's Celebrity Portraits — *Ray, Man*
Man to Man — *Korda, Michael*
A Man Under Authority — *Mitchell, Reid*
The Man Who Came to a Village — *Tizon, Hector*
The Man Who Cast Two Shadows — *O'Connell,
  Carol*
The Man Who Cast Two Shadows (Burton). Audio
  Version — *O'Connell, Carol*
y The Man Who Counted — *Tahan, Malba*
y The Man Who Created Narnia — *Coren, Michael*
A Man Who Does Not Exist — *Fleming, Deborah*
The Man Who Grew Two Breasts and Other True
  Tales of Medical Detection — *Roueche, Berton*
The Man Who Listens to Horses — *Roberts, Monty*
c The Man Who Lived Alone — *Hall, Donald, 1928-*
The Man Who Loved God — *Kienzle, William X*
The Man Who Loved Women to Death — *Handler,
  David*
c The Man Who Painted Indians — *Plain, Nancy*
The Man Who Painted Women — *Newton, John Sefton*
The Man Who Rode the Tiger — *Mitgang, Herbert*
y The Man Who Was Poe — *Avi*
The Man Who Was Thursday — *Chesterton, Gilbert T*
Man without a Face — *Wolf, Markus*
y Man without Medicine — *Haseloff, Cynthia*
The Man without Qualities. Vols. 1-2 — *Musil, Robert*
Manadufur — *Olafsson, Einar*
Managed Care Contracting — *Conrad, Doug*

The Managed Care Handbook. 2nd Ed. — *Lyle, James R*

p Management (University of Split)

Management Accounting in Support of Manufacturing Excellence — *Jenson, Richard L*

Management Consulting. 3rd Ed. — *Kubr, Milan*

Management Education and Competitiveness — *Amdam, Rolv Petter*

Management for a Small Planet — *Stead, W Edward*

Management for Privatization — *Prokopenko, Joseph*

Management in Engineering. 2nd Ed. — *Freeman-Bell, Gail*

Management in the USA — *Lawrence, Peter*

Management, Labour, and Industrial Politics in Modern Europe — *Melling, Joseph*

The Management Methods of Jesus — *Briner, Bob*

A Management Odyssey — *Haas, J M*

The Management of a Multicultural Workforce — *Tayeb, Monir H*

The Management of a Student Research Project. 2nd Ed. — *Sharp, John A*

Management of Alcohol- and Drug-Related Issues in the Workplace

The Management of Burns and Fire Disasters — *International Conference on Burns and Fire Disasters (2nd)*

Management of Developing Economies in Transition — *Lin, Wuu-Long*

Management of Epilepsy — *Chokroverty, Sudhansu*

The Management of Ethnic Secessionist Conflict — *Navaratna-Bandara, Abeysinghe M*

Management of Federally Sponsored Libraries — *Missar, Charles D*

The Management of Forests on Reserve

Management of Health Information — *Mattingly, Rozella*

The Management of Human Resources in Chinese Industry — *Warner, Malcolm*

The Management of Mentoring — *Glover, Derek*

Management of Offenders — *Ireland. Dept. of Justice*

Management of Sediment — *International Symposium on River Sedimentation (6th: 1995: New Delhi, India)*

Management of Temporomandibular Joint Degenerative Diseases — *Stegenga, B*

Management of the Absurd — *Farson, Richard*

Management of the Absurd (Farson). Audio Version — *Farson, Richard*

The Management of the Severely Disturbed Adolescent — *Easson, William M*

Management of Trauma. 2nd Ed. — *Wilson, Robert F*

Management of Water Treatment Plant Residuals

Management of Wild Horses by Fertility Control — *Kirkpatrick, Jay F*

Management Policies in Local Government Finance. 4th Ed. — *Aronson, J Richards*

Management Redeemed — *Hilmer, Frederick G*

Managerial Finance in the Corporate Economy — *Ghosh, Dilip K*

Managers and Workers. 2nd Ed. — *Nelson, Daniel, 1941-*

Managers as Mentors — *Bell, Chip R*

r The Manager's Desk Reference. 2nd Ed. — *Berryman-Fink, Cynthia*

The Manager's Guide to Benchmarking — *Finnigan, Jerome P*

A Manager's Guide to Globalization. 2nd Ed — *Rhinesmith, Stephen H*

Manager's Guide to Software Engineering — *Pressman, Roger*

Managers vs. Owners — *Kaufman, Allen*

Managing Arms in Peace Processes — *Ginifer, Jeremy*

Managing Arms in Peace Processes: Cambodia — *Wang, Chien-Wei*

Managing Arms in Peace Processes: Croatia and Bosnia-Herzegovina — *Ekwall-Uebelhart, Barbara*

Managing by Values — *Blanchard, Kenneth H*

Managing Capital Flows in East Asia

Managing Change in Academic Libraries — *Branin, Joseph*

Managing Change in the Nonprofit Sector — *Bergman, Jed I*

Managing Chaos and Complexity in Government — *Kiel, L Douglas*

Managing Children with Problems — *Varma, Ved*

Managing Command and Control in the Persian Gulf War — *Mandeles, Mark D*

Managing Conventions and Group Business — *Hoyle, Leonard H*

Managing Cultural Differences. 4th Ed. — *Harris, Philip R*

Managing Derivative Risks — *Chew, Lillian*

Managing for Dummies — *Nelson, Bob*

Managing Global Chaos — *Crocker, Chester A*

Managing Global Operations — *Young, Scott T*

Managing Heart Failure in Primary Care — *Dargie, Henry*

Managing Information for the Competitive Edge — *Auster, Ethel*

Managing Internet Information Services — *Liu, Cricket*

Managing Language in Piers Plowman — *Rudd, Gillian*

Managing Legal Uncertainty — *Shamir, Ronen*

Managing Price Risk in the Pakistan Wheat Market — *Faruqee, Rashid*

Managing Prison Health Care and Costs — *McDonald, Douglas C*

Managing Risk — *Johnstone-Bryden, Ian M*

Managing Saskatchewan Rangeland. Rev. Ed.

Managing Squeegeeing — *Kelling, George L*

Managing Sustainable Development in South Africa — *FitzGerald, Patrick*

Managing Technical People — *Humphrey, Watts S*

Managing the British Economy in the 1960s — *Cairncross, Alec*

Managing the Change Process — *Carr, David K*

Managing the Data Warehouse — *Inmon, W H*

Managing the Global Commons — *Nordhaus, William D*

Managing the Global Supply Chain — *Schary, Philip B*

Managing the Information Ecology — *Hasenyager, Bruce W*

Managing the Interview — *Curzon, Susan Carol*

Managing the Practice — *Huntington, June*

Managing Traumatic Stress through Art — *Cohen, Barry M*

Managing Wilderness Regions — *Chaffey, John*

Managing without Traditional Methods — *Flood, Patrick C*

Managing Your Band — *Marcone, Stephen*

Managing Your Business with QuickBooks — *Rubin, Charles*

Managing Your Inheritance — *Card, Emily W*

Manana Es San Peron — *Plotkin, Mariano Ben*

c Manatees and Dugongs — *Harman, Amanda*

Manchester Pieces — *Driver, Paul*

Manchu Palaces — *Larsen, Jeanne*

y Mandarin Plaid — *Rozan, S J*

y Mandela: An Illustrated Autobiography — *Mandela, Nelson*

c Mandela: From the Life of the South African Statesman (Illus. by Floyd Cooper) — *Cooper, Floyd*

r Mandela's Five Years of Freedom — *Schoeman, Elna*

The Mandelstam and Der Nister Files — *Maggs, Peter B*

c Mandie and the Courtroom Battle — *Leppard, Lois Gladys*

Manet — *Pickvance, Ronald*

Manet and the Painters of Contemporary Life — *Krell, Alan*

Manet's Modernism — *Fried, Michael*

c Mangaboom (Illus. by Anita Lobel) — *Pomerantz, Charlotte*

Manganese Ores of Supergene Zone — *Varentsov, I M*

The Mangle of Practice — *Pickering, Andrew*

r The Mangum Star Weekly 1898-1900 — *Martin, Jodean McGuffin*

Manhattan Music — *Alexander, Meena*

Manhattan Nocturne — *Harrison, Colin*

Manhattan Nocturne (Rubenstein). Audio Version — *Harrison, Colin*

r Manhattan User's Guide — *Suisman, Charles A*

Manhattan, When I Was Young — *Cantwell, Mary*

Manhole Covers — *Melnick, Mimi*

Manhood at Harvard — *Townsend, Kim*

Manhood in America — *Kimmel, Michael S*

Mania and Literary Style — *Hawes, Clement*

c Maniac Magee — *Spinelli, Jerry*

The Manichaean Nous — *Tongerloo, Alois Van*

Manifest Your Destiny — *Dyer, Wayne W*

Manifesto for a New Medicine — *Gordon, James S*

p Manifold

Manifolds and Geometry — *De Bartolomeis, Paolo*

The Manikin — *Scott, Joanna, 1960-*

Manipulation on Trial — *Williams, Jeffrey, 1953-*

Manitoba Lottery Policy Review Working Group Report

y The Manitous: The Supernatural World of the Ojibway — *Johnston, Basil*

Manliness and Civilization — *Bederman, Gail*

Der Mann Mit Dem Rasiermesser — *Putik, Jaroslav*

Mann Und Weib, Und Weib Und Mann — *Frevert, Ute*

c Manners (Illus. by Aliki) — *Aliki*

Manners, Morals, and Class in England 1774-1858 — *Morgan, Marjorie*

Mann's Buddenbrooks and the Magic Mountain — *Ridley, Hugh*

Manny — *Rosen, Isaac*

Manor House — *Rense, Paige*

r I Manoscritti Polifonici Della Biblioteca Musicale L. Feininger — *Lunelli, Clemente*

r A Man's Guide to Coping with Disability

A Man's Life — *Boyles, Denis*

A Man's World — *Cose, Ellis*

A Man's World — *Humphries, Steve*

Mansfield and Vietnam — *Olson, Gregory Allen*

Mansfield College Oxford — *Kaye, Elaine*

Mansfield Park — *Austen, Jane*

Mansfield Park. Audio Version — *Austen, Jane*

The Mansion House — *Jeffery, Sally*

The Mansion on the Hill — *Goodman, Fred*

Mansions of Darkness — *Yarbro, Chelsea Quinn*

The Manson Impact Structure, Iowa — *Koeberland, Christian*

Mantle Remembered — *Creamer, Robert W*

Manual Del Perfecto Idiota Latinoamericano — *Mendoza, Plinio Apuleyo*

Manual for Clinical Psychology Trainees. 3rd Ed. — *Choca, James P*

r A Manual for Planning and Implementing the Living Standards Measurement Study Survey — *Grosh, Margaret E*

yr A Manual for Writers of Term Papers, Theses, and Dissertations. 6th Ed. — *Turabian, Kate L*

r Manual of Bulbs — *Bryan, John*

A Manual of California Vegetation — *Sawyer, John O*

Manual of Diagnosis and Professional Practice in Mental Retardation — *Jacobson, John W*

Manual of Environmental Microbiology — *Hurst, Christon J*

Manual of Gerontologic Nursing — *Eliopoulos, Charlotte*

Manual of GM-CSF — *Marty, Michael*

Manual of Oculoplastic Surgery. 2nd Ed. — *Levine, Mark R*

Manual of Psittacine Birds — *Beynon, Peter H*

Manual of Raptors, Pigeons and Waterfowl — *Beynon, Peter H*

Manual of Small Animal Neurology. 2nd Ed. — *Wheeler, Simon J*

Manual on Bookselling. 5th Ed. — *Whouley, Kate*

Manual on Elastic-Plastic Fracture — *Joyce, James A*

r Manuale Enciclopedico Della Bibliofilia

c Manuelita (Illus. by Sara Facio) — *Walsh, Maria Elena*

The Manufactured Crisis — *Berliner, David C*

r Manufacturing and Business Excellence — *Warnock, Ian*

Manufacturing and the Internet — *Mathieu, Richard G*

Manufacturing Bad Mothers — *Swift, Karen J*

Manufacturing Desire — *Berger, Arthur Asa*

Manufacturing for Export in the Developing World — *Helleiner, G K*

Manufacturing Inequality — *Downs, Laura Lee*

Manufacturing Science and Engineering 1996

r Manufacturing Worldwide. 1st Ed.

The Manuscript Found in Saragossa — *Potocki, Jan*

The Manuscript Library of Sir Robert Cotton — *Tite, Colin G C*

Manuscript, Print, and the English Renaissance Lyric — *Marotti, Arthur F*

Manuscript Sources of Medieval Medicine — *Schleissner, Margaret R*

Manuscripts and Government Records in the United Kingdom and Ireland Relating to Canada — *Wilson, Bruce G*

Manuscripts and the Text of the New Testament — *Elliott, Keith*

Manx Crosses — *Kermode, P M C*

Many Are Chosen — *Hutchinson, William R*

Many Faces, Many Voices — *Manna, Anthony L*

The Many Faces of Gay — *Kahn, Arthur D*

Many Faces of Mexico — *Ruiz, Octavio Madigan*

p Many Mountains Moving

c Many Rivers to Cross — *Lloyd, Errol*

Many Things to Tell You — *Heinzen, Thomas E*

The Mao Game — *Miller, Joshua*

y Mao Zedong: Founder of the People's Republic of China — *Stefoff, Rebecca*

Maoist Insurgency since Vietnam — *Marks, Thomas A*
Mao's Military Romanticism — *Zhang, Shu Guang*
Mao's Road to Power. Vol. 2 — *Schram, Stuart R*
Mao's Road to Power. Vol. 3 — *Mao, Tse-Tung*
The Map-Building and Exploration Strategies of a Simple Sonar-Equipped Mobile Robot — *Lee, David, 1956-*
y A Map of the World — *Hamilton, Jane*
A Map with Utopia — *Price, Jody*
c Mapas Y Globos Terraqueos (Illus. by Harriett Barton) — *Knowlton, Jack*
y Maphead — *Howarth, Lesley*
Maple: A Comprehensive Introduction — *Nicolaides, Roy*
r The Maple Handbook: Maple V Release 4 — *Redfern, Darren*
Maple Talk — *Adams, Steven G*
c Maples in the Mist (Illus. by Jean Tseng)
A Mapmaker's Dream — *Cowan, James*
y Mapp v. Ohio — *Persico, Deborah A*
Mappa Mundi — *Harvey, P D A*
Mapping American Culture — *Franklin, Wayne*
yr Mapping America's Past — *Carnes, Mark C*
Mapping Fate — *Wexler, Alice*
Mapping Multiculturalism — *Gordon, Avery F*
The Mapping of California as an Island — *McLaughlin, Glen*
The Mapping of New Spain — *Mundy, Barbara E*
The Mapping of the Heavens — *Whitfield, Peter*
Mapping the Faerie Queens — *Erickson, Wayne*
Mapping the Farm — *Hildebrand, John*
Mapping the Future — *St. John-Brooks, Caroline*
Mapping the Invisible Landscape — *Ryden, Kent C*
Mapping the Nation — *Balakrishnan, Gopal*
Mapping the Terrain — *Lacy, Suzanne*
r Mapping the UK — *Perkins, C R*
c Mapping the Unknown — *Chrisp, Peter*
Mapplethorpe: A Biography — *Morrisroe, Patricia*
Mapplethorpe Altars — *White, Edmund*
c Maps — *Bowles, Rachel*
c Maps — *Haslam, Andrew*
Maps and Civilization — *Thrower, Norman J W*
c Maps and the Landscape — *Greenlees, John*
Maps as Territories — *Turnbull, David*
Maps of Heaven, Maps of Hell — *Ingebretsen, Edward J*
Al-Maqasid: Imam Nawawi's Manual of Islam — *Nawawi*
Marabou Stork Nightmares — *Welsh, Irvine*
The Marabout and the Muse — *Harrow, Kenneth W*
Marathas, Marauders, and State Formation in Eighteenth-Century India — *Gordon, Stewart, 1945-*
Marauders — *Green, Tim, 1963-*
c The Marble Crusher (Illus. by Frances Thatcher) — *Morpurgo, Michael*
Marc Bloch, Sociology and Geography — *Friedman, Susan W*
Marcel Proust: Biographie — *Tadie, Jean-Yves*
Marcel Pursued by the Hounds — *Tremblay, Michel*
March of the Machines — *Warwick, Kevin*
c The March on Washington 1963 — *Andryszewski, Tricia*
The March to Monterrey — *Dilworth, Rankin*
Marchen Und Marchenforschung In Europa — *Roth, Diether*
y Marching through Georgia — *Kennett, Lee*
Marching to Glory. 2nd Ed., Rev. and Expanded — *McKinley, Edward H*
y Marching to Valhalla — *Blake, Michael*
Marching to Valhalla (Blake). Audio Version — *Blake, Michael*
Marco Polo, If You Can — *Buckley, William F*
c Marco's Monster — *Willis, Meredith Sue*
c Marduk the Mighty and Other Stories of Creation (Illus. by Sheila Moxley) — *Matthews, Andrew*
Margaret Atwood's Novels — *Staels, Hilde*
y Margaret Bourke-White: A Photographer's Life — *Keller, Emily*
Margaret Cape — *Dunbar, Wylene*
Margaret Cavendish: Sociable Letters — *Newcastle, Margaret Cavendish*
Margaret Fishback Powers Boxed Set — *Powers, Margaret Fishback*
c Margaret, Frank, and Andy — *Rylant, Cynthia*
Margaret Fuller: Visionary of the New Age — *Urbanski, Marie Mitchell Olesen*
Margaret Mead and the Heretic — *Freeman, Derek*
Margaret Mee: Return to the Amazon — *Stiff, Ruth*
Margaret Oliphant: Critical Essays on a Gentle Subversive — *Trela, D J*

Margery Kempe: A Study in Early English Feminism — *Neuberger, Verena E*
Margery Kempe's Dissenting Fictions — *Staley, Lynn*
Margin of Error — *Buchanan, Edna*
Marginal Cost Rate Design and Wholesale Water Markets — *Hall, Darwin C*
A Marginal Jew. Vols. 1-2 — *Meier, John P*
Marginal Worth — *Lewis, Lionel S*
Marginalia — *Larson, Doran*
Marginality and Dissent in Twentieth-Century American Sociology — *Galliher, John F*
Marginalized in the Middle — *Wolfe, Alan*
Margins — *Pena, Terri De La*
Margins: A Naturalist Meets Long Island Sound — *Buckles, Mary Parker*
Margins and Mainstreams — *Okihiro, Gary Y*
Margins and Marginality — *Tribble, Evelyn B*
c Margo's House — *Griffin, Peni R*
Marguerite Porete: The Mirror of Simple Souls — *Porete, Marguerite*
y Margy Misunderstood — *Smith, Margaret*
Maria Irene Fornes and Her Critics — *Kent, Assunta Bartolomucci*
y Maria Mitchell: The Soul of an Astronomer — *Gormley, Beatrice*
y Maria Montessori: Teacher of Teachers — *Shephard, Marie Tennent*
y Maria Tallchief: America's Prima Ballerina — *Tallchief, Maria*
Maria Theresa — *Crankshaw, Edward*
The Marian Icons of the Painter Fre Seyon — *Heldman, Marilyn E*
Marianne Faithfull's Year One — *Faithfull, Marianne*
Marianne Moore and the Visual Arts — *Leavell, Linda*
Marianne Moore: Questions of Authority — *Miller, Cristanne*
Mariano Matamoros, Segundo De Morelos Y Terror De Los LLamados Gachupines — *Escamilla Torres, Rogelio Javier*
c Marie: An Invitation to Dance (Illus. by Lyn Durham) — *Kudlinski, Kathleen V*
c Marie Curie — *Fisher, Leonard Everett*
Marie Curie: A Life — *Quinn, Susan*
y Marie Curie and the Science of Radioactivity — *Pasachoff, Naomi*
y Marie Curie in 90 Minutes — *Gribbin, John*
c Marie in Fourth Position (Illus. by Ian Schoenherr) — *Littlesugar, Amy*
Marie Sen — *Pham, Thi Hoai*
y Marijuana — *Schleichert, Elizabeth*
Mariken Van Nieumghen — *Decker, Therese*
Marilyn: Her Life in Her Own Words — *Monroe, Marilyn*
y Marilyn Monroe — *Woog, Adam*
Marilyn: Story of a Woman — *Hyatt, Kathryn*
Marilyn: The Niagara Photographs — *Carroll, Jock*
Marinades: The Secret of Great Grilling — *Barnard, Melanie*
Marine: A Guided Tour of a Marine Expeditionary Unit — *Clancy, Tom*
r Marine Animals of Southern New England and New York — *Weiss, Howard M*
Marine Biology — *Levinton, Jeffrey S*
Marine Conservation for the 21st Century — *Viders, Hillary*
The Marine Corps' Search for a Mission 1880-1898 — *Shulimson, Jack*
Marine Geology — *Erickson, Jon*
Marine Invertebrates of the Pacific Northwest — *Kozloff, Eugene N*
y Mario Andretti — *Prentzas, G S*
Mario Bellini, Architecture 1984-1995 — *Bellini, Mario*
c Mario Lemieux: Beating the Odds — *Hughes, Morgan E*
c Mario Scumbini and the Big Pig Swipe (Illus. by David Simonds) — *Brennan, Herbie*
p Marion Zimmer Bradley's Fantasy Magazine
c La Mariposa Bailarina (Illus. by Francisco N Mora) — *Ruvalcaba, Carlos*
Mariposa Blanca — *Mosley, Walter*
c Marisol and the Yellow Messenger — *Smith-Ayala, Emilie*
Marital Instability — *Veroff, Joseph*
Marital Power in Dickens' Fiction — *Lubitz, Rita*
The Marital-Relationship Therapy Casebook — *Weeks, G R*
Maritime — *Mews, Peter*
Maritime India in the Seventeenth Century — *Arasaratnam, Sinnappah*

Maritime Security and Peacekeeping — *Pugh, Michael*
r Marjorie Kinnan Rawlings: A Descriptive Bibliography — *Tarr, Rodger L*
Mark — *Hare, Douglas R A*
Mark — *Telford, W R*
Mark and Q — *Fleddermann, Harry T*
Mark Bunting's Virtual Power — *Bunting, Mark*
Mark: Images of an Apostolic Interpreter — *Black, C Clifton*
Mark My Words — *Twain, Mark*
y Mark of the Bear — *Schullery, Paul*
yr Mark Twain A to Z — *Rasmussen, R Kent*
Mark Twain and William James — *Horn, Jason Gary*
Mark Twain in the Company of Women — *Skandera-Trombley, Laura E*
Mark Twain: Letters from the Earth (Layne). Audio Version — *Twain, Mark*
Mark Twain Made Me Do It and Other Plains Adventures — *Jones, Bryan L*
Mark Twain on the Loose — *Michelson, Bruce*
Mark Twain's America — *DeVoto, Bernard*
Mark Twain's Letters. Vol. 4 — *Twain, Mark*
Mark Twain's Library of Humor. Audio Version — *Twain, Mark*
c Market! (Illus. by Ted Lewin) — *Lewin, Ted*
Market-Based Control — *Clearwater, Scott H*
Market Capitalism and Moral Values — *Brittan, Samuel*
c Market Day (Illus. by Holly Berry) — *Bunting, Eve*
c Market Days (Illus. by Marti Shohet) — *Jaffrey, Madhur*
Market Dominance and Antitrust Policy — *Utton, M A*
Market-Driven Health Care — *Herzlinger, Regina E*
cr The Market Guide for Young Writers. 5th Ed.
r Market Information 1995/96
Market Orientation in Food and Agriculture — *Grunert, Klaus G*
Market Power and Business Strategy — *Morris, David Joseph*
The Market Research Toolbox — *McQuarrie, Edward F*
The Market Revolution in America — *Stokes, Melvyn*
Market Smarter Not Harder — *Truax, Pamela Larson*
The Market Structure of Sports — *Scully, Gerald W*
The Market Tells Them So — *Mihevc, John*
Market Unbound — *Bryan, Lowell*
Marketing. 7th Ed. — *Evans, Joel R*
Marketing across Cultures. 2nd Ed. — *Usunier, Jean-Claude*
Marketing and Selling A/E and Other Engineering Services — *Gladden, Scott C*
Marketing Channel Management — *McCalley, Russell W*
Marketing for Nonprofit Organizations. 2nd Ed. — *Rados, David L*
Marketing Health Care into the Twenty-First Century — *Vitberg, Alan K*
Marketing in Asia Pacific and Beyond — *Taylor, Charles R*
Marketing Madness — *Jacobson, Michael F*
Marketing Management. 9th Ed. — *Kotler, Philip*
Marketing Modernism in Fin-De-Siecle Europe — *Jensen, Robert*
Marketing on the Internet. 2nd Ed. — *Mathiesen, Michael*
Marketing Straight to the Heart — *Feig, Barry*
Marketing to the Mind — *Maddock, Richard C*
Marketing Your Practice — *American Psychological Association. Practice Directorate*
Marketization, Restructuring and Competition in Transition Industries of Central and Eastern Europe — *Jackson, Marvin*
Markets and Mortality — *Dorman, Peter*
r Markets of the U.S. for Business Planners. 2nd Ed., Vols. 1-2 — *Conroy, Thomas F*
Markets, States, and Public Policy — *Zahariadis, Nikolaos*
Marking Our Times — *Quaill, Avril*
Markov Decision Processes — *Puterman, Martin L*
Markov Processes and Differential Equations — *Freidlin, Mark I*
r Marks' Electronic Handbook for Mechanical Engineers. Electronic Media Version
Marks of Civilization — *Rubin, Arnold*
r Marks' Standard Handbook for Mechanical Engineers. 10th Ed.
Marlon Brando: Portraits and Film Stills 1946-1995 — *Schirmer, Lothar*
c Marmaduke the Magic Cat — *West, Colin*

Title Index

c Marmouset Compte De Un A Dix — *Tourneur, Dina Kathelyn*
Maror: Les Regles Del Genere — *Sirera, Rodolf*
The Marquis De Sade's Elements of Style — *Pell, Derek*
Marranen in Madrid 1600-1670 — *Schrieber, Markus*
Marranisme Et Hebraisme Dans L'Oeuvre De Proust — *Hassine, Juliette*
Marrano as Metaphor — *Marks, Elaine*
Marriage Alliance in Late Medieval Florence — *Molho, Anthony*
r Marriage and Death Notices from the South Western Baptist Newspaper — *Kelsey, Michael*
The Marriage Bed — *Saville, Diana*
Marriage, Debt and the Estates System — *Habakkuk, John*
Marriage, Family, and Law in Medieval Europe — *Sheehan, Michael M*
The Marriage in the Trees — *Plumly, Stanley*
Marriage in the Western Church — *Reynolds, Phillip L*
y Marriage Is Murder (Bernard). Audio Version — *Pickard, Nancy*
Marriage, Kinship, and Power in Northern China — *Holmgren, Jennifer*
r Marriage Notices from Washington County, New York Newspapers 1799-1880 — *Jackson, Mary S*
A Marriage of Convenience — *Wills, Gale*
c Marriage of the Rain Goddess (Illus. by Clifford Alexander Parms) — *Wolfson, Margaret Olivia*
Marriage or Celibacy? — *Robson, John M*
Marriage, Property and Law in Late Imperial Russia — *Wagner, William G*
Marriage Shock — *Heyn, Dalma*
The Marriage Wager — *Ashford, Jane*
r Marriages of Amelia County, Virginia 1735-1815 — *Williams, Kathleen*
Married to the Church — *Hedin, Raymond*
The Marrying Kind — *Stirling, Jessica*
y Marrying Malcolm Murgatroyd — *Farrell, Mame*
Marrying Mom — *Goldsmith, Olivia*
Marrying Mom (Goldsmith). Audio Version — *Goldsmith, Olivia*
The Mars Effect — *Benski, Claude*
Mars Underground — *Hartmann, William K*
Marsalis on Music — *Wynton, Marsalis*
Marsigli's Europe 1680-1730 — *Stoye, John*
y Martha Black: Gold Rush Pioneer — *Martin, Carol*
c Martha Blah Blah (Illus. by Susan Meddaugh) — *Meddaugh, Susan*
c Martha Calling (Illus. by Susan Meddaugh) — *Meddaugh, Susan*
c Martha Washington Goes to War (Illus. by Dave Gibbons) — *Miller, Frank*
Martha's Ark — *Moore, Charlotte*
Martial in English — *Martial*
Martian Deathtrap — *Archer, Nathan*
Martin Aircraft 1909-1960 — *Breihan, John R*
Martin Buber: Prophet of Religious Secularism — *Moore, Donald J*
Martin Bucer: Reforming Church and Community — *Wright, David F*
Martin Dressler: The Tale of an American Dreamer — *Millhauser, Steven*
A Martin Genealogy Tied to the History of Germanna, Virginia — *Martin, William A, 1946-*
r Martin Heidegger II: A Bibliography — *Nordquist, Joan*
Martin Luther: Faith in Christ and the Gospel — *Gritsch, Eric W*
c Martin Luther King, Jr., Leader for Civil Rights — *Schuman, Michael*
Martin Luther Und Die Reformation In Ostdeutschland Und Sudosteuropa — *Hutter, Ulrich*
Martin Luthers Kreuzestheologie — *Blaumeiser, Hubertus*
Martin Salander: Politik Und Poesie In Gottfried Kellers Grunderzeitroman — *Graef, Eva*
y Martina — *Blue, Adrianne*
c Martine Chez Tante Lucie — *Delahaye, Gilbert*
Martinique, Charmeuse De Serpents — *Breton, Andre*
c Martin's Mice (Illus. by Jez Alborough) — *King-Smith, Dick*
The Martinsville Seven — *Rise, Eric W*
Marton Partjelzo Fazik — *Hamvai, Kornel*
Martyrdom and Rome — *Bowersock, G W*
Martyrdom and the Politics of Religion — *Peterson, Anna Lisa*
Martyrs: Contemporary Writers on Modern Lives of Faith — *Bergman, Susan*
The Martyrs of Cordoba — *Coope, Jessica A*

c Marushka and the Month Brothers (Illus. by Anna Vojtech) — *Vojtech, Anna*
y Marvel Universe — *Sanderson, Peter*
The Marvellous Land of Snergs — *Wyke-Smith, E A*
c The Marvelous Market on Mermaid (Illus. by Maryann Kovalski) — *Melmed, Laura Krauss*
c The Marvelous Maze (Illus. by Patricia Dewitt-Grush) — *Schur, Maxine Rose*
c The Marvelous Toy (Illus. by Elizabeth Sayles) — *Paxton, Tom*
Marvels — *Busiek, Kurt*
c Marvin and the Mean Words (Illus. by Blanche Sims) — *Kline, Suzy*
Marx and Non-Equilibrium Economics — *Freeman, Alan*
Marx, Deceased — *Djerassi, Carl*
Marx, Durkheim, Weber — *Morrison, K*
The Marx Family Saga — *Goytisolo, Juan*
Marx, Hayek, and Utopia — *Sciabarra, Chris M*
Marx Toys — *Pinsky, Maxine A*
Marxian Socialism in the United States — *Bell, Daniel*
Marxism and Human Sociobiology — *Chang, Po-Shu*
Marxism and the City — *Katznelson, Ira*
Marxism and the Leap to the Kingdom of Freedom — *Walicki, Andrzej*
A Marxist Reading of Fuentes, Vargas Llosa and Puig — *Duran, Victor Manuel*
c Mary Alice Peale, Philadelphia 1777 — *Duey, Kathleen*
c Mary and Martha (Illus. by Cat Bowman Smith) — *Figley, Marty Rhodes*
A Mary Austin Reader — *Austin, Mary Hunter*
Mary Barton — *Gaskell, Elizabeth*
Mary Berry's Complete Cookbook — *Berry, Mary*
c Mary Carter Smith, African American Storyteller — *Hajdusiewicz, Babs Bell*
Mary Curzon — *Nicolson, Nigel*
Mary Emmerling's New Country Collecting — *Emmerling, Mary*
Mary Engelbreit: The Art and the Artist — *Regan, Patrick*
Mary Garden — *Turnbull, Michael*
Mary: Glimpses of the Mother of Jesus — *Gaventa, Beverly Roberts*
Mary Jane: Living through Anorexia and Bulimia Nervosa — *Robinson, Sancia*
y Mary Lincoln's Dressmaker — *Rutberg, Becky*
Mary Magdalen: Myth and Metaphor — *Haskins, Susan*
Mary Magdalene and Many Others — *Ricci, Carla*
Mary Magdalene in the New Testament Gospels and Early Tradition — *Atwood, Richard*
c Mary Margaret's Tree (Illus. by Blair Drawson) — *Drawson, Blair*
Mary Newcomb — *Andreae, Christopher*
c Mary: The Mother of Jesus (Illus. by Tomie De Paola) — *De Paola, Tomie*
Mary through the Centuries — *Pelikan, Jaroslav*
y Mary Tyler Moore — *Finn, Margaret L*
A Mary Wilkins Freeman Reader — *Freeman, Mary Wilkins*
y Mary Wolf — *Grant, Cynthia D*
Mary Wollstonecraft and the Language of Sensibility — *Conger, Syndy McMillen*
c Mary Wore Her Red Dress and Henry Wore His Green Sneakers — *Peek, Mary*
c Marya's Emmets — *Cooper, Claire*
Maryland Freedom Papers. Vol. 1 — *Hynson, Jerry M*
Maryland: The South's First Casualty — *Talbert, Bart Rhett*
Mary's Miracles and Prophecies — *Shaw, Connie*
Mas Alla De La Isla
Mas Alla Del Puente — *Bonomini, Angel*
r Masaccio — *Spike, John T*
Masacres De La Selva — *Falla, Ricardo*
The Masada Myth — *Ben-Yehuda, Nachman*
Masada: The Yigael Yadin Excavations 1963-1965. Vols. 1-5 — *Aviram, J*
c Masai and I (Illus. by Nancy Carpenter) — *Kroll, Virginia*
Masaryk A Benes Ve Svych Dopisech Z Doby Parizskych Mirovych Jednani V Roce 1919. Vols. 1-2 — *Masaryk, T G*
Maschinen Fur Die Massenfertigung — *Ruby, Jurgen*
The Masculine Marine — *Zeeland, Steven*
The Masculine Masquerade — *Perchuk, Andrew*
Masculinities — *Connell, R W*
Masculinities in Organizations — *Cheng, Cliff*
Masculinities in Victorian Painting — *Kestner, Joseph A*

Masculinity and the British Organization Man since 1945 — *Roper, Michael*
Masculinity in Crisis — *Horrocks, Roger*
Masculinity, Law, and the Family — *Collier, Richard*
Mask Arts of Mexico — *Lechuga, Ruth D*
The Mask of Enlightenment — *Rosen, Stanley*
A Mask of Stone — *Scanlon, Tony*
Mask of the Sorcerer — *Schweitzer, Darrell*
Masked Performance — *Emigh, John*
c Masks — *Doney, Meryl*
c Masks! — *Flanagan, Alice K*
y Masks — *Hatrick, Gloria*
c Masks: From Countries around the World — *Frank, Vivien*
Masks of Difference — *Richards, David, 1953-*
The Masks of Hamlet — *Rosenberg, Marvin*
The Masks of Menander — *Wiles, David*
Masolino Da Panicale — *Roberts, Perri Lee*
Mason and Dixon — *Pynchon, Thomas*
Mason's Coin and Stamp Collector's Magazine. Vols. 1-2
y Mason's Retreat — *Tilghman, Christopher*
Mason's Retreat (Long). Audio Version — *Tilghman, Christopher*
Das Masoretische Und Alexandrinische Sondergut Des Jeremiabuches — *Stipp, Hermann-Josef*
Masquerade — *Hoff, B J*
Masquerade — *Lynds, Gayle*
Mass and Charge Transport in Ceramics — *Koumoto, Kunihito*
Mass Culture and Modernism in Egypt — *Armbrust, Walter*
Mass Enlightenment — *Simon, Julia*
The Mass Flights of Italo Balbo — *Lana, Robert E*
Mass Hate — *Kressel, Neil J*
Mass Immigration and the National Interest. 2nd Ed. — *Briggs, Vernon M*
Mass Media and Environmental Conflict — *Neuzil, Mark*
Mass Media and Popular Culture, Version 2 — *Duncan, Barry*
Mass Media and Tiananmen Square — *He, Zhou*
Mass Media for the Nineties — *De Beer, Arrie S*
Mass Media in the Middle East — *Kamalipour, Yahya R*
Mass Media, Modernity, and Development — *Kazan, Fayad E*
Mass Mediauras — *Weber, Samuel*
Mass Migration in Europe — *King, Russell*
The Mass Ornament — *Kracauer, Siegfried*
Mass-Participatory Economy. Rev. Ed. — *Kim, Dae Jung*
Mass Politics in the People's Republic — *Liu, Alan P L*
Mass Privatization in Central and Eastern Europe and the Former Soviet Union — *Lieberman, Ira W*
Mass Production, the Stock Market Crash, and the Great Depression — *Beaudreau, Bernard C*
The Mass Psychology of Ethnonationalism — *Kecmanovic, Dusan*
Mass Resistance in Kashmir — *Amin, Tahir*
Mass Spectrometry for Chemists and Biochemists. 2nd Ed. — *Johnstone, Robert A W*
Mass Spectrometry of Soils — *Boutton, Thomas W*
r Massachusetts and Maine Families in the Ancestry of Walter Goodwin Davis 1885-1966. Vols. 1-3 — *Davis, Walter Goodwin*
r Massachusetts Community Profiles. Vols. 1-5
Massachusetts Congregationalist Political Thought 1760-1790 — *Kuehne, Dale S*
The Massachusetts Historical Society — *Tucker, Louis Leonard*
Massenet: A Chronicle of His Life and Times — *Irvine, Demar*
Masted Structures in Architecture — *Harris, James B*
Master and Fool — *Jones, J V*
The Master and Minerva — *Solterer, Helen*
The Master Builders — *Blake, Peter*
Master Builders of Modern Psychology — *Keehn, J D*
c Master Bun the Bakers' Boy (Illus. by Fritz Wegner) — *Ahlberg, Allan*
Master Dogen's Shobogenzo. Vol. 2 — *Dogen*
Master Drawings Rediscovered — *Ilatovskaya, Tatiana*
The Master Letters — *Brock-Broido, Lucie*
c Master Money the Millionaire (Illus. by Andre Amstutz) — *Ahlberg, Allan*
Master of Death — *Camille, Michael*
The Master of Petersburg — *Coetzee, J M*
y The Master of Petersburg (Case). Audio Version — *Coetzee, J M*
A Master of Surprise — *Juel, Donald H*

c Master Salt the Sailors' Son (Illus. by Andre Amstutz)
— *Ahlberg, Allan*

Master Tung's Western Chamber Romance — *Tung, Chieh-Yuan*

Mastering AS/400 Performance — *Arnold, Alan*

Mastering British Politics — *Forman, F N*

r Mastering Italian Vocabulary — *Feinler-Torriani, Luciana*

Mastering Miracles — *Liu, Hong*

Mastering Network Management — *Swisher, Valerie M*

Mastering Prolog — *Lucas, Robert J*

Mastering Slavery — *Fleischner, Jennifer*

Mastering Space — *Agnew, John*

r Mastering Spanish Vocabulary — *Navarro, Jose Maria*

r Mastering the Internet. 2nd Ed. — *Cady, Glee*

Mastering the Sky — *Harrison, James P*

Mastering the Zone — *Sears, Barry*

Mastering the Zone (Sears). Audio Version — *Sears, Barry*

Mastering WordPerfect 7 for Windows 95 — *Simpson, Alan*

The Masterless Men — *Mayo, J K*

Masterpiece of Murder — *Kruger, Mary*

Masterpieces in Little — *Lloyd, Christopher, 1945-*

Masterpieces of American Indian Art — *Vincent, Gilbert Tapley*

r Masterplots II: Short Story Series. Vols. 7-10
— *Magill, Frank Northen*

yr Masterplots: 1,801 Plot Stories and Critical Evaluations of the World's Finest Literature. Rev. 2nd Ed., Vols. 1-12 — *Magill, Frank Northen*

Masters and Managers — *Sullivan, Norma*

Masters and Miniatures — *Congress on Medieval Manuscript Illumination in the Northern Netherlands (1989: Utrecht, Netherlands)*

Masters of Battle — *Wilcox, John*

Masters of Bedlam — *Scull, Andrew*

Masters of Deception — *Mizell, Louis R, Jr.*

Masters of English Landscape — *Meyer, Laure*

Masters of Illusion — *Caufield, Catherine*

The Masters of Meditation and Miracles — *Thondup, Tulku*

Masters of Small Worlds — *McCurry, Stephanie*

The Masters of the Spirit — *Fisher, Anne Kinsman*

The Masters of Truth in Archaic Greece — *Detienne, Marcel*

Masters of War — *Buzzanco, Robert*

The Masters Revealed — *Johnson, K Paul*

Masterworks in Berlin — *Eisler, Colin*

Masterworks in Lithography — *Weston, William*

Masterworks of Asian Literature in Comparative Perspective — *Miller, Barbara Stoler*

Masterworks of Latin American Short Fiction — *Canfield, Cass, Jr.*

Mastery and Escape — *Brooker, Jewel Spears*

c The Mastodon Mystery — *Perkins, Dorothy*

The Matachines Dance — *Rodriguez, Sylvia*

Matadorens Hand — *Carling, Finn*

Matando Dinosaurios Con Tirachinas — *Maestre, Pedro*

c Mateo Y Los Reyes Magos (Illus. by Alberto Urdiales) — *Alonso, Fernando*

Material Christianity — *McDannell, Colleen*

Material Concerns — *Jackson, Tim*

Material Culture and People's Art among Norwegians in America — *Nelson, Marion J*

p Material for Thought

Material Girls — *Walters, Suzanna Danuta*

Material Witness — *Tanenbaum, Robert K*

y Material World — *Menzel, Peter*

Material World. Electronic Media Version — *Menzel, Peter*

A Materialist Critique of English Romantic Drama — *Watkins, Daniel P*

c Materials — *Bryant-Mole, Karen*

y Materials — *Stone, Philip*

Materials for Optoelectronics — *Quillec, Maurice*

Materials Reliability in Microelectronics VI

r Materials Research Centres. 6th Ed.

Materials Selection for Hydrocarbon and Chemical Plants — *Hansen, David A*

Materials Theory, Simulations, and Parallel Algorithms — *Kaxiras, Efthimios*

Maternal Ethics and Other Slave Moralities — *Willett, Cynthia*

Maternal Justice — *Freedman, Estelle B*

c Math-a-Magic (Illus. by Ray Brockel) — *White, Laurence B*

y Math and Logic Puzzles for PC Enthusiasts — *Clessa, J J*

c The Math Chef (Illus. by Tina Cash-Walsh) — *D'Amico, Joan*

y Math Curse (Illus. by Lane Smith) — *Scieszka, Jon*

c Math in the Bath and Other Fun Places, Too! — *Atherly, Sara*

Math into LATEX — *Grotzes, George*

c Math Logic Puzzles — *Smith, Kurt*

r Math on File — *Day, Trevor*

Math Solutions — *Phillips, Jan*

r The Math Teacher's Book of Lists — *Muschla, Judith A*

c Math Tricks, Puzzles and Games — *Blum, Raymond*

Math without Fear — *Martinez, Joseph G R*

The Mathematica Book. 3rd Ed. — *Wolfram, Stephen*

Mathematica in Theoretical Physics — *Baumann, Gerd*

r Mathematical Algorithms in Visual Basic for Scientists and Engineers — *Shammas, Namir C*

Mathematical and Numerical Modelling in Electrical Engineering Theory and Applications — *Krizek, Michal*

The Mathematical Career of Pierre De Fermat 1601-1665. 2nd Ed. — *Mahoney, Michael Sean*

y Mathematical Challenge — *Gardiner, Tony*

y Mathematical Circles — *Genkin, S A*

Mathematical Cranks — *Underwood, Dudley*

Mathematical Encounters of the Second Kind — *Davis, Philip J*

Mathematical Go — *Berlekamp, Elwyn*

Mathematical Methods for Geo-Electromagnetic Induction — *Weaver, J T*

Mathematical Methods for Scientists and Engineers — *Kahn, Peter B*

Mathematical Methods in Artificial Intelligence — *Bender, Edward A*

Mathematical Methods in Biomedical Image Analysis — *Workshop on Mathematical Methods in Biomedical Image Analysis (1996: San Francisco, Calif.)*

p Mathematical Methods of Operations Research

Mathematical Modeling and Numerical Techniques in Drying Technology — *Turner, Ian*

y Mathematical Modelling — *Burghes, David*

Mathematical Models for Structural Reliability Analysis — *Casciati, Fabio*

Mathematical Morphology and Its Applications to Image and Signal Processing — *Maragos, Petros*

y A Mathematical Mosaic (Illus. by Taisa Kelly) — *Vakil, Ravi*

Mathematical Mysteries — *Clawson, Calvin C*

Mathematical Perspectives on Neural Networks — *Smolensky, Paul*

Mathematical Population Dynamics — *Arino, Ovide*

Mathematical Problems in the Theory of Water Waves — *Dias, F*

Mathematical Programming for Industrial Engineers — *Avriel, Mordecai*

Mathematical Programs with Equilibrium Constraints — *Luo, Zhi-Quan*

r Mathematical Statistics for Economics and Business — *Mittelhammer, Ron C*

A Mathematical Theory of Hints — *Kohlas, Jurg*

Mathematical Theory of Reliability — *Barlow, Richard E*

Mathematical Thinking and Problem Solving — *Schoenfeld, Alan H*

Mathematical Topics in Fluid Mechanics. Vol. 1 — *Lions, P L*

y The Mathematical Traveller — *Clawson, Calvin C*

y A Mathematical Word Search Puzzle Book — *Hechler, Ellen*

y Mathematics 1 — *Kodaira, Kunihiko*

y Mathematics 2 — *Kodaira, Kunihiko*

Mathematics and Politics — *Taylor, Alan D, 1947-*

Mathematics for Economics and Finance — *Anthony, Martin*

Mathematics for Tomorrow's Young Children — *Mansfield, Helen*

y Mathematics: From the Birth of Numbers — *Gullberg, Jan*

Mathematics of Dependable Systems — *Mitchell, Chris*

Mathematics of Microstructure Evolution — *Chen, Long-Qing*

The Mathematics of Numerical Analysis — *AMS-SIAM Summer Seminar in Applied Mathematics (1995: Park City, Utah)*

Mathematics of the 19th Century — *Kolmogorov, A N*

Les Mathematiques Japonaises A L'Epoque D'Edo — *Horiuchi, Annick*

y Maths in Action. Rev. Ed., Bks. 1-4B

y Maths in Action Plus. Bks. 1-4

y Matieres Premieres — *Stroud, Mark*

c Matilda the Moocher (Illus. by Diana Cain Bluthenthal) — *Bluthenthal, Diana Cain*

c Matisse from A to Z — *Sellier, Marie*

Matisse's War — *Everett, Peter*

Matlock's System — *Hill, Reginald*

c Matreshka (Illus. by Alexi Natchev) — *Ayres, Becky Hickox*

Matrices of Sign-Solvable Linear Systems — *Brualdi, Richard A*

Les Matricules Universitaires — *Pacquet, Jacques*

The Matrifocal Family — *Smith, Raymond T*

Il Matrimonio Puo Morire? — *Petra, Basilio*

Matrix Analysis for Statistics — *Schott, James R*

Matrix-Analytic Methods in Stochastic Models — *Chakravarthy, Srinivas R*

Matrix Computations. 3rd Ed. — *Golub, Gene H*

Matroid Theory — *AMS-IMS-SIAM Joint Summer Research Conference on Matroid Theory (1995: University of Washington)*

r Matrology: A Bibliography of Writings by Christian Women from the First to the Fifteenth Centuries — *Kadel, Andrew*

Matsushita Leadership — *Kotter, John P*

c Matter and Materials (Illus. by Terry Hadler) — *Kerrod, Robin*

A Matter of Choices — *Ajzenberg-Selove, Fay*

A Matter of Faith — *Sullivan, Robert*

r Matter of Fax — *British Library. Information Sciences Service*

A Matter of Honor — *Izzi, Eugene*

A Matter of Interpretation — *Scalia, Antonin*

The Matter of Revolution — *Rogers, John, 1961-*

y A Matter of Style — *Leuzzi, Linda*

Matter's End — *Benford, Gregory*

Matters of Choice — *Gordon, Noah*

Matters of Life and Death — *Cairns, John*

Matters of Mind — *McKillop, A B*

The Matthean Parables — *Jones, Ivor H*

Matthew — *Riches, John*

Matthew in History, Interpretation, Influence, and Effects — *Luz, Ulrich*

Matthew: Storyteller, Interpreter, Evangelist — *Carter, Warren*

c Matthew Wheelock's Wall — *Weller, Frances Ward*

Matthew's Christian-Jewish Community — *Saldarini, Anthony J*

Matthew's Transfiguration Story and Jewish-Christian Controversy — *Moses, A D A*

c Matt's Million (Illus. by Richard Jones) — *Norriss, Andrew*

Mature Christianity in the 21st Century. Expanded and Rev. Ed. — *Beck, Norman A*

Mature Money — *Gruber, Joan M*

r The Mature Traveler's Book of Deals — *Malott, Gene*

A Mature Woman — *Maruya, Saiichi*

y The Matzo Mitzvah (Illus. by Jan Golden) — *Kantor, Herman I*

c Maud in France (Illus. by Alain Cheneviere) — *Cheneviere, Alain*

c Maudie and the Green Children (Illus. by Sigune Hamann) — *Mitchell, Adrian*

c Maui and the Sun (Illus. by Gavin Bishop) — *Bishop, Gavin*

The Maui Onion Cookbook — *Santos, Barbara*

Maulwurfsarchaologie: Zum Verhaltnis Von Geschichte Und Anthropologie In Wilhelm Raabes Historischen Erzahltexten — *Bertschik, Julia*

Maupassant and the American Short Story — *Fusco, Richard*

Maupassant: Espaces Du Roman — *Giacchetti, Claudine*

Maurice (Firth). Audio Version — *Forster, E M*

Maurice Blanchot and the Literature of Transgression — *Gregg, John*

Maurice Blanchot: L'Ecriture Comme Experience Du Dehors — *Schulte Nordholt, Annelies*

Maurice Blanchot: The Demand of Writing — *Gill, Carolyn Bailey*

Maurice Ravel — *Larner, Gerald*

The Maverick Mindset — *Hall, Doug, 1959-*

Mavis — *Marshall, Brenda K*

Mawdudi and the Making of Islamic Revivalism — *Nasr, Seyyed Vali Reza*

r Mawsuat Mustalahat Al-Hasub — *Hammad, Alam Al-Huda*

c Max and Ruby's Midas (Illus. by Rosemary Wells) — *Wells, Rosemary*

Max Beckmann — *Selz, Peter*

Max Beckmann in Exile

c Max Bonker and the Howling Thieves (Illus. by Bruce Van Patter) — *Weidensaul, Scott*

Max Jamison — *Sheed, Wilfrid*
Max Ophuls in the Hollywood Studios — *Bacher, Lutz*
Max: The Life and Music of Peter Maxwell Davies
    — *Seabrook, Mike*
Max Weber: Politics and the Spirit of Tragedy
    — *Diggins, John Patrick*
c Maxie's Music — *Dale, Elizabeth*
Maxime Le Confesseur: Essence Et Energies De Dieu
    — *Karayiannis, Vasilios*
r Maximov's Companion to Who Governs the Russian
    Federation. Vol. 2, No. 1
Maximum Achievement — *Tracy, Brian*
Maximum Entropy and Bayesian Methods
    — *International Workshop on Maximum Entropy and
    Bayesian Methods (13th: 1993: Santa Barbara, Calif.)*
Maximum Security — *Devine, John*
Maximum Velocity — *Jones, Bruce*
c Max's Dragon Shirt — *Wells, Rosemary*
c Max's First Word — *Wells, Rosemary*
Maxwell Anderson: A Research and Production
    Sourcebook — *Horn, Barbara Lee*
r Maxwell Anderson on the European Stage 1929-1992
    — *Engle, Ron*
Maxwell on Heat and Statistical Mechanics
    — *Maxwell, James Clerk*
Maxwell: The Final Verdict — *Bower, Tom*
May out West — *Swenson, May*
May Sarton: A Biography — *Peters, Margot*
y May Sky — *De Cristoforo, Violet Kazue*
May the Lord in His Mercy Be Kind to Belfast
    — *Parker, Tony*
c Maya Angelou: Journey of the Heart — *Pettit, Jayne*
y Maya Angelou: More than a Poet — *Lisandrelli,
    Elaine Slivinski*
y Maya Angelou's I Know Why the Caged Bird Sings
    — *Bloom, Harold*
Maya in Exile — *Burns, Allan F*
c Maya Lin — *Ling, Bettina*
Maya Maritime Trade, Settlement, and Populations on
    Ambergris Caye, Belize — *Guderjan, Thomas H*
Maya Quest — *Buettner, Dan*
r Maya Sculpture of Copan — *Baudez, Claude-Francois*
The Maya Textile Tradition — *Schevill, Margot Blum*
Mayan Drifter — *Herrera, Juan Felipe*
c Maya's Children (Illus. by Maria Baca) — *Anaya,
    Rudolfo*
c Maybelle the Cable Car (Illus. by Virginia Lee
    Burton) — *Burton, Virginia Lee*
Maye and Faye's Building and Loan — *Smith, Maye*
Mayflower Deeds and Probates — *Roser, Susan E*
r The Mayflower Descendant. Vols. 17-18
Mayflower Families in Progress — *Wakefield, Robert S*
Mayflower Families though Five Generations. Vol. 9
Mayflower Increasings. 2nd Ed. — *Roser, Susan E*
The Mayflower Murder — *Kemprecos, Paul*
p The Maynooth University Record
r Mayo Clinic Complete Book of Pregnancy and Baby's
    First Year
r The Mayo Clinic Family Health Book. 1996 Ed. Book
    and Electronic Media Version
yr Mayo Clinic Family Health Book. 1996 Ed. Electronic
    Media Version
The Mayo Clinic Manual of Nuclear Medicine
    — *O'Connor, Michael K*
p Mayo Clinic Women's Healthsource
Mayo Del 68 — *Rodriguez, Jesus Antonio*
c Mayor: In the Company of Norman Rice, Mayor of
    Seattle — *Sobol, Richard*
Mazarin: The Crisis of Absolutism in France
    — *Treasure, G R R*
The Maze — *Coulter, Catherine*
y Mazel — *Goldstein, Rebecca*
p Mazel-Tov Cocktail
Mazurka for Two Dead Men — *Cela, Camilo Jose*
Mazzini — *Mack Smith, Denis*
McCarthyism and New York's Hearst Press — *Tuck,
    Jim*
r McCarthy's Desk Encyclopedia of Intellectual
    Property. 2nd Ed. — *McCarthy, J Thomas*
McCartney: Yesterday and Today — *Coleman, Ray*
r McDonald County, Missouri 1870 Federal Census
    — *Looney, Janice Soutee*
y McDonald's — *Gould, William*
McDonald's Happy Meal Toys around the World
    — *Losonsky, Terry*
c McDuff Moves In (Illus. by Susan Jeffers) — *Wells,
    Rosemary*
The McFarlane Legacy — *Britnell, R H*
McGill Medicine. Vol. 1 — *Hanaway, Joseph*
r McGraw-Hill Circuit Encyclopedia and
    Troubleshooting Guide. Vol. 3 — *Lenk, John D*

r The McGraw-Hill Dictionary of International Trade
    and Finance — *Gipson, Carolyn Renee*
r McGraw-Hill Encyclopedia of Astronomy. 2nd Ed.
    — *Parker, Sybil P*
r McGraw-Hill Encyclopedia of Personal Computing
    — *Gibilisco, Stan*
McGraw-Hill High-Speed LANs Handbook
    — *Saunders, Stephen*
yr The McGraw-Hill PC Programmer's Desk Reference
    — *Canton, Maria P*
The McGraw-Hill World Wide Web Training Manual
    — *Wagner, Ronald L*
r McGraw-Hill Yearbook of Science and Technology
    1996
McGraw-Hill's National Electrical Code Handbook.
    22nd Ed.
r McKinley Internet Yellow Pages — *Maxwell, Christine*
McLuhan, or Modernism in Reverse — *Willmott,
    Glenn*
McLuhan's Children — *Dale, Stephen*
McNally's Puzzle — *Sanders, Lawrence*
McNeil NYPD 2 — *Featherstone, Ivy*
MCQs for the Paediatric MRCP Part 1 — *Winrow, A
    P*
MCSE Study Guide — *McLaren, Tim*
c Me and Mary Kangaroo — *Gilbert, Kevin*
c Me and My World (Illus. by Teri Gower) — *Parsons,
    Alexandra*
c Me, Dad and Number 6 (Illus. by Goro Sasaki)
    — *Jennings, Dana Andrew*
c Me on the Map (Illus. by Annette Cable) — *Sweeney,
    Joan*
The Meadow — *Galvin, James*
Meadowlands — *Gluck, Louise*
The Meagre Harvest — *Kaplan, Gisela*
Meals That Heal — *Turner, Lisa*
Meals That Heal for Babies, Toddlers and Children
    — *Behan, Eileen*
Mean Business — *Dunlap, Albert J*
y Mean High Tide (Muller). Audio Version — *Hall, Jim,
    1947-*
Mean Streak — *Wheat, Carolyn*
p Mean Streets
Meaning and Form — *Berry, Margaret*
Meaning and Interpretation — *Hagberg, G L*
The Meaning of Mind — *Szasz, Thomas*
The Meaning of Nucleocytoplasmic Transport
    — *Agutter, Paul S*
The Meaning of Race — *Malik, Kenan*
The Meaning of Religious Freedom — *Gamwell,
    Franklin I*
The Meanings of Age — *Neugarten, Bernice L*
Meanings of Work — *Gamst, Frederick C*
y Means and Probabilities — *Krieger, Melanie Jacobs*
The Measurable World — *Coles, Katharine*
The Measure of California Agriculture — *Carter,
    Harold O*
A Measure of Defiance — *Harcourt, Mike*
A Measure of Memory — *Aarons, Victoria*
y A Measure of My Days — *Loxterkamp, David*
The Measure of Reality — *Crosby, Alfred W*
Measured Lies — *Kincheloe, Joe L*
The Measured Man — *Owen, Howard*
Measurement and Analysis of Job Vacancies
    — *Muysken, J*
The Measurement of Starlight — *Hearnshaw, J B*
Measures and Probabilities — *Simonnet, Michel*
c Measuring — *Hewitt, Sally*
Measuring and Controlling Interest Rate Risk
    — *Fabozzi, Frank J*
Measuring and Managing Customer Satisfaction
    — *Kessler, Sheila*
Measuring and Managing Patient Satisfaction. 2nd Ed.
    — *Krowinski, William J*
Measuring Economic Benefits for Water Investments
    and Policies — *Young, Robert A*
Measuring Inequality. 2nd Ed. — *Cowell, Frank A*
Measuring Lives — *Foley, Tom*
Measuring Movement and Locomotion — *Ossenkopp,
    Klaus-Peter*
Measuring Poverty — *Citro, Constance F*
Measuring the Effectiveness of Image and Linkage
    Advertising — *Woodside, Arch G*
Measuring the Employment Effects of Regulation
    — *Zank, Neal S*
Measuring the Mind — *Wooldridge, Adrian*
Measuring Up — *Rothman, Robert*
c Meat-Eating Plants — *Aaseng, Nathan*
Meatless Mexican Home Cooking — *Zaslavsky, Nancy*

Meatpackers: An Oral History of Black Packinghouse
    Workers and Their Struggle for Racial and
    Economic Equality — *Halpern, Rick*
Meaty, Beaty, Big and Bouncy — *Jones, Dylan*
Mecca: A Literary History of the Muslim Holy Land
    — *Peters, F E*
De Mechanica Van Het Liegen — *Krol, Gerrit*
Mechanical Behaviour of Materials at High
    Temperature — *NATO Advanced Study Institute on
    Mechanical Behaviour of Materials at High
    Temperature (1995: Sesimbra, Portugal)*
Mechanical Connections in Wood Structures
    — *American Society of Civil Engineers. Task
    Committee on Fasteners*
r Mechanical Design Handbook — *Rothbart, Harold A*
The Mechanical Design Process. 2nd Ed. — *Ullman,
    David G*
Mechanical Properties and Phase Transformation of
    Multiphase Intermetallic Alloys — *Giamei, Anthony
    F*
r Mechanical Properties of Ceramics — *Wachtman, J B*
The Mechanical Song — *Miller Frank, Felicia*
Mechanics Day — *Shadwick, William F*
c Mechanics FUNdamentals (Illus. by Rick Brown)
    — *Wood, Robert W*
Mechanics of Liquids and Gases. 6th Ed.
    — *Loitsianskii, L G*
Mechanics of Materials — *Craig, Roy R*
Mechanics of Materials — *Roylance, David*
Mechanics of Materials. 3rd Ed. — *Hibbeler, R C*
Mechanics of Solids — *Ross, C T F*
Mechanics of Sport — *Carr, Gerry*
Mechanics of Transformation Toughening and Related
    Topics — *Karihaloo, B L*
Mechanics Problems in Geodynamics. Pt. 1 — *Wang,
    Jen*
Die Mechanisierung Des Herzens — *Fuchs, Thomas*
Die Mechanisierung Des Ruhrbergbaus 1890-1930
    — *Burghardt, Uwe*
The Mechanisms of Governance — *Williamson, Oliver
    E*
Mechanisms of Lymphocyte Activation and Immune
    Regulation VI — *Gupta, Sudhir*
Mechthild Von Magdeburg: A Medieval Mystic in
    Modern Eyes — *Tobin, Frank*
Mecox Road — *Cohen, Marc*
Medea: Essays on Medea in Myth, Literature,
    Philosophy, and Art — *Clauss, James J*
Medea: Stimmen — *Wolf, Christa*
La Medecine Dans L'Oeuvre De J.K. Huysmans
    — *Maingon, Charles*
The Media and Modernity — *Thompson, John B*
Media and Public Policy — *Spitzer, Robert J*
The Media and the Persian Gulf War — *Denton,
    Robert E, Jr.*
Media at War — *Jackaway, Gwenyth L*
Media beyond Socialism — *Splichal, Slavko*
r Media Courses UK 1996
Media Culture — *Kellner, Douglas*
Media Effects on Voters — *Cavanaugh, John William*
The Media Equation — *Reeves, Byron*
Media Guide to the New Parliament Constituencies
    — *Ralling, Colin*
Media Law for Producers. 2nd Ed. — *Miller, Philip*
Media Marathon — *Barnouw, Erik*
r Media Review Digest 1996
Media Science before the Great War — *Broks, Peter*
y Media Stories for GCSE — *Wall, Peter*
The Media Student's Book — *Branston, Gill*
Mediaeval Isma'ili History and Thought — *Daftary,
    Farhad*
Mediated Messages and African-American Culture
    — *Berry, Venise T*
Mediating and Negotiating Marital Conflicts — *Ellis,
    Desmond*
Mediating Interpersonal Conflicts — *Umbreit, Mark S*
Mediation in Contemporary Native American Fiction
    — *Ruppert, James*
Mediators between Human and Divine — *Macquarrie,
    John*
Medicaid and the Limits of State Health Reform
    — *Sparer, Michael S*
r The Medical Advisor — *Time-Life Books*
Medical and Surgical Management of Prostate Cancer
    — *Middleton, Richard G*
Medical Applications of Titanium and Its Alloys
    — *Brown, Stanley A*
Medical Blunders — *Youngson, R M*
Medical Consequences of the Chernobyl Nuclear
    Accident — *Ramzaev, P V*
Medical Crisis Counseling — *Pollin, Irene*

Medical Curiosities — *Youngson, R M*

The Medical Device Quality Assurance Manual — *Montanez, Jose*

r Medical Dictionary in Six Languages — *Spilker, Bert*

r Medical Emergency — *Lynn, Stephen G*

Medical Ethics in the Renaissance — *Schleiner, Winfried*

Medical Ethnobiology of the Highland Maya of Chiapas, Mexico — *Berlin, Elois Ann*

Medical Evaluation of Physically and Sexually Abused Children — *Jenny, Carole*

Medical Genetics — *Jorde, Lynn B*

Medical Informatics — *De Dombal, F T*

Medical Management of Heart Disease — *Sobel, Burton E*

The Medical Mandarins — *Weisz, George*

Medical Nutrition and Disease — *Morrison, Gail*

Medical Protestants — *Haller, John S, Jr.*

Medical School Admissions. 3rd Rev. Ed. — *Zebala, John*

r Medical School Admissions. 4th Rev. Ed. — *Zebala, John*

Medical Terminology — *Willis, Marjorie Canfield*

Medicare and Graduate Medical Education — *Baumgardner, James*

Medicare Made Simple — *Knaus, Denise*

The Medici Wedding of 1589 — *Saslow, James*

Medicinal Resources of the Tropical Forest — *Balick, Michael J*

Medicine — *Axford, J S*

Medicine and Medical Ethics in Medieval and Early Modern Spain — *Kottek, Samuel S*

Medicine and the Family — *Candib, Lucy M*

Medicine and Western Civilization — *Rothman, David J*

Medicine, Health and Risk — *Gabe, Jonathon*

Medicine Men — *Adams, Alice*

Medicine, Monopolies, and Malice — *Wilk, Chester A*

The Medicine of ER — *Ross, Alan Duncan*

Medicine of the Earth — *Fischer-Rizzi, Susanne*

Medicine, Philosophy and Religion in Ancient China — *Sivin, Nathan*

Medicine: Self-Assessment Picture Tests. Vols. 1-4 — *Bouloux, Pierre-Marc*

Medicine, Society, and Faith in the Ancient and Medieval Worlds — *Amundsen, Darrel W*

Medicine Worth Paying For — *Frazier, Howard S*

Medicine's Dilemma — *Kissick, William L*

Medicolegal Issues for Radiographers. 3rd Ed. — *Parelli, Robert J*

Medicos, Maleantes, Y Maricas — *Salessi, Jorge*

Medieval Agriculture and Islamic Science — *Varisco, Daniel Martin*

r Medieval and Renaissance Manuscript Books in the Library of Congress. Vol. 1 — *Library of Congress*

r Medieval and Renaissance Manuscripts at the University of California, Los Angeles. Vol. 2 — *Ferrari, Mirella*

r Medieval and Renaissance Manuscripts in the Walters Art Gallery. Vol. 2 — *Walters Art Gallery (Baltimore, Md.)*

Medieval and Renaissance Spanish Literature — *Whinnom, Keith*

r Medieval Art — *Ross, Leslie*

Medieval Bestiaries — *Hassig, Debra*

y Medieval Britain — *Laing, Lloyd*

Medieval Canon Law — *Brundage, James A*

c Medieval Castle — *Pipe, Jim*

Medieval Christian Perceptions of Islam — *Tolan, John Victor*

c A Medieval Christmas — *Bible. N.T. English. Luke. Tyndale. Selections. 1996*

The Medieval Cult of Saints — *Abou-El-Haj, Barbara Fay*

Medieval Death — *Binski, Paul*

Medieval Dutch Literature in Its European Context — *Kooper, Erik*

Medieval Ecclesiastical Studies in Honour of Dorothy M. Owen — *Franklin, M J*

Medieval England — *Miller, Edward, 1915-*

Medieval English Medicine — *Rubin, Stanley*

r Medieval France — *Kibler, William W*

The Medieval Hall — *Thompson, M W*

Medieval Illuminators and Their Methods of Work — *Alexander, Jonathan J G*

Medieval in L.A. — *Paul, Jim*

Medieval Knighthood V

c Medieval Life (Illus. by Geoff Dann) — *Langley, Andrew*

Medieval Listening and Reading — *Green, D H*

Medieval Lives — *Cantor, Norman F*

Medieval London Widows 1300-1500 — *Barron, Caroline M*

The Medieval Medea — *Morse, Ruth*

A Medieval Mercantile Community — *Nightingale, Pamela*

y Medieval Monarchs — *Smith, Nigel, 1947-*

Medieval Mythography — *Chance, Jane*

Medieval Pageant — *Wagner, Anthony*

The Medieval Poet as Voyeur — *Spearing, A C*

Medieval Religious Houses — *Knowles, David*

Medieval Religious Women. Vol. 3, Bks. 1-2 — *Nichols, John A*

Medieval Russian Culture. Vol.2 — *Flier, Michael S*

Medieval Scotland — *Grant, Alexander*

A Medieval Semiotic — *Furton, Edward*

Medieval Ships and Shipping — *Hutchinson, Gillian*

Medieval Society and the Manor Court — *Razi, Zvi*

Medieval Southwark — *Carlin, Martha*

The Medieval Stage — *Chambers, E K*

The Medieval Super-Companies — *Hunt, Edwin S*

The Medieval Theater in Castile — *Stern, Charlotte*

c Medieval Times (Illus. by Richard Berridge) — *Mason, Antony*

The Medieval Town — *Holt, Richard*

Medieval Towns — *Schofield, John*

Medieval Venuses and Cupids — *Tinkle, Theresa*

Medieval Wales — *Carr, A D*

Medieval Warfare Source Book. Vol. 1 — *Nicolle, David*

The Medieval Warhorse from Byzantium to the Crusades — *Hyland, Ann*

Medieval Women — *Leyser, Henrietta*

Medieval Women Monastics — *Schmitt, Miriam*

r Medieval Wordbook — *Cosman, Madeleine Pelner*

The Medieval Year Diary 1997

The Medievalist Impulse in American Literature — *Moreland, Kim Ileen*

c Mediopollito (Illus. by Kim Howard) — *Ada, Alma Flor*

Meditation: The First and Last Freedom — *Osho*

A Meditation to Help You Recover from Alcohol and Other Drugs. Audio Version — *Naparstek, Belleruth*

A Meditation to Help You Recover from Smoking. Audio Version — *Naparstek, Belleruth*

A Meditation to Help You Recover from Weight Loss. Audio Version — *Naparstek, Belleruth*

Meditations of a Flawed Bridegroom — *Hopkirk, Vivian*

Meditations on the Book of Psalms — *Crafton, Barbara Cawthorne*

Meditations on the Soul — *Ficino, Marsilio*

y The Mediterranean Caper (Greenwood). Audio Version — *Cussler, Clive*

The Mediterranean Cat — *Silvester, Hans*

The Mediterranean Debt Crescent — *Henry, Clement M*

A Mediterranean Emporium — *Abulafia, David*

r Mediterranean France Insider's Guide — *Burke, David*

p Mediterranean Politics

Mediterranean Strategies

A Mediterranean Valley — *Barker, Graeme*

Medizin Und Wissenschaftstheorie — *Reckenfelderbaumer, Alfred*

r Die Medizinische Fakultat Der Universitat Helmstedt 1576-1810 — *Triebs, Michaela*

Medjugorje: Religion, Politics, and Violence in Rural Bosnia — *Bax, Mart*

The Medusa Tree — *Dressler, Mylene*

y Medusa's Child — *Nance, John J*

Das Meer Unter Meinem Kopfkissen — *Zornack, Annemarie*

c Meet Matt and Roxy (Illus. by Susan Huszar) — *Huszar, Karen*

Meet Me at the Morgue — *Macdonald, Ross*

c Meet the Arthropods (Illus. by Len Rubenstein) — *Doris, Ellen*

c Meet the Friends — *Whalen, Sharla*

c Meet the Monsters (Illus. by Patricia Ludlow) — *Yolen, Jane*

A Meeting about Laughter — *Erdman, Nikolai*

Meeting Legal Challenges — *Beckham, Joseph*

A Meeting of Minds — *Aron, Lewis*

Meeting of the Minds — *Barabba, Vincent P*

The Meeting of Two Worlds — *Bray, Warwick*

The Meeting Place — *Hocking, Mary*

Meeting Special Needs in Mainstream Schools — *Stakes, Richard*

Meeting the Challenges of Local Government: Final Report

Meeting the Great Bliss Queen — *Klein, Anne Carolyn*

Meeting the Madwoman — *Leonard, Linda Schierse*

Meeting the Master — *Wald, Elissa*

Meeting the Minotaur — *Dawson, Carol*

Meeting the Tree of Life — *Tallmadge, John*

Meetings with Remarkable Trees — *Pakenham, Thomas, 1933-*

Meg — *Alten, Steve*

Mega-City Growth and the Future — *Fuchs, Roland J*

The Mega-Urban Regions of Southeast Asia — *McGee, T G*

c The Megamogs and the Dangerous Doughnut (Illus. by Peter Haswell) — *Haswell, Peter*

c Megan's Two Houses (Illus. by Freya Tanz) — *Jong, Erica*

El Megaterio De Bru Y El Presidente Jefferson — *Lopez Pinero, Jose Maria*

Megatrends Asia — *Naisbitt, John*

c Meg's Monkey (Illus. by Anthea Sieveking) — *MacKinnon, Debbie*

c Mei Lin's Message (Illus. by Frances Luke) — *Jacobson, Kerri*

y MEI Structured Mathematics: Mechanics 5-6

y MEI Structured Mathematics: Pure Mathematics 3-4

The Meiji Unification through the Lens of Ishikawa Prefecture — *Baxter, James C*

Mein Heiliger Stein — *Laxness, Halldor*

Mein Kampf — *Levinthal, David*

Meister Eckhart and the Beguine Mystics — *McGinn, Bernard*

Mejor Dicho — *Garcia, Carmen*

The Mekong Delta — *Brocheux, Pierre*

Mekruh Kadinlar Mezarligi — *Kutlu, Ayla*

Melancholy Dialectics — *Pensky, Max*

The Melancholy Muse — *Heffernan, Carol Falvo*

c Melanie (Illus. by Alisher Dianov) — *Carrick, Carol*

c Melanie Jane (Illus. by Isabelle Dervaux) — *Couture, Susan Arkin*

Melanogenesis and Malignant Melanoma — *International Symposium on Melanogenesis and Malignant Melanoma (1995: Fukuoka-Shi, Japan)*

Melchizedek — *Traylor, Ellen Gunderson*

Meletij Smotryc'kyj — *Frick, David*

c Melinda and Nock and the Magic Spell (Illus. by Alex De Wolf) — *Uebe, Ingrid*

Melissa — *Hylton, Sara*

Les Melkites: Grecs-Orthodoxes Et Grecs-Catholiques Des Patriarcats D'Antioche, D'Alexandrie Et De Jerusalem — *Dick, Ignace*

c The Mellion Moon Mystery (Illus. by Patrice Aggs) — *Blackman, Malorie*

The Melnikov House, Moscow 1927-1929 — *Pallasmaa, Juhani*

Melodrama and Meaning — *Klinger, Barbara*

Melodrama: Stage, Picture, Screen — *Bratton, Jacky*

Melodrama: The Cultural Emergence of a Genre — *Hays, Michael*

Melodramatic Tactics — *Hadley, Elaine*

c Melody Mooner Takes Lessons (Illus. by John Bianchi) — *Edwards, Frank B*

Melt-Spinning, Strip Casting and Slab Casting — *Matthys, Eric F*

The Melungeons: The Resurrection of a Proud People — *Kennedy, N Brent*

Melville: A Biography — *Robertson-Lorant, Laurie*

Melville and His Circle — *Dillingham, William B*

Melville and Turner — *Wallace, Robert K*

Melville, Shame, and the Evil Eye — *Adamson, Joseph*

Melville's City — *Kelley, Wyn*

Melville's Muse — *Wenke, John Paul*

c Melvin and the Deadheads — *Apps, Roy*

Member of the Club — *Graham, Lawrence*

r Members of Congress — *Goehlert, Robert U*

Memento Mori — *Lewitt, Shariann*

Memnoch the Devil — *Rice, Anne*

p Memo #70

Memo: Wortschatz- Und Fertigkeitstraining Zum Zertifikat Deutsch Als Fremdsprache — *Haublein, Gernot*

Memoir in Two Voices — *Mitterrand, Francois*

y Memoir of the Bookie's Son — *Offit, Sidney*

La Memoire Ensanglantee — *Pean, Stanley*

Memoiren Und Aufsatze Gegen Den Nationalsozialismus 1933-1938 — *Von Hildebrand, Dietrich*

Memoires. Vol. 1 — *Vidal-Naquet, Pierre*

Memoires Interrompus — *Mitterand, Francois*

Memoires Sur Les Cent-Jours — *Constant, Benjamin*

Memoirs — *Gorbachev, Mikhail Sergeevich*

Memoirs A Deux Voix — *Wiesel, Elie*

Memoirs of a Mountain Guide — *Whittaker, Lou*

The Memoirs of Cleopatra — *George, Margaret*

The Memoirs of Elizabeth Frankenstein — *Roszak, Theodore*

Memoirs of Emma Courtney. 1st Annotated Ed. — *Hays, Mary*

The Memoirs of Lady Hyegyong — *Hyegyonggung Hong Ssi*

Memoirs of Senator Joseph Connelly 1885-1961 — *Connelly, Joseph*

The Memoirs of the Dean of Wall Street — *Graham, Benjamin*

La Memoria Enclaustrada — *Bracamonte Y Sosa, Pedro*

El Memorial Portugues De 1494 — *Leaon-Borja, Istvan Szaszdi*

Memorials of the Spanish Civil War — *Williams, Colin*

Memorias — *Schindler, Emilie*

Memorias De Mi Viaje — *Torres, Olga Beatriz*

Memories: My Life as an International Leader in Health, Suffrage, and Peace — *Jacobs, Aletta*

Memories of a Revolution — *Muhyi Al-Din, Khaled*

Memories of a Revolution — *Muhyi Al-Din, Khalid*

Memories of Chicano History — *Garcia, Mario T*

Memories of God — *Bondi, Roberta C*

Memories of Migration — *Friedman-Kasaba, Kathie*

Memories of My Ghost Brother — *Fenkl, Heinz Insu*

Memories of My Life — *Escoffier, Auguste*

Memories of Resistance — *Mangini, Shirley*

Memories of Revolt — *Swedenburg, Ted*

Memories of Summer — *Kahn, Roger*

r Memories of the Land — *Hall-Patton, Mark P*

Memories of the Mick — *Allen, Maury*

Memory — *Bjork, Elizabeth Ligon*

y Memory — *Bujold, Lois McMaster*

y Memory — *Yount, Lisa*

Memory and Hope — *Priestley, David T*

Memory at These Speeds — *Miller, Jane*

The Memory Bird — *Malone, Caroline*

c The Memory Book (Illus. by Malcolm Cullen) — *Spencer, Anne*

The Memory Cathedral — *Dann, Jack*

Memory Distortion — *Schacter, Daniel L*

The Memory Game — *French, Nicci*

Memory Gardens — *Creeley, Robert*

Memory in Oral Traditions — *Rubin, David C*

Memory in the Cerebral Cortex — *Fuster, Joaquin M*

Memory Lane — *Gough, Laurence*

Memory Mambo — *Obejas, Achy*

Memory, Narrative, and Identity — *Singh, Amritjit*

The Memory of Birds in Times of Revolution — *Breytenbach, Breyten*

Memory of Childhood Trauma — *Reviere, Susan L*

y The Memory of Earth — *Card, Orson Scott*

The Memory of Water — *Schiff, Michel*

c The Memory Quilt — *Hulbert, Elizabeth*

Memory Slips — *Cutting, Linda Katherine*

Memory, the Holocaust, and French Justice — *Golsan, Richard J*

The Memphis Diary of Ida B. Wells — *Wells-Barnett, Ida B*

Men among the Mammoths — *Van Riper, A Bowdoin*

Men and Women at Toulouse in the Age of the Cathars — *Mundy, John Hine*

Men and Women in Interaction — *Aries, Elizabeth*

Men and Women Writers of the 1930s — *Montefiore, Janet*

Men Are from Mars, Women Are from Venus — *Gray, John, 1951-*

Men Are from Mars, Women Are from Venus. Electronic Media Version — *Gray, John, 1951-*

y Men at Arms — *Pratchett, Terry*

Men at Work — *Woodward, Donald*

Men before Ten A.M. — *Houston, Pam*

Men Down West — *Lincoln, Kenneth*

The Men from the Boys — *Mann, William J*

Men, Ideas and Tanks — *Harris, J P*

Men in Black — *Harvey, John Robert*

Men in Groups — *Andronico, Michael P*

y The Men in Sheepskin Coats (Illus. by Paul McCusker) — *Berton, Pierre*

Men in Women's Clothing — *Levine, Laura*

y Men, Makeup and Monsters — *Timpone, Anthony*

Men, Masculinities and Social Welfare — *Pringle, Keith*

Men on Divorce — *Kaganoff, Penny*

Men on Men 6

The Men Out There — *Shapiro, Susan R*

Men Own the Fields, Women Own the Crops — *Goheen, Miriam*

The Men Stood lIke Iron — *Herdegen, Lance J*

Men Talk — *Bowen, Jan*

The Men Who Made the Monsters — *Jensen, Paul M*

The Men Who Murdered Marilyn — *Smith, Matthew*

Men Will Be Boys — *Jenkins, Sally*

Men, Women, and God(s) — *Malti-Douglas, Fedwa*

Men, Women, and Madness — *Busfield, Joan*

Men Working — *Faulkner, John*

y The Menace of Multiculturalism — *Schmidt, Alvin J*

The Menace of the Corporate Newspaper — *Demers, David Pearce*

The Menace of the Sublime to the Individual Self — *Marie, Linda*

Menaechmi — *Plautus, Titus Maccius*

Menander and the Making of Comedy — *Walton, J Michael, 1939-*

Mencken: A Life — *Hobson, Fred*

A Mencken Chrestomathy — *Mencken, H L*

The MEND Clinic Guide to Natural Medicine for Menopause and Beyond — *Maas, Paula*

Mending Fences — *Ganguly, Sumit*

Mennonite Entrepreneurs — *Redekop, Calvin*

Mennonites in Canada 1939-1970 — *Regehr, T D*

c Mennyms Alive — *Waugh, Sylvia*

y Mennyms Alone — *Waugh, Sylvia*

c Mennyms under Siege — *Waugh, Sylvia*

r Menopause and Midlife Health — *Notelovitz, Morris*

Menopause, Naturally. 4th Ed. — *Greenwood, Sadja*

r Men's Fashion — *Peacock, John*

r Men's Travel in Your Pocket. 13th Ed.

Mental Causation — *Heil, John*

r Mental Health and the Built Environment — *Halpern, David*

r Mental Health Disorders Sourcebook — *Bellenir, Karen*

Mental Health in a Multi-Ethnic Society — *Fernando, Suman*

Mental Health in Black America — *Neighbors, Harold W*

Mental Health in Europe — *Ramon, Shulamit*

Mental Health in Remote Rural Developing Areas — *Group for the Advancement of Psychiatry. Committee on Therapeutic Care*

Mental Health Policy in Britain — *Rogers, Anne*

y Mental Illness — *Sherrow, Victoria*

Mental Illness in the Family — *Abosh, Beverley*

c Mental Maths — *Straker, Anita*

Mental Reality — *Strawson, Galen*

Mental Retardation — *Hickson, Linda*

Mental Wellness for Women — *Baron-Faust, Rita*

The Mental World of the Jacobean Court — *Peck, Linda Levy*

La Mentalidad Religiosa En Antioquia — *Arango, Gloria Mercedes*

Mentor Program

c O Mercador De Coisa Nenhuma (Illus. by Angela Melo) — *Torrado, Antonio*

Mercenaries of the Ancient World — *Yalichev, Serge*

Mercenaries, Pirates, and Sovereigns — *Thomson, Janice E*

Mercer Commentary on the Bible

Merchant Capital and Economic Decolonization — *Fieldhouse, D K*

Merchant Culture in Fourteenth-Century Venice

Merchant Enterprise in Britain — *Chapman, Stanley*

Merchant Networks in the Early Modern World — *Subrahmanyam, Sanjay*

The Merchant of Venice — *Holmer, Joan Ozark*

Merchants and Faith — *Risso, Patricia*

Merchants and Luxury Markets — *Sargentson, Carolyn*

Merchants and Shopkeepers — *Gulliver, P H*

The Merchants of Venus — *Grescoe, Paul*

Mercury Free — *Hardy, James E*

Mercury: The King of Queen — *Jackson, Laura*

Mercy and Eagleflight — *Phillips, Michael, 1946-*

Mercy of a Rude Stream. Vol. 3 — *Roth, Henry*

Mere Christianity — *Lewis, C S*

Mere Creatures of the State? — *Ball, William Bentley*

Meret Oppenheim: Beyond the Teacup — *Burckhardt, Jacqueline*

Mergers, Acquisitions, and Corporate Restructurings — *Gaughan, Patrick A*

Ha-Merhak Ha-Nakhoni — *Gur, Batya*

c Merlin and the Dragons (Illus. by Li Ming) — *Yolen, Jane*

The Merlin Chronicles — *Ashley, Mike*

c Merlin: The Young Merlin Trilogy — *Yolen, Jane*

Mermaid — *Gould, Alan*

c The Mermaid and Other Sea Poems (Illus. by Sophie Windham) — *Windham, Sophie*

Mermaids: Nymphs of the Sea — *Gachot, Theodore*

c The Mermaid's Purse — *Estes, Kathleen*

The Mermaids Singing — *McDermid, Val*

The Mermaid's Song — *Willman, Marianne*

cr The Merriam-Webster Dictionary. Home and Office Ed.

r Merriam-Webster's Collegiate Dictionary. Deluxe Electronic Ed. Electronic Media Version

r Merriam-Webster's Crossword Puzzle Dictionary. 2nd Ed.

r Merriam-Webster's Dictionary of Law

Merriam-Webster's Medical Office Handbook. 2nd Ed. — *Hamburg, Joseph*

r Merriam-Webster's Pocket Biographical Dictionary

r Merriam-Webster's Pocket Geographical Dictionary

Merrill Markoe's Guide to Love — *Markoe, Merrill*

c Merry Birthday, Nora Noel (Illus. by Mark Graham) — *Dixon, Ann*

c Merry Christmas, Baby — *Woods, Paula L*

c The Merry Christmas Postcard Story Book (Illus. by Emily Grossman) — *Lampl, Patricia Ryan*

The Merry Heart — *Davies, Robertson*

Merry-Making in Old Russia — *Popov, Eugeny*

The Mersey Sound (Henri). Audio Version — *Henri, Adrian*

A Merseyside Town in the Industrial Revolution — *Barker, Theo*

Ha-Meruts: Behirot 96 — *Neubach, Keren*

Mervyn Stockwood: A Lonely Life — *De-La-Noy, Michael*

c Mes Premiers Chiffres — *Audry-Llyic, Francoise*

p Mesechabe

Mesilla Valley Pioneers 1823-1912 — *Price, Paxton P*

Mesopotamia and the East — *Potts, Timothy C*

Mesopotamian Civilization — *Potts, D T*

The Message — *Peterson, Eugene H*

c A Message from the Match Girl — *Lisle, Janet Taylor*

y Message from Venus — *Krailing, Tessa*

The Message Is the Medium — *Koch, Tom*

Message, Messenger, and Response — *Lewis, Gladys Sherman*

Messages from My Father — *Trillin, Calvin*

y Messages from My Father (Trillin). Audio Version — *Trillin, Calvin*

Messengers of the Lost Battalion — *Orfalea, Gregory*

c Messes of Dresses (Illus. by Tova Leff) — *Pertzig, F*

The Messiaen Companion — *Hill, Peter*

The Messiah: Developments in Earliest Judaism and Christianity — *Charlesworth, James H*

c Messipes (Illus. by Susan Synarski) — *Gordon, Lynn*

Mest' Zhenshchiny — *Kalinina, Natallia*

Mestari: Eino Leinon Elama Ja Kuolema — *Makela, Hannu*

La Mesure De Son Siecle — *Haydn, Joseph*

Meta-Heuristics: Theory and Applications — *Osman, Ibrahim H*

Meta-Modeling: Performance and Information Modeling — *Berge, Jean-Michel*

Metabolic Regulation — *Frayn, Keith N*

Metafiction — *Currie, Mark*

Metafiction, Moving Pictures, Moving Histories — *Irmer, Thomas*

Metal-Containing Polymeric Materials — *Pittman, C U, Jr.*

r Metal Cutting Theory and Practice — *Stephenson, David A*

Metal Surface Electron Physics — *Kiejna, A*

Metalwork in Early America — *Henry Francis Du Pont Winterthur Museum*

r Metalworking in Africa South of the Sahara — *Lawal, Ibironke O*

Die Metamorphosen Des Messianismus In Den Iberischen Kulturen — *Delgado, Mariano*

The Metamorphoses of Apuleius — *Schlam, Carl C*

The Metamorphoses of Ovid — *Ovid*

c Metamorphosis (Illus. by Francisco Arredondo) — *Llamas Ruiz, Andres*

Metamorphosis: Postembryonic Reprogramming of Gene Expression in Amphibian and Insect Cells — *Gilbert, Lawrence I*

The Metamorphosis: The Translation, Backgrounds and Contexts, Criticism — *Kafka, Franz*

Metaphilosophy and Free Will — *Double, Richard*

Metaphors of Genre — *Fishelov, David*

Metaphysical Community — *Urban, Greg*

Metaphysical Delusion — *Cowley, Fraser*

Metaphysical Myths, Mathematical Practice — *Azzouni, Jody*

Metaphysical Personalism — *Conti, Charles*

Metaphysics as Rhetoric — *Parens, Joshua*

The Metaphysics of Free Will — *Fischer, John Martin*

The Metaphysics of Morals — *Kant, Immanuel*

The Metaphysics of Sound in Wallace Stevens — *Rosu, Anca*

Metaphysik Und Mathematik Bei Giordano Bruno — *Bonker-Vallon, Angelika*

Metapoesis: The Russian Tradition from Pushkin to Chekhov — *Finke, Michael C*

r Metapopulation Biology — *Hanski, Ilkka*

Metastable Phases and Microstructures — *Bormann, Rudiger*

c Meteorite Spoon — *Ridley, Philip*

Meteorites — *Hutchison, Robert*

Meteorology. 7th Ed. — *Anthes, Richard A*

c Meteors: The Truth behind Shooting Stars — *Aronson, Billy*

Meter in English — *Baker, David, 1954-*

r Methane and Its Derivatives — *Lee, Sunggyu*

Method in Ecumenical Theology — *Evans, G R*

The Methodists — *Kirby, James E*

Methodists and Women's Education in Ontario 1836-1925 — *Selles, Johanna M*

Methodological Issues and Strategies in Clinical Research — *Kazdin, Alan E*

The Methodologies of Art — *Adams, Laurie Schneider*

The Methodology of Macroeconomic Thought. 2nd Ed. — *Dow, Sheila C*

Methods and Applications of Linear Models — *Hocking, Ronald R*

Methods in Comparative Psychoacoustics — *Klump, G M*

Methods in Enzymology. Vol. 273

Methods in Renal Toxicology — *Zalups, Rudolfs K*

Methods in Stereochemical Analysis — *Dodziuk, Helena*

Methods in Stream Ecology — *Hauer, F Richard*

Methods in the Mediterranean — *Small, David B*

Methods of Confinement — *Maginn, Simon*

p Metre: A Magazine of International Poetry

Metre, Rhythm and Verse Form — *Hobsbaum, Philip*

p Metrika

y Metropolis: Ten Cities, Ten Centuries — *Lorenz, Albert*

Metropolitan America — *Frieden, Bernard J*

c Metropolitan Cow (Illus. by Tim Egan) — *Egan, Tim*

Metropolitan Governance — *Rothblatt, Donald N*

Metropolitan Governance Handbook

Metropolitan Lives — *Zurier, Rebecca*

Metropolitan Maternity — *Marks, Lara V*

The Metropolitan Opera Stories of the Great Operas. Vol. 2 — *Freeman, John W*

Metropolitan Organization

Metropolitics: A Regional Agenda for Community and Stability — *Orfield, Myron*

r Mexican American Labor 1790-1990 — *Gomez-Quinones, Juan*

Mexican American Youth Organization — *Navarro, Armando*

Mexican Americans and the Catholic Church 1900-1965 — *Dolan, Jay P*

Mexican Anarchism after the Revolution — *Hodges, Donald Clark*

Mexican Birds — *Peterson, Roger Tory*

Mexican Cinema — *Paranagua, Paulo Antonio*

Mexican Cinema/Mexican Woman 1940-1950 — *Hershfield, Joanne*

The Mexican Corrido — *Herrera-Sobek, Maria*

Mexican Devotional Retablos from the Peters Collection — *Chorpenning, Joseph F*

Mexican Folk Tales — *Campos, Anthony Hohn*

Mexican Hat — *McGarrity, Michael*

Mexican Light — *Shulman, Martha Rose*

The Mexican Peso Crisis — *Roett, Riordan*

Mexican Politics. 3rd Ed. — *Needler, Martin C*

y The Mexican Revolution — *Frost, Mary Pierce*

The Mexican Shock — *Castaneda, Jorge G*

Mexican Studies in the History and Philosophy of Science — *Ramirez, Santiago*

y The Mexican War of Independence

Mexican Workers and American Dreams — *Guerin-Gonzales, Camille*

Mexicans at Arms — *Santoni, Pedro*

Mexicans in the Midwest 1900-1932 — *Garcia, Juan R*

c Mexico — *Alcraft, Rob*

r Mexico — *Collis, John*

c Mexico — *Lewington, Anna*

c Mexico — *Morrison, Marion*

y Mexico: A Landscape Revisited — *Smithsonian Institution. Traveling Exhibition Service*

Mexico and the Survey of Public Lands — *Holden, Robert H*

y Mexico and the United States — *Pascoe, Elaine*

Mexico at the Crossroads — *Tangeman, Michael*

Mexico at the World's Fairs — *Tenorio-Trillo, Mauricio*

Mexico: Biography of Power — *Krauze, Enrique*

c Mexico City — *Stein, R Conrad*

r Mexico Environmental Report — *Wolfson, Paulette S*

Mexico Faces the 21st Century — *Schulz, Donald E*

Mexico: From Montezuma to NAFTA, Chiapas, and Beyond — *Suchlicki, Jaime*

r Mexico Handbook — *Cummings, Joe*

Mexico in the Age of Democratic Revolutions 1750-1850 — *Rodriguez O, Jaime E*

Mexico: Paso A Paso Guia Turistica — *Camargo Espriu, Rosario*

Mexico Profundo — *Bonfil Batalla, Guillermo*

c Mexico: Rich in Spirit and Tradition — *Kent, Deborah*

Mexico Trilogy — *Stuefloten, D N*

Mexico's Sierra Tarahumara — *Raat, W Dirk*

Meyerhold: A Revolution in Theatre — *Braun, Edward*

Meyerhold at Work — *Schmidt, Paul, 1934-*

Meyerhold, Eisenstein and Biomechanics — *Law, Alma*

The Mezzanine — *Baker, Nicholson*

Mfantsipim and the Making of Ghana — *Boahen, A Adu*

MFC Smartlabs

Mi Hermano Mayor (Illus. by Mati Lepp) — *Stark, Ulf*

Mi Musica Extremada — *Cabrera Infante, G*

c Mi Pequeno Libro De Numeros (Illus. by Judy Ziegler) — *Amerikaner, Susan*

Mia Nihta Me Tin Kokkini — *Ghimosoulis, Kostis*

c Mia the Beach Cat (Illus. by Kirsten Hocker) — *Hanel, Wolfram*

Miami Blues — *Willeford, Charles*

Miami: City of Dreams — *Maltz, Alan S*

c Miami-Nanny Stories (Illus. by Oki S Han) — *Milstein, Linda*

Miami: Trends and Traditions — *Dunlop, Beth*

c Mice — *Potter, Beatrix*

c The Mice of Mousehole — *Cartlidge, Michelle*

The Mice Will Play — *Phillips, Edward, 1931-*

Michael Collins: A Life — *Mackay, James*

Michael Collins: The Man Who Made Ireland — *Coogan, Tim Pat*

y Michael Crichton: A Critical Companion — *Trembley, Elizabeth A*

Michael Faraday — *Cantor, Geoffrey*

Michael Harrington: Speaking American — *Gorman, Robert A*

Michael Heseltine: A Biography — *Crick, Michael*

Michael Jackson's Beer Companion — *Jackson, Michael, 1942-*

r Michael Jackson's World Beer Hunter. Electronic Media Version — *Jackson, Michael, 1942-*

c Michael Jordan — *Rambeck, Richard*

Michael Lucero: Sculpture 1976-1995 — *Leach, Mark Richard*

Michael O'Meara's View from the Funny Farm — *Ryan, John, 1941-*

Michael Robartes and the Dancer — *Yeats, W B*

c Michael Rosen's ABC (Illus. by Bee Willey) — *Rosen, Michael, 1946-*

c Michael's Monsters (Illus. by Gus Clarke) — *Clarke, Gus*

Michel De Certeau: Interpretation and Its Other — *Ahearne, Jeremy*

Michel Foucault Et Ses Contemporains — *Eribon, Didier*

Michel Leiris: Dualisme Et Totalite — *Poitry, Guy*

Michel Tournier — *Gascoigne, David*

Michel Tournier — *Worton, Michael*

Michel Tournier: Bricolage and Cultural Mythology — *Roberts, Martin*

Michel Tournier: Le Coq De Bruyere — *Redfern, Walter*

c Michelangelo (Illus. by Simone Boni) — *Di Cagno, Gabriella*

Michelangelo: A Biography — *Bull, George*

y Michelangelo and His Times — *Milande, Veronique*

Michelangelo and His World — *Poeschke, Joachim*

Michelangelo and Raphael in the Vatican — *Botticelli, Sandro*

y Michelangelo: Master of the Italian Renaissance (Illus. by Sergio) — *Di Cagno, Gabriella*

Michelangelo: Selected Scholarship in English. Vols. 1-5

Michelangelo: The Sistine Chapel Ceiling, Rome — *Partridge, Loren*

Michelangelo: The Vatican Frescoes — *De Vecchi, Pierluigi*

Michelangelo Unterperger 1695-1758 — *Kronbichler, Johann*

r Michelin Canada

r Michelin's In Your Pocket Guide Books

p Michigan Quarterly Review

r The Michigan State Constitution — *Fino, Susan P*

y Mick — *Lynch, Chris*

Mickey Mouse History and Other Essays on American Memory — *Wallace, Mike*

Micro-Electronics: The Structure and Operation of Microprocessor-Based Systems — *Boniface, Douglas M*

Micro Fiction — *Stern, Jerome*

Micro-Macro Dilemmas in Political Science — *Eulau, Heinz*

y Microbes, Bugs and Wonder Drugs — *Balkwill, Fran*

Microbial Diversity in Time and Space — *Colwell, Rita R*

p Microbial Drug Resistance

Microbial Physiology. 3rd Ed. — *Moat, A G*

Microbial Physiology and Metabolism — *Caldwell, D R*

Microbial Quality of Water Supply in Distribution Systems — *Geldreich, Edwin E*

Microbiology for the Analytical Chemist — *Dart, R K*

Microcirculatory Approach to Asian Traditional Medicine — *Niimi, Hideyuki*

Microclimatic Landscape Design — *Brown, Robert D*

r Microcomputer Servicing. 3rd Ed. — *Asser, Stuart M*

r Microcomputer Theory and Servicing. 3rd Ed. — *Asser, Stuart M*

Microelectromechanical Systems — *Kim, C*

Microelectronic Switched-Capacitor Filters with ISICAP — *Baher, H*

Microelectronics: An Integrated Approach — *Howe, Roger T*

Microelectronics Technology — *Reichmanis, Elsa*

Microfiltration and Ultrafiltration — *Zeman, Leos J*

Microfinance and Poverty Reduction — *Johnson, Susan*

Microhistories: Demography, Society and Culture in Rural England 1800-1930 — *Reay, Barry*

Micrologus: Natura, Scienze E Societa Medievali. Vol. 2

Micromechanics of Advanced Materials — *Chu, S N G*

Micromechanics of Composites — *Stellbrink, Kuno K U*

Microorganisms and Autoimmune Diseases — *Friedman, Herman*

Microparticulate Systems for the Delivery of Proteins and Vaccines — *Cohen, Smadar*

The Micropolitics of Educational Leadership — *Blase, Joseph*

Microporous and Macroporous Materials — *Lobo, Raul F*

The Microprocessor: A Biography — *Malone, Michael S, 1954-*

Microprocessors and Microcomputers. 4th Ed. — *Tocci, Ronald J*

Microregional Fragmentation — *Persson, Lars Olof*

c The Microscope Book (Illus. by David Sovka) — *Levine, Shar*

The Microscope in the Dutch Republic — *Ruestow, Edward G*

Microscopic Anatomy of Invertebrates. Vol. 6, Pts. A-B

Microsimulation Modelling of the Corporate Firm — *Tongeren, F W Van*

Microsoft Access 2.0 How-To CD — *Getz, Ken*

Microsoft Access 95 How To — *Getz, Ken*

Microsoft Access for Windows 95 Step by Step — *Catapult, Inc.*

Microsoft BackOffice. Pt. 1

yr Microsoft Bookshelf 1996-97. Electronic Media Version

r Microsoft Bookshelf Internet Directory. 1996-1997 Ed.

cr Microsoft Encarta 96 World Atlas. Electronic Media Version

yr Microsoft Encarta 97 World Atlas. Electronic Media Version

The Microsoft Exchange Guide — *Foley, Todd*

Microsoft Exchange Server — *Redmond, Tony*

Microsoft Internet Explorer 3.0 Frontrunner — *Taylor, Mary*

Microsoft Office 95 Unleashed — *Charlesworth, Sue*

r Microsoft Office 97 Professional 6-in-One — *Aitken, Peter*

Microsoft Powerpoint for Windows 95 Step by Step — *Perspection, Inc.*

r Microsoft Press Programmer's Bookshelf for Windows 95. Electronic Media Version
Microsoft Project for Windows 95 Step by Step — *Catapult, Inc.*
r Microsoft Project/Visual Basic Reference — *Microsoft Corporation*
Microsoft Publisher by Design. 3rd Ed. — *Simone, Luisa*
Microsoft Secrets — *Cusumano, Michael A*
Microsoft Visual Basic Workshop — *Craig, John Clark*
The Microsoft Way — *Stross, Randall E*
Microsoft Windows NT Server One Step at a Time — *Brandt, Brian*
r Microsoft Wine Guide. Electronic Media Version
r Microsoft Word for Windows 95 — *Campbell, Mary*
Microsoft Word for Windows 95 Made Easy — *Neibauer, Alan*
Microsoft Word for Windows 95 Step by Step — *Catapult, Inc.*
Microsoft Works for Windows 95 — *Beatty, Grace Joely*
The Microstructure of Foreign Exchange Markets — *Frankel, Jeffrey A*
Microwave and Optical Wageguide Analysis by the Finite Element Method — *Fernandez, F Anibal*
Microwave Aquametry — *Kraszewski, Andrzej*
Microwave Processing of Materials V
Microwaves: Theory and Application in Materials Processing III
Midas Investing — *Steinberg, Jonathan*
The Midden — *Sharpe, Tom*
Middens of the Tribe — *Hoffman, Daniel*
yr The Middle Ages. Vols. 1-4 — *Jordan, William C*
The Middle Ages Reconsidered — *Keller, Barbara G*
Middle Class Dreams. Rev. and Updated Ed. — *Greenberg, Stanley B*
yr The Middle East — *Hiro, Dilip*
The Middle East — *Krooth, Richard*
The Middle East: A Brief History of the Last 2,000 Years — *Lewis, Bernard*
The Middle East after Iraq's Invasion of Kuwait — *Freedman, Robert O*
The Middle East after the Cold War — *Harris, William*
r The Middle East and North Africa 1996
r The Middle East and North Africa 1997
The Middle East and the United States — *Lesch, David W*
r Middle East Contemporary Survey. Vol. 17
The Middle East Economy — *Issawi, Charles Philip*
Middle East Imbroglio — *Link, P S*
c The Middle East in Search of Peace. Updated Ed. — *Long, Cathryn J*
The Middle East in the New World Order — *Jawad, H A*
The Middle East into the 21st Century — *Mallat, Chibli*
Middle East Oil and Gas — *International Energy Agency*
c The Middle East: Struggle for a Homeland (Illus. by John Isaac) — *Isaac, John*
The Middle Heart — *Lord, Bette Bao*
r Middle Level Education — *Totten, Samuel*
The Middle Paleolithic Site of Combe-Capelle Bas — *Dibble, Harold*
y The Middle Passage (Illus. by Tom Feelings) — *Feelings, Tom*
The Middle Passage — *Hollis, James*
y Middle Son — *Iida, Deborah*
y The Middle Window — *Goudge, Elizabeth*
The Middleground: The American Public and the Abortion Debate — *Sitaraman, Bhavani*
Middlemarch — *Eliot, George*
Middletown Jews — *Rottenberg, Dan*
The Middling Sort — *Hunt, Margaret R*
Midlife Journeys — *Olson, Richard P*
c A Midnight Clear — *Paterson, Katherine*
c The Midnight Detectives — *Lloyd, Carole*
c The Midnight Feast (Illus. by Tony Ross) — *Camp, Lindsay*
c The Midnight Gang (Illus. by Ann James) — *Wild, Margaret*
c The Midnight Horse (Illus. by Peter Sis) — *Fleischman, Sid*
c The Midnight Hour — *Edgers, Geoff*
Midnight in Sicily — *Robb, Peter*
Midnight in the City of Clocks — *Hill, Tobias*
y Midnight in the Garden of Good and Evil (Woodman). Audio Version — *Berendt, John*

The Midnight Meal and Other Essays about Doctors, Patients, and Medicine — *Lowenstein, Jerome*
c Midnight Rescue — *Johnson, Lois Walfrid*
Midnight Tales — *Stoker, Bram*
c Midnight Teddies — *Kubick, Dana*
Midrash and Theory — *Stern, David*
Midrass Tanhuma-Yelammedenu — *Berman, Samuel A*
y Midshipman's Hope — *Feintuch, David*
Midstream — *Schreiber, Le Anne*
y A Midsummer Night's Dream. Electronic Media Version
A Midsummer Night's Dream — *Griffiths, Trevor R*
y A Midsummer Night's Dream — *Olster, Fredi*
Midterm: The Elections of 1994 in Context — *Klinkner, Philip A*
r Midwest Weekends — *Gauper, Beth*
y The Midwife's Apprentice — *Cushman, Karen*
y The Midwife's Apprentice (Sterlin). Audio Version — *Cushman, Karen*
c Midwinter — *Henry, Maeve*
Midwinter: An Education Resource Pack for the Winter Term on British Traditions — *Rowe, Doc*
y Midwives — *Bohjalian, Chris*
c A Mien Family — *Gogol, Sara*
Mieter, Hausbesitzer, Staat Und Wohnungsmarkt — *Fuhrer, Karl Christian*
MiG Pilot — *Wise, Alan R*
Mightier than the Sword — *Streitmatter, Rodger*
A Mighty Baptism — *Juster, Susan*
The Mighty Bears! — *Moore, Andrew*
c Mighty Dinosaurs — *Simpson, Judith*
The Mighty Eighth — *Astor, Gerald*
c Mighty Giants of the Wild — *Donnelly, Jane*
c Mighty Max and the Castle of Doom (Illus. by Bernat Serrat) — *Razzi, Jim*
c The Mighty Ocean — *Berger, Melvin*
y The Mighty Skink — *Shipton, Paul*
Migraine: Pharmacology and Genetics — *Sandler, Merton*
Migrancy, Culture, Identity — *Chambers, Iain*
c Migrant Worker (Illus. by Lawrence Migdale) — *Hoyt-Goldsmith, Diane*
p Migrants against HIV/AIDS
Migrants, Emigrants and Immigrants — *Pooley, Colin F*
Migrants West — *Woolsey, Ronald C*
Migrating to Windows 95 — *Andrews, Mark*
Migration and Economic Integration in the Nordic Common Labour Market — *Fischer, Peter A*
Migration and European Integration — *Miles, Robert*
Migration and the Interindustry Wage Structure in Germany — *Haisken-DeNew, John P*
Migration and Transformations — *Strathern, Andrew J*
Migration, Citizenship and Ethno-National Identities in the European Union — *Martiniello, Marco*
La Migration Des Coeurs — *Conde, Maryse*
Migration, Jihad, and Muslim Authority in West Africa — *Hanson, John H*
Migration: The Asian Experience — *Brown, Judith M*
Migrations and Cultures — *Sowell, Thomas*
c Mike Mulligan and His Steam Shovel. Electronic Media Version — *Burton, Virginia Lee*
c Mike's Bulldozer and the Big Flood — *Bodsworth, Nan*
Mikhail Bakhtin — *Clark, Katerina*
Mikhail Bakhtin: Between Phenomenology and Marxism — *Bernard-Donals, Michael F*
Mikhail Bakhtin: Creation of a Prosaics — *Morson, Gary Saul*
The Mi'kmaq: Resistance, Accommodation, and Cultural Survival — *Prins, Harald E L*
Milagro De La Paz — *Argueta, Manlio*
Milchstrasse, Nebel, Galaxien — *Wolfschmidt, Gudrun*
The Milepost: Alaska. Spring '96-Spring '97
Miles and Flora — *Bailey, Hilary*
y Miles Davis — *Crisp, George R*
Miles to Go — *Moynihan, Daniel Patrick*
r Milestones: A Chronology of American Women's History — *Weatherford, Doris L*
Milestones in Rock Engineering
Milestones in the British Accounting Literature — *Parker, R H*
Militancy, Market Dynamics, and Workplace Authority — *Zetka, James R, Jr.*
Militant and Triumphant — *O'Toole, James M*
The Militarization of the U.S.-Mexico Border 1978-1992 — *Dunn, Timothy J*
yr The Military 100 — *Lanning, Michael Lee*

The Military and the Media 1968-1973 — *Hammond, William M*
Military Flying Activities in Labrador and Quebec — *Canadian Environmental Assessment Agency*
r A Military History of Ireland — *Bartlett, Thomas*
r The Military History of the Third World since 1945 — *Sturgill, Claude C*
The Military in British India — *Heathcote, T A*
The Military in Politics and Society in France and Germany in the Twentieth Century — *Muller, Klaus-Jurgen*
The Military in the Making of Modern South Africa — *Seegers, Annette*
Military Innovation in the Interwar Period — *Murray, Williamson*
Military Institutions on the Welsh Marches — *Suppe, Frederick C*
Military Orders and Crusades — *Forey, Alan*
Military R&D after the Cold War — *Gummett, Philip*
Military Readiness — *Betts, Richard K*
Military Rebellion in Argentina — *Norden, Deborah L*
The Military Revolution. 2nd Ed. — *Parker, Geoffrey*
The Military Revolution Debate — *Rogers, Clifford J*
The Military Revolution in Sixteenth-Century Europe — *Eltis, David*
The Military Uses of Literature — *Hooker, Mark T*
y The Militia Movement — *Cozic, Charles P*
y The Militia Movement and Hate Groups in America — *McCuen, Gary*
y The Militia Movement in America — *Andryszewski, Tricia*
Militiamen, Rangers, and Redcoats — *Johnson, James M*
yr Militias in America — *Hamilton, Neil A, 1949-*
c Milk and Honey (Illus. by Louise August) — *Yolen, Jane*
Milk, Money, and Madness — *Baumslag, Naomi*
Milk of Human Kindness (Haddon). Audio Version — *Ferrars, Elizabeth*
Milky Way Railroad — *Miyazawa, Kenji*
The Mill Iron Site — *Frison, George C*
y The Mill on the Floss — *Edmundson, Helen*
The Mill on the Floss — *Eliot, George*
Mill Valley — *Spitz, Barry*
Millennium: A History of the Last Thousand Years — *Fernandez-Armesto, Felipe*
Das Millennium — *Heiss, Gernot*
The Millennium Hotel — *Rudman, Mark*
A Millennium of the Book — *Myers, Robin*
y Millennium Rage — *Lamy, Philip*
Miller, Bukowski, and Their Enemies — *Joyce, William, 1945-*
Miller's Bolt — *Stirr, Thomas*
c Millie and the Mermaid — *Ives, Penny*
c Millie Cooper and Friends (Illus. by Helen Cogancherry) — *Herman, Charlotte*
Million Dollar Mouths — *Bruce, Stephen D*
The Million-Dollar Tattoo — *Emerson, Earl*
c A Million Fish...More or Less — *McKissack, Pat*
c A Million Visions of Peace — *Garrison, Jennifer*
The Millionaire Next Door — *Stanley, Thomas J*
The Millionaire's Secrets — *Fisher, Mark*
Millrat — *Casey, Michael*
c Milly of the Rovers (Illus. by Christyan Fox) — *Castor, Harriet*
c Milton (Illus. by Kristy Chu) — *Massey, Ed*
Milton and the Culture of Violence — *Lieb, Michael*
Milton and the Hermeneutic Journey — *Carrithers, Gale H, Jr.*
Milton and the Revolutionary Reader — *Achinstein, Sharon*
Milton in America — *Ackroyd, Peter*
Milton in Government — *Fallon, Robert Thomas*
r Milton, Spenser, and the Epic Tradition — *Cook, Patrick J*
Milton Studies. Vol. 29
Milton, the Metaphysicals, and Romanticism — *Low, Lisa*
Milton Unbound — *Rumrich, John P*
Milton's Burden of Interpretation — *Haskin, Dayton*
Milton's House of God — *Honeygosky, Stephen R*
Milton's Imperial Epic — *Evans, J Martin*
Milwaukee Road 1850-1960 Photo Archive — *Letourneau, P A*
Mimbres Mogollon Archaeology — *Woosley, Anne I*
Mimes Et Parades — *Boulad-Ayoub, Josiane*
c Mimi and Jean-Paul's Cajun Mardi Gras (Illus. by Marilyn Carter Rougelot) — *Moore, Elizabeth*
c Mimi's Tutu (Illus. by Jan Spivey Gilchrist) — *Thomassie, Tynia*
Mimologics — *Genette, Gerard*

Min Cui Wang Tai Lun — *Huang, Kuang-Kuo*
Mina P. Shaughnessy: Her Life and Work — *Maher, Jane*
c Minas and the Fish (Illus. by Olga Pastuchiv) — *Pastuchiv, Olga*
c The Mincing Machine (Illus. by Dee Shulman) — *Wooderson, Philip*
c The Mind (Illus. by Ross Collins) — *Barber, Nicola*
A Mind Always in Motion — *Segre, Emilio*
Mind and Morality — *Bricke, John*
Mind and Morals — *May, Larry*
The Mind and the Physical World — *Snyder, Douglas M*
Mind-Body Deceptions — *Dubovsky, Steven L*
Mind/Body Health — *Hafen, Brent Q*
r Mind-Body Wellness — *Polidora, Jim*
c Mind-Boggling Machines and Amazing Mazes — *Davis, Edmond*
Mind Games — *Baker, Robert A*
Mind Games — *Kindler, Seth*
Mind Grenades — *Plunkett, John*
The Mind of David Hume — *Johnson, Oliver*
The Mind of John Locke — *Harris, Ian*
Mind over Golf — *Coop, Richard H*
y Mind Riot — *Hirsch, Karen D*
Mind Set — *Doster, Paul W*
Mind Slash (Auberjonois). Audio Version — *Wellen, Edward*
c Mind the Door (Illus. by Tony Ross) — *Barlow, Steve*
Mind Your Musical Manners. 3rd Ed. — *Sorel, Claudette*
c Mind Your Own Business (Illus. by Quentin Blake) — *Rosen, Michael, 1946-*
Minderheden In Westeuropese Steden 16de-20ste Eeuw — *Soly, Hugh*
Minding Her Own Business — *Zobel, Jan*
Minding My Own Business — *Muir, Percy*
Minding Nature — *Macauley, David*
Minding the Children — *Youcha, Geraldine*
Minding the Sun — *Pack, Robert*
c Mindmaster — *Gifford, Clive*
y Mindquakes: Stories to Shatter Your Brain — *Shusterman, Neal*
c Mind's Eye — *French, Jackie*
The Minds of Birds — *Skutch, Alexander Frank*
yr Mindscape Student Reference Library. Electronic Media Version
Mindstar Rising — *Hamilton, Peter F*
y Mindstorms: Stories to Blow Your Mind — *Shusterman, Neal*
Mine Eyes Have Seen — *Goldstein, Richard*
A Mine of Her Own — *Zanjani, Sally*
Minefields in Their Hearts — *Apfel, Roberta J*
Mineral Resources Development and Investment Opportunities
r The Mineralogical Record Index: Vols. 1-25 — *Clopton, Edwin L*
Mineralogy of Arizona. 3rd Ed. — *Anthony, John W*
r Mineralogy of Maine. Vol. 1 — *King, Vandall T*
Mineralogy Tutorials. Electronic Media Version — *Klein, Cornelis*
Minerals Bioprocessing II — *Holmes, David S*
The Miner's Flame Light Book — *Pohs, Henry A*
The Miners of Windber — *Beik, Mildred Allen*
Miners, Unions, and Politics 1910-47 — *Campbell, Alan*
Minerva and the Muse — *Von Mehren, Joan*
c Minerva Louise at School (Illus. by Janet Morgan Stoeke) — *Stoeke, Janet Morgan*
c Mine's the Best — *Bonsall, Crosby*
Miniature Vertebrates — *Miller, P J*
r Miniature Victorian Lamps — *Hulsebus, Marjorie*
Miniatury: Catalogue of Miniatures
Minimal Art — *Colpitt, Frances*
Minimalism: Origins — *Strickland, Edward*
Minimalism, Scope, and VP Structure — *Stroik, Thomas S*
Minimalists — *Schwarz, K Robert*
Minimax Theorems — *Willem, Michel*
Minimum — *Pawson, John*
Minimum Wages in Central and Eastern Europe — *Standing, Guy*
Mining Environment — *World Mining Environment Congress (1st: 1995: New Delhi, India)*
y Mining the Sky — *Lewis, John S*
Ministerial Conference Summary — *G7 Ministerial Conference on the Global Information Society (1995: Brussels, Belgium)*
Ministry and Meaning — *Kauffman, Christopher J*
Ministry and Theology in Global Perspective — *Pittman, Don A*

Ministry for the Homebound — *Miller, Kent C*
The Ministry of Hope — *Heath, Roy*
The Ministry of Illusion — *Rentschler, Eric*
Minkowski Geometry — *Thompson, Anthony C*
Minnesota and the Global Community
MinnowKnits: Uncommon Clothes to Knit for Kids — *Eaton, Jill*
The Minoan Buildings on the West Side of Area A — *Betancourt, Philip P*
y Minor Players, Major Dreams — *Mandel, Brett H*
Minority Rights in Europe — *Miall, Hugh*
Mintha Elnel — *Garaczi, Laszlo*
c Minty: A Story of Young Harriet Tubman (Illus. by Jerry Pinkney) — *Schroeder, Alan*
Minute Meditations — *Peltz, Carl F*
Minutes of the Lead Pencil Club — *Henderson, Bill*
c Mira Las Flores, Teo (Illus. by Violeta Denou) — *Denou, Violeta*
Mirabile Dictu — *Biow, Douglas*
Miracle at Kitty Hawk — *Wright, Wilbur*
Miracle at St. Bruno's (White). Audio Version — *Carr, Philippa*
Le Miracle De Laon — *Backus, Irena*
A Miracle Mirrored — *Davids, Karel*
The Miracle of Change — *Wholey, Dennis*
y The Miracle of Life — *D'Oyen, F M*
Miracle of the Saints — *Ghezzi, Bert*
Miracle on the 17th Green — *Patterson, James*
Miracle on the 17th Green (Linden). Audio Version — *Patterson, James*
Miracles and the Modern Religious Imagination — *Mullin, Robert Bruce*
Miracles Happen When You Pray — *Sherrer, Quin*
Miracles on the Border — *Durand, Jorge*
Miraculous Living — *Labowitz, Shoni*
Miradas, Versiones Y Escrituras — *Flawia De Fernandez, Nilda Maria*
Mirage — *Khashoggi, Soheir*
y Mirage — *Wilson, F Paul*
Mirage (Mettey). Audio Version — *Wilson, F Paul*
Mirage: The False Promise of Desert Agriculture — *Clemings, Russell Allan*
Mirage: Why Neither Democrats nor Republicans Can Balance the Budget, End the Deficit, and Satisfy the Public — *Hager, George*
Miramar — *Mahfouz, Naguib*
c Miranda the Castaway (Illus. by James Mayhew) — *Mayhew, James*
y Miranda v. Arizona — *Wice, Paul B*
c Mirandy and Brother Wind (Illus. by Jerry Pinkney) — *McKissack, Pat*
Mirbeau's Fictions — *Lloyd, Christopher, 1945-*
c Miremos Donde Voy — *Ribas, Teresa*
c Miremos El Campo — *Ribas, Teresa*
c Miremos El Fin De Semana — *Ribas, Teresa*
c Miremos El Hipermercado — *Ribas, Teresa*
c Miremos La Casa — *Ribas, Teresa*
c Miremos La Ciudad — *Ribas, Teresa*
c Miremos La Fiesta — *Ribas, Teresa*
c Miremos Las Tiendas — *Ribas, Teresa*
c Mirette on the High Wire — *McCully, Emily Arnold*
c Miriam — *Sommerfelt, Aimee, 1892-*
c Miro in the Kingdom of the Sun (Illus. by David Frampton) — *Kurtz, Jane*
Le Miroir Des Idees — *Tournier, Michel*
Le Miroir: Naissance D'un Genre Litteraire — *Jonsson, Einar Mar*
Le Miroir Qui Revient — *Robbe-Grillet, Alain*
c Mirror (Illus. by Alexandra Day) — *Darling, Christina*
The Mirror and the Killer-Queen — *Schwab, Gabriele*
The Mirror and the Word — *Williams, Eric B*
y Mirror Game — *Foon, Dennis*
Mirror Machine — *Marchessault, Janine*
The Mirror of Alchemy — *Roberts, Gareth*
The Mirror of Confusion — *Kirk, Andrew M*
A Mirror to the Cage — *Gyorgyey, Clara*
Mirrors Blink — *Kucharski, Lisa*
Mirrors in Mind — *Gregory, Richard*
Mirrors of Celestial Grace — *Weatherby, Harold L*
Mis Memorias — *Duque Miyar, Evelio*
La Misa De Baroja — *Molina-Foix, Vicente*
Miscellania De Textos Medievals. Vol. 7 — *Ferrer I Mallol, Maria Teresa*
A Miscellany on Nicholas of Cusa — *Hopkins, Jasper*
Mischief — *Quick, Amanda*
c Mischief, Mad Mary, and Me — *Knight, Dawn*
Misery — *King, Stephen*
The Misfortunes of Prosperity — *Cohen, Daniel, 1953-*
Mismanaged Trade? — *Flamm, Kenneth*
Mismapping the Underworld — *Kleiner, John*

The Mismeasure of Man. Rev. and Expanded Ed. — *Gould, Stephen Jay*
Misogynies — *Smith, Joan, 1953-*
Misreading Jane Eyre — *Beaty, Jerome*
Misrepresentations: Shakespeare and the Materialists — *Bradshaw, Graham*
c Miss Bindergarten Gets Ready for Kindergarten (Illus. by Ashley Wolff) — *Slate, Joseph*
c Miss Brick the Builders' Baby (Illus. by Colin McNaughton) — *Ahlberg, Allan*
Miss Bunting — *Thirkell, Angela*
The Miss Dennis School of Writing and Other Lessons from a Woman's Life — *Steinbach, Alice*
c Miss Dirt the Dustman's Daughter (Illus. by Tony Ross) — *Ahlberg, Allan*
c Miss Dose the Doctor's Daughter (Illus. by Faith Jaques) — *Ahlberg, Allan*
c Miss Emma's Wild Garden (Illus. by Anna Grossnickle Hines) — *Hines, Anna Grossnickle*
c Miss Fischer's Jewels (Illus. by Michael Reid) — *Alexander, Jenny*
Miss Gomez and the Brethren — *Trevor, William*
c Miss Jump the Jockey (Illus. by Andre Amstutz) — *Ahlberg, Allan*
Miss Kendall Sets Her Cap — *Devon, Marian*
c Miss Malarkey Doesn't Live in Room 10 (Illus. by Kevin O'Malley) — *Finchler, Judy*
Miss Manners Basic Training: Communication — *Martin, Judith*
Miss Manners on (Painfully Proper) Weddings — *Martin, Judith*
Miss Manners Rescues Civilization — *Martin, Judith*
c Miss Nelson Is Missing! (Illus. by James Marshall) — *Allard, Harry*
Miss O — *Oliphant, Betty*
Miss Rhythm — *Brown, Ruth, 1928-*
c Miss Rumphius — *Cooney, Barbara*
c Miss Spider's Tea Party (Illus. by David Kirk) — *Kirk, David*
c Miss Spider's Wedding — *Kirk, David*
c Miss Wire and the Three Kind Mice (Illus. by Emma Chichester Clark) — *Whybrow, Ian*
Miss Zukas and the Raven's Dance — *Dereske, Jo*
Missadot Sheba'emek Ad Rekhov Hamasger — *Mazor, Yair*
Misschien Wisten Zij Alles — *Tellegen, Toon*
Missed Chances — *Denman, Roy*
Misselthwaite — *Moody, Susan*
The Missile and Space Race — *Levine, Alan J*
The Missing — *O'Hagan, Andrew*
y Missing Angel Juan — *Block, Francesca Lia*
c The Missing Cat (Illus. by Chris Demarest). Book and Audio Version
Missing Eden — *Lee, W W*
c The Missing Fossil Mystery (Illus. by Andrew Glass) — *Herman, Emily*
Missing Links — *Reilly, Rick*
Missing Links — *United Nations Commission on Science and Technology for Development. Gender Working Group*
y Missing May — *Rylant, Cynthia*
c Missing May (Rogers). Audio Version — *Rylant, Cynthia*
Missing Pieces — *Fielding, Joy*
y Missing Pieces — *Mazer, Norma Fox*
c The Missing Sunflowers (Illus. by Donna Ruff) — *Stern, Maggie*
y Missing the Piano — *Rapp, Adam*
Missiology: An Ecumenical Introduction — *Camps, A*
Mission Critical — *Picken, Joseph C*
Mission Culture on the Upper Amazon — *Block, David*
c Mission, Earth — *English, June A*
Mission in a Pluralist World — *Lande, Aasulv*
Mission Legacies — *Anderson, Gerald H*
Mission Possible — *Blanchard, Kenneth H*
Mission Possible: 200 Ways to Strengthen the Nonprofit Sector's Infrastructure — *Chieco, Kate*
Mission to the Planets — *Moore, Patrick*
The Missionary and the Libertine — *Buruma, Ian*
Missionary Conquest — *Tinker, George E*
The Missionary Movement in Christian History — *Walls, Andrew F*
The Missionary Position — *Hitchens, Christopher*
The Missionary's Wife — *Jeal, Tim*
Missionnaires Au Quotidien A Tahiti — *Toullelan, Pierre-Yves*
c Missions of the Central Coast — *Behrens, June*
c Missions of the Los Angeles Area — *MacMillan, Dianne*
c Missions of the Monterey Bay Area — *Abbink, Emily*

Title Index

c Missions of the San Francisco Bay Area — *White, Tekla N*

c Missions of the Southern Coast — *Lemke, Nancy*

Mississippi: An American Journey — *Walton, Anthony*

Mississippi Currents — *Malcolm, Andrew H*

The Mississippi Delta and the World — *Cohn, David L*

c Mississippi Going North (Illus. by Bill Farnsworth) — *Baker, Sanna Anderson*

c Mississippi Mud (Illus. by Robert J Blake) — *Turner, Ann Warren*

A Mississippi Rebel in the Army of Northern Virginia — *Cockrell, Thomas D*

y Mississippi Treasure Hunt — *Cannon, Taffy*

Mississippian Communities and Households — *Rogers, J Daniel*

r Missouri Nature Viewing Guide — *Daniels, Martha*

r Missouri's Conservation Atlas — *Overby, Charlotte*

c Mist over the Mountains (Illus. by Raymond Bial) — *Bial, Raymond*

y Mister Christian — *Kinsolving, William*

Mister Roberts — *Heggen, Thomas*

Mister Rogers' Neighborhood — *Collins, Mark*

Mister Sandman — *Gowdy, Barbara*

La Mistica De Sandino — *Bendana, Alejandro*

The Mistress of Spices — *Divakaruni, Chitra Banerjee*

Mistress of the House, Mistress of Heaven — *Capel, Anne K*

The Mistresses of King George IV — *Levy, M J*

Mists of Regret — *Andrew, Dudley*

y Misty of Chincoteague (McDonough). Audio Version — *Henry, Marguerite*

Misunderstanding Science? — *Irwin, Alan*

c Mitchell Is Moving (Illus. by Jose Aruego) — *Sharmat, Marjorie Weinman*

Mithras — *Cooper, D Jason*

Mitosenes and Related Antitumor Drugs — *Maliepaard, Marc*

Mitsrayim Be-Petah Ha-Idan Ha-Moderni — *Toledano, Ehud*

Mitsuaki Iwago's Penguins — *Iwago, Mitsuaki*

Die Mittelalterlichen Grabmaler In Rom Und Latium Vom 13. Bis Zum 15. Jahrhundert. Vol. 2 — *Garms, J*

Mitteleuropa and German Politics 1848 to the Present — *Brechtefeld, Jorg*

c The Mitten: A Ukrainian Folktale (Illus. by Jan Brett) — *Brett, Jan*

p Mix: The Magazine of Artist-Run Culture

Mixed Company — *Shapiro, Alan*

Mixing in Estuaries and Coastal Seas — *Pattiaratchi, Charitha*

Mixing Messages — *Lupton, Ellen*

Mixteca-Puebla: Discoveries and Research in Mesoamerican Art and Archaeology — *Nicholson, H B*

c Miz Fannie Mae's Fine New Easter Hat (Illus. by Yong Chen) — *Milich, Melissa*

ML for the Working Programmer. 2nd Ed. — *Paulson, Lawrence C*

r MLA International Bibliography of Books and Articles on the Modern Languages and Literatures 1922-

Mo Ri Zhi Men. Vols. 1-2 — *Qiao, Liang*

c Mo Vaughn: Big Mo — *Santella, Andrew*

r Moanin' Low — *Laird, Ross*

Mobile and Personal Communications — *Joint COST 227/231 Workshop on Mobile and Personal Communications (2nd: 1995: Florence, Italy)*

Mobile and Rapidly Assembled Structures II — *International Conference on Mobile and Rapidly Assembled Structures (2nd: 1996: Seville, Spain)*

Mobile and Wireless Networks — *Black, Uyless*

Mobile Capital and Latin American Development — *Mahon, James E*

r Mobile Communications — *Mazda, Fraidoon*

Mobile Computing — *Imielinski, Tomasz*

Mobile Farmers — *Graham, Martha*

Mobile Guerrilla Force — *Donahue, James C*

Mobile Pastoralists — *Chatty, Dawn*

Mobility and Migration — *Thompson, Roger, 1933-*

The Mobilization of Intellect — *Hanna, Martha*

The Mobilization of Muslim Women in Egypt — *Talhami, Ghada Hashem*

Mobilizing the Masses — *Wou, Odoric Y K*

Mobilizing the Organization — *Litwin, George*

Mobius on Emerging Markets — *Mobius, J Mark*

y Moby-Dick (Illus. by Victor G Ambrus) — *McCaughrean, Geraldine*

Mockery of Justice — *Cooper, Cynthia L*

MODA4--Advances in Model-Oriented Data Analysis — *Kitsos, Christos P*

Modalities: Philosophical Essays — *Marcus, Ruth Barcan*

The Model City of the New South — *Gates, Grace Hooten*

Model Guide — *Heinen, Renata*

Model Mothers — *Marks, Lara V*

The Model Occupation — *Bunting, Madeleine*

A Model of Human Occupation. 2nd Ed. — *Kielhofner, Gary*

A Model of the Universe — *McCall, Storrs*

Model Strategies in Bilingual Education — *Leighton, Mary S*

Model: The Ugly Business of Beautiful Women — *Gross, Michael*

c Modela Con Barro — *Bohera, Carme*

Le Modele Et L'Enquete — *Gerard-Varet, Louis-Andre*

Modeling, Analysis and Control of Dynamic Elastic Multi-Link Structures — *Lagnese, J E*

Modeling and Analysis of Reservoir System Operations — *Wurbs, Ralph Allen*

Modeling and Optimization of the Lifetime of Technologies — *Hritonenko, Natali*

Modeling and Simulation of Mixed Analog-Digital Systems — *Antao, Brian*

Modeling Biological Systems — *Haefner, James W*

Modeling Change in Environmental Systems — *Jakeman, A J*

Modeling Dynamic Transportation Networks. 2nd Ed. — *Ran, Bin*

Modeling Economic Management and Policy Issues of Water in Irrigated Agriculture — *Dinar, Ariel*

Modeling Methods for Environmental Engineers — *Abd Al-Majid, Isam Mohammed*

Modeling North American Economic Integration — *Kehoe, Patrick J*

Modeling of Casting, Welding and Advanced Solidification Processes VII — *Conference in a Series on Modeling Casting and Welding Processes (7th: 1995: London, England)*

Modeling of Composites — *Chen, Shao Ping*

Modeling Prehistoric Agricultural Productivity in Southwestern Colorado — *Van West, Carla R*

Modelling Early Christianity — *Esler, Philip F*

Modelling Marine Processes — *Dyke, Phil*

Modelling Mathematical Methods and Scientific Computation — *Bellomo, Nicola*

Modelling Molecular Structures — *Hindcliffe, Alan*

Modelling Techniques for Financial Markets and Bank Management — *Bertocchi, Marida*

Modelling the Early Human Mind — *Mellars, Paul*

Modelling the Economy and the Environment — *Madsen, Bjarne*

Models for Assessing Drug Absorption and Metabolism — *Borchardt, Ronald T*

Models for Energy Policy — *Lesourd, Jean-Baptiste*

Models for Infectious Human Diseases — *Isham, Valerie*

Models for Interpretation of Scripture — *Goldingay, John*

Models for Scripture — *Goldingay, John*

Models of Confirmation and Baptismal Affirmation — *Browning, Robert L*

Models of Democracy. 2nd Ed. — *Held, David*

Models of Management — *Guillen, Mauro E*

Models of Matter — *Wiegand, Gayl H*

Models of My Life — *Simon, Herbert Alexander*

Models of Random Processes — *Kovalenko, Igor Nikolaevich*

Models of Sustainable Development — *Faucheux, Sylvie*

Models of Visual Spatial Cognition — *De Vega, Manuel*

Models That Work — *Tucker, Alan C*

Modem Nation — *Bowen, Charles*

Moderate Realism and its Logic — *Mertz, D W*

Modern Algebra and the Rise of Mathematical Structures — *Corry, Leo*

Modern American Houses — *Pearson, Clifford A*

Modern American Music — *Karolyi, Otto*

r Modern American Popular Religion — *Lippy, Charles H*

Modern American Religion. Vol. 3 — *Marty, Martin E*

Modern American Short Story Sequences — *Kennedy, J Gerald*

A Modern Approach to Probability Theory — *Fristedt, Bert*

Modern Arabic Drama — *Jayyusi, Salma Khadra*

Modern Architecture since 1900. 3rd Ed. — *Curtis, William J R*

The Modern Ark — *Croke, Vicki*

Modern Art in the Common Culture — *Crow, Thomas*

Modern Aspects of Electrochemistry. No. 28

Modern Aspects of Electrochemistry. No. 30

Modern Astrometry — *Kovalevsky, Jean*

Modern Austrian Literature — *Markolin, Caroline*

Modern Baptists — *Wilcox, James*

Modern Black Nationalism — *Van Deburg, William L*

The Modern Book of Stretching — *Rush, Anne Kent*

Modern Britain — *Glynn, Sean*

Modern British Jewry — *Alderman, Geoffrey*

Modern by Tradition — *Bernstein, Bruce*

Modern Chinese Literary Thought — *Denton, Kirk A*

y Modern Classics of Fantasy — *Dozois, Gardner*

r Modern Collector's Dolls — *Smith, Patricia R*

Modern Control Engineering. 3rd Ed. — *Ogata, Katsuhiko*

Modern Control Systems Engineering — *Gajic, Zoran*

The Modern Corporation and American Political Thought — *Bowman, Scott R*

r Modern Dictionary of Electronics. 6th Ed. — *Graf, Rudolf F*

Modern Drama by Women 1880s-1930s — *Kelly, Katherine E*

r Modern Electronic Communication. 5th Ed. — *Miller, Gary M*

Modern Elementary Statistics. 9th Ed. — *Freund, John E*

Modern Environmentalism — *Pepper, David*

The Modern Epic — *Moretti, Franco*

The Modern Epidemic — *Johnston, William, 1955-*

Modern Europe in the Making — *Fasel, George*

The Modern Functional Building — *Behne, Adolf*

Modern Greece — *Legg, Keith R*

Modern Hernia Repair. 2nd Ed. — *Skandalakis, Lee John*

A Modern History of Southeast Asia — *Christie, Clive J*

A Modern History of the Kurds — *McDowall, David*

Modern Indonesia — *Cribb, Robert*

Modern Investment Theory. 4th Ed. — *Haugen, Robert A*

Modern Irish Literature — *Mercier, Vivian*

r Modern Irish Lives — *McRedmond, Louis*

Modern Irish Poetry — *Crotty, Patrick*

Modern Italy 1871-1995 — *Clark, Martin*

Modern Japanese Diaries — *Keene, Donald*

Modern Japanese Tanka — *Ueda, Makoto*

Modern Judaism — *Cohn-Sherbok, Dan*

Modern Law — *Blumrosen, Alfred W*

Modern Lives — *Dolan, Marc*

y Modern Mathematicians — *Henderson, Harry*

Modern Mathematics in the Light of the Fields Medals — *Monastysky, Michael*

A Modern Mephistopheles (Herbert). Audio Version — *Alcott, Louisa May*

Modern Music and After — *Griffiths, Paul*

The Modern Practice of Adult Education — *Briton, Derek*

The Modern Presidency and Economic Policy — *Frendreis, John P*

Modern Questions about Medieval Sermons — *Beriou, Nicole*

Modern Regression Methods — *Ryan, Thomas P*

Modern Skeletons in Postmodern Closets — *Sosnoski, James J*

r Modern Solder Technology for Competitive Electronics Manufacturing — *Hwang, Jennie S*

The Modern Spanish Economy — *Salmon, Keith G*

Modern Spectroscopy. 3rd Ed. — *Hollas, J Michael*

Modern Spectroscopy of Solids, Liquids, and Gases

Modern Spectrum Analysis of Time Series — *Naidu, Prabhakar S*

The Modern Subject — *Ameriks, Karl*

Modern Techniques in Electroanalysis — *Vanysek, Petr*

Modern Techniques in Raman Spectroscopy — *Laserna, J J*

The Modern Temper — *Dumenil, Lynn*

Modern Times — *Li, Po-Yuan*

y Modern Tyrants — *Chirot, Daniel*

Modern Ukrainian Short Stories — *Luckyj, George S N*

The Modern Voice in American Poetry — *Doreski, William*

Modern Wales — *Morgan, Kenneth O*

Modern Well Design — *Aadnoy, Bernt S*

r Modern Women Writers. Vols. 1-4 — *Robinson, Lillian S*

y The Modern World — *Kelly, Nigel*

y The Modern World — *Lancaster, Tony*

y Modern World History — *McAleavy, Tony*
Moderne Makrookonomik — *Flemmig, Jorg*
Moderne Zeiten — *Schildt, Axel*
Moderni Revue 1894-1925 — *Urban, Otto M*
Modernism — *Weston, Richard*
Modernism and Feminism — *Topliss, Helen*
Modernism and Mass Politics — *Tratner, Michael*
Modernism and the Theater of Censorship — *Parkes, Adam*
Modernism from Right to Left — *Filreis, Alan*
El Modernismo Argentino Incognito En La Ondina Del Plata Y Revista Literaria 1875-1880 — *Marun, Gioconda*
r Modernisms: A Literary Guide — *Nicholls, Peter*
Modernism's Body — *Froula, Christine*
Modernist Alchemy — *Materer, Timothy*
Modernist Quartet — *Lentricchia, Frank*
Modernity and Beyond — *Sabapathy, T K*
Modernity and Nostalgia — *Golan, Romy*
Modernity and Power — *Ninkovich, Frank*
Modernity and the State — *Offe, Claus*
Modernizacion Economica vs. Modernizacion Social — *Saenz Rovner, Eduardo*
Modernization and Postmodernization — *Inglehart, Ronald*
Modernization and the Structure of Societies. Vols. 1-2 — *Levy, Marion J*
The Modernization of Fatherhood — *LaRossa, Ralph*
Modest Musorgsky and Boris Godunov — *Emerson, Caryl*
Modules and Group Algebras — *Carlson, J F*
Moe Berg: Athlete, Scholar, Spy — *Kaufman, Louis*
y Moe Berg: The Spy behind Home Plate — *Grey, Vivian*
La Moglie Estatica — *Terzi, Antonio*
The Mojave: A Portrait of the Definitive American Desert — *Darlington, David*
c Mola: Cuna Life Stories and Art — *Presilla, Maricel E*
Molding the Good Citizen — *Lerner, Robert*
Molecular and Genetic Aspects of Obesity — *Bray, George A*
Molecular Basis of Virus Evolution — *Gibbs, Adrian J*
The Molecular Biology of Gaia — *Williams, George Ronald*
Molecular Biology of Hematopoiesis 5 — *Abraham, Nader G*
Molecular Biology of Membrane Transport Disorders — *Schultz, Stanley G*
Molecular Biology of Pseudomonads — *Nakazawa, Teruko*
Molecular Biotechnology — *Maulik, Sunil*
p Molecular Breeding: New Strategies in Plant Improvement
Molecular, Cellular, and Clinical Aspects of Angiogenesis — *Maragoudakis, Michael E*
Molecular Diagnosis of Cancer — *Cotter, Finbarr E*
Molecular Diagnosis of Genetic Diseases — *Elles, Rob*
Molecular Diagnostics — *Coleman, William B*
Molecular Diversity and Combinatorial Chemistry — *Chaiken, Irwin M*
Molecular Evolution of Viruses — *Becker, Yechiel*
Molecular Genetics and Colorectal Neoplasia — *Church, James M*
Molecular Genetics and Therapy of Leukemia — *Freireich, Emil J*
Molecular Level Artificial Photosynthetic Materials — *Meyer, Gerald J*
Molecular Magnetism — *Coronado, Eugenio*
Molecular Microbial Ecology Manual — *Akkermans, Antoon D L*
Molecular Modeling of Inorganic Compounds — *Comba, Peter*
Molecular Physics and Elements of Quantum Chemistry — *Haken, Hermann*
Molecular Physics and Hypersonic Flows — *Molecular Physics and Hypersonic Flows (1995: Maratea, Italy)*
Molecular Physiology and Pharmacology of Cardiac Ion Channels and Transporters — *Morad, Martin*
Molecular Politics — *Wright, Susan, 1939-*
r Molecular Zoology — *Ferraris, Joan D*
Molecule-Based Magnetic Materials — *Turnbull, Mark M*
Moliere: Don Juan — *Whitton, David*
Moliseide: Songs and Ballads in the Molisan Dialect — *Rimanelli, Giose*
y Moll Flanders (Leishman). Audio Version — *Defoe, Daniel*
c Molly — *Drinkwater, Carol*
c Molly Brown Is Not a Clown (Illus. by Rick Van Krugel) — *Rogers, Linda*

c Molly Limbo (Illus. by Elizabeth Miles) — *Hodges, Margaret*
Molnfri Bombnatt — *Olsson, Vibeke*
r Molotov and Soviet Government — *Watson, Derek*
Molyneux's Problem — *Degenaar, Marjolein*
c Mom and Me — *Kaplan, John*
The Moment: A History, Typology and Theory of the Moment in Philosophy and Literature — *Wagenbaur, Thomas*
A Moment on the Earth — *Easterbrook, Gregg*
A Moment's Monument — *Wagner, Jennifer Ann*
A Moment's Notice — *Greenhouse, Carol J*
Moments of Crisis in Jewish-Christian Relations — *Saperstein, Marc*
Moments of Grace — *Gaines, Patrice*
Moments of Vision and Miscellaneous Verses — *Hardy, Thomas*
c Mommi Watta (Illus. by Theodocia Swecker) — *Castleman, Virginia*
c Mommies (Illus. by Mary Morgan) — *Regan, Dian Curtis*
Mommy and the Money — *Goldstone, Nancy*
c Mommy Got Hurt — *Sylwester, Kathy*
c Mommy, Who Does God Love? (Illus. by Mary Melcher) — *Melcher, Mary*
c Mommy, Would You Love Me — *Dijs, Carla*
c Mommy's Briefcase (Illus. by Aliki) — *Low, Alice*
c Mommy's in the Hospital Having a Baby (Illus. by Robert Maass) — *Rosenberg, Maxine B*
Mompreneurs: A Mother's Practical Step-by-Step Guide to Work-at-Home Success — *Parlapiano, Ellen H*
y Mon Pere Et Moi — *Ruel, Francine*
Mona in the Promised Land — *Jen, Gish*
c Mona Lisa: The Secret of a Smile (Illus. by Letizia Galli) — *Galli, Letizia*
Monad to Man — *Ruse, Michael*
c Monarchs at Risk — *Pageler, Elaine*
Monarchy and Incest in Renaissance England — *Boehrer, Bruce Thomas*
The Monarchy and the Constitution — *Bogdanor, Vernon*
A Monarchy Transformed — *Kishlansky, Mark*
Monasteries of Greece — *Hellier, Chris*
A Monastic Year — *D'Avila-Latourrette, Victor-Antoine*
Monchskonig Und Rex Idiota — *Hoffmann, Hartmut*
Mondays Are Yellow, Sundays Are Gray — *Prescott, Ellen*
Mondays on the Dark Night of the Moon — *Narayan, Kirin*
c Monday's Troll (Illus. by Peter Sis) — *Prelutsky, Jack*
c Monday's Troll (Prelutsky). Audio Version — *Prelutsky, Jack*
y Mondo Canuck — *Pevere, Geoff*
c Monerans and Protists — *Silverstein, Alvin*
Monet — *Forge, Andrew*
r Monet: Catalogue Raisonne. Vols. 1-4 — *Wildenstein, Daniel*
Monet on the Normandy Coast — *Herbert, Robert L*
Monetarism and the Methodology of Economics — *Hoover, Kevin D*
Monetary Interpretations of the Great Depression — *Steindl, Frank G*
Monetary Policy, a Market Price Approach — *Johnson, Manuel H*
Monetary Policy and the Design of Financial Institutions in China 1978-90 — *Jin, Leroy*
Monetary Policy in a Converging Europe — *Alders, Koos*
Monetary Policy in the European Monetary System — *Loureiro, Joao*
y Money: A History — *Williams, Jonathan, Dr.*
Money: A History (CCNB)
c A Money Adventure (Illus. by Rany Verougstraete) — *Godfrey, Neale S*
Money and Markets in the Americas — *Dorn, James A*
Money and Morals Worldwide: First Annual Report
Money, Banking, and Financial Markets in China — *Yi, Gang*
r Money Coach Guide to Top Funds 1997
Money, Exchange Rates, and Output — *Calvo, Guillermo A*
Money for Change — *Ostrander, Susan A*
r Money for Graduate Students in the Humanities 1996-1998
r Money for Graduate Students in the Sciences 1996-1998
r Money for Graduate Students in the Social Sciences 1996-1998
Money, Heart and Mind — *Bloom, William*

Money in Motion — *Deleplace, Ghislain*
Money, Interest, and Stagnation — *Ono, Yoshiyasu*
c Money Madness — *Davis, Gibbs*
Money Matters — *Guyer, Jane I*
Money Matters — *Hoge, Dean R*
c Money, Money, Money (Illus. by Nancy Winslow Parker) — *Parker, Nancy Winslow*
Money, Power and Space — *Corbridge, Stuart*
Money, Price, and Power in Poland, Sixteenth and Seventeenth Centuries — *Maczak, Antoni*
Money Sings — *Ruble, Blair*
The Money Supply in the Economic Process — *Musella, Marco*
y Money to Burn — *Goldman, E M*
Money to Burn — *Jenish, D'Arcy*
c The Money Tree Myth — *Vaz-Oxlade, Gail*
Money While You Sleep — *Bly, R D*
Money: Who Has How Much and Why — *Hacker, Andrew*
Mongols and Mamluks — *Amitai-Preiss, Reuven*
c Monica Seles — *Rambeck, Richard*
Monitored Peril — *Hamamoto, Darrell Y*
Monitoring Economic Transition — *Blazyca, George*
Monitoring Report: Berkeley Measure O Service Programs — *Wittman, Friedner D*
Monitoring the World Economy 1820-1992 — *Maddison, Angus*
The Monk Who Dared — *Tabrah, Ruth M*
c The Monkey and the Mango (Illus. by Ilka Jerabek) — *Easwaran, Eknath*
c The Monkey Bridge (Illus. by Fahimeh Amiri) — *Martin, Rafe*
The Monkey, Chinese Horoscopes for Lovers — *Reid, Lori*
The Monkey House — *Fullerton, John*
The Monkey House (Charles). Audio Version — *Fullerton, John*
Monkey King — *Chao, Patricia*
The Monkey's Fist — *Pease, William D*
Monkey's Wedding — *Freiman, Marcelle*
Monkfish Moon — *Gunesekera, Romesh*
A Monk's Confession — *Guibert, Abbot of Nogent-Sous-Coucy*
Monnew — *Kourouma, Ahmadou*
Monnikewerk — *Hugo, Daniel*
Monogamy — *Phillips, Adam*
Monolith — *Corry, Matt*
r Monolithic Phase-Locked Loops and Clock Recovery Circuits — *Razavi, Behzad*
y Monomotapa, Zulu, Basuto — *Mann, Kenny*
Monopoly Television — *Banks, Jack*
Monotone Operators in Banach Space and Nonlinear Partial Differential Equations — *Showalter, R E*
r Monroe Township Cemeteries, Nodaway County, Missouri 1960 — *Nodaway County Genealogical Society*
Monsieur De Phocas — *Lorrain, Jean*
Monsieur D'Eon Is a Woman — *Kates, Gary*
Monsieur Malaussene — *Pennac, Daniel*
Monsoon History — *Lim, Shirley*
c Monster Boy (Illus. by Christine M Winn) — *Winn, Christine M*
c Monster Bugs (Illus. by Pamela Johnson) — *Penner, Lucille Recht*
c Monster Faces
c Monster Film — *Hoban, Russell*
Monster in a Box (Gray). Audio Version — *Gray, Spalding*
Monster: Living Off the Big Screen — *Dunne, John Gregory*
c Monster Manners (Illus. by Andrew Glass) — *Roberts, Bethany*
yr Monster Manual — *Ballinger, Erich*
c Monster Math (Illus. by Marge Hartelius) — *Maccarone, Grace*
c Monster Maze (Illus. by S Holmes) — *Forsyth, Ann*
c The Monster Party (Illus. by Nigel McMullen) — *Laslett, Stephanie*
c Monster Trucks — *Savage, Jeff*
c Monsters (Hologram World)
c Monsters and Animals. 2nd Ed. — *Siembieda, Kevin*
Monsters and Other Lovers — *Glatt, Lisa*
The Monsters and the Critics — *Tolkien, J R R*
c Monsters in Cyberspace (Illus. by Melissa Sweet) — *Regan, Dian Curtis*
c Monsters in the Garden (Illus. by Christopher Brook) — *Brook, Christopher*
y The Monster's Legacy (Illus. by Jody A Lee) — *Norton, Andre*
c The Monsters' Test (Illus. by Sal Murdocca) — *Heinz, Brian J*

Monsters, Tricksters, and Sacred Cows — *Arnold, A James*

Monstrous Imagination — *Huet, Marie-Helene*

y A Monstrous Regiment of Women — *King, Laurie R*

y A Monstrous Regiment of Women (Follows). Audio Version — *King, Laurie R*

La Montagne R — *Jouet, Jacques*

Montaigne: A Collection of Essays. Vols. 1-5 — *Berven, Dikka*

Montaigne: Espace, Voyage, Ecriture — *Samaras, Zoe*

Montaigne Et La Rhetorique — *Tournon, Andre*

Montaigne Et L'Histoire Des Hellenes — *Christodoulou, Kyriaki*

Montaigne, Quelques Anciens Et L'Ecriture Des Essais — *Coleman, Dorothy Gabe*

Montaigne: Une Vie, Une Oeuvre 1533-1592 — *Frame, Donald*

Montaigne's Unruly Brood — *Regosin, Richard L*

Montana 1948 — *Watson, Larry*

r Montana Handbook. 3rd Ed. — *McRae, W C*

r Montana Handbook. 3rd Rev. Ed. — *McRae, W C*

Monte Carlo and Molecular Dynamics Simulations in Polymer Science — *Binder, K*

Monte Irvin: Nice Guys Finish First — *Irvin, Monte*

Monte Verde — *Dillehay, Tom D*

Montesquieu: Lettres Persanes — *Betts, Christopher*

Monteverdi — *Fabbri, Paolo*

y Montezuma and the Aztecs — *Helly, Mathilde*

r Montgomery Clift: A Bio-Bibliography — *Kalfatovic, Mary C*

A Month and a Day — *Saro-Wiwa, Ken*

A Month-by-Month Guide to Entertaining Angels — *Boyer, Mark*

A Month in the Country (Williams). Audio Version — *Carr, J L*

r The Monthly Sky Guide. 4th Ed. — *Ridpath, Ian*

Montreal Protocol on Substances That Deplete the Ozone Layer: 1994 Report of the Methyl Bromide Technical Options Committee

Montreal Protocol on Substances That Deplete the Ozone Layer: 1994 Report of the Solvents, Coatings, and Adhesives Technical Options Committee

Montrose — *Wedgwood, C V*

c Monty (Illus. by James Stevenson) — *Stevenson, James*

Monument: Antichi Di Roma Nei Disegni Di Alberto Alberti — *Forni, Giovanna Maria*

Monumental Brasses as Art and History — *Bertram, Jerome*

Monumentality in Early Chinese Art and Architecture — *Wu Hung*

Monuments Illustrating New Comedy. 2nd Ed., Rev. and Enlarged, Vols. 1-2 — *Webster, T B L*

Moo — *Smiley, Jane*

c Moo-Ha! — *Most, Bernard*

A Mood Apart — *Whybrow, Peter C*

Mooi Street and Other Moves — *Slabolepszy, Paul*

c Mookie Goes Fishing (Illus. by Korky Paul) — *Tzannes, Robin*

c The Moon Book (Illus. by Gail Gibbons) — *Gibbons, Gail*

Moon Country — *Armitage, Simon*

c Moon Frog (Illus. by Sarah Fox-Davies) — *Edwards, Richard*

y Moon Handbook — *Koppeschaar, Carl*

The Moon in Your Life — *Cunningham, Donna*

The Moon Is a Harsh Mistress — *Heinlein, Robert A*

c Moon Lake (Illus. by Ivan Gantschev) — *Gantschev, Ivan*

The Moon of Hoa Binh. Vols. 1-2 — *Pensinger, William L*

c Moon Rope (Illus. by Lois Ehlert) — *Ehlert, Lois*

r Moon Travel Handbooks

c Moon Window — *Curry, Jane Louise*

c Moonbathing (Illus. by Stephen Lambert) — *Rosenberg, Liz*

c Moonbear's Pet — *Asch, Frank*

Moonbird Boy — *Padgett, Abigail*

Mooncranker's Gift — *Unsworth, Barry*

Moonlight Becomes You — *Clark, Mary Higgins*

c Moonlight Kite (Illus. by Elise Primavera) — *Buckley, Helen E*

Moonlit Days and Nights — *Toole, D H*

p Moonrabbit Review: Asian Pacific American Voices

Moonrise — *Bova, Ben*

c Moonstruck: The True Story of the Cow Who Jumped over the Moon (Illus. by Paul Yalowitz) — *Choldenko, Gennifer*

y The Moorchild — *McGraw, Eloise*

r Moorhead-Bear Ancestry — *Moorhead, Rex K*

The Moor's Last Sigh — *Rushdie, Salman*

c Moosetache (Illus. by Henry Cole) — *Palatini, Margie*

y Moosewood Restaurant Low-Fat Favorites — *Moosewood Collective*

Moral Action and Christian Ethics — *Porter, Jean*

Moral and Political Essays — *Seneca, Lucius Annaeus*

The Moral Animal — *Wright, Robert*

The Moral Challenge of Alzheimer Disease — *Post, Stephen Garrard*

Moral Codes and Social Structure in Ancient Greece — *Bryant, Joseph M*

Moral Demands and Personal Obligations — *Fuchs, Joseph S J*

Moral Desperado — *Heffer, Simon*

Moral Dilemmas and Moral Theory — *Mason, H E*

The Moral Dimension of Man in the Age of Computers — *Drozdek, Adam*

Moral Dimensions of American Foreign Policy — *Thompson, Kenneth W*

The Moral Foundations of Canadian Federalism — *Laselva, Samuel V*

The Moral Gap — *Hare, John E*

Moral Grandeur and Spiritual Audacity — *Heschel, Abraham Joshua*

Moral Imagination — *Johnson, Mark*

The Moral Intelligence of Children — *Coles, Robert*

The Moral Intelligence of Children. Audio Version — *Coles, Robert*

Moral Issues — *Palmer-Fernandez, Gabriel*

Moral Judgment — *Wilson, James Q*

Moral Knowledge — *Sinnott-Armstrong, Walter*

The Moral Limitations of Capitalism — *Michelman, Irving S*

Moral Luck — *Statman, Daniel*

Moral Nexus — *Nelson, James B*

Moral Opposition to Authoritarian Rule in Chile 1973-90 — *Lowden, Pamela*

Moral Panic — *Fekete, John*

Moral Passages — *Addelson, Kathryn Pyne*

Moral Politics — *Lakoff, George*

The Moral Problem — *Smith, Michael*

Moral Relativism and Moral Objectivity — *Harman, Gilbert*

Moral Responsibility and the Boundaries of Community — *Smiley, Marion*

Moral Rights and Political Freedom — *Smith, Tara*

The Moral Sex — *Steinbrugge, Liselotte*

Moral Strangers, Moral Acquaintance, and Moral Friends — *Loewy, Erich H*

Moral Theology and Suffering — *MacDonald, Sebastian K*

The Moral Tradition of American Constitutionalism — *Powell, H Jefferson*

The Moral Vision of the New Testament — *Hays, Richard B*

Moral Voices, Moral Selves — *Hekman, Susan J*

Moral Wisdom and Good Lives — *Kekes, John*

Morale De La Foi Et Morale Autonome — *Gaziaux, Eric*

Moralists and Modernizers — *Mintz, Steven*

Morality and Action — *Quinn, Warren*

Morality and International Relations — *Wright, Moorhead*

r Morality and Social Order in Television Crime Drama — *Sumser, John*

Morality and the New Genetics — *Gert, Bernard*

Morality, Culture and Philosophy — *Moody-Adams, Michelle*

Morality, Normativity, and Society — *Copp, David*

The Morality of Abortion — *Noonan, John T*

The Morality of the Fallen Man — *Saastamoinen, Kari*

Morality Play — *Unsworth, Barry*

Morality Play (Maloney). Audio Version — *Unsworth, Barry*

The Morals of Modernity — *Larmore, Charles*

The Morbid Kitchen — *Melville, Jennie*

Morbus Kitahara — *Ransmayr, Christoph*

Mordecai Kaplan's Thought in a Postmodern Age — *Breslauer, S Daniel*

Malcolm Lowry's La Mordida. Scholarly Ed. — *Lowry, Malcolm*

More and Better Jobs for Women — *Lim, Lin Lean*

c More Animal Heroes — *Bradford, Karleen*

More Beautiful Lies — *Papaellinas, George*

More Books Kids Will Sit Still For — *Freeman, Judy*

More Choice Menus — *Hollands, Marjorie*

More Effective C++ — *Meyers, Scott*

c More Errata (Illus. by Hemesh Alles) — *Roland-Entwistle, Theodore*

More Games to Play with Toddlers — *Silberg, Jackie*

r More Generals in Gray — *Allardice, Bruce S*

More Heartsmart Cooking — *Stern, Bonnie*

c More Help! (Illus. by Scott Nash) — *Holyoke, Nancy*

More Irish County Towns — *Simms, Anngret*

More Letters from the American Farmer — *Moore, Dennis D*

c More Letters to Uncle Albert — *Stannard, Russell*

More Market Plays — *Kani, John*

More Maya Missions — *Perry, Richard D*

More Microsoft Windows 95 Step by Step — *Catapult, Inc.*

y More Minds — *Matas, Carol*

r More Names and Naming — *Lawson, Edwin D*

r More Opening Nights on Broadway — *Suskin, Steven*

c More or Less a Mess! (Illus. by Patrick Girouard) — *Keenan, Sheila*

More Passages — *McLeRoy, Sherrie*

A More Perfect Legacy — *Armstrong, Philip*

More Quizzes for Great Children's Books — *Wickstrom, Polly Jeanne*

More Random Acts of Kindness (Asner). Audio Version — *Conari Press*

c More Rapid Math Tricks and Tips — *Julius, Edward H*

More San Francisco Memoirs — *Barker, Malcolm E*

c More Scary Stories for Stormy Nights (Illus. by Eric Angeloch) — *Ingram, Scott*

More Scott Operas — *Mitchell, Jerome*

More Stepping Stones to Jewish-Christian Relations — *Croner, Helga*

c More Stories Huey Tells (Illus. by Lis Toft) — *Cameron, Ann*

c More than a Horse — *Adler, C S*

More than a Muckraker — *Tarbell, Ida Minerva*

c More than Anything Else (Illus. by Chris K Soentpiet) — *Bradby, Marie*

More than Chattel — *Gaspar, David Barry*

y More than Friends — *Baer, Judy*

y More Than Graphs — *Specht, Jim*

c More than Moccasins — *Carlson, Laurie M*

c More than One (Illus. by Donald Crews) — *Schlein, Miriam*

More than One Way? — *Hick, John*

More than the Truth — *Wolf, Dennie Palmer*

More than Victims — *Downs, Donald Alexander*

More than You Know — *Kelman, Judith*

More's Utopia and the Utopian Inheritance — *Cousins, A D*

Morgane — *D'Haen, Christine*

Morgentaler: A Difficult Hero — *Dunphy, Catherine*

Morley Callaghan: Literary Anarchist — *Boire, Gary*

r Mormon Americana — *Whittaker, David*

The Mormon Hierarchy — *Quinn, D Michael*

The Mormon Trail — *Hill, William E*

y The Mormons — *Williams, Jean Kinney*

y The Morning After — *Kosinski, Dahlia*

Morning All Day — *Paling, Chris*

Morning Becomes the Law — *Rose, Gillian*

Morning Dew and Roses — *Toelken, Barre*

Morning Glory, Evening Shadow — *Ichihashi, Yamato*

Morning Glory Mother — *Pearson, Carol Lynn*

c Morning Has Broken (Illus. by Tim Ladwig) — *Farjeon, Eleanor*

c Morning in the Meadow (Illus. by Holly Keller) — *Buck, Nola*

c Morning, Noon, and Night (Illus. by Nancy Doniger) — *Taberski, Sharon*

Morning Poems — *Bly, Robert*

The Morning River — *Gear, W Michael*

Morning Watch — *Reibetanz, John*

c Morningtown Ride (Illus. by Michael Leeman) — *Reynolds, Malvina*

Morocco Modern — *Ypma, Herbert*

p Morocco: The Journal of the Society for Moroccan Studies

Morphologic Behaviour of a Barred Coast Over a Period of Decades — *Wijnberg, K M*

A Morphology of New Testament Greek — *Brooks, James A*

c Morris and the Cat Flap — *French, Vivian*

c Morris and the Kingdom of Knoll (Illus. by Jeff Colson) — *Hill, T L*

c Morris Macmillipede (Illus. by Satoshi Kitamura) — *Fitzmaurice, Mick*

y The Morrow Anthology of Great Western Short Stories — *Tuska, Jon*

c Morse's Greatest Mystery and Other Stories (Davidson). Audio Version — *Dexter, Colin*

y Morse's Greatest Mystery and Other Stories (Nelson). Audio Version — *Dexter, Colin*

y Morse's Greatest Mystery and Other Stories (Tull). Audio Version — *Dexter, Colin*

Mort Au Champ D'Honneur — *Roy, Jules*

La Mort D'Un Juste — *Chessex, Jacques*

La Mort Lente De Torcello — *Crouzet-Pavan, Elisabeth*
Mortal Fear — *Iles, Greg*
The Mortal Nuts — *Hautman, Pete*
Mortal Pages, Literary Lives — *Newey, Vincent*
Mortal Peril — *Epstein, Richard Allen*
The Mortal Sickness — *Taylor, Andrew*
Mortal Sin — *Levine, Paul*
Mortal Sins — *McLaurin, David*
Mortality and Migration in the Modern World — *Shlomowitz, Ralph*
Mortality and Morality — *Jonas, Hans*
Mortally Wounded — *Kearney, Michael*
Mortgage Lending, Racial Discrimination, and Federal Policy — *Goering, John*
Mortgage Lifter and Other Stories — *Lockhart, Olive*
Mortgaging the Earth — *Rich, Bruce*
Mortgaging Women's Lives — *Sparr, Pamela*
The Morton Years — *Halse, Elizabeth*
Mortuary Practices and Skeletal Remains at Teotihuacan — *Sempowski, Martha L*
Mortuary Variability and Status Differentiation on the Columbia-Fraser Plateau — *Schulting, Rick J*
Morvern Callar — *Warner, Alan*
Mosaic. Audio Version — *Taylor, Jeri*
The Mosaic Book — *Vance, Peggy*
Mosaic: Memoirs — *Kirstein, Lincoln*
The Mosaic of Economic Growth — *Landau, Ralph*
Mosaics and Mirrors — *Harrison, Jennifer*
Mosaics and Wallpaintings in Roman Churches — *Osborne, Jon*
Mosaics of Meaning — *Vandergrift, Kay E*
Mosaics of Roman Africa — *Blanchard-Lemee, Michele*
r Mosby's Complete Drug Reference 1997
r Mosby's Critical Care Nursing Reference — *Stillwell, Susan B*
r Mosby's Medical, Nursing, and Allied Health Dictionary. 4th Ed.
r Mosby's Medical Surfari — *Gibbs, Scott R*
r Mosby's Pediatric Nursing Reference. 3rd Ed. — *Betz, Cecily*
Mosby's USMLE Step 1 Reviews: Microbiology and Immunology — *Rosenthal, Ken S*
Mosby's USMLE Step 1 Reviews: Pharmacology — *Enna, S J*
Mosby's USMLE Step 2 Reviews--General Clinical Sciences — *Bollet, Alfred J*
Moscou Aller-Retour — *Derrida, Jacques*
r Moscow and St. Petersburg (Essential Travel Guides)
Moscow: Governing the Socialist Metropolis — *Colton, Timothy J*
Moscow Stations — *Erofeev, Venedikt*
Moscow Yankee — *Page, Myra*
Mose — *Graham, Loren*
c Moses (Illus. by Leonard Everett Fisher) — *Fisher, Leonard Everett*
Moses and Civilization — *Paul, Robert A*
c Moses Austin and Stephen F. Austin — *Warren, Betsy*
Moses Mendelssohn and the Religious Enlightenment — *Sorkin, David*
The Moses Mystery — *Greenberg, Gary*
Moses Supposes — *Greenberg, Dan*
y Mosh — *Parry, Glyn*
Moshe Safdie: Buildings and Projects 1967-1992 — *Murray, Irena Zantovska*
Moshe Sharett: Biography of a Political Moderate — *Sheffer, Gabriel*
y The Mosquito Coast — *Theroux, Paul*
Mosquitoes — *Faulkner, William*
Moss Gardening — *Schenk, George*
Mossbauer Spectroscopy Applied to Magnetism and Materials Science. Vol. 2 — *Long, Gary J*
y Mossflower (Keith). Audio Version — *Jacques, Brian*
The Most Beautiful Christmas — *Snow, Jonathan*
The Most Beautiful Gift (Wood). Audio Version — *Snow, Jonathan*
c The Most Beautiful Kid in the World (Illus. by Susan Meddaugh) — *Ericsson, Jennifer A*
c The Most Beautiful Roof in the World (Illus. by Christopher G Knight) — *Lasky, Kathryn*
The Most Beautiful Villages of the Dordogne — *Bentley, James*
The Most Dangerous Man in America — *Boston, Robert*
The Most Dangerous Man in Detroit — *Lichtenstein, Nelson*
A Most Dangerous Method — *Kerr, John*
A Most Deadly Retirement — *Michaels, Laura*
c The Most Excellent Book of How to Be a Clown (Illus. by Rob Shone) — *Perkins, Catherine*

c The Most Excellent Book of How to Be a Magician (Illus. by Rob Shone) — *Eldin, Peter*
c The Most Excellent Book of How to Be a Puppeteer (Illus. by Rob Shone) — *Lade, Roger*
c The Most Excellent Book of How to Do Card Tricks (Illus. by Rob Shone) — *Eldin, Peter*
The Most Excellent Historie of The Merchant of Venice — *Shakespeare, William*
The Most High — *Blanchot, Maurice*
A Most Indispensable Art — *Petersen, James B*
Most Likely to Die — *Girdner, Jaqueline*
The Most Monstrous of Wars — *Finley, Milton*
r Most Popular Web Sites — *English, Katharine*
A Most Satisfactory Man — *Bryan, Charles S*
The Most Solitary of Afflictions — *Scull, Andrew*
c The Most Wonderful Movie in the World — *Ford, Barbara*
y Mostly Ghostly Stories (Holt). Audio Version — *Holt, David*
p Mostly Murder: Your Guide to Reading Mysteries
Mot Ngay Co 26 Gio — *Nguyen, Vu*
Mot Pour Mot. Book and Electronic Media Version — *Aaron, William*
The Motel in America — *Jakle, John A*
Motel Nirvana — *McGrath, Melanie*
Mother — *Olausen, Judy*
c Mother and Daughter Tales (Illus. by Helen Cann) — *Evetts-Secker, Josephine*
The Mother-Daughter Book Club — *Dodson, Shireen*
Mother Doesn't Know about Kissing — *Templeman, Corinne*
Mother Donit Fore the Best — *Dulberger, Judith A*
y Mother Earth, Father Sky (Illus. by Jennifer Hewitson) — *Yolen, Jane*
c Mother Goose: A Canadian Sampler
c Mother Goose Magic (Illus. by Kay Chorao) — *Chorao, Kay*
c Mother Hubbard's Christmas (Illus. by John O'Brien) — *O'Brien, John*
p Mother Jones
c Mother Jones — *Horton, Madelyn*
y Mother Jones: Fierce Fighter for Workers' Rights — *Josephson, Judith Pinkerton*
c Mother Jones: One Woman's Fight for Labor — *Kraft, Betsey Harvey*
Mother Mary Speaks to Us — *Steiger, Brad*
Mother Nature — *Andrews, Sarah*
Mother Nature's Herbal — *Griffin, Judy*
Mother of God — *Ambrose, David*
y Mother of Winter — *Hambly, Barbara*
Mother Said — *Sirowitz, Hal*
Mother Superior — *Biggs, Vicki*
y Mother Teresa: The Authorized Biography — *Chawla, Navin*
Mother Tongue — *Ozdamar, Emine Sevgi*
Mother Tongue — *Wilde-Menozzi, Wallis*
Motherfuckers: The Auschwitz of Oz — *Britton, David*
Motherguilt: How Our Culture Blames Mothers for What's Wrong with Society — *Eyer, Diane*
Motherhood Reconceived — *Umansky, Lauri*
Mothering: Ideology, Experience, and Agency — *Glenn, Evelyn Nakano*
Mothers and Daughters — *L'Engle, Madeleine*
y Mothers and Daughters — *Saline, Carol*
Mothers and Daughters of Invention — *Stanley, Autumn*
Mothers and Other Lovers — *Briscoe, Joanna*
y Mothers and Other Strangers — *Wilson, Budge*
Mothers and Others — *Lasner, Mark Samuels*
y Mothers and Sons — *Cook, Mariana Ruth*
Mothers and Work in Popular American Magazines — *Keller, Kathryn*
Mother's Daily Scream (Krapf). Audio Version — *Pilling, Ann*
Mother's First-Born Daughters — *Humez, Jean M*
y Mothers of Invention — *Faust, Drew Gilpin*
Mothers of Invention — *Vare, Ethlie Ann*
Mothers of the Revolution — *Staunton, Irene*
MotherTongue — *Martinez, Demetria*
c Moths, Butterflies, Insects, and Spiders — *Vansant, Rhonda*
Moths to a Flame — *Ash, Sarah*
Moths to the Flame — *Rawlins, Gregory J E*
Motive for Murder — *Fraser, Anthea*
A Motive for Murder — *Gray, Gallagher*
Motives and Goals in Groups — *Zander, Alvin*
The Motley Fool Investment Guide — *Gardner, David*
Motorcycle Collectibles — *Dunbar, Leila*
The Motorcycle Diaries — *Guevara, Ernesto*
Les Mots Des Femmes — *Ozouf, Mona*
Les Mots Du Corps — *Prat, Marie-Helene*

Les Mouches — *Sartre, Jean Paul*
Mould's Medical Anecdotes — *Mould, Richard F*
Mould's Medical Anecdotes Omnibus Edition — *Mould, Richard F*
Mount Dragon — *Preston, Douglas*
y Mount Dragon (Colacci). Audio Version — *Preston, Douglas*
c Mount Everest and Beyond — *Hacking, Sue Muller*
Mount Misery — *Shem, Samuel*
y Mount St. Helens (Illus. by Geff Hinds) — *Carson, Rob*
Mount Sinai — *Hobbs, Joseph J*
Mount Soledad — *Polkinhorn, Harry*
y The Mountain — *Ab Hugh, Dafydd*
c A Mountain Alphabet (Illus. by Andrew Kiss) — *Ruurs, Margriet*
r Mountain Bike Adventures in Washington's North Cascades and Olympics. 2nd Ed. — *Kirkendall, Tom*
r Mountain Bike Adventures in Washington's South Cascades and Puget Sound. 2nd Ed. — *Kirkendall, Tom*
Mountain Country Cooking — *Sohn, Mark F*
Mountain Environments and Geographic Information Systems — *Price, Martin F*
Mountain Environments in Changing Climates — *Beniston, Martin*
Mountain Goats Never Say Cheese. Audio Version — *McManus, Patrick*
The Mountain King — *Hautala, Rick*
The Mountain Massacres — *Champion, David*
Mountain Meadows Witness — *Backus, Anna Jean*
c The Mountain Men — *Collins, James L*
y The Mountain on the Mile — *King, Stephen*
c Mountain Ranges (Illus. by Vanessa Card) — *Morris, Neil*
c Mountain Wedding (Illus. by Ted Rand) — *Gibbons, Faye*
r Mountaineering First Aid. 4th Ed. — *Carline, Jan D*
The Mountainous West — *Wyckoff, William*
c Mountains — *Morris, Neil*
c Mountains — *Murray, Peter, 1952, Sep., 9-*
c Mountains — *Sauvain, Philip*
c Mountains — *Stronach, Neil*
Mountains and Mesas — *Bengeyfield, Pete*
y Mountains and Rivers without End — *Snyder, Gary*
Mountains of Fire, Lands That Shake — *Feldman, Lawrence H*
c Mountains of Quilt (Illus. by Tomie De Paola) — *Willard, Nancy*
The Mountains of the Mediterranean World — *McNeill, J R*
y Mountains Touched with Fire (Sevra). Audio Version — *Sword, Wiley*
Mourir Pour Jerusalem — *Lartaguy, Jean*
Mourn Not Your Dead — *Crombie, Deborah*
Mourning Gloria — *Christmas, Joyce*
Mourning into Joy — *Connolly, Thomas*
c The Mouse and the Motorcycle (Roberts). Audio Version — *Cleary, Beverly*
r The Mouse Brain in Stereotaxic Coordinates — *Franklin, Keith B J*
c The Mouse Bride (Illus. by David Christiana) — *Cowley, Joy*
c Mouse Count — *Walsh, Ellen Stoll*
c Mouse Creeps (Illus. by Reg Cartwright) — *Harris, Peter*
c A Mouse in the House! (Illus. by Uli Waas) — *Wagener, Gerda*
c Mouse in the Manger (Illus. by Elaine Blier) — *Wynne-Jones, Tim*
c A Mouse in Winter — *Merrick, Anne*
y The Mouse on the Mile — *King, Stephen*
c Mouse Paint — *Walsh, Ellen Stoll*
c Mouse Party (Illus. by Sue Heap) — *Durant, Alan*
c A Mouse Told His Mother (Illus. by Maryjane Begin) — *Roberts, Bethany*
c Mouse TV — *Novak, Matt*
y Mouse under Glass — *Koenig, David*
c The Mousehole Cat (Illus. by Nicola Bayley) — *Barber, Antonia*
c Mouse's Christmas — *Baker, Alan*
Mousterian Lithic Technology — *Kuhn, Steven L*
p Mouth: The Voice of Disability Rights
Mouth to Mouth — *Gander, Forrest*
Mova Dilovykh Paperiv — *Palamar, Larysa*
Movement Stories for Children Ages 3-6 — *Landalf, Helen*
Movements in Chicano Poetry — *Perez-Torres, Rafael*
y The Moves Make the Man — *Brooks, Bruce*
y The Moves Make the Man (James). Audio Version — *Brooks, Bruce*

The Movie Book of the Western — *Cameron, Ian*
Movie Censorship and American Culture
— *Couvares, Francis G*
Movie-Made America — *Sklar, Robert*
c Movie Magic — *Cross, Robin*
y Movie Magic — *Scott, Elaine*
y Movie Magic (Runger). Audio Version — *Scott, Elaine*
The Movie of the Week — *Rapping, Elayne*
r Movie Time — *Brown, Gene*
Movieland: Hollywood and the Great American
Dream Culture — *Charyn, Jerome*
Movies in the Mind — *Rae, Colleen Mariah*
Moving Away from Silence — *Turino, Thomas*
c The Moving Book (Illus. by Sue Dennen) — *Davis,
Gabriel*
c Moving Day (Illus. by Yossi Abolafia) — *Kalan,
Robert*
Moving Finite Elements — *Baines, M J*
Moving for Work — *Hendershott, Anne B*
Moving Images — *Buckingham, David*
Moving Loads on Ice Plates — *Squire, Vernon A*
c Moving Mama to Town — *Young, Ronder Thomas*
Moving Medicine — *Liskin, Jack*
Moving Mountains — *Pagonis, William G*
Moving On — *Coleman, Jane Candia*
Moving On — *Fein, Jessica*
Moving On — *Kissel, Susan S*
r The Moving Picture Boy — *Holmstrom, John*
The Moving Target — *Macdonald, Ross*
Moving to a Small Town — *Urbanska, Wanda*
Moving to Market — *Strong, John S*
Moving toward Life — *Halprin, Anna*
y Moving toward Maturity — *St. Clair, Barry*
y Moving Violations — *Hockenberry, John*
Moving Words — *Morris, Gay*
r Mozambique, the Quest for Peace — *Strachan, Beth*
y Mozart — *Nardo, Don*
Mozart: A Life — *Solomon, Maynard*
Mozart: A Musical Biography — *Kuster, Konrad*
Mozart: Clarinet Concerto — *Lawson, Colin*
r The Mozart Compendium — *Landon, H C Robbins*
MPI Developer's Conference — *MPI Developer's
Conference (2nd: 1996: Notre Dame, Indiana)*
c Mr. and Mrs. Hay the Horse (Illus. by Colin
McNaughton) — *Ahlberg, Allan*
c Mr. and Mrs. Pig's Evening Out — *Rayner, Mary*
c Mr. Bear to the Rescue — *Gliori, Debi*
c Mr. Bear's Picnic — *Gliori, Debi*
c Mr. Biff the Boxer (Illus. by Janet Ahlberg)
— *Ahlberg, Allan*
Mr. Bligh's Bad Language — *Dening, Greg*
Mr. Blue — *Poulin, Jacques*
Mr. Bristol's Barn — *Szarkowski, John*
Mr. Brooks and the Australian Trade — *Broeze,
Franklin J A*
c Mr. Brown Can Moo! Can You? — *Seuss, Dr.*
c Mr. Buzz the Beeman (Illus. by Faith Jaques)
— *Ahlberg, Allan*
c Mr. Carey's Garden (Illus. by G Brian Karas)
— *Cutler, Jane*
c Mr. Chips! (Illus. by Laura McGee Kvasnosky)
— *Kvasnosky, Laura McGee*
Mr. Clive and Mr. Page — *Bartlett, Neil, 1958-*
c Mr. Cool (Illus. by Stephen Lewis) — *Wilson,
Jacqueline*
c Mr. Cosmo the Conjuror (Illus. by Joe Wright)
— *Ahlberg, Allan*
c Mr. Creep the Crook (Illus. by Andre Amstutz)
— *Ahlberg, Allan*
c Mr. Davies and the Baby (Illus. by Charlotte Voake)
— *Voake, Charlotte*
c Mr. Dunfilling and the Denture Adventure — *Lewis,
Rob*
Mr. Food — *Ginsberg, Art*
c Mr. Gumpy's Outing — *Burningham, John*
Mr. Ives' Christmas — *Hijuelos, Oscar*
c Mr. Knuckles (Illus. by Leigh Hobbs) — *Dumbleton,
Mike*
c Mr. Lincoln's Whiskers (Illus. by Karen B Winnick)
— *Winnick, Karen B*
c Mr. Lunch Takes a Plane Ride — *Seibold, J Otto*
c Mr. MacMurdo's Guide to Ghostkeeping — *Hawksley,
Gerald*
y Mr. Majestyk (Muller). Audio Version — *Leonard,
Elmore*
c Mr. Merlin and the Turtle (Illus. by Seymour Chwast)
— *Chwast, Seymour*
Mr. Nice — *Marks, Howard*
c Mr. Pak Buys a Story (Illus. by Benrei Huang)
— *Farley, Carol*

c Mr. Potato Head's Mix'n Match Book (Illus. by Rick
Farley)
c Mr. Potter's Pet (Illus. by Mark Teague)
— *King-Smith, Dick*
Mr. President, Mr. President! — *McClendon, Sarah*
c Mr. Putter and Tabby Fly the Plane (Illus. by Arthur
Howard) — *Rylant, Cynthia*
c Mr. Putter and Tabby Pick the Pears (Illus. by Arthur
Howard) — *Rylant, Cynthia*
c Mr. Putter and Tabby Row the Boat (Illus. by Arthur
Howard) — *Rylant, Cynthia*
c Mr. Revere and I (Porter). Audio Version — *Lawson,
Robert*
c Mr. Semolina-Semolinus (Illus. by Giselle Potter)
— *Manna, Anthony L*
Mr. Skylight — *Brunner, Ernst*
c Mr. Tick the Teacher (Illus. by Faith Jaques)
— *Ahlberg, Allan*
Mr. Truman's War — *Moskin, J Robert*
Mr. Tubbs' Civil War — *Brandt, Nat*
y Mr. Tucket — *Paulsen, Gary*
y Mr. Was — *Hautman, Pete*
y Mr. Wilson's Cabinet of Wonder — *Weschler,
Lawrence*
r MRI Bankers' Guide to Foreign Currency, Spring
1997
r MRI Bankers' Guide to Foreign Currency, Winter
1996
MRI of Musculoskeletal Masses — *Laorr, Alan*
Mridula Sarabhai: Rebel with a Cause — *Basu,
Aparna*
MRP and Beyond — *Ptak, Carol A*
Mrs. Alexander: A Life of the Hymn Writer
— *Wallace, Valerie*
c Mrs. Brown Went to Town — *Yee, Wong Herbert*
c Mrs. Donald's Dog Bun and His Home Away from
Home (Illus. by James Stevenson) — *Maxwell,
William, 1908-*
c Mrs. Hen's Secret! (Illus. by Cathy Beylon)
Mrs. Hornstien — *Wagman, Fredrica*
Mrs. Ike: Memories and Reflections on the Life of
Mamie Eisenhower — *Eisenhower, Susan*
c Mrs. Jolly's Joke Shop (Illus. by Colin McNaughton)
— *Ahlberg, Allan*
Mrs. Keppel and Her Daughter — *Souhami, Diana*
c Mrs. Lather's Laundry (Illus. by Andre Amstutz)
— *Ahlberg, Allan*
Mrs. Malory: Death of a Dean — *Holt, Hazel*
c Mrs. Merriwether's Musical Cat (Illus. by Petra
Mathers) — *Purdy, Carol*
c Mrs. Meyer the Bird (Illus. by Wolf Erlbruch)
— *Erlbruch, Wolf*
Mrs. Oliphant: A Fiction to Herself — *Jay, Elisabeth*
c Mrs. Peachtree and the Eighth Avenue Cat
— *Silverman, Erica*
c Mrs. Peachtree's Bicycle (Illus. by Ellen Beier)
— *Silverman, Erica*
c Mrs. Pig Gets Cross — *Rayner, Mary*
c Mrs. Plug the Plumber (Illus. by Joe Wright)
— *Ahlberg, Allan*
Mrs. Pollifax and the Lion Killer — *Gilman, Dorothy*
y Mrs. Pollifax, Innocent Tourist — *Gilman, Dorothy*
c Mrs. Potter's Pig (Illus. by Russell Ayto) — *Root,
Phyllis*
c Mrs. Rose's Garden (Illus. by Elaine Greenstein)
— *Greenstein, Elaine*
Mrs. Spring Fragrance and Other Writings — *Sui Sin
Far*
Mrs. Ted Bliss — *Elkin, Stanley*
c Mrs. Vole the Vet (Illus. by Emma Chichester Clark)
— *Ahlberg, Allan*
Mrs. Whaley and Her Charleston Garden — *Whaley,
Emily*
c Mrs. Wobble the Waitress (Illus. by Janet Ahlberg)
— *Ahlberg, Allan*
c Ms. Davison, Our Librarian (Illus. by Christine
Osinski) — *Flanagan, Alice K*
c Ms. MacDonald Has a Class (Illus. by Jan Ormerod)
— *Ormerod, Jan*
Ms. Thang, Real Knights Don't Show Up at 3 in the
Morning — *Elliott, Max*
r MSA Profile 1996
MSI-2000: Multivariate Statistical Analysis in Honor
of Professor Minoru Siotani. Vol. 34
Much Ado about Nothing. Audio Version
— *Shakespeare, William*
y Much Ado about Prom Night — *McCants, William*
Mucha: The Triumph of Art Nouveau — *Ellridge,
Arthur*
Mucosal Vaccines — *Kiyono, Hiroshi*
c Mud (Illus. by Lauren Stringer) — *Ray, Mary Lyn*

c Mud Racing — *Savage, Jeff*
c Muddle Cuddle (Illus. by Vlasta Van Kampen)
— *Gugler, Laurel Dee*
Muddling Through — *Hennessy, Peter*
Mudrist' Vikiv — *Chubyns'kyi, Pavlo*
c Muffin Pigdoom and the Keeper — *Warren, Paul*
c Muggsy Bogues: Tall on Talent — *Reiser, Howard*
Al-Mughtaribun: American Law and the
Transformation of Muslim Life in the United States
— *Moore, Kathleen M*
Mugshots: Celebrities under Arrest — *Seminara,
George*
c Muhamad's Desert Night (Illus. by Ian Schoenherr)
— *Kessler, Cristina*
c Muhammad Ali: Champion — *Schulman, Arlene*
Muhammad Ali: In Perspective — *Hauser, Thomas*
Muhammad Ali, the Peoples Champ — *Gorn, Elliott J*
Muhammad and Jesus — *Phipps, William E*
Muhammad and the Golden Bough — *Stetkevych,
Jaroslav*
Muhammad and the Origins of Islam — *Peters, F E*
Mujerista Theology — *Isasi-Diaz, Ada Maria*
Mukiwa: A White Boy in Africa — *Godwin, Peter*
c The Mulberry Bird (Illus. by Diana L Stanley)
— *Brodzinsky, Anne Braff*
The Mulching of America — *Crews, Harry*
y Mule Deer — *Bauer, Erwin A*
Mules, Jackasses, and Other Misconceptions
— *Burkhart, James A*
Multi-Objective Programming and Goal Programming
— *Tamiz, Mehrdad*
Multi-Output Production and Duality — *Fare, Rolf*
Multi-Storey Precast Concrete Framed Structures
— *Elliott, Kim S*
Multi-Track Diplomacy — *Diamond, Louise*
Multi-User Smalltalk — *Almarode, Jay*
Multiaccess, Mobility and Teletraffic for Personal
Communications — *Jabbari, Bijan*
r The Multiage Handbook — *Grant, Jim, 1942-*
y MultiAmerica: Essays on Cultural Wars and Cultural
Peace — *Reed, Ishmael*
Multibody Dynamics with Unilateral Contacts
— *Pfeiffer, Friedrich*
Multichip Modules with Integrated Sensors — *Jones,
W Kinzy*
Multicriteria Evaluation in a Fuzzy Environment
— *Munda, Giuseppe*
Multicultural AIDS Prevention Programs — *Trotter,
Robert T*
Multicultural Aspects of Sociolinguistics in Deaf
Communities — *Lucas, Ceil*
Multicultural Celebrations — *Orenstein, Gloria Feman*
r Multicultural Children's Literature — *Lind, Beth
Beutler*
Multicultural Citizenship — *Kymlicka, Will*
Multicultural Clients — *Lassiter, Sybil M*
Multicultural Counseling in a Divided and
Traumatized Society — *Hickson, Joyce*
r The Multicultural Dictionary of Proverbs — *Cordry,
Harold V*
r Multicultural Education — *Mitchell, Bruce M*
Multicultural Education as Social Activism — *Sleeter,
Christine E*
r The Multicultural Education Directory — *Washburn,
David E*
Multicultural Education in the U.S. — *Washburn,
David E*
Multicultural Education, Transformative Knowledge,
and Action — *Banks, James A*
r Multicultural Folktales for the Feltboard and Readers'
Theater — *Sierra, Judy*
Multicultural Literatures through Feminist/
Poststructuralist Lenses — *Waxman, Barbara Frey*
Multicultural Manners — *Dresser, Norine*
The Multicultural Math Classroom — *Zaslavsky,
Claudia*
Multicultural Perspectives in Music Education. 2nd
Ed. — *Anderson, William M*
c Multicultural Plays for Children. Vol. 1 — *Gerke,
Pamela*
c Multicultural Plays for Children. Vol. 2 — *Gerke,
Pamela*
c Multicultural Plays for Children. Vols. 1-2 — *Gerke,
Pamela*
y A Multicultural Portrait of Immigration — *Press,
Petra*
y A Multicultural Portrait of the American Revolution
— *Zell, Fran*
y A Multicultural Portrait of the Great Depression
— *Rensberger, Susan*

y A Multicultural Portrait of the Vietnam War
— *Wright, David K*

y A Multicultural Portrait of World War I — *Uschan, Michael V*

Multicultural Teaching in the University — *Schoem, David*

r Multicultural Voices in a Contemporary Literature
— *Day, Frances Ann*

Multiculturalism from the Margins — *Harris, Dean A*

r Multiculturalism in Academe — *Morris, Libby V*

Multidimensional Systems Signal Processing Algorithms and Applications Techniques. Vol. 77

Multigrid Methods for Finite Elements — *Shaidurov, V V*

Multigrid Methods for Process Simulation — *Joppich, W*

Multilateral Treaties Deposited with the Secretary-General 1995

The Multilevel Design — *Huttner, Harry J M*

r A Multilingual Glossary of Biotechnological Terms
— *Leuenberger, Hans Georg W*

r Multilingual Thesaurus of Geosciences. 2nd Ed.
— *Gravesteijn, J*

Multilingualism — *Edwards, John R*

Multilingualism for All — *Skutnabb-Kangas, Tove*

r The Multimedia and CD-ROM Directory 1996 on CD-ROM. Electronic Media Version

Multimedia and CD-ROMs for Dummies. 2nd Ed.
— *Rathbone, Andy*

Multimedia and Communications Technology
— *Heath, Steve*

cr The Multimedia Bird Book. Electronic Media Version

Multimedia Business Presentations — *Heller, David*

Multimedia Communications and Video Coding
— *Wang, Yao*

Multimedia Computing and System — *International Conference on Multimedia Computing and Systems (1996: Hiroshima, Japan)*

Multimedia Database Systems — *Nwosu, Kingsley C*

r The Multimedia Directory. 4th Ed. — *Samsel, Jon*

r The Multimedia Encyclopedia of Science Fiction. Electronic Media Version

Multimedia Graphics — *Velthoven, Willem*

The Multimedia I Ching. Electronic Media Version

Multimedia Information Storage and Management
— *Chung, Soon M*

Multimedia Network Integration and Management
— *Ball, Larry*

Multimedia Scriptwriting Workshop — *Varchol, Douglas*

yr Multimedia Shakespeare. Electronic Media Version
— *Shakespeare, William*

Multimedia Systems and Techniques — *Furht, Borko*

yr Multimedia: The Complete Guide

Multimedia Tools and Applications — *Furht, Borko*

Multimedia Tools for Managers — *Szuprowicz, Bohdan O*

r The Multimedia Yearbook 1996

Multimodal Therapy in Oncology Nursing
— *Liebman, Marcia C*

Multinational Companies in United States International Trade — *Hipple, F Steb*

Multinational Enterprise and Economic Analysis. 2nd Ed. — *Caves, Richard E*

Multinational Investment and Economic Structure
— *Narula, Rajneesh*

Multinationality and Firm Performance
— *Riahi-Belkaoui, Ahmed*

Multinationals in North America — *Eden, Lorraine*

Multiparty Politics in Mississippi 1877-1902
— *Cresswell, Stephen*

Multiphase Flow 1995 — *International Conference on Multiphase Flow (2nd: 1995: Kyoto, Japan)*

Multiphase Reactor and Polymerization System Hydrodynamics — *Cheremisinoff, Nicholas P*

The Multiple Effects of Rainshadow — *Astley, Thea*

Multiple Personality — *Martinez-Taboas, Alfonso*

Multiple Pregnancy and Delivery — *Gall, Stanley A*

Multiple Sclerosis — *Kalb, Rosalind C*

Multiple Voices in Feminist Film Criticism — *Carson, Diane*

Multiple Wounds — *Russell, Alan*

c Multiplication (Illus. by Richard Maccabe)
— *Stienecker, David*

Multiply Bonded Main Group Metals and Metalloids
— *West, Robert*

Multiracial Couples — *Rosenblatt, Paul C*

r Multistate Payroll Guide — *Buckley, John F*

Multithreaded Processor Design — *Moore, Simon W*

Multivariable Analysis — *Feinstein, Alvan R*

Multivariable Control System Design Techniques
— *Bryant, G F*

Multivariate Analysis of Data in Sensory Science
— *Naes, Tormod*

Multivendor Networking — *Fortino, Andres*

c Mum and Dad and Me (Illus. by Jan Ormerod)
— *Ormerod, Jan*

Mumbo Jumbo — *Reed, Ishmael*

y The Mummers' Curse — *Roberts, Gillian*

c Mummies — *Knapp, Ron*

c Mummies (Illus. by Susan Swan) — *Milton, Joyce*

y Mummies, Dinosaurs, Moon Rocks (Illus. by Bruce Hiscock) — *Jespersen, James*

The Mummy! A Tale of the Twenty-Second Century
— *Loudon, Jane*

c Mums the Word — *Morpurgo, Michael*

y Munch (Faerna) — *Munch, Edvard*

y The Munchkins of Oz — *Cox, Stephen*

El Mundo Alucinante — *Arenas, Reinaldo*

cr El Mundo De Los Ninos. Vols. 1-16

Municipal Benchmarks — *Ammons, David N*

A Municipal Mother — *Myers, Gloria E*

Das Municipio In Mexiko Zwischen Tradition Und Modernisierung — *Sagawe, Thorsten*

y Murals: Cave, Cathedral, to Street — *Capek, Michael*

Murchison in Moray — *Collie, Michael*

c Los Murcielagos (Illus. by Estudio Marcel Socias)
— *Julivert, Maria Angels*

Murder among the Angels — *Matteson, Stefanie*

Murder and Sullivan — *Frommer, Sara Hoskinson*

Murder at Fenway Park — *Soos, Troy*

The Murder at Hazelmoor — *Christie, Agatha*

c Murder at Hockey Camp — *MacGregor, Roy*

Murder at Midnight — *Roosevelt, Elliott*

Murder at San Simeon — *Hearst, Patty*

Murder at the Baseball Hall of Fame — *Daniels, David*

Murder at the Farm — *Foot, Paul*

Murder at the Movies — *Eddenden, A E*

Murder at the National Gallery — *Truman, Margaret*

Murder at the Races — *Haining, Peter*

Murder Benign — *Hunt, Richard*

r Murder...by Category — *Mackler, Tasha*

y Murder by the Book — *Manson, Cynthia*

r Murder Cases of the Twentieth Century — *Frasier, David K*

Murder Crossed — *Boylan, Eleanor*

Murder Done to Death — *Melling, John Kennedy*

Murder for Love — *Penzler, Otto*

Murder for Love. Audio Version — *Penzler, Otto*

Murder in a Cathedral — *Edwards, Ruth Dudley*

Murder in America — *Lane, Roger*

Murder in Brentwood — *Fuhrman, Mark*

Murder in Cormyr — *Williamson, Chet*

y Murder in Perspective — *Miles, Keith*

Murder in Scorpio — *Lawrence, Martha C*

Murder in the Central Committee — *Vazquez Montalban, Manuel*

Murder in the Chateau — *Roosevelt, Elliott*

y Murder in the House — *Truman, Margaret*

Murder in the Museum of Man — *Alcorn, Alfred*

Murder in the Solid State — *McCarthy, Wil*

Murder Intercontinental — *Manson, Cynthia*

y The Murder Lover — *Rawlings, Ellen*

Murder Makes an Entree — *Myers, Amy*

Murder of a Dead Man — *John, Katherine*

A Murder of Crows — *Shepard, Steve*

y The Murder of Edgar Allan Poe — *Hatvary, George Egon*

Murder Ole! — *Sawyer, Corinne Holt*

A Murder on the Appian Way — *Saylor, Steven*

A Murder on the Appian Way (Harrison). Audio Version — *Saylor, Steven*

Murder on the Flying Scotsman — *Dunn, Carola*

Murder on the Links — *Logue, John*

Murder on the Net — *Ellison, Julian*

y Murder on the Orient Express — *Christie, Agatha*

Murder on Theatre Row — *Jahn, Michael*

Murder Runs in the Family — *George, Anne*

y Murder, She Meowed — *Brown, Rita Mae*

Murder under the Palms — *Matteson, Stefanie*

The Murderer's Tale — *Frazer, Margaret*

Murdering to Dissect — *Marshall, Tim*

Murderous Schemes — *Westlake, Donald E*

The Murders of Richard III — *Peters, Elizabeth*

y Murphy's Ambush (Dietz). Audio Version — *Paulsen, Gary*

y Murphy's Trail — *Paulsen, Gary*

The Murrow Boys — *Cloud, Stanley*

Musa Lapidaria — *Courtney, E*

Muscarinic Agonists and the Treatment of Alzheimer's Disease — *Fisher, Abraham*

The Muscle Memory Method — *Jaffe, Marjorie*

Muscles, Nerves, and Movement. 2nd Ed.
— *Tyldesley, Barbara*

Muscovy and Sweden in the Thirty Years' War 1630-1635 — *Porshney, B F*

Muscular Christianity — *Hall, Donald E, 1960-*

r Musculoskeletal Examination — *Gross, Jeffrey*

Musculoskeletal Pain Emanating from the Head and Neck — *Allen, Murray E*

cp Muse

Il Museo Di San Martino De Napoli — *Fittipaldi, Teodoro*

The Muses — *Nancy, Jean-Luc*

Muses from Chaos and Ash — *Vaucher, Andrea R*

The Muses, the Masses, and the Massey Commission
— *Litt, Paul*

Museum Culture — *Sherman, Daniel J*

Museum Librarianship — *Bierbaum, Esther Green*

The Museum of Bad Art — *Jackson, Marie*

The Museum of Love — *Weiner, Steve*

c Museum of Science Activities for Kids (Illus. by Julie Fraenkel) — *Gregoire, Tanya*

r Museum Premieres and Exhibitions, Special Events 1996

r Museums and Galleries of New York — *Wright, Carol*

r Museums and Galleries of San Francisco and the Bay Area — *Carber, Kristine*

Museums and Money — *Alexander, Victoria D*

Museums and the First World War — *Kavanagh, Gaynor*

Museums of the Mind — *Spitz, Ellen Handler*

r The Mushri-English Pronouncing Dictionary — *Stray, Christopher*

r The Mushroom Book — *Laessoe, Thomas*

c The Mushroom Man — *Pochocki, Ethel*

Mushrooms of North America in Color — *Bessette, Alan E*

c Music — *Grimshaw, Caroline*

Music among the Zu'Wa-Si and Related Peoples of Namibia, Botswana and Angola — *England, Nicholas M*

r Music and Culture in Eighteenth-Century Europe
— *Fubini, Enrico*

r The Music and Dance of the World's Religions
— *Rust, Ezra Gardner*

c Music and Drum (Illus. by Debra Lill) — *Robb, Laura*

Music and Irish Cultural History — *Gillen, Gerard*

Music and Menus for Christmas — *Elsener, Willi*

r Music and Poetry in the Middle Ages — *Switten, Margaret L*

Music and Spectacle in Baroque Rome — *Hammond, Frederick*

Music and the Occult — *Godwin, Joscelyn*

Music and the Origins of Language — *Thomas, Downing A*

Music and Women — *Drinker, Sophie*

A Music behind the Wall. Vol. 1 — *Ortese, Anna Maria*

The Music Box — *Bunn, T Davis*

c Music Box (Illus. by Zoe Figg) — *Clark, Veronica*

Music Connections — *Buchanan, Kate*

Music, Culture and Experience — *Blacking, John*

Music Cultures of the Pacific, the Near East, and Asia. 3rd Ed. — *Malm, William P*

r Music Festivals from Bach to Blues — *Clynes, Tom*

c Music from a Place Called Half Moon — *Oughton, Jerrie*

Music from the Heart — *Quigley, Colin*

Music, in a Foreign Language — *Crumey, Andrew*

The Music in African American Fiction — *Cataliotti, Robert H*

Music in Eighteenth-Century Austria — *Jones, David Wyn*

Music in Human Life — *Kaemmer, John E*

Music in Renaissance Lyons — *Dobbins, Frank*

Music in the Castle — *Gallo, F Alberto*

Music in the English Courtly Masque 1604-1640
— *Walls, Peter*

Music in the Jewish Community of Palestine 1880-1948 — *Hirshberg, Jehoash*

Music in the Medieval English Liturgy — *Rankin, Susan*

Music in the Theater — *Petrobelli, Pierluigi*

Music in the Third Reich — *Levi, Erik*

Music Matters — *Elliott, David J*

Music Minus One — *Shore, Jane*

The Music of Alban Berg — *Headlam, Dave*

The Music of Anthony Braxton — *Heffley, Mike*

The Music of Black Americans. 3rd Ed. — *Southern, Eileen*
y The Music of Dolphins — *Hesse, Karen*
r The Music of Francis Poulenc 1899-1963 — *Schmidt, Carl B*
The Music of Gershwin — *Gilbert, Steven E*
The Music of Israel. 2nd Ed., Rev. and Expanded — *Gradenwitz, Peter*
The Music of Morton Feldman — *DeLio, Thomas*
The Music of Per Norgard — *Beyer, Anders*
The Music of Reason — *Pappas, Theoni*
The Music of Stuart Saunders Smith — *Welsh, John P*
Music of the Earth — *Morton, Ron L*
The Music of the Troubadours — *Aubrey, Elizabeth*
Music of the Twentieth Century. 2nd Ed. — *Simms, Bryan R*
Music of the Warao of Venezuela — *Olsen, Dale A*
Music of Yes — *Martin, Bill, 1956-*
Music Performance during the Weimar Republic — *Gilliam, Bryan*
Music, Politics, and the Academy — *Van Den Toorn, Pieter C*
Music, Print and Culture in Early Sixteenth-Century Italy — *Fenlon, Iain*
Music Publishing and Collecting — *Hunter, David*
The Music: Stories — *Hamilton-Paterson, James*
The Music Teacher — *Starer, Robert*
Music, the Brain, and Ecstasy — *Jourdain, Robert*
Music: The New Age Elixir — *Summer, Lisa*
y Music to My Ears — *White, Timothy*
Music Universe, Music Mind — *Sweet, Robert E*
Music, Value, and the Passions — *Ridley, Aaron*
La Musica A Roma Attraverso Le Fonti D'Archivio — *Antoloni, Bianca Maria*
Musica E Liturgia Nella Riforma Tridentina — *Curti, Danilo*
Musica Enchiriadis and Scolica Enchiriadis — *Palisca, Claude V*
Musicage: Cage Muses on Words, Art, Music — *Retallack, Joan*
Musical! A Grand Tour — *Flinn, Denny Martin*
r Musical Anthologies for Analytical Study — *Perone, James E*
Musical Blunders and Other Musical Curiosities — *Spiegl, Fritz*
Musical Creativity in Twentieth-Century China — *Stock, Jonathan P J*
The Musical from the Inside Out — *Citron, Stephen*
The Musical Idea and the Logic, Technique, and Art of Its Presentation — *Schoenberg, Arnold*
Musical Instrument Design — *Hopkin, Bart*
c Musical Instruments — *Doney, Meryl*
c Musical Instruments — *Tythacott, Louise*
Musical Life in a Changing Society — *Blaukopf, Kurt*
The Musical Life of the Crystal Palace — *Musgrave, Michael*
Musical Poetics — *Burmeister, Joachim*
Musical Repercussions of 1492 — *Robertson, Carol E*
c Musical Tales (Robinson). Audio Version — *Robinson, Tony*
The Musical Temperament — *Kemp, Anthony E*
Musical Theatre at the Court of Louis XIV — *Harris-Warrick, Rebecca*
r MusicHound Rock — *Graff, Gary*
Musicians and the Prevention of Hearing Loss — *Chasin, Marshall*
c The Musicians of Bremen (Illus. by John Segal) — *Yolen, Jane*
Musique Et Societe — *Signorile, Marc*
La Musique Oubliee — *Pautrot, Jean-Louis*
c Muskrat Will Be Swimming (Illus. by Robert Hynes) — *Savageau, Cheryl*
c Muslim — *Tames, Richard*
r The Muslim Almanac — *Nanji, Azim*
A Muslim and a Christian in Dialogue — *Kateregga, Badru D*
Muslim Communities in North America — *Haddad, Yvonne Yasbeck*
Muslim Communities in the New Europe — *Nonneman, Gerd*
Muslim Communities of South Asia. Rev. and Enlarged Ed. — *Madan, T N*
Muslim Devotions — *Padwick, Constance E*
Muslim Eurasia — *Ro'i, Yaacov*
Muslim Politics — *Eickelman, Dale F*
Muslim Resistance to the Tsar — *Gammer, Moshe*
Muslim Writers on Judaism and the Hebrew Bible — *Adang, Camilla*
Muslims — *Mercier, S C*
Muslims in Western Europe. 2nd Ed. — *Nielsen, Jorgen S*

Muslims, Jews and Pagans — *Lecker, Michael*
The Muslims of Bosnia-Herzegovina. 2nd Ed. — *Pinson, Mark*
Muslims through Discourse — *Bowen, John R*
Mustang — *Curtin, Sharon*
y The Mustang Herder (Osborne). Audio Version — *Brand, Max*
r Muster Rolls of the Soldiers of the War of 1812 — *North Carolina. Adjutant-General's Dept.*
c The Musubi Man (Illus. by Pat Hall) — *Takayama, Sandi*
c Mute Swans (Illus. by Wendy Pfeffer) — *Pfeffer, Wendy*
The Muted Conscience — *Bird, Frederick Bruce*
A Muted Fury — *Ross, William G*
y Mutiny on the Bounty (Reed). Audio Version — *Nordhoff, Charles*
Mutts: America's Dogs — *Kilcommons, Brian*
Mutual Fund Investing on the Internet — *Crane, Peter*
Muy Macho — *Gonzalez, Ray*
r The MVR Book Motor Sources Guide 1996
Mwalimu: The Influence of Nyerere — *Legum, Colin*
c My ABC Signs of Animal Friends (Illus. by Patricia Pearson) — *Bahan, Ben*
y My Aces, My Faults — *Bollettieri, Nick*
My Alexandria — *Doty, Mark*
My American Century — *Terkel, Studs*
My American Journey — *Powell, Colin*
My Ancestors Were Londoners — *Webb, Cliff*
c My Arctic 1,2,3 (Illus. by Vladyana Krykorka) — *Kusugak, Michael*
c My Baby Brother Has Ten Tiny Toes (Illus. by Clara Vulliamy) — *Leuck, Laura*
c My Backpack (Illus. by Maryann Cocca-Leffler) — *Bunting, Eve*
c My Barmy Aunt Boomerang, the Coolest Act in School (Illus. by Jamie Smith) — *Apps, Roy*
My Beautiful Laundrette and Other Writings — *Kureishi, Hanif*
y My Best Defense — *Riggs, Bob*
c My Best Friends (Illus. by Margaret Miller) — *Miller, Margaret*
c My Big Book of Everything — *Priddy, Roger*
My Black Horse — *Gallagher, Tess*
y My Blue Country — *Melling, O R*
My Body. My Blood — *Kirby, Margaret*
c My Body, Your Body — *Manning, Mick*
c My Book about Me (Illus. by Grahame Corbett) — *Jenkins, Sandra*
My Boyfriend's Father — *Winch, Ben*
c My Brother, Ant (Illus. by Marc Simont) — *Byars, Betsy*
c My Brother Is a Superhero (Illus. by Derek Brazell) — *Sheldon, Dyan*
c My Brother Is from Outer Space (Illus. by Eric Brace) — *Ostrow, Vivian*
My Brother Michael — *Owens, Janis*
c My Brother, My Enemy — *Harrah, Madge*
y My Brother Sam Is Dead (Brown). Audio Version — *Collier, James*
c My Brother, the Brat (Illus. by Joan Holub) — *Hall, Kirsten*
My Buddhist Life — *St. Pierre, Meg*
c My Busy Day (Illus. by Philippe Dupasquier) — *Dupasquier, Philippe*
c My Cats Nick and Nora (Illus. by Barry Moser) — *Harper, Isabelle*
My Children, My Gold — *Taylor, Debbie*
My Christian Life — *Seaman, Alison*
c My Crayons Talk (Illus. by G Brian Karas) — *Hubbard, Patricia*
c My Dad Has HIV (Illus. by Ronnie Walter Shipman) — *Alexander, Earl*
c My Dad's a Wizard! (Illus. by Chris Fisher) — *Roche, Hannah*
My Dark Places — *Ellroy, James*
My Dark Places (Ellroy). Audio Version — *Ellroy, James*
c My Day with Anka (Illus. by Bill Farnsworth) — *Nelson, Nan Ferring*
c My Denali (Illus. by Roy Corral) — *Corral, Kimberly*
c My Dinosaur (Illus. by Mark Alan Weatherby) — *Weatherby, Mark Alan*
c My Dog Never Says Please (Illus. by Tedd Arnold) — *Williams, Suzanne*
c My Dog Rosie (Illus. by Barry Moser) — *Harper, Isabelle*
c My Dream of Martin Luther King — *Ringgold, Faith*
My Drowning — *Grimsley, Jim*

c My Elephant Can Do Almost Anything (Illus. by Ilia Walraven) — *Vries, Anke De*
My Enemy's Enemy — *Eisenberg, Laura Zittrain*
c My Family and Other Natural Disasters — *Feeney, Josephine*
c My Family Tree — *Laden, Nina*
My Father, My Son — *Cohen, Max*
y My Father's Scar — *Cart, Michael*
My Father's War — *Dis, Adriaan Van*
My Father's War — *Richmond, Peter*
My Favorite War — *Farley, Christopher John*
c My Fellow Americans — *Provensen, Alice*
c My First Action Word Book (Illus. by Susanna Price) — *Bunting, Jane*
c My First Book of How Things Are Made — *Jones, George*
cr My First Canadian Science Encyclopedia (Illus. by Teresa Foster) — *Scarborough, Kate*
cr My First Oxford Dictionary — *Goldsmith, Evelyn*
c My First Stamp and Learn Book (Illus. by Cathy Beylon) — *Tomaselli, Doris*
My First Summer in the Sierra — *Muir, John*
My First White Friend — *Raybon, Patricia*
My Five Cambridge Friends — *Modin, Yuri*
c My Five Senses — *Aliki*
c My Five Senses — *Miller, Margaret*
My Foot's in the Stirrup... — *Bly, Stephen A, 1944-*
My Foreign Country — *Fishlock, Trevor*
c My Friends That Rhyme with Orange (Illus. by Peggy Trabalka) — *Rudner, Barry*
c My G-r-r-r-reat Uncle Tiger (Illus. by Alex Ayliffe) — *Riordan, James, 1936-*
My Gal Sunday — *Clark, Mary Higgins*
My Gal Sunday (Follows). Audio Version — *Clark, Mary Higgins*
My Garden Visits — *Matott, Justin*
c My Grandad — *Isherwood, Sheila*
c My Grandfather's House (Illus. by Henri Sorensen) — *Coville, Bruce*
c My Grandma Is Great! (Illus. by Chris Fisher) — *Roche, Hannah*
c My Great-Aunt Arizona (Illus. by Susan Condie Lamb) — *Houston, Gloria*
My Hair Turning Gray among Strangers — *Quintana, Leroy*
c My Happy Birthday Book — *Jahn-Clough, Lisa*
My Happy Life — *Milhaud, Darius*
My, Haven't the Flowers Been? — *Zinnes, Harriet*
c My Heart Is Full of Wishes (Illus. by Lane Yerkes) — *Grishaw, Joshua*
My Hindu Life — *Kadodwala, Dilip*
c My Home (Illus. by Cliff Wright) — *Hunt, Roderick*
c My Home Is the Desert — *Tracqui, Valerie*
c My Home Is the Farm — *Tracqui, Valerie*
c My Home Is the Mountains — *Tracqui, Valerie*
c My Home Is the Polar Regions — *Tracqui, Valerie*
c My Home Is the Sea — *Tracqui, Valerie*
c My House Has Stars (Illus. by Peter Catalanotto) — *McDonald, Megan*
My Jerusalem — *Drainie, Bronwyn*
My Jewish Life — *Clark, Anne*
My Kantian Ways — *Bencivenga, Ermanno*
My Kenya Days — *Thesiger, Wilfred*
My Kid's Allergic to Everything Dessert Cookbook — *Harris, Mary*
r My Kind of Town
y My Lead Dog Was a Lesbian — *O'Donoghue, Brian*
My Life — *Duncan, Isadora*
c My Life among the Aliens — *Gauthier, Gail*
My Life as a Boy — *Chernin, Kim*
My Life as a Radical Lawyer (Kunstler). Audio Version — *Kunstler, William Moses*
My Life as an Explorer — *Hedin, Sven*
My Life in the Irish Brigade — *McCarter, William*
My Life, Starring Dara Falcon — *Beattie, Ann*
My Life with Noel Coward — *Payn, Graham*
c My Little House Cookbook (Illus. by Holly Jones) — *Cotler, Amy*
c My Little Sister Ate One Hare (Illus. by Kevin Hawkes) — *Grossman, Bill*
c My Little Supermarket (Illus. by Claire Henley) — *Repchuk, Caroline*
y My Lone Star Summer — *Love, D Anne*
c My Love for You (Illus. by Susan L Roth) — *Roth, Susan L*
My Lucky Stars — *Maclaine, Shirley*
My Mama Always Said — *Klam, Marillyn Taylor*
c My Mama Had a Dancing Heart (Illus. by Raul Colon) — *Gray, Libba Moore*
My Manifold City — *Gomori, George*

c My Many Colored Days (Illus. by Steve Johnson) — *Seuss, Dr.*
c My Map Book — *Fanelli, Sara*
c My Mexico (Illus. by F John Sierra) — *Johnston, Tony*
My Micheline — *Drevet, Patrick*
My Mind Set on Freedom — *Salmond, John A*
c My Mother's Ghost — *Buffie, Margaret*
My Mother's Keeper — *Holley, Tara Elgin*
c My Mum Is Magic! (Illus. by Chris Fisher) — *Roche, Hannah*
My Music Is My Flag — *Glasser, Ruth*
My Name Escapes Me — *Guinness, Alec*
c My Name Is Seepeetza — *Sterling, Shirley*
c My Napoleon (Illus. by Catherine Brighton) — *Brighton, Catherine*
c My Navajo Sister (Illus. by Eleanor Schick) — *Schick, Eleanor*
My New Life — *Molen, Ron*
c My New Sandbox (Illus. by Julia Gorton) — *Jakob, Donna*
c My Nose, My Toes! (Illus. by Sandra Lousada)
c My Ol' Man — *Polacco, Patricia*
y My Old Man and the Sea — *Hays, David*
y My Old Man and the Sea (Guidall). Audio Version — *Hays, David*
My Other Life — *Theroux, Paul*
My Other Life (Dukes). Audio Version — *Theroux, Paul*
My Outlaw — *Miller, Linda Lael*
My Own Backyard — *Dalton, Greg*
My Own Country — *Verghese, Abraham*
My Own Private Germany — *Santner, Eric L*
y My Own Two Feet — *Cleary, Beverly*
c My Oxford Pop-Up Surprise 123 (Illus. by Robert Crowther) — *Crowther, Robert*
c My Oxford Pop-up Surprise ABC (Illus. by Robert Crowther) — *Crowther, Robert*
c My Oxford Surprise Pop-Up 123 — *Crowther, Robert*
c My Oxford Surprise Pop-Up 123 (Illus. by Robert Crowther) — *Crowther, Robert*
c My Oxford Surprise Pop-up ABC — *Crowther, Robert*
c My Oxford Surprise Pop-Up ABC (Illus. by Robert Crowther) — *Crowther, Robert*
c My Painted House, My Friendly Chicken and Me — *Angelou, Maya*
c My Palace of Leaves in Sarajevo (Illus. by Herbert Tauss) — *Lorbiecki, Marybeth*
c My Pen Pal Scrapbook (Illus. by Shelley Aliotti) — *Aliotti, Shelley*
My Psychosis, My Bicycle, and I — *Simon, Fritz B*
y My Remembers — *Stimpson, Eddie, Jr.*
My Russian Love — *Franck, Dan*
y My Sergei — *Gordeeva, Ekaterina*
My Sergei (Gordeeva). Audio Version — *Gordeeva, Ekaterina*
My Shining Archipelago — *Ansel, Talvikki*
My Silver Shoes — *Dunn, Nell*
c My Sister Is Super! (Illus. by Chris Fisher) — *Roche, Hannah*
y My Sister's Bones — *Hanauer, Cathi*
c My Sister's Rusty Bike (Illus. by Richard Hull) — *Aylesworth, Jim*
y My So-Called Boyfriend — *Winfrey, Elizabeth*
My Soul Magnifies the Lord — *Gabriele, Edward Francis*
My Soul to Keep — *Hawkes, Judith*
My Spirit Rejoices — *Leseur, Elisabeth*
My Steadfast Heart — *Goodman, Jo*
c My Steps (Illus. by Adjoa J Burrowes) — *Derby, Sally*
My Story — *York, Sarah Mountbatten-Windsor, Duchess of*
My Story. Audio Version — *York, Sarah Mountbatten-Windsor, Duchess of*
My Story of the War — *Livermore, Mary*
My Struggle — *Zhirinovsky, Vladimir*
My Summer with George — *French, Marilyn*
My Sweet Folly — *Kinsale, Laura*
c My Teacher the Ghost (Illus. by Antony Lewis) — *Fischel, Emma*
c My Teacher's Secret Life (Illus. by JoAnn Adinolfi) — *Krensky, Stephen*
c My Tooth Is about to Fall Out (Illus. by Betsy Lewin) — *Maccarone, Grace*
My Town — *Lee, David, 1944, Aug., 8-*
My Trouble Is My English — *Fu, Danling*
My Two Wars — *Thomsen, Moritz*
My Uncle Napoleon — *Pezeshkzad, Iraj*
My Vagabond Lover — *Vallee, Eleanor*
My Vegetable Love — *Klaus, Carl H*
c My Very First Mother Goose (Illus. by Rosemary Wells) — *Opie, Iona Archibald*

c My Very First Nature Craft Book (Illus. by Anna Curti) — *Curti, Anna*
c My Very Own Birthday (Illus. by Jackie Urbanovic) — *West, Robin*
c My Very Own Mother's Day (Illus. by Jackie Urbanovic) — *West, Robin*
My View of Shakespeare — *Rowse, A L*
c My Wartime Summers — *Cutler, Jane*
My Worst Date — *Leddick, David*
My Years in Theresienstadt — *Spies, Gerty*
My Years with Apu — *Ray, Satjavit*
My Years with Gorbachev and Shevardnadze — *Palazchenko, Pavel*
r Myanmar (Burma). 6th Ed. — *Cummings, Joe*
Mycenaean Athens — *Mountjoy, P A*
r Mycenaean Civilization — *Feuer, Bryan*
y Myfanwy's Demon — *Katz, Louise*
Mykola Kostomarov: A Biography — *Prymak, Thomas M*
Myocardial Ischemia — *Karmazyn, M*
Myocardial Preconditioning — *Wainwright, Cherry L*
Myoe the Dreamkeeper — *Tanabe, George J, Jr.*
y Myra Bradwell: First Woman Lawyer — *Wheaton, Elizabeth*
c Myself — *Bryant-Mole, Karen*
Le Mystere Apocryphe — *Kaestli, Jean-Daniel*
Le Mystere De Judith Et Holofernes — *Molinet, Jean*
Mysteries — *Hamsun, Knut*
Mysteries of Ancient China — *Rawson, Jessica*
y Mysteries of Animal Intelligence — *Steiger, Sherry Hansen*
c Mysteries of Harris Burdick — *Van Allsburg, Chris*
The Mysteries of London — *Reynolds, G W M*
c Mysteries of Lost Civilizations — *Millard, Anne*
y Mysteries of Prehistoric Life (Illus. by Francis Phillipps) — *Unwin, David*
The Mysteries of Research. 2nd Ed. — *Cohen, Sharron*
c Mysteries of Sherlock Holmes (Illus. by Paul Bachem) — *Doyle, Arthur Conan, Sir*
Mysteries of the Home — *Meehan, Paula*
c Mysteries of the Ocean Deep — *Dipper, Frances*
cr Mysteries through the Ages — *Millard, Anne*
y The Mysterious Affair at Styles (May). Audio Version — *Christie, Agatha*
y The Mysterious Affair at Styles (Suchet). Audio Version — *Christie, Agatha*
The Mysterious Death of Mary Rogers — *Srebnick, Amy Gilman*
Mysterious Erotic Tales
The Mysterious Fayum Portraits — *Doxiadis, Euphrosyne*
c The Mysterious Jungles (Illus. by Luis Rizo) — *Llamas, Andreu*
The Mysterious Science of Law — *Boorstin, Daniel J*
Mysterious Skin — *Heim, Scott*
y Mysterious Skin (Ciccolini). Audio Version — *Heim, Scott*
c Mysterious Tales of Japan (Illus. by Tatsuro Kiuchi) — *Martin, Rafe*
c The Mysterious Visitor (Illus. by Elivia Savadier) — *Jaffe, Nina*
p Mysterious Women
Mystery! A Celebration — *Miller, Ron*
c Mystery at Winklesea (Illus. by Susan Winter) — *Cresswell, Helen*
c Mystery History of a Medieval Castle — *Pipe, Jim*
c Mystery History of a Pirate Galleon (Illus. by Mike Bell) — *Finney, Fred*
c The Mystery of King Karfu (Illus. by Doug Cushman) — *Cushman, Doug*
Mystery of Love — *Beckett, Wendy*
The Mystery of Men — *Bellamy, Guy*
The Mystery of Romans — *Nanos, Mark D*
The Mystery of the Acts of John — *Schneider, Paul G*
The Mystery of the Campden Wonder — *Potter, Jeremy*
The Mystery of the Eucharist in the Anglican Tradition — *McAdoo, H R*
c The Mystery of the Missing Money — *Riehecky, Janet*
c Mystery of the Tooth Gremlin (Illus. by Paige Billin-Frye) — *Graves, Bonnie*
c The Mystery of the UFO (Illus. by Lydia Halverson) — *Riehecky, Janet*
The Mystery Roast — *Gadol, Peter*
r The Mystery Science Theater 3000 Amazing Colossal Episode Guide — *Beaulieu, Trace*
y Mystery Stories (Illus. by Adrian Reynolds) — *Cresswell, Helen*
The Mystery to a Solution — *Irwin, John T*
Mystic Tales from the Zohar — *Wineman, Aryeh*
The Mystical Arts of Tibet — *Mullin, Glenn*

Mystical Bedlam — *MacDonald, Michael*
Mystical Christianity — *Sanford, John A*
Mystical Delights — *Huttner, Hilary*
Mystical Healing — *Horn, John*
Mystical Theology — *Johnston, William, 1925-*
Mystical Union in Judaism, Christianity and Islam — *Idel, Moshe*
Mysticism and the Mystical Experience — *Bishop, Donald H*
Mysticism, Buddhist and Christian — *Mommaers, Paul*
Mysticism: Holiness East and West — *Carmody, Denise Lardner*
y Mystifying Math Puzzles — *Ryan, Steve*
Myth and Fiction in Early Norse Lands — *Dronke, Ursula*
Myth and Metropolis — *Gilloch, Graeme*
Myth and Mobilization in Revolutionary Iran — *Ram, Haggay*
Myth, Magic, and Mystery — *Clark, Trinkett*
c Myth Maker (Illus. by Brad Weinman) — *Neimark, Anne E*
Myth, Meaning and Memory on Roman Sarcophagi — *Koortbojian, Michael*
yr Myth: Myths and Legends of the World Explored — *McLeish, Kenneth*
The Myth of A.S. Pushkin in Russia's Silver Age — *Horowitz, Brian*
The Myth of American Individualism — *Shain, Barry Alan*
The Myth of Apollo and Marsyas in the Art of the Italian Renaissance — *Wyss, Edith*
The Myth of Aunt Jemima — *Roberts, Diane*
The Myth of Constitutionalism in Pakistan — *Maluka, Zulfikar Khalid*
The Myth of Democracy — *Lindbom, Tage*
The Myth of Democratic Failure — *Wittman, Donald A*
The Myth of Mondragon — *Kasmir, Sharryn*
The Myth of Political Correctness — *Wilson, John K*
The Myth of Repressed Memory — *Loftus, Elizabeth*
The Myth of Santa Fe — *Wilson, Chris*
The Myth of the Framework — *Popper, Karl Raimund, Sir*
The Myth of the Male Breadwinner — *Safa, Helen I*
The Myth of the Renaissance in Nineteenth-Century Writing — *Bullen, J B*
Myth of the Welfare Queen — *Zucchino, David*
The Myth of the West — *Schulte Nordholt, J W*
The Myth of Wild Africa — *Adams, Jonathan S*
Myth, Symbol, and Colonial Encounter — *Reid, Jennifer*
Mythes Grecs Et Sources Orientales — *Duchemin, Jacqueline*
Mythic Archetypes in Ralph Waldo Emerson — *O'Keefe, Richard R*
The Mythic Path — *Feinstein, David*
c Mythical Birds and Beasts from Many Lands (Illus. by Jane Ray) — *Mayo, Margaret*
The Mythical Quest — *Kerven, Rosalind*
Mythical Trickster Figures — *Hynes, William H*
Mythisches Denken Zwischen Romantik Und Realismus — *Winkler, Markus*
Mythologies of the Heart — *Malanga, Gerard*
The Mythology of Dogs — *Hausman, Gerald*
The Mythology of Sex — *Dening, Sarah*
r Mythology of the Lenape — *Bierhorst, John*
The Mythology of Transgression — *Highwater, Jamake*
Mythomania: Fantasies, Fables, and Sheer Lies in Contemporary American Popular Art — *Welt, Bernard*
y Myths and Legends from around the World — *Shepherd, Sandy*
c Myths and Legends of the World. Vol. 2 (Illus. by Bee Willey) — *McCaughrean, Geraldine*
Myths and Tales of the White Mountain Apache — *Goodwin, Greenville*
Myths of Modern Individualism — *Watt, Ian*
Myths of the Emergent — *Higgins, James*
r Mytsi Ukrainy — *Kudryts'kyi, Anatolii*

N

N: A Romantic Mystery — Edwards, Louis

N.E.W.S: A Model for the Evaluation of Non-Life Insurance Companies — Kramer, Bert

Na Cherta Nam Chuzhie — Tokareva, Viktoria

The Na+/H+ Exchanger — Fliegel, Larry

Na Perekhidnomu Etapi — Kamins'kyi, Anatol'

Na Prelomu — Jankovic, Sava

c Nabulela (Illus. by Fiona Moodie) — Moodie, Fiona

Nach Dem Holocaust — Brenner, Michael

Nachgelassene Schriften. Vol. 10 — Fichte, Johann Gottlieb

Nachts, Unter Baumen — Kruger, Michael

La Nada Cotidiana — Valdes, Zoe

Nadar — Hambourg, Maria Morris

Nadya: The Wolf Chronicles — Murphy, Pat, 1955-

NAFTA and Beyond — Norton, Joseph J

r A NAFTA Bibliography — Metz, Allan

NAFTA in Transition — Randall, Stephen J

NAFTA: Poverty and Free Trade in Mexico — Coote, Belinda

Nagasaki Journey — Yamahata, Yosuke

Nagging Questions — Bushnell, Dana E

Nagybanya Muveszete — Csorba, Geza

Naissance Et Mort Des Entreprises En Europe XIXe-XXe Siecles — Ross, Michael

Najstarsze Druki Cerkiewnoslowianskie I Ich Stosunek Do Tradycji Rekopismiennej

Naked — Sedaris, David

Naked (Sedaris). Audio Version — Sedaris, David

Naked as Water — Azzopardi, Mario

Naked Babies — Kelsh, Nick

Naked Came the Manatee — Hiaasen, Carl

The Naked City — Willett, Ralph

y Naked Earth — Vogel, Shawna

The Naked Heart — Gay, Peter

Naked Instinct — Sanello, Frank

y Naked Justice — Bernhardt, William

The Naked Madonna — Wiese, Jan

y The Naked Mole-Rat Mystery (Illus. by Raymond A Mendez) — Jarrow, Gail

y Naked Mole-Rats — Jarrow, Gail

Naked Racial Preference — Cohen, Carl

Naked Science — Nader, Laura

Naked Sleeper — Nunez, Sigrid

Naked to the Bone — Kevles, Bettyann

The Naked Tree — Pak, Wan-So

The Name of a Bullfighter — Sepulveda, Luis

Name Witheld — Jance, J A

The Names: A Memoir — Momaday, N Scott

The Names of the Dead — O'Nan, Stewart

The Names of Things — Morrow, Susan Brind

Names We Call Home — Thompson, Becky W

Namibia: The Wall of Silence — Groth, Siegfried

Namibia's Liberation Struggle — Leys, Colin

Naming Canada — Rayburn, Alan

c Naming Colors — Dewey, Ariane

Naming Grace — Hilkert, Mary Catherine

Naming Our Truth — Ware, Ann Patrick

Naming Properties — Miner, Earl

Naming Rumpelstiltskin — Finlayson, Ann

Naming the Antichrist — Fuller, Robert C

Naming the Light — Deen, Rosemary

y Naming the New World — Baker, Calvin

y Naming the Spirits — Thornton, Lawrence

Nampeyo and Her Pottery — Kramer, Barbara, 1926-

Nan Goldin: I'll Be Your Mirror — Sussman, Elisabeth

c Nana Hannah's Piano (Illus. by Diana Cain Bluthenthal) — Bottner, Barbara

Nana's Gift — Oke, Janette

Nancy Spero — Bird, Jon

Nang Qua Pho Cu — Nguyen, Ngoc Ngan

c Nanny Fox and the Christmas Surprise (Illus. by Selina Young) — Adams, Georgie

c Nanny Fox and the Three Little Pigs (Illus. by Selina Young) — Adams, Georgie

Nanomaterials: Synthesis, Properties, and Applications — Edelstein, A S

c Nanook and Naoya (Illus. by Fred Bruemmer) — Delaunois, Angele

Nanotechnology: Molecular Speculations on Global Abundance — Crandall, B C

Nanotechnology: Molecularly Designed Materials — National Meeting of the American Chemical Society (210th: 1995: Chicago, IL)

Nantucket Recipes — Dawson, Mark

Naomi — Campbell, Naomi

Naples in the Time of Cholera 1884-1911 — Snowden, Frank M

Napoleon — Ellis, Geoffrey

Napoleon and English Romanticism — Bainbridge, Simon

Napoleon and His Artists — Wilson-Smith, Timothy

Napoleon and His Marshals — Macdonell, A G

Napoleon and Josephine — Bruce, Evangeline

Napoleon Conquers Austria — Arnold, James R

Napoleon: Europe and the Empire. Electronic Media Version

Napoleon: The Final Verdict — Haythornthwaite, Philip

Napoleonic Wars: Napoleon's Army — Chartrand, Rene

Napoleonic Wars: Wellington's Army — Fletcher, Ian

Napoleon's Jailer — Desmond, Gregory

c The Napping House (Illus. by Don Wood) — Wood, Audrey

c Nappy Hair (Illus. by Joe Cepeda) — Herron, Carolivia

Nar Fabrikerna Tystnar — Greider, Goran

Naranjo the Muse — Castaneda, Omar S

Narcissism and Philanthropy — Freund, Gerald

Narcissism and the Literary Libido — Alcorn, Marshall W, Jr.

NarcoDiplomacy: Exporting the U.S. War on Drugs — Friman, H Richard

Narodynyi Kalendarl — Mishchenko, Mykola

Narrating Our Pasts — Tonkin, Elizabeth

Narrating the Thirties — Baxendale, John

Narration and Description in the French Realist Novel — Reid, James H

Narrative and Freedom — Morson, Gary Saul

Narrative and the Natural Law — Hall, Pamela M

Narrative Art, Political Rhetoric — Dutcher-Walls, Patricia

Narrative as Rhetoric — Phelan, James

Narrative, Authority, and Power — Scanlon, Larry

r A Narrative Bibliography of the African American Frontier — Hardaway, Roger D

Narrative Ethics — Newton, Adam Zachary

The Narrative Fiction of Heinrich Boll — Butler, Michael

Narrative Policy Analysis — Roe, Emery

The Narrative Secret of Flannery O'Connor — Johansen, Ruthann Knechel

Narrative Solutions in Brief Therapy — Eron, Joseph B

Narrative Therapy — Freedman, Jill

Narrative Therapy in Practice — Monk, Gerald

Narratives in Popular Culture, Media, and Everyday Life — Berger, Arthur Asa

Narratology: An Introduction — Onega, Susana

The Narrow Bridge — Brettschneider, Marla

Narrow Roads of Gene Land. Vol. 1 — Hamilton, W D

Narziss and Goldmund — Hesse, Hermann

r The NASA Atlas of the Solar System — Greeley, Ronald

Nashville 1864 — Jones, Madison

Nat Sherman's Passion for Cigars — Sherman, Joel

Natalie on the Street — Nietzke, Ann

Natasha: Vygotskian Dialogues — Lipman, Matthew

c Nate the Great and the Crunchy Christmas (Illus. by Marc Simont) — Sharmat, Marjorie Weinman

Nathalie Sarraute and the Feminist Reader — Barbour, Sarah

y Nathaniel Hawthorne: American Storyteller — Whitelaw, Nancy

c Nathaniel's Violin (Illus. by Marlene Watson) — Lohans, Alison

y Nathan's Run — Gilstrap, John

y Nathan's Run (Glover). Audio Version — Gilstrap, John

The Nation and Its City — Lessoff, Alan

Nation and State in Late Imperial Russia — Weeks, Theodore R

A Nation of Adversaries — Garry, Patrick M

A Nation of Beggars? — Kerr, Donal

A Nation of Fliers — Fritzsche, Peter

The Nation of Islam — Lee, Martha F

A Nation of Steel — Misa, Thomas J

Une Nation Peut-Elle Se Donner La Constitution De Son Choix? — Seymour, Michael

y A Nation Torn — Ray, Delia

A Nation under Lawyers — Glendon, Mary Ann

r National 5-Digit Zip Code and Post Office Directory 1996. Vols. 1-2

National Accounts and the Environment — Musu, Ignazio

National Accounts Studies of the ESCWA Region

r National Ag Safety Disc (NASD). Electronic Media Version

The National Archives Preparing for a New Records Age

National Assessments — Murphy, Paud

r National Audubon Society Field Guide to North American Mammals. Rev. Ed. — Whitaker, John O

cr National Audubon Society Interactive CD-ROM Guide to North American Birds. Electronic Media Version

The National Audubon Society: The Bird Garden — Kress, Stephen W

r National Bank Notes. 3rd Ed. — Kelly, Don C

National Character — Inkeles, Alex

National Competitiveness in a Global Economy — Rapkin, David P

National Conference of Intermodalism — National Conference on Intermodalism (1994: New Orleans, Louisiana)

The National Conference on Legal Information Issues — Coggins, Timothy

National Culture and the New Global System — Buell, Frederick

A National Curriculum for the Early Years — Anning, Angela

c The National Debt — Sandak, Cass R

National Defense and the Environment — Dycus, Stephen

National Development Planning and the Regions of Namibia

r The National Directory of Addresses and Telephone Numbers 1996

r National Directory of Grantmaking Public Charities. 1st Ed.

r National Directory of Woman-Owned Business Firms. 8th Ed.

National Diversity and Global Capitalism — *Berger, Suzanne*

National Education Longitudinal Study of 1988: High School Seniors' Instructional Experiences in Science and Mathematics

r The National Electronic Library — *Pitkin, Gary M*

r National Fax Directory 1996

National Gallery Companion Guide — *Langmuir, Erika*

r The National Gallery Complete Illustrated Catalogue — *National Gallery (Great Britain)*

National Gallery of Art, Washington. New and Rev. Ed. — *Walker, John, 1906-*

cp National Geographic World

r The National Guide to Educational Credit for Training Programs. 1996 Ed. — *Swinerton, E Nelson*

r National Guide to Funding for Children, Youth, and Families. 3rd Ed.

r National Guide to Funding for Community Development — *Rich, Elizabeth H*

r National Guide to Funding for Elementary and Secondary Education. 3rd Ed. — *Baumgartner, James E*

r National Guide to Funding for Libraries and Information Services. 3rd Ed. — *Baumgartner, James E*

r National Guide to Funding for the Environment and Animal Welfare. 3rd Ed. — *Rich, Elizabeth H*

r National Guide to Funding in Religion. 3rd Ed. — *Baumgartner, James E*

r National Health Directory 1996

National Histories and European History — *Fulbrook, Mary*

National Identity and Democratic Prospects in Socialist China — *Friedman, Edward*

National Innovation Systems — *Nelson, Richard R*

National Intelligencer and Washington Advertiser Newspaper Abstracts 1800-1805 — *Dixon, Joan M*

National Interest and Foreign Aid — *Hook, Steven W*

National Interests in International Society — *Finnemore, Martha*

National Libraries 3 — *Line, Maurice B*

r The National Literacy Trust's Guide to Books on Literacy Published during 1995

National Military Establishments and the Advancement of Science and Technology — *Forman, Paul*

cr The National Museum of American Art. Electronic Media Version

National Parks and Protected Areas — *Wright, R Gerald*

National Parks and the Woman's Voice — *Kaufman, Polly Welts*

r National Party Conventions 1831-1992

National Popular Politics in Early Independent Mexico 1820-1847 — *Di Tella, Torcuato S*

The National Question — *Berberoglu, Berch*

National Redeemer — *Henken, Elissa R*

National Report for the Fourth World Conference on Women

National Rights, International Obligations — *Caney, Simon*

National School Policy — *Docking, Jim*

National Science Education Standards

National Security — *United States. General Accounting Office*

r National Security Directives of the Reagan and Bush Administrations — *Simpson, Christopher*

National Sovereignty and International Organizations — *Martin Martinez, Magdalena M*

The National Space Transportation Policy

National Sports Policies — *Chalip, Laurence*

National Standards for United States History — *National Center for History in the Schools*

National Standards in American Education — *Ravitch, Diane*

r National Storytelling Directory 1996

National Systems for Financing Innovation

National Television Violence Study. Vol. 1

r National Trade and Professional Associations of the United States. 31st Ed.

The National Trust Guide to Art Deco in America — *Gebhard, David*

The National Trust Guide to Great Opera Houses in America — *Zietz, Karyl Lynn*

r The National Trust Guide to Historic Bed and Breakfasts, Inns, and Small Hotels. 4th Ed.

r National Union Catalog of Manuscript Collections 1959/61-

r The National Union Catalog: Pre-1956 Imprints. Vols. 1-754 — *Library of Congress*

The National Wildlife Federation's Guide to Gardening for Wildlife — *Tufts, Craig*

Nationalising Femininity — *Gledhill, Christine*

Nationalism and Federalism in Australia — *McMinn, W G*

Nationalism and Language in Kurdistan 1918-1985 — *Hassanpour, Amir*

Nationalism and Rationality — *Breton, Albert*

y Nationalism and Unionism — *Brennan, Eilis*

Nationalism, Ethnicity, and Identity — *Farnen, Russell F*

Nationalism, Politics, and the Practice of Archaeology — *Kohl, Philip L*

Nationalism Reframed — *Brubaker, Rogers*

Nationen, Nationalitaten, Minderheiten — *Heuberger, Valeria*

Nationhood and Political Theory — *Canovan, Margaret*

Nations against the State — *Keating, Michael*

Nations and Nationalism since 1780. 2nd Ed. — *Hobsbawm, Eric*

Nations, Nationalism and Patriotism in the European Past — *Bjorn, Claus*

A Nation's Shame — *United States. Advisory Board on Child Abuse and Neglect*

r Nations without States — *Minahan, James*

yr Native America in the 20th Century — *Davis, Mary B*

Native American Autobiography — *Krupat, Arnold*

Native American Communities in Wisconsin 1600-1960 — *Bieder, Robert E*

Native American Cultural and Religious Freedoms — *Wunder, John R*

Native American Gardening — *Caduto, Michael J*

r Native American Genealogical Sourcebook — *Byers, Paula K*

yr The Native American in Long Fiction — *Beam, Joan*

r Native American Issues — *Thompson, William Norman*

Native American Law and Colonialism before 1776 to 1903 — *Wunder, John R*

y Native American Literature — *Gleason, Katherine*

c The Native American Look Book — *Sullivan, Missy*

Native American Perspectives on Literature and History — *Velie, Alan R*

r Native American Political Systems and the Evolution of Democracy — *Johansen, Bruce E*

Native American Postcolonial Psychology — *Duran, Eduardo*

y Native American Religion — *Bonvillain, Nancy*

Native American Sovereignty — *Wunder, John R*

Native American Verbal Art — *Clements, William M*

y Native Americans and the Reservation in American History — *McCormick, Anita Louise*

Native Americans, Crime, and Justice — *Nielsen, Marianne O*

r Native Americans in Children's Literature — *Stott, Jon C*

Native Americans in the News — *Weston, Mary Ann*

y Native Americans of the West — *Smith, C Carter*

The Native Americans (Turner Publishing). Electronic Media Version

Native and Newcomer — *Robertson, Jennifer*

Native Canadiana — *Scofield, Gregory*

Native in a Strange Land — *Coleman, Wanda*

yr Native North American Biography. Vols. 1-2 — *Malinowski, Sharon*

Native People of Southern New England 1500-1650 — *Bragdon, Kathleen J*

r Native Peoples of the Northwest — *Halliday, Jan*

Native Place, City, and Nation — *Goodman, Bryna*

The Native Plant Primer — *Ottesen, Carole*

Native Speaker — *Lee, Chang-Rae*

Natives and Newcomers — *Tindall, George Brown*

Nativism Reborn? — *Tatalovich, Raymond*

c The Nativity (Illus. by Juan Wijngaard) — *Wijngaard, Juan*

c The Nativity: From the Gospels of Matthew and Luke (Illus. by Ruth Sanderson) — *Bible. N.T. Matthew. English. Revised Standard. Selections. 1993*

NATO in the New European Order — *Carr, Fergus*

NATO in the Post-Cold War Era — *Papacosma, S Victor*

NATO's Eastern Dilemmas — *Haglund, David G*

Nattering on the Net — *Spender, Dale*

The Natufian Chipped Lithic Assemblage — *Pedersen, Charlott Hoffman*

Natural and Artificial Parallel Computation — *Waltz, David L*

Natural Beauty for All Seasons — *Cox, Janice*

Natural Bridges — *McCampbell, Debbie Lynn*

Natural Climate Variability on Decade-to-Century Time Scales — *National Research Council (U.S.). Climate Research Committee*

Natural Connections — *Chamlee, Paula*

Natural Convection in a Horizontal Circular Cylinder — *Pepper, D W*

Natural Draught Cooling Towers — *International Symposium on Natural Draught Cooling Towers (4th: Kaiserslautern, Germany)*

c Natural Foods and Products — *Chandler, Gary*

r Natural Gardening — *Boring, John Kadel*

Natural Gas Vehicles — *Ingersoll, John G*

Natural Grace — *Fox, Matthew*

Natural Hazard Phenomena and Mitigation 1996

Natural Healing for Schizophrenia — *Edelman, Eva*

Natural Histories of Discourse — *Silvestein, Michael*

A Natural History of Amphibians — *Stebbins, Robert C*

A Natural History of Homosexuality — *Mondimore, Francis Mark*

y The Natural History of Insects — *Preston-Mafham, Rod*

c The Natural History of Make-Believe — *Goldthwaite, John*

The Natural History of Mania, Depression, and Schizophrenia — *Winokur, George*

The Natural History of Monitor Lizards — *De Lisle, Harold F*

y A Natural History of Parenting — *Allport, Susan*

The Natural History of Pollination — *Proctor, Michael*

Natural History of the Colorado Plateau and Great Basin — *Harper, Kimball T*

The Natural History of the Long Expedition to the Rocky Mountains 1819-1820 — *Evans, Howard Ensign*

y A Natural History of the Senses (Porter). Audio Version — *Ackerman, Diane*

Natural Hormone Replacement for Women over 45 — *Wright, Jonathan V*

The Natural House Catalog — *Pearson, David, 1940-*

Natural Law and Moral Philosophy — *Haakonssen, Knud*

Natural Masques — *Campbell, Jill*

Natural Prozac — *Robertson, Joel C*

The Natural Rate of Unemployment — *Cross, Rod*

Natural Recipes for the Good Life — *Levine, Hedi*

The Natural Remedies for Common Ailments Handbook — *White, Celeste*

Natural Rights and the New Republicanism — *Zuckert, Michael P*

The Natural Science of the Human Species — *Lorenz, Konrad*

The Natural Selection of the Chemical Elements — *Williams, R J P*

Natural Theology — *Paley, William*

Natural Toxins 2 — *Singh, B R*

cr Natural Treasures Field Guide for Kids (Illus. by Elizabeth Biesiot) — *Biesiot, Elizabeth*

The Natural Water Garden — *Burrell, C Colston*

Natural Woman, Natural Menopause — *Laux, Marcus*

Natural Women's Health — *Wharton, Lynda*

yr Natural World — *Parker, Steve*

Natural Worlds — *Bateman, Robert*

Naturaliser L'Intentionnalite — *Pacherie, Elisabeth*

Naturalist — *Wilson, Edward Osborne*

A Naturalist along the Jersey Shore — *Burger, Joanna*

A Naturalist in Florida — *Carr, Archie*

The Naturalistic Inner-City Novel in America — *Giles, James R*

The Naturalistic Novel of the New World — *Sedycias, Joao*

The Naturalist's Garden. 3rd Ed. — *Ernst, Ruth Shaw*

Naturalizing the Mind — *Dretske, Fred*

Naturally Occurring Radioactive Material — *Underhill, Philip T*

The Naturalness of Religious Ideas — *Boyer, Pascal*

The Nature and Functions of Law. 5th Ed. — *Berman, Harold J*

Nature and Properties of Refractory Carbides — *Upadhyaya, G S*

Nature and the Greeks. Science and Humanism — *Schrodinger, Erwin*

Nature and Treatment of Stuttering. 2nd Ed. — *Curlee, Richard F*

c Nature Crafts for Kids — *Diehn, Gwen*

c Nature Cross-Sections (Illus. by Richard Orr) — *Orr, Richard*

Nature, Culture, Imperialism — *Arnold, David*

c Nature Got There First — *Gates, Phil*

Nature, Justice, and Rights in Aristotle's Politics
— Miller, Fred D, Jr.
p Nature Medicine
The Nature of Blood — Phillips, Caryl
The Nature of Buddhist Ethics — Keown, Damien
The Nature of Confession — Phillips, Timothy R
The Nature of Doctrine — Lindbeck, George
The Nature of Emotion — Ekman, Paul
The Nature of God — Hughes, Gerard J
y The Nature of Horses — Budiansky, Stephen
y The Nature of Smoke — Harris, Anne
The Nature of Space and Time — Hawking, Stephen
y The Nature of the Beast — Campion, Isaac
c The Nature of the Beast (Illus. by G Brian Karas)
— Carr, Jan
The Nature of the Place — Quantic, Diane Dufva
The Nature of Value — Lemos, Ramon M
Nature Photography — Fitzharris, Tim
Nature: Poems Old and New — Swenson, May
r Nature Travel — Holing, Dwight
Nature Walks of Central Park — Burton, Dennis
c Nature Watch (Illus. by Brita Granstrom)
— Manning, Mick
Nature Writing — Scheese, Don
Nature Writings — Muir, John
Nature's Ban — McLennan, Karen Jacobsen
Nature's Body — Schiebinger, Londa
r Nature's Cures — Castleman, Michael
Nature's Keeper — Wenz, Peter S
Nature's Keepers — Budiansky, Stephen
y Nature's Numbers — Stewart, Ian
The Natures of John and William Bartram
— Slaughter, Thomas P
Nature's Prozac — Sachs, Judith
c The Naughty Boy and the Strawberry Horse (Illus. by
G Patterson) — Patterson, Geoffrey
Nautical Instruction 1587 — Garcia De Palacio, Diego
Navajo and Tibetan Sacred Wisdom — Gold, Peter
The Navajo-Hopi Land Dispute — Brugge, David M
Navajo Kinship and Marriage — Witherspoon, Gary
Navajo Multi-Household Social Units — Rocek,
Thomas R
Navajo Rugs. 2nd Rev. Ed. — Dedera, Don
Navajo Sacred Places — Kelley, Klara Bonsack
y Navajo: Visions and Voices across the Mesa (Illus. by
Shonto Begay) — Begay, Shonto
Naval Aviation in the First World War — Layman, R
D
r Naval Documents of the American Revolution. Vol. 10
— United States. Naval History Division
The Naval Institute Guide to Combat Fleets of the
World. Book and Electronic Media Version
— Baker, A D, III
r The Naval Institute Guide to Combat Fleets of the
World. Electronic Media Version — Baker, A D, III
r The Naval Institute Guide to World Military Aviation
1996. Electronic Media Version
The Naval Policy of Austria-Hungary 1867-1918
— Sondhaus, Lawrence
Naval Power in the Twentieth Century — Rodger, N A
M
Naval Warfare in the Baltic 1939-1945 — Koburger,
Charles W
Ha-Navi Me-Rehov Eser — Keller, Tsipi
Navicelle — Trucillo, Luigi
Navier-Stokes Equations and Nonlinear Functional
Analysis. 2nd Ed. — Temam, Roger
Navier-Stokes Equations and Related Nonlinear
Problems — Sequeira, A
Navies and Nations. Vols. 1-2 — Glete, Jan
Navies and Shipbuilding Industries — Todd, Daniel
Navigating the Microsoft Network — Snell, Ned
Navigating the Mortgage Maze — Turnauer, Andrew E
Navigatio — Croggon, Alison
The Nazi Connection — Kuhl, Stefan
The Nazi Economic Recovery 1932-1938. 2nd Ed.
— Overy, R J
Nazi Germany — Fischer, Klaus P
Nazi Germany 1933-1945 — Dulffer, Jost
Nazi Germany and the American Germanists
— Lauwers-Rech, Magda
Nazi Germany and the Jews. Vol. 1 — Friedlander,
Saul
Nazi Germany at War — Kitchen, Martin
Nazi Justiz — Miller, Richard Lawrence
Nazi Science — Walker, Mark
The Nazification of an Academic Discipline — Dow,
James R
The Nazification of Russia — Reznik, Semyon
Nazimova: A Biography — Lambert, Gavin

Nazism, Fascism and the Working Class — Mason,
Timothy W
y NBA at 50 — Vancil, Mark
y NBA Basketball Basics — Vancil, Mark
y NBA Basketball Offense Basics — Vancil, Mark
c NBA by the Numbers — Brooks, Bruce
NBA Hoop Shots — Bernstein, Andrew D
NBER Macroeconomics Annual 1995
r NCAA Basketball 1997
r NCAA Final Four 1997
r NCEA/Ganley's Catholic Schools in America 1995
The NCSA Guide to PC and LAN Security — Cobb,
Stephen
NDE Engineering Codes and Standards and Materials
Characterization — Cook, J F
c Ndito Runs (Illus. by Anita Van Der Merwe)
— Anderson, Laurie Halse
Ne Dam Se, Ljubavi — Lazic, Momir
Nea Nikomedeia. Vol. 1 — Pyke, Gillian
y The Neandertal Enigma — Shreeve, James
Neanderthal — Darnton, John
The Neandertal Legacy — Mellars, Paul
The Near Death Experience — Bailey, Lee
The Near East since the First World War — Yapp, M
E
r Near-Field Optics — Paesler, Michael A
c Near Myths — Kraus, Robert
c Near Water — Wale, Carole
y Nearer Nature (Illus. by Jim Arnosky) — Arnosky,
Jim
Nearer the Moon — Nin, Anais
y The Nearest Faraway Place — White, Timothy
The Nearest Place That Wasn't Ireland — Harris,
Ruth-Ann M
c The Nearly Ghost Baby (Illus. by David William)
— Huddy, Delia
Nearly Roadkill — Sullivan, Caitlin
y The Nearness of You — Edgar, Christopher
The Neatest Little Guide to Mutual Fund Investing
— Kelly, Jason
Nebraska Alternative Transportation Fuels Handbook
Nebraska: An Illustrated History — Luebke, Frederick
C
r Nebraska Merchant Trade Tokens, Town/Place Rarity
Listing, and Other Exonumia. 6th Ed. — Hosek,
George
Nebraska Moments — Hickey, Donald R
Nebula Awards 30
y Nebula Awards 31
Nebulous Earth — Brush, Stephen G
A Necessary Evil? — Kaminski, John P
Necessary Evil — Van Meter, David A
Necessary Fraud — Taniguchi, Nancy J
The Necessary Hunger — Revoyr, Nina
Necessary Madness — Crowell, Jenn
y Necessary Roughness — Lee, Marie G
The Necessity of Experience — Reed, Edward S
Necessity or Contingency — Vuillemin, Jules
c Necklace of Stars (Illus. by Veronica Martenova
Charles) — Charles, Veronica Martenova
p Necrofile
NecronomicoN. Bk. 1
La Necropoli Protoeneolitica Di Piano Vento Nel
Territorio Di Palma Di Montechiaro — Castellana,
Giuseppe
Necroscope: Resurgence — Lumley, Brian
Need — Cohn, Nik
Needlework Animals — Bradley, Elizabeth
Needs Assessments in Public Policy — Percy-Smith,
Janie
c Neeny Coming, Neeny Going (Illus. by Synthia Saint
James) — English, Karen
Negao Et Doralice — Kokis, Sergio
Negation and Utopia — Jones, Calvin N
Negation, Subjectivity, and the History of Rhetoric
— Vitanza, Victor
The Neglected War — Hiery, Hermann Joseph
Negotiated Authorities — Greene, Jack P
Negotiating Competitiveness — Wever, Kirsten
Negotiating Cooperation — Ross, Robert S
Negotiating Democracy — Casper, Gretchen
Negotiating Identity — Buckley, Anthony D
Negotiating Performance — Taylor, Diana
Negotiating Rapture — Francis, Richard
The Negotiation Process and the Resolution of
International Conflicts — Hopmann, P Terrence
Negotiators of Change — Shoemaker, Nancy
Negritude and Literary Criticism — Jack, Belinda
Elizabeth
Negro: An Anthology — Cunard, Nancy
The Negro Baseball Leagues — Dixon, Phil

El Negro Esclavo En Nueva Espana — Aguirre
Beltran, Gonzalo
The Negro in Virginia — Virginia Writers' Project
c The Negro Leagues — Riley, James A
Negro Musicians and Their Music — Cuney Hare,
Maud
Nehru: A Tryst with Destiny — Wolpert, Stanley
Nei Zhan — Zhao, Shilin
Neighbor — Simak, Clifford D
Neighbor Blood — Frost, Richard
Neighborhood Watch — Andrus, Jeff
r Neikirk, Newkirk, Nikirk and Related Families. Vol. 1
— Hurley, W N
Neither Cargo nor Cult — Kaplan, Martha
Neither Gods nor Emperors — Calhoun, Craig
Neither King nor Prelate — Gaustad, Edwin S
Neither Kingdom nor Nation — York, Neil Longley
Neither Man nor Beast — Adams, Carol J
Neither Victim nor Enemy — Simon, Rita J
Neither Wolf nor Dog — Lewis, David Rich
Neither World — Angel, Ralph
Nejimaki Tori Kuronikuru — Murakami, Haruki
Nel Segno Di Galileo — Caroti, Stefano
c Nell Nugget and the Cow Caper (Illus. by Paul
Yalowitz) — Enderle, Judith Ross
y Nellie Bishop — Clark, Clara Gillow
c Nellie Bly's Monkey (Illus. by Catherine Stock)
— Blos, Joan W
Nellie Brown or, the Jealous Wife — Detter, Thomas
Nelson: A Personal History — Hibbert, Christopher
r Nelson Canadian Dictionary of the English Language
— Harkness, Jan
c Nelson Spelling — Kosnik, Clare
Nelson: The Life and Letters of a Hero — Morriss,
Roger
Nelson's Battles — Tracy, Nicholas
Neo-Impressionism and the Search for Solid Ground
— Hutton, John G
Neo-Liberalism with a Human Face? — Hojman,
David E
The Neo-Nazis and German Unification — Lewis,
Rand C
The Neo-Thomists — McCool, Gerald A
Neoclassical History and English Culture — Hicks,
Philip
Neocolonialism American Style 1960-2000
— Blanchard, William H
Neoconservatism: The Autobiography of an Idea
— Kristol, Irving
The Neoconservative Vision — Gerson, Mark
The Neon Smile — Lochte, Dick
r Neotropical Birds — Stotz, Douglas F
r Neotropical Migratory Birds — DeGraaf, Richard M
c Nepal — Heinrichs, Ann
The Nepal Cookbook — Association of Nepalis in the
Americas
r Nepal Handbook — Moran, Kerry
r Nepal Handbook. 2nd Ed. — Moran, Kerry
The Neppi Modona Diaries — Cohen, Kate
Neptune, and the Quest for Redemption — Greene,
Liz
Neptune and Triton — Cruikshank, Dale P
c The Neptune Fountain (Illus. by Taylor Morrison)
— Morrison, Taylor
Neptune's Gift — Multhauf, Robert P
c Nerd No More — Franklin, Kristine L
Nero — Wishart, David
Nerve (Britton). Audio Version — Francis, Dick
p Nerve Cowboy
Nerve Growth and Guidance — McCaig, C D
The Nerves of State — Braddick, M J
Nervous — Dangarembga, Tsitsi
y The Nervous System (Illus. by Antonio Munoz
Tenllado) — Roca, Nuria
Nesuah: Ela Mah? — Bar-El, Dalyah
y Net Bandits — Coleman, Michael
y A Net Full of Honey — Pinney, Estelle Runcie
Net Gain — Hagel, John
The Net-Head Handbook — Rosen, Nick
Net Learning — Serim, Ferdi
The Net of Dreams — Salamon, Julie
c A Net to Catch Time (Illus. by Scott Cook) — Banks,
Sara Harrell
NetActivism: How Citizens Use the Internet
— Schwartz, Edward
r NetDoctor: Your Guide to Health and Medical Advice
on the Internet and Online Services — Wolff,
Michael

Netherlandish Drawings of the 15th and 16th Centuries and Flemish Drawings of the 17th and 18th Centuries in Pierpont Morgan Library — *Stampfle, Felice*

NetLove: The 75 Most Erogenous Zones in Cyberspace — *Grippo, Alison*

r NetMusic: Your Guide to Rock and More on the Internet and Online Services — *Greenman, Ben*

r NetPages: The Internationally Renowned Resource Guide to the Internet. 3rd Ed.

Netscape 2 Unleashed — *Oliver, Dick*

Netscape 3 for Windows — *Castro, Elizabeth*

r The Netscape LiveWire Sourcebook — *Coombs, Ted*

Netscape Navigator 3.0, Macintosh — *Pfaffenberger, Bryan*

Netscape Navigator 3.0, Windows — *Pfaffenberger, Bryan*

Netsci Fi: — *Wolff, Michael*

y Netstudy: Your Guide to Getting Better Grades Using the Internet and Online Services

Netware Login Scripts — *Held, Gilbert*

NetWare to Internet Gateways — *Gaskin, James E*

Network and Internet Security — *Ahuja, Vijay*

Network Competition for European Telecommunications — *Stehmann, Oliver*

Network Models of the Diffusion of Innovations — *Valente, Thomas W*

Network Planning, Procurement, and Management — *Muller, Nathan J*

Network Reengineering — *Geier, James T*

Network Security — *Simonds, Fred*

Networking: Breaking Down the Walls of the Learning Environment — *Epler, Doris*

Networking CD-ROMs — *Elshami, Ahmed M*

Networking in the Humanities — *Kenna, Stephanie*

Networking Technologies — *Fortino, Andres*

Networking Windows 95 — *Collin, Simon*

Networks and Resource Sharing in the 21st Century — *Huston-Somerville, Mary*

Networks in Marketing — *Iacobucci, Dawn*

Networks, Infrastructure, and the New Task for Regulation — *Sichel, Werner*

Networks of Dissolution — *Simons, Anna*

Neue Machtzentren In Der Deutschen Kriegswirtschaft 1942-1945 — *Naasner, Walter*

Das Neue Testament Im Rahmen Der Antiken Literatur-Geschichte — *Dormeyer, Detlev*

Neural Bases of Motor Behaviour — *Lacquaniti, Francesco*

Neural Fuzzy Systems — *Lin, C T*

Neural Network Perception for Mobile Robot Guidance — *Pomerleau, Dean A*

Neural Networks in Bioprocessing and Chemical Engineering — *Baughman, D R*

Neural Networks in Finance and Investing. Rev. Ed. — *Trippi, Robert R*

Neural Networks in Robotics — *Bekey, George A*

Neuro-Fuzzy and Soft Computing — *Jang, Jyh-Shing Roger*

r Neuroanatomy of the Zebrafish Brain — *Wullimann, Mario F*

Neurobiological Mechanisms of Opiate Withdrawal — *Maldonado, Rafael*

r The Neurobiology of an Insect Brain — *Burrows, Malcolm*

Neuroethological Studies of Cognitive and Perceptual Processes — *Moss, Cynthia E*

Neuroimaging. Vol. 1 — *Bigler, Erin D*

Neuroimaging. Vol. 2 — *Bigler, Erin D*

p Neuroimmunomodulation

Neurological Disorders — *Brandt, Thomas*

Neurological Physiotherapy — *Edwards, Susan*

Neurology--What Shall I Do?. 2nd Ed. — *Thomas, Dafydd*

Neuronal Adaptation Theory — *Carmesin, Hans-Otto*

Neuropathology: The Practical Approach — *Klutzow, F W*

Neuropeptide Protocols — *Irvine, G Brent*

Neuropeptides: Basic and Clinical Advances — *Crawley, Jacqueline N*

Neuropsychiatry, Neuropsychology, and Clinical Neuroscience — *Joseph, Rhawn*

Neuropsychiatry of Personality Disorders — *Ratey, John J*

Neuroradiology. 3rd Ed. — *Taveras, Juan M*

Neuroscience: Exploring the Brain — *Bear, Mark F*

Neuroscience, Memory and Language — *Broadwell, Richard*

The Neuroscience of Mental Health II — *Koslow, Stephen H*

p The Neuroscientist: A Review Journal Bridging Neurobiology, Neurology and Psychiatry

r Neurotoxic Side Effects of Prescription Drugs — *Brust, John C M*

Neurotransmitter Transporters — *Reith, Maarten E A*

The Neutered Mother, the Sexual Family and Other Twentieth Century Tragedies — *Fineman, Martha Albertson*

Neutral Corner — *Liebling, A J*

Neutrino Mass, Dark Matter, Gravitational Waves, Monopole Condensation, and Light Cone Quantization — *Kursunoglu, Behram N*

r Nevada County, Arkansas United States Census of 1880

Nevada Youth Risk Behavior Survey 1995

Never a Normal Man — *Farson, Daniel*

y Never Again Goodbye — *Blackstock, Terri*

Never Be Afraid — *Mednicki, Bernard*

y Never Cry Arp! and Other Great Adventures — *McManus, Patrick F*

Never Drink Coffee from Your Saucer — *Long, Sheila M*

r Never Eat More than You Can Lift, and Other Food Quotes and Quips — *Herbst, Sharon Tyler*

Never Eat Your Heart Out — *Moore, Judith*

c The Never-Ending Greenness (Illus. by Neil Waldman) — *Waldman, Neil*

Never Fear, Never Quit — *Tye, Joe*

y Never Fight Fair! — *Kelly, Orr*

y Never in a Hurry — *Nye, Naomi Shihab*

Never Marry in Morocco — *Dale, Virginia*

Never Pay Retail — *Kirchheimer, Sid*

The Never-Resting Mind — *Whiting, Anthony*

c Never Ride Your Elephant to School (Illus. by Abby Carter) — *Johnson, Doug*

Never Street — *Estleman, Loren D*

y Never Too Late — *Baer, Judy*

Never Too Late to Remember — *Saidel, Rochelle G*

Never without a Song — *Newman, Katherine D*

Never without Heroes — *Vetter, Lawrence C*

Nevermore — *Redonnet, Marie*

y Neverwhere — *Gaiman, Neil*

Neveryona — *Delany, Samuel R*

New Advances in Financial Economics — *Ghosh, Dilip K*

The New African American Urban History — *Goings, Kenneth W*

r The New Age Information Guide to the Federal Government 1995

The New Age Movement — *Heelas, Paul*

y The New Age of Communications — *Green, John O, 1945-*

New Amazonia — *Corbett, Elizabeth Burgoyne*

The New American Diet Cookbook — *Connor, Sonja L*

The New American Ghetto — *Vergara, Camilo Jose*

The New American Kitchen Cookbook — *Geise, Judie*

The New American Politics — *Jones, Bryan D*

The New American Reality — *Farley, Reynolds*

The New American Voter — *Miller, Warren E*

New and Collected Poems — *Wilbur, Richard*

New and Improved — *Tedlow, Richard S*

New and Selected Poems — *Bonnefoy, Yves*

New and Selected Poems — *Galvin, Patrick*

New and Selected Poems — *Justice, Donald*

New and Selected Poems — *Padgett, Ron*

New and Selected Poems 1956-1996 — *Appleman, Philip*

New and Selected Poems 1962-92 — *Lieberman, Laurence*

New and Selected Poems 1971-1993 — *Duggan, Laurie*

The New Apartment Book — *Michael, Michele*

New Approaches to Development Cooperation — *Griffin, Keith*

New Approaches to Family Practice — *Vosler, Nancy R*

New Approaches to Poverty Analysis and Policy. Vols. 1-3

A New Archetype for Competitive Intelligence — *McGonagle, John J*

New Arenas for Violence — *Kelleher, Michael D*

A New Art — *Boom, Mattie*

New Artists' Video — *Battcock, Gregory*

The New Asian Immigration in Los Angeles and Global Restructuring — *Ong, Paul*

The New Astronomy. 2nd Ed. — *Henbest, Nigel*

New Automation Technology for Acquisitions and Collection Development — *Bazirjian, Rosann*

New Baby Owner's Manual — *Weinberg, Horst D*

r The New Beacon Book of Quotations by Women — *Maggio, Rosalie*

The New Bedding Plant Expert — *Hessayon, D G*

New Beginnings — *Grossman, Grace Cohen*

r New Bible Dictionary. 3rd Ed. — *Marshall, I Howard*

A New Birth of Freedom — *Black, Charles L, Jr.*

r The New Blackwell Guide to Recorded Blues — *Cowley, John*

cr The New Book of Knowledge 1996. Vols. 1-21

New-Born Child Murder — *Jackson, Mark*

New Boy — *Sutcliffe, William*

New Britain — *Blair, Tony*

New Broadways — *Berkowitz, Gerald*

New Business Opportunities in Latin America — *Nevaer, Louis E V*

c A New Butterfly (Illus. by Heather Collins) — *Hickman, Pamela M*

The New Cairn Terrier — *Marcum, Betty E*

The New Cambridge History of India. Vol. 3, Pt. 4

The New Cambridge Medieval History. Vol. 2 — *McKitterick, Rosamond*

r The New Cancer Sourcebook — *Cook, Allan R*

y New Candanian Kid. Invisible Kids — *Foon, Dennis*

The New Catastrophism — *Ager, Derek*

The New Challenge of Direct Democracy — *Budge, Ian*

The New Child — *Steward, James Christian*

y The New Chili Cuisine — *Hughes, Nancy S*

New Chinese Cinemas — *Browne, Nick*

r New Choices in Natural Healing — *Gottleib, Bill*

A New Class of Art — *Tovell, Rosemarie*

New Cloak, Old Dagger — *Smith, Michael, 1952, May, 5-*

The New Color Line — *Roberts, Paul Craig*

The New Colored People — *Spencer, Jon Michael*

New Communication Technologies in Developing Countries — *Hanson, Jarice*

The New Communitarians and the Crisis of Modern Liberalism — *Frohnen, Bruce*

New Community Networks — *Schuler, Douglas*

New Comparative Grammar of Greek and Latin — *Sihler, Andrew L*

cr The New Comparative World Atlas — *Hammond Incorporated*

A New Context, A New Vision

r The New Country Music Encyclopedia — *Richards, Tad*

p The New Criterion

New Critical Perspectives on Martin Walser — *Pilipp, Frank*

The New Crusades, the New Holy Land — *Morgan, David T*

New Danish Plays — *Andersen, Hans Christian*

A New Day Rising — *Snelling, Lauraine*

y The New Deal — *Stewart, Gail B*

r The New Deal Fine Arts Projects 1933-1992 — *Kalfatovic, Martin R*

r A New Deal for Southeastern Archaeology — *Lyon, Edwin A*

New Deals — *Gordon, Colin*

The New Decorating Book. 7th Ed. — *Caringer, Denise L*

p New Delta Review

The New Democracy — *Naylor, James*

New Developments in Heat Exchangers — *Afgan, Naim*

New Developments in Transmission and Driveline Design

The New Diabetic Cookbook. 4th Ed. — *Cavaiani, Mabel*

r New Dictionary of Christian Ethics and Pastoral Theology — *Atkinson, David J*

r A New Dictionary of Religions. Rev. Ed. — *Hinnells, John R*

New Directions for Equity in Mathematics Education — *Secada, Walter G*

New Directions for Lotteries and Gaming — *Alberta. Lotteries Review Committee*

New Directions in Mediation — *Folger, Joseph P*

New Directions in Vestibular Research — *Highstein, Stephen M*

The New Division of Labour — *Littek, Wolfgang*

The New Dynamics of Goal Setting — *Waitley, Denis*

The New Dynamics of Goal Setting (Waitley). Audio Version — *Waitley, Denis*

New Easy Basics Cookbook — *DiVecchio, Jerry Anne*

The New Ecological Order — *Ferry, Luc*

The New Economic Model in Latin America and Its Impact on Income Distribution and Poverty — *Bulmer-Thomas, Victor*

The New Economics of Human Behavior — *Tommasi, Mariano*

r The New Encyclopaedia Britannica. Vols. 1-32

r The New Encyclopedia of Home Repair. Rev. and Updated Ed. — *Worthington, Julian*
r New Encyclopedia of Zionism and Israel. Vols. 1-2 — *Wigoder, Geoffrey*
The New Engineering Contract — *Eggleston, Brian*
r New England: A Lonely Planet Travel Survival Kit — *Brosnahan, Tom*
A New England Fish Tale — *Murphy, Martha Watson*
r The New England Historical and Genealogical Register: Index of Persons, Volumes 51-148. Vols. 1-4 — *Fiske, Jane Fletcher*
New England Planters in the Maritime Provinces of Canada 1759-1800 — *Norton, Judith A*
r New England: Travel-Smart Trip Planner — *Wright, Anne E*
c New England Whaler (Illus. by Richard Erickson) — *Baldwin, Robert F*
New England's Gothic Literature — *Ringel, Faye*
New Epigraphic Evidence from the Biblical Period — *Deutsch, R*
New Essays on Call It Sleep — *Wirth-Nesher, Hana*
New Essays on F. Scott Fitzgerald's Neglected Stories — *Bryer, Jackson R*
New Essays on Go Down, Moses — *Wagner-Martin, Linda*
New Essays on The Crying of Lot 49 — *O'Donnell, Patrick, 1948-*
New Essays on the Maternal Voice in the Nineteenth Century — *Thaden, Barbara*
New Essays on Wise Blood — *Kreyling, Michael*
The New Ethnic Mobs — *Kleinknecht, William*
New Ethnicities — *Back, Les*
The New Etiquette — *Stewart, Marjabelle Young*
The New European Automobile Industry — *Wells, Peter*
New European Orders 1919 and 1991 — *Wells, Samuel F*
The New European Security Disorder — *Duke, Simon*
c New Faces (Illus. by Elspeth Lacey) — *Stewart, Robin E*
y The New Field Guide to the U.S. Economy — *Folbre, Nancy*
The New Finance — *Edwards, Franklin R*
The New Flower Arranging from Your Garden — *MacQueen, Sheila*
New Forces in the World Economy — *Roberts, Brad*
r The New Fowler's Modern English Usage. 3rd Ed. — *Fowler, H W*
The New French Poetry — *Kelley, David*
New French Thought — *Lilla, Mark*
New Frontiers in Hyperstructures — *Vougiouklis, Thomas*
New Frontiers in Physics. Vols. 1-2 — *Gill, Tepper L*
New Frontiers in Relativities — *Gill, Tepper L*
New Frontiers in Theoretical Biology — *Dreissmann, C A C*
New Frontiers in Women's Studies — *Maynard, Mary*
The New Gambler's Bible — *Reber, Arthur S*
New Game, New Rules — *Gray, Adele*
The New Genetics — *Shinn, Roger Lincoln*
The New Geopolitics of Central Asia and Its Borderlands — *Banuazizi, Ali*
The New Georgia — *Gachechiladze, R G*
r The New Georgia Guide
The New Germany — *Jones, Alun*
The New Girl — *Mitchell, Sally, 1937-*
y New Girl in Town — *Baer, Judy*
y The New Girls — *Gutcheon, Beth*
The New Golden Rule — *Etzioni, Amitai*
The New Good Cake Book — *Dalsass, Diana*
New Governance for Rural America — *Radin, Beryl A*
The New Great Vintage Wine Book. Rev. Ed. — *Broadbent, Michael*
The New Grove Book of Operas — *Sadie, Stanley*
r New Hacker's Dictionary. 3rd Ed. — *Raymond, Eric*
The New Handbook for Electricians: Based on the 1996 NEC. 2nd Ed. — *Clifford, Martin*
r A New Handbook of Living Religions — *Hinnells, John R*
r New Handbook of Texas. Vols. 1-6 — *Tyler, Ron*
The New Historicism Reader — *Veeser, H Aram*
New History in France — *Dosse, Francois*
A New History of Christianity — *Green, Vivian Hubert Howard*
A New History of Kentucky — *Harrison, Lowell H*
The New Home Buying Strategy — *Sullivan, Marilyn D*
c New Hope (Illus. by Henri Sorensen) — *Sorensen, Henri*
The New Hotel — *Kaplan, Mike*

yr New Immigrant Literatures in the United States — *Knippling, Alpana Sharma*
The New Informants — *Bollas, Christopher*
The New Information Industry — *Klingler, Richard*
r The New Information Revolution — *Gay, Martin, 1950-*
The New Inn — *Jonson, Ben*
The New Institutional Economics and Third World Development — *Harriss, John*
The New Internet Business Book — *Ellsworth, Jill H*
The New Interpreter's Bible. Vol. 1
The New Interpreter's Bible. Vol. 4
The New Interpreter's Bible. Vols. 9-10
The New Interventionism 1991-1994 — *Mayall, James*
A New Introduction to Bibliography — *Gaskell, Philip*
r The New Islamic Dynasties. Enl. and Updated Ed. — *Bosworth, Clifford Edmund*
The New Italian Novel — *Baranski, Zygmunt G*
The New Italian Republic — *Gundle, Stephen*
c New Jersey — *Thompson, Kathleen*
New Jersey Architecture — *Hand, Susanne C*
r New Jersey Books 1801-1860 — *Felcone, Joseph J*
r New Jersey's Women Legislators 1921-1995
c The New King — *Rappaport, D*
New Kingdom of the Saints — *Frank, Larry*
The New Kitchen Garden — *Pavord, Anna*
The New Knighthood — *Barber, Malcolm*
The New Labor Press — *Pizzigati, Sam*
The New Latin American Mission History — *Langer, Erick D*
The New Left and Labor in the 1960s — *Levy, Peter B*
New Left, New Right, and the Legacy of the Sixties — *Lyons, Paul*
p New Left Review
y New Legends — *Bear, Greg*
The New Lesbian Studies — *Zimmerman, Bonnie*
A New Life — *Harris, Alex*
The New Life — *Pamuk, Orhan*
New Light at the Cape of Good Hope — *McCracken, J L*
New Lincoln Cent Book
The New Living Heart — *DeBakey, Michael E*
r The New Loyalist Index. Vol. 2 — *Bunnell, Paul J*
The New Macroeconomics — *Dixon, Huw David*
The New Making of a Cook — *Kamman, Madeleine*
The New Man — *Bruce, H C*
The New Management — *Halal, William E*
The New Maritime History of Devon. Vol. 2 — *Duffy, Michael*
y New Math Workbook for SAT I — *Leff, Lawrence S*
The New Maximarketing — *Rapp, Stan*
The New Meat Lover's Cookbook — *Sarlin, Janeen*
New Media Technology — *Pavlik, John V*
New Methods in Quantum Theory — *Tsipis, Constantinos A*
New Methods, Old Problems — *Maschner, Herbert D G*
r New Mexican Tinwork 1840-1940 — *Coulter, Lane*
r The New Mexico State Constitution — *Smith, Chuck*
New Migrants in the Marketplace — *Halter, Marilyn*
The New Military in Russia — *Staar, Richard F*
The New Modern Times — *Bills, David B*
New Monologues for Mature Actors — *McDonough, Ann*
cp New Moon
New Moon — *Grossinger, Richard*
c New Moon (Illus. by Cathryn Falwell) — *Shea, Pegi Deitz*
c A New Move — *Lowell, Melissa*
The New Multilateralism in Japan's Foreign Policy — *Yasutomo, Dennis T*
A New Name for Peace — *Shabecoff, Philip*
y New Native American Cooking — *Carson, Dale*
The New Natural Family Doctor — *Stanway, Andrew*
The New Niagara — *Irwin, William*
The New Nineteenth Century — *Harman, Barbara Leah*
A New North America — *Doran, Charles F*
The New Novel in Latin America — *Swanson, Philip*
New Novel, New Wave, New Politics — *Higgins, Lynn A*
New Old-Fashioned Ways — *Santino, Jack*
The New Older Woman — *Downes, Peggy*
A New Order for Gas in Europe? — *Stoppard, Michael*
The New Orleans Cabildo — *Din, Gilbert C*
r The New Our Right to Love — *Vida, Ginny*
c The New Oxford Book of Children's Verse — *Philip, Neil*
y New Oxford English 2 — *Powling, Anne*

c New Oxford Treasury of Children's Poems — *Harrison, Michael*
The New Pacific Community — *Lasater, Martin L*
The New Pacific Community in the 1990s — *Kim, Young Jeh*
The New Painting. Vols. 1-2 — *Berson, Ruth*
r The New Parents' Sourcebook — *Wagner, Hilory*
The New Parliaments of Central and Eastern Europe — *Olson, David M*
A New Partnership — *Hamilton, A C*
New Patterns in Global Television — *Sinclair, John, 1944-*
The New Pediatrics — *Pawluch, Dorothy*
r The New Penguin Dictionary of Geology — *Kearey, Philip*
The New Perennial Garden — *Kingsbury, Noel*
New Personality Self-Portrait — *Oldham, John M*
New Perspectives for U.S.-Asia Pacific Security Strategy — *Alves, Dora*
New Perspectives in Historical Theology — *Nassif, Bradley*
New Perspectives in Indian Literature in English — *Yaravintelimath, C R*
New Perspectives on Margaret Laurence — *Coger, Greta M*
New Perspectives on the Chinese Communist Revolution — *Saich, Tony*
New Perspectives on the Holocaust — *Millen, Rochelle L*
New Perspectives on the Seventeenth-Century English Religious Lyric — *Roberts, John R*
A New Philosophy of History — *Ankersmit, Frank*
New Pioneers — *Jacob, Jeffrey*
y New Plays from A.C.T.'s Young Conservatory. Vol. 2 — *Slaight, Craig*
New Plays from the Abbey Theatre 1993-1995 — *Harding, Michael P*
The New Poetry of Japan--the 70s and 80s — *Fitzsimmons, Thomas*
New Poets of West Africa — *Sallah, Tijan M*
The New Politics of Public Policy — *Landy, Marc K*
New Poverty — *Cheal, David J*
The New Poverty — *DaCosta Nunez, Ralph*
New Promising Electrochemical Systems for Rechargeable Batteries — *International Conference on New Promising Electrochemical Systems for Rechargeable Batteries (1995: Kiev, Ukraine)*
The New Psychiatry — *Gorman, Jack M*
A New Psychology of Men — *Levant, Ronald F*
New Refrigerants for Air Conditioning and Refrigeration Systems — *Wylie, David*
The New Republic of Childhood — *Egoff, Sheila*
The New Resource Wars — *Gedicks, Al*
The New Role of Women — *Blossfeld, Hans-Peter*
r The New Rolling Stone Encyclopedia of Rock and Roll. Completely Rev. and Updated Ed. — *Romanowski, Patricia*
The New Rules — *Kotter, John P*
The New Russian Space Programme — *Harvey, Brian M A*
New Science out of Old Books — *Beadle, Richard*
p New Scientist
New Scottish Writing — *Ritchie, Harry*
The New Second Generation — *Portes, Alejandro*
New Selected Poems 1968-1994 — *Muldoon, Paul, 1951-*
r New Serial Titles 1953-
The New Shape of World Affairs
The New Simonides (Boedeker) — *Simonides, of Amorgos*
r A New Social Atlas of Britain — *Dorling, Daniel*
New Social Movements in Western Europe — *Kriesi, Hanspeter*
New Song and Dance from the Central Pacific — *Thomas, Allan*
The New South 1945-1980 — *Bartley, Numan V*
New South--New Law — *Woodman, Harold D*
The New Sovereignty — *Chayes, Abram*
r The New Specialized Catalogue of Canadian Post Official First Day Covers — *Chung, Andrew*
yr New Standard Encyclopedia 1996. Vols. 1-20
New States, New Politics — *Bremmer, Ian*
p New Statesman
The New Statesman — *Smith, Adrian*
New Stories from the South: The Year's Best 1996
The New Struggle for Democracy in Africa — *Wiseman, John A*
The New Superconductors — *Owens, Frank J*
New Swedish Style — *Waddell, Sasha*
The New System of National Accounts — *Kendrick, John W*

A New System of Philosophy-Science from the Biological Standpoint — *Dural, Teoman*

New Taiwan, New China — *Klintworth, Gary*

New Teacher Orientation

The New Teaching Elementary Science — *Wassermann, Selma*

New Technologies for the Humanities — *Mullings, Christine*

The New Television — *Davis, Douglas*

The New Testament — *Bible. N.T. English. Lattimore. 1996*

The New Testament and Psalms — *Bible. N.T. English. New Revised Standard. 1995*

The New Testament and the People of God — *Wright, N T*

New Testament Ethics — *Matera, Frank J*

New Testament Greek Manuscripts. Vols. 1-4 — *Bible. N.T. Greek. 1995*

r New Testament Introduction — *Porter, Stanley E*

The New Testament: Its Background and Message — *Lea, Thomas D*

r New Thinking in Design — *Mitchell, C Thomas*

A New Time for Mexico — *Fuentes, Carlos*

r The New Trek Program Guide — *Cornell, Paul*

c New Tricks I Can Do! (Illus. by Robert Lopshire) — *Lopshire, Robert*

The New Typography — *Tschichold, Jan*

The New Unblocked Manager. Rev. Ed. — *Francis, Dave*

The New Unionism — *Heckscher, Charles C*

The New Unofficial X-Files Companion II — *Genge, Ngaire*

The New Untouchables — *Harris, Nigel, 1935-*

The New Uprooted — *Mulroy, Elizabeth A*

New Urban Strategies in Advanced Regional Economies — *Norton, R D*

New Uses for New Phylogenies — *Harvey, Paul*

y The New Vegetarian Epicure — *Thomas, Anna*

The New Vegetarian Gourmet — *Ayanoglu, Byron*

New Venture Formations in United States Manufacturing — *Dean, Thomas J*

y The New Victorians — *Denfeld, Rene*

yr The New View Almanac (Illus. by David C Bell) — *Tesar, Jenny E*

New Visions for Metropolitan America — *Downs, Anthony*

New Visions for the Americas — *Batstone, David*

New Visions, New Perspectives — *Voigt, Anna*

New Voices in the Nation — *Hart, Janet*

The New War — *Kerry, John*

The New Water — *Jacobsen, Roy*

c New Way

New Ways in Teaching Writing — *White, Ronald V*

New Ways of Making Babies — *Cohen, Cynthia B*

New Westers — *Johnson, Michael L*

The New Winter Soldiers — *Moser, Richard*

A New Woman of Japan — *Hopper, Helen M*

New Women's Writing from Israel — *Domb, Risa*

The New World — *Banks, Russell*

y New World — *Cross, Gillian*

A New World — *Norris, Ken*

New World — *Stavans, Ilan*

The New World Border — *Gomez-Pena, Guillermo*

A New World in a Small Place — *Brentano, Robert*

A New World of Words — *Spengemann, William C*

New World Primates — *Kinzey, Warren S*

New World Regionalism — *Jordan, David M*

The New World Tattoo — *Hawke, John*

New World Vistas. Vols. 1-14 — *United States. USAF Scientific Advisory Board*

New Worlds for All — *Calloway, Colin G*

New Worlds, New Animals — *Hoage, R J*

New Writing 6

New Writing from Southern Africa — *Ngara, Emmanuel*

New Writing Scotland 14

New Year's Eve — *Grunwald, Lisa*

c New York — *Schomp, Virginia*

c New York — *Thompson, Kathleen*

New York 1954-55 — *Klein, William*

r New York 1960 — *Stern, Robert A M*

r New York and New Jersey. 1996 Ed. — *Sinotte, Barbara*

The New York Approach — *Schwartz, Joel*

c New York City — *Kent, Deborah*

New York City Methodist Marriages 1785-1893. Vols. 1-2 — *Fisher, William Scott*

New York Fictions — *Brooker, Peter*

The New York Giants Base Ball Club — *Hardy, James D*

r New York Giving Guide 1996-1997

The New York Intellectuals — *Wilford, Hugh*

The New York Irish — *Bayor, Ronald H*

New York Jews and the Great Depression — *Wenger, Beth S*

The New York Musicals of Comden and Green — *Comden, Betty*

New York, New York — *Silbert, Layle*

yr The New York Public Library Amazing Space (Illus. by Jessica Wolk-Stanley) — *Campbell, Ann*

yr The New York Public Library Incredible Earth (Illus. by Jessica Wolk-Stanley) — *Campbell, Ann*

r The New York Public Library's Books of the Century — *Diefendorf, Elizabeth*

r The New York State Directory 1996/1997

The New York Times Book of Health — *Brody, Jane E*

y The New York Times Book of Science Questions and Answers — *Ray, C Claiborne*

r The New York Times Film Reviews 1993-1994

r The New York Times Season-by-Season Guide to Home Maintenance — *Warde, John*

p The New Yorker

r New Zealand: A Lonely Planet Travel Survival Kit. 8th Ed. — *Turner, Peter*

The New Zealand Macroeconomy. 2nd Ed. — *Dalziel, Paul*

The Newbery and Caldecott Awards. 1996 Ed.

r The Newbery Companion — *Gillespie, John T, 1928-*

Newborn Intensive Care — *Zaichkin, Jeanette*

y Newcomers to America — *Greenberg, Judith E*

The Newfoundland National Convention 1946-1948. Vols. 1-2 — *Hiller, J K*

r Newnes C++ Pocket Book. 2nd Ed. — *Sexton, Conor*

r Newnes Computer Engineer's Pocket Book. 4th Ed. — *Tooley, Michael H*

Newnes Digital Logic IC Pocket Book — *Marston, R M*

News and Newsmaking — *Hess, Stephen*

News Coverage of Violence against Women — *Meyers, Marian*

News for All — *Leonard, Thomas C*

r News from Marion — *Moore, Sharon*

News from Nowhere or, An Epoch of Rest — *Morris, William, 1834-1896*

The News Media, Civil War, and Humanitarian Action — *Minear, Larry*

News of a Kidnapping — *Garcia Marquez, Gabriel*

News of the Plains and Rockies 1803-1865. Vol. 1 — *White, David A*

News Revolution — *Alleyne, Mark D*

The News Revolution in England — *Sommerville, C John*

p Newsletter Inago

Newspaper Days 1899-1906 — *Mencken, H L*

r A Newspaper Index and Guide for Genealogy in Wahkiakum County and Naselle Area of Pacific County — *Martin, Irene*

Newspaper Power — *Tunstall, Jeremy*

The Newspaper Publishing Industry — *Picard, Robert G*

r Newspapers in Microform: U.S. Newspapers 1948-1983. Vols. 1-2

Newsplan: Report of the Newsplan Project in the London and South Eastern Library Region (Laser), January 1992-December 1995

Newsworkers: Toward a History of the Rank and File — *Hardt, Hanno*

c Newt — *Novak, Matt*

Newton's Optical Writings — *Sepper, Dennis L*

Newton's Principia — *Newton, Isaac, Sir*

Newton's Principia for the Common Reader — *Chandrasekhar, Subrahmanyan*

Newton's Sleep — *Tallis, Raymond*

The Next 500 Years — *Berry, Adrian*

The Next American Nation — *Lind, Michael*

The Next Cold War? — *Hanson, Jim M*

c Next-Door Neighbors — *Ellis, Sarah*

The Next Fifty Years — *Barry, Tom*

p Next Generation

Next Generation Computing — *Fingar, Peter*

y Next in Line — *Feinberg, Barbara Silberdick*

Next of Kin — *Dingus, Lowell*

The Next Pope — *Hebblethwaite, Peter*

Next Season — *Blakemore, Michael*

The Next War — *Weinberger, Caspar*

y Next Year in Cuba — *Perez Firmat, Gustavo*

c Next Year in Jerusalem (Illus. by Neil Waldman) — *Schwartz, Howard*

c Le Nez De Marmouset — *Kathelyn, Dina*

Nez Perce Women in Transition 1877-1990 — *James, Caroline*

Nga Uruora — *Park, Geoff*

Ngon Co Bong Toan Tap — *Nguyen, Ba Trac*

Ngon Ngu Van Tu Viet Nam — *Ha, Mai Phuong*

NGOs and Environmental Policies — *Potter, David, 1931-*

Nguoi Hoa Tai Vietnam — *Nguyen, Van Huy*

Nguyen Trung Truc — *Ly, Minh Hao*

Nhin Lai Mot Thap Nien — *Nguyen, Ngoc Ngan*

Nhu Ao Nhu Thuc — *Luu, Kim Loan*

Nhung Con Chuot Thoi Tho Au — *Hoang, Khoi Phong*

Nhung Dua Tre Con My Ham Hiu — *Duyen Anh*

Nhung Truyen Can Duoc Ke Lai — *Phan, Nhat Nam*

Niagara: A History of the Falls — *Berton, Pierre*

y Niagara Falls — *Fisher, Leonard Everett*

Nian Hua — *Mo, Shen*

A Nice Change — *Bawden, Nina*

Nice Girls Finish Last — *Hayter, Sparkle*

y Nice Jewish Girls — *Marks, Marlene Adler*

Nice Little Stories Jam-Packed with Depraved Sex and Violence — *Hemmingson, Michael*

Nice Work — *Dodge, David*

Niche Markets as a Rural Development Strategy

Nichecraft — *Falkenstein, Lynda*

Nicholas of Autrecourt: His Correspondence with Master Giles and Bernard of Arezzo — *Nicolaus, De Autricuria*

c Nicholas Pipe (Illus. by David Shannon) — *San Souci, Robert D*

Nicholas Ray: An American Journey — *Eisenschitz, Bernard*

Nick Cave: The Birthday Party and Other Epic Adventures — *Brokenmouth, Robert*

Nick Stellino's Mediterranean Flavors — *Stellino, Nick*

Nickel Dreams — *Tucker, Tanya*

cp Nickelodeon

c Nicki Palin's Hidden Pictures — *Wood, A J*

Nicklaus — *Shaw, Mark*

c Nick's Mission — *Blatchford, Claire H*

c Nicky — *Ross, Tony*

Nico — *Ladenis, Nico*

c Nicola's Floating Home — *Kalman, Bobbie*

r Nicolas Poussin 1594-1665. Vols. 1-2 — *Rosenberg, Pierre*

Nicolas Poussin: Friendship and the Love of Painting — *Cropper, Elizabeth*

Nicolas Poussin: Masterpieces 1594-1665 — *Rosenberg, Pierre*

c Nicole's Story (Illus. by Lillian S Kossacoff) — *Aldape, Virginia Tortorica*

Nicomachean Ethics — *Aristotle*

Nie Yu — *He, Jingwen*

Niederlandische Gemalde Im Stadel 1400-1550 — *Sander, Jochen*

Nietzsche: A Critical Reader — *Sedgwick, Peter R*

Nietzsche: A Novel — *Krell, David Farrell*

Nietzsche and Metaphysics — *Haar, Michel*

Nietzsche and Modern Times — *Lampert, Laurence*

Nietzsche and Schiller — *Martin, Nicholas*

Nietzsche and Soviet Culture — *Rosenthal, Bernice Glatzer*

Nietzsche and the Modern Crisis of the Humanities — *Levine, Peter*

r The Nietzsche Canon — *Schaberg, William H*

Nietzsche Et La Musique — *Liebert, Georges*

Nietzsche, God and the Jews — *Santaniello, Weaver*

Nietzsche, Heidegger, and the Transition to Postmodernity — *Smith, Gregory Bruce*

y Nietzsche in 90 Minutes — *Strathern, Paul*

Nietzsche in American Literature and Thought — *Putz, Manfred, 1938-*

Nietzsche in Turin — *Chamberlain, Lesley*

Nietzsche, Politics and Modernity — *Owen, David, 1964-*

Nietzsche: The Ethics of an Immoralist — *Berkowitz, Peter*

A Nietzschean Defense of Democracy — *Hatab, Lawrence J*

Nietzsche's French Legacy — *Schrift, Alan D*

Nietzsche's Genealogy — *Havas, Randall*

Nietzsche's System — *Richardson, John, 1951-*

Het Nieuwe Gebouw Van De Universiteitsbibliotheek Te Groningen — *Koops, W R H*

The Nigel Lawson Diet Book — *Lawson, Nigel*

c Nigeria — *Tenquist, Alasdair*

p Nigeria Democracy Action Update

c Nigeria: One Nation, Many Cultures — *Adeeb, Hassan*

Nigerian Women in Historical Perspective — *Awe, Bolanle*

The Nigger of the Narcissus — *Conrad, Joseph*

Night, Again — *Dinh, Linh*
The Night (Alone) — *Meltzer, Richard*
Night and Day — *Leslie, John, 1944-*
A Night at the Opera — *Smith, Ray*
c The Night before Christmas (Illus. by Howard
   Finster) — *Finster, Howard*
c The Night before Christmas (Illus. by Nan Brooks)
   — *Moore, Clement Clarke*
c The Night before Christmas (Illus. by Howard
   Finster) — *Moore, Clement Clarke*
c The Night before Christmas (Illus. by Anita Lobel)
   — *Moore, Clement Clarke*
c The Night before Christmas (Streep) (Illus. by
   William Cone). Book and Audio Version — *Moore,
   Clement Clarke*
c Night Birds — *Flanagan, Alice K*
Night Bites — *Brownworth, Victoria A*
y Night Calls — *Kimbriel, Katharine Eliska*
Night Cover — *Lewin, Michael Z*
y The Night Crew — *Sandford, John*
Night Departure. No Place — *Bove, Emmanuel*
Night Dogs — *Anderson, Kent*
Night Drawings — *Stelmach, Marjorie*
c Night Driving (Illus. by Peter McCarty) — *Coy, John*
c Night Fell at Harry's Farm (Illus. by Carey Hedlund)
   — *Hedlund, Carey*
y Night Flight — *Hausman, Gerald*
c Night Fright — *Ure, Jean*
c Night Gliders (Illus. by Melissa Bay Mathis) — *Ryder,
   Joanne*
c Night House, Bright House (Illus. by Monica
   Wellington) — *Wellington, Monica*
c The Night I Was Chased by a Vampire (Illus. by
   Keren Ludlow) — *Umansky, Kaye*
y The Night in Question — *Wolff, Tobias*
The Night in Question (Wolff). Audio Version
   — *Wolff, Tobias*
c A Night in Terror Tower. Audio Version — *Stine, R L*
c Night in the Barn (Illus. by Erick Ingraham)
   — *Gibbons, Faye*
The Night Is Large — *Gardner, Martin, 1914-*
c The Night Journey (Illus. by Paul Dowling)
   — *Dowling, Paul*
y Night Journey — *King, Stephen*
c Night Knight (Illus. by Richard Brown) — *Ziefert,
   Harriet*
y Night Lamp — *Vance, Jack*
Night Letters — *Dessaix, Robert*
c Night Letters (Illus. by Normand Chartier)
   — *LoMonaco, Palmyra*
c Night Life of the Yucca (Illus. by Kay Sather)
   — *Hauth, Katherine B*
c Night Lights (Illus. by Denys Cazet) — *Cazet, Denys*
c The Night Mare — *Westall, Robert*
Night of Broken Souls — *Monteleone, Thomas F*
y Night of the Cruel Moon — *Hoig, Stan*
Night of the Dragon's Blood — *Pridgen, William*
c Night of the Five Aunties (Illus. by Kate Salley
   Palmer) — *Somer, Mesa*
Night of the Panther — *Ayres, E C*
Night Open — *Jacobsen, Rolf*
The Night Remembers — *Eagle, Kathleen*
y The Night Riders of Harpers Ferry — *Ernst, Kathleen*
y The Night Room — *Goldman, E M*
The Night Side of Dickens — *Stone, Harry*
The Night-Side: Seven Years in the Kingdom of the
   Sick — *Skloot, Floyd*
c The Night Sky (Illus. by Terry Hadler) — *Kerrod,
   Robin*
y Night Sky Mine — *Scott, Melissa*
c Night Sounds (Illus. by Randall F Ray) — *Grambling,
   Lois G*
The Night Stalker (Aiello). Audio Version — *Carlo,
   Philip*
Night Summons — *Gentry, Anita*
Night Surfing — *Capp, Fiona*
Night Swimmer — *Olshan, Joseph*
y Night Terrors — *Duncan, Lois*
y Night Terrors — *Sumner, Mark*
y The Night the Heads Came — *Sleator, William*
c The Night the Moon Blew Kisses (Illus. by Robin
   Spowart) — *Manuel, Lynn*
c The Night the Reindeer Rocked. Book and Audio
   Version — *Albrecht, Sally K*
c A Night the Stars Danced for Joy (Illus. by Tim
   Jonke) — *Hartman, Bob*
A Night to Remember — *Lord, Walter*
Night Train Blues — *Hower, Edward*
The Night Trilogy — *Wiesel, Elie*
Night Vision — *Levine, Paul*
c Night Visitors (Illus. by Ed Young) — *Young, Ed*

Night Whispers — *Erickson, Lynn*
Night Wrestling — *Williams, Leslie*
Nightflowers — *Stewart, Kathleen*
The Nightingale's Song — *Power, Jo-Ann*
The Nightingale's Song — *Timberg, Robert*
y Nightjohn — *Paulsen, Gary*
Nightland — *Owens, Louis*
Nightline: History in the Making and the Making of
   Television — *Koppel, Ted*
Nightlines — *Jordan, Neil*
y Nightmare — *Roberts, Willo Davis*
The Nightmare Factory — *Ligotti, Thomas*
Nightmare of Ecstasy — *Grey, Rudolph*
Nightmare Syndrome — *Marshall, William*
Nightmare: The Birth of Horror — *Frayling,
   Christopher*
y A Nightmare's Dozen (Illus. by Michael Hussar)
   — *Stearns, Michael*
Nightmover: How Aldrich Ames Sold the CIA to the
   KGB for $4.6 Million — *Wise, David*
NightShade — *Williams, Karen, 1959-*
Nightshift and Other Stories — *Zimunya, Musaemura
   B*
Nightsong: Performance, Power, and Practice in South
   Africa — *Erlmann, Veit*
c Nightwalkers — *Morris, Judy K*
c Nightwatch — *Palmer, Frank*
Nightwatch: New and Selected Poems 1968-1996
   — *Lee, Dennis, 1939-*
Nightwork — *Schutt, Christine*
Nihilism before Nietzsche — *Gillespie, Michael Allen*
Niji No Misaki — *Tsujii, Takashi*
Die Nike Von Samothrake — *Knell, Heiner*
Nikita's Shadows — *Vira, Soma*
Nikolaikirche — *Loest, Erich*
The Nile: Sharing a Scarce Resource — *Howell, P P*
c Nim and the War Effort (Illus. by Yangsook Choi)
   — *Lee, Milly*
The Nimble Reader — *McGillis, Roderick*
Nimbus: Technology Serving the Arts — *Griffiths,
   John Charles*
Nimes at War — *Zaretsky, Robert*
y Nimitz Class — *Robinson, Patrick*
p Nimrod: The City
c Nina Bonita (Illus. by Rosana Faria) — *Machado, Ana
   Maria*
c Nina's Machines — *Firmin, Peter*
c Nine Candles (Illus. by Amanda Schaffer) — *Testa,
   Maria*
c Nine for California (Illus. by Cat Bowman Smith)
   — *Levitin, Sonia*
Nine Ghosts — *Malden, R H*
Nine Lives to Live — *Messmer, Otto*
Nine Medieval Latin Plays — *Dronke, Peter*
c The Nine Tasks of Mistry — *McEwan, Chris*
c The Nine-Ton Cat — *Thomson, Peggy*
y Nineteen Eighty-Four (West). Audio Version
   — *Orwell, George*
r Nineteenth- and Twentieth-Century Harpists
   — *Govea, Wenonah Milton*
yp Nineteenth Avenue
Nineteenth-Century American Poetry — *Spengemann,
   William C*
Nineteenth-Century American Women Writers
   — *Kilcup, Karen L*
r Nineteenth Century Baseball — *Wright, Marshall D*
The Nineteenth-Century Church and English Society
   — *Knight, Frances*
Nineteenth-Century English Religious Traditions
   — *Paz, D G*
Nineteenth Century French Drawings and Some
   Sculpture
r Nineteenth-Century Literature Criticism. Vols. 47-52
r Nineteenth-Century Literature Criticism Annual
   Cumulative Title Index for 1996
Nineteenth-Century Piano Music — *Witten, David*
r Nineteenth Century Short Title Catalogue Series III.
   Electronic Media Version
Nineteenth-Century Women Learn to Write — *Hobbs,
   Catherine*
Nineteenth-Century Women Poets — *Armstrong,
   Isobel*
Ninety-Nine Days — *Colling, Herb*
Ninna Nanna Del Lupo — *Grasso, Silvana*
c Nino Cuervo — *Yashima, Taro*
c El Nino Que No Creia En La Primavera (Illus. by
   Brinton Turkle) — *Clifton, Lucille*
c Los Ninos Alfabeticos (Illus. by Kathryn Shoemaker)
   — *Lourdes, Ayala*
The Ninth Amendment and the Politics of Creative
   Jurisprudence — *DeRosa, Marshall L*

Ninth Conference on Software Engineering Education
   — *Conference on Software Engineering Education
   (9th: 1996: Daytona Beach, Fla.)*
Nip the Buds, Shoot the Kids — *Oe, Kenzaburo*
r Nishapur: Glass of the Early Islamic Period
   — *Kroger, Jens*
Nitrates in Groundwater — *Canter, Larry W*
Nitration: Recent Laboratory and Industrial
   Developments — *National Meeting of the American
   Chemical Society (209th: 1995: Anaheim, CA)*
Nitric Oxide — *Lancaster, Jack*
Nitric Oxide and the Lung — *Zapol, Warren M*
Nitric Oxide Synthase — *Maines, Mahin D*
Nitty Gritty — *Burns, Ben*
The Nixon Administration and the Making of U.S.
   Nuclear Strategy — *Terriff, Terry*
y Nixon off the Record — *Crowley, Monica*
Nixon's Piano — *O'Reilly, Kenneth*
NKVD I Pol'Skoe Podpol'e 1944-1945. Vol. 1
   — *Noskova, Albina F*
NMR as a Structural Tool for Macromolecules
   — *Nageswara Rao, B D*
NMR Data Processing — *Hoch, Jeffrey C*
The No B.S. Guide to Windows 95 — *Spanbauer, Scott*
c No Bajes Al Sotano! — *Stine, R L*
y No Big Deal — *McClain, Ellen Jaffe*
No Birds Sing — *Bannister, Jo*
No-Body — *Foreman, Richard*
No Brakes — *Gould, Lois*
No Casual Traveller — *Hergenhan, Laurie*
c No Cats Allowed (Illus. by Cynthia Nugent)
   — *Simmie, Lois*
No Contest — *Nader, Ralph*
y No Crystal Stair — *Sarsfield, Mairuth*
No Daughter of the South — *Webb, Cynthia*
No Discouragement — *Halsey, A H, 1923-*
No Distinction of Sex? — *Dyhouse, Carol*
y No Easy Victories — *Lusane, Clarence*
No Faith in the System — *Clarke, Sarah*
No Fat Chicks — *Poulton, Terry*
No Fear — *Ashworth, Sherry*
No Free Ride — *Mfume, Kweisi*
No Free Ride (Mfume). Audio Version — *Mfume,
   Kweisi*
No Friend like a Sister — *Alpert, Barbara*
r No Germs Allowed! — *Weinberg, Winkler G*
No Graven Image? — *Mettinger, Tryggve N D*
No Greater Love — *Teresa, Mother*
c No Gun for Asmir — *Mattingley, Christobel*
No Hands — *Crown, Judith*
No Hiding Place — *Barnie, John*
c No Howling in the House (Illus. by Mercer Mayer)
   — *Farber, Erica*
No Intermissions — *Easton, Carol*
y No Justice — *Brewer, James D*
No King, No Popery — *Cogliano, Francis D*
No Laughing Matter — *Cronin, Anthony*
No Lie like Love — *Rawlins, Paul*
No Longer Dead to Me — *Woodhead, Sally*
No Man's Land — *Gerson, Kathleen*
No Man's Land. Vol. 3 — *Gilbert, Sandra M*
y No Matter How Loud I Shout — *Humes, Edward*
No Me Esperen En Abril — *Bryce Echenique, Alfredo*
y No Mercy — *O'Hanlon, Redmond*
y No Mercy — *Stefancic, Jean*
y No More Dodos — *Nirgiotis, Nicholas*
c No More Nice (Illus. by Cat Bowman Smith)
   — *MacDonald, Amy*
No More Wacos — *Kopel, David B*
c No More Water in the Tub (Illus. by Tedd Arnold)
   — *Arnold, Tedd*
No More Worthy — *Chalmers, William*
No Mountain High Enough — *Ehrhart-Morrison,
   Dorothy*
No Name — *Collins, Wilkie*
No Nature — *Snyder, Gary*
No Neutral Ground? — *O'Connor, Karen, 1952-*
No New Jokes — *Bloom, Steven*
y No One Noticed the Cat — *McCaffrey, Anne*
c No One Told the Aardvark (Illus. by Jim Spence)
   — *Eaton, Deborah*
c No One Walks on My Father's Moon (Illus. by
   Rebecca Hyland) — *Curtis, Chara M*
c No Orchids for Andrea! (Illus. by Nathalie Gagnon)
   — *Brouillet, Chrystine*
No Ordinary Princess — *Morsi, Pamela*
No Ordinary Time — *Goodwin, Doris Kearns*
No Passion Spent — *Steiner, George*
No Place for Death — *Lewis, Sherry*
No Place for Sovereignty — *Wright, R K McGregor*
No Place like Utopia — *Blake, Peter*

No Place to Hide — *Carroll, Gerry*
No Place to Hide — *Nichols, Michael P*
No Previous Experience — *Cameron, Elspeth*
No Price Too High — *Copp, Terry*
y No Quarter — *Huff, Tanya*
No Rattling of Sabers
No Respect — *Ross, Andrew, 1956-*
No Safe Place — *MacColl, Mary-Rose*
c No! Said Joe — *Prater, John*
c No Se Salta En La Cama! (Illus. by Tedd Arnold) — *Arnold, Tedd*
No Shit — *Corman, Cid*
No Sorrow like Our Sorrow — *Chesebrough, David B*
No Stone Unturned — *Peters, E K*
y No Strange Fire — *Wojtasik, Ted*
c No Such Thing (Illus. by Betsy Lewin) — *Koller, Jackie French*
No Sweetness Here and Other Stories — *Aidoo, Ama Ata*
No Thanks or Regrets — *Kent, Jacqueline*
c No-Thanks Thanksgiving — *Cooper, Ilene*
No Time for an Everyday Woman — *Morrone, Wenda Wardell*
No Time for Family History? — *McLaughlin, Eve*
No Time for Heroes — *Freemantle, Brian*
c No Time to Cry — *McDaniel, Lurlene*
No Time to Say Goodbye — *Fine, Carla*
No Time to Sew — *Betzina, Sandra*
No Truce with the Furies — *Thomas, R S*
No Truer Love — *Gray, Ginna*
y No Turning Back — *Baer, Judy*
y No Turning Back — *Naidoo, Beverley*
c No Turning Back — *Peterson, Beth*
No Victor, No Vanquished — *O'Ballance, Edgar*
No Word for Time — *Pritchard, Evan T*
c Noah and the Ark (McGillis). Book and Audio Version
c Noah's Ark (Illus. by Lucy Cousins) — *Cousins, Lucy*
c Noah's Ark (Illus. by Kathy Rusynyk) — *Daniels, Patricia*
c Noah's Ark — *Ray, Jane*
c Noah's Ark of Animals (Little Moorings)
Noah's Choice — *Mann, Charles C*
Noah's Flood — *Cohn, Norman Rufus Colin*
Noah's Garden — *Stein, Sara Bonnett*
Noam Chomsky: A Life of Dissent — *Barsky, Robert F*
Noble Bondsmen — *Freed, John B*
Noble Government — *Stater, Victor L*
Noble Outlaw — *Braun, Matt*
The Noble Savage — *Cranston, Maurice*
r Noble's International Guide to the Law Reports. 1995 Ed. — *Noble, Scott*
Nobles, Knights and Men-at-Arms in the Middle Ages — *Keen, Maurice*
Noblesse Et Pouvoir Royal En France XIIIe-XVIe Siecle — *Caron, Marie-Therese*
Noblesse Oblige — *Smith, Cynthia*
r Les Noblesses Espagnoles Au Moyen Age XIe-XV Siecle — *Gerbet, Marie-Claude*
Nobody Home — *Neidermeier, Otto*
c Nobody Owns the Sky (Illus. by Pamela Paparone) — *Lindbergh, Reeve*
Nobody Roots for Goliath — *Champion, David*
Nobody Wants to Hear Our Truth — *Ralston, Meredith L*
Nobody's Angels — *Langland, Elizabeth*
Nobody's Baby but Mine — *Phillips, Susan Elizabeth*
Nobody's Story — *Gallagher, Catherine*
Noces De Sable — *Cauwelaert, Didier Van*
c Noche De Paz...O Casi (Illus. by Federico Delicado) — *Sierra I Fabra, Jordi*
Las Noches De Ventura — *Aguilera Garramuno, Marco Tulio*
Noci U Bijelom Satenu — *Luksic, Irena*
c The Noctuary of Narcissus Batt (Illus. by Marketa Prachaticka) — *Muldoon, Paul*
Nocturne — *McBain, Ed*
Nocturnes for the King of Naples — *White, Edmund*
c Nodding Farm — *Markey, Peter*
c Nodding Safari — *Markey, Peter*
c The Nodland Express (Illus. by Martin Rowson) — *Clarke, Anna*
Noel Coward: A Biography — *Hoare, Philip*
Noel Coward and Radclyffe Hall — *Castle, Terry*
c Noel the First (Illus. by Jim McMullan) — *McMullan, Kate*
Nog — *Wurlitzer, Rudolph*
c Noguchi the Samurai (Illus. by Johnny Wales) — *Konzak, Burt*
Nohow On — *Beckett, Samuel*

A Noise of War (Blake). Audio Version — *Langguth, A J*
Noises in the Blood — *Cooper, Carolyn*
c A Noisy Noise Annoys — *Curry, Jennifer*
c Noisy Nora (Illus. by Rosemary Wells) — *Wells, Rosemary*
p Nolo News
Nolo's Everyday Law Book — *Irving, Shae*
Le Nom Des Singes — *Volodine, Antoine*
Nomadaime — *Bouraoui, Hedi*
Die Nomadiese Oomblik — *Naude, Charl-Pierre*
Nombres, Astres, Plantes Et Visceres — *Ang, Isabelle*
Nomenclator: The First Printed Catalogue of Leyden University Library 1595 — *Bertius, P*
Nominal Compounds in Old English — *Terasawa, Jun*
c Nomo: The Tornado Who Took America by Storm — *Rodman, Edmon J*
r Noms Et Lieux De Quebec — *Quebec (Province). Commission De Toponymie*
Non De Code — *Anglads, Edouard*
Non Destructive Testing — *Hemelrijck, Danny Van*
Non-Government Organizations and Democratic Participation in Indonesia — *Eldridge, Philip J*
Non-Governmental Organizations and Rural Poverty Alleviation — *Riddell, Roger*
The Non-Jewish Origins of the Sephardic Jews — *Wexler, Paul*
Non-Retaliation in Early Jewish and New Testament Texts — *Zerbe, G M*
Non-Violence to Animals, Earth, and Self in Asian Traditions — *Chapple, Christopher Key*
Nonanticoagulant Actions of Glycosaminoglycans — *Harenberg, Job*
Nonconformity: Writing on Writing — *Algren, Nelson*
Nondestructive Testing Handbook. 2nd Ed. — *Ness, Stanley*
y Nonfiction for the Classroom — *Meltzer, Milton*
Nongovernmental Organizations as Policy Entrepreneurs — *Najam, Adil*
Noninfectious Diseases of Wildlife. 2nd Ed. — *Fairbrother, Anne*
r Nonionic Surfactants — *Nace, Vaughn M*
Nonlethal Weapons — *Morehouse, David A*
Nonlinear Control Systems Design 1995. Vol. 1-2 — *Krener, A J*
Nonlinear Dynamical Systems and Chaos — *Broer, H W*
Nonlinear Dynamics — *Solari, Hernan G*
Nonlinear Dynamics and Controls — *Bajaj, Anil K*
Nonlinear Dynamics and Pattern Formation in the Natural Environment — *Doelman, A*
Nonlinear Dynamics and Stochastic Mechanics — *Kliemann, W H*
Nonlinear Dynamics and Time Series — *Cutler, Colleen D*
Nonlinear Dynamics in Economics — *Finkenstadt, Barbel*
Nonlinear Effects in Fluids and Solids — *Carroll, Michael M*
Nonlinear Filters. 2nd Ed. — *Tanizaki, Hisashi*
Nonlinear Integral Equations in Abstract Spaces — *Guo, Dajun*
Nonlinear Mathematics and Its Applications — *Aston, Philip J*
Nonlinear Microwave Circuits — *Maas, Stephen A*
Nonlinear Optical Materials — *Karna, Shashi P*
Nonlinear Optics — *Sauter, E G*
Nonlinear Optimization and Applications — *International School of Mathematics G. Stampacchia Workshop on Nonlinear Optimization and Application (21st: 1995: Erice, Italy)*
Nonlinear Partial Differential Equations — *Benkirane, A*
Nonlinear Process Control — *Henson, Michael A*
Nonmammalian Genomes Analysis — *Birren, Bruce*
Nonparametric Methods for Quantitative Analysis. 3rd Ed. — *Gibbons, Jean Dickinson*
r Nonprofit Almanac 1996-1997
r The Nonprofit Manager's Resource Directory — *Landskroner, Ronald A*
The Nonprofit Sector in Hungary — *Kuti, Eva*
c Nonsense Songs (Illus. by Bee Willey) — *Lear, Edward*
c Noodles (Illus. by David Carter) — *Weeks, Sarah*
c Nora Normal and the Great Shark Rescue — *Asquith, Ros*
y Norby and the Court Jester — *Asimov, Janet*
Norddeutscher Lloyd Bremen 1857-1970. Vol. 2 — *Drechsel, Edwin*
Nordisk Smukkekunst — *Funder, Lise*
Norfolk Airfields in the Second World War — *Smith, Graham*

r Norge: Helpostkatalog. 1996/97 Ed. — *Arne, Finn*
The Normal Chaos of Love — *Beck, Ulrich*
Normal Child and Adolescent Development — *Gemelli, Ralph*
Normal Modes and Localization in Nonlinear Systems — *Vakakis, Alexander F*
Normal Service Won't Be Resumed — *Williams, Robyn*
Normal: Stories — *Nevai, Lucia*
y The Norman Conquest — *Chrisp, Peter*
Norman Lewis Omnibus — *Lewis, Norman*
y Norman Rockwell — *Durrett, Deanne*
c Norman Rockwell's Four Freedoms — *Murray, Stuart*
The Normandy Diary of Marie-Louise Osmont 1940-1944 — *Osmont, Marie-Louise*
Die Normannen In Osteuropa — *Heller, Klaus*
The Normative Constitution — *Sherlock, Richard*
Norms and the State in China — *Huang, Chun-Chieh*
Norms in International Relations — *Klotz, Audie*
North — *Celine, Louis-Ferdinand*
North Africa: Development and Reform in a Changing Global Economy — *Vandewalle, Dirk*
North American Auto Unions in Crisis — *Green, William C*
r North American Bird Folknames and Names — *Sayre, James Kedzie*
r North American Brewers Resource Directory 1996-1997
North American Cities and the Global Economy — *Kresl, Peter Karl*
r North American Coins and Prices 1997
c North American Indians (Illus. by Bryn Barnard) — *Viola, Herman J*
r North American Landscape Trees — *Jacobson, Arthur Lee*
c North American Peoples — *Haslam, Andrew*
The North American Railroad — *Vance, James E, Jr.*
r North American Shortwave Frequency Guide. Vol. 3 — *Pickard, James D*
The North American Trajectory — *Inglehart, Ronald*
North American Tunneling '96. Vols. 1-2 — *International Conference on North American Tunneling and the General Assembly of the International Tunneling Association (22nd: 1996)*
North American Water and Environment Congress and Destructive Water. Electronic Media Version — *North American Water and Environment Congress (1996: Anaheim, Calif.)*
North Carolina Environmental Indicators — *North Carolina. State Center for Health and Environmental Statistics*
r North Carolina History — *Jones, H G*
r North Carolina Tracings — *Morgan, Janet*
p North Coast Review
North Country — *Mosher, Howard Frank*
c North Country Spring (Illus. by Liz Sivertson) — *Lindbergh, Reeve*
p North Dakota Quarterly
North Enough — *Grover, Jan Zita*
North from Texas — *Shaw, James C*
North German Church Music in the Age of Buxtehude — *Webber, Geoffrey*
North Gladiola — *Wilcox, James*
North: Landscape of the Imagination — *Martin, Carol*
The North Light Artist's Guide to Materials and Techniques — *Metzger, Phil*
The North of England in the Age of Richard III — *Pollard, A J*
North of Havana — *White, Randy Wayne*
North Oxford — *Hinchcliffe, Tanis*
c The North Sea and the Baltic Sea — *Morgan, Nina*
The North-South Divide — *Jewell, Helen M*
North-South Linkages and International Macroeconomic Policy — *Vines, David*
North Spirit — *Jiles, Paulette*
y North Star to Freedom — *Gorrell, Gena K*
North to Aztlan — *Griswold Del Castillo, Richard*
North to the Bitterroot — *Compton, Ralph*
North Wind — *Jones, Gwyneth*
North with Lee and Jackson — *Kegel, James A*
Northanger Abbey — *Austen, Jane*
The Northeast Shelf Ecosystem — *Sherman, Kenneth*
Northeastern Indian Lives 1632-1816 — *Grumet, Robert S*
Northern City — *Pearson, Lynn F*
The Northern Copper Inuit — *Condon, Richard G*
Northern English Books, Owners, and Makers in the Late Middle Ages — *Friedman, John B*
Northern Frights 3 — *Hutchison, Don*
The Northern Gold Fleet — *Spence, Clark C*

The Northern Ireland Peace Process 1993-1996 — *Brew, Paul*
Northern Ireland Politics — *Aughey, Arthur*
Northern Justice — *Morrow, William G*
c Northern Lights — *Pullman, Philip*
c A Northern Nativity (Illus. by William Kurelek) — *Kurelek, William*
r Northern Portugal — *Anderson, Brian*
The Northern Region Economy — *Evans, Lynne*
Northern Sandlots — *Howell, Colin D*
Northern Tales — *Norman, Howard*
Northwest Exposures — *Alt, David*
The Northwest Necropolis of Satricum — *Waarsenburg, Demetrius J*
y Northwest Passage — *Dietrich, William*
y Northwest Passage — *Ketchum, Robert Glenn*
Northwest Passage Solo — *Cowper, David S*
The Northwest Salmon Crisis — *Cone, Joseph*
c Northwest Territories — *Daitch, Richard W*
c Northwoods Cradle Song (Illus. by Lisa Desimini) — *Wood, Douglas*
y The Norton Anthology of African American Literature
Norton Anthology of Poetry. 4th Ed.
The Norton Book of Interviews — *Silvester, Christopher*
The Norton Book of Personal Essays — *Epstein, Joseph*
r The Norton/Grove Dictionary of Women Composers — *Sadie, Julie Anne*
The Norton History of Astronomy and Cosmology — *North, John D*
The Norton History of Technology — *Cardwell, Donald*
The Norton History of the Environmental Sciences — *Bowler, Peter J*
r Norton's Star Atlas and Reference Handbook. 17th Ed. — *Norton, Arthur P*
c Norway — *Kagda, Sakina*
Norwegian Folk Art — *Nelson, Marion J*
Norwich Cathedral — *Atherton, Ian*
r Nose, Throat, and Ear (Coding Illustrated)
c The Nose Tree and Other Grimms' Fairy Tales (Ringenberg). Audio Version — *Grimm, Jacob*
Nosotros, Los Nicaraguenses — *Solorzano, Carlos Jose*
y Nostromo (Pennington). Audio Version — *Conrad, Joseph*
c Not a Nibble! (Illus. by Elizabeth Honey) — *Honey, Elizabeth*
Not a Prairie River — *Jansen, Walfried*
Not a Tame Lion — *Glaspey, Terry W*
Not All Black and White — *Edley, Christopher F*
Not All of Us Are Saints — *Hilfiker, David*
Not Ashamed of the Gospel — *Hooker, Morna D*
Not at Home — *Reed, Christopher*
Not Bad for a Foreigner — *Evans, Jean*
Not between Brothers — *Wilkinson, D Marion*
y Not Black and White — *Hebert, Mary*
Not Entitled — *Kermode, Frank*
Not Even Wrong — *Orans, Martin*
Not Every Spirit — *Morse, Christopher*
Not Exactly What I Had in Mind — *Breslin, Rosemary*
Not for America Alone — *Mitchell, George J*
c Not Home — *Grifalconi, Ann*
Not June Cleaver — *Meyerowitz, Joanne*
y Not like Other Boys — *Shyer, Marlene Fanta*
Not like Us — *Pells, Richard*
Not Much Fun — *Parker, Dorothy*
Not My Own — *Schlossberg, Terry*
Not Out of Africa — *Lefkowitz, Mary R*
Not Quite an Angel — *Edmonds, Lucinda*
Not Quite Straight — *Smart, Jeffrey*
c The Not-So-Minor Leagues — *Gay, Douglas*
c Not-So-Perfect Rosie — *Giff, Patricia Reilly*
Not So Simple — *Harper, Donna Akiba Sullivan*
A Not-So-Tender Offer — *Barmash, Isadore*
c Not the Piano, Mrs. Medley!. Book and Audio Version — *Levine, Evan*
A Not Unsightly Building — *Richardson, Douglas*
Not without a Struggle — *McKenzie, Vashti*
Not Without Honor — *Powers, Richard Gid*
Not Yet Home — *Cartwright, Justin*
r Notable American Women 1607-1950. Vols. 1-3
r Notable Americans. 4th Ed. — *Hubbard, Linda S*
yr Notable Black American Women. Bk. 2 — *Smith, Jessie Carney*
r Notable Latino Americans — *Meier, Matt S*
r Notable Twentieth-Century Pianists. Vols. 1-2 — *Gillespie, John, 1921-*
yr Notable Women in the Life Sciences — *Shearer, Benjamin F*
Notches — *Bowen, Peter*

The Notebook — *Sparks, Nicholas*
The Notebook (Nelligan). Audio Version — *Sparks, Nicholas*
Notebook of a Return to My Native Land — *Cesaire, Aime*
Notebooks 1960-1994 — *Dudek, Louis*
y Notes across the Aisle — *Carver, Peter*
Notes from a Kidwatcher — *Goodman, Yetta*
Notes from a Small Island — *Bryson, Bill*
Notes from an Incomplete Revolution — *Maran, Meredith*
Notes from the Minefield — *Gendzier, Irene L*
Notes from the Shore — *Ackerman, Jennifer*
Notes from Underground — *Cushman, Thomas*
Notes of a Piano Tuner — *Campbell, Denele Pitts*
Notes of a Racial Caste Baby — *Fair, Bryan K*
y Notes on Fermat's Last Theorem — *Van Der Poorten, A J*
Notes on the Greek Text of Deuteronomy — *Wevers, John William*
c Nothing (Illus. by Mick Inkpen) — *Inkpen, Mick*
c Nothing (Holm) (Illus. by Mick Inkpen). Book and Audio Version — *Inkpen, Mick*
Nothing beyond the Necessary — *Nilson, Jon*
Nothing but Net — *Walton, Bill*
Nothing but the Blues — *Cohn, Lawrence*
Nothing but the Girl — *Bright, Susie*
y Nothing but the Truth — *Smith, Ronn*
c Nothing but Trouble (Illus. by Jacqueline Rogers) — *Wright, Betty Ren*
Nothing but You — *Angell, Roger*
Nothing Diplomatic — *Leonard, Richard G*
c Nothing Ever Happens on 90th Street (Illus. by Kyrsten Brooker) — *Schotter, Roni*
y Nothing Interesting about Cross Street — *Yahp, Beth*
Nothing, Nobody — *Poniatowska, Elena*
Nothing on My Mind — *Storlie, Erik Fraser*
Nothing Risque, Nothing Gained — *Lederer, Richard*
Nothing to Read — *Mondak, Jeffrey J*
Nothungs Modernitat — *Kopnick, Lutz*
Noticia De Un Secuestro — *Garcia Marquez, Gabriel*
The Notion of Equilibrium in the Keynesian Theory — *Sebastiani, Mario*
Notions Et Perceptions Du Changement En Chine — *Alleton, Viviane*
Notitia Experimentalis Dei--Erfahrungserkenntis Gottes — *Walach, Harald*
y Notorious (Larson). Audio Version — *Dailey, Janet*
The Notorious Life of Gyp — *Silverman, Willa Z*
Notorious Voices — *Selvidge, Marla J*
Notre-Dame, Cathedral of Amiens — *Murray, Stephen, 1945-*
p Notre Dame Review
Notre Siecle Au Miroir Des Limbes — *Moatti, Christiane*
Die Notwendige Reise — *Graf, Johannes*
Noucentisme, Mediterraneisme I Classicisme — *Vallcorba, Jaume*
Le Nouveau French for Business. 3rd Ed. — *Le Goff, Claude*
Nouveau Monde, Autres Mondes, Surrealisme Et Ameriques — *Chenieux-Gendron, Jacqueline*
La Nouvelle-Caledonie Au Tournant Des Annees 1990 — *Arreghini, Louis*
Nouvelles Cantates — *Supervielle, Silvia Baron*
Les Nouvelles Formes De La Mobilite Spatiale Dans Le Monde Arabe. Vol. 2 — *Escallier, Robert*
Nouvelles Histoires Tragiques — *Poissenot, Benigne*
Nova Scotia: Shaped by the Sea — *Choyce, Lesley*
Novak's Gynecology. 12th Ed. — *Berek, Jonathan S*
Novalis: Signs of Revolution — *O'Brien, William Arctander*
Nove Canterburske Povidky A Jine Pribehy — *Skvorecky, Josef*
r Novel and Short Story Writer's Market 1996
The Novel and the Globalization of Culture — *Moses, Michael Valdez*
r A Novel Approach to the Theatre — *Sarver, Linda*
Novel Arguments — *Walsh, Richard*
The Novel in the Ancient World — *Schmeling, Gareth*
Novel Molecular Approaches to Anti-Inflammatory Therapy — *Pruzanski, W*
The Novel of Female Adultery — *Overton, Bill*
r Novel Optical Materials and Applications — *Khoo, Iam-Choon*
Novel Possibilities — *Childers, Joseph W*
Novel Therapeutic Agents for the Treatment of Autoimmune Diseases — *Strand, Vibeke*
Novel to Film — *McFarlane, Brian, 1934-*
La Novela De Un Pintor — *Alperi, Victor*

La Novela Moderna En Venezuela — *Hidalgo De Jesus, Amarilis*
Novell CNA/CNE Study Guide. 2nd Ed. — *Mueller, John, 1958-*
Novels 1955-1962 — *Nabokov, Vladimir Vladimirovich*
Novels 1969-1974 — *Nabokov, Vladimir Vladimirovich*
Novels and Memoirs 1941-1951 — *Nabokov, Vladimir Vladimirovich*
The Novels and Selected Works of Mary Shelley. Vols. 1-8 — *Shelley, Mary Wollstonecraft*
Novels and the Nation — *Birbalsingh, Frank*
Novels behind Glass — *Miller, Andrew H*
Novels behind Glass — *Miller, Andrew H, 1964-*
The Novels of Mrs. Oliphant — *Rubik, Margarete*
November Veil — *Hall, Linda, 1950-*
Novemberland: Selected Poems 1956-1993 — *Grass, Gunter*
The Novice Insomniac — *Warn, Emily*
y Novio Boy — *Soto, Gary*
Now and Then — *Castle, Roy*
Now and Then — *Corlett, William*
Now Face to Face — *Koen, Karleen*
y Now Face to Face (Hart). Audio Version — *Koen, Karleen*
r Now Hiring! — *Canfield, Clarke*
c Now I Know Better — *Children's Hospital at Yale-New Haven. Pediatric Emergency Dept.*
Now I Lay Me Down to Sleep — *Rushford, Patricia H*
c Now I Will Never Leave the Dinner Table (Illus. by Roz Chast) — *Martin, Jane Read*
c Now I'm Big (Illus. by Margaret Miller) — *Miller, Margaret*
c Now Let Me Fly (Illus. by Dolores Johnson) — *Johnson, Dolores*
Now More than Ever — *Aldous Huxley Centenary Symposium (1994: University of Munster)*
Now or Never — *Adler, Elizabeth*
c Now, Soon, Later (Illus. by Jane Johnson) — *Grunwald, Lisa*
Now That I Am Old — *Reilly, Maria*
Now That I'm Out, What Do I Do? — *McNaught, Brian*
Now the Wolf Has Come — *White, Christine Schultz*
c Now You See Them, Now You Don't (Illus. by Francois Caumartin) — *Caumartin, Francois*
Now You're Cooking for Company — *Corn, Elaine*
Nowhere to Hide — *Elliott, James*
Nowhere to Run — *Daley, Robert*
Nowhere to Run — *Priest, John Michael*
Nowle's Passing — *Forbes, Edith*
Nox — *Hettche, Thomas*
y Noyaya Iskra-1
NPO Webmaster — *Jamieson, Doug*
The NPR Interviews 1996
r NTC's Dictionary of China's Cultural Code Words — *De Mente, Boye*
r NTC's Dictionary of Folksy, Regional, and Rural Sayings — *Bertram, Anne*
r NTC's Dictionary of Mexican Cultural Code Words — *De Mente, Boye*
r NTC's Multilingual Dictionary of American Sign Language — *Proctor, Claude O*
r NTC's New College Russian and English Dictionary — *Arakin, Vladimir Dmitrievich*
r NTC's Romanian and English Dictionary — *Bantas, Andrei*
r NTC's Vietnamese-English Dictionary. New Updated Ed. — *Nguyen, Dinh Hoa*
Nu Non Tren Nhanh Kho — *Tran, Quan Niem*
Nua The Ky Pham Duy — *Le, My Huong*
c The Nubbler — *Ayres, Pam*
The Nubians of West Aswan — *Jennings, Anne M*
Nuclear Annihilation and Contemporary American Poetry — *Gery, John*
Nuclear Designs — *Larkin, Bruce D*
Nuclear Energy — *Bodansky, David*
c Nuclear Energy — *Holland, Gini*
The Nuclear Freeze Campaign — *Hogan, J Michael*
Nuclear Magnetic Resonance — *Canet, Daniel*
The Nuclear Matrix and Spatial Organization of Chromosomal DNA Domains — *Razin, Sergey V*
r Nuclear Movies — *Broderick, Mick*
The Nuclear Peninsula — *Zonabend, Francoise*
Nuclear Politics in South Asia — *Jain, B M*
Nuclear Rites — *Gusterson, Hugh*
Nuclear Rivalry and International Order — *Gjelstad, Jorn*
Nuclear Safeguards and the International Atomic Energy Agency
Nuclear Structure and Gene Expression — *Bird, R Curtis*

r Nuclear Test Ban: Glossary in English, French, and Arabic

r Nuclear Wastelands — *Makhijani, Arjun*

Nuclear Wastes — *National Research Council (U.S.). Committee on Separations Technology and Transmutation Systems*

Nuclear Wastes in the Arctic

Nuclear Weapons after the Comprehensive Test Ban — *Arnett, Eric*

Nuclear Weapons in Israel — *Nashif, Taysir N*

Nuer Prophets — *Johnson, Douglas H*

Nueva Granada — *Gish, Robert*

Nueva Guia Del Embarazo Y Cuidado Del Bebe — *Stanway, Penny*

La Nueva Mujer En La Escritura De Autoras Hispanicas — *Arancibia, Juana Alcira*

Los Nuevos Limenos — *Portocarrero, Gonzalo*

Nuff Respect — *Edwards, D J*

y Nuffield-BP Business and Economics for GCSE — *Wall, Nancy*

y Nuffield National Curriculum Mathematics (Levels 7 and 8): Number and Algebra 4

y Nuffield National Curriculum Mathematics (Levels 7 and 8): Shape, Space and Measures 4

c Nugget and Darling (Illus. by Sue Truesdell) — *Joosse, Barbara M*

Nugget City — *Overholser, Wayne*

La Nuit De La Saint-Barthelemy — *Crouzet, Denis*

La Nuit La Neige — *Pujade-Renaud, Claude*

La Nuit Sauvage — *Dib, Mohammed*

Null Models in Ecology — *Gotelli, Nicholas J*

Number at Key Stage 2 — *Askew, Mike*

Number Grids and Tiles

c Number the Stars — *Lowry, Lois*

Number Theory — *Redmond, Don*

Numbered Voices — *Herbst, Susan*

c Numbers — *Hewitt, Sally*

Numbers — *Olson, Dennis T*

c Numbers (Illus. by Richard Maccabe) — *Stienecker, David*

y Numbers and Shapes Revisited — *Cofman, Judita*

Numbers: Based on the Revised Standard Version — *Davies, Eryl W*

r Numbers: How Many, How Far, How Long, How Much — *Sutcliffe, Andrea*

Numbers in the Dark and Other Stories — *Calvino, Italo*

Numerical Algorithms with C — *Engeln-Mullges, Gisela*

Numerical Algorithms with Fortran — *Engeln-Mullges, Gisela*

Numerical Analysis. 2nd Ed. — *Kincaid, David*

Numerical Analysis of Ordinary Differential Equations and Its Applications — *Mitsui, T*

Numerical Methods and Error Bounds — *IMACS-GAMM International Symposium on Numerical Methods and Error Bounds (1995: Oldenburg, Germany)*

Numerical Methods for Differential Equations — *Dormand, John R*

Numerical Methods for Least Squares Problems — *Bjorck, Ake*

Numerical Methods in Structural Mechanics — *Bittnar, Zdenek*

Numerical Recipes in Fortran 90 — *Press, William H*

Numerical Solutions for Partial Differential Equations — *Ganzha, Victor G*

Numismatica Mexicana Hecha Facil — *Alva, Mike*

y Nunca Sere Como Te Quiero — *Gandara, Alejandro*

The Nun's Tale — *Robb, Candace M*

Nuntiaturberichte Aus Deutschland — *Wijnhoven, Joseph*

Nuoruuden Kolmas Naytos — *Vartio, Marja-Liisa*

Nuptial Arithmetic — *Allen, Michael J B*

Nuremberg: The Last Battle — *Irving, David*

y The Nuremberg Trials — *Rice, Earle*

The Nursery — *Culbertson, Judi*

c Nursery Rhyme Songbook — *Hooper, Caroline*

c Nursery Rhyme Time (Illus. by Nancy Story) — *Huffman, Ru Story*

c The Nursery Storybook (Illus. by Peter Utton) — *Adams, Georgie*

c Nursery Tales around the World (Illus. by Stefano Vitale) — *Sierra, Judy*

r Nurse's Clinical Guide to Psychiatric and Mental Health Care — *Copel, Linda Carman*

Nurses Counselling — *Burnard, Philip*

r Nursing Diagnosis Pocket Manual — *Sparks, Sheila M*

A Nursing Home and Its Organizational Climate — *Farmer, Bonnie Cashin*

r Nursing Home Statistical Yearbook 1995

Nursing Informatics — *Ball, Marion J*

Nursing Management in the New Paradigm — *Loveridge, Catherine E*

Nursing Models for Practice. 2nd Ed. — *Pearson, Alan*

Nursing Mother, Working Mother — *Pryor, Gale*

Nursing Negligence — *Beckmann, Janet Pitts*

Nursing Praxis — *Thorne, Sally E*

Nursing Research — *Polit, Denise F*

Nursing Staff Development. 2nd Ed. — *Abruzzese, Roberta Straessle*

Nursing Staff in Hospitals and Nursing Homes — *Wunderlich, Gooloo S*

Nursing Wounds — *Fisher, Sue, 1936-*

r Nursing96 Drug Handbook

Nurture by Nature — *Tieger, Paul D*

Nurturing Peace — *Hampson, Fen Osler*

c The Nut Map — *Gretz, Susanna*

c The Nutcracker (Illus. by Nan Brooks) — *Hoffmann, E T A*

c Nutcracker (Illus. by Roberto Innocenti) — *Hoffmann, E T A*

c The Nutcracker and the Mouse King (Reed). Audio Version — *Hoffmann, E T A*

Nutrient Management of Food Animals to Enhance and Protect the Environment — *Kornegay, E T*

c Nutrients: Superstars of Good Health — *Patten, Barbara J*

Nutrition and Health — *Bronner, Felix*

Nutrition, Cancer and You — *Calhoun, Susan*

r The Nutrition Desk Reference. 3rd Ed. — *Garrison, Robert, Jr.*

Nutrition in Primary Care — *Thomas, Briony*

Nutrition Secrets for Optimal Health — *Kurleto, Betsey*

The Nutrition Superbook. Vol. 2 — *Barilla, Jean*

Nutritional Concerns of Women — *Wolinsky, Ira*

Nutritional Management of Renal Disease — *Kopple, Joel D*

c Nuts — *Chambers, Catherine*

Nuts! Southwest Airlines' Crazy Recipe for Business and Personal Success — *Freiberg, Kevin*

c Nutshell Library — *Sendak, Maurice*

Nutty as a Fruitcake — *Daheim, Mary*

NVQ Handbook — *Walton, John*

NVQs and How to Get Them — *Dean, Hazel*

O

O Beulah Land — *Settle, Mary Lee*
O Brave New People — *Moffitt, John F*
c O Christmas Tree (Illus. by Frane Lessac)
    — *Rahaman, Vashanti*
O Come Emmanuel — *Marshall, W J*
O D — *Pepperell, Robert*
O Holy Night — *Moser, Johann M*
r O.J. A to Z — *Linedecker, Clifford*
y The O.J. Simpson Trial — *Aaseng, Nathan*
O.J. Unmasked — *Rantala, M L*
O Jerusalem — *Barkan, Stanley H*
c O Jerusalem (Illus. by John Thompson) — *Yolen,
    Jane*
O Mot Noi De Tim Thay Thien Duong — *Huynh, Van
    Phu*
O Mot Noi Nao — *Bui, Vinh Phuc*
O Pioneers! — *Cather, Willa*
O Tatline — *Punin, Nikolai*
Oak Ridge National Laboratory — *Johnson, Leland*
y Oasis — *Maguire, Gregory*
Oasis: What's the Story? — *Robertson, Ian*
The Oath — *Peretti, Frank E*
The Oath (Davidson). Audio Version — *Wiesel, Elie*
The Oatmeal Ark — *MacLean, Rory*
Obabakoak — *Atxaga, Bernardo*
Obedient Sons — *Wallach, Glenn*
c Obee and Mungedeech — *Martin, Trude*
r Obituaries in the Performing Arts 1994
r Obituaries in the Performing Arts 1995
r Obituaries of Benton County, Arkansas. Vol. 6
    — *Easley, Barbara P*
r Obituary Index 1859 to 1920 — *Waukesha County
    Genealogical Society*
The Object as Subject — *Lowenthal, Anne W*
Object Lessons — *Boland, Eavan*
The Object of Labor — *Lampland, Martha*
Object of Your Love — *Speak, Dorothy*
Object Orientation with Parallelism and Persistence
    — *Freitag, Burkhard*
Object-Oriented Application Development with Visual
    Age for C++ for OS/2 — *Carrel-Billiard, Marc*
Object-Oriented Behavioral Specifications — *Kilov,
    Haim*
Object-Oriented COBOL — *Arranga, Edmund C*
Object-Oriented Development Process and Metrics
    — *De Champeaux, Dennis*
An Object-Oriented Introduction to Computer Science
    Using Eiffel — *Wiener, Richard S*
Object-Oriented Modeling — *Berge, Jean-Michel*
Object-Oriented Neural Networks in C++ — *Rogers,
    Joey*
Object-Oriented Simulation — *Zobrist, George W*
Object-Oriented Test and Measurement Software
    Development in C++ — *Atchison, Lee*
Object Persistence — *Sessions, Roger*
Object Programming with Visual Basic 4 — *Dehlin,
    Joel*
Object REXX for OS/2 Warp — *Turton, Trevor*
The Object Stares Back — *Elkins, James*
Object Technology Strategies and Tactics — *Singer,
    Gilbert L*
Objectif France — *Rosenthal, Alan*
y Objective: Bajor — *Peel, John*
The Objectivists — *McAllister, Andrew*
Objectivity and Its Other — *Natter, Wolfgang*
Objects of Desire — *Holm, Pamela*
Objects of Enquiry — *Cannon, Garland*
Objects: Signs of Africa — *Heusch, Luc De*
The Oblate Assault on Canada's Northwest
    — *Choquette, Robert*
Oblivion — *Hart, Josephine*

Oblivion: The Mystery of West Point Cadet Richard
    Cox — *Maihafer, Harry J*
La Obra Narrativa De Jose Maria Merino — *Candau,
    Antonio*
Obras Completas. Vol. 1, Bks. 1-5 — *Sepulveda, Juan
    Gines De*
Obscene Bodies — *Benabib, Kim*
Observational Studies — *Rosenbaum, Paul R*
Observations on Cumberland and Westmoreland 1786
    — *Gilpin, William*
p Observatory Techniques
An Observer's Guide to Comet Hale-Bopp
    — *Machholz, Don*
r Observer's Handbook. 1st Ed.-
Observing Children in Their Natural Worlds
    — *Pellegrini, Anthony D*
The Obsession — *Cookson, Catherine*
Obsession and Culture — *Brink, Andrew*
Obsession and Release — *Upton, Lee*
An Obsession with Anne Frank — *Graver, Lawrence*
An Obsession with History — *Wachtel, Andrew Baruch*
Obstetric and Gynecologic Milestones Illustrated. 2nd
    Ed. — *Speert, Harold*
Obstetrics: Normal and Problem Pregnancies. 3rd Ed.
    — *Gabbe, Steven G*
The Obstruction of Peace — *Aruri, Naseer H*
Obtaining Resources for Technology
An Occasion for War — *Fawaz, Leila Tarazi*
An Occasional Hell — *Silvis, Randall*
Gli Occhi Colore Del Tempo — *Astrologo, Sergio*
L'Occhio Del Tiempo — *Bonito, Vitaniello*
Occidentalism: A Theory of Counter-Discourse in
    Post-Mao China — *Chen, Xiao-Mei*
Occidentalism: Images of the West — *Carrier, James
    G*
The Occult Roots of Nazism — *Goodrick-Clarke,
    Nicholas*
Occupation and Disease — *Dembe, Allard E*
The Occupation of Alcatraz Island — *Johnson, Troy R*
Occupation of France and Annexation of Alsace-
    Lorraine by Germany — *Bournique, Jean-Pierre*
Occupational Ergonomics — *Bhattacharya, Amit*
r The Occupational Outlook Handbook. 1996-97 Ed.
Occupational Therapy and Physical Dysfunction. 4th
    Ed. — *Turner, Ann*
Occupational Therapy for Physical Dysfunction. 4th
    Ed. — *Trombly, Catherine A*
r Occupazioni Ed Annessioni Italiane Nella Seconda
    Guerra Mondiale — *Astolfi, Valter*
c Ocean — *Ricciuti, Edward R*
c Ocean — *Sayre, April Pulley*
Ocean Acoustic Tomography — *Munk, Walter H*
The Ocean Basins and Margins. Vol. 8 — *Nairn, Alan
    E M*
Ocean Bridge — *Christie, Carl A*
c Ocean Buddies (Illus. by Dabney Miller Philabaum)
    — *Philabaum, Dabney Miller*
The Ocean Circulation Inverse Problem — *Wunsch,
    Carl*
Ocean Circulation Theory — *Pedlosky, Joseph*
The Ocean inside Kenji Takezo — *Noguchi, Rick*
c The Ocean of Story (Illus. by Jacqueline Mair)
    — *Ness, Caroline*
An Ocean of Time — *Mathiasen, Patrick*
Ocean of Words — *Jin, Ha*
Ocean Thermal Energy Conversion — *Takahashi,
    Patrick*
Ocean Warrior — *Watson, Paul*
r Oceanographic and Marine Resources. Vol. 1.
    Electronic Media Version

Oceanography: An Illustrated Guide — *Summerhayes,
    C P*
c Oceans — *Morris, Neil*
c Oceans — *Rothaus, Don P*
c Oceans: A Fold-Out Book (Illus. by Peter David Scott)
    — *Harris, Nicholas*
c Oceans and Rivers — *Dipper, Frances*
c Oceans and Seas — *McLeish, Ewan*
Ochagi Trevogi V Vostochnoi Europe
October 1964 — *Halberstam, David*
y October Moon — *Scott, Michael, 1959-*
The October Palace — *Hirshfield, Jane*
c October Smiled Back (Illus. by Ed Young) — *Peters,
    Lisa Westberg*
The October Twelve — *Rizzuto, Phil*
c Octopus — *Stefoff, Rebecca*
The Octopus: Europe in the Grip of Organized Crime
    — *Freemantle, Brian*
c The Octopus: Phantom of the Sea (Illus. by Jeffrey L
    Rotman) — *Cerullo, Mary M*
y The Octopus's Garden — *Van Dover, Cindy*
r Ocular Differential Diagnosis. 6th Ed. — *Roy,
    Frederick Hampton*
r Ocular Disease. 2nd Ed. — *Roberts, Daniel K*
Odd Fish and Englishmen — *Francis, Sarah*
Odd Girl Out — *Howard, Elizabeth Jane*
c The Odd Job Man and the Thousand Mile Boots
    (Illus. by Val Biro) — *Kenward, Jean*
Odd Man Out — *Dmytryk, Edward*
Odd Mercy — *Stern, Gerald*
y Oddballs — *Sleator, William*
Oddity Odyssey — *Chenoweth, James*
y Oddly Enough — *Coville, Bruce*
Odds and Gods — *Holt, Tom*
The Odds Must Be Crazy — *Ragozin, Len*
Ode to the Cold War — *Allen, Dick*
Odes A Pasithee — *Tagaut, Jean*
The Odessans — *Ratushinskaya, Irina*
Odile Decq Benoit Cornette — *Melhuish, Clare*
r Odilon Redon: Catalogue Raisonne De L'Oeuvre Peint
    Et Dessine. Vol. 2 — *Wildenstein, Alec*
c Odin's Family (Illus. by Maryclare Foa) — *Philip,
    Neil*
r Odysseus '96
c Odysseus Goes through Hell (Illus. by Chris Smedley)
    — *Robinson, Tony*
c Odysseus Super Hero (Illus. by Chris Smedley)
    — *Robinson, Tony*
The Odyssey — *Homer*
c The Odyssey (Illus. by Victor G Ambrus) — *Homer*
y The Odyssey (Bodkin). Audio Version — *Homer*
The Odyssey (Fagles) — *Homer*
y The Odyssey (Jacobi). Audio Version — *Homer*
The Odyssey (McKellen). Audio Version — *Homer*
Odyssey Now — *Grove, Nicola*
The Odyssey of a Manchurian — *Yang, Belle*
The Odyssey of a New Religion — *Lucas, Phillip
    Charles*
Odyssey of Exile — *Morris, Katherine*
The Odyssey Re-Formed — *Ahl, Frederick*
p Odyssey: The Glaxo Wellcome Journal of Innovation
    in Healthcare
Odyssey with the Goddess — *Christ, Carol*
r OECD Statistical Compendium 1996/1. Electronic
    Media Version
Oedipe A L'Universite — *Lafortune, Monique*
Oedipus: A Folklore Casebook — *Edmunds, Lowell*
L'Oeil De La Sultane — *Bensoussan, Albert*
L'Oeuvre De Pierre Charron 1541-1603. Rev. Ed.
    — *Belin, Christian*
Oeuvre Romanesque — *Cluny, Claude Michel*

Oeuvres II — *Sade, Marquis De*
Oeuvres Chretiennes — *Coignard, Gabrielle De*
Oeuvres Completes — *Sarraute, Nathalie*
Oeuvres Completes. Vol. 1 — *Blondel, Maurice*
Oeuvres Completes. Vols. 1-2 — *Segalen, Victor*
Oeuvres Poetiques. Vol. 1 — *Belleau, Remy*
r Of a Certain Age — *Rubin, Rhea Joyce*
Of Bicycles, Bakelites, and Bulbs — *Bijker, Wiebe E*
Of Bridles and Burnings — *Burford, E J*
Of Dreams Deferred, Dead or Alive — *Ojo-Ade, Femi*
Of Good Laws and Good Men — *Offutt, William M, Jr.*
y Of Kings and Fools — *Parent, Michael*
Of Life and Death — *Canada. Parliament. Senate. Special Committee on Euthanasia and Assisted Suicide*
Of Life and Death — *Hepburn, Elizabeth*
y Of Love and Other Demons — *Garcia Marquez, Gabriel*
Of Making Many Books — *Burlingame, Roger*
Of Marshes and Maize — *Huckell, Bruce B*
Of Men and Numbers — *Muir, Jane*
y Of Mice and Men. Electronic Media Version — *Steinbeck, John*
y Of Mind and Body — *Smith, Linda Wasmer*
Of Nawabs and Nightingales and Other Episodes — *Raza, Moosa*
Of Passionate Intensity — *Harrison, Trevor*
Of People, of Places — *Basu, Kaushik*
Of Permanent Value — *Kilpatrick, Andrew*
Of Poles and Zeros — *Scherbaum, Frank*
Of Sluts and Bastards — *Armstrong, Louise*
r Of Spirituality — *Fischer, Clare B*
Of the Laws of Ecclesiastical Polity. Pts. 1-2 — *Hooker, Richard*
r Of the People, by the People, for the People, and Other Quotations from Abraham Lincoln — *Lincoln, Abraham*
Of the Sublime — *Courtine, Jean-Francois*
Of Tigers and Men — *Ives, Richard*
Of Wee Sweetie Mice and Men — *Bateman, Colin*
c Off and Running (Illus. by Eric Velasquez) — *Soto, Gary*
Off Limits — *Datlow, Ellen*
The Off Season — *Cady, Jack*
Off Side — *Vazquez Montalban, Manuel*
y Off the Air — *Trout, Mike*
Off the Map — *Philo, Chris*
Off the Rag — *Lynch, Lee*
Off the Road — *Cooper, Elisha*
Off the Wall — *Bodhidharma*
Off the Wall! — *Frankel, Ken*
Off Track — *Spear-Swerling, Louise*
Office 97 for Busy People. 2nd Ed. — *Nelson, Stephen L*
Office Hysteroscopy — *Isaacson, Keith B*
Office Politics — *Mogensen, Vernon L*
The Office Relocation Sourcebook — *Attwood, Dennis A*
c Officer Buckle and Gloria (Illus. by Peggy Rathmann) — *Rathmann, Peggy*
c The Officers' Ball (Illus. by Wong Herbert Yee) — *Yee, Wong Herbert*
Officers in Flight Suits — *Sherwood, John Darrell*
r Official 1996 National Football League Record and Fact Book
Official and Doubtful — *Close, Ajay*
r The Official Country Music Directory 1994
The Official Dog Codependents Handbook — *Sellers, Ronnie*
Official Duke Nukem 3D Strategies and Secrets — *Mendoza, Jonathan*
r The Official Gamelan Java Directory — *Tapley, Rebecca*
The Official Gladiators Training Programme — *Anderson, John*
r The Official Guide to American Attitudes — *Mitchell, Susan, 1958-*
r The Official Guide to Household Spending. 3rd Ed. — *Tran, Hoai Huong*
r The Official Guide to Racial and Ethnic Diversity — *Russell, Cheryl*
r The Official Guide to the Generations — *Mitchell, Susan, 1958-*
y Official Heartbreak High Book
r Official License Plate Book — *Murray, Thomson C*
Official Methods of Analysis of the AOAC International. 16th Ed., Vols. 1-2
Official Microsoft Internet Explorer Book — *Pfaffenberger, Bryan*
Official Multimedia Publishing for Netscape — *Bouton, Gary David*

Official Papers of Alfred Marshall: A Supplement — *Marshall, Alfred*
r Official Railway Equipment Register
Official Records of the Human Rights Committee 1989/90. Vol. 2
The Official Rules at Home — *Dickson, Paul*
The Official UEFA Euro '96
r Les Officiers De Milice Du Bascanada 1812-1815 — *Lepine, Luc*
Offshore Breakwaters and Shore Evolution Control — *Pilarczyk, Krystian W*
Offshore Mechanics and Arctic Engineering. Vol. 1, Pts. 1-2; Vols. 2-6 — *International Conference on Offshore Mechanics and Arctic Engineering (15th: 1996: Florence, Italy)*
Offside: The Battle for Control of Maple Leaf Gardens — *Tedesco, Theresa*
Offsides — *Madden-Lunsford, Kerry*
Den Ofullbordade Himlen — *Werup, Jacques*
c Ogbo: Sharing Life in an African Village (Illus. by Ifeoma Onyefulu) — *Onyefulu, Ifeoma*
L'Oggetto Libro '96
The Oglala People 1841-1879 — *Price, Catherine*
The Ogre — *Tournier, Michel*
c Oh, Cats! (Illus. by Nadine Bernard Westcott) — *Buck, Nola*
c Oh, Freedom! — *King, Casey*
c Oh, Grow Up! (Illus. by Nadine Bernard Westcott) — *Heide, Florence Parry*
c Oh, No, Toto! (Illus. by Colin Bootman) — *Tchana, Katrin Hyman*
c Oh, the Places You'll Go! — *Seuss, Dr.*
y Oh, What a Feeling — *Malhuish, M*
The Ohio Frontier — *Foster, Emily*
Ohio Place Names — *Miller, Larry L*
Ohio Short Fiction — *Saari, Jon*
Ohio Star Quilts — *Faoro, Victoria*
c El Oido (Illus. by Francisco Arredondo) — *Sanchez, Isidro*
r Oil and Gas on the Internet — *Crowley, William R*
Oil and Socioeconomic Crisis in Nigeria — *Nnadozie, Emmanuel U*
Oil, Banks, and Politics — *Hall, Linda B, 1939-*
Oil, Gas and Coal Supply Outlook — *International Energy Agency*
Oil, Gas, and Government. Vols. 1-2 — *Bradley, Robert L*
Oil on the Edge — *Gramling, Robert*
Oil Painting for the Serious Beginner — *Allrich, Steve*
Oils — *Parramon, Jose M*
Oinaru Hi Ni — *Oe, Kenzaburo*
c Oink-Ha! — *Most, Bernard*
r Ojibwa Chiefs 1690-1890 — *Ilko, John A*
The Ojibwa of Western Canada 1780-1970 — *Peers, Laura*
y Ojos Saltones — *Fine, Anne*
Ok! Stage 2 — *Finnie, Sue*
Okinawa 1945 — *Foster, Simon*
y Okinawa: The Last Battle of World War II — *Leckie, Robert*
Okkupation Und Kollaboration 1938-1945 — *Rohr, Werner*
Okno V Ianvare — *Novikov, Denis*
Okoboji Wetlands — *Lannoo, Michael J*
c Oksana: My Own Story — *Baiul, Oksana*
An Olaf Stapledon Reader — *Stapledon, Olaf*
Olaus Magnus. Vol. 1 — *Magnus, Olaus*
Old Abe's Jokes — *Swank, Walbrook*
Old Age in Late Medieval England — *Rosenthal, Joel Thomas*
Old and Homeless--Double-Jeopardy — *Rich, Diane Wiatt*
Old and New Testaments — *Powell, Lynn*
c Old Bag of Bones (Illus. by Janet Stevens) — *Stevens, Janet*
Old Bank Notes — *Souster, Raymond*
Old Believers in Modern Russia — *Robson, Roy R*
Old Books in the Old World — *Rostenberg, Leona*
Old Books, Rare Friends — *Rostenberg, Leona*
The Old Boys — *Trevor, William*
Old Christmas — *Irving, Washington*
c The Old Dog (Illus. by James Ransome) — *Zolotow, Charlotte*
The Old English Lives of St. Margaret — *Clayton, Mary*
Old English Minor Heroic Poems — *Hill, Joyce*
The Old English Version of the Gospels. Vol. 1 — *Bible. N.T. Gospels. English (Old English). 1994*
The Old Farmer's Almanac Book of Garden Wisdom — *Van Hazinga, Cynthia*

The Old Forest and Other Stories — *Taylor, Peter Hillsman*
r The Old Free State. Vols. 1-2 — *Bell, Landon C*
Old Garden, New Gardener — *Search, Gay*
The Old Gents — *Yglesias, Jose*
Old Glory and the Stars and Bars — *Koon, George William*
c Old Growler's Last Match — *Richardson, John*
Old Hickory's War — *Heidler, David S*
c Old Home Day (Illus. by Emily Arnold McCully) — *Hall, Donald, 1928-*
p Old House Journal
c Old Howl Hall (Illus. by Mercer Mayer)   *Mayer, Mercer*
c Old Ironsides (Illus. by David Weitzman) — *Weitzman, David*
The Old Kingdom Cemetery at Hamara Dom — *Save-Soderbergh, Torgny*
The Old Left in History and Literature — *Dietrich, Julia*
c Old Letivia and the Mountain of Sorrows (Illus. by Rudy Gutierrez) — *Mohr, Nicholasa*
The Old Life — *Hall, Donald, 1928-*
c Old MacDonald — *Souhami, Jessica*
c Old Magic (Illus. by Di Wu) — *Baillie, Allan*
c The Old Man and His Door (Illus. by Joe Cepeda) — *Soto, Gary*
c The Old Man Who Loved Cheese (Illus. by Anne Wilsdorf) — *Keillor, Garrison*
c The Old Man Who Loved to Sing — *Winch, John*
r Old Masters — *Castagno, John*
Old Masters, New Subjects — *Wojciehowski, Dolora A*
Old Masters Repainted — *Stanley-Baker, Joan*
Old Media/New Media. 2nd Ed. — *Dizard, Wilson, Jr.*
c Old Meshikee and the Little Crabs (Illus. by John Hart) — *Spooner, Michael*
c Old Mr. Bannerjee (Illus. by Vaughan Duck) — *Clayton, Sandra*
r The Old New York Frontier — *Halsey, Francis Whiting*
Old Norse Images of Women — *Jochens, Jenny*
The Old Patagonian Express — *Theroux, Paul*
c Old Pig (Illus. by Ron Brooks) — *Wild, Margaret*
Old Problems in New Times — *Byrum, Oliver E*
c Old Salt, Young Salt (Illus. by Todd L W Doney) — *London, Jonathan*
The Old Service — *Newman, P R*
Old Ship of Zion — *Pitts, Walter F, Jr.*
Old Soldiers Never Die — *Perret, Geoffrey*
r Old South (Insight Guides)
Old Swedish Quilts — *Wettre, Asa*
The Old Testament — *Bible. O.T. English. Authorized. 1996*
r Old Testament Commentary Survey. 2nd Ed. — *Longman, Tremper, III*
The Old Testament in Fiction and Film — *Kreitzer, Larry J*
Old Testament Interpretation — *Mays, James Luther*
r Old Testament Introduction — *Hostetter, Edwin C*
Old Testament Theology. Vols. 1-2 — *Preuss, Horst Dietrich*
c Old-Time Toys (Illus. by Barbara Bedell) — *Kalman, Bobbie*
c Old Turtle (Wood). Audio Version — *Wood, Douglas*
Old Way to Fold New Paper — *Lowitz, Leza*
c Old Winter (Illus. by R W Alley) — *Richardson, Judith Benet*
Old Wisdom in the New World — *Numrich, Paul David*
c The Old Woman and Her Pig — *Litzinger, Rosanne*
c Old Woman Who Lived in a Vinegar Bottle (Illus. by Nancy Dunaway) — *MacDonald, Margaret Read*
c The Old Woman Who Loved to Read (Illus. by John Winch) — *Winch, John*
c The Old Woman Who Named Things (Illus. by Kathryn Brown) — *Rylant, Cynthia*
Oldcat and Ms. Puss — *Taylor, Joe*
c Older Adult Education — *Manheimer, Ronald J*
Older Adults' Decision-Making and the Law — *Smyer, Michael*
Older and Active — *Bass, Scott A*
c Older Brother, Younger Brother (Illus. by Wenhai Ma) — *Jaffe, Nina*
The Oldest Ally — *Stone, Glyn*
The Oldest Dead White European Males and Other Reflections on the Classics — *Knox, Bernard*
c The Oldest Elf (Illus. by James Stevenson) — *Stevenson, James*
The Oldest Sin — *Hart, Ellen*
Oldtown Folks — *Stowe, Harriet Beecher*
Olduvai Gorge. Vol. 5 — *Leakey, M D*

OLE-Remote Automation Visual Basic 4 — *Spencer, Kenneth L*
Olfaction in Mosquito-Host Interactions — *Bock, Gregory R*
c El Olfato (Illus. by Francisco Arredondo) — *Sanchez, Isidro*
Olga — *Zocchi, Chiara*
Oliver Cromwell — *Gaunt, Peter*
c Oliver Twist (Illus. by Christian Birmingham) — *Baxter, Lesley*
c Oliver Twist (Illus. by Chris Mould) — *Dickens, Charles*
Oliver Twist (Margolyes). Audio Version — *Dickens, Charles*
c Oliver's Vegetables (Illus. by Alison Bartlett) — *French, Vivian*
c Oliver's Wood (Illus. by Sue Hendra) — *Hendra, Sue*
The Olives Table — *English, Todd*
Olives: The Life and Lore of a Noble Fruit — *Rosenblum, Mort*
Olivi and Franciscan Poverty — *Burr, David*
Olivier De Clisson and Political Society in France under Charles V and Charles VI — *Henneman, John Bell*
Olivier Messiaen Music and Color — *Samuel, Claude*
Olivier Messiaen, the Musical Mediator — *Hsu, Madeleine*
Olivi's Peaceable Kingdom — *Burr, David*
c Ollie All Over (Illus. by Denis Roche) — *Roche, Denis*
Olmec Art of Ancient Mexico — *Benson, Elizabeth P*
Olvidame: Novelas De Amor Para La Monja Portuguesa — *Fernandez, Sergio*
Olvidando Olvidos — *Nieto, Adelaida*
c Olympic Black Women (Illus. by Ronald Jones) — *Plowden, Martha Ward*
y Olympic Dream (Illus. by Karen Meyer) — *Christopher, Matt*
Olympic Dreams — *Collins, Douglas*
c Olympic Jokes (Illus. by Viki Woodworth) — *Rothaus, James R*
yr Olympic National Park — *McNulty, Tim*
Olympic Politics. 2nd Ed. — *Hill, Christopher R*
Olympic Portraits — *Leibovitz, Annie*
c The Olympic Spirit — *Barrett, Norman S*
Olympic Winners — *Lund, Marcia*
c Olympics! (Illus. by Michael Chesworth) — *Hennessy, B G*
The O'Malley Saga. Bk. 1 — *Austin, Tom*
Oman and the World — *Kechichian, Joseph A*
Omega 3 Oils — *Rudin, Donald*
An Omelette and a Glass of Wine — *David, Elizabeth*
Omelie Sui Salmi — *Prinzivalli, Emanuela*
Omens of Millennium — *Bloom, Harold*
Omensetter's Luck — *Gass, William H*
Omeros — *Walcott, Derek*
c Omnibombulator (Illus. by Jim Kavanagh) — *King-Smith, Dick*
Omnivores — *Millet, Lydia*
Omon Ra — *Pelevin, Viktor*
The OMRI Annual Survey of Eastern Europe and the Former Soviet Union 1995
Omul Nou — *Zografi, Vlad*
On a Clear Day — *Blunkett, David*
c On a Clear Day (Thorne). Audio Version — *Blunkett, David*
y On a Pale Horse (Guidall). Audio Version — *Anthony, Piers*
On a Street Called Easy, in a Cottage Called Joye — *Smith, Gregory White*
On Aristotle's On Interpretation 1-8 — *Ammonius, Hermiae*
On Becoming a Biologist — *Janovy, John, Jr.*
On Becoming a Servant-Leader — *Greenleaf, Robert K*
On Behalf of the Wolf and the First Peoples — *Marshall, Joe*
On Being Jewish — *Neuberger, Julia*
On Being the Church in the United States — *Hollar, Barry Penn*
On Best Behavior — *Walden, Gregory S*
On Blindness — *Magee, Bryan*
y On Board the Titanic (Illus. by Ken Marschall) — *Tanaka, Shelley*
On Burning Ground — *Dybikowski, James*
c On Call Back Mountain (Illus. by Barry Moser) — *Bunting, Eve*
On Call in Bone Marrow Transplantation — *Burt, Richard K*
On Chinese Women — *Kristeva, Julia*
On Christian Government — *James of Viterbo, Archbishop of Naples*

c On Christmas Eve (Illus. by Nancy Edwards Calder) — *Brown, Margaret Wise*
c On Christmas Eve — *Collington, Peter*
On Collecting — *Pearce, Susan M*
On Constitutional Ground — *Ely, John Hart*
On Crimes and Punishments and Other Writings — *Beccaria, Cesare, Marchese Di*
On Criminalization — *Schonsheck, Jonathan*
On Depiction. Rev. Ed. — *Arikha, Avigdor*
On Dialogue — *Grudin, Robert*
On Eagle's Wings — *Veerman, David R*
On Entering the Sea — *Qabbani, Nizar*
On Est Si Serieux Quand On A Dix-Neuf Ans — *Green, Julien*
On Evil — *Thomas, Aquinas, Saint*
r On Evolution — *Darwin, Charles*
On Fashion — *Benstock, Shari*
On Fire (Sala). Audio Version — *Brown, Larry*
On First Looking into Arden's Goethe — *Mengel, Ewald*
On Flirtation — *Phillips, Adam*
y On Gold Mountain — *See, Lisa*
On Government and Law in Roman Egypt — *Lewis, Naphtali*
On Grief and Reason — *Brodsky, Joseph*
c On Guard — *Napoli, Donna Jo*
On Gwendolyn Brooks — *Wright, Stephen Caldwell*
On Heidegger's Nazism and Philosophy — *Rockmore, Tom*
y On Holiday — *Central Office of Information*
On Humane Governance — *Falk, Richard*
On Issues (Heath) — *Hermogenes*
On Jordan's Stormy Banks — *Sparks, Randy J*
On Kissing — *Blue, Adrianne*
On Knowing and the Known — *Lucey, Kenneth G*
c The On-Line Spaceman and Other Cases (Illus. by S D Schindler) — *Simon, Seymour*
On Literature and Society — *Candido, Antonio*
On Mahler and Britten — *Reed, Philip*
On Managing — *McCormack, Mark H*
On Many a Bloody Field — *Gaff, Alan D*
On Marriage — *Hippel, Theodor Gottlieb Von*
On McLhan — *McLuhan, Marshall*
r On Monsters and Marvels — *Pare, Ambroise*
On Moral Business — *Stackhouse, Max L*
On Mozart — *Morris, James*
c On My Honor — *Bauer, Marion Dane*
c On My Horse (Illus. by Jan Spivey Gilchrist) — *Greenfield, Eloise*
y On My Own — *Alexander, Sally Hobart*
On My Own at 107 — *Delany, Sarah Louise*
On Naming the Present — *Tracy, David*
On Nationality — *Miller, David Leslie*
On Native Ground — *Barnes, Jim*
On or about December 1910 — *Stansky, Peter*
On Original Sin — *Odo, of Tournai*
c On Passover (Illus. by Melanie W Hall) — *Fishman, Cathy Goldberg*
On Persephone's Island — *Simeti, Mary Taylor*
On Politics — *Mencken, H L*
On Quine — *Leonardi, Paolo*
On Reading — *Goodman, Ken*
On Reading Prophetic Texts — *Becking, Bob*
On Reduplication — *Back, Allan*
On Religion — *Schleiermacher, Friedrich*
On Ruins of Empire — *Mirsky, Georgiy I*
c On Sally Perry's Farm (Illus. by Cat Bowman Smith) — *Komaiko, Leah*
On Silence — *Guillevic, Eugene*
On-Site Inspections under the INF Treaty — *Harahan, Joseph P*
On Social Research and Its Language — *Lazarsfeld, Paul F*
On Social Structure and Science — *Merton, Robert King*
p On Spec
On Stage, America! — *Meserve, Walter J*
On the Art of Doing Field Studies — *Andersen, Ib*
On the Basis of Morality — *Schopenhauer, Arthur*
On the Boulevard of Galleons — *Farrell, Wallace B*
On the Brink — *Winik, Jay*
c On the Bus with Joanna Cole — *Cole, Joanna*
On the Causes of War — *Suganami, Hidemi*
On the Challenges of Unemployment in a Regional Europe — *Verhaar, C H A*
On the Couch — *Kates, Erica*
c On the Court with...Grant Hill — *Christopher, Matt*
c On the Court with...Michael Jordan — *Christopher, Matt*
On the Cultural Achievements of Negroes — *Gregoire, Henri*

c On the Day I Was Born (Illus. by Melodye Rosales) — *Chocolate, Deborah M Newton*
c On the Day You Were Born (Illus. by Debra Frasier) — *Frasier, Debra*
On the Demon-Mania of Witches — *Bodin, Jean*
On the Edge — *Etue, Elizabeth*
On the Edge — *Poverman, C E*
On the Edge of America — *Karlstrom, Paul J*
On the Form of the American Mind — *Voegelin, Eric*
On the Frontier — *Seitz, Frederick*
On the Genealogy of Morality and Other Writings — *Nietzsche, Friedrich*
On the Genre and Message of Revelation — *Malina, Bruce J*
On the Great Atlantic Rainway — *Koch, Kenneth*
c On the Ice with...Wayne Gretzky — *Christopher, Matt*
On the Level Everyday — *Berrigan, Ted*
On the Life of Christ — *Romanus, Melodus, Saint*
On the Limits of the Law — *Halpern, Stephen C*
On the Line at Subaru-Isuzu — *Graham, Laurie, 1949-*
On the Loose — *Button, John*
On the Margins — *Haidar, Aziz*
c On the Mayflower (Illus. by Russ Kendall) — *Waters, Kate*
On the Moral Nature of the Universe — *Murphy, Nancey*
c On the Move (Illus. by Lizzy Rockwell) — *Heiligman, Deborah*
c On the Move — *Sage, Angie*
On the Name — *Derrida, Jacques*
On the Nature of Consciousness — *Hunt, Harry T*
On the Nature of the Universe — *Lucretius Carus, Titus*
On the New Frontiers of Genetics and Religion — *Nelson, J Robert*
On the Notion of Mental Illness — *Svensson, Tommy*
On the Origins of Classical Economics — *Aspromourgos, Tony*
On the Origins of War and the Preservation of Peace — *Kagan, Donald*
On the Other Side of the Camera — *Crane, Arnold*
On the Outside Looking Out — *Shoptaw, John*
On the Padres' Trail — *Vecsey, Christopher*
On the Plains with Custer and Hancock — *Coates, Isaac*
On the Reliability of Economic Models — *Little, Daniel*
c On the Road — *Wale, Carole*
r On the Road around New England — *Morgan, Stephen*
r On the Road around Normandy, Brittany, and the Loire Valley — *Thomas, Roger*
On the Road to EU Accession — *Borish, Michael S*
On the Road to Tara — *Harmetz, Aljean*
On the Road to the Wolf's Lair — *Hamerow, Theodore S*
y On the Rocks — *Chick, Sandra*
On the Rocks — *Dickey, John S*
On the Ropes — *Beattie, Geoffrey*
c On the Run — *Cooling, Wendy*
On the Shoulders of Merchants — *Hadden, Richard W*
On the Side of My People — *DeCaro, Louis A, Jr.*
On the Streets — *McCarthy, Bill*
On the Teaching and Writing of History — *Bailyn, Bernard*
On the Track of Unknown Animals. Rev. 3rd Ed. — *Heuvelmans, Bernard*
c On the Wing — *Blacker, Terence*
c On the Wing (Illus. by Douglas Florian) — *Florian, Douglas*
y On the Wings of Peace — *Hamanaka, Sheila*
On Their Side — *Strachota, Bob*
r On These Walls — *Cole, John Y*
On This Delightful Morn — *Russell, Ian*
On This Site — *Sternfeld, Joel*
On Toleration — *Walzer, Michael*
On Top Down Under — *Robinson, Ray, 1905-1982*
On Voluntary Servitude — *Rosen, Michael*
On What Gives Value to Life — *Schleiermacher, Friedrich*
On What Is History? — *Jenkins, Keith*
c On Winter's Wind — *Hermes, Patricia*
On with the Story — *Barth, John*
On World History — *Herder, Johann Gottfried*
c On Your Own — *Wale, Carole*
Once a Dancer... — *Kent, Allegra*
y Once a Hero — *Moon, Elizabeth*
Once a Jolly Bagman — *McAlpine, Alistair*
Once a Warrior — *Monk, Karyn*
Once and Forever — *Miyazawa, Kenji*

L'Oppidum De Saint-Blaise Du Ve Au VIIe S. (Bouches-Du-Rhone) — *Demians D'Archimbaud, Gabrielle*
The Opponents of Third Isaiah — *Schramm, Brooks*
Opportunities for English in the Primary School — *Lockwood, Michael*
Opportunities for Mathematics in the Primary School — *Comer, Tom*
y Opportunities in Airline Careers — *Paradis, Adrian A*
y Opportunities in Chemistry Careers — *Woodburn, John H*
y Opportunities in Electrical Trades — *Wood, Robert B*
Opportunity-to-Learn Standards for Music Instruction, Grades PreK-12 — *Music Educators National Conference (U.S.)*
Opposing Ambitions — *Kleinman, Sherryl*
Opposing the System — *Reich, Charles A*
Opposite the Lion's Den — *Huygens, Daniel Johannes*
c Opposites: A Beginner's Book of Signs — *Bednarczyk, Angela*
Oprawy Zabytkowe I Artystyczne XIII-XIX Wieku W Zbiorach Biblioteki Gdanskiej Polskiej Akademii Nauk — *Ogonowska, Ewa*
Optical Communication Receiver Design — *Alexander, Stephen B*
Optical Diagnostics of Thin Film Processing — *Herman, Irving P*
Optical Fiber Communication Systems — *Kazovsky, Leonid G*
Optical Fiber Sensors. Vol. 3 — *Culshaw, Brian*
c Optical Illusions — *Muir, D*
y Optical Illusions in Art — *Sturgis, Alexander*
Optical Line Systems — *Maclean, D J H*
Optical Metrology. 2nd Ed. — *Gasvik, Kjell J*
Optical Scattering. 2nd Ed. — *Stover, John C*
Optical Storage and Retrieval — *Yu, Francis T S*
r Optical Thin Films — *Rancourt, James D*
Optics and Focus for Camera Assistants — *Hershey, Fritz Lynn*
Optics at the Nanometer Scale — *Nieto-Vesperinas, M*
Optima for Animals. Rev. Ed. — *Alexander, R McNeill*
Optimal Control — *Whittle, Peter*
Optimal Design and Control — *Workshop on Optimal Design and Control (1994: Blacksburg, Va.)*
An Optimal Foraging Model of Hunter-Gatherer Land Use in the Carson Desert — *Zeanah, David W*
Optimal Imperfection? — *Downs, George W*
The Optimist — *Stephenson, John*
Optimization and Dynamical Systems — *Helmke, Uwe*
Optimization of Stochastic Models — *Pflug, Georg Ch.*
Optimizing Windows 95 — *Nelson, Kay Yarborough*
Optimum and Equilibrium for Regional Economies — *Sakashita, Noboru*
Option-Embedded Bonds — *Nelken, Israel*
Options for Britain — *Halpern, David*
Options for Consolidation of Health Benefits Purchasing for State Employees
Options, Futures, and Other Derivatives. 3rd Ed. — *Hull, John C*
Options, Perception and Deception — *Cottle, Charles M*
Optoelectronic Materials — *Jones, Eric D*
Optometric Management of Reading Dysfunction — *Griffin, John R*
Opus 100 — *Moses, Emmanuel*
Opus Maledictorum — *Aman, Reinhold*
L'Or Des Iles — *Jaham, Marie-Reine De*
L'Or Du Maniema — *Ziegler, Jean*
Or, Monnaie, Echange Dans La Culture De La Renaissance — *Tournon, Andre*
...Or Not to Be — *Etkind, Marc*
p OR Spektrum
L'Ora Preferita Della Sera — *Vigano, Valeria*
Oral History in Social Work — *Martin, Ruth R*
An Oral History of Abraham Lincoln — *Nicolay, John G*
Oral Mucosal Drug Delivery — *Rathbone, Michael J*
Oral Tradition and Hispanic Literature — *Caspi, Mishael M*
The Orange Cat Bistro — *Linde, Nancy*
Orange County Grand Jury Final Report 1994-95
c An Orange Poetry Paintbox — *Foster, John*
Orange Rhymes with Everything — *McKinty, Adrian*
Oranges Are Not the Only Fruit — *Winterson, Jeanette*
Orbit: NASA Astronauts Photograph the Earth — *Apt, Jay*
y Orca: Visions of the Killer Whale — *Knudtson, Peter*
The Orchard — *Robertson, Adele Crockett*
y The Orchard (Gallagher) . Audio Version — *Robertson, Adele Crockett*

c The Orchard Book of Funny Poems (Illus. by Amanda Vesey) — *Cope, Wendy*
c The Orchard Book of Irish Fairy Tales and Legends (Illus. by Susan Field) — *Leavy, Una*
c Orchard Book of Mythical Birds and Beasts (Illus. by Jane Ray) — *Mayo, Margaret*
c The Orchard Book of Poems — *Mitchell, Adrian*
c The Orchard Book of Stories from the Ballet — *McCaughrean, Geraldine*
c The Orchard Book of Stories from the Seven Seas (Illus. by Sheila Moxley) — *Clayton, Pomme*
The Orchard on Fire — *Mackay, Shena*
The Orchestration of the Media — *Goban-Klas, Tomasz*
r Orchestration Theory — *Perone, James E*
The Orchid House — *Shand, Phyllis*
y Ordeal — *Mills, Deanie Francis*
The Ordeal: My Ten Years in a Malaysian Prison — *Saubin, Beatrice*
Orden Y Virtud — *Myers, Jorge*
Order and Disorder after the Cold War — *Roberts, Brad*
The Order of Terror — *Sofsky, Wolfgang*
yr The Order of Things — *Kipfer, Barbara Ann*
Ordered Phases in Metallic Systems — *Matveeva, N M*
Ordered Universes — *Klass, Morton*
Ordering and Phase Transitions in Charged Colloids — *Arora, A K*
The Ordering of Time — *Borst, Arno*
r OrderNow CD-ROM. Electronic Media Version
y Orders of Affection — *Smith, Arthur, 1948-*
The Orders of Light — *Lang-Westcott, Martha*
Ordinary Americans — *Monk, Linda R*
Ordinary Differential Equations in Theory and Practice — *Mattheij, R M M*
c Ordinary Jack — *Beattie, Andrew*
c Ordinary Life — *Conway, Kathlyn*
Ordinary Life, Festival Days — *Prosterman, Leslie*
The Ordinary Seaman — *Goldman, Francisco*
Ordinary Social Occasions, Sandcastles, and Structural Reproduction — *Boughey, Howard Nathaniel*
y Ordinary Things (Illus. by Walter Lyon Krudop) — *Fletcher, Ralph*
The Ordinary Transformed — *Reno, Russell Ronald*
L'Ordine Giuridico Medievale — *Grossi, Paolo*
Ordine Pubblico — *Camarca, Claudio*
Ordines Coronationis Franciae — *Jackson, Richard A*
Ordinul Masonic Roman — *Nastorescu-Balcesti, Horia*
r The Ordnance Survey Interactive Atlas of Great Britain. Electronic Media Version
Ordnung Und Bruch — *Schupp, Ulrike*
r Oregon 1920 Deschutes County Census
The Oregon Health Plan Economic Impact Analysis for the Employer Mandate
The Oregon Trail (Muller). Audio Version — *Parkman, Francis*
Oregon's Watershed Health Program. Vols. 1-2
Orf Effendi, Chroniqueur — *Belanger, Marcel*
L'Orfevrerie Parisienne De La Renaissance — *Bimbenet-Privat, Michele*
Organ and Tissue Donation — *Spielman, Bethany*
The Organ in Western Culture 750-1250 — *Williams, Peter F*
Organ Pipe Cactus National Monument Ecological Monitoring Program Monitoring Protocol Manual
Organ Sonatas — *Bach, C P E*
Organ Transplantation — *Youngner, Stuart J*
r Organelles in Tumor Diagnosis — *Eyden, Brian*
Organic Additives and Ceramic Processing. 2nd Ed. — *Shanefield, Daniel J*
Organic Chemistry — *Bruice, Paula Yurkanis*
Organic Chemistry — *Ouellette, Robert J*
Organic Chemistry. 3rd Ed. — *Carey, Francis A*
Organic Chemistry. 6th Ed. — *Solomons, T W Graham*
Organic Chemistry. Vol. 1 — *Macomber, Roger*
Organic Chemistry. Vol. 2 — *Macomber, Roger*
Organic Chemistry. Vols. 1-2 — *Macomber, Roger*
Organic Chemistry in Action. 2nd Ed. — *Serratosa, Felix*
The Organic Chemistry Survival Manual — *Marbrouk, S T*
The Organic Machine — *White, Richard*
Organic Pest and Disease Control — *Ellis, Barbara*
Organic Reactions. Vol. 49
Organic Reactions, Simplicity and Logic — *Laszlo, Pierre*
The Organic Rose Garden — *Druitt, Liz*
Organic Synthesis — *Willis, Christine*
Organic Vegetable Gardening — *Time-Life Books*
Organic Voice Disorders — *Brown, Wm. S*

Organisation of Science and Technology at the Watershed — *Reger, Guido*
p Organised Sound
An Organised Woman — *Toner, Barbara*
Organising Voluntary Help in the School Library — *Dubber, Geoff*
The Organism: A Holistic Approach to Biology Derived from Pathological Data in Man — *Goldstein, Kurt*
The Organization of American States — *Sheinin, David*
The Organization of Europe — *Harrison, D M*
The Organization of International Business — *Casson, Mark*
The Organization of Local Public Economies — *Oakerson, Ronald J*
The Organization of the Future — *Hesselbein, Frances*
Organization Theories and Public Administration — *Davis, Charles R*
Organizational Ethics and the Good Life — *Hartman, Edwin M*
Organizations and the Psychological Contract — *Makin, Peter J*
Organizations in Action — *Thompson, James D*
Organizations in America — *Kalleberg, Arne L*
Organized and Corporate Crime in Europe — *Ruggiero, Vincenzo*
Organizing a Christian Mind — *Carmody, Denise Lardner*
Organizing Civil Society — *Oxhorn, Philip D*
Organizing Corporate Contributions — *Clark, Sylvia*
Organizing for Equality — *Minkoff, Debra C*
Organizing Genius — *Bennis, Warren*
Organizing Jainism in India and England — *Banks, Marcus*
Organizing the Unemployed — *Lorence, James J*
Organizing to Count — *Norwood, Janet L*
Organizing Your Practice through Automation — *American Psychological Association. Practice Directorate*
Organometallic Chemistry — *Spessard, Gary O*
Oriental Medicine: An Illustrated Guide to the Asian Arts of Healing
Oriental Porcelain — *Jorg, C J A*
Orientalism and Modernism — *Qian, Zhaoming*
Orientalism and the Postcolonial Predicament — *Breckenridge, Carol A*
Orientations 3 — *Boer, Inge*
Orienting Masculinity, Orienting Nation — *Holden, Philip*
Origene Et Plotin — *Crouzel, Henri*
The Origenist Controversy — *Clark, Elizabeth A*
The Origin and Evolution of Birds — *Feduccia, Alan*
The Origin and Evolution of the Universe — *Zuckerman, Ben*
An Origin like Water — *Boland, Eavan*
y The Origin of Humankind — *Leakey, Richard*
The Origin of Language — *Ruhlen, Merritt*
The Origin of Modern Humans and the Impact of Chronometric Dating — *Aitken, M J*
The Origin of Perspective — *Damisch, Hubert*
The Origin of Satan — *Pagels, Elaine*
The Origin of the Arab-Israeli Arms Race — *Ilan, Amitzur*
The Origin of the Concept of Nuclear Forces — *Brown, Laurie M*
The Origin of the Modern Jewish Woman Writer — *Galchinsky, Michael*
The Origin of Waves — *Clarke, Austin*
Original Ambivalence — *Schneider, Matthew*
Original Bliss — *Kennedy, A L*
Original Color — *Kennedy, Hugh*
Original Dwelling Place — *Aitken, Robert*
c The Original Freddie Ackerman — *Irwin, Hadley*
c The Original Freddie Ackerman (McDonough). Audio Version — *Irwin, Hadley*
The Original Jesus — *Wright, Tom*
Original Love — *Peacock, Molly*
y An Original Man — *Clegg, Claude Andrew*
Original Meanings — *Rakove, Jack N*
Original Mediterranean Cuisine — *Santich, Barbara*
y The Original Olympics — *Ross, Stewart*
Original Sin — *James, P D*
y Original Sin — *Sheahan, Robyn*
Original Six — *Quarrington, Paul*
Les Origines Du Missel Des Chartreux — *Devaux, Dom Augustin*
Origins and Destinies — *Pedraza, Silvia*
y Origins of a Catastrophe — *Zimmermann, Warren*
Origins of a Spontaneous Revolution — *Opp, Karl-Dieter*

y The Origins of American Slavery — Wood, Betty
The Origins of Beowulf — Newton, Sam
The Origins of Christian Morality — Meeks, Wayne A
The Origins of Complex Societies in Late Prehistoric Iberia — Lillios, Katina T
The Origins of Desire — Masoliver, Juan Antonio
The Origins of Free Verse — Kirby-Smith, H T
The Origins of French Art Criticism — Wrigley, Richard
The Origins of Grammar — Hirsch-Pasek, Kathy
The Origins of Industrial Capitalism in India — Chandavarkar, Rajnarayan
The Origins of Japanese Industrial Power — Abe, Etsuo
The Origins of Japanese Trade Supremacy — Howe, Christopher
The Origins of Lonergan's Notion of Dialectic of History — Shute, Michael
Origins of Mankind. Electronic Media Version
The Origins of Middle-Class Culture — Smail, John
The Origins of Military Thought — Gat, Azar
Origins of Modern Japanese Literature — Kojin, Karatani
Origins of Narrative — Prickett, Stephen
The Origins of Nazi Genocide — Friedlander, Henry
The Origins of Renaissance Art — Paolucci, Antonio
The Origins of the American Civil War — Reid, Brian Holden
The Origins of the American High School — Reese, William J
Origins of the American Navy — O'Connor, Raymond G
The Origins of the Authoritarian Welfare State in Prussia — Beck, Hermann
Origins of the Bronze Age Civilization in Central Asia — Hiebert, Fredrik Talmage
The Origins of the Cold War 1941-1949 — McCauley, Martin
The Origins of the Cold War in Europe — Reynolds, David
The Origins of the Crimean War — Goldfrank, David M
The Origins of the Eucharistic Prayer — Mazza, Enrico
The Origins of the Great Leap Forward — Domenach, Jean-Luc
The Origins of the Greek Civil War — Close, David H
Origins of the Human Mind (Riggenbach). Audio Version — Lumsden, Charles J
The Origins of the Inquisition in Fifteenth Century Spain — Netanyahu, Benzion
Origins of the Modern Mind — Donald, Merlin
Origins of the Modern State in Europe 13th-18th Centuries — Bonney, Richard
The Origins of the Russian Civil War — Swain, Geoffrey
Origins of the Salvation Army — Murdoch, Norman H
The Origins of the South African War 1899-1902 — Smith, Iain R
The Origins of the State in Italy 1300-1600 — Kirshner, Julius
The Origins of Violence in Mexican Society — Johns, Christina Jacqueline
The Origins of Virtue — Ridley, Matt
The Origins of Walter Rauschenbusch's Social Ethics — Smucker, Donovan E
r The Origins of War Prevention — Ceadel, Martin
The Origins of Western Warfare — Dawson, Doyne
The Oriki of a Grasshopper and Other Plays — Osofisan, Femi
Orioles, Blackbirds, and Their Kin — Skutch, Alexander Frank
y Orion's Dagger — McAllister, P K
Orion's Legacy — Bergman, Charles
Orishatukeh Faduma: Liberal Theology and Evangelical Pan-Africanism 1857-1946 — Moore, Moses Nathaniel
Orlando Di Lasso's Imitation Magnificats for Counter-Reformation Munich — Crook, David
Orlando's Sleep — Spry, Jennifer
Ornament: A Social History since 1450 — Snodin, Michael
Ornament and Silence — Fraser, Kennedy
y The Ornament Tree — Thesman, Jean
c Ornithomimids, the Fastest Dinosaur (Illus. by Donna Bragenitz) — Lessem, Don
c The Orphan of Ellis Island — Woodruff, Elvira
Orphan of the Cold War — Anstee, Margaret Joan
c Orphan Train Rider — Warren, Andrea
Orphans of Petrarch — Navarrete, Ignacio
y Orphans of the Living — Toth, Jennifer

Orphans of the Storm — Cowasjee, Saros
y The Orphan's Tent — De Haven, Tom
Les Orphelins — Pauwels, Louis
Orpheus and Power — Hanchard, Michael George
The Orphic Moment — McGahey, Robert
p The Orrery
Orson Welles. Vol. 1 — Callow, Simon
y Orson Welles: A Biography (Conlin). Audio Version — Leaming, Barbara
Orthodox Christians and Jews on Continuity and Renewal — Lowe, Malcolm
The Orthodox Church — Fitzgerald, Thomas E
The Orthodox Corruption of Scripture — Ehrman, Bart D
r Orthodox Judaism in America — Sherman, Moshe D
Orthodox Visions of Ecumenism — Limouris, Gennadios
Orthodoxies in Massachusetts — Knight, Janice
Orthopaedic Decision Making. 2nd Ed. — Bucholz, Robert W
Orthopaedic Knowledge Update 5
Orthopaedic Practice — Yeoman, P M
The OS/2 Warp Toolkit for Software Developers — Viscuso, Maurice J
Os Sertoes — Cunha, Euclides Da
Oscar Wilde: A Life in Letters, Writings and Wit — Gardiner, Juliet
Oscar Wilde: A Long and Lovely Suicide — Knox, Melissa
Oscar Wilde and the Poetics of Ambiguity — Gillespie, Michael Patrick
Oscar Wilde: Myths, Miracles, and Imitations — Stokes, John
Oscar Wilde's The Importance of Being Earnest — Donohue, Joseph
Oscar Zeta Acosta: The Uncollected Works — Acosta, Oscar
c Osceola: Seminole Warrior — Sanford, William R
Oscillation Theory for Functional Differential Equations — Erbe, L H
OSHA Inspections — Kaletsky, Richard
c El Osito Polar Y Su Nueva Amiga — De Beer, Hans
Oskar Kokoschka: Die Gemalde 1906-1929 — Winkler, Johann
c Oskar Schindler — Roberts, Jack L
Osler's Web — Johnson, Hillary
Osobaia Papka I.V. Stalina — Kozlov, V A
c Los Osos (Illus. by Estudio Marcel Socias) — Julivert, Maria Angels
OSS Agents in Hitler's Heartland — Schwab, Gerald
OSS in China — Yu, Maochun
Osseous Reconstruction of the Maxilla and the Mandible — Boyne, Philip J
Ostarbeiter Mail in World War II — Werbizky, George G
Ostavte Moiu Dushu V Pokoe — Erofeev, Venedikt
Ostend — Gravel, Francois
r Osteoporosis — Marcus, Robert
Osteoporosis: Diagnosis and Treatment — Sartoris, David J
Osteoporosis: Diagnostic and Therapeutic Principles — Rosen, Clifford J
Osteoporosis: Medical Blunders and Treatment Strategies — Taylor, William N
Osterreich Und Die Europaische Integration 1945-1993 — Gehler, Michael
c Ostriches — Maynard, Thane
Oswald's Tale — Mailer, Norman
y Othello — Lester, Julius
Othello (Ridley) — Shakespeare, William
Othello: A Contextual History — Vaughan, Virginia Mason
Othello Blues — Jaffe, Harold
The Other Americans — Jackson, Charles O
The Other Argentina — Sawers, Larry
Other Britain, Other British — Lee, A Robert
The Other Carl Sandburg — Yannella, Philip R
Other Dimensions 3
y The Other End of Time — Pohl, Frederik
Other Entertainment — Rorem, Ned
The Other Face of Love — Pollard, Miriam
y The Other Family — Carey, Jacqueline
Other Followers of Jesus — Williams, Joel F
The Other Greeks — Hanson, Victor Davis
The Other Islands of New York City — Seitz, Sharon
Other Lives — Woodhouse, Sarah
Other Minds — Nagel, Thomas
The Other Modernism — Blum, Cinzia Sartini
Other People's Blood — Kahn, Robert S
Other People's Gardens — Lloyd, Christopher, 1921-
Other People's Words — Purcell-Gates, Victoria

The Other Rebecca — Freely, Maureen
Other Selves — Schollmeier, Paul
The Other Side — Alvarez, Julia
c The Other Side (Illus. by Julia Gukova) — Aura, Alejandro
The Other Side of Heaven — Karlin, Wayne
The Other Side of the Asian American Success Story — Walker-Moffat, Wendy
c The Other Side of the Bridge (Illus. by Alex De Wolf) — Hanel, Wolfram
Other Suns, Other Worlds? — Mammana, Dennis
The Other Taiwan — Rubinstein, Murray A
The Other Tuscany — Blomquist, Thomas W
p Other Voices
The Other War — Vale, Geoffrey
The Other within Us — Pearsall, Marilyn
The Other Woman — Silvera, Makeda
The Other Writing — Kadir, Djelal
Otherland. Vol. 1 — Williams, Tad
Otherness and Media — Naficy, Hamid
y Otherwere: Stories of Transformation — Gilman, Laura Anne
y Otherwise: New and Selected Poems — Kenyon, Jane
c Otherworlds: Poems of the Mysterious (Illus. by Shirley Felts) — Nicholls, Judith
I Othoni Ton Onomaton — Evanghelatos, Kostas
Otilia's Body — Galindo, Sergio
Otsar Ha-Milim Shel Ha-Shalom — Hareven, Shulamith
c The Ottawa — Landau, Elaine
Ottawa and the Outer Provinces — Tomblin, Stephen G
Otters — Tulloch, Bobby
Otto Klemperer: His Life and Times. Vol. 2 — Heyworth, Peter
Otto Klemperer: His Life and Times. Vols. 1-2 — Heyworth, Peter
Otto Neurath: Philosophy between Science and Politics — Cartwright, Nancy
An Ottoman Century — Ze'evi, Dror
The Ottoneum Theater — Adams, Graham C
Oudheteri Zoni — Kariotis, Manthos
Oum — Nassib, Selim
An Ounce of Preservation — Tuttle, Craig A
Our Age — Bemporad, Jack
Our America — Jones, LeAlan
Our America — Michaels, Walter Benn
c Our Baby from China (Illus. by Nancy D'Antonio) — D'Antonio, Nancy
c Our Beckoning Borders (Illus. by Paul Conklin) — Ashabranner, Brent
Our Bones Are Scattered — Ward, Andrew
Our Boots — Oakes, Jill
Our Bravest and Our Best — Bishop, Arthur
c Our Brother Has Down's Syndrome — Cairo, Shelley
c Our Changing Planet
Our Changing White House — Garrett, Wendell
Our Children's Toxic Legacy — Wargo, John
Our Coastal Seas, What Is Their Future? — Brooks, Anathea
Our Common Affairs — Cashin, Joan E
Our Cry for Life — Aquino, Maria Pilar
Our Earliest Ancestors — Kurten, Bjorn
Our Ecological Footprint — Wackernagel, Mathis
Our Evolving Universe — Longair, Malcolm S
y Our Experience
y Our Fascinating Earth. Rev. Ed. — Seff, Philip
Our Father Abraham — Wilson, Marvin R
c Our Favorite Stories from around the World (Illus. by Barnabas Kindersley) — Gavin, Jamila
c Our Field (Illus. by Robin Bell Corfield) — Doherty, Berlie
Our Game (Davidson). Audio Version — Le Carre, John
Our Gift of Love
Our Global Environment. 4th Ed. — Nadakavukaren, Anne
Our Glorious Century
Our Grandmothers' Lives as Told in Their Own Words — Ahenakew, Freda
Our Guerrilas, Our Sidewalks — Braun, Herbert
Our Guys — Lefkowitz, Bernard
c Our House (Illus. by Brian Selznick) — Conrad, Pam
Our Irish Presbyterian Heritage — Holmes, Finlay
Our Lady of Babylon — Rechy, John
Our Lady of Guadalupe — Poole, Stafford
Our Lady of the Potatoes — Sprott, Duncan
Our Landlady — Baum, L Frank
Our Living Resources — LaRoe, Edward T
Our Molecular Nature — Goodsell, David S
c Our Most Dear Friend — Vishaka

Our Mothers — *Esders, Viviane*
Our National Park System — *Rettie, Dwight F*
Our National Wetland Heritage. 2nd Ed. — *Kusler, Jon*
Our Natural History — *Botkin, Daniel B*
c Our Natural Homes (Illus. by James M Needham) — *Collard, Sneed B*
c Our New Puppy (Illus. by Barry Moser) — *Harper, Isabelle*
Our People. 3rd Ed. — *Magocsi, Paul Robert*
y Our Poisoned Waters — *Dolan, Edward F*
Our Politics, Our Selves? — *Digeser, Peter*
Our Racist Legacy — *Beals, Ivan A*
Our Religions — *Sharma, Arvind*
Our Right to Choose — *Harrison, Beverly Wildung*
Our Rightful Share — *Helg, Aline*
r Our Scientific Heritage — *Williams, Trevor I*
Our Secret Century. Electronic Media Version
Our Selves, Our Souls and Bodies — *Hefling, Charles*
Our Sisters' Promised Land — *Emmett, Ayala*
Our Son the Arson — *Ziolkowski, Thad*
Our Southern Zion — *Clarke, Erskine*
y Our Stolen Future — *Colborn, Theo*
y Our Stories — *Bauer, Marion Dane*
Our Stories of Miscarriage — *Faldet, Rachel*
r Our Sunday Visitor's 1997 Catholic Almanac
Our Tempestuous Day — *Erickson, Carolly*
y Our Times — *Sullivan, Mark, 1874-1952*
Our Town — *Kirp, David L*
Our Town — *Pace, DeWanna*
c Our Universe — *Stannard, Russell*
Our Vampires, Ourselves — *Auerbach, Nina*
Our War — *Harris, David*
c Our World in Danger
Our World, Our Rights — *Brown, Margot*
y Our World This Century — *Heater, Derek, 1931-*
r Out and About Gay Travel Guides — *Kolber-Stuart, Billy*
c Out and about with Anthony Ant — *Philpot, Lorna*
Out El Kouloub — *Atiya, Nayra*
Out from Behind the Eight-Ball — *Elder, Donald C*
Out from Underdevelopment Revisited — *Mittelman, James H*
Out in Force — *Herek, Gregory M*
Out in the Cold — *Haricombe, Lorraine J*
Out in the Field — *Lewin, Ellen*
Out of Afghanistan — *Cordovez, Diego*
Out of America — *Richburg, Keith B*
Out of Body — *Baum, Thomas*
Out of Character — *Russell, Mark, 1954-*
Out of Control — *Brzezinski, Zbigniew*
Out of Control — *Harris, Sally*
Out of Control — *Kelly, Kevin*
y Out of Darkness — *Baksh, Ishmael*
c Out of Darkness (Illus. by Kate Kiesler) — *Freedman, Russell*
Out of Eden — *Lehrer, Kate*
Out of Eden — *Stratton, Beverly J*
Out of Egypt — *Aciman, Andre*
Out of Galileo — *Maffioli, Cesare S*
Out of Inferno — *Carlson, Harry G*
Out of My Head — *Jowitt, Susannah*
Out of My Mind — *Neville, Richard*
c Out of Nowhere — *Sebestyen, Ouida*
Out of Nowhere, the Body's Shape — *Simon, Beth*
Out of Order — *Patterson, Thomas E*
Out of Order, Out of Sight. Vols. 1-2 — *Piper, Adrian*
Out of Sheer Rage — *Dyer, Geoff*
y Out of Sight — *Leonard, Elmore*
y Out of Sight (Mantegna). Audio Version — *Leonard, Elmore*
Out of Sight, Out of Mind — *Vissing, Yvonne M*
c Out of the Ark (Illus. by Jackie Morris) — *Ganeri, Anita*
c Out of the Blue — *Ellis, Sarah*
Out of the Blue — *Hanson, Mark Victor*
Out of the Blue — *Moss, Kevin*
Out of the Class Closet — *Penelope, Julia*
r Out of the Closet and into the Classroom. 2nd Ed. — *Lobban, Marjorie*
Out of the Crisis — *Deming, W Edward*
y Out of the Dark (Illus. by Martin Springett) — *Katz, Welwyn Wilton*
c Out of the Dump — *Franklin, Kristine L*
Out of the Garden — *Buchanan, Christina*
Out of the Garden — *Kline, Stephen*
Out of the Ordinary — *Walker, Barbara*
Out of the Red Shadows — *Kostyrchenko, Gennadi*
Out of the Shadows — *Elson Roessler, Shirley*
y Out of the Shadows (Bron). Audio Version — *Sutherland, Titia*

Out of the Shadows — *Torrey, E Fuller*
y Out of the Storm — *Willis, Patricia*
Out of the Sun — *Goddard, Robert*
Out of the Wilderness — *Warren, Preston*
Out of This World — *Gudgeon, Chris*
y Out of Time — *Cooney, Caroline B*
Out of Time — *Thomas, Nicholas*
Out Our Way — *Riordon, Michael*
Out-Smarting Your Karma and Other Preordained Conditions — *Kaufman, Barry Neil*
Out the Window. Audio Version — *Block, Lawrence*
Out to Canaan — *Karon, Jan*
Out West — *Dale, John*
Out West — *Leebron, Fred G*
y Out with It — *Kay, Philip*
r Outback Australia Handbook. 2nd Ed. — *Johnson, Marael*
The Outbreak of the Irish Rebellion of 1641 — *Perceval-Maxwell, M*
y The Outcast of Redwall (Illus. by Allan Curless) — *Jacques, Brian*
Outcome Assessment in Residential Treatment — *Pfeiffer, Steven I*
Outcome-Based Evaluation — *Schalock, R L*
Outcomes of Community Care for Users and Carers — *Nocon, Andrew*
y The Outdoor Adventure Handbook — *McManners, Hugh*
c Outdoor Safety (Illus. by Penny Dann) — *Loewen, Nancy*
r Outdoor Writers Association of America Style Manual — *Kersavage, Carol J*
c Outer Space (Illus. by Kuo Kang Chen) — *Hall, Godfrey*
The Outfit — *Brown, J P S*
Outing Goethe and His Age — *Kuzniar, Alice A*
Outlaw Culture — *Hooks, Bell*
The Outlaw Legend — *Seal, Graham*
The Outlaw Trail — *Kelly, Charles*
Outlaws — *Green, Tim, 1963-*
Outlaws, Renegades, and Saints — *Midge, Tiffany*
Outlines of Scepticism (Annas) — *Empiricus, Sextus*
Outlive Your Enemies — *Sanford, Terry*
Outlooks: Lesbian and Gay Sexualities and Visual Cultures — *Horne, Peter*
Outpatient Management of HIV Infection. 2nd Ed. — *Masci, Joseph R*
Outposts of Empire — *Lee, Steven Hugh*
Output Measures and More — *Walter, Virginia A*
Outrage and Insight — *Walker, David H*
Outrage: The Five Reasons Why O.J. Simpson Got Away with Murder — *Bugliosi, Vincent*
c Outrageous, Bodacious Boliver Boggs! (Illus. by JoAnn Adinolfi) — *Harper, Jo*
The Outrageous Idea of Christian Scholarship — *Marsden, George M*
Outrageous Women, Outrageous God — *Saunders, Ross*
y Outrageously Alice — *Naylor, Phyllis Reynolds*
Outside Agency — *Daly, Conor*
c Outside and inside Sharks — *Markle, Sandra*
Outside History — *Boland, Eavan*
Outside In — *D'Arnuk, Nanisi Barrett*
Outside in the Teaching Machine — *Spivak, Gayatri Chakravorty*
c Outside, Inside (Illus. by Linnea Asplind Riley) — *Crimi, Carolyn*
Outside Looking In — *Apraku, Kofi K*
r Outside Magazine Adventure Guide to Northern California*
y Outside Permission — *Nilsson, Eleanor*
Outside the Law — *Shreve, Susan*
y Outside the Walls — *Bransby, Lawrence*
The Outsider — *Williamson, Penelope*
Outsider Features — *Ferncase, Richard K*
Outsiders in 19th-Century Press History — *Hutton, Frankie*
Outsiders' Response to European Integration — *Hirsch, Seev*
Outsourcing Library Technical Services — *Hirshon, Arnold*
yr Outstanding Books for the College Bound — *Young Adults Library Services Association*
The Ovary: Regulation, Dysfunction, and Treatment — *Symposium on the Ovary: Regulation, Dysfunction, and Treatment (1996: Florida)*
Ovation by Death — *Yeager, Dorian*
c Over on the Farm (Illus. by Christopher Gunson) — *Gunson, Christopher*
Over the Door — *Yang, John*
Over the Hills — *Lamb, David*

Over the Ivy Walls — *Gandara, Patricia*
Over the Misty Mountains — *Morris, Gilbert*
c Over the Moon
Over the Next Hill — *Counts, Dorothy Ayers*
c Over the River and through the Wood (Illus. by David Catrow) — *Child, Lydia Maria Francis*
Over the River and through the Woods — *Simak, Clifford D*
Over the River and through the Woods (Frakes). Audio Version — *Simak, Clifford D*
c Over the Top of the World (Illus. by Will Steger) — *Steger, Will*
y Over the Water — *Casey, Maude*
Over There — *Jarrard, Kyle*
c Over under in the Garden (Illus. by Pat Schories) — *Schories, Pat*
Over What Hill? — *Wilder, Effie Leland*
Overcoming Anxiety — *Peurifoy, Reneau*
Overcoming Dyslexia in Children, Adolescents, and Adults. 2nd Ed. — *Jordon, Dale R*
Overcoming Fear between Christians and Jews — *Charlesworth, James H*
Overcoming Global Hunger — *Conference on Actions to Reduce Hunger Worldwide (1993: American University)*
Overcoming Law — *Posner, Richard A*
An Overcrowded World? — *Sarre, Philip*
Overdentures Made Easy — *Preiskel, Harold W*
Overdrive: Bill Gates and the Race to Control Cyberspace — *Wallace, James, 1947-*
Overland: The California Emigrant Trail of 1841-1870 — *MacGregor, Greg*
The Overland Trail — *Lee, W W*
Overseas Chinese Business Networks in Asia — *East Asia Analytical Unit*
Overstekend Wild — *Vanhole, Kamiel*
Overstory--Zero — *Heilman, Robert Leo*
Overtones and Undertones — *Brown, Royal S*
Overtones of War — *Blunden, Edmund*
The Overwhelmed Person's Guide to Time Management — *Eisenberg, Ronni*
Ovid's Causes — *Myers, K Sara*
c Owen Foote, Second Grade Strongman (Illus. by Dee DeRosa) — *Greene, Stephanie*
c The Owl and the Pussy Cat (Illus. by Ian Beck) — *Lear, Edward*
The Owl at Dawn — *Cutrofello, Andrew*
c Owl Babies (Illus. by Patrick Benson) — *Waddell, Martin*
y The Owl in the Mask of the Dreamer — *Haines, John*
y Owl Light — *Pearson, Maggie*
c Owl Moon — *Yolen, Jane*
c The Owl Who Became the Moon (Illus. by Ted Rand) — *London, Jonathan*
c Owls: Whoo Are They? (Illus. by Leslie Leroux) — *Jarvis, Kila*
Own or Other Culture — *Okely, John*
An Owner's Manual for the Unfinished Soul — *Miller, Calvin*
Ownership and Control — *Blair, Margaret M*
Ownership and Performance in Electric Utilities — *Pollitt, Michael G*
c The Ox-Cart Man (Illus. by Barbara Cooney) — *Hall, Donald, 1928-*
Oxcart Catholicism on Fifth Avenue — *Diaz-Stevens, Ana Maria*
r The Oxfam Handbook of Development and Relief
r The Oxfam Handbook of Development and Relief. Vols. 1-2 — *Eade, Deborah*
cr Oxford 3-in-1 Bilingual Dictionary on CD-Rom. Electronic Media Version
r Oxford Advanced Learner's Dictionary of Current English. 5th Ed. — *Hornby, A S*
r Oxford Atlas of the World. 4th Ed.
The Oxford Book of American Detective Stories — *Hillerman, Tony*
y The Oxford Book of Australian Ghost Stories — *Gelder, Ken*
The Oxford Book of Australian Travel Writing — *Pesman, Ros*
The Oxford Book of Classical Verse in Translation — *Poole, Adrian*
The Oxford Book of Creatures — *Adcock, Fleur*
The Oxford Book of English Mystical Verse — *Nicholson, D H S*
The Oxford Book of Hebrew Short Stories — *Abramson, Glenda*
The Oxford Book of Letters — *Kermode, Frank*
The Oxford Book of London — *Bailey, Paul*
The Oxford Book of Modern Australian Verse — *Porter, Peter*

The Oxford Book of Nature Writing — *Mabey, Richard*

c Oxford Book of Poetry for Children (Illus. by Brian Wildsmith) — *Blishen, Edward*

c The Oxford Book of Scary Tales — *Pepper, Dennis*

The Oxford Book of Scottish Short Stories — *Dunn, Douglas*

y The Oxford Book of Spy Stories — *Cox, Michael*

y The Oxford Book of the American South — *Ayers, Edward L*

The Oxford Book of the Supernatural — *Enright, D J*

The Oxford Book of Travel Stories — *Craig, Patricia*

y The Oxford Book of Twentieth-Century Ghost Stories — *Cox, Michael*

c The Oxford Children's A to Z of Mathematics — *Glover, David, 1953, Sep., 9-*

cr The Oxford Children's A to Z of Science — *Jennings, Terry*

y The Oxford Children's Book of Science — *Taylor, Charles*

cr Oxford Children's Encyclopedia. 2nd Ed., Vols. 1-9

cr Oxford Children's Encyclopedia. Rev. Ed. Electronic Media Version

yr The Oxford Classical Dictionary. 3rd Ed. — *Hornblower, Simon*

r The Oxford Companion to African American Literature — *Andrews, William L*

r The Oxford Companion to American Literature, 6th Ed. — *Hart, James D*

r The Oxford Companion to Archaeology — *Fagan, Brian M*

The Oxford Companion to Australian Cricket — *Cashman, Richard*

r The Oxford Companion to Australian Military History — *Dennis, Peter*

r The Oxford Companion to Christian Art and Architecture — *Murray, Peter, 1920-*

The Oxford Companion to English Literature. Rev. Ed. — *Drabble, Margaret*

r The Oxford Companion to Irish Literature — *Welch, Robert*

r The Oxford Companion to Local and Family History — *Hey, David*

r Oxford Companion to Medicine — *Walton, John Nicholas*

r The Oxford Companion to Philosophy — *Honderich, Ted*

yr The Oxford Companion to the English Language — *McArthur, Tom*

yr The Oxford Companion to Twentieth-Century Literature in English — *Stringer, Jenny*

r The Oxford Companion to Wine — *Robinson, Jancis*

r Oxford Companion to Women's Writing in the United States — *Davidson, Cathy N*

r The Oxford Companion to World War II — *Dear, C B*

r The Oxford Dictionary and Thesaurus

r The Oxford Dictionary of Current English. 2nd Ed.

r The Oxford Dictionary of Humorous Quotations — *Sherrin, Ned*

r The Oxford Dictionary of Modern Slang — *Ayto, John*

r The Oxford Dictionary of Philosophy — *Blackburn, Simon*

r The Oxford Dictionary of Political Quotations — *Jay, Antony*

r The Oxford Dictionary of Sports Science and Medicine — *Kent, Michael*

r The Oxford Dictionary of the Jewish Religion — *Werblowsky, R J Zwi*

r The Oxford Dictionary of the World — *Munro, David*

r The Oxford Dictionary of World Religions — *Bowker, John Westerdale*

yr The Oxford-Duden Pictorial Spanish and English Dictionary. 2nd Ed.

r The Oxford Encyclopedia of Archaeology in the Near East. Vols. 1-5

r The Oxford Encyclopedia of the Reformation. Vols. 1-4

yr Oxford Encyclopedic World Atlas. 3rd Ed.

r Oxford English Dictionary. 2nd Ed. Electronic Media Version

The Oxford English Grammar — *Greenbaum, Sidney*

r The Oxford English-Hebrew Dictionary

r The Oxford English Reference Dictionary. 2nd Ed. — *Pearsall, Judy*

c Oxford First Ancient History (Illus. by Peter Connolly) — *Burrell, Roy*

c The Oxford Funny Story Book — *Pepper, Dennis*

The Oxford Group, Group Revivalism, and the Churches in Northern Europe 1930-1940 — *Jarlet, Anders*

r The Oxford Guide to Contemporary Writing — *Sturrock, John*

The Oxford Guide to Family History — *Hey, David*

r The Oxford-Hachette Concise French Dictionary — *Correard, Marie-Helene*

r The Oxford-Hachette French Dictionary — *Correard, Marie-Helene*

r Oxford Handbook of Clinical Dentistry. 2nd Ed. — *Mitchell, David A*

The Oxford History of Australia. Vol. 5

yr The Oxford History of the American West — *Milner, Clyde A*

The Oxford History of the Prison — *Morris, Norval*

r The Oxford History of World Cinema — *Nowell-Smith, Geoffrey*

The Oxford Illustrated History of Ireland — *Foster, R F*

y The Oxford Illustrated History of Modern Europe — *Blanning, T C W*

The Oxford Illustrated History of Roman Britain — *Salway, Peter*

The Oxford Illustrated History of the British Army — *Chandler, David*

The Oxford Illustrated History of Theatre — *Brown, John Russell*

The Oxford Illustrated History of Tudor and Stuart Britain — *Morrill, John*

cr Oxford Junior Dictionary. 3rd Rev. Ed. — *Sansome, Rosemary*

r The Oxford Large Print Dictionary. 2nd Ed.

The Oxford Mark Twain. Vols. 1-29 — *Twain, Mark*

y Oxford Mathematics: Intermediate Link for Year 9

yr The Oxford Mathematics Study Dictionary — *Tapson, Frank*

Oxford Mourning — *Stallwood, Veronica*

The Oxford Movement in Context — *Nockles, Peter B*

c The Oxford Nursery Book (Illus. by Ian Beck) — *Beck, Ian*

r The Oxford Paperback French Dictionary and Grammar — *Rowlinson, William*

r The Oxford Paperback Spanish Dictionary — *Lea, Christine*

c Oxford Primary Geography: Pupils' Book 3

cr Oxford Primary School Dictionary — *Augarde, A J*

Oxford Reading Tree Teacher's Guide 4 — *Franks, Tim*

Oxford Readings in Aristophanes — *Segal, Erich*

cr Oxford School Dictionary — *Hawkins, Joyce*

yr The Oxford School Thesaurus — *Spooner, A*

cr Oxford Shorter School Dictionary — *Hawkins, Joyce*

cr Oxford Study Dictionary — *Hawkins, Joyce*

c The Oxford Treasury of Children's Stories

y The Oxford Treasury of Classic Poems — *Harrison, Michael*

yr Oxford Visual Dictionary

Oxfordshire — *Steane, John*

Oxygen Transport to Tissue XVII — *Ince, C*

Oxytocin: Cellular and Molecular Approaches in Medicine and Research — *Ivell, Richard*

Oyayubi P No Shugyo Jidal — *Matsuura, Rieko*

c Oyo, Benin, Ashanti — *Mann, Kenny*

The Oyster — *Brooks, William*

Oyster — *Hospital, Janette Turner*

c Oyster Moon (Illus. by Marcy Dunn Ramsey) — *Meacham, Margaret*

The Oystercatcher: From Individuals to Populations — *Goss-Custard, John D*

Oz and Beyond — *Riley, Michael O*

r Oz Clarke's Wine Advisor 1997

r Oz Clarke's Wine Atlas — *Clarke, Oz*

The Ozone Project — *Saugier, Philippe*

P

p P-Form: A Journal of Interdisciplinary and Performance Art

c P.J. and Puppy (Illus. by Cathryn Falwell) — *Falwell, Cathryn*

P.K. Page: Poems Selected and New — *Page, P K*

P.S.: A Memoir — *Salinger, Pierre*

Paare Passanten — *Strauss, Botho*

Pablo Neruda: Absence and Presence — *Poirot, Luis*

y Pablo Picasso (Illus. by Simone Boni) — *Loria, Stefano*

c Pablo Picasso — *Meadows, Matthew*

Pablo Picasso: Academic and Anti-Academic 1895-1900 — *Palau I Fabre, Josep*

Pacific 2010: Challenging the Future — *Cole, Rodney V*

Pacific 2010: Urbanisation in Polynesia — *Connell, John*

Pacific 2010: Women's Education and Economic Development in Melanesia — *Gannicott, K G*

The Pacific Basin since 1945 — *Thompson, Roger C, 1941-*

p Pacific Coast Journal

r The Pacific Coast League — *Snelling, Dennis*

Pacific Defense — *Calder, Kent E*

Pacific Island — *Ypma, Herbert*

Pacific Island Economies

The Pacific Northwest. Rev. and Enl. Ed. — *Schwantes, Carlos A*

The Pacific Northwest Travel-Smart Trip Planner — *Harris, Richard, 1947-*

c The Pacific Ocean — *Lambert, David*

Pacific Passage — *Cohen, Warren I*

The Pacific Raincoast — *Bunting, Robert*

The Pacific War — *Levine, Alan J*

Pacific War Diary — *Fahey, James J*

Pacifism and Revolution 1916-18 — *Russell, Bertrand*

The Pacifist Impulse in Historical Perspective — *Dyck, Harvey L*

Packaging. 4th Ed. — *Leonard, Edmund A*

r Packet Based Communications — *Mazda, Fraidoon*

PACS: Picture Archiving and Communication Systems in Biomedical Imaging — *Huang, H K*

The Pact — *Norman, Hilary*

El Pacto — *Palma, Milagros*

r A Pada Index and Reverse Pada Index to Early Jain Canons — *Yamazaki, Moriichi*

c Paddington's 1 2 3 — *Bond, Michael*

Paddle to the Arctic — *Starkell, Don*

Padinnia Davn'oi Stolytsi — *Lupii, Oles'*

Padyavand. Vol. 1 — *Netzer, Amnon*

Paediatric MCOs for Postgraduate Examinations. Vol. 2 — *Attard-Montalto, Simon*

Paediatric Osteology — *International Workshop on Paediatric Osteology (1st: 1995: Cologne, Germany)*

Paenitentialia Franciae, Italiae Et Hispaniae Saeculi VIII-XI. Vol. 1 — *Korntgen, Ludger*

The Pagan Path — *Farrar, Janet*

Paganism in Arthurian Romance — *Darrah, John*

Pagan's Father — *Arditti, Michael*

y Pagan's Scribe — *Jinks, Catherine*

Page after Page — *Page, Tim*

The Page as a Stage Set — *Spaulding, Amy E*

c Page to Jane Seymour (Illus. by Pauline Hazelwood) — *Trease, Geoffrey*

Pagemill 2 for Macintosh — *Langer, Maria*

Pages from My Diary 1986-1995 — *Baliozian, Ara*

Pagnol's Provence — *More, Julian*

Pain and Polemic — *Smiga, George M*

Pain and Touch — *Kruger, Lawrence*

Pain, Distress, and the Newborn Baby — *Sparshott, Margaret*

Pain Relief! — *Cowles, Jane*

Pain Treatment Centers at a Crossroads — *Bristol-Myers Squibb Symposium on Pain Research (6th: 1995: Baltimore, Md.)*

Painfreak — *Houarner, Gerard Daniel*

y Paint: A Manual of Pictorial Thought and Practical Advice — *Camp, Jeffery*

Paint: Decorating with Water-Based Paints — *Sutcliffe, John*

Paint It Black — *Timlin, Mark*

Paint Your House with Powdered Milk — *Green, Joey*

p Painted Bride Quarterly

Painted Desert — *Barthelme, Frederick*

y Painted Devil — *Bedard, Michael*

Painted Diaries — *Zabbia, Kim Howes*

Painted Faces on the Renaissance Stage — *Drew-Bear, Annette*

A Painted Field — *Robertson, Robin, 1955-*

The Painted Page — *Alexander, Jonathan J G*

The Painted Photograph 1839-1914 — *Henisch, Heinz K*

A Painter of Our Time — *Berger, John*

y Painters Painting. Electronic Media Version — *De Antonio, Emile*

Painters, Paintings and Books — *Porter, Yves*

The Painter's Practice in Renaissance Tuscany — *Thomas, Anabel*

Painting Acrylics — *Lord, Vicki*

Painting and Decorating Bird Houses — *Egan, Dorothy*

Painting and Illumination in Early Renaissance Florence 1300-1450 — *Kanter, Laurence B*

Painting and the Journal of Eugene Delacroix — *Hannoosh, Michele*

c Painting Dreams — *Lyons, Mary E*

y Painting Expressive Portraits in Oil — *Leveille, Paul*

Painting for Money — *Solkin, David H*

Painting Greeting Cards in Watercolor — *Penney, Jacqueline*

Painting in Renaissance Venice — *Humfrey, Peter*

Painting Nature's Details — *Jelbert, Wendy*

Painting on the Page — *Feal, Rosemary Geisdorfer*

Painting Outside Painting

Painting Place — *Silcox, David P*

y Painting the Black — *Deuker, Carl*

Painting the Tower of Babel — *Russo, Albert*

c Painting the Wind (Illus. by Kevin Hawkes) — *Dionetti, Michelle*

Painting Wildlife Textures Step by Step — *Lawrence, Rod*

Painting Women — *Cherry, Deborah*

c Paintings (Illus. by Tony Ross) — *Delafosse, Claude*

Paintings by Masami Teraoka — *Teraoka, Masami*

Paintings in the Vatican — *Pietrangeli, Carlo*

r The Paintings of Paul Cezanne. Vols. 1-2 — *Rewald, John*

Paintings, Sculpture, Architecture — *Goldscheider, Ludwig*

c A Pair of Socks (Illus. by Lois Ehlert) — *Murphy, Stuart J*

y Pairin' Up — *Littleton, Mark*

yr PAIS Select. Electronic Media Version

Paita, Outpost of Empire — *Lofstrom, William L*

Une Paix A Vivre — *Mimouni, Rachid*

Une Paix Royale — *Mertens, Pierre*

c Pak in Indonesia (Illus. by Alain Cheneviere) — *Cheneviere, Alain*

c Pakistan — *Clayton, Elspeth*

y Pakistan — *Rumalshah, Mano*

Pakistan 1995

Pakistan: A Country Study — *Blood, Peter R*

r Pakistan (Handbooks of the World)

Pakistan: Tradition and Change — *Mumtaz, Khawar*

c Pal the Pony — *Herman, R A*

Palace — *Kerr, Katharine*

Palaces of Florence — *Gurrieri, Francesco*

Palaeoecology and Palaeoenvironments of Late Cenozoic Mammals — *Stewart, Kathlyn M*

Palaeopathology of Aboriginal Australians — *Webb, Stephen*

Pale Blue Dot — *Sagan, Carl*

Pale Grace — *Johnson, Sherry*

Paleface — *Boyle, Charles*

The Paleo-Indian of Southern St. Louis Co., Minnesota — *Harrison, Christina*

Paleoclimate and Evolution — *Vrba, Elisabeth S*

Le Paleolithique Moyen Dans Le Nord Du Senonoais (Yonne) — *Deloze, Valerie*

Le Paleolithique Superieur De L'Abri Pataud (Dordogne) — *Bricker, Harry M*

Paleoseismology — *McCalpin, James P*

Palestine and the Arab-Israeli Conflict. 3rd Ed. — *Smith, Charles D*

Palestine in Crisis — *Usher, Graham*

The Palestinian Dwelling in the Roman-Byzantine Period — *Hirschield, Yizhar*

Palestinian Identity — *Khalidi, Rashid*

Palestinian Peasants and Ottoman Officials — *Singer, Amy*

The Palestinians between Terrorism and Statehood — *Inbari, Pinhas*

Der Palestrina-Stil Als Satzideal In Der Musiktheorie Zwischen 1750 Und 1900 — *Luttig, Peter*

Palimpsest: A Memoir — *Vidal, Gore*

Palinuro of Mexico — *Paso, Fernando Del*

Palissy Ware — *Katz, Marshall P*

Palladium — *Fulton, Alice*

Palladium Reagents and Catalysts — *Tsuji, Jiro*

Palliative Care Ethics — *Randall, Fiona*

c The Palm of My Heart (Illus. by Gregory Christie) — *Adedjouma, Davida*

Palm-of-the-Hand Stories — *Kawabata, Yasunari*

Palmerston and Africa — *Braithwaite, Roderick*

r Palms throughout the World — *Jones, David L*

Palynological Correlation of Major Pennsylvanian (Middle and Upper Carboniferous) Chronostratigraphic Boundaries in the Illinois and Other Coal Basins — *Peppers, Russel A*

Pamela — *Richardson, Samuel*

c Pamela's First Musical (Illus. by Andrew Jackness) — *Wasserstein, Wendy*

Pampa Grande and the Mochica Culture — *Shimada, Izumi*

The Pamphlets of Lewis Carroll. Vol. 2 — *Dodgson, Charles Lutwidge*

Pan — *Hamsun, Knut*

r Pan-African Chronology — *Jenkins, Everett, Jr.*

The Pan-American Dream — *Harrison, Lawrence E*

Pan Asian Express — *Witt, Barbara*

Pan-Turkism: From Irredentism to Cooperation. 2nd Rev. and Updated Ed. — *Landau, Jacob M*

Panaflex User's Manual. 2nd Ed. — *Samuelson, David W*

c Panama — *Hassig, Susan M*

Panama — *Zencey, Eric*

y Panama (Gaines). Audio Version — *Zencey, Eric*

Panama: La Integracion Con Los Otros Paises Del Istmo Centroamericano — *Ossa, Alvaro De La*

Panamanian Militarism — *Guevara Mann, Carlos*

Pancakes: From Morning to Midnight — *Greenspan, Dorie*

c Pancho Villa — *Carroll, Bob*

Panda Ray — *Kandel, Michael*

Pandaemonium — *Epstein, Leslie*
c Pandora (Illus. by Dietlind Blech) — *Mayne, William*
Pandora: Women in Classical Greece — *Reeder, Ellen D*
Pandora's Box — *Tubb, E C*
y Pandora's Clock — *Nance, John J*
Panentheism in Hartshorne and Tillich — *Nikkel, David H*
Pangeia — *Tellermann, Esther*
The Panic Hand — *Carroll, Jonathan*
y The Panorama of the Renaissance — *Aston, Margaret*
p Panoramiques
The Pantanal of Mato Grosso (Brazil) — *Por, Francis Dov*
Panter Ba-Martef — *Oz, Amos*
c Panther in Argyll — *Tuttle, Lisa*
The Pantomine Book — *Harris, Paul*
Paolo Giovio: The Historian and the Crisis of Sixteenth-Century Italy — *Zimmerman, T C Price*
c Papa Gatto (Illus. by Ruth Sanderson) — *Sanderson, Ruth*
c Papa, Please Get the Moon for Me — *Carle, Eric*
Papal Art and Cultural Politics — *Johns, Christopher M S*
Papal Patronage and the Music of St. Peter's 1380-1513 — *Reynolds, Christopher A*
y Papa's Angels — *Wilcox Paxton, Collin*
c Papa's Latkes (Illus. by Jane Breskin Zalben) — *Zalben, Jane Breskin*
Pape Junsland En Utopia — *Bejczy, Istvan*
Le Pape Pie XI Et L'Opinion 1922-1939 — *Agostino, Marc*
Papeles Que Fueron Vidas — *Cunqueiro, Alvaro*
Paper and Composites from Agro-Based Resources — *Rowell, Roger M*
c Paper and Fabric Mache — *Cusick, Dawn*
Paper and Iron — *Ferguson, Niall*
c Paper Animal Masks from Northwest Tribal Tales — *Rudolph, Nancy Lyn*
c The Paper Bag Prince (Illus. by Colin Thompson) — *Thompson, Colin*
p Paper Boat
Paper Boat — *Chao, Sheng*
Paper Bullets — *Weber, Harold M*
Paper Chemistry. 2nd Ed. — *Roberts, J C*
c Paper Clip Science — *Moje, Steven W*
y Paper Doll — *Feuer, Elizabeth*
Paper Fish — *De Rosa, Tina*
Paper Laws, Steel Bayonets — *O'Neill, William G*
Paper Museum — *Graham-Dixon, Andrew*
The Paper Trail — *Straus, Dorothea*
Paper Wings — *Swick, Marly A*
r Paperback Books for Children
Paperbound: A Showcase of Contemporary Papermakers and Bookbinders
c Paperboy (Illus. by Ted Lewin) — *Kroeger, Mary Kay*
c The Paperboy (Illus. by Dav Pilkey) — *Pilkey, Dav*
c Papercrafts around the World — *Fiarotta, Phyllis*
The Papers — *Phillips, Newk*
Papers and Journals — *Kierkegaard, Soren*
Papers from the Headmaster — *Hawley, Richard A*
Papers in Hellenistic Philosophy — *Brunschwig, Jacques*
p Papers in Regional Science
The Papers of George Catlett Marshall. Vol. 4 — *Marshall, George Catlett*
The Papers of George Washington — *Washington, George*
The Papers of George Washington: Colonial Series. Vols. 7-10 — *Washington, George*
The Papers of James Madison: Presidential Series. Vol. 3 — *Madison, James*
The Papers of John C. Calhoun. Vol. 23 — *Calhoun, John C*
The Papers of John Marshall. Vol. 8 — *Marshall, John, 1755-1835*
The Papers of Martin Luther King, Jr. Vol. 3 — *King, Martin Luther, Jr.*
The Papers of Robert Morris 1781-1784. Vol. 8 — *Morris, Robert*
The Papers of Robert Morris 1781-1784. Vols. 7-8 — *Morris, Robert*
The Papers of Thomas A. Edison. Vol. 3 — *Edison, Thomas A*
The Papers of Thomas Jefferson. Vol. 26 — *Jefferson, Thomas*
The Papers of Will Rogers. Vol. 1 — *Rogers, Will*
Papers of William Thornton. Vol. 1 — *Thornton, William*
The Papers of Zebulon Baird Vance. Vol. 2 — *Vance, Zebulon Baird*

The Paper's Papers — *Shepard, Richard F*
Papers Sobre Carles Riba — *Ferrarte, Joan*
Papiers De Famille — *Lever, Maurice*
y Papillon (Guidall). Audio Version — *Charriere, Henri*
Par Ici — *Ariew, Robert*
p Para-Doxa: Studies in World Literary Genres
Para Uma Nova Politica Externa Brasileira — *Seitenfus, Ricardo*
Parable and Story in Judaism and Christianity — *Thoma, Clemens*
The Parable of Fire — *Reiss, James*
c The Parable of the Lily (Illus. by Nancy Munger) — *Higgs, Liz Curtis*
Parables as Subversive Speech — *Herzog, William R, II*
Parables of Possibility — *Martin, Terence*
Paracelsus: Speculative Theory and the Crisis of the Early Reformation — *Weeks, Andrew*
Paradigm Lost? — *Jablonsky, David*
Parading through History — *Hoxie, Frederick E*
c Parading with Piglets — *Hansen, Biruta Akerbergs*
Paradis — *Eriksson, Ulf*
The Paradise Complex — *Lockhart, Douglas*
r Paradise Lost — *Klemp, P J*
Paradise Lost — *Milton, John, 1608-1674*
Paradise Lost and the Romantic Reader — *Newlyn, Lucy*
The Paradise Snare — *Crispin, A C*
Paradise Transformed — *Cooper, Guy*
Paradise Valley, Nevada — *Marshall, Howard Wright*
Paradox Lost — *Wallace, Philip R*
The Paradox of Progress — *McKenzie, Richard B*
The Paradox of Revolution — *Middlebrook, Kevin J*
The Paradox Principles — *Price Waterhouse (Firm). Change Integration Team*
Paradoxes of Gender — *Lorber, Judith*
Paradoxes of Modernity — *Schluchter, Wolfgang*
The Paradoxical Vision — *Benne, Robert*
The Parafaith War — *Modesitt, L E, Jr.*
y Paragons: Twelve Master Science Fiction Writers Ply Their Craft — *Wilson, Robin Scott*
El Paraguay Bajo Los Lopez — *Cooney, Jerry W*
c The Parakeet Girl (Illus. by Roger Bollen) — *Sadler, Marilyn*
Parallel and Distributed Computing Handbook — *Zomaya, Albert Y*
Parallel and Distributed Processing — *Proceedings of the IEEE Symposium on Parallel and Distributed Processing*
Parallel Computational Fluid Dynamics — *International Conference on Parallel Computational Fluid Dynamics (1995: Pasadena, Calif.)*
Parallel Expeditions — *Railsback, Brian E*
y Parallel Journeys — *Ayer, Eleanor H*
Parallel Paths — *Rotman, Leonard Ian*
c Parallel Poems — *Royston, Mike*
Parallel Processing. Vols. 1-4 — *International Conference on Parallel Processing (1996: Cornell University, Ithaca, NY)*
Parallel Programming Using C++ — *Wilson, Gregory V*
Parallel Tracks — *Kirby, Lynne*
Parallel Views — *French-American Foundation*
Parametric Statistical Inference — *Lindsey, J K*
Parametric Statistical Theory — *Pfanzagl, Johann*
y The Paranormal: A Guide to the Unexplained — *North, Anthony*
Paraphrase on Acts — *Erasmus, Desiderius*
Paraphrase on the Acts of the Apostles — *Erasmus, Desiderius*
Paraphrases on the Epistles to Timothy, Titus and Philemon; the Epistles of Peter and Jude; the Epistle of James; the Epistles of John... — *Erasmus, Desiderius*
r Parasitic Infections of Domestic Animals — *Kaufmann, Johannes*
Parastoo: Stories and Poems — *Yalfani, Mehri*
The Paratroopers of the French Foreign Legion — *Simpson, Howard R*
y A Parcel of Patterns (Forsyth). Audio Version — *Paton Walsh, Jill*
y A Parcel of Trees (Illus. by Margery Gill) — *Mayne, William*
The Pardon of Saint Anne — *Palmer, William, 1945-*
c Las Paredes Hablan (Illus. by Anne Sibley O'Brien) — *Knight, Margy Burns*
Parent-School Collaboration — *Henry, Mary E*
c The Parent Thief (Illus. by Mitra Modarressi) — *Modarressi, Mitra*

Parentage and Inheritance in the Novels of Charles Dickens — *Sadrin, Anny*
The Parental Experience in Midlife — *Ryff, Carol D*
Parental Involvement and the Political Principle — *Sarason, Seymour B*
r Parenting A to Z — *Franck, Irene*
Parenting Adolescents — *Huggins, Kevin*
The Parenting Cookbook — *Gunst, Kathy*
Parenting Teens with Love and Logic — *Cline, Foster*
Parenting the Fussy Baby and High-Need Child — *Sears, William*
Parenting the Strong-Willed Child — *Forehand, Rex*
Parenting toward Solutions — *Metcalf, Linda*
Parenting Your Teenager in the 1990s — *Elkind, David*
p Parents and Computers
Parents and Primary Mathematics — *Loewenstein, Jane*
Parents and the Dynamics of Child Rearing — *Holden, George W*
r Parents' Complete Special Education Guide — *Pierangelo, Roger*
The Parent's Crash Course in Career Planning — *Harris, Marcia B*
Parents' Cultural Belief Systems — *Harkness, Sara*
The Parents' Guide to Alternatives in Education — *Koetzsch, Ronald E*
Parent's Guide to Literacy for the 21st Century — *Hydrick, Janie*
Parents' Guide to Special Needs Schooling — *Cantor, Ruth F*
The Parent's Journal Guide to Raising Great Kids — *Conner, Bobbi*
Parents Magazine's It Worked for Me! — *Murphy, Ann Pleshette*
r The Parents' Resource Almanac — *DeFrancis, Beth*
A Pariah People — *Maccoby, Hyam*
Paribas 1872-1992 — *Bussiere, Eric*
c Paris — *Stein, R Conrad*
Paris: An Architectural History — *Sutcliffe, Anthony*
Paris and the Anarchists — *Varias, Alexander*
Paris: Artistic Life in the Twenties and Thirties — *Mann, Carol*
Paris as Revolution — *Ferguson, Priscilla Parkhurst*
Paris Babylon — *Christiansen, Rupert*
Paris: Capital of Europe — *Willms, Johannes*
The Paris Codex — *Love, Bruce*
Paris Flea Market — *Ypma, Herbert*
Paris in the Twentieth Century — *Verne, Jules*
Paris Noir — *Stovall, Tyler*
Paris out of Hand — *Gordon, Karen Elizabeth*
y Paris Quest — *Allen, Judy*
r Paris, Tightwad, and Peculiar — *McMillen, Margot Ford*
r Paris (Travelers' Tales)
r Parish Activities Handbook — *Meredith, Owen*
Parish Boundaries — *McGreevy, John T*
Parish Liturgy — *Duggan, Robert D*
Parish School — *Walch, Timothy*
Parishes, Tithes and Society in Earlier Medieval Poland c. 1100-c. 1250 — *Gorecki, Piotr*
Parisian Fields — *Sheringham, Michael*
A Parisian from Kansas — *Tapon, Philippe*
The Park and the People — *Rosenzweig, Roy*
Park Prisoners — *Waiser, Bill*
Parker and Hulme — *Glamuzina, Julie*
r Parker's Wine Buyer's Guide. 4th Ed. — *Parker, Robert M, Jr.*
Parking — *Bon, Francois*
y Parkland — *Kelleher, Victor*
The Parkman Dexter Howe Library. Pt. 10
Le Parler Lyonnais — *Vurpas, Anne-Marie*
r The Parliament and Government Pocket Book 1996
The Parliamentary Diary of Sir Richard Cocks 1698-1702 — *Cocks, Richard*
Parliamentary Politics in Revolutionary Iran — *Baktiari, Bahman*
Parliamentary Taxation in Seventeenth-Century England — *Braddick, M J*
Parliamo Insieme — *Docker, Julie*
Parlor Radical — *Pfaelzer, Jean*
Parmenide (Brisson) — *Plato*
Parmenides (Gill) — *Plato*
La Parodie — *Sangsue, Daniel*
A Parody — *Connor, Tom*
Parody in the Middle Ages — *Bayless, Martha*
Parrains, Marraines — *Fine, Agnes*
y Parrot in the Oven — *Martinez, Victor*
c Parrots — *Horton, Casey*
c Parrots — *Rauzon, Mark J*
The Parsimonious Universe — *Hildebrandt, Stefan*

Parsley, Sage, Rosemary, and Crime — *Myers, Tamar*
Parson and Parish in Eighteenth-Century Hampshire
— *Ward, W R*
Parson and Parish in Eighteenth-Century Surrey
— *Ward, W R*
La Part De L'Ombre — *Dumont, Fernand*
Part of His Story — *Corn, Alfred*
Part of Nature — *Lloyd, Genevieve*
Part of the Furniture — *Wesley, Mary*
c A Part of the Ribbon — *Hunter, Ruth*
Part-Time Public Relations with Full-Time Results
— *Karp, Rashelle S*
The Parthenon and Its Impact in Modern Times
— *Tournikiotis, Panayotis*
Partial Differential Equations — *Taylor, Michael E*
Partial Differential Equations and Applications
— *Marcellini, Paolo*
Partial Differential Equations and Functional Analysis
— *Cea, Jean*
Partial Differential Equations and Mathematica
— *Kythe, Prem K*
Partial Differential Equations and Mathematical
Physics — *Hormander, Lars*
Participation and Partnership in Urban Infrastructure
Management — *Schubeler, Peter*
Participation and Substantiality in Thomas Aquinas
— *Velde, Rudi A Te*
Participation in Congress — *Hall, Richard L*
Participatory Design — *Schuler, Douglas*
Participatory Financing through Investment Banks
and Commercial Banks — *Gafoor, A L M Abdul*
Particle Bombardment for Genetic Engineering of
Plants — *Christou, Paul*
Particle Detectors — *Grupen, Claus*
The Particle Garden — *Kane, Gordon*
The Particle Hunters. 2nd Ed. — *Ne'eman, Yuval*
r Particle Physics — *Ezhela, V V*
Particle Physics at the New Millennium — *Roe, Byron
P*
Particle Strengthening of Metals and Alloys
— *Nembach, Eckhard*
Particle Theory — *Gathorne-Hardy, Jonathan*
Particles in Our Air — *Wilson, Richard*
A Particular Condition in Life — *Burley, David G*
A Particuler Discourse Concerninge the Greate
Necessitie and Manifolde Commodyties That Are
like to Growe to This Realme of England
— *Hakluyt, Richard*
A Particuler Discourse Concerninge the Greate
Necessitie and Manifolde Commodyties That Are
like to Growe to This Realme of Englande
— *Hakluyt, Richard*
Partida De Pocher — *Neagu, Fanus*
El Partido Nationalista Vasco Ante La Guerra De
Espana 1936-1937 — *Meer Lecha-Marzo, Fernando
De*
La Partie Et Le Tout — *Malenfant, Paul Chanel*
Parties: A Literary Companion — *Johnston, Susanna*
Parties and Democracy in the Post-Soviet Republics
— *Arter, David*
Parties and Politics in Post-1989 Poland — *Tworzecki,
Hubert*
Parties, Policies, and Democracy — *Klingemann,
Hans-Dieter*
Parting Gestures — *Pedrero, Paloma*
Parting the Curtain — *Hixson, Walter L*
The Partings of the Ways between Christianity and
Judaism and Their Significance for the Character of
Christianity — *Dunn, James D G*
A Partisan Century — *Kurzweil, Edith*
Partisan Politics, Divided Government, and the
Economy — *Alesina, Alberto*
A Partisan's Memoir — *Schulman, Faye*
The Partition Principle — *McAlpine, Trevor*
The Partner — *Grisham, John*
Partners in Change — *Read, Edward M*
y Partners in Power — *Morris, Roger*
Partners in Revolution — *Elliott, Marianne*
A Partnership for Disorder — *Liu, Xiaoyuan*
Partnerships Can Kill — *Shelton, Connie*
Partnerships in Birds — *Black, Jeffrey M*
Party Conflict and Community Development
— *Eldersveld, Samuel J*
Party Decline in America — *Coleman, John J*
A Party of Mad Fellows — *Boyle, Frank A*
The Party of Unbelief — *Luukkanen, Arto*
Party, Parliament and Personality — *Jones, Peter,
1945-*
Party Pieces — *MacAndrew, Amanda*
Party Politics and Decolonization — *Murphy, Philip*
The Party Train — *Alexander, Robert, 1949-*

Party Tricks — *Bedell, Geraldine*
The Party's Not Over — *Faux, Jeff*
c Pas De Bruit Julie — *Ray, Helene*
Pasado Meridiano — *Aguirre, Erick*
Pascal and Disbelief — *Wetsel, David*
Paschal Beverly Randolph: A Nineteenth-Century
Black American Spiritualist, Rosicrucian, and Sex
Magician — *Deveney, John Patrick*
c Pascual's Magic Pictures (Illus. by Karen Dugan)
— *Gage, Amy Glaser*
Paseo De La Reforma — *Poniatowska, Elena*
Paseos En El Horizonte — *Sanjines, Jose*
Pasion Y Farsa — *Aviles Farre, Juan*
Pass CCRN! — *Dennison, Robin*
c Pass It On (Illus. by Floyd Cooper) — *Hudson, Wade*
y Pass the Butterworms — *Cahill, Tim*
Passage to Ararat — *Arlen, Michael J*
c Passage to Freedom (Illus. by Dom Lee) — *Mochizuki,
Ken*
Passage to Modernity — *Dupre, Louis*
Passage to the New World — *Hollett, David*
Passage to Union — *Gordon, Sarah*
Passage to Vietnam. Electronic Media Version
— *Smolan, Rick*
y Passager: The Young Merlin Trilogy — *Yolen, Jane*
Passavamo Sulla Terra Leggeri — *Atzeni, Sergio*
Passchendaele: The Untold Story — *Prior, Robin*
r Passenger and Immigration Lists Index. 1996 Suppl.
The Passenger Train in the Motor Age — *Thompson,
Gregory Lee*
r Passengers and Ships Prior to 1684 — *Sheppard,
Walter Lee, Jr.*
Passing By — *Gardner, Carol Brooks*
y Passing for Black — *Kidd, Mae Street*
y Passing Higher History — *Matheson, Ian*
Passing Judgment — *Ferrell, Keith*
The Passing of Starr Faithfull — *Goodman, Jonathan*
Passing Off — *LeClair, Tom*
Passing Remarks — *Hodgman, Helen*
Passing Strange — *Citro, Joseph A*
Passing the Fictions of Identity — *Ginsberg, Elaine K*
Passing Through — *Kunitz, Stanley*
Passion and Principle — *Hodge, Jane Aiken*
y Passion and Reason — *Lazarus, Richard S*
La Passion De Charles Bovary — *Girard, Marc*
The Passion Dream Book — *Otto, Whitney*
The Passion Dream Book (Brown). Audio Version
— *Otto, Whitney*
Passion Flowers — *Vanderplank, John*
A Passion for Justice — *Solomon, Robert C*
A Passion for Life — *Chittister, Joan*
A Passion for Living — *Somersall, Alan*
A Passion for Success — *Inamori, Kazuo*
Passion for the Earth — *McDonagh, Sean*
A Passion for Wings — *Wohl, Robert*
y A Passion for Wisdom — *Solomon, Robert C*
Passion Fruit — *Limb, Sue*
y The Passion of Alice — *Grant, Stephanie*
The Passion of Chocolate — *Caton, Patrick*
The Passion of Dellie O'Barr — *Bonner, Cindy*
The Passion of Meter — *O'Donnell, Brennan*
The Passion of Pier Paolo Pasolini — *Rohdie, Sam*
Passion of the People? — *Mason, Tony*
A Passion to Oppose — *Kennedy, Brian*
y The Passion to Skate — *Bezic, Sandra*
Passionate Enlightenment — *Shaw, Miranda*
A Passionate Life — *Caldicott, Helen*
A Passionate Pen — *Downie, Jill*
Passione Dlinverno — *Salvalaggio, Nantas*
Passions and Constraints — *Holmes, Stephen F*
Passions between Women — *Donoghue, Emma*
Passions of the Voice — *Kahane, Claire*
Il Passo Del Giorno — *Deidier, Roberto*
c The Passover Journey (Illus. by Neil Waldman)
— *Goldin, Barbara Diamond*
The Passover Murder — *Harris, Lee*
r Passport Mexico — *Malat, Randy*
Passport Pour La France. 2nd Ed. — *Rouxeville,
Annie*
The Passport Society — *Matthews, Mervyn*
c Passport to Russia — *Lye, Keith*
The Past and Future of Medieval Studies — *Van
Engen, John H*
p Past and Present
The Past and the Punishments — *Yu, Hua*
The Past as Future — *Habermas, Jurgen*
y Past Forgiving — *Miklowitz, Gloria*
Past Glacial Environments — *Menzies, John*
Past Imperfect
Past Imperfect — *Carnes, Mark C*

The Past in the Present — *British and Cultural Studies
Conference (5th: 1994: Oldenburg, Germany)*
Past Lives, Future Lives — *Cockell, Jenny*
Past, Space, and Self — *Campbell, John, 1956-*
Past Tense — *Greenleaf, Stephen*
c Pasta — *Powell, Jillian*
The Pasta Bible — *Rizzi, Silvio*
The Paston Family in the Fifteenth Century. Vol. 2
— *Richmond, Colin*
Pastor Daniels Ekarte and the African Churches
Mission — *Sherwood, Marika*
Pastoral and the Poetics of Self-Contradiction
— *Haber, Judith*
The Pastoral Epistles — *Davies, Margaret*
Los Pastores: History and Performance in the
Mexican Shepherd's Play of South Texas — *Flores,
Richard R*
Pastors and Parishioners in Wurttemberg during the
Late Reformation 1581-1621 — *Tolley, Bruce*
y Pastwatch: The Redemption of Christopher Columbus
— *Card, Orson Scott*
y Pat Conroy: A Critical Companion — *Burns, Landon
C*
Pat Summerall's Sports in America — *Summerall, Pat*
c Patch and His Favorite Things — *Lodge, Jo*
c Patch Bakes a Cake — *Lodge, Jo*
c Patch Goes to the Park — *Lodge, Jo*
c Patch Grows Flowers — *Lodge, Jo*
c Patch in the Garden — *Lodge, Jo*
A Patch of Eden — *Hynes, H Patricia*
c Patch Takes a Vacation — *Lodge, Jo*
y Patches of Fire — *French, Albert*
c The Patchwork House (Illus. by Dean Griffiths)
— *Fitz-Gibbon, Sally*
Patchwork of Dreams — *Sklar, Morty*
y A Patchwork of Ghosts — *Bull, Angela*
c The Patchwork Quilt (Illus. by Jerry Pinkney)
— *Flournoy, Valerie*
r Patent, Copyright, and Trademark — *Elias, Stephen*
Patent Strategy for Researchers and Research
Managers — *Knight, H Jackson*
Patents in Imperial Russia — *Aer, Anneli*
Paterson Ewen — *Teitelbaum, Matthew*
The Path of Beauty — *Li, Tse-Hou*
c The Path of the Quiet Elk — *Stroud, Virginia A*
The Path to a Successful Retirement — *Smith, James
F*
The Path to Christian Democracy — *Cary, Noel D*
The Path to Freedom — *Collins, Michael, 1890-1922*
The Path to Love — *Chopra, Deepak*
Pathologies of Rational Choice Theory — *Green,
Donald P*
The Pathology of Drug Abuse. 2nd Ed. — *Karch,
Steven B*
Pathology of Lymph Nodes — *Weiss, Lawrence M*
Paths of a Prodigal — *Young, Richard G*
Paths of Continuity — *Lehmann, Hartmut*
Paths of Emancipation — *Birnbaum, Pierre*
Paths of Fire — *Adams, Robert McCormick*
Paths to Homelessness — *Timmer, Doug A*
A Pathway into the Holy Scripture — *Satterthwaite,
Philip E*
Pathways: Jews Who Return — *Greenberg, Richard H*
Pathways of Addiction — *Committee on Opportunities
in Drug Abuse Research*
Pathways to Literacy — *Cairney, Trevor H*
Pathways to Manhood — *Billson, Janet Mancini*
Pathways to Maturity — *Flint, Betty M*
Pathways to Paul Celan — *Rosenthal, Bianca*
Pathways to Re-Creating Religious Communities
— *Wittberg, Patricia*
y The Patience of Maigret (Norgate). Audio Version
— *Simenon, Georges*
r Patient Care Standards. 6th Ed. — *Tucker, Susan M*
Patient Confidentiality — *Saunders, Janet McGee*
The Patient in the Family — *Nelson, Hilde Lindemann*
Patient: The True Story of a Rare Illness — *Watt, Ben*
El Patio De Atras — *Gorostiza, Carlos*
Patio Gardening — *Phillips, Sue*
Patriarch: George Washington and the New American
Nation — *Smith, Richard Norton*
Patriarchal Desire and Victorian Discourse — *Walton,
Priscilla L*
Patriarchy and Economic Development — *Moghadam,
Valentine M*
r Patricia Smith's Doll Values. 12th Ed.
Patricia Wells at Home in Provence — *Wells, Patricia*
Patricians and Parvenus — *Augustine, Dolores L*
c Patrick Doyle Is Full of Blarney (Illus. by Krista
Brauckmann-Towns) — *Armstrong, Jennifer*
c Patrick Ewing — *Wiener, Paul*

Patrick Modiano — *Morris, Alan*
Patrick Pearse and the Politics of Redemption — *Moran, Sean Farrell*
Patrick White — *During, Simon*
Patrimony: A True Story — *Roth, Philip*
The Patriot: An Exhortation to Liberate America from the Barbarians — *Hart, Gary*
The Patriot Opposition to Walpole — *Gerrard, Christine*
Patriot Royal — *Pottle, Russ*
y Patriotism in America — *Leinwand, Gerald*
Patriots — *Drake, David*
The Patriot's Handbook — *Grant, George, 1954-*
Patron Behavior in Libraries — *McNeil, Beth*
Patron Saints — *Weber, Nicholas Fox*
Patronage in Renaissance Italy from 1400 to the Early Sixteenth Century — *Hollingsworth, Mary*
Patronage in Sixteenth-Century Italy — *Hollingsworth, Mary*
Patronage, Practice, and the Culture of American Science — *Slotten, Hugh Richard*
Patsy: The Life and Times of Patsy Cline — *Jones, Margaret*
y The Pattern — *Peart, Jane*
The Pattern Book — *Pickover, Clifford A*
Pattern Formation — *Chadam, John*
Pattern Formation and Lattice Gas Automata — *Lawniczak, Anna T*
Pattern-Oriented Software Architecture — *Buschmann, Frank*
Pattern Recognition. Vols. 1-4
Pattern Recognition and Image Analysis — *Gose, Earl*
Pattern Recognition and Neural Networks — *Ripley, B D*
Pattern Recognition and Prediction with Applications to Signal Characterization — *Kil, David H*
c Patterns (Illus. by Richard Maccabe) — *Stienecker, David*
Patterns in Evolution — *Levin, Roger*
Patterns in Fungal Development — *Chiu, Siu-Wai*
Patterns of Development — *Auty, Richard M*
Patterns of European Industrialization — *Sylla, Richard*
Patterns of Software Systems Failure and Success — *Jones, Capers*
Patterns of Stylistic Changes in Islamic Architecture — *Meinecke, Michael*
Patterns That Connect — *Schuster, Carl*
Patton: A Genius for War — *D'Este, Carlo*
c Patty Cat. Book and Audio Version — *DeRubertis, Barbara*
Patty Jane's House of Curl — *Landvik, Lorna*
Patty Jane's House of Curl (Landvik). Audio Version — *Landvik, Lorna*
Patty McCormick's Pieces of an American Quilt — *McCormick, Patty*
y Patty's Journey — *Norling, Donna Scott*
Paugvik: A Nineteenth-Century Native Village on Bristol Bay, Alaska — *Dumond, Don E*
Paul: A Critical Life — *Murphy-O'Connor, Jerome*
Paul among Jews and Gentiles and Other Essays — *Stendahl, Krister*
Paul and the Law — *Thielman, Frank*
Paul and the Nations — *Scott, James M*
c Paul and the Wolf (Illus. by Bill Nelson) — *Lemieux, Margo*
Paul between Damascus and Antioch — *Hengel, Martin*
Paul Bowles, Music — *Bowles, Paul*
c Paul Bunyan on the West Coast (Illus. by Kim La Fave) — *Henry, Tom, 1961-*
Paul Celan: Poet, Survivor, Jew — *Felstiner, John*
Paul Cezanne: A Life in Art — *Cahn, Isabelle*
Paul Cezanne: Portrait of My World. Electronic Media Version
Paul Gauguin: A Life — *Sweetman, David*
Paul Gauguin: Pages from the Pacific — *Druick, Douglas*
Paul in His Hellenistic Context — *Engberg-Pedersen, Troels*
Paul J. Stankard: Homage to Nature — *Dietz, Ulysses Grant*
Paul Matt Scale Airplane Drawings. Vols. 1-2 — *Matt, Paul*
Paul Metcalf: Collected Works 1956-1976 — *Metcalf, Paul*
Paul Miliukov and the Quest for a Liberal Russia 1880-1918 — *Stockdale, Melissa Kirschke*
Paul Muldoon — *Kendall, Tim*
Paul Nash: Aerial Creatures — *Hall, Charles*
Paul Newman: A Biography — *Lax, Eric*

Paul Newman: The Unauthorized Biography — *Quirk, Lawrence J*
Paul on Marriage and Celibacy — *Deming, Will*
Paul on the Mystery of Israel — *Harrington, Daniel J*
y Paul Revere's Ride (Estell). Audio Version — *Fischer, David Hackett*
Paul Ricoeur: His Life and His Work — *Reagan, Charles E*
Paul the Apostle. Vols. 1-2 — *Penna, Romano*
Paul: The Mind of the Apostle — *Wilson, A N*
Paul Valery: Charmes — *Gifford, Paul*
Paula — *Allende, Isabel*
r Paulding County, Ohio Census Index 1830, 1840, 1850, 1860
Paulina 1880 — *Jouve, Pierre Jean*
Paul's Idea of Community. Rev. Ed. — *Banks, Robert*
Paul's Letter to the Philippians — *Fee, Gordon D*
Paul's Letter to the Romans — *Stuhlmacher, Peter*
Paul's Rhetoric in 1 Corinthians 15 — *Saw, Insawn*
c Paul's World — *Shirrefs, Mark*
Pausanias' Greece — *Arafat, K W*
Pavement for My Pillow — *Kitch, Chris*
Pavilions of Plenty — *Haddow, Robert H*
c Pavlova's Gift (Illus. by Victoria Berdichevsky) — *Trottier, Maxine*
c The Paw Thing (Illus. by Keith McEwan) — *Jennings, Paul*
Pawa Na Pipel! — *Matane, Paulias*
y The Pawnee — *Lacey, Theresa Jensen*
Pay Any Price — *Gardner, Lloyd C*
Pay Dirt — *Brown, Rita Mae*
Pay for Results — *Jorgensen, Karen*
Pay or Play — *Boorstin, Jon*
Pay Severance or Die — *Erickson, Tyler*
Payback — *Kelly, Thomas*
Payback: The Conspiracy to Destroy Michael Milken and His Financial Revolution — *Fischel, Daniel*
Payback: The Logic of Retribution in Melanesian Religions — *Trompf, G W*
Paying for Inequality — *Glyn, Andrew*
Paying the Price of Freedom — *Hunefeldt, Christine*
PBS: Behind the Screen — *Jarvik, Laurence*
p PBS Teacher Connex
PC Buyer's Handbook: Summer 1996 — *Foreman, Gordon P*
r PC Magazine 1997 Computer Buyer's Guide
r PC Magazine Network Buyer's Guide — *Strategic Research Corporation*
PC Magazine Visual Basic Programmer's Guide to the Win32 API — *Appleman, Daniel*
PC Multimedia — *Botto, Francis*
PCR Cloning Protocols — *White, Bruce A*
PCR Protocols for Emerging Infectious Diseases — *Persing, David H*
PCR Sequencing Protocols — *Rapley, Ralph*
y PCs for Busy People — *Einstein, David*
y PCs for Dummies. 4th Ed.
The PDMA Handbook of New Product Development — *Rosenau, Milton*
Peace after Abortion — *Torre-Bueno, Ava*
Peace and Disarmament — *Fanning, Richard W*
Peace and Its Discontents — *Said, Edward*
Peace by Peaceful Means — *Galtung, Johan*
The Peace Dividend — *Gleditsch, Nils P*
Peace-Keeping in a Peace Process — *Amer, Ramses*
y Peace, Land, Bread — *Vail, John J*
Peace of Heart — *Kirvan, John*
Peace Operations — *United States. General Accounting Office*
The Peace Powers Act (S.5) and the National Security Revitalization Act (H.R. 7) — *United States. Congress. Senate. Committee on Foreign Relations*
The Peace Progressives and American Foreign Relations — *Johnson, Robert David*
Peace Support Operations and the U.S. Military — *Quinn, Dennis J*
Peace without Victory for the Allies 1918-1932 — *Moore, Sara*
c Peacebound Trains (Illus. by Chris K Soentpiet) — *Balgassi, Haemi*
A Peaceful and Working People — *French, William E*
Peacekeeping and the Role of Russia in Eurasia — *Jonson, Lena*
The Peacemaker's Journey (Swamp). Audio Version
Peacemaking and Peacekeeping in Yugoslavia — *Rossanet, Bertrand De*
Peacemaking, Peacekeeping and Coalition Warfare — *Mokhtari, Fariborz L*
The Peacock Rider — *Gordon, Katharine*
c Peacocks (Illus. by Richard R Hewett) — *Berman, Ruth*

The Peale Family — *Miller, Lillian B*
c The Peanut Butter Gang (Illus. by Catherine Siracusa) — *Siracusa, Catherine*
Pearl — *Bigsby, Christopher*
Pearl — *Crosbie, Lynn*
Pearl: An Edition with Verse Translation
The Pearl Book — *Matlins, Antoinette L*
Pearl from the Dragon's Mouth — *Sun, Cecile Chu-Chin*
c Pearl Harbor Child — *Nicholson, Dorinda Makanaonalani*
Pearl S. Buck: A Cultural Biography — *Conn, Peter*
yr The Pearl. The Red Pony. Electronic Media Version — *Steinbeck, John*
c Pearl's First Prize Plant (Illus. by A Delaney) — *Delaney, A*
c Pearls of Lutra (Illus. by Allan Curless) — *Jacques, Brian*
The Pearls on Coromandel — *Bhattacharya, Keron*
Pears, Lake, Sun — *Solomon, Sandy*
Peasant and French — *Lehning, James R*
Peasant and Nation — *Mallon, Florencia E*
Peasant Economic Development within the English Manorial System — *Raftis, J A*
The Peasant in Economic Thought — *Forget, Evelyn L*
Peasant Metropolis — *Hoffmann, David L*
Peasant Power in China — *Kelliher, Daniel*
Peasantry to Capitalism — *Hoppe, Goran*
Peasants and Landlords in Later Medieval England — *Fryde, E B*
Peasants and Monks in British India — *Pinch, William R*
Peasants and Tobacco in the Dominican Republic 1870-1930 — *Baud, Michiel*
Peasants into Frenchmen — *Weber, Eugen Joseph*
Peasants, Politics, and the Formation of Mexico's National State — *Guardino, Peter F*
c Peau D'Ane — *Perrault, Charles*
La Peau De Chagrin — *Balzac, Honore De*
c The Pebble in My Pocket (Illus. by Chris Coady) — *Hooper, Meredith*
Peccato, Penitenza, Perdono — *Di Simplicio, Oscar*
Le Pecheur D'Eau — *Goffette, Guy*
c Peck, Slither and Slide (Illus. by Suse MacDonald) — *MacDonald, Suse*
Pecking Order — *Berthoud, Joy*
Peckinpah: The Western Films: A Reconsideration — *Seydor, Paul*
A Peculiar Humanism — *Wiethoff, William E*
A Peculiar People — *Clapp, Rodney*
Peculiar Power — *Levenduski, Cristine*
Pedagogy of Praxis — *Gadotti, Moacir*
Pedagogy, Praxis, Ulysses — *Newman, Robert D, 1951-*
Pedagogy, Symbolic Control, and Identity — *Bernstein, Basil B*
c Pedal Power — *Hautzig, David*
c Pedaling Along — *Otfinoski, Steve*
Pederasty and Pedagogy in Archaic Greece — *Percy, William Armstrong*
Pediatric Behavioral Neurology — *Frank, Yitzchak*
Pediatric GI Problems — *Hyman, Paul E*
Pediatric Neoplasia — *Parham, David M*
Pediatric Otolaryngology for the General Otolaryngologist — *Hotaling, Andrew J*
Pedophiles and Priests — *Jenkins, Philip*
c Pedrito's Day (Illus. by Luis Garay) — *Garay, Luis*
c Pedro and the Monkey (Illus. by Michael Hays) — *San Souci, Robert D*
Pedro Calderon De La Barca's The Fake Astrologer — *Calderon De La Barca, Pedro*
r Pedro Menendez De Aviles — *Lyon, Eugene*
Pedro Nunes 1502-1578 — *Martyn, John R C*
Pedro the Cruel of Castile 1350-1369 — *Estow, Clara*
c Peekaboo Babies — *Leneouanic, Lionel*
y Peeling the Onion — *Orr, Wendy*
The Peenemunde Wind Tunnels — *Wegener, Peter P*
Peep O'Day Boys and Defenders — *Miller, David W*
c Peeping Beauty. Book and Audio Version — *Auch, Mary Jane*
Peer Mediation — *Ferrara, Judith M*
Peer Mediation. Rev. Ed. — *Schrumpf, Fred*
Pegaz Zdebiat — *Baranczak, Stanislaw*
Peggy Guggenheim: A Collector's Album — *Tacou-Rumney, Laurence*
Les Peintures Des Necropoles Romaines D'Abila Et Du Nord De La Jordanie. Vols. 1-2 — *Barbet, Alix*
r Les Peintures Flamande, Hollandaise Et Allemande XVe, XVIe, XVIIe Siecles — *Foucart, Jacques*
Peirce Et La Signification — *Chauvire, Christiane*
Peirce, Science, Signs — *Kevelson, Roberta*

Peirce's Philosophical Perspectives — *Potter, Vincent G*

Peking Story — *Kidd, David*

Pel and the Parked Car — *Hebden, Mark*

Pel Bell Nord Glacat — *Pi De Cabanyes, Oriol*

Pelagonius and Latin Veterinary Terminology in the Roman Empire — *Adams, J N*

Pellegrino Tibaldi E Il S Fedele Di Milano — *Della Torre, Stefano*

Il Pellicano Di Pietra — *Prisco, Michele*

Pelon Maantiede — *Kauranen, Anja*

Pelot Family Genealogy — *Colket, Meredith B, Jr.*

Peltse and Pentameron — *Dibrova, Volodymyr*

Pelvic Locomotor Dysfunction — *DeFranca, George G*

Pelzdamen: Weiblichkeitsbilder Bei Thomas Mann Und Leopold Von Sacher-Masoch — *Rudloff, Holger*

The Pena Files — *Pena, Octavio G*

c Penalty Shot — *Christopher, Matt*

Penance — *Housewright, David*

c Pencils, Poems and Princesses — *Parvin, Joy*

y Pendragon (Davidson). Audio Version — *Lawhead, Stephen R*

Pendragon's Banner — *Hollick, Helen*

y Penelope — *Farmer, Penelope*

Penelope Voyages — *Lawrence, Karen R*

c Penguin — *Newton, Jill*

r The Penguin Atlas of African History. New Ed., Rev. Ed. 1995 — *McEvedy, Colin*

Penguin Book of Food and Drink — *Levy, Paul, 1941-*

y The Penguin Book of Historic Speeches — *MacArthur, Brian*

The Penguin Book of International Gay Writing — *Mitchell, Mark*

The Penguin Book of International Women's Stories — *Figes, Kate*

The Penguin Book of Irish Comic Writing — *Mac Anna, Ferdia*

y The Penguin Book of Modern Fantasy by Women — *Williams, A Susan*

y The Penguin Book of Scottish Folktales — *Philip, Neil*

y The Penguin Book of Women's Humor — *Barreca, Regina*

yr The Penguin Dictionary of Jokes — *Metcalf, Fred*

r The Penguin Dictionary of Music. 6th Ed. — *Jacobs, Arthur*

r The Penguin Dictionary of Saints. 3rd Ed. — *Attwater, Donald*

r The Penguin Dictionary of Symbols — *Chevalier, Jean*

yr The Penguin Dictionary of Twentieth-Century Quotations — *Cohen, J M*

yr The Penguin Encyclopedia of Classical Civilizations — *Cotterell, Arthur*

Penguin English Verse. Vol. 1. Audio Version — *Driver, Paul*

Penguin English Verse. Vol. 3. Audio Version

Penguin English Verse. Vols. 1-6. Audio Version — *Driver, Paul*

r The Penguin Guide to Compact Discs — *March, Ivan*

r The Penguin Guide to Jazz on CD — *Cook, Richard*

yr The Penguin Historical Atlas of Ancient Egypt — *Manley, Bill*

yr The Penguin Historical Atlas of Ancient Greece — *Morkot, Robert*

r The Penguin Historical Atlas of Ancient Rome — *Scarre, Chris*

yr The Penguin Historical Atlas of the Dinosaurs — *Benton, M J*

Penguin Modern Poets 8

c Penguin Pete (Illus. by Marcus Pfister) — *Pfister, Marcus*

c Penguin Pete's New Friends (Illus. by Marcus Pfister) — *Pfister, Marcus*

Penguin Portrait — *Hare, Steve*

c Penguins — *Kalman, Bobbie*

c Penguins — *Love, John*

c Penguins — *Mettler, Rene*

Pennies from Heaven — *Sanjek, Russell*

The Penninsula Campaign of 1862 — *Miller, William J*

The Pennsy in the Steel City — *Kobus, Ken*

The Pennsy Middle Division in HO Scale — *Frary, Dave*

c Pennsylvania — *Thompson, Kathleen*

r Pennsylvania Births Lebanon County 1714-1800 — *Humphrey, John T*

c A Penny for a Hundred (Illus. by Mary Beth Owens) — *Pochocki, Ethel*

c Penny Hen. Book and Audio Version — *DeRubertis, Barbara*

The Penny Whistle Any Day Is a Holiday Party Book — *Brokaw, Meredith*

Penological Esperanto and Sentencing Parochialism — *Davies, Malcolm*

Pensamiento De La Liberacion — *Gomez-Martinez, Jose Luis*

Pensee, Langage Et Communaute — *Seymour, Michel*

Pension Schemes and Pension Funds in the United Kingdom — *Blake, David, 1954-*

Der Pentateuch: Die Geschichte Seiner Erforschung Neben Einer Auswertung — *Houtman, Cees*

Pentecost Alley — *Perry, Anne*

Penthesilea — *Kleist, Heinrich Von*

c People (Illus. by Sallie Alane Reason) — *Perham, Molly*

c The People (Illus. by Ted Finger) — *Pickering, Robert*

People and Environment — *Morse, Stephen*

People and Other Animals

c People and the Planet — *Wasserman, Pamela*

A People Apart — *Frank, Daniel H*

c A People Apart (Illus. by Andrew Stawicki) — *Kenna, Kathleen*

People for Lunch. Spoilt — *Hammick, Georgina*

The People from Heaven — *Sanford, John B*

c People in the Country — *Bryant-Mole, Karen*

y People in the News 1996

c People in the Town — *Bryant-Mole, Karen*

People, Land, and Community — *Hannum, Hildegarde*

c People of Corn (Illus. by Carla Golembe) — *Gerson, Mary-Joan*

People of Legend — *Annerino, John*

The People of Providence — *Parker, Tony*

c People of Salmon and Cedar (Illus. by Deborah Cooper) — *Hirschi, Ron*

People of Sunlight, People of Starlight — *Gordon, Bryan C*

c People of the Bible (Illus. by Letizia Galli) — *Ziefert, Allison*

People of the Book — *Jeffrey, David Lyle*

People of the Book — *Rubin-Dorsky, Jeffrey*

People of the Dalles — *Boyd, Robert*

People of the Great Ocean — *Houghton, Philip*

People of the Great Plains — *Miller, Peter, 1934-*

People of the Peyote — *Schaefer, Stacy B*

People of the Plow — *McCann, James C*

y People of the Silence — *Gear, Kathleen O'Neal*

People of the Silence. Audio Version — *Gear, Kathleen O'Neal*

y People of the West — *Duncan, Dayton*

People on the Prowl — *Collyer, Jaime*

People, Plans, and Policies — *Gans, Herbert J*

y People Power — *Terkel, Susan Neiburg*

People Skills for Library Managers — *Wilson, Lucile*

A People Starved — *Murphy, Ignatius*

People, the Environment and Responsibility — *Amalric, F*

The People vs. Larry Flynt — *Alexander, Scott*

The People Who Discovered Columbus — *Keegan, William F*

People Who Lived in Big Houses — *Coupland, Gary*

y People with AIDS — *Stewart, Gail B*

People with Dirty Hands — *Chotzinoff, Robin*

c People with Disabilities — *Sanders, Pete*

yr The Peoplepedia: The Ultimate Reference on the American People — *Krantz, Les*

y The People's Choice — *Greenfield, Jeff*

The People's Church — *MacEoin, Gary*

People's Companion to the Breviary. Vols. 1-2 — *Carmelites of Indianapolis*

A People's Conquest — *Paludan, Philip Shaw*

A People's Game — *Moorhouse, Geoffrey*

r The People's Guide to Deadly Drug Interactions — *Graedon, Joe*

The People's Health — *Henig, Robin Marantz*

The People's Historian — *Brundage, Anthony*

People's Initiatives for Sustainable Development — *Samad, Syed Abdus*

r The Peoples of Africa — *Olson, James Stuart*

c Peoples of the Arctic — *Low, Robert*

c Peoples of the Desert — *Low, Robert*

c Peoples of the Mountains — *Low, Robert*

c Peoples of the Rain Forest — *Low, Robert*

c Peoples of the Savanna — *Low, Robert*

People's Playground — *Barnard, Jill*

A People's Tragedy — *Figes, Orlando*

The People's Welfare — *Novak, William J*

The People's Writer — *Mixon, Wayne*

Peopling Indiana — *Taylor, Robert M, Jr.*

The Peopling of Africa — *Newman, James L*

Peopling the Plains — *Shortridge, James R*

Peopling the Purple Land — *Kleinpenning, Jan M G*

c Pepe's Dog (Illus. by Martin Salisbury) — *Santos, Helen*

Pepita Jimenez — *Valera, Juan*

c Peppe the Lamplighter (Illus. by Ted Lewin) — *Bartone, Elisa*

c El Pequeno Rey De Las Flores — *Pacovska, Kveta*

The Pequot War — *Cave, Alfred A*

Per Una Letteratura Giustificata — *Pustianaz, Marco*

Per Via Di Sguardo — *Ramous, Mario*

r Perceived Exertion — *Noble, Bruce J*

Perception and Reality — *Yolton, John W*

Le Pere Vaincu, La Meduse Et Les Fils Castres — *Vanasse, Andre*

Perec Ou La Cicatrice — *Duvignaud, Jean*

y The Peregrine Reader — *Vause, Mikel*

Peregrine's Rest — *Gostin, Jennifer*

Pereira Declares — *Tabucchi, Antonio*

Peremena Mest — *Gurskii, Lev*

Perennial Ground Covers — *MacKenzie, David S*

r Perennials (Eyewitness Handbooks)

Perennials for the Lower Midwest — *Haggard, Ezra*

Perfect Angel — *Margolis, Seth*

The Perfect Baby — *McGee, Glenn*

Perfect Country Rooms — *O'Reilly, Emma-Louise*

Perfect Enemies — *Gallagher, John*

A Perfect Execution — *Binding, Tim*

Perfect Happiness — *Billington, Rachel*

Perfect Happiness. Audio Version — *Billington, Rachel*

Perfect Happiness (Beckinsale). Audio Version — *Billington, Rachel*

A Perfect Harmony — *Caras, Roger A*

y The Perfect Match — *Anderson, Wayne*

A Perfect Match — *Lisle, Julia*

c Perfect Pancakes if You Please (Illus. by Richard Egielski) — *Wise, William*

Perfect Plants — *Phillips, Roger*

c The Perfect Present (Illus. by Michael Hague) — *Hague, Michael*

The Perfect Recipe Baking Book — *Jaffe, Murray*

The Perfect Storm — *Junger, Sebastian*

The Perfect Vehicle — *Pierson, Melissa Holbrook*

The Perfect Yankee — *Larsen, Don*

The Perfectible Body — *Dutton, Kenneth R*

Perfection in New Testament Theology — *Walters, John R*

The Perfection of Solitude — *Jotischky, Andrew*

Perfection of the Morning — *Butala, Sharon*

Perfectly Criminal — *Edwards, Martin*

Perfils Cruels — *Simo, Isabel-Clara*

Performance: A Critical Introduction — *Carlson, Marvin*

Performance and Cultural Politics — *Diamond, Elin*

Performance Assessment in Academic Libraries — *Morgan, Steve*

Performance-Based Curriculum for Science — *Burz, Helen L*

Performance Breakthroughs for Adolescents with Learning Disabilities or ADD — *Markel, Geraldine*

The Performance of Conviction — *Graham, Kenneth J E*

Performance Poems — *Moses, Brian*

Performance Power — *Kruger, Irtraud Tarr*

Performance Standards for Music — *MENC Committee on Performance Standards*

Performances — *Dening, Greg*

y Performing and Responding — *Howard, John*

Performing Arts: Music — *Newsom, Iris*

Performing Music — *Dunsby, Jonathan*

Performing Nostalgia — *Bennett, Susan*

y Performing Rites — *Frith, Simon*

Perheen Vuosisata — *Haggman, Kai*

The Pericardium: A Comprehensive Textbook — *Spodick, David H*

The Perilous Cemetery — *Black, Nancy B*

Perilous Friends — *Epstein, Carole*

Perilous Prospects — *Cordesman, Anthony H*

c The Period Book (Illus. by Debbie Palen) — *Gravelle, Karen*

Period Costume for Stage and Screen — *Hunnisett, Jean*

r The Period House — *Lawrence, Richard Russell*

Period Rooms in the Metropolitan Museum of Art — *Peck, Amelia*

The Periodic Kingdom — *Atkins, P W*

Periodical Literature in Nineteenth-Century America — *Price, Kenneth M*

r Periodicals in Print 1996

Periodicity and Stochastic Trends in Economic Time Series — *Franses, Philip Hans*

Peripatetic Rhetoric after Aristotle — *Fortenbaugh, William W*

y Les Peripeties De P. Le Prophete — *Duchesne, Christiane*

Peripheral Migrants — *Martinez, Samuel*
Peripheral Vision — *Green, Charles*
Peripheral Visions — *Bateson, Mary Catherine*
Perks and Parachutes — *Tarrant, John*
Perl 5 How-To — *Glover, Mike*
Perl 5 Interactive Course — *Orwant, Jon*
The Permanence of the Political — *Schwartz, Joseph M*
r Permanent Magnet Motor Technology — *Gieras, Jacek F*
Permanent Midnight — *Stahl, Jerry*
Permanent Pilgrims — *Yamba, C Bawa*
Permanently Bard — *Harrison, Tony*
The Peroxisome: A Vital Organelle — *Masters, Colin*
Perpetual Mirage — *Castleberry, May*
Perpetuating the Pork Barrel — *Stein, Robert M*
La Perruque De Dom Juan — *May, Georges*
Perry Mason: The Authorship and Reproduction of a Popular Hero — *Bounds, J Dennis*
c Perry Poops! (Illus. by Bernadette Gervais) — *Pittau, Francesco*
Persecuting Zeal — *Cooke, Dennis*
y El Perseguidor De La Luz — *Swaan, Bram De*
Persephone Returns — *Wilkinson, Tanya*
Perseus 2.0. Comprehensive Ed. Electronic Media Version
Perseus 2.0. Concise Ed. Electronic Media Version
y The Persian Empire — *Zeinert, Karen*
The Persian Gulf Region in the Twenty First Century — *Alaolmolki, Nozar*
c Persian Gulf War — *Gay, Kathlyn*
The Persian Pickle Club — *Dallas, Sandra*
y The Persian Pickle Club (Kelly). Audio Version — *Dallas, Sandra*
Persians (Hall) — *Aeschylus*
Persistence and Change in the Protestant Establishment — *Pyle, Ralph E*
The Persistence of Purgatory — *Fenn, Richard K*
The Persistence of Unemployment — *Jones, Stephen R G*
A Persistent Spirit — *Stephenson, Peter H*
Persistent Underdevelopment — *Mandle, Jay R*
Person-Centered Leadership — *Plas, Jeanne M*
Personal and Wireless Communications — *Park, Kun Il*
The Personal Correspondence of Sam Houston. Vol. 1 — *Houston, Sam*
Personal Existence after Death — *Geis, Robert J*
Personal History — *Graham, Katharine*
Personal History (Graham). Audio Version — *Graham, Katharine*
Personal Memoirs of U.S. Grant — *Grant, Ulysses S*
Personal Pronouns in Present-Day English — *Wales, Katie*
The Personal Rule of Charles I — *Sharpe, Kevin*
Personal Speech-Ethics in the Epistle of James — *Baker, William R*
The Personal Touch — *Williams, Terrie*
Personal Videoconferencing — *Rosen, Evan*
Personal Writings — *Ignatius, of Loyola, Saint*
Personalism and the Politics of Culture — *Grant, Patrick*
r The Personalities of Melvin Hill Cemetery, Phelps, Ontario County, New York — *Burnisky, David L*
Personality and Belief — *Magill, Gerard*
Personality in Greek Epic, Tragedy, and Philosophy — *Gill, Christopher*
The Personality of Ireland — *Evans, E Estyn*
Personality: Theory and Research. 7th Ed. — *Pervin, Lawrence A*
Personhood: Orthodox Christianity and the Connection Between Body, Mind, and Soul — *Chirban, John T*
Personnel Economics — *Lazear, Edward P*
Personnel Management. 3rd Ed. — *Torrington, Derek*
Persons, Animals, and Fetuses — *Forrester, Mary Gore*
Persons with Disabilities — *Wiener, Joshua M*
Perspectivas: Hispanic Ministry — *Deck, Allan Figueroa*
Perspectives De La Recherche Sur Le XVIIe Siecle Francais Aujourd'hui — *Dotoli, Giovanni*
Perspectives in Quantum Hall Effects — *Sarma, Sankar Das*
Perspectives in Urban Ecology — *Webb, Elizabeth A*
Perspectives of Oil and Gas — *Colitti, Marcello*
Perspectives on Akira Kurosawa — *Goodwin, James*
Perspectives on Arabic Linguistics VII
Perspectives on Case Management Practice — *Austen, Carol D*
Perspectives on Pacifism — *Smock, David R*

Perspectives on Philippine Policy towards China — *Carino, Theresa C*
Perspectives on Philippine Poverty — *Balisacan, Arsenio M*
Perspectives on Quantum Reality — *Clifton, Rob*
Perspectives on Stanley Kubrick — *Falsetto, Mario*
Persuasion — *Austen, Jane*
Persuasion (Scacchi). Audio Version — *Austen, Jane*
r Persuasive Fictions — *Walker, Greg*
Perturbation Methods in the Computer Age — *Wilcox, David C*
c Peru — *Allard, Denise*
c Peru — *Falconer, Kieran*
c Peru — *Parker, Edward*
r Peru (Insight Guides)
The Peru Reader — *Starn, Orin*
Peru Y Ecuador — *Denegri Luna, Felix*
A Peruvian Psychiatric Hospital — *Stein, William W*
Perversion and Utopia — *Whitebrook, Joel*
The Perversion of Autonomy — *Gaylin, Willard*
El Peso De La Lengua Espanola En El Mundo
Peso Perfecto — *Chopra, Deepak*
Pest Control — *Fitzhugh, Bill*
Pest Management at the Crossroads — *Benbrook, Charles M*
Pesticide Formulation and Adjuvant Technology — *Foy, Chester L*
Pesticides and the Immune System — *Repetto, Robert*
Pesticides in Ground Water — *Barbash, Jack E*
c Pet Detectives — *Hunter, Jana*
c Pet Parade (Illus. by Blanche Sims) — *Giff, Patricia Reilly*
c The Pet Person (Illus. by Tony Ross) — *Willis, Jeanne*
c The Pet-Sitters (Illus. by Bob Dorsey) — *Schecter, Ellen*
c The Pet That I Want (Illus. by John Magino) — *Packard, Mary*
c Pete Sampras — *Rambeck, Richard*
c Pete the Puppy — *Buck, Gisela*
Peter: Apostle for the Whole Church — *Perkins, Pheme*
Peter Brook — *Hunt, Albert*
Peter De Vries and Surrealism — *Campion, Dan*
Peter Des Roches: An Alien in English Politics 1205-1238 — *Vincent, Nicholas*
The Peter Martyr Library. Vol. 1 — *Vermigli, Pietro Martire*
The Peter Martyr Library. Vols. 1-2 — *Vermigli, Pietro Martire*
Peter Mettler: Making the Invisible Visible — *Pitschen, Salome*
r Peter Milton: Complete Prints 1960-1996 — *Johnson, Robert Flynn*
Peter Munk: The Making of a Modern Tycoon — *Rumball, Donald*
Peter Nevsky and the True Story of the Russian Moon Landing — *Batchelor, John Calvin*
Peter Norton's Guide to Windows 95/NT 4 Programming with MFC — *McGregor, Rob*
c Peter Piglet (Illus. by John A Rowe) — *Rowe, John A*
c Peter Rabbit and Friends Study Guide — *Ward, Ann*
c The Peter Rabbit and Friends Treasury — *Potter, Beatrix*
c Peter Rabbit's Math Garden. Electronic Media Version
c Peter Spier's Rain — *Spier, Peter*
y Peter the Great (Kandinsky). Audio Version — *Troyat, Henri*
c Peter's Chair (Illus. by Ezra Jack Keats) — *Keats, Ezra Jack*
c Peter's Place (Illus. by Michael Foreman) — *Grindley, Sally*
Petersburg, Crucible of Cultural Revolution — *Clark, Katerina*
yr Peterson's Distance Learning 1997
r Peterson's Internships 1996
yr Peterson's Paying Less for College 1996
yr Peterson's Study Abroad 1996
r Peterson's Summer Opportunities for Kids and Teenagers 1996
yr Peterson's Top Colleges for Science. 1st Ed.
c Pete's Puddles (Illus. by Pierre Pratt) — *Roche, Hannah*
Le Petit Aigle A Tete Blanche — *Lalonde, Robert*
The Petite Bourgeoisie in Europe 1780-1914 — *Crossick, Geoffrey*
La Petite Phrase Et La Longue Phrase — *Bonnefoy, Yves*
Petrarch: The Canzoniere — *Petrarca, Francesco*
Petrarch's Songbook — *Petrarca, Francesco*
c Petrified Forest National Park — *Petersen, David*

y Petrified Lightning and More Amazing Stories from Our Fascinating Earth — *Seff, Philip*
y Petroleum Geochemistry and Geology. 2nd Ed. — *Hunt, John M*
Petrolio — *Pasolini, Pier Paolo*
Petrus Alfonsi and His Medieval Readers — *Tolan, John Victor*
Petrus Christus: Renaissance Master of Bruges — *Ainsworth, Maryan W*
Pets — *Burgess, Lynne*
c Pets (Illus. by Tony Ross) — *Ross, Tony*
c Pets (Time-Life)
Il Pettine — *Pariani, Laura*
c El Pez Arco Iris (Illus. by Marcus Pfister) — *Pfister, Marcus*
c El Pez Arco Iris Al Rescate! (Illus. by Marcus Pfister) — *Pfister, Marcus*
Pezsdules — *Kabdebo, Tamas*
r The PFA Footballers Factfile — *Hagman, Barry*
The PGA Manual of Golf — *Wren, Gary*
Phage Display of Peptides and Proteins — *Kay, Brian K*
Phanerozoic Faunal and Floral Realms of the Earth — *Meyerhoff, Arthur A*
y Phantom — *Pike, Christopher*
The Phantom Church and Other Stories from Romania — *Farnoaga, Georgiana*
The Phantom Father — *Gifford, Barry*
Phantom Formations — *Redfield, Marc*
The Phantom Gringo Boat — *Kane, Stephanie C*
Phantom Islands of the Atlantic — *Johnson, Donald S*
Phantom of the Opera — *Leroux, Gaston*
Phantom Pain — *Sherman, Richard A*
c The Phantom Tollbooth (Illus. by Jules Feiffer) — *Juster, Norton*
y Phantoms of the Night — *Gilliam, Richard*
Pharaoh, Pharaoh — *Andrews, Claudia Emerson*
Pharaoh's Daughter — *Ni Dhomhnaill, Nuala*
Pharisees, Scribes and Sadducees — *Saldarini, Anthony J*
Pharmaceutical Calculations. 10th Ed. — *Stoklosa, Mitchell J*
Pharmaceutical Dosage Forms: Disperse Systems. 2nd Ed., Vols. 1-2 — *Lieberman, Herbert A, 1920-*
p Pharmaceutical News
The Pharmacologic Management of Heart Disease — *Kupersmith, Joel*
r PharmFacts for Nurses
Phase Equilibria Diagrams. Vol. 12
r Phase Equilibria Diagrams: 1996 Cumulative Indexes to Annuals '91-'93 — *Clevinger, Mary A*
The Pheasant Cap Master — *Defoort, Carine*
y A Phenomenally Phrank History of Philosophy — *Farman, John*
Phenomenology, Interpretation, and Community — *Langsdorf, Lenore*
The Phenomenon of Teilhard — *Lane, David H*
y Phil Simms on Passing — *Simms, Phil*
Philadelphia Flowers — *Whiteman, Roberta Hill*
Philadelphia Mental Health and Mental Retardation Program
p The Philatelic Exporter
Philip Hart: The Conscience of the Senate — *O'Brien, Michael, 1943-*
Philip Johnson: Recent Work — *Kipnis, Jeffrey*
Philip K. Dick: Contemporary Critical Interpretations — *Umland, Samuel J*
Philip Larkin: A Writer's Life — *Motion, Andrew*
Philip Larkin and His Bibliographer
Philip Neri: The Fire of Joy — *Turks, Paul*
Philip Roth and the Jews — *Cooper, Alan*
Philipp Melanchthon: Eine Gestalt Der Reformationszeit — *Scheible, Heinz*
Philipp Melanchthons Sicht Der Rhetorik — *Berwald, Olaf*
Philipp Otto Runge, Caspar David Friedrich — *Bluhm, Andreas*
Philippe De Commynes: Un Historien A L'Aube Des Temps Modernes — *Dufournet, Jean*
Philippe Djian: 37° 2 Le Matin — *Platten, David*
Philippe Egalite — *Lever, Evelyne*
Philippi. Vol. 1 — *Pilhofer, Peter*
Philippians — *Thielman, Frank*
Philippicae I-VII. Vols. 1-2 — *Cochlaeus, Johannes*
The Philippine Economy — *Vos, Rob*
The Philippine Temptation — *San Juan, E*
r Philippines Business — *Hinkelman, Edward G*
r The Philippines in World War II and to Independence (December 8, 1941-July 4, 1946). 2nd Ed., Vols. 1-2 — *Netzorg, Morton J*

c Philipp's Birthday Book (Illus. by Hanne Turk)
— *Clements, Andrew*

r Philip's Atlas of the Oceans — *Pernetta, John*

Philo and the Church Fathers — *Runia, David T*

Philo Judaeus: His Universe of Discourse — *Cohen, Naomi G*

Philodemus and Poetry — *Obbink, Dirk*

Philology and Philosophy — *Diels, Hermann*

Philosophers Who Believe — *Clark, Kelly James*

Philosophical Foundations of the Social Sciences — *Kincaid, Harold*

Philosophical Foundations of Tort Law — *Owen, David G*

Philosophical Historicism and the Betrayal of First Philosophy — *Page, Carl*

Philosophical Idealism and Christian Belief — *Sell, Alan P F*

Philosophical Naturalism — *Papineau, David*

The Philosophical Papers of Alan Donagan. Vols. 1-2 — *Donagan, Alan*

Philosophical Perspectives on Computer-Mediated Communication — *Ess, Charles*

Philosophical Perspectives on Language — *Stainton, Robert J*

Philosophical Problems in Health Care — *Greaves, David*

A Philosophical Testament — *Grene, Marjorie*

Philosophical Writings — *Nietzsche, Friedrich*

La Philosophie Dans Le Boudoir — *Sade, Marquis De*

r Die Philosophie Des 17. Jahrhunderts. Pt. 2, Vols. 1-2 — *Schobinger, Jean-Pierre*

La Philosophie Et Son Histoire — *Boss, Gilbert*

La Philosophie Medievale — *Libera, Alain De*

La Philosophie Negro-Africaine — *Bidima, Jean Godefroy*

Philosophies of Music in Medieval Islam — *Shehadi, Fadlou*

Philosophy and the Belief in a Life after Death — *Paterson, R W K*

Philosophy and the Grammar of Religious Belief — *Tessin, Timothy*

Philosophy and the Mirror of Nature — *Rorty, Richard*

Philosophy in Christian Antiquity — *Stead, Christopher*

Philosophy in Experience — *Hart, Richard E*

Philosophy in the Mass Age — *Grant, George Parkin*

Philosophy of a Concerned Academic — *Simpson, William Brand*

The Philosophy of Artificial Life — *Boden, Margaret A*

The Philosophy of Classical Yoga — *Feuerstein, Georg*

r The Philosophy of Education — *Chambliss, J J*

The Philosophy of Jonathan Edwards — *Daniel, Stephen H*

The Philosophy of Law — *Schauer, Frederick*

The Philosophy of Mathematics — *Hart, W D*

Philosophy of Mathematics and Mathematical Practice in the Seventeenth Century — *Mancosu, Paolo*

Philosophy of Mind — *Kim, Jaegwon*

Philosophy of Religion — *Stewart, Melville Y*

The Philosophy of Religion: A Buddhist Perspective — *Sharma, Arvind*

The Philosophy of Religion and Advaita Vedanta — *Sharma, Arvind*

The Philosophy of Science — *Papineau, David*

Philosophy of Sexuality — *Marietta, Don E*

The Philosophy of Simone De Beauvoir — *Bergoffen, Debra B*

The Philosophy of Social Science — *Hollis, Martin*

Philosophy of Technology — *Ferre, Frederick*

Philosophy, Science and Ideology in Political Thought — *Morrice, David*

Phineas F. Bresee: His Life in Methodism, the Holiness Movement, and the Church of the Nazarene — *Bangs, Carl*

Phineas Finn — *Trollope, Anthony*

The Phishing Manual — *Budnick, Dean*

y Phobias: Everything You Wanted to Know, but Were Afraid to Ask — *Monroe, Judy*

c Phoebe's Fabulous Father (Illus. by Bridget Starr Taylor) — *Campbell, Louisa*

y Phoebe's Folly — *Karr, Kathleen*

r The Phoenix Award of the Children's Literature Association 1990-1994 — *Helbig, Alethea*

Phoenix Cafe — *Jones, Gwyneth*

A Phoenix in the Ashes — *Mollenkopf, John*

Phoenix Irish Short Stories 1996

The Phoenix of Prague — *Skeggs, Douglas*

A Phoenix Rising — *Schramm-Evans, Zoe*

y The Phoenix Solution (Campanella). Audio Version — *Bugliosi, Vincent*

y Phoenix, Upside Down — *Scarboro, Elizabeth*

Phog Allen: The Father of Basketball Coaching — *Kerkhoff, Blair*

r Phonetic Symbol Guide. 2nd Ed. — *Pullum, Geoffrey K*

The Phonetics of English and Dutch. 3rd Ed. — *Collins, Beverly*

Phonic Awareness 1 and 2 — *Green, Mary*

Phonological Development — *Vihman, Marilyn May*

Phosgene and Related Carbonyl Halides — *Ryan, T Anthony*

The Phospholipase C Pathway — *Tobin, Andrew B*

r Photo Marketing Guidebook '96-'97 — *Gould, Peter L*

Photo-Textualities: Reading Photographs and Literature — *Bryant, Marsha*

p Photo Work: Art and Technique

Photoactive Organic Materials — *NATO Advanced Research Workshop on Photoactive Organic Materials: Science and Applications (1995: Avignon, France)*

Photoassimilate Distribution in Plants and Crops — *Zamski, Eli*

Photocopies — *Berger, John*

The Photograph — *Clarke, Graham*

y The Photograph — *Porcelli, Joe*

Photographer's Digital Studio — *Farace, Joe*

y Photographers: History and Culture through the Camera — *Jackson, Nancy*

The Photographer's Sweethearts — *Hartog, Diana*

r Photographic Atlas of Civil War Injuries — *Bengtson, Bradley P*

A Photographic Garden History — *Phillips, Roger*

A Photographic Guide to North American Raptors — *Clark, William S*

r Photographic Guide to the Shorebirds of the World — *Rosair, David*

y A Photographic Tour of the Universe — *Vanin, Gabriele*

Photographing Minerals, Fossils and Lapidary Materials — *Scovil, Jeffrey A*

Photographing the Landscape — *Fielder, John*

Photographs and Notebooks — *Chatwin, Bruce*

The Photographs of Dorothea Lange — *Davis, Keith F*

c Photography (Make It Work!)

y Photography — *Dunn, Chris*

c Photography — *Holland, Gini*

Photography and the Body — *Pultz, John*

Photography, Vision, and the Production of Modern Bodies — *Lalvani, Suren*

r Photonics Rules of Thumb — *Miller, John Lester*

PhotoOp — *Kennerly, David H*

Photoshop in 4 Colors — *Nyman, Mattias*

Photosynthesis — *International Photosynthesis Congress (10th: 1995: Montpellier, France)*

Photothermal Spectroscopy Methods for Chemical Analysis — *Bialkowski, Stephen E*

Phthalocyanines: Properties and Applications. Vol. 4 — *Leznoff, C C*

Phuong Van No Ben Troi Ha Noi — *Nguyen, Thi Ngoc Dung*

Phya Khankhaak, the Toad King

Phyllis Shand Allfrey: A Caribbean Life — *Paravisini-Gebert, Lizabeth*

Phyllo: Easy Recipes for Sweet and Savory Treats — *O'Connor, Jill*

Die Physica Und Der Liber De Causis Im 12 Jahrhundert — *Ricklin, Thomas*

r Physical Activity in Human Experience — *Curtis, James E*

The Physical and the Moral — *Williams, Elizabeth A*

Physical Attractiveness and the Theory of Sexual Selection — *Jones, Doug*

The Physical Basis of Mind — *Lewes, George Henry*

Physical Ceramics — *Chiang, Yet-Ming*

Physical Chemistry. 2nd Ed. — *Alberty, Robert A*

Physical Chemistry from Ostwald to Pauling — *Servos, John W*

The Physical Geography of Africa — *Adams, W M*

Physical Metallurgy. 4th Ed., Vols. 1-3 — *Cahn, Robert W*

Physical Modalities — *Hooper, Paul D*

Physical Origin of Homochirality in Life — *Cline, David B*

The Physical Origins of Time Asymmetry — *Halliwell, Jonathan*

Physical Processes — *Byrne, David*

y Physical Processes — *Tracy, Charles*

r Physical Properties of Polymers Handbook — *Mark, James E*

r Physical Properties of Polymers Handbook. Electronic Media Version — *Mark, James E*

Physical Rehabilitation Outcome Measures — *Cole, B*

Physical Science. 3rd Ed. — *Tillery, Bill W*

The Physical Sciences — *Hazen, Robert M*

Physical Supramolecular Chemistry — *Echegoyen, Luis*

Physicalism: The Philosophical Foundations — *Poland, Jeffrey*

Physician-Assisted Suicide — *Weir, Robert F*

The Physician-Manager Alliance — *Davidson, Stephen M*

The Physician of London — *Cowell, Stephanie*

The Physician Strategist — *Swayne, Linda E*

Physicians, Colonial Racism, and Diaspora in West Africa — *Patton, Adell*

r Physician's Guide to Arthropods of Medical Importance. 2nd Ed. — *Goddard, Jerome*

y A Physician's Guide to Herbal Wellness — *Cammarata, John*

r Physician's Guide to Rare Diseases. 2nd Ed. — *Theone, Jess G*

Physics and Chemistry at Oxide Surfaces — *Noguera, Claudine*

Physics and Chemistry of Low-Dimensional Inorganic Conductors — *NATO Advanced Study Institute on Physics and Chemistry of Low-Dimensional Inorganic Conductors (1995: Les Houches, Frances)*

Physics and Chemistry of Mineral Surfaces — *Brady, Patrick V*

Physics and Fractal Structures — *Gouyet, Jean-Francois*

Physics and National Socialism — *Hentschel, Klaus*

Physics for Scientists and Engineers — *Lerner, Lawrence S*

c Physics Lab in a Hardware Store (Illus. by Joe Hosking) — *Friedhoffer, Robert*

c Physics Lab in a Housewares Store (Illus. by Joe Hosking) — *Friedhoffer, Bob*

c Physics Lab in a Housewares Store (Illus. by Joe Hosking) — *Friedhoffer, Robert*

The Physics of Angels — *Fox, Matthew*

Physics of Biomaterials — *Riste, T*

Physics of Cryocrystals — *Manzhelii, Vadim G*

The Physics of Immortality — *Tipler, Frank J*

The Physics of Polymers — *Strobl, Gert R*

The Physics of Skiing — *Lind, David*

The Physics of Star Trek — *Krauss, Lawrence Maxwell*

y The Physics of Star Trek (Krauss). Audio Version — *Krauss, Lawrence Maxwell*

Physics of the Aurora and Airglow — *Chamberlain, Joseph W*

Physics over Easy — *Azaroff, Leonid V*

r The Physics Quick Reference Guide — *Cohen, E Richard*

Physiologia: Natural Philosophy in Late Aristotelian and Cartesian Thought — *Des Chene, Dennis*

Physiologic and Pharmacologic Bases of Anesthesia — *Collins, Vincent J*

The Physiologic Basis of Surgery. 2nd Ed. — *O'Leary, J Patrick, 1941-*

The Physiology and Biochemistry of Prokaryotes — *White, David C*

Physiology of Cephalopod Molluscs — *Portner, Hans O*

Physiology of Domestic Animals. 2nd Ed. — *Reece, William O*

The Physiology of Taste — *Brillat-Savarin, Jean Anthelme*

Physiology of Woody Plants. 2nd Ed. — *Kozlowski, Theodore T*

Physique Quantique Mesoscopique — *Akkermans, E*

Phytochemical Diversity and Redundancy in Ecological Interactions — *Romeo, John T*

I Piaceri E Le Grazie. Vols. 1-2 — *Cifani, Arabella*

Piaget--Vygotsky — *Tryphon, Anastasia*

Piaget's Conception of Evolution — *Messerly, John G*

Piano: A Photographic History of the World's Most Celebrated Instrument — *Crombie, David*

Piano Lessons — *Adams, Noah*

c Piano Lessons Can be Murder — *Stine, R L*

The Piano Man's Daughter — *Findley, Timothy*

Piano Music for One Hand — *Edel, Theodore*

Piano Pieces — *Sherman, Russell*

The Piano Quartet and Quintet — *Smallman, Basil*

The Piazza Tales — *Melville, Herman*

The Picador Book of Contemporary New Zealand Fiction — *Barrowman, Fergus*

The Picador Book of Sports Writing — *Coleman, Nick*

The Picaresque: A Symposium on the Rogue's Tale — *Benito-Vessels, Carmen*

Picasso and Els 4 Gats — *Ocana, Maria Teresa*

Picasso and Portraiture — *Rubin, William*

Picasso and the Spanish Tradition — *Brown, Jonathan, 1939-*
Picasso at the Lapin Agile and Other Plays — *Martin, Steve, 1945-*
Picasso Bon Vivant — *Herscher, Ermine*
Picasso Et Apollinaire — *Read, Peter*
Picasso Et Le Portrait — *Rubin, William*
r Picasso's Paintings, Watercolors, Drawings and Sculpture. Vols. 3-4
Picasso's Variations on the Masters — *Galassi, Susan Grace*
Pick a Better Country — *Hamblin, Ken*
c The Pick and Shop Marketplace (Illus. by Fran Thatcher)
c Picker McClikker (Illus. by Stephen Hanson) — *Johnson, Allen, Jr.*
Pickett, Leader of the Charge — *Longacre, Edward G*
r Picking the Right Bible Study Program — *Scott, Macrina*
y Pickups: Classic American Trucks — *Moses, Harry*
c Picnic in the Park — *Albert, Marjorie*
Pictorial Effect/Naturalistic Vision — *Handy, Ellen*
r The Pictorial Guide to the Living Primates — *Rowe, Noel*
A Pictorial History of Psychology — *Bringman, Wolfgang*
r A Pictorial History of World War II Veterans from Laurel County, Kentucky — *Laurel County Historical Society*
Pictorial Metaphor in Advertising — *Forceville, Charles*
Pictorialism in the Fictional Miniatures of Albert Paris Gutersloh — *Laue, Ingrid E*
Picture Beaded Earrings for Beginners — *Steil, Starr*
c A Picture Book of Davy Crockett (Illus. by John Wallner) — *Adler, David A*
c A Picture Book of Sojourner Truth (Illus. by Gershom Griffith) — *Adler, David A*
c A Picture Book of Thomas Alva Edison (Illus. by John Wallner) — *Adler, David A*
Picture Framing Made Easy — *Stokes, Penelope*
The Picture of Dorian Gray — *Gillespie, Michael Patrick*
c A Picture of Freedom — *McKissack, Pat*
cr Picture Reference Atlas — *Pickering, Mel*
c The Picture That Mom Drew (Illus. by Bruce McMillan) — *Mallat, Kathy*
Picture This — *Gore, Tipper*
cr Picture Word Book
Pictured in My Mind — *Trechsel, Gail Andrews*
Pictures from an Institution — *Jarrell, Randall*
y Pictures in the Dark — *Cross, Gillian*
Pictures of the Heart — *Mostow, Joshua S*
Picturing a Nation — *Lubin, David M*
Picturing an Exhibition — *Sandeen, Eric J*
Picturing Casablanca — *Ossman, Susan*
Picturing Health and Illness — *Gilman, Sander L*
Picturing Knowledge — *Baigrie, Brian S*
Picturing the Past — *Harper, Sue*
Picturing the South 1860 to the Present — *Dugan, Ellen*
Picturing the Wreck — *Shapiro, Dani*
y Picturing Us — *Willis-Thomas, Deborah*
PIDE's Research Programme for 1993-96 — *Naqvi, Syed Nawab Haider*
Pie Every Day — *Willard, Pat*
c Pie Magic (Illus. by Laura Cornell) — *Forward, Toby*
y Piece by Piece (Trillin). Audio Version — *Trillin, Calvin*
c A Piece of Cake — *Murphy, Jill*
c A Piece of Home (Illus. by Juan Wijngaard) — *Levitin, Sonia*
y A Piece of Justice (Forsyth). Audio Version — *Paton Walsh, Jill*
A Piece of the Action — *Nocera, Joseph*
Pieces of Heaven — *Phelan, Nancy*
Piecework — *Hamill, Pete*
The Piedmont Conspiracy — *Washburn, James*
La Piel Y La Mascara — *Diaz, Jesus*
y Pierced by a Ray of Sun — *Gordon, Ruth*
Pierpaolo Vergerio the Elder — *McManamon, John M*
c Pierre Auguste Renoir — *Parsons, Tom*
c Pierre Auguste Renoir (Illus. by Mike Venezia) — *Venezia, Mike*
Pierre Boulle — *Becker, Lucille Frackman*
Pierre De Berulle Et Les Carmelites De France — *Morgain, Stephane-Marie*
Pierre De Bourdeille, Seigneur De Brantome — *Lazard, Madeleine*
Pierre Franey Cooks with His Friends — *Franey, Pierre*

Pierre Lalande: Special Agent — *Zembsch-Schreve, Guido*
Pierre, or, The Ambiguities — *Melville, Herman*
Piers Gaveston: Edward II's Adoptive Brother — *Chaplais, Pierre*
Piers Plowman. Vol. 1 — *Langland, William*
Piers Plowman: A Facsimile of the Z-Text in Bodleian Library, Oxford, MS Bodley 851 — *Langland, William*
c Pie's in the Oven (Illus. by Holly Meade) — *Birney, Betty G*
Piet Stockmans (Uitgeverij Lannoo) — *Stockmans, Piet*
The Pieta in French Late Gothic Sculpture — *Forsyth, William H*
Pietari Suuri Hatun Polki — *Huovinen, Veikko*
c Pieter Bruegel — *Butler, Daphne*
Pieter Bruegel the Elder: Two Studies — *Gibson, Walter S*
Piety and Charity in Late Medieval Florence — *Henderson, John*
Piety and Poverty — *McLeod, Hugh*
The Piety of Afrikaans Women — *Landman, Christina*
y Pig — *Cowan, Andrew*
The Pig and the Python — *Cork, David*
A Pig Called Francis Bacon — *Measday, Stephen*
c Pig, Horse, or Cow, Don't Wake Me Now — *Alda, Arlene*
c The Pig in the Pond (Illus. by Jill Norton) — *Waddell, Martin*
Pig Tales — *Darrieussecq, Marie*
c Pigasus (Illus. by Graham Percy) — *Murphy, Pat*
c Pigeon Summer — *Turnbull, Ann*
c Piggie Pie! (Illus. by Howard Fine) — *Palatini, Margie*
c Piggies (Illus. by Don Wood) — *Wood, Don*
y The Pigman and Me — *Zindel, Paul*
c Pignic (Illus. by Rosekrans Hoffman) — *Miranda, Anne*
c Pigou, Fiflard Et Compagnie (Illus. by Pierre Leon) — *Leon, Pierre*
c Pigs Ahoy! (Illus. by David McPhail) — *McPhail, David*
c Pigs Aplenty, Pigs Galore! — *McPhail, David*
c Pigs from 1 to 10 — *Geisert, Arthur*
c Pigs from A to Z — *Geisert, Arthur*
Pigs in Heaven — *Kingsolver, Barbara*
c Pigs in the Mud in the Middle of the Rud (Illus. by John Schoenherr) — *Plourde, Lynn*
c Pigs in the Pantry (Illus. by Sharon McGinley-Nally) — *Axelrod, Amy*
c Pigs on a Blanket (Illus. by Sharon McGinley-Nally) — *Axelrod, Amy*
Pigskin: The Early Years of Pro Football — *Peterson, Robert W*
Pigtown — *Caunitz, William J*
Pilger, Mirakel Und Alltag — *Krotzl, Christian*
c Pilgrim Voices (Illus. by Shelley Pritchett) — *Roop, Connie*
The Pilgrimage of Grace — *Bush, Michael*
Pilgrimage: Past and Present in the World Religions — *Coleman, Simon*
Pilgrimage to Beethoven and Other Essays — *Wagner, Richard, 1813-1883*
Pilgrimage to Mecca — *Pearson, M N, 1941-*
c The Pilgrims at Plymouth (Illus. by S D Schindler) — *Penner, Lucille Recht*
Pilgrims from the Sun — *Palmer, Ransford W*
Pilgrims in Lotus Land — *Burkinshaw, Robert K*
c The Pilgrims of Plimoth (Illus. by Marcia Sewall) — *Sewall, Marcia*
A Pilgrim's Progress (Topping). Audio Version — *Bunyan, John*
Pilgrim's Progress, Puritan Progress — *Swaim, Kathleen M*
A Pillar of Society — *Hamilton, Julia*
The Pillars of Hercules — *Theroux, Paul*
Pillars of Salt — *Faqir, Fadia*
The Pillow Boy of the Lady Onogoro — *Fell, Alison*
The Pillow Friend — *Tuttle, Lisa*
Pills, Petticoats and Plows — *Clark, Thomas D*
Pillsbury Best Chicken Cookbook
Pillsbury Best of the Bake-Off Cookbook
Pilot Judgment and Crew Resource Management — *Jensen, Richard S*
c Pilots — *Peacock, Lindsay T*
The Pilot's Daughter — *McFall, Gardner*
c Pilots Fly Planes — *Robinson, Fay*
Pimeasta Maasta — *Verronen, Maarit*
Pimps, Whores and Welfare Brats — *Parker, Star*
The Pinball Effect — *Burke, James*
y The Pinball Effect (Burke). Audio Version — *Burke, James*

c The Pinballs — *Byars, Betsy*
c El Pinguino Pedro (Illus. by Marcus Pfister) — *Pfister, Marcus*
c El Pinguino Pedro Y Sus Nuevos Amigos (Illus. by Marcus Pfister) — *Pfister, Marcus*
c Pink and Say — *Polacco, Patricia*
Pink Balloons and Other Deadly Things — *Tesler, Nancy*
The Pink Glass Swan — *Lippard, Lucy*
c The Pink Hare (Illus. by Ken Brown) — *Willis, Jeanne*
Pink Therapy — *Davies, Dominic*
Pink Triangle — *Morris, Miranda*
Pink Water Down — *Green, Bill*
Pinktoes — *Himes, Chester*
c Pinky and Rex and the Bully (Illus. by Melissa Sweet) — *Howe, James*
c Pinky and Rex and the New Neighbors (Illus. by Melissa Sweet) — *Howe, James*
c A Pinky Is a Baby Mouse and Other Baby Animal Names (Illus. by Diane DeGroat) — *Ryan, Pam Munoz*
Pino Grande. 2nd Ed. — *Polkinghorn, R S*
c Pinocchio (Illus. by Ed Young) — *Collodi, Carlo*
c Pinocchio (Illus. by Victor G Ambrus) — *Riordan, James*
Pinocchio in Venice — *Coover, Robert*
c Pinocchio: The Classic Italian Tale (Illus. by Brian Ajhar). Book and Audio Version — *Metaxas, Eric*
Pinocchio's Progeny — *Segel, Harold B, 1930-*
Pinochet's Economists — *Valdes, Juan Gabriel*
La Pintura Holandesa Y Flamenca (Siglos XVI Al XVIII) En El Museo Nacional De Bellas Artes De Buenos Aires — *Navarro, Angel M*
Pioneer Children on the Journey West — *Werner, Emmy E*
c Pioneer Crafts (Illus. by Heather Collins) — *Greenwood, Barbara*
A Pioneer of American Folklore — *Schamschula, Eleonore*
Pioneer Women — *Peavy, Linda*
Pioneering Americana — *Amsler, Cory*
c Pioneering Frozen Worlds — *Markle, Sandra*
Pioneering Venus — *Fimmel, Richard O*
Pioneers in Historical Archaeology — *South, Stanley*
Pioneers of Islamic Revival — *Rahnema, Ali*
The Pioneers of NMR and Magnetic Resonance in Medicine — *Mattson, James*
c Pipe Cleaners Gone Crazy — *Torres, Laura*
Pipe Drafting and Design — *Parisher, Roy A*
Pipeline Crossings — *American Society of Civil Engineers. Task Committee on Pipeline Crossings*
Pipeline Crossings 1996 — *Catalano, Lawrence F*
Pipeline Risk Management Manual. 2nd Ed. — *Muhlbauer, W Kent*
c Pippa's Puppy (Illus. by Anthea Sieveking) — *MacKinnon, Debbie*
c Pippi in the South Seas — *Lindgren, Astrid*
c Pippi Longstocking's After-Christmas Party (Illus. by Michael Chesworth) — *Lindgren, Astrid*
Pirandello and Film — *Nichols, Nina Da Vinci*
Pirandello's Love Letters to Marta Abba — *Pirandello, Luigi*
c Piratas En La Casa De Al Lado (Illus. by Korby Paul) — *Tabern, Peter*
y Pirate — *Platt, Richard*
c The Pirate and the Pig — *Rodgers, Frank*
c Pirate Plunder's Treasure Hunt (Illus. by Iain Smyth) — *Smyth, Iain*
c The Pirate Queen (Illus. by Emily Arnold McCully) — *McCully, Emily Arnold*
c Pirate Trouble for Wiggy and Boa — *Fienberg, Anna*
p Pirate Writings
c Pirates (Illus. by Nicholas Hewetson) — *Steedman, Scott*
c Pirates (Illus. by McRae Books) — *Ross, Stewart*
The Pirates and the People — *Greer, Allan*
The Pirate's Daughter — *Girardi, Robert*
The Pirate's Daughter. Audio Version — *Girardi, Robert*
c A Pirate's Life for Me! (Illus. by Patrick O'Brien) — *Thompson, Julie*
c The Pirates of Bat Cave Island (Illus. by Margeaux Lucas) — *Albert, Burton*
Pirates of the Heart — *Kraus, Jim*
y Pirates of the Universe — *Bisson, Terry*
y Pirates: Terror on the High Seas from the Caribbean to the South China Sea
Pisanello: Le Peintre Aux Sept Vertus — *Cordellier, Dominique*

yr Pisces Guide to Venomous and Toxic Marine Life of
the World — Cunningham, Patricia
r Pissarro, Neo-Impressionism, and the Spaces of the
Avant-Garde — Ward, Martha
Pistils — Mapplethorpe, Robert
Pistols and Politics — Hyde, Samuel C
Pit Ghosts, Padfeet and Poltergeists — Linaham, Liz
The Pitcairn Islands — Benton, Tim
The Pitcher Is Broken — Holloway, Steven W
c Pitcher Plants — Gentle, Victor
Pitfalls, Variants, and Artifacts in Body MR Imaging
— Mirowitz, Scott A
Pitied but Not Entitled — Gordon, Linda
Pitirim A. Sorokin: An Intellectual Biography
— Johnston, Barry V
y The Pits — Howarth, Lesley
c Pitschi (Illus. by Hans Fischer) — Fischer, Hans
The Pitt Rivers Museum — Cousins, Julia
Il Pittore Felice — Job, Enrico
The Pittsburgh Poems — Locklin, Gerald
Le Pitture Erotiche Delle Terme Suburbane Di
Pompei — Jacobelli, Lucianna
La Piu Semplice Macchina — Amigoni, Ferdinando
c Pizza Fun — Bastyra, Judy
y Pizza Presto — Kolpas, Norman
c The Pizza Puzzle — Pfeffer, Susan Beth
c A Pizza the Size of the Sun (Illus. by James
Stevenson) — Prelutsky, Jack
Placchette, Secoli XV-XVIII Nel Museo Nazionale Del
Bargello — Toderi, Giuseppe
Place and Displacement in the Renaissance — Vos,
Alvin
A Place Apart — Friedland, Martin L
A Place Beyond — Jans, Nick
A Place Called Grand Canyon — Morehouse, Barbara
J
A Place Called Heaven — Foster, Cecil
A Place Called Home — Pearlman, Mickey
A Place for Kathy — Denker, Henry
A Place in El Paso — Lopez-Stafford, Gloria
A Place in Normandy — Kilmer, Nicholas
A Place in Space — Snyder, Gary
c A Place in the Sun — Rubalcaba, Jill
A Place in the World? — Massey, Doreen B
The Place Is Too Small for Us — Gordon, Robert P
Place Matters — Morgan, Susan
r Place Names of Atlantic Canada — Hamilton, William
B
r The Place Names of New Mexico — Julyan, Robert
r Place Names of the White Mountains. Rev. Ed.
— Julyan, Robert
y A Place Not Home — Wiseman, Eva
A Place of My Own — Pollan, Michael
y A Place of Safety — Lisson, Deborah
The Place of the Stage — Mullaney, Steven
A Place on the Glacial Till — Sherman, Thomas
Fairchild
y A Place to Call Home — Koller, Jackie French
A Place to Call Home — Smith, Deborah
y The Place Within — Daynard, Jodi
r Placenames of Russia and the Former Soviet Union
— Room, Adrian
Places of Inquiry — Clark, Burton R
Placido Domingo — Schnauber, Cornelius
Placing the Gods — Alcock, Susan E
c Plague — Roden, Katie
Plague Doctors — Feldman, Jamie L
Plague? Jesuit Accounts of Epidemic Disease in the
16th Century — Martin, A Lynn
Plague of Strangers — Marcus, Alan I
Plagues: Their Origin, History and Future — Wills,
Christopher
y Plain City — Hamilton, Virginia
Plain Pictures — Kinsey, Joni L
Plains Indian Drawings 1865-1935 — Berlo, Janet
Catherine
y The Plains Indian Wars — Marker, Sherry
c The Plains People — Hewitt, Sally
Plains Song — Morris, Wright
y Plains Warrior — Marrin, Albert
Plainsongs — Darrell
Plaire Et Instruire — Scavillo, Anthony
Les Plaisirs Et Les Jours, De Marcel Proust — Daum,
Pierre
Plan and Purpose in Nature — Williams, George C
Plan and Section Drawing. 2nd Ed. — Wang, Thomas
C
A Plan for a Research Program on Aerosol Radiative
Forcing and Climate Change — National Research
Council (U.S.). Panel on Aerosol Radiative Forcing
and Climate Change

Plan Nacional De Desarrollo 1994/1998 — Orlich,
Francisco J
c Plane (Illus. by Chris L Demarest) — Demarest, Chris
L
c Plane (Illus. by George Fryer) — Oxlade, Chris
Plane Death — Dooley, Anne M
c Planes and Other Flying Things — Temko, Florence
c Planet Dexter's Calculator Mania! (Illus. by Jack
Keely) — Planet Dexter
Planet Dora — Beon, Yves
yr Planet Earth. Electronic Media Version
c Planet Earth/Inside Out (Illus. by Gail Gibbons)
— Gibbons, Gail
y The Planet Mars — Sheehan, William
c Planet Monster (Illus. by Alan Rowe) — Maisner,
Heather
The Planet Neptune — Moore, Patrick
y Planet of Twilight — Hambly, Barbara
c A Planet with One Mind (Pinder). Audio Version
Planetary Symbolism in the Horoscope
— Hamaker-Zondag, Karen
Planetary Volcanism. 2nd Ed. — Cattermole, Peter
y Planetology: Comparing Other Worlds to Our Own
— Schaaf, Fred
r The Planets. Electronic Media Version
c The Planets (Illus. by Paul Doherty) — Moore, Patrick
c Planets (Illus. by Tom LaPadula) — Schecter, Darrow
Planets: A Smithsonian Guide — Watters, Thomas R
Planets in Peril — Downing, David C
Planets, Stars and Orbs — Grant, Edward
r The Planned Parenthood Women's Health
Encyclopedia
Planning and Designing Libraries for Children and
Young People — Dewe, Michael
Planning and Designing the Data Warehouse
— Barquin, Ramon C
Planning and Managing ATM Networks — Minoli,
Daniel
Planning, Delivering and Assessing GNVQs — Ollin,
Ros
Planning Estuaries — Westen, C J Van
Planning for a Wage-Goods Economy
— Brahmananda, P R
Planning for Change — Vestal, James E
Planning for Library Development — Evans, John A
Planning for the Indian Power Sector — Canadian
Energy Research Institute
Planning Global Information Infrastructure — Chen,
Ching-Chih
Planning, Implementing, and Evaluating Health
Promotion Programs. 2nd Ed. — McKenzie, James
F
Planning Primary Design and Technology
— Richardson, Roy
Planning Programs for Adult Learners — Caffarella,
Rosemary
Planning the Twentieth-Century American City
— Sies, Mary Corbin
Plans, Pragmatism and People — French, R A
Plant Alkaloids — Raffauf, Robert F
Plant Hormone Signal Perception and Transduction
— Smith, A R
Plant Operation and Optimization — Nalven, Gail
Plant Response to Air Pollution — Yunus, Mohammad
Plant Species Composition of Wisconsin Prairies
— Henderson, Richard A
r Plant Stems — Gartner, Barbara L
y Plant Survival — Capon, Brian
Plant Systems/Components Aging Management 1996
Plant Tissue Culture Concepts and Laboratory
Exercises — Trigiano, Robert N
Plantagenet Ancestry of Seventeenth-Century
Colonists — Faris, David
c Plantas Del Mar (Illus. by Luis Rizo) — Sanchez,
Isidro
Planters, Containers, and Raised Beds — Crandall,
Chuck
A Planters' Republic — Ragsdale, Bruce A
Planting Noah's Garden — Stein, Sara Bonnett
Planting Planner — Rice, Graham
r Plants for American Landscapes — Odenwald, Neil G
Plants for the Future — Malitz, Jerome
y Plants of the Desert (Illus. by Luis Rizo) — Llamas,
Andreu
y Plants of the Forest (Illus. by Miquel Ferron)
— Llamas, Andreu
y Plants, People, and Culture — Balick, Michael J
r Plants That Merit Attention. Vol. 2 — Garden Club of
America
y Plants under the Sea (Illus. by Luis Rizo) — Llamas,
Andreu

Plasma Astrophysics — Kirk, J G
Plasma Surface Modification and Plasma
Polymerization — Inagaki, N
c Plastic Component Design — Campbell, Paul D Q
c Plastic Cups (Illus. by Sarah-Jane Neaves) — Connor,
Nikki
Plastic: The Making of a Synthetic Century
— Fenichell, Stephen
Plasticity in the Central Nervous System — McGaugh,
James L
The Plate Flaws of the Hermes Heads of Greece
1861-1886 — Asimakopulos, N
Platinum by Cartier — Cologni, Franco
The Platinum Rule — Alessandra, Tony
The Platinum Rule (Alessandra). Audio Version
— Alessandra, Tony
Plato and the Republic — Pappas, Nickolas
y Plato in 90 Minutes — Strathern, Paul
Plato Rediscovered — Seung, T K
Platonism and the English Imagination — Baldwin,
Anna
Plato's Apology of Socrates — Stryker, E De
Plato's Craft of Justice — Parry, Richard D
Plato's Ethics — Irwin, Terence
Plato's Euthyphro, Apology and Crito — Emery, S W
Plato's Literary Garden — Sayre, Kenneth M
Plato's Statesman — Rosen, Stanley
Plato's Third Eye — Allen, Michael J B
Plato's World — Cropsey, Joseph
Les Plats Qui Ont Fait La France — Couderc,
Philippe
Platt Brothers and Company — Roth, Matthew W
Platteland: Images from Rural South Africa
— Ballen, Roger
c Play Ball, Amelia Bedelia (Illus. by Wallace Tripp)
— Parish, Peggy
Play Better Golf — Rankin, Judy
c Play Cleaning (Dorling Kindersley)
c Play Garage (Dorling Kindersley)
c Play Garden (Dorling Kindersley)
Play Great Golf — Palmer, Arnold
Play in Family Therapy — Gil, Eliana
The Play in the Mirror — Stroud, Matthew D
y Play It for Real — Barrett, Stan
c Play Kitchen (Dorling Kindersley)
The Play of Paradox — Crockett, Bryan
The Play of Terror in Nineteenth-Century France
— Booker, John T
Play On! — McNaspy, Clement J
Play with a Tiger and Other Plays — Lessing, Doris
May
The Players: A Novel of the Young Shakespeare
— Cowell, Stephanie
Playing Better Baseball — Wolff, Rick
Playing for Dollars. 3rd Ed. — Staudohar, Paul D
Playing for Scotland — Campbell, Donald
Playing for Stakes — Kuhn, Anna K
Playing for Thrills — Wang, Shuo
Playing God? — Peters, Ted, 1941-
Playing Happy Families (Shelley). Audio Version
— Symons, Julian
Playing in the Dark — Morrison, Toni
Playing Nice — Festle, Mary Jo
Playing Off the Rail — McCumber, David
Playing out of the Deep Woods — Hawkes, G W
The Playing Self — Melucci, Alberto
Playing the Bones — Redd, Louise
Playing the Future — Rushkoff, Douglas
Playing the Game — Birley, Derek
Playing the Harlot or Mostly Coffee — Avis, Patricia
Playing the Other — Zeitlin, Froma I
Playing with the Edge — Danto, Arthur C
Playing with Time — Arnoldi, Mary Jo
Playing with Time — Newlands, Carole E
Playing with Truth — Hammond, Nicholas
Plays and Petersburg Tales — Gogol, Nikolai
Plays and Playwrights from Ireland in International
Perspective — Kosok, Heinz
Plays by French and Francophone Women
— Makward, Christiane P
r Plays for Children and Young Adults. 1st Suppl.
— Karp, Rashelle S
c Plays of America from American Folklore for
Children Grades K-6 — McCullough, L E
y Plays of America from American Folklore for Young
Actors — McCullough, L E
The Plays of Ernst Toller — Davies, Cecil
The Plays of Heinrich Von Kleist — Allan, Sean
c The Plays of the Songs of Christmas — McCullough, L
E
Plays, Prose Writings and Poems — Wilde, Oscar

Playtexts: Ludics in Contemporary Literature
— *Motte, Warren*
c Playtime Poems (Illus. by Nick Sharratt) — *Bennett, Jill*
Playtime Pottery and Porcelain from Europe and Asia
— *Punchard, Lorraine*
c Playtime Rhymes. Audio Version — *Gardener, Sally*
Playwright versus Director — *Luere, Jeane*
The Playwright's Art — *Bryer, Jackson R*
A Plea for Purity — *Arnold, Johann Christoph*
r Pleasant Weather Ratings — *Whitmore, Thomas*
Please Don't Eat My Garden! — *McCord, Nancy*
Please Don't Wish Me a Merry Christmas
— *Feldman, Stephen M*
c Please Keep off the Dinosaur (Crane). Pts. 1-2. Audio Version — *Wilson, David Henry*
Please Kill Me — *McNeil, Legs*
c Pleasing the Ghost (Illus. by Stacey Schuett)
— *Creech, Sharon*
y Pleasure of Believing — *Hobbet, Anastasia*
The Pleasure of the Play — *States, Bert O*
The Pleasure of Your Company — *O'Neill, Molly*
r Pleasure Paradises — *Radulski, John P*
The Pleasure Police — *Shaw, David, 1943-*
The Pleasure Prescription — *Pearsall, Paul*
Pleasures and Pains — *Milligan, Barry*
The Pleasures of Aesthetics — *Levinson, Jerrold*
The Pleasures of Children's Literature — *Nodelman, Perry*
The Pleasures of Conquest — *Gooneratne, Yasmine*
The Pleasures of Counting — *Korner, Tom*
The Pleasures of Reading — *Alter, Robert*
The Pleasures of Virtue — *Ruderman, Anne Crippen*
Pleasures Taken — *Mavor, Carol*
y The Pledge — *Peart, Jane*
Pledging Allegiance — *Samuel, Lawrence R*
Pleistocene Amphibians and Reptiles in North America — *Holman, J Alan*
Plessy v. Ferguson — *Thomas, Brook*
Pleuropulmonary and Bronchial Infections
— *Mandell, Gerald L*
The Plight of Emulation — *Gotlieb, Marc*
The Plimoth Plantation New England Cookery Book
— *Hornblower, Malabar*
Pliny on Art and Society — *Isager, Jacob*
Plotinus — *Gerson, Lloyd P*
Plotinus on the Origin of Matter — *O'Brien, Denis*
Plotinus, or, The Simplicity of Vision — *Hadot, Pierre*
y Plotting Hitler's Death — *Fest, Joachim*
Plotting the Past — *Della Coletta, Cristina*
p Plotz: The Zine for the Vaclempt
The Plough and the Pen — *Youmans, Vance Joseph*
Plough Monday to Hocktide — *Rowe, Doc*
c Ploumette Et Ploum Partagent Leurs Jouets — *Marin, Lise*
Plowing Ground in Washington — *Gardner, B Delworth*
Plows, Prosperity, and Cooperation at Agbassa
— *Farnham, Dana A*
Plug In — *Gurley, Ted*
Plugged In and Turned On — *McCain, Charles H*
Plum Island — *DeMille, Nelson*
Plums and Ashes — *Moolten, David*
Plunder and Preservation — *Murphy, J David*
Plundering Africa's Past — *Schmidt, Peter R*
y Plundering Paradise — *McCaughrean, Geraldine*
r Plunkett's Financial Services Industry Almanac
— *Plunkett, Jack W*
r Plunkett's Health Care Industry Almanac — *Plunkett, Jack W*
r Plunkett's InfoTech Industry Almanac — *Plunkett, Jack W*
Pluralism — *McLennan, Gregor*
Pluralism, Justice, and Equality — *Miller, David Leslie*
The Pluralist Game — *Canavan, Francis*
The Pluralist State — *Nicholls, David*
The Pluralistic Philosophy of Stephen Crane
— *Dooley, Patrick K*
The Pluralistic Vision — *Coalter, Milton J*
La Plus Longue Des Republiques 1870-1940
— *Mollier, Jean-Yves*
Plutarch's Lives of Galba and Otho — *Little, Douglas*
Plutarch's Sertorius — *Konrad, Christoph F*
Plutonium and the Rio Grande — *Graf, William L*
The Plutonium Story — *Seaborg, Glenn Theodore*
Plutot Que D'En Pleurer — *Jouanard, Gil*
r Plymouth Colony Records. Vol. 1 — *Simmons, C H*
PM&R Secrets — *O'Young, Brian*
La Poblacion De America Latina — *Sanchez-Albornoz, Nicolas*

Pocahontas: The Evolution of an American Narrative
— *Tilton, Robert S*
A Pocket Book of Spiritual Poems — *Godden, Rumer*
c Pocket Bunny (Illus. by P Adams) — *Twinn, M*
r The Pocket Factfile of 20th Century Events
r The Pocket Factfile of 20th Century People
c Pocket Frog (Illus. by P Adams) — *Twinn, M*
r Pocket Guide to ECG Diagnosis — *Chung, Edward K*
Pocket Guide to Managed Care — *La Puma, John*
Pocket Guide to Shamanism — *Cowan, Tom*
Pocket Guide to the Internet — *Gach, Gary*
Pocket Handbook of Primary Care Psychiatry
— *Kaplan, Harold I*
c Pocket Kitten (Illus. by P Adams) — *Twinn, M*
y Pocket Poems — *Janeczko, Paul*
c Pocket Puppy (Illus. by P Adams) — *Twinn, M*
r A Pocket Reference for Psychiatrists. 2nd Ed.
— *Jenkins, Susan C*
The Pocket Watchmaker — *Dawkins, Richard*
A Pocketful of Paradise — *Kane, Kathleen*
c Pocketful of Stars (Illus. by Michael Martchenko)
— *Williams, Felicity*
Pod Almighty — *Podmore, Dave*
y A Poem a Day — *McCosker, Karen*
r Poem Finder 95. Electronic Media Version
Poemas De Las Madres — *Mistral, Gabriela*
Poemas Invisibles — *Baquero, Gaston*
The Poems (Ryan) — *Michelangelo Buonarroti*
Pocms — *Milton, John, 1608-1674*
The Poems (Lee) — *Propertius, Sextus*
Poems — *Rossetti, Christina*
Poems. Vol. 1 — *Mangan, James Clarence*
Poems 1892 — *Wilde, Oscar*
Poems 1895 — *Yeats, W B*
Poems 1923-1941 — *Rakosi, Carl*
Poems 1938-1993 — *Smith, Bernard*
Poems and Adolphe 1920 — *Rodker, John*
Poems and Fragments — *Holderlin, Friedrich*
The Poems and Prose of Mary, Lady Chudleigh
— *Chudleigh, Mary Lee, Lady*
Poems by Marjorie Kinnan Rawlings — *Rawlings, Marjorie Kinnan*
y Poems Deep and Dangerous — *Phillips, Jo*
c Poems for Christmas (Illus. by Ian Beck) — *Bennett, Jill*
c Poems for Christmas (Illus. by John Lawrence)
— *Philip, Neil*
Poems for the Millennium. Vol. 1 — *Rothenberg, Jerome*
y Poems for Youth (Illus. by Thomas B Allen)
— *Dickinson, Emily*
Poems from Captured Documents — *Nguyen, Thanh T*
Poems from the Blue Horizon — *McLennan, Rob*
The Poem's Heartbeat — *Corn, Alfred*
The Poems of Aemilia Lanyer — *Lanyer, Aemilia*
Poems of Ambrose Bierce — *Bierce, Ambrose*
c Poems of Childhood (Illus. by Joan Walsh Anglund)
— *Anglund, Joan Walsh*
c Poems of Childhood (Illus. by Maxfield Parrish)
— *Field, Eugene*
Poems of Color — *Keele, Wendy*
The Poems of Emily Bronte — *Bronte, Emily*
The Poems of Hafez — *Hafiz, Reza*
The Poems of John Dryden. Vols. 1-2 — *Dryden, John*
Poems of Nazim Hikmet — *Hikmet, Nazim*
The Poems of Ossian and Related Works
— *Macpherson, James*
Poems of the Middle Period 1822-1837. Vols. 1-2
— *Clare, John*
Poe's Mother — *Barnes, Djuna*
Poesia E Lettori In Roma Antica — *Citroni, Mario*
Poesia Espanola De Vanguardia 1918-1936 — *Diez De Revenga, Francisco Javier*
Poesia Y Antipoesia — *Parra, Nicanor*
Poesie — *Sereni, Vittorio*
La Poesie Au Miroir — *Bizer, Marc*
Poesie D'Afrique Au Sud Du Sahara 1945-1995
— *Magnier, Bernard*
La Poesie De Baudelaire Et La Poesie Francaise
1838-1852 — *Robb, Graham*
La Poesie Du Ciel En France Dans La Seconde Moitie
Du Seizieme Siecle — *Pantin, Isabelle*
La Poesie Eclatee De Rene Char — *Lancaster, Rosemary*
Poesie, Etcetera — *Roubaud, Jacques*
La Poesie Malgre Tout — *Maulpoix, Jean-Michel*
Poesie, Revolte Und Revolution — *Kienberger, Silvia*
The Poet — *Connelly, Michael*
The Poet (Schirner). Audio Version — *Connelly, Michael*
The Poet as Thinker — *Lernout, Geert*

The Poet in Socialist Cuba — *Cuadra, Angel*
El Poeta Y La Ciudad — *Canas, Dionisio*
Poetaster — *Jonson, Ben*
The Poetic Art of Aldhelm — *Orchard, Andy*
The Poetic Craft of Bella Akhmadulina — *Ketchian, Sonia I*
The Poetic Edda — *Larrington, Caroline*
Poetic Justice — *Nussbaum, Martha Craven*
Poetic Justice — *Tranter, Nigel*
r Poetic Madness and the Romantic Imagination
— *Burwick, Frederick*
Poetic Process — *Kudszus, Winfried*
Poetic Realism in Scandinavia and Central Europe
1820-1895 — *Bernd, Clifford Albrecht*
Poetic Voices — *Austin, Timothy R*
Poetic Voices of the Maritimes — *Mitcham, Allison*
The Poetical Works of Mark Akenside — *Akenside, Mark*
The Poetical Works of Robert Browning. Vol. 5
— *Browning, Robert*
The Poetics of Alfarabi and Avicenna — *Kemal, Salim*
The Poetics of Authorship in the Later Middle Ages
— *Kimmelman, Burt*
The Poetics of Death — *Guenther, Beatrice Martina*
The Poetics of Personification — *Paxson, James J*
The Poetics of Resistance — *Roth, Michael*
The Poetics of Scepticism — *Swales, Erika*
The Poetics of Sensibility — *McGann, Jerome*
Poetik Der Autoren — *Lutzeler, Paul Michael*
La Poetique De La Chasse Au Moyen Age — *Strubel, Armand*
La Poetique Des Troubadours — *Thiolier-Mejean, Suzanne*
Poetiques De La Modernite — *Filteau, Claude*
Poetisierung--Politisierung — *Gossmann, Wilhelm*
Poetry and Jacobite Politics in Eighteenth-Century
Britain and Ireland — *Pittock, Murray G H*
The Poetry and Poetics of Constantine P. Cavafy
— *Anton, John P*
The Poetry and Poetics of Nishiwaki Junzaburo
— *Hirata, Hosea*
Poetry and Purgatory — *Giovinazzo, Buddy*
Poetry and the Practical — *Simms, William Gilmore*
Poetry and the Realm of Politics — *Erskine-Hill, Howard*
Poetry as Performance — *Nagy, Gregory*
c The Poetry Book (Illus. by Caroline Crossland)
— *Waters, Fiona*
The Poetry Break — *Bauer, Caroline Feller*
p Poetry Flash
y Poetry in Motion — *Paschen, Elise*
Poetry into Song — *Stein, Deborah*
Poetry like Bread — *Espada, Martin*
Poetry My Arse — *Kennelly, Brendan*
p Poetry Now
The Poetry of Anne Finch — *Hinnant, Charles H*
The Poetry of Fifteenth-Century France. Vols. 1-2
— *Fox, John Howard*
The Poetry of George Gissing — *Gissing, George*
The Poetry of Healing — *Campo, Rafael*
The Poetry of Jane Austen and the Austen Family
— *Austen, Jane*
The Poetry of Julia Uceda — *Uceda, Julia*
Poetry of Opposition and Revolution — *Erskine-Hill, Howard*
The Poetry of Pain — *Martinson, Linda*
The Poetry of Saint Therese of Lisieux — *Therese, De Lisieux, Saint*
Poetry of the American West — *Deming, Alison Hawthorne*
Poetry of the People — *Whisenhunt, Donald W*
A Poetry Reading — *Jones, Seaborn*
p Poetry Review
Poetry, Space, Landscape — *Fitter, Chris*
The Poet's Notebook — *Kuusisto, Stephen*
Poets of Hope and Despair — *Hellman, Ben*
Poets, Patrons, and Printers — *Brown, Cynthia J*
Poets, Princes, and Private Citizens — *Knippenberg, Joseph M*
Poets Teaching Poets — *Orr, Gregory*
Poeziia — *Atencia, Maria Victoria*
Poincare and the Three Body Problem
— *Barrow-Green, June*
Point and Click Investor — *Godin, Seth*
Point Counter Point — *Huxley, Aldous*
Point Last Seen — *Nyala, Hannah*
The Point of Points and Other Stories — *Fox, Hugh*
The Point: Stories — *D'Ambrosio, Charles*
The Point Where All Things Meet — *Andrews, Tom*
Point Zero Bliss — *Legacy, Sean*
Points of Departure — *Williams, Miller*

Poison — *Harrison, Kathryn*
y Poison! How to Handle the Hazardous Substances in Your Home — *Morelli, Jim*
Poison Mind — *Good, Jeffrey*
Poison Pen — *Moskowitz-Mateu, Lysa*
y The Poison Tree — *O'Rourke, F M*
Poisoned Ivy — *McNaron, Toni A H*
The Pol Pot Regime — *Kiernan, Ben*
c Poland — *Allard, Denise*
c Poland: A Troubled Past, a New Start — *Ayer, Eleanor H*
r Poland (Rough Guide). 3rd Ed.
Poland since 1944 — *Karpiski, Jakub*
Poland's Permanent Revolution — *Curry, Jane Leftwich*
c Polar Animals (Illus. by Paul Hess) — *Hess, Paul*
c The Polar Bear Family Book — *Larsen, Thor*
Polar Bears — *Ovsyanikov, Nikita*
c Polar Bears — *Pfeffer, Wendy*
Polar Dance — *Mangelsen, Thomas D*
c The Polar Express (Illus. by Chris Van Allsburg) — *Van Allsburg, Chris*
c The Polar Express (Illus. by Chris Van Allsburg). Electronic Media Version — *Van Allsburg, Chris*
Polar Peoples — *Minority Rights Group*
Polar Pioneers — *Ross, M J*
c Polar Regions — *Bonner, Nigel*
Polar Tourism — *Hall, C M*
Polaroids from the Dead — *Coupland, Douglas*
y Pole Stars — *Maekawa, Takeshi*
The Polemics of Imagination — *Abbs, Peter*
Polenta — *Binns, Brigit Legere*
Polenta: 100 Innovative Recipes, from Appetizers to Desserts — *Jordan, Michele Anna*
Poles Apart — *Rowell, Galen*
The Police-Mental Health Partnership — *Marans, Steven*
c Police Officers Protect People — *Greene, Carol*
c Police Patrol (Illus. by John S Winkleman) — *Winkleman, Katherine K*
Police Violence — *Geller, William A*
Policing. Vols. 1-2 — *Reiner, Robert*
Policing Gender, Class and Family — *Mahood, Linda*
Policing Morals — *Petrow, Stefan*
Policing Public Sex — *Dangerous Bedfellows*
Policing Shanghai 1927-1937 — *Wakeman, Frederic, Jr.*
Le Policratique De Jean De Salisbury 1372. Bks. 1-3 — *John, of Salisbury, Bishop of Chartres*
Policy Adjustment in Africa — *Milner, Chris*
Policy and Practice in Bilingual Education — *Garcia, Ofelia*
The Policy Implications of U.S. Involvement in Bosnia — *United States. Congress. House. Committee on Armed Services*
Policy Innovation in State Government — *Nice, David C, 1952-*
Policy-Making in Britain — *Mullard, Maurice*
Policy-Making in the European Union. 3rd Ed. — *Wallace, Helen*
The Policy-Making Process in Contemporary Japan — *Nakano, Minoru*
Policy Options for Reform of Chinese State-Owned Enterprises — *Broadman, Harry G*
Policy, Practice, and Provision for Children with Specific Learning Difficulties — *Duffield, Jill*
Policy Responses to the Globalization of American Banking — *Dombrowski, Peter*
Policy Studies in Canada — *Dobuzinskis, Laurent*
Policymaking for Conservation in Latin America — *Hopkins, Jack W*
Polio's Legacy — *Sass, Edmund J*
The Polis and the Divine Order — *Zak, William F*
A Polish Renaissance — *Jacobson, Bernard*
Polite Landscapes — *Williamson, Tom*
Politeia: Society and State in the Aegean Bronze Age. Vols. 1-2 — *Laffineur, Robert*
Politica — *Althusius, Johannes*
r La Politica Italiana — *Pasquino, Gianfranco*
Political Alignment in the French National Assembly 1789-1791 — *Applewhite, Harriet B*
Political and Economic Liberalization — *Nonneman, Gerd*
Political and Economic Trends in Central Asia — *Akiner, Shirin*
r A Political Approach to Pacifism. Bks. 1-2 — *Morrisey, Will*
Political Bribery in Japan — *Mitchell, Richard H*
Political Catholicism and the Czechoslovak People's Party in Czechoslovakia 1918-1938 — *Trapl, Milos*

Political Change in Southeast Asia — *Vatikiotis, Michael R J*
The Political Classics — *Forsyth, Murray*
r Political Commentators in the United States in the 20th Century — *Nimmo, Dan*
A Political Companion to American Film — *Crowdus, Gary*
Political Correctness — *Feldstein, Richard*
Political Correctness — *Friedman, Marilyn*
Political Corruption in Europe and Latin America — *Little, Walter*
Political Culture and Civil Society in Russia and the New States of Eurasia — *Tismaneanu, Vladimir*
Political Culture in the Nineteenth-Century South — *Bond, Bradley G*
y Political Death (Hodge). Audio Version — *Fraser, Antonia*
Political Economy and the Labour Party — *Thompson, Noel*
Political Economy for the 21st Century — *Whalen, Charles J*
A Political Economy of Agricultural Markets in South India — *Harriss-White, Barbara*
The Political Economy of American Trade Policy — *Krueger, Anne O*
The Political Economy of Central-Bank Independence — *Eijffinger, Sylvester C W*
The Political Economy of Conflict and Appropriation — *Garfinkel, Michelle R*
The Political Economy of Democratic Transitions — *Haggard, Stephan*
The Political Economy of Diversity — *Delorme, Robert*
The Political Economy of Environmental Protection — *Congleton, Roger D*
The Political Economy of European Monetary Unification — *Eichengreen, Barry*
Political Economy of Fairness — *Zajac, Edward E*
The Political Economy of Hunger — *Dreze, Jean*
The Political Economy of Industrial Promotion — *Sridharan, Eswaran*
The Political Economy of International Labour Migration — *Gardezi, Hassan N*
The Political Economy of Japan Money — *Nakao, Shigeo*
The Political Economy of Nationalisation in Britain 1920-1950 — *Millward, Robert*
The Political Economy of Policy Coordination — *Webb, Michael C*
The Political Economy of Poverty, Equity, and Growth — *Lal, Deepak*
The Political Economy of Power — *Gadzey, Anthony Tuo-Kofi*
The Political Economy of Privatization and Deregulation — *Bailey, Elizabeth E*
The Political Economy of Public Administration — *Horn, Murray J*
The Political Economy of Racism — *Leiman, Melvin M*
The Political Economy of Regional Cooperation — *Axline, W Andrew*
The Political Economy of Socialism — *Horvat, Branko*
The Political Economy of Syria under Asad — *Perthes, Volker*
A Political Economy of the Middle East. 2nd Ed. — *Richards, Alan*
The Political Economy of the Minimal State — *Rowley, Charles K*
The Political Economy of the World Trading System — *Hoekman, Bernard M*
The Political Economy of Trade Integration — *Fratzscher, Oliver*
The Political Economy of Trade Protection — *Krueger, Anne O*
Political Economy of U.S.-Taiwan Trade — *Baldwin, Robert E*
The Political Education of Henry Adams — *Simpson, Brooks D*
Political Essays — *Hume, David*
r Political Geography — *Sukhwal, B L*
Political Geography of the United States — *Shelley, Fred M*
r Political Handbook of the World 1995-1996
The Political History of Economic Reform in Russia 1985-1994 — *Mau, Vladimir*
Political Ideas and Institutions in Imperial Russia — *Raeff, Marc*
Political Incorrections (Maher). Audio Version — *Maher, Bill*
Political Incorrectness — *Goldsmith, Marlene Herbert*
Political Institutions in Europe — *Colomer, Josep M*
Political Interaction in the Old Regime — *Gustafsson, Harald*

Political Inversions — *Hewitt, Andrew*
Political Islam — *Beinin, Joel*
Political Issues in America Today — *Davies, Philip John*
Political Judgment — *Lodge, Milton*
Political Judgments — *Howard, Dick*
y Political Leaders — *Lindop, Laurie*
r Political Leaders and Military Figures of the Second World War — *Chambers, Steven D*
Political Legitimacy in Southeast Asia — *Alagappa, Muthiah*
Political Liberalism — *Rawls, John*
Political Liberalization and Democratization in the Arab World. Vol. 1 — *Brynen, Rex*
Political Life in Medieval England 1300-1450 — *Ormrod, W M*
Political Order — *Shapiro, Ian*
y Political Parties — *Lindop, Edmund*
Political Parties and the European Union — *Gaffney, John, 1950-*
Political Parties and the State — *Shefter, Martin*
y Political Parties of the United States — *Kronenwetter, Michael*
Political Partisanship in the American Middle Colonies 1700-1776 — *Newcomb, Benjamin H*
Political Persuasion and Attitude Change — *Mutz, Diana C*
Political Philosophy and the Human Soul — *Palmer, Michael, 1952-*
Political Power in Alabama — *Permaloff, Anne*
Political Protest and Social Change — *Andrain, Charles F*
Political Realism in International Theory — *Spegele, Roger D*
Political Recruitment across Two Centuries — *Camp, Roderic Ai*
Political Reformism in Mexico — *Morris, Stephen D*
Political Rhetoric, Power, and Renaissance Women — *Levin, Carole*
The Political Role of the Military — *Danopoulos, Constantine P*
Political Science — *Scott, Gregory M*
Political Science in History — *Farr, James, 1950-*
Political Science in Theory and Practice — *Lane, Ruth*
Political Style — *Hariman, Robert*
r Political Systems of the World. 2nd Ed. — *Derbyshire, J Denis*
Political Theory and the Displacement of Politics — *Honig, Bonnie*
Political Theory for Mortals — *Seery, John E*
Political Theory, Modernity, and Postmodernity — *Rengger, N J*
The Political Thought of Karl Popper — *Shearmur, Jeremy*
y Political Timber — *Lynch, Chris*
The Political World of Thomas Wentworth, Earl of Strafford 1621-1641 — *Merritt, J F*
y Politically Correct Bedtime Stories — *Garner, James Finn*
Politically Correct Bedtime Stories (French). Audio Version — *Garner, James Finn*
The Politically Correct Guide to American History — *Moser, Edward P*
The Politically Correct Guide to the Bible — *Moser, Edward P*
Politically Correct Parables — *Walker, Robert Martin*
Politically Speaking — *Rebick, Judy*
Politicheskaia Istoriia Sovremennoi Rossii 1985-1994 — *Sogrin, Vladimir V*
y Politicians and Ethics — *Cozic, Charles P*
Politician's Dilemma — *Geddes, Barbara*
Politics after Hitler — *Rogers, Daniel E*
The Politics and Aesthetics of New Negro Literature — *Wintz, Cary D*
Politics and Corruption in Africa — *Kpundeh, Sahr John*
Politics and Development in the Caribbean Basin — *Grugel, Jean*
Politics and Elections in Nineteenth-Century Liverpool — *Collins, Neil*
Politics and Form in Postmodern Poetry — *Blasing, Mutlu Konuk*
Politics and Ideology in the Italian Workers' Movement — *Bedani, Gino*
Politics and Industrialization — *Dunlavy, Colleen A*
Politics and Judgment in Federal District Courts — *Rowland, C K*
Politics and Justice in Russia — *Feofanov, Yuri*
Politics and Narratives of Birth — *Mossman, Carol A*
Politics and Opinion in Crisis 1678-81 — *Knights, Mark*

Politics and Policy Implementation — *Lazin, Frederick A*

The Politics and Processes of Scholarship — *Moxley, Joseph M*

Politics and Rationality — *Booth, William James*

Politics and Religion in Central and Eastern Europe — *Swatos, William H*

Politics and Religious Authority — *Gelm, Richard J*

Politics and Scholarship — *McDermott, Patrice*

Politics and Society in Great Yarmouth 1660-1722 — *Gauci, Perry*

Politics and Society in Scotland — *Brown, Alice*

Politics and Space — *Brynes, Mark E*

Politics and Symbols — *Kertzer, David I*

Politics and the Class Divide — *Croteau, David*

Politics and the Constitution — *Bogdanor, Vernon*

Politics and the Parlement of Paris under Louis XV 1754-1774 — *Swann, Julian*

Politics and the People — *Vernon, James*

Politics and the Pound — *Stephens, Philip*

Politics and Welfare in Birmingham 1900-1975 — *LaMonte, Edward Shannon*

Politics, Censorship and the English Reformation — *Loades, D M*

Politics, Death, and the Devil — *Goldman, Harvey*

Politics for People — *Mathews, David*

Politics, Gender, and the Islamic Past — *Spellberg, D A*

Politics, Ideology, and Literary Discourse in Modern China — *Liu, Kang*

Politics, Ideology and the Law in Early Modern Europe — *Bakos, Adrinna E*

Politics in Black and White — *Sonenshein, Raphael*

Politics in Indonesia — *Ramage, Douglas E*

Politics in Performance — *Stuart, Ian*

Politics in the Impasse — *Martin, Bill, 1956-*

Politics, Law and Order in Nineteenth-Century Ireland — *Crossman, Virginia*

The Politics of a Popular Uprising — *Roy, Tapti*

The Politics of Africa's Economic Recovery — *Sandbrook, Richard*

The Politics of American Economic Policy Making. 2nd Ed. — *Peretz, Paul*

The Politics of Bargaining — *Waddington, Jeremy*

The Politics of Bavaria--an Exception to the Rule — *James, Peter, 1946-*

The Politics of Child Abuse in America — *Costin, Lela B*

The Politics of Clientelism — *Martz, John D*

Politics of Climate Change — *O'Riordan, Tim*

The Politics of Codification — *Young, Brian*

Politics of Conscience — *Wallace, Patricia Ward*

The Politics of Conversion — *Clark, Christopher M*

The Politics of Deafness — *Wrigley, Owen*

The Politics of Democratic Consolidation — *Gunther, Richard*

The Politics of Democratization — *Friedman, Edward*

The Politics of Denial — *Milburn, Michael A*

The Politics of Diversity — *Horton, John*

The Politics of Dreaming in the Carolingian Empire — *Dutton, Paul Edward*

The Politics of Economic Reform in Zimbabwe — *Skalnes, Tor*

The Politics of Economic Restructuring — *Cook, Maria Lorena*

The Politics of Educators' Work and Lives — *Ginsburg, Mark B*

The Politics of English Jacobinism — *Thelwall, John*

The Politics of Environmental Discourse — *Hajer, Maarten A*

The Politics of Expertise in Congress — *Bimber, Bruce A*

The Politics of Faith and the Politics of Scepticism — *Oakeshott, Michael*

The Politics of Garbage — *Luton, Larry S*

The Politics of German Child Welfare from the Empire to the Federal Republic — *Dickinson, Edward Ross*

The Politics of Global Atmospheric Change — *Rowlands, Ian H*

The Politics of Gun Control — *Spitzer, Robert J*

The Politics of Health Legislation. 2nd Ed. — *Feldstein, Paul J*

The Politics of Historical Vision — *Best, Steven*

The Politics of Hope — *Sacks, Jonathan*

The Politics of Industrialization in Tsarist Russia — *McCaffray, Susan P*

The Politics of Jerusalem since 1967 — *Dumper, Michael*

Politics of Liberation — *McLaren, Peter L*

The Politics of Manhood — *Kimmel, Michael S*

The Politics of Marriage — *Loades, D M*

The Politics of Marxism — *Townshend, Jules*

The Politics of Meaning — *Lerner, Michael, 1943-*

The Politics of Memory — *Hilberg, Raul*

The Politics of Memory — *Kramer, Jane*

The Politics of Minority Coalitions — *Rich, Wilbur C*

The Politics of Motherhood — *Bowers, Toni*

The Politics of My Heart — *Slaughter, William*

The Politics of Pan-Islam — *Landau, Jacob M*

The Politics of Pessimism — *Grubb, Alan*

The Politics of Philosophy — *Davis, Michael*

The Politics of Pictures — *Hartley, John*

The Politics of Population — *Johnson, Stanley*

The Politics of Power — *Freeman, Neil B*

The Politics of Presence — *Phillips, Anne*

The Politics of Protest — *Kaminer, Reuven*

The Politics of Punishment — *Adams, Bruce F*

The Politics of Rage — *Carter, Dan T*

The Politics of Readjustment — *Scott, Wilbur J*

The Politics of Redistributing Urban Aid — *Watson, Douglas J*

The Politics of Religion in Russia and the New States of Eurasia — *Bourdeaux, Michael*

The Politics of Revelation and Reason — *West, John G*

The Politics of Sensibility — *Ellis, Markman*

The Politics of Social Protest — *Jenkins, J Craig*

The Politics of Space — *Von Bencke, Matthew J*

The Politics of Structural Adjustment in Nigeria — *Olukoshi, Adebayo*

The Politics of Symbolism in the Mixtec Codices — *Pohl, John M D*

Politics of Technology in Latin America — *Bastos, Maria Ines*

The Politics of the Body in Weimar Germany — *Usborne, Cornelie*

The Politics of the Electronic Text — *Chernaik, Warren*

The Politics of the People in Eighteenth-Century Britain — *Dickinson, H T*

The Politics of the Reformation in Germany — *Brady, Thomas A*

Politics of the Theological — *Harvey, Barry*

The Politics of the Unpolitical — *Craig, Gordon A*

The Politics of Time — *Osborne, Peter*

The Politics of Torah — *Mittleman, Alan L*

The Politics of Unease in the Plays of John Fletcher — *McMullan, Gordon*

The Politics of Warfare — *Cimbala, Stephen J*

The Politics of Water — *Bennett, Vivienne*

The Politics of Women's Work — *Coffin, Judith G*

Politics on the Endless Frontier — *Kleinman, Daniel Lee*

Politics on the Net — *Mann, Bill*

Politics on the Nets — *Rash, Wayne*

Politics or Principle? — *Binder, Sarah A*

Politics, Philosophy, and the Production of Romantic Texts — *Hoagwood, Terence Allan*

Politics, Postmodernity and Critical Legal Studies — *Douzinas, Costas*

Politics, Religion and Diplomacy in Early Modern Europe — *Thorp, Malcolm R*

Politics, Society, and Christianity in Vichy France — *Halls, W D*

Politics, Sociology and Social Theory — *Giddens, Anthony*

Polities: Authority, Identities, and Change — *Ferguson, Yale H*

Politik Der Illusionen — *Larres, Klaus*

Politik Und Gelehrsamkeit In Der Zeit Der Han 202 V. Chr.-220 N. Chr. — *Ess, Hans Van*

La Politique Imaginaire — *Duhamel, Alain*

Politique Pour Le Developpement Rural

Polity and Society in Contemporary North Africa — *Zartman, I William*

Pollen — *Noon, Jeff*

r Polling and Survey Research Methods 1935-1979 — *Walden, Graham R*

Polling for Democracy — *Camp, Roderic Ai*

The Polliticke Courtier — *Dixon, Michael F N*

Pollution Prevention and Waste Minimization in Laboratories — *Reinhardt, Peter A*

Pollution Prevention for Chemical Processes — *Allen, David T*

Pollution Science — *Pepper, Ian L*

c Polly Pocket's Pajama Party (Illus. by Emilie Kong) — *Razzi, Jim*

c Pollyanna (Gordon). Audio Version — *Porter, Eleanor H*

La Pologne Dans L'Eglise Medievale — *Kloczowski, Jerzy*

Polska Prasa Studencka W II Rzeczypospolitej — *Magowska, Anita*

y Poltergeist — *Masters, Anthony*

Polyamines in Cancer — *Nishioka, Kenji*

Polycrystalline Thin Films — *Frost, Harold J*

y Polyethylene Terphthalate in Plastic Pop Bottles — *Jones, Judy*

Polygamous Families in Contemporary Society — *Altman, Irwin*

Polygnotos and Vase Painting in Classical Athens — *Matheson, Susan B*

c Polygons (Illus. by Richard Maccabe) — *Stienecker, David*

Polyhedral Virions and Bipartite RNA Genomes — *Harrison, B D*

r Polyimides: Fundamentals and Applications — *Ghosh, Malay K*

Polykleitos, the Doryphoros, and Tradition — *Moon, Warren G*

Polymer Devolatilization — *Albalak, Ramon J*

Polymer Microscopy. 2nd Ed. — *Sawyer, Linda C*

r Polymer Syntheses. 2nd Ed., Vol. 3 — *Sandler, Stanley R*

Polymer Technology. 3rd Ed. — *Miles, D C*

Polymeric Compatibilizers — *Datta, Sudhin*

Polymeric Systems — *Prigogine, I*

A Polynomial Approach to Linear Algebra — *Fuhrmann, Paul Abraham*

Polynomials and Polynomial Inequalities — *Borwein, P*

Polyominoes: Puzzles, Patterns, Problems, and Packings — *Golomb, Solomon W*

Polyphony and Symphony in Prophetic Literature — *Biddle, Mark E*

Polyphony in Portugal c. 1530-c. 1620 — *Rees, Owen*

Polypropylene Handbook — *Moore, Edward P*

Polysaccharides in Medicinal Applications — *Dumitriu, Severian*

Pombal: Paradox of the Enlightenment — *Maxwell, Kenneth, 1941-*

c The Pomegranate Seeds (Illus. by Leonid Gore) — *Geringer, Laura*

p Pomp and Circumstantial Evidence

y Pompeii — *Andrew, Ian*

c Pompeii and Herculaneum — *Hicks, Peter*

Pompeij: Stadtbild Und Wohngeschmack — *Zanker, Paul*

c Pond Water Zoo (Illus. by Jean Jenkins) — *Loewer, H Peter*

c Pond Year (Illus. by Mike Bostock) — *Lasky, Kathryn*

c Pongee Goes to Paris — *Noel, Rhya*

c Pongwiffy and the Holiday of Doom. Audio Version — *Ymansky, Kaye*

Pontiffs: Popes Who Shaped History — *Hughes, John Jay*

Il Pontificale Di Ravenna — *Benericetti, Ruggero*

c Pony Club Rider — *Leitch, Patricia*

c The Pony Express — *Anderson, Peter*

c Pony Express! (Illus. by Dan Andreasen) — *Kroll, Steven*

c Pony Express Riders of the Wild West — *Savage, Jeff*

The Pony Fish's Glow and Other Clues to Plan and Purpose in Nature — *Williams, George C*

c A Pony for Jeremiah (Illus. by Nneka Bennett) — *Miller, Robert H*

c Pooh and Some Bees (Illus. by Ernest H Shepard) — *Milne, A A*

c The Pooh Bedside Reader (Illus. by Ernest H Shepard) — *Melrose, A R*

cr The Pooh Dictionary (Illus. by Ernest H Shepard) — *Melrose, A R*

c Pooh Goes Visiting (Illus. by Ernest H Shepard) — *Milne, A A*

c Pooh's Little Etiquette Book (Illus. by Ernest H Shepard) — *France, Melissa Dorfman*

c Pooh's Parade. retold (Illus. by Ernest H Shepard) — *Milne, A A*

y Pool Party — *Cargill, Linda*

Poor Butterfly (Parker). Audio Version — *Kaminsky, Stuart M*

Poor Discipline — *Simon, Jonathan*

Poor Policy — *Schansberg, D Eric*

Poor Relations — *Hawes, C J*

Poor Richard's Principle — *Wuthnow, Robert*

Poor, Sinning Folk — *Myers, W David*

Poor Women and Children in the European Past — *Henderson, John*

Poor Women, Poor Children. 3rd Ed. — *Rodgers, Harrell R, Jr.*

r Pop Culture Landmarks — *Cantor, George*

Pop Culture Wars — *Romanowski, William D*

Pop Internationalism — *Krugman, Paul*
c Pop-o-Mania: How to Create Your Own Pop-Ups
   — *Valenta, Barbara*
Pop Out — *Doyle, Jennifer*
y Pope Joan — *Cross, Donna Woolfolk*
Pope John Paul II on Jews and Judaism 1979-1986
   — *John Paul II, Pope*
y Pope John Paul II: The Biography — *Szulc, Tad*
Pope Patrick — *De Rosa, Peter*
Pope, Swift, and Women Writers — *Mell, Donald C*
The Pope's Rhinoceros — *Norfolk, Lawrence*
c Poppleton (Illus. by Mark Teague) — *Rylant, Cynthia*
c Pepposites: A Lift, Pull, and Pop Book of Opposites
   — *Yoon, Jung-Huyn*
c Poppy (Illus. by Brian Floca) — *Avi*
y Poppy — *Rushton, Rosie*
r Popular American Housing — *Brent, Ruth*
Popular Anatomy — *Fraser, Keath*
Popular and Practical Science of Medieval England
   — *Matheson, Lister M*
Popular Anti-Catholicism in Mid-Victorian England
   — *Paz, D G*
Popular Arts of Mexico 1850-1950 — *McMenamin,*
Donna
Popular Contention in Great Britain 1758-1834
   — *Tilly, Charles*
Popular Culture, Crime, and Social Control in 18th-
Century Wurttemberg — *Wegert, Karl H*
Popular Culture in England c. 1500-1850 — *Harris,*
Tim
Popular Culture in Medieval Cairo — *Shoshan, Boaz*
The Popular Culture of Modern Art — *Weiss, Jeffrey*
r A Popular Dictionary of Judaism — *Cohn-Sherbok,*
Lavinia
Popular Fiction by Women 1660-1730
   — *Backscheider, Paula R*
Popular Government and the Supreme Court
   — *Sunderland, Lane V*
p Popular Mechanics
Popular Music and Society — *Longhurst, Brian*
Popular Music and the Underground — *Mancuso,*
Chuck
r Popular Physics and Astronomy — *Smith, Roger,*
1953, Apr., 4-
Popular Piety in Late Medieval England — *Brown,*
Andrew D
Popular Politics and British Anti-Slavery — *Oldfield,*
J R
Popular Radicalism in Nineteenth-Century Britain
   — *Belchem, John*
Popular Religion and Modernization in Latin America
   — *Parker G, Cristian*
Popular Religion in Germany and Central Europe
1400-1800 — *Scribner, Bob*
yr Popular YA Reading — *Estes, Sally*
The Popularization of Images — *Chu, Petra Ten-*
Doesschate
Popularizing Pennsylvania — *Bronner, Simon J*
Population and Development — *Cliquet, Robert*
Population and Development Transformations in the
Arab World — *Sirageldin, Ismail*
Population and the Environment — *Cartledge, Bryan*
Population Biology of the Florida Manatee — *O'Shea,*
Thomas J
Population Dynamics — *Cappuccino, Naomi*
Population Dynamics in Ecological Space and Time
   — *Rhodes, Olin E*
y Population Ecology. 3rd Ed. — *Begon, Michael*
Population Economics — *Razin, Assaf*
y Population Growth — *Jacobsen, Judith E*
r Population History of Western U.S. Cities and Towns
1850-1990 — *Moffat, Riley Moore*
Population in Asia — *Sanderson, Warren C*
Population Migration and the Changing World Order
   — *Gould, W T S*
Population Policy in Turkey — *Franz, Erhard*
Population: The Complex Reality — *Population*
Summit (1993: New Delhi, India)
The Populist Persuasion — *Kazin, Michael*
Poquosin: A Study of Rural Landscape and Society
   — *Kirby, Jack Temple*
Por La Libertad De Cuba — *Carbonell Cortina, Nestor*
y Pornography — *Wekesser, Carol*
Pornography: The Other Side — *Christensen, F M*
Le Port Interieur — *Volodine, Antoine*
cr The Portable Baker's Biographical Dictionary of
Musicians — *Slonimsky, Nicolas*
Portable C++ — *Giencke, Patricia*
y The Portable College Adviser — *Robbins, Wendy H*
The Portable Jack Kerouac — *Kerouac, Jack*

The Portable Pediatrician's Guide to Kids
   — *Nathanson, Laura Walther*
yr The Portable World Factbook — *Lye, Keith*
The Portable Writer's Conference — *Mettee, Stephen*
Blake
Portage Lake — *Kegg, Maude*
Il Portale Maggiore Di San Marco A Venezia
   — *Tigler, Guido*
I Portali Della Cattedrale Di Genova E Il Gotico
Europeo — *Cervini, Fulvio*
y Portent — *Herbert, James*
Le Porteur De Jeunes Mariees — *Pingwa, Jia*
Portfolios across the Curriculum and Beyond — *Cole,*
Donna
The Portobello Cookbook — *Czarnecki, Jack*
y Portofino: A Novel — *Schaeffer, Frank*
A Portrait in Letters — *Stape, J H*
Portrait Mummies from Roman Egypt (I-IV Centuries
A.D.) — *Corcoran, Lorelei Hilda*
Portrait of a Lady — *James, Henry*
The Portrait of a Lady — *Jones, Laura*
Portrait of a Lady (Bloom). Audio Version — *James,*
Henry
Portrait of a Young Man Drowning — *Perry, Charles*
Portrait of American Jews — *Heilman, Samuel C*
Portrait of an Abolitionist — *Heller, Charles E*
Portrait of an Appeaser — *Michie, Lindsay W*
Portrait of an Artist — *Varley, Frederick H*
y Portrait of an Artist (Conlin). Audio Version — *Lisle,*
Laurie
Portrait of California — *Jones, DeWitt*
A Portrait of Leni Riefenstahl — *Salkeld, Audrey*
Portrait of Mary — *Grimes, Nikki*
Portrait of My Body — *Lopate, Phillip*
Portrait of Picasso as a Young Man — *Mailer,*
Norman
Portrait of the Artist as a Bad Character — *Ozick,*
Cynthia
Portrait of the Walrus by a Young Artist — *Foos,*
Laurie
Portraits — *Holm, Stef Ann*
c Portraits — *King, Penny*
Portraits: A Gallery of Intellectuals — *Shils, Edward*
Portraits from the Age of Exploration — *Thevet,*
Andre
Portraits of Love — *Rogers, Susan Fox*
Portraits of Recovery — *Gaynor, Adam*
Portraits of Women — *Thomas, Alison*
Portrat Und Gesellschaft In Der Romischen Welt
   — *Balty, Jean Charles*
Ports of Entry — *Sobieszek, Robert A*
c Portugal, 8 Seculos Em Banda Desenhada (Illus. by
Jose Morim) — *Fernandes, Maria Da Conceicao*
Portugal E A NATO — *Telo, Antonio Jose*
Portugal, Spain, and the African Atlantic 1343-1490
   — *Russell, P E, 1913-*
The Portuguese Economy — *Neves, Joao Luis Cesar*
Das
The Portuguese in India — *Pearson, M N, 1941-*
c Posh Watson — *Cross, Gillian*
The Posing of Questions — *Wisniewski, Andrzej*
Positioning Subjects — *Appel, Stephen*
Positions Concerning the Training Up of Children
   — *Mulcaster, Richard*
Positive Behavioral Support — *Koegel, Lynn Kern*
Positive Cooking — *McMillan, Lisa*
Positively Women. Rev. and Updated Ed.
   — *O'Sullivan, Sue*
Positivist Republic — *Harp, Gillis J*
Positron Annihilation in Chemistry — *Mogensen, Ole*
Erik
Posmodernidad En La Periferia — *Herlinghaus,*
Hermann
Possessed by the Past — *Lowenthal, David*
Possessed: The True Story of an Exorcism — *Allen,*
Thomas B
Possessing Nature — *Findlen, Paula*
Possessing the Land — *Stalls, Clay*
y Possessing the Past — *Kuo Li Ku Kung Po Wu Yuan*
The Possessions of a Lady — *Gash, Jonathan*
Possibilities and Constraints of GIS Applications in
Developing Countries — *GISDECO Seminar (1991:*
Utrecht University)
Possible Dreams — *Bryant, Chris*
y Possible Lives — *Rose, Mike*
Possible Worlds — *Schroeder, Ralph*
Possible Worlds in Literary Theory — *Ronen, Ruth*
Possible Worlds of the Fantastic — *Traill, Nancy H*
c Possibles — *Nelson, Vaunda Micheaux*
c Possum's Harvest Moon (Illus. by Anne Hunter)
   — *Hunter, Anne*

The Post-Colonial Literature of Lusophone Africa
   — *Chabal, Patrick*
r Post-Colonial Literatures in English: Australia
1970-1992 — *Lever, Richard*
r Post-Colonial Literatures in English: Southeast Asia,
New Zealand, and the Pacific 1970-1992
   — *Williams, Mark*
Post Colonial Novel — *Juneja, Om P*
The Post-Human Condition — *Pepperell, Robert*
Post-Intellectualism and the Decline of Democracy
   — *Wood, Donald N*
Post-Keynesian Economic Theory — *Wells, Paul*
r Post Keynesian Economics — *King, J E*
Post Keynesian Economics — *Palley, Thomas I*
Post-Modernism for Beginners (Appignanesi). Audio
Version — *Appignanesi, Richard*
The Post Office — *Tagore, Rabindranath*
Post Office Jobs — *Damp, Dennis V*
Post-Passage Politics — *Van Beek, Stephen D*
y The Post-Rapture Diner — *Barresi, Dorothy*
Post-Shoa Religious Metaphors — *Rudnick, Ursula*
r The Post-Soviet Handbook — *Ruffin, M Holt*
Post-Soviet Perspectives on Russian Psychology
   — *Koltsova, Vera A*
Post-Soviet Puzzles. Vols. 1-4 — *Segbers, Klaus*
Post-Theory: Reconstructing Film Studies
   — *Bordwell, David*
Post-Totalitarian Spanish Fiction — *Spires, Robert C*
The Post-War Generation and Establishment Religion
   — *Roof, Wade Clark*
Post-War Wales — *Herbert, Trevor*
The Postal History and Markings of the Forwarding
Agents — *Rowe, Kenneth*
Postcards from France — *Libby, Megan McNeill*
Postcards from the Country — *Marren, Peter*
Postcards from the Net — *Casimir, Jon*
Postcards in the Library — *Stevens, Norman D*
Postcolonial Discourse and Changing Cultural
Contexts — *Rajan, Gita*
Postcolonial Subjects — *Green, Mary Jean*
Postcommunism: Four Perspectives — *Mandelbaum,*
Michael
Postera Crescam Laude
Posterior Circulation Disease — *Caplan, Louis R*
Postethnic America — *Hollinger, David A*
r Postgraduate Engineering and Technology Studies in
Europe, the CIS and North America: 1996/97
Academic Year
Posthuman Bodies — *Halberstam, Judith*
c Postman Pat's Holiday Packing (Illus. by J Hickson)
   — *Cunliffe, John*
The Postmodern Bible — *Bible and Culture Collective*
Postmodern Cities and Spaces — *Watson, Sophie*
Postmodern Environmental Ethics — *Oelschlager,*
Max
Postmodern Ethics — *Bauman, Zygmunt*
Postmodern Gaming — *Kuchler, Tilman*
The Postmodern in Latin and Latino American
Cultural Narratives — *Ferman, Claudia*
The Postmodern Novel in Latin America — *Williams,*
Raymond L
Postmodern Platos — *Zuckert, Catherine H*
Postmodern Public Administration — *Fox, Charles F*
Postmodern Representations — *Brown, Richard*
Harvey
Postmodern Semiotics — *Gottdiener, Mark*
Postmodern Socialism — *Beilharz, Peter*
Postmodern Theologies — *Tilley, Terrence W*
Postmodern Theory and Biblical Theology
   — *Ingraffia, Brian D*
Postmodern War — *Gray, Chris Hables*
Postmodernism across the Ages — *Readings, Bill*
Postmodernism and Islam — *Ahmed, Akbar S*
Postmodernism and Popular Culture — *McRobbie,*
Angela
Postmodernism and the Quebec Novel — *Paterson,*
Janet M
The Postmodernism Debate in Latin America
   — *Beverley, John*
Postmodernism: Local Effects, Global Flows — *Leitch,*
Vincent B
The Postmodernist Allegories of Thomas Pynchon
   — *Madsen, Deborah L*
Postmodernity in Latin America — *Colas, Santiago*
Postmortem: The O.J. Simpson Case — *Abramson,*
Jeffrey
Postnationalist Ireland — *Kearney, Richard*
Postscript to Murder — *Meek, M R D*
Poststructuralism, Politics and Education — *Peters,*
Michael, 1948-
Die Posttaxen Der Schweiz Ab 1875. Vol. 2

The Posture of Meditation — *Johnson, Will*
The Postwar Japanese System — *Tabb, William K*
Postwar Politics in the G-7 — *Shafer, Byron E*
Potash: Deposits, Processing, Properties and Uses
  — *Garrett, Donald E*
c Potato: A Tale from the Great Depression (Illus. by
  Lisa Campbell Ernst) — *Lied, Kate*
The Potato Factory — *Courtenay, Bryce*
c Potatoes — *Powell, Jillian*
A Potencie of Life — *Barker, Nicolas*
The Potential Effect of Two New Biotechnologies on
  the World Dairy Industry — *Jarvis, Lovell S*
I Poteri Dei Canossa Da Reggio Emilia All'Europa
  Golinelli, Paolo
c Potions to Pulsars — *Bursztynski, Sue*
c Potlatch: A Tsimshian Celebration — *Hoyt-Goldsmith,
  Diane*
p Potpourri
Potpourri and Fragrant Crafts — *Williams, Betsy*
Potshot — *Boyle, Gerry*
Potter's Fields — *Roderus, Frank*
The Potter's Palette — *Constant, Christine*
Potter's Pathology of the Fetus and Infant. Vols. 1-2
  — *Gilbert-Barnes, Enid*
r Poultry Diseases and Meat Hygiene — *Herenda,
  Drago C*
Pound/Cummings: The Correspondence of Ezra
  Pound and E.E. Cummings — *Pound, Ezra*
Pound, Thayer, Watson and The Dial — *Sutton,
  Walter*
Poundemonium — *Rios, Julian*
Pour Guy Debord — *Guilbert, Cecile*
Pour Lire Le Clezio — *Onimus, Jean*
Pour Sartre — *Brochier, Jean-Jacques*
Pour Une Histoire Des Traites De Savoir-Vivre En
  Europe — *Montandon, Alain*
Pourquoi Suis-Je Moi? — *Green, Julien*
Le Pouvoir Des Fables. Vol. 1 — *Grimm, Jurgen*
Poverty--A Global Review — *Oyen, Else*
Poverty: A History — *Geremek, Bronislaw*
Poverty and Deviance in Early Modern Europe
  — *Jutte, Robert*
Poverty and Place — *Jargowsky, Paul A*
Poverty and Political Culture — *Gouda, Frances*
Poverty and Power — *Cameron, John*
Poverty and Power — *Imig, Douglas A*
Poverty, Chastity, and Change — *Rogers, Carole
  Garibaldi*
Poverty in Canada. 2nd Ed. — *Sarlo, Christopher A*
Poverty, Inequality and Rural Development — *Lloyd,
  Tim*
Poverty, Inequality and Social Welfare in Australia
  — *Johnson, David Thomas*
Poverty, Inequality, and the Future of Social Policy
  — *McFate, Katherine*
Poverty Is Not a Vice — *Lindenmeyr, Adele*
The Poverty of Welfare Reform — *Handler, Joel F*
Povidky Z Rajskeho Udoli — *Skvorecky, Josef*
Powder Keg in the Middle East — *Kemp, Geoffrey*
Power across the Pacific — *Nester, William R*
Power Amp Book — *Dell, Edward, Jr.*
Power and Christian Ethics — *Mackey, James P*
Power and Compassion — *Price, Jerome A*
Power and Decision — *Sen, Gita*
c Power and Glory (Illus. by Geoff Kelly) — *Rodda,
  Emily*
Power and Pauperism — *Driver, Felix*
Power and Politics in Old Regime France 1720-1745
  — *Campbell, Peter R*
Power and Prosperity — *Shirk, Susan L*
y The Power and the Darkness — *Ribowsky, Mark*
Power and the Professions in Britain 1700-1850
  — *Corfield, Penelope J*
The Power and Value of Philosophical Skepticism
  — *Whitman, Jeffrey P*
Power and Violence in the Colonial City — *Cornblit,
  Oscar*
Power, Culture and Conflict in the Coalfields
  — *Fagge, Roger*
Power Curve — *Herman, Richard*
Power Cycles and Energy Efficiency — *Hoffman, E J*
r Power Electronics and Variable Frequency Drives
  — *Bose, Bimal K*
Power from Wind — *Hills, Richard L*
Power, Gender, and Christian Mysticism — *Jantzen,
  Grace*
Power Hybrid Circuit Design and Manufacture
  — *Taraseiskey, Haim*
Power in Motion — *Winters, Jeffrey A*
Power in Struggle — *Cooper, Davina*
Power in the Party — *Gill, Graeme*

Power in Transition — *Dosal, Paul J*
Power Lines — *Bendana, Alejandro*
The Power of Beauty — *Friday, Nancy*
The Power of Black Music — *Floyd, Samuel A, Jr.*
The Power of Color — *Marberry, Sara O*
The Power of Commerce — *Koehn, Nancy F*
The Power of Feminist Art — *Broude, Norma*
The Power of Influence — *Lambert, Tom*
The Power of Lies — *Kucich, John*
The Power of Mindful Learning — *Langer, Ellen*
The Power of Music (Campbell). Audio Version
  — *Campbell, Don*
The Power of News — *Schudson, Michael*
The Power of Place — *Hayden, Dolores*
The Power of Politics — *Duyvendak, Jan Willem*
Power of Raven, Wisdom of Spirit — *Jones, Noragh*
The Power of Separation — *Korn, Jessica*
The Power of Storytelling — *Mason, Harriet*
The Power of Style — *Tapert, Annette*
The Power of the Story — *Hanne, Michael*
The Power of Their Ideas — *Meier, Deborah*
The Power of Women — *Smith, Susan L*
Power on the Job — *Yates, Michael*
Power, Pasta, and Politics — *D'Amato, Alfonse*
Power Play — *Fleming, Dan*
Power, Politics, and Pentecostals in Latin America
  — *Cleary, Edward L*
Power Pricing — *Dolan, Robert J*
The Power Principle — *Lee, Blaine*
Power Programming in HP Openview — *Caruso,
  Raymond*
Power Restructuring in China and Russia — *Lupher,
  Mark*
Power Rules — *Duffield, John S*
Power Sharing and International Mediation in Ethnic
  Conflicts — *Sisk, Timothy D*
The Power Struggle — *Shannon, William T*
The Power to Care — *Hopps, June Gary*
The Power to Get In — *Boylan, Michael A*
The Power to Harm — *Cornwell, John*
The Power to Prevent Suicide — *Nelson, Richard E*
Power to Rise — *Neufeld, James*
y Power to the People — *Haskins, James*
Power to the People — *Thompson, Tommy G*
Power, Trust, and Meaning — *Eisenstadt, S N*
y Power Unseen — *Dixon, Bernard*
Power Up Your Library — *Salmon, Sheila*
Powerbuilder 5 How-To — *Biberdorf, Daryl*
r Powerful Black Women — *Smith, Jessie Carney*
c Powerhouse: Inside a Nuclear Power Plant (Illus. by
  Jerry Boucher) — *Wilcox, Charlotte*
Powering Apollo — *Lambright, W Henry*
Powerless: Selected Poems 1973-1990 — *Dlugos, Tim*
PowerPC: An Inside View — *Koerner, Michael*
PowerPC Microprocessor Common Hardware
  Reference Platform
PowerPoint for Windows 95 for Busy People
  — *Mansfield, Ron*
Powers and Prospects — *Chomsky, Noam*
Powers of Congress — *Fulton, Alice*
Powers of Evil — *Page, Sydney H T*
Powers of Horror — *Kristeva, Julia*
Powers of the Press — *Jones, Aled*
The Powers That Punish — *Bright, Charles*
Powersharing: White House-Cabinet Relations in the
  Modern Presidency — *Warshaw, Shirley Anne*
Powertown — *Lind, Michael*
y Powwow: Images Along the Red Road — *Marra, Ben*
c Powwow Summer (Illus. by Cheryl Walsh Bellville)
  — *Rendon, Marcie R*
PR! A Social History of Spin — *Ewen, Stuart*
A Practical Approach to Microsoft Word for Windows
  95 — *Morrison, Connie*
Practical Aspects of the Transfusion Service
  — *Anstall, Harold B*
Practical Decision Making in Health Care Ethics
  — *Devettere, Raymond J*
Practical Design and Production of Optical Thin Films
  — *Willey, Ronald R*
Practical Diagnosis of Hematologic Disorders. 2nd Ed.
  — *Kjeldsberg, Carl R*
The Practical Director. 2nd Ed. — *Crisp, Mike*
Practical Dispersion — *Conley, Robert F*
Practical Education. Vols. 1-3 — *Edgeworth, Maria*
Practical Electromyography. 3rd Ed. — *Johnson,
  Ernest W*
Practical Electronic Fault Finding and
  Troubleshooting — *Pain, Robin*
Practical Electronics — *Cook, Nigel P*
Practical Ethics for Roman Gentlemen — *Skidmore,
  Clive*

Practical Exotic Animal Medicine — *Rosenthal, Karen
  L*
Practical Flexible Sigmoidoscopy — *Cohen, Lawrence
  B*
Practical Gastrointestinal Endoscopy. 4th Ed.
  — *Cotton, Peter B*
A Practical Guide to Business Process Re-Engineering
  — *Robson, Mike*
Practical Guide to Experimental Design — *Frigon,
  Normand L*
Practical Guide to Grouting of Underground
  Structures — *Henn, Raymond W*
Practical Guide to Interviewing Teachers
Practical Guide to Occupational Health and Safety
  — *Erickson, Paul A*
r Practical Guide to Planned Giving 1996
yr The Practical Guide to Practically Everything 1997
Practical Guide to Software Quality Management
  — *Horch, John W*
Practical Guilt — *Greenspan, Patricia*
The Practical Handbook of Clinical Gerontology
  — *Carstensen, Laura L*
Practical Handbook of Genetic Algorithms. Vols. 1-2
  — *Chambers, Lance*
Practical Handbook of Processing and Recycling of
  Municipal Waste — *Manser, A G R*
Practical Handbook of Spatial Statistics — *Arlinghaus,
  Sandra Lach*
Practical Horticulture. 3rd Ed. — *Williams, Laura
  Rice*
r Practical HTML — *Tennant, Roy*
Practical Intuition — *Day, Laura*
Practical Lessons for Africa from East Asia in
  Industrial and Trade Policies — *Harrold, Peter*
Practical Management of Hypertension. 2nd Ed.
  — *Birkenhager, Willem H*
Practical Management of the Balance Disorder Patient
  — *Shepard, Neil T*
Practical Manual of Wastewater Chemistry
  — *Hauser, Barbara A*
Practical Neurology of the Elderly — *Sage, Jacob L*
Practical NLP for Managers — *McDermott, Ian*
Practical Numerical Analysis — *Evans, Gwynne A*
r Practical Paediatric Ophthalmology — *Taylor, David,
  1942-*
Practical Parallel Programming — *Wilson, Gregory V*
Practical Parenting — *Lipsitz, Gail Josephson*
r The Practical Pediatrician — *Markel, Howard*
Practical Praying — *Martin, Linette*
Practical Public Affairs in an Era of Change
  — *Dennis, Lloyd B*
Practical Realism and Moral Psychology — *Jacobs,
  Jonathan A*
Practical Reasoning about Final Ends — *Richardson,
  Henry S*
Practical Sociology — *Bryant, Christopher G A*
The Practical SQL Handbook. 3rd Ed. — *Bowman,
  Judith S*
Practical Strategies for Family-Centered Early
  Intervention — *McWilliam, P J*
Practical Strategies for the Modern Academic Library
  — *Heery, Mike*
Practical Thermoforming — *Florian, John*
A Practical View of Christianity — *Wilberforce,
  William*
Practical Ways to Teach Phonics — *Redfern, Angela*
c Practically Perfect (Illus. by H Offen) — *McKay,
  Hilary*
Practice and Progress in Cardiac Pacing and
  Electrophysiology — *Oto, Ali M*
Practice Management for the Dental Team. 4th Ed.
  — *Finkbeiner, Betty Ladley*
The Practice of Confessional Subscription — *Hall,
  David W*
The Practice of Diplomacy — *Hamilton, Keith*
The Practice of Emotionally Focused Marital Therapy
  — *Johnson, Susan M*
The Practice of Forensic Neuropsychology
  — *McCaffrey, Robert J*
The Practice of Management — *Drucker, Peter
  Ferdinand*
r The Practice of Multinational Banking. 2nd Ed.
  — *Khambata, Dara*
The Practice of Perfection — *Aitken, Robert*
The Practice of Performance — *Rink, John*
The Practice of Power — *Foot, Rosemary*
The Practice of Silviculture. 9th Ed. — *Smith, David
  Martyn*
The Practice of Theory — *Moxey, Keith*
The Practice of Writing — *Lodge, David*

Practice Parameters for the Psychiatric Assessment of Children and Adolescents
Practicing Our Faith — *Bass, Dorothy C*
Practicing Responsible Tourism — *Harrison, Lynn C*
Practicing What We Teach — *Martin, Renee J*
c Practise Your Language Skills Series — *Howard, Peter*
r Practitioner's Guide to Clinical Neuropsychology — *Anderson, Robert M, Jr.*
r A Practitioner's Guide to RISC Microprocessor Architecture — *Stakem, Patrick H*
The Pragmatics of Discourse Anaphora in English — *Geluykens, Ronald*
Pragmatism and Feminism — *Seigfried, Charlene Haddock*
Pragmatism and Social Theory — *Joas, Hans*
Pragmatism and the Political Economy of Cultural Revolution 1850-1940 — *Livingston, James, 1949-*
Pragmatism: From Progressivism to Postmodernism — *Hollinger, Robert*
r Prague and the Best of the Czech Republic
Prague in Black and Gold — *Demetz, Peter*
Prague Tales — *Neruda, Jan*
c A Prairie Boy's Summer (Illus. by William Kurelek) — *Kurelek, William*
c A Prairie Boy's Winter (Illus. by William Kurelek) — *Kurelek, William*
y The Prairie Chicken Kill — *Crider, Bill*
Prairie Conservation — *Samson, Fred B*
c The Prairie Dog (Illus. by Graham Allen) — *Crewe, Sabrina*
La Prairie En Nouvelle-France 1647-1760 — *Lavallee, Louis*
Prairie Night — *Miller, Brian*
Prairie Nights to Neon Lights — *Carr, Joe*
c Prairie Primer (Illus. by Susan Condie Lamb) — *Stutson, Caroline*
Prairie Reunion — *Scot, Barbara J*
y Prairie Rose — *Kirby, Susan*
The Prairie Schoolhouse — *Campbell, John Martin, 1927-*
y Prairie Songs — *Conrad, Pam*
The Prairie Winnows Out Its Own — *Nelson, Paula M*
c Prairies — *Murray, Peter, 1952, Sep., 9-*
c Prairies (Illus. by William Munoz) — *Patent, Dorothy Hinshaw*
Praise Jerusalem! — *Trobaugh, Augusta*
Praises to a Formless God — *Lorenzen, David N*
Prayer, Despair, and Drama — *Kaufman, Peter Iver*
c Prayer for a Child (Illus. by Elizabeth Orton Jones) — *Field, Rachel*
c A Prayer for the Earth (Illus. by Bethanne Andersen) — *Sasso, Sandy Eisenberg*
Prayer in the New Testament — *Cullmann, Oscar*
Prayer Is Good Medicine — *Dossey, Larry*
Prayer: The Mission of the Church — *Danielou, Jean*
Prayers for Bobby — *Aarons, Leroy*
Prayers for the Dead — *Kellerman, Faye*
y Prayers for the Dead (Schirner). Audio Version — *Kellerman, Faye*
Prayers for the Dead Ventriloquist — *Smith, D J*
Prayers of Faith — *Sand, Faith Annette*
Prayers of the Hours — *Lahman, James R*
Prayers of the Saints — *Koenig-Bricker, Woodeene*
Prayers to She Who Is — *Cleary, William*
Praying for Sleep — *Deaver, Jeffrey*
Praying Jesus' Way — *Dodd, Brian J*
c Praying Mantis — *Stefoff, Rebecca*
A Praying People — *Morrison, Dane*
Praying the Eucharist — *Miller, Charles*
Praying with Icons — *Forest, Jim*
Praying with the Word — *Haas, David*
Pre-Harvest Sprouting in Cereals 1995 — *Noda, Kaz*
The Pre-Industrial Urban System — *Lepetit, Bernard*
Pre-Law Companion — *Coleman, Ronald*
The Pre-Raphaelites — *Marsh, Jan*
y Pre: The Story of America's Greatest Running Legend, Steve Prefontaine. 2nd Ed. — *Jordan, Tom*
The Preacher King — *Lischer, Richard*
Preaching Friars and the Civic Ethos — *Paton, Bernadette*
Preaching the Crusades — *Maier, Christoph T*
Preaching the Epistles — *Collins, Raymond F*
Preaching the Hard Sayings of Jesus — *Carroll, John T*
Preaching the Just Word — *Burghardt, Walter J*
Preaching the Rites of Christian Initiation. Vol. 4 — *Joncas, Jan Michael*
Precarious Dependencies — *Gill, Leslie*
y Precious and Few — *Breithaupt, Don*

c The Precious Gift (Illus. by Woodleigh Marx Hubbard) — *Jackson, Ellen*
Precoat Filtration. 2nd Ed.
Precursori Di Cristoforo Colombo
p Predator: Big Game — *Arcudi, John*
Predatory Marketing — *Beemer, C Britt*
Prediction and Performance in Rock Mechanics and Rock Engineering. Vols. 1-3 — *Barla, G*
Prediction of Polymer Properties. 2nd Ed. — *Bicerano, Jozef*
Predictions for a New Millennium — *Tyl, Noel*
Predictors of Treatment Response in Mood Disorders — *Goodnick, Paul J*
Predigt In Der Alten Kirche — *Muhlenberg, Ekkehard*
The Preface to Luke's Gospel — *Alexander, Loveday*
A Preface to Shakespeare's Comedies 1594-1603 — *Mangan, Michael*
A Preface to Theology — *Gilpin, Clark*
y Pregnant? Adoption Is an Option — *Lindsay, Jeanne Warren*
Pregnant Men, Practice, Theory and the Law — *Colker, Ruth*
Prehistoire De La Geometrie — *Keller, Olivier*
Prehistoric Britain from the Air — *Darvill, Timothy*
Prehistoric Bulgaria — *Bailey, Douglass W*
Prehistoric Cultural Ecology and Evolution — *Henry, Donald O*
The Prehistoric Exploration and Colonisation of the Pacific — *Irwin, Geoffrey*
Prehistoric Farmers of the Susquehanna Valley — *Stewart, R Michael*
Prehistoric Japan — *Imamura, Keiji*
c Prehistoric Life — *Dixon, Dougal*
cr Prehistoric Life Explained — *Johnson, Jinny*
c Prehistoric People of North America — *Childress, Diana*
The Prehistory of Sex — *Taylor, Timothy*
Prehistory of the Central Mississippi Valley — *McNutt, Charles H*
The Prehistory of the Chickamauga Basin in Tennessee. Vols. 1-2 — *Lewis, Thomas M N*
The Prehistory of the Mind — *Mithen, Steven*
The Prehistory of the Netherlands — *Broeke, P W Van Den*
Prehistory to Politics — *Bonyhady, Tim*
Prehistorya Yazilari
Prejudices: A Selection — *Mencken, H L*
A Preliminary Edition of the Unpublished Dead Sea Scrolls. Vols. 1-4 — *Dead Sea Scrolls. 4Q. Selections*
Prelude for a Beginner Trombonist. Vols. 1-2 — *Borderes, Yves*
Prelude to Death — *Zukowski, Sharon*
Prelude to Trade Wars — *Kaplan, Edward S*
Premature Infatuation — *Peters, Lynn*
Premeditated Murder — *Selenic, Slobodan*
The Premier See — *Spalding, Thomas W*
Les Premieres Centuries Ou Propheties — *Nostradamus*
c Premiers Mots Pour Bebes De 12-18 Mois
c Premlata and the Festival of Lights (Illus. by Ian Andrew) — *Godden, Rumer*
r The Prentice Hall Directory of Online Business Information 1997
r The Prentice Hall Good Reading Guide — *McLeish, Kenneth*
Prepare to Be Healed. Audio Version — *Moran, Michael*
Preparing Convicts for Law-Abiding Lives — *Glaser, Daniel*
y Preparing for Adolescence — *Dobson, James C*
Preparing for Crises in the Schools — *Brock, Stephen E*
Preparing for the 21st Century
Preparing for the Urban Future — *Cohen, Michael A*
Preparing Staff to Serve Patrons with Disabilities — *Deines-Jones, Courtney*
Preparing to Teach Writing — *Williams, James D*
Prepositions and Complement Clauses — *Rudanko, Martti Juhani*
c Preposterous Pete (Illus. by Emma Chichester Clark) — *Cecil, Laura*
Prerequisites for Peace in the Middle East — *Taylor, Mark Adams*
Pres: The Story of Lester Young — *Delannoy, Luc*
The Presbyterian Conflict — *Rian, Edwin H*
Presbyterian Missions and Cultural Interaction in the Far Southwest 1850-1950 — *Banker, Mark T*
Presbyterian Women in America. 2nd Ed. — *Boyd, Lois A*
r Preschool Education in America — *Beatty, Barbara*

Preschoolers: Questions and Answers — *Furman, Erna*
The Prescott Street Reader — *Gale, Vi*
Prescription for Nutritional Healing. 2nd Ed. — *Black, James*
Prescription for Profits — *Marsa, Linda*
The Presence Is in Exile, Too — *Ayalti, Hanan J*
The Presence of Camoes — *Monteiro, George*
The Presence of God in the Christian Life — *Knight, Henry H, III*
Presence of Mind — *Brand, Alice Garden*
Present — *Corn, Alfred*
Present Fears — *Taylor, Elisabeth Russell*
c A Present for Paul (Illus. by David Mitchell) — *Ashley, Bernard*
Present Imperfect — *Kagal, Ayesha*
Present Tense — *Duncan, Dave*
Present Tense — *Reaman, Micki*
Presente, Pasado, Y Futuro De Las Chinampas — *Rojas Rabiela, Teresa*
The Presented Past — *Stone, Peter G*
Presenting ActiveX — *Warren, Ernst*
Presently a Beast — *Brewer, Gay*
Presenza Verbale Di Dante Nella Letteratura Italiana Del Novecento — *Scorrano, Luigi*
Preservation Management — *Feather, John*
Preservation Microfilming. 2nd Ed. — *Fox, L L*
Preservation of Surfactant Formulations — *Morpeth, F F*
Preserving — *Schwartz, Oded*
Preserving Digital Information — *Task Force on Archiving of Digital Information*
A Preserving Grace — *Cromartie, Michael*
Preserving Historic New England — *Lindgren, James M*
Preserving Library Materials. 2nd Ed. — *Swartzburg, Susan G*
Preserving Memory — *Linenthal, Edward T*
Preserving Ontario's Harvest by Foodland Ontario
Preserving the Family Farm — *Neth, Mary*
Preserving the Monarchy — *Price, Munro*
Preserving the Present — *Bikson, T K*
The Presidency and the Rhetoric of Foreign Crisis — *Bostdorff, Denise M*
The Presidency in a Separated System — *Jones, Charles O*
The Presidency of Gerald R. Ford — *Greene, John Robert*
The Presidency of James Monroe — *Cunningham, Noble E, Jr.*
y The Presidency of the United States — *Judson, Karen*
The President — *Hudson, Parker*
y The President Has Been Shot! — *Jones, Rebecca C*
The President Is at Camp David — *Nelson, W Dale*
The President We Deserve — *Walker, Martin*
The Presidential Archive — *Griffiths, John, 1940-*
The Presidential Commission on the Assignment of Women in the Armed Forces — *United States. Presidential Commission on the Assignment of Women in the Armed Forces*
c Presidential Conventions — *Henry, Christopher*
c Presidential Elections — *Henry, Christopher*
r Presidential Elections 1789-1992
Presidential Leadership — *Fisher, James L*
Presidential Leadership from Eisenhower to Clinton — *Blakesley, Lance*
r Presidential Libraries and Museums — *Hyland, Pat*
r The Presidential Medal of Freedom — *Wetterau, Bruce*
c Presidential Medal of Freedom Winners — *Bredeson, Carmen*
Presidential Polls and the News Media — *Lavrakas, Paul J*
The Presidential Republic — *Gregg, Gary L*
Presidential War Power — *Fisher, Louis*
r The Presidents: A Reference History. 2nd Ed. — *Graff, Henry F*
The President's Daughter — *Higgins, Jack*
yr The Presidents, First Ladies and Vice Presidents — *Diller, Daniel C*
The President's Man — *Weiss, Stuart L*
Presidents of Central America, Mexico, Cuba, and Hispaniola — *Alexander, Robert J*
r Presidents of the United States--Their Written Measure — *Sayler, James*
r The Presidents Speak — *United States. President*
Presocratic Reflexivity — *Sandywell, Barry*
The Press and the Bush Presidency — *Rozell, Mark J*
The Press in Ghana — *Asante, Clement E*
The Press in the Arab Middle East — *Ayalon, Ami*
Press Law in South Korea — *Youm, Kyu Ho*

The Press of the Young Republic 1783-1833
— *Humphrey, Carol Sue*
Pressepolitik Und Staatsreform — *Hofmeister-Hunger, Andrea*
Pressure-Sensitive Adhesives Technology — *Benedek, Istvan*
Pressure Vessels and Piping Codes and Standards. Vols. 1-2
Pressure Vessels and Piping Design, Analysis, and Severe Accidents — *Dermenjian, Artin A*
The Prestige — *Priest, Christopher*
Presto Con Fuoco — *Cotroneo, Roberto*
The Presumption of Culture — *Henighan, Tom*
Pretend You Don't See Her — *Clark, Mary Higgins*
c Pretend You're a Cat (Illus. by Jerry Pinkney) — *Marzollo, Jean*
Pretending and Meaning — *Henry, Richard*
Preternatural — *Bonanno, Margaret Wander*
Pretexts of Authority — *Dunn, Kevin*
c Pretty Brown Face (Illus. by Brian Pinkney) — *Pinkney, Andrea Davis*
y Pretty in Pink — *Bernstein, Jon*
Die Preussenreisen Des Europaischen Adels. Vol. 2 — *Paravicini, Werner*
Prevent, Repent, Reform, Revenge — *Diver-Stamnes, Ann C*
Preventing and Mitigating AIDS in Sub-Saharan Africa — *Cohen, Barney*
Preventing Childhood Disorders, Substance Abuse, and Delinquency — *Peters, Ray DeV*
Preventing Conflict in the Post-Communist World — *Chayes, Abram*
Preventing Heterosexism and Homophobia — *Rothblum, Esther D*
Preventing Illness among People with Coronary Heart Disease — *Piette, John D*
Preventing Misdiagnosis of Women — *Klonoff, Elizabeth A*
Preventing Patient Falls — *Morse, Janice M*
r Preventing Substance Abuse — *Stoil, Michael J*
Preventing Violence in America — *Hampton, Robert L*
Preventing Violent Conflicts — *Lund, Michael S*
Prevention and Management of Complications in Minimally Invasive Surgery — *Lanzafame, Raymond J*
Prevention in Psychiatry — *Paykel, Eugene S*
Prevention, Response, and Oversight Five Years after the Exxon Valdez Oil Spill
r Prevention's Healing with Vitamins — *Prevention Magazine Health Books*
Prevention's the Healthy Cook — *Prevention Magazine Health Books*
Preventive Diplomacy — *Cahill, Kevin M*
Previous Convictions — *Sayre, Nora*
Prezente Romanesti In Italia — *Lazarescu, George*
Price Caps for Telecommunications
r Price Funeral Home Records 1960 — *Nodaway County Genealogical Society*
r Price Guide and Bibliographic Check List for Children's and Illustrated Books 1880-1960. 1996 Ed. — *Baumgarten, E Lee*
The Price of a Child — *Cary, Lorene*
The Price of a Dream — *Bornstein, David*
The Price of a Horse — *Cotton, Ralph*
The Price of Blood — *Logan, Chuck*
The Price of Excellence — *Neusner, Jacob*
The Price of Federalism — *Peterson, Paul E*
The Price of Freedom — *Whitman, T Stephen*
The Price of Honor — *Goodwin, Jan*
The Price of Land in Shelby — *Alberts, Laurie*
The Price of Meat — *Penman, Danny*
The Price of Prophecy. 2nd Ed. — *Webster, Alexander F C*
The Price of the Past — *Gaddy, Clifford G*
Price Rigidity — *Andersen, Torben M*
r The Price Waterhouse Guide to TIN Compliance. 1996-1997 Ed.
The Price You Pay — *Randall, Margaret*
r Prices and Financial Statistics in the ESCWA Region. 13th Ed.
Prices, Cycles, and Growth — *Nikaido, Hukukane*
Prices, Food, and Wages in Scotland 1550-1780 — *Gibson, A J S*
Pricing the Planet — *May, Peter Herman*
Pricing, Valuation and Systems — *Tool, Marc R*
c Prickety Prackety (Illus. by Caroline Crossland) — *Ross, Diana*
c Prickly and Poisonous — *Ganeri, Anita*
c Pride and Penalties — *Blacker, Terence*
Pride and Prejudice — *Austen, Jane*
y Pride of Lions — *Llywelyn, Morgan*

Priest and Partisan — *Worsnip, Michael*
Priestess, Mother, Sacred Sister — *Sered, Susan Starr*
Priesthood Imperiled — *Haring, Bernard*
Priestly Fictions — *Candy, Catherine*
c Prietita and the Ghost Woman (Illus. by Christina Gonzalez) — *Anzaldua, Gloria*
Prikliucheniia Maiora Zviagina — *Veller, Mikhail Iosifovich*
The Primacy of Practical Reason — *Marsonet, Michele*
Primal-Dual Interior-Point Methods — *Wright, Stephen J*
The Primary Assembly File
Primary Behaviour File — *Gordon, Rory*
Primary Care — *Donaldson, Molla S*
Primary Care for the Obstetrician and Gynecologist — *Thornton, Yvonne S*
Primary Care in Gynecology — *Ling, Frank W*
Primary Care of the Child with a Chronic Condition. 2nd Ed. — *Jackson, Patricia Ludder*
Primary Care Optometry. 3rd Ed. — *Grosvenor, Theodore P*
Primary Colors — *Anonymous*
The Primary Colors — *Theroux, Alexander*
y Primary Colors (James). Audio Version — *Anonymous*
Primary English — *Sainsbury, Marian*
Primary Prevention Works — *Albee, George W*
Primary Pulmonary Hypertension — *Rubin, Lewis J*
Primary Science — *Kennedy, Jenny*
y The Prime Minister — *Clarke, Austin*
y The Prime Ministers of Canada — *Donaldson, Gordon*
Prime-Time Feminism — *Dow, Bonnie J*
r Prime-Time Religion — *Melton, J Gordon*
A Primer for Health Care Ethics — *DeBlois, Jean*
A Primer of Population Dynamics — *Namboodiri, N Krishnan*
A Primer of Real Functions. 4th Ed. — *Boas, Ralph P*
A Primer on German Enlightenment — *Roehr, Sabine*
A Primer on Postmodernism — *Grenz, Stanley J*
Primer on the Autonomic Nervous System — *Robertson, David, 1947-*
A Primer to Mechanism in Organic Chemistry — *Sykes, Peter*
Primeras Doctrinas Del Nuevo Mundo — *Gil, Fernando*
Primero Sueano — *Juana Ines De La Cruz, Sister*
The Primitive Church in the Modern World — *Hughes, Richard T*
Primitive Passions — *Torgovnick, Marianna*
Primitives, Patriarchy, and the Picaresque in Blasco Ibanez's Canas Y Barro — *Anderson, Christopher L*
y The Primrose Path — *Matas, Carol*
y The Primrose Way — *Koller, Jackie French*
Prin Lume — *Lupu, N*
c The Prince and the Pauper (Reiner). Audio Version — *Twain, Mark*
The Prince and the Professor — *Blake, L L*
c Prince Edward Island — *Campbell, Kumari*
Prince John Magruder: His Life and Campaigns — *Casdorph, Paul D*
Prince of the People — *Silva, Eduardo Da*
c The Prince of the Pond — *Napoli, Donna Jo*
The Prince of West End Avenue — *Isler, Alan*
Prince, People, and Confession — *Nischan, Bodo*
Princes of the Trenches — *Linder, Ann P*
y The Princess and the God — *Orgel, Doris*
c The Princess and the Pea (Illus. by Emily Bolam) — *Ziefert, Harriet*
c The Princess and the Perfect Dish (Illus. by Armin Greder) — *Gleeson, Libby*
c The Princess and the Pirate King — *Gliori, Debi*
c The Princess Book (Illus. by Jan Palmer) — *Loehr, Mallory*
Princess Charming — *Heller, Jane*
c Princess Florecita and the Iron Shoes (Illus. by K Wendy Popp) — *Stewig, John*
c A Princess in Boxland (Illus. by Tanja Szekessy) — *Szekessy, Tanja*
Princess in Love — *Pasternak, Anna*
Princess Margaret: A Biography — *Aronson, Theo*
Princess of Hollywood — *Gehman, Pleasant*
c Princess Penelope's Parrot (Illus. by Lynn Munsinger) — *Lester, Helen*
c Princess Prunella and the Purple Peanut — *Atwood, Margaret*
c Princess Stinky-Toes and the Brave Frog Robert (Illus. by Leslie Fitzgerald Watts) — *Watts, Leslie Fitzgerald*
The Princessa: Machiavelli for Women — *Rubin, Harriet*
La Princesse De Cleves — *La Fayette, Madame De*
p Princeton Arts Review

r The Princeton Field Guide to the Birds of Australia. 5th Ed. — *Simpson, Ken*
r The Princeton Handbook of Multicultural Poetries — *Brogan, T V F*
yr The Princeton Review College Advisor. 1997 Ed. Electronic Media Version
y The Princeton Review College Companion — *Sponholz, Melanie*
y The Princeton Review Grammar Smart Junior — *Buffa, Liz*
r The Princeton Review Guide to Your Career. 1997 Ed.
yr The Princeton Review Student Access Guide to the Best Business Schools. 1996 Ed.
yr The Princeton Review Student Advantage Guide to Summer Programs. 1997 Ed.
y The Princeton Review Word Smart Junior — *Brantley, C L*
y The Princeton Review Writing Smart Junior — *Brantley, C L*
The Principal: Creative Leadership for Effective Schools. 3rd Ed. — *Ubben, Gerald C*
Principal Products of Portugal — *Hall, Donald, 1928-*
Il Principe E L'Antichristo — *Barbuto, Gennaro Maria*
Les Principia De Newton — *Blay, Michel*
The Principle of Duty — *Selbourne, David*
The Principle of Mercy — *Sobrino, Jon*
The Principle of Provenance — *Abukhanfusa, Kerstin*
Principles and Applications of Inorganic, Organic, and Biological Chemistry. 2nd Ed. — *Caret, Robert L*
Principles and Applications of Optical Communications — *Ming-Kang Liu, Max*
Principles and Politics in Contemporary Britain — *Garnett, Mark*
Principles and Practice of Dermatology. 2nd Ed. — *Sams, W Mitchell*
The Principles and Practice of Electrical Epilation. 2nd Ed. — *Godfrey, Sheila*
Principles and Practice of Mathematics — *Consortium for Mathematics and Its Applications (U.S.)*
Principles and Practice of Pediatric Infectious Diseases — *Long, Sarah S*
Principles and Privilege — *Kemble, Frances A*
Principles and Techniques of Vibrations — *Meirovitch, Leonard*
Principles of Antineoplastic Drug Development and Pharmacology — *Schilsky, Richard L*
Principles of Asymmetric Synthesis — *Gawley, Robert E*
Principles of Bibliographical Description — *Bowers, Fredson*
Principles of Biochemistry. 2nd Ed. — *Horton, H Robert*
Principles of Bone Biology — *Bilezikian, John P*
Principles of Brain Functioning — *Haken, Hermann*
Principles of Condensed Matter Physics — *Chaikin, P M*
Principles of Contaminant Hydrogeology. 2nd Ed. — *Palmer, Christopher M*
Principles of Cost-Benefit Analysis for Developing Countries — *Dinwiddy, Caroline*
Principles of Digital Design — *Gajski, Daniel D*
Principles of Drug Development in Transplantation and Autoimmunity — *Lieberman, Ronald*
Principles of Ecotoxicology — *Walker, C H*
Principles of Electric Circuits. 5th Ed. — *Floyd, Thomas L*
Principles of Fluoroscopic Image Intensification and Television Systems — *Parelli, Robert J*
Principles of Gardening. Rev. Ed. — *Johnson, Hugh*
Principles of High-Resolution Radar — *Rihaczek, August W*
Principles of Information Systems Management — *Ward, John*
Principles of Lightware Communications — *Einarsson, Goran*
Principles of Logic and Logic Programming — *Metakides, George*
Principles of Marketing. European Ed. — *Kotler, Philip*
The Principles of Mathematics Revisited — *Hintikka, Jaakko*
Principles of Microwave Technology — *Harsany, Stephen C*
Principles of Mobile Communication — *Stuber, Gordon L*
Principles of Pharmacology. Rev. Ed. — *Munson, Paul L*
Principles of Polymer Systems. 4th Ed. — *Rodriguez, Ferdinand*

Principles of Precambrian Geology — *Goodwin, Alan M*

r Principles of Radio Communication — *Mazda, Fraidoon*

Principles of Seed Pathology. 2nd Ed. — *Agarwal, V K*

The Principles of the Most Ancient and Modern Philosophy — *Conway, Anne*

Principles of Toxicology — *Stine, Karen E*

Principles of Wet End Chemistry. 2nd Ed. — *Scott, William E*

PRINS and In Situ PCR Protocols — *Gosden, John R*

Print and Broadcast Journalism — *Applegate, Edd*

Print Culture in Renaissance Italy — *Richardson, Brian*

yr The Print in the Western World — *Hults, Linda C*

Print, Power and People in 17th-Century France — *Martin, Henri-Jean*

r Print Quarterly: Index to Vols. 1-10 — *Pollak, Felix*

Print Style — *Hinchcliffe, John*

r The Printed Catalogues of the Harvard College Library 1723-1790 — *Bond, W H*

Printed Circuit Board Design Techniques for EMC Compliance — *Montrose, Mark I*

r Printed Circuits Handbook. 4th Ed. — *Coombs, Clyde F, Jr.*

Printed Commonplace-Books and the Structuring of Renaissance Thought — *Moss, Ann*

The Printed Press and Television in the Regions of Europe — *Musso, Pierre*

Le Printemps N'En Sera Que Plus Beau — *Mimouni, Rachid*

Printers and Men of Capital — *Remer, Rosalind*

y Printer's Devil to Publisher — *Faber, Doris*

c Printing — *Gibson, Ray*

Printing a Book at Verona in 1622 — *Fahy, Conor*

Printing, Propaganda, and Martin Luther — *Edwards, Mark U*

Prints and Printmaking. 2nd Ed. — *Griffiths, Antony*

Prion Diseases — *Baker, Harry F*

Prions Prions Prions — *Prusiner, S B*

Priority One — *California Public Education Partnership*

c Priscilla Twice (Illus. by Judith Caseley) — *Caseley, Judith*

Prison Letters — *Gramsci, Antonio*

p Prison Life

Prison Meditations on Psalms 51 and 31 — *Savonarola, Girolamo*

Prison Notebooks. Vol. 2 — *Gramsci, Antonio*

Prisoned Chickens, Poisoned Eggs — *Davis, Karen*

The Prisoner — *Zaman, Fakhar*

Prisoner for Polygamy — *Clawson, Rudger*

Prisoner of Dunes — *Eberhardt, Isabelle*

Prisoner of History — *Henry, Madeleine M*

Prisoner of Hope — *Prywes, Moshe*

Prisoners of Myth — *Hargrove, Erwin C*

Prisoners of the Japanese — *Daws, Gavan*

Prisons — *Settle, Mary Lee*

Prisons and AIDS — *Braithwaite, Ronald L*

y Prisons: Inside the Big House — *Hjelmeland, Andy*

Prisons of Light — *Ferguson, Kitty*

Privacy and Its Invasion — *McLean, Deckle*

Private and Public School Partnerships — *Madsen, Jean*

Private Banking in Europe — *Bicker, Lyn*

Private Business and Economic Reform in China — *Young, Susan*

Private Confessions — *Bergman, Ingmar*

Private Consciences and Public Reasons — *Greenawalt, Kent*

Private Correspondence — *Lewis, Trudy*

The Private Diary of an O.J. Juror — *Knox, Michael*

r Private Libraries in Renaissance England. Vols. 1-2 — *Fehrenbach, R J*

The Private Life of Chairman Mao — *Li, Zhisui*

The Private Life of Plants — *Attenborough, David*

The Private Lives of the Three Tenors — *Lewis, Marcia*

Private Lives, Public Spirit — *Harris, Jose*

Private Markets in Health and Welfare — *Johnson, Norman*

Private Matters — *Smith, Janna Malamud*

Private Matters and Public Culture in Post-Reformation England — *Orlin, Lena Cowen*

A Private Mythology — *Sarton, May*

Private Myths — *Stevens, Anthony*

c The Private Notebook of Katie Roberts, Age 11 (Illus. by Sonja Lamut) — *Hest, Amy*

The Private Parts of Women — *Glaister, Lesley*

Private Poets, Worldly Acts — *Stein, Kevin*

The Private Regulation of American Health Care — *Leyerle, Betty*

The Private Science of Louis Pasteur — *Geison, Gerald L*

Private Sector Development during Transition — *Borish, Michael S*

Private Sector Development in Egypt — *Giugale, Marcelo M*

Private Sector Development in Low-Income Countries — *World Bank*

Private Sector Participation in the Water Supply and Wastewater Sector — *Rivera, Daniel*

Private Truths, Public Lies — *Kuran, Timur*

A Private View (Whale). Audio Version — *Brookner, Anita*

Private Voices — *Gaskell, Elizabeth*

Private Voices, Public Lives — *Nelson, Nancy Owen*

Private Voluntary Organizations in Egypt — *Sullivan, Denis Joseph*

Private Welfare Insurance and Social Security — *Hills, John*

The Private World of the Duke and Duchess of Windsor — *Vickers, Hugo*

The Private Worlds of Marcel Duchamp — *Seigel, Jerrold*

Privatisation and Regulation — *Jackson, Peter M*

r Privatisation Policy and Performance — *Cook, Paul, 1944-*

Privatising the Public Interest — *Skogerboe, Eli*

Privatization and Capital Market Development — *McLindon, Michael P*

Privatization and Political Change in Mexico — *Teichman, Judith A*

Privatization, Deregulation and the Macroeconomy — *Bergeijk, Peter A G Van*

Privatization in Central and Eastern Europe — *Estrin, Saul*

Privatization in Eastern Europe — *Frydman, Roman*

Privatization in the Ancient Near East and Classical World — *Hudson, Michael*

The Privatization of Public Utilities — *Hyman, Leonard S*

The Privatization Process — *Anderson, Terry J*

Privatization: Social Science Themes and Perspectives — *Braddon, Derek*

Privatizing Africa's Infrastructure — *Kerf, Michel*

Privatizing Monopolies — *Ramamurti, Ravi*

The Privats: Lore, Legends and Facts 1600-1995 — *Privat, John Pierre*

Privilege Revealed — *Wildman, Stephanie M*

Privileged Anonymity — *Green, Anne*

Privileged Conversation (Whitener). Audio Version — *Hunter, Evan*

Privileged Hands — *Vermeij, Geerat*

Privileged to Kill — *Havill, Steven F*

Privileging Gender in Early Modern England — *Brink, Jean R*

The Prize — *Yergin, Daniel*

Prize Stories 1996

y Prize Winners — *Yunghans, Penelope*

The Prizefighters: An Intimate Look at Champions and Contenders — *Schulman, Arlene*

r Pro-Choice/Pro-Life Issues in the 1990s — *Fitzsimmons, Richard*

Pro-Choice vs. Pro-Life — *Morton, F L*

r Pro Football Guide. 1996 Ed.

y Pro Sports Halls of Fame. Vols. 1-8

A Probabilistic Analysis of the Sacco and Vanzetti Evidence — *Kadane, Joseph B*

Probabilistic Mechanics and Structural Reliability — *Specialty Conference on Probabilistic Mechanics and Structural Reliability (7th: 1996: Worcester, Mass.)*

Probability: A Survey of the Mathematical Theory. 2nd Ed. — *Lamperti, John W*

Probability and Statistical Inference — *Bartoszynski, Robert*

Probability in Economics — *Hamouda, Omar F*

Probability Theory — *Borkar, Vivek S*

Probability Theory and Combinatorial Optimization — *Steele, J Michael*

p Probable Cause

Le Probable, Le Possible Et Le Virtuel — *Granger, Gilles-Gaston*

r Probate Death Records, Wood County, Ohio. Vol. 1

Probation and Parole. 6th Ed. — *Abadinsky, Howard*

Probes: Genetic Studies in Joyce — *Hayman, David*

Probing the Foundations — *Pailin, David A*

Probing the Limits of Representation — *Freidlander, Saul*

c Probity Jones and the Fear Not Angel (Illus. by Tim Ladwig) — *Wangerin, Walter*

The Problem of American Realism — *Bell, Michael Davitt*

The Problem of Consciousness — *McGinn, Colin*

The Problem of Democracy in Cuba — *Bengelsdorf, Carolee*

A Problem of Evidence — *Bosco, Joseph*

The Problem of Hell — *Kvanvig, Jonathan L*

The Problem of Humanity — *Tiainen-Anttila, Kaija*

The Problem of Ireland in Tudor Foreign Policy 1485-1603 — *Palmer, William, 1951-*

The Problem of Nature — *Arnold, David*

The Problem of the Rational Soul in the Thirteenth Century — *Dales, Richard C*

Problem Pictures — *Nunn, Pamela Gerrish*

Problem Solving — *German, O V*

y Problem Solving in Environmental Biology — *Ennos, A R*

The Problem That Won't Go Away — *Aaron, Henry J*

The Problem with Pornography — *Easton, Susan M*

La Problematique Du Sujet Chez Montaigne — *Kushner, Eva*

Le Probleme Feminin Et Les Portraits De Femmes Dans L'Oeuvre De Nikolaj Leskov — *Muller De Morogues, Ines*

Problems and Exercises in Discrete Mathematics — *Gavrilov, G P*

Problems in Equilibrium Theory — *Aliprantis, Charalambos D*

Problems in Philosophy — *McGinn, Colin*

Problems in the Life and Writings of A.E. Housman — *Naiditch, P G*

Problems of Democratic Transition and Consolidation — *Linz, Juan J*

Problems of Economic and Political Transformation in the Balkans — *Jeffries, Ian*

Problems of Reducing the Exhaustive Search — *Kreinovich, V*

The Proboscidea: Evolution and Palaeoecology of Elephants and Their Relatives — *Shoshani, Jeheskel*

Proceedings: 11th Annual Knowledge-Based Software Engineering Conference

Proceedings 1996 International Conference on Parallel and Distributed Systems — *International Conference on Parallel and Distributed Systems (1996: Tokyo, Japan)*

Proceedings 1996 Symposium on Logic in Computer Science

Proceedings: International Workshop on Neural Networks for Identification, Control, Robotics, and Signal/Image Processing — *International Workshop on Neural Networks for Identification, Control, Robotics, and Signal/Image Processing (1996: Venice, Italy)*

Proceedings of the 2nd International Symposium on Parallel Architectures, Algorithms, and Networks (ISPAN)

Proceedings of the 3rd International Symposium on Intelligent Robotic Systems '95 — *Colombo, Carlo*

Proceedings of the 4th International Workshop on Parallel and Distributed Real-Time Systems, April 15-16, 1996, Honolulu, Hawaii

Proceedings of the 4th Israeli Symposium on the Theory of Computing and Systems

Proceedings of the 7th ASME International Transmission and Gearing Committee — *Karvelis, Albert*

Proceedings of the 8th International Conference on Pressure Vessel Technology. Vols. 1-2 — *International Conference on Pressure Vessel Technology (8th: 1996: Montreal, Quebec)*

Proceedings of the 9th International Symposium on Insect-Plant Relationships — *International Symposium on Insect-Plant Relationships (9th: 1995: Gwatt, Switzerland)*

Proceedings of the 10th Workshop on Parallel and Distributed Simulation — *Workshop on Parallel and Distributed Simulation (10th: 1996: Philadelphia, Penn.)*

Proceedings of the 15th Symposium on Reliable Distributed Systems

Proceedings of the 26th International Symposium on Multiple-Valued Logic — *International Symposium on Multiple-Valued Logic*

Proceedings of the 1995 Total Life Cycle Conference

Proceedings of the 1996 Annual Symposium on Foundations of Computer Science

Proceedings of the 1996 Asian Test Symposium — *Asian Test Symposium*

Proceedings of the 1996 Conference on Parallel Architectures and Compilation Techniques

Proceedings of the 1996 IEEE/ASME Joint Railroad Conference

Proceedings of the 1996 International Symposium on Fault-Tolerant Computing — *International Symposium on Fault-Tolerant Computing*

Proceedings of the 1996 International Symposium on High Performance Distributed Computing — *IEEE International Symposium on High Performance Distributed Computing (5th: 1996: Syracuse, NY)*

Proceedings of the 1997 Annual ACM-SIAM Symposium on Discrete Algorithms

Proceedings of the Annual IEEE Symposium on Computer-Based Medical Systems (9th: 1996: Ann Arbor, MI)

Proceedings of the ASME Advanced Energy Systems Division — *Duncan, A B*

Proceedings of the ASME Fluids Engineering Division — *Rediniotis, Othon K*

Proceedings of the ASME Fluids Engineering Division Summer Meeting. Vols. 1-4 — *American Society of Mechanical Engineers Fluids Engineering Division. Summer Meeting (1996: San Diego, CA)*

Proceedings of the ASME Noise Control and Acoustics Division 1996

Proceedings of the Danish Institute at Athens I

Proceedings of the Exxon Valdez Oil Spill Symposium — *Rice, Stanley D*

Proceedings of the Fifth Biennial Conference of the International Society for Scientometrics and Informetrics

Proceedings of the Fifth Workshop on Enabling Technologies

Proceedings of the First Euromicro Workshop on Advanced Mobile Robots — *Euromicro Workshop on Advanced Mobile Robots (1st: 1996: Kaiserslautern, Germany)*

Proceedings of the First International Conference on Differential Equations — *Elaydi, Saber N*

Proceedings of the Fourth International Symposium on Assessment of Software Tools, May 22-24, 1996, Toronto, Canada — *International Symposium on Assessment of Software Tools (4th: 1996: Toronto, Ont.)*

Proceedings of the IEEE Second International Workshop on Systems Management, June 19-21, 1996, Toronto, Ontario, Canada — *IEEE International Workshop on Systems Management (2nd: 1996: Toronto, Ont.)*

Proceedings of the International COADS Winds Workshop, Kiel, Germany, 31 May-2 June 1994 — *International COADS Winds Workshop (1994: Kiel, Germany)*

Proceedings of the International Conference on Greek Architectural Terracottas of the Classical and Hellenistic Periods, December 12-15, 1991 — *International Conference on Greek Architectural Terracottas of the Classical and Hellenistic Periods (1991: American School of Classical Studies)*

Proceedings of the SCOPE Workshop on Soil and Groundwater Pollution — *SCOPE Workshop on Soil and Groundwater Pollution (1994: Cesky Krumlov, Czech Republic)*

Proceedings of the Second Biennial Conference on Research in Colorado Plateau National Parks

Proceedings of the Second International Conference on Requirements Engineering — *International Conference on Requirements Engineering (2nd: 1996: Colorado Springs, CO)*

Proceedings of the Seventh Annual International Symposium on Information Storage and Processing Systems

Proceedings of the Seventh Israeli Conference on Computer Systems and Software Engineering, June 12-13, 1996, Herzliya, Israel — *Israel Conference on Computer Systems and Software Engineering (7th: 1996: Hertseliyah, Israel)*

Proceedings of the Third International Conference on Massively Parallel Processing Using Optical Interconnections

Proceedings of WORDS'96 — *Workshop on Object-Oriented Real-Time Dependable Systems (2nd: 1996: Laguna Beach, Calif.)*

Proceedings: The First Conference on Emerging Technologies and Applications in Communications — *Conference on Emerging Technologies and Applications in Communications (1st: 1996: Portland, Or.)*

Le Proces De Canonisation De Saint Louis 1272-1297 — *Carolus-Barre, Louis*

Process Dynamics in Environmental Systems — *Weber, Walter J*

Process Improvement — *Cook, Sarah*

Process Industry Procedures and Training Manual — *Sawers, James R*

Process Metaphysics — *Rescher, Nicholas*

Process Redesign — *Tenner, Arthur R*

Processing and Properties of Nanocrystalline Materials — *Suryanarayana, C*

Il Processo — *Arlacchi, Pino*

Il Processo Inquisitoriale Del Cardinal Giovanni Morone. Vol. 6 — *Firpo, Massimo*

ProCite in Libraries — *Biggs, Deb R*

Proclaiming Shalom — *Cunningham, Philip A*

r Proctor and Hughes' Chemical Hazards of the Workplace. 4th Ed. — *Proctor, Nick H*

The Prodigal Daughter — *Lane, Allison*

The Prodigal Father — *Bryan, Mark*

Produced Water 2 — *Reed, Mark*

Producer Cooperatives and Labor-Managed Systems. Vols. 1-2 — *Prychitko, David L*

Producers versus Capitalists — *Freyer, Tony A*

Producing a Quality Family History — *Hatcher, Patricia Law*

Producing a School Newsletter Parents Will Read! — *Jones, Rhonda*

Producing Hegemony — *Rupert, Mark*

Producing Power — *Yelvington, Kevin A*

Producing the Sacred — *Wuthnow, Robert*

y Product Design — *Jones, Judy*

Product Design Review — *Ichida, Takashi*

Product Development and the Environment — *Burall, Paul*

Production and Neutralization of Negative Ions and Beams — *Prelec, Kresto*

Production and Operations Management — *Martinich, Joseph Stanislaus*

Production D'Armement — *Hebert, Jean-Paul*

The Production of English Renaissance Culture — *Miller, David Lee*

Production Planning in Automated Manufacturing. 2nd Ed. — *Crama, Yves*

Productive Performance in Chinese Enterprises — *Wu, Yanrui*

Productivity Analysis — *Wang, Doris Yi-Hsin*

Productivity Change, Public Goods and Transaction Costs — *Barzel, Yoram*

Produzione E Fruizione Del Libro Nel Basso Medioevo — *Scalon, Cesare*

Professing Feminism — *Patai, Daphne*

Profession of Conscience — *Sprinkle, Robert Hunt*

The Profession of Dietetics — *Payne-Palacio, June*

Professional Academic Writing in the Humanities and Social Sciences — *MacDonald, Susan Peck*

r Professional Beverage Management — *Lipinski, Robert A*

r Professional Codes of Conduct in the United Kingdom. 2nd Ed. — *Harris, Nigel G E, 1940-*

Professional Competence and Higher Education — *Winter, Richard*

Professional Development through Action Research in Educational Settings — *O'Hanlon, Christine*

r Professional Guide to Diseases. 5th Ed.

The Professional Knowledge Economy — *Tordoir, Pieter P*

The Professional Pastry Chef — *Friberg, Bo*

r Professional Periodicals in International Children's Literature. 3rd Rev. Ed. — *Reetz, Marianne*

r The Professional Secretary's Book of Lists and Tips — *De Vries, Mary Ann*

Professionalism and Community — *Louis, Karen Seashore*

Professionals against Populism — *Keren, Michael*

Professional's Guide to Robust Spreadsheets — *Richardson, Ronny*

Professional's Guide to Systems Analysis. 2nd Ed. — *Modell, Martin E*

Professions of Desire — *Haggerty, George*

c Professor Protein's Fitness, Health, Hygiene and Relaxation Tonic (Illus. by Rob Shone) — *Parker, Steve*

c Professor Sniff and the Lost Spring Breezes (Illus. by Tony Kenyon) — *Shearer, Alex*

Professors, Politics and Pop — *Wiener, Jon*

r Profile of Courts in Canada

A Profile of the American High School Senior in 1992 — *Green, Patricia J*

r Profile of Western North America — *Burgess, Philip M*

r Profiles in Business and Management. Electronic Media Version

Profiles in Character — *Hernon, Joseph Martin*

cr Profiles in World History. Vols. 1-8 — *Moss, Joyce*

y Profiles of Black Success — *Landrum, Gene N*

Profiles of Women — *Rodden, Lois*

y Profiles of Women Past and Present. Vol. 2 — *American Association of University Women. Thousand Oaks California Branch*

r Profiles of Worldwide Government Leaders — *Leeuwenburgh, Todd*

Profili: Saba, Cardarelli, Ungaretti, Montale — *Piccioni, Leone*

Profils Des Principaux Groupes Religieux De Quebec

Profit Sharing — *Kruse, Douglas L*

Profits and Morality — *Cowan, Robin*

Profits of Peace — *Newton, Scott*

Program Applicants as a Comparison Group in Evaluating Training Programs — *Bell, Stephen H*

r Program-Based Literacy Materials Catalogue. 2nd Ed. — *Churchill, Kevin*

Programmable Logic Devices and Logic Controllers — *Mandado, Enrique*

Programming for the Newton Using Windows — *McKeehan, Julie*

Programming for Young Children — *Fiore, Carole D*

Programming Intelligent Agents for the Internet — *Watson, Mark*

Programming Perl. 2nd Ed. — *Wall, Larry*

Programming Windows 95. 4th Ed. — *Petzold, Charles*

Programming Windows 95 with MFC — *Prosise, Jeff*

Programming with Java! Beta 2.0 — *Ritchey, Tim*

Programming with MFC for Windows 95 — *Broquard, Vic*

Progress and Poverty — *Daunton, M J*

Progress and Privilege — *Tucker, William, 1942-*

Progress and Problems in Medieval England — *Britnell, Richard H*

Progress: Fact or Illusion? — *Marx, Leo*

Progress in Algebraic Combinatorics — *Bannai, E*

Progress in Cell Cycle Research. Vol. 2 — *Meijer, Laurent*

Progress in Durability Analysis of Composite Systems — *International Conference Duracosys (1995: Brussels, Belgium)*

Progress in Environmental Remote Sensing Research and Applications — *EARSeL Symposium on Progress in Environmental Remote Sensing Research and Applications (15th: 1995: Basel, Switzerland)*

Progress in Inorganic Chemistry. Vol. 45

Progress in Partial Differential Equations — *Chipot, M*

Progress in Unity? — *Brinkman, Martien E*

The Progress of Romance — *Richter, David H*

Prohibition: Thirteen Years That Changed America — *Behr, Edward*

The Project — *Chafets, Zev*

Project Appraisal and Valuation of the Environment — *Abelson, Peter*

The Project Cool Guide to HTML — *Martin, Teresa A*

Project Death — *Bertematti, Richard*

c Project Earth Science — *Ford, Brent A*

Project Finance at the World Bank — *Benoit, Philippe*

Project Leadership. 2nd Ed. — *Briner, Wendy*

Project Libra — *Craddock, John*

Project Management. 6th Ed. — *Lock, Dennis*

Project Management in Construction. 3rd Ed. — *Walker, Anthony*

Project Management in Manufacturing and High Technology Operations. 2nd Ed. — *Badiru, Adedeji Bodunde*

Projecting the Shadow — *Rushing, Janice Hocker*

Projections 3

Projections 6

Projective Genogramming — *Kaslow, Florence*

Projektionen Des Weiblichen — *Scheifele, Sigrid*

Prolegomena to a Middlebrow Arithmetic of Curves of Genus 2 — *Cassels, J W S*

Prolegomena to Religious Pluralism — *Byrne, Peter*

Prolog Programming in Depth — *Covington, Michael A*

Prologue to History — *Van Seters, John*

Prologue to Manifest Destiny — *Jones, Howard*

The Prologues and Epilogues of the Eighteenth Century. Pt. 2 — *Danchin, Pierre*

Prolonged Wars — *Magyar, Karl P*

La Promeneuse D'Oiseaux — *Decoin, Didier*

Promesas De La Nueva Historia — *Araya Monge, Rolando*

The Prometheus Complex — *Braak, Hans Van De*

Prominent Sisters — *Polowetzky, Michael*

cr Prominent Women of the 20th Century. Vols. 1-4 — *Saari, Peggy*

y Promiscuities: The Secret Struggle for Womanhood — *Wolf, Naomi*

y The Promise — *Peart, Jane*

y Promise Me the Moon — *Barnes, Joyce Annette*

The Promise of Rest — *Price, Reynolds*

The Promise of the Land as Oath — *Booorer, Suzanne*

The Promise of Your Touch — *Carter, Annee*

y Promise Song — *Holeman, Linda*

Promised Land — *Adriance, Madeleine Cousineau*

Promised Land — *Felice, Cynthia*

c The Promised Land — *Holland, Isabelle*

Promised Land, Crusader State — *McDougall, Walter A*

Promised Lands — *Rogers, Jane*

Promises — *Plain, Belva*

Promises Broken — *Frost, Ginger S*

Promises Lost — *Howard, Audrey*

Promises to Keep — *Carter, Marshall N*

Promises to Keep — *Popenoe, David*

Promising the Earth — *Lamb, Robert*

Promoting Food Security in Rwanda through Sustainable Agricultural Productivity — *Clay, Daniel C*

Promoting Issues and Ideas. Rev. Ed. — *M. Boothe and Associates*

Promoting Polyarchy — *Robinson, William I*

Promoting Risk — *Stallings, Robert A*

Promotion and Tenure — *Tierney, William G*

Pronghorn: Portrait of the American Antelope — *Turbak, Gary*

Proofs and Theories — *Gluck, Louise*

y Propa Propaganda — *Zephaniah, Benjamin*

Propaganda — *Jackall, Robert*

Propaganda and Censorship during Canada's Great War — *Keshen, Jeffrey A*

Propaganda and the Role of the State in Inter-War Britain — *Grant, Mariel*

Propaganda for War — *Ross, Stewart Halsey*

r Propaganda in Twentieth Century War and Politics — *Cole, Robert*

Propaganda, Politics and Violence in Cambodia — *Heder, Steven R*

The Propaganda Warriors — *Laurie, Clayton D*

The Propensity of Things — *Jullien, Francois*

A Propensity to Self-Subversion — *Hirschman, Albert O*

Proper Confidence — *Newbigin, Lesslie*

Proper Name and Other Stories — *Mayer, Bernadette*

The Proper Study of Mankind — *Berlin, Isaiah*

The Properties of Water — *Hood, Ann*

Properties of Writing — *Dombroski, Robert S*

Property and Inequality in Victorian Ontario — *Darroch, Gordon*

Property, Bureaucracy and Culture — *Savage, Mike*

Property Matters — *DeLong, James V*

Property Rights and the Environment — *Hanna, Susan*

Property Taxes and Local Economic Development — *Kish-Goodling, Donna M*

Property Taxes and Tax Revolts — *O'Sullivan, Arthur*

Property to the People — *Nelson, Lynn D, 1943-*

The Prophecies — *Hogue, John*

Prophecy and Apocalypticism — *Cook, Stephen L*

Prophecy and Dissent 1914-16 — *Russell, Bertrand*

Prophecy and Power among the Dogrib Indians — *Helm, June*

Prophecy in Carthage — *Robeck, Cecil M, Jr.*

Prophecy in the Cotswolds 1803-1947 — *Derrett, J D M*

Prophecy of Berchan — *Hudson, Benjamin T*

A Prophet from amongst You — *Silberman, Neil Asher*

Prophet of Management — *Follett, Mary Parker*

Prophet of Rage — *Magida, Arthur J*

y The Prophetess (Breck). Audio Version — *Wood, Barbara*

Prophetic Inspiration after the Prophets — *Heschel, Abraham J*

Prophetic Song — *Kuczynski, Michael P*

p Prophetic Voices

Prophetic Writings of Lady Eleanor Davies — *Eleanor, Lady*

Prophets — *Dawes, Kwame*

Prophets and Emperors — *Potter, D S*

Prophets and Professors — *Bawer, Bruce*

Prophets of Agroforestry — *Reed, Richard K*

The Prophets of Old and the Day of the End — *Tigchelaar, Eibert J C*

Propietarios Y Esclavos Negros En Valladolid De Michoacan 1600-1650 — *Chavez Carbajal, Guadalupe*

Proportional Representation and Election Reform in Ohio — *Barber, Kathleen L*

The Proposal — *Hunt, Angela Elwell*

Proposal Savvy — *Parsigian, Elise K*

Proposed Recovery Plan for Snake River Salmon

Proposed Recovery Plan for Snake River Salmon: Summary

The Pros Talk Microsoft Visual FoxPro 3 — *Hentzen, Whil*

Prose and Poetry (Hall). Audio Version — *Hall, Donald, 1928-*

The Prose and the Passion — *Rapport, Nigel*

Prose and Travel Books in Prose and Verse. Vol. 1 — *Auden, W H*

Prose by Victorian Women — *Broomfield, Andrea*

Prose E Racconti — *Montale, Eugenio*

The Prosecution of International Crimes — *Clark, Roger S*

The Prosecution Responds — *Goldberg, Hank M*

Prosimetrum: Tradition Und Wandel Einer Literaturform Zwischen Spatantike Und Spatmittelalter. Vols. 1-2 — *Pabst, Bernhard*

Prosody at the Cafe Du Coin — *Bien, Jeff*

The Prosody of Greek Speech — *Devine, A M*

p Prospect

The Prospect before Her. Vol. 1 — *Hufton, Olwen*

Prospect of Death — *Duffy, Margaret*

Prospect: The Journal of an Artist — *Truitt, Anne*

The Prospects for Nuclear Power in the UK

Prospects: The Congressionally Mandated Study of Educational Growth and Opportunity — *Moss, Marc*

Prosperity's Promise — *Barham, Bradford L*

Prospero: Muistelmat Vuosilta 1967-1995 — *Haavikko, Paavo*

Prospero's Cell — *Durrell, Lawrence*

Prostate Cancer — *Bostick, David G*

Prostate Cancer — *Kantoff, Philip*

The Prostitute and the Prophet — *Sherwood, Yvonne*

Protect Your Achilles Heel — *Roberts, Wess*

Protecting Competition from the Postal Monopoly — *Sidak, J Gregory*

Protecting Human Rights in Africa — *Welch, Claude E*

y Protecting Marie — *Henkes, Kevin*

y Protecting Our Air, Land, and Water — *Chandler, Gary*

Protecting the Right to Read — *Symons, Ann*

Protecting Trade Secrets under the Uniform Trade Secrets Act — *Budden, Michael Craig*

Protecting Women — *Wikander, Ulla*

r The Protection of Children. 2nd Ed. — *Dingwall, Robert*

Protection or Liberalization? — *Forster, Elke M*

Protection, Power and Display — *Tavarelli, Andrew*

The Protection Racket State — *Stanley, William*

Protectors or Praetorians? — *Petry, Carl F*

Protein Analysis and Purification — *Rosenberg, Ian M*

Protein and Amino Acid Metabolism in Cancer Cachexia — *Pisters, Peter W T*

Protein and Peptide Analysis by Mass Spectrometry — *Chapman, John R*

Protein Electron Transfer — *Bendall, Derek S*

Protein Engineering and Design — *Carey, Paul R*

Protein Kinesis

Protein Motions — *Subbiah, S*

The Protein Protocols Handbook — *Walker, John M, 1948-*

Protein Sequencing Protocols — *Smith, Bryan John*

Protein Structure-Function Relationship — *Zaidi, Zafar H*

Protein Toxin Structure — *Parker, Michael W, 1959-*

Protektor — *Platt, Charles*

y Protest! — *Kronenwetter, Michael*

Protest: Photographs 1963-1995 — *Fernandez, Benedict J*

Protestant Dissent and Controversy in Ireland 1660-1714 — *Kilroy, Phil*

The Protestant Evangelical Awakening — *Ward, W R*

Protestant History and Identity in Sixteenth-Century Europe. Vols. 1-2 — *Gordon, Bruce*

Protestant Nonconformity and Roman Catholicism — *Shorney, David*

Protestant Politics — *Brady, Thomas A*

Protestantism and Patriotism — *Pincus, Steven C A*

Protestantism and Patriotism — *Pincus, Steven*

Protestantismos Y Modernidad Latinoamericana — *Bastian, Jean-Pierre*

Protestants and the Formation of Modern Korean Nationalism 1885-1920 — *Kim, In-Su*

The Protocol of the Gods — *Grapard, Allan G*

Protocols for Neural Cell Culture. 2nd Ed. — *Fedoroff, Sergey*

Die Protokolle Des Osterreichischen Ministerrates 1848-1867 — *Malfer, Stefan*

Protozoology. 2nd Ed. — *Hausmann, Klaus*

The Proud Highway — *Thompson, Hunter S*

Proudly We Served — *Kelly, Mary Pat*

Proust: Lecture Du Narrataire — *Solomon, Julie*

Prove the Nameless — *Faherty, Terence*

r Provenance Research in Book History — *Pearson, David, 1955-*

r Provence — *Feess, Susanne*

r Provence and the Cote D'Azur. 3rd Ed. — *Baillie, Kate*

Provenience Studies and Bronze Age Cyprus — *Knapp, A Bernard*

Proverbs — *Martin, James D*

Proversity: Getting Past Face Value and Finding the Soul of People — *Graham, Lawrence*

Providence Island 1630-1641 — *Kupperman, Karen Ordahl*

Providing for Young People — *Maychell, Karen*

Providing Health Care Benefits in Retirement — *Mazo, Judith F*

The Provincial: Calvin Coolidge and His World 1885-1895 — *Booraem, Hendrik, 1939-*

A Provincial Elite in Early Modern Tuscany — *Benadusi, Giovanna*

Provincial Families of the Renaissance — *Grubb, James S*

Provincial Passages — *Yeh, Wen-Hsin*

y The Proving Ground — *Davis, W E*

Provvisioni Concernenti L'Ordinamento Della Repubblica Fiorentina 1494-1512. Vol. 1 — *Florence (Duchy)*

c Prudence of Plymouth Plantation — *Reese, Colleen L*

Prudent Practices in the Laboratory — *National Research Council (U.S.). Committee on Prudent Practices for Handling, Storage, and Disposal of Chemicals in Laboratories*

The Prudential Regulation of Banks — *Dewatripont, Mathias*

Prufer Domains — *Fontana, Marco*

Pruning — *Medic, Kris*

The Pruning Book — *Reich, Lee*

The Pruning Handbook — *Bradley, Steve*

Psalm at Journey's End — *Hansen, Erik Fosnes*

Psalm Journal for Lent. Vols. 1-2 — *Chittister, Joan*

The Psalm Killer — *Petit, Chris*

Psalm Refrains — *Lehman, Charles*

Psalmodia Christiana — *Sahagun, Bernardino De*

The Psalms and the Life of Faith — *Brueggemann, Walter*

Psalms for All Occasions with Accompanying Prayers — *Peltz, Carl F*

Psalms for Praying — *Merrill, Nan C*

The Psalms in English — *Bible. O.T. Psalms. English. 1996*

The Psalms of Herod — *Friesner, Esther*

The Pseudepigrapha and Early Biblical Interpretation — *Charlesworth, James H*

Pseudo-Martyr — *Donne, John*

r Psilocybin Mushrooms of the World — *Stamets, Paul*

Psiquiatras Y Locos — *Ruiz Zevallos, Augusto*

y Psmith in the City (Davidson). Audio Version — *Wodehouse, P G*

y Psmith Journalist (Davidson). Audio Version — *Wodehouse, P G*

Psychedelic Prayers and Other Meditations — *Leary, Timothy*

r The Psychedelic Sourcebook — *Beifuss, Will*

r Psychedelics Encyclopedia. 3rd Ed. — *Stafford, Peter G*

The Psychiatric Persuasion — *Lunbeck, Elizabeth*

Psychiatry and Religion — *Bhugra, Dinesh*

r Psychic New York — *Collins, Patricia*

c Psychic Pets — *Sutton, John*

Psychic Warrior — *Morehouse, David*

Psycho Cat — *Hansen, Derek*

Psychoanalysis and Ethics — *Wallwork, Ernest*

Psychoanalysis at the Political Border — *Rangell, Leo*

Psychoanalysis, Language, and the Body of the Text — *Gliserman, Martin*

A Psychoanalytic History of the Jews — *Falk, Avner*

Psychoanalytic Pioneers — *Alexander, Franz*

r Psychoanalytic Studies of Religion — *Beit-Hallahmi, Benjamin*

The Psychoanalytic Theory of Neurosis — *Fenichel, Otto M*

Psychodynamic Concepts in General Psychiatry — *Schwartz, Harvey J*

Psychological and Spiritual Evolution — *Twiggs, Dennis G*

Psychological Anthropology — *Bock, Philip K*

Psychological Approaches to Pain Management — *Gatchel, Robert J*

Psychological Aspects of Women's Reproductive Health — *O'Hara, Michael W*

Psychological Management of Schizophrenia — *Birchwood, Max*

Psychological Reflections on Cinematic Terror — *Iaccino, James F*

Psychological Research — *Haworth, John*

Psychological Testing. 4th Ed. — *Kaplan, Robert M*

Psychological Treatment of Older Adults — *Hersen, Michel*

Psychological Writings and Letters — *Freud, Sigmund*

r Psychology: An Introductory Bibliography — *Salem Press*

Psychology and Health in African Cultures — *Peltzer, Karl*

Psychology and Nihilism — *Evans, Fred J*

Psychology and Policing — *Brewer, Neil*

Psychology Applied to Work. 5th Ed. — *Muchinsky, Paul M*

Psychology: Contexts of Behavior. 2nd Ed. — *Halonen, Jane S*

Psychology for Performing Artists — *Wilson, Glenn D*

Psychology in Action — *Canter, David V*

Psychology in Action. 4th Ed. — *Huffman, Karen*

The Psychology of Action — *Gollwitzer, Peter M*

The Psychology of Adversity — *Feldman, Robert S*

The Psychology of Back Pain — *Drukteinis, Albert M*

Psychology of Dance — *Taylor, Jim*

A Psychology of Difference — *Rank, Otto*

The Psychology of Freedom — *Pink, Thomas*

The Psychology of Intimacy — *Prager, Karen J*

The Psychology of Kundalini Yoga — *Jung, C G*

The Psychology of Language — *Harley, Trevor A*

The Psychology of Religion — *Spilka, Bernard*

The Psychology of Religion. 2nd Ed. — *Hood, Ralph W*

Psychology of the Youthful Offender. 3rd Ed. — *Walker, Robert N*

The Psychology of Vandalism — *Goldstein, Arnold P*

The Psychology of Women's Health — *Stanton, Annette L*

The Psychology Research Handbook — *Leong, Frederick T L*

Psychology: The Adaptive Mind — *Nairne, James S*

Psychology: The Hope of a Science — *Kimble, Gregory A*

Psychology: Themes and Variations. 3rd Ed. — *Weiten, Wayne*

Psychopathology and Psychotherapy. 2nd Ed. — *Sperry, Len*

The Psychopharmacologists — *Healy, David*

Psychopharmacology and Psychotherapy — *Sperry, Len*

Psychophysiology: The Mind-Body Perspective — *Hugdahl, Kenneth*

Psychoses and Pervasive Developmental Disorders in Childhood and Adolescence — *Volkmar, Fred R*

Psychosis and Power — *Glass, James M*

Psychosocial Approaches to Deeply Disturbed Persons — *Breggin, Peter R*

Psychosocial Development during Adolescence — *Adams, Gerald R*

Psychosocial Interventions in HIV Disease — *Crawford, Isiaah*

Psychosocial Treatment for Child and Adolescent Disorders — *Hibbs, Euthymia D*

Psychosomatic Disorders — *Asaad, Ghazi*

Psychotherapy Abbreviation — *Pekarik, Gene*

Psychotherapy and Buddhism — *Rubin, Jeffrey B*

r The Psychotronic Video Guide — *Weldon, Michael J*

r Psychotropic Drug Use in the Medically Ill — *Silver, Paul A*

Psychoville — *Fowler, Christopher*

Pthreads Programming — *Nichols, Bradford*

Public Access to the Internet — *Kahin, Brian*

Public Administration and Law. 2nd Ed. — *Rosenbloom, David H*

r Public Administration Dictionary — *Fox, William, 1935-*

Public Affairs — *Hammond, William M*

Public and Private Ownership of British Industry 1820-1990 — *Foreman-Peck, James*

Public and Private Roles in Maintaining Military Equipment at the Depot Level — *Clay-Mendez, Deborah*

Public and Private Secondary Education in Developing Countries — *Jimenez, Emmanuel*

Public and Specialised Libraries — *England, Len*

Public Archaeology in Annapolis — *Potter, Parker B, Jr.*

Public Attitudes toward Church and State — *Jelen, Ted G*

Public Catholicism. 2nd Ed. — *O'Brien, David J*

Public Deliberation — *Bohman, James*

Public Disputation, Power, and Social Order in Late Antiquity — *Lim, Richard*

Public Economics — *Myles, Gareth D*

Public Economics in Action — *Atkinson, A B*

Public Education in a Multicultural Society — *Fullinwider, Robert K*

Public Enterprise Management — *Farazmand, Ali*

Public Et Litterature En France Au XVIIe Siecle — *Merlin, Helene*

Public Expenditure Decision Making — *Basu, Anuradha*

Public Finances, Stabilization, and Structural Reform in Latin America — *Perry, Guillermo*

Public Goods, Public Enterprise, Public Choice — *Stretton, Hugh*

Public Health in British India — *Harrison, Mark*

Public Integrity Annual 1996

r Public Interest Profiles 1996-1997

Public Investment Programme 1994-1996

Public Lands and Private Rights — *Nelson, Robert H*

Public Libraries, Communities, and Technology — *Council on Library Resources*

Public Library Legislation in Europe — *Granheim, Else*

Public Library Planning — *Sutton, Brett*

Public Lives — *Benn, Melissa*

Public Management as Art, Science, and Practice — *Lynn, Lawrence E, Jr.*

Public Morality and Liberal Society — *Clor, Harry M*

Public Opinion and American Foreign Policy — *Holsti, Ole R*

Public Opinion and the Communication of Consent — *Glasser, Theodore L*

Public Opinion in America and Japan — *Ladd, Everett Carll*

Public Order in Ancient Rome — *Nippel, Wilfried*

Public Policies Towards Financial Liberalization — *Sak, Guven*

Public Policy and the Quality of Life — *Holcombe, Randall G*

Public Radio and Television in America — *Engelman, Ralph*

Public Reading and the Reading Public in Late Medieval England and France — *Coleman, Joyce*

Public Religions in the Modern World — *Casanova, Jose*

Public Sector Deficits and Macroeconomic Performance — *Easterly, William*

Public Sector Reform in Hong Kong — *Lee, Jane C Y*

Public Services and Market Mechanisms — *Walsh, Kieron*

Public Spending and the Poor — *Van De Walle, Dominique*

Public Spirit in the Thrift Tragedy — *Rom, Mark C*

The Public Treasury of the Muslims — *Abu Shouk, Ahmad Ibrahim*

Public Trust — *Gregory, Sarah*

The Public Trust and the First Americans — *Knudson, Ruthann*

Public Values, Private Lands — *Lehman, Tim*

Public Works Administration — *Brewer, Lucy*

Publish and Perish — *Hynes, James*

Publish and Perish — *Wright, Sally S*

Publish It on the Web — *Pfaffenberger, Bryan*

r Publishers, Distributors, and Wholesalers of the United States 1996-97. Vols. 1-2

r Publishing and Book Development in Sub-Saharan Africa — *Zell, Hans M*

Publishing Lives — *Gold, Jerome*

Publishing on the Internet — *Arnold, Stephen E*

The Puck Starts Here — *Vaughan, Garth*

c Puddle Jumpers (Illus. by Patti Delmonte) — *Gillis, Jennifer Storey*

c The Puddle Pail (Illus. by Elisa Kleven) — *Kleven, Elisa*

c Puddles (Illus. by G Brian Karas) — *London, Jonathan*

c Pueblo Indian (Illus. by Richard Erickson) — *Cory, Steven*

Pueblo Indian Painting — *Brody, J J*

The Pueblo Revolt of 1680 — *Knaut, Andrew L*

Pueblos Y Jornadas Boyacenses — *Camargo Perez, Gabriel*

Puerto Real — *Deagan, Kathleen*

Puerto Rican and Cuban Catholics in the U.S. 1900-1965 — *Dolan, Jay P*

Puerto Rican Women and Work — *Ortiz, Altagracia*

yr Puerto Ricans — *Press, Petra*

c Puerto Rico — *Levy, Patricia Marjorie*

Puerto Rico: Culture, Politics, and Identity — *Morris, Nancy*

y Puerto Rico: Deciding Its Future — *Harlan, Judith*

Puerto Vallarta Squeeze — *Waller, Robert James*

c The Puffin Book of Christmas Poems (Illus. by Jill Bennett) — *Magee, Wes*

c The Puffin Book of Classic Children's Stories (Illus. by Diz Wallis) — *Carpenter, Humphrey*

c The Puffin Book of Classic Verse (Illus. by Diz Wallis) — *Wilson, Raymond*

c The Puffin Book of Nonsense Verse (Illus. by Quentin Blake) — *Blake, Quentin*

c The Puffin Book of Stories for Eight-Year-Olds (Illus. by S Cox) — *Cooling, Wendy*

c The Puffin Book of Stories for Five-Year Olds — *Cooling, Wendy*

c The Puffin Book of Stories for Seven-Year-Olds (Illus. by S Cox) — *Cooling, Wendy*

c The Puffin Treasury of Children's Stories — *Trenter, Anna*

Pugin: A Gothic Passion — *Pugin, Augustus Welby Northmore*

Le Puits D'Exil — *Gobry-Valle, Armande*

Puka Ola — *Ezera, Regina*

The Pulitzer Diaries — *Hohenberg, John*

The Pull of the Moon — *Berg, Elizabeth*

c Pulleys (Illus. by Mike Gordon) — *Rush, Caroline*

y Pulling the Moves — *Clark, Margaret*

c Pulling the Plug on the Universe — *Prince, Maggie*

Pulmonary Embolism — *Stein, Paul D*

Pulmonary Function Testing. 2nd Ed. — *Wanger, Jack*

Pulmonary Rehabilitation — *Bach, John R*

Pulmonary Rehabilitation — *Fishman, Alfred P*

Pulmonary Rehabilitation Administration and Patient Education Manual — *Morris, Kathleen V*

Pulp Bleaching — *Dence, Carlton W*

Pulp Culture — *Haut, Woody*

Pulp Election — *St. Keeldare, Carmen*

Pulping the South — *Carrere, Ricardo*

Pulpit Politics — *Vinz, Warren L*

Pulpit, Table, and Song — *Elkins, Heather Murray*

y Pulse — *Cardillo, Joe*

Pulsed Metal Vapour Lasers — *NATO Advanced Research Workshop (ARW) Pulsed Metal Vapour Lasers, Physics and Emerging Applications (1995: University of St. Andrews)*

Pulsion Et Desir Dans Les Romans Et Nouvelles De Guy De Maupassant — *Danger, Pierre*

Pump Application Desk Book. 3rd Ed. — *Garay, Paul N*

c Pumpkin Carving — *Palmer, Edward*

c Pumpkin Painting — *McKinney, Jordan*

Pumpu: Centro Administrativo Inka De La Puna De Junin — *Matos Mendieta, Ramiro*

y Pun and Games — *Lederer, Richard*

Punctuation and Its Dramatic Value in Shakespearean Drama — *Graham-White, Anthony*

y Punctuation Repair Kit (Illus. by David Farris) — *Vandyck, William*

The Pundits: British Exploration of Tibet and Central Asia — *Waller, Derek*

c Punia and the King of Sharks (Illus. by Felipe Davalos) — *Wardlaw, Lee*

y The Punic Wars — *Nardo, Don*

Punishment and Social Control — *Blomberg, Thomas G*

Punishment for Profit — *Shichor, David*

Punishment: Social Control and Coercion — *Sistare, Christine T*

r Punjab — *Tatla, Darshan Singh*

Punjabi Bal Sahit Da Aalochanatmak Muhandra — *Aasht, Darshan Singh*

y Punk: The Illustrated History of a Music Revolution — *Boot, Adrian*

Pupil Behaviour and Teacher Culture — *Miller, Andy*

Puppet for a Corpse (Hardiman). Audio Version — *Simpson, Dorothy*

c Puppet Theater (Illus. by Emma Carlow) — *James, Susan Niner*

c Puppets — *Doney, Meryl*

Puppets and Popular Culture — *Shershow, Scott Cutler*
y Puppies, Dogs, and Blue Northers (Illus. by Ruth Wright Paulsen) — *Paulsen, Gary*
y Puppy Fat — *Gleitzman, Morris*
c The Puppy Sister (Illus. by Jacqueline Rogers) — *Hinton, S E*
c Puppy Training and Critters, Too! (Illus. by Darryl Bush) — *Peterson-Fleming, Judy*
Purana Perennis — *Doniger, Wendy*
Purcell: A Biography — *Keates, Jonathan*
Purcell Remembered — *Burden, Michael*
Purcell Studies — *Price, Curtis*
Purchasing for Manufacturing — *Hough, Harry E*
Purchasing Power — *Frank, Dana*
Pure Justice — *Ledbetter, Suzann*
Pure Kingdom — *Chilton, Bruce*
Pure Prairie — *Fertig, Judith*
Pure Selling — *Vanwyck, Wayne*
c Purely Rosie Pearl — *Cochrane, Patricia A*
Purgatory Road — *Reiss, Bob*
Purging Racism from Christianity — *Edwards, Jefferson D, Jr.*
The Purification Ceremony — *Sullivan, Mark T*
Purification of Laboratory Chemicals. 4th Ed. — *Armarego, W L F*
Purify Your Body — *Diamond, Nina L*
Purines and Myocardial Protection — *Abd-Elfattah, Anwar-Saad A*
The Puritan Conscience and Modern Sexuality — *Leites, Edmund*
Puritans at Play — *Daniels, Bruce C*
Puritans in Babylon — *Kuklick, Bruce*
Purity and Exile — *Malkki, Liisa H*
y Purity under Pressure — *Anderson, Neil T*
The Purloined Clinic — *Malcolm, Janet*
Purloined Letters — *Riddel, Joseph N*
Purple America — *Moody, Rick*
c The Purple Hat (Illus. by Tracey Campbell Pearson) — *Pearson, Tracey Campbell*
c A Purple Poetry Paintbox — *Foster, John*
The Purpose of Playing — *Montrose, Louis*
c Purr--: Children's Book Illustrators Brag about Their Cats — *Rosen, Michael J*
Pursued by Furies — *Bowker, Gordon*
The Pursuit of Power — *Johnson, Ellwood*
The Pursuit of Power — *McNeil, William Hardy*
The Pursuit of Prime — *Adizes, Ichak*
The Pursuit of Reason — *Edwards, Ruth Dudley*
Pursuits Amateur and Academic — *Pratt, E J*
Push — *Sapphire*
c Push and Pull — *Challoner, Jack*
y The PUSH Guide to Which University 1997
The Pushcart Prize XX
The Pushcart Prize XXI
c Pushes and Pulls — *Jennings, Terry*
Pushing Boundaries — *Vasquez, Olga A*
y Pushing the Bear — *Glancy, Diane*
Pushkin and Romantic Fashion — *Greenleaf, Monika*
Pushkin: Poet and Man of Letters and His Prose — *Shaw, J Thomas*
Pushkin's Poetics of the Unexpected — *Shaw, J Thomas*
c Puss in Boots (Illus. by Hans Fischer) — *Fischer, Hans*
Pussy, King of the Pirates — *Acker, Kathy*
c A Pussycat's Christmas (Illus. by Anne Mortimer) — *Brown, Margaret Wise*
c Put on a Show! (Illus. by Colin McNaughton) — *Ahlberg, Allan*
La Putain Du Diable — *Clement, Catherine*
Putevoditel'. Vol. 1 — *Rossiiskii Gosudarstvennyi Arkhiv Ekonomiki*
Putevoditel': Arkhivnye Dokumenty Po Istorii Evreev V Rossii V XIX-Nachale XX vv. — *Deych, Genrich M*
Puti Istorii — *D'iakonov, I M*
c Putt-Putt and Pep
The Puttermesser Papers — *Ozick, Cynthia*
Putting America's House in Order — *Abshire, David*
Putting Choice before Democracy — *Hauptmann, Emily*
Putting Consumers First — *Mintz, Jack M*
Putting Foreign Policy to Work — *Roberts, John W*
c Putting on a Play (Illus. by Katy Keck Arnsteen) — *Bentley, Nancy*
The Putting on the Brakes Activity Book for Young People with ADHD — *Quinn, Patricia O*
Putting Popular Music in Its Place — *Hamm, Charles*
Putting Your Mouth Where the Money Is — *Douthitt, Chris*

c The Puzzle Arcade — *Slocum, Jerry*
The Puzzle of Evil — *Vardy, Peter*
The Puzzle of God — *Vardy, Peter*
The Puzzle of Strikes — *Franzosi, Roberto*
c The Puzzle of the Dinosaur-Bird (Illus. by Mark Hallett) — *Schlein, Miriam*
c Puzzles — *Hewitt, Sally*
c Puzzles (Illus. by Cornelius Van Wright) — *Walker, Dava*
c Puzzles, Mazes and Numbers — *Snape, Charles*
c A Puzzling Day in the Land of the Pharaohs (Illus. by Scoular Anderson) — *Anderson, Scoular*
PWA: Looking AIDS in the Face — *Moore, Oscar*
PWA: Looking AIDS in the Face (Moore). Audio Version — *Moore, Oscar*
Pygmalion (L.A. Theatre Works). Audio Version — *Shaw, Bernard*
Pygmalion: Shaw's Spin on Myth and Cinderella — *Berst, Charles A*
Pyke Koch — *Schoom, Talitha*
Pynchon's Poetics — *Berressem, Hanjo*
c Pyne — *Guy, Jonathan*
The Pyramid and the Urn — *Lawrence, William*
c Pyramids — *Millard, Anne*
c Pyramids and Temples — *Parker, Jane*
Pyramids of Tucume — *Heyerdahl, Thor*
Pyrrhonian Reflections on Knowledge and Justification — *Fogelin, Robert J*
Pythagoras' Trousers — *Wertheim, Margaret*
The Pythagorean Golden Verses

Q R

Q Auf Dem Prufstand — *Bergemann, Thomas*
Q-Synopsis: The Double Tradition Passages in Greek. Rev. Ed. — *Neirynck, Frans*
p Q-Zine: A Rocket to the Unknown
Qaddafi Und Die Islamistische Opposition In Libyen — *Mattes, Hanspeter*
Qadhafi's Libya 1969-1994 — *Vandewalle, Dirk*
The Qadi and the Fortune Teller — *Saleh, Nabil*
Qian Shan Du Xing — *Wang, Shi-Ch'un*
Oin Al De Bao Jun — *Zuo, Qingwen*
Qing Tai — *Lin, Pai*
QS-9000 Implementation and Registration — *Naroola, Gurmeet*
QS-9000 Pioneers — *Chowdhury, Subir*
Qua Bong Tuoi Tho — *Ngoc, Thuy*
y Quaaludes — *Ziemer, Maryann*
Quaderni Dell' Istituto Italiano Di Cultura. New Ser., No. 1
p Quaderni Musicali Marchigiani
Quadratics — *Mollin, Richard A*
Quaestiones. Vol. 2 — *Alexander, of Aphrodisias*
Quake City — *Spencer, John B*
Quake: Stories — *Van Winckel, Nance*
Quaker Crosscurrents — *Barbour, Hugh*
Qualitative Educational Research in Developing Countries — *Crossley, Michael*
Qualitative Interviewing — *Rubin, Herbert J*
Qualitative Problems for Differential Equations and Control Theory — *Corduneanu, C*
Qualitative Research Design — *Maxwell, Joseph Alex*
Qualitative Research for Nurses — *Holloway, Immy*
Qualitative Research in Nursing — *Streubert, Helen J*
Qualitative Studies in Education — *Salisbury, Jane*
Qualitative Topics in Integer Linear Programming — *Shevchenko, V N*
Quality — *Summers, Donna C S*
Quality and Accessibility of Food-Related Data — *International Food Data Base Conference (1st: 1993: Sydney, Australia)*
Quality Assurance. 2nd Ed. — *Hughes, Terry*
Quality Assurance in Construction. 2nd Ed. — *Thorpe, Brian*
Quality Circle Time in the Primary Classroom — *Mosley, Jenny*
Quality in the Veterans Health Administration — *Barbour, Galen L*
Quality Management for Information and Library Managers — *Brophy, Peter*
Quality Measurement in Economics — *Payson, Stephen*
Quality of Ground Water — *American Society of Civil Engineers. Committee on Ground Water Quality*
Quality of Life and Mental Health Services — *Oliver, Joseph*
Quality of Life in Long-Term Care — *Coons, Dorothy H*
The Quality of Mercy — *Harper, Keith*
The Quality Technician's Handbook. 3rd Ed. — *Griffith, Gary K*
r Quamran Cave 4. Vol. 5 — *Dead Sea Scrolls. 4Q. Selections*
c Quanah Parker: Comanche Warrior — *Sanford, William R*
The Quango Debate — *Ridley, F F*
Quantification and the Quest for Medical Certainty — *Matthews, J Rosser*
Quantification of Brain Function Using PET — *Myers, Ralph*
Quantifying Language — *Scholfield, Phil*
Quantitative Development Policy Analysis, with Diskettes — *Sadoulet, Elisabeth*

Quantitative Electron-Probe Microanalysis. 2nd Ed. — *Scott, V D*
Quantitative Risk Assessment of Hazardous Materials Transport Systems — *Nicolet-Monnier, Michel*
Quantitative Trading and Money Management — *Gehm, Fred*
The Quantity Theory of Money — *Blaug, Mark*
Quantrill's War — *Schultz, Duane*
Quantum 1/f Noise and Other Low Frequency Fluctuations in Electronic Devices — *Handel, Peter H*
Quantum Business — *DePorter, Bobbi*
r Quantum Companies II — *Silver, A David*
The Quantum Dot — *Turton, Richard*
Quantum Dynamics of Simple Systems — *Scottish Universities' Summer School in Physics (44th: 1994: Stirling, Scotland)*
Quantum Field Theory and Critical Phenomena. 3rd Ed. — *Zinn-Justin, Jean*
Quantum Field Theory in Condensed Matter Physics — *Tsvelik, Alexi M*
Quantum Groups in Two-Dimensional Physics — *Gomez, Cesar*
Quantum Mechanics — *Robinett, Richard W*
Quantum Mechanics — *Singh, Jasprit*
y Quantum Moon — *Vitola, Denise*
Quantum Non-Locality and Relativity — *Maudlin, Tim*
Quantum Optics of Confined Systems — *Ducloy, Martial*
Quantum Physics. 2nd Ed. — *Gasiorowicz, Stephen*
The Quantum Society — *Zohar, Danah*
Quantum Statistical Theory of Superconductivity — *Fujita, Shigeji*
Quantum Technology — *Milburn, Gerard*
Quantum Theology — *O'Murchu, Diarmuid*
Quantum Theory — *Peres, Asher*
Quantum Theory, Black Holes, and Inflation — *Moss, Ian G*
The Quantum Theory of Fields. Vol. 2 — *Weinberg, Steven*
Quantum Theory of Matter — *Modinos, A*
Quantum Transport in Semiconductor Submicron Structures — *Kramer, B*
La Quarantaine — *Le Clezio, J-M G*
Quarantine! East European Jewish Immigrants and the New York City Epidemics of 1892 — *Markel, Howard*
The Quarry: Stories by Harvey Grossinger — *Grossinger, Harvey*
p Quarry West
Quarterdeck and Bridge — *Bradford, James C*
Quartet — *Rhys, Jean*
y Quartet of Stories — *Gerschel, Liz*
c The Quasar Quartz Quest (Illus. by Patrice Aggs) — *Blackman, Malorie*
Quase Memoria — *Cony, Carlos Heitor*
Quasidifferentiability and Nonsmooth Modelling in Mechanics, Engineering and Economics — *Dem'yanov, Vladimir F*
The Quaternary History of Scandinavia — *Donner, Joakim*
Quatre Presidents Et L'Afrique — *Wauthier, Claude*
Quatre Siecles De Reliure Belgique 1500-1900. Vol. 2 — *Culot, Paul*
Quattrocento Adriatico — *Dempsey, Charles*
Le Quatuor De L'Errance Suivi De La Traversee Du Desert — *Thibodeau, Serge Patrice*
cr Que Es Que
Que Huong Yen Dau — *Xuan, Vu*
Que Nha Bon Muoi Nam Tro Lai — *Phan, Lac Tiep*
c Quebec — *Hamilton, Janice*

The Queen: A Biography of Elizabeth II — *Pimlott, Ben*
Queen Elizabeth and the Making of Policy 1572-1603 — *MacCaffrey, Wallace T*
Queen Elizabeth the Queen Mother at Clarence House — *Cornforth, John*
y The Queen of Dreamland — *Tomey, Ingrid*
y Queen of Swords — *Tarr, Judith*
c Queen Victoria — *Netzley, Patricia D*
Queen Victoria's Gene — *Potts, D M*
Queen Victoria's Secrets — *Munich, Adrienne*
y The Queen's Man — *Penman, Sharon Kay*
c The Queen's Museum and Other Fanciful Tales. Audio Version — *Stockton, Frank R*
Queensboro Bridge and Other Poems — *Paolucci, Anne*
A Queer Book — *Hogg, James, 1770-1835*
Queer Looks — *Gever, Martha*
Queer Noises — *Gill, John*
Queer Science — *LeVay, Simon*
Queer Space — *Betsky, Aaron*
Queer Spirits — *Roscoe, Will*
Queer View Mirror
Queer View Mirror 2
Queerly Classed — *Raffo, Susan*
Que(e)rying Religion — *Comstock, Gary David*
Quellen Zur Geschichte Der Juden Im Hessischen Staatsarchiv Darmstadt 1080-1650 — *Battenberg, Friedrich*
c Quentin Blake Book of Nonsense Stories (Illus. by Quentin Blake) — *Blake, Quentin*
Quentin Tarantino — *Clarkson, Wensley*
Querdenken: Dissens Und Toleranz Im Wandel Der Geschichte — *Erbe, Michael*
Qu'est-Ce Qu'on Dit? — *Manley, Joan H*
Quest for Answers — *Akhtar, Salman*
The Quest for Becket's Bones — *Butler, John*
Quest for Conception — *Inhorn, Marcia Claire*
The Quest for Cure — *Maddox, Sam*
Quest for Freedom — *Clymer, Kenton J*
A Quest for Glory — *Schneller, Robert J*
The Quest for God — *Johnson, Paul, 1928-*
The Quest for Hegemony in the Arab World — *Podeh, Elie*
Quest for Kim — *Hopkirk, Peter*
A Quest for Life — *McHarg, Ian L*
The Quest for Longitude — *Longitude Symposium (1993: Harvard University)*
The Quest for Loyalty — *Reichheld, Frederick F*
The Quest for Moral Foundations — *Brown, Montague, 1952-*
Quest for Perfection — *Maranto, Gina*
The Quest for Security in the Caribbean — *Griffith, Ivelaw Lloyd*
Quest for the Golden Circle — *Gomez, Arthur R*
c Quest for the Lost Prince (Illus. by Julian Jackson) — *Jackson, Dave*
The Quest for the Nazi Personality — *Zillmer, Eric A*
The Quest for the Other — *Van Den Berghe, Pierre L*
A Quest for the Post-Historical Jesus — *Hamilton, William*
The Quest for Three Abbots — *Lehane, Brendan*
The Quest of the Folk — *McKay, Ian*
The Question of Food Security in Cuban Socialism — *Enriquez, Laura J*
A Question of Labour — *Laurence, K O*
The Question of Namibia — *Kaela, Laurent C W*
A Question of Priorities — *Boehling, Rebecca L*
The Question of Style in Philosophy and the Arts — *Eck, Caroline Van*
y A Question of Timing — *Moe, Barbara A*

c A Question of Trust — *Bauer, Marion Dane*
Questioning Development — *Kohler, Gabriele*
Questioning Slavery — *Walvin, James*
Questioning the Secular State — *Westerlund, David*
Questions and Answers on AIDS. 3rd Ed. — *Frumkin, Lyn R*
Questions and Uncertainties in Prostate Cancer — *Peeling, W B*
Questions De Rhetorique — *Meyer, Michel*
Questions for Ecclesiastes — *Jarman, Mark*
Questions of Cultural Identity — *Hall, Stuart*
Questions of Heaven — *Ehrlich, Gretel*
Questions of Judgement — *Low-Beer, F H*
Questions of Travel — *Kaplan, Caren*
La Quete De La Race — *Conte, Edouard*
c Quetzal: Sacred Bird of the Cloud Forest (Illus. by Neil Waldman) — *Patent, Dorothy Hinshaw*
c Qui Est Mon Meilleur Ami — *Tenaille, Marie*
Qui Perd Gagne — *Knee, Philip*
The Quick: A Novella and Stories — *Rossi, Agnes*
The Quick after Work Indian Vegetarian Cookbook — *Shah, Kumud*
Quick, Now, Always — *Irwin, Mark*
cr Quick Reference Atlas. Electronic Media Version
Quick Sewing Projects from Placemats — *Beck, Susan P*
c Quick-Solve Whodunit Puzzles — *Sukach, Jim*
Quick-Turnaround ASIC Design in VHDL — *Romdhane, Mohamed S Ben*
Quicken 6 for Windows — *Schwartz, Steven*
Quicken 6 for Windows for Busy People — *Weverka, Peter*
The Quicken Tree — *Knott, Bill*
y Quicker than the Eye — *Bradbury, Ray*
Quicksand: Israel, the Intifada, and the Rise of Political Evil in Democracies — *Gordon, Haim*
The Quiet American — *Greene, Graham*
y The Quiet Center — *Ross, Katherine Ball*
The Quiet Child — *Collins, Janet*
A Quiet Country — *Henderson, Sally*
A Quiet Courage — *Skoglund, Elizabeth R*
Quiet Flows the Don — *Sholokhov, Mikhail Aleksandrovich*
A Quiet Life — *Oe, Kenzaburo*
r Quiet Places of Massachusetts — *Tougias, Michael*
Quilted for Christmas. Bk. 3
y Quilted Landscape — *Strom, Yale*
A Quilter's Wisdom — *Hall, Eliza Calvert*
Quilts of Provence — *Berenson, Kathryn*
Quimica, Botanica Y Farmacia En La Nueva Espana A Finales Del Siglo XVII — *Pastrana, Patricia Aceves*
r Quinlan's Illustrated Directory of Film Character Actors — *Quinlan, David*
Quinolones in Pulmonary Tuberculosis Management — *LaScolea, Len J*
Quis Deum? — *Sauron, Gilles*
Quisine — *Thompson, Antony Worrall*
c The Quite Remarkable Adventures of the Owl and the Pussycat (Illus. by Edward Lear) — *Idle, Eric*
Qumran Prayer and Religious Poetry — *Nitzan, Bilha*
The Quotable Einstein — *Einstein, Albert*
The Quotable Feline — *Dratfield, Jim*
Quotations from Chairman Mao Tse-Tung — *Mao, Tse-Tung*
Qur'an Liberation and Pluralism — *Esack, Farid*
R and D, Innovation and Industrial Structure — *Maurer, Boris*
R and R for American Schools — *Washington State Association for Supervision and Curriculum Development*
c R.C. Gorman, Navajo Artist — *Hermann, Spring*
R.D. Laing: A Divided Self — *Clay, John*
R.I.P.: The Complete Book of Death and Dying — *Jones, Constance, 1961-*
c R.L. Stine's Ghosts of Fear Street. Audio Version — *Stine, R L*
r R.W. Ketton-Cremer: A Summary Catalogue of His Manuscripts, Notebooks, Correspondence and Related Papers — *Clarke, Stephen*
r R.W. Ketton-Cremer: An Annotated Bibliography — *Clarke, Stephen*
Rabbinic Literature and the New Testament — *Neusner, Jacob*
c Rabbit (Illus. by Diana Magnuson) — *Birchfield, D L*
c The Rabbit and the Tigerdile — *Rowe, W W*
c Rabbit Hill (Caruso). Audio Version — *Lawson, Robert*
c Rabbit Moon (Illus. by John A Rowe) — *Rowe, John A*

c Rabbits and Raindrops (Illus. by Jim Arnosky) — *Arnosky, Jim*
c The Rabbit's Escape (Illus. by Yumi Heo) — *Han, Suzanne Crowder*
Rabelais — *Heath, Michael J*
Rabelais Et L'Humanisme Civil — *Desrosiers-Bonin, Diane*
Rabelais: Oeuvres Completes — *Rabelais, Francois*
Rabelais Revisited — *Zegura, Elizabeth Chesney*
Rabelais: Tiers Livre, Quart Livre, Ve Livre — *Morrison, Ian R*
The Rabelaisian Mythologies — *Gauna, Max*
Rabi'a the Mystic and Her Fellow Saints — *Smith, Margaret, 1884-*
Rabin of Israel — *Slater, Robert*
y Rabin: Our Life, His Legacy — *Rabin, Leah*
Rabinal Achi — *Breton, Alain*
Rabu Ando Poppu — *Murakami, Ryu*
The Race against Lethal Microbes — *Howard Hughes Medical Institute*
c Race against Time — *Elliot, Ginny*
y Race: An Anthology in the First Person — *Schneider, Bart*
Race and Democracy — *Fairclough, Adam*
Race and Educational Reform in the American Metropolis — *Lewis, Dan A*
Race and Ethnicity in America — *Thomas, Gail E*
Race and Gender Discrimination across Urban Labor Markets — *Schmitz, Susanne*
Race and Human Evolution — *Wolpoff, Milford*
Race and Justice — *Gibbs, Jewelle Taylor*
Race and Labor in Western Copper — *Mellinger, Philip J*
Race and the Shaping of Twentieth-Century Atlanta — *Bayor, Ronald H*
Race, Campaign Politics, and the Realignment in the South — *Glaser, James M*
c Race Car — *Bingham, Caroline, 1962-*
The Race Card — *Collier, Peter*
Race, Class, and Community in Southern Labor History — *Fink, Gary M*
Race, Crime, and Justice — *Hudson, Barbara A*
Race, Crime, and the Law — *Kennedy, Randall*
Race, Discourse, and the Origin of the Americas — *Hyatt, Vera Lawrence*
Race, Ethnicity, and Entrepreneurship in Urban America — *Light, Ivan*
The Race Gallery — *Kohn, Marek*
Race, Gender, and Class in Criminology — *Schwartz, Martin J*
Race, Gender, and Health — *Bayne-Smith, Marcia*
Race, Gender, and Rank — *Horowitz, Maryanne Cline*
Race in the Making — *Hirschfeld, Lawrence A*
Race, Modernity, Postmodernity — *Hogue, W Lawrence*
Race, Multiculturalism, and the Media. 2nd Ed. — *Wilson, Clint C, II*
Race, Myth and the News — *Campbell, Christopher P*
Race of Angels — *Waters, John*
c The Race of the Golden Apples (Illus. by Leo Dillon) — *Martin, Claire*
c The Race of Toad and Deer (Illus. by M I Brooks) — *Mora, Pat*
Race, Poverty, and American Cities — *Boger, John Charles*
Race, Rape, and Lynching — *Gunning, Sandra*
Race Relations Litigation in an Age of Complexity — *Wasby, Stephen L*
Race Relations within Western Expansion — *Levine, Alan J*
Race Rules — *Dyson, Michael Eric*
Race Rules (Dyson). Audio Version — *Dyson, Michael Eric*
Race: The History of an Idea in the West — *Hannaford, Ivan*
Racechanges: White Skin, Black Face in American Culture — *Gubar, Susan*
c Racers and Roadsters (Illus. by Richard Chasemore) — *Atkinson, Mary*
c Racetrack Robbery (Illus. by Bill Basso) — *Leroe, Ellen*
c Rachel Carson (Illus. by William Accorsi) — *Accorsi, William*
y Rachel Carson: Voice for the Earth (Hughes). Audio Version — *Wadsworth, Ginger*
Rachel Whiteread: Shedding Life — *Whiteread, Rachel*
Racial Fault Lines — *Almaguer, Tomas*
Racial Healing — *Dutton, Harlon L*
y Racial Prejudice — *Pascoe, Elaine*

The Racialisation of British Policing — *Holdaway, Simon*
Racine Et Heidegger — *Bonzon, Alfred*
Racine: Language and Theatre — *Phillips, Henry*
Racine, Phedre — *James, E D*
c Racing a Ghost Ship — *Wilson, Rich*
c Racing Drivers — *Wood, Tim*
Racing to the Beginning of the Road — *Weinberg, Robert A*
y Racism — *Garg, Samidha*
Racism and Anti-Racism in World Perspective — *Bowser, Benjamin*
Racism and Child Protection — *Jackson, Valerie*
Racism and Society — *Solomos, John*
Racism and the Labour Market — *Linden, Marcel Van Der*
Racism, Ethnicity and Politics in Contemporary Europe — *Hargreaves, Alec G*
Racism: From Slavery to Advanced Capitalism — *Wilson, Carter A*
Racism, Health, and Post-Industrialism — *Semmes, Clovis*
Racism in Canada — *McKague, Ormond*
Racism in Children's Lives — *Troyna, Barry*
r Racism in Contemporary America — *Weinberg, Meyer*
Racism, Sexism, and the University — *Marchak, M Patricia*
Racismo Y Mestizaje — *Portocarrero, Gonzalo*
p Racunovodstvo I Financije
r Radiation Shielding — *Shultis, J Kenneth*
Radiation Therapy for Head and Neck Neoplasms. 3rd Ed. — *Wang, C C*
Radical Artifice — *Perloff, Marjorie*
The Radical Choice and Moral Theory — *Zhai, Zhenming*
Radical Christianity and the Flesh of Jesus — *Vogel, Arthur A*
Radical Culture — *Worrall, David*
Radical Democracy — *Lummis, C Douglas*
The Radical Enlightenments of Benjamin Franklin — *Anderson, Douglas*
Radical Evil on Trial — *Nino, Carlos Santiago*
Radical Expression — *Epstein, James A*
The Radical Faces of Godard and Bertolucci — *Loshitzky, Yosefa*
A Radical Jew — *Boyarin, Daniel*
Radical Philosophy — *Gottlieb, Roger S*
Radical Politicians and Poets in Early Victorian Britain — *Roberts, Stephen*
Radical Realism — *Pols, Edward*
Radical Religion in America — *Kaplan, Jeffrey*
Radical Revisions — *Mullen, Bill*
The Radical Right in Western Europe — *Kitschelt, Herbert*
Radical Right-Wing Populism in Western Europe — *Betz, Hans-Georg*
Radical Satire and Print Culture 1790-1822 — *Wood, Marcus*
y Radical Son — *Horowitz, David, 1939-*
Radicalism and Education Reform in 20th-Century China — *Pepper, Suzanne*
r Radicalism in Minnesota 1900-1960
Radically Gay — *Hay, Harry*
Radically Speaking — *Bell, Diane*
Radicals, Reformers, and Reactionaries — *Cohen, Youssef*
Radio Comedy 1938-1968 — *Foster, Andy*
Radio Corpse — *Tiffany, Daniel*
Radio Diplomacy and Propaganda — *Rawnsley, Gary D*
Radio-Frequency Electronics — *Hagen, Jon B*
Radio Hole-in-the-Head/Radio Liberty — *Critchlow, James*
y Radio On — *Vowell, Sarah*
Radio Priest — *Warren, Donald*
r Radio Stars — *DeLong, Thomas A*
Radio Voices — *Hilmes, Michele*
Radiodiffusion Et Societe Distincte — *Filion, Michel*
Radioecology and the Restoration of Radioactive-Contaminated Sites — *Luykx, Felix F*
A Radiologic Approach to Diseases of the Chest. 2nd Ed. — *Freundlich, Irwin M*
c Radiology — *Winkler, Kathy*
r Radio's Morning Show Personalities — *Lieberman, Philip A*
Rafael Arevalo Martinez: Biografia De 1926 Hasta Su Muerte En 1975 — *Arevalo, Teresa*
y The Raft (Parker). Audio Version — *Trumbull, Robert*
Rag Rug Inspirations — *Bawden, Juliet*
The Ragas of Early Indian Music — *Widdess, Richard*
La Ragazza Del Ghetto — *Acquaviva, Sabino*

Rage for Fame — *Morris, Sylvia Jukes*
A Rage for Justice — *Jacobs, John*
A Rage for Love — *Merini, Alda*
y Rage of a Demon King — *Feist, Raymond E*
The Rage of Angels — *Fisher, Alan*
Rage of Spirits — *Hynd, Noel*
The Rage of the Vulture — *Unsworth, Barry*
c Ragged Bear (Illus. by Alan Marks) — *Weninger, Brigitte*
c The Raggly Scraggly No-Soap No-Scrub Girl (Illus. by Guy Portirio) — *Birchman, David F*
Ragion Di Stato — *Borrelli, Gianfranco*
The Ragman's Memory — *Mayor, Archer*
c Ragtime Tumpie (Illus. by Bernie Fuchs) — *Schroeder, Alan*
Die Rahmenerzahlung Im 19. Jahrhundert — *Jaggi, Andreas*
Rahner and Metz — *Guenther, Titus F*
The Raid — *Eickhoff, Randy Lee*
y The Raiders — *Kilworth, Garry*
The Raiders — *Robbins, Harold*
The Raiders of 1862 — *Brewer, James D*
Rail Transportation 1996
Railroad Crossing — *Deverell, William*
Railroad Postcards in the Age of Steam — *Grant, H Roger*
Railroad Radio — *Reh, Vincent*
Railway Engineering — *Profillidis, V A*
y The Railway Man — *Lomax, Eric*
y The Railway Man (Paterson). Audio Version — *Lomax, Eric*
y The Railway Pathfinders (Illus. by Paul McCusker) — *Berton, Pierre*
c The Rain (Illus. by Jeffrey Greene) — *Laser, Michael*
c Rain (Illus. by Luis Rizo) — *Llamas Ruiz, Andres*
y The Rain Catchers — *Thesman, Jean*
y Rain Dance — *Moody, Skye Kathleen*
c Rain Forest (Illus. by Carolyn Scrace) — *Clarke, Penny*
c Rain Forest (Illus. by Colin Woolf) — *Harris, Nicholas*
c Rain Forest Babies (Illus. by Tara Darling) — *Darling, Kathy*
c Rain Forests (Illus. by Still Pictures Firm) — *Oldfield, Sara*
c Rain Forests and Reefs (Illus. by Stan Rullman) — *Maynard, Caitlin*
Rain Men — *Berkmann, Marcus*
Rain of Iron and Ice — *Lewis, John S*
The Rain on Macy's Parade — *Trachtenberg, Jeffrey A*
c Rain Player — *Wisniewski, David*
c Rain Player. Book and Audio Version — *Wisniewski, David*
The Rain Tree — *Cook, Will*
c Rain, Where Do You Come From? (Illus. by Chiara Carrer) — *Grazzini, Francesca*
Rain without Thunder — *Francione, Gary L*
c Rainbabies — *Melmed, Laura Krauss*
Rainbow — *Mao, Tun*
c A Rainbow at Night — *Hucko, Bruce*
c The Rainbow Fairy Book (Illus. by Michael Hague) — *Lang, Andrew*
c The Rainbow Fish — *Pfister, Marcus*
c Rainbow Fish to the Rescue! (Illus. by Marcus Pfister) — *Pfister, Marcus*
The Rainbow People of God — *Tutu, Desmond*
c Rainforest — *Ricciuti, Edward R*
c The Rainforest — *Wood, Selina*
c Rainforest Animals (Illus. by Paul Hess) — *Hess, Paul*
c The Rainforest Indians — *Thomson, Ruth*
c Rainforests — *Murray, Peter, 1952, Sep., 9-*
c Rainy Day Play! (Illus. by Loretta Trezzo Braren) — *Castaldo, Nancy Fusco*
y Rainy Lake — *Rockcastle, Mary Francois*
y Rainy Season — *Griffin, Adele*
c Rainy, Windy, Snowy, Sunny Days — *Perry, Phyllis J*
y Raise the Red Lantern — *Su, T'ung*
Raised by Wolves — *Goldberg, Jim, 1953-*
Raising Abel — *Alison, James*
Raising Arizona's Dams — *Rogge, A E*
Raising Children in a Socially Toxic Environment — *Garbarino, James*
Raising Educational Standards in the Inner Cities — *Barber, Michael*
y Raising Holy Hell — *Olds, Bruce*
y Raising Issues. Bks. 1-2 — *West, Keith*
Raising Kane and Other Essays — *Kael, Pauline*
Raising Low-Fat Kids in a High-Fat World — *Shaw, Judith*
Raising My Titanic — *Sheldon, Mary*
r Raising Our Future

Raising Spiritual Children in a Material World — *Catalfo, Phil*
Raja Rammohan Ray: The Father of Modern India — *Robertson, Bruce Carlisle*
Rajahdyksen Pelko Ja Kaipuu, Nobel — *Vakkuri, Juha*
Rajani Palme Dutt: A Study of British Stalinism — *Callaghan, John*
Rajiv Gandhi and Rama's Kingdom — *Mehta, Ved*
The Rakehell's Reform — *Fairchild, Elizabeth*
A Rake's Reform — *Barbour, Anne*
Rakkasans: The Combat History of the 187th Airborne Infantry — *Flanagan, E M, Jr.*
Raku: A Review of Contemporary Work — *Andrews, Tim*
Rallying the Whole Village — *Comer, James P*
Ralph Adams Crum: Life and Architecture. Vol. 1 — *Shand-Tucci, Douglass*
Ralph Albert Blakelock — *Davidson, Abraham A*
Ralph J. Bunche: Selected Speeches and Writings — *Bunche, Ralph J*
c Ralph S. Mouse (Roberts). Audio Version — *Cleary, Beverly*
Ram with Red Horns — *Davies, Rhys*
c Rama (Guidall). Audio Version — *Highwater, Jamake*
c Ramachandra in India — *Cheneviere, Alain*
c Ramadan (Illus. by Omar Rayyan) — *Ghazi, Suhaib Hamid*
Ramadan and Id-Al-Fitr — *MacMillan, Dianne M*
c The Ramayana — *Mitchell, Pratima*
The Ramayana of Valmiki. Vol. 4 — *Valmiki*
y Ramblin' Robots — *Wickelgren, Ingrid*
Ramblin' Rose — *Whiteside, Jonny*
Rameau's Niece — *Schine, Cathleen*
Ramon Maria Del Valle-Inclan: Questions of Gender — *Maier, Carol*
c Ramona La Chinche (Illus. by Louis Darling) — *Cleary, Beverly*
Ramona: The Heart and Conscience of Early California (Martin). Audio Version — *Jackson, Helen Hunt*
y The Ramsay Scallop — *Temple, Frances*
y Ramses II and Egypt — *Tiano, Olivier*
y Ran Van — *Wieler, Diana*
The Ranch — *Steel, Danielle*
Randalls Round — *Scott, Eleanor*
R&D and Technology Transfer by Multinational Enterprises — *Fors, Gunnar*
y The Randle Report — *Randle, Kevin D*
y Random Acts of Kindness. Audio Version — *Conari Press*
A Random Gospel — *Helwig, David*
r Random House Compact Unabridged Dictionary. Special 2nd Ed. Book and Electronic Media Version
r Random House Concise Encyclopedia
yr Random House Dictionary of Popular Proverbs and Sayings — *Titelman, Gregory Y*
r Random House Personal Computer Dictionary. 2nd Ed. — *Margolis, Philip E*
r Random House Russian-English Dictionary of Idioms — *Lubensky, Sophia*
r Random House Unabridged Electronic Dictionary: Version 1.7 for Windows. Electronic Media Version
r Random House Webster's College Dictionary. Newly Rev. and Updated Ed.
r Random House Webster's College Thesaurus. Rev. and Updated Ed. — *Stein, Jess*
r Random House Webster's Dictionary of American English — *Dalgish, Gerard M*
r Random House Webster's Unabridged Dictionary. Book and Electronic Media Version
r Random House Webster's Unabridged Dictionary CD-ROM Version 2.0. Electronic Media Version
Random Summation — *Gnedenko, Boris V*
y Random Winds (Fairman). Audio Version — *Plain, Belva*
r Randomised Controlled Clinical Trials. 2nd Ed. — *Bulpitt, Christopher J*
Range of Motion — *Berg, Elizabeth*
cp Ranger Rick
y Ransom — *Duncan, Lois*
Ransom for Our Sins — *Hunter, Fred W*
Rantaravintola — *Salmi, Vexi*
The Rap Factor — *Delacorta*
r Rap Whoz Who — *Stancell, Steven*
Rape: A Philosophical Investigation — *Burgess-Jackson, Keith*
The Rape of Sita — *Collen, Lindsey*
The Rape of the American Constitution — *Shiver, Chuck*
Rape on Trial — *Cuklanz, Lisa M*
Raphael and France — *Rosenberg, Martin R*

Rapid Application Development with Oracle Designer/2000 — *Billings, Chris*
Rapid Prototyping — *Reilly, John*
Rapid System Prototyping — *IEEE International Workshop on Rapid System Prototyping (7th: 1996: Thessaloniki, Greece)*
Rapid Thermal and Integrated Processing V
Rapport Des Resultats Officiels Du Scrutin
y Raptor Red — *Bakker, Robert T*
c Raptor Rescue (Illus. by Ron Winch) — *Johnson, Sylvia A*
c Raptors, Fossils, Fins and Fangs (Illus. by Ray Troll) — *Troll, Ray*
yr Raptors: The Birds of Prey — *Weidensaul, Scott*
c Raptors! The Nastiest Dinosaurs (Illus. by David Peters) — *Lessem, Don*
Rapture — *Sosnowski, David*
y The Rapture of Canaan — *Reynolds, Sheri*
The Rapture of Politics — *Bruce, Steve*
c Rapunzel (Illus. by Maja Dusikova) — *Grimm, Jacob*
c Rapunzel (Illus. by Kelvin Steinberger) — *Steinberger, Kelvin*
Rare and Endangered Biota of Florida. Vol. 5 — *Rodgers, James A*
A Rare Bird — *Dutton, Geoffrey*
r Rare Birds Day by Day — *Dudley, Steve*
p Rare Breed
A Rare Breed — *Leech, Ben*
Rare Earth Doped Semiconductors II — *Coffa, Salvatore*
Rare Lilies of California — *Fiedler, Peggy Lee*
y The Rarest of the Rare — *Ackerman, Diane*
p Raritan
Rascally Signs in Sacred Places — *Whisnant, David E*
Rasero — *Rebolledo, Francisco*
The Rashaayda Bedouin — *Young, William A*
Rastafari: Roots and Ideology — *Chevannes, Barry*
Rastalmacirea Lui Tepes — *Ungheanu, Mihai*
Rat Bohemia — *Schulman, Sarah*
r The Rate Reference Guide to the U.S. Treasury Market 1984-1995 — *Ricchiuto, Steven R*
Rating Scales and Checklists — *Aiken, Lewis R*
The Rational and the Moral Order — *Baier, Kurt*
Rational Choice and Moral Agency — *Schmidtz, David*
The Rational Factory — *Biggs, Lindy*
Rational Fears — *Jancovich, Mark*
The Rational Foundations of Economic Behaviour — *Arrow, Kenneth J*
Rational Recovery — *Trimpey, Jack*
Rational Suicide? — *Werth, James L*
Rationality, Allocation, and Reproduction — *Walsh, Vivian*
Rationality and Coordination — *Bicchieri, Cristina*
Rationality and Ethics in Agriculture — *Lehman, Hugh*
Rationality in Greek Thought — *Frede, Michael*
Rationality in Science, Religion, and Everyday Life — *Stenmark, Mikael*
The Rationality of the Welfare State — *Eriksen, Erik Oddvar*
Rationalizing Culture — *Born, Georgina*
Rationalizing Parliament — *Huber, John D*
Ratite Management, Medicine, and Surgery — *Tully, Thomas N*
y The Ratpackers — *Blake, Chris*
c Rats! (Illus. by Tracey Campbell Pearson) — *Cutler, Jane*
RATS Handbook for Econometric Time Series — *Enders, Walter*
y Rats Saw God — *Thomas, Rob*
c Rattle and Hum, Robot Detectives — *Rodgers, Frank*
y Rattler! A Natural History of Rattlesnakes — *Mattison, Chris*
c Rattlesnake Dance (Illus. by Jennifer Owings Dewey) — *Dewey, Jennifer Owings*
Raum Und Bewegung — *Beck, Hartmut*
Raunds Furnells, Northants — *Boddington, Andy*
y Rave On — *Norman, Philip, 1943-*
y The Raven — *Landesman, Peter*
p Raven: A Journal of Vexillology
c Raven and River (Illus. by Jon Van Zyle) — *Carlstrom, Nancy White*
y The Raven's Knot — *Jarvis, Robin*
The Raven's Moon — *King, Susan*
Le Ravin — *Princeau, Gerard M*
Ravished: Sexual Violence in Victorian Australia — *Bavin-Mizzi, Jill*
Raw Creation — *Maizels, John*
Raw Feeling — *Kirk, Robert*
Rawhide: A Western Quintet — *Flynn, T T*

r Rawson's Dictionary of Euphemisms and Other Doubletalk. Rev. Ed. — *Rawson, Hugh*
c Ray Charles: Soul Man — *Turk, Ruth*
Ray Gun — *Kuipers, Dean*
Raymond Carver: An Oral Biography — *Halpert, Sam*
Raymond Chandler: A Biography — *Hiney, Tom*
Raymond Chandler in Hollywood — *Clark, Al*
Raymond Chandler Speaking — *Chandler, Raymond*
Raymond Chandler's Philip Marlowe
Raymond Williams — *Inglis, Fred*
Ray's a Laugh — *Billingham, Richard*
RCRA Hazardous Waste Sourcedisk. Electronic Media Version
Re-Create Your Life — *Lefkoe, Morty*
Re-Discovering the Sacred — *Tickle, Phyllis*
The Re-Enchantment of Everyday Life — *Moore, Thomas, 1940-*
The Re-Enchantment of Everyday Life. Audio Version — *Moore, Thomas, 1940-*
Re-Engineering the Manufacturing System — *Stein, Robert E, 1949-*
Re-Imagining the Modern American West — *Etulain, Richard W*
Re-Inventing the Jewish Past — *Myers, David*
Re-Presenting the City — *King, Anthony D*
Re-Reading Cultural Geography — *Foote, Kenneth E*
Re-Reading Leavis — *Day, Gary*
Re-Searching Black Music — *Spencer, Jon Michael*
Re-Stating Social and Political Change — *Hay, Colin*
Re-Viewing Reception — *Joyrich, Lynne*
Re-Viewing Reviewing — *Satpathy, Sumanyu*
Re-Visioning Romanticism — *Wilson, Carol Shiner*
Re-Visioning the Earth — *Devereux, Paul*
y Re-Zoom (Illus. by Istvan Banyai) — *Banyai, Istvan*
The Reach of Rome — *Williams, Derek*
Reaching for a Better Standard — *Wilson, Thomas A, 1938-*
Reaching for the Stars — *Bond, Peter*
Reaching into Thought — *Russon, Anne E*
Reaching Out without Dumbing Down — *Dawn, Marva J*
Reaching Standards — *Lindquist, Mary M*
Reaction Kinetics — *Pilling, Michael J*
Reactivity of Solids — *Boldyrev, V V*
r Read All Your Life — *Davis, Barbara Kerr*
c Read and Learn with Dr. Seuss (Illus. by Dr. Seuss) — *Seuss, Dr.*
c Read for Me, Mama (Illus. by Lori McElrath-Eslick) — *Rahaman, Vashanti*
Read Me First — *Sun Technical Publications*
Read My Lips — *Parris, Matthew*
c Read On — *Ray, Rita*
Read This and Tell Me What It Says — *Ansay, A Manette*
r Read Up on It, Out of This World 1995
Reader (Runger). Audio Version — *McPhee, John*
Reader Response in the Classroom — *Karolides, Nicholas J*
r The Reader's Adviser on CD-ROM. Electronic Media Version
r Readers' Advisory Service in the Public Library — *Saricks, Joyce G*
Readers and Books in Majorca 1229-1550. Vols. 1-2 — *Hillgarth, J N*
Reader's Block — *Markson, David*
r The Reader's Catalog. 2nd Ed., Vols. 1-2 — *O'Brien, Geoffrey*
A Reader's Companion to Crossing the Threshold of Hope — *Honea, Charla H*
yr The Reader's Companion to Military History — *Cowley, Robert*
c Reader's Digest Bible for Children (Illus. by Ulises Wensell) — *Delval, Marie-Helene*
Reader's Digest Book of Skills and Tools
cr The Reader's Digest Children's World Atlas — *Day, Malcolm*
r The Reader's Digest Complete Book of Perennials — *Rice, Graham*
r Reader's Digest Complete Do-It-Yourself Guide. Electronic Media Version
Reader's Digest New Complete Do-It-Yourself Manual. Rev. Ed. — *Reader's Digest Association*
Reader's Digest New Fix-It-Yourself Manual
The Reader's Eye — *Esrock, Ellen J*
A Reader's Guide to Finnegans Wake — *Tindall, William York*
r Reader's Guide to Literature in English — *Hawkins-Dady, Mark*
Reader's Guide to Murder — *Jeffers, H Paul*
r Reader's Guide to Periodical Literature 1901-

r A Reader's Guide to the American Novel of Detection — *Lachman, Marvin*
r A Reader's Guide to the Classic British Mystery — *Oleksiw, Susan*
r Reader's Guide to the Private Eye Novel — *Niebuhr, Gary Warren*
r A Reader's Guide to the Twentieth-Century Novel — *Parker, Peter*
r Readers Guide to Twentieth-Century Science Fiction — *Fletcher, Marilyn*
yr A Reader's Guide to Twentieth-Century Writers — *Parker, Peter*
r A Reader's Guide to Writers' Britain — *Varlow, Sally*
Readin' Country Music — *Tichi, Cecelia*
Reading, a Comparative View — *IFLA Round Table on Research in Reading (1993: Haifa, Israel). Mid-Term Seminar*
Reading an Erased Code — *Despland, Michel*
Reading and Wisdom — *English, Edward D*
Reading and Writing — *Tickoo, Makhan L*
Reading and Writing. 2nd Ed. — *Harp, Bill*
Reading Andreas Gryphius — *Metzger, Erika A*
Reading Aristotle's Ethics — *Tessitore, Aristide*
Reading Asian American Literature — *Wong, Sau-Ling Cynthia*
Reading Berlin 1900 — *Fritzsche, Peter*
y Reading between the Bones — *Clinton, Susan*
Reading Beyond Words — *Brown, Jennifer S H*
Reading by Starlight — *Broderick, Damien*
Reading Colossians, Ephesians and 2 Thessalonians — *Thurston, Bonnie*
Reading Dialogics — *Pearce, Lynne*
The Reading Environment — *Chambers, Aidan*
Reading Esther — *Craig, Kenneth M*
Reading for Information — *Ennew, Craig*
Reading from This Place. Vol. 2 — *Segovia, Fernando*
Reading Greek Death — *Sourvinou-Inwood, Christiane*
r The Reading Group Handbook — *Jacobsohn, Rachel W*
Reading Heidegger from the Start — *Kisiel, Theodore*
r Reading Holinshed's Chronicles — *Patterson, Annabel*
Reading Houses and Building Books — *Sweeting, Adam W*
Reading Images — *Kress, Gunther*
Reading in Bed — *Gilbar, Steven*
y Reading in the Dark — *Deane, Seamus*
Reading in Tudor England — *Kintgen, Eugene R*
Reading Jazz — *Gottlieb, Robert*
Reading Jazz — *Meltzer, David*
Reading John — *Talbert, Charles H*
Reading Kristeva — *Oliver, Kelly*
y Reading Lists for College-Bound Students. 2nd Ed. — *Estell, Doug*
Reading Literacy in the United States — *Binkley, Marilyn R*
Reading Marx Writing — *Kemple, Thomas M*
Reading Matthew — *Garland, David E*
Reading Medieval Latin — *Sidwell, Keith*
r Reading New Testament Greek: Complete Word Lists and Reader's Guide — *Scott, Bernard Brandon*
Reading North by South — *Larsen, Neil*
Reading Seminars I and II — *Feldstein, Richard*
Reading Shakespeare Historically — *Jardine, Lisa*
The Reading Terminal Market Cookbook — *Hazan, Ann*
Reading the Apostolic Fathers — *Jefford, Clayton N*
Reading the Fractures of Genesis — *Carr, David M*
Reading the Gospels with the Church — *Brown, Raymond Edward*
Reading the Ground — *John, Brian*
Reading the Rabbis — *Kraemer, David*
Reading the Renaissance — *Hart, Jonathan*
Reading the Rhythm — *Scott, Clive*
Reading the Social Body — *Burroughs, Catherine B*
Reading the Voice — *Zolbrod, Paul*
Reading the West — *Kowalewski, Michael*
r Reading Therapy for Children. Vol. 2 — *Schlenther, Elizabeth*
Reading Together. 2nd Ed. — *Krahnke, K*
Reading Tudor-Stuart Texts through Cultural Historicism — *Tricomi, Albert H*
Reading with a Passion — *Staley, Jeffrey L*
r Reading with Feeling — *Feagin, Susan L*
Reading Women's Magazines — *Hermes, Joke*
Reading World Literature — *Lawall, Sarah*
Reading, Writing, and Race — *Douglas, Davison M*
Readings for Meditation and Reflection — *Lewis, C S*
Readings in Christian Ethics — *Wogaman, J Philip*
Readings in Medieval English Romance — *Meale, Carol M*
Readings in Modern Theology — *Gill, Robin*

Readings in True and Fair — *Parker, R H*
Readings on Equal Education. Vol. 13
y Readings on Herman Melville — *Szumski, Bonnie*
yr Readings on John Steinbeck — *Swisher, Clarice*
y Readings on Mark Twain — *De Koster, Katie*
yr Readings on Nathaniel Hawthorne — *Swisher, Clarice*
y Readings on Sophocles — *Nardo, Don*
y Readings on The Canterbury Tales — *Nardo, Don*
y Readings on the Sonnets — *Swisher, Clarice*
y Readings on the Tragedies of William Shakespeare — *Swisher, Clarice*
README.1ST: SGML for Writers and Editors — *Turner, Ronald C*
Ready for Sea — *Allston, Frank J*
y Ready or Not — *Macleod, Mark*
Ready, Set, Count — *Barron, Marlene*
c Ready, Set, Go! (Illus. by John Stadler) — *Stadler, John*
c Ready, Set, Grow! with the Earth Buddies (Illus. by Jane Kurisu) — *Pearson, Debora*
c Ready, Set, Hop! (Illus. by Jon Buller) — *Murphy, Stuart J*
Ready, Set, Read and Write — *Barron, Marlene*
c Ready, Steady, Go, Cheetah — *Moon, Pat*
c Ready, Steady, Read! Series
Readymade — *Liehu, Rakel*
The Reagan Doctrine — *Lagon, Mark P*
c The Reagan Way — *Morris, Jeffrey*
r The Reagan Years A to Z — *Kurz, Kenneth Franklin*
Real Analysis — *Bruckner, Andrew M*
The Real Balti Cookbook — *Baljekar, Mridula*
Real China — *Gittings, John*
p Real Crime Book Digest
Real Estate Issues in the Health Care Industry — *Health Care Real Estate Institute Conference (1st: 1995: Los Angeles, Calif.)*
Real Events Revisited — *Scott, Ann, 1930-*
Real Freedom for All — *Parijs, Philippe Van*
Real Gardener's True Confessions — *Stone, Pat*
The Real Goods Independent Builder — *Clark, Sam*
The Real Jesus — *Johnson, Luke Timothy*
Real Knowing — *Alcoff, Linda Martin*
Real Life — *Daigle, France*
Real-Life Math Problem Solving — *Illingworth, Mark*
The Real Life of Laurence Olivier — *Lewis, Roger*
The Real Life of Mary Ann Evans — *Bodenheimer, Rosemarie*
c Real-Life Stories — *Byars, Betsy*
Real Matter — *Robertson, David, 1937-*
Real Options — *Trigeorgis, Lenos*
yr Real People Working in Communications — *Goldberg, Jan*
yr Real People Working in Health Care — *Camenson, Blythe*
yr Real People Working in Sales and Marketing — *Camenson, Blythe*
yr Real People Working in Service Businesses — *Camenson, Blythe*
y The Real Plato Jones — *Bawden, Nina*
Real Process — *Burbidge, John W*
Real Rights — *Wellman, Carl*
y The Real Taste of Jamaica — *Donaldson, Enid*
Real-Time Imaging — *Laplante, Phillip A*
The Real, True Angel — *Lippincott, Robin*
c Real Vampires — *Cohen, Daniel, 1936-*
Real Vegetarian Thai — *McDermott, Nancie*
The Real War on Crime — *Donziger, Steven R*
Real Women — *Oudot, Susan*
REAL: Yearbook of Research in English and American Literature. Vol. 11
Realignments in the Welfare State — *Ruggie, Mary*
Realism and Invention in the Prints of Albrecht Durer — *Smith, David R*
Realism and Representation — *Levine, George*
Realism and the American Dramatic Tradition — *Demastes, William W*
Realism and the Birth of the Modern United States — *Corkin, Stanley*
A Realist Conception of Truth — *Alston, William P*
Realist Social Theory — *Archer, Margaret S*
A Realistic Theory of Categories — *Chisholm, Roderick M*
Der Realistische Weg — *Geppert, Hans Vilmar*
Realities and Relationships — *Gergen, Kenneth J*
Reality and Dreams — *Spark, Muriel*
Reality and Illusion in New Testament Scholarship — *Meyer, Ben F*
Reality and Research — *Galster, George*
y Reality Check — *Anderson, Neil T*
y Reality Check — *Trapani, Margi*
Reality Check — *Wieners, Brad*

The Reality Dysfunction — *Hamilton, Peter F*
The Reality of Aid 1996
r The Realization and Suppression of the Situationist
   International — *Ford, Simon*
Realizing Rights — *Oorschot, Wim Van*
c The Really Amazing Animal Book (Illus. by Peter
   Anderson) — *Sirett, Dawn*
Really Existing Nationalisms — *Benner, Erica*
cr The Really Fearsome Blood-Loving Vampire Bat and
   Other Creatures with Strange Eating Habits
   — *Greenaway, Theresa*
cr The Really Hairy Scary Spider and Other Creatures
   with Lots of Legs (Illus. by F Greenaway)
   — *Greenaway, Theresa*
cr The Really Horrible Horned Toad and Other Cold,
   Clammy Creatures — *Greenaway, Theresa*
c Really Weird Animals (Illus. by Christopher Hartley)
   — *Everts, Tammy*
c Really Weird News Stories (Illus. by Granger Davis)
   — *Del Prado, Dana*
cr The Really Wicked Droning Wasp and Other Things
   That Bite and Sting — *Greenaway, Theresa*
The Realm of the Word — *Landau, Paul Stuart*
The Realms of Apollo — *Anselment, Raymond A*
Realms of Memory. Vol. 1 — *Kritzman, Lawrence D*
y The Realms of the Gods — *Pierce, Tamora*
Reaping the Bounty — *Heikkonen, Esko*
The Rear View — *Hennig, Jean-Luc*
y Rear View Mirrors — *Fleischman, Paul*
Rearview Mirror — *Feldman, Ellen*
Reason and Passion — *Rosenkranz, E Joshua*
Reason and Religious Faith — *Penelhum, Terence*
Reason and Rhetoric in the Philosophy of Hobbies
   — *Skinner, Quentin*
Reason and the Heart — *Wainwright, William J*
Reason, History, and Politics — *Ingram, David*
Reason in Action — *Hollis, Martin*
Reason in the Balance — *Johnson, Phillip E*
The Reason of Following — *Scharlemann, Robert P*
Reason, Reality, and Speculative Philosophy
   — *Murphy, Arthur Edward*
Reason, Ridicule and Religion — *Redwood, John*
Reason to Believe — *Cuomo, Mario*
The Reason Why — *Rendell, Ruth*
Reasonable Accommodation — *Spechler, Jay W*
Reasonable Children — *Pritchard, Michael S*
Reasonable Democracy — *Chambers, Simone*
Reasonable Doubts — *Dershowitz, Alan M*
Reasoning about Knowledge — *Fagin, Ronald*
Reasoning about Luck — *Ambegaokar, Vinay*
Reasonings in Chemistry — *Marsella, Gail B C*
Reasons for Knocking at an Empty House — *Viola,
   Bill*
Reassessing Anglo-Saxon England — *John, Eric*
Reassessing the Sixties — *Macedo, Stephen*
A Reassessment of Weimar Classicism — *Hoffmeister,
   Gerhart*
Rebecca (Stevenson). Audio Version — *Du Maurier,
   Daphne*
Rebecca West: A Life — *Rollyson, Carl*
Rebecca West: A Saga of the Century — *Rollyson,
   Carl*
Rebel — *Graham, Heather*
c Rebel (Illus. by John Schoenherr) — *Schoenherr, John*
Rebel (Morse). Audio Version — *Cornwell, Bernard*
Rebel against Injustice — *Buckingham, Peter H*
The Rebel and the Redcoat — *Monk, Karyn*
Rebel Angels — *Jarman, Mark*
y Rebel Angels — *Malcolm, Jahnna N*
Rebel Baseball — *Perlstein, Steve*
Rebel Bishop — *Gannon, Michael*
Rebel Brothers — *Williams, Edward B*
Rebel Daughter — *Anderson, Doris*
Rebel Hearts — *Toolis, Kevin*
Rebel Private — *Fletcher, William A*
Rebel Storehouse — *Taylor, Robert A*
Rebel: The Life and Legend of James Dean — *Spoto,
   Donald*
Rebel with a Cause — *Eysenck, H J*
Rebel without a Car — *Mednick, Fred*
Rebel without a Crew — *Rodriguez, Robert*
Rebellion — *Schull, Joseph*
y Rebellion: A Novel of Upper Canada (Illus. by G
   Brender A Brandis) — *Brandis, Marianne*
The Rebellious Body — *Wittenberg, Janice Strubbe*
y Rebels against Slavery — *McKissack, Pat*
Rebels against the Future — *Sale, Kirkpatrick*
The Rebel's Dilemma — *Lichbach, Mark Irving*
Rebels of Highland Guatemala — *Carmack, Robert M*
y Rebels of the Heavenly Kingdom (Guidall). Audio
   Version — *Paterson, Katherine*

y A Rebel's Recollections — *Eggleston, George Cary*
The Rebirth of Russian Democracy — *Petro, Nicolai
   N*
Rebirth of the Small Family Farm — *Gregson, Bob*
The Rebirth of the West — *Duignan, Peter*
Reborn in the Light — *Sutherland, Cherie*
Rebuilding Inner City Airports — *International Air
   Transportation Conference (24th: 1996: Louisville, KY)*
Rebuilding Romania — *Patterson, Walt*
Rebuilding the Inner City — *Halpern, Robert*
Rebuilding the State — *Serrano, Monica*
c Rebus Riot (Illus. by Bonnie Christensen)
   — *Christensen, Bonnie*
Recast Dreams — *Livingstone, D W*
Recasting Persian Poetry — *Karimi-Hakkak, Ahmad*
Recasting Social Values in the Work of Virginia Woolf
   — *Reese, Judy S*
Recasting the Imperial Far East — *Xiang, Lanxin*
Received Wisdom? — *Hoose, Bernard*
Receiving the Vision — *Bird, David*
Recent Advances in Cellular and Molecular Aspects of
   Angiotensin Receptors — *Raizada, Mohan K*
Recent Advances in Clinical Neurophysiology
   — *International Congress of EMG and Clinical
   Neurophysiology (10th: 1995: Kyoto, Japan)*
Recent Advances in Event-Related Brain Potential
   Research — *International Conference on Event-
   Related Potentials of the Brain (11th: 1995: Okinawa-
   Shi, Japan)*
Recent Advances in Reinforcement Learning
   — *Kaelbling, Leslie Pack*
Recent Advances in Robot Learning — *Franklin, Judy
   A*
Recent Advances in Solids/Structures and Applications
   of Metallic Materials 1996
Recent Advances in Tryptophan Research
   — *Filippini, Graziella Allegri*
Recent Developments in Alcoholism. Vol. 12
Recent Developments in Applied Demand Analysis
   — *Selvanathan, E A*
Recent Developments in Forensic Linguistics
   — *Kniffka, Hannes*
Recent Developments in Geotextile Filters and
   Prefabricated Drainage Geocomposites — *Bhatia,
   Shobha K*
Recent Developments in Optimization — *Durier,
   Roland*
Recent Developments on Engine Emissions. Vols. 1-3
   — *Spring Technical Conference of the ASME Internal
   Combustion Engine Division (1996: Youngstown, OH)*
Recent Excavations in Israel — *Gitin, Seymour*
Recent Legal Issues for American Indians 1968 to the
   Present — *Wunder, John R*
Recent Marxian Theory — *Sitton, John F*
r Recent Reference Books in Religion — *Johnston,
   William M, 1936-*
r Recent Work in Critical Theory 1989-1995 — *Baker,
   William, 1944-*
La Reception D'Agrippa D'Aubigne XVIe-XXe Siecles
   — *Schrenck, Gilbert*
The Reception of Myth in English Romanticism
   — *Harding, Anthony John*
c Recess Mess (Illus. by Betsy Lewin) — *Maccarone,
   Grace*
Recharting the Thirties — *Quinn, Patrick J*
Recherche De L'Ironie Et Ironie De La Recherche
   — *Schoentjes, Pierre*
Recipes 1-2-3 — *Gold, Rozanne*
Recipes from Central Market — *Good, Phyllis
   Pellman*
Recipes from Ireland — *Asala, Joanne*
Recipes from the Dump — *Stone, Abigail*
Reciprocity and Retaliation in U.S. Trade Policy
   — *Bayard, Thomas O*
Reciprocity and Ritual — *Seaford, Richard*
Le Recit Au Cinema — *Masson, Alain*
y Reckless — *Bates, Michael*
Reckoning Infinity — *Stith, John E*
Reckoning with the Dead — *Bray, Tamara L*
c Reclaim It — *Oliver, Geoff*
Reclaiming Democracy — *Mendel-Reyes, Meta*
Reclaiming Herstory — *Bell-Gadsby, Cheryl*
Reclaiming Higher Ground — *Secretan, Lance H K*
Reclaiming Male Sexuality — *Ryan, George*
Reclaiming Myths of Power — *Jenkins, Ruth Y*
Reclaiming Our Health — *Robbins, John*
Reclaiming Rhetoric — *Lunsford, Andrea A*
Reclaiming the American Library Past
   — *Hildenbrand, Suzanne*
Reclaiming the Arid West — *Rowley, William D*

Reclaiming the Dead Sea Scrolls — *Schiffman,
   Lawrence H*
Reclaiming the Heartland — *Osborne, Karen Lee*
Reclaiming the Jesus of History — *Eckardt, A Roy*
Reclaiming Truth — *Norris, Christopher*
Reclaiming William Morris — *Weinroth, Michelle*
y Reclamation — *Zettel, Sarah*
Reclamos Y Representaciones — *Garrido, Margarita*
Recognition: Advancing Ecumenical Thinking
   — *Kelly, Gerard*
Recognizing European Modernities — *Pred, Allan*
Recollected Words of Abraham Lincoln
   — *Fehrenbacher, Don Edward*
Recollections of Anais Nin by Her Contemporaries
   — *Franklin, Benjamin, 1939-*
Recombinant FSH (Puregon) — *Out, H J*
Recommendations for the Primary Prevention of
   Cancer
r Recommended Books in Spanish for Children and
   Young Adults 1991-1995 — *Schon, Isabel*
r Recommended Reading — *Salem Press*
r Recommended Reference Books for Small and
   Medium-Sized Libraries and Media Centers 1996
Reconceiving Experience — *Kearns, John T*
Reconceiving Mathematics Instruction — *Borasi,
   Rafaella*
Reconceiving, Writing, Rethinking Writing Instruction
   — *Petraglia, Joseph*
Reconceptualizing American Literary/Cultural Studies
   — *Cain, William E*
Reconciliation and Revival — *Margulies, Herbert F*
Reconciliation of National Income and Expenditure
   — *Sefton, James*
Reconciling Economic Reform and Sustainable Human
   Development — *Taylor, Lance*
Reconfigured Spheres — *Higonnet, Margaret R*
Reconfiguring Truth — *Ward, Steven C*
Reconsidering American Liberalism — *Young, James
   P*
Reconsidering Tu Fu — *Chou, Eva Shan*
Reconstructing Architecture — *Dutton, Thomas A*
Reconstructing Biology — *Vandermeer, John*
Reconstructing Christian Theology — *Chopp, Rebecca
   S*
Reconstructing Eliade — *Rennie, Bryan S*
Reconstructing Foucault — *Miguel-Alfonso, Ricardo*
Reconstructing Gender — *Disch, Estelle*
Reconstructing Literature in an Ideological Age
   — *Ritchie, Daniel E*
Reconstructing Political Pluralism — *Eisenberg,
   Avigail I*
r Reconstructing Proto-Afroasiatic — *Ehret, Christopher*
Reconstructing the Black Past — *Myers, Norma*
Reconstructing the Christ Symbol — *Stevens,
   Maryanne*
Reconstructing the History of Basin and Range
   Extension Using Sedimentology and Stratigraphy
   — *Beratan, Kathi K*
Reconstructing the Household — *Bardaglio, Peter W*
Reconstructing the Subject — *Heibel, Yule F*
Reconstructing Theory — *Roberts, David, 1937-*
Reconstructing Urban Regime Theory — *Lauria,
   Mickey*
The Reconstruction — *Casper, Claudia*
The Reconstruction of the International Economy
   1945-1960 — *Eichengreen, Barry*
r Record of Deaths in the First Church in Rowley,
   Massachusetts 1696-1777 — *Blodgett, George B*
The Records Continuum — *McKemmish, Sue*
Records of Early English Drama: Shropshire. Vols.
   1-2 — *Somerset, J Alan B*
r Records of Indentured Servants and of Certificates for
   Land, Northumberland County, Virginia 1650-1795
   — *Haynie, W Preston*
r Records of Randolph County, Missouri 1833-1964
   — *Eddlemon, Sherida K*
Records of the 1996 IEEE International Workshop on
   Memory Technology, Design and Testing
The Records of the Medieval Ecclesiastical Courts. Pt.
   2 — *Donahue, Charles, Jr.*
The Records of the Virginia Company of London. Vol.
   4 — *Virginia Company of London*
Recovered Memories of Abuse — *Pope, Kenneth S*
The Recovered Memory/False Memory Debate
   — *Pezdek, Kathy*
Recovered Roots — *Zerubavel, Yael*
Recovering Shakespeare's Theatrical Vocabulary
   — *Dessen, Alan C*
The Recovery of Black Presence — *Bailey, Randall C*
The Recovery of Race in America — *Greeson, Aaron
   David, III*

The Recovery of Self — *Fauteux, Kevin*

The Recovery of Unconscious Memories — *Erdelyi, Matthew Hugh*

Recovery Plan for the Mexican Spotted Owl: Draft — *Block, William M*

r Recreating the Past — *Adamson, Lynda G*

y Recreation Can Be Risky — *Gutman, Bill*

Recruiters' Internet Survival Guide — *Sumser, John*

c Rectangles (Illus. by Richard Maccabe) — *Stienecker, David*

The Rector's Wife — *Trollope, Joanna*

Recueil De Farces 1450-1550. Vol. 9

Recueil De Timbres Sur Amphores Romaines 1987-1988 — *Carre, M B*

Recueil Des Actes De Louis VI, Roi De France 1108-1137. Vols. 1-4

Recuento De Incertidumbres — *Castellanos Moya, Horacio*

The Recurrence of Fate — *Golub, Spencer*

The Recurring Dream of Equality — *Ozinga, James R*

y Recycled, Re-Seen — *Cerny, Charlene*

c Recycling — *Chandler, Gary*

c Red — *Bryant-Mole, Karen*

The Red and the Black — *Stendhal*

y Red as Blood — *Lee, Tanith*

c Red Bird (Illus. by Todd L W Doney) — *Mitchell, Barbara*

c Red, Blue and Yellow Yarn — *Kosman, Miriam*

r The Red Book. Electronic Media Version

The Red Camp — *Diaz, Debra*

Red Card — *Hoyt, Richard*

Red Cat, White Cat — *Weil, Robert*

p The Red Cedar Review

Red China Blues — *Wong, Jan*

c Red Cloud: Sioux Warrior — *Sanford, William R*

y Red Cloud: Warrior-Statesman of the Lakota Sioux — *Larson, Robert W*

c Red Cross, Red Crescent — *Burger, Leslie*

Red Diaper Baby — *Kornbluth, Josh*

The Red Drum — *Coleman, Jane Candia*

Red Dwarf Backwards — *Grant, Rob*

c The Red-Eared Ghosts — *Alcock, Vivien*

Red Earth and Pouring Rain — *Chandra, Vikram*

Red Emma Speaks — *Goldman, Emma*

Red Flag Over Hong Kong — *Bueno De Mesquita, Bruce*

Red Flags and Red Tape — *Leier, Mark*

Red Fox — *Henry, J David*

c Red Fox and the Baby Bunnies (Illus. by Alan Baron) — *Baron, Alan*

c Red Fox Dances — *Baron, Alan*

c The Red Fox Monster (Illus. by Alan Baron) — *Baron, Alan*

c Red Fox Running (Illus. by Wendell Minor) — *Bunting, Eve*

y The Red-Haired Khumalo — *Bregin, Elana*

y The Red Heels (Illus. by Gary Kelley) — *San Souci, Robert D*

c The Red Herring Mystery — *Adshead, Paul*

Red, Hot and Blue — *Henderson, Amy*

Red Hot Mamas — *Dowling, Colette*

The Red Jews — *Gow, Andrew Colin*

y A Red Kite in a Pale Sky — *Hofmeyr, Dianne*

y Red Leaves — *Simons, Paullina*

Red Light — *Plachy, Sylvia*

Red Mars — *Robinson, Kim Stanley*

The Red Mirror — *Wen, Chihua*

Red Moon Passage — *Horrigan, Bonnie J*

p Red Pepper

c The Red Poppy (Illus. by Irmgard Lucht) — *Lucht, Irmgard*

c The Red Racer (Illus. by Audrey Wood) — *Wood, Audrey*

Red, Red Robin — *Gallagher, Stephen*

A Red River — *Heron, Liz*

Red River Women — *McLeRoy, Sherrie*

Red Scare or Red Menace? — *Haynes, John E*

y The Red Scream (Critt). Audio Version — *Walker, Mary Willis*

Red Signature — *Leader, Mary*

Red Sky at Night — *Hall, Jim, 1947-*

Red Sorghum — *Mo, Yen*

Red Star Over China — *Snow, Edgar*

c The Red String — *Blair, Margot*

y Red-Tail Angels — *McKissack, Pat*

Red Tails, Black Wings — *Holway, John B*

Red Tempest — *Vogelfanger, Isaac J*

Red Trousseau — *Muske, Carol*

c A Red Wagon Year (Illus. by Laura McGee Kvasnosky) — *Appelt, Kathi*

y Red, White and Blue — *Leeson, Robert*

Red, White and Greens — *Willinger, Faith*

Red, White, and Oh So Blue — *Blakely, Mary Kay*

Red Wind and Thunder Moon — *Brand, Max*

Red Wing Art Pottery 1920s-1960s — *Dollen, B L*

Red-Winged Blackbirds — *Beletsky, Les*

c Red Wolf Country (Illus. by Daniel San Souci) — *London, Jonathan*

Redeem the Time — *Frost, Sue*

Redeeming America — *Johnson, Curtis D*

Redeeming Creation — *Van Dyke, Fred*

Redeeming Culture — *Gilbert, James*

Redeeming the Republic — *Brown, Roger H*

Redeeming the Time — *Scharper, Stephen Bede*

Redeeming the Wasteland — *Curtin, Michael*

Redefining a Public Health System — *Barbour, Galen L*

r Redefining American History Painting — *Burnham, Patricia M*

Redefining Diversity — *Thomas, R Roosevelt*

Redefining Family Support — *Singer, George H S*

Redefining Moral Education — *Wayne, Kathryn Ross*

Redefining the American Dream — *Harvey, Sally Peltier*

Redefining the Church — *Lennan, Richard*

Redefining the Egyptian Nation 1930-1945 — *Gershoni, Israel*

Redefining the Place to Learn — *Programme on Educational Building*

Redefining the Self — *Markowe, Laura A*

The Redemption of the Cannibal Woman — *Denevi, Marco*

Redemption Trail — *Ledbetter, Suzann*

Redesigning School — *McDonald, Joseph P*

Redesigning the Work of Human Services — *O'Looney, John*

Redeye: A Western — *Edgerton, Clyde*

Rediscoveries and Reformulations — *Alker, Hayward R*

Rediscovering Antiquity — *Parslow, Christopher Charles*

Rediscovering Nancy Drew — *Dyer, Carolyn Stewart*

Rediscovering Palestine — *Doumani, Beshara*

Rediscovering Public Library Management — *Usherwood, Bob*

Rediscovering Russia in Asia — *Kotkin, Stephen*

Rediscovery of the Mind — *Searle, John*

Redliners — *Drake, David*

Redneck Heaven — *Bultman, Bethany*

The Redneck Manifesto — *Goad, Jim*

c Redoute: The Man Who Painted Flowers (Illus. by Carolyn Croll) — *Croll, Carolyn*

Redrawing the Boundaries — *Greenblatt, Stephen*

The Redress of Poetry — *Heaney, Seamus*

Reducing Earthquake Losses

Reducing Poverty in America — *Darby, Michael R*

Reducing Space Mission Cost — *Wertz, James R*

Reducing Unemployment — *Ottosen, Garry K*

Reductions in Organic Chemistry. 2nd Ed. — *Hudlicky, Milos*

c Redwall (Keith). Audio Version — *Jacques, Brian*

c Redwoods — *Murray, Peter, 1952, Sep., 9-*

y The Reef (Underwood). Audio Version — *Wharton, Edith*

The Reel Cowboy — *Rainey, Buck*

Reel Justice — *Bergman, Paul*

Reel to Real — *Hooks, Bell*

Reenchanted Science — *Harrington, Anne*

Reengineering Nursing and Health Care — *Blancett, Suzanne Smith*

Reference and Collection Development on the Internet — *Thomsen, Elizabeth*

r Reference and Information Services. 2nd Ed. — *Bopp, Richard E*

r Reference and Price Guide for MicroTrains N Scale Rolling Stock

The Reference Assessment Manual — *American Library Association. Evaluation of Reference and Adult Service Committee*

r Reference Books Bulletin 1994-1995

r Reference Books Bulletin 1995-1996

r Reference Books for Children's Collections. 3rd Ed.

r Reference Encyclopedia of the American Indian. 7th Ed. — *Klein, Barry T*

yr A Reference Guide for Botany and Horticulture — *Simon, Ronald G*

r Reference Guide to World Literature. 2nd Ed., Vols. 1-2 — *Henderson, Lesley*

The Reference Realist in Library Academia — *Gebhard, Patricia*

r Reference Reviews Europe Annual 1995

Reference Services for the Unserved — *Zipkowitz, Fay*

r Reference Sources for Children's and Young Adult Literature — *Rollins, Deborah*

r The Reference Sources Handbook. 4th Ed. — *Lea, Peter W*

Reference Work in School Library Media Centers — *Job, Amy G*

The Referendum Experience in Europe — *Gallagher, Michael, 1951-*

Refiguring Life — *Keller, Evelyn Fox*

Refiguring Modernism. Vols. 1-2 — *Scott, Bonnie Kime*

The Refiner's Fire — *Brooke, John L*

The Refining Fire — *Davis, W E*

Reflected Glory — *Smith, Sally Bedell*

y Reflected Values — *Blatchford, Roy*

Reflecting a Prairie Town — *Hokanson, Drake*

Reflecting Senses — *Pape, Walter*

y Reflections and Refractions — *Silverberg, Robert*

Reflections from a Garden — *Hill, Susan, 1942-*

Reflections from the Dead — *Prohaszka, Marianne*

Reflections in a Golden Eye — *McCuller, Carson*

Reflections in Dark Glass — *McGinnis, Bruce*

Reflections of a Cold Warrior — *Bissell, Richard M*

Reflections of a Radical Moderate — *Richardson, Elliot*

Reflections of Eden — *Galdikas, Birute Marija Filomena*

y Reflections of the Dream 1975-1994 — *Williams, Clarence G*

Reflections on Economic Development — *Todaro, Michael P*

Reflections on Human Development — *Haq, Mahbub Ul*

Reflections on Jesus and Socrates — *Gooch, Paul W*

Reflections on Violence — *Keane, John*

Reflexionen Der Fackel — *Krolop, Kurt*

Reflexive Communication in the Culturally Diverse Workplace — *Kikoski, John F*

Reflexive Modernization — *Beck, Ulrich*

Reform and Counterreform — *Hawley, John C*

Reform and Reconstruction — *Brooke, Stephen*

Reform in Modern Russian History — *Taranovski, Theodore*

The Reform of King Josiah and the Composition of the Deuteronomistic History — *Eynikel, Erik*

Reform, Revolution and Reaction — *McNally, Vincent J*

Reforma Y Fraude Fiscal En El Reinado De Carlos II — *Caarceles, Beatriz*

y The Reformation — *Flowers, Sarah*

Reformation and Latin Literature in Northern Europe — *Ekrem, Inger*

The Reformation and Rural Society — *Dixon, C Scott*

Reformation: Christianity and the World 1500-2000 — *Fernandez-Armesto, Felipe*

The Reformation in National Context — *Scribner, Bob*

The Reformation of Machismo — *Brusco, Elizabeth E*

The Reformation of the Bible, the Bible of the Reformation — *Pelikan, Jaroslav*

The Reformation of the Subject — *Gregerson, Linda*

Reformations: A Radical Interpretation of Christianity and the World 1500-2000 — *Fernandez-Armesto, Felipe*

Reformationstheorien: Ein Kirchenhistorischer Disput Uber Einheit Und Vielfalt Der Reformation — *Hamm, Berndt*

Reformatorisches Profil — *Zur Meuhlen, Karl-Heinz*

La Reforme De La Dynamique — *Leibniz, Gottfried Wilhelm, Freiherr Von*

Reforming Asian Socialism — *McMillan, John*

Reforming Health Care Systems — *Culyer, A J*

Reforming Mexico's Agrarian Reform — *Randall, Laura*

Reforming Planned Economies in an Integrating World Economy — *Bosworth, Barry*

Reforming Popular Piety in Sixteenth-Century Strasbourg — *McKee, Elsie Anne*

The Reforming Power of the Scriptures — *Trammell, Mary Metzner*

Reforming Protestantism — *Ottati, Douglas F*

Reforming Sex — *Grossmann, Atina*

r Reforms of Statistical System under Socio-Economic Changes — *Mizoguchi, Toshiyuki*

The Reforms of the Council of Constance 1414-1418 — *Stump, Philip H*

Refounding Democratic Public Administration — *Wamsley, Gary L*

Refractive Surgery — *Serdarevic, Olivia N*

Reframing and Reform — *Carlson, Robert V*

Reframing Educational Policy — *Kahne, Joseph*

Reframing the Renaissance — *Farago, Claire*

Reframings: New American Feminist Photographies
— *Neumaier, Diane*
Refreshed by the Word. Vol. 2 — *O'Brien, John E*
y **Refugees** — *Warner, Rachel*
Refugees, Immigration and Gender
r **Refugees in America in the 1990s** — *Haines, David W*
Refugees in Inter-War Europe — *Skran, Claudena M*
Refugees into Citizens — *Arzt, Donna E*
Refugees unto the Third Generation — *Schiff, Benjamin N*
y **Refuse to Lose** — *Calipari, John*
Regaining Marxism — *Post, Ken*
Regaining Paradise Lost — *Corns, Thomas N*
c **El Regalo Magico (Illus. by Rudy Gutierrez)** — *Mohr, Nicholasa*
Regarding Animals — *Arluke, Arnold*
Regarding Penelope — *Felson-Rubin, Nancy*
Regendering the School Story — *Clark, Beverly Lyon*
The Regenerate Lyric — *New, Elisa*
Regeneration — *Barker, Pat*
y **Regeneration (Crossley). Audio Version** — *Barker, Pat*
Regeneration of the Coalfield Areas — *Critcher, C*
p **Regeneration Quarterly**
y **Reggie Miller: Basketball Sharpshooter** — *Cox, Ted*
Regiam Sibi Bibliothecam Instruxit — *Malaguzzi, Francesco*
El Regimen De La Encomienda En Barquisimeto Colonial 1530-1810 — *Rojas, Reinaldo*
Region, Religion, Caste, Gender and Culture in Contemporary India — *Sathyamurthy, T V*
Regional Conflicts — *Goodby, James E*
The Regional Dimension in Agricultural Economics and Policies — *Sotte, Franco*
The Regional Dimension of Unemployment in Transition Countries
Regional Excellence — *Dodge, Bill*
Regional Futures and Transatlantic Economic Relations — *Kahler, Miles*
A Regional History of England — *Phillips, C B*
Regional Impacts of Global Climate Change — *Ghan, S J*
Regional Library Development--Where Next? — *Wressell, Pat*
Regional Politics — *Savitch, H V*
Regional Satellite Oceanography — *Victorov, S V*
r **Regional Theatre Directory 1996-97**
Regionalism and the Global Economy — *Teunissen, Jan Joost*
Regionalism and the World Trading System
Regionalism and World Order — *Gamble, Andrew*
Regionalism, Multilateralism, and Deeper Integration — *Lawrence, Robert Z*
Regionalismus Und Staatsintegration Im Widerstreit — *Bahlke, Joachim*
The Regions and the New Europe — *Rhodes, Martin*
yr **The Regions of France** — *Northcutt, Wayne*
yr **The Regions of Spain** — *Kern, Robert W*
The Register of John Kirkby, Bishop of Carlisle 1332-1352 and the Register of John Ross, Bishop of Carlisle 1325-1332. Vol. 2 — *Catholic Church. Diocese of Carlisle (England)*
The Register of John Kirkby, Bishop of Carlisle 1332-1352 and the Register of John Ross, Bishop of Carlisle 1325-1332. Vols. 1-2 — *Catholic Church. Diocese of Carlisle (England)*
The Register of John Waltham, Bishop of Salisbury 1388-1395 — *Waltham, John*
The Register of Walter Bronescombe, Bishop of Exeter 1258-1280. Vol. 1 — *Catholic Church. Diocese of Exeter (England). Bishop (1257-1280: Bronescombe)*
Registre Des Conclusions De La Faculte De Theologie De L'Universite De Paris. Vol. 2 — *Farge, James K*
Registres De La Compagnie Des Pasteurs De Geneve. Vol. 12 — *Cahier, Gabriella*
Registres De La Compagnie Des Pasteurs De Geneve. Vols. 10-11 — *Cahier, Gabriella*
The Regla Papers — *Guido, John F*
A Regular Guy — *Simpson, Mona*
Regularization of Inverse Problems — *Engl, Heinz W*
Regulating a New Society — *Keller, Morton*
Regulating Media — *Hoffmann-Riem, Wolfgang*
Regulating Reproduction in India's Population — *Srinivasan, K*
Regulating the Lives of Women. Rev. Ed. — *Abramovitz, Mimi*
Regulating the Social — *Steinmetz, George*
Regulation and Macroeconomic Performance — *Goff, Brian*
Regulation and Protectionism under GATT — *Schmitz, Andrew*

Regulation and the Revolution in United States Farm Productivity — *Clarke, Sally H*
Regulation in the Reagan-Bush Era — *Friedman, Barry D*
Regulation of Body Weight — *Dahlem Workshop on Regulation of Body Weight: Biological and Behavioral Mechanisms (1995: Berlin)*
Regulation of Gene Expression in Escherichia Coli — *Lin, E C C*
The Regulation of International Trade — *Trebilcock, Michael J*
The Regulation of Private Schools in America — *Williams, L Patricia*
Regulations, Institutions, and Commitment — *Levy, Brian*
The Regulators — *Bachman, Richard*
y **The Regulators (Nelligan). Audio Version** — *Bachman, Richard*
Regulatory Proteins — *Cummings, Hugh C, Jr.*
Regulatory Reform — *Armstrong, Mark*
Regulatory Takings — *Fischel, William A*
Rehabilitation Activities Profile — *Lankhorst, G J*
Rehabilitation Engineering — *United Nations. Economic Commission for Europe*
Rehabilitation of Degraded Forests in Asia — *Banerjee, Ajit K*
Reichsidee Und Liebesethik — *Borgstedt, Thomas*
Reichstag Uns Aussenpolitik Im Ersten Weltkrieg — *Oppellund, Torsten*
The Reign of Cnut — *Rumble, Alexander R*
The Reign of Elizabeth I — *Guy, J A*
The Reign of Henry VIII — *MacCulloch, Diarmaid*
The Reign of Ideology — *Goodheart, Eugene*
y **Reign of Shadows** — *Chester, Deborah*
The Reign of the Brown Magician — *Watt-Evans, Lawrence*
Reimagining Denominationalism — *Mullin, Robert Bruce*
Reimagining God — *Van Wijk-Bos, Johanna W H*
Reincarnation: A Critical Examination — *Edwards, Paul, 1923-*
r **Reincarnation: A Selected Annotated Bibliography** — *Kear, Lynn*
The Reincarnation of Russia — *Lowenhardt, John*
Una Reincarnazione Di Pico Ai Tempi Di Pomponazzi — *Zambelli, Paola*
Reinforced Concrete. 3rd Ed. — *MacGregor, James G*
Reinforcement and Reconstruction of Foundations — *Shvets, V B*
Reinhold Messner, Free Spirit — *Messner, Reinhold*
Reinhold Niebuhr and Christian Realism — *Lovin, Robin W*
Reinventing Africa — *Coombes, Annie E*
Reinventing Anarchy Again — *Ehrlich, Howard J*
Reinventing Biology — *Birke, Lynda*
Reinventing Germany — *Glees, Anthony*
Reinventing Government — *Schachter, Hindy Lauer*
Reinventing Government and the Problem of Bureaucracy — *Libecap, Gary D*
Reinventing Human Services — *Adams, Paul*
Reinventing Marxism — *Sherman, Howard J*
Reinventing the American People — *Royal, Robert*
Reinventing the Business — *Harmon, Roy L*
Reinventing the Enemy's Language — *Harjo, Joy*
Reinventing the Soviet Self — *Turpin, Jennifer E*
Reinventing the Workplace — *Levine, David I*
The Reinvention of Love — *Low, Anthony*
The Reinvention of the World — *Chambers, Douglas*
Reinvestment of Defense Resources for Economic Growth — *United States. Congress. House. Committee on Armed Services*
Reis Nei De Kalkman — *Ploeg, Durk Van Der*
Der Reisebericht: Die Entwicklung Einer Gattung In Der Deutschen Literatur — *Brenner, Peter J*
Reisen In Die Neue Welt — *Brenner, Peter J*
Reisen Wir — *Muhringer, Doris*
Reiver Blues — *Murray, James*
The Rejected Body — *Wendell, Susan*
Rekindling the Word — *Thiede, Carsten Peter*
Relaciones Geograficas De Oaxaca 1777-1778 — *Esparza, Manuel*
Relational Database Design for Mere Mortals — *Hernandez, Michael J*
Relationship Dynamics — *Musgrave, James*
Relationship Morality — *Kellenberger, James*
The Relationship of Calvin to Process Theology as Seen through His Sermons — *Reynolds, Blair*
Relationships in Chronic Illness and Disability — *Lyons, Renee F*
Relativistic Atomic Collisions — *Eichler, Jorg*
Relativity and Gravitation — *Tourrenc, Philippe*

Releasing the Imagination — *Greene, Maxine*
The Relentlessly Practical Guide to Raising Serious Money — *Lansdowne, David*
The Relevance of Philosophy to Life — *Lachs, John*
Relevant Translations — *Muschard, Jutta*
Reliability and Degradation of III-V Optical Devices — *Ueda, Osamu*
Reliability Engineering — *Elsayed, Elsayed A*
r **Reliability Evaluation of Power Systems. 2nd Ed.** — *Billinton, Roy*
Reliability, Stress Analysis, and Failure Prevention Issues in Fastening and Joining, Composite and Smart Structures, Numerical and SEA Methods — *Sancaktar, Erol*
y **Relic** — *Preston, Douglas*
Relic, Icon, or Hoax? — *Gove, H E*
Reliefs Und Epigramme Griechischer Privatgrabmaler — *Breuer, Christine*
Relieving Pain — *Schafer, Donald W*
c **Religion** — *Langley, Myrtle*
r **Religion: A Cross Cultural Encyclopedia** — *Levinson, David*
Religion and American Culture — *Hackett, David G*
Religion and American Education — *Nord, Warren A*
Religion and Art — *Wagner, Richard, 1813-1883*
Religion and Creation — *Ward, Keith*
Religion and Democracy in Latin America — *Swatos, William H*
Religion and Devotion in Europe c. 1215-c. 1515 — *Swanson, R N*
Religion and Globalization — *Beyer, Peter*
Religion and Guerrilla Warfare in Modern Africa — *Weigert, Stephen L*
Religion and Justice in the War over Bosnia — *Davis, Scott*
y **Religion and Life** — *Watton, Victor*
r **Religion and Mass Media** — *Stout, Daniel A*
Religion and Medical Ethics — *Verhey, Allen*
Religion and Mental Health — *Schumaker, John F*
Religion and Modernity — *Repstad, Pal*
Religion and Morality — *Sagi, Avi*
Religion and Political Culture in Britain and Ireland from the Glorious Revolution to the Decline of Empire — *Hempton, David*
Religion and Politics in America — *Fowler, Robert Booth, 1940-*
Religion and Politics in Nigeria — *Kastfelt, Niels*
Religion and Politics in the Early Republic — *Dreisbach, Daniel L*
Religion and Power — *Edwards, Douglas R*
Religion and Practical Reason — *Reynolds, Frank E*
r **Religion and Psychoactive Sacraments** — *Roberts, Thomas*
Religion and Psychology in Transition — *Jones, James W*
Religion and Rational Theology — *Kant, Immanuel*
Religion and Revelation — *Ward, Keith*
Religion and Science — *Richardson, W Mark*
Religion and Social Justice — *Thakur, Shivesh C*
Religion and Society in 19th-Century Ireland — *Connolly, S J*
r **Religion and Society in Early Modern England** — *Cressy, D*
Religion and Society in England 1850-1914 — *McLeod, Hugh*
Religion and Society in Kent 1640-1914 — *Yates, Nigel*
Religion and Society in Post-Emancipation Jamaica — *Stewart, Robert J*
Religion and Society in Spain — *Edwards, John, 1949-*
Religion and the Clinical Practice of Psychology — *Shafranske, Edward P*
Religion and the Decline of Magic — *Thomas, Keith*
Religion and the Public Schools in 19th Century America — *Power, Edward J*
Religion and the Racist Right — *Barkun, Michael*
Religion and the Rise of Democracy — *Maddox, Graham*
Religion and the Working Class in Antebellum America — *Lazerow, Jama*
Religion and Wine — *Fuller, Robert C*
Religion, Commerce, and the Integration of the Mandingo in Liberia — *Konneh, Augustine*
Religion, Culture and Society in Early Modern Britain — *Fletcher, Anthony*
Religion, Economics, and Revolution — *Waterman, A M C*
Religion, Ethnicity, and Politics — *Ireland, Owen S*
The Religion Factor — *Green, William Scott*
y **Religion for Today**
Religion in Antebellum Kentucky — *Boles, John B*
Religion in Australia — *Thompson, Roger C, 1944-*

Religion in Industrial Society — *Smith, Mark*
Religion in Public Life — *Thiemann, Ronald F*
Religion in the Age of Decline — *Green, S J D*
Religion in the Age of Exploration — *LeBeau, Bryan F*
Religion in the Ancient Greek City — *Zaidman, Louise Bruit*
Religion in the Contemporary South — *White, O Kendall, Jr.*
Religion in the Megacity — *Berryman, Phillip*
Religion in the Modern World — *Bruce, Steve*
The Religion of the People — *Hempton, David*
Religion Paysanne Et Religion Urbaine En Toscane (c. 1250-c. 1450) — *De La Ronciere, Charles M*
Religion, Politics, and Preferment in France since 1890 — *Larkin, Maurice*
Religion, Public Life, and the American Polity — *Lugo, Luis E*
Religion, Science and Naturalism — *Drees, Willem B*
Religion, the Missing Dimension of Statecraft — *Johnston, Douglas*
Religion vs. Television — *Newman, Jay*
Religionem Significare — *Drager, Olaf*
c Religions Explained — *Ganeri, Anita*
Religions of China in Practice — *Lopez, Donald S*
Religions of India in Practice — *Lopez, Donald S*
c Religions of the World (Illus. by L R Galante) — *Elliot, Jason*
Religions of Tibet in Practice — *Lopez, Donald S*
The Religious and Romantic Origins of Psychoanalysis — *Kirschner, Suzanne R*
Religious and Social Ritual — *Aune, Michael B*
Religious Education at a Crossroads — *Darcy-Berube, Francoise*
Religious Experience and Lay Society in T'ang China — *Dudbridge, Glen*
r Religious Higher Education in the United States — *Hunt, Thomas C*
Religious Human Rights in Global Perspective: Legal Perspectives — *Witte, John*
Religious Human Rights in Global Perspective: Religious Perspectives — *Witte, John*
Religious Imagination and Language in Emerson and Nietzsche — *Makarushka, Irena S M*
Religious Liberty — *Ford, John T*
Religious Melancholy and Protestant Experience in America — *Rubin, Julius H*
Religious Nationalism — *Veer, Peter Van Der*
Religious Orders of the Catholic Reformation — *DeMolen, Richard L*
The Religious Origins of the French Revolution — *Van Kley, Dale K*
Religious Pluralism and Truth — *Dean, Thomas*
Religious Regimes in Peru — *Spier, Fred*
yr The Religious Right — *Utter, Glenn H*
Religious Routes to Gladstonian Liberalism — *Ellens, J P*
Religious Studies — *Capps, Walter H*
Religious Thought in the Victorian Age. 2nd Ed. — *Reardon, Bernard M G*
The Religious World of Jesus — *Murphy, Frederick J*
y Reliquary — *Preston, Douglas*
La Reliure: Recherches Historiques, Techniques Et Biographiques Sur La Reliure Francaise — *Devauchelle, Roger*
Relocating Eden — *Marcus, Alan Rudolph*
The Relocation of the North American Indian — *Dunn, John M*
The Reluctant Emperor — *Nicol, Donald M*
Reluctant Expatriate — *Myers, Robert M*
The Reluctant Metropolis — *Fulton, William*
The Reluctant Modernist — *Keys, Roger*
Reluctant Warrior — *Hodgins, Michael C*
The Reluctant Welfare State. 3rd Ed. — *Jansson, Bruce S*
Reluctant Witnesses — *Haynes, Stephen R*
c REM--Rapid Eye Movement (Illus. by Istvan Banyai) — *Banyai, Istvan*
The Remake: As Time Goes By — *Bogart, Stephen Humphrey*
Remaking Congress — *Thurber, James A*
The Remaking of France — *Fitzsimmons, Michael P*
Remaking the Agrarian Dream — *Cannon, Brian Q*
Remaking the Argentine Economy — *Balze, Felipe A M De La*
c Remaking the Earth (Illus. by Paul Goble) — *Goble, Paul*
Remaking the Italian Economy — *Locke, Richard M*
Remaking the Labour Party — *Jones, Tudor*
Remapping China — *Hershatter, Gail*
The Remarkable Beatrix Potter — *Grinstein, Alexander*

y Remarkable Jewish Women — *Taitz, Emily*
Remarkable Recovery — *Hirshberg, Caryle*
y Rembrandt and Seventeenth-Century Holland (Illus. by Sergio) — *Pescio, Claudio*
The Remedy: Class, Race, and Affirmative Action — *Kahlenberg, Richard D*
Remember Goliad! — *Roell, Craig H*
Remember Laughter — *Grauer, Neil A*
Remember Me, God of Love — *Penna, Sandro*
Remember Reno — *McConnell, William F*
c Remember That (Illus. by Karen Ritz) — *Newman, Leslea*
c Remembering — *Mayo, Virginia*
Remembering and Forgetting — *Gong, Gerrit W*
Remembering Anna O. — *Borch-Jacobsen, Mikkel*
Remembering Babylon — *Malouf, David*
Remembering Elizabeth Bishop — *Fountain, Gary*
Remembering Kings Past — *Remensnyder, Amy G*
Remembering Laughter — *Stegner, Wallace Earle*
y Remembering Mog — *Rodowsky, Colby*
Remembering Mr. Fox — *Wiseman, Christopher*
Remembering our Past — *Rubin, David C*
Remembering Stalin's Victims — *Smith, Kathleen E*
Remembering the Christian Past — *Wilken, Robert L*
Remembering the Future — *Grossman, Wendy*
Remembering the Harlem Renaissance — *Wintz, Cary D*
Remembering the Maine — *Samuels, Peggy*
Remembering the Present — *Fabian, Johannes*
Remembering War the American Way — *Piehler, G Kurt*
Remembering Weary — *Geddes, Margaret*
Remembrance and Imagination — *Leerssen, Joep*
Remembrance of Things Past (Rowe). Vol. 1. Audio Version — *Proust, Marcel*
y Remnant Population — *Moon, Elizabeth*
Remnants of the First Earth — *Young Bear, Ray A*
Remodel! An Architect's Advice on Home Remodeling — *Gibson, Greg*
Remote — *Shields, David*
Remote Access Essentials — *Robbins, Margaret*
Remote Control — *Kruger, Barbara*
Remote Control — *White, Stephen Walsh*
Remote Control (Muller). Audio Version — *White, Stephen Walsh*
The Remote Control in the New Age of Television — *Walker, James R*
The Remote Country of Women — *Pai, Hua*
Remote Intrusion — *Olgin, Howard*
Removing Anti-Judaism from the Pulpit — *Kee, Howard Clark*
Remus: A Roman Myth — *Wiseman, T P*
Renaissance — *Holmes, George, 1927-*
Renaissance and Revolution — *Field, J V*
The Renaissance Antichrist — *Riess, Jonathan B*
The Renaissance Bible — *Shuger, Debora Kuller*
Renaissance Drama by Women — *Cerasano, S P*
The Renaissance in Scotland — *MacDonald, A A*
Renaissance Moon — *Nevins, Linda*
The Renaissance of American Steel — *Ahlbrandt, Roger S*
The Renaissance of Jewish Culture in Weimar Germany — *Brenner, Michael*
Renaissance Painting in Manuscripts — *Kren, Thomas, 1950-*
The Renaissance Print 1470-1550 — *Landau, David*
Renaissance Warrior and Patron — *Knecht, R J*
Renaissances Europeennes Et Renaissance Francaise — *Gadoffre, Gilbert*
Renal Biopsy Interpretation — *Silva, Fred G*
Rena's Promise — *Gelissen, Rena Kornreich*
Renata Leoa — *Rangel, Paulo*
Rencontres Avec La Grece Antique — *Romilly, Jacqueline De*
Render Me, Gender Me — *Weston, Kath*
Le Rendez-vous — *Levy, Justine*
Rendezvous: Reliving the Fur Trade Era of 1825-1840 — *Rhody, Kurt*
Renegades: Hitler's Englishmen — *Weale, Adrian*
Renegotiating Health Care — *Marcus, Leonard J*
Renewable Energy — *Boyle, Godfrey*
Renewable Energy Development in India — *Ramana, P Venkata*
Renewable Energy Systems in Southeast Asia — *Green, Joanta H*
p Renewal
Renewal through Suffering — *Harvey, A E*
Renewing American Compassion — *Olasky, Marvin*
Renewing America's Soul — *Butt, Howard E, Jr.*
Renewing Our Energy Future
Renewing Presidential Politics — *Buchanan, Bruce*

Renewing the Left — *Teres, Harvey M*
Renniks Australian Coin and Banknote Values. 17th Ed. — *Pitchfork, Colin E*
Renovating and Restyling Vintage Homes — *Dworin, Lawrence*
Renovating Old Houses — *Nash, George*
Renovating Woman — *Bennett, Allegra*
Renovation: A Complete Guide. 2nd Ed. — *Litchfield, Michael W*
Rentas Y Patrimonios De La Nobleza Valenciana En El Siglo XVIII — *Catala Sanz, Jorge Antonio*
Reordering Marriage and Society in Reformation Germany — *Harrington, Joel F*
Reorientations/Arabic and Persian Poetry — *Stetkevych, Suzanne Pinckney*
Repairing Pottery and Porcelain — *Acton, Lesley*
Repairing the Breach — *National Task Force on African-American Men and Boys*
Reparations to Poverty — *Loesche-Scheller, Brigitta*
The Repeal of Reticence — *Gurstein, Rochelle*
Repeated Games with Incomplete Information — *Aumann, Robert J*
Repentance in Jewish Ethics — *Shokek, Shimon*
r Repertoire Des Etudes, Enquetes Et Seminaires Socio-Economiques Sur Le Benin 1988-1993
Repertoire Des Imprimeurs Parisiens Libraires Et Fondeurs De Caracteres Au XVIIe Siecle — *Renouard, Phillipe*
Repertoire Des Series, Feuilletons Et Teleromans Quebecois — *Croteau, Jean-Yves*
Repertoires and Cycles of Collective Action — *Traugott, Mark*
Repetition of the Possessive Pronouns in the Septuagint — *Sollamo, Raija*
Replacement of Renal Function by Dialysis. 4th Ed. — *Jacobs, Claude*
Replicant Night — *Jeter, K W*
Replication Techniques in Distributed Systems — *Helal, Abdelsalam A*
Replications: A Robotic History of the Science Fiction Film — *Telotte, J P*
Replications: Archaeology, Art History, Psychoanalysis — *Davis, Whitney*
Report III. Pts. 4A-4B — *International Labour Conference, 83rd Session, 1996*
Report V — *International Labour Conference, 83rd Session, 1996*
Report VI — *International Labour Conference, 83rd Session, 1996*
Report Card on Report Cards — *Azwell, Tara*
Report from Part Two — *Brooks, Gwendolyn*
Report of the American Workforce
Report of the Board of Banking Supervision Inquiry into the Circumstances of the Collapse of Barings
Report of the Commission Nationale Sur L'Avenir Du Quebec
Report of the Council on the Functioning of the Treaty on European Union — *Council of the European Union*
Report of the Efficiency Review Team, Correctional Services Division, Department of Justice
Report of the Gove Inquiry into Child Protection in British Columbia. Vol. 3 — *Gove Inquiry into Child Protection (B.C.)*
Report of the Health Crisis Task Force
Report of the Inquiry into the Export of Defence Equipment and Dual-Use Goods to Iraq and Related Prosecutions. Vols. 1-5 — *Scott, Richard*
Report of the Joint Interim Study Committee on Violence Prevention
Report on Effects of Aircraft Overflights on the National Park System
Report on Object Analysis and Design 1994-1996. Electronic Media Version
Report on Public Consultation
A Report on the New Post-Modern World — *Drucker, Peter Ferdinand*
Report to the Governor's Hemp and Related Fiber Crops Task Force (Kentucky) — *McNulty, Sara*
Report to the Minister of Health (Urban Health Planning Partnership Committee, Canada)
Report to the Minister of Presidential Affairs and Public Administration on the General Election 1994 (Botswana)
Report Writing for Architects and Project Managers. 3rd Ed. — *Chappell, David*
The Reportage of Urban Culture — *Linder, Rolf*
Reported Miracles — *Houston, J*
y A Reporter's Life — *Cronkite, Walter*
A Reporter's Life (Cronkite). Audio Version — *Cronkite, Walter*

Reporting the Kennedy Assassination — *Hlavach, Laura*

Reporting the News from China — *Porter, Robin*

Repossession — *Thorne, Nicola*

Repossessions: Selected Essays on the Irish Literary Heritage — *O Tuama, Sean*

Representation and Retrieval of Visual Media in Multimedia Systems — *Zhang, HongJiang*

Representation from Above — *Esaiasson, Peter*

Representation in Crisis — *Ryden, David K*

Representation in Ethnography — *Van Maanen, John*

Les Representations De L'Autre Du Moyen Age Au XVIIe Siecle — *Winn, Colette H*

Representations L-Modulaires D'un Groupe Reductif P-Adique Avec 1-P — *Vigneras, Marie-France*

Representations of Discrete Functions — *Sasao, Tsutomu*

Representations of Infinite-Dimensional Groups — *Ismagilov, R S*

Representations of Preferences Orderings — *Bridges, Douglas S*

RePresenting Bisexualities — *Hall, Donald E, 1960-*

Representing Black Culture — *Merelman, Richard M*

Representing Black Men — *Blount, Marcellus*

Representing Hinduism — *Dalmia, Vasudha*

Representing Ireland — *Bradshaw, Brendan*

Representing Jazz — *Gabbard, Krin*

Representing the Holocaust — *LaCapra, Dominick*

Reproducing Persons — *Purdy, Laura M*

Reproducing the Future — *Strathern, Marilyn*

Reproducing the Womb — *Adams, Alice E*

Reproduction, Ethics and the Law — *Callahan, Joan C*

Reproduction, Technology, and Rights — *Humber, James M*

Reptile Journalism — *Dobroszycki, Lucjan*

Reptile Keeper's Handbook — *Barnard, Susan M*

c Reptiles (Illus. by James Field) — *Chatfield, June*

c Reptiles — *Creagh, Carson*

c Reptiles — *Lovett, Sarah, 1953-*

c Reptiles and Amphibians (Illus. by Ali Garousi) — *Llamas Ruiz, Andres*

Reptiles and Herbivory — *King, Gillian*

The Republic of Letters — *Goodman, Dena*

The Republic of Letters. Vols. 1-3 — *Jefferson, Thomas*

Republican and Fascist Germany — *Hiden, John*

The Republican Crown — *Jacob, Joseph M*

The Republican Moment — *Nord, Philip*

y The Republicans: From Lincoln to Bush — *Rutland, Robert Allen*

Republik Ohne Chance? — *Asmuss, Burkhard*

Republikschutz: Masstabe Fur Die Verteidigung Der Demokratie — *Leggewie, Claus*

Reputation and International Politics — *Mercer, Jonathan*

Reputation: Realizing Value from the Corporate Image — *Fombrun, Charles J*

Requiem — *Joyce, Graham*

Requiem for a Glass Heart — *Lindsey, David L*

Requiem for a People — *Beckham, Stephen Dow*

A Requiem for Karl Marx — *Manuel, Frank E*

Requiem for Moses — *Kienzle, William X*

Requiem for the Sudan — *Burr, J Millard*

Requiem Pour Une Avant-Garde — *Duteurtre, Benoit*

Rereading — *Calinescu, Matei*

Rereading Jack London — *Cassuto, Leonard*

Rereading Modernism — *Rado, Lisa*

A Rereading of Romans — *Stowers, Stanley K*

Resandes Ensak — *Ardelius, Lars*

Rescheduling, Credit-Worthiness and Market Prices — *Palac-McMiken, Evanor D*

Rescue as Resistance — *Lazare, Lucien*

y Rescue Josh McGuire (Sala). Audio Version — *Mikaelsen, Ben*

c Rescue! True Life Survival Stories — *Robinson, Karen*

y Rescued by Upgrading Your PC. 2nd Ed. — *Jamsa, Kris*

Rescuers of Cypress — *Stuhlmiller, Cynthia M*

c Rescuing a Neighborhood (Illus. by Porter Gifford) — *Fleming, Robert*

Rescuing History from the Nation — *Duara, Prasenjit*

y Rescuing Little Roundhead — *Jones, Syl*

Resculpting — *Bramkamp, Maura Alia*

Research and Evaluation in Recreation, Parks and Leisure Studies. 2nd Ed. — *Kraus, Richard G*

Research Design — *Creswell, John W*

r Research-Doctorate Programs in the United States — *Goldberger, Marvin L*

Research Ethics — *Penslar, Robin Levin*

Research Ethics — *Stanley, Barbara H*

r Research Guide to the Turner Movement in the United States — *Pumroy, Eric*

Research in Collegiate Mathematics Education — *Kaput, Jim*

Research in Domestic and International Agribusiness Management. Vol. 12

Research in Economic History. Vol. 16 — *Field, Alexander J*

Research in Experimental Economics. Vol. 6

Research in Finance. 2nd Suppl.

Research in Finance. Vol. 13

Research in Governmental and Nonprofit Accounting. Vol. 9 — *Chan, James L*

Research in International Business and Finance — *Doukas, John*

Research in Organizational Behavior. Vol. 18

Research in Personnel and Human Resources Management. Vol. 14

Research in Physical Education, Exercise Science, and Sport — *Cicciarella, Charles F*

Research in Politics and Society. Vol. 5 — *Ratcliff, Richard E*

Research in Population Economics. Vol. 8 — *Schultz, T Paul*

Research in the History of Economic Thought and Methodology. Vol.14

Research in the History of Economic Thought and Methodology: Archival Supplement 5

Research Libraries — *Welsh, William J*

Research Methods in Family Therapy — *Sprenkle, Douglas H*

r Research on Group Treatment Methods — *Lubin, Bernard*

Research Priorities in Indian Agriculture — *Jha, Dayanatha*

y Research Reports — *Sullivan, Helen*

r Research Services Directory 1995

Research Strategies for Small Businesses — *Gudmundson, Donald E*

Research Strategies in Human Communication Disorders. 2nd Ed. — *Doehring, Donald G*

Research Strategies in Technical Communication — *Porter, Lynnette*

Research Techniques for the Health Sciences. 2nd Ed. — *Neutens, James J*

The Research University in a Time of Discontent — *Cole, Jonathan R*

Researchers Hooked on Teaching — *Andre, Rae*

Researching Culture — *Alasuutari, Pertti*

cr Researching People — *Schrecengost, Maity*

Researching School-Based Teacher Education — *Blake, David*

y Reservation Blues — *Alexie, Sherman*

Reserve and Guard Effectiveness — *United States. Congress. House. Committee on Armed Services*

Reservoirs in River Basin Development. Vol. 2 — *ICOLD Symposium on Reservoirs in River Basin Development (1995: Oslo, Norway)*

Reshaping Government in Metropolitan Areas — *Committee for Economic Development*

Reshaping the World Trading System — *Croome, John*

Resident Alien — *Crisp, Quentin*

Resident Alien — *Wolff, Janet*

Residential Treatment of Adolescents and Children — *Stein, John A*

Residents of the Mississippi Territory. Bk. 3 — *Strickland, Jean*

Residents: The Perils and Promise of Educating Young Doctors — *Duncan, David Ewing*

Residual Stresses in Design, Fabrication, Assessment and Repair

Resist and Masking Techniques — *Beard, Peter*

Resistance — *Shreve, Anita*

Resistance and Reform in Tibet — *Barnett, Robert*

Resistance and Reformation in Nineteenth-Century African-American Literature — *Ernest, John*

Resistance of the Heart — *Stoltzfus, Nathan*

Resisting Reagan — *Smith, Christian*

Resisting State Violence — *James, Joy*

Resituating Writing — *Janangelo, Joseph*

Resolution of Prison Riots — *Useem, Bert*

Resolution Proof Systems — *Stachniak, Zbigniew*

Resolutions: A Critique of Video Art — *Podesta, Patti*

Resolutions Adopted by the General Assembly during the First Part of Its Fiftieth Session, from 19 September to 23 December 1995 — *United Nations. General Assembly*

Resolutions: Contemporary Video Practices — *Renov, Michael*

A Resolvable Conflict? — *Pankhurst, Donna*

Resolving Africa's Multilateral Debt Problem — *Mistry, Percy S*

Resolving Disputes over Life-Sustaining Treatment — *Hafemeister, Thomas L*

Resource Allocation in Divisionalized Groups — *Segelod, Esbjorn*

Resource Allocation in Higher Education — *Massy, William F*

p Resource Links

Resource Management for Distributed Multimedia Systems — *Wolf, Lars Christian*

Resources, Deprivation and Poverty — *Nolan, Brian*

r Resources for Elders with Disabilities. 3rd Ed.

Resources for Learning in College Libraries — *Hamm, Tricia*

r Resources for People with Disabilities and Chronic Conditions. 3rd Ed.

r Resources for Teaching Elementary School Science — *National Science Resources Center (U.S.)*

The Resourcing of Special Educational Needs — *Fletcher-Campbell, Felicity*

Respect — *Foreman, Freddie*

Respect and Protect — *Remboldt, Carole*

y The Respiratory System (Illus. by Antonio Munoz Tenllado) — *Roca, Nuria*

Responding to Low-Intensity Challenges — *Blank, Stephen*

Responding to Young Adult Literature — *Monseau, Virginia R*

Response Surfaces. 2nd Ed. — *Khuri, Andre I*

r The Response to Allen Ginsberg 1926-1994 — *Morgan, Bill*

Responses to 101 Questions on Business Ethics — *Devine, George*

Responses to 101 Questions on the Biblical Torah — *Murphy, Roland E*

Responses to 101 Questions on the Church — *McBrien, Richard P*

Responsibility and Christian Ethics — *Schweiker, William*

Responsibility and the Moral Sentiments — *Wallace, R Jay*

c Responsibility: Annie Shows Off — *Canning, Shelagh*

Responsibility as Paradox — *Harmon, Michael M*

The Responsible Conduct of Research — *Beach, Dore*

Rest for the Wicked — *Maxwell, Glyn*

The Rest Is Silence — *Watson, Robert N*

Restitution and the Conflict of Laws — *Rose, Francis*

Restitution Law in Australia — *Mason, Keith*

Restless Nation — *Clements, Alan*

Restless Spirits — *Lundie, Catherine A*

Restless: The Memoirs of Labor and Consumer Activist Esther Peterson — *Peterson, Esther*

Restless Youth 1922-1929 — *Green, Julien*

Restoration and Rehabilitation of the Desert Environment — *Al-Awadhi, N*

Restoring Balance to the American Federal System — *Moyes, Howard A*

Restoring Diversity — *Falk, Donald A*

Restoring Hope in America — *Beard, Sam*

Restoring Pride — *Taylor, Richard, 1919-*

Restoring Prosperity — *Wilms, Wellford W*

Restoring Vision — *Zasloff, Tela*

Restrained Trade — *Tilton, Mark*

The Restraint of Trade — *Shaffer, Butler*

Restructuring Higher Education — *MacTaggart, Terrence J*

The Restructuring of International Relations Theory — *Neufeld, Mark A*

Resume with Monsters — *Spencer, William Browning, 1946-*

Resumes and Cover Letters That Have Worked for Military Professionals — *McKinney, Anne*

Resumes and Job Hunting — *King, Julie*

Resumes for Dummies — *Kennedy, Joyce Lain*

The Resurgence of the Real — *Spretnak, Charlene*

Resurgent Evangelicalism in the United States — *Shibley, Mark A*

Resurrection — *Tolstoy, Leo, Graf*

Resurrection and Discipleship — *Lorenzen, Thorwald*

Resurrection from the Underground — *Girard, Rene*

Resurrection Man — *McNamee, Eoin*

The Resurrection of Jesus — *Luedemann, Gerd*

The Resurrection of the Body in Western Christianity 200-1336 — *Bynum, Caroline Walker*

Resurrection: Poems — *Cooley, Nicole*

Resurrection Reconsidered — *Riley, Gregory J*

Resurrection: The Struggle for a New Russia — *Remnick, David*

Resurrection Update — *Galvin, James*

Rethinking Abortion — *Graber, Mark A*

y Rethinking America — *Smith, Hedrick*
Rethinking Architecture — *Leach, Neil*
Rethinking Borders — *Welchman, John C*
Rethinking C.L.R. James — *Farred, Grant*
Rethinking Democratic Education — *Steiner, David*
Rethinking Federalism — *Knop, Karen*
Rethinking Hypermedia — *Hall, Wendy*
Rethinking Liberal Education — *Farnham, Nicholas H*
Rethinking Literary Biography — *Pagan, Nicholas O*
Rethinking Local Democracy — *King, Desmond*
Rethinking Los Angeles — *Dear, Michael J*
Rethinking Management Accountability Systems
   Workshop, May 23, 1995 — *Pumphrey, Lela D*
Rethinking Materialism — *Wuthnow, Robert*
Rethinking Media Literacy — *McLaren, Peter*
Rethinking Metaphysics — *Jones, L Gregory*
Rethinking Race — *Williams, Vernon J, Jr.*
Rethinking Restructuring — *Bakker, Isabella*
Rethinking Social History — *Wilson, Adrian*
Rethinking the Borderlands — *Gutierrez-Jones, Carl*
Rethinking the Constitution — *Peacock, Anthony*
Rethinking the Development Experience — *Rodwin, Lloyd*
Rethinking the Political — *Laslett, Barbara*
Rethinking Tradition in Modern Islamic Thought
   — *Brown, Daniel W*
Rethinking Unionism — *Porter, Norman*
The Retreat — *Sherman, Jason*
The Retreat of Scientific Racism — *Barkan, Elazar*
A Retreat with Francis and Clare of Assisi — *Bodo, Murray*
A Retreat with Francis De Sales, Jane De Chantal and
   Aelred of Rievaulx — *Wright, Wendy M*
A Retreat with Gerard Manley Hopkins and
   Hildegard of Bingen — *Hutchinson, Gloria*
A Retreat with Pope John XXIII — *McBride, Alfred*
A Retreat with Thomas Merton — *Padovano, Anthony T*
Retreating from the Cold War — *Cox, David*
Retribution (Whitener). Audio Version — *Pineiro, R J*
Retrieved Riches — *Englander, David*
Retroviral Reverse Transcriptases — *Litvak, Simon*
Retsah Be-Layl Ha-Skadim — *Mazel, Michelle*
The Return — *Tubb, E C*
The Return of Cultural Treasures. 2nd Ed.
   — *Greenfield, Jeanette*
The Return of Culture and Identity in IR Theory
   — *Lapid, Yosef*
Return of No Return and Other Poems — *Brew, Kwesi*
The Return of Pleasure — *Elizabeth, Martha*
c The Return of the Buffaloes (Illus. by Paul Goble)
   — *Goble, Paul*
The Return of the God of Wealth — *Ikels, Charlotte*
The Return of the Gods — *Daniken, Erich Von*
Return of the Indian — *Wearne, Phillip*
Return of the Jedi — *Daley, Brian*
The Return of the Native — *Thomas, Brian*
The Return of the Native (Rickman). Audio Version
   — *Hardy, Thomas*
The Return of the Political — *Mouffe, Chantal*
The Return of the Prodigal Son — *Nouwen, Henri J M*
The Return of the Real — *Foster, Hal*
The Return of the Wolf — *Grooms, Steve*
y The Return of the Wolf to Yellowstone — *McNamee, Thomas*
r The Return of Thematic Criticism — *Sollors, Werner*
y Return to Harmony — *Oke, Janette*
The Return to Incomes Policy — *Dore, Ronald*
Return to Resistance — *Robinson, Raoul A*
y Return to Sodom and Gomorrah (Davidson). Audio
   Version — *Pellegrino, Charles*
Return to the House of Usher — *Poe, Robert*
Return to the Promised Land — *Schnarr, Grant R*
Return to the Same City — *Taibo, Paco Ignacio, II*
Return to Zork — *Spear, Peter*
Return with Honor — *O'Grady, Scott*
Returning a Borrowed Tongue — *Carbo, Nick*
Returning: A Spiritual Journey — *Wakefield, Dan*
Returning the Gift — *Bruchac, Joseph*
Returning to Learning — *Brem, Caroline*
Returning to Nothing — *Read, Peter, 1945-*
Returning to the Teachings — *Ross, Rupert*
The Returns — *Barone, Dennis*
c Reuben and the Blizzard (Illus. by P Buckley Moss)
   — *Moss, P Buckley*
Reunion: The Extraordinary Story of a Messenger of
   Love and Healing — *Ezell, Jessica*
The Reuniting of America — *Roy, Donald H*
Reusing Old Graves — *Davies, Douglas*
Revealing Difference — *Allison, Jenene J*

Revelation and Revolution — *Muntzer, Thomas*
The Revelation of Ares — *Michel, Frere*
Revelation of the Unknowable God — *King, Karen L*
Revelation, Redemption, and Response — *Butin, Philip Walker*
Revelation: The Torah and the Bible — *Neusner, Jacob*
Revelations — *Winter, Douglas E*
Revelations: American History, American Myths
   — *Huggins, Nathan Irvin*
Revelations of a Spanish Infanta — *Muirden, Sallie*
y Revelations: The Medieval World — *Harpur, James*
Revenance — *Blacker, Terence*
Revenge of the Barbeque Queens — *Temple, Lou Jane*
Revenge of the Christmas Box — *Crimmins, Cathy*
Revenge of the Cootie Girls — *Hayter, Sparkle*
Revenge Tragedy — *Kerrigan, John*
Revenue Management — *Cross, Robert G*
Revenue Management (Cross). Audio Version
   — *Cross, Robert G*
Reversals of Fortune — *Mucciaroni, Gary*
Reverse Engineering — *Wills, Linda*
Reversing Asthma — *Firshein, Richard N*
Reversing Course — *Skidmore, David*
Reversing Underachievement among Gifted Black
   Students — *Ford, Donna Y*
Des Reves Et Des Assassins — *Mokeddem, Malika*
Review and Outlook for the World Oil Market
   — *Streifel, Shane S*
Review of Colombia's Agriculture and Rural
   Development Strategy
p Review of Derivatives Research
Review of Ophthalmology — *Chern, Kenneth C*
Review of Progress in Quantitative Nondestructive
   Evaluation. Vol. 15, Pts. A-B
Review of Psychiatry. Vol. 15
Review of Pulmonary and Critical Care Medicine
   — *Cherniack, Reuben M*
p Review of Urban and Regional Development Studies
Reviewing Sex — *Thompson, Nicola Diane*
Reviews in Computational Chemistry. Vol. 8
Revising Herself — *Josselson, Ruthellen*
Revising Wilde — *Eltis, Sos*
Revision and Romantic Authorship — *Leader, Zachary*
Revisioning History — *Rosenstone, Robert A*
Revisioning the Political — *Hirschmann, Nancy J*
y Revisitations — *Weinstein, Howard*
Revisiting The Culture of the School and the Problem
   of Change — *Sarason, Seymour B*
p Revista De La Facultad De Ciencias Economicas
Revitalizing Historic Urban Quarters — *Tiesdell, Steven*
Revitalizing Urban Neighborhoods — *Keating, W Dennis*
Revival and Revivalism — *Murray, Iain H*
Revivals and Roller Rinks — *Marks, Lynne*
Reviving Ophelia — *Pipher, Mary Bray*
Reviving Ophelia (Pipher). Audio Version — *Pipher, Mary Bray*
Reviving the Ancient Faith — *Hughes, Richard T*
Reviving the European Union — *Henning, Randall*
Reviving the Spirit — *Lawrence, Beverly Hall*
The Revolt — *Bauer, S Wise*
Revolt against Modernity — *McAllister, Ted V*
Revolt in Prerevolutionary France — *Woodbridge, John D*
The Revolt of Owain Glyn Dwr — *Davies, R R*
Revolt of the Admirals — *Barlow, Jeffrey G*
Revolt of the Provinces — *Dorman, Robert L*
Revolucion Cientifica, Renacimiento E Historia De La
   Ciencia — *Beltran, Antonio*
Revolucion Y Fiscalidad Municipal — *Martinez Neira, Manuel*
Revolution: 500 Years of Struggle for Change
   — *Almond, Mark*
Revolution and Ideology — *Britton, John A*
Revolution and Religion — *Griffin, Keith L*
Revolution and Restoration — *Szuchman, Mark D*
Revolution and Subjectivity in Postwar Japan
   — *Koschmann, J Victor*
Revolution and the Form of the British Novel
   1790-1825 — *Watson, Nicola*
Revolution and the Multiclass Coalition in Nicaragua
   — *Everingham, Mark*
Revolution and War — *Walt, Stephen M*
Revolution at the Roots — *Eggers, William D*
Revolution Betrayed — *Tucker, Janet G*
Revolution by Decree — *Kruijt, Dirk*
Revolution in El Salvador — *Montgomery, Tommie Sue*
c Revolution in Europe 1989 — *Burke, Patrick*

Revolution in Ireland — *Kostick, Conor*
Revolution in Poetic Language — *Kristeva, Julia*
A Revolution in Progress — *Bruton, Alastair*
The Revolution in Provincial France — *Forrest, Alan*
Revolution in the Balance — *Evenson, Debra*
Revolution in the Head — *McDonald, Ian*
Revolution in the Village — *Luong, Hy V*
The Revolution in the Visual Arts and the Poetry of
   William Carlos Williams — *Halter, Peter*
Revolution of Conscience — *Moses, Greg*
The Revolution of the Candles — *Swoboda, Jorg*
y Revolution of the Heart — *Shore, Bill*
Revolution of the Mind — *Polizzotti, Mark*
Revolution, Romanticism, and the Afro-Creole Protest
   Tradition in Louisiana 1718-1868 — *Bell, Caryn Cosse*
y The Revolutionaries — *Time-Life Books*
r Revolutionary America 1763 to 1800 — *Purvis, Thomas L*
Revolutionary Brotherhood — *Bullock, Steven C*
Revolutionary Justice in Paris 1789-1790 — *Shapiro, Barry M*
The Revolutionary Mission — *O'Brien, Thomas F*
Revolutionary Outlaws — *Bellesiles, Michael A*
r Revolutionary Soldiers in Kentucky — *Quisenberry, Anderson Chenault*
r Revolutionary War Bounty Land Grants Awarded by
   State Governments — *Bockstruck, Lloyd DeWitt*
r Revolutionary War Veterans of Greene County, Ohio
   — *Overton, Julie*
The Reward Plan Advantage — *McAdams, Jerry L*
Rewind and Search — *Miller, Mary Jane*
Rewind: Video Art and Alternative Media in the
   United States — *Hill, Chris*
Rewolucja: Russian Poland 1904-1907 — *Blobaum, Robert E*
Reworking Authority — *Hirschhorn, Larry*
Rewrites: A Memoir — *Simon, Neil*
Rewrites: A Memoir (Simon). Audio Version
   — *Simon, Neil*
Rewriting Family Scripts — *Byng-Hall, John*
Rewriting Reality — *Fiddler, Allyson*
Rewriting Resemblance in Medieval French Romance
   — *Rockwell, Paul Vincent*
Rewriting the Self — *Porter, Roy*
Rewriting the Soul — *Hacking, Ian*
c Rex and Lilly Schooltime (Illus. by Marc Brown)
   — *Brown, Laurene Krasny*
Die Rezeption Des Matthausevangeliums Im 1.
   Petrusbrief — *Metzner, Rainer*
A Rhanna Mystery — *Fraser, Christine Marion*
Rhapsody — *Mason, Felicia*
Rheology and Fluid Mechanics of Nonlinear Materials
   1996 — *Siginer, Dennis A*
Rheology for Polymer Melt Processing — *Piau, J-M*
Rhetoric and Marxism — *Aune, James Arnt*
Rhetoric and Pluralism — *Antczak, Frederick J*
Rhetoric and Redaction in Trito-Isaiah — *Smith, Paul A*
Rhetoric and the Arts of Design — *Kaufer, David S*
Rhetoric and Theology — *Hoffmann, Manfred*
Rhetoric in the New World — *Abbott, Don Paul*
A Rhetoric of Bourgeois Revolution — *Sewell, William H, Jr.*
The Rhetoric of Church and State — *Gedicks, Frederick Mark*
The Rhetoric of Concealment — *Kegl, Rosemary*
The Rhetoric of Curse in Galatians — *Morland, Kjell Arne*
The Rhetoric of Empiricism — *Law, Jules David*
The Rhetoric of Eugenics in Anglo-American Thought
   — *Hasian, Marouf Arif*
The Rhetoric of Science — *Gross, Alan G*
A Rhetoric of Silence and Other Selected Writings
   — *Block De Behar, Lisa*
The Rhetoric of Vision — *Huttar, Charles A*
Rhetoric, Reason and Society — *Myerson, George*
Rhetoric-Rhetoriqueurs-Rederijkers — *Koopmans, Jelle*
Rhetoric, Sophistry, Pragmatism — *Mailloux, Steven*
Rhetorical Criticism — *Trible, Phyllis*
Rhetorical Hermeneutics — *Gross, Alan G*
The Rhetorical Logic of Henry James — *Teahan, Sheila*
Rhetorical Spaces — *Code, Lorraine*
Rhetorical Traditions and British Romantic Literature
   — *Bialostosky, Don H*
The Rhetorics of Life-Writing in Early Modern
   Europe — *Mayer, Thomas F*
Rhetorique Speculative — *Quignard, Pascal*

The Rhine as Musical Metaphor — *Porter, Cecelia Hopkins*
c Rhino (Illus. by Richard Hewett) — *Arnold, Caroline*
c Rhinoceroses — *Harman, Amanda*
cr Rhinos (Illus. by Gerry Ellis) — *Walker, Sally M*
c Rhinos Who Surf — *Mammano, Julie*
r Rhode Island Jobs Outlook to 2000
　 Rhode Island Public Library Trustees Handbook. Rev. and Updated Ed. — *Iacono, Frank P*
　 Rhode Island Red — *Carter, Charlotte*
　 Rhodes — *Millin, Sarah Gertrude*
r Rhodes and the Dodecanese plus the East Aegean — *Dubin, Marc S*
　 Rhodes: The Race for Africa — *Thomas, Antony*
c Rhyme and Analogy — *Kirtley, Clare*
　 The Rhymers' Club — *Alford, Norman*
c Rhymes for Annie Rose (Illus. by Shirley Hughes) — *Hughes, Shirley*
　 Rhythm and Noise — *Gracyk, Theodore*
　 The Rhythm Book. 2nd Ed. — *Kazez, Daniel*
　 Rhythms of Academic Life — *Frost, Peter J*
　 Rhythms: On the Work, Translation, and Psychoanalysis — *Abraham, Nicolas*
　 Ri Ben Te Wu Zai Zhong Guo
c Riana's World — *Shirrefs, Mark*
c Ribbons — *Yep, Laurence*
　 Ribstone Pippins — *Wykham, Helen*
c Rice — *Powell, Jillian*
　 Rice — *Su, T'ung*
　 The Rice Cookbook — *Denny, Roz*
　 Rice Research in Asia — *Evenson, R E*
　 Rice (St. Martin's Press) — *Rice, Jerry*
　 Ricerche Su Francesco Sansovino Imprenditore Librario E Letterato — *Bonora, Elena*
　 Ricerche Sulla Tradizione Di Rufino Del De Principiis Di Origene — *Pace, Nicola*
　 The Rich Are Different — *Winokur, Jon*
c Rich Lizard and Other Poems — *Chandra, Deborah*
　 The Rich Man and the Kingdom — *Schenkel, Albert F*
　 Rich Nations, Poor Nations — *Aldcroft, Derek H*
　 Rich Relations — *Reynolds, David*
　 Richard II — *Saul, Nigel*
　 Richard II. Audio Version — *Shakespeare, William*
　 Richard A. McCormick and the Renewal of Moral Theology — *Odozor, Paulinus Ikechukwu*
　 Richard Brinsley Sheridan: A Life — *Kelly, Linda*
　 Richard Brown's New England — *Brown, Richard W*
　 Richard Coeur De Lion — *Gillingham, John*
　 Richard J. Daley: Politics, Race, and the Governing of Chicago — *Biles, Roger*
c Richard M. Nixon, Jimmy Carter, Ronald Reagan — *Lindop, Edmund*
　 Richard M. Weaver 1910-1963 — *Young, Fred Douglas*
　 Richard Meier Houses — *Goldberger, Paul*
　 Richard Owen: Victorian Naturalist — *Rupke, Nicolaas A*
c Richard Petty — *Frankl, Ron*
　 Richard Rogers Partnership — *Rogers, Richard*
　 Richard Ronan — *VanStavern, Jan*
c Richard Scarry's Best Reading Program Ever. Electronic Media Version — *Scarry, Richard*
c Richard Scarry's Pop-Up Colors (Illus. by Renee Jablow) — *Scarry, Richard*
c Richard Scarry's Pop-Up Numbers (Illus. by Renee Jablow) — *Scarry, Richard*
c Richard Scarry's Pop-Up Wheels (Illus. by Bruce Reifel) — *Scarry, Richard*
　 Richard Shute of Boston, Massachusetts 1631-1703 and Selected Progeny — *Shute, Alan H*
　 The Richard Simmons Farewell to Fat Cookbook — *Simmons, Richard*
　 Richard Thompson: Strange Affair — *Humphries, Patrick*
　 Richard Thompson: The Biography — *Humphries, Patrick*
　 Richard Wagner and the Anti-Semitic Imagination — *Weiner, Marc A*
　 Richard Wright and Racial Discourse — *Hakutani, Yoshinobu*
r Richards/Cox and Barbee — *Richards, James D*
　 Richardus Tertius — *Legge, Thomas*
y The Richer, the Poorer — *West, Dorothy*
　 Riches and Poverty — *Winch, Donald*
　 Riches and Renunciation — *Laidlaw, James*
y The Riches of the West — *Smith, C Carter*
　 Richthofen: Beyond the Legend of the Red Baron — *Kilduff, Peter*
c Ricitos Dorados Y Los Tres Osos (Illus. by James Marshall) — *Marshall, James*
　 Rick Bayless's Mexican Kitchen — *Bayless, Rick*

　 Ricordanze II — *Castellani, Francesco Di Matteo*
　 Ricorso and Revelation — *Smith, Evans Lansing*
　 The Riddle and the Knight — *Milton, Giles*
c Riddle-icious (Illus. by Debbie Tilley) — *Lewis, J Patrick*
　 The Riddle of Grace — *Hoezee, Scott*
　 The Riddle of the Titanic — *Gardiner, Robin*
c Riddle Rhymes (Illus. by Julia Gorton) — *Ghigna, Charles*
　 Riddles in Stone — *Hayman, Richard*
y Ride against the Wind — *Bowers, Terrell L*
　 Ride for the High Points — *Bramlett, Jim*
　 Ride of the Second Horseman — *O'Connell, Robert L*
c A Ride on Mother's Back (Illus. by Durga Bernhard) — *Bernhard, Emery*
　 Ride the Lightning — *Mitchell, Robert H*
c Ride the Wind (Illus. by Elsa Warnick) — *Simon, Seymour*
　 Rider — *Wolbers, Marian Frances*
y Rider at the Gate — *Cherryh, C J*
　 The Riders — *Winton, Tim*
　 Riders to the Sea. The Shadow of the Glen. The Tinker's Wedding. The Well of the Saints... — *Synge, J M*
c Ridgeback Joe and the Boy — *McClain, Liz*
c Ridiculous! (Illus. by Gwyneth Williamson) — *Coleman, Michael*
　 Riding Astride — *Dunlap, Patricia Riley*
　 Riding for a Fall — *Roberts, Lillian M*
　 Riding Shotgun — *Brown, Rita Mae*
c Riding Silver Star (Illus. by Margaret Miller) — *Cole, Joanna*
c Riding the Ferry with Captain Cruz (Illus. by Christine Osinski) — *Flanagan, Alice K*
c Riding the Rails — *Otfinoski, Steve*
　 Riding the Rap — *Leonard, Elmore*
　 Riding the Tiger — *Davidson, Alistair*
　 Riding the Tiger — *Leon Carpio, Ramiro De*
　 Riemannian Geometry — *Lovric, Miroslav*
y The Rifle — *Paulsen, Gary*
c The Rifle (Dietz). Audio Version — *Paulsen, Gary*
　 Rifleman Dodd — *Forester, C S*
　 The Right and the Righteous — *Oldfield, Duane Murray*
y Right from Wrong — *McDowell, Josh*
y Right in the Old Gazoo — *Simpson, Alan K*
　 The Right in the Twentieth Century — *Girvin, Brian*
　 The Right Man for the Job — *Magnuson, Mike*
　 Right Practical Reason — *Westberg, Daniel*
　 The Right Thing — *Friedman, Emily*
　 Right Thinking and Sacred Oratory in Counter-Reformation Rome — *McGinness, Frederick J*
　 The Right to Be King — *Nenner, Howard*
　 The Right to Privacy — *Alderman, Ellen*
c The Right to Speak Out — *King, David C*
　 Right Turn — *Wolters, Raymond*
　 Righteous Discontent — *Higginbotham, Evelyn Brooks*
y Righteous Gentile. Rev. Ed. — *Bierman, John*
　 The Righteous Gentiles of the Holocaust — *Gushee, David P*
　 Righteous Religion — *Ritter, Kathleen*
　 Rightness and Reasons — *Krausz, Michael*
　 Rights — *Jones, Peter, 1945-*
　 Rights across Borders — *Jacobson, David*
　 Rights and the Common Good — *Etzioni, Amitai*
　 The Rights of Man. Common Sense — *Paine, Thomas*
　 The Rights of Minority Cultures — *Kymlicka, Will*
　 Rights of Passage — *Herman, Didi*
　 Rights of Passage, Social Change and the Transition from Youth to Adulthood — *Irwin, Sarah*
　 The Rights of People Who Are HIV Positive — *Rubenstein, William B*
　 Rights of the Terminally Ill Act
　 The Rights of Women in Islam — *Engineer, Asghar Ali*
　 Rigorous Global Search — *Kearfott, R Baker*
　 Rilke on Black — *Bruen, Ken*
　 Rilke's Duino Elegies — *Paulin, Roger*
　 La Rima En La Lirica Medieval — *Torruella I Casanas, Joan*
　 Rimbaud 1891-1991
y Rimwalkers — *Grove, Vicki*
c Rinaldo on the Run — *Scheffler, Ursel*
c The Ring (Illus. by Lisa Maizlish) — *Maizlish, Lisa*
c Ring-a-Ring O'Roses and a Ding, Dong, Bell (Illus. by Alan Marks) — *Marks, Alan*
　 The Ring of Brightest Angels around Heaven — *Moody, Rick*
c The Ring of Truth (Illus. by Omar Rayyan) — *Bateman, Teresa*

　 Das Ringen Um Den Nationalen Staat — *Mommsen, Wolfgang J*
　 Rings: Five Passions in World Art — *Brown, J Carter*
　 Rings, Groups, and Algebras — *Cao, X H*
　 Rings, Modules, and Algebras in Stable Homotopy Theory — *Elmendorf, Anthony D*
　 Rings: The Alice and Louis Koch Collection. Vols. 1-2 — *Chadour, Anna Beatriz*
　 Ringside: A Knockout Collection of Fights and Fighters — *Corris, Peter*
y Ringworld (Parker). Audio Version — *Niven, Larry*
　 The Ringworld Throne — *Niven, Larry*
c Rio De Janeiro — *Kent, Deborah*
　 Rio Del Norte — *Riley, Carroll L*
　 Rio Grande Fall — *Anaya, Rudolfo*
　 Riobard Bheldon: Amhrain Agus Danta — *Bheldon, Riobard*
　 Riopelle in Conversation — *Riopelle, Jean-Paul*
c Los Rios Y Los Lagos (Illus. by Luis Rizo) — *Sanchez, Isidro*
c Riot — *Casanova, Mary*
　 Riot — *Moodie, Andrew*
　 Rioting in America — *Gilje, Paul A*
　 The Ripening of Pinstripes — *Torreson, Rodney*
　 RISC Systems and Applications — *Tabak, Daniel*
　 Il Riscatto D'Adamo Nella Morte Di Gesu Cristo — *Orioles, Filippo*
　 Risco Da Vida — *Guzik, Alberto*
　 The Rise and Crisis of Psychoanalysis in the United States — *Hale, Nathan G, Jr.*
　 The Rise and Decline of Catholic Religious Orders — *Wittberg, Patricia*
　 The Rise and Decline of the British Motor Industry — *Church, Roy*
　 The Rise and Fall of an Urban School System — *Mirel, Jeffrey*
　 The Rise and Fall of Development Theory — *Leys, Colin*
　 The Rise and Fall of Economic Liberalism — *Clairmont, Frederic F*
　 The Rise and Fall of Gay Culture — *Harris, Daniel*
　 The Rise and Fall of Merry England — *Hutton, Ronald*
　 The Rise and Fall of Palestine — *Finkelstein, Norman G*
　 The Rise and Fall of Popular Music — *Clarke, Donald*
　 The Rise and Fall of Renaissance France 1483-1610 — *Knecht, R J*
　 The Rise and Fall of Revolutionary England — *MacLachlan, Alastair*
　 The Rise and Fall of State Socialism — *Lane, David Stuart*
　 The Rise and Fall of the Grenvilles — *Beckett, John*
　 The Rise and Fall of the Sportswoman — *Stanley, Gregory Kent*
　 The Rise and Fall of Weimar Democracy — *Mommsen, Hans*
　 Rise and Resurrection of the American Programmer — *Yourdon, Edward*
c Rise and Shine (Illus. by Eugenie Fernandes) — *Raffi*
　 The Rise, Corruption, and Coming Fall of the House of Saud — *Aburish, Said K*
　 The Rise of Christianity — *Stark, Rodney*
　 The Rise of Confucian Ritualism in Late Imperial China — *Chow, Kai-Wing*
　 The Rise of Consumer Society in Britain 1880-1980 — *Benson, John*
　 The Rise of Early Modern Science — *Huff, Toby E*
　 The Rise of Fishes — *Long, John A, 1957-*
　 The Rise of Islam and the Bengal Frontier 1204-1760 — *Eaton, Richard M*
　 The Rise of Marginal Voices — *Statham, Anne*
　 The Rise of Modern Egypt — *Annesley, George*
　 The Rise of Neoconservatism — *Ehrman, John, 1959-*
r The Rise of Robert Dodsley — *Solomon, Harry M*
　 The Rise of Sinclair Lewis 1920-1930 — *Hutchisson, James M*
　 Rise of the Bourgeoisie, Demise of Empire — *Gocek, Fatma Muge*
　 The Rise of the Imperial Self — *Dworkin, Ronald William*
　 The Rise of the Islamic Empire and the Threat to the West — *Dennis, Anthony J*
　 The Rise of the Network Society — *Castells, Manuel*
　 Rise of the New York Skyscraper 1865-1913 — *Landau, Sarah Bradford*
　 The Rise of the Russian Democrats — *Devlin, Judith*
　 The Rise of the Rustbelt — *Cooke, Philip*
　 The Rise of the Sixties — *Crow, Thomas*
　 The Rise of Western Christendom — *Brown, Peter Robert Lamont*

The Rise to Power of the Chinese Communist Party — *Saich, Tony*
A Rising Public Voice — *Brill, Alida*
Rising Tension in Eastern Europe and the Former Soviet Union — *Carlton, David*
Rising Tide — *Barry, John M*
Rising Wind — *Plummer, Brenda Gayle*
Risk — *Adams, John, 1938-*
Risk and Redemption — *Kent, Arthur*
Risk-Based Decision Making in Water Resources VII
Risk-Based Inservice Testing. Vol. 2
Risk: Evaluation, Management and Sharing — *Eeckhoudt, Louis*
Risk Management — *Higson, Nigel*
Risk Management — *Vaughan, Emmett J*
Risk Management in Volatile Financial Markets — *Bruni, Franco*
The Risk of Being Alive — *Francis, Dylan*
The Risk of Heaven — *Berger, Bob*
The Risk of His Music — *Weltner, Peter*
Risk, Science, and Politics — *Harrison, Kathryn, 1958-*
Risk versus Risk — *Graham, John D*
y Risking Elizabeth — *McCloskey, Walter*
Risking Free Trade — *Lusztig, Michael*
Risks and Rewards — *Walsh, Julia Montgomery*
Risks, Costs, and Lives Saved — *Hahn, Robert W*
Risks to Students in School
Risky Business — *McClure, Lynne Falkin*
Risky Rivers — *Chibnik, Michael*
c Rita the Rescuer — *Offen, Hilda*
Ritalin-Free Kids — *Reichenberg-Ullman, Judyth*
The Rites of Labor — *Truant, Cynthia Maria*
Rites of Passage — *Crowley, Walt*
El Ritmo Ludico Y Los En Bogota — *Peralta, Victoria*
Il Ritorno Di Andrea — *Micheli, Enrico*
I Ritratti Di Agrippina Maggiore — *Tansini, Raffaella*
Die Ritterwurde In Mittelitalien Zwischen Mittelalter Und Fruher Neuzeit — *Boninger, Lorenz*
Ritual and Ethnic Identity — *Lightston, Jack N*
Ritual and Rubbish in the Iron Age of Wessex — *Hill, J D*
Ritual and Scripture in Chinese Popular Religion — *Johnson, David G*
Rituales Agricolas Y Otras Costumbres Guerrences Siglos XVI-XX — *Matias Alonso, Marcos*
Rituals for Home and Parish — *Rathschmidt, Jack*
Rituals in Babism and Baha'ism — *MacEoin, Denis*
Rituals of Childhood — *Marcus, Ivan G*
Rituals of Retribution — *Evans, Richard J*
Rituals of Rule, Rituals of Resistance — *Beezley, William H*
Rituals of Self-Revelation — *Hijiya-Kirschnereit, Irmela*
Rival States, Rival Firms — *Grunberg, Isabelle*
A Rivalry of Genius — *Hirshman, Marc*
Rivals for Power — *Thurber, James A*
c River and Stream — *Sayre, April Pulley*
The River at the Center of the World — *Winchester, Simon*
The River at the Centre of the World — *Winchester, Simon*
c The River Bank and Other Stories from The Wind in the Willows (Illus. by Inga Moore) — *Grahame, Kenneth*
The River beyond the World — *Peery, Janet*
River Biota — *Petts, Geoffrey*
The River Cafe Cook Book — *Gray, Rose*
c A River Dream — *Say, Allen*
River Flows and Channel Forms — *Petts, Geoffrey*
River Hydraulics
A River Lost — *Harden, Blaine*
c River My Friend (Illus. by Ken Campbell) — *Bell, William*
A River No More — *Fradkin, Philip L*
River of Fire — *Putney, Mary Jo*
River of Life, Channel of Death — *Petersen, Keith*
River of Mirrors — *Huss, Judson*
River of Promise, River of Peril — *Thorson, John E*
River of Stars — *Akiko, Yosano*
River of Stone — *Wiebe, Rudy*
River of Time — *Swain, Jon*
River: One Man's Journey Down the Colorado, Source to Sea — *Fletcher, Colin*
River out of Eden — *Dawkins, Richard*
y River Rats — *Stevermer, Caroline*
River Restoration — *Petts, Geoffrey*
A River Runs through It and Other Stories — *Maclean, Norman*
y The River Sorrow (Ferrone). Audio Version — *Holden, Craig*

c The River That Went to the Sky (Illus. by Ademola Akintola) — *Medicott, Mary*
The River to Pickle Beach — *Betts, Doris*
A River Town — *Keneally, Thomas*
Riverrun Trilogy — *Somtow, S P*
c Rivers — *Haslam, Andrew*
c Rivers (Illus. by Francisco Arredondo) — *Llamas Ruiz, Andres*
c Rivers — *Martin, Fred*
c Rivers (Illus. by Vanessa Card) — *Morris, Neil*
c Rivers and Valleys — *Sauvain, Philip*
Rivers of Blood — *Uekert, Brenda K*
Rivers of History — *Jackson, Harvey H, III*
Rivers West — *McCarthy, Gary*
The Riverview Murders — *Raleigh, Michael*
Riverwalking — *Moore, Kathleen Dean*
The Riviera: Off Season and On — *Lehman, Doris*
RL's Dream — *Mosley, Walter*
y RL's Dream (Kramer). Audio Version — *Mosley, Walter*
p RNA
The Roaches Have No King — *Weiss, Daniel Evan*
The Road Ahead — *Gates, Bill*
y The Road Ahead. Completely Rev. and Up-to-Date — *Gates, Bill*
The Road Ahead (Adamson). Completely Rev. and Up-to-Date. Audio Version — *Gates, Bill*
The Road Back — *Thompson, Dorothy Davis*
y Road from Home — *Kherdian, David*
The Road from Serfdom — *Skidelsky, Robert*
The Road Home — *Thomas, Eliza*
y The Road Home — *White, Ellen Emerson*
The Road Less Traveled — *Peck, M Scott*
The Road Less Traveled and Beyond — *Peck, M Scott*
The Road Less Traveled and Beyond (Peck). Audio Version — *Peck, M Scott*
Road Stories and Recipes — *Nix, Don*
The Road That Is Not a Road and the Open City, Ritoque, Chile — *Pendleton-Jullian, Ann M*
y The Road to Auschwitz — *Fried, Hedi*
Road to Divorce — *Stone, Lawrence*
The Road to Elizabeth — *Ridgway, John*
The Road to Guilford Courthouse — *Buchanan, John*
The Road to Hell — *Liberatore, Paul*
The Road to Hell — *Maren, Michael*
c The Road to Irriyan — *Lawrence, Louise*
The Road to Judgement — *Stacey, Robin Chapman*
The Road to Love Canal — *Colten, Craig E*
The Road to Memphis (Thigpen). Audio Version — *Taylor, Mildred D*
The Road to Notown — *Foley, Michael, 1947-*
The Road to Nowhere — *Hacker, Jacob S*
The Road to Redemption — *Parfitt, Tudor*
c The Road to Seneca Falls (Illus. by Mary O'Keefe Young) — *Swain, Gwenyth*
Road to Survival — *Vogt, William*
The Road to West 43rd Street — *Burger, Nash K*
Road Transport Informatics — *Camus, Jean-Pierre*
r Road Trip USA
Road Trips, Head Trips and Other Car-Crazed Writings — *Lindamood, Jean*
Road Warriors — *Burstein, Daniel*
y A Road We Do Not Know — *Chiaventone, Frederick J*
c Roads and Tunnels — *Pollard, Michael*
The Roads between the Worlds — *Moorcock, Michael*
The Roads of Chinese Childhood — *Stafford, Charles*
Roads to Dominion — *Diamond, Sara*
Roads to Rome — *Franchot, Jenny*
Roads to Santiago — *Nooteboom, Cees*
Roadside Geology of Louisiana — *Spearing, Darwin*
Roadside Geology of South Dakota — *Gries, John Paul*
Roadside Geology of Vermont and New Hampshire — *VanDiver, Bradford B*
Roadworks — *McCartney, Linda*
c The Roald Dahl Quiz Book (Illus. by Quentin Blake) — *Maher, Richard*
Roald Dahl's Book of Ghost Stories
c Roar! (Illus. by Woody) — *Hoggarth, Peter*
y The Roaring Boy — *Marston, Edward*
Roaring Days — *Mouat, Jeremy*
The Roaring Girl — *Hollingshead, Greg*
The Roaring Stream — *Foster, Nelson*
Rob Parr's Post-Pregnancy Workout — *Parr, Rob*
y Robber Barons and Radicals — *Stiles, T J*
c Robbers of the Giant Cactus — *Pageler, Elaine*
Robber's Wine — *Hart, Ellen*
c Robbie Rabbit and the Little Ones (Illus. by Catherine Walters) — *Sykes, Julie*
Robert A.M. Stern Buildings — *Stern, Robert A M*
y Robert Bateman: Natural Worlds — *Archbold, Rick*

r Robert Benchley: An Annotated Bibliography — *Ernst, Gordon E, Jr.*
Robert Boyle Reconsidered — *Hunter, Michael Cyril William*
Robert Browning — *Woolford, John*
Robert Browning and Twentieth-Century Criticism — *O'Neill, Patricia*
Robert Browning's Rondures Brave — *Bright, Michael*
c Robert Burns: Maker of Rhymes (Illus. by Scoular Anderson) — *McNair, Elisabeth Jane*
Robert Capa: Photographs — *Capa, Robert*
Robert Clarke: To B or Not to B — *Clarke, Robert*
y Robert Crowther's Pop-Up Olympics — *Crowther, Robert*
Robert De Cotte and the Perfection of Architecture in Eighteenth-Century France — *Neuman, Robert*
y Robert E. Lee: A Biography — *Thomas, Emory M*
y Robert E. Lee: A Biography (Davidson). Audio Version — *Thomas, Emory M*
r Robert E. Lee: Gentleman General/Ulysses S. Grant: Unlikely Hero. Electronic Media Version
y Robert Frost: A Biography — *Meyers, Jeffrey*
Robert Frost: Selected Poems — *Frost, Robert*
Robert Frost's Star in a Stone Boat — *Ingebretsen, Edward J*
Robert Graves and the White Goddess 1940-85 — *Graves, Richard Perceval*
Robert Kennedy: The Final Years — *Dooley, Brian*
Robert Louis Stevenson and the Appearance of Modernism — *Sandison, Alan*
Robert Louis Stevenson: Interviews and Recollections — *Terry, R C*
y Robert Louis Stevenson: Teller of Tales — *Gherman, Beverly*
Robert Lowell and the Sublime — *Hart, Henry*
r Robert Morris Crenshaw and Blanche Rowe Crenshaw — *De Moss, Geri Crenshaw*
Robert Motherwell: What Art Holds — *Caws, Mary Ann*
Robert Musil and the Tradition of the German Novelle — *O'Connor, Kathleen*
Robert Penn Warren: A Biography — *Blotner, Joseph*
Robert Persons: The Biography of an Elizabethan Jesuit 1546-1610 — *Edwards, Francis*
Robert Remak 1815-1865 — *Schmiedebach, Heinz-Peter*
Robert Runcie: The Reluctant Archbishop — *Carpenter, Humphrey, 1946-*
Robert Schumann: Herald of a New Poetic Age — *Daverio, John*
Robert Smithson: The Collected Writings — *Smithson, Robert*
Robert Wilson — *Bertoni, Franco*
Roberts' Rules of Lesbian Living — *Roberts, Shelly*
Robertson Davies: Man of Myth — *Grant, Judith Skelton*
Robin Boyd: A Life — *Serle, Geoffrey*
c Robin Hood (Illus. by Margaret Early) — *Early, Margaret*
Robin Hood — *Knight, Stephen Thomas*
c Robin Hood (Illus. by Nick Harris) — *Philip, Neil*
c Robin Hood and Little John (Illus. by David Ray) — *Cohen, Barbara*
y Robin of Sherwood (Illus. by Michael Foreman) — *Morpurgo, Michael*
c The Robins in Your Backyard — *Willis, Nancy Carol*
Robinson Crusoe — *Defoe, Daniel*
Robinson Crusoe — *Spaas, Lieve*
c Robinson Crusoe (Baker). Audio Version — *Defoe, Daniel*
Robinson Crusoe Revisited 1996 — *Suarez, Maria Luz*
Robinson Jeffers and a Galaxy of Writers — *Thesing, William B*
Robinson Jeffers: Dimensions of a Poet — *Brophy, Robert*
Robinson Jeffers: Poet of California. Rev. Ed. — *Karman, James*
Robot Blues — *Weis, Margaret*
Robot Evolution — *Rosheim, Mark E*
c The Robot King (Illus. by Brian Selznick) — *Selznick, Brian*
Robotic Observatories — *Bode, Michael F*
Robotics for Challenging Environments — *ASCE Specialty Conference on Robotics for Challenging Environments (2nd: 1996: Albuquerque, N.M.)*
The Robot's Dilemma Revisited — *Ford, Kenneth M*
Robust Control System Design — *Tsui, Chia-Chi*
Robust Nonlinear Control Design — *Freeman, Randy A*
y Roc and a Hard Place — *Anthony, Piers*

Rocas Alijos — *Schmieder, Robert W*
Rock and Roll — *Friedlander, Paul*
r The Rock and Roll Almanac — *Bego, Mark*
The Rock Art of Texas Indians — *Kirkland, Forrest*
Rock Art Studies in the Americas — *Steinbring, Jack*
Rock Bottom — *Des Barres, Pamela*
Rock Fractures and Fluid Flow — *National Research Council (U.S.). Committee on Fracture Characterization and Fluid Flow*
The Rock Garden Month-by-Month — *Jefferson-Brown, Michael*
y Rock Hardware — *Trynka, Paul*
Rock Island Color Guide to Freight and Passenger Equipment — *Hile, Steve*
Rock Jocks, Wall Rats, and Hang Dogs — *Long, John, 1954, Apr.-*
Rock Mechanics Tools and Techniques. Vols. 1-2 — *North American Rock Mechanics Symposium (2nd: 1996: Montreal, Quebec)*
r Rock Music in American Popular Culture — *Cooper, B Lee*
r Rock Music Scholarship — *Gatten, Jeffrey N*
Rock n Roll Babes from Outer Space — *Jaivin, Linda*
c Rock n' Roll Rainforest — *Platt, Pamela*
Rock, Rhythm and Reels — *Fleming, Lee*
r Rock Stars/Pop Stars — *Leyser, Brady J*
yr Rock: The Rough Guide — *Buckley, Jonathan*
r The Rock Who's Who. 2nd Ed. — *Helander, Brock*
Rockbridge County Artists and Artisans — *Crawford, Barbara*
Rockenwagner — *Rockenwagner, Hans*
The Rocket and the Reich — *Neufeld, Michael J*
y A Rocket at Heart — *Tomjanovich, Rudy*
r Rocket Man — *Bernardin, Claude*
c Rockets — *Fox, Mary Virginia*
y The Rockford Files — *Kaminsky, Stuart M*
r The Rockies (Insight Guides). New Ed.
c Rockin' Reptiles (Illus. by Lynn Munsinger) — *Calmenson, Stephanie*
Rocking the Ages — *Smith, J Walker*
Rocking the Babies — *Raymond, Linda*
Rocking the Boat — *O'Farrell, Brigid*
Rocking the Classics — *Macan, Edward L*
The Rockingham Connection and the Second Founding of the Whig Party 1768-1773 — *Elofson, W M*
c Rocks — *Jennings, Terry*
yr Rocks and Fossils — *Busbey, Arthur Bresnahan*
yr Rocks and Minerals — *O'Donoghue, Michael*
Rocks and Minerals of Kentucky — *Anderson, Warren H*
c Rocks and Soil (Illus. by Mike Gordon) — *Gordon, Maria*
Rocks from Space — *Norton, O Richard*
r Rockspeak: The Language of Rock and Pop — *Warner, Simon*
y The Rocky and Bullwinkle Book — *Chunovic, Louis*
c Rocky Bobocky, the Pizza Man (Illus. by Vickey Bolling) — *Ellison, Emily*
Rocky Mountain Home — *Flood, Elizabeth Clair*
The Rococo Interior — *Scott, Katie*
Rodale's Garden Answers — *Bradley, Fern Marshall*
Rodef Shalom Neome Ha-Shalom Shel Ha-Memshalah Yitshak Rabin — *Rabin, Yitzhak*
Rodent Angel — *Weinstein, Debra*
Rodents of the World — *Alderton, David*
c Rodeo (Illus. by Ken Robbins) — *Robbins, Ken*
Rodeo in America — *Wooden, Wayne S*
c Rodeos: The Greatest Show on Dirt — *Alter, Judy*
Roderick Hudson — *James, Henry*
y Rodin: A Biography (Vance). Pts. 1-2. Audio Version — *Grunfeld, Frederic V*
Rodinny Sjezd — *Kraus, Ivan*
Rodrigo Carazo Y La Utopia De La Dignidad 1970-1983 — *Abarca Vasquez, Carlos*
y Roe v. Wade — *Tompkins, Nancy*
y Roger Ebert's Book of Film — *Ebert, Roger*
A Roger Fry Reader — *Fry, Roger Eliot*
c Roger Tory Peterson's ABC of Birds (Illus. by Roger Tory Peterson) — *Peterson, Roger Tory*
Roger Williams' Dream for America — *Skaggs, Donald*
The Rogers Gray Italian Country Cookbook — *Rogers, Ruth*
Rogers Hornsby: A Biography — *Alexander, Charles C*
Roget's International Thesaurus — *Chapman, Robert L*
Rogue Asteroids and Doomsday Comets — *Steel, Duncan*
Rogue Lion Safaris — *Barnes, Simon*

Rogue States and Nuclear Outlaws — *Klare, Michael*
Rogue Tory — *Smith, Denis, 1932-*
Rogue Warrior--Designation Gold — *Marcinko, Richard*
Rogue Warrior--Task Force Blue — *Marcinko, Richard*
The Rogue Warrior's Strategy for Success — *Marcinko, Richard*
y Rogue Wave and Other Red-Blooded Sea Stories — *Taylor, Theodore*
Rogue's Justice — *Briody, Thomas Gately*
Le Roi Du Bois — *Michon, Pierre*
Le Roi: Mythes Et Symboles — *Roux, Jean-Paul*
c Roland Harvey's Drawing Book — *Harvey, Roland*
Role Et Fonctionnement De L'Anaphore Dans La Dynamique Textuelle — *Apotheloz, Denis*
The Role of Art in the Late Anglo-Saxon Church — *Gameson, Richard*
Role of Ceramics in Advanced Electrochemical Systems — *Kumta, Prashant N*
The Role of European Naval Forces after the Cold War — *Nooy, G C De*
The Role of the Bacterial Membrane in Chromosome Replication and Partition — *Funnell, Barbara E*
The Role of the Ocean in the 21st Century — *Law of the Sea Institute. Conference (27th: 1993: Seoul, Korea)*
The Role of the State in Economic Change — *Chang, Ha-Joon*
Role of the State in the Economy — *Siddiqi, Muhammad Nejatullah*
Role Play — *Melville, Anne*
The Roles of Reference Librarians — *Low, Kathleen*
Rolf Armstrong: The Dream Girls — *Stevens, Ben*
p Roll Call: The Newspaper of Capitol Hill
c Roll of Thunder, Hear My Cry — *Taylor, Mildred D*
c Roll of Thunder, Hear My Cry (Thigpen). Audio Version — *Taylor, Mildred D*
Roll the Dice — *Guppy, Darius*
Die Rolle Des Konigs Und Seiner Familie Nach Den Texten Von Ugaret — *Aboud, Jehad*
c Roller Hockey (Illus. by Bruce Curtis) — *Millar, Cam*
Rollerderby: The Book — *Carver, Lisa*
The Rolling Stone Book of Women in Rock — *O'Dair, Barbara*
The Rolling Stone Film Reader — *Travers, Peter*
c The Rolling Store (Illus. by Peter Catalanotto) — *Johnson, Angela*
c Rollow and Tweedy and the Ghost at Dougal Castle. Book and Audio Version — *Allen, Laura Jean*
c Roly-Poly Puppies (Illus. by Jacqueline Rogers) — *Moore, Elaine*
c Rolypolyology (Illus. by Brian Grogan) — *Ross, Michael Elsohn*
Rom Und Der Romische Adel In Der Spaten Stauferzeit — *Thumser, Matthias*
r Roma Capitale 1447-1527 — *Gensini, Sergio*
Roman Bridges — *O'Connor, Colin*
Roman Catholic Worship — *White, James F*
Roman Catholics and Evagelicals — *Geisler, Norman L*
Le Roman D'Adam Et Eve — *Noel, Bernard*
Le Roman De Chaireas Et Callirhoe — *Chariton*
Le Roman De La Rose, ou, De Guillaume De Dole De Jean Renart — *Andrieu, Gabriel*
Le Roman De Troyle. Vols. 1-2 — *Bianciotto, Gabriel*
Roman Defeat, Christian Response, and the Literary Construction of the Jew — *Olster, David M*
cr The Roman Empire — *Chrisp, Peter*
y The Roman Empire — *Whittock, Martyn*
c The Roman Fort — *Connolly, Peter*
c Roman Fort — *McNeill, Sarah*
The Roman Goddess Ceres — *Spaeth, Barbette Stanley*
The Roman Imperial Coinage. Vol. 10 — *Kent, J P C*
Roman Literary Culture — *Fantham, Elaine*
The Roman Near East 31 B.C.-A.D. 337 — *Millar, Fergus*
c The Roman News — *Langley, Andrew*
c Roman Numerals I to MM (Illus. by Arthur Geisert) — *Geisert, Arthur*
Roman Popes and German Patriots — *Stadtwald, Kurt*
Roman Portraits. Vols. 1-3 — *Johansen, Flemming*
Roman Portraiture — *Bazant, Jan*
Roman Theater and Society — *Slater, William J*
Romance — *McBain, Ed*
Romance and Aretine Humanism in Sienese Comedy — *Clubb, Louise George*
Romance and Revolution — *Duff, David*
p Romance Forever
The Romance Languages — *Posner, Rebecca*

The Romance of American Psychology — *Herman, Ellen*
The Romance of Crime — *Roberts, Gareth*
The Romance of Origins — *Margherita, Gayle*
Romance of the Mission — *Baca, Elmo*
Romance of the Road — *Primeau, Ronald*
The Romance of the Rose and Its Medieval Readers — *Hunt, Sylvia*
The Romance of the Rose or of Guillaume De Dole — *Jean Renart*
Romance, Poetry, and Surgical Sleep — *Papper, E M*
y The Romance Reader — *Abraham, Pearl*
r Romance Writer's Sourcebook. 1st Ed. — *Borcherding, David H*
Romance Writings — *Montagu, Mary Wortley, Lady*
Romances of the Republic — *Samuels, Shirley*
Romancing the Grail — *Groos, Arthur*
Romancing the Holy — *Farrington, Debra K*
Romanesque Manuscripts. Vols. 1-2 — *Cahn, Walter*
Romania — *Morton, Jerry*
y Romania — *Sanborne, Mark*
Romania after Ceausescu — *Gallagher, Tom*
Romania In Lumea Sportului
Romanian Cassandra — *Watts, Larry L*
The Romanians 1774-1866 — *Hitchins, Keith*
y The Romanovs: The Final Chapter — *Massie, Robert K*
c The Romans — *Allard, Denise*
Romans — *Byrne, Brendan*
c The Romans — *Dineen, Jacqueline*
c The Romans — *Haywood, John*
Romans — *Hepplewhite, Peter*
r Romans — *Mills, Watson E*
c Romans in Britain — *Howard, Coltia*
The Romans in Spain — *Richardson, J S*
Romantic Days and Nights in San Francisco — *Peck, Donna*
The Romantic Generation — *Rosen, Charles, 1927-*
r Romantic Hearts — *Jaegly, Peggy J*
Romantic Motives — *Stocking, George W*
r The Romantic Movement 1995
Romantic Outlaws, Beloved Prisons — *Duncan, Martha Grace*
Romantic Passion — *Jankowiak, William*
Romantic Relationships — *Robbins, Paul R*
Romantic Stages — *Finkel, Alicia*
p Romantic Times Magazine
Romantic Vagrancy — *Langan, Celeste*
Romantic Wedding Destinations. 2nd Ed. — *Carrington, Jackie*
Romantic Women Writers — *Feldman, Paula R*
Romanticism — *Day, Aidan*
Romanticism: A Critical Reader — *Wu, Duncan*
Romanticism: An Anthology — *Wu, Duncan*
Romanticism and Contemporary Criticism — *De Man, Paul*
Romanticism and the Androgynous Sublime — *Stevenson, Warren*
Romanticism and the Anglican Newman — *Goslee, David*
Romanticism and the Rise of History — *Bann, Stephen*
Romanticism, Nationalism, and the Revolt against Theory — *Simpson, David*
Il Romanziere E L'Archivista — *Povolo, Claudio*
Rome and Baetica — *Fear, A T*
Rome and the Western Greeks 350 B.C.-A.D. 200 — *Lomas, Kathryn*
Rome Reborn — *Grafton, Anthony*
Rome the Sorceress — *Frenaud, Andre*
Rome: Time and Eternity — *Woodward, Anthony*
y Romeo and Juliet — *Olster, Fredi*
y Romeo and Juliet. Electronic Media Version — *Shakespeare, William*
c Romeo and Juliet — *Whitesides, Nigel*
y Romeo and Juliet: Center Stage. Electronic Media Version
Der Romerbriefkommentar Des Origenes — *Bammel, Caroline P Hammond*
Romische Kardinalshaushalte Des 17. Jahrhunderts — *Volkel, Markus*
Romulo Betancourt Y El Partido Comunista De Costa Rica — *Gomez, Alejandro*
r Ronald Firbank: An Annotated Bibliography of Secondary Materials 1905-1995 — *Moore, Steven*
Ronald Johnson — *Stratton, Dirk*
c Ronald Morgan Goes to Camp (Illus. by Susanna Natti) — *Giff, Patricia Reilly*
Ronald Reagan in Hollywood — *Vaughn, Stephen*
Ronald Reagan's Crusade — *Wymbs, Norman*
Ronsard and Du Bellay versus Beze — *Smith, Malcolm*

Roof Gardens, Balconies and Terraces — *Stevens, David*

y The Roof of Voyaging — *Kilworth, Garry*

Rook — *Masterton, Graham*

Rookery Blues — *Hassler, Jon*

y The Rookie — *Jenkins, Jerry B*

y Room for a Stranger — *Turnbull, Ann*

The Room In-Between — *Delgado, Ana Maria*

y A Room of One's Own (Atkins). Audio Version — *Woolf, Virginia*

A Room with a Different View — *Ostrow, Jill*

A Room with a View. Audio Version — *Forster, E M*

Rooms for Rent in the Outer Planets — *Purdy, Al*

The Rooms in My Mother's House — *Lorenzo, Olga*

The Rooms We Make Our Own — *Mirosevich, Toni*

Roosevelt and the French — *Rossi, Mario*

Roosevelt's Warrior — *Clarke, Jeanne Nienaber*

The Rooster's Egg — *Williams, Patricia J*

c The Rooster's Gift (Illus. by Eric Beddows) — *Conrad, Pam*

c The Root Cellar (Illus. by Scott Cameron) — *Lunn, Janet*

The Root of All Evil — *Farrow, David A*

Rooted against the Wind — *Wade-Gayles, Gloria*

Rooted in the Land — *Vitek, William*

Rooted Sorrow — *Doebler, Bettie Anne*

Roots and Branches — *Campbell, Patricia Shehan*

r The Roots and Branches of Daniel Roman Young and Ann Maria Beck, Delaware County, Iowa 1755-1996 — *Williams-Taylor, Helen Sue Young*

Roots and Recipes — *Berry, Vern*

Roots in the Air — *Kaufman, Shirley*

Roots of American Racism — *Vaughan, Alden T*

Roots of Bitterness. 2nd Ed. — *Cott, Nancy F*

Roots of Black Music. 2nd Ed. — *Kebede, Ashenafi*

The Roots of Christian Mysticism — *Clement, Olivier*

Roots of Identity — *King, Linda*

The Roots of Organic Development — *Desmurs, Jean-Roger*

The Roots of Power — *Johnstone, Maxine Sheets*

Roots of the Future — *Frow, Mayerlene*

yr Roots of the Republic. Vols. 1-6 — *Quinn, C Edward*

Roots of Wisdom — *Westermann, Claus*

The Rorschach: A Developmental Perspective — *Leichtman, Martin*

c Rosa and Her Singing Grandfather (Illus. by Marcia Sewall) — *Rosselson, Leon*

Rosa Gallica — *Verrier, Suzanne*

Rosa Lee: A Mother and Her Family in Urban America — *Dash, Leon*

Rosa Luxemburg and the Noble Dream — *Shepardson, Donald E*

c Rosa Moves to Town (Illus. by Eva Eriksson) — *Lindgren, Barbro*

Rosa Ponselle: A Centenary Biography — *Drake, James A*

Rosa T' Oniro — *Hristofis, Hristoforos*

Rosario Ferre: A Search for Identity — *Hintz, Suzanne S*

Rosas De Fuego — *Janes, Clara*

r Roscoe Fatty Arbuckle: A Bio-Bibliography — *Young, Robert, 1927-*

Roscoe Fatty Arbuckle: A Biography of the Silent Film Comedian 1887-1933 — *Oderman, Stuart*

Roscommon before the Famine — *Gacquin, William*

c Rose (Illus. by Lynne Woodcock Cravath) — *Leverich, Kathleen*

Rose — *Smith, Martin Cruz*

The Rose Crossing — *Jose, Nicholas*

The Rose Engagement — *Brown, Richard E*

c Rose in Bloom — *Alcott, Louisa May*

Rose Mellie Rose — *Redonnet, Marie*

c Rose Red and Snow White (Illus. by Ruth Sanderson) — *Sanderson, Ruth*

Rose Reisman's Enlightened Kitchen — *Reisman, Rose*

Rosebud: The Story of Orson Welles — *Thomson, David*

Rosemary Remembered — *Albert, Susan Wittig*

Rosemary Verey's English Country Gardens — *Verey, Rosemary*

c Rosemary's Witch — *Warren, Ann*

r Roses (Eyewitness Handbooks)

c Roses Are Pink, Your Feet Really Stink — *De Groat, Diane*

c Roses for Gita (Illus. by Alice Priestley) — *Gilmore, Rachna*

y The Rosewood Casket (Darling). Audio Version — *McCrumb, Sharyn*

y The Rosewood Casket (Herbert). Audio Version — *McCrumb, Sharyn*

c Rosie and Michael — *Viorst, Judith*

c Rosie No-Name and the Forest of Forgetting — *Owen, Gareth*

y Rosie O'Donnell: Her True Story — *Mair, George*

c Rosie Plants a Radish (Illus. by Axel Scheffler) — *Petty, Kate*

y Rosie: Rosie O'Donnell's Biography — *Parish, James Robert*

y Rosie the Riveter — *Colman, Penny*

y Rosie's Bakery All-Butter, Fresh Cream, Sugar-Packed, No-Holds-Barred Baking Book — *Rosenberg, Judy*

Rosie's Bakery Chocolate-Packed, Jam-Filled, Butter-Rich, No-Holds-Barred Cookie Book — *Rosenberg, Judy*

c Rosie's Ballet Slippers (Illus. by Maria Teresa Meloni) — *Hampshire, Susan*

c Rosie's Fiddle (Illus. by Kevin O'Malley) — *Root, Phyllis*

c Rosie's Nutcracker Dreams (Illus. by Julie Durrell) — *Giff, Patricia Reilly*

r Ross and Wilson Anatomy and Physiology in Health and Illness. 8th Ed. — *Wilson, Kathleen J W*

r Ross Lee Finney: A Bio-Bibliography — *Hitchens, Susan Hayes*

Rosso in Italy — *Franklin, David, 1961-*

Un Rostro Encubierto — *Ruz, Mario Humberto*

The Roswell Report — *Weaver, Richard L*

y The Roswell UFO Crash — *Korff, Kal K*

The Rosy Future of War — *Delmas, Philippe*

y Rosy Is My Relative (Glover). Audio Version — *Durrell, Gerald*

r Rotating Electrical Machines and Power Systems. 2nd Ed. — *Patrick, Dale R*

r Rotational Moulding of Plastics. 2nd Ed. — *Crawford, R J*

Les Rothschild: Batisseurs Et Mecenes — *Prevost-Marchilhacy, Pauline*

The Rothschild Gardens — *Rothschild, Miriam*

The Rothschilds: Essays on the History of a European Family — *Heuberger, Georg*

c Rotten Ralph's Rotten Romance (Illus. by Nicole Rubel) — *Gantos, Jack*

Roubiliac and the Eighteenth-Century Monument — *Bindman, David*

Rouge Decante — *Brouwers, Jeroen*

Le Rouge Et Le Noir — *Crouzet, Michel*

The Rouge Mysteries — *Swan, John*

Rough Mix — *Bowen, Jimmy*

Rough Music — *Digges, Deborah*

The Rough Road to Renaissance — *Teaford, Jon C*

c Rough Sketch Beginning (Illus. by Robert Florczak) — *Berry, James*

Rough Skin — *Hynes, Maureen*

Roughing It — *Twain, Mark*

Round about Midnight. Updated Ed. — *Nisenson, Eric*

c Round Buildings, Square Buildings, and Buildings that Wiggle like a Fish — *Isaacson, Philip M*

r Round the Year with the World's Religions — *Pike, Royston*

The Roundtable Talks and the Breakdown of Communism — *Elster, Jon*

Rousseau — *Wokler, Robert*

Rousseau and Liberty — *Wokler, Robert*

Rousseau and the Politics of Ambiguity — *Morgenstern, Mira*

p Route One

Routes: Travel and Translation in the Late Twentieth Century — *Clifford, James*

r Routledge Dictionary of Economics — *Rutherford, Donald, 1942-*

r Routledge Dictionary of Language and Linguistics — *Bussmann, Hadumod*

r Routledge German Technical Dictionary. Vols. 1-2

The Routledge Reader in Caribbean Literature — *Donnell, Alison*

Rov: Folkelivsskildring — *Fjelheim, Freddy O*

The Roving Editor — *Redpath, James*

y Rowan and the Travellers — *Rodda, Emily*

Rowntree and the Marketing Revolution 1862-1969 — *Fitzgerald, Robert*

Roxanna's Children — *Bonfield, Lynn*

Roy Acuff: The Smoky Mountain Boy. 2nd Ed. — *Schlappi, Elizabeth*

Roy DeCarava: A Retrospective — *DeCarava, Roy*

r Roy Fuller: A Bibliography — *Smith, Steven E*

Roy Fuller: Writer and Society — *Powell, Neil*

The Royal and Ancient Golfer's Handbook 1996

The Royal and Republican Sovereignty in Early Modern Europe — *Oresko, Robert*

y Royal Assassin — *Hobb, Robin*

Royal Blue — *Oxenberg, Christina*

Royal Bounty — *Prochaska, Frank*

c The Royal Drum (Illus. by Carol O'Malia) — *Lake, Mary Dixon*

The Royal French State 1460-1610 — *Le Roy Ladurie, Emmanuel*

Royal Insignia — *Patterson, Stephen*

The Royal Marsden NHS Trust Manual of Clinical Nursing Procedures. 4th Ed. — *Mallett, Jane*

A Royal Passion — *Berger, Robert W*

c The Royal Raven — *Wilhelm, Hans*

r The Royal Society of Medicine's Dictionary of Symptoms — *Youngson, R M*

c The Royal Switch (Illus. by Jacqueline Rogers) — *York, Sarah Mountbatten-Windsor, Duchess of*

Royal Tombs of Sipan — *Alva, Walter*

Royalist Political Thought during the French Revolution — *Osen, James L*

The Royalscope Fe-As-Ko — *Platt, Randall Beth*

RPG IV by Example — *Farr, George*

Rrugetimi I Mbrame I Ago Ymerit — *Shehu, Bashkim*

Ru He Tou Zi — *Tang, Qinghua*

c Rub-a-Dub-Dub (Illus. by Val Biro) — *Biro, Val*

c Rubber-Band Banjos and a Java Jive Bass — *Sabbeth, Alex*

Rubber Bullets — *Ezrahi, Yaron*

Rubber Processing — *White, James Lindsay*

Rubber Up! — *King, Edward*

The Rubbish on Our Plates — *Perucca, Fabien*

Rubens's Landscapes — *Brown, Christopher, 1948-*

Ruby — *Andrews, V C*

Ruby of Cochin: An Indian Jewish Woman Remembers — *Daniel, Ruby*

y Ruby Slippers, Golden Tears — *Datlow, Ellen*

y Ruby's Low-Fat Soul Food Cookbook — *Banks-Payne, Ruby*

Ruchome Schody — *Romanowiczowa, Zofia*

Der Ruckblick Auf Die Vergangenheit Wird Sich Nicht Vermeiden Lassen — *Dudek, Peter*

Ruckblicke Auf Personen Und Zustande — *Gans, Eduard*

Ruddlemoor — *Thompson, E V*

Ruddy Ducks and Other Stifftails — *Johnsgard, Paul A*

Rudolf — *Pankowski, Marian*

y Rue Ordener, Rue Labat — *Kofman, Sarah*

Rueful Death — *Albert, Susan Wittig*

c Ruff — *Hissey, Jane*

Ruffo: My Parabola — *Ruffo, Titta*

Rufus Woods, the Columbia River, and the Building of Modern Washington — *Ficken, Robert E*

c Rugby and Rosie (Illus. by Nan Parson Rossiter) — *Rossiter, Nan Parson*

Ruger and His Guns — *Wilson, R L*

Rugs and Carpets — *Middleton, Andrew*

Ruin — *Phillips, Patrick*

The Ruin of Kasch — *Calasso, Roberto*

Ruin the Sacred Truths — *Bloom, Harold*

Ruined by Reading — *Schwartz, Lynne Sharon*

c A Ruined House — *Manning, Mick*

y Ruins — *Anderson, Kevin J*

Rule Britannia — *David, Deirdre*

The Rule of Benedict — *Holzherr, George*

y Rule of the Bone — *Banks, Russell*

The Rule of the Many — *Christiano, Thomas*

The Rules — *Schneider, Sherrie*

Rules of Civility — *Washington, George*

Rules of Engagement — *Harris, Lis*

The Rules of Insanity — *Elliot, Carl*

The Rules of the Game — *Gordon, G A H*

The Rules of the Game — *McKinnon, Ronald I*

Rules, Routines and Regimentation — *Sherman, Ann*

The Rules: Time-Tested Secrets for Capturing the Heart of Mr. Right — *Fein, Ellen*

The Rules: Time-Tested Secrets for Capturing the Heart of Mr. Right. Audio Version — *Fein, Ellen*

The Ruling Passion — *Lane, Christopher*

c Rum-a-Tum-Tum (Illus. by James E Ransome) — *Medearis, Angela Shelf*

Rumania 1866-1947 — *Hitchins, Keith*

Rumba: Dance and Social Change in Contemporary Cuba — *Daniel, Yvonne*

A Rumor of Bones — *Connor, Beverly*

A Rumor of War — *Caputo, Philip*

Rumors and Stones — *Karlin, Wayne*

Rumors of Change — *Hassan, Ihab*

The Rumour of Calcutta — *Hutnyk, John*

c Rumpelstiltskin (Illus. by Bernadette Watts) — *Grimm, Jacob*

c Rumpelstiltskin's Daughter (Illus. by Diane Stanley) — *Stanley, Diane*

c Rumply Crumply Stinky Pin (Illus. by Arthur Robin) — *Anholt, Laurence*
Rumpole and the Angel of Death — *Mortimer, John*
Rumpole and the Angel of Death (May). Audio Version — *Mortimer, John*
y Run for Your Life — *Levy, Marilyn*
The Run of His Life — *Toobin, Jeffrey*
c Run, Zan, Run — *McPhail, Catherine*
Runamok: A Novel about the Realities of Small Business — *Park, Tom*
y Runaway — *Lau, Evelyn*
y Runaway — *Wartski, Maureen*
The Runaway Jury — *Grisham, John*
The Runaway Jury (Beck). Abridged Version. Audio Version — *Grisham, John*
y The Runaway Jury (Muller). Unabridged Version. Audio Version — *Grisham, John*
c Runaway Ralph (Roberts). Audio Version — *Cleary, Beverly*
Runaway Religious in Medieval England c. 1240-1540 — *Logan, F Donald*
c The Runaway Train (Illus. by Benedict Blathwayt) — *Blathwayt, Benedict*
Runaway Wedding — *Dale, Ruth Jean*
Rune Power — *Meadows, Kenneth*
y Runemaker — *Nunnally, Tiina*
y Runner — *Hawkins, Elizabeth*
c Runnery Granary (Illus. by Jos. A Smith) — *Farmer, Nancy*
Running a School — *Gold, Richard*
Running a School--Legal Duties and Responsibilities. 1996/1997 Ed.
Running a Team for Disabled Children and Their Families — *Robards, Martin F*
y Running Away — *Fremon, David K*
c Running Away from Home (Illus. by Gregory Rogers) — *Gray, Nigel*
Running for Shelter — *Spring, Michelle*
Running from the Law — *Scottoline, Lisa*
Running from the Law (Rosenblat). Audio Version — *Scottoline, Lisa*
Running in the Family (Ondaatje). Audio Version — *Ondaatje, Michael*
Running Linux. 2nd Ed. — *Welsh, Matt*
Running Linux Companion CD-ROM. 2nd Ed. — *Ewing, Marc*
Running Microsoft Excel for Windows 95 — *Dodge, Mark*
Running Microsoft Word for Windows 95 — *Borland, Russell*
y Running Out of Time — *Haddix, Margaret Peterson*
Running Out of Time — *Struthers, Betsy*
y Running Scared — *King, Anthony Stephen*
c Running the Road to ABC (Illus. by Reynold Ruffins) — *Lauture, Denize*
Running to Paradise — *Rosenthal, M L*
y Running Wild — *Dygard, Thomas J*
y Running Wild — *McNutt, John*
Runs, Hits and an Era — *Zingg, Paul J*
y Runs with Horses — *Burks, Brian*
c The Runton Werewolf and the Big Match — *Perry, Ritchie*
Rural Crime in the Eighteenth Century — *Davey, B J*
Rural Democracy — *Watkins, Marilyn P*
Rural Development in the United States — *Galston, William A*
Rural Development Research — *Rowley, Thomas D*
Rural Development Strategies — *Sears, David W*
Rural Energy and Development
Rural Europe — *Hoggart, K*
Rural Guatemala 1760-1940 — *McCreery, David*
Rural Images — *Buisseret, David*
Rural Industrialization in Indonesia — *Mizuno, Kosuke*
Rural Ireland, Real Ireland? — *Genet, Jacqueline*
Rural Libraries and Internetworking — *Senkevitch, Judith*
Rural Life in Eighteenth-Century English Poetry — *Goodridge, John*
Rural Poverty in Developing Asia. Vol. 2 — *Quibria, M G*
Rural Protest in the Weimar Republic — *Osmond, Jonathan*
Rural Radicals — *Stock, Catherine McNicol*
Rural Rides — *Dashwood, Henry*
Rural Society and the Search for Order in Early Modern Germany — *Robisheaux, Thomas*
c Rush Hour (Illus. by Mari Takabayashi) — *Loomis, Christine*
Rush Limbaugh Is a Big Fat Idiot and Other Observations — *Franken, Al*

The Rush to German Unity — *Jarausch, Konrad H*
Rush to Union — *McKay, David*
Rushing to Paradise — *Ballard, J G*
Ruskin and Environment — *Wheeler, Michael*
Ruskin's Letters in the Mikimoto Collection: A Facsimile Edition — *Ruskin, John*
Die Russen In Amerika — *Gerigk, Horst-Jurgen*
Russia: A Return to Imperialism? — *Ra'anan, Uri*
Russia and Azerbaijan — *Swietochowski, Tadeusz*
Russia and Beyond — *Gheissari, Nick*
Russia and Eastern Europe after Communism — *Kraus, Michael, 1949-*
y Russia and the USSR 1900-95 — *Radway, Richard*
Russia and the World Economy — *Smith, Alan*
c Russia: Building Democracy — *Bradley, John*
Russia: Creating Private Enterprises and Efficient Markets — *Lieberman, Ira W*
Russia Goes Dry — *White, Stephen, 1945-*
c Russia--New Freedoms, New Challenges — *Schomp, Virginia*
Russia: People and Empire 1552-1917 — *Hosking, Geoffrey*
Russia through Women's Eyes — *Clyman, Toby W*
Russia under the Old Regime — *Pipes, Richard*
Russia--Women--Culture — *Goscilo, Helena*
y Russia: Yesterday, Today, Tomorrow — *Pavlenkov, Victor*
Russian-American Dialogue on the American Revolution — *Wood, Gordon S*
Russian-American Seminar on Critical Thinking and the Library — *Oberman, Cerise*
yr Russian Americans — *Ferry, Steven*
The Russian Army and Fleet in the Nineteenth Century — *Beskrovny, L G*
Russian Beauty — *Erofeev, V V*
The Russian Concept of Work — *Leibovich, Anna Feldman*
Russian Contributions to Invertebrate Behavior — *Abramson, Charles I*
Russian Corporate Capitalism from Peter the Great to Perestroika — *Owen, Thomas C*
Russian Critics on the Cinema of Glasnost — *Brashinsky, Michael*
Russian Culture at the Crossroads — *Shalin, Dmitri N*
Russian Currency and Finance — *Hanke, Steve H*
Russian Economic Reform — *Leitzel, Jim*
Russian Economic Reform at Risk — *Aslund, Anders*
The Russian Economy in Crisis and Transition — *Sutela, Pekka*
Russian Education — *Holmes, Brian*
r A Russian-English Collocational Dictionary of the Human Body — *Iordanskaia, L N*
The Russian Far East — *Khisamutdinov, Amir*
The Russian Far East in Transition — *Valencia, Mark J*
Russian Federation
Russian Foreign Policy after the Cold War — *Buszynski, Leszek*
A Russian Grammar Workbook — *Wade, Terence*
Russian Imperialism — *Cohen, Ariel*
Russian in the United States — *Brecht, Richard D*
Russian Jewish Artists in a Century of Change 1890-1990 — *Goodman, Susan Tumarkin*
c A Russian Jewish Family — *Leder, Jane Mersky*
y Russian Language and People. New Ed. — *Culhane, Terry*
The Russian Language in the Twentieth Century. 2nd Ed. — *Comrie, Bernard*
r Russian Literature 1988-1994 — *Shneidman, N N*
Russian Literature and Empire — *Layton, Susan*
Russian Literature and the Classics — *Barta, Peter I*
A Russian Mother — *Bosquet, Alain*
Russian Overseas Commerce with Great Britain during the Reign of Catherine II — *Kaplan, Herbert H*
The Russian Question — *Solzhenitsyn, Aleksandr Isaevich*
Russian Religious Thought — *Kornblatt, Judith Deutsch*
c The Russian Revolution — *Gilbert, Adrian*
r The Russian Revolution 1917-1921 — *White, James D, 1941-*
The Russian Revolutions — *Weber, Max*
Russian Rightists and the Revolution of 1905 — *Rawson, Don C*
Russian Society and the Greek Revolution — *Prousis, Theophilus C*
Russian Unemployment and Enterprise Restructuring — *Standing, Guy*
Russian Women in Politics and Society — *Rule, Wilma*
Russian Women's Shorter Fiction

Russian Writers on Russian Writers — *Wigzell, Faith*
Russian Youth — *Finckenauer, James O*
Russians and Dutchmen — *Braat, J*
Russians as the New Minority — *Chinn, Jeff*
Russians beyond Russia — *Melvin, Neil*
The Russians in Germany — *Naimark, Norman*
Russians in the Former Soviet Republics — *Kolstoe, Paul*
Russia's First Modern Jews — *Fishman, David E*
Russia's Muslim Frontiers — *Eickelman, Dale F*
Die Russische Abteilung Des Auswartigen Amtes In Der Weimarer Republik — *Sutterlin, Ingmar*
r Russkaia Lubochnaia Kniga XVII-XIX Vekov — *Naumuk, O M*
Russkaia Ruletka — *Gorodnikov, Sergei*
Russkie Mify — *Druzhnikov, Yuri*
Rust on the Razor — *Zubro, Mark Richard*
The Rustic Furniture Companion — *Mack, Daniel*
A Rusty Needle — *Lalic, Ivan V*
c Rusty's Red Vacation (Illus. by Kelly Asbury) — *Asbury, Kelly*
Ruth and Esther — *Larkin, Katrina J A*
c Ruth Law Thrills a Nation (Illus. by Don Brown) — *Brown, Don, 1949-*
Rutherford B. Hayes: Warrior and President — *Hoogenboom, Ari*
y Ruth's Journey — *Gold, Ruth Glasberg*
Ruze Pro Josefa Sudka 1896-1976 — *Rezac, Jan*
The RVer's Bible — *Baker, Kim*
c Rwanda (Illus. by John Isaac) — *Greenberg, Keith Elliot*
Rwanda: An Agenda for International Action — *Vassall-Adams, Guy*
The Rwanda Crisis — *Prunier, Gerard*
c Rwanda: Fierce Clashes in Central Africa (Illus. by John Isaac) — *Isaac, John*
RX for Murder — *Horowitz, Renee B*
Ryan Giggs: My Story — *Giggs, Ryan*
Ryan's Mammoth Collection — *Sky, Patrick*
Ryan's Return — *Freethy, Barbara*

S

S/He — *Pratt, Minnie Bruce*
S/He Brain — *Nadeau, Robert L*
S.J.V. Chelvanayakam and the Crisis of Sri Lankan
Tamil Nationalism 1947-1977 — *Wilson, A
Jeyaratnam*
S.L. Frank: The Life and Work of a Russian
Philosopher 1877-1950 — *Boobbyer, Philip*
S, M, L, XL — *Koolhaas, Rem*
Saadyllinen Murhenaytelma — *Hamalainen, Helvi*
Saare Gan Eden
Saatchi and Saatchi — *Fendley, Alison*
Sab. Autobiography — *Gomez De Avellaneda Y
Arteaga, Gertrudis*
Sabbath's Theater — *Roth, Philip*
Sabbatical: A Romance — *Barth, John*
Sabine R. Ulibarri: Critical Essays — *Duke Dos
Santos, Maria I*
Sabino's Map — *Usner, Don J*
y The Sable Doughboys — *Willard, Tom*
r SABR Presents the Home Run Encyclopedia
— *McConnell, Bob*
Sabre — *Follett, James*
y Sabriel — *Nix, Garth*
Sabriya — *Idilbi, Ulfat*
c Sacagawea: Native American Hero — *Sanford,
William R*
y Sacagawea: Westward with Lewis and Clark
— *White, Alana J*
Sachsischer Serpentin — *Hoyer, Eva Maria*
The Sacralization of Politics in Fascist Italy
— *Gentile, Emilio*
y Sacrament — *Barker, Clive*
y Sacrament (Keith). Audio Version — *Barker, Clive*
Sacrament of Salvation — *McPartlan, Paul*
Les Sacramentaires — *Metzger, Marcel*
Sacramento Army Depot Reuse Plan
Sacred and Secular — *Markus, R A*
Sacred Art of the Earth — *Korp, Maureen*
The Sacred Chain — *Cantor, Norman F*
Sacred Cow — *Eltit, Diamela*
Sacred Cows Make the Best Burgers — *Kriegel,
Robert*
Sacred Dust — *Hill, David*
The Sacred Fire of Liberty — *Banning, Lance*
A Sacred Heart — *Watson, Ron*
Sacred Hunger — *Unsworth, Barry*
The Sacred Image East and West — *Ousterhout,
Robert*
A Sacred Journey — *Elcott, David M*
Sacred Magic of the Angels — *Goddard, David*
The Sacred Mountains of Asia — *Einarsen, John*
y Sacred Myths — *McFarlane, Marilyn*
y Sacred Origins of Profound Things — *Panati, Charles*
Sacred Pampering Principles — *Gandy, Debrena
Jackson*
The Sacred Place — *Olsen, W Scott*
c Sacred Places (Illus. by David Shannon) — *Yolen,
Jane*
Sacred Plant Medicine — *Buhner, Stephen Harrod*
Sacred Practices for Conscious Living — *Napier,
Nancy J*
Sacred Reading — *Casey, Michael, Monk of
Tarrawarra*
Sacred Realm — *Fine, Steven*
The Sacred Rules of Management — *Smith, Stanley E*
Sacred Seasons — *Isaacs, Ronald H*
Sacred Sites of the West — *Barlow, Bernyce*
Sacred Song from the Byzantine Pulpit — *Schork, R J*
A Sacred Union of Citizens — *Spalding, Matthew*
Sacrifice — *Smith, Mitchell*
The Sacrifice — *Wiseman, Adele*

Sacrifice of Fools — *McDonald, Ian*
Sacrifice of Isaac — *Gordon, Neil*
Sacrificed for Honor — *Kertzer, David I*
Sacrificed Wife/Sacrificer's Wife — *Jamison,
Stephanie W*
Sacrificial Logics — *Weir, Allison*
Sacrificing Commentary — *Goodhart, Sandor*
c The Sad Story of Veronica Who Played the Violin
— *McKee, David*
c Sad Underwear and Other Complications (Illus. by
Richard Hull) — *Viorst, Judith*
y Saddam Hussein: Absolute Ruler of Iraq — *Stefoff,
Rebecca*
Saddlepoint Approximations — *Jensen, Jens Ledet*
Sade and the Narrative of Transgression — *Allison,
David B*
Sade's Wife — *Crosland, Margaret*
c Sadie the Shrew — *Buck, Gisela*
Sadness — *Yang, William*
Safad — *Ben David, Arieh*
Safe and Easy Lawn Care — *Ellis, Barbara*
Safe House — *Shulman, Burton*
y Safe in America — *Hershman, Marcie*
c Safe in the Spotlight (Runger). Audio Version
— *Scott, Elaine*
y Safe People — *Cloud, Henry*
c The Safe Place — *Peterseil, Tehila*
c A Safe Place — *Vigna, Judith*
c Safe Return — *Dexter, Catherine*
Safe Schools — *Stephens, Ronald D*
r The Safe Shopper's Bible — *Steinman, David*
Safe Surfing — *McKeehan, Julie*
Safe Uses of Cortisol. 2nd Ed. — *Jefferies, William
McK.*
c Safety City (Illus. by Roger DeKlerk) — *Rodman,
Edmon J*
Safety Engineering and Risk Analysis — *Mintz, F J*
Safety in the Handling of Cryogenic Fluids
— *Edeskuty, Frederick J*
Safety Management — *Gustin, Joseph F*
Safety Management — *Pybus, Roger*
Safety Net — *Coll, Blanche D*
Safety, Systems and People — *Cox, Sue*
Safeware: System Safety and Computers — *Leveson,
Nancy G*
The Saga of Anthropology in China — *Guldin,
Gregory Eliyu*
p Sage Range Review
Sage, Saint, and Sophist — *Anderson, Graham*
La Sagesse Et Le Monde — *Fedou, Michel*
Saggi. Vols. 1-2 — *Calvino, Italo*
y Sahara Unveiled — *Langewiesche, William*
Sai Gon Nang Nho Mua Thuong — *Nguyen, Thi Ngoc
Dung*
c Sailaway Home (Illus. by Bruce Degen) — *Degen,
Bruce*
Sailing at the U.S. Naval Academy — *McNitt, Robert
W*
Sailing in a Spoonful of Water — *Coomer, Joe*
Sailing on a Budget — *Johnson, Anne M*
Sailing on the Ice — *Stevens, C A*
r Sailing on the Silver Screen — *Suid, Lawrence H*
Sailing to Australia — *Hassam, Andrew*
Sailing with Byzantium from Europe to America
— *Weitzmann, Kurt*
c Sailor — *Church, Caroline*
c Sailor Bear (Illus. by Virginia Austin) — *Waddell,
Martin*
Sailors Guide to the Windward Islands. 8th Ed.
— *Doyle, Chris*
Sails Full and By — *Degnon, Dom*

r The Saint: A Complete History in Print, Radio, Film
and Television of Leslie Charteris' Robin Hood of
Modern Crime, Simon Templar 1928-1992
— *Barer, Burl*
r St. Bernard Church Records, Alpena, Michigan 1864-
1925
St. Burl's Obituary — *Akst, Daniel*
St. Catherine's Parish Dublin 1840-1900 — *Crawford,
John*
Saint Ephrem's Commentary on Tatian's Diatessaron
— *McCarthy, Carmel*
St. Famous — *Dee, Jonathan*
Saint Foucault — *Halperin, David M*
c Saint Francis (Illus. by Brian Wildsmith)
— *Wildsmith, Brian*
r The St. Gall Tractate — *Grotans, Anna A*
c Saint George and the Dragon — *Hodges, Margaret*
St. Gregory of Nyssa and the Tradition of the Fathers
— *Azkoul, Michael*
Saint Hysteria — *Mazzoni, Cristina*
St. James Episcopal Church, Baton Rouge — *Bond,
Edward L*
yr St. James Guide to Fantasy Writers — *Pringle, David*
r St. James Guide to Science Fiction Writers. 4th Ed.
— *Pederson, Jay P*
St. Katherine of Alexandria — *Nevanlinna, Saara*
The St. Kitts Monkey Feuds — *Lieberman, Laurence*
r St. Lucia — *Momsen, Janet Henshall*
r St. Lucia — *Philpott, Don*
St. Martin De Porres: The Little Stories and the
Semiotics of Culture — *Garcia-Rivera, Alex*
Saint Mary Mazzarello: The Spirit of Joy — *Agasso,
Domenico*
St. Mary's of Natchez. Vols. 1-2 — *Nolan, Charles E*
St. Paul versus St. Peter — *Goulder, Michael*
St. Paul's Theology of Proclamation — *Litfin, A Duane*
Saint Peter's Fair. Audio Version — *Peters, Ellis*
St. Petersburg: A Cultural History — *Volkov, Solomon*
St. Petersburg: Architecture of the Tsars
— *Shvidkovskii, D O*
St. Petersburg Dialogues — *Maistre, Joseph Marie,
Comte De*
Saint-Porchaire Ceramics — *Barbour, Daphne*
St. Teresa of Avila: Author of a Heroic Life — *Slade,
Carole*
Saint Thomas Aquinas. Vol. 1 — *Torrell, Jean-Pierre*
St. Vincent De Paul of Baltimore — *Spalding, Thomas
W*
y Saint Vitus' Dance — *Rubalcaba, Jill*
Saint Vitus Dances Eternity — *Von Allmen, Stewart*
Sainte Jeanne De Chantal: Correspondance. Vols. 1-5
— *Chantal, Jeanne-Francoise De, Saint*
Saintre. Vols. 1-2 — *La Sale, Antoine De*
c Saints — *Sauvain, Philip*
Saints Alive — *Schreiber, Gayle*
Saints in Exile — *Sanders, Cheryl J*
The Saints in Iceland — *Cormack, Margaret*
c Saints of Scotland (Illus. by Adrienne Salgado)
— *Dunlop, Eileen*
Saints Rest — *Gifford, Thomas*
Une Saison En Banlieue — *Jazouli, Adil*
Les Saisons De Passage — *Chedid, Andree*
Salad Suppers — *Chesman, Andrea*
c Salamanders — *Maruska, Edward*
Salammbo — *Flaubert, Gustave*
Salem Story — *Rosenthal, Bernard*
Salli Koistisen Talvisota — *Skiftesvik, Joni*
Sally — *North, Freya*
c Sally Ann Thunder Ann Whirlwind Crockett (Illus. by
Steven Kellogg) — *Kellogg, Steven*
c Sally Arnold — *Ryan, Cheryl*

c Sally's Christmas Miracle (Illus. by Charles M Schulz) — Schulz, Charles M

c The Salmon (Illus. by Colin Newman) — Crewe, Sabrina

Salo Wittmayer Baron: Architect of Jewish History — Liberles, Robert

Salome of the Tenements — Yezierska, Anzia

El Salon Dorado — Corral Lafuente, Jose Luis

The Saloon on the Rocky Mountain Mining Frontier — West, Elliott

Salsa! Havana Heat, Bronx Beat — Calvo Ospina, Hernando

Salse Di Pomodoro — Della Croce, Julia

Salt — Lovelace, Earl

c The Salt and Pepper Boys — Willis, Jean

Salt Dancers — Hegi, Ursula

p Salt Hill Journal

Salt of the Earth — Olsen, Jack

Salt of the Earth (Bottino). Audio Version — Olsen, Jack

Salt Water — Motion, Andrew

c Salta, Ranita, Salta! (Illus. by Byron Barton). Book and Audio Version — Kalan, Robert

c Salta Y Brinca (Illus. by Ellen Stoll Walsh) — Walsh, Ellen Stoll

c Saltarin (Illus. by Marcus Pfister) — Pfister, Marcus

Saluti Da Palermo — Russo, Enzo

Salvador Dali: Masterpieces from the Collection of the Salvador Dali Museum — Wach, Kenneth

Salvador Dali's Art and Writing 1927-1942 — Finkelstein, Haim

Salvation on Sand Mountain — Covington, Dennis

Salvator Rosa: His Life and Times — Scott, Jonathan

Sam and Angie — Sweatman, Margaret

Sam and His Brother Len — Manderino, John

c Sam and the Lucky Money (Illus. by Cornelius Van Wright) — Chinn, Karen

c Sam and the Tigers (Illus. by Jerry Pinkney) — Lester, Julius

Sam Golod: A Novel of St. Petersburg — Creswell, Sophia

c Sam Houston: Texas Hero — Sanford, William R

Sam Peckinpah: If They Move, Kill 'Em — Weddle, David

c Sam Plants a Sunflower (Illus. by Axel Scheffler) — Petty, Kate

Sam Shepard — DeRose, David J

c Sam Sunday and the Mystery at the Ocean Beach Hotel (Illus. by Will Hillenbrand) — Supraner, Robyn

c Sam the Garbage Hound (Illus. by Gary Bialke) — Simon, Charnan

c Samantha (Illus. by Ellen Stoll Walsh) — Walsh, Ellen Stoll

y Samantha Crane on the Run — Cooney, Linda A

Samareia: Antike Quellen Zur Geschichte Und Kultur Der Samaritaner In Deutscher Ubersetzung — Zangenberg, Jurgen

Les Samaritains: Histoire D'Une Legende Israel Et La Province De Samarie — Macchi, Jean-Daniel

Samarkand: A Novel — Maalouf, Amin

Samba: Resistance in Motion — Browning, Barbara

The Same and Not the Same — Hoffmann, Roald

Same Blue Chevy — Walden, Gale Renee

Same Place, Same Things — Gautreaux, Tim

The Same River Twice — Walker, Alice

Same-Sex Dynamics among Nineteenth-Century Americans — Quinn, D Michael

Same-Sex Marriage — Baird, Robert M

Same-Sex Marriage, Pro and Con — Sullivan, Andrew

Same-Sex Unions in Premodern Europe — Boswell, John

r Same Time...Same Station — Lackmann, Ron

p Samizdat

Samlede Dikt 1973-1994 — Aamodt, Bjorn

Sammy Davis Jr., My Father — Davis, Tracey

The Samoa Islands. Vol. 2 — Kramer, Augustine

Samovar — Koval, Ramona

Sampling in Digital Signal Processing and Control — Feuer, Arie

r Sampling Systems for Process Analysers. 2nd Ed. — Carr-Brion, K G

Sampling the Book — Losse, Deborah N

Sampras: A Legend in the Works — Branham, H A

c Sam's Duck (Illus. by Keith Bowen) — Morpurgo, Michael

c Sam's Pizza — Pelham, David

c Sam's Wild West Show (Illus. by Simms Taback) — Antle, Nancy

Samtliche Werke — Nestroy, Johann

Samtliche Werke Und Briefe. Vols. 1-3 — Holderlin, Friedrich

Samuel Beckett: The Complete Short Prose 1929-1989 — Beckett, Samuel

Samuel Beckett: The Last Modernist — Cronin, Anthony

Samuel Beckett's Mal Vu Mal Dit — Beckett, Samuel

Samuel Hartlib and Universal Reformation — Greengrass, Mark

r Samuel Johnson: A Dictionary of the English Language. Electronic Media Version

r The Samuel Johnson Encyclopedia — Rogers, Pat

Samuel Johnson: Literature, Religion and English Cultural Politics from the Restoration to Romanticism — Clark, J C D

Samuel Marsden: The Great Survivor — Yarwood, A T

r Samuel Taylor Coleridge: An Annotated Bibliography of Criticism and Scholarship. Vol. 3, Pts. 1-2 — Crawford, Walter B

Samuel Von Pufendorf: Naturrecht Und Staat — Behme, Thomas

The Samurai — Endo, Shusaku

c A Samurai Castle (Illus. by David Antram) — Macdonald, Fiona

Samurai from Outer Space — Levi, Antonia

San Antonio De Bexar — Teja, Jesus F De La

San Cristobal: Voices and Visions of the Galisteo Basin — Mednick, Christina Singleton

r San Francisco — O'Reilly, James

r San Francisco Almanac. Rev. Ed. — Hansen, Gladys

The San Francisco Chronicle Cookbook — Bauer, Michael

The San Francisco School of Abstract Expressionism — Landauer, Susan

r San Marino — Edwards, Adrian

San Mythistorima — Kiourtsakis, Yannis

Sancta Sanctorum — Pietrangeli, Carlo

The Sanctified South — Brasher, J Lawrence

Sanctity of Life and Human Dignity — Bayertz, Kurt

The Sanctity of Rural Life — Baranowski, Shelley

Le Sanctuaire Grec — Schachter, A

Sanctuaries of Spanish New Mexico — Treib, Marc

y Sanctuary — De Goldi, Kate

Sanctuary — Roberts, Nora

Sanctuary: A Tale of Life in the Woods — Monette, Paul

The Sanctuary Man — Beven, A R

Sanctuary Stories — Smith, Michael, 1943-

Sand — James, Will

y Sand and Fog — Brandenburg, Jim

The Sandinista Legacy — Luciak, Ilja A

Sandino's Daughter Revisited — Randall, Margaret

The Sandlot Game — Wimme, Dick

Sandlot Seasons — Ruck, Rob

c The Sandman — Poortvliet, Rien

Sandman Blues — Bourguignon, Stephane

y The Sandman: Book of Dreams — Gaiman, Neil

y Sandra Day O'Connor, Independent Thinker — Herda, D J

Sandra Nichols Found Dead (Esmo). Audio Version — Higgins, George V

c Sandra's Sun Hat (Illus. by Pierre Pratt) — Roche, Hannah

Sands of the Well — Levertov, Denise

y The Sandy Bottom Orchestra — Keillor, Garrison

Sandy Dennis: A Personal Memoir — Dennis, Sandy

Sankofa: African Thought and Education — Tedla, Ellini

Sankofa: Stories, Proverbs and Poems of an African Childhood — Abdulai, David

y Sans Signature — Bell, William

Santa and Son — Logan, Leandra

p Santa Barbara Review

c Santa Calls Gift Box — Joyce, William

Santa Evita — Martinez, Tomas Eloy

y Santa Evita (Grifasi). Audio Version — Martinez, Tomas Eloy

The Santa Fe Trail — Crutchfield, James A

c Santa through the Window — Gomi, Taro

c Santa's Busy Christmas (Illus. by Delana Bettoli) — Chambers, Julie

c Santa's New Reindeer (Illus. by Dan Rodriguez) — Schrecker, Judie

c Santa's Sackful of Best Christmas Ideas — Robins, Deri

c Santa's Twin (Illus. by Phil Parks) — Koontz, Dean

y Santa's Twin (Sanders). Audio Version — Koontz, Dean

c Santa's Workshop (Illus. by Paul Stickland) — Stickland, Paul

c The Santasaurus (Illus. by Bartt Warburton) — Sheldon, Mary, 1955-

y The Santee Sioux — Bonvillain, Nancy

Santeria Aesthetics in Contemporary Latin American Art — Lindsay, Arturo

Il Santo Peccatore — Crovi, Raffaele

Santos and Saints — Steele, Thomas J

Sap Rising — Gill, A A

Sapientie Immarcessibilis — Mingroot, Erik Van

Saponins Used in Food and Agriculture — Waller, George R

Saponins Used in Traditional and Modern Medicine — Waller, George R

Sappho Is Burning — Dubois, Page

Sappho through English Poetry — Jay, Peter

Sappho's Lyre

Saraband for Two Sisters (Sandison). Audio Version — Carr, Philippa

y Sarah and the People of Sand River (Illus. by Ian Wallace) — Valgardson, W D

y Sarah Bishop (Haas). Audio Version — O'Dell, Scott

Sarah Fielding — Bree, Linda

y Sarah on Her Own — Coombs, Karen M

y Sarah Royce and the American West — Shuter, Jane

y Sarah with an H — Irwin, Hadley

c Sarah's House — Thomas, Eric

Sarah's Psalm — Ladd, Florence

c Sarah's Shovel (Illus. by Anthea Sieveking) — MacKinnon, Debbie

y Sarah's Song — Burns, Janice A

c Sarah's Story (Illus. by Eve Aldridge) — Harley, Bill

Sarajevo Days, Sarajevo Nights — Softic, Elma

y Saratoga — Friedman, Michael Jan

r I Sarcofagi Romani in Sicilia — Tusa, Vincenzo

Sardonic Smile — Lateiner, Donald

Sari Dialect — Yoshie, Satoko

The Sari: Styles, Patterns, History, Techniques — Lynton, Linda

c Sarn, the Story of an Otter (Illus. by Kenneth Lilly) — Potter, Tessa

Sartre — Howells, Christina

p Sartre Studies International

c Sasha and the Wind (Illus. by Helene Desputeaux) — Tregebov, Rhea

The Saskatchewan Air Quality Task Force

Saskatchewan's Protected Areas — Appleby, A

y The Saskiad — Hall, Brian

Sassafrass, Cypress, and Indigo — Shange, Ntozake

Satanic Ritual Abuse — Ross, Colin

Satan's Fire — Doherty, P C

Satan's Silence — Matthews, Alex

Satan's Silence — Nathan, Debbie

Satan's Stones — Ravanipur, Moniru

c Satchmo's Blues (Illus. by Floyd Cooper) — Schroeder, Alan

c Satchmo's Blues (James). Audio Version — Schroeder, Alan

The Satellite Communication Applications Handbook — Elbert, Bruce R

Satellite Projects Handbook — Harris, Lawrence

c Satellites — Fox, Mary Virginia

c Satellites — Parker, Steve

Sati, the Blessing and the Curse — Hawley, John Stratton

Satie Remembered — Orledge, Robert

Satire and Sentiment 1660-1830 — Rawson, Claude

Satires. Bk. 1 — Juvenal

Satiric Impersonations — Schechter, Joel

Satirical Apocalypse — Cook, Jonathan A

y Satisfied with Nothin' — Hill, Ernest

SATs, the Inside Story — Sainsbury, Marian

c Saturday Sancocho (Illus. by Leyla Torres) — Torres, Leyla

Saturday's Child — Fairclough, Ellen Louks

Saturn Rukh — Forward, Robert L

Saturn's Child — Nichols, Nichelle

Satyrica (Branham) — Petronius Arbiter

The Satyricon (Walsh) — Petronius Arbiter

Sau Con Mua — Nguyen, Duc An

Sauces: Sweet and Savory, Classic and New — Roux, Michel

Saudades Do Brasil — Levi-Strauss, Claude

Saudi Arabia: The Coming Storm — Wilson, Peter W

Sauja Medaus — Keleras, Julius

Saul Bellow and the Struggle at the Center — Hollahan, Eugene

Saule Merktie — Bels, Alberts

Saul's Book — Rogers, Paul T

Saunders Interactive General Chemistry CD-ROM. Electronic Media Version — Kotz, John C

Savage Art — Polito, Robert

Title Index

Savage Cut — *Dereske, Jo*
The Savage Freud and Other Essays on Possible and Retrievable Selves — *Nandy, Ashis*
Savage Pilgrims — *Shukman, Henry*
Savages — *Kane, Joe*
The Savannah River Chiefdoms — *Anderson, David G*
c Save Brave Ted (Illus. by Charlotte Hard) — *Maisner, Heather*
c Save My Rainforest — *Zak, Monica*
c Save the Rain Forests — *Fowler, Allan*
The Save Your Heart Wine Guide — *Jones, Frank*
Saved by the Telling — *Tihanyi, Eva*
Saving Biodiversity
Saving Face — *Schneiderman, Stuart*
A Saving Grace — *Crozier, Lorna*
y Saving Grace — *Smith, Lee*
y Saving Jessica — *McDaniel, Lurlene*
Saving Old Glory — *Goldstein, Robert Justin*
Saving Our Sons — *Golden, Marita*
c Saving Places
The Saving Remnant — *Cowing, Cedric B*
Saving St. Germ — *Muske, Carol*
c Saving Sweetness (Illus. by G Brian Karas) — *Stanley, Diane*
Saving the Constitution from the Courts — *Gangi, William*
y Saving the Environment — *Gay, Kathlyn*
Saving the Oceans — *MacInnis, Joseph*
Saving the Salmon — *Mighetto, Lisa*
Saving Work — *Chopp, Rebecca S*
Saving Your Skin — *Kenet, Barney J*
c The Savior Is Born (Freeman) (Illus. by Robert Van Nutt). Book and Electronic Media Version — *Gleeson, Brian*
Savoldos Sogenanntes Bildnis Des Gaston De Foix — *Martin, Andrew John*
Savoring the Day — *Hurley, Judith Benn*
Savory Suppers and Fashionable Feasts — *Williams, Susan, 1948-*
Sawai Jai Singh and His Astronomy — *Sharma, Virendra Nath*
c Sawgrass Poems (Illus. by Ted Levin) — *Asch, Frank*
y The Sawtooth Wolves (Illus. by Jim Dutcher) — *Dutcher, Jim*
Saxophone Dreams — *Royle, Nicholas, 1963-*
r Sax's Dangerous Properties of Industrial Materials. 9th Ed., Vols. 1-3 — *Lewis, Richard J*
c Say Cheese! (Illus. by Tim Archbold) — *Owen, Gareth*
y Say Goodnight, Gracie — *Deaver, Julie Reece*
c Say Hola to Spanish (Illus. by Loretta Lopez) — *Elya, Susan Middleton*
c Say Please — *Austin, Virginia*
Say You Love Me — *Lindsey, Johanna*
Saying Grace — *Gutcheon, Beth*
Saying the Right Thing — *DiZazzo, Raymond*
c Sayonara, Mrs. Kackleman (Illus. by Maira Kalman) — *Kalman, Maira*
Scaasi: A Cut Above — *Scaasi, Arnold*
Scale in Conscious Experience — *King, Joseph*
Scaling and Renormalization in Statistical Physics — *Cardy, John*
Scaling the Ivory Tower — *Cyr, Dianne J*
c Scaly Things — *Lamprell, Klay*
Scam — *Hall, Parnell*
Scandal in the Ink — *Robinson, Christopher*
The Scandal of Pleasure — *Steiner, Wendy*
The Scandal of the Gospels — *McCracken, David*
A Scandalous Providence — *Tupper, E Frank*
r Scandinavian Atlas of Historic Towns. Vols. 1-8 — *Stromstad, Triis*
Scandinavian Cross Stitch Designs — *Lindberg, Jana Hauschild*
c Scandinavian Ghost Stories and Other Tales of the Supernatural — *Asala, Joanne*
Scandinavian Immigrants and Education in North America — *Anderson, Philip J*
r Scandinavian Immigrants in New York 1630-1674 — *Evjen, John O*
r Scandinavian Personal Names in Norfolk — *Insley, John*
The Scandinavian Reformation — *Grell, Ole Peter*
The Scapegoat — *Settle, Mary Lee*
Scapegoat: General Percival of Singapore — *Kinvig, Clifford*
The Scapegoat Generation — *Males, Mike A*
A Scapegoat in the New Wilderness — *Jaher, Frederic Cople*
Lo Scapigliato In Archivio — *Tamiozzo Goldmann, Silvana*
c The Scarecrow of Oz (Illus. by John R Neill) — *Baum, L Frank*

The Scared Child — *Brooks, Barbara*
c Scared of a Bear — *Offen, Hilda*
c Scaredy Cat (Illus. by Joan Rankin) — *Rankin, Joan*
c Scaredy Dog (Illus. by Marilyn Mets) — *Thomas, Jane Resh*
The Scarlet Landscape — *Tettman, Elizabeth*
The Scarlet Letter — *Hawthorne, Nathaniel*
Scarlet Memorial — *Cheng, I*
Scarlet Music — *Ohanneson, Joan*
The Scarlet Rider — *Sussex, Lucy*
Scarlet Women — *Christilian, J D*
Scars — *Meinke, Peter*
c Scary Howl of Fame — *Scarborough, Sheryl*
c Scary Science (Illus. by Dusan Petricic) — *Funston, Sylvia*
c Scary Sights and Funny Frights (Illus. by Nathan Young Jarvis) — *Tomaselli, Doris*
y Scatter His Ashes (Stafford). Audio Version — *Ferrars, Elizabeth*
Scatter Matrix — *Child, Abigail*
Scattered among the Nations — *Rubin, Alexis*
Scattered Hegemonies — *Grewal, Inderpal*
A Scattering of Salts — *Merrill, James*
Scavengers, Recyclers, and Solutions for Solid Waste Management in Indonesia — *Sicular, Daniel T*
Scenario Studies for the Rural Environment — *Symposium Scenario Studies for the Rural Environment (1994: Wageningen, Netherlands)*
Scenarios of Power. Vol. 1 — *Wortman, Richard S*
Scenes for Mandarins — *Birch, Cyril*
y Scenes from a Sistah — *Files, Lolita*
c Scenes from Peter Rabbit — *Potter, Beatrix*
y Scenes from Plays — *Marland, Michael*
Scenes from the Life of a City — *Homberger, Eric*
c Scenes from Tom Kitten — *Potter, Beatrix*
The Scenic Daguerreotype — *Wood, John*
The Scent of Dried Roses — *Lott, Tim*
The Scent of Power — *Mitchell, Susan, 1945-*
r Scented Geraniums — *Becker, Jim*
Scented Treasures — *Donaldson, Stephanie*
The Scepter and the Star — *Collins, John J*
Scepticism in the History of Philosophy — *Popkin, Richard H*
A Sceve Celebration — *Nash, Jerry C*
Schaduwboksen — *Koevoets, Pamela*
Schedule Two — *Dold, Gaylord*
Scheduling Algorithms — *Brucker, Peter*
Scheduling Divisible Loads in Parallel and Distributed Systems — *Bharadwaj, Veeravalli*
Der Scheidungsprozess Von Gottfried Kellers Mutter — *Wurgau, Rainer*
Scheler's Critique of Kant's Ethics — *Blosser, Philip*
Schelling and the End of Idealism — *Snow, Dale E*
Schelling's Philosophy of Mythology and Revelation — *Schelling, Friedrich Wilhelm Joseph Von*
Scherenschnitte: Designs and Techniques for Traditional Papercutting — *Schlapfer-Geiser, Susanne*
Schillers Dramen — *Guthke, Karl S*
Schismatrix Plus — *Sterling, Bruce*
Schizophrenia: Exploring the Spectrum of Psychosis — *Ancill, R J*
Schliemann of Troy — *Traill, David A*
Schmitz, Svevo, Zeno — *Palmieri, Giovanni*
Schneider on Schneider — *Schneider, David M*
c Schnitzel Von Krumm Forget-Me-Not (Illus. by Lynley Dodd) — *Dodd, Lynley*
c Schnorky the Wave Puncher! (Illus. by Jeff Raglus) — *Raglus, Jeff*
The Schocken Book of Jewish Mystical Testimonies — *Jacobs, Louis*
Scholar of Decay — *Huff, Tanya*
Scholarly Editing — *Greetham, D C*
Scholarly Publishing — *Peek, Robin P*
The Scholar's Courtesy — *Cronin, Blaise*
yr Scholarships, Grants, Fellowships, and Endowments — *Johnson, Loretta*
cr Scholastic Atlas of Exploration — *Starkey, Dinah*
cr Scholastic Children's Dictionary
cr Scholastic Encyclopedia of the North American Indian — *Ciment, James*
cr Scholastic Encyclopedia of Women in the United States — *Keenan, Sheila*
Scholastic Guide to Balanced Reading — *Baltas, Joyce*
Scholastic Humanism and the Unification of Europe. Vol. 1 — *Southern, R W*
yp Scholastic Update
c Scholastic's The Magic School Bus Explores the Human Body. Electronic Media Version
c Scholastic's The Magic School Bus Explores the Solar System. Electronic Media Version

r The Schomberg Center Guide to Black Literature from the Eighteenth Century to the Present — *Valade, Roger M, III*
Schones Deutschland — *Becker, Thorsten*
Schonheit Des Lebens — *Dannenberg, Matthias*
School Administration — *Jacobson, Stephen L*
The School Bag — *Heaney, Seamus*
School-Based Prevention for Children at Risk — *Cowen, Emory L*
School-Based Reform — *Quellmalz, Edys*
c School Campout — *Citra, Becky*
School Days — *Chamoiseau, Patrick*
School Figures — *Song, Cathy*
c A School for Pompey Walker (Illus. by Aminah Brenda Lynn Robinson) — *Rosen, Michael J*
School for Women — *Miller, Jane*
A School in the Hills — *Stewart, Katharine*
School Library Journal's Best — *Gerhardt, Lillian*
c The School Mouse (Illus. by Cynthia Fisher) — *King-Smith, Dick*
The School Music Program — *MENC Task Force for National Standards in the Arts*
y School News Shows — *Wallace, Virginia*
School of Hard Knocks — *Murray, Donna Huston*
c School Safety (Illus. by Penny Dann) — *Loewen, Nancy*
c School Supplies (Illus. by Renee Flower) — *Hopkins, Lee Bennett*
School Talk — *Eder, Donna*
A School Teacher in Old Alaska — *Breece, Hannah*
The School Tradition of the Old Testament — *Heaton, E W*
c School Trouble (Illus. by Lesley Harker) — *Bruce, Lisa*
School Wars — *Gaddy, Barbara B*
School Work — *Biklen, Sari Knopp*
Schooling the Generations in the Politics of Prison
Schooling the New South — *Leloudis, James L*
c The Schoolmasters — *Fisher, Leonard Everett*
Schools as Learning Communities — *Clark, David*
r Schools, Communities, and the Arts
Schools Count — *Heneveld, Ward*
c Schools in Victorian Times — *Stephen, Margaret*
Schools of Thought in International Relations — *Thompson, Kenneth W*
Schools, Violence, and Society — *Hoffman, Allan M*
The Schools We Need and Why We Don't Have Them — *Hirsch, E D*
A Schoolteacher in Old Alaska — *Breece, Hannah*
The Schooner Bertha L. Downs — *Greenhill, Basil*
Schopenhauer on the Character of the World — *Atwell, John E*
Schotenkloster: Irische Benediktinerkonvente Im Hochmittelalterlichen Deutschland — *Flachenecker, Helmut*
Schriftlichkeit Im Fruhen Mittelalter — *Schaefer, Ursula*
Schrodinger Diffusion Processes — *Aebi, Robert*
Schrodinger's Kittens and the Search for Reality — *Gribbin, John*
Schubert: The Music and the Man — *Newbould, Brian*
Schubert's Complete Song Texts. Vol. 1 — *Schubert, Franz*
Schubert's Poets and the Making of Lieder — *Youens, Susan*
Die Schulpolitik Des Faschistischen Regimes In Italien 1922-1943 — *Charnitzky, Jurgen*
p Schumann Studien
Schumpeter in the History of Ideas — *Shionoya, Yuichi*
r Schweizer Briefmarken Katalog 1996
Schweizer Theologen Im Zarenreich 1700-1917 — *Schneider, Harry*
p Schweizerische Nationalbank Quartalsheft
Science and Civilisation in China. Vol. 5, Pt. 6 — *Needham, Joseph*
Science and Civilisation in China. Vol. 6, Pt. 3 — *Needham, Joseph*
Science and Dissent in Post-Mao China — *Miller, H Lyman*
Science and Ecosystem Management in the National Parks — *Halvorson, William L*
p Science and Engineering Ethics
The Science and Engineering of Microelectronic Fabrication — *Campbell, Stephen A*
Science and Innovation as Strategic Tools for Industrial and Economic Growth — *NATO Advanced Research Workshop on Science and Innovation as Strategic Tools for Industrial and Economic Growth (1994: Moscow, Russia)*

Science and Instruments in Seventeenth-Century Italy — *Bedini, Silvio A*

The Science and Politics of Racial Research — *Tucker, William H, 1940-*

Science and Religion in the Era of William James. Vol. 1 — *Croce, Paul Jerome*

Science and Social Status — *Sturdy, David J*

r Science and Technical Writing

r Science and Technology: A Purchase Guide for Libraries 1995

r Science and Technology Firsts — *Bruno, Leonard C*

Science and Technology in a Multicultural World — *Hess, David J*

Science and the Endangered Species Act — *National Research Council (U.S.). Committee on Scientific Issues in the Endangered Species Act*

Science and the Founding Fathers — *Cohen, I Bernard*

Science and the Perception of Nature — *Klonk, Charlotte*

Science and the Practice of Medicine in the Nineteenth Century — *Bynum, W F*

Science and the Quiet Art — *Weatherall, David*

Science and the Raj 1857-1905 — *Kumar, Deepak*

Science and the Secrets of Nature — *Eamon, William*

Science and the Shape of Orthodoxy — *Hunter, Michael Cyril William*

c Science around the World (Illus. by Laurel Aiello) — *Levine, Shar*

Science as a Questioning Process — *Sanitt, Nigel*

Science at the Bar — *Jasanoff, Sheila*

c The Science Book of Color — *Ardley, Neil*

c The Science Book of the Senses — *Ardley, Neil*

r Science Books and Films' Best Books for Children 1992-1995 — *Gath, Tracy*

r Science Books for Young People — *Phelan, Carolyn*

c The Science Chef (Illus. by Tina Cash-Walsh) — *D'Amico, Joan*

c The Science Chef Travels around the World (Illus. by Tina Cash-Walsh) — *D'Amico, Joan*

Science Communication and Development — *Vilanilam, J V*

Science Economique — *Meidinger, Claude*

cr Science Experiments Index for Young People. 2nd Ed. — *Pilger, Mary Anne*

y Science Experiments You Can Eat. Rev. and Updated Ed. — *Cobb, Vicki*

y Science Explained — *Ronan, Colin A*

c The Science Explorer (Illus. by Jason Gorski) — *Murphy, Pat*

y Science Fair Projects with Electricity and Electronics (Illus. by Karen McKee) — *Bonnet, Bob*

yr Science Fiction: A Visual Encyclopedia — *Clute, John*

Science Fiction after 1900 — *Landon, Brooks*

r Science Fiction and Fantasy Literature 1975-1991 — *Reginald, Robert*

Science Fiction and the Theatre — *Willingham, Ralph*

Science Fiction Audiences — *Jenkins, Henry*

y The Science Fiction Century — *Hartwell, David G*

Science Fiction Fandom — *Sanders, Joe*

r Science Fiction Television Series — *Phillips, Mark*

r Science Fiction: The Illustrated Encyclopedia

yr Science Fiction: The Multimedia Encyclopedia of Science Fiction. Electronic Media Version

Science for a Polite Society — *Sutton, Geoffrey V*

Science for All — *Brock, William H*

Science for All Children — *National Science Resources Center (U.S.)*

Science Framework for the 1996 National Assessment of Educational Progress

r Science Frontiers and Biological Anomalies — *Corliss, William R*

y Science Handbook for Students, Writers and Science Buffs

Science Has No National Borders — *Yoshikawa, Hideo*

c Science in Action Books 1-4 — *Harrison, Patricia*

Science in Primary Schools — *Harris, Sue*

Science in the Field — *Kuklick, Henrika*

Science in the Making. Vol. 1 — *Davis, E A*

Science in the Pleasure Ground — *Hay, Ida*

Science, Industry, and the Social Order in Post-Revolutionary France — *Fox, Robert*

Science, Jews, and Secular Culture — *Hollinger, David A*

Science Lessons — *New, W H*

Science, Medicine, and the State in Germany — *Tuchman, Arleen Marcia*

Science, Nonscience, and Nonsense — *Zimmerman, Michael, 1953-*

Science Now! — *Richardson, Ian*

The Science of Emotion — *Cornelius, Randolph R*

The Science of Empire — *Baber, Zaheer*

r Science of Flexibility. 2nd Ed. — *Alter, Michael J*

y The Science of Jurassic Park and the Lost World — *DeSalle, Rob*

The Science of the Mind — *Solso, Robert L*

The Science of the X-Files — *White, Michael*

Science of Whitewares — *Henkes, Victoria E*

y The Science of Words — *Miller, George A*

Science on the Run — *Bowker, Geoffrey C*

r Science on the Web — *Renehan, Edward J*

Science on Trial — *Angell, Marcia*

Science, Paradox, and the Moebius Principle — *Rosen, Steven M*

Science, Reason and Rhetoric — *Krips, Henry*

p Science Spectra: The International Magazine of Contemporary Scientific Thought

Science, Technology and Commercialization of Powder Synthesis and Shape Forming Processes — *Kingsley, J J*

Science, Technology, and Ecopolitics in the USSR — *Rezun, Miron*

r Science, Technology, and Society in the Third World — *Shrum, Wesley*

Science, Technology and the British Industrial Decline 1870-1970 — *Edgerton, David*

Science/Technology/Society as Reform in Science Education — *Yager, Robert E*

Science, Theology and the Transcendental Horizon — *Morrison, Roy D*

Science Today — *Levinson, Ralph*

cr Science Year 97

The Sciences of the Artificial. 3rd Ed. — *Simon, Herbert Alexander*

r The Scientific 100 — *Simmons, John*

Scientific Advances in Alternative Demilitarization Technologies — *NATO Advanced Research Workshop on Scientific Advances in Alternative Demilitarization Technologies (1995: Warsaw, Poland)*

r Scientific American Library: The Planets. Electronic Media Version

Scientific and Statistical Database Systems — *International Conference on Scientific and Statistical Database Systems (8th: 1996: Stockholm, Sweden)*

Scientific and Technical Communication — *Collier, James H*

Scientific Aspects of European Expansion — *Storey, William K*

Scientific Basis for Nuclear Waste Management. Vol. 19

Scientific Computing and Validated Numerics — *Alefeld, G*

Scientific Deception — *Grayson, Lesley*

The Scientific Education of Girls — *Commission De La Republique Francaise Pour L'Education, La Science Et La Culture*

Scientific Elite — *Zuckerman, Harriet*

The Scientific Enterprise in America — *Numbers, Ronald L*

The Scientific Foundations of Neurology — *Guthkelch, A Norman*

Scientific Knowledge — *Barnes, Barry*

The Scientific Letters and Papers of James Clerk Maxwell. Vol. 2 — *Maxwell, James Clerk*

Scientific Method — *Gower, Barry*

The Scientific Names of the British Lepidoptera — *Emmet, A Maitland*

Scientific Practice — *Buchwald, Jed Z*

Scientific Practice and Ordinary Action — *Lynch, Michael, 1948-*

Scientific Racism in Modern South Africa — *Dubow, Saul*

The Scientific Revolution — *Cohen, H F*

y The Scientific Revolution — *Henderson, Harry*

r The Scientific Revolution — *Jayawardene, S A*

The Scientific Revolution — *Shapin, Steven*

The Scientific Survey of Puerto Rico and the Virgin Islands — *Figueroa, Julio C*

Scientific Uncertainty and Environmental Problem Solving — *Lemons, John*

Scientific Unit Conversion — *Cardarelli, Francois*

The Scientific Voice — *Montgomery, Scott L*

A Scientist Speaks Out — *Seaborg, Glenn Theodore*

c The Scientist within You. Vol. 1, Rev. Ed. — *Warren, Rebecca Lowe*

yr The Scientist within You. Vol. 1, Rev. Ed.; Vol. 2 — *Warren, Rebecca Lowe*

c Scientists and Inventors (Illus. by John Dillow) — *Clarke, Danny*

Scientists and the Development of Nuclear Weapons — *Badash, Lawrence*

y Scientists in 90 Minutes — *Gribbin, John*

cr Scientists: The Lives and Works of 150 Scientists. Vols. 1-3 — *Saari, Peggy*

Scipione Borghese E L'Architettura — *Antinori, Aloisio*

r SciTech Reference PLUS 1995-1996. Electronic Media Version

SCO Companion — *Mohr, James*

Scoop (Cadell). Audio Version — *Waugh, Evelyn*

The Scope of Government — *Borre, Ole*

y The Scopes Trial — *Nardo, Don*

p Score

Scorn — *Parris, Matthew*

SCORP: Continuing the Tradition — *Indiana. Division of Outdoor Recreation*

y Scorpion Shards — *Shusterman, Neal*

c Scorpions — *Murray, Peter, 1952, Sep., 9-*

y Scorpions — *Myers, Walter Dean*

The Scorsese Connection — *Stern, Lesley*

Scotichronicon. Vol. 4 — *Bower, Walter*

r Scotland — *Brooke, Marcus*

c Scotland — *Bruycker, Daniel De*

r Scotland. 2nd Ed. — *Abram, Dave*

Scotland after Enlightenment — *Beveridge, Craig*

Scotland before the Industrial Revolution — *Whyte, Ian D*

Scotland County Emerging 1750-1900 — *Gibson, Joyce M*

c Scotland's Changing Landscapes — *Maclean, Kenneth*

Scots and Its Literature — *McClure, J Derrick*

The Scots and Parliament — *Jones, Clyve*

r The Scots Herbal — *Darwin, Tess*

r Scott 1996 Classic Specialized Catalogue

The Scott Report

The Scott Report and Its Appendices on CD-ROM. Electronic Media Version — *Scott, Richard*

c Scottie Pippen — *McMane, Fred*

Scottie, the Daughter of-- — *Lanahan, Eleanor Anne*

Scottish Ballads — *Lyle, Emily*

Scottish Elites — *Devine, T M*

The Scottish High Church Tradition in America — *Fisk, William Lyons*

Scottish Literature. Vols. 1-2 — *McCordick, David*

r The Scottish Nation. Vols G-S — *Anderson, William, 1805-1866*

The Scottish Regency of the Earl of Arran — *Franklin, David Byrd*

Scottish Theatre since the Seventies — *Stevenson, Randall*

Scottish Wild Plants — *Lusby, Philip*

The Scourging of Iraq — *Simons, Geoff*

Scrambled Eggs and Whiskey — *Carruth, Hayden*

Scrambles amongst the Alps — *Whymper, Edward*

Scraps — *Leiris, Michel*

Scratch an Actor — *Sherrin, Ned*

c Scratch and the Sniffs — *Lynch, Chris*

c Scratch City — *Gross, Philip*

c Scratch 'n' Sniff (Illus. by Gus Clarke) — *Clarke, Gus*

c Scream, Team! — *Stone, Tom*

c Screech Owl at Midnight Hollow (Komisar) (Illus. by Joel Snyder). Book and Audio Version — *Lamm, C Drew*

c The Screech Owl's Northern Adventure — *MacGregor, Roy*

Screen Smarts — *Degaetano, Gloria*

Screen Violence — *French, Karl*

Screening the Sacred — *Martin, Joel W*

Screw: Observations and Revelations of a Prison Officer — *Merlo, Pat*

Scribal Publication in Seventeenth-Century England — *Love, Harold*

Scribbling Women — *Showalter, Elaine*

Scribes and Illuminators — *De Hamel, Christopher*

Scribes and Translators — *Fernandez Marcos, Natalio*

Scribner's Best of the Fiction Workshops 1997

The Script of Decadence — *Donato, Eugenio*

Scripture and Community — *Folkert, Kendall W*

Scripture and Discernment — *Johnson, Luke Timothy*

Scripture and Ethics — *Siker, Jeffrey S*

Scripture and Homosexuality — *Soards, Marion L*

Scripture and the Church — *Sasse, Hermann*

Scripture and Translation — *Buber, Martin*

The Scripture on the Ten Kings and the Making of Purgatory in Medieval Chinese Buddhism — *Teiser, Stephen*

Scritti E Frammenti Autobiografici — *Leopardi, Giacomo*

Le Scritture Ai Tempi Di Gesu' — *Carbone, Sandro Paolo*

Scritture Private — *Sereni, Vittorio*

Scrivere La Storia — *Fumagalli, Vito*

c Scruffy: A Wolf Finds His Place in the Pack (Illus. by Jim Brandenburg) — Brandenburg, Jim
Scrutton on Charterparties and Bills of Lading. 20th Ed. — Scrutton, Thomas Edward, Sir
SCTV: Behind the Scenes — Thomas, Dave
Sculpted Stones — Montejo, Victor
Sculpting in Time — Tarkovskii, Andrei Arsen'evich
Sculpting with the Environment — Oakes, Baile
Sculptors and Physicians in Fifth-Century Greece — Metraux, Guy P R
c Sculpture (Illus. by Jean-Philippe Chabot)
y Sculpture and Ceramics — Dunn, Chris
Sculpture of Compassion — Ziegler, Joanna E
r The Sculpture of Jacques Lipchitz. Vol. 1 — Wilkinson, Alan G
The Sculpture of Ursula Von Rydingsvard — Von Rydingsvard, Ursula
Scurta Istorie A Cartii Romanesti — Simionescu, Dan
Scurta Istorie A Literaturii Romane — Micu, Dumitru
SDP: The Birth, Life and Death of the Social Democratic Party — Crewe, Ivor
c The Sea Baby (Illus. by Peter Bailey) — Dickinson, Susan
Sea Change — Earle, Sylvia
Sea Change — Nichols, Peter
y Sea Change — Purkis, Christine
Sea-Dumped Chemical Weapons — Kaffka, Alexander V
The Sea Family — Raymond, Diana
r Sea Fiction Guide — Smith, Myron J
The Sea Floor. 3rd Ed. — Seibold, Eugen
c Sea Horse — Stefoff, Rebecca
y The Sea Hunters — Cussler, Clive
The Sea Hunters (Naughton). Audio Version — Cussler, Clive
Sea-Level Rise and Coastal Subsidence — Milliman, John D
c The Sea Maidens of Japan (Illus. by Erin McGonigle Brammer) — Bell, Lili
y Sea Monkey Summer — Ware, Cheryl
The Sea of Galilee Boat — Wachsmann, Shelley
c The Sea of Tranquillity (Illus. by Christian Birmingham) — Haddon, Mark
The Sea of Trees — Murphy, Yannick
cr The Sea Otter — Silverstein, Alvin
c Sea Otters — Kalman, Bobbie
c Sea Searcher's Handbook — Armstrong, Pam
c Sea Stars and Dragons — Perry, Phyllis J
c Sea Sums (Illus. by Carol Schwartz) — Hulme, Joy N
c Sea Turtles — Lepthien, Emilie U
c Sea Watch (Illus. by Ted Lewin) — Yolen, Jane
c Seabirds — Flanagan, Alice K
c Seabirds — Rauzon, Mark J
Seabirds on Islands — Seabird Specialist Group Workshop (1990: Hamilton, New Zealand)
Seafaring in the Contemporary Pacific Islands — Feinberg, Richard
Seagull Beach — Metras, Gary
c Seal Surfer (Illus. by Michael Foreman) — Foreman, Michael
Sealed in Parchment — Hindman, Sandra
Sealed in Struggle — Vulpe, Nicola
c Seals — Woodward, John
Seamless Networks — Grinberg, Arkady
Seamus Heaney: A Celebration — Haviaras, Stratis
r Seamus Heaney: A Reference Guide — Durkan, Michael J
Seamus Heaney: The Shaping Spirit — Malloy, Catharine
r Sean O'Casey: A Research and Production Sourcebook — Schrank, Bernice
Sean Scully: Twenty Years 1979-1995 — Rifkin, Ned
Seapower: Theory and Practice — Till, Geoffrey
Seaquake — Neruda, Pablo
Search and Destroy — Miller, Jerome G
Search and Destroy #1-6 — Vale, V
Search and Seizure in the Public Schools. 2nd Ed. — Rossow, Lawrence F
The Search for Anti-Inflammatory Drugs — Merluzzi, Vincent J
The Search for Corporate Strategic Credibility — Higgins, Richard B
The Search for David — Schwimmer, George
c The Search for Dinosaurs — Dixon, Dougal
r The Search for Economics as a Science — Turgeon, Lynn
The Search for God's Law — Weiss, Bernard G
The Search for Intimacy — Storkey, Elaine
The Search for Justice — Shapiro, Robert L
The Search for Liberty — Wright, Esmond

r The Search for Missing Friends. Vol. 4 — Harris, Ruth-Ann M
The Search for Peace in Afghanistan — Rubin, Barnett R
The Search for Political Space — Magnusson, Warren
r Search for Security. 3rd Ed. — Lord, Mary E
The Search for Simplicity — Brinch Hansen, Per
A Search for Solitude — Merton, Thomas
The Search for the Perfect Language — Eco, Umberto
The Search for the Perfect Swing — Cochran, Alastair
y Search for the Shadowman — Nixon, Joan Lowery
Search for the Tourette Syndrome and Human Behavior Genes — Comings, David E
The Search for Thomas F. Ward, Teacher of Frederick Delius — Gillespie, Don C
Search Out the Land — Godfrey, Sheldon J
r The Searchable Internet Bibliography. Electronic Media Version — Johnson, Peggy
Searching Electronic Resources — Pappas, Marjorie L
Searching for Everardo — Harbury, Jennifer K
Searching for Memory — Schacter, Daniel L
Searching for Saleem — Gauhari, Farooka
Searching for the Snowy — Seddon, George
c Searching for Velociraptor — Dingus, Lowell
Searching Multimedia Databases by Content — Faloutsos, Christos
c Seashore — Sayre, April Pulley
c Seashore Babies (Illus. by Tara Darling) — Darling, Kathy
Seashore Gardening — Tenenbaum, Frances
The Season — Kelly, Tom
r Season Feasts and Festivals — James, E O
y A Season for Goodbye — McDaniel, Lurlene
A Season in Heaven — Tomory, David
c A Season in the Rodeo (Illus. by Robert Crum) — Crum, Robert
Season of Adventure — Gould, Jean
Season of Apples — Copeland, Ann
y Season of Blood — Keane, Fergal
c A Season of Comebacks — Mackel, Kathy
The Season of Comfort — Vidal, Gore
Season of High Adventure — Thomas, S Bernard
A Season of Knives — Chisholm, P F
Season of New Beginnings — Finley, Mitch
Season of Promises — Finley, Mitch
y Season of Storms — Foxxe, Ellen
Season of the Vigilante. Bks. 1-2 — Jonas, Kirby
Seasoned Timber — Fisher, Dorothy Canfield
Season's End — Grimes, Tom
c Seasons (Illus. by Luis Rizo) — Llamas Ruiz, Andres
The Seasons of a Woman's Life — Levinson, Daniel J
The Seasons of Beento Blackbird — Busia, Akosua
Seasons of Change — Reinert, Paul
Seasons of Grace — Crawford, Michael J
The Seasons of Rome — Hofmann, Paul
Seasons of the Senses — Worboys, Anne
Seasons of the Sun — Telesco, Patricia
Seasons of War — Sutherland, Daniel E
c The Seasons Sewn (Illus. by Michael McCurdy) — Paul, Ann Whitford
c The Seattle Space Needle — Doherty, Craig A
c The Seaweed Book — Treat, Rose
Sebastiano Serlio on Architecture. Vol. 1, Bks. 1-5 — Serlio, Sebastiano
The Second Battle of New Orleans — Baker, Liva
y The Second Bend in the River — Rinaldi, Ann
r Second Bibliographic Guide to the History of Computing, Computers, and the Information Processing Industry — Cortada, James W
y Second Chance — Baer, Judy
A Second Chicago School? — Fine, Gary Alan
Second Coming — Rozell, Mark J
The Second Creation. Rev. Ed. — Crease, Robert P
The Second Curve — Morrison, J Ian
y Second Daughter — Walter, Mildred Pitts
The Second Four Books of Poems — Merwin, W S
Second Gold Rush — Johnson, Marilynn S
Second IEEE International Conference on Engineering of Complex Computer Systems — IEEE International Conference on Engineering of Complex Computer Systems (2nd: 1996: Montreal, Quebec)
Second Impression — Kaye, Barbara
Second Impressions — Adams, Clinton
y A Second Infinity — Weaver, Michael D
y The Second Jewish Book of Why (Bikel). Audio Version — Kolatch, Alfred J
Second Language Practice — Duquette, Georges
The Second Law. Rev. Ed. — Atkins, P W
Second Life — Gunn, Janet Varner
Second Lives — Wheeler, Richard S
Second Nature — Pollan, Michael

y Second Nature — Robinson, Nigel
The Second Part of King Henry VI (Hattaway) — Shakespeare, William
The Second Punic War — Cornell, Tim
The Second Set. Vol. 2 — Feinstein, Sascha
Second Sight — Stuart, Dabney
The Second Ten Commandments — Kopelman, Orion Moshe
Second Time Around — Sleem, Patty
Second to None. Vols. 1-2 — Moynihan, Ruth Barnes
Le Second Traite Du Gouvernement — Locke, John
Secondary Adjustments and Related Aspects of Transfer Pricing Corrections
The Secondary Assembly File
The Secondary Colors — Theroux, Alexander
r La Seconde Guerre Mondiale, Guide Des Sources Conservees En France 1939-1945
Secrecy and Deceit — Gitlitz, David M
c The Secret — Masson, Sophie
The Secret — Victor, Cynthia
A Secret Affair — Bradford, Barbara Taylor
Secret Agencies — Johnson, Loch K
y The Secret Agent (Jennings). Audio Version — Conrad, Joseph
Secret and Sanctioned — Knott, Stephen F
c The Secret Box — Pearson, Gaye
The Secret Chain — Bradie, Michael
c Secret Dawn (Illus. by Yolaine Lefebvre) — Chase, Edith Newlin
y The Secret Diary of Adrian Mole, Age 13 3/4 — Townsend, Sue
The Secret Diary of Anne Boleyn — Maxwell, Robin
Secret Empire — Waller, J Michael
Secret Flotillas — Richards, Brooks
c Secret Friends (Illus. by Jason Cockcroft) — Laird, Elizabeth
c The Secret Garden — Burnett, Frances Hodgson
c The Secret Garden (Illus. by Kathy Mitchell) — Burnett, Frances Hodgson
c The Secret Garden. Audio Version — Burnett, Frances Hodgson
Secret Gardens in Venice — Moldi-Ravenna, Cristiana
The Secret Gospels — Hoffmann, R Joseph
Secret History — Tartt, Donna
The Secret History of Gender — Stern, Steve J
The Secret Holy War of Santiago De Chile — Parra, Marco Antonio De La
y Secret Life — Ryan, Michael
The Secret Life of Aphra Behn — Todd, Janet M, 1942-
c The Secret Life of Billie's Uncle Myron — Jenkin, Len
The Secret Life of Jesse James — Knight, Arthur Winfield
The Secret Life of Money — Crawford, Tad
The Secret Life of Nature — Tompkins, Peter
The Secret Life of Santa Claus — Solotareff, Gregoire
The Secret Life of Wilkie Collins — Clarke, William C
Secret Lives of Sgt. John Wilson — Simmie, Lois
The Secret Love of Sons — Weinstock, Nicholas
The Secret Malady — Merians, Linda E
The Secret Marriage of Sherlock Holmes and Other Eccentric Readings — Atkinson, Michael
Secret Muses — Kavanagh, Julie
The Secret Museum — Kendrick, Walter
y Secret of Gumbo Grove — Tate, Eleanora E
The Secret of Healing — Holzer, Hans
y The Secret of Sentinel Rock — Silverthorne, Judith
y Secret of the Best Choice — Johnson, Lois Walfrid
The Secret of the Bulls — Bernardo, Jose Raul
The Secret of the Incas — Sullivan, William
The Secret of the Villa Mimosa — Adler, Elizabeth
y The Secret of Two Brothers — Hernandez, Irene Beltran
Secret Paths — Apter, Terri
c Secret Place (Illus. by Ted Rand) — Bunting, Eve
Secret Place of Thunder — Morris, Lynn
Secret Police — Benjaminson, Peter
The Secret Reader — Barnstone, Willis
The Secret Room — Laughlin, James
The Secret School — Strieber, Whitley
Secret Sexualities — McCormick, Ian
c The Secret Shortcut (Illus. by Mark Teague) — Teague, Mark
c Secret Signs (Illus. by Anita Riggio) — Riggio, Anita
Secret Sins — Cresswell, Jasmine
c Secret Societies — Hite, Kenneth
c Secret Societies (Illus. by McRae Books) — Ross, Stewart
Secret Society Inside--and Outside--the Conservative Party — Nicholson, Emma
Secret Soldier — Betser, Muki

y Secret Star — *Springer, Nancy*
The Secret State — *Thurlow, Richard*
Secret Thoughts of an Adoptive Mother — *Wolff, Jana*
c The Secret under the Whirlpool — *Hammond, Elaine Breault*
y Secret Vampire — *Smith, L J*
Secret Vow — *Cecala, Kathy*
The Secret War against the Jews — *Loftus, John*
The Secret War for the Falklands — *West, Nigel*
The Secret War for the Union — *Fishel, Edwin C*
Secret War in the Middle East — *Rathmell, Andrew*
Secret Weapon — *Williams, Kathleen Broome*
c The Secret Wish of Nannerl Mozart — *Nickel, Barbara Kathleen*
The Secret Woman — *O'Connor, Garry*
The Secret World of American Communism — *Klehr, Harvey*
The Secretary of the Interior's Standards for the Treatment of Historic Properties — *Weeks, Kay D*
c Secrets — *Ferguson, Alane*
Secrets: A Writer in the Cold War — *Brodeur, Paul*
c Secrets at Hidden Valley — *Roberts, Willo Davis*
Secrets from a Vegetarian Kitchen — *Abensur, Nadine*
Secrets in Satin — *Smith, Haywood*
The Secrets of a Fire King — *Edwards, Kim*
c The Secrets of Animal Flight (Illus. by Nic Bishop) — *Bishop, Nic*
The Secrets of Barneveld Calvary — *Schaap, James Calvin*
y The Secrets of Cain's Castle — *Murphy, T M*
c The Secrets of Cranberry Beach — *Murphy, T M*
Secrets of Fat-Free Chinese Cooking — *Compestine, Ying Chang*
Secrets of Fat-Free Italian Cooking — *Woodruff, Sandra*
Secrets of Life and Death — *Siebert, Renate*
y The Secrets of Mariko — *Bumiller, Elisabeth*
y The Secrets of Sarah Byrnes — *Crutcher, Chris*
The Secrets of Star Wars — *Vaz, Mark Cotta*
Secrets of Successful Grantsmanship — *Golden, Susan L*
The Secrets of Successful Parents — *Rolfe, Randy*
Secrets of the Super Net Searchers — *Basch, Reva*
y Secrets of Walden Rising — *Baillie, Allan*
Le Secteur Forestier National — *Benin. Direction Des Forets Et Des Ressources Naturelles*
Sector Investing. 1996 Ed.
Sects and Scrolls — *Davies, Philip R*
Secular Bioethics in Theological Perspective — *Shelp, Earl E*
The Secular City — *Hemming, T D*
The Secularization of the Academy — *Marsden, George M*
Secure Commerce on the Internet — *Ahuja, Vijay*
Secure the Shadow — *Ruby, Jay*
Secure UNIX — *Samalin, Samuel*
Securing Client/Server Computer Networks — *Davis, Peter T*
Securing Employer-Based Pensions — *Bodie, Zvi*
Securing Religious Liberty — *Choper, Jesse H*
Securing Stability and Growth in Latin America — *Hausmann, Ricardo*
Securing the Covenant — *Reich, Bernard*
Security and Privacy — *IEEE Symposium on Security and Privacy (1996: Oakland, CA)*
Security Challenges in the Mediterranean Region — *Aliboni, Roberto*
Security, Democracy, and Development in U.S.-Latin American Relations — *Schoultz, Lars*
Security in Computing. 2nd Ed. — *Pfleeger, Charles P*
Security Issues for the Internet and the World Wide Web — *Cameron, Debra*
Security Issues in the Post-Cold War World — *Davis, M Jane*
Security Metaphors — *Chilton, Paul A*
The Security of Turkey and Adjacent Areas — *Ambraseys, Nicolas*
Security Threatened — *Arian, Asher*
Sedimentary Environments. 3rd Ed. — *Reading, H G*
y Sedimentary Geology — *Prothero, Donald R*
Seduced — *George, Nelson*
Seduced by Death — *Hendin, Herbert*
Seduction and Repetition in Ovid's Ars Amatoria 2 — *Sharrock, Alison*
The Seduction of Hillary Rodham — *Brock, David*
The Seduction of Mrs. Caine — *Ryan, Mary*
Seduction Theory — *Beller, Thomas*
The Seductions of Emily Dickinson — *Smith, Robert McClure*
See — *Roth, Gerhard*
p See: A Journal of Visual Culture

r See and Enjoy the Great Comet — *Burnham, Robert*
See How They Ran — *Troy, Gil*
y See How They Run — *McRobbie, David*
See Naples and Die — *Ellis, Robert B*
See No Evil — *Finkelstein, Jay*
See No Evil — *Shapiro, Barbara*
y See Rock City — *Davis, Donald*
See Through — *Boyack, Neil*
c See You Around, Sam! (Illus. by Diane De Groat) — *Lowry, Lois*
c See You Later, Alligator — *Kvasnosky, Laura McGee*
Seeable Signs — *Nichols, Ann Eljenholm*
c The Seed Bunny (Illus. by Jennifer Selby) — *Selby, Jennifer*
c A Seed Grows (Illus. by Heather Collins) — *Hickman, Pamela M*
The Seed Is Mine — *Van Onselen, Charles*
Seedbeds of Virtue — *Glendon, Mary Ann*
Seedborne Diseases and Their Control — *Maude, R B*
c Seedfolks (Illus. by Judy Pedersen) — *Fleischman, Paul*
Seedings and Other Poems — *Rothenberg, Jerome*
c Seeds and Seedlings (Illus. by Dwight Kuhn) — *Pascoe, Elaine*
Seeds in the Heart — *Keene, Donald*
Seeds of Crisis — *Rury, John L*
The Seeds of Speech — *Aitchison, Jean*
The Seeds of Time — *Jameson, Fredric*
The Seeds of Time — *Kenyon, Kay*
Seedtime for the Modern Civil Rights Movement — *Reed, Merl E*
c Seeing (Illus. by Barrie Watts) — *Walpole, Brenda*
y Seeing a Large Cat — *Peters, Elizabeth*
Seeing and Believing — *Kacmarcik, Frank*
Seeing and Believing — *Miles, Margaret R*
Seeing Calvin Coolidge in a Dream — *Derbyshire, John*
Seeing Canada Whole — *Pickersgill, J W*
Seeing Double — *Kaplan, Carola M*
The Seeing Glass — *Gorman, Jacquelin*
Seeing God Everywhere — *Shraddhananda, Swami*
Seeing in the Dark — *States, Bert O*
Seeing Is Deceiving — *North, Suzanne*
Seeing Language in Sign — *Maher, Jane*
Seeing New Worlds — *Walls, Laura Dassow*
Seeing Pittsburgh — *Fifield, Barringer*
c Seeing Red (Illus. by Tony Ross) — *Garland, Sarah*
Seeing Red — *Shaughnessy, Dan*
c Seeing Stars — *Collicott, Sharleen*
Seeing the Crab — *Middlebrook, Christina*
Seeing the Light — *Toner, Michael*
Seeing the Lord — *Sawicki, Marianne*
Seeing through the Eighties — *Feuer, Jane*
Seeing through the Mother Goose Tales — *Lewis, Philip E*
Seeing Together — *Luftig, Victor*
Seeing Women as Men — *Sprechman, Ellen Lew*
Seek the Welfare of the City — *Winter, Bruce*
The Seeker's Guide to Being Catholic — *Finley, Mitch*
r Seeking Common Ground — *Anderson, Andrew D M*
Seeking Ezekiel — *Halperin, David J*
Seeking Strategic Advantage through Health Policy Analysis — *Longest, Beaufort B*
Seeking Structure from Nature — *Cook, Jeffrey*
Seeking the Highest Good — *Burke, Sara Z*
Seeking Western Waters — *Strong, Emory*
r Seen That, Now What? — *Shaw, Andrea*
The Seer King — *Bunch, Chris*
Seers of God — *Winship, Michael P*
c Sees behind Trees — *Dorris, Michael*
y Seesaw — *Foon, Dennis*
c Sefer Ha-Aggadah (Illus. by Judy Dick) — *Rossel, Seymour*
Segu — *Conde, Maryse*
Die Sehnsucht Fahrt Schwarz — *Schami, Rafik*
Sei Ruoli Per Solisti — *Mitropulu, Costula*
Seigniorage and Burdens of Government Debt — *Kun, Janos*
c Seiji Ozawa — *Tan, Sheri*
Seismic Design and Retrofit of Bridges — *Priestley, M J N*
Seismic Engineering 1996
Seismic, Shock, and Vibration Isolation 1996
c Seismosaurus: The Longest Dinosaur (Illus. by Donna Braginetz) — *Lessem, Don*
Seize Paroles Voilees — *Stetie, Salah*
Seize the Initiative — *Colvin, Gregory L*
Seizures of the Will in Early Modern English Drama — *Whigham, Frank*
c Selby Spacedog (Illus. by Allan Stomann) — *Ball, Duncan*

c Selby: The Secret Adventures of a Talking Dog (Illus. by M K Brown) — *Ball, Duncan*
Selected Cronicas — *Lispector, Clarice*
Selected Essays and Reviews — *Carruth, Hayden*
The Selected Essays of Shigeto Tsuru — *Tsuru, Shigeto*
Selected Letters — *Thomas, Edward*
Selected Letters. Vol. 1 — *Sarton, May*
Selected Letters of Berlioz — *Berlioz, Hector*
The Selected Letters of D.H. Lawrence — *Lawrence, D H*
Selected Letters of Edith Sitwell — *Sitwell, Edith*
Selected Letters of Ezra Pound and William Carlos Williams — *Pound, Ezra*
Selected Letters of John Gould Fletcher — *Fletcher, John Gould*
Selected Letters of Leslie Stephen. Vols. 1-2 — *Stephen, Leslie*
The Selected Letters of Lewis Carroll — *Carroll, Lewis*
The Selected Letters of Louisa May Alcott — *Alcott, Louisa May*
Selected Letters of Mary Wollstonecraft Shelley — *Shelley, Mary Wollstonecraft*
The Selected Papers of Charles Willson Peale and His Family. Vol. 4 — *Peale, Charles Willson*
Selected Papers of Freeman Dyson. Vol. 5 — *Dyson, Freeman*
Selected Papers on Computer Science — *Knuth, Donald E*
Selected Plays — *Nash, N Richard*
Selected Poems — *Ammons, A R*
Selected Poems — *Ash, John*
Selected Poems — *Ashbery, John*
Selected Poems — *Bertolucci, Attilio*
Selected Poems — *Celan, Paul*
Selected Poems — *Creeley, Robert*
Selected Poems — *Enzensberger, Hans Magnus*
Selected Poems — *Guest, Barbara*
Selected Poems — *Logue, Christopher*
Selected Poems — *Lomas, Herbert*
Selected Poems — *Mandelstam, Osip*
Selected Poems — *Merrill, James*
Selected Poems — *Nelligan, Emile*
Selected Poems — *Sisson, C H*
Selected Poems — *Strand, Mark*
Selected Poems. Rev. Ed. — *Duncan, Robert*
Selected Poems 1933-1993 — *Ewart, Gavin*
Selected Poems 1947-1995 — *Ginsberg, Allen*
Selected Poems 1954-1992 — *Brown, George Mackay*
Selected Poems 1960-1990 — *Kumin, Maxine*
Selected Poems 1963-1983 — *Simic, Charles*
Selected Poems 1965-1990 — *Hacker, Marilyn*
Selected Poems 1965-1993 — *Wilmer, Clive*
Selected Poems 1972-1997 — *Schmidt, Michael*
Selected Poems 1976-1996 — *Szirtes, George*
Selected Poems and Prose of John Davidson — *Davidson, John*
Selected Poems of Rita Dove — *Dove, Rita*
Selected Poems of Shmuel HaNagid — *Samuel, Ha-Nagid*
Selected Poems of Su Tung-Po — *Su, Shih*
The Selected Poetry of Yehuda Amichai — *Amichai, Yehuda*
Selected Prose Works — *Ephraem, Syrius, Saint*
Selected Social Safety Net Programs in the Philippines — *Subbarao, Kalanidhi*
Selected Stories — *Dubus, Andre*
Selected Stories — *Munro, Alice*
The Selected Stories of Mavis Gallant — *Gallant, Mavis*
The Selected Stories of Richard Bausch — *Bausch, Richard*
Selected Topics on Electron Physics — *Campbell, Murray*
Selected Verse — *Carducci, Giosue*
Selected Verse Translations — *Gascoyne, David*
Selected Works. Vol. 3 — *Eisenstein, S M*
Selected Works in Applied Mechanics and Mathematics — *Reissner, Eric*
Selected Works of Edythe Mae Gordon — *Gordon, Edythe Mae*
Selected Works of George McCready Price — *Price, George McCready*
Selected Works of I.L. Peretz — *Peretz, Isaac Leib*
Selected Writings. Vol. 1 — *Benjamin, Walter*
Selected Writings of Judith Sargent Murray — *Murray, Judith Sargent*
Selected Writings of Madame De Villedieu — *Villedieu, Madame De*

Selected Writings of Rosemary Ellis — *Ellis, Rosemary*

Selecting Development Projects for the World Bank — *Baneth, Jean*

Selecting the Right Form of Business — *Bernard, Bruce D*

A Selection of the Poems of Laura Riding — *Riding, Laura*

Selection: The Mechanism of Evolution — *Bell, Graham*

r A Selective Checklist of the Published Work of Aubrey Beardsley — *Lasner, Mark Samuels*

Selena's Secret — *Arraras, Maria Celeste*

Self — *Martel, Yann*

Self and Deception — *Ames, Roger T*

Self and Interpersonal Insight — *London, Manuel*

The Self and the Other — *Serageldin, Ismail*

Self-Assessment Color Review of Reptiles and Amphibians — *Frye, Fredric L*

Self-Assessment in Accident and Emergency Medicine — *Burke, Derek*

Self-Care Nursing in a Multicultural Context — *Lipson, Juliene G*

Self-Conscious Emotions — *Tangney, June Price*

c Self-Control (Illus. by Mechelle Ann) — *Gambill, Henrietta*

Self-Determination: International Perspectives — *Clark, Donald*

r Self-Determination of Peoples — *Cassese, Antonio*

Self-Determination, Terrorism, and the International Humanitarian Law of Armed Conflict — *Chadwick, Elizabeth*

r Self-Directed Behavior — *Watson, David*

Self-Directed RRSPs — *Woods, S E*

Self-Esteem and Adjusting with Blindness. 2nd Ed. — *Tuttle, Dean W*

Self Expressions — *Flanagan, Owen*

Self-Knowledge in the Age of Theory — *Hartle, Ann*

The Self-Made Map — *Conley, Tom*

Self-Ownership, Freedom and Equality — *Cohen, G A*

Self-Portrait in a Convex Mirror — *Ashbery, John*

Self-Portrait in Words — *Beckmann, Max*

Self-Rule: A Cultural History of American Democracy — *Wiebe, Robert H*

Self, Struggle, and Change — *Cohen, Norman J*

Self-Study Course for Optometric Assisting. 2nd Ed. — *Jameson, Mary*

The Self-Taught Gardener — *Eddison, Sydney*

Self-Traps: The Elusive Quest for Higher Self-Esteem — *Swann, William B*

The Selfish Brain — *DuPont, Robert L*

c Selina and the Bear Paw Quilt (Illus. by Janet Wilson) — *Smucker, Barbara Claassen*

Selinunte: Le Metope Dell'Heraion — *Marconi, Clemente*

Selling Black History for Carter G. Woodson — *Greene, Lorenzo J*

Selling Culture — *Ohmann, Richard*

Selling Free Enterprise — *Fones-Wolf, Elizabeth A*

Selling Illusions — *Bissoondath, Neil*

Selling on the Net — *Lewis, Herschell*

Selling Out (Green). Audio Version — *Green, Joey*

Selling Radio — *Smulyan, Susan*

Selling Sin — *Davidson, D Kirk*

Selling the Air — *Streeter, Thomas*

Selling the Invisible — *Beckwith, Harry*

Selling the Sea — *Dickinson, Robert H*

Selling War — *Cull, Nicholas John*

Selling with Integrity — *Morgen, Sharon Drew*

Sellos Medievales De Navarra — *Menendez Pidal De Navascues, Faustino*

Sellout: Aldrich Ames and the Corruption of the CIA — *Adams, James, 1951-*

La Selva: Ecology and Natural History of a Neotropical Rain Forest — *McDade, Lucinda A*

c Las Selvas Misteriosas (Illus. by Luis Rizo) — *Sanchez, Isidro*

Semantic Indexicality — *Cresswell, M J*

Semantics and Experience — *Alverson, Hoyt*

The Semantics of Syntax — *Bouchard, Denis*

y El Sembrador De Salud — *Rojas, Jose Antonio*

Il Seme Della Violenza — *Niccoli, Ottavia*

Semiconductor Characterization — *Bullis, W Murray*

Semiconductor Optoelectronic Devices. 2nd Ed. — *Bhattacharya, Pallab*

Semigroup Theory and Its Applications — *Hofmann, Karl H*

Semigroups and Their Subsemigroup Lattices — *Shevrin, L N*

Seminaire Robert Challe — *Weil-Bergougnoux, Michele*

Seminary Education and Christian Jewish-Relations. 2nd, Rev. Ed. — *Fisher, Eugene J*

Seminary or University? — *Maag, Karin*

Seminole Burning — *Littlefield, Daniel F, Jr.*

Seminole Song — *Munn, Vella*

Semiotic Investigations — *McHoul, A W*

Semiotica E Linguaggio Nella Scolastica — *Marmo, Constantino*

Semiotics 1994

Seml Vozhdei. Vols. 1-2 — *Volkogonov, Dmitrii Antonovich*

Senator Alan Bible and the Politics of the New West — *Elliott, Gary E*

Senator Allen Ellender of Louisiana — *Becnel, Thomas A*

The Senator's Daughter — *Gotti, Victoria*

Senators on the Campaign Trail — *Fenno, Richard F*

y Send Me Down a Miracle — *Nolan, Han*

r Sendero Luminoso — *Stern, Peter A*

Sendiboo Ur Djupunum — *Egilsson, Egill*

c Seneca (Illus. by Karen Lee Baker) — *Baker, Karen Lee*

y Seneca's Troades (Boyle) — *Seneca, Lucius Annaeus*

c Senegal — *Brownlie, Alison*

Seniority and Employment Equity for Women — *Dulude, Louise*

Senor Bajo Los Arboles O Brevisima Relacion De La Destruccion De Los Indios — *Morales, Maino R*

c Senor Cat's Romance and Other Favorite Stories from Latin America (Illus. by Lulu Delacre) — *Gonzalez, Lucia M*

Senora De La Miel — *Buitrago, Fanny*

Senora Honeycomb — *Buitrago, Fanny*

Senora Rodriguez and Other Worlds — *Cerda, Martha*

Los Senorios De Los Montes De Torozos — *Reglero De La Fuente, Carlos M*

c The Sensational Samburger (Illus. by Chris Moore) — *Pelham, David*

Sensational Soups — *Wright, Jeni*

y Sensational TV — *Day, Nancy*

Sense and Sensibility — *Austen, Jane*

y Sense and Sensibility (Harker). Audio Version — *Austen, Jane*

The Sense and Sensibility Screenplay and Diaries — *Thompson, Emma*

A Sense of Common Ground — *Sheikh, Fazal*

The Sense of Reality — *Berlin, Isaiah*

A Sense of Self — *Sheffer, Susannah*

The Sense of the People — *Wilson, Kathleen*

r Sensible Self-Help — *Grudermeyer, David*

Sensing, Modeling and Simulation in Emerging Electronic Packaging — *Yeh, Chao-Pin*

Senso: The Japanese Remember the Pacific War — *Gibney, Frank*

Sensor Materials — *Mosley, Pat*

Sensual Healing — *Kennedy, Teresa*

Sensual Math — *Fulton, Alice*

Sensuous Horizons — *Maniam, K S*

Sentences of Earth and Stone — *De Paor, Louis*

A Sentimental Economy — *Salazar, Carles*

Sentimental Narrative and the Social Order in France 1760-1820 — *Denby, David*

Sentimental Twain — *Camfield, Gregg*

El Sentimiento — *Guelbenzu, Jose Maria*

Sentinels — *Pronzini, Bill*

Sentinels — *Weis, Margaret*

Separate and Unequal — *King, Desmond*

y A Separate Battle — *Chang, Ina*

The Separate City — *Silver, Christopher*

A Separate Creation — *Burr, Chandler*

Separated by Death — *Axler, Leo*

Separations — *Hall, Oakley*

Separatism and Women's Community — *Shugar, Dana R*

Sephardi and Middle Eastern Jewries — *Goldberg, Harvey E*

Sephardi Religious Responses to Modernity — *Stillman, Norman A*

Sephardic American Voices — *Matza, Diane*

The Sephardic Kitchen — *Sternberg, Robert*

c Septimouse. Supermouse and Septimouse. Big Cheese (Lambert). Audio Version — *Jungman, Ann*

r Sequels: An Annotated Guide to Novels in Series. 2nd Ed. — *Husband, Janet*

Sequence Data Analysis Guidebook — *Swindell, Simon R*

Sequence Stratigraphy — *Emery, Dominic*

The Serbs: History, Myth, and the Destruction of Yugoslavia — *Judah, Tim*

Serene Compassion — *Carmody, Denise Lardner*

Serenity, Courage, Wisdom — *Clark, Henry B*

Sergeant Major, U.S. Marines — *Norton, Bruce H*

y Sergei Rachmaninov: An Essential Guide to His Life and Work — *Haylock, Julian*

Sergei Radlov: The Shakespearean Fate of a Soviet Director — *Zolotnitsky, David*

Serial Killer Days — *Prill, David*

Serial Networked Field Instrumentation — *Jordan, J R*

r Serials on British Television 1950-1994 — *Baskin, Ellen*

Serials to the Tenth Power — *Sheble, Mary Ann*

r Series Books and the Media — *Farah, David*

A Series for New York — *Kelly, Rob*

y Serious Business — *Kanfer, Stefan*

y Serious Intent (Rodska). Audio Version — *Yorke, Margaret*

Serious Money — *Brown, Clifford W*

Serious Pig — *Thorne, John*

Serious Talk — *Polkinghorne, John*

Seriously Funny — *Jacobson, Howard*

The Sermon Notebook of Samuel Parris 1689-1694 — *Parris, Samuel*

The Sermon on the Mount — *Betz, Hans Dieter*

Le Sermon Sur La Montagne — *Dumais, Marcel*

Sermones — *Thomas De Chobham*

The Serpent Garden — *Riley, Judith Merkle*

Serpent-Handling Believers — *Burton, Thomas*

Serpent Kills — *Millan, Jim*

Serpent on the Rock — *Eichenwald, Kurt*

Serpent on the Rock — *Ellis, Alice Thomas*

The Serpentine Cave — *Paton Walsh, Jill*

Serpents in the Sand — *Brown, Courtney*

The Serpents of Paradise — *Abbey, Edward*

Serpins: Structure, Function and Biology — *Gettins, Peter G W*

Sertorius, or, The Roman Patriot — *Brown, David Paul*

Servant of the Bones — *Rice, Anne*

Servant of the Bones (Cumpsty). Audio Version — *Rice, Anne*

Servant of the Bones (Prichard). Audio Version — *Rice, Anne*

Servants: English Domestics in the Eighteenth Century — *Hill, Bridget*

Servants of the People — *Williams, Lea E*

Service Experience and Design in Pressure Vessels and Piping — *Bamford, W H*

Service Industries in the World Economy — *Daniels, P W*

The Service Productivity and Quality Challenge — *Harker, Patrick T*

The Service Profit Chain — *Heskett, James L*

Service Provision under Stress in East Africa — *Semboja, Joseph*

Service Quality in Academic Libraries — *Hernon, Peter*

The Service Sector — *Felli, Ernesto*

Servicing the Middle Classes — *Gregson, Nicky*

Serving Families and Children through Partnerships — *Feinberg, Sandra*

Serving Print Disabled Library Patrons — *Massis, Bruce Edward*

Servitude and Grandeur of Arms — *Vigny, Alfred De*

Il Servo: Storia Di Una Carriera Nel Settecento — *Arru, Angiolina*

cp Sesame Street

Sesir Od Riblje Koze — *Pavic, Milorad*

Set in Authority — *Duncan, Sara Jeannette*

The Set-Up — *Erdman, Paul Emil*

The Set-Up (Campanella). Audio Version — *Erdman, Paul Emil*

Seta — *Baricco, Alessandro*

c Seth and Samona (Illus. by Colin Bootman) — *Hyppolite, Joanne*

Sets in Motion — *Affron, Charles*

Il Settimo Senso — *Forabosco, Giovannantonio*

Setting Foot on the Shores of Connemara and Other Writings — *Robinson, Tim*

Setting the Gospel Free — *Taylor, Brian C*

Setting the Record Straight — *Fix, Michael*

Setting the Stage for Strategic Planning for Alberta's Continued Response to HIV/AIDS to the Year 2000 — *Blair, Carol*

Setting the Stage for the Next Century

r Setting the Tempo — *Piazza, Tom*

Setting the Virgin on Fire — *Becker, Marjorie*

Settlement and Politics in Three Classic Maya Polities — *De Montmollin, Olivier*

Settlement and Social Organization — *Halsall, Guy*

y Shadows on a Sword — *Bradford, Karleen*
Shadows on the Past — *Grindon, Leger*
Shadows: The Depiction of Cast Shadows in Western Art — *Gombrich, E H*
y The Shadowsmith — *Gravel, Geary*
y Shadrach Minkins: From Fugitive Slave to Citizen — *Collison, Gary Lee*
Shaft Seals for Dynamic Applications — *Horve, Leslie A*
Shaftesbury and the Culture of Politeness — *Klein, Lawrence*
Shaka's Children — *Taylor, Stephen*
c Shake It to the One That You Love the Best (Illus. by Warren-Mattox) — *Mattox, Cheryl Warren*
Shake Them 'Simmons Down — *Lembke, Janet*
Shakedown: How the New Economy Is Changing Our Lives — *Reid, Angus*
c Shaker Children — *Thorne-Thomsen, Kathleen*
c Shaker Hearts (Illus. by Wendell Minor) — *Turner, Ann Warren*
The Shaker Herb and Garden Book — *Buchanan, Rita*
A Shaker Hymnal
Shakespeare: An Illustrated Stage History — *Bate, Jonathan*
Shakespeare and Classical Comedy — *Miola, Robert S*
Shakespeare and Cultural Traditions — *Kishi, Tetsuo*
Shakespeare and Multiplicity — *Gibbons, Brian*
Shakespeare and Ovid — *Bate, Jonathan*
Shakespeare and the Constant Romans — *Miles, Geoffrey*
Shakespeare and the English Romantic Imagination — *Bate, Jonathan*
Shakespeare and the Geography of Difference — *Gillies, John*
Shakespeare and the Jews — *Shapiro, James*
Shakespeare and the Nature of Women. 2nd Ed. — *Dusinberre, Juliet*
The Shakespeare Conspiracy — *Phillips, Graham*
Shakespeare from the Margins — *Parker, Patricia*
Shakespeare in China — *Zhang, Hsiao Yang*
Shakespeare in Performance — *Cousin, Geraldine*
Shakespeare Interactive: Romeo and Juliet. Electronic Media Version — *Shakespeare, William*
Shakespeare: Poet and Citizen — *Kiernan, V G*
Shakespeare Reread — *McDonald, Russ*
Shakespeare Reshaped 1606-1623 — *Taylor, Gary*
c Shakespeare Stories II (Illus. by Michael Foreman) — *Garfield, Leon*
Shakespeare Survey 47
Shakespeare: The Jacobean Plays — *McGuire, Philip C*
Shakespeare, the King's Playwright — *Kernan, Alvin*
Shakespeare, Theory, and Performance — *Bulman, James C*
Shakespearean Constitutions — *Bates, Jonathan*
Shakespearean Pragmatism — *Engle, Lars*
Shakespearean Suspect Texts — *Mcguire, Laurie E*
Shakespeare's Christian Dimension — *Battenhouse, Roy*
Shakespeare's Earliest Tragedy — *Metz, G Harold*
Shakespeare's Edward III — *Sams, Eric*
Shakespeare's Landlord — *Harris, Charlaine*
r Shakespeare's Language — *Shewmaker, Eugene F*
Shakespeare's Theory of Drama — *Kiernan, Pauline*
The Shakespearian Playing Companies — *Gurr, Andrew*
Shaking a Fist at God — *Dell, Katharine*
Shaky Ground — *Brewer, Steve*
Shalom, Friend — *Horovitz, David Phillip*
c Shalom, Haver — *Sofer, Barbara*
Shalom, Japan — *Horn, Shifra*
y The Shaman — *Stasheff, Christopher*
The Shaman Laughs — *Doss, James D*
Shamanism as a Spiritual Practice for Daily Life — *Cowan, Tom*
Shamans and Elders — *Humphrey, Caroline*
y Shaman's Circle (Illus. by Frank Howell) — *Wood, Nancy*
The Shaman's Secret — *Gillette, Douglas*
Shamans, Software, and Spleens — *Boyle, James*
r The Shambhala Dictionary of Taoism — *Fischer-Schreiber, Ingrid*
Shame: A Faith Perspective — *Albers, Robert H*
Shame and Grace — *Smedes, Lewis B*
Shame and Humiliation — *Steinberg, Blema S*
Shame and Necessity — *Williams, Bernard*
Shame and Pride — *Nathanson, Donald L*
Shame, Exposure, and Privacy — *Schneider, Carl D*
r Shan-English Dictionary — *Tern Moeng, Sao*
Shan Fei Qing Hua
Shane — *Schaefer, Jack*

Shang Xin — *Wang, An-I*
Shanghai: From Market Town to Treaty Port 1074-1858 — *Johnson, Linda Cooke*
The Shanghai Green Gang — *Martin, Brian G*
Shanghai on Strike — *Perry, Elizabeth J*
Shanghaied in San Francisco — *Pickelhaupt, Bill*
Shangri-La — *Cooney, Eleanor*
Shank — *Anscombe, Roderick*
c Shannon: A Chinatown Adventure, San Francisco 1880 (Illus. by Bill Farnsworth) — *Kudlinski, Kathleen V*
c Shannon, Lost and Found — *Kudlinski, Kathleen V*
c Shannon Miller: American Gymnast — *Green, Septima*
Shantytown Protest in Pinochet's Chile — *Schneider, Cathy Lisa*
The Shape of Biblical Language — *Breck, John*
The Shape of Life — *Raff, Rudolf A*
The Shape of Texas — *Francaviglia, Richard V*
The Shape of the Holy — *Grabar, Oleg*
Shape Selective Catalysis in Industrial Applications. 2nd Ed. — *Chen, N Y*
c Shapes — *Hewitt, Sally*
c Shapes (Illus. by Tony Ross) — *Ross, Tony*
y Shapes — *Steiber, Ellen*
The Shapes of Revenge — *Keyishian, Harry*
c Shapes, Sizes and More Surprises! (Illus. by Loretta Trezzo Braren) — *Tomczyk, Mary*
Shaping a City — *Boal, Frederick W*
y Shaping a Nation — *Morton, Desmond*
Shaping America — *Watson, George L*
Shaping China's Future in World Affairs — *Sutter, Robert G*
Shaping Constitutional Values — *Devins, Neal E*
Shaping National Responses to Climate Change — *Lee, Henry*
The Shaping of a Community — *Kumin, Beat A*
r The Shaping of a Profession — *Larsen, Oivind*
The Shaping of America. Vol. 2 — *Meinig, D W*
The Shaping of the Elizabethan Regime — *MacCaffrey, Wallace T*
Shaping Suburbia — *Lewis, Paul G*
Shaping the Culture of Schooling — *Desmond, Cheryl Taylor*
Shaping the Eighteenth Amendment — *Hamm, Richard F*
y Shaping U.S. Foreign Policy — *Dolan, Edward F*
c Shaquille O'Neal — *Ungs, Tim*
c Shaquille O'Neal: Star Center — *Macnow, Glen*
Shards — *Piccirilli, Tom*
y Shards of Alderaan — *Anderson, Kevin J*
y Shards of Empire — *Shwartz, Susan*
Shards of Honor (Cowan). Audio Version — *Bujold, Lois McMaster*
Shards of Love — *Menocal, Maria Rosa*
Shards of Memory — *Jhabvala, Ruth Prawer*
c Share Bear — *Stickland, Paul*
c A Share of Freedom — *Wood, June Rae*
Shared Anxiety — *Walker, George F*
Shared Creation — *Bottenberg, Joanna*
Shared Differences — *Carson, Diane*
r A Shared Heritage — *Taylor, William E*
Shared Responsibilities in Higher Education
Shares — *Gray, William*
Sharing Responsibility — *May, Larry*
y Sharing Sam — *Applegate, Katherine*
Sharing Secrets with Stalin — *Smith, Bradley F*
Sharing the Ganges — *Crow, Ben*
Sharing the Promised Land — *Hiro, Dilip*
c Sharing Time Troubles (Illus. by Betsy Lewin) — *Maccarone, Grace*
Sharing Your Good Ideas — *Sharp, Peggy*
Sharing Your Space — *Stukel, Eileen Dowd*
A Shark in the House — *Heffron, Dorris*
c Shark in the Sea (Illus. by Michael Rothman) — *Ryder, Joanne*
Shark of the Confederacy — *Robinson, Charles M*
c Sharks — *Harman, Amanda*
c Sharks (Illus. by Tony Kenyon) — *Parker, Steve*
c Sharks (Illus. by Seymour Simon) — *Simon, Seymour*
c Sharks! True Stories and Legends — *Gourley, Catherine*
c Sharon, Keep Your Hair On (Illus. by David Mackintosh) — *Rubinstein, Gillian*
y The Sharp Teeth of Love — *Betts, Doris*
Sharpening the Warrior's Edge — *Siddle, Bruce K*
y Sharpe's Regiment (Davidson). Audio Version — *Cornwell, Bernard*
y Sharpe's Revenge (Davidson). Audio Version — *Cornwell, Bernard*

Sharpe's Siege (Davidson). Audio Version — *Cornwell, Bernard*
y A Sharpness on the Neck — *Saberhagen, Fred*
Sharpshooter: A Novel of the Civil War — *Madden, David*
Shattered Rainbows — *Putney, Mary Jo*
Shattering Air — *Biespiel, David*
Shattering Glass — *Rotstein, Nancy-Gay*
Shaw 16
c The Shawnee Indians — *Dolan, Terrance*
Shaw's People — *Weintraub, Stanley*
y She (Williams). Audio Version — *Haggard, H Rider*
She Came to the Castro — *Wings, Mary*
c She Dared to Fly — *Johnson, Dolores*
She Has Reddish Hair and Her Name Is Sabina — *Campos, Julieta*
She Made Friends and Kept Them — *Cowles, Fleur*
She Must Have Known — *Masters, Brian*
She Took My Arm as if She Loved Me — *Gold, Herbert*
She Wields a Pen — *Grey, Jane*
She Works/He Works — *Barnett, Rosalind C*
Ad She-Yaaleh Amud Ha-Shahar — *Appelfeld, Aron*
Shedding Skin — *Ward, Robert*
Sheep — *Maginn, Simon*
c Sheep Dogs — *Bedson, Jack*
c Sheep in Wolves' Clothing (Illus. by Satoshi Kitamura) — *Kitamura, Satoshi*
c Sheep Take a Hike (Illus. by Margo Apple) — *Shaw, Nancy*
c Sheepish Riddles (Illus. by R W Alley) — *Hall, Katy*
Sheer Gall — *Kahn, Michael A*
c Sheila Rae, the Brave. Electronic Media Version — *Henkes, Kevin*
y Sheila's Dying — *Carter, Alden R*
Shekhinah/Spirit: Divine Presence in Jewish and Christian Religion — *Lodahl, Michael E*
Sheldon Jacobs' Guide to Successful No Load Investing — *Jacobs, Sheldon*
c The Shell Book (Illus. by Barbara Hirsch Lember) — *Lember, Barbara Hirsch*
Shell Game — *Mantle, Peter*
Shelley and Scripture — *Shelley, Bryan*
Shelley and the Revolution in Taste — *Morton, Timothy*
Shelley and the Romantics — *Catlin, Alan*
Shelley: Poet and Legislator of the World — *Bennett, Betty T*
Shelley's 1821-1822 Huntington Notebook — *Shelley, Percy Bysshe*
Shelley's Satire — *Jones, Steven E*
c Shells — *Chambers, Catherine*
Shells: Treasures of the Sea — *Hill, Leonard*
Shelter for the Spirit — *Moran, Victoria*
Shelter: Human Habitats from Around the World — *Knevitt, Charles*
The Shelter of Each Other — *Pipher, Mary Bray*
y The Shelter of Each Other (Pipher). Audio Version — *Pipher, Mary Bray*
Shelter Provision and Employment Generation
Sheltering the Jews — *Paldiel, Mordecai*
r Shenandoah County, Virginia. Vol. 3 — *Vann, Marvin J*
Shenandoah: Daughter of the Stars — *Niemeyer, Lucian*
y Shepherd — *Thompson, Julian F*
r Shepherd Family Genealogy — *Peck, Patricia D*
The Shepherd's Calendar — *Hogg, James, 1770-1835*
r Sheppard's International Directory of Ephemera Dealers 1996
Sherlock Holmes — *Doyle, Arthur Conan, Sir*
Sherlock Holmes and the Red Demon — *Millett, Larry*
Sherlock Holmes and the Titanic Tragedy — *Seil, William B*
r The Sherlock Holmes Encyclopedia — *Bunson, Matthew*
y Sherlock Holmes: Tales of Avarice (Hardwicke). Audio Version — *Doyle, Arthur Conan, Sir*
Sherlock Holmes: Tales of Betrayal (Hardwicke). Audio Version — *Doyle, Arthur Conan, Sir*
Sherlock Holmes: Tales of Intrigue (Hardwicke). Audio Version — *Doyle, Arthur Conan, Sir*
y Sherlock Holmes: Tales of Suspense (Hardwicke). Audio Version — *Doyle, Arthur Conan, Sir*
Sherman's Horsemen — *Evans, David, 1952, Sep., 9-*
Sherrin's Year — *Sherrin, Ned*
Sherwood Anderson's Winesburg, Ohio — *Anderson, Sherwood*
She's Come Undone — *Lamb, Wally*
She's Fantastical — *Sussex, Lucy*

Settlement Development in the North Jazira, Iraq — Wilkinson, T J

Settlement Ecology — Stone, Glenn Davis

c Settlements — Martin, Fred

Settlements in the Americas — Bennett, Ralph

c Settler Sayings (Illus. by Barbara Bedell) — Kalman, Bobbie

Settlers of the Beekman Patent, Dutchess County, New York. Vol. 3 — Doherty, Frank J

Settling the Canadian-American West 1890-1915 — Bennett, John W

Settling the Score — Kalinak, Kathryn

Settling the West — Arnold, James R

Setup Reduction through Effective Workholding — Hoffman, Edward G

c Seuss-Isms: Wise and Witty Prescriptions for Living from the Good Doctor — Seuss, Dr.

The Seven A.M. Practice — MacGregor, Roy

Seven Cats and the Art of Living — Coudert, Jo

The Seven Concertos of Beethoven — Hopkins, Antony

The Seven Cultures of Capitalism — Hampden-Turner, Charles

The Seven Days of Man — Qasim, Abd Al-Hakim

Seven Doors to Islam — Renard, John

The Seven Dumbest Relationship Mistakes Smart People Make — Bushong, Carolyn N

y Seven Experiments That Could Change the World — Sheldrake, Rupert

Seven Figure Selling — Kennedy, Danielle

c Seven Great Explorations (Illus. by Celia King) — King, Celia

Seven Japanese Tales — Tanizaki, Junichiro

The Seven League Boots — Murray, Albert

y The Seven Magpies — Hughes, Monica

Seven Minutes — Klein, Norman M

Seven Mountains — Mason, Marilyn

Seven Moves — Anshaw, Carol

c Seven Seas of Billy's Bathtub — Nelson, Ray

c The Seven Silly Eaters (Illus. by Marla Frazee) — Hoberman, Mary Ann

Seven Sixes Are Forty-Three — Nagarkar, Kiran

The Seven States of California — Fradkin, Philip L

Seven Story Mountain — Thievel, Philip M

y Seven Strange and Ghostly Tales (Jacques). Audio Version — Jacques, Brian

Seven Tales and a Fable — Jones, Gwyneth

Seven Tattoos — Trachtenberg, Peter

Seven Theories of Religion — Pals, Daniel L

yr Seven Trails West — Peters, Arthur King

The Seven-Year Atomic Make-Over Guide and Other Stories — Bell, Christine

The Seven-Year Stretch — Kastner, Laura S

y Seventeen against the Dealer — Voigt, Cynthia

Seventeen and J — Oe, Kenzaburo

y The Seventeen Guide to Sex and Your Body — Solin, Sabrina

Seventeenth-Century Spanish Poetry — Terry, Arthur

Seventeenth Texas Symposium on Relativistic Astrophysics and Cosmology — Texas Symposium on Relativistic Astrophysics (17th: 1994: Munich, Germany)

cr Seventh Book of Junior Authors and Illustrators — Holtze, Sally Holmes

Seventh-Day Adventist Attitudes toward Roman Catholicism 1845-1965 — Bruinsma, Reinder

Seventy Facets — Gorenberg, Gershom

The Several Lives of Chester Himes — Margolies, Edward

Severe Storm Engineering for Structural Design — Melaragno, Michele

Severe Stress and Mental Disturbance in Children — Pfeffer, Cynthia R

Severi Episcopi Malacitani (?) in Evangelia Libri XII — Severus, Bishop of Malaga

Severing the Ties That Bind — Pettipas, Katherine

Sewer, Gas and Electric — Ruff, Matt

The Sewing Circle — Madsen, Axel

Sewing Tools and Trinkets — Thompson, Helen Lester

Sewing Victorian Doll Clothes — Hamilton, Michelle

Sex and Anarchy — Coombs, Anne

Sex and Conquest — Trexler, Richard C

Sex and Danger in Buenos Aires — Guy, Donna J

Sex and Revolution — Smith, Lois M

Sex and Sensibility — Pally, Marcia

Sex and Sensibility — Stein, Arlene

Sex and Society in Graeco-Roman Egypt — Montserrat, Dominic

Sex and the City — Bushnell, Candace

Sex and the Origins of Death — Clark, William R

yr Sex and Zen and a Bullet in the Head — Hammond, Stefan

Sex at Work. Rev. Ed. — Hearn, Jeff

Sex between Men — Sadownick, Douglas

The Sex Box

Sex Crimes — Shute, Jenefer

Sex Crimes — Spear, Peta

Sex, Culture, and Modernity in China — Dikotter, Frank

Sex, Death, Enlightenment — Matousek, Mark

Sex Discrimination in the Labor Market — Perlman, Richard

Sex, Gender, and Christian Ethics — Cahill, Lisa Sowle

Sex in America — Michael, Robert T

Sex in Georgian England — Harvey, A D

Sex in the Head — Williams, Linda Ruth

Sex in the Snow — Adams, Michael

Sex in the Time of Generation X — Morrissey, Gabrielle

Sex Is Not a Four-Letter Word! — Miller, Patricia Martens

Sex, Laws, and Cyberspace — Wallace, Jonathan

Sex, Marriage and the Church — Porter, Muriel

c Sex Matters — Cohen, Julian

The Sex of Architecture — Agrest, Diana

Sex of the Stars — Proulx, Monique

Sex Offender Treatment — Coleman, Eli

Sex, Priests, and Power — Sipe, A W Richard

Sex, Race, and Science — Larson, Edward J

The Sex Revolts — Reynolds, Simon

Sex, Scams, and Street Life — McNamara, Robert P

Sex Scandal — Cohen, William A

The Sex Side of Life — Chen, Constance M

Sex Signs. Rev. and Updated Ed. — Bennett, Judith

Sex: The Catholic Experience — Greeley, Andrew M

Sex under Socialism — Pynsent, Robert B

Sex, Violence and Power in Sports — Messner, Michael A

Sex Work on the Streets — McKeganey, Neil

Sexing the Mind — Ender, Evelyne

Sexplorations: Journeys to the Erogenous Frontier — Radakovich, Anka

Sextet — Beauman, Sally

Sexual Abuse and Eating Disorders — Schwartz, Mark F

y The Sexual Abuse of Children and Adolescents — Hyde, Margaret O

Sexual Abuse Recalled — Alpert, Judith L

Sexual Behaviour and AIDS in the Developing World — Cleland, John

Sexual Coercion in Dating Relationships — Byers, E Sandra

Sexual Cultures and the Construction of Adolescent Identities — Irvine, Janice M

Sexual Ecology — Rotello, Gabriel

Sexual Freedom in Restoration Literature — Chernaik, Warren

r Sexual Harassment — Hartel, Lynda Jones

r Sexual Harassment — Jones, Constance

y Sexual Harassment — Nash, Carol Rust

Sexual Harassment in the Workplace and Academia — Shrier, Diane K

Sexual Harassment on College Campuses — Paludi, Michele Antoinette

Sexual Healing — De Paoli, Carlo

Sexual Investigations — Soble, Alan

Sexual Knowledge, Sexual Science — Porter, Roy

Sexual Nature, Sexual Culture — Abramson, Paul R, 1949-

A Sexual Odyssey — Maxwell, Kenneth E, 1908-

Sexual Orientation and Human Rights — Wintemute, Robert

The Sexual Perspective. New Ed. — Cooper, Emmanuel

Sexual Politics — Jones, Amelia

Sexual Politics in Cuba — Leiner, Marvin

The Sexual Politics of Disability — Shakespeare, Tom

Sexual Power in British Romantic Poetry — Watkins, Daniel P

The Sexual Revolution in Russia — Kon, Igor S

Sexual Selection — Gould, James L

The Sexual Tensions of William Sharp — Meyers, Terry L

Sexualitat, Macht Und Moral — Kienitz, Sabine

Sexualities — Hall, Marny

Sexuality and Authority in the Catholic Church — Miller, Monica Migliorino

Sexuality and Catholicism — Fox, Thomas C

Sexuality and Human Bonding — World Congress of Sexology (12th: 1995: Yokohama-Shi, Japan)

Sexuality and Modern Western Culture — Dean, Carolyn J

Sexuality and the Reading Encounter — Wilson, Emma

Sexuality in the Confessional — Haliczer, Stephen

The Sexuality of Christ in Renaissance Art and in Modern Oblivion. 2nd Ed., Rev. and Expanded — Steinberg, Leo

Sexuality, State, and Civil Society in Germany 1700-1815 — Hull, Isabel V

Sexualizing Power in Naturalism — Gammel, Irene

Sexualizing the Social — Adkins, Lisa

Sexy Bodies — Grosz, E A

c Seymour and Opal (Illus. by Ana Lopez Escriva) — Jussek, Nicole

Seymour/Carraher's Polymer Chemistry. 4th Ed. — Carraher, Charles E, Jr.

The SGML Implementation Guide — Travis, Brian E

Sha Ying — Yi, Li

c Shabanu, Daughter of the Wind — Staples, Suzanne Fisher

Shabby Chic — Ashwell, Rachel

Shackled — Garton, Ray

The Shade — Hogan, Judy

y Shade and Shadow — Woodbury, Francine G

Shades of Blue and Gray — Hattaway, Herman

Shades of Freedom — Higginbotham, A Leon

Shades of Grace — Delinsky, Barbara

y Shades of L.A. — Cole, Carolyn Kozo

Shades of Mao — Barme, Geremie

Shades of Twilight — Howard, Linda

Shadow behind the Heart — McCauley, Shane

The Shadow Box — Maxim, John R

y Shadow Boxer — Lynch, Chris

The Shadow Bride — Heath, Roy

y The Shadow Catcher — Szczypiorski, Andrzej

Shadow Dance — Carter, Angela

y Shadow Dawn (Auberjonois). Audio Version — Claremont, Chris

The Shadow Economy in Denmark 1994 — Mogensen, Gunnar Viby

Shadow Lines — Martens, Lorna

Shadow Maker — Sullivan, Rosemary

The Shadow Man — Gordon, Mary

Shadow Man — Scott, Melissa

y Shadow of a Star — Mann, Alfred K

Shadow of Ashland — Green, Terence M

y The Shadow of August — Welford, Sue

r Shadow of Death — Prunckun, Henry W, Jr.

The Shadow of Desire — Stowe, Rebecca

y Shadow of Fear — Peart, Jane

y The Shadow of Mordican — Lawrence, Louise

The Shadow of the Galilean — Theissen, Gerd

Shadow of the Plantation — Johnson, Charles S

c Shadow of the Red Moon (Illus. by Christopher Myers) — Myers, Walter Dean

Shadow of the Wolf — Plumlee, Harry James

The Shadow of Ulysses — Boitani, Piero

The Shadow of Wings — Knox-Mawer, June

c Shadow over Second (Illus. by Anna Dewdney) — Christopher, Matt

y Shadow over Shangri-La — Pokhrel, Durga

Shadow Play — Klaber, William F

The Shadow President — Hersh, Burton

Shadow Shoguns — Schlesinger, Jacob M

Shadow Syndromes — Ratey, John J

The Shadow: Thirteen Stories in Opposition — Jaramillo Levi, Enrique

y Shadow War — Chester, Deborah

Shadow War — Conboy, Kenneth

y The Shadow Warriors — Judd, Cameron

Shadow Woman — Perry, Thomas

Shadowcatchers: A Journey in Search of the Teachings of Native American Elders (Toms). Audio Version — Wall, Steve

The Shadowed Hills — Howard, Audrey

Shadowlands (Suchet). Audio Version — Sibley, Brian

ShadowLight: A Photographer's Life — Patterson, Freeman

Shadows and Enlightenment — Baxandall, Michael

Shadows in the Sea — Allen, Thomas B

Shadows of Empire — Sears, Laurie J

y Shadows of Olive Trees — Gervay, Susanne

Shadows of Realism — Kindelan, Nancy

y Shadows of Steel (Foxworth). Audio Version — Brown, Dale

Shadows of Tender Fury — Marcos, Subcomandante

Shadows of the Empire — Perry, Steve

Shadows of the Future — Parrinder, Patrick

Shadows of the Heart — Grant, Tracy

Shadows of the Mind — Penrose, Roger

y Shadows of Time — Wrightson, Patricia

Shadows of Vietnam — Vandiver, Frank E

She's Got the Blues

c She's Wearing a Dead Bird on Her Head (Illus. by David Catrow) — *Lasky, Kathryn*

c Shhh! (Illus. by Tim Warnes) — *Sykes, Julie*

Shi Nian De Lu — *Wu, Jiang*

Shi'a Islam — *Halm, Heinz*

y Shield of Lies — *Kube-McDowell, Michael P*

y Shield of Lies (Heald). Audio Version — *Kube-McDowell, Michael P*

The Shift — *Foy, George*

Shift — *Merrin, Jeredith*

The Shifting Realities of Philip K. Dick — *Dick, Philip K*

Shiite Islam — *Richard, Yann*

c Shiloh — *Naylor, Phyllis Reynolds*

y Shiloh — *Time-Life Books*

Shiloh Autumn — *Thoene, Bodie*

y Shiloh Season — *Naylor, Phyllis Reynolds*

y Shiloh: The Battle That Changed the Civil War — *Daniel, Larry J*

Shimmer — *Tunstrom, Goran*

y The Shimmering Door — *Kerr, Katharine*

y Shimmy Shimmy Shimmy like My Sister Kate — *Giovanni, Nikki*

Shine: The Screenplay — *Sardi, Jan*

Shingwauk's Vision — *Miller, J R*

A Shining City on a Hill — *Kiewe, Amos*

A Shining Reflection — *Rogers, Annie G*

Shinju — *Rowland, Laura Joh*

c Shinkei — *Rubenstein, Gillian*

c Shin's Tricycle (Illus. by Noriyuki Ando) — *Kodama, Tatsuharu*

Shiny Water — *Salter, Anna*

c Ship (Illus. by Chris L Demarest) — *Demarest, Chris L*

Ship Ashore! — *Mobley, Joe A*

The Ship Avenged — *Stirling, S M*

r The Ship Captain's Medical Guide. 21st Ed.

Ship Fever and Other Stories — *Barrett, Andrea*

Ship of the Hunted — *Elberg, Yehuda*

The Ship That Held the Line — *Rose, Lisle A*

The Shipbuilders of Essex — *Story, Dana*

Shipbuilding on Prince Edward Island — *De Jong, Nicolas J*

Shipbuilding Technology and Education — *National Research Council (U.S.). Committee on National Needs in Maritime Technology*

r Shipping Business and Maritime Economics — *McConville, James*

The Shipping Forecast — *Powers, Mark*

y The Shipping News (Schraf). Audio Version — *Proulx, E Annie*

c Ships — *Humble, Richard*

c Ships (Illus. by Gerald Wood) — *Kerr, Daisy*

Ship's Doctor — *Riley, Terrence L*

Ships of Our Ancestors — *Anuta, Michael J*

c Ships of the Air (Illus. by Lynn Curlee) — *Curlee, Lynn*

The Shipwreck of Their Hopes — *Cozzens, Peter*

Shipwrecks — *Yoshimura, Akira*

yr Shipwrecks: An Encyclopedia of the World's Worst Disasters at Sea — *Ritchie, David*

Shirley — *Bronte, Charlotte*

Shirts of Steel — *Birand, Mehmet Ali*

Shivers for Christmas — *Dalby, Richard*

Shkaba — *Kadare, Ismail*

Shliakhom Burkhlyvym — *Babenko, Hry Horri*

c Sho and the Demons of the Deep (Illus. by Annouchka G Galouchko) — *Galouchko, Annouchka G*

Shoah: The Paradigmatic Genocide — *Garber, Zev*

The Shobies' Story (Bruce). Audio Version — *Le Guin, Ursula K*

Shock Compression of Condensed Matter 1995. Pts. 1-2 — *Schmidt, Steve*

Shock, from Molecular and Cellular Level to Whole Body — *Okada, Kazuo*

The Shock of Arrival — *Alexander, Meena*

Shock Radio — *Clark, Leigh*

A Shock to the System — *Brennan, Timothy J*

Shock Wave — *Cussler, Clive*

y Shock Wave (Prichard). Audio Version — *Cussler, Clive*

c Shock Waves through Los Angeles — *Vogel, Carole Garbuny*

y A Shocker on Shock Street. Audio Version — *Stine, R L*

The Shocking Ballad Picture Show — *Cheesman, Tom*

Shocking Crimes of Postwar Japan — *Schreiber, Mark*

y Shocking Science (Illus. by John Kelly) — *Parker, Steve*

Shocking the Web — *Clarke, Cathy*

Shocks and Rocks — *Oliver, Jack*

Shockwave Power Solutions — *Rabinowitz, Noel*

c Shoebag Returns — *James, Mary*

Shoes: A Celebration of Pumps, Sandals, Slippers and More — *O'Keeffe, Linda*

Shoes in the Freezer, Beer in the Flower Bed and Other Down-Home Tips for House and Garden — *Wilen, Joan*

c Shoes like Miss Alice's (Illus. by Ken Page) — *Johnson, Angela*

c Shoes: Their History in Words and Pictures (Illus. by David Yue) — *Yue, Charlotte*

The Shona and Their Neighbours — *Beach, D N*

Shoot! — *Bowering, George*

Shoot! — *Cronley, Jay*

Shoot/Don't Shoot (Critt). Audio Version — *Jance, J A*

Shooters — *Lankford, Terrill*

The Shooters — *Metz, Leon Claire*

Shooters: TV News Photographers and Their Work — *Lindekugel, D M*

Shooting at Loons (Critt). Audio Version — *Maron, Margaret*

Shooting at the Moon — *Warner, Roger*

Shooting Elvis — *Eversz, Robert M*

Shooting from the Hip — *Fordham, John*

The Shooting Gallery — *Tsushima, Yuko*

Shooting Sports for Women — *Morrow, Laurie*

c Shooting Star   *Blacker, Terence*

c Shooting Star (Illus. by Scott Goto) — *Dadey, Debbie*

c A Shooting Star — *Klass, Sheila Solomon*

A Shooting Star — *Stegner, Wallace Earle*

y The Shop on Danforth Avenue — *Barclay, Tony*

c The Shopping Basket — *Burningham, John*

Shopping for Buddhas — *Greenwald, Jeff*

r Shopping LA

yr The Shoresaver's Handbook — *Coombe, Tucker*

c Short Cut (Illus. by Donald Crews) — *Crews, Donald*

A Short Discourse on the Tyrannical Government — *William, of Ockham*

A Short Guide to the Retention of Documents — *Hamer, Andrew*

y A Short History of Africa (Howard). Audio Version — *Oliver, Roland*

A Short History of Ancient Egypt — *James, T G H*

A Short History of Byzantium — *Norwich, John Julius*

c A Short History of God, Me and the Universe — *Stannard, Russell*

y A Short History of Planet Earth — *Macdougall, J D*

A Short History of Renaissance and Reformation Europe — *Zophy, Jonathan W*

y A Short History of the Civil War — *Stokesbury, James L*

A Short History of the Universe — *Silk, Joseph*

yr The Short Oxford History of English Literature. Rev. Ed. — *Sanders, Andrew*

y Short Plays for Young Actors — *Slaight, Craig*

Short Stories — *Hughes, Langston*

Short Stories — *Knauff, Robert E*

Short Stories 1895-1926 — *De La Mare, Walter*

y Short Stories by Guy De Maupassant — *Maupassant, Guy De*

y Short Stories by Katherine Mansfield — *Mansfield, Katherine*

y Short Stories by Thomas Hardy — *Hardy, Thomas*

The Short Stories of F. Scott Fitzgerald — *Fitzgerald, F Scott*

r Short Story Criticism. Vols. 18-19

r Short Story Criticism. Vols. 20-21

The Short Swift Time of Gods on Earth — *Bahr, Donald*

Short Tails and Treats from Three Dog Bakery — *Dye, Daniel*

y Short Takes — *Kulpa, Kathryn*

Short-Term Couples Therapy — *Luquet, Wade*

Short-Term Losses — *Lindensmith, Mark*

r Short-Title Catalogue of Hungarian Books Printed before 1851 in the British Library — *British Library*

c A Short Walk around the Pyramids and through the World of Art — *Isaacson, Philip M*

Shortchangers: A Story of the Near Future — *Silver, Arnold*

Shortcuts to Beginning Reading — *Myers, Marie L*

A Shorter Illustrated History of Ulster — *Bardon, Jonathan*

The Shorter Science and Civilisation in China. Vol. 5 — *Needham, Joseph*

c A Shorter Shakespeare Series (Illus. by Cal Williams) — *Shakespeare, William*

Shorter Works and Fragments. Vols. 1-2 — *Coleridge, Samuel Taylor*

The Shortest Day — *Langton, Jane*

y The Shortest Day (Reading). Audio Version — *Langton, Jane*

The Shortest Distance between You and a Published Book — *Page, Susan*

r Shortwave Listening on the Road — *Yoder, Andrew R*

Shostakovich Studies — *Fanning, David*

A Shot in the Cathedral — *Bencastro, Mario*

Should Developing Countries Have Central Banks? — *Schuler, Kurt*

Should We Burn Babar? — *Kohl, Herbert*

Shoulder Injuries in Sport — *Ciullo, Jerome V*

c Show and Tell Day (Illus. by Lizzy Rockwell) — *Rockwell, Anne F*

Show Me a Hero — *Schinto, Jeanne*

c Show-Me-How I Can Make Music — *Purton, Michael*

c The Show-Off Mouse (Illus. by Val Biro) — *Benjamin, A H*

Showdown: The Lithuanian Rebellion and the Breakup of the Soviet Empire — *Krickus, Richard J*

Showdown: The Struggle between the Gingrich Congress and the Clinton White House — *Drew, Elizabeth*

Showgirls — *Stuart, Andrea*

Showing America a New Way Home — *Johnson, James A*

y Showing My Color — *Page, Clarence*

Showing Signs of Violence — *George, Kenneth M*

Showtune: A Memoir — *Herman, Jerry*

A Shriek in the Forest Night — *Lawrence, R D*

The Shrine — *Odone, Cristina*

c Shrinking Mouse (Illus. by Pat Hutchins) — *Hutchins, Pat*

c Shrinking Pains — *Goldman, E M*

A Shrinking World? — *Allen, John*

Shroud for the Archbishop — *Tremayne, Peter*

y Shrouds of Glory (Whitener). Audio Version — *Groom, Winston*

r Shrubs and Climbers (Eyewitness Handbooks)

Shupton's Fancy — *Schullery, Paul*

Shutout: The Legend of Terry Sawchuk — *Kendall, Brian*

The Shuttered Eye — *Copus, Julia*

Si Prega Di Non Disturbare — *D'Eramo, Luce*

Si Shi Nian Lai Zhong Guo Wen Xue

The Sibelius Companion — *Goss, Glenda Dawn*

Siberia and Other Plays — *Mitterer, Felix*

Siberia, Siberia — *Rasputin, Valentin Grigor'evich*

The Siberian Iris — *McEwen, Currier*

Sibling Relationships across the Life Span — *Cicirelli, Victor G*

The Sibling Society — *Bly, Robert*

The Sibling Society (Bly). Audio Version — *Bly, Robert*

r Sicily: The Rough Guide. 3rd Ed. — *Andrews, Robert*

Sick Heart River — *Buchan, John*

Sicken and So Die — *Brett, Simon*

Sicken and So Die (Brett). Audio Version — *Brett, Simon*

The Sickening Mind — *Martin, Paul*

c Sickle Cell Anemia — *Silverstein, Alvin*

Sickness and Healing — *Kahn, Robert A*

The Sickroom in Victorian Fiction — *Bailin, Miriam*

c Sid and Sam (Illus. by G Brian Karas) — *Buck, Nola*

En Sida Av Himlen — *Born, Heidi Von*

El SIDA Y El Trabajo — *Vasquez, Priscilla*

c Side by Side (Illus. by Romi Caron) — *Baillie, Marilyn*

Side by Side French and English Grammar — *Farrell, Edith R*

Side Show 1997

r Sideline Help — *Steele, Marshall K*

Sidelines Activist — *Robbins, Richard*

Sideshow War — *Botjer, George F*

c Sidewalk Games around the World — *Erlbach, Arlene*

c Sideways Arithmetic from Wayside School — *Sachar, Louis*

The Sidney Family Romance — *Waller, Gary*

Sidney Lumet — *Boyer, Jay*

Sidney Rigdon: A Portrait of Religious Excess — *Van Wagoner, Richard S*

Sidonius Apollinaris and the Fall of Rome A.D. 407-485 — *Harries, Jill*

Sieches Volk Macht Siechen Staat — *Burg, Thomas N*

Le Siecle De Louis XIV — *Goubert, Pierre*

Un Siecle De Sculpture Anglaise

Le Siecle Des Platter. Vol. 1 — *Le Roy Ladurie, Emmanuel*

The Siege of Fort Cumberland 1776 — *Clarke, Ernest*

A Siegel Film — *Siegel, Don*

Siegfried Sassoon: Scorched Glory — *Moeyes, Paul*

r Sieg's Montkatalog. 1997 Ed.
Siena and the Sienese in the Thirteenth Century — *Waley, Daniel Philip*
Siena, Florence and Padua. Vols. 1-2 — *Norman, Diana*
y Sierra: A Novel of the California Gold Rush — *Wheeler, Richard S*
r The Sierra Club Green Guide — *Feldman, Andrew J*
The Sierra Club Nature Writing Handbook — *Murray, John A*
The Sierra Club Wetlands Reader — *Wilson, Sam*
r A Sierra Nevada Flora. 4th Ed. — *Weeden, Norman*
c Sight (Illus. by Francisco Arredondo) — *Llamas, Andreu*
r Sight and Sound Film Review Volume: January 1994 to December 1994
Sight Unseen and Other Plays — *Margulies, Donald*
Sightings: Beyond Imagination Lies the Truth — *Michaels, Susan*
Sights Unseen — *Gibbons, Kaye*
Sigmar Polke Photoworks — *Ferguson, Russell*
c The Sign in Mendel's Window (Illus. by Margot Zemach) — *Phillips, Mildred*
The Sign of Four — *Doyle, Arthur Conan, Sir*
The Sign of the Cross — *Toibin, Colm*
c Sign of the Dove — *Fletcher, Susan*
The Sign of the Golden Grasshopper — *Gresham, Perry S*
c The Sign of the Seahorse — *Base, Graeme*
A Sign of the Times — *Calabrese, Omar*
Sign, Symbol, Code (Lopez-Morillas). Audio Version — *Eco, Umberto*
Sign Wars — *Goldman, Robert*
The Signal Companion — *Moss, Elaine*
Signal Processing for Industrial Diagnostics — *Romberg, T M*
Signal Treatment and Signal Analysis in NMR — *Rutledge, D N*
Signaling by the Hematopoietic Cytokine Receptors — *Silvennoinen, Olli*
Signaling from Mars — *Ransome, Arthur*
Signals and Systems. 2nd Ed. — *Oppenheim, Alan V*
r Signals Intelligence in World War II — *Sexton, Donal J*
Signals of Distress — *Crace, Jim*
Un Signe Des Temps — *Michaud, Francine*
Signes and Sothe — *Barr, Helen*
Significant Incident — *Bercuson, David Jay*
Significant Others — *Chadwick, Whitney*
Signo Y Memoria — *Bou, Enric*
Il Signor Leprotti E Sensibile — *Gnocchi, Gene*
Signs Grow — *Merrell, Floyd*
Signs of Arrival — *Harrison, Jeffrey*
Signs of Borges — *Molloy, Sylvia*
Signs of Grace — *Brown, David, 1948, July, 7-*
Signs of Life — *Brookes, Tim*
y Signs of Life — *Wilder, Cherry*
Signs of Nations — *Hedetoft, Ulf*
Signs of Performance — *Counsell, Colin*
Signs of Writing — *Harris, Roy*
Siirin Vaktine Mezmur — *Demirag, Fikret*
c Sikh — *Chambers, Catherine*
c Sikhism — *Prior, Lesley*
Sikhism — *Richards, Chris*
y Sikhism: A New Approach — *Draycott, Pamela*
Silas Marner — *Eliot, George*
Silas Talbot: Captain of Old Ironsides — *Fowler, William M, Jr.*
The Silence — *Maclean, Charles*
Un Silence D'Environ Une Demiheure — *Schreiber, Boris*
Silence in the Novels of Elie Wiesel — *Sibelman, Simon P*
The Silence of Memory — *Gregory, Adrian*
The Silence of the Body — *Ceronetti, Guido*
Silence of the Hams — *Churchill, Jill*
The Silence of the Langford — *Langford, Dave*
Silencer — *Armstrong, Campbell*
Silencing a People — *Americas Watch Committee (U.S.)*
The Silent Dialogue — *Hackett, David G*
The Silent Feminists — *Slide, Anthony*
r Silent Film Performers — *Liebman, Roy*
r Silent Films on Video — *Klepper, Robert K*
The Silent Garden — *Ogden, Paul W*
Silent Honor — *Steel, Danielle*
Silent Honor. Audio Version — *Steel, Danielle*
p Silent Invasion, Bk. 3: The Tarnished Dreams — *Cherkas, Michael*
p Silent Invasion, Bk. 4: The Great Fear — *Cherkas, Michael*
c Silent Night (Illus. by Belinda Downes)

Silent Night — *Clark, Mary Higgins*
c Silent Night (Illus. by Susan Jeffers) — *Mohr, Joseph*
c Silent Night (Illus. by Alexandra Wallner) — *Wallner, Alexandra*
Silent Revolution — *Green, Duncan*
Silent Rights — *Massey, Calvin R*
The Silent Subject — *Stetson, Brad*
y Silent Tears No More — *Baer, Judy*
Silent Travelers — *Kraut, Alan M*
Silent Witness — *Patterson, Richard North*
y Silent Words — *Drury, Joan M*
Silicon Carbide and Related Materials 1995 — *Nakashima, S*
Silicon Embrace — *Shirley, John*
y Silicon Snake Oil — *Stoll, Clifford*
The Silicone Breast Implant Story — *Vanderford, Marsha L*
Silk — *Anquetil, Jacques*
Silk — *Baricco, Alessandro*
Silk and Bamboo Music in Shanghai — *Witzleben, J Lawrence*
Silk and Religion — *Liu, Hsin-Ju*
c Silk Peony, Parade Dragon (Illus. by Carol Inouye) — *Steckman, Elizabeth*
Silk Stockings and Ballot Boxes — *Tyler, Pamela*
Silk: Stories — *Mazur, Grace Dane*
Silk Tree, Guanacaste, Monkey's Earring. Pt. 1 — *Barneby, Rupert C*
c La Silla De Pedro (Illus. by Ezra Jack Keats) — *Keats, Ezra Jack*
c Silly Heads (Illus. by Cathie Shuttleworth) — *Wickings, Ruth*
c Silly Times with Two Silly Trolls (Illus. by Lisa Thiesing) — *Jewell, Nancy*
The Silo: A Pastoral Symphony — *Kinsella, John*
Silver Bells (Illus. by Gwynne Forster)
c Silver Berries and Christmas Magic (Illus. by Steven Morris) — *Gaffington, Urslan Judith*
The Silver Castle — *James, Clive*
The Silver Chariot Killer — *Lupoff, Richard A*
The Silver Cloud Cafe — *Vea, Alfredo, Jr.*
The Silver Coins of Medieval France 476-1610 A.D. — *Roberts, James N*
The Silver Cord — *Armstrong, David*
Silver Dollar — *Russell, Carol Ann*
y The Silver Gryphon — *Lackey, Mercedes*
Silver: History and Design — *Glanville, Philippa*
Silver Holloware for Dining Elegance — *Osterberg, Richard*
Silver Jewelry Designs — *Schiffer, Nancy N*
y The Silver Kiss — *Klause, Annette Curtis*
y Silver Rights — *Curry, Constance*
The Silver Rubles and Yefimoks of Romanov Russia 1654-1915 — *Zander, Randolph*
Silver Seasons — *Mandelaro, Jim*
The Silver Stone — *Rosenberg, Joel*
c Silver Threads (Illus. by Michael Martchenko) — *Skrypuch, Marsha Forchuk*
c The Silver Treasure (Illus. by Bee Willey) — *McCaughrean, Geraldine*
Silverman's Game — *Heuer, Gerald A*
c The Silversmiths — *Fisher, Leonard Everett*
y Silvestre Y Los Ladrones De Suenos — *Ferrer Bermejo, Jose*
Simenon: A Biography — *Assouline, Pierre*
Simeon's Bride — *Taylor, Alison G*
c Similon — *Cave, Kathryn*
Simisola — *Rendell, Ruth*
y Simisola (Peters). Audio Version — *Rendell, Ruth*
c Simon and Schuster Children's Guide to Birds — *Johnson, Jinny*
c Simon and Schuster Children's Guide to Insects and Spiders — *Johnson, Jinny*
r The Simon and Schuster Pocket Guide to Beer — *Jackson, Michael, 1942-*
Simon Said — *Shaber, Sarah R*
y Simon Wiesenthal: A Life in Search of Justice — *Pick, Hella*
Simone De Beauvoir: The Making of an Intellectual Woman — *Moi, Toril*
Simone Weil — *Plant, Stephen*
Simple Abundance — *Ban Breathnach, Sarah*
Simple Annals — *Allen, James*
A Simple Approach to Digital Signal Processing — *Marven, Craig*
A Simple Celebration — *Bragg, Ginna Bell*
c Simple Earth Science Experiments with Everyday Materials (Illus. by Frances Zweifel) — *Loeschnig, Louis V*
Simple Gifts — *Coulter, William*

c Simple Gifts of Christmas. Book and Audio Version — *Kupferschmid, Steve*
A Simple Heart — *Flaubert, Gustave*
Simple Justice — *Wilson, John Morgan*
c Simple Kaleidoscopes! — *Newlin, Gary*
c Simple Machines (Illus. by Ray Boudreau) — *Hodge, Deborah*
Simple Methods for Identification of Plastics. 3rd, Rev. Ed. — *Braun, Dietrich*
c Simple Nature Experiments with Everyday Materials (Illus. by Frances Zweifel) — *Fredericks, Anthony D*
Simple Passion — *Ernaux, Annie*
A Simple Program — *W., Bill*
c Simple Puppets from Everyday Materials (Illus. by Barbara MacDonald Buetter) — *Buetter, Barbara MacDonald*
Simple Rules for a Complex World — *Epstein, Richard Allen*
c Simple Science Experiments (Illus. by Lynn Adams) — *McLoughlin, Andrea*
y The Simple Science of Flight — *Tennekes, H*
Simple Simon. Audio Version — *Pearson, Ryne Douglas*
y Simple Simon (Morton). Audio Version — *Pearson, Ryne Douglas*
Simple Skin Surgery. 2nd Ed. — *Burge, Susan B*
Simple Spells for Success — *Dolnick, Barrie*
Simple Statistics for Library and Information Professionals — *Stephen, Peter*
A Simple Story — *Inchbald, Elizabeth*
Simple Theory, Hard Reality — *Wicharaya, Tamasak*
The Simple Truth — *Levine, Philip*
Simple Upholstery and Slipcovers — *Parks, Carol*
Simpler Times — *Butler, J George*
A Simpler Way — *Wheatley, Margaret J*
La Simplicite Du Principe — *Gilbert, Paul*
Simplicity — *Stone, Ruth*
A Simplified Approach to Image Processing — *Crane, Randy*
Simplified Design of Concrete Structures. 7th Ed. — *Ambrose, James E*
Simplified Design of IC Amplifiers — *Lenk, John D*
A Simplified Guide to Custom Stairbuilding and Tangent Handrailing — *Di Cristina, George R*
Simply AIX — *Cannon, Casey*
y Simply Italian — *Harris, Valentina*
Simply Love — *Anderson, Catherine*
Simply Stars — *Anderson, Alex*
Simply Surrender — *Kirvan, John*
c Simply the Best
r Simpson's Contemporary Quotations — *Simpson, James B*
Simulating Workplace Safety Policy — *Kniesner, Thomas J*
Simulation Modelling in Bioengineering — *Cerrolaza, M*
The Simultaneous Treatment of Parent and Child — *Chazan, Saralea E*
Das Simultaneum: Ein Staatskirchenrechtliches, Politisches Und Theologisches Problem Des Alten Reiches — *Schafer, Christoph*
Sin and Censorship — *Walsh, Frank*
Sin and Self-Consciousness in the Thought of Friedrich Schleiermacher — *Vance, Robert Lee*
Sin and the Calvinists — *Mentzer, Raymond A*
y The Sin Eater — *Schmidt, Gary D*
Sin-Itiro Tomonaga: Life of a Japanese Physicist — *Matsui, Makinosuke*
Sin, Organized Charity and the Poor Law in Victorian England — *Humphreys, Robert*
c Sinbad the Sailor (Illus. by Marcia Williams) — *Williams, Marcia*
Since the Noon Mail Stopped — *Prunty, Wyatt*
The Sincere Cafe — *Becker, Leslee*
Sindh Revisited — *Ondaatje, Christopher*
c Sing a New Song (Illus. by Bijou Le Tord) — *Bible. O.T. Psalms. English. Le Tord. Selections. 1997*
Sing a New Song — *Spencer, Jon Michael*
c Sing a Song of Circus (Illus. by Ward Schumaker) — *Schumaker, Ward*
c Sing, Elvis, Sing! (Illus. by Steve Bjorkman) — *Spinner, Stephanie*
r Sing Glory and Hallelujah! — *Rogal, Samuel J*
c Sing 'n Learn Chinese. Book and Audio Version — *Jeng, Trio Jan*
c Sing 'n Learn Korean. Book and Audio Version — *Kim, Bo-Kyung*
c Sing Noel (Illus. by Nancy Sippel Carpenter) — *Yolen, Jane*
c Sing, Sophie! (Illus. by Rosanne Litzinger) — *Dodds, Dayle Ann*

y Sing the Warmth — *Marley, Louise*
y Sing to Me, Dreamer (Howley). Audio Version — *Koea, Shonagh*
Sing unto God a New Song — *Levine, Herbert J*
r Sing Your Heart Out, Country Boy. Newly Rev. and Expanded Ed. — *Horstman, Dorothy*
The Singapore Economy — *Peebles, Gavin*
Singapore: The Global City-State — *Murray, Geoffrey*
The Singer of Tales in Performance — *Foley, John Miles*
r Singers of the Century — *Steane, J B*
Singing Early Music — *McGee, Timothy J*
Singing for Your Supper — *Hazard, Edith*
Singing of the Source — *Chaves, Jonathan*
Singing Professionally — *Young, Arabella Hong*
The Singing Sword — *Whyte, Jack*
Singing the Chaos — *Pratt, William*
Single Firing — *Tristram, Fran*
Single Minding! — *Lederer, Helen*
y Single-Parent Families — *Swisher, Karin L*
A Single Shot — *Jones, Matthew F*
A Single Shot (Choate). Audio Version — *Jones, Matthew F*
Singular Impressions — *Moser, Joann*
Singular Semi-Riemannian Geometry — *Kupeli, Demir N*
Singular Spectrum Analysis — *Elsner, James B*
Singular Voices — *Diamonstein, Barbaralee*
Singular Voices — *Humill, Tony*
Singularity — *Glazner, Greg*
Sink or Swim — *Hammond, Gerald*
r Sinkler/Sinclair/St. Clair. Update 1996 — *Grigsby, Jean*
Sinners and the Righteous — *Winninge, Mikael*
Sins — *Jose, F Sionil*
The Sins of Childhood and Other Stories — *Prus, Boleslaw*
Sintaxis De Un Signo — *Urbina, Nicasio*
Sintering Technology — *German, Randall M*
Sintesis E Indice De Los Mandamientos Virreinales 1548-1553 — *Gerhard, Peter*
c A Sip of Aesop (Illus. by Karen Barbour) — *Yolen, Jane*
c Sip, Slurp, Soup, Soup (Illus. by Alex Pardo DeLange) — *Bertrand, Diane Gonzales*
p Sipaz Report
r Sir Arthur Sullivan: A Resource Book — *Dillard, Philip H*
r Sir Banister Fletcher's A History of Architecture. 20th Ed. — *Fletcher, Banister, Sir*
Sir Charles Grey, First Earl Grey — *Nelson, Paul David*
y Sir Edmund Hillary: To Everest and Beyond (Illus. by Anne B Keiser) — *Stewart, Whitney*
Sir Ernest MacMillan: The Importance of Being Canadian — *Schabas, Ezra*
Sir Francis Drake — *Sugden, John*
Sir Francis Drake as Seen by His Contemporaries — *Quinn, David B*
Sir Gawain and the Green Knight and French Arthurian Romance — *Putter, Ad*
Sir Hans Sloane: Collector, Scientist, Antiquary, Founding Father of the British Museum — *MacGregor, Arthur*
Sir Harry Gibbs: Without Fear or Favour — *Priest, Joan*
Sir James Pennethorne and the Making of Victorian London — *Tyack, Geoffrey*
Sir John Everett Millais — *Ash, Russell*
Sir John Soane: Enlightenment Thought and the Royal Academy Lectures — *Watkin, David*
Sir Joshua Reynolds: The Painter in Society — *Wendorf, Richard*
Sir Joshua Reynolds: The Subject Pictures — *Postle, Martin*
Sir Matthew Hale 1609-1676 — *Cromartie, Alan*
Sir Richard Westmacott, Sculptor — *Busco, Marie*
r Sir Robert Peel 1788-1850 — *Cowie, Leonard W*
r Sir Thomas More in the English Renaissance — *Boswell, Jackson Campbell*
Sir Wilfrid Laurier and the Romance of Canada — *LaPierre, Laurier L*
Sir William Chambers: Architect to George III — *Harris, John, 1931-*
Sir William Jones — *Franklin, Michael J, 1949-*
Sir William Jones: Selected Poetical and Prose Works — *Jones, William, Sir*
y Siren Song — *Welford, Sue*
Siren's Lullaby — *Kennedy, William P*
The Sirius Connection — *Hope, Murry*
Sirk on Sirk — *Sirk, Douglas*

Det Sista Ljuset — *Kallifatides, Theodor*
El Sistema Defensivo Americano — *Gomez Perez, Maria Del Carmen*
Sister — *Ansay, A Manette*
Sister Brother — *Wineapple, Brenda*
Sister CEO — *Broussard, Cheryl D*
c Sister Cities — *Burger, Leslie*
Sister Jamaica — *Bolles, A Lynn*
Sister Power — *Reid-Merritt, Patricia*
c Sister Shako and Kolo the Goat — *Dalokay, Vedat*
Sister, Sister — *Dickey, Eric Jerome*
y Sister Stories — *Peterson, Brenda*
y Sister to Sister — *Foster, Patricia*
y Sister Wendy's Grand Tour — *Beckett, Wendy*
Sisters in Arms — *McNamara, Jo Ann Kay*
y Sisters in Fantasy 2 — *Shwartz, Susan*
Sisters in Solitude — *Tsomo, Karma Lekshe*
Sisters in the Resistance — *Weitz, Margaret Collins*
Sisters Listening to Sisters — *Andrews, Peggy*
Sisters: Lives of Devotion and Defiance — *Lieblich, Julia*
Sisters of Gore — *Franceschina, John*
Sisters of the Brush — *Garb, Tamar*
c A Sister's Wish (Illus. by Nancy Carpenter) — *Jacobs, Kate*
The Sistine Chapel — *Mancinelli, Fabrizio*
c Sit Still! — *Carlson, Nancy*
Sit: Zen Teachings of Master Taisen Deshimaru — *Deshimaru, Taisen*
Site Destruction in Georgia and the Carolinas — *Anderson, David G*
Sites of Memory, Sites of Mourning — *Winter, J M*
Un Sitio De Guangala Temprano En El Suroeste Del Ecuador — *Stothert, Karen E*
c Sitting Bull: Sioux Warrior — *Sanford, William R*
c Sitting Down to Eat (Illus. by Kitty Harvill) — *Harley, Bill*
Sitting In. Expanded Ed. — *Carruth, Hayden*
Situado and Sabana — *Bushnell, Amy Turner*
Situating College English — *Carton, Evan*
Situating Selves — *Carbaugh, Donal A*
y Situation Tragedy (Howard). Audio Version — *Brett, Simon*
The Sitwells and the Arts of the 1920s and 1930s — *Skipwith, Joanna*
Siuzhet Gogolia — *Vaiskopf, Mikhail*
Siva and Her Sisters — *Kapadia, Karin*
Six Circles, One Dewdrop — *Thornhill, Arthur H, III*
Six Contemporary Dramatists — *Wu, Duncan*
The Six-Day War — *Parker, Richard B*
Six Degrees of Kevin Bacon — *Fass, Craig*
Six Generation Charts. Vol. 1
Six Improvisations on the River — *Tsaloumas, Dimitris*
Six Masters of the Spanish Sonnet — *Barnstone, Willis*
The Six-Minute Fraternity — *Wallenfeldt, E C*
c Six-Minute Science Experiments (Illus. by Kim Whittingham) — *Brynie, Faith Hickman*
y Six Months to Live — *McDaniel, Lurlene*
Six Myths of Our Time — *Warner, Marina*
Six-Pack: Plays for Scotland — *McGrath, John*
c The Six Servants (Illus. by Sergei Goloshapov) — *Grimm, Jacob*
Six Years of Hell — *Hearn, Chester G*
Sixteen Songs — *Mendelssohn, Fanny*
r Sixteenth-Century British Nondramatic Writers: Third Series — *Richardson, David A*
Sixteenth-Century Ireland — *Lennon, Colm*
A Sixteenth-Century Spanish Bookstore — *Pettas, William*
y The Sixth Extinction — *Leakey, Richard*
Sixth Form Options — *Schagen, Sandie*
The Sixth Shotgun. Audio Version — *L'Amour, Louis*
The Sixties — *Stine, Peter*
The Sixties and the End of Modern America — *Steigerwald, David*
Sixties Design — *Garner, Philippe*
Sixties Going on Seventies — *Sayre, Nora*
Sixties Radicals, Then and Now — *Chepesuik, Ron*
Sixty Miles from Contentment — *Dunlop, M H*
Sixty-One Psalms of David — *Bible. O.T. Psalms. English. Slavitt. Selections. 1996*
Sixty Years of American Poetry
Sixty Years of Biology — *Bonner, John Tyler*
Size, Function and Life History — *Calder, William*
The Size of Thoughts — *Baker, Nicholson*
Sizing Down — *Illes, Louise Moser*
The Sjovold Site — *Dyck, Ian*
Skate: 100 Years of Figure Skating — *Milton, Steve*
c Skating on Sand (Illus. by Ann James) — *Gleeson, Libby*

Skazki O Liubvi — *Vasilleva, Larisa*
Skeletal Muscle — *McComas, Alan J*
Skeletal Radiology. 2nd Ed. — *Chew, Felix S*
c Skeleton — *Parker, Steve*
c Skeleton Closet (Illus. by Steven Guarnaccia) — *Guarnaccia, Steven*
c The Skeleton Club — *Sefton, Catherine*
A Skeptical Biochemist — *Fruton, Joseph S*
Skeptical Selves — *Russo, Elena*
A Skeptic's Guide to the New Age — *Edwards, Harry*
A Sketch of the Life and Character of Daniel Boone — *Houston, Peter*
Sketching Stories, Stretching Minds — *Whitin, Phyllis*
r Skibspost Til Og Fra Danmark I Midten Af 1800-Tallet — *Hansen, Kurt*
Skill Acquisition and Human Performance — *Proctor, Robert W*
Skill and Occupational Change — *Penn, Roger*
Skills, Qualifications and Utilisation — *Parsons, David*
Skills Training for Children with Behavior Disorders — *Bloomquist, Michael L*
Skin — *Briscoe, Joanna*
Skin Cancer — *Leigh, I M*
y Skin Deep — *Featherston, Elena*
y Skin Deep — *Golden, Marita*
r Skin Deep — *Ruby, Lois*
r Skin Deep — *Turkington, Carol*
y Skin Deep and Other Teenage Reflections (Illus. by Michael Bryant) — *Medearis, Angela Shelf*
Skin Deep, Blood Red — *Skinner, Robert E*
y Skin. Liars — *Foon, Dennis*
Skin: Sensual Tales — *Hiller, Catherine*
Skin Shows — *Halberstam, Judith*
c Skin, Teeth and Hair (Illus. by Ian Thompson) — *Sandeman, Anna*
Skin Trade — *DuCille, Ann*
Skinheads: Shaved for Battle — *Moore, Jack B*
Skinner's Ordeal — *Jardine, Quintin*
Skinner's Round — *Jardine, Quintin*
Skinner's Trail — *Jardine, Quintin*
Skinning Time — *Webster, Graeme*
Skinny Comfort Foods — *Spitler, Sue*
Skinny Feasts — *Hobsbawn-Smith, Dees*
Skinny Italian Cooking — *Glick, Ruth*
c Skinny Melon and Me (Illus. by Chris Fisher) — *Ure, Jean*
Skinny Vegetarian Entrees — *Magida, Phyllis*
Skinprint — *Marwood, Lorraine*
Skins — *Louis, Adrian C*
c Skip across the Ocean (Illus. by Sheila Moxley) — *Benjamin, Floella*
Skip All That — *Robinson, Robert*
The Skull Measurer's Mistake and Other Portraits of Men and Women Who Spoke Out against Racism — *Lindqvist, Sven*
Sky — *Purcell, Deirdre*
y Sky: A True Story of Resistance during World War II — *Ippisch, Hanneke*
Sky and Island Light — *Galvin, Brendan*
c Sky Dancer (Illus. by Jan Ormerod) — *Bushnell, Jack*
The Sky Fisherman — *Lesley, Craig*
The Sky Fisherman (Sala). Audio Version — *Lesley, Craig*
c A Sky Full of Kites (Illus. by Helen Hipshman) — *Molarsky, Osmond*
y The Sky in Silver Lace — *Klein, Robin*
c The Sky Is Not So Far Away (Illus. by Thomas Werner) — *Hillert, Margaret*
The Sky Never Changes — *Reed, Thomas F*
The Sky of the Heart — *Nityananda, Swami*
Sky over El Nido — *Mayo, C M*
The Sky People — *Grace, Patricia*
c Sky Pioneer — *Szabo, Corrine*
c Sky Scrape/City Scape (Illus. by Ken Condon) — *Yolen, Jane*
c Sky Tree (Illus. by Thomas Locker) — *Locker, Thomas*
y Sky Trillium — *May, Julian*
y Skydive! (Woodman). Audio Version — *Paulsen, Gary*
Skylar in Yankeeland — *Mcdonald, Gregory*
Skylark — *Kosztolanyi, Dezso*
c Skylark — *MacLachlan, Patricia*
c Skymaze — *Rubenstein, Gillian*
The Skyscraper Bioclimatically Considered — *Yeang, Ken*
c Skyscrapers and Towers — *Oxlade, Chris*
Skyscrapers Higher and Higher — *Mierop, Caroline*
y The Skystone — *Whyte, Jack*
Skywatchers, Shamans, and Kings — *Krupp, E C*
r Skywatching — *Levy, David H*
y Slam! — *Myers, Walter Dean*

c Slam Dunk (Illus. by Bill James) — *Morrison, Lillian*
Slam the Door Gently — *Glater, Ruth Ann Bobrov*
The Slammer: The Crisis in Canada's Prisons
 — *Marron, Kevin*
Slander — *Le, Linda*
r Slang and Sociability — *Eble, Connie*
The Slap — *McDonald, Roger*
SLAPPs: Getting Sued for Speaking Out — *Pring, George W*
Slashback — *Levine, Paul*
Slaughter among Neighbors — *Human Rights Watch (Organization)*
Slaughterhouse: Bosnia and the Failure of the West
 — *Rieff, David*
Slave Cultures and the Cultures of Slavery — *Palmie, Stephan*
c The Slave Dancer (MacNicol). Audio Version — *Fox, Paula*
y Slave Day — *Thomas, Rob*
Slave Laws in Virginia — *Schwarz, Philip J*
Slave-Mistress of Vixania — *Baron, Morgana*
Slave Population and Economy in Jamaica 1807-1834
 — *Higman, Barry W*
Slave Songs of the United States — *Allen, William Francis*
The Slave Soul of Russia — *Rancour-Laferriere, Daniel*
Slavery and Antislavery in Mauritius 1810-33
 — *Barker, Anthony J*
Slavery and Freedom in Delaware 1639-1865
 — *Williams, William H*
Slavery and Freedom in the Rural North — *Hodges, Graham Russell*
r Slavery and Slaving in World History — *Miller, Joseph C*
Slavery and the Catholic Tradition — *Brett, Stephen F*
Slavery and the Founders — *Finkelman, Paul*
Slavery, Capitalism, and Politics in the Antebellum Republic. Vol. 1 — *Ashworth, John*
Slavery in Early Mediaeval England — *Pelteret, David A E*
Slavery in North Carolina 1748-1775 — *Kay, Marvin L Michael*
Slaves into Workers — *Sikainga, Ahmad Alawad*
Slaves of the Machine — *Rawlins, Gregory J E*
Slavic and Baltic Library Resources at the New York Public Library — *Davis, Robert H, Jr.*
y Slay and Rescue — *Moore, John*
Slaying the Dragon — *Johnson, Michael*
Sleaze: Politicians, Private Interests and Public Raction — *Ridley, F F*
Sleaze: The Corruption of Parliament — *Leigh, David*
Sleep — *Hobson, J Allan*
c Sleep — *Newson, Lesley*
Sleep Deep — *Kenton, Leslie*
Sleep No More — *Rolt, L T C*
The Sleep of Reason — *Connelly, Frances S*
c Sleep, Sleep, Sleep (Illus. by Holly Meade) — *Van Laan, Nancy*
Sleep Thieves — *Coren, Stanley*
Sleeper Spy — *Safire, William*
y Sleeping at the Starlight Motel and Other Adventures on the Way Back Home — *White, Bailey*
Sleeping Beauty — *Macdonald, Ross*
Sleeping, Dreaming and Dying — *Varela, Francisco*
The Sleeping Giant — *Kaufmann, J E*
y Sleeping Lady — *Henry, Sue*
Sleeping Partner — *Paul, William*
Sleeping Preacher — *Kasdorf, Julia*
c Sleepless Beauty (Illus. by G Brian Karas) — *Minters, Frances*
c The Sleepy Men (Illus. by Robert Rayevsky)
 — *Brown, Margaret Wise*
y A Slender Thread — *Ackerman, Diane*
c A Slice through a City (Illus. by Peter Kent) — *Kent, Peter*
A Slice through Time — *Baillie, Michael G L*
r Slick Spins and Fractured Facts — *Rivers, Caryl*
Slicky Boys — *Limon, Martin*
Slide Collection Management in Libraries and Information Units — *Sutcliffe, Glyn*
Slide, Kelly, Slide — *Appel, Marty*
Slide Mountain — *Steinberg, Theodore*
Sling Blade — *Thornton, Billy Bob*
Slip-Shod Sibyls — *Greer, Germaine*
c Slither McCreep and His Brother Joe (Illus. by Victoria Chess) — *Johnston, Tony*
y A Sliver of Glass and Other Uncommon Tales
 — *Mazer, Anne*
Slogan Postmarks of Canada — *Coutts, Cecil C*
c Slopes (Illus. by Mike Gordon) — *Rush, Caroline*
The Slopes of Lebanon — *Oz, Amos*

Sloss Furnaces and the Rise of the Birmingham District — *Lewis, W David*
y Slot Machine — *Lynch, Chris*
r Slouching towards Gomorrah — *Bork, Robert H*
r Slovenia — *Carmichael, Cathie*
Slovo I Dilo Hosudareve — *Horban', Mykola*
Slow Birds (Bond). Audio Version — *Watson, Ian, 1943-*
Slow Dance — *Klein, Bonnie Sherr*
y Slow Dance Heart Break Blues (Illus. by William Cotton) — *Adoff, Arnold*
Slow Dancing with the Angel of Death — *Chappell, Helen*
Slow Death — *Home, Stewart*
Slow Emergencies — *Huston, Nancy*
Slow Fuse — *Togawa, Masako*
Slow Hand — *Slung, Michele*
Slow Reckoning — *Athanasiou, Tom*
y Slow River — *Griffith, Nicola*
Slow Train to Paradise — *Veenendaal, Augustus J, Jr.*
Slowness — *Kundera, Milan*
c Slug (Illus. by Karen Duncan) — *Robb, Jackie*
c Slumber Party! (Illus. by Judith Caseley) — *Caseley, Judith*
c The Slumber Party Secret — *Keene, Carolyn*
Smachnoho! Starovynni Ta Suchasni Retsepty Strav
 — *Charykova, Svitlana*
c Small Acts of Kindness (Illus. by Christopher Fay)
 — *Vollbracht, James*
Small Astronomical Observatories — *Moore, Patrick*
c Small Bear Lost (Illus. by Virginia Austin)
 — *Waddell, Martin*
The Small Business Start-Up Guide — *Sullivan, Robert, 1940-*
Small Ceremonies and the Box Garden — *Shields, Carol*
y A Small Civil War — *Neufeld, John*
Small Countries, Big Lessons — *Root, Hilton L*
Small Farmers and the Protection of the Watersheds
 — *Edwards, David T*
Small Firm Formation and Regional Economic Development — *Danson, Michael W*
Small Firms and Economic Growth. Vols. 1-2 — *Acs, Zoltan J*
Small Firms and Local Economic Development
 — *Ozcan, Gul Berna*
A Small Gathering of Bones — *Powell, Patricia*
The Small Hands of Slavery — *Tucker, Lee*
Small Holdings — *Barker, Nicola*
Small Hours of the Night — *Dalton, Roque*
Small Is Powerful — *Papworth, John*
Small Islands, Big Politics — *Amirahmadi, Hooshang*
Small Media, Big Revolution — *Sreberny-Mohammadi, Annabelle*
Small Spaces — *Brown, Azby*
Small States, Open Markets and the Organization of Business Interests — *McCann, Dermot*
y Small Steps — *Kehret, Peg*
A Small Target — *Andreae, Christine*
Small Town Girl — *Spencer, LaVyrle*
Small-Town Heroes — *Davis, Hank*
Small Towns in Early Modern Europe — *Clark, Peter*
c A Small Treasury of Easter Poems and Prayers (Illus. by Susan Spellman)
Small Vices — *Parker, Robert B*
Small Wars. 3rd Ed. — *Callwell, C E*
The Small Words in My Body — *Connelly, Karen*
Small Worlds — *Hoffman, Allen*
Small Worlds, Large Questions — *Rutman, Darrett P*
c The Smallest Whale (Illus. by Susan Field)
 — *Beresford, Elisabeth*
Smalltalk, Objects, and Design — *Liu, Chamond*
Smalltime — *Raine, Jerry*
Smart Actors, Foolish Choices — *Mayfield, Katherine*
c Smart Art — *Mayes, Susan*
Smart Cards — *Allen, Catherine A*
Smart Cards — *Kaplan, Jack*
Smart Cooking. 10th Anniversary Ed. — *Lindsay, Anne*
r Smart Funds 1997
r The Smart Gardener's Guide to Growing Vegetables
 — *Gough, Bob*
Smart Jews — *Gilman, Sander L*
r Smart Medicine for a Healthier Child — *Zand, Janet*
Smart Money Moves for African Americans
 — *Boston, Kelvin E*
Smart Moves — *Hannaford, Carla*
Smart Moves — *McCollum, Audrey*
The Smart Shopper's Guide to the Best Buys for Kids
 — *Robinson, Sue*
The Smart Take from the Strong — *Carril, Pete*

Smart Verse — *Smart, Ninian*
The Smart Woman's Guide to Starting a Business
 — *Montgomery, Vickie L, 1956-*
Smarter than You Think — *Loeb, Paul*
Smarter Trading — *Kaufman, Perry*
Smashed: Australian Drinking Stories — *Condon, Matthew*
Smashing Pots — *Barley, Nigel*
c Smell (Illus. by Francisco Arredondo) — *Llamas, Andreu*
c Smell and Taste (Illus. by Barrie Watts) — *Walpole, Brenda*
The Smell of Books — *Rindisbacher, Hans J*
c Smelly Old History: Roman Aromas — *Dobson, Mary*
c Smelly Old History: Tudor Odours — *Dobson, Mary*
c Smelly Old History: Victorian Vapours — *Dobson, Mary*
Smiatenie Chuvstv — *Berseneva, Anna*
c Smiffy Blue: Ace Crime Detective (Illus. by David J A Sims) — *Myers, Walter Dean*
Smile of the Medusa — *San Juan, E*
Smiley's People (Jayston). Audio Version — *Le Carre, John*
Smilla's Sense of Snow — *Hoeg, Peter*
Smith and Nephew in the Health Care Industry
 — *Foreman-Peck, James*
y Smithereens — *Chehak, Susan Taylor*
r Smithers' Mammals of Southern Africa — *Apps, Peter*
The Smithsonian and the American Indian — *Hinsley, Curtis M*
y The Smithsonian Book of the First Ladies
r The Smithsonian Guides to Natural America: Central Appalachia — *Hopkins, Bruce*
yr The Smithsonian Guides to Natural America: Southern New England — *Finch, Robert*
r The Smithsonian Guides to Natural America: The Far West — *Holing, Dwight*
r The Smithsonian Guides to Natural America: The Great Lakes — *Strutin, Michele*
yr The Smithsonian Guides to Natural America: The Mid-Atlantic States — *Walters, Eugene*
y The Smithsonian Guides to Natural America: The Northern Plains — *Shepard, Lansing*
y The Smithsonian Guides to Natural America: The South-Central States — *White, Mel*
r Smithsonian's Great Battles and Battlefields of the Civil War — *Wertz, Jay*
Smoke — *Macken, Deirdre*
Smoke — *Westlake, Donald E*
y Smoke (Kramer). Audio Version — *Westlake, Donald E*
Smoke and Mirrors — *Baum, Dan*
y Smoke and Mirrors — *Leonard, John*
Smoke and Mirrors — *Lindskold, Jane*
y Smoke Jumpers — *Sasser, Charles W*
The Smoke of Satan — *Cuneo, Michael W*
Smoke Proofs — *Taylor, James, 1952-*
Smokejumpers '49 — *Jenkins, Starr*
Smokescreen: The Truth behind the Tobacco Industry Cover-Up — *Hilts, Philip J*
Smokestack Lightning — *Elie, Lolis Eric*
Smokey O — *Cohen, Celia*
c Smoking (Illus. by Mike Lacey) — *Sanders, Pete*
y Smoking — *Wekesser, Carol*
c Smoking: A Risky Business — *Pringle, Laurence*
c Smoky Mountain Rose (Illus. by Brad Sneed)
 — *Schroeder, Alan*
c Smoky Night — *Bunting, Eve*
c Smoky's Special Easter Present (Illus. by Christa Unzner) — *Lachner, Dorothea*
Smoldering City — *Sawislak, Karen*
Smooth Talkers — *Kuiper, Koenrad*
Smoothing Methods in Statistics — *Simonoff, Jeffrey S*
c Smugglers' Island (Guidall). Audio Version — *Avi*
c Snail Started It! (Illus. by Angeli Von Roehl)
 — *Reider, Katja*
c Snailology (Illus. by Brian Grogan) — *Ross, Michael Elsohn*
c The Snake — *Crewe, Sabrina*
Snake — *Jennings, Kate*
c The Snake Book (Illus. by Frank Greenaway) — *Ling, Mary*
The Snake of God — *Young, Bard, 1941-*
y The Snake-Stone — *Doherty, Berlie*
c The Snake-Stone (Crowley). Audio Version
 — *Doherty, Berlie*
Snakebite Sonnet — *Phillips, Max*
Snakes and Ladders — *Mehta, Gita*
Snake's Daughter — *Gilberg, Gail Hosking*
y Snakes in Question — *Ernst, Carl H*

c Snakes, Salamanders, and Lizards (Illus. by Linda Garrow) — *Burns, Diane L*

Snakes: The Evolution of Mystery in Nature — *Greene, Harry W*

c Snap! (Illus. by Sascha Hutchinson) — *Vaughan, Marcia*

c Snap! Snap! — *Hawkins, Colin*

c Snappy Jazzy Jewelery — *Gayle, Katie*

c Snappy Jazzy Jewelry — *Gayle, Katie*

y Snapshot: America Discovers the Camera — *Czech, Kenneth P*

c Snapshots from the Wedding (Illus. by Stephanie Garcia) — *Soto, Gary*

A Sniper in the Tower — *Lavergne, Gary M*

The Snitch — *Leuci, Robert*

Snitch Factory — *Plate, Peter*

SNMP, SNMPv2, and RMON. 2nd Ed. — *Stallings, William*

c Snoopy's Christmas Tree (Illus. by Charles M Schulz) — *Schulz, Charles M*

Snow Angel — *Racina, Thom*

Snow Angels — *O'Nan, Stewart*

c Snow Day (Illus. by Moira Fain) — *Fain, Moira*

Snow Falling on Cedars — *Guterson, David*

y Snow Falling on Cedars (Guidall). Audio Version — *Guterson, David*

Snow Falling on Cedars (Marinker). Audio Version — *Guterson, David*

Snow in August — *Hamill, Pete*

Snow Job? — *Riley, Kevin Jack*

c The Snow Lambs (Illus. by Debi Gliori) — *Gliori, Debi*

The Snow Leopard — *Matthiessen, Peter*

The Snow Tree — *Walker, Elizabeth*

c The Snow Walker (Illus. by Mary O'Keefe Young) — *Wetterer, Margaret K*

c The Snow Whale (Illus. by Jackie Morris) — *Pitcher, Caroline*

c Snow White and Rose Red (Illus. by Bernadette Watts) — *Grimm, Jacob*

y Snow White, Blood Red — *Datlow, Ellen*

Snow Wolf — *Meade, Glenn*

y Snow Wolf (Michael). Audio Version — *Meade, Glenn*

c The Snowball (Illus. by Jean Pidgeon) — *Armstrong, Jennifer*

c Snowballs (Illus. by Lois Ehlert) — *Ehlert, Lois*

c Snowboarding: A Complete Guide for Beginners — *Sullivan, George*

Snowboarding to Nirvana — *Lenz, Frederick*

Snowboarding to Nirvana (Hawkins). Audio Version — *Lenz, Frederick*

c Snowbound: The Tragic Story of the Donner Party — *Lavender, David*

Snowdon on Stage — *Snowdon, Anthony Armstrong-Jones, Earl of*

r Snowdonia Rocky Rambles — *Lynas, Bryan*

Snowfire (Harper). Audio Version — *Whitney, Phyllis A*

The Snowflake on the Belfry — *Balakian, Anna*

Snowflakes in the Sun — *Buffong, Jean*

c A Snowman on Sycamore Street (Illus. by Melissa Sweet) — *Christiansen, C B*

c Snowpaws (Illus. by Kathryn Naylor) — *Downie, Mary Alice*

c The Snowy Day (Illus. by Ezra Jack Keats) — *Keats, Ezra Jack*

The Snowy Road and Other Stories — *Sallee, Hyunjae Yee*

c Snowy: The Christmas Dog (Illus. by Susan Scott) — *Lavelle, Sheila*

c Snuffles (Illus. by Judith Russell) — *Anson-Weber, Joan*

c Snuffles and Snouts (Illus. by Steven Kellogg) — *Robb, Laura*

So Close to Heaven — *Crossette, Barbara*

So Dear to Wicked Men — *Iakovou, Takis*

So Dearly Loved, So Much Admired — *Birdwood, Vere*

So Fine a Prospect — *Emmet, Alan*

So Forth — *Brodsky, Joseph*

So Good — *Berry, Venise T*

So I Am Glad — *Kennedy, A L*

So Incredibly Idaho! — *Schwantes, Carlos A*

So It Goes — *Grennan, Eamon*

So Little Done — *Dalrymple, Theodore*

So Long, See You Tomorrow — *Maxwell, William, 1908-*

y So Loud a Silence — *Jenkins, Lyll Becerra De*

c So Many Dynamos! and Other Palindromes — *Agee, Jon*

So Many Worlds — *Bachmann, Dieter*

c So Much (Illus. by Helen Oxenbury) — *Cooke, Trish*

y So Much to Live For — *McDaniel, Lurlene*

y So Much to Tell You — *Marsden, John*

So Ordered — *Hopkins, Ann Branigar*

So Shall I Tell You a Story — *Taylor, Judy*

So We Believe, So We Pray — *Best, Thomas F*

r So Who the Heck Was Oscar Mayer? — *Gelbert, Doug*

So Wide the Sky — *Grayson, Elizabeth*

So Wise Were Our Elders — *McDowell, John Holmes*

cr So You Love to Draw (Illus. by Michel Bisson) — *Seary, Michael*

So You Want to Be a Lesbian? — *Tracey, Liz*

Soap Fans — *Harrington, C Lee*

Soaps and Detergents — *Spitz, Luis*

y Soaring above Setbacks — *Bragg, Janet Harmon*

A Soaring Eagle — *Groenewegen, Peter*

y The Soaring Twenties — *Gilbert, Thomas*

Soaring Underground — *Orbach, Larry*

Sobre Gobernadores Y Residencias En La Provincia De Venezuela Siglos XVI, XVII, XVIII — *Vaccari De Venturini, Letizia*

Sobre Literatura Y Otras Complejidades — *Dominguez, Maria*

c Soccer — *Loveloch, Damien*

The Soccer Handbook for Players, Coaches and Parents — *Luongo, Albert M*

c Soccer Mad (Illus. by Aiden Potts) — *Childs, Rob*

Social Action and Non-Violence — *Gupta, R K*

Social and Economic Reform in Ecuador — *Pineo, Ronn F*

Social and Ethical Effects of the Computer Revolution — *Kizza, Joseph Migga*

Social and Political Change in Literature and Film — *Chapple, Richard L*

Social and Political Philosophy — *Sterba, James P*

The Social and Religious Designs of J.S. Bach's Brandenburg Concertos — *Marissen, Michael*

Social Approaches to Communication — *Leeds-Hurwitz, Wendy*

Social Aspects and Country Reviews of Population Aging — *Stolnitz, George J*

Social Blunders — *Sandlin, Tim*

Social Capitalism — *Kersbergen, Kees Van*

Social Care Markets — *Wistow, Gerald*

r Social Cartography — *Paulston, Rolland G*

The Social Causes of Environmental Destruction in Latin America — *Painter, Michael*

Social Causes of Violence — *Levine, Felice J*

c Social Change — *Hepplewhite, Peter*

Social Change and Social Policy in Contemporary China — *Wong, Linda*

Social Change and the Family in Taiwan — *Thornton, Arland*

Social Change and the Middle Classes — *Butler, Tim, 1949-*

Social Change in the Age of Enlightenment — *Houston, R A*

Social Choice, Welfare, and Ethics — *Barnett, William A*

Social Citizenship for Whom? — *Faist, Thomas*

Social Citizenship Rights — *Espada, Joao Carlos*

Social Class and Marxism — *Kirk, Neville*

Social Complexity and the Development of Towns in Iberia — *Cunliffe, Barry*

The Social Construction of Nature — *Eder, Klaus*

The Social Construction of Virtue — *Noblit, George W*

Social Contract. Discourse on the Virtue Most Necessary for a Hero. Political Fragments. Geneva Manuscript — *Rousseau, Jean-Jacques*

Social Control in China — *Shaw, Victor N*

The Social Control of Religious Zeal — *Miller, Jon*

Social Currents in Eastern Europe. 2nd Ed. — *Ramet, Sabrina Petra*

Social Democracy and Rational Choice — *Milner, Henry*

The Social Democratic State — *Rothstein, Bo*

Social Differentiation and Social Inequality — *Baron, James N*

Social Dimensions of Adjustment — *Jayarajah, Carl*

Social Divisions — *Morris, Lydia*

The Social Dynamics of Pottery Style in the Early Puebloan Southwest — *Hegmon, Michelle*

Social Ecology — *O'Boyle, Edward J*

Social Gospel Liberalism and the Ministry of Ernest Fremont Tittle — *Evans, Christopher Hodge*

The Social History of Labor in the Middle East — *Goldberg, Ellis Jay*

A Social History of Truth — *Shapin, Steven*

r Social Indicators of Development 1996

Social Issues in Technology. 2nd Ed. — *Alcorn, Paul A*

Social Justice and Political Change — *Kluegel, James R*

Social Justice in the Ancient World — *Irani, K D*

Social Learning in Animals — *Heyes, Cecilia M*

Social Limits to Economic Theory — *Mulberg, Jon*

The Social Misconstruction of Reality — *Hamilton, Richard F*

Social Motivation — *Juvonen, Jaana*

Social Movements and Cultural Change — *D'Anjou, Leo*

Social Movements and Culture — *Johnston, H*

Social Movements and Social Classes — *Maheu, Louis*

Social Movements, Political Violence, and the State — *Della Porta, Donatella*

Social Network Analysis — *Wasserman, Stanley*

Social Networks and Social Influences in Adolescence — *Cotterell, John*

The Social Networks of Older People — *Litwin, Howard*

The Social Organization of Mental Illness — *Prior, Lindsay*

The Social Organization of Sexuality — *Laumann, Edward O*

The Social Origins of the Iran-Iraq War — *Workman, W Thom*

Social Phobia — *Stein, Murray B*

Social Policies for Children — *Garfinkel, Irwin*

Social Policy and Economic Transformation in Uzbekistan — *Griffin, Keith*

Social Policy in the United States — *Skocpol, Theda*

Social Practices — *Schatzki, Theodore R*

Social Problem Solving — *Elias, Maurice J*

Social Problems and Social Contexts in Adolescence — *Hurrelmann, Klaus*

Social Problems and Social Movements — *Bash, Harry H*

Social Psychiatry across Cultures — *Price, Rumi Kato*

Social Psychology — *Higgins, E Tory*

Social Psychology. 8th Ed. — *Baron, Robert A*

The Social Psychology of Interpersonal Discrimination — *Lott, Bernice*

The Social Psychology of Organizing — *Weick, Karl E*

Social Reconstructions of the World Automobile Industry — *Deyo, Frederic C*

Social Revolutions in the Modern World — *Skocpol, Theda*

Social Rituals and the Verbal Art of Zora Neale Hurston — *Hill, Lynda Marion*

The Social Role of Higher Education — *Kempner, Ken*

Social Rules — *Braybrooke, David*

r The Social Science Encyclopedia. 2nd Ed. — *Kuper, Adam*

Social Science in the Crucible — *Smith, Mark C*

r Social Science Index 1974-

r The Social Sciences. 2nd Ed. — *Herron, Nancy L*

r Social Sciences Citation Index 1979-

Social Security — *Diamond, Peter A*

Social Security in the 21st Century — *Kingson, Eric R*

Social Security Programs — *Dixon, John*

The Social Semiotics of Mass Communication — *Jensen, Klaus Bruhn*

Social Services and the Ethnic Community — *Iglehart, Alfreda P*

c Social Smarts (Illus. by Martha Weston) — *James, Elizabeth*

Social Struggles and the City — *Kowarick, Lucio*

Social Support in Couples — *Cutrona, Carolyn E*

Social Systems — *Luhmann, Niklas*

Social Theory and Social Policy — *Sorensen, Aage B*

Social Theory and the Crisis of State Socialism — *Ray, Larry J*

Social Theory and the Environment — *Goldblatt, David*

Social Theory and the Global Environment — *Redclift, Michael*

The Social Theory of Practices — *Turner, Stephen P*

Social Transformations — *Sanderson, Stephen K*

r Social Trends 1970-1995. Electronic Media Version

p Social Watch

Social Welfare. 4th Ed. — *DiNitto, Diana M*

Social Work Interventions — *Henderson, George*

Social Work Practice and People of Color. 3rd Ed. — *Lum, Doman*

Social Work Practice with Children — *Webb, Nancy Boyd*

Socialism after Communism — *Pierson, Christopher*

Socialism and Marginalism in Economics 1870-1930 — *Steedman, Ian*

Socialism and the Common Good — *King, Preston*

Socialism, Capitalism, Transformation — *Balcerowicz, Leszek*

Socialisms: Old and New — *Wright, Tony*
Socialist Ensembles — *Martin, Randy*
The Socialist Movement in Turkey 1960-1980 — *Lipovsky, Igor P*
The Socialist Revolutionaries and the Russian Anti-War Movement 1914-17 — *Melancon, Michael*
Socialist Unemployment — *Woodward, Susan L*
A Socialist Utopia in the New South — *Brundage, W Fitzhugh*
The Socially Responsible Guide to Smart Investing — *Case, Samuel*
Societat Catalana D'Economia. Vol. 12
Une Societe Rurale En Milieu Rhenan. Vols. 1-3 — *Boehler, Jean-Michel*
Societies and Military Power — *Rosen, Stephen Peter*
Societies, Cultures and Kinship 1580-1850 — *Phythian-Adams, Charles*
Societies in Space — *Rudoff, Alvin*
Society and Museum — *Goodyear, George F*
Society and Politics in the Plays of Thomas Middleton — *Chakravorty, Swapan*
Society and Psyche — *Leledakis, Kanakis*
Society and the Professions in Italy 1860-1914 — *Malatesta, Maria*
A Society Based on Responsibility and Solidarity — *Conference on the Course of Social and Economic Change in Quebec (1996: Quebec, Quebec)*
Society, Culture and Technology in Africa — *Childs, S Terry*
Society, Culture, and the State in Germany 1870-1930 — *Eley, Geoff*
Society in Prehistory — *Megarry, Tim*
A Society of Wolves — *McIntyre, Rick*
Society on the Run — *Peters, Werner*
Society's Impact on Television — *Selnow, Gary W*
r Socio-Economic Statistical Profiles of British Columbia Regions. 3rd Ed.
A Sociocritique of Translation — *Brisset, Annie*
Sociolinguistic Metatheory — *Figueroa, Esther*
Sociological Reasoning — *Stones, Rob*
Sociological Theory — *Mouzelis, Nicos*
Sociological Writings — *Weber, Max*
Sociologies of Food and Nutrition — *McIntosh, Wm. Alex*
Sociology after the Crisis — *Lemert, Charles*
Sociology and Development — *Kiely, Ray*
Sociology, Environmentalism, Globalization — *Yearley, Steven*
The Sociology of Development. Vols. 1-2 — *Roberts, Bryan R*
The Sociology of Law — *Trevino, A Javier*
The Sociology of Medicine — *Cockerham, William C*
The Sociology of Religion. Vols. 1-2 — *Bruce, Steve*
A Sociology of Sex and Sexuality — *Hawkes, Gail*
The Sociology of the Environment. Vols. 1-3 — *Redclift, Michael*
The Sociology of Urban Communities. Vols. 1-3 — *Harloe, Michael*
Sociology, Work and Industry. 3rd Ed. — *Watson, Tony J*
c Sodbuster (Illus. by Richard Erickson) — *Toht, David W*
c Sody Salleratus (Illus. by Alan Daniel) — *Davis, Aubrey*
c Sody Sallyratus (Illus. by Teri Sloat) — *Sloat, Teri*
Soft Ground Improvement in Lowland Environment — *Bergado, D T*
Soft Systems Analysis and Its Application in Libraries, Information Services and Resources Centres — *Underwood, Peter G*
Soft Tissue Rheumatic Pain. 3rd Ed. — *Sheon, Robert P*
Software Change Impact Analysis — *Bohner, Shaw A*
r Software Directory for Fibre Artists. 3rd Ed. — *Larson, Lois*
r The Software Encyclopedia 1996. Vols. 1-2
Software Engineering — *Dorfman, Merlin*
Software Engineering — *International Conference Software Engineering; Education and Practice (1996: Dunedin, New Zealand)*
Software Engineering and Environment — *Sheu, Phillip C Y*
Software Engineering Guides — *Fairclough, Jon*
Software Engineering with B — *Wordsworth, J B*
Software for Electrical Engineering Analysis and Design — *International Conference on Software for Electrical Engineering Analysis and Design (3rd: 1996: Pisa, Italy)*
Software Inspection — *Wheeler, David A*
Software Measurement Guidebook — *Gaffney, John E*
Software Metrics — *Kitchenham, Barbara*

Software Patterns — *Coplien, James O*
Software Performability — *Tai, Ann T*
Software Portability with Imake. 2nd Ed. — *DuBois, Paul*
Software Reuse — *International Conference on Software Reuse (4th: 1996: Orlando, FL)*
Software Rx — *Wilson, Rodney C*
Software Synthesis from Dataflow Graphs — *Battacharyya, Shuvra S*
y SOG: The Secret Wars of America's Commandos in Vietnam — *Plaster, John L*
Soho Square Seven
c Soil (Illus. by Barrie Watts) — *Bryant-Mole, Karen*
Soil Behaviour in Earthquake Geotechnics — *Ishihara, Kenji*
Soil Biochemistry. Vol. 9 — *Bollag, Jean-Marc*
The Soil Conservation Service Responds to the 1993 Midwest Floods — *Phillips, Steven*
Soil Erosion and Conservation. 2nd Ed. — *Morgan, R P C*
Soil Mechanics in Engineering Practice. 3rd Ed. — *Terzaghi, Karl*
Soil Microbiology and Biochemistry. 2nd Ed. — *Paul, Eldor A*
Soil Salinity and Water Quality — *Chhabra, Ranbir*
Soil Science and Sustainable Land Management in the Tropics — *Syers, J K*
Soil Survey — *Zinck, J Alfred*
Soil, Water, Biology, and Belief in Prehistoric and Traditional Southwestern Agriculture — *Toll, Henry Wolcott*
Soiled Doves — *Seagraves, Anne*
Soils: A New Global View — *Paton, T R*
Soils and Environment — *Ellis, S*
y Soils, Sustainability and the Natural Heritage — *Taylor, A G*
y Sojourner Truth: A Life, a Symbol — *Painter, Nell Irvin*
y Sojourner Truth: Ain't I a Woman? — *McKissack, Pat*
Sojourner Truth: Slave, Prophet, Legend — *Mabee, Carleton*
Sojourners in the Sun — *Karras, Alan L*
Sojourners: The Return of German Jews and the Question of Identity — *Borneman, John*
Sol Power — *Behling, Sophia*
Sol White's History of Colored Baseball — *Malloy, Jerry*
Sola Scriptura! — *Kistler, Don*
The Solace of Food — *Clark, Robert*
Solar and Astrophysical Magnetohydrodynamic Flows — *Tsinganos, Kanaris C*
Solar Astronomy Handbook — *Beck, Rainer*
Solar Energy in Architecture and Urban Planning — *Herzog, Thomas*
Solar Engineering 96
Solar Polarization — *Stenflo, Jan Olof*
Solar Returns in Your Face — *Penfield, Marc*
Solar Storms — *Hogan, Linda*
Solar System Astronomy in America — *Doel, Ronald E*
Solar Wind Eight — *Winterhalter, Daniel*
The Soldier — *Binstock, R C*
Soldier and Society in Roman Egypt — *Alston, Richard*
y Soldier Boy — *Burks, Brian*
Soldier Boy — *Popchock, Barry*
Soldier in Buckskin — *Hogan, Ray*
y Soldier Life — *Woodhead, Henry*
Soldiers, Civilians, and Democracy — *Aguero, Felipe*
Soldiers for Peace — *Benton, Barbara*
Soldier's Heart — *Ames, John Edward*
Soldiers of Christ — *Noble, Thomas F X*
y The Soldiers of Fear — *Smith, Dean Wesley*
Soldiers of the King — *Gray, W M, 1953-*
Soldiers on the Steppe — *Stevens, Carol Belkin*
Soldiers' Pay — *Faulkner, William*
Soldiers Serving the Nation — *Sullivan, Gordon R*
Soldiers, Society, and National Security — *Sarkesian, Sam C*
The Soldiers' Story — *Heinamaa, Anna*
y The Soldiers' Tale — *Hynes, Samuel*
y The Soldiers' Voice — *O'Connor, Barbara*
Soldner Im Nordwestdeutschland Des 16. Und 17. Jahrhunderts — *Burschel, Peter*
y Sole Survivor — *Koontz, Dean*
Sole Survivor (Birney). Audio Version — *Koontz, Dean*
Soledad Women — *Girshick, Lori B*
Solemn Duty — *Scott, Leonard B*

c The Soles of Your Feet (Illus. by Genichiro Yagyu) — *Yagyu, Genichiro*
A Solid Investment
Solid-Liquid Filtration and Separation Technology — *Rushton, A*
Solidarity in the Conversation of Humankind — *Geras, Norman*
Solidarity of Strangers — *Dean, Jodi*
y The Solitaire Mystery — *Gaarder, Jostein*
y The Solitaire Mystery. Abridged Ed. Audio Version — *Gaarder, Jostein*
y The Solitaire Mystery. Unabridged Ed. Audio Version — *Gaarder, Jostein*
The Solitary Self — *Cranston, Maurice*
Solitude of Illusions — *Khan, Adib*
c Solo (Illus. by Paul Geraghty) — *Geraghty, Paul*
The Solo Chef — *Wylie, Betty Jane*
Solo Dolci — *Benson, Anna Bruni*
Solomon Kane — *Howard, Robert E*
Solution of Crack Problems — *Hills, D A*
The Solution: The 6 Causes and 6 Cures of Weight Problems — *Mellin, Laurel*
Solutions Handbook for PC Programmers. 2nd Ed. — *Sanchez, Julio*
Solved by Sunset — *Orsborn, Carol*
Solvent Effects and Chemical Reactivity — *Tapia, Orlando*
Solvents and Self-Organization of Polymers — *Webber, Stephen E*
c Solving International Crime — *Roden, Katie*
Solving Problems in Environmental Engineering and Geosciences with Artificial Neural Networks — *Dowla, Farid U*
Solymitana Clades — *Legge, Thomas*
The Solzhenitsyn Files — *Scammell, Michael*
Soma Blues — *Sheckley, Robert*
c Somalia — *Fox, Mary Virginia*
c Somalia — *Hassig, Susan M*
Somalia: The Missed Opportunities — *Sahnoun, Mohammed*
Somatic Fictions — *Vrettos, Athena*
Some Appointed Work to Do — *Colby, Robin B*
r Some Early Citizens of Marion County, Texas — *Cawthon, Juanita Davis*
Some Far and Distant Place — *Addleton, Jonathan S*
c Some Fine Grandpa! (Illus. by Dirk Zimmer) — *Arkin, Alan*
Some Foul Play — *Quinton, Ann*
c Some Friend — *Warner, Sally*
Some Instructions to My Wife Concerning the Upkeep of the House and Marriage and to My Son and Daughter Concerning the Conduct of Their Childhood — *Crawford, Stanley*
r Some Joe You Don't Know — *Slide, Anthony*
Some Love, Some Pain, Sometime — *Cooper, J California*
Some Men Are Lookers — *Mordden, Ethan*
Some of Me — *Rossellini, Isabella*
c Some of the Kinder Planets — *Wynne-Jones, Tim*
Some Other Frequency — *McCaffery, Larry*
Some Other Kind of Mission — *Jarnot, Lisa*
Some Questions of Differential Geometry in the Large — *Shikin, E V*
Some Remarkable Men — *Lord, James*
Some Remembered Words — *Shoenfeld, Oscar*
Some Seed Fell on Good Ground — *Dolan, Timothy Michael*
c Some Sleep Standing Up — *Stockdale, Susan*
c Some Smug Slug (Illus. by Henry Cole) — *Edwards, Pamela Duncan*
Some Tame Gazelle (McKenzie). Audio Version — *Pym, Barbara*
Some Trouble with Cows — *Roy, Beth*
Somebody Else's Child — *Grimes, Terris McMahan*
Somebody Else's Children — *Hubner, John*
y Somebody Else's Mama — *Haynes, David*
c Somebody Loves You, Mr. Hatch — *Spinelli, Eileen*
Somebody's Daughter — *Jessome, Phonse*
c Somebody's New Pajamas (Illus. by David Soman) — *Jackson, Isaac*
c The Someday House (Illus. by Rosanne Litzinger) — *Shelby, Anne*
Somehow a Past — *Hartley, Marsden*
c Someone Came Knocking — *Merrick, Anne*
y Someone Else's Baby — *Kaye, Geraldine*
Someone or Nothing? — *Bowers, Russell H*
y Someone to Love — *Lantz, Francess Lin*
c Someplace to Go (Illus. by Karen Ritz) — *Testa, Maria*
Somesthesis and the Neurobiology of the Somatosensory Cortex — *Franzen, O*

yr Something about the Author. Vols. 81-85
Something Borrowed — *Marshall, Alexandra*
c Something Else (Illus. by Chris Riddell) — *Cave,*
   Kathryn
c Something Fishy at MacDonald Hall — *Korman,*
   Gordon
c Something for James (Illus. by Neil Reed)
   — *Isherwood, Shirley*
c Something from Nothing — *Gilman, Phoebe*
Something like Fire — *Cook, Lin*
c Something Might Be Hiding (Illus. by Paul Zwolak)
   — *Lottridge, Celia Barker*
y Something Old, Something New — *Baer, Judy*
c Something Special (Illus. by Alex Ayliffe) — *Moon,*
   Nicola
y Something Terrible Happened — *Porte, Barbara Ann*
Something That a Cowboy Knows — *Griffin, L L*
Something That Happens to Other People
   — *Feldman, Susan*
Something to Draw On — *Ross, Carol*
y Something Very Sorry — *Bohlmeijer, Arno*
c Something's Buggy? (Illus. by Heather Anne Bausch)
   — *Bausch, Heather Anne*
Sometimes My Heart Goes Numb — *Garfield, Charles*
y Sometimes They Bite and Other Stories (Weitz).
   Audio Version — *Block, Lawrence*
Sometimes You Just Want to Feel like a Human Being
   — *Blotzer, M A*
c Somewhere (Illus. by Trish Hill) — *Baskwill, Jane*
Somewhere I'll Find You — *Kleypas, Lisa*
c Somewhere in Africa (Illus. by Nicolaas Maritz)
   — *Mennen, Ingrid*
Somewhere in France — *Nott, Lewis Windermere*
Somewhere in the Night — *Christopher, Nicholas*
c Somewhere in the World Right Now — *Schuett, Stacey*
Somewhere New — *Wilding, Michael*
Somnium Viridarii. Vols. 1-2 — *Schnerb-Lievre,*
   Marion
Somos Iglesia — *Mejia, Maria*
y The Son of Summer Stars — *Pierce, Meredith Ann*
Son of the Morning — *Howard, Linda*
Son of Two Bloods — *Mendoza, Vincent L*
Sonette An Orpheus — *Rilke, Rainer Maria*
Song — *Kelly, Brigit Pegeen*
c Song and Dance (Illus. by Cheryl Munro Taylor)
   — *Hopkins, Lee Bennett*
c Song and Dance Man — *Ackerman, Karen*
r Song Finder — *Ferguson, Gary Lynn*
c A Song for Lena (Illus. by Leslie Baker) — *Hippely,*
   Hilary Horder
c A Song for Little Toad (Illus. by Barbara Firth)
   — *French, Vivian*
y A Song for the Asking — *Gannon, Steve*
A Song for the Asking (Sanders). Audio Version
   — *Gannon, Steve*
A Song in the Dark — *Barrios, Richard*
y Song in the Silence — *Kerner, Elizabeth*
c Song Lee and the Leech Man (Illus. by Frank
   Remkiewicz) — *Kline, Suzy*
Song Ni Qi Zhi Huo Wang Ba
The Song of Earth — *Mor, Caiseal*
c The Song of El Coq and Other Tales of Puerto Rico
   — *Mohr, Nicholasa*
Song of Rita Joe — *Joe, Rita*
Song of Solomon — *Morrison, Toni*
The Song of Songs — *Bible. O.T. Song of Solomon.*
   Hebrew. 1994
Song of Songs — *Sholem Aleichem*
c Song of the Chirimia — *Volkmer, Jane Anne*
y The Song of the Dodo — *Quammen, David*
c Song of the Hermit Thrush (Illus. by Charles
   Reasoner) — *Dominic, Gloria*
Song of the Hummingbird — *Limon, Graciela*
y The Song of the Magdalene — *Napoli, Donna Jo*
Song of the Phoenix — *Fairchilde, Lily*
y Song of the Sea — *Ferris, Jean*
Song of the Simple Truth — *Burgos, Julia De*
y Song of the Turtle — *Allen, Paula Gunn*
A Song to the Creator — *Ackerman, Lillian A*
Song Troi — *Thuyet Ngu*
r Song Writer's Market 1997
c Songbirds — *Flanagan, Alice K*
Songbirds in Your Garden — *Terres, John K*
r SongCite: An Index to Popular Songs — *Goodfellow,*
   William D
Songdogs — *McCann, Colum*
Songe Que Je Bouge — *Cyr, Gilles*
r The Songmakers' Almanac — *Johnson, Graham*
Songs about Work — *Green, Archie*
Songs and Musicians in the Fifteenth Century
   — *Fallows, David*

Songs and Rhymes — *Sharp, Ian*
c Songs for Survival (Illus. by Bernard Lodge)
   — *Siegen-Smith, Nikki*
Songs My Neighbours Taught Me — *Anstey, Robert G*
c The Songs My Paddle Sings (Illus. by Michael
   Foreman) — *Riordan, James, 1936-*
The Songs of Ascents (Psalms 120-134) — *Crow,*
   Loren D
y Songs of Earth and Power — *Bear, Greg*
Songs of Life — *Lawler, Jennifer*
The Songs of Scotland — *Paterson, Wilma*
Songs of Sunrise, Seeds of Prayer — *Simsic, Wayne*
Songs of the Sons and Daughters of Buddha
   — *Tipitaka. Suttapitaka. Khuddakanikaya.*
   Theragatha. English. Selections
Songs of Zion — *Campbell, James T*
r Songwriting and the Creative Process — *Gillette, Steve*
Sonia's Daughters — *Bernstein, Laurie*
c Los Sonidos A Mi Alrededor (Illus. by Aliki)
   — *Showers, Paul*
Sonlka Zolotaia Ruchka — *Drozdetskii, Aleks*
Sonne Du Cor! — *Barakat, Salim*
Sonnet: One Woman's Voyage from Maryland to
   Greece — *Bird, Lydia*
y Sonnets from the Puerto Rican — *Agueros, Jack*
The Sonnets of Michelangelo (Jennings)
   — *Michelangelo Buonarroti*
p Sonora Review
Sons and Mothers — *Glendinning, Matthew*
y Sons from Afar — *Voigt, Cynthia*
Sons of the Revolution — *Stone, Judith F, 1946-*
A Son's Return — *Brown, Sterling A*
The Sooner Spy — *Lehrer, Jim*
Soos Honde Van Die Hemel — *Leroux-Van Der Boon,*
   Marzanne
c Sophie and the New Baby (Illus. by Catherine Anholt)
   — *Anholt, Catherine*
Sophie Mereau-Brentano: Freiheit, Liebe, Weiblichkeit
   — *Von Hammerstein, Katharina*
c Sophie's Lucky (Illus. by David Parkins)
   — *King-Smith, Dick*
y Sophie's World — *Gaarder, Jostein*
y Sophie's World (Needleman). Audio Version
   — *Gaarder, Jostein*
The Sophie's World Workbook — *Olsen, Peer*
Sophistical Rhetoric in Classical Greece — *Poulakos,*
   John
Sophocles: The Classical Heritage — *Dawe, R D*
Sophocles' Tragic World — *Segal, Charles*
y Sophomores: Tales of Reality, Conflict, and the Road
   by Tenth Grade Writers — *Lord, Christine*
Sopra I Porti Di Mare. Vols. 1-2 — *Simoncini, Giorgio*
y The Soprano Sorceress — *Modesitt, L E*
Soranus' Gynecology — *Soranus, of Ephesus*
Sorbets and Granitas — *Maeda, Seiji*
The Sorcerer's Apprentice — *Rolfs, Richard W*
La Sorciere — *Ndiaye, Marie*
Sorgegondolen — *Transtromer, Tomas*
Sorokin and Civilization — *Ford, Joseph B*
The Sorrows of Satan — *Corelli, Marie*
The Sorrows of the Quaker Jesus — *Damrosch, Leo*
Sorry I Didn't Quite Catch That... — *Sharpley, G D A*
A Sort of Virtue — *Symons, Julian*
c Sorting and Sets — *Hewitt, Sally*
y SOS Titanic — *Bunting, Eve*
So's Your Old Man — *Cross, Peter*
Sostiene Pereira — *Tabucchi, Antonio*
Sotnyky: Istorychnyi Romankhronika — *Korbach,*
   Ivan
Soto Zen in Medieval Japan — *Bodiford, William M*
r Sotrudniki Rossiiskoi Natsional'noi Biblioteki — *Grin,*
   Ts. I
Sotsial'naia Istoriia Rossii 1917-1941 — *Holmes, Larry*
Une Soudaine Solitude — *Chapsal, Madeleine*
The Soul as Virgin Wife — *Hollywood, Amy*
Soul at Work — *Smith-Moran, Barbara*
Soul in Management — *America, Richard F*
Soul in Society — *Dorrien, Gary*
The Soul Is Here for Its Own Joy — *Bly, Robert*
Soul Kiss — *Youngblood, Shay*
r Soul Music A-Z. Rev. Ed. — *Gregory, Hugh*
The Soul of a New Machine — *Kidder, Tracy*
The Soul of Celtic Spirituality in the Lives of Its
   Saints — *Mitton, Michael*
The Soul of Golf — *Hallberg, William*
The Soul of Shamanism — *Noel, Daniel C*
The Soul of the American University — *Marsden,*
   George M
The Soul of the Night — *Raymo, Chet*
Soul of the World — *Weigel, George*
Soul Rebels — *Lewis, William F*

Soul Says — *Vendler, Helen*
Soul Searching — *Humphrey, Nicholas*
Soul Survivor — *Martin, Stephen Hawley*
y The Soul Thieves — *Fisher, Catherine*
Soul Weaving — *Klug, Lyn*
Soulages: Noir Lumiere — *Andral, Jean-Louis*
y Soulfire — *Hewett, Lorri*
The Soul's Code — *Hillman, James*
Souls in Anguish — *Cueto, Ronald*
The Soul's Journey — *Jones, Alan W*
The Souls of Black Folk — *DuBois, W E B*
Souls Raised from the Dead — *Betts, Doris*
Sound and Form in Modern Poetry. 2nd Ed.
   — *Gross, Harvey*
Sound Choices — *Machover, Wilma*
c A Sound of Leaves (Illus. by Erik Blegvad)
   — *Blegvad, Lenore*
The Sound of Living Things — *Turcotte, Elise*
The Sound of My Voice — *Butlin, Ron*
The Sound of the City. 2nd Ed., Newly Illustrated and
   Expanded — *Gillett, Charlie*
The Sound of the Dove — *Patterson, Beverly Bush*
The Sound of the Trumpet — *Moody, Bill*
The Sound of the Whistle — *Ericson, Steven J*
The Sound of Virtue — *Worden, Blair*
Sound-on-Film — *LoBrutto, Vincent*
Sound Transmission through Buildings — *Craik,*
   Robert J M
Soundbites — *Karin, Roberta*
Soundbites and Spin Doctors — *Jones, Nicholas*
Sounding Boards — *Marcombe, David*
Sounding the Whale — *Sten, Christopher*
p Soundings
y Sounds and Silences — *Peck, Richard*
Sounds and Society — *Martin, Peter J*
Sounds, Feelings, Thoughts — *Szymborska, Wislawa*
Sounds from the Heart — *Barbieri, Maureen*
The Sounds of People and Places — *Carney, George O*
c Soup 1776 (Illus. by Charles Robinson) — *Peck,*
   Robert Newton
The Soup Bible — *Larousse, David Paul*
c Soup Pot (Illus. by Mary Beth Owens) — *Pochocki,*
   Ethel
r The Source: A Guidebook of American Genealogy.
   Rev. Ed. — *Szucs, Loretto Dennis*
r A Source Book for the Community of Religions
r Source Book of American Architecture — *Smith, G E*
   Kidder
Source Readings in American Choral Music
   — *DeVenney, David P*
r Sourcebook for Jewish Genealogies and Family
   Histories. 2nd Ed. — *Zubatsky, David S*
r The Sourcebook of Federal Courts. 2nd Ed.
r Sourcebook of Korean Civilization. Vol. 2 — *Lee,*
   Peter H
r The Sourcebook of Online Public Record Experts
   — *Ernst, Carl R*
r The Sourcebook of State Public Records. 2nd Ed.
r Sources and Methods. 2nd Ed., Vol. 2
The Sources and Sitz Im Leben of Matthew 23
   — *Newport, Kenneth G C*
Les Sources De La Pensee Philosophique De Raimond
   Sebond (Ramon Sibiuda) — *Puig, Jaume De*
r Sources for American Studies — *Kellogg, Jefferson*
Sources for the Poetry of T.S. Eliot — *Hands, Anthony*
The Sources of Christian Ethics — *Pinckaers, Servais*
The Sources of Economic Growth — *Nelson, Richard*
   R
Sources of Hyperbolic Geometry — *Stillwell, John*
r Sources of London English — *Wright, Laura*
The Sources of Moral Agency — *Deigh, John*
The Sources of Normativity — *Korsgaard, Christine M*
Sources of Productivity Growth — *Mayes, David G*
Sources of the Pentateuch — *Campbell, Antony F*
Sourcing Prehistoric Ceramics at Chodistaas Pueblo,
   Arizona — *Zedeno, Maria Nieves*
La Souris, La Mouche Et L'Homme — *Jacob,*
   Francois
The South — *Hall, B Clarence*
c South Africa — *Barraclough, John*
c South Africa — *Flint, David*
South Africa — *Stedman, Stephen John*
c South Africa: A Tapestry of Peoples and Traditions
   — *Meisel, Jacqueline Drobis*
c South Africa: Free at Last — *Lewis, Peter*
South Africa: The Dynamics and Prospects of
   Transformation — *Buthelezi, Sipho*
r South African Bibliography. 3rd Ed. — *Musiker,*
   Reuben
South African Feminisms — *Daymond, M J*
South African Media Policy — *Louw, P Eric*

r South African Women — *Durban Women's Bibliography Group*

South Africa's Defence and Security into the 21st Century — *Gutteridge, William*

r South America, Central America, and the Caribbean 1997

r South American Cinema — *Barnard, Timothy*

South American Consumer Protection Laws — *Jaffe, David B*

r South American Handbook 1997

c South American Monkeys — *Harman, Amanda*

The South as an American Problem — *Griffin, Larry J*

r South Asian Cultural Studies — *Lal, Vinay*

South Asian Love Poetry — *Sareen, S K*

r South Asian Religions in the Americas — *Fenton, John Y*

South Atlantic Conflict — *Hinds, James R*

r South Carolina Directory of Services for Women, Children and Families

r South Carolina, off the Beaten Path — *Cox, William Price*

South Dakota Native American Youth Risk Behavior Survey Report 1994 — *Schubot, David B*

r South-East Asia. 8th Ed. — *Cummings, Joe*

South-East Asia's Environmental Future — *Brookfield, Harold*

South Florida Folklife — *Bucuvalas, Tina*

The South in Modern America — *Grantham, Dewey W*

South Korea Environmental Report — *Yi, Sin-Bom*

y South of Heaven — *French, Thomas*

r South Pacific Handbook. 6th Ed. — *Stanley, David*

South Pacific Oral Traditions — *Finnegan, Ruth*

South Pass 1868 — *Chisholm, James*

r South Slavic Folk Culture — *Roth, Klaus*

The South through Time. Vols. 1-2 — *Boles, John B*

Southeast Asian Art Today

The Southeast Asian Economic Miracle — *Kim, Young C*

r Southeast Asian Languages and Literatures — *Kratz, E Ulrich*

Southeast Asian Security in the New Millennium — *Ellings, Richard J*

r Southern Africa Bibliography — *Musiker, Reuben*

Southern African Literatures — *Chapman, Michael*

Southern Cheyenne Women's Songs — *Giglio, Virginia*

Southern China, Hong Kong, and Taiwan — *Khanna, Jane*

Southern City, National Ambition — *Gillette, Howard*

Southern Cross — *Heyrman, Christine Leigh*

y A Southern Exposure — *Adams, Alice*

Southern Fires — *Baxter, Mary Lynn*

y Southern Fried Rat and Other Gruesome Tales — *Cohen, Daniel, 1936-*

The Southern Heirloom Garden — *Welch, William C*

Southern Horrors and Other Writings — *Wells-Barnett, Ida B*

r Southern Illinois Birds — *Robinson, W Douglas*

y Southern Journey — *Dent, Tom*

The Southern Lady — *Scott, Anne Firor*

r Southern Mountaineers in Silent Films — *Williamson, J W, 1944-*

Southern Pamphlets on Secession November 1860-April 1861 — *Wakelyn, Jon L*

p The Southern Quarterly

Southern Slavery and the Law 1619-1860 — *Morris, Thomas D*

Southern Thunder — *Campbell, R Thomas*

The Southern Tradition — *Genovese, Eugene D*

y Southern Vampires — *Zweifel, Karyn*

A Southern Weave of Women — *Tate, Linda*

Southern Women's Writing — *Weaks, Mary Louise*

Southern Writers and Their Worlds — *Morris, Christopher*

Southernmost and Other Stories — *Brodsky, Michael*

c The Southernmost Cat (Illus. by Kathy Osborn) — *Cech, John*

The Southpaw — *Harris, Mark, 1922-*

The Southwest in the American Imagination — *Baxter, Sylvester*

yr The Southwest Pacific Campaign 1941-1945 — *Rasor, Eugene L*

Southwestern Pottery — *Hayes, Allan*

Southwestern Virginia's Railroad — *Noe, Kenneth W*

The Souvenir — *Carlon, Patricia*

p Sou'wester

Sovereign Creations — *Mufti, Malik*

The Sovereign Individual — *Davidson, James Dale*

Sovereign Nations or Reservations? — *Anderson, Terry Lee*

The Sovereign State and Its Competitors — *Spruyt, Hendrik*

Sovereignty and Intelligence — *Archer, John Michael*

Sovereignty as Responsibility — *Deng, Francis M*

Sovetnik Korolevy--Superagent Kremlia — *Popov, V I*

Soviet and Post-Soviet Telecommunications — *Campbell, Robert W*

r The Soviet Armed Forces 1918-1992 — *Erickson, John*

Soviet Dissident Artists — *Baigell, Renee*

The Soviet Economy and the Red Army 1930-1945 — *Dunn, Walter S, Jr.*

Soviet Hieroglyphics — *Condee, Nancy*

Soviet Jewish Aliyah 1989-1992 — *Jones, Clive*

Soviet Media in Transition — *Androunas, Elena*

The Soviet Photograph 1924-1937 — *Tupitsyn, Margarita*

The Soviet Socialist Republic of Iran 1920-1921 — *Chaqueri, Cosroe*

The Soviet Union and the Origins of the Second World War — *Roberts, Geoffrey*

The Soviet Union and the Vietnam War — *Gaiduk, Ilya V*

Soviet Workers and the Collapse of Perestroika — *Filtzer, Donald*

Sowa's Ark — *Sowa, Michael*

y Sowieso: A German Course for Young People — *Funk, Hermann*

Sowing the Dragon's Teeth — *McGeer, Eric*

Sowing the Seeds of Democracy in China — *Goldman, Merle*

Soziale Traditionen In Zieten Des Wandels — *Ehmer, Josef*

Sozialgeschichte Serbiens 1815-1941 — *Calic, Marie-Janine*

c Space (Illus. by Jon Barnes) — *Haslam, Andrew*

c Space — *Snedden, Robert*

The Space between Us — *Josselson, Ruthellen*

Space Charge Dominated Beams and Applications of High Brightness Beams — *Space Charge Dominated Beams and Applications of High Brightness Beams (1995: Bloomington, IN)*

c Space Demons — *Rubenstein, Gillian*

Space: Discovery and Exploration — *Collins, Martin J*

cr Space Explained — *Scagell, Robin*

The Space of Appearance — *Baird, George*

The Space of Poetry. Vol. 3 — *McCredden, Lyn*

A Space on the Side of the Road — *Stewart, Kathleen*

Space Opera — *McCaffrey, Anne*

Space, Place and Gender — *Massey, Doreen B*

Space Power Interests — *Hayes, Peter*

Space Safety and Rescue 1993

y Space Stories — *Ashley, Mike*

Space, Structure and Form — *Newman, Rochelle*

c Space Technology

Space, Time, and Perversion — *Grosz, E A*

Space-Time of the Bororo of Brazil — *Fabian, Stephen Michael*

c Spacebaby (Illus. by Ellis Nadler) — *Branford, Henrietta*

Spacecraft-Environment Interactions — *Hastings, Daniel*

r Spaceflight and Rocketry — *Baker, David, 1944-*

Spaceflight Revolution — *Hansen, James R*

c Spaceman — *Cutler, Jane*

The Spaces between Birds — *McPherson, Sandra*

Spaces, Worlds, and Grammar — *Fauconnier, Gilles*

La Spada E La Luna — *Pariani, Laura*

Spadework — *Pronzini, Bill*

Spain and the Early Stuarts 1585-1655 — *Loomie, Albert J*

Spain at War — *Esenwein, George*

Spain, Europe, and the Spanish Miracle 1700-1900 — *Ringrose, David R*

r Spain (Eyewitness Travel Guides)

Spain's First Democracy — *Payne, Stanley G*

Spain's Forgotten Novelist — *Dendle, Brian J*

p SPAN Connection

Spanish Agriculture — *Simpson, James*

The Spanish American Roots of William Carlos Williams — *Marzan, Julio*

The Spanish-American War at Sea — *Feuer, A B*

The Spanish Avantgarde — *Harris, Derek*

The Spanish Balance of Payments 1995

Spanish Blood — *Blakely, Mike*

r Spanish, Catalan, and Galician Literary Authors of the Eighteenth and Nineteenth Centuries — *Zubatsky, David S*

r The Spanish Civil War in Literature, Film, and Art — *Monteath, Peter*

Spanish Comedies and Historical Contexts in the 1620s — *Blue, William R*

Spanish Composition through Literature. 3rd Ed. — *Ayllon, Candido*

The Spanish Economy — *Harrison, Joseph*

Spanish Expeditions into Texas 1689-1768 — *Foster, William C*

Spanish Golden Age Autobiography in Its Context — *Goetz, Rainer*

Spanish Hours — *Courtauld, Simon*

Spanish in Four Continents — *Silva-Corvalan, Carmen*

A Spanish Lover — *Trollope, Joanna*

c Spanish Missions (Illus. by Barbara Bedell) — *Kalman, Bobbie*

Spanish New Mexico. Vols. 1-2 — *Pierce, Donna*

r Spanish Protestants and Reformers in the Sixteenth Century. 1st Suppl. — *Kinder, A Gordon*

Spanish Romances of the Sixteenth Century — *Binkley, Thomas*

Spanish Sculpture — *Trusted, Marjorie*

Spanish Still Life from Velazquez to Goya — *Jordan, William B*

Spanish Traditional Ballads from Aragon — *Cruz-Saenz, Michele S De*

Spanish Women in the Golden Age — *Sanchez, Magdalena S*

Spanish Women on the Threshold of the 21st Century

Spare the Child — *Greven, Philip*

Spared Angola — *Suarez, Virgil*

Spares — *Smith, Michael Marshall*

c The Spark Gap — *Bertagna, Julie*

Sparks of Reform — *Leach, J H C*

Sparring with Charlie — *Hunt, Christopher*

y The Sparrow — *Russell, Mary Doria*

y The Sparrow (Colacci). Audio Version — *Russell, Mary Doria*

r Sparrows and Buntings — *Byers, Clive*

Spartacus — *Fast, Howard*

r Spartacus: International Gay Guide 96-97

Spatial Electric Load Forecasting — *Willis, H Lee*

Spatial Microeconomics — *Greenhut, Melvin L*

Spatial Search — *Maier, Gunther*

SPD Und Grune — *Berger, Rainer*

c Speak Chinese, Fang Fang (Illus. by Sally Rippin) — *Rippin, Sally*

y Speak for Yourself! — *Rushton, Rosie*

Speak Low (When You Speak Love) — *Weill, Kurt*

Speak Now against the Day — *Egerton, John*

Speak Silence — *Greenberg, Mark L*

Speak the Speech — *Shakespeare, William*

Speak Truth to Power — *Hine, Darlene Clark*

The Speaker: Leadership in the U.S. House of Representatives — *Peters, Ronald M, Jr.*

Speaking of Reading — *Rosenthal, Nadine*

Speaking of Sadness — *Karp, David A*

Speaking on Stage — *Kolin, Philip C*

Speaking Pictures — *Bath, Michael*

Speaking Silences — *Ettin, Andrew Vogel*

Speaking the Unspeakable — *Michelson, Peter*

Speaking to Power — *Wilson, Lynn B*

c Speaking Up, Speaking Out (Illus. by Carol Nicklaus) — *Otfinoski, Steve*

Speaking with the Devil — *Goldberg, Carl*

The Spears of Twilight — *Descola, Philippe*

r Special Collections in Children's Literature. 3rd Ed. — *Jones, Dolores Blythe*

r Special Collections in the Library of Congress — *Library of Congress*

Special Delivery — *James, C L R*

Special Educational Needs and the Law — *Oliver, Simon*

Special Events from A to Z — *Jasso, Gayle*

The Special Guest — *Allen, Lee*

y Special Kind of Love — *Baer, Judy*

c A Special Kind of Love — *King, Stephen Michael*

Special Olympics — *Bueno, Ana*

c A Special Place for Charlee (Illus. by Karen Cannon) — *Morehead, Debby*

Special Sorrows — *Jacobson, Matthew Frye*

r Specialized Catalog of U.S. Non-Pictorial Waterfowl Stamps 1996

r Specialized Catalogue of U.S. Stamps 1996

yr Specialty Occupational Outlook: Trade and Technical. 1st Ed.

Species — *Giger, H R*

Species Diversity in Space and Time — *Rosenzweig, Michael L*

Species, Species Concepts and Primate Evolution — *Kimbel, William H*

Specific Techniques for the Psychotherapy of Schizophrenic Patients — *Lotterman, Andrew*

c The Speckled Rose of Oz — *Abbott, Donald*

The Spectacle of History — *Lynch, Michael, 1948-*

Stedman's Radiology and Oncology Words. 2nd Ed.
— *Baxter, Catherine S*
y Steel across the Shield (Illus. by Paul McCusker)
— *Berton, Pierre*
r Steel Castings Handbook. 6th Ed. — *Blair, Malcolm*
Steel City — *Tweedale, Geoffrey*
The Steel Cricket — *Berg, Stephen*
Steel Designer's Handbook. 6th Ed. — *Gorenc, B*
c Steel Drums and Ice Skates (Illus. by Ho Che
Anderson) — *McLean, Dirk*
r The Steel Market in 1995 and Prospects for 1996
Steel Phoenix — *Hall, Christopher G L*
Steel, State, and Labor — *Daley, Anthony*
Steels: Microstructure and Properties. 2nd Ed.
— *Honeycombe, Robert*
Steepland Geomorphology — *Slaymaker, Olav*
c Steffi Graf: Tennis Champ — *Brooks, Philip*
Stein Og Speil — *Ulven, Tor*
Steina and Woody Vasulka and Machine Media
— *Riley, Robert R*
Steinbeck's Typewriter — *DeMott, Robert*
Steinway and Sons — *Lieberman, Richard K*
The Steinway Saga — *Fostle, D W*
c Stellaluna — *Cannon, Janell*
c Stellaluna. Electronic Media Version — *Cannon,
Janell*
c Stellaluna (Holt). Audio Version — *Cannon, Janell*
Stellar Surface Structure — *International Astronomical
Union. Symposium (176th: 1995: Vienna, Austria)*
Stemming Middle-Class Decline — *Leigh, Nancey
Green*
Stendhal — *Keates, Jonathan*
Stendhal Et La Hollande — *Stendhal*
Stendhal: Le Rouge Et Le Noir — *Bolster, Richard*
Stendhal Tra Letteratura E Musica — *Dotoli,
Giovanni*
Stendhal's Italy — *Greaves, A E*
Stengel: His Life and Times — *Creamer, Robert W*
Steno: Life, Science, Philosophy — *Kardel, Troels*
Step 1 Exam — *Underdown, Emma D*
c Step by Step — *Russell, Ginny*
Step by Step. Rev. and Expanded Ed. — *McNee,
Mona*
y Step-by-Step Guide to Painting Realistic Watercolors
— *Heim, Dawn McLeod*
Step-by-Step Plumbing — *Allen, Benjamin W*
y Step by Wicked Step — *Fine, Anne*
Step-Growth Polymers for High-Performance
Materials — *Hedrick, James L*
Step Right Up. Rev. Ed. — *McNamara, Brooks*
Stepfamilies: The Step by Step Model of Brief
Therapy — *Burt, Mala S*
Stepfamilies: Who Benefits? Who Does Not? — *Booth,
Alan, 1935-*
c Stephanie's Ponytail (Illus. by Michael Martchenko)
— *Munsch, Robert*
y Stephen Biesty's Incredible Explosions (Illus. by
Stephen Biesty) — *Biesty, Stephen*
y Stephen Gets Even — *Pascal, Francine*
y Stephen Hawking: Quest for a Theory of the Universe
— *Ferguson, Kitty*
c Stephen Hawking: Understanding the Universe
— *Sakurai, Gail*
Stephen J. Gould and Immanuel Velikovsky
— *Pearlman, Dale Ann*
Stephen King: A Critical Companion — *Russell,
Sharon A*
Stephen Pollan's Foolproof Guide to Renovating Your
Kitchen — *Pollan, Stephen M*
Stephen R. Donaldson's Chronicles of Thomas
Covenant — *Senior, W A*
The Stepman — *Margolis, David*
Steppin' on the Blues — *Malone, Jacqui*
c Stepping on the Cracks — *Hahn, Mary Downing*
y Stepping over the Color Line — *Wells, Amy Stuart*
Stepping Stones (Pennington). Audio Version
— *Heaney, Seamus*
Stepping Stones to Further Jewish-Christian Relations
— *Croner, Helga*
Stepping Stones to Further Jewish-Lutheran
Relationships — *Ditmanson, Harold H*
Steps of the Sun — *Thaddeus, Eva*
Steps under Water — *Kozameh, Alicia*
Stereochemistry of Coordination Compounds
— *Zelewsky, Alexander Von*
r Stereochemistry of Organic Compounds — *Eliel,
Ernest L*
Stereoselective Synthesis — *Atkinson, Robert S*
Stereotype Accuracy — *Lee, Yueh-Ting*
Stereotyped Movements — *Sprague, Robert L*
Stereotypes and Stereotyping — *Macrae, C Neil*

The Stern Gang — *Heller, Joseph*
r Stern's Guide to the Cruise Vacation. 6th Ed.
— *Stern, Steven B*
Steuern, Abgaben Und Dienste Vom Mittelalter Bis
Zur Gegenwart — *Schremmer, Eckart*
c Steve Young — *Bock, Hal*
c Steve Young — *Rambeck, Richard*
c Steve Young — *Stewart, Mark*
c Steve Young: Forever Young (Illus. by Doug Keith)
— *Young, Steve*
c Steve Young: NFL Passing Wizard — *Gutman, Bill*
c Steve Young: Star Quarterback — *Knapp, Ron*
c Steven Kellogg's Yankee Doodle (Illus. by Steven
Kellogg) — *Bangs, Edward*
Steven Spielberg — *Baxter, John*
y Steven Spielberg — *Ferber, Elizabeth*
Steven Spielberg — *McBride, Joseph*
Steven Spielberg: A Biography — *McBride, Joseph*
y Steven Spielberg: Hollywood Filmmaker — *Meachum,
Virginia*
The Stevensons: A Biography of an American Family
— *Baker, Jean H*
c Stevie — *Steptoe, John*
Stewart MacFarlane: Riddles of Life
— *Helmridge-Marsillian, Veronique*
Stick (Muller). Audio Version — *Leonard, Elmore*
Stickeen — *Muir, John*
c Sticking It Out — *O'Connor, Jim*
c Sticks — *Bauer, Joan*
y Sticks (Paris). Audio Version — *Bauer, Joan*
c Sticky — *Warbrick, Sarah*
c Sticky Fingers — *Collinson, Roger*
c Sticky Little Fingers (Illus. by Bettina Paterson)
— *Frere, Jane*
Stiff Lips — *Billson, Anne*
The Still — *Feintuch, David*
Still a Man's World — *Williams, Christine L*
Still Catholic after All These Years — *Stivender, Ed*
Still Life — *Hanson, Rick*
Still Life in Harlem — *Harris, Eddy L*
Still Life in Real Time — *Dienst, Richard*
Still Life with Rice — *Lee, Helie*
Still Lives — *Bigsby, Christopher*
Still Looking — *Durstin, Larry*
A Still Small Voice — *Schmidt, Frederick W, Jr.*
Still the Promised City? — *Waldinger, Roger*
y Still Unequal — *Dusky, Lorraine*
Still Wild, Always Wild — *Zwinger, Susan*
Stillborn Crusade — *Somin, Ilya*
y Stink Bomb Mom — *Freeman, Martha*
c Stinkerbell (Illus. by Tony Blundell) — *Murhall, J J*
The Stinking Rose — *Bhatt, Sujata*
c The Stinky Cheese Man and Other Fairly Stupid
Tales (Illus. by Lane Smith) — *Scieszka, Jon*
The Stirring of Soul in the Workplace — *Briskin, Alan*
Stirring the Chalkdust — *Wasley, Patricia A*
Stirrup High — *Coburn, Walt*
Stitch Charted Designs — *Hasler, Julie*
c A Stitch in Rhyme (Illus. by Belinda Downes)
— *Downes, Belinda*
Stitches for Effect — *Howren, Suzanne*
Stochastic Analysis — *Fouque, Jean-Pierre*
Stochastic Calculus — *Durrett, Richard*
Stochastic Decomposition — *Higle, Julia L*
Stochastic Geometry and Its Applications. 2nd Ed.
— *Stoyan, Dietrich*
Stochastic Hydraulics 1996 — *IAHR International
Symposium on Stochastic Hydraulics (7th: 1996:
Mackay, Queensland, Australia)*
Stochastic Programming — *Kall, Peter*
Stochastic Programming — *Marti, Kurt*
Stochastic Programming Problems with Probability
and Quantile Functions — *Kibzun, A I*
Stock Assessment in Inland Fisheries — *Cowx, I G*
Stock Market Crashes and Speculative Manias
— *White, Eugene N*
r Stokes Beginner's Guide to Birds: Eastern Region
— *Stokes, Donald W*
r Stokes Beginner's Guide to Birds: Western Region
— *Stokes, Donald W*
r Stokes Field Guide to Birds: Eastern Region
— *Stokes, Donald W*
r Stokes Field Guide to Birds: Western Region
— *Stokes, Donald W*
Stolen Childhood — *King, Wilma*
Stolen China — *Fraser, John*
Stolen Hearts — *Martin, Michelle*
A Stolen Tongue — *Holman, Sheri*
Stolen Years — *Floyd, Maita*
c The Stomach and Digestive System — *Ballard, Carol*
Stomata. 2nd Ed. — *Willmer, Colin*

Stone — *Sallis, John*
Stone: A Biography of Oliver Stone — *Riordan, James*
c Stone Age Farmers beside the Sea (Illus. by Arthur P
Arnold) — *Arnold, Caroline*
The Stone and the Scorpion — *Mitchell, Judith*
r The Stone and the Thread — *Paternosto, Cesar*
y Stone, Bone, Antler and Shell (Illus. by Hilary
Stewart) — *Stewart, Hilary*
The Stone Boy and Other Stories — *Nhat Hanh, Thich*
The Stone Canal — *McLeod, Ken*
c Stone Cold — *Swindells, Robert*
The Stone Diaries (Bresnahan). Audio Version
— *Shields, Carol*
y The Stone Diaries (Shields). Audio Version — *Shields,
Carol*
Stone Horses — *Gallegos, Sallie*
Stone Kingdoms — *Park, David*
c The Stone Lion (Illus. by Bill Slavin) — *Slavin, Bill*
Stone Magic of the Ancients — *Cunkle, James R*
The Stone of Laughter — *Barakat, Huda*
y Stone of Tears — *Goodkind, Terry*
A Stone of the Heart — *McEldowney, Eugene*
c The Stone Orchard — *Merritt, Susan E*
c The Stone That Grew (Illus. by Derek Brazell)
— *Richemont, Enid*
The Stone That Shines — *Brand, Max*
Stone: The Controversies, Excesses, and Exploits of a
Radical Filmmaker — *Riordan, James*
Stone Tools — *Odell, George H*
Stone Tools and Mobility in the Illinois Valley
— *Odell, George H*
The Stone Trumpet — *Gibboney, Richard A*
Stone Vessels of the Cyclades in the Early Bronze Age
— *Getz-Gentle, Pat*
y Stone Water — *Gilbert, Barbara Snow*
Stone Work — *Jerome, John*
The Stonecutter's Hand — *Tillinghast, Richard*
Stonehenge: Neolithic Man and the Cosmos — *North,
John David*
Stonekiller — *Janes, J Robert*
c Stones — *Chambers, Catherine*
Stones and Fires — *Fuller, John*
Stones from the River — *Hegi, Ursula*
c Stonestruck — *Cresswell, Helen*
y Stonewall Jackson — *Pflueger, Lynda*
Stonewall Jackson at Gettysburg — *Gibboney,
Douglas Lee*
Stonewall Jackson--The Man, the Soldier, the Legend
— *Robertson, James I*
Stonewall of the West — *Symonds, Craig L*
Stoneware of Southwestern Pennsylvania
— *Schaltenbrand, Phil*
Stony Ground — *Chambers, Douglas*
Stop Being Mean to Yourself — *Beattie, Melody*
Stop Committing Voice Suicide — *Cooper, Morton*
c Stop, Look and Listen (Illus. by Loretta Trezzo
Braren) — *Williamson, Sarah, 1974-*
Stop Osteoarthritis Now! — *McIlwain, Harris H*
r Stop the Violence
Stopping and Seeing — *Cleary, Thomas*
y Stopping for Death (Illus. by Trisha Rafferty)
— *Duffy, Carol Ann*
Stora Scenen — *Harding, Gunnar*
Storage Projects You Can Build — *Stiles, David*
Store Wars — *Monod, David*
Storia Della Biblioteca Universitaria Di Napoli Dal
Viceregno Spagnolo All'Unita D'Italia — *Trombetta,
Vincenzo*
La Storia Dell'Alto Medioevo Italiano (VI-X Secolo)
Alla Luce Dell'Archeologia — *Francovich, Ricardo*
r Storia Delle Biblioteche Fra Settecento E Novecento
— *Del Bono, Gianna*
Storia Delle Origini Del Fascismo. Vols. 1-2
— *Vivarelli, Roberto*
Storia Dello Stato Italiano Dall'Unita A Oggi
— *Romanelli, Raffaele*
Storie Della Citta Di Dio — *Pasolini, Pier Paolo*
c Stories — *King, Penny*
Stories (Hughes). Audio Version — *Cather, Willa*
The Stories Children Tell — *Engel, Susan*
Stories for All Seasons — *Fuller, Gerald*
Stories for Thinking — *Fisher, Robert*
Stories from a Siberian Village — *Shukshin, Vasily*
Stories from an Open Country — *Lang, William L*
y Stories from Europe — *Barton, Geoff*
Stories from Home — *Clower, Jerry*
Stories from Response-Centered Classrooms
— *Livdahl, Barbara Smith*
Stories from Shakespeare — *Chute, Marchette*
Stories from the Heart — *Meyer, Richard J*

y A Starfarer's Dozen — *Stearns, Michael*
c Starfish — *Stefoff, Rebecca*
The Starfleet Academy Entrance Exam — *Robin, Peggy*
y Starlight 1
Starlight Passage — *Bunkley, Anita R*
c A Starlit Somersault Downhill (Illus. by Jerry Pinkney) — *Willard, Nancy*
Staroobriadcheskaia Kniga V Rossii Vo Vtoroi Polovine XVII v. — *Bubnov, N Iu*
Starplex — *Sawyer, Robert J*
c Starring Alice MacKenzie — *Dhami, Narinder*
Starring John Wayne as Genghis Khan — *Bona, Damien*
c Starring Mirette and Bellini (Illus. by Emily Arnold McCully) — *McCully, Emily Arnold*
c Starring Rosie (Illus. by Julie Durrell) — *Giff, Patricia Reilly*
c Starry Messenger (Illus. by Peter Sis) — *Sis, Peter*
Starry Night — *Agosin, Marjorie*
c Stars (Illus. by Mavis Smith) — *Dussling, Jennifer*
c Stars (Illus. by Ali Garousi) — *Llamas Ruiz, Andres*
c The Stars (Illus. by Paul Doherty) — *Moore, Patrick*
y Stars — *Walters, Eric*
y Stars and Planets — *Levy, David H*
c Stars and Planets (Discoveries)
Stars and Their Spectra — *Kaler, James B*
Stars as Laboratories for Fundamental Physics — *Raffelt, Georg G*
The Stars Dispose — *Roessner, Michaela*
The Stars down to Earth and Other Essays on the Irrational in Culture — *Adorno, Theodor W*
Stars in De Elements — *James, Willis Laurence*
Stars in My Pocket like Grains of Sand — *Delany, Samuel R*
c Stars in the Sky — *Fowler, Allan*
c Stars in Your Eyes — *Cooling, Wendy*
The Stars My Destination — *Bester, Alfred*
The Stars of the South — *Green, Julien*
The Stars, the Earth, the River — *Le, Minh Khue*
Stars without Garters — *Carpenter, C Tyler*
y Starstruck — *Cusick, Richie Tankersley*
Start Up Marketing — *Nulman, Philip*
Start with a Scan — *Ashford, Janet*
Start Your Own Business for $1,000 or Less — *Davis, Will*
Starting and Operating a Business in New York. 4th Ed.
Starting and Running a Nonprofit Organization. 2nd Ed. — *Hummel, Joan M*
Starting and Running a Successful Newsletter or Magazine — *Woodard, Cheryl*
Starting from Food — *Clarke, Peter*
Starting from Houses and Homes — *Connor, Kim*
Starting from Scratch — *Levy, Steven*
Starting from Shops and Markets — *Henley, Tricia*
Starting from Toys
Starting from Transport — *Clarke, Peter*
c Starting Gardening (Illus. by T Gower) — *Meredith, Susan*
Starting Out — *Hymer, Dian*
Starting Over — *Newton, Judith*
c Starting Painting (Illus. by T Burton) — *Mayes, Susan*
Starting Right — *Kamerman, Sheila*
Startup: A Silicon Valley Adventure — *Kaplan, Jerry*
Starvation Heights — *Olsen, Gregg*
The State against Society — *Ekiert, Grzegorz*
The State and Capital in Chile — *Silva, Eduardo, 1950-*
The State and Educational Change — *Simon, Brian*
The State and Its Servants — *Hanna, Nelly*
State and Local Public Finance. 2nd Ed. — *Fisher, Ronald C*
State and Party in America's New Deal — *Finegold, Kenneth*
State and Peasant in the Ottoman Empire — *Islamoglu-Inan, Huri*
r State and Regional Associations of the United States. 8th Ed.
State and Society in China's Political Economy — *Shih, Chih-Yu*
State and Society in Contemporary Korea — *Koo, Hagen*
State and Society in Early Modern Austria — *Ingrao, Charles W*
State and Society in Francophone Africa since Independence — *Kirk-Greene, Anthony*
State and Society in Pre-Colonial Asante — *McCaskie, T C*
State and Society in Syria and Lebanon — *Choueiri, Youssef M*

State and Society in the Dominican Republic — *Betances, Emelio*
State and Status — *Clark, Samuel, 1945-*
The State and the Economic Process — *Naastepad, C W M*
The State and the Family — *Gauthier, Anne Helene*
The State and the Provision of Social Services in Sierra Leone since Independence 1961-1991 — *Fyle, C Magbaily*
The State and the Rule of Law — *Kriegel, Blandine*
The State and the Tributary Mode of Production — *Haldon, John*
The State as a Monster — *Carlson, Benny*
State Autonomy or Class Dominance? — *Domhoff, G William*
State Building and Democracy in Southern Africa — *Du Toit, P Van Der P*
The State, Bureaucracy, and the Cuban Schools — *Lutjens, Sheryl*
c State by State with the State — *State (Comedy Group)*
State, Capitalism, and Democracy in Latin America — *Boron, Atilio A*
State Educator — *Midwinter, Eric*
State Fair — *Stong, Phil*
The State in Early Modern France — *Collins, James B*
The State in India 1000-1700 — *Kulke, Hermann*
State, Labor, Capital — *Buchanan, Paul G*
r State Labor Proceedings — *Fink, Gary M*
r State Legislative Sourcebook 1996
State, Market and Civil Organizations — *De Janvry, Alain*
State, Nation and Ethnicity in Contemporary South Asia — *Ahmed, Ishtiaq*
The State of Academic Freedom in Africa 1995
The State of Americans — *Bronfenbrenner, Urie*
The State of Canada's Climate
The State of Families. Vol. 4 — *Curtis, Lynn A*
The State of Humanity — *Simon, Julian Lincoln*
The State of Juvenile Justice — *Missouri. Dept. of Public Safety*
State of Mind — *Katzenbach, John*
The State of Public Management — *Kettl, Donald F*
State of Rebellion — *Zuczek, Richard*
State of the Art in Global Optimization — *Floudas, C A*
r State of the City 1995: Hartford, Conn.
The State of the Cybernation — *Barrett, Neil*
The State of the Nation — *Bok, Derek*
State of the Union — *Callahan, David*
State of the Union. Vols. 1-2 — *Farley, Reynolds*
r State of the World 1984-
r State of the World 1997
r State Parks of the South — *DeHaan, Vici*
r State Party Profiles — *Appleton, Andrew M*
State Perfectionism and Personal Freedom — *Rijpkema, Peter*
State Power and Black Politics in South Africa 1912-51 — *Rich, Paul B*
State Power and Social Forces — *Migdal, Joel S*
State, Society, and Law in Islam — *Gerber, Haim*
The State, Society, and Limited Nuclear War — *Mlyn, Eric*
State, Society, and Privatization in Turkey 1979-1990 — *Shaker, Sallama*
State-Society Relations in Yugoslavia 1945-1992 — *Bokovoy, Melissa K*
State Solid Waste Management Plan 1995
State Sovereignty as Social Construct — *Biersteker, Thomas J*
State Strategies in the Global Political Economy — *Palan, Ronen*
State Troops and Volunteers. Vol. 1 — *Mast, Greg*
State Trust Lands — *Souder, Jon A*
A State under Siege — *Follis, Bryan A*
State under Siege — *Mauceri, Philip*
The State under Stress — *Foster, Christopher*
The State, War, and the State of War — *Holsti, K J*
The State We're In — *Hutton, Will*
The Stateless Market — *Kapteyn, Paul*
The Statement — *Moore, Brian*
y The Statement (Sachs). Audio Version — *Moore, Brian*
States and the Reemergence of Global Finance — *Helleiner, Eric*
States, Nations, and Nationalism — *Schulze, Hagen*
States of Desire — *White, Edmund*
States of Disarray — *United Nations Research Institute for Social Development*
States of Fantasy — *Rose, Jacqueline*
States of Injury — *Brown, Wendy*

States, Social Knowledge, and the Origins of Modern Social Policies — *Rueschemeyer, Dietrich*
The States System of Europe 1640-1990 — *Osiander, Andreas*
r The Statesman's Year Book 1996-1997
Statics and Kinematics with Applications to Robotics — *Duffy, Joseph*
Stations of the Divided Subject — *Gray, Richard T*
The Stations of the Sun — *Hutton, Ronald*
Statistical Applications in Process Control — *Keats, J Bert*
Statistical Computing Environments for Social Research — *Stine, Robert*
Statistical Digital Signal Processing and Modeling — *Hayes, Mason H*
r Statistical Handbook 1995: States of the Former USSR
r The Statistical Handbook of Social and Economic Indicators for the Former Soviet Union — *Commonwealth of Independent States. Statistical Committee*
r Statistical Handbook on Adolescents in America — *Chadwick, Bruce A*
r Statistical Handbook on Violence in America — *Dobrin, Adam*
r Statistical Handbook on Women in America. 2nd Ed. — *Taeuber, Cynthia M*
Statistical Mechanics. 2nd Ed. — *Pathria, R K*
Statistical Methods — *Williams, John Delane*
Statistical Methods. Rev. Ed. — *Freund, Rudolf J*
Statistical Methods for Non-Precise Data — *Viertl, Reinhard*
Statistical Optimization for Geometric Computation — *Kanatani, Kenichi*
p Statistical Papers
Statistical Process Control. 2nd Ed. — *Doty, Leonard A*
Statistical Quality Control for the Food Industry. 2nd Ed. — *Hubbard, Merton R*
Statistical Theory and Computational Aspects of Smoothing — *Hardle, Wolfgang*
Statistical Tools for Nonlinear Regression — *Huet, Sylvie*
r Statistically Speaking — *Gaither, Carl C*
Statistics as Principled Argument — *Abelson, Robert P*
Statistics for Petroleum Engineers and Geoscientists — *Jensen, Jerry L*
Statistics for the Behavioral Sciences. 3rd Ed. — *Jaccard, James*
r Statistics of Quality — *Ghosh, Subir*
r Statistics on Crime and Punishment — *Gall, Timothy L*
r Statistics on Weapons and Violence — *Gall, Timothy L*
r Statlas UK — *Great Britain. Ordinance Survey*
c The Statue of Liberty — *Doherty, Craig A*
c The Statue Walks at Night (Illus. by Kathleen Collins Howell) — *Nixon, Joan Lowery*
Stature, Living Conditions, and Economic Development — *Komlos, John*
Status and Identity in West Africa — *Conrad, David C*
Status and Sacredness — *Milner, Murray, Jr.*
The Status of Black Atlanta 1993
The Status of Black Atlanta 1994
The Status of Black Atlanta 1995
Staub Von Stadten — *Krommer, Anna*
Stauffenberg: A Family History 1905-1944 — *Hoffmann, Peter*
y Stay Away from That City...They Call It Cheyenne — *Bly, Stephen A, 1944-*
Stay Here with Me — *Olmstead, Robert*
c Stay in Line — *Slater, Teddy*
Stay Tuned — *Murphy, Jane*
y Staying Fat for Sarah Byrnes — *Crutcher, Chris*
Staying Is Nowhere — *Knox, Ann B*
Staying Put — *Lanspery, Susan*
y Staying Safe on Dates — *Chaiet, Donna*
Staying the Distance — *McMahon, Franci*
c The Steadfast Tin Soldier (Illus. by Rachel Isadora) — *Isadora, Rachel*
c Steadfast Tin Soldier (Illus. by Jonathan Heale) — *Mitchell, Adrian*
Steak Lover's Cookbook — *Rice, William*
Steal Away — *Watts, Timothy*
y Stealing Home — *Robinson, Sharon*
Stealing Midnight — *Simone, Sonia*
r Steam Powered Video's Comprehensive Railroad Atlas of North America: Great Lakes West Including Chicago and St. Louis — *Walker, Mike*
r Stedman's OB-GYN Words. 2nd Ed. — *Littrell, Helen E*

c Stories from the Old Testament — *Bible. O.T. English. Authorized. Selections. 1996*

c Stories from the Sea (Illus. by Amanda Hall) — *Riordan, James, 1936-*

c Stories from the Stars (Illus. by Jackie Morris) — *Burke, Juliet Sharman*

c The Stories Huey Tells (Illus. by Lis Toft) — *Cameron, Ann*

y Stories I Ain't Told Nobody Yet — *Carson, Jo*

Stories in My Pocket — *Hamilton, Martha*

c Stories in Stone (Illus. by Richard Hewett) — *Arnold, Caroline*

Stories in Stone — *Rose, Martial*

Stories in the Worst Way — *Lutz, Gary*

The Stories of David Bergelson — *Bergelson, David*

The Stories of John Edgar Wideman — *Wideman, John Edgar*

The Stories of Raymond Carver — *Nesset, Kirk*

The Stories of Vladimir Nabokov — *Nabokov, Vladimir Vladimirovich*

Stories on Stage — *Shepard, Aaron*

c Stories on Stone (Illus. by Jennifer Owings Dewey) — *Dewey, Jennifer Owings*

The Stories (So Far) of Deborah Eisenberg — *Eisenberg, Deborah*

The Stories That Shape Us — *Jordan, Teresa*

Stories to Gather All Those Lost — *Siporin, Ona*

c Stories to Share (Illus. by Caroline Jayne Church) — *Eccleshare, Julia*

c Stories to Sleep On (Illus. by Kelly Pulley) — *Taylor, Charron E*

Stories to Tell a Five-Year-Old — *Low, Alice*

The Stories We Are — *Randall, William Lowell*

Stories We Live — *Rodriguez, Jeanette*

The Stork and the Plow — *Ehrlich, Paul R*

Storm at Arberth — *James, Sian*

c Storm Boy — *Lewis, Paul Owen*

y Storm Breaking — *Lackey, Mercedes*

y Storm Chaser — *Faidley, Warren*

c Storm on the Desert (Illus. by Ted Rand) — *Lesser, Carolyn*

Storm over Mono — *Hart, John, 1948-*

Storm Over Rhanna (Heilbron). Audio Version — *Fraser, Christine Marion*

The Storm Passed By — *Allen, Trevor*

y Storm Rising — *Lackey, Mercedes*

Storm: Short Stories — *Slater, Peter*

p Storm Warning

Storming the Desert — *Coughlin, Sean T*

Storming the Gates — *Balz, Dan*

c Storms and Hurricanes — *Gemmell, Kathy*

The Stormy Search for the Self — *Grof, Christina*

Stormy Weather — *Hiaasen, Carl*

A Story about Mr. Silberstein — *Josephson, Erland*

Story and Space in Renaissance Art — *Andrews, Lew*

c The Story Dance (Illus. by Fran Gregory) — *Satterfield, Barbara*

y The Story Knife — *Reynolds, Brad*

Story of a City — *Munif, Abd Al-Rahman*

y The Story of a Shipwrecked Sailor — *Garcia Marquez, Gabriel*

The Story of an Affinity — *Lampman, Archibald*

The Story of Art. 16th Ed. — *Gombrich, E H*

The Story of Astronomy — *Motz, Lloyd*

y The Story of B — *Quinn, Daniel*

The Story of B (Heald). Audio Version — *Quinn, Daniel*

The Story of Big Bend National Park — *Jameson, John*

The Story of Britain — *Strong, Roy*

c The Story of Christmas (Illus. by Loretta Krupinski) — *Cooney, Barbara*

The Story of Creation — *Carmichael, Calum M*

y The Story of David — *Howells, Dion*

The Story of Digby and Marie — *Shure, Robert*

c The Story of Doctor Doolittle (Illus. by Hugh Lofting) — *Kleinbaum, N H*

c The Story of Dusty (Illus. by Tom Morse-Brown) — *Svendsen, Elisabeth D*

c The Story of Easter (Illus. by Stefano Vitale) — *Fisher, Aileen*

c The Story of Flight

c The Story of Gold — *Hellman, Hal*

The Story of Henri Tod — *Buckley, William F*

The Story of Jane — *Kaplan, Laura*

The Story of Junk — *Yablonsky, Linda*

The Story of King Kabul the First and Gawain the Kitchen-Boy — *Jacob, Max*

c The Story of Kwanzaa (Illus. by Stephen Taylor) — *Washington, Donna L*

c The Story of Little Babaji (Illus. by Fred Marcellino) — *Bannerman, Helen*

c The Story of Little Black Sambo — *Bannerman, Helen*

c The Story of Little Black Sambo — *Russell, Judith*

The Story of Lynx — *Levi-Strauss, Claude*

c The Story of Money — *Orna-Ornstein, John*

The Story of My Life — *Darrow, Clarence*

c The Story of Numbers and Counting — *Ganeri, Anita*

c The Story of Oxygen — *Fitzgerald, Karen*

c The Story of Passover (Illus. by Erika Weihs) — *Simon, Norma*

c The Story of Printmaking — *Marchand, Pierre*

c The Story of Religion (Illus. by Giulio Maestro) — *Maestro, Betsy*

The Story of Rose O'Neill — *O'Neill, Rose Cecil*

c The Story of Ruby Bridges (Illus. by George Ford) — *Coles, Robert*

y A Story of Scorpions — *Everett, Gabriel*

c The Story of Sculpture (Illus. by Giacinto Gaudenzi) — *Romei, Francesca*

c The Story of Stagecoach Mary Fields (Illus. by Cheryl Hanna) — *Miller, Robert H*

The Story of the Church — *McBride, Alfred*

c The Story of the Milky Way (Illus. by Virginia A Stroud) — *Bruchac, Joseph*

The Story of the Night — *Toibin, Colm*

y The Story of the Olympics — *Anderson, Dave*

c The Story of the Three Kingdoms (Illus. by Ashley Bryan) — *Myers, Walter Dean*

c The Story of the Tooth Fairy (Illus. by Robert Sauber) — *Paxton, Tom*

The Story of the Voyage — *Edwards, Philip*

The Story of Worker Sport — *Kruger, Arnd*

The Story of Writing — *Robinson, Andrew*

c The Story of Writing and Printing — *Ganeri, Anita*

c The Story Snail (Illus. by Theresa Smith) — *Rockwell, Anne F*

The Story the Soldiers Wouldn't Tell — *Lowry, Thomas P*

Storyman — *Kelleher, Victor*

Storyteller. 3rd Ed. — *Ross, Ramon Royal*

Storyteller, Story-Teacher — *Gillard, Marni*

The Storyteller's Guide — *Mooney, William*

r Storytellers' Research Guide — *Sierra, Judy*

Storytellers to the Nation — *Stempel, Tom*

c Storytelling Adventures — *Dubrovin, Vivian*

r Storytelling: Art and Technique. 3rd Ed. — *Greene, Ellin*

Storytelling, Narrative, and the Thematic Apperception Test — *Cramer, Phebe*

Storytelling the Word — *Bausch, William J*

Stowaway — *Cordoba, Carol*

c The Stowaway: A Tale of California Pirates — *Gregory, Kristiana*

The Stowe Debate — *Lowance, Mason I, Jr.*

Strafford CD-ROM. Electronic Media Version

Straight Man — *Bingham, Sallie*

Straight Man — *Russo, Richard*

Straight News — *Alwood, Edward*

Straight Out of View — *Sutphen, Joyce*

Straight Razor — *Jaffe, Harold*

y Straight Talk about Post-Traumatic Stress Disorder — *Porterfield, Kay Marie*

Straight Talk on Stuttering — *Hulit, Lloyd M*

y Straight Up! — *Taylor-Gerdes, Elizabeth*

Straitjacket Society — *Miyamoto, Masao*

y Stranded — *Mikaelsen, Ben*

y Stranded in Harmony — *Shoup, Barbara*

Strandloper — *Garner, Alan*

y A Strange and Distant Shore — *Ashabranner, Brent*

yr Strange and Unexplained Happenings. Vols. 1-3 — *Clark, Jerome*

Strange Attractors — *Butz, Michael R*

The Strange Career of Legal Liberalism — *Kalman, Laura*

Strange Case of Dr. Jekyll and Mr. Hyde — *Stevenson, Robert Louis*

Strange City — *Krause, Staley*

The Strange Death of Mistress Coffin — *Begiebing, Robert J*

The Strange Deaths of President Harding — *Ferrell, Robert H*

Strange Dislocations — *Steedman, Carolyn*

Strange Multiplicity — *Tully, James*

c Strange Mysteries from around the World. Rev. Ed. — *Simon, Seymour*

y Strange New Land — *Wood, Peter H*

Strange Phenomena in Convex and Discrete Geometry — *Zong, Chuanming*

Strange Rain — *Armanno, Venero*

Strange Relation — *Hall, Daniel*

Strange Sites — *Christy, Jim*

Strange Weather — *Ross, Andrew, 1956-*

c The Stranger — *Van Allsburg, Chris*

Stranger among Friends — *Mixner, David B*

A Stranger at My Table — *Braid, Helen*

Stranger Danger — *Cope, Carol Soret*

A Stranger for Christmas — *Pearson, Carol Lynn*

A Stranger Here — *Bouras, Gillian*

y A Stranger Here — *Wyss, Thelma Hatch*

y Stranger in a Strange Land (Hurt). Audio Version — *Heinlein, Robert A*

Stranger in Our Midst — *Segel, Harold B, 1930-*

Stranger in the Midst — *Fink, Nan*

c Stranger in the Mirror (Illus. by Allen Say) — *Say, Allen*

Stranger to the Game — *Gibson, Bob*

The Stranger Who Bore Me — *March, Karen*

The Stranger Wilde — *Schmidgall, Gary*

The Stranger within Your Gates — *Porton, Gary G*

Strangers among Us — *Wright, Laurali*

Strangers and Sojourners — *O'Brien, Michael D*

Strangers in Paradise — *Abbott, Lee K*

Strangers in Paradise — *Ryan, Jake*

Strangers in Their Own Land — *Hezel, Francis X*

Strangers Settled Here amongst Us — *Yungblut, Laura Hunt*

Strangers to Ourselves — *Kristeva, Julia*

c The Strangest Halloween (Illus. by Kathryn Mitter) — *Barkan, Joanne*

Strassenpolitik: Zur Sozialgeshichte Der Offentlichen Ordnung In Berlin 1900 Bis 1914 — *Lindenberger, Thomas*

Strategic Analysis and the Management of Power — *Knudsen, Olav F*

Strategic Appraisal 1996

Strategic Approaches to the International Economy — *Hamada, Koichi*

Strategic Assessment 1995 — *National Defense University. Institute for National Strategic Studies*

Strategic Assessment 1996

Strategic Board Recruitment — *Kile, Robert W*

Strategic Choice and Path-Dependency in Post-Socialism — *Hausner, Jerzy*

Strategic Disagreement — *Gilmour, John B*

Strategic Environmental Management — *Wever, Grace*

Strategic Involvement and International Partnership — *Ngaosyvathn, Pheuiphanh*

Strategic IS/IT Planning — *Tozer, Edwin*

r Strategic Management for Public Libraries — *Hayes, Robert Mayo*

Strategic Management in the Global Economy. 3rd Ed. — *Vernon-Wortzel, Heidi*

Strategic Management of the China Venture — *Steidlmeier, Paul*

Strategic Negotiations — *Walton, Richard E*

Strategic Networking — *Henry, Paul David*

Strategic Planning in Technology Transfer to Less Developed Countries — *Madu, Christian N*

Strategic Pragmatism — *Schein, Edgar*

The Strategic Presidency. 2nd Ed., Rev. — *Pfiffner, James P*

Strategic Views from the Second Tier — *Hopkins, John C*

r Strategie Missionnaire Du Saint-Siege Sous Leon XIII 1878-1903 — *Prudhomme, Claude*

Strategies and Policies for Air Pollution Abatement: 1994 Major Review

Strategies for Asia Pacific — *Lasserre, Philippe*

Strategies for Business in Mexico — *Nevaer, Louis E V*

Strategies for Cultural Change — *Bate, Paul*

Strategies for International Legitimacy — *Steiner, Kristian*

Strategies for Learning Spanish — *Saz, Sara M*

Strategies for Mars — *Stoker, Carol R*

Strategies for Safer Communities in Prince Edward Island

y Strategies for Studying

Strategies for Teaching Learners with Special Needs. 6th Ed. — *Polloway, Edward A*

Strategies of Arms Control — *Croft, Stuart*

Strategies of Economic Order — *Tribe, Keith*

Strategies to Combat Poverty in Latin America — *Raczynski, Dagmar*

Strategy in Advertising. 3rd Ed. — *Bogart, Leo*

The Strategy of the Lloyd George Coalition 1916-1918 — *Dockrill, M L*

Strategy through People — *Hendry, Chris*

Stratification and Power — *Scott, John*

Stravinsky and the Russian Traditions. Vols. 1-2 — *Taruskin, Richard*

Strawberry Fields — *Wells, Miriam J*
c The Stray (Illus. by Wayne Parmenter) — *King-Smith, Dick*
Stray Dogs — *Ridley, John*
r Streamkeeper's Field Guide. 5th Ed. — *Murdoch, Tom*
Streams of Silver — *Flori, Monica*
y Street Child — *Doherty, Berlie*
Street Gallery — *Dunitz, Robin J*
c Street of Tall People — *Gibbons, Alan*
Street Smarts — *Major, Devorah*
Street Smarts and Critical Theory — *McLaughlin, Thomas*
y Street Soldier (Marshall). Audio Version — *Marshall, Joseph, Jr.*
Street Talk 3 — *Burke, David, 1956-*
y Streets: A Memoir of the Lower East Side — *Spewack, Bella*
Streets and Alleys — *Liberman, Syd*
Streets and the Shaping of Towns and Cities — *Southworth, Michael*
Streets of Fire — *Santiago, Soledad*
Streetwise — *Maddocks, John*
c Strega Nona (Illus. by Tomie De Paola) — *De Paola, Tomie*
Streisand: A Biography — *Edwards, Anne*
Streisand: Her Life — *Spada, James*
Streisand: It Only Happens Once — *Edwards, Anne*
r Strength in Numbers — *Brelin, Christa*
y Strength in Numbers — *Stein, Sherman K*
The Strength of a People — *Brown, Richard D*
Strengthening Aging Families — *Smith, Gregory C*
Strengthening National Agricultural Research Systems in the Humid and Sub-Humid Zones of West and Central Africa — *Taylor, Ajibola*
Stress — *Estleman, Loren D*
Stress: 63 Ways to Relieve Tension and Stay Healthy — *Inlander, Charles B*
Stress and Human Performance — *Driskell, James E*
Stress and Marriage — *Miller, Lyle H*
Stress, Coping, and Resiliency in Children and Families — *Hetherington, E Mavis*
Stress, Culture and Aggression — *Linsky, Arnold S*
Stress-Induced Phenomena in Metallization — *Ho, Paul S*
Stresses in Special Educational Needs Teachers — *Upton, Graham*
Stretching at Your Computer or Desk — *Anderson, Bob*
Strictly Business — *Cheape, Charles W*
Strike Swiftly! — *Jensen, Marvin*
Strike through the Mask — *Renker, Elizabeth*
Strike Zone — *Bouton, Jim*
Strikeout: A Celebration of the Art of Pitching — *Curran, William*
Striking In — *Dickey, James*
c Striking It Rich (Illus. by Anna DiVito) — *Krensky, Stephen*
c Striking It Rich (Davidson). Audio Version — *Krensky, Stephen*
y Striking Out — *Weaver, Will*
Striking the Balance — *Gammie, Malcolm*
String of Beads — *Shikishi, Princess, Daughter of Goshirakawa, Emperor of Japan*
String Too Short to Be Saved — *Hall, Donald, 1928-*
p Strings
Strip Tease (Asner). Audio Version — *Hiaasen, Carl*
Strip the Willow — *Marshall, Sybil*
The Striped Bass Chronicles — *Reiger, George*
c Stripes — *Fatus, Sophie*
Stripes in Quilts — *Mashuta, Mary*
Striving toward Virtue — *Olitzky, Kerry M*
Striving towards Being — *Merton, Thomas*
Strofy Veka — *Yevtushenko, Yevgenii*
Stroke: A Practical Guide to Management — *Warlow, Charles*
Strong and Free — *Griffiths, Franklyn*
Strong Arts, Strong Schools — *Fowler, Charles*
y Strong as Death — *Newman, Sharan*
Strong Brew — *Saks, Claude M*
Strong Hearts, Inspired Minds — *Mayor, Anne*
Strong Hearts, Wounded Souls — *Holm, Tom*
Strong Managers, Weak Owners — *Roe, Mark J*
Strong Mothers, Strong Sons — *Caron, Ann F*
Strong Parties and Lame Ducks — *Coppedge, Michael*
A Strong Showing — *Tanner, Rolf*
A Strong Supporting Cast — *Wilson, F M G*
Strong Women Stay Young — *Nelson, Miriam E*
Strong Words, Brave Deeds — *Klaus, H Gustav*
y Strongbow: The Story of Richard and Aoife — *Llywelyn, Morgan*

c Strongheart Jack and the Beanstalk (Illus. by Joe Shlichta) — *DeSpain, Pleasant*
Structural Adjustment and Socio-Economic Change in Sub-Saharan Africa — *Gibbon, Peter*
Structural Adjustment in Sub-Saharan Africa — *Lensink, Robert*
Structural Adjustment, World Trade and Third World Tourism — *Ramesh, K T*
Structural Analysis. 3rd Ed., Rev. — *Hibbeler, R C*
Structural Analysis in Microelectronics and Fiber Optics 1996
Structural Aspects of Manufacturing in Sub-Saharan Africa — *Biggs, Tyler*
Structural Competitiveness in the Pacific — *Boyd, Gavin*
Structural Funding and Employment in the European Union — *Harrop, Jeffrey*
y Structural Geology of Rocks and Regions. 2nd Ed. — *Davis, George H*
Structural Integrity, NDE, Risk and Material Performance for Petroleum, Process and Power — *Prager, M*
Structural Steel Design. 2nd Ed. — *Smith, J C, 1933-*
The Structure and Composition of Jeremiah 50:2-51:58 — *Bellis, Alice Ogden*
Structure and Identity — *Fouli, Janet*
Structure and Interpretation of Computer Programs. 2nd Ed. — *Abelson, Harold*
Structure and Policy in Japan and the United States — *Cowhey, Peter F*
Structure and Strategy of Small and Medium Size Enterprises since the Industrial Revolution — *Mueller, Margrit*
r Structure in Protein Chemistry — *Kyte, Jack*
The Structure of Paul's Theology — *Davis, Christopher A*
The Structure of Petrarch's Canzoniere — *Jones, Frederic J*
y The Structure of the Universe — *Halpern, Paul*
Structure-Property Correlations in Drug Research — *Waterbeemd, Han Van De*
Structured Biological Modelling — *Kraus, Michael, 1965-*
Structured Exercises for Promoting Family and Group Strengths — *McManus, Ron*
Structures and Categories for the Representation of Meaning — *Potts, Timothy C*
Structures in the Stream — *Shallat, Todd*
Structures of Power — *Peavler, Terry J*
Structures of Society — *Wirtschafter, Elise Kimerling*
Structures Rurales Et Societes Antiques — *Doukellis, P N*
Structures under Extreme Loading Conditions 1996 — *Shin, Y S*
Structures under Shock and Impact IV
Structuring Diversity — *Lamphere, Louise*
c Struggle and Hope — *Yee, Paul*
Struggle, Defeat or Rebirth — *Dubost, Thierry*
The Struggle for Australian Industrial Relations — *Dabscheck, Braham*
The Struggle for Canadian Sport — *Kidd, Bruce*
Struggle for Domination in the Middle East — *Har-El, Shai*
A Struggle for Fame — *Casteras, Susan P*
y The Struggle for Freedom — *Wepman, Dennis*
The Struggle for Land in Southern Somalia — *Besteman, Catherine*
The Struggle for Modern Tibet — *Goldstein, Melvyn C*
y The Struggle for Peace 1918-1989 — *Traynor, John*
The Struggle for Peace in Central America — *Moreno, Dario*
A Struggle for Power — *Draper, Theodore*
The Struggle for Power in Syria — *Dam, Nikolaos Van*
The Struggle for Recognition — *Honneth, Axel*
The Struggle for the American Curriculum 1893-1958. 2nd Ed. — *Kliebard, Herbert M*
The Struggle for the Breeches — *Clark, Anna*
The Struggle for the Georgia Coast — *Worth, John E*
Struggle for the Spirit — *Lehmann, David*
The Struggle for Theology's Soul — *Thompson, William M*
The Struggle for Utopia — *Margolin, Victor*
Struggle of the Magicians — *Patterson, William Patrick*
The Struggle over the Past — *Shea, William H*
Struggle to Unite Europe — *Zurcher, Arnold*
Struggles in the Promised Land — *Salzman, Jack*
Struttura E Lingua — *Porcelli, Bruno*
The Stuart Age. 2nd Ed. — *Coward, Barry*
The Stuart Court in Exile and the Jacobites — *Cruickshanks, Eveline*

Stuart: The Life and Art of Stuart Sutcliffe — *Williams, Kay*
Stubble over the Soil — *Lamarca, Carlos Crovetto*
Stubborn Hope — *Berryman, Phillip*
Stuck Rubber Baby — *Cruse, Howard*
c Stuck with Baby (Illus. by Geoff Kelly) — *Kelly, Geoff*
Stud: Architectures of Masculinity — *Sanders, Joel*
Stud Rites — *Conant, Susan*
Studebaker: The Life and Death of an American Corporation — *Critchlow, Donald T*
Student-Led Parent Conferences — *Picciotto, Linda Pierce*
Student Nationalism in China 1924-1949 — *Li, Lincoln*
r Student Reference Library. Electronic Media Version
y Student Writing and Research Center. Electronic Media Version
The Student's Cookbook — *Baker, Jenny*
yr A Student's Guide to African American Genealogy — *Johnson, Anne E*
yr A Student's Guide to British American Genealogy — *Johnson, Anne E*
yr A Student's Guide to Chinese American Genealogy — *She, Colleen*
yr A Student's Guide to German American Genealogy — *Robl, Gregory*
cr A Student's Guide to Irish American Genealogy — *McKenna, Erin*
yr A Student's Guide to Italian American Genealogy — *Brockman, Terra Castiglia*
A Student's Guide to Jewish American Genealogy — *Schleifer, Jay*
yr A Student's Guide to Mexican American Genealogy — *Ryskamp, George R*
yr A Student's Guide to Native American Genealogy — *Kavasch, E Barrie*
yr A Student's Guide to Scandinavian American Genealogy — *Paddock, Lisa Olson*
A Student's Guide to the IEP — *McGabee-Kovac, Marcy*
y A Student's Guide to the Internet — *Marshall, Elizabeth L*
The Student's Guide to the Internet — *Winship, Ian*
Studia Ietina IV — *Dalcher, Katharina*
Studien Zur Darstellung Des Menschen In Der Minoischen Kunst Der Alteren Und Jungeren Palastzeit — *Wingerath, Halina*
Studien Zur Fruhgeschichte Der Jesus-Bewegung — *Hoffmann, Paul*
Studien Zur Komposition Des Pentateuch — *Blum, Erhard*
Studien Zur Neutestament-Lichen Theologie — *Thusing, Wilhelm*
Studies in Accounting History — *Tsuji, Atsuo*
Studies in Biblical Law — *Brin, Gershon*
r Studies in Bibliography. Vol. 48
r Studies in Bibliography. Vol. 49
Studies in Early Muslim Jurisprudence — *Calder, Norman*
Studies in Economic Instability and Change — *Lundberg, Erik*
Studies in Eighteenth-Century Culture. Vol. 24
Studies in Eighteenth-Century Culture. Vol. 25
Studies in Entertainment — *Modleski, Tania*
Studies in Global Econometrics — *Theil, Henri*
Studies in Greek Philosophy. Vols. 1-2 — *Vlastos, Gregory*
Studies in Immersion Education — *Day, Elaine M*
Studies in Italian American Folklore — *Del Giudice, Lusia*
Studies in Jaina Art and Iconography and Allied Subjects — *Vyas, R T*
Studies in Legal Systems — *Orucu, Esin*
Studies in Newspaper and Periodical History 1994
Studies in Pharmaceutical Economics — *Smith, Mickey C*
Studies in Religion — *Richards, Glyn*
Studies in Scottish Fiction 1945 to the Present — *Hagemann, Susanne*
Studies in Stemmatology — *Reenen, Pieter Th. Van*
Studies in the American Renaissance 1995
Studies in the Economics of Aging — *Wise, David A*
Studies in the Greek New Testament — *Porter, Stanley E*
Studies in the Jewish Background of Christianity — *Schwartz, Daniel R*
Studies in the Logic of Charles Sanders Peirce — *Houser, Nathan*
Studies in the Sermon on the Mount — *Chambers, Oswald*
p Studies in Weird Fiction

Studies of High Temperature Superconductors. Vol. 18, Pt. 2

Studio Affairs — *Sherman, Vincent*

The Studios of Frances and Margaret Macdonald — *Helland, Janice*

Studs Terkel: A Life in Words — *Parker, Tony*

r Study Guide and Self-Examination Review for Kaplan and Sadock's Synopsis of Psychiatry. 5th Ed. — *Pataki, Caroly S*

Study Guide to the American Psychiatric Press Textbook of Psychiatry. 2nd Ed. — *Berman, Jude*

Study of Civil War Sites in the Shenandoah Valley of Virginia — *United States. National Park Service. Interagency Resources Division*

A Study of National Vocational Qualification Achievement through Open and Flexible Routes — *Calder, Judith*

The Study of Religion in British Columbia — *Fraser, Brian J*

The Study of Urban Geography. 4th Ed. — *Carter, Harold*

Study Skills — *Hutchings, Merry*

Studying John — *Ashton, John*

Studying the Cost and Value of Library Services: Final Report — *Kantor, Paul B*

Studying the Life of Saint Francis of Assisi — *Hugo, William R*

y Studywise 1 — *Foster, John*

Stuff — *Connolly, Joseph*

Stuff: The Materials the World Is Made Of — *Amato, Ivan*

Stumpwork Embroidery — *Nicholas, Jane*

c Stunt Performers — *Ware, Derek*

c Stunt Woman (Illus. by Tim Sanders) — *Greenberg, Keith Elliot*

The Stuntman's Daughter and Other Stories — *Blanchard, Alice*

The Stupefaction: Stories and a Novella — *Williams, Diane*

Stupid Boys Are Good to Relax With — *Swan, Susan*

Der Sturz Der Generale — *Janssen, Karl-Heinz*

Stuttering: A Life Bound Up in Words — *Jezer, Marty*

Style and the Man — *Flusser, Alan*

Style, Society, and Person — *Carr, Christopher*

Style Surfing — *Polhemus, Ted*

Styles of Scientific Thought — *Harwood, Jonathan*

Stylistics: Rethinking the Artforms after Hegel — *Winfield, Richard Dien*

Styrofoam Benchwork for Model Railroads — *Turner, Paul W*

The Sub — *Jazz, Jimmy*

Sub Specie Deae — *Mikocki, Tomasz*

Subcellular Biochemistry. Vol. 26

Subcellular Biochemistry. Vol. 27

Subhuman Redneck Poems — *Murray, Les*

The Subject Approach to Information. 5th Ed. — *Foskett, A C*

r Subject Collections. 7th Ed., Vols. 1-2 — *Ash, Lee*

r Subject Guide to U.S. Government Reference Sources. 2nd Ed. — *Hardy, Gayle J*

r Subject Guide to Women of the World — *Phenix, Katharine Joan*

r Subject Headings for School and Public Libraries. 2nd Ed. — *Fountain, Joanna*

r Subject Index — *Cockerell, Carol*

Subject Indexing. Vol. 15 — *Holley, Robert P*

r The Subject Is Murder. Vols. 1-2 — *Menendez, Albert J*

The Subject of Desire — *Baker, Deborah Lesko*

Subject to Change — *Boyle, Deirdre*

Subject to Ourselves — *Elliott, Anthony*

Subjected to Science — *Lederer, Susan E*

Subjectivity in English — *Pelyvas, Peter*

Subjects and Citizens — *Moon, Michael*

Subjects of Experience — *Lowe, E J*

Subjects on the World's Stage — *Allen, David G*

Subjects or Citizens? — *Ens, Adolf*

Das Subjekt Als Kind — *Schindler, Stephan K*

The Sublime: Poems — *Holden, Jonathan*

Sublime Thoughts/Penny Wisdom — *Teichgraeber, Richard F*

Subnational Movements in South Asia — *Mitra, Subrata K*

Subsistence and Stone Tool Technology — *Vierra, Bradley J*

r Substance Abuse Sourcebook — *Bellenir, Karen*

Substance and Separation in Aristotle — *Spellman, Lynne*

Substance and Shadow — *Kandall, Stephen R*

The Substance of Spinoza — *Harris, Errol E*

y The Substance of Things Hoped For (Proctor). Audio Version — *Proctor, Samuel DeWitt*

Substate Regionalism and the Federal System — *United States. Advisory Commission on Intergovernmental Relations*

The Subtext of Form in the English Renaissance — *Heninger, S K, Jr.*

Subtilisin Enzymes — *Bott, Richard*

The Subtlety of Sameness — *French, Robert M*

c Subtraction (Illus. by Richard Maccabe) — *Wells, Alison*

The Subtropical Garden — *Walker, Jacqueline*

Suburban Guerrillas — *Freda, Joseph*

Suburbs under Siege — *Haar, Charles M*

Subversion as Foreign Policy — *Kahin, Audrey R*

Subversive Discourse — *Kranidis, Rita S*

Subversive Laughter — *Jenkins, Ronald Scott*

The Subversive Psyche — *Kantaris, Elia Geoffrey*

Subversive Words — *Farge, Arlette*

Subverting Patriarchy — *Lewis, Alison*

Succeeding Generations — *Haveman, Robert*

y Succeeding with LD — *Lauren, Jill*

Succeeding with the Booch and OMT Methods — *Quatrani, Terry*

c Success (Illus. by Mechelle Ann) — *McDonnell, Janet*

Success at the Enquiry Desk — *Owen, Tim*

The Success Ethic, Education, and the American Dream — *DeVitis, Joseph L*

y The Success of Caroline Jones Advertising, Inc. (Illus. by Michael Harris) — *Fleming, Robert*

y The Success of Gordon H. Chong and Associates (Illus. by Kim Komenich) — *Chin, Steven A*

y The Success of Hispanic Magazine (Illus. by Ricardo Vargas) — *Garcia, John*

y The Success of the Navajo Arts and Crafts Enterprise (Illus. by Monty Roessel) — *Trahant, LeNora Begay*

Success Runs in Our Race — *Fraser, George*

Success Skills Curriculum for Teen Single Parents — *Hendon, Sarah*

Success while Others Fail — *Johnston, Paul, 1951-*

Success with Windows 95 — *Jamsa, Kris*

Successful Adoptive Families — *Groze, Victor*

Successful C for Commercial UNIX Developers — *Osman, Mohamed*

Successful Diversity Management Initiatives — *Arredondo, Patricia*

r Successful Gardening Journal

Successful Intelligence — *Sternberg, Robert J*

Successful Scientific Writing — *Matthews, Janice R*

Successful Staff Development — *Trotta, Marcia*

Successful Use of Teaching Portfolios — *Seldin, Peter*

Successfully Self-Employed — *Brennan, Gregory*

A Succession of Honorable Victories — *Sauers, Richard A*

The Succession to Muhammad — *Madelung, Wilferd*

The Succulent Garden — *Cave, Yvonne*

Sucesos Argentinos — *Battista, Vicente*

Such a Big Yearning and Other Stories — *Verma, Nirmal*

Such Good People — *Hickman, Martha Whitmore*

Die Suche: Das Andere Lehrwerk Fur Deutsch Als Fremdsprache — *Eismann, Volker*

Die Suche Nach Der Letzten Zahl — *Rytcheu, Juri*

Suche Werkis To Werche — *Vaughan, Miceal F*

Sud-Estul European In Vremea — *Dutu, Alexandra*

The Sudan — *Daly, M W*

c Sudan — *Levy, Patricia Marjorie*

Il Sudario Delle Caligini — *Giannetto, Nella*

A Sudden and Unprovided Death — *Hey, Stan*

A Sudden, Fearful Death (Porter). Audio Version — *Perry, Anne*

Sudden Fiction (Continued) — *Shapard, Robert*

Sudden Glory — *Sanders, Barry, 1938-*

Sudden Shakespeare — *Davis, Philip*

c Suddenly! — *McNaughton, Colin*

Suddenness: On the Moment of Aesthetic Appearance — *Bohrer, Karl Heinz*

Sudnyi Step — *Barka, Vasyl*

Sue Dolman's Book of Animal Toys — *Dolman, Sue*

El Sueno De America — *Santiago, Esmeralda*

Los Suenos De Un Portugues Y Otras Historias — *Alperi, Victor*

Suenos Y Discursos — *Quevedo, Francisco De*

Suenos Y Discursos. Vols. 1-2 — *Quevedo, Francisco De*

Suffering in Luke's Gospel — *Scheffler, Eben*

Suffering Made Real — *Lindee, M Susan*

The Suffering of God According to Martin Luther's Theologia Crucis — *Ngien, Dennis*

Suffolk Airfields in the Second World War — *Smith, Graham*

Suffrage Days — *Holton, Sandra Stanley*

The Suffragettes in Pictures — *Atkinson, Diane*

p Suffusion

Sufism and Islamic Reform in Egypt — *Johansen, Julian*

Sufism, Mystics, and Saints in Modern Egypt — *Hoffman, Valerie J*

Sugar Among the Freaks — *Nordan, Lewis*

Sugar and Other Stories — *Byatt, A S*

Sugar and Slavery — *Sheridan, Richard B*

Sugar and Slavery, Family and Race — *Dessalles, Pierre*

Sugar and Spice — *Bloom, Carole*

Sugar Dynasty — *Wade, Michael G*

y Sugar in the Raw — *Carroll, Rebecca*

Sugar Island Slavery in the Age of Enlightenment — *Stinchcombe, Arthur L*

The Sugar Mill Caribbean Cookbook — *Morgan, Jinx*

Sugar Mouth

c Sugaring (Illus. by Jos. A Smith) — *Haas, Jessie*

c The Sugaring-Off Party (Illus. by Gilles Pelletier) — *London, Jonathan*

Sui Sin Far/Edith Maude Eaton — *White-Parks, Annette*

The Suicidal Mind — *Shneidman, Edwin S*

y Suicide — *Woog, Adam*

Suicide across the Life Span. 2nd Ed. — *Stillion, Judith M*

Suicide Charlie — *Russell, Norman L*

Suicide Prevention — *Silverman, Morton M*

c The Suitcase Kid (Illus. by Nick Sharratt) — *Wilson, Jacqueline*

y A Suitcase of Seaweed and Other Poems (Illus. by Janet S Wong) — *Wong, Janet S*

y The Suitcase: Refugee Voices from Bosnia and Croatia — *Mertus, Julie*

c Suki's Sun Hat (Illus. by Pierre Pratt) — *Roche, Hannah*

Sula — *Morrison, Toni*

Suleyman the Magnificent and His Age — *Kunt, Metin*

c Sulky Suzy. Jittery Jack (Illus. by Jacqui Thomas) — *Lingard, Joan*

p Sulpher River Review

Sultan Omar Ali Saifuddin III and Britain — *Hussainmiya, B A*

The Sultanate of Aceh — *Lee, Kam Hing*

The Sultan's Daughter — *Chamberlin, Ann*

Suma Y Epiloga De Toda La Desripcion De Tlaxcala — *Martinez Baracs, Andrea*

r Sumatra: Island of Adventure. 2nd Ed. — *Caldwell, Ian*

Die Sumerischen Und Akkadischen Briefen — *Kienast, Burkhart*

Summary of Public Comments on the Inland Native Fish Strategy Environmental Assessment 1995

c Summer (Illus. by Kim Woolley) — *Baxter, Nicola*

Summer at the Lake — *Greeley, Andrew M*

Summer Bird Feeding — *Dennis, John V*

Summer Cooking — *David, Elizabeth*

Summer Garden Glory — *Bloom, Adrian*

The Summer House — *McLeay, Alison*

c Summer Ice — *McMillan, Bruce*

y A Summer Life — *Soto, Gary*

Summer of Betrayal — *Lao-Hung*

The Summer of Black Widows — *Alexie, Sherman*

y Summer of Secrets — *Cusick, Richie Tankersley*

c The Summer of Stanley (Illus. by Donald Gates) — *Kinsey-Warnock, Natalie*

c The Summer of the Great Divide — *High, Linda Oatman*

y The Summer of the Hand — *Moore, Ishbel L*

c The Summer of the Swans (Moore). Audio Version — *Byars, Betsy*

A Summer of Tigers — *Daruwalla, Keki N*

c Summer on the Farm — *Powell, Jillian*

c Summer on Wheels — *Soto, Gary*

A Summer Plague — *Gould, Tony*

c The Summer Sisters and the Dance Disaster (Illus. by Tony Kenyon) — *Shearer, Alex*

c Summer Spy — *Wilson, Linda*

yr Summer Stargazing — *Dickinson, Terence*

r Summer Theatre Directory 1996

c Summer Tunes (Illus. by Peter Simon) — *McMahon, Patricia*

The Summer Walkers — *Neat, Timothy*

Summer Will End — *Yeager, Dorian*

c Summerland — *French, Jackie*

Summer's End — *Ryan, Mary*

y Summerspell — *Thesman, Jean*

c Summertime in the Big Woods (Illus. by Renee Graef) — *Wilder, Laura Ingalls*

c A Summertime Song (Illus. by Irene Haas) — Haas, Irene
Summon Spirit's Cry — Mary Francis, Mother
Summoning: Ideas of the Covenant and Interpretive Theory — Spolsky, Ellen
Sumner Locke Elliott: Writing Life — Clarke, Sharon
Sumter Is Avenged — Schiller, Herbert M
c The Sun — Vogt, Gregory L
p The Sun: A Magazine of Ideas
c The Sun and Moon (Illus. by Paul Doherty) — Moore, Patrick
c The Sun and Other Stars (Illus. by Dennis Davidson) — Harris, Richard, 1942-
c Sun and the Solar System — Branley, Franklyn Mansfield
The Sun as a Star — Taylor, Roger
The Sun at Midday — Alhadeff, Gini
Sun Dancer — London, David
Sun, Earth and Sky — Lang, Kenneth R
y The Sun Hath Looked upon Me — Beyala, Calixthe
c Sun Is Falling, Night Is Calling (Illus. by Ora Eitan) — Leuck, Laura
c The Sun Is Rising — Masson, Sophie
c The Sun Is So Quiet (Illus. by Ashley Bryan) — Giovanni, Nikki
c The Sun Is Up (Illus. by Jane Chambless Wright) — Smith, William Jay
Sun on the Stubble — Thiele, Colin
Sun Pin: Military Methods — Sun, Pin
Sun Stories — Edwards, Carolyn McVickar
y The Sun, the Moon, and the Stars — Brust, Steven
y The Sun, the Sea, a Touch of the Wind — Guy, Rosa
c Sun through the Window — Ridlon, Marci
Sun Tzu and the Art of Business — McNeilly, Mark
Sun under Wood — Hass, Robert
c Sun, Where Do You Go? (Illus. by Chiara Carrer) — Grazzini, Francesca
Sun Yat-Sen — Bergere, Marie-Claire
Sunbelt Working Mothers — Lamphere, Louise
c A Sunburned Prayer — Talbert, Marc
c Sunday (Illus. by Synthia Saint James) — Saint James, Synthia
The Sunday Macaroni Club — Lopez, Steve
The Sunday Service of the Methodists — Tucker, Karen B Westerfield
Sundays at Seven — Pickett, James Carroll
Sundenzucht Und Sozialer Wandel — Friedeburg, Robert Von
Sunder Oder Ubertreter — Bachmann, Michael
c Sundew Stranglers — Wexler, Jerome
c Sundews: A Sweet and Sticky Death — Gentle, Victor
Sundials Australia — Folkard, Margaret
y Sundials: History, Theory, and Practice — Rohr, Rene R J
c The Sunflower Family (Illus. by Sherry Shahan) — Winner, Cherie
c Sunflower House (Illus. by Kathryn Hewitt) — Bunting, Eve
The Sunflower: On the Possibilities and Limits of Forgiveness. Rev. and Expanded Ed., 2nd Ed. — Wiesenthal, Simon
Sunflower Seeds and Seoul Food — Klein, Frederick C
c Sunflowers — McDonald, Mary Ann
The Sunken Road — Disher, Garry
c Sunny Days and Starry Nights (Illus. by Loretta Trezzo Braren) — Castaldo, Nancy Fusco
c Sunny Goes to School (Illus. by Lavona Keskey) — Juusola, Detta
Sunny Side Plucked — Higgins, Rita Ann
Sunnybrook: A True Story with Lies — Blackbridge, Persimmon
Sunrise Shows Late — Mekler, Eva
Sunrise Song — Eagle, Kathleen
Sunscreens: Development, Evaluation, and Regulatory Aspects. 2nd Ed. — Love, Nicholas J
Sunset and Santiago — White, Gloria
Sunset Express — Crais, Robert
y Sunset Express (Stuart). Audio Version — Crais, Robert
c Sunshine Home (Illus. by Diane De Groat) — Bunting, Eve
c Sunshine, Moonshine (Illus. by Lucia Washburn) — Armstrong, Jennifer
Super Heroes — Reynolds, Richard
Super-Learning 2000 — Ostrander, Sheila
c Super Paper Flyers Book and Kit — Schmidt, Norman
Super-Radiance: Multiatomic Coherent Emission — Benedict, M G
c Super Science Concoctions — Hauser, Jill Frankel
yr Super Science Fair Sourcebook — Iritz, Maxine Haren
c Super Senses (Snapshot)

c Super Skaters — Milton, Steve
c Super Structures (Illus. by Andy Crawford) — Wilkinson, Philip
Super Vixens' Dymaxion Lounge — Johnson, H
Superchefs: Signature Recipes from America's New Royalty — Zahler, Karen Gantz
Supercommunity Banking Strategies — Bird, Anat
Superconductivity — Poole, C P, Jr.
c Supercross Motorcycle Racing — Savage, Jeff
Superdistribution — Cox, Brad J
c Superfudge — Blume, Judy
Superfund Risk Assessment in Soil Contamination Studies. Vol. 2 — Hoddinott, Keith B
Superior Force — Miller, Geoffrey
The Superlative Man — Thomas, Herbert, 1957-
Superman's Song — Ostick, Stephen
The Supermen: The Story of Seymour Cray and the Technical Wizards behind the Supercomputer — Murray, Charles J
Supermodell V Luchakh Smerti — Rogozhin, Mikhail
c The Supernatural — Powell, Jillian
r Supernatural Britain — Hough, Peter
yr Supernatural Fiction for Teens. 2nd Ed. — Kies, Cosette
y Supernatural Sleuths — Waugh, Charles G
c Supernatural Stories (Illus. by Martin Salisbury) — Maynes, William
The Supernova Story — Marschall, Laurence
Supernovae and Nucleosynthesis — Arnett, David
Superplasticity and Superplastic Forming 1995 — Conference on Superplasticity and Superplastic Forming (1995: Las Vegas, NV)
c Superpooch — Thomson, Pat
y Superquake; Why Earthquakes Occur and When the Big One Will Hit Southern California — Ritchie, David
c Superstars on Ice — Cranston, P
c Superstitions — Corbishley, Mike
Supersymmetry in Disorder and Chaos — Efetov, Konstantin
Supplement to India's Family Welfare Program — Measham, Anthony R
r The Supplement to The Modern Encyclopedia of Russian, Soviet, and Eurasian History. Vol. 1 — Rhyne, George N
Supply Chain Optimization — Poirier, Charles C
Supplying the Nuclear Arsenal — Carlisle, Rodney P
Supporting Special Needs in the Secondary School Library — Ball, Frances
Supposed to Fly — Holub, Miroslav
A Supposedly Fun Thing I'll Never Do Again — Wallace, David Foster
p Supramolecular Science
The Supreme Court. 5th Ed. — Baum, Lawrence
The Supreme Court and Individual Rights. 3rd Ed. — Biskupic, Joan
r The Supreme Court CD-ROM. Electronic Media Version
r The Supreme Court Compendium. 2nd Ed. — Epstein, Lee
The Supreme Court in the Early Republic — Casto, William R
yr The Supreme Court Justices. 2nd Ed. — Cushman, Clare
y The Supreme Court of the United States — Kronenwetter, Michael
The Supreme Court Reborn — Leuchtenburg, William Edward
r The Supreme Court Yearbook 1995-1996
Supremely Abominable Crimes — Burman, Edward
c Suprising Science — De Waard, Nancy
Surely There Is a Future — Hamlin, E John
Surely You're Joking, Mr. Feynman — Feynman, Richard
Surface Activities of Proteins — Magdassi, Shlomo
Surface Coatings. 2nd Ed. — Paul, Swaraj
Surface/Interface and Stress Effects in Electronic Material Nanostructures — Prokes, S M
Surface Modification Technologies IX — International Conference on Surface Modification Technologies (9th: 1995: Cleveland, Ohio)
Surfaces and Interfaces of Solid Materials — Luth, Hans
Surfaces, Vacuum, and Their Applications — Hernandez-Calderon, I
Surfactants in Solution — Chattopadhyay, Arun K
A Surfeit of Guns — Chisholm, P F
SurferGrrrls: Look Ethel! An Internet Guide for Us! — Gilbert, Laurel
Surfers, Soulies, Skinheads, and Skaters — De La Haye, Amy

r Surfin' Guitars. 2nd Ed. — Dalley, Robert J
y Surfing the Himalayas — Lenz, Frederick
A Surgeon's Civil War — Holt, Daniel M
Surgeons, Smallpox, and the Poor — Marble, Allan Everett
Surgery and Prosthetic Voice Restoration after Total and Subtotal Laryngectomy — International Congress on Surgical and Prosthetic Voice Restoration after Total Laryngectomy (6th: 1995: San Sebastian, Spain)
r The Surgery Book — Youngson, R M
Surgery of Disorders of the Foot and Ankle — Helal, Basil
Surgery of the Upper Respiratory System. 3rd Ed. — Montgomery, William W
Surgery on My Soul — Kolumban, Nicholas
Surgical Anatomy of the Ocular Adnexa — Jordan, David R
Surgical Dermatology — Eedy, David J
Surgical Restoration of the Aging Face — Bernard, Robert W
r The Surnames of Wales — Rowlands, John
Surplus Population and the Poor Law Bill — Cobbett, William
c Surprise! Surprise! (Illus. by Michael Foreman) — Foreman, Michael
Surprised by Laughter — Lindvall, Terry
c Surprising Science Puzzles — Brecher, Erwin
Surrealism — Levy, Julien
Surrealism in Exile and the Beginning of the New York School — Sawin, Martica
Le Surrealisme Autour Du Monde 1929-1947 — Chenieux-Gendron, Jacqueline
Surrealist Vision and Technique — Poling, Clark V
Surrendering to Motherhood — Krasnow, Iris
r Surveillance of Agricultural Price and Trade Policies — Valdes, Alberto
r The Survey Kit. Vols. 1-9 — Fink, Arlene
A Survey of Bhuddist Thought — Scheepers, Alfred
The Survey of Early Byzantine Sites in Oludeniz Area (Lycia, Turkey) — Tsuji, Shigebumi
r Survey of English Dialects — Upton, Clive
A Survey of Geographic Information Systems in Government 1994
Survey of Routine Maternity Care and Practices in Canadian Hospitals — Levitt, Cheryl
Survey Research for Public Administration — Folz, David H
Surveyors of Persian Art — Gluck, Jay
Surveys in Applied Mathematics — Keller, Joseph B
Survival Guide to Computer Contracts — Monassebian, Jeff
Survival Instincts — Piesman, Marissa
c The Survival of Arno Mostyn — Garland, Sarah
Survived to Tell — Keonjian, Edward
Surviving Debt — Sheldon, Jonathon
c Surviving Homework (Illus. by Anne Canevari Green) — Nathan, Amy
Surviving Indonesia's Gulag — Budiardjo, Carmel
y Surviving Teen Pregnancy. Rev. Ed. — Arthur, Shirley
Surviving the Americans — Hilliard, Robert L
Surviving the Breakup — Wallerstein, Judith S
Surviving the Swastika — Macrakis, Kristie
The Survivor — Champlin, Tim
Survivor — King, Tabitha
Survivor from a Dead Age — Lozowick, Louis
Survivors: How to Keep Your Best People on Board after Downsizing — Caplan, Gayle
c Su's Snowgirl (Illus. by Pierre Pratt) — Roche, Hannah
r Susan B. Anthony Slept Here — Sherr, Lynn
y Susan Butcher and the Iditarod Trail — Dolan, Ellen M
Susan Sontag: Mind as Passion — Kennedy, Liam, 1961-
c Susannah and the Sandman (Illus. by Monika Laimgruber) — Laimgruber, Monika
Susie Bright's Sexual State of the Union — Bright, Susie
Susie Cooper: An Elegant Affair — Youds, Bryn
Suspects — Berger, Thomas
Suspended Music — Falkenhausen, Lothar Von
Un Suspens De Cristal — Stetie, Salah
Suspicion — McCrum, Robert
Suspicion — Pappano, Marilyn
Suspicious River — Kasischke, Laura
p Sustain: A Journal of Environmental and Sustainability Issues
Sustainability and Policy — Common, Michael
Sustainability of a Government Targeted Credit Program — Khandker, Shahidur R

Sustainability of Irrigated Agriculture — *International Conference on Sustainability of Irrigated Agriculture (1994: Vimeiro, Portugal)*

Sustainability, the Environment and Urbanization — *Pugh, Cedric*

Sustainable America — *President's Council on Sustainable Development*

Sustainable Cities — *Haughton, Graham*

Sustainable Community Development — *Maser, Chris*

Sustainable Democracy — *Buell, John*

Sustainable Development and Poverty Alleviation in Sub-Saharan Africa — *Perrings, Charles*

Sustainable Development of Small Island Economies — *Kakazu, Hiroshi*

Sustainable Development or Malignant Growth? — *Emberson-Bain, Atu*

Sustainable Dryland Farming — *Chatterton, Lynne*

Sustainable Financing Mechanisms for Coral Reef Conservation — *Hooten, Anthony J*

Sustainable Reconstruction of Highland and Headwater Regions — *International Symposium on Headwater Control (3rd: 1995: New Delhi)*

Sustainable Settlement in the Brazilian Amazon — *Almeida, Anna Luiza Ozorio De*

Sustainable Transport

Sustaining the Common Good — *Cobb, John B, Jr.*

Sut Lovingood's Nat'ral Born Yarnspinner — *Caron, James E*

Suzanne Somers' Eat Great, Lose Weight — *Somers, Suzanne*

Svensk Ingenjorskonst Under Stormaktstiden — *Dahl, Per*

Svensk Posthistorisk 1855-1925 — *Billgren, Jan*

Svezho Predanie — *Grekova, I*

Swag (Muller). Audio Version — *Leonard, Elmore*

c The Swallow — *Crewe, Sabrina*

c The Swallow Summer (Illus. by K M Peyton) — *Peyton, K M*

c The Swallow Tale — *Peyton, K M*

c Swallows in the Birdhouse (Illus. by Robin Brickman) — *Swinburne, Stephen R*

Swami Sahajanand and the Peasants of Jharkhand — *Hauser, Walter*

Swamp Cats — *Love, Jeff*

c Swamp Stomp! — *Stickland, Paul*

Swamplands of the Soul — *Hollis, James*

Swan Song — *Seddon, George*

Swan: The Second Voyage — *Moore, Jim*

Swann's Way (Jason). Audio Version — *Proust, Marcel*

Swann's Way. Swann in Love (Jason). Audio Version — *Proust, Marcel*

c Swaziland — *Blauer, Ettagale*

Sweat Equity — *Lynch, Allan*

Swedish Mentality — *Daun, Ake*

y Sweet and Natural Baking — *Niall, Mani*

c Sweet Corn Poems — *Stevenson, James*

Sweet Diamond Dust — *Ferre, Rosario*

c Sweet Dreams (Illus. by Vicki Wehrman) — *Lansky, Bruce*

c Sweet Dreams (Illus. by Sue Porter) — *Porter, Sue*

c Sweet Dreams of the Wild (Illus. by Katharine Dodge) — *Dotlich, Rebecca Kai*

c Sweet Dried Apples (Illus. by Deborah Kogan Ray) — *Breckler, Rosemary*

The Sweet Everlasting — *Mitcham, Judson*

Sweet Liberty — *O'Connor, Joseph*

Sweet Lorain — *Weigl, Bruce*

Sweet Maple — *Lawrence, James*

c Sweet Memories Still (Illus. by Laurie Harden) — *Kinsey-Warnock, Natalie*

Sweet Miss Seeton — *Crane, Hamilton*

c Sweet Potato Pie — *Rockwell, Anne F*

Sweet Reason — *Wells, Susan*

The Sweet Smell of Psychosis — *Self, Will*

c Sweet, Sweet Fig Banana (Illus. by Fritz Millvoix) — *Gershator, Phillis*

Sweet Tea with Cardamom — *Thornhill, Teresa*

cr Sweet Words So Brave (Illus. by Jerry Butler) — *Curry, Barbara K*

c Sweetapple Farm — *Smith, Wendy*

Sweetbitter — *Gibbons, Reginald*

c Sweetgrass — *Hudson, Jan*

The Sweetheart Season — *Fowler, Karen Joy*

y Sweetness and Light — *Wilcox, Kip*

c The Sweetwater Run (Illus. by Andrew Glass) — *Glass, Andrew*

c The Sweetwater Run (Guidall). Audio Version — *Glass, Andrew*

Swift and Sure — *Cornelius, William J*

c Swift as the Wind (Illus. by Jean Cassels) — *Esbensen, Barbara Juster*

y A Swiftly Tilting Planet (L'Engle). Audio Version — *L'Engle, Madeleine*

Swift's Politics — *Higgins, Ian*

c Swim! (Illus. by Marisabina Russo) — *Rice, Eve*

c Swim, Polar Bear, Swim! (Illus. by Meg Rutherford) — *Stimson, Joan*

Swim with the Dolphins. Audio Version — *Glaser, Connie*

c Swimming (Illus. by Art Seiden) — *Wilner, Barry*

y Swimming across the Hudson — *Henkin, Joshua*

Swimming in the Congo — *Meyers, Margaret*

Swimming Lessons — *Willard, Nancy*

Swimming Lessons and Other Stories from Firozsha Baag — *Mistry, Rohinton*

The Swimming Pool Library — *Hollinghurst, Alan*

Swimming the Channel — *Friedman, Sally*

Swimming Underground — *Woronov, Mary*

Swindler, Spy, Rebel — *De Grave, Kathleen*

The Swine's Wedding — *Weiss, Daniel Evan*

Swing Low — *Carroll, Rebecca*

Swing Low, Sweet Chariot — *McDaniel, Antonio*

The Swing: Mastering the Principles of the Game — *Price, Nick*

The Swing Tree — *Andrychuk, Kristin*

c Swinging on a Rainbow (Illus. by Thomas Hamilton) — *Perkins, Charles*

c Swings and Shadows — *Harvey, Anne*

y The Switch — *Horowitz, Anthony*

y Switch — *McColley, Kevin*

Switch Hitters — *Queen, Carol*

r Switching Systems and Applications — *Mazda, Fraidoon*

c Switching Well — *Griffin, Peni R*

r Switzerland — *Heusler, Eugen E*

c Switzerland--in Pictures — *Lerner Publications Company. Geography Dept.*

y Sword and Sorceress XIII

The Sword of General Englund — *Honig, Donald*

y Sword of Ice and Other Tales of Valdemar — *Lackey, Mercedes*

The Sword of Imagination — *Kirk, Russell*

The Swordfish — *Claus, Hugo*

Sworn on the Altar of God — *Gaustad, Edwin S*

p The Sycamore Review

r Sydney (Eyewitness Travel Guides)

The Sylvan Path — *Ferguson, Gary, 1956-*

c Sylvette Sous La Tente Bleue — *Daveluy, Paule*

Sylvia Pankhurst: Sexual Politics and Political Activism — *Winslow, Barbara, 1945-*

Symbiosis: An Intercultural Anthology of Poetry — *Diaz, Luciano*

Symbol and Sacrament — *Chauvet, Louis-Marie*

The Symbolic Earth — *Cantrill, James G*

Symbolic Exchange and Death — *Baudrillard, Jean*

Symbolism in the Fourth Gospel — *Koester, Craig R*

Symbolist Aesthetics and Early Abstract Art — *Reynolds, Dee*

The Symbolist Prints of Edvard Munch — *Prelinger, Elizabeth*

Symbols and Meanings in School Mathematics — *Pimm, David*

y Symbols of Judaism — *Ouaknin, Marc-Alain*

Symmetric Inverse Semigroups — *Lipscomb, Stephen*

Symmetries and Integrability of Difference Equations — *Levi, Decio*

Symmetries in Science VIII

Symmetries of Nature — *Mainzer, Klaus*

Symmetry — *Moriarty, Laura*

Symmetry in Chaos — *Field, Michael*

Sympathetic Attractions — *Fara, Patricia*

Symphony — *Grant, Charles L*

The Symphony: A Listener's Guide — *Steinberg, Michael, 1928-*

c A Symphony for the Sheep (Illus. by Mary Azarian) — *Millen, C M*

The Symptom-Context Method — *Luborsky, Lester*

r Symptoms and Early Warning Signs — *Apple, Michael*

Synaesthesia — *Baron-Cohen, Simon*

The Synagogue Survival Kit — *Wagner, Jordan Lee*

The Synagogues and Churches of Ancient Palestine — *Hoppe, Leslie J*

The Synagogues of Kentucky — *Weissbach, Lee Shai*

Synchronic or Diachronic? — *De Moor, Johannes C*

r Syndicated Comic Strips and Artists 1924-1995 — *Strickler, Dave*

Syndicats, Nous Voila! — *Le Crom, Jean-Pierre*

The Synergy Myth and Other Ailments of Business Today — *Geneen, Harold*

Synonym for Love — *Moore, Alison*

Synopsis of Neuropsychiatry — *Yudofsky, Stuart C*

The Synoptic Gospels — *Evans, Craig A*

Syntactic Structures — *Chomsky, Noam*

Syntax and the Literary System — *Ayres-Bennett, Wendy*

Synthesis and Application of Lanthanide-Doped Materials — *Potter, B G*

y Synthesis and Other Virtual Realities — *Rosenblum, Mary*

Synthesis and Processing of Nanocrystalline Powder — *Bourell, David Lee*

Synthesis of Porous Materials — *Occelli, Mario L*

Synthesis of Power Distribution to Manage Signal Integrity in Mixed-Signal ICs — *Stanisic, Balsha R*

Synthesis/Processing of Lightweight Metallic Materials — *Froes, F H*

Synthetic and Natural Phenols — *Tyman, J H P*

Synthetic Polymers — *Feldman, Dorel*

System Dynamics — *Rowell, Derek*

System for Ophthalmic Dispensing. 2nd Ed. — *Brooks, Clifford W*

A System of Social Science. 2nd Ed. — *Skinner, Andrew Stewart*

The System: The American Way of Politics at the Breaking Point — *Johnson, Haynes*

Systematic Theology — *Sobrino, Jon*

Systematic Theology. Vol. 2 — *McClendon, James William*

Systematic Theology. Vol. 2 — *Pannenberg, Wolfhart*

Le Systeme Politique De La Chine Populaire — *Cabestan, Jean-Pierre*

Systemic Treatment of Families Who Abuse — *Gil, Eliana*

Systems of War and Peace — *Caplow, Theodore*

Szinhaz Az Egesz Vilag — *Sarkozi, Matyas*

r Szycher's Dictionary of Medical Devices — *Szycher, Michael*

T

c T-Backs, T-Shirts, Coat, and Suit — *Konigsburg, E L*
T.C. Cannon: He Stood in the Sun — *Frederick, Joan*
T.M. Healy — *Callanan, Frank*
r The T.Q.M. Toolkit — *Waller, Jenny*
T. Rex and the Crater of Doom — *Alvarez, Walter*
T.S. Eliot and Ideology — *Asher, Kenneth*
T.S. Eliot and the Ideology of Four Quartets — *Cooper, John Xiros*
T.S. Eliot, Anti-Semitism, and Literary Form — *Julius, Anthony*
T.S. Eliot at the Turn of the Century — *Thormahlen, Marianne*
T.S. Eliot: The Modernist in History — *Bush, Ronald*
Tabac — *Franck, Dan*
c Tabitha: The Fabulous Flying Feline (Illus. by Laura Kelly) — *Timmel, Carol Ann*
Table Flowers — *Connolly, Shane*
Table of Integrals, Series, and Products. 5th Ed. Electronic Media Version — *Gradshteyn, I S*
Tablets of Stone, Hearts of Flesh — *Caserta, Thomas G*
Tabloid Dreams — *Butler, Robert Olen*
r Tabloid Journalism — *Greenberg, Gerald S*
Tabooed Jung — *Gallant, Christine*
Taboos in German Literature — *Jackson, David*
Tabu I — *Ruhmkorf, Peter*
Tacachale: Essays on the Indians of Florida and Southeastern Georgia during the Historic Period — *Milanich, Jerald T*
Tackling Racism and Xenophobia
c El Tacto (Illus. by Francisco Arredondo) — *Sanchez, Isidro*
Tadao Ando: Complete Works — *Dal Co, Francesco*
c Tadpole to Frog — *Rodger, Elizabeth*
c Tadpoles (Illus. by Dwight Kuhn) — *Pascoe, Elaine*
Tafelrunde Und Gral — *Pratelidis, Konstantin*
The Taft Museum — *Sullivan, Edward J*
y Tag against Time — *Vick, Helen Hughes*
Tagebuch 1920-1922 — *Schnitzler, Arthur*
Tagebucher 1906 Bis 1913 — *Hauptmann, Gerhart*
Tagebucher 1953-55 — *Mann, Thomas*
Tagebucher Nebst Aufsatzen Und Entwurfen Bis 1923. Vol. 1 — *Scholem, Gershom*
The T'ai-Chi Ch'uan Experience — *Delza, Sophia*
Tai Chi Chuan Martial Applications — *Yang, Jwing-Ming*
Tai Chi Theory and Martial Power — *Yang, Jwing-Ming*
c Taiga — *Kaplan, Elizabeth*
y The Tailor of Panama — *Le Carre, John*
c Tailypo! (Illus. by Wil Clay) — *Wahl, Jan*
c Tailypo: A Newfangled Tall Tale (Illus. by Sterling Brown) — *Medearis, Angela Shelf*
The Tainos: Rise and Decline of the People Who Greeted Columbus — *Rouse, Irvin*
Tainted Greatness — *Harrowitz, Nancy A*
Tainted Justice 1914 — *Newton, David, 1933-*
The Tainted Source — *Laughland, John*
Taipei — *Selya, Mark*
c Taiwan — *Moiz, Azra*
The Taiwan-China Connection — *Leng, Tse-Kang*
Taiwan: Nation-State or Province. 2nd Ed. — *Copper, John F*
Taiwan: National Identity and Democratization — *Wachman, Alan M*
Taiwan's Democratization — *Wu, Jaushieh Joseph*
Taiwan's Electoral Politics and Democratic Transition — *Tien, Hung-Mao*
Tajkep Fohasszal — *Baka, Istvan*
Take a Look at a Good Book — *Kahan, Steven*

c Take a Look, It's in a Book (Illus. by Christopher Hornsby) — *Krauss, Ronnie*
c Take a Stand! (Illus. by Jack Keely) — *Weizmann, Daniel*
Take Action! — *Bixler, Susan*
Take and Make Holy — *Zimmerman, Mari West*
r Take and Read — *Peterson, Eugene H*
Take Care — *Rhodes, Ann*
Take Charge of Your Career — *Moreau, Daniel*
Take My Word — *Goldman, Anne*
Take the Rich Off Welfare — *Zepezauer, Mark*
Take Three 2 — *Melnyczuk, Askold*
c Take to the Sky — *Lawlor, Laurie*
Takedown: The Pursuit and Capture of Kevin Mitnick, America's Most Wanted Computer Outlaw--By the Man Who Did It — *Shimomura, Tsutomu*
y Taken Captive — *Shohei, Ooka*
Taken to the Stage — *Kennedy, Mimi*
Takeoff: The Pilot's Lore — *Del Giudice, Daniele*
The Takeover (Stinton). Audio Version — *Frey, Stephen W*
Takeover: How Euroman Changed the World — *Niehoff, Arthur*
Takes One to Know One — *Allen, Kate*
y Takes: Stories for Young Adults — *MacIntyre, R P*
Takin' Back My Name — *Turner, Ike*
Taking a Bite out of Crime — *O'Keefe, Garrett J*
Taking Animals Seriously — *DeGrazia, David*
Taking Back Our Streets — *Williams, Willie L*
c Taking Care of the Earth (Illus. by Bobbie Moore) — *Pringle, Laurence*
Taking Charge — *Lester, Joan Steinau*
Taking Charge — *Schiffer, Michael Brian*
y Taking Charge of My Mind and Body — *Folkers, Gladys*
Taking Charge of Your Career Direction — *Lock, Robert D*
Taking Humour Seriously — *Palmer, Jerry*
y Taking It — *Cadnum, Michael*
Taking Judaism Personally — *Petsonk, Judy*
Taking Lives. 4th Ed., Expanded and Rev. — *Horowitz, Irving Louis*
Taking Measures across the American Landscape — *Corner, James*
Taking Money out of Your Corporation — *Storey, M John, 1943-*
y The Taking of Room 114 — *Glenn, Mel*
c Taking Off — *Otfinoski, Steve*
y Taking Off and Other Coming of Age Stories by American Teen Writers — *Kulpa, Kathryn*
y Taking Off and Other Coming of Age Stories by American Teen Writers. Audio Version — *Kulpa, Kathryn*
Taking on the World — *Merry, Robert W*
Taking Our Time — *Donaldson, Mike*
Taking Pictures for Profit — *Frost, Lee*
y Taking Sides. 2nd Ed. — *Easton, Thomas A*
Taking Stock — *Chalmers, Malcolm*
Taking Stock — *Green, David*
Taking Stock — *Tobin, Lad*
Taking Suffering Seriously — *Felice, William F*
Taking Tea with Clarice Cliff — *Griffin, Leonard*
Taking the Hard Road — *Maynes, Mary Jo*
Taking the Stage — *Zimmerman, Cynthia*
Taking the Tide — *Barber, Anthony*
y Taking the World in for Repairs (Gray). Audio Version — *Selzer, Richard*
y Taking Time Off — *Hall, Colin*
Taking Up Serpents — *Kimbrough, David L*

Takings: Land-Development Conditions and Regulatory Takings after Dolan and Lucas — *Callies, David L*
Talaq-I-Tafwid: The Muslim Woman's Contractual Access to Divorce — *Carroll, Lucy*
c The Tale of Ali Baba and the Forty Thieves (Illus. by Will Hillenbrand) — *Kimmel, Eric A*
The Tale of Beatrix Potter — *Lane, Margaret*
c The Tale of Hilda Louise (Illus. by Olivier Dunrea) — *Dunrea, Olivier*
c The Tale of Jemima Puddle-Duck (Illus. by Beatrix Potter) — *Potter, Beatrix*
c The Tale of Mucky Mabel (Illus. by Margaret Chamberlain) — *Willis, Jeanne*
c The Tale of One Bad Rat — *Talbot, Bryan*
c The Tale of Peter Rabbit. Electronic Media Version — *Potter, Beatrix*
The Tale of the Incomparable Prince — *Tshe-Rin-Dban-Rgyal, Mdo-Mkhar Zabs-Drun*
c The Tale of the Monstrous Toad (Illus. by Ruth Brown) — *Brown, Ruth*
The Tale of the Next Great War 1871-1914 — *Clarke, I F*
c Tale of the Terrible Teeth (Illus. by Russell Ayto) — *Townson, Hazel*
c The Tale of Tobias (Illus. by Rachel Merriman) — *Mark, Jan*
y The Tale of Tsar Saltan (Illus. by Gennady Spirin) — *Pushkin, Aleksandr Sergeevich*
A Tale of Two Cities — *Loader, J A*
A Tale of Two Cities — *Taylor, Ian*
A Tale of Two Continents — *Pais, Abraham*
A Tale of Two Gardens — *Paz, Octavio*
A Tale of Two Utopias — *Berman, Paul*
p Talebones
A Talent for Trouble — *Herman, Jan*
c Tales Alive! (Illus. by Michael A Donato) — *Milord, Susan*
Tales as Tools — *Weaver, Mary C*
Tales for Heart and Mind — *Silo*
c Tales from Agrabah (Illus. by Fred Marvin) — *Applegate, Katherine*
c Tales from Grandad's Attic (Illus. by Bruce Whatley) — *Whatley, Bruce*
y Tales from Other Times — *Hall, Christine*
Tales from Tartarus — *Russell, R B*
c Tales from the Brothers Grimm and the Sisters Weird (Illus. by Brad Weinman) — *Vande Velde, Vivian*
y Tales from the Crypt — *Diehl, Digby*
Tales from the Dena — *De Laguna, Frederica*
Tales from the Dugout — *Shannon, Mike*
c Tales from the Empty Notebook (Illus. by Joe Servello) — *Kotzwinkle, William*
c Tales from the Homeplace — *Burandt, Harriet*
Tales from the Irish Club — *Goran, Lester*
Tales from Two Pockets — *Capek, Karel*
y Tales from Watership Down — *Adams, Richard*
y Tales from Wide Ruins — *Engels, Mary Tate*
c Tales of a Fourth Grade Nothing (Blume). Audio Version — *Blume, Judy*
Tales of a Grandfather — *Scott, Walter, Sir*
Tales of Burning Love — *Erdrich, Louise*
Tales of Love — *Kristeva, Julia*
Tales of Mean Streets — *Morrison, Arthur*
Tales of Mendele the Book Peddler — *Mendele Mokher Sefarim*
Tales of Neveryon — *Delany, Samuel R*
c Tales of Real Adventure — *Dowswell, Paul*
c Tales of Real Heroism — *Dowswell, Paul*
c Tales of St. Patrick — *Dunlop, Eileen*
Tales of Tears and Laughter

Tales of Terror from Blackwood's Magazine — *Morrison, Robert*
Tales of the Bounty Hunters — *Anderson, Kevin J*
Tales of the Old North Shore — *Siverton, Howard*
c Tales of the Shimmering Sky (Illus. by JoAnn E Kitchel) — *Milord, Susan*
Tales of the Slav Peasants and Herdsmen — *Asala, Joanne*
Tales of the South — *Simms, William Gilmore*
c Tales of the Wicked Witch (Illus. by Annemarie Van Haeringen) — *Kraan, Hanna*
c Tales of Trotter Street (Illus. by Shirley Hughes) — *Hughes, Shirley*
Tales of Two Cities — *Milani, Abbas*
Tales of Zothique — *Smith, Clark Ashton*
Tales Out of School — *Taylor, Benjamin*
Tales, Rumors, and Gossip — *De Vos, Gail*
y Tales to Scary to Tell at Camp — *Stone, Tom*
y Talion Revenant — *Stackpole, Michael A*
Talk about Trouble — *Martin-Perdue, Nancy J*
Talk at Work — *Drew, Paul*
Talk of Angels — *O'Brien, Kate*
Talk of the Devil — *Guilliatt, Richard*
The Talk Show Defense — *Gross, Ken*
y Talk That Talk — *Goss, Linda*
y Talk to Me — *Dines, Carol*
Talked to Death — *Shaffer, Louise*
Talking about Genesis — *Moyers, Bill D*
Talking About Genesis — *Public Affairs Television (Firm)*
Talking about Leaving — *Seymour, Elaine*
Talking about Machines — *Orr, Julian E*
Talking about William Faulkner — *Faulkner, Jim*
Talking Animals — *Ziolkowski, Jan M*
y Talking Back to Poems — *Alderson, Daniel*
Talking Back to Shakespeare — *Rozett, Martha Tuck*
c Talking Birds — *Flanagan, Alice K*
c The Talking Cloth (Illus. by Rhonda Mitchell) — *Mitchell, Rhonda*
The Talking Cure — *Hoskyns, Tam*
The Talking Cure — *Shattuc, Jane M*
The Talking Cure — *Vaughan, Susan C*
Talking Cures — *Bankart, C Peter*
Talking Difference — *Crawford, Mary*
Talking Dollars and Making Sense — *Stephens, Brooks*
Talking from 9 to 5 — *Tannen, Deborah*
Talking Gender — *Hewitt, Nancy*
y The Talking Head — *Pewsey, Elizabeth*
Talking Horse — *Cheuse, Alan*
Talking Horse — *Malamud, Bernard*
y Talking in Animal — *Farish, Terry*
Talking in Bed — *Nelson, Antonya*
Talking Mathematics — *Corwin, Rebecca B*
Talking Pictures — *Watson, Victor*
Talking Proper — *Mugglestone, Lynda*
Talking Tidewater — *Harwood, Richard*
Talking to Angels — *Perkins, Robert F*
c Talking to Angels — *Watson, Esther*
Talking to Ghosts — *Gardner, Philip*
Talking to My Body — *Swir, Anna*
Talking to Strangers — *Stearns, Monteagle*
Talking to the Dead — *Dunmore, Helen*
Talking to the Ground — *Preston, Douglas*
c Talking Turkeys — *Zephaniah, Benjamin*
Talking Union — *Stepan-Norris, Judith*
Talking up a Storm — *Morris, Gregory L*
c Talking Walls (Illus. by Anne Sibley O'Brien) — *Knight, Margy Burns*
c Talking with Artists. Vol. 2 — *Cummings, Pat*
Talking with Confidence for the Painfully Shy — *Gabor, Don*
Tall Stories? — *Morison, John*
Tallchief — *McCall, Dinah*
Tallgrass — *Coldsmith, Don*
Tallulah Bankhead: A Scandalous Life — *Brett, David*
Talons of the Eagle — *Smith, Peter H*
y Tam Lin — *Dean, Pamela*
Tamara: Memoirs of St. Petersburg, Paris, Oxford and Byzantium — *Rice, Tamara Talbot*
Tamarind Mem — *Badami, Anita Rau*
Tame the Wild Wind — *Bittner, Rosanne*
A Tamil Asylum Diaspora — *McDowell, Christopher*
Taming Democracy — *Yunis, Harvey*
The Taming of the Samurai — *Ikegami, Eiko*
The Taming of the Shrew — *Dolan, Frances E*
y The Taming of the Shrew — *Olster, Fredi*
The Taming of the Shrew (Morris) — *Shakespeare, William*
Tammy: Telling It My Way — *Messner, Tammy Faye*

c Tam's Slipper. Book and Audio Version — *Palazzo-Craig, Janet*
Tang Thu Song Chet — *Rinpoche, Sogyal*
y Tangerine — *Bloor, Edward*
Tangible Visions — *Wardwell, Allen*
c Tangle Town (Illus. by Kurt Cyrus) — *Cyrus, Kurt*
c Tanglebird (Illus. by Bernard Lodge) — *Lodge, Bernard*
Tangled Loyalties — *Rubenstein, Joshua*
Tangled Memories — *Sturken, Marita*
Tangled Tassels — *Eastman, Richard*
The Tangled Web — *Hoff, B J*
c Tangletalk (Illus. by Jessica Clerk) — *Nikola-Lisa, W*
Tango and the Political Economy of Passion — *Savigliano, Marta E*
y Tango's Baby — *Waddell, Martin*
c Tanks (Illus. by Richard Chasemore) — *Chasemore, Richard*
Tanks and Industry — *Thornton, Kevin*
Tantalizing Tomatoes — *Cutler, Karan D*
Tanten Och Krokodilen — *Mazzarella, Merete*
c Tanya Steps Out (Illus. by Satomi Ichikawa) — *Gauch, Patricia Lee*
c Tanya's Reunion (Illus. by Jerry Pinkney) — *Flournoy, Valerie*
r Tanzania. Rev. Ed. — *Darch, Colin*
The Tanzanian Peasantry — *Forster, Peter G*
y Tanzit: A Bridge to Advanced Russian Language Studies — *West, Daphne*
Tao and Method — *LaFargue, Michael*
The Tao of Jung — *Rosen, David*
The Tao of Muhammad Ali — *Miller, Davis*
The Tao of Muhammad Ali (Miller). Audio Version — *Miller, Davis*
The Tao of Natural Breathing — *Lewis, Dennis*
The Tao of Unity. Audio Version — *Barrette, Greg*
Tap, Tap — *Martin, David Lozell, 1946-*
c Tap-Tap (Taylor). Book and Audio Version — *Williams, Karen Lynn*
The Tape-Recorded Interview. 2nd Ed. — *Ives, Edward D*
c Tapenum's Day (Illus. by Russ Kendall) — *Waters, Kate*
Tapestries for the Courts of Federico II Ercole and Ferrante Gonzaga 1522-63 — *Brown, Clifford M*
Tapestries of Hope, Threads of Love — *Agosin, Marjorie*
A Tapestry of Murders — *Doherty, P C*
Tapices Y Cartones De Goya — *Herrero, Concha*
cp Tapori: A Children's Newsletter
r TAPR Software Library. Vol. 1. Electronic Media Version
p Taproot Reviews
Tapu: A Novel — *Corbalis, Judy*
Tar Baby — *Morrison, Toni*
c Tar Beach — *Ringgold, Faith*
c The Tarantula in My Purse and 172 Other Wild Pets (Illus. by Jean Craighead George) — *George, Jean Craighead*
Target Costing — *Ansari, Shahid L*
y Target Earth — *Perry, Steve*
y Target Geography. Bks. 1-2 — *Goddard, Peter*
Target Language, Collaborative Learning and Autonomy — *Macaro, Ernesto*
Targeting Inflation — *Haldane, Andrew G*
Targeting of Drugs 5 — *Gregoriadis, Gregory*
The Tariff Question in the Gilded Age — *Reitano, Joanne*
y Tarka the Otter (Maloney). Audio Version — *Williamson, Henry*
Tarnished Brass — *Taylor, Scott*
The Tartar Step — *Buzzati, Dino*
c Tashi and the Ghosts (Illus. by Kim Gamble) — *Fienberg, Anna*
y Task Maths. Bks. 1-3 — *Ball, Barbara*
r Tassie Terms — *Brooks, Maureen*
c Taste (Illus. by Francisco Arredondo) — *Llamas, Andreu*
Taste and Power — *Auslander, Leora*
A Taste of Indochina — *Castorina, Jan*
A Taste of Madras — *Kingman, Rani*
A Taste of the Gulf Coast — *Tirsch, Jessie*
c A Taste of the Mexican Market — *Tabor, Nancy*
Taste of the Pacific — *Parkinson, Susan*
The Taste of Wine. 2nd Ed. — *Peynaud, Emile*
Tasting Food, Tasting Freedom — *Mintz, Sidney W*
Tasting the Dish — *Satlow, Michael L*
Tata: A Voice from the Rio Puerco — *Garcia, Nasario P*
Tattoo — *Britto, Anthony*
The Tattooed Map — *Hodgson, Barbara*

Tattooed on Their Tongues — *Escott, Colin*
Taurine 2 — *Huxtable, Ryan J*
The Tavern Lamps Are Burning — *Carmer, Carl*
Taverna — *Goldstein, Joyce*
Tax Accounting for Small Business — *Gelb, Joseph*
Tax Compliance Costs — *Sandford, Cedric*
Tax Credits for Low Income Housing. 9th Ed. — *Guggenheim, Joseph*
Taxation in an Integrating World — *Tanzi, Vito*
c The Taxi Navigator — *Mosher, Richard*
To Taxidi 1963-1992. Vols. 1-2 — *Tsaloumas, Dimitris*
Taxing America — *Brown, Karen B*
Taxing Bads by Taxing Goods — *Eskeland, Gunnar S*
Taxing Ourselves — *Slemrod, Joel*
Taxing Women — *McCaffery, Edward J*
The Taxpayers of Medieval Gloucestershire — *Franklin, Peter*
Taylored Lives — *Banta, Martha*
r Taylor's Guide to Fruits and Berries — *Holmes, Roger*
r Taylor's Guide to Heirloom Vegetables — *Watson, Benjamin*
Tchaikovsky — *Holden, Anthony*
Tchaikovsky: A Biography — *Holden, Anthony*
Tchaikovsky's Last Days — *Poznansky, Alexander*
Tchipayuk, or the Way of the Wolf — *Lavallee, Ronald*
Te Ao Marama. Vol. 5 — *Ihimaera, Witi*
Te Di La Vida Entera — *Valdes, Zoe*
r Te Matatiki: Contemporary Maori Words. New, Rev. Ed. — *New Zealand. Maori Language Commission*
Te Pup In Fund Conductor Iubit! — *Banulescu, Daniel*
r The Tea Companion — *Pettigrew, Jane*
c Teach Me Chinese (Illus. by Amy Xiaomin Wang). Book and Audio Version — *Mahoney, Judy*
Teach to Reach — *Mitchell, Craig*
c Teach Us, Amelia Bedelia (Illus. by Lynn Sweat) — *Parish, Peggy*
Teach Yourself Computers and the Internet Visually — *Maran, Ruth*
Teach Yourself Java in 21 Days — *Lemay, Laura*
Teach Yourself New Testament Greek — *Macnair, Ian*
Teach Yourself the Simplified Zone System of Light Measurement — *Farzad, Bahman*
Teach Yourself...Corel WordPerfect 7 — *Weingarten, Jan*
Teacher Education in America — *Lucas, Christopher J*
Teacher Research and Urban Literacy Education — *Hollingsworth, Sandra*
Teacher Thinking in Cultural Contexts — *Rios, Francisco*
Teachers and Mentors — *Kridel, Craig*
Teachers and Technology
The Teachers and Writers Guide to Frederick Douglass — *Brown, Wesley*
The Teacher's Book of Wit — *Ortman, Mark*
Teachers, Discourses, and Authority in the Postmodern Composition Classroom — *Gale, Xin Lui*
Teachers Guide to Cyberspace
A Teacher's Introduction to Composition and the Rhetorical Tradition — *Winterowd, W Ross*
Teachers of the Inner Chambers — *Ko, Dorothy*
Teachers, Pupils and Primary Schooling — *Croll, Paul*
Teaching about International Conflict and Peace — *Merryfield, Merry M*
r Teaching about the Holocaust
Teaching Adolescents with Mild Disabilities — *Platt, Jennifer M, 1945-*
Teaching American Ethnic Literatures — *Maitino, John R*
r Teaching and Learning in the Early Years — *Whitebread, David*
Teaching and Testimony — *Carey-Webb, Allen*
Teaching Art — *Goldstein, Carl*
Teaching Bibliographic Skills in History — *D'Aniello, Charles A*
Teaching Business English — *Ellis, Mark*
Teaching Children to Love — *Childre, Doc Lew*
r Teaching Children's Literature — *Lundin, Anne*
Teaching Christian Children about Judaism — *Levine, Deborah J*
Teaching Christianity — *Augustinus, Aurelius*
Teaching Democracy by Being Democratic — *Becker, Theodore L*
r Teaching English/Japan — *O'Sullivan, Jerry*
Teaching for Justice in the Age of the Good Universities Guide
Teaching Grammar in Context — *Weaver, Constance*

Teaching in the Real World — *Simola, Robert*
Teaching Information Literacy Using Electronic
 Resources for Grades 6-12 — *Anderson, Mary Alice*
Teaching Information Literacy Using Electronic
 Resources for Grades K-6 — *Skeele, Linda*
Teaching Information Retrieval Skills to Education
 Students and Practitioners — *Libutti, Patricia
 O'Brien*
Teaching Introductory Physics — *Arons, Arnold B*
Teaching Introductory Physics — *Swartz, Clifford E*
Teaching Kids with Learning Difficulties in the
 Regular Classroom — *Winebrenner, Susan*
Teaching Literature in Middle School
Teaching Malcolm X — *Perry, Theresa*
Teaching Mathematically Able Children — *Kennard,
 Roy*
Teaching Mathematics — *Davis, A Brent*
Teaching Nursing. 2nd Ed. — *Ewan, Christine*
The Teaching of Arabic as a Foreign Language
 — *Al-Batal, Mahmoud*
The Teaching of Organizational Behavior across
 Discipline and National Boundaries — *Whiteley,
 Alma M*
The Teaching of Poetry — *Thompson, Linda*
Teaching Patients with Low Literacy Skills. 2nd Ed.
 — *Doak, Cecilia Conrath*
Teaching Physical Education — *Williams, Anne*
Teaching Physical Science through Children's
 Literature — *Gertz, Susan E*
Teaching Pigs to Sing — *Strube, Cordelia*
The Teaching Portfolio — *Seldin, Peter*
Teaching Problem Students — *Brophy, Jere E*
Teaching Science for All Children. 2nd Ed. — *Martin,
 Ralph*
c Teaching the Bairns to Cook — *Ashworth, Liz*
Teaching the New Basic Skills — *Murnane, Richard J*
Teaching the New Library — *LaGuardia, Cheryl*
c Teaching the Parrot (Illus. by John Lawrence)
 — *Edwards, Richard*
Teaching the World's Children — *Ashworth, Mary*
Teaching to Transgress — *Hooks, Bell*
Teaching Tolerance — *Bullard, Sara*
Teaching Translation and Interpreting 2 — *Dollerup,
 Cay*
Teaching Translation from Spanish to English
 — *Lonsdale, Allison Beeby*
Teaching under Pressure — *Cockburn, Anne*
The Teaching Voice — *Martin, Stephanie*
Teaching with a Multicultural Perspective
 — *Davidman, Leonard*
Teaching with Children's Books — *Sorensen, Marilou*
Teaching with Shakespeare — *McIver, Bruce*
Teaching Writing as Reflective Practice — *Hillocks,
 George, Jr.*
Teachings from the Worldly Philosophy
 — *Heilbroner, Robert*
Teachings of the Tao
Team Management — *Bluck, Robert*
Team Member's Survival Guide — *George, Jill A*
y Team Picture — *Hughes, Dean*
Team Talk — *Donnellon, Anne*
Team Think — *Butler, Ava S*
Team Toyota — *Besser, Terry L*
Teaming Up — *Edwards, Paul, 1940-*
c Teammates (Illus. by Paul Bacon) — *Golenbock, Peter*
Teams and Technology — *Mankin, Don*
r Teapots — *Tippett, Paul*
Tear This Heart Out — *Mastretta, Angeles*
Tearing the Silence — *Hegi, Ursula*
Tears and Saints — *Cioran, E M*
y Tears of a Tiger — *Draper, Sharon M*
The Tears of Narcissus — *Enterline, Lynn*
y Tears of the Heart (Weideman). Audio Version
 — *Paine, Lauran*
Tears of the Madonna — *Herman, George*
y The Tears of Things — *McInerny, Ralph*
Teatro: 5 Autores Cubanos — *Leal, Rine*
c Teatro As Tres Pancadas (Illus. by Joao Caetano)
 — *Torrado, Antonio*
El Teatro Campesino — *Broyles-Gonzalez, Yolanda*
Teatro! Hispanic Plays for Young People — *Vigil,
 Angel*
r Teatro Hispano! — *De La Roche, Elisa*
Tebaldi: The Voice of an Angel — *Casanova,
 Carlamaria*
Technical Change and the World Economy
 — *Hagedoorn, John*
Technical Change, Human Capital, and Spillovers in
 United States Agriculture 1949-1985 — *Deininger,
 Klaus W*

Technical Communication. 4th Ed. — *Markel, Michael
 H*
Technical Communication and Its Applications
 — *Borowick, Jerome N*
Technical Issues in Large-Scale Performance
 Assessment — *Phillips, Gary W*
Technical Knowledge in American Culture
 — *Cravens, Hamilton*
Technical Services Management 1965-1990 — *Smith,
 Linda C*
Technical Writing. 2nd Ed. — *Gerson, Sharon J*
r Technics and Architecture — *Elliott, Cecil D*
The Technique of Film and Video Editing. 2nd Ed.
 — *Dancyger, Ken*
The Technique of Pseudodifferential Operators
 — *Cordes, H O*
Techniques and Equipment for Gathering Visitor Use
 Data on Recreation Sites — *Yuan, Susan*
Techniques and Standards for Image, Video, and
 Audio Coding — *Rao, K R*
r Techniques for Analyzing Food Aroma — *Marsili,
 Ray*
Techniques in Apoptosis — *Cotter, T G*
Techniques in Aquatic Toxicology — *Ostrander, Gary
 K*
Techniques of Event History Modeling — *Blossfeld,
 Hans-Peter*
Techniques of Satire — *Draitser, Emil*
Technohistory: Using the History of American
 Technology in Interdisciplinary Research — *Gray,
 Chris Hables*
Technological Capabilities and Learning in African
 Enterprises — *Biggs, Tyler*
Technological Change — *Fox, Robert*
Technological Collaboration — *Coombs, Rod*
Technological Development and Industrial Exhibitions
 1850-1914 — *Ahlstrom, Goran*
Technological Evolution, Variety and the Economy
 — *Saviotti, Paolo*
Technological Infrastructure Policy — *Teubal, Morris*
Technological Innovation and the Great Depression
 — *Szostak, Rick*
The Technological Reshaping of Metropolitan America
The Technological Transformation of Japan
 — *Morris-Suzuki, Tessa*
The Technological Unemployment and Structural
 Unemployment Debates — *Woirol, Gregory R*
Technologies for Detection of DNA Damage and
 Mutations — *Pfeifer, Gerd P*
Technologies for Rainfed Agriculture in
 Mediterranean Climates — *Oram, Peter A*
Technologies of the Gendered Body — *Balsamo, Anne*
Technology — *Boyle, David*
c Technology — *Kerrod, Robin*
Technology and Copyright Law — *Bielefield, Arlene*
Technology and Creativity — *Dasgupta, Subrata*
Technology and Enterprise Development — *Lall,
 Sanjaya*
Technology and European Overseas Enterprises
 — *Adas, William Michael*
Technology and Industrial Progress — *Von
 Tunzelmann, G N*
Technology and the Dynamics of Specialization in
 Open Economies — *Stolpe, Michael*
Technology Education in the Classroom — *Raizen,
 Senta A*
Technology in the Hospital — *Howell, Joel D*
The Technology Link to Economic Development
 — *Raymond, Susan U*
Technology of Thermoforming — *Throne, James L*
Technology, Pessimism, and Postmodernism
 — *Ezrahi, Yaron*
y Technology Projects for the Classroom — *Kaufman,
 Allan*
Technology Transfer — *Williams, Frederick*
Technology Trendlines — *Keyes, Jessica*
yr Technology's Past — *Karwatka, Dennis*
Technology's School — *Waks, Leonard J*
Technopols: Freeing Politics and Markets in Latin
 America in the 1990s — *Domainguez, Jorge I*
Tecnicas Narrativas De La Novelistica De Sergio
 Galindo — *Garcia, Connie*
Tecnologia Moderna En Los Andes — *Contreras,
 Manuel E*
The Tectonic Evolution of Asia — *Yin, An*
c Teddies and Machines — *Haldane, Suzanne*
c Teddies and Trucks — *Haldane, Suzanne*
Teddy Bear Figurines — *Murray, Jesse*
c Teddy Bear Tears (Illus. by Jo Ellen
 McAllister-Stammen) — *Aylesworth, Jim*

c Teddy Bear, Teddy Bear (Illus. by Michael Hague)
 — *Hague, Michael*
c The Teddy Bears' Picnic (Illus. by Bruce Whatley)
 — *Garcia, Jerry*
c The Teddy Bears' Picnic (Illus. by Bruce Whatley).
 Book and Audio Version — *Kennedy, Jimmy*
Ted's Travelling Circus — *Stewart, Carroll*
Tee Times — *Burnett, Jim*
Teed Off — *Furlong, Nicola*
y Teen Addiction — *Winters, Paul A*
Teen Mothers — *Horowitz, Ruth*
y Teen Mothers — *Stewart, Gail B*
y Teen Runaways — *Stewart, Gail B*
y Teen Sexuality — *Nardo, Don*
yr The Teen Trip — *Kimball, Gayle*
yp Teen Voices Magazine
y Teenage Couples: Expectations and Reality
 — *Lindsay, Jeanne Warren*
y Teenage Health Care — *Slap, Gail B*
y The Teenage Q and A Book — *McDowell, Josh*
y Teenage Suicide — *Goldman, Nikkie*
y The Teenage Worrier's Christmas Survival Guide
 — *Asquith, Ros*
Teenagers: An American History — *Palladino, Grace*
y Teens and Gambling — *Haddock, Patricia*
y Teens and Tobacco — *Lang, Susan S*
y A Teen's Guide to Going Vegetarian — *Krizmanic,
 Judy*
y Teens in Prison — *Stewart, Gail B*
y Teens with Physical Disabilities — *Cheney, Glenn Alan*
y Teenspeak — *Meyer, Linda*
The Teeth Are Smiling — *Vasta, Ellie*
Tejano Religion and Ethnicity — *Matovina, Timothy M*
Tejanos and Texas Under the Mexican Flag 1821-1836
 — *Tijerina, Andres*
Tek Kill — *Shatner, William*
Tek Money — *Shatner, William*
Telecom Made Easy. 2nd Ed. — *Langhoff, June*
r Telecommunication Networks — *Mazda, Fraidoon*
Telecommunication System Engineering. 3rd Ed.
 — *Freeman, Roger L*
r Telecommunication Systems and Applications
 — *Mazda, Fraidoon*
r Telecommunication Transmission Principles
 — *Mazda, Fraidoon*
Telecommunications: A Bridge to the 21st Century
 — *Jussawalla, Meheroo*
Telecommunications and Geography — *Kellerman,
 Aharon*
Telecommunications and the City — *Graham, Stephen,
 1965-*
Telecommunications, Mass Media, and Democracy
 — *McChesney, Robert W*
Telecommunications Technology and Native
 Americans
Telecommunications Wiring for Commercial Buildings
 — *Gilbert, Elliot M*
Telecommute! Go to Work without Leaving Home
 — *Shaw, Lisa*
r Telecommuters: The Workforce of the Twenty-First
 Century — *Switzer, Teri R*
Telecommuting Pluses and Pitfalls — *Thompson,
 Brenda B*
To Telefteo Kanarini — *Kotsias, Telemahos*
Telegrams from the Soul — *Barker, Andrew*
Telematics and Transport Behaviour — *Nijkamp,
 Peter*
Telemedicine: A Guide to Assessing
 Telecommunications in Health Care — *Institute of
 Medicine (U.S.). Committee on Evaluating Clinical
 Applications of Telemedicine*
c Telephone (Illus. by Vladimir Radunsky)
 — *Chukovsky, Kornei*
c The Telephone (Illus. by J-M Poissenot) — *Delafosse,
 Claude*
c Telephone (Illus. by Vladimir Radunsky) — *Gambrell,
 Jamey*
c Telephones — *Holland, Gini*
Teletheory: Grammatology in the Age of Video
 — *Ulmer, Gregory*
c Television — *Riehecky, Janet*
Television and the Public Sphere — *Dahlgren, Peter*
Television and the Remote Control — *Bellamy, Robert
 V*
Television Culture and Women's Lives — *Heide,
 Margaret*
Television, Ethnicity, and Cultural Change
 — *Gillespie, Marie*
Television Fundamentals — *Watkinson, John*
Television IC Data Files — *Edwards, John*
Television News. 3rd Ed. — *Yorke, Ivor*

The Theory and Practice of Political Communication Research — *Stuckey, Mary E*

Theory and Practice of Water and Wastewater Treatment — *Droste, Ronald L*

Theory-Based Assessment, Treatment and Prevention of Sexual Aggression — *Hall, Gordon C Nagayama*

Theory-Building in the Business Sciences — *Elfring, Tom*

A Theory for Everything — *Bernstein, Jeremy*

Theory Groups and the Study of Language in North America — *Murray, Stephen O*

Theory in Its Feminist Travels — *King, Katie*

Theory in the Practice of the Nicaraguan Revolution — *Wright, Bruce E*

The Theory of Absence — *Fuery, Patrick*

A Theory of Cognitive Dissonance — *Festinger, Leon*

Theory of Combustion of Powder and Explosives — *Lipanov, Aleksei M*

A Theory of Conceptual Intelligence — *Li, Rex*

The Theory of Corporate Finance. Vols. 1-2 — *Brennan, Michael J*

Theory of Electron-Atom Collisions. Pt. 1 — *Burke, Philip G*

The Theory of Externalities, Public Goods, and Club Goods. 2nd Ed. — *Cornes, Richard*

A Theory of Full Employment — *Brenner, Y S*

Theory of History in Ortega y Gasset — *Graham, John T*

Theory of Incomplete Markets. Vol. 1 — *Magill, Michael*

A Theory of Individual Behavior — *Wichers, Robert*

The Theory of Institutional Design — *Goodin, Robert E*

The Theory of Intermolecular Forces — *Stone, A J*

Theory of Markets — *Roehner, Bertrand M*

Theory of Mind — *O'Connell, Sanjida*

Theory of Moves — *Brams, Steven J*

A Theory of Multicultural Counseling and Therapy — *Sue, Derald Wing*

Theory of Population Genetics and Evolutionary Ecology — *Roughgarden, Jonathan*

Theory of Production — *Kurz, Heinz D*

The Theory of Value, Capital and Interest — *Horvat, Branko*

Theory, Policy and Dynamics in International Trade — *Ethier, Wilfred J*

Theory Rules — *Berland, Jody*

Theory, Text, Context — *Johnstone, Christopher Lyle*

Therapeutic Astrology — *Bogart, Greg*

Therapeutic Immunology — *Austen, K Frank*

The Therapeutic Narrative — *Almond, Barbara*

Therapeutic Touch Inner Workbook — *Krieger, Dolores*

Therapeutic Uses of Trace Elements — *Naeve, Jean*

The Therapeutic Uses of Writing — *Hunter, Allan*

The Therapist as a Person — *Gerson, Barbara*

Therapy — *Lodge, David*

y Therapy (Clarke). Audio Version — *Lodge, David*

Therapy Abatement, Autonomy and Futility — *Lamb, David, 1942-*

Therapy and How to Avoid It! — *Planer, Nigel*

The Therapy of Desire — *Nussbaum, Martha Craven*

Therapy with Stepfamilies — *Visher, Emily B*

There Are No Accidents — *Hopcke, Robert H*

There but for Fortune — *Schumacher, Michael*

There Goes the Neighborhood — *Harris, Sidney*

There Is a Season — *Chittister, Joan*

There Is a Tomorrow — *Nazar, David*

There Is Hope — *Oldham, Doug*

There Was No Path So I Trod One — *Gateley, Edwina*

y There Will Be Wolves — *Bradford, Karleen*

There You Are — *Simpson, Louis*

c There's a Pig in the Closet! — *Anderson, Kate*

c There's a Square (Illus. by David A Carter) — *Serfozo, Mary*

c There's an Owl in the Shower (Illus. by Christine Herman Merrill) — *George, Jean Craighead*

There's No Business like Your Business — *Nadel, Jack*

c There's No Such Thing as a Dragon (Illus. by Jack Kent) — *Kent, Jack*

There's No Such Thing as Free Speech, and It's a Good Thing, Too — *Fish, Stanley*

Thermal Field Theory — *Le Bellac, Michel*

Thermal Infrared Characterization of Ground Targets and Backgrounds — *Jacobs, Pieter A*

Thermal Transport in Laser-Materials Interaction — *Laving, A S*

The Thermal Warriors — *Heinrich, Bernd*

Thermodynamics. 2nd Ed. — *Gokcen, N A*

Thermodynamics and Kinetics of Phase Transformations — *Im, James S*

Thermodynamics of Extremes — *Lavenda, Bernard H*

Thermodynamics of Molecular Species — *Grunwald, Ernest*

Thermoelastic Deformations — *Iesan, Dorin*

Thermomechanical Fatigue Behavior of Materials. Vol. 2 — *Verrilli, Michael J*

Thermoplastic Elastomers. 2nd Ed. — *Holden, Geoffrey*

r Thermoplastic Melt Rheology and Processing — *Shenoy, A V*

Theropithecus: The Rise and Fall of a Primate Genus — *Jablonski, Nina G*

r Thesaurus Linguae Gallicae — *Billy, Pierre-Henri*

y These Are the Rules — *Many, Paul*

These Demented Lands — *Warner, Alan*

These High, Green Hills — *Karon, Jan*

c Theseus and the Minotaur — *Fisher, Leonard Everett*

c Theseus, Monster Killer! (Illus. by Chris Smedley) — *Robinson, Tony*

Thesiger: A Biography — *Asher, Michael*

Thessalonica — *Turtledove, Harry*

Theurgy and the Soul — *Shaw, Gregory*

They Built Utopia — *Reiter, Frederick J*

They Called Her the Baroness — *Duquin, Lorene Hanley*

They Called It Prairie Light — *Lomawaima, K Tsianina*

They Came to Teach — *Raiche, Annabelle*

They Can Kill You, but They Can't Eat You — *Steel, Dawn*

They Cried to the Lord — *Miller, Patrick D*

They Eat from Their Labor — *Zulawski, Ann*

They Forged the Signature of God — *Sencion, Viriato*

They Fought in the Fields — *Tyrer, Nicola*

y They Had a Dream — *Archer, Jules*

They Heard Georgia Singing — *Miller, Zell*

They Must Be Represented — *Rabinowitz, Paula*

y They Never Knew — *Cheney, Glenn Alan*

They Only Look Dead — *Dionne, E J*

They Say You're Crazy — *Caplan, Paula J*

c They Sought a New World (Illus. by William Kurelek) — *Kurelek, William*

They Still Call Me Junior — *Coghlan, Frank*

They Still Play Baseball the Old Way — *Stout, Robert Joe*

c They Thought They Saw Him (Illus. by Jose Aruego) — *Strete, Craig Kee*

y They Would Never Be Friends — *Walsh, Lawrence*

They're Cows, We're Pigs — *Boullosa, Carmen*

c They're Off! (Illus. by Cheryl Harness) — *Harness, Cheryl*

c They've Escaped out of His Mind! — *Davenport, Roger*

A Thick and Darksome Veil — *Moore, Thomas R*

y Thick as Thieves — *Quinn, Patrick, 1957-*

c Thief — *Blackman, Malorie*

y The Thief — *Turner, Megan Whalen*

Thief of Light — *Ramus, David*

The Thief of Reason — *Pine, Richard*

Thief of Souls — *North, Darian*

Thin Air (Dukes). Audio Version — *Parker, Robert B*

A Thin Dark Line — *Hoag, Tami*

Thin Films and Surfaces for Bioactivity and Biomedical Applications — *Cotell, Catherine M*

Thin Films for Photovoltaic and Related Device Applications — *Ginley, David*

Thin He Was and Filthy-Haired — *Llewellyn, Robert*

Thin Ice — *McCall, Bruce*

Thin Ice — *Silver, Jim*

Thin-Walled Structures with Structural Imperfections — *Godoy, Luis A*

Thine Is the Kingdom — *Townsend, Eileen*

The Thing in the Gap-Stone Stile — *Oswald, Alice*

c The Thing on Two Legs — *Hendry, Diana*

A Thing That Is — *Lax, Robert*

Things I Wish I'd Known Sooner — *Edwards, Jaroldeen*

Things of Darkness — *Hall, Kim F*

c Things That Grow (Snapshot Books)

Things That Happen Because They Should — *Stout, Rowland*

Things that Happen Once — *Jones, Rodney, 1950-*

Things Will Be Different for My Daughter — *Bingham, Mindy*

cr Things with Wings — *Creagh, Carson*

Think out of the Box — *Vance, Mike*

r Think Tank Directory. 1st Ed.

Thinking about Beowulf — *Earl, James W*

Thinking about Children — *Winnicott, D W*

Thinking about Development — *Streeten, Paul Patrick*

y Thinking about God — *Harrison, Maureen*

Thinking about Matter — *Brooke, John Hedley*

Thinking about the Earth — *Oldroyd, D R*

Thinking about the Environment — *Cahn, Matthew Alan*

Thinking about the Longstanding Problems of Virtue and Happiness — *Kushner, Tony*

y Thinking Black — *Wickham, DeWayne*

Thinking Class — *Kadi, Joanna*

Thinking from A-Z — *Warburton, Nigel*

Thinking German Translation — *Hervey, Sandor*

Thinking in Pictures and Other Reports from My Life with Autism — *Grandin, Temple*

Thinking in the Future Tense — *James, Jennifer*

c Thinking Matters — *Fox, Richard, 1945*

Thinking Passover — *Kamin, Ben*

The Thinking Person's Guide to God — *Harpur, Tom*

Thinking Sound Music — *Shere, Charles*

Thinking Spanish Translation — *Hervey, Sandor*

Thinking the Difference — *Irigaray, Luce*

Thinking the Unthinkable — *Cockett, Richard*

Thinking Through — *Bannerji, Himani*

Thinking through the Body of the Law — *Cheah, Pheng*

Thinking with Demons — *Clark, Stuart*

Thinner at Last — *Lamm, Steven*

y Thinning the Predators (Garber). Audio Version — *Graziunas, Diana*

y Third and Indiana — *Lopez, Steve*

The Third and Only Way — *Bevington, Helen*

The Third Culture — *Brockman, John*

The Third Day at Gettysburg and Beyond — *Gallagher, Gary W*

y The Third Day, the Frost — *Marsden, John*

The Third Force — *Laidlaw, Marc*

Third International Conference on the Economics of Design, Test, and Manufacturing — *International Conference on the Economics of Design, Test, and Manufacturing (3rd: 1994: Austin, TX)*

Third International Symposium, Recycling of Metals and Engineered Materials — *International Symposium, Recycling of Metals and Engineered Materials (3rd: 1995: Point Clear, Ala.)*

Third International Workshop on Services in Distributed and Networked Environments — *International Workshop on Services in Distributed and Networked Environments (3rd: 1996: Macau)*

Third International Workshop on Temporal Representation and Reasoning — *International Workshop on Temporal Representation and Reasoning (3rd: 1996: Key West, FL)*

The Third Lie — *Kristof, Agota*

The Third Millennium — *Meier, Paul*

The Third Miracle — *Vetere, Richard*

The Third Pandemic — *Ouellette, Pierre*

Third Parties — *Sebba, Leslie*

The Third Policeman — *O'Brien, Flann*

The Third Revolution — *Perkin, Harold*

The Third Revolution in the Chinese Countryside — *Garnaut, Ross*

y The Third Sister — *Barrett, Julia*

y The Third Twin — *Follett, Ken*

The Third Twin (Venora). Audio Version — *Follett, Ken*

Third World Cities in Global Perspective — *Smith, David A*

p Third World Economics: Trends and Analysis

The Third World in Global Environmental Politics — *Miller, Marian A L*

Third World in the First — *Young, Elspeth*

p Third World Resurgence

The Third World Security Predicament — *Ayoob, Mohammed*

p Third World Viewpoint

r Third World Women's Literature — *Fister, Barbara*

A Thirst for Glory — *Pocock, Tom*

Thirst: The Desert Trilogy — *Hareven, Shulamith*

y Thirsty — *Anderson, M T*

Thirteen: A Journey into the Number — *Cott, Jonathan*

y Thirteen Miles from Suncrest — *Davis, Donald*

Thirteen Ways — *Harbison, Robert*

Thirteen Ways of Looking at a Black Man — *Gates, Henry Louis*

Thirteenth Century England V

The Thirteenth Hour — *Sofer, Barbara*

Thirty-Five Years of Newspaper Work — *Mencken, H L*

The Thirty Seven Practices of Bodhisattvas — *Rgyal-Sras Thogs-Med-Dpal Bzacn-Po-Dpal*

Thirty Years of Computer Assisted Language Instruction — *Sanders, Ruth H*
Thirty Years On — *Benn, Caroline*
The Thirty Years' War — *Kopkind, Andrew*
The Thirty Years War — *Wedgwood, C V*
c This and That (Illus. by Tanya Linch) — *Sykes, Julie*
This Book of Starres — *White, James Boyd, 1938-*
y This Boy's Life — *Wolff, Tobias*
This Business of Books — *Suzanne, Claudia*
This Chosen Place — *Evans, Max*
This Christmas — *Abbot, Laura*
This Dark Embrace — *Stuewe, Paul*
y This Dog for Hire — *Benjamin, Carol Lea*
This Earth of Mankind — *Toer, Pramoedya Ananta*
This Far, No Further — *Wessel, John*
This Fine Place So Far from Home — *Dews, C L Barney*
c This for That (Illus. by Victoria Chess) — *Aardema, Verna*
This Game of Ghosts — *Simpson, Joe*
This Game's the Best! So Why Don't They Quit Screwing with It? — *Karl, George*
This Great Calamity — *Kinealy, Christine*
y This House on Fire — *Awmiller, Craig*
y This I Believe — *Marsden, John*
r This Is a Thriller — *Warren, Alan*
This Is Biology — *Mayr, Ernst*
This Is How We Live — *International Movement ATD Fourth World*
c This Is Me — *King, Dave*
c This Is Me, Laughing (Illus. by Walter Gaffney-Kessell) — *Bowdish, Lynea*
c This Is Our House (Illus. by Bob Graham) — *Rosen, Michael, 1946-*
c This Is Rhythm — *Jenkins, Ella*
c This Is the Baby (Illus. by Rick Incrocci) — *Weisheit, Eldon*
c This Is the Bear (Illus. by Helen Craig) — *Hayes, Sarah*
c This Is the Bird (Illus. by David Soman) — *Shannon, George*
This Is the Place — *Rock, Peter*
y This Is the Sound! — *Reisfeld, Randi*
c This Is the Star (Illus. by Gary Blythe) — *Dunbar, Joyce*
c This Is the Way We Pull a Face — *Lodge, Jo*
This Is True — *Cassingham, Randy*
This Jesus — *Bockmuehl, Markus*
r This Land Is Our Land — *Helbig, Alethea*
This Land Is Our Land — *Pombo, Richard*
This Land Is Your Land — *Bridges, Marilyn*
c This Little Piggy (Illus. by Jane Manning)
c This Little Piggy (Illus. by Sonja Lamut) — *Heller, Nicholas*
This Mad Masquerade — *Studlar, Gaylyn*
This Man Bernardin — *Kennedy, Eugene*
This Man Bernardin — *White, John H*
This Man Cries — *Hosey, Henry P, II*
This Matter of Marriage — *Macomber, Debbie*
This Meadow of Time — *Smock, Frederick*
This Nervous Breakdown Is Driving Me Crazy — *Reiner, Annie*
This Noble Land — *Michener, James A*
This Noble Land. Audio Version — *Michener, James A*
This Ol' Drought Ain't Broke Us Yet — *Garry, Jim*
p This Old House
This Place on Earth — *Durning, Alan Thein*
This Present Darkness (Sondericker). Audio Version — *Peretti, Frank E*
This Ragged Place — *Glavin, Terry*
This Rebellious House — *Keillor, Steven J*
This Side of Cooperstown — *Moffi, Larry*
This Side of Paradise — *Fitzgerald, F Scott*
This Thing of Darkness — *Aho, James A*
This Time We Knew — *Cushman, Thomas*
This Wild Darkness — *Brodkey, Harold*
This Year in Jerusalem — *Richler, Mordecai*
This Year It Will Be Different — *Binchy, Maeve*
c Thistle (Illus. by Bryna Waldman) — *Wangerin, Walter*
y Thomas Alva Edison: Inventing the Electric Age — *Adair, Gene*
Thomas and Beulah — *Dove, Rita*
Thomas Aquinas and His Legacy — *Gallagher, David M*
Thomas Aquinas: Spiritual Master — *Barron, Robert*
Thomas Bernhard — *Mittermayer, Manfred*
Thomas Bradwardine: A View of Time and a Vision of Eternity in Fourteenth-Century Thought — *Dolnikowski, Edith Wilks*
Thomas Cranmer: A Life — *MacCulloch, Diarmaid*

Thomas Eakins: The Rowing Pictures — *Cooper, Helen A*
Thomas Gray: Contemporary Essays — *Hutchings, W B*
Thomas Hardy — *Hands, Timothy*
Thomas Hardy: A Literary Life — *Gibson, James*
Thomas Hardy and the Church — *Jedrzejewski, Jan*
Thomas Hobbes — *Martinich, A P*
Thomas Hobbes and the Natural Law Tradition — *Bobbio, Norberto*
Thomas Hobbes and the Science of Moral Virtue — *Boonin-Vail, David*
Thomas Hornsby Ferril and the American West — *Ferril, Thomas Hornsby*
Thomas Jefferson and Sally Hemings — *Gordon-Reed, Annette*
Thomas Jefferson's Travels in Europe 1784-1789 — *Shackleford, George Green*
Thomas K. Beecher: Minister to a Changing America 1824-1900 — *Glenn, Myra C*
Thomas Mann: A Biography — *Hayman, Ronald*
Thomas Mann: A Life — *Prater, Donald*
Thomas Mann: Doctor Faustus — *Beddow, Michael*
Thomas Mann: Eine Biographie — *Harpprecht, Klaus*
Thomas Mann: Eros and Literature — *Heilbut, Anthony*
c Thomas Merton: Poet, Prophet, Priest — *Bryant, Jennifer Fisher*
A Thomas Merton Reader. Rev. Ed. — *Merton, Thomas*
Thomas Moran: The Field Sketches 1856-1923 — *Moran, Thomas, 1837-1926*
Thomas More — *Murphy, Anne*
Thomas Paine: Apostle of Freedom — *Fruchtman, Jack, Jr.*
Thomas Pynchon: Allusive Parables of Power — *Dugdale, John*
Thomas Reid on the Animate Creation — *Reid, Thomas*
Thomas Stearns Eliot: Poet. 2nd Ed. — *Moody, A David*
r Thomas Wolfe: An Annotated Critical Bibliography — *Bassett, John Earl*
The Thor Conspiracy — *Burkett, Larry*
Thoreau's Garden — *Loewer, H Peter*
yr Thorndike-Barnhart Junior Dictionary — *Bready, Richard*
cr Thorndike-Barnhart Junior Dictionary. Rev. Ed.
Thorns and Thistles — *Hotle, C Patrick*
c Those Calculating Crows! (Illus. by Christy Hale) — *Wakefield, Ali*
c Those Can-Do Pigs (Illus. by David McPhail) — *McPhail, David*
y Those Darn Dithers — *Hite, Sid*
Those of Little Note — *Scott, Elizabeth M*
y Those Remarkable Women of the American Revolution — *Zeinert, Karen*
c Those Summers (Illus. by Aliki) — *Aliki*
Those Who Can — *Wilson, Robin Scott*
y Those Who Hunt the Night — *Hambly, Barbara*
y Those Who Love the Game — *Rivers, Glenn*
Thought Contagion — *Lynch, Aaron*
A Thousand Blunders — *Leonard, Frank*
c A Thousand Cousins (Illus. by Betsy Lewin) — *Harrison, David L*
Thousand Cranes — *Kawabata, Yasunari*
The Thousand Faces of the Virgin Mary — *Tavard, George H*
...A Thousand Graceful Subtleties — *Beers, Terry*
c A Thousand Lights — *Benton, Hope*
A Thousand Tears Falling — *Krall, Yung*
A Thousand Years of Czech Culture
The Thread of Life — *Aldridge, Susan*
The Thread of Life — *Hollan, Douglas W*
Thread of the Silkworm — *Chang, Iris*
Threads of Arctic Prehistory — *Morrison, David*
y Threads of Evidence — *Silverstein, Herma*
Threads of Experience — *Martz, Sandra Haldeman*
The Threat of Life — *Brueggemann, Walter*
c Threat to the Sea Otters — *Pageler, Elaine*
Threatened Peoples, Threatened Borders — *Teitelbaum, Michael S*
c Threatened Planet — *Juniper, Tony*
The Three-Arched Bridge — *Kadare, Ismail*
Three Artists (Three Women) — *Wagner, Anne Middleton*
c Three Baby Chicks (Illus. by Ernie Eldredge) — *Patrick, Ellen*
The Three Big Bangs — *Dauber, Philip M*
c Three Cheers for Tacky (Illus. by Lynn Munsinger) — *Lester, Helen*

Three Chinese Economies — *Ng, Linda Fung-Yee*
Three Chords and the Truth — *Leamer, Laurence*
c Three Cool Kids (Illus. by Rebecca Emberley) — *Emberley, Rebecca*
Three Decades of Peace Education around the World — *Burns, Robin J*
Three-Dimensional Analysis of Crack Growth — *Mi, Yaoming*
Three-Dimensional Electron Microscopy of Macromolecular Assemblies — *Frank, Joachim*
Three-Dimensional Image Reconstruction in Radiology and Nuclear Medicine — *Grangeat, Pierre*
c Three-Dimensional Shapes (Illus. by Richard Maccabe) — *Stienecker, David*
Three-Dimensional Velocity and Vorticity Measuring and Image Analysis Techniques — *Dracos, Th. A*
Three Discourses — *Hobbes, Thomas*
Three Discourses — *Reynolds, Noel B*
Three Essays on Style — *Panofsky, Erwin*
y The Three Faces of Mind — *De Beauport, Elaine*
c Three Freckles Past a Hair (Illus. by Sally Bourgeois) — *Hallinan, P K*
Three French Comedies — *Coleman, C B*
Three Frontiers — *May, Dean L*
Three Generations of Chilean Cuisine — *Umana-Murray, Mirtha*
Three Gospels — *Bible. N.T. Mark. English. Price. 1996*
Three Gospels — *Price, Reynolds*
Three in the Back, Two in the Head — *Sherman, Jason*
The Three-Inch Golden Lotus — *Feng, Chi-Tsai*
c Three Kind Mice (Illus. by Rodger Wilson) — *Sathre, Vivian*
Three Kingdoms — *Lo, Kuan-Chung*
c Three Little Pigs — *Langley, Jonathan*
c The Three Little Pigs and the Fox (Illus. by S D Schindler) — *Hooks, William H*
c The Three Little Wolves and the Big Bad Pig (Illus. by Helen Oxenbury) — *Trivizas, Eugene*
y The Three Lives of Harris Harper — *Cullen, Lynn*
The Three Lives of Littleton Blue — *Bowman, Doug*
y Three Men on Third and Other Wacky Events from the World of Sports — *Sifakis, Carl*
Three Messengers for One God — *Arnaldez, Roger*
Three Moons in Vietnam — *Coffey, Maria*
y Three Mothers, Three Daughters — *Gorkin, Michael*
c The Three Musketeers (Homewood). Audio Version — *Dumas, Alexandre*
c The Three Musketeers (Ward). Audio Version — *Dumas, Alexandre*
Three Paths to the Lake — *Bachmann, Ingeborg*
c Three Perfect Peaches (Illus. by Irene Trivas) — *DeFelice, Cynthia C*
The Three Perils of Woman — *Hogg, James, 1770-1835*
The Three Pillars of Liberty — *Klug, Francesca*
Three Plays by Mae West — *West, Mae*
Three Renaissance Travel Plays — *Parr, Anthony*
The Three Roads — *Macdonald, Ross*
Three Steps on the Ladder of Writing — *Cixous, Helene*
The Three Stigmata of Palmer Eldritch — *Dick, Philip K*
Three Stories and a Reflection — *Suskind, Patrick*
c Three Stories You Can Read to Your Cat (Illus. by True Kelley) — *Miller, Sara Swan*
c Three Stories You Can Read to Your Dog (Illus. by True Kelley) — *Miller, Sara Swan*
Three Strikes and You're Out — *Shichor, David*
r Three Studies — *Longhi, Roberto*
Three Studies in Medieval Religious and Social Thought — *Constable, Giles*
c Three Terrible Trins (Whitfield). Audio Version — *King-Smith, Dick*
Three to Get Deadly — *Evanovich, Janet*
Three Tragic Actresses — *Booth, Michael R*
Three Wogs — *Theroux, Alexander*
The Threefold Paradise of Cotton Mather — *Mather, Cotton*
y Three's a Crowd — *Baer, Judy*
Threshold of Fire — *Haasse, Hella S*
The Threshold of the Visible World — *Silverman, Kaja*
Thresholds — *Alegria, Claribel*
Thrombopoiesis and Thrombopoietins — *Kuter, David J*
Throne of Gold — *Edwards, Anne*
The Throne of the Third Heaven of the Nations Millennium General Assembly — *Johnson, Denis*
Through a Glass Darkly — *Mulryan, John*

Through a Gold Eagle — *Monfredo, Miriam Grace*
Through a Reporter's Eyes — *Kaluza, Roman*
Through a Speculum That Shines — *Wolfson, Elliot R*
Through a Universe Darkly — *Bartusiak, Marcia*
Through Amazonian Eyes — *Moran, Emilio F*
Through Fire and Water — *Loewen, Harry*
Through Fortress and Rock — *Jones, J D F*
Through French Windows — *Corbett, James*
Through Green-Colored Glasses — *Beckerman, Wilfred*
Through Indian Eyes
Through Jackie Robinson — *Robinson, Rachel*
Through Jaundiced Eyes — *Puette, William J*
c Through My Window (Illus. by Eileen Browne) — *Bradman, Tony*
Through Students' Eyes — *Donaldson, Karen B McLean*
Through Sunshine and Shadow — *Cook, Sharon Anne*
Through the Dark Labyrinth — *Bowker, Gordon*
Through the Forest — *Kaplinski, Jaan*
Through the Kitchen Window — *Avakian, Arlene Voski*
c Through the Medicine Cabinet (Illus. by Jack E Davis) — *Greenburg, Dan*
Through the Northern Gate — *Banerjee, Jacqueline P*
Through the Woods — *Bates, H E*
Throwaway Angels — *Richler, Nancy*
y Throwaways — *Strachan, Ian*
Throwing the Emperor from His Horse — *Seybolt, Peter J*
Throwing the House out of the Window — *Richards, Ben*
Thru — *Brooke-Rose, Christine*
Thrum — *Evans, Leef*
c Thumbelina (Illus. by Emma Chichester Clark) — *Falloon, Jane*
c Thump, Thump, Rat-a-Tat-Tat (Illus. by Lois Ehlert) — *Baer, Gene*
c Thunder Bunny (Illus. by Rodney Alan Greenblat) — *Greenblat, Rodney Alan*
c Thunder Cave — *Smith, Roland*
y Thunder Ice — *Acheson, Alison*
Thunder in the Heartland — *Schmidlin, Thomas W*
Thunder Moon and the Sky People — *Brand, Max*
y Thunderbird: Ford's High Flier — *Schleifer, Jay*
r The Thunderbird Guide to International Business Resources on the World Wide Web — *Deans, Candace*
c Thunderbird Spirit — *Brouwer, Sigmund*
c Thunderbolt's Waxwork — *Pullman, Philip*
c The Thunderherd (Illus. by Elizabeth Sayles) — *Appelt, Kathi*
y Thundering Hooves (Illus. by Victor Ambrus) — *Pullein-Thompson, Christine*
Thuo Sen Hong Phuong Tham — *Ho, Truong An*
r The Thurgarton Cartulary — *Foulds, Trevor*
y Thurgood Marshall: A Life for Justice — *Haskins, James*
y Thurgood Marshall, Civil Rights Champion — *Herda, D J*
Thus Was Adonis Murdered — *Caudwell, Sarah*
y Thwonk — *Bauer, Joan*
Thy Kingdom Come — *Meissner, W W*
Thyestes (Heywood) — *Seneca, Lucius Annaeus*
La Tia Agueda — *Garcia Morales, Adelaida*
Tiao Zhan Zhong Guo — *Hu, An-Kang*
Tiberius (Lindsay) — *Suetonius*
c Tibet — *Bruycker, Daniel De*
c Tibet — *Heinrichs, Ann*
y Tibet — *Levy, Patricia Marjorie*
Tibet: Abode of the Gods, Pearl of the Motherland — *Erickson, Barbara*
Tibet: On the Paths of the Gentlemen Brigands — *Baldizzone, Tiziana*
Tibetan Nation — *Smith, Warren W*
Tibetan Portraits — *Borges, Phil*
y The Tick Omnibus. Vol. 1
c Tick-Tock (Illus. by David Parkins) — *Browne, Eileen*
c Tick Tock — *Dunbar, James*
r The Ticker Symbol Book. 1997 Ed.
A Ticket for a Seamstitch — *Harris, Mark, 1922-*
The Ticket: Recollections of 50 Years of Sports Classics — *Newcomb, Jack*
r Ticket to the Opera — *Goulding, Phil G*
Ticking Time Bombs — *Kuttner, Robert*
Tickle the Public — *Engel, Matthew*
Tickled to Death to Go — *Clouting, Ben*
Tickling the Dragon — *Brandon, Ruth*
c Tickling Tigers — *Currey, Anna*
Ticktock — *Koontz, Dean*
Tidal Waves of Reform — *Mitchell, Samuel*

Tidecraft: The Boats of South Carolina, Georgia and Northeastern Florida 1550-1950. 2nd Ed. — *Fleetwood, William C, Jr.*
Tides of History — *Howe, K R*
The Tides of Reform — *Light, Paul C*
Tidewater Families of the New World and Their Westward Migrations — *Chatham, Anne Bassett Stanley*
Tidings of the King — *Wagoner, Phillip B*
c The Tie Man's Miracle (Illus. by Stephen T Johnson) — *Schnur, Steven*
y Tie My Bones to Her Back — *Jones, Robert F*
Tiempo De Guerras Perdidas — *Caballero Bonald, Jose Manuel*
Tiempo De Silencio — *Martin-Santos, Martin*
Tiempos Del Cantar — *Garcia, Dionisia*
Tiepolo and His Circle — *Aikema, Bernard*
Tiepolo in Wurzburg. Vols. 1-2 — *Kruckmann, Peter O*
Tiepolo: Masterpieces of the Wurzburg Years — *Kruckmann, Peter O*
La Tierra De Soria — *Diez Sanz, Enrique*
Tierra, Gobierno Local, Y Actividad Misionera En La Comunidad Indigena Del Oriente Venezolano — *Laserna Gaitan, Antonio Ignacio*
Ties-Ties-Ties: Traditional Quilts from Neckties — *Elwin, Janet B*
y Tiffany — *Ellis, Joyce*
The Tiffany Fortune and Other Chronicles of a Connecticut Family — *Bingham, Alfred M*
Tiffin Glass 1914-1940 — *Pina, Leslie*
Tiger: A Biography of Tiger Woods — *Strege, John*
c The Tiger Child (Illus. by Joanna Troughton) — *Troughton, Joanna*
Tiger in a Lion's Den — *Brown, Dale*
The Tiger in the Grass — *Doerr, Harriet*
y The Tiger in the Grass (Schraf). Audio Version — *Doerr, Harriet*
y Tiger Tiger — *Burgess, Melvin*
c The Tiger Who Lost His Stripes (Illus. by Michael Foreman) — *Paul, Anthony*
c Tiger Woods — *Boyd, Aaron*
Tiger Woods: The Makings of a Champion (Addison). Audio Version — *Rosaforte, Tim*
c Tigers (Illus. by Lynn M Stone) — *DuTemple, Lesley A*
c Tigers — *Harman, Amanda*
Tigers Burning — *Evers, Crabbe*
c Tiger's New Cowboy Boots (Illus. by Georgia Graham) — *Morck, Irene*
The Tigers of '68 — *Cantor, George*
Tiger's Tail — *Lee, Gus*
c Tigger Has Breakfast (Illus. by Ernest H Shepard) — *Milne, A A*
The Tightwad Gazette III — *Dacyczyn, Amy*
c Tik-Tok of Oz (Illus. by John R Neill) — *Baum, L Frank*
p Tikkun: A Bimonthly Jewish Critique of Politics, Culture and Society
c Tiktala (Illus. by Laszlo Gal) — *Shaw-MacKinnon, Margaret*
c Tikvah Means Hope — *Polacco, Patricia*
'Til I Come Marching Home — *Larson, C Kay*
Tile — *Herbers, Jill*
Till We Meet Again — *Stokes, Penelope J*
r Tiller's Guide to Indian Country — *Tiller, Veronica E Velarde*
Tim Boxer's Jewish Celebrity Anecdotes — *Boxer, Tim*
The Tim-Tim Man — *Collison, Kerry B*
c Timber! — *Jaspersohn, William*
Timber. 7th Ed. — *Desch, H E*
p Timber Creek Review
c The Timbertoes 123 Counting Book (Illus. by Judith Hunt) — *Highlights for Children, Inc.*
c The Timbertoes ABC Alphabet Book (Illus. by Judith Hunt) — *Highlights for Children, Inc.*
c Time (Illus. by Jon Barnes) — *Haslam, Andrew*
c Time — *Hewitt, Sally*
c Time — *Newson, Lesley*
c Time — *Snedden, Robert*
y Time and Again (Hecht). Audio Version — *Finney, Jack*
Time and Chance — *Campbell, Kim*
Time and Money — *Matthews, William*
Time and Sense — *Kristeva, Julia*
Time and Space in Chinese Culture — *Huang, Chun-Chieh*
c The Time and Space of Uncle Albert — *Stannard, Russell*
Time and Temporal Structure in Chekhov — *Turner, C J G*

Time and the Erotic in Horace's Odes — *Ancona, Ronnie*
Time and the Island — *Dunne, Sean*
Time as History — *Grant, George Parkin*
A Time before Deception — *Cooper, Thomas W*
y The Time before History — *Tudge, Colin*
The Time Bind — *Hochschild, Arlie Russell*
Time, Change and Freedom — *Smith, Quentin*
Time Changes in the World — *Doane, Doris Chase*
Time-Constrained Transaction Management — *Soparkar, Nandit R*
Time, Culture, and Identity — *Thomas, Julian*
Time, Desire and Horror — *Corbin, Alain*
Time-Effective Psychotherapy — *Friedman, Steven*
A Time Far Past — *Le, Luu*
A Time for Action
Time for Bed — *Baddiel, David*
c Time for Bed — *Obi, Alexis*
c Time for Christmas (Illus. by Tony Linsell) — *Wood, A J*
y A Time for Dancing — *Hurwin, Davida Wills*
Time for Life — *Robinson, John P*
Time for Meaning — *Bomer, Randy*
y A Time for War — *Schulzinger, Robert D*
Time, Freedom, and the Common Good — *Sherover, Charles M*
y Time Ghost — *Katz, Welwyn Wilton*
The Time in Aderra — *Schlee, Ann*
Time in the Black Consciousness — *Adjaye, Joseph K*
Time-Limited Dynamic Psychotherapy — *Levenson, Hanna*
cp Time Machine
The Time Machine — *Wells, H G*
The Time Machine. Centennial Ed. — *Wells, H G*
c Time (Make It Work!)
y A Time of Angels — *Hesse, Karen*
The Time of Feasting — *Farren, Mick*
c A Time of Fire — *Westall, Robert*
y The Time of Murder at Mayerling — *Dukthas, Ann*
y The Time of the Ghost — *Jones, Diana Wynne*
The Time of the Tribes — *Maffesoli, Michel*
y The Time of the Vampires — *Elrod, P N*
c The Time of the Wolf — *MacDonald, Thomas A*
The Time of Theory — *Ffrench, Patrick*
Time of Your Life — *Lyons, Steve*
Time on Fire — *Handler, Evan*
Time on My Hands — *Delacorte, Peter*
r Time Out Budapest Guide
yr Time Out Film Guide. 5th Ed.
Time-Out for Children — *Hill, Barbara Albers*
r Time Out New York Guide. 4th Ed.
The Time-Out Prescription — *Corwin, Donna G*
r Time Out Rome Guide. 2nd Ed.
Time Present, Time Past — *Bradley, Bill*
Time Release — *Smith, Martin J*
Time Sanctified — *Wieck, Roger S*
Time Series Analysis — *Tanaka, Katsuto*
Time-Series-Based Econometrics — *Hatanaka, Michio*
y Time Station London — *Evans, David*
A Time to Be Born — *Powell, Dawn*
A Time to Be Born — *Shullenberger, Bonnie*
Time-to-Build: Interrelated Investment and Labour Demand Modelling with Applications to Six OECD Countries — *Peeters, Marga*
A Time to Dance — *Sullivan, Walter*
y Time to Depart — *Davis, Lindsey*
c A Time to Fight Back — *Pettit, Jayne*
Time to Go — *Hawkins, Anne Hunsaker*
c A Time to Keep (Illus. by Tasha Tudor) — *Tudor, Tasha*
A Time to Kill — *Skelton, Douglas*
A Time to Live — *Raines, Robert*
A Time to Speak — *Rudin, A James*
c Time to Tell Time — *Rutman, Shereen*
Time Travel — *Savage, Jon*
c The Time Trekkers Visit the Middle Ages — *Needham, Kate*
c The Time Trekkers Visit the Stone Age — *Mason, Antony*
Time-Varying Discrete Linear Systems — *Halanay, Aristide*
c The Time Warp Virus — *Gifford, Clive*
Time, Will, and Mental Process — *Brown, Jason W*
Time Will Darken It — *Maxwell, William, 1908-*
Time within Time — *Tarkovskii, Andrei Arsen'evich*
y Time Wreck — *Alcock, Vivien*
The Timekeeper — *Ferguson, Trevor*
Timeless Healing — *Benson, Herbert*
r Timelines of American Women's History — *Heinemann, Sue*

r Timelines of Native American History
   — *Hazen-Hammond, Susan*
A Timely Death — *Neel, Janet*
Timely Meditations — *Thiele, Leslie Paul*
Time's Arrow and Archimedes' Point — *Price, Huw*
Time's Cycle and National Military Strategy
   — *Jablonsky, David*
Time's Purpled Masquers — *Fowler, Alastair*
The Times Square Gym — *Hamill, Pete*
The Times Square Hustler — *McNamara, Robert P*
The Times Were Strange and Stirring — *Hildebrand,
   Reginald F*
Time's Witness — *Malone, Michael*
Timeshift: On Video Culture — *Cubitt, Sean*
The Timetables of African-American History
   — *Harley, Sharon*
r The Timetables of Women's History — *Greenspan,
   Karen*
Timewalkers: The Prehistory of Global Colonization
   — *Gamble, Clive*
c Timewatch: Stories of Past and Future — *Cooling,
   Wendy*
Timnah: A Biblical City in the Sorek Valley — *Kelm,
   George L*
TIMSS Monograph. No. 2 — *Robitaille, David F*
The Timucua — *Milanich, Jerald T*
The Tin-Pan Man — *Bechko, P A*
c Tina's Diner (Illus. by JoAnn Adinolfi) — *Adinolfi,
   JoAnn*
Tinder-Box Criminal Aggression — *Pallone, Nathaniel
   J*
c Tingleberries, Tuckertubs, and Telephones (Illus. by
   Robert Staermose) — *Mahy, Margaret*
Tinisima — *Poniatowska, Elena*
Tinker, Tailor, Soldier, Spy (Jayston). Audio Version
   — *Le Carre, John*
y Tinker v. Des Moines — *Farish, Leah*
Tinkering toward Utopia — *Tyack, David*
c The Tinker's Daughter — *Hayes, Sheila*
c The Tiny Kite of Eddie Wing (Illus. by Al Van Mil)
   — *Trottier, Maxine*
c The Tiny Seed (Illus. by Eric Carle) — *Carle, Eric*
c Tiny Talks (Illus. by Ann S Hogue) — *Morgan, Robert
   J*
c The Tip at the End of the Street (Illus. by Tohby
   Riddle) — *Riddle, Tohby*
Tipperary: A Treasure Chest — *Houlihan, Elaine
   Burke*
Tippett on Music — *Tippett, Michael*
TIPS: Transjugular Intrahepatic Portalsystemic
   Shunts — *Conn, Harold O*
Tirso De Molina: El Condenado Por Desconfiado
   — *Oakley, R J*
Tissot: The Life and Work of Jacques Joseph Tissot
   1846-1902 — *Wood, Christopher*
Tissue Expansion — *Nordstrom, Rolf E A*
Tissue Oxygen Deprivation — *Haddad, Gabriel G*
Titanic at Two A.M. — *Quinn, Paul J*
Titans — *Green, Tim, 1963-*
c Titch and Daisy (Illus. by Pat Hutchins) — *Hutchins,
   Pat*
r The Tithe Maps of England and Wales — *Kain, Roger
   J P*
Titian: Nymph and Shepherd — *Berger Andreadakis,
   Katya*
Titian's Portraits through Aretino's Lens
   — *Freedman, Luba*
Title Output in the UK — *Bryant, Philip*
r The Title to the Poem — *Ferry, Anne*
Tituba, Reluctant Witch of Salem — *Breslaw, Elaine
   G*
Titus — *Salmon, Elon*
Titus Andronicus — *Shakespeare, William*
Titus Crow. Vol. 1 — *Lumley, Brian*
Titus Crow. Vol. 2 — *Lumley, Brian*
Tiwanaku and Its Hinterland — *Kolata, Alan L*
Tiziano Y La Monarquia Hispanica — *Checa,
   Fernando*
Tjanarinnan — *Gustafsson, Lars*
r TLA Film and Video Guide 1996-1997
To Appomattox and Beyond — *Logue, Larry M*
To Ask the Suffrages of the Patrons — *Laycock,
   Thomas*
To Awaken My Afflicted Brethren — *Hinks, Peter P*
c To Baby with Love — *Ormerod, Jan*
To Be a Teacher — *Henry, Eric*
y To Be an American — *Hing, Bill Ong*
r To Be Continued — *Jacob, Merle*
To Be Mayor of New York — *McNickle, Chris*
To Be There with You — *Reid, Gayla*
To Boldy Go... — *Fiske, Peter*

To Build a Bridge — *Moore, David*
To Build a Wall — *Ivers, Gregg*
To Bury the Dead — *Laird, Brian Andrew*
To Change Them Forever — *Ellis, Clyde*
To Comfort the Heart — *Treckel, Paula A*
y To Dance at the Palais Royale — *McNaughton, Janet*
To Dance with the Devil — *Stabiner, Karen*
r To Die Gallantly — *Runyan, Timothy J*
To Dream of Dreams — *O'Brien, David M*
To Everest Via Antarctica — *Anderson, Robert Mads*
To Fathom More — *Jenkins, Edward Sidney*
To Foreign Shores — *Lorelli, John A*
To Have and Have Not — *Marshall, Jonathan*
To Hell with Picasso and Other Essays — *Johnson,
   Paul, 1928-*
To 'Joy My Freedom — *Hunter, Tera W*
To Keep and Bear Arms — *Malcolm, Joyce Lee*
To Lie Abroad — *Shea, Michael*
To Lie with Lions — *Dunnett, Dorothy*
To Live Is to Think — *Goetz, Hans*
To Live Within — *Reymond, Lizelle*
To Love, Honour and Betray — *West-Meads, Zelda*
To Make a Spotless Orange — *Sawyer, Richard C*
To Make My Bread — *Lumpkin, Grace*
c To My Father's Village (Illus. by William Kurelek)
   — *Kurelek, William*
y To Race a Dream — *Savage, Deborah*
To Remember the Faces of the Dead — *Maschio,
   Thomas*
To Rule Jerusalem — *Friedland, Roger*
To Secure These Rights — *Gerber, Scott Douglas*
To See a Promised Land — *Vogel, Lester I*
To See Ourselves — *Pan, Zhongdang*
c To See the Moon (Illus. by David Ray) — *Bacon,
   Ethel*
y To See with the Heart — *St. George, Judith*
c To Seek a Better World (Illus. by Paul Conklin)
   — *Ashabranner, Brent*
To Serve Other Gods — *Harbin, Michael A*
To Set before the King — *Champe, Gertrud Graubart*
To Settle the Succession of the State — *Downie, J A*
To Sing with Pigs Is Human — *Goodale, Jane C*
To Speak for the Dead — *Levine, Paul*
To Steal a Book Is an Elegant Offense — *Alford,
   William P*
To the Bone — *Lea, Sydney*
To the Heart of Spain — *Walker, Ann*
y To the Hilt — *Francis, Dick*
To the Hilt (Britton). Audio Version — *Francis, Dick*
To the Hoop — *Berkow, Ira*
To the Lighthouse — *Woolf, Virginia*
To the Lighthouse (Atkins). Audio Version — *Woolf,
   Virginia*
c To the Mountains by Morning — *Wieler, Diana*
To the North — *Bowen, Elizabeth*
To the Other — *Peperzak, Adriaan Theodoor*
c To the Rescue — *Otfinoski, Steve*
c To the Rescue! (Illus. by Patrick Merrell) — *St.
   Pierre, Stephanie*
To the Royal Crown Restored — *Vargas, Diego De*
To the Summit — *Chisholm, Margo*
c To the Tub (Illus. by Peggy Perry Anderson)
   — *Anderson, Peggy Perry*
To the Wedding — *Berger, John*
To the White Sea — *Dickey, James*
y To the Young Scientist — *Bortz, Fred*
To Timbuktu — *Jenkins, Mark*
To Touch the Past — *Brody, J J*
p To Turn the Tide: Newsletter for the World Council
   of Churches Climate Change Petition Campaign
To Us, All Flowers Are Roses — *Goodison, Lorna*
To Wake the Nations — *Sundquist, Eric J*
To Write like a Woman — *Russ, Joanna*
c Toad (Illus. by Ruth Brown) — *Brown, Ruth*
c Toad Overload (Illus. by Jan Davey Ellis) — *Seibert,
   Patricia*
c Toad Takes Off — *Schade, Susan*
y Toad Triumphant (Illus. by Patrick Benson)
   — *Horwood, William*
c Toads and Diamonds (Illus. by Anita Lobel) — *Huck,
   Charlotte*
Toamna Diplomatica — *Iliescu, Ion*
The Toastmasters International Guide to Successful
   Speaking — *Slutsky, Jeff*
Tobacco — *Gold, Mark S*
Tobacco Advertising — *Petrone, Gerard S*
r Tobacco and Health Network Directory 1996
Tobacco in Atlantic Trade — *Price, Jacob M*
y Tobacco Road (MacDonald). Audio Version
   — *Caldwell, Erskine*

y Tobacco Road (Schirner). Audio Version — *Caldwell,
   Erskine*
The Tobin Tax — *Haq, Mahbub Ul*
c Toby — *Wild, Margaret*
Toby Tyler (Purinton). Audio Version — *Kaler, James
   Otis*
c Toby, Where Are You? (Illus. by Teryl Euvremer)
   — *Steig, William*
Tocqueville and the Nature of Democracy — *Manent,
   Pierre*
Tocqueville's Civil Religion — *Kessler, Sanford*
c Today Is Monday (Illus. by Eric Carle) — *Carle, Eric*
c Today Is the Day (Illus. by Catherine Stock)
   — *Riecken, Nancy*
r Today's English Dictionary — *Sinclair, John*
Toddler-Hunting and Other Stories — *Kono, Taeko*
c Toddlerobics — *Newcome, Zita*
c Toenails, Tonsils, and Tornadoes (Illus. by Helen
   Cogancherry) — *Pryor, Bonnie*
Toeplitz Operators and Index Theory in Several
   Complex Variables — *Upmeier, Harald*
Together as a Companionship — *Padberg, John W*
Together We Were Eleven Foot Nine — *Palmer, Jim*
r Togo Murano: Master Architect of Japan — *Botond,
   Bognar*
Togo: The Postal History of the Anglo-French
   Occupation 1914-1922 — *Martin, Jeremy*
c The Token Gift (Illus. by Scott Cameron)
   — *McKibbon, Hugh William*
Token Professionals and Master Critics — *Sosnoski,
   James J*
p Tokenews
Tokens of Affection — *Bleser, Carol*
Tokens of Affection — *Connell, Maria Bryan Harford*
Tokugawa Confucian Education — *Kassel, Marleen*
Tokugawa Village Practice — *Ooms, Herman*
c Tokyo — *Kent, Deborah*
r Tokyo: ANA's City Guide
r Tokyo (Insight Guides) 1991-
r Tokyo Journal's Tokyo Restaurant Guide
   — *Kennerdell, John*
Tokyo Life, New York Dreams — *Sawada, Mitziko*
c Told in Greece — *Haviland, Virginia*
c Told in Italy — *Haviland, Virginia*
c Told in Norway — *Haviland, Virginia*
Tolerance and Community — *Tinder, Glenn*
Tolerance and Transformation — *Lubarsky, Sandra B*
Toleration: An Elusive Virtue — *Heyd, David*
c The Toll-Bridge Troll (Illus. by Kimberly Bulcken
   Root) — *Wolff, Patricia Rae*
Tolstoi and Britain — *Jones, W Gareth*
Tolstoy and the Genesis of War and Peace — *Feuer,
   Kathryn B*
Tolstoy's Diaries — *Tolstoy, Leo, Graf*
Tolstoy's Dictaphone — *Birkerts, Sven*
c Tom (Illus. by Daniel Torres) — *Torres, Daniel*
Tom Bass: Totem Maker — *Bass, Tom*
Tom Lea: An Oral History — *Lea, Tom*
Tom Paine: A Political Life — *Keane, John*
y Tom Paine: Voice of Revolution — *Meltzer, Milton*
y Tom Sawyer Abroad (Dietz). Audio Version — *Twain,
   Mark*
Tom: The Unknown Tennessee Williams — *Leverich,
   Lyle*
Tomato Blessings and Radish Teachings — *Brown,
   Edward Espe*
The Tomato Handbook — *Bennett, Jennifer*
c Tomatoes, Potatoes, Corn, and Beans — *Johnson,
   Sylvia A*
The Tomb of God — *Andrews, Richard, 1953-*
Tombs for the Living — *Dillehay, Tom D*
Tombs, Graves and Mummies — *Bahn, Paul G*
c Tomie's Little Mother Goose (Illus. by Tomie De
   Paola) — *De Paola, Tomie*
Tommaso Campanella En France — *Lerner, Michel-
   Pierre*
Tommaso E Il Fotografo Cieco — *Bufalino, Gesualdo*
c Tommy's Mommy's Fish (Illus. by Thomas Aldren
   Dingman Watson) — *Watson, Nancy Dingman*
y Tomorrow and Tomorrow — *Sheffield, Charles*
Tomorrow by Design — *Lewis, Philip H*
Tomorrow, God Willing — *Wikan, Unni*
Tomorrow in the Battle Think on Me — *Marias,
   Javier*
Tomorrow Is Another Country — *Sparks, Allister*
The Tomorrow of Malaria — *Litsios, Socrates*
y Tomorrow, When the War Began — *Marsden, John*
c Tomorrow's Alphabet (Illus. by Donald Crews)
   — *Shannon, George*
Tomorrow's Hospital — *Ginzberg, Eli*
cp Tomorrow's Morning

y Tomorrow's Promise — *Baer, Judy*
Tomorrow's War — *Shukman, David*
c Tom's Hats (Illus. by Andre Amstutz) — *Amstutz, Andre*
c Tom's Train (Illus. by Anthea Sieveking) — *MacKinnon, Debbie*
Le Ton Beau De Marot — *Hofstadter, Douglas R*
Tone Vigeland — *Thue, Anniken*
The Tongue Is Fire — *Scheub, Harold*
Tongues of the Children — *Lee, John B*
Toni Morrison — *Peach, Linden*
y Toni Morrison: Nobel Prize-Winning Author — *Kramer, Barbara*
Toni Morrison's Fiction — *Furman, Jan*
c Tonight, by Sea — *Temple, Frances*
y Toning the Sweep — *Johnson, Angela*
c Tonio's Cat (Illus. by Edward Martinez) — *Calhoun, Mary*
c Tonka Big Book of Trucks (Illus. by Tom LaPadula) — *Relf, Patricia*
Tonkin Gulf and the Escalation of the Vietnam War — *Moise, Edwin E*
Tonnacour: Life in Grosse Pointe and along the Shores of Lake St. Clair — *Woodford, Arthur M*
Tony Bennett: What My Heart Has Seen — *Bennett, Tony, 1926-*
Tony Blair — *Rentoul, John*
Tony Cragg — *Celant, Germano*
Tony O'Malley (Lynch) — *O'Malley, Tony*
r Tony Richardson: A Bio-Bibliography — *Radovich, Don*
The Too Bright Sun — *O'Flynn, Mark*
Too Hot to Cool Down — *Cummings, Terrance*
Too Jewish? — *Kleeblatt, Norman L*
Too Late for Man — *Ospina, William*
Too Loud a Solitude — *Hrabal, Bohumil*
Too Many Blondes — *Henderson, Lauren*
c Too Many Kangaroo Things to Do! (Illus. by Kevin O'Malley) — *Murphy, Stuart J*
Too Many Notes, Mr. Mozart — *Bastable, Bernard*
c Too Many Pumpkins (Illus. by Megan Lloyd) — *White, Linda*
c Too Many Suns (Illus. by Martin Springett) — *Lawson, Julie*
Too Much a Good Thing — *Curry, Ramona*
Too Much Is Never Enough — *Lapidus, Morris*
c Too Much Talk (Illus. by Stefano Vitale) — *Medearis, Angela Shelf*
Too Soon Dead — *Kurland, Michael*
Too Soon to Panic — *Forbes, Gordon*
Too Soon To Tell — *Trillin, Calvin*
Toolbox — *Morabito, Fabio*
c Tools — *Barton, Byron*
c Tools — *Bryant-Mole, Karen*
Tools and Environments for Parallel and Distributed Systems — *Zaky, Amr*
Tools for Team Excellence — *Huszczo, Gregory E*
Tools of the Trade — *Taylor, Jeff*
c Tooth Truth (Illus. by Patti Delmonte) — *Gillis, Jennifer Storey*
c Toots and the Upside Down House — *Hughes, Carol*
Toots in Solitude — *Yount, John*
y Top 10 Basketball Slam Dunkers — *Bjarkman, Peter C*
r The Top 10 of Everything — *Ash, Russell*
r The Top 100 Morgan Dollar Varieties — *Fey, Michael S*
c Top Banana (Illus. by Erika Oller) — *Best, Cari*
r Top Birding Spots in Britain and Ireland — *Tipling, David*
Top Dog — *Carroll, Jerry Jay*
Top Guns — *McManners, Hugh*
y Top Lawyers and Their Famous Cases — *Emert, Phyllis Raybin*
c Top Secret — *Cooling, Wendy*
c Top Secret (Illus. by Ted Dewan) — *Dewan, Ted*
Top Secret Exchange — *Zimmerman, David*
y Top Secret/MAJIC — *Friedman, Stanton T*
Top Secret Restaurant Recipes — *Wilbur, Todd*
y The Top Ten of Everything 1997
Topics in Clinical Cardiology — *Raizner, Albert E*
Topics in Geometry — *Gindikin, Simon*
Topics in Statistical and Theoretical Physics — *Dobrushin, R L*
The Topkapi Scroll — *Necipoglu, Gulru*
Toplu Siirler — *Turan, Guven*
r A Topographical Dictionary of England — *Lewis, Samuel*
Topographies — *Miller, J Hillis*
Topological Algorithms for Digital Image Processing — *Kong, T Yung*

c Tops and Bottoms (Illus. by Janet Stevens) — *Stevens, Janet*
Topspin: Ups and Downs in Big-Time Tennis — *Berry, Elliot*
c Topsy and Tim Have Itchy Heads — *Adamson, Jean*
c Topsy and Tim Meet the Ambulance Crew — *Adamson, Jean*
c The Topsy-Turvies (Illus. by Keren Ludlow) — *Simon, Francesca*
c The Topsy-Turvy Emperor of China (Illus. by Julian Jusim) — *Singer, Isaac Bashevis*
Tora Fur Israel, Tora Fur Die Volker — *Fischer, Irmtraud*
Die Tora: Theologie Und Sozialgeschichte Des Alttestamentlichen Gesetzes — *Crusemann, Frank*
Torah Studies. Rev. Ed. — *Schneerson, Menachem M*
y The Torc and the Ring — *Joy, Margaret*
The Torchbearers: Women and Their Amateur Arts Associations in America 1890-1930 — *Blair, Karen J*
The Torments of Love — *Crenne, Helisenne De*
y Torn Away — *Heneghan, James*
c Tornado (Illus. by Doron Ben-Ami) — *Byars, Betsy*
y Tornado Alley — *Lehman, Yvonne*
Toronto's Girl Problem — *Strange, Carolyn*
A Torrent of Words — *Souter, Gavin*
Torrents of Spring — *Turgenev, Ivan*
Torrid Zones — *Nussbaum, Felicity A*
The Tortilla Curtain — *Boyle, T Coraghessan*
y The Tortilla Curtain (Rosenblat). Audio Version — *Boyle, T Coraghessan*
c The Tortilla Factory (Illus. by Ruth Wright Paulsen) — *Paulsen, Gary*
c Tortoise Brings the Mail (Illus. by Jillian Lund) — *Lillegard, Dee*
Torvill and Dean — *Torvill, Jayne*
The Tory View of Landscape — *Everett, Nigel*
c Tot Shabbat (Illus. by Camille Kress) — *Kress, Camille*
Total Control — *Baldacci, David*
Total Control (Dukes). Audio Version — *Baldacci, David*
Total Manufacturing Solutions — *Basu, Ron*
The Total Package — *Hine, Thomas*
Total Quality and Organization Development — *Lindsay, William M*
Total Quality in Information Systems and Technology — *Woodall, Jack*
Total Quality Management — *James, Paul T J*
Total-Reflection X-Ray Fluorescence Spectrometry — *Klockenkamper, Reinhold*
r Total Television. 4th Ed. — *McNeil, Alex*
Totalitarian and Post-Totalitarian Law — *Podgorecki, Adam*
Totalitarian Science and Technology — *Josephson, Paul R*
Totalitarianism: The Inner History of the Cold War — *Gleason, Abbott*
y A Totally Alien Life-Form — *Lewis, Sydney*
Totally Awesome 80s — *Rettenmund, Matthew*
Totally Fit Living — *Kronmeyer, Robert*
y Totally Private and Personal — *Wilber, Jessica*
Totally Unauthorized Guide to Doom II — *Waring, Robert*
Totally Unauthorized Myst — *Kempker, Debra*
Totally Unauthorized the 11th Hour — *Davis, H Leigh*
Totem and Taboo — *Freud, Sigmund*
The Totem Ship — *Gould, Alan*
Touch — *Josipovici, Gabriel*
c Touch (Illus. by Francisco Arredondo) — *Llamas, Andreu*
The Touch — *Myerson, Julie*
c Touch (Illus. by Barrie Watts) — *Walpole, Brenda*
Touch and Go — *Stein, Eugene*
y Touch and Go (Phillips). Audio Version — *Berridge, Elizabeth*
c Touch and Tell — *Brown, Marcia*
y A Touch of Classic Soul — *Taylor, Marc*
Touch of Enchantment — *Medeiros, Teresa*
A Touch of Mortality — *Granger, Ann*
The Touch of Your Shadow, the Whisper of Your Name — *Barrett, Neal*
Touch the Dragon — *Connelly, Karen*
Touched — *Haines, Carolyn*
y Touched by an Angel — *Williamson, Martha*
Touched by Fire — *Barnett, Louise*
Touched with Fire — *Bergerud, Eric*
Touched with Fire — *Jamison, Kay Redfield*
c Touching All the Bases — *Mackay, Claire*
y Touching Earth Lightly — *Lanagan, Margo*
Touching Liberty — *Sanchez-Eppler, Karen*
Touching Spirit — *Stratton, Elizabeth K*

Touching the Past — *Curtis, Elizabeth*
Touching the Void. Audio Version — *Simpson, Joe*
Touching the World — *Eakin, Paul John*
The Touchstone — *Horsfall, Paul*
Tough Calls — *Gordon, Josh*
Tough Choices — *Brown, Lester Russell, 1934-*
Tough Daisies — *Haywood, C Robert*
c Tough Loser — *DeClements, Barthe*
The Tough-on-Crime Myth — *Elikann, Peter T*
Tough to Tackle. Audio Version — *Christopher, Matt*
Toughened Plastics II — *Riew, C Keith*
y Toulouse-Lautrec: A Life (Schraf). Audio Version — *Frey, Julia*
Toulouse-Lautrec in the Metropolitan Museum of Art — *Ives, Colta*
c Toulouse: The Story of a Canada Goose (Illus. by A R Cohen) — *Cummings, Priscilla*
A Tour of the Calculus — *Berlinski, David*
A Tour through the Whole Island of Great Britain — *Defoe, Daniel*
Le Tourbillon De La Vie — *Flugge, Manfred*
r Touring in Wine Country — *Pigott, Stuart*
r Touring in Wine Country: Loire — *Duijker, Hubrecht*
r Touring in Wine Country: Northwest Italy — *Ashley, Maureen*
Tourism Development — *Gartner, William C*
Tourism in China — *Lew, Alan A*
Tourism in Europe. 1995 Ed.
Tourism: The State of the Art — *Seaton, A V*
Tourists: How Our Fastest Growing Industry Is Changing the World — *Krotz, Larry*
Tournaments of Value — *Meneley, Anne*
Tournier Elementaire — *Krell, Jonathan F*
c Toussaint L'Ouverture: The Fight for Haiti's Freedom (Illus. by Jacob Lawrence) — *Myers, Walter Dean*
Tout Etait Dans Montesquieu — *Bergeron, Gerard*
Touvier, Vichy Et Le Crime Contre L'Humanite — *Bedarida, Francois*
Toward 2015 — *Kew, Richard*
Toward a Catholic Constitution — *Swidler, Leonard*
Toward a Competitive Telecommunication Industry — *Brock, Gerald W*
Toward a Definition of Antisemitism — *Langmuir, Gavin I*
Toward a History of Chinese Communist Foreign Relations 1920s-1960s — *Hunt, Michael H*
Toward a New Common Sense — *Santos, Boaventura De Sousa*
Toward a Postpositivist World — *Rogers, Katrina S*
Toward a Reassessment of the Shepherd of Hermas — *Wilson, J Christian*
Toward a Science of Consciousness — *Hameroff, Stuart R*
Toward a Simpler Way of Life — *Winter, Robert*
Toward a Theological Encounter — *Klenicki, Leon*
Toward a Theory of Radical Origin — *Pizer, John*
Toward a Working-Class Canon — *Murphy, Paul Thomas*
Toward Amnesia — *Van Arsdale, Sarah*
Toward an African Christianity — *Hillman, Eugene*
Toward an Intellectual History of Women — *Kerber, Linda K*
Toward Anti-Adhesion Therapy for Microbial Diseases — *Kahane, Itzhak*
Toward Civil Society in the Middle East? — *Schwedler, Jillian*
Toward Gender Equality
Toward God — *Casey, Michael, Monk of Tarrawarra*
Toward Participatory Research — *Narayan, Deepa*
Toward the Beloved Community — *Baldwin, Lewis V*
y Toward the Sunrising — *Morris, Lynn*
Toward Wholeness in Paule Marshall's Fiction — *Pettis, Joyce*
Toward Wisdom — *Macdonald, Copthorne*
Towards a Civic Society — *Hoyer, Svennik*
Towards a Competent Workforce — *Mansfield, Bob*
Towards a Feminist Christology — *Hopkins, Julie M*
Towards a Modern Art World — *Allen, Brian*
Towards a New Europe — *Schneider, Gerald*
Towards a New Liberal Internationalism — *Long, David*
Towards a Rapid Reaction Capability for the United Nations — *Canada*
Towards a Semiotics of Ideology — *Reis, Carlos*
Towards a Sociology of Schizophrenia — *Doubt, Keith*
Towards a Tax Free Society — *Kumar, Devendra*
Towards Consensus? — *Vowles, Jack*
Towards Drama as Method in the Foreign Language Classroom — *Schewe, Manfred*
Towards Evening — *Hope, Mary*
y Towards Freedom — *Alexander, Ken*

Towards Gender Equity in Mathematics Education
— Hanna, Gila
Towards Global Multilingualism — Khoo, Rosemary
Towards Holistic Wellness
Towards Illiberal Democracy in Pacific Asia — Bell,
Daniel A
Towards Sustainable Architecture — Edwards, Brian
Towards Welfare Pluralism — Rao, Nirmala
Tower of Dreams — Abdul-Baki, Kathryn K
c The Tower to the Sun (Illus. by Colin Thompson)
— Thompson, Colin
y Towers in the Mist — Goudge, Elizabeth
A Town Abandoned — Dandaneau, Steven P
c Town Mouse, Country Mouse (Illus. by Jan Brett)
— Brett, Jan
The Town of No. My Brother Running — McNair,
Wesley
Town on Trial — Harrington, William
The Towneley Plays. Vols. 1-2
Towns in Transition — Christie, Neil
y Toxic Deception — Fagin, Dan
Toxic Sludge Is Good for You — Stauber, John
Toxic Work — Reinhold, Barbara Bailey
Toxicological and Performance Aspects of Oxygenated
Motor Vehicle Fuels — National Research Council
(U.S.) Committee on Toxicological and Performance
Aspects of Oxygenated Motor Vehicle Fuels
r Toxicology Desk Reference. 3rd Ed., Vols. 1-3
— Ryan, Robert P
Toxicology of Industrial Compounds — Thomas,
Helmut
Toxicology of Metals — Chang, Louis W
Toxicology: Principles and Applications — Niesink,
Raymond J M
Toxics and Health — Silver, Cheryl Simon
c The Toy Brother (Illus. by William Steig) — Steig,
William
The Toy Soldier's Heart — Hufford, Charlie
c Toybox Tales (Illus. by Andy Ellis) — Grindley, Sally
c Toyin Fay (Illus. by Paul Hunt) — Wilkins, Verna
Allette
c Toys — Bryant-Mole, Karen
c Toys — Doney, Meryl
Toys — Leach, Barbara J
Toys Ahoy! — Baker, Felicity
Toys and Designs from the World of Beatrix Potter
— Wilkinson, Anne
Toys and Reasons — Erikson, Erik H
y Toys with Nine Lives — McClary, Andrew
Tra Riforma Ed Eresea, La Giovinezza Di Martin
Borrhaus 1499-1528 — Felici, Lucia
Trace Analysis — Prichard, E
Traces behind the Esmeraldas Shore — Deboer,
Warren R
Traces of an Omnivore — Shepard, Paul
Tracing Chains-of-Thought — Juliano, Benjoe A
r Tracing Your Ancestors — Saul, Pauline
Tracing Your Ancestors in the Public Record Office
— Cox, Jane
r Tracing Your West Indian Ancestors — Grannum,
Guy
r Track and Field Record Holders — Baldwin, David
Track Conditions — Klein, Michael
Track Down Your Ancestors — Catlett, Estelle
Tracking the Vanishing Frogs — Phillips, Kathryn
c Tracks (Illus. by Tedd Arnold) — Galef, David
c Tracks, Scats, and Signs (Illus. by Linda Garrow)
— Dendy, Leslie
c Tractor (Illus. by Craig McFarland Brown) — Brown,
Craig McFarland
c Tractor (Snapshot Books)
c Tractors and Trucks — Crowther, Robert
c Tracy's Mess (Illus. by Iza Trapani) — Petersen, Elise
Trade, Aid and Global Interdependence — Cho,
George
Trade and Development Report 1996
Trade and Investment in the 1990s — Sato, Ryuzo
Trade and the American Dream — Aaronson, Susan
Ariel
Trade and the Industrial Revolution 1700-1850. Vols.
1-2 — Engerman, Stanley L
Trade and Traders in Muslim Spain — Constable,
Olivia Remie
Trade and Transformation in Korea 1876-1945
— McNamara, Dennis L
Trade and Urban Development in Poland — Carter, F
W
r Trade Data Elements Directory. Vol. 3 — United
Nations. Economic Commission for Europe
Trade in the Pre-Modern Era 1400-1700. Vols. 1-2
— Irwin, Douglas A

Trade, Industrialization, and Integration in Twentieth-
Century Central America — Tirado De Alonso, Irma
Trade, Investment and Pacific Economic Integration
— Kojima, Kiyoshi
Trade Issues in the Caribbean — Tirado De Alonso,
Irma
A Trade Like Any Other — Nieuwkerk, Karin Van
Trade, Markets and Welfare — Lancaster, Kelvin
A Trade Policy for Free Societies — McGee, Robert W
Trade Protection in the United States — Rowley,
Charles K
Trade Secret — Parkin, Stuart
Trade, Technology, and International Competitiveness
— Irfan-Ul-Haque
Trade Union Politics — Perusek, Glenn
r Trade Union Publications. Vols. 1-3 — Reynolds,
Lloyd George
Trade Unionism in Recession — Duncan, Gallie
Trade Warriors — Dryden, Steve
y Trader — De Lint, Charles
Traders in a Brave New World — Preeg, Ernest H
Trading in Choppy Markets — Barnes, Robert M
Trading in Santa Fe — Elder, Jane Lenz
Trading in Santa Fe — Kingsbury, John M
Trading Partners — Tweedie, Sandra
Trading Places — Chilton, Bruce
Trading Reality — Ridpath, Michael
Trading Up — Vogel, David
Trading with the Environment — Andersson, Thomas
Tradition in Late Antique Sculpture — Hannestad,
Niels
r The Tradition of Technology — Bruno, Leonard C
A Tradition That Has No Name — Belenky, Mary
Field
Tradition Transformed — Sorin, Gerald
Tradition versus Democracy in the South Pacific
— Lawson, Stephanie
y Traditional Africa — Minks, Louise
Traditional Beluga Drives of the Inupiat of Kotzebue
Sound — Lucier, Charles V
Traditional Chinese Medicine — McNamara, Sheila
Traditional Country Style — Wilhide, Elizabeth
c Traditional Crafts from Africa (Illus. by Diane Wolfe)
— Temko, Florence
c Traditional Crafts from Mexico and Central America
(Illus. by Randall Gooch) — Temko, Florence
Traditional Healers and Childhood in Zimbabwe
— Reynolds, Pamela
The Traditional Homelands of the Tamils. Rev. 2nd
Ed. — De Silva, K M
Traditional Hymns — Fordham, David
The Traditional Literature of Cambodia — Jacob,
Judith M
Traditional Metalworking in Kenya — Brown, Jean
Traditional Pasta — Middione, Carlo
Traditional Politics and Regime Change in Brazil
— Hagopian, Frances
Traditional Religion and Guerrilla Warfare in
Modern Africa — Wiegert, Stephen L
Traditional Textiles of Central Asia — Harvey, Janet
Traditionalists, Militants and Liberals in Present
Islam — Chamieh, Jebran
Traditions and Transitions
Traditions of Bread and Violence — Sasanov,
Catherine
Traditions, Voices, and Dreams — Friedman, Melvin J
Traductrice De Sentiments — Rioux, Helen
Trafalgar Square (Holiday Geology Guides)
Traffic and Politics — Yates, Nigel
c Traffic Safety (Illus. by Penny Dann) — Loewen,
Nancy
The Tragedie of Anthonie, and Cleopatra
— Shakespeare, William
Tragedies Grecques Au Fil Des Ans — Romilly,
Jacqueline De
Tragedies of Our Own Making — Neely, Richard
Tragedy in Paradise — Hart, Gail K
The Tragedy of Coriolanus (Parker) — Shakespeare,
William
The Tragedy of Lin Biao — Teiwes, Frederick C
The Tragedy of Mariam, the Fair Queen of Jewry
— Cary, Elizabeth
The Tragedy of Origins — Lyons, John D
Tragedy's End — Dunn, Francis M
Tragic Failure — Wicker, Tom
Tragic Lucidity — Hansen, Keith W
The Tragic Mission of Bishop Paul Juusten to Tsar
Ivan the Terrible — Kajanto, Iiro
The Tragic Muse — James, Henry
Tragic Posture and Tragic Vision — Ruprecht, Louis
A, Jr.

Les Tragiques. Vols. 1-2 — D'Aubigne, Agrippa
Die Tragodie Des Oberleutnants Zur See Oskar Kusch
— Walle, Heinrich
The Tragoedie of Othello, the Moore of Venice
— Shakespeare, William
c Trail Drive (Illus. by James Rice) — Rice, James
Trail Fever — Lewis, Michael
y Trail of Darkness — Bolesny, Darlene B
Trail of Secrets — Goudge, Eileen
y Trail of Stones — Strauss, Gwen
The Trail of Time — Bedini, Silvio A
Trail to the Klondike — McCune, Don
Trail to Vicksburg — Patten, Lewis B
y Trails across America — Miller, Arthur P, Jr.
Trails of Yesterday — Bratt, John
Trails Plowed Under — Russell, Charles
c Train (Illus. by Chris L Demarest) — Demarest, Chris
L
c Train (Illus. by Larry Johnson) — Temple, Charles
Train Country — MacKay, Donald
Train Go Sorry — Cohen, Leah Hager
c The Train Ride (Illus. by Stephen Lambert)
— Crebbin, June
c Train to Somewhere (Illus. by Ronald Himler)
— Bunting, Eve
A Trainer's Companion to Advanced Automotive
Emissions Systems — Andrew, Douglas
Training a Tiger — Woods, Earl
r Training and Development Yearbook 1996/1997
Training the Body for China — Brownell, Susan
Trains, Tracks and Tall Timber — Coleman, Matt
Trainspotting — Welsh, Irvine
Trainspotting: A Screenplay — Hodge, John
Traits of American Life — Hale, Sarah Josepha
Trance and Recalcitrance
Trans-Atlantyk — Gombrowicz, Witold
The Trans-Mississippi West 1804-1912. Pts. 1-3
— Kvasnicka, Robert M
Transaction Cost Economics and Beyond
— Groenewegen, John
Transactions of the Canadian Numismatic Research
Society. Vol. 32
Transbluesency: The Selected Poems of Amiri Baraka/
LeRoi Jones 1961-1995 — Baraka, Imamu Amiri
Transcaucasian Boundaries — Wright, John F R
The Transcaucasus in Transition — Hunter, Shireen T
The Transcendent Child — Rubin, Lilian
Transcendental Utopias — Francis, Richard, 1945-
Transcendental Wife — Barton, Cynthia H
Transcending the Talented Tenth — James, Joy
c The Transcontinental Railroad — Anderson, Peter
The Transcription of Primary Textual Sources Using
SGML — Robinson, Peter
Transfigurations of the Maghreb — Woodhull,
Winifred
Transformation and Emerging Markets — Macesich,
George
Transformation: Awakening to the Sacred in
Ourselves — Cochran, Tracy
Transformation from Below — Gibson, John
The Transformation of British Politics 1860-1995
— Harrison, Brian
The Transformation of Communist Systems
— Chavance, Bernard
The Transformation of Natural Philosophy
— Kusukawa, Sachiko
The Transformation of Property Rights in the Gold
Coast — Firmin-Sellers, Kathryn
The Transformation of Rural Life — Adams, Jane
The Transformation of Rural Scotland — Devine, T M
The Transformation of Security in the Asia/Pacific
Region — Ball, Desmond
The Transformation of the World Economy 1980-93
— Solomon, Robert
The Transformation of Wall Street. Rev. Ed.
— Seligman, Joel
Transformational Leadership in Government
— Koehler, Jerry W
Transformations: Immigration, Family Life, and
Achievement Motivation among Latino Adolescents
— Suarez-Orozco, Carola
Transformations in Cleveland Art 1796-1946
— Robinson, William H
Transformations in Irish Culture — Gibbons, Luke
Transformations of Circe — Yarnell, Judith
Transformative Curriculum Leadership — Henderson,
James G
Transformed by the Light — Morse, Melvin
y Transformer — Gross, Philip
Transforming Computer Technology — Norberg,
Arthur L

Transforming Desire — *Silberman, Lauren*
Transforming Development — *Snyder, Margaret*
The Transforming Hand of Revolution — *Hoffman, Ronald, 1941-*
p Transforming Libraries
Transforming Men — *Dench, Geoff*
Transforming Paris — *Jordan, David P*
Transforming Power — *Kellow, Aynsley*
Transforming Qualitative Data — *Wolcott, Harry F*
Transforming Rural Life — *McMurry, Sally Ann*
Transforming School Cultures — *Maehr, Martin L*
Transforming the Bottom Line — *Hope, Tony*
Transforming the Core — *Ernst, Maurice*
Transforming Tradition — *Rosenberg, Neil V*
Transforming Trauma — *Parnell, Laurel*
Transforming Women's Work — *Dublin, Thomas, 1946-*
The Transforms and Applications Handbook — *Poularikas, Alexander D*
Transgender Warriors — *Feinberg, Leslie*
Transgenic Organisms — *Tomiuk, J*
Transgenic Xenopus — *Seidman, Shlomo*
Transgressions of Reading — *Newman, Robert D, 1951-*
p Transit
Transition and Students with Learning Disabilities — *Patton, James R*
The Transition from War to Peace in Sub-Saharan Africa — *Colletta, Nat J*
The Transition from Work to Retirement
The Transition in Eastern Europe. Vol. 1 — *Blanchard, Olivier Jean*
Transition Metal Sulfur Chemistry — *Stiefel, Edward*
The Transition of H.P. Lovecraft — *Lovecraft, H P*
The Transition to Democracy in Latin America — *Farcau, Bruce W*
Transition to Democracy in Latin America — *Stotzky, Irwin P*
Transitional Objects and Potential Spaces — *Rudnytsky, Peter L*
Transitions in Land and Housing — *Strong, Ann Louise*
r Transitions through Adolescence — *Graber, Julia A*
Transitions: Unlocking the Creative Quilter Within — *Balosky, Andrea*
The Translatability of Cultures — *Budick, Sanford*
Translating by Factors — *Gutknecht, Christoph*
Translating History — *Korchilov, Igor*
Translating Ireland — *Cronin, Michael*
Translating Slavery — *Kadish, Doris Y*
Translating the Enlightenment — *Oz-Salzberger, Fania*
Translating Woman — *Behar, Ruth*
Translatio Religionis — *Heither, Theresia*
Translation and Taboo — *Robinson, Douglas*
The Translation Begins — *Risset, Jacqueline*
Translation Horizons beyond the Boundaries of Translation Spectrum — *Rose, Marilyn Gaddis*
A Translation of Jerome's Chronicon with Historical Commentary — *Jerome, Saint*
Translation, Power, Subversion — *Alvarez, Roman*
Translations of Power — *Bellamy, Elizabeth J*
The Translator in the Text — *May, Rachel*
r The Translator's Handbook — *Sofer, Morry*
The Translator's Invisibility — *Venuti, Lawrence*
Translators through History — *Delisle, Jean*
Transmission Electron Microscopy — *Williams, David B*
The Transmission-Line Modeling Method TLM — *Christopolous, Christos*
Transmissions: Theory and Practice for a New Video Aesthetics — *D'Agostino, Peter*
Transmuted Past — *Brush, Stephen G*
r Transnational Accounting. Vols. 1-2 — *Ordelheide, Dieter*
Transnational Citizenship — *Baubock, Rainer*
p Transnational Corporations
Transnational Religion and Fading States — *Rudolph, Susanne Hoebert*
Transpersonal Development — *Assagioli, Roberto*
Transpersonal Psychotherapy. 2nd Ed. — *Boorstein, Seymour*
The Transpersonal: Psychotherapy and Counselling — *Rowan, John*
Transplantation of Ovarian and Testicular Tissues — *Gosden, Roger G*
Transport and Storage of Radioactive Materials 1996
c Transport in Art — *Micklethwait, Lucy*
Transport Infrastructure in Central and Eastern European Countries

Transport Phenomena and Materials Processing — *Kou, Sindo*
Transport Systems, Policy and Planning — *Tolley, Rodney*
Transport: The Way Forward — *Great Britain. Dept. of Transport*
c Transportation: Automobiles to Zeppelins — *English, June A*
r Transportation Expressions — *O'Leary, Pamela*
Transportation Planning on Trial — *Garrett, Mark*
Transportation-Related Air Quality and Energy
Transportation Tunnels — *Ponnuswamy, S*
Transports: Travel, Pleasure and Imaginative Geography 1600-1830 — *Chard, Chloe*
The Trap — *Matute, Ana Maria*
The Trap — *Velde, Rink Van Der*
Trap Door to Heaven — *Choyce, Lesley*
Traplines: Stories — *Robinson, Eden*
Trapped in the Net — *Rochlin, Gene I*
Tras El Dorado Vegetal — *Frias Nunez, Marcelo*
c Trash Trucks! (Illus. by Daniel Kirk) — *Kirk, Daniel*
Trattato Sulla Febre — *Alexander, of Aphrodisias*
Der Traum Vom Gluck. Vols. 1-2 — *Fillitz, Hermann*
Trauma and Dreams — *Barrett, Deirdre*
Trauma and Self — *Strozier, Charles B*
Trauma and Survival — *Waites, Elizabeth*
Trauma and the Therapist — *Pearlman, Laurie A*
Trauma and Transformation — *Tedeschi, Richard G*
Trauma Research Methodology — *Carlson, Eve B*
Traumatic Stress — *Van Der Kolk, Bessel A*
Travel Air — *Bissonette, Bruce*
Travel Alone and Love It — *Wingler, Sharon B*
r The Travel Dictionary. New Ed. — *Dervaes, Claudine*
Travel, Gender and Imperialism — *Blunt, Alison*
r A Travel Guide to Jewish Europe. 2nd Ed. — *Frank, Ben G*
Travel in Early Modern Europe — *Maczak, Antoni*
y Travel Writing — *Marsh, Linda*
Traveler's and TV Viewer's Golf Tournament Guide — *McCord, Robert*
r Traveler's Guide to Art Museum Exhibitions. 9th Ed. — *Rappaport, Susan S*
A Traveler's Guide to Pioneer Jewish Cemeteries of the California Gold Rush — *Morris, Susan*
r Traveler's Guide to the Great Sioux War — *Hedren, Paul L*
r The Traveler's Reading Guide. Rev. Ed. — *Simony, Maggy*
r The Traveler's Sourcebook — *Smith, Darren L*
r Travelers' Tales Brazil — *Haddad, Annette*
r Travelers' Tales Food — *Sterling, Richard*
r Traveler's Tales Hong Kong
Travelers' Tales India — *O'Reilly, James*
The Traveler's Tree — *Bontempelli, Bruno*
Traveling in Notions — *Rosen, Michael J*
y Traveling on into the Light — *Brooks, Martha*
Traveller's Literary Companion to the Indian Sub-Continent — *Weightman, Simon*
Travelling Hopefully — *Makepeace, Maggie*
Travelling in the Family — *Andrade, Carlos Drummond De*
c The Travelling Pillow (Illus. by Margot Jane Ott) — *Brown, Beverly*
Travels and Other Writings — *Bartram, William*
y Travels in Alaska (Waterman). Audio Version — *Muir, John*
Travels of the Mind — *Vasconcelos, Renato Silva De Mendonca E*
Travels with Lizbeth — *Eighner, Lars*
c Travels with Rainie Marie — *Martin, Patricia*
Travers Corners — *Waldie, Scott*
Traverse Theatre Presents the World Premiere of Reader — *Dorfman, Ariel*
La Travesia Secreta — *Victoria, Carlos*
La Travesia Solitaria De Juan Cabrera — *Fraxedas, J Joaquin*
c Travis and the Better Mousetrap (Illus. by Theresa Burns) — *Dennard, Deborah*
Treading in the Past — *Kankainen, Kathy*
Treading Softly — *Clark, George B*
Treading Softly, Speaking Low — *Durczak, Joanna*
Treading the Maze — *King, Susan Elizabeth*
Treadwell: Photographs — *Modica, Andrea*
Treason of the Intellectuals — *Mathews, Robin*
Treasure Box — *Card, Orson Scott*
The Treasure Chest — *Hebel, Johann Peter*
c The Treasure Hunt (Illus. by Nick Butterworth) — *Butterworth, Nick*
c Treasure Island (Illus. by Fernando Fernandez) — *Norby, Lisa*

y Treasure Island (Illus. by Francois Place) — *Stevenson, Robert Louis*
c Treasure Island (Cummings). Audio Version — *Stevenson, Robert Louis*
c Treasure Island (O'Herlihy). Audio Version — *Stevenson, Robert Louis*
c The Treasure of El Patron — *Paulsen, Gary*
The Treasure of Timbuktu — *Palmer, Catherine*
Treasured Earth — *Davis, Carolyn O'Bagy*
Treasures from the Ob'Basin — *Marshak, Boris*
Treasures New and Old — *Bauer, David R*
Treasures of the Keio University — *Takamiya, Toshiyuki*
r The Treasures of the Parthenon and Erechtheion — *Harris, Diane*
Treasures of the Uffizi Florence — *Asher, Abigail*
The Treasury and Whitehall — *Thain, Colin*
A Treasury of American-Jewish Folklore — *Koppman, Lion*
r Treasury of Barbie Doll Accessories 1961-1995 — *Rupp, Rebecca Ann*
c Treasury of Children's Folklore — *Sockin, Brian Scott*
c A Treasury of Christmas Stories — *Hardy, Sian*
c A Treasury of Flannelboard Stories — *Bay, Jeanette Graham*
c A Treasury of Ghost Stories (Illus. by Tony Morris) — *Ireland, Kenneth*
c Treasury of Irish Stories (Illus. by Ian Newsham) — *Riordan, James, 1936-*
c A Treasury of Jewish Stories (Illus. by Jane Cope) — *Geras, Adele*
c A Treasury of Old Testament Stories (Illus. by Kate Aldous) — *Pearson, Maggie*
A Treasury of Pennsylvania Tales — *Garrison, Webb*
c A Treasury of Pony Stories (Illus. by Anthony Lewis) — *Jennings, Linda*
c A Treasury of Prayers
c A Treasury of Princesses (Illus. by Ruth Sanderson) — *Climo, Shirley*
Treasury of Spanish Love Poems, Quotations and Proverbs — *Serrano, Juan*
c A Treasury of Stories from Hans Christian Andersen (Illus. by Robin Lawrie) — *Korlek, Jenny*
c A Treasury of Stories from the Brothers Grimm (Illus. by Robin Lawrie) — *Korlek, Jenny*
A Treasury of Tennessee Tales — *Ewing, James*
A Treasury of the Great Children's Book Illustrators — *Meyer, Susan E*
c Treasury of Wise Action
y Treating Abused Adolescents — *Gil, Eliana*
Treating Adolescents — *Steiner, Hans*
Treating Children and Adolescents in Residential and Inpatient Settings — *Lyman, Robert D*
Treating Couples — *Kessler, Hilda*
Treating Difficult Personality Disorders — *Rosenbluth, Michael*
Treating Sexual Disorders — *Charlton, Randolph S*
Treating Sexually Abused Children and Their Nonoffending Parents — *Deblinger, Esther*
Treating the Elderly — *Sheikh, Javaid I*
A Treatise on Carriages — *Felton, William*
Treatment of Behavior Problems in Dogs and Cats — *Askew, Henry R*
The Treatment of Dual Diagnosis
r The Treatment of Epilepsy. 2nd Ed. — *Wyllie, Elaine*
Treatment of Functional Somatic Symptoms — *Mayou, Richard*
Treatment of Suicidal People — *Leenaars, Antoon A*
Treatment Outcomes in Psychotherapy and Psychiatric Interventions — *Sperry, Len*
Treatment Strategies for Abused Children — *Karp, Cheryl L*
Treatment Wetlands — *Kadlec, Robert H*
Treatment with GnRH Analogs — *Filicori, Marco*
Treaty Making in the Spirit of Co-Existence — *Canada. Royal Commission on Aboriginal Peoples*
Tredici Canti Del Floridoro — *Fonte, Moderata*
The Tree and the Canoe — *Bonnemaison, Joel*
The Tree and the Vine — *De Jong, Dola*
Tree Huggers — *Durbin, Kathie*
c A Tree Is Growing (Illus. by S D Schindler) — *Dorros, Arthur*
Tree Kangaroos — *Flannery, T F*
Tree of Heaven — *Binstock, R C*
The Tree of Life — *Bencastro, Mario*
The Tree. The Nature of Nature — *Fowles, John*
Treehouse: New and Selected Poems — *Kloefkorn, William*
c Trees (Illus. by Barrie Watts) — *Bryant-Mole, Karen*
Trees — *Gates, Galen*
Trees — *Joyce, Kristin*

c Trees (Illus. by Francisco Arredondo) — *Llamas Ruiz, Andres*
r Trees and Shrubs of British Columbia — *Brayshaw, T Christopher*
c Trees, Leaves, and Bark (Illus. by Linda Garrow) — *Burns, Diane L*
c The Trees of the Dancing Goats (Illus. by Patricia Polacco) — *Polacco, Patricia*
c A Tree's Tale (Illus. by Lark Carrier) — *Carrier, Lark*
r Trekking in Africa — *Ardito, Stefano*
Trekways of the Wind — *Valkeapaa, Nils-Aslak*
Tren Song Hong Cuon Cuon — *Nguyen, Tuong Bach*
Trends 2000 — *Celente, Gerald*
Trends in Developing Economies 1996
Trends in Educational Technology 1995
r Trends in Europe and North America 1995
Trends in Hospital Diagnoses for Black Patients and White Patients 1980-87 — *Elixhauser, A*
Trends in the Health of Older Americans — *Cohen, R A*
p The Trends Journal
Trent Frayne's All Stars — *Frayne, Trent*
c Tres Dias Salvajes (Illus. by Federico Delicado) — *Sierra I Fabra, Jordi*
c Los Tres Osos (Illus. by Paul Galdone) — *Galdone, Paul*
c Tres Semanas Com A Avo (Illus. by Cristina Malaquias) — *Saldanha, Ana*
y The Trespassers — *Snyder, Zilpha Keatley*
c The Trev Series (Illus. by Craig Smith) — *Negus, George*
y The Trevarton Inheritance — *Macdonald, Malcolm*
p Tri-quarterly (Northwester University)
y The Triad Worlds — *Busby, F M*
y Trial by Fire (Crouse). Audio Version — *Rosenberg, Nancy Taylor*
c The Trial of Anna Cotman — *Alcock, Vivien*
The Trial of Elizabeth Cree — *Ackroyd, Peter*
Trials — *Wallach, Anne Tolstoi*
The Trials and Tribulations of Little Red Riding Hood. 2nd Ed. — *Zipes, Jack*
Trials of an Ordinary Doctor — *Cook, Harold J*
The Trials of Ezra Pound — *Findley, Timothy*
The Trials of Maria Barbella — *Pucci, Idanna*
c Triangles (Illus. by Richard Maccabe) — *Riggs, Sandy*
Trianon and East Central Europe — *Kiraly, Bela K*
Tribal and Chiefly Warfare in South America — *Redmond, Elsa M*
A Tribal Fever — *Sweetman, David*
A Tribe of Warrior Women — *Springer, Melissa*
Tribes — *Wolfe, Art*
Tribes and Tribulations — *Hauptman, Laurence M*
Tribiblos Astronomique. Bk. 2, Vols. 1-2 — *Meliteniote, Theodore*
Tribulation Force — *LaHaye, Tim*
A Tribute to Robert A. Koch — *Clark, Gregory T*
Tribute to Teddy Bear Artists. 2nd Ser. — *Mullins, Linda*
Tributyltin: Case Study of an Environmental Contaminant — *De Mora, S J*
Tricia Guild in Town — *Guild, Tricia*
The Trick of Singularity — *Osborne, Laurie E*
Trick of the Light — *Dawson, Jill*
c Trick or Eeek! and Other Ha Ha Halloween Riddles (Illus. by R W Alley) — *Hall, Katy*
c Trick or Treat, Great Pumpkin (Illus. by Charles M Schulz) — *Schulz, Charles M*
Trick or Treat Murder — *Meier, Leslie*
Trick Question — *Dunbar, Tony*
Tricks — *Camus, Renaud*
Tricks of the Floor Trader — *Weintraub, Neal*
Trickster in the Land of Dreams — *Papanikolas, Zeese*
c Trickster Tales (Illus. by David Boston) — *Sherman, Josepha*
Tricksterism in Turn-of-the-Century American Literature — *Ammons, Elizabeth*
r A Triduum Sourcebook. Vols. 1-3 — *Halmo, Joan*
Die Trierer Kartause St. Alban Von Der Grundung 1330/31 Bis Zur Mitte Des 15. Jahrhunderts — *Oldenburg, Manfred*
Triet Ly Ve Su Vuot Bien — *Pham, Cong Thien*
Trigg County 1880 Families — *Taylor, Pete*
Trigg County, Kentucky Deeds. Vol. 1 — *Willis, Laura*
r Trigg County, Kentucky Newspaper Abstracts. Vol. 28 — *Taylor, Pete*
Trigger Factors in Transfusion Medicine — *International Symposium on Blood Transfusion (20th: 1995: Groningen, Netherlands)*

Triggering of Acute Coronary Syndromes — *Willich, Stefan N*
The Triggerman's Dance — *Parker, T Jefferson*
De Triginta Sex Decanis — *Hermes, Trismegistus*
Trigonometric Fourier Series and Their Conjugates — *Zhizhiashvili, Levan V*
Trilateral Perspectives on International Legal Issues — *Young, Michael K*
Trim and Terrific One-Dish Favorites — *Clegg, Holly*
Trimdas Lugas. Vols. 1-2 — *Hausmanis, Viktors*
Trinitarian Perspectives — *Torrance, Thomas F*
Trinity and Incarnation — *Studer, Basil*
The Trinity in Asian Perspective — *Lee, Jung Young*
r A Trip East in 1888 — *Covington, Mary Hamilton*
c A Trip to the Moon
The Triple Cord — *Mazor, Yair*
Triple Feature — *Bagshawe, Louise*
Triple-Helical Nucleic Acids — *Soyfer, Valery N*
Triple Jeopardy — *Parloff, Roger*
Triple-X International — *Pander Brothers*
Tripolitania — *Mattingly, David J*
Tripwire: Korea and U.S. Foreign Policy in a Changed World — *Bandow, Doug*
Triton — *Delany, Samuel R*
The Triumph of Corporate Capitalism in France 1867-1914 — *Freedeman, Charles E*
The Triumph of Propaganda — *Hoffmann, Hilmar*
Triumph of the Laity — *Westerkamp, Marilyn J*
Triumph of the Market — *Herman, Edward S*
Triumphant Capitalism — *Warren, Kenneth*
y The Triumphant Spirit — *Del Calzo, Nick*
The Trivialization of God — *McCullough, Donald W*
Troilus and Cressida — *Shakespeare, William*
Troilus and Criseyde — *Chaucer, Geoffrey*
Les Trois Minutes Du Diable — *Sallenave, Daniele*
Les Trois Premiers Livres Des Odes De 1559 — *Magny, Olivier De*
Le Troisieme Faust — *Petit, Marc*
c The Trojan Horse (Illus. by Warwick Hutton) — *Hutton, Warwick*
c Trojans — *Adorian, Simon*
y The Trokeville Way — *Hoban, Russell*
Trolley Wars — *Molloy, Scott*
Trollope and Women — *Markwick, Margaret*
c Troodon: The Smartest Dinosaur — *Lessem, Don*
The Trophies of Time — *Parry, Graham*
y Trophy Wife (David). Audio Version — *Thorne, Nicola*
Tropical Animal Health — *Seifert, Horst S H*
Tropical Archaeobotany — *Hather, Jon G*
Tropical Classical — *Iyer, Pico*
Tropical Deforestation — *Sponsel, Leslie E*
Tropical Depression — *Shames, Laurence*
c The Tropical Forest — *Massa, Renato*
Tropical Forest Plant Ecophysiology — *Mulkey, Stephen S*
Tropical Freshwater Wetlands — *Roggeri, Henri*
Tropical Gardening — *Bar-Zvi, David*
Tropical Rainforest Research — *Edwards, D S*
Trotsky: The Eternal Revolutionary — *Volkogonov, Dmitrii Antonovich*
c Troubadour's Storybag — *Livo, Norma J*
c Trouble (Illus. by Durga Bernhard) — *Kurtz, Jane*
c Trouble Dolls (Illus. by Lambert Davis) — *Buffet, Jimmy*
Trouble Follows Me — *Macdonald, Ross*
c Trouble for Alberta (Illus. by Jacqueline East) — *Krailing, Tessa*
Trouble-Free Travel — *Colwell, Stephen D*
Trouble in the Town Hall — *Dams, Jeanne M*
Trouble in Your Tank?. 3rd Ed. — *Durney, Lawrence J*
Trouble No More — *Grooms, Anthony*
c Trouble on the Day — *Clarke, Norma*
c Trouble on the T-Ball Team (Illus. by Irene Trivas) — *Bunting, Eve*
c Trouble on the Tracks — *Napoli, Donna Jo*
y Trouble the Water — *Ward, Jerry W*
y Trouble with a Capital T — *Baer, Judy*
The Trouble with Blame — *Lamb, Sharon*
The Trouble with Computers — *Landauer, Thomas K*
The Trouble with Friendship — *DeMott, Benjamin*
The Trouble with Prosperity — *Grant, James*
The Trouble with Testosterone and Other Essays on the Biology of the Human Predicament — *Sapolsky, Robert M*
c Trouble with Trucks — *Jenner, Caryn*
c The Trouble with Wishes (Illus. by Jennifer Plecas) — *Pfeffer, Susan Beth*
Troubled Bodies — *Komesaroff, Paul A*
Troubled Industries — *Uriu, Robert M*

Troubled Pleasures — *Beekman, E M*
Troubled Waters — *Sweel, Pat*
Troublemaker: One Man's Crusade against China's Cruelty — *Wu, Harry*
c Troubles in the Rain Forest — *Pageler, Elaine*
The Troubles: Ireland's Ordeal 1966-1996, and the Search for Peace — *Coogan, Tim Pat*
Troubleshooting and Repairing Compact Disc Players. 3rd Ed. — *Davidson, Homer L*
Troubleshooting and Repairing Computer Printers. 2nd Ed. — *Bigelow, Stephen J*
Troubleshooting TCP/IP. 2nd Ed. — *Miller, Mark*
Troublesome Children — *Shamsie, Jalal*
Trout: An Illustrated History — *Prosek, James*
Trout Fishing in America — *Brautigan, Richard*
y Trout Summer — *Conly, Jane Leslie*
c Troy Aikman — *Rosenblatt, Richard*
c Troy Aikman: Super Quarterback — *Gutman, Bill*
c Troy and Knossos — *Hicks, Peter*
c Truck and Tractor Pullers — *Savage, Jeff*
Truck: On Rebuilding a Worn-Out Pickup and Other Post-Technological Adventures — *Jerome, John*
c Truck Talk (Illus. by Bobbi Katz) — *Katz, Bobbi*
c Trucks (Illus. by Nicholas Hewetson) — *Llewellyn, Claire*
Trudeau and Our Times. Vol. 2 — *McCall, Christina*
Trudeau and the End of a Canadian Dream — *Laforest, Guy*
c The True Adventure of Daniel Hall (Illus. by Diane Stanley) — *Stanley, Diane*
True and Fair — *Jones, Edgar*
True and False Romances — *Vega, Ana Lydia*
True Beauty — *Emme*
True Beauty — *Paisner, Emme*
A True Believer — *Gordon, Michael*
y True Betrayals (Shansky). Audio Version — *Roberts, Nora*
c True Blue (Illus. by DyAnne DiSalvo-Ryan) — *Elste, Joan*
True Blue — *Milch, David*
True Colors — *Haden-Guest, Anthony*
y The True Colors of Caitlynne Jackson — *Williams, Carol Lynch*
y The True Confessions of Charlotte Doyle (Illus. by Ruth E Murray) — *Avi*
True Crime — *Klavan, Andrew*
True Crime Astrology — *Rowland, Edna*
True Faith and Allegiance — *Toner, James H*
True Faith in the True God — *Schwarz, Hans, 1939-*
y True Ghost Stories (Illus. by David Wyatt) — *Deary, Terry*
True Grit — *Carlyon, Les*
True Heart — *Lamb, Arnette*
The True History of Chocolate — *Coe, Sophie D*
y True Horror Stories — *Deary, Terry*
True Joy — *Francis, of Assisi, Saint*
The True Law of Kingship — *Burns, J H*
c True Lies (Illus. by John O'Brien) — *Shannon, George*
True Love — *Fulghum, Robert*
True Love Waits — *Kaminer, Wendy*
y True Myths — *Andrews, Nigel*
True Names — *O'Hara, James J*
y True North — *Lasky, Kathryn*
True North — *Strickland, Stephanie*
y True North (Reading). Audio Version — *Conway, Jill K*
True Patriot — *Bercuson, David Jay*
True Professionalism — *Maister, David H*
True Prosperity — *Knouse, K C*
y True Romance — *Gask, Marina*
True Romance — *Zahavi, Helen*
True Selves — *Brown, Mildred L*
True Serenity — *Kirvan, John*
c True Stories — *Masters, Anthony*
c True Stories — *Razgon, Lev*
c True Stories Series
r The True Story of the Novel — *Doody, Margaret Anne*
c The True Story of the Three Little Pigs (Illus. by Lane Smith) — *Scieszka, Jon*
p True Swamp: The Memoirs of Lenny the Frog — *Lewis, Jon*
The True World — *Reeves, Catherine*
c Trueno — *Armstrong, William H*
The Truest Pleasure — *Morgan, Robert*
y Truly Grim Tales — *Galloway, Priscilla*
Truman (McCullough). Audio Version — *McCullough, David*
Truman and the Hiroshima Cult — *Newman, Robert P*
Trumpets from the Tower — *Sprunger, Keith L*
Trung Ky Dan Bjen 1908 — *Tran, Gia Phung*

Trunk Music — *Connelly, Michael*
Trunk Music (Hill). Audio Version — *Connelly, Michael*
y **Trust and Betrayal** — *Bode, Janet*
Trust, Ethnicity, and Identity — *Landa, Janet Tai*
Trust in Modern Societies — *Misztal, Barbara A*
Trust in Numbers — *Porter, Theodore M*
Trust No One — *Schwarz, Ted*
Trust the Force — *Davidson, Todd*
Trust: The Social Virtues and the Creation of Prosperity — *Fukuyama, Francis*
Trust Your Children — *West, Mark*
Trusted Criminals — *Friedrichs, David O*
Trusting the People — *Dole, Bob*
The Truth about Catalogers — *Manley, Will*
c **The Truth about Cats (Illus. by Alan Snow)** — *Snow, Alan*
c **The Truth about Cousin Ernie's Head (Illus. by Matthew McElligott)** — *McElligott, Matthew*
The Truth about Everything — *Stewart, Matthew*
The Truth about Money — *Edelman, Ric*
The Truth about Reference Librarians — *Manley, Will*
The Truth about the National Debt — *Cavanaugh, Francis X*
Truth and Power — *Parker, J I*
Truth and Rationality — *Villanueva, Enrique*
Truth and Textuality in Chaucer's Poetry — *Kiser, Lisa J*
Truth and Trust — *Navran, Frank*
Truth, Fiction, and Literature — *Lamarque, Peter*
Truth in Nursing Inquiry — *Kikuchi, June F*
The Truth in the Light — *Fenwick, Peter*
y **Truth, Lies and Homework** — *Feeney, Josephine*
y **The Truth Machine** — *Halperin, James L*
The Truth of Broken Symbols — *Neville, Robert C*
Truth Serum — *Cooper, Bernard*
The Truth Teller — *Simons, Margaret, 1960-*
The Truth under Lock and Key? — *Berger, Klaus*
Truthfully Yours — *Hango, Angeline*
c **The Truthsinger** — *Haworth-Attard, Barbara*
Trutor and the Balloonist — *Wesselmann, Debbie Lee*
Tryin' to Sleep in the Bed You Made — *DeBerry, Virginia*
Trying to Get Some Dignity — *Rhodes, Ginger*
y **Trying to Get the Toothpaste Back into the Tube** — *Peterson, Lorraine*
y **Trying to Save Piggy Sneed** — *Irving, John*
Tsar: The Lost World of Nicholas and Alexandra — *Kurth, Peter*
The Tsarist Secret Police in Russian Society 1880-1917 — *Zuckerman, Fredric S*
r **The TSCA Compliance Handbook. 3rd Ed.** — *Griffin, Ginger L*
T'shuva — *Paul, Carolyn Keiler*
Tsongkhapa's Six Yogas of Naropa — *Tsongkhapa Lobzang Drakpa*
Tsvetaeva's Orphic Journeys in the Worlds of the Word — *Hasty, Olga Peters*
Tu Felix Austria Nube — *Sommer-Mathis, Andrea*
Tu, La Oscuridad — *Montero, Mayra*
r **Tu Then Tin Hoc Tong Hop** — *Do, Thong Minh*
c **The Tub Grandfather (Illus. by Richard Egielski)** — *Conrad, Pam*
c **Tub People (Sallley) (Illus. by Richard Egielski). Book and Audio Version** — *Conrad, Pam*
r **The Tuba Source Book** — *Morris, R Winston*
y **Tube: The Invention of Television** — *Fisher, David E*
c **Tubman: Harriet Tubman and the Underground Railroad** — *Sadlier, Rosemary*
c **Tubu the Friendly Tokolosh** — *Ferguson, Gail*
c **Tuck-Me-In Tales (Illus. by Yvonne Davis)** — *MacDonald, Margaret Read*
c **Tucket's Ride** — *Paulsen, Gary*
The Tudor and Stuart Monarchy. Vol. 1 — *Strong, Roy*
The Tudor and Stuart Town — *Barry, Jonathan*
Tudor and Stuart Women Writers — *Schleiner, Louise*
Tudor Frontiers and Noble Power — *Ellis, Steven G, 1950-*
Tudor Political Culture — *Hoak, Dale*
Tudor Times — *Moorcroft, Christine*
Tudor Times — *Tonge, Neil*
c **Tudor Warship** — *Newbery, Elizabeth*
Tudor's Soiree Musicale — *Tudor, Anthony*
Tuer Etc. — *Clerc, Philippe*
Tuesday — *Wiesner, David*
y **The Tuesday Cafe** — *Trembath, Don*
c **Tufty Bear (Illus. by Peter Melnyczuk)** — *Gardam, Jane*

Tug of War — *Erdman, Paul Emil*
c **Tug, Tug** — *Wildsmith, Brian*
y **Tularosa** — *McGarrity, Michael*
The Tulip Sacrament — *Sobelman, 'Annah*
y **The Tulip Touch** — *Fine, Anne*
c **Tulips (Illus. by Debrah Santini)** — *O'Callahan, Jay*
Tullio Lombardo and Ideal Portrait Sculpture in Renaissance Venice 1490-1530 — *Luchs, Alison*
c **Tumble Bumble (Illus. by Felicia Bond)** — *Bond, Felicia*
Tumble Home — *Hempel, Amy*
c **Tumblebugs and Hairy Bears (Illus. by Preston Neel)** — *Samson, Suzanne Marie*
c **Tumbleweed Christmas (Illus. by Tom Sully)** — *Ferguson, Alane*
TumbleWords: Writers Reading the West — *Fox, William L, 1949-*
Tumbling — *McKinney-Whetstone, Diane*
Tumbling in the Hay — *Gogarty, Oliver St. John*
c **Tundra** — *Kaplan, Elizabeth*
c **Tundra** — *Shepherd, Donna Walsh*
Tunisia's Global Integration and Sustainable Development
The Tunnel — *Gass, William H*
Tunnel Boring Machines — *International Lecture Series TBM Tunnelling Trends (1995: Hagenberg, Austria)*
The Tunnel: The Underground Homeless of New York City — *Morton, Margaret*
Tunnel to Canto Grande — *Alegria, Claribel*
Tunnel Vision — *Walter, James*
Tunnetteko Tyypin? — *Seppala, Juha*
c **Turandot (Illus. by Winslow Pels)** — *Mayer, Marianna*
Turbulence and Transition Modelling — *Hallback, M*
Turbulence, Coherent Structures, Dynamical Systems and Symmetry — *Holmes, Philip*
Turbulence: The Legacy of A.N. Kolmogorov — *Frisch, U*
Turbulent Decade — *Yan, Jiaqi*
Turbulent Shear Layers in Supersonic Flow — *Smits, Alexander J*
Turbulent Skies — *Heppenheimer, T A*
Turfgrasses: Their Management and Use in the Southern Zone. 2nd Ed. — *Duble, Richard L*
Turin 1564-1680 — *Pollak, Martha D*
Das Turkenbild in Der Neueren Deutschen Literatur 1970-1990 — *Akbulut, Nazire*
Turkey: A Country Study — *Metz, Helen Chapin*
Turkey between East and West — *Mastny, Vojtech*
c **The Turkey Girl (Illus. by Ed Young)** — *Pollock, Penny*
c **Turkey Pox (Illus. by Dorothy Donohue)** — *Anderson, Laurie Halse*
A Turkish Folktale — *Mahir, Behcet*
Turlupin — *Perutz, Leo*
Turmoil to Turning Points — *Kagan, Richard*
The Turn of the Millennium — *Sobosan, Jeffrey G*
y **Turn on the Lights from Bed! (Illus. by Rick Brown)** — *Carrow, Robert*
The Turn to Experience in Contemporary Theology — *Gelpi, Donald L*
The Turn to the Native — *Krupat, Arnold*
Turnaround: The Untold Story of Bear Bryant's First Year as Head Coach at Alabama — *Stoddard, Tom*
Turnaway — *Browner, Jesse*
The Turnbull: A Library and Its World — *Barrowman, Rachel*
Turncoats: Changing Party Allegiance by British Politicians — *Leach, Robert*
Turned On — *Dow, Roger*
Turner — *Lloyd, Michael*
Turner in the North — *Hill, David, 1953-*
The Turner Journals — *Leigh, Robert*
Turner Syndrome in a Life Span Perspective — *International Symposium on Turner Syndrome (4th: 1995: Goteborg, Sweden)*
Turner: The Fighting Temeraire — *Egerton, Judy*
Turning Back — *Steinberg, Stephen*
Turning Point — *Townsend, Helen*
Turning Points in Social Security — *Tynes, Sheryl R*
Turning Right in the Sixties — *Brennan, Mary C*
y **Turning Stones** — *Parent, Marc*
Turning toward the World — *Merton, Thomas*
The Turning Word — *Riddel, Joseph N*
c **The Turnip (Illus. by Laura Rader)** — *Ziefert, Harriet*
La Turquie En Mouvement — *Vaner, Semih*
c **Turtle Knows Your Name (Illus. by Ashley Bryan)** — *Bryan, Ashley*
c **The Turtle Who Lost His Shell (Illus. by Rick Grayson)** — *Levy, Paul*
c **Turtles** — *Baskin-Salzberg, Anita*

Tuscan Poetry of the Duecento — *Jensen, Frede*
The Tuscan Table — *Newdick, Jane*
y **Tusk and Stone** — *Bosse, Malcolm*
y **The Tuskegee Airmen** — *Harris, Jacqueline L*
c **Tut, Tut (Illus. by Lane Smith)** — *Scieszka, Jon*
y **Tutankhamun** — *Green, Robert*
r **Tuttle Dictionary of the Martial Arts of Korea, China and Japan** — *Kim, Sun-Jin*
The TUXEDO System — *Andrade, Juan M*
c **The TV Book (Illus. by Lorraine Tuson)** — *Wallace, Shelagh*
TV I Kulturhistorisk Perspektiv 1954-1994 — *Sepstrup, Preben*
TV Sets — *Bennett, Mark*
TV's Biggest Hits — *Burlingame, Jon*
c **TV's Forgotten Hero** — *McPherson, Stephanie Sammartino*
TVTV: The Debate — *Anderson, Robert*
Twas Only an Irishman's Dream — *Williams, William A*
c **'Twas the Night b'fore Christmas (Illus. by Melodye Rosales)** — *Rosales, Melodye*
Twelfe Night, or, What You Will — *Shakespeare, William*
r **The Twelfth Mental Measurements Yearbook**
Twelfth Night — *Llewellyn, Michael*
c **The Twelve Circus Rings** — *Chwast, Seymour*
c **The Twelve Dancing Princesses (Illus. by Jane Ray)** — *Ruy, June*
c **The Twelve Days of Christmas (Illus. by Angel Dominguez)** — *Dominguez, Angel*
c **The Twelve Days of Christmas** — *Duntze, Dorothee*
The Twelve Days of Christmas — *Geddes, Anne*
c **The Twelve Days of Christmas (Illus. by Robert Sabuda)** — *Sabuda, Robert*
c **The Twelve Days of Christmas (Illus. by Janis Jones)** — *Sexton, Margot*
Twelve Lessons in Personal Spirituality — *Todeschi, Kevin J*
Twelve Months of Monastery Soups — *Latourrette, Victor*
c **The Twelve Poodle Princesses** — *Pancheri, Jan*
c **Twelve Snails to One Lizard (Illus. by Matt Novak)** — *Hightower, Susan*
y **The Twentieth Century** — *DeMarco, Neil*
r **Twentieth-Century American Music for the Dance** — *Emerson, Isabelle Putnam*
r **Twentieth-Century Artists on Art. 2nd Enl. Ed.** — *Robertson, Jack S*
Twentieth-Century Britain — *Johnson, Paul, 1956-*
r **Twentieth-Century Britain** — *Leventhal, F M*
Twentieth-Century Building Materials — *Jester, Thomas C*
r **Twentieth-Century Caribbean and Black African Writers: Third Series** — *Lindfors, Bernth*
r **Twentieth-Century Crime and Mystery Writers. 3rd Ed.**
Twentieth-Century Dictatorship — *Brooker, Paul*
r **Twentieth-Century Dictionary of Christian Biography** — *Douglas, J D*
r **A Twentieth-Century History of United States Population** — *Wright, Russell O*
Twentieth-Century Latin American Poetry — *Tapscott, Stephen*
r **Twentieth-Century Literary Criticism. Vol. 58**
r **Twentieth-Century Literary Criticism. Vol. 61**
r **Twentieth-Century Literary Criticism. Vols. 59-60**
r **Twentieth-Century Literary Criticism Annual Cumulative Title Index for 1996**
r **The Twentieth-Century Newspaper Press in Britain** — *Linton, David*
Twentieth Century Performance Reader — *Huxley, Mike*
Twentieth Century Physics. Vols. 1-3 — *Brown, Laurie M*
Twentieth-Century Pittsburgh. Vol. 2 — *Lubove, Roy*
Twentieth-Century Poetry — *Verdonk, Peter*
r **Twentieth-Century Romance and Historical Writers. 3rd Ed.**
The Twentieth Century Russian Novel — *Gillespie, David C*
r **Twentieth-Century Science Fiction Writers. 3rd Ed.**
Twentieth Century Type Designers. New Ed. — *Carter, Sebastian*
r **Twentieth-Century Western Writers. 2nd Ed.**
y **Twentieth-Century Women Scientists** — *Yount, Lisa*
y **Twentieth-Century Writers 1950-1990** — *Verde, Tom*
Twenty Blue Devils — *Elkins, Aaron*
The Twenty-First Century Will Be American — *Valladao, Alfredo G A*

c The Twenty-Five Mixtec Cats (Illus. by L Martinez) — *Gollub, Matthew*

Twenty-Four Ways of Looking at Mary McCarthy — *Stwertka, Eve*

c Twenty Mini Mysteries You Can Solve (Illus. by Kevin Faerber) — *Anastasio, Dina*

c The Twenty-One Balloons (Illus. by William Pene Du Bois) — *Du Bois, William Pene*

The Twenty-Seventh City — *Franzen, Jonathan*

Twenty Years of Jewish-Catholic Relations — *Fisher, Eugene J*

Twenty Years On — *Swannell, John*

Twice a Hero — *Krinard, Susan*

y Twice Taken — *Pfeffer, Susan Beth*

Twice the Work of Free Labor — *Lichtenstein, Alex*

Twilight at the Equator — *Manrique, Jaime*

y Twilight in Grace Falls — *Honeycutt, Natalie*

Twilight in Italy and Other Essays — *Lawrence, D H*

Twilight Memories — *Huyssen, Andreas*

The Twilight of Common Dreams — *Gitlin, Todd*

Twilight of Heroes — *Peters, Ralph*

Twilight of Majesty — *Petry, Carl F*

Twilight of the Celtic Gods — *Clarke, David*

The Twilight of the Early Helladics — *Forsen, Jeannette*

The Twilight of the Goddesses — *Gutwirth, Madelyn*

Twilight of the Habsburgs — *Palmer, Alan Warwick*

A Twilight Struggle — *Kagan, Robert*

y Twilight Warriors — *Arostegui, Martin C*

The Twin Earth Chronicles — *Pessin, Andrew*

Twin Peaks Cherry Pie — *Peters, Robert*

c Twin Pickle (Illus. by Clare Mackie) — *Doro, Ann*

Twin Rivers — *Nesbitt, John*

c Twin Trouble (Illus. by Liz Roberts) — *Farmer, Penelope*

The Twins, the Dream — *Bellessi, Diana*

c Twist with a Burger, Jitter with a Bug (Illus. by Pat Dypold) — *Lowery, Linda*

Twisted Cross — *Bergen, Doris L*

The Twisted Muse — *Kater, Michael H*

y Twisted Summer — *Roberts, Willo Davis*

Twisted Tales — *Spady, James G*

Twister: The Original Screenplay — *Crichton, Michael*

y Twister: The Science of Tornadoes and the Making of an Adventure Movie — *Davidson, Keay*

c Twisters! (Illus. by Kazushige Nitta) — *Penner, Lucille Recht*

The Two Alberts — *Owen, Gordon R*

Two Americans within the Gates — *Mizrachi, Eli*

Two Armies and One Fatherland — *Schonbohm, Jorg*

c Two Bad Boys (Illus. by Gail E Haley) — *Haley, Gail E*

Two Below Zero — *McIntyre, Don*

c The Two Brothers (Illus. by Jean Tseng) — *Ho, Minfong*

Two by George — *Boyd, George Elroy*

y Two Centuries — *Barton, Geoff*

Two Cities — *Zagajewski, Adam*

c Two Cool Cows (Illus. by Barry Root) — *Speed, Toby*

y The Two Dead Girls — *King, Stephen*

The Two Deaths of George Wallace — *Healey, Thomas S*

Two East Anglian Diaries 1641-1729 — *Archer, Isaac*

Two Ends of Sleep — *Jones, Lizard*

Two Essays on Virgil — *Penwill, John*

The Two Faces of Economics — *Dawson, Anthony Dalston*

The Two Faces of Political Apathy — *DeLuca, Tom*

Two Fat Ladies — *Paterson, Jennifer*

c Two for Stew (Illus. by Sal Murdocca) — *Numeroff, Laura Joffe*

Two for the Dough — *Evanovich, Janet*

y Two for the Dough (Petty). Audio Version — *Evanovich, Janet*

Two Generation Programs for Families in Poverty — *Smith, Sheila*

Two Gentlemen of Verona — *Schlueter, June*

y The Two Georges — *Dreyfuss, Richard*

Two Great Scouts and Their Pawnee Battalion — *Grinnell, George Bird*

Two Guadalupes — *Weigle, Marta*

The Two-Headed Deer — *Williams, Joanna*

The Two-Headed Eagle — *Biggins, John*

Two Hearts Desire — *Lassell, Michael*

Two Lands on One Soil — *Wright, Frank*

Two Late Medieval Love Treatises — *Brook, Leslie C*

c Two Little Witches (Illus. by Simms Taback) — *Ziefert, Harriet*

Two Lives — *Trevor, William*

Two Loves — *Boice, James Montgomery*

The Two Majorities — *Shafer, Byron E*

c Two-Minute Teddy Bear Tales (Gordon). Book and Audio Version

Two Months in the Confederate States — *Corsan, W C*

The Two Mr. Gladstones — *Crosby, Travis L*

c Two Mrs. Gibsons (Illus. by Daryl Wells) — *Igus, Toyomi*

Two Novels — *Oe, Kenzaburo*

c The Two of Them — *Aliki*

y Two Old Women (Means). Audio Version — *Wallis, Velma*

Two, or, The Book of Twins and Doubles — *Farmer, Penelope*

y Two or Three Things I Know for Sure — *Allison, Dorothy*

The Two-Party Line — *Goodale, Jane C*

Two Paths to Women's Equality — *Giele, Janet Zollinger*

Two Perfectly Marvellous Cats — *Young, Rosamond M*

Two Shores — *Vuong-Riddick, Thuong*

The Two Siblings and Other Stories — *Levinson, Luisa Mercedes*

Two Strand River — *Maillard, Keith*

The Two Tipperarys — *Murphy, Donal A*

Two Towns in Germany — *Dannhaeuser, Norbert*

Two Tudor Subsidy Assessment Rolls for the City of London 1541 and 1582 — *Lang, R G*

c Two under Par (Illus. by Kevin Henkes) — *Henkes, Kevin*

The Two Versions of Malory's Morte D'Arthur — *Tieken-Boon Van Ostade, Ingrid*

Two Voices — *Doyle, Jim*

Two Wheels — *Moody, Greg*

Two Worlds Merging — *Hoekstra, Rik*

Two Years behind the Mast — *McCormick, Harold J*

c Two's Company (Illus. by Oxford Scientific Films) — *Greenway, Shirley*

Tycho Brahes Urania Titani — *Zeeberg, Peter*

Tycoon — *Robbins, Harold*

Tydverdryf — *Eybers, Elisabeth*

Tyndale's New Testament — *Bible. N.T. English. Tyndale. 1995*

Type A Behavior — *Friedman, Meyer*

r Type Two Double Eagles 1866-1876 — *Winter, Douglas*

Typesense: Making Sense of Type on the Computer — *Wheeler, Susan*

Typhoid Mary: Captive to the Public's Health — *Leavitt, Judith Walzer*

y Typing Tutor 7. Electronic Media Version

Typographers on Type — *McLean, Ruari*

Tyranny of Kindness — *Funiciello, Theresa*

The Tyranny of Taste — *Lubbock, Jules*

Tyranny of the Bottom Line — *Estes, Ralph*

The Tyranny of the Market — *Vickers, Douglas*

The Tyranny of the Normal — *Donley, Carol*

Tyranny of the Normal — *Fiedler, Leslie*

y Tyrant's Test — *Kube-McDowell, Michael P*

The Tyrant's Writ — *Steiner, Deborah*

c Tyrone and the Swamp Gang — *Wilhelm, Hans*

U

U Potpalublju — *Arsenijevic, Vladimir*
c The U.S.A. — *Davies, Kath*
U.S.A. — *Dos Passos, John*
The UAE: Formative Years 1965-75 — *Shukla, Ramesh*
The UAW and the Heyday of American Liberalism 1945-1968 — *Boyle, Kevin*
Uber Die Sprache Und Weisheit Der Indier — *Schlegel, Friedrich*
Uberall Blicke Ich Nacheinem, Heimatlichen Boden Aus — *Hedgepeth, Sonia M*
Die Uberfliegerin — *Krauss, Angela*
r UC Davis Book of Horses — *Siegal, Mordecai*
Ucheniye O Simvolakh I Chislakh V Kitaiskoi Klassicheskoi Filosofii — *Kobzev, Artyom I*
The Ufa Story — *Kreimeier, Klaus*
Ufficiali E Gentiluomini — *Castelnuovo, Guido*
y The UFO Invasion — *Frazier, Kendrick*
r Uganda. Rev. Ed. — *Nyeko, Balam*
Uganda: The Challenge of Growth and Poverty Reduction
c The Ugly Duckling (Illus. by Bert Kitchen) — *Grindley, Sally*
The Ugly Duckling — *Johansen, Iris*
c The Ugly Menorah (Illus. by Marissa Moss) — *Moss, Marissa*
c Uh Oh! Gotta Go! (Illus. by Shelley Dieterichs) — *McGrath, Bob*
c Uh-Oh! It's Mama's Birthday! (Illus. by Keinyo White) — *Thomas, Naturi*
The UK Economy (Prest and Coppock). 14th Ed. — *Artis, M J*
UK Eyes Alpha — *Urban, Mark*
The UK School Internet Primer — *Mailer, Nicholas*
UK Solar Eclipses from Year 1 — *Williams, Sheridan*
r UK Stamp Shops Directory 1994-95
r Ukolug Quick Guide to CD-Rom Networking — *Bradley, Phil*
Ukolug Quick Guide to the Internet — *Bradley, Phil*
r Ukraina — *Zinkevych, Osyp*
c Ukraine: A New Independence — *Clay, Rebecca*
Ukraine's Economic Reform — *Shen, Raphael*
c Ukrainian Folk Tales — *Oparenko, Christina*
r Ukrainian Postage Stamps — *Kuzych, Ingert*
Ukrainian Security Policy — *Kuzio, Taras*
y Ukrainians in America — *Kuropas, Myron B*
Ukrains'ka Brafika XI Pochatky XX St.
Ukrains'ka Vyshyvka — *Kara-Vasyleva, Tat'iana*
Ukraintsi V Sviti. 2nd Ed. — *Kardash, Peter*
The Ukulele: A Visual History — *Beloff, Jim*
The Ulcer Story — *Thompson, W Grant*
Ulisse: Il Mito E La Memoria
r Ulrich's International Periodicals Directory 1932-
r Ulrich's International Periodicals Directory 1997. Vols. 1-5
r Ulrich's Plus. Electronic Media Version
Ulster 1641 — *Mac Cuarta, Brian*
r Ulster County, New York Probate Records — *Anjou, Gustave*
Ulster Unionism and British National Identity since 1885 — *Loughlin, James*
y The Ultimate Book of Cross-Sections
Ultimate Christmas — *Newdick, Jane*
y The Ultimate Classic Car Book — *Willson, Quentin*
r The Ultimate Einstein. Electronic Media Version
r The Ultimate Encyclopedia of Extreme Sports — *Tomlinson, Joe*
c The Ultimate Game — *Dicks, Terrance*
r The Ultimate Garden Book for North America — *Stevens, David*
Ultimate Golf Techniques — *Campbell, Malcolm*

r The Ultimate Guide to Lesbian and Gay Film and Video — *Olson, Jenni*
r The Ultimate Guide to Science Fiction. 2nd Ed. — *Pringle, David*
c Ultimate Hockey Trivia — *Weekes, Don*
r The Ultimate Hollywood Tour Book — *Gordon, William A*
yr The Ultimate Human Body 2.0. Electronic Media Version
Ultimate Intimacy — *Ostow, Mortimer*
y The Ultimate Kids' Club Book — *Maupin, Melissa*
y Ultimate Makeup and Beauty — *Quant, Mary*
r The Ultimate Movie Thesaurus — *Case, Christopher*
r The Ultimate Multimedia Handbook. 2nd Ed. — *Keyes, Jessica*
cr The Ultimate Ocean Book — *Mudd-Ruth, Maria*
Ultimate Office Book. 2nd Ed. — *Stroo, Eric*
y The Ultimate On-Line Homework Helper — *Salzman, Marian*
The Ultimate Planting Guide — *Kingsbury, Noel*
The Ultimate Pressure Cooker Cookbook — *LaCalamita, Tom*
The Ultimate Resource 2 — *Simon, Julian Lincoln*
The Ultimate Sin — *Karpf, Ronald J*
The Ultimate Spin Doctor — *Hollingsworth, Mark*
yr The Ultimate Spy Book — *Melton, H Keith*
r The Ultimate Stress Handbook for Women — *Markham, Ursula*
Ultra Lounge — *Jones, Dylan*
Ultrafast Dynamics of Chemical Systems — *Simon, John D*
Ultrasound and the Fallopian Tube — *Timor-Tritschi, Ilan E*
Ultrasound and the Fetal Heart — *Wladimiroff, J W*
Ultrasound Angioplasty — *Siegel, Robert J*
Ultrasound for Surgeons — *Machi, Junji*
Ultraviolet Reflections — *Nilsson, Annika*
Ulysses — *Joyce, James*
Umbrales — *Alegria, Claribel*
Umbria: A Cultural History — *Ross, Ian Campbell*
Umgang Mit Jacob Burckhardt — *Guggisberg, Hans*
Umkehr Und Sunde Im Hebraerbrief — *Lohr, Hermut*
Umpires: Classic Baseball Stories from the Men Who Made the Calls — *Skipper, John*
The UN and the Bretton Woods Institutions — *Haq, Mahbub Ul*
The UN at 50
UN Peacekeeping — *Harrison, Selig S*
UN Peacekeeping, American Politics, and the Uncivil Wars of the 1990s — *Durch, William J*
UN Peacekeeping in Cambodia — *Doyle, Michael W*
Unanswered Questions — *Brooks, Roger*
Unaufhorlich Lenz Gelesen... — *Stephan, Inge*
The Unauthorized Teacher's Survival Guide — *Warner, Jack*
y Unbearable! More Bizarre Stories — *Jennings, Paul*
c The Unbeatable Bread (Illus. by Brad Sneed) — *Hoopes, Lyn Littlefield*
r Unbelievably Good Deals That You Absolutely Can't Get Unless You're a Teacher — *Harrington, Barry*
r UNBIS Thesaurus. English Ed. — *Dag Hammarskjold Library*
Unbound: A Book of AIDS — *Shurin, Aaron*
Unbound Feet — *Yung, Judy*
The Unbounded Community — *Caferro, William*
c The Unbreakable Code (Illus. by Julia Miner) — *Hunter, Sara Hoagland*
Unbridled Power — *Davis, Shelley L*
Unbroken Poetry II — *Eluard, Paul*
Uncertain Belief — *Bartholomew, David J*
Uncertain Glory — *McKenzie, John D*

Uncertain Knowledge — *Dolby, R G A*
Uncertain Partners — *Goncharov, Sergei*
y Uncertain Seasons — *Morgan, Elizabeth Shelfer*
Uncertain Unions and Broken Lives — *Stone, Lawrence*
Uncertainty — *Larsen, Michael*
Uncertainty in Economic Thought — *Schmidt, Christian*
Uncertainty in the Geologic Environment. Vols. 1 2 — *Uncertainty '96 (1996: Madison, Wis.)*
The Uncertainty Principle — *Brandon, Ruth*
Unchained Voices — *Carretta, Vincent*
Uncivil Rites — *Detweiler, Robert*
Unclaimed Experience — *Caruth, Cathy*
c Uncle Albert and the Quantum Quest — *Stannard, Russell*
y Uncle Comanche — *Benner, J A*
Uncle Fred in Springtime (Cecil). Audio Version — *Wodehouse, P G*
c Uncle Jed's Barbershop — *Mitchell, Margaree King*
c Uncle Magic — *Gauch, Patricia Lee*
y Uncle Ronald — *Doyle, Brian*
c Uncle Snake (Illus. by Leovigildo Martinez) — *Gollub, Matthew*
c Uncle Switch (Illus. by John O'Brien) — *Kennedy, X J*
Uncle Tom's Cabin — *Stowe, Harriet Beecher*
The Uncollected Critical Writings — *Wharton, Edith*
The Uncollected Oscar Wilde — *Wilde, Oscar*
Uncollected Poems — *Rilke, Rainer Maria*
Uncommon Calling — *Glaser, Chris*
Uncommon Common Women — *Butler, Anne M, 1938-*
Uncommon Ground — *Cronon, William*
y An Uncommon Soldier — *Burgess, Lauren Cook*
The Uncommon Wisdom of Oprah Winfrey — *Winfrey, Oprah*
An Uncommon Woman — *Pakula, Hannah*
Unconditional Surrender — *Humphreys, Emyr*
Unconquerable Rebel — *Andrade, Ernest*
Unconquered — *Howell, Hannah*
The Unconscious Civilization — *Saul, John Ralston*
The Unconscious Civilization (Saul). Audio Version — *Saul, John Ralston*
The Unconscious Quantum — *Stenger, Victor J*
The Unconsoled — *Ishiguro, Kazuo*
Unconventional Flying Objects — *Hill, Paul R*
Unconventional Warfare — *Marquis, Susan*
c Uncovered! Weird, Weird Stories — *Jennings, Paul*
Uncovering Lives — *Elms, Alan C*
Uncovering the Past — *Stiebing, William H, Jr.*
Uncrowned King — *Weintraub, Stanley*
r UNCTAD Commodity Yearbook 1995
y Undaunted Courage — *Ambrose, Stephen E*
y Undaunted Courage (Smith). Audio Version — *Ambrose, Stephen E*
The Under 35 Guide to Starting and Running Your Business — *Shaw, Lisa*
y Under a Different Sky — *Savage, Deborah*
Under African Skies — *Larson, Charles R*
Under an English Heaven — *Williams, Kay*
Under Cover of Daylight — *Hall, Jim, 1947-*
Under Crescent and Cross — *Cohen, Mark R*
Under Glass — *Buday, Grant*
Under His Spell — *Archer, Ellen*
c Under My Nose (Illus. by Carlo Ontal) — *Ehlert, Lois*
Under My Skin — *Dunant, Sarah*
Under My Skin — *Lessing, Doris May*
Under Northern Eyes — *Berger, Mark T*
Under-Studied Relationships — *Wood, Julia T*
Under the Beetle's Cellar (Fields). Audio Version — *Walker, Mary Willis*

y Under the Black Flag — *Cordingly, David*
c Under the Blood-Red Sun (Woodman). Audio Version
— *Salisbury, Graham*
Under the Burning Sun — *Derosso, H A*
c Under the Cherry Blossom Tree (Illus. by Allen Say)
— *Say, Allen*
Under the Lake (Stechschulte). Audio Version
— *Woods, Stuart*
y Under the Mermaid Angel — *Moore, Martha*
Under the Rainbow — *Kantrowitz, Arnie*
c Under the Sea — *Rothman, Cynthia*
c Under the Sea in 3-D! — *Sammon, Rick*
c Under the Shadow of Wings — *Banks, Sara Harrell*
Under the Sign — *Bann, Stephen*
Under the Spell of God — *Cannon, Makeda*
Under the Stars — *Gray, Lois S*
c Under the Table (Illus. by Marisabina Russo)
— *Russo, Marisabina*
Under the Tuscan Sun — *Mayes, Frances*
Under Western Eyes — *Conrad, Joseph*
Under Western Eyes — *Hongo, Garret Kaoru*
Underboss: Sammy the Bull Gravano's Story of Life
in the Mafia — *Maas, Peter*
The Underdevelopment of Development — *Chew, Sing
C*
y Undergraduate Commutative Algebra — *Reid, Miles*
Undergraduate Teaching of the History of Technology
— *Olsson, Lars O*
y The Underground CD-ROM Handbook for the SAT.
Electronic Media Version
The Underground Guide to Teenage Sexuality
— *Basso, Michael J*
Underground Harmonies — *Tanenbaum, Susie J*
The Underground Man — *Jackson, Mick*
The Underground Man — *Macdonald, Ross*
y The Underground Railroad — *Bial, Raymond*
Underground River and Other Stories — *Arredondo,
Ines*
c Underground to Canada — *Smucker, Barbara
Claassen*
y Underrunners — *Mahy, Margaret*
c Understanding (Illus. by Mechelle Ann) — *Ziegler,
Sandra*
Understanding ActiveX and OLE — *Chappell, David*
y Understanding Adventures of Huckleberry Finn
— *Johnson, Claudia Durst*
Understanding Aggressive Behavior in Children
— *Ferris, Craig F*
Understanding AIDS — *Kalichman, Seth C*
Understanding Alzheimer's Disease — *Cutler, Neal R*
Understanding and Managing Children's Classroom
Behavior — *Goldstein, Sam*
Understanding and Preventing HIV Risk Behavior
— *Oskamp, Stuart*
Understanding and Preventing Sexual Harassment
— *Rutter, Peter*
Understanding and Using Baptismal Records
— *Humphrey, John T*
Understanding Arthur Miller — *Griffin, Alice*
Understanding ATM — *Schatt, Stan*
Understanding Attitudes about War — *Brunk,
Gregory G*
Understanding Biological Psychiatry — *Hedaya,
Robert J*
Understanding China — *Chu, Yen-An*
Understanding Christian Spirituality — *Downey,
Michael*
Understanding Classical Sociology — *Hughes, J A,
1941-*
Understanding Differences between Divorced and
Intact Families — *Simons, Ronald L*
Understanding Digital Signal Processing — *Lyons,
Richard G*
Understanding Diverse Families — *Okun, Barbara F*
Understanding DNA and Gene Cloning. 3rd Ed.
— *Drlica, Karl*
Understanding Drug Treatment in Mental Health
Care — *Bond, Alyson J*
Understanding Drugs — *Emmett, David*
Understanding Economics — *Allsopp, Vicky*
Understanding Engineering Thermo — *Levenspiel,
Octave*
Understanding Eugene Ionesco — *Lane, Nancy*
r Understanding Europeans. 2nd Rev. Ed. — *Miller,
Stuart*
Understanding Federico Garcia Lorca — *Newton,
Candelas*
Understanding Fiction — *Taylor, Henry*
Understanding Flannery O'Connor — *Whitt, Margaret
Earley*
Understanding Fossils — *Doyle, Peter*

Understanding French Poetry — *Metzidakis, Stamos*
Understanding Geographical and Environmental
Education — *Williams, Michael, 1935-*
r Understanding Greek Sculpture — *Spivey, Nigel*
Understanding Health Care Financial Management.
2nd Ed. — *Gapenski, Louis C*
Understanding Human Rights — *Gearty, Conor*
Understanding Illuminated Manuscripts — *Brown,
Michelle P*
Understanding in Human Context — *Sinha, Debabrata*
Understanding Ingeborg Bachmann — *Achberger,
Karen R*
Understanding Interdependence — *Kenen, Peter B*
y Understanding Jewish History. Vol. 1 — *Scharfstein,
Sol*
Understanding John Dewey — *Campbell, James, 1948-*
Understanding Juan Goytisolo — *Pope, Randolph D*
Understanding Justice — *Hudson, Barbara A*
Understanding Latino Families — *Zambrana, Ruth E*
Understanding Masculinities — *Mac An Ghaill,
Mairtin*
r Understanding McLuhan. Electronic Media Version
Understanding Molecular Simulation — *Frenkel, Daan*
Understanding NAFTA — *Orme, Will A, Jr.*
r Understanding Networking Technology — *Norris,
Mark*
c Understanding Opposites
Understanding Peter Weiss — *Cohen, Robert, 1941,
Apr., 4-*
Understanding Policy Fiascoes — *Bovens, Mark*
Understanding Rainer Werner Fassbinder — *Watson,
Wallace Steadman*
Understanding Relativity — *Sartori, Leo*
Understanding Reynolds Price — *Schiff, James A*
Understanding Risk — *Stern, Paul C*
Understanding Scripture — *Thoma, Clemens*
Understanding Second Language Learning Difficulties
— *Ehrman, Madeline Elizabeth*
Understanding Sport Organizations — *Slack, Trevor*
Understanding the American Revolution — *Greene,
Jack P*
r Understanding the Census — *Lavin, Michael R*
Understanding the Developing World — *Yamaguchi,
Hiroichi*
Understanding the I Ching — *Wilhelm, Hellmut*
Understanding the Infinite — *Lavine, Shaughan*
Understanding the Internet
Understanding the Jewish Experience — *Fisher,
Eugene J*
Understanding the Media — *Smith, Joel*
Understanding the Self-Help Organization — *Powell,
Thomas J*
Understanding Third World Politics — *Smith, B C*
Understanding Violence against Women — *Crowell,
Nancy A*
y Understanding Your Horse — *Bayley, Lesley*
The Undertaking: Life Studies from the Dismal Trade
— *Lynch, Thomas*
The Undertow: New and Selected Poems — *Kinsella,
John*
c Underwater Animals — *Cooney, Helen*
Underwater Archaeology — *Blot, Jean-Yves*
The Underwater Photographer — *Edge, Martin*
Underwater Robots — *Yuh, Junku*
Underwater Warriors — *Kemp, Paul*
yr Underwater Wilderness — *Seaborn, Charles*
y Underwear — *Ruby, Jennifer*
The Underwharf — *Naher, Gaby*
Underworlds: Organized Crime in the Netherlands
1650-1800 — *Egmond, Florike*
The Undetected Enemy — *Nordell, John R, Jr.*
Undiplomatic Observations — *Baliozian, Ara*
Undone — *Kimball, Michael*
Undying Love — *Harrison, Ben*
The Uneasy Case for Equalization Payments
— *Usher, Dan*
The Uneasy Center — *Conkin, Paul Keith*
Uneasy Partners — *Cuninggim, Merrimon*
Uneasy Rider — *Bryan, Mike*
Uneasy Sensations — *Douglas, Aileen*
Unemployment: Choices for Europe — *Alogoskoufis,
George*
Unemployment in Capitalist, Communist and Post-
Communist Economies — *Porket, J L*
Unemployment, Restructuring, and the Labor Market
in Eastern Europe and Russia — *Commander,
Simon*
Uneven Development in the Third World. 2nd (Rev.
and Enlarged) Ed. — *Bhalla, A S*
Unfinished Conquest — *Perera, Victor*
y Unfinished Dreams — *Zalben, Jane Breskin*

The Unfinished Gospel — *Powell, Evan*
Unfinished Journey — *Menuhin, Yehudi*
Unfinished Peace — *International Commission on the
Balkans*
Unfinished People — *Gay, Ruth*
The Unfinished Universe — *Young, Louise*
Unforgettable — *Sawyer, Meryl*
y The Unforgiving Land — *Sullivan, Paul*
Unfortunate Emigrants — *Johnson, Kristin*
y Unheard Voices — *Baer, Judy*
An Unholy Alliance — *Gregory, Susanna*
Unholy Angels — *Gallison, Kate*
Unholy Loves — *Oates, Joyce Carol*
r The Unicode Standard, Version 2.0 — *Unicode
Consortium*
y The Unicorn Sonata — *Beagle, Peter S*
Unicorn Variation (Auberjonois). Audio Version
— *Zelazny, Roger*
c Unidentified Flying Objects and Extraterrestrial Life
— *Marsh, Carole*
Unification of Law in the Field of International
Industrial Property — *Lontai, Endre*
Unified Action Armed Forces (UNAAF) — *United
States. Joint Chiefs of Staff*
Unified Constitutive Laws of Plastic Deformation
— *Krausz, A S*
Uniform Commercial Law in the Twenty-First
Century
Unifying Biology — *Smocovitis, Vassiliki Betty*
r UNILEX: International Case Law and Bibliography
on the UN Convention on Contracts for the
International Sale of Goods — *Bonell, Michael
Joachim*
Unimolecular Reactions. 2nd Ed. — *Holbrook,
Kenneth A*
r Union List of Serials in Libraries of the United States
and Canada. 3rd Ed., Vols. 1-5
Union Mergers in Hard Times — *Chaison, Gary N*
c The Union of 1707 — *Rose, Iain*
Union of Words — *Fields, Wayne*
Union Pacific Modeler. Vol. 2
The Union, the Confederacy, and the Atlantic Rim
— *May, Robert E*
Union with Christ — *Tamburello, Dennis E*
Unions and Public Policy — *Flood, Lawrence*
Unions and Workplace Change in Canada — *Kumar,
Pradeep*
r Unique Oregon — *Harris, Richard, 1947-*
The Unique Voice of Hillary Rodham Clinton
— *Clinton, Hillary Rodham*
Unisex'd Revolutionaries — *Ty, Eleanor*
r Unit Operations for the Food Industries — *Gould,
Wilbur A*
United Artists — *Rosenstock, S X*
The United Irishmen — *Curtin, Nancy J*
The United Irishmen — *Dickson, David*
y The United Kingdom — *Burnett, Chris*
The United Mine Workers of America — *Laslett, John
H M*
United Nations — *Meisler, Stanley*
y The United Nations — *Swisher, Karin L*
The United Nations and Apartheid 1948-1994
— *United Nations*
The United Nations and Cambodia 1991-1995
The United Nations and El Salvador 1990-1995
The United Nations and Human Rights 1945-1995
— *United Nations*
The United Nations and International Peacekeeping
— *Zacarias, Agostinho*
The United Nations and Mozambique 1992-1995
The United Nations and Nuclear Non-Proliferation
The United Nations and Rwanda 1993-1996
The United Nations and Somalia 1992-1996
The United Nations and the Advancement of Women
1945-1995 — *United Nations*
The United Nations and the Advancement of Women
1945-1996. Rev. Ed.
r The United Nations and the Iraq-Kuwait Conflict
1990-1996
The United Nations at Fifty — *Thakur, Ramesh*
The United Nations Disarmament Yearbook 1995
y United Nations High Commissioner for Refugees
— *Burger, Leslie*
c The United Nations: Its History and the Canadians
Who Shaped It — *Morton, Desmond*
r United Nations Women's Indicators and Statistics
CD-ROM Database (WISTAT): Version 3.
Electronic Media Version
c The United States — *Allard, Denise*
c United States — *Brooks, Philip*

United States — *Dumm, Thomas L*
c The United States — *Sandak, Cass R*
The U.S. Air Service in the Great War 1917-1919 — *Cooke, James J*
The United States and Arab Nationalism — *Saunders, Bonnie F*
The United States and Cuba under Reagan and Shultz — *Skoug, Kenneth N*
The United States and Europe after the Cold War — *Holmes, John W*
The United States and Northeast Asia — *Puckett, Robert H*
The United States and the Integration of Europe — *Heller, Francis H*
The United States and the Struggle for Southeast Asia 1945-1975 — *Levine, Alan J*
The United States and the Use of Force in the Post-Cold War Era
The United States and the World Court as a Supreme Court of the Nations — *Pomerance, Michla*
The United States and Viet Nam from War to Peace — *Slabey, Robert M*
The U.S. Army in the West 1870-1880 — *McChristian, Douglas C*
United States Army Logistics — *Waddell, Steve R*
U.S. Civil-Military Relations — *Snider, Don M*
r U.S. Coast Guard and Revenue Cutters 1790-1935 — *Canney, Donald L*
r The United States Congress — *Goehlert, Robert U*
r U.S. Consumer Interest Groups — *Bykerk, Loree*
r U.S. Electric Industry Phone and Fax Directory 1996
United States: Essays 1952-1992 — *Vidal, Gore*
r U.S. Flea Market Directory. 2nd Ed. — *LaFarge, Albert*
U.S. Foreign Policy and the United Nations System — *Maynes, Charles William*
U.S. Foreign Policy in Transition — *Winkates, James E*
r U.S. Global Trade Outlook 1995-2000
The U.S. Government and the Vietnam War. Pt. 4 — *Gibbons, William Conrad*
r The United States Government Manual 1996/1997
r U.S. Half Cent Quickfinder. 3rd Ed. — *Heim, Greg*
r United States History — *Merriam, Louise A*
U.S. History as Women's History — *Kerber, Linda K*
c The United States Holocaust Memorial Museum — *Brooks, Philip*
r United States Immigration — *Miller, E Willard*
cr The United States in the 19th Century — *Rubel, David*
r The United States in the First World War — *Venzon, Anne Cipriano*
The United States in the Pacific — *Johnson, Donald D*
U.S. Intelligence at the Crossroads — *Godson, Roy*
The U.S. Intelligence Community. 3rd Ed. — *Richelson, Jeffrey T*
U.S. Interests in the New Taiwan — *Lasater, Martin L*
r U.S. International Postal Rates 1872-1996 — *Wawrukiewicz, Anthony S*
The United States, Japan, and the Future of Nuclear Weapons — *Harrison, Selig S*
r The U.S. Labor Movement — *Stern, Robert N*
U.S.-Latin American Policymaking — *Dent, David W*
The U.S. Military NGO Relationship in Humanitarian Interventions — *Seiple, Chris*
U.S. Nuclear Policy — *United States. Congress. House. Committee on Foreign Affairs*
The United States of Jasper Johns — *Yau, John*
y The United States of Poetry — *Blum, Joshua*
U.S. Official Propaganda during the Vietnam War 1965-1973 — *Page, Caroline*
U.S. Oil Import Vulnerability
U.S. Participation in Somalia Peacekeeping — *United States. Congress. Senate. Committee on Foreign Relations*
U.S.-PLO Dialogue — *Rabie, Mohamed*
United States Policy in Latin America — *Martz, John D*
U.S. Policy on Palestine — *Suleiman, Michael W*
U.S. Post Cold War Foreign Policy — *United States. Congress. House. Committee on Foreign Affairs*
United States Postage Stamps of 1869 — *Rose, Jon*
r U.S. Presidential Candidates and the Elections. Vols. 1-2 — *Havel, James T*
U.S.-Russian Cooperation in Space
U.S.-Sandinista Diplomatic Relations — *Ryan, David*
r United States Senate Election, Expulsion and Censure Cases 1793-1990 — *Butler, Anne M, 1938-*
United States Shipping Policies and the World Market — *Lovett, William A*
The U.S. Soccer Sports Medicine Book — *Garrett, William E*

c The U.S. Space Camp Book of Astronauts — *Baird, Anne*
United States Special Operations Forces Posture Statement 1994
United States-Taiwan Security Ties — *Hickey, Dennis Van Vranken*
U.S. Trade Policy and Global Growth — *Blecker, Robert A*
y United States v. Nixon — *Herda, D J*
r U.S. Virgin Islands — *Philpott, Don*
r U.S. Women's Interest Groups — *Slavin, Sarah*
Uniting the Kingdom? — *Grant, Alexander*
Unity in the Church or the Principle of Catholicism — *Mohler, Johann Adam*
The Unity of Reason — *Henrich, Dieter*
The Unity of the Common Law — *Brudner, Alan*
Unity Temple — *Siry, Joseph M*
L'Univers Des Conquistadores — *Grunberg, Bernard*
Universal Access to E-mail — *Anderson, Robert H*
Universal Banking — *Saunders, Anthony*
The Universal Donor — *Nova, Craig*
Universal Grammar and Narrative Form — *Herman, David*
The Universal Kitchen — *Rozin, Elisabeth*
Universe. 4th Ed. — *Kaufmann, William J, III*
The Universe Below — *Broad, William J*
Universe Down to Earth — *Tyson, Neil De Grasse*
y The Universe Explained — *Ronan, Colin A*
The Universe In a Handkerchief — *Gardner, Martin, 1914-*
Universes — *Leslie, John, 1940-*
La Universidad Americana Y La Ilustracion — *Siebzehner, Batia B*
Universities in the Twenty-First Century — *Muller, Steven*
r University and College Museums, Galleries, and Related Facilities — *Danilov, Victor J*
The University in Ruins — *Readings, Bill*
The University-Industry Relationship in Science and Technology — *Doutriaux, Jerome*
University Life in Eighteenth-Century Oxford — *Midgley, Graham*
The University of Glasgow 1451-1996 — *Brown, A L, 1927-*
r The University of Michigan Index to Labor Union Periodicals 1960-
y University Places. 1996 Ed.
The University Wine Course. 2nd Ed. — *Baldy, Marian W*
r The UNIX Dictionary of Commands, Terms, and Acronyms — *Levine, John*
UNIX for MVS Programmers — *Singh, Harry*
UNIX System Programming Using C++ — *Chan, Terrence*
UNIX Systems Programming for SVR4 — *Curry, David A*
Unkind to Unicorns — *Housman, A E*
The Unkindest Cut — *Queenan, Joe*
c The Unknown Arthur (Illus. by Mark Robertson) — *Matthews, John*
The Unknown Lenin — *Lenin, Vladimir Ilich*
The Unknown Navy — *Halford, Robert G*
p Unknown Public
y Unknown Regions — *Holdstock, Robert*
The Unknown Shore — *O'Brian, Patrick*
The Unknown Soldiers — *Barbeau, Arthur E*
The Unknown Virginia Woolf. 4th Ed. — *Poole, Roger*
Unlearning Violence
Unleashing Rights — *Silverstein, Helena*
Unless the Wind Turns — *Walker, Mildred*
Unlike Normal Women — *Fuller, Vernella*
(Un)like Subjects — *Meaney, Gerardine*
y The Unlikely Romance of Kate Bjorkman — *Plummer, Louise*
y The Unlikely Spy — *Silva, Daniel*
The Unlikely Spy (Rees). Audio Version — *Silva, Daniel*
Unlimited Access — *Aldrich, Gary*
y Unlimited Power — *Robbins, Anthony*
y Unlived Affections — *Shannon, George*
Unlocking Mallarme — *Robb, Graham*
y Unlocking the Air and Other Stories — *Le Guin, Ursula K*
The Unloved: From the Diary of Perla S. — *Lustig, Arnost*
The Unlucky Seven — *Boyle, Alistair*
The Unmaking of Adolf Hitler — *Davidson, Eugene*
Unmasking Japan — *Matsumoto, David*
Unmasking Japan Today — *Kumagai, Fumie*

Unmentionables: A Brief History of Underwear — *Benson, Elaine*
The Unnatural — *Prill, David*
Unnatural Acts — *Jones, Dylan*
Unnatural Disasters — *Panter, Nicole*
Unnatural Exposure — *Cornwell, Patricia Daniels*
The Unnatural Lottery — *Card, Claudia*
Unnatural Murder — *Somerset, Anne*
Unnecessary Debts — *Osberg, Lars*
An Unnecessary Man — *Dowler, Wayne*
The Unnecessary War — *Meehan, Patricia*
c Uno, Dos, Tres (Illus. by Barbara Lavallee) — *Mora, Pat*
The Unofficial X-Files Companion — *Genge, Ngaire*
Unopened Letters — *Zisquit, Linda*
An Unordinary Man — *Hecht, Robert A*
Unorthodox Freud — *Lohser, Beate*
Unpacking Duchamp — *Judovitz, Dalia*
Unpainted to the Last — *Schultz, Elizabeth A*
Unplanned Suburbs — *Harris, Richard, 1952-*
Unplugged Kitchen — *La Place, Viana*
The Unpredictable Certainty — *National Research Council (U.S.). NII 2000 Steering Committee*
Unpublishable! Rejected Writers from Jane Austen to Zane Grey — *Borish, Elaine*
Unpublishable Works — *Warkentin, Erwin J*
Unpublished Philosophical Essays — *Godel, Kurt*
r The Unpublished Roll of Honor — *Hughes, Mark*
Unpublished Shaw — *Shaw, Bernard*
The Unquiet Ghost — *Hochschild, Adam*
An Unquiet Mind — *Jamison, Kay Redfield*
c Unraveling Fibers — *Keeler, Patricia*
Unraveling Piltdown — *Walsh, John Evangelist*
Unraveling Global Apartheid — *Alexander, Titus*
Unravelling the Asian Miracle — *Lele, Jayant*
The Unreal America — *Huxtable, Ada Louise*
Unreal City — *Kennedy, Thomas E*
r Unreal! Hennepin County Library Subject Headings for Fictional Characters and Places. 2nd Ed. — *Hennepin County Library*
Unreasonable Men — *Seidler, Victor J*
The Unredeemed Captive — *Demos, John*
Unrelated Kin — *Etter-Lewis, Gwendolyn*
Unrepentant Leftist — *Rabinowitz, Victor*
Unrepentant, Self-Affirming, Practicing — *Comstock, Gary David*
The Unriddling of Christian Origins — *Carmichael, Joel*
Unrugged Individualism — *Kelley, D*
Unruly Gods — *Shahar, Meir*
The Unruly Queen — *Fraser, Flora*
The Unruly Voice — *Gruesser, John Cullen*
The Unruly Woman — *Rowe, Kathleen*
Unsecular Media — *Silk, Mark*
An Unseemly Man — *Flynt, Larry*
c The Unseen: Scary Stories — *Lunn, Janet*
The Unseen War in Europe — *Waller, John H*
Unseen Warhol — *O'Connor, John*
Unselected Poems — *Levine, Philip*
c The Unsers — *Bentley, Karen*
Unsettled States, Disputed Lands — *Lustick, Ian*
Unsettling Settler Societies — *Stasiulis, Daiva*
Unsettling Statecraft — *Conaghan, Catherine M*
Unshackling the Private Sector — *Holden, Paul*
Unsichtbare Frauen — *Schlag, Evelyn*
Unsolved Problems of the Milky Way — *Blitz, Leo*
Unspeakable Acts — *Pryor, Douglas W*
An Unspeakable Sadness — *Wishart, David J*
Unspeakable: The Rise of the Gay and Lesbian Press in America — *Streitmatter, Rodger*
An Unspoken Promise — *Bockoven, Georgia*
Unstable Bodies — *Matus, Jill L*
Unstable Frontiers — *Erni, John Nguyet*
Unsubmissive Women — *Tong, Benson*
The Untamed — *Michaels, Kasey*
Unthinkable Tenderness — *Gelman, Juan*
Unthinking Eurocentrism — *Shohat, Ella*
Until Death Do Us Part — *McGuire, Christine*
Until It Hurts — *Whitney, Polly*
Until the End — *Coyle, Harold*
Until the End (Lewis). Audio Version — *Coyle, Harold*
Until the Karma Ends — *Adireks, Paul*
The Untimely Death of a Nihilist — *Bluett, Rick*
Unto the Soul — *Appelfeld, Aharon*
The Untouchable — *Banville, John*
Untouchable: A Biography of Robert De Niro — *Dougan, Andy*
The Unusual Life of Tristan Smith — *Carey, Peter*
Unusual Suspects — *Grady, James*
The Unwelcome Companion — *Fowler, Rick*

Unwrapping Christmas — *Miller, Daniel*
Un Uomo Di Carattere — *Capriolo, Paola*
Up against the Corporate Wall. 6th Ed. — *Sethi, S Prakash*
Up, Down, and Sideways — *Patton, Robert H*
y Up from Conservatism — *Lind, Michael*
c Up in the Air — *Hart, Philip S*
Up in the Air — *Jarman, Derek*
Up in the Old Hotel — *Mitchell, Joseph*
Up Island — *Siddons, Anne Rivers*
y Up Jumps the Devil — *Maron, Margaret*
c Up Pop the Monsters 1,2,3! (Illus. by Carla Dijs) — *Dijs, Carla*
y Up River — *Pierce, Olive*
c Up to the Plate — *Galt, Margot Fortunato*
r Updates/2000 Forecasts Edition Demographic 1995. Electronic Media Version
r Updating Wilkinson — *Cole, James H*
y Upgrade Chemistry A-Level — *Lister, Ted*
Upgrade: The High-Tech Road to School Success — *Wirths, Claudine G*
Upgrade Your Own PC — *Rohrbough, Linda*
r Upgrading and Repairing Networks — *Zacker, Craig*
Upgrading and Repairing PCs. 5th Ed.
r Upgrading and Repairing PCs. 6th Ed.
Upholding the Common Life — *Mukta, Parita*
r UPI Stylebook. 3rd Ed. — *McNeill, Robert*
The Upland Bird Art of Maynard Reece — *Reece, Maynard*
Uplifting the Race — *Gaines, Kevin K*
Upon a Mystic Tide — *Barrett, Victoria*
y Upon the Head of the Goat (Moore). Audio Version — *Siegal, Aranka*
Upon This Rock — *Freedman, Samuel G*
Uppark Restored — *Rowell, Christopher*
Uppkomlingarna: Kanslitjanstemannen I 1600-Talets — *Norrhem, Svante*
Uproar at Dancing Rabbit Creek — *Crawford, Colin*
Uprooted in Old Age — *Litwin, Howard*
c The Upside-Down Mice and Other Animal Stories — *Merer, Jane*
The Upstairs Room — *Reiss, Johanna*
Upstate Arcadia — *Hugill, Peter J*
Upstream — *Butala, Sharon*
Upstream: Salmon and Society in the Pacific Northwest — *National Research Council (U.S.). Committee on Protection and Management of Pacific Northwest Anadromous Salmonids*
Urantia: The Great Cult Mystery — *Gardner, Martin, 1914-*
Uranus — *Dondeyne, Desire*
Urban Agglomeration and Economic Growth — *Giersch, Herbert*
Urban Design — *Moughtin, Cliff*
Urban Disorder and the Shape of Belief — *Smith, Carl*
Urban Economics and Real Estate Markets — *DiPasquale, Denise*
Urban Enclaves — *Abrahamson, Mark*
Urban Environments in Emerging Economies — *McKee, David L*
The Urban Frontier — *Wade, Richard C*
Urban Geoscience — *McCall, G J H*
Urban Girls — *Leadbeater, Bonnie J Ross*
Urban Health in Developing Countries — *Harpham, Trudy*
The Urban Image of Augustan Rome — *Favro, Diane*
Urban Leviathan — *Davis, Diane E*
Urban Odyssey — *Cary, Francine Curro*
Urban Oracles — *Santos Febres, Mayra*
Urban Patronage and Social Authority — *Proudfoot, Lindsay J*
Urban Planning and the African American Community — *Thomas, June Manning*
Urban Spaces in Contemporary China — *Davis, Deborah*
y Urban Terrorism — *Sadler, A E*
Urban Tourism — *Berg, Leo Van Den*
The Urban Transformation of the Developing World — *Gugler, Josef*
Urban Transport and the Environment II — *Baldasano, J M*
Urban Travel and Sustainable Development
Urban Usurpation — *McAndrew, John P*
Urban Verbs — *McNamara, Kevin R*
Urbanising Britain — *Kearns, Gerry*
Urbanization and Crime — *Johnson, Eric A*
An Urbanizing World — *United Nations Centre for Human Settlements*
Urgings of the Heart — *Au, Wilkie*
Urinary Continence — *Palmer, Mary H*
Urinary Tract Infections. 5th Ed. — *Kunin, Calvin M*

Urkrains'ka Kukhnia — *Dotsiak, Vira*
Urn Burial — *Greenwood, Kerry*
Les Urnes Scellees — *Ollivier, Emile*
r Urogynecology and Urodynamics. 4th Ed. — *Ostergard, Donald R*
Urological Pathology — *Anatomic Pathology Slide Seminar (60th: 1994: Washington, D.C.)*
L'URSS Et Sa Television — *Feigelson, Kristian*
The Uruguay Round — *Finger, J Michael*
The Uruguay Round — *Schott, Jeffrey J*
The Uruguay Round and the Developing Economies — *Martin, Will*
Uruk: Die Graber — *Boehmer, Rainer Michael*
Urwind — *Carpelan, Bo*
y Us and Them (Illus. by Herbert Tauss) — *Carnes, Jim*
Us Mob — *Mudrooroo*
The USA and the New Europe 1945-1993 — *Duignan, Peter*
USA Cookbook — *Lukins, Sheila*
r USA in Space. Vols. 1-3 — *Magill, Frank Northen*
Usages De La Poesie — *Dumont, Francois*
c The Usborne Big Book of Experiments — *Smith, Alastair*
c The Usborne Big Book of Papercraft — *Smith, Alastair*
cr Usborne First Dictionary — *Wardley, Rachel*
c The Usborne French Songbook for Beginners — *Marks, Anthony*
cr The Usborne Illustrated Atlas of the 20th Century
cr Usborne Illustrated Dictionary — *Bingham, Jane*
cr The Usborne Illustrated Encyclopaedia of Science and Technology
The Use of Arthurian Legend in Hollywood Film — *Umland, Rebecca A*
The Use of Benchmark Dose Approach in Health Risk Assessment — *Crump, Kenny*
Use of Inter-Regional Input-Output Models in Economic Analysis, Economic Development Planning and Project Appraisal — *Kizilyalli, Husnu*
Use of Neuroleptics in Children — *Richardson, Mary Ann*
The Use of Recovery Factors in Trace Analysis — *Parkany, M*
The Use of Scripture in the Damascus Document 1-8, 19-20 — *Campbell, Jonathan*
y Use Your Computer — *Fry, Ronald W*
Used and Rare — *Goldstone, Lawrence*
r The Used Book Lover's Guide to the Pacific Coast States — *Siegel, David S*
Useful Adversaries — *Christensen, Thomas J*
The Useful Cobbler — *Conniff, James*
Useful Toil — *Burnett, John, 1925-*
User-Driven Innovation — *Caminer, David*
A User's Guide to Federal Architect-Engineer Contracts. 2nd Ed. — *Goodowens, James B*
A User's Guide to Operator Algebras — *Fillmore, Peter A*
A User's Guide to the Millennium — *Ballard, J G*
Uses and Abuses — *Busi, Aldo*
The Uses of Literary History — *Brown, Marshall*
The Uses of Reform — *Graham, Michael F*
The Uses of Tradition — *Branch, Michael*
Using and Managing UUCP. 2nd Ed. — *Ravin, Ed*
Using Assessment to Drive School Change — *Maine Association for Supervision and Curriculum Development*
Using Cointegration Analysis in Econometric Modelling — *Harris, R I D*
Using Corel WordPerfect 7 — *Nossiter, Joshua C*
Using Europe, Abusing the Europeans — *Kaiser, Wolfram*
Using Information Technology Effectively in Teaching and Learning — *Somekh, Bridget*
Using MATLAB, SIMULINK and Control System Toolbox — *Cavallo, Alberto*
Using Microsoft FrontPage. Special Ed. — *Randall, Neil*
Using Microsoft Works 4.0 for Windows 95 — *Christoph, Richard T*
Using OCLC under PRISM — *Warwick, Robert T*
Using Secondary Data in Marketing Research — *Patzer, Gordon L*
r Using Spanish Synonyms — *Batchelor, R E*
Using Subject Headings for Online Retrieval — *Drabenstott, Karen Markey*
r Using the Biological Literature. 2nd Ed. — *Davis, Elisabeth B*
Using the Internet in Your Job Search — *Jandt, Fred E*

Using the Internet, Online Services and CD-ROMs for Writing Research and Term Papers — *Harmon, Charles*
Using the M68HC11 Microcontroller — *Skroder, John C*
Using the World Wide Web — *Eager, Bill*
Using the World Wide Web and Creating Home Pages — *Metz, Ray E*
Using Visual Basic — *Sprague, Michael W*
y Using Your PC. 2nd Ed. — *O'Mara, Michael*
Using Z — *Woodcock, Jim*
c USKids History (Illus. by D J Simison) — *Egger-Bovet, Howard*
USMLE Step 1 Review — *Goldberg, Joel S*
r USSC CD-ROM. Electronic Media Version
r Utah (Frommer's Guides)
Utah: A Portrait — *Smart, William B*
r Utah Energy: Statistical Abstract. 5th Ed.
Utah, the Right Place — *Alexander, Thomas G*
Utah: The Struggle for Statehood — *Verdoia, Ken*
c Utahraptor: The Deadliest Dinosaur (Illus. by Donna Braginetz) — *Lessem, Don*
Utilitarianism as a Public Philosophy — *Goodin, Robert E*
The Utility of Splendor — *Klingensmith, Samuel John*
Utmost Savagery — *Alexander, Joseph H*
Uto — *De Carlo, Andrea*
Utopia — *More, Thomas*
Utopia and Dissent — *Smith, Richard Candida*
Utopia and History in Mexico — *Baudot, Georges*
Utopia in the Present Tense — *Camboni, Marina*
Utopia in Zion — *Russell, Raymond*
Utopia Parkway — *Solomon, Deborah*
A Utopian Experiment in Kentucky — *Sears, Richard D*
Utopias, Dolphins and Computers — *Midgley, Mary*
UV Lasers — *Duley, W W*
Uwe Johnson — *Neumann, Bernd*
yr UXL Biographies. Electronic Media Version
r Uzbekistan — *Macleod, Calum*

V

V.C. Andrews: A Critical Companion — *Huntley, E D*
y V Is for Vampire — *Skal, David J*
V Labirinte Doktriny — *Tsakunov, S V*
V.O. Kliuchevskii, Historian of Russia — *Byrnes, Robert F*
V.S. Naipaul — *Mustafa, Fawzia*
Va Savoir — *Ducharme, Rejean*
r Vacations That Can Change Your Life — *Lederman, Ellen*
Vaccines 96 (Illus. by Maurice Sendak)
Vad Du Vill — *Radstrom, Niklas*
Vagabond of Verse — *Mackay, James*
Vagabonds (Ollerenshaw). Audio Version — *Cox, Josephine*
r Vaginal Operations. 2nd Ed. — *Reiffenstuhl, Gunther*
A Valentine Bouquet — *Girard, Paula Tanner*
Valentine Delights
Valentine for Mr. Wonderful — *Frankenthaler, Helen*
Valentine Place — *Lehman, David, 1948-*
Valentine Treasury — *Brenner, Robert*
Valerius Flaccus, Argonautica, Book V — *Wijsman, H J W*
Validation Practices for Biotechnology Products — *Shillenn, James K*
Valle-Inclan and the Theatre — *Vila, Xavier*
Valley Forge — *Treese, Lorett*
A Valley in Italy — *St. Aubin De Teran, Lisa*
The Valley of Decision — *Davenport, Marcia*
c The Valley of the Kings — *Clayton, Peter A*
Valley of the Shadow — *Helfert, Erich Anton*
Valley of the Spirits — *Kolata, Alan L*
Valley of the Thousand Smokes — *Cushman, Dan*
Valois Guyenne — *Harris, Robin*
Valuation of Interest-Sensitive Financial Instruments — *Babbel, David F*
Value at Risk — *Jorion, Philippe*
Value Change in Global Perspective — *Abramson, Paul R*
Value for Money — *Iacobucci, Edward*
Value in Ethics and Economics — *Anderson, Elizabeth*
The Value in the Valley — *Vanzant, Iyanla*
Value Judgement — *Griffin, James*
The Value of Family — *Westheimer, Ruth K*
The Value of Life — *Kellert, Stephen R*
The Value to Libraries of Special Services Provided by Library Suppliers — *Capital Planning Information*
Values, Nature, and Culture in the American Corporation — *Frederick, William C*
Values of Art, Pictures, Poetry and Music — *Budd, Malcolm*
The Values of Precision — *Wise, M Norton*
Valuing Climate Change — *Fankhauser, Samuel*
Valuing Diversity in the School System — *Bellanca, James*
Valuing the Environment — *Malnes, Raino*
Vamp: The Rise and Fall of Theda Bara — *Golden, Eve*
c The Vampire — *Rice, Bebe Faas*
The Vampire State and Other Myths and Fallacies about the U.S. Economy — *Block, Fred L*
Vampires — *Konstantinos*
y Vampires — *Scavone, Daniel C*
Vampires, Mummies, and Liberals — *Glover, David*
c The Vampire's Visit — *Poulsen, David A*
y Vampires, Wine and Roses — *Stephens, John Richard*
c Van Gogh (Illus. by Jean-Philippe Chabot)
c Van Gogh — *Crispino, Enrica*
y Van Gogh (Illus. by Francesca D'Ottavi) — *Pescio, Claudio*
c The Van Gogh Cafe — *Rylant, Cynthia*

Van Gogh's Bad Cafe — *Tuten, Frederic*
Van Gogh's Progress — *Zemel, Carol*
r Van Nostrand's Scientific Encyclopedia. 8th Ed., Vols. 1-2 — *Considine, Douglas M*
Vanadium Compounds — *Srivastava, Aschok K*
Vancouver Island Letters of Edmund Hope Verney 1862-65 — *Verney, Edmund Hope*
Vancouver's Chinatown — *Anderson, Kay J*
Vand Til Torstig Jord — *Michelsen, I*
Vanilla Blood — *Martin, Nancy*
Vanished Churches of the City of London — *Huelin, Gordon*
c Vanished! The Mysterious Disappearance of Amelia Earhart (Illus. by Ying-Hwa Hu) — *Kulling, Monica*
y The Vanishing American Jew — *Dershowitz, Alan M*
c Vanishing Clues — *Morris, Gilbert*
Vanishing Flora — *Stermer, Dugald, 1936-*
Vanishing Point — *West, Morris*
Vanishing Songbirds — *Porter, Eliot*
y Vanishing Star — *Baer, Judy*
The Vanishing Vision — *Day, James*
Vanitas — *Somtow, S P*
y Vanity — *Power, Vicki*
Vanity Fair — *Harden, Edgar F*
c Los Vaqueros: Our First Cowboys — *Munson, Sammye*
Vaquita and Other Stories — *Pearlman, Edith*
Variability in Human Fertility — *Rosetta, Lyliane*
Variable Cloud — *Gaite, Carmen Martin*
y Variations on a Dream — *Paul, Bette*
Varieties of Protestantism — *Marty, Martin E*
Varieties of Southern History — *Clayton, Bruce*
The Variorum Edition of the Poetry of John Donne. Vol. 8 — *Donne, John*
Various Atwoods — *York, Lorraine M*
Various Positions — *Nadel, Ira Bruce*
Varner, Verner, Werner Families of America — *Palmer, Janice B*
Vascular Technology — *Rumwell, Claudia*
Vasiliy Grossman: The Genesis and Evolution of a Russian Heretic — *Ellis, Frank*
Vasily Kandinsky: A Colourful Life — *Barnett, Vivian Endicott*
Vaste Est La Prison — *Djebar, Assia*
Vatican Radio — *Matelski, Marilyn J*
The Vatican Vergil — *Wright, David H*
Vatmaar: 'N Lewendagge Verhaal Van 'N Tyd Wat Nie Meer Is Nie — *Scholtz, A H M*
Vdekja Lexon Gazeten — *Marku, Rudolf*
Vdekje Pa Emer — *Kraja, Mehmet*
Ve Bien Dong — *Trang, Chan*
Vector Mechanics for Engineers. 6th Ed. — *Beer, Ferdinand Pierre*
Vectors in Physics and Engineering — *Durrant, A V*
Veda and Torah — *Holdrege, Barbara A*
Vedhuggaren I Natten — *Sandelin, Peter*
Vega — *Dondeyne, Desire*
Vegas Heat — *Michaels, Fern*
Vegas Rich (Merlington). Audio Version — *Michaels, Fern*
De Vegetabilibus. Bk. 6, Pts. 1-2 — *Albertus, Magnus, Saint*
Vegetables — *Joyce, Kristin*
c Vegetables and Herbs (Illus. by Cecilia Fitzsimmons) — *Fitzsimmons, Cecilia*
The Vegetarian Bistro — *Spieler, Marlena*
The Vegetarian Child — *Moll, Lucy*
Vegetarian Cookbook — *Ridgway, Judy*
y Vegetarian Cooking of the Mediterranean — *Schinharl, Cornelia*

c Vegetarian Factfinder (Illus. by Adrienne Hartman) — *Klavan, Ellen*
The Vegetarian Hearth — *Goldstein, Darra*
Vegetarian Planet — *Emmons, Didi*
Vegetarian Soups for All Seasons — *Atlas, Nava*
The Vegetarian Table: India — *Devi, Yamuna*
r The Vegetarian Traveler — *Civic, Jed*
y The Vegetation of Rivers, Lakes, and Swamps (Illus. by Luis Rizo) — *Llamas, Andreu*
Vehicle for God — *Zimany, Roland D*
Vehicle Security Systems — *Brown, A L*
Veiled Desire — *Power, Kim*
Veiled Half-Truths — *Mabro, Judy*
y The Veiled One (Wilding). Audio Version — *Rendell, Ruth*
Veiled Threats — *Carroll, Michael P*
Veiled Threats — *Simon, Frank*
The Vein of Gold — *Cameron, Julia*
The Vein of Gold (Cameron). Audio Version — *Cameron, Julia*
Vejgaze — *Liepa, Anita*
Velazquez in Seville — *Davies, David, 1937-*
Velazquez, Los Borrachos, and Painting at the Court of Philip IV — *Orso, Steven N*
Velda Newman: A Painter's Approach to Quilt Design — *Newman, Velda*
Velocities: New and Selected Poems — *Dobyns, Stephen*
The Velvet Horn — *Lytle, Andrew*
The Velvet Years — *Shore, Stephen*
c The Velveteen Rabbit (Illus. by Donna Green) — *Williams, Margery*
Vendetta: Lucky's Revenge — *Collins, Jackie*
The Veneration of Divine Justice — *Rosenberg, Roy A*
The Venetian's Wife — *Bantock, Nick*
Venezuela and the United States — *Ewell, Judith*
Venezuela: The Challenge of Competitiveness — *Enright, Michael J*
Venezuela: The Political Economy of Oil — *Boue, Juan Carlos*
Venezuelan Democracy under Stress — *McCoy, Jennifer*
Venice and Antiquity — *Brown, Patricia Fortini*
Venice and the Grand Tour — *Redford, Bruce*
Venice's Hidden Enemies — *Martin, John*
Venona: Soviet Espionage and the American Response 1939-1957 — *Benson, Obert Louis*
Le Vent Majeur — *Gagnon, Madeleine*
Le Ventilateur — *Detambel, Regine*
Ventilation and Indoor Air Quality in Hospitals — *NATO Advanced Research Workshop on Ventilation and Indoor Air Quality in Hospitals (1996: Milan, Italy)*
Venture Capital and the Indian Financial Sector — *Ramesh, S*
Ventures into Greek History — *Worthington, Ian*
y Venus among the Fishes — *Hall, Elizabeth*
Venus and Don Juan — *Frost, Carol*
c Venus Flytraps and Waterwheels — *Gentle, Victor*
y Venus Revealed — *Grinspoon, David Harry*
Venus to the Hoop — *Corbett, Sara*
Vera Brittain: A Feminist Life — *Gorham, Deborah*
Vera Brittain: A Life — *Berry, Paul*
The Veracruz Blues — *Winegardner, Mark*
y The Veracruz Blues. Audio Version — *Winegardner, Mark*
Un Verano Incesante — *De La Paz, Luis*
Verbal Aspect in the Greek of the New Testament — *Porter, Stanley E*
c Verdi (Illus. by Janell Cannon) — *Cannon, Janell*
Verdict Unsafe — *McGown, Jill*

Verdilak — *Hampton, Bo*
Verfruhte Tierliebe — *Lange-Muller, Katja*
Verfuhrungen — *Streeruwitz, Marlene*
Das Vergangene Reich — *Hildebrand, Klaus*
y Vergil's Aeneid — *Bloom, Harold*
Vergil's Eclogues — *Virgil*
Verification 1995
Verification 1996
The Verilog Hardware Description Language. 3rd Ed.
  — *Thomas, D E*
A Veritable Dynamo — *Holt, Stephen*
Veritas — *Lashner, William*
Veritas (Howard). Audio Version — *Lashner, William*
La Verite Chretienne A L'Age Du Pluralisme
  Religieux — *O'Leary, Joseph S*
Vermeer and the Art of Painting — *Wheelock, Arthur
  K*
Vermeer: Faith in Painting — *Arasse, Daniel*
Vermont Recollections — *Beck, Jane*
Vernunftkritik Und Patriarchatskritik — *Waschescio,
  Petra*
Veronica — *Christopher, Nicholas*
c Veronica's First Year (Illus. by Kay Life)
  — *Rheingrover, Jean Sasso*
Versailles: The History of the Gardens and Their
  Sculpture — *Pincas, Stephane*
Verse with Prose from Petronius to Dante — *Dronke,
  Peter*
Versed in Country Things — *Frost, Robert*
Versions of Deconversion — *Barbour, John D*
Versohnung Und Progression — *Ferner, Jurgen*
c Versos De Palmo E Meio (Illus. by Helena Fernandes)
  — *Viana, Antonio Manuel Couto*
Die Verspatete Stadt. Pts. 1-2 — *Reif, Heinz*
Die Verspielte Freiheit — *Mommsen, Hans*
Vertamae Cooks in the Americas' Family Kitchen
  — *Grosvenor, Vertamae*
c Vertebrates — *Silverstein, Alvin*
Vertigo: A Memoir — *DeSalvo, Louise A*
c The Very Best Book (Illus. by Vitaliy Romanenko)
  — *Rosenfeld, Dina*
The Very Best Men — *Thomas, Evan*
c The Very Best of Aesop's Fables (Illus. by Charlotte
  Voake) — *Clark, Margaret*
The Very Bloody History of Britain (Jones). Audio
  Version — *Farman, John*
c The Very Busy Spider (Illus. by Eric Carle) — *Carle,
  Eric*
Very Close to Trouble — *Grant, Johnny*
y The Very First Light — *Mather, John C*
c The Very Hungry Caterpillar (Illus. by Eric Carle)
  — *Carle, Eric*
c The Very Hungry Lion (Illus. by Indrapramit Roy)
  — *Wolf, Gita*
c A Very Important Day (Illus. by Catherine Stock)
  — *Herold, Maggie Rugg*
The Very Inside — *Lim-Hing, Sharon*
A Very Large Soul — *Laurence, Margaret*
c Very Little Duck (Illus. by Ernie Eldredge) — *Patrick,
  Ellen*
c The Very Lonely Firefly (Illus. by Eric Carle)
  — *Carle, Eric*
A Very Long Engagement — *Japrisot, Sebastien*
A Very Long Weekend — *Berebitsky, William*
c The Very Quiet Cricket — *Carle, Eric*
y The Very Real Ghost Book of Christina Rose
  — *Deem, James M*
A Very Short War — *Guilmartin, John F, Jr.*
A Very Violent Rebel — *House, Ellen Renshaw*
Vesicles — *Rosoff, Morton*
Vessels of Time — *Ostor, Akos*
The Vest-Pocket CPA. 2nd Ed. — *Dauber, Nicky*
Vet Xuoc Dau Doi — *Tran, Doan Nho*
Veterinaires — *Lamarche-Vadel, Bernard*
c Veterinarians Help Animals — *Greene, Carol*
r Veterinary Drug Handbook. 2nd Ed. — *Plumb,
  Donald C*
r Veterinary Management of Tortoises and Turtles
  — *McArthur, Stuart*
Veterinary Parasitology. 2nd Ed. — *Urquhart, G M*
r Viacheslav Ivanov: A Reference Guide — *Davidson,
  Pamela*
Vibrations and Waves. 2nd Ed. — *Gough, William*
y The Vicar of Sorrows (Davidson). Audio Version
  — *Wilson, A N*
y The Vicar of Wakefield (Tull). Audio Version
  — *Goldsmith, Oliver*
The Vicar of Wrexhill — *Trollope, Fanny*
yr The Vice Presidents — *Waldrup, Carole Chandler*
Vichy Law and the Holocaust in France — *Weisberg,
  Richard H*

A Vicious Circle — *Craig, Amanda*
Vicky's Supermac — *Weisz, Victor*
The Victim — *Bellow, Saul*
Victimized Daughters — *Jacobs, Janet Liebman*
Victims and the Postmodern Narrative — *Ledbetter,
  Mark*
Victims of Memory — *Pendergrast, Mark*
y Victims of Teen Violence — *Zeinert, Karen*
Victims or Criminals? — *Singh, Priyam*
Victor Griffuelhes and French Syndicalism 1895-1922
  — *Vandervort, Bruce*
Victor Hugo Ou Le Calcul Des Profondeurs
  — *Seebacher, Jacques*
Victor Schoelcher Et L'Abolition De L'Esclavage
  — *Schmidt, Nelly*
Victoria — *Hamsun, Knut*
Victoria and Albert — *Hough, Richard*
y Victoria and Her Times — *Chiflet, Jean-Loup*
The Victoria History of the County of Essex. Vol. 9
Victoria Victorious (Franklin). Audio Version
  — *Plaidy, Jean*
r Victorian America 1876 to 1913 — *Shifflett, Crandall
  A*
Victorian Biography — *Amigoni, David*
r Victorian Biography — *Bell, Peter, 1944-*
c Victorian Christmas — *Kalman, Bobbie*
A Victorian Christmas — *Wolf, Jill*
Victorian Churches — *Curl, James Stevens*
The Victorian City — *Morris, R J*
Victorian Contexts — *Roston, Murray*
r Victorian Database on CD-ROM 1970-1995. Electronic
  Media Version — *Chandhuri, Brahma*
Victorian Explorer — *Stairs, William G*
c Victorian Factory — *Tolhurst, Marilyn*
Victorian Fiction — *Sutherland, John*
Victorian Girls — *Fletcher, Sheila*
c The Victorian Home (Illus. by Barbara Bedell)
  — *Kalman, Bobbie*
Victorian Icon — *Dunstan, David*
Victorian Identities — *Robbins, Ruth*
Victorian Illustration — *Goldman, Paul*
Victorian Insolvency — *Lester, V Markham*
Victorian Literature and Culture — *Maynard, John*
Victorian Love Stories — *Flint, Kate*
Victorian Majolica — *Bockol, Leslie*
Victorian Masculinities — *Sussman, Herbert*
A Victorian Naturalist — *Jay, Eileen*
The Victorian Nude — *Smith, Alison*
Victorian Periodicals and Victorian Society — *Vann, J
  Don*
Victorian Photography, Painting, and Poetry — *Smith,
  Lindsay*
Victorian Poetry — *Armstrong, Isobel*
r Victorian Poetry — *Mazzeno, Laurence W*
A Victorian Seaside Resort — *Marsden, Vera*
The Victorian Social-Problem Novel — *Guy, Josephine
  M*
Victorian Urban Settings — *Mancoff, Debra N*
The Victorian Watercolours and Drawings in the
  Collection of Her Majesty the Queen. Vols. 1-2
  — *Millar, Delia*
Victorian Women Poets — *Bristow, Joseph*
Victorian Women Poets — *Leighton, Angela*
The Victorians and the Stuart Heritage — *Lang,
  Timothy*
The Victorians: British Painting 1837-1901 — *Warner,
  Malcolm, 1953-*
c Victoria's a Star (Illus. by Cathy Wilcox) — *Gervay,
  Susanne*
The Victorious Christ — *Sleeper, C Freeman*
c Victor's Quest (Illus. by Kim Gamble) — *Freeman,
  Pamela*
Victory: An Island Tale — *Conrad, Joseph*
Victory at Any Cost — *Currey, Cecil B*
Victory in the East — *France, John*
Vicus — *Makowski, Krzysztof*
La Vida Cotidiana En La Galicia Del Antiguo
  Regimen — *Saavedra, Pegerto*
La Vida De Guarnicion En Las Ciudades Americanas
  De La Ilustracion — *Marchena Fernandez, Juan*
Vida Y Milagros De La Farandula De Cuba — *Rosell,
  Rosendo*
c Video — *Biel, Jackie*
Video — *Payant, Rene*
Video Acquisitions and Cataloging — *Scholtz, James C*
Video Art — *Schneider, Ira*
Video Art — *University of Pennsylvania Institute of
  Contemporary Art*
Video by Artists — *Gale, Peggy*
Video by Artists 2 — *Town, Elke*
Video Coding — *Torres, Luis*

Video Culture — *Hanhardt, John G*
Video Engineering. 2nd Ed. — *Inglis, Andrew F*
y Video Games — *Erlbach, Arlene*
p Video Librarian
Video Production for Elementary and Middle Schools
  — *Kyker, Keith*
Video-Visions — *Price, Jonathan*
Videocassette Instructor's Manual with Script for Con
  Mucho Gusto
Videoconferencing and Videotelephony — *Schaphorst,
  Richard*
Videography: Video Medium as Art and Culture
  — *Cubitt, Sean*
r VideoHound's Complete Guide to Cult Flicks and
  Trash Pics
p Videomaker
r Videos of African and African-Related Performance
  — *Lems-Dworkin, Carol*
La Vie Courante — *Peju, Pierre*
La Vie De Saint Alexis (Hemming)
La Vie Interpretee — *Broussard, Yves*
c La Vieja Letivia Y El Monte De Los Pesares (Illus. by
  Rudy Gutierrez) — *Mohr, Nicholasa*
Las Viejas Fantasiosas — *Orphee, Elvira*
c La Viejecita Que No Le Tenia Miedo A Nada (Illus.
  by Megan Lloyd) — *Williams, Linda D*
r Vienna. 2nd Ed. — *Klein, Wilhelm*
La Vierge Du Grand Retour — *Confiant, Raphael*
De Vierplichte Tewerkstelling In Duitsland 1942-1945
Viet Len Troi Xanh — *Hoang, Khoi Phong*
Viet Nam Theo Duong Nao Vao The Ky 21? — *Pham,
  Kim Vinh*
Viet Nam Van Hoc Su Viet Van — *Pham, The Ngu*
The Viet Nam War/The American War
  — *Christopher, Renny*
c Vietnam — *Allard, Denise*
Vietnam — *Balaban, John*
c Vietnam — *Hansen, Ole Steen*
c Vietnam — *Simmons, Pat*
Vietnam 1945 — *Marr, David*
Vietnam: A Book of Changes — *Epstein, Mitch*
Vietnam: A Kick Start Guide for Business Travellers
  — *Brooks, Guy*
Vietnam: A Portrait of Its People at War — *Chanoff,
  David*
Vietnam Protest Theatre — *Alter, Nora M*
Vietnam: Revolution in Transition — *Duiker, William
  J*
Vietnam: The Australian Dilemma — *Burstall, Terry*
c Vietnam: The Boat People Search for a Home (Illus.
  by John Isaac) — *Isaac, John*
c Vietnam: The Culture — *Kalman, Bobbie*
c Vietnam: The Land — *Kalman, Bobbie*
c Vietnam: The People — *Kalman, Bobbie*
y Vietnam War — *Gay, Kathlyn*
The Vietnam War — *Gilbert, Marc Jason*
r The Vietnam War — *Olson, James Stuart*
r Vietnam War Literature. 2nd Ed. — *Newman, John,
  1942-*
Vietnam, We've All Been There — *Schroeder, Eric
  James*
Vietnamerica — *Bass, Thomas A*
y The View from Here — *Jackson, Brian Keith*
y The View from Saturday — *Konigsburg, E L*
y View from the Air (Illus. by Richard Brown)
  — *Lindbergh, Reeve*
A View from the Ridge — *West, Morris*
The View from the Top — *Barker, Paul*
A View to a Death in the Morning — *Cartmill, Matt*
View with a Grain of Sand — *Szymborska, Wislawa*
The Viewfinder — *Lawrence, Anthony*
Viewing Violence — *Levine, Madeline*
Vigil — *Panych, Morris*
The Vigil — *Williams, C K*
The Vigilant God — *Davies, Horton*
Los Vigilantes — *Eltit, Diamela*
Les Vignes De Sainte Colombe — *Signol, Christian*
c Viking — *Morley, Jacqueline*
The Viking-Age Gold and Silver of Scotland A.D.
  850-1100 — *Graham-Campbell, James*
c Viking Explorers (Illus. by Claudia Saraceni)
  — *Pruneti, Luigi*
c A Viking Town (Illus. by Mark Bergin) — *Macdonald,
  Fiona*
c The Viking Treasury of Children's Stories — *Trenter,
  Anna*
c The Vikings — *Allard, Denise*
c Vikings — *Davies, Kath*
c The Vikings in Scotland — *Dargie, Richard*
Viktor Frankl--Recollections — *Frankl, Viktor Emil*
Den Vilde Jomfru — *Hansen, Anne Chaplin*

Vile Bodies — *Waugh, Evelyn*
La Villa In Italia — *Visentini, Margherita Azzi*
c The Village Basket Weaver (Illus. by George Crespo) — *London, Jonathan*
The Village in Court — *Schulte, Regina*
A Village in France — *Clergeau, Louis*
Village Life in Late Tsarist Russia — *Semyonova Tian-Shanskaia, Olga*
Village Matters — *Shaw, Rebecca*
The Village of Cannibals — *Corbin, Alain*
The Village of Silwan — *Ussishkin, David*
c The Village Sings — *Fitzmaurice, Gabriel*
The Village That Died for England — *Wright, Patrick*
Villagers of the Maros — *O'Shea, John M*
Villanova University 1842-1992 — *Contosta, David R*
Villeneuve: My First Season in Formula 1 — *Villeneuve, Jacques*
Villon's Last Will — *Hunt, Tony*
Vim and Vinegar — *Moore, Melodie*
Vincent D'Indy and His World — *Thomson, Andrew*
c Vincent Van Gogh — *Harrison, Peter*
c Vincent Van Gogh — *Malam, John*
c Vincent Van Gogh (Illus. by Jean Philippe Chabot) — *Sorbier, F*
y Vincent Van Gogh: A Life — *Callow, Philip*
y Vincent Van Gogh: Artist — *Tyson, Peter*
Vincent Van Gogh: Drawings. Vol. 1 — *Heugten, Sjraar Van*
Vincentius Lauro 1572-1578. Bk. 1 — *Korolko, Miroslaw*
The Vinegar Jar — *Doherty, Berlie*
The Vineland Papers — *Green, Geoffrey*
Vineyard Tales — *Asher, Gerald*
Vingt Etudes Sur Prevost D'Exiles — *Sgard, Jean*
The Vintage Book of Classic Crime — *Dibdin, Michael*
y The Vintage Book of Contemporary World Poetry — *McClatchy, J D*
The Vintage Book of Historical Feminism — *Schneir, Miriam*
Vintage Farm Tractors — *Sanders, Ralph W*
Vintage Fashions for Women 1920s-1940s — *Harris, Kristina*
Vintage Feasting — *Sterling, Joy*
Vintage Illustration — *Martin, Rick*
Vintage Talk — *Schaefer, Dennis*
Violence against Women and Children — *Adams, Carol J*
Violence and Mediation in Contemporary Culture — *Bogue, Ronald*
Violence and Miracle in the Fourteenth Century — *Goodich, Michael E*
Violence and Religion — *Sproxton, Judy*
yr Violence and the Media — *Newton, David E*
y Violence and the Media — *Sherrow, Victoria*
Violence as Obscenity — *Saunders, Kevin W*
Violence in America — *Goldstein, Arnold P*
Violence in Argentine Literature — *Foster, David William*
y Violence in Schools — *Day, Nancy*
Violence in the Black Patch of Kentucky and Tennessee — *Marshall, Suzanne*
The Violence of Our Lives — *Parker, Tony*
Violence: Our Deadly Epidemic and Its Causes — *Gilligan, James*
Violence: Reflections on a National Epidemic — *Gilligan, James*
Violence, Silence and Anger — *Lashgari, Dierdre*
Violence: The Unrelenting Assault on Human Dignity — *Huber, Wolfgang*
Violence Unveiled — *Bailie, Gil*
Violencia En La Region Andina — *Gonzalez, Fernan E*
The Violent Bear It Away — *O'Connor, Flannery*
The Violent Couple — *Stacey, William A*
Violent Crimes — *Holton, Hugh*
Violent Land — *Courtwright, David T*
A Violent Life — *Pasolini, Pier Paolo*
The Violent Muse — *Howlett, Jana*
c Violet (Illus. by Lynne Woodcock Cravath) — *Leverich, Kathleen*
Violet: Life and Loves of Violet Gordon Woodhouse — *Douglas-Home, Jessica*
Violet Twilights — *Sodergran, Edith*
Violette Leduc: Mothers, Lovers, and Language — *Hughes, Alex*
Violette's Embrace — *Zackheim, Michele*
The Violin — *Menuhin, Yehudi*
r The Violin Family and Its Makers in the British Isles — *Harvey, Brian W*
r Violin Virtuosos — *Roth, Henry, 1916-*
Violinernes Kemi — *Christensen, Karsten Brejnbjerg*
The Vipers' Club — *Richardson, John H*

The Virago Book of Spirituality — *Anderson, Sarah*
The Virago Book of Women Gardeners — *Kellaway, Deborah*
y Viral Sex — *Goudsmit, Jaap*
Virgil and the Moderns — *Ziolkowski, Theodore*
Virgil as Orpheus — *Lee, M Owen*
Virgil Earp: Western Peace Officer — *Chaput, Donald*
Virgil in English (Gransden) — *Virgil*
Virgil in Medieval England — *Baswell, Christopher*
Virgil Thomson: Composer on the Aisle — *Tommasini, Anthony*
Virgil's Aeneid — *Putnam, Michael C J*
The Virgin and the Bride — *Cooper, Kate*
The Virgin and the Dinosaur — *Garcia Y Robertson, R*
The Virgin Blue — *Chevalier, Tracy*
The Virgin Goddess — *Benko, Stephen*
Virgin Heat — *Shames, Laurence*
y The Virgin in the Rose Bower (McDonough). Audio Version — *Oates, Joyce Carol*
Virgin Land — *Smith, Henry Nash*
Virgin Mother, Maiden Queen — *Hackett, Helen*
The Virgin of the Andes — *Damian, Carol*
c Virginia — *Barrett, Tracy*
r Virginia Landmarks of Black History — *Loth, Calder*
Virginia Woolf — *Hanson, Clare*
Virginia Woolf — *King, James*
Virginia Woolf — *Lee, Hermione*
Virginia Woolf: A Biography — *Bell, Quentin*
r Virginia Woolf A to Z — *Hussey, Mark*
Virginia Woolf against Empire — *Phillips, Kathy J*
Virginia Woolf and Samuel Johnson — *Rosenberg, Beth Carole*
Virginia Woolf: Texts and Contexts — *Conference on Virginia Woolf (5th: 1995: Otterbein College)*
Virginia Woolf's Subject and the Subject of Ethics — *Schroeder, Steven*
y Virginia's General — *Marrin, Albert*
Virgins of God — *Elm, Susanna*
Virtual Archaeology — *Forte, Maurizio*
Virtual Classrooms — *Hobbs, Vicki*
The Virtual Community — *Rheingold, Howard*
Virtual Connections — *Warschauer, Mark*
Virtual Destruction — *Anderson, Kevin J*
Virtual Equality — *Vaid, Urvashi*
Virtual Help Desk — *Thomas, Andrew*
Virtual Individuals, Virtual Groups — *Oravec, Jo Ann*
Virtual Justice — *Uviller, H Richard*
Virtual Muse — *Hartman, Charles O*
The Virtual Office Survival Handbook — *Bredin, Alice*
y Virtual Reality — *Weiss, Ann E*
The Virtual School Library — *Kuhlthau, Carol Collier*
y Virtual Sexual Reality — *Rayban, Chloe*
c Virtual World — *Westwood, Chris*
Virtually Normal — *Sullivan, Andrew*
y Virtually Now — *Schinto, Jeanne*
Virtue, Corruption, and Self-Interest — *Matthews, Richard H*
Virtues and Reasons — *Hursthouse, Rosalind*
Virtue's Faults — *Alliston, April*
Virtues of the Will — *Kent, Bonnie*
Virtue's Own Feature — *Beauregard, David N*
Virtuosity, Charisma, and Social Order — *Silber, Ilana Friedrich*
Virtuous Lives — *Salitan, Lucille*
Virtuous Reality — *Katz, J*
A Virtuous Woman — *Gibbons, Kaye*
Virus — *Buchanan, Bill*
y Virus — *Hoh, Diane*
Virus Detection and Elimination — *Skardhamar, Rune*
y Virus Ground Zero — *Regis, Ed*
y Virus Hunter — *Peters, C J*
y Virus X — *Ryan, Frank*
Visible and Apostolic — *Cornwall, Robert D*
Visible and Invisible Realms — *Wiener, Margaret J*
y The Vision — *Johnson, Pete*
Vision 2001 — *Flanagan, Jana Ricketts*
A Vision Achieved — *Lemmon, David*
Vision and Textuality — *Melville, Stephen*
A Vision Betrayed — *Ross, Andrew*
A Vision for the World Economy — *Lawrence, Robert Z*
y Vision Magica — *Ditzinger, Thomas*
The Vision of Kings — *Brand, Michael*
The Vision of Richard Weaver — *Scotchie, Joseph*
The Vision of the Anointed — *Sowell, Thomas*
Vision Quest. Electronic Media Version — *Doll, Don*
Vision/Re-Vision: Adapting Contemporary American Fiction by Women to Film — *Lupack, Barbara T*
c The Vision Seeker (Illus. by Paul Morin) — *Whetung, James*

Vision: Variations on Some Berkeleian Themes — *Schwartz, Robert*
Visionaries — *Mosher, Bill*
Visionaries: The Spanish Republic and the Reign of Christ — *Christian, William A, 1944-*
The Visionary D.H. Lawrence — *Montgomery, Robert E*
Visionary Experience in the Golden Age of Spanish Art — *Stoichita, Victor Ieronim*
Visionary Fictions — *Ahearn, Edward J*
Visionary Worlds — *Irwin, Lee*
Visions and Longings — *Furlong, Monica*
p Visions International
Visions of Arcadia — *Woods, May*
Visions of Cody (Parker). Audio Version — *Kerouac, Jack*
Visions of Empire — *Miller, David Philip*
Visions of Modernity — *Nolan, Mary*
Visions of New York State — *Tantillo, Leonard F*
Visions of Power — *Faure, Bernard*
Visions of Presence in Modern American Poetry — *Scott, Nathan A*
Visions of Roses — *Beales, Peter*
The Visions of Sor Maria De Agreda — *Colahan, Clark*
Visions of Sound — *Diamond, Beverley*
Visions of the East — *Bernstein, Matthew*
Visions of the Modern — *Golding, John*
Visions of the Past — *Rosenstone, Robert A*
Visions of the People — *Joyce, Patrick*
Visions of the Sociological Tradition — *Levine, Donald N*
Visions of Wonder — *Hartwell, David G*
A Visit to Strangers — *Swan, Gladys*
c A Visit to William Blake's Inn (Illus. by Alice Provensen) — *Willard, Nancy*
c A Visit with Great-Grandma — *Addy, Sharon H*
The Visitation — *Reidy, Sue*
Visitation Articles and Injunctions of the Early Stuart Church. Vol. 1 — *Fincham, Kenneth*
Visitation of England and Wales. Vols. 7-9 — *Howard, Joseph Jackson*
Visiting the Mino Kilns — *Barriskill, Janet*
Visitor Profile Study
c La Vista (Illus. by Francisco Arredondo) — *Sanchez, Isidro*
La Viste Des Eglises Du Diocese De Lausanne En 1453. Vols. 1-2 — *Wildermann, Ansgar*
Visual and Active Supervision — *Williams, Antony*
Visual Arts in the Twentieth Century — *Lucie-Smith, Edward*
Visual Basic 4.0 Internet Programming — *Franklin, Carl*
Visual Basic Programming — *Gersting, Judith L*
Visual dBASE Programming — *Irwin, Michael R*
r Visual Dictionary: English-French-German-Spanish — *Corbeil, Jean-Claude*
yr The Visual Dictionary of Chemistry — *Challoner, Jack*
yr The Visual Dictionary of Human Anatomy
Visual Display — *Cooke, Lynne*
Visual Explanations — *Tufte, Edward R*
r The Visual Food Encyclopedia
Visual Interface Design for Windows — *Howlett, Virginia*
The Visual J++ Handbook — *Murray, William H*
Visual Modeling Technique — *Tkach, Daniel*
Visual Persuasion — *Messaris, Paul*
Visual Programming with HP VEE — *Helsel, Robert*
r Visual QuickStart Guide to Internet Explorer for Windows 95/NT — *Schwarz, Steven*
Visual Resources for Design — *Godfrey, Jenny*
Visual Servoing — *Hashimoto, Koichi*
Visualization and Optimization — *Jones, Christopher V*
Visualization Techniques in Space and Atmospheric Sciences — *Szuszczewicz, E P*
Visuelle Poesie Aus Den USA — *Andryczuk, Hartmut*
Vita Di Federico Di Montefeltro — *De'Rossi, Giovangirolamo*
Vita Mathematica — *Calinger, Ronald*
Vital Crises in Italian Cinema — *Sitney, P Adams*
Vital Dust — *De Duve, Christian*
yr The Vital Guide to Combat Guns and Infantry Weapons — *Bishop, Chris*
yr The Vital Guide to Fighting Aircraft of World War II — *Leverington, Karen*
The Vital Minute — *Ormerod, Roger*
r Vital Records of Sandwich, Massachusetts to 1885. Vols. 1-3 — *Kardell, Caroline Lewis*

Title Index

r Vital Records of the Towns of Barnstable and Sandwich — *Smith, Leonard H, Jr.*

Vital Signs — *Coalter, Milton J*

Vital Signs — *Tuttleton, James W*

Vitale E Agricola — *Fasoli, Gina*

Vitamania: Vitamins in American Culture — *Apple, Rima D*

Vitamins in Human Health and Disease — *Basu, Tapan K*

Viva: Women and Popular Protest in Latin America — *Radcliffe, Sarah A*

La Vivandiere Pas De Six — *Saint-Leon, Arthur*

The Vivien Greene Doll's House Collection — *Greene, Vivien*

Vivienne Westwood: Fashion, Perversity and the Sixties Laid Bare — *Vermorel, Fred*

The Vixen: Poems — *Merwin, W S*

Vladimir Nabokov: The American Years — *Boyd, Brian*

Vladimir Nabokov: The Russian Years — *Boyd, Brian*

Vnutri I Vne Bollshogo Domall — *Berezhkov, Vasilii*

r Vocabulaire Trilingue Des Vehicules De Transport Routier

Vocal Fold Physiology — *Davis, Pamela J*

Vocal Pathologies — *Dworkin, James Paul*

Vodka, Tears, and Lenin's Angel — *Gould, Jennifer*

The Vogue of Revolution in Poor Countries — *Colburn, Forrest D*

Voice and Data Communications Handbook — *Bates, Bud*

Voice and Equality — *Verba, Sidney*

Voice for the Mad — *Gollaher, David L*

Voice from the Desert — *Gaillot, Jacques*

Voice in the Mirror — *Shargel, Lee*

Voice into Text — *Worthington, Ian*

The Voice of Nations — *Eyck, F Gunther*

The Voice of the Child — *Davie, Ronald*

Voice of the Old Wolf — *Evans, Steven Ross*

The Voice of the People — *Fishkin, James S*

c The Voice of the People — *Maestro, Betsy*

A Voice of Thunder — *Stephens, George E*

y The Voice on the Radio — *Cooney, Caroline B*

y Voices: Canadian Writers of African Descent — *Black, Ayanna*

Voices from Indenture — *Carter, Marina*

Voices from Jerusalem — *Burrell, David B*

Voices from the Century Before — *Berry, Mary Clay*

Voices from the Japanese Women's Movement — *Ampo*

y Voices from the Streets — *Atkin, S Beth*

c Voices from the Wild (Illus. by Ron Parker) — *Bouchard, Dave*

y Voices from Vietnam — *Denenberg, Barry*

Voices in the Wilderness — *Payne, Daniel G*

p Voices Israel 1995

y Voices of AIDS — *Ford, Michael Thomas*

Voices of Authority — *Poteau-Tralie, Mary L*

y Voices of D-Day — *Drez, Ronald J*

Voices of Diversity — *Andrews, Pat*

The Voices of Eden — *Schutz, Albert J*

y Voices of Feminism — *Guernsey, JoAnn Bren*

Voices of Feminist Therapy — *Williams, Elizabeth Friar*

Voices of Ferrier — *O'Coileain, Seamas*

Voices of Fire — *Barber, Bruce*

Voices of Freedom

y Voices of Hope — *Feintuch, David*

r Voices of Multicultural America — *Straub, Deborah Gillan*

Voices of Sibyls

y The Voices of Silence — *Mooney, Bel*

Voices of the 55th — *Trudeau, Noah Andre*

c Voices of the Dream — *Johnson, Venice*

y Voices of the Heart (Illus. by Ed Young) — *Young, Ed*

Voices of the Marketplace — *Rose, Anne C*

Voices of the Song Lyric in China — *Yu, Pauline*

Voices of Their Own — *Ordonez, Elizabeth J*

Voices Off — *Styles, Morag*

Voicing America — *Looby, Christopher*

Voicing Women — *Chedgzoy, Kate*

La Voie Jaina — *Shanta, N*

c Les Voix Truquees (Illus. by Caroline Merola) — *Sarfati, Sonia*

Les Volailles — *Vergne, Elisa*

Volatile Bodies — *Grosz, E A*

Volatile Capital Flows — *Hausmann, Ricardo*

Volatile Organic Compounds (VOCs) in the Environment — *Wang, Wun-Cheng*

The Volatile Powder Kegs — *Larrabee, F Stephen*

Volcanic Heaven — *Edwards, Paul, 1950-*

y Volcano: A Memoir of Hawai'i — *Hongo, Garrett Kaoru*

Volcano and Miracle — *Herling, Gustaw*

Volcano Instability on the Earth and Other Planets — *McGuire, W J*

y Volcano: The Search for Vesuvius — *Hoffer, William*

r Volcanoes. Electronic Media Version

c Volcanoes — *Green, Jen*

c Volcanoes — *Morris, Neil*

c Volcanoes: Mountains That Blow Their Tops (Illus. by Michael Radencich) — *Nirgiotis, Nicholas*

Volcanoes of the Solar System — *Frankel, Charles*

Ein Volk, Ein Reich, Ein Glaube — *Lachele, Rainer*

Volk Und Herrscher In Der Historischen Sage — *Kompatscher, Gottfried*

Volksbucher: Prosaromane, Renaissancenovellen, Versdichtungen Und Schwankbucher. Pt. 2 — *Gotzkowsky, Bodo*

Volume and Open Interest. Rev. Ed. — *Shaleen, Kenneth H*

The Voluntary Sector, the State and Social Work in Britain — *Lewis, Jane*

The Voluptuous Gardener — *Rosenblatt, Joe*

Vom Generalplan Ost Zum Generalsiedlungsplan — *Madajczyk, Czeslaw*

Vom Privaten Motivkomplex Zum Poetischen Weltentwurf — *Stolz, Dieter*

Vom Schaffenden Zum Edierten Nestroy — *Yates, W Edgar*

Vom Sinn Aller Metaphorie Zur Funktion Komplexer Bildgestaltungen In Heimito Von Doderers Roman Die Strudlhofstiege — *Sommer, Gerald*

Von Bek — *Moorcock, Michael*

The Vonnegut Chronicles — *Reed, Peter*

r The Vonnegut Encyclopedia — *Leeds, Marc*

Een Voortreffelijke Ridder — *Brakman, Willem*

Voracious Idols and Violent Hands — *Wandel, Lee Palmer*

Der Vorleser — *Schlink, Bernhard*

The Voronezh Notebooks — *Mandelstam, Osip*

c Vorsprung. Bk. 1 — *Corney, Kate*

Vortex of Indian Fevers — *Louis, Adrian C*

Vospominaniia O Mikhaile Zoshchenko

Votes and Budgets — *Healey, John*

Votes for Women! — *Wheeler, Marjorie Spruill*

y Voting Behavior — *Winters, Paul A*

Voting for Reform — *Haggard, Stephan*

Votre Tres Humble Et Tres Obeissant Serviteur — *Troyat, Henri*

y A Vow of Poverty — *Black, Veronica*

Vows: Weddings of the Nineties from the New York Times — *Brady, Lois Smith*

yr Vox: Diccionario Esencial De Sinonimos Y Antonimos. Rev. Ed.

Vox Mystica — *Bartlett, Anne Clark*

cr Vox Spanish and English School Dictionary

Voyage — *Baxter, Stephen*

The Voyage — *MacNeil, Robert*

The Voyage of HMS Herald to Australia and the South-West Pacific 1852-1861 under the Command of Captain Henry Mangles Denham — *David, Andrew*

Voyage of Rediscovery — *Finney, Ben*

y Voyage of the Basset (Illus. by James Christensen) — *Christensen, James*

y The Voyage of the Frog — *Paulsen, Gary*

y Voyage of the Lucky Dragon — *Bennett, Jack*

Voyage to Honor — *Fowler, Robert H*

Voyage to the Great Attractor — *Dressler, Alan*

Voyage to the Sonorous Land. The Hour We Knew Nothing of Each Other — *Handke, Peter*

Voyager — *Gabaldon, Diana*

y Voyager (James). Audio Version — *Gabaldon, Diana*

Voyages Au Pays Du Reel — *Segalen, Vincent*

c The Voyages of Doctor Doolittle (Illus. by Hugh Lofting) — *Kleinbaum, N H*

The Voyages of the Morning — *Doorly, Gerald S*

c Voyages Series

The Voyeur — *Moriarty, Michael*

De Vrek Van Missenburg — *Nolens, Leonard*

De Vriendschap — *Palmen, Connie*

The VRML 2.0 Sourcebook. 2nd Ed. — *Ames, Andrea L*

VRML: Bringing Virtual Reality to the Internet — *Vacca, John*

VRML: Exploring Virtual Words on the Internet — *Goralski, Walter*

The VRML Sourcebook — *Ames, Andrea L*

Vuk Karadzic Im Europaischen Kontext — *Potthoff, Wilfried*

The Vulgarization of Art — *Dowling, Linda*

Vulnerability and Adaptation Assessments — *Benioff, Ron*

The Vulnerable Child — *Weissbourd, Richard*

The Vulnerable Fortress — *Taylor, James R, 1928-*

The Vulnerable Observer — *Behar, Ruth*

c Vulpes, the Red Fox (Illus. by Jean Craighead George) — *George, Jean Craighead*

The Vulture Fund — *Frey, Stephen W*

The Vulture Fund (Guidall). Audio Version — *Frey, Stephen W*

Vung Da Ngam — *Ha, Ky Lam*

Vuot Bien — *Huyen, Chau Nu*

VUV and Soft X-Ray Photoionization — *Becker, Uwe*

Vyrishal'ni Zustichi — *Nyzhankivs'kyi, Bohdan*

Vznik Ceskoslovenska 1918 — *Klimek, Antonin*

W

W.A. Mozart: Cosi Fan Tutte — *Brown, Bruce Alan*
W.B. Yeats: A Life. Vol. 1 — *Foster, R F*
W.B. Yeats, Man and Poet. 3rd Ed. — *Jeffares, A Norman*
W.B. Yeats: The Man and the Milieu — *Alldritt, Keith*
c W.E.B. DuBois: Civil Rights Leader — *Moss, Nathaniel*
W.E.H. Lecky: Historian and Politician 1838-1903 — *McCartney, Donal*
W.H. Auden: Prose 1926-1938 — *Mendelson, Edward*
W Pogoni Za Sienkiewiczem — *Mikos, Michal Jacek*
W.S. Gilbert: A Classic Victorian and His Theatre — *Stedman, Jane W*
r Wabash County, Indiana Marriages 1835-1899 — *Scheuer, Larry*
Das Wachstum Des Gottesvolkes — *Reinhardt, Wolfgang*
Wachstum Und Differenzierung Der Deutschen Universitaten 1830-1945 — *Titze, Hartmut*
c Waddle Giggle Gargle (Illus. by Pamela Allen) — *Allen, Pamela*
The Wage Curve — *Blanchflower, David G*
Wage Determination and Distribution in Japan — *Tachibanaki, Toshiaki*
Wage Differentials between Men and Women — *Paci, Pierella*
Wage Hunters and Gatherers — *Breman, Jan*
Wage Slave No More — *Fishman, Stephen*
Wage Workers in Agriculture — *Tripartite Meeting Improving Conditions of Employment and Work of Agricultural Wage Workers in Context of Economic Restructuring (1996: Geneva, Switz)*
Wages, Manufacturers, and Workers in the Nineteenth Century Factory — *Scholliers, Peter*
The Wages of Conquest — *Nutini, Hugo G*
The Wages of Globalism — *Brands, H W*
The Wages of Motherhood — *Mink, Gwendolyn*
Waging Peace in Our Schools — *Lantieri, Linda*
Wagner — *Tanner, Michael*
Wagner and Russia — *Bartlett, Rosamund*
Wagner/Artaud — *Delany, Samuel R*
Wagner: Race and Revolution — *Rose, Paul Lawrence*
c The Wagner Whacker — *Romain, Joseph*
Wagner's Ring — *Holman, J K*
c The Wagon (Illus. by James E Ransome) — *Johnston, Tony*
c Wagon Train 911 — *Gilson, Jamie*
The Wagon Wars — *Ritchie, James A*
Wagon Wheels — *Moulton, Candy*
c A Wagonload of Fish (Illus. by Alexi Natchev) — *Bodnar, Judit Z*
c Wagons West! (Illus. by Roy Gerrard) — *Gerrard, Roy*
c Wagons West — *Wiggins, VeraLee*
y Waist-High in the World — *Mairs, Nancy*
Wait for Me at the Bottom of the Pool — *Smith, Jack*
c Wait until Dark — *Shahan, Sherry*
Waiting at the Altar — *Frazier, Amy*
c Waiting for Anya — *Morpurgo, Michael*
Waiting for Bardot — *Martin, Andy*
c Waiting for Christmas (Illus. by Jan Spivey Gilchrist) — *Greenfield, Monica*
c Waiting for Filippo — *Bender, Michael*
Waiting for Godot — *Beckett, Samuel*
Waiting for Katie — *Webster, Elizabeth*
Waiting for the Healer — *Sweeney, Eamonn*
Waiting for the Light — *Silversides, Brock V*
Waiting for the Sea to Be Blue — *Blake, Philippa*
Waiting for the Snow — *Scanlon, Thomas J*
The Waiting Time — *Price, Eugenia*
Waiting to Forget — *Moorman, Margaret*

The Wake of Deconstruction — *Johnson, Barbara*
Wake Up and Cook — *Tonkinson, Carole*
Wake Up and Smell the Coffee! — *Landers, Ann*
c Wake Up, Grizzly! (Illus. by Gustavo Rosemffet) — *Bittner, Wolfgang*
c Wake Up, It's Midnight — *Schutte, David*
c Wake Up, Little Children (Illus. by Walter Lyon Krudop) — *Aylesworth, Jim*
c Wake Up Piglet — *Barger, Ian*
c Wake Up, Santa Claus! (Illus. by Marcus Pfister) — *Pfister, Marcus*
Wake Up to Murder — *Allen, Steve*
c The Wakening — *Stewart, Paul*
Waking Beauty — *Witcover, Paul*
Waking the Tempests — *Randolph, Eleanor*
Waking the World — *Chinen, Allan B*
Waking Up, Fighting Back — *Altman, Roberta*
Waking Up Screaming from the American Dream — *Garfield, Bob*
c Waking Upside Down (Illus. by Dwight Been) — *Heckman, Philip*
Walden — *Thoreau, Henry David*
y Wales and Britain in the Early Modern World c. 1500 - c. 1760 — *Turvey, Roger*
Wales and the Wars of the Roses — *Evans, H T*
r Walford's Guide to Reference Material. 7th Ed., Vol. 1
Walk Around P-51D — *Davis, Larry*
Walk on the Wild Side — *Rodman, Dennis*
y A Walk through the Heavens — *Heifetz, Milton D*
c Walk Twenty, Run Twenty — *Disher, Garry*
y Walk Two Moons — *Creech, Sharon*
c The Walker Book of First Rhymes
Walker Percy: A Life — *Samway, Patrick H*
Walker Percy: The Last Catholic Novelist — *Quinlan, Kieran*
Walker Percy's Feminine Characters — *Lawson, Lewis A*
r The Walker's Companion (Illus. by Cathy Johnson) — *Ferber, Elizabeth*
Walkers Gleichung — *Wackwitz, Stephan*
r Walker's Manual of Unlisted Stocks 1996
r Walking Amsterdam — *Gauldie, Robin*
Walking Back the Cat — *Littell, Robert*
The Walking Dead — *Parker, John*
A Walking Guide to Melbourne's Monuments — *Ridley, Ronald T*
r Walking in Switzerland — *Lindenmayer, Clem*
Walking in the Same Direction — *Hinton, Jeanne*
Walking on Lotus Flowers — *Batchelor, Martine*
y Walking Point — *Watson, James, Chief*
Walking Possession — *Hamilton, Ian*
y The Walking Stones — *Hunter, Mollie*
y Walking the Black Cat — *Simic, Charles*
Walking the Dog and Other Stories — *MacLaverty, Bernard*
Walking the Labyrinth — *Goldstein, Lisa*
Walking the Tightrope — *Gokhale, Vibha Bakshi*
Walking the Twilight II — *Wilder, Kathryn*
Walking the Victorian Streets — *Nord, Deborah Epstein*
Walking to La Milpa — *Villatoro, Marcos McPeek*
Walking to Mercury — *Starhawk*
Walking towards Walden — *Mitchell, John Hanson*
y Walking Up a Rainbow — *Taylor, Theodore*
Walking with Presidents — *Poinsett, Alex*
Walking Words — *Galeano, Eduardo*
Walking Wounded — *Deveraux, Robert*
The Wall in My Backyard — *Dodds, Dinah*
The Wall of the Sky, the Wall of the Eye — *Lethem, Jonathan*

The Wall Street Journal Lifetime Guide to Money — *Wall Street Journal (Firm). Personal-Finance Staff*
Wall Street Money Machine (Cook). Audio Version — *Cook, Wade B*
Wall Street's Picks for 1997
c Wallace and Gromit in A Close Shave — *Marks, Graham*
c Wallace and Gromit in The Wrong Trousers — *Marks, Graham*
Wallace Stegner: His Life and Work — *Benson, Jackson J*
Wallace Stegner: Man and Writer — *Rankin, Charles E*
Wallace Stevens and Modern Art — *MacLeod, Glen*
The Walled-Up Wife — *Dundes, Alan*
c Wallpaper from Space (Illus. by Jill Pinkwater) — *Pinkwater, Daniel*
c Walls (Illus. by Steve Shott) — *Pluckrose, Henry*
Walls and Mirrors — *Gutierrez, David G*
The Walls Came Tumbling Down — *Stokes, Gale*
The Walls of Jericho — *Land, Jon*
The Walls of Jericho — *Mann, Robert*
Wally Hammond: The Reasons Why — *Foot, David*
c Walt Disney: Creator of Mickey Mouse — *Cole, Michael D*
c Walt Disney: His Life in Pictures — *Schroeder, Russell*
y Walt Disney Imagineering — *Imagineers (Group)*
Walt Whitman and Sir William Osler — *Leon, Philip W*
Walt Whitman and the World — *Allen, Gay Wilson*
Walt Whitman Bathing — *Wagoner, David*
Walt Whitman in Hell — *Hummer, T R*
Walt Whitman of Mickle Street — *Sill, Geoffrey M*
r Walt Whitman: The Contemporary Reviews — *Price, Kenneth M*
y Walt Whitman's America — *Reynolds, David S*
Walter Benjamin: A Biography — *Brodersen, Momme*
Walter Benjamin and the Bible — *Britt, Brian*
Walter Benjamin and the Demands of History — *Steinberg, Michael P*
Walter Benjamin: Theoretical Questions — *Ferris, David S*
Walter Francis Dillingham 1875-1963 — *Melendy, H Brett*
Walter Hasenclever: Eine Biographie Der Deutschen Moderne — *Kasties, Bert*
Walter Lippmann--Odyssey of a Liberal — *Riccio, Barry D*
Walter Pater 1839-1894 — *Bizzotto, Elisa*
Walter Pater: Lover of Strange Souls — *Donoghue, Denis*
Walter Sickert: Drawings — *Robins, Anna Gruetzner*
c Walter the Baker (Illus. by Eric Carle) — *Carle, Eric*
Walter Wanger, Hollywood Independent — *Bernstein, Matthew*
c Walter's Tail — *Ernst, Lisa Campbell*
The Waltham Chronicle — *Watkiss, Leslie*
Waltz into Darkness — *Woolrich, Cornell*
Waltzing in Ragtime — *Charbonneau, Eileen*
Der Wanderer of St. Paul — *Kulas, John S*
The Wanderer of the Subconscious Realm — *Wood, Sebastian*
Wanderers of the Wolfways — *Horwood, William*
c The Wanderings of Odysseus (Illus. by Alan Lee) — *Sutcliff, Rosemary*
Wandjuk Marika: Life Story — *Marika, Wandjuk*
Wang Shiwei and Wild Lilies — *Tai, Ching*
The Waning of the Communist State — *Walder, Andrew G*
y Wannabe — *Stoehr, Shelley*

c Wanted: Best Friend (Illus. by Lynn Munsinger) — Monson, A M
Wanted Dead or Alive — Aquila, Richard
c Wanted...Mud Blossom (Illus. by Jacqueline Rogers) — Byars, Betsy
Wantok — Botha, W P B
y War — Foon, Dennis
The War After — Karpf, Anne
The War against the Kitchen Sink — Guare, John
The War against the Poor — Gans, Herbert J
War and American Women — Breuer, William B
War and Anti-War — Toffler, Alvin
War and Chivalry — Strickland, Matthew
War and Peas — Churchill, Jill
War and Popular Culture — Hung, Chang-Tai
War and Reason — Bueno De Mesquita, Bruce
War and Society in the Greek World — Rich, John, 1944-
War and Society in the Roman World — Rich, John, 1944-
War and the City — Ashworth, Gregory J
War and the Economy in the Third Reich — Overy, Richard
War Baby Express — Lloyd, Roseann
War before Civilization — Keeley, Lawrence H
War beneath the Sea — Padfield, Peter
y War between Brothers — Time-Life Books
c The War between the Vowels and the Consonants (Illus. by Whitney Turner) — Turner, Priscilla
War by Other Means — Fialka, John J
War by Stealth — Powell, Alan
War, Chaos, and History — Beaumont, Roger
The War Diaries of Eddie Allan Stanton — Stanton, Eddie Allan
War, Diplomacy, and Development — Niblo, Stephen R
War, Diplomacy and Informal Empire — McLean, David
y War Dog — Booth, Martin
War Games — Hunter, Douglas
The War in American Culture — Erenberg, Lewis A
y The War in Georgia — Oughton, Jerrie
The War in Heaven — Nussey, Kent
y War in Italy (Howard). Audio Version — Lamb, Richard
r The War in North Africa 1940-1943 — Baxter, Colin F
War in the Air — Coonts, Stephen
The War in the Pacific — Gailey, Harry A
War in the Tribal Zone — Ferguson, R Brian
The War in Vietnam. Electronic Media Version
p War Literature and the Arts
The War Lover — Craig, Leon Harold
War Minus the Shooting — Marqusee, Mike
War, Nationalism and Peasants — Sato, Shigeru
The War North of Rome June 1944-May 1945 — Brooks, Thomas R
The War of Desire and Technology at the Close of the Mechanical Age — Stone, Allucquere Rosanne
The War of Gods — Lowy, Michael
y The War of Jenkins' Ear — Morpurgo, Michael
The War of the Fatties and Other Stories from Aztec History — Novo, Salvador
The War of the Fists — Davis, Robert C
The War of the Roses — Seward, Desmond
r The War of the Spanish Succession 1702-1713 — Dickinson, W Calvin
y War of the Worlds — Anderson, Kevin J
y War of the Worlds — Slouka, Mark
y The War on the Poor — Albelda, Randy
War or Peace? — Burg, Steven L
War Powers — Westerfield, Donald L
War, Revolution, and the Bureaucratic State — Brown, Howard G
y War Scare — Pry, Peter Vincent
War Stories — Pedelty, Mark
r War Story Guide — Smith, Myron J
y War, Terrible War — Hakim, Joy
War Voices — Curtis, Tony
War, Wings, and a Western Youth 1925-1945 — Hinckley, Ted C
War with Japan. Vols. 1-4 — Great Britain. Ministry of Defence (Navy)
War without Bloodshed — Clift, Eleanor
r Warblers of the Americas — Curson, Jon
y The Warding of Witch World — Norton, Andre
Warehouse and Distribution Automation Handbook — Adams, Nicholas D
Warfare in Roman Europe AD 350-425 — Elton, Hugh
r Warfare in the Classical World — Warry, John

Warfare in the Western World. Vols. 1-2 — Doughty, Robert A
Warfare under the Anglo-Norman Kings 1066-1135 — Morillo, Stephen
Warhogs: A History of War Profits in America — Brandes, Stuart D
Warhol — Bourdon, David
Warhost of Vastmark — Wurts, Janny
y Warleggan (Britton). Audio Version — Graham, Winston
Warlock — Hall, Oakley
Warlords: Ancient-Celtic-Medieval — Newark, Tim
r Warlords of the Ancient Americas: Central America — Tsouras, Peter G
y The Warm Place — Farmer, Nancy
Warman's Coins and Currency. 2nd Ed. — Berman, Allen G
r Warman's Country Antiques and Collectibles. 3rd Ed. — Morykan, Dana Gehman
Warming to the Issue — National Greenhouse Advisory Committee
Warning Shot — Egleton, Clive
The Warp of Ulster's Past — Cohen, Marilyn
Warpaths, Invasions of North America — Steele, Ian K
The Warren Court — Schwartz, Bernard
Warrigal's Way — Anderson, Warrigal
Warrior Dreams — Gibson, James William
y Warrior Enchantresses — Massie-Ferch, Kathleen M
Warrior: One Man's Environmental Crusade — Wilkinson, Pete
y The Warrior Returns — Cole, Allan
The Warrior Who Would Rule Russia — Lambeth, Benjamin S
The Warrior Within — Little, John
Warriors and Wildmen — Wicks, Stephen
c Warriors, Warthogs, and Wisdom (Illus. by Keith West) — Watson, Lyall
r Wars in the Third World Since 1945. 2nd Ed. — Arnold, Guy
Wars, Internal Conflicts, and Political Order — Barzilai, Gad
The Wars of Eduard Shevardnadze — Ekedahl, Carolyn M
The Wars of Frederick the Great — Showalter, Dennis E
The Wars of French Decolonization — Clayton, Anthony
y The Wars of the Roses — Lace, William W
The Wars of the Roses — Pollard, A J
The Wars of the Roses — Seward, Desmond
r The Wars of the Roses in Fiction — Murph, Roxane C
War's Other Voices — Cooke, Miriam
The Wars We Took to Vietnam — Bates, Milton J
Wartime America — Jeffries, John W
c Warts (Illus. by Gregg Thorkelson) — Shreve, Susan
Was Heisst Osterreich? — Plaschka, Richard G
Was Ich Erlebte. Vols. 1-2 — Steffens, Henrich
p Wasafiri
Washing the Great Unwashed — Williams, Marilyn Thornton
c Washing the Willow Tree Loon (Illus. by Nancy Carpenter) — Martin, Jacqueline Briggs
r Washington 96
r The Washington Almanac of International Trade and Business 1995/96
Washington Babylon — Cockburn, Alexander
c Washington City Is Burning — Robinet, Harriette Gillem
The Washington Club — Corris, Peter
Washington County — Bourke, Paul
Washington County, Kentucky Court Order Book 1792-1800 — Sanders, Faye Sea
r The Washington Post Dining Guide — Richman, Phyllis C
r Washington Representatives 1996
Washington Square — James, Henry
Washington's Partisan War 1775-1783 — Kwasny, Mark V
Al-Washm — Rubaie, Abd Al-Rahman Majid
c Wasp (Illus. by Lee Montgomery) — Hawcock, David
Wassily Kandinsky and Gabriele Munter — Kandinsky, Wassily
The Waste Land — Eliot, T S
Waste Management — Bilitewski, Bernd
A Wasteland of Strangers — Pronzini, Bill
Wasting America's Future — Sherman, Arloc
Wasting Away — Armstrong, Pat
The Watch Below — White, James, 1928-
y The Watch House — Westall, Robert
A Watch in the Night — Wilson, A N

Watch Me — Holt, A J
c Watch Out for the Giant-Killers! — McNaughton, Colin
c Watch Out for Witches! (Illus. by Hilda Offen) — Offen, Hilda
c Watch Out, Fred's About! (Illus. by C Crossland) — Sefton, Catherine
A Watch over Mortality — Raley, Harold C
Watch the Skies! — Peebles, Curtis
c Watch the Stars Come Out — Levinson, Riki
c Watch William Walk (Illus. by Ann Jonas) — Jonas, Ann
y The Watcher — Howe, James
c The Watchers: A Mystery at Alton Towers (Rodska). Audio Version — Cresswell, Helen
Watchfiends and Rack Screams — Artaud, Antonin
y Watching Our Crops Come In — Taulbert, Clifton L
Watching Race — Gray, Herman
Watching the River Flow — Williams, Paul, 1948-
y Watching the Watcher — Hicyilmaz, Gaye
Watching the Watchers — Monks, Robert A G
Watching the Weather — Gribbin, John
Watching Vanessa — Tiffin, Patricia M
Watching Wildlife — LaTourrette, Joe
The Watchman: The Twisted Life and Crimes of Serial Hacker Kevin Poulsen — Littman, Jonathan
c Water — Bryant-Mole, Karen
c Water (Illus. by Sallie Alane Reason) — Perham, Molly
c Water — Valat, Pierre-Marie
y Water: A Natural History — Outwater, Alice
Water Allocation and Water Markets — Hearne, Robert R
Water and Power — Lowi, Miriam R
Water and the Quest for Sustainable Development in the Ganges Valley — Chapman, G P
Water and Womanhood — Feldhaus, Anne
c The Water-Babies (Illus. by Jessie Willcox Smith) — Kingsley, Charles
c The Water-Babies. Audio Version — Kingsley, Charles
c The Water Babies (Illus. by Jan Ormerod) — Poole, Josephine
c Water Dance (Illus. by Thomas Locker) — Locker, Thomas
Water Disinfection and Natural Organic Matter — Minear, Roger A
Water from the Well — McLarey, Myra
Water Gardening — Slocum, Perry D
Water in the Middle East — Allan, J A
Water, Land, and Law in the West — Pisani, Donald J
c Water Life (Illus. by Helen Ward) — Fitzsimmons, Cecilia
Water Lilies — Kaminsky, Amy Katz
Water on Mars — Carr, Michael H
Water, Peace, and the Middle East — Allan, J A
Water Quality — Perry, James A
Water Relations of Plants and Soils. 2nd Ed. — Kramer, Paul J
r Water Resources Handbook — Mays, Larry W
Water Resources Management — Grigg, Neil S
Water Resources Management in the Face of Climatic/Hydrologic Uncertainties — Kaczmarek, Zdzislaw
c Water Safety (Illus. by Penny Dann) — Loewen, Nancy
c Water Science, Water Fun — Fiarotta, Noel
c Water, the Source of Life
Water Under the Bridge — Sallis, Susan
Water Waves — Rahman, Matiur
Water Witches — Bohjalian, Chris
y Waterborn — Keyes, J Gregory
y Waterbound — Stemp, Jane
c Waterbugs and Dragonflies — Stickney, Doris
Watercolor: A Step-by-Step Guide to Watercolor Techniques — Gair, Angela
The Watercolor Painter's Handbook — Monahan, Patricia
The Waterfront Journals — Wojnarowicz, David
Waterfront Workers of New Orleans — Arnesen, Eric
Waterloo (Davidson). Audio Version — Cornwell, Bernard
c Waterman's Child (Illus. by Daniel San Souci) — Mitchell, Barbara
c The Watermelon Boys — McCall Smith, Alexander
c The Watermelon Boys (Illus. by Lis Toft) — McCall Smith, Alexander
c Watermelon Day (Illus. by Dale Gottlieb) — Appelt, Kathi
Waters of Zion — McCool, Daniel C
Watershed — Everett, Percival

c The Watertower (Illus. by Steven Woolman) — *Crew, Gary*

y Watery Grave — *Alexander, Bruce*

y The Watsons Go to Birmingham--1963 — *Curtis, Christopher Paul*

y The Watsons Go to Birmingham--1963 (Burton). Audio Version — *Curtis, Christopher Paul*

Watsuji Tetsuro's Rinrigaku — *Watsuji, Tetsuro*

yr The Watts Teen Health Dictionary — *Isler, Charlotte*

The Wave — *Scott, Evelyn*

c Wave Goodbye (Illus. by Lorraine Williams) — *Reid, Rob*

Wave-Rings in the Water — *Johnson, Carmen*

Wavelets: An Analysis Tool — *Ilolschneider, M*

Wavelets in Medicine and Biology — *Aldroubi, Akram*

Wavelets, Theory and Applications — *Erlebacher, Gordon*

Waves and Nonlinear Processes in Hydrodynamics — *Grue, John*

c Waves in the Bathtub — *Fernandez, Eugenie*

c Waves: The Electromagnetic Universe — *Skurzynski, Gloria*

Wavewalker — *Duffy, Stella*

Waving the Flag — *Higson, Andrew*

c The Wax Museum (Illus. by Donald Cook) — *Speregen, Devra*

c Way Cool Web Sites — *Raucci, Richard*

Way Down Deep in the Belly of the Beast — *Fetherling, Douglas*

The Way Home — *Benson, Angela*

c Way Home (Illus. by Gregory Rogers) — *Hathorn, Libby*

The Way Home Is Longer — *Renino, Christopher*

The Way I Remember It — *Rudin, Walter*

The Way Life Works — *Hoagland, Mahlon*

The Way Microsoft Word for Windows 95 Works — *Gloster, Peter*

The Way of an Eagle — *Darden, Robert*

A Way of Looking at Things — *Erikson, Erik H*

The Way of Silent Love

The Way of the Bodhisattva — *Shantideva*

The Way of the Cross Leads Home — *Schneider, A Gregory*

The Way of the English Mystics — *Miller, Gordon L*

The Way of the Explorer (Mitchell). Audio Version — *Mitchell, Edgar*

The Way of the Guerrilla — *Levinson, Jay Conrad*

The Way of the Heavenly Sword — *Humphreys, Leonard A*

The Way of the Human — *Wolinsky, Stephen H*

The Way of the Leader — *Krause, Donald G*

The Way of the Owl — *Rivers, Frank*

The Way of the Traitor — *Rowland, Laura Joh*

c The Way of the Willow Branch (Illus. by Durga Bernhard) — *Bernhard, Emery*

y A Way out of No Way — *Woodson, Jacqueline*

c The Way Science Works

The Way She Looks Tonight — *Fowler, Marian*

The Way Some People Die — *Macdonald, Ross*

r Way Stations to Heaven — *Gurvis, Sandra*

The Way That Water Enters Stone — *Dufresne, John*

yr The Way Things Work. Electronic Media Version — *Macaulay, David*

cr The Way Things Work 2. Electronic Media Version — *Macaulay, David*

A Way through the Wilderness — *Davis, William C*

The Way to Rainy Mountain — *Momaday, N Scott*

The Way to the West — *West, Elliott*

The Way We Live Now — *Hoggart, Richard*

The Way We Really Are — *Coontz, Stephanie*

c A Way with Horses — *McPhee, Peter*

Wayfarer: New Fiction by Korean Women — *Fulton, Bruce*

cr The Wayland Atlas of Rain Forests — *Lewington, Anna*

cr Wayland Atlas of Threatened Cultures

Waylon: An Autobiography — *Jennings, Waylon*

y Waylon: An Autobiography (Jennings). Audio Version — *Jennings, Waylon*

c Wayne Anderson's Horrorble Book — *Anderson, Wayne*

Ways in Mystery — *Askeland, Luther*

Ways into the Logic of Alexander of Aphrodisias — *Flannery, Kevin L*

The Ways of Confucianism — *Nivison, David S*

The Ways of God — *Thomas, Aquinas, Saint*

Ways of Telling — *Royston, Mike*

Ways of War and Peace — *Doyle, Michael W*

c Wayside School Gets a Little Stranger (Illus. by Joel Schick) — *Sachar, Louis*

We — *Zamyatin, Yevgeny*

We All Got History — *Salvatore, Nick*

We All Lost the Cold War — *Stein, Janice Gross*

c We Animals Would Like a Word with You (Illus. by Satoshi Kitamura) — *Agard, John*

We Are All Multiculturalists Now — *Glazer, Nathan*

We Are Free — *Ebert, Myrtle V*

c We Are Monsters (Illus. by John Magine) — *Packard, Mary*

y We Are Witnesses — *Boas, Jacob*

We Ask for British Justice — *Tabili, Laura*

We Called Each Other Comrade — *Ruff, Allen*

We Cannot Escape History — *McPherson, James M*

c We Couldn't Provide Fish Thumbs (Illus. by Colin McNaughton) — *Berry, James*

We Dance Because We Can — *Contreras, Don*

c We Didn't Mean to Go to Sea — *Ransome, Arthur*

y We Flew over the Bridge — *Ringgold, Faith*

y We Have Conquered Pain — *Fradin, Dennis Brindell*

We Have Just Begun to Not Fight — *Frazer, Heather T*

y We Have Marched Together — *Currie, Stephen*

We Have No Leaders — *Smith, Robert Charles*

We Live at the End of the 20th Century — *McLennan, Rob*

We Made a Garden — *Fish, Margery*

We Now Know — *Gaddis, John Lewis*

We Paid Our Dues — *Bolles, A Lynn*

We People Here — *Lockhart, James*

c We Rode the Wind — *Katz, Jane B*

We Scholars — *Damrosch, David*

c We Shake in a Quake (Illus. by David Uttal) — *Givon, Hannah Gelman*

y We Shall Not Be Moved — *Dash, Joan*

We Should Know Better — *Walden, George*

c We Sing the City (Illus. by Donna Perrone) — *Lundgren, Mary Beth*

We So Seldom Look on Love — *Gowdy, Barbara*

We, the Dangerous — *Mirikitani, Janice*

We Were Baptized Too — *Alexander, Marilyn Bennett*

We Were Each Other's Prisoners — *Carlson, Lewis H*

We Were the Mulvaneys — *Oates, Joyce Carol*

y We Won't Go Back — *Lawrence, Charles, 1943-*

y We Wrecked the Place — *Stevenson, Jonathan*

r Weakley County, Tennessee Register Survey Books. Vol. 2

Weakness of the Will in Medieval Thought — *Saarinen, Risto*

Wealth as Peril and Obligation — *Wheeler, Sondra Ely*

Wealth from Diversity — *Vence-Deza, Xavier*

Wealth, Kinship and Culture — *Larminie, Vivienne*

r The Wealth Management Index — *Levin, Ross*

The Wealth of Poor Nations. 2nd Ed. — *Suriyakumaran, C*

The Wealth of Shrewsbury in the Early Fourteenth Century — *Cromarty, D*

y Weapons and Warfare (Illus. by Sergio Martinez) — *Meltzer, Milton*

Weapons Decisions — *Elworthy, Scilla*

Weapons for Victory — *Maddox, Robert James*

Weapons of Liberation — *Barber, Stephen*

Weapons of Mass Destruction — *Lewis, William H*

Weapons Proliferation and World Order — *Roberts, Brad*

Weapons without a Cause — *Farrell, Theo*

The Wearing of Costume — *Green, Ruth M*

Wearing Purple — *Alexander, Lydia Lewis*

Wearing the Morning Star — *Swann, Brian*

c Weasel — *DeFelice, Cynthia C*

yr Weather — *Burroughs, William James*

c Weather — *Martin, Fred*

c Weather — *Morgan, Sally*

c Weather (Illus. by Tony Ross) — *Ross, Tony*

r Weather America — *Garwood, Alfred N*

The Weather and Climate of Australia and New Zealand — *Sturman, A P*

Weather Central — *Kooser, Ted*

y Weather Eye — *Howarth, Lesley*

Weather in the Garden — *Taylor, Jane*

r Weather of U.S. Cities. 5th Ed. — *Wood, Richard A*

c Weather Watch — *Kahl, Jonathan D*

r Weather Wisdom — *Kingsbury, Stewart A*

c The Weather's Getting Verse (Illus. by Alan Larkins) — *Peters, Andrew*

The Weaver-God, He Weaves — *Sten, Christopher*

c Weaving a California Tradition (Illus. by Dugan Aguilar) — *Yamane, Linda*

Weaving a Tapestry of Resistance — *Sutton, Sharon E*

Weaving a World — *Willink, Roseann Sandoval*

Weaving the Corporate Web — *Bernard, Ryan*

The Web — *Kellerman, Jonathan*

Web Advertising and Marketing — *Testerman, Joshua O*

The Web after Work for Dummies — *Ellsworth, Jill H*

Web-Based Instruction — *Khan, Badrul*

p Web Bound

Web Developer's Guide to Multimedia and Video — *Johnson, Nel*

r Web Graphics Sourcebook — *Tittel, Ed*

The Web of Friendship — *Schulze, Robin G*

The Web of Inclusion — *Helgesen, Sally*

y The Web of Life — *Capra, Fritjof*

The Web of Life (Prichard). Audio Version — *Capra, Fritjof*

The Web Page Recipe Book — *Sosinsky, Barrie*

Web Programming — *Jamsa, Kris*

Web Publisher's Construction Kit with Netscape Plug-Ins — *Angel, Jonathan*

Web Publishing with Netscape for Busy People — *Crumlish, Christian*

Web Search Strategies — *Pfaffenberger, Bryan*

The Web Server Handbook — *Palmer, Pete*

Web Site Construction Kit for Windows NT — *Brown, Christopher L T*

yr Web Site Source Book 1996

Web Site Stats — *Stout, Rick*

c Web Weaver — *Coburn, Ann*

c Web Weavers and Other Spiders — *Kalman, Bobbie*

Webbing with Literature. 2nd Ed. — *Bromley, Karen D'Angelo*

Weber's Electrodynamics — *Assis, Andre Koch Torres*

p WebMaster

Webmaster in a Nutshell — *Spainhour, Stephen*

Webmaster Strategies — *Sullivan-Trainor, Michael*

r Webmaster's Professional Reference — *Buhle, E Loren*

Webonomics: The Nine Essential Principles for Growing Your Business on the World Wide Web — *Schwartz, Evan I*

c Webster's Leap — *Dunlop, Eileen*

cr Webster's New American Dictionary

yr Webster's New Biographical Dictionary. Electronic Media Version

r Webster's New World Dictionary of Media and Communications. Rev. and Updated Ed. — *Weiner, Richard*

p WEBTechniques

The Wedding — *West, Dorothy*

The Wedding (Crossley). Audio Version — *Garwood, Julie*

The Wedding: New Pictures from the Continuing Living Room Series — *Waplington, Nick*

Wedding Night — *Devon, Gary*

Wedding Photographer's Handbook — *Hurth, Robert*

Wedding Pictures — *Osborn, Kathy*

The Wedding Raffle — *Dawson, Geralyn*

Wedekinds Lulu — *Florack, Ruth*

c The Wednesday Surprise — *Bunting, Eve*

c Wee G. (Illus. by Donald Saaf) — *Ziefert, Harriet*

Wee Girls — *Murphy, Lizz*

c Wee Mouse Christmas (Illus. by Linda Birkinshaw) — *Capucilli, Alyssa Satin*

Wee Sing Baby (Illus. by Tammy Daniel-Biske). Book and Audio Version — *Beall, Pamela Conn*

c Wee Sing Baby Band Sounds and Songs (Illus. by Tammy Daniel-Biske). Book and Audio Version — *Beall, Pamela Conn*

c Wee Sing Farm Animals (Illus. by Kurt R Kress). Book and Audio Version — *Beall, Pamela Conn*

c Wee Sing Toys (Illus. by Patrick O Chapin). Book and Audio Version — *Beall, Pamela Conn*

c Wee Sing Wheels (Illus. by Diana Fisher). Book and Audio Version — *Beall, Pamela Conn*

c A Weed Is a Seed (Illus. by Janet Pedersen) — *Wolff, Ferida*

Weeding and Maintenance of Reference Collections — *Pierce, Sydney J*

Weeding Out the Tears — *White, Jeanne*

Weeds — *Kelley, Edith Summers*

r Weeds of the Northeast — *Uva, Richard H*

The Week of Salvation — *Monti, James*

A Week on the Concord and Merrimack Rivers — *Thoreau, Henry David*

Weekend De Chasse A La Mere — *Brisac, Genevieve*

Weekly Themes for Assemblies — *Grice, Phil*

Weeping for Lost Babylon — *Beach, Eric*

Weeping Violins — *Alt, Betty*

y Weetzie Bat (Bresnahan). Audio Version — *Block, Francesca Lia*

Der Weg In Die Geschichte — *Fried, Johannes*

Wegbereiders Der Revolutie — *Sap, J W*

Wege In Die Schriftlichkeit — *Holznagel, Franz-Josef*

Title Index

c **Wegman's Mother Goose (Illus. by William Wegman)** — *Wegman, William*

Wei Jingsheng and the Prospects for Democracy in China — *Hart, Tom*

The Weigh Down Diet — *Shamblin, Gwen*

Weighed in the Balance — *Perry, Anne*

Weighed in the Balance (Jones). Audio Version — *Perry, Anne*

The Weight of the Yen — *Murphy, R Taggart*

y **The Weight of Water** — *Shreve, Anita*

Die Weihreliefs Aus Dem Athener Pankrates-Heiligtum Am Ilissos — *Vikela, Eugenia*

Weimar 1918-1933 — *Winkler, Heinrich August*

Weimar Germany — *Bookbinder, Paul*

The Weimar Republic Sourcebook — *Kaes, Anton*

c **Weird and Wonderful** — *Cooling, Wendy*

y **Weird on the Inside** — *Stoehr, Shelley*

c **Weird Parents** — *Wood, Audrey*

Weird Rooms — *Sharpe, Mal*

Weird Water and Fuzzy Logic — *Gardner, Martin, 1914-*

y **The Weirdo** — *Taylor, Theodore*

y **The Weirdo (Guidall). Audio Version** — *Taylor, Theodore*

y **Weirdo's War** — *Coleman, Michael*

Die Weisheit Israels--Ein Fremdkorper Im Alten Testament — *Steiert, Franz-Josef*

Weisheit Und Pradestination — *Lange, Armin*

Ein Weites Feld — *Grass, Gunter*

c **Welcome Back to Pokeweed Public School** — *Bianchi, John*

The Welcome Table — *Harris, Jessica*

c **Welcome to Bayou Town! (Illus. by Ann Biedenharn Jones)** — *Schadler, Cherie D*

c **Welcome to Chillsville Elementary** — *King, Jane*

Welcome to Heights High — *Tittle, Diana*

Welcome to Hell — *Arriens, Jan*

Welcome to My Country — *Slater, Lauren*

Welcome to My Country (Slater). Audio Version — *Slater, Lauren*

Welcome to Tangier — *Lurie, Morris*

y **Welcome to the Ark** — *Tolan, Stephanie S*

r **Welcome to the Catholic Church. Electronic Media Version**

Welcome to the Revolution — *Cannon, Tom*

c **Welcome to the Sea of Sand (Illus. by Laura Regan)** — *Yolen, Jane*

y **Welcome to the World** — *Siegen-Smith, Nikki*

c **Welcome to the World of Whales** — *Swanson, Diane*

c **Welcome to the World of Wolves** — *Swanson, Diane*

Welcome to Your Facelift — *Bransford, Helen*

A Welcoming Life — *Fisher, M F K*

Welcoming the Undesirables — *Lesser, Jeffrey*

Welding and Weld Automation in Shipbuilding — *DeNale, Robert*

y **Welfare** — *Cozic, Charles P*

Welfare Economics and the Theory of Economic Policy — *Walker, Donald*

Welfare Effects of Value-Added Tax Harmonization in Europe — *Fehr, Hans*

Welfare, Happiness, and Ethics — *Sumner, L W*

Welfare Justice — *Gilbert, Neil*

Welfare, Law and Citizenship — *Dean, Hartley*

The Welfare of Children — *Lindsey, Duncan*

Welfare or Welfare State? — *Marsland, David*

y **Welfare Reform** — *Cozic, Charles P*

r **Welfare Reform** — *Hombs, Mary Ellen*

y **Welfare Reform** — *McCuen, Gary*

y **The Well: David's Story** — *Taylor, Mildred D*

c **Well Dazzled** — *Robinson, Sue*

The Well-Heeled Murders — *Hartman, Cherry*

The Well of Loneliness — *Hall, Radclyffe*

y **A Well Regulated Militia** — *Weir, William*

Well Rounded — *Lippincott, Catherine*

r **The Well-Tempered Announcer** — *Fradkin, Robert A*

The Well-Tempered Self — *Miller, Toby*

c **Well Wished** — *Billingsley, Franny*

r **The Wellcome Trust History of Tropical Diseases** — *Cox, F E G*

The Wellcome Trust Illustrated History of Tropical Diseases — *Cox, F E G*

Wellington: A Personal History — *Hibbert, Christopher*

Wellness at Work — *O'Hara, Valerie*

y **Wells of Glory** — *McReynolds, Mary*

The Wellspring — *Olds, Sharon*

The Wellspring: Poems — *Olds, Sharon*

Wellsprings of Achievement — *Gouk, Penelope*

r **The Welsh Academy English-Welsh Dictionary** — *Griffiths, Bruce*

A Welsh Childhood — *Ellis, Alice Thomas*

The Welsh Fairy Book — *Thomas, W Jenkyn*

r **Weltmunzkatalog 19. Jahrhundert. 13th Ed.** — *Schon, Gunter*

r **Weltmunzkatalog 20. Jahrhundert. 1996 Ed.** — *Schon, Gunter*

Wen Xuan. Vol. 3 — *Hsiao, T'ung*

Wendy Perrin's Secrets Every Smart Traveler Should Know — *Perrin, Wendy*

Wendy Stavrianos — *Cree, Laura Murray*

Wer Ist Wie Du, Herr, Unter De Gottern? — *Kottsieper, Ingo*

c **We're Going on a Bear Hunt (Illus. by Helen Oxenbury)** — *Rosen, Michael, 1946-*

c **We're Making Breakfast for Mother (Illus. by Nancy Winslow Parker)** — *Neitzel, Shirley*

We're Poor Little Lambs — *Andrews, Paul M*

We're Ready for You, Mr. Grodin — *Grodin, Charles*

We're Right, They're Wrong — *Carville, James*

Were They Pushed or Did They Jump? — *Gambetta, Diego*

Were You There? — *Goatley, David Emmanuel*

De Wereld Aan Boeken — *Rijksuniversiteit Te Groningen. Bibliotheek*

c **Werewolves** — *Cohen, Daniel, 1936-*

Werewolves — *Greenberg, Martin Harry*

Die Werke Von Daniel Bernoulli. Vol. 7 — *Bernoulli, Daniel*

r **Werner and Ingbar's The Thyroid. 7th Ed.** — *Braverman, Lewis E*

Werner Sombart 1863-1941 — *Lenger, Friedrich*

Werner Von Siemens: Inventor and International Entrepreneur — *Feldenkirchen, Wilfried*

Die Wesenslogik In Hegels Wissenschaft Der Logic — *Wolfle, Gerhard Martin*

Wesley and the People Called Methodists — *Heitzenrater, Richard P*

West 47th — *Browne, Gerald A*

The West (Ward). Audio Version — *Ward, Geoffrey C*

The West: An Illustrated History — *Ward, Geoffrey C*

y **The West: An Illustrated History for Children** — *Duncan, Dayton*

The West beyond the West. 2nd Ed. — *Barman, Jean*

p **West Branch**

West Coast Seafood Recipes — *Freer, Blaine*

y **West End Shuffle** — *Prior, Natalie Jane*

West European Drawings of XVI-XX Centuries

West Indian Workers and the United Fruit Company in Costa Rica 1870-1940 — *Chomsky, Aviva*

c **The West Indies** — *Arnold, Helen*

West (Montana Shootout. Bones, Bullets, and Badmen) — *Hullar, Link*

West of Venus — *Troy, Judy*

The West Pole — *Glancy, Diane*

West Virginia Women — *Hannah, Karen L*

West with the Night (Harris). Audio Version — *Markham, Beryl*

r **Westbrook, Maine Cemeteries** — *Ketover, Karen Sherman*

The Westerbork Observatory, Continuing Adventure in Radio Astronomy — *Raimond, Ernst*

r **Western American Novelists. Vol. 1** — *Kich, Martin*

r **Western and Frontier Film and Television Credits 1903-1995. Vols. 1-2** — *Lentz, Harris M*

The Western Canon — *Bloom, Harold*

r **Western Civilization** — *Heyman, Neil M*

Western Civilization through Muslim Eyes — *Lari, Sayyid*

Western Dominance and Political Islam — *Bin Sayeed, Khalid*

Western Electric — *Zancanella, Don*

y **Western Europe** — *Dornberg, John*

Western Europe in Transition — *Fontenay, Patrick De*

r **Western Europe since 1945** — *Higbee, Joan F*

Western Furniture 1350 to the Present Day — *Wilk, Christopher*

The Western Greeks — *Pugliese Carratelli, Giovanni*

The Western Home — *Overland, Orm*

Western Lights — *Birnie, Lisa Hobbs*

r **Western Lore and Language** — *Clark, Thomas L*

r **Western Mail and South Wales Echo and Wales on Sunday on CD-Rom. Electronic Media Version**

The Western Medical Tradition 800 B.C. to A.D. 1800 — *Conrad, Lawrence I*

Western New York Land Transactions 1825-1835 — *Livsey, Karen E*

Western Philosophy — *Cottingham, John*

r **Western Sahara** — *Pazzanita, Anthony G*

The Western San Juan Mountains — *Blair, Rob*

r **Western Series and Sequels. 2nd Ed.** — *Drew, Bernard A*

Western Skyline — *Peattie, Noel*

Western Society in Transition — *Bornschier, Volker*

r **Western Water Rights** — *Wolfe, Mary Ellen*

Western Women Working in Japan — *Napier, Nancy K, 1952-*

Westerns: Making the Man in Fiction and Film — *Mitchell, Lee Clark*

r **Westfalischer Stadteatlas. Vols. 1-4** — *Stoob, H*

Westminster Abbey and the Plantagenets — *Binski, Paul*

The Westminster Corridor — *Sullivan, David*

r **Westminster Dictionary of Theological Terms** — *McKim, Donald K*

r **Westminster Guide to the Books of the Bible** — *Ramsay, William M*

y **Westminster West** — *Haas, Jessie*

Westmoreland Glass — *Wilson, Charles West*

y **Westward (Erickson). Audio Version** — *Ross, Dana Fuller*

c **Westward Ho!** — *Carlson, Laurie M*

c **Westward, Ho, Ho, Ho! (Illus. by Anne Canevari Green)** — *Roop, Peter*

c **Wet and Dry** — *Challoner, Jack*

The Wet and the Dry — *Kirch, Patrick Vinton*

Wet H2S Cracking of Carbon Steels and Weldments — *Kane, Russell D*

Wet: On Painting, Feminism, and Art Culture — *Schor, Mira*

Wet Scrubbers. 2nd Ed. — *Schiffiner, Kenneth C*

Wetenschap Tussen Universiteit En Industrie — *Heijmans, H G*

c **Wetland** — *Sayre, April Pulley*

y **Wetlands** — *Lisowski, Marylin*

Wetlands: Archaeology and Nature Conservation — *Cox, Margaret*

Wetlands: Environmental Gradients, Boundaries, and Buffers — *Mulamoottil, George*

y **Wetlands: The Web of Life** — *Rezendes, Paul*

c **Whaddaya Doin' in There?**

c **The Whale** — *Crewe, Sabrina*

Whale: Giant of the Ocean — *Grace, Eric S*

y **Whaleroad** — *Greenwood, Kerry*

c **Whales** — *DuTemple, Lesley A*

c **Whales** — *Harman, Amanda*

c **The Whales (Illus. by Cynthia Rylant)** — *Rylant, Cynthia*

Whales, Ice and Men — *Bockstoce, John R*

c **Whales: Killer Whales, Blue Whales and More (Illus. by Pat Stephens)** — *Hodge, Deborah*

Whaling Will Never Do for Me — *Busch, Briton Cooper*

Wharton Esherick 1887-1970 — *Edwards, Robert*

What a Book! — *Hall, Tom T*

What a Carve Up! — *Coe, Jonathan*

c **What a Doll!** — *Corbett, Sara*

What a Woman Ought to Be and to Do — *Shaw, Stephanie J*

c **What a Wonderful World (Illus. by Ashley Bryan)** — *Weiss, George David*

What a Writer Needs — *Fletcher, Ralph*

What about America's Homeless Children? — *Shane, Paul G*

c **What about Emma? (Illus. by Ken Rush)** — *Rush, Ken*

What about Us? — *Freely, Maureen*

c **What Am I? (Illus. by Leo Dillon)** — *Charles, N N*

c **What Am I? (Illus. by Anthea Sieveking)** — *MacKinnon, Debbie*

c **What Am I Doing?** — *Garland, Sarah*

What Americans Know about Politics and Why It Matters — *Delli Carpini, Michael X*

What Are Big Girls Made Of? — *Piercy, Marge*

What Are Freedoms For? — *Garvey, John H*

y **What Are Hyenas Laughing At, Anyway? (Illus. by Kassie Schwan)** — *Feldman, David, 1950-*

c **What Are Roses For? (Illus. by Jacqueline Chwast)** — *Stoddard, Sandol*

What Are They Saying about Matthew?. Rev. Ed. — *Senior, Donald*

What Are We Going to Do Now? — *Molloy, William*

What Children Bring to Light — *Shapiro, Bonnie*

c **What Color Is Camouflage? (Illus. by Megan Lloyd)** — *Otto, Carolyn*

c **What Color Was the Sky Today? (Illus. by Sally Noll)** — *Ford, Miela*

What Did You Do in the War, Auntie? — *Hickman, Tom*

What Did You Do in the War, Mummy? — *Nicholson, Mavis*

c **What Do Authors Do? (Illus. by Eileen Christelow)** — *Christelow, Eileen*

yr **What Do I Read Next?. Electronic Media Version**

r What Do I Read Next? 1990-

c What Do the Fairies Do with All Those Teeth?
— *Luppens, Michel*

c What Do We Do with Dawson? (Illus. by Terry Denton) — *Greenwood, Ted*

c What Do We Know about Hinduism? — *Ganeri, Anita*

c What Do We Know about Islam? (Illus. by Celia Hart) — *Shahrukh Husain*

c What Do We Know about Judaism? — *Fine, Doreen*

c What Do We Know about Plains Indians? — *Taylor, Colin*

c What Do We Know about Prehistoric People? — *Corbishley, Mike*

c What Do We Know about Sikhism? — *Dhanjal, Beryl*

c What Do We Know about the Middle Ages? — *Howarth, Sarah*

What Do Women Want from Men?. Audio Version — *True, Dan*

c What Do You Hear When Cows Sing? And Other Silly Riddles (Illus. by Giulio Maestro) — *Maestro, Marco*

c What Do You Mean I Have Attention Deficit Disorder? (Illus. by Gregg A Flory) — *Dwyer, Kathleen M*

c What Do You See in a Cloud? — *Fowler, Allan*

c What Do You See under the Sea? (Illus. by Christopher Hartley) — *Kalman, Bobbie*

yr What Do Young Adults Read Next?. Vol. 1 — *Spencer, Pam*

What Does a Woman Want? — *Felman, Shoshana*

What Does Your Wife Do? — *Beeghley, Leonard*

What Else but Love? — *Weinstein, Philip M*

r What Else Should I Read?. Vol. 2 — *Berman, Matt*

What Employers Want — *Holzer, Harry J*

What Ever Happened to Baby Peggy? — *Cary, Diana Serra*

What Every Jew Needs to Know about God — *Levin, Michael*

What Falls Away — *Farrow, Mia*

What Falls Away (Farrow). Audio Version — *Farrow, Mia*

c What Faust Saw (Illus. by Matt Ottley) — *Ottley, Matt*

c What Food Is This? — *Hausherr, Rosmarie*

What Freud Really Said — *Stafford-Clark, David*

y What Girls Learn — *Cook, Karin*

What God Allows — *Shapiro, Ivor*

What Goes around Comes Around — *Bliss, Michael, 1947-*

c What Goes around Comes Around (Illus. by Richard McGuire) — *McGuire, Richard*

What Goes without Saying — *Jacobsen, Josephine*

What Happened to You? — *Keith, Lois*

r What Happened Where — *Cook, Chris*

c What Happens to Your Food? — *Smith, Alastair*

c What Happens When...? (Illus. by Steve Fricker) — *Farndon, John*

c What Happens When Fire Burns? — *Butler, Daphne*

c What Happens When Flowers Grow? — *Butler, Daphne*

c What Happens When Food Cooks? — *Butler, Daphne*

c What Happens When People Talk? — *Butler, Daphne*

c What Happens When Rain Falls? — *Butler, Daphne*

c What Happens When Volcanoes Erupt? — *Butler, Daphne*

c What Happens When Wheels Turn? — *Butler, Daphne*

c What Happens When Wind Blows? — *Butler, Daphne*

c What Have You Done, Davy? (Illus. by Eve Tharlet) — *Weninger, Brigitte*

c What I Believe (Illus. by Robert Crum) — *Birdseye, Debbie Holsclaw*

y What I Believe (Hardiman). Audio Version — *Russell, Bertrand*

y What I Did for Roman — *Conrad, Pam*

c What I Eat (Illus. by Christopher Wormell) — *Wormell, Christopher*

What I Hope to Leave Behind — *Black, Allida M*

y What I Know Now — *Larson, Rodger*

What I Know So Far — *Lish, Gordon*

What I Really Want to Do Is Direct — *Frolick, Billy*

c What If! (Illus. by Jane Chapman) — *Benjamin, A H*

y What If You Could Unscramble an Egg? — *Ehrlich, Robert*

cr What in the Word? — *Muschell, David*

cr What in the World Is a Homophone? — *Presson, Leslie*

What Is a Human Being? — *Olafson, Frederick A*

What Is Appropriation? — *Butler, Rex*

What Is Art? — *Tolstoy, Leo, Graf*

What Is Counseling? — *Feltham, Colin*

What Is Creativity? (Lopez-Morillas). Audio Version — *Weisberg, Robert W*

p What Is Enlightenment?

What Is History Teaching? — *Husbands, Christopher*

What Is Intelligence? — *Khalfa, Jean*

What Is Japan? — *Sakaiya, Taichi*

What Is Jewish Literature? — *Wirth-Nesher, Hana*

What Is Life? — *Murphy, Michael P*

What Is Literature? — *Cornilliat, Francois*

What Is Pastoral? — *Alpers, Paul J*

What Is Philosophy? — *Deleuze, Gilles*

What Is Secret — *Agosin, Marjorie*

c What Is That? (Illus. by Tana Hoban) — *Hoban, Tana*

c What Is the Sun? (Illus. by Stephen Lambert) — *Lindbergh, Reeve*

What Is Your Will, O God? — *Toner, Jules J*

y What It Means to Be a Libertarian — *Murray, Charles A*

What It Means to Be a Libertarian (Murray). Audio Version — *Murray, Charles A*

y What Jamie Saw — *Coman, Carolyn*

What Katy Read — *Foster, Shirley*

What Keeps Me Here — *Brown, Rebecca*

y What Kind of Love? — *Cole, Sheila*

y What Labour Can Do — *Layard, P R G*

y What Life Was like on the Banks of the Nile — *Time-Life Books*

y What Love Sees (Stephens). Audio Version — *Vreeland, Susan*

What Made Gertie Gallop? — *Kharbanda, O P*

What Made the South Different? — *Gispen, Kees*

c What Makes a Bird a Bird? (Illus. by Trish Hill) — *Garelick, May*

c What Makes a Magnet? (Illus. by True Kelley) — *Branley, Franklyn Mansfield*

What Makes Life Worth Living? — *Mathews, Gordon*

c What Makes Popcorn Pop?

What Makes the Great Great — *Kimbro, Dennis P*

What Makes Women Sick — *Doyal, Lesley*

r What Mystery Do I Read Next? — *Stilwell, Steven A*

What Needs to Change — *Radice, Giles*

c What Newt Could Do for Turtle (Illus. by Louise Voce) — *London, Jonathan*

What On Earth Are We Doing? — *Fischer, John, 1947-*

c What on Earth Is a Bustard? — *Tesar, Jenny E*

c What on Earth Is a Hyrax? — *Ricciuti, Edward R*

c What on Earth Is a Pout? — *Ricciuti, Edward R*

c What on Earth Is a Quokka? — *Tesar, Jenny E*

c What on Earth? Series

What Parents Need to Know about Dating Violence — *Levy, Barrie*

What Parish Are You From? — *McMahon, Eileen M*

What Passes for Love — *Rogal, Stan*

r What Plant Where? — *Lancaster, Roy*

c What Rhymes with Eel? (Illus. by Rick Brown) — *Ziefert, Harriet*

c What Rot! (Illus. by Dwight Kuhn) — *Ring, Elizabeth*

c What Sadie Saw — *King-Smith, Dick*

What Saint Paul Really Said — *Wright, Tom*

c What Shall I Dream? (Illus. by Judith Byron Schachner) — *Kvasnosky, Laura McGee*

What She Wanted — *Singer, Nicky*

What the Animals Tell Me — *Fitzpatrick, Sonya*

What the Body Told — *Campo, Rafael*

What the Darkness Proposes — *Martin, Charles, 1942-*

What the Deaf-Mute Heard (Whitener). Audio Version — *Gearino, G D*

c What the Painter Sees

y What the Parrot Told Alice (Illus. by John Bardwell) — *Smith, Dale*

What the Scarecrow Said — *Ikeda, Stewart David*

What They Didn't Teach You about the Civil War — *Wright, Mike*

c What They Don't Tell You about Shakespeare (Illus. by Alan Rowe) — *Ganeri, Anita*

What to Do About... — *Kozodoy, Neal*

c What to Do When a Bug Climbs in Your Mouth and Other Poems to Drive You Buggy (Illus. by Nancy Carlson) — *Walton, Rick*

What to Do When Someone You Love Is Depressed — *Golant, Mitch*

What to Eat if You Have Cancer — *Keane, Maureen*

The What to Eat if You Have Cancer Cookbook — *Keane, Maureen*

r What to Read — *Pearlman, Mickey*

c What Use Is a Moose? (Illus. by Arthur Robins) — *Waddell, Martin*

What Was Shakespeare — *Pechter, Edward*

What Was Socialism, and What Comes Next? — *Verdery, Katherine*

What We Talk about When We Talk about Love — *Carver, Raymond*

What Wild Ecstasy — *Heidenry, John*

What Will Be — *Dertouzos, Michael L*

y What Will My Mother Say — *Ugwu-Oju, Dympna*

What Women Need to Know — *Legato, Marianne*

What Women Want — *Ireland, Patricia*

What Works for Whom? — *Roth, Anthony*

c What You Do Is Easy, What I Do Is Hard (Illus. by Anna Dewdney) — *Wolf, Jake*

c What You Know First (Illus. by Barry Moser) — *MacLachlan, Patricia*

What You Should Know about Angels — *Altemose, Charlene*

What You Should Know about Homeopathic Remedies — *Mindell, Earl*

What Your Clients Won't Tell You...and Your Managers Don't Know — *Gamble, John*

What Your Travel Agent Knows That You Don't

c What Zeesie Saw on Delancey Street (Illus. by Marjorie Priceman) — *Rael, Elsa*

y Whatever Happened to Janie — *Cooney, Caroline B*

c Whatever Happened to Katy-Jane? — *Ure, Jean*

c Whatever Happened to the Dinosaurs? (Illus. by Bernard Most) — *Most, Bernard*

Whatever It Takes — *Drew, Elizabeth*

c Whatever You Do, Don't Go Near That Canoe! (Illus. by Werner Zimmermann) — *Lawson, Julie*

What's a Nice Republican Girl Like Me Doing in the ACLU? — *Kennedy, Sheila Suess*

What's Bred in the Bone (Davidson). Audio Version — *Davies, Robertson*

r What's Cooking in Multicultural America — *Wertsman, Vladimir F*

c What's for Lunch? (Illus. by Jill Dubin) — *Chang, Cindy*

What's Happened to the Humanities? — *Kernan, Alvin*

c What's He Doing Now? (Illus. by Janet Wilson) — *Farmer, Patti*

r What's in a Name? — *Dickson, Paul*

c What's in Aunt Mary's Room? (Illus. by Cedric Lucas) — *Howard, Elizabeth Fitzgerald*

What's It All About? — *Van Wert, William F*

c What's It like to Be a Fish? (Illus. by Holly Keller) — *Pfeffer, Wendy*

r What's News in Coos County?. Vol. 1 — *Kenney, Milli S*

What's on the Internet. 3rd Ed. — *Gagnon, Eric*

What's Right — *Frum, David*

What's So Funny? — *Cart, Michael*

c What's So Terrible about Swallowing an Apple Seed? (Illus. by Catharine O'Neill) — *Lerner, Harriet*

c What's That Noise? (Illus. by David Melling) — *Simon, Francesca*

y What's That Pig Outdoors? — *Kisor, Henry*

c What's That Sound, Woolly Bear? (Illus. by Joan Paley) — *Sturges, Philemon*

c What's the Matter, Kelly Beans? (Illus. by Blanche Sims) — *Enderle, Judith Ross*

What's the Worst That Could Happen? — *Westlake, Donald E*

c What's to Be Scared Of, Suki? — *Adler, C S*

y What's Tuesday? — *Dale, Mitzi*

c What's Under the Bed? — *Manning, Mick*

What's Up Girlfriend? — *Peltier-Draine, Elsaida*

c What's Up the Coconut Tree? (Illus. by Val Biro) — *Benjamin, A H*

c What's What? (Illus. by Keiko Narahashi) — *Serfozo, Mary*

c What's Wrong Now, Millicent? (Illus. by David Scott Meier) — *Alexander, Sue*

c What's Wrong with Grandma? (Illus. by Jeffrey K Bagby) — *Shawver, Margaret*

c What's Wrong with This Book? (Illus. by Richard McGuire) — *McGuire, Richard*

What's Your Friends I.Q.? — *Spignesi, Stephen J*

What's Your Mad About You I.Q.? — *Spignesi, Stephen J*

r Wheater's Basic Histopathology. 3rd Ed. — *Burkitt, George*

y Wheel of Dreams — *Tyson, Salinda*

The Wheel of Life — *Kubler-Ross, Elisabeth*

c Wheels! — *Cobb, Annie*

Wheels: A Season on NASCAR's Winston Cup Circuit — *Hemphill, Paul*

c Wheels and Cogs (Illus. by Mike Gordon) — *Rush, Caroline*

Wheels in Motion — *Perschbacher, Gerald*

Wheels in the Head — *Spring, Joel*

When a Loose Cannon Flogs a Dead Horse, There's the Devil to Pay — *Isil, Olivia A*
When a Parent Has Cancer — *Harpham, Wendy S*
When Abortion Was a Crime — *Reagan, Leslie J*
When Are You Entitled to New Underwear and Other Major Financial Decisions — *Michaels, Eileen*
c When Artie Was Little (Illus. by Thomas B Allen) — *Schwartz, Harriet Berg*
c When Aunt Lena Did the Rhumba (Illus. by Diane Greenseid) — *Kurtis-Kleinman, Eileen*
c When Birds Could Talk and Bats Could Sing (Illus. by Barry Moser) — *Hamilton, Virginia*
When Capitalists Collide — *Vitalis, Robert*
When Catholics Speak about Jews — *Pawlikowski, John T*
c When Chickens Grow Teeth (Illus. by Wendy Anderson Halperin) — *Halperin, Wendy Anderson*
When Children Want Children — *Dash, Leon*
When Coyote Howls — *Gish, Robert*
When Cultures Collide — *Lewis, Richard D*
c When Daddy Took Us Camping — *Brillhart, Julie*
When Dempsey Fought Tunney — *Evensen, Bruce J*
c When Dinosaurs Die (Illus. by Marc Brown) — *Brown, Laurene Krasny*
When Dinosaurs Roamed New Jersey — *Gallagher, William B*
When Dreams Came True — *Bennett, Michael J*
When Dreams Cross — *Blackstock, Terri*
y When Elephants Weep — *Masson, J Moussaieff*
c When Frank Was Four — *Lester, Alison*
When God Becomes Goddess — *Grigg, Richard*
y When God Doesn't Make Sense — *Dobson, James C*
When Hens Crow — *Hoffert, Sylvia D*
c When Hitler Stole Pink Rabbit (Illus. by Judith Kerr) — *Kerr, Judith*
c When I Grow Up I Want to Be... (Illus. by Tania Hurt-Newton) — *Douglas, Blaise*
c When I Left My Village (Illus. by Brian Pinkney) — *Schur, Maxine Rose*
c When I Was Five (Illus. by Arthur Howard) — *Howard, Arthur*
y When I Was Puerto Rican — *Santiago, Esmeralda*
y When I Was Your Age — *Ehrlich, Amy*
c When I'm Sleepy (Illus. by Lynne Cherry) — *Howard, Jane R*
When Indians Became Cowboys — *Iverson, Peter*
c When It Is Night, When It Is Day — *Tyers, Jenny*
When Lean Enterprises Collide — *Cooper, Robin*
When Life and Choice Collide — *Mall, David*
When Life Becomes Precious — *Babcock, Elise NeeDell*
When Love Is Not Enough — *Piazza, Donna*
When Madness Comes Home — *Secunda, Victoria*
c When Martha's Away — *Ingman, Bruce*
When Memory Dies — *Sivanandan, A*
c When Mom Turned into a Monster — *Harrison, Joanna*
y When Nobody's Home — *Gorog, Judith*
When Passion Reigned — *Anderson, Patricia J*
When People Play People — *Mda, Zakes*
y When Plague Strikes (Illus. by David Frampton) — *Giblin, James Cross*
When Sacred and Secular Mix — *Monsma, Stephen V*
y When She Hollers — *Voigt, Cynthia*
c When Snow Lay Soft on the Mountain (Illus. by Leslie Baker) — *Hermes, Patricia*
c When Someone in the Family Drinks Too Much (Illus. by Nicole Rubel) — *Langsen, Richard C*
c When Someone You Know Has AIDS — *Forbes, Anna*
When Someone You Love Has Alzheimer's — *Grollman, Earl A*
When Someone You Love Is Depressed — *Rosen, Laura Epstein*
When Sons and Daughters Choose Alternative Lifestyles — *Caplan, Mariana*
c When Stories Fell like Shooting Stars (Illus. by Stefano Vitale) — *Gregory, Valiska*
When Strikes Make Sense--And Why — *Cohn, Samuel*
c When Sun Ruled the Land (Illus. by Dave Albers) — *Palazzo-Craig, Janet*
c When Sun Ruled the Land (Illus. by Dave Alpers). Book and Audio Version — *Palazzo-Craig, Janet*
When the Air Hits Your Brain — *Vertosick, Frank*
c When the Big Dog Barks (Illus. by Susan Avishai) — *Curtis, Munzee*
When the Bough Breaks — *Bernstein, Judith*
y When the Boys Came Back — *Turner, Frederick W*
c When the Circus Came to Town — *Horvath, Polly*
When the Colts Belonged to Baltimore — *Gildea, William*

When the Devil Came to Endless — *Boeckman, Charles*
When the Drummers Were Women — *Redmond, Layne*
When the Game Was Black and White — *Chadwick, Bruce*
When the Giants Were Giants — *Williams, Peter, 1937, Jan., 1-*
When the Lamp Is Shattered — *Janan, Micaela*
When the Land Was Young — *Russell, Sharman*
When the Music Stopped — *Lebrecht, Norman*
When the North Was Red — *Bartels, Dennis A*
When the Odds Were Even — *Bonn, Keith E*
When the Sons of Heaven Meet the Daughters of the Earth — *Eberstadt, Fernanda*
When the Soviet Union Entered World Politics — *Jacobson, Jon*
c When the Sun Rose (Illus. by Barbara Berger) — *Berger, Barbara*
c When the Teddy Bears Came (Illus. by Penny Dale) — *Waddell, Martin*
When the Tunnels Meet — *Fairleigh, John*
c When the Whippoorwill Calls (Illus. by Kimberley Bulcken Root) — *Ransom, Candice F*
c When the Wind Stops (Illus. by Stefano Vitale) — *Zolotow, Charlotte*
When the Wind Was a River — *Kohlhoff, Dean*
c When the World Was Young (Illus. by Louise Brierley) — *Mayo, Margaret*
When the Yankees Came — *Ash, Stephen V*
When They Came to Take My Father — *Kahn, Leora*
y When They Invited Me to FellowShip... — *Littleton, Mark*
When Things Fall Apart — *Chodron, Pema*
c When This Box Is Full (Illus. by Donald Crews) — *Lillie, Patricia*
y When This Cruel War Is Over — *Damon, Duane*
y When Thunders Spoke — *Sneve, Virginia Driving Hawk*
When Time Shall Be No More — *Boyer, Paul*
When Titans Clashed — *Glantz, David M*
y When Wallflowers Die — *Prowell, Sandra West*
y When Wallflowers Die (Breck). Audio Version — *Powell, Sandra West*
c When We Married Gary (Illus. by Anna Grossnickle Hines) — *Hines, Anna Grossnickle*
When We Were Good — *Cantwell, Robert*
When We Were Young — *Mclean, Stuart*
c When Whales Exhale and Other Poems (Illus. by Judy LaBrasca) — *Levy, Constance*
y When Will This Cruel War Be Over? — *Denenberg, Barry*
c When Willard Met Babe Ruth (Illus. by Barry Moser) — *Hall, Donald, 1928-*
When Women Call the Shots — *Seger, Linda*
When Women Kill — *Mann, Coramae Richey*
When Words Are Not Enough — *Raskin, Valerie Davis*
When Work Disappears — *Wilson, William Julius*
When You Look Like Your Passport Photo, It's Time to Go Home (Rosenblat). Audio Version — *Bombeck, Erma*
When You Worry About the Child You Love — *Hallowell, Edward*
c When You're Happy and You Know It (Illus. by Mits Katayama) — *Crary, Elizabeth*
c When You're Mad and You Know It (Illus. by Mits Katayama) — *Crary, Elizabeth*
c When You're Not Looking (Illus. by Maggie Kneen) — *Kneen, Maggie*
c When You're Shy and You Know It (Illus. by Mits Katayama) — *Crary, Elizabeth*
c When You're Silly and You Know It (Illus. by Mits Katayama) — *Crary, Elizabeth*
Where a Nickel Costs a Dime — *Perdomo, Willie*
Where Am I? — *Beeman, Marsha Lynn*
Where Angels Fear to Tread (Fry). Audio Version — *Forster, E M*
Where Angels Walk — *Anderson, Joan Wester*
c Where Are You, Little Zack? (Illus. by Brian Floca) — *Enderle, Judith Ross*
Where Coyotes Howl and Wind Blows Free — *Haslam, Alexandra R*
Where Did AIDS Come From? — *Forbes, Anna*
c Where Did All the Dragons Go? (Illus. by Victor Lee) — *Robinson, Fay*
c Where Do Babies Come From? (Illus. by Steve Gorton) — *Royston, Angela*
r Where Do I Go from Here? — *Thomas, Randy Ann*
c Where Do I Live? (Illus. by Ann Iosa) — *Chesanow, Neil*

c Where Do You Get Your Great Ideas? — *Bell, Krista*
y Where Do You Stand? — *Higgins, Gregory C*
c Where Does God Live? (Illus. by Kim Howard) — *Bea, Holly*
Where Does the Weirdness Go? — *Lindley, David, 1956-*
Where Every Breath Is a Prayer — *Ortner, Jon*
Where Evil Sleeps — *Wesley, Valerie Wilson*
y Where Have You Been, Billy Boy? — *Hughes, Monica*
c Where Have You Gone, Davy? (Illus. by Eve Tharlet) — *Weninger, Brigitte*
c Where I Live (Illus. by Christopher Wormell) — *Wormell, Christopher*
Where I Stopped — *Ramsey, Martha*
c Where in the USA Is Carmen Sandiego?. Electronic Media Version
Where Is Everybody? — *Ashpole, Edward*
Where Is Our Responsibility? — *Hartford, William F*
c Where Is the Night Train Going? (Illus. by Cyd Moore) — *Spinelli, Eileen*
Where Is Your Body? and Other Essays on Race, Gender, and the Law — *Matsuda, Mari J*
y Where It Stops, Nobody Knows — *Ehrlich, Amy*
c Where Jamaica Go? (Illus. by Dale Gottlieb) — *Gottlieb, Dale*
Where Masks Still Dance — *Rainier, Chris*
Where Nobody Dies — *Wheat, Carolyn*
y Where on Earth Am I? — *Gardner, Robert, 1929-*
c Where Once There Was a Wood (Illus. by Denise Fleming) — *Fleming, Denise*
Where Only Love Can Go — *Kirvan, John*
Where Past Meets Present — *Hemesath, James B*
Where Peachtree Meets Sweet Auburn — *Pomerantz, Gary M*
Where Resident Aliens Live — *Hauerwas, Stanley*
Where Rivers Meet — *Marshall, Muriel*
Where Shall Wisdom Be Found? — *Schreiner, Susan E*
Where Something Catches — *Munoz, Victoria I*
Where the Body Meets Memory — *Mura, David*
Where the Girls Are — *Douglas, Susan*
y Where the Heart Is — *Letts, Billie*
r Where the Information Is — *Bergan, Helen*
Where the Morning Light's Still Blue — *Studebaker, William*
Where the Oceans Meet — *Mandava, Bhargavi C*
y Where the Red Fern Grows — *Rawls, Wilson*
Where the Roads Met — *Zanier, Claudio*
c Where the Wild Things Are — *Sendak, Maurice*
c Where There Is No Name for Art — *Hucko, Bruce*
Where This Lake Is — *Lodge, Jeff*
r Where to Find the Best Soul Food, Blues and Jazz in the Southeast — *Rudison, Ron*
c Where to Look for a Dinosaur — *Most, Bernard*
r Where to Ski — *Gill, Chris*
r Where to Watch Birds in Africa — *Wheatley, Nigel*
r Where to Watch Birds in South America — *Wheatley, Nigel*
Where Two or Three Are Gathered — *Smith, Harmon L*
Where We've Been — *Simons, Michael*
y Where White Men Fear to Tread — *Means, Russell*
c Where Will This Shoe Take You? — *Lawlor, Laurie*
Where Wizards Stay Up Late — *Hafner, Katie*
Where Wonders Prevail — *Anderson, Joan Wester*
Where You Are — *Constable, George*
y Where You Belong — *McGuigan, Mary Ann*
Where You Find It — *Galloway, Janice*
c Where's Caterpillar? (Illus. by Louise Batchelor) — *Godwin, Sarah*
c Where's Molly? (Illus. by Mary Collier) — *Weiss, Ellen*
c Where's My Kitten? (Illus. by Michele Coxon) — *Coxon, Michele*
c Where's My Mum (Illus. by Priscilla Lamont) — *Rosselson, Leon*
c Where's My Teddy? — *Alborough, Jez*
c Where's Spot? — *Hill, Eric*
c Where's the Big Dipper? (Illus. by Dean Lindberg) — *Rosen, Sidney*
c Where's the Cat? (Illus. by Debbie Harter) — *Blackstone, Stella*
c Where's the Duckie? (Illus. by Stef De Reuver)
c Where's the Fly? (Illus. by Nancy Barnet) — *Cohen, Caron Lee*
c Where's the Mouse? (Illus. by Jill Dubin) — *Chang, Cindy*
Wherever That Great Heart May Be — *Wetherell, W D*

Whether Secular Government Has the Right to Wield the Sword in Matters of Faith — *Estes, James Martin*

p Whetstone

Which Reminds Me — *Sharp, Mitchell*

y Which Way Did the Bicycle Go? and Other Intriguing Mathematical Mysteries — *Konhauser, Joseph D E*

y Which Way Is Home? — *Strachan, Ian*

While England Sleeps — *Leavitt, David*

c While the Candles Burn (Illus. by Elaine Greenstein) — *Goldin, Barbara Diamond*

While the Music Lasts — *Bulger, William M*

While the Music Plays — *Austell, Diane*

While the Women Only Wept — *Potter-MacKinnon, Janice*

c While You Sleep (Illus. by Lyn Gilbert) — *Moore, Julia*

y Whip Hand (Ford). Audio Version — *Francis, Dick*

c The Whipping Boy (Illus. by Peter Sis) — *Fleischman, Sid*

Whirling Round the Sun — *Noguere, Suzanne*

The Whirlwind War

c Whisker's Great Adventure (Illus. by William Geldart) — *Doney, Meryl*

A Whisper of Black — *Harvey, Clay*

y Whispered Silences — *Okihiro, Gary Y*

c The Whispering Cloth (Illus. by Anita Riggio) — *Shea, Pegi Deitz*

The Whispering Pond — *Laszlo, Ervin*

c The Whispering Room (Illus. by Justin Todd) — *Clarke, Gillian*

Whispering the Lyrics — *Long, Thomas G*

The Whispering Wall — *Carlon, Patricia*

y Whispers (King). Audio Version — *Plain, Belva*

y Whispers from the Dead — *Nixon, Joan Lowery*

Whispers in the Dark — *Keyser, Elizabeth Lennox*

c Whispers in the Graveyard — *Breslin, Theresa*

Whispers of the Mountain — *Hron, Tom*

Whistle Down the Wind — *Bell, Mary Hayley*

y Whistle Me Home — *Wersba, Barbara*

Whistle up the Devil — *Smith, Derek*

Whistlejacket: A Novel — *Hawkes, John, 1925-*

Whistler and Montesquiou — *Munhall, Edgar*

Whistler on Art — *Whistler, James McNeill*

c Whistling Dixie (Illus. by Barry Moser) — *Vaughan, Marcia*

The Whistling Thorn — *Sugunasiri, Suwanda*

y The Whistling Toilets — *Powell, Randy*

Whit: Or, Isis amongst the Unsaved — *Banks, Iain*

c The Whitby Witches (McKenzie). Audio Version — *Jarvis, Robin*

The White Abacus — *Broderick, Damien*

The White beyond the Forest — *Rinkewich, Mindy*

The White Blackbird — *Moore, Honor*

The White Boy Shuffle — *Beatty, Paul*

White Boys and River Girls — *Gover, Paula K*

The White Buddhist — *Prothero, Stephen*

White by Law — *Haney-Lopez, Ian*

White-Collar Blues — *Heckscher, Charles C*

White Crane Spreads Wings — *Hyland, Gary*

White Crosses — *Watson, Larry*

The White Death — *Cribb, Julian*

White Elephants — *Vazirani, Reetika*

c White Fang (Hagon). Audio Version — *London, Jack*

y White Fang (Hootkins). Audio Version — *London, Jack*

White Fire — *Edwards, Cassie*

c The White Goblin — *De Rico, Ul*

White Horse, Red Rider — *Brierley, Barry*

The White House — *Freidel, Frank*

c The White House — *Quiri, Patricia Ryon*

The White House Garden — *Seale, William*

y White House Horrors — *Greenberg, Martin Harry*

White House Landscapes — *McEwan, Barbara*

The White House Speaks — *Smith, Craig Allen*

White House to Your House — *Diamond, Edwin*

White Leg — *Martinez, Max*

White Lies, White Power — *Novick, Michael*

White Linen Remembered — *Fiamengo, Marya*

y White Male Applicant — *Whitaker, William A*

White Man's Burden — *Leob, Kurt*

White Man's Grave — *Dooling, Richard*

White Man's Wicked Water — *Unrau, William E*

A White Merc with Fins — *Hawes, J M*

White Nights, Red Mornings — *Pella, Judith*

White Noise — *DeLillo, Don*

y White on White (White). Audio Version — *White, E B*

White Paper on Transport Policy (Namibia). Vol. 1

y White Peak Farm — *Doherty, Berlie*

The White Peril — *Brawley, Sean*

White Pine — *Oliver, Mary*

y The White Pine Chronicles — *Stahl, Hilda*

White Queen — *Jones, Gwyneth*

White Rabbit — *Phillips, Kate*

White Rajah — *Pybus, Cassandra*

r The White Ravens 1995

The White Rose — *Bromley, Theodore Norbert*

White Sands — *Gandolfi, Simon*

White Shroud — *Ginsberg, Allen*

White Smoke — *Greeley, Andrew M*

y White Smoke. Audio Version — *Greeley, Andrew M*

c White Socks Only (Illus. by Tyrone Geter) — *Coleman, Evelyn*

White Soul — *Sample, Tex*

A White Sports Coat and Other Plays — *Lyssiotis, Tess*

The White T — *Harris, Alice*

y The White-Tailed Deer — *Hiller, Ilo*

The White Tecumseh — *Hirshson, Stanley P*

White Trash — *Wray, Matt*

White Viper — *Strong, Terence*

White Walls, Designer Dresses — *Wigley, Mark*

c White Wave (Illus. by Ed Young) — *Wolkstein, Diane*

White Widow — *Lehrer, Jim*

The White Woman's Other Burden — *Jayawardena, Kumari*

Whiteley: An Unauthorised Life — *Hilton, Margot*

Whiteout — *Walker, Sage*

Whitetails: Behavior, Ecology, Conservation — *Bauer, Erwin A*

Whitewash: Pablo Escobar and the Cocaine Wars — *Strong, Simon*

Whitewashing Britain — *Paul, Kathleen*

Whither Environmental Archaeology? — *Luff, Rosemary*

Whither Jerusalem? — *Hirsch, Moshe*

Whither Marxism? — *Magnus, Bernd*

r Whitman Juvenile Books — *Brown, David, 1953-*

Whitman, Slavery, and the Emergence of Leaves of Grass — *Klammer, Martin*

Whitman's and Dickinson's Contemporaries — *Bain, Robert*

The Whitsun Weddings (Bennett). Audio Version — *Larkin, Philip*

Whittaker Chambers: A Biography — *Tanenhaus, Sam*

r Whittington's Dictionary of Plastics. 3rd Ed. Electronic Media Version — *Carley, James E*

The Whiz Kids and the 1950 Pennant — *Roberts, Robin, 1926-*

Who Adjusts? — *Simmons, Beth A*

c Who Am I? (Illus. by Robin Davies) — *Nicholls, Judith*

Who Are the Macedonians? — *Poulton, Hugh*

Who Are the People of God? — *Kee, Howard Clark*

Who Are the Promise Keepers? — *Abraham, Ken*

c Who Are You? (Illus. by Debbie Harter) — *Blackstone, Stella*

c Who Can I Be? — *Garland, Sarah*

c Who Can Tell? (Illus. by Wayne Anderson) — *Henson, Stuart*

Who Controls Public Lands? — *Klyza, Christopher McGrory*

Who Deliberates? — *Page, Benjamin I*

Who Did Jesus Think He Was? — *O'Neill, J C*

Who Do You Say I Am? — *Barry, William A*

Who Do You Say That I Am? — *Porges, Vivette*

c Who Drives This? (Illus. by Charles Reasoner) — *Reasoner, Charles*

c Who Eats What? (Illus. by Holly Keller) — *Lauber, Patricia*

Who Elected the Bankers? — *Pauly, Louis W*

r Who Else Writes Like...?. 2nd Ed. — *Huse, Roy*

WHO Expert Committee on Biological Standardization: Forty-Fifth Report

Who Gave Pinta to the Santa Maria? — *Desowitz, Robert S*

Who in Hell — *Kelly, Sean*

Who in Hell Is Wanda Fuca? — *Ford, G M*

c Who Is Ben? (Illus. by Kathryn Jacobi) — *Zolotow, Charlotte*

Who Is Fourier?

Who Is This Jesus? — *Green, Michael, 1930-*

Who Killed Classical Music? — *Lebrecht, Norman*

Who Killed Confederation Life? — *McQueen, Rod*

Who Killed Father Christmas? and Other Unseasonable Demises — *Moyes, Patricia*

Who Killed George Polk? — *Vlanton, Elias*

y Who Killed Mr. Chippendale? — *Glenn, Mel*

Who Knows — *Cavoukian, Ann*

c Who Likes Wolfie? (Illus. by Tim Warnes) — *Scamell, Ragnhild*

c Who Lives Here? (Illus. by Maggie Silver) — *Silver, Maggie*

c Who Made This Big Mess? (Illus. by Sally Schaedler) — *Gutelle, Andrew*

Who Owns the Sun? — *Berman, Daniel M*

Who Owns the West? — *Kittredge, William*

Who Pays and When?

Who Pays for the Kids? — *Folbre, Nancy*

c Who Plays This Sport? (Illus. by Charles Reasoner) — *Reasoner, Charles*

c Who Pretends? (Illus. by Charles Reasoner) — *Reasoner, Charles*

Who Rules Japan? — *Kerbo, Harold R*

Who Said It Would Be Easy? — *Holtzman, Elizabeth*

c Who Said That? (Illus. by David Catrow) — *Burleigh, Robert*

c Who Sank the Boat? (Illus. by Pamela Allen) — *Allen, Pamela*

Who Says? — *Birch, Carol L*

y Who Shall Live — *Oliner, Samuel P*

Who Should We Treat? — *Newdick, Christopher*

Who Speaks for God? — *Wallis, Jim*

Who Stole Feminism? — *Sommers, Christina Hoff*

c Who Stole the Cookies? (Illus. by Judith Moffatt) — *Moffatt, Judith*

c Who Stole the Pie? (Illus. by Colin McNaughton) — *Ahlberg, Allan*

Who Succeeds in Science? — *Sonnert, Gerhard*

Who the Devil Made It — *Bogdanovich, Peter*

y Who Took Henry and Mr. Z? — *Glaze, Dave*

c Who Wakes Rooster? (Illus. by Megan Halsey) — *Meeker, Clare Hodgson*

c Who Wants One? (Illus. by Keiko Narahashi) — *Serfozo, Mary*

r Who Was Who. Vol. 9

r Who Was Who in America. Vols. 1-12. Book and Electronic Media Version

y Who Were the Founding Fathers? — *Jaffe, Steven H*

Who Will Feed China? — *Brown, Lester Russell, 1934-*

Who Wrote Shakespeare? — *Michell, John*

y Who Wrote That? — *Dicks, Terrance*

Who Wrote the New Testament? — *Mack, Burton L*

y Whodunit--You Decide! — *Conrad, Hy*

The Whole Book — *Nichols, Stephen G*

The Whole Child. 6th Ed. — *Hendrick, J*

Whole Effluent Toxicity Testing — *Pellston Workshop on Whole Effluent Toxicity (1995: University of Michigan Biological Station, Douglas Lake)*

r The Whole Foods Companion — *Onstad, Dianne*

A Whole-School Behaviour Policy — *Lund, Roy*

The Whole Shebang — *Ferris, Timothy*

r The Whole Story — *Simkin, John E*

The Whole Tooth — *Schissel, Marvin J*

The Whole Truth — *Kaplan, Janice*

The Whole Way to Natural Detoxification — *Krohn, Jacqueline*

r Wholesale and Retail Trade USA 1995

y Who'll Catch the Nightmares? — *Kempton, Linda*

Whom God Wishes to Destroy... — *Lewis, Jon, 1955-*

Whom Gods Destroy — *Padel, Ruth*

Whom Shall I Fear? — *Dickson, Athol*

c Whoopi Goldberg — *Katz, Sandor*

c Whoosh! Went the Wish (Illus. by Barry Root) — *Speed, Toby*

Whores of the Court — *Hagen, Margaret A*

Who's a Pretty Boy Then? — *Gardiner, James*

c Who's Afraid? (Illus. by Carla Dijs) — *Dijs, Carla*

Who's Afraid of C++? — *Heller, Steve, 1949, Apr., 4-*

Who's Afraid of Feminism? — *Oakley, Ann*

y Who's Afraid of Schrodinger's Cat? — *Marshall, Ian*

c Who's Afraid of the Dark? (Illus. by Doris Barrette) — *Duchesne, Christiane*

Who's Afraid of the Religious Right? — *Feder, Don*

c Who's at Home with Anthony Ant? — *Philpot, Lorna*

r Who's Buying for the Home — *Wellner, Alison Stein*

c Who's Got Gertie? and How Do We Get Her Back? — *Bailey, Linda*

Who's in Control? — *Darman, Richard*

c Who's That Jumbun in the Log? (Illus. by Grace Fielding) — *McRobbie, Narelle*

yr Who's Who 1897-1996. Electronic Media Version

c Who's Who at the Zoo (Illus. by Patricia Mullins) — *Walters, Celeste*

r Who's Who in Classical Mythology — *Room, Adrian*

r Who's Who in Finance and Industry 1996-1997

r Who's Who in Korean Literature

r Who's Who in Labor 1946- (Dryden)

r Who's Who in Labor (Arno)

r Who's Who in Lebanon 1997-1998

r Who's Who in Military History from 1453 to the Present Day — *Keegan, John*

The Wiles of Women/The Wiles of Men — *Goldman, Shalom*

c Wiley and the Hairy Man — *Bang, Molly*

c Wiley and the Hairy Man (Illus. by Brian Pinkney) — *Sierra, Judy*

r The Wiley Dictionary of Civil Engineering and Construction: English-Spanish, Spanish-English — *Kennedy, Felicitas*

r Wiley Encyclopedia of Energy and the Environment. Vols. 1-2 — *Bisio, Attilio*

Wilhelm II. Vol. 2 — *Cecil, Lamar*

Wilhelm II: Die Jugend Des Kaisers 1859-1888 — *Rohl, John C G*

Wilhelmi: The Clay's the Thing — *Holland, Ben*

Wilkie Collins to the Forefront — *Smith, Nelson*

Will America Grow Up before It Grows Old? — *Peterson, Peter G*

r Will H. Bradley: His Work — *Bambace, Anthony*

Will Power! — *Weinberg, George*

c Will Rogers (Illus. by David Charles Brandon) — *Schott, Jane A*

c Will Rogers: Cowboy Philosopher — *Malone, Mary*

y Will the Dollars Stretch? — *Pollock, Sudie*

The Will to Believe and Other Essays — *James, William*

Will to Murder — *Sorrells, Walter*

Will We Be Smart Enough? — *Hunt, Earl*

Will You Always Love Me? and Other Stories — *Oates, Joyce Carol*

y Will You Always Love Me? and Other Stories (Guidall). Audio Version — *Oates, Joyce Carol*

y Will You Be My Brussels Sprout? — *Frank, Lucy*

Will You Hold Me? — *Kenworthy, Christopher*

c Will You Mind the Baby, Davy? (Illus. by Eve Tharlet) — *Weninger, Brigitte*

Willa Cather (Seldes). Audio Version — *Cather, Willa*

Willa Cather and the Art of Conflict — *Shaw, Patrick W*

Willa Cather and the Myth of American Migration — *Urgo, Joseph R*

Willa Cather in Context — *Reynolds, Guy*

Willard L. Sperry: The Quandaries of a Liberal Protestant Mind 1914-1939 — *Fox, William L, 1953-*

Willem De Kooning: Sculpture — *Forge, Andrew*

William III and the Godly Revolution — *Claydon, Tony*

William and Henry James — *James, William*

William Appleman Williams: The Tragedy of Empire — *Buhle, Paul M*

William Bartram on the Southeastern Indians — *Waselkov, Gregory A*

r William Booton (1712-1787) of Culpeper County, Virginia and His Descendants — *Dieterle, Diane*

William Burke and Francisco De Miranda — *Rodriguez, Mario*

William Cobbett: The Politics of Style — *Nattrass, Leonora*

r William Congreve: An Annotated Bibliography 1978-1994 — *Bartlett, Laurence*

William Cooper's Town — *Taylor, Alan, 1955-*

William Corby, C.S.C.: Memoirs of Chaplain Life — *Corby, William*

William Crolly: Archbishop of Armagh 1835-49 — *Macaulay, Ambrose*

William Ellerby and James Pigott Pritchett — *Royle, Edward*

William Faulkner and Southern History — *Williamson, Joel*

William Faulkner and the Tangible Past — *Hines, Thomas S*

William Friday: Power, Purpose, and American Higher Education — *Link, William A*

William Glackens — *Gerdts, William H*

William Goyen: Selected Letters from a Writer's Life — *Goyen, William*

r William Grant Still: A Bio-Bibliography — *Still, Judith Anne*

c William Hall — *Pachai, Bridglal*

William Harvey's Natural Philosophy — *French, R K*

William I. Myers and the Modernization of American Agriculture — *Slaybaugh, Douglas*

William James on Consciousness beyond the Margin — *Taylor, Eugene*

William James Remembered — *Simon, Linda*

William John Leech: An Irish Painter Abroad — *Ferran, Denise*

William Lindsay White 1900-1973 — *Jernigan, E Jay*

William Morris — *Parry, Linda*

William Morris: A Life for Our Times — *MacCarthy, Fiona*

William Morris: Artifacts/Glass — *Blonston, Gary*

r The William Morris Chronology — *Salmon, Nicholas*

William Morris Revisited

y William Parker: Rebel without Rights — *Rosenburg, John*

The William Powell and Myrna Loy Murder Case — *Baxt, George*

William Shakespeare: Writing for Performance — *Brown, John Russell*

y William Shakespeare's A Midsummer Night's Dream (Illus. by Dennis Nolan) — *Coville, Bruce*

y William Tecumseh Sherman: Defender and Destroyer — *Whitelaw, Nancy*

c William Tell (Illus. by Leonard Everett Fisher) — *Fisher, Leonard Everett*

William Thomas, Architect 1799-1860 — *McArthur, Glenn*

William Tyndale: A Biography — *Daniell, David*

William Tyndale and the Law — *Dick, John A R*

William Tyndale on Priests and Preachers — *Brown, Andrew J*

William Waynflete: Bishop and Educationalist — *Davis, Virginia*

c William Wegman's Farm Days (Illus. by William Wegman) — *Wegman, William*

c William Wegman's Mother Goose (Illus. by William Wegman) — *Wegman, William*

William Wordsworth: A Literary Life — *Williams, John, 1946-*

William Wordsworth: A Poetic Life — *Mahoney, John L*

Williams Sassine Ecrivain De La Marginalite — *Chevrier, Jacques*

y The Williamson Effect — *Zelazny, Roger*

Willie Brown: A Biography — *Richardson, James, 1953-*

Willie Nelson Lyrics 1957-1994 — *Nelson, Willie*

Willie: Raising and Loving a Child with Attention Deficit Disorder — *Colin, Ann*

c Willie Takes a Hike (Illus. by Ted Rand) — *Rand, Gloria*

c Willie Was Different (Illus. by Norman Rockwell) — *Rockwell, Norman*

The Willing Spirit — *Anthony, Piers*

A Willing Spirit — *Stover, Deb*

c Willis and the Echo (Illus. by Cheryl Lloyd) — *Wellington, Craig*

c Willow Chase — *Duey, Kathleen*

The Willow Grove — *Sheck, Laurie*

p Willow Springs

c The Willows in Winter — *Horwood, William*

c Willy and Hugh — *Brown, Anthony*

c Willy and May (Illus. by Judith Byron Schachner) — *Schachner, Judith Byron*

Willy Slater's Lane — *Wieland, Mitch*

c Willy the Wizard (Illus. by Anthony Browne) — *Browne, Anthony*

c Willy's Silly Grandma (Illus. by Shelley Jackson) — *DeFelice, Cynthia C*

c Wilma Mankiller (Illus. by Janice Lee Porter) — *Lowery, Linda*

c Wilma Unlimited (Illus. by David Diaz) — *Krull, Kathleen*

c Wilmot and Chips — *Shearer, Alex*

Wilsonian Idealism in America — *Steigerwald, David*

The Wilsonian Impulse — *Hampton, Mary N*

c The Wilsons, a House-Painting Team (Illus. by Christine Osinski) — *Flanagan, Alice K*

Wilson's Island — *Blanchard, Stephen*

Win, Lose or Die — *Manson, Cynthia*

Win, Lose, or Draw — *Stam, Allan C*

The Winchcombe Sacramentary — *Davril, Anselme*

Wind against the Mountain — *Davis, Richard L, 1951-*

The Wind among the Reeds — *Yeats, W B*

Wind and Lies — *Parrish, Richard*

r Wind Chamber Music — *Secrist-Schmedes, Barbara*

Wind Effects on Structures. 3rd Ed. — *Simiu, Emil*

Wind Energy in America — *Righter, Robert W*

The Wind Ensemble and Its Repertoire — *Cipolla, Frank J*

Wind from a Foreign Sky — *Reimann, Katya*

c The Wind Harp and Other Angel Tales — *Pochocki, Ethel*

c The Wind in the Willows — *Grahame, Kenneth*

c The Wind in the Willows. Audio Version — *Grahame, Kenneth*

y Wind Shifter — *Smith, Linda, 1949-*

Wind Water — *Williams, Jeanne*

c Wind, What Makes You Move? (Illus. by Chiara Carrer) — *Grazzini, Francesca*

Windfall — *Stevenson, Helen*

c The Windigo's Return (Illus. by Greg Couch) — *Wood, Douglas*

The Winding Road to West Egg — *Roulson, Robert*

The Winding Stair 1929 — *Yeats, W B*

Windmill: Essays from Four Mile Ranch — *Romtvedt, David*

y The Window — *Ingold, Jeanette*

Window Boxes — *Martin, Tovah*

r A Window into History — *MacDonald, Eleanor Kay*

c A Window of Time (Illus. by Rhonda Kyrias) — *Leighton, Audrey O*

Window on a Catholic Parish — *Kelly, Francis*

Windows 95 and NT Programming with the Microsoft Foundation Class Library — *Murray, William H*

Windows 95 API How-To — *Telles, Matthew A*

The Windows 95 Bible — *Davis, Frederic E*

Windows 95 Clear and Simple — *McBride, Peter*

Windows 95 for Busy People. 2nd Ed. — *Mansfield, Ron*

Windows 95 Games Programming — *Trujillo, Stan*

Windows 95 Is Driving Me Crazy — *Nelson, Kay Yarborough*

Windows 95 Power Toolkit — *Mansfield, Richard*

Windows and Doors — *Time-Life Books*

c Windows for Beginners — *Dungworth, Richard*

Windows into the Infinite — *Powell, Barbara*

Windows NT 4 for Busy People — *Nelson, Stephen L*

Windows NT for Open VMS Professionals — *Solomon, David A*

Windows NT Training Guide — *Turley, James*

Windows NT Versus NetWare — *Korzeniowski, Paul*

Windows NT Web Server Handbook — *Sheldon, Tom*

Windows on Mathematical Meanings — *Noss, Richard*

Windows on the World Complete Wine Course. Rev. Ed. — *Zraly, Kevin*

c Windowsill Science Centers — *Kepler, Lynne*

r Winds of Change — *Gros, Daniel*

The Winds of Change — *Ray, Himanshu P*

Winds of Change — *Royle, Trevor*

Winds of the Spirit — *Hodgson, Peter C*

Windswept House — *Martin, Malachi*

Windy City Blues — *Paretsky, Sara*

y Windy City Blues (Cassidy). Audio Version — *Paretsky, Sara*

c Windy Day — *Feller, Carline*

Windy Gap — *Silkensen, Gregory M*

Wine and Dine — *Breitstein, Ron*

Wine Appreciation. 2nd Ed. — *Vine, Richard P*

r Wine Country Bike Rides — *Emmery, Lena*

Wine for Dummies — *McCarthy, Ed*

Wine for Dummies — *Mulligan, Mary*

p Wine Spectator

r Wine Spectator's Guide to Great Wine Values $10 and Under

r Wine Spectator's Ultimate Guide to Buying Wine. 5th Ed.

Wine with Food — *Simon, Joanna*

y Winesburg, Ohio (Guidall). Audio Version — *Anderson, Sherwood*

The Wing of Madness — *Burston, Daniel*

r Wing Short-Title Catalogue 1641-1700. Electronic Media Version

The Wingate Anaerobic Test — *Inbar, Omri*

c The Winged Cat — *Lattimore, Deborah Nourse*

y Winged Magic — *Herbert, Mary H*

y Winging It — *Malcolm, Jahnna N*

Wings for Victory — *Dunmore, Spencer*

Wings from Cover — *Gray, Ed*

Wings Guide to British Birds — *Cozens, Dominic*

y Wings of Fury — *Wilcox, Robert*

y Wings of Morning — *Childers, Thomas*

Wings of Paradise — *Cody, John*

c Wings on Things — *Brown, Marc*

c Wings, Stings, and Wriggly Things (Illus. by Sandra Doyle) — *Jenkins, Martin*

The Winner-Take-All Society — *Frank, Robert H*

r Winners: A Collection of Cooperatively Developed Teaching Units for Resource-Based Learning — *Knight, Linda*

Winners and Losers

c Winnie in Winter (Illus. by K Paul) — *Thomas, V*

c Winnie the Pooh's 1,2,3

c Winnie-the-Pooh's 1,2,3 (Illus. by Ernest H Shepard)

c Winnie the Pooh's ABC

c Winnie-the-Pooh's Cookie Book (Illus. by Ernest H Shepard)

c Winnie-the-Pooh's Picnic Cookbook (Illus. by Ernest H Shepard)

Winning Can Be Murder — *Crider, Bill*

c Winning Checkers for Kids

Winning Hearts and Minds — *Carruthers, Susan L*

Winning Passion — *Priddy, Laurance L*
Winning People Over — *Kaplan, Burton*
Winning Solutions — *Lozansky, Edward*
y The Winning Stroke — *Wyeth, Sharon Dennis*
Winning the Peace — *Ruggie, John Gerard*
Winning the Race for Value — *Sheehy, Barry*
Winning the West for Christ — *Bender, Norman J*
Winning through Innovation — *Tushman, Michael L*
y Winning Ways — *Macy, Sue*
y Winning's Only Part of the Game — *Bowden, Bobby*
Winnipeg Development Agreement 1995-2000
The Winnipeg General Strike of 1919 — *Bumsted, J M*
Winona's Web — *Cogan, Priscilla*
Winslow Homer — *Cikovsky, Nicolai, Jr.*
Winslow Homer in the Adirondacks — *Tatham, David*
y Winston Churchill: Soldier, Statesman, Artist
    — *Severance, John B*
Winston Churchill's Last Campaign — *Young, John W*
c Winter (Illus. by Kim Woolley) — *Baxter, Nicola*
Winter Butterfly — *Renton, Alice*
Winter Chill — *Cleary, Jon*
Winter Fire — *Lowell, Elizabeth*
Winter Fruit — *Randall, Dale B J*
Winter Games — *Feinstein, John*
y The Winter Hare — *Goodman, Joan Elizabeth*
Winter in July — *Barley, Janet Crane*
The Winter King — *Cornwell, Bernard*
Winter Numbers — *Hacker, Marilyn*
y The Winter of Red Snow — *Gregory, Kristiana*
c Winter on the Farm — *Powell, Jillian*
c Winter on the Farm (Illus. by Jody Wheeler)
    — *Wilder, Laura Ingalls*
Winter Quarters — *Richards, Mary Haskin Parker*
y Winter Rose — *McKillip, Patricia A*
Winter Tales — *Brown, George Mackay*
The Winter Wolf — *Parry, Richard, 1942-*
Winterflight — *Bayly, Joseph*
Wintergras — *Bydlinski, Georg*
Eine Winterliche Reise Zu Den Flussen Donau, Save,
    Morawa Und Drina Oder Gerechtigkeit Fur Serbien
    — *Handke, Peter*
Winter's Edge — *Miner, Valerie*
Winter's Gold — *Heffernan, William*
The Winter's Hero — *Aksyonov, Vassily*
Wintersong: Christmas Readings — *L'Engle,
    Madeleine*
The Wired Neighborhood — *Doheny-Farina, Stephen*
r Wired Style — *Hale, Constance*
Wired Women — *Cherny, Lynn*
Wireless Communications in Developing Countries
    — *Schwartz, Rachel E*
Wireless LANs — *Wenig, Raymond*
Wireless Radio — *Coe, Lewis*
Wiring a House — *Cauldwell, Rex*
Die Wirtschaftsfuhrung Des Deutschen Ordens In
    Preussen 1382-1454 — *Sarnowsky, Jurgen*
Wisdom and Creation — *Perdue, Leo G*
Wisdom and Innocence — *Pearce, Joseph*
The Wisdom of Religious Commitment — *Tilley,
    Terrence W*
Wisdom of the African World — *McKnight, Reginald*
The Wisdom of the Body — *Nuland, Sherwin B*
The Wisdom of the Bones — *Walker, Alan, 1938-*
Wisdom of the Earth. Vol. 1 — *Miller, Gordon L,
    1954-*
The Wisdom of the Elders — *Fleming, Robert, 1950-*
Wisdom of the Gurus — *Bowman, Charles F*
The Wisdom of the Word: Faith — *Ponder, Rhinold
    Lamar*
The Wisdom of the Word: Love — *Ponder, Rhinold
    Lamar*
Wisdom Sits in Places — *Basso, Keith H*
c Wisdom Tales from around the World — *Forest,
    Heather*
Wise as Serpents, Innocent as Doves — *Miller, Keith
    Graber*
A Wise Extravagance — *Neal, Kenneth*
Wise Moves in Hard Times — *Leslie, David W*
y Wise Poison — *Rivard, David*
Wise Up to Teens — *Zollo, Peter*
c The Wise Washerman (Illus. by Wang Kui) — *Froese,
    Deborah L*
A Wise Woman — *Mynors, Lavinia*
y Wise Women — *Cahill, Susan*
Wiser Than Despair — *Faulkner, Quentin*
The Wish for Kings — *Lapham, Lewis H*
y Wish Me Luck — *Heneghan, James*
Wish You Were Here — *Kirkpatrick, Peter*
c Wish You Were Here (Illus. by Amy Schwartz)
    — *Krull, Kathleen*
The Wishbones — *Perrotta, Tom*

c Wishing (Illus. by Debrah Santini) — *Tiller, Ruth*
c Wishing Moon (Illus. by Lesley Harker). Book and
    Audio Version — *Harker, Lesley*
Wishing on the Moon — *Clarke, Donald*
Wisps of Violence — *Sypher, Eileen*
y The Wit and Wisdom of the Founding Fathers
    — *Zall, Paul M*
The Wit of Seventeenth-Century Poetry — *Summers,
    Claude J*
The Witch Doctors — *Micklethwait, John*
Witch Hunt in the B.C. Woods — *Robinson, A B*
The Witch in History — *Purkiss, Diane*
c Witch Mama (Illus. by Judith Caseley) — *Caseley,
    Judith*
c Witch Music and Other Stories — *Rubinstein, Gillian*
c The Witch of Blackbird Pond — *Speare, Elizabeth
    George*
The Witch of Exmoor — *Drabble, Margaret*
Witchcraft at Salem — *Hansen, Chadwick*
Witchcraft in Celestina — *Severin, Dorothy Sherman*
Witchcraze: A New History of the European Witch
    Hunts — *Barstow, Anne Llewellyn*
Witches and Jesuits — *Wills, Gary*
Witches and Neighbors — *Briggs, Robin*
Witches and Neighbours — *Briggs, Robin*
y Witches' Brew — *Brooks, Terry*
Witches, Devils, and Doctors in the Renaissance
    — *Weyer, Johann*
c Witches (Illus. by McRae Books) — *Ross, Stewart*
y Witchlight — *Bradley, Marion Zimmer*
The Witch's Kitchen — *Prokhoris, Sabine*
c The Witch's Tears (Illus. by Paul Howard) — *Nimmo,
    Jenny*
With a Moon in Transit — *Osherow, Jacqueline*
y With a Tangled Skein (Guidall). Audio Version
    — *Anthony, Piers*
With an Extreme Burning — *Pronzini, Bill*
With Bleeding Footsteps — *Thomas, Robert David*
With Broadax and Firebrand — *Dean, Warren*
With Chatwin — *Clapp, Susannah*
With Child — *King, Laurie R*
With Courage — *Nalty, Bernard C*
With Custer on the Little Bighorn — *Taylor, William
    O*
y With Every Drop of Blood — *Collier, James Lincoln*
With Faith and Physic — *Pollock, Linda*
With Friends like These — *Coleridge, Nicholas*
With Friends like These — *Jentleson, Bruce W*
y With God on Our Side — *Martin, William C, 1937-*
With Kindest Regards — *Freer, Charles Lang*
y With Love, Amanda — *Ritthaler, Shelly*
With Malice toward Some — *Marcus, George E*
With Musket, Cannon, and Sword — *Nosworthy,
    Brent*
With My Soul amongst Lions — *Patterson, Gareth*
With My Trousers Rolled — *Epstein, Joseph*
y With Needle and Thread — *Bial, Raymond*
c With One White Wing (Illus. by Erik Blegvad)
    — *Spires, Elizabeth*
With Our Own Eyes — *Mosley, Don*
With Pen and Saber — *Trout, Robert J*
With Rod and Line in Colorado Waters — *France, L
    B*
With Roots and Wings — *McDaniel, Jay B*
y With the Indians in the Rockies — *Schultz, James
    Willard*
With Undefending Heart — *McGowan, Susan*
With Walt Whitman in Camden. Vols. 8-9 — *Traubel,
    Horace*
With Wounds Still Wet — *Sallee, Wayne Allen*
Within a Budding Grove (Jason). Audio Version
    — *Proust, Marcel*
y Within a Painted Past (Illus. by Ruth Ohi)
    — *Hutchins, Hazel*
Within Context — *Efroymson, David P*
Within the Context of No Context — *Trow, George W
    S*
Within the Human Realm — *Schmidt, J D*
Within the Wall of Denial — *Kearney, Robert J*
Without a Guide — *Govier, Katherine*
Without a Name — *Vera, Yvonne*
Without a Prayer — *Alley, Robert S*
Without Blare of Trumpets — *Fine, Sidney*
Without Consent — *Fyfield, Frances*
Without Lying Down — *Beauchamp, Cari*
Without Miracles — *Cziko, Gary*
c Without Words (Illus. by Barbara Sonneborn)
    — *Ryder, Joanne*
Witness: 25 Years on the Environmental Front Line
    — *Mulvaney, Kieran*
The Witness of the Brothers — *Oved, Iaacov*

Witness to Injustice — *Frost, David, Jr.*
Witnessed: The True Story of the Brooklyn Bridge
    UFO Abductions — *Hopkins, Budd*
Witnessing America — *Rae, Noel*
Witnessing for Sociology — *Jenkins, Pamela*
Witnessing Insanity — *Eigen, Joel Peter*
A Wittenberg University Library Catalogue of 1536
    — *Kusukawa, Sachiko*
Wittgenstein: A Religious Point of View? — *Malcolm,
    Norman*
Wittgenstein: A Way of Seeing — *Genova, Judith*
Wittgenstein and the Mystical — *Sontag, Frederick*
r A Wittgenstein Dictionary — *Glock, Hans-Johann*
y Wittgenstein in 90 Minutes — *Strathern, Paul*
Wittgenstein: Mind and Will — *Hacker, P M S*
Wittgenstein Reads Freud — *Bouveresse, Jacques*
Wittgensteinian Themes — *Malcolm, Norman*
Wittgenstein's Ladder — *Perloff, Marjorie*
Wittgenstein's Place in Twentieth-Century Analytic
    Philosophy — *Hacker, P M S*
Wives and Daughters (Scales). Audio Version
    — *Gaskell, Elizabeth*
Wives and Mothers, Schoolmistresses and Scullery
    Maids — *Errington, Elizabeth Jane*
y The Wizard and Me — *Luckett, Dave*
y The Wizard and the Floating City — *Rowley,
    Christopher*
A Wizard in Peace — *Stasheff, Christopher*
c The Wizard of Oz (Illus. by Lisbeth Zwerger)
    — *Baum, L Frank*
Wizard of the Wind — *Keith, Don*
Wizard of the Winds — *Cole, Allan*
Wizard: The Life and Times of Nikola Tesla — *Seifer,
    Marc J*
c Wizard's Hall (Yolen). Audio Version — *Yolen, Jane*
Wo De Jie Jie — *Zhang, Zijing*
Wo Es War — *Drawert, Kurt*
Wo Kan Ying Dai Er — *Yu, Youcheng*
Wo Liang — *Fangfang, Li*
Woe Is I — *O'Conner, Patricia T*
Wogfood: An Oral History with Recipes (Illus. by
    Grenville Turner) — *Newton, John Sefton*
Woke Me up This Morning — *Young, Alan*
c The Wolf — *Bour, Laura*
c Wolf (Illus. by Sara Fanelli) — *Fanelli, Sara*
c Wolf Country I — *Robbins, Barbara H*
Wolf Creek Station — *Miner, Craig*
p Wolf Head Quarterly
Wolf Kahn — *Spring, Justin*
Wolf Mountain Moon — *Johnston, Terry C*
Wolf, No Wolf — *Bowen, Peter*
y Wolf Rider — *Avi*
The Wolf Strain — *Brand, Max*
The Wolf, the Woman, the Wilderness — *Martino,
    Teresa Tsimmu*
Wolf Tourist — *Elhard, Jay Robert*
Wolf Walking — *Rideout, Judi*
c The Wolf Watcher (Illus. by Andy DaVolls) — *Hood,
    Alison*
y Wolf-Woman — *Jordan, Sherryl*
Wolfe Tone: Prophet of Irish Independence — *Elliott,
    Marianne*
Wolfgang Tillmans (Taschen) — *Tillmans, Wolfgang*
c The Wolfhound (Illus. by Kris Waldherr) — *Franklin,
    Kristine L*
c Wolfman Sam — *Levy, Elizabeth*
y Wolfpack: U-Boats at War 1939-1945 — *Kaplan,
    Philip*
Wolfram Von Eschenbach: Parzival. Vols. 1-2
    — *Wolfram, Von Eschenbach*
y Wolves — *Gibson, Nancy*
c The Wolves (Illus. by Bernie Fuchs) — *Heinz, Brian J*
c Wolves — *Horton, Casey*
Wolves from the Sea — *Whitehead, Neil L*
c Wolves in Yellowstone (Illus. by Randy Houk). Book
    and Audio Version — *Houk, Randy*
The Wolves of Isle Royale — *Peterson, Rolf O*
The Wolves of Yellowstone — *Phillips, Michael K*
The Woman and the Ape — *Hoeg, Peter*
y The Woman and the Ape (Guidall). Audio Version
    — *Hoeg, Peter*
Woman and the Infinite — *Hartfield-Mendez, Vialla*
The Woman and the Myth. Rev. and Expanded Ed.
    — *Fuller, Margaret*
A Woman Doctor's Guide to Depression — *Ferber,
    Jane S*
A Woman Doctor's Guide to Miscarriage
    — *Friedman, Lynn*
Woman in a Special House — *Little, Geraldine*
y A Woman in Amber — *Nesaule, Agate*
A Woman in History — *Berg, Maxine*

Woman in the Dark — *Phillips, T J*

c The Woman in the Moon (Illus. by Carla Golembe) — *Rattigan, Jama Kim*

The Woman in the Oil Field — *Daugherty, Tracy*

y The Woman in the Wall — *Kindl, Patrice*

The Woman in White (Holm). Audio Version — *Collins, Wilkie*

A Woman of Air — *Hargrave, Margaret Packham*

Woman of Color, Daughter of Privilege — *Leslie, Kent Anderson*

The Woman of Ideas in French Art 1830-1848 — *Bergman-Carton, Janis*

A Woman of Means — *Taylor, Peter Hillsman*

The Woman of Reason — *Green, Karen*

Woman on the Edge of Time — *Piercy, Marge*

Woman Police Officer in Elevator — *Lasdun, James*

The Woman Reader 1837-1914 — *Flint, Kate*

A Woman Scorned — *Sanday, Peggy Reeves*

Woman Suffrage and the New Democracy — *Graham, Sara Hunter*

Woman the Hunter — *Stange, Mary Zeiss*

Woman to Woman — *Thornton, Yvonne S*

The Woman Who Died in Her Sleep — *Gregerson, Linda*

y The Woman Who Lives in the Earth — *Wolfe, Swain*

c The Woman Who Outshone the Sun (Illus. by F Olivera) — *Cruz Martinez, Alejandro*

y The Woman Who Ran for President — *Underhill, Lois Beachy*

c The Woman Who Rides Like a Man — *Pierce, Tamora*

The Woman Who Rode Away and Other Stories — *Lawrence, D H*

The Woman Who Spilled Words All over Herself — *Daniell, Rosemary*

The Woman Who Walked into Doors — *Doyle, Roddy*

The Woman Who Walked into Doors (Ryan). Audio Version — *Doyle, Roddy*

The Woman Who Walked on Water — *Tuck, Lily*

The Woman Without Experiences — *Dienstfrey, Patricia*

WomanGifts: Biblical Models for Forming Church — *Smith, Pamela*

Womanist and Feminist Aesthetics — *Allan, Tuzyline Jita*

Woman's Best Friend — *Cohen, Barbara, 1949-*

A Woman's Book of Life — *Borysenko, Joan*

A Woman's Constitution? — *Irving, Helen*

The Woman's Day Book of Holiday Crafts — *Woman's Day (New York, N.Y.)*

r The Woman's Encyclopedia of Natural Healing — *Null, Gary*

Woman's Face of Resistance — *Kerschbaumer, Marie-Therese*

r A Woman's Guide to Coping with Disability

The Woman's Guide to Hysterectomy — *Haas, Adelaide*

A Woman's Guide to Starting a Small Business — *Saxon, Ro*

The Woman's Hand — *Schalow, Paul Gordon*

A Woman's Place — *Delinsky, Barbara*

A Woman's Place — *Juster, Norton*

A Woman's Place — *Roberts, Elizabeth*

Woman's Theatrical Space — *Scolnicov, Hanna*

c Wombat Divine (Illus. by Kerry Argent) — *Fox, Mem*

c A Wombat Named Bosco (Illus. by Bettina Guthridge) — *French, Jackie*

The Women — *Als, Hilton*

Women according to Men — *Hull, Suzanne W*

Women against Hitler — *Thomas, Theodore N*

Women and AIDS — *O'Leary, Ann*

Women and Alcohol in a Highland Maya Town — *Eber, Christine*

Women and Arthurian Literature — *Wynne-Davies, Marion*

Women and Autobiography in the Twentieth Century — *Anderson, Linda*

Women and Discourse in the Fiction of Marguerite Duras — *Cohen, Susan D*

Women and Drugs

Women and Families — *Roberts, Elizabeth*

Women and Fundamentalism — *Gerami, Shahin*

Women and Gender in Early Modern Europe — *Wiesner, Merry E*

Women and Group Psychotherapy — *DeChant, Betsy*

Women and Industrialization in Asia — *Horton, Susan*

Women and Lawyers in the Mid-Nineteenth Century English Novel — *DeCicco, Lynne Marie*

Women and Leadership — *Klenke, Karin*

yr Women and Men at Work — *Reskin, Barbara*

yr Women and Men in Europe and North America 1995

Women and Men in Namibia — *Namibia. National Planning Commission*

Women and Men in the European Union — *Statistical Office of the European Communities*

Women and Mental Health — *Sechzer, Jeri A*

Women and Minorities in American Professions — *Tang, Joyce*

r Women and Music — *Ericson, Margaret D*

Women and Philanthropy in Nineteenth-Century Ireland — *Luddy, Maria*

Women and Political Insurgency — *Barry, David*

Women and Politics in the Third World — *Afshar, Haleh*

Women and Politics Worldwide — *Nelson, Barbara J*

Women and Power in Native North America — *Klein, Laura F*

r Women and Religion in Britain and Ireland — *Johnson, Dale A*

Women and Religion in Medieval and Renaissance Italy — *Bornstein, Daniel Ethan*

Women and Revolution in Africa, Asia, and the New World — *Tetreault, Mary Ann*

r Women and Science — *Ogilvie, Marilyn Bailey*

Women and Senior Management — *Poland, F*

Women and Sexuality in China — *Evans, Harriet*

Women and Sport — *Costa, D Margaret*

Women and Sustainable Development in Africa — *James, Valentine Udoh*

Women and Terrorism — *De Cataldo Neuburger, Luisella*

Women and the Common Life — *Lasch, Christopher*

yr Women and the Military — *Sherrow, Victoria*

Women and the Ownership of PMS — *Figert, Anne E*

Women and the Political Process in Twentieth-Century Iran — *Paidar, Parvin*

Women and the Religious Life in Premodern Europe — *Ranft, Patricia*

Women and the Use of Military Force — *Howes, Ruth H*

Women and the War Story — *Cooke, Miriam*

Women and War — *Elshtain, Jean Bethke*

Women and Words in Saudi Arabia — *Arebi, Saddeka*

r Women and Work — *Dubeck, Paula J*

Women and Work in Developing Countries — *Ghorayshi, Parvin*

Women and Work in Eighteenth-Century Edinburgh — *Sanderson, Elizabeth C*

Women, Art and Society — *Chadwick, Whitney*

Women Artists and the Parisian Avant-Garde — *Perry, Gill*

Women at Risk — *O'Leary, Ann*

Women at the Center — *Todd, Helen*

The Women at the Pump — *Hamsun, Knut*

Women before the Bar — *Dayton, Cornelia Hughes*

Women Breaking Through — *Swiss, Deborah J*

r Women Composers. Vol. 1 — *Schleifer, Martha Furman*

r Women Composers. Vols. 1-2 — *Schleifer, Martha Furman*

r Women Composers and Songwriters — *Claghorn, Gene*

Women Creating Women — *Haberstroh, Patricia Boyle*

Women, Crime and the Courts in Early Modern England — *Walker, Garthine*

Women Critics 1660-1820 — *Folger Collective on Early Women Critics (Scholarly Group)*

Women, Culture, and Development — *Nussbaum, Martha Craven*

Women Editing Modernism — *Marek, Jayne E*

Women, Education, and Development in Asia — *Mak, Grace C L*

Women Encounter God — *Moody, Linda A*

p Women Envision

Women, Family and Society in Medieval Europe — *Herlihy, David*

Women, Feminism, and Social Change in Argentina, Chile, and Uruguay 1890-1940 — *Lavrin, Asuncion*

Women for Hire — *Corbin, Alain*

y Women for Peace — *Brill, Marlene Targ*

Women, Gender, and World Politics — *Beckman, Peter R*

Women, Guerrillas, and Love — *Rodriguez, Ileana*

Women, Identity and Private Life in Britain 1900-50 — *Giles, Judy*

Women in a Changing Global Economy — *United Nations. Dept. for Policy Coordination and Sustainable Development*

r Women in Agriculture — *Maman, Marie*

c Women in America's Wars — *Sheafer, Silvia Anne*

Women in Ancient Greece — *Blundell, Sue*

Women in Ancient Persia 559-331 BC — *Brosius, Maria*

Women in Antiquity — *Hawley, Richard, 1963-*

Women in Antiquity — *McAuslan, Ian*

Women in Brazil — *Caipora (Organization)*

Women in Britain — *Great Britain. Central Office of Information*

Women in Celtic Law and Culture — *Thompson, Jack George*

r Women in Christian History — *Blevins, Carolyn DeArmond*

r Women in Communication — *Signorielli, Nancy*

Women in England 1500-1760 — *Laurence, Anne*

Women in Exile — *Afkhami, Mahnaz*

Women in Islam — *Walther, Wiebke*

Women in Islamic Biographical Collections from Ibn Sa'd to Who's Who — *Roded, Ruth*

cr Women in Law — *Salokar, Rebecca Mae*

Women in Love — *Lawrence, D H*

Women in Medical Education — *Wear, Delese*

y Women in Medicine — *Garza, Hedda*

Women in Medieval England — *Jewell, Helen M*

r Women in Modern American Politics — *Cox, Elizabeth M*

Women in Music. Rev. Ed. — *Neuls-Bates, Carol*

Women in Myth — *Knapp, Bettina L*

r Women in Nigeria — *Azikiwe, Uche*

Women in Old Norse Society — *Jochens, Jenny*

Women in Prison. Rev. Ed. — *Watterson, Kathryn*

Women in Russian History from the Tenth to the Twentieth Century — *Pushkareva, Natalia*

r Women in Southern Literature — *Sweeney, Patricia*

Women in the Age of Economic Transformation — *Aslanbeigui, Nahid*

Women in the American Theatre — *Dudden, Faye E*

Women in the American Welfare Trap — *Kingfisher, Catherine Pelissier*

Women in the Background — *Humphries, Barry*

r Women in the Biblical World. Vol. 1 — *Gruber, Mayer I*

Women in the Church — *Kostenberger, Andreas J*

Women in the Civil Rights Movement — *Crawford, Vicki L*

Women in the Latin American Development Process — *Bose, Christine E*

y Women in the Material World — *D'Aluisio, Faith*

y Women in the Middle East — *Harik, Ramsay M*

Women in the Mines — *Moore, Marat*

r Women in the Netherlands

Women in the Presence — *Davie, Jody Shapiro*

Women in the Qur'an Traditions, and Interpretation — *Stowasser, Barbara Freyer*

Women in the Trees — *Koppelman, Susan*

r Women in the United States Military 1901-1995 — *Friedl, Vicki L*

Women in the Victorian Art World — *Orr, Clarissa Campbell*

Women in Their Beds — *Berriault, Gina*

Women in World Politics — *D'Amico, Francine*

Women, Information, and the Future — *Moseley, Eva Steiner*

y Women Inventors — *Altman, Linda Jacobs*

Women, Jews, and Muslims in the Texts of Reconquest Castile — *Mirrer, Louise*

Women: Looking beyond 2000

Women Love Sex — *Johnson, S*

Women, Media, and Politics — *Norris, Pippa*

Women, Men, and Gender — *Walsh, Mary Roth*

Women, Men, and Language — *Coates, Jennifer*

Women of Belize — *McClaurin, Irma*

The Women of Ben Jonson's Poetry — *Smith, Barbara, 1949, Dec., 12-*

Women of Color — *Brown-Guillory, Elizabeth*

r Women of Color — *Nordquist, Joan*

r Women of Congress — *Kaptur, Marcy*

Women of Fire and Spirit — *Hoehler-Fatton, Cynthia*

r Women of Ireland — *O Ceirin, Kit*

Women of Japan and Korea — *Gelb, Joyce*

Women of Mark — *Treadway, Sandra Gioia*

Women of Mongolia — *Avery, Martha*

Women of Prague — *Iggers, Wilma Abeles*

The Women of Royaumont — *Crofton, Eileen*

Women of Sand and Myrrh — *Shaykh, Hanan*

r Women of Strength — *Baldwin, Louis*

Women of the Anti-Slavery Movement — *Taylor, Clare*

Women of the Beat Generation — *Knight, Brenda*

Women of the Beat Generation (Weiss). Audio Version — *Knight, Brenda*

Women of the Commonwealth — *Porter, Susan L*

Women of the Earth Lodges — *Peters, Virginia Bergman*
Women of the Far Right — *Jeansonne, Glen*
c Women of the Lights (Illus. by James Watling) — *Fleming, Candace*
Women of the Place — *Jolly, Margaret*
Women of the Raj — *MacMillan, Margaret*
Women of the Street — *Herera, Sue*
The Women of Tijucopapo — *Felinto, Marilene*
y Women of Valor — *Segal, Sheila*
Women of Value — *Dimand, Mary Ann*
Women on a Wire — *Jones, Georgia*
Women on Divorce — *Kaganoff, Penny*
y The Women on the Bridge — *Dagg, Mel*
Women on the Case — *Paretsky, Sara*
y Women on the Hill — *Bingham, Clara*
y Women on the Hill — *Pollack, Jill S*
Women on the Margins — *Davis, Natalie Zemon*
Women on the Threshold — *Hayes, Kathleen*
Women on Women 3 — *Nestle, Joan*
Women Playwrights — *Smith, Marisa*
Women Playwrights 1995
r Women Playwrights in England, Ireland, and Scotland 1660-1823 — *Mann, David D*
r Women Playwrights of Diversity — *Peterson, Jane T*
Women Politicians and the Media — *Braden, Maria*
Women, Politics, and Reproduction — *Makus, Ingrid*
Women, Politics, and the United Nations — *Winslow, Anne*
Women, Power and Consciousness in Nineteenth Century Ireland — *Cullen, Mary*
Women, Property and Islam — *Moors, Annelies*
Women Readers and the Ideology of Gender in Old French Verse Romance — *Krueger, Roberta L*
Women Reading, Women Writing — *Keating, AnaLouise*
Women Religious and the Intellectual Life — *Puzon, Bridget*
Women Reshaping Human Rights — *Bouvard, Marguerite Guzman*
Women Resisting AIDS — *Schneider, Beth E*
Women Scientists in America — *Rossiter, Margaret W*
Women Shapeshifters — *Shinn, Thelma J*
Women Singing in the Snow — *Rebolledo, Tey Diana*
Women, Sport, and Culture — *Birrell, Susan*
Women Stage Directors Speak — *Daniels, Rebecca*
r Women State and Territorial Legislators 1895-1995 — *Cox, Elizabeth M*
Women Strike for Peace — *Swerdlow, Amy*
Women Struggling for a New Life — *Kim, Ai Ra*
Women Teachers and Feminist Politics 1900-1939 — *Oram, Alison*
Women, the Book and the Godly — *Smith, Lesley*
Women, the Environment and Sustainable Development — *Braidotti, Rosi*
Women, the Family, and Divorce Laws in Islamic History — *Sonbol, Amira El Azhary*
Women Transforming Communications — *Allen, Donna*
Women under the Bo Tree — *Bartholomeusz, Tessa*
Women vs. Capital — *Samara, Adel*
y Women Warriors — *Jones, David E*
The Women We Become — *Thomas, Ann G*
Women Who Changed the Heart of the City — *Burger, Dolores*
Women with Men — *Ford, Richard*
Women, Work, and Gender Relations in Developing Countries — *Ghorayshi, Parvin*
r Women Workers: An Annotated Bibliography 1983-94
r Women Writers in the United States — *Davis, Cynthia J*
Women Writers in Twentieth-Century Spain and Spanish America — *Davies, Catherine*
Women Writers of the English Renaissance — *Walker, Kim*
Women, Writing, and Revolution 1790-1827 — *Kelly, Gary*
Women Writing Culture — *Behar, Ruth*
Women Writing Culture — *Olson, Gary*
The Women's Awakening in Egypt — *Baron, Beth*
Women's Bodies in Classical Greek Science — *Dean-Jones, Lesley*
Women's Business — *Kenny, Chris*
r The Women's Complete Healthbook — *Epps, Roselyn Payne*
Women's Education, Autonomy, and Reproductive Behaviour — *Jejeebhoy, Shireen J*
Women's Fiction of the Second World War — *Plain, Gill*
r Women's Firsts — *Zilboorg, Caroline*

Women's Guide to Financial Self-Defense — *Mays, June*
Women's Health — *Falik, Marilyn M*
Women's Health — *Lewis, Judith A*
Women's Health in Primary Care — *Rosenfeld, Jo Ann*
Women's Health--Missing from U.S. Medicine — *Rosser, Sue Vilhauer*
Women's History — *Purvis, June*
r Women's Legal Guide — *Hauser, Barbara R*
The Women's Movement in Latin America. 2nd Ed. — *Jaquette, Jane S*
Women's Orients — *Melman, Billie*
r Women's Periodicals in the United States — *Endres, Kathleen L*
y Women's Rights (Illus. by Andrew McIntyre) — *Parker, Victoria*
y The Women's Rights Movement — *Stalcup, Brenda*
Women's Spirituality, Women's Lives — *Ochshorn, Judith*
r Women's Travel in Your Pocket. 16th Ed.
yr Women's Voices. Vols. 1-2 — *McElroy, Lorie Jenkins*
Women's Voices in Russia Today — *Rotkirch, Anna*
c Women's Voting Rights — *Harvey, Miles*
Women's Wages and Employment in Korea — *Pae, Mu-Gi*
r Women's Words — *Biggs, Mary*
Women's Work — *Barber, Elizabeth Wayland*
Women's Work 1840-1940 — *Roberts, Elizabeth*
Women's Work, Men's Work — *Wood, Betty*
c A Wonder Book for Girls and Boys (Illus. by Walter Crane) — *Hawthorne, Nathaniel*
The Wonder Book of the Air — *Shearer, Cynthia*
Wonder Bread and Ecstasy — *Isherwood, Charles*
c The Wonder Child and Other Jewish Fairy Tales (Illus. by Stephen Fieser) — *Schwartz, Howard*
The Wonder of Boys — *Gurian, Michael*
Wonder Tales — *Warner, Marina*
c The Wonder Thing (Illus. by Peter Gouldthorpe) — *Hathorn, Libby*
c Wondercrump Poetry — *Curry, Jennifer*
Wonderful Flying Machines — *Beard, Barrett Thomas*
c Wonderful Nature, Wonderful You (Illus. by Christopher Canyon) — *Ireland, Karin*
Wonderful Women by the Water — *Fagerholm, Monika*
The Wonderful World of Cookie Jars — *Supnick, Mark*
c Wood — *Chambers, Catherine*
Wood — *Goldsworthy, Andy*
The Wood Beyond — *Hill, Reginald*
Wood Destroying Insects — *Creffield, J W*
The Wood Duck and the Mandarin — *Shurtleff, Lawton L*
Wood of the Cradle, Wood of the Cross — *Houselander, Caryll*
Wood Play — *Henderson, Ann*
y The Wood Wife — *Windling, Terri*
Wooden: A Lifetime of Observations On and Off the Court — *Wooden, John*
y Wooden Fish Songs — *McCunn, Ruthanne Lum*
c Wooden Teeth and Jelly Beans — *Nelson, Ray*
The Wooden World — *Rodger, N A M*
y Woodholme: A Black Man's Story of Growing Up Alone — *Wickham, DeWayne*
c Woodland Christmas — *Angel, Marie*
c Woodland Christmas (Illus. by Frances Tyrrell) — *Tyrrell, Frances*
The Woodlanders (Rowe). Audio Version — *Hardy, Thomas*
c Woodleigh Marx Hubbard's Twelve Days of Christmas (Illus. by Woodleigh Hubbard) — *Twelve Days of Christmas (English Folk Song)*
c Woodpeckers — *McDonald, Mary Ann*
r Woodpeckers: An Identification Guide to the Woodpeckers of the World — *Winkler, Hans*
y Woodrow Wilson: Visionary for Peace — *Rogers, James T*
c Woods (Illus. by Patricia J Wynne) — *Silver, Donald M*
y Woodsong — *Paulsen, Gary*
Woody Allen on Woody Allen — *Allen, Woody*
Woody Allen's Angst — *Lee, Sander H*
Woody, Cisco, and Me — *Longhi, Jim*
Woody Gwyn — *Sacks, Peter M*
y Woody: Movies from Manhattan — *Fox, Julian*
Woolf and Lessing — *Saxton, Ruth*
A Word after Dying — *Granger, Ann*
Word and Image in Arthurian Literature — *Busby, Keith*
Word and Silence — *Gawronski, Raymond*

y Word by Word (Lamott). Audio Version — *Lamott, Anne*
The Word Encountered — *Kavanaugh, John F*
The Word for Everything — *Mitchell, Roger*
Word for Windows 95 Clear and Simple — *Brindley, Keith*
Word for Windows 95 for Busy People — *Crumlish, Christian*
A Word in Season — *Newbigin, Lesslie*
The Word Made Flesh — *Bliss, Michael, 1947-*
The Word of God and the Languages of Man. Vol. 1 — *Bono, James*
Word of Mouth — *Farrant, M A C*
Word of Mouth — *Welter, Matt*
The Word of the Lord. Vol. 2 — *McBrien, Philip J*
Word of Windows Project Book — *Copestake, Stephen*
Word, Sound, Image — *Kersenboom, Saskia*
y Word Watch — *Soukhanov, Anne H*
c A Wordful Child (Illus. by Ann W Olson) — *Lyon, George Ella*
WordPerfect 7 for Windows 95 and Windows NT Essentials — *Acklen, Laura*
r WordPerfect 7 for Windows 95 Bible — *Harris, Stephen E*
Words about Wizards — *Parrish, Robert*
Words across the Taiwan Strait — *Copper, John F*
c Words and Pictures — *Shorrock-Kelly, Kerry*
Words Apart — *Green, Jonathon*
Words Are Something Else — *Albahari, David*
c Words by Heart — *Sebestyen, Ouida*
Words for the Taking — *Bowers, Neal*
Words like Freedom — *Newman, Richard*
y Words of Stone — *Henkes, Kevin*
Words of Welfare — *Schram, Sanford*
Words, Script, and Pictures — *Schapiro, Meyer*
Words That Bind — *Arthur, John*
r Words That Make America Great — *Agel, Jerome*
Words That Matter — *Anderson, Judith H*
Words, Thoughts, and Theories — *Gopnik, Alison*
Words under the Words — *Nye, Naomi Shihab*
The Words We Live By — *Burrell, Brian*
The Words We Use — *O Muirithe, Diarmaid*
Words, Words, Words — *Anderman, Gunilla M*
Wordsworth and the Geologists — *Wyatt, John*
Wordsworth and the Question of Romantic Religion — *Easterlin, Nancy*
Wordsworth and the Zen Mind — *Rudy, John G*
Wordsworthian Errancies — *Collings, David*
r Wordsworth's Reading 1800-1815 — *Wu, Duncan*
Work — *Ritts, Herb*
Work Abuse — *Wyatt, Judith*
The Work Alternative — *Nightingale, Demetra Smith*
Work and Employment in Europe — *Cressey, Peter*
Work and Inequality in Urban China — *Bian, Yanjie*
Work and Its Inhibitions — *Socarides, Charles W*
Work and Welfare — *Stabile, Donald R*
r Work-at-Home Sourcebook. 6th Ed. — *Arden, Lynie*
Work Clothes — *Omelianuk, J Scott*
Work Concepts for the Future — *Estess, Patricia Schiff*
Work-Family Role Choices for Women in Their 20s and 30s — *Granrose, Cherlyn S*
Work for a Living and Still Be Free to Live — *McDargh, Eileen*
Work, Gender, and Family in Victorian England — *Ittmann, Karl*
Work in Towns 850-1850 — *Corfield, Penelope J*
Work It Out — *Hirsh, Sandra Krebs*
The Work Lives of First-Year Assistant Principals — *Hartzell, Gary N*
The Work of Antonio Sant'Ella — *Meyer, Esther Da Costa*
The Work of Charles Samuel Keene — *Houfe, Simon*
The Work of Democracy — *Keppel, Ben*
The Work of Nature — *Baskin, Yvonne*
The Work of Words — *Thurston, John*
The Work of Work — *Frantzen, Allen J*
r Work Patterns and Capital Utilisation — *Anxo, Dominique*
Work-Place: The Social Regulation of Labor Markets — *Peck, Jamie*
Work, Recreation, and Culture — *Blatt, Martin Henry*
r Work Related Abstracts 1973-
Work Songs — *Silverman, Jerry*
Work without Hope — *Burt, John*
Workbook and Laboratory Manual for Con Mucho Gusto. 4th Ed. — *Valette, Jean-Paul*
Workbook for Quality Mammography. 2nd Ed. — *Kimme-Smith, Carolyn*
Worker-Writer in America — *Wixson, Douglas*
Workers against Lenin — *Aves, Jonathan*

Workers and Canadian History — *Kealey, Gregory S*
Workers' Financial Participation
  — *Vaughan-Whitehead, Daniel*
p Workers' Health International Newsletter
The Workers' Movement in Russia — *Clarke, Simon*
The Workers of Nations — *Jacoby, Sanford M*
Workfare or Fair Work — *Rose, Nancy E*
Workgroup Computing — *Simon, Alan R*
Working-Class Cultures in Britain 1890-1960
  — *Bourke, Joanna*
Working Class Movements in India 1885-1975 — *Sen, Sunil Kumar*
Working-Class Self-Help in Nineteenth-Century
  England — *Hopkins, Eric*
c Working Cotton (Illus. by Carole Byard) — *Williams, Sherley Anne*
Working Cowboy — *Holmes, Ray*
Working from the Margins — *Schein, Virginia E*
Working in English — *Murray, Heather*
y Working in Health Care and Wellness — *Lee, Barbara*
y Working in Music — *Lee, Barbara*
y Working in Sports and Recreation — *Lee, Barbara*
Working in the Service Society — *Macdonald, Cameron Lynne*
Working Light — *Rooney, Frances*
Working Memory and Human Cognition
  — *Richardson, John T E*
Working on the Bomb — *Sanger, S L*
Working Papers on Disaster Management — *Revill, Don*
The Working Parents Handbook — *Sale, June Solnit*
Working Parts — *Bledsoe, Lucy Jane*
Working People of California — *Cornford, Daniel*
Working Sex — *Macy, Marianne*
Working Smarter from Home — *Struck, Nancy*
Working Sober — *Sonnenstuhl, William J*
Working Solo — *Lonier, Terri*
r Working Stiffs, Union Maids, Reds, and Riffraff
  — *Zaniello, Tom*
Working the Stone — *Milligan, Bryce*
c Working Together against Crime — *Adint, Victor*
c Working Together against Drinking and Driving
  — *Grosshandler-Smith, Janet*
c Working Together against Gang Violence — *Trapani, Margi*
y Working Together against School Violence — *Klee, Sheila*
y Working Together against Violence against Women
  — *Sherman, Aliza*
Working toward Freedom — *Hudson, Larry E, Jr.*
y Working with Animals — *Lee, Barbara*
Working with Child Abuse and Neglect — *Wiehe, Vernon R*
Working with Dreams in Psychotherapy — *Hill, Clara E*
Working with Mr. Wright — *Besinger, Curtis*
Working with Relationship Triangles — *Guerin, Philip J*
Working with Soft Furnishings — *Dunkerley, Charlotte*
Working with Your Foreign Language Assistant
  — *Page, Robin*
Workplace Violence — *Heskett, Sandra L*
r Works about John Dewey 1886-1995 — *Levine, Barbara*
Works Councils — *Rogers, Joel*
Works for Piano — *Chabrier, Emmanuel*
The Works of Aphra Behn. Vols. 5-7 — *Behn, Aphra*
Works of John Ruskin. Electronic Media Version
The Works of Jonathan Edwards. Vol. 13 — *Edwards, Jonathan*
Works of Love — *Kierkegaard, Soren*
y Works of Love Are Works of Peace — *Collopy, Michael*
A Workshop of the Possible — *Hubbard, Ruth*
Workshops on Particles and Fields and
  Phenomenology of Fundamental Interactions
  — *D'Olivo, Juan C*
c Worksong (Illus. by Ruth Wright Paulsen) — *Paulsen, Gary*
WORKTypes — *Kummerow, Jean M*
p The World
r The World: A Third World Guide 1995/96
r World Academic Database. Electronic Media Version
The World according to Hollywood 1918-1939
  — *Vasey, Ruth*
The World according to Mike Leigh — *Coveney, Michael*
The World according to Wavelets — *Hubbard, Barbara Burke*

r The World Affairs Companion. 5th Ed. — *Segal, Gerald*
r The World, Afghanistan to Zimbabwe — *Rand McNally and Company*
The World after Communism — *Skidelsky, Robert*
World Agriculture and Climate Change — *Darwin, Roy*
World Agriculture in a Post-GATT Environment
  — *Gray, Richard Stanley*
yr The World Almanac and Book of Facts 1996
cr The World Almanac for Kids 1997
r The World Almanac Job Finder's Guide 1997
The World and Yugoslavia's Wars — *Ullman, Richard H*
p World Art
The World at Night — *Furst, Alan*
r World Authors 1900-1950. Vols. 1-4 — *Seymour-Smith, Martin*
yr World Authors 1985-1990 — *Colby, Vineta*
r World Awaits — *Otteson, Paul*
The World Bank and Non-Governmental
  Organizations — *Nelson, Paul J*
The World Bank Annual Report 1996
r The World Bank Glossary: English-Spanish, Spanish-English
World Bank Lending for Small Enterprises 1989-1993
  — *Webster, Leila*
The World Bank Participation Sourcebook
r The World Bank Research Program 1996
The World Bank's Strategy for Reducing Poverty and
  Hunger — *Binswanger, Hans P*
r A World Bibliography of Bibliographies 1964-1974.
  Vols. 1-2 — *Toomey, Alice*
r A World Bibliography of Bibliographies and of
  Bibliographical Catalogues, Calenders, Abstracts,
  Digests, Indexes, and the Like. 4th Ed., Rev. and
  Greatly Enl. Throughout, Vols. 1-5 — *Besterman, Theodore*
r World Biographical Index. 2nd Ed. Electronic Media
  Version
cr The World Book Atlas — *World Book, Inc.*
cr The World Book Encyclopedia. 1996 Ed., Vols. 1-22
cr The World Book Encyclopedia of People and Places.
  Vols. 1-6
r The World Book Encyclopedia of Science. Vols. 1-8
cr The World Book Health and Medical Annual 1997
yr The World Book Multimedia Encyclopedia. Electronic
  Media Version
r The World Book/Rush-Presbyterian-St. Luke's
  Medical Center Medical Encyclopedia. Updated and
  Expanded 7th Ed.
World-Building: A Writer's Guide to Constructing
  Star Systems and Life Supporting Planets — *Gillett, Stephen L*
World Cinema: Hungary — *Burns, Bryan*
World Cinema: Israel — *Kronish, Amy*
World Cities in a World-System — *Knox, Paul L*
World Citizenship and Government — *Heater, Derek Benjamin*
World Class Manufacturing — *Schonberger, Richard J*
r World Communication — *Hamelink, Cees*
r The World Competitiveness Yearbook 1996
r World Databases in Agriculture — *Armstrong, C J*
r World Databases in Biosciences and Pharmacology
  — *Armstrong, C J*
r World Databases in Chemistry — *Armstrong, C J*
r World Databases in Company Information
  — *Armstrong, C J*
r World Databases in Humanities — *Armstrong, C J*
r World Databases in Social Sciences — *Armstrong, C J*
r World Debt Tables. Electronic Media Version
World Debt Tables 1996. Vols. 1-2
World Development Report 1996
r World Directory of Business Information Libraries.
  2nd Ed.
r World Directory of Country Environmental Studies.
  3rd Ed.
r World Directory of Defence and Security — *Kerr, Donald*
r World Directory of Human Rights Research and
  Training Institutions. 3rd Ed.
r World Directory of Non-Official Statistical Sources
r World Directory of Trade and Business Associations
r World Directory of Trade and Business Journals
World Disasters Report 1995
The World Doesn't End — *Simic, Charles*
c World-Eater — *Swindells, Robert*
World Economic and Social Survey 1996
r The World Economic Factbook 1996/97
World Economic Primacy 1500-1990 — *Kindleberger, Charles P*

The World Economy — *Svetlicic, Marjan*
The World Economy and National Finance in
  Historical Perspective — *Kindleberger, Charles P*
The World Economy in Transition — *Hinshaw, Randall*
World Economy Macroeconomics — *Whitmore, Harland William*
World Employment 1995
The World Encompassed — *Scammell, G V*
r The World Encyclopedia of Contemporary Theatre.
  Vol. 2 — *Rubin, Don*
r The World Encyclopedia of Wine — *Walton, Stuart*
r World Energy and Nuclear Directory. 3rd Ed., Vols.
  1-2
r World Engineering Industries and Automation 1994-
  1996
r The World Factbook 1996-97
yr The World Factbook 1997-98
r World Geographical Encyclopedia. Vols. 1-5
  — *Parker, Sybil P*
A World Growing Old — *Callahan, Daniel*
r World Guide to Religious and Spiritual Organizations.
  1st Ed.
r World Guide to Religious and Spiritual Organizations
  1996
r World Guide to Trade Associations. 4th Ed.
The World Health Report 1995
r World Historical Fiction Guide. 2nd Ed. — *McGarry, Daniel D*
World History — *Thomas, Hugh*
A World History of Art. 4th Ed. — *Honour, Hugh*
y A World History of Photography. 3rd Ed.
  — *Rosenblum, Nancy*
The World in 2020 — *McRae, Hamish*
The World in a Bowl of Tea — *Vitell, Bettina*
A World in Need of Leadership — *Urquhart, Brian*
World Industrial Robots 1995
World Industrial Robots 1996
c The World Is Big and I'm So Small (Illus. by Joe
  Servello) — *Kotzwinkle, William*
c The World Is Full of Babies! (Illus. by Mick Manning)
  — *Manning, Mick*
p World Letter
r World Librarianship — *Huq, A M Abdul*
A World Lit Only by Fire — *Manchester, William*
A World Lost — *Berry, Wendell*
The World Made New — *Merricks, Linda*
r World Marketing Data and Statistics 1996 on CD-
  ROM. Electronic Media Version
r World Media Handbook. 1995 Ed.
World Military and Social Expenditures 1996
World, Mind, and Ethics — *Altham, J E J*
World Musics in Education — *Floyd, Malcolm*
r World Mythology — *Sienkewicz, Thomas J*
y World Mythology — *Willis, Roy*
The World News Prism. 4th Ed. — *Hachten, William A*
c World of 1001 Mysteries — *Stannard, Russell*
c The World of Castles and Forts — *Day, Malcolm*
The World of Classical Myth — *Ruck, Carl A P*
r World of Economic Models — *Uebe, Gotz*
y The World of Edward Gorey — *Ross, Clifford*
The World of Emily Dickinson — *Longsworth, Polly*
The World of Fashion. 2nd Ed. — *Diamond, Jay*
c World of Festivals — *Steele, Philip*
The World of Hannah More — *Demers, Patricia*
The World of Jewish Cooking — *Marks, Gil*
The World of Jimmy Carter — *Maga, Timothy P*
The World of John Taylor the Water Poet 1578-1653
  — *Capp, Bernard*
c The World of Little House (Illus. by Deborah Maze)
  — *Collins, Carolyn Strom*
A World of Love — *Conroy, Maggie Francis*
c The World of Reptiles — *Murawski, Darlyne*
The World of Rozome — *Benjamin, Betsy Sterling*
The World of Rural Dissenters 1520-1725 — *Spufford, Margaret*
The World of Samuel Beckett 1906-1946 — *Gordon, Lois*
The World of Shakespeare — *Claybourne, Anna*
c World of Soccer — *Nevin, Michael*
The World of Suzie Wong — *Mason, Richard*
The World of the Manager — *Yaney, George*
c The World of the Medieval Knight (Illus. by Brett
  Breckon) — *Gravett, Christopher*
The World of the Oratorio — *Pahlen, Kurt*
The World of the Paris Cafe — *Haine, W Scott*
y The World of the Penguin — *Chester, Jonathan*
The World of the Ploughwoman — *Rey-Henningsen, Marisa*

c The World of the Polar Bear (Illus. by Norbert Rosing) — *Rosing, Norbert*
y The World of the Shorebirds — *Thurston, Harry*
The World of the Ten Thousand Things — *Wright, Charles*
The World of the Troubadours — *Paterson, Linda M*
y The World of the Wolf — *Savage, Candace*
A World of Their Own Making — *Gillis, John R*
c The World of Weather
A World of Widows — *Owen, Margaret*
The World of William and Mary — *Hoak, Dale*
The World of Work — *Auerbach, Alan*
The World on a String — *Goodman, Al*
The World on Blood — *Nasaw, Jonathan*
The World on Paper — *Olson, David R*
The World on Time — *Wetherbe, James C*
y The World Out There — *Ford, Michael Thomas*
World Philosophies — *Cooper, David Edward*
World Politics since 1945. 7th Ed. — *Calvocoressi, Peter*
World Population — *Johnson, Stanley*
World Population Monitoring 1993
World Press Photo 1995
r World Radio TV Handbook. 1996 Ed.
r The World Reacts to the Holocaust — *Wyman, David S*
c The World Record Paper Airplane Book — *Blackburn, Ken*
r World Religions — *Bowker, John Westerdale*
yr World Religions — *Jacobs, William Jay*
World Religions — *Self, David*
World Religions in America — *Neusner, Jacob*
r World Resources 1994-1995
r World Resources 1996-1997
r World Resources 1996-1997 Data Diskette. Electronic Media Version
r World Retail Directory and Sourcebook. 2nd Ed.
World Sound Matters — *Stock, Jonathan P J*
r World Statistics in Brief 1976-
r World Stock Exchange Fact Book. 1st Ed.
World Surfactants Congress. Vols. 1-4 — *World Surfactants Congress (4th: 1996: Barcelona, Spain)*
World Survey of Economic Freedom 1995-1996
The World the Cold War Made — *Cronin, James E*
The World the Railways Made — *Faith, Nicolas*
The World, the World — *Lewis, Norman*
p The World Today
World Trade after the Uruguay Round — *Sander, Harald*
r World Trade Almanac 1996-1997
r World Trade Almanac and the Dictionary of International Trade. 1997 Ed. Electronic Media Version
The World Trade Organization — *Qureshi, Asif H*
World Travel — *Baker, Christopher P*
r World Travel Guide 1996/97
The World Turned Right Side Up — *Hodgson, Godfrey*
A World Turned Upside Down — *Towles, Louis P*
The World Upside Down — *Ramirez, Susan Elizabeth*
World Vegetables. 2nd Ed. — *Rubatzky, Vincent E*
y World War II — *Dudley, William*
r World War II — *Polmar, Norman*
World War II and the American Dream — *Albrecht, Donald*
World War II, Film, and History — *Chambers, John Whiteclay*
yr World War II (News Multimedia). Electronic Media Version
yr World War One (YITM). Electronic Media Version
yr World War Two (YITM). Electronic Media Version
r World Watch List for Domestic Animal Diversity. 2nd Ed. — *Scherf, Beate D*
The World Wide Web — *Handley, Mark*
r World Wide Web — *Stout, Rick*
World Wide Web and Other Internet Information Services in the Health Sciences — *Lingle, Virginia*
World Wide Web Bible. 2nd Ed. — *Pfaffenberger, Bryan*
The World Wide Web for Busy People — *Nelson, Stephen L*
The World Wide Web for Teachers — *Williams, Bard*
World Wide Web Handbook — *Flynn, Peter*
p The World Wide Web Journal
World Wide Web Marketing — *Sterne, Jim*
r World Wide Web Pocket Dictionary — *Campbell, Mary*
World Wide Web Searching for Dummies — *Hill, Brad*
r World Wide Web Yellow Pages. 1997 Ed.
World without End — *Cochran, Molly*

Worlda Mirth — *Croll, Su*
Worlding Women — *Pettman, Jan Jindy*
Worldling — *Spires, Elizabeth*
A Worldly Art — *Westermann, Mariet*
Worldly Goods — *Jardine, Lisa*
Worldmaking — *Pencak, William*
yr Worldmark Encyclopedia of the Nations. 8th Ed., Vols. 1-5
Worlds Apart — *Miller, Daniel*
c Worlds Apart — *Murphy, Jill*
Worlds Between — *Davidoff, Leonore*
r The World's Columbian Exposition — *Bertuca, David J*
The World's Easiest Guide to Using the APA — *Amato, Carol J*
World's End — *Boyle, T Coraghessan*
World's Finest — *Gibbons, Dave*
The World's Game — *Murray, Bill*
The World's Healthiest Food — *Marshall, Anne*
Worlds in Interaction — *Rickman, H*
The World's Most Dangerous Places — *Pelton, Robert Young*
c World's Most Perplexing Puzzles — *Townsend, Charles*
Worlds of Exile and Illusion — *Le Guin, Ursula K*
Worlds of Hurt — *Tal, Kali*
The Worlds of P'otsunu — *Shutes, Jeanne*
The World's Parliament of Religions — *Seager, Richard Hughes*
The World's Regions and Weather — *Perry, Phyllis J*
c World's Weirdest Birds — *Roberts, M L*
The World's Women 1995
c The World's Worst Fairy Godmother (Illus. by Katherine Coville) — *Coville, Bruce*
The World's Worst Medical Mistakes — *Fido, Martin*
r The World's Writing Systems — *Daniels, Peter T*
Worldviews and Ecology — *Tucker, Mary Evelyn*
y Worldviews: The Challenge of Choice — *Bradley, Ken*
Worldwar: Striking the Balance — *Turtledove, Harry*
y Worldwar: Upsetting the Balance — *Turtledove, Harry*
Worldwide Advances in Structural Concrete and Masonry — *International Conference on Worldwide Advances in Structural Concrete and Masonry (14th: 1996: Chicago, Ill.)*
r Worldwide Government Directory 1996
r Worldwide Guide to Equivalent Nonferrous Metals and Alloys. 3rd Ed. — *Mack, William C*
r Worldwide Offshore Contractors and Equipment Directory 1996
Worldwide Trends in Youth Sport — *De Knop, Paul*
c Worm (Illus. by Tim Hayward) — *Wiseman, Stella*
c Worm Pie — *Scudamore, Beverly*
c Worm Songs — *Coburn, Ann*
y The Wormholers — *Gavin, Jamila*
c Wormology (Illus. by Brian Grogan) — *Ross, Michael Elsohn*
c The Worry Stone (Illus. by Sibyl Graber Gerig) — *Dengler, Marianna*
Worse than Slavery — *Oshinsky, David M*
Worship and Theology in England. Vols. 1-3 — *Davies, Horton*
Worship in Transition — *Fenwick, John R K*
Worst Case Scenario — *Bowen, Michael*
The Worst Desert on Earth — *Blackmore, Charles*
Worst Fears — *Weldon, Fay*
Worst Fears (Porter). Audio Version — *Weldon, Fay*
The Worst Tax? — *Fisher, Glenn W*
r Worth a Thousand Words — *Ammon, Bette DeBruyne*
The Worth Book of Softball — *Dickson, Paul*
The Worth of a Child — *Murray, Thomas H, 1946-*
Would-Be Worlds — *Casti, John L*
c Would My Fortune Cookie Lie? — *Pevsner, Stella*
c Would You Love Me? (Illus. by Andrea Wayne-Von-Konigslow) — *Von Konigslow, Andrea Wayne*
c Wouldn't You Like to Know (Illus. by Quentin Blake) — *Rosen, Michael, 1946-*
y The Wound-Dresser's Dream — *Stainer, Pauline*
The Wounded Heart of God — *Park, Andrew Sung*
The Wounded Jung — *Smith, Robert C*
Wounded Libraries in Croatia — *Aparac-Gazivoda, Tatjana*
Wounded Titans — *Lerner, Max*
Wounding Words — *Accad, Evelyne*
Woven Gods — *Hereniko, Vilsoni*
c Wow! I'm a Whale (Illus. by Clive Scruton) — *Bradman, Tony*
Woza Shakespeare! — *Sher, Antony*
The WPA Oklahoma Slave Narratives — *Baker, T Lindsay*

Das Wrack: Die Antike Schiffsfund Von Mahdia. Vols. 1-2 — *Salies, G Hellenkemper*
Wrapped in Wishes — *Bicos, Olga*
c Wrapper Rockets and Trombone Straws — *Sobey, Ed*
Wrasse: Biology and Use in Aquaculture — *Sayer, M D J*
Wreath Magic — *Dierks, Leslie*
The Wreck of the Isabella — *Miller, David M O*
c The Wreck of the Zanzibar (Illus. by Christian Birmingham) — *Morpurgo, Michael*
y The Wrecked, Blessed Body of Shelton Lafleur — *Brown, John Gregory*
y Wrecked! Mysteries and Disasters at Sea — *Bassett, Jan*
The Wrestling — *Garfield, Simon*
Wrestling Angels into Song — *Beavers, Herman*
y Wrestling Sturbridge — *Wallace, Rich*
Wrestling until Daybreak — *Schweid, Eliezer*
Wrestling with Angels — *Rosenblatt, Naomi H*
Wrestling with God — *Fiand, Barbara*
c The Wright Brothers — *Freedman, Russell*
Wrigleyville: A Magical History Tour of the Chicago Cubs — *Golenbock, Peter*
c A Wrinkle in Time — *L'Engle, Madeleine*
Wriston: Walter Wriston, Citibank, and the Rise and Fall of American Financial Supremacy — *Zweig, Phillip L*
Writ in Blood — *Yarbro, Chelsea Quinn*
Write to Be Read — *Smalzer, William R*
Write Your Own User Guide — *Ramsay, Jim*
The Writer Got Screwed (but Didn't Have to Go) — *Wharton, Brooke*
The Writer in Politics — *Gass, William H*
The Writer's Book of Memory — *Rider, Janine*
yr A Writer's Companion — *Rubin, Louis Decimus*
The Writer's Desk — *Krementz, Jill*
r The Writer's Digest Dictionary of Concise Writing — *Fiske, Robert Hartwell*
r Writer's Encyclopedia. 3rd Ed. — *Writer's Digest*
yr The Writer's Guide to Everyday Life in Renaissance England — *Emerson, Kathy Lynn*
The Writer's Guide to the Internet — *Groves, Dawn*
Writers Harvest 2
The Writer's Journal — *Bender, Sheila*
r Writer's Market 1997: The Electronic Edition. Electronic Media Version
A Writer's Nightmare — *Narayan, R K*
r Writers of Multicultural Fiction for Young Adults — *Kutzer, M Daphne*
Writers on Organizations. 5th Ed. — *Pugh, Derek S*
r The Writer's Ultimate Research Guide — *Metter, Ellen*
yp Writes of Passage: The Literary Journal for Teenagers
yr Writing 101 — *Sorsby, Claudia*
r Writing-across-the-Curriculum and the Academic Library — *Sheridan, Jean*
Writing against God — *McMullen, Joanne Halleran*
Writing and Being — *Gordimer, Nadine*
Writing and Literacy in Chinese, Korean, and Japanese — *Taylor, Insup*
Writing and Orality — *Fielding, Penny*
Writing and Rebellion — *Justice, Steven*
Writing and Reporting News. 2nd Ed. — *Rich, Carole*
Writing and the English Renaissance — *Zunder, William*
Writing and the Rise of Finance — *Nicholson, Colin*
Writing Center Perspectives — *Stay, Byron L*
r Writing Centers — *Murphy, Christina*
r Writing Changes Everything — *Brodie, Deborah*
Writing Chicago — *Cappetti, Carla*
Writing East — *Higgins, Iain Macleod*
Writing Ethnographic Fieldnotes — *Emerson, Robert M*
Writing Family Histories and Memoirs — *Polking, Kirk*
Writing for Science — *Silyn-Roberts, Heather*
Writing for Video — *Bjerke, Gene*
Writing from Life — *Albert, Susan Wittig*
Writing from the Center — *Sanders, Scott Russell*
Writing Ground Zero — *Treat, John Whittier*
r Writing Handbook. 2nd Ed. — *Streicher, Bernard J*
Writing Histories of Rhetoric — *Vitanza, Victor*
Writing Home — *Bennett, Alan*
Writing Horror and the Body — *Badley, Linda*
Writing in Dante's Cult of Truth from Borges to Boccaccio — *Menocal, Maria Rosa*
Writing in Hope and Fear — *McLaren, John*
Writing in Parts — *McLaughlin, Kevin*
Writing in the Shadow — *Stone, Harry*
Writing India 1757-1990 — *Moore-Gilbert, Bart*

Writing Long-Running Television Series — *Friedman, Julian*

Writing Mothers, Writing Daughters — *Burstein, Janet Handler*

Writing on the Renaissance Stage — *Kiefer, Frederick*

The Writing on the Wall — *Wood, Mary Elene*

Writing OpenVMS Alpha Device Drivers in C — *Sherlock, Margie*

Writing Out My Heart — *Willard, Frances E*

The Writing Path 2

Writing Pynchon — *McHoul, A W*

Writing Rome — *Edwards, Catharine*

Writing S.E/Asia in English — *Lim, Shirley*

Writing Selves — *Perreault, Jeanne*

Writing Skills for Parents — *Yates, Irene*

Writing: Teachers and Children at Work — *Graves, Donald H*

The Writing Teacher's Companion — *Peterson, Rai*

Writing the Australian Child — *Bradford, Clare*

Writing the Memoir — *Barrington, Judith*

Writing the Orgy — *Frappier-Mazur, Lucienne*

Writing the Private Eye Novel — *Randisi, Robert J*

Writing the Range — *Jameson, Elizabeth*

Writing the Southwest — *Dunaway, David King*

Writing Their Nations — *Lichtenstein, Diane*

Writing through Repression — *Levine, Michael G*

Writing to Communicate — *Webster, Chris*

Writing to the Moment — *Paulin, Tom*

Writing toward Home — *Heard, Georgia*

Writing Was Everything — *Kazin, Alfred*

c **Writing with Style** — *Young, Sue*

Writing Women in Jacobean England — *Lewalski, Barbara Kiefer*

Writing Women in Late Medieval and Early Modern Spain — *Surtz, Ronald E*

Writings — *Washington, George*

Writings and Drawings — *Thurber, James*

The Writings of a Savage — *Gauguin, Paul*

y **The Writings of Carlos Fuentes** — *Williams, Raymond L*

The Writings of Christine De Pizan — *Christine, De Pisan*

The Writings of John Evelyn — *Evelyn, John*

The Writings of Koda Aya, a Japanese Literary Daughter — *Tansman, Alan*

The Writings of William Carlos Williams — *Morris, Daniel*

r **Writings on African Archives** — *McIlwaine, John*

r **Writings on American History 1902-1961**

r **Writings on American History: A Subject Bibliography of Articles 1962-1990**

Writings on Glass — *Kostelanetz, Richard*

y **Written by Herself. Vol. 2** — *Conway, Jill K*

Written in Water, Written in Stone — *Lammen, Michael*

y **Written on Memory** — *Wolin, Jeffrey A*

Written on the Body — *Winterson, Jeanette*

r **Written Out of Television** — *Lance, Steven*

The Written Wars — *Cox, Joseph T*

Written with a Spoon — *Fay, Nancy*

Wrong for All the Right Reasons — *MacInnes, Gordon*

The Wrong Kind of Money — *Birmingham, Stephen*

y **The Wrong Stuff** — *Moore, John*

c **The Wrong Trousers** — *Park, Nick*

Wrongful Death — *Gilbert, Sandra M*

Wry Martinis — *Buckley, Christopher*

Wuthering Heights — *Bronte, Emily*

Wuthering Heights — *Knoepflmacher, U C*

y **Wuthering Heights (McCaddon). Audio Version** — *Bronte, Emily*

WWW.Security: How to Build a Secure World Wide Web Connection — *MacGregor, Robert S*

The Wycherly Woman — *Macdonald, Ross*

c **Wynton Marsalis: Gifted Trumpet Player** — *Awmiller, Craig*

Wyrm — *Fabi, Mark*

Wystan and Chester — *Clark, Thekla*

c **Wyvern Fall** — *Forward, Toby*

X Y Z

The X-Files Book of the Unexplained. Vol. 2 — *Goldman, Jane*
yp The X-Files Collection. Vol. 1 — *Petrucha, Stefan*
The X-Files Companion. Vol. 2 — *Edwards, Ted*
r X-Files Confidential — *Edwards, Ted*
X-Rays: The First Hundred Years — *Michette, Alan*
X-Texts — *Pell, Derek*
X Window System — *Scheifler, Robert W*
X Windows on the World — *McFarland, Thomas C*
X20 — *Beard, Richard*
y Xanadu 2 — *Yolen, Jane*
O Xango De Baker Street — *Soares, Jo*
Xbo — *Fourcade, Dominique*
Xenophon and the History of His Times — *Dillery, John*
Xenophon, Oeconomicus — *Pomeroy, Sarah B*
Xenophon of Ephesus: His Compositional Technique and the Birth of the Novel — *O'Sullivan, J N*
Xenophon's Cyropaedia — *Gera, Deborah Levine*
Xenotransplantation: Science, Ethics, and Public Policy
Xeriscape Plant Guide — *Denver (Colo.). Water Dept.*
Xiang Gang Gu Dai Shi — *Xiao, Jianguo*
Xiang Gang Yin Yuan — *Liu, Shaoming*
Xie Ji Tai Yang Qi — *Liu, Feng*
Xing Bie Bei Ju
Xue Shang — *Xin, Shi*
Xunzi--A Translation and Study of the Complete Works. Vol. 3 — *Hsun-Tzu*
XXX: A Woman's Right to Pornography — *McElroy, Wendy*
XY: On Masculine Identity — *Badinter, Elisabeth*
Y Tu, Que Dices. 3rd Ed. — *Kupferschmid, Gene S*
The Yahwist's Landscape — *Hiebert, Theodore*
y Yak Butter and Black Tea — *Brackenbury, Wade*
Yakuza Diary — *Seymour, Christopher*
r The Yale Guide to Children's Nutrition
Yamsi: A Year in the Life of a Wilderness Ranch — *Hyde, Dayton*
c Yancy and Bear (Illus. by Ruth Ohi) — *Hutchins, Hazel*
c Yang the Third and Her Impossible Family (Illus. by Kees De Kiefte) — *Namioka, Lensey*
c Yang the Youngest and His Terrible Ear — *Namioka, Lensey*
Yangban: Ri Chosen Shakai No Tokken Kaiso — *Hiroshi, Miyajima*
A Yankee Ace in the RAF — *Rogers, Bogart*
Yankee Correspondence — *Silber, Nina*
c Yankee Doodle — *Kellogg, Steven*
Yankee Doodle Days — *Diamant, Lincoln*
r The Yankee Encyclopedia — *Gallagher, Mark*
Yankee Go Home? — *Granatstein, J L*
Yankee Magazine's Make It Last — *Proulx, Earl*
Yankee Sailors in British Gaols — *Cohen, Sheldon S*
A Yankee Spy in Richmond — *Van Lew, Elizabeth L*
r Yankee Talk — *Hendrickson, Robert*
The Yankee West — *Gray, Susan E*
Yanomami Warfare — *Ferguson, R Brian*
Yao Ya Yao Yao Dao Wai Po Qiao — *Bi, Feiyu*
p Yapi Kredi Economic Review
c Yard Sale (Illus. by James Stevenson) — *Stevenson, James*
y Ybor City Chronicles — *Pacheco, Ferdie*
Ye Jian Ying Zhuan
The Year 2000 Computing Crisis — *Murray, Jerome T*
y The Year 2000 Problem Solver — *Ragland, Bryce*
A Year at North Hill (Illus. by Joe Eck) — *Eck, Joe*
y A Year Between. 2nd Ed.
The Year Book of Psychiatry and Applied Mental Health 1995

r Year Book of the Muslim World 1996
c A Year Full of Poems — *Harrison, Michael*
A Year in Figure Skating — *Smith, Beverley*
c A Year in the City (Illus. by Paul Howard) — *Henderson, Kathy*
A Year in the Life of a Rose — *Reddell, Rayford Clayton*
A Year in the Life of a Shinto Shrine — *Nelson, John K*
y A Year in the Maine Woods — *Heinrich, Bernd*
A Year of Lesser — *Bergen, David*
A Year of Roses — *Scanniello, Stephen*
The Year of the Flood — *Mendoza, Eduardo*
The Year of the Hare — *Paasilinna, Arto*
A Year of the Hunter — *Milosz, Czeslaw*
c The Year of the Ranch (Illus. by Kimberly Bulcken Root) — *McLerran, Alice*
y Year of the Tiger — *Higgins, Jack*
The Year of the Whale — *Scheffer, Victor B*
c The Year-Round Book of Fun Stuff (Illus. by Michael Chesworth) — *Spider Magazine*
The Year the Dragon Came — *Sang, Ye*
The Year the Dream Died — *Witcover, Jules*
c A Year with Molly and Emmett (Illus. by Marylin Hafner) — *Hafner, Marylin*
A Year with Swollen Appendices — *Eno, Brian*
Yearbook of Cell and Tissue Transplantation 1996-1997
r Yearbook of English Festivals — *Spicer, Dorothy Gladys*
r Yearbook of Labour Statistics 1995
The Yearbook of Langland Studies. Vols. 6-7
The Year's 25 Finest Crime and Mystery Stories. 5th Ed.
The Year's Best Fantasy and Horror: Eighth Annual Collection
The Year's Best Fantasy and Horror: Ninth Annual Collection
The Year's Best Science Fiction: Thirteenth Annual Collection
Years Like Brief Days — *Dobles, Fabian*
The Year's Midnight — *Benzie, Alex*
Years of Estrangement — *Leyens, Erich*
Years of Infamy. Updated Ed. — *Weglyn, Michi Nishiura*
Years of Promise — *Carnegie Task Force on Learning in the Primary Grades*
A Year's Turning — *Viney, Michael*
Yeats and Alchemy — *Gorski, William T*
The Yeats Sisters — *Hardwick, Joan*
Yeats's Political Identities — *Allison, Jonathan*
Yeats's Worlds — *Pierce, David*
c Yellow — *Bryant-Mole, Karen*
The Yellow Admiral — *O'Brian, Patrick*
The Yellow Admiral (Tull). Audio Version — *O'Brian, Patrick*
The Yellow Arrow — *Pelevin, Viktor*
Yellow Dogs, Hushpuppies, and Bluetick Hounds — *Howorth, Lisa*
Yellow Fever and Public Health in the New South — *Ellis, John H*
Yellow Fever and the South — *Humphreys, Margaret*
Yellow Fever, Black Goddess — *Wills, Christopher*
The Yellow Lady — *Broinowski, Alison*
y A Yellow Raft in Blue Water — *Dorris, Michael*
The Yellow Sofa — *Queiros, Eca De*
The Yellow Wall Paper and Other Stories — *Gilman, Charlotte Perkins*
The Yellow Wallpaper (Phillips). Audio Version — *Gilman, Charlotte Perkins*

The Yellow Wallpaper. To Build a Fire. Audio Version — *Gilman, Charlotte Perkins*
Yellow Woman and a Beauty of the Spirit — *Silko, Leslie*
Yellowstone Place Names — *Haines, Aubrey L*
The Yellowstone Story. Rev. Ed., Vols. 1-2 — *Haines, Aubrey L*
The Yellowstone Wolf — *Schullery, Paul*
Yemen — *Wald, Peter*
Yerkes Observatory 1892-1950 — *Osterbrock, Donald E*
Yerushalayim Ve-Svivoteyah — *Kark, Ruth*
y Yes, We Have No Neutrons — *Dewdney, A K*
y Yesterday's Child — *Levitin, Sonia*
c Yesterday's Children (Illus. by Kevin Sollows) — *Barkhouse, Joyce*
y Yesterday's Dream — *Baer, Judy*
Yesterday's Stories — *Raub, Patricia*
Yesterday's Tomorrows — *Corn, Joseph J*
Yesterday's Train — *Pindell, Terry*
The Yetzer: A Kabbalistic Psychology of Eroticism and Human Sexuality — *Rotenberg, Mordechai*
Yew and Non-Yew — *Bartholomew, James*
Yi Ge Nu Ren De Bei Ju — *Wei, Tzu-Yun*
Yi Ge Tai Wan Xiao Liu Xue Sheng Dao Ha Fo Zhi Lu — *Wang, Chih-Hung*
r Yiddish Linguistics — *Bunis, Davis M*
c Yike! Yike! Where's My Trike? — *Berenstain, Stan*
c Yikes! In Seven Wild Adventures, Who Would You Be? (Illus. by Alison Lester) — *Lester, Alison*
Yindiao Weiding De Chuantong — *Zhu, Weizheng*
The Yishuv in the Shadow of the Holocaust — *Edelheit, Abraham J*
y Yitzhak Rabin: Israel's Soldier Statesman — *Kort, Michael*
Yksityisia Asioita — *Haavikko, Paavo*
Yo! — *Alvarez, Julia*
c Yo Ho Ho! — *Newman, Marjorie*
c Yob (Illus. by Abigail Pizer) — *King-Smith, Dick*
Yocandra in the Paradise of Nada — *Valdes, Zoe*
Yoga: Discipline of Freedom — *Patanjali*
y Yoga: The Spirit and Practice of Moving into Stillness — *Schiffmann, Erich*
The Yoke of Christ — *Burnett, Amy Nelson*
c Yolanda's Yellow School (Illus. by Kelly Asbury) — *Asbury, Kelly*
c Yolonda's Genius — *Fenner, Carol*
y Yon Ill Wind — *Anthony, Piers*
The Yoni Rocks — *Morrissey, Stephen*
Yorghos Seferis-Kypros Hrysanthis Ke I Ghates T'Ai Nikola — *Dhimitrakopoulos, Fotis*
The Yoruba Artist — *Abiodun, Rowland*
r Yoruba-English/English-Yoruba Concise Dictionary — *Yai, Olabiyi Babalola*
c The Yoruba of West Africa — *Hetfield, Jamie*
y Yorubaland: The Flowering of Genius — *Koslow, Philip*
c Yoshiko and the Foreigner (Illus. by Mimi Otey Little) — *Little, Mimi Otey*
Yoter Muzar Meha-Dimayon 6
You Alone Are Dancing — *Flanagan, Brenda*
c You and Me, Little Bear (Illus. by Barbara Firth) — *Waddell, Martin*
You and No Other — *Maxwell, Cathy*
You and Your Only Child — *Nachman, Patricia*
c You Animal! (Illus. by Nancy King) — *Booth, Jerry*
y You Are a Mathematician — *Wells, D G*
y You Are More than What You Weigh — *Sward, Sharon*
c You Are the President — *Aaseng, Nathan*
c You Are the President II — *Aaseng, Nathan*

c You Are Very Special (Illus. by Susie Poole) — *Box, Su*
y You Are Wonderfully Made! — *Johnson, Lois Walfrid*
cr You Asked? — *Farris, Katherine*
You Bright and Risen Angels — *Vollmann, William T*
You Can Be a Philanthropist — *Clough, David G*
You Can Be a Stock Market Genius Even if You're Not Too Smart — *Greenblatt, Joel*
c You Can Be a Woman Cardiologist (Illus. by David Katz) — *Redberg, Rita F*
c You Can Do Great Lettering — *Gamble, Kim*
c You Can Do Thousands of Things with String (Illus. by David Miller) — *Miller, David*
You Can Have It All — *Patent, Arnold M*
You Can Make It Happen — *Graham, Stedman*
c You Can Make Mobiles — *Novak, Jiri Tibor*
c You Can Surf the Net! — *Gascoigne, Marc*
You Can Teach Yourself Guitar. Electronic Media Version — *Bay, William*
You Cannot Unsneeze a Sneeze and Other Tales from Liberia — *Dendel, Esther W*
c You Can't Catch Me! (Illus. by Quentin Blake) — *Rosen, Michael, 1946-*
You Can't Catch Me — *Smith, Rosamond*
You Can't Do Both (Shelley). Audio Version — *Amis, Kingsley*
c You Can't Eat Your Chicken Pox, Amber Brown (Illus. by Tony Ross) — *Danziger, Paula*
c You Can't Smell a Flower with Your Ear — *Cole, Joanna*
You Can't Take It with You — *Foster, Sandra*
You Couldn't Make It Up — *Littlejohn, Richard*
You Do Teach Atoms, Don't You? — *Lyons, Lyman*
c You Don't Always Get What You Hope For (Illus. by Heidi Stetson Mario) — *Walton, Rick*
You Don't Have to Suffer — *Lang, Susan S*
You Gotta Believe — *Shinn, George*
You Have Stept out of Your Place — *Lindley, Susan Hill*
You Have the Wrong Man — *Flook, Maria*
You Just Don't Duct Tape a Baby — *Weinberger, Norman*
You Just Fight for Your Life — *Buchmann-Moller, Frank*
c You Little Monkey! (Illus. by Jan Lewis) — *Foster, John*
You Might as Well Laugh — *Shelton, Sandi Kahn*
c You Never Sausage Love (Illus. by Rick Dupre) — *Cleary, Brian P*
You Send Me — *Wolff, Daniel*
You Shall Not Abhor an Edomite for He Is Your Brother — *Edelman, Diana Viklander*
You Shall Not Want — *Chilson, Richard*
You Should Have Been Here Yesterday — *Eff, Elaine*
c You Wait till I'm Older than You! (Illus. by Shoo Rayner) — *Rosen, Michael, 1946-*
You Went Away — *Findley, Timothy*
You'll Never Make Love in This Town Again — *Frankel, Jennie Louise*
c Young Abe Lincoln — *Harness, Cheryl*
Young Adam — *Trocchi, Alexander*
r Young Adult Fiction by African American Writers 1968-1993 — *Kutenplon, Deborah*
c Young Cam Jansen and the Dinosaur Game (Illus. by Susanna Natti) — *Adler, David A*
c Young Cam Jansen and the Lost Tooth (Illus. by Susanna Natti) — *Adler, David A*
c Young Cam Jansen and the Missing Cookie (Illus. by Susanna Natti) — *Adler, David A*
Young Children, Parents and Professionals — *Henry, Margaret*
y Young Citizen's Passport — *Thorpe, Tony*
The Young Disraeli — *Ridley, Jane*
c Young Explorer's Guide to Undersea Life (Illus. by Ket Tom Conway) — *Conway, Ket Tom*
y Young George Washington — *Rosenburg, John*
c Young Guinevere (Illus. by Jamichael Henterly) — *San Souci, Robert D*
c Young Guinevere (Leishman). Audio Version — *San Souci, Robert D*
c The Young Inline Skater — *Edwards, Chris*
y Young Joan — *Dana, Barbara*
The Young Jonathan Edwards — *Morris, William Sparkes*
c Young Lancelot (Illus. by Jamichael Henterly) — *San Souci, Robert D*
c Young Lancelot (Leishman). Audio Version — *San Souci, Robert D*
c The Young Life of Mother Teresa of Calcutta (Illus. by Jane Robbins) — *Mohan, Claire Jordan*
The Young Man — *Strauss, Botho*

Young Man from the Provinces — *Helms, Alan*
Young Man Luther — *Erikson, Erik H*
y Young Men and Fire — *Maclean, Norman*
Young Men in the Street — *Snell, Cudore L*
y Young Merlin (Leishman). Audio Version — *San Souci, Robert D*
c Young Mouse and Elephant (Illus. by Valeri Gorbachev) — *Farris, Pamela J*
c Young Mozart (Illus. by Rachel Isadora) — *Isadora, Rachel*
c The Young Oxford Book of Archaeology — *Moloney, Norah*
yr The Young Oxford Book of Astronomy — *Mitton, Simon*
yr The Young Oxford Book of Ecology — *Scott, Michael M*
c The Young Oxford Book of the Human Being — *Glover, David M*
yr The Young Oxford Book of the Prehistoric World — *Bailey, Jill*
y The Young Oxford History of Britain and Ireland — *Corbishley, Mike*
y A Young Patriot — *Murphy, Jim*
The Young Paul Robeson — *Brown, Lloyd L*
y Young People from Bosnia Talk about War — *Fireside, Harvey*
cr The Young People's Atlas of the United States. Rev. 1996, New Ed. — *Harrison, James*
yr A Young Person's Guide to Music — *Ardley, Neil*
c The Young Person's Guide to the Orchestra — *Ganeri, Anita*
c The Young Person's Guide to the Orchestra. Book and Electronic Media Version — *Ganeri, Anita*
yr Young Person's Occupational Outlook Handbook
y The Young Tennis Player — *Sanchez Vicario, Arantxa*
c The Young Track and Field Athlete — *Jackson, Colin*
The Young Turks in Opposition — *Hanioglu, M Sukru*
Young v. Old — *MacManus, Susan A*
y The Young Vegetarian's Companion (Illus. by Sarah Durham) — *Parr, Jan*
The Younger Pitt: The Consuming Struggle — *Ehrman, John*
Younger than Springtime — *Williams, Greg*
y The Youngest Parents — *Coles, Robert*
c Your Amazing Brain — *Bryan, Jenny*
Your Backyard Wildlife Garden — *Schneck, Marcus*
Your Bank Is Ripping You Off — *Mrkvicka, Edward F, Jr.*
Your Body Can Talk — *Levy, Susan L*
Your Child with Arthritis — *Tucker, Lori B*
Your Complete Guide to Money Happiness — *Brock, Henry S*
Your Dieting Daughter — *Costin, Carolyn*
Your Father, Your Self — *Gordon, Barry H*
y Your First Horse — *Dwelle, Jacqueline*
c Your First Step — *Sorensen, Henri*
Your First Year of Teaching and Beyond — *Kronowitz, Ellen L*
y Your Future Career in Education — *Ryan, Michael J*
y Your Heart's Desire — *Choquette, Sonia*
Your Intuition Is Wrong — *Simon, Marc T*
Your John — *Hall, Radclyffe*
Your Life as Story — *Rainer, Tristine*
Your Mother's Tongue — *Burgen, Stephen*
Your Name Is Hughes Hannibal Shanks — *Shanks, Lela Knox*
Your Name Shall Be Tanga — *Beyala, Calixthe*
Your Oasis on Flame Lake — *Landvik, Lorna*
c Your Own ABC (Illus. by June Bradford) — *Baron, Marcie*
Your Personal Netspy — *Wolff, Michael*
yr Your Reading. 1995-96 Ed. — *Samuels, Barbara G*
Your Role as a Primary School Subject Coordinator — *Briggs, Mary*
Your Sixth Sense — *Naparstek, Belleruth*
c You're a Genius, Blackboard Bear (Illus. by Martha Alexander) — *Alexander, Martha*
c You're Aboard Spaceship Earth (Illus. by Holly Keller) — *Lauber, Patricia*
c You're Dead, David Borelli — *Brown, Susan M*
c You're Invited to Bruce Lansky's Poetry Party! (Illus. by Stephen Carpenter) — *Lansky, Bruce*
c You're Kidding, Ms. Wiz (Illus. by Tony Ross) — *Blacker, Terence*
y You're My Best Friend--I Hate You — *Rushton, Rosie*
c You're Safe Now, Waterdog (Illus. by Sophy Williams) — *Edwards, Richard*
You're So Beautiful — *FitzGerald, Eileen*
c You're Special, Too — *Parsons, Alexandra*
y You're Worth More than You Think — *Johnson, Lois Walfrid*

Yours, Isaac Asimov — *Asimov, Isaac*
Youth, AIDS, and Sexually Transmitted Diseases — *Moore, Susan*
Youth and Authority — *Griffiths, Paul*
Youth and Other Stories — *Ogai, Mori*
Youth and the Welfare State in Weimar Germany — *Harvey, Elizabeth*
The Youth Corridor — *Imber, Gerald*
The Youth Gang Problem — *Spergel, Irving A*
Youth, Murder, Spectacle — *Acland, Charles R*
y Youth Violence — *Guernsey, JoAnn Bren*
You've Always Been Wrong — *Daumal, Rene*
You've Only Got Three Seconds — *Lavington, Camille*
Yuan Si Zhong Sheng Sui — *Su, Hsiao-K'ang*
Yucatan's Maya Peasantry and the Origins of the Caste War — *Rugeley, Terry*
y Yuck! A Big Book of Little Horrors — *Snedden, Robert*
The Yugoslav Drama. 2nd Ed. — *Crnobrnja, Mihailo*
Yugoslavia: Death of a Nation — *Silber, Laura*
Yugoslavia Dismembered — *Samary, Catherine*
Yugoslavia's Bloody Collapse — *Bennett, Christopher*
Yul Brynner, Photographer — *Brynner, Yul*
Yves Saint Laurent: A Biography — *Rawsthorn, Alice*
Z: A Dave Riley Novel — *Mayer, Bob*
y Z for Zachariah — *O'Brien, Robert C*
Za Kulisami — *Vertinskii, A*
c Zack's Story (Illus. by Carol Halebian) — *Greenberg, Keith Elliot*
r Zagat Survey: America's Best Meal Deals — *Zagat, Eugene H*
Zai Hai De Bao Zhui Ru Qing Wang — *Long, Yingtai*
Zai Jian Cheng Du — *Tian, Wenyi*
La Zandunga: Of Fieldwork and Friendship in Southern Mexico — *Chinas, Beverly*
Zang Hun — *Teng, Wei*
Zanouba — *Out El Kouloub*
Zanzotto — *Hand, Vivienne*
c Zap! I'm a Mind Reader (Illus. by Jack E Davis) — *Greenburg, Dan*
Zapinette Video — *Russo, Albert*
Zapotec Civilization — *Marcus, Joyce*
Zapp! The Lightning of Empowerment — *Byham, William*
Zariskian Filtrations — *Li, Huishi*
Der Zauberberg — *Mann, Thomas*
Das Zauberberg-Symposium 1994 In Davos — *Sprecher, Thomas*
p Zbornik Radova
Zealotry and Academic Freedom — *Hamilton, Neil W*
c Zeb, the Cow's on the Roof Again! and Other Tales of Early Texas Dwellings (Illus. by Scott Arbuckle) — *Arbuckle, Scott*
The Zebra Finch — *Zann, Richard A*
A Zebra in Lion Country — *Wanger, Ralph*
c The Zebra-Riding Cowboy (Illus. by Maria Cristina Brusca) — *Medearis, Angela Shelf*
The Zebra Striped Hearse — *Macdonald, Ross*
c Zebulon Pike: Explorer of the Southwest — *Sanford, William R*
Zechariah 9-14 and Malachi — *Petersen, David L*
Zeena — *Cooke, Elizabeth*
Zefania Und Das Israel Der Armen — *Weigl, Michael*
Zeh Yigamer Be-Bekhi — *Asheri, Ehud*
Zeitgeist
Zeitgeschichte In Lebensbildern. Vol. 7 — *Aretz, Jurgen*
The Zeitroman of the Late Weimar Republic — *Matijevich, Elke*
Zeke and Ned — *McMurtry, Larry*
y Zel — *Napoli, Donna Jo*
y Zelda: An Illustrated Life — *Kurth, Peter*
y Zen and the Art of Motorcycle Maintenance (Pressman). Audio Version — *Pirsig, Robert M*
Zen at Work — *Kaye, Les*
Zen Combat — *Gluck, Jay*
The Zen Detective — *Talbot, Colin*
Zen Fixtures — *Luce, Solomon*
Zen Guitar — *Sudo, Philip Toshio*
Zen in the Art of Rhetoric — *McPhail, Mark Lawrence*
The Zen of Cooking — *Naimer, Lucille*
A Zen Romance — *Boehm, Deborah Boliver*
Zen Spirit, Christian Spirit — *Kennedy, Robert E*
Zen Zulu — *Yamamoto, Georgia*
Zenkoji and Its Icon — *McCallum, Donald F*
Zenobia — *Naum, Gellu*
c Zenon: Girl of the 21st Century (Illus. by Roger Bollen) — *Sadler, Marilyn*
Zenzele: A Letter for My Daughter — *Maraire, J Nozipo*

Zephaniah: A New Translation with Introduction and Commentary — *Bible. O.T. Zephaniah. English. Berlin. 1994*

Zephaniah's Oracles against the Nations — *Ryou, Daniel Hojoon*

y Zero at the Bone — *Cadnum, Michael*

Zero at the Bone — *Walker, Mary Willis*

Zero Fighter — *Yoshimura, Akira*

The Zero Hour — *Finder, Joseph*

The Zero Hour (Charles). Audio Version — *Finder, Joseph*

Zero Minus Ten — *Benson, Raymond*

y Zero to Lazy Eight — *Humez, Alexander*

Zero Tolerance — *Emberley, Peter*

Zero Tolerance — *Richards, Thomas, 1956-*

Der Zeuge — *Mitrofanow, Ilja*

Zhan: Tai Wan De Zui Hou Shi Ke — *Xu, Bing*

Zhenskaia Filosofiia — *Suvorov, Oleg*

Zhirnovsky: Russian Fascism and the Making of a Dictator — *Solovyov, Vladimir*

Zhizn' Russkoi Kubistki — *Udal'tsova, Nadezhda*

Zhiznl I Reformy. Vols. 1-2 — *Gorbachev, Mikhail Sergeevich*

Zhong Guo Kang Ri Zhan Zheng Duan Pian J Ing Cui

Zhong Guo Ke Yi Shuo Bu

Zhong Guo Ren She Chao — *Liu, Ning-Jung*

r Zhongguo Zhiqing Shidian — *Xiaomeng, Liu*

Zhou Enlai and the Foundations of Chinese Foreign Policy — *Shao, Kuo-kang*

Zhu Ming Wai Jiao Jia Yan Jiang Jian Shang

Zhukov. Rev. Ed. — *Chaney, Otto Preston*

Zhukov: The Rise and Fall of a Great Captain — *Spahr, William J*

Zi Ji De Gu Shi — *Zhang, Min*

Zigzag Street — *Earls, Nick*

Zikadengeschrei — *Wellershoff, Dieter*

c Zilla Sasparilla and the Mud Baby (Illus. by Amanda Harvey) — *Gorog, Judith*

Zima U Hercegovini — *Bratic, Radoslav*

Der Zimmerspringbrunnen: Ein Heimatroman — *Sparschuh, Jens*

p Zinj

Zion City, Illinois — *Cook, Philip L*

Zionist Culture and West European Jewry before the First World War — *Berkowitz, Michael*

r The Zionist Ideology — *Shimoni, Gideon*

Zip Six — *Gantos, Jack*

Zipper — *Friedel, Robert*

Zivilization Und Barbarei — *Bajohr, Frank*

c Zoe and Columbo — *Shreve, Susan*

y Zoe Rising — *Conrad, Pam*

Zoe Trope — *Prantera, Amanda*

Zola: A Life — *Brown, Frederick, 1934-*

Zola Et Les Genres — *Baguley, David*

Zombie — *Oates, Joyce Carol*

y Zone Soldiers — *Ransom, Daniel*

Zones of Contention — *Becker, Carol*

Zoo — *Jaschinski, Britta*

c Zoo Animals — *Barton, Byron*

c The Zoo at Night (Illus. by Bee Willey) — *Rosen, Michael, 1946-*

c Zoo Dreams (Illus. by Cor Hazelaar) — *Hazelaar, Cor*

y A Zoo in My Luggage (Davenport). Audio Version — *Durrell, Gerald*

c Zoo-Looking (Illus. by Candace Whitman) — *Fox, Mem*

c A Zooful of Animals (Illus. by Lynn Musinger) — *Cole, William*

Zoogeomorphology: Animals as Geomorphic Agents — *Butler, David R*

c Zookeepers Care for Animals — *Moses, Amy*

Zoology. 3rd Ed. — *Miller, Stephen A*

Zoolutions: A Mathematical Expedition — *Burgunder, Anne*

c Zoom (Illus. by Istvan Banyai) — *Banyai, Istvan*

c Zoom: Resources for Struggling Readers: Sets A-C

c Zora Hurston and the Chinaberry Tree (Illus. by Cornelius Van Wright) — *Miller, William*

Zora Neale Hurston, Eulalie Spence, Marita Bonner, and Others — *Burton, Jennifer*

y Zora Neale Hurston: Southern Storyteller — *Yannuzzi, Della A*

Zora Neale Hurston: Stories (Joshua-Porter). Audio Version — *Hurston, Zora Neale*

c Zorah's Magic Carpet — *Czernecki, Stefan*

y Zorba the Greek (Guidall). Audio Version — *Kazantzakis, Nikos*

Zoroaster: Life and Work of the Forerunner in Persia. 2nd Ed.

y El Zorro (Illus. by Javier Zabala) — *Sechan, Olivier*

c Zorro and Quwi (Illus. by Kim Howard) — *Hickox, Rebecca*

c Zorro En La Escuela (Illus. by James Marshall) — *Marshall, Edward*

Die Zunge Als Lohn — *Exner, Richard*

Zuni: A Village of Silversmiths — *Ostler, James*

Zuni and the Courts — *Hart, E Richard*

The Zuni Man-Woman — *Roscoe, Will*

Zuppa! A Tour of the Many Regions of Italy and Their Soups — *Romagnoli, Margaret*

Zuppa! Soups from the Italian Countryside — *Bianchi, Anne*

Zur Bedeutung Mystischer Denktradition Im Werk Von Hermann Broch — *Grabowsky-Hotamanidis, Anja*

Zur Frughgeschichte Des Elektronenmikroskops — *Quing, Lin*

Zwanzig Und Ein Tag — *Tschinag, Galsan*

Zwei Einsamkeiten — *Makanin, Vladimir*

Zwischen Hoffnung Und Ernuchterung — *Lendvai, Paul*

Zwischen Marktwirtschaft Und Dirigismus — *Kopper, Christopher*

Zwischen Wirklichkeit Und Traum — *Strelka, Joseph P*